中华人民共和国
海关进出口税则

十三位编码·监管条件·出口退税·检验检疫·海关代征税一览表

2022年中英文对照版

中华人民共和国海关进出口税则 编委会 编

Customs Import and Export Tariff
of the People's Republic of China

Coding of HS, Customs Control Conditions, Export Drawback, CIQ, Customs Duties Levied on Commission Basis

Compiled by the Editorial Department of the Customs
Import and Export Tariff of the People's Republic of China

经济日报出版社
Economic Daily Press

图书在版编目(CIP)数据

中华人民共和国海关进出口税则. 2022 年 ：汉英对照 / 中华人民共和国海关进出口税则编委会编. —— 北京：经济日报出版社，2022.1

ISBN 978－7－5196－1022－7

Ⅰ. ①中… Ⅱ. ①中… Ⅲ. ①海关税则－中国－2022－汉、英 Ⅳ. ①F752.50

中国版本图书馆 CIP 数据核字(2021)第 262563 号

中华人民共和国海关进出口税则(2022 年中英文对照版)

编　　者	中华人民共和国海关进出口税则编委会
责任编辑	门　睿
责任校对	王施义
出版发行	经济日报出版社
地　　址	北京市西城区白纸坊东街 2 号（邮政编码：100054）
电　　话	010－85843117（总编室）
	010－63584556（财经编辑部）
	010－63567687（企业与企业家史编辑部）
	010－63567683（经济与管理学术编辑部）
	010－51393396（发行部）
网　　址	www. edpbook. com. cn
E － mail	edpbook@126. com
经　　销	全国新华书店
印　　刷	北京盛通印刷股份有限公司
	大厂回族自治县益利印刷有限公司
开　　本	850×1168mm　1/16
印　　张	75
字　　数	2200 千字
版　　次	2022 年 1 月第一版
印　　次	2022 年 1 月第一次印刷
书　　号	ISBN 978－7－5196－1022－7
定　　价	400. 00 元

关于增值服务的说明

为答谢本版《税则》的新老用户，我们为您花重金统一购买了易通网(www. i—tong. cn)通关查询服务及权威专家归类、关务咨询服务等增值服务。

2022 年新增服务栏目：

税号定制服务：客户通过关注易通网公众号，在税号定制栏目下输入您关注的税号，当该税号项下品名、申报要素、最惠国、普通、增值、协定、特惠、暂定、消费、信息技术、反倾销反补贴等税率、3C 认证、出口退税、监管条件、报检等信息发生变动都会主动推送给用户。

增值服务内容包括：

1. 提供包括申报要素填写实例、反倾销反补贴税、检验检疫类别、报检查询、3C 认证、危险化学品目录等增值查询服务。

2. 网站对特惠、普通、最惠国、出口退税、检验检疫类别、监管条件等信息将进行实时维护更，新保证您查询的税率的准确性。

3. 免费提供三次权威专家线上归类咨询和关务咨询服务。

4. 提供与海关计算结果一致的模拟计税服务。

5. 提供通关状态查询等。

增值服务的使用方法：

1. 刮开封面上的“扫码获取增值服务”标签中的涂层，可以得到两行数字（第一行是登录账号，第二行是密码）。

2. 激活账号，登录（www. i—tong. cn)后，在网站的左上角注册页面找到激活按钮，点击激活，按照提示填写相关信息，完成后提交。

3. 提交激活信息后，系统会给您的注册邮箱中发送一封邮件，打开后点击激活，完成激活程序。

4. 在登录页面输入账号和密码即可登录使用。

特别申明：

凡是图书上未贴增值服务防伪标，或不能正常激活提供数据更新查询服务的一律为盗版图书。

提　　示：

此二维码为易通网微信公众服务号，您只需要添加关注，并将防伪标上的账号进行绑定，即可使用微信端进行查询使用。(此账号必须先在网站上激活后才能正常使用)

对照表编排图例及说明

斜杠前面的监管条件代码含义详见本书“3. 常用代码表”中监管证件代码表；斜杠后面的特殊证件代码含义详见本书“3. 常用代码表”中特殊证件代码表。

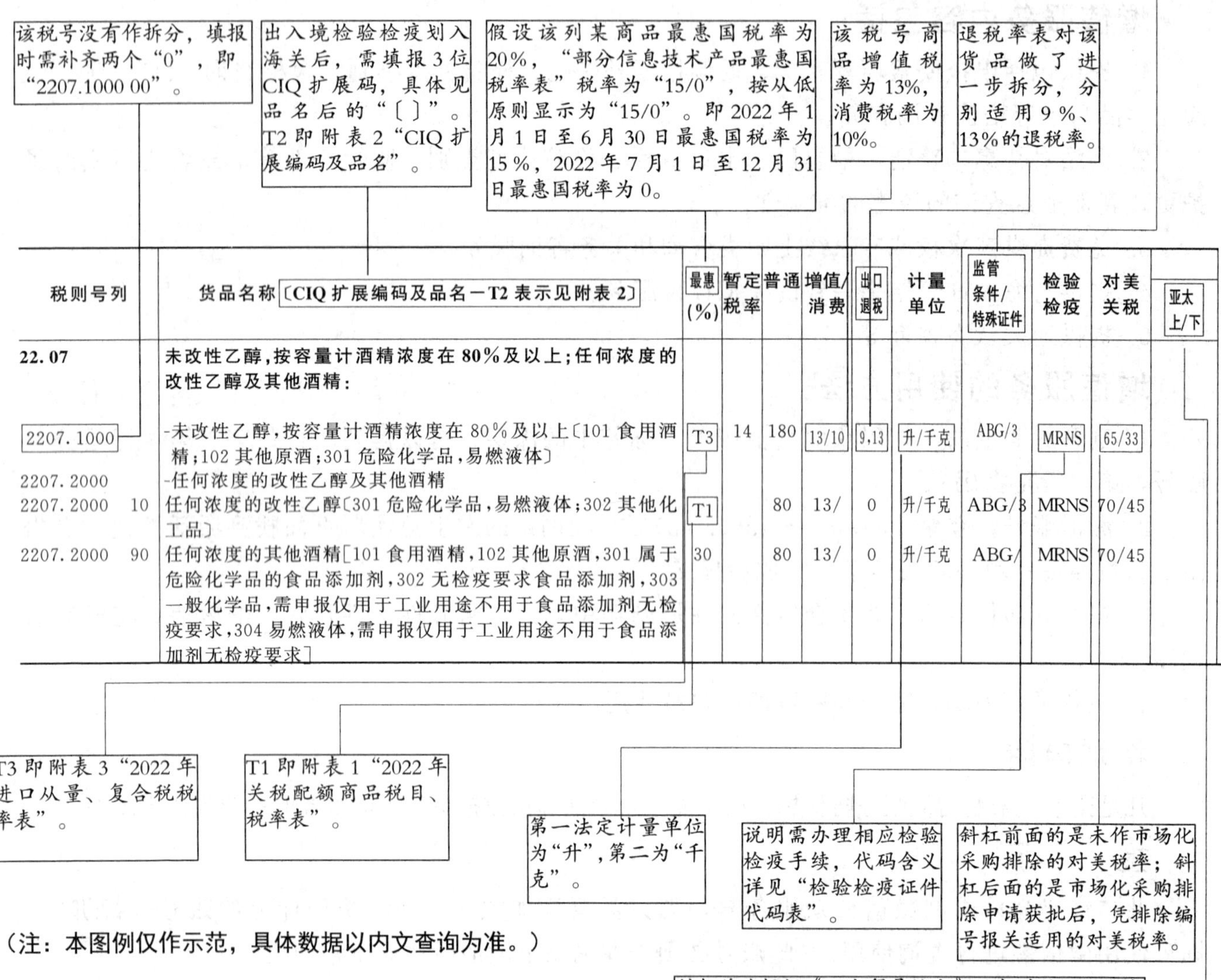

斜杠前为根据《亚太贸易协定》及相关协议，上半年实施的协定税率；斜杠后为下半年自7月1日起针对部分信息技术协定扩围产品降低的协定税率。

（注：本图例仅作示范，具体数据以内文查询为准。）

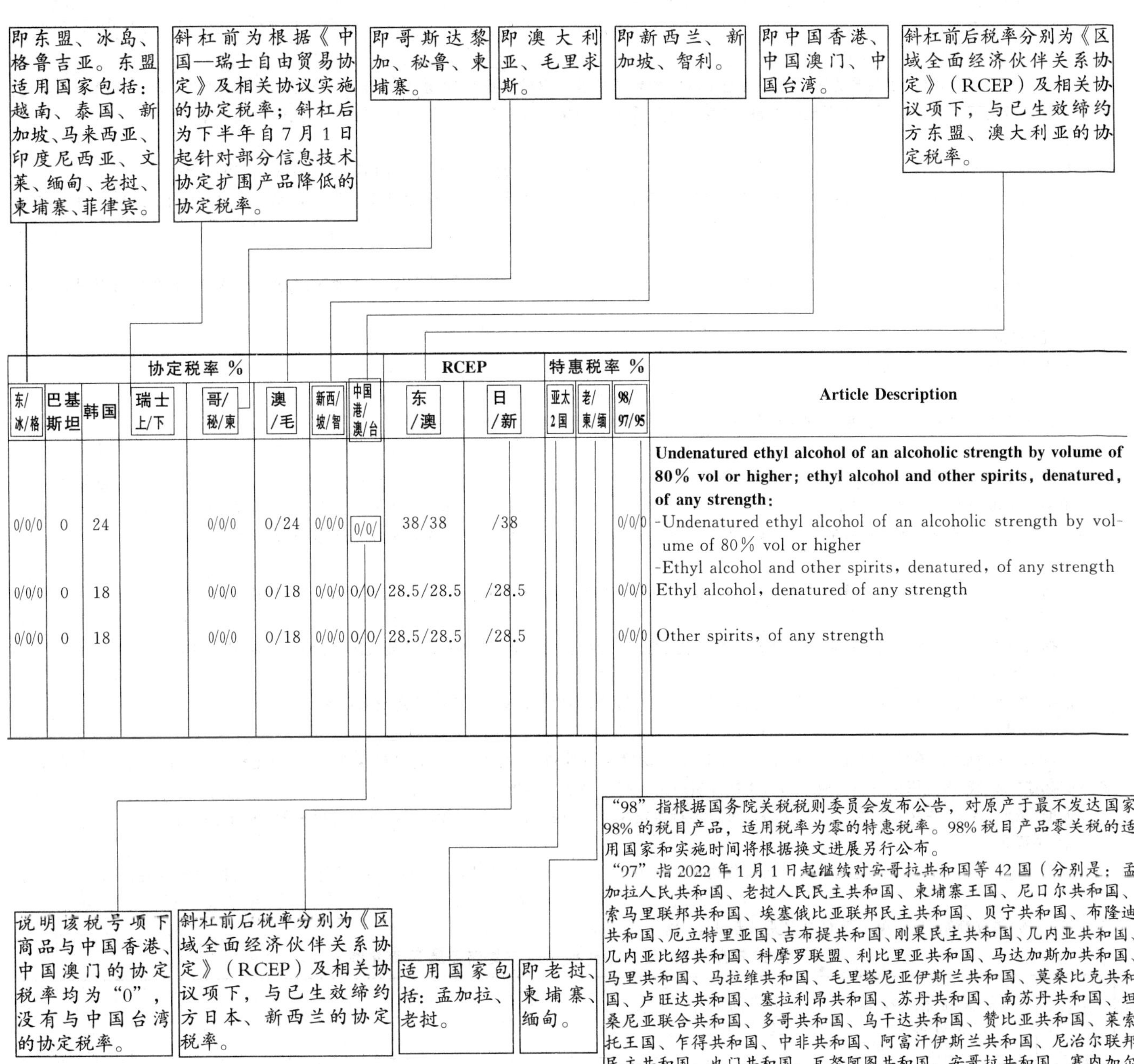

协定税率 %								RCEP		特惠税率 %			Article Description
东/冰/格	巴基斯坦	韩国	瑞士上/下	哥/秘/柬	澳/毛	新西/坡/智	中国港/澳/台	东/澳	日/新	亚太2国	老/柬/缅	98/97/95	
													Undenatured ethyl alcohol of an alcoholic strength by volume of 80% vol or higher; ethyl alcohol and other spirits, denatured, of any strength:
0/0/0	0	24		0/0/0	0/24	0/0/0	0/0/	38/38	/38			0/0/0	-Undenatured ethyl alcohol of an alcoholic strength by volume of 80% vol or higher
													-Ethyl alcohol and other spirits, denatured, of any strength
0/0/0	0	18		0/0/0	0/18	0/0/0	0/0/	28.5/28.5	/28.5			0/0/0	Ethyl alcohol, denatured of any strength
0/0/0	0	18		0/0/0	0/18	0/0/0	0/0/	28.5/28.5	/28.5			0/0/0	Other spirits, of any strength

税率适用说明

一、进口税则

进口税则商品分类目录采用《商品名称及编码协调制度》。进口税则税目税率设置税则号列、货品中文名称、最惠国税率、普通税率、增值税税率、出口退税率、计量单位、监管条件、货品英文名称等栏目。

(一)正文税率使用说明

1. 最惠国税率

根据《条例》规定,原产于共同适用最惠国待遇条款的世界贸易组织成员的进口货物,原产于与中华人民共和国签订含有互给予最惠国待遇条款的双边贸易协定的国家或者地区的进口货物,以及原产于中华人民共和国境内的进口货物,适用最惠国税率。

2. 暂定税率

根据《条例》规定,适用最惠国税率、协定税率、特惠税率、关税配额税率的进口货物在一定期限内可以实行暂定税率。

适用最惠国税率、协定税率、特惠税率的进口货物有暂定税率的,应当从低适用税率;适用关税配额税率的进口货物有暂定税率的,应当适用暂定税率。适用普通税率的进口货物,不适用暂定税率。

3. 普通税率

根据《条例》规定,原产于除适用最惠国税率、协定税率、特惠税率国家或地区以外的国家或者地区的进口货物,以及原产地不明的进口货物,适用普通税率。

4. 增值税税率

海关代征的进口货物法定增值税税率,栏目空白时为免征。

5.消费税率

进口环节海关代征的消费税率,依照《消费税暂行条例》所附的《消费税税目税率表》执行。

6.出口退税率

国家为鼓励出口对出口商品已征收的国内税部分或全部退还给出口企业的税率。本书收录截止到 2021 年 12 月前实施的退税率。因出口税率在年度内调整频繁,所以本书所列出口退税率仅供企业参考,若年度内出口税率有调整,请参照最新出台的税率政策。其中部分税号项下存在同一税号退税率不一致的情况,退税率一栏会出现一个或以上退税率,按商品不同情况分别退税。

7. 协定税率

根据我国与有关国家或地区签署的贸易或关税优惠协定,对有关国家或地区实施协定税率。具体见图例说明。

8. 特惠税率

根据我国与有关国家或地区签署的贸易或关税优惠协定,双边换文情况,以及国务院有关决定,对相关国家实施特惠税率。

9. 配额税率

根据《条例》规定,按照国家规定实行关税配额管理的进口货物,关税配额内的,适用关税配额税率。

二、出口税则

出口税则的商品分类目录与进口税则相同。出口税则设置税则号列、货品中文名称、出口税率、出口暂定税率、货品英文名称等栏目。税号前标注“ex”,表示适用该税率的应税出口货物以货品名称栏中的描述为准。

根据《条例》规定,对出口货物在一定期限内可以实行暂定税率;适用出口税率的出口货物有暂定税率的,应当适用暂定税率。

三、关税减免

特定地区、特定企业或者特定用途的进出口货物减征或者免征关税的,以及其他依法减征或者免征关税的,按照国务院的有关规定执行。

四、2022 年反倾销、反补贴商品对应海关商品编号调整

2022 年反倾销、反补贴商品对应海关商品编号调整表

序号	海关商品编号(2021 年)	海关商品编号(2022 年)	商品名称
1	3907209010	3907299010	聚 2,6－二甲基－1,4－苯醚(包括化学改性或物理改性 的)
2	7318140001	7318140001 9021100010 9021290010	钢铁制自攻螺钉(不包括不锈钢紧固件)
3	7318151001	7318151001 9021100020 9021290020	抗拉强度≥800 兆帕,杆径＞6mm 的其他钢铁制螺钉及螺栓(不包括不锈钢紧固件)
4	7318159001	7318159001 9021100030 9021290030	杆径＞6mm 的其他钢铁制螺钉及螺栓(不包括不锈钢紧固件)
5	7318220001	7318220001 9021100040 9021290040	钢铁制垫圈(不包括不锈钢紧固件)(不包括弹簧垫圈及其他防松垫圈)

编者按

为方便海关等有关管理部门、从事进出口的企业、报关企业、预录入企业和其他单位及个人了解最新的进出口税则税率、进口环节代征税税率和海关监管条件，准确地将外贸单证中的英文商品名称翻译成规范的中文名称，及时办理报关手续，我们编写了2022版《中华人民共和国海关进出口税则》(中英文对照版)(以下简称《税则》)。

2022版《税则》内容根据国务院关税税则委员会2022年最新调整的进出口关税税率编制而成。2022年1月1日起，我国将对954项商品实施低于最惠国税率的进口暂定税率。2022年1月1日起，根据国内产业发展和供需情况变化，在我国加入世界贸易组织承诺范围内，提高部分商品进出口关税。2022年7月1日起，我国还将对62项信息技术产品的最惠国税率实施第七步降税。调整后我国关税总水平继续维持7.4%。协定税率方面，根据我国与有关国家或地区签署的自贸协定和优惠贸易安排，2022年将对原产于29个国家或地区的部分商品实施协定税率。其中，《区域全面经济伙伴关系协定》(RCEP)、中国—柬埔寨自贸协定自2022年1月1日起生效并实施降税。2022年继续对与我国建交并完成换文手续的最不发达国家实施特惠税率。此外，根据世界海关组织修订的《商品名称及编码协调制度》内容及世界贸易组织有关规则，2022年还将对税则税目税率进行技术性转换。

我们对上述变化涉及的最新税率及商品编码等进行了认真修订。在此基础上，为了便于读者使用，我们还增加了检验检疫CIQ扩展编码及品名，收录了“进口反倾销、反补贴税清单”、《进出口商品规范申报目录》等。此外，还对增值税、退税税率，以及最新对美关税税率进行了修改和补充。

由于作者水平的限制和时间仓促，本书不足之处在所难免，恳请社会各界和广大读者批评指正。其中不准确和不全面之处敬请以发布的规范性文件为准！

Editor's Note

Aiming at assisting Customs and other governing bodies, enterprises participating import and export, Customs brokers, other trading partners and persons to query up-to-date tariff rates, other rates related to import and Custom supervision conditions, translate English commodity names in trade documents into standard Chinese names and go through declaring procedures to Customs, this Press compiles this Customs Import and Export Tariff of the People's Republic of China (Chinese-English Version , referred to as Chinese-English Tariff later)

2022 Tariff Regulations are prepared according to the latest adjusted import and export tariff rate in 2022 by the Tariff Commission of the State Council. From January 1, 2022, China will implement a provisional import tax rate lower than the MFN tax rate for 954 commodities. From January 1, 2022, according to the changes of domestic industrial development and supply and demand, the import and export tariffs of some commodities will be increased within the scope of China's commitment to join the world trade organization. From July 1, 2022, China will also implement the seventh step of tax reduction on the MFN tax rate of 62 information technology products. After adjustment, China's total tariff level will continue to maintain 7.4%. In terms of agreed tax rate, according to the free trade agreements and preferential trade arrangements signed between China and relevant countries or regions, the agreed tax rate will be implemented on some commodities originating from 29 countries or regions in 2022. Among them, The regional comprehensive economic partnership agreement (RCEP) and the China Cambodia free trade agreement will enter into force on January 1, 2022 and implement tax reduction. In 2022, preferential tax rates will continue to be implemented for the least developed countries that have established diplomatic relations with China and completed the exchange of letters. In addition, according to the Harmonized Commodity and Code System (HS) revised by the world customs organization Contents and relevant rules of the world trade organization. In 2022, technical conversion of tax items and tax rates will be carried out.

We have carefully revised the latest tax rates and HS codes involved in these changes. On this basis, in order to facilitate the reader's use, we have also added the CIQ expansion code and the article Description , including the "import anti—dumping, countervailing duty list" and the " Index Catalogue on Essential Standard Data Required by China Customs for the Declaration of Import and Export Goods ", etc.In addition, VAT, rebate rates and the latest US to China tariff rates have been revised and supplemented.

Due to limits of time and the knowledge of the author, some weaknesses in this book should be inevitable. Here I am open to readers' corrections and comments with great sincerity. If there is any inaccuracy and inadequacy, the official documents prevail.

总目录

Table of Contents

1

中华人民共和国海关进口税则

（2022 年 1 月 1 日起实施）

Customs Import Tariff of the People's Republic of China

（Enforced from January 1，2022）

目　录

INDEX

归类总规则

货品在本税则目录上的归类，应遵循以下原则：

规则一 类、章及分章的标题，仅为查找方便而设；具有法律效力的归类，应按税目条文和有关类注或章注确定，如税目、类注或章注无其他规定，按以下规则确定。

规则二 （一）税目所列货品，应视为包括该项货品的不完整品或未制成品，只要在报验时该项不完整品或未制成品具有完整品或制成品的基本特征；还应视为包括该项货品的完整品或制成品（或按本款可作为完整品或制成品归类的货品）在报验时的未组装件或拆散件。

（二）税目中所列材料或物质，应视为包括该种材料或物质与其他材料或物质混合或组合的物品。税目所列某种材料或物质构成的货品，应视为包括全部或部分由该种材料或物质构成的货品。由一种以上材料或物质构成的货品，应按规则三归类。

规则三 当货品按规则二（二）或由于其他原因看起来可归入两个或两个以上税目时，应按以下规则归类：

（一）列名比较具体的税目，优先于列名一般的税目。但是，如果两个或两个以上税目都仅述及混合或组合货品所含的某部分材料或物质，或零售的成套货品中的某些货品，即使其中某个税目对该货品描述得更为全面、详细，这些货品在有关税目的列名应视为同样具体。

（二）混合物、不同材料构成或不同部件组成的组合物以及零售的成套货品，如果不能按照规则三（一）归类时，在本款可适用的条件下，应按构成货品基本特征的材料或部件归类。

（三）货品不能按照规则三（一）或（二）归类时，应按号列顺序归入其可归入的最末一个税目。

规则四 根据上述规则无法归类的货品，应归入与其最相类似的货品的税目。

规则五 除上述规则外，本规则适用于下列货品的归类：

（一）制成特殊形状，适用于盛装某个或某套物品并适合长期使用的照相机套、乐器盒、枪套、绘图仪器盒、项链盒及类似容器，如果与所装物品同时报验，并通常与所装物品一同出售的，应与所装物品一并归类。但本款不适用于本身构成整个货品基本特征的容器。

（二）除规则五（一）规定的以外，与所装货品同时报验的包装材料或包装容器，如果通常是用来包装这类货品的，应与所装货品一并归类。但明显可重复使用的包装材料和包装容器可不受本款限制。

规则六 货品在某一税目项下各子目的法定归类，应按子目条文或有关的子目注释以及以上各条规则来确定，但子目的比较只能在同一数级上进行。除本税则目录条文另有规定的以外，有关的类注、章注也适用于本规则。

第一类
活动物；动物产品

注释：

一、本类所称的各属种动物，除条文另有规定的以外，均包括其幼仔在内。

二、除条文另有规定的以外，本协调制度所称干的产品，均包括经脱水、蒸发或冷冻干燥的产品。

第一章
活 动 物

注释：

本章包括所有活动物，但下列各项除外：

一、税目 03.01、03.06、03.07 或 03.08 的鱼、甲壳动物、软体动物及其他水生无脊椎动物；

二、税目 30.02 的培养微生物及其他产品；

三、税目 95.08 的动物。

GENERAL RULES FOR THE INTERPRETATION OF THE HARMONIZED SYSTEM

Classification of goods in the Nomenclature shall be governed by the following Ruks:

1. The titles of Sections, Chapters and sub-Chapters are provided for easeof reference only; for legal purposes, classification shall be determined according to the terms of the headings and any relative Section or Chapter Notes andprovided such headings or Notes do not otherwise require, according to the following provisions.
2. (a) Any reference in a heading to an article shall be taken to include a reference to that article incomplete or unfinished, provided that, as presented, the incomplete or unfinished article has the essential character of the complete or finished article. It shall also be taken to include a reference to that article complete or finished (or falling to be classified as complete or finished by virtue of this Rule), presented unassembled or disassembled.

   (b) Any reference in a heading to a material or substance shall be taken toinclude a reference to mixtures or combinations of that material or substance with other materials or substances. Any reference to goods of a given material or-substance shall be taken to include a reference to goods consisting wholly or partly of such material or substance. The classification of goods consisting ofmore than one material or substance shall be according to the principles of Rule3.
3. When by application of Rule 2(b) or for any other reason, goods are, *prima facie*, classifiable under two or more headings, classification shall beeffected as follows:

   (a) The heading which provides the most specific description shall be preferred to headings providing a more general description. However, when two or moreheadings each refer to part only of the materials or substances contained in mixed or composite goods or to part only of the items in a set put up for retail sale, those headings are to be regarded as equally specific in relation to thosegoods, even if one of them gives a more complete or precise description of the goods.

   (b) Mixtures, composite goods consisting of different materials or made up of different components, and goods put up in sets for retail sale, which cannot be classified by reference to Rule 3(a), shall be classified as they consisted of the material or component which gives them their essential character, insofar as this criterion is applicable.

   (c) When goods cannot be classified by reference to Rule 3(a) or Rule 3(b), they shall be classified under the heading which occurs last in numerical order among those which equally merit consideration.
4. Goods which cannot be classified in accordance with the above Rules shall be classified under the heading appropriate to the goods to which they are most akin.
5. In addition to the foregoing Rules, the following Rules shall applyin respect of the goods referred to therein:

   (a) Camera cases, musical instrument cases, gun cases, drawing instrument cases, necklace cases and similar containers, specially shaped or fitted to contain a specific article or set of articles, suitable for long-term use and presented with the articles for which they are intended, shall be classified with sucharticles when of a kind normally sold therewith. This Rule does not, however, apply to containers which give the whole its essential character;

   (b) Subject to the provisions of Rule 5(a) above, packing materials and packing containers presented with the goods therein shall be classified with the goods if they are of a kind normally used for packing such goods. However, this provision is not binding when such packing matcrials or packing containers are clearly suitable for repetitive use.
6. For legal purposes, the classification of goods in the subheadings of aheading shall be determined according to the terms of those subheadings and anyrelated Subheading Notes and, *mutatis mutandis*, to the above Rules, on the understanding that only subheadings at the same level are comparable. For the purposes of this Rule the relative Section and Chapter Notes also apply, unless the context otherwise requires.

SECTION I
LIVE ANIMALS; ANIMAL PRODUCTS

Notes:

1. Any reference in this Section to a particular genus or species of ananimal, except where the context otherwise requires, includes a reference to theyoung of that genus or species.
2. Except where the context otherwise requires, throughout the Nomenclature any reference to "dried" products also covers products which have beendehydrated, evaporated or freeze-dried.

Chapter 1
Live animals

Notes:

This Chapter covers all live animals except:

1. Fish and crustaceans, molluscs and other aquatic invertebrates, of heading No. 03. 01, 03. 06, 03. 07 or 03. 08
2. Cultures of micro-organisms and other products of heading No. 30. 02;
3. Animals of heading No. 95. 08.

税则号列	货品名称〔CIQ扩展编码及品名－T2表示见附表2〕	最惠(%)	暂定税率	普通	增值/消费	出口退税	计量单位	监管条件/特殊证件	检验检疫	对美关税	亚太上/下
01.01	马、驴、骡：										
	-马：										
0101.2100	--改良种用										
0101.2100 10	改良种用的濒危野马〔999〕	0		0	9/	0	千克/头	AFEB/	PQ		
0101.2100 90	改良种用马(濒危野马除外)〔999〕	0		0	0/	9	千克/头	AB/	PQ		
0101.2900	--其他										
0101.2900 10	非改良种用濒危野马〔999〕	10		30	9/	0	千克/头	AFEB/	PQ	40	
0101.2900 90	非改良种用其他马〔101屠宰马，102赛马，103其他用途马〕	10		30	9/	9	千克/头	AB/	PQ	40	
	-驴：										
0101.3010	---改良种用										
0101.3010 10	改良种用的濒危野驴〔999〕	0		0	9/	0	千克/头	AFEB/	PQ		
0101.3010 90	改良种用驴(濒危野驴除外)〔999〕	0		0	0/	9	千克/头	AB/	PQ		
0101.3090	---其他										
0101.3090 10	非改良种用濒危野驴〔999〕	10		30	9/	0	千克/头	AFEB/	PQ	12.5	
0101.3090 90	非改良种用其他驴〔999〕	10		30	9/	9	千克/头	AB/	PQ	12.5	
0101.9000	-其他〔999〕	10		30	9/	9	千克/头	AB/	PQ	12.5	
01.02	牛：										
	-家牛：										
0102.2100	--改良种用〔101种牛，102屠宰牛，103其他用途牛〕	0		0	0/	9	千克/头	AB/	PQ		
0102.2900	--其他〔101种牛，102屠宰牛，103其他用途牛〕	10		30	9/	9	千克/头	4xAB/	PQ	12.5	
	-水牛：										
0102.3100	--改良种用										
0102.3100 10	改良种用濒危水牛〔999〕	0		0	9/	0	千克/头	ABEF/	PQ		
0102.3100 90	改良种用水牛(濒危水牛除外)〔999〕	0		0	0/	9	千克/头	AB/	PQ		
0102.3900	--其他										
0102.3900 10	非改良种用濒危水牛〔999〕	10		30	9/	0	千克/头	4ABEFx/	PQ	12.5	
0102.3900 90	非改良种用其他水牛〔999〕	10		30	9/	9	千克/头	4ABx/	PQ	12.5	
	-其他：										
0102.9010	---改良种用										
0102.9010 10	改良种用濒危野牛〔999〕	0		0	9/	0	千克/头	AFEB/	PQ		
0102.9010 90	其他改良种用牛〔101种牛，102屠宰牛，103其他用途牛，104水牛，105牦牛〕	0		0	9/	9	千克/头	AB/	PQ		
0102.9090	---其他										
0102.9090 10	非改良种用濒危野牛〔999〕	10		30	9/	0	千克/头	4xABFE/	PQ	12.5	
0102.9090 90	非改良种用其他牛〔101种牛，102屠宰牛，103其他用途牛，104水牛，105牦牛〕	10		30	9/	9	千克/头	4xAB/	PQ	12.5	
01.03	猪：										
0103.1000	-改良种用										
0103.1000 10	改良种用的鹿豚、姬猪〔999〕	0		0	9/	9	千克/头	AFEB/	PQ		
0103.1000 90	改良种用猪(鹿豚、姬猪除外)〔999〕	0		0	0/	9	千克/头	AB/	PQ		
	-其他：										
	--重量在50千克以下：										
0103.9110	---重量在10千克以下										
0103.9110 10	重量在10千克以下的其他野猪(改良种用的除外)〔999〕	10		50	9/	9	千克/头	4xABFE/	PRQ	12.5	
0103.9110 90	重量在10千克以下的其他猪(改良种用的除外)〔101屠宰猪，102其他用途猪〕	10		50	9/	9	千克/头	4xAB/	PRQ	12.5	
0103.9120	---重量在10千克及以上，但在50千克以下										
0103.9120 10	10千克≤重量＜50千克的其他野猪(改良种用的除外)〔999〕	10		50	9/	9	千克/头	4xABFE/	PRQ	12.5	
0103.9120 90	10千克≤重量＜50千克的其他猪(改良种用的除外)〔101屠宰猪；102其他用途猪〕	10		50	9/	9	千克/头	4xAB/	PRQ	12.5	
0103.9200	--重量在50千克及以上										
0103.9200 10	重量在50千克及以上的其他野猪(改良种用的除外)〔999〕	10		50	9/	9	千克/头	4xABFE/	PRQ	12.5	
0103.9200 90	重量在50千克及以上的其他猪(改良种用的除外)〔101屠宰猪，102其他用途猪〕	10		50	9/	9	千克/头	4xAB/	PRQ	12.5	
01.04	绵羊、山羊：										
	-绵羊：										
0104.1010	---改良种用绵羊〔999〕	0		0	0/	9	千克/头	AB/	PQ		
0104.1090	---其他〔101屠宰绵羊，102其他用途绵羊〕	10		50	9/	9	千克/头	AB/	PRQ	12.5	
	-山羊：										
0104.2010	---改良种用〔101种山羊，102种野山羊〕	0		0	0/	9	千克/头	AB/	PQ		
0104.2090	---其他〔101屠宰山羊，102其他用途山羊，103屠宰野山羊，104其他用途野山羊〕	10		50	9/	9	千克/头	AB/	PQ	12.5	
01.05	家禽，即鸡、鸭、鹅、火鸡及珍珠鸡：										

协定税率 %								RCEP		特惠税率 %			Article Description
东/冰/格	巴基斯坦	韩国	瑞士 上/下	哥/秘/柬	澳/毛	新西/坡/智	中国港/澳/台	东盟及马来/澳/韩	日/新	亚太2国	老/柬/缅	98/97/95	
													Live horses, asses, mules and hinnies:
													-Horses:
													--Pure-bred breeding
0/0/0	0	0	0/0	0/0/0	0/0	0//0	0/0/	0/0/0	0/0			0/0/0	Endangered wild horses, pure-bred breeding
0/0/0	0	0	0/0	0/0/0	0/0	0//0	0/0/	0/0/0	0/0			0/0/0	Other horses, pure-bred breeding
													--Other
0/0/0	3.5	2	0/0	0/0/0	0/0	0//0	0/0/	0/0/9	9.1/0			0/0/0	Endangered wild horses, not for breeding
0/0/0	3.5	2	0/0	0/0/0	0/0	0//0	0/0/	0/0/9	9.1/0			0/0/0	Other horses, not for breeding
													-Asses:
													---Pure-bred breeding
0/0/0	0	0	0/0	0/0/0	0/0	0//0	0/0/	0/0/0	0/0			0/0/0	Endangered wild asses, pure-bred breeding
0/0/0	0	0	0/0	0/0/0	0/0	0//0	0/0/	0/0/0	0/0			0/0/0	Other asses, pure-bred breeding
													---Other
0/0/0	3.5	2	0/0	0/0/0	0/0	0//0	0/0/	0/0/9	9.1/0			0/0/0	Endangered wild asses, not for breeding
0/0/0	3.5	2	0/0	0/0/0	0/0	0//0	0/0/	0/0/9	9.1/0			0/0/0	Other asses, not for breeding
0/0/0	3.5	2	0/0	0/0/0	0/0	0//0	0/0/	0/0/9	9.1/0			0/0/0	-Other
													Live bovine animals:
													-Cattle:
0/0/0	0	0	0/0	0/0/0	0/0	0//0	0/0/	0/0/0	0/0			0/0/0	--Pure-bred breeding
0/0/0	3.5	2	0/0	0/0/0	0/0	0//0	0/0/	0/0/9	9.1/0		0/0/0	0/0/0	--Other
													-Buffalo:
													--Pure-bred breeding
0/0/0	0	0	0/0	0/0/0	0/0	0//0	0/0/	0/0/0	0/0			0/0/0	Endangered buffalo, pure-bred breeding
0/0/0	0	0	0/0	0/0/0	0/0	0//0	0/0/	0/0/0	0/0			0/0/0	Other buffalo, prue-bred breeding
													--Other
0/0/0	3.5	2	0/0	0/0/0	0/0	0//0	0/0/	0/0/9	9.1/0		0/0/0	0/0/0	Endangered buffalo, not for breeding
0/0/0	3.5	2	0/0	0/0/0	0/0	0//0	0/0/	0/0/9	9.1/0		0/0/0	0/0/0	Other buffalo, not for breeding
													-Other:
													---Pure-bred breeding
0/0/0	0	0	0/0	0/0/0	0/0	0//0	0/0/	0/0/0	0/0			0/0/0	Endangered wild bovine, pure-bred breeding
0/0/0	0	0	0/0	0/0/0	0/0	0//0	0/0/	0/0/0	0/0			0/0/0	Other bovine pure-bred breeding
													---Other
0/0/0	3.5	2	0/0	0/0/0	0/0	0//0	0/0/	0/0/9	9.1/0		0/0/0	0/0/0	Endangered wild bovine, not for breeding
0/0/0	3.5	2	0/0	0/0/0	0/0	0//0	0/0/	0/0/9	9.1/0		0/0/0	0/0/0	Other bovine not for breeding
													Live swine:
													-Pure-bred breeding
0/0/0	0	0	0/0	0/0/0	0/0	0//0	0/0/	0/0/0	0/0			0/0/0	Pig-deer (*Babyrousa*)、pygmy pig (*Porcula*), pure-bred breeding
0/0/0	0	0	0/0	0/0/0	0/0	0//0	0/0/	0/0/0	0/0			0/0/0	Other swine, pure-bred breeding
													-Other:
													--Weighing less than 50kg:
													---Weighing less than 10kg
0/0/0	3.5	2	0/0	0/0/0	0/0	0//0	0/0/	0/0/9	9.1/0		/0/0	0/0/0	Other wild swine, weighing＜10kg (other than pure-bred breeding)
0/0/0	3.5	2	0/0	0/0/0	0/0	0//0	0/0/	0/0/9	9.1/0		/0/0	0/0/0	Other swine, weighing＜10kg (other than pure-bred breeding)
													---Weighing 10kg or more, but less than 50kg
0/0/0	3.5	2	0/0	0/0/0	0/0	0//0	0/0/	0/0/9	9.1/0		/0/0	0/0/0	Other wild swine, 10kg≤weighing＜50kg (other than pure-bred breeding)
0/0/0	3.5	2	0/0	0/0/0	0/0	0//0	0/0/	0/0/9	9.1/0		/0/0	0/0/0	Other swine, 10kg≤weighing＜50kg (other than pure-bred breeding)
													--Weighing 50kg or more
0/0/0	3.5	2	0/0	0/0/0	0/0	0//0	0/0/	0/0/9	9.1/0		0/0/0	0/0/0	Other wild swine, weighing≥50kg (other than pure-bred breeding)
0/0/0	3.5	2	0/0	0/0/0	0/0	0//0	0/0/	0/0/9	9.1/0		0/0/0	0/0/0	Other swine, weighing≥50kg (other than pure-bred breeding)
													Live sheep and goats:
													-Sheep:
0/0/0	0	0	0/0	0/0/0	0/0	0//0	0/0/	0/0/0	0/0			0/0/0	---Pure-bred breeding
0/0/0	5	2	0/0	0/0/0	0/0	0//0	0/0/	0/0/9	9.1/0			0/0/0	---Other
													-Goats:
0/0/0	0	0	0/0	0/0/0	0/0	0//0	0/0/	0/0/0	0/0			0/0/0	---Pure-bred breeding
0/0/0	5	2	0/0	0/0/0	0/0	0//0	0/0/	0/0/9	9.1/0			0/0/0	---Other
													Live poultry, that is to say, fowls of the species *Gallus domesticus*, ducks, geese, turkeys and guinea fowls:

税则号列	货品名称〔CIQ 扩展编码及品名－T2 表示见附表 2〕	最惠(%)	暂定税率	普通	增值/消费	出口退税	计量单位	监管条件/特殊证件	检验检疫	对美关税	亚太上/下
	-重量不超过 185 克：										
	--鸡：										
0105.1110	---改良种用〔101 肉种鸡，102 蛋种鸡〕	0		0	0/	9	千克/只	AB/	PQ		
0105.1190	---其他〔101 屠宰鸡，102 其他用途鸡〕	10		50	9/	9	千克/只	AB/	PRQ	12.5	
	--火鸡：										
0105.1210	---改良种用〔999〕	0		0	0/	9	千克/只	AB/	PQ		
0105.1290	---其他〔999〕	10		50	9/	9	千克/只	AB/	PRQ	12.5	
	--鸭：										
0105.1310	---改良种用〔999〕	0		0	0/	9	千克/只	AB/	PQ		
0105.1390	---其他〔999〕	10		50	9/	9	千克/只	AB/	PRQ	12.5	
	--鹅：										
0105.1410	---改良种用〔999〕	0		0	0/	9	千克/只	AB/	PQ		
0105.1490	---其他〔999〕	10		50	9/	9	千克/只	AB/	PRQ	12.5	
	--珍珠鸡：										
0105.1510	---改良种用〔999〕	0		0	0/	9	千克/只	AB/	PQ		
0105.1590	---其他〔999〕	10		50	9/	9	千克/只	AB/	PRQ	12.5	
	-其他：										
	--鸡：										
0105.9410	---改良种用〔101 肉种鸡，102 蛋种鸡〕	0		0	0/	9	千克/只	4xAB/	PQ		
0105.9490	---其他〔101 屠宰鸡，102 其他用途鸡〕	10		50	9/	9	千克/只	4xAB/	PRQ	12.5	
	--其他：										
0105.9910	---改良种用〔101 珍珠鸡，102 其他饲养鸡形目禽鸟，103 鹅，104 鸭，105 其他饲养雁形目禽鸟，106 鸽，107 其他饲养禽鸟〕	0		0	0/	9	千克/只	AB/	PQ		
	---其他：										
0105.9991	----鸭〔999〕	10		50	9/	9	千克/只	AB/	PQ	12.5	
0105.9992	----鹅〔999〕	10		50	9/	9	千克/只	AB/	PQ	12.5	
0105.9993	----珍珠鸡〔999〕	10		50	9/	9	千克/只	4xAB/	PQ	12.5	
0105.9994	----火鸡〔999〕	10		50	9/	9	千克/只	AB/	PQ	12.5	
01.06	**其他活动物：**										
	-哺乳动物：										
	--灵长目：										
0106.1110	---改良种用〔101 猴，102 猿，103 猩猩，104 狒狒，105 山魈，106 其他野生灵长动物〕	0		0	9/	9	千克/只	AFEB/	PQ		
0106.1190	---其他〔101 猴，102 猿，103 猩猩，104 狒狒，105 山魈，106 其他野生灵长动物〕	10		50	9/	9	千克/只	AFEB/	PQ	12.5	
	--鲸、海豚及鼠海豚(鲸目哺乳动物)；海牛及儒艮(海牛目哺乳动物)；海豹、海狮及海象(鳍足亚目哺乳动物)：										
	---鲸、海豚及鼠海豚(鲸目哺乳动物)；海牛及儒艮(海牛目哺乳动物)：										
0106.1211	----改良种用〔101 海豚，102 鲸，103 海牛，104 其他野生哺乳动物〕	10	0	50	9/	9	千克/只	AFEB/	PQ		
0106.1219	----其他〔101 海豚，102 鲸，103 海牛，104 其他野生哺乳动物〕	10		50	9/	9	千克/只	AFEB/	PQ	12.5	
	---海豹、海狮及海象(鳍足亚目哺乳动物)：										
0106.1221	----改良种用〔101 海豹，102 海狮，103 海象，104 其他野生哺乳动物〕	0		0	9/	9	千克/只	AFEB/	PQ		
0106.1229	----其他〔102 海狮，101 海豹，103 海象，104 其他野生哺乳动物〕	10		50	9/	9	千克/只	ABEF/	PQ	12.5	
	--骆驼及其他骆驼科动物：										
0106.1310	---改良种用										
0106.1310 10	改良种用濒危骆驼及其他濒危骆驼科动物(包括人工驯养、繁殖的)〔101 骆驼，102 其他野生偶蹄动物〕	0		0	9/	0	千克/只	ABFE/	PQ		
0106.1310 90	改良种用骆驼及其他骆驼科动物(濒危骆驼及其他濒危骆驼科动物除外)〔101 骆驼，102 其他饲养偶蹄动物〕	0		0	0/	9	千克/只	AB/	PQ		
0106.1390	---其他										
0106.1390 10	其他濒危骆驼及其他濒危骆驼科动物(包括人工驯养、繁殖的)〔101 骆驼，102 其他饲养偶蹄动物〕	10		50	9/	0	千克/只	AFEB/	PRQ	12.5	
0106.1390 90	其他骆驼及其他骆驼科动物〔101 骆驼，102 其他饲养偶蹄动物〕	10		50	9/	9	千克/只	AB/	PRQ	12.5	
	--家兔及野兔：										
0106.1410	---改良种用										
0106.1410 10	改良种用濒危野兔(包括人工驯养、繁殖的)〔999〕	0		0	9/	0	千克/只	ABEF/	PQ		
0106.1410 90	改良种用家兔及野兔(濒危除外)〔999〕	0		0	0/	9	千克/只	AB/	PQ		
0106.1490	---其他										

协定税率 %								RCEP		特惠税率 %			Article Description
东/冰/格	巴基斯坦	韩国	瑞士上/下	哥/秘/柬	澳/毛	新西/坡/智	中国港/澳/台	东盟及马来/澳/韩	日/新	亚太2国	老/柬/缅	98/97/95	
													-Weighing not more than 185g:
													--Fowls of the species *Gallus domesticus*:
0/0/0	0	0	0/0	0/0/0	0/0	0//0	0/0/	0/0/0	0/0			0/0/0	---Pure-bred breeding
0/0/0	3.5	2	0/0	0/0/0	0/0	0//0	0/0/	0/0/9	9.1/0		0//0	0/0/0	---Other
													--Turkeys:
0/0/0	0	0	0/0	0/0/0	0/0	0//0	0/0/	0/0/0	0/0			0/0/0	---Pure-bred breeding
0/0/0	3.5	2	0/0	0/0/0	0/0	0//0	0/0/	0/0/9	9.1/0			0/0/0	---Other
													--Ducks:
0/0/0	0	0	0/0	0/0/0	0/0	0//0	0/0/	0/0/0	0/0			0/0/0	---Pure-bred breeding
0/0/0	3.5	2	0/0	0/0/0	0/0	0//0	0/0/	0/0/9	9.1/0		0//	0/0/0	---Other
													--Geese:
0/0/0	0	0	0/0	0/0/0	0/0	0//0	0/0/	0/0/0	0/0			0/0/0	---Pure-bred breeding
0/0/0	3.5	2	0/0	0/0/0	0/0	0//0	0/0/	0/0/9	9.1/0		0//	0/0/0	---Other
													--Guinea fowls:
0/0/0	0	0	0/0	0/0/0	0/0	0//0	0/0/	0/0/0	0/0			0/0/0	---Pure-bred breeding
0/0/0	3.5	2	0/0	0/0/0	0/0	0//0	0/0/	0/0/9	9.1/0		0//	0/0/0	---Other
													-Other:
													--Fowls of the species *Gallus domesticus*:
0/0/0	0	0	0/0	0/0/0	0/0	0//0	0/0/	0/0/0	0/0			0/0/0	---Pure-bred breeding
0/0/0	3.5	2	0/0	0/0/0	0/0	0//0	0/0/	0/0/9	9.1/0			0/0/0	---Other
													--Other:
0/0/0	0	0	0/0	0/0/0	0/0	0//0	0/0/	0/0/0	0/0			0/0/0	---Pure-bred breeding
													---Other:
0/0/0	3.5	2	0/0	0/0/0	0/0	0//0	0/0/	0/0/9	9.1/0			0/0/0	----Ducks
0/0/0	3.5	2	0/0	0/0/0	0/0	0//0	0/0/	0/0/9	9.1/0			0/0/0	----Geese
0/0/0	3.5	2	0/0	0/0/0	0/0	0//0	0/0/	0/0/9	9.1/0			0/0/0	----Guinea fowls
0/0/0	3.5	2	0/0	0/0/0	0/0	0//0	0/0/	0/0/9	9.1/0			0/0/0	----Turkeys
													Other live animals:
													-Mammals:
													--Primates:
0/0/0	0	0	0/0	0/0/0	0/0	0//0	0/0/	0/0/0	0/0			0/0/0	---pure-bred breeding
0/0/0	3.5	2	0/0	0/0/0	0/0	0//0	0/0/	0/0/9	9.1/0			0/0/0	---Other
													--Whales, dolphins and porpoises (mammals of the order Cetacea); manatees and dugongs (mammals of the order Sirenia); seal、sea lion and walruses (mammals of the suborder Pinnipedia):
													---Whales, dolphins and porpoises (mammals of the order Cetacea); manatees and dugongs (mammals of the order Sirenia):
0/0/0	3.5	0	0/0	0/0/0	0/0	0//0	0/0/	0/0/0	/0			0/0/0	----Pure-bred breeding
0/0/0	3.5	2	0/0	0/0/0	0/0	0//0	0/0/	0/0/9	9.1/0			0/0/0	----Other
													---Seal、sea lion and walruses (mammals of the suborder Pinnipedia):
0/0/0	0	0	0/0	0/0/0	0/0	0//0	0/0/	0/0/0	0/0			0/0/0	----Pure-bred breeding
0/0/0	3.5	2	0/0	0/0/0	0/0	0//0	0/0/	0/0/9	9.1/0			0/0/0	----Other
													--Camel and other camelids (camelidae):
													---Pure-bred breeding
0/0/0	0	0	0/0	0/0/0	0/0	0//0	0/0/	0/0/0	0/0			0/0/0	Endangered camel and other endangered camel familia animals, pure-bred breeding (including domesticated and artificially bred)
0/0/0	0	0	0/0	0/0/0	0/0	0//0	0/0/	0/0/0	0/0			0/0/0	Other camel and other camel familia animals, pure-bred brdding
													---Other
0/0/0	3.5	2	0/0	0/0/0	0/0	0//0	0/0/	0/0/9	9.1/0			0/0/0	Endangered camel and other endangered camel familia animals (including domesticated and artificially bred)
0/0/0	3.5	2	0/0	0/0/0	0/0	0//0	0/0/	0/0/9	9.1/0			0/0/0	Other camel and other camel familia animals
													--Rabbits and hares:
													---Pure-bred breeding
0/0/0	0	0	0/0	0/0/0	0/0	0//0	0/0/	0/0/0	0/0			0/0/0	Endangered hares, pure-bred breeding (including donesticatd and artificiauy bred)
0/0/0	0	0	0/0	0/0/0	0/0	0//0	0/0/	0/0/0	0/0			0/0/0	Rabbits and Other hares, pure-bred breeding
													---Other

税则号列	货品名称〔CIQ扩展编码及品名—T2表示见附表2〕	最惠(%)	暂定税率	普通	增值/消费	出口退税	计量单位	监管条件/特殊证件	检验检疫	对美关税	亚太上/下
0106.1490 10	其他濒危野兔(包括人工驯养、繁殖的)〔999〕	10		50	9/	0	千克/只	AFEB/	PRQ	12.5	
0106.1490 90	其他家兔及野兔〔999〕	10		50	9/	9	千克/只	AB/	PRQ	12.5	
	--其他:										
0106.1910	---改良种用										
0106.1910 10	其他改良种用濒危哺乳动物(包括人工驯养、繁殖的)[T2]	0		0	9/	0	千克/只	ABFE/	PQ		
0106.1910 20	改良种用梅花鹿、马鹿、驯鹿、水貂、银狐、北极狐、貉(濒危除外)〔101 其他饲养偶蹄动物,102 其他饲养食肉动物〕	0		0	0/	9	千克/只	AB/	PQ		
0106.1910 90	其他改良种用哺乳动物[T2]	0		0	9/	9	千克/只	AB/	PQ		
0106.1990	---其他										
0106.1990 10	其他濒危哺乳动物(包括人工驯养、繁殖的)[T2]	10		50	9/	0	千克/只	AFEB/	PRQ	22.5	
0106.1990 90	其他哺乳动物[T2]	10		50	9/	9	千克/只	AB/	PRQ	22.5	
	-爬行动物(包括蛇及龟鳖):										
	---改良种用:										
0106.2011	----鳄鱼苗〔999〕	0		0	9/	9	千克/只	AFEB/	PQ		
0106.2019	----其他[T2]	0		0	9/	9	千克/只	FEAB/	PQ		
0106.2020	---食用										
0106.2020 10	食用蛇(包括人工驯养、繁殖的)〔999〕	10		50	9/	9	千克/只	AFEB/	PRQ	12.5	
0106.2020 21	食用濒危龟鳖(包括人工驯养、繁殖的)〔101 乌龟,102 草龟,103 绿毛龟,104 鳖(甲鱼、团鱼),105 玳瑁,106 鳄龟,107 其他龟鳖〕	10		50	9/	0	千克/只	ABFE/	PRQ	12.5	
0106.2020 29	其他食用龟鳖(包括人工驯养、繁殖的)〔101 乌龟,102 草龟,103 绿毛龟,104 鳖(甲鱼、团鱼),105 玳瑁,106 鳄龟,107 其他龟鳖〕	10		50	9/	9	千克/只	AB/	PRQ	12.5	
0106.2020 91	其他食用濒危爬行动物(包括人工驯养、繁殖的)〔999〕	10		50	9/	0	千克/只	FEAB/	PRQ	12.5	
0106.2020 99	其他食用爬行动物(包括人工驯养、繁殖的)〔999〕	10		50	9/	9	千克/只	AB/	PRQ	12.5	
0106.2090	---其他										
0106.2090 10	其他濒危爬行动物(包括人工驯养、繁殖的)〔999〕	10		50	9/	0	千克/只	FEAB/	PQ	22.5	
0106.2090 90	其他爬行动物(包括人工驯养、繁殖的)[T2]	10		50	9/	9	千克/只	AB/	PQ	22.5	
	-鸟:										
	--猛禽:										
0106.3110	---改良种用〔101 鹰,102 其他野生禽鸟〕	0		0	9/	9	千克/只	AFEB/	PQ		
0106.3190	---其他〔101 鹰,102 其他野生禽鸟〕	10		50	9/	9	千克/只	ABFE/	PQ	12.5	
	--鹦形目(包括普通鹦鹉、长尾鹦鹉、金刚鹦鹉及美冠鹦鹉):										
0106.3210	---改良种用[999]	0		0	9/	9	千克/只	ABFE/	PQ		
0106.3290	---其他[999]	10		50	9/	9	千克/只	ABFE/	PQ	12.5	
	--鸵鸟;鸸鹋:										
0106.3310	---改良种用										
0106.3310 10	改良种用濒危鸵鸟(包括人工驯养、繁殖的)〔999〕	0		0	9/	0	千克/只	ABFE/	PQ		
0106.3310 90	改良种用鸵鸟;鸸鹋(濒危鸵鸟除外)〔101 鸵鸟,102 鸸鹋〕	0		0	0/	9	千克/只	AB/	PQ		
0106.3390	---其他										
0106.3390 10	其他濒危鸵鸟(包括人工驯养、繁殖的)〔999〕	10		50	9/	0	千克/只	ABFE/	PRQ	12.5	
0106.3390 90	其他鸵鸟、鸸鹋〔101 鸵鸟,102 鸸鹋〕	10		50	9/	9	千克/只	AB/	PRQ	12.5	
	--其他:										
0106.3910	---改良种用										
0106.3910 10	其他改良种用濒危鸟(包括人工驯养、繁殖的)[T2]	0		0	9/	0	千克/只	ABFE/	PQ		
0106.3910 20	改良种用鸽、鹌鹑〔999〕	0		0	0/	9	千克/只	AB/	PQ		
0106.3910 90	其他改良种用的鸟〔999〕	0		0	9/	9	千克/只	AB/	PQ		
	---食用:										
0106.3921	----乳鸽〔999〕	10		50	9/	9	千克/只	AB/	PRQ	12.5	
0106.3923	----野鸭〔999〕	10		50	9/	9	千克/只	FEAB/	PRQ	12.5	
0106.3929	----其他										
0106.3929 10	其他食用濒危鸟(包括人工驯养、繁殖的)〔101 鹌鹑,102 鹧鸪,103 雉(山鸡),104 乌骨鸡,105 其他野生鸡形目禽鸟〕	10		50	9/	0	千克/只	ABFE/	PRQ	12.5	
0106.3929 90	其他食用鸟〔101 其他饲养鸡形目禽鸟,102 其他饲养雁形目禽鸟,103 其他饲养禽鸟〕	10		50	9/	9	千克/只	AB/	PRQ	12.5	
0106.3990	---其他										

协定税率 %								RCEP		特惠税率 %			Article Description
东/冰/格	巴基斯坦	韩国	瑞士上/下	哥/秘/柬	澳/毛	新西/坡/智	中国港/澳/台	东盟及马来/澳/韩	日/新	亚太2国	老/柬/缅	98/97/95	
0/0/0	3.5	2	0/0	0/0/0	0/0	0//0	0/0/	0/0/9	9.1/0			0/0/0	Other endangered hares(including domes ticatedandan tifi-ciauy bred)
0/0/0	3.5	2	0/0	0/0/0	0/0	0//0	0/0/	0/0/9	9.1/0			0/0/0	Other rabbits and hares
													--Other:
													---Pure-bred breeding
0/0/0	0	0	0/0	0/0/0	0/0	0//0	0/0/	0/0/0	0/0			0/0/0	Other endangered mammals, pure-bred breeding(including domesticated and artificially bred)
0/0/0	0	0	0/0	0/0/0	0/0	0//0	0/0/	0/0/0	0/0			0/0/0	Improved sika deer, red deer, reindeer, mink, silver fox, arctic fox and raccoon dog (except endangered)
0/0/0	0	0	0/0	0/0/0	0/0	0//0	0/0/	0/0/0	0/0			0/0/0	Other mammals, pure-bred breeding
													---Other
0/0/0	3.5	2	0/0	0/0/0	0/0	0//0	0/0/	0/0/9	9.1/0			0/0/0	Other endangered mammals, including domesticated and artificially bred
0/0/0	3.5	2	0/0	0/0/0	0/0	0//0	0/0/	0/0/9	9.1/0			0/0/0	Other mammals
													-Reptiles(including snakes and turtles):
													---Pure-bred breeding:
0/0/0	0	0	0/0	0/0/0	0/0	0//0	0/0/	0/0/0	0/0			0/0/0	----Crocodiles for cultivation
0/0/0	0	0	0/0	0/0/0	0/0	0//0	0/0/	0/0/0	0/0			0/0/0	----Other
													---For human consumption
0/0/0	3.5	2	0/0	0/0/0	0/0	0//0	0/0/	0/0/9	9.1/0		//0	0/0/0	Snakes, for human consumption(including domesticated and artificially bred)
0/0/0	3.5	2	0/0	0/0/0	0/0	0//0	0/0/	0/0/9	9.1/0		//0	0/0/0	Endangered turtle (including domestication and artificial breeding)
0/0/0	3.5	2	0/0	0/0/0	0/0	0//0	0/0/	0/0/9	9.1/0		//0	0/0/0	Other eating a turtle (including domestication and artificial breeding)
0/0/0	3.5	2	0/0	0/0/0	0/0	0//0	0/0/	0/0/9	9.1/0		//0	0/0/0	Other endangered reptiles, for human consumption (including domesticated and artificially propagated)
0/0/0	3.5	2	0/0	0/0/0	0/0	0//0	0/0/	0/0/9	9.1/0		//0	0/0/0	Other reptiles, for human consumption (including domesticated and artificially propagated)
													---Other
0/0/0	3.5	2	0/0	0/0/0	0/0	0//0	0/0/	0/0/9	9.1/0			0/0/0	Other endangered reptiles (including domesticated and artificially propagated)
0/0/0	3.5	2	0/0	0/0/0	0/0	0//0	0/0/	0/0/9	9.1/0			0/0/0	Other reptiles (including domesticated and artificially propagated)
													-Birds:
													--Birds of prey:
0/0/0	0	0	0/0	0/0/0	0/0	0//0	0/0/	0/0/0	0/0			0/0/0	---Pure-bred breeding
0/0/0	3.5	2	0/0	0/0/0	0/0	0//0	0/0/	0/0/9	9.1/0			0/0/0	---Other
													--Psittaciformes(including parrots, parakeets, macaws and cockatoos):
0/0/0	0	0	0/0	0/0/0	0/0	0//0	0/0/	0/0/0	0/0			0/0/0	---Pure bred breeding
0/0/0	3.5	2	0/0	0/0/0	0/0	0//0	0/0/	0/0/9	9.1/0			0/0/0	---Other
													--Ostriches;emus(Dromaius novaehollandiae):
													---Pure-bred breeding
0/0/0	0	0	0/0	0/0/0	0/0	0//0	0/0/	0/0/0	0/0			0/0/0	Endangered ostriches,pure-bred breeding(including domesticated and artificially bred)
0/0/0	0	0	0/0	0/0/0	0/0	0//0	0/0/	0/0/0	0/0			0/0/0	Other ostriches and emus,pure-bred breeding
													---Other
0/0/0	3.5	2	0/0	0/0/0	0/0	0//0	0/0/	0/0/9	9.1/0			0/0/0	Other endangered ostriches(including domesticated and artificially bred)
0/0/0	3.5	2	0/0	0/0/0	0/0	0//0	0/0/	0/0/9	9.1/0			0/0/0	Other ostriches and emus
													--Other:
													---Pure-bred breeding
0/0/0	0	0	0/0	0/0/0	0/0	0//0	0/0/	0/0/0	0/0			0/0/0	Other endangered birds, pure-bred breeding(including domesticated and artificially bred)
0/0/0	0	0	0/0	0/0/0	0/0	0//0	0/0/	0/0/0	0/0			0/0/0	Improved breeding pigeon and quail
0/0/0	0	0	0/0	0/0/0	0/0	0//0	0/0/	0/0/0	0/0			0/0/0	Other birds, pure-bred breeding
													---For human consumption:
0/0/0	3.5	2	0/0	0/0/0	0/0	0//0	0/0/	0/0/9	9.1/0		//0	0/0/0	----Squabs
0/0/0	3.5	2	0/0	0/0/0	0/0	0//0	0/0/	0/0/9	9.1/0		//0	0/0/0	----Teals
													----Other
0/0/0	3.5	2	0/0	0/0/0	0/0	0//0	0/0/	0/0/9	9.1/0		//0	0/0/0	Other endangered birds, for human consumption(including domesticated and artificially bred)
0/0/0	3.5	2	0/0	0/0/0	0/0	0//0	0/0/	0/0/9	9.1/0		//0	0/0/0	Other birds for human consumption
													---Other

税则号列	货品名称〔CIQ 扩展编码及品名—T2 表示见附表 2〕	最惠(%)	暂定税率	普通	增值/消费	出口退税	计量单位	监管条件/特殊证件	检验检疫	对美关税	亚太上/下
0106.3990 10	其他濒危鸟(包括人工驯养、繁殖的)[T2]	10		50	9/	0	千克/只	ABFE/	PRQ	12.5	
0106.3990 90	其他鸟〔101 其他饲养鸡形目禽鸟,102 其他饲养雁形目禽鸟,103 其他饲养禽鸟〕	10		50	9/	9	千克/只	AB/	PRQ	12.5	
	-昆虫:										
	--蜂:										
0106.4110	---改良种用〔999〕	0		0	0/	9	千克/只	AB/	PQ		
0106.4190	---其他〔101 蜜蜂,102 其他昆虫(其他动物)〕	10		50	9/	9	千克/只	AB/	PQ	12.5	9/9
	--其他:										
0106.4910	---改良种用										
0106.4910 10	其他改良种用濒危昆虫(包括人工驯养、繁殖的)〔101 有害昆虫;102 媒介昆虫;103 其他昆虫(害虫)〕	0		0	9/	0	千克/只	ABFE/	PQ		
0106.4910 90	其他改良种用非濒危昆虫〔101 有害昆虫;102 媒介昆虫;103 其他昆虫(害虫)〕	0		0	9/	9	千克/只	AB/	PQ		
0106.4990	---其他										
0106.4990 10	其他濒危昆虫(包括人工驯养、繁殖的)〔999〕	10		50	9/	0	千克/只	ABFE/	PQ	22.5	9/9
0106.4990 90	其他非濒危昆虫〔101 有害昆虫;102 媒介昆虫;103 其他昆虫(害虫)〕	10		50	9/	9	千克/只	AB/	PQ	22.5	9/9
	-其他:										
	---改良种用:										
0106.9011	----蛙苗										
0106.9011 10	改良种用濒危蛙苗〔101 牛蛙苗,102 青蛙苗,103 金线蛙苗,104 棘胸蛙苗,105 其他蛙苗〕	0		0	9/	0	千克/只	ABFE/	PQ		
0106.9011 90	其他改良种用蛙苗〔101 牛蛙苗,102 青蛙苗,103 金线蛙苗,104 棘胸蛙苗,105 其他蛙苗〕	0		0	9/	9	千克/只	AB/	PQ		
0106.9019	----其他										
0106.9019 10	其他改良种用濒危动物(包括人工驯养、繁殖的)[T2]	0		0	9/	0	千克/只	ABFE/	PQ		
0106.9019 90	其他改良种用动物[T2]	0		0	9/	9	千克/只	AB/	PQ		
0106.9090	---其他										
0106.9090 10	其他濒危动物(包括人工驯养、繁殖的)[T2]	10		50	9/	0	千克/只	ABFE/	PQ	37.5	9/9
0106.9090 90	其他动物[T2]	10		50	9/	9	千克/只	AB/	PQ	37.5	9/9

协定税率 %								RCEP		特惠税率 %			Article Description
东/冰/格	巴基斯坦	韩国	瑞士 上/下	哥/秘/柬	澳/毛	新西/坡/智	中国港/澳/台	东盟及马来/澳/韩	日/新	亚太2国	老/柬/缅	98/97/95	
0/0/0	3.5	2	0/0	0/0/0	0/0	0//0	0/0/	0/0/9	9.1/0			0/0/0	Other endangered bird, including domesticated and artificially bred
0/0/0	3.5	2	0/0	0/0/0	0/0	0//0	0/0/	0/0/9	9.1/0			0/0/0	Other birds
													-Insects:
													--Bees:
0/0/0	0	0	0/0	0/0/0	0/0	0//0	0/0/	0/0/0	0/0			0/0/0	---Pure-bred breeding
0/0/0	3.5	0	0/0	0/0/0	0/0	0//0	0/0/	0/0/0	9.1/0			0/0/0	---Other
													--Other:
													---Pure-bred breeding
0/0/0	0	0	0/0	0/0/0	0/0	0//0	0/0/	0/0/0	0/0			0/0/0	Other endangered insects, pure-bred breeding (including domesticated and artificially bred)
0/0/0	0	0	0/0	0/0/0	0/0	0//0	0/0/	0/0/0	0/0			0/0/0	Other insects, pure-bred breeding
													---Other
0/0/0	3.5	0	0/0	0/0/0	0/0	0//0	0/0/	0/0/0	9.1/0			0/0/0	Other endangered insects (including domesticated and artificially bred)
0/0/0	3.5	0	0/0	0/0/0	0/0	0//0	0/0/	0/0/0	9.1/0			0/0/0	Other insects
													-Other:
													---Pure-bred breeding:
													----Tadpole and young frogs
0/0/0	0	0	0/0	0/0/0	0/0	0//0	0/0/	0/0/0	0/0			0/0/0	Endangered tadpole and young frogs, pure-bred breeding
0/0/0	0	0	0/0	0/0/0	0/0	0//0	0/0/	0/0/0	0/0			0/0/0	Other tadpole and young frogs, pure-bred breeding
													----Other
0/0/0	0	0	0/0	0/0/0	0/0	0//0	0/0/	0/0/0	0/0			0/0/0	Other endangered animals, pure-bred breeding (including domesticated and artificially bred)
0/0/0	0	0	0/0	0/0/0	0/0	0//0	0/0/	0/0/0	0/0			0/0/0	Other animals, pure-bred breeding
													---Other
0/0/0	3.5	2	0/0	0/0/0	0/0	0//0	0/0/	0/0/9	9.1/0			0/0/0	Other endangered animals, purebred breeding (including domesticated and artificially bred)
0/0/0	3.5	2	0/0	0/0/0	0/0	0//0	0/0/	0/0/9	9.1/0			0/0/0	Other animals

第二章
肉及食用杂碎

注释：

本章不包括：

一、税目 02.01 至 02.08 或 02.10 的不适合供人食用的产品；

二、可食用的死昆虫(税目 04.10)；

三、动物的肠、膀胱、胃(税目 05.04)或动物血(税目 05.11、30.02)；

四、税目 02.09 所列产品以外的动物脂肪(第十五章)。

税则号列	货品名称〔CIQ 扩展编码及品名－T2 表示见附表 2〕	最惠(%)	暂定税率	普通	增值/消费	出口退税	计量单位	监管条件/特殊证件	检验检疫	对美关税	亚太上/下
02.01	鲜、冷牛肉：										
0201.1000	-整头及半头										
0201.1000 10	整头及半头鲜或冷藏的野牛肉〔101 鲜的，102 冷藏〕	20		70	9/	9	千克	4ABEFx/	PRQS	45	
0201.1000 90	其他整头及半头鲜或冷藏的牛肉〔101 鲜的；102 冷藏；103 冷藏(30 月龄以下)〕	20		70	9/	9	千克	4ABx/	PRQS	45	
0201.2000	-带骨肉										
0201.2000 10	鲜或冷藏的带骨野牛肉〔101 鲜的，102 冷藏〕	12		70	9/	9	千克	47ABEFx/	PRQ	42	
0201.2000 90	其他鲜或冷藏的带骨牛肉〔101 鲜的；102 冷藏；103 冷藏(30 月龄以下)〕	12		70	9/	9	千克	47ABx/	PRQ	42	
0201.3000	-去骨肉										
0201.3000 10	鲜或冷藏的去骨野牛肉〔101 鲜的，102 冷藏〕	12		70	9/	9	千克	47ABEFx/	PRQS	42	
0201.3000 90	其他鲜或冷藏的去骨牛肉〔101 鲜的，102 冷藏，103 冷藏(12 月龄以下)，104 冷藏(30 月龄以下)，105 冷藏(冰鲜牛绞肉(30 月龄以下)，106 冷藏牛绞肉，107 冷藏牛肉饼〕	12		70	9/	9	千克	47ABx/	PRQS	42	
02.02	冻牛肉：										
0202.1000	-整头及半头										
0202.1000 10	冻藏的整头及半头野牛肉〔999〕	25		70	9/	9	千克	4ABEFx/	PRQS	50	
0202.1000 90	其他冻藏的整头及半头牛肉〔10130 月龄以下，102 不含脊柱和头骨，103 不含脊柱和头骨，30 月龄以下，999〕	25		70	9/	9	千克	4ABx/	PRQS	50	
0202.2000	-带骨肉										
0202.2000 10	冻藏的带骨野牛肉〔999〕	12		70	9/	9	千克	47ABEFx/	PRQS	42	
0202.2000 90	其他冻藏的带骨牛肉〔10130 月龄以下，102 不含脊柱和头骨，103 不含脊柱和头骨，30 月龄以下，999〕	12		70	9/	9	千克	47ABx/	PRQS	42	
0202.3000	-去骨肉										
0202.3000 10	冻藏的去骨野牛肉〔999〕	12		70	9/	9	千克	47ABEFx/	PRQS	42	
0202.3000 90	其他冻藏的去骨牛肉〔101：12 月龄以下，102：30 月龄以下，103：冷冻牛绞肉，30 月龄以下，104：冷冻牛绞肉，105：冷冻牛肉饼，999：其他〕	12		70	9/	9	千克	47ABx/	PRQS	42	
02.03	鲜、冷、冻猪肉：										
	-鲜或冷的：										
	--整头及半头：										
0203.1110	---乳猪										
0203.1110 10	鲜或冷藏的整头及半头野乳猪肉〔101 鲜的，102 冷藏〕	20		70	9/	9	千克	4ABEFx/	PRQS	45	
0203.1110 90	其他鲜或冷藏的整头及半头乳猪肉〔101 鲜的，102 冷藏〕	20		70	9/	9	千克	4ABx/	PRQS	45	
0203.1190	---其他										
0203.1190 10	其他鲜或冷藏的整头及半头野猪肉〔101 鲜的，102 冷藏〕	20		70	9/	9	千克	4ABEFx/	PRQS	45	
0203.1190 90	其他鲜或冷藏的整头及半头猪肉〔101 鲜的，102 冷藏〕	20		70	9/	9	千克	4ABx/	PRQS	45	
0203.1200	--带骨的前腿、后腿及其肉块										
0203.1200 10	鲜或冷的带骨野猪前腿、后腿及肉块〔101 鲜的，102 冷藏〕	20		70	9/	9	千克	47ABEFx/	PRQS	75/45	
0203.1200 90	鲜或冷的带骨猪前腿、后腿及其肉块〔101 鲜的，102 冷藏〕	20		70	9/	9	千克	47ABx/	PRQS	75/45	
0203.1900	--其他										
0203.1900 10	其他鲜或冷藏的野猪肉〔101 鲜的，102 冷藏〕	20		70	9/	9	千克	47ABEFx/	PRQS	75/45	
0203.1900 90	其他鲜或冷藏的猪肉〔101 鲜的，102 冷藏，103 冷藏猪肉馅〕	20		70	9/	9	千克	47ABx/	PRQS	75/45	
	-冻的：										
	--整头及半头：										
0203.2110	---乳猪										
0203.2110 10	冻整头及半头野乳猪肉〔999〕	12		70	9/	9	千克	4ABEFx/	PRQS	37	
0203.2110 90	冻整头及半头乳猪肉〔999〕	12		70	9/	9	千克	4ABx/	PRQS	37	
0203.2190	---其他										
0203.2190 10	其他冻整头及半头野猪肉〔999〕	12		70	9/	9	千克	47ABEFx/	PRQS	62/37	
0203.2190 90	其他冻整头及半头猪肉〔999〕	12		70	9/	9	千克	47ABx/	PRQS	62/37	
0203.2200	--带骨的前腿、后腿及其肉块										

Chapter 2
Meat and edible meat offal

Notes:

This Chapter does not cover:

1. Products of the kinds described in headings No. 02.01 to 02.08 or 02.10, unfit or unsuitable for human consumption;
2. Edible, non—living insects (heading No.04.10);
3. Guts, bladders or stomachs of animals (heading No. 05.04) or animal blood (heading No. 05.11 or 30.02);
4. Animal fat, other than products of heading No. 02.09(Chapter15).

协定税率 %								RCEP		特惠税率 %			Article Description
东/冰/格	巴基斯坦	韩国	瑞士 上/下	哥/秘/柬	澳/毛	新西/坡/智	中国港/澳/台	东盟及马来/澳/韩	日/新	亚太2国	老/柬/缅	98/97/95	
													Meat of bovine animals, fresh or chilled:
													-Carcasses and half-carcasses
0/0/0		9.3	2/2	4/2.7/0	4/0	0//0	0/0/	18//18	/18		0/0/	0/0/0	Meat of wild bovine animals, carcasses and half-carcasses, fresh or chilled
0/0/0		9.3	2/2	4/2.7/0	4/0	0//0	0/0/	18//18	/18		0/0/	0/0/0	Other meat of bovine animals, carcasses and half-carcasses, fresh or chilled
													-Other cuts with bone in
0/0/0	0	5.6	1.2/1.2	2.4/2.8/0	2.4/0	0//0	0/0/	11.4//11.4	/11.4		0/0/	0/0/0	Meat of wild bovine animals, with bone in, fresh or chilled
0/0/0	0	5.6	1.2/1.2	2.4/2.8/0	2.4/0	0//0	0/0/	11.4//11.4	/11.4		0/0/	0/0/0	Other meat of bovine animals, with bone in, fresh or chilled
													-Boneless
0/0/0	0	5.6	1.2/1.2	2.4/2.8/0	2.4/0	0//0	0/0/	11.4//11.4	/11.4		/0/	0/0/0	Meat of wild bovine animals, boneless, fresh or chilled
0/0/0	0	5.6	1.2/1.2	2.4/2.8/0	2.4/0	0//0	0/0/	11.4//11.4	/11.4		/0/	0/0/0	Other meat of bovine animals, boneless, fresh or chilled
													Meat of bovine animals, frozen:
													-Carcasses and half-carcasses
0/0/	0	15	2.5/2.5	0/3.3/0	5/15	0//0	0/0/	23.8//23.8	/23.8		0/0/	0/0/0	Meat of wild bovine animals, carcasses and half-carcasses, frozen
0/0/	0	15	2.5/2.5	0/3.3/0	5/15	0//0	0/0/	23.8//23.8	/23.8		0/0/	0/0/0	Other meat of bovine animals, carcasses and half-carcasses, frozen
													-Other cuts with bone in
0/0/	0	5.6	1.2/1.2	0/2.8/0	2.4/0	0//0	0/0/	11.4//11.4	/11.4		0/0/	0/0/0	Meat of wild bovine animals, with bone in, frozen
0/0/	0	5.6	1.2/1.2	0/2.8/0	2.4/0	0//0	0/0/	11.4//11.4	/11.4		0/0/	0/0/0	Other meat of bovine animals, with bone in, frozen
													-Boneless
0/0/	0	5.6	1.2/1.2	0/2.8/0	2.4/0	0//0	0/0/	11.4//11.4	/11.4		/0/	0/0/0	Meat of wild bovine animals, boneless, frozen
0/0/	0	5.6	1.2/1.2	0/2.8/0	2.4/0	0//0	0/0/	11.4//11.4	/11.4		/0/	0/0/0	Other meat of bovine animals, boneless, frozen
													Meat of swine, fresh, chilled or frozen:
													-Fresh or chilled:
													--Carcasses and half-carcasses:
													---Sucking pig
0/0/0		9.3	2/2	0/0/0	0/0	0//0	0/0/	18/18/18	18.8/18		0/0/	0/0/0	Meat of wild sucking pig, carcasses and half-carcasses, fresh or chilled
0/0/0		9.3	2/2	0/0/0	0/0	0//0	0/0/	18/18/18	18.8/18		0/0/	0/0/0	Meat of other sucking pig, carcasses and half-carcasses, fresh or chilled
													---Other
0/0/0		9.3	2/2	0/0/0	0/0	0//0	0/0/	18/18/18	18.8/18		0/0/	0/0/0	Other meat of wild swine, carcasses and half-carcasses, fresh or chilled
0/0/0		9.3	2/2	0/0/0	0/0	0//0	0/0/	18/18/18	18.8/18		0/0/	0/0/0	Other meat of swine, carcasses and half-carcasses, fresh or chilled
													--Hams, shoulders and cuts thereof, with bone in
0/0/0		9.3	2/2	0/0/0	0/0	0//0	0/0/	18/18/18	18.8/18		0/0/	0/0/0	Hams, shoulders and cuts thereof, with bone in, of wild swine, fresh or chilled
0/0/0		9.3	2/2	0/0/0	0/0	0//0	0/0/	18/18/18	18.8/18		0/0/	0/0/0	Hams, shoulders and cuts thereof, with bone in, of swine, fresh or chilled
													--Other
0/0/0		9.3	2/2	0/0/0	0/0	0//0	0/0/	18/18/18	18.8/18		0/0/	0/0/0	Other meat of wild swine, fresh or chilled
0/0/0		9.3	2/2	0/0/0	0/0	0//0	0/0/	18/18/18	18.8/18		0/0/	0/0/0	Other meat of swine, fresh or chilled
													-Frozen:
													--Carcasses and half-carcasses:
													---Sucking pig
0/0/0	6	2.4	1.2/1.2	0/0/0	0/0	0//0	0/0/	0/0/10.8	10.9/0		0/0/	0/0/0	Meat of wild sucking pig, carcasses and half-carcasses, frozen
0/0/0	6	2.4	1.2/1.2	0/0/0	0/0	0//0	0/0/	0/0/10.8	10.9/0		0/0/	0/0/0	Meat of sucking pig, carcasses and half-carcasses, frozen
													---Other
0/0/0	6	2.4	1.2/1.2	0/0/0	0/0	0//0	0/0/	0/0/10.8	10.9/0		0/0/	0/0/0	Other meat of wild swine, carcasses and half-carcasses, frozen
0/0/0	6	2.4	1.2/1.2	0/0/0	0/0	0//0	0/0/	0/0/10.8	10.9/0		0/0/	0/0/0	Other meat of swine, carcasses and half-carcasses, frozen
													--Hams, shoulders and cuts thereof, with bone in

税则号列	货品名称〔CIQ 扩展编码及品名—T2 表示见附表 2〕	最惠(%)	暂定税率	普通	增值/消费	出口退税	计量单位	监管条件/特殊证件	检验检疫	对美关税	亚太上/下
0203.2200 10	冻带骨野猪前腿、后腿及肉〔999〕	12		70	9/	9	千克	47ABEFx/	PRQS	67/37	
0203.2200 90	冻藏的带骨猪前腿、后腿及其肉块〔999〕	12		70	9/	9	千克	47ABx/	PRQS	67/37	
0203.2900	--其他										
0203.2900 10	冻藏野猪其他肉〔999〕	12		70	9/	9	千克	47ABEFx/	PRQS	67/37	
0203.2900 90	其他冻藏猪肉〔101 冷冻猪肉馅,999 其他〕	12		70	9/	9	千克	47ABx/	PRQS	67/37	
02.04	**鲜、冷、冻绵羊肉或山羊肉:**										
0204.1000	-鲜或冷的整头及半头羔羊〔101 鲜的绵羊肉,102 冷藏绵羊肉,103 鲜的山羊肉,104 冷藏山羊肉,105 鲜的野羊肉,106 冷藏野羊肉,107 冷藏绵羊肉,6 月龄以下,108 冷藏山羊肉,6 月龄以下〕	15		70	9/	9	千克	7AB/	PRQS		
	-其他鲜或冷的绵羊肉:										
0204.2100	--整头及半头〔101 鲜的绵羊肉,102 冷藏绵羊肉,103 鲜的野羊肉,104 冷藏野羊肉,105 冷藏绵羊肉,6 月龄以下〕	23		70	9/	9	千克	7AB/	PRQ		
0204.2200	--带骨肉〔101 鲜的绵羊肉,102 冷藏绵羊肉,103 鲜的野羊肉,104 冷藏野羊肉,105 冷藏绵羊肉,6 月龄以下〕	15		70	9/	9	千克	7AB/	PRQS	45	
0204.2300	--去骨肉〔101 鲜的绵羊肉,102 冷藏绵羊肉,103 鲜的野羊肉,104 冷藏野羊肉,105 冷藏绵羊肉,6 月龄以下〕	15		70	9/	9	千克	7AB/	PRQS		
0204.3000	-冻的整头及半头羔羊〔101 绵羊肉,102 山羊肉,103 野羊肉,104 绵羊肉,6 月龄以下 105 山羊肉,6 月龄以下〕	15		70	9/	9	千克	7AB/	PRQS		
	-其他冻的绵羊肉:										
0204.4100	--整头及半头〔101 绵羊肉,102 野羊肉,103 绵羊肉,6 月龄以下〕	23		70	9/	9	千克	7AB/	PRQS		
0204.4200	--带骨肉〔101 绵羊肉,102 野羊肉,103 绵羊肉,6 月龄以下〕	12		70	9/	9	千克	7AB/	PRQS		
0204.4300	--去骨肉〔101 绵羊肉,102 野羊肉,103 绵羊肉,6 月龄以下〕	15		70	9/	9	千克	7AB/	PRQS		
0204.5000	-山羊肉[T2]	20		70	9/	9	千克	7AB/	PRQS		
02.05	**鲜、冷、冻马、驴、骡肉:**										
0205.0000	鲜、冷、冻马、驴、骡肉										
0205.0000 10	鲜、冷或冻的濒危野马、野驴肉[T2]	20		70	9/	0	千克	ABFE/	PRQS		
0205.0000 90	鲜、冷或冻的马、驴、骡肉[T2]	20		70	9/	9	千克	AB/	PRQS		
02.06	**鲜、冷、冻牛、猪、绵羊、山羊、马、驴、骡的食用杂碎:**										
0206.1000	-鲜、冷牛杂碎[T2]	12		70	9/	9	千克	4ABx/	PRQS		
	-冻牛杂碎:										
0206.2100	--舌〔101:冻牛舌;102:冻野牛舌;103:30 月龄以下〕	12		70	9/	9	千克	47ABx/	PRQS		
0206.2200	--肝〔101:冻牛肝;102:冻野牛肝;103:30 月龄以下〕	12		70	9/	9	千克	47ABx/	PRQS		
0206.2900	--其他[T2]	12		70	9/	9	千克	47ABx/	PRQS	42	
0206.3000	-鲜、冷猪杂碎[T2]	20		70	9/	9	千克	4ABx/	PRQS	50	
	-冻猪杂碎:										
0206.4100	--肝〔101 冻猪肝,102 冻野猪肝〕	20		70	9/	9	千克	47ABx/	PRQS	75/45	
0206.4900	--其他[T2]	12		70	9/	9	千克	47ABx/	PRQS	67/37	
0206.8000	-其他鲜或冷杂碎										
0206.8000 10	鲜或冷的羊杂碎[T2]	20		70	9/	9	千克	AB/	PRQS		
0206.8000 90	鲜或冷的马、驴、骡杂碎[T2]	20		70	9/	9	千克	AB/	PRQS		
0206.9000	-其他冻杂碎										
0206.9000 10	冻藏的羊杂碎[T2]	18		70	9/	9	千克	7AB/	PRQS		
0206.9000 90	冻藏的马、驴、骡杂碎[T2]	18		70	9/	9	千克	AB/	PRQS		
02.07	**税目 01.05 所列家禽的鲜、冷、冻肉及食用杂碎:**										
	-鸡:										
0207.1100	--整只,鲜或冷的〔101 鲜的整只鸡,102 冷藏整只鸡〕	20		70	9/	9	千克	4xAB/	PRQS	50	
0207.1200	--整只,冻的〔101 冻的整只鸡(不包括内脏及胃肠等消化道器官),999〕	T3		T3	9/	9	千克	4x7AB/	PRQS	T3	
	--块及杂碎,鲜或冷的:										
	---块:										
0207.1311	----带骨的〔101 鲜的带骨的鸡块,102 冷藏带骨的鸡块〕	20		70	9/	9	千克	4xAB/	PRQS	50	
0207.1319	----其他〔101 其他鲜的鸡块,102 其他冷藏鸡块〕	20		70	9/	9	千克	4xAB/	PRQS	50	
	---杂碎:										
0207.1321	----翼(不包括翼尖)	20		70	10/	10	千克	4xAB	PRQS		
0207.1321 01	鲜或冷的鸡整翅(翼)(沿肩关节将鸡翅从整鸡上分割下来的部位)〔101 鲜的;102 冷藏〕	20		70	9/	9	千克	4xAB/	PRQS	50	
0207.1321 02	鲜或冷的鸡翅(翼)根(将整翅从肘关节处切开,靠近根部的部分)〔101 鲜的;102 冷藏〕	20		70	9/	9	千克	4xAB/	PRQS	50	
0207.1321 03	鲜或冷的鸡翅(翼)中(将整翅从肘关节和腕关节处切开,中间的部分)〔101 鲜的;102 冷藏〕	20		70	9/	9	千克	4xAB/	PRQS	50	
0207.1321 04	鲜或冷的鸡两节翅(翼)(翅中和翅尖相连的部分,或翅根和翅中相连的部分)〔101 鲜的,102 冷藏〕	20		70	9/	9	千克	4xAB/	PRQS	50	
0207.1329	----其他	20		70	10/	6	千克	AB4x	PRQS		

协定税率 %								RCEP		特惠税率 %			Article Description
东/冰/格	巴基斯坦	韩国	瑞士上/下	哥/秘/柬	澳/毛	新西/坡/智	中国港/澳/台	东盟及马来/澳/韩	日/新	亚太2国	老/柬/缅	98/97/95	
0/0/0	6	2.4	1.2/1.2	0/0/0	0/0	0//0	0/0/	0/0/10.8	10.9/0		0/0/	0/0/0	Hams, shoulders and cuts thereof, with bone in, of wild swine, frozen
0/0/0	6	2.4	1.2/1.2	0/0/0	0/0	0//0	0/0/	0/0/10.8	10.9/0		0/0/	0/0/0	Hams, shoulders and cuts thereof, with bone in, of swine, frozen
													--Other
0/0/0	6	2.4	1.2/1.2	0/1.6/0	0/0	0//0	0/0/	0/0/10.8	10.9/0		/0/	0/0/0	Other meat of wild swine, frozen
0/0/0	6	2.4	1.2/1.2	0/1.6/0	0/0	0//0	0/0/	0/0/10.8	10.9/0		/0/	0/0/0	Other meat of swine, frozen
													Meat of sheep or goats, fresh, chilled or frozen:
0/0/0	12	3	1.5/1.5	3/2/0	1.7/0	0//0	0/0/	0/13.5/13.5	13.6/0			0/0/0	-Carcasses and half-carcasses of lamb, fresh or chilled
													-Other meat of sheep, fresh or chilled:
0/0/0		13.8	2.3/2.3	4.6/3.1/0	2.6/13.8	0//0	0/0/	22.4/22.4/	/22.4			0/0/0	--Carcasses and half-carcasses
0/0/0	12	3	1.5/1.5	3/2/0	1.7/0	0//0	0/0/	0/13.5/13.5	13.6/0			0/0/0	--Other cuts with bone in
0/0/0	12	3	1.5/1.5	3/0/0	1.7/0	0//0	0/0/	0/13.5/13.5	13.6/0			0/0/0	--Boneless
0/0/0	12	3	1.5/1.5	3/3.5/0	1.7/0	0//0	0/0/	0/13.5/13.5	13.6/0			0/0/0	-Carcasses and half-carcasses of lamb, frozen
													-Other meat of sheep, frozen:
0/0/0		13.8	2.3/2.3	4.6/5.4/0	2.6/13.8	0//0	0/0/	21.9/21.9/21.9	/21.9			0/0/0	--Carcasses and half-carcasses
0/0/0	6	2.4	1.2/1.2	2.4/2.8/0	1.3/0	0//0	0/0/	0/10.8/10.8	10.9/0			0/0/0	--Other cuts with bone in
0/0/0	12	3	1.5/1.5	3/3.5/0	1.7/0	0//0	0/0/	13.5/13.5/13.5	13.6/13.5			0/0/0	--Boneless
0/0/0	0	9.3	2/2	4/0/0	2.2/0	0//0	0/0/	18.7/19/18.7	18.8/19			0/0/0	-Meat of goats
													Meat of horses, asses, mules or hinnies, fresh, chilled or frozen:
													Meat of horses, asses, mules or hinnies, fresh, chilled or frozen
0/0/0		9.3	2/2	0/0/0	0/0	0//0	0/0/	18/18/18	18.8/18			0/0/0	Meat of endangered wild horses and asses, fresh, chilled or frozen
0/0/0		9.3	2/2	0/0/0	0/0	0//0	0/0/	18/18/18	18.8/18			0/0/0	Other meat of horses, asses, mules or hinnies, fresh, chilled or frozen
													Edible offal of bovine animals, swine, sheep, goats, horses, asses, mules or hinnies, fresh, chilled or frozen:
0/0/0	6	2.4	1.2/1.2	0/0/0	0/0	0//0	0/0/	0/0/10.8	10.9/0		0/0/	0/0/0	-Of bovine animals, fresh or chilled
													-Of bovine animals, frozen:
0/0/0	6	2.4	1.2/1.2	0/0/0	0/0	0//0	0/0/	0/0/10.8	10.9/0		0/0/	0/0/0	--Tongues
0/0/0	6	2.4	1.2/1.2	0/0/0	0/0	0//0	0/0/	0/0/10.8	10.9/0		0/0/	0/0/0	--Livers
0/0/0	0	2.4	1.2/1.2	0/0/0	0/0	0//0	0/0/	10.8/10.8/10.8	10.9/10.8		0/0/	0/0/0	--Other
0/0/0		9.3	2/2	0/0/0	0/0	0//0	0/0/	18/18/18	18.8/18		0/0/0	0/0/0	-Of swine, fresh or chilled
													-Of swine, frozen:
0/0/0		9.3	2/2	0/0/0	0/0	0//0	0/0/	18/18/18	18.8/18		0/0/	0/0/0	--Livers
0/0/0	6	2.4	1.2/1.2	0/0/0	0/0	0//0	0/0/	0/0/10.8	10.9/0		0/0/	0/0/0	--Other
													-Other, fresh or chilled
0/0/0		9.3	2/2	0/0/0	4/0	0//0	0/0/	18/18/18	18.8/18		/0/	0/0/0	Edible offal of sheep or goats, fresh or chilled
0/0/0		9.3	2/2	0/0/0	4/0	0//0	0/0/	18/18/18	18.8/18		/0/	0/0/0	Edible offal of horses, asses, mules or hinnies, fresh or chilled
													-Other, frozen
0/0/0	14.4	8.4	1.8/1.8	0/4.2/0	0/0	0//0	0/0/	16.8/17.1/16.8	16.9/17.1		/0/	0/0/0	Edible offal of sheep or goats, frozen
0/0/0	14.4	8.4	1.8/1.8	0/4.2/0	0/0	0//0	0/0/	16.8/17.1/16.8	16.9/17.1		/0/	0/0/0	Edible offal of horses, asses, mules or hinnies, frozen
													Meat and edible offal, of the poultry of heading No. 01.05, fresh, chilled or frozen:
													-Of fowls of the species *Gallus domesticus*:
0/0/0		9.3	2/2	0/0/0	0/0	0//0	0/0/	18/18/18	18.8/18		0/0/0	0/0/0	--Not cut in pieces, fresh or chilled
0/0/0		0.6元/千克	2/2	0/0/0	0/0	0//0	0/0/	18/18/18	18.8/18		0/0/0	0/0/0	--Not cut in pieces, frozen
													--Cuts and offal, fresh or chilled:
													---Cuts:
0/0/0		9.3	2/2	0/0/0	0/0	0//0	0/0/	18/18/18	18.8/18		0/0/0	0/0/0	----With bone
0/0/0		9.3	2/2	0/0/0	0/0	0//0	0/0/	18/18/18	18.8/18		0/0/0	0/0/0	----Other
													Offal:
0/0/12		13.3	8	0	0	0	0//0	0/0/			0/0/0	0/0	----Midjoint wing
0/0/0		9.3	2/2	0/0/0	0/0	0//0	0/0/	18/18/18	18.8/18		0/0/0	0/0/0	Whole Wings, fresh or chilled
0/0/0		9.3	2/2	0/0/0	0/0	0//0	0/0/	18/18/18	18.8/18		0/0/0	0/0/0	Wing root, fresh or chilled
0/0/0		9.3	2/2	0/0/0	0/0	0//0	0/0/	18/18/18	18.8/18		0/0/0	0/0/0	Midjoint wing, fresh or chilled
0/0/0		9.3	2/2	0/0/0	0/0	0//0	0/0/	18/18/18	18.8/18		0/0/0	0/0/0	2—joint wings, fresh or chilled
0/0/12		13.3	8	0	0	0	0//0	0/0/			0/0/0	0/0	----Other

税则号列		货品名称〔CIQ扩展编码及品名－T2表示见附表2〕	最惠(%)	暂定税率	普通	增值/消费	出口退税	计量单位	监管条件/特殊证件	检验检疫	对美关税	亚太上/下
0207.1329	01	鲜或冷的鸡翅(翼)尖〔101 鲜的鸡翼翼尖，102 冷藏鸡翼翼尖〕	20		70	9/	9	千克	AB4x/	PRQS	50	
0207.1329	02	鲜或冷的鸡膝软骨(鸡膝部连接小腿和大腿的软骨)〔101 鲜的;102 冷藏〕	20		70	9/	9	千克	AB4x/	PRQS	50	
0207.1329	90	其他鲜或冷的鸡杂碎〔101 鲜的鸡胸、鸡腿，102 冷藏的鸡胸、鸡腿，103 鲜的鸡爪，104 冷藏鸡爪，105 鲜的鸡肫、胃，106 冷藏鸡肫、胃，107 其他鲜的鸡杂碎，108 其他冷藏鸡杂碎〕	20		70	9/	9	千克	AB4x/	PRQS	50	
		--块及杂碎，冻的：										
		---块：										
0207.1411		----带骨的〔101 冷冻带骨鸡肉，除鸡胸、鸡腿，102 鸡胸、鸡腿〕	T3		T3	9/	9	千克	7AB4x/	PRQS	T3	
0207.1419		----其他〔101 冷冻不带骨鸡肉，除鸡胸、鸡腿，102 鸡胸、鸡腿〕	T3		T3	9/	9	千克	7AB4x/	PRQS	T3	
		---杂碎：										
0207.1421		----翼(不包括翼尖)										
0207.1421	01	冻的鸡整翅(翼)(沿肩关节将鸡翅从整鸡上分割下来的部位)〔999〕	T3		T3	9/	9	千克	7AB4x/	PRQS	T3	
0207.1421	02	冻的鸡翅(翼)根(将整翅从肘关节处切开，靠近根部的部分)〔999〕	T3		T3	9/	9	千克	7AB4x/	PRQS	T3	
0207.1421	03	冻的鸡翅(翼)中(将整翅从肘关节和腕关节处切开，中间的部分)〔999〕	T3		T3	9/	9	千克	7AB4x/	PRQS	T3	
0207.1421	04	冻的鸡两节翅(翼)(翅中和翅尖相连的部分，或翅根和翅中相连的部分)〔101 冻鸡两节翅(翼)不包括翅(翼)尖，999〕	T3		T3	9/	9	千克	7AB4x/	PRQS	T3	
0207.1422		----鸡爪〔999〕	T3		T3	9/	9	千克	7AB4x/	PRQS	T3	
0207.1429		----其他										
0207.1429	01	冻的鸡翅(翼)尖〔999〕	T3		T3	9/	9	千克	7AB4x/	PRQS	T3	
0207.1429	02	冻的鸡膝软骨(鸡膝部连接小腿和大腿的软骨)〔999〕	T3		T3	9/	9	千克	7AB4x/	PRQS	T3	
0207.1429	90	其他冻的食用鸡杂碎[T2]	T3		T3	9/	9	千克	7AB4x/	PRQS	T3	
		-火鸡：										
0207.2400		--整只，鲜或冷的〔101 鲜的整只火鸡，102 冷藏整只火鸡〕	20		70	9/	9	千克	AB/	PRQS	50	
0207.2500		--整只，冻的〔101 冻的整只火鸡(不包括内脏及胃肠等消化道器官，999〕	20		70	9/	9	千克	AB/	PRQS	50	
0207.2600		--块及杂碎，鲜或冷的[T2]	20		70	9/	9	千克	AB/	PRQS	50	
0207.2700		--块及杂碎，冻的[T2]	10		70	9/	9	千克	AB/	PRQS	40	
		-鸭：										
0207.4100		--整只，鲜或冷的〔101 鲜的，102 冷的〕	20		70	9/	9	千克	AB/	PRQS	50	
0207.4200		--整只，冻的〔101 不包括内脏及胃肠等消化道器官，999 其他〕	20		70	9/	9	千克	AB/	PRQS	50	
0207.4300		--肥肝，鲜或冷的〔101 鲜的，102 冷的〕	20		70	9/	9	千克	AB/	PRQS	50	
0207.4400		--其他，鲜或冷的[T2]	20		70	9/	9	千克	AB/	PRQS	50	
0207.4500		--其他，冻的[T2]	20		70	9/	9	千克	AB/	PRQS	50	
		-鹅：										
0207.5100		--整只，鲜或冷的〔101 鲜的，102 冷藏〕	20		70	9/	9	千克	AB/	PRQS	50	
0207.5200		--整只，冻的〔999〕	20		70	9/	9	千克	AB/	PRQS	50	
0207.5300		--肥肝，鲜或冷的〔101 鲜的，102 冷藏〕	20		70	9/	9	千克	AB/	PRQS	50	
0207.5400		--其他，鲜或冷的[T2]	20		70	9/	9	千克	AB/	PRQS	50	
0207.5500		--其他，冻的[T2]	20		70	9/	9	千克	AB/	PRQS	50	
0207.6000		-珍珠鸡[T2]	20		70	9/	9	千克	AB/	PRQS		
02.08		**其他鲜、冷、冻肉及食用杂碎：**										
		-家兔或野兔的：										
0208.1010		---鲜、冷兔肉，兔头除外〔101 鲜的家兔肉，102 冷藏家兔肉〕	20		70	9/	9	千克	AB/	PRQS		
0208.1020		---冻兔肉，兔头除外〔999〕	20		70	9/	9	千克	AB/	PRQS		
0208.1090		---其他										
0208.1090	10	鲜、冷或冻濒危野兔肉及其食用杂碎(不包括兔头)〔101 鲜的野兔肉，102 冷藏野兔肉，103 冻藏野兔肉，104 鲜的野兔杂碎，105 冷藏野兔杂碎，106 冻藏野兔杂碎〕	20		70	9/	0	千克	ABFE/	PRQS		
0208.1090	90	鲜、冷或冻家兔食用杂碎〔101 鲜的，102 冷藏，103 冻藏〕	20		70	9/	9	千克	AB/	PRQS		
0208.3000		-灵长目的〔101 鲜的，102 冷藏，103 冻藏〕	23		70	9/	9	千克	ABFE/	PRQS		
0208.4000		-鲸、海豚及鼠海豚(鲸目哺乳动物)的；海牛及儒艮(海牛目哺乳动物)的；海豹、海狮及海象(鳍足亚目哺乳动物)的〔101 鲜、冷的，102 冻的〕	23		70	9/	9	千克	ABFE/	PRQS		
0208.5000		-爬行动物(包括蛇及龟鳖)的[T2]	23		70	9/	9	千克	ABFE/	PRQS		
0208.6000		-骆驼及其他骆驼科动物的										
0208.6000	10	鲜、冷或冻的濒危野生骆驼及其他濒危野生骆驼科动物的肉及食用杂碎〔101 鲜的，102 冷藏，103 冻藏〕	23		70	9/	0	千克	ABFE/	PRQS		
0208.6000	90	其他鲜、冷或冻骆驼及其他骆驼科动物的肉及食用杂碎〔101 鲜的，102 冷藏，103 冻藏〕	23		70	9/	9	千克	AB/	PRQS		
		-其他：										

协定税率 %								RCEP		特惠税率 %			Article Description
东/冰/格	巴基斯坦	韩国	瑞士 上/下	哥/秘/柬	澳/毛	新西/坡/智	中国港/澳/台	东盟及马来/澳/韩	日/新	亚太2国	老/柬/缅	98/97/95	
0/0/0		9.3	2/2	0/0/0	0/0	0//0	0/0/	18/18/18	18.8/18		0/0/0	0/0/0	chicken wing tips,fresh or chilled
0/0/0		9.3	2/2	0/0/0	0/0	0//0	0/0/	18/18/18	18.8/18		0/0/0	0/0/0	Chicken knee cartilage,fresh or chilled
0/0/0		9.3	2/2	0/0/0	0/0	0//0	0/0/	18/18/18	18.8/18		0/0/0	0/0/0	Other chicken edible offal ,fresh or chilled
													--Cuts and offal, frozen:
													---Cuts:
0/0/0	0	0.1元/千克	0/0	0/0/0	0/0	0//0	0/0/	0/0/9	9.1/0		0/0/0	0/0/0	----With bone
0/0/0	0	0.1元/千克	0/0	0/0/0	0/0	0//0	0/0/	0/0/9	9.1/0		0/0/0	0/0/0	----Other
													---Offal:
													----Midjoint wing
0/0/0	0	0.1元/千克	0/0	0/0/0	0/0	0//0	0/0/	0/0/9	9.1/0		0/0/0	0/0/0	Whole Wings,frozen
0/0/0	0	0.1元/千克	0/0	0/0/0	0/0	0//0	0/0/	0/0/9	9.1/0		0/0/0	0/0/0	Drumettes,frozen
0/0/0	0	0.1元/千克	0/0	0/0/0	0/0	0//0	0/0/	0/0/9	9.1/0		0/0/0	0/0/0	Midjoint Wings,frozen
0/0/0	0	0.1元/千克	0/0	0/0/0	0/0	0//0	0/0/	0/0/9	9.1/0		0/0/0	0/0/0	2—Joint Wings,frozen
0/0/0	0	0.1元/千克	0/0	0/0/0	0/0	0//0	0/0/	0/0/9	9.1/0		0/0/0	0/0/0	----Chicken claw
													----Other
0/0/0	0	0.1元/千克	0/0	0/0/0	0/0	0//0	0/0/	0/0/9	9.1/0		0/0/0	0/0/0	Wing Tips,frozen
0/0/0	0	0.1元/千克	0/0	0/0/0	0/0	0//0	0/0/	0/0/9	9.1/0		0/0/0	0/0/0	Chicken knee cartilage,frozen
0/0/0	0	0.1元/千克	0/0	0/0/0	0/0	0//0	0/0/	0/0/9	9.1/0		0/0/0	0/0/0	Other chicken edible offal,frozen
													-Of turkeys:
0/0/0		9.3	2/2	0/0/0	0/0	0//0	0/0/	18/18/18	18.8/18		0//	0/0/0	--Not cut in pieces, fresh or chilled
0/0/0		9.3	2/2	0/0/0	0/0	0//0	0/0/	18/18/18	18.8/18		0//	0/0/0	--Not cut in pieces, frozen
0/0/0		9.3	2/2	0/0/0	0/0	0//0	0/0/	18/18/18	18.8/18		0//	0/0/0	--Cuts and offal, fresh or chilled
0/0/0	3.5	2	0/0	0/0/0	0/0	0//0	0/0/	0/0/9	9.1/0		0//	0/0/0	--Cuts and offal, frozen
													-Of ducks:
0/0/0		9.3	2/2	0/0/0	0/0	0//0	0/0/	18/18/18	18.8/18		0/0/0	0/0/0	--Not cut in pieces,fresh or chilled
0/0/0		9.3	2/2	0/0/0	0/0	0//0	0/0/	18/18/18	18.8/18		0/0/0	0/0/0	--Not cut in pieces,frozen
0/0/0		9.3	2/2	0/0/0	0/0	0//0	0/0/	18/18/18	18.8/18		0/0/	0/0/0	--Fatty livers,fresh or chilled
0/0/0		9.3	2/2	0/0/0	0/0	0//0	0/0/	18/18/18	18.8/18		0/0/0	0/0/0	--Other,fresh or chilled
0/0/0		12	2/2	0/0/0	0/0	0//0	0/0/	19/19/	19/19		0/0/0	0/0/0	--Other,frozen
													-Of geese
0/0/0		9.3	2/2	0/0/0	0/0	0//0	0/0/	18/18/18	18.8/18		0/0/0	0/0/0	--Not cut in pieces,fresh or chilled
0/0/0		9.3	2/2	0/0/0	0/0	0//0	0/0/	18/18/18	18.8/18		0/0/0	0/0/0	--Not cut in pieces,frozen
0/0/0		9.3	2/2	0/0/0	0/0	0//0	0/0/	18/18/18	18.8/18		0/0/	0/0/0	--Fatty livers,fresh or chilled
0/0/0		9.3	2/2	0/0/0	0/0	0//0	0/0/	18/18/18	18.8/18		0/0/0	0/0/0	--Other,fresh or chilled
0/0/0		9.3	2/2	0/0/0	0/0	0//0	0/0/	18/18/18	18.8/18		0/0/0	0/0/0	--Other,frozen
0/0/0		9.3	2/2	0/0/0	0/0	0//0	0/0/	18/18/18	18.8/18		0/0/	0/0/0	-Of guinea fowls
													Other meat and edible meat offal, fresh, chilled or frozen:
													-Of rabbits or hares:
0/0/0		9.3	2/2	0/0/0	0/0	0//0	0/0/	18/18/18	18.8/18			0/0/0	---Meat of rabbits, fresh or chilled,excluding head
0/0/0		9.3	2/2	0/0/0	0/0	0//0	0/0/	18/18/18	18.8/18			0/0/0	---Meat of rabbits, frozen,excluding head
													---Other
0/0/0		9.3	2/2	0/0/0	0/0	0//0	0/0/	18/18/18	18.8/18			0/0/0	Meat and offal,of endangered wild hares (other than head), fresh、chilled or frozen
0/0/0		9.3	2/2	0/0/0	0/0	0//0	0/0/	18/18/18	18.8/18			0/0/0	Edible offal of rabbits,fresh、chilled or frozen
0/0/0		4.6	2.3/2.3	0/0/0	0/13.8	0//0	0/0/	0/0/20.7	20.9/0			0/0/0	-Of primates
0/0/0		4.6	2.3/2.3	0/0/0	0/13.8	0//0	0/0/	0/0/20.7	20.9/0			0/0/0	-Of whales, dolphins and porpoises(mammals of the order Cetacea);of manatees and dugongs(mammals of the order Sirenia);of seal、sea lion and walrus(mammals of the suborder Pinnipedia)
0/0/0		4.6	2.3/2.3	0/0/0	0/13.8	0//0	0/0/	0/0/20.7	20.9/0			0/0/0	-Of reptiles(including snakes and turtles)
													-Of camel and other camelids(camelidae):
0/0/0		4.6	2.3/2.3	0/0/0	0/13.8	0//0	0/0/	0/0/20.7	20.9/0			0/0/0	Meat and offal of endangered wild camel and other endangered camel familia animals,fresh,chilled or frozen
0/0/0		4.6	2.3/2.3	0/0/0	0/13.8	0//0	0/0/	0/0/20.7	20.9/0			0/0/0	Meat and offal of other camel and other camel familia animals, fresh, chilled or frozen
													-Other:

税则号列	货品名称〔CIQ扩展编码及品名—T2表示见附表2〕	最惠(%)	暂定税率	普通	增值/消费	出口退税	计量单位	监管条件/特殊证件	检验检疫	对美关税	亚太上/下
0208.9010	---乳鸽的〔101鲜的乳鸽肉,102冷藏的乳鸽肉,103冻藏的乳鸽肉,104鸽杂碎,105其它鸽肉及杂碎〕	20		70	9/	9	千克	AB/	PRQS		
0208.9090	---其他										
0208.9090 10	其他鲜、冷或冻的濒危野生动物肉[T2]	23		70	9/	0	千克	ABFE/	PRQS		
0208.9090 90	其他鲜、冷或冻肉及食用杂碎[T2]	23		70	9/	9	千克	AB/	PRQS		
02.09	**未炼制或用其他方法提取的不带瘦肉的肥猪肉、猪脂肪及家禽脂肪,鲜、冷、冻、干、熏、盐腌或盐渍的:**										
0209.1000	-猪的[T2]	20		70	9/	9	千克	AB/	PRQ	45	
0209.9000	-其他[T2]	20		70	9/	9	千克	AB/	PRQ		
02.10	**肉及食用杂碎,干、熏、盐腌或盐渍的;可供食用的肉或杂碎的细粉、粗粉:**										
	-猪肉:										
	--带骨的前腿、后腿及其肉块:										
0210.1110	---带骨的腿										
0210.1110 10	干、熏、盐制的带骨鹿豚、姬猪腿101干、熏、盐制带骨姬猪腿(猪蹄);102带骨熟制猪肉制品〕	25		80	9/	9	千克	ABFE/	PRQS	55	
0210.1110 90	其他干、熏、盐制的带骨猪腿〔101其他盐制带骨猪腿、带骨腌制猪腿(猪蹄),102带骨熟制猪肉制品〕	25		80	9/	9	千克	AB/	PRQS	55	
0210.1190	---其他										
0210.1190 10	干、熏、盐制的带骨鹿豚、姬猪腿肉块〔101干、熏、盐制带骨姬猪腿肉块(猪蹄),102带骨熟制猪肉制品〕	25		80	9/	9	千克	ABFE/	PRQS	55	
0210.1190 90	其他干、熏、盐制的带骨猪腿肉〔101其他盐制带骨猪腿肉、带骨腌制猪腿肉(猪蹄),102带骨熟制猪肉制品〕	25		80	9/	9	千克	AB/	PRQS	55	
0210.1200	--腹肉(五花肉)										
0210.1200 10	干、熏、盐制的鹿豚、姬猪腹肉(指五花肉)〔101干、熏制鹿豚腹肉,102去骨熟制猪肉制品,103盐制鹿豚腹肉〕	25		80	9/	9	千克	ABFE/	PRQS	55	
0210.1200 90	其他干、熏、盐制的猪腹肉(指五花肉)〔101其他盐制猪腹肉、腌制猪腹肉,102去骨熟制猪肉制品〕	25		80	9/	9	千克	AB/	PRQS	55	
0210.1900	--其他										
0210.1900 10	干、熏、盐制的鹿豚、姬猪其他肉〔101干、熏、盐制姬猪其他肉,102干、熏鹿豚其他肉,103盐制鹿豚其他肉〕	25		80	9/	9	千克	ABFE/	PRQS	55	
0210.1900 90	其他干、熏、盐制的其他猪肉〔101其他干制其他猪肉,102去骨熟制猪肉制品,104去骨腌制猪肉制品,105以上述产品为原料制成的腌制(干、熏、盐制)猪肉产品〕	25		80	9/	9	千克	AB/	PRQS	55	
0210.2000	-牛肉										
0210.2000 10	干、熏、盐制的濒危野牛肉〔101干、熏制野牛肉,102盐制带骨野牛肉、腌制带骨牛肉,103盐制去骨野牛肉、腌制去骨牛肉,104去骨熟制牛肉制品〕	25		80	9/	0	千克	ABFE/	PRQS	55	
0210.2000 90	干、熏、盐制的其他牛肉〔101干、熏制牛肉;102盐制带骨牛肉、腌制带骨牛肉;103盐制去骨牛肉、腌制去骨牛肉;104去骨熟制牛肉制品;106以上述产品为原料制成的腌制(干、熏、盐制)牛肉产品〕	25		80	9/	9	千克	AB/	PRQS	55	
	-其他,包括可供食用的肉或杂碎的细粉、粗粉:										
0210.9100	--灵长目的〔101干、熏、盐制灵长目动物肉,102干、熏、盐制灵长目动物食用杂碎〕	25		80	9/	9	千克	ABFE/	PRQS		
0210.9200	--鲸、海豚及鼠海豚(鲸目哺乳动物)的;海牛及儒艮(海牛目哺乳动物)的;海豹、海狮及海象(鳍足亚目哺乳动物)的〔101干、熏、盐制鲸目海牛目动物肉,102干、熏、盐制鲸目海牛目动物食用杂碎,103熏拷的灌肠类熟肉制品,104腌制的灌肠类熟肉制品〕	25		80	9/	9	千克	ABFE/	PRQS		
0210.9300	--爬行动物(包括蛇及龟鳖)的〔105养殖干制,106野生干制,107养殖盐腌及盐渍等,108野生盐腌及盐渍等,109养殖其他制作及保藏,110野生其他制作及保藏〕	25		80	9/	9	千克	ABFE/	PRQS		
0210.9900	--其他										
0210.9900 10	干、熏、盐制的其他濒危动物肉及杂碎(包括可供食用的肉或杂碎的细粉、粗粉)〔101干、熏、盐制其他濒危动物肉,102干、熏、盐制其他濒危动物食用杂碎〕	25		80	9/	0	千克	ABFE/	PRQS	50	
0210.9900 90	干、熏、盐制的其他肉及食用杂碎(包括可供食用的肉或杂碎的细粉、粗粉)〔101腌制马肉,102腌制绵羊肉,103腌制山羊肉,104腌制鹿肉,105干、熏、盐制其他肉,106干、熏、盐制其他食用杂碎,107去骨熟制猪肉制品〕	25		80	9/	9	千克	AB/	PRQS	50	

协定税率 %								RCEP		特惠税率 %			Article Description
东/冰/格	巴基斯坦	韩国	瑞士 上/下	哥/秘/柬	澳/毛	新西/坡/智	中国港/澳/台	东盟及马来/澳/韩	日/新	亚太2国	老/柬/缅	98/97/95	
0/0/0		9.3	2/2	0/0/0	0/0	0//0	0/0/	18/18/18	/18			0/0/0	---Of squabs
													---Other
0/0/0		13.8	2.3/2.3	0/0/0	0/13.8	0//0	0/0/	21.9/21.9/21.9	/21.9			0/0/0	Other meat of endangered wild animals, fresh, chilled or frozen
0/0/0		13.8	2.3/2.3	0/0/0	0/13.8	0//0	0/0/	21.9/21.9/21.9	/21.9			0/0/0	Other meat and edible offal, fresh、chilled or frozen
													Pig fat free of lean meat and poultry fat not rendered or otherwise extracted, fresh, chilled, frozen, salted, in brine, dried or smoked:
0/0/0		9.3	2/2	0/0/0	0/0	0//0	0/0/	18/18/18	18.8/18			0/0/0	-Of pigs
0/0/0		9.3	2/2	0/0/0	0/0	0//0	0/0/	18/18/18	18.8/18			0/0/0	-Other
													Meat and edible meat offal, salted, in brine, dried or smoked; edible flours and meals of meat or meat offal:
													-Meat of swine:
													--Hams, shoulders and cuts thereof, with bone in:
													---Hams and shoulders, with bone in
0/0/0		15		0/0/0	0/15	0//0	0/0/	23.8/23.8/23.8	23.8/23.8		0/0/	0/0/0	Hams and shoulders of pig-deer (*Babyrousa*), pygmy pig (*Porcula*), with bone in, salted, in brine, dried or smoked
0/0/0		15		0/0/0	0/15	0//0	0/0/	23.8/23.8/23.8	23.8/23.8		0/0/	0/0/0	Other hams and shoulders of swine, with bone in, salted, in brine, dried or smoked
													---Other
0/0/0		15		0/0/0	0/15	0//0	0/0/	23.8/23.8/23.8	23.8/23.8		0/0/	0/0/0	Cuts of pig-deer (*Babyrousa*), pygmy pig (*Porcula*), with bone in, salted, in brine, dried or smoked
0/0/0		15		0/0/0	0/15	0//0	0/0/	23.8/23.8/23.8	23.8/23.8		0/0/	0/0/0	Other meat of hams and shoulders, with bone in, salted, in brine, dried or smoked
													--Bellies (streaky) and cuts thereof
0/0/0		15		0/0/0	0/15	0//0	0/0/	23.8/23.8/23.8	23.8/23.8		0/0/	0/0/0	Bellies (streaky) and cuts thereof, of pig-deer (*Babyrousa*), pygmy pig (*Porcula*), salted, in brine, dried or smoked
0/0/0		15		0/0/0	0/15	0//0	0/0/	23.8/23.8/23.8	23.8/23.8		0/0/	0/0/0	Other bellies (streaky) and cuts thereof of swine, salted, in brine, dried or smoked
													--Other
0/0/0		15		0/0/0	0/15	0//0	0/0/	23.8/23.8/23.8	23.8/23.8		/0/0	0/0/0	Other meat of pig-deer (*Babyrousa*), pygmy pig (*porcula*), salted, in brine, dried or smoked
0/0/0		15		0/0/0	0/15	0//0	0/0/	23.8/23.8/23.8	23.8/23.8		/0/0	0/0/0	Other meat of swine, salted, in brine, dried or smoked
													-Meat of bovine animals
0/0/0		15	0/0	0/0/0	5/15	0//0	0/0/	23.8/23.8/23.8	23.8/23.8		0/0/	0/0/0	Meat of endangered wild bovine animals, salted, in brine, dried or smoked
0/0/0		15	0/0	0/0/0	5/15	0//0	0/0/	23.8/23.8/23.8	23.8/23.8		0/0/	0/0/0	Other meat of bovine animals, salted, in brine, dried or smoked
													-Other, including edible flours and meals of meat and meat offal:
0/0/0		5	2.5/2.5	0/0/0	0/15	0//0	0/0/	0/0/22.5	22.7/0		0/0/	0/0/0	--Of primates
0/0/0	17.5	5	2.5/2.5	0/0/0	0/15	0//0	0/0/	0/0/22.5	22.7/0		0/0/	0/0/0	--Of whales, dolphins and porpoises (mammals of the order Cetacea); of manatees and dugongs (mammals of the order Sirenia); of seal、sea lion and walrus (mammals of the sub-order Pinnipedia)
0/0/0		5	2.5/2.5	0/0/0	0/15	0//0	0/0/	0/0/22.5	22.7/0		0/0/	0/0/0	--Of reptiles (including snakes and turtles)
													--Other
0/0/0		15	2.5/2.5	0/0/0	0/15	0//0	0/0/	23.8/23.8/23.8	23.8/23.8		0/0/	0/0/0	Meat and edible offal of other endangered wild animals (including edible flours and meals of meat and meat offal), salted, in brine, dried or smoked
0/0/0		15	2.5/2.5	0/0/0	0/15	0//0	0/0/	23.8/23.8/23.8	23.8/23.8		0/0/	0/0/0	Other meat and edible offal (including edible flours and meals of meat and meat offal), salted, in brine, dried or smoked

第三章
鱼、甲壳动物、软体动物及其他水生无脊椎动物

注释：

一、本章不包括：

(一)税目 01.06 的哺乳动物；

(二)税目 01.06 的哺乳动物的肉(税目 02.08 或 02.10)；

(三)因品种或鲜度不适合供人食用的死鱼(包括鱼肝、鱼卵及鱼精等)、死甲壳动物、死软体动物及其他死水生无脊椎动物(第五章)；不适合供人食用的鱼、甲壳动物、软体动物、其他水生无脊椎动物的粉、粒(税目 23.01)；或

(四)鲟鱼子酱及用鱼卵制成的鲟鱼子酱代用品(税目 16.04)。

二、本章所称“团粒”，是指直接挤压或加入少量黏合剂制成的粒状产品。

三、税目 03.05 至 03.08 不包括适合供人食用的细粉、粗粉及团粒(税目 03.09)。

税则号列	货品名称〔CIQ 扩展编码及品名－T2 表示见附表 2〕	最惠(%)	暂定税率	普通	增值/消费	出口退税	计量单位	监管条件/特殊证件	检验检疫	对美关税	亚太上/下
03.01	**活鱼：**										
	-观赏鱼：										
0301.1100	--淡水鱼										
0301.1100 10	观赏用濒危淡水鱼〔101 淡水养殖热带鱼，102 淡水捕捞热带鱼，103 其他观赏鱼〕	10		80	9/	0	千克	ABFE/	PQ	35	
0301.1100 20	淡水鱼观赏鱼种苗(濒危除外)〔101 淡水养殖热带鱼，102 淡水捕捞热带鱼，103 其他观赏鱼〕	10		80	0/	9	千克	AB/	PQ		
0301.1100 90	观赏用其他淡水鱼(种苗除外)〔101 淡水养殖热带鱼，102 淡水捕捞热带鱼，103 其他观赏鱼〕	10		80	9/	9	千克	AB/	PQ	35	
0301.1900	--其他										
0301.1900 10	观赏用濒危非淡水鱼〔101 海水养殖热带鱼，102 海水捕捞热带鱼，103 其他观赏鱼〕	10		80	9/	0	千克	ABFE/	PQ	35	
0301.1900 20	非淡水观赏鱼种苗(濒危除外)〔101 海水养殖热带鱼，102 海水捕捞热带鱼，103 其他观赏鱼〕	10		80	0/	9	千克	AB/	PQ		
0301.1900 90	观赏用其他非淡水鱼(种苗除外)〔101 海水养殖热带鱼，102 海水捕捞热带鱼，103 其他观赏鱼〕	10		80	9/	9	千克	AB/	PQ	35	
	-其他活鱼：										
	--鳟鱼(河鳟、虹鳟、克拉克大麻哈鱼、阿瓜大麻哈鱼、吉雨大麻哈鱼、亚利桑那大麻哈鱼、金腹大麻哈鱼)：										
0301.9110	---鱼苗〔999〕	0		0	0/	9	千克	AB/	PQ		
0301.9190	---其他〔999〕	10		40	9/	9	千克	AB/	PRQ	15	7.6/7.6
	--鳗鱼(鳗鲡属)：										
0301.9210	---鱼苗										
0301.9210 10	花鳗鲡鱼苗〔999〕	0		0	9/	0	千克	ABE/	PNQ		
0301.9210 20	欧洲鳗鲡鱼苗〔999〕	0		0	9/	0	千克	ABEF/	PNQ		
0301.9210 90	鳗鱼(鳗鲡属)鱼苗(濒危除外)〔101 种用鳗鲡，102 海鳗〕	0		0	0/	0	千克	AB/	PNQ		
0301.9290	---其他										
0301.9290 10	花鳗鲡〔999〕	7		40	9/	9	千克	ABE/	PRQS	12	4.7/4.7
0301.9290 20	欧洲鳗鲡〔999〕	7		40	9/	9	千克	ABEF/	PRQS	12	4.7/4.7
0301.9290 90	其他活鳗鱼(鳗鲡属)〔101 种用鳗鲡，102 食用鳗鲡，103 海鳗〕	7		40	9/	9	千克	AB/	PRQS	12	4.7/4.7
	--鲤科鱼(鲤属、鲫属、草鱼、鲢属、鲮属、青鱼、卡特拉鲃、野鲮属、哈氏纹唇鱼、何氏细须鲃、鲂属)										
0301.9310	---鱼苗										
0301.9310 10	鲤属鱼鱼苗〔999〕	0		0	0/	9	千克	AB/	PQ		
0301.9310 90	其他鲤科鱼(鲫属、草鱼、鲢属、鲮属、青鱼、卡特拉鲃、野鲮属、哈氏纹唇鱼、何氏细须鲃、鲂属)鱼苗〔999〕	0		0	9/	9	千克	AB/	PQ		
0301.9390	---其他〔999〕	7		40	9/	9	千克	AB/	PRQS	12	5.3/5.3
	--大西洋及太平洋蓝鳍金枪鱼：										
0301.9410	---鱼苗〔999〕	0		0	0/	9	千克	AB/	PQ		
	---其他：	10.5									
0301.9491	----大西洋蓝鳍金枪鱼〔999〕	7		40	9/	9	千克	AB/	PNQ	12	5.3/5.3
0301.9492	----太平洋蓝鳍金枪鱼〔999〕	7		40	9/	9	千克	AB/	PNQ	12	5.3/5.3
	--南方蓝鳍金枪鱼：										
0301.9510	---鱼苗〔999〕	0		0	0/	9	千克	AB/	PQ		
0301.9590	---其他〔999〕	7		40	9/	9	千克	AB/	PNQ	12	5.3/5.3
	--其他：										
	---鱼苗：										
0301.9911	----鲈鱼〔101 淡水鲈鱼，102 海水鲈鱼〕	0		0	0/	9	千克	AB/	PQ		
0301.9912	----鲟鱼〔999〕	0		0	9/	9	千克	ABFE/	PQ		
0301.9919	----其他										

Chapter 3
Fish and crustaceans, molluscs and other aquatic invertebrates

Notes:

1. This Chapter does not cover:
   (a) Mammals of heading No. 01. 06;
   (b) Meat of mammals of heading No. 01. 06(heading No. 02. 08 or 02. 10);
   (c) Fish (including livers, roes thereof and nilt) or crustaceans, molluscs or other aquatic invertebrates, dead and unfit or unsuitable for human consumption by reason of either their species or their condition (Chapter 5); flours, meals or pellets of fish or of crustaceans, molluscs or other aquatic invertebrates, unfit for human consumption (heading No. 23. 01); or
   (d) Caviar or caviar substitutes prepared from fish eggs (heading No. 16. 04).
2. In this Chapter the term "pellets" means products which have been agglomerated either directly by compression or by the addition of a small quantity of binder.
3. Headings No.03.05 to 03.08 do not cover flours, meals and pellets, fit for human consumption (heading No.03.09).

协定税率 %								RCEP		特惠税率 %			Article Description
东/冰/格	巴基斯坦	韩国	瑞士上/下	哥/秘/柬	澳/毛	新西/坡/智	中国港/澳/台	东盟及马来/澳/韩	日/新	亚太2国	老/柬/缅	98/97/95	
													Live fish:
													-Ornamental fish:
													--Freshwater
0/0/0	14	8.1	1.8/1.8	0/0/0	0/0	0//0	0/0/	16.6/16.6/16.6	/16.6			0/0/0	Ornamental endangered freshwater fish
0/0/0	14	8.1	1.8/1.8	0/0/0	0/0	0//0	0/0/	16.6/16.6/16.6	/16.6			0/0/0	Freshwater fish and ornamental fish fry (except endangered)
0/0/0	14	8.1	1.8/1.8	0/0/0	0/0	0//0	0/0/	16.6/16.6/16.6	/16.6			0/0/0	Ornamental other freshwater fish
													--Other
0/0/0	14	8.1	1.8/1.8	0/0/0	0/0	0//0	0/0/	15.8/15.8/15.8	/15.8			0/0/0	Ornamental endangered not freshwater fish
0/0/0	14	8.1	1.8/1.8	0/0/0	0/0	0//0	0/0/	15.8/15.8/15.8	/15.8			0/0/0	Non—freshwater ornamental fish fry (except endangered)
0/0/0	14	8.1	1.8/1.8	0/0/0	0/0	0//0	0/0/	15.8/15.8/15.8	/15.8			0/0/0	Ornamental other not fresh water fish(other than fry)
													-Other live fish:
													--Trout (*Salmo trutta*, *Oncorhynchus my kiss*, *Oncorhynchus clarki*, *Oncorhynchus aguabonita*, *Oncorhynchus gilae*, *Oncorhynchus apache* and *Oncorhynchus chrysogaster*):
0/0/0	0	0	0/0	0/0/0	0/0	0//0	0/0/	0/0/0	0/0			0/0/0	---Fry
0/0/0	3.5	2.1	1.1/1.1	0/0/0	0/0	0//0	0/0/	0/0/9.5	9.5/0			0/0/0	---Other
													--Eels (*Anguilla spp.*):
													---Fry
0/0/0	0	0	0/0	0/0/0	0/0	0//0	0/0/	0/0/0	0/0			0/0/0	Fry of marbled eels (*Anguilla marmorata*)
0/0/0	0	0	0/0	0/0/0	0/0	0//0	0/0/	0/0/0	0/0			0/0/0	Fry eruopean eels
0/0/0	0	0	0/0	0/0/0	0/0	0//0	0/0/	0/0/0	0/0			0/0/0	Fry ofeels (*Anguilla marmorata*) (other than endangered fry)
													---Other
0/0/0	3.5	2	0/0	0/0/0	0/0	0//0	0/0/	0/0/9	9.1/0		/0/0	0/0/0	Marbled eels (*Anguilla marmorata*)
0/0/0	3.5	2	0/0	0/0/0	0/0	0//0	0/0/	0/0/9	9.1/0		/0/0	0/0/0	European eels
0/0/0	3.5	2	0/0	0/0/0	0/0	0//0	0/0/	0/0/9	9.1/0		/0/0	0/0/0	Other live eels (*Anguilla marmorata*)
													--Carp (*Cyprinus spp.*, *Caras— sius spp.*, *Ctenopharyngodon idellus*, *Hypophthalmichthys spp.*, *Cirrhinus spp.*, *Mylo— pharyngodon piceus*, *Catla catla*, *Labeo spp.*, *Osteochi—lus hasselti*, *Leptobarbus ho—eveni*, *Megalobrama spp.*)
													---Fry
0/0/0	0	0	0/0	0/0/0	0/0	0//0	0/0/	0/0/0	0/0			0/0/0	Carp fry
0/0/0	0	0	0/0	0/0/0	0/0	0//0	0/0/	0/0/0	0/0			0/0/0	Fry of other Cyprinidae fishes (crucian carp, grass carp, silver carp, dace, herring, catrabibarbus, wild dace, Haliotis, Spinibarbus Ho and Megalobrama)
0/0/0	3.5	2.1	1.1/1.1	0/0/0	0/0	0//0	0/0/	0/0/9.5	9.5/0		/0/0	0/0/0	---Other
													--Atlantic and pacific bluefin tunas(Thunnus thynnus, Thunnus orientalis):
0/0/0	0	0	0/0	0/0/0	0/0	0//0	0/0/	0/0/0	0/0			0/0/0	---Fry
													---Other:
0/0/0	3.5	2.1	1.1/1.1	0/0/0	0/0	0//0	0/0/	0/0/9.5	9.5/0		/0/0	0/0/0	----Atlantic bluefin tunas(Thunnus thynnus)
0/0/0	3.5	2.1	1.1/1.1	0/0/0	0/0	0//0	0/0/0	0/0/9.5	9.5/0		/0/0	0/0/0	----Pacific bluefin tunas(Thunnus orientalis)
													--Southern bluefin tunas(*thunnus maccoyii*):
0/0/0	0	0	0/0	0/0/0	0/0	0//0	0/0/	0/0/0	0/0			0/0/0	---Fry
0/0/0	3.5	2.1	1.1/1.1	0/0/0	0/0	0//0	0/0/	0/0/9.5	9.5/0		/0/0	0/0/0	---Other
													--Other:
													---Fry:
0/0/0	0	0	0/0	0/0/0	0/0	0//0	0/0/	0/0/0	0/0			0/0/0	----Of perches
0/0/0	0	0	0/0	0/0/0	0/0	0//0	0/0/	0/0/0	0/0			0/0/0	----Of sturgeon
													----Other

税则号列	货品名称〔CIQ 扩展编码及品名－T2 表示见附表 2〕	最惠(%)	暂定税率	普通	增值/消费	出口退税	计量单位	监管条件/特殊证件	检验检疫	对美关税	亚太上/下
0301.9919 10	其他濒危鱼苗〔101 其他淡水鱼,102 其他海水鱼,103 其他观赏鱼,104 其他鱼〕	0		0	9/	0	千克	ABFE/	PQ		
0301.9919 90	其他鱼苗(濒危除外)〔101 草鱼,102 鳙鱼(胖头鱼),103 鲢鱼,104 青鱼,105 鲶鱼(鲇鱼),106 武昌鱼,107 大马哈鱼,108 黄鳝,109 泥鳅,110 鲫鱼,111 牛头鮰鱼,112 斑点叉尾鮰鱼,113 黄蜡鲳鱼(狮鼻鲳鱼参),114 多瑙哲罗鱼,115 其他淡水鱼,116 海鳗,117 鲽鱼,118 红鱼(似石首鱼),119 牙鲆鱼,120 石斑鱼,121 大鲮鲆鱼,122 带鱼,123 鳎鱼,124 鲑鱼,125 金枪鱼,126 鲱鱼,127 鲣鱼,128 沙丁鱼,129 黄鱼,130 鲨鱼,131 鲭鱼,132 鳀鱼,133 鳕鱼,134 鲳鱼,135 卡拉白鱼,136 其他海水鱼,137 金鱼,138 锦鲤,139 其他鱼,140 其他受精卵〕	0		0	0/	9	千克	AB/	PQ		
	---其他:										
0301.9991	----罗非鱼〔999〕	7		40	9/	9	千克	AB/	PRQS	12	
0301.9992	----鲀〔101 其他淡水鱼,102 其他海水鱼,103 其他观赏鱼〕	10		40	9/	9	千克	AB/	PNQ	15	7.6/7.6
0301.9993	----其他鲤科鱼										
0301.9993 10	活的濒危鲤科鱼〔999〕	7		40	9/	0	千克	ABFE/	PNQ	12	5.3/5.3
0301.9993 90	活的其他鲤科鱼[鲤科鱼(鲤属、鲫属、草鱼、鲢属、鲮属、青鱼、卡特拉鲃、野鲮属、哈氏纹唇鱼、何氏细须鲃、鲂属)除外]〔999〕	7		40	9/	9	千克	AB/	PRQS	12	5.3/5.3
0301.9999	----其他										
0301.9999 10	其他濒危活鱼〔101 其他淡水鱼,102 其他海水鱼,103 其他观赏鱼,104 其他鱼〕	7		40	9/	0	千克	ABFE/	PNQ	12	5.3/5.3
0301.9999 90	其他活鱼〔T2〕	7		40	9/	9	千克	AB/	PRQS	12	5.3/5.3
03.02	**鲜、冷鱼,但税目 03.04 的鱼片及其他鱼肉除外:**										
	-鲑科鱼,但子目 0302.91 至 0302.99 的可食用鱼杂碎除外:										
0302.1100	--鳟鱼(河鳟、虹鳟、克拉克大麻哈鱼、阿瓜大麻哈鱼、吉雨大麻哈鱼、亚利桑那大麻哈鱼、金腹大麻哈鱼)[T2]	10		40	9/	9	千克	AB/	PRQS		
0302.1300	--大麻哈鱼[红大麻哈鱼、细鳞大麻哈鱼、大麻哈鱼(种)、大鳞大麻哈鱼、银大麻哈鱼、马苏大麻哈鱼、玫瑰大麻哈鱼][T2]	10		40	9/	9	千克	ABU/	PRQS		
	--大西洋鲑鱼及多瑙哲罗鱼:										
0302.1410	---大西洋鲑鱼〔101 养殖(非生食),102 养殖(可能用于生食),103 野生(非生食),104 野生(可能用于生食)〕	10	7	40	9/	9	千克	AB/	PRQS		
0302.1420	---多瑙哲罗鱼〔101 养殖,102 野生〕	7		40	9/	9	千克	AB/	PRQS		
0302.1900	--其他										
0302.1900 10	鲜或冷川陕哲罗鲑(子目 0302.91 至 0302.99 的可食用鱼杂碎除外)〔101 养殖,102 野生〕	10		40	9/	9	千克	AB/	PRQS		6.7/6.7
0302.1900 20	鲜或冷秦岭细鳞鲑(子目 0302.91 至 0302.99 的可食用鱼杂碎除外)〔101 养殖,102 野生〕	10		40	9/	9	千克	AB/	PRQS		6.7/6.7
0302.1900 90	其他鲜或冷鲑科鱼(子目 0302.91 至 0302.99 的可食用鱼杂碎除外)〔101 养殖,102 野生〕	10		40	9/	9	千克	AB/	PRQS		6.7/6.7
	-比目鱼(鲽科、鲆科、舌鳎科、鳎科、菱鲆科、刺鲆科),但子目 0302.91 至 0302.99 的可食用鱼杂碎除外:										
0302.2100	--庸鲽鱼(马舌鲽、庸鲽、狭鳞庸鲽)										
0302.2100 10	鲜或冷大西洋庸鲽(庸鲽)(子目 0302.91 至 0302.99 的可食用鱼杂碎除外)〔101 养殖,102 野生〕	7		40	9/	9	千克	ABU/	PRQS		5.3/5.3
0302.2100 20	鲜或冷马舌鲽(子目 0302.91 至 0302.99 的可食用鱼杂碎除外)〔101 养殖,102 野生〕	7		40	9/	9	千克	ABU/	PRQS		5.3/5.3
0302.2100 90	其他鲜或冷庸鲽鱼(子目 0302.91 至 0302.99 的可食用鱼杂碎除外)〔101 养殖,102 野生〕	7		40	9/	9	千克	AB/	PRQS		5.3/5.3
0302.2200	--鲽鱼(鲽)〔101 养殖,102 野生〕	7		40	9/	9	千克	AB/	PRQS		5.3/5.3
0302.2300	--鳎鱼(鳎属)〔101 养殖,102 野生〕	7		40	9/	9	千克	AB/	PRQS		5.3/5.3
0302.2400	--大菱鲆(瘤棘鲆)〔101 养殖,102 野生〕	7		40	9/	9	千克	AB/	PRQS		3.5/3.5
0302.2900	--其他										
0302.2900 10	鲜或冷的亚洲箭齿鲽(子目 0302.91 至 0302.99 的可食用鱼杂碎除外)〔101 养殖,102 野生〕	7		40	9/	9	千克	ABU/	PRQS		3.5/3.5
0302.2900 90	其他鲜或冷比目鱼(鲽科、鲆科、舌鳎科、鳎科、菱鲆科、刺鲆科)(子目 0302.91 至 0302.99 的可食用鱼杂碎除外)〔101 养殖,102 野生〕	7		40	9/	9	千克	AB/	PRQS		3.5/3.5
	-金枪鱼(金枪鱼属)、鲣,但子目 0302.91 至 0302.99 的可食用鱼杂碎除外:										
0302.3100	--长鳍金枪鱼〔101:野生(非生食); 102:野生(可能用于生食)〕	7		40	9/	9	千克	AB/	PRQS		5.3/5.3

协定税率 %								RCEP		特惠税率 %			Article Description
东/冰/格	巴基斯坦	韩国	瑞士 上/下	哥/秘/柬	澳/毛	新西/坡/智	中国港/澳/台	东盟及马来/澳/韩	日/新	亚太2国	老/柬/缅	98/97/95	
0/0/0	0	0	0/0	0/0/0	0/0	0//0	0/0/	0/0/0	0/0			0/0/0	Other endangered fry
0/0/0	0	0	0/0	0/0/0	0/0	0//0	0/0/	0/0/0	0/0			0/0/0	Other fry
													---Other:
0/0/0	3.5	2.1	1.1/1.1	0/0/0	0/0	0//0	0/0/	0/0/9.5	9.5/0		/0/0	0/0/0	----Tilapia
0/0/0	3.5	2.1	1.1/1.1	0/0/0	0/0	0//0	0/0/	0/0/9.5	9.5/0		/0/0	0/0/0	----Puffer fish
													----Other carp
0/0/0	3.5	2.1	1.1/1.1	0/0/0	0/0	0//0	0/0/	0/0/9.5	9.5/0		/0/0	0/0/0	Other live endangered carp
0/0/0	3.5	2.1	1.1/1.1	0/0/0	0/0	0//0	0/0/	0/0/9.5	9.5/0		/0/0	0/0/0	Other live carp(Carp(excluding Cyprinus spp., Carassius spp., Ctenopharyngodon idellus, Hypophthalmichthys spp., Cirrhinus spp., Mylopharyngodon piceus, Catla catla, Labeo spp., Osteochilus hasselti, Leptobarbus hoeveni, Megalobrama spp.)
													----Other
0/0/0	3.5	2.1	1.1/1.1	0/0/0	0/0	0//0	0/0/0	9.5/9.5/9.5	9.5/9.5		/0/0	0/0/0	Other live endangered fish
0/0/0	3.5	2.1	1.1/1.1	0/0/0	0/0	0//0	0/0/0	9.5/9.5/9.5	9.5/9.5		/0/0	0/0/0	Other live fish
													Fish, fresh or chilled, excluding fish fillets and other fish meat of heading No. 03. 04:
													-Salmonoid, excluding edible fish offal of subheading 0302. 91to 0302.99.
0/0/0	6	2.4	1.2/1.2	0/0/0	0/0	0//0	0/0/	0/0/10.8	10.9/0			0/0/0	--Trout (*Salmo trutta*, *Oncorhynchus my-kiss*, *Oncorhynchus clarki*, *Oncorhynchus aguabonita*, *Oncorhynchus gilae*, *Oncorhynchus apache* and *Oncorhynchus chrysogaster*)
0/0/0	3.5	2	0/0	0/0/0	0/0	0//0	0/0/	0/0/9	9.1/0			0/0/0	--Pacific salmon(Oncorhynchus nerka, Oncorhynchus gorbuscha, Oncorhynchus keta, Oncorhynchus tschawytscha, Oncorhynchus kisutch, Oncorhynchus masou and Oncorhynchus rhodurus)
													--Atlantic salmon(salmo salar) and Danube salmon(Hucho hucho):
0/0/0	3.5	2	0/0	0/0/0	0/0	0//0	0/0/	0/0/9	9.1/0			0/0/0	---Atlantic salmon(salmo salar)
0/0/0	3.5	2	0/0	0/0/0	0/0	0//0	0/0/	0/0/9	9.1/0			0/0/0	---Danube salmon(Hucho hucho)
													--Other
0/0/0	3.5	2.4	1.2/1.2	0/0/0	0/0	0//0	0/0/	0/0/10.8	10.9/0			0/0/0	Hucho bleekeri, fresh or chilled(excluding edible fish offal of subheading 0302.91 to 0302.99)
0/0/0	3.5	2.4	1.2/1.2	0/0/0	0/0	0//0	0/0/	0/0/10.8	10.9/0			0/0/0	Brachymystax lenck(Tslinling lenok), fresh or chilled(excluding edible fish offal of subheading 0302.91 to 0302.99)
0/0/0	3.5	2.4	1.2/1.2	0/0/0	0/0	0//0	0/0/	0/0/10.8	10.9/0			0/0/0	Other salmon, fresh or chilled(excluding edible fish offal of subheading 0302.91 to 0302.99)
													-Flat fish(pleuronectidae, Bothidae, Cynoglosside, Soleidae, Scophthalmidae and Citharidae), excluding edible fish offal of subheading NO.0302.91 to 0302.99:
													--Halibut (*Reinhardtius hippo-glossoides*, *Hippoglossush ippo-glossus*, *Hippoglossus stenole-pis*)
0/0/0	3.5	2.4	1.2/1.2	0/0/0	0/0	0//0	0/0/	0/0/10.8	10.9/0			0/0/0	Atlantic halibut(halibut), fresh or chilled(excluding edible fish offal of subheading 0302.91 to 0302.99)
0/0/0	3.5	2.4	1.2/1.2	0/0/0	0/0	0//0	0/0/	0/0/10.8	10.9/0			0/0/0	Reinhardtius, fresh or chilled(excluding edible fish offal of subheading 0302.91 to 0302.99)
0/0/0	3.5	2.4	1.2/1.2	0/0/0	0/0	0//0	0/0/	0/0/10.8	10.9/0			0/0/0	Other halibut, fresh or chilled(excluding edible fish offal of subheading 0302.91 to 0302.99)
0/0/0	3.5	2.4	1.2/1.2	0/0/0	0/0	0//0	0/0/	0/0/10.8	10.9/0			0/0/0	--Plaice (*Pleuronectes platessa*)
0/0/0	3.5	2.4	1.2/1.2	0/0/0	0/0	0//0	0/0/	0/0/10.8	10.9/0			0/0/0	--Sole (*Solea spp.*)
0/0/0	3.5	2.4	1.2/1.2	0/0/0	0/0	0//0	0/0/	0/0/10.8	10.9/0		/0/	0/0/0	--Turbot(Psetta maxima)
													--Other
0/0/0	3.5	2.4	1.2/1.2	0/0/0	0/0	0//0	0/0/	0/0/10.8	10.9/0		/0/	0/0/0	Arrowtooth halibut, fresh or chilled(excluding edible fish offal of subheading 0302.91 to 0302.99)
0/0/0	3.5	2.4	1.2/1.2	0/0/0	0/0	0//0	0/0/	0/0/10.8	10.9/0		/0/	0/0/0	Other flat fish ,fresh or chilled(excluding edible fish offal of subheading 0302.91 to 0302.99)
													-Tunas (*of the genus Thunnus*), skipjack tuna (stripe-bellied bonito) (*Katsuwonus pelamis*), excluding edible fish offal of subheading 0302. 91 to 0302. 99:
0/0/0	3.5	2.4	1.2/1.2	0/0/0	0/0	0//0	0/0/	0/0/10.8	10.9/0		/0/	0/0/0	--Albacore or longfinned tunas (*Thunnus alalunga*)

税则号列	货品名称〔CIQ 扩展编码及品名－T2 表示见附表 2〕	最惠(%)	暂定税率	普通	增值/消费	出口退税	计量单位	监管条件/特殊证件	检验检疫	对美关税	亚太上/下
0302.3200	--黄鳍金枪鱼〔101:野生(非生食);102:野生(可能用于生食)〕	7		40	9/	9	千克	AB/	PRQS		5.3/5.3
0302.3300	--鲣〔999〕	7		40	9/	9	千克	AB/	PRQS		4.7/4.7
0302.3400	--大眼金枪鱼〔101:野生(非生食);102:野生(可能用于生食)〕	7		40	9/	9	千克	AB/	PRQS		
	--大西洋及太平洋蓝鳍金枪鱼:										
0302.3510	---大西洋蓝鳍金枪鱼〔101:野生(非生食);102:野生(可能用于生食)〕	7		40	9/	9	千克	ABU/	PRQS		
0302.3520	---太平洋蓝鳍金枪鱼〔101 野生(非生食),102 野生(可能用于生食)〕	7		40	9/	9	千克	AB/	PRQS		4.7/4.7
0302.3600	--南方蓝鳍金枪鱼〔101:野生(非生食);102:野生(可能用于生食)〕	7		40	9/	9	千克	AB/	PRQS		
0302.3900	--其他〔101 野生(非生食),102 野生(可能用于生食),103 养殖〕	7		40	9/	9	千克	AB/	PRQS		4.7/4.7
	-鲱鱼(大西洋鲱鱼、太平洋鲱鱼)、鳀鱼(鳀属)、沙丁鱼(沙丁鱼、沙瑙鱼属)、小沙丁鱼属、黍鲱或西鲱、鲭鱼[大西洋鲭、澳洲鲭(鲐)、日本鲭(鲐)]、印度鲭(羽鳃鲐属)、马鲛鱼(马鲛属)、对称竹荚鱼、新西兰竹荚鱼及竹荚鱼(竹荚鱼属)、鲹鱼(鲹属)、军曹鱼、银鲳(鲳属)、秋刀鱼、圆鲹(圆鲹属)、多春鱼(毛鳞鱼)、剑鱼、鲔鱼、狐鲣(狐鲣属)、枪鱼、旗鱼、四鳍旗鱼(旗鱼科),但子目 0302.91 至 0302.99 的可食用鱼杂碎除外:										
0302.4100	--鲱鱼(大西洋鲱鱼、太平洋鲱鱼)										
0302.4100 10	鲜或冷太平洋鲱鱼(子目 0302.91 至 0302.99 的可食用鱼杂碎除外)〔101:鲜或冷养殖太平洋鲱鱼(养殖);102:鲜或冷野生太平洋鲱鱼(野生)〕			40	9/	9	千克	ABU/	PRQS		4.7/4.7
0302.4100 90	鲜或冷大西洋鲱鱼(子目 0302.91 至 0302.99 的可食用鱼杂碎除外)〔101:鲜或冷养殖大西洋鲱鱼(养殖);102:鲜或冷野生大西洋鲱鱼(野生)〕	7		40	9/	9	千克	AB/	PRQS		4.7/4.7
0302.4200	--鳀鱼(鳀属)〔101 饲料用其他海水鱼,102 鲜或冷养殖鳀鱼(鳀属),103 鲜或冷野生鳀鱼(鳀属)〕	7		40	9/	9	千克	AB/	PRQS		4.7/4.7
0302.4300	--沙丁鱼(沙丁鱼、沙瑙鱼属)、小沙丁鱼属、黍鲱或西鲱[T2]	7		40	9/	9	千克	AB/	PRQS		4.7/4.7
0302.4400	--鲭鱼[大西洋鲭、澳洲鲭(鲐)、日本鲭(鲐)]〔101 饲料用鲭鱼,102 养殖日本鲭(鲐),103 大西洋鲭,104 澳洲鲭(鲐),105 野生日本鲭(鲐)〕	7		40	9/	9	千克	AB/	PRQS		4.7/4.7
0302.4500	--对称竹荚鱼、新西兰竹荚鱼及竹荚鱼(竹荚鱼属)〔101 饲料用其他海水鱼,102 养殖对称竹荚鱼,103 养殖新西兰竹荚鱼及竹荚鱼(竹荚鱼属),104 野生对称竹荚鱼,105 野生新西兰竹荚鱼及竹荚鱼(竹荚鱼属)〕	7		40	9/	9	千克	AB/	PRQS		4.7/4.7
0302.4600	--军曹鱼〔101 饲料用其他海水鱼,102 食用〕	7		40	9/	9	千克	AB/	PRQS		4.7/4.7
0302.4700	--剑鱼〔999〕	7		40	9/	9	千克	ABU/	PRQS		4.7/4.7
	--其他:										
0302.4910	---银鲳(鲳属)〔999〕	7		40	9/	9	千克	AB/	PRQS		4.7/4.7
0302.4990	---其他〔101 鲜或冷印度鲭(羽鳃鲐属);102 鲜或冷马鲛鱼(马鲛属);103 鲜或冷鲹鱼(鲹属);104 鲜或冷秋刀鱼;105 鲜或冷圆鲹(圆鲹属);106 鲜或冷多春鱼(毛鳞鱼);107 鲜或冷鲔鱼;108 鲜或冷狐鲣(狐鲣属);109 鲜或冷枪鱼;110 鲜或冷旗鱼;111 鲜或冷四鳍旗鱼(旗鱼科)〕	7		40	9/	9	千克	AB/	PRQS		4.7/4.7
	-犀鳕科、多丝真鳕科、鳕科、长尾鳕科、黑鳕科、无须鳕科、深海鳕科及南极鳕科鱼,但子目 0302.91 至 0302.99 的可食用鱼杂碎除外:										
0302.5100	--鳕鱼(大西洋鳕鱼、格陵兰鳕鱼、太平洋鳕鱼)〔101 大西洋鳕鱼,102 太平洋鳕鱼,103 格陵兰鳕鱼〕	7		40	9/	9	千克	AB/	PRQS		4.7/4.7
0302.5200	--黑线鳕鱼(黑线鳕)〔999〕	7		40	9/	9	千克	AB/	PRQS		4.7/4.7
0302.5300	--绿青鳕鱼〔999〕	7		40	9/	9	千克	AB/	PRQS		4.7/4.7
0302.5400	--狗鳕鱼(无须鳕属、长鳍鳕属)〔101 饲料用其他海水鱼,102 无须鳕属,103 长鳍鳕属〕	7		40	9/	9	千克	AB/	PRQS		4.7/4.7
0302.5500	--阿拉斯加狭鳕鱼〔101 饲料用其他海水鱼,102 食用〕	7		40	9/	9	千克	ABU/	PRQS		4.7/4.7
0302.5600	--蓝鳕鱼(小鳍鳕、南蓝鳕)〔101 饲料用其他海水鱼,102 小鳍鳕,103 南蓝鳕〕	7		40	9/	9	千克	AB/	PRQS		4.7/4.7
0302.5900	--其他[T2]	7		40	9/	9	千克	AB/	PRQS		4.7/4.7

协定税率 %								RCEP		特惠税率 %			Article Description
东/冰/格	巴基斯坦	韩国	瑞士 上/下	哥/秘/柬	澳/毛	新西/坡/智	中国港/澳/台	东盟及马来/澳/韩	日/新	亚太2国	老/柬/缅	98/97/95	
0/0/0	3.5	2.4	1.2/1.2	0/0/0	0/0	0//0	0/0/	0/0/10.8	10.9/0			0/0/0	--Yellowfin tunas (*Thunnus albacares*)
0/0/0	3.5	2.4	1.2/1.2	0/0/0	0/0	0//0	0/0/	0/0/10.8	10.9/0			0/0/0	--Bonito
0/0/0	6	2.4	1.2/1.2	0/0/0	0/0	0//0	0/0/	0/0/10.8	10.9/0		/0/0	0/0/0	--Bigeye tunas (*Thunnus obesus*)
													--Atlantic and pacific bluefin tunas(Thunnus thynnus, Thunnus orientalis):
0/0/0	6	2.4	1.2/1.2	0/0/0	0/0	0//0	0/0/	0/0/10.8	10.9/0		/0/0	0/0/0	---Atlantic bluefin tunas(Thunnus thynnus)
0/0/0	3.5	2.4	1.2/1.2	0/0/0	0/0	0//0	0/0/	0/0/10.8	10.9/0		/0/0	0/0/0	---Pacific bluefin tunas(Thunnus orientalis)
0/0/0	6	2.4	1.2/1.2	0/0/0	0/0	0//0	0/0/	0/0/10.8	10.9/0		/0/0	0/0/0	--Southern bluefin tunas(Thunnus maccoyii)
0/0/0	3.5	2.4	1.2/1.2	0/0/0	0/0	0//0	0/0/	0/0/10.8	10.9/0		/0/0	0/0/0	--Other
													-Herrings (*Clupea harengus*, *Clupea pallasii*), *anchovies* (*Engraulis spp.*), sardines (*Sardina pilchardus*, *Sardinops spp*), sardinella (*sardinella spp.*), brisling or sprats (*Sprattus Sprattus*), mackerel (*Scomber Scombrus*, *Scomber australasicus*, *Scom-ber japonicus*), Indian macker-els (*Rastrelliger spp.*), seerfi-shes (*Scomberomorus spp.*), jack and horse mackerel (*Tra-churus spp.*), jacks, crevalles (*Caranx spp.*), cobia (*Rachy-centron canadum*), silver pom-frets (*Pampus spp.*), Pacific saury (*Cololabis saira*), scad s (*Decapterus spp.*), capelin (*Mallotus villosus*), swordfish (*Xiphias gladius*), Kawakawa (*Euthynnus affinis*), bonitos (*Sarda spp.*), marlins, sail-fishes, spearfish (*Istiophori-dae*), excluding edible fish offal of subheading 0302. 91 to 0302. 99:)
													--Herring(Clupea harengus, clupea pallasii)
0/0/0	3.5	2.4	1.2/1.2	0/0/0	0/0	0//0	0/0/	0/0/10.8	10.9/0			0/0/0	Clupea pallasii, fresh or chilled(excluding edible fish offal of subheading 0302.91 to 0302.99)
0/0/0	3.5	2.4	1.2/1.2	0/0/0	0/0	0//0	0/0/	0/0/10.8	10.9/0			0/0/0	Herrings(Clupea harengus), fresh or chilled(excluding edible fish offal of subheading 0302.91 to 0302.99)
0/0/0	3.5	2.4	1.2/1.2	0/0/0	0/0	0//0	0/0/0	0/0/10.8	10.9/0		/0/0	0/0/0	--anchovies(Engraulis spp.)
0/0/0	3.5	2.4	1.2/1.2	0/0/0	0/0	0//0	0/0/	0/0/10.8	10.9/0			0/0/0	--sardines (Sardina pilchardus, Sardinops spp.), sardinella (Sardinella spp.), brisling or sprats(Sprattus sprattus)
0/0/0	3.5	2.4	1.2/1.2	0/0/0	0/0	0//0	0/0/	0/0/10.8	10.9/0			0/0/0	--mackerel(Scomber scombrus, Scomber australasicus, Scomber japonicus)
0/0/0	3.5	2.4	1.2/1.2	0/0/0	0/0	0//0	0/0/0	11.2/11.4/11.2	11.3/11.4		/0/0	0/0/0	--jack and horse mackerel(Trachurus spp.)
0/0/0	3.5	2.4	1.2/1.2	0/0/0	0/0	0//0	0/0/0	0/0/10.8	10.9/0		/0/0	0/0/0	--Cobia(Rachycentron canadum)
0/0/0	3.5	2.4	1.2/1.2	0/0/0	0/0	0//0	0/0/	0/0/10.8	10.9/0			0/0/0	--Swordfish(Xiphias gladius)
													--Other:
0/0/0	3.5	2.4	1.2/1.2	0/0/0	0/0	0//0	0/0/0	0/0/10.8	10.9/0		/0/0	0/0/0	---Silver pomfret (Pampus spp.)
0/0/0	3.5	2.4	1.2/1.2	0/0/0	0/0	0//0	0/0/0	0/0/10.8	10.9/0		/0/0	0/0/0	---Other
													-Fish of the families Bregmacer-otidae, Euclichthyidae, Gadidae, Macrouridae, Melanoni-dae, Merlucciidae, Moridae and Muraenolepididae, excluding edible fish offal of subheading 0303.91 to 0303.99:
0/0/0	3.5	2.4	1.2/1.2	0/0/0	0/0	0//0	0/0/	0/0/10.8	10.9/0			0/0/0	--Cod(Gadus morhua, Gadus ogac, Gadus macrocephalus)
0/0/0	3.5	2.4	1.2/1.2	0/0/0	0/0	0//0	0/0/	0/0/10.8	10.9/0			0/0/0	--Haddock(Melanogrammus aeglefinus)
0/0/0	3.5	2.4	1.2/1.2	0/0/0	0/0	0//0	0/0/	0/0/10.8	10.9/0			0/0/0	--Coalfish(Pollachius virens)
0/0/0	3.5	2.4	1.2/1.2	0/0/0	0/0	0//0	0/0/0	0/0/10.8	10.9/0		/0/0	0/0/0	--Hake(Merluccius spp., Urophycis spp.)
0/0/0	3.5	2.4	1.2/1.2	0/0/0	0/0	0//0	0/0/0	0/0/10.8	10.9/0		/0/0	0/0/0	--Alaska Pollock(*Theragra chalcogramma*)
0/0/0	3.5	2.4	1.2/1.2	0/0/0	0/0	0//0	0/0/0	0/0/10.8	10.9/0		/0/0	0/0/0	--Blue whitings (Micromesistius poutassou, Micromesistius australis)
0/0/0	3.5	2.4	1.2/1.2	0/0/0	0/0	0//0	0/0/0	0/0/10.8	10.9/0		/0/0	0/0/0	--Other

税则号列	货品名称〔CIQ 扩展编码及品名－T2 表示见附表 2〕	最惠(%)	暂定税率	普通	增值/消费	出口退税	计量单位	监管条件/特殊证件	检验检疫	对美关税	亚太上/下
	-罗非鱼(口孵非鲫属)、鲶鱼(𩷶鲶属、鲶属、胡鲶属、真鮰属)、鲤科鱼(鲤属、鲫属、草鱼、鲢属、鲮属、青鱼、卡特拉鲃、野鲮属、哈氏纹唇鱼、何氏细须鲃、鲂属)、鳗鱼(鳗鲡属)、尼罗河鲈鱼(尼罗尖吻鲈)及黑鱼(鳢属),但子目 0302.91 至 0302.99 的可食用鱼杂碎除外:										
0302.7100	--罗非鱼(口孵非鲫属)〔101 养殖罗非鱼(口孵非鲫属),102 野生罗非鱼(口孵非鲫属)〕	7		40	9/	9	千克	AB/	PRQS		
0302.7200	--鲶鱼(𩷶鲶属、鲶属、胡鲶属、真鮰属)〔101 饲料用其他海水鱼,102 养殖(鱼芒)鲶属,103 养殖胡鲶属,104 养殖真鮰属,105 野生(鱼芒)鲶属,106 野生胡鲶属,107 野生真鮰属〕	10		40	9/	9	千克	AB/	PRQS		6.7/6.7
0302.7300	--鲤科鱼(鲤属、鲫属、草鱼、鲢属、鲮属、青鱼、卡特拉鲃、野鲮属、哈氏纹唇鱼、何氏细须鲃、鲂属)[T2]	7		40	9/	9	千克	AB/	PRQS		4.7/4.7
0302.7400	--鳗鱼(鳗鲡属)										
0302.7400 10	鲜或冷花鳗鲡(子目 0302.91 至 0302.99 的可食用鱼杂碎除外)〔101 养殖非生食,102 养殖可能用于生食,103 野生非生食,104 野生可能用于生食〕	7		40	9/	9	千克	ABE/	PRQS		4.7/4.7
0302.7400 20	鲜或冷欧洲鳗鲡(子目 0302.91 至 0302.99 的可食用鱼杂碎除外)〔101 养殖非生食,102 养殖可能用于生食,103 野生非生食,104 野生可能用于生食〕	7		40	9/	9	千克	ABEF/	PRQS		4.7/4.7
0302.7400 90	其他鲜或冷鳗鱼(鳗鲡属)(子目 0302.91 至 0302.99 的可食用鱼杂碎除外)〔101 养殖非生食,102 养殖可能用于生食,103 野生非生食,104 野生可能用于生食〕	7		40	9/	9	千克	AB/	PRQS		4.7/4.7
0302.7900	--其他										
0302.7900 01	鲜或冷尼罗河鲈鱼(尼罗尖吻鲈)(子目 0302.91 至 0302.99 的可食用鱼杂碎除外)〔101 养殖非生食,102 养殖可能用于生食,103 野生非生食,104 野生可能用于生食〕	7		40	9/	9	千克	AB/	PRQS		4.7/4.7
0302.7900 90	鲜或冷的黑鱼(鳢属)(子目 0302.91 至 0302.99 的可食用鱼杂碎除外)〔101 养殖非生食,102 养殖可能用于生食,103 野生非生食,104 野生可能用于生食〕	7		40	9/	9	千克	AB/	PRQS		4.7/4.7
	-其他鱼,但子目 0302.91 至 0302.99 的可食用鱼杂碎除外:										
0302.8100	--角鲨及其他鲨鱼										
0302.8100 10	鲜或冷濒危鲨鱼(子目 0302.91 至 0302.99 的可食用鱼杂碎除外)〔999〕	7		40	9/	0	千克	ABEF/	PRQS		5.3/5.3
0302.8100 90	鲜或冷其他鲨鱼(子目 0302.91 至 0302.99 的可食用鱼杂碎除外)〔999〕	7		40	9/	9	千克	AB/	PRQS		5.3/5.3
0302.8200	--魟鱼及鳐鱼(鳐科)〔101 饲料用其他海水鱼,102 食用〕	7		40	9/	9	千克	AB/	PRQS		4.7/4.7
0302.8300	--南极犬牙鱼(南极犬牙鱼属)〔999〕	7		40	9/	9	千克	ABU/	PRQS		4.7/4.7
0302.8400	--尖吻鲈鱼(舌齿鲈属)〔999〕	7		40	9/	9	千克	AB/	PRQS		4.7/4.7
0302.8500	--菱羊鲷(鲷科)〔应为:101 饲料用其他海水鱼,102 养殖非生食,103 养殖可能用于生食,104 野生非生食,105 野生可能用于生食〕	7		40	9/	9	千克	AB/	PRQS		4.7/4.7
	--其他:										
0302.8910	---带鱼〔999〕	7		40	9/	9	千克	AB/	PRQS		4.7/4.7
0302.8920	---黄鱼〔101 养殖,102 野生〕	7		40	9/	9	千克	AB/	PRQS		4.7/4.7
0302.8930	---鲳鱼(银鲳除外)〔101 养殖;102 野生〕	7		40	9/	9	千克	AB/	PRQS		4.7/4.7
0302.8940	---鲀〔999〕	10		40	9/	9	千克	AB/	PRQS		6.7/6.7
0302.8990	---其他										
0302.8990 01	鲜或冷的其他鲈鱼(子目 0302.91 至 0302.99 的可食用鱼杂碎除外)〔101 养殖非生食,102 养殖可能用于生食,103 野生非生食,104 野生可能用于生食〕	7		40	9/	9	千克	AB/	PRQS		4.7/4.7
0302.8990 10	其他未列名濒危鲜或冷鱼(子目 0302.91 至 0302.99 的可食用鱼杂碎除外)〔999〕	7		40	9/	0	千克	ABFE/	PRQS		4.7/4.7
0302.8990 20	鲜或冷的平鲉属(子目 0302.91 至 0302.99 的可食用鱼杂碎除外)〔101 养殖,102 野生〕	7		40	9/	9	千克	ABU/	PRQS		4.7/4.7
0302.8990 30	鲜或冷的鲪鲉属(叶鳍鲉属)(子目 0302.91 至 0302.99 的可食用鱼杂碎除外)〔101 养殖,102 野生〕	7		40	9/	9	千克	ABU/	PRQS		4.7/4.7
0302.8990 90	其他鲜或冷鱼(子目 0302.91 至 0302.99 的可食用鱼杂碎除外)[T2]	7		40	9/	9	千克	AB/	PRQS		4.7/4.7
	-鱼肝、鱼卵、鱼精、鱼鳍、鱼头、鱼尾、鱼鳔及其他可食用鱼杂碎:										
0302.9100	--鱼肝、鱼卵及鱼精										
0302.9100 10	鲜或冷濒危鱼种的肝、鱼卵及鱼精[T2]	7		50	9/	0	千克	ABFE/	PRQS		
0302.9100 20	鲜、冷的鱼卵(濒危除外)〔101 其他鲜或冷养殖鱼鱼卵,102 其他鲜或冷野生鱼鱼卵〕	7		50	0/	9	千克	AB/	PQ		

协定税率 %								RCEP		特惠税率 %			Article Description
东/冰/格	巴基斯坦	韩国	瑞士 上/下	哥/秘/柬	澳/毛	新西/坡/智	中国港/澳/台	东盟及马来/澳/韩	日/新	亚太2国	老/柬/缅	98/97/95	
													-Tilapias (*Oreochromis spp.*), catfish (*Pangasius spp.*, *Si-lu-rus spp.*, *Clarias spp.*, *Icta-lurus spp.*), carp (*Cypri-nus spp.*, *Carassius spp.*, *Cteno-pharyngodon idellus*, *Hy-po-phthalmichthys spp.*, *Cirrhi-nus spp.*, *Mylopharyng-odon piceus*, *Catla catla*, *Labeo spp*,. *Osteochilus hasselti*, *Leptobarbus hoeveni*, *Megalo-brama spp*), eels (*Anguilla spp.*), Nile perch (*Lates niloticus*) and snakeheads (*Cham-ma spp.*), excluding edi-ble fish offal of subheading 0303.91 to 0303.99:
0/0/0	6	2.4	1.2/1.2	0/0/0	0/0	0//0	0/0/	0/0/10.8	10.9/0		/0/0	0/0/0	--Tilapia(oreochromis spp.)
0/0/0	3.5	2.4	1.2/1.2	0/0/0	0/0	0//0	0/0/0	0/0/10.8	10.9/0		/0/0	0/0/0	--catfish(Pangasius spp., Silurus spp., Clarias spp., Ictalurus spp.)
0/0/0	3.5	2.4	1.2/1.2	0/0/0	0/0	0//0	0/0/0	0/0/10.8	10.9/0		/0/0	0/0/0	--Carp (*Cyprinus spp.*, *Caras- sius spp.*, *Ctenopharyng-odon idellus*, *Hypophthalmichthys spp.*, *Cirrhinus spp.*, *Mylo- pharyngodon piceus*, *Catla catla*, *Labeo spp.*, *Os-teochi-lus hasselti*, *Leptobarbus ho-eveni*, *Megalobrama spp.*)
													--Eel(anguilla spp.)
0/0/0	3.5	2.4	1.2/1.2	0/0/0	0/0	0//0	0/0/	0/0/10.8	10.9/0		//0	0/0/0	Marbled eels, fresh or chilled(excluding edible fish offal of subheading 0302.91 to 0302.99)
0/0/0	3.5	2.4	1.2/1.2	0/0/0	0/0	0//0	0/0/	0/0/10.8	10.9/0		//0	0/0/0	European eels, fresh or chilled(excluding edible fish offal of subheading 0302.91 to 0302.99)
0/0/0	3.5	2.4	1.2/1.2	0/0/0	0/0	0//0	0/0/	0/0/10.8	10.9/0		//0	0/0/0	Other eels, fresh or chilled(excluding edible fish offal of sub-heading 0302.91 to 0302.99)
													--Other
0/0/0	3.5	2.4	1.2/1.2	0/0/0	0/0	0//0	0/0/0	0/0/10.8	10.9/0		/0/0	0/0/0	Nile perch(Lates niloticus) , fresh or chilled(excluding edible fish offal of subheading 0302.91 to 0302.99)
0/0/0	3.5	2.4	1.2/1.2	0/0/0	0/0	0//0	0/0/0	0/0/10.8	10.9/0		/0/0	0/0/0	Snakeheads(Channa spp.), fresh or chilled(excluding edible fish offal of subheading 0302.91 to 0302.99)
													-Other fish excluding edible fish offal of subheading 0302. 91 to 0302. 99:
													--Dogfish and other sharks
0/0/0	3.5	2.4	1.2/1.2	0/0/0	0/0	0//0	0/0/	0/0/10.8	10.9/0			0/0/0	Endangered shark, fresh or chilled(excluding edible fish offal of subheading 0302.91 to 0302.99)
0/0/0	3.5	2.4	1.2/1.2	0/0/0	0/0	0//0	0/0/	0/0/10.8	10.9/0			0/0/0	Other sharks, fresh or chilled excluding livers and roes
0/0/0	3.5	2.4	1.2/1.2	0/0/0	0/0	0//0	0/0/0	0/0/10.8	10.9/0		/0/0	0/0/0	--Rays and skates(Rajidae)
0/0/0	3.5	2.4	1.2/1.2	0/0/0	0/0	0//0	0/0/	0/0/10.8	10.9/0		/0/0	0/0/0	Toothfish(dissostichus spp.)
0/0/0	3.5	2.4	1.2/1.2	0/0/0	0/0	0//0	0/0/0	0/0/10.8	10.9/0		/0/0	0/0/0	--Seabass(Dicentrarchus spp.)
0/0/0	3.5	2.4	1.2/1.2	0/0/0	0/0	0//0	0/0/0	0/0/10.8	10.9/0		/0/0	0/0/0	--Seabream(Sparidae)
													--Other:
0/0/0	0	2.4	1.2/1.2	0/0/0	0/0	0//0	0/0/	0/0/10.8	10.9/0			0/0/0	---Scabber fish(Trichurius)
0/0/0	3.5	2.4	1.2/1.2	0/0/0	0/0	0//0	0/0/	0/0/10.8	10.9/0			0/0/0	---Yellow croaker(Pseudosicaena)
0/0/0	4	2.4	1.2/1.2	0/0/0	0/0	0//0	0/0/	0/0/10.8	10.9/0			0/0/0	---Butterfish (pamus), excluding Silver pomfret
0/0/0	3.5	2.4	1.2/1.2	0/0/0	0/0	0//0	0/0/	0/0/10.8	10.9/0		/0/0	0/0/0	---Puffer fish
													---Other
0/0/0	3.5	2.4	1.2/1.2	0/0/0	0/0	0//0	0/0/0	0/0/10.8	10.9/0		/0/0	0/0/0	Other perch, fresh or chilled(excluding edible fish offal of subheading 0302.91 to 0302.99)
0/0/0	3.5	2.4	1.2/1.2	0/0/0	0/0	0//0	0/0/0	0/0/10.8	10.9/0		/0/0	0/0/0	Other endangered fish, fresh or chilled(excluding edible fish offal of subheading 0302.91 to 0302.99)
0/0/0	3.5	2.4	1.2/1.2	0/0/0	0/0	0//0	0/0/0	0/0/10.8	10.9/0		/0/0	0/0/0	Fresh and cold flat scorpionfish genera(excluding edible fish offal of subheading 0302.91 to 0302.99)
0/0/0	3.5	2.4	1.2/1.2	0/0/0	0/0	0//0	0/0/0	0/0/10.8	10.9/0		/0/0	0/0/0	Fresh and cold Jun scorpionfish genera (leaf scorpionfish fins)(excluding edible fish offal of subheading 0302. 91 to 0302.99)
0/0/0	3.5	2.4	1.2/1.2	0/0/0	0/0	0//0	0/0/0	0/0/10.8	10.9/0		/0/0	0/0/0	Other fish, fresh or chilled(excluding edible fish offal of sub-heading 0302.91 to 0302.99)
													Livers, roes, milt, fins, heads, tails, maws and other edible fish offal:
													--Livers, roes, and milt
0/0/0	6	2.4	1.2/1.2	0/0/0	0/0	0//0	0/0/	0/0/10.8	10.9/0		/0/	0/0/0	Livers, roes and milt of endangered fish, cold or chilled
0/0/0	6	2.4	1.2/1.2	0/0/0	0/0	0//0	0/0/	0/0/10.8	10.9/0		/0/	0/0/0	Fresh and cold fish eggs (except endangered)

税则号列	货品名称〔CIQ 扩展编码及品名－T2 表示见附表 2〕	最惠(%)	暂定税率	普通	增值/消费	出口退税	计量单位	监管条件/特殊证件	检验检疫	对美关税	亚太上/下
0302.9100 90	其他鲜或冷鱼肝及鱼精〔101 其他鲜或冷养殖鱼鱼肝，102 其他鲜或冷野生鱼鱼肝，103 其他鲜或冷养殖鱼鱼精，104 其他鲜或冷野生鱼鱼精〕	7		50	9/	9	千克	AB/	PRQS		
0302.9200	--鲨鱼翅										
0302.9200 10	鲜或冷濒危鲨鱼翅〔999〕	12		40	9/	0	千克	ABFE/	PRQS		9/9
0302.9200 90	其他鲜或冷鲨鱼翅〔999〕	12		40	9/	9	千克	AB/	PRQS		9/9
0302.9900	--其他										
0302.9900 10	其他鲜或冷可食用濒危鱼杂碎〔101 养殖，102 野生〕	7		40	9/	0	千克	ABFE/	PRQS		
0302.9900 20	鲜或冷的大菱鲆、比目鱼、鲱鱼、鲭鱼、鲳鱼、带鱼、尼罗河鲈鱼、尖吻鲈鱼、其他鲈鱼的可食用其他鱼杂碎〔101 养殖，102 野生〕	7		40	9/	9	千克	AB/	PRQS		
0302.9900 90	其他鲜或冷可食用其他鱼杂碎〔101 养殖，102 野生〕	7		40	9/	9	千克	AB/	PRQS		
03.03	**冻鱼，但税目 03.04 的鱼片及其他鱼肉除外：**										
	-鲑科鱼，但子目 0303.91 至 0303.99 的可食用鱼杂碎除外：										
0303.1100	--红大麻哈鱼〔101 冻养殖红大麻哈鱼，102 冻野生红大麻哈鱼〕	7		40	9/	9	千克	ABU/	PRQS	37	4.7/4.7
0303.1200	--其他大麻哈鱼[细鳞大麻哈鱼、大麻哈鱼(种)、大鳞大麻哈鱼、银大麻哈鱼、马苏大麻哈鱼、玫瑰大麻哈鱼][T2]	7		40	9/	9	千克	ABU/	PRQS	37	4.7/4.7
	--大西洋鲑鱼及多瑙哲罗鱼：										
0303.1310	---大西洋鲑鱼〔101 养殖大西洋鲑鱼(非生食)；102 养殖大西洋鲑鱼(可能用于生食)；103 野生大西洋鲑鱼(非生食)；104 野生大西洋鲑鱼(可能用于生食)〕	7	5	40	9/	9	千克	AB/	PRQS	35	
0303.1320	---多瑙哲罗鱼〔101 养殖多瑙哲罗鱼；102 野生多瑙哲罗鱼〕	7		40	9/	9	千克	AB/	PRQS	37	
0303.1400	--鳟鱼(河鳟、虹鳟、克拉克大麻哈鱼、阿瓜大麻哈鱼、吉雨大麻哈鱼、亚利桑那大麻哈鱼、金腹大麻哈鱼)[T2]	12		40	9/	9	千克	AB/	PRQS	42	
0303.1900	--其他										
0303.1900 10	冻川陕哲罗鲑(但子目 0303.91 至 0303.99 的可食用鱼杂碎除外)〔101 养殖，102 野生〕	10		40	9/	9	千克	AB/	PRQS	40	6.7/6.7
0303.1900 20	冻秦岭细鳞鲑(但子目 0303.91 至 0303.99 的可食用鱼杂碎除外)〔101 养殖，102 野生〕	10		40	9/	9	千克	AB/	PRQS	40	6.7/6.7
0303.1900 90	其他冻鲑科鱼(但子目 0303.91 至 0303.99 的可食用鱼杂碎除外)〔101 养殖，102 野生〕	10		40	9/	9	千克	AB/	PRQS	40	6.7/6.7
	-罗非鱼(口孵非鲫属)、鲶鱼(鲑鲶属、鲶属、胡鲶属、真鮰属)、鲤科鱼(鲤属、鲫属、草鱼、鲢属、鲮属、青鱼、卡特拉鲃、野鲮属、哈氏纹唇鱼、何氏细须鲃、鲂属)、鳗鱼(鳗鲡属)、尼罗河鲈鱼(尼罗尖吻鲈)及黑鱼(鳢属)，但子目 0303.91 至 0303.99 的可食用鱼杂碎除外：										
0303.2300	--罗非鱼(口孵非鲫属)〔101 养殖，102 野生〕	7		40	9/	9	千克	AB/	PRQS	37	3.5/3.5
0303.2400	--鲶鱼(鲑鲶属、鲶属、胡鲶属、真鮰属)[T2]	10		40	9/	9	千克	AB/	PRQS	40	5/5
0303.2500	--鲤科鱼(鲤属、鲫属、草鱼、鲢属、鲮属、青鱼、卡特拉鲃、野鲮属、哈氏纹唇鱼、何氏细须鲃、鲂属)[T2]	10		40	9/	9	千克	AB/	PRQS	40	5/5
0303.2600	--鳗鱼(鳗鲡属)										
0303.2600 10	冻花鳗鲡(但子目 0303.91 至 0303.99 的可食用鱼杂碎除外)〔101 养殖，102 野生〕	10		40	9/	9	千克	ABE/	PRQS	40	6.7/6.7
0303.2600 20	冻欧洲鳗鲡(但子目 0303.91 至 0303.99 的可食用鱼杂碎除外)〔101 养殖，102 野生〕	10		40	9/	9	千克	ABEF/	PRQS	40	6.7/6.7
0303.2600 90	其他冻鳗鱼(鳗鲡属)(但子目 0303.91 至 0303.99 的可食用鱼杂碎除外)〔101 养殖，102 野生〕	10		40	9/	9	千克	AB/	PRQS	40	6.7/6.7
0303.2900	--其他										
0303.2900 01	冻尼罗河鲈鱼(尼罗尖吻鲈)(但子目 0303.91 至 0303.99 的可食用鱼杂碎除外)〔101 养殖，102 野生〕	7		40	9/	9	千克	AB/	PRQS	37	3.5/3.5
0303.2900 90	冻黑鱼(鳢属)(但子目 0303.91 至 0303.99 的可食用鱼杂碎除外)〔101 养殖，102 野生〕	7		40	9/	9	千克	AB/	PRQS	37	3.5/3.5
	-比目鱼(鲆科、鲽科、舌鳎科、鳎科、菱鲆科、刺鲆科)，但子目 0303.91 至 0303.99 的可食用鱼杂碎除外：										
	--庸鲽鱼(马舌鲽、庸鲽、狭鳞庸鲽)：										
0303.3110	---马舌鲽(格陵兰庸鲽鱼)〔999〕	7	2	40	9/	9	千克	ABU/	PRQS	32	4.7/4.7

协定税率 %								RCEP		特惠税率 %			Article Description
东/冰/格	巴基斯坦	韩国	瑞士上/下	哥/秘/柬	澳/毛	新西/坡/智	中国港/澳/台	东盟及马来/澳/韩	日/新	亚太2国	老/柬/缅	98/97/95	
0/0/0	6	2.4	1.2/1.2	0/0/0	0/0	0//0	0/0/	0/0/10.8	10.9/0		/0/	0/0/0	Other fish livers and milt, cold or chilled
													--Shark fins
0/0/0	3.5	2.4	1.2/1.2	0/0/0	0/	0//0	0/0/	0/0/10.8	10.9/0			0/0/0	Endangered Shark fins, cold or chilled
0/0/0	3.5	2.4	1.2/1.2	0/0/0	0/	0//0	0/0/	0/0/10.8	10.9/0			0/0/0	Other Shark fins, cold or chilled
													--Other
0/0/0	3.5	2	0/0	0/0/0	0/0	0//0	0/0/	0/0/9	9.1/0			0/0/0	Other edible endangered fish offals, cold or chilled
0/0/0	3.5	2	0/0	0/0/0	0/0	0//0	0/0/	0/0/9	9.1/0			0/0/0	Other edible fish offals of Turbots, flatfish, herring, mackerel, Pomfret, hairtail, Nile perch and other perch, fresh or chilled
0/0/0	3.5	2	0/0	0/0/0	0/0	0//0	0/0/	0/0/9	9.1/0			0/0/0	Other edible fish offals of other fish , cold or chilled
													Fish, frozen, excluding fish fillets and other fish meat of heading No. 03. 04:
													-Salmonidae, excluding edible fish offal of subheading 0303. 91 to 0303. 99:
0/0/0	3.5	2	0/0	0/0/0	0/0	0//0	0/0/	0/0/9	9.1/0		/0/	0/0/0	--Sockeye salmon(red salmon)(*Oncorhynchus nerka*)
0/0/0	3.5	2	0/0	0/0/0	0/0	0//0	0/0/	9/9/9	9.5/9		/0/	0/0/0	--Other Pacific salmon(Oncorhynchus gorbuscha, Oncorhynchus keta, Oncorhynchus tschawytscha, Oncorhynchus kisutch, Oncorhynchus masou and Oncorhynchus rhodurus)
													--Atlantic salmon (salmo salar) and Danube salmon (Hucho hucho):
0/0/0	3.5	2	0/0	0/0/0	0/0	0//0	0/0/	0/0/9	9.1/0			0/0/0	---Atlantic salmon (salmo salar)
0/0/0	3.5	2	0/0	0/0/0	0/0	0//0	0/0/	0/0/9	9.1/0			0/0/0	---Danube salmon (Hucho hucho)
0/0/0	6	2.4	1.2/1.2	0/0/0	0/0	0//0	0/0/	0/0/10.8	10.9/0			0/0/0	--Trout(Salmo trutta, Oncorhynchus mykiss, Oncorhynchus clarki, Oncorhynchus aguabonita, Oncorhynchus gilae, Oncorhynchus apache and Oncorhynchus chrysogaster)
													--Other
0/0/0	3.5	2	0/0	0/0/0	0/0	0//0	0/0/	0/0/9	9.1/0			0/0/0	Hucho bleekeri (excluding edible fish offal of subheading 0302.91 to 0302.99), frozen
0/0/0	3.5	2	0/0	0/0/0	0/0	0//0	0/0/	0/0/9	9.1/0			0/0/0	Tslinling lenok(Brachymystax lenck)(excluding edible fish offal of subheading 0302.91 to 0302.99), frozen
0/0/0	3.5	2	0/0	0/0/0	0/0	0//0	0/0/	0/0/9	9.1/0			0/0/0	Other salmon, frozen(excluding edible fish offal of subheading 0302.91 to 0302.99)
													-Tilapias (*Oreochromis spp.*), catfish (*Pangasius spp.*, *Si-lu-rus spp.*, *Clarias spp.*, *Icta-lurus spp.*), carp (*Cyprinus spp.*, *Carassius spp.*, *Cteno-pharyngodon idellus*, *Hy-po-phthalmichthys spp.*, *Cirrhi-nus spp.*, *Mylopharyngodon piceus*, *Catla catla*, *Labeo spp*,. *Osteochilus hasselti*, *Leptobarbus hoeveni*, *Megalo-brama spp*), eels (*Anguilla spp.*), Nile perch (*Lates niloticus*) and snakeheads (*Channa spp.*), excluding cdi-blc fish offal of subheading 0303.91 to 0303.99:
0/0/0	3.5	2	0/0	0/0/0	0/0	0//0	0/0/	0/0/9	9.1/0	0	/0/0	0/0/0	--Tilapia(oreochromis spp.)
0/0/0	5	0	0/0	0/0/0	0/0	0//0	0/0/0	0/0/0	9.1/0	0	/0/0	0/0/0	--Catfish(Pangasius spp., Silurus spp., Clarias spp., Ictalurus spp.)
0/0/0	0	0	0/0	0/0/0	0/0	0//0	0/0/0	0/0/0	9.1/0	0	/0/0	0/0/0	--Carp (*Cyprinus spp.*, *Caras- sius spp.*, *Ctenopharyngodon idellus*, *Hypophthalmichthys spp.*, *Cirrhinus spp.*, *Mylo- pharyngodon piceus*, *Catla catla*, *Labeo spp.*, *Osteochi-lus hasselti*, *Leptobarbus ho-eveni*, *Megalobrama spp.*)
													--Eel(Anguilla spp.)
0/0/0	8	2.4	1.2/1.2	0/0/0	0/0	0//0	0/0/	0/0/10.8	10.9/0			0/0/0	Marbled eels(Anguilla marmorata), frozen(excluding edible fish offal of subheading 0302.91 to 0302.99)
0/0/0	8	2.4	1.2/1.2	0/0/0	0/0	0//0	0/0/	0/0/10.8	10.9/0			0/0/0	European eels, frozen (excluding edible fish offal of subheading 0302.91 to 0302.99)
0/0/0	8	2.4	1.2/1.2	0/0/0	0/0	0//0	0/0/	0/0/10.8	10.9/0			0/0/0	Other eels(Anguilla spp.(excluding edible fish offal of subheading 0302.91 to 0302.99); frozen
													--Other
0/0/0	5	0	0/0	0/0/0	0/0	0//0	0/0/0	0/0/0	9.1/0	0	/0/0	0/0/0	Nile perch(Lates niloticus) , frozen(excluding edible fish offal of subheading 0302.91 to 0302.99)
0/0/0	5	0	0/0	0/0/0	0/0	0//0	0/0/0	0/0/0	9.1/0	0	/0/0	0/0/0	Snakeheads(Channa spp.), frozen(excluding edible fish offal of subheading 0302.91 to 0302.99)
													-Flat fish (*Pleuronectidae*, *Bothidae*, *Cynoglossidae*, *Soleidae*, *Scophthalmidae and Citharidae*), excluding edible fish offal of subheading 0303.91 to 0303.99:
													--Halibut (*Reinhardtius hippo-glossoides*, *Hippoglossus hip-poglossus*, *Hippoglossus stenolepis*):
0/0/0	3.5	2	0/0	0/0/0	0/0	0//0	0/0/	0/0/9	/0			0/0/0	---Greenland halibut(Reinhardtius hippoglossoides)

税则号列	货品名称〔CIQ 扩展编码及品名—T2 表示见附表 2〕	最惠(%)	暂定税率	普通	增值/消费	出口退税	计量单位	监管条件/特殊证件	检验检疫	对美关税	亚太上/下
0303.3190	---其他										
0303.3190 10	冻大西洋庸鲽(庸鲽)(但子目 0303.91 至 0303.99 的可食用鱼杂碎除外)〔101 养殖,102 野生〕	10		40	9/	9	千克	ABU/	PRQS	40	6.7/6.7
0303.3190 90	其他冻庸鲽鱼(但子目 0303.91 至 0303.99 的可食用鱼杂碎除外)〔101 养殖,102 野生〕	10		40	9/	9	千克	AB/	PRQS	40	6.7/6.7
0303.3200	--鲽鱼(鲽)〔101 养殖,102 野生〕	7	2	40	9/	9	千克	AB/	PRQS	32	4.7/4.7
0303.3300	--鳎鱼(鳎属)〔101 养殖,102 野生〕	7		40	9/	9	千克	AB/	PRQS	37	4.7/4.7
0303.3400	--大菱鲆(瘤棘鲆)〔101 养殖,102 野生〕	7		40	9/	9	千克	AB/	PRQS	37	5.6/5.6
0303.3900	--其他										
0303.3900 10	冻亚洲箭齿鲽(但子目 0303.91 至 0303.99 的可食用鱼杂碎除外)〔101 养殖,102 野生〕	7		40	9/	9	千克	ABU/	PRQS	37	5.6/5.6
0303.3900 90	其他冻比目鱼(鲽科、鲆科、舌鳎科、鳎科、菱鲆科、刺鲆科)(但子目 0303.91 至 0303.99 的可食用鱼杂碎除外)[T2]	7		40	9/	9	千克	AB/	PRQS	37	5.6/5.6
	-金枪鱼(金枪鱼属)、鲣,但子目 0303.91 至 0303.99 的可食用鱼杂碎除外:										
0303.4100	--长鳍金枪鱼〔999〕	7	6	40	9/	9	千克	AB/	PRQS	36	5.3/5.3
0303.4200	--黄鳍金枪鱼〔999〕	7	6	40	9/	9	千克	AB/	PRQS	36	5.3/5.3
0303.4300	--鲣〔999〕	7		40	9/	9	千克	AB/	PRQS	37	5.3/5.3
0303.4400	--大眼金枪鱼〔999〕	7	6	40	9/	9	千克	ABU/	PRQS	36	
	--大西洋及太平洋蓝鳍金枪鱼:										
0303.4510	---大西洋蓝鳍金枪鱼〔999〕	7	6	40	9/	9	千克	ABU/	PRQS	36	
0303.4520	---太平洋蓝鳍金枪鱼〔999〕	7	6	40	9/	9	千克	AB/	PRQS	36	5.3/5.3
0303.4600	--南方蓝鳍金枪鱼〔999〕	7	6	40	9/	9	千克	AB/	PRQS	36	
0303.4900	--其他〔101 养殖,102 野生〕	7		40	9/	9	千克	AB/	PRQS	37	5.3/5.3
	-鲱鱼(大西洋鲱鱼、太平洋鲱鱼)、鳀鱼(鳀属)、沙丁鱼(沙丁鱼、沙瑙鱼属)、小沙丁鱼属、黍鲱或西鲱、鲭鱼[大西洋鲭、澳洲鲭(鲐)、日本鲭(鲐)]、印度鲭(羽鳃鲐属)、马鲛鱼(马鲛属)、对称竹荚鱼、新西兰竹荚鱼及竹荚鱼(竹荚鱼属)、鲹鱼(鲹属)、军曹鱼、银鲳(鲳属)、秋刀鱼、圆鲹(圆鲹属)、多春鱼(毛鳞鱼)、剑鱼、鲔鱼、狐鲣(狐鲣属)、枪鱼 、旗鱼、四鳍旗鱼(旗鱼科),但子目 0303.91 至 0303.99 的可食用鱼杂碎除外:										
0303.5100	--鲱鱼(大西洋鲱鱼、太平洋鲱鱼)										
0303.5100 10	冻太平洋鲱鱼(但子目 0303.91 至 0303.99 的可食用鱼杂碎除外:)〔101 养殖,102 野生〕	7	2	40	9/	9	千克	ABU/	PRQS	32	4.7/4.7
0303.5100 90	冻大西洋鲱鱼(但子目 0303.91 至 0303.99 的可食用鱼杂碎除外:)〔101 养殖,102 野生〕	7	2	40	9/	9	千克	AB/	PRQS	32	4.7/4.7
0303.5300	--沙丁鱼(沙丁鱼、沙瑙鱼属)、小沙丁鱼属、黍鲱或西鲱[T2]	7		40	9/	9	千克	AB/	PRQS	37	4.7/4.7
0303.5400	--鲭鱼[大西洋鲭、澳洲鲭(鲐)、日本鲭(鲐)]〔101 饲料用鲭鱼,102 养殖日本鲭(鲐),103 野生日本鲭(鲐),104 大西洋鲭,105 澳洲鲭(鲐)〕	7		40	9/	9	千克	AB/	PRQS	37	4.7/4.7
0303.5500	--对称竹荚鱼、新西兰竹荚鱼及竹荚鱼(竹荚鱼属)[T2]	7		40	9/	9	千克	AB/	PRQS	37	3.5/3.5
0303.5600	--军曹鱼〔101 饲料用其他海水鱼,102 食用鱼〕	7		40	9/	9	千克	AB/	PRQS	37	3.5/3.5
0303.5700	--剑鱼〔999〕	7		40	9/	9	千克	ABU/	PRQS	37	3.5/3.5
	--其他:										
0303.5910	---银鲳(鲳属)〔999〕	7		40	9/	9	千克	AB/	PRQS	37	3.5/3.5
0303.5990	---其他										
0303.5990 10	冻毛鳞鱼,但食用杂碎除外〔999〕	7	5	40	9/	9	千克	AB/	PRQS	35	3.5/3.5
0303.5990 90	其他冻 0303.5 项下的鱼(鳀鱼(鳀属)、印度鲭(羽鳃鲐属)、马鲛鱼(马鲛属)、鲹鱼(鲹属)、秋刀鱼、圆鲹(圆鲹属)、鲔鱼、狐鲣(狐鲣属)、枪鱼 、旗鱼、四鳍旗鱼(旗鱼科),但子目 0303.91 至 0303.99 的可食用鱼杂碎除外:)〔101 冻的鳀鱼(鳀属),102 冻的印度鲭(羽鳃鲐属),103 冻的马鲛鱼(马鲛属),104 冻的鲹鱼(鲹属),106 冻的秋刀鱼,107 冻的圆鲹(圆鲹属),108 冻的鲔鱼,109 冻的狐鲣(狐鲣属),110 冻的枪鱼,111 冻的旗鱼,112 冻的四鳍旗鱼(旗鱼科)〕	7		40	9/	9	千克	AB/	PRQS	37	3.5/3.5
	-犀鳕科、多丝真鳕科、鳕科、长尾鳕科、黑鳕科、无须鳕科、深海鳕科及南极鳕科鱼,但子目 0303.91 至 0303.99 的可食用鱼杂碎除外:										
0303.6300	--鳕鱼(大西洋鳕鱼、格陵兰鳕鱼、太平洋鳕鱼)〔101 大西洋鳕鱼,102 太平洋鳕鱼,103 格陵兰鳕鱼〕	7	2	40	9/	9	千克	AB/	PRQS	32	4.7/4.7
0303.6400	--黑线鳕鱼(黑线鳕)〔999〕	7		40	9/	9	千克	AB/	PRQS	37	4.7/4.7
0303.6500	--绿青鳕鱼〔999〕	7		40	9/	9	千克	AB/	PRQS	37	4.7/4.7

协定税率 %								RCEP		特惠税率 %			Article Description
东/冰/格	巴基斯坦	韩国	瑞士上/下	哥/秘/柬	澳/毛	新西/坡/智	中国港/澳/台	东盟及马来/澳/韩	日/新	亚太2国	老/柬/缅	98/97/95	
													---Other
0/0/0	3.5	2	0/0	0/0/0	0/0	0//0	0/0/	0/0/9	9.1/0			0/0/0	Frozen Atlantic agent sole (commonplace sole)(excluding edible fish offal of subheading 0302.91 to 0302.99)
0/0/0	3.5	2	0/0	0/0/0	0/0	0//0	0/0/	0/0/9	9.1/0			0/0/0	Frozen horse tongue sole(excluding edible fish offal of subheading 0302.91 to 0302.99)
0/0/0	8	2.4	1.2/1.2	0/0/0	0/0	0//0	0/0/	0/0/10.8	/0			0/0/0	--Plaice (*Pleuronectes platessa*)
0/0/0	8	2.4	1.2/1.2	0/0/0	0/0	0//0	0/0/	0/0/10.8	10.9/0			0/0/0	--Sole (*Solea spp.*)
0/0/0	8	2	0/0	0/0/0	0/0	0//0	0/0/	0/0/9	9.1/0			0/0/0	--Turbots(Psetta maxima)
													--Other
0/0/0	0	2	0/0	0/0/0	0/0	0//0	0/0/	0/0/9	/0			0/0/0	Frozen arrow tooth sole in Asia(excluding edible fish offal of subheading 0302.91 to 0302.99)
0/0/0	0	2	0/0	0/0/0	0/0	0//0	0/0/	0/0/9	/0			0/0/0	Other flatfish(Pleuronectidae, Bothidae, Cynoglossidae, Soleidae, Scophthalmidae and Citharidae) frozen(excluding edible fish offal of subheading 0302.91 to 0302.99)
													-Tunas (*of the genus Thun-nus*), bonito , excluding edible fish offal of subheading 0303.91 to 0303.99:
0/0/0	3.5	2.4	1.2/1.2	0/0/0	0/0	0//0	0/0/	0/0/10.8	10.9/0			0/0/0	--Albacore or longfinned tunas (*Thunnus alalunga*)
0/0/0	3.5	2.4	1.2/1.2	0/0/0	0/7.2	0//0	0/0/	0/0/10.8	10.9/0			0/0/0	--Yellowfin tunas (*Thunnus albacares*)
0/0/0	3.5	7.2	1.2/1.2	0/0/0	0/0	0//0	0/0/	11.4/11.4/	/11.4			0/0/0	--Bonito
0/0/0	6	2.4	1.2/1.2	0/0/0	0/7.2	0//0	0/0/	0/0/10.8	10.9/0		/0/0	0/0/0	--Bigeye tunas(*Thunnus obesus*)
													--Atlantic and pacific bluefin tunas(Thunnus thynnus, Thunnus orientalis):
0/0/0	6	2.4	1.2/1.2	0/0/0	0/0	0//0	0/0/	0/0/10.8	10.9/0		/0/0	0/0/0	---Atlantic bluefin tunas(Thunnus thynnus)
0/0/0	3.5	2.4	1.2/1.2	0/0/0	0/0	0//0	0/0/	0/0/10.8	10.9/0		/0/0	0/0/0	---pacific bluefin tunas(Thunnus Orientalis)
0/0/0	6	2.4	1.2/1.2	0/0/0	0/0	0//0	0/0/	0/0/10.8	10.9/0		/0/0	0/0/0	--Southern bluefin tunas(*Thunnus maccoyii*)
0/0/0	3.5	2.4	1.2/1.2	0/0/0	0/0	0//0	0/0/	0/0/10.8	10.9/0		/0/0	0/0/0	--Other
													-Herrings (*Clupea harengus*, *Clupea pallasii*), anchovies (*Engraulis spp.*), sardines (*Sardina pilchardus*, *Sardinops spp.*), sardinella (*Sardinella spp.*), brisling or sprats (*Sprattus sprattus*), mackerel (*Scomber scombrus*, *Scomber australasicus*, *Scom-her japonicus*), Indian macker-els (*Rastrelliger spp.*), seerfi-shes(*Scomberomorus spp.*), jack and horse mackerel (*Tra-churus spp.*), jacks, crevalles (*Caranx spp.*), cobia (*Rachy-centron canadum*), silver pom-frets(*Pampus spp.*), Pacific saury(*Cololabis saira*), scads(*Decapterus spp.*), capelin(*Mallotus villosus*), swordfish(*Xiphias gladius*), Kawakawa(*Euthymus affinis*), bonitos(*Sarda spp.*), marlins, sail-fishes, spearfish (*Istiophori-dae*), excluding edible fish offal of subheadin9 0303.91 to 0303.99:
													--Herrings(Clupea harengus, Clupea pallosii)
0/0/0	3.5	2	0/0	0/0/0	0/0	0//0	0/0/	0/0/9	9.1/0			0/0/0	Frozen Pacific herring (excluding edible fish offal of subheading 0302.91 to 0302.99)
0/0/0	3.5	2	0/0	0/0/0	0/0	0//0	0/0/	0/0/9	9.1/0			0/0/0	Herrings(Clupea harengus) Frozen(excluding edible fish offal of subheading 0302.91 to 0302.99)
0/0/0	0	2.4	1.2/1.2	0/0/0	0/0	0//0	0/0/	0/0/10.8	10.9/0			0/0/0	--Sardines (Sardina pilchardus, Sardinops spp.), sardinella (Sardinella spp.), brisling or sprats(Sprattus sprattus)
0/0/0	0	2	0/0	0/0/0	0/0	0//0	0/0/	0/0/9	9.1/0			0/0/0	--Mackerel(Scomber scombrus, Scomber australasicus, Scomber japonicus)
0/0/0	5	0	0/0	0/0/0	0/0	0//0	0/0/0	0/0/0	9.1/0	0	/0/0	0/0/0	-Jack and horse mackerel(Trachurus spp.)
0/0/0	5	0	0/0	0/0/0	0/0	0//0	0/0/0	0/0/0	9.1/0	0	/0/0	0/0/0	--Cobia(Rachycentron canadum)
0/0/0	5	2	0/0	0/0/0	0/0	0//0	0/0/	0/0/9	9.1/0	0		0/0/0	--Swordfish(Xiphias gladius)
													--Other:
0/0/0	0	4.6	0/0	0/0/0	0/0	0//0	0/0/0	9.3/9.5/9.3	9.4/9.5	0	/0/0	0/0/0	---Silver pomfret (Pampus spp.)
													---Other
0/0/0	0	4.6	0/0	0/0/0	0/0	0//0	0/0/0	9.3/9.5/9.3	9.4/9.5	0	/0/0	0/0/0	Frozen capelin, but edible offal except
0/0/0	0	4.6	0/0	0/0/0	0/0	0//0	0/0/0	9.3/9.5/9.3	9.4/9.5	0	/0/0	0/0/0	Other frozen fish of the subheading 0303.5 , including anchovies $ (Engraulisspp.) $ $, Indian mackerel(feather gill danio genus), mackerel, horse mackerel(mackerel)(trevally), pomfret, saury, round trevally(butterfish) trevally(circle), spring(capelin), tuna fish, bonito (bonito) four fin sailfish, marlin, swordfish (swordG fish), excluding the edible fish offal of the subheading 0303.91 to 0303.99
													-Fish of the families Bregmacer-otidae, Euclichthyidae, Gadidae, Macrouridae, Melanoni-dae, Merlucciidae, Moridae and Muraenolepididae, excluding edible fish offal of subheading 0303.91 to 0303.99:
0/0/0	3.5	2	0/0	0/0/0	0/0	0//0	0/0/	0/0/9	9.1/0			0/0/0	--Cod(Gadus morhua, Gadus ogac, Gadus macrocep halus)
0/0/0	3.5	2.4	1.2/1.2	0/0/0	0/0	0//0	0/0/	0/0/10.8	10.9/0			0/0/0	--Haddock(melanogrammus aeglefinus)
0/0/0	3.5	2.4	1.2/1.2	0/0/0	0/0	0//0	0/0/	0/0/10.8	10.9/0			0/0/0	--Coalfish(Pollachius virens)

税则号列	货品名称〔CIQ 扩展编码及品名—T2 表示见附表 2〕	最惠(%)	暂定税率	普通	增值/消费	出口退税	计量单位	监管条件/特殊证件	检验检疫	对美关税	亚太上/下
0303.6600	--狗鳕鱼(无须鳕属、长鳍鳕属)〔101 无须鳕属,102 长鳍鳕属〕	7		40	9/	9	千克	AB/	PRQS	37	
0303.6700	--阿拉斯加狭鳕鱼〔101 饲料用其他海水鱼,102 食用鱼〕	7	2	40	9/	9	千克	ABU/	PRQS	32	3.5/3.5
0303.6800	--蓝鳕鱼(小鳍鳕、南蓝鳕)〔101 饲料用其他海水鱼,102 小鳍鳕,103 南蓝鳕,104 蓝鳕〕	7		40	9/	9	千克	AB/	PRQS	37	3.5/3.5
0303.6900	--其他〔101 饲料用其他海水鱼,102 犀鳕科,103 多丝真鳕科,104 鳕科,105 长尾鳕科,106 黑鳕科,107 无须鳕科,108 深海鳕科,109 南极鳕科鱼〕	7		40	9/	9	千克	AB/	PRQS	37	3.5/3.5
	-其他鱼,但子目 0303.91 至 0303.99 的可食用鱼杂碎除外:										
0303.8100	--角鲨及其他鲨鱼										
0303.8100 10	冻濒危鲨鱼(但子目 0303.91 至 0303.99 的可食用鱼杂碎除外:)〔999〕	7		40	9/	0	千克	ABFE/	PRQS	37	5.3/5.3
0303.8100 90	冻其他鲨鱼(但子目 0303.91 至 0303.99 的可食用鱼杂碎除外:)〔999〕	7		40	9/	9	千克	AB/	PRQS	37	5.3/5.3
0303.8200	--魟鱼及鳐鱼(鳐科)〔101 饲料用其他海水鱼,102 食用鱼〕	7		40	9/	9	千克	AB/	PRQS	37	3.5/3.5
0303.8300	--南极犬牙鱼(南极犬牙鱼属)〔999〕	7		40	9/	9	千克	ABU/	PRQS	37	3.5/3.5
0303.8400	--尖吻鲈鱼(舌齿鲈属)〔999〕	7		40	9/	9	千克	AB/	PRQS	37	4.7/4.7
	--其他:										
0303.8910	---带鱼〔999〕	7	5	40	9/	9	千克	AB/	PRQS	35	3.5/3.5
0303.8920	---黄鱼〔101 养殖,102 野生〕	7		40	9/	9	千克	AB/	PRQS	37	3.5/3.5
0303.8930	---鲳鱼(银鲳除外)〔101 养殖;102 野生〕	7		40	9/	9	千克	AB/	PRQS	37	3.5/3.5
0303.8990	---其他										
0303.8990 01	其他冻鲈鱼(但子目 0303.91 至 0303.99 的可食用鱼杂碎除外:)〔101 养殖,102 野生〕	7		40	9/	9	千克	AB/	PRQS	37	3.5/3.5
0303.8990 10	其他未列名濒危冻鱼(但子目 0303.91 至 0303.99 的可食用鱼杂碎除外:)〔999〕	7		40	9/	0	千克	ABFE/	PRQS	37	3.5/3.5
0303.8990 20	冻平鲉属鱼(但子目 0303.91 至 0303.99 的可食用鱼杂碎除外:)〔101 养殖,102 野生〕	7	5	40	9/	9	千克	ABU/	PRQS	35	3.5/3.5
0303.8990 30	冻鲉属(叶鳍鲉属)(但子目 0303.91 至 0303.99 的可食用鱼杂碎除外:)〔101 养殖,102 野生〕	7		40	9/	9	千克	ABU/	PRQS	37	3.5/3.5
0303.8990 90	其他未列名冻鱼(但子目 0303.91 至 0303.99 的可食用鱼杂碎除外:)[T2]	7		40	9/	9	千克	AB/	PRQS	37	3.5/3.5
	-鱼肝、鱼卵、鱼精、鱼鳍、鱼头、鱼尾、鱼鳔及其他可食用鱼杂碎:										
0303.9100	--鱼肝、鱼卵及鱼精										
0303.9100 10	冻濒危鱼种的肝、鱼卵及鱼精[T2]	7		50	9/	0	千克	ABFE/	PRQS	37	6.3/6.3
0303.9100 20	冻的鱼卵(濒危除外)〔101 养殖冷冻鱼鱼卵,102 野生冷冻鱼鱼卵〕	7		50	0/	9	千克	AB/	PRQS		6.3/6.3
0303.9100 90	其他冻鱼肝及鱼精〔101 养殖冷冻鱼鱼肝,102 野生冷冻鱼鱼肝,103 养殖冷冻鱼鱼精,104 野生冷冻鱼鱼精〕	7		50	9/	9	千克	AB/	PRQS	37	6.3/6.3
0303.9200	--鲨鱼翅										
0303.9200 10	冻濒危鲨鱼翅〔999〕	12		40	9/	0	千克	ABFE/	PRQS	42	9/9
0303.9200 90	其他冻鲨鱼翅〔999〕	12		40	9/	9	千克	AB/	PRQS	42	9/9
0303.9900	--其他										
0303.9900 10	其他冻可食用濒危鱼杂碎〔101 其他养殖冷冻鱼,102 其他野生冷冻鱼〕	7		40	9/	0	千克	ABFE/	PRQS	37	4.7/4.7
0303.9900 20	冻的大菱鲆、比目鱼、鲱鱼、鲭鱼、鲳鱼、带鱼、尼罗河鲈鱼、尖吻鲈鱼、其他鲈鱼的可食用其他鱼杂碎〔101 其他养殖冷冻鱼,102 其他野生冷冻鱼〕	7		40	9/	9	千克	AB/	PRQS	37	4.7/4.7
0303.9900 90	其他冻可食用其他鱼杂碎〔101 其他养殖冷冻鱼,102 其他野生冷冻鱼〕	7		40	9/	9	千克	AB/	PRQS	37	4.7/4.7
03.04	**鲜、冷、冻鱼片及其他鱼肉(不论是否绞碎):**										
	-鲜或冷的罗非鱼(口孵非鲫属)、鲶鱼(鲶鲶属、鲶属、胡鲶属、真鮰属)、鲤科鱼(鲤属、鲫属、草鱼、鲢属、鲮属、青鱼、卡特拉鲃、野鲮属、哈氏纹唇鱼、何氏细须鲃、鲂属)、鳗鱼(鳗鲡属)、尼罗河鲈鱼(尼罗尖吻鲈)及黑鱼(鳢属)的鱼片:										
0304.3100	--罗非鱼(口孵非鲫属)〔101 养殖,102 野生〕	7		70	9/	9	千克	AB/	PRQS		5.3/5.3
0304.3200	--鲶鱼(鲶鲶属、鲶属、胡鲶属、真鮰属)〔101 养殖(鱼芒)鲶属,102 养殖胡鲶属,103 养殖真鮰属,104 野生(鱼芒)鲶属,105 野生胡鲶属,106 野生真鮰属〕	7		70	9/	9	千克	AB/	PRQS		5.3/5.3
0304.3300	--尼罗河鲈鱼(尼罗尖吻鲈)〔999〕	7		70	9/	9	千克	AB/	PRQS		5.3/5.3
0304.3900	--其他										
0304.3900 10	鲜或冷的花鳗鲡鱼片〔101 养殖,102 野生〕	7		70	9/	9	千克	ABE/	PRQS		5.3/5.3
0304.3900 20	鲜或冷的欧洲鳗鲡鱼片〔101 养殖,102 野生〕	7		70	9/	9	千克	ABEF/	PRQS		5.3/5.3

协定税率 %								RCEP		特惠税率 %			Article Description
东/冰/格	巴基斯坦	韩国	瑞士上/下	哥/秘/柬	澳/毛	新西/坡/智	中国港/澳/台	东盟及马来/澳/韩	日/新	亚太2国	老/柬/缅	98/97/95	
0/0/0	6	2.4	1.2/1.2	0/0/0	0/0	0//0	0/0/	0/0/10.8	10.9/0			0/0/0	--Hake(Merluccius spp. ,urophycis spp.)
0/0/0	5	2	0/0	0/0/0	0/0	0//0	0/0/0	9/9/9	9.5/9	0	/0/0	0/0/0	--Alaska pollock(*Theragra chalcogramma*)
0/0/0	5	0	0/0	0/0/0	0/0	0//0	0/0/0	0/0/0	9.1/0	0	/0/0	0/0/0	--Blue whitings (Micromesistius poutassou, Micromesistius australis)
0/0/0	5	0	0/0	0/0/0	0/0	0//0	0/0/0	9/9/9	9.1/9	0	/0/0	0/0/0	--Other
													-Other fish, excluding edible fish offal of subheading 0303.91 to 0303.99:
													--Dogfish and other sharks
0/0/0	9	2.4	1.2/1.2	0/0/0	0/0	0//0	0/0/	0/0/10.8	10.9/0			0/0/0	Endangered shark(excluding edible fish offal of subheading 0302.91 to 0302.99), frozen
0/0/0	9	2.4	1.2/1.2	0/0/0	0/0	0//0	0/0/	0/0/10.8	10.9/0			0/0/0	Other sharks(excluding edible fish offal of subheading 0302. 91 to 0302.99), frozen
0/0/0	5	0	0/0	0/0/0	0/0	0//0	0/0/0	0/0/0	9.1/0	0	/0/0	0/0/0	--Rays and skates(Rajidae)
0/0/0	5	2	0/0	0/0/0	0/0	0//0	0/0/	0/0/9	9.1/0	0	/0/0	0/0/0	--Toothfish(Dissostichus spp.)
0/0/0	3.5	2.4	1.2/1.2	0/0/0	0/0	0//0	0/0/	0/0/10.8	10.9/0			0/0/0	--Seabass(Dicentrarchus spp.)
													--Other:
0/1.9/0	0	2	0/0	0/0/0	0/0	0//0	0/0/	0/0/9	9.1/0	0	/0/0	0/0/0	---Scabber fish(Trichurius)
0/0/0	0	2	0/0	0/0/0	0/0	0//0	0/0/	0/0/9	9.1/0	0	/0/0	0/0/0	---Yellow croaker(Pseudosicaena)
0/0/0	0	2	0/0	0/0/0	0/0	0//0	0/0/	0/0/9	9.1/0	0	/0/0	0/0/0	---Butterfish (pamus),excluding Silver pomfret
													---Other
0/0/0	0	4.6	0/0	0/0/0	0/6	0//0	0/0/0	9.3/9.5/9.3	9.4/9.5	0	/0/0	0/0/0	Other perch, frozen (excluding edible fish offal of subheading 0302.91 to 0302.99)
0/0/0	0	4.6	0/0	0/0/0	0/6	0//0	0/0/0	9.3/9.5/9.3	9.4/9.5	0	/0/0	0/0/0	Other endangered fish frozen, not elsewhere specified or included(excluding edible fish offal of subheading 0302. 91 to 0302.99)
0/0/0	0	4.6	0/0	0/0/0	0/6	0//0	0/0/0	9.3/9.5/9.3	9.4/9.5	0	/0/0	0/0/0	Frozen flat scorpionfish genera(excluding edible fish offal of subheading 0302.91 to 0302.99)
0/0/0	0	4.6	0/0	0/0/0	0/6	0//0	0/0/0	9.3/9.5/9.3	9.4/9.5	0	/0/0	0/0/0	Frozen Jun scorpionfish belongs to fin (leaf scorpionfish)(excluding edible fish offal of subheading 0302.91 to 0302.99)
0/0/0	0	4.6	0/0	0/0/0	0/6	0//0	0/0/0	9.3/9.5/9.3	9.4/9.5	0	/0/0	0/0/0	Other fish frozen, not elsewhere specified or included(excluding edible fish offal of subheading 0302.91 to 0302.99)
													-Livers, roes, milt, fish fins, heads, tails, maws and other edible fish offal:
													--Livers, roes,and milt
0/0/0	3.5	2	0/0	0//0	0/0	0//0	0/0/	0/0/9	9.1/0			0/0/0	Forzen livers,roes and milt of endangered fish
0/0/0	3.5	2	0/0	0//0	0/0	0//0	0/0/	0/0/9	9.1/0			0/0/0	Frozen fish eggs (except endangered)
0/0/0	3.5	2	0/0	0//0	0/0	0//0	0/0/	0/0/9	9.1/0			0/0/0	Other forze nlivers, and milt
													--Shark fins
0/0/0	9	2.4	1.2/1.2	0/0/0	0/	0//0	0/0/	0/0/10.8	10.9/0			0/0/0	Frozen endangered Shark fins
0/0/0	9	2.4	1.2/1.2	0/0/0	0/	0//0	0/0/	0/0/10.8	10.9/0			0/0/0	Other frozen Shark fins
													--Other
0/0/0	0	2	0/0	0/0/0	0/0	0//0	0/0/	0/0/0	9.1/0		/0/	0/0/0	Other edible offals of endangered fish
0/0/0	0	2	0/0	0/0/0	0/0	0//0	0/0/	0/0/0	9.1/0		/0/	0/0/0	Frozen edible fish offals of Turbots, flatfish, herring, mackerel, Pomfret, hairtail, Nile perch and other perch?
0/0/0	0	2	0/0	0/0/0	0/0	0//0	0/0/	0/0/0	9.1/0		/0/	0/0/0	Other frozen edible offals of other fish
													Fish fillets and other fish meat (whether or not minced), fresh, chilled or frozen:
													-Fresh or chilled fillets of tilapias (*Oreochromis spp.*), catfish (*Pangasius spp.*, *Silurus spp.*, *Clarias spp.*, *Ictalurus spp.*), carp (*Cyprin us spp.*, *Carassius spp.*, *Ctenopharyn-godon idellus* , *Hypophthal-michthys spp.* , *Cirrhins spp.* , *Mylopharyngodon pi-ceus* , *Catla catla* , *Labeo spp.* , *Osteochilus hasselti* , *Leptobar-bus hoeveni*, *Megalobrama spp.*) , eels (*Anguilla spp.*) , Nile perch (*Lates niloticus*) and snakeheads (*Channa spp.*) :
0/0/0	3.5	2.4	1.2/1.2	0/0/0	0/0	0//0	0/0/	0/0/10.8	10.9/0		//0	0/0/0	--Tilapia(oreochromis spp.)
0/0/0	3.5	2.4	1.2/1.2	0/0/0	0/0	0//0	0/0/	0/0/10.8	10.9/0		//0	0/0/0	--Catfish(pangasius spp. 、silurus spp. 、clarias spp. 、ictalurus spp.)
0/0/0	3.5	2.4	1.2/1.2	0/0/0	0/0	0//0	0/0/	0/0/10.8	10.9/0		//0	0/0/0	--Nile perch(lates niloticus)
													--Other
0/0/0	3.5	2.4	1.2/1.2	0/0/0	0/0	0//0	0/0/	0/0/10.8	10.9/0		//0	0/0/0	Fresh or chilled fillets of marbled eels
0/0/0	3.5	2.4	1.2/1.2	0/0/0	0/0	0//0	0/0/	0/0/10.8	10.9/0		//0	0/0/0	Fresh or chilled fillets of european eels

税则号列	货品名称〔CIQ 扩展编码及品名—T2 表示见附表 2〕	最惠(%)	暂定税率	普通	增值/消费	出口退税	计量单位	监管条件/特殊证件	检验检疫	对美关税	亚太上/下
0304.3900 90	鲜或冷的鲤科鱼(鲤属、鲫属、草鱼、鲢属、鲮属、青鱼、卡特拉鲃、野鲮属、哈氏纹唇鱼、何氏细须鲃、鲂属)、其他鳗鱼(鳗鲡属)及黑鱼(鳢属)的鱼片[T2]	7		70	9/	9	千克	AB/	PRQS		5.3/5.3
	-鲜或冷的其他鱼片:										
0304.4100	--大麻哈鱼[红大麻哈鱼、细鳞大麻哈鱼、大麻哈鱼(种)、大鳞大麻哈鱼、银大麻哈鱼、马苏大麻哈鱼、玫瑰大麻哈鱼]、大西洋鲑鱼及多瑙哲罗鱼〔101 非生食,102 可能用于生食〕	7		70	9/	9	千克	AB/	PRQS		5.3/5.3
0304.4200	--鳟鱼(河鳟、虹鳟、克拉克大麻哈鱼、阿瓜大麻哈鱼、吉雨大麻哈鱼、亚利桑那大麻哈鱼、金腹大麻哈鱼)〔999〕	7		70	9/	9	千克	AB/	PRQS		5.3/5.3
0304.4300	--比目鱼(鲽科、鲆科、舌鳎科、鳎科、菱鲆科、刺鲆科)[T2]	7		70	9/	9	千克	AB/	PRQS		5.3/5.3
0304.4400	--犀鳕科、多丝真鳕科、鳕科、长尾鳕科、黑鳕科、无须鳕科、深海鳕科及南极鳕科鱼〔101 犀鳕科,102 多丝真鳕科,103 鳕科,104 长尾鳕科,105 黑鳕科,106 无须鳕科,107 深海鳕科,108 南极鳕科鱼〕	7		70	9/	9	千克	AB/	PRQS		5.3/5.3
0304.4500	--剑鱼〔999〕	7		70	9/	9	千克	ABU/	PRQS		5.3/5.3
0304.4600	--南极犬牙鱼(南极犬牙鱼属)〔999〕	7		70	9/	9	千克	ABU/	PRQS		5.3/5.3
0304.4700	--角鲨及其他鲨鱼										
0304.4700 10	鲜或冷的濒危鲨鱼的鱼片〔999〕	7		70	9/	0	千克	ABFE/	PRQS		5.3/5.3
0304.4700 90	鲜或冷的其他鲨鱼的鱼片〔999〕	7		70	9/	9	千克	AB/	PRQS		5.3/5.3
0304.4800	--魟鱼及鳐鱼(鳐科)										
0304.4800 10	鲜或冷的濒危魟鱼及鳐鱼的鱼片〔999〕	7		70	9/	0	千克	ABFE/	PRQS		5.3/5.3
0304.4800 90	鲜或冷的其他魟鱼及鳐鱼的鱼片〔999〕	7		70	9/	9	千克	AB/	PRQS		5.3/5.3
0304.4900	--其他										
0304.4900 10	鲜或冷的其他濒危鱼的鱼片〔999〕	7		70	9/	0	千克	ABFE/	PRQS		5.3/5.3
0304.4900 90	鲜或冷的其他鱼的鱼片〔999〕	7		70	9/	9	千克	AB/	PRQS		5.3/5.3
	-其他,鲜或冷的:										
0304.5100	--罗非鱼(口孵非鲫属)、鲶鱼(鲑鲶属、鲶属、胡鲶属、真鮰属)、鲤科鱼(鲤属、鲫属、草鱼、鲢属、鲮属、青鱼、卡特拉鲃、野鲮属、哈氏纹唇鱼、何氏细须鲃、鲂属)、鳗鱼(鳗鲡属)、尼罗河鲈鱼(尼罗尖吻鲈)及黑鱼(鳢属)										
0304.5100 10	鲜或冷的花鳗鲡的鱼肉(不论是否绞碎)〔101 养殖,102 野生〕	7		70	9/	9	千克	ABE/	PRQS		5.3/5.3
0304.5100 20	鲜或冷的欧洲鳗鲡的鱼肉(不论是否绞碎)〔101 养殖,102 野生〕	7		70	9/	9	千克	ABEF/	PRQS		5.3/5.3
0304.5100 90	鲜或冷的罗非鱼(口孵非鲫属)、鲶鱼(鲑鲶属、鲶属、胡鲶属、真鮰属)、鲤科鱼(鲤属、鲫属、草鱼、鲢属、鲮属、青鱼、卡特拉鲃、野鲮属、哈氏纹唇鱼、何氏细须鲃、鲂属)、其他鳗鱼(鳗鲡属)、尼罗河鲈鱼(尼罗尖吻鲈)及黑鱼(醴属)的鱼肉[T2]	7		70	9/	9	千克	AB/	PRQS		5.3/5.3
0304.5200	--鲑科鱼〔101 养殖,102 野生〕	7		70	9/	9	千克	AB/	PRQS		5.3/5.3
0304.5300	--犀鳕科、多丝真鳕科、鳕科、长尾鳕科、黑鳕科、无须鳕科、深海鳕科及南极鳕科鱼[T2]	7		70	9/	9	千克	AB/	PRQS		5.3/5.3
0304.5400	--剑鱼〔999〕	7		70	9/	9	千克	ABU/	PRQS		5.3/5.3
0304.5500	--南极犬牙鱼(南极犬牙鱼属)〔999〕	7		70	9/	9	千克	ABU/	PRQS		5.3/5.3
0304.5600	--角鲨及其他鲨鱼										
0304.5600 10	鲜或冷的濒危鲨鱼肉(不论是否绞碎)〔999〕	7		70	9/	0	千克	ABEF/	PRQS		5.3/5.3
0304.5600 90	鲜或冷的其他鲨鱼肉(不论是否绞碎)〔999〕	7		70	9/	9	千克	AB/	PRQS		5.3/5.3
0304.5700	--魟鱼及鳐鱼(鳐科)										
0304.5700 10	鲜或冷的濒危魟鱼及鳐鱼的鱼肉(不论是否绞碎)〔999〕	7		70	9/	0	千克	ABEF/	PRQS		5.3/5.3
0304.5700 90	鲜或冷的其他魟鱼及鳐鱼的鱼肉(不论是否绞碎)〔999〕	7		70	9/	9	千克	AB/	PRQS		5.3/5.3
0304.5900	--其他										
0304.5900 10	鲜或冷的其他濒危鱼的鱼肉(不论是否绞碎)〔999〕	7		70	9/	0	千克	ABEF/	PRQS		5.3/5.3
0304.5900 90	鲜或冷的其他鱼的鱼肉(不论是否绞碎)[T2]	7		70	9/	9	千克	AB/	PRQS		5.3/5.3

协定税率 %								RCEP		特惠税率 %			Article Description
东/冰/格	巴基斯坦	韩国	瑞士上/下	哥/秘/柬	澳/毛	新西/坡/智	中国港/澳/台	东盟及马来/澳/韩	日/新	亚太2国	老/柬/缅	98/97/95	
0/0/0	3.5	2.4	1.2/1.2	0/0/0	0/0	0//0	0/0/	0/0/10.8	10.9/0		//0	0/0/0	Fresh or chilled fillets of Carp (Cyprinus spp., Carassius spp., Ctenopharyngodon idellus, Hypophthalmichthys spp., Cirrhinus spp., Mylopharyngodon piceus, Catla catla, Labeo spp., Osteochilus hasselti, Leptobarbus hoeveni, Megalobrama spp.), Mylopharyngodon piceus) and snakeheads (Channa spp).
													-Fresh or chilled fillets of other fish:
0/0/0	3.5	2.4	1.2/1.2	0/0/0	0/0	0//0	0/0/	0/0/10.8	10.9/0		//0	0/0/0	--Pacific salmon (Oncorhynchus nerka, Oncorhynchus gorbuscha, Oncorhynchus keta, Oncorhynchus tschawytscha, Oncorhynchus kisutch, Oncorhynchus masou and Oncorhynchus rhodurus), Atlantic salmon (Salmo salar) and Danube salmon (Hucho hucho)
0/0/0	3.5	2.4	1.2/1.2	0/0/0	0/0	0//0	0/0/	0/0/10.8	10.9/0		//0	0/0/0	--Trout (Salmo trutta, Oncorhynchus mykiss, Oncorhynchus clarki, Oncorhynchus aguabonita, Oncorhynchus gilae, Oncorhynchus apache and Oncorhynchus chrysogaster)
0/0/0	3.5	2.4	1.2/1.2	0/0/0	0/0	0//0	0/0/	0/0/10.8	10.9/0		//0	0/0/0	--Flat fish (Pleuronectidae, Bothidae, Cynoglossidae, Soleidae, Scophthalmidae and Citharidae)
0/0/0	3.5	2.4	1.2/1.2	0/0/0	0/0	0//0	0/0/	0/0/10.8	10.9/0		//0	0/0/0	--Fish of the families Bregmacerotidae, Euclichthyidae, Gadidae, Macrouridae, Melanonidae, Merlucciidae, Moridae and Muraenolepididae
0/0/0	3.5	2.4	1.2/1.2	0/0/0	0/0	0//0	0/0/	0/0/10.8	10.9/0		//0	0/0/0	--Swordfish (Xiphias gladius)
0/0/0	3.5	2.4	1.2/1.2	0/0/0	0/0	0//0	0/0/	0/0/10.8	10.9/0		//0	0/0/0	--Toothfish (Dissostichus spp.)
													--Dogfish and other sharks
0/0/0	3.5	2.4	1.2/1.2	0/0/0	0/0	0//0	0/0/	0/0/10.8	10.9/0		//0	0/0/0	Fresh or chilled fillets of endangered Shark
0/0/0	3.5	2.4	1.2/1.2	0/0/0	0/0	0//0	0/0/	0/0/10.8	10.9/0		//0	0/0/0	Fresh or chilled fillets of other Shark
													--Ray and skates (*Rajidae*)
0/0/0	3.5	2.4	1.2/1.2	0/0/0	0/0	0//0	0/0/	0/0/10.8	10.9/0		//0	0/0/0	Fresh or chilled fillets of endangered Ray and skates
0/0/0	3.5	2.4	1.2/1.2	0/0/0	0/0	0//0	0/0/	0/0/10.8	10.9/0		//0	0/0/0	Fresh or chilled fillets of other Ray and skates
													--Other
0/0/0	3.5	2.4	1.2/1.2	0/0/0	0/0	0//0	0/0/	0/0/10.8	10.9/0		//0	0/0/0	Fresh or chilled fillets of Other endangered fish
0/0/0	3.5	2.4	1.2/1.2	0/0/0	0/0	0//0	0/0/	0/0/10.8	10.9/0		//0	0/0/0	Fresh or chilled fillets of fish
													-Other, fresh and chilled:
													--Tilapias (*Oreochromis spp.*), catfish (*Pangasius spp.*, *Silurus spp.*, *Cla rias spp.*, *Ic-talurus spp.*), carp (*Cyprinus spp.*, *Carassius spp.*, *Ctenopharyngodon idellus*, *Hypophthalmichthys spp.*, *Cirrhinus spp.*, *Mylopharyngodon piceus*, *Catla catla*, *Labeo spp.*, *Osteochilus hasselti*, *Leptobarbus hoeveni*, *Megalobrama spp.*), eels (*Anguilla spp.*), Nile perch (*Lates niloticus*) and snake-heads (*Channa spp.*)
0/0/0	3.5	2.4	1.2/1.2	0/0/0	0/0	0//0	0/0/	0/0/10.8	10.9/0		//0	0/0/0	Marbled eels, fresh or chilled (whether or not minced)
0/0/0	3.5	2.4	1.2/1.2	0/0/0	0/0	0//0	0/0/	0/0/10.8	10.9/0		//0	0/0/0	Meat of european eels, fresh or chilled (whether or not minced)
0/0/0	3.5	2.4	1.2/1.2	0/0/0	0/0	0//0	0/0/	0/0/10.8	10.9/0		//0	0/0/0	Fresh or chilled fish meat of Tilapias (*Oreochromis spp.*), catfish (*Pangasius spp.*, *Silurus spp.*, *Clarias spp.*, *Ictalurus spp.*), carp (*Cyprinus spp.*, *Carassius spp.*, *Ctenopharyngodon idellus* *Hypophthalmichthys spp.*, *Cirrhinus spp.*, *Mylopharyngodon piceus*, *Catla catla*, *Labeo spp.*, *Osteochilus hasselti*, *Leptobarbus hoeveni*, *Megalobrama spp.*), eels (*Anguilla spp.*), Nile perch (*Lates niloticus*) and snakeheads (*Channa spp.*)
0/0/0	3.5	2.4	1.2/1.2	0/0/0	0/0	0//0	0/0/	0/0/10.8	10.9/0		//0	0/0/0	--Salmonoids
0/0/0	3.5	2.4	1.2/1.2	0/0/0	0/0	0//0	0/0/	0/0/10.8	10.9/0		//0	0/0/0	--Fish of the families bregmacerotidae、euclichthyidae、gadidae、macrouridae、melanonidae、merluccidae、moridae and Muraenolepididae
0/0/0	3.5	2.4	1.2/1.2	0/0/0	0/0	0//0	0/0/	0/0/10.8	10.9/0		//0	0/0/0	--Swordfish (Xiphias gladius)
0/0/0	3.5	2.4	1.2/1.2	0/0/0	0/0	0//0	0/0/	0/0/10.8	10.9/0		//0	0/0/0	--Toothfish (Dissostichus spp.)
													--Dogfish and other sharks
0/0/0	3.5	2.4	1.2/1.2	0/0/0	0/0	0//0	0/0/	0/0/10.8	10.9/0		//0	0/0/0	Fresh or chilled fish meat of endangered Shark, whether or not minced
0/0/0	3.5	2.4	1.2/1.2	0/0/0	0/0	0//0	0/0/	0/0/10.8	10.9/0		//0	0/0/0	Fresh or chilled fish meat of other Shark, whether or not minced
													--Ray and skates (*Rajidae*)
0/0/0	3.5	2.4	1.2/1.2	0/0/0	0/0	0//0	0/0/	0/0/10.8	10.9/0		//0	0/0/0	Fresh or chilled fish meat of endangered Ray and skates, whether or not minced
0/0/0	3.5	2.4	1.2/1.2	0/0/0	0/0	0//0	0/0/	0/0/10.8	10.9/0		//0	0/0/0	Fresh or chilled fish meat of other Ray and skates, whether or not minced
													--Other
0/0/0	3.5	2.4	1.2/1.2	0/0/0	0/0	0//0	0/0/	0/0/10.8	10.9/0		//0	0/0/0	Other endangered fish meat, fresh or chilled (whether or not minced)
0/0/0	3.5	2.4	1.2/1.2	0/0/0	0/0	0//0	0/0/	0/0/10.8	10.9/0		//0	0/0/0	Other fish meat, fresh or chilled (whether or not minced)

税则号列		货品名称〔CIQ扩展编码及品名—T2表示见附表2〕	最惠(%)	暂定税率	普通	增值/消费	出口退税	计量单位	监管条件/特殊证件	检验检疫	对美关税	亚太上/下
		-冻的罗非鱼(口孵非鲫属)、鲶鱼(鮰鲶属、鲶属、胡鲶属、真鮰属)、鲤科鱼(鲤属、鲫属、草鱼、鲢属、鲮属、青鱼、卡特拉鲃、野鲮属、哈氏纹唇鱼、何氏细须鲃、鲂属)、鳗鱼(鳗鲡属)、尼罗河鲈鱼(尼罗尖吻鲈)及黑鱼(鳢属)的鱼片:										
0304.6100		--罗非鱼(口孵非鲫属)〔999〕	7		70	9/	9	千克	AB/	PRQS	37	
		--鲶鱼(鮰鲶属、鲶属、胡鲶属、真鮰属):										
		---叉尾鮰鱼(真鮰属):										
0304.6211		----斑点叉尾鮰鱼〔101养殖,102野生〕	7		70	9/	9	千克	AB/	PRQS	37	
0304.6219		----其他〔101养殖,102野生〕	7		70	9/	9	千克	AB/	PRQS	37	
0304.6290		---其他[T2]	7		70	9/	9	千克	AB/	PRQS	37	
0304.6300		--尼罗河鲈鱼(尼罗尖吻鲈)〔999〕	7		70	9/	9	千克	AB/	PRQS	37	
0304.6900		--其他										
0304.6900	10	冻的花鳗鲡鱼片〔101养殖,102野生〕	7		70	9/	9	千克	ABE/	PRQS	37	
0304.6900	20	冻的欧洲鳗鲡鱼片〔101养殖,102野生〕	7		70	9/	9	千克	ABEF/	PRQS	37	
0304.6900	90	冻的鲤科鱼(鲤属、鲫属、草鱼、鲢属、鲮属、青鱼、卡特拉鲃、野鲮属、哈氏纹唇鱼、何氏细须鲃、鲂属)、其他鳗鱼(鳗鲡属)及黑鱼(鳢属)的鱼片[T2]	7		70	9/	9	千克	AB/	PRQS	37	
		-冻的犀鳕科、多丝真鳕科、鳕科、长尾鳕科、黑鳕科、无须鳕科、深海鳕科及南极鳕科鱼的鱼片:										
0304.7100		--鳕鱼(大西洋鳕鱼、格陵兰鳕鱼、太平洋鳕鱼)〔101大西洋鳕鱼,102太平洋鳕鱼,103格陵兰鳕鱼〕	7		70	9/	9	千克	AB/	PRQS	37	
0304.7200		--黑线鳕鱼(黑线鳕)〔999〕	7		70	9/	9	千克	AB/	PRQS	37	
0304.7300		--绿青鳕鱼〔999〕	7		70	9/	9	千克	AB/	PRQS	37	
0304.7400		--狗鳕鱼(无须鳕属、长鳍鳕属)〔101无须鳕属,102长鳍鳕属〕	7		70	9/	9	千克	AB/	PRQS	37	
0304.7500		--阿拉斯加狭鳕鱼〔999〕	7		70	9/	9	千克	AB/	PRQS	37	
0304.7900		--其他〔101犀鳕科,102多丝真鳕科,103鳕科,104长尾鳕科,105黑鳕科,106无须鳕科,107深海鳕科,108南极鳕科〕	7		70	9/	9	千克	AB/	PRQS	37	
		-其他冻鱼片:										
0304.8100		--大麻哈鱼[红大麻哈鱼、细鳞大麻哈鱼、大麻哈鱼(种)、大鳞大麻哈鱼、银大麻哈鱼、马苏大麻哈鱼、玫瑰大麻哈鱼]、大西洋鲑鱼及多瑙哲罗鱼[T2]	7		70	9/	9	千克	AB/	PRQS	37	
0304.8200		--鳟鱼(河鳟、虹鳟、克拉克大麻哈鱼、阿瓜大麻哈鱼、吉雨大麻哈鱼、亚利桑那大麻哈鱼、金腹大麻哈鱼)[T2]	7		70	9/	9	千克	AB/	PRQS	37	
0304.8300		--比目鱼(鲽科、鲆科、舌鳎科、鳎科、菱鲆科、刺鲆科)[T2]	7		70	9/	9	千克	AB/	PRQS	37	
0304.8400		--剑鱼〔999〕	7		70	9/	9	千克	ABU/	PRQS	37	
0304.8500		--南极犬牙鱼(南极犬牙鱼属)〔999〕	7		70	9/	9	千克	ABU/	PRQS	37	
0304.8600		--鲱鱼(大西洋鲱鱼、太平洋鲱鱼)〔101大西洋鲱鱼,102太平洋鲱鱼〕	7		70	9/	9	千克	AB/	PRQS	37	
0304.8700		--金枪鱼(金枪鱼属)、鲣〔101:金枪鱼(金枪鱼属));102:鲣鱼或狐鲣(鲣)〕	7		70	9/	9	千克	AB/	PRQS	37	
0304.8800		--角鲨、其他鲨鱼、魟鱼及鳐鱼(鳐科)										
0304.8800	10	冻的濒危鲨鱼、魟鱼及鳐鱼的鱼片〔999〕	7		70	9/	0	千克	ABEF/	PRQS	37	
0304.8800	90	冻的其他鲨鱼、魟鱼及鳐鱼的鱼片〔999〕	7		70	9/	9	千克	AB/	PRQS	37	
0304.8900		--其他										
0304.8900	10	冻的其他濒危鱼片〔999〕	7		70	9/	0	千克	ABEF/	PRQS	37	
0304.8900	90	冻的其他鱼片〔999〕	7		70	9/	9	千克	AB/	PRQS	37	
		-其他,冻的:										
0304.9100		--剑鱼〔999〕	7		70	9/	9	千克	ABU/	PRQS	37	
0304.9200		--南极犬牙鱼(南极犬牙鱼属)〔999〕	7		70	9/	9	千克	ABU/	PRQS	37	
0304.9300		--罗非鱼(口孵非鲫属)、鲶鱼(鮰鲶属、鲶属、胡鲶属、真鮰属)、鲤科鱼(鲤属、鲫属、草鱼、鲢属、鲮属、青鱼、卡特拉鲃、野鲮属、哈氏纹唇鱼、何氏细须鲃、鲂属)、鳗鱼(鳗鲡属)、尼罗河鲈鱼(尼罗尖吻鲈)及黑鱼(鳢属)										
0304.9300	10	冻的花鳗鲡鱼肉(不论是否绞碎)〔101养殖,102野生〕	7		70	9/	9	千克	ABE/	PRQS	37	
0304.9300	20	冻的欧洲鳗鲡鱼肉(不论是否绞碎)〔101养殖,102野生〕	7		70	9/	9	千克	ABEF/	PRQS	37	

协定税率 %								RCEP		特惠税率 %			Article Description
东/冰/格	巴基斯坦	韩国	瑞士上/下	哥/秘/柬	澳/毛	新西/坡/智	中国港/澳/台	东盟及马来/澳/韩	日/新	亚太2国	老/柬/缅	98/97/95	
													-Frozen fillets of tilapias (*Oreo-chromis spp.*),catfish(*Pan-gasi us spp.*, *Silurus spp.*,*Clarias spp.*, *Ictalurus spp.*), carp(*Cyp rin us spp.*,*Carassius spp.*,*Ctenopharyn-godon idellus*, *Hypophthal-michthys spp.* , *Cirrh inus spp.*, *Mylopharyngodon pi-ceus*, *Catla catla*, *Labeo spp.*, *Os-teochilus hasselti*, *Leptobar-bus hoeveni*, *Megalobrama spp.*),eels (*Anguilla spp.*),Nile perch (*Lares niloticus*) and snakeheads (*Channa spp.*):
0/0/0	3.5	2	0/0	0/0/0	0/0	0//0	0/0/	0/0/9	9.1/0		/0/0	0/0/0	--Tilapia(oreochromis spp.)
													--catfish(Pangasius spp.,Silurus spp.,Clarias spp.,Ictalurus spp.):
													---Ictalurus:
0/0/0	3.5	2	0/0	0/0/0	0/0	0//0	0/0/	0/0/9	9.1/0			0/0/0	----Channel catfish(ictalurus punctatus)
0/0/0	3.5	2	0/0	0/0/0	0/0	0//0	0/0/	0/0/9	9.1/0			0/0/0	----Other
0/0/0	3.5	2	0/0	0/0/0	0/0	0//0	0/0/0	0/0/9	9.1/0		/0/0	0/0/0	---Other
0/0/0	3.5	2	0/0	0/0/0	0/0	0//0	0/0/0	0/0/9	9.1/0		/0/0	0/0/0	--Nile perch(Lates niloticus)
													--Other
0/0/0	3.5	2	0/0	0/0/0	0/0	0//0	0/0/0	0/0/9	9.1/0		/0/0	0/0/0	Frozen fillets of marbled eels
0/0/0	3.5	2	0/0	0/0/0	0/0	0//0	0/0/0	0/0/9	9.1/0		/0/0	0/0/0	Frozen fillets of european eels
0/0/0	3.5	2	0/0	0/0/0	0/0	0//0	0/0/0	0/0/9	9.1/0		/0/0	0/0/0	Frozen fillets of Carp(Cyprinus spp., Carassius spp., Cteno-pharyngodon idellus, Hypophthalmichthys spp., Cirrhinus spp., Mylopharyngodon piceus, Catla catla,Labeo spp., Os-teochilus hasselti, Leptobarbus hoeveni, Megalobrama spp.), Mylopharyngodon piceus) and snakeheads (Channa spp).
													-Frozen fillets of fish of the families Bregmacerotidae, Eucli-chthyidae, Gadidae, Macrouridae, Melanonidae, Merlucci-idae,Moridae and Muraenolepididae:
0/0/0	3.5	2	0/0	0/0/0	0/0	0//0	0/0/0	0/0/9	9.1/0		/0/0	0/0/0	--Cod(Gadus morhua,Gadus ogac,Gadus macrocephalus)
0/0/0	3.5	2	0/0	0/0/0	0/0	0//0	0/0/0	0/0/9	9.1/0		/0/0	0/0/0	--Haddock(Melanogrammus aeglefinus)
0/0/0	3.5	2	0/0	0/0/0	0/0	0//0	0/0/0	0/0/9	9.1/0		/0/0	0/0/0	--Coalfish(Pollachius virens)
0/0/0	3.5	2	0/0	0/0/0	0/0	0//0	0/0/0	0/0/9	9.1/0		/0/0	0/0/0	--Hake(Merluccius spp. Urophycis spp.)
0/0/0	3.5	2	0/0	0/0/0	0/0	0//0	0/0/0	0/0/9	9.1/0		/0/0	0/0/0	--Alaska pollock(*Theragra chalcogramma*)
0/0/0	3.5	2	0/0	0/0/0	0/0	0//0	0/0/0	0/0/9	9.1/0		/0/0	0/0/0	--Other
													-Frozen fillets of other fish:
0/0/0	3.5	2	0/0	0/0/0	0/0	0//0	0/0/0	0/0/9	9.1/0		/0/0	0/0/0	--Pacific salmon(Oncorhynchus nerka, Oncorhynchus gor-buscha, Oncorhynchus keta, Oncorhynchus tschawytscha, Oncorhynchus kisutch, Oncorhynchus masou and On-corhynchus rhodurus), Atlantic salmon(Salmo salar) and Danube salmon(Hucho hucho)
0/0/0	3.5	2	0/0	0/0/0	0/0	0//0	0/0/0	0/0/9	9.1/0		/0/0	0/0/0	--Trout(Salmo trutta, Oncorhynchus mykiss, Oncorhynchus clarki, Oncorhynchus aguabonita, Oncorhynchus gilae, On-corhynchus apache and Oncorhynchus chrysogaster)
0/0/0	3.5	2	0/0	0/0/0	0/0	0//0	0/0/0	0/0/9	9.1/0		/0/0	0/0/0	--Flat fish(Pleuronectidae, Bothidae, Cynoglossidae, Solei-dae, Scophthalmidae and Citharidae)
0/0/0	3.5	2	0/0	0/0/0	0/0	0//0	0/0/	0/0/9	9.1/0		/0/0	0/0/0	--Swordfish(Xiphias gladius)
0/0/0	3.5	2	0/0	0/0/0	0/0	0//0	0/0/	0/0/9	9.1/0		/0/0	0/0/0	--Toothfish(Dissostichus spp.)
0/0/0	3.5	2	0/0	0/0/0	0/0	0//0	0/0/0	0/0/9	9.1/0		/0/0	0/0/0	--Herring(Clupea harengus,clupea pallasii)
0/0/0	3.5	2	0/0	0/0/0	0/6	0//0	0/0/0	0/0/9	9.1/0		/0/0	0/0/0	--Tunas(of the genus *Thunnus*),skipjack tuna (stripe-bellied bonito)(*Katsuwonus pelamis*)
													--Dogfish,other sharks,rays and skates(*Rajidae*)
0/0/0	3.5	2	0/0	0/0/0	0/0	0//0	0/0/0	0/0/9	9.1/0		/0/0	0/0/0	Frozen fillets of endangered Shark,Ray and skates
0/0/0	3.5	2	0/0	0/0/0	0/0	0//0	0/0/0	0/0/9	9.1/0		/0/0	0/0/0	Frozen fillets of other Shark,Ray and skates
													--Other
0/0/0	3.5	2	0/0	0/0/0	0/0	0//0	0/0/0	0/0/9	9.1/0		/0/0	0/0/0	Other endangered fish fillets
0/0/0	3.5	2	0/0	0/0/0	0/0	0//0	0/0/0	0/0/9	9.1/0		/0/0	0/0/0	Other fish fillets
													-Other,frozen:
0/0/0	3.5	2	0/0	0/0/0	0/0	0//0	0/0/	0/0/9	9.1/0	0	//0	0/0/0	--Swordfish(Xiphias gladius)
0/0/0	3.5	2	0/0	0/0/0	0/0	0//0	0/0/	0/0/9	9.1/0	0	//0	0/0/0	--Toothfish(Dissostichus spp.)
													--Tilapias (*Oreochromis spp.*),catfish (*Pangasius spp.*,*Si-lurus spp.*, *Clarias spp.*,*Ictalurus spp.*),carp (*Cypri-nus spp.*,*Carassius spp.*,*Ctenopharyngodon idellus Hypoph-thalmichthys spp.*,*Cirrhinus spp.*,*Mylopharyn-godon pi-ceus* , *Catla catla* , *Labeo spp.*,*Osteochilus has-selti* ,*Lepto-barbus hoeveni*, *Megalobrama spp.*), eels (*Anguilla spp.*), Nile perch (*Lates niloticus*) and snake-heads (*Channa spp.*)
0/0/0	0	2	0/0	0/0/0	0/0	0//0	0/0/	0/0/9	9.1/0	0	//0	0/0/0	Frozen meat of marbled eels(whether or not minced)
0/0/0	0	2	0/0	0/0/0	0/0	0//0	0/0/	0/0/9	9.1/0	0	//0	0/0/0	Frozen meat of european eels(whether or not minced)

税则号列		货品名称〔CIQ扩展编码及品名－T2表示见附表2〕	最惠(%)	暂定税率	普通	增值/消费	出口退税	计量单位	监管条件/特殊证件	检验检疫	对美关税	亚太上/下
0304.9300	90	冻的罗非鱼(口孵非鲫属)、鲶鱼(鲑鲶属、鲶属、胡鲶属、真鮰属)、鲤科鱼(鲤属、鲫属、草鱼、鲢属、鲮属、青鱼、卡特拉鲃、野鲮属、哈氏纹唇鱼、何氏细须鲃、鲂属)、其他鳗鱼(鳗鲡属)、尼罗河鲈鱼(尼罗尖吻鲈)及黑鱼(鳢属)鱼肉(不论是否绞碎)〔T2〕	7		70	9/	9	千克	AB/	PRQS	37	
0304.9400		--阿拉斯加狭鳕鱼〔999〕	7		70	9/	9	千克	AB/	PRQS	37	
0304.9500		--犀鳕科、多丝真鳕科、鳕科、长尾鳕科、黑鳕科、无须鳕科、深海鳕科及南极鳕科鱼，阿拉斯加狭鳕鱼除外〔101犀鳕科，102多丝真鳕科，103鳕科，104长尾鳕科，105黑鳕科，106无须鳕科，107深海鳕科，108南极鳕科鱼〕	7		70	9/	9	千克	AB/	PRQS	37	
0304.9600		--角鲨及其他鲨鱼										
0304.9600	10	冻的濒危鲨鱼肉(不论是否绞碎)〔999〕	7		70	9/	0	千克	ABFE/	PRQS	37	
0304.9600	90	冻的其他鲨鱼肉(不论是否绞碎)〔999〕	7		70	9/	9	千克	AB/	PRQS	37	
0304.9700		--魟鱼及鳐鱼(鳐科)										
0304.9700	10	冻的濒危魟鱼及鳐鱼的鱼肉(不论是否绞碎)〔999〕	7		70	9/	0	千克	ABFE/	PRQS	37	
0304.9700	90	冻的其他魟鱼及鳐鱼的鱼肉(不论是否绞碎)〔999〕	7		70	9/	9	千克	AB/	PRQS	37	
0304.9900		--其他										
0304.9900	10	冻的其他濒危鱼的鱼肉(不论是否绞碎)〔999〕	7		70	9/	0	千克	ABFE/	PRQS	37	
0304.9900	90	其他冻鱼肉(不论是否绞碎)［T2］	7		70	9/	9	千克	AB/	PRQS	37	
03.05		**干、盐腌或盐渍的鱼；熏鱼，不论在熏制前或熏制过程中是否烹煮：**										
0305.2000		-干、熏、盐腌或盐渍的鱼肝、鱼卵及鱼精	7		80	9/	9,13	千克	AB/	PRQS	37	
0305.2000	10	干、熏、盐制的濒危鱼种肝、卵及鱼精［T2］	7		80	9/	0	千克	ABFE/	PRQS	37	
0305.2000	90	其他干、熏、盐制的鱼肝、鱼卵及鱼精［T2］	7		80	9/	9,13	千克	AB/	PRQS	37	
		-干、盐腌或盐渍的鱼片，但熏制的除外：										
0305.3100		--罗非鱼(口孵非鲫属)、鲶鱼(鲑鲶属、鲶属、胡鲶属、真鮰属)、鲤科鱼(鲤属、鲫属、草鱼、鲢属、鲮属、青鱼、卡特拉鲃、野鲮属、哈氏纹唇鱼、何氏细须鲃、鲂属)、鳗鱼(鳗鲡属)、尼罗河鲈鱼(尼罗尖吻鲈)及黑鱼(鳢属)										
0305.3100	10	干、盐腌或盐渍的花鳗鲡鱼片(熏制的除外)〔101干制的养殖花鳗鲡，102盐腌或盐渍的养殖花鳗鲡，103干制的野生花鳗鲡，104盐腌或盐渍的野生花鳗鲡〕	7		80	9/	9,13	千克	ABE/	PRQS		5.5/5.5
0305.3100	20	干、盐腌或盐渍的欧洲鳗鲡鱼片(熏制的除外)〔101干制的养殖欧洲鳗鲡；102盐腌或盐渍的养殖欧洲鳗鲡；103干制的野生欧洲鳗鲡；104盐腌或盐渍的野生欧洲鳗鲡鱼片(熏制的除外)〕	7		80	9/	9,13	千克	ABEF/	PRQS		5.5/5.5
0305.3100	90	干、盐腌或盐渍的罗非鱼(口孵非鲫属)、鲶鱼(鲑鲶属、鲶属、胡鲶属、真鮰属)、鲤科鱼(鲤属、鲫属、草鱼、鲢属、鲮属、青鱼、卡特拉鲃、野鲮属、哈氏纹唇鱼、何氏细须鲃、鲂属)、鳗鱼(鳗鲡属)、尼罗河鲈鱼(尼罗尖吻鲈)及黑鱼(鳢属)的鱼片(熏制的除外)〔161干制的养殖鱼，162干制的野生鱼，163盐腌或盐渍的养殖鱼，164盐腌或盐渍的野生鱼〕	7		80	9/	9,13	千克	AB/	PRQS		5.5/5.5
0305.3200		--犀鳕科、多丝真鳕科、鳕科、长尾鳕科、黑鳕科、无须鳕科、深海鳕科及南极鳕科鱼［T2］	7		80	9/	9,13	千克	AB/	PRQS		5.5/5.5
0305.3900		--其他										
0305.3900	10	干、盐腌或盐渍的濒危鱼类的鱼片(熏制的除外)〔999〕	7		80	9/	0	千克	ABEF/	PRQS		5.5/5.5
0305.3900	90	其他干、盐腌或盐渍的鱼片(熏制的除外)［T2］	7		80	9/	9,13	千克	AB/	PRQS		5.5/5.5
		-熏鱼，包括鱼片，但食用杂碎除外：										

协定税率 %								RCEP		特惠税率 %			Article Description
东/冰/格	巴基斯坦	韩国	瑞士 上/下	哥/秘/柬	澳/毛	新西/坡/智	中国港/澳/台	东盟及马来/澳/韩	日/新	亚太2国	老/柬/缅	98/97/95	
0/0/0	0	2	0/0	0/0/0	0/0	0//0	0/0/	0/0/9	9.1/0	0	//0	0/0/0	Fresh or chilled fish meat of Tilapias (*Oreochromis spp.*), catfish (*Pangasius spp.*,*Silurus spp.*, *Clarias spp.*,*Ictalurus spp.*), carp (*Cyprinus spp.*,*Carassius spp.*,*Ctenopharyngodon idellus Hypophthalmichthys spp.*, *Cirrhinus spp.*,*Mylopharyngodon piceus* , *Catla catla*, *Labeo spp.*, *Osteochilus hasselti*, *Leptobarbus hoeveni*, *Megalobrama spp.*),eels (*Anguilla spp.*),Nile perch (*Lates niloticus*)and snakeheads (*Channa spp.*)
0/0/0	3.5	2	0/0	0/0/0	0/0	0//0	0/0/	0/0/9	9.1/0	0	//0	0/0/0	--Alaska Pollock(*Theragra chalcogramma*)
0/0/0	3.5	2	0/0	0/0/0	0/0	0//0	0/0/	0/0/9	9.1/0	0	//0	0/0/0	--Fish of the families Bregmacerotidae, Euclichthyidae, Gadidae, Macrouridae, Melanonidae, Merlucciidae, Moridae and Muraenolepididae, other than Alaska Pollock (*Theragra chalcogramma*)
													--Dogfish and other sharks
0/0/0	0	2	0/0	0/0/0	0/0	0//0	0/0/	9/9/9	9.1/9	0	//0	0/0/0	Forzen endangered Shark meat,whether or not minced
0/0/0	0	2	0/0	0/0/0	0/0	0//0	0/0/	9/9/9	9.1/9	0	//0	0/0/0	Forzen other Shark meat,whether or not minced
													--Ray and skates(*Rajidae*)
0/0/0	0	2	0/0	0/0/0	0/0	0//0	0/0/	9/9/9	9.1/9	0	//0	0/0/0	Forzen meat of endangered Ray and skates, whether or not minced
0/0/0	0	2	0/0	0/0/0	0/0	0//0	0/0/	9/9/9	9.1/9	0	//0	0/0/0	Forzen meat of other Ray and skates, whether or not minced
													--Other
0/0/0	0	2	0/0	0/0/0	0/0	0//0	0/0/	9/9/9	9.1/9	0	//0	0/0/0	Other meat of endangered fish(whether or not minced)frozen
0/0/0	0	2	0/0	0/0/0	0/0	0//0	0/0/	9/9/9	9.1/9	0	//0	0/0/0	Other fish meat(whether or not minced)frozen
													Fish, dried, salted or in brine; smoked fish, whether or not cooked before or during the smoking process:
0/0/0	4	3	0	0	0	0/0	0//0	0/0/					
													-Livers ,roes and milt of fish, dried, smoked, salted or in brine
0/0/0	3.5	2		0//0	0/0	0//0	0/0/	0/0/9	9.1/0			0/0/0	Livers, roes and milt of endangered fish, dried, smoked, salted or in brine
0/0/0	3.5	2		0//0	0/0	0//0	0/0/	0/0/9	9.1/0			0/0/0	Livers,roes and milt of other fish, dried, smoked, salted or in brine
													-Fish fillets, dried, salted or in brine, but not smoked:
													--Tilapias (*Oreochromis spp.*),catfish (*Pangasius spp.*,*Silurus spp.*, *Clarias spp.*,*Ictalurus spp.*),carp (*Cypri-nus spp.*,*Carassius spp.*,*Ctenopharyngodon idellus Hypophthalmichthys spp.*,*Cirrhinus spp.*,*Mylopharyn-godon piceus* , *Catla catla*, *Labeo spp.*,*Osteochilus has-selti*,*Leptobarbus hoeveni*, *Megalobrama spp.*), eels (*Anguilla spp.*), Nile perch (*Lates niloticus*) and snake-heads (*Channa spp.*)
0/0/0	3.5	2		0/0/0	0/0	0//0	0/0/	0/0/9	9.1/0	0	//0	0/0/0	Fillets of marbled eels(Anguilla marmorata),dried, smoked, salted or in brine(excluding smoked)
0/0/0	3.5	2		0/0/0	0/0	0//0	0/0/	0/0/9	9.1/0	0	//0	0/0/0	Fillets of Tilapias (*Oreochromis spp.*),catfish (*Pangasius spp.*, *Silurus spp.*, *Clarias spp.*,*Ictalurus spp.*),carp (*Cyprinus spp.*, *Carassius spp.*, *Ctenopharyngodon idellus Hypophthalmichthys spp.*,*Cirrhinus spp.*,*Mylopharyngodon piceus* , *Catla catla*, *Labeo spp.*, *Osteochilus hasselti*, *Leptobarbus hoeveni*, *Megalobrama spp.*), eels (*Anguilla spp.*), Nile perch (*Lates niloticus*) and snakeheads (*Channa spp.*), dried, salted or in brine(excluding smoked)
0/0/0	3.5	2		0/0/0	0/0	0//0	0/0/	0/0/9	9.1/0	0	//0	0/0/0	Fish fillets of tilapia(oreochromis spp.), catfish(Pangasius spp.,Silurus spp.,Clarias spp.,Ictalurus spp.),carp(Cyprinus carpio,Carassius carassius,Ctenopharyngodon idellus, Hypophthalmichthys spp., Cirrhinus spp., Mylopharyngodon piceus), eels(Aguilla spp.), nile perch(Lates niloticus) and snakeheads(Channa spp.), dried, salted or in brine, but not smoked
0/0/0	3.5	2		0/0/0	0/0	0//0	0/0/	0/0/9	9.1/0	0	//0	0/0/0	--Fish of the families Bregmacerotidae, Euclichthyidae, Gadidae, Macrouridae, Melanonidae, Merlucciidae, Moridae and Muraenolepididae
													--Other
0/0/0	3.5	2		0/0/0	0/0	0//0	0/0/	0/0/9	9.1/0	0	//0	0/0/0	Endangered fish fillets, dried, salted or in brine (other than smoked)
0/0/0	3.5	2		0/0/0	0/0	0//0	0/0/	0/0/9	9.1/0	0	//0	0/0/0	Fish fillets, dried, salted or in brine (excluding smoked)
													-Smoked fish, including fillets,but excluding offal for human consumption:

税则号列	货品名称〔CIQ 扩展编码及品名－T2 表示见附表 2〕	最惠(%)	暂定税率	普通	增值/消费	出口退税	计量单位	监管条件/特殊证件	检验检疫	对美关税	亚太上/下
	--大麻哈鱼[红大麻哈鱼、细鳞大麻哈鱼、大麻哈鱼(种)、大鳞大麻哈鱼、银大麻哈鱼、马苏大麻哈鱼、玫瑰大麻哈鱼]、大西洋鲑鱼及多瑙哲罗鱼：										
0305.4110	---大西洋鲑鱼〔101 养殖,102 野生〕	14		80	9/	9	千克	AB/	PRQ		
0305.4120	---大麻哈鱼及多瑙哲罗鱼〔101 养殖大麻哈鱼,102 养殖多瑙哲罗鱼,103 野生大麻哈鱼,104 野生多瑙哲罗鱼〕	7		80	9/	9	千克	AB/	PRQ	37	
0305.4200	--鲱鱼(大西洋鲱鱼、太平洋鲱鱼)[T2]	7		80	9/	9	千克	AB/	PRQ		
0305.4300	--鳟鱼(河鳟、虹鳟、克拉克大麻哈鱼、阿瓜大麻哈鱼、吉雨大麻哈鱼、亚利桑那大麻哈鱼、金腹大麻哈鱼)[T2]	14		80	9/	9	千克	AB/	PRQS		
0305.4400	--罗非鱼(口孵非鲫属)、鲶鱼(鲑鲶属、鲶属、胡鲶属、真鮰属)、鲤科鱼(鲤属、鲫属、草鱼、鲢属、鲮属、青鱼、卡特拉鲃、野鲮属、哈氏纹唇鱼、何氏细须鲃、鲂属)、鳗鱼(鳗鲡属)、尼罗河鲈鱼(尼罗尖吻鲈)及黑鱼(鳢属)										
0305.4400 10	熏制花鳗鲡及鱼片(食用杂碎除外)〔101 养殖,102 野生〕	7		80	9/	9	千克	ABE/	PRQS		
0305.4400 20	熏制欧洲鳗鲡及鱼片(食用杂碎除外)〔101 养殖,102 野生〕	7		80	9/	9	千克	ABEF/	PRQS		
0305.4400 90	熏制罗非鱼(口孵非鲫属)、鲶鱼(鲑鲶属、鲶属、胡鲶属、真鮰属)、鲤科鱼(鲤属、鲫属、草鱼、鲢属、鲮属、青鱼、卡特拉鲃、野鲮属、哈氏纹唇鱼、何氏细须鲃、鲂属)、鳗鱼(鳗鲡属)、尼罗河鲈鱼(尼罗尖吻鲈)及黑鱼(鳢属)(食用杂碎除外)〔131 熏制的养殖鱼,132 熏制的野生鱼〕	7		80	9/	9	千克	AB/	PRQS		
0305.4900	--其他										
0305.4900 20	熏制其他濒危鱼及鱼片(食用杂碎除外)〔999〕	7		80	9/	0	千克	ABEF/	PRQS		
0305.4900 90	其他熏鱼及鱼片(食用杂碎除外)[T2]	7		80	9/	9	千克	AB/	PRQS		
	-干鱼(不包括食用杂碎),不论是否盐腌,但熏制的除外：										
0305.5100	--鳕鱼(大西洋鳕鱼、格陵兰鳕鱼、太平洋鳕鱼)〔101 干制的大西洋鳕鱼,102 干制的太平洋鳕鱼,103 干制的格陵兰鳕鱼〕	7		80	9/	9	千克	AB/	PRQS		
0305.5200	--罗非鱼(口孵非鲫属)、鲶鱼(鲑鲶属、鲶属、胡鲶属、真鮰属)、鲤科鱼(鲤属、鲫属、草鱼、鲢属、鲮属、青鱼、卡特拉鲃、野鲮属、哈氏纹唇鱼、何氏细须鲃、鲂属)、鳗鱼(鳗鲡属)、尼罗河鲈鱼(尼罗尖吻鲈)及黑鱼(鳢属)〔101 养殖干制鱼类制品,102 野生干制鱼类制品〕	7		80	9/	9	千克	AB/	PRQS		
0305.5300	--犀鳕科、多丝真鳕科、鳕科、长尾鳕科、黑鳕科、无须鳕科、深海鳕科及南极鳕科鱼,鳕鱼(大西洋鳕鱼、格陵兰鳕鱼、太平洋鳕鱼)除外〔101〕	7		80	9/	9	千克	AB/	PRQS		
	--鲱鱼(大西洋鲱鱼、太平洋鲱鱼)、鳀鱼(鳀属)、沙丁鱼(沙丁鱼、沙瑙鱼属)、小沙丁鱼属、黍鲱或西鲱、鲭鱼[大西洋鲭、澳洲鲭(鲐)、日本鲭(鲐)]、印度鲭(羽鳃鲐属)、马鲛鱼(马鲛属)、对称竹荚鱼、新西兰竹荚鱼及竹荚鱼(竹荚鱼属)、鲹鱼(鲹属)、军曹鱼、银鲳(鲳属)、秋刀鱼、圆鲹(圆鲹属)、多春鱼(毛鳞鱼)、剑鱼、鲔鱼、狐鲣(狐鲣属)、枪鱼、旗鱼、四鳍旗鱼(旗鱼科)：										
0305.5410	---银鲳(鲳属)〔101 养殖干制鱼类制品;102 野生干制鱼类制品〕	7		80	9/	9	千克	AB/	PRQS		
0305.5490	---其他〔101 养殖干制鱼类制品;102 野生干制鱼类制品〕	7		80	9/	9	千克	AB/	PRQS		
	--其他：										
0305.5910	---海龙、海马〔101 干制的海马,102 干制的海龙,103 药用海马,104 药用海龙〕	2		20	9/	9	千克	FEAB/	PRQ		
0305.5990	---其他										
0305.5990 10	其他濒危干鱼,食用杂碎除外(不论是否盐腌,但熏制的除外)〔999〕	7		80	9/	0	千克	AFEB/	PRQS		

协定税率 %								RCEP		特惠税率 %			Article Description
东/冰/格	巴基斯坦	韩国	瑞士上/下	哥/秘/柬	澳/毛	新西/坡/智	中国港/澳/台	东盟及马来/澳/韩	日/新	亚太2国	老/柬/缅	98/97/95	
													--Pacific salmon(Oncorhynchus nerka, Oncorhynchus gorbuscha, Oncorhynchus keta, Oncorhynchus tschawytscha, Oncorhynchus kisutch, Oncorhynchus masou and Oncorhynchus rhodurus), Altantic salmon(salmo salar) and Danube salmon(hucho hucho):
0/0/0	7	2.8		0/0/0	0/0	0//0	0/0/	0/0/12.6	12.7/0			0/0/0	---Atlantic salmon
0/0/0	11.2	2.8		0/0/0	0/0	0//0	0/0/	0/0/12.6	12.7/0			0/0/0	---Pacific salmon and Danube salmon
0/0/0	12.8	7.4		0/0/0	0/0	0//0	0/0/	14.4/14.4/14.4	/14.4			0/0/0	--Herrings(Clupea harengus, clupea pallasii)
0/0/0	11.2	2.8		0/0/0	0/0	0//0	0/0/	0/0/12.6	12.7/0	0	//0	0/0/0	--Trout(Salmo trutta, Oncorhynchus mykiss, Oncorhynchus clarki, Oncorhynchus aguabonita, Oncorhynchus gilae, Oncorhynchus apache and Oncorhynchus chrysogaster)
													--Tilapias (*Oreochromis spp.*), catfish (*Pangasius spp.*, *Silurus spp.*, *Clarias spp.*, *Ictalurus spp.*), carp (*Cypri-nus spp.*, *Carassius spp.*, *Ctenopharyngodon idellus Hypophthalmichthys spp.*, *Cirrhinus spp.*, *Mylopharyn-godon piceus* , *Catla catla*, *Labeo spp.*, *Osteochilus has-selti*, *Leptobarbus hoeveni*, *Megalobrama spp.*), eels (*Anguilla spp.*), Nile perch (*Lates niloticus*) and snake-heads (*Channa spp.*)
0/0/0	11.2	2.8		0/0/0	0/0	0//0	0/0/	0/0/12.6	12.7/0	0	//0	0/0/0	Marbled eels and fillets, smoked(other than edible for human consumption)
0/0/0	11.2	2.8		0/0/0	0/0	0//0	0/0/	0/0/12.6	12.7/0	0	//0	0/0/0	European eels and fillets, smoked (other than edible for human consumption)
0/0/0	11.2	2.8		0/0/0	0/0	0//0	0/0/	0/0/12.6	12.7/0	0	//0	0/0/0	smoked Tilapias (*Oreochromis spp.*), catfish (*Pangasius spp.*, *Silurus spp.*, *Clarias spp.*, *Ictalurus spp.*), carp (*Cyprinus spp.*, *Carassius spp.*, *Ctenopharyngodon idellus Hypophthalmichthys spp.*, *Cirrhinus spp.*, *Mylopharyngodon piceus* , *Catla catla*, *Labeo spp.*, *Osteochilus hasselti*, *Leptobarbus hoeveni*, *Megalobrama spp.*), eels (*Anguilla spp.*), Nile perch (*Lates niloticus*) and snakeheads (*Channa spp.*), dried, salted or in brine(excluding smoked)(other than edible fish offal)
													--Other
0/0/0	11.2	2.8		0/0/0	0/0	0//0	0/0/	0/0/12.6	12.7/0	0	//0	0/0/0	Other endangered fish and its fillets, smoked
0/0/0	11.2	2.8		0/0/0	0/0	0//0	0/0/	0/0/12.6	12.7/0	0	//0	0/0/0	Other fish and their fillets, smoked
													-Dried fish, other than edible fish offal, whether or not salted but not smoked:
0/0/0	12.8	7.4	1.6/1.6	0/0/0	0/0	0//0	0/0/	14.4/14.4/14.4	15/14.4			0/0/0	--Cod(Gadus morhua, Gadus ogac, Gadus macrocephalus)
0/0/0		7.4	1.6/1.6	0/0/0	0/0	0//0	0/0/	14.4/14.4/14.4	15/14.4	0	//0	0/0/0	--Tilapias (*Oreochromis spp.*), catfish (*Pangasius spp.*, *Silurus spp.*, *Clarias spp.*, *Ictalurus spp.*), carp (*Cypri-nus spp.*, *Carassius spp.*, *Ctenopharyngodon idellus Hypophthalmichthys spp.*, *Cirrhinus spp.*, *Mylopharyn-godon piceus* , *Catla catla*, *Labeo spp.*, *Osteochilus has-selti*, *Leptobarbus hoeveni*, *Megalobrama spp.*), eels (*Anguilla spp.*), Nile perch (*Lates niloticus*) and snake-heads (*Channa spp.*)
0/0/0		7.4	1.6/1.6	0/0/0	0/0	0//0	0/0/	14.4/14.4/14.4	15/14.4	0	//0	0/0/0	--Fish of the families Bregmacerotidae, Euclichthyidae, Gadidae, Macrouridae, Melanonidae, Merlucciidae, Moridae and Muraenolepididae, other than cod (*Gadusmorhua*, *Gadus ogac*, *Gadus macrocephalus*)
													--Herrings (Clupeaharengus, Clupeapallasii), anchovies (Engraulis spp.), sardines (Sardina pilchardus, Sardinops spp.), sardinella (Sardinella spp.), brisling or sprats (Sprattus sprattus), mackerel(Scomber scombrus, Scomber australasicus, Scomber japonicus), Indian mackerels(Rastrelliger spp.), seerfishes (Scomberomorus spp.), jack and horse mackerel(Trachurus spp.), jacks, crevalles(Caranx spp.), cobia(Rachycentron canadum), silver pomfrets(Pampus spp.), Pacific saury(Cololabis saira), scads (Decapterus spp.), capelin(Mallotus villosus), swordfish(Xiphias gladius), Kawakawa(Euthymus affinis), bonitos(Sarda spp.), marlins, sailfishes, spearfish(Istiophoridae)
0/0/0		7.4	1.6/1.6	0/0/0	0/0	0//0	0/0/	14.4/14.4/14.4	15/14.4	0	//0	0/0/0	---Silver pomfret (Pampus spp.)
0/0/0		7.4	1.6/1.6	0/0/0	0/0	0//0	0/0/	14.4/14.4/14.4	15/14.4	0	//0	0/0/0	---Other
													--Other:
0/0/0	0	0	0/0	0/0/0	0/0	0//0	0/0/	0/0/0	0/0	0	/0/0	0/0/0	---Pipefish and hippocampi
													---Other
0/0/0		7.4	1.6/1.6	0/0/0	0/0	0//0	0/0/	14.4/14.4/14.4	15/14.4	0	//0	0/0/0	Other endangered fish other than edible for human consumption, dried (whether or not salted but not smoked)

税则号列	货品名称〔CIQ扩展编码及品名－T2表示见附表2〕	最惠(%)	暂定税率	普通	增值/消费	出口退税	计量单位	监管条件/特殊证件	检验检疫	对美关税	亚太上/下
0305.5990 90	其他干鱼，食用杂碎除外（不论是否盐腌，但熏制的除外）[T2]	7		80	9/	9	千克	AB/	PRQS		
	-盐腌及盐渍的鱼（不包括食用杂碎），但干或熏制的除外：										
0305.6100	--鲱鱼（大西洋鲱鱼、太平洋鲱鱼）〔101 盐腌及盐渍的大西洋鲱鱼，102 盐腌及盐渍的太平洋鲱鱼〕	7		80	9/	9	千克	AB/	PRQ		4.8/4.8
0305.6200	--鳕鱼（大西洋鳕鱼、格陵兰鳕鱼、太平洋鳕鱼）〔101 盐腌及盐渍的大西洋鳕鱼，102 盐腌及盐渍的太平洋鳕鱼，103 盐腌及盐渍的格陵兰鳕鱼〕	7		80	9/	9	千克	AB/	PRQS		5.3/5.3
0305.6300	--鳀鱼（鳀属）〔999〕	7		80	9/	9	千克	AB/	PRQ		5.3/5.3
0305.6400	--罗非鱼（口孵非鲫属）、鲶鱼（𩷶鲶属、鲶属、胡鲶属、真鮰属）、鲤科鱼（鲤属、鲫属、草鱼、鲢属、鲮属、青鱼、卡特拉鲃、野鲮属、哈氏纹唇鱼、何氏细须鲃、鲂属）、鳗鱼（鳗鲡属）、尼罗河鲈鱼（尼罗尖吻鲈）及黑鱼（鳢属）										
0305.6400 10	盐腌及盐渍的花鳗鲡，食用杂碎除外（干或熏制的除外）〔101 盐腌及盐渍的养殖花鳗鲡，102 盐腌及盐渍的野生花鳗鲡〕	10		80	9/	9	千克	ABE/	PRQS		
0305.6400 20	盐腌及盐渍的欧洲鳗鲡，食用杂碎除外（干或熏制的除外）〔101 盐腌及盐渍的养殖，102 盐腌及盐渍的野生〕	10		80	9/	9	千克	ABEF/	PRQS		
0305.6400 90	盐腌及盐渍的罗非鱼（口孵非鲫属）、鲶鱼（𩷶鲶属、鲶属、胡鲶属、真鮰属）、鲤科鱼（鲤属、鲫属、草鱼、鲢属、鲮属、青鱼、卡特拉鲃、野鲮属、哈氏纹唇鱼、何氏细须鲃、鲂属）、其他鳗鱼（鳗鲡属）、尼罗河鲈鱼（尼罗尖吻鲈）及黑鱼（鳢属），食用杂碎除外（干或熏制的除外）〔131 盐腌及腌渍的养殖鱼类制品，132 盐腌及腌渍的野生鱼类制品〕	10		80	9/	9	千克	AB/	PRQS		
	--其他：										
0305.6910	---带鱼〔999〕	7		80	9/	9	千克	AB/	PRQS		
0305.6920	---黄鱼〔101 盐腌及盐渍的养殖黄鱼，102 盐腌及盐渍的野生黄鱼〕	10		80	9/	9	千克	AB/	PRQS		
0305.6930	---鲳鱼（银鲳除外）〔101 盐腌及盐渍的养殖鲳鱼；102 盐腌及盐渍的野生鲳鱼〕	7		80	9/	9	千克	AB/	PRQS		
0305.6990	---其他										
0305.6990 10	盐腌及盐渍的其他濒危鱼，食用杂碎除外（干或熏制的除外）〔999〕	7		80	9/	0	千克	ABFE/	PRQS		
0305.6990 90	盐腌及盐渍的其他鱼，食用杂碎除外（干或熏制的除外）[T2]	7		80	9/	9	千克	AB/	PRQS		
	-鱼鳍、鱼头、鱼尾、鱼鳔及其他可食用杂碎：										
0305.7100	--鲨鱼翅										
0305.7100 10	濒危鲨鱼鱼翅（不论是否干制、盐腌、盐渍和熏制）〔999〕	15		80	9/	0	千克	ABEF/	PRQS		
0305.7100 90	其他的鲨鱼鱼翅（不论是否干制、盐腌、盐渍和熏制）〔999〕	15		80	9/	9	千克	AB/	PRQS		
0305.7200	--鱼头、鱼尾、鱼鳔										
0305.7200 10	濒危鱼的鱼头、鱼尾、鱼鳔（不论是否干制、盐腌、盐渍和熏制）〔999〕	7		80	9/	0	千克	ABEF/	PRQS		
0305.7200 90	其他鱼的鱼头、鱼尾、鱼鳔（不论是否干制、盐腌、盐渍和熏制）〔101 养殖，102 野生〕	7		80	9/	9	千克	AB/	PRQS		
0305.7900	--其他										
0305.7900 10	其他濒危可食用鱼杂碎（不论是否干制、盐腌、盐渍和熏制）〔999〕	7		80	9/	0	千克	ABEF/	PRQS		
0305.7900 90	其他可食用鱼杂碎（不论是否干制、盐腌、盐渍和熏制）〔101 养殖，102 野生〕	7		80	9/	9	千克	AB/	PRQS		
03.06	**带壳或去壳的甲壳动物，活、鲜、冷、冻、干、盐腌或盐渍的；熏制的带壳或去壳甲壳动物，不论在熏制前或熏制过程中是否烹煮；蒸过或用水煮过的带壳甲壳动物，不论是否冷、冻、干、盐腌或盐渍的：**										
	-冻的：										
0306.1100	--岩礁虾和其他龙虾（真龙虾属、龙虾属、岩龙虾属）〔101 养殖大螯虾，102 养殖小龙虾，103 野生大螯虾，104 野生小龙虾〕	7		70	9/	9	千克	AB/	PRQS	37	
0306.1200	--螯龙虾（螯龙虾属）〔101 养殖，102 野生〕	7		70	9/	9	千克	AB/	PRQS	37	5/5
	--蟹：										
0306.1410	---梭子蟹〔101 饲料用梭子蟹，102 养殖，103 野生〕	7		70	9/	9	千克	AB/	PRQS	37	
0306.1490	---其他										

协定税率 %								RCEP		特惠税率 %			Article Description
东/冰/格	巴基斯坦	韩国	瑞士上/下	哥/秘/柬	澳/毛	新西/坡/智	中国港/澳/台	东盟及马来/澳/韩	日/新	亚太2国	老/柬/缅	98/97/95	
0/0/0		7.4	1.6/1.6	0/0/0	0/0	0//0	0/0/	14.4/14.4/14.4	15/14.4	0	//0	0/0/0	Other fish other than edible for human consumption, dried (whether or not salted but not smoked)
													-Fish, salted but not dried or smoked and fish in brine, other than edible fish offal:
0/0/0	8	7.4	1.6/1.6	0/0/0	0/0	0//0	0/0/	14.4/14.4/14.4	15/14.4			0/0/0	--Herrings (clupea harengus, clupea pallasii)
0/0/0	8	7.4	1.6/1.6	0/0/0	0/0	0//0	0/0/	14.4/14.4/14.4	15/14.4			0/0/0	--Cod(Gadus morhua, Gadus ogac, Gadus Macrocephalus)
0/0/0	8	7.4	1.6/1.6	0/0/0	0/0	0//0	0/0/	14.4/14.4/14.4	15/14.4			0/0/0	--Anchovies (*Engraulis spp.*)
													--Tilapias (*Oreochromis spp.*), catfish (*Pangasius spp., Silurus spp., Cla rias spp., Ic-talurus spp.*), carp (*Cyprinus spp., Carassius spp., Ctenopharyngodon idellus, Hypophthalmichthys spp., Cirrhinus spp., Mylopharyngodon piceus, Catla catla, Labeo spp., Osteochilus hasselti, Leptobarbus hoeveni, Megalobrama spp.*), eels (*Anguilla spp.*), Nile perch (*Lates niloticus*) and snake-heads (*Channa spp.*)
0/0/0	12.8	7.4	1.6/1.6	0/0/0	0/0	0//0	0/0/	14.4/14.4/14.4	15/14.4	0	//0	0/0/0	Marbled eels, dried, salted or in brine, other than deible for human consumption, but not smoked
0/0/0	12.8	7.4	1.6/1.6	0/0/0	0/0	0//0	0/0/	14.4/14.4/14.4	15/14.4	0	//0	0/0/0	European eels, dried, salted or in brine, other than deible for human consumption, but not smoked
0/0/0	12.8	7.4	1.6/1.6	0/0/0	0/0	0//0	0/0/	14.4/14.4/14.4	15/14.4	0	//0	0/0/0	Tilapias (*Oreochromis spp.*), catfish (*Pangasius spp., Silurus spp., Clarias spp., Ictalurus spp.*), carp (*Cyprinus spp., Carassius spp., Ctenopharyngodon idellus Hypophthalmichthys spp., Cirrhinus spp., Mylopharyngodon piceus, Catla catla, Labeo spp., Osteochilus hasselti, Leptobarbus hoeveni, Megalobrama spp.*), eels (*Anguilla spp.*), Nile perch (*Lates niloticus*) and snakeheads (*Channa spp.*), dried, salted or in brine(excluding smoked)(other than edible fish offal), salted or in brine
													--Other:
0/0/0	12.8	7.4	1.6/1.6	0/0/0	0/0	0//0	0/0/	14.4/14.4/14.4	15/14.4	0	//0	0/0/0	---Scabber fish (*Trichurius*)
0/0/0	12.8	7.4	1.6/1.6	0/0/0	0/0	0//0	0/0/	14.4/14.4/14.4	15/14.4	0	//0	0/0/0	---Yellow croaker (*Pseudosicaena*)
0/0/0	12.8	7.4	1.6/1.6	0/0/0	0/0	0//0	0/0/	14.4/14.4/14.4	15/14.4	0	//0	0/0/0	---Butterfish (pamus), excluding Silver pomfret
													---Other
0/0/0	12.8	7.4	1.6/1.6	0/0/0	0/0	0//0	0/0/	14.4/14.4/14.4	15/14.4	0	//0	0/0/0	Other endangered fish, other than edible for human consuption, salted or in brine (not dried nor smoked)
0/0/0	12.8	7.4	1.6/1.6	0/0/0	0/0	0//0	0/0/	14.4/14.4/14.4	15/14.4	0	//0	0/0/0	Other fish, other than edible for human consuption salted or in brine (not dried nor smoked)
													-Fish fins, heads, tails, maws and other edible fish offfal:
													--Shark fin
0/0/0			1.5/1.5	0/0/0		0//0	0/0/	14.3/14.3/	/14.3	0	/0/0	0/0/0	Sharks fins of whale(Rhincodon), man-eating shark(Carcharodon), basking shark(Cetorhinus), whether or not dried, salted, in brine and smoked
0/0/0			1.5/1.5	0/0/0		0//0	0/0/	14.3/14.3/	/14.3	0	/0/0	0/0/0	Other sharks fins, whether or not dried, salted, in brine and smoked, whether or not dried, salted, in brine and smoked
													--Fish heads, tails and maws
0/0/0	12.8	7.4		0/0/0	0/0	0//0	0/0/	14.4/14.4/14.4	15/14.4			0/0/0	Endangered fish of fish heads, tails and maws, whether or not dried, salted, in brine and smoked
0/0/0	12.8	7.4		0/0/0	0/0	0//0	0/0/	14.4/14.4/14.4	15/14.4			0/0/0	Other fish of fish heads, tails and maws, whether or not dried, salted, in brine and smoked
													--Other
0/0/0	12.8	7.4		0/0/0	0/0	0//0	0/0/	14.4/14.4/14.4	15/14.4			0/0/0	Other endangered fish edible for human consumption, whether or not dried, salted, in brine and smoked
0/0/0	12.8	7.4		0/0/0	0/0	0//0	0/0/	14.4/14.4/14.4	15/14.4			0/0/0	Other fish edible for human consumption, whether or not dried, salted, in brine and smoked
													Crustaceans, whether in shell or not, live, fresh, chilled, frozen, dried, salted or in brine; smoked crustaceans, whether or not cooked before or during the smoking process; crustaceans, in shell, cooked by steaming or by boiling in water, whether or not chilled, frozen, dried, salted or in brine:
													-Frozen:
0/0/0	3.5	2	0/0	0/0/0	0/0	0//0	0/0/	0/0/9	9.1/0		/0/0	0/0/0	--Rock lobster and other sea crawfish (palinurus spp., panulirus spp., Jasus spp.)
0/0/0	3.5	2	0/0	0/0/0	0/0	0//0	0/0/	0/0/9	9.1/0		/0/	0/0/0	--Lobster (Homarus SPP.)
													--Crabs:
0/0/0	3.5	2	0/0	0/0/0	0/0	0//0	0/0/	0/0/9	9.1/0	0	/0/0	0/0/0	---Swimming crab
													---Other

税则号列	货品名称〔CIQ 扩展编码及品名－T2 表示见附表 2〕	最惠(%)	暂定税率	普通	增值/消费	出口退税	计量单位	监管条件/特殊证件	检验检疫	对美关税	亚太上/下
0306.1490 10	冻的金霸王蟹(帝王蟹)、毛蟹、仿石蟹(仿岩蟹)、堪察加拟石蟹、短足拟石蟹、扁足拟石蟹、雪蟹、日本雪蟹〔101 养殖冻的金霸王蟹(帝王蟹),102 野生冻的金霸王蟹(帝王蟹),103 冻的养殖毛蟹,104 冻的养殖仿石蟹(仿岩蟹),105 冻的养殖堪察加拟石蟹,106 冻的养殖短足拟石蟹,107 冻的养殖扁足拟石蟹,108 冻的养殖雪蟹,109 冻的养殖日本雪蟹,110 冻的野生毛蟹,111 冻的野生仿石蟹(仿岩蟹),112 冻的野生堪察加拟石蟹,113 冻的野生短足拟石蟹,114 冻的野生扁足拟石蟹,115 冻的野生雪蟹,116 冻的野生日本雪蟹〕	7	5	70	9/	9	千克	ABU/	PRQS	35	
0306.1490 90	其他冻蟹[T2]	7	5	70	9/	9	千克	AB/	PRQS	35	
0306.1500	--挪威海螯虾〔101 养殖,102 野生〕	7		70	9/	9	千克	AB/	PRQS	37	
	--冷水小虾及对虾(长额虾属、褐虾):										
0306.1630	---虾仁〔101 其他养殖冷冻虾,102 其他野生冷冻虾,103 其他养殖冷冻虾,104 其他野生冷冻虾〕	7		70	9/	9	千克	AB/	PRQS	37	3.5/3.5
0306.1640	---其他,北方长额虾〔101 其他养殖冷冻虾,102 其他野生冷冻虾〕	5	2	70	9/	9,13	千克	AB/	PRQS	32	2.5/2.5
0306.1690	---其他〔101 其他养殖冷冻虾,102 其他野生冷冻虾,103 其他养殖冷冻虾,104 其他野生冷冻虾〕	5		70	9/	9	千克	AB/	PRQS	35	2.5/2.5
	--其他小虾及对虾:										
0306.1730	---虾仁〔101 养殖河虾,102 养殖罗氏沼虾,103 养殖其他小虾,104 野生河虾,105 野生红虾,106 野生罗氏沼虾,107 野生其他小虾,108 养殖对虾,109 野生对虾〕	7		70	9/	9	千克	AB/	PRQS	37	3.5/3.5
0306.1790	---其他										
0306.1790 10	其他冻小虾(对虾属除外)(虾仁除外)〔101 养殖河虾,102 养殖罗氏沼虾,103 养殖其他小虾,104 野生河虾,105 野生红虾,106 野生罗氏沼虾,107 野生其他小虾〕	5	2	70	9/	9	千克	AB/	PRQS	32	2.5/2.5
0306.1790 90	冻对虾(对虾属)(虾仁除外)〔101 养殖斑节对虾(虎虾),102 养殖南美白对虾,103 养殖草虾,104 养殖其他对虾,105 野生斑节对虾(虎虾),106 野生南美白对虾,107 野生草虾,108 野生其他对虾〕	5	2	70	9/	9	千克	AB/	PRQS	32	2.5/2.5
	--其他:										
	---淡水小龙虾:										
0306.1911	----虾仁〔101 养殖,102 野生〕	7		70	9/	9	千克	AB/	PRQS	37	
0306.1919	----其他〔101 养殖,102 野生〕	7		70	9/	9	千克	AB/	PRQS	37	
0306.1990	---其他〔101 养殖,102 野生〕	7		70	9/	9	千克	AB/	PRQS	37	
	-活、鲜或冷的:										
	--岩礁虾及其他龙虾(真龙虾属、龙虾属、岩龙虾属):										
0306.3110	---种苗〔999〕	0		0	0/	9	千克	AB/	PQ		
0306.3190	---其他[T2]	7	5	70	9/	9	千克	AB/	PRQS	35	
	--螯龙虾(螯龙虾属):										
0306.3210	---种苗〔999〕	0		0	0/	9	千克	AB/	PQ		
0306.3290	---其他〔101 活螯虾,102 鲜或冷的带壳或去壳养殖螯龙虾(螯龙虾属),103 鲜或冷的带壳或去壳野生螯龙虾(螯龙虾属)〕	7		70	9/	9	千克	AB/	PRQS	37	
	--蟹:										
0306.3310	---种苗〔101:青蟹;102:梭子蟹;103:其他海水虾蟹;104:中华绒螯蟹(大闸蟹);105:其他淡水虾蟹〕	0		0	0/	9	千克	AB/	PQ		
	---其他:										
0306.3391	----中华绒螯蟹〔101 活的中华绒螯蟹(大闸蟹),102 其他野生鲜或冷蟹,103 野生鲜或冷中华绒螯蟹〕	7		70	9/	9	千克	AB/	PRQS	37	
0306.3392	----梭子蟹〔101:活的梭子蟹;102:饲料用梭子蟹;103:鲜或冷的养殖梭子蟹;104:鲜或冷的野生梭子蟹〕	14		70	9/	9	千克	AB/	PRQS	44	
0306.3399	----其他										
0306.3399 10	活、鲜或冷的金霸王蟹(帝王蟹)、毛蟹、仿石蟹(仿岩蟹)、堪察加拟石蟹、短足拟石蟹、扁足拟石蟹、雪蟹、日本雪蟹〔101 其他海水虾蟹,102 鲜或冷的养殖毛蟹,103 鲜或冷的养殖仿石蟹(仿岩蟹),104 鲜或冷的养殖堪察加拟石蟹,105 鲜或冷的养殖短足拟石蟹,106 鲜或冷的养殖扁足拟石蟹,107 鲜或冷的养殖雪蟹,108 鲜或冷的养殖日本雪蟹,109 鲜或冷的养殖金霸王蟹(帝王蟹),110 鲜或冷的野生毛蟹,111 鲜或冷的野生仿石蟹(仿岩蟹),112 鲜或冷的野生堪察加拟石蟹,113 鲜或冷的野生短足拟石蟹,114 鲜或冷的野生扁足拟石蟹,115 鲜或冷的野生雪蟹,116 鲜或冷的野生日本雪蟹,117 鲜或冷的野生金霸王蟹(帝王蟹),118 活的金霸王蟹(帝王蟹)〕	7		70	9/	9	千克	ABU/	PRQS	37	
0306.3399 90	其他活、鲜或冷的带壳或去壳蟹[T2]	7		70	9/	9	千克	AB/	PRQS	37	
	--挪威海螯虾:										
0306.3410	---种苗〔999〕	0		0	9/	9	千克	AB/	PQ	25	
0306.3490	---其他〔101:活挪威海螯虾;102:养殖;103:野生〕	7		70	9/	9	千克	AB/	PRQS	37	
	--冷水小虾及对虾(长额虾属、褐虾):										
0306.3510	---种苗〔101:长额虾属种苗;102:褐虾种苗〕	0		0	0/	9	千克	AB/	PQ		
0306.3590	---其他										

协定税率 %								RCEP		特惠税率 %			Article Description
东/冰/格	巴基斯坦	韩国	瑞士上/下	哥/秘/柬	澳/毛	新西/坡/智	中国港/澳/台	东盟及马来/澳/韩	日/新	亚太2国	老/柬/缅	98/97/95	
0/0/0	3.5	4.6	0/0	0/0/0	0/0	0//0	0/0/	9.5/9.5/9.5	/9.5	0	/0/0	0/0/0	Frozen King Crab (king crab), hairy crab, imitation stone crab (imitation rock crab), Kamchatka pseudostone crab, short－footed pseudostone crab, flat－footed pseudostone crab, snow crab, Japanese snow crab
0/0/0	3.5	4.6	0/0	0/0/0	0/0	0//0	0/0/	9.5/9.5/9.5	/9.5	0	/0/0	0/0/0	Other crab,frozen
0/0/0	12.8	7.4	1.6/1.6	0/0/0	0/0	0//0	0/0/	14.4/14.4/14.4	15/14.4		/0/	0/0/0	--Norway Lobsters(Nehrops norvegicus)
													--Cold-water shrimp and prawns (pandalus、spp., Crangon crangon):
0/0/0	0	0	0/0	0/0/0	0/0	0//0	0/0/	0/0/0	7.3/0		/0/0	0/0/0	---Shelled
0/0/0	0	0	0/0	0/0/0	0/0	0//0	0/0/	0/0/0	0/0		/0/0	0/0/0	---Other, northerm pandalus(pandalus)
0/0/0	0	0	0/0	0/0/0	0/0	0//0	0/0/	0/0/0	0/0		/0/0	0/0/0	---Other
													--Other shrimps and prawns:
0/0/0	0	0	0/0	0/0/0	0/0	0//0	0/0/	0/0/0	7.3/0		/0/0	0/0/0	---Shellde
													---Other:
0/0/0	0	0	0/0	0/0/0	0/0	0//0	0/0/	0/0/0	0/0		/0/0	0/0/0	Other frozen shrimps (except prawn) (except shrimp meat)
0/0/0	0	0	0/0	0/0/0	0/0	0//0	0/0/	0/0/0	0/0		/0/0	0/0/0	Frozen shrimp (prawn) (excluding shrimp meat)
													--Other
													---Freshwater crawfish:
0/0/0	12.8	7.4	1.6/1.6	0/0/0	0/0	0//0	0/0/	14.4/14.4/14.4	15/14.4		/0/	0/0/0	----Shelled
0/0/0	12.8	7.4	1.6/1.6	0/0/0	0/0	0//0	0/0/	14.4/14.4/14.4	15/14.4		/0/	0/0/0	----Other
0/0/0	0	7.4	1.6/1.6	0/0/0	0/0	0//0	0/0/	14.9/15.2/14.9	15/15.2		/0/	0/0/0	---Other
													-Live,fresh or chilled:
													--Rock lobster and other sea crawfish (*Palinurus spp.* , *Panulirus spp.* , *Jasus spp.*):
0/0/0	0	0	0/0	0/0/0	0/0	0//0	0/0/	0/0/0	0/0			0/0/0	---For cultivation
0/0/0	0	3	1.5/1.5	0/0/0	0/0	0//0	0/0/	0/0/13.5	13.6/0		/0/0	0/0/0	---Other
													--Lobsters (*Homarus spp.*):
0/0/0	0	0	0/0	0/0/0	0/0	0//0	0/0/	0/0/0	0/0			0/0/0	---For cultivation
0/0/0	12	3	1.5/1.5	0/0/0	0/0	0//0	0/0/	0/0/13.5	13.6/0		/0/0	0/0/0	---Other
													--Crabs:
0/0/0	0	0	0/0	0/0/0	0/0	0//0	0/0/	0/0/0	0/0			0/0/0	---For cultivation
													---Other:
0/0/0	4.9	2.8	1.4/1.4	0/0/0	0/0	0//0	0/0/	0/0/12.6	12.7/0		/0/	0/0/0	----Freshwater crabs, live
0/0/0	0	2.8	1.4/1.4	0/0/0	0/0	0//0	0/0/	0/0/12.6	12.7/0		/0/	0/0/0	----Swimming crab
													----Other
0/0/0	0	2.8	1.4/1.4	0/0/0	0/0	0//0	0/0/	0/0/12.6	12.7/0		/0/	0/0/0	Live, fresh or cold golden overlord crab (emperor crab), hairy crab, imitation stone crab (imitation rock crab), Kamchatka imitation stone crab, short foot imitation stone crab, flat foot imitation stone crab, snow crab and Japanese snow crab
0/0/0	0	2.8	1.4/1.4	0/0/0	0/0	0//0	0/0/	0/0/12.6	12.7/0		/0/	0/0/0	Other live,fresh or cold crab,in shell or not
													--Norway lobsters (*Nephrops norvegicus*)
0/0/0	0	0	0/0	0/0/0	0/0	0//0	0/0/	0/0/0	0/0			0/0/0	---For cultivation
0/0/0	11.2	2.8	1.4/1.4	0/0/0	0/0	0//0	0/0/	0/0/12.6	12.7/0		/0/0	0/0/0	---Other
													--Cold－water shrimps and prawns (*Pandalus spp.* , *Crangon crangon*):
0/0/0	0	0	0/0	0/0/0	0/0	0//0	0/0/	0/0/0	0/0			0/0/0	---For cultivation
													---Other

税则号列	货品名称〔CIQ 扩展编码及品名—T2 表示见附表 2〕	最惠(%)	暂定税率	普通	增值/消费	出口退税	计量单位	监管条件/特殊证件	检验检疫	对美关税	亚太上/下
0306.3590 10	鲜、冷的冷水小虾及对虾(长额虾属、褐虾)(种苗除外)〔101 养殖对虾,102 野生对虾,103 饲料用海水虾,104 饲料用淡水虾,105 养殖的冷水小虾,106 野生的冷水小虾〕	10		70	9/	9	千克	AB/	PRQS	40	
0306.3590 90	活的冷水小虾及对虾(长额虾属、褐虾)(种苗除外)〔101 活的南美白对虾,102 活的斑节对虾,103 活的其他对虾,104 活的其他海水虾蟹,105 活的日本沼虾(青虾),106 活的罗氏沼虾(马来沼虾),107 活的其他淡水虾蟹,108 活的虾蛄,109 活的糠虾,110 活的其他甲壳动物〕	10		70	9/	9	千克	AB/	PRQS	40	
	--其他小虾及对虾:										
0306.3610	---种苗〔101:南美白对虾;102:斑节对虾;103:其他对虾;104:其他海水虾蟹〕	0		0	0/	9	千克	AB/	PQ		
0306.3690	---其他										
0306.3690 10	其他鲜、冷的小虾(对虾属除外)(种苗除外)〔101 其他养殖鲜或冷虾,102 其他野生鲜或冷虾,103 饲料用海水虾,104 饲料用淡水虾〕	12		70	9/	9	千克	AB/	PRQS	42	
0306.3690 90	活、鲜或冷的对虾(对虾属);其他活的小虾(对虾属除外)(种苗除外)〔101 其他养殖鲜或冷虾,102 其他野生鲜或冷虾,103 饲料用海水虾,104 饲料用淡水虾,105 活的南美白对虾,106 活的斑节对虾,107 活的其他对虾,108 活的其他海水虾蟹,109 活的日本沼虾(青虾),110 活的罗氏沼虾(马来沼虾),111 活的其他淡水虾蟹,112 活的虾蛄,113 活的糠虾,114 活的其他甲壳动物〕	12		70	9/	9	千克	AB/	PRQS	42	
	--其他:										
0306.3910	---种苗[T2]	0		0	0/	9	千克	AB/	PQ		
0306.3990	---其他										
0306.3990 10	其他甲壳动物的卵〔101 未列出的饲料用其他淡水产品,102 其他养殖鲜或冷动物水产品,103 其他野生鲜或冷动物水产品〕	7		70	0/	9	千克	AB/	PRQS		
0306.3990 90	其他活、鲜、冷的带壳或去壳甲壳动物〔101 其他淡水虾蟹,102 未列出的饲料用其他淡水产品,103 其他养殖鲜或冷动物水产品,104 其他野生鲜或冷动物水产品〕	7		70	9/	9	千克	AB/	PRQS	37	
	-其他:										
0306.9100	--岩礁虾及其他龙虾(真龙虾属、龙虾属、岩龙虾属)〔101 养殖干制虾类制品,102 野生干制虾类制品,105 养殖盐腌及盐渍虾类制品,106 野生盐腌及盐渍虾类制品〕〔101 养殖干制虾类制品,102 野生干制虾类制品,103 养殖盐腌及盐渍虾类制品,104 野生盐腌及盐渍虾类制品〕	7		70	9/	9	千克	AB/	PRQS	37	
0306.9200	--螯龙虾(螯龙虾属)〔101 养殖干制虾类制品,102 野生干制虾类制品,103 养殖盐腌及盐渍虾类制品,104 野生盐腌及盐渍虾类制品〕	7		70	9/	9	千克	AB/	PRQS	37	
	--蟹:										
0306.9310	---中华绒螯蟹[T2]	7		70	9/	9	千克	AB/	PRQS	37	
0306.9320	---梭子蟹[T2]	7		70	9/	9	千克	AB/	PRQS	37	
0306.9390	---其他〔101 养殖干制蟹类制品,102 野生干制蟹类制品,103 养殖盐腌及盐渍蟹类制品,104 野生盐腌及盐渍蟹类制品〕	7		70	9/	9	千克	AB/	PRQS	37	
0306.9400	--挪威海螯虾[T2]	7		70	9/	9,13	千克	AB/	PRQS	37	
	--小虾及对虾:										
0306.9510	---冷水小虾及对虾(长额虾属、褐虾)〔101 养殖干制虾类制品,102 野生干制虾类制品,103 养殖盐腌及盐渍虾类制品,104 野生盐腌及盐渍虾类制品〕	10		70	9/	9	千克	AB/	PRQS	40	
0306.9590	---其他小虾及对虾〔101 养殖干制虾类制品,102 野生干制虾类制品,103 养殖盐腌及盐渍虾类制品,104 野生盐腌及盐渍虾类制品〕	10		70	9/	9	千克	AB/	PRQS	40	
0306.9900	--其他[T2]	7		70	9/	9,13	千克	AB/	PRQS	37	
03.07	**带壳或去壳的软体动物,活、鲜、冷、冻、干、盐腌或盐渍的;熏制的带壳或去壳软体动物,不论在熏制前或熏制过程中是否烹煮:**										
	-牡蛎(蚝):										
	--活、鲜或冷的:										
0307.1110	---种苗〔999〕	0		0	0/	9	千克	AB/	PQ		
0307.1190	---其他〔101 活的牡蛎(蚝),102 非生食的鲜、冷的养殖牡蛎(蚝),103 可用于生食的鲜、冷的养殖牡蛎(蚝),104 非生食的鲜、冷的野生牡蛎(蚝),105 可用于生食的鲜、冷的野生牡蛎(蚝)〕	7		70	9/	9	千克	AB/	PRQS	37	
0307.1200	--冻的〔101 养殖,102 野生〕	10		70	9/	9	千克	AB/	PRQS	40	
0307.1900	--其他〔101 干制的养殖牡蛎(蚝),102 干制的野生牡蛎(蚝),103 盐腌或盐渍的养殖牡蛎(蚝),104 盐腌或盐渍的野生牡蛎(蚝)〕	10		70	9/	9	千克	AB/	PRQS	40	
	-扇贝及其他扇贝科的软体动物										
	--活、鲜或冷的:										
0307.2110	---种苗〔101 养殖,102 野生〕	0		0	0/	9	千克	AB/	PQ		
	---其他:										

协定税率 %								RCEP		特惠税率 %			Article Description
东/冰/格	巴基斯坦	韩国	瑞士 上/下	哥/秘/柬	澳/毛	新西/坡/智	中国港/澳/台	东盟及马来/澳/韩	日/新	亚太2国	老/柬/缅	98/97/95	
0/0/0	8.1	2.7	1.4/1.4	0/0/0	0/0	0//0	0/0/	0/0/10.8	10.9/0		/0/0	0/0/0	Fresh and cold cold water shrimps and prawns (prawns, brown shrimp) (excluding seedlings)
0/0/0	8.1	2.7	1.4/1.4	0/0/0	0/0	0//0	0/0/	0/0/10.8	10.9/0		/0/0	0/0/0	Other live cold water prawns
													--Other shrimps and prawns:
0/0/0	0	0	0/0	0/0/0	0/0	0//0	0/0/	0/0/0	0/0			0/0/0	---For cultivation
													---Other
0/0/0	8.1	2.7	1.4/1.4	0/0/0	0/0	0//0	0/0/	0/0/10.8	10.9/0		/0/0	0/0/0	Other fresh and cold shrimps (except prawn) (except seedlings)
0/0/0	8.1	2.7	1.4/1.4	0/0/0	0/0	0//0	0/0/	0/0/10.8	10.9/0		/0/0	0/0/0	Live, fresh or cold prawns (Penaeus); Other live shrimps (except prawn) (except seedlings)
													--Other:
0/0/0	0	0	0/0	0/0/0	0/0	0//0	0/0/	0/0/0	0/0			0/0/0	---For cultivation
													---Other
0/0/0	11.2	2.8	1.4/1.4	0/0/0	0/0	0//0	0/0/	12.6/12.6/12.6	12.7/12.6		/0/0	0/0/0	Eggs of other crustaceans
0/0/0	11.2	2.8	1.4/1.4	0/0/0	0/0	0//0	0/0/	12.6/12.6/12.6	12.7/12.6		/0/0	0/0/0	Other live, fresh and cold shelled or shelled crustaceans
													-Other:
0/0/0	0	3	1.5/1.5	0/0/0	0/0	0//0	0/0/	0/0/13.5	13.6/0		/0/0	0/0/0	--Rock lobster and other sea crawfish (*Palinurus spp.* , *Panulirus spp.* , *Jasus spp.*)
0/0/0	12	3	1.5/1.5	0/0/0	0/0	0//0	0/0/	0/0/13.5	13.6/0		/0/0	0/0/0	--Lobsters (*Homarus spp.*)
													--Crabs:
0/0/0	4.9	2.8	1.4/1.4	0/0/0	0/0	0//0	0/0/	0/0/12.6	12.7/0		/0/	0/0/0	---Freshwater crabs, live
0/0/0	0	2.8	1.4/1.4	0/0/0	0/0	0//0	0/0/	0/0/12.6	12.7/0		/0/	0/0/0	---Swimming crab
0/0/0	0	2.8	1.4/1.4	0/0/0	0/0	0//0	0/0/	0/0/12.6	12.7/0		/0/	0/0/0	---Other
0/0/0	11.2	2.8	1.4/1.4	0/0/0	0/0	0//0	0/0/	0/0/12.6	12.7/0		/0/0	0/0/0	--Norway lobsters (*Nephrops norvegicus*)
													--Shrimps and prawns:
0/0/0	4.2	2.4	1.2/1.2	0/0/0	0/0	0//0	0/0/	0/0/10.8	10.9/0		/0/0	0/0/0	---Cold-water shrimps and prawns (*Pandalus spp.* , *Crangon crangon*):
0/0/0	4.2	2.4	1.2/1.2	0/0/0	0/0	0//0	0/0/	10.8/10.8/10.8	10.9/10.8		/0/0	0/0/0	---Other shrimps and prawns
0/0/0	11.2	2.8	1.4/1.4	0/0/0	0/0	0//0	0/0/	12.6/12.6/12.6	12.7/12.6		/0/0	0/0/0	--Other
													Molluscs, whether in shell or not, live, fresh, chilled, frozen, dried, salted or in brine; smoked molluscs, whether in shell or not, whether or not cooked before or during the smoking process:
													-Oysters:
													--Live, fresh or chilled:
0/0/0	0	0	0/0	0/0/0	0/0	0//0	0/0/	0/0/0	0/0			0/0/0	---For cultivation
0/0/0	11.2	2.8	1.4/1.4	0/0/0	0/0	0//0	0/0/	0/0/12.6	12.7/0		//0	0/0/0	---Other
0/0/0	11.2	2.8	1.4/1.4	0/0/0	0/0	0//0	0/0/	0/0/12.6	12.7/0		//0	0/0/0	--Frozen
0/0/0	11.2	2.8	1.4/1.4	0/0/0	0/0	0//0	0/0/	0/0/12.6	12.7/0		//0	0/0/0	--Other
													-Scallops and other molluscs of the family Pectinidae
													--Live, fresh or chilled:
0/0/0	0	0	0/0	0/0/0	0/0	0//0	0/0/	0/0/0	0/0			0/0/0	---For cultivation
													---Other:

税则号列	货品名称〔CIQ 扩展编码及品名—T2 表示见附表 2〕	最惠(%)	暂定税率	普通	增值/消费	出口退税	计量单位	监管条件/特殊证件	检验检疫	对美关税	亚太上/下
0307.2191	----扇贝(扇贝属、栉孔扇贝属、巨扇贝属)〔101 活的扇贝,102 非生食的鲜、冷的养殖扇贝,103 可用于生食的鲜、冷的养殖扇贝,104 非生食的鲜、冷的野生扇贝,105 可用于生食的鲜、冷的野生扇贝〕	10		70	9/	9	千克	AB/	PRQS	40	
0307.2199	----其他〔101 鲜、冷养殖扇贝科的软体动物,102 鲜、冷养殖扇贝科的软体动物,103 鲜、冷野生扇贝科的软体动物〕	7		70	9/	9	千克	AB/	PRQS	37	
	--冻的:										
0307.2210	---扇贝(扇贝属、栉孔扇贝属、巨扇贝属)〔101 养殖冷冻扇贝,102 野生冷冻扇贝〕	10		80	9/	9	千克	AB/	PRQS	40	
0307.2290	---其他〔101 其他养殖冷冻动物水产品,102 其他野生冷冻动物水产品〕	7		70	9/	9	千克	AB/	PRQS	37	
	--其他:										
0307.2910	---扇贝(扇贝属、栉孔扇贝属、巨扇贝属)〔101 养殖干制贝类制品,102 野生干制贝类制品,103 养殖盐腌及盐渍贝类制品,104 野生盐腌及盐渍贝类制品〕	10		80	9/	9	千克	AB/	PRQS	40	
0307.2990	---其他〔101 养殖干制头足类制品,102 野生干制头足类制品,103 养殖盐腌及盐渍头足类制品,104 野生盐腌及盐渍头足类制品〕	7		70	9/	9,13	千克	AB/	PRQS	37	
	-贻贝:										
	--活、鲜或冷的:										
0307.3110	---种苗〔999〕	0		0	0/	9	千克	AB/	PQ		
0307.3190	---其他										
0307.3190 01	鲜、冷贻贝〔101 养殖,102 野生〕	10		70	9/	9	千克	AB/	PRQS	40	
0307.3190 90	其他活贻贝〔999〕	10		70	9/	9	千克	AB/	PRQS	40	
0307.3200	--冻的〔101 养殖冷冻贻贝,102 其他野生冷冻双壳贝〕	10		70	9/	9	千克	AB/	PRQS	40	7/7
0307.3900	--其他〔101 养殖干制贝类制品,102 野生干制贝类制品,103 养殖盐腌及盐渍贝类制品,104 野生盐腌及盐渍贝类制品〕	10		70	9/	9	千克	AB/	PRQS	40	7/7
	-墨鱼及鱿鱼:										
	--活、鲜或冷的:										
0307.4210	---种苗〔101 乌贼(墨鱼),102 鱿鱼〕	0		0	0/	9	千克	AB/	PQ		
	---其他:										
0307.4291	----墨鱼(乌贼属、巨粒僧头乌贼、耳乌贼属)及鱿鱼(柔鱼属、枪乌贼属、双柔鱼属、拟乌贼属)[T2]	12		70	9/	9	千克	AB/	PRQS	42	
0307.4299	----其他[T2]	14		70	9/	9	千克	AB/	PRQS	44	
	--冻的:										
0307.4310	---墨鱼(乌贼属、巨粒僧头乌贼、耳乌贼属)及鱿鱼(柔鱼属、枪乌贼属、双柔鱼属、拟乌贼属)[T2]	12		70	9/	9	千克	AB/	PRQS	42	10/10
0307.4390	---其他〔101 其他冻的养殖墨鱼,102 其他冻的野生墨鱼,103 其他冻的养殖鱿鱼,104 其他冻的野生鱿鱼〕	10		70	9/	9	千克	AB/	PRQS	40	
	--其他:										
0307.4910	---墨鱼(乌贼属、巨粒僧头乌贼、耳乌贼属)及鱿鱼(柔鱼属、枪乌贼属、双柔鱼属、拟乌贼属)[T2]	12		70	9/	9	千克	AB/	PRQS	42	10/10
0307.4990	---其他[T2]	10		70	9/	9,13	千克	AB/	PRQS	40	
	-章鱼:										
0307.5100	--活、鲜或冷的〔101 活的章鱼,102 饲料用章鱼,103 非生食的,104 可用于非生食的〕	7		70	9/	9	千克	AB/	PRQS	37	
0307.5200	--冻的〔101 养殖,102 野生〕	7		70	9/	9	千克	AB/	PRQS	37	
0307.5900	--其他〔101 饲料用章鱼,102 干制的章鱼,103 盐制的章鱼〕	7		70	9/	9	千克	AB/	PRQS	37	
	-蜗牛及螺,海螺除外:										
0307.6010	---种苗										
0307.6010 10	濒危蜗牛及螺种苗,海螺除外〔101 田螺,102 蜗牛〕	0		0	9/	0	千克	ABFE/	PQ	25	
0307.6010 90	蜗牛及螺种苗,海螺除外(濒危除外)〔101 田螺,102 蜗牛〕	0		0	0/	9	千克	AB/	PQ		
0307.6090	---其他										
0307.6090 10	其他濒危蜗牛及螺,海螺除外〔101 田螺,102 蜗牛,103 其他软体〕	7		70	9/	0	千克	ABFE/	PRQS	37	
0307.6090 90	其他活、鲜、冷、冻、干、盐腌或盐渍的蜗牛及螺,海螺除外(包括熏制的带壳或去壳的,不论在熏制前或熏制过程中是否烹煮)[T2]	7		70	9/	9	千克	AB/	PRQS	37	
	-蛤、鸟蛤及舟贝(蚶科、北极蛤科、鸟蛤科、斧蛤科、缝栖蛤科、蛤蜊科、中带蛤科、海螂科、双带蛤科、截蛏科、竹蛏科、砗磲科、帘蛤科):										
	--活、鲜或冷的:										
0307.7110	---种苗										
0307.7110 10	砗磲的种苗〔999〕	0		0	9/	9	千克	ABEF/	PQ	25	
0307.7110 90	蛤、鸟蛤及舟贝种苗(濒危除外)〔999〕	0		0	0/	9	千克	AB/	PQ		
	---其他:										
0307.7191	----蛤[T2]	10		70	9/	9	千克	AB/	PRQS	40	
0307.7199	----其他										

协定税率 %								RCEP		特惠税率 %			Article Description
东/冰/格	巴基斯坦	韩国	瑞士 上/下	哥/秘/柬	澳/毛	新西/坡/智	中国港/澳/台	东盟及马来/澳/韩	日/新	亚太2国	老/柬/缅	98/97/95	
0/0/0	11.2	2.8	1.4/1.4	0/0/0	0/0	0//0	0/0/	0/0/12.6	12.7/0		//0	0/0/0	----Scallop (scallop, Chlamys farreri, giant scallop)
0/0/0	11.2	2.8	1.4/1.4	0/0/0	0/0	0//0	0/0/	0/0/12.6	12.7/0		/0/0	0/0/0	----Other
													--Frozen:
0/0/0	11.2	2.8	1.4/1.4	0/0/0	0/0	0//0	0/0/	13.3/13.3/13.3	13.3/13.3		//0	0/0/0	---Scallop (scallop, Chlamys farreri, giant scallop)
0/0/0		6	0/0	0/0/0	0/0	0//0	0/0/	9.5/9.5/	/9.5		/0/0	0/0/0	---Other
													--Other:
0/0/0	11.2	2.8	1.4/1.4	0/0/0	0/0	0//0	0/0/	13.3/13.3/13.3	13.3/13.3		//0	0/0/0	---Scallop (scallop, Chlamys farreri, giant scallop)
0/0/0		6	0/0	0/0/0	0/0	0//0	0/0/	9.5/9.5/	/9.5		/0/0	0/0/0	---Other
													-Mussels (*Mytilus spp.*, *Perna spp.*):
													--Live, fresh or chilled:
0/0/0	0	0	0/0	0/0/0	0/0	0//0	0/0/	0/0/0	0/0			0/0/0	---For cultivation
													---Other
0/0/0	11.2	2.8	1.4/1.4	0/0/0	0/0	0//0	0/0/	0/0/12.6	12.7/0		/0/0	0/0/0	Mussels, fresh or chilled
0/0/0	11.2	2.8	1.4/1.4	0/0/0	0/0	0//0	0/0/	0/0/12.6	12.7/0		/0/0	0/0/0	Other mussels, live
0/0/0	4.9	2.8	1.4/1.4	0/0/0	0/0	0//0	0/0/	0/0/12.6	12.7/0		/0/0	0/0/0	--Frozen
0/0/0	4.9	2.8	1.4/1.4	0/0/0	0/0	0//0	0/0/	0/0/12.6	12.7/0		/0/0	0/0/0	--Other
													-Cuttle fish and squid:
													--Live, fresh or chilled:
0/0/0	0	0	0/0	0/0/0	0/0	0//0	0/0/	0/0/0	0/0			0/0/0	--For cultivation
													---Other
0/0/0	4.2	2.4	1.2/1.2	0/0/0	0/0	0//0	0/0/	0/0/10.8	10.9/0		/0/0	0/0/0	----Cuttle fish (*Sepia of fici-nalis*, *Rossia macrosoma*, *Se-piola spp.*) and squid (*Ommastrephes spp.*, *Loli-go spp.*, *Nototodarus spp.*, *Sepioteuthis spp.*)
0/0/0	11.2	2.8	1.4/1.4	0/0/0	0/0	0//0	0/0/	0/0/12.6	12.7/0		/0/0	0/0/0	----Other
													--Frozen:
0/0/0	10	7.2	1.2/1.2	0/0/0	0/0	0//0	0/0/	11.4/11.4/11.4	11.4/11.4		/0/0	0/0/0	---Cuttle fish (*Sepia of ficina-lis*, *Rossia macrosoma*, *Sepi-ola spp.*) and squid (*Om-mastrephes spp.*, *Loligo spp.*, *Nototodarus spp.*, *Se-pioteuthis spp.*)
0/0/0		6	0/0	0/0/0	0/0	0//0	0/0/	9.5/9.5/	/9.5		/0/0	0/0/0	---Other
													--Other
0/0/0	10	7.2	1.2/1.2	0/0/0	0/0	0//0	0/0/	11.4/11.4/11.4	11.4/11.4		/0/0	0/0/0	---Cuttle fish (*Sepia of fici-nalis*, *Rossia macrosoma*, *Sepi-ola spp.*) and squid (*Ommastrephes spp.*, *Loli-go spp.*, *No-totodarus spp.*, *Sepioteuthis spp.*)
0/0/0		6	0/0	0/0/0	0/0	0//0	0/0/	9.5/9.5/	/9.5		/0/0	0/0/0	---Other
													-Octopus (*Octopus spp.*):
0/0/0	13.6	7.9	1.7/1.7	0/0/0	0/0	0//0	0/0/	15.3/15.3/15.3	/15.3			0/0/0	--Live, fresh or chilled
0/0/0	13.6	7.9	1.7/1.7	0/0/0	0/0	0//0	0/0/	16.2/16.2/16.2	/16.2			0/0/0	--Frozen
0/0/0	13.6	7.9	1.7/1.7	0/0/0	0/0	0//0	0/0/	16.2/16.2/16.2	/16.2			0/0/0	--Other
													-Snails, other than sea snails:
													---For cultivation
0/0/0	0	0	0/0	0/0/0	0/0	0//0	0/0/	0/0/0	0/0			0/0/0	Endangered snails, other than sea snails, for cultivation
0/0/0	0	0	0/0	0/0/0	0/0	0//0	0/0/	0/0/0	0/0			0/0/0	Other snails, other than sea snails, for cultivation
													---Other
0/0/0	11.2	2.8	1.4/1.4	0/0/0	0/0	0//0	0/0/	0/0/12.6	12.7/0		/0/	0/0/0	Other endangered snails (other than sea snails), for cultiva-tion
0/0/0	11.2	2.8	1.4/1.4	0/0/0	0/0	0//0	0/0/	0/0/12.6	12.7/0		/0/	0/0/0	Other snails, other than sea snails, live, fresh, chilled, frozen, dried, salted or in brine(including smoked, in whether in shell or not, whether or not cooked before or during the smoking process)
													-Clam, cockle and ark shell(families arcidae, arcticidae, cardi-idae, donacidae, hiatellidae, mactridae, mesodesmatidae, myi-dae, semelidae, solecurtidae, solenidae, tridacnidae, veneri-dae):
													--Live, fresh or chilled:
													---For cultivation
0/0/0	0	0	0/0	0/0/0	0/0	0//0	0/0/	0/0/0	0/0			0/0/0	Tridacindae for cultivation
0/0/0	0	0	0/0	0/0/0	0/0	0//0	0/0/	0/0/0	0/0			0/0/0	Clam, cockles and ark shells, for cultivation, other than en-dangered
													---Other:
0/0/0	11.2	2.8	1.4/1.4	0/0/0	0/0	0//0	0/0/	0/0/12.6	12.7/0			0/0/0	----Clam
													----Other

税则号列	货品名称〔CIQ 扩展编码及品名—T2 表示见附表 2〕	最惠(%)	暂定税率	普通	增值/消费	出口退税	计量单位	监管条件/特殊证件	检验检疫	对美关税	亚太上/下
0307.7199 10	活、鲜、冷砗磲〔101 活的砗磲,102 鲜、冷的养殖砗磲,103 鲜、冷的野生砗磲〕	10		70	9/	9	千克	ABEF/	PRQS	40	
0307.7199 20	活、鲜、冷的粗饰蚶〔101 活的,102 鲜、冷的〕	10		70	9/	9	千克	ABU/	PRQS	40	
0307.7199 90	活、鲜、冷鸟蛤及舟贝(蚶科、北极蛤科、鸟蛤科、斧蛤科、缝栖蛤科、蛤蜊科中带蛤科、海螂科、双带蛤科、截蛏科、竹蛏科、帘蛤科)[T2]	10		70	9/	9	千克	AB/	PRQS	40	
0307.7200	--冻的										
0307.7200 10	冻的砗磲〔999〕	10		70	9/	9	千克	ABEF/	PRQS	40	
0307.7200 20	冻的粗饰蚶〔999〕	10		70	9/	9	千克	ABU/	PRQS	40	
0307.7200 90	冻的其他蛤、鸟蛤及舟贝(蚶科、北极蛤科、鸟蛤科、斧蛤科、缝栖蛤科、蛤蜊科、中带蛤科、海螂科、双带蛤科、截蛏科、竹蛏科、帘蛤科)[T2]	10		70	9/	9	千克	AB/	PRQS	40	
0307.7900	--其他										
0307.7900 10	干、盐制的砗磲(包括熏制的带壳或去壳的,不论在熏制前或熏制过程中是否烹煮)〔101 干制的砗磲,102 盐制的砗磲〕	10		70	9/	9,13	千克	ABEF/	PRQS	40	
0307.7900 20	干、盐制的粗饰蚶(包括熏制的带壳或去壳的,不论在熏制前或熏制过程中是否烹煮)〔101 干制的粗饰蚶,102 盐制的粗饰蚶〕	10		70	9/	9,13	千克	ABU/	PRQS	40	
0307.7900 90	干、盐制其他蛤、鸟蛤及舟贝(蚶科、北极蛤科、鸟蛤科、斧蛤科、缝栖蛤科、蛤蜊科、中带蛤科、海螂科、双带蛤科、截蛏科、竹蛏科、帘蛤科)(包括熏制的带壳或去壳的,不论在熏制前或熏制过程中是否烹煮)[T2]	10		70	9/	9,13	千克	AB/	PRQS	40	
	-鲍鱼(鲍属)及凤螺(凤螺属):										
	--活、鲜或冷的鲍鱼(鲍属):										
0307.8110	---种苗〔999〕	0		0	0/	9	千克	AB/	PQ		
0307.8190	---其他〔101 活的鲍鱼鲍鱼,102 鲜、冷养殖的鲍鱼,103 鲜、冷野生的鲍鱼〕	10	7	80	9/	9	千克	AB/	PRQS	37	
	--活、鲜或冷的凤螺(凤螺属):										
0307.8210	---种苗〔999〕	0		0	0/	9	千克	AB/	PQ		
0307.8290	---其他〔101 活的,102 鲜或冷的其他养殖凤螺(凤螺属),103 鲜或冷的其他野生凤螺(凤螺属)〕	10		70	9/	9	千克	AB/	PRQS	40	
0307.8300	--冻的鲍鱼(鲍属)〔101 养殖,102 野生〕	10		80	9/	9	千克	AB/	PRQS	40	
0307.8400	--冻的凤螺(凤螺属)〔101 养殖,102 野生〕	10		70	9/	9	千克	AB/	PRQS	40	
0307.8700	--其他鲍鱼(鲍属)〔101 干制的养殖鲍鱼(鲍属),102 干制的野生鲍鱼(鲍属),103 盐腌或盐渍的养殖鲍鱼(鲍属),104 盐腌或盐渍的野生鲍鱼(鲍属)〕	10		80	9/	9	千克	AB/	PRQS	40	
0307.8800	--其他凤螺(凤螺属)〔101 干制的养殖凤螺(凤螺属),102 干制的野生凤螺(凤螺属)),103 盐腌或盐渍的养殖凤螺(凤螺属),104 盐腌或盐渍的野生凤螺(凤螺属)〕	10		70	9/	9,13	千克	AB/	PRQS	40	
	-其他:										
	--活、鲜或冷的:										
0307.9110	---种苗										
0307.9110 11	大珠母贝的种苗〔101 其他海水贝,102 其他淡水贝〕	0		0	9/	9	千克	ABE/	PQ	25	
0307.9110 19	其他濒危软体动物的种苗(大珠母贝除外)〔101 其他海水贝,102 其他淡水贝,103 其他棘皮动物,104 其他软体及其他水生无脊椎动物〕	0		0	9/	0	千克	ABEF/	PQ	25	
0307.9110 90	其他软体动物的种苗[T2]	0		0	9/	9	千克	AB/	PQ	25	
0307.9190	---其他										
0307.9190 11	活、鲜、冷大珠母贝(种苗除外)〔999〕	7		70	9/	9	千克	ABE/	PRQS	37	
0307.9190 19	活、鲜、冷的其他濒危软体动物(种苗除外)〔999〕	7		70	9/	0	千克	ABEF/	PRQS	37	
0307.9190 20	活、鲜、冷蚬属(种苗除外)〔101 活的,102 鲜、冷的蚬属〕	7		70	9/	9	千克	ABU/	PRQS	37	
0307.9190 90	其他活、鲜、冷的软体动物(种苗除外)〔101 活的软体动物,102 鲜、冷非生食的养殖北极贝,103 鲜、冷可用于生食的养殖北极贝,104 鲜、冷非生食的野生北极贝,105 鲜、冷可用于生食的野生北极贝,106 鲜、冷的其他养殖双壳贝类,107 鲜、冷的其他野生双壳贝类,108 鲜、冷的其他养殖单壳贝类,109 鲜、冷的其他野生单壳贝类,110 鲜、冷的养殖头足类,111 鲜、冷的其他野生头足类,112 鲜、冷的其他养殖软体动物,113 鲜、冷的其他野生软体动物,114 活的有害软体动物,115 活的海螺〕	7		70	9/	9	千克	AB/	PRQS	37	
0307.9200	--冻的										
0307.9200 11	冻的大珠母贝〔101 其他养殖冷冻动物水产品,102 其他野生冷冻动物水产品〕	7		80	9/	9	千克	ABE/	PRQS	37	
0307.9200 19	冻的其他濒危软体动物〔101 其他养殖冷冻动物水产品,102 其他野生冷冻动物水产品〕	7		70	9/	0	千克	ABEF/	PRQS	37	
0307.9200 20	冻的蚬属〔101 养殖,102 野生〕	7		70	9/	9	千克	ABU/	PRQS	37	
0307.9200 90	其他冻的软体动物〔101 养殖,102 野生〕	7		70	9/	9	千克	AB/	PRQS	37	
0307.9900	--其他										

协定税率 %								RCEP		特惠税率 %			Article Description
东/冰/格	巴基斯坦	韩国	瑞士上/下	哥/秘/柬	澳/毛	新西/坡/智	中国港/澳/台	东盟及马来/澳/韩	日/新	亚太2国	老/柬/缅	98/97/95	
0/0/0	11.2	2.8	1.4/1.4	0/0/0	0/0	0//0	0/0/	0/0/12.6	12.7/0		/0/0	0/0/0	Tridacnidae, live, fresh or chilled
0/0/0	11.2	2.8	1.4/1.4	0/0/0	0/0	0//0	0/0/	0/0/12.6	12.7/0		/0/0	0/0/0	Live, fresh, cold coarse act the role of cockle
0/0/0	11.2	2.8	1.4/1.4	0/0/0	0/0	0//0	0/0/	0/0/12.6	12.7/0		/0/0	0/0/0	Clam、cockle and ark shell (arcidae、arcticidae、cardiidae、donacidae、hiatellidae、mactridae、mesodesmatidae、myidae、mesodesmatidae、solecurtidae、solenidae、tridacnidae、veneridae), live, fresh or chilled
													--Frozen
0/0/0		2	0/0	0//0	0/0	0//0	0/0/	0/0/9	9.1/0			0/0/0	Frozen Tridacindae
0/0/0		2	0/0	0//0	0/0	0//0	0/0/	0/0/9	9.1/0			0/0/0	Frozen Anadara
0/0/0		2	0/0	0//0	0/0	0//0	0/0/	0/0/9	9.1/0			0/0/0	Other frozen Clam, cockles and ark shells(famillies Arcidae, Arcticidae, Cardiidae, Donacidae, Hiatellidae, Mactridae, Mesodesmatidae, Myidae, Semelidae, Solecutidae, Solenidae, Tridacnidae and Veneridae)
													--Other
0/0/0		4.6	0/0	0/0/0	0/0	0//0	0/0/	0/0/9	9.1/0		/0/0	0/0/0	Tridacindae, dried, salted or in brine
0/0/0		4.6	0/0	0/0/0	0/0	0//0	0/0/	0/0/9	9.1/0		/0/0	0/0/0	Anadara, dried, salted or in brine (smoked crustaceans, whether in shell or not, whether or not cooked before or during the smoking processother crustaceans, in shell, cooked by steaming or boiling in water)
0/0/0		4.6	0/0	0/0/0	0/0	0//0	0/0/	0/0/9	9.1/0		/0/0	0/0/0	Other Clam, cockles and ark shells(famillies Arcidae, Arcticidae, Cardiidae, Donacidae, Hiatellidae, Mactridae, Mesodesmatidae, Myidae, Semelidae, Solecutidae, Solenidae, Tridacnidae and Veneridae), dried or salted
													-Abalone(*Haliotis spp.*) and stromboid conchs (*Strombus spp*):
													--Abalone (*Haliotis spp.*), live, fresh or chillde:
0/0/0	0	0	0/0	0/0/0	0/0	0//0	0/0/	0/0/0	0/0			0/0/0	---For cultivation
0/0/0	11.2	2.8	1.4/1.4	0/0/0	0/0	0//0	0/0/	12.6/12.6/12.6	12.7/12.6		/0/0	0/0/0	---Other
													--Stromboid conchs (*Haliotis spp.*), live, fresh or chillde:
0/0/0	0	0	0/0	0/0/0	0/0	0//0	0/0/	0/0/0	0/0			0/0/0	---For cultivation
0/0/0	11.2	2.8	1.4/1.4	0/0/0	0/0	0//0	0/0/	0/0/12.6	12.7/0		/0/0	0/0/0	---Other
0/0/0	3.5	2	0/0	0//0	0/0	0//0	0/0/	0/0/9	9.1/0		/0/0	0/0/0	--Abalone (*Haliotis spp.*), fro-zen
0/0/0		6	0/0	0/0/0	0/0	0//0	0/0/	9.5/9.5/	/9.5		/0/0	0/0/0	--Stromboid conchs (*Strombus spp.*), frozen
0/0/0	3.5	2	0/0	0//0	0/0	0//0	0/0/	0/0/9	9.1/0		/0/0	0/0/0	--Other abalone (*Haliotis spp.*)
0/0/0		6	0/0	0/0/0	0/0	0//0	0/0/	9.5/9.5/	/9.5		/0/0	0/0/0	--Other stromboid conchs (*Strombus spp.*)
													-Other:
													--Live, fresh or chilled:
													---For cultivation
0/0/0	0	0	0/0	0/0/0	0/0	0//0	0/0/	0/0/0	0/0			0/0/0	Seedlings of pearl oyster
0/0/0	0	0	0/0	0/0/0	0/0	0//0	0/0/	0/0/0	0/0			0/0/0	Seedlings of other endangered molluscs (except pearl oyster)
0/0/0	0	0	0/0	0/0/0	0/0	0//0	0/0/	0/0/0	0/0			0/0/0	Other molluscs, for cultivation
													---Other
0/0/0	11.2	2.8	1.4/1.4	0/0/0	0/0	0//0	0/0/	0/0/12.6	12.7/0		/0/0	0/0/0	Live, fresh and cold pearl oyster (excluding seedlings)
0/0/0	11.2	2.8	1.4/1.4	0/0/0	0/0	0//0	0/0/	0/0/12.6	12.7/0		/0/0	0/0/0	Live, fresh and cold other endangered molluscs (excluding seedlings)
0/0/0	11.2	2.8	1.4/1.4	0/0/0	0/0	0//0	0/0/	0/0/12.6	12.7/0		/0/0	0/0/0	Live, fresh, cold clam
0/0/0	11.2	2.8	1.4/1.4	0/0/0	0/0	0//0	0/0/	0/0/12.6	12.7/0		/0/0	0/0/0	Other molluscs, live, fresh, or chilled
													--Frozen
0/0/0		6	0/0	0/0/0	0/0	0//0	0/0/	9.5/9.5/	/9.5		/0/0	0/0/0	Frozen pearl oyster
0/0/0		6	0/0	0/0/0	0/0	0//0	0/0/	9.5/9.5/	/9.5		/0/0	0/0/0	Frozen other endangered molluscs
0/0/0		6	0/0	0/0/0	0/0	0//0	0/0/	9.5/9.5/	/9.5		/0/0	0/0/0	Frozen clam
0/0/0		6	0/0	0/0/0	0/0	0//0	0/0/	9.5/9.5/	/9.5		/0/0	0/0/0	Other frozen Molluscs
													--Other

税则号列		货品名称〔CIQ 扩展编码及品名－T2 表示见附表 2〕	最惠(%)	暂定税率	普通	增值/消费	出口退税	计量单位	监管条件/特殊证件	检验检疫	对美关税	亚太上/下
0307.9900	11	干、盐腌或盐渍的大珠母贝(包括熏制的带壳或去壳的,不论在熏制前或熏制过程中是否烹煮)〔101 养殖干制贝类制品,102 野生干制贝类制品,103 养殖盐腌及盐渍贝类制品,104 野生盐腌及盐渍贝类制品〕	7		80	9/	9	千克	ABE/	PRQS	37	
0307.9900	19	干、盐腌或盐渍的其他濒危软体动物(包括熏制的带壳或去壳的,不论在熏制前或熏制过程中是否烹煮)〔999〕	7		70	9/	0	千克	ABEF/	PRQS	37	
0307.9900	20	干、盐腌或盐渍蚬属(包括供人食用的软体动物粉、团粒,甲壳动物除外;包括熏制的带壳或去壳的,不论在熏制前或熏制过程中是否烹煮)〔101 冻的,102 干的,103 盐腌或盐渍〕	7		70	9/	9,13	千克	ABU/	PRQS	37	
0307.9900	90	其他干、盐腌或盐渍软体动物(包括熏制的带壳或去壳的,不论在熏制前或熏制过程中是否烹煮)〔101 干制的养殖软体动物,102 干制的野生软体动物,103 盐腌或盐渍的养殖软体动物,104 盐腌或盐渍的野生软体动物〕	7		70	9/	9,13	千克	AB/	PRQS	37	
03.08		**不属于甲壳动物及软体动物的水生无脊柱动物,活、鲜、冷、冻、干、盐腌或盐渍的;熏制的不属于甲壳动物及软体动物的水生无脊柱动物,不论在熏制前或熏制过程中是否烹煮:**										
		-海参(仿刺参、海参纲):										
		--活、鲜或冷的:										
0308.1110		---种苗										
0308.1110	10	暗色刺参的种苗〔999〕	0		0	9/	9	千克	ABEF/	PQ	25	
0308.1110	90	海参(仿刺参、海参纲)种苗(濒危除外)〔999〕	0		0	0/	9	千克	AB/	PQ		
0308.1190		---其他										
0308.1190	10	活、鲜或冷的暗色刺参〔101 活的暗色刺参,102 鲜或冷的养殖暗色刺参,103 鲜或冷的野生暗色刺参〕	10		70	9/	9	千克	ABEF/	PRQS	40	
0308.1190	20	活、鲜或冷的刺参〔101 活的其他海参,102 鲜或冷的养殖其他海参,103 鲜或冷的野生其他海参〕	10		70	9/	9	千克	ABU/	PRQS	40	
0308.1190	90	活、鲜或冷的其他海参(仿刺参、海参纲)〔101 活的其他海参,102 鲜或冷的养殖其他海参,103 鲜或冷的野生其他海参〕	10		70	9/	9	千克	AB/	PRQS	40	
0308.1200		--冻的										
0308.1200	10	冻的暗色刺参〔101 养殖冷冻海参,102 野生冷冻海参〕	10		80	9/	9	千克	ABEF/	PRQS	40	
0308.1200	20	冻的其他刺参〔101 养殖冷冻海参,102 野生冷冻海参〕	10		80	9/	9	千克	ABU/	PRQS	40	
0308.1200	90	冻的其他海参(仿刺参、海参纲)〔101 养殖冷冻海参,102 野生冷冻海参〕	10		80	9/	9	千克	AB/	PRQS	40	
0308.1900		--其他										
0308.1900	10	干、盐腌或盐渍暗色刺参(包括熏制的,不论在熏制前或熏制过程中是否烹煮)〔101 干制的养殖暗色刺参,102 干制的野生暗色刺参,103 盐腌或盐渍的养殖暗色刺参,104 盐腌或盐渍的野生暗色刺参〕	10		80	9/	9	千克	ABEF/	PRQS	40	
0308.1900	20	干、盐腌或盐渍的其他刺参(包括熏制的,不论在熏制前或熏制过程中是否烹煮)〔101 干制的其他养殖刺参,102 干制的其他野生刺参,103 盐腌或盐渍的其他养殖刺参,104 盐腌或盐渍的其他野生刺参〕	10		80	9/	9	千克	ABU/	PRQS	40	
0308.1900	90	干、盐腌或盐渍的其他海参(仿刺参、海参纲)(包括熏制的,不论在熏制前或熏制过程中是否烹煮)〔101 干制的其他养殖海参(仿刺参、海参纲),102 干制的其他野生海参(仿刺参、海参纲),103 盐腌或盐渍的其他养殖海参(仿刺参、海参纲),104 盐腌或盐渍的其他野生海参(仿刺参、海参纲)〕	10		80	9/	9	千克	AB/	PRQS	40	
		-海胆(球海胆属、拟球海胆、智利海胆、食用正海胆):										
		--活、鲜或冷的:										
0308.2110		---种苗〔999〕	0		0	0/	9	千克	AB/	PQ		
0308.2190		---其他										
0308.2190	10	活、鲜或冷的食用海胆纲〔101 活的海胆纲,102 鲜或冷的养殖海胆纲,103 鲜或冷的野生海胆纲〕	10		70	9/	9	千克	ABU/	PRQS	40	
0308.2190	90	其他活、鲜或冷的海胆〔101 活的海胆,102 鲜或冷的养殖海胆,103 鲜或冷的野生海胆〕	10		70	9/	9	千克	AB/	PRQS	40	
0308.2200		--冻的										
0308.2200	10	冻食用海胆纲〔101 养殖冷冻海胆,102 野生冷冻海胆〕	10		70	9/	9	千克	ABU/	PRQS	40	
0308.2200	90	其他冻海胆〔101 养殖冷冻海胆,102 野生冷冻海胆〕	10		70	9/	9	千克	AB/	PRQS	40	
0308.2900		--其他										
0308.2900	10	干、盐制食用海胆纲(包括熏制的,不论在熏制前或熏制过程中是否烹煮)〔101 干制的养殖海胆纲,102 干制的野生海胆纲,103 盐制的养殖海胆纲,104 盐制的野生海胆纲〕	10		70	9/	9,13	千克	ABU/	PRQS	40	
0308.2900	90	其他干、盐制海胆(包括熏制的,不论在熏制前或熏制过程中是否烹煮)〔101 干制的养殖海胆,102 干制的野生海胆,103 盐制的养殖海胆,104 盐制的野生海胆〕	10		70	9/	9,13	千克	AB/	PRQS	40	
		-海蜇(海蜇属):										
		---活、鲜或冷的:										
0308.3011		----种苗〔999〕	0		0	0/	9	千克	AB/	PQ		

协定税率 %								RCEP		特惠税率 %			Article Description
东/冰/格	巴基斯坦	韩国	瑞士 上/下	哥/秘/柬	澳/毛	新西/坡/智	中国港/澳/台	东盟及马来/澳/韩	日/新	亚太2国	老/柬/缅	98/97/95	
0/0/0		6	0/0	0/0/0	0/0	0//0	0/0/	9.5/9.5/	/9.5		/0/0	0/0/0	Dried, salted or salted pearl oysters (including smoked shelled or shelled, whether or not cooked before or during smoking)
0/0/0		6	0/0	0/0/0	0/0	0//0	0/0/	9.5/9.5/	/9.5		/0/0	0/0/0	Other endangered molluscs, dried, salted or salted (including smoked shelled or shelled, whether or not cooked before or during smoking)
0/0/0		6	0/0	0/0/0	0/0	0//0	0/0/	9.5/9.5/	/9.5		/0/0	0/0/0	dried, salted or in brine clam(including flours, meals and pellets of molluscs , fit for human consumption; including smoked, whether in shell or not, whether or not cooked before or during the smoking process)
0/0/0		6	0/0	0/0/0	0/0	0//0	0/0/	9.5/9.5/	/9.5		/0/0	0/0/0	Other dried, salted or salted mollusks (including smoked shelled or shelled, whether or not cooked before or during smoking)
													Aquatic invertebrates other than crustaceans and molluscs, live, fresh, chilled, frozen, dried, salted or in brine; smoked aquatic invertebrates other than crustaceans and molluscs, whether or not cooked before or during the smoking process:
													-Sea cucumbers(Stichopus japonicus、holothurioidea):
													--Live, fresh and chilled:
													---For cultivation
0/0/0	0	0	0/0	0/0/0	0/0	0//0	0/0/	0/0/0	0/0			0/0/0	Isostichopus fuscus, for cultivation
0/0/0	0	0	0/0	0/0/0	0/0	0//0	0/0/	0/0/0	0/0			0/0/0	Sea cucumber (Apostichopus japonicus and sea cucumber class) seedlings (except endangered)
													---Other
0/0/0	11.2	2.8	1.4/1.4	0/0/0	0/0	0//0	0/0/	0/0/12.6	12.7/0		/0/0	0/0/0	Isostichopus fuscus, live, fresh or chilled
0/0/0	11.2	2.8	1.4/1.4	0/0/0	0/0	0//0	0/0/	0/0/12.6	12.7/0		/0/0	0/0/0	Live, fresh trepang or cold(exceptisostichopus fuscus)
0/0/0	11.2	2.8	1.4/1.4	0/0/0	0/0	0//0	0/0/	0/0/12.6	12.7/0		/0/0	0/0/0	Other sea cucumbers(Stichopus japonicus, holothurioidea), live, fresh or chilled
													--Frozen
0/0/0		2	0/0	0/0/0	0/0	0//0	0/0/	0/0/9	/0		/0/0	0/0/0	Frozen Isostichopus fuscus
0/0/0		2	0/0	0/0/0	0/0	0//0	0/0/	0/0/9	/0		/0/0	0/0/0	Other frozen sea cucumbers
0/0/0		2	0/0	0/0/0	0/0	0//0	0/0/	0/0/9	/0		/0/0	0/0/0	Other frozensea cucumbers (Stichopus japonicus, Holothurioidea)
													--Other
0/0/0		2	0/0	0/0/0	0/0	0//0	0/0/	0/0/9	/0		/0/0	0/0/0	Dried, salted or salted sea cucumber (including smoked, whether cooked or not before or during smoking)
0/0/0		2	0/0	0/0/0	0/0	0//0	0/0/	0/0/9	/0		/0/0	0/0/0	Other sea cucumber, dried, salted or salted (including smoked, whether or not cooked before or during smoking)
0/0/0		2	0/0	0/0/0	0/0	0//0	0/0/	0/0/9	/0		/0/0	0/0/0	Dried, salted or salted sea cucumber (sea cucumber, sea cucumber class) (including smoked, whether cooked or not before or during smoking)
													-Sea urchin(strongylocentrotus spp., paracentrotus lividus, Loxechinus albus, Echichinus esculentus):
													--Live, fresh or chilled:
0/0/0	0	0	0/0	0/0/0	0/0	0//0	0/0/	0/0/0	0/0			0/0/0	---For cultivation
													---Other
0/0/0	11.2	2.8	1.4/1.4	0/0/0	0/0	0//0	0/0/	0/0/12.6	12.7/0		/0/0	0/0/0	Live, fresh and cold edible echinoidea
0/0/0	11.2	2.8	1.4/1.4	0/0/0	0/0	0//0	0/0/	0/0/12.6	12.7/0		/0/0	0/0/0	OtherSea urchins, live, fresh, chilled, not for cultivation.
													--Frozen
0/0/0		4.6	0/0	0/0/0	0/0	0//0	0/0/	9/9/9	9.4/9		/0/0	0/0/0	Frozen edible echinoidea
0/0/0		4.6	0/0	0/0/0	0/0	0//0	0/0/	9/9/9	9.4/9		/0/0	0/0/0	Other frozen Sea urchins
													--Other
0/0/0		4.6	0/0	0/0/0	0/0	0//0	0/0/	9/9/9	9.4/9		/0/0	0/0/0	Dried and salted edible sea urchins (including smoked, whether cooked or not before or during smoking)
0/0/0		4.6	0/0	0/0/0	0/0	0//0	0/0/	9/9/9	9.4/9		/0/0	0/0/0	Other dried and salted sea urchins (including smoked, whether cooked or not before or during smoking)
													-Jellyfish(Rhopilema spp.):
													---Live, fresh or chilled:
0/0/0	0	0	0/0	0/0/0	0/0	0//0	0/0/	0/0/0	0/0			0/0/0	----For cultivation

税则号列		货品名称〔CIQ 扩展编码及品名—T2 表示见附表 2〕	最惠(%)	暂定税率	普通	增值/消费	出口退税	计量单位	监管条件/特殊证件	检验检疫	对美关税	亚太上/下
0308.3019		----其他〔101 活的海蜇,102 鲜或冷的养殖海蜇,103 鲜或冷的野生海蜇〕	7		70	9/	9	千克	AB/	PRQS	37	
0308.3090		---其他〔101 冻的养殖海蜇(海蜇属),103 冻的野生海蜇(海蜇属),105 干制的养殖海蜇(海蜇属),106 干制的野生海蜇(海蜇属),107 盐制的养殖海蜇(海蜇属),108 盐制的野生海蜇(海蜇属)〕	10		70	9/	9,13	千克	AB/	PRQS	40	
		-其他:										
		---活、鲜或冷的:										
0308.9011		----种苗										
0308.9011	10	活、鲜或冷的其他濒危水生无脊椎动物的种苗(甲壳动物及软体动物除外)〔999〕	0		0	9/	0	千克	ABFE/	PQ	25	
0308.9011	90	其他水生无脊椎动物的种苗(甲壳动物及软体动物和其他濒危水生无脊椎动物除外)(甲壳动物及软体动物除外)〔999〕	0		0	0/	9	千克	AB/	PQ		
0308.9012		----沙蚕,种苗除外〔999〕	7		70	9/	9	千克	AB/	PRQS	37	
0308.9019		----其他										
0308.9019	10	活、鲜或冷的其他濒危水生无脊椎动物(甲壳动物及软体动物除外)〔999〕	7		70	9/	0	千克	ABFE/	PRQS	37	
0308.9019	90	活、鲜或冷的其他水生无脊椎动物(甲壳动物及软体动物除外)[T2]	7		70	9/	9	千克	AB/	PRQS	37	
0308.9090		---其他										
0308.9090	10	其他冻、干、盐制濒危水生无脊椎动物(包括熏制的,不论在熏制前或熏制过程中是否烹煮)〔111 其他冻的养殖濒危水生无脊椎动物,112 其他冻的野生濒危水生无脊椎动物,113 其他干制的养殖濒危水生无脊椎动物,114 其他干制的野生濒危水生无脊椎动物,115 其他盐制的养殖濒危水生无脊椎动物,116 其他盐制的野生濒危水生无脊椎动物〕	7		70	9/	0	千克	ABFE/	PRQS	37	
0308.9090	90	其他冻、干、盐制水生无脊椎动物(包括熏制的,不论在熏制前或熏制过程中是否烹煮)〔105 其他冷冻的养殖棘皮类,106 其他冷冻的野生棘皮类,111 其他冻的养殖水生无脊椎动物,112 其他冻的野生水生无脊椎动物,113 其他干制的养殖水生无脊椎动物,114 其他干制的野生水生无脊椎动物,115 其他盐制的养殖水生无脊椎动物,116 其他盐制的野生水生无脊椎动物〕	7		70	9/	9,13	千克	AB/	PRQS	37	
03.09		**适合供人食用的鱼、甲壳动物、软体动物和其他水生 无脊椎动物的细粉、粗粉及团粒:**										
0309.1000		-鱼的										
0309.1000	10	适合供人食用的濒危鱼的细粉、粗粉及团粒〔101 其他养殖水产制品,102 其他野生水产制品〕	7		80	9/	0	千克	ABEF/	PRQS	37	
0309.1000	90	适合供人食用的其他鱼的细粉、粗粉及团粒〔101 其他养殖水产制品,102 其他野生水产制品〕	7		80	9/	9,13	千克	AB/	PRQS	37	
0309.9000		-其他										
0309.9000	10	适合供人食用的濒危甲壳动物、软体动物和其他水生无脊椎动物的细粉、粗粉及团粒〔101 养殖濒危虾类甲壳动物,102 野生濒危虾类甲壳动物,103 养殖濒危蟹类甲壳动物,104 野生濒危蟹类甲壳动物,105 养殖濒危软体动物,106 野生濒危软体动物,107 其他养殖濒危水生无脊椎动物,108 其他野生濒危水生无脊椎动物〕	7		70	9/	0	千克	ABEF/	PRQS	37	
0309.9000	90	适合供人食用的其他甲壳动物、软体动物和其他水生无脊椎动物的细粉、粗粉及团粒〔101 养殖虾类甲壳动物,102 野生虾类甲壳动物,103 养殖蟹类甲壳动物,104 野生蟹类甲壳动物,105 养殖软体动物,106 野生软体动物,107 其他养殖水生无脊椎动物,108 其他野生水生无脊椎动物〕	7		70	9/	9,13	千克	AB/	PRQS	37	

协定税率 %								RCEP		特惠税率 %			Article Description
东/冰/格	巴基斯坦	韩国	瑞士上/下	哥/秘/柬	澳/毛	新西/坡/智	中国港/澳/台	东盟及马来/澳/韩	日/新	亚太2国	老/柬/缅	98/97/95	
0/0/0	9	2.8	1.4/1.4	0/0/0	0/0	0//0	0/0/	0/0/12.6	12.7/0		/0/0	0/0/0	----Other
0/0/0		4.6	0/0	0/0/0	0/0	0//0	0/0/	9.5/9.5/9.5	/9.5		/0/0	0/0/0	---Other
													-Other:
													---Live, fresh or chilled:
													----For cultivation
0/0/0	0	0	0/0	0/0/0	0/0	0//0	0/0/	0/0/0	0/0			0/0/0	Other endangered aquatic invertebrates, other than crustaceans and molluscs, for cultivation
0/0/0	0	0	0/0	0/0/0	0/0	0//0	0/0/	0/0/0	0/0			0/0/0	Seedlings of other aquatic invertebrates (except crustaceans and mollusks and other endangered aquatic invertebrates) (except crustaceans and mollusks)
0/0/0	9	2.8	1.4/1.4	0/0/0	0/0	0//0	0/0/	0/0/12.6	12.7/0		/0/0	0/0/0	----Clamworm, other than for cultivation
													----Other
0/0/0	11.2	2.8	1.4/1.4	0/0/0	0/0	0//0	0/0/	0/0/12.6	12.7/0		/0/0	0/0/0	Other endangered aquatic invertebrates, live, fresh or chilled (other than crustaceans and molluscs)
0/0/0	11.2	2.8	1.4/1.4	0/0/0	0/0	0//0	0/0/	0/0/12.6	12.7/0		/0/0	0/0/0	Other aquatic invertebrates, live, fresh or chilled (other than crustaceans and molluscs)
													---Other
0/0/0		4.6	0/0	0/0/0	0/0	0//0	0/0/	9/9/9	9.4/9		/0/0	0/0/0	Other endangered aquatic invertebrates, frozen, dried and salted (including those smoked, whether or not cooked before or during smoking)
0/0/0		4.6	0/0	0/0/0	0/0	0//0	0/0/	9/9/9	9.4/9		/0/0	0/0/0	Other frozen, dried, salted aquatic invertebrates (including those smoked, whether or not cooked before or during smoking)
													Flours, meals and pellets of fish, crustaceans, molluscs and other aquatic invertebrates, fit for human consumption:
													-Of fish
0/0/0	3.5	2	0/0	0/0/0	0/0	0//0	0/0/	0/0/9	9.1/0			0/0/0	Fine powder, coarse powder and pellets of endangered fish suitable for human consumption
0/0/0	3.5	2	0/0	0/0/0	0/0	0//0	0/0/	0/0/9	9.1/0			0/0/0	Fine powder, coarse powder and pellets of other fish suitable for human consumption
													-Other
0/0/0	11.2	4.4	0.9/0.9	0/0/0	0/0	0//0	0/0/	0/0/9	9.1/0		/0/0	0/0/0	Fine powder, coarse powder and pellets of endangered crustaceans, molluscs and other aquatic invertebrates suitable for human consumption
0/0/0	11.2	4.4	0.9/0.9	0/0/0	0/0	0//0	0/0/	0/0/9	9.1/0		/0/0	0/0/0	Fine powder, coarse powder and pellets of other crustaceans, molluscs and other aquatic invertebrates suitable for human consumption

第四章
乳品；蛋品；天然蜂蜜；其他食用动物产品

注释：

一、所称“乳”，是指全脂乳及半脱脂或全脱脂的乳。

二、税目 04.03 所称“酸乳”可以浓缩或调味，可以含糖或其他甜味物质、水果、坚果、可可、巧克力、调味香料、咖啡或咖啡提取物、其他植物或植物的部分、谷物或面包制品，但添加的任何物质不能用于全部或部分取代任何乳成分，而且产品需保留酸乳的基本特征。

三、税目 04.05 所称：

(一)“黄油”，仅指从乳中提取的天然黄油、乳清黄油及调制黄油(新鲜、加盐或酸败的，包括罐装黄油)，按重量计乳脂含量在 80%及以上，但不超过 95%，乳的无脂固形物最大含量不超过 2%，以及水的最大含量不超过 16%。黄油中不含添加的乳化剂，但可含有氯化钠、食用色素、中和盐及无害乳酸菌的培养物。

(二)“乳酱”是一种油包水型可涂抹的乳状物，乳脂是该制品所含的唯一脂肪，按重量计其含量在 39%及以上，但小于 80%。

四、乳清经浓缩并加入乳或乳脂制成的产品，若同时具有下列三种特性，则视为乳酪归入税目 04.06：

(一)按干重计乳脂含量在 5%及以上的；

(二)按重量计干质成分至少为 70%，但不超过 85%的；

(三)已成形或可以成形的。

五、本章不包括：

(一)不适宜供人食用的死昆虫(税目 05.11)；

(二)按重量计乳糖含量(以干燥无水乳糖计)超过 95%的乳清制品(税目 17.02)；

(三)以一种物质(例如，油酸酯)代替乳中一种或多种天然成分(例如，丁酸酯)而制得的产品(税目 19.01 或 21.06)；

(四)白蛋白(包括按重量计干质成分的乳清蛋白含量超过 80%的两种或两种以上的乳清蛋白浓缩物)(税目 35.02)及球蛋白(税目 35.04)。

六、税目 04.10 所称“昆虫”是指全部或部分食用的死昆虫，新鲜的、冷藏的、冷冻的、干燥的、烟熏的、盐腌或盐渍的；以及适合供人食用的昆虫的细粉和粗粉。但本税目不包括用其他方法制作或保藏的食用的死昆虫（第四类）。

子目注释：

一、子目 0404.10 所称“改性乳清”，是指由乳清成分构成的制品，即全部或部分去除乳糖、蛋白或矿物质的乳清、加入天然乳清成分的乳清及由混入天然乳清成分制成的产品。

二、子目 0405.10 所称“黄油”，不包括脱水黄油及印度酥油(子目号 0405.90)。

税则号列	货品名称〔CIQ 扩展编码及品名－T2 表示见附表 2〕	最惠(%)	暂定税率	普通	增值/消费	出口退税	计量单位	监管条件/特殊证件	检验检疫	对美关税	亚太上/下
04.01	**未浓缩及未加糖或其他甜物质的乳及稀奶油：**										
0401.1000	-脂肪含量≤1%未浓缩的乳及稀奶油(脂肪含量按重量计，本编号货品不得加糖和其他甜物质)〔101 巴氏杀菌乳，102 超高温灭菌乳，103 保持灭菌乳，104 巴氏杀菌工艺调制乳，105 其他乳与乳制品，106 灭菌工艺调制乳，107 其他调制乳〕	15		40	9/	9,13	千克	7AB/	PRQS	42.5	
0401.2000	-1%<脂肪含量≤6%的未浓缩的乳及稀奶油(脂肪含量按重量计，本编号货品不得加糖和其他甜物质)[T2]	15		40	9/	9,13	千克	7AB/	PRQS	42.5	
0401.4000	-6%<脂肪含量≤10%的未浓缩的乳及稀奶油(脂肪含量按重量计，本编号货品不得加糖和其他甜物质)[T2]	15		40	13/	9,13	千克	7AB/	PRQS	42.5	
0401.5000	-脂肪含量>10%未浓缩的乳及稀奶油(脂肪含量按重量计，本编号货品不得加糖和其他甜物质)[T2]	15		40	13/	9,13	千克	7AB/	PRQS	42.5	
04.02	**浓缩、加糖或其他甜物质的乳及稀奶油：**										
0402.1000	-脂肪含量≤1.5%固状乳及稀奶油(指粉状、粒状或其他固体状态，浓缩，加糖或其他甜物质)〔101 脱脂乳粉，102 儿童调制乳粉，103 其他乳与乳制品，104 孕产妇调制乳粉，105 其他调制乳粉〕	10		40	13/	13	千克	7AB/	MPRQS	35	7/7
	-粉状、粒状或其他固体形状，按重量计脂肪含量超过 1.5%：										
0402.2100	--脂肪量>1.5%未加糖固状乳及稀奶油(指粉状、粒状或其他固体状态，浓缩，未加糖或其他甜物质)[T2]	10		40	13/	13	千克	7AB/	MPRQS	35	7/7
0402.2900	--其他〔101 儿童调制乳粉，102 其他乳与乳制品，103 孕产妇调制乳粉，104 其他调制乳粉〕	10		40	13/	13	千克	7AB/	PRQS	35	
	-其他：										
0402.9100	--浓缩但未加糖的非固状乳及稀奶油(未加其他甜物质)[T2]	10		90	13/	9,13	千克	AB/	PRQS	35	
0402.9900	--浓缩并已加糖的非固状乳及稀奶油(加其他甜物质)[T2]	10		90	13/	9,13	千克	AB/	PRQS	35	
04.03	**酸乳；酪乳、结块的乳及稀奶油、酸乳、酸乳酒及其他发酵或酸化的乳和稀奶油，不论是否浓缩、加糖、加其他甜物质、加香料、加水果、加坚果或加可可：**										
	-酸乳：	10		90	13/	13	千克	AB/	PRQS	37.5	

Chapter 4
Dairy produce; birds eggs; natural honey; edible products of animal origin, not elsewhere specified or included

Notes:

1. The expression "milk" means full cream milk or partially or completely skimmed milk.
2. For the purposes of heading No. 04.03, yogurt may be concentrated or flavoured and may contain added sugar or other sweetening matter, fruit, nuts, cocoa, chocolate, spices, coffee or coffee extracts, plants, parts of plants, cereals or bakers' wares, provided that any added substance is not used for the purpose of replacing, in whole or in part, any milk constituent, and the product retains the essential character of yogurt.
3. For the purposes of heading No. 04. 05:
   (a) The term "butter" means natural butter, whey butter or recombined butter (fresh, salted or rancid, including canned butter) derived exclusively from milk, with a milkfat content of 80% or more but not more than 95% by weight, a maximum milk solids-not-fvat content of 2% by weight and a maximum water content of 16% by weight. Butter does not contain added emulsifiers, but may contain sodium chloride, food colours, neutralising salts and cultures of harmless lactic-acid-producing bacteria.
   (b) The expression "dairy spreads" means a spreadable emulsion of the water-in-oil type, containing milkfat as the only fat in the product, with a milkfat content of 39% or more but less than 80% by weight.
4. Products obtained by the concentration of whey and with the addition of milk or milkfat are to be classified as cheese in heading No. 04. 06. Provided that they have the three following characteristics:
   (a) A milkfat content, by weight of the dry matter, of 5% or more;
   (b) A dry matter content, by weight, of at least 70% but not exceeding 85%; and
   (c) They are moulded or capable of being moulded.
5. This Chapter does not cover:
   (a) Non—living insects, unfit for human consumption (heading 05.11);
   (b) Products obtained from whey, containing by weight more than 95% lactose, expressed as anhydrous lactose calculated on the dry matter (heading No. 17. 02);
   (c) A product made of a substance (e.g., oleic acid ester) instead of one or more natural ingredients (e.g., butyrate) in milk.
   (d) Albumins (including concentrates of two or more whey proteins, containing by weight more than 80% whey proteins, calculated on the dry matter) (heading No. 35. 02) or globulins(heading No. 35. 04)
6. For the purposes of heading No. 04.10, the term "insects" means ediblenon— living insects, whole or in parts, fresh, chilled, frozen, dried, smoked, salted or in brine, as well as flours and meals of insects, fit for human consumption. However, it does not cover edible non—living insects otherwise prepared or preserved (generally Section IV).

Subheading Notes:

1. For the purpose of subheading No. 0404. 10, the expression "modified whey" means products consisting of whey constituents, that is, whey from which all or part of the lactose, proteins or minerals have been removed, whey to which natural whey constituents have been added and products obtained by mixing natural whey constituents.
2. For the purposes of subheading No. 0405. 10 the term "butter" does not include dehydrated butter or ghee (subheading No. 0405. 90)

协定税率 %								RCEP		特惠税率 %			Article Description
东/冰/格	巴基斯坦	韩国	瑞士上/下	哥/秘/柬	澳/毛	新西/坡/智	中国港/澳/台	东盟及马来/澳/韩	日/新	亚太2国	老/柬/缅	98/97/95	
													Milk and thin cream, not concentrated nor containing added sugar or other sweetening matter:
0/0/0	12		1.5/1.5	3/0/0	3/0	0//0	0/0/	14.3/14.3/	/14.3			0/0/0	-Of a fat content, by weight, not exceeding 1%
0/0/0	0		1.5/1.5	3/0/0	3/0	0//0	0/0/	14.3/15/	/15			0/0/0	-Of a fat content, by weight, exceeding 1% but not exceeding 6%
0/0/0	12		1.5/1.5	3/0/0	3/0	0//0	0/0/	14.3/15/	/15			0/0/0	-Of a fat content, by weight, exceeding 6%, but not exceeding 10%
0/0/0	12		1.5/1.5	3/0/0	3/0	0//0	0/0/	14.3/15/	/15			0/0/0	-Of a fat content, by weight, exceeding 10%
													Milk and thin cream, concentrated or containing added sugar or other sweetening matter:
0/0/0	5		0/0	2/2.4/0	3.3/0	0//0	0/0/	9.5/10/	/10			0/0/0	-In powder, granules or other solid forms, of a fat content, by weight, not exceeding 1.5%
													-In powder, granules or other solid forms, of a fat content, by weight, exceeding 1.5%:
0/0/0	0			2/2.4/0	3.3/0	0//0	0/0/	9.5//	/10			0/0/0	--Not containing added sugar or other sweetening matter
0/0/0	5		0/0	2/2.4/0	3.3/0	0//0	0/0/	9.5//	/10			0/0/0	--Other
													-Other:
0/0/0	5			2/0/0	3.3/0	0//0	0/0/	9.5/10/	/10			0/0/0	--Not containing added sugar or other sweetening matter
0/0/0	5			2/2.4/0	3.3/0	0//0	0/0/	9.5/9.5/	/9.5			0/0/0	--Other
													Yogurt; buttermilk, curdled milk and cream, kephir and other fermented or acidified milk and cream, whether or not concentrated or containing added sugar or other sweetening matter or flavoured or containing added fruit, nuts or cocoa:
0/0/2	5		3.3	2.7	0	3/0	0//0	0/0/				0/0	-Yogurt:

税则号列		货品名称〔CIQ 扩展编码及品名—T2 表示见附表 2〕	最惠(%)	暂定税率	普通	增值/消费	出口退税	计量单位	监管条件/特殊证件	检验检疫	对美关税	亚太上/下
0403.2010		---不论是否浓缩,除允许添加的添加剂外,仅可含糖或其他甜味物质、香料、水果、坚果、可可〔101 发酵乳,102 风味发酵乳〕	10		90	13/	13	千克	AB/	PRQS	37.5	
0403.2090		---其他〔101 发酵乳,102 风味发酵乳〕	10		80	13/	13	千克	AB/	PRQS	35	
0403.9000		-其他	20		90	13/	13	千克	AB/	PRQ	47.5	
04.04		**乳清,不论是否浓缩、加糖或其他甜物质;其他税目未列名的含天然乳的产品,不论是否加糖或其他甜物质:**										
0404.1000		-乳清及改性乳清,不论是否浓缩、加糖或其他甜物质[T2]	6	2	30	13/	13	千克	AB	PRQ	/27	
0404.1000	10	饲料用乳清(按重量计蛋白含量 2—7%,乳糖含量 76—88%)(不论是否浓缩、加糖或其他甜物质)〔101 饲料用乳粉,102 饲料用乳清粉〕	6	2	30	13/	13	千克	AB/	PRQ		
0404.1000	90	其他乳清及改性乳清(不论是否浓缩、加糖或其他甜物质)〔101 脱盐乳清粉,102 非脱盐乳清粉,103 乳清蛋白粉,104 其他乳清粉,105 其他乳与乳制品,106 饲料用乳粉,107 饲料用乳清粉〕	6	2	30	13/	13	千克	AB/	PRQ	27	
0404.9000		-其他〔999〕	20		90	13/	13	千克	AB/	PRQ	45	
04.05		**黄油及其他从乳中提取的脂和油;乳酱:**										
0405.1000		-黄油〔101 奶油,102 无水奶油,103 其他奶油〕	10		90	13/	13	千克	AB/	PRQS	35	
0405.2000		-乳酱〔101 调制淡炼乳,102 其他乳与乳制品〕	10		90	13/	13	千克	AB/	PRQS	35	8.1/8.1
0405.9000		-其他〔101 其他奶油,102 其他乳与乳制品〕	10		90	13/	13	千克	AB/	PRQS	35	
04.06		**乳酪及凝乳:**										
0406.1000		-鲜乳酪(未熟化或未固化的),包括乳清乳酪;凝乳〔101 非熟化干酪,102 其他干酪〕	12		90	13/	13	千克	AB/	PRQ	39.5	
0406.2000		-各种磨碎或粉化的乳酪〔101 霉菌成熟干酪,102 其他熟化干酪,103 非熟化干酪,104 其他干酪〕	12	8	90	13/	13	千克	AB/	PRQS	35.5	
0406.3000		-经加工的乳酪,但磨碎或粉化的除外〔101 再制干酪,102 其他干酪〕	12	8	90	13/	13	千克	AB/	PRQ	35.5	
0406.4000		-蓝纹乳酪和娄地青霉生产的带有纹理的其他乳酪〔101 霉菌成熟干酪,102 其他干酪〕	15	8	90	13/	13	千克	AB/	PRQ	35.5	
0406.9000		-其他乳酪〔999〕	12	8	90	13/	13	千克	AB/	PRQ	35.5	
04.07		**带壳禽蛋,鲜、腌制或煮过的:**										
		-孵化用受精禽蛋:										
0407.1100		--鸡的										
0407.1100	10	孵化用受精的濒危鸡的蛋〔999〕	0		0	9/	0	千克/个	AFEB/	PQ		
0407.1100	90	孵化用受精的鸡的蛋(濒危除外)〔999〕	0		0	0/	9	千克/个	AB/	PQ		
0407.1900		--其他										
0407.1900	10	其他孵化用受精濒危禽蛋〔101 鸭种蛋,102 鹅种蛋,103 鸵鸟种蛋,104 火鸡种蛋,105 鸽种蛋,106 其他种蛋〕	0		0	9/	0	千克/个	AFEB/	PQ		
0407.1900	90	其他孵化用受精禽蛋(濒危禽蛋除外)〔101 鸭种蛋,102 鹅种蛋,103 鸵鸟种蛋,104 火鸡种蛋,105 鸽种蛋,106 其他种蛋〕	0		0	0/	9	千克/个	AB/	PQ		
		-其他鲜蛋:										
0407.2100		--鸡的〔999〕	20		80	9/	9	千克/个	AB/	PRQS		
0407.2900		--其他										
0407.2900	10	其他鲜的带壳濒危禽蛋〔999〕	20		80	9/	0	千克/个	ABFE/	PRQS		
0407.2900	90	其他鲜的带壳禽蛋[T2]	20		80	9/	9	千克/个	AB/	PRQS		
		-其他:										
0407.9010		---咸蛋〔999〕	20		90	9/	9	千克/个	AB/	PRQS		
0407.9020		---皮蛋〔999〕	20		90	9/	9	千克/个	AB/	PRQS		
0407.9090		---其他										
0407.9090	10	其他腌制或煮过的带壳濒危野鸟蛋〔999〕	20		90	9/	0	千克/个	ABFE/	PRQS		
0407.9090	90	其他腌制或煮过的带壳禽蛋〔999〕	20		90	9/	9,13	千克/个	AB/	PRQS		
04.08		**去壳禽蛋及蛋黄,鲜、干、冻、蒸过或水煮、制成型或用其他方法保藏的,不论是否加糖或其他甜物质:**										
		-蛋黄:										
0408.1100		--干的〔999〕	20		90	9/	9,13	千克	AB/	PRQS		
0408.1900		--其他〔101 咸蛋黄,102 食用蛋黄粉〕	20		90	9/	9	千克	AB/	PRQS	32.5	
		-其他:										
0408.9100		--干的〔101 食用全蛋粉,102 食用蛋白粉(片),103 干的其他食用蛋制品〕	20		90	9/	9,13	千克	AB/	PRQS		
0408.9900		--其他[T2]	20		90	9/	9,13	千克	AB/	PRQS		
04.09		**天然蜂蜜:**										
0409.0000		天然蜂蜜〔101 药用蜂蜜,102 食用蜂蜜〕	15		80	9/	9	千克	AB/	PRQS	45	
04.10		**其他税目未列名的昆虫及其他食用动物产品:**										
0410.1000		-昆虫										
0410.1000	10	食用濒危昆虫〔999〕	20		70	13/	0	千克	ABFE/	PRQS	50	
0410.1000	90	其他食用昆虫〔999〕	20		70	13/	9	千克	AB/	PRQS	50	

协定税率 %								RCEP		特惠税率 %			Article Description
东/冰/格	巴基斯坦	韩国	瑞士 上/下	哥/秘/柬	澳/毛	新西/坡/智	中国港/澳/台	东盟及马来/澳/韩	日/新	亚太2国	老/柬/缅	98/97/95	
0/0/0	5		2.5/2.5	2/0/0	2/0	0//0	0/0/	9.5/9.5/	/9.5			0/0/0	---Whether or not concentrated, other than the additives allowed to be added, only containing added sugar or other sweetening matter or flavoured or containing added fruit, nuts or cocoa
0/0/0	0	4.6	0/0	0/0/0	0/0	0/0/0	0/0/	9.3/9.5/9.3	9.4/9.5			0/0/0	---Other
0/0/0				4/0/0	4/0	0//0	0/0/	19/19/	/19			0/0/0	-Other
													Whey, whether or not concentrated or containing added sugar or other sweetening matter; products consisting of natural milk constituents, whether or not containing added sugar or other sweetening matter, not elsewhere specified or included:
0/0/3.6	5	4		2.4	0	0	0//0	0/0/				0/0/	-Whey and modified whey, whether or not concentrated or containing added sugar or other sweetening matter
0/0/0	5	2.8		1.2/0/0	0/0	0//0	0/0/	5.4/5.4/5.4	5.6/5.4		//	0/0/0	Whey for feed (2－7% protein by weight, 76－88% lactose) (whether or not concentrated, sweetened or otherwise)
0/0/0	5	2.8		1.2/0/0	0/0	0//0	0/0/	5.4/5.4/5.4	5.6/5.4		//	0/0/0	Other whey and modified whey (whether concentrated, sweetened or otherwise)
0/0/0		9.3		4/0/0	4/0	0//0	0/0/	18.7/19/18.7	18.8/19			0/0/0	-Other
													Butter and other fats and oils derived from milk; dairy spreads:
0/0/0	5	4.6	0/0	2/0/0	2/0	0//0	0/0/	9.3/10/9.3	9.4/10			0/0/0	-Butter
0/0/0	5	4.6	0/0	2/0/0	0/0	0//0	0/0/	9/9/9	9.4/9			0/0/0	-Dairy spreads
0/0/0	5	4.6		2/0/0	2/0	0//0	0/0/	9.3/10/9.3	9.4/10			0/0/0	-Other
													Cheese and curd:
0/0/0	6	5.6	5/5	2.4/0/0	2.4/0	0//0	0/0/	11.2/12/11.2	11.3/12			0/0/0	-Fresh (unripened or uncured) cheese, including whey cheese, and curd
0/0/0	6	5.6	5/5	2.4/1.6/0	2.4/0	0//0	0/0/	11.2/11.4/11.2	11.3/11.4			0/0/	-Grated or powdered cheese, of all kinds
0/0/0	6	5.6	5/5	2.4/1.6/0	2.4/0	0//0	0/0/	11.2/12/11.2	11.3/12			0/0/0	-Processed cheese, not grated or powdered
0/0/0	12	7		3/0/0	0/0	0//0	0/0/	13.5/13.5/13.5	14.1/13.5			0/0/0	-Blue-veined cheese and other cheese containing veins produced by *Penicillium roqueforti*
0/0/0	6	5.6	5/5	2.4/0/0	2.4/0	0//0	0/0/	11.2/12/11.2	11.3/12			0/0/0	-Other cheese
													Birds' eggs, in shell, fresh, preserved or cooked:
													-Fertilised eggs for incubation:
													--Of fowls of the species Gallus domesticus
0/0/0	0	0	0/0	0/0/0	0/0	0//0	0/0/	0/0/0	0/0			0/0/0	Of endangered hen's fertilised eggs for incubation
0/0/0	0	0	0/0	0/0/0	0/0	0//0	0/0/	0/0/0	0/0			0/0/0	Of hen's fertilised eggs for incubation
													--Other
0/0/0	0	0	0/0	0/0/0	0/0	0//0	0/0/	0/0/0	0/0			0/0/0	Other fertilised endangered eggs for incubation
0/0/0	0	0	0/0	0/0/0	0/0	0//0	0/0/	0/0/0	0/0			0/0/0	Other fertilised eggs for incubation
													-Other fresh eggs:
0/0/0		9.3	2/2	0/0/0	0/0	0//0	0/0/	18/18/18	18.8/18		/0/0	0/0/0	--Of fowls of the species Gallus domesticus
													--Other
0/0/0		9.3	2/2	0/0/0	0/0	0//0	0/0/	18/18/18	18.8/18		/0/0	0/0/0	Other endangered birds' eggs, in shell, fresh
0/0/0		9.3	2/2	0/0/0	0/0	0//0	0/0/	18/18/18	18.8/18		/0/0	0/0/0	Other birds' eggs, in shell, fresh
													-Other:
0/0/0		9.3	2/2	0/0/0	0/0	0//0	0/0/	18/18/18	18.8/18		//0	0/0/0	---Salted eggs
0/0/0		9.3	2/2	0/0/0	0/0	0//0	0/0/	18/18/18	18.8/18			0/0/0	---Lime-preserved eggs
													---Other
0/0/0		9.3	2/2	0/0/0	0/0	0//0	0/0/	18/18/18	18.8/18			0/0/0	Other endangered wild birds' eggs, in shell, preserved or cooked
0/0/0		9.3	2/2	0/0/0	0/0	0//0	0/0/	18/18/18	18.8/18			0/0/0	Other birds' eggs, in shell, preserved or cooked
													Birds' eggs, not in shell, and egg yolks, fresh, dried, cooked by steaming or by boiling in water, moulded, frozen or otherwise preserved, whether or not containing added sugar or other sweetening matter:
													-Egg yolks:
0/0/0		9.3	2/2	0/0/0	0/0	0//0	0/0/	18/18/18	18.8/18			0/0/0	--Dried
0/0/0		9.3	2/2	0/0/0	0/0	0//0	0/0/	18/18/18	18.8/18			0/0/0	--Other
													-Other:
0/0/0		9.3	2/2	0/0/0	0/0	0//0	0/0/	18/18/18	18.8/18			0/0/0	--Dried
0/0/0		9.3	2/2	0/0/0	0/0	0//0	0/0/	18/18/18	18.8/18			0/0/0	--Other
													Natural honey:
0/0/0	0	7	1.5/1.5	0/0/0	0/0	0//0	0/0/	14/14.3/14	14.1/14.3		0/0/	0/0/0	Natural honey
													Insects and other edible products of animal origin, not elsewhere specified or included:
													-Insects
0/0/0		9.3	2/2	0/0/0	0/0	0//0	0/0/0	18.7/19/20	18.8/19		//0	0/0/0	Eating endangered insects
0/0/0		9.3	2/2	0/0/0	0/0	0//0	0/0/0	18.7/19/20	18.8/19		//0	0/0/0	Other edible insects

税则号列	货品名称〔CIQ 扩展编码及品名—T2 表示见附表 2〕	最惠(%)	暂定税率	普通	增值/消费	出口退税	计量单位	监管条件/特殊证件	检验检疫	对美关税	亚太上/下
	-其他：										
0410.9010	---燕窝〔101 毛燕，102 食用燕窝，103 燕窝制品，104 具有保健食品批准文号〕	25		80	13/	9	千克	AB/	PRQS		
	---蜂产品：										
0410.9021	----鲜蜂王浆〔999〕	15		70	9/	9	千克	AB/	PRQS		
0410.9022	----鲜蜂王浆粉〔999〕	15		70	13/	9	千克	AB/	PRQS		
0410.9023	----蜂花粉〔999〕	20		70	13/	9	千克	AB/	PRQS		
0410.9029	----其他〔101 药用蜂房，102 药用蜂胶，103 蜂胶，104 其他蜂产品，105 蜂胶乙醇提取物〕	20		70	13/	9	千克	AB/	PRQS	50	
0410.9090	---其他										
0410.9090 10	其他编号未列名的食用濒危动物产品〔101 动物源性新食品原料食品，102 其他未列出的动物源性食品〕	20		70	13/	0	千克	ABFE/	PRQS	50	
0410.9090 90	其他编号未列名的食用动物产品〔101 食用龟蛋，102 食用鳖蛋，103 其他两栖类动物食用蛋品，104 其他爬行类动物食用蛋品，105 批准为新食品原料，106 其他未列出的动物源性食品〕	20		70	13/	9	千克	AB/	PRQS	50	

协定税率 %								RCEP		特惠税率 %			Article Description
东/冰/格	巴基斯坦	韩国	瑞士上/下	哥/秘/柬	澳/毛	新西/坡/智	中国港/澳/台	东盟及马来/澳/韩	日/新	亚太2国	老/柬/缅	98/97/95	
													- Other:
0/0/0		5	2.5/2.5	0/0/0	0/15	0//0	0/0/	0/0/22.5	22.7/0		/0/0	0/0/0	---Salanganes' nests
													---Bee products
0/0/0	12	3	1.5/1.5	0/0/0	0/0	0//0	0/0/	0/0/13.5	13.6/0			0/0/0	----Pure royal jelley
0/0/0	12	3	1.5/1.5	0/0/0	0/0	0//0	0/0/	0/0/13.5	13.6/0			0/0/0	----Pure royal jelley, in powder
0/0/0		9.3	2/2	0/0/0	0/0	0//0	0/0/	18/18/18	18.8/18			0/0/0	----Bee pollen
0/0/0		9.3	2/2	0/0/0	0/0	0//0	0/0/	18/18/18	18.8/18			0/0/0	----Other
													---Other
0/0/0		9.3	2/2	0/0/0	0/0	0//0	0/0/0	18.7/19/20	18.8/19		//0	0/0/0	Other food endangered animal products not listed
0/0/0		9.3	2/2	0/0/0	0/0	0//0	0/0/0	18.7/19/20	18.8/19		//0	0/0/0	Other food animal products not listed

第五章
其他动物产品

注释：

一、本章不包括：

(一)食用产品(整个或切块的动物肠、膀胱和胃以及液态或干制的动物血除外)；

(二)生皮或毛皮(第四十一章、第四十三章)，但税目 05.05 的货品及税目 05.11 的生皮或毛皮的边角废料仍归入本章；

(三)马毛及废马毛以外的动物纺织原料(第十一类)；

(四)供制帚、制刷用的成束、成簇的材料(税目 96.03)。

二、仅按长度而未按发根和发梢整理的人发，视为未加工品，归入税目 05.01。

三、本协调制度所称"兽牙"，是指象、河马、海象、一角鲸和野猪的长牙、犀角及其他动物的牙齿。

四、本协调制度所称"马毛"，是指马科、牛科动物的鬃毛和尾毛。税目 05.11 主要包括马毛及废马毛，不论是否制成带衬垫或不带衬垫的毛片。

税则号列	货品名称〔CIQ 扩展编码及品名－T2 表示见附表 2〕	最惠(%)	暂定税率	普通	增值/消费	出口退税	计量单位	监管条件/特殊证件	检验检疫	对美关税	亚太上/下
05.01	**未经加工的人发，不论是否洗涤；废人发：**										
0501.0000	未经加工的人发，不论是否洗涤；废人发〔999〕	15		90	13/	13	千克	9B/	VW	17.5	
05.02	**猪鬃、猪毛；獾毛及其他制刷用兽毛；上述鬃毛的废料：**										
	-猪鬃、猪毛及其废料：										
0502.1010	---猪鬃〔999〕	20		90	9/	9,13	千克	AB/	PQ	25	
0502.1020	---猪毛〔999〕	20		90	9/	9,13	千克	AB/	PQ	25	
0502.1030	---废料〔101 猪毛，102 猪鬃〕	20		90	9/	9	千克	9B/	PQ	25	
	-其他：										
	---獾毛及其他制刷用兽毛：										
0502.9011	----山羊毛〔999〕	20		90	9/	9,13	千克	AB/	PQ	25	
0502.9012	----黄鼠狼尾毛〔999〕	20		90	9/	9,13	千克	ABEF/	PQ	25	
0502.9019	----其他										
0502.9019 10	濒危獾毛及其他制刷用濒危兽毛[T2]	20		90	9/	0	千克	ABFE/	PQ	25	
0502.9019 90	其他獾毛及其他制刷用兽毛[T2]	20		90	9/	9,13	千克	AB/	PQ	25	
0502.9020	---废料										
0502.9020 10	濒危獾毛及其他制刷濒危兽毛废料[T2]	20		90	9/	0	千克	BEF/	PQ	25	
0502.9020 90	其他獾毛及其他制刷用兽毛的废料[T2]	20		90	9/	9	千克	9B/	PQ	25	
05.04	**整个或切块的动物(鱼除外)的肠、膀胱及胃，鲜、冷、冻、干、熏、盐腌或盐渍的：**										
	---肠衣：										
0504.0011	----盐渍猪肠衣(猪大肠头除外)〔999〕	20		90	9/	9	千克	AB/	PRQS	50	10/10
0504.0012	----盐渍绵羊肠衣〔999〕	18		90	9/	9	千克	AB/	PRQS	48	9/9
0504.0013	----盐渍山羊肠衣〔999〕	18		90	9/	9	千克	AB/	PRQS	23	9/9
0504.0014	----盐渍猪大肠头〔999〕	20		90	9/	9	千克	AB/	PRQS	25	10/10
0504.0019	----其他[T2]	18		90	9/	9	千克	AB/	PRQS	23	9/9
	---胃：										
0504.0021	----冷、冻的鸡胗〔101 冷藏的鸡胗、胃，102 冻藏的鸡胗、胃〕	T3		T3	9/	9	千克	7AB/	PRQS	T3	10/10
0504.0029	----其他[T2]	20		90	9/	9	千克	AB/	PRQS	50	10/10
0504.0090	---其他[T2]	20		80	9/	9	千克	AB/	PRQS	25	10/10
05.05	**带有羽毛或羽绒的鸟皮及鸟体其他部分；羽毛及不完整羽毛(不论是否修边)、羽绒，仅经洗涤、消毒或为了保藏而作过处理，但未经进一步加工；羽毛或不完整羽毛的粉末及废料：**										
0505.1000	-填充用羽毛；羽绒										
0505.1000 10	填充用濒危野生禽类羽毛、羽绒(仅经洗涤、消毒等处理，未进一步加工)〔999〕	10	2	100	9/	0	千克	ABFE/	PQ	24.5	7.5/7.5
0505.1000 90	其他填充用羽毛；羽绒(仅经洗涤、消毒等处理，未进一步加工)〔999〕	10	2	100	9/	9,13	千克	AB/	PQ	24.5	7.5/7.5
	-其他：										
0505.9010	---羽毛或不完整羽毛的粉末及废料[T2]	10		35	9/	9	千克	9AB/	PQ	12.5	
0505.9090	---其他										
0505.9090 10	其他濒危野生禽类羽毛、羽绒(包括带有羽毛或羽绒的鸟皮及鸟体的其他部分)〔101 野生禽鸟毛(绒)(未经加工鸭毛除外)，102 其他禽鸟羽毛，103 未经加工鸭毛〕	10		90	9/	0	千克	AFEB/	PQ	22.5	
0505.9090 90	其他羽毛、羽绒(包括带有羽毛或羽绒的鸟皮及鸟体的其他部分)[T2]	10		90	9/	9,13	千克	AB/	PQ	22.5	
05.06	**骨及角柱，未经加工或经脱脂、简单整理(但未切割成形)、酸处理或脱胶；上述产品的粉末及废料：**										

Chapter 5
Products of animal origin, not elsewhere specified or included

Notes:

1. This Chapter does not cover:
   (a) Edible products (other than guts, bladders and stomachs of animals, whole and pieces thereof, and animal blood, liquid or dried);
   (b) Hides or skins (including furskins) other than goods of heading No. 05.05 and parings and similar waste of raw hides or skins of heading No. 05.11 (Chapter 41 or 43)
   (c) Animal textile materials, other than horsehair and horsehair waste (Section XI); or
   (d) Prepared knots or tufts for broom or brush making (heading No. 96.03).
2. For the purposes of heading No. 05.01, the sorting of human hair by length (provided the root ends and tip ends respectively are not arranged together) shall be deemed not to constitute working.
3. Throughout the Nomenclature, elephant, hippopotamus, walrus, narwhal and wild boar tusks, rhinoceros horns and the teeth of all animals are regarded as "ivory".
4. Throughout the Nomenclature, the expression"horsehair" means hair of the manes or tails of equine or bovine animals. Heading No.05.11 mainly include horsehair and horsehair waster, whether or not put up as a layer with or without supporting material.

协定税率 %								RCEP		特惠税率 %			Article Description
东/冰/格	巴基斯坦	韩国	瑞士上/下	哥/秘/柬	澳/毛	新西/坡/智	中国港/澳/台	东盟及马来/澳/韩	日/新	亚太2国	老/柬/缅	98/97/95	
													Human hair, unworked, whether or not washed or scoured; waste of human hair:
0/0/0	8.4	3	1.5/1.5	0/0/0	0/0	0//0	0/0/	0/0/13.5	13.6/0			0/0/0	Human hair, unworked, whether or not washed or scoured; waste of human hair
													Pigs', hogs', or boars', bristles and hair; badger hair and other brush making hair; waste of such bristles or hair:
													-Pigs', hogs', or boars', bristles and hair and waste thereof:
0/0/0	14	9.3	2/2	0/0/0	0/0	0//0	0/0/	18/18/18	18.2/18			0/0/0	---Bristles
0/0/0	14	9.3	2/2	0/0/0	0/0	0//0	0/0/	18/18/18	18.2/18			0/0/0	---Hair
0/0/0	14	9.3	2/2	0/0/0	0/0	0//0	0/0/	18/18/18	18.2/18			0/0/0	---Waste
													-Other:
													---Badger hair and other brush making hair:
0/0/0		9.3	2/2	0/0/0	0/0	0//0	0/0/	18/18/18	18.8/18			0/0/0	----Goat hair
0/0/0		9.3	2/2	0/0/0	0/0	0//0	0/0/	18/18/18	18.8/18			0/0/0	----Weasel tail hair
													----Other
0/0/0		9.3	2/2	0/0/0	0/0	0//0	0/0/	18/18/18	18.8/18			0/0/0	Endangered badger hair and other brush making hair of endangered animals
0/0/0		9.3	2/2	0/0/0	0/0	0//0	0/0/	18/18/18	18.8/18			0/0/0	Other badger hair and other brush making hair of other animal
													---Waste
0/0/0		9.3	2/2	0/0/0	0/0	0//0	0/0/	18/18/18	18.8/18			0/0/0	Waste of endangered badger hair and other brush making hair of endangered animals
0/0/0		9.3	2/2	0/0/0	0/0	0//0	0/0/	18/18/18	18.8/18			0/0/0	Waste of badger hair and other brush making hair of other animals
													Guts, bladders and stomachs of animals (other than fish), whole and pieces thereof, fresh, chilled, frozen, salted, in brine, dried or smoked:
													---Casings:
0/0/0	10	9.3	0/0	0/0/0	0/0	0//0	0/0/	18.7/19/20	18.8/19			0/0/0	----Hog casings, salted(excluding hog fat-ends)
0/0/0	9	8.4	1.8/1.8	0/0/0	0/0	0//0	0/0/	16.8/17.1/16.8	16.9/17.1			0/0/0	----Sheep casings, salted
0/0/0	9	8.4	1.8/1.8	0/0/0	0/0	0//0	0/0/	16.2/16.2/16.2	16.9/16.2			0/0/0	----Goat casings, salted
0/0/0	10	9.3	2/2	0/0/0	0/0	0//0	0/0/	18/18/18	18.8/18			0/0/0	----Hog fat-ends, salted
0/0/0	9	8.4	1.8/1.8	0/0/0	0/0	0//0	0/0/	16.8/17.1/16.8	16.9/17.1			0/0/0	----Other
													---Gizzard:
0/0/0	0.65元/千克	0.6元/十克	2/2	0/0/0	0/0	0//0	0/0/	18/18/18	18.8/18			0/0/0	----Cold, frozen gizzard
0/0/0	10	9.3	2/2	0/0/0	0/0	0//0	0/0/	18/18/18	18.8/18			0/0/0	----Other
0/0/0	10	9.3	0/0	0/0/0	0/0	0//0	0/0/	18/18/18	18.8/18			0/0/0	---Other
													Skins and other parts of birds, with their feathers or down; feathers and parts of feathers (whether or not with trimmed edges) and down, not further worked than cleaned, disinfected or treated for preservation; powder and waste of feathers or parts of feathers:
													-Feathers of a kind used for stuffing; down
0/0/0	3.5	2	0/0	0/0/0	0/0	0//0	0/0/	9/9/9	9.1/9			0/0/0	Feathers of endangered wild birds, of a kind used for stuffing; down(not further worked than cleaned, disinfected or treated for preservation)
0/0/0	3.5	2	0/0	0/0/0	0/0	0//0	0/0/	9/9/9	9.1/9			0/0/0	Feathers of other birds, of a kind used for stuffing; down (not further worked than cleaned, disinfected or treated for preservation)
													-Other:
0/0/0	3.5	2	0/0	0/0/0	0/0	0//0	0/0/	0/0/9	9.1/0			0/0/0	---Powder and waste of feathers or parts of feathers
													---Other
0/0/0	3.5	2	0/0	0/0/0	0/0	0//0	0/0/	0/0/9	9.1/0			0/0/0	Feathers and down of endangered wild birds (including skins and other parts of birds, with their feathers or down)
0/0/0	3.5	2	0/0	0/0/0	0/0	0//0	0/0/	0/0/9	9.1/0			0/0/0	Feathers and down of other birds (including skins and other parts of birds, with their feathers or down)
													Bones and horn-cores, unworked, defatted, simply prepared (but not cut to shape), treated with acid or degelatinized; powder and waste of these products:

税则号列	货品名称〔CIQ 扩展编码及品名—T2 表示见附表 2〕	最惠(%)	暂定税率	普通	增值/消费	出口退税	计量单位	监管条件/特殊证件	检验检疫	对美关税	亚太上/下
0506.1000	-经酸处理的骨胶原及骨[T2]	12		50	13/	0	千克	AB/	PQ	14.5	
	-其他:										
	---骨粉、骨废料:										
0506.9011	----含牛羊成分的										
0506.9011 10	含牛羊成分的骨废料(未经加工或仅经脱脂等加工的)〔999〕	12		35	13/	0	千克	9AB/	PQ	14.5	
0506.9011 90	含牛羊成分的骨粉(未经加工或仅经脱脂等加工的)[T2]	12		35	13/	0	千克	AB/	MPQ	14.5	
0506.9019	----其他										
0506.9019 10	其他骨废料(未经加工或仅经脱脂等加工的)〔999〕	12		35	13/	0	千克	9AB/	PQ	14.5	
0506.9019 90	其他骨粉(未经加工或仅经脱脂等加工的)[T2]	12		35	13/	0	千克	AB/	MPQ	14.5	
0506.9090	---其他										
0506.9090 11	已脱胶的虎骨(指未经加工或经脱脂等加工的)〔999〕	12	12	50	9/	0	千克	89AB/	PQ	14.5	
0506.9090 19	未脱胶的虎骨(指未经加工或经脱脂等加工的)〔999〕	12		50	9/	0	千克	89AB/	PQ	14.5	
0506.9090 21	已脱胶的豹骨(指未经加工或经脱脂等加工的)〔999〕	12	12	50	9/	0	千克	ABFE/	PQ	14.5	
0506.9090 29	未脱胶的豹骨(指未经加工或经脱脂等加工的)〔999〕	12		50	9/	0	千克	ABFE/	PQ	14.5	
0506.9090 31	已脱胶的濒危野生动物的骨及角柱(不包括虎骨、豹骨,指未经加工或经脱脂等加工的)〔101 其他野生偶蹄动物骨、蹄、角,102 未列出的其他动物骨、蹄、角,103 工业用牛软骨,104 工业用羊软骨,105 工业用猪软骨,106 工业用烘干鹿骨〕	12	12	50	9/	0	千克	AFEB/	PQ	14.5	
0506.9090 39	未脱胶的濒危野生动物的骨及角柱(不包括虎骨、豹骨,指未经加工或经脱脂等加工的)〔101 工业用牛软骨,102 工业用羊软骨,103 工业用猪软骨,104 工业用烘干鹿骨,999 未列出的其他动物骨、蹄、角〕	12		50	9/	0	千克	AFEB/	PQ	14.5	
0506.9090 91	已脱胶的其他骨及角柱(不包括虎骨、豹骨,指未经加工或经脱脂等加工的)[T2]	12	12	50	9/	0	千克	AB/	PQ	14.5	
0506.9090 99	未脱胶的其他骨及角柱(不包括虎骨、豹骨,指未经加工或经脱脂等加工的)[T2]	12		50	9/	0	千克	AB/	PQ	14.5	
05.07	**兽牙、龟壳、鲸须、鲸须毛、角、鹿角、蹄、甲、爪及喙,未经加工或仅简单整理但未切割成形;上述产品的粉末及废料:**										
0507.1000	-兽牙;兽牙粉末及废料										
0507.1000 10	犀牛角〔999〕	10		30	9/	9	千克	89AB/	PQ	12.5	
0507.1000 20	其他濒危野生兽牙、兽牙粉末及废料〔101 其他野生偶蹄动物骨、蹄、角(河马牙除外),102 象牙,103 未列出的其他动物骨、蹄、角,104 河马牙〕	10		30	9/	0	千克	AFEB/	PQ	12.5	
0507.1000 30	其他兽牙[T2]	10		30	9/	9	千克	AB/	PQ	12.5	
0507.1000 90	其他兽牙粉末及废料[T2]	10		30	9/	9	千克	9AB/	PQ	12.5	
	-其他:										
0507.9010	---羚羊角及其粉末和废料〔101 羚羊角,102 药用羚羊角〕	3		14	9/	9	千克	ABFE/	PQ		
0507.9020	---鹿茸及其粉末[T2]	11		30	9/	9	千克	ABFE/	PQ	13.5	
0507.9090	---其他										
0507.9090 10	龟壳、鲸须、鲸须毛、鹿角及其他濒危动物角(包括蹄,甲,爪及喙及其粉末和废料)[T2]	10		50	9/	0	千克	AFEB/	PQ	12.5	
0507.9090 90	其他动物角(包括蹄,甲,爪及喙及其粉末和废料)[T2]	10		50	9/	9	千克	AB/	PQ	12.5	
05.08	**珊瑚及类似品,未经加工或仅简单整理但未经进一步加工;软体动物壳、甲壳动物壳、棘皮动物壳、墨鱼骨,未经加工或仅简单整理但未切割成形,上述壳、骨的粉末及废料:**										
0508.0010	---粉末及废料										
0508.0010 10	濒危珊瑚及濒危水产品的粉末、废料(包括介、贝、棘皮动物壳,不包括墨鱼骨的粉末、废料)〔101:未经加工虾蟹壳;999:除未经加工虾蟹壳外〕	12		35	9/	0	千克	AFEB/	PQ	39.5	
0508.0010 90	其他水产品壳、骨的粉末及废料(包括介、贝、棘皮动物壳、墨鱼骨的粉末及废料)[T2]	12		35	9/	9	千克	AB/	PQ	39.5	
0508.0090	---其他										
0508.0090 10	濒危珊瑚及濒危水产品的壳、骨(包括介、贝、棘皮动物的壳,不包括墨鱼骨)〔101 未经加工虾蟹壳,999 除未经加工虾蟹壳外〕	12		50	9/	0	千克	AFEB/	PQ	39.5	
0508.0090 90	其他水产品的壳、骨(包括介、贝、棘皮动物的壳,墨鱼骨)〔101 未经加工虾蟹壳,999 除未经加工虾蟹壳外〕	12		50	9/	9	千克	AB/	PQ	39.5	

协定税率 %								RCEP		特惠税率 %			Article Description
东/冰/格	巴基斯坦	韩国	瑞士上/下	哥/秘/柬	澳/毛	新西/坡/智	中国港/澳/台	东盟及马来/澳/韩	日/新	亚太2国	老/柬/缅	98/97/95	
0/0/0	4.2	2.4	1.2/1.2	0/0/0	0/0	0//0	0/0/	0/0/10.8	10.9/0		0//	0/0/0	-Ossein and bones treated with acid
													-Other:
													---Powder and waste of bones:
													----Of bovine and sheep
0/0/0	4.2	2.4	1.2/1.2	0/0/0	0/0	0//0	0/0/	0/0/10.8	10.9/0		0//	0/0/0	Waste of bones, containing bovine composition or sheep and goats composition(unworked, defatted, simply prepared)
0/0/0	4.2	2.4	1.2/1.2	0/0/0	0/0	0//0	0/0/	0/0/10.8	10.9/0		0//	0/0/0	Powder of bones, containing bovine composition or sheep and goats composition(unworked, defatted, simply prepared)
													----Other
0/0/0	4.2	2.4	1.2/1.2	0/0/0	0/0	0//0	0/0/	0/0/10.8	10.9/0		0//	0/0/0	Other waste of bones(unworked, defatted, simply prepared)
0/0/0	4.2	2.4	1.2/1.2	0/0/0	0/0	0//0	0/0/	0/0/10.8	10.9/0		0//	0/0/0	Other powder of bones(unworked, defatted, simply prepared)
													---Other
0/0/0	4.8	2.4	1.2/1.2	0/0/0	0/0	0//0	0/0/	0/0/10.8	10.9/0		0//	0/0/0	Tiger-bone (*as tigris*), degelatinized(unworked, defatted, simply prepared)
0/0/0	4.8	2.4	1.2/1.2	0/0/0	0/0	0//0	0/0/	0/0/10.8	10.9/0		0//	0/0/0	Tiger-bone (*as tigirs*), not degelatinized(unworked, defatted, simply prepared)
0/0/0	4.8	2.4	1.2/1.2	0/0/0	0/0	0//0	0/0/	0/0/10.8	10.9/0		0//	0/0/0	Leopard-bone, degelatinized (unworked, defatted, simply prepared)
0/0/0	4.8	2.4	1.2/1.2	0/0/0	0/0	0//0	0/0/	0/0/10.8	10.9/0		0//	0/0/0	Leopard-bone, not degelatinized(unworked, defatted, simply prepared)
0/0/0	4.8	2.4	1.2/1.2	0/0/0	0/0	0//0	0/0/	0/0/10.8	10.9/0		0//	0/0/0	Bones and horn-cores of endangered wild animals, degelatinized (other than tiger-bone, leopard-bone, unworked, defatted, simply prepared)
0/0/0	4.8	2.4	1.2/1.2	0/0/0	0/0	0//0	0/0/	0/0/10.8	10.9/0		0//	0/0/0	Bones and horn-cores of endangered wild animals, not degelatinized (other than tiger-bone, leopard-bone, unworked, defatted, simply prepared)
0/0/0	4.8	2.4	1.2/1.2	0/0/0	0/0	0//0	0/0/	0/0/10.8	10.9/0		0//	0/0/0	Bones and horn-cores of other animals, degelatinized (other than tiger-bone, leopard-bone, unworked, defatted, simply prepared)
0/0/0	4.8	2.4	1.2/1.2	0/0/0	0/0	0//0	0/0/	0/0/10.8	10.9/0		0//	0/0/0	Bones and horn-cores of other animals, not degelatinized (other than tiger-bone, leopard-bone, unworked, defatted, simply prepared)
													Ivory, tortoise-shell, whalebone and whalebone hair, horns, antlers, hooves, nails, claws and beaks, unworked or simply prepared but not cut to shape; powder and waste of these products:
													-Ivory; ivory powder and waste
0/0/0	3.5	2	0/0	0/0/0	0/0	0//0	0/0/	0/0/9	9.1/0			0/0/0	Rhinocerus horn (*cornu rhinocerotis*)
0/0/0	3.5	2	0/0	0/0/0	0/0	0//0	0/0/	0/0/9	9.1/0			0/0/0	Ivory, ivory powder and waste thereof of other endangered wild animals
0/0/0	3.5	2	0/0	0/0/0	0/0	0//0	0/0/	0/0/9	9.1/0			0/0/0	Other ivory
0/0/0	3.5	2	0/0	0/0/0	0/0	0//0	0/0/	0/0/9	9.1/0			0/0/0	Other ivory powedr and waste thereof
													-Other:
0/0/0	0	0	0/0	0/0/0	0/0	0//0	0/0/	0/0/0	0/0			0/0/0	---Antelope horns and powder or waste thereof
0/0/0	3.5	2.2	1.1/1.1	0/0/0	0/0	0//0	0/0/	0/0/9.9	10/0			0/0/0	---Pilose antlers and powder thereof
													---Other
0/0/0	3.5	2	0/0	0/0/0	0/0	0//0	0/0/	0/0/9	9.1/0			0/0/0	Tortoise-shell, whalebone and whalebone hair, horns and other endangered antlers, hooves, nails, claws and beaks, unworked or simply prepared but not cut to shape; powder and waste of these products
0/0/0	3.5	2	0/0	0/0/0	0/0	0//0	0/0/	0/0/9	9.1/0			0/0/0	Other animal antlers, hooves, nails, claws and beaks, unworked or simply prepared but not cut to shape; powder and waste of these products
													Coral and similar materials, unworked or simply prepared but not otherwise worked; shells of molluscs, crustaceans or echinoderms and cuttle-bone, unworked or simply prepared but not cut to shape, powder and waste thereof:
													---Powder and waste
0/0/0		2.4	1.2/1.2	0/0/0	0/0	0//0	0/0/	0/0/10.8	10.9/0			0/0/0	Powder and waste of endangered aquatic product(including shells of molluscs, crustaceans or echinoderms and cuttle-bone)
0/0/0		2.4	1.2/1.2	0/0/0	0/0	0//0	0/0/	0/0/10.8	10.9/0			0/0/0	Powder and waste of other aquatic products (including shells of molluscs, crustaceans or echinoderms and cuttle-bone)
													---Other
0/0/0	6	2.4	1.2/1.2	0/0/0	0/0	0//0	0/0/	0/0/10.8	/0			0/0/0	Shells , bone of endangered coral and endangered aquatic products(including shells of molluscs, crustaceans or echinoderms and cuttle-bone)
0/0/0	6	2.4	1.2/1.2	0/0/0	0/0	0//0	0/0/	0/0/10.8	/0			0/0/0	Shells and bone of other aquatic products(including shells of molluscs, crustaceans or echinoderms and cuttle-bone)

税则号列	货品名称〔CIQ扩展编码及品名－T2表示见附表2〕	最惠(%)	暂定税率	普通	增值/消费	出口退税	计量单位	监管条件/特殊证件	检验检疫	对美关税	亚太上/下
05.10	**龙涎香、海狸香、灵猫香及麝香；斑蝥；胆汁，不论是否干制；供配制药用的腺体及其他动物产品，鲜、冷、冻或用其他方法暂时保藏的：**										
0510.0010	---黄药										
0510.0010 10	牛黄[T2]	3		14	9/	9	千克	8A/	PQ		
0510.0010 20	猴枣〔999〕	3		14	9/	9	千克	QAFEB/	PQ		
0510.0010 90	其他黄药(不包括牛黄)〔999〕	3		14	9/	9	千克	AFEB/	PQ		
0510.0020	---龙涎香、海狸香、灵猫香										
0510.0020 10	海狸香、灵猫香〔999〕	7		50	9/	9	千克	AFEB/	PQ	9.5	
0510.0020 20	龙涎香〔999〕	7		50	9/	9	千克	AB/	PQ	9.5	
0510.0030	---麝香〔999〕	7		20	9/	0	千克	8AF/	PQ	9.5	
0510.0040	---斑蝥〔999〕	7		50	9/	9	千克	QAB/	PQ	9.5	
0510.0090	---其他										
0510.0090 10	其他濒危野生动物胆汁及其他产品(不论是否干制；鲜、冷、冻或用其他方法暂时保藏的)〔101〕	6		20	9/	0	千克	AFEB/	PQ	8.5	
0510.0090 90	胆汁，配药用腺体及其他动物产品(不论是否干制；鲜、冷、冻或用其他方法暂时保藏的)[T2]	6		20	9/	9	千克	AB/	PQ	8.5	
05.11	**其他税目未列名的动物产品；不适合供人食用的第一章或第三章的死动物：**										
0511.1000	-牛的精液										
0511.1000 10	濒危野生牛的精液〔999〕	0		0	9/	0	千克/支	ABFE/	PQ		
0511.1000 90	牛的精液(濒危野牛的精液除外)〔101 牛精液，102 其他精液〕	0		0	0/	9	千克/支	AB/	PQ		
	-其他：										
	--鱼、甲壳动物、软体动物、其他水生无脊椎动物的产品；第三章的死动物：										
	---鱼的：										
0511.9111	----受精鱼卵										
0511.9111 10	濒危鱼的受精卵〔999〕	12	0	35	9/	0	千克	ABFE/	PQ		
0511.9111 90	受精鱼卵(包括发眼卵，濒危除外)〔101 鲈鱼卵，102 鲑鱼卵，103 鲟鱼卵，104 牙鲆鱼卵，105 虹鳟鱼卵，106 河豚鱼卵，107 大鲮鲆鱼卵，108 其他受精卵〕	12	0	35	0/	9	千克	AB/	PQ		
0511.9119	----其他										
0511.9119 10	濒危鱼的非食用产品(包括鱼肚)〔101 受精卵，102 用作鱼饵的海水鱼，103 用作鱼饵的淡水鱼〕	12		35	9/	0	千克	ABFE/	PQ	14.5	
0511.9119 90	其他鱼的非食用产品(包括鱼肚)〔101 受精卵，102 用作鱼饵的海水鱼，103 用作鱼饵的淡水鱼〕	12		35	9/	9	千克	AB/	PQ	14.5	
0511.9190	---其他										
0511.9190 10	濒危水生无脊椎动物产品(包括甲壳动物、软体动物、第三章死动物)〔101 头索类，102 头索类以外〕	12		35	9/	0	千克	ABFE/	PQ	24.5	
0511.9190 20	丰年虫卵(丰年虾卵)〔999〕	12	6	35	9/	9	千克	AB/	PQ	18.5	
0511.9190 90	其他水生无脊椎动物产品(包括甲壳动物、软体动物、第三章死动物)〔101 头索类；102 头索类以外；201 头索类；202 头索类以外；203 头索类以外〕	12		35	9/	9	千克	AB/	PQ	24.5	
	--其他：										
0511.9910	---动物精液(牛的精液除外)										
0511.9910 10	濒危野生动物精液(牛的精液除外)〔999〕	0		0	9/	0	千克	AFEB/	PQ		
0511.9910 90	其他动物精液(牛的精液和其他濒危动物精液除外)〔101 猪精液，102 绵羊精液，103 山羊精液，104 马精液，105 其他精液〕	0		0	0/	9	千克	AB/	PQ		
0511.9920	---动物胚胎										
0511.9920 10	濒危野生动物胚胎〔999〕	0		0	9/	0	千克	AFEB/	PQ		
0511.9920 20	猪、牛、山羊、绵羊胚胎〔101 猪胚胎，102 牛胚胎，103 山羊胚胎，104 绵羊胚胎〕	0		0	0/	9	千克	AB/	PQ		
0511.9920 90	其他动物胚胎[T2]	0		0	9/	9	千克	AB/	PQ		
0511.9930	---蚕种〔999〕	0		0	9/	9	千克	AB/	PQ		
0511.9940	---马毛及废马毛，不论是否制成有或无衬垫的毛片										
0511.9940 10	废马毛(不论是否制成有或无衬垫的毛片)[T2]	15		90	9/	9,13	千克	9B/	PQ	17.5	
0511.9940 90	其他马毛(不论是否制成有或无衬垫的毛片)[T2]	15		90	9/	9,13	千克	AB/	PQ	17.5	
0511.9990	---其他										
0511.9990 10	其他编号未列名濒危野生动物产品(包括不适合供人食用的第一章的死动物)[T2]	12		35	9/	0	千克	AFEB/	PQ	39.5	
0511.9990 90	其他编号未列名的动物产品(包括不适合供人食用的第一章的死动物)[T2]	12		35	9/	9	千克	AB/	PQ	39.5	

协定税率 %								RCEP		特惠税率 %			Article Description
东/冰/格	巴基斯坦	韩国	瑞士 上/下	哥/秘/柬	澳/毛	新西/坡/智	中国港/澳/台	东盟及马来/澳/韩	日/新	亚太2国	老/柬/缅	98/97/95	
													Ambergris, castoreum, civet and musk; cantharides; bile, whether of not dried; glands and other animal products used in the preparation of pharmaceutical products, fresh, chilled, frozen or otherwise provisionally preserved:
													---Bezoar
0/0/0	0	0	0/0	0/0/0	0/0	0//0	0/0/	0/0/0	0/0			0/0/0	Calculus bovis
0/0/0	0	0	0/0	0/0/0	0/0	0//0	0/0/	0/0/0	0/0			0/0/0	Calculus macaca mulatta
0/0/0	0	0	0/0	0/0/0	0/0	0//0	0/0/	0/0/0	0/0			0/0/0	Other bezoar (excluding calculus bovis)
													---Ambergris, castoreum and civet
0/0/0	2	0	0/0	0/0/0	0/0	0//0	0/0/	0/0/0	0/0			0/0/0	castoreum and civet
0/0/0	2	0	0/0	0/0/0	0/0	0//0	0/0/	0/0/0	0/0			0/0/0	Ambergris
0/0/0	2	0	0/0	0/0/0	0/0	0//0	0/0/	0/0/0	0/0			0/0/0	---Musk
0/0/0	2	0	0/0	0/0/0	0/0	0//0	0/0/	0/0/0	0/0			0/0/0	---Cantharides
													---Other
0/0/0	4	0	0/0	0/0/0	0/0	0//0	0/0/	0/0/0	0/0			0/0/0	Bile and other products of other endangered wild animals (whether or not dried, fresh, chilled, frozen or otherwise provisionally preserved)
0/0/0	4	0	0/0	0/0/0	0/0	0//0	0/0/	0/0/0	0/0			0/0/0	Bile, glands and other animal products used in the preparation of pharmaceutical products (whether or not dried, fresh, chilled, frozen or otherwise provisionally preserved)
													Animal products not elsewhere specified or included; dead animals of Chapter 1 or 3, unfit for human consumption:
													-Bovine semen
0/0/0	0	0	0/0	0/0/0	0/0	0//0	0/0/	0/0/0	0/0			0/0/0	Semen of endangered wild bovine
0/0/0	0	0	0/0	0/0/0	0/0	0//0	0/0/	0/0/0	0/0			0/0/0	Other bovine semen
													-Other:
													--Products of fish or crustaceans, molluscs or other aquatic invertebrates; dead animals of Chapter 3:
													---Fish:
													----Fertilized fish eggs
0/0/0	6	0	1.2/1.2	0/0/0	0/0	0//0	0/0/	0/0/0	10.9/0			0/0/0	Fertilized eggs of endangered fish
0/0/0	6	0	1.2/1.2	0/0/0	0/0	0//0	0/0/	0/0/0	10.9/0			0/0/0	Other fertilized fish eggs
													----Other
0/2.1/0		2.4	1.2/1.2	0/0/0	0/0	0//0	0/0/	0/0/10.8	10.9/0			0/0/0	Products of endangered fish(including fish maw)unfit for human consumption
0/2.1/0		2.4	1.2/1.2	0/0/0	0/0	0//0	0/0/	0/0/10.8	10.9/0			0/0/0	Products of other fish(including fish maw) unfit for human consumption
													---Other
0/0/0	4.2	2.4	1.2/1.2	0/0/0	0/0	0//0	0/0/	0/0/10.8	10.9/0			0/0/0	Products of endangererd crustaceans molluscs or other aquatic invertebrates; dead animals of Chapter 3
0/0/0	4.2	2.4	1.2/1.2	0/0/0	0/0	0//0	0/0/	0/0/10.8	10.9/0		//	0/0/0	Abundant eggs(Shrimp eggs in harvest)
0/0/0	4.2	2.4	1.2/1.2	0/0/0	0/0	0//0	0/0/	0/0/10.8	10.9/0			0/0/0	Other products of crustaceans, molluscs or other aquatic invertebrates; dead animals of Chapter 3
													Other:
													---Animal semen, other than bovine semen
0/0/0	0	0	0/0	0/0/0	0/0	0//0	0/0/	0/0/0	0/0			0/0/0	Semen of endangered wild animals(other than bovine semen)
0/0/0	0	0	0/0	0/0/0	0/0	0//0	0/0/	0/0/0	0/0			0/0/0	Semen of other animals (other than bovine semen)
													---Animal embryo
0/0/0	0	0	0/0	0/0/0	0/0	0//0	0/0/	0/0/0	0/0			0/0/0	Embryo of endangered wild animals
0/0/0	0	0	0/0	0/0/0	0/0	0//0	0/0/	0/0/0	0/0			0/0/0	Pig, cow, goat, sheep embryo
0/0/0	0	0	0/0	0/0/0	0/0	0//0	0/0/	0/0/0	0/0			0/0/0	Embryo of other animals
0/0/0	0	0	0/0	0/0/0	0/0	0//0	0/0/	0/0/0	0/0			0/0/0	---Silkworm graine
													---Horsehair and horsehair waster, whether or not put up as a layer with or without supporting material
0/0/0	8.4	3	1.5/1.5	0/0/0	0/0	0//0	0/0/	0/0/13.5	13.6/0			0/0/0	Horsehair waster(whether or not put up as a lalyer with or without supporting material)
0/0/0	8.4	3	1.5/1.5	0/0/0	0/0	0//0	0/0/	0/0/13.5	13.6/0			0/0/0	Other horsehair (whether or not put up as a lalyer with or without supporting material)
													Other
0/0/0	4.2	2.4	1.2/1.2	0/0/0	0/0	0//0	0/0/	0/0/10.8	10.9/0			0/0/0	Products of endangered wild animals, not elsewhere specified or included(including dead animals of Chapter 1, unfit for human consumption)
0/0/0	4.2	2.4	1.2/1.2	0/0/0	0/0	0//0	0/0/	0/0/10.8	10.9/0			0/0/0	Animal products not elsewhere specified or included (including dead animals of Chapter 1, unfit for human consumption)

第二类
植物产品

注释：

本类所称“团粒”，是指直接挤压或加入按重量计比例不超过3%的黏合剂制成的粒状产品。

第六章
活树及其他活植物；鳞茎、根及类似品；插花及装饰用簇叶

注释：

一、除税号06.01的菊苣植物及其根以外，本章包括通常由苗圃或花店供应为种植或装饰用的活树及其他货品（包括植物秧苗）；但不包括马铃薯、洋葱、青葱、大蒜及其他第七章的产品。

二、税号06.03、06.04的各种货品，包括全部或部分用这些货品制成的花束、花篮、花圈及类似品，不论是否有其他材料制成的附件。但这些货品不包括税号97.01的拼贴画或类似的装饰板。

税则号列	货品名称〔CIQ扩展编码及品名－T2表示见附表2〕	最惠(%)	暂定税率	普通	增值/消费	出口退税	计量单位	监管条件/特殊证件	检验检疫	对美关税	亚太上/下
06.01	**鳞茎、块茎、块根、球茎、根颈及根茎，休眠、生长或开花的；菊苣植物及其根，但税目12.12的根除外：**										
	-休眠的鳞茎、块茎、块根、球茎、根颈及根茎：										
0601.1010	---番红花球茎〔999〕	4		14	0/	9	个/千克	AB/	PQ		2/2
	---百合球茎：										
0601.1021	----种用〔999〕	0		0	0/	0	个/千克	AB/	PQ		
0601.1029	----其他〔999〕	5		40	9/	0	个/千克	AB/	PQ	7.5	2.5/2.5
	---其他：										
0601.1091	----种用										
0601.1091 10	种用休眠的兰花块茎(包括球茎、根颈及根茎)〔999〕	0		0	9/	9	个/千克	AFEB/	PQ	2.5	
0601.1091 91	种用休眠其他濒危植物鳞茎等(包括球茎、根颈、根茎、鳞茎、块茎、块根)〔999〕	0		0	9/	0	个/千克	ABFE/	PQ	2.5	
0601.1091 99	种用休眠的鳞茎、块茎、块根、球茎、根颈及根茎(濒危除外)〔101球根海棠，102其他观赏花木，103洋葱(鳞球块根茎)，104蒜(种用)，105芋艿(种用)，106郁金香球茎，107朱顶兰球茎，108睡莲块根，109水仙花球茎，110其他鳞球块根茎〕	0		0	0/	9	个/千克	AB/	PQ		
0601.1099	----其他										
0601.1099 10	其他休眠的兰花块茎(包括球茎、根颈及根茎)〔999〕	5		40	9/	9	个/千克	AFEB/	PQ	7.5	2.5/2.5
0601.1099 91	其他休眠濒危植物鳞茎等(包括球茎、根颈、根茎、鳞茎、块茎、块根)〔999〕	5		40	9/	0	个/千克	AFEB/	PQ	7.5	2.5/2.5
0601.1099 99	其他休眠的其他鳞茎、块茎、块根(包括球茎、根颈及根茎)〔101水仙花球茎，102其他鳞球块根茎〕	5		40	9/	9	个/千克	AB/	PQ	7.5	2.5/2.5
0601.2000	-生长或开花的鳞茎、块茎、块根、球茎、根颈及根茎；菊苣植物及其根										
0601.2000 10	生长或开花的兰花块茎(包括球茎、根颈及根茎)〔999〕	15		80	9/	9	个/千克	AFEB/	PQ	20	7.5/7.5
0601.2000 20	生长或开花的仙客来鳞茎〔999〕	15		80	9/	9	个/千克	AFEB/	PQ	20	7.5/7.5
0601.2000 91	生长或开花的其他濒危植物鳞茎等(包括球茎、根颈、根茎、鳞茎、块茎、块根、菊苣植物)〔999〕	15		80	9/	0	个/千克	AFEB/	PQ	20	7.5/7.5
0601.2000 99	生长或开花的鳞茎、块茎、块根、球茎、根颈及根茎；菊苣植物及其根(濒危除外)(包括块茎、块根、球茎、根颈及根茎，税目1212的根除外)〔101洋葱(鳞球块根茎)，102蒜(种用)，103芋艿(种用)，104甘薯块茎，105百合球茎，106郁金香球茎，107朱顶兰球茎，108睡莲块根，109水仙花球茎，110其他鳞球块根茎〕	15		80	0/	9	个/千克	AB/	PQ		7.5/7.5
06.02	**其他活植物(包括其根)、插枝及接穗；蘑菇菌丝：**										
0602.1000	-无根插枝及接穗										
0602.1000 10	濒危植物的无根插枝及接穗〔101营养体，102其他组培苗〕	0		0	9/	0	株/千克	ABFE/	PQ	2.5	
0602.1000 90	无根插枝及接穗(濒危除外)〔101其他观赏花木，102营养体〕	0		0	0/	9	株/千克	AB/	PQ		
	-食用水果或食用坚果的树、灌木，不论是否嫁接：										
0602.2010	---种用苗木[T2]	0		0	0/	0	株/千克	AB/	PQ		
0602.2090	---其他〔999〕	10		80	9/	9	株/千克	AB/	PQ	32.5	5/5
	-杜鹃，不论是否嫁接：										
0602.3010	---种用〔101杜鹃(观赏花木)，102其他组培苗，103营养体〕	0		0	9/	9	株/千克	AB/	PQ	2.5	
0602.3090	---其他〔999〕	15		80	9/	9	株/千克	AB/	PQ	17.5	
	-玫瑰，不论是否嫁接：										
0602.4010	---种用〔101玫瑰，102其他组培苗，103营养体〕	0		0	9/	9	株/千克	AB/	PQ		
0602.4090	---其他〔999〕	15		80	9/	9	株/千克	AB/	PQ	17.5	

SECTION Ⅱ
VEGETABLE PRODUCTS

Notes:

In this Section the term "pellets" means products which have been agglomerated either directly by compression or by the addition of a binder in a proportion not exceeding 3% by weight.

Chapter 6
Live trees and other plants; bulbs, roots and the like; cut flowers and ornamental foliage

Notes:

1. Subject to the second part of heading No. 06.01 this Chapter covers only live trees and goods (including seeding vegetables) of a kind commonly supplied by nursery gardeners or florists for planting or for ornamental use; nevertheless it does not include potatoes, onions, shallots, garlic or other products of Chapter 7.
2. Any reference in heading No. 06.03 or 06.04 to goods of any kind shall be construed as including a reference to bouquets, floral baskets, wreaths and similar articles made wholly or partly of goods of that kind, account not being taken of accessories of other materials. However, these headings do not include collages or similar decorative plaques of heading No. 97.01.

协定税率 %								RCEP		特惠税率 %			Article Description
东/冰/格	巴基斯坦	韩国	瑞士上/下	哥/秘/柬	澳/毛	新西/坡/智	中国港/澳/台	东盟及马来/澳/韩	日/新	亚太2国	老/柬/缅	98/97/95	
													Bulbs, tubers, tuberous roots, corms, crowns and rhizomes, dormant, in growth or in flower; chicory plants and roots other than roots of heading No. 12.12:
													-Bulbs, tubers, tuberous roots, corms, crowns and rhizomes, dormant:
0/0/0	0	0	0/0	0/0/0	0/0	0//0	0/0/	0/0/0	0/0		0//	0/0/0	---Stigma croci corms
													---lily corms:
0/0/0	0	0	0/0	0/0/0	0/0	0//0	0/0/	0/0/0	0/0			0/0/0	----Seed
0/0/0	0	0	0/0	0/0/0	0/0	0//0	0/0/	0/0/0	0/0		0//	0/0/0	----Other
													---Other:
													----Seed
0/0/0	0	0	0/0	0/0/0	0/0	0//0	0/0/	0/0/0	0/0			0/0/0	Orchid tubers, dormant, seed (including corms, crowns and rhizomes)
0/0/0	0	0	0/0	0/0/0	0/0	0//0	0/0/	0/0/0	0/0			0/0/0	Bulbs, tubers, tuberous roots, dormant, seed (including corms, crowns and rhizomes) of endaergered plants
0/0/0	0	0	0/0	0/0/0	0/0	0//0	0/0/	0/0/0	0/0			0/0/0	Dormant bulbs, tubers, tubers, corms, root necks and rhizomes for species (except wild orchids and other endangered plants)
													----Other
0/0/0	0	0	0/0	0/0/0	0/0	0//0	0/0/	0/0/0	0/0		0//	0/0/0	Other orchid tubers, dormant(including corms, crowns and rhizomes)
0/0/0	0	0	0/0	0/0/0	0/0	0//0	0/0/	0/0/0	0/0		0//	0/0/0	Other endangered plants bulbs (including corms, crowns, rhizomes, bulbs, tuber, tuberous roots, dormant)
0/0/0	0	0	0/0	0/0/0	0/0	0//0	0/0/	0/0/0	0/0		0//	0/0/0	Other bulbs, tubers, tuberous roots, dormant, seed (including corms, crowns and rhizomes), dormant
													-Bulbs, tubers, tuberous roots, corms, crowns and rhizomes, in growth or in flower; chicory plants and roots
0/0/0	5.3	3	1.5/1.5	0/0/0	0/0	0//0	0/0/	0/0/13.5	13.6/0			0/0/0	Orchid tubers, in growth or in flower (in-cluding corms, crowns and rhizomes)
0/0/0	5.3	3	1.5/1.5	0/0/0	0/0	0//0	0/0/	0/0/13.5	13.6/0			0/0/0	Cyclamen tubers, in growth or in flower
0/0/0	5.3	3	1.5/1.5	0/0/0	0/0	0//0	0/0/	0/0/13.5	13.6/0			0/0/0	Other endangered plants bulbs(including corms, crowns, rhizomes, bulbs, tubers, tuberous roots, chicory plants) in growth or in flower
0/0/0	5.3	3	1.5/1.5	0/0/0	0/0	0//0	0/0/	0/0/13.5	13.6/0			0/0/0	Bulbs, tubers, tubers, corms, root necks and rhizomes growing or flowering; Chicory plants and their roots (except endangered) (including tubers, tubers, corms, root necks and rhizomes, except those of heading 1212)
													Other live plants (including their roots) cuttings and slips; mushroom spawn:
													-Unrooted cuttings and slips
0/0/0	0	0	0/0	0/0/0	0/0	0//0	0/0/	0/0/0	0/0			0/0/0	Unrooted cuttings and slips of endangered pl-ants
0/0/0	0	0	0/0	0/0/0	0/0	0//0	0/0/	0/0/0	0/0			0/0/0	Other unrooted cuttings and slips
													-Trees, shrubs and bushes, grafted or not, of kinds which bear edible fruit or nuts:
0/0/0	0	0	0/0	0/0/0	0/0	0//0	0/0/	0/0/0	0/0			0/0/0	---Seedlings
0/0/0	3.5	2	0/0	0/0/0	0/0	0//0	0/0/	0/0/9	9.1/0			0/0/0	---Other
													-Rhododendrons and azaleas, grafted or not:
0/0/0	0	0	0/0	0/0/0	0/0	0//0	0/0/	0/0/0	0/0			0/0/0	---Seedlings
0/0/0	9.6	3	1.5/1.5	0/0/0	0/0	0//0	0/0/	13.5/13.5/13.5	/13.5			0/0/0	---Other
													-Roses, grafted or not:
0/0/0	0	0	0/0	0/0/0	0/0	0//0	0/0/	0/0/0	0/0			0/0/0	---Seedlings
0/0/0	9.6	3	1.5/1.5	0/0/0	0/0	0//0	0/0/	0/0/13.5	13.6/0			0/0/0	---Other

税则号列	货品名称〔CIQ 扩展编码及品名－T2 表示见附表 2〕	最惠(%)	暂定税率	普通	增值/消费	出口退税	计量单位	监管条件/特殊证件	检验检疫	对美关税	亚太上/下
	-其他：										
0602.9010	---蘑菇菌丝〔999〕	0		0	9/	9	千克	AB/	PQ		
	---其他：										
0602.9091	----种用苗木										
0602.9091 10	种用兰花[T2]	0		0	9/	0	株/千克	AFEB/	PQ	2.5	
0602.9091 20	种用红豆杉苗木〔999〕	0		0	9/	0	株/千克	AFEB/	PQ	2.5	
0602.9091 91	其他濒危植物种用苗木[T2]	0		0	9/	0	株/千克	AFEB/	PQ	2.5	
0602.9091 99	其他种用苗木(濒危除外)〔101 白腊槭苗木，102 长叶松苗木，103 岛松苗木，104 其他松属苗木，105 黄檀苗木，106 柳苗木，107 榆苗木，108 杉属苗木，109 梧桐苗木，110 棕榈苗木，111 栎树苗木，112 槟榔苗木，113 其他林木苗木，114 牡丹，115 安祖花，116 其他观赏花木，117 其他组培苗，118 营养体〕	0		0	0/	0	株/千克	AB/	PQ		
0602.9092	----兰花〔101 蝴蝶兰，102 兰花〕	10		80	9/	9	株/千克	ABFE/	PQ	12.5	
0602.9093	----菊花〔999〕	10		80	9/	0,9	株/千克	AB/	PQ	12.5	
0602.9094	----百合										
0602.9094 10	芦荟(种用除外)〔999〕	10		80	9/	9	株/千克	ABEFQ/	PQ	12.5	
0602.9094 90	其他百合(种用除外)〔101 观赏花木，102 药用百合〕	10		80	9/	0	株/千克	AB/	PQ	12.5	
0602.9095	----康乃馨〔999〕	10		80	9/	9	株/千克	AB/	PQ	12.5	
0602.9099	----其他										
0602.9099 10	苏铁(铁树)类〔999〕	10		80	9/	9	株/千克	ABFE/	PQ	37.5	5/5
0602.9099 20	仙人掌(包括仙人球、仙人柱、仙人指)〔999〕	10		80	9/	9	株/千克	ABFE/	PQ	37.5	5/5
0602.9099 30	红豆杉(种用除外)〔999〕	10		80	9/	0	株/千克	ABFE/	PQ	37.5	5/5
0602.9099 91	其他濒危活植物(种用除外)[T2]	10		80	9/	0	株/千克	AFEB/	PQ	37.5	5/5
0602.9099 99	其他活植物(种用除外)[T2]	10		80	9/	9	株/千克	AB/	PQ	37.5	5/5
06.03	**制花束或装饰用的插花及花蕾，鲜、干、染色、漂白、浸渍或用其他方法处理的：**										
	-鲜的：										
0603.1100	--玫瑰〔999〕	10		100	9/	9	千克/枝	AB/	PQ	12.5	5/5
0603.1200	--康乃馨〔999〕	10		100	9/	9	千克/枝	AB/	PQ	12.5	5/5
0603.1300	--兰花〔101 洋兰切花，102 鹤望兰切花，103 其他切花〕	10		100	9/	9	千克/枝	ABEF/	PQ	12.5	5/5
0603.1400	--菊花〔999〕	10		100	9/	9	千克/枝	AB/	PQ	12.5	5/5
0603.1500	--百合花(百合属)〔999〕	10		100	9/	9	千克/枝	AB/	PQ	12.5	5/5
0603.1900	--其他										
0603.1900 10	鲜的濒危植物插花及花蕾(制花束或装饰用的)〔999〕	10		100	9/	0	千克/枝	ABFE/	PQ	37.5	5/5
0603.1900 90	其他鲜的插花及花蕾(制花束或装饰用的)〔999〕	10		100	9/	9	千克/枝	AB/	PQ	37.5	5/5
0603.9000	-其他										
0603.9000 10	干或染色等加工濒危植物的插花及花蕾(制花束或装饰用的，鲜的除外)〔999〕	23		100	13/	0	千克/枝	ABFE/	PQ	53	11.5/11.5
0603.9000 90	其他干或染色等加工的插花及花蕾(制花束或装饰用的，鲜的除外)〔999〕	23		100	13/	9	千克/枝	AB/	PQ	53	11.5/11.5
06.04	**制花束或装饰用的不带花及花蕾的植物枝、叶或其他部分，草、苔藓及地衣，鲜、干、染色、漂白、浸渍或用其他方法处理的：**										
	-鲜的：										
0604.2010	---苔藓及地衣〔101 苔藓及地衣，102 苔藓(栽培介质)，103 泥炭藓(栽培介质)〕	23		100	9/	9	千克	AB/	PQ	53	
0604.2090	---其他										
0604.2090 10	其他鲜濒危植物枝、叶或其他部分，草(枝、叶或其他部分是指制花束或装饰用并且不带花及花蕾)〔999〕	10		100	9/	0	千克	ABFE/	PQ	37.5	
0604.2090 90	其他鲜植物枝、叶或其他部分，草(枝、叶或其他部分是指制花束或装饰用并且不带花及花蕾)〔101 其他林木苗木，102 其他观赏花木，103 富贵竹切花，104 未列出的其他植物〕	10		100	9/	9	千克	AB/	PQ	37.5	
	-其他：										
0604.9010	---苔藓及地衣[T2]	23		100	9/	9	千克	AB/	PQ	28	
0604.9090	---其他										
0604.9090 10	其他染色或经加工濒危植物枝、叶、草等(枝、叶或其他部分是指制花束或装饰用并且不带花及花蕾)〔999〕	10		100	13/	0	千克	ABFE/	PQ	37.5	
0604.9090 90	其他染色或加工的植物枝、叶、草等(枝、叶或其他部分是指制花束或装饰用并且不带花及花蕾)〔101：干花；102：未列出的其他植物产品〕	10		100	13/	9	千克	AB/	PQ	37.5	

协定税率 %								RCEP		特惠税率 %			Article Description
东/冰/格	巴基斯坦	韩国	瑞士上/下	哥/秘/柬	澳/毛	新西/坡/智	中国港/澳/台	东盟及马来/澳/韩	日/新	亚太2国	老/柬/缅	98/97/95	
													-Other:
0/0/0	0	0	0/0	0/0/0	0/0	0//0	0/0/	0/0/0	0/0			0/0/0	---Mushroom spawn
													---Other:
													----Seedlings
0/0/0	0	0	0/0	0/0/0	0/0	0//0	0/0/	0/0/0	0/0			0/0/0	Orchid, seedlings
0/0/0	0	0	0/0	0/0/0	0/0	0//0	0/0/	0/0/0	0/0			0/0/0	Chinese yew, seeding
0/0/0	0	0	0/0	0/0/0	0/0	0//0	0/0/	0/0/0	0/0			0/0/0	Other seedlings of endangered plants
0/0/0	0	0	0/0	0/0/0	0/0	0//0	0/0/	0/0/0	0/0			0/0/0	Seedlings for other species (except endangered)
0/0/0	3.5	2	0/0	0/0/0	0/0	0//0	0/0/	0/0/9	9.1/0			0/0/0	----Orchid
0/0/0	3.5	2	0/0	0/0/0	0/0	0//0	0/0/	0/0/9	9.1/0			0/0/0	----Chrysathemum
													----Lily
0/0/0	3.5	2	0/0	0/0/0	0/0	0//0	0/0/	0/0/9	9.1/0			0/0/0	Aloe(other than seedlings)
0/0/0	3.5	2	0/0	0/0/0	0/0	0//0	0/0/	0/0/9	9.1/0			0/0/0	Other lily(other than seedling)
0/0/0	3.5	2	0/0	0/0/0	0/0	0//0	0/0/	0/0/9	9.1/0			0/0/0	----Carnation
													----Other
0/0/0	3.5	2	0/0	0/0/0	0/0	0//0	0/0/	9/9/9	/9			0/0/0	Sago cycas (*Cycas revoluta*)
0/0/0	3.5	2	0/0	0/0/0	0/0	0//0	0/0/	9/9/9	/9			0/0/0	Cactus (including ball cactus, column cactus, finger cactus)
0/0/0	3.5	2	0/0	0/0/0	0/0	0//0	0/0/	9/9/9	/9			0/0/0	Chinese yew(other than seeding)
0/0/0	3.5	2	0/0	0/0/0	0/0	0//0	0/0/	9/9/9	/9			0/0/0	Other live endangered plants(other than seedlings)
0/0/0	3.5	2	0/0	0/0/0	0/0	0//0	0/0/	9/9/9	/9			0/0/0	Other live plants (other than seedlings)
													Cut flowers and flower buds of a kind suitable for bouquets or for ornamental purposes, fresh, dried, dyed, bleached, impregnated or otherwise prepared:
													-Fresh:
0/0/0	3.5	2	0/0	0/0/0	0/0	0//0	0/0/	0/0/9	9.1/0		0//	0/0/0	--Roses
0/0/0	3.5	2	0/0	0/0/0	0/0	0//0	0/0/	0/0/9	9.1/0		0//	0/0/0	--Carnations
0/0/0	3.5	2	0/0	0/0/0	0/0	0//0	0/0/0	0/0/9	9.1/0		0//	0/0/0	--Orchids
0/0/0	3.5	2	0/0	0/0/0	0/0	0//0	0/0/	0/0/9	9.1/0		0//	0/0/0	--Chrysanthemums
0/0/0	3.5	2	0/0	0/0/0	0/0	0//0	0/0/	0/0/9	9.1/0		0//	0/0/0	--Lilies(Lilium spp.)
													--Other
0/0/0	3.5	2	0/0	0/0/0	0/0	0//0	0/0/	0/0/9	9.1/0		0//	0/0/0	Cut flowers and flower buds of endangered plants(of a kind suitable for bouquets or for ornamental purposes)fresh
0/0/0	3.5	2	0/0	0/0/0	0/0	0//0	0/0/	0/0/9	9.1/0		0//	0/0/0	Other cut flower and flower buds(of a kind suitable for bouquets or for ornamental purposes)fresh
													-Other
0/0/0	8.1	13.8	2.3/2.3	0/0/0	0/13.8	0//0	0/0/	21.9/21.9/23	21.9/21.9		0//	0/0/0	Cut flowers and flower buds of endangered plants(of a kind suitable for bouquets or for ornamental purposes), other than fresh dried, dyed or otherwise prepared, other than fresh
0/0/0	8.1	13.8	2.3/2.3	0/0/0	0/13.8	0//0	0/0/	21.9/21.9/23	21.9/21.9		0//	0/0/0	Other cut flowers and flower buds(of a kind suitable for bouquets or for ornamental purposes) dried, dyed or otherwise prepared, other than fresh
													Foliage, branches and other parts of plants, without flowers or flower-buds, and grasses, mosses and lichens, being goods of a kind suitable for bouquets or for ornamental purposes, fresh, dried, dyed, bleached, impregnated or otherwise prepared:
													-Fresh:
0/0/0	18.4	4.6	2.3/2.3	0/0/0	0/13.8	0//0	0/0/	0/0/20.7	20.9/0			0/0/0	---Mosses and lichens
													---Other
0/0/0	3.5	2	0/0	0/0/0	0/0	0//0	0/0/	0/0/9	9.1/0			0/0/0	Other foliage, branches and other parts of endangered plants, fresh, and grasses, without flowers or flower buds (being goods of a kind suitable for bouquets or for ornamental purposes)
0/0/0	3.5	2	0/0	0/0/0	0/0	0//0	0/0/	0/0/9	9.1/0			0/0/0	Other foliage, branches or other parts of plants, fresh, and grasses, without flowers or flower buds(being good of a kind suitable for bouquets or for ornamental prposes)
													-Other:
0/0/0	18.4	4.6	2.3/2.3	0/0/0	0/13.8	0//0	0/0/	0/0/20.7	20.9/0			0/0/0	---Mosses and liehens:
													---Other
0/0/0	3.5	2	0/0	0/0/0	0/0	0//0	0/0/	0/0/9	9.1/0			0/0/0	Other foliage, branches and other parts of endangered plants, and grasses without flowers or flower buds, (being goods of a kind suitable for bouquets or for ornamental purposes)
0/0/0	3.5	2	0/0	0/0/0	0/0	0//0	0/0/	0/0/9	9.1/0			0/0/0	Other foliage, branches and other parts of plants, and grasses without flowers or flower buds, (being goods of a kind sitable for banquets or for ornamental purposes)

第七章
食用蔬菜、根及块茎

注释：

一、本章不包括税号12.14的草料。

二、税号07.09、07.10、07.11及07.12所称"蔬菜"，包括食用的蘑菇、块菌、油橄榄、刺山柑、菜葫芦、南瓜、茄子、甜玉米、辣椒、茴香菜、欧芹、细叶芹、龙蒿、水芹、甜茉乔栾那。

三、税号07.12包括干制的归入税号07.01至07.11的各种蔬菜，但下列各项除外：
(一)作蔬菜用的脱荚干豆(税号07.13)；
(二)税目11.02至11.04所列形状的甜玉米；
(三)马铃薯细粉、粗粉、粉末、粉片、颗粒及团粒(税号11.05)；
(四)用税目07.13的干豆制成的细粉、粗粉及粉末(税目11.06)。

四、本章不包括辣椒干及辣椒粉(税目09.04)。

五、税目07.11适用于使用前在运输或贮存时仅为暂时保藏而进行处理（例如，使用二氧化硫气体、盐水、亚硫酸水或其他防腐液）的蔬菜，但不适于直接食用。

税则号列	货品名称〔CIQ扩展编码及品名－T2表示见附表2〕	最惠(%)	暂定税率	普通	增值/消费	出口退税	计量单位	监管条件/特殊证件	检验检疫	对美关税	亚太上/下
07.01	**鲜或冷藏的马铃薯：**										
0701.1000	-种用〔101种质资源；102种质资源除外〕	13		70	9/	0	千克	AB/	PQ	40.5	
0701.9000	-其他〔101替代种植；102替代种植除外；999〕	13		70	9/	0	千克	AB/	PRQS	43	9/9
07.02	**鲜或冷藏的番茄：**										
0702.0000	鲜或冷藏的番茄〔999〕	13		70	9/	0	千克	AB/	PRQS	43	
07.03	**鲜或冷藏的洋葱、青葱、大蒜、韭葱及其他葱属蔬菜：**										
	-洋葱及青葱：										
0703.1010	---洋葱〔999〕	13		70	9/	0	千克	AB/	PRQS	43	6.5/6.5
0703.1020	---青葱〔999〕	13		70	9/	0	千克	AB/	PRQS	43	6.5/6.5
	-大蒜：										
0703.2010	---蒜头〔101大蒜，102药用大蒜(蒜头)〕	13		70	9/	0	千克	AB/	PRQS	43	6.5/6.5
0703.2020	---蒜薹及蒜苗(青蒜)〔101蒜苔，102蒜苗，103青蒜〕	13		70	9/	0	千克	AB/	PRQS	43	6.5/6.5
0703.2090	---其他〔999〕	13		70	9/	0	千克	AB/	PRQS	43	6.5/6.5
	-韭葱及其他葱属蔬菜：										
0703.9010	---韭葱〔999〕	13		70	9/	0	千克	AB/	PRQS	43	
0703.9020	---大葱〔999〕	13		70	9/	0	千克	AB/	PRQS	43	
0703.9090	---其他〔101分葱，102荞头，999分葱、荞头除外〕	13		70	9/	0	千克	AB/	PRQS	43	
07.04	**鲜或冷藏的卷心菜、菜花、球茎甘蓝、羽衣甘蓝及类似的食用芥菜类蔬菜：**										
	-菜花及西兰花：										
0704.1010	---菜花〔999〕	10		70	9/	0	千克	AB/	PRQS	40	
0704.1090	---其他										
0704.1090 10	鲜或冷的硬花甘蓝〔101羽衣甘蓝，102羽衣甘蓝除外〕	11		70	9/	0	千克	AB/	PRQS	41	
0704.1090 90	鲜或冷的西兰花〔999〕	11		70	9/	0	千克	AB/	PRQS	41	
0704.2000	-抱子甘蓝〔999〕	13		70	9/	0	千克	AB/	PRQS	43	
	-其他：										
0704.9010	---卷心菜〔999〕	13		70	9/	0	千克	AB/	PRQS	43	
0704.9090	---其他										
0704.9090 01	鲜、冷其他甘蓝〔999〕	13		70	9/	0	千克	AB/	PRQS	43	
0704.9090 90	鲜或冷藏的其他食用芥菜类蔬菜〔101芥蓝，999芥蓝除外〕	13		70	9/	0	千克	AB/	PRQS	43	
07.05	**鲜或冷藏的莴苣及菊苣：**										
	-莴苣：										
0705.1100	--结球莴苣(包心生菜)〔999〕	10		70	9/	0	千克	AB/	PRQS	40	
0705.1900	--其他〔101莴苣，999莴苣除外〕	10		70	9/	0	千克	AB/	PRQS	40	
	-菊苣：										
0705.2100	--维特罗夫菊苣〔999〕	13		70	9/	0	千克	AB/	PRQ	43	
0705.2900	--其他〔101莴苣，999莴苣除外〕	13		70	9/	0	千克	AB/	PRQ	43	
07.06	**鲜或冷藏的胡萝卜、芜菁、色拉甜菜根、婆罗门参、块根芹、萝卜及类似的食用根茎：**										
0706.1000	-胡萝卜及芜菁										
0706.1000 01	鲜、冷胡萝卜〔999〕	13		70	9/	0	千克	AB/	PRQS	43	
0706.1000 90	鲜或冷藏的芜菁〔999〕	13		70	9/	0	千克	AB/	PRQS	43	
0706.9000	-其他〔101小萝卜，102小萝卜类似食用根茎(芜菁)，103其他鲜或冷藏的小萝卜及类似食用根茎〕	13		70	9/	0	千克	AB/	PRQS	43	
07.07	**鲜或冷藏的黄瓜及小黄瓜：**										
0707.0000	鲜或冷藏的黄瓜及小黄瓜〔999〕	13		70	9/	0	千克	AB/	PRQS	43	6.5/6.5
07.08	**鲜或冷藏的豆类蔬菜，不论是否脱荚：**										
0708.1000	-豌豆〔999〕	13		70	9/	0	千克	AB/	PRQS	43	6.5/6.5
0708.2000	-豇豆属及菜豆属〔101豇豆，102菜豆〕	13		70	9/	0	千克	AB/	PRQS	43	6.5/6.5
0708.9000	-其他豆类蔬菜〔101：蚕豆；102：毛豆；103：四棱豆；104：豆苗；105：豆芽；106：其他豆科蔬菜〕	13		70	9/	0	千克	AB/	PRQS	43	6.5/6.5
07.09	**鲜或冷藏的其他蔬菜：**										
0709.2000	-芦笋〔999〕	13		70	9/	0	千克	AB/	PRQS	43	6.5/6.5
0709.3000	-茄子〔999〕	13		70	9/	0	千克	AB/	PRQS	43	6.5/6.5
0709.4000	-芹菜，但块根芹除外〔101欧芹，999欧芹除外〕	10		70	9/	0	千克	AB/	PRQS	40	
	-蘑菇及块菌：										
0709.5100	--伞菌属蘑菇〔999〕	13		90	9/	0	千克	AB/	PRQS	43	

Chapter 7
Edible vegetables and certain roots and tubers

Notes:

1. This Chapter does not cover forage products of heading 12.14.
2. In headings No. 07.09, 07.10, 07.11 and 07.12 the word "vegetables" includes edible mushrooms, truffles, olives, capers, marrows, pumpkins, aubergines, sweet corn (*Zea maysvar. saccharata*), fruits of the genus *Capsicum* or of the genus *Pimenta*, fennel, parsley, chervil, tarragon, cress and sweet marjoram (*Majorana hortensis or Origanum majorana*).
3. Heading No. 07.12 covers all dried vegetables of the kinds falling in headings No. 07.01 to 07.11, other than:
   (a) dried leguminous vegetables, shelled (heading No. 07.13);
   (b) sweet corn in the forms specified in headings No. 11.02 to 11.04;
   (c) flour, meal, powder, flakes, granules and pellets of potatoes (heading No. 11.05);
   (d) flour, meal and powder of the dried leguminous vegetables of heading No. 07.13 (heading No. 11.06).
4. However, dried or crushed or ground fruits of the genus *Capsicum* or of the genus *Pimenta* are excluded from this Chapter (heading No. 09.04).
5. Heading No.07.11 applies to vegetables which have been treated solely to ensure their provisional preservation during transport or storage prior to use (for example, by sulphur dioxide gas, in brine, in sulphur water or in other preservative solutions), provided they remain unsuitable for immediate consumption in that state.

协定税率 %								RCEP		特惠税率 %			Article Description
东/冰/格	巴基斯坦	韩国	瑞士上/下	哥/秘/柬	澳/毛	新西/坡/智	中国港/澳/台	东盟及马来/澳/韩	日/新	亚太2国	老/柬/缅	98/97/95	
													Potatoes, fresh or chilled:
0//0	4.6	2.6	1.3/1.3	0/0/0	0/0	0//0	0/0/	0/0/11.7	11.8/0			0/0/0	-Seeds
0/0/0	3.5	2.6	1.3/1.3	0/0/0	0/0	0//0	0/0/	0/0/11.7	11.8/0		/0/	0/0/0	-Other
													Tomatoes, fresh or chilled:
0/0/0	4.6	2.6	1.3/1.3	0/0/0	0/0	0//0	0/0/	0/0/11.7	11.8/0			0/0/0	Tomatoes, fresh or chilled
													Onions, shallots, garlic, leeks and other alliaceous vegetables, fresh or chilled:
													-Onions and shallots:
0/0/0	3.5	2.6	1.3/1.3	0/0/0	0/0	0//0	0/0/	0/0/11.7	11.8/0		/0/0	0/0/0	---Onions
0/0/0	3.5	2.6	1.3/1.3	0/0/0	0/0	0//0	0/0/	0/0/11.7	11.8/0		/0/0	0/0/0	---Shallots
													-Garlic:
0/0/0	0	2.6	1.3/1.3	0/0/0	0/0	0//0	0/0/	0/0/11.7	11.8/0			0/0/0	---Garlic bulbs
0/0/0	0	2.6	1.3/1.3	0/0/0	0/0	0//0	0/0/	0/0/11.7	11.8/0			0/0/0	---Garlic stems, garlic seedlings
0/0/0	0	2.6	1.3/1.3	0/0/0	0/0	0//0	0/0/	0/0/11.7	11.8/0			0/0/0	---Other
													-Leeks and other alliaceous vegetables:
0/0/0	4.6	2.6	1.3/1.3	0/0/0	0/0	0//0	0/0/	0/0/11.7	11.8/0		/0/	0/0/0	---Leeks
0/0/0	4.6	2.6	1.3/1.3	0/0/0	0/0	0//0	0/0/	0/0/11.7	11.8/0		/0/	0/0/0	---Scallion
0/0/0	4.6	2.6	1.3/1.3	0/0/0	0/0	0//0	0/0/	0/0/11.7	11.8/0		/0/	0/0/0	---Other
													Cabbages, cauliflowers, kohlrabi, kale and similar edible brassicas, fresh or chilled:
													-Cauliflowers and broccoli:
0//0	3.5	2	0/0	0/0/0	0/0	0//0	0/0/	0/0/9	9.1/0			0/0/0	---Cauliflowers
													---Other
0/0/0	4.1	2.3	0.7/0.7	0/0/0	0/0	0//0	0/0/	0/0/9	9.1/0		0//	0/0/0	Fresh or cold Kale
0/0/0	4.1	2.3	0.7/0.7	0/0/0	0/0	0//0	0/0/	0/0/9	9.1/0		0//	0/0/0	Fresh or cold broccoli
0/0/0	4.6	2.6	1.3/1.3	0/0/0	0/0	0//0	0/0/	0/0/11.7	11.8/0			0/0/0	-Brussels sprouts
													-Other:
0/0/0	4.6	2.6	1.3/1.3	0/0/0	0/0	0//0	0/0/	0/0/11.7	11.8/0		0//	0/0/0	---Cabbage(Brassica oleracea var.capitata)
													---Other
0/0/0	4.6	2.6	1.3/1.3	0/0/0	0/0	0//0	0/0/	0/0/11.7	11.8/0		0//	0/0/0	Other Cabbage, fresh or chilled
0/0/0	4.6	2.6	1.3/1.3	0/0/0	0/0	0//0	0/0/	0/0/11.7	11.8/0		0//	0/0/0	Other edible brassicas, fresh or chilled
													Lettuce(*lactuca sativa*) and chicory (*Cichorium spp.*), fresh or chilled:
													-Lettuce:
0/0/0	0	2	0/0	0/0/0	0/0	0//0	0/0/	0/0/9	9.1/0			0/0/0	--Cabbage lettuce (head lettuce)
0/0/0	0	2	0/0	0/0/0	0/0	0//0	0/0/	0/0/9	9.1/0			0/0/0	--Other
													-Chicory:
0/0/0	0	2.6	1.3/1.3	0/0/0	0/0	0//0	0/0/	0/0/11.7	11.8/0			0/0/0	--Witloof chicory (*Cichoriym intybus var. foliosum*)
0/0/0	0	2.6	1.3/1.3	0/0/0	0/0	0//0	0/0/	0/0/11.7	11.8/0			0/0/0	--Other
													Carrots, turnips, salad beetroot, salsify, celeriac, radishes and similar edible roots, fresh or chilled:
													-Carrots and turnips
0//0	4.6	2.6	1.3/1.3	0/0/0	0/0	0//0	0/0/	0/0/11.7	11.8/0			0/0/0	Carrots, fresh or chilled
0//0	4.6	2.6	1.3/1.3	0/0/0	0/0	0//0	0/0/	0/0/11.7	11.8/0			0/0/0	Turnips, fresh or chilled
0/0/0	4.6	2.6	1.3/1.3	0/0/0	0/0	0//0	0/0/	0/0/11.7	11.8/0			0/0/0	-Other
													Cucumbers and gherkins, fresh or chilled:
0/0/0	3.5	2.6	1.3/1.3	0/0/0	0/0	0//0	0/0/	0/0/11.7	11.8/0		/0/	0/0/0	Cucumbers and gherkins, fresh or chilled
													Leguminous vegetables, shelled or unshelled, fresh or chilled:
0/0/0	0	2.6	1.3/1.3	0/0/0	0/0	0//0	0/0/	0/0/11.7	11.8/0		/0/	0/0/0	-Peas (*Pisum sativum*)
0/0/0	0	2.6	1.3/1.3	0/0/0	0/0	0//0	0/0/	0/0/11.7	11.8/0		0/0/	0/0/0	-Beans (*Vigna spp.*, *Phaseolus spp.*)
0/0/0	0	2.6	1.3/1.3	0/0/0	0/0	0//0	0/0/	0/0/11.7	11.8/0		/0/	0/0/0	-Other leguminous vegetables
													Other vegetables, fresh or chilled:
0/0/0	0	2.6	1.3/1.3	0/0/0	0/0	0//0	0/0/	0/0/11.7	11.8/0			0/0/0	-Asparagus
0/0/0	0	2.6	1.3/1.3	0/0/0	0/0	0//0	0/0/	0/0/11.7	11.8/0			0/0/0	-Aubergines (egg-plants)
0/0/0	0	2	0/0	0/0/0	0/0	0//0	0/0/	0/0/9	9.1/0			0/0/0	-Celery, other than celeriac
													-Mushrooms and truffles:
0/0/0	0	2.6	1.3/1.3	0/0/0	0/0	0//0	0/0/	0/0/11.7	11.8/0		/0/	0/0/0	--Mushrooms of the genus *Agaricus*

税则号列	货品名称〔CIQ 扩展编码及品名－T2 表示见附表 2〕	最惠(%)	暂定税率	普通	增值/消费	出口退税	计量单位	监管条件/特殊证件	检验检疫	对美关税	亚太上/下
0709.5200	--牛肝菌属蘑菇〔999〕	13		90	9/	0	千克	AB/	PRQS	43	
0709.5300	--鸡油菌属蘑菇〔999〕	13		90	9/	0	千克	AB/	PRQS	43	
0709.5400	--香菇〔999〕	13		90	9/	0	千克	AB/	PRQS	43	
0709.5500	--松茸(松口蘑、美洲松口蘑、雪松口蘑、甜味松口蘑、欧洲松口蘑)〔999〕	13		90	9/	0	千克	ABE/	PRQS	43	
0709.5600	--块菌(松露属)〔999〕	13		90	9/	9	千克	AB/	PRQS	43	
	--其他：										
0709.5910	---其他松茸〔999〕	13		90	9/	0	千克	ABE/	PRQS	43	
0709.5930	---金针菇〔999〕	13		90	9/	0	千克	AB/	PRQS	43	
0709.5940	---草菇〔999〕	13		90	9/	0	千克	AB/	PRQS	43	
0709.5950	---口蘑〔999〕	13		90	9/	0	千克	AB/	PRQS	43	
0709.5960	---其他块菌〔101 银耳,102 木耳,103 其他块菌〕	13		90	9/	9	千克	AB/	PRQS	43	
0709.5990	---其他〔101 杏鲍菇,102 猴头菇,103 姬菇,104 平菇,105 秀珍菇,107 其他食用菌,108 双孢菇〕	13		90	9/	0	千克	AB/	PRQS	43	
0709.6000	-辣椒属及多香果属的果实(包括甜椒)〔999〕	13		70	9/	0	千克	AB/	PRQS	43	6.5/6.5
0709.7000	-菠菜〔999〕	13		70	9/	0	千克	AB/	PRQS	43	
	-其他：										
0709.9100	--洋蓟〔999〕	13		70	9/	9	千克	AB/	PRQS	43	
0709.9200	--油橄榄〔999〕	13		70	9/	9	千克	AB/	PRQS	43	
0709.9300	--南瓜、笋瓜及瓠瓜(南瓜属)〔101 南瓜,102 笋瓜,103 瓠瓜〕	13		70	9/	0	千克	AB/	PRQS	43	
	--其他：										
0709.9910	---竹笋										
0709.9910 10	鲜或冷藏的酸竹笋〔999〕	13		70	9/	0	千克	ABE/	PRQS	43	
0709.9910 90	鲜或冷藏的其他竹笋〔999〕	13		70	9/	0	千克	AB/	PRQS	43	
0709.9990	---其他										
0709.9990 01	鲜或冷藏的丝瓜〔999〕	13		70	9/	0	千克	AB/	PRQS	43	
0709.9990 02	鲜或冷藏的青江菜〔999〕	13		70	9/	0	千克	AB/	PRQS	43	
0709.9990 03	鲜或冷藏的小白菜〔999〕	13		70	9/	0	千克	AB/	PRQS	43	
0709.9990 04	鲜或冷藏的苦瓜〔999〕	13		70	9/	0	千克	AB/	PRQS	43	
0709.9990 05	鲜或冷藏的山葵〔999〕	13		70	9/	0	千克	AB/	PRQS	43	
0709.9990 10	鲜或冷藏的莼菜〔999〕	13		70	9/	0	千克	ABE/	PRQS	43	
0709.9990 90	鲜或冷藏的其他蔬菜[T2]	13		70	9/	0	千克	AB/	PRQS	43	
07.10	**冷冻蔬菜(不论是否蒸煮)：**										
0710.1000	-马铃薯〔999〕	13		70	9/	0,9	千克	AB/	PRQS	28	
	-豆类蔬菜,不论是否脱荚：										
0710.2100	--豌豆〔999〕	13		70	9/	0,9	千克	AB/	PRQS	43	
	--豇豆属及菜豆属：										
0710.2210	---红小豆(赤豆)〔999〕	13		70	9/	0,9	千克	AB/	PRQS	15.5	
0710.2290	---其他〔101 豇豆,102 菜豆〕	13		70	9/	0,9	千克	AB/	PRQS	28	
0710.2900	--其他〔999〕	13		70	9/	0,9	千克	AB/	PRQS	43	
0710.3000	-菠菜〔999〕	13		70	9/	0,9	千克	AB/	PRQS	43	
0710.4000	-甜玉米〔999〕	10		70	9/	0,9	千克	AB/	PRQS	25	
	-其他蔬菜：										
0710.8010	---松茸〔999〕	13		70	9/	0,9	千克	ABE/	PRQS	15.5	
0710.8020	---蒜薹及蒜苗(青蒜)〔101 蒜苔,102 蒜苗,103 青蒜〕	13		70	9/	0,9	千克	AB/	PRQS	15.5	
0710.8030	---蒜头〔999〕	13		70	9/	0,9	千克	AB/	PRQS	15.5	
0710.8040	---牛肝菌〔999〕	13		70	9/	0,9	千克	AB/	PRQS	15.5	
0710.8090	---其他										
0710.8090 10	冷冻的大蒜瓣(不论是否蒸煮)〔999〕	13		70	9/	0,9	千克	AB/	PRQS	28	
0710.8090 20	冷冻的香菇(不论是否蒸煮)〔999〕	13		70	9/	0,9	千克	AB/	PRQS	28	
0710.8090 30	冷冻莼菜(不论是否蒸煮)〔999〕	13		70	9/	0,9	千克	ABE/	PRQS	28	
0710.8090 90	冷冻的未列名蔬菜(不论是否蒸煮)[T2]	13		70	9/	0,9	千克	AB/	PRQS	28	
0710.9000	-什锦蔬菜〔999〕	10		70	9/	0,9	千克	AB/	PRQS	25	
07.11	**暂时保藏的蔬菜,但不适于直接食用的：**										
0711.2000	-油橄榄〔999〕	13		70	9/	9	千克	AB/	PRQS	15.5	
0711.4000	-黄瓜及小黄瓜〔999〕	13		70	9/	9	千克	AB/	PRQS	15.5	
	-蘑菇及块菌：										
	--伞菌属蘑菇：										
	---盐水的：										
0711.5112	----白蘑菇〔999〕	13		90	9/	9	千克	AB/	PRQS	15.5	
0711.5119	----其他〔101 腌渍草菇,102 腌渍姬菇,103 腌渍口蘑,104 腌渍其他食用菌〕	13		90	9/	9	千克	AB/	PRQS	15.5	
0711.5190	---其他〔101 腌渍草菇,102 腌渍姬菇,103 腌渍口蘑,104 腌渍其他食用菌〕	13		90	9/	9	千克	AB/	PRQS	15.5	
	--其他：										
	---盐水的：										
0711.5911	----松茸〔999〕	13		90	9/	9	千克	EAB/	PRQS	15.5	
0711.5919	----其他										

协定税率 %								RCEP		特惠税率 %			Article Description
东/冰/格	巴基斯坦	韩国	瑞士上/下	哥/秘/柬	澳/毛	新西/坡/智	中国港/澳/台	东盟及马来/澳/韩	日/新	亚太2国	老/柬/缅	98/97/95	
0/0/0	0	2.6	1.3/1.3	0/0/0	0/0	0//0	0/0/	0/0/11.7	11.8/0		/0/	0/0/0	-- Mushrooms of the genus Boletus
0/0/0	0	2.6	1.3/1.3	0/0/0	0/0	0//0	0/0/	0/0/11.7	11.8/0		/0/	0/0/0	-- Mushrooms of the genus Cantharellus
0/0/0	0	2.6	1.3/1.3	0/0/0	0/0	0//0	0/0/	0/0/11.7	11.8/0		/0/	0/0/0	-- Shiitake (Lentinus edodes)
0/0/0	0	2.6	1.3/1.3	0/0/0	0/0	0//0	0/0/	0/0/11.7	11.8/0		/0/	0/0/0	-- Matsutake (Tricholoma matsutake, Tricholoma magnivelare, Tricholoma anatolicum, Tricholoma dulciolens, Tricholoma caligatum)
0/0/0	0	2.6	1.3/1.3	0/0/0	0/0	0//0	0/0/	0/0/11.7	11.8/0			0/0/0	--Truffles (truffles)
													--Other:
0/0/0	0	2.6	1.3/1.3	0/0/0	0/0	0//0	0/0/	0/0/11.7	11.8/0		/0/	0/0/0	---Other Sungmo
0/0/0	0	2.6	1.3/1.3	0/0/0	0/0	0//0	0/0/0	0/0/11.7	11.8/0		/0/	0/0/0	---Winter mushroom
0/0/0	0	2.6	1.3/1.3	0/0/0	0/0	0//0	0/0/	0/0/11.7	11.8/0		/0/	0/0/0	---Paddy straw mushroom
0/0/0	0	2.6	1.3/1.3	0/0/0	0/0	0//0	0/0/	0/0/11.7	11.8/0		/0/	0/0/0	---Tricholoma mongolicum Imai
0/0/0	0	2.6	1.3/1.3	0/0/0	0/0	0//0	0/0/	0/0/11.7	11.8/0			0/0/0	---Other Truffle
0/0/0	0	2.6	1.3/1.3	0/0/0	0/0	0//0	0/0/	0/0/11.7	11.8/0		/0/	0/0/0	---Other
0/0/0	0	2.6	1.3/1.3	0/0/0	0/0	0//0	0/0/	0/0/11.7	11.8/0		/0/	0/0/0	-Fruits of the genus *Capsicum* or of the genus *Pimenta*
0/0/0	0	2.6	1.3/1.3	0/0/0	0/0	0//0	0/0/	0/0/11.7	11.8/0			0/0/0	-Spinach, New Zealand spinach and orache spinach (garden spinach)
													-Other:
0/0/0	0	2.6	1.3/1.3	0/0/0	0/0	0//0	0/0/	0/0/11.7	11.8/0		/0/	0/0/0	--Globe artichokes
0/0/0	0	2.6	1.3/1.3	0/0/0	0/0	0//0	0/0/	0/0/11.7	11.8/0		/0/	0/0/0	--Olives
0/0/0	0	2.6	1.3/1.3	0/0/0	0/0	0//0	0/0/	0/0/11.7	11.8/0		/0/	0/0/0	--Pumpkin, squash and gourd (cucurbita spp.)
													--Other:
													---Bamboo shoots
0/0/0	0	2.6	1.3/1.3	0/0/0	0/0	0//0	0/0/	0/0/11.7	11.8/0		0/0/	0/0/0	Acidosasa shoots, fresh or chilled
0/0/0	0	2.6	1.3/1.3	0/0/0	0/0	0//0	0/0/	0/0/11.7	11.8/0		0/0/	0/0/0	Other bamboo shoots, fresh or chilled
													---Other
0/0/0	0	2.6	1.3/1.3	0/0/0	0/0	0//0	0/0/	0/0/11.7	11.8/0		/0/	0/0/0	Loofah, fresh or chilled
0/0/0	0	2.6	1.3/1.3	0/0/0	0/0	0//0	0/0/	0/0/11.7	11.8/0		/0/	0/0/0	Bok choy, fresh or chilled
0/0/0	0	2.6	1.3/1.3	0/0/0	0/0	0//0	0/0/	0/0/11.7	11.8/0		/0/	0/0/0	Pakchoi, fresh or chilled
0/0/0	0	2.6	1.3/1.3	0/0/0	0/0	0//0	0/0/	0/0/11.7	11.8/0		/0/	0/0/0	Balsum pear, fresh or chilled
0/0/0	0	2.6	1.3/1.3	0/0/0	0/0	0//0	0/0/	0/0/11.7	11.8/0		/0/	0/0/0	Horseradish, fresh or chilled
0/0/0	0	2.6	1.3/1.3	0/0/0	0/0	0//0	0/0/	0/0/11.7	11.8/0		/0/	0/0/0	Water shield, fresh or chilled
0/0/0	0	2.6	1.3/1.3	0/0/0	0/0	0//0	0/0/	0/0/11.7	11.8/0		/0/	0/0/0	Other vegetables, fresh or chilled
													Vegetables (uncooked or cooked by steaming or boiling in water), frozen:
0//0	4.6	2.6	1.3/1.3	0/0/0	0/0	0//0	0/0/	0/0/11.7	11.8/0			0/0/0	-Potatoes
													-Leguminous vegetables, shelled or unshelled:
0/0/0	4.6	2.6	1.3/1.3	0/0/0	0/0	0//0	0/0/	0/0/11.7	11.8/0			0/0/0	--Peas (*Pisum sativum*)
													--Beans (*Vigna spp.*, *Phaseolus spp.*):
0/0/0	4.6	2.6	1.3/1.3	0/0/0	0/0	0//0	0/0/	0/0/11.7	11.8/0		/0/	0/0/0	---Adzuki beans
0/0/0	4.6	2.6	1.3/1.3	0/0/0	0/0	0//0	0/0/	0/0/11.7	11.8/0		/0/	0/0/0	---Other
0/0/0	4.6	2.6	1.3/1.3	0/0/0	0/0	0//0	0/0/	0/0/11.7	11.8/0		/0/	0/0/0	--Other
0/0/0	4.6	2.6	1.3/1.3	0/0/0	0/0	0//0	0/0/	0/0/11.7	11.8/0			0/0/0	-Spinach, New Zealand spinach and orache spinach (garden spinach)
0/0/0	3.5	2	0/0	0/0/0	0/0	0//0	0/0/	0/0/9	9.1/0			0/0/0	-Sweet corn
													-Other vegetables:
0/0/0	4.6	2.6	1.3/1.3	0/0/0	0/0	0//0	0/0/	0/0/11.7	11.8/0		/0/	0/0/0	---Sungmo
0/0/0	4.6	2.6	1.3/1.3	0/0/0	0/0	0//0	0/0/	0/0/11.7	11.8/0		/0/	0/0/0	---Garlic stems, garlic seedlings
0/0/0	4.6	2.6	1.3/1.3	0/0/0	0/0	0//0	0/0/	0/0/11.7	11.8/0		/0/	0/0/0	---Garlic bulbs
0/0/0	4.6	2.6	1.3/1.3	0/0/0	0/0	0//0	0/0/	0/0/11.7	11.8/0		/0/	0/0/0	---Boletus (Porcini)
													---Other
0/0/0	4.6	2.6	1.3/1.3	0/0/0	0/0	0//0	0/0/	0/0/11.7	11.8/0		/0/	0/0/0	Garlic cloves, frozen (uncooked or cooked by steaming or boiling in water)
0/0/0	4.6	2.6	1.3/1.3	0/0/0	0/0	0//0	0/0/	0/0/11.7	11.8/0		/0/	0/0/0	Shiitake, frozen (uncooked or cooked by steaming or boiling in water)
0/0/0	4.6	2.6	1.3/1.3	0/0/0	0/0	0//0	0/0/	0/0/11.7	11.8/0		/0/	0/0/0	Water shield, frozen (uncooked or cooked by steaming or boiling in water)
0/0/0	4.6	2.6	1.3/1.3	0/0/0	0/0	0//0	0/0/	0/0/11.7	11.8/0		/0/	0/0/0	Vegetables, frozen, not elsewhere specified or included (uncooked or cooked by steaming or boiling in water)
0/0/0	3.5	2	0/0	0/0/0	0/0	0//0	0/0/	0/0/9	9.1/0		/0/	0/0/0	-Mixtures of vegetables
													Vegetables provisionally preserved, but unsuitable in that state for immediate consumption:
0/0/0	0	2.6	1.3/1.3	0/0/0	0/0	0//0	0/0/	0/0/11.7	11.8/0			0/0/0	-Olives
0/0/0	0	2.6	1.3/1.3	0/0/0	0/0	0//0	0/0/	0/0/11.7	11.8/0			0/0/0	-Cucumbers and gherkins
													-Mushrooms and truffles:
													--Mushrooms of the genus *Agaricus*:
													---In brine:
0/0/0	0	2.6	1.3/1.3	0/0/0	0/0	0//0	0/0/	0/0/11.7	11.8/0			0/0/0	----White mushroom
0/0/0	0	2.6	1.3/1.3	0/0/0	0/0	0//0	0/0/	0/0/11.7	11.8/0			0/0/0	----Other
0/0/0	0	2.6	1.3/1.3	0/0/0	0/0	0//0	0/0/	0/0/11.7	11.8/0			0/0/0	---Other
													--Other:
													---In brine:
0/0/0	0	2.6	1.3/1.3	0/0/0	0/0	0//0	0/0/	0/0/11.7	11.8/0			0/0/0	----Sungmo
													----Other

税则号列		货品名称〔CIQ 扩展编码及品名－T2 表示见附表 2〕	最惠(%)	暂定税率	普通	增值/消费	出口退税	计量单位	监管条件/特殊证件	检验检疫	对美关税	亚太上/下
0711.5919	10	盐水的香菇(不适于直接食用的)〔999〕	13		90	9/	9	千克	AB/	PRQS	15.5	
0711.5919	90	盐水的其他非伞菌属蘑菇及块菌(不适于直接食用的)〔101 腌渍牛肝菌,102 腌渍其他块菌〕	13		90	9/	9	千克	AB/	PRQS	15.5	
0711.5990		---其他										
0711.5990	10	暂时保藏的香菇(不适于直接食用的)〔999〕	13		90	9/	9	千克	AB/	PRQS	15.5	
0711.5990	90	暂时保藏的蘑菇及块菌(不适于直接食用的)〔101 腌渍蘑菇,102 腌渍其他块菌〕	13		90	9/	9	千克	AB/	PRQS	15.5	
		-其他蔬菜;什锦蔬菜:										
		---盐水的:										
0711.9031		----竹笋										
0711.9031	10	盐水酸竹笋(不适于直接食用的)〔999〕	13		70	9/	9	千克	ABE/	PRQS	15.5	6.5/6.5
0711.9031	90	其他盐水竹笋(不适于直接食用的)〔999〕	13		70	9/	9	千克	AB/	PRQS	15.5	6.5/6.5
0711.9034		----大蒜										
0711.9034	10	盐水简单腌制的大蒜头、大蒜瓣(无论是否去皮,但不适于直接食用)〔999〕	13		70	9/	9	千克	AB/	PRQS	15.5	6.5/6.5
0711.9034	90	盐水简单腌制的其他大蒜(不含蒜头、蒜瓣,无论是否去皮,但不适于直接食用)〔999〕	13		70	9/	9	千克	AB/	PRQS	15.5	6.5/6.5
0711.9039		----其他[T2]	13		70	9/	9	千克	AB/	PRQS	15.5	6.5/6.5
0711.9090		---其他[T2]	13		90	9/	9	千克	AB/	PRQS	15.5	6.5/6.5
07.12		**干蔬菜,整个、切块、切片、破碎或制成粉状,但未经进一步加工的:**										
0712.2000		-洋葱〔999〕	13		80	9/	0,9	千克	AB/	PRQS	43	
		-蘑菇、木耳、银耳及块菌:										
0712.3100		--伞菌属蘑菇〔101 脱水杏鲍菇,102 脱水姬菇,103 脱水秀珍菇,104 脱水姬松茸〕	13		80	9/	0,9	千克	AB/	PRQS	43	9/9
0712.3200		--木耳〔999〕	13		100	9/	0,9,13	千克	AB/	PRQS	43	
0712.3300		--银耳〔999〕	13		90	9/	0,9,13	千克	AB/	PRQS	43	
0712.3400		--香菇〔999〕	13		100	9/	0,9,13	千克	AB/	PRQS	43	9/9
		--其他:										
0712.3920		---金针菇〔999〕	13		100	9/	0,9	千克	AB/	PRQS	43	9/9
0712.3950		---牛肝菌〔999〕	13		100	9/	0,9	千克	AB/	PRQS	43	9/9
		---其他:										
0712.3991		----羊肚菌〔999〕	13		100	9/	0,9	千克	AB/	PRQS	43	9/9
0712.3999		----其他										
0712.3999	10	干制松茸(整个,切块,切片,破碎或制成粉状,但未经进一步加工的)〔999〕	13		100	9/	0,9	千克	ABE/	PRQS	43	9/9
0712.3999	90	其他干制蘑菇及块菌(整个,切块,切片,破碎或制成粉状,但未经进一步加工的)〔101 脱水蘑菇,102 脱水猴头菇,103 脱水平菇,104 脱水其他块菌,105 脱水竹荪,106 脱水其他食用菌,107 干制榛蘑〕	13		100	9/	0,9	千克	AB/	PRQS	43	9/9
		-其他蔬菜;什锦蔬菜:										
0712.9010		---笋干丝										
0712.9010	10	酸竹笋干丝〔999〕	13		80	9/	0	千克	ABE/	PRQS	43	
0712.9010	90	其他笋干丝〔999〕	13		80	9/	0	千克	AB/	PRQS	43	
0712.9020		---紫萁(薇菜干)〔999〕	13		80	9/	0,9	千克	AB/	PRQS	43	
0712.9030		---金针菜(黄花菜)〔999〕	13		80	9/	0,9	千克	AB/	PRQS	43	
0712.9040		---蕨菜〔999〕	13		80	9/	0,9	千克	AB/	PRQS	43	
0712.9050		---大蒜										
0712.9050	10	干燥或脱水的大蒜头、大蒜瓣(无论是否去皮)〔999〕	13		80	13/	0	千克	AB/	PRQS	43	
0712.9050	90	干燥或脱水的其他大蒜(不含蒜头、蒜瓣,无论是否去皮)〔999〕	13		80	13/	0,9,13	千克	AB/	PRQS	43	
		---其他:										
0712.9091		----辣根〔999〕	13		80	9/	0,9,13	千克	AB/	PRQS	43	
0712.9099		----其他										
0712.9099	10	干莼菜(整个、切块、切片、破碎或制成粉状,但未经进一步加工的)〔999〕	13		80	9/	0,9	千克	ABE/	PRQS	43	
0712.9099	90	干制的其他蔬菜及什锦蔬菜(整个、切块、切片、破碎或制成粉状,但未经进一步加工的)[T2]	13		80	9/	0,9,13	千克	AB/	PRQS	43	
07.13		**脱荚的干豆,不论是否去皮或分瓣:**										
		-豌豆:										
0713.1010		---种用〔101 种质资源;102 种质资源除外〕	0		0	0/	0	千克	AB/	PNQ		
0713.1090		---其他〔101 食用,201 饲用〕	5		20	9/	0	千克	AB/	PRQS	32.5	
		-鹰嘴豆:										
0713.2010		---种用〔101 种质资源;102 种质资源除外〕	0		0	9/	9	千克	AB/	PNQ	25	
0713.2090		---其他〔999〕	7		20	9/	9	千克	AB/	PRQS	34.5	
		-豇豆属及菜豆属:										
		--绿豆:										

协定税率 %								RCEP		特惠税率 %			Article Description
东/冰/格	巴基斯坦	韩国	瑞士 上/下	哥/秘/柬	澳/毛	新西/坡/智	中国港/澳/台	东盟及马来/澳/韩	日/新	亚太2国	老/柬/缅	98/97/95	
0/0/0	0	2.6	1.3/1.3	0/0/0	0/0	0//0	0/0/	0/0/11.7	11.8/0			0/0/0	Shiitake, in brine(unsuitable in that state for immediate consumption)
0/0/0	0	2.6	1.3/1.3	0/0/0	0/0	0//0	0/0/	0/0/11.7	11.8/0			0/0/0	Other mushroom except the genus *Agaricus* and truffles, in brine, (unsuitable in that state for immediate consumption)
													---Other
0/0/0	0	2.6	1.3/1.3	0/0/0	0/0	0//0	0/0/	0/0/11.7	11.8/0			0/0/0	Temporarily preserved Lentinus edodes (not suitable for direct consumption)
0/0/0	0	2.6	1.3/1.3	0/0/0	0/0	0//0	0/0/	0/0/11.7	11.8/0			0/0/0	Temporarily preserved mushrooms and truffles (not suitable for direct consumption)
													-Other vegetables; mixtures of vegetables:
													---In brine:
													----Bamboo shoots
0/0/0	0	2.6	1.3/1.3	0/0/0	0/0	0//0	0/0/	0/0/11.7	11.8/0			0/0/0	Acidosasa chinensis shoots, in brine(unsuitable in that state for immediate consumption)
0/0/0	0	2.6	1.3/1.3	0/0/0	0/0	0//0	0/0/	0/0/11.7	11.8/0			0/0/0	Other bamboo shoots, in brine(unsuitable in that state for immediate consumption)
													----Garlic
0/0/0	0	2.6	1.3/1.3	0/0/0	0/0	0//0	0/0/	0/0/11.7	11.8/0			0/0/0	Garlic bulbs and garlic cloves, in brine(but unsuitable in that state for immediate consumption, whether skinned or not)
0/0/0	0	2.6	1.3/1.3	0/0/0	0/0	0//0	0/0/	0/0/11.7	11.8/0			0/0/0	Other garlic in brine (other than garlic bulbs, garlic cloves, whether or not skinned, but unsuitable in that state for immediate consumption)
0/0/0	0	2.6	1.3/1.3	0/0/0	0/0	0//0	0/0/	0/0/11.7	11.8/0			0/0/0	----Other
0/0/0	0	2.6	1.3/1.3	0/0/0	0/0	0//0	0/0/	0/0/11.7	11.8/0			0/0/0	---Other
													Dried vegetables, whole, cut, sliced, broken or in powder, but not further prepared:
0/0/0	4.6	2.6	1.3/1.3	0/0/0	0/0	0//0	0/0/	0/0/11.7	11.8/0			0/0/0	-Onions
													-Mushrooms, wood ears (*Auricularia spp.*), jelly fungi (*Tremella spp.*) and truffles:
0/0/0	3.5	2.6	1.3/1.3	0/0/0	0/0	0//0	0/0/	0/0/11.7	11.8/0			0/0/0	--Mushrooms of the genus *Agaricus*
0/0/0	4.6	2.6	1.3/1.3	0/0/0	0/0	0//0	0/0/	0/0/11.7	11.8/0			0/0/0	--Wood ears(*Auricularia spp.*)
0/0/0	4.6	2.6	1.3/1.3	0/0/0	0/0	0//0	0/0/	0/0/11.7	11.8/0			0/0/0	--Jelly fungi (*Tremella spp.*)
0/0/0	3.5	2.6	1.3/1.3	0/0/0	0/0	0//0	0/0/	0/0/11.7	11.8/0			0/0/0	--Shiitake
													--Other:
0/0/0	3.5	2.6	1.3/1.3	0/0/0	0/0	0//0	0/0/	0/0/11.7	11.8/0			0/0/0	---Winter mushroom
0/0/0	3.5	2.6	1.3/1.3	0/0/0	0/0	0//0	0/0/	0/0/11.7	11.8/0			0/0/0	---Boletus; Porcini
													---Other:
0/0/0	9	2.6	1.3/1.3	0/0/0	0/0	0//0	0/0/	0/0/11.7	11.8/0			0/0/0	----Toadsiool
													----Other
0/0/0	9	2.6	1.3/1.3	0/0/0	0/0	0//0	0/0/	0/0/11.7	11.8/0			0/0/0	Dried sungmo (whole, cut, sliced, broken or in powder, but not further prepared)
0/0/0	9	2.6	1.3/1.3	0/0/0	0/0	0//0	0/0/	0/0/11.7	11.8/0			0/0/0	Other dried Mushrooms and truffles (whole, cut, sliced, broken or in powder, but not further prepared)
													-Other vegetables; mixtures of vegetables:
													---Bamboo shoots
0/0/0	4.6	2.6	1.3/1.3	0/0/0	0/0	0//0	0/0/	0/0/11.7	11.8/0			0/0/0	Dried acidosasa chinensis shoots
0/0/0	4.6	2.6	1.3/1.3	0/0/0	0/0	0//0	0/0/	0/0/11.7	11.8/0			0/0/0	Other bamboo shoots
0/0/0	4.6	2.6	1.3/1.3	0/0/0	0/0	0//0	0/0/	0/0/11.7	11.8/0			0/0/0	---Osmund
0/0/0	4.6	2.6	1.3/1.3	0/0/0	0/0	0//0	0/0/	0/0/11.7	11.8/0			0/0/0	---Day lily flowers
0/0/0	4.6	2.6	1.3/1.3	0/0/0	0/0	0//0	0/0/	0/0/11.7	11.8/0			0/0/0	---Wild brake
													---Garlic
0/0/0	4.6	2.6	1.3/1.3	0/0/0	0/0	0//0	0/0/	0/0/11.7	11.8/0			0/0/0	Dried or dewatered garlic bulbs or garlic cloves(whether or not skinned)
0/0/0	4.6	2.6	1.3/1.3	0/0/0	0/0	0//0	0/0/	0/0/11.7	11.8/0			0/0/0	Other dried or dewatered garlic (other than garlic bulbs garlic cloves, whether or not skinned)
													---Other:
0/0/0	4.6	2.6	1.3/1.3	0/0/0	0/0	0//0	0/0/	0/0/11.7	11.8/0			0/0/0	----Horseradish
													----Other
0/0/0	4.6	2.6	1.3/1.3	0/0/0	0/0	0//0	0/0/	0/0/11.7	11.8/0			0/0/0	Dried water shield(whole, cut, sliced, broken or in powder, but not further prepared)
0/0/0	4.6	2.6	1.3/1.3	0/0/0	0/0	0//0	0/0/	0/0/11.7	11.8/0			0/0/0	Other dried vegetable and mixtures of vegetables(whole, cut, sliced, broken or in powder, but not further prepared)
													Dried leguminous vegetables, shelled, whether or not skinned or split:
													-Peas (*Pisum sativum*):
0/0/0	0	0	0/0	0/0/0	0/0	0//0	0/0/	0/0/0	0/0			0/0/0	---Seed
0/0/0	0	0	0/0	0/0/0	0/0	0//0	0/0/	0/0/0	0/0			0/0/0	---Other
													-Chickpeas (garbanzos):
0/0/0	0	0	0/0	0/0/0	0/0	0//0	0/0/	0/0/0	0/0			0/0/0	Seed
0/0/0	2	0	0/0	0/0/0	0/0	0//0	0/0/	0/0/0	0/0			0/0/0	---Other
													-Beans(Vigna spp., Phaseolus spp.):
													--Beans of the species *Vigna mungo* (*L.*) *Hepper or Vigna radiata* (*L.*) *Wilczek*:

税则号列	货品名称〔CIQ 扩展编码及品名—T2 表示见附表 2〕	最惠(%)	暂定税率	普通	增值/消费	出口退税	计量单位	监管条件/特殊证件	检验检疫	对美关税	亚太上/下
0713.3110	---种用〔101 种质资源;102 种质资源除外〕	0		0	9/	9	千克	AB/	PNQ	25	
0713.3190	---其他〔999〕	3		11	9/	9	千克	AB/	PRQS	30.5	1.5/1.5
	--红小豆(赤豆):										
0713.3210	---种用〔101 种质资源;102 种质资源除外〕	0		0	9/	9	千克	AB/	PNQ	25	
0713.3290	---其他〔101 干赤豆,102 药用赤小豆〕	3		14	9/	9	千克	AB/	PRQS	30.5	
	--芸豆:										
0713.3310	---种用〔101 种质资源;102 种质资源除外〕	0		0	0/	0	千克	AB/	PNQ		
0713.3390	---其他〔999〕	7.5		20	9/	0	千克	AB/	PRQS	37.5	
0713.3400	--巴姆巴拉豆〔999〕	7		20	9/	9	千克	AB/	PRQS	34.5	3.5/3.5
0713.3500	--牛豆(豇豆)〔101 豇豆,102 脱水豇豆〕	7		20	9/	9	千克	AB/	PRQS	34.5	3.5/3.5
0713.3900	--其他〔101 非种用豇豆;102 脱水豇豆;103 脱水菜豆;104 种用豇豆〕	7		20	9/	0	千克	AB/	PRQS	34.5	3.5/3.5
	-扁豆:										
0713.4010	---种用〔101 种质资源;102 种质资源除外〕	0		0	9/	0	千克	AB/	PNQ	25	
0713.4090	---其他〔101 干扁豆,102 药用白扁豆〕	7		20	9/	0	千克	AB/	PRQS	34.5	
	-蚕豆:										
0713.5010	---种用〔101 种质资源;102 种质资源除外〕	0		0	0/	9	千克	AB/	PNQ		
0713.5090	---其他〔999〕	7		20	9/	9	千克	AB/	PRQS	34.5	
	-木豆(木豆属):										
0713.6010	---种用〔999〕	0		0	9/	9	千克	AB/	PNQ	25	
0713.6090	---其他〔999〕	7		20	9/	9	千克	AB/	PRQS	34.5	
	-其他:										
0713.9010	---种用干豆〔101 种质资源;102 种质资源除外〕	0		0	0/	0	千克	AB/	PNQ		
0713.9090	---其他〔101 其他实用豆类,102 药用黑豆,103 红腰豆,104 角豆,105 眉豆,106 饭豆,107 黑豆,108 竹豆,109 珍珠豆,110 白豆,111 瓜尔豆,112 白凤豆〕	7		20	9/	0,9	千克	AB/	PRQS	34.5	
07.14	**鲜、冷、冻或干的木薯、竹芋、兰科植物块茎、菊芋、甘薯及含有高淀粉或菊粉的类似根茎,不论是否切片或制成团粒;西谷茎髓:**										
	-木薯:										
0714.1010	---鲜的〔999〕	10		30	9/	9	千克	7AB/	PRQS	37.5	
0714.1020	---干的〔101 饲用,替代种植除外;102 食品加工,替代种植除外;103 工业用,替代种植除外;104 替代种植〕	5		30	9/	9	千克	7AB/	PRQS	30	
0714.1030	---冷或冻的〔999〕	10		80	9/	9	千克	7AB/	PRQ	12.5	
	-甘薯:										
	---鲜的:										
0714.2011	----种用〔101 种质资源;102 种质资源除外〕	0		50	9/	0	千克	AB/	PQ	25	
0714.2019	----其他〔999〕	13		50	9/	0	千克	AB/	PRQS	43	6.5/6.5
0714.2020	---干的〔999〕	13		50	9/	0	千克	AB/	PRQS	43	6.5/6.5
0714.2030	---冷或冻的〔101 冷藏甘薯,102 冻藏甘薯〕	13		80	9/	0	千克	AB/	PRQS	38	6.5/6.5
0714.3000	-山药〔101 鲜、冷的山药,102 冷冻山药,103 脱水山药,104 药用山药〕	13		50	9/	0	千克	AB/	PRQ	43	6.5/6.5
0714.4000	-芋头(芋属)										
0714.4000 01	鲜、冷的芋头(芋属)(不论是否切片或制成团粒;芋头又称芋艿,为天南星科芋属植物,分旱芋、水芋)〔999〕	13		50	9/	0	千克	AB/	PRQ	43	6.5/6.5
0714.4000 90	冻、干的芋头(芋属)(不论是否切片或制成团粒;芋头又称芋艿,为天南星科芋属植物,分旱芋、水芋)〔101 冷冻芋头,102 脱水芋头〕	13		50	9/	0	千克	AB/	PRQ	43	6.5/6.5
0714.5000	-箭叶黄体芋(黄肉芋属)〔101 鲜、冷箭叶黄体芋,102 冷冻箭叶黄体芋,103 脱水箭叶黄体芋〕	13		50	9/	9	千克	AB/	PRQ	43	6.5/6.5
	-其他:										
0714.9010	---荸荠〔101 鲜、冷的马蹄(荸荠),102 冷冻马蹄(荸荠),103 脱水马蹄(荸荠)〕	13		50	9/	0	千克	AB/	PRQS	43	6.5/6.5
	---藕:										
0714.9021	----种用〔999〕	0		0	9/	0	千克	AB/	PNQ	25	
0714.9029	----其他〔101 鲜、冷的莲藕,102 冷冻莲藕,103 脱水莲藕〕	13		50	9/	0	千克	AB/	PRQS	43	6.5/6.5
0714.9090	---其他										
0714.9090 10	鲜、冷、冻、干的兰科植物块茎〔101:鲜、冷、干的兰科植物块茎;999:冻的兰科植物块茎〕	13		50	9/	0	千克	ABFE/	PRQ	43	6.5/6.5
0714.9090 91	含高淀粉或菊粉其他濒危类似根茎(包括西谷茎髓,不论是否切片或制成团粒,鲜、冷、冻或干的)〔101:鲜、冷的;102:冷冻的;103:干的;104:腌渍的;999:其他鳞球块根茎〕	13		50	9/	0	千克	ABFE/	PRQ	43	6.5/6.5
0714.9090 99	含有高淀粉或菊粉的其他类似根茎(包括西谷茎髓,不论是否切片或制成团粒,鲜、冷、冻或干的)〔101 鲜、冷的,102 冷冻的,103 干的,104 腌渍的,999 其他鳞球块根茎〕	13		50	9/	0	千克	AB/	PRQ	43	6.5/6.5

协定税率 %								RCEP		特惠税率 %			Article Description
东/冰/格	巴基斯坦	韩国	瑞士上/下	哥/秘/柬	澳/毛	新西/坡/智	中国港/澳/台	东盟及马来/澳/韩	日/新	亚太2国	老/柬/缅	98/97/95	
0/0/0	0	0	0/0	0/0/0	0/0	0//0	0/0/	0/0/0	0/0			0/0/0	---Seed
0/0/0	0	0	0/0	0/0/0	0/0	0//0	0/0/	0/2.7/0	0/2.7		/0/0	0/0/0	---Other
													--Small red (Adzuki) beans (*Phaseolus* or *Vigna angularis*):
0/0/0	0	0	0/0	0/0/0	0/0	0//0	0/0/	0/0/0	0/0			0/0/0	---Seed
0/0/0	0	0	0/0	0/0/0	0/0	0//0	0/0/	0/0/0	0/0		/0/	0/0/0	---Other
													--Kidney beans, including white pea-beans (*Phaseolus vulgaris*):
0/0/0	0	0	0/0	0/0/0	0/0	0//0	0/0/	0/0/0	0/0			0/0/0	---Seed
0/0/0	2	0	0/0	0/0/0	0/0	0//0	0/0/	0/0/0	0/0		/0/	0/0/0	---Other
0/0/0	0	0	0/0	0/0/0	0/0	0//0	0/0/	0/0/0	0/0		/0/	0/0/0	--Bambara beans (Vigna subterranea or Voandzeia subterranea)
0/0/0	0	0	0/0	0/0/0	0/0	0//0	0/0/	0/0/0	0/0		/0/	0/0/0	--Cow peas(Vigna unguiculata)
0/0/0	0	0	0/0	0/0/0	0/0	0//0	0/0/	0/0/0	0/0		/0/	0/0/0	--Other
													-Lentils:
0/0/0	0	0	0/0	0/0/0	0/0	0//0	0/0/	0/0/0	0/0			0/0/0	---Seed
0/0/0	2	0	0/0	0/0/0	0/0	0//0	0/0/	0/0/0	0/0			0/0/0	---Other
													-Broad beans (*Vicia faba var. Major*) and horse beans (*Vicia faba var. equina*, *Vicia faba var. minor*):
0/0/0	0	0	0/0	0/0/0	0/0	0//0	0/0/	0/0/0	0/0			0/0/0	---Seed
0/0/0	2	0	0/0	0/0/0	0/0	0//0	0/0/	0/0/0	0/0			0/0/0	---Other
													-Pigeon peas(Cajanus cajan):
0/0/0	0	0	0/0	0/0/0	0/0	0//0	0/0/	0/0/0	0/0			0/0/0	---Seed
0/0/0	2	0	0/0	0/0/0	0/0	0//0	0/0/	0/0/0	0/0			0/0/0	---Other
													-Other:
0/0/0	0	0	0/0	0/0/0	0/0	0//0	0/0/	0/0/0	0/0			0/0/0	---Seed
0/0/0	5	0	0/0	0/0/0	0/0	0//0	0/0/	0/0/0	0/0			0/0/0	---Other
													Manioc, arrowroot, salep, Jerusalem artichokes, sweet potatoes and similar roots and tubers with high starch or inulin content, fresh, chilled, frozen or dried, whether or not sliced or in the form of pellets; sago pith:
													-Manioc(cassava):
0/0/0	3.5	0	0/0	0/0/0	0/0	0//0	0/0/	0/0/0	9.1/0		0/0/	0/0/0	---Fresh
0/0/0	0	0	0/0	0/0/0	0/0	0//0	0/0/	0/0/0	0/0		0/0/	0/0/0	---Dried
0/0/0	3.5	2	0/0	0/0/0	0/0	0//0	0/0/	0/0/9	9.1/0		0/0/	0/0/0	---Chilled or frozen
													-Sweet potatoes:
													---Fresh:
0/0/0	0	0	0/0	0/0/0	0/0	0//0	0/0/	0/0/0	0/0		0/0/	0/0/0	----For Cultivation
0/0/0	3.5	2.6	1.3/1.3	0/0/0	0/0	0//0	0/0/	0/0/11.7	11.8/0		0/0/	0/0/0	----Other
0/0/0	3.5	2.6	1.3/1.3	0/0/0	0/0	0//0	0/0/	0/0/11.7	11.8/0		0/0/	0/0/0	---Dried
0/0/0	3.5	2.6	1.3/1.3	0/0/0	0/0	0//0	0/0/	0/0/11.7	11.8/0		0/0/	0/0/0	---Chilled or frozen
0/0/0	3.5	2.6	1.3/1.3	0/0/0	0/0	0//0	0/0/	0/0/11.7	11.8/0		0/0/	0/0/0	-Yams(*dioscoreae spp.*)
													-Taros(*colocasia spp.*)
0/0/0	3.5	2.6	1.3/1.3	0/0/0	0/0	0//0	0/0/	0/0/11.7	11.8/0			0/0/0	Fresh,chilled taros(colocasia spp.)(whether or not sliced or made granule;taros are also called yunai belong to Spath hyttum of the Araceae vegetables,classified into ground taros and river taros)
0/0/0	3.5	2.6	1.3/1.3	0/0/0	0/0	0//0	0/0/	0/0/11.7	11.8/0			0/0/0	Frozen,dried taros(colocasia spp.)(whether or not sliced or made granule;taros are also called yunai belong to Spath hyttum of the Araceae vegetables,classified into ground taros and river taros)
0/0/0	3.5	2.6	1.3/1.3	0/0/0	0/0	0//0	0/0/	0/0/11.7	11.8/0		0/0/	0/0/0	-Yautia(Xanthosoma spp.)
													-Other:
0/0/0	3.5	2.6	1.3/1.3	0/0/0	0/0	0//0	0/0/	0/0/11.7	11.8/0		0/0/	0/0/0	---Water chestnut
													---Lotus(*Nelumbo nucifera*) rootstock:
0/0/0	0	0	0/0	0/0/0	0/0	0//0	0/0/	0/0/0	0/0			0/0/0	----For cultivation
0/0/0	3.5	2.6	1.3/1.3	0/0/0	0/0	0//0	0/0/	0/0/11.7	11.8/0		0/0/	0/0/0	----Other
													---Other
0/0/0	3.5	2.6	1.3/1.3	0/0/0	0/0	0//0	0/0/	0/0/11.7	11.8/0		0/0/	0/0/0	Tubers of orchid family, fresh, chilled, frozen or dried
0/0/0	3.5	2.6	1.3/1.3	0/0/0	0/0	0//0	0/0/	0/0/11.7	11.8/0		0/0/	0/0/0	Other endangered similar roots and tubers with high starch or inulin content(including sago pith,whether or not sliced or made gramule,fresh,chilled,frozen,dried)
0/0/0	3.5	2.6	1.3/1.3	0/0/0	0/0	0//0	0/0/	0/0/11.7	11.8/0		0/0/	0/0/0	Other similar roots and tubers with high starch or inulin content(including sago pith whether or not sliced or in the form of pellets fresh,chilled,frozen,dried)

第八章
食用水果及坚果；
柑橘属水果或甜瓜的果皮

注释：

一、本章不包括非供食用的坚果或水果。
二、冷藏的水果和坚果应按相应的鲜果税目归类。
三、本章的干果可以部分复水或为下列目的进行其他处理，但必须保持干果的特征。

（一）为保藏或保持其稳定性（例如，经适度热处理或硫化处理、添加山梨酸或山梨酸钾）；

（二）为改进或保持其外观（例如，添加植物油或少量葡萄糖浆）。

四、税目08.12适用于使用前在运输或贮存时仅为暂时保藏而进行处理（例如，使用二氧化硫气体、盐水、亚硫酸水或其他防腐液）的水果及坚果，但不适于直接食用。

税则号列	货品名称〔CIQ扩展编码及品名－T2表示见附表2〕	最惠(%)	暂定税率	普通	增值/消费	出口退税	计量单位	监管条件/特殊证件	检验检疫	对美关税	亚太上/下
08.01	**鲜或干的椰子、巴西果及腰果，不论是否去壳或去皮：**										
	-椰子：										
0801.1100	--干的〔101其他工艺，102蜜饯，103提取（晒干的除外）、压榨、烹制、烘焙、冻干、脱水、裹糖屑、发酵、冷冻、（经漂汤和杀青，并在－18度以下冷冻）、浸酸、腌渍、炒制等工艺进行加工处理的〕	12	7	80	9/	9	千克	AB/	PRQS	52/22	6/6
0801.1200	--未去内壳（内果皮）〔101：椰青；102：加工用去皮老椰子；999：椰青和加工用去皮老椰子除外〕	12		80	9/	9	千克	AB/	PRQS	57/27	6/6
	--其他：										
0801.1910	---种用〔999〕	0		0	9/	9	千克	AB/	PQN	25	
0801.1990	---其他〔999〕	12		80	9/	9	千克	AB/	PRQS	57/27	6/6
	-巴西果：										
0801.2100	--未去壳〔101提取（晒干的除外）、压榨、烹制、烘焙、冻干、脱水、裹糖屑、发酵、冷冻（经漂汤和杀青，并在－18度以下冷冻）、浸酸、腌渍、炒制等工艺进行加工处理的，999：其他工艺〕	10	7	80	9/	9	千克	AB/	PRQ	52/22	
0801.2200	--去壳〔101提取（晒干的除外）、压榨、烹制、烘焙、冻干、脱水、裹糖屑、发酵、冷冻（经漂汤和杀青，并在－18度以下冷冻）、浸酸、腌渍、炒制等工艺进行加工处理的，999：其他工艺〕	10	7	80	9/	9	千克	AB/	PRQ	52/22	
	-腰果：										
0801.3100	--未去壳〔101提取（晒干的除外）、压榨、烹制、烘焙、冻干、脱水、裹糖屑、发酵、冷冻（经漂汤和杀青，并在－18度以下冷冻）、浸酸、腌渍、炒制等工艺进行加工处理的，999：其他工艺〕	20	7	70	9/	9	千克	AB/	PRQS	52/22	
0801.3200	--去壳〔101提取（晒干的除外）、压榨、烹制、烘焙、冻干、脱水、裹糖屑、发酵、冷冻（经漂汤和杀青，并在－18度以下冷冻）、浸酸、腌渍、炒制等工艺进行加工处理的，999：其他工艺〕	10	7	70	9/	9	千克	AB/	PRQS	52/22	
08.02	**鲜或干的其他坚果，不论是否去壳或去皮：**										
	-扁桃核及仁：										
0802.1100	--未去壳〔101提取（晒干的除外）、压榨、烹制、烘焙、冻干、脱水、裹糖屑、发酵、冷冻（经漂汤和杀青，并在－18度以下冷冻）、浸酸、腌渍、炒制等工艺进行加工处理的，999：其他工艺〕	24	10	70	9/	9	千克	AB/	PRQS	55/25	
0802.1200	--去壳〔101巴旦木（其他工艺），102其他蜜饯，103巴旦木（提取（晒干的除外）、压榨、烹制、烘焙、冻干、脱水、裹糖屑、发酵、冷冻（经漂汤和杀青，并在－18度以下冷冻）、浸酸、腌渍、炒制等工艺进行加工处理的）〕	10		70	9/	9	千克	AB/	PRQS	55/25	
	-榛子：										
0802.2100	--未去壳〔101提取（晒干的除外）、压榨、烹制、烘焙、冻干、脱水、裹糖屑、发酵、冷冻（经漂汤和杀青，并在－18度以下冷冻）、浸酸、腌渍、炒制等工艺进行加工处理的，999：其他工艺〕	25		70	9/	9	千克	AB/	PRQS	65/40	
0802.2200	--去壳〔101提取（晒干的除外）、压榨、烹制、烘焙、冻干、脱水、裹糖屑、发酵、冷冻（经漂汤和杀青，并在－18度以下冷冻）、浸酸、腌渍、炒制等工艺进行加工处理的，999：其他工艺〕	10		70	9/	9	千克	AB/	PRQS	55/25	
	-核桃：										
0802.3100	--未去壳〔101提取（晒干的除外）、压榨、烹制、烘焙、冻干、脱水、裹糖屑、发酵、冷冻（经漂汤和杀青，并在－18度以下冷冻）、浸酸、腌渍、炒制等工艺进行加工处理的，999：其他工艺〕	25		70	9/	9	千克	AB/	PRQS	70/40	
0802.3200	--去壳〔101提取（晒干的除外）、压榨、烹制、烘焙、冻干、脱水、裹糖屑、发酵、冷冻（经漂汤和杀青，并在－18度以下冷冻）、浸酸、腌渍、炒制等工艺进行加工处理的，999：其他工艺〕	20		70	9/	9	千克	AB/	PRQS	65/35	
	-栗子：										
	--未去壳：										
0802.4110	---板栗〔101提取（晒干的除外）、压榨、烹制、烘焙、冻干、脱水、裹糖屑、发酵、冷冻（经漂汤和杀青，并在－18度以下冷冻）、浸酸、腌渍、炒制等工艺进行加工处理的，999：其他工艺〕	25		70	9/	9	千克	AB/	PRQS	70/40	

Chapter 8
Edible fruit and nuts; peel of citrus fruit or melons

Notes:

1. This Chapter does not cover inedible nuts or fruits.
2. Chilled fruits and nuts are to be classified in the same headings as the corresponding fresh fruits and nuts.
3. Dried fruit or dried nuts of this Chapter may be partially rehydrated, or treated for the following purposes, provided that they retain the character of dried fruit or dried nuts.
   (a) For additional preservation or stabilization (for example, bymoderate heat treatment, sulphuring, the addition of sorbic acid or potassium sorbate).
   (b) To improve or maintain their appearance (for example., bythe addition of vegetable oil or small quantities of glucose syrup),
4. Heading No.08.12 applies to fruit and nuts which have been treated solely to ensure their provisional preservation during transport or storage prior to use (for example, by sulphur dioxide gas, in brine, in sulphur water or in other preservative solutions), provided they remain unsuitable for immediate consumption in that state.

协定税率 %								RCEP		特惠税率 %			Article Description
东/冰/格	巴基斯坦	韩国	瑞士 上/下	哥/秘/柬	澳/毛	新西/坡/智	中国港/澳/台	东盟及马来/澳/韩	日/新	亚太2国	老/柬/缅	98/97/95	
													Coconuts, Brazil nuts and cashew- nuts, fresh or dried, whether or not shelled or peeled:
													-Coconuts:
0/0/0	3.5	0	1.2/1.2	2.4/0/0	0/0	0//0	0/0/	0/0/0	10.9/0		/0/	0/0/0	--Desiccated
0/0/0	3.5	0	1.2/1.2	2.4/0/0	0/0	0//0	0/0/	10.8/10.8/10.8	10.9/10.8		/0/	0/0/0	--In the inner shell(endocarp)
													--Other:
0/0/0	0	0	0/0	0/0/0	0/0	0//0	0/0/	0/0/0	0/0			0/0/0	---Seedlings
0/0/0	3.5	0	1.2/1.2	2.4/0/0	0/0	0//0	0/0/	0/0/0	10.9/0		/0/	0/0/0	---Other
													-Brazil nuts:
0/0/0	3.5	0	0/0	2/0/0	0/0	0//0	0/0/	0/0/0	9.1/0			0/0/0	--In shell
0/0/0	3.5	0	0/0	2/0/0	0/0	0//0	0/0/	0/0/0	9.1/0			0/0/0	--Shelled
													-Cashew nuts:
0/0/0		4	2/2	4/0/0	0/0	0//0	0/0/	0/0/18	18.2/0		/0/	0/0/0	--In shell
0/0/0	3.5	2	0/0	2/0/0	0/0	0//0	0/0/	9/9/9	9.1/9		/0/0	0/0/0	--Shelled
													Other nuts, fresh or dried, whether or not shelled or peeled:
													-Almonds:
0/0/0		4.8	2.4/2.4	4.8/0/0	0/14.4	0//0	0/0/	0/0/21.6	21.8/0			0/0/0	--In shell
0/0/0	3.5	2	0/0	2/0/0	0/0	0//0	0/0/	0/0/9	9.1/0			0/0/0	--Shelled
													-Hazelnuts or filberts (*Corylus spp.*):
0/0/0		15	2.5/2.5	5/0/0	0/15	0//0	0/0/	23.8/23.8/23.8	23.8/23.8			0/0/0	--In shell
0/0/0	3.5	2	0/0	2/0/0	0/0	0//0	0/0/	0/0/9	9.1/0			0/0/0	--Shelled
													-Walnuts:
0/0/0		15	2.5/2.5	5/0/0	0/15	0//0	0/0/	23.8/23.8/23.8	/23.8			0/0/0	--In shell
0/0/0		9.3	2/2	4/0/0	0/0	0//0	0/0/	18/19/18	18.2/19			0/0/0	--Shelled
													-Chestnuts (*Castanea spp.*):
													-In shell:
0/0/0			2.5/2.5	5/0/0	0/15	0//0	0/0/	23.8/23.8/	/23.8			0/0/0	---Chestnuts(Castanea spp.)

税则号列	货品名称〔CIQ 扩展编码及品名－T2 表示见附表 2〕	最惠(%)	暂定税率	普通	增值/消费	出口退税	计量单位	监管条件/特殊证件	检验检疫	对美关税	亚太上/下
0802.4190	---其他〔101 提取(晒干的除外)、压榨、烹制、烘焙、冻干、脱水、裹糖屑、发酵、冷冻(经漂汤和杀青,并在－18 度以下冷冻)、浸酸、腌渍、炒制等工艺进行加工处理的,102 其他工艺〕	25	20	70	9/	9	千克	AB/	PRQS	50	
	--去壳:										
0802.4210	---板栗〔101(提取(晒干的除外)、压榨、烹制、烘焙、冻干、脱水、裹糖屑、发酵、冷冻(经漂汤和杀青,并在－18 度以下冷冻)、浸酸、腌渍、炒制等工艺进行加工处理的),999 其他工艺〕	25		70	9/	9	千克	AB/	PRQS	55	
0802.4290	---其他〔101 提取(晒干的除外)、压榨、烹制、烘焙、冻干、脱水、裹糖屑、发酵、冷冻(经漂汤和杀青,并在－18 度以下冷冻)、浸酸、腌渍、炒制等工艺进行加工处理的,102 其他工艺〕	25	20	70	9/	9	千克	AB/	PRQS	65/35	
	-阿月浑子果(开心果):										
0802.5100	--未去壳〔101:提取(晒干的除外)、压榨、烹制、烘焙、冻干、脱水、裹糖屑、发酵、冷冻(经漂汤和杀青,并在－18 度以下冷冻)、浸酸、腌渍、炒制等工艺进行加工处理的;999:其他工艺〕	10	5	70	9/	9	千克	AB/	PRQS	50/20	
0802.5200	--去壳〔101:提取(晒干的除外)、压榨、烹制、烘焙、冻干、脱水、裹糖屑、发酵、冷冻(经漂汤和杀青,并在－18 度以下冷冻)、浸酸、腌渍、炒制等工艺进行加工处理的;999:其他工艺〕	10	5	70	9/	9	千克	AB/	PRQS	50/20	
	-马卡达姆坚果(夏威夷果):										
	--未去壳:										
0802.6110	---种用〔999〕	0		70	9/	9	千克	AB/	PQ	25	
0802.6190	---其他〔101 提取(晒干的除外)、压榨、烹制、烘焙、冻干、脱水、裹糖屑、发酵、冷冻(经漂汤和杀青,并在－18 度以下冷冻)、浸酸、腌渍、炒制等工艺进行加工处理的,999:其他工艺〕	24	12	70	9/	9	千克	AB/	PRQS	57/27	
0802.6200	--去壳〔101 提取(晒干的除外)、压榨、烹制、烘焙、冻干、脱水、裹糖屑、发酵、冷冻(经漂汤和杀青,并在－18 度以下冷冻)、浸酸、腌渍、炒制等工艺进行加工处理的,999:其他工艺〕	24	12	70	9/	9	千克	AB/	PRQS	57/27	
0802.7000	-可乐果(可乐果属)〔101 提取(晒干的除外)、压榨、烹制、烘焙、冻干、脱水、裹糖屑、发酵、冷冻(经漂汤和杀青,并在－18 度以下冷冻)、浸酸、腌渍、炒制等工艺进行加工处理的,999:其他工艺〕	24		70	9/	9	千克	AB/	PRQS	54	
0802.8000	-槟榔果										
0802.8000 01	鲜的槟榔果(不论是否去壳或去皮)〔999〕	10		30	9/	9	千克	AB/	PRQS	55/25	5/5
0802.8000 90	干的槟榔果(不论是否去壳或去皮)〔101 其他工艺,102 其他蜜饯,103 提取(晒干的除外)、压榨、烹制、烘焙、冻干、脱水、裹糖屑、发酵、冷冻(经漂汤和杀青,并在－18 度以下冷冻)、浸酸、腌渍、炒制等工艺进行加工处理的〕	10		30	9/	9	千克	AB/	PRQS	55/25	5/5
	-其他:										
0802.9100	--未去壳松子										
0802.9100 10	鲜或干的未去壳红松子〔101 提取(晒干的除外)、压榨、烹制、烘焙、冻干、脱水、裹糖屑、发酵、冷冻(经漂汤和杀青,并在－18 度以下冷冻)、浸酸、腌渍、炒制等工艺进行加工处理的,102 其他工艺〕	24	10	70	9/	9	千克	ABE/	PRQS	55/25	
0802.9100 20	鲜或干的未去壳其他濒危松子〔101 提取(晒干的除外)、压榨、烹制、烘焙、冻干、脱水、裹糖屑、发酵、冷冻(经漂汤和杀青,并在－18 度以下冷冻)、浸酸、腌渍、炒制等工艺进行加工处理的,102 其他工艺〕	24	10	70	9/	0	千克	ABEF/	PRQS	55/25	
0802.9100 90	鲜或干的未去壳其他松子〔101 提取(晒干的除外)、压榨、烹制、烘焙、冻干、脱水、裹糖屑、发酵、冷冻(经漂汤和杀青,并在－18 度以下冷冻)、浸酸、腌渍、炒制等工艺进行加工处理的,102 其他工艺,103 白皮松子(其他工艺)〕	24	10	70	9/	9	千克	AB/	PRQS	55/25	
0802.9200	--去壳松子										
0802.9200 10	鲜或干的去壳红松子〔101 提取(晒干的除外)、压榨、烹制、烘焙、冻干、脱水、裹糖屑、发酵、冷冻(经漂汤和杀青,并在－18 度以下冷冻)、浸酸、腌渍、炒制等工艺进行加工处理的,102 其他工艺〕	25	10	70	9/	9	千克	ABE/	PRQS	55/25	
0802.9200 20	鲜或干的去壳其他濒危松子〔101 提取(晒干的除外)、压榨、烹制、烘焙、冻干、脱水、裹糖屑、发酵、冷冻(经漂汤和杀青,并在－18 度以下冷冻)、浸酸、腌渍、炒制等工艺进行加工处理的,102 其他工艺〕	25	10	70	9/	0	千克	ABEF/	PRQS	55/25	
0802.9200 90	鲜或干的去壳其他松子〔101 提取(晒干的除外)、压榨、烹制、烘焙、冻干、脱水、裹糖屑、发酵、冷冻(经漂汤和杀青,并在－18 度以下冷冻)、浸酸、腌渍、炒制等工艺进行加工处理的,102 其他工艺〕	25	10	70	9/	9	千克	AB/	PRQS	55/25	
	--其他:										
0802.9910	---白果〔101 药用白果,102(白果)其他工艺,103(白果)提取(晒干的除外)、压榨、烹制、烘焙、冻干、脱水、裹糖屑、发酵、冷冻(经漂汤和杀青,并在－18 度以下冷冻)、浸酸、腌渍、炒制等工艺进行加工处理的〕	25	20	70	9/	9	千克	ABE/	PRQ	50	

协定税率 %								RCEP		特惠税率 %			Article Description
东/冰/格	巴基斯坦	韩国	瑞士 上/下	哥/秘/柬	澳/毛	新西/坡/智	中国港/澳/台	东盟及马来/澳/韩	日/新	亚太2国	老/柬/缅	98/97/95	
0/0/0		15	2.5/2.5	5/0/0	0/15	0//0	0/0/	23.8/23.8/23.8	23.8/23.8			0/0/0	---Other
													--Shelled:
0/0/0		15	2.5/2.5	5/0/0	0/15	0//0	0/0/	23.8/23.8/23.8	23.8/23.8			0/0/0	---Chestnuts(castanea spp.)
0/0/0		15	2.5/2.5	5/0/0	0/15	0//0	0/0/	23.8/23.8/23.8	23.8/23.8			0/0/0	---Other
													-Pistachios:
0/0/0	3.5	2	0/0	2/0/0	0/0	0//0	0/0/	0/0/9	9.1/0			0/0/0	--In shell
0/0/0	3.5	2	0/0	2/0/0	0/0	0//0	0/0/	0/0/9	9.1/0			0/0/0	--Shelled
													-Macadamia nuts:
													--In shell:
0/0/0	0	0	0/0	0/0/0	0/0	0//0	0/0/	0/0/0	0/0			0/0/0	---For cultivation
0/0/0		4.8	2.4/2.4	4.8/0/0	0/14.4	0//0	0/0/	0/0/21.6	21.8/0			0/0/0	---Other
0/0/0		4.8	2.4/2.4	4.8/0/0	0/14.4	0//0	0/0/	0/0/21.6	21.8/0			0/0/0	--Shelled
0/0/0		14.4	2.4/2.4	4.8/0/0	0/14.4	0//0	0/0/	22.8/22.8/22.8	22.9/22.8			0/0/0	-Kola nuts(Cola spp.)
													-Areca nut
0/0/0	3.5	2	0/0	2/0/0	0/0	0//0	0/0/	0/0/9	9.1/0			0/0/0	Areca nuts,fresh(whether or not shelled or peeled)
0/0/0	3.5	2	0/0	2/0/0	0/0	0//0	0/0/	0/0/9	9.1/0			0/0/0	Areca nuts,dried(whether or not shelled or peeled)
													-Other:
													-- Pine nuts, in shell
0/0/0	0	14.4	2.4/2.4	4.8/0/0	0/14.4	0//0	0/0/	22.8/22.8/22.8	/22.8			0/0/0	Raw red pine nuts, fresh or dry
0/0/0	0	14.4	2.4/2.4	4.8/0/0	0/14.4	0//0	0/0/	22.8/22.8/22.8	/22.8			0/0/0	Other endangered pine nuts, fresh or dried, not shelled
0/0/0	0	14.4	2.4/2.4	4.8/0/0	0/14.4	0//0	0/0/	22.8/22.8/22.8	/22.8			0/0/0	Other pine nuts, fresh or dry, not shelled
													-- Pine nuts, shelled
0/0/0	0	15	2.5/2.5	5/0/0	0/15	0//0	0/0/	23.8/23.8/23.8	23.8/23.8			0/0/0	Shelled red pine nuts, fresh or dry
0/0/0	0	15	2.5/2.5	5/0/0	0/15	0//0	0/0/	23.8/23.8/23.8	23.8/23.8			0/0/0	Shelled other endangered pine nuts, fresh or dried
0/0/0	0	15	2.5/2.5	5/0/0	0/15	0//0	0/0/	23.8/23.8/23.8	23.8/23.8			0/0/0	Shelled other pine nuts, fresh or dry
													-- Other:
0/0/0		15	2.5/2.5	5/0/0	0/15	0//0	0/0/	23.8/23.8/23.8	23.8/23.8			0/0/0	---Ginkgo

税则号列	货品名称〔CIQ 扩展编码及品名—T2 表示见附表 2〕	最惠(%)	暂定税率	普通	增值/消费	出口退税	计量单位	监管条件/特殊证件	检验检疫	对美关税	亚太上/下
0802.9990	---其他										
0802.9990 10	鲜或干的榧子(不论是否去壳或去皮，不包括人工培植的)〔101 药用榧子，102 提取(晒干的除外)、压榨、烹制、烘焙、冻干、脱水、裹糖屑、发酵、冷冻(经漂汤和杀青，并在－19 度以下冷冻)、浸酸、腌渍、炒制等工艺进行加工处理的，103 其他工艺〕	24		70	9/	9	千克	ABE/	PRQS	69/39	
0802.9990 20	鲜或干的巨籽棕(海椰子)果仁〔101 提取(晒干的除外)、压榨、烹制、烘焙、冻干、脱水、裹糖屑、发酵、冷冻(经漂汤和杀青，并在－18 度以下冷冻)、浸酸、腌渍、炒制等工艺进行加工处理的，102 其他工艺〕	24		70	9/	9	千克	ABEF/	PRQS	69/39	
0802.9990 30	鲜或干的碧根果(不论是否去壳或去皮)〔101 提取(晒干的除外)、压榨、烹制、烘焙、冻干、脱水、裹糖屑、发酵、冷冻(经漂汤和杀青，并在－18 度以下冷冻)、浸酸、腌渍、炒制等工艺进行加工处理的，102 其他工艺〕	24	7	70	9/	9	千克	AB/	PRQS	52/22	
0802.9990 90	鲜或干的其他坚果(不论是否去壳或去皮)〔101 干的其他瓜子，102(其他坚果)其他工艺，103(巴西坚果)其他工艺，104(鲍鱼果)其他工艺，105(干橡子仁)其他工艺，106 提取(晒干的除外)、压榨、烹制、烘焙、冻干、脱水、裹糖屑、发酵、冷冻(经漂汤和杀青，并在－18 度以下冷冻)、浸酸、腌渍、炒制等工艺进行加工处理的〕	24		70	9/	9	千克	AB/	PRQS	69/39	
08.03	**鲜或干的香蕉，包括芭蕉：**										
0803.1000	-芭蕉〔101 鲜芭蕉，102 干的芭蕉(其他工艺)，103 其他蜜饯，104 干的芭蕉(提取(晒干的除外)、压榨、烹制、烘焙、冻干、脱水、裹糖屑、发酵、冷冻(经漂汤和杀青，并在－18 度以下冷冻、浸酸、腌渍、炒制等工艺进行加工处理的))〕	10		40	9/	9	千克	AB/	PRQS	55/25	6.9/6.9
0803.9000	-其他〔101 鲜香蕉，替代种植除外；102 干的香蕉(其他工艺)；103 其他蜜饯；104 干的香蕉(提取(晒干的除外)、压榨、烹制、烘焙、冻干、脱水、裹糖屑、发酵、冷冻(经漂汤和杀青，并在－18 度以下冷冻)、浸酸、腌渍、炒制等工艺进行加工处理的)；105 鲜香蕉，替代种植〕	10		40	9/	9	千克	AB/	PRQS	55/25	6.9/6.9
08.04	**鲜或干的椰枣、无花果、菠萝、鳄梨、番石榴、芒果及山竹果：**										
0804.1000	-椰枣〔101 提取(晒干的除外)压榨、烹制、烘焙、冻干、脱水、裹糖屑、发酵、冷冻(经漂汤和杀青，并在－18 度以下冷冻)、浸酸、腌渍、炒制等工艺进行加工处理的，999 其他工艺〕	15		40	9/	9	千克	AB/	PRQ	60/30	
0804.2000	-无花果〔101 鲜的无花果，102 干的无花果(其他工艺)，103 其他蜜饯，104 干的无花果(提取(晒干的除外)、压榨、烹制、烘焙、冻干、脱水、裹糖屑、发酵、冷冻(经漂汤和杀青，并在－18 度以下冷冻)、浸酸、腌渍、炒制等工艺进行加工处理的)〕	30		70	9/	9	千克	AB/	PRQ	75/45	
0804.3000	-菠萝										
0804.3000 01	鲜菠萝〔999〕	12		80	9/	9	千克	AB/	PRQS	57/27	7.9/7.9
0804.3000 90	干菠萝〔101 干菠萝(其他工艺)，102 其他蜜饯，103(干菠萝)提取(晒干的除外)、压榨、烹制、烘焙、冻干、脱水、裹糖屑、发酵、冷冻(经漂汤和杀青，并在－18 度以下冷冻)、浸酸、腌渍、炒制等工艺进行加工处理的〕	12		80	9/	9	千克	AB/	PRQS	57/27	7.9/7.9
0804.4000	-鳄梨〔101 鲜的鳄梨，102 干的鳄梨(其他工艺)，103 其他蜜饯，104 干的鳄梨(提取(晒干的除外)、压榨、烹制、烘焙、冻干、脱水、裹糖屑、发酵、冷冻(经漂汤和杀青，并在－18 度以下冷冻)、浸酸、腌渍、炒制等工艺进行加工处理的)〕	25	7	80	9/	9	千克	AB/	PRQ	52/22	12.5/12.5
	-番石榴、芒果及山竹果：										
0804.5010	---番石榴										
0804.5010 01	鲜番石榴〔999〕	15		80	9/	9	千克	AB/	PRQ	60/30	7.5/7.5
0804.5010 90	干番石榴〔101 干番石榴(其他工艺)，102 其他蜜饯，103(干番石榴)提取(晒干的除外)、压榨、烹制、烘焙、冻干、脱水、裹糖屑、发酵、冷冻(经漂汤和杀青，并在－18 度以下冷冻)、浸酸、腌渍、炒制等工艺进行加工处理的〕	15		80	9/	9	千克	AB/	PRQ	60/30	7.5/7.5
0804.5020	---芒果										
0804.5020 01	鲜芒果〔999〕	15		80	9/	9	千克	AB/	PRQ	60/30	10.7/10.7
0804.5020 90	干芒果〔101 干芒果(其他工艺)，102 其他蜜饯，103(干芒果)提取(晒干的除外)、压榨、烹制、烘焙、冻干、脱水、裹糖屑、发酵、冷冻(经漂汤和杀青，并在－18 度以下冷冻)、浸酸、腌渍、炒制等工艺进行加工处理的〕	15		80	9/	9	千克	AB/	PRQ	60/30	10.7/10.7
0804.5030	---山竹果〔101 鲜的山竹果，102 干的山竹果(其他工艺)，103 其他蜜饯，104 干的山竹果提取(晒干的除外)、压榨、烹制、烘焙、冻干、脱水、裹糖屑、发酵、冷冻(经漂汤和杀青，并在－18 度以下冷冻)、浸酸、腌渍、炒制等工艺进行加工处理的〕	15		80	9/	9	千克	AB/	PRQ	60/30	7.5/7.5
08.05	**鲜或干的柑橘属水果：**										

协定税率 %								RCEP		特惠税率 %			Article Description
东/冰/格	巴基斯坦	韩国	瑞士上/下	哥/秘/柬	澳/毛	新西/坡/智	中国港/澳/台	东盟及马来/澳/韩	日/新	亚太2国	老/柬/缅	98/97/95	
													---Other
0/0/0	0	14.4	2.4/2.4	4.8/0/0	0/14.4	0//0	0/0/	22.8/22.8/22.8	/22.8			0/0/0	Torreya grandis, fresh or dried (whether or not shelled or peeled, excluding artificially cultivated)
0/0/0	0	14.4	2.4/2.4	4.8/0/0	0/14.4	0//0	0/0/	22.8/22.8/22.8	/22.8			0/0/0	Fresh or dried giant seed palm (sea coconut) kernel
0/0/0	0	14.4	2.4/2.4	4.8/0/0	0/14.4	0//0	0/0/	22.8/22.8/22.8	/22.8			0/0/0	Bigen fruit, fresh or dried (whether or not shelled or peeled)
0/0/0	0	14.4	2.4/2.4	4.8/0/0	0/14.4	0//0	0/0/	22.8/22.8/22.8	/22.8			0/0/0	Other nuts, fresh or dried (whether or not shelled or peeled)
													Bananas, including plantains, fresh or dried:
0/0/0	3.5	2	0/0	2/0/0	0/0	0//0	0/0/0	0/0/9	9.1/0		0/0/	0/0/0	-Plantains
0/0/0	3.5	2	0/0	2/0/0	0/0	0//0	0/0/0	0/0/9	9.1/0		0/0/	0/0/0	-Other
													Dates, figs, pineapples, avocados, guavas, mangoes and mangosteens, fresh or dried:
0/0/0	0	3	1.5/1.5	3/0/0	0/0	0//0	0/0/	0/0/13.5	13.6/0			0/0/0	-Dates
0/0/0	0	18	12.6/12.6	6/0/0	0/18	0//0	0/0/	28.5/28.5/28.5	28.6/28.5			0/0/0	-Figs
													-Pineapples
0/0/0	0	2.4	1.2/1.2	2.4/0/0	0/0	0//0	0/0/	10.8/10.8/10.8	10.9/10.8		/0/	0/0/0	Pineapples, fresh
0/0/0	0	2.4	1.2/1.2	2.4/0/0	0/0	0//0	0/0/	10.8/10.8/10.8	10.9/10.8		/0/	0/0/0	Pineapples, dried
0/0/0	0	15	2.5/2.5	5/0/0	0/15	0//0	0/0/	23.8/23.8/23.8	23.8/23.8		/0/	0/0/0	-Avocados
													-Guavas, mangoes and mangosteens:
													---Guavas
0/0/0	0	3	1.5/1.5	3/0/0	0/0	0//0	0/0/	0/0/13.5	13.6/0			0/0/0	Guavas, fresh
0/0/0	0	3	1.5/1.5	3/0/0	0/0	0//0	0/0/	0/0/13.5	13.6/0			0/0/0	Guavas, dried
													---Mangoes
0/0/0	0	3	1.5/1.5	3/0/0	0/0	0//0	0/0/	0/0/13.5	13.6/0			0/0/0	Mangoes, fresh
0/0/0	0	3	1.5/1.5	3/0/0	0/0	0//0	0/0/	0/0/13.5	13.6/0			0/0/0	Mangoes, dried
0/0/0	0	3	1.5/1.5	3/0/0	0/0	0//0	0/0/	0/0/13.5	13.6/0			0/0/0	---Mangosteens
													Citrus fruit, fresh or dried:

税则号列	货品名称〔CIQ扩展编码及品名—T2表示见附表2〕	最惠(%)	暂定税率	普通	增值/消费	出口退税	计量单位	监管条件/特殊证件	检验检疫	对美关税	亚太上/下
0805.1000	-橙〔101 鲜的橙,102 干的橙其他工艺,103 其他蜜饯,104 干的橙(提取(晒干的除外)、压榨、烹制、烘焙、冻干、脱水、裹糖屑、发酵、冷冻(经漂汤和杀青,并在−18度以下冷冻)、浸酸、腌渍、炒制等工艺进行加工处理的)〕	11		100	9/	9	千克	AB/	PRQS	56/26	
	-柑橘(包括小蜜橘及萨摩蜜柑橘);克里曼丁橘、韦尔金橘及类似的杂交柑橘:										
	--柑橘(包括小蜜橘及萨摩蜜柑橘):										
0805.2110	---蕉柑〔101 鲜的蕉柑,102 干的蕉柑(提取(晒干的除外)、压榨、烹制、烘焙、冻干、脱水、裹糖屑、发酵、冷冻(经漂汤和杀青,并在−18度以下冷冻)、浸酸、腌渍、炒制等工艺进行加工处理的),999:干的蕉柑(其他工艺)〕	12		100	9/	9	千克	AB/	PRQS	42	
0805.2190	---其他〔101 鲜的柑橘,102 干的柑橘(提取(晒干的除外)、压榨、烹制、烘焙、冻干、脱水、裹糖屑、发酵、冷冻(经漂汤和杀青,并在−18度以下冷冻)、浸酸、腌渍、炒制等工艺进行加工处理的),999:干的柑橘(其他工艺)〕	12		100	9/	9	千克	AB/	PRQS	57/27	
0805.2200	--克里曼丁橘〔101 鲜的克里曼丁橘,102 干的克里曼丁橘(提取(晒干的除外)、压榨、烹制、烘焙、冻干、脱水、裹糖屑、发酵、冷冻(经漂汤和杀青,并在−18度以下冷冻)、浸酸、腌渍、炒制等工艺进行加工处理的),999:干的克里曼丁橘(其他工艺)〕	12		100	9/	9	千克	AB/	PRQS	57/27	
0805.2900	--其他〔101 鲜的韦尔金橘及其他类似的杂交柑橘,102 干的韦尔金橘及其他类似的杂交柑橘)(提取(晒干的除外)、压榨、烹制、烘焙、冻干、脱水、裹糖屑、发酵、冷冻(经漂汤和杀青,并在−18度以下冷冻)、浸酸、腌渍、炒制等工艺进行加工处理的),999 干的韦尔金橘及其他类似的杂交柑橘(其他工艺)〕	12		100	9/	9	千克	AB/	PRQS	57/27	
0805.4000	-葡萄柚及柚										
0805.4000 10	鲜的葡萄柚及柚〔101 柚,102 葡萄柚〕	12		100	9/	9	千克	AB/	PRQS	57/27	
0805.4000 90	干的葡萄柚及柚〔101 干的萄柚,包括干柚(提取(晒干的除外)、压榨、烹制、烘焙、冻干、脱水、裹糖屑、发酵、冷冻(经漂汤和杀青,并在−18度以下冷冻)、浸酸、腌渍、炒制等工艺进行加工处理的),102(干的萄柚,包括干柚)(其他工艺),103 其他蜜饯〕	12		100	9/	9	千克	AB/	PRQS	57/27	
0805.5000	-柠檬及酸橙〔101 鲜的柠檬,102 鲜的酸橙,103 干的酸橙(其他工艺),104 其他蜜饯,105 柠檬干(其他工艺),106 干的酸橙(提取(晒干的除外)、压榨、烹制、烘焙、冻干、脱水、裹糖屑、发酵、冷冻(经漂汤和杀青,并在−18度以下冷冻)、浸酸、腌渍、炒制等工艺进行加工处理的),107 柠檬干(提取(晒干的除外)、压榨、烹制、烘焙、冻干、脱水、裹糖屑、发酵、冷冻(经漂汤和杀青,并在−19度以下冷冻)、浸酸、腌渍、炒制等工艺进行加工处理的)〕	11		100	9/	9	千克	AB/	PRQS	56/26	5.5/5.5
0805.9000	-其他〔102 鲜的其他柑桔,103 干的其他柑桔属水果(其他工艺),104 其他蜜饯,105 干的其他柑桔属水果(提取(晒干的除外)、压榨、烹制、烘焙、冻干、脱水、裹糖屑、发酵、冷冻(经漂汤和杀青,并在−18度以下冷冻)、浸酸、腌渍、炒制等工艺进行加工处理的〕	30		100	9/	9	千克	AB/	PRQS	75/45	15/15
08.06	**鲜或干的葡萄:**										
0806.1000	-鲜的〔999〕	13		80	9/	9	千克	AB/	PRQS	58/28	
0806.2000	-干的〔101 提取(晒干的除外)、压榨、烹制、烘焙、冻干、脱水、裹糖屑、发酵、冷冻(经漂汤和杀青,并在−18度以下冷冻)、浸酸、腌渍、炒制等工艺进行加工处理的,999:其他工艺〕	10		80	9/	9	千克	AB/	PRQS	55/25	
08.07	**鲜的甜瓜(包括西瓜)及番木瓜:**										
	-甜瓜,包括西瓜:										
0807.1100	--西瓜〔101 替代种植;102 替代种植除外;999〕	25		70	9/	9	千克	AB/	PRQS	70/40	12.5/12.5
	--其他:										
0807.1910	---哈密瓜〔999〕	12		70	9/	9	千克	AB/	PRQS	57/27	6/6
0807.1920	---罗马甜瓜及加勒比甜瓜〔999〕	12		70	9/	9	千克	AB/	PRQS	42	6/6
0807.1990	---其他〔101 其他甜瓜,102 香瓜〕	12		70	9/	9	千克	AB/	PRQS	42	6/6
0807.2000	-番木瓜〔101 鲜番木瓜除外;102 鲜番木瓜;999 鲜番木瓜〕	25		70	9/	9	千克	AB/	PRQS	70/40	
08.08	**鲜的苹果、梨及榅桲:**										
0808.1000	-苹果〔999〕	10		100	9/	9	千克	AB/	PRQS	55/25	
	-梨:										
0808.3010	---鸭梨及雪梨〔101 鸭梨,102 其它梨〕	12		100	9/	9	千克	AB/	PRQS	57/27	10/10
0808.3020	---香梨〔999〕	12		100	9/	9	千克	AB/	PRQS	42	10/10
0808.3090	---其他〔101 砂梨属,102 中国梨,103 其它梨〕	10		100	9/	9	千克	AB/	PRQS	55/25	
0808.4000	-榅桲〔999〕	16		100	9/	9	千克	AB/	PRQ	46	
08.09	**鲜的杏、樱桃、桃(包括油桃)、李及黑刺李:**										
0809.1000	-杏										
0809.1000 10	鲜杏(梅)〔999〕	25		70	9/	9	千克	AB/	PRQ	55	
0809.1000 90	其他鲜杏(杏属)〔999〕	25		70	9/	9	千克	AB/	PRQ	55	

协定税率 %								RCEP		特惠税率 %			Article Description
东/冰/格	巴基斯坦	韩国	瑞士上/下	哥/秘/柬	澳/毛	新西/坡/智	中国港/澳/台	东盟及马来/澳/韩	日/新	亚太2国	老/柬/缅	98/97/95	
0/0/0	0	2.2	1.1/1.1	2.2/0/0	1.2/0	0//0	0/0/0	0/9.9/9.9	10/0			0/0/0	-Oranges
													-Mandarins (*including tange-rines and satsumas*); clementines, wilkings and similar cit-rus hybrids:
													--Mandarins (*including tange-rines and satsumas*):
0/0/0	0	2.4	1.2/1.2	2.4/0/0	1.3/0	0//0	0/0/	0/10.8/10.8	10.9/0			0/0/0	---Chiao-Kan
0/0/0	0	2.4	1.2/1.2	2.4/0/0	1.3/0	0//0	0/0/	0/10.8/10.8	10.9/0			0/0/0	---Other
0/0/0	0	2.4	1.2/1.2	2.4/0/0	1.3/0	0//0	0/0/	0/10.8/10.8	10.9/0			0/0/0	--Clementines
0/0/0	0	2.4	1.2/1.2	2.4/0/0	1.3/0	0//0	0/0/	0/10.8/10.8	10.9/0			0/0/0	--Other
													-Grapefruit and pomelos
0/0/0	0	2.4	1.2/1.2	2.4/0/0	1.3/0	0//0	0/0/	0/10.8/10.8	10.9/0			0/0/0	Fresh grapefruit and grapefruit
0/0/0	0	2.4	1.2/1.2	2.4/0/0	1.3/0	0//0	0/0/	0/10.8/10.8	10.9/0			0/0/0	Dried grapefruit and grapefruit
0/0/0	0	2.2	1.1/1.1	2.2/0/0	1.2/0	0//0	0/0/0	0/9.9/9.9	10/0			0/0/0	-Lemons (*Citrus limon*, *Citrus limonum*) and limes (*Citrus aurantifolia*)
0/0/0	0	18	12.6/12.6	6/0/0	3.3/18	0//0	0/0/	28.5/28.5/28.5	28.6/28.5			0/0/0	-Other
													Grapes, fresh or dried:
0/0/0	4.6	2.6	1.3/1.3	0/0/0	0/0	0//0	0/0/	0/0/11.7	11.8/0			0/0/0	-Fresh
0/0/0	3.5	2	0/0	0/0/0	0/0	0//0	0/0/	0/0/9	9.1/0			0/0/0	-Dried
													Melons (including watermelons) and papaws (papayas), fresh:
													-Melons (including watermelons):
0/0/0	8.8	15	2.5/2.5	0/0/0	0/15	0//0	0/0/	23.8/23.8/23.8	/23.8			0/0/	--Watermelons
													--Other:
0/0/0	3.5	2.4	1.2/1.2	0/0/0	0/0	0//0	0/0/0	0/0/10.8	10.9/0			0/0/0	---Hami melons
0/0/0	3.5	2.4	1.2/1.2	0/0/0	0/0	0//0	0/0/	0/0/10.8	10.9/0			0/0/0	---Cantaloupe and Galia melons
0/0/0	3.5	2.4	1.2/1.2	0/0/0	0/0	0//0	0/0/	0/0/10.8	10.9/0			0/0/0	---Other
0/0/0	17.5	5	2.5/2.5	0/0/0	0/15	0//0	0/0/	0/0/22.5	22.7/0		/0/	0/0/0	-Papaws(papayas)
													Apples, pears and quinces, fresh:
0/0/0	3.5	2	0/0	0/0/0	0/0	0//0	0/0/	0/0/9	9.1/0			0/0/0	-Apples
													-Pears:
0/0/0	3.5	2.4	1.2/1.2	0/0/0	0/0	0//0	0/0/	0/0/10.8	10.9/0			0/0/0	---Ya pears and hsueh pears
0/0/0	3.5	2.4	1.2/1.2	0/0/0	0/0	0//0	0/0/	0/0/10.8	10.9/0			0/0/0	---Xiang pear
0/0/0	3.5	2	0/0	0/0/0	0/0	0//0	0/0/	0/0/9	9.1/0			0/0/0	---Other
0/0/0	10.2	7.4	1.6/1.6	0/0/0	0/0	0//0	0/0/	14.4/14.4/14.4	15/14.4			0/0/0	-Quinces
													Apricots, cherries, peaches (including nectarines), plums and sloes, fresh:
													-Apricots
0/0/0	20	15	2.5/2.5	0/0/0	0/15	0//0	0/0/	23.8/23.8/23.8	23.8/23.8			0/0/0	Fresh apricot (plum)
0/0/0	20	15	2.5/2.5	0/0/0	0/15	0//0	0/0/	23.8/23.8/23.8	23.8/23.8			0/0/0	Other fresh apricots (apricot)

税则号列	货品名称〔CIQ扩展编码及品名—T2表示见附表2〕	最惠(%)	暂定税率	普通	增值/消费	出口退税	计量单位	监管条件/特殊证件	检验检疫	对美关税	亚太上/下
	-樱桃：										
0809.2100	--欧洲酸樱桃〔999〕	10		70	9/	9	千克	AB/	PRQ	55/25	
0809.2900	--其他〔999〕	10		70	9/	9	千克	AB/	PRQ	55/25	
0809.3000	-桃，包括油桃〔101：鲜油桃除外；102：鲜油桃〕	10		70	9/	9	千克	AB/	PRQS	55/25	
0809.4000	-李及黑刺李										
0809.4000 10	鲜梅(樱桃李)〔999〕	10		70	9/	9	千克	AB/	PRQS	55/25	
0809.4000 90	其他鲜李子及黑刺李〔999〕	10		70	9/	9	千克	AB/	PRQS	55/25	
08.10	**其他鲜果：**										
0810.1000	-草莓〔999〕	14		80	9/	9	千克	AB/	PRQ	59/29	
0810.2000	-木莓、黑莓、桑葚及罗甘莓〔101 树莓(木莓)，102 其他瓜果〕	25		80	9/	9	千克	AB/	PRQ	70/40	
0810.3000	-黑、白或红的穗醋栗(加仑子)及醋栗〔999〕	25		80	9/	9	千克	AB/	PRQ	55	
0810.4000	-蔓越橘、越橘及其他越橘属植物果实〔101 鲜蔓越橘，102 鲜越橘，103 鲜蓝莓，104 其他越橘属果实〕	30	15	80	9/	9	千克	AB/	PRQ	60/30	
0810.5000	-猕猴桃〔999〕	20		80	9/	9	千克	AB/	PRQS	65/35	16.4/16.4
0810.6000	-榴莲〔999〕	20		80	9/	9	千克	AB/	PRQ	65/35	
0810.7000	-柿子〔999〕	20		80	9/	9	千克	AB/	PRQS	65/35	16.4/16.4
	-其他：										
0810.9010	---荔枝〔999〕	30		80	9/	9	千克	AB/	PRQS	75/45	20.1/20.1
0810.9030	---龙眼〔999〕	12		80	9/	9	千克	AB/	PRQS	57/27	
0810.9040	---红毛丹〔999〕	20		80	9/	9	千克	AB/	PRQS	65/35	
0810.9050	---番荔枝〔999〕	20		80	9/	9	千克	AB/	PRQS	65/35	
0810.9060	---杨桃〔999〕	20		80	9/	9	千克	AB/	PRQS	65/35	
0810.9070	---莲雾〔999〕	20		80	9/	9	千克	AB/	PRQS	65/35	16.4/16.4
0810.9080	---火龙果〔999〕	20		80	9/	9	千克	AB/	PRQS	65/35	16.4/16.4
0810.9090	---其他										
0810.9090 01	鲜枣〔101：毛叶枣，替代种植；102：其他；999〕	20		80	9/	9	千克	AB/	PRQS	65/35	16.4/16.4
0810.9090 02	鲜枇杷〔999〕	20		80	9/	9	千克	AB/	PRQS	65/35	16.4/16.4
0810.9090 10	鲜的翅果油树果〔999〕	20		80	9/	9	千克	ABE/	PRQS	65/35	16.4/16.4
0810.9090 90	其他鲜果〔101 杨梅，104 巴旦杏(水果)，106 山楂，107 余甘子，108 西番莲，替代种植除外，109 石榴，110 菱角，111 橄榄，112 菠萝蜜，114 其他瓜果，115 罗望子，116 人心果，117 蛇皮果，118 椰色果，119 蓝靛果，120 鲜木瓜，122 西番莲，替代种植，123 百香果〕	20		80	9/	9	千克	AB/	PRQS	65/35	16.4/16.4
08.11	**冷冻水果及坚果，不论是否蒸煮、加糖或其他甜物质：**										
0811.1000	-草莓〔999〕	30		80	9/	9	千克	AB/	PRQS	70/45	
0811.2000	-木莓、黑莓、桑葚、罗甘莓、黑、白或红的穗醋栗(加仑子)及醋栗〔101 冷冻木莓，102 冷冻黑莓，103 冷冻桑葚 ，104 黑、白或红的穗醋栗(加仑子)及醋栗，105 罗甘莓〕	30		80	9/	9	千克	AB/	PRQ	75/45	
	-其他：										
0811.9010	---栗子，未去壳〔999〕	30		80	9/	9	千克	AB/	PRQS		
0811.9090	---其他										
0811.9090 10	冷冻的白果〔999〕	30		80	9/	9	千克	ABE/	PRQS	75/45	
0811.9090 21	冷冻的红松子(不论是否去壳或去皮)〔999〕	30		80	9/	9	千克	ABE/	PRQS	75/45	
0811.9090 22	冷冻的其他濒危松子(不论是否去壳或去皮)〔999〕	30		80	9/	0	千克	ABEF/	PRQS	75/45	
0811.9090 30	冷冻的榧子〔999〕	30		80	9/	9	千克	ABE/	PRQS	75/45	
0811.9090 40	冷冻的翅果油树果〔999〕	30		80	9/	9	千克	ABE/	PRQS	75/45	
0811.9090 50	冷冻的巨籽棕(海椰子)果仁〔999〕	30		80	9/	9	千克	ABEF/	PRQS	75/45	
0811.9090 60	冷冻的鳄梨〔999〕	30	7	80	9/	9	千克	AB/	PRQS	52/22	
0811.9090 90	其他未列名冷冻水果及坚果[T2]	30		80	9/	9	千克	AB/	PRQS	75/45	
08.12	**暂时保藏的水果及坚果，但不适于直接食用的：**										
0812.1000	-樱桃〔999〕	30		80	9/	9	千克	AB/	PRQ	45/45	
0812.9000	-其他										
0812.9000 60	暂时保存的白果、红松子、榧子、翅果油树果(不适于直接食用的，不包括人工培植的)〔101 白果，102 红松子，103 榧子，104 翅果油树果〕	25		80	9/	9	千克	ABE/	PRQS	40/40	
0812.9000 70	暂时保存的其他濒危松子、巨籽棕(海椰子)果仁(但不适于直接食用的)〔101 其他濒危松子，102 巨籽棕(海椰子)果仁〕	25		80	9/	0，9	千克	ABEF/	PRQS	40/40	
0812.9000 90	暂时保存的其他水果及坚果(但不适于直接食用的)〔999〕	25		80	9/	9	千克	AB/	PRQS	40/40	
08.13	**税目 08.01 至 08.06 以外的干果；本章的什锦坚果或干果：**										

协定税率 %								RCEP		特惠税率 %			Article Description
东/冰/格	巴基斯坦	韩国	瑞士 上/下	哥/秘/柬	澳/毛	新西/坡/智	中国港/澳/台	东盟及马来/澳/韩	日/新	亚太2国	老/柬/缅	98/97/95	
													-Cherries:
0/0/0	3.5	2	0/0	0/0/0	0/0	0//0	0/0/	0/0/9	9.1/0			0/0/0	--Sour cherries(Prunus cerasus)
0/0/0	0	2	0/0	0/0/0	0/0	0//0	0/0/	0/0/9	9.1/0			0/0/0	--Other
0/0/0	3.5	2	0/0	0/0/0	0/0	0//0	0/0/	0/0/9	9.1/0			0/0/0	-Peaches, including nectarines
													-Plums and sloes
0/0/0	3.5	2	0/0	0/0/0	0/0	0//0	0/0/	0/0/9	9.1/0			0/0/0	Fresh plum (cherry plum)
0/0/0	3.5	2	0/0	0/0/0	0/0	0//0	0/0/	0/0/9	9.1/0			0/0/0	Other fresh plums and black thorn plums
													Other fruit, fresh:
0/0/0	9.8	2.8	1.4/1.4	0/0/0	0/0	0//0	0/0/	0/0/12.6	12.7/0			0/0/0	-Strawberries
0/0/0	20	15	2.5/2.5	0/0/0	0/15	0//0	0/0/	23.8/23.8/23.8	23.8/23.8			0/0/0	-Raspberries, blackberries, mulberries and loganberries
0/0/0	20	15	2.5/2.5	0/0/0	0/15	0//0	0/0/	23.8/23.8/23.8	23.8/23.8			0/0/0	-Black, white or red currant and gooseberries
0/0/0	24	18	12.6/12.6	0/0/0	0/18	0//0	0/0/	28.5/28.5/28.5	28.6/28.5			0/0/	-Cranberries, bilberries and other fruits of the genus *Vaccinium*
0/0/0	16	9.3	2/2	0/0/0	0/0	0//0	0/0/	19/19/19	/19			0/0/0	-Kiwifruit
0/0/0	14	4	2/2	0/0/0	0/0	0//0	0/0/	0/0/18	18.2/0		/0/	0/0/0	-Durian
0/0/0	12.8	9.3	2/2	0/0/0	0/0	0//0	0/0/	18/18/18	/18			0/0/0	-Persimmons
													-Other:
0/0/0	14	18	12.6/12.6	0/0/0	0/18	0//0	0/0/	28.5/28.5/28.5	/28.5			0/0/0	---Lychee
0/0/0	4.2	2.4	1.2/1.2	0/0/0	0/0	0//0	0/0/	0/0/10.8	10.9/0		/0/	0/0/0	---Longan
0/0/0	14	4	2/2	0/0/0	0/0	0//0	0/0/	0/0/18	18.2/0			0/0/0	---Rambutan
0/0/0	14	4	2/2	0/0/0	0/0	0//0	0/0/	0/0/18	18.2/0			0/0/0	---Sugar apple
0/0/0	14	9.3	2/2	0/0/0	0/0	0//0	0/0/	18/18/18	18.8/18			0/0/0	---Carambola
0/0/0	11.2	4	2/2	0/0/0	0/0	0//0	0/0/	0/0/18	18.2/0			0/0/0	---Wax apple
0/0/0	12.8	4	2/2	0/0/0	0/0	0//0	0/0/0	0/0/18	18.2/0			0/0/0	---Dragon fruit
													---Other
0/0/0	0	9.3	2/2	0/0/0	0/0	0//0	0/0/	18.7/19/18.7	18.8/19			0/0/0	Chinese date, fresh
0/0/0	0	9.3	2/2	0/0/0	0/0	0//0	0/0/	18.7/19/18.7	18.8/19			0/0/0	Loquat, fresh
0/0/0	0	9.3	2/2	0/0/0	0/0	0//0	0/0/	18.7/19/18.7	18.8/19			0/0/0	Fruit of elaeagnus mollis diels
0/0/0	0	9.3	2/2	0/0/0	0/0	0//0	0/0/	18.7/19/18.7	18.8/19			0/0/0	Other fruit, fresh
													Fruit and nuts, uncooked or cooked by steaming or boiling in water, frozen, whether or not containing added sugar or other sweetening matter:
0/0/0	0	18		0/0/0	0/18	0//0	0/0/	28.5/28.5/28.5	28.6/28.5			0/0/0	-Strawberries
0/0/0		18		0/0/0	0/18	0//0	0/0/	28.5/28.5/28.5	/28.5			0/0/0	-Raspberries, blackberries, mulberries, loganberries, black, white or red currants and gooseberries
													-Other:
0/0/0		18		0/0/0	0/18	0//0	0/0/	28.5/28.5/28.5	28.6/28.5			0/0/0	---Chestnuts, in shell
													---Other
0/0/0		18		0/0/0	0/18	0//0	0/0/	28.5/28.5/28.5	/28.5			0/0/	Ginkgo, frozen
0/0/0		18		0/0/0	0/18	0//0	0/0/	28.5/28.5/28.5	/28.5			0/0/	Korean pine nuts, shelled, frozen(whethe or not shelled or peeled)
0/0/0		18		0/0/0	0/18	0//0	0/0/	28.5/28.5/28.5	/28.5			0/0/	Other endangered pine-nuts, shelled(whethe or not shelled or peeled)
0/0/0		18		0/0/0	0/18	0//0	0/0/	28.5/28.5/28.5	/28.5			0/0/	Semen torreyae, frozen
0/0/0		18		0/0/0	0/18	0//0	0/0/	28.5/28.5/28.5	/28.5			0/0/	Fruit of wingfruit elaeagus (Elaeagus mollis Diels), frozen
0/0/0		18		0/0/0	0/18	0//0	0/0/	28.5/28.5/28.5	/28.5			0/0/	Lodoicea maldivica nut, frozen
0/0/0		18		0/0/0	0/18	0//0	0/0/	28.5/28.5/28.5	/28.5		//	0/0/	Frozen avocado
0/0/0		18		0/0/0	0/18	0//0	0/0/	28.5/28.5/28.5	/28.5			0/0/	Other fruit and nuts, frozen, not elsewhere specified or included
													Fruit and nuts, provisionally preserved , but unsuitable in that state for immediate consumption:
0/0/0		18		0/0/0	0/18	0//0	0/0/	28.5/28.5/28.5	/28.5			0/0/	-Cherries
													-Other
0/0/0		15	2.5/2.5	0/0/0	0/15	0//0	0/0/	23.8/23.8/23.8	23.8/23.8			0/0/0	Temporarily preserved ginkgo, red pine nut, Torreya grandis, Samara and oil tree fruit (not suitable for direct consumption, excluding artificially cultivated)
0/0/0		15	2.5/2.5	0/0/0	0/15	0//0	0/0/	23.8/23.8/23.8	23.8/23.8			0/0/0	Other endangered pine nuts, giant seed palm (sea coconut) nuts temporarily preserved (but not suitable for direct consumption)
0/0/0		15	2.5/2.5	0/0/0	0/15	0//0	0/0/	23.8/23.8/23.8	23.8/23.8			0/0/0	Other fruits and nuts temporarily preserved (but not suitable for direct consumption)
													Fruit, dried, other than that of headings No. 08. 01 to 08. 06; mixtures of nuts or dried fruits of this Chapter:

税则号列		货品名称〔CIQ 扩展编码及品名—T2 表示见附表 2〕	最惠(%)	暂定税率	普通	增值/消费	出口退税	计量单位	监管条件/特殊证件	检验检疫	对美关税	亚太上/下
0813.1000		-杏〔101:杏干(其他工艺);102:其他蜜饯;103:杏干 提取(晒干的除外)、压榨、烹制、烘焙、冻干、脱水、裹糖屑、发酵、冷冻(经漂汤和杀青,并在-18 度以下冷冻)、浸酸、腌渍、炒制等工艺进行加工处理的〕	25		70	9/	9	千克	AB/	PRQS	70/40	
0813.2000		-梅及李〔101:药用乌梅;102:李干(其他工艺);103:梅干(其他工艺);104:话梅;105:其他蜜饯;106:李干 提取(晒干的除外)、压榨、烹制、烘焙、冻干、脱水、裹糖屑、发酵、冷冻(经漂汤和杀青,并在-18 度以下冷冻)、浸酸、腌渍、炒制等工艺进行加工处理的 107(梅干)(提取(晒干的除外)、压榨、烹制、烘焙、冻干、脱水、裹糖屑、发酵、冷冻(经漂汤和杀青,并在-18 度以下冷冻)、浸酸、腌渍、炒制等工艺进行加工处理的)〕	25		70	9/	9	千克	AB/	PRQS	70/40	
0813.3000		-苹果〔101:提取(晒干的除外)、压榨、烹制、烘焙、冻干、脱水、裹糖屑、发酵、冷冻(经漂汤和杀青,并在-18 度以下冷冻)、浸酸、腌渍、炒制等工艺进行加工处理的);999:其他工艺〕	25		70	9/	9	千克	AB/	PRQS	70/40	
		-其他干果:										
0813.4010		---龙眼干、肉〔101:药用龙眼肉;102:龙眼干(其他工艺);103:其他蜜饯;104:提取(晒干的除外)、压榨、烹制、烘焙、冻干、脱水、裹糖屑、发酵、冷冻(经漂汤和杀青,并在-18 度以下冷冻)、浸酸、腌渍、炒制等工艺进行加工处理的)〕	20		70	9/	9	千克	AB/	PRQS	65/35	
0813.4020		---柿饼〔101 柿饼(其他工艺),102 其他蜜饯 ,103(柿饼)提取(晒干的除外)、压榨、烹制、烘焙、冻干、脱水、裹糖屑、发酵、冷冻(经漂汤和杀青,并在-18 度以下冷冻)、浸酸、腌渍、炒制等工艺进行加工处理的)〕	25		70	9/	9	千克	AB/	PRQS	70/40	
0813.4030		---红枣〔101:药用大枣;102:(干枣)(其他工艺);103:其他蜜饯;104:提取(晒干的除外)、压榨、烹制、烘焙、冻干、脱水、裹糖屑、发酵、冷冻(经漂汤和杀青,并在-18 度以下冷冻)、浸酸、腌渍、炒制等工艺进行加工处理的)〕	25		70	9/	9	千克	AB/	PRQS	70/40	
0813.4040		---荔枝干〔101:提取(晒干的除外)、压榨、烹制、烘焙、冻干、脱水、裹糖屑、发酵、冷冻(经漂汤和杀青,并在-18 度以下冷冻)、浸酸、腌渍、炒制等工艺进行加工处理的);999:其他工艺〕	25		70	9/	9	千克	AB/	PRQS	70/40	
0813.4090		---其他										
0813.4090	10	翅果油树干果〔101:提取(晒干的除外)、压榨、烹制、烘焙、冻干、脱水、裹糖屑、发酵、冷冻(经漂汤和杀青,并在-18 度以下冷冻)、浸酸、腌渍、炒制等工艺进行加工处理的);999:其他工艺〕	25		70	9/	9	千克	ABE/	PRQS	70/40	
0813.4090	20	蔓越橘干〔101:提取(晒干的除外)、压榨、烹制、烘焙、冻干、脱水、裹糖屑、发酵、冷冻(经漂汤和杀青,并在-18 度以下冷冻)、浸酸、腌渍、炒制等工艺进行加工处理的);999:其他工艺〕	25	15	70	9/	9	千克	AB/	PRQS	60/30	
0813.4090	90	其他干果(税目 08.01 至 08.06 的干果除外)[T2]	25		70	9/	9	千克	AB/	PRQS	70/40	
0813.5000		-本章的什锦坚果或干果〔101:提取(晒干的除外)、压榨、烹制、烘焙、冻干、脱水、裹糖屑、发酵、冷冻(经漂汤和杀青,并在-18 度以下冷冻)、浸酸、腌渍、炒制等工艺进行加工处理的);999:其他工艺〕	18		70	9/	9	千克	AB/	PRQS	63/33	
08.14		**柑橘属水果或甜瓜(包括西瓜)的果皮,鲜、冻、干或用盐水、亚硫酸水或其他防腐液暂时保藏的:**										
0814.0000		柑橘属水果或甜瓜(包括西瓜)的果皮鲜、冻、干或用盐水、亚硫酸水或其他防腐液暂时保藏的〔101 果脯,102 其他蜜饯,103 药用陈皮(橘皮),104 冻的、干的,105(鲜或暂时保藏的)提取(晒干的除外)、压榨、烹制、烘焙、冻干、脱水、裹糖屑、发酵、冷冻(经漂汤和杀青,并在-18 度以下冷冻)、浸酸、腌渍、炒制等工艺进行加工处理的),106(鲜或暂时保藏的)橘子皮(其他工艺),107(鲜或暂时保藏的)柠檬皮(其他工艺),108(鲜或暂时保藏的)蓝莓皮(其他工艺),109(鲜或暂时保藏的)山竹果皮(其他工艺)〕	25		70	9/	9	千克	AB/	PRQS	50	

协定税率 %								RCEP		特惠税率 %			Article Description
东/冰/格	巴基斯坦	韩国	瑞士上/下	哥/秘/柬	澳/毛	新西/坡/智	中国港/澳/台	东盟及马来/澳/韩	日/新	亚太2国	老/柬/缅	98/97/95	
0/0/0		15	2.5/2.5	0/0/0	0/15	0//0	0/0/	23.8/23.8/23.8	/23.8			0/0/0	-Apricots
0/0/0		15	2.5/2.5	0/0/0	0/15	0//0	0/0/	23.8/23.8/23.8	/23.8			0/0/0	-Prunes
0/0/0		15	2.5/2.5	0/0/0	0/15	0//0	0/0/	23.8/23.8/23.8	/23.8			0/0/0	-Apples
0/0/0	0	4	2/2	0/0/0	0/0	0//0	0/0/	0/0/18	18.2/0		/0/	0/0/0	-Other: ---Longans and longan pulps
0/0/0	0	15	2.5/2.5	0/0/0	0/15	0//0	0/0/	23.8/23.8/23.8	/23.8		/0/	0/0/0	---Persimmons
0/0/0		15	2.5/2.5	0/0/0	0/15	0//0	0/0/	23.8/23.8/25	23.8/23.8		/0/	0/0/0	---Red jujubes
0/0/0		5	2.5/2.5	0/0/0	0/15	0//0	0/0/	0/0/22.5	22.7/0		/0/	0/0/0	---Preserved litchi
0/0/0	0	15	2.5/2.5	0/0/0	0/15	0//0	0/0/	23.8/23.8/23.8	/23.8		/0/	0/0/0	---Other Fruit of wingfruit elaeagus (*Elaeagus mollis Diels*), dried
0/0/0	0	15	2.5/2.5	0/0/0	0/15	0//0	0/0/	23.8/23.8/23.8	/23.8		/0/	0/0/0	Dried Cranberry
0/0/0	0	15	2.5/2.5	0/0/0	0/15	0//0	0/0/	23.8/23.8/23.8	/23.8		/0/	0/0/0	Other fruit, dried(other than that of headings No. 08.01 to 08.06)
0/0/0	14.4	8.4	1.8/1.8	0/0/0	0/0	0//0	0/0/	16.2/16.2/16.2	/16.2			0/0/0	-Mixtures of nuts or dried fruits of this Chapter
0/0/0		15	2.5/2.5	0/0/0	0/15	0//0	0/0/	23.8/23.8/23.8	/23.8			0/0/0	**Peel of citrus fruit or melons (including watermelons), fresh, frozen, dried or provisionally preserved in brine, in sulphur water or in other preservative solutions:** Peel of citrus fruit or melons (including watermelons), fresh, frozen, dried or provisionally preserved in brine, in sulphur water or in other preservative solutions

第九章
咖啡、茶、马黛茶及调味香料

注释：

一、税目 09.04 至 09.10 所列产品的混合物，应按下列规定归类：

(一)同一税目的两种或两种以上产品的混合物仍应归入该税目；

(二)不同税目的两种或两种以上产品的混合物应归入税目 09.10。

税目 09.04 至 09.10 的产品[或上述(一)或(二)项的混合物]如添加了其他物质，只要所得的混合物保持了原产品的基本特性，其归类应不受影响。基本特性已经改变的，则不应归入本章；构成混合调味品的，应归入税目 21.03。

二、本章不包括荜澄茄椒或税目 12.11 的其他产品。

税则号列	货品名称〔CIQ 扩展编码及品名—T2 表示见附表 2〕	最惠(%)	暂定税率	普通	增值/消费	出口退税	计量单位	监管条件/特殊证件	检验检疫	对美关税	亚太上/下
09.01	**咖啡，不论是否焙炒或浸除咖啡碱；咖啡豆荚及咖啡豆皮；含咖啡的咖啡代用品：**										
	-未焙炒的咖啡：										
0901.1100	--未浸除咖啡碱〔101 提取(晒干的除外)、压榨、烹制、烘焙、冻干、脱水、裹糖屑、发酵、冷冻(经漂汤和杀青，并在－18 度以下冷冻)、浸酸、腌渍、炒制等工艺进行加工处理的，999：其他工艺〕	8		50	13/	9	千克	AB/	PRQS	33	
0901.1200	--已浸除咖啡碱〔101 提取(晒干的除外)、压榨、烹制、烘焙、冻干、脱水、裹糖屑、发酵、冷冻(经漂汤和杀青，并在－18 度以下冷冻)、浸酸、腌渍、炒制等工艺进行加工处理的，999：其他工艺〕	8		50	13/	9	千克	AB/	PRQS	33	
	-已焙炒的咖啡：										
0901.2100	--未浸除咖啡碱〔101 咖啡粉，999：经焙烤后的咖啡豆〕	15		80	13/	13	千克	AB/	PRQS	40	
0901.2200	--已浸除咖啡碱〔999〕	15		80	13/	13	千克	AB/	PRQS	40	
	-其他：										
0901.9010	---咖啡豆荚及咖啡豆皮〔999〕	10		30	13/	9	千克	AB/	PRQS	22.5	
0901.9020	---含咖啡的咖啡代用品〔999〕	30		80	13/	13	千克	AB/	PRQ		
09.02	**茶，不论是否加香料：**										
	-绿茶(未发酵)，内包装每件净重不超过 3 千克：										
0902.1010	---花茶〔999〕	15		100	9/	9,13	千克	AB/	PRS	40	7.5/7.5
0902.1090	---其他〔101 绿茶，102 白茶〕	15		100	9/	9,13	千克	AB/	PRS	40	7.5/7.5
	-其他绿茶(未发酵)：										
0902.2010	---花茶〔999〕	15		100	9/	9,13	千克	AB/	PRS		7.5/7.5
0902.2090	---其他〔101 绿茶，102 白茶〕	15		100	9/	9,13	千克	AB/	PRS	40	7.5/7.5
	-红茶(已发酵)及部分发酵茶，内包装每件净重不超过 3 千克：										
0902.3010	---乌龙茶〔999〕	15		100	9/	9,13	千克	AB/	PRS	40	7.5/7.5
	---黑茶：										
0902.3031	----普洱茶(熟茶)〔999〕	15		100	9/	9,13	千克	AB/	PRS		7.5/7.5
0902.3039	----其他〔999〕	15		100	9/	9,13	千克	AB/	PRS	40	7.5/7.5
0902.3090	----其他〔999〕	15		100	9/	9,13	千克	AB/	PRS	40	7.5/7.5
	-其他红茶(已发酵)及部分发酵茶：										
0902.4010	---乌龙茶〔999〕	15		100	9/	9,13	千克	AB/	PRS		7.5/7.5
	---黑茶：										
0902.4031	----普洱茶(熟茶)〔999〕	15		100	9/	9,13	千克	AB/	PRS		7.5/7.5
0902.4039	----其他〔999〕	15		100	9/	9,13	千克	AB/	PRS	40	7.5/7.5
0902.4090	----其他〔999〕	15		100	9/	9,13	千克	AB/	PRS	40	7.5/7.5
09.03	**马黛茶：**										
0903.0000	马黛茶〔999〕	10		100	9/	13	千克	AB/	PRQ		
09.04	**胡椒；辣椒干及辣椒粉：**										
	-胡椒：										
0904.1100	--未磨										
0904.1100 10	毕拨〔101 药用荜茇，102 调味料〕	20		70	9/	9	千克	QAB/	PRQS	45	
0904.1100 90	未磨胡椒(毕拨除外)〔101 药用未磨胡椒，102 调味料〕	20		70	9/	9	千克	AB/	PRQS	45	
0904.1200	--已磨〔101 药用已磨胡椒，102 调味料〕	20		70	9/	13	千克	AB/	PRQS	45	10/10
	-辣椒：										
0904.2100	--干，未磨〔101 药用辣椒(干)，102 辣椒干〕	20		70	9/	0	千克	AB/	PRQS		10/10
0904.2200	--已磨〔999〕	20		70	9/	9,13	千克	AB/	PRQS	45	10/10
09.05	**香子兰豆：**										
0905.1000	-未磨〔999〕	15		50	9/	9	千克	AB/	PRQ		
0905.2000	-已磨〔999〕	15		50	9/	9	千克	AB/	PRQ		
09.06	**肉桂及肉桂花：**										

Chapter 9
Coffee, tea, mate and spices

Notes:

1. Mixtures of the products of headings No. 09. 04 to 09. 10 are to be classified as follows:
   (a) Mixtures of two or more of the products of the same heading are to be classified in that heading;
   (b) Mixtures of two or more of the products of different headings are to be classified in heading No. 09. 10.
   The addition of other substances to the products of headings No. 09. 04 to 09. 10 (or to the mixtures referred to in paragraph (a) or (b) above) shall not affect their classification provided the resulting mixtures retain the essential character of the goods of those headings. Otherwise such mixtures are not classified in this Chapter; those constituting mixed condiments or mixed seasonings are classified in heading No. 21. 03.
2. This Chapter does not cover Cubeb pepper (*Piper cubeba*) or other products of heading No. 12. 11.

协定税率 %								RCEP		特惠税率 %			Article Description
东/冰/格	巴基斯坦	韩国	瑞士 上/下	哥/秘/柬	澳/毛	新西/坡/智	中国港/澳/台	东盟及马来/澳/韩	日/新	亚太2国	老/柬/缅	98/97/95	
													Coffee, whether or not roasted or decaffeinated; coffee husks and skins; coffee substitutes containing coffee in any proportion:
													-Coffee, not roasted:
5/0/		0	0/0	0//0	0/4.8	0//0	0/0/	5/5/	/5		0/0/	0/0/0	--Not decaffeinated
5/0/		0	0/0	//0	0/4.8	0//0	0/0/	5/5/	/5		0/0/	0/0/0	--Decaffeinated
													-Coffee, roasted:
5/0/		3	6.9/6.9	0//0	0/9	0//0	0/0/				0/0/	0/0/0	--Not decaffeinated
0/0/	12	3	1.5/1.5	//0	0/9	0//0	0/0/	0/0/	13.6/0		0/0/	0/0/0	--Decaffeinated
													-Other:
0/0/	3.5	2	0/0	0/0/0	0/6	0/0/0	0/0/	0/0/9	9.1/0		0/0/	0/0/0	---Coffee husks and skins
0/0/		18		//0	0/18	0/0/0	0/0/	28.5/28.5/28.5	28.6/28.5		0/0/	0/0/0	---Coffee substitutes containing coffee
													Tea, whether or not flavoured:
													-Green tea (not fermented) in immediate packings of a content not exceeding 3kg:
0/0/0	7.5	3	1.5/1.5	0/0/0	0/	0/0/0	0/0/	0/0/13.5	13.6/0			0/0/0	---Flavoured
0/0/0	7.5	3	1.5/1.5	0/0/0	0/	0/0/0	0/0/0	0/0/13.5	13.6/0			0/0/0	---Other
													-Other green tea (not fermented):
0/0/0	7.5	3	1.5/1.5	0/0/0	0/	0/0/0	0/0/	0/0/13.5	13.6/0			0/0/0	---Flavoured
0/0/0	7.5	3	1.5/1.5	0/0/0	0/	0/0/0	0/0/0	0/0/13.5	13.6/0			0/0/0	---Other
													-Black tea (fermented) and partly fermented tea, in immediate packings of a content not exceeding 3 kg:
0/0/0	7.5	3	1.5/1.5	0/0/0	0/	0/0/0	0/0/0	0/0/13.5	13.6/0			0/0/0	---Oolong tea
													Black tea:
0/0/0	7.5	3	1.5/1.5	0/0/0	0/10.7	0/0/0	0/0/	0/0/13.5	13.6/0			0/0/0	----Pu—er tea (Ripe)
0/0/0	7.5	3	1.5/1.5	0/0/0	0/10.7	0/0/0	0/0/0	0/0/13.5	13.6/0			0/0/0	----Other
0/0/0	7.5	3	1.5/1.5	0/0/0	0/10.7	0/0/0	0/0/0	0/0/13.5	13.6/0			0/0/0	---Other
													-Other black tea (fermented) and other partly fermented tea:
0/0/0	7.5	3	1.5/1.5	0/0/0	0/	0/0/0	0/0/0	0/0/13.5	13.6/0		0/0/0	0/0/0	---Oolong tea
													---Black tea:
0/0/0	7.5	3	1.5/1.5	0/0/0	0/10.7	0/0/0	0/0/	0/0/13.5	13.6/0		0/0/0	0/0/0	----Pu—er tea (Ripe)
0/0/0	7.5	3	1.5/1.5	0/0/0	0/10.7	0/0/0	0/0/0	0/0/13.5	13.6/0		0/0/0	0/0/0	----Other
0/0/0	7.5	3	1.5/1.5	0/0/0	0/10.7	0/0/0	0/0/0	0/0/13.5	13.6/0		0/0/0	0/0/0	---Other
													Mate:
0/0/0	3.5	2	0/0	0/0/0	0/0	0/0/0	0/0/	0/0/9	9.1/0			0/0/0	Mate
													Pepper of the genus Piper; dried or crushed or ground fruits of the genus Capsicum or of the genus Pimenta:
													-Pepper:
													--Neither crushed nor ground
5/0/0		9.3	2/2	0/0/18	0/12	0//0	0/0/	19/19.5/19	/19.5			0/0/0	Piper longum
5/0/0		9.3	2/2	0/0/18	0/12	0//0	0/0/	19/19.5/19	/19.5			0/0/0	Pepper of the genus *Piper*, neither crushed nor ground (other than piper longum)
5/0/0	10	9.3	2/2	0/0/5	0/0	0//0	0/0/					0/0/0	--Crushed or ground
													-Fruit of the genus capsicum or of the genus pimenta:
0/0/0	10	9.3	2/2	0/0/0	0/0	0/0/0	0/0/	0/0/11.7	11.8/0			0/0/0	--Dried, neither crushed nor ground
0/0/0	10	9.3	2/2	0/0/0	0/0	0/0/0	0/0/	0/0/11.7	11.8/0			0/0/0	--Crushed or ground
													Vanilla:
0/0/0	12	3	1.5/1.5	0/0/0	0/0	0/0/0	0/0/	0/0/13.5	13.6/0			0/0/0	-Neither crushed nor ground
0/0/0	12	3	1.5/1.5	0/0/0	0/0	0/0/0	0/0/	0/0/13.5	13.6/0			0/0/0	-Crushed or ground
													Cinnamon and cinnamon-tree flowers:

税则号列	货品名称〔CIQ 扩展编码及品名—T2 表示见附表 2〕	最惠(%)	暂定税率	普通	增值/消费	出口退税	计量单位	监管条件/特殊证件	检验检疫	对美关税	亚太上/下
	-未磨:										
0906.1100	--锡兰肉桂〔999〕	5		50	9/	9	千克	AB/	PRQS		
0906.1900	--其他〔101 药用未磨肉桂(桂枝),102 调味料〕	5		50	9/	9	千克	AB/	PRQS	30	
0906.2000	-已磨〔101 药用已磨肉桂(桂枝),102 调味料,103 调味料(玉桂)〕	15		50	9/	13	千克	QAB/	PRQS		
09.07	**丁香(母丁香、公丁香及丁香梗):**										
0907.1000	-未磨〔101 药用未磨丁香,102 调味料〕	3		14	9/	9	千克	QAB/	PRQ		
0907.2000	-已磨〔101 药用已磨丁香,102 调味料〕	3		14	9/	9	千克	QAB/	PRQ		
09.08	**肉豆蔻、肉豆蔻衣及豆蔻:**										
	-肉豆蔻:										
0908.1100	--未磨〔101 药用未磨肉豆蔻,102 调味料〕	8		30	9/	9	千克	QABE/	PRQ		
0908.1200	--已磨〔101 药用已磨肉豆蔻,102 调味料〕	8		30	9/	9	千克	QABE/	PRQ		
	-肉豆蔻衣:										
0908.2100	--未磨〔999〕	8		30	9/	9	千克	ABE/	PRQ		
0908.2200	--已磨〔999〕	8		30	9/	9	千克	ABE/	PRQ		
	-豆蔻:										
0908.3100	--未磨〔101 药用未磨豆蔻,102 调味料〕	3		14	9/	9	千克	QABE/	PRQ		
0908.3200	--已磨〔101 药用已磨豆蔻,102 调味料〕	3		14	9/	13	千克	QABE/	PRQ		
09.09	**茴芹子、八角茴香、小茴香子、芫荽子、枯茗子及贳蒿子;杜松果:**										
	-芫荽子:										
0909.2100	--未磨〔999〕	15		50	9/	9	千克	AB/	PRQ		
0909.2200	--已磨〔999〕	15		50	9/	13	千克	AB/	PRQ		
	-枯茗子:										
0909.3100	--未磨〔999〕	15		50	9/	9	千克	AB/	PRQ		7.5/7.5
0909.3200	--已磨〔999〕	15		50	9/	13	千克	AB/	PRQ	40	7.5/7.5
	-茴芹子或八角茴香、贳蒿子或小茴香子;杜松果:										
	--未磨:										
0909.6110	---八角茴香〔101 药用未磨八角茴香,102 调味料〕	20		90	9/	9	千克	QAB/	PRQS		
0909.6190	---其他										
0909.6190 10	未磨的小茴香子;未磨的杜松果〔101 药用未磨小茴香,102 调味料〕	15		50	9/	9	千克	QAB/	PRQS		
0909.6190 90	未磨的茴芹子;未磨的贳蒿子〔101 茴芹子,102 贡蒿子〕	15		50	9/	9	千克	AB/	PRQ		
	--已磨:										
0909.6210	---八角茴香〔101 药用已磨八角茴香,102 调味料〕	20		90	9/	13	千克	QAB/	PRQS		
0909.6290	---其他										
0909.6290 10	已磨的小茴香子;已磨的杜松果〔101 药用已磨小茴香,102 调味料〕	15		50	9/	13	千克	QAB/	PRQS	27.5	
0909.6290 90	已磨的茴芹子;已磨的贳蒿子〔101 茴芹子,102 贡蒿子〕	15		50	9/	13	千克	AB/	PRQ	27.5	
09.10	**姜、番红花、姜黄、麝香草、月桂叶、咖喱及其他调味香料:**										
	-姜:										
0910.1100	--未磨〔101 药用未磨干姜,102 药用未磨生姜,103 调味料〕	15		50	9/	0	千克	AB/	PRQS		7.5/7.5
0910.1200	--已磨〔101 药用已磨干姜,102 调味料〕	15		50	9/	9	千克	AB/	PRQS	40	7.5/7.5
0910.2000	-番红花〔101 药用番红花(西红花),102 调味料〕	2		14	9/	9,13	千克	QAB/	PRQS		
0910.3000	-姜黄〔102:药用姜黄;103:调味料;104:姜黄浸膏(有检疫要求食品添加剂)〕	15		50	9/	9	千克	QAB/	PRQS		7.5/7.5
	-其他调味香料:										
0910.9100	--本章注释一(二)所述的混合物〔101:五香;102:咖喱粉;999:其他〕	15		50	13/	13	千克	AB/	PRQS	40	7.5/7.5
0910.9900	--其他〔101 药用花椒,102 调味料,103 奥勒岗,104 龙蒿,105 咖喱粉,106 百里香叶、百里香叶粉,107 干薄荷叶,108 香草,109 花椒,110 芥末粉,111 多香果,112 罗勒粉,113 莳萝子粉,114 芹菜子,115 葫芦巴子,116 牛至叶 、牛至叶粉,117 月桂,118 众香子,119 洋苏叶,120 墨角兰,121 迷迭香,122 香叶,123 草果〕	15		50	13/	9,13	千克	AB/	PRQS	40	

协定税率 %								RCEP		特惠税率 %			Article Description
东/冰/格	巴基斯坦	韩国	瑞士上/下	哥/秘/柬	澳/毛	新西/坡/智	中国港/澳/台	东盟及马来/澳/韩	日/新	亚太2国	老/柬/缅	98/97/95	
													-Neither crushed nor ground:
0/0/0	0	0	0/0	0/0/0	0/0	0//0	0/0/	0/0/0	0/0			0/0/0	--Cinnamon(*Cinnamomum zeylan-icum blume*)
0/0/0	0	0	0/0	0/0/0	0/0	0//0	0/0/	0/0/0	0/0			0/0/0	--Other
0/0/0	12	3	1.5/1.5	0/0/0	0/0	0/0/0	0/0/	0/0/13.5	13.6/0			0/0/0	-Crushed or ground
													Cloves (whole fruit, cloves and stems):
0/0/0	0	0	0/0	0/0/0	0/0	0//0	0/0/	0/0/0	0/0		/0/	0/0/0	-Neither crushed nor ground
0/0/0	0	0	0/0	0/0/0	0/0	0//0	0/0/	0/0/0	0/0		/0/	0/0/0	-Crushed or ground
													Nutmeg, mace and cardamoms:
													-Nutmeg:
0/0/0	2	0	0/0	0/0/0	0/0	0//0	0/0/	0/0/0	7.3/0		0/0/	0/0/0	--Neither crushed nor ground
0/0/0	2	0	0/0	0/0/0	0/0	0//0	0/0/	0/0/0	7.3/0		0/0/	0/0/0	--Crushed or ground
													-Mace:
0/0/0	2	0	0/0	0/0/0	0/0	0//0	0/0/	0/0/0	7.3/0		0/0/	0/0/0	--Neither crushed nor ground
0/0/0	2	0	0/0	0/0/0	0/0	0//0	0/0/	0/0/0	7.3/0		0/0/	0/0/0	--Crushed or ground
													-Cardamoms:
0/0/0	0	0	0/0	0/0/0	0/0	0//0	0/0/	0/0/0	0/0		0/0/	0/0/0	--Neither crushed nor ground
0/0/0	0	0	0/0	0/0/0	0/0	0//0	0/0/	0/0/0	0/0		0/0/	0/0/0	--Crushed or ground
													Seeds of anise, star anise, fennel, coriander, cumin or caraway; juniper berries:
													-Seeds of coriander:
0/0/0	12	3	1.5/1.5	0/0/0	0/0	0/0/0	0/0/	0/0/13.5	13.6/0			0/0/0	--Neither crushed nor ground
0/0/0	12	3	1.5/1.5	0/0/0	0/0	0/0/0	0/0/	0/0/13.5	13.6/0			0/0/0	--Crushed or ground
													-Seeds of cumin:
0/0/0	5.3	3	1.5/1.5	0/0/0	0/0	0/0/0	0/0/	0/0/13.5	13.6/0			0/0/0	--Neither crushed nor ground
0/0/0	5.3	3	1.5/1.5	0/0/0	0/0	0/0/0	0/0/	0/0/13.5	13.6/0			0/0/0	--Crushed nor ground
													-Seeds of anise;juniper berries:
													--Neither crushed nor ground:
0/0/0		9.3	2/2	0/0/0	0/0	0/0/0	0/0/	18/18/18	18.8/18			0/0/0	---Star anises
													---Other
0/0/0	12	3	1.5/1.5	0/0/0	0/0	0/0/0	0/0/	0/0/13.5	13.6/0			0/0/0	Seed of fennel, seed of juniper berries, neither crushed nor ground
0/0/0	12	3	1.5/1.5	0/0/0	0/0	0/0/0	0/0/	0/0/13.5	13.6/0			0/0/0	Seed of pimpinella, seed of caraway, neither crushed nor ground
													--Crushed nor ground:
0/0/0		9.3	2/2	0/0/0	0/0	0/0/0	0/0/	18/18/18	18.8/18			0/0/0	---Star anises
													---Other
0/0/0	12	3	1.5/1.5	0/0/0	0/0	0/0/0	0/0/	0/0/13.5	13.6/0			0/0/0	Seed of fennel, seed of juniper berries, crushed or ground
0/0/0	12	3	1.5/1.5	0/0/0	0/0	0/0/0	0/0/	0/0/13.5	13.6/0			0/0/0	Seed of pimpinella, seed of caraway, crushed or ground
													Ginger, saffron, turmeric (curcuma), thyme, bay leaves, curry and other spices:
													Ginger:
0/0/0	5.3	3	1.5/1.5	0/0/0	0/0	0/0/0	0/0/	0/0/13.5	13.6/0		0/0/	0/0/0	--Neither crushed nor ground
0/0/0	5.3	3	1.5/1.6	0/0/0	0/0	0/0/0	0/0/	0/0/13.5	13.6/0		0/0/	0/0/0	--Crushed or ground
0/0/0	0	0	0/0	0/0/0	0/0	0//0	0/0/	0/0/0	0/0			0/0/0	-Saffron
0/0/0	5.3	3	1.5/1.5	0/0/0	0/0	0/0/0	0/0/	0/0/13.5	13.6/0		/0/	0/0/0	-Turmeric (curcuma)
													-Other spices:
0/0/0	0	3	1.5/1.5	0/0/0	0/0	0/0/0	0/0/	0/0/13.5	13.6/0			0/0/0	--Mixtures referred to in Note 1(b) to this Chapter
0/0/0	0	3	1.5/1.5	0/0/0	0/0	0/0/0	0/0/	0/0/	13.6/0			0/0/0	--Other

第十章
谷 物

注释：

一、(一)本章各税目所列产品必须带有谷粒，不论是否成穗或带杆。

(二)本章不包括已去壳或经其他加工的谷物。但去壳、碾磨、磨光、上光、半熟或破碎的稻米仍应归入税目10.06。同样，已全部或部分去皮以分离皂苷，但没有经过任何其他加工的昆诺阿藜仍应归入税目10.08。

二、税目10.05不包括甜玉米(第七章)。

子目注释：

所称“硬粒小麦”，是指硬粒小麦属的小麦及以该属具有相同染色体数目(28)的小麦种间杂交所得的小麦。

税则号列	货品名称〔CIQ扩展编码及品名－T2表示见附表2〕	最惠(%)	暂定税率	普通	增值/消费	出口退税	计量单位	监管条件/特殊证件	检验检疫	对美关税	亚太上/下
10.01	**小麦及混合麦：**										
	-硬粒小麦：										
1001.1100	--种用										
1001.1100 01	种用硬粒小麦(配额内)〔999〕	1		180	9/	0	千克	4xABty/	PQ		
1001.1100 90	种用硬粒小麦(配额外)〔101种质资源；102种质资源除外〕	65		180	9/	0	千克	4xABy/	PQ		
1001.1900	--其他										
1001.1900 01	其他硬粒小麦(配额内)〔101食用小麦，102工业用小麦，103饲用小麦〕	1		180	9/	0	千克	4xABty/	PRQS	26	
1001.1900 90	其他硬粒小麦(配额外)〔101食用小麦，102工业用小麦，103饲用小麦〕	65		180	9/	0	千克	4xABy/	PRQS	90	
	-其他：										
1001.9100	--种用										
1001.9100 01	其他种用小麦及混合麦(配额内)〔999〕	1		180	9/	0	千克	4xABty/	PQ		
1001.9100 90	其他种用小麦及混合麦(配额外)〔999〕	65		180	9/	0	千克	4xABy/	PQ		
1001.9900	--其他										
1001.9900 01	其他小麦及混合麦(配额内)〔101食用小麦，102工业用小麦，103饲用小麦〕	1		180	9/	0	千克	4xABty/	PRQS	26	
1001.9900 90	其他小麦及混合麦(配额外)〔101食用小麦，102工业用小麦，103饲用小麦〕	65		180	9/	0	千克	4xABy/	PRQS	90	
10.02	**黑麦：**										
1002.1000	-种用〔999〕	0		0	9/	0	千克	AB/	PQ	5	
1002.9000	-其他〔201：食用；202：饲用〕	3		8	9/	0	千克	AB/	PRQ	8	
10.03	**大麦：**										
1003.1000	-种用〔101种质资源；102种质资源除外〕	0		160	0/	0	千克	7AB/	PQ		
1003.9000	-其他〔101食用，102饲料用〕	3		160	9/	0	千克	7AB/	PRQS	8	0/0
10.04	**燕麦：**										
1004.1000	-种用〔101种质资源；102种质资源除外〕	0		0	0/	0	千克	AB/	PQ		
1004.9000	-其他〔201：食用；202：饲用〕	2		8	9/	0	千克	AB/	PRQ	7	
10.05	**玉米：**										
1005.1000	-种用										
1005.1000 01	种用玉米(配额内)〔999〕	1		180	0/	0	千克	4xAByt/	PQ		
1005.1000 90	种用玉米(配额外)〔101种质资源；102种质资源除外〕	20		180	0/	0	千克	4xABy/	PQ		
1005.9000	-其他										
1005.9000 01	其他玉米(配额内)〔101食用玉米，替代种植除外；102工业用玉米，替代种植除外；103饲用玉米，替代种植除外；104替代种植〕	1		180	9/	0	千克	4xAByt/	PRQS	26	
1005.9000 90	其他玉米(配额外)〔101食用玉米，102工业用玉米，103饲用玉米〕	65		180	9/	0	千克	4xABy/	PRQS	90	
10.06	**稻谷、大米：**										
	-稻谷：										
	---种用：										
1006.1021	----长粒米										
1006.1021 01	种用长粒米稻谷(配额内)〔999〕	1		180	9/	0	千克	4xAByt/	PNQ	26	
1006.1021 90	种用长粒米稻谷(配额外)〔101种质资源；102种质资源除外〕	65		180	9/	0	千克	4xABy/	PNQ	90	
1006.1029	----其他										
1006.1029 01	其他种用稻谷(配额内)〔999〕	1		180	9/	0	千克	4xAByt/	PNQ	26	
1006.1029 90	其他种用稻谷(配额外)〔101种质资源；102种质资源除外〕	65		180	9/	0	千克	4xABy/	PNQ	90	
	---其他：										
1006.1081	----长粒米										
1006.1081 01	其他长粒米稻谷(配额内)〔101替代种植；102替代种植除外；999〕	1		180	9/	0	千克	4xAByt/	PRQS	26	
1006.1081 90	其他长粒米稻谷(配额外)〔999〕	65		180	9/	0	千克	4xABy/	PRQS	90	
1006.1089	----其他										

Chapter 10
Cereals

Notes:

1. (a) The products specified in the headings of this Chapter are to be classified in those headings only if grains are present, whether or not in the ear or on the stalk.

   (b) The Chapter does not cover grains which have been hulled or otherwise worked. However, rice, husked, milled, polished, glazed, parboiled or broken remains classified in heading No. 10.06. Similarly, quinoa from which the pericarp has been wholly or partly removed in order to separate the saponin, but which has not undergone any other processes, remains classified in heading No.10.08.

2. Heading No. 10.05 does not cover sweet corn (Chapter 7).

Subheading Note:

The term "durum wheat" means wheat of the *Triticum durum* species and the hybrids derived from the inter-specific crossing of *Triticum durum* which have the same number (28) of chromosomes as that species.

协定税率 %								RCEP		特惠税率 %			
东/冰/格	巴基斯坦	韩国	瑞士上/下	哥/秘/柬	澳/毛	新西/坡/智	中国港/澳/台	东盟及马来/澳/韩	日/新	亚太2国	老/柬/缅	98/97/95	Article Description
													Wheat and maslin:
													-Durum wheat:
													--Seed
5//							0/0/						Durum wheat, seed(in-quota)
5//							0/0/						Durum wheat, seed(out-quota)
													--Other
5//							0/0/						Other durum wheat(in-quota)
5//							0/0/						Other durum wheat(out-quota)
													-Other:
													--Seed
5//							0/0/						Other wheat, seed and maslin(in-quota)
5//							0/0/						Other wheat, seed and maslin(out-quota)
													--Other
5//							0/0/						Other wheat and maslin (in-quota)
5//							0/0/						Other wheat and maslin (out-quota)
													Rye:
0/0/0	0	0	0/0	0/0/0	0/0	0//0	0/0/	0/0/0	0/0			0/0/0	-Seed
0/0/0	0	0	0/0	0/0/0	0/0	0//0	0/0/	0/0/0	2.7/0			0/0/0	-Other
													Barley:
0/0/0	0	0	0/0	0/0/0	0/0	0//0	0/0/	0/0/0	0/0			0/0/0	-Seed
0/0/0	0	0	0/0	0/0/0	0/0	0//0	0/0/	0/0/0	2.7/0			0/0/0	-Other
													Oats:
0/0/0	0	0	0/0	0/0/0	0/0	0//0	0/0/	0/0/0	0/0			0/0/0	-Seed
0/0/0	0	0	0/0	0/0/0	0/0	0//0	0/0/	1.8/1.8/1.8	1.8/1.8			0/0/0	-Other
													Maize (corn):
													Seed
							0/0/						Maize (corn) seed (in-quota)
							0/0/						Maize (corn) seed (out-quota)
													-Other
50//							0/0/						Other maize (corn) (in-quota)
50//							0/0/						Other maize (corn) (out-quota)
													Rice:
													-Rice in husk (paddy or rough):
													---Seed:
													----Long grain rice
50//							0/0/						rice in husk(paddy or rough), Long grain rice, seed(in-quota)
50//							0/0/						rice in husk(paddy or rough), Long grain rice, seed(out-quota)
													----Other
50//							0/0/						Other rice in husk(paddy or rough), seed(in-quota)
50//							0/0/						Other rice in husk(paddy or rough), seed(out-quota)
													---Other:
													----Long grain rice
50//							0/0/						Other rice in husk(paddy or rough), Long grain rice(in-quota)
50//							0/0/						Other rice in husk(paddy or rough), Long grain rice(out-quota)
													----Other

税则号列		货品名称〔CIQ 扩展编码及品名－T2 表示见附表 2〕	最惠(%)	暂定税率	普通	增值/消费	出口退税	计量单位	监管条件/特殊证件	检验检疫	对美关税	亚太上/下
1006.1089	01	其他稻谷(配额内)〔101 替代种植;102 替代种植除外;999〕	1		180	9/	0	千克	4xAByt/	PRQS	26	
1006.1089	90	其他稻谷(配额外)〔999〕	65		180	9/	0	千克	4xABy/	PRQS	90	
		-糙米:										
1006.2020		---长粒米										
1006.2020	01	长粒米糙米(配额内)〔999〕	1		180	9/	0	千克	4xAByt/	PRQS	26	
1006.2020	90	长粒米糙米(配额外)〔999〕	65		180	9/	0	千克	4xABy/	PRQS	90	
1006.2080		---其他										
1006.2080	01	其他糙米(配额内)〔999〕	1		180	9/	0	千克	4xAByt/	PRQS	26	
1006.2080	90	其他糙米(配额外)〔999〕	65		180	9/	0	千克	4xABy/	PRQS	90	
		-精米,不论是否磨光或上光:										
1006.3020		---长粒米										
1006.3020	01	长粒米精米(不论是否磨光或上光(配额内))〔201 食用白米,202 食用蒸煮米,203 食用其他加工米〕	1		180	9/	0	千克	4xAByt/	PRQS	26	
1006.3020	90	长粒米精米(不论是否磨光或上光(配额外))〔201 食用白米,202 食用蒸煮米,203 食用其他加工米〕	65		180	9/	0	千克	4xABy/	PRQS	90	
1006.3080		---其他										
1006.3080	01	其他精米(不论是否磨光或上光(配额内))〔201 食用白米,202 食用蒸煮米,203 食用其他加工米〕	1		180	9/	0	千克	4xAByt/	PRQS	26	
1006.3080	90	其他精米(不论是否磨光或上光(配额外))〔201 食用白米,202 食用蒸煮米,203 食用其他加工米〕	65		180	9/	0	千克	4xABy/	PRQS	90	
		-碎米:										
1006.4020		---长粒米										
1006.4020	01	长粒米碎米(配额内)〔201 食用白米,202 食用蒸煮米,203 食用其他加工米〕	1		180	9/	0	千克	4xAByt/	PRQS	26	
1006.4020	90	长粒米碎米(配额外)〔201 食用白米,202 食用蒸煮米,203 食用其他加工米〕	10		180	9/	0	千克	4xABy/	PRQS	35	
1006.4080		---其他										
1006.4080	01	其他碎米(配额内)〔201 食用白米,202 食用蒸煮米,203 食用其他加工米〕	1		180	9/	0	千克	4xAByt/	PRQS	26	
1006.4080	90	其他碎米(配额外)〔201 食用白米,202 食用蒸煮米,203 食用其他加工米〕	10		180	9/	0	千克	4xABy/	PRQS	35	
10.07		**食用高粱:**										
1007.1000		-种用〔101 种用,种质资源除外;102 食用、带壳,种质资源除外;103 食用、去壳,种质资源除外;104 种质资源〕	0		0	0/	0	千克	7AB/	PNQ		
1007.9000		-其他〔101 饲用,102 食用、带壳,103 食用、去壳〕	2		8	9/	0	千克	7AB/	PRQS	27	
10.08		**荞麦、谷子及加那利草子;其他谷物:**										
1008.1000		-荞麦〔101 食用、带壳,102 食用、去壳〕	2		8	9/	0	千克	AB/	PRQS	7	
		-谷子:										
1008.2100		--种用〔101 种质资源;102 种质资源除外〕	2		8	9/	0	千克	AB/	PQ	7	
1008.2900		--其他〔101 食用、带壳,102 食用、去壳〕	2		8	9/	0	千克	AB/	PRQS	7	
1008.3000		-加那利草子〔999〕	2		8	9/	9	千克	AB/	PRQ	7	
		-直长马唐(马唐属):										
1008.4010		---种用〔999〕	0		0	9/	0	千克	AB/	PNQ	5	
1008.4090		---其他〔999〕	3		8	9/	0	千克	AB/	PRQS	8	
		-昆诺阿藜:										
1008.5010		---种用〔999〕	0		0	9/	0	千克	AB/	PNQ	5	
1008.5090		---其他〔999〕	3		8	9/	0	千克	AB/	PRQS	8	
		-黑小麦:										
1008.6010		---种用〔999〕	0		0	9/	0	千克	AB/	PNQ	5	
1008.6090		---其他〔101 食用,102 工业用,103 饲用〕	3		80	9/	0	千克	AB/	PRQS	8	
		-其他谷物:										
1008.9010		---种用 101 粟种子,种质资源除外;102 荞麦种子,种质资源除外;103 其他谷物种子,种质资源除外;104 种质资源〕	0		0	9/	0	千克	AB/	PNQ	5	
1008.9090		---其他〔101 饲用其他粮谷,102 食用、去壳黍子,103 食用、带壳黍子,104 食用谷穗,105 食用其他粮谷,106 野米,107 薏米,108 藜麦〕	3		8	9/	0	千克	AB/	PRQS	8	

协定税率 %								RCEP		特惠税率 %			Article Description
东/冰/格	巴基斯坦	韩国	瑞士上/下	哥/秘/柬	澳/毛	新西/坡/智	中国港/澳/台	东盟及马来/澳/韩	日/新	亚太2国	老/柬/缅	98/97/95	
50//							0/0/						Other rice in husk(paddy or rough)(in-quota)
50//							0/0/						Other rice in husk(paddy or rough),(out-quota)
													-Husked (brown) rice:
													---Long grain rice
50//							0/0/						Husked(brown) rice,long grain rice(in-quota)
50//							0/0/						Husked(brown) rice,long grain rice(out-quota)
													---Other
50//							0/0/						Other husked(brown) rice(in-quota)
50//							0/0/						Other husked(brown) rice(out-quota)
													-Semi-milled or wholly missed rice, whether or not polished or glazed:
													---Long grain rice
50//							0/0/						Semi-milled or wholly milled rice,long grain rice(whether or not polished or glazed(in-quota))
50//							0/0/						Semi-milled or wholly milled rice,long grain rice(whether or not polished or glazed(out-quota))
													---Other
50//							0/0/						Other semi-milled or wholly milled rice(whether or not polished or glazed(in-quota))
50//							0/0/						Other semi-milled or wholly milled rice(whether or not polished or glazed(out-quota))
													-Broken rice:
													---Long grain rice
5//							0/0/						Broken rice,long grain rice(in-quota)
5//							0/0/						Broken rice,long grain rice(out-quota)
													---Other
5//							0/0/						Other broken rice(in-quota)
5//							0/0/						Other broken rice(out-quota)
													Grain sorghum:
0/0/0	0	0	0/0	0/0/0	0/0	0//0	0/0/	0/0/0	0/0			0/0/0	-Seed
0/0/0	0	0	0/0	0/0/0	0/0	0//0	0/0/	0/0/0	1.8/0			0/0/0	-Other
													Buckwheat, millet and canary seed; other cereals:
0/0/0	0	0	0/0	0/0/0	0/0	0//0	0/0/	0/0/0	1.8/0			0/0/0	-Buckwheat
													-Millet:
0/0/0	0	0	0/0	0/0/0	0/0	0//0	0/0/	0/0/0	0/0		0//	0/0/0	--Seed
0/0/0	0	0	0/0	0/0/0	0/0	0//0	0/0/	0/0/0	1.8/0		0//	0/0/0	--Other
0/0/0	0	0	0/0	0/0/0	0/0	0//0	0/0/	0/0/0	0/0		0//	0/0/0	-Canary seed
													-Fonio(Digitaria spp.):
0/0/0	0	0	0/0	0/0/0	0/0	0//0	0/0/	0/0/0	0/0			0/0/0	---Seed
0/0/0	0	0	0/0	0/0/0	0/0	0//0	0/0/	0/0/0	0/0		0//	0/0/0	---Other
													-Quinoa(Chenopodium quinoa):
0/0/0	0	0	0/0	0/0/0	0/0	0//0	0/0/	0/0/0	0/0			0/0/0	---Seed
0/0/0	0	0	0/0	0/0/0	0/0	0//0	0/0/	0/0/0	0/0		0//	0/0/0	---Other
													-Triticale:
0/0/0	0	0	0/0	0/0/0	0/0	0//0	0/0/	0/0/0	0/0			0/0/0	---Seed
0/0/0	0	0	0/0	0/0/0	0/0	0//0	0/0/	0/0/0	0/0		0//	0/0/0	---Other
													-Other cereals:
0/0/0	0	0	0/0	0/0/0	0/0	0//0	0/0/	0/0/0	0/0			0/0/0	---Seed
0/0/0	0	0	0/0	0/0/0	0/0	0//0	0/0/	0/0/0	2.7/0		0//	0/0/0	---Other

第十一章
制粉工业产品;麦芽;淀粉;菊粉;面筋

注释:

一、本章不包括:

(一)作为咖啡代用品的焙制麦芽(税目09.01或21.01);

(二)税目19.01的经制作的细粉、粗粒、粗粉或淀粉;

(三)税目19.04的玉米片及其他产品;

(四)税目20.01、20.04或20.05的经加工或保藏的蔬菜;

(五)药品(第三十章);

(六)具有芳香料制品或化妆盥洗品性质的淀粉(第三十三章)。

二、(一)下表所列谷物碾磨产品按干制品重量计如果同时符合以下两个条件,应归入本章;但是,整粒、滚压、制片或磨碎的谷物胚芽均应归入税目11.04:

1. 淀粉含量(按修订的尤艾斯旋光法测定)超过表列第(2)栏的比例;

2. 灰分含量(除去任何添加的矿物质)不超过表列第(3)栏的比例。

否则,应归入税目23.02。

(二)符合上述规定归入本章的产品,如果用表列第(4)或第(5)栏规定孔径的金属丝网筛过筛,其通过率按重量计不低于表列比例的,应归入税目11.01或11.02。

否则,应归入税目11.03或11.04。

谷　物 (1)	淀粉含量 (2)	灰分含量 (3)	通过下列孔径筛子的比率	
			315微米 (4)	500微米 (5)
小麦及黑麦	45%	2.5%	80%	—
大　麦	45%	3%	80%	—
燕　麦	45%	5%	80%	—
玉米及高粱	45%	2%	—	90%
大　米	45%	1.6%	80%	—
荞　麦	45%	4%	80%	—

三、税目11.03所称"粗粒"及"粗粉",是指谷物经碾碎所得的下列产品:

(一)玉米产品,用2毫米孔径的金属丝网筛过筛后通过率按重量计不低于95%的;

(二)其他谷物产品,用1.25毫米孔径的金属丝网筛过筛,通过率按重量计不低于95%的。

税则号列	货品名称〔CIQ扩展编码及品名—T2表示见附表2〕	最惠(%)	暂定税率	普通	增值/消费	出口退税	计量单位	监管条件/特殊证件	检验检疫	对美关税	亚太上/下
11.01	**小麦或混合麦的细粉:**										
1101.0000	小麦或混合麦的细粉										
1101.0000 01	小麦或混合麦的细粉(配额内)〔999〕	6		130	9/	9	千克	4ABtxy/	PRQS	31	
1101.0000 90	小麦或混合麦的细粉(配额外)〔999〕	65		130	9/	9	千克	4ABxy/	PRQS	90	
11.02	**其他谷物细粉,但小麦或混合麦的细粉除外:**										
1102.2000	-玉米细粉										
1102.2000 01	玉米细粉(配额内)〔999〕	9		130	9/	0	千克	4ABtxy/	PRQS	34	
1102.2000 90	玉米细粉(配额外)〔999〕	40		130	9/	0	千克	4ABxy/	PRQS	65	
	-其他:										
	---大米细粉:										
1102.9021	----长粒米的										
1102.9021 01	长粒米大米细粉(配额内)〔999〕	9		130	9/	0	千克	4ABtxy/	PRQS	34	
1102.9021 90	长粒米大米细粉(配额外)〔999〕	40		130	9/	0	千克	4ABxy/	PRQS	65	
1102.9029	----其他										
1102.9029 01	其他大米细粉(配额内)〔201食用米粉,202食用其他粮食加工产品〕	9		130	9/	0	千克	4ABtxy/	PRQS	34	
1102.9029 90	其他大米细粉(配额外)〔201食用米粉,202食用其他粮食加工产品〕	40		130	9/	0	千克	4ABxy/	PRQS	65	

Chapter 11
Products of the milling industry; malt; starches; inulin; wheat gluten

chorpterr Notes:

1. This Chapter does not cover:
   (a) Roasted malt put up as coffee substitutes (heading No. 09.01 or 21.01);
   (b) Prepared flours, groats, meals or starches of heading No. 19.01;
   (c) Corn flakes or other products of heading No. 19.04;
   (d) Vegetables, prepared or preserved, of heading No. 20.01, 20.04 or 20.05;
   (e) Pharmaceutical products (Chapter 30);
   (f) Starches having the character of perfumery, cosmetic or toilet preparations (Chapter 33).
2. (A) Products from the milling of the cereals listed in the table below fall in this Chapter if they have, by weight on the dry product. However, germ of cereals, whole, rolled, flaked or ground is always classified in heading No. 11.04.
   (ⅰ) a starch content (determined by the modified Ewers polarimetric method) exceeding that indicated in Column (2); and
   (ⅱ) an ash content (after deduction of any added minerals) not exceeding that indicated in Column (3).
   Otherwise, they fall in heading No. 23.02
   (B) Products falling in this Chapter under the above provisions shall be classified in heading No. 11.01 or 11.02 if the percentage passing through a woven metal wire cloth sieve with the aperture indicated in Column (4) or (5) is not less, by weight, than that shown against the cereal concerned.
   Otherwise, they fall in heading No. 11.03 or 11.04.

Cereal (1)	Starch content (2)	Ash content (3)	Rate of passage through a sieve with an aperture of	
			315 micrometres (microns) (4)	500 micrometres (microns) (5)
Wheat and rye	45%	2.5%	80%	-
Barley	45%	3%	80%	-
Oats	45%	5%	80%	-
Maize(corn) and grain Sorghum	45%	2%	-	90%
Rice	45%	1.6%	80%	-
Buckwheat	45%	4%	80%	-

3. For the purposes of heading No. 11.03, the terms "groats" and "meal" mean products obtained by the fragmentation of cereal grains, of which:
   (a) in the case of maize (corn) products, at least 95% by weight passes through a woven metal wire cloth sieve with an aperture of 2mm.
   (b) in the case of other cereal products, at least 95% by weight passes through a woven metal wire cloth sieve with an aperture of 1.25mm.

协定税率 %								RCEP		特惠税率 %			Article Description
东/冰/格	巴基斯坦	韩国	瑞士上/下	哥/秘/柬	澳/毛	新西/坡/智	中国港/澳/台	东盟及马来/澳/韩	日/新	亚太2国	老/柬/缅	98/97/95	
													Wheat or maslin flour:
													Wheat or maslin flour
50//							0/0/						Wheat or maslin flour (in-quota)
50//							0/0/						Wheat or maslin flour (out-quota)
													Cereal flours other than of wheat or maslin:
													-Maize (corn) flour
							0/0/						Maize (corn) flour (in-quota)
							0/0/						Maize(corn) flour(out-quota)
													-Other:
													---Rice flour
													----Of long grain
							0/0/						Long grain rice flour(in—quota)
							0/0/						Long grain rice flour(out—quota)
													----Other
40//							0/0/						Other rice flour(in—quota)
40//							0/0/						Other rice flour(out—quota)

税则号列	货品名称〔CIQ 扩展编码及品名—T2 表示见附表 2〕	最惠(%)	暂定税率	普通	增值/消费	出口退税	计量单位	监管条件/特殊证件	检验检疫	对美关税	亚太上/下
1102.9090	---其他〔101 食用荞麦仁、粉,102 食用其他面粉类,103 食用其他粮食加工产品,104 黑麦粉〕	5		14	9/	0	千克	AB/	PRQS	30	
11.03	**谷物的粗粒、粗粉及团粒:**										
	-粗粒及粗粉:										
1103.1100	--小麦的										
1103.1100 01	小麦粗粒及粗粉(配额内)〔999〕	9		130	9/	9	千克	4ABtxy/	PRQS	34	
1103.1100 90	小麦粗粒及粗粉(配额外)〔999〕	65		130	9/	9	千克	4ABxy/	PRQS	90	
1103.1300	--玉米的										
	--其他:										
1103.1300 01	玉米粗粒及粗粉(配额内)〔999〕	9		130	9/	0	千克	4ABtxy/	PRQS	14	
1103.1300 90	玉米粗粒及粗粉(配额外)〔999〕	65		130	9/	0	千克	4ABxy/	PRQS	70	
1103.1910	---燕麦的〔999〕	5		14	9/	0	千克	AB/	PRQ	10	
	---大米的:										
1103.1931	----长粒米的										
1103.1931 01	长粒米大米粗粒及粗粉(配额内)〔999〕	9		70	9/	0	千克	4ABtxy/	PRQS	34	
1103.1931 90	长粒米大米粗粒及粗粉(配额外)〔999〕	10		70	9/	0	千克	4ABxy/	PRQS	35	
1103.1939	----其他										
1103.1939 01	其他大米粗粒及粗粉(配额内)〔201 食用米粉,202 食用其他粮食加工产品〕	9		70	9/	0	千克	4ABtxy/	PRQS	34	
1103.1939 90	其他大米粗粒及粗粉(配额外)〔201 食用,202 食用米粉,203 食用其他粮食加工产品〕	10		70	9/	0	千克	4ABxy/	PRQS	35	
1103.1990	---其他〔101 食用荞麦仁、粉,102 食用黑麦粉,103 食用其他粮食加工产品〕	5		14	9/	0	千克	AB/	PRQS	10	
	-团粒:										
1103.2010	---小麦的										
1103.2010 01	小麦团粒(配额内)〔999〕	10		180	9/	9	千克	4ABtxy/	PRQ	15	
1103.2010 90	小麦团粒(配额外)〔999〕	65		180	9/	9	千克	4ABxy/	PRQ	70	
1103.2090	---其他〔101 食用荞麦仁、粉,102 食用黑麦粉,103 食用燕麦粉,104 食用其他面粉类〕	20		50	9/	0	千克	AB/	PRQ	25	
11.04	**经其他加工的谷物(例如,去壳、滚压、制片、制成粒状、切片或粗磨),但税目 10.06 的稻谷、大米除外;谷物胚芽,整粒、滚压、制片或磨碎的:**										
	-滚压或制片的谷物:										
1104.1200	--燕麦的〔999〕	20		50	13/	0	千克	AB/	PRQ	45	
	--其他:										
1104.1910	---大麦的〔999〕	20		50	13/	0	千克	AB/	PRQ	25	
1104.1990	---其他										
1104.1990 10	滚压或制片的玉米〔999〕	20		50	13/	0	千克	4ABxy/	PRQ	30	
1104.1990 90	滚压或制片的其他谷物〔999〕	20		50	13/	0	千克	AB/	PRQ	30	
	-经其他加工的谷物(例如,去壳、制成粒状、切片或粗磨):										
1104.2200	--燕麦的〔999〕	20		50	13/	0	千克	AB/	PRQ	45	
1104.2300	--玉米的										
1104.2300 01	经其他加工的玉米(配额内)〔101 食用玉米粉,102 食用其他粮食加工产品〕	10		180	9/	0	千克	4ABtxy/	PRQ	15	
1104.2300 90	经其他加工的玉米(配额外)〔101 食用玉米粉,102 食用其他粮食加工产品〕	65		180	9/	0	千克	4ABxy/	PRQ	70	
	--其他:										
1104.2910	---大麦的〔999〕	65		114	9/	0	千克	AB/	PRQS	70	
1104.2990	---其他〔101 食用小麦粉,102 食用荞麦仁、粉,103 食用燕麦粉,104 食用其他粮食加工产品,105 黑麦粉,106 野米,107 薏仁米〕	20		50	9/	0	千克	AB/	PRQS	45	
1104.3000	-谷物胚芽,整粒、滚压、制片或磨碎的〔101 食用其他麦芽,102 食用其他粮食加工产品〕	20		50	9/	0	千克	AB/	PRQ	40	
11.05	**马铃薯的细粉、粗粉、粉末、粉片、颗粒及团粒:**										
1105.1000	-细粉、粗粉及粉末〔999〕	15		50	13/	13	千克	AB/	PRQ	27.5	
1105.2000	-粉片、颗粒及团粒〔999〕	15		50	13/	13	千克	AB/	PRQ	40	
11.06	**用税目 07.13 的干豆或税目 07.14 的西谷茎髓及植物根茎、块茎制成的细粉、粗粉及粉末;用第八章的产品制成的细粉、粗粉及粉末:**										
1106.1000	-用税目 07.13 的干豆制成的〔999〕	10		30	13/	13	千克	AB/	PRQS	22.5	
1106.2000	-用税目 07.14 的西谷茎髓及植物根茎、块茎制成的〔999〕	20		50	13/	13	千克	AB/	PRQS	25	

协定税率 %								RCEP		特惠税率 %			Article Description
东/冰/格	巴基斯坦	韩国	瑞士上/下	哥/秘/柬	澳/毛	新西/坡/智	中国港/澳/台	东盟及马来/澳/韩	日/新	亚太2国	老/柬/缅	98/97/95	
0/0/0	0	0	0/0	0/0/0	0/0	0//0	0/0/	0/0/0	4.5/0		/0/	0/0/0	---Other
													Cereal groats, meal and pellets:
													-Groats and meal:
													--Of wheat
50//							0/0/						Wheat groats and meal (in-quota)
50//							0/0/						Wheat groats and meal (out-quota)
													--Of maize (corn)
													--Other:
50//							0/0/						Maize(corn) groats and meal (in-quota)
50//							0/0/						Maize (corn) groats and meal (out-quota)
0/0/0	0	0	0/0	0/0/0	0/0	0//0	0/0/	0/0/0	4.5/0		//	0/0/0	---Of oat
													---Of rice
													----Of long grain rice
5//							0/0/						long grain rice groats and meal(in—quota)
5//							0/0/						long grain rice groats and meal(out—quota)
													----Other
5//							0/0/						Other rice groats and meal(in—quota)
5//							0/0/						Other rice groats and meal(out—quota)
0/0/0	0	0	0/0	0/0/0	0/0	0//0	0/0/	0/0/0	4.5/0		/0/	0/0/0	---Other
													-Pellets:
													---Of wheat
50//							0/0/						Wheat pellets (in-quota)
50//							0/0/						Wheat pellets (out-quota)
0/0/		9.3	2/2	0/0/0	0/0	0/0/0	0/0/	18/18/18	18.8/18			0/0/0	---Of other cereals
													Cereal grains otherwise worked (for example, hulled, rolled, flaked, pearled, sliced or kibbled), except rice of heading No. 10.06; germ of cereals, whole, rolled, flaked or ground:
													-Rolled or flaked grains:
0/0/		9.3	2/2	0/0/0	0/0	0/0/0	0/0/	18/18/18	18.8/18			0/0/0	--Of oats
													--Other:
0/0/		9.3	2/2	0/0/0	0/0	0/0/0	0/0/	18/18/18	18.8/18			0/0/0	---Of barley
													---Other
0/0/		9.3	2/2	0/0/0	0/0	0/0/0	0/0/	18/18/18	18.8/18			0/0/0	Rolled or flaked maize
0/0/		9.3	2/2	0/0/0	0/0	0/0/0	0/0/	18/18/18	18.8/18			0/0/0	Rolled or flaked other corns
													-Other worked grains (for example, hulled, pearled, sliced or kibbled):
0/0/		9.3	2/2	0/0/0	0/0	0/0/0	0/0/	18/18/18	18.8/18			0/0/0	--Of oats
													--Of maize (corn)
50//							0/0/						Maize (corn) otherwise worked (in-quota)
50//							0/0/						Maize (corn) otherwise worked (out-quota)
													--Other:
0//				0/0/0	0/39	0/0/0	0/0/	61.8/63.4/65	61.9/63.4			0/0/0	---Of barley
0/0/		9.3	2/2	0/0/0	0/0	0/0/0	0/0/	18.7/19/18.7	18.8/19			0/0/0	---Other
0/0/0		9.3	2/2	0/0/0	0/0	0/0/0	0/0/	18/18/18	18.8/18			0/0/0	-Germ of cereals, whole, rolled, flaked or ground
													Flour, meal, powder, flakes, granules and pellets of potatoes:
0/0/	12	3	1.5/1.5	0/0/0	0/0	0/0/0	0/0/	0/0/13.5	13.6/0			0/0/0	-Flour, meal and powder
0/0/	12	3	1.5/1.5	0/0/0	0/0	0/0/0	0/0/	0/0/13.5	13.6/0			0/0/0	-Flakes, granules and pellets
													Flour, meal and powder of the dried leguminous vegetables of heading No. 07.13, of sago or of roots or tubers of heading No. 07.14; or of the products of Chapter 8:
0/0/0		2	0/0	0/0/0	0/0	0/0/0	0/0/	0/0/9	9.1/0		/0/	0/0/0	-Of the dried leguminous vegetables of heading No. 07.13
0/0/0		9.3	2/2	0/0/0	0/0	0/0/0	0/0/	18.7/19/18.7	18.8/19		0/0/0	0/0/0	-Of sago or of roots or tubers of heading No. 07.14

税则号列	货品名称〔CIQ 扩展编码及品名—T2 表示见附表 2〕	最惠(%)	暂定税率	普通	增值/消费	出口退税	计量单位	监管条件/特殊证件	检验检疫	对美关税	亚太上/下
1106.3000	-用第八章的产品制成的〔101:其他籽仁为坚硬外壳包被的籽实提取(晒干的除外)、压榨、烹制、烘焙、冻干、脱水、裹糖屑、发酵、冷冻(经漂汤和杀青,并在-18 度以下冷冻)、浸酸、腌渍、炒制等工艺进行加工处理的);102:其他籽仁为皮或衣等包的籽实提取(晒干的除外)、压榨、烹制、烘焙、冻干、脱水、裹糖屑、发酵、冷冻(经漂汤和杀青,并在-19 度以下冷冻)、浸酸、腌渍、炒制等工艺进行加工处理的);103:其他籽仁为坚硬外壳包被的籽实(扁桃仁粉)其他工艺;104:其他籽仁为坚硬外壳包被的籽实(椰子粉、椰壳粉、椰浆粉)其他工艺 ;105:其他籽仁为坚硬外壳包被的籽实(杏仁粉)其他工艺;106:其他籽仁为坚硬外壳包被的籽实(巴旦杏粉)其他工艺 ;107:其他籽仁为坚硬外壳包被的籽实(榴莲粉)其他工艺;108:其他籽仁为坚硬外壳包被的籽实(榛子粉)其他工艺;109:其他籽仁为坚硬外壳包被的籽实(罗望子粉)其他工艺;110:其他籽仁为皮或衣等包被的籽实(蓝莓粉)其他工艺;111:其他籽仁为皮或衣等包被的籽实(香蕉粉)(其他工艺);112:其他籽仁为皮或衣等包被的籽实(樱桃粉)(其他工艺);113:其他籽仁为皮或衣等包被的籽实(阿萨伊果粉)(其他工艺);114:其他籽仁为皮或衣等包被的籽实(竹芋果粉)(其他工艺);115:其他籽仁为皮或衣等包被的籽实(蔓越莓粉)(其他工艺);116:其他籽仁为皮或衣等包被的籽实(柠檬粉、柠檬皮粉)(其他工艺);117:其他籽仁为皮或衣等包被的籽实(柑橘粉、桔子粉)(其他工艺);118:其他籽仁为皮或衣等包被的籽实(梅粉)(其他工艺);998:其他籽仁为坚硬外壳包被的籽实(其他工艺);999:其他籽仁为皮或衣等包被的籽实(其他工艺)〕	20		80	13/	9,13	千克	AB/	PRQS	45	10/10
11.07	**麦芽,不论是否焙制:**										
1107.1000	-未焙制〔101 食用,102 药用未焙制麦芽〕	10		50	13/	13	千克	AB/	PRQS	35	
1107.2000	-已焙制〔101 食用,102 食用其他粮食加工产品,103 药用已焙制麦芽,104 其他粮食制品〕	10		50	13/	13	千克	AB/	PRQS	35	
11.08	**淀粉;菊粉:**										
	-淀粉:										
1108.1100	--小麦淀粉〔999〕	20		50	13/	0	千克	AB/	PRQS	25	
1108.1200	--玉米淀粉〔101 饲用,102 工业用,999:食用〕	20		50	13/	9,13	千克	AB/	PRQS	30	
1108.1300	--马铃薯淀粉〔999〕	15		50	13/	13	千克	AB/	PRQS	40	
1108.1400	--木薯淀粉〔999〕	10		50	13/	13	千克	AB/	PRQS	35	
1108.1900	--其他〔101 其他粮食加工产品不包括马铃薯及木薯淀粉(其他粮食加工产品),102 其他粮食制品,103 其他淀粉制品,104 淀粉〕	20		50	13/	13	千克	AB/	PRQ	45	
1108.2000	-菊粉〔999〕	20		50	13/	13	千克	AB/	PRQS	25	
11.09	**面筋,不论是否干制:**										
1109.0000	面筋,不论是否干制〔101 面筋,102 其他粮食制品〕	18		80	13/	13	千克	AB/	PRQS	43	

协定税率 %								RCEP		特惠税率 %			Article Description
东/冰/格	巴基斯坦	韩国	瑞士上/下	哥/秘/柬	澳/毛	新西/坡/智	中国港/澳/台	东盟及马来/澳/韩	日/新	亚太2国	老/柬/缅	98/97/95	
0/0/0	10	9.3	2/2	0/0/0	0/0	0/0/0	0/0/	18.7/19/18.7	18.8/19			0/0/0	-Of the products of Chapter 8
													Malt, whether or not roasted:
0/0/0	3.5	2	0/0	0/0/0	0/0	0/0/0	0/0/	0/0/9	9.1/0			0/0/0	-Not roasted
0/0/0	3.5	2	0/0	0/0/0	0/0	0/0/0	0/0/	0/0/9	9.1/0			0/0/0	-Roasted
													Starches; inulin:
													-Starches:
0/0/		9.3	2/2	0/0/0	0/0	0/0/0	0/0/	18/18/18	18.8/18			0/0/0	--Wheat starch
0/0/		9.3	2/2	0/0/0	0/0	0/0/0	0/0/	18/18/18	18.8/18			0/0/0	--Maize (corn) starch
0/0/	12	3	1.5/1.5	0/0/0	0/0	0/0/0	0/0/	0/0/13.5	13.6/0			0/0/0	--Potato starch
0/0/	5	2	0/0	0/0/0	0/0	0/0/0	0/0/	0/0/9	9.1/0			0/0/0	--Manioc (cassava) starch
0/0/		9.3	2/2	0/0/0	0/0	0/0/0	0/0/	18/18/18	18.8/18			0/0/0	--Other starches
0/0/0		4	2/2	0/0/0	0/0	0/0/0	0/0/	0/0/18	18.2/0			0/0/0	-Inulin
													Wheat gluten, whether or not dried:
0/0/0	14.4	8.4	1.8/1.8	0/0/0	0/0	0/0/0	0/0/	16.2/16.2/16.2	16.9/16.2			0/0/0	Wheat gluten, whether or not dried

第十二章
含油子仁及果实;杂项子仁及果实;
工业用或药用植物;
稻草、秸杆及饲料

注释:

一、税目 12.07 主要包括油棕果及油棕仁、棉子、蓖麻子、芝麻、芥子、红花子、罂粟子、牛油树果。但不包括税目 08.01 或 08.02 的产品及油橄榄(第七章或第二十章)。

二、税目 12.08 不仅包括未脱脂的细粉和粗粉,而且包括部分或全部脱脂以及用其本身的油料全部或部分复脂的细粉和粗粉。但不包括税目 23.04 至 23.06 的残渣。

三、甜菜子、草子及其他草本植物种子、观赏用花的种子、蔬菜种子、林木种子、果树种子、巢菜子(蚕豆除外)、羽扇豆属植物种子,可一律视为种植用种子,归入税目 12.09。

但下列各项即使用作种子用,也不归入税目12.09:
(一)第七章的豆类蔬菜或甜玉米;
(二)第九章的调味香料及其他产品;
(三)第十章的谷物;
(四)税目 12.01 至 12.07 或 12.11 的产品。

四、税目 12.11 主要包括下列植物或这些植物的某部分:
罗勒、琉璃苣、人参、海索草、甘草、薄荷、迷迭香、芸香、鼠尾草及苦艾。
但税目 12.11 不包括:
(一)第三十章的药品;
(二)第三十三章的芳香料制品及化妆盥洗品;
(三)税目 38.08 的杀虫剂、杀菌剂、除草剂、消毒剂及类似产品。

五、税目 12.12 的"海草及其他藻类"不包括:
(一)税目 21.02 的已死的单细胞微生物;
(二)税目 30.02 的培养微生物;
(三)税目 31.01 或 31.05 的肥料。

子目注释:

子目 1205.10 所称"低芥子酸油菜子",是指所榨取的固定油中芥子酸含量按重量计低于 2%,以及所得的固体成分每克葡萄糖苷酸(酯)含量低于 30 微摩尔的油菜子。

税则号列	货品名称〔CIQ 扩展编码及品名－T2 表示见附表 2〕	最惠(%)	暂定税率	普通	增值/消费	出口退税	计量单位	监管条件/特殊证件	检验检疫	对美关税	亚太上/下
12.01	**大豆,不论是否破碎:**										
1201.1000	-种用〔101 种质资源;102 种质资源除外〕	0		180	9/	0	千克	7AB/	PQ	5	
	-其他:										
	---黄大豆:										
1201.9011	----非转基因〔101 大豆(榨油用),102 大豆(饲料用),103 大豆(食品加工用)〕	3		180	9/	0	千克	7AB/	PRQS	30.5	0/0
1201.9019	----其他〔101 大豆(榨油用),102 大豆(饲料用),103 大豆(食品加工用)〕	3		180	9/	0	千克	7AB/	PRQS	30.5	0/0
1201.9020	---黑大豆〔101 榨油用,102 饲料用,103 食品加工用〕	3		180	9/	0	千克	7AB/	PRQS	28	0/0
1201.9030	---青大豆〔101 榨油用,102 饲料用,103 食品加工用〕	3		180	9/	0	千克	7AB/	PRQS	8	0/0
1201.9090	---其他〔101 榨油用,102 饲料用,103 食品加工用〕	3		180	9/	0	千克	7AB/	PRQS	8	0/0
12.02	**未焙炒或未烹煮的花生,不论是否去壳或破碎:**										
1202.3000	-种用〔999〕	0		0	9/	0	千克	AB/	PNQ	5	
	-其他:										
1202.4100	--未去壳〔101 提取(晒干的除外)、压榨、烹制、烘焙、冻干、脱水、裹糖屑、发酵、冷冻(经漂汤和杀青,并在－18 度以下冷冻)、浸酸、腌渍、炒制等工艺进行加工处理的),999 其他工艺〕	15		70	9/	0	千克	AB/	PRQS	25	
1202.4200	--去壳,不论是否破碎〔101:提取(晒干的除外)、压榨、烹制、烘焙、冻干、脱水、裹糖屑、发酵、冷冻(经漂汤和杀青,并在－18 度以下冷冻)、浸酸、腌渍、炒制等工艺进行加工处理的);999:其他工艺〕	15		70	9/	0	千克	AB/	PRQS	40	
12.03	**干椰子肉:**										
1203.0000	干椰子肉〔101:提取(晒干的除外)、压榨、烹制、烘焙、冻干、脱水、裹糖屑、发酵、冷冻(经漂汤和杀青,并在－18 度以下冷冻)、浸酸、腌渍、炒制等工艺进行加工处理的);999:其他工艺〕	15		30	9/	9	千克	AB/	PRQ	20	7.5/7.5
12.04	**亚麻子,不论是否破碎:**										
1204.0000	亚麻子,不论是否破碎										
1204.0000 10	亚麻种子(不论是否破碎)〔999〕	15		70	0/	9	千克	AB/	PRQ		
1204.0000 90	其他亚麻子(种用除外)(不论是否破碎)〔999〕	15		70	9/	9	千克	AB/	PRQ	40	
12.05	**油菜子,不论是否破碎:**										

Chapter 12
Oil seeds and oleaginous fruits; miscellaneous grains, seeds and fruit; industrial or medicinal plants; straw and fodder

Notes:

1. Heading No. 12.07 applies, *inter alia*, to palm nuts and kernels, cotton seeds, castor oil seeds, sesamum seeds, mustard seeds, safflower seeds, poppy seeds and shea nuts (karite nuts). It does not apply to products of heading No. 08.01 or 08.02 or to olives (Chapter 7 or Chapter 20).
2. Heading No. 12.08 applies not only to non-defatted flours and meals but also to flours and meals which have been partially defatted or defatted and wholly or partially refatted with their original oils. It does not, however, apply to residues of headings No. 23.04 to 23.06
3. For the purposes of heading No. 12.09, beet seeds, grass and other herbage seeds, seeds of ornamental flowers, vegetable seeds, seeds of forest trees, seeds of fruit trees, seeds of vetches (other than those of the species *Vicia faba*) or of lupines are to be regarded as "seeds of a kind used for sowing".
   Heading No. 12.09 does not, however, apply to the following even if for sowing:
   (a) Laguminous vegetables or sweet corn(Chapter 7);
   (b) Spices or other products of Chapter 9;
   (c) Cereals (Chapter 10); or
   (d) Products of headings No. 12.01 to 12.07 or 12.11
4. Heading No. 12.11 applies, *inter alia*, to the following plants or parts thereof:
   Basil, borage, ginseng, hyssop, liquorice, all species of mint, rosemary, rue, sage and wormwood.
   Heading No. 12.11 does not, however, apply to:
   (a) Medicaments of Chapter 30;
   (b) Perfumery, cosmetic or toilet preparations of Chapter 33;
   (c) Insecticides, fungicides, herbicides, disinfectants or similar products of heading No. 38.08.
5. For the purposes of heading No. 12.12, the term "seaweeds and other algae" does not include:
   (a) Dead single-cell micro-organisms of heading No. 21.02;
   (b) Cultures of micro-organisms of heading No. 30.02;
   (c) Fertillizers of heading No. 31.01 or 31.05.

Subheading Notes:

For the purposes of subheading No. 1205.10, the expression "low erucic acid rape or colza seeds" means rape or colza seeds yielding a fixed oil which has an erucic acid content of less than 2% by weight and yielding a solid component which contains less than 30 micromoles of glucosinolates per gram.

协定税率 %								RCEP		特惠税率 %			Article Description
东/冰/格	巴基斯坦	韩国	瑞士上/下	哥/秘/柬	澳/毛	新西/坡/智	中国港/澳/台	东盟及马来/澳/韩	日/新	亚太2国	老/柬/缅	98/97/95	
													Soya beans, whether or not broken:
0/0/0	0	0	0/0	0/0/0	0/0	0//0	0/0/	0/0/0	0/0			0/0/0	-Seed
													-Other:
													---Yellow soya beans:
0/0/	0	0	0/0	0/0/0		0//0	0/0/				0/0/	0/0/0	----Non—GMO
0/0/	0	0	0/0	0/0/0		0//0	0/0/				0/0/	0/0/0	----Other
0/0/	0	0	0/0	0/0/0		0//0	0/0/				0/0/	0/0/0	---Black soya beans
0/0/	0	0	0/0	0/0/0		0//0	0/0/				0/0/	0/0/0	---Green soya beans
0/0/	0	0	0/0	0/0/0		0//0	0/0/					0/0/0	---Other
													Ground-nuts, not roasted or otherwise cooked, whether or not shelled or broken:
0/0/0	0	0	0/0	0/0/0	0/0	0//0	0/0/	0/0/0	0/0			0/0/0	-Seed
													-Other:
0/0/	0	3	1.5/1.5	0/0/0	0/0	0/0/0	0/0/	0/0/13.5	13.6/0		0//	0/0/0	--In shell
0/0/	0	3	1.5/1.5	0/0/0	0/0	0/0/0	0/0/	0/0/13.5	13.6/0		0//	0/0/0	--Shell, whether or not broken
													Copra:
0/0/0	5.3	3	1.5/1.5	0/0/0	0/0	0/0/0	0/0/	0/0/13.5	13.6/0		/0/	0/0/0	Copra
													Linseed, whether or not broken:
													Linseed, whether or not broken
0/0/	12	3	1.5/1.5	0/0/0	0/0	0/0/0	0/0/	0/0/13.5	13.6/0			0/0/0	Flax seeds (whether or not broken)
0/0/	12	3	1.5/1.5	0/0/0	0/0	0/0/0	0/0/	0/0/13.5	13.6/0			0/0/0	Other linseed (other than seed) (whether or not broken)
													Rape or colza seeds, whether or not broken:

税则号列	货品名称〔CIQ 扩展编码及品名—T2 表示见附表 2〕	最惠(%)	暂定税率	普通	增值/消费	出口退税	计量单位	监管条件/特殊证件	检验检疫	对美关税	亚太上/下
	-低芥子酸油菜子:										
1205.1010	---种用〔999〕	0		80	0/	0	千克	7AB/	PNQ		
1205.1090	---其他〔999〕	9		80	9/	9	千克	7AB/	PRQS	14	0/0
	-其他:										
1205.9010	---种用〔999〕	0		80	0/	0	千克	7AB/	PNQ		
1205.9090	---其他〔999〕	9		80	9/	9	千克	7AB/	PRQS	14	0/0
12.06	**葵花子,不论是否破碎:**										
1206.0010	---种用〔999〕	0		0	9/	9	千克	AB/	PNQ		
1206.0090	---其他〔101 非熟制(其他工艺),102 熟制,103 非熟制(提取(晒干的除外)、压榨、烹制、烘焙、冻干、脱水、裹糖屑、发酵、冷冻(经漂汤和杀青,并在－18 度以下冷冻)、浸酸、腌渍、炒制等工艺进行加工处理的)〕	15		70	9/	9	千克	AB/	PRQS	40	
12.07	**其他含油子仁及果实,不论是否破碎:**										
	-棕榈果及棕榈仁:										
1207.1010	---种用										
1207.1010 10	种用濒危棕榈果及棕榈仁〔999〕	0		0	9/	0	千克	ABEF/	PNQ	5	
1207.1010 90	其他种用棕榈果及棕榈仁〔999〕	0		0	9/	9	千克	AB/	PNQ	5	
1207.1090	---其他										
1207.1090 10	其他濒危棕榈果及棕榈仁(不论是否破碎)〔999〕	10		70	9/	0	千克	ABEF/	PRQS	20	
1207.1090 90	其他棕榈果及棕榈仁(不论是否破碎)〔999〕	10		70	9/	9	千克	AB/	PRQS	20	
	-棉子:										
1207.2100	--种用〔999〕	0		0	9/	9	千克	AB/	PNQ	5	
1207.2900	--其他〔999〕	15		70	9/	9	千克	AB/	PRQS	20	
	-蓖麻子:										
1207.3010	---种用〔999〕	0		0	0/	9	千克	AB/	PNQ		
1207.3090	---其他〔999〕	15		70	9/	9	千克	AB/	PRQS	20	
	-芝麻:										
1207.4010	---种用〔999〕	0		0	9/	9	千克	AB/	PNQ	5	
1207.4090	---其他〔101 食用,102 药用黑芝麻〕	10		70	9/	9	千克	AB/	PRQS	15	9/9
	-芥子:										
1207.5010	---种用〔999〕	0		0	9/	9	千克	AB/	PNQ	5	
1207.5090	---其他〔999〕	15		70	9/	9	千克	AB/	PRQ	40	
	-红花子:										
1207.6010	---种用〔999〕	0		0	9/	9	千克	AB/	PNQ	5	
1207.6090	---其他〔999〕	20		70	9/	9	千克	AB/	PRQS	25	
	-甜瓜的子:										
1207.7010	---种用〔101 西瓜种子,102 哈密瓜种子,103 甜瓜种子〕	0		0	0/	0	千克	AB/	PQ		
	---其他:										
1207.7091	----黑瓜子〔101 非熟制(其他工艺),102 熟制,103 非熟制(提取(晒干的除外)、压榨、烹制、烘焙、冻干、脱水、裹糖屑、发酵、冷冻(经漂汤和杀青,并在－18 度以下冷冻)、浸酸、腌渍、炒制等工艺进行加工处理的)〕	20		80	9/	9	千克	AB/	PRQS	25	
1207.7092	----红瓜子〔101 提取(晒干的除外)、压榨、烹制、烘焙、冻干、脱水、裹糖屑、发酵、冷冻(经漂汤和杀青,并在－18 度以下冷冻)、浸酸、腌渍、炒制等工艺进行加工处理的),999 其他工艺〕	20		80	9/	9	千克	AB/	PRQS	25	
1207.7099	----其他〔101:提取(晒干的除外)、压榨、烹制、烘焙、冻干、脱水、裹糖屑、发酵、冷冻(经漂汤和杀青,并在－18 度以下冷冻)、浸酸、腌渍、炒制等工艺进行加工处理的);999:其他工艺〕	30		70	9/	9	千克	AB/	PRQS	35	
	-其他:										
1207.9100	--罂粟子〔999〕	20		70	9/	9	千克	AB/	PQ	25	
	--其他:										
1207.9910	---种用										
1207.9910 10	大麻子〔999〕	0		0	0/	9	千克	AB/	PNQ		
1207.9910 90	其他种用含油子仁及果实〔101 亚麻种子,102 蓖麻种子,103 油棕果种子,104 红花籽,105 其他油料种子〕	0		0	9/	9	千克	AB/	PNQ	5	
	---其他:										
1207.9991	----牛油树果〔999〕	20		70	9/	9	千克	AB/	PRQ	25	
1207.9999	----其他[T2]	10		70	9/	9	千克	AB/	PRQS	35	
12.08	**含油子仁或果实的细粉及粗粉,但芥子粉除外:**										
1208.1000	-大豆粉〔999〕	9		70	13/	0	千克	AB/	PRQS	14	
1208.9000	-其他〔999〕	15		80	13/	13	千克	AB/	PRQS	20	
12.09	**种植用的种子、果实及孢子:**										
1209.1000	-糖甜菜子〔999〕	0		0	0/	9	千克	AB/	PQ		
	-饲料植物种子:										
1209.2100	--紫苜蓿子〔999〕	0		0	9/	0	千克	AB/	PQ		

协定税率 %								RCEP		特惠税率 %			Article Description
东/冰/格	巴基斯坦	韩国	瑞士上/下	哥/秘/柬	澳/毛	新西/坡/智	中国港/澳/台	东盟及马来/澳/韩	日/新	亚太2国	老/柬/缅	98/97/95	
													-Low erucic acid rape or colza seeds:
0/0/0	0	0	0/0	0/0/0	0/	0//0	0/0/	0/0/0	0/0			0/0/0	---Seed
0/0/	0	0	0/0	0/0/0		0//0	0/0/					0/0/0	---Other
													-Other:
0/0/0	0	0	0/0	0/0/0	0/0	0//0	0/0/	0/0/0	0/0			0/0/0	---Seed
0/0/	0	0	0/0	0/0/0	/0	0//0	0/0/					0/0/0	---Other
													Sunflower seeds, whether or not broken:
0/0/0	0	0	0/0	0/0/0	0/0	0//0	0/0/	0/0/0	0/0			0/0/0	---Seed
0/0/	12	3	1.5/1.5	0/0/0	0/0	0/0/0	0/0/	0/0/13.5	13.6/0			0/0/0	---Other
													Other oil seeds and oleaginous fruits, whether or not broken:
													-Palm nuts and kernels:
													---Seed
0/0/0	0	0	0/0	0/0/0	0/0	0//0	0/0/	0/0/0	0/0			0/0/0	Endangered palm fruit and palm nut, seed
0/0/0	0	0	0/0	0/0/0	0/0	0//0	0/0/	0/0/0	0/0			0/0/0	Other palm fruit and palm nut, seed
													---Other
0/0/0	3.5	2	0/0	0/0/0	0/0	0/0/0	0/0/	0/0/9	9.1/0		/0/	0/0/0	Other endangered palm fruit and palm nut(whether or not broken)
0/0/0	3.5	2	0/0	0/0/0	0/0	0/0/0	0/0/	0/0/9	9.1/0		/0/	0/0/0	Other palm fruit and palm nut(whether or not broken)
													-Cotton seeds:
0/0/0	0	0	0/0	0/0/0	0/0	0//0	0/0/	0/0/0	0/0			0/0/0	--Seeds
0/0/	12	3	1.5/1.5	0/0/0	0/0	0/0/0	0/0/	0/0/13.5	13.6/0			0/0/0	--Other
													-Castor oil seeds:
0/0/0	0	0	0/0	0/0/0	0/0	0//0	0/0/	0/0/0	0/0			0/0/0	---Seed
0/0/		3	1.5/1.5	0/0/0	0/0	0/0/0	0/0/	0/0/13.5	13.6/0		0/0/0	0/0/0	---Other
													-Sesamum seeds:
0/0/0	0	0	0/0	0/0/0	0/0	0//0	0/0/	0/0/0	0/0			0/0/0	---Seed
0/0/	0	2	0/0	0/0/0	0/0	0/0/0	0/0/	0/0/9	9.1/0		0/0/0	0/0/0	---Other
													-Mustard seeds:
0/0/0	0	0	0/0	0/0/0	0/0	0//0	0/0/	0/0/0	0/0			0/0/0	---Seed
0/0/0	12	3	1.5/1.5	0/0/0	0/0	0/0/0	0/0/	0/0/13.5	13.6/0			0/0/0	---Other
													-Safflower seeds(carthamus tinctorius):
0/0/0	0	0	0/0	0/0/0	0/0	0//0	0/0/	0/0/0	0/0			0/0/0	---Seed
0/0/0		9.3	2/2	0/0/0	0/0	0/0/0	0/0/	18/18/18	18.8/18			0/0/0	---Other
													-Melon seeds:
0/0/0	0	0	0/0	0/0/0	0/0	0//0	0/0/	0/0/0	0/0			0/0/0	---Seed
													---Other:
0/0/0		9.3	2/2	0/0/0	0/0	0/0/0	0/0/	18/18/18	18.8/18			0/0/0	----Black watermelon seeds
0/0/0		9.3	2/2	0/0/0	0/0	0/0/0	0/0/	18/18/18	18.8/18			0/0/0	----Red watermelon seeds
0/0/0		18		0/0/0	0/18	0//0	0/0/	28.5/28.5/28.5	28.6/28.5			0/0/0	----Other
													-Other:
0/0/0		9.3	2/2	0/0/0	0/0	0/0/0	0/0/	18/18/18	18.8/18			0/0/0	--Poppy seeds
													--Other:
													---Seed
0/0/0	0	0	0/0	0/0/0	0/0	0//0	0/0/	0/0/0	0/0			0/0/0	Hemp seed
0/0/0	0	0	0/0	0/0/0	0/0	0//0	0/0/	0/0/0	0/0			0/0/0	Oilseed kernels and fruits for other species
													---Other:
0/0/0		9.3	2/2	0/0/0	0/0	0/0/0	0/0/	18/18/18	18.8/18		//0	0/0/0	----Shea nuts(*karite nuts*)
0/0/	5	2	0/0	0/0/0	0/0	0/0/0	0/0/	0/0/9	9.1/0		0/0/0	0/0/0	----Other
													Flours and meals of oil seeds or oleaginous fruits, other than those of mustard:
0/0/0	5	0	0/0	0/0/0	0/0	0//0	0/0/	0/0/0	8.2/0		/0/	0/0/0	-Of soya beans
0/0/	12	3	1.5/1.5	0/0/0	0/0	0/0/0	0/0/	0/0/13.5	13.6/0		/0/	0/0/0	-Other
													Seeds, fruit and spores, of a kind used for sowing:
0/0/0	0	0	0/0	0/0/0	0/0	0//0	0/0/	0/0/0	0/0			0/0/0	-Sugar beet seed
													-Seeds of forage plants:
0/0/0	0	0	0/0	0/0/0	0/0	0//0	0/0/	0/0/0	0/0			0/0/0	--Lucerne (alfalfa) seed

税则号列	货品名称〔CIQ 扩展编码及品名－T2 表示见附表 2〕	最惠(%)	暂定税率	普通	增值/消费	出口退税	计量单位	监管条件/特殊证件	检验检疫	对美关税	亚太上/下
1209.2200	--三叶草子〔999〕	0		0	9/	0	千克	AB/	PQ		
1209.2300	--羊茅子〔999〕	0		0	9/	0	千克	AB/	PQ		
1209.2400	--草地早熟禾子〔999〕	0		0	9/	0	千克	AB/	PQ		
1209.2500	--黑麦草种子〔999〕	0		0	9/	0	千克	AB/	PQ		
	--其他：										
1209.2910	---甜菜子，糖甜菜子除外〔999〕	0		0	0/	9	千克	AB/	PQ		
1209.2990	---其他[T2]	0		0	0/	0	千克	AB/	PQ		
1209.3000	-草本花卉植物种子										
1209.3000 10	濒危草本花卉植物种子〔999〕	0		0	9/	0	千克	AFEB/	PQ		
1209.3000 90	草本花卉植物种子（濒危除外）〔T2〕	0		0	0/	0	千克	AB/	PQ		
	-其他：										
1209.9100	--蔬菜种子[T2]	0		0	0/	0	千克	AB/	PQ		
1209.9900	--其他										
1209.9900 10	其他种植用濒危种子、果实及孢子〔101 其他花卉种子，102 其他林木种子，103 其他经济类植物种子〕	0		0	9/	0	千克	AFEB/	PQ		
1209.9900 20	黄麻种子、红麻种子、柴胡种子、当归种子、白芷种子、林木种子（濒危除外）〔T2〕	0		0	0/	0	千克	AB/	PQ		
1209.9900 90	其他种植用的种子、果实及孢子[T2]	0		0	9/	0	千克	AB/	PQ		
12.10	**鲜或干的啤酒花，不论是否研磨或制成团粒；蛇麻腺：**										
1210.1000	-啤酒花，未经研磨也未制成团粒〔101：提取（晒干的除外）、压榨、烹制、烘焙、冻干、脱水、裹糖屑、发酵、冷冻（经漂汤和杀青，并在－18 度以下冷冻）、浸酸、腌渍、炒制等工艺进行加工处理的）；999：其他工艺〕	20		50	13/	13	千克	AB/	PRQS	25	
1210.2000	-啤酒花，经研磨或制成团粒；蛇麻腺〔101：提取（晒干的除外）、压榨、烹制、烘焙、冻干、脱水、裹糖屑、发酵、冷冻（经漂汤和杀青，并在－18 度以下冷冻）、浸酸、腌渍、炒制等工艺进行加工处理的）；999：其他工艺〕	10		50	13/	13	千克	AB/	PRQS	30	
12.11	**主要用作香料、药料、杀虫、杀菌或类似用途的植物或这些植物的某部分（包括子仁及果实），鲜、冷、冻或干的，不论是否切割、压碎或研磨成粉：**										
	-人参：										
	---西洋参：	7.5		70	9/	9	千克	AQBFE/	MPRQS	32.5/22.5	
1211.2011	----鲜的或干的〔999〕	7.5		70	9/	9	千克	AQBFE/	PRQS	32.5/22.5	
1211.2019	----其他〔999〕	7.5		70	9/	9	千克	AQBFE/	PRQS	32.5/22.5	
	---野山参（西洋参除外）：										
1211.2021	----鲜的或干的										
1211.2021 10	鲜或干的野山参（仅限俄罗斯属，西洋参除外）（不论是否切割、压碎或研磨成粉）〔101 药用野山参，102 食用野山参〕	20		90	9/	9	千克	ABEF/	PRQS	25	16.4/16.4
1211.2021 90	鲜或干的野山参（俄罗斯属除外，西洋参除外）（不论是否切割、压碎或研磨成粉）〔999〕	20		90	9/	9	千克	AB/	PRQS	25	16.4/16.4
1211.2029	----其他										
1211.2029 10	冷或冻的野山参（仅限俄罗斯属，西洋参除外）（不论是否切割、压碎或研磨成粉）〔101 药用野山参，102 食用野山参〕	20		90	9/	9	千克	ABEF/	PRQS	25	16.4/16.4
1211.2029 90	冷或冻的野山参（俄罗斯属除外，西洋参除外）（不论是否切割、压碎或研磨成粉）〔999〕	20		90	9/	9	千克	AB/	PRQS	25	16.4/16.4
	---其他：										
1211.2091	----鲜的	20		50	9/	9	千克	AB	PRQS	/45	
1211.2091 10	其他鲜的人参（仅限俄罗斯属）（不论是否切割、压碎或研磨成粉）〔101 药用野山参，102 食用野山参〕	20		50	9/	9	千克	ABEF/	PRQS	40/35	
1211.2091 90	其他鲜的人参（俄罗斯属除外）（不论是否切割、压碎或研磨成粉）〔101 药用野山参，102 食用野山参〕	20		50	9/	9	千克	AB/	PRQS	40/35	
1211.2092	----干的										
1211.2092 10	其他干的人参（仅限俄罗斯属）（不论是否切割、压碎或研磨成粉）〔101 药用人参，102 药用红参，103 食用人参〕	20		50	9/	9	千克	ABEFQ/	PRQS	40/35	
1211.2092 90	其他干的人参（俄罗斯属除外）（不论是否切割、压碎或研磨成粉）〔101 药用人参，102 药用红参，103 食用人参〕	20		50	9/	9	千克	ABQ/	PRQS	40/35	
1211.2099	----其他	20		50	9/	9	千克	ABQ	PRQS	/45	

协定税率 %								RCEP		特惠税率 %			Article Description
东/冰/格	巴基斯坦	韩国	瑞士上/下	哥/秘/柬	澳/毛	新西/坡/智	中国港/澳/台	东盟及马来/澳/韩	日/新	亚太2国	老/柬/缅	98/97/95	
0/0/0	0	0	0/0	0/0/0	0/0	0//0	0/0/	0/0/0	0/0			0/0/0	--Clover (*Trifolium spp.*) seed
0/0/0	0	0	0/0	0/0/0	0/0	0//0	0/0/	0/0/0	0/0			0/0/0	--Fescue seed
0/0/0	0	0	0/0	0/0/0	0/0	0//0	0/0/	0/0/0	0/0			0/0/0	--Kentucky blue grass (*Poa-pratensis L.*) seed
0/0/0	0	0	0/0	0/0/0	0/0	0//0	0/0/	0/0/0	0/0			0/0/0	--Rye grass (*Lolium multiflorum Lam.*, *Lolium perenne L.*) seed
													--Other:
0/0/0	0	0	0/0	0/0/0	0/0	0//0	0/0/	0/0/0	0/0			0/0/0	---Beet seed, excluding sugar beet seed
0/0/0	0	0	0/0	0/0/0	0/0	0//0	0/0/	0/0/0	0/0			0/0/0	---Other
													-Seeds of herbaceous plants cultivated principally for their flowers
0/0/0	0	0	0/0	0/0/0	0/0	0//0	0/0/	0/0/0	0/0			0/0/0	Seeds of endangered herbaceous plants cultivated principally for their flowers
0/0/0	0	0	0/0	0/0/0	0/0	0//0	0/0/	0/0/0	0/0			0/0/0	Other seeds of herbaceous plants cultivated principally for their flowers
													-Other:
0/0/0	0	0	0/0	0/0/0	0/0	0//0	0/0/	0/0/0	0/0			0/0/0	--Vegetable seeds
													--Other
0/0/0	0	0	0/0	0/0/0	0/0	0//0	0/0/	0/0/0	0/0			0/0/0	Other endangered seeds, fruit and spores, of a kind used for sowing
0/0/0	0	0	0/0	0/0/0	0/0	0//0	0/0/	0/0/0	0/0			0/0/0	Jute seeds, kenaf seeds, bupleurum seeds, angelica seeds, Angelica dahurica seeds, forest seeds
0/0/0	0	0	0/0	0/0/0	0/0	0//0	0/0/	0/0/0	0/0			0/0/0	Other seeds, fruit and spores, of a kind used for sowing
													Hop cones, fresh or dried, whethr or not ground, powdered or in the form of pellets; lupulin:
0/0/0	16	9.3	2/2	0/0/0	0/0	0/0/0	0/0/	18/18/18	18.8/18			0/0/0	-Hop cones, neither ground nor powdered nor in the form of pellets
0/0/0	3.5	2	0/0	0/0/0	0/0	0/0/0	0/0/	0/0/9	9.1/0			0/0/0	-Hop cones, ground, powdered or in the form of pellets; lupulin
													Plants and parts of plants (including seeds and fruits), of a kind used primarily in perfumery, in pharmacy or for insecticidal, fungicidal or similar purposes, fresh or dried, whether or not cut, crushed or powdered:
													-Ginseng roots:
0/0/0	3	0	0	0	0	0/0	0/0/0	0/0/				0/0	---American ginseng:
0/0/0	2	0	0/0	0/0/0	0/0	0/0/0	0/0/	0/0/0	0/0			0/0/0	----Fresh or dried
0/0/0	2	0	0/0	0/0/0	0/0	0/0/0	0/0/	0/0/13.5	13.6/0			0/0/0	----Other
													Wild ginseng (other than American ginseng)
													----Fresh or dried
0/0/0	16	9.3	2/2	0/0/0	0/0	0/0/0	0/0/	18/18/18	18.8/18			0/0/0	Wild ginseng, fresh or dried (Russian only, except American ginseng) (whether or not cut, crushed or ground into powder)
0/0/0	16	9.3	2/2	0/0/0	0/0	0/0/0	0/0/	18/18/18	18.8/18			0/0/0	Wild ginseng, fresh or dried (other than Russian ginseng and American ginseng) (whether or not cut, crushed or ground into powder)
													----Other
0/0/0	16	9.3	2/2	0/0/0	0/0	0/0/0	0/0/	0/0/13.5	13.6/0			0/0/0	Cold or frozen wild ginseng (Russian only, except American ginseng) (whether or not cut, crushed or ground into powder)
0/0/0	16	9.3	2/2	0/0/0	0/0	0/0/0	0/0/	0/0/13.5	13.6/0			0/0/0	Cold or frozen wild ginseng (except Russian ginseng and American ginseng) (whether or not cut, crushed or ground into powder)
													---Other:
0/0/0		12	6	0	0	0	0/0/0	0/0/				0/0/	----Fresh
0/0/0		9.3	2/2	0/0/0	0/0	0/0/0	0/0/	18.7/19/	18.8/19		//	0/0/0	Other fresh ginseng (Russian ginseng only) (whether or not cut, crushed or ground into powder)
0/0/0		9.3	2/2	0/0/0	0/0	0/0/0	0/0/	18.7/19/	18.8/19		//	0/0/0	Other fresh ginseng (other than Russian ginseng) (whether or not cut, crushed or ground into powder)
													----Dried
0/0/0			2/2	0/0/0	0/0	0/0/0	0/0/	19/19/	/19			0/0/0	Other dried ginseng (Russian only) (whether or not cut, crushed or ground into powder)
0/0/0			2/2	0/0/0	0/0	0/0/0	0/0/	19/19/	/19			0/0/0	Other dried ginseng (other than Russian ginseng) (whether or not cut, crushed or ground into powder)
0/0/0			6	0	0	0	0/0/0	0/0/				0/0/	----Other

税则号列	货品名称〔CIQ 扩展编码及品名—T2 表示见附表 2〕	最惠(%)	暂定税率	普通	增值/消费	出口退税	计量单位	监管条件/特殊证件	检验检疫	对美关税	亚太上/下
1211.2099 10	其他冷、冻的人参(仅限俄罗斯属)(不论是否切割、压碎或研磨成粉)〔101 药用人参,102 药用红参,103 食用人参〕	20		50	9/	9	千克	ABEFQ/	PRQS	40/35	
1211.2099 90	其他冷、冻的人参(俄罗斯属除外)(不论是否切割、压碎或研磨成粉)〔101 药用人参,102 药用红参,103 食用人参〕	20		50	9/	9	千克	ABQ/	PRQS	40/35	
1211.3000	-古柯叶										
1211.3000 10	药用古柯叶(不论是否切割、压碎或研磨成粉)〔999〕	9		50	9/	9	千克	ABI/	PQ	14	
1211.3000 20	做香料用古柯叶(不论是否切割、压碎或研磨成粉)〔999〕	9		50	9/	9	千克	AB/	PQ	14	
1211.3000 90	杀虫杀菌用古柯叶(不论是否切割、压碎或研磨成粉)〔999〕	9		50	9/	9	千克	AB/	PQ	14	
1211.4000	-罂粟秆										
1211.4000 10	药用罂粟秆(不论是否切割、压碎或研磨成粉)〔999〕	9		50	9/	9	千克	AB/	PQ	14	
1211.4000 20	做香料用罂粟秆(不论是否切割、压碎或研磨成粉)〔999〕	9		50	9/	9	千克	AB/	PQ	14	
1211.4000 90	杀虫杀菌用罂粟秆(不论是否切割、压碎或研磨成粉)〔999〕	9		50	9/	9	千克	AB/	PQ	14	
1211.5000	-麻黄										
1211.5000 11	药料用麻黄草粉〔999〕	9		30	9/	9	千克	23AQB/	PQ	14	4.5/4.5
1211.5000 12	药料用人工种植麻黄草〔999〕	9		30	9/	9	千克	4ABQxy/	PQ	14	4.5/4.5
1211.5000 19	其他药料用麻黄草〔999〕	9		30	9/	9	千克	ABQ/	PQ	14	4.5/4.5
1211.5000 21	香料用麻黄草粉〔999〕	9		30	9/	9	千克	23AB/	PRQ	14	4.5/4.5
1211.5000 29	香料用麻黄草〔999〕	9		30	9/	9	千克	8A/	R	14	4.5/4.5
1211.5000 91	其他用麻黄草粉〔999〕	9		30	9/	9	千克	23AB/	PQ	14	4.5/4.5
1211.5000 99	其他用麻黄草〔999〕	9		30	9/	9	千克	8A/	PQ	14	4.5/4.5
1211.6000	-非洲李的皮〔999〕	6		20	9/	0	千克	ABFE/	PQ	31	3/3
	-其他:										
	---主要用作药料的植物及其某部分:										
1211.9011	----当归〔101 药用当归,102 药用三七〕	6		30	9/	9	千克	AQB/	PRQ	11	3/3
1211.9012	----三七(田七)〔101 药用田七,102 药用党参〕	6		20	9/	9	千克	AQB/	PRQ	11	3/3
1211.9013	----党参〔999〕	6		20	9/	9	千克	AQB/	PRQ	11	3/3
1211.9014	----黄连〔999〕	6		20	9/	9	千克	AQB/	PQ	11	3/3
1211.9015	----菊花〔101 药用野菊花,102 药用菊花,103 食用菊花〕	6		20	9/	0,9	千克	AQB/	PRQS	11	3/3
1211.9016	----冬虫夏草〔999〕	6		20	9/	9	千克	AQBE/	PQ	11	3/3
1211.9017	----贝母〔999〕	6		20	9/	9	千克	AQB/	PRQ	11	3/3
1211.9018	----川芎〔101〕	6		20	9/	9	千克	AQB/	PRQ	11	3/3
1211.9019	----半夏〔999〕	6		20	9/	9	千克	AQB/	PQ	11	3/3
1211.9021	----白芍〔101〕	6		20	9/	9	千克	AQB/	PRQ	11	3/3
1211.9022	----天麻〔101〕	6		20	9/	9	千克	AQBFE/	PRQ	11	3/3
1211.9023	----黄芪〔101〕	6		30	9/	9	千克	AQB/	PRQ	11	3/3
1211.9024	----大黄、籽黄〔999〕	6		20	9/	9	千克	AQB/	PRQ	11	3/3
1211.9025	----白术〔101〕	6		20	9/	9	千克	AQB/	PRQ	11	3/3
1211.9026	----地黄〔101〕	6		20	9/	9	千克	AQB/	PRQ	11	3/3
1211.9027	----槐米〔101 药用槐米,102 食用槐米〕	6		20	9/	9	千克	AQB/	PRQS	11	3/3
1211.9028	----杜仲〔999〕	6		20	9/	9	千克	ABQ/	PRQ	11	3/3
1211.9029	----茯苓〔101 药用茯苓,102 食用茯苓〕	6		20	9/	9	千克	AQB/	PRQS	11	3/3
1211.9031	----枸杞〔101 药用枸杞子,102 食用枸杞子〕	6		30	9/	9	千克	AQB/	PRQS	11	3/3
1211.9032	----大海子〔101 药用大海子(胖大海),102 食用大海子(胖大海)〕	6		20	9/	9	千克	AQB/	PRQS	11	3/3
1211.9033	----沉香〔999〕	3		20	9/	9	千克	AQFEB/	PQ	8	1.5/1.5
1211.9034	----沙参〔999〕	6		20	9/	9	千克	AQB/	PRQ	11	3/3
1211.9035	----青蒿〔999〕	6		20	9/	0	千克	AB/	PQ	11	
1211.9036	----甘草〔101 药用甘草,103 食用甘草〕	6	0	30	9/	9	千克	AQB4xy/	PRQS	5	
1211.9037	----黄芩〔999〕	6		20	9/	9	千克	ABQ/	PQ	11	3/3
1211.9038	----椴树(欧椴)花及叶										
1211.9038 10	海南椴、紫椴(籽椴)花及叶(不论是否切割、压碎或研磨成粉)〔999〕	6		30	9/	9	千克	ABEQ/	PQ	11	3/3
1211.9038 90	其他椴树(欧椴)花及叶〔999〕	6		30	9/	9	千克	ABQ/	PQ	11	3/3
1211.9039	----其他										
1211.9039 30	大麻〔999〕	6		20	9/	9	千克	ABI/	PQ	31	3/3
1211.9039 40	罂粟壳〔999〕	6		20	9/	9	千克	ABI/	PQ	31	3/3
1211.9039 50	鲜、冷、冻或干的木香(不论是否切割,压碎或研磨成粉)〔999〕	6		20	9/	9	千克	ABFE/	PQ	31	3/3
1211.9039 60	鲜、冷、冻或干的黄草及枫斗(石斛)(不论是否切割,压碎或研磨成粉)〔101〕	6		20	9/	9	千克	ABFE/	PQ	31	3/3
1211.9039 70	鲜、冷、冻或干的苁蓉(不论是否切割,压碎或研磨成粉)〔999〕	6		20	9/	9	千克	ABFE/	PQ	31	3/3

协定税率 %								RCEP		特惠税率 %			Article Description
东/冰/格	巴基斯坦	韩国	瑞士上/下	哥/秘/柬	澳/毛	新西/坡/智	中国港/澳/台	东盟及马来/澳/韩	日/新	亚太2国	老/柬/缅	98/97/95	
0/0/0			2/2	0/0/0	0/0	0/0/0	0/0/	0/0/13.5	13.6/0		//	0/0/0	Other cold and frozen ginseng (Russian only) (whether or not cut, crushed or ground into powder)
0/0/0			2/2	0/0/0	0/0	0/0/0	0/0/	0/0/13.5	13.6/0		//	0/0/0	Other cold and frozen ginseng (other than Russian ginseng) (whether or not cut, crushed or ground into powder)
													-Coca leaf
0/0/0	2	0	0/0	0/0/0	0/0	0//0	0/0/	0/0/0	8.2/0		/0/	0/0/0	Coca leaf of a kind used primarily in pharmacy(whether or not cut, crushed or powdered)
0/0/0	2	0	0/0	0/0/0	0/0	0//0	0/0/	0/0/0	8.2/0		/0/	0/0/0	Coca leaf of a kind used primarily in perfumery(whether or not cut, crushed or powdered)
0/0/0	2	0	0/0	0/0/0	0/0	0//0	0/0/	0/0/0	8.2/0		/0/	0/0/0	Coca leaf of a kind used for insecticidal(fungicidal, whether or not cut, crushed or powdered)
													-Poppy straw
0/0/0	2	0	0/0	0/0/0	0/0	0//0	0/0/	0/0/0	8.2/0		/0/	0/0/0	Poppy straw of a kind used primarily in pharmacy(whether or not cut, crushed or powdered)
0/0/0	2	0	0/0	0/0/0	0/0	0//0	0/0/	0/0/0	8.2/0		/0/	0/0/0	Poppy straw of a kind used primarily in perfumery(whether or not cut, crushed or powdered)
0/0/0	2	0	0/0	0/0/0	0/0	0//0	0/0/	0/0/0	8.2/0		/0/	0/0/0	Poppy straw of a kind used for insecticidal, fungicidal(whether or not cut, crushed or powdered)
													-Ephedra
0/0/0	0	0	0/0	0/0/0	0/0	0//0	0/0/	0/0/0	8.2/0		/0/	0/0/0	Ephedra powder, used in pharmacy
0/0/0	0	0	0/0	0/0/0	0/0	0//0	0/0/	0/0/0	8.2/0		/0/	0/0/0	Medicinal materials are artificially planted ephedra
0/0/0	0	0	0/0	0/0/0	0/0	0//0	0/0/	0/0/0	8.2/0		/0/	0/0/0	Ephedra sinica, used in pharmacy
0/0/0	0	0	0/0	0/0/0	0/0	0//0	0/0/	0/0/0	8.2/0		/0/	0/0/0	Ephedra powder, of a kind used in perfumery
0/0/0	0	0	0/0	0/0/0	0/0	0//0	0/0/	0/0/0	8.2/0		/0/	0/0/0	Ephedra sinica, of a kind used in perfumery
0/0/0	0	0	0/0	0/0/0	0/0	0//0	0/0/	0/0/0	8.2/0		/0/	0/0/0	Other ephedra powder
0/0/0	0	0	0/0	0/0/0	0/0	0//0	0/0/	0/0/0	8.2/0		/0/	0/0/0	Other ephedra
0/0/0	0	0	0/0	0/0/0	0/0	0//0	0/0/	0/0/0	0/0		0/0/0	0/0/0	-Bark of African cherry (prunus africana)
													-Other:
													---Of a kind used primarily in pharmacy:
0/0/0	0	0	0/0	0/0/0	0/0	0//0	0/0/	0/0/0	0/0		/0/	0/0/0	----Radix angelicae sinensis
0/0/0	0	0	0/0	0/0/0	0/0	0//0	0/0/	0/0/0	0/0		/0/	0/0/0	----Radix pseudoginseng
0/0/0	0	0	0/0	0/0/0	0/0	0//0	0/0/	0/0/0	0/0			0/0/0	----Radix codonopsitis
0/0/0	0	0	0/0	0/0/0	0/0	0//0	0/0/	0/0/0	0/0			0/0/0	----Rhizoma coptidis
0/0/0	0	0	0/0	0/0/0	0/0	0//0	0/0/	0/0/0	0/0		/0/	0/0/0	----Flos chrysanthemi
0/0/0	0	0	0/0	0/0/0	0/0	0//0	0/0/	0/0/0	0/0		/0/	0/0/0	----Cordyceps sinensis
0/0/0	0	0	0/0	0/0/0	0/0	0//0	0/0/	0/0/0	0/0		/0/	0/0/0	----Bulbs fritillariae thunbergii
0/0/0	0	0	0/0	0/0/0	0/0	0//0	0/0/	0/0/0	0/0		/0/	0/0/0	----Rhizoma ligustici
0/0/0	0	0	0/0	0/0/0	0/0	0//0	0/0/	0/0/0	0/0		/0/	0/0/0	----Rhizoma pinelliae
0/0/0	0	0	0/0	0/0/0	0/0	0//0	0/0/	0/0/0	0/0		/0/	0/0/0	----Radix paeoniae lactiflorae
0/0/0	0	0	0/0	0/0/0	0/0	0//0	0/0/	0/0/0	0/0		/0/	0/0/0	----Rhizoma gastrodiae
0/0/0	0	0	0/0	0/0/0	0/0	0//0	0/0/	0/0/0	0/0		/0/	0/0/0	----Radix astragali
0/0/0	0	0	0/0	0/0/0	0/0	0//0	0/0/	0/0/0	0/0		/0/	0/0/0	----Rhubarb
0/0/0	0	0	0/0	0/0/0	0/0	0//0	0/0/	0/0/0	0/0		/0/	0/0/0	----Rhizoma atractylodis macrocephalae
0/0/0	0	0	0/0	0/0/0	0/0	0//0	0/0/	0/0/0	0/0		/0/	0/0/0	----Radix rehmanniae
0/0/0	0	0	0/0	0/0/0	0/0	0//0	0/0/	0/0/0	0/0		/0/	0/0/0	----Flos sophorae
0/0/0	0	0	0/0	0/0/0	0/0	0//0	0/0/	0/0/0	0/0		/0/	0/0/0	----Cortex eucommiae
0/0/0	0	0	0/0	0/0/0	0/0	0//0	0/0/	0/0/0	0/0		0/0/0	0/0/0	----Poria
0/0/0	0	0	0/0	0/0/0	0/0	0//0	0/0/	0/0/0	0/0		/0/	0/0/0	----Fructus lycii
0/0/0	0	0	0/0	0/0/0	0/0	0//0	0/0/	0/0/0	0/0		/0/	0/0/0	----Bantaroi seeds
0/0/0	0	0	0/0	0/0/0	0/0	0//0	0/0/	0/0/0	0/0		/0/	0/0/0	----Aloes wood
0/0/0	0	0	0/0	0/0/0	0/0	0//0	0/0/	0/0/0	0/0		/0/	0/0/0	----Adenophora axilliflora
0/0/0	5	0	0/0	0/0/0	0/0	0//0	0/0/	0/0/0	0/0		/0/	0/0/0	----Southernwood
0/0/0	0	0	0/0	0/0/0	0/0	0//0	0/0/	0/0/0	5.5/0			0/0/0	----Liquorice roots
0/0/0	0	0	0/0	0/0/0	0/0	0//0	0/0/	0/0/0	0/0		0/0/0	0/0/0	----Radix scutellariae
													----Flower and leaves of linden tree (tilia europaea)
0/0/0	0	0	0/0	0/0/0	0/0	0//0	0/0/	0/0/0	0/0		0/0/0	0/0/0	Flower and leaves of hainan linden, amur linden(whether or not cut, crushed or powdered)
0/0/0	0	0	0/0	0/0/0	0/0	0//0	0/0/	0/0/0	0/0		0/0/0	0/0/0	Flower and leaves of other linden tree(lindens)
													----Other
0/0/0	0	0	0/0	0/0/0	0/0	0//0	0/0/	0/0/0	0/0		0/0/0	0/0/0	Hemp
0/0/0	0	0	0/0	0/0/0	0/0	0//0	0/0/	0/0/0	0/0		0/0/0	0/0/0	Poppy pod
0/0/0	0	0	0/0	0/0/0	0/0	0//0	0/0/	0/0/0	0/0		0/0/0	0/0/0	Costustoot, fresh, chilled, frozen or dried, whether or not cut, crushed or powdered
0/0/0	0	0	0/0	0/0/0	0/0	0//0	0/0/	0/0/0	0/0		0/0/0	0/0/0	Herba dendrobii and Dendrobium, fresh, chilled, frozen or dried, whether or not cut, crushed or powdered
0/0/0	0	0	0/0	0/0/0	0/0	0//0	0/0/	0/0/0	0/0		0/0/0	0/0/0	Cistanche, fresh, chilled, frozen or dried, whether or not cut, crushed or powdered

税则号列	货品名称〔CIQ扩展编码及品名—T2表示见附表2〕	最惠(%)	暂定税率	普通	增值/消费	出口退税	计量单位	监管条件/特殊证件	检验检疫	对美关税	亚太上/下
1211.9039 81	鲜或干的红豆杉皮、枝叶(不论是否切割,压碎或研磨成粉)〔999〕	6	0	20	9/	9	千克	ABFE/	PQ	25	3/3
1211.9039 89	冷或冻的红豆杉皮、枝叶(不论是否切割,压碎或研磨成粉)〔999〕	6		20	9/	9	千克	ABFE/	PQ	31	3/3
1211.9039 91	其他主要用作药料鲜、冷、冻或干的濒危植物(包括其某部分,不论是否切割、压碎或研磨成粉)〔101 其他药用濒危植物中药材,102 食用濒危植物中药材,103 药用黄柏〕	6		20	9/	0	千克	ABFE/	PQ	31	3/3
1211.9039 92	加纳籽、车前子壳粉、育亨宾皮(包括其某部分,不论是否切割、压碎或研磨成粉)〔999〕	6		20	9/	9	千克	AB/	PQ	31	3/3
1211.9039 93	恰特草(Cathaedulis Forssk;包括其某部分,不论是否切割、压碎或研磨成粉)〔999〕	6		20	9/	9	千克	ABI/	PQ	31	3/3
1211.9039 99	其他主要用作药料的鲜、冷、冻或干的植物(包括其某部分,不论是否切割,压碎或研磨成粉)〔T2〕	6		20	9/	9	千克	ABQ/	PQ	31	3/3
1211.9050	---主要用作香料的植物及其某部分										
1211.9050 30	香料用沉香木及拟沉香木(包括其某部分,不论是否切割、压碎或研磨成粉)〔999〕	8		50	9/	0	千克	ABFE/	PRQ	33	4/4
1211.9050 91	其他主要用作香料的濒危植物(包括其某部分,不论是否切割、压碎或研磨成粉)〔101 香辛料,102 其他调味料〕	8		50	9/	0	千克	ABFE/	PRQ	33	4/4
1211.9050 99	其他主要用作香料的植物(包括其某部分,不论是否切割、压碎或研磨成粉)〔111 香辛料,112 其他调味料,113 干薄荷叶,114 罗勒粉,115 香叶,116 牛至叶(包括牛至叶粉),117 洋苏叶,118 野生墨角兰,119 迷迭香〕	8		50	9/	9	千克	AB/	MPRNQ	33	4/4
	---其他:										
1211.9091	----鱼藤根、除虫菊〔999〕	3		11	9/	9	千克	AB/	MPNQ	8	1.5/1.5
1211.9099	----其他										
1211.9099 91	其他鲜、冷、冻或干的杀虫、杀菌用濒危植物(不论是否切割,压碎或研磨成粉)〔999〕	9		30	9/	0	千克	ABFE/	PQ	34	4.5/4.5
1211.9099 99	其他鲜、冷、冻或干的杀虫、杀菌用植物(不论是否切割,压碎或研磨成粉)〔999〕	9		30	9/	9	千克	AB/	PQ	34	4.5/4.5
12.12	**鲜、冷、冻或干的刺槐豆、海草及其他藻类、甜菜及甘蔗,不论是否碾磨;主要供人食用的其他税目未列名的果核、果仁及植物产品(包括未焙制的菊苣根):**										
	-海草及其他藻类:										
	--适合供人食用的:										
1212.2110	---海带										
1212.2110 10	不超过10厘米的海带种苗及其配子或孢子(不论是否碾磨)〔101 鲜、冷的养殖海带,102 冻的养殖海带,103 干的养殖海带,104 鲜、冷的野生海带,105 冻的野生海带,106 干的野生海带〕	20		70	0/	0	千克	AB/	PRQS		10/10
1212.2110 90	适合供人食用的鲜、冷、冻或干的海带(不论是否碾磨)〔101 鲜、冷的养殖海带,102 冻的养殖海带,103 干的养殖海带,104 鲜、冷的野生海带,105 冻的野生海带,106 干的野生海带,107 药用昆布〕	20		70	9/	0	千克	AB/	PRQS	25	10/10
1212.2120	---发菜〔101 鲜、冷的养殖发菜,102 冻的养殖发菜,103 干的养殖发菜,104 鲜、冷的野生发菜,105 冻的野生发菜,106 干的野生发菜〕	20		70	9/	9	千克	8A/	PRQS	25	10/10
	---裙带菜:										
1212.2131	----干的〔101 干的养殖裙带菜,102 干的野生裙带菜〕	15		70	9/	9	千克	AB/	PRQS	20	7.5/7.5
1212.2132	----鲜的										
1212.2132 10	不超过10厘米的裙带菜种苗及其配子或孢子(不论是否碾磨)〔101 养殖鲜或冷裙带菜,102 野生鲜或冷裙带菜〕	15		70	0/	9	千克	AB/	PRQS		7.5/7.5
1212.2132 90	适合供人食用的鲜的裙带菜(不论是否碾磨)〔101 养殖鲜或冷裙带菜,102 野生鲜或冷裙带菜〕	15		70	9/	9	千克	AB/	PRQS	20	7.5/7.5
1212.2139	----其他〔101 冷藏养殖裙带菜,102 冻藏养殖裙带菜,103 冷藏野生裙带菜,104 冻藏野生裙带菜〕	15		70	9/	9	千克	AB/	PRQS	20	7.5/7.5
	---紫菜:										
1212.2141	----干的〔101 干的养殖紫菜,102 干的野生紫菜〕	15		70	9/	0	千克	AB/	PRQS	20	7.5/7.5
1212.2142	----鲜的										
1212.2142 10	不超过5厘米的紫菜种苗及其配子或孢子(不论是否碾磨)〔101 养殖鲜或冷紫菜,102 野生鲜或冷紫菜〕	15		70	0/	0	千克	AB/	PRQS		7.5/7.5

协定税率 %								RCEP		特惠税率 %			Article Description
东/冰/格	巴基斯坦	韩国	瑞士上/下	哥/秘/柬	澳/毛	新西/坡/智	中国港/澳/台	东盟及马来/澳/韩	日/新	亚太2国	老/柬/缅	98/97/95	
0/0/0	0	0	0/0	0/0/0	0/0	0//0	0/0/	0/0/0	0/0		0/0/0	0/0/0	Bark, branch and leaf of Chinese yew (Taxus chinensis), fresh or dried, whether or not cut, crushed or powdered
0/0/0	0	0	0/0	0/0/0	0/0	0//0	0/0/	0/0/0	0/0		0/0/0	0/0/0	Bark, branch and leaf of Chinese yew (Taxus chinensis), cold or frozen, whether or not cut, crushed or powdered
0/0/0	0	0	0/0	0/0/0	0/0	0//0	0/0/	0/0/0	0/0		0/0/0	0/0/0	Other endangered plants and parts of plants, of a kind used primarily in pharmacy, fresh, chilled, frozen or dried, whether or not cut, crushed or powdered
0/0/0	0	0	0/0	0/0/0	0/0	0//0	0/0/	0/0/0	0/0		0/0/0	0/0/0	Carbon Ghana seeds, plantago shell powder, yohimbe bark (including part of its, whether or not cut, crushed or ground to powder)
0/0/0	0	0	0/0	0/0/0	0/0	0//0	0/0/	0/0/0	0/0		0/0/0	0/0/0	Catha edulis forssk(Cathaedulis Forssk; including part of its, whether or not cut, ccrushed or powdered)
0/0/0	0	0	0/0	0/0/0	0/0	0//0	0/0/	0/0/0	0/0		0/0/0	0/0/0	Other plants and parts of plants, of a kind used primarily in pharmacy, fresh, chilled, frozen or drie, whether or not cut, crushed or powdered
													---Of a kind used primarily in perfumery
0/0/0	0	0	0/0	0/0/0	0/5.7	0//0	0/0/	0/0/0	7.3/0		/0/	0/0/0	Spices(including part of its, whether or not cutccrushed or powdered)
0/0/0	0	0	0/0	0/0/0	0/5.7	0//0	0/0/	0/0/0	7.3/0		/0/	0/0/0	Other endangered plants, of a kind used primarily in perfumery(including parts of its, whether or not cut, crushed or powdered)
0/0/0	0	0	0/0	0/0/0	0/5.7	0//0	0/0/	0/0/0	7.3/0		/0/	0/0/0	Other plants, of a kind used primarily in perfumery(including parts of its, whether or not cut, crushed or powdered)
													---Other:
0/0/0	0	0	0/0	0/0/0	0/0	0//0	0/0/	0/0/0	0/0		/0/	0/0/0	----Derris roots and pyrethrum
													----Other
0/0/0	1.8	0	0/0	0/0/0	0/0	0//0	0/0/	0/0/0	8.2/0		/0/	0/0/0	Other endangered plants of a kind used for insecticidal or fungicidal, fresh, chilled, frozen or drie, whether or not cut, crushed or powdered
0/0/0	1.8	0	0/0	0/0/0	0/0	0//0	0/0/	0/0/0	8.2/0		/0/	0/0/0	Other plants, of a kind used for insecticidal or fungicidal, fresh, chilled, frozen or drie, whether or not cut, crushed or powdered
													Locust beans, seaweeds and other algae, sugar beet and sugar cane, fresh, chilled, frozen or dried, whether or not ground; fruit stones and kernels and other vegetable products(including unroasted chicory roots of the variety *Cichorium intybus sativum*) of a kind used primarily for human consumption, not elsewhere specified or included:
													-Seaweeds and other algae:
													--Fit for human consumption:
													---Sea tangle
0/0/0	7	9.3	2/2	0/0/0	0/0	0/0/0	0/0/	18.7/19/	18.8/19			0/0/0	Kelp seedlings not exceeding 1 cm and their gametes or spores (whether or not ground)
0/0/0	7	9.3	2/2	0/0/0	0/0	0/0/0	0/0/	18.7/19/	18.8/19			0/0/0	Fresh, cold, frozen or dried kelp (whether or not ground) suitable for human consumption
0/0/0	7	9.3	2/2	0/0/0	0/0	0/0/0	0/0/	18/18/18	18.8/18			0/0/0	---Black moss
													---Pinnatifida:
0/0/0	5.3	3	1.5/1.5	0/0/0	0/0	0/0/0	0/0/	0/0/13.5	13.6/0			0/0/0	----Dried
													----Fresh
0/0/0	5.3	3	1.5/1.5	0/0/0	0/0	0/0/0	0/0/	0/0/13.5	13.6/0			0/0/0	Undaria pinnatifida seedlings not exceeding 1 cm and their gametes or spores (whether or not ground)
0/0/0	5.3	3	1.5/1.5	0/0/0	0/0	0/0/0	0/0/	0/0/13.5	13.6/0			0/0/0	Undaria pinnatifida fresh for human consumption (whether or not ground)
0/0/0	5.3	3	1.5/1.5	0/0/0	0/0	0/0/0	0/0/	0/0/13.5	13.6/0			0/0/0	----Other
													---Laver:
0/0/0	5.3	3	1.5/1.5	0/0/0	0/0	0/0/0	0/0/	0/0/13.5	13.6/0			0/0/0	----Dried
													----Fresh
0/0/0	5.3	3	1.5/1.5	0/0/0	0/0	0/0/0	0/0/	0/0/13.5	13.6/0			0/0/0	Porphyra seedlings not exceeding 5 cm and their gametes or spores (whether or not ground)

税则号列		货品名称〔CIQ 扩展编码及品名—T2 表示见附表 2〕	最惠(%)	暂定税率	普通	增值/消费	出口退税	计量单位	监管条件/特殊证件	检验检疫	对美关税	亚太上/下
1212.2142	90	适合供人食用的鲜的紫菜(不论是否碾磨)〔101 养殖鲜或冷紫菜,102 野生鲜或冷紫菜〕	15		70	9/	0	千克	AB/	PRQS	20	7.5/7.5
1212.2149		----其他〔101 冷藏养殖紫菜,102 冻藏养殖紫菜,103 冷藏野生紫菜,104 冻藏野生紫菜〕	15		70	9/	0	千克	AB/	PRQS	20	7.5/7.5
		---麒麟菜:										
1212.2161		----干的〔101 干的养殖麒麟菜,102 干的野生麒麟菜〕	15		70	9/	9	千克	AB/	PRQS	20	7.5/7.5
1212.2169		----其他										
1212.2169	10	麒麟菜种苗及其配子或孢子(不论是否碾磨)〔101 养殖鲜或冷麒麟菜,102 养殖冷冻麒麟菜,103 野生鲜或冷麒麟菜,104 野生冷冻麒麟菜〕	15		70	0/	9	千克	AB/	PRQS		7.5/7.5
1212.2169	90	适合供人食用的鲜、冷或冻的麒麟菜(不论是否碾磨)〔101 养殖鲜或冷麒麟菜,102 养殖冷冻麒麟菜,103 野生鲜或冷麒麟菜,104 野生冷冻麒麟菜〕	15		70	9/	9	千克	AB/	PRQS	20	7.5/7.5
		---江蓠:										
1212.2171		----干的〔101 干的养殖江蓠,102 干的野生江蓠〕	15		70	9/	9	千克	AB/	PRQS	20	7.5/7.5
1212.2179		----其他										
1212.2179	10	江篱种苗及其配子或孢子(不论是否碾磨)〔101 养殖鲜或冷江蓠,102 养殖冷冻江蓠,103 野生鲜或冷江蓠,104 野生冷冻江蓠〕	15		70	0/	9	千克	AB/	PRQS		7.5/7.5
1212.2179	90	适合供人食用的鲜、冷或冻的江蓠(不论是否碾磨)〔101 养殖鲜或冷江蓠,102 养殖冷冻江蓠,103 野生鲜或冷江蓠,104 野生冷冻江蓠〕	15		70	9/	9	千克	AB/	PRQS	20	7.5/7.5
1212.2190		---其他										
1212.2190	10	其他适合供人食用的藻类(石花菜、羊栖菜、苔菜等)种苗及其配子或孢子(不论是否碾磨)〔101 其他养殖鲜或冷海藻,102 其他养殖冷冻海藻,103 养殖干制藻类制品,104 其他野生鲜或冷海藻,105 其他野生冷冻海藻,106 野生干制藻类制品〕	15	2	70	0/	9	千克	AB/	PRQS		7.5/7.5
1212.2190	90	其他适合供人食用的海草及藻类(不论是否碾磨)〔101 其他养殖鲜或冷海藻,102 其他养殖冷冻海藻,103 养殖干制藻类制品,104 其他野生鲜或冷海藻,105 其他野生冷冻海藻,106 野生干制藻类制品〕	15	2	70	9/	9	千克	AB/	PRQS	27	7.5/7.5
		--其他:										
1212.2910		---马尾藻〔999〕	15	2	70	9/	9	千克	AB/	PQ	7	7.5/7.5
1212.2990		---其他〔999〕	15	2	70	9/	9	千克	AB/	PQ	7	7.5/7.5
		-其他:										
1212.9100		--甜菜〔999〕	20		70	9/	9	千克	AB/	PRQ	30	
1212.9200		--刺槐豆〔999〕	20		70	9/	9	千克	AB/	PRQ	25	10/10
1212.9300		--甘蔗〔101 替代种植;102 替代种植除外;999〕	20		70	9/	9	千克	AB/	PRQ	25	
1212.9400		--菊苣根〔101〕	20		70	9/	9	千克	AB/	PRQS	25	
		--其他:										
		---杏、桃(包括油桃)、梅或李的核及核仁:										
1212.9911		----苦杏仁〔101 药用苦杏仁,102 非药用(其他工艺),103 非药用(提取(晒干的除外)、压榨、烹制、烘焙、冻干、脱水、裹糖屑、发酵、冷冻(经漂汤和杀青,并在—18 度以下冷冻)、浸酸、腌渍、炒制等工艺进行加工处理的)〕	20		80	9/	9	千克	QAB/	PRQS	25	
1212.9912		----甜杏仁〔101:提取(晒干的除外)、压榨、烹制、烘焙、冻干、脱水、裹糖屑、发酵、冷冻(经漂汤和杀青,并在—18 度以下冷冻)、浸酸、腌渍、炒制等工艺进行加工处理的);999:其他工艺〕	20		80	9/	9	千克	AB/	PRQS	45	
1212.9919		----其他〔101 药用桃仁,102 非熟制(其他工艺),103 熟制,104 非熟制(提取(晒干的除外)、压榨、烹制、烘焙、冻干、脱水、裹糖屑、发酵、冷冻(经漂汤和杀青,并在—18 度以下冷冻)、浸酸、腌渍、炒制等工艺进行加工处理的)〕	20		80	9/	9	千克	AB/	PRQS	30	
		---其他:										
1212.9993		----白瓜子〔101 非熟制(其他工艺),102 熟制,103 饲用,104 非熟制(提取(晒干的除外)、压榨、烹制、烘焙、冻干、脱水、裹糖屑、发酵、冷冻(经漂汤和杀青,并在—18 度以下冷冻)、浸酸、腌渍、炒制等工艺进行加工处理的)〕	20		80	9/	9	千克	AB/	PRQS	25	
1212.9994		----莲子〔101 药用莲子心,102 药用莲子,103 非药用〕	20		80	9/	9	千克	AB/	PRQS	25	
1212.9996		----甜叶菊叶〔999〕	30		70	9/	9	千克	AB/	PRQS	35	
1212.9999		----其他										
1212.9999	10	其他供人食用濒危植物产品(包括未焙制的菊苣根,包括果核、仁等)〔101 其他干坚果其他工艺,102 供制食品或医药用的植物产品,103 批准为新食品原料,104 其他干坚果提取晒干的除外、压榨、烹制、烘焙、冻干、脱水、裹糖屑、发酵、冷冻经漂汤和杀青,并在—18 度以下冷冻、浸酸、腌渍、炒制等工艺进行加工处理的〕	30		70	9/	0	千克	ABFE/	PRQS	55	

协定税率 %								RCEP		特惠税率 %			Article Description
东/冰/格	巴基斯坦	韩国	瑞士上/下	哥/秘/柬	澳/毛	新西/坡/智	中国港/澳/台	东盟及马来/澳/韩	日/新	亚太2国	老/柬/缅	98/97/95	
0/0/0	5.3	3	1.5/1.5	0/0/0	0/0	0/0/0	0/0/	0/0/13.5	13.6/0			0/0/0	Fresh seaweed (whether or not ground) suitable for human consumption
0/0/0	5.3	3	1.5/1.5	0/0/0	0/0	0/0/0	0/0/	0/0/13.5	13.6/0			0/0/0	----Other
													---Eucheuma:
0/0/0	5.3	3	1.5/1.5	0/0/0	0/0	0/ /0	0/0/	0/0/13.5	13.6/0			0/0/0	----Dried
													----Other
0/0/0	5.3	3	1.5/1.5	0/0/0	0/0	0/ /0	0/0/	0/0/13.5	13.6/0			0/0/0	Eucheuma seedlings and their gametes or spores (whether or not ground)
0/0/0	5.3	3	1.5/1.5	0/0/0	0/0	0/ /0	0/0/	0/0/13.5	13.6/0			0/0/0	Fresh, cold or frozen Eucheuma (whether or not ground) suitable for human consumption
													----Garcilaria:
0/0/0	5.3	3	1.5/1.5	0/0/0	0/0	0/ /0	0/0/	0/0/13.5	13.6/0			0/0/0	----Dried
													----Other
0/0/0	5.3	3	1.5/1.5	0/0/0	0/0	0/ /0	0/0/	0/0/13.5	13.6/0			0/0/0	Hedgerow seedlings and their gametes or spores (whether or not ground)
0/0/0	5.3	3	1.5/1.5	0/0/0	0/0	0/ /0	0/0/	0/0/13.5	13.6/0			0/0/0	Fresh, cold or frozen Gracilaria (whether or not ground) suitable for human consumption
													---Other
0/0/0	5.3	3	1.5/1.5	0/0/0	0/0	0/0/0	0/0/	0/0/13.5	13.6/0			0/0/0	Other algae suitable for human consumption (cauliflower, Sargassum fusiforme, Carex, etc.) seedlings and their gametes or spores (whether or not ground)
0/0/0	5.3	3	1.5/1.5	0/0/0	0/0	0/0/0	0/0/	0/0/13.5	13.6/0			0/0/0	Other seaweed and algae suitable for human consumption (whether or not ground)
													-Other:
0/0/0	5.3	0	1.5/1.5	0/0/0	0/0	0/0/0	0/0/	13.5/13.5/13.5	/13.5			0/0/0	---Sargassun
0/0/0	5.3	0	1.5/1.5	0/0/0	0/0	0/0/0	0/0/	13.5/13.5/13.5	/13.5			0/0/0	---Other
													-Other:
0/0/0		9.3	2/2	0/0/0	0/0	0/0/0	0/0/	18/18/18	18.8/18			0/0/0	--Sugar beet
0/0/0	10	9.3	2/2	0/0/0	0/0	0/0/0	0/0/	18/18/18	18.8/18			0/0/0	--Locust beans(carob)
0/0/0		4	2/2	0/0/0	0/0	0/ /0	0/0/	18/18/18	18.2/18		0/0/0	0/0/0	--Sugar cane
0/0/0		9.3		0/0/0	0/0	0/ /0	0/0/	18/18/18	18.8/18			0/0/0	--Chicory roots
													--Other:
													---Apricot, peach(including nectarine) or plum stones and kernels:
0/0/0		9.3	2/2	0/0/0	0/0	0/0/0	0/0/	18/18/18	18.8/18			0/0/0	----Bitter
0/0/0		9.3	2/2	0/0/0	0/0	0/0/0	0/0/	18/18/18	18.8/18			0/0/0	----Sweet
0/0/0		9.3	2/2	0/0/0	0/0	0/0/0	0/0/	18/18/18	18.8/18			0/0/0	----Other
													---Other:
0/0/0		9.3	2/2	0/0/0	0/0	0/0/0	0/0/	18/18/18	18.8/18			0/0/0	----Pumpkin seeds
0/0/0		9.3	2/2	0/0/0	0/0	0/0/0	0/0/	18/18/18	18.8/18			0/0/0	----Lotus seeds(*Semen Nelumbinis*)
0/0/0				0/0/0	0/18	0/0/0	0/0/	28.5/28.5/	/28.5			0/0/0	----leaf of steviol
													----Other
0/0/0				0/0/0	0/18	0/0/0	0/0/	28.5/28.5/	/28.5			0/0/0	Other endangered vegetable products (including unroasted chicory roots of the variety *Cichorium intybus sativum*) of a kind used primarily for human consumption

税则号列		货品名称〔CIQ扩展编码及品名－T2表示见附表2〕	最惠(%)	暂定税率	普通	增值/消费	出口退税	计量单位	监管条件/特殊证件	检验检疫	对美关税	亚太上/下
1212.9999	90	其他供人食用果核、仁及植物产品(包括未焙制的菊苣根)〔T2〕	30		70	9/	9	千克	AB/	PRQS	55	
12.13		**未经处理的谷类植物的茎、秆及谷壳,不论是否切碎、碾磨、挤压或制成团粒:**										
1213.0000		未经处理的谷类植物的茎、秆及谷壳,不论是否切碎、碾磨、挤压或制成团粒[101其他饲用粮谷,102稻草及其制品,103其他草及草制品,104饲用燕麦草,105饲用稻草,106其他饲草,107饲用其他淀粉,108饲用植物颗粒和植物粉,109其他植物饲料]	12		35	9/	9	千克	AB/	PQ	17	
12.14		**芜菁甘蓝、饲料甜菜、饲料用根、干草、紫苜蓿、三叶草、驴喜豆、饲料羽衣甘蓝、羽扇豆、巢菜及类似饲料,不论是否制成团粒:**										
1214.1000		-紫苜蓿粗粉及团粒〔201:苜蓿草;202:苜蓿草颗粒;999:除苜蓿草和苜蓿草颗粒外〕	5		35	0/	0	千克	AB/	PQ		
1214.9000		-其他										
1214.9000	01	其他紫苜蓿(粗粉及团粒除外)〔T2〕	9	7	35	0/	0	千克	AB/	PQ		
1214.9000	02	以除紫苜蓿外的禾本科和豆科为主的多种混合天然饲草〔T2〕	9	4	35	0/	0	千克	AB/	PQ	29	
1214.9000	90	芜菁甘蓝、饲料甜菜、其他植物饲料(包括饲料用根、干草、三叶草、驴喜豆等,不论是否制成团粒)〔101其他饲草,102饲用其他淀粉,103饲用植物颗粒和植物粉,104其他植物饲料,105燕麦草,106梯牧草,107羊草,108小叶草,109狼尾草,110稻草,111碱草〕	9		35	0/	0	千克	AB/	PQ	34	

协定税率 %								RCEP		特惠税率 %			Article Description
东/冰/格	巴基斯坦	韩国	瑞士上/下	哥/秘/柬	澳/毛	新西/坡/智	中国港/澳/台	东盟及马来/澳/韩	日/新	亚太2国	老/柬/缅	98/97/95	
0/0/0				0/0/0	0/18	0/0/0	0/0/	28.5/28.5/	/28.5			0/0/0	Other fruit stones and kernels and vegetable products (including unroasted chicory roots of the variety *Cichorium intybus sativum*) of a kind used primarily for human consumption
													Cereal straw and husks, unprepared, whether or not chopped, ground, pressed or in the form of pellets:
0/0/0	4.2	2.4	1.2/1.2	0/0/0	0/0	0/0/0	0/0/	0/0/10.8	10.9/0		/0/	0/0/0	Cereal straw and husks, unprepared, whether or not chopped, ground, pressed or in the form of pellets
													Swedes, mangolds, fodder roots, hay, lucerne (alfalfa), clover, sainfoin, forage kale, lupines, vetches and similar forage products, whether or not in the form of pellets:
0/0/0	0	0	0/0	0/0/0	0/0	0//0	0/0/	0/0/0	0/0		/0/	0/0/0	-Lucerne (alfalfa) meal and pellets
													-Other
0/0/0	2	0	0/0	0/0/0	0/0	0//0	0/0/	0/0/0	8.2/0		/0/	0/0/0	Other lucerne(other than meal and pellets)
0/0/0	2	0	0/0	0/0/0	0/0	0//0	0/0/	0/0/0	8.2/0		/0/	0/0/0	In addition to alfalfa variety of graminaceous and leguminous based mixed natural forage grass
0/0/0	2	0	0/0	0/0/0	0/0	0//0	0/0/	0/0/0	8.2/0		/0/	0/0/0	Swedes, mangolds, other vegetable fodder (including fodder roots, hay, clover, sainfoin, whether or not in the form of pellets)

第十三章
虫胶;树胶、树脂
及其他植物液、汁

注释:

税目13.02主要包括甘草、除虫菊、啤酒花、芦荟的浸膏及鸦片,但不包括:

一、按重量计蔗糖含量在10%以上或制成糖食的甘草浸膏(税目17.04);
二、麦芽膏(税目19.01);
三、咖啡精、茶精、马黛茶精(税目21.01);
四、构成含酒精饮料的植物汁、液(第二十二章);
五、樟脑、甘草甜及税目29.14或29.38的其他产品;
六、按重量计生物碱含量不低于50%的罂粟秆的浓缩物(税目29.39);
七、税目30.03或30.04的药品及税目38.22的血型试剂;
八、鞣料或染料的浸膏(税目32.01或32.03);
九、精油、浸膏、净油、香膏提取的油树脂或精油的水馏液及水溶液;饮料制造业用的以芳香物质为基料的制剂(第三十三章);

十、天然橡胶、巴拉塔胶、古塔波胶、银胶菊胶、糖胶树胶或类似的天然树胶(税目40.01)。

本国注释:

子目1302.1100的鸦片,我国禁止进口。

税则号列	货品名称〔CIQ扩展编码及品名—T2表示见附表2〕	最惠(%)	暂定税率	普通	增值/消费	出口退税	计量单位	监管条件/特殊证件	检验检疫	对美关税	亚太上/下
13.01	**虫胶;天然树胶、树脂、树胶脂及油树脂(例如,香树脂):**										
1301.2000	-阿拉伯胶〔101饲料添加剂,102有检疫要求食品添加剂,301需申报仅用于工业用途不用于食品添加剂有检疫要求的化学品〕	15		40	9/	9	千克	AB/	PRQ	35	
	-其他:										
1301.9010	---胶黄蓍树胶(卡喇杆胶),〔101〕	15		40	9/	9	千克	AB/	PQ		
1301.9020	---乳香、没药及血竭〔101植物产品,102药用乳香,103药用没药,104药用血竭〕	3		17	9/	9	千克	ABQ/	PQ	8	
1301.9030	---阿魏〔101植物产品,102药用阿魏〕	3		17	9/	9	千克	AB/	PQ	8	
1301.9040	---松脂										
1301.9040 10	濒危松科植物的松脂〔301危险化学品,不用作食品添加剂;302危险化学品,用作食品添加剂;303其他化工品,不用作食品添加剂;304其他化工品,用作食品添加剂;999未列出的其他植物产品〕	15		45	9/	0	千克	ABE/3	MPNQ		
1301.9040 90	其他松脂〔301危险化学品,不用作食品添加剂;302危险化学品,用作食品添加剂;303其他化工品,不用作食品添加剂;304其他化工品,用作食品添加剂;999未列出的其他植物产品〕	15		45	9/	9	千克	AB/3	MPRNQ		
1301.9090	---其他										
1301.9090 10	龙血树脂、大戟脂、愈疮树脂〔999〕	15		45	9/	9	千克	ABFE/	PQ	35	
1301.9090 20	大麻脂〔999〕	15		45	9/	9	千克	ABI/	PQ	35	
1301.9090 91	其他濒危植物的天然树胶、树脂[包括天然树胶、树脂及其他油树脂(例如:香树脂)]〔301属于危险化学品的食品添加剂,999未列出的其他植物产品〕	15		45	9/	0	千克	ABFE/	PQ	35	
1301.9090 99	其他天然树胶、树脂[包括天然树胶、树脂及其他油树脂(例如:香树脂)]〔101药用干漆,102药用安息香,103药用苏合香,104药用枫香脂,117其他植物产品,301属于危险化学品的食品添加剂〕	15		45	9/	9	千克	AB/	PQ	35	
13.02	**植物液汁及浸膏;果胶、果胶酸盐及果胶酸酯;从植物产品制得的琼脂、其他胶液及增稠剂,不论是否改性:**										
	-植物液汁及浸膏:										
1302.1100	--鸦片〔101供制食品或医药用的植物提取物,301其他危险化学品〕	0		0	0/	13	千克	9BI/3	PQ	5	
1302.1200	--甘草的〔101供制食品或医药用的植物提取物,102甘草提取物(粉)(有检疫要求食品添加剂)103甘草流浸膏(有检疫要求食品添加剂)〕	6	0	20	13/	13	千克	4xAy/	R	25	
1302.1300	--啤酒花的〔301有检疫要求食品添加剂,999啤酒花制品〕	10		80	13/	13	千克	AB/	PRQS	22.5	
1302.1400	--麻黄的										
1302.1400 11	供制农药用麻黄浸膏及浸膏粉〔999〕	9.5		80	13/	13	千克	23AB/	PQ	12	7.1/7.1
1302.1400 12	供制医药用麻黄浸膏及浸膏粉〔101〕	9.5		80	13/	13	千克	Q23AB/	PQ	12	7.1/7.1
1302.1400 19	其他麻黄浸膏及浸膏粉〔101〕	9.5		80	13/	13	千克	23AB/	PQ	12	7.1/7.1
1302.1400 20	麻黄液汁〔101〕	9.5		80	13/	13	千克	Q23AB/	PQ	12	7.1/7.1
	--其他:										

Chapter 13
Lac; gums, resins and other vegetable saps and extracts

Notes:

Heading No. 13.02 applies, *inter alia*, to liquorice extract and extract of pyrethrum, extract of hops, extract of aloes and opium. The heading does not apply to:

(1) Liquorice extract containing more than 10% by weight of sucrose or putup as confectionery (heading No. 17.04);
(2) Malt extract (heading No. 19.01);
(3) Extracts of coffee, tea or mate (heading No. 21.01);
(4) Vegetable saps or extracts constituting alcoholic beverages (Chapter22);
(5) Camphor, glycyrrhizin or other products of heading No. 29.14 or 29.38;
(6) Concentrates of poppy straw containing not less than 50% by weight of alkaloids(heading No. 29.39);
(7) Medicaments of heading No. 30.03 or 30.04 or bloodgrouping reagents (heading No. 38.22);
(8) Tanning or dyeing extracts (heading No. 32.01 or 32.03);
(9) Essential oils, concretes, absolutes, resinoids, extracted oleoresins, aqueous distillates or aqueous solutions of essential oils or preparations basedon odoriferous substances of a kind used for the manufacture of beverages (Chapter 33);
(10) Natural rubber, balata, gutta-percha, guayule, chicle or similar natural gums (heading No. 40.01).

National note:

Opium of Subheading No. 1302.1100 is subject to import ban.

协定税率 %								RCEP		特惠税率 %			Article Description
东/冰/格	巴基斯坦	韩国	瑞士上/下	哥/秘/柬	澳/毛	新西/坡/智	中国港/澳/台	东盟及马来/澳/韩	日/新	亚太2国	老/柬/缅	98/97/95	
													Lac; natural gums, resins, gum-resins and oleoresins (for example, balsams):
0/0/0	0	3	1.5/1.5	0/0/0	0/0	0/0/0	0/0/	0/0/13.5	13.6/0			0/0/0	-Gum Arabic
													-Other:
0/0/0	0	3	1.5/1.5	0/0/0	0/0	0/0/0	0/0/	0/0/13.5	13.6/0			0/0/0	---Gum tragacanth
0/0/0	0	0	0/0	0/0/0	0/0	0//0	0/0/	0/0/0	0/0			0/0/0	---Olibanum, myrrh and dragon's blood
0/0/0	0	0	0/0	0/0/0	0/0	0//0	0/0/	0/0/0	0/0			0/0/0	---Asafoetida
													---Pine-resin
0/0/0	0	3	1.5/1.5	0/0/0	0/0	0/0/0	0/0/	0/0/13.5	13.6/0			0/0/0	Pine-resin of endangered plants of pine family
0/0/0	0	3	1.5/1.5	0/0/0	0/0	0/0/0	0/0/	0/0/13.5	13.6/0			0/0/0	Other pine-resin
													---Other
0/0/0	0	3	1.5/1.5	0/0/0	0/0	0/0/0	0/0/	0/0/13.5	13.6/0			0/0/0	Resin of daemonorops draco, resin of euphorbia, resin of lignum vitae
0/0/0	0	3	1.5/1.5	0/0/0	0/0	0/0/0	0/0/	0/0/13.5	13.6/0			0/0/0	Charas, churrus
0/0/0	0	3	1.5/1.5	0/0/0	0/0	0/0/0	0/0/	0/0/13.5	13.6/0			0/0/0	Other natural gums, resins, gum-resins and oleoresins (for example, balsams) of endangered plants
0/0/0	0	3	1.5/1.5	0/0/0	0/0	0/0/0	0/0/	0/0/13.5	13.6/0			0/0/0	Other natural gums, resins, gum-resins and oleoresins (for example, balsams)
													Vegetable saps and extracts; pectic substances, pectinates and pectates; agar-agar and other mucilages and thickeners, whether or not modified, derived from vegetable products:
													-Vegetable saps and extracts:
0/0/0	0	0	0/0	0/0/0	0/0	0//0	0/0/	0/0/0	0/0			0/0/0	--Opium
0/0/0	0	0	0/0	0/0/0	0/0	0//0	0/0/	0/0/0	0/0			0/0/0	--Of liquorice
0/0/0	3.5	2	0/0	0/0/0	0/0	0/0/0	0/0/	0/0/9	9.1/0			0/0/0	--Of hops
													--Of ephedra
0/0/0	0	9.3	0/0	0/0/0	0/0	0/0/0	0/0/	18.7/19/18.7	18.8/19			0/0/0	Ephedra extracts powder used in pesticide
0/0/0	0	9.3	0/0	0/0/0	0/0	0/0/0	0/0/	18.7/19/18.7	18.8/19			0/0/0	Ephedra extracts powder used in medical
0/0/0	0	9.3	0/0	0/0/0	0/0	0/0/0	0/0/	18.7/19/18.7	18.8/19			0/0/0	Other Ephedra extracts powder
0/0/0	0	9.3	0/0	0/0/0	0/0	0/0/0	0/0/	18.7/19/18.7	18.8/19			0/0/0	Saps and extracts of Ephedra
													--Other:

税则号列	货品名称〔CIQ 扩展编码及品名—T2 表示见附表 2〕	最惠(%)	暂定税率	普通	增值/消费	出口退税	计量单位	监管条件/特殊证件	检验检疫	对美关税	亚太上/下
1302.1910	---生漆〔101 植物产品;301 其他危险化学品〕	20		90	13/	9	千克	AB/3	MPNQ		
1302.1920	---印楝素〔999〕	3		11	13/	9	千克	ABS/	PQ	8	
1302.1930	---除虫菊的或含鱼藤酮植物根茎的										
1302.1930 10	除虫菊的液汁及浸膏〔999〕	3		11	13/	13	千克	ABS/	MPNQ	8	
1302.1930 90	含鱼藤酮植物根茎的液汁及浸膏〔999〕	3		11	13/	13	千克	AB/	MPNQ	8	
1302.1940	---银杏的〔999〕	9.5		80	13/	13	千克	ABE/	PQ	12	7.1/7.1
1302.1990	---其他										
1302.1990 01	苦参碱〔999〕	9.5		80	13/	13	千克	ABS/	PQ	29.5	7.1/7.1
1302.1990 13	供制农药用的濒危植物液汁及浸膏〔999〕	9.5		80	13/	0	千克	ABFE/	PQ	29.5	7.1/7.1
1302.1990 19	供制农药用的其他植物液汁及浸膏〔101〕	9.5		80	13/	13	千克	AB/	PRQ	29.5	7.1/7.1
1302.1990 95	红豆杉液汁及浸膏〔101 供工业用的植物及植物提取物(包括液汁等),102 供制食品或医药用的植物提取物〕	9.5		80	13/	13	千克	ABFE/	PQ	29.5	7.1/7.1
1302.1990 96	黄草汁液及浸膏〔101 供工业用的植物及植物提取物,102 供制食品或医药用的植物提取物〕	9.5		80	13/	13	千克	ABFE/	PQ	29.5	7.1/7.1
1302.1990 97	其他濒危植物液汁及浸膏〔101 供工业用的植物及植物提取物,102 供制食品或医药用的植物提取物,103 批准为新食品原料〕	9.5		80	13/	0	千克	ABFE/	PQ	29.5	7.1/7.1
1302.1990 99	其他植物液汁及浸膏[T2]	9.5		80	13/	13	千克	AB/	MPRNQS	29.5	7.1/7.1
1302.2000	-果胶、果胶酸盐及果胶酸酯〔999〕	20		80	13/	13	千克	A/	R	45	
	-从植物产品制得的胶液及增稠剂,不论是否改性:										
1302.3100	--琼脂〔101 饲料添加剂,102 有检疫要求食品添加剂〕	10		80	13/	13	千克	A/	R	37.5	
1302.3200	--从刺槐豆、刺槐豆子或瓜尔豆制得的胶液及增稠剂,不论是否改性〔101 饲料添加剂,301 有检疫要求食品添加剂,302 其他化工品,不用作食品添加剂〕	10		80	13/	13	千克	A/	R	32.5	6.7/6.7
	--其他:										
	---海草及其他藻类制品:										
1302.3911	----卡拉胶〔101:硒化卡拉胶(有检疫要求食品添加剂);102:卡拉胶(有检疫要求食品添加剂);301:需申报仅用于工业用途不用于食品添加剂有检疫要求的化学品〕	8		80	13/	13	千克	A/	R	18	
1302.3912	----褐藻胶〔999〕	8		80	13/	13	千克	AB/	PQ	10.5	
1302.3919	----其他〔103〕	8		80	13/	13	千克	AB/	PQ	28	
1302.3990	---其他										
1302.3990 10	未列名濒危植物胶液及增稠剂(有机过氧化物)〔101〕	8		80	13/	0	千克	ABFE/	PQ	33	
1302.3990 90	其他未列名植物胶液及增稠剂〔101 土荆芥油,301 有检疫要求食品添加剂〕	8		80	13/	13	千克	AB/	MPRQ	33	

协定税率 %								RCEP		特惠税率 %			Article Description
东/冰/格	巴基斯坦	韩国	瑞士上/下	哥/秘/柬	澳/毛	新西/坡/智	中国港/澳/台	东盟及马来/澳/韩	日/新	亚太2国	老/柬/缅	98/97/95	
0/0/0		9.3	2/2	0/0/0	0/0	0/0/0	0/0/	18/18/18	18.8/18			0/0/0	---Crude lacquer
0/0/0	0	0	0/0	0/0/0	0/0	0//0	0/0/	0/0/0	0/0			0/0/0	---Azadirachtin
													---Of pyrethrum or of the roots of plants containing rotenone
0/0/0	0	0	0/0	0/0/0	0/0	0//0	0/0/	0/0/0	0/0			0/0/0	Liquid and extract of pyrethrum
0/0/0	0	0	0/0	0/0/0	0/0	0//0	0/0/	0/0/0	0/0			0/0/0	Juice and extract of plant rhizome containing rotenone
0/0/0	15	9.3	0/0	0/0/0	0/0	0/0/0	0/0/	18/18/18	18.8/18			0/0/0	---Ginkgo biloba
													---Other
0/0/0	0	9.3	0/0	0/0/0	0/0	0/0/0	0/0/	18.7/19/18.7	18.8/19			0/0/0	Matrine
0/0/0	0	9.3	0/0	0/0/0	0/0	0/0/0	0/0/	18.7/19/18.7	18.8/19			0/0/0	Endangered vegetable saps and extracts for used primarily in pesticide
0/0/0	0	9.3	0/0	0/0/0	0/0	0/0/0	0/0/	18.7/19/18.7	18.8/19			0/0/0	Other vegetable saps and extracts used primarily in pharmacy
0/0/0	0	9.3	0/0	0/0/0	0/0	0/0/0	0/0/	18.7/19/18.7	18.8/19			0/0/0	Saps and extracts of taxusl
0/0/0	0	9.3	0/0	0/0/0	0/0	0/0/0	0/0/	18.7/19/18.7	18.8/19			0/0/0	Saps and extracts of herba dendroii
0/0/0	0	9.3	0/0	0/0/0	0/0	0/0/0	0/0/	18.7/19/18.7	18.8/19			0/0/0	Saps and extracts of other endangered vegetable
0/0/0	0	9.3	0/0	0/0/0	0/0	0/0/0	0/0/	18.7/19/18.7	18.8/19			0/0/0	Other vegetable saps and extracts
0/0/0		9.3	2/2	0/0/0	0/0	0/0/0	0/0/	18/18/18	18.8/18			0/0/0	-Pectic substances, pectinates and pectates
													-Mucilages and thickeners, whether or not modified, derived from vegetable products:
0/0/0	3.5	2	0/0	0/0/0	0/0	0/0/0	0/0/	0/0/9	9.1/0			0/0/0	--Agar-agar
0/0/0	0	3	1.5/1.5	0/0/0	0/0	0/0/0	0/0/	13.5/13.5/13.5	13.6/13.5			0/0/0	--Mucilages and thickeners, whether or not modified, derived from locust beans, locust bean seeds or guar seeds
													--Other:
													---Preparations of seaweeds and other algae:
0/0/0	12	3	1.5/1.5	0/0/0	0/0	0/0/0	0/0/	0/0/13.5	13.6/0			0/0/0	----Carrageenan
0/0/0	12	3	1.5/1.5	0/0/0	0/0	0/0/0	0/0/	0/0/13.5	13.6/0			0/0/0	----Algin
0/0/0	12	3	1.5/1.5	0/3.5/0	0/0	0/0/0	0/0/	0/0/13.5	13.6/0			0/0/0	----Other
													---Other
0/0/0	12	3	1.5/1.5	0/0/0	0/0	0/0/0	0/0/	0/0/13.5	13.6/0			0/0/0	Mucilages and thickeners, derived from endangered vegetable products, not elsewhere specified or included
0/0/0	12	3	1.5/1.5	0/0/0	0/0	0/0/0	0/0/	0/0/13.5	13.6/0			0/0/0	Other mucilages and thickeners, derived from vegetable products, not elsewhere specified or included

第十四章
编结用植物材料；
其他植物产品

注释：

一、本章不包括归入第十一类的下列产品：

主要供纺织用的植物材料或植物纤维，不论其加工程度如何；或经过处理使其只能作为纺织原料用的其他植物材料。

二、税目14.01主要包括竹（不论是否劈开、纵锯、切段、圆端、漂白、磨光、染色或进行不燃处理）、劈开的柳条、芦苇及类似品和藤心、藤丝、藤片。但不包括木片条（税目44.04）。

三、税目14.04不包括木丝（税目44.05）及供制帚、制刷用成束、成簇的材料（税目96.03）。

税则号列	货品名称〔CIQ扩展编码及品名—T2表示见附表2〕	最惠(%)	暂定税率	普通	增值/消费	出口退税	计量单位	监管条件/特殊证件	检验检疫	对美关税	亚太上/下
14.01	**主要作编结用的植物材料（例如，竹、藤、芦苇、灯芯草、柳条、酒椰叶，已净、漂白或染色的谷类植物的茎秆，椴树皮）：**										
1401.1000	-竹										
1401.1000 10	酸竹〔999〕	10		70	9/	9	千克	ABE/	PQ	35	
1401.1000 90	其他竹〔101原竹，102其他竹及竹制品〕	10		70	9/	9	千克	AB/	PQ	35	
1401.2000	-藤										
1401.2000 10	濒危藤〔999〕	10		35	9/	0	千克	ABFE/	PQ	15	
1401.2000 90	其他藤〔999〕	10		35	9/	9	千克	AB/	PQ	15	
	-其他：										
1401.9010	---谷类植物的茎秆（麦秸除外）〔999〕	10		70	9/	9	千克	AB/	PQ	15	
1401.9020	---芦苇〔999〕	10		70	9/	9	千克	AB/	PQ	15	
	---灯芯草属：										
1401.9031	----蔺草〔999〕	10		70	9/	9	千克	AB4xy/	PQ	15	
1401.9039	----其他〔999〕	10		70	9/	9	千克	AB/	PQ	15	
1401.9090	---其他〔999〕	10		70	9/	9	千克	AB/	PQ	15	
14.04	**其他税目未列名的植物产品：**										
1404.2000	-棉短绒〔999〕	4		30	9/	9	千克	AB/	PQ	29	
	-其他：										
1404.9010	---主要供染料、鞣料用的植物原料〔999〕	5		45	9/	9	千克	AB/	PQ	10	4.3/4.3
1404.9090	---其他										
1404.9090 10	椰糠（条/块）〔999〕	15	4	70	9/	9	千克	AB/	PQ	29	
1404.9090 90	其他编号未列名植物产品［101其他竹及竹制品，102藤及藤制品，103柳及柳制品，104其他草及草制品，105芦苇及芦苇制品，106棕及棕制品，107葵及葵制品，108其他竹藤柳草类，109软木（栽培介质），110木屑（栽培介质），111稻壳（栽培介质），112花生壳（栽培介质），113棉子壳（栽培介质），114其他有机栽培介质，115植物标本，116未列出的其他植物产品］	15		70	9/	9,13	千克	AB/	PQ	40	

Chapter 14
Vegetable plaiting materials; vegetable products not elsewhere specified or included

Notes:

1. This Chapter does not cover the following products which are to be classified in Section Ⅺ:
   Vegetable materials or fibres of vegetable materials of a kind used primarily in the manufacture of textiles, however prepared, or other vegetable materials which have undergone treatment so as to render them suitable for use only as textile materials.
2. Heading No. 14.01 applies, *inter alia*, to bamboos (whether or not split, sawn lengthwise, cut to length, rounded at the ends, bleached, rendered non-inflammable, polished or dyed), split osier, reeds and the like, to rattan cores and to drawn or split rattans. The heading does not apply to chipwood (heading No. 44.04).
3. Heading No. 14.04 does not apply to wood wool (heading No. 44.05) and prepared knots or tufts for broom or brush making (heading No.96.03).

协定税率 %								RCEP		特惠税率 %			Article Description
东/冰/格	巴基斯坦	韩国	瑞士上/下	哥/秘/柬	澳/毛	新西/坡/智	中国港/澳/台	东盟及马来/澳/韩	日/新	亚太2国	老/柬/缅	98/97/95	
													Vegetable materials of a kind used primarily for plaiting (for example, bamboos, rattans, reeds, rushes, osier, raffia, cleaned, bleached or dyed cereal straw, and lime bark):
													-Bamboos
0/0/0	3.5	2	0/0	0/0/0	0/0	0/0/0	0/0/	0/0/9	9.1/0		0/0/	0/0/0	Acidosasa chinensis(*Raphia vinifera*)
0/0/0	3.5	2	0/0	0/0/0	0/0	0/0/0	0/0/	0/0/9	9.1/0		0/0/	0/0/0	Other bamboos
													-Rattans
0/0/0	3.5	2	0/0	0/0/0	0/0	0/0/0	0/0/	9/9/9	9.1/9		0/0/	0/0/0	Endangered rattans
0/0/0	3.5	2	0/0	0/0/0	0/0	0/0/0	0/0/	9/9/9	9.1/9		0/0/	0/0/0	Other rattans
													-Other:
0/0/0	3.5	2	0/0	0/0/0	0/0	0/0/0	0/0/	0/0/9	9.1/0		/0/	0/0/0	---Cereal straw (other than wheat straw)
0/0/0	3.5	2	0/0	0/0/0	0/0	0/0/0	0/0/	0/0/9	9.1/0		/0/	0/0/0	---Reeds
													---Rushes:
0/0/0	3.5	2	0/0	0/0/0	0/0	0/0/0	0/0/	0/0/9	9.1/0		/0/	0/0/0	----Juncaceae
0/0/0	3.5	2	0/0	0/0/0	0/0	0/0/0	0/0/	0/0/9	9.1/0		/0/	0/0/0	----Other
0/0/0	3.5	2	0/0	0/0/0	0/0	0/0/0	0/0/	0/0/9	9.1/0		/0/	0/0/0	---Other
													Vegetable products not elsewhere specified or included:
0/0/0	0	0	0/0	0/0/0	0/0	0//0	0/0/	0/3.6/0	0/3.6			0/0/0	-Cotton linters
													-Other:
0/0/0	0	0	0/0	0/0/0	0/0	0//0	0/0/	0/0/0	4.5/0			0/0/0	---Raw vegetable materials of a kind used primarily in dyeing or tanning
													---Other
0/0/0	0	3	1.5/1.5	0/0/0	0/0	0/0/0	0/0/	13.5/13.5/13.5	13.6/13.5			0/0/0	coco coir(sripe/piece)
0/0/0	0	3	1.5/1.5	0/0/0	0/0	0/0/0	0/0/	13.5/13.5/13.5	13.6/13.5			0/0/0	Other vegetable products not elsewhere specified or included

第三类
动、植物或微生物油、脂及其分解产品;精制的食用油脂;动、植物蜡

第十五章
动、植物或微生物油、脂及其分解产品;精制的食用油脂;动、植物蜡

注释:

一、本章不包括:

(一)税目02.09的猪脂肪及家禽脂肪;

(二)可可脂、可可油(税目18.04);

(三)按重量计税目04.05所列产品的含量超过15%的食品(通常归入第二十一章);

(四)税目23.01的油渣或税目23.04至23.06的残渣;

(五)第六类的脂肪酸、精制蜡、药品、油漆、清漆、肥皂、芳香料制品、化妆盥洗品、磺化油及其他货品;

(六)从油类提取的油膏(税目40.02)。

二、税目15.09不包括用溶剂提取的橄榄油(税目15.10)。

三、税目15.18不包括变性的油、脂及其分离品,这些货品应归入其相应的未变性油、脂及其分离品的税目。

四、皂料、油脚、硬脂沥青、甘油沥青及羊毛脂残渣,归入税目15.22。

子目注释:

一、子目1509.30所称"初榨油橄榄油",游离酸度(以油酸计)不超过2.0克/100克,可根据《食品法典标准》(33—1981)与其他初榨油橄榄油类别加以区分。

二、子目1514.11及1514.19所称"低芥子酸菜子油",是指按重量计芥子酸含量低于2%的固定油。

税则号列	货品名称〔CIQ扩展编码及品名—T2表示见附表2〕	最惠(%)	暂定税率	普通	增值/消费	出口退税	计量单位	监管条件/特殊证件	检验检疫	对美关税	亚太上/下
15.01	**猪脂肪(包括已炼制的猪油)及家禽脂肪,但税目02.09及15.03的货品除外:**										
1501.1000	-猪油〔101工业用猪油脂,102饲料用猪油脂,103饲料用野生猪、牛、羊油脂,104未炼制的食用猪油(脂),105已炼制的食用猪油(脂)〕	10		35	13/	13	千克	AB/	MPRQS	15	
1501.2000	-其他猪脂肪〔101工业用猪油脂,102饲料用猪油脂,103饲料用野生猪、牛、羊油脂,104未炼制的食用猪油(脂),105已炼制的食用猪油(脂)〕	10		35	13/	13	千克	AB/	MPRQS	15	
1501.9000	-其他〔101工业用禽油脂,102饲料用禽油脂,103未炼制的食用家禽油(脂),104已炼制的食用家禽油(脂)〕	10		35	13/	13	千克	AB/	MPRQS	15	
15.02	**牛、羊脂肪,但税目15.03的货品除外:**										
1502.1000	-牛、羊油脂[101工业用牛油脂,102工业用羊油脂,103工业用野生猪、牛、羊油脂,104饲料用牛油脂,105饲料用羊油脂,106饲料用野生猪、牛、羊油脂,107未炼制的食用牛油(脂),108未炼制的食用羊油(脂),109已炼制的食用牛油(脂),110已炼制的食用羊油(脂)]	8	2	30	13/	13	千克	AB/	MPRQS	7	0/0
1502.9000	-其他[T2]〔101:工业用牛油脂;102:工业用羊油脂;103:工业用野生猪、牛、羊油脂;104:饲料用牛油脂;105:饲料用羊油脂;106:饲料用野生猪、牛、羊油脂;107:未炼制的食用牛脂肪;108:未炼制的食用羊脂肪;109:已炼制的食用牛油(脂);110:已炼制的食用羊油(脂);111:未炼制的食用牛脂肪(冰鲜未炼制牛脂肪(食用,不包括内脏脂肪);112:未炼制的食用牛脂肪(冰鲜未炼制牛脂肪(食用,不包括内脏脂肪,12月龄以下);113:未炼制的食用牛脂肪(冰鲜未炼制牛脂肪(食用,不包括内脏脂肪,30月龄以下));114:未炼制的食用牛脂肪(冷冻未炼制牛脂肪(食用,不包括内脏脂肪));115:未炼制的食用牛脂肪(冷冻未炼制牛脂肪(食用,不包括内脏脂肪,12月龄以下));116:未炼制的食用牛脂肪(冷冻未炼制牛脂肪(食用,不包括内脏脂肪,30月龄以下));117:未炼制的食用羊脂肪(冰鲜未炼制绵羊脂肪(食用,不包括内脏脂肪));118:未炼制的食用羊脂肪(冰鲜未炼制山羊脂肪(食用,不包括内脏脂肪));119:未炼制的食用羊脂肪(冷冻未炼制绵羊脂肪(食用,不包括内脏脂肪));120:未炼制的食用羊脂肪(冷冻未炼制山羊脂肪(食用,不包括内脏脂肪));121:冷冻未炼制绵羊羔羊脂肪(食用,不包括内脏脂肪);122:(冷冻未炼制山羊羔羊脂肪(食用,不包括内脏脂肪)〕	8	4	70	13/	9	千克	AB/	MPRQS	9	0/0

SECTION Ⅲ
ANIMAL, VEGETABLE OR MICROBIAL FATS AND OILS AND THEIR CLEAVAGE PRODUCTS; PREPARED EDIBLE FATS; ANIMAL OR VEGETABLE WAXES

Chapter 15

Animal, vegetable or microbial fats and oils and their cleavage products; prepared edible fats; animal or vegetable waxes

Notes:

1. This Chapter does not cover:
   (a) Pig fat or poultry fat of heading No. 02.09;
   (b) Cocoa butter, fat or oil (heading No. 18.04);
   (c) Edible preparations containing by weight more than 15% of the products of heading No. 04.05 (generally Chapter 21);
   (d) Greaves (heading No. 23.01) or residues of headings No. 23.04 to 23.06;
   (e) Fatty acids, prepared waxes, medicaments, paints, varnishes, soap, perfumery, cosmetic or toilet preparations, sulphonated oils or other goods of Section Ⅵ;
   (f) Factice derived from oils (heading No. 40.02).
2. Heading No. 15.09 does not apply to oils obtained from olives by solvent extraction (heading No. 15.10).
3. Heading No. 15.18 does not cover fats or oils or their fractions, merely denatured, which are to be classified in the heading appropriate to the corresponding undenatured fats and oils and their fractions.
4. Soap-stocks, oil foots and dregs, stearin pitch, glycerol pitch and wool grease residues fall in heading No. 15.22.

Subheading Note:

1. For the purposes of subheading No.1509.30, virgin olive oil has a free acidity expressed as oleic acid not exceeding 2.0 g/ 100 g and can be distinguished from the other virgin olive oil categories according to the characteristics indicated in the Codex Alimentarius Standard 33—1981.
2. For the purposes of subheadings No. 1514.11 and 1514.19, the expression "low erucic acid rape or colza oil" means the fixed oil which has an erucic acid content of less than 2% by weight.

协定税率 %								RCEP		特惠税率 %			Article Description
东/冰/格	巴基斯坦	韩国	瑞士上/下	哥/秘/柬	澳/毛	新西/坡/智	中国港/澳/台	东盟及马来/澳/韩	日/新	亚太2国	老/柬/缅	98/97/95	
													Pig fat (including lard) and poultry fat, other than that of heading No. 02.09 or 15.03:
0/0/0		2	0/0	0/0/0	0/0	0/0/0	0/0/	0/0/9	9.1/0			0/0/0	-Lard
0/0/0		2	0/0	0/0/0	0/0	0/0/0	0/0/	0/0/9	9.1/0			0/0/0	-Other pig fat
0/0/0		2	0/0	0/0/0	0/0	0/0/0	0/0/	0/0/9	9.1/0			0/0/0	-Other
													Fats of bovine animals, sheep or goats, other than those of heading No. 15.03:
0/0/0	0	0	0/0	0/0/0	0/0	0//0	0/0/	0/0/0	7.3/0			0/0/0	-Tallow
0/0/0	0	0	0/0	0/0/0	0/0	0//0	0/0/	7.2/7.2/7.2	7.3/7.2			0/0/0	-Other

税则号列	货品名称〔CIQ 扩展编码及品名—T2 表示见附表 2〕	最惠(%)	暂定税率	普通	增值/消费	出口退税	计量单位	监管条件/特殊证件	检验检疫	对美关税	亚太上/下
15.03	**猪油硬脂、液体猪油、油硬脂、食用或非食用脂油,未经乳化、混合或其他方法制作:**										
1503.0000	猪油硬脂、液体猪油、油硬脂、食用或非食用脂油,未经乳化、混合或其他方法制作[101 工业用猪油脂,102 工业用其他野生偶蹄动物油脂,103 未列出的工业用其他动物油脂,104 饲料用猪油脂,105 饲料用其他野生偶蹄动物油脂,106 未炼制的食用猪油(脂))]	10		30	13/	13	千克	AB/	PRQS	15	
15.04	**鱼或海生哺乳动物的油、脂及其分离品,不论是否精制,但未经化学改性:**										
1504.1000	-鱼肝油及其分离品										
1504.1000 10	濒危鱼鱼肝油及其分离品〔101〕	12		30	13/	0	千克	ABEF/	PRQS	37	
1504.1000 90	其他鱼鱼肝油及其分离品〔101 工业用鱼油脂,102 未列出的工业用其他动物油脂,103 饲料用鱼油脂,104 未列出的饲料用其他动物油脂,201 保健食品〕	12		30	13/	13	千克	AB/	PRQS	37	
1504.2000	-除鱼肝油以外的鱼油、脂及其分离品										
1504.2000 11	濒危鱼油软胶囊(鱼肝油除外)〔101 保健食品,102 除保健食品以外〕	12	6	50	13/	0	千克	ABEF/	PRQS	26	
1504.2000 19	濒危鱼其他鱼油、脂及其分离品(鱼肝油除外)[101 工业用鱼油脂,102 未列出的工业用其他动物油脂,103 饲料用鱼油脂,104 未列出的饲料用其他动物油脂,105 养殖鱼鱼油,106 野生鱼鱼油,107 保健食品]	12		50	13/	0	千克	ABEF/	PRQS	32	
1504.2000 91	其他鱼油软胶囊(鱼肝油除外)〔101 保健食品,102 除保健食品以外〕	12	6	50	13/	13	千克	AB/	PRQS	26	
1504.2000 99	其他鱼油、脂及其分离品(鱼肝油除外)[101 工业用鱼油脂,102 未列出的工业用其他动物油脂,103 饲料用鱼油脂,104 未列出的饲料用其他动物油脂,105 养殖鱼鱼油,106 野生鱼鱼油,107 保健食品]	12		50	13/	13	千克	AB/	PRQS	32	
1504.3000	-海生哺乳动物的油、脂及其分离品										
1504.3000 10	濒危哺乳动物的油、脂及其分离品(仅指海生)〔101 工业用海生哺乳动物油脂,102 未列出的工业用其他动物油脂,103 饲料用海生哺乳动物油脂,104 野生鱼鱼油〕	14		50	13/	0	千克	ABFE/	PRQS	16.5	
1504.3000 90	其他海生哺乳动物油、脂及其分离品〔101 工业用海生哺乳动物油脂,102 未列出的工业用其他动物油脂,103 饲料用海生哺乳动物油脂,104 野生鱼鱼油〕	14		50	13/	13	千克	AB/	PRQS	16.5	
15.05	**羊毛脂及从羊毛脂制得的脂肪物质(包括纯净的羊毛脂):**										
1505.0000	羊毛脂及从羊毛制得的脂肪物质(包括纯净的羊毛脂)〔101 工业用羊毛脂,102 饲料用羊毛脂〕	20		70	13/	13	千克	AB/	PQS	25	
15.06	**其他动物油、脂及其分离品,不论是否精制,但未经化学改性:**										
1506.0000	其他动物油、脂及其分离品,不论是否精制,但未经化学改性										
1506.0000 10	其他濒危动物为原料制取的脂肪(包括河马、熊、野兔、海龟为原料的及海龟蛋油)[101 工业用其他野生偶蹄动物油脂,102 未列出的工业用其他动物油脂,103 饲料用其他野生偶蹄动物油脂,104 未列出的饲料用其他动物油脂,105 未炼制的食用濒危动物油(脂),106 已炼制的食用濒危动物油(脂)]	20		70	13/	0	千克	ABFE/	PRQS	45	
1506.0000 90	其他动物油、脂及其分离品(不论是否精制,但未经化学改性)[T2]	20		70	13/	13	千克	AB/	PRQS	45	
15.07	**豆油及其分离品,不论是否精制,但未经化学改性:**										
1507.1000	-初榨的,不论是否脱胶〔999〕	9		190	9/	0	千克	7AB/	MPRQS	34	
1507.9000	-其他〔101 初榨食用大豆油,102 食用豆油〕	9		190	9/	0	千克	7AB/	MRS	34	
15.08	**花生油及其分离品,不论是否精制,但未经化学改性:**										
1508.1000	-初榨的〔999〕	10		100	9/	0	千克	AB/	PRQS	35	
1508.9000	-其他〔999〕	10		100	9/	0	千克	AB/	MRS	35	
15.09	**油橄榄油及其分离品,不论是否精制,但未经化学改性:**										
1509.2000	-特级初榨油橄榄油〔999〕	10		30	9/	0	千克	7AB/	PRQS	35	
1509.3000	-初榨油橄榄油〔999〕	10		30	9/	0	千克	7AB/	PRQS	35	
1509.4000	-其他初榨油橄榄油〔999〕	10		30	9/	0	千克	7AB/	PRQS	35	
1509.9000	-其他〔999〕	10		30	13/	0	千克	7AB/	RS	35	
15.10	**其他橄榄油及其分离品,不论是否精制,但未经化学改性,包括掺有税目 15.09 的油或分离品的混合物:**										
1510.1000	-粗提油橄榄果渣油〔999〕	10		30	13/	0	千克	7AB/	PRQS	15	

协定税率 %								RCEP		特惠税率 %			Article Description
东/冰/格	巴基斯坦	韩国	瑞士 上/下	哥/秘/柬	澳/毛	新西/坡/智	中国港/澳/台	东盟及马来/澳/韩	日/新	亚太2国	老/柬/缅	98/97/95	
													Lard stearin, lard oil, oleostearin, oleooil and tallow oil, not emulsified or mixed or otherwise prepared:
0/0/0		2	0/0	0/0/0	0/0	0/0/0	0/0/	0/0/9	9.1/0			0/0/0	Lard stearin, lard oil, oleostearin, oleooil and tallow oil, not emulsified or mixed or otherwise prepared
													Fats and oils and their fractions, of fish or marine mammals, whether or not refined, but not chemically modified:
													-Fish-liver oils and their fractions
0/0/0		2.4	1.2/1.2	0/0/0	0/0	0/0/0	0/0/	0/0/10.8	10.9/0			0/0/0	Endangered species of fish cod-liver oil and its fractions
0/0/0		2.4	1.2/1.2	0/0/0	0/0	0/0/0	0/0/	0/0/10.8	10.9/0			0/0/0	Other fish cod-liver oil and its fractions
													-Fats and oils and their fractions, of fish, other than liver oils
0/0/0		2.4	5/5	0/0/0	0/7.2	0/0/0	0/0/	10.8/10.8/10.8	10.9/10.8			0/0/0	Endangered fish oil capsules,other than liver oils
0/0/0		2.4	5/5	0/0/0	0/7.2	0/0/0	0/0/	10.8/10.8/10.8	10.9/10.8			0/0/0	Fats and oils and their fractions, of endangerd fish, other than liver oils
0/0/0		2.4	5/5	0/0/0	0/7.2	0/0/0	0/0/	10.8/10.8/10.8	10.9/10.8			0/0/0	Other fish oil capsules,other than liver oils
0/0/0		2.4	5/5	0/0/0	0/7.2	0/0/0	0/0/	10.8/10.8/10.8	10.9/10.8			0/0/0	Fats and oils and their fractions, of other fish, other than liver oils
													-Fats and oils and their fractions, of marine mammals
0/0/0		2.8	1.4/1.4	0/0/0	0/0	0/0/0	0/0/	0/0/13	13.1/0			0/0/0	Fats and oils and their fractions, of endangered marine mammals
0/0/0		2.8	1.4/1.4	0/0/0	0/0	0/0/0	0/0/	0/0/13	13.1/0			0/0/0	Other fats and oils and their fractions of marine mammals
													Wool grease and fatty substances derived therefrom (including lanolin):
0/0/0		9.3	2/2	0/0/0	0/0	0/0/0	0/0/	18/18/18	18.8/18			0/0/0	Wool grease and fatty substances derived therefrom (including lanolin)
													Other animal fats and oils and their fractions, whether or not refined, but not chemically modified:
													Other animal fats and oils and their fractions, whether or not refined, but not chemically modified
0/0/0		9.3	2/2	0/0/0	0/0	0/0/0	0/0/	18/18/18	18.8/18			0/0/0	Fats made of materials of endangered wild animals (including hippo, bear, hare, green turtle and green turtle egg)
0/0/0		9.3	2/2	0/0/0	0/0	0/0/0	0/0/	18/18/18	18.8/18			0/0/0	Fats and oils and their fractions, of other animals(whether or not refined, but not chemically modified)
													Soya-bean oil and its fractions, whether or not refined, but not chemically modified:
							0/0/						-Crude oil,whether or not degummed
							0/0/						-Other
													Ground-nut oil and its fractions, whether or not refined, but not chemically modified:
0//				//0		/0/	0/0/					0//	-Crude oil
0//				//0		/0/	0/0/					0//	-Other
													Olive oil and its fractions, whether or not refined, but not chemically modified:
0/0/		2	0/0	0/0/0		0/0/0	0/0/					0/0/0	- Extra virgin olive oil
0/0/		2	0/0	0/0/0		0/0/0	0/0/					0/0/0	- Virgin olive oil
0/0/		2	0/0	0/0/0		0/0/0	0/0/					0/0/0	- Other virgin olive oils
0/0/		2	0/0	0/0/0		0/0/0	0/0/					0/0/0	-Other
													Other oils and their fractions, obtained solely from olives, whether or not refined, but not chemically modified, including blends of these oils or fractions with oils or fractions of heading No.15. 09:
0/0/		2	0/0	0/0/0		0/0/0	0/0/					0/0/0	- Crude olive pomace oil

税则号列	货品名称〔CIQ扩展编码及品名－T2表示见附表2〕	最惠(%)	暂定税率	普通	增值/消费	出口退税	计量单位	监管条件/特殊证件	检验检疫	对美关税	亚太上/下
1510.9000	-其他〔101 初榨食用橄榄油,102 其他初榨植物食用油,103 食用橄榄油〕	10		30	13/	0	千克	7AB/	PRQS	15	
15.11	**棕榈油及其分离品,不论是否精制,但未经化学改性:**										
1511.1000	-初榨的〔999〕	9		60	9/	0	千克	7AB/	MPRQS	14	
	-其他:										
1511.9010	---棕榈液油(熔点19～24度)〔999〕	9		60	9/	0	千克	7AB/	MRS	14	
1511.9020	---棕榈硬脂液油(熔点44～56度)										
1511.9020 01	固态棕榈硬脂(50摄氏度≤熔点≤56摄氏度)(未经化学改性)〔999〕	8	2	60	9/	0	千克	7AB/	MRS	7	
1511.9020 90	其他棕榈硬脂(44摄氏度≤熔点＜50摄氏度)(未经化学改性)〔999〕	8		60	9/	0	千克	AB/	MRS	13	
1511.9090	---其他〔999〕	9		60	13/	0	千克	7AB/	MRS	14	
15.12	**葵花油、红花油或棉子油及其分离品,不论是否精制,但未经化学改性:**										
	-葵花油或红花油及其分离品:										
1512.1100	--初榨的〔101 初榨食用葵花油,102 初榨食用红花油,103 其他食用植物油〕	9		160	9/	0	千克	AB/	PRQS	34	
1512.1900	--其他〔101 食用葵花籽油,102 其他食用植物油〕	9		160	13/	0	千克	AB/	RS	34	
	-棉子油及其分离品:										
1512.2100	--初榨的,不论是否去除棉子酚〔999〕	10		70	9/	0	千克	AB/	PRQS	15	
1512.2900	--其他〔999〕	10		70	13/	0	千克	AB/	RS	20	
15.13	**椰子油、棕榈仁油或巴巴苏棕榈果油及其分离品,不论是否精制,但未经化学改性:**										
	-椰子油及其分离品:										
1513.1100	--初榨的〔999〕	9		40	9/	0	千克	AB/	MPRQS	34	4.5/4.5
1513.1900	--其他〔999〕	9		40	9/	0	千克	AB/	MPRQS	34	4.5/4.5
	-棕榈仁油或巴巴苏棕榈果油及其分离品:										
1513.2100	--初榨的〔101 初榨食用棕榈油,102 其他初榨植物食用油〕	9		40	9/	0	千克	AB/	MPRQS	14	
1513.2900	--其他〔999〕	9		40	13/	0	千克	AB/	MRS	14	
15.14	**菜子油或芥子油及其分离品,不论是否精制,但未经化学改性:**										
	-低芥子酸菜子油及其分离品:										
1514.1100	--初榨的〔999〕	9		170	9/	0	千克	7AB/	MPRQS	34	
1514.1900	--其他〔999〕	9		170	9/	0	千克	7AB/	MPRQS	14	
	-其他:										
	--初榨的:										
1514.9110	---菜子油〔999〕	9		170	9/	0	千克	7AB/	MPRQS	14	
1514.9190	---芥子油〔999〕	9		170	9/	0	千克	7AB/	MPRQS	14	
1514.9900	--其他〔101 食用菜籽油,102 其他食用植物油〕	9		170	13/	0	千克	7AB/	MRS	34	
15.15	**其他固定植物或微生物油、脂(包括希蒙得木油)及其分离品,不论是否精制,但未经化学改性:**										
	-亚麻子油及其分离品:										
1515.1100	--初榨的〔999〕	15		30	9/	0	千克	AB/	MPRQS	40	
1515.1900	--其他〔999〕	15		30	13/	0	千克	AB/	RS	25	
	-玉米油及其分离品:										
1515.2100	--初榨的〔999〕	10		160	9/	0	千克	AB/	PRQS	15	
1515.2900	--其他〔999〕	10		160	13/	0	千克	AB/	RS	35	
1515.3000	-蓖麻油及其分离品〔301 有检疫要求食品添加剂;302 需申报仅用于工业用途不用于食品添加剂有检疫要求的化学品〕	10		70	13/	13	千克	AB/	MPQS	35	
1515.5000	-芝麻油及其分离品〔101 初榨食用芝麻油,102 食用芝麻油〕	12		20	9/	0	千克	AB/	PRQS	37	
1515.6000	-微生物油、脂及其分离品〔999〕	20		70	13/	0	千克	AB/	MPRNQS	40	
	-其他:										
1515.9010	---希蒙得木油(霍霍巴油)及其分离品〔102〕	20		70	13/	13	千克	AB/	PRQS	45	
1515.9020	---印楝油及其分离品〔999〕	20		70	13/	13	千克	ABS/	PRQS	25	
1515.9030	---桐油及其分离品〔999〕	20		70	13/	13	千克	AB/	PRQS	25	
1515.9040	---茶籽油及其分离品〔101 食用茶油,102 其他食用植物油〕	20		70	13/	0	千克	AB/	MPRNQS	40	
1515.9090	---其他										
1515.9090 10	红松子油(不论是否精制,但未经化学改性)〔101 其他初榨植物食用油,102 其他食用植物油〕	20		70	13/	0	千克	ABE/	PRQS	40	
1515.9090 90	其他固定植物油、脂及其分离品(不论是否精制,但未经化学改性)[T2]	20		70	13/	0	千克	AB/	MPRNQS	40	
15.16	**动、植物或微生物油、脂及其分离品,全部或部分氢化、相互酯化、再酯化或反油酸化,不论是否精制,但未经进一步加工:**										
1516.1000	-动物油、脂及其分离品〔999〕	5		70	13/	13	千克	AB/	RS	30	

协定税率 %								RCEP		特惠税率 %			Article Description
东/冰/格	巴基斯坦	韩国	瑞士 上/下	哥/秘/柬	澳/毛	新西/坡/智	中国港/澳/台	东盟及马来/澳/韩	日/新	亚太2国	老/柬/缅	98/97/95	
0/0/		2	0/0	0/0/0		0/0/0	0/0/					0/0/0	- Other
													Palm oil and its fractions, whether or not refined, but not chemically modified:
							0/0/						-Crude oil
													-Other:
							0/0/						---Palm olein(cmelting point 19℃～24℃)
							0/0/						---Palm stearin(cmelting point 44℃～56℃) Solid plam stearin(cmelting point 50℃～56℃, not chemically modified)
							0/0/						Palm Stearin(melting point 44℃～50℃, not chemically modified)
							0/0/						---Other
													Sunflower-seed, safflower or cotton-seed oil and fractions thereof, whether or not refined, but not chemically modified:
													-Sunflower-seed or safflower oil and fractions thereof:
0//				//0			0/0/					0//	--Crude oil
0//				//0			0/0/					0//	--Other
													-Cotton-seed oil and its fractions:
0//				//0		/0/	0/0/					0//	--Crude oil, whether or not gossypol has been removed
0//				//0		/0/	0/0/					0//	--Other
													Coconut (copra), palm kernel or babassu oil and fractions thereof, whether or not refined, but not chemically modified:
													-Coconut (copra) oil and its fractions:
0/0/	4.5	0	0/0	0/0/0		0//0	0/0/	8.6/8.8/8.6	8.6/8.8			0/0/0	--Crude oil
0/0/	4.5	0	0/0	0/0/0		0//0	0/0/	8.6/8.8/8.6	8.6/8.8			0/0/0	--Other
													-Palm kernel or babassu oil and fractions thereof:
0/0/		0	0/0	0/0/0		0//0	0/0/					0/0/0	--Crude oil
0/0/		0	0/0	0/0/0		0//0	0/0/					0/0/0	--Other
													Rape, colza or mustard oil and fractions thereof, whether or not refined, but not chemically modified:
													-Low erucic acid rape of colza oil and its fractions:
							0/0/						--Crude oil
							0/0/						--Other
													-Other:
													--Crude oil:
9//							0/0/						---Rape oil
							0/0/						---Mustard oil
9//							0/0/						--Other
													Other fixed vegetable or microbial fats and oils (including jojoba oil) and fractions thereof, whether or not refined, but not chemically modified:
													-Linseed oil and its fractions:
0/0/		3	1.5/1.5	0/0/0		0/0/0	0/0/					0/0/0	--Crude oil
0/0/		3	1.5/1.5	0/0/0		0/0/0	0/0/					0/0/0	--Other
													-Maize (corn) oil and its fractions:
0//				//0		/0/	0/0/				0/0/	0/0/0	--Crude oil
0//				//0		/0/	0/0/				0/0/	0/0/0	--Other
0/0/		2	0/0	0/0/0	0/	0/0/0	0/0/	0/0/10	9.1/0		0/0/	0/0/0	-Castor oil and its fractions
0/0/		2.4	1.2/1.2	0/0/0	0/	0/0/0	0/0/	0/0/10.8	10.9/0		0/0/	0/0/0	-Sesame oil and its fractions
0/0/			2/2	0//0	0/	0/0/0	0/0/	5/5/	/5		0/0/0	0/0/0	- Microbial fats and oils and their fractions
													-Other:
0/0/		9.3	2/2	0//0	0/	0/0/0	0/0/	18/18/18	18.8/18		/0/	0/0/0	---Jojoba oil and its fractions
0/0/		9.3	2/2	0//0	0/	0/0/0	0/0/	18/18/18	18.8/18			0/0/0	---Neem oil and its fractions
0/0/		9.3	2/2	0//0	0/	0/0/0	0/0/	18/18/18	18.8/18		/0/	0/0/0	---Tung oil and its fractions
0/0/			2/2	0//0	0/	0/0/0	0/0/	5/5/	/5		0/0/0	0/0/0	---Tea seed oil and fractions thereof
													---Other
0/0/			2/2	0//0	0/	0/0/0	0/0/	5/5/	/5		0/0/0	0/0/0	Korean pine seed oil (whether or not refined, but not chemical modified)
0/0/			2/2	0//0	0/	0/0/0	0/0/	5/5/	/5		0/0/0	0/0/0	Other fixed vegetable fats and oils and fraction thereof oil (whether or not refined, but not chemically modified)
													Animal or vegetable or microbial fats and oils and fractions thereof, partly or wholly hydrogenated, inter-esterified, reesterified or elaidinized, whether or not refined, but not further prepared:
0/0/0		0	0/0	0/0/0	0/0	0//0	0/0/	0/0/0	0/0			0/0/0	-Animal fats and oils and fractions thereof

税则号列	货品名称〔CIQ 扩展编码及品名－T2 表示见附表 2〕	最惠(%)	暂定税率	普通	增值/消费	出口退税	计量单位	监管条件/特殊证件	检验检疫	对美关税	亚太上/下
1516.2000	-植物油、脂及其分离品〔101 其他食用植物油；103 食用起酥油；104 食用其他加工油脂；301 氢化植物油(无检疫要求食品添加剂)；302 氢化植物油(需申报仅用于工业用途不用于食品添加剂无检疫要求的化学品)〕	25		70	13/	0	千克	AB/	RS	50	
1516.3000	-微生物油、脂及其分离品〔101 其他化工品，不用做食品添加剂，102 其他化工品，用做食品添加剂〕	25		70	13/	0	千克	AB/	RS	50	
15.17	**人造黄油；本章各种动、植物或微生物油、脂及其分离品混合制成的食用油、脂或制品，但税目 15.16 的食用油、脂及其分离品除外：**										
1517.1000	-人造黄油，但不包括液态的〔101 食用植物奶油，102 食用其他加工油脂，301 无检疫要求食品添加剂〕	30		80	13/	0	千克	AB/	MRS	55	
	-其他：										
1517.9010	---起酥油										
1517.9010 01	动物油脂制造的起酥油(税目 15.16 的食用油、脂及其分离品除外)〔301 无检疫要求食品添加剂，999 动物油脂制造的食用起酥油〕	25		70	13/	13	千克	AB/	RS	50	
1517.9010 02	植物油脂制造的起酥油(品目 1516 的食用油、脂及其分离品除外)〔101 食用植物调和油，102 食用其他加工油脂，301 无检疫要求食品添加剂〕	25		70	9/	0	千克	AB/	RS	50	
1517.9010 90	微生物油脂制造的起酥油(税目 1516 的食用油、脂及其分离品除外)〔101 食用植物调和油，102 食用其他加工油脂，301 无检疫要求食品添加剂〕	25		70	9/	0	千克	AB/	RS	50	
1517.9090	---其他										
1517.9090 01	其他混合制成的动物质食用油脂或制品(税目 15.16 的食用油、脂及其分离品除外)〔101 混合制成的动物质食用油脂或制品，102 食用其他加工油脂，301 无检疫要求食品添加剂〕	25		70	13/	13	千克	AB/	RS	50	
1517.9090 02	其他混合制成的植物质食用油脂或制品(品目 1516 的食用油、脂及其分离品除外)〔101 食用植物调和油，102 其他食用植物油，103 食用其他加工油脂，301 无检疫要求食品添加剂〕	25		70	9/	0	千克	AB/	RS	50	
1517.9090 90	其他混合制成的微生物质食用油脂或制品(税目 1516 的食用油、脂及其分离品除外)〔101 食用植物调和油，102 其他食用植物油，103 食用其他加工油脂，301 无检疫要求食品添加剂〕	25		70	9/	0	千克	AB/	RS	50	
15.18	**动、植物或微生物油、脂及其分离品，经过熟炼、氧化、脱水、硫化、吹制或在真空、惰性气体中加热聚合及用其他化学方法改性的，但税目 15.16 的产品除外；本章各种油、脂及其分离品混合制成的其他税目未列名的非食用油、脂或制品：**										
1518.0000	动、植物或微生物油、脂及其分离品，经过熟炼、氧化、脱水、硫化、吹制或在真空、惰性气体中加热聚合及用其他化学方法改性的，但税目 15.16 的产品除外；本章各种油、脂及其分离品混合制成的其他税目未列名的非食用油、脂或制品[T2]	10		70	13/	13	千克	AB/	MRS	30	
15.20	**粗甘油；甘油水及甘油碱液：**										
1520.0000	粗甘油，甘油水及甘油碱液〔301 无检疫要求食品添加剂，302 需申报仅用于工业用途不用于食品添加剂无检疫要求的化学品〕	20	6	50	13/	13	千克	AB/	MRS	31	
15.21	**植物蜡(甘油三酯除外)、蜂蜡、其他虫蜡及鲸蜡，不论是否精制或着色：**										
1521.1000	-植物蜡										
1521.1000 10	小烛树蜡〔999〕	20		80	13/	13	千克	ABEF/	PRQ	40	
1521.1000 90	其他植物蜡〔101 吗啉脂肪酸盐果蜡，102 巴西棕榈蜡〕	20		80	13/	13	千克	AB/	PRQS	40	
	-其他：										
1521.9010	---蜂蜡〔101 其他动物产品，104 工业用未经加工蜂蜡〕	20		80	13/	13	千克	AB/	PRQS	30	
1521.9090	---其他										
1521.9090 10	鲸蜡(不论是否精制或着色)〔999〕	20		80	13/	13	千克	AFEB/	PQ	25	
1521.9090 90	其他虫蜡(不论是否精制或着色)〔101 其他动物产品，102 药用五倍子〕	20		80	13/	13	千克	AB/	PQ	25	
15.22	**油鞣回收脂；加工处理油脂物质及动、植物蜡所剩的残渣：**										
1522.0000	油鞣回收脂；加工处理油脂物质及动、植物蜡所剩的残渣〔999〕	20		50	13/	13	千克	9/		25	

协定税率 %								RCEP		特惠税率 %			Article Description
东/冰/格	巴基斯坦	韩国	瑞士 上/下	哥/秘/柬	澳/毛	新西/坡/智	中国港/澳/台	东盟及马来/澳/韩	日/新	亚太2国	老/柬/缅	98/97/95	
0/0/	0			0/0/0	0/15	0//0	0/0/	5/5/	/5			0/0/0	-Vegetable fats and oils and fractions thereof
0/0/	0			0/0/0	0/15	0//0	0/0/	5/5/	/5			0/0/0	- Microbial fats and oils and their fractions
													Margarine; edible mixtures or preparations of animal or vegetable or microbial fats or oils or of fractions of different fats or oils of this Chapter, other than edible fats or oils or their fractions of heading No. 15. 16:
0//				0//0	0/18	0/0/0	0/0/	28.5/28.5/30	28.6/28.5			0//	-Margarine, excluding liquid margarine
													-Other:
													---Shortening
0/0/			2.5/2.5	0/0/0	0/15	0//0	0/0/	23.8/23.8/25	23.8/23.8			0/0/0	Shortening made of animal grease(other than edible fats or oils or their fractions of heading No.1516)
0/0/			2.5/2.5	0/0/0	0/15	0//0	0/0/	23.8/23.8/25	23.8/23.8			0/0/0	Shortening made from vegetable oils (except edible oils, fats and their fractions of heading 1516)
0/0/			2.5/2.5	0/0/0	0/15	0//0	0/0/	23.8/23.8/25	23.8/23.8			0/0/0	Shortening made from microbial oils (except edible oils, fats and their isolates of heading 1516)
													---Other
0/0/			10.5/10.5	0/0/0		0//0	0/0/					0/0/0	Edible mixtures or preparations of animal fats or oil or of fractions (Other than edible fats or oil or their fractions of heading No. 15.16)
0/0/			10.5/10.5	0/0/0		0//0	0/0/					0/0/0	Other vegetable edible oils and fats or products made by mixing (except edible oils, fats and their isolates of heading 1516)
0/0/			10.5/10.5	0/0/0		0//0	0/0/					0/0/0	Other mixed microbial substances, edible oils and fats or products (other than edible oils, fats and their isolates of heading 1516)
													Animal or vegetable or microbial fats and oils and fractions thereof, boiled, oxidized, dehydrated, sulphurized, blown, polymerized by heat in vacuum or in inert gas or otherwise chemically modified, excluding those of heading No. 15. 16; inedible mixtures or preparations of animal or vegetable fats or oils or of fractions of different fats or oils of this Chapter, not elsewhere specified or included:
0/0/		6	0/0	0/0/0	/0	0/0/0	0/0/					0/0/0	Animal or vegetable or microbial fats and oils and fractions thereof, boiled, oxidized, dehydrated, sulphurized, blown, polymerized by heat in vacuum or in inert gas or otherwise chemically modified, excluding those of heading No. 15. 16; inedible mixtures or preparations of animal or vegetable fats or oils or of fractions of different fats or oils of this Chapter, not elsewhere specified or included
													Glycerol, crude; glycerol waters and glycerol lyes:
0/0/0		9.3	2/2	0/0/0	0/0	0/0/0	0/0/	18.7/19/18.7	18.8/19			0/0/0	Glycerol, crude; glycerol waters and glycerol lyes
													Vegetable waxes (other than triglycerides), beeswax, other insect waxes and spermaceti, whether or not refined or coloured:
													-Vegetable waxes
0/0/0		9.3	2/2	0/0/0	0/0	0/0/0	0/0/	18/19/18	18.2/19			0/0/0	Candelilla waxes
0/0/0		9.3	2/2	0/0/0	0/0	0/0/0	0/0/	18/19/18	18.2/19			0/0/0	Other vegetable waxes
													-Other:
0/0/0		9.3	2/2	0/0/0	0/0	0/0/0	0/0/	18/18/18	18.8/18			0/0/0	---Beeswax
													---Other
0/0/0		9.3	2/2	0/0/0	0/0	0/0/0	0/0/	19/19/20	19/19			0/0/0	Spermaceti(whether or not refined or coloured)
0/0/0		9.3	2/2	0/0/0	0/0	0/0/0	0/0/	19/19/20	19/19			0/0/0	Other insect waxes(whether or not refined or coloured)
													Degras; residues resulting from the treatment of fatty substances of animal or vegetable waxes:
0/0/0		9.3	2/2	0/0/0	0/0	0/0/0	0/0/	18/18/18	18.8/18			0/0/0	Degras; residues resulting from the treatment of fatty substances of animal or vegetable waxes

第四类
食品;饮料、酒及醋;烟草、烟草及烟草代用品的制品;非经燃烧吸用的产品,不论是否含有尼古丁;其他供人体摄入尼古丁的含尼古丁的产品

注释:

本类所称"团粒",是指直接挤压或加入按重量计比例不超过3%的黏合剂制成的粒状产品。

第十六章
肉、鱼、甲壳动物,软体动物及其他水生无脊椎动物、以及昆虫的制品

注释:

一、本章不包括用第二章、第三章、第四章注释六及税目05.04所列方法制作或保藏的肉、食用杂碎、鱼、甲壳动物、软体动物或其他水生无脊椎动物及昆虫。

二、本章的食品按重量计必须含有20%以上的香肠、肉、食用杂碎、动物血、昆虫、鱼、甲壳动物、软体动物或其他水生无脊椎动物及其混合物。对于含有两种或两种以上前述产品的食品,则应按其中重量最大的产品归入第十六章的相应税目。但本条规定不适用于税目19.02的包馅食品和税目21.03及21.04的食品。

子目注释:

一、子目1602.10的"均化食品",是指用肉、食用杂碎、动物血或昆虫经精细均化制成适合供婴幼儿食用或营养用的零售包装食品(每件净重不超过250克)。为了调味、保藏或其他目的,均化食品中可以加入少量其他配料,还可以含有少量可见的肉粒或食用杂碎粒。归类时该子目优先于税目16.02的其他子目。

二、税目16.04或16.05项下各子目所列的是鱼、甲壳动物、软体动物及其他水生无脊柱动物的俗名,它们与第三章中相同名称的鱼、甲壳动物、软体动物及其水生无脊柱动物种类范围相同。

税则号列	货品名称〔CIQ扩展编码及品名一T2表示见附表2〕	最惠(%)	暂定税率	普通	增值/消费	出口退税	计量单位	监管条件/特殊证件	检验检疫	对美关税	亚太上/下
16.01	**肉、食用杂碎、动物血或昆虫制成的香肠及类似产品;用香肠制成的食品:**										
1601.0010	---用天然肠衣做外包装的香肠及类似产品										
1601.0010 10	濒危野生动物肉、杂碎、血或昆虫制天然肠衣香肠(含税目02.08的野生动物,包括类似品)〔101未列出的其他动物肉脏及杂碎制品,102其他熟制禽肉制品,103其他去骨熟制畜肉制品,104未列出的其他动物肉脏及杂碎制品〕	5		90	13/	0	千克	ABFE/	PRQS	30	
1601.0010 90	其他动物肉、杂碎、血或昆虫制天然肠衣香肠(包括类似品)〔101未列出的其他动物肉脏及杂碎制品,102其他熟制禽肉制品,103其他去骨熟制畜肉制品,104未列出的其他动物肉脏及杂碎制品〕	5		90	13/	13	千克	AB/	PRQS	30	
1601.0020	---其他香肠及类似产品										
1601.0020 10	濒危野生动物肉、杂碎、血或昆虫制其他肠衣香肠(含税目02.08的野生动物,包括类似品)〔101未列出的其他动物肉脏及杂碎制品,102其他熟制禽肉制品,103其他去骨熟制畜肉制品,104未列出的其他动物肉脏及杂碎制品〕	5		90	13/	0	千克	ABFE/	PRQS	30	
1601.0020 90	其他动物肉、杂碎、血或昆虫制其他肠衣香肠(包括类似品)〔101未列出的其他动物肉脏及杂碎制品,102其他熟制禽肉制品,103其他去骨熟制畜肉制品,104其他养殖制作及保藏水产制品,105其他野生制作及保藏水产制品,106未列出的其他动物肉脏及杂碎制品〕	5		90	13/	13	千克	AB/	PRQS	30	
1601.0030	---用香肠制成的食品										
1601.0030 10	用含濒危野生动物或昆虫成分的香肠制的食品(含税目02.08的野生动物)〔101其他熟制禽肉制品,102其他去骨熟制畜肉制品,103未列出的其他动物肉脏及杂碎制品〕	5		90	13/	0	千克	ABFE/	PRQS	7.5	
1601.0030 90	用含其他动物或昆虫成分的香肠制的食品〔101其他熟制禽肉制品,102其他去骨熟制畜肉制品,103未列出的其他动物肉脏及杂碎制品〕	5		90	13/	9,13	千克	AB/	PRQS	7.5	
16.02	**其他方法制作或保藏的肉、食用杂碎、动物血或昆虫:**										
1602.1000	-均化食品										
1602.1000 10	含濒危野生动物或昆虫成分的均化食品(指用肉、食用杂碎或动物血经精细均化制成,零售包装)〔101其他熟制禽肉制品,102其他去骨熟制畜肉制品,103其他带骨熟制畜肉制品,104未列出的其他动物肉脏及杂碎制品〕	5		90	13/	0	千克	ABFE/	RS	30	
1602.1000 90	其他动物肉、食用杂碎、血或昆虫的均化食品(指用肉、食用杂碎、动物血或昆虫经精细均化制成,零售包装)〔101其他熟制禽肉制品,102其他去骨熟制畜肉制品,103其他带骨熟制畜肉制品,104熟制猪肉制品,105熟制牛肉制品,106未列出的其他动物肉脏及杂碎制品〕	5		90	13/	13	千克	AB/	RS	30	
1602.2000	-动物肝										

SECTION Ⅳ
PREPARED FOODSTUFFS; BEVERAGES, SPIRITS AND VINEGAR, TOBACCO AND MANUFACTURED TOBACCO SUBSTITUTES; PRODUCTS, WHETHER OR NOT CONTAINING NICOTINE, INTENDED FOR INHALATION WITHOUT COMBUSTION; OTHER NICOTINE CONTAINING PRODUCTS INTENDED FOR THE INTAKE OF NICOTINE INTO THE HUMAN BODY

Note:

In this Section the term "pellets" means products which have been agglomerated either directly by compression or by the addition of a binder in a proportion not exceeding 3% by weight.

Chapter 16
Preparations of meat, of fish, of crustaceans, molluscs or other aquatic invertebrates, or of insects

Notes:

1. This Chapter does not cover meat, meat offal, fish, crustaceans, molluscs or other aquatic invertebrates and insects, prepared or preserved by the processes specified in Chapter 2 or 3, Note 6 to chapter 4 or heading No. 05.04.
2. Food preparations fall in this Chapter provided that they contain more than 20% by weight of sausage, meat, meat offal, blood, insects, fish or crustaceans, molluscs or other aquatic invertebrates, or any combination thereof. In cases where the preparation contains two or more of the products mentioned above, it is classified in the heading of Chapter 16 corresponding to the component or components which predominate by weight. These provisions do not apply to the stuffed products of heading No. 19.02 or to the preparations of heading No. 21.03 or 21.04.

Subheading Notes:

1. For the purposes of subheading No. 1602.10, the expression "homogenized preparations" means preparations of meat, meat offal, blood or insects, finely homogenized, put up for retail sale Suitable for infants to eat or for dietetic purposes, in containers of a net weight content not exceeding 250g. For the application of this definition no account is to be taken of small quantities of any ingredients which may have been added to the preparation for seasoning, preservation or other purposes. These preparations may contain a small quantity of visible pieces of meat or meat offal. This subheading takes precedence over all other subheadings of heading No.16.02.
2. Ther fish、crustaceans、Molluscs and other aquatic invertebrates specified in the subheadings of heading No.16.04 or 16.05 under their common names only, are of the same species as those mentionde in Chpapter 3 under the same name.

协定税率 %								RCEP		特惠税率 %			Article Description
东/冰/格	巴基斯坦	韩国	瑞士上/下	哥/秘/柬	澳/毛	新西/坡/智	中国港/澳/台	东盟及马来/澳/韩	日/新	亚太2国	老/柬/缅	98/97/95	
													Sausages and similar products, of meat, meat offal, blood or insects; food preparations based on these products:
													---Sausages and similar products, coated with natural casings
0/0/0	12	3	1.5/1.5	0/0/0	0/0	0/0/0	0/0/	0/0/13.5	13.6/0			0/0/0	Natural sausage casings made from meat, offal, blood or insects of endangered wild animals (including wild animals of heading 02.08, including analogues)
0/0/0	12	3	1.5/1.5	0/0/0	0/0	0/0/0	0/0/	0/0/13.5	13.6/0			0/0/0	Natural sausage casings (including analogues) of other animal meat, offal, blood or insects
													---Other sausages and similar products
0/0/0	12	3	1.5/1.5	0/0/0	0/0	0/0/0	0/0/	0/0/13.5	13.6/0			0/0/0	Other sausage casings of meat, offal, blood or insects of endangered wild animals (including wild animals of heading 02.08, including analogues)
0/0/0	12	3	1.5/1.5	0/0/0	0/0	0/0/0	0/0/	0/0/13.5	13.6/0			0/0/0	Other sausage casings (including analogues) of meat, offal, blood or insects of other animals
													---Sausage based food products
0/0/0	12	3	1.5/1.5	0/0/0	0/0	0/0/0	0/0/	0/0/13.5	13.6/0			0/0/0	Food prepared from sausages containing ingredients of endangered wild animals or insects (including wild animals of heading 02.08)
0/0/0	12	3	1.5/1.5	0/0/0	0/0	0/0/0	0/0/	0/0/13.5	13.6/0			0/0/0	Food made from sausages containing other animal or insect ingredients
													Other Prepared or preserved meat, meat offal, blood or insects:
													-Homogenized preparations
0/0/0	12	3	1.5/1.5	0/0/0	0/0	0/0/0	0/0/	0/0/13.5	13.6/0			0/0/0	Homogenized food containing endangered wild animals or insects (refers to finely homogenized meat, edible offal or animal blood, retail packaging)
0/0/0	12	3	1.5/1.5	0/0/0	0/0	0/0/0	0/0/	0/0/13.5	13.6/0			0/0/0	Homogenized food of other animal meat, edible offal, blood or insects (refers to finely homogenized meat, edible offal, animal blood or insects, retail packaging)
													-Of liver of any animal

税则号列	货品名称〔CIQ 扩展编码及品名－T2 表示见附表 2〕	最惠(%)	暂定税率	普通	增值/消费	出口退税	计量单位	监管条件/特殊证件	检验检疫	对美关税	亚太上/下
1602.2000 10	制作或保藏的濒危动物肝(第 2、3 章所列方法制作或保藏的除外)[T2]	5		90	13/	0	千克	ABEF/	PRQS	7.5	
1602.2000 90	制作或保藏的其他动物肝(第 2、3 章所列方法制作或保藏的除外)[T2]	5		90	13/	13	千克	AB/	PRQS	7.5	
	-税目 01.05 的家禽的：										
1602.3100	--火鸡的[T2]	5		90	13/	13	千克	AB/	PRQS	15	
	--鸡的：										
1602.3210	---罐头〔999〕	5		90	13/	13	千克	AB/	PRQS	7.5	
	---其他：										
1602.3291	----鸡胸肉[T2]	5		90	13/	13	千克	AB/	PRQS	15	
1602.3292	----鸡腿肉[T2]	5		90	13/	13	千克	AB/	PRQS	7.5	
1602.3299	----其他[T2]	5		90	13/	13	千克	AB/	PRQS	7.5	
	--其他：										
1602.3910	---罐头[T2]	5		90	13/	13	千克	AB/	PRQS	7.5	
	---其他：										
1602.3991	----鸭的[T2]	5		90	13/	9,13	千克	AB/	PRQS	7.5	
1602.3999	----其他[T2]	5		90	13/	13	千克	AB/	PRQS	7.5	
	-猪的：										
1602.4100	--后腿及其肉块										
1602.4100 10	制作或保藏的鹿豚、姬猪后腿及肉块〔101 猪蹄，102 去骨熟制猪肉制品，103 带骨熟制猪肉制品〕	5		90	13/	13	千克	ABFE/	PRQS	30	
1602.4100 90	制作或保藏的猪后腿及其肉块〔101 猪蹄，102 去骨熟制猪肉制品，103 带骨熟制猪肉制品，104 以上述产品为原料制成的熟制猪肉产品〕	5		90	13/	13	千克	AB/	PRQS	30	
1602.4200	--前腿及其肉块										
1602.4200 10	制作或保藏的鹿豚，姬猪前腿及其肉块〔101 猪蹄，102 去骨熟制猪肉制品，103 带骨熟制猪肉制品〕	5		90	13/	13	千克	ABFE/	PRQS	7.5	
1602.4200 90	制作或保藏的猪前腿及其肉块[T2]	5		90	13/	13	千克	AB/	PRQS	7.5	
	--其他，包括混合的肉：										
1602.4910	---罐头										
1602.4910 10	其他含鹿豚、姬猪肉及杂碎的罐头〔999〕	5		90	13/	13	千克	ABFE/	PRQS	7.5	
1602.4910 90	其他猪肉及杂碎的罐头〔101 猪肉罐头，102 午餐肉罐头，103 火腿午餐肉罐头，104 火腿罐头，105 云腿罐头〕	5		90	13/	13	千克	AB/	PRQS	7.5	
1602.4990	---其他										
1602.4990 10	制作或保藏的其他鹿豚、姬猪肉、杂碎(包括血等)〔101 其他猪杂碎，102 去骨熟制猪肉制品，103 带骨熟制猪肉制品〕	5		90	13/	13	千克	ABFE/	PRQS	7.5	
1602.4990 90	制作或保藏的其他猪肉、杂碎、血〔101：猪杂碎；102：去骨熟制猪肉制品；103：带骨熟制猪肉制品〕	5		90	13/	13	千克	AB/	PRQS	7.5	
	-牛的：										
1602.5010	---罐头										
1602.5010 10	含濒危野牛肉的罐头〔999〕	5		90	13/	0	千克	ABFE/	PRQS	7.5	
1602.5010 90	其他牛肉及牛杂碎罐头(含野牛肉的除外)〔999〕	5		90	13/	13	千克	AB/	PRQS	7.5	
1602.5090	---其他										
1602.5090 10	其他制作或保藏濒危野牛肉、杂碎(包括血等)〔101 野牛肉及杂碎，102 去骨熟制牛肉制品，103 带骨熟制牛肉制品〕	5		90	13/	0	千克	ABFE/	PRQS	30	
1602.5090 90	其他制作或保藏的牛肉、杂碎、血〔101 其他牛杂碎，102 去骨熟制牛肉制品，103 带骨熟制牛肉制品，104 以上述产品为原料制成的熟制牛肉产品〕	5		90	13/	13	千克	AB/	PRQS	30	
	-其他，包括动物血的食品：										
1602.9010	---罐头										
1602.9010 10	其他濒危动物肉、杂碎、血或昆虫罐头〔999〕	5		90	13/	0	千克	ABFE/	PRQS	7.5	
1602.9010 90	其他动物肉、杂碎、血或昆虫的罐头〔101 鸟肉罐头，102 香肠罐头，103 羊肉罐头，104 鹿肉罐头，105 袋鼠肉罐头，106 马肉罐头，107 食用〕	5		90	13/	13	千克	AB/	PRQS	7.5	
1602.9090	---其他										
1602.9090 10	制作或保藏的其他濒危动物肉、杂碎、血或昆虫〔101 其他动物肉脏及杂碎，102 其他熟制禽肉制品，103 其他去骨熟制畜肉制品，104 其他带骨熟制畜肉制品〕	5		90	13/	0	千克	ABFE/	PRQS	7.5	
1602.9090 90	制作或保藏的其他动物肉、杂碎、血或昆虫〔101 其他动物肉脏及杂碎，102 去骨熟制羊肉制品，103 带骨熟制羊肉制品，104 去骨熟制鹿肉制品，105 带骨熟制鹿肉制品，106 去骨熟制马肉制品，107 带骨熟制马肉制品，108 其他熟制禽肉制品，109 其他去骨熟制畜肉制品，110 其他带骨熟制畜肉制品〕	5		90	13/	13	千克	AB/	PRQS	7.5	
16.03	**肉、鱼、甲壳动物、软体动物或其他水生无脊椎动物的精及汁：**										
1603.0000	肉、鱼、甲壳动物、软体动物或其他水生无脊椎动物的精及汁										

协定税率 %								RCEP		特惠税率 %			Article Description
东/冰/格	巴基斯坦	韩国	瑞士 上/下	哥/秘/柬	澳/毛	新西/坡/智	中国港/澳/台	东盟及马来/澳/韩	日/新	亚太2国	老/柬/缅	98/97/95	
0/0/0	12	3	1.5/1.5	0/0/0	0/0	0/0/0	0/0/	0/0/13.5	13.6/0			0/0/0	Liver of endangered animal, prepared or preserved(other than prepared or preserved of Chapter 2 and 3)
0/0/0	12	3	1.5/1.5	0/0/0	0/0	0/0/0	0/0/	0/0/13.5	13.6/0			0/0/0	eiver of other animals, prepared or preserved(other than prepared or preserved of Chapter 2 and 3)
													-Of poultry of heading No. 01.05:
0/0/0	12	3	1.5/1.5	0/0/0	0/0	0/0/0	0/0/	0/0/13.5	13.6/0			0/0/0	--Of turkeys
													--Of fowls of the species *Gallus domesticus*:
0/0/0	12	3	1.5/1.5	0/0/0	0/0	0/0/0	0/0/	0/0/13.5	13.6/0			0/0/0	---In airtight containers
													---Other:
0/0/0	12	3	1.5/1.5	0/0/0	0/0	0/0/0	0/0/	0/0/13.5	13.6/0			0/0/0	----Chicken breast filets
0/0/0	12	3	1.5/1.5	0/0/0	0/0	0/0/0	0/0/	0/0/13.5	13.6/0			0/0/0	----Chicken leg meat
0/0/0	12	3	1.5/1.5	0/0/0	0/0	0/0/0	0/0/	0/0/13.5	13.6/0			0/0/0	----Other
													--Other:
0/0/0	12	3	1.5/1.5	0/0/0	0/0	0/0/0	0/0/	0/0/13.5	13.6/0			0/0/0	---In airtight containers
													---Other:
0/0/0	12	3	1.5/1.5	0/0/0	0/0	0/0/0	0/0/	0/0/13.5	13.6/0			0/0/0	----Of duck
0/0/0	12	3	1.5/1.5	0/0/0	0/0	0/0/0	0/0/	0/0/13.5	13.6/0			0/0/0	----Other
													-Of swine:
													--Hams and cuts thereof
0/0/0	12	3	1.5/1.5	0/0/0	0/0	0/0/0	0/0/	0/0/13.5	13.6/0			0/0/0	Prepared or preserved hams and cuts of pig-deer (*Babyrousa*)、pygmy pig (*Porcula*)
0/0/0	12	3	1.5/1.5	0/0/0	0/0	0/0/0	0/0/	0/0/13.5	13.6/0			0/0/0	Prepared or preserved hams and cuts of swine
													--Shoulders and cuts thereof
0/0/0	12	3	1.5/1.5	0/0/0	0/0	0/0/0	0/0/	0/0/13.5	13.6/0			0/0/0	Prepared or preserved shoulders and cuts of pig-deer (*Babyrousa*)、pygmy pig (*Porcula*)
0/0/0	12	3	1.5/1.5	0/0/0	0/0	0/0/0	0/0/	0/0/13.5	13.6/0			0/0/0	Prepared or preserved shoulders and cuts of swine
													--Other, including mixtures:
													---In airtight containers
0/0/0	12	3	1.5/1.5	0/0/0	0/0	0/0/0	0/0/	0/0/13.5	13.6/0			0/0/0	Other meat, meat offal of pig-deer (*Babyrousa*)、pygmy pig (*Porcula*), tinned
0/0/0	12	3	1.5/1.5	0/0/0	0/0	0/0/0	0/0/	0/0/13.5	13.6/0			0/0/0	Other meat, meat offal of swine, tinned
													---Other
0/0/0	12	3	1.5/1.5	0/0/0	0/0	0/0/0	0/0/	0/0/13.5	13.6/0			0/0/0	Prepared or preserved meat, meat offal or blood of pig-deer (*Babyrousa*)、pygmy pig (*Porcula*)
0/0/0	12	3	1.5/1.5	0/0/0	0/0	0/0/0	0/0/	0/0/13.5	13.6/0			0/0/0	Prepared or preserved meat, meat offal or blood of swine
													-Of bovine animals:
													---In airtight containers
0/0/0	6	2.4	1.2/1.2	0/0/0	0/0	0/0/0	0/0/	0/0/10.8	10.9/0			0/0/0	Meat of endangered wild bovine animals, tinned
0/0/0	6	2.4	1.2/1.2	0/0/0	0/0	0/0/0	0/0/	0/0/10.8	10.9/0			0/0/0	Other meat, meat offal of bovine animals, tinned(other than meat of wild bovine animals)
													---Other
0/0/0	6	2.4	1.2/1.2	0/0/0	0/0	0/0/0	0/0/	0/0/10.8	10.9/0			0/0/0	Other prepared or preserved meat, meat offal or blood of endangered wild bovine animals
0/0/0	6	2.4	1.2/1.2	0/0/0	0/0	0/0/0	0/0/	0/0/10.8	10.9/0			0/0/0	Other prepared or preserved meat, meat offal or blood of bovine animals
													-Other, including preparations of blood of any animal:
													---In airtight containers
0/0/0	12	3	1.5/1.5	0/0/0	0/0	0/0/0	0/0/	0/0/7.2	7.3/0			0/0/0	Canned meat, offal, blood or insects of other endangered animals
0/0/0	12	3	1.5/1.5	0/0/0	0/0	0/0/0	0/0/	0/0/7.2	7.3/0			0/0/0	Cans of other animal meat, offal, blood or insects
													---Other
0/0/0	12	3	1.5/1.5	0/0/0	0/0	0/0/0	0/0/	0/0/7.2	7.3/0			0/0/0	Meat, offal, blood or insects of other endangered animals prepared or preserved
0/0/0	12	3	1.5/1.5	0/0/0	0/0	0/0/0	0/0/	0/0/7.2	7.3/0			0/0/0	Meat, offal, blood or insects of other animals prepared or preserved
													Extracts and juices of meat, fish or crustaceans, molluscs or other aquatic invertebrates:
													Extracts and juices of meat, fish or crustaceans, molluscs or other aquatic invertebrates

税则号列		货品名称〔CIQ扩展编码及品名－T2表示见附表2〕	最惠(%)	暂定税率	普通	增值/消费	出口退税	计量单位	监管条件/特殊证件	检验检疫	对美关税	亚太上/下
1603.0000	10	含濒危野生动物及鱼类成分的肉(指税目02.08及子目0301.92野生动物及鱼类)〔101其他野生水产制品,102野生鱼类罐头〕	5		90	13/	0	千克	ABFE/	PRQS	30	
1603.0000	90	肉及水产品的精、汁(水产品指鱼、甲壳动物、软体动物或其他水生无脊椎动物)〔101其他养殖水产制品,102其他野生水产制品〕	5		90	13/	13	千克	AB/	PRQS	30	
16.04		**制作或保藏的鱼;鲟鱼子酱及鱼卵制的鲟鱼子酱代用品:**										
		-鱼,整条或切块,但未绞碎:										
		--鲑鱼:										
1604.1110		---大西洋鲑鱼[T2]	10		90	13/	13	千克	AB/	PRQS	35	
1604.1190		---其他										
1604.1190	10	制作或保藏的川陕哲罗鲑鱼(整条或切块,但未绞碎)〔101水产制品,102野生鱼类罐头〕	10		90	13/	13	千克	AB/	PRQS	35	
1604.1190	20	制作或保藏的秦岭细鳞鲑鱼(整条或切块,但未绞碎)〔101水产制品,102野生鱼类罐头〕	10		90	13/	13	千克	AB/	PRQS	35	
1604.1190	90	制作或保藏的其他鲑鱼〔101水产制品,102野生鱼类罐头〕	10		90	13/	13	千克	AB/	PRQS	35	
1604.1200		--鲱鱼〔101水产制品,102野生鱼类罐头〕	5		90	13/	13	千克	AB/	PRQS	30	
1604.1300		--沙丁鱼、小沙丁鱼属、黍鲱或西鲱[T2]	5		90	13/	13	千克	AB/	PRQS	30	
1604.1400		--金枪鱼、鲣及狐鲣(狐鲣属)[T2]	5		90	13/	13	千克	AB/	PRQS	30	
1604.1500		--鲭鱼〔101养殖水产制品,102野生水产制品,103养殖鱼类罐头,104野生鱼类罐头〕	5		90	13/	13	千克	AB/	PRQS	30	
1604.1600		--鳀鱼〔101养殖水产制品,102野生水产制品,103养殖鱼类罐头,104野生鱼类罐头〕	5		90	13/	13	千克	AB/	PRQS	30	
1604.1700		--鳗鱼										
1604.1700	10	制作或保藏的花鳗鲡(整条或切块,但未绞碎)[T2]	5		90	13/	13	千克	ABE/	PRQS	30	4.1/4.1
1604.1700	20	制作或保藏的欧洲鳗鲡(整条或切块,但未绞碎)[T2]	5		90	13/	13	千克	ABEF/	PRQS	30	4.1/4.1
1604.1700	90	其他制作或保藏的鳗鱼(整条或切块,但未绞碎)[T2]	5		90	13/	13	千克	AB/	PRQS	30	4.1/4.1
1604.1800		--鲨鱼翅										
1604.1800	10	制作或保藏的濒危鲨鱼鱼翅(整条或切块,但未绞碎)〔999〕	12		90	13/	0	千克	AFEB/	PRQS	37	9.8/9.8
1604.1800	90	制作或保藏的其他鲨鱼鱼翅(整条或切块,但未绞碎)〔999〕	12		90	13/	13	千克	AB/	PRQS	37	9.8/9.8
		--其他:										
1604.1920		---罗非鱼〔101养殖水产制品,102野生水产制品,103养殖鱼类罐头,104野生鱼类罐头〕	5		90	13/	13	千克	AB/	PRQS	30	
		---叉尾鮰鱼:										
1604.1931		----斑点叉尾鮰鱼〔101养殖水产制品,102野生水产制品,103养殖鱼类罐头,104野生鱼类罐头〕	5		90	13/	13	千克	AB/	PRQS	30	4.1/4.1
1604.1939		----其他〔101养殖水产制品,102野生水产制品,103养殖鱼类罐头,104野生鱼类罐头〕	5		90	13/	13	千克	AB/	PRQS	30	4.1/4.1
1604.1990		---其他										
1604.1990	10	制作或保藏的濒危鱼类(整条或切块,但未绞碎)〔101野生水产制品,102野生鱼类罐头〕	5		90	13/	0	千克	AFEB/	PRQS	30	4.1/4.1
1604.1990	90	制作或保藏的其他鱼(整条或切块,但未绞碎)[T2]	5		90	13/	13	千克	AB/	PRQS	30	4.1/4.1
		-其他制作或保藏的鱼:										
		---罐头:										
1604.2011		----鱼翅										
1604.2011	10	濒危鲨鱼鱼翅罐头〔999〕	12		90	13/	0	千克	ABFE/	PRQS	37	9.8/9.8
1604.2011	90	其他鲨鱼鱼翅罐头〔999〕	12		90	13/	13	千克	AB/	PRQS	37	9.8/9.8
1604.2019		----其他										
1604.2019	10	非整条或切块的濒危鱼罐头(鱼翅除外)〔999〕	5		90	13/	0	千克	ABFE/	PRQS	30	4.1/4.1
1604.2019	90	非整条或切块的其他鱼罐头(鱼翅除外)[T2]	5		90	13/	13	千克	AB/	PRQS	30	4.1/4.1
		---其他:										
1604.2091		----鱼翅										
1604.2091	10	制作或保藏的濒危鲨鱼鱼翅(非整条、非切块、非罐头)〔999〕	12		90	13/	0	千克	ABFE/	PRQS	37	9.8/9.8
1604.2091	90	制作或保藏其他鲨鱼鱼翅(非整条、非切块、非罐头)〔999〕	12		90	13/	13	千克	AB/	PRQS	37	9.8/9.8
1604.2099		----其他										
1604.2099	10	其他制作或保藏的濒危鱼(非整条、非切块、非罐头,鱼翅除外)〔999〕	5		90	13/	0	千克	ABFE/	PRQS	30	4.1/4.1

协定税率 %								RCEP		特惠税率 %			Article Description
东/冰/格	巴基斯坦	韩国	瑞士 上/下	哥/秘/柬	澳/毛	新西/坡/智	中国港/澳/台	东盟及马来/澳/韩	日/新	亚太2国	老/柬/缅	98/97/95	
0/0/0		13.8	2.3/2.3	0/0/0	0/13.8	0/0/0	0/0/	21.9/21.9/23	21.9/21.9			0/0/0	Meat containing compositions of endangered wild animals and fish of heading No. 0208 or of subheading No. 030192
0/0/0		13.8	2.3/2.3	0/0/0	0/13.8	0/0/0	0/0/	21.9/21.9/23	21.9/21.9			0/0/0	Extracts and juices of meat, fish or crustaceans, molluscs or other aquatic invertebrates
													Prepared or preserved fish; caviar and caviar substitutes prepared from fish eggs:
													-Fish, whole or in pieces, but not minced:
													--Salmon:
0/0/0	4.2	2.4		0//0	0/0	0/0/0	0/0/	0/0/10.8	10.9/0			0/0/0	---Atlantic Salmon
													---Other
0/0/0	4.2	2.4		0//0	0/0	0/0/0	0/0/	0/0/10.8	10.9/0			0/0/0	Prepared or preserved sichuan tamen(*Hucho taimen*)(whole or in pieces, but not minced)
0/0/0	4.2	2.4		0//0	0/0	0/0/0	0/0/	0/0/10.8	10.9/0			0/0/0	Prepared or preserved Qinling lenok (*Brachymystax lenok*) (whole or in pieces, but not minced)
0/0/0	4.2	2.4		0//0	0/0	0/0/0	0/0/	0/0/10.8	10.9/0			0/0/0	Prepared or preserved other salmon
0/0/0	4.2	2.4	1.2/1.2	0/0/0	0/0	0/0/0	0/0/	0/0/10.8	10.9/0			0/0/0	--Herrings
0/0/0	0	0	0/0	0/0/0	0/0	0//0	0/0/	0/0/0	0/0		/0/	0/0/0	--sardines, sardinella, and brisling or sprats
0/0/0	0	0	0/0	0/0/0	0/0	0//0	0/0/	0/0/0	0/0		/0/	0/0/0	--Tunas, skipjack and bonito(*Sarda spp.*)
0/0/0	4.2	2.4	1.2/1.2	0/0/0	0/0	0/0/0	0/0/	0/0/10.8	10.9/0			0/0/0	--Mackerel
0/0/0	4.2	2.4	1.2/1.2	0/0/0	0/0	0/0/0	0/0/	0/0/10.8	10.9/0			0/0/0	--Anchovies
													--Eels
0/0/0	3.5	2.4	1.2/1.2	0//0	0/0	0/0/0	0/0/	0/0/10.8	10.9/0			0/0/0	Preared or preserved marbled eels(whole or in pieces, but not minced)
0/0/0	3.5	2.4	1.2/1.2	0//0	0/0	0/0/0	0/0/	0/0/10.8	10.9/0			0/0/0	Preared or preserved europea eels(whole or in pieces, but not minced)
0/0/0	3.5	2.4	1.2/1.2	0//0	0/0	0/0/0	0/0/	0/0/10.8	10.9/0			0/0/0	Preared or preserved other eels(whole or in pieces, but not minced)
													--Shark fins
0/0/0	3.5	2.4	1.2/1.2	0//0	0/	0/0/0	0/0/	0/0/10.8	10.9/0			0/0/0	Endangered shark's fins , prepared or preserved, whole nor in pieces, not not minced
0/0/0	3.5	2.4	1.2/1.2	0//0	0/	0/0/0	0/0/	0/0/10.8	10.9/0			0/0/0	Other shark's fins , prepared or preserved, whole nor in pieces, not not minced
													--Other:
0/0/0	4.2	2.4	1.2/1.2	0//0	0/0	0/0/0	0/0/	0/0/10.8	10.9/0			0/0/0	---Tilapia
													---Of Ictalurus:
0/0/0	3.5	2.4	1.2/1.2	0//0	0/0	0/0/0	0/0/	0/0/10.8	10.9/0			0/0/0	----Channel catfish(*Ictalurus punctatus*)
0/0/0	3.5	2.4	1.2/1.2	0//0	0/0	0/0/0	0/0/	0/0/10.8	10.9/0			0/0/0	----Other
													Other
0/0/0	3.5	2.4	1.2/1.2	0//0	0/0	0/0/0	0/0/	0/0/10.8	10.9/0			0/0/0	Prepared or preserved endangered fish(whole or in pieces, but not minced)
0/0/0	3.5	2.4	1.2/1.2	0//0	0/0	0/0/0	0/0/	0/0/10.8	10.9/0			0/0/0	Prepared or preserved other fish(whole or in pieces, but not minced)
													-Other prepared or preserved fish:
													---In airtight containers:
													----Shark's fin
0/0/0	3.5		1.2/1.2	0/0/0	/0	0/0/0	0/0/	11.4/11.7/12	11.4/11.7			0/0/0	Shark's fins of endangered shark (Cetorhinus) in airtight containers
0/0/0	3.5		1.2/1.2	0/0/0	/0	0/0/0	0/0/	11.4/11.7/12	11.4/11.7			0/0/0	Other shark's fins in airtight containers
													----Other
0/0/0	3.5	2.4	1.2/1.2	0/0/0	0/0	0/0/0	0/0/	0/0/10.8	10.9/0			0/0/0	Endangered fish in airtight containers, other than whole or in pieces(other than shark's fins)
0/0/0	3.5	2.4	1.2/1.2	0/0/0	0/0	0/0/0	0/0/	0/0/10.8	10.9/0			0/0/0	Other fish in airtight containers, other than whole or in pieces (other than shark's fins)
													---Other:
													----Shark's fin
0/0/0	3.5		1.2/1.2	0/0/0	/0	0/0/0	0/0/	11.4/11.7/12	11.4/11.7			0/0/0	Prepared or preserved shark's fins of endangered shark(Cetorhinus)(other than whole or in pieces, not in airtight containers)
0/0/0	3.5		1.2/1.2	0/0/0	/0	0/0/0	0/0/	11.4/11.7/12	11.4/11.7			0/0/0	Prepared or preserved other shark's fins(other than whole or in pieces, not in airtight containers)
													----Other
0/0/0	3.5	2.4	1.2/1.2	0/0/0	0/0	0/0/0	0/0/	10.8/10.8/10.8	10.9/10.8			0/0/0	Prepared or preserved engdangered fish(other than whole or in pieces, not in airtight containers, other than shark's fins)

税则号列	货品名称〔CIQ 扩展编码及品名—T2 表示见附表 2〕	最惠(%)	暂定税率	普通	增值/消费	出口退税	计量单位	监管条件/特殊证件	检验检疫	对美关税	亚太上/下
1604.2099 90	其他制作或保藏的鱼（非整条、非切块、非罐头，鱼翅除外）[T2]	5		90	13/	13	千克	AB/	PRQS	30	4.1/4.1
	-鲟鱼子酱及鲟鱼子酱代用品：										
1604.3100	--鲟鱼子酱〔999〕	5		90	13/	13	千克	ABFE/	PRQS	30	
1604.3200	--鲟鱼子酱代用品〔999〕	5		90	13/	13	千克	AB/	PRQS	30	
16.05	**制作或保藏的甲壳动物、软体动物及其他水生无脊椎动物：**										
1605.1000	-蟹〔101 养殖水产制品，102 野生水产制品，103 养殖甲壳类罐头，104 野生甲壳类罐头〕	5		90	13/	13	千克	AB/	PRQS	35	
	-小虾及对虾：										
1605.2100	--非密封包装〔101 养殖水产制品，102 野生水产制品，103 养殖甲壳类罐头，104 野生甲壳类罐头〕	5		90	13/	13	千克	AB/	PRQS	30	
1605.2900	--其他〔101 养殖水产制品，102 野生水产制品，103 养殖甲壳类罐头，104 野生甲壳类罐头〕	5		90	13/	13	千克	AB/	PRQS	30	
1605.3000	-龙虾〔101 养殖水产制品，102 野生水产制品，103 养殖甲壳类罐头，104 野生甲壳类罐头〕	5		90	13/	13	千克	AB/	PRQS	30	
	-其他甲壳动物：										
	---淡水小龙虾：										
1605.4011	----虾仁[T2]	5		90	13/	13	千克	AB/	PRQS	30	
1605.4019	----其他[T2]	5		90	13/	13	千克	AB/	PRQS	35	
1605.4090	---其他[T2]	5		90	13/	13	千克	AB/	PRQS	30	
	-软体动物：										
1605.5100	--牡蛎（蚝）〔101 养殖水产制品，102 野生水产制品，103 养殖贝类罐头，104 野生贝类罐头〕	5		90	13/	13	千克	AB/	PRQS	30	3.9/3.9
1605.5200	--扇贝，包括海扇										
1605.5200 10	制作或保藏的大珠母贝〔101 养殖水产制品，102 野生水产制品，103 养殖贝类罐头，104 野生贝类罐头〕	5		90	13/	13	千克	ABE/	PRQS	30	3.9/3.9
1605.5200 90	其他制作或保藏的扇贝，包括海扇〔101 养殖水产制品，102 野生水产制品，103 养殖贝类罐头，104 野生贝类罐头〕	5		90	13/	13	千克	AB/	PRQS	30	3.9/3.9
1605.5300	--贻贝〔101 养殖水产制品，102 野生水产制品，103 养殖贝类罐头，104 野生贝类罐头〕	5		90	13/	13	千克	AB/	PRQS	30	3.9/3.9
1605.5400	--墨鱼及鱿鱼〔101 养殖水产制品，102 野生水产制品，103 养殖水产罐头，104 野生水产罐头〕	5		90	13/	13	千克	AB/	PRQS	30	3.9/3.9
1605.5500	--章鱼〔101 养殖水产制品，102 野生水产制品，103 养殖水产罐头，104 野生水产罐头〕	5		90	13/	13	千克	AB/	PRQS	30	3.9/3.9
	--蛤、鸟蛤及舟贝：										
1605.5610	---蛤〔101 养殖水产制品，102 野生水产制品，103 养殖贝类罐头，104 野生贝类罐头〕	5		90	13/	9,13	千克	AB/	PRQS	30	3.9/3.9
1605.5620	---鸟蛤及舟贝										
1605.5620 10	制作或保藏的砗磲〔101 养殖水产制品，102 野生水产制品，103 养殖贝类罐头，104 野生贝类罐头〕	5		90	13/	13	千克	ABEF/	PRQS	30	3.9/3.9
1605.5620 90	其他制作或保藏的鸟蛤及舟贝〔101 养殖水产制品，102 野生水产制品，103 养殖贝类罐头，104 野生贝类罐头〕	5		90	13/	13	千克	AB/	PRQS	30	3.9/3.9
1605.5700	--鲍鱼〔101 养殖水产制品，102 野生水产制品，103 养殖贝类罐头，104 野生贝类罐头〕	5		90	13/	13	千克	AB/	PRQS	30	3.9/3.9
1605.5800	--蜗牛及螺，海螺除外										
1605.5800 10	制作或保藏的濒危蜗牛及螺，海螺除外[T2]	5		90	13/	0	千克	ABFE/	PRQS	30	3.9/3.9
1605.5800 90	其他制作或保藏的蜗牛及螺，海螺除外[T2]	5		90	13/	13	千克	AB/	PRQS	30	3.9/3.9
1605.5900	--其他										
1605.5900 10	其他制作或保藏的濒危软体动物〔101 野生水产制品，102 野生水产罐头〕	5		90	13/	0	千克	ABFE/	PRQS	30	3.9/3.9
1605.5900 90	其他制作或保藏的软体动物〔101 养殖水产制品，102 野生水产制品，103 养殖水产罐头，104 野生水产罐头〕	5		90	13/	13	千克	AB/	PRQS	30	3.9/3.9
	-其他水生无脊柱动物：										
1605.6100	--海参										
1605.6100 10	制作或保藏的暗色刺参〔101 养殖水产制品，102 野生水产制品，103 养殖水产罐头，104 野生水产罐头〕	5		90	13/	13	千克	ABFE/	PRQS	35	3.9/3.9
1605.6100 90	其他制作或保藏的海参〔101 养殖水产制品，102 野生水产制品，103 养殖水产罐头，104 野生水产罐头〕	5		90	13/	13	千克	AB/	PRQS	35	3.9/3.9
1605.6200	--海胆〔101 野生水产制品，102 野生水产罐头〕	5		90	13/	13	千克	AB/	PRQS	30	3.9/3.9
1605.6300	--海蜇[T2]	5		90	13/	9,13	千克	AB/	PRQS	30	
1605.6900	--其他										
1605.6900 10	其他制作或保藏的濒危水生无脊椎动物[T2]	5		90	13/	0	千克	ABFE/	PRQS	30	3.9/3.9
1605.6900 90	其他制作或保藏的水生无脊椎动物[T2]	5		90	13/	13	千克	AB/	PRQS	30	3.9/3.9

协定税率 %								RCEP		特惠税率 %			Article Description
东/冰/格	巴基斯坦	韩国	瑞士 上/下	哥/秘/柬	澳/毛	新西/坡/智	中国港/澳/台	东盟及马来/澳/韩	日/新	亚太2国	老/柬/缅	98/97/95	
0/0/0	3.5	2.4	1.2/1.2	0/0/0	0/0	0/0/0	0/0/	10.8/10.8/10.8	10.9/10.8			0/0/0	Other prepared or preserved fish (other than whole or in pieces, not in airtight containers, other than shark's fins)
													-Caviar and caviar substitutes:
0/0/0	4.2	2.4	1.2/1.2	0/0/0	0/0	0/0/0	0/0/	0/0/10.8	10.9/0			0/0/0	--Caviar
0/0/0	4.2	2.4	1.2/1.2	0/0/0	0/0	0/0/0	0/0/	0/0/10.8	10.9/0			0/0/0	--Caviar substiutes
													Crustaceans, molluscs and other aquatic invertebrates, prepared or preserved:
0/0/0	0	0	0/0	0/0/0	0/0	0//0	0/0/	0/0/0	0/0			0/0/0	-Crab
													-Shrimps and prawns:
0/0/0	0	0	0/0	0/0/0	0/0	0//0	0/0/	0/0/0	0/0		/0/	0/0/0	--Not in airtight container
0/0/0	0	0	0/0	0/0/0	0/0	0//0	0/0/	0/0/0	0/0		/0/	0/0/0	--Other
0/0/0	0	0	0/0	0/0/0	0/0	0//0	0/0/	0/0/0	0/0		/0/	0/0/0	-Lobster
													-Other crustaceans:
													---Freshwater crawfish:
0/0/0	0	0	0/0	0/0/0	0/0	0//0	0/0/	0/0/0	0/0		/0/	0/0/0	----Shelled
0/0/0	0	0	0/0	0/0/0	0/0	0//0	0/0/	0/0/0	0/0		/0/	0/0/0	----Other
0/0/0	0	0	0/0	0/0/0	0/0	0//0	0/0/	0/0/0	0/0		/0/	0/0/0	---Other
													-Molluscs:
0/0/0	0	0	0/0	0/0/0	0/0	0//0	0/0/	0/0/0	0/0			0/0/0	--Oysters
													--Scallops, including queen scallops
0/0/0	0	0	0/0	0/0/0	0/0	0//0	0/0/	0/0/0	0/0			0/0/0	Pinctada maxima, prepared or preserved
0/0/0	0	0	0/0	0/0/0	0/0	0//0	0/0/	0/0/0	0/0			0/0/0	Other scallops, including queen scallops, prepared or preserved
0/0/0	0	0	0/0	0/0/0	0/0	0//0	0/0/	0/0/0	0/0			0/0/0	--Mussels
0/0/0	0	0	0/0	0/0/0	0/0	0//0	0/0/	0/0/0	0/0			0/0/0	--Cuttle fish and squid
0/0/0	0	0	0/0	0/0/0	0/0	0//0	0/0/	0/0/0	0/0			0/0/0	--Octopus
													--Clams, cockles and arkshells:
0/0/0	0	0	0/0	0//0	0/0	0//0	0/0/	0/0/0	4.5/0			0/0/0	---Clam
													---Cockles and ark shells
0/0/0	0	0	0/0	0/0/0	0/0	0//0	0/0/	0/0/0	0/0			0/0/0	Tridacna stone, prepared or preserved
0/0/0	0	0	0/0	0/0/0	0/0	0//0	0/0/	0/0/0	0/0			0/0/0	Other cockles and ark shells, prepared or preserved
0/0/0	0	0	0/0	0/0/0	0/0	0//0	0/0/	0/0/0	0/0			0/0/0	--Abalone
													--Snails, other than sea snails
0/0/0	0	0	0/0	0/0/0	0/0	0//0	0/0/	0/0/0	0/0			0/0/0	Endangered snails, other than sea snails, prepared or preserved
0/0/0	0	0	0/0	0/0/0	0/0	0//0	0/0/	0/0/0	0/0			0/0/0	Other snails, other than sea snails, prepared or preserved
													--Other
0/0/0	0	0	0/0	0/0/0	0/0	0//0	0/0/	0/0/0	0/0			0/0/0	Endangered molluscs, prepared or preserved
0/0/0	0	0	0/0	0/0/0	0/0	0//0	0/0/	0/0/0	0/0			0/0/0	Other molluscs, prepared or preserved
													-Other aquatic invertebrates:
													--Sea cucumbers
0/0/0	0	0	0/0	0/0/0	0/0	0//0	0/0/	0/0/0	0/0			0/0/0	Isostichopus fuscus, prepared or preserved
0/0/0	0	0	0/0	0/0/0	0/0	0//0	0/0/	0/0/0	0/0			0/0/0	Other sea cucumbers, prepared or preserved
0/0/0	0	0	0/0	0/0/0	0/0	0//0	0/0/	0/0/0	0/0			0/0/0	--Sea urchin
0/0/0	12	3	1.5/1.5	0//0	0/0	0/0/0	0/0/	0/0/13.5	13.6/0			0/0/0	--Jellyfish
													--Other
0/0/0	0	0	0/0	0/0/0	0/0	0//0	0/0/	0/0/0	0/0			0/0/0	Endangered aquatic invertebrates, prepared or preserved
0/0/0	0	0	0/0	0/0/0	0/0	0//0	0/0/	0/0/0	0/0			0/0/0	Other aquatic invertebrates, prepared or preserved

第十七章
糖及糖食

注释：

本章不包括：

一、含有可可的糖食(税目18.06)；

二、税目29.40的化学纯糖(蔗糖、乳糖、麦芽糖、葡萄糖及果糖除外)及其他产品；

三、第三十章的药品及其他产品。

子目注释：

一、子目号1701.12、1701.13及1701.14所称"原糖"，是指按重量计干燥状态的蔗糖含量对应的旋光读数低于99.5°的糖。

二、子目1701.13仅包括非离心甘蔗糖，其按重量计干燥状态的蔗糖含量对应的旋光读数不低于69°但低于93°。该产品仅含肉眼不可见的不规则形状天然他形微晶，外被糖蜜残余及其他甘蔗成分。

税则号列	货品名称〔CIQ扩展编码及品名—T2表示见附表2〕	最惠(%)	暂定税率	普通	增值/消费	出口退税	计量单位	监管条件/特殊证件	检验检疫	对美关税	亚太上/下
17.01	**固体甘蔗糖、甜菜糖及化学纯蔗糖：**										
	-未加香料或着色剂的原糖：										
1701.1200	--甜菜糖										
1701.1200 01	未加香料或着色剂的甜菜原糖[按重量计干燥状态的糖含量低于旋光读数99.5度(配额内)]〔999〕	15		125	13/	13	千克	ABt/	MPRQS	20	
1701.1200 90	未加香料或着色剂的甜菜原糖[按重量计干燥状态的糖含量低于旋光读数99.5度(配额外)]〔999〕	50		125	13/	13	千克	7AB/	MPRQS	55	
1701.1300	--本章子目注释二所述的甘蔗糖										
1701.1300 01	未加香料或着色剂的本章子目注释二所述的甘蔗原糖[按重量计干燥状态的蔗糖含量对应的旋光读数不低于69度，但低于93度(配额内)]〔101冰糖，102冰片糖，103原糖〕	15		125	13/	13	千克	ABt/	MPRQS	20	
1701.1300 90	未加香料或着色剂的本章子目注释二所述的甘蔗原糖[按重量计干燥状态的蔗糖含量对应的旋光读数不低于69度，但低于93度(配额外)]〔101冰糖，102冰片糖，103原糖〕	50		125	13/	13	千克	7AB/	PRQS	55	
1701.1400	--其他甘蔗糖										
1701.1400 01	未加香料或着色剂其他甘蔗原糖[按重量计干燥状态的糖含量低于旋光读数99.5度(配额内)]〔101冰糖，102冰片糖，103原糖〕	15		125	13/	13	千克	ABt/	PRQS	40	
1701.1400 90	未加香料或着色剂其他甘蔗原糖[按重量计干燥状态的糖含量低于旋光读数99.5度(配额外)]〔101冰糖，102冰片糖，103原糖〕	50		125	13/	13	千克	7AB/	PRQS	75	
	-其他：										
1701.9100	--加有香料或着色剂										
1701.9100 01	加有香料或着色剂的糖[指甘蔗糖、甜菜糖及化学纯蔗糖(配额内)]〔999〕	15		125	13/	13	千克	ABt/	RS	25	
1701.9100 90	加有香料或着色剂的糖[指甘蔗糖、甜菜糖及化学纯蔗糖(配额外)]〔999〕	50		125	13/	13	千克	7AB/	RS	60	
	--其他：										
1701.9910	---砂糖										
1701.9910 10	砂糖(配额内)〔101白砂糖，102冰砂糖〕	15		125	13/	13	千克	ABt/	MRS	40	
1701.9910 90	砂糖(配额外)〔101白砂糖，102冰砂糖〕	50		125	13/	13	千克	7AB/	MRS	75	
1701.9920	---绵白糖										
1701.9920 01	绵白糖(配额内)〔999〕	15		125	13/	13	千克	BAt/	RS	20	
1701.9920 90	绵白糖(配额外)〔999〕	50		125	13/	13	千克	7AB/	RS	55	
1701.9990	---其他										
1701.9990 01	其他精制糖(配额内)〔101方糖，102冰糖，103红塘，104冰片糖内，105糖浆，106糖霜，107其他食糖〕	15		125	13/	13	千克	ABt/	RS	35	
1701.9990 90	其他精制糖(配额外)〔101方糖，102冰糖，103红塘，104冰片糖内，105糖浆，106糖霜，107其他食糖〕	50		125	13/	13	千克	7AB/	RS	70	
17.02	**其他固体糖，包括化学纯乳糖、麦芽糖、葡萄糖及果糖；未加香料或着色剂的糖浆；人造蜜，不论是否掺有天然蜂蜜；焦糖：**										

① 国别关税配额税率：15

Chapter 17
Sugars and sugar confectionery

Note:

This Chapter does not cover:

(1)Sugar confectionery containing cocoa (heading No. 18.06);

(2)Chemically pure sugars (other than sucrose, lactose, maltose, glucose and fructose) or other products of heading No.29.40;

(3)Medicaments or other products of Chapter 30.

Subheading Note:

1. For the purposes of subheadings No. 1701.12、1701.13 及 1701.14, "raw sugar" means sugar whose content of sucrose by weight, in the dry state, corresponds to a polarimeter reading of less than 99.5°.
2. Subheading 1701.13 covers only cane sugar obtained without centrifugation, whose content of sucrose by weight, in the dry state, corresponds to a polarimeter reading of 69°or more but less than 93°. The product contains only natural anhedral microcrystals, of irregular shape, not visible to the naked eye, which are surrouded by residues of molasses and other constituents of sugar cane

协定税率 %								RCEP		特惠税率 %			Article Description
东/冰/格	巴基斯坦	韩国	瑞士上/下	哥/秘/柬	澳/毛	新西/坡/智	中国港/澳/台	东盟及马来/澳/韩	日/新	亚太2国	老/柬/缅	98/97/95	
													Cane or beet sugar and chemically pure sucrose, in solid form:
													-Raw sugar not containing added flavouring or colouring matter:
													--Beet sugar
					①		0/0/						Raw beet sugar not containing added flavouring or colouring matter[sugar whose content of sucrose by weight, in the dry state, corresponds to a polarimeter reading of less than 99.5° (in-quota)]
					/①		0/0/						Raw beet sugar not containing added flavouring or colouring matter[sugar whose content of sucroseby weight, in the dry state, corresponds to a polarimeter reading of less than 99.5° (out-quota)]
													--Cane sugar specified in subheading Note 2 to this chapter
					/①		0/0/						Of cane sugar in subheading Note 2 to this chapter not containing added flavouring or colouring matter[whose content of sucrose by weight, in the dry state, corresponds to a polarimeter reading of 69°or more but less 93°(in-quota)]
					/①		0/0/						Of cane sugar in subheading Note 2 to this chapter not containing added flavouring or colouring matter[whose content of sucrose by weight, in the dry state, corresponds to a polarimeter reading of 69°or more but less 93°(out-quota)]
													--Other cane sugar
					/①		0/0/						Other cane sugar not containing added flavouring or colouring matter[sugar whose content of sucrose by weight, in the dry state, corresponds to a polarimeter reading of less than 99.5° (in-quota)]
					/①		0/0/						Other cane sugar not containing added flavouring or colouring matter[sugar whose content of sucrose by weight, in the dry state, corresponds to a polarimeter reading of less than 99.5° (out-quota)]
													-Other:
													--Containing added flavouring or colouring matter
					/①		0/0/						Cane or beet sugar and chemically pure sucrose, containing added flavouring or colouring matter (in-quota)
					/①		0/0/						Cane or beet sugar and chemically pure sucrose, containing added flavouring or colouring matter (out-quota)
													--Other:
													---Granulated sugar
					/①		0/0/						Granulated sugar (in-quota)
					/①		0/0/						Granulated sugar (out-quota)
													---Superfine sugar
					/①		0/0/						Superfine sugar (in-quota)
					/①		0/0/						Superfine sugar (out-quota)
													---Other
					/①		0/0/						Other refined sugar (in-quota)
					/①		0/0/						Other refined sugar (out-quota)
													Other sugars, including chemically pure lactose, maltose, glucose and fructose, in solid form; sugar syrups not containing added flavouring or colouring matter; artificial honey, whether or not mixed with natural honey; caramel:

税则号列	货品名称〔CIQ 扩展编码及品名－T2 表示见附表 2〕	最惠(%)	暂定税率	普通	增值/消费	出口退税	计量单位	监管条件/特殊证件	检验检疫	对美关税	亚太上/下
	-乳糖及乳糖浆：										
1702.1100	--按重量计干燥无水乳糖含量在 99％及以上〔999〕	10	5	80	13/	13	千克	AB/	RS	15	
1702.1900	--其他〔111 其他乳糖及乳糖浆，301 可溶性大豆多糖（无检疫要求食品添加剂），302 异构化乳糖液（无检疫要求食品添加剂）〕	10		80	13/	13	千克	AB/	RS	20	
1702.2000	-槭糖及槭糖浆〔101 槭糖浆，102 槭糖，301 需申报仅用于工业用途不用于食品添加剂无检疫要求的化学品〕	30		80	13/	13	千克	AB/	RS	55	
1702.3000	-葡萄糖及葡萄糖浆，不含果糖或按重量计干燥状态的果糖含量在 20％以下〔101 葡萄糖浆，102 葡萄糖，103 变性淀粉，301 无检疫要求食品添加剂〕	30		80	13/	13	千克	BA/	RS	55	
1702.4000	-葡萄糖及葡萄糖浆，按重量计干燥状态的果糖含量在 20％及以上，但在 50％以下，转化糖除外〔101 葡萄糖浆，102 葡萄糖〕	30		80	13/	13	千克	BA/	RS	35	
1702.5000	-化学纯果糖〔101 合成糖，102 阿思巴甜无检疫要求食品添加剂，301 需申报仅用于工业用途不用于食品添加剂无检疫要求的化学品〕	30		80	13/	13	千克	AB/	RS	55	
1702.6000	-其他果糖及果糖浆，按重量计干燥状态的果糖含量在 50％以上，转化糖除外〔101 冰糖，102 糖浆，103 其他食糖，104 合成糖，105 其他糖果，106 低聚果糖无检疫要求食品添加剂〕	30		80	13/	13	千克	BA/	RS	50	
	-其他，包括转化糖及其他按重量计干燥状态的果糖含量为 50％的糖及糖浆混合物：										
	---甘蔗糖或甜菜糖水溶液；蔗糖含量超过 50％的甘蔗糖、甜菜糖与其他糖的简单固体混合物：										
1702.9011	----甘蔗糖或甜菜糖水溶液〔999〕	30		80	13/	13	千克	AB/	RS	50	
1702.9012	----蔗糖含量超过 50％的甘蔗糖、甜菜糖与其他糖的简单固体混合物〔999〕	30		80	13/	13	千克	AB/	RS	50	
1702.9090	---其他										
1702.9090 10	人造蜜〔101 人造糖浆，102 合成糖，103 阿思巴甜（无检疫要求食品添加剂）〕	30		80	13/	13	千克	AB/	RS	50	
1702.9090 90	其他固体糖、糖浆及焦糖（包括转化糖及按重量计干燥状态果糖含量 50％的糖、糖浆）〔101 合成糖，102 其他糖果，301 无检疫要求食品添加剂〕	30		80	13/	13	千克	AB/	RS	50	
17.03	**制糖后所剩的糖蜜：**										
1703.1000	-甘蔗糖蜜〔101 冰片糖，102 糖浆，103 糖霜，104 其他食糖，105 废糖蜜，301 需申报仅用于工业用途不用于食品添加剂无检疫要求的化学品〕	8		50	13/	13	千克	9B/	RS	13	
1703.9000	-其他[101 冰片糖，102 糖浆，103 糖霜，104 其他食糖，106 废糖蜜，301 糖蜜提取物无检疫要求食品添加剂，302 需申报仅用于工业用途不用于食品添加剂无检疫要求的化学品]	8		50	13/	13	千克	9B/	RS	13	
17.04	**不含可可的糖食（包括白巧克力）：**										
1704.1000	-口香糖，不论是否裹糖〔102 凝胶口香糖，103 胶基口香糖〕	12		50	13/	13	千克	AB/	RS	37	9.5/9.5
1704.9000	-其他〔101 合成糖，107 胶基糖果，111 其他糖果，112 巧克力，不适用非可可脂添加量超过 5％的产品，113 其他糖与糖果，巧克力与可可制品〕	10		50	13/	13	千克	AB/	RS	35	8.2/8.2

协定税率 %								RCEP		特惠税率 %			
东/冰/格	巴基斯坦	韩国	瑞士上/下	哥/秘/柬	澳/毛	新西/坡/智	中国港/澳/台	东盟及马来/澳/韩	日/新	亚太2国	老/柬/缅	98/97/95	Article Description
													-Lactose and lactose syrup:
0//0	5	2	0/0	0/0/0	0/0	0/0/0	0/0/	0/0/9	9.1/0			0/0/0	--Containing by weight 99% or more lactose, expressed as anhydrous lactose, calculated on the dry matter
0//0	5	2	0/0	0/0/0	0/0	0/0/0	0/0/	0/0/9	9.1/0			0/0/0	--Other
0//		18		0/0/0	0/18	0/0/0	0/0/	28.5/28.5/28.5	28.6/28.5			0/0/	-Maple sugar and maple syrup
0//	0			0/0/0	0/18	0/0/0	0/0/	5/5/	/5			0/0/	-Glucose and glucose syrup, not containing fructose or containing in the dry state less than 20% by weight of fructose
0//				0/0/0	0/18	0/0/0	0/0/	5/5/	/5			0/0/	-Glucose and glucose syrup, containing in the dry state at least 20% but less than 50% by weight of fructose
0/0/				0/0/0	0/18	0/0/0	0/0/	5/5/	/5			0/0/	-Chemically pure fructose
0/0/				0/0/0	0/18	0/0/0	0/0/	5/5/	/5			0/0/	-Other fructose and fructose syrup, containing in the dry state more than 50% by weight of fructose
													-Other, including invert sugar and other sugar and sugar syrup bends containing in the dry state 50% by weight of fructose:
													---Cane sugar or beet sugar solution; Cane sugar, beet sugar and other sugars in imple solid mixture with more than 50% by weight of cane sucrose
0/0/			12.6/12.6	0/7.1/0	0/18	0/0/0	0/0/	5/5/	/5			0/0/0	----Cane sugar or beet sugar solution
0/0/			12.6/12.6	0/7.1/0	0/18	0/0/0	0/0/	5/5/	/5			0/0/0	----Cane sugar, beet sugar and other sugars in imple solid mixture with more than 50% by weight of cane sucrose
													---Other
0/0/			12.6/12.6	0/7.1/0	0/18	0/0/0	0/0/	5/5/	/5		//	0/0/0	Artificial honey
0/0/			12.6/12.6	0/7.1/0	0/18	0/0/0	0/0/	5/5/	/5		//	0/0/0	Other sugars, syrup and caramel (including invert sugar, in the dry state 50%
													Molasses resulting from the extraction or refining or sugar:
0/0/0	5	0	0/0	0/0/0	0/0	0//0	0/0/	0/0/0	7.3/0			0/0/0	-Cane molasses
0/0/0	5	0	0/0	0/0/0	0/0	0//0	0/0/	0/0/0	7.3/0			0/0/0	-Other
													Sugar confectionery (including white chocolate), not containing cocoa:
0/0/0	0		1.2/1.2	0/2.8/0	0/0	0/0/0	0/0/	11.4/11.4/	/11.4			0/0/0	-Chewing gum, whether or not sugarcoated
0/0/0	0	6	0/0	0/0/0	0/0	0/0/0	0/0/	9.5/9.5/	/9.5			0/0/0	-Other

第十八章
可可及可可制品

注释:

一、本章不包括:

(一)按重量计含香肠、肉、食用杂碎、动物血、昆虫、鱼、甲壳动物、软体动物或其他水生无脊椎动物及其混合物超过 20%的食品(第十六章);

(二)税目 04.03、19.01、19.02、19.04、19.05、21.05、22.02、22.08 、30.03、30.04 的制品。

二、税目 18.06 包括含有可可的糖食及注释一以外的其他含可可的食品。

税则号列	货品名称〔CIQ 扩展编码及品名－T2 表示见附表 2〕	最惠(%)	暂定税率	普通	增值/消费	出口退税	计量单位	监管条件/特殊证件	检验检疫	对美关税	亚太上/下
18.01	**整颗或破碎的可可豆,生的或焙炒的:**										
1801.0000	整颗或破碎的可可豆,生的或焙炒的〔101 生的(提取(晒干的除外)、压榨、烹制、烘焙、冻干、脱水、裹糖屑、发酵、冷冻(经漂汤和杀青,并在－18 度以下冷冻)、浸酸、腌渍、炒制等工艺进行加工处理的),102 焙炒的,999 生的(其他工艺)〕	8	0	30	13/	9,13	千克	AB/	MPRQS	25	
18.02	**可可荚、壳、皮及废料:**										
1802.0000	可可荚、壳、皮及废料〔999〕	10		30	13/	9	千克	AB/	PQS	15	
18.03	**可可膏,不论是否脱脂:**										
1803.1000	-未脱脂〔999〕	10		30	13/	13	千克	AB/	RS	35	
1803.2000	-全脱脂或部分脱脂〔999〕	10		30	13/	13	千克	AB/	RS	15	
18.04	**可可脂、可可油:**										
1804.0000	可可脂、可可油										
1804.0000 10	可可脂〔999〕	22		70	13/	13	千克	AB/	RS	47	
1804.0000 90	可可油〔101 可可油,102 可可壳酊(无检疫要求食品添加剂),103 可可酊(无检疫要求食品添加剂)〕	22		70	13/	13	千克	AB/	RS	47	
18.05	**未加糖或其他甜物质的可可粉:**										
1805.0000	未加糖或其他甜物质的可可粉〔101〕	15		40	13/	13	千克	AB/	PRQS	40	
18.06	**巧克力及其他含可可的食品:**										
1806.1000	-加糖或其他甜物质的可可粉〔101 可可粉,102 可可粉固体饮料〕	10		50	13/	13	千克	AB/	PRQS	20	
1806.2000	-其他重量超过 2 千克的块状或条状含可可食品,或液状、膏状、粉状、粒状或其他散装形状的含可可食品,容器包装或内包装每件净重超过 2 千克的〔102 巧克力,不适用非可可脂添加量超过 5%的产品,103 可可粉固体饮料,104 巧克力〕	10		50	13/	13	千克	AB/	RS	35	7.7/7.7
	-其他块状或条状的含可可食品:										
1806.3100	--夹心〔102 巧克力,不适用非可可脂添加量超过 5%的产品,103 巧克力,适用非可可脂添加量超过 5%的产品〕	8		50	13/	13	千克	AB/	RS	33	6.4/6.4
1806.3200	--不夹心〔101 巧克力,不适用非可可脂添加量超过 5%的产品,102 其他糖与糖果,巧克力与可可制品,103 巧克力,适用非可可脂添加量超过 5%的产品〕	10		50	13/	13	千克	AB/	RS	35	7.7/7.7
1806.9000	-其他[101 巧克力,不适用非可可脂添加量超过 5%的产品,102 其他可可制品,103 其他糖与糖果,巧克力与可可制品,104 巧克力,适用非可可脂添加量超过 5%的产品]	8		50	13/	13	千克	AB/	RS	33	6.4/6.4

Chapter 18
Cocoa and cocoa preparations

Notes:

1. This Chapter does not cover :
   (a) Food preparations containing more than 20 % by weight of sausage, meat, meat offal, blood, insects, fish or crustaceans, molluscs or other aquatic invertebrates, or any combination thereof (Chapter 16);
   (b) Preparations of headings 04.03, 19.01, 19.02, 19.04, 19.05, 21.05, 22.02, 22.08, 30.03 or 30.04.
2. Heading No. 18. 06 includes sugar confectionery containing cocoa and, subject to Note 1 to this Chapter, other food preparations containing cocoa.

协定税率 %								RCEP		特惠税率 %			Article Description
东/冰/格	巴基斯坦	韩国	瑞士上/下	哥/秘/柬	澳/毛	新西/坡/智	中国港/澳/台	东盟及马来/澳/韩	日/新	亚太2国	老/柬/缅	98/97/95	
													Cocoa beans, whole or broken, raw or roasted:
0/0/0	2	0	0/0	0/0/0	0/0	0//0	0/0/	7.2/7.2/7.2	7.3/7.2			0/0/0	Cocoa beans, whole or broken, raw or roasted
													Cocoa shells, husks, skins and other cocoa waste:
0/0/0	3.5	2	0/0	0/0/0	0/0	0/0/0	0/0/	0/0/9	9.1/0			0/0/0	Cocoa shells, husks, skins and other cocoa waste
													Cocoa paste, whether or not defatted:
0/0/0	3.5	2	0/0	0/0/0	0/0	0//0	0/0/	9/9/9	9.1/9			0/0/0	-Not defatted
0/0/0	3.5	2	0/0	0/0/0	0/0	0//0	0/0/	0/0/9	9.1/0			0/0/0	-Wholly or partly defatted
													Cocoa butter, fat and oil:
													Cocoa butter, fat and oil
0/0/0		13.2	2.2/2.2	0/0/0	0/13.2	0//0	0/0/	20.9/20.9/20.9	/20.9			0/0/0	Cocoa fat
0/0/0		13.2	2.2/2.2	0/0/0	0/13.2	0//0	0/0/	20.9/20.9/20.9	/20.9			0/0/0	Cocoa oil
													Cocoa powder, not containing added sugar or other sweetening matter:
0/0/0	12	3	1.5/1.5	0/0/0	0/0	0//0	0/0/	0/0/13.5	13.6/0			0/0/0	Cocoa powder, not containing added sugar or other sweetening matter
													Chocolate and other food preparations containing cocoa:
0/0/0	3.5	2	0/0	0/0/0	0/0	0//0	0/0/	0/0/9	9.1/0			0/0/0	-Cocoa powder, containing added sugar or other sweetening matter
0/0/0	3.5	2	0/0	0/0/0	0/0	0/0/0	0/0/	0/0/9	9.1/0			0/0/0	-Other preparations in blocks, slabs or bars weighing more than 2kg or in liquid, paste, powder, granular or other bulk form in containers or immediate packings, of a content exceeding 2kg
													-Other, in blocks, slabs or bars:
0/0/0	4	3.7	0/0	0/0/0	0/0	0//0	0/0/	7.5/7.6/7.5	7.5/7.6			0/0/0	--Filled
0/0/0	4	4.6	0/0	0/0/0	0/0	0/0/0	0/0/	9.3/9.5/9.3	9.4/9.5			0/0/0	--Not filled
0/0/0	4	3.7	0.8/0.8	0/0/0	0/0	0//0	0/0/	7.5/7.6/7.5	7.5/7.6			0/0/0	-Other

第十九章
谷物、粮食粉、淀粉或乳的制品；糕饼点心

注释：

一、本章不包括：

(一)按重量计含香肠、肉、食用杂碎、动物血、昆虫、鱼、甲壳动物、软体动物、其他水生无脊椎动物及其混合物超过20%的食品(第十六章)，但税目19.02的包馅食品除外；

(二)用粮食粉或淀粉制的专作动物饲料用的饼干及其他制品(税目23.09)；

(三)第三十章的药品及其他产品。

二、税目19.01所称：

(一)“粗粒”是指第十一章的谷物粗粒；

(二)“细粉”及“粗粉”，是指：

1. 第十一章谷物的细粉及粗粉；

2. 其他章植物的细粉、粗粉及粉末，但不包括干蔬菜、马铃薯和干豆类的细粉、粗粉及粉末(应分别归入税目07.12、11.05和11.06)。

三、税目19.04不包括按重量计全脱脂可可含量超过6%或用巧克力完全包裹的食品以及税目18.06的其他含可可食品(税目18.06)。

四、税目19.04所称“其他方法制作的”，是指制作或加工程度超过第十章或第十一章各税目或注释所规定范围的。

税则号列	货品名称〔CIQ扩展编码及品名—T2表示见附表2〕	最惠(%)	暂定税率	普通	增值/消费	出口退税	计量单位	监管条件/特殊证件	检验检疫	对美关税	亚太上/下
19.01	**麦精；细粉、粗粒、粗粉、淀粉或麦精制的其他税目未列名的食品，不含可可或按重量计全脱脂可可含量低于40%；税目04.01至04.04所列货品制的其他税目未列名的食品，不含可可或按重量计全脱脂可可含量低于5%：**										
	-适合供婴幼儿食用的零售包装食品：										
1901.1010	---配方奶粉										
1901.1010 10	早产/低出生体重婴儿配方(乳基)、母乳营养补充剂(乳基)特殊婴幼儿配方食品(按重量计全脱脂可可含量<5%乳品制)〔101早产儿/低出生体重婴儿配方(乳基)食品，102母乳营养补充剂(乳基)特殊婴幼儿配方食品〕	15	0	40	13/	13	千克	7AB/	RS	25	
1901.1010 90	供婴幼儿食用的零售包装配方奶粉〔早产/低出生体重婴儿配方(乳基)、母乳营养补充剂(乳基)特殊婴幼儿配方食品除外〕(按重量计全脱脂可可含量<5%乳品制)〔101乳基婴儿配方食品，102乳基较大婴儿配方食品，103乳基幼儿配方食品，104乳基婴儿配方食品，105乳基较大婴儿配方食品，106乳基幼儿配方食品〕	15	5	40	13/	13	千克	7AB/	RS	30	
1901.1090	---其他〔101其他含肉速冻粮食制品，102其他不含肉速冻粮食制品，103其他不含馅速冻粮食制品，104豆基婴儿配方食品，105豆基较大婴儿和幼儿配方食品，106婴幼儿谷类辅助食品，107婴幼儿罐装辅助食品，108乳基婴幼儿配方食品，109豆基较大婴儿和幼儿配方食品〕	15	2	40	13/	13	千克	AB/	RS	12	
1901.2000	-供烘焙税目19.05所列面包糕饼用的调制品及面团〔101速食粮食产品，102其他粮食制品，103其他含肉速冻粮食制品，104其他不含肉速冻粮食制品，105其他不含馅速冻粮食制品〕	10		80	13/	9,13	千克	AB/	RS	35	
1901.9000	-其他[T2]	10	5	80	13/	13	千克	AB/	RS	30	
19.02	**面食，不论是否煮熟、包馅(肉馅或其他馅)或其他方法制作，例如，通心粉、面条、汤团、馄饨、饺子、奶油面卷；古斯古斯面食，不论是否制作：**										
	-生的面食，未包馅或未经其他方法制作：										
1902.1100	--含蛋〔101生面食，102面条(如挂面等)，103通心粉，104速食粮食产品，105其他粮食制品〕										
1902.1100 10	未包馅或未制作的含蛋生面食，非速冻的〔101生面食，102面条(如挂面等)，103通心粉，104速食粮食产品，105其他粮食制品〕	10		80	13/	9	千克	AB/	PRQS	35	
1902.1100 90	其他未包馅或未制作的含蛋生面食〔101生面食，102面条(如挂面等)，103通心粉，104速食粮食产品，105其他粮食制品〕	10		80	13/	9	千克	AB/	PRQS	35	
1902.1900	--其他〔101生面食，102面条(如挂面等)，103通心粉，104湿面，105速食粮食产品，106其他粮食制品，107馒头〕										
1902.1900 10	其他未包馅或未制作的生面食，非速冻的〔101生面食，102面条(如挂面等)，103通心粉，104湿面，105速食粮食产品，106其他粮食制品，107馒头〕	10		80	13/	9,13	千克	AB/	PRQS	33	

Chapter 19
Preparations of cereals, flour, starch or milk; pastrycooks' products

Notes:

1. This Chapter does not cover:
   (a) Except in the case of stuffed products of heading No. 19.02, food preparations containing more than 20% by weight of sausage, meat, meat offal, blood, insects, fish or crustaceans, molluscs or other aquatic invertebrates, or any combination thereof (Chapter 16);
   (b) Biscuits or other articles made from flour or from starch, specially prepared for use in animal feeding (heading No. 23.09);
   (c) Medicaments or other products of Chapter 30.
2. For the purposes of heading No. 19.01:
   (a) The term "groats" means cereal groats of Chapter 11;
   (b) The terms "flour" and "meal" mean:
      (1) Cereal flour and meal of Chapter 11, and
      (2) Flour, meal and powder of vegetable origin of any Chapter, other than flour, meal or powder of driedvegetables (heading No. 07.12), of potatoes(heading No. 11.05) or of dried leguminous vegetables (heading No. 11.06).
3. Heading No. 19.04 does not cover preparations containing more than 6% by weight of cocoa calculated on a totally defatted basis or completely coated with chocolate or other food preparations containing cocoa of heading 18.06 (heading No.18.06).
4. For the purposes of heading No.19.04, the expression "otherwise prepared" means preparedor or processed to an extent beyond that provided for in the headings of or Notes to Chapter 10 or 11.

协定税率 %								RCEP		特惠税率 %			Article Description
东/冰/格	巴基斯坦	韩国	瑞士上/下	哥/秘/柬	澳/毛	新西/坡/智	中国港/澳/台	东盟及马来/澳/韩	日/新	亚太2国	老/柬/缅	98/97/95	
													Malt extract; food preparations of flour, groats, meal, starch or malt extract, not containing cocoa or containing less than 40% by weight of cocoa calculated on a totally defatted basis, not elsewhere specified or included; food preparations of goods of headings No. 04.01 to 04.04, not containing cocoa or containing less than 5% by weight of cocoa calculated on a totally defatted basis, not elsewhere specified or included:
													-Preparations for infant use, put up for retail sale:
													---Formula milk powder
0/0/	0		1.5/1.5	0/0/0	0/0	0/0/0	0/0/	5/5/	/5		//	0/0/0	premature infant /Low birth weight infant formula (milk based)、Breast milk supplements (milk based)、Special infant formula (containing less than 5% by weight of cocoacal calculated on a totally defatted basis)
0/0/	0		1.5/1.5	0/0/0	0/0	0/0/0	0/0/	5/5/	/5		//	0/0/0	Other retail packaged formula for infants(containing less than 5% by weight of cocoacal calculated on a totally defatted basis)
0/0/	0		1.5/1.5	0/0/0	0/0	0/0/0	0/0/	5/5/	/5			0/0/0	---Other
0/0/0		15	2.5/2.5	0/0/0	0/15	0/0/0	0/0/	23.8/23.8/	23.8/23.8			0/0/0	-Mixes and doughs for the preparation of bakers' wares of heading No. 19.05
0/0/0	0	4.6	0/0	0/0/0	0/0	0/0/0	0/0/	9.3/9.5/9.3	9.4/9.5			0/0/0	-Other
													Pasta, whether or not cooked or stuffed (with meat or other substances) or otherwise prepared, such as, macaroni, noodles, lasagne, gnocchi, ravioli, cannelloni; couscous, whether or not prepared:
													-Uncooked pasta, not stuffed or otherwise prepared:
													--Containing eggs
0//0	12	3	1.5/1.5	0/0/0	0/0	0/0/0	0/0/	0/0/13.5	13.6/0			0/0/0	Raw pasta with eggs, not stuffed or prepared, not frozen
0//0	12	3	1.5/1.5	0/0/0	0/0	0/0/0	0/0/	0/0/13.5	13.6/0			0/0/0	Other raw pasta, containing eggs without stuffing or preparation
													--Other
0//0	0	7	1.5/1.5	0/0/0	0/0	0/0/0	0/0/	14/14.3/14	14.1/14.3			0/0/0	Other raw pasta, without stuffing or preparation, not frozen

税则号列	货品名称〔CIQ 扩展编码及品名—T2 表示见附表 2〕	最惠(%)	暂定税率	普通	增值/消费	出口退税	计量单位	监管条件/特殊证件	检验检疫	对美关税	亚太上/下
1902.1900 90	其他未包馅或未制作的生面食〔101 生面食,102 面条(如挂面等),103 通心粉,104 湿面,105 速食粮食产品,106 其他粮食制品,107 馒头〕	10		80	13/	9,13	千克	AB/	PRQS	33	
1902.2000	-包馅面食,不论是否烹煮或经其他方法制作[101 月饼,102 蛋糕,103 其他糕点,104 饼干,107 面包,108 膨化食品,109 生面食,110 其他糕点饼干,111 速食粮食产品,112 其他粮食制品,113 含肉包子,114 不含肉包子,115 含肉饺子,116 不含肉饺子,117 含肉春卷,118 不含肉春卷,119 其他含肉速冻粮食制品,120 其他不含肉速冻粮食制品]	10		80	13/	9,13	千克	AB/	PRQS	35	
	-其他面食:										
1902.3010	---米粉干〔101 方便米、粉,102 米粉,103 其他粮食制品,104 其他不含馅速冻粮食制品〕	10		80	13/	9	千克	AB/	PRQS	20	
1902.3020	---粉丝〔101 粉丝,102 其他粮食制品〕	10		80	13/	13	千克	AB/	PRQS	12.5	
1902.3030	---即食或快熟面条〔101 快熟面条,102 即食面条,103 面条如挂面等,104 方便面,105 方便米、粉,106 速食通粉〕	10		80	13/	9,13	千克	AB/	RS	35	8.7/8.7
1902.3090	---其他[101 面食罐头,102 其他糕点饼干,103 面条如挂面等,104 方便面,105 方便米、粉,106 通心粉,107 即食通粉沙律,108 湿面,109 速食粮食产品,110 其他粮食制品,111 馒头,112 其他含肉速冻粮食制品,113 其他不含肉速冻粮食制品,114 其他不含馅速冻粮食制品]	10		80	13/	9,13	千克	AB/	PRQS	35	8.7/8.7
1902.4000	-古斯古斯面食〔101 其他糕点饼干,102 速食粮食产品,103 其他粮食制品〕	10		80	13/	9,13	千克	AB/	RS	12.5	
19.03	**珍粉及淀粉制成的珍粉代用品,片、粒、珠、粉或类似形状的:**										
1903.0000	珍粉及淀粉制成的珍粉代用品,片、粒、珠、粉或类似形状的〔101 其他糕点饼干,102 速食粮食产品,103 其他粮食制品,104 其他淀粉制品〕	10		80	13/	13	千克	AB/	RS	12.5	
19.04	**谷物或谷物产品经膨化或烘炒制成的食品(例如,玉米片);其他税目未列名的预煮或经其他方法制作的谷粒(玉米除外)、谷物片或经其他加工的谷粒(细粉、粗粒及粗粉除外):**										
1904.1000	-谷物或谷物产品经膨化或烘炒制成的食品[101 熟制谷物坚果炒货,102 膨化食品,103 纯麦片,104 速食粮食产品,105 其他粮食制品,106 其他纯谷物的冲调谷物制品,107 含其他原料的谷物类冲调谷物制品,108 淀粉质类冲调谷物制品]	10		80	13/	13	千克	AB/	RS	35	
1904.2000	-未烘炒谷物片制成的食品及未烘炒的谷物片与烘炒的谷物片或膨化的谷物混合制成的食品[101 其他糕点饼干,102 纯麦片,103 湿粉,104 速食粮食产品,105 其他粮食制品,106 其他含肉速冻粮食制品,107 其他不含肉速冻粮食制品,108 其他不含馅速冻粮食制品,109 其他纯谷物的冲调谷物制品,110 含其他原料的谷物类冲调谷物制品,111 淀粉质类冲调谷物制品]	10		80	13/	13	千克	AB/	PRQS	35	
1904.3000	-碾碎的干小麦〔101 食用小麦粉,102 其他粮食制品〕	10		80	13/	13	千克	AB/	PRQS	20	
1904.9000	-其他[T2]	10		80	13/	13	千克	AB/	PRQS	35	
19.05	**面包、糕点、饼干及其他烘焙糕饼,不论是否含可可;圣餐饼、装药空囊、封缄、糯米纸及类似制品:**										
1905.1000	-黑麦脆面包片〔999〕	10		80	13/	13	千克	AB/	RS	12.5	
1905.2000	-姜饼及类似品〔101 姜饼,102 姜饼类似品〕	10		80	13/	13	千克	AB/	RS	12.5	
	-甜饼干;华夫饼及圣餐饼:										
1905.3100	--甜饼干〔101 饼干,102 婴幼儿谷类辅助食品〕	10		80	13/	13	千克	AB/	RS	35	8.2/8.2
1905.3200	--华夫饼及圣餐饼〔101 华夫饼干,102 圣餐饼,103 饼干〕	10		80	13/	13	千克	AB/	RS	35	8.2/8.2
1905.4000	-面包干、吐司及类似的烤面包〔999〕	10		80	13/	13	千克	AB/	RS	35	
1905.9000	-其他〔101 未列出的其他熟制坚果炒货,103 月饼,104 蛋糕,105 其他糕点,106 饼干,109 面包,110 膨化食品,111 其他糕点饼干,112 发酵豆制品,113 其他含肉速冻粮食制品,114 其他不含肉速冻粮食制品,115 其他不含馅速冻粮食制品,116 其他淀粉制品,117 非发酵豆制品,118 婴幼儿谷类辅助食品〕	10		80	13/	13	千克	AB/	RS	35	8.6/8.6

协定税率 %								RCEP		特惠税率 %			Article Description
东/冰/格	巴基斯坦	韩国	瑞士 上/下	哥/秘/柬	澳/毛	新西/坡/智	中国港/澳/台	东盟及马来/澳/韩	日/新	亚太2国	老/柬/缅	98/97/95	
0//0	0	7	1.5/1.5	0/0/0	0/0	0/0/0	0/0/	14/14.3/14	14.1/14.3			0/0/0	Other raw pasta, without stuffing or preparation
0/0/0	12	7		0/0/0	0/0	0/0/0	0/0/	14/14.3/14	14.1/14.3			0/0/0	-Stuffed pasta, whether or not cooked or otherwise prepared
													-Other pasta:
0/0/0	12	3	1.5/1.5	0/0/0	0/0	0/0/0	0/0/	0/0/13.5	13.6/0			0/0/0	---Rice vermicelli, cooked
0/0/0	12	3	1.5/1.5	0/0/0	0/0	0/0/0	0/0/	0/0/13.5	13.6/0			0/0/0	---Bean vermicelli, cooked
0/0/0	7.5	9	1.5/1.5	0/0/0	0/0	0/0/0	0/0/	14.3/14.3/	/14.3			0/0/0	---Instant noodle
0/0/0	7.5	7		0/0/0	0/0	0/0/0	0/0/	14/14.3/14	14.1/14.3			0/0/0	---Other
0/0/0		15	2.5/2.5	0/0/0	0/15	0/0/0	0/0/	23.8/23.8/23.8	23.8/23.8			0/0/0	-Couscous
													Tapioca and substitutes therefor prepared from starch, in the form of flakes, grains, pearls, siftings or in similar forms:
0/0/0	12	3	1.5/1.5	0/0/0	0/0	0/0/0	0/0/	0/0/13.5	13.6/0			0/0/0	Tapioca and substitutes therefor prepared from starch, in the form of flakes, grains, pearls, siftings or in similar forms
													Prepared foods obtained by the swelling or roasting of cereals or cereal products (for example, corn flakes); cereals (other than maize (corn)) in grain form or in the form of flakes or other worked grains (except flour, groats and meal), precooked or otherwise prepared, not elsewhere specified or included:
0/0/0		15	6.3/6.3	0/0/0	0/15	0/0/0	0/0/	23.8/23.8/	23.8/23.8			0/0/0	-Prepared foods obtained by the swelling or roasting of cereals or cereal products
0/0/0		18	0/0	0/4/0	0/18	0/0/0	0/0/	28.5/28.5/28.5	/28.5			0/0/	-Prepared foods obtained from unroasted cereal flakes or from mixtures of unroasted cereal flakes and roasted cereal flakes or swelled cereals
0/0/0		18		0/4/0	0/18	0/0/0	0/0/	28.5/28.5/28.5	28.6/28.5			0/0/	-Bulgur wheat
0/0/0		18	0/0	0/0/0	0/18	0/0/0	0/0/	28.5/28.5/	28.6/28.5			0/0/	-Other
													Bread, pastry, cakes, biscuits and other bakers' wares, whether or not containing cocoa; communion wafers, empty cachets of a kind suitable for pharmaceutical use, sealing wafers, rice paper and similar products:
0/0/0		9.3	2/2	0/0/0	0/0	0/0/0	0/0/	18/18/18	18.8/18			0/0/0	-Crispbread
0/0/0		9.3	2/2	0/0/0	0/0	0/0/0	0/0/	18/18/18	18.8/18			0/0/0	-Gingerbread and the like
													-Sweet biscuits; waffles and wafers:
0/0/0	0	7	3.8/3.8	0/0/0	0/0	0/0/0	0/0/	14/14.3/14	14.1/14.3	5		0/0/0	--Sweet biscuits
0/0/0	7.5	7	0/0	0/0/0	0/0	0/0/0	0/0/	14/14.3/14	14.1/14.3	5		0/0/0	--Waffles and wafers
0//0		9.3	2/2	0/0/0	0/0	0/0/0	0/0/	18.7/19/18.7	18.8/19			0/0/0	-Rusks, toasted bread and similar toasted products
0/0/0	0	12	2/2	0/0/0	0/0	0/0/0	0/0/	19/19/	19/19	5		0/0/0	-Other

第二十章
蔬菜、水果、坚果或植物其他部分的制品

注释：

一、本章不包括：

(一)用第七章、第八章或第十一章所列方法制作或保藏的蔬菜、水果或坚果；

(二)植物油、脂(第十五章)；

(三)按重量计含香肠、肉、食用杂碎、动物血、昆虫、鱼、甲壳动物、软体动物、其他水生无脊椎动物及其混合物超过20%的食品(第十六章)；

(四)税目19.05的烘焙糕饼及其他制品；

(五)税目21.04的均化混合食品。

二、税目20.07及20.08不包括制成糖食的果冻、果膏、糖衣杏仁或类似品(税目17.04)及巧克力糖食(税目18.06)。

三、税目20.01、20.04及20.05仅酌情包括用本章注释一(一)以外的方法制作或保藏的第七章或税目11.05、11.06的产品(第八章产品的细粉、粗粉除外)。

四、干重量在7%及以上的番茄汁归入税目20.02。

五、税目20.07所称"烹煮制成的"，是指在常压或减压下，通过减少水分或其他方法增加产品粘稠度的热处理制得的。

六、税目20.09所称"未发酵及未加酒精的水果汁"，是指按容量计酒精浓度(标准见第二十二章注释二)不超过0.5%的水果汁。

子目注释：

一、子目2005.10所称"均化蔬菜"，是指蔬菜经精细均化制成适合供婴幼儿食用或营养用的零售包装食品(每件净重不超过250克)。为了调味、保藏或其他目的，均化蔬菜中可以加入少量其他配料，还可以含有少量可见的蔬菜粒。归类时，子目2005.10优先于税目20.05的其他子目。

二、子目2007.10所称"均化食品"，是指果实经精细均化制成适合供婴幼儿食用或营养用的零售包装食品(每件净重不超过250克)。为了调味、保藏或其他目的，均化食品中可以加入少量其他配料，还可以含有少量可见的果粒。归类时，子目2007.10优先于税目20.07的其他子目。

三、子目2009.12、2009.21、2009.31、2009.41、2009.61及2009.71所称"白利糖度值"，是指在20℃时直接从白利糖度计读取的度数或从折射计读取的以蔗糖百分比含量计的折射率，在其他温度下读取的数值应折算为20℃时的折射率。

税则号列	货品名称〔CIQ扩展编码及品名－T2表示见附表2〕	最惠(%)	暂定税率	普通	增值/消费	出口退税	计量单位	监管条件/特殊证件	检验检疫	对美关税	亚太上/下
20.01	蔬菜、水果、坚果及植物的其他食用部分，用醋或醋酸制作或保藏的：										
2001.1000	-黄瓜及小黄瓜〔999〕	5		70	13/	9,13	千克	AB/	RS	30	
	-其他：										
2001.9010	---大蒜										
2001.9010 10	用醋或醋酸腌制的大蒜头、大蒜瓣(无论是否加糖或去皮)〔999〕	5		70	13/	9,13	千克	AB/	RS	10	
2001.9010 90	用醋或醋酸腌制的其他大蒜(不含蒜头、蒜瓣，无论是否加糖或去皮)〔999〕	5		70	13/	9,13	千克	AB/	RS	10	
2001.9090	---其他										
2001.9090 10	用醋或醋酸制作或保藏的松茸〔999〕	5		70	13/	9	千克	ABE/	RS	30	
2001.9090 20	用醋或醋酸制作或保藏的酸竹笋〔999〕	5		70	13/	9	千克	ABE/	RS	30	
2001.9090 30	用醋或醋酸制作或保藏的芦荟〔999〕	5		70	13/	9	千克	ABFE/	RS	30	
2001.9090 40	用醋或醋酸制作或保藏的仙人掌植物〔999〕	5		70	13/	9	千克	ABFE/	RS	30	
2001.9090 50	用醋或醋酸制作或保藏的莼菜〔999〕	5		70	13/	9	千克	ABE/	RS	30	
2001.9090 90	用醋制作的其他果、菜及食用植物(包括用醋酸制作或保藏的)〔101腌渍蘑菇，102腌渍其他未列出蔬菜〕	5		70	13/	9,13	千克	AB/	RS	30	

Chapter 20
Preparations of vegetables, fruit, nuts or other parts of plants

Notes:

1. This Chapter does not cover:
   (a) Vegetables, fruit or nuts, prepared or preserved by the processes specified in Chapter 7,8 or 11;
   (b) Vegetable fats and oils (Chapter 15);
   (c) Food preparations containing more than 20% by weight of sausage, meat, meat offal, blood, insects, fish or crustaceans, molluscs or other aquatic invertebrates, or any combination thereof (Chapter 16);
   (d) Bakers' wares and other products of heading No. 19.05;
   (e) Homogenized composite food preparations of heading No. 21.04.
2. Headings No. 20.07 and 20.08 do not apply to fruit jellies, fruit pastes, sugar-coated almonds or the like in the form of sugar confectionery (heading No. 17.04) or chocolate confectionery (heading No. 18.06).
3. Headings No. 20.01, 20.04 and 20.05 cover, as the case may be, only those products of Chapter 7 or of heading No. 11.05 or 11.06 (other than flour, meal and powder of the products of Chapter 8) which have been prepared or preserved by processes other than those referred to in Note 1 (a).
4. Tomato juice the dry weight content of which is 7% or more, is to be classified in heading No. 20.02.

5. For the purposes of heading No. 20.07, the expression "obtained by cooking" means obtained by heat treatment at atmospheric pressure or under reduced pressure to increase the viscosity of a product through reduction of water content or other means.
6. For the purposes of heading No. 20.09, the expression "juices, unfermented and not containing added spirit" means juices of an alcoholic strength by volume (see Note 2 to Chapter 22) not exceeding 0.5% vol.

Subheading Notes:

1. For the purposes of subheading No. 2005.10, the expression "homogenized vegetables" means preparations of vegetables, finely homogenized, put up for retail sale Suitable for infants to eat or for dietetic purposes, in containers of a net weight content not exceeding 250g. For the application of this definition no account is to be taken of small quantities of any ingredients which may have been added to the preparation for seasoning, preparation or other purposes. These preparations may contain a small quantity of visible pieces of vegetables. Subheading No. 2005.10 takes precedence over all other subheadings of heading No. 20.05.
2. For the purposes of subheading No. 2007.10, the expression "homogenized preparations" means preparations of fruit, finely homogenized, put up for retail sale Suitable for infants to eat or for dietetic purposes, in containers of a net weight content not exceeding 250g. For the application of this definition no account is to be taken of small quantities of any ingredients which may have been added to the preparation for seasoning, preservation or other purposes. These preparations may contain a small quantity of visible pieces of fruit. Subheading No. 2007.10 takes precedence over all other subheadings of heading No. 20.07.
3. For the purposes of subheadings No. 2009.12, 2009.21, 2009.31, 2009.41, 2009.61 and 2009.71, the expression "Brix value" means the direct reading of degrees Brix obtained from a Brix hydrometer or of refractive index expressed in terms of percentage sucrose content obtained from a refractometer, at a temperature of 20℃ or corrected for 20℃ if the reading is made at a different temperature.

协定税率 %								RCEP		特惠税率 %			Article Description
东/冰/格	巴基斯坦	韩国	瑞士 上/下	哥/秘/柬	澳/毛	新西/坡/智	中国港/澳/台	东盟及马来/澳/韩	日/新	亚太2国	老/柬/缅	98/97/95	
													Vegetagbles, fruit, nuts and other edible parts of plants, prepared or preserved by vinegar or acetic acid:
0/0/0	17.5	15	2.5/2.5	0/0/0	0/15	0/0/0	0/0/	23.8/23.8/23.8	23.8/23.8			0/0/0	-Cucumbers and gherkins
													-Other:
													---Garlic
0/0/0	20	15	2.5/2.5	0/0/0	0/15	0/0/0	0/0/	23.8/23.8/23.8	23.8/23.8	2.5		0/0/0	Garlic bulbs, garlic cloves, prepared by vinegar or acetic acid (whether or not added sugars or skinned)
0/0/0	20	15	2.5/2.5	0/0/0	0/15	0/0/0	0/0/	23.8/23.8/23.8	23.8/23.8	2.5		0/0/0	Other garlic prepared by vinegar or acetic acid (whether or not added sugars or skinned other than garlic bulbs, galic cloves)
													---Other
0/0/0		15	2.5/2.5	0/0/0	0/15	0/0/0	0/0/	23.8/23.8/23.8	23.8/23.8	2.5		0/0/0	Matsutske, prepared or preserved by vinegar or acetic acid
0/0/0		15	2.5/2.5	0/0/0	0/15	0/0/0	0/0/	23.8/23.8/23.8	23.8/23.8	2.5		0/0/0	Acidosasa chinensis shoots, prepared or preserved by vinegar or acetic acid
0/0/0		15	2.5/2.5	0/0/0	0/15	0/0/0	0/0/	23.8/23.8/23.8	23.8/23.8	2.5		0/0/0	Aloe, prepared or preserved by vinegar or acetic acid
0/0/0		15	2.5/2.5	0/0/0	0/15	0/0/0	0/0/	23.8/23.8/23.8	23.8/23.8	2.5		0/0/0	Cactus, prepared or preserved by vinegar or acetic acid
0/0/0		15	2.5/2.5	0/0/0	0/15	0/0/0	0/0/	23.8/23.8/23.8	23.8/23.8	2.5		0/0/0	Water shield, prepared or preserved by vinegar or acetic acid
0/0/0		15	2.5/2.5	0/0/0	0/15	0/0/0	0/0/	23.8/23.8/23.8	23.8/23.8	2.5		0/0/0	Vegetagbles, fruit, nuts and other edible parts of plants, prepared or preserved by vinegar or acetic acid

税则号列	货品名称〔CIQ扩展编码及品名—T2表示见附表2〕	最惠(%)	暂定税率	普通	增值/消费	出口退税	计量单位	监管条件/特殊证件	检验检疫	对美关税	亚太上/下
20.02	**番茄,用醋或醋酸以外的其他方法制作或保藏的:**										
	-番茄,整个或切片:										
2002.1010	---罐头〔999〕	5		80	13/	13	千克	AB/	RS	30	
2002.1090	---其他〔101 冷冻番茄,102 脱水番茄〕	5		70	13/	9,13	千克	AB/	PRQ	10	
	-其他:										
	---番茄酱罐头:										
2002.9011	----重量不超过5千克的番茄酱罐头〔999〕	5		80	13/	13	千克	AB/	RS	17.5	
2002.9019	----重量超过5千克的番茄酱罐头〔999〕	5		80	13/	13	千克	AB/	RS	17.5	
2002.9090	---其他〔101 冷冻番茄,102 脱水番茄〕	5		70	13/	9,13	千克	AB/	PRQS	15	
20.03	**蘑菇及块菌,用醋或醋酸以外的其他方法制作或保藏的:**										
	-伞菌属蘑菇:										
	---罐头:										
2003.1011	----小白蘑菇〔999〕	5		90	13/	13	千克	AB/	RS	30	
2003.1019	----其他〔101 草菇罐头,102 金针菇罐头,103 其他食用菌罐头〕	5		90	13/	13	千克	AB/	RS	10	
2003.1090	---其他〔101 冷冻其他伞菌属蘑菇,102 脱水其他伞菌属蘑菇,103 腌渍蘑菇,104 腌渍其他伞菌属蘑菇〕	5		90	13/	9,13	千克	AB/	RS	10	
	-其他:										
2003.9010	---罐头										
2003.9010 10	非用醋制作的香菇罐头[用醋或醋酸以外其他方法制作或保藏的(非伞菌属蘑菇)]〔999〕	5		90	13/	13	千克	AB/	RS	30	
2003.9010 20	非用醋制作的松茸罐头(用醋或醋酸以外其他方法制作或保藏的)〔999〕	5		90	13/	13	千克	ABE/	RS	30	
2003.9010 90	非用醋制作的其他蘑菇罐头[用醋或醋酸以外其他方法制作或保藏的(非伞菌属蘑菇)]〔101 滑子蘑罐头,102 猴头菇罐头,103 鸡油菌罐头,104 牛肝菌罐头,105 姬菇罐头,106 鲍鱼菇罐头,107 白灵菇罐头,108 平菇罐头,109 茶树菇罐头,110 凤尾菇罐头,111 灰树花菇罐头,112 黑木耳罐头,113 球盖菇罐头,114 鸡腿菇罐头,115 松茸罐头,116 什锦菇罐头,117 其他蘑菇类罐头,118 其他木耳类罐头,119 其他食用菌罐头〕	5		90	13/	13	千克	AB/	RS	30	
2003.9090	---其他										
2003.9090 10	非用醋制作的其他香菇[用醋或醋酸以外其他方法制作或保藏的(非伞菌属蘑菇)]〔101 冷冻香菇,102 脱水香菇,103 腌渍香菇〕	5		90	13/	9,13	千克	AB/	PRQS	10	
2003.9090 20	非用醋制作的其他松茸(用醋或醋酸以外其他方法制作或保藏的)〔101 冷冻松茸,102 脱水松茸,103 腌渍松茸〕	5		90	13/	9,13	千克	ABE/	PRQS	10	
2003.9090 90	非用醋制作的其他蘑菇[用醋或醋酸以外其他方法制作或保藏的(非伞菌属蘑菇)]〔101 冷冻其他非伞菌属蘑菇,102 脱水其他非伞菌属蘑菇,103 腌渍其他非伞菌属蘑菇〕	5		90	13/	9,13	千克	AB/	PRQS	10	
20.04	**其他冷冻蔬菜,用醋或醋酸以外的其他方法制作或保藏的,但税目20.06的产品除外:**										
2004.1000	-马铃薯〔999〕	5		70	13/	9,13	千克	AB/	PRQS	15	
2004.9000	-其他蔬菜及什锦蔬菜										
2004.9000 10	非用醋制作的冷冻松茸〔999〕	5		70	13/	9,13	千克	ABE/	PRQS	30	
2004.9000 20	非用醋制作的冷冻酸竹笋〔999〕	5		70	13/	9,13	千克	ABE/	PRQS	30	
2004.9000 30	非用醋制作的冷冻芦荟〔999〕	5		70	13/	9,13	千克	ABFE/	PRQS	30	
2004.9000 40	非用醋制作的冷冻仙人掌植物〔999〕	5		70	13/	9,13	千克	ABFE/	PRQS	30	
2004.9000 90	非用醋制作的其他冷冻蔬菜(税目20.06的货品除外)〔101 其它冷冻植物产品,102 其他含肉速冻粮食制品,103 其他不含肉速冻粮食制品,104 冷冻其他未列出蔬菜〕	5		70	13/	9,13	千克	AB/	PRQS	30	
20.05	**其他未冷冻蔬菜,用醋或醋酸以外的其他方法制作或保藏的,但税目20.06的产品除外:**										
2005.1000	-均化蔬菜〔999〕	5		70	13/	13	千克	AB/	PRQS	15	
2005.2000	-马铃薯〔999〕	5		70	13/	9,13	千克	AB/	PRQS	30	
2005.4000	-豌豆〔101 青豆罐头,102 即食豌豆沙律,103 熟制豌豆炒货,104 发酵豆制品,105 非发酵豆制品〕	5		70	13/	9,13	千克	AB/	PRQS	30	
	-豇豆属及菜豆属:										

协定税率 %								RCEP		特惠税率 %			Article Description
东/冰/格	巴基斯坦	韩国	瑞士 上/下	哥/秘/柬	澳/毛	新西/坡/智	中国港/澳/台	东盟及马来/澳/韩	日/新	亚太2国	老/柬/缅	98/97/95	
													Tomatoes prepared or preserved otherwise than by vinegar or acetic acid:
													-Tomatoes, whole or in pieces:
0/0/0	15.2	8.8	1.9/1.9	0/0/0	0/0	0/0/0	0/0/	17.1/17.1/17.1	17.8/17.1			0/0/0	---In airtight containers
0/0/0	20	15	2.5/2.5	0/0/0	0/15	0/0/0	0/0/	23.8/23.8/23.8	23.8/23.8			0/0/0	---Other
													-Other:
													---Tomato paste, in airtight containers:
0/0/0	16	9.3	2/2	0/0/0	0/0	0/0/0	0/0/	18/18/18	18.8/18			0/0/0	----Weighing not more than 5kg
0/0/0	16	4	2/2	0/0/0	0/0	0/0/0	0/0/	0/0/18	18.2/0			0/0/0	----Weighing more than 5kg
0/0/0	11.5	8.4	1.8/1.8	0/0/0	0/0	0/0/0	0/0/	16.2/16.2/16.2	16.9/16.2			0/0/0	---Other
													Mushrooms and truffles, prepared or preserved otherwise than by vinegar or acetic acid:
													-Mushrooms of the genus Agaricus:
													---In airtight containers:
0/0/0		5	2.5/2.5	0/0/0	0/15	0/0/0	0/0/	0/0/22.5	22.7/0			0/0/0	----Small white agaric
0/0/0		5	2.5/2.5	0/0/0	0/15	0/0/0	0/0/	0/0/22.5	22.7/0			0/0/0	----Other
0/0/0		5	2.5/2.5	0/0/0	0/15	0/0/0	0/0/	0/0/22.5	22.7/0			0/0/0	---Other
													-Other:
													---In airtight containers
0/0/0		5	2.5/2.5	0/0/0	0/15	0/0/0	0/0/	0/0/22.5	22.7/0			0/0/0	Shiitake in airtight continiers, not prepared by vinegar [prepared or preserved otherwise than by vinegar or acetic(not mushrooms of the genera agaricus)]
0/0/0		5	2.5/2.5	0/0/0	0/15	0/0/0	0/0/	0/0/22.5	22.7/0			0/0/0	Matsutske in airtight continiers, not prepared by vinegar [prepared or preserved otherwise than by vinegar or acetic (not mushrooms of the genera agaricus)]
0/0/0		5	2.5/2.5	0/0/0	0/15	0/0/0	0/0/	0/0/22.5	22.7/0			0/0/0	Other mushrooms in airtight continiers, not prepared by vinegar [prepared or preserved otherwise than by vinegar or acetic (not mushrooms of the genera agaricus)]
													---Other
0/0/0		5	2.5/2.5	0/0/0	0/15	0/0/0	0/0/	0/0/22.5	22.7/0			0/0/0	Other Matsutske mushroom, prepared or preserved otherwise than by vinegar(not mushrooms of the genera agaricus)
0/0/0		5	2.5/2.5	0/0/0	0/15	0/0/0	0/0/	0/0/22.5	22.7/0			0/0/0	Other sungmo, not prepared by vinegar (prepared or preserved otherwise than by vinegar or acetic)
0/0/0		5	2.5/2.5	0/0/0	0/15	0/0/0	0/0/	0/0/22.5	22.7/0			0/0/0	Other mushrooms, not prepared by vinegar or [prepared or preserved otherwise than by vinegar or acetic(not mushrooms of the genera agaricus)]
													Other Frozen vegetables prepared or preserved otherwise than by vinegar or acetic acid, other than products of heading No. 20.06:
0//0	4.6	2.6	1.3/1.3	0/0/0	0/0	0/0/0	0/0/	0/0/11.7	11.8/0			0/0/0	-Potatoes
													-Other vegetables and mixtures of vegetables
0/0/0		5	2.5/2.5	0/0/0	0/15	0/0/0	0/0/	0/0/22.5	22.7/0			0/0/0	Sungmo, not prepared by vinegar or acetic acid, frozen
0/0/0		5	2.5/2.5	0/0/0	0/15	0/0/0	0/0/	0/0/22.5	22.7/0			0/0/0	Acidosasa chinensis shoots, frozen, not prepared by vinegar
0/0/0		5	2.5/2.5	0/0/0	0/15	0/0/0	0/0/	0/0/22.5	22.7/0			0/0/0	Aloe, frozen, not prepared by vinegar
0/0/0		5	2.5/2.5	0/0/0	0/15	0/0/0	0/0/	0/0/22.5	22.7/0			0/0/0	Cactus, frozen, not prepared by vinegar
0/0/0		5	2.5/2.5	0/0/0	0/15	0/0/0	0/0/	0/0/22.5	22.7/0			0/0/0	Other vegetables, not prepared by vinegar(other than products of heading No. 2006)
													Other vegetables prepared or preserved otherwise than by vinegar or acetic acid, not frozen, other than products of heading No. 20.06:
0/0/0		5	2.5/2.5	0/0/0	0/15	0/0/0	0/0/	0/0/22.5	22.7/0			0/0/0	-Homogenized vegetables
0//0	0	3	1.5/1.5	0/0/0	0/0	0/0/0	0/0/	0/0/13.5	13.6/0			0/0/0	-Potatoes
0/0/0		5	2.5/2.5	0/0/0	0/15	0/0/0	0/0/	0/0/22.5	22.7/0			0/0/0	-Peas (*Pisum sativum*)
													-Beans (*Vigna spp.*, *Phaseolus spp.*):

税则号列	货品名称〔CIQ 扩展编码及品名—T2 表示见附表 2〕	最惠(%)	暂定税率	普通	增值/消费	出口退税	计量单位	监管条件/特殊证件	检验检疫	对美关税	亚太上/下
	--脱荚的：										
	---罐头：										
2005.5111	----赤豆馅〔101 红豆罐头，102 豆类罐头〕	5		80	13/	13	千克	AB/	RS	10	
2005.5119	----其他〔999〕	5		80	13/	13	千克	AB/	RS	30	
	---其他：										
2005.5191	----赤豆馅〔101 红豆馅，102 其他粮食制品〕	5		70	13/	13	千克	AB/	PRQS	10	
2005.5199	----其他〔101 冷冻脱荚豇豆，102 冷冻脱荚菜豆〕	5		70	13/	9,13	千克	AB/	PRQS	10	
	--其他：										
2005.5910	---罐头〔999〕	5		80	13/	13	千克	AB/	RS	30	
2005.5990	---其他〔101 腌渍豇豆，102 腌渍菜豆〕	5		70	13/	9,13	千克	AB/	PRQS	10	
	-芦笋：										
2005.6010	---罐头〔999〕	5		80	13/	13	千克	AB/	RS		
2005.6090	---其他〔101 冷冻芦笋，102 脱水芦笋，103 腌渍芦笋〕	5		70	13/	9,13	千克	AB/	PRQS	10	
2005.7000	-油橄榄〔999〕	5		70	13/	9,13	千克	AB/	PRQS	30	
2005.8000	-甜玉米〔101〕	5		80	13/	9,13	千克	AB/	PRQS	30	
	-其他蔬菜及什锦蔬菜：										
	--竹笋：										
2005.9110	---竹笋罐头										
2005.9110 10	非用醋制作的酸竹笋罐头〔999〕	5		80	13/	13	千克	ABE/	RS	10	
2005.9110 90	非用醋制作的其他竹笋罐头〔999〕	5		80	13/	13	千克	AB/	RS	10	
2005.9190	---其他										
2005.9190 10	非用醋制作的酸竹笋〔999〕	5		70	13/	9,13	千克	ABE/	PRQS	10	
2005.9190 90	非用醋制作的其他竹笋〔101 冷冻竹笋，102 腌渍竹笋，103 脱水竹笋〕	5		70	13/	9,13	千克	AB/	PRQS	10	
	--其他：										
2005.9920	---蚕豆罐头〔999〕	5		80	13/	13	千克	AB/	RS	10	
2005.9940	---榨菜〔999〕	5		70	13/	9,13	千克	AB/	RS	10	
2005.9950	---咸蕨菜〔999〕	5		70	13/	9,13	千克	AB/	RS	10	
2005.9960	---咸蕌头〔999〕	5		70	13/	9,13	千克	AB/	RS	10	
2005.9970	---蒜制品〔999〕	5		70	13/	9,13	千克	AB/	RS	30	
	---其他：										
2005.9991	----罐头[T2]	5		70	13/	13	千克	AB/	RS	30	
2005.9999	----其他										
2005.9999 10	非用醋制作的仙人掌〔101 冷冻仙人掌，102 脱水仙人掌，103 腌渍仙人掌〕	5		70	13/	9,13	千克	ABFE/	PRQS	30	
2005.9999 20	非用醋制作的芦荟〔101 冷冻芦荟，102 脱水芦荟，103 腌渍芦荟〕	5		70	13/	9,13	千克	ABFE/	PRQS	30	
2005.9999 90	非用醋制作的其他蔬菜及什锦蔬菜〔999〕	5		70	13/	9,13	千克	AB/	PRQS	30	
20.06	**糖渍蔬菜、水果、坚果、果皮及植物的其他部分(沥干、糖渍或裹糖的)：**										
2006.0010	---蜜枣〔999〕	5		90	13/	13	千克	AB/	RS		
2006.0020	---橄榄〔999〕	5		90	13/	13	千克	AB/	RS	30	
2006.0090	---其他										
2006.0090 10	糖渍制松茸〔999〕	5		90	13/	13	千克	ABE/	RS	30	
2006.0090 90	其他糖渍蔬菜、水果、坚果、果皮(包括糖渍植物的其他部分)〔101 红豆馅，102 果脯，103 话梅，104 其他蜜饯〕	5		90	13/	13	千克	AB/	RS	30	
20.07	**烹煮的果酱、果冻、柑橘酱、果泥及果膏，不论是否加糖或其他甜物质：**										
2007.1000	-均化食品〔201：非罐头工艺生产的果酱；999：果酱罐头〕	5		80	13/	13	千克	AB/	RS	27.5	
	-其他：										
2007.9100	--柑橘属水果的〔201：非罐头工艺生产的果酱；999：果酱罐头〕	5		80	13/	13	千克	AB/	RS	30	
	--其他：										
2007.9910	---罐头〔101 什锦果酱罐头，102 杏酱罐头，103 菠萝酱罐头，104 苹果酱罐头，105 西瓜酱罐头，106 猕猴桃酱罐头，107 其他果酱罐头，108 果冻罐头，109 婴幼儿罐装辅助食品〕	5		80	13/	13	千克	AB/	RS	30	
2007.9990	---其他〔201：非罐头工艺生产的果酱；999：果脯〕	5		80	13/	13	千克	AB/	RS	30	

协定税率 %								RCEP		特惠税率 %			Article Description
东/冰/格	巴基斯坦	韩国	瑞士 上/下	哥/秘/柬	澳/毛	新西/坡/智	中国港/澳/台	东盟及马来/澳/韩	日/新	亚太2国	老/柬/缅	98/97/95	
													--Beans, shelled:
													---In airtight containers:
0/0/0		5	2.5/2.5	0/0/0	0/15	0/0/0	0/0/	0/0/22.5	22.7/0			0/0/0	----Red bean paste
0/0/0		15	2.5/2.5	0/0/0	0/15	0/0/0	0/0/	23.8/23.8/23.8	23.8/23.8			0/0/0	----Other
													---Other:
0/0/0		5	2.5/2.5	0/0/0	0/15	0/0/0	0/0/	0/0/22.5	22.7/0			0/0/0	----Red bean paste
0//0		15	2.5/2.5	0/0/0	0/15	0/0/0	0/0/	23.8/23.8/23.8	23.8/23.8			0/0/0	----Other
													--Other:
0//0		5	2.5/2.5	0/0/0	0/15	0/0/0	0/0/	0/0/22.5	22.7/0			0/0/0	---In airtight containers
0//0		5	2.5/2.5	0/0/0	0/15	0/0/0	0/0/	0/0/22.5	22.7/0			0/0/0	---Other
													-Asparagus:
0//0		5	2.5/2.5	0/0/0	0/15	0/0/0	0/0/	0/0/22.5	22.7/0			0/0/0	---In airtight containers
0/0/0		5	2.5/2.5	0/0/0	0/15	0/0/0	0/0/	0/0/22.5	22.7/0			0/0/0	---Other
0/0/0	3.5	2	0/0	0/0/0	0/0	0/0/0	0/0/	0/0/9	9.1/0			0/0/0	-Olives
0/0/0	3.5	2	0/0	0/0/0	0/0	0/0/0	0/0/	0/0/9	9.1/0			0/0/0	-Sweet corn (*Zea mays var. saccharata*)
													-Other vegetables and mixtures of vegetables:
													--Bamboo shoots:
													---Bamboo shoots in airtight containers
0/0/0		5	2.5/2.5	0/0/0	0/15	0/0/0	0/0/	0/0/22.5	22.7/0			0/0/0	Acidosasa chinensis shoots in airtight containers, not preserved by vinegar
0/0/0		5	2.5/2.5	0/0/0	0/15	0/0/0	0/0/	0/0/22.5	22.7/0			0/0/0	Other bamboo shoots in airtight containers, not preserved by vinegar
													---Other
0/0/0		5	2.5/2.5	0/0/0	0/15	0/0/0	0/0/	0/0/22.5	22.7/0			0/0/0	Acidosasa chinensis shoots, not preserved by vinegar
0/0/0		5	2.5/2.5	0/0/0	0/15	0/0/0	0/0/	0/0/22.5	22.7/0			0/0/0	Other bamboo shoots, not prepared or preserved by vinegar
													--Other:
0/0/0	17.5	5	2.5/2.5	0/0/0	0/15	0/0/0	0/0/	0/0/22.5	22.7/0			0/0/0	---Broad beans, in airtight containers
0/0/0	17.5	5	2.5/2.5	0/0/0	0/15	0/0/0	0/0/	0/0/22.5	22.7/0			0/0/0	---Hot pickled mustard tubers
0/0/0	17.5	5	2.5/2.5	0/0/0	0/15	0/0/0	0/0/	0/0/22.5	22.7/0			0/0/0	---Chueh tsai (fiddle-head), salted
0/0/0	17.5	5	2.5/2.5	0/0/0	0/15	0/0/0	0/0/	0/0/22.5	22.7/0			0/0/0	---Scallion, salted
0/0/0		15	5/5	0/0/0	0/15	0/0/0	0/0/	23.8/23.8/23.8	23.8/23.8			0/0/0	---Garlic products
													---Other:
0/0/0		15	2.5/2.5	0/0/0	0/15	0/0/0	0/0/	23.8/23.8/23.8	23.8/23.8			0/0/0	----In airtight containers
													----Other
0/0/0		15	5/5	0/0/0	0/15	0/0/0	0/0/	23.8/23.8/	/23.8			0/0/0	Cactus, not preserved by vinegar
0/0/0		15	5/5	0/0/0	0/15	0/0/0	0/0/	23.8/23.8/	/23.8			0/0/0	Aloe, not preserved by vinegar
0/0/0		15	5/5	0/0/0	0/15	0/0/0	0/0/	23.8/23.8/	/23.8			0/0/0	Other vegetables and mixtures of vegetables, not preserved by vinegar
													Vegetables, fruit, nuts, fruit-peel and other parts of plants, preserved by sugar (drained, glac or crystallized):
0/0/0		18		0/0/0	0/18	0/0/0	0/0/	28.5/28.5/28.5	28.6/28.5		//0	0/0/0	---Preserved jujubes
0/0/0		18		0/7.1/0	0/18	0/0/0	0/0/	28.5/28.5/28.5	28.6/28.5		//0	0/0/0	---Preserved olives
													---Other
0/0/0		18	0/0	0/7.1/0	0/18	0/0/0	0/0/	28.5/28.5/	/28.5		//0	0/0/0	Matsutske, preserved by sugar
0/0/0		18	0/0	0/7.1/0	0/18	0/0/0	0/0/	28.5/28.5/	/28.5		//0	0/0/0	Other vegetables, fruit, nuts, fruit-peel (including other parts of plants) preserved by sugar
													Jams, fruit jellies, marmalades, fruit or nut puree and fruit or nut pastes, being cooked preparations, whether or not containing added sugar or other sweetening matter:
0/0/0		18	0/0	0/7.1/0	0/18	0/0/0	0/0/	28.5/28.5/28.5	28.6/28.5			0/0/	-Homogenized preparations
													-Other:
0/0/0		18	0/0	0/0/0	0/18	0/0/0	0/0/	28.5/28.5/28.5	28.6/28.5		//0	0/0/0	--Citrus fruit
													--Other:
0/0/0	0	0	0/0	0/0/0	0/0	0//0	0/0/	0/0/0	0/0	2.5		0/0/0	---In airtight containers
0/0/0	0	0	0/0	1/0/0	0/0	0//0	0/0/	0/0/0	4.5/0	2.5		0/0/0	---Other

税则号列	货品名称〔CIQ扩展编码及品名—T2表示见附表2〕	最惠(%)	暂定税率	普通	增值/消费	出口退税	计量单位	监管条件/特殊证件	检验检疫	对美关税	亚太上/下
20.08	**用其他方法制作或保藏的其他税目未列名水果、坚果及植物的其他食用部分,不论是否加酒、加糖或其他甜物质:**										
	-坚果、花生及其他子仁,不论是否混合:										
	--花生:										
2008.1110	---花生米罐头〔999〕	5		90	13/	13	千克	AB/	RS	27.5	
2008.1120	---烘焙花生〔999〕	5		80	13/	13	千克	AB/	PRQS	20	
2008.1130	---花生酱〔999〕	5		90	13/	13	千克	AB/	RS	20	
2008.1190	---其他〔101 熟制,102 花生罐头〕	5		80	13/	9,13	千克	AB/	PRQS	30	
	--其他,包括什锦坚果及其他子仁:										
2008.1910	---核桃仁罐头〔999〕	5		90	13/	13	千克	AB/	RS	7.5	2.5/2.5
2008.1920	---其他果仁罐头〔999〕	5		90	13/	13	千克	AB/	RS	15	2.5/2.5
	---其他:										
2008.1991	----栗仁〔999〕	5		80	13/	9,13	千克	AB/	PRQS	7.5	2.5/2.5
2008.1992	----芝麻〔101 芝麻罐头,102 即食芝麻沙律,103 熟制芝麻炒货,104 芝麻酱〕	5		80	13/	9,13	千克	AB/	PRQS	7.5	2.5/2.5
2008.1999	----其他										
2008.1999 10	其他方法制作保藏的红松子仁(用醋或醋酸以外其他方法制作或保藏的)〔101 熟制红松子仁,102 其他红松子仁炒货〕	5		80	13/	0	千克	ABE/	PRQS	30	2.5/2.5
2008.1999 90	未列名制作或保藏坚果及其他子仁(用醋或醋酸以外其他方法制作或保藏的)[101:杏仁罐头;102:银杏罐头;103:板栗罐头;104:腰果罐头;105:其他坚果罐头; 106:熟制杏仁;107:熟制开心果 ;108:熟制松子; 109:熟制夏威夷果; 110:熟制南瓜子; 111:熟制西瓜子; 112:未列名的即食坚果沙律; 113:未列出的其他熟制坚果炒货; 114:榛子酱; 115:扁桃仁酱; 116:其他坚果及籽类的泥(酱);]	5		80	13/	9,13	千克	AB/	PRQS	30	2.5/2.5
	-菠萝:										
2008.2010	---罐头〔101 马口铁菠萝罐头,102 玻璃瓶菠萝罐头,103 复合塑料袋菠萝罐头,104 其他材质菠萝罐头〕	5		90	13/	13	千克	AB/	RS	7.5	
2008.2090	---其他〔999〕	5		80	13/	9,13	千克	AB/	PRQ	7.5	
	-柑橘属水果:										
2008.3010	---罐头〔101 桔子罐头,102 糖水橘子罐头,103 橘子囊胞罐头,104 其他橘子罐头〕	5		90	13/	13	千克	AB/	RS	7.5	
2008.3090	---其他〔101 食品工业用浓缩液(汁、浆),999 果脯〕	5		80	13/	9,13	千克	AB/	PRQS	15	
	-梨:										
2008.4010	---罐头〔101 梨罐头,102 糖水梨罐头,103 糖水洋梨罐头,104 其他梨罐头〕	5		90	13/	13	千克	AB/	RS	7.5	
2008.4090	---其他〔999〕	5		80	13/	9,13	千克	AB/	PRQ	7.5	
2008.5000	-杏〔101 杏子罐头,102 果脯〕	5		90	13/	9,13	千克	AB/	PRQS	30	
	-樱桃:										
2008.6010	---罐头〔101 樱桃罐头,102 果脯〕	5		90	13/	13	千克	AB/	PRQS	30	
2008.6090	---其他〔101 果脯,102 其他蜜饯〕	5		90	13/	9,13	千克	AB/	PRQS	17.5	
	-桃,包括油桃:										
2008.7010	---罐头〔999〕	5		90	13/	13	千克	AB/	RS	30	
2008.7090	---其他〔101 其他桃罐头,102 果脯〕	5		80	13/	9,13	千克	AB/	PRQS	7.5	
2008.8000	-草莓〔101 果脯,102 其他蜜饯〕	5		90	13/	9,13	千克	AB/	PRQS	30	
	-其他,包括子目 2008.19 以外的什锦果实:										
2008.9100	--棕榈芯〔999〕	5		80	13/	9,13	千克	AB/	PRQS	10	
2008.9300	--蔓越橘(大果蔓越橘、小果蔓越橘)、越橘〔999〕	15		80	13/	9,13	千克	AB/	PRQS	45	
2008.9700	--什锦果实〔101 马口铁什锦水果罐头,102 玻璃瓶什锦水果罐头,103 复合塑料袋什锦水果罐头,104 其他材质什锦水果罐头,105 果脯〕	5		80	13/	9,13	千克	AB/	PRQS	30	
	--其他:										
2008.9910	---荔枝罐头〔101 马口铁荔枝罐头,102 玻璃瓶荔枝罐头,103 复合塑料袋荔枝罐头,104 其他材质荔枝罐头〕	5		90	13/	13	千克	AB/	RS	7.5	
2008.9920	---龙眼罐头〔101 马口铁龙眼罐头,102 玻璃瓶龙眼罐头,103 复合塑料袋龙眼罐头,104 其他材质龙眼罐头〕	5		80	13/	13	千克	AB/	RS	7.5	
	---海草及其他藻类制品:										
2008.9931	----调味紫菜〔101 养殖,102 野生〕	15		90	13/	13	千克	AB/	RS	40	13.8/13.8

协定税率 %								RCEP		特惠税率 %			Article Description
东/冰/格	巴基斯坦	韩国	瑞士 上/下	哥/秘/柬	澳/毛	新西/坡/智	中国港/澳/台	东盟及马来/澳/韩	日/新	亚太 2国	老/柬/缅	98/97/95	
													Fruit, nuts and other edible parts of plants, otherwise prepared or preserved, whether or not containing added sugar or other sweetening matter or spirit, not elsewhere specified or included:
													-Nuts, groundnuts and other seeds, whether or not mixed together:
													--Ground-nuts:
0/0/0		18		0//0	0/18	0/0/0	0/0/	28.5/28.5/28.5	/28.5			0/0/	---Ground-nuts kernels, in airtight containers
0/0/0		18		0//0	0/18	0/0/0	0/0/	28.5/28.5/28.5	/28.5		/0/	0/0/0	---Roasted ground-nuts
0/0/0		18		0//0	0/18	0/0/0	0/0/	28.5/28.5/28.5	28.6/28.5			0/0/	---Ground-nut butter
0/0/0		18		0//0	0/18	0/0/0	0/0/	28.5/28.5/28.5	28.6/28.5			0/0/	---Other
													--Other, including mixtures:
0/0/0	10	9.3	2/2	0/0/0	0/0	0/0/0	0/0/	18/18/18	18.8/18		0/0/	0/0/0	---Walnut meats, in airtight containers
0/0/0	3.5	2.6	1.3/1.3	0/0/0	0/0	0/0/0	0/0/	0/0/11.7	11.8/0		0/0/	0/0/0	---Other nuts, in airtight containers
													---Other:
0/0/0	3.5	2	4.2/4.2	0/0/0	0/0	0/0/0	0/0/	0/0/9	9.1/0		0/0/	0/0/0	----Chestnut seed
0//0	3.5	2	0/0	0/0/0	0/0	0/0/0	0/0/	0/0/9	9.1/0			0/0/0	----Sesame
													----Other
0/0/0	3.5	2	0/0	0/0/0	0/0	0/0/0	0/0/	0/0/9	9.1/0		0/0/	0/0/0	Korean pine-nuts, shelled,(not prepared or preserved by vinegar or acetic acid)
0/0/0	3.5	2	0/0	0/0/0	0/0	0/0/0	0/0/	0/0/9	9.1/0		0/0/	0/0/0	Nuts and other seeds,(not prepared or preserved by vinegar or acetic acid)not elsewhere specified or included
													-Pineapples:
5/0/0		3	1.5/1.5	3/0/13.5	0/0	0//0	0/0/	14.3/14.6/14.3	/14.6		0//	0/0/0	---In airtight containers
5/0/0		3	1.5/1.5	3/0/13.5	0/0	0//0	0/0/	14.3/14.6/14.3	/14.6		0//	0/0/0	---Other
													-Citrus fruit:
0/0/0		9.3	2/2	4/0/0	0/0	0/0/0	0/0/	18/19/18	18.2/19		0//	0/0/0	---In airtight containers
0/0/0		12	2/2	0/0/0	0/0	0/0/0	0/0/	19/19/	/19		0//	0/0/0	---Other
													-Pears:
0/0/0		9.3	2/2	0/0/0	0/0	0/0/0	0/0/	18/18/18	18.8/18		0//	0/0/0	---In airtight containers
0/0/0		9.3	2/2	0/0/0	0/0	0/0/0	0/0/	18/18/18	18.8/18		0//	0/0/0	Other
0/0/0		9.3	2/2	0/0/0	0/0	0/0/0	0/0/	18/18/18	18.8/18			0/0/0	-Apricots
													Cherries.
0/0/0		9.3	2/2	0/0/0	0/0	0/0/0	0/0/	18/18/18	18.8/18			0/0/0	---In airtight containers
0/0/0		9.3	2/2	0/0/0	0/0	0/0/0	0/0/	18/18/18	18.8/18			0/0/0	---Other
													-Peaches, including nectarines:
0/0/0	3.5	2	0/0	0/0/0	0/0	0/0/0	0/0/	0/0/9	9.1/0		0//	0/0/0	---In airtight containers
0/0/0		9.3	2/2	0/0/0	0/0	0/0/0	0/0/	18/18/18	18.8/18		0//	0/0/0	---Other
0/0/0	12	3	1.5/1.5	0/0/0	0/0	0/0/0	0/0/	0/0/13.5	13.6/0			0/0/0	-Strawberries
													-Other, including mixtures other than those of subheading No.2008. 19:
0/0/0	0	0	0/0	0/0/0	0/0	0//0	0/0/	0/0/0	0/0		/0/	0/0/0	--Palm hearts
0/0/0	12	3	0/0	0/0/0	0/0	0/0/0	0/0/	0/0/13.5	13.6/0		/0/	0/0/0	--Cranberry(Vaccinium macrocarpon, vaccinium oxycoccos), vaccinium vitis-idaea
0/0/0	3.5	2	0/0	0/0/0	0/0	0/0/0	0/0/	0/0/9	9.1/0		/0/	0/0/0	--Mixtures
													--Other:
0/0/0		9.3	2/2	0/0/0	0/0	0/0/0	0/0/	18/18/18	18.8/18			0/0/0	---Lychee can
5/0/0		3	1.5/1.5	0/0/0	0/0	0//0	0/0/	14.6/14.6/	/14.6		/0/	0/0/0	---Longan can
													---Seaweeds and other alga product:
0/0/0	0	9	1.5/1.5	0/0/0	0/0	0/0/0	0/0/	14.3/14.3/	/14.3		/0/	0/0/0	----Seasoned laver

税则号列	货品名称〔CIQ 扩展编码及品名—T2 表示见附表 2〕	最惠(%)	暂定税率	普通	增值/消费	出口退税	计量单位	监管条件/特殊证件	检验检疫	对美关税	亚太上/下
2008.9932	----盐腌海带〔101 养殖,102 野生〕	10		80	13/	9,13	千克	AB/	PRQS	12.5	
2008.9933	----盐腌裙带菜〔101 养殖,102 野生〕	10		80	13/	9,13	千克	AB/	PRQS	12.5	
2008.9934	----烤紫菜〔998 养殖,999 野生〕	10		80	13/	13	千克	AB/	RS	12.5	
2008.9939	----其他〔104 养殖水产制品,105 野生水产制品〕	10		80	13/	9,13	千克	AB/	PRQS	12.5	
2008.9940	---清水荸荠(马蹄)罐头〔999〕	5		80	13/	13	千克	AB/	RS	10	
2008.9990	---其他[T2]	5		80	13/	9,13	千克	AB/	PRQS	15	
20.09	**未发酵及未加酒精的水果汁或坚果汁(包括酿酒葡萄汁及椰子水)、蔬菜汁,不论是否加糖或其他甜物质:**										
	-橙汁:										
2009.1100	--冷冻的〔999〕	7.5		90	13/	13	千克	AB/	PRQS	32.5	
2009.1200	--非冷冻的,白利糖度值不超过 20 的	30		90	13/	13	千克	AB	PRQS	/55	
2009.1200 10	白利糖度值不超过 20 的非冷冻橙汁,最小独立包装净重≥180 千克(未发酵及未加酒精的,不论是否加糖或其他甜物质)〔101 可直接饮用的蔬菜果汁类饮料。102 浓缩蔬菜果汁饮料包括冷冻的,103 食品工业用浓缩液汁、浆〕	30	18	90	13/	13	千克	AB/	PRQS	43	
2009.1200 90	其他白利糖度值不超过 20 的非冷冻橙汁(未发酵及未加酒精的,不论是否加糖或其他甜物质)〔101 可直接饮用的蔬菜果汁类饮料,102 浓缩蔬菜果汁饮料(包括冷冻的),103 食品工业用浓缩液(汁、浆)〕	30		90	13/	13	千克	AB/	PRQS	55	
2009.1900	--其他	30		90	13/	13	千克	AB	RS	/40	
2009.1900 10	白利糖度值超过 20 的非冷冻橙汁,最小独立包装净重≥180 千克(未发酵及未加酒精的,不论是否加糖或其他甜物质)〔101 可直接饮用的蔬菜果汁类饮料,102 浓缩蔬菜果汁饮料(包括冷冻的),103 食品工业用浓缩液(汁、浆)〕	30	18	90	13/	13	千克	AB/	RS	28	
2009.1900 90	其他白利糖度值超过 20 的非冷冻橙汁(未发酵及未加酒精的,不论是否加糖或其他甜物质)〔101 可直接饮用的蔬菜果汁类饮料,102 浓缩蔬菜果汁饮料(包括冷冻的),103 食品工业用浓缩液(汁、浆)〕	30		90	13/	13	千克	AB/	RS	40	
	-葡萄柚汁;柚汁:										
2009.2100	--白利糖度值不超过 20 的〔101 可直接饮用的蔬菜果汁类饮料,102 浓缩蔬菜果汁饮料(包括冷冻的),103 食品工业用浓缩液(汁、浆)〕	5		90	13/	13	千克	AB/	PRQS	30	
2009.2900	--其他〔101 可直接饮用的蔬菜果汁类饮料,102 浓缩蔬菜果汁饮料(包括冷冻的),103 食品工业用浓缩液(汁、浆)〕	5		90	13/	13	千克	AB/	RS	30	
	-其他未混合的柑橘属水果汁:										
	--白利糖度值不超过 20 的:										
2009.3110	---柠檬汁〔101 可直接饮用的蔬菜果汁类饮料,102 浓缩蔬菜果汁饮料(包括冷冻的),103 食品工业用浓缩液(汁、浆)〕	5		90	13/	13	千克	AB/	PRQS	30	4.7/4.7
2009.3190	---其他〔101 可直接饮用的蔬菜果汁类饮料,102 浓缩蔬菜果汁饮料包括冷冻的,103 食品工业用浓缩液汁、浆〕	5		90	13/	13	千克	AB/	PRQS	7.5	4.7/4.7
	--其他:										
2009.3910	---柠檬汁〔101:浓缩蔬菜果汁饮料(包括冷冻的);102:可直接饮用的蔬菜果汁类饮料;103:食品工业用浓缩液(汁、浆)〕	5		90	13/	13	千克	AB/	RS	30	4.7/4.7
2009.3990	---其他〔999〕	5		90	13/	13	千克	AB/	RS	7.5	4.7/4.7
	-菠萝汁:										
2009.4100	--白利糖度值不超过 20 的〔101 可直接饮用的蔬菜果汁类饮料,102 浓缩蔬菜果汁饮料(包括冷冻的)〕	5		90	13/	13	千克	AB/	PRQS	30	
2009.4900	--其他〔101 可直接饮用的蔬菜果汁类饮料,102 浓缩蔬菜果汁饮料(包括冷冻的)〕	5		90	13/	13	千克	AB/	RS	30	
2009.5000	-番茄汁〔101 可直接饮用的蔬菜果汁类饮料,102 浓缩蔬菜果汁饮料(包括冷冻的)〕	5		80	13/	13	千克	AB/	RS	20	
	-葡萄汁,包括酿酒葡萄汁:										
2009.6100	--白利糖度值不超过 30 的〔101 浓缩蔬菜果汁饮料(包括冷冻的),102 未发酵葡萄酒,103 可直接饮用的蔬菜果蔬汁类饮料〕	5		90	13/	13	千克	AB/	PRQS	30	
2009.6900	--其他〔101 浓缩蔬菜果汁饮料包括冷冻的,102 未发酵葡萄酒〕	5		90	13/	13	千克	AB/	RS	30	
	-苹果汁:										
2009.7100	--白利糖度值不超过 20 的〔101 可直接饮用的蔬菜果汁类饮料,102 浓缩蔬菜果汁饮料包括冷冻的〕	5		90	13/	13	千克	AB/	PRQS	30	

协定税率 %								RCEP		特惠税率 %			Article Description
东/冰/格	巴基斯坦	韩国	瑞士上/下	哥/秘/柬	澳/毛	新西/坡/智	中国港/澳/台	东盟及马来/澳/韩	日/新	亚太2国	老/柬/缅	98/97/95	
0/0/0	12	3	1.5/1.5	0/0/0	0/0	0//0	0/0/	0/0/13.5	13.6/0		/0/	0/0/0	----Salted,sea tangle
0/0/0	0	3	1.5/1.5	0/0/0	0/0	0//0	0/0/	0/0/13.5	13.6/0		/0/	0/0/0	----Salted undaria pinnatifida
0/0/0	8.4	3	1.5/1.5	0/0/0	0/0	0//0	0/0/	0/0/13.5	13.6/0		/0/	0/0/0	----Roasted laver
0/0/0	8.4	3	1.5/1.5	0/0/0	0/0	0//0	0/0/	0/0/13.5	13.6/0		/0/	0/0/0	----Other
0/0/0	17.5	5	2.5/2.5	0/0/0	0/15	0/0/0	0/0/	0/0/22.5	22.7/0			0/0/0	---Water chestnut(Eleocharis dulcis),in airtight containers
0/0/0	0	3	0/0	0/0/0	0/0	0/0/0	0/0/	0/0/13.5	13.6/0		/0/	0/0/0	---Other
													Fruit or nut juices (including grape must and coconut water) and vegetable juices, unfermented and not containing added spirit, whether or not containing added sugar or other sweetening matter:
													-Orange juice:
0/0/0	2	0	0/0	0/0/0	0/0	0//0	0/0/	0/6.8/0	6.8/0		0/0/	0/0/0	--Frozen
0/0/0		22.5	0		0	11.3	0/0/0	0/0/			0/0/	0/0/0	--Not frozen, of a Brix value not exceeding 20
0/0/0		18	0/0	/0/0	0/	0/0/0	0/0/	28.5/28.5/28.5	/28.5		0/0/	0/0/0	Non frozen orange juice with Brix value no more than 20, with minimum net weight of independent package ≥ 180kg (unfermented and without alcohol, whether or not added with sugar or other sweet substances)
0/0/0		18	0/0	/0/0	0/	0/0/0	0/0/	28.5/28.5/28.5	/28.5		0/0/	0/0/0	Other orange juices (unfermented and not containing alcohol, whether or not containing sugar or other sweet substances) of not more than 20 unfrozen Brix concentrations
0/0/0		22.5			0	11.3	0/0/0	0/0/			0/0/	0/0/0	--Other
0/0/0		18		/0/0	0/	0/0/0	0/0/	28.5/28.5/28.5	/28.5		0/0/	0/0/0	Non frozen orange juice with a Brix value of more than 20, with a minimum net weight of independent packaging ≥ 180 kg (unfermented and non－alcoholic, with or without sugar or other sweet substances)
0/0/0		18		/0/0	0/	0/0/0	0/0/	28.5/28.5/28.5	/28.5		0/0/	0/0/0	Orange juice (unfermented and not containing alcohol, whether or not containing sugar or other sweet substances) with a concentration of non frozen Baili sugar exceeding 20
													-Grapefruit juice; pomelo juice:
0/0/0	12	3	1.5/1.5	0/0/0	0/0	0/0/0	0/0/	0/0/13.5	13.6/0		0//	0/0/0	--Of a Brix value not exceeding 20
0/0/0	12	3	1.5/1.5	0/0/0	0/0	0/0/0	0/0/	0/0/13.5	13.6/0		0//	0/0/0	--Other
													-Juice of any other single citrus fruit:
													--Of a Brix value not exceeding 20:
0/0/0	14.4	8.4	1.8/1.8	0/0/0	0/0	0/0/0	0/0/	16.2/16.2/16.2	16.9/16.2	2.5	/0/	0/0/0	---Lemon Juice
0/0/0	14.4	8.4	1.8/1.8	0/0/0	0/0	0/0/0	0/0/	16.8/17.1/16.8	16.9/17.1	2.5	/0/	0/0/0	---Other
													--Other:
0/0/0	14.4	8.4	1.8/1.8	0/0/0	0/0	0/0/0	0/0/	16.2/16.2/16.2	16.9/16.2	2.5	/0/	0/0/0	---Lemon juice
0/0/0	14.4	8.4	1.8/1.8	0/0/0	0/0	0/0/0	0/0/	16.2/16.2/16.2	16.9/16.2	2.5	/0/	0/0/0	---Other
													-Pineapple juice:
5/0/0		2	0/0	0/0/9	0/0	0//0	0/0/	9.5/9.8/9.5	/9.8		0/0/	0/0/0	--Of a Brix value not exceeding 20
5/0/0		2	0/0	0/0/9	0/	0//0	0/0/	9.5/9.8/9.5	/9.8		0/0/	0/0/0	--Other
0/0/0		18		0/0/0	0/	0/0/0	0/0/	28.5/28.5/28.5	28.6/28.5	2.5	0//	0/0/0	-Tomato juice
													-Grape juice(including grape must):
0/0/0		9.3	2/2	0/0/0	0/0	0/0/0	0/0/	18.7/19/18.7	18.8/19			0/0/0	--Of a Brix value not exceeding 30
0/0/0		9.3	2/2	0/0/0	0/0	0/0/0	0/0/	18/18/18	18.8/18			0/0/0	--Other
													-Apple juice:
0/0/0		9.3	2/2	0/0/0	0/0	0/0/0	0/0/	18/18/18	18.8/18			0/0/0	--Of a Brix value not exceeding 20

税则号列	货品名称〔CIQ 扩展编码及品名—T2 表示见附表 2〕	最惠(%)	暂定税率	普通	增值/消费	出口退税	计量单位	监管条件/特殊证件	检验检疫	对美关税	亚太上/下
2009.7900	--其他〔101 可直接饮用的蔬菜果汁类饮料，102 浓缩蔬菜果汁饮料包括冷冻的〕	10		90	13/	13	千克	AB/	RS	35	
	-其他未混合的水果汁、坚果汁或蔬菜汁：										
2009.8100	--蔓越橘汁(大果蔓越橘、小果蔓越橘)、越橘汁〔101 可直接饮用的蔬菜果汁类饮料，102 浓缩蔬菜果汁饮料(包括冷冻的)，103 食品工业用浓缩液(汁、浆)〕	5		90	13/	13	千克	AB/	PRQS	17.5	2.5/2.5
	--其他：										
	---水果汁或坚果汁：										
2009.8912	----芒果汁〔101：可直接饮用的蔬菜果汁类饮料；102：浓缩蔬菜果汁饮料(包括冷冻的)；103：食品工业用浓缩液(汁、浆)〕	5		90	13/	13	千克	AB/	PRQS	30	4.4/4.4
2009.8913	----西番莲果汁〔101：可直接饮用的蔬菜果汁类饮料；102：浓缩蔬菜果汁饮料(包括冷冻的)；103：食品工业用浓缩液(汁、浆)〕	5		90	13/	13	千克	AB/	PRQS	30	4.4/4.4
2009.8914	----番石榴果汁〔101：可直接饮用的蔬菜果汁类饮料；102：浓缩蔬菜果汁饮料(包括冷冻的)；103：食品工业用浓缩液(汁、浆)〕	5		90	13/	13	千克	AB/	PRQS	30	4.4/4.4
2009.8915	----梨汁〔101：可直接饮用的蔬菜果汁类饮料；102：浓缩蔬菜果汁饮料(包括冷冻的)；103：食品工业用浓缩液(汁、浆)〕	5		90	13/	13	千克	AB/	PRQS	7.5	2.5/2.5
2009.8916	----沙棘汁〔101 可直接饮用的蔬菜果汁类饮料，102 浓缩蔬菜果汁饮料(包括冷冻的)，103 食品工业用浓缩液(汁、浆)〕	5		90	13/	13	千克	AB/	PRQS	17.5	2.5/2.5
2009.8919	----其他〔101：可直接饮用的蔬菜果汁类饮料；102：浓缩蔬菜果汁饮料(包括冷冻的)；103：食品工业用浓缩液(汁、浆)〕	5		90	13/	13	千克	AB/	PRQS	17.5	2.5/2.5
2009.8920	---蔬菜汁〔101：可直接饮用的蔬菜果汁类饮料；102：浓缩蔬菜果汁饮料(包括冷冻的)；103：食品工业用浓缩液(汁、浆)〕	5		80	13/	13	千克	AB/	PRQS	30	2.5/2.5
	-混合汁：										
2009.9010	---水果汁〔101 可直接饮用的蔬菜果汁类饮料，102 浓缩蔬菜果汁饮料(包括冷冻的)，103 食品工业用浓缩液(汁、浆)〕	5		90	13/	13	千克	AB/	PRQS	30	4.4/4.4
2009.9090	---其他〔101 可直接饮用的蔬菜果汁类饮料，102 浓缩蔬菜果汁饮料包括冷冻的，103 食品工业用浓缩液汁、浆〕	5		80	13/	13	千克	AB/	PRQS	30	

协定税率 %								RCEP		特惠税率 %			Article Description
东/冰/格	巴基斯坦	韩国	瑞士上/下	哥/秘/柬	澳/毛	新西/坡/智	中国港/澳/台	东盟及马来/澳/韩	日/新	亚太2国	老/柬/缅	98/97/95	
0/0/0		9.3	2/2	0/0/0	0/0	0/0/0	0/0/	18/18/18	18.8/18			0/0/0	--Other
													-Juice of any other single fruit, nut or vegetable:
0/0/0	10	9.3	2/2	0/0/0	0/0	0/0/0	0/0/	18/18/18	18.8/18		0//0	0/0/0	--Cranberry(Vaccinium macrocarpon, Vaccinium oxycoccos) juice; Lingonberry (Vaccinium vitis-idaea)juice
													--Other:
													---Fruit juice or nut juice:
0/0/0	0	9.3	2/2	0/0/0	0/0	0/0/0	0/0/	18.7/19/18.7	18.8/19		0//0	0/0/0	----Mango juice
0/0/0	16	9.3	2/2	0/0/0	0/0	0/0/0	0/0/	18/18/18	18.8/18		0//0	0/0/0	----Passion-fruit juice
0/0/0	16	9.3	2/2	0/0/0	0/0	0/0/0	0/0/	18/18/18	18.8/18		0//0	0/0/0	----Guva juice
0/0/0	0	9.3	2/2	0/0/0	0/0	0/0/0	0/0/	18/18/18	18.8/18		0//0	0/0/0	----Pear Juice
0/0/0	0	9.3	2/2	0/0/0	0/0	0/0/0	0/0/	18/18/18	18.8/18		0//0	0/0/0	----Seabuckthorn juice
0/0/0	0	9.3	2/2	0/0/0	0/0	0/0/0	0/0/	18/18/18	18.8/18		0//0	0/0/0	----Other
0/0/0	10	9.3	2/2	0/0/0	0/0	0/0/0	0/0/	18/18/18	18.8/18		//0	0/0/0	---Vegetable juice
													-Mixtures of juices:
0/0/0	0	9.3	2/2	0/0/0	0/0	0/0/0	0/0/	18.7/19/18.7	18.8/19	2.5	0/0/	0/0/0	---Of fruit juices
0/0/0	0	9.3	2/2	0/0/0	0/0	0/0/0	0/0/	18/18/18	18.8/18	2.5	0/0/	0/0/0	---Other

第二十一章
杂 项 食 品

注释：

一、本章不包括：

(一)税目07.12的什锦蔬菜；

(二)含咖啡的焙炒咖啡代用品(税目09.01)；

(三)加香料的茶(税目09.02)；

(四)税目09.04至09.10的调味香料或其他产品；

(五)按重量计含香肠、肉、食用杂碎、动物血、昆虫、鱼、甲壳动物、软体动物、其他水生无脊椎动物及其混合物超过20%的食品(第十六章)，但税目21.03或21.04的产品除外；

(六)税目20.04的产品；

(七)税目30.03或30.04的药用酵母及其他产品；

(八)税目35.07的酶制品。

二、上述注释一(二)所述咖啡代用品的精汁归入税目21.01。

三、税目21.04所称"均化混合食品"，是指两种或两种以上的基本配料，例如，肉、鱼、蔬菜或果实等，经精细均化制成适合供婴幼儿食用或营养用的零售包装食品(每件净重不超过250克)。为了调味、保藏或其他目的，可以加入少量其他配料，还可以含有少量可见的小块配料。

税则号列	货品名称〔CIQ扩展编码及品名—T2表示见附表2〕	最惠(%)	暂定税率	普通	增值/消费	出口退税	计量单位	监管条件/特殊证件	检验检疫	对美关税	亚太上/下
21.01	**咖啡、茶、马黛茶的浓缩精汁及以其为基本成分或以咖啡、茶、马黛茶为基本成分的制品；烘焙菊苣和其他烘焙咖啡代用品及其浓缩精汁：**										
	-咖啡浓缩精汁及以其为基本成分或以咖啡为基本成分的制品：										
2101.1100	--浓缩精汁〔101速溶咖啡，102其他咖啡，103植脂末咖啡伴侣，104未列出的其他饮料、冷冻饮品、咖啡、果冻〕	12		130	13/	13	千克	AB/	RS	37	
2101.1200	--以浓缩精汁或咖啡为基本成分的制品〔101茶饮料，102咖啡粉，103速溶咖啡，104其他咖啡，105未列出的其他饮料、冷冻饮品、咖啡、果冻〕	12		130	13/	13	千克	AB/	RS	37	
2101.2000	-茶、马黛茶浓缩精汁及以其为基本成分或以茶、马黛茶为基本成分的制品〔999〕	12		130	13/	13	千克	AB/	RS	37	6/6
2101.3000	-烘焙菊苣和其他烘焙咖啡代用品及其浓缩精汁〔101其他咖啡，102植脂末(咖啡伴侣)，103未列出的其他饮料、冷冻饮品、咖啡、果冻〕	12		130	13/	13	千克	AB/	RS	17	
21.02	**酵母(活性或非活性)；已死的其他单细胞微生物(不包括税目30.02的疫苗)；发酵粉：**										
2102.1000	-活性酵母〔101饲料添加剂，104食品加工用酵母制品活性酵母〕	25		80	13/	13	千克	AB/	PRQS	50	
2102.2000	-非活性酵母；已死的其他单细胞微生物〔201：食品加工用酵母制品(非活性酵母)；301：有检疫要求食品添加剂；999：其他饲料添加剂〕	25		70	9/	13	千克	AB/	PRQS	50	
2102.3000	-发酵粉〔101饲料添加剂，102其他粮食制品，103食品加工用酵母制品(活性酵母)，104食品加工用酵母制品(非活性酵母)，105食品加工用酵母衍生制品，106食品加工用其他酵母产品〕	25		70	13/	13	千克	AB/	PRQS	50	
21.03	**调味汁及其制品；混合调味品；芥子粉及其调制品：**										
2103.1000	-酱油〔101酿造酱油，102配制酱油，103鲜味汁，104其他酱油〕	12		90	13/	13	千克	AB/	RS	37	
2103.2000	-番茄沙司及其他番茄调味汁〔101番茄沙司，102番茄调味汁〕	12		90	13/	13	千克	AB/	RS	22	
2103.3000	-芥子粉及其调制品〔999香辛料，998未列出的其他调味品〕	12		70	13/	13	千克	AB/	PRQS	22	
	-其他：										
2103.9010	---味精〔999〕	12		130	13/	13	千克	AB/	RS	14.5	10.4/10.4
2103.9020	---别特酒(Aromatic bitters)，按体积计酒精含量44.2%～49.2%，按重量计含1.5%～6%的香料、各种配料以及4%～10%的糖〔999〕	12		90	13/	13	千克	AB/	RS	14.5	
2103.9090	---其他[T2]	12		90	13/	9,13	千克	AB/	RS	37	10.6/10.6

Chapter 21
Miscellaneous edible preparations

Notes:

1. This Chapter does not cover:
   (a) Mixed vegetables of heading No. 07.12;
   (b) Roasted coffee substitutes containing coffee in any proportion (heading No. 09.01);
   (c) Flavoured tea (heading No. 09.02);
   (d) Spices or other products of headings No. 09.04 to 09.10;
   (e) Food preparations, other than the products described in heading No. 21.03 or 21.04, containing more than 20% by weight of sausage, meat, meat offal, blood, insects, fish or crustaceans, molluscs or other aquatic invertebrates, or any combination thereof (Chapter 16);
   (f) Products of headings No. 20.04;
   (g) Yeast put up as a medicament or other products of heading No. 30.03 or 30.04; or
   (h) Prepared enzymes of heading No. 35.07.
2. Extracts of the substitutes referred to in Note 1(b) above are to be classified in heading No. 21.01.

3. For the purposes of heading No. 21.04, the expression "homogenized composite food preparations" means preparations consisting of a finely homogenized mixture of two or more basic ingredients such as meat, fish, vegetables or fruit, put up for retail sale Suitable for infants to eat or for dietetic purposes, in containers of a net weight content not exceeding 250g. For the application of this definition, no account is to betaken of small quantities of any ingredients which may be added to the mixture for seasoning, preservation or other purposes. Such preparations may contain a small quantity of visible pieces of ingredients.

协定税率 %								RCEP		特惠税率 %			Article Description
东/冰/格	巴基斯坦	韩国	瑞士上/下	哥/秘/柬	澳/毛	新西/坡/智	中国港/澳/台	东盟及马来/澳/韩	日/新	亚太2国	老/柬/缅	98/97/95	
													Extracts, essences and concentrates, of coffee, tea or maté and preparations with a basis of these products or with a basis of coffee, tea or maté; roasted chicory and other roasted coffee substitutes, and extracts, essences and concentrates thereof:
													-Extracts, essences and concentrates of coffee, and preparations with a basis of these extracts, essences or concentrates or with a basis of coffee:
0/0/0	13.6	7.9		0//0	0/0	0/0/0	0/0/	15.9/16.2/	15.9/16.2			0/0/0	--Extracts, essences and concentrates
0/0/0		18		0//0	0/18	0/0/0	0/0/	28.5/28.5/	/28.5			0/0/	--Preparations with a basis of extracts, essences or concentrates or with a basis of coffee
0/0/0	16		0/0	0/0/0	0/19.2	0/0/0	0/0/	30.4/30.4/	/30.4			0/0/0	-Extracts, essences and concentrates, of tea or maté, and preparations with a basis of these extracts, essences or concentrates or with a basis of tea or mate
0//0		19.2		0//0	0/19.2	0/0/0	0/0/	30.4/30.4/	30.5/30.4			0/0/0	-Roasted chicory and other roasted coffee substitutes, and extracts, essences and concentrates thereof
													Yeasts (active or inactive); other singlecell micro-organisms, dead (but not including vaccines of heading No. 30.02); prepared baking powders:
0/0/0	20	15	0/0	0/0/0	0/15	0/0/0	0/0/	23.8/23.8/	/23.8			0/0/0	Active yeasts
0/0/0	17.5	15	0/0	0/0/0	0/15	0/0/0	0/0/	23.8/23.8/23.8	/23.8			0/0/0	-Inactive yeasts; other single-cell microorganisms, dead
0/0/0	17.5	15		0/0/0	0/15	0/0/0	0/0/	23.8/23.8/23.8	23.8/23.8			0/0/0	-Prepared baking powders
													Sauces and preparations therefor; mixed condiments and mixes seasonings; mustard flour and meal and prepared mustard:
0/0/0	19.6	16.8	2.8/2.8	0/0/0	0/16.8	0/0/0	0/0/	26.6/26.6/	26.7/26.6		/0/	0/0/0	-Soya sauce
0//0	12	3	1.5/1.5	0/0/0	0/0	0/0/0	0/0/	0/0/13.5	13.6/0		/0/	0/0/0	-Tomato ketchup and other tomato sauces
0//0	12	3	1.5/1.5	0/0/0	0/0	0/0/0	0/0/	0/0/13.5	13.6/0		/0/	0/0/0	-Mustard flour and meal and prepared mustard
													-Other:
0/0/0	12.7	12.6	2.1/2.1	0/0/0	0/0	0/0/0	0/0/	20.5/20.5/	/20.5			0/0/0	---Gourmet powder
0/0/0		12.6	2.1/2.1	0/4.9/0	0/0	0/0/0	0/0/	20/20/20	20/20			0/0/0	---Aromatic bitters, 44.2%~49.2% of which is alcoholic strength by volume, 1.5%~6% of which is spiles and various ingredients by weight and 4%~10% of which is sugar by weight
0/0/0	18.4	12.6	5.3/5.3	0/0/0	0/0	0/0/0	0/0/	20/20/	20/20			0/0/0	---Other

税则号列		货品名称〔CIQ 扩展编码及品名－T2 表示见附表 2〕	最惠(%)	暂定税率	普通	增值/消费	出口退税	计量单位	监管条件/特殊证件	检验检疫	对美关税	亚太上/下
21.04		**汤料及其制品；均化混合食品：**										
2104.1000		-汤料及其制品〔101 制汤调料，102 其他含肉速冻粮食制品，103 其他不含肉速冻粮食制品〕	12		90	13/	13	千克	AB/	PRQS	37	
2104.2000		-均化混合食品〔101 汤料，102 混合调味品，103 未列出的其他调味品，104 具有保健食品批准文号，105 婴幼儿罐装辅助食品〕	12		90	13/	13	千克	AB/	RS	22	
21.05		**冰淇淋及其他冰制食品，不论是否含可可：**										
2105.0000		冰淇淋及其他冰制食品，不论是否含可可〔101 冰淇淋，102 冷冻饮品制作料，104 食用冰，105 其他冷冻饮品〕	12		90	13/	13	千克	AB/	RS	37	
21.06		**其他税号未列名的食品：**										
2106.1000		-浓缩蛋白质及组织化蛋白质[T2]	10		90	13/	9,13	千克	AB/	RS	20	
		-其他：										
2106.9010		---制造碳酸饮料的浓缩物〔102 果香型固体饮料（如菊花精、柠檬茶、果珍），103 未列出的其他饮料、冷冻饮品、咖啡、果冻〕	12		100	13/	13	千克	AB/	RS		
2106.9020		---制造饮料用的复合酒精制品〔999〕	12		180	13/5	13	千克	AB/	RS	14.5	
2106.9030		---蜂王浆制剂										
2106.9030	10	含濒危植物成分的蜂王浆制剂〔101 具有保健食品批准文号，102 蜂王浆及制品〕	3		80	13/	0	千克	ABFE/	RS	8	
2106.9030	90	其他蜂王浆制剂〔101 具有保健食品批准文号，102 蜂王浆及制品〕	3		80	13/	13	千克	AB/	RS	8	
2106.9040		---椰子汁〔999〕	10		90	13/	13	千克	AB/	PRQS	35	9/9
2106.9050		---海豹油胶囊										
2106.9050	10	濒危海豹油胶囊〔999〕	5		90	13/	0	千克	ABEF/	RS	7.5	4.6/4.6
2106.9050	90	其他海豹油胶囊〔999〕	5		90	13/	13	千克	AB/	RS	7.5	4.6/4.6
		---含香料或着色剂的甘蔗糖或甜菜糖水溶液；蔗糖含量超过50%的甘蔗糖、甜菜糖与其他食品原料的简单固体混合物：										
2106.9061		----含香料或着色剂的甘蔗糖或甜菜糖水溶液〔999〕	12		90	13/	13	千克	AB/	RS	22	11/11
2106.9062		----蔗糖含量超过 50%的甘蔗糖、甜菜糖与其他食品原料的简单固体混合物〔999〕	12		90	13/	13	千克	AB/	RS	22	11/11
2106.9090		---其他										
2106.9090	01	无乳糖配方或低乳糖配方、乳蛋白部分水解配方、乳蛋白深度水解配方或氨基酸配方、早产/低出生体重婴儿配方（非乳基）、氨基酸代谢障碍配方、母乳营养补充剂（非乳基）特殊婴幼儿配方食品[101 乳基婴儿配方食品，102 乳基较大婴儿配方食品，103 氨基酸代谢障碍配方特殊医学用途婴儿配方食品，104 无乳糖配方特殊医学用途婴儿配方食品，105 乳蛋白部分水解配方特殊医学用途婴儿配方食品，106 乳蛋白深度水解配方特殊医学用途婴儿配方食品，107 乳基幼儿配方食品]	12	0	90	13/	13	千克	AB/	RS	10	11/11
2106.9090	11	含濒危鱼软骨素胶囊〔999〕	12		90	13/	0	千克	ABEF/	RS	22	11/11
2106.9090	19	含濒危动植物成分的其他编号未列名食品[101 蛋白型固体饮料，102 果香型固体饮料（如菊花精、柠檬茶、果珍），103 未列出的其他饮料、冷冻饮品、咖啡、果冻，104 发酵豆制品，105 红豆馅，106 其他粮食制品，107 具有保健食品批准文号，108 非发酵豆制品，109 婴幼儿谷类辅助食品，110 婴幼儿罐装辅助食品，111 特殊医学用途配方食品]	12		90	13/	0	千克	ABEF/	RS	22	11/11
2106.9090	90	其他编号未列名的食品[T2]	12		90	13/	9,13	千克	AB/	RS	22	11/11

协定税率 %								RCEP		特惠税率 %			Article Description
东/冰/格	巴基斯坦	韩国	瑞士 上/下	哥/秘/柬	澳/毛	新西/坡/智	中国港/澳/台	东盟及马来/澳/韩	日/新	亚太2国	老/柬/缅	98/97/95	
													Soups and broths and preparations therefor; homogenized composite food preparations:
0/0/0	12	3	1.5/1.5	0/0/0	0/0	0/0/0	0/0/	0/0/13.5	13.6/0			0/0/0	-Soups and broths and preparations therefor
0//0		19.2		0/0/0	0/19.2	0/0/0	0/0/	30.4/30.4/	30.5/30.4			0/0/0	-Homogenized composite food preparations
													Ice cream and other edible ice, whether or not containing cocoa:
0/0/0	0		0/0	0/0/0	0/0	0/0/0	0/0/	18.1/18.1/	/18.1			0/0/0	Ice cream and other edible ice, whether or not containing cocoa
													Food preparations not elsewhere specified or included:
0/0/0	3.5	2	0/0	0/0/0	0/0	0/0/0	0/0/	0/0/9	9.1/0			0/0/0	-Protein concentrates and textured protein substances
													-Other:
0/0/0		21		0/0/0	0/21	0/0/0	0/0/	33.3/33.3/33.3	/33.3			0/0/0	---Beverage bases
0/0/0		9.3	2/2	0/0/0	0/0	0/0/0	0/0/	18/18/18	18.8/18			0/0/0	---Compound alcoholic preparations of a kind used for the manufacture of beverages
													---Royal jelly, put up as tonic essences
0/0/0	0	0	0/0	0/0/0	0/0	0//0	0/0/	0/0/0	0/0		0//	0/0/0	Royal jelly, put up as tonic essences containing composition of endangered plants
0/0/0	0	0	0/0	0/0/0	0/0	0//0	0/0/	0/0/0	0/0		0//	0/0/0	Other royal jelly, put up as tonic essences
5/0/0	9	2	0/0	0/0/9	0/0	0//0	0/0/	9.5/9.8/9.5	/9.8		0//0	0/0/0	---Coconut juice
													---Seal oil capsules
0/0/0	18.4	18.4	5/5	0/0/0	0/0	0/0/0	0/0/	19/19/	/19			0/0/0	Endangered seal oil capsules
0/0/0	18.4	18.4	5/5	0/0/0	0/0	0/0/0	0/0/	19/19/	/19			0/0/0	Other seal oil capsules
													---Cane sugar or beet sugar solution containing added flavouring or colouring matter; Cane sugar, beet sugar and other food ingredients in imple solid mixture with more than 50% by weight of cane sucrose
0/0/	0	18.4	5/5	0/0/0	0/12	0/0/0	0/0/	19/19/20	19/19			0/0/0	----Cane sugar or beet sugar solution containing added flavouring or colouring matter
0/0/	0	18.4	5/5	0/0/0	0/12	0/0/0	0/0/	19/19/20	19/19			0/0/0	----Cane sugar, beet sugar and other food ingredients in imple solid mixture with more than 50% by weight of cane sucrose
													---Other
0/0/	0	18.4	5/5	0/0/0	0/12	0/0/0	0/0/	19/19/20	19/19			0/0/0	Milk protein partial hydrolysate formula, milk protein hydrolysis amino acid formula special depth formula, infant milk powder
0/0/	0	18.4	5/5	0/0/0	0/12	0/0/0	0/0/	19/19/20	19/19			0/0/0	Endangered species of fish cartilage capsules
0/0/	0	18.4	5/5	0/0/0	0/12	0/0/0	0/0/	19/19/20	19/19			0/0/0	Other food preparations containing composition of endangered plants, not eleswhere specified or included
0/0/	0	18.4	5/5	0/0/0	0/12	0/0/0	0/0/	19/19/20	19/19			0/0/0	Other food preparations, not eleswhere specified or included

第二十二章
饮料、酒及醋

注释：

一、本章不包括：

(一)本章的产品(税目 22.09 的货品除外)经配制后，用于烹饪而不适于作为饮料的制品(通常归入税目 21.03)；

(二)海水(税目 25.01)；

(三)蒸馏水、导电水及类似的纯净水(税目 28.53)；

(四)按重量计浓度超过 10%的醋酸(税目 29.15)；

(五)税目 30.03 或 30.04 的药品；

(六)芳香料制品及盥洗品(第三十三章)。

二、本章及第二十章和第二十一章所称“按容量计酒精浓度”，应是温度在 20℃时测得的浓度。

三、税目 22.02 所称“无酒精饮料”，是指按容量计酒精浓度不超过 0.5%的饮料。含酒精饮料应分别归入税目 22.03 至 22.06 或税目 22.08。

子目注释：

子目 2204.10 所称“汽酒”，是指温度在 20℃时装在密封容器中超过大气压力 3 巴及以上的酒。

税则号列	货品名称〔CIQ 扩展编码及品名－T2 表示见附表 2〕	最惠(%)	暂定税率	普通	增值/消费	出口退税	计量单位	监管条件/特殊证件	检验检疫	对美关税	亚太上/下
22.01	**未加糖或其他甜物质及未加味的水，包括天然或人造矿泉水及汽水；冰及雪：**										
	-矿泉水及汽水：										
2201.1010	---矿泉水〔999〕	5		90	13/	0	升/千克	AB/	RS	30	
2201.1020	---汽水〔101〕	5		90	13/	13	升/千克	AB/	RS	30	
	-其他：										
	---天然水：										
2201.9011	----已包装〔999〕	5		30	13/	0	千升/千克	AB/	RS	30	
2201.9019	----其他〔999〕	5		30	13/	0	千升/千克	/		30	
2201.9090	---其他[T2]	5		30	13/	0	千升/千克	AB/	RS	30	
22.02	**加味、加糖或其他甜物质的水，包括矿泉水及汽水，其他无酒精饮料，但不包括税目 20.09 的水果汁、坚果汁或蔬菜汁：**										
2202.1000	-加味、加糖或其他甜物质的水，包括矿泉水及汽水										
2202.1000 10	含濒危动植物成分的加味、加糖或其他甜物质的水（包括矿泉水及汽水）[T2]	5		100	13/	0	升/千克	ABEF/	RS	30	
2202.1000 90	其他加味、加糖或其他甜物质的水(包括矿泉水及汽水)[T2]	5		100	13/	13	升/千克	AB/	RS	30	
	-其他：										
2202.9100	--无醇啤酒										
2202.9100 11	含濒危动植物成份散装无醇啤酒〔999〕	5		100	13/	0	升/千克	ABEF/	RS	32.5	4.2/4.2
2202.9100 19	其他散装无醇啤酒〔999〕	5		100	13/	13	升/千克	AB/	RS	32.5	4.2/4.2
2202.9100 91	含濒危动植物成份其他包装无醇啤酒〔999〕	5		100	13/	0	升/千克	ABEF/	RS	32.5	4.2/4.2
2202.9100 99	其他包装无醇啤酒〔999〕	5		100	13/	13	升/千克	AB/	RS	32.5	4.2/4.2
2202.9900	--其他										
2202.9900 11	其他含濒危动植物成份散装无酒精饮料(不包括税目 20.09 的水果汁、坚果汁或蔬菜汁)〔101 碳酸饮料，102 含乳饮料，103 植物蛋白饮料，104 茶饮料，105 运动饮料，106 其他软饮料，107 未列出的其他饮料、冷冻饮品、咖啡、果冻，108 具有保健食品批准文号，109 植物饮料，110 乳酸菌饮料〕	5		100	13/	0	升/千克	ABEF/	RS	32.5	4.2/4.2
2202.9900 19	其他散装无酒精饮料(不包括税目 20.09 的水果汁、坚果汁或蔬菜汁)〔101 碳酸饮料，102 含乳饮料，103 植物蛋白饮料，104 茶饮料，105 运动饮料，106 其他软饮料，107 未列出的其他饮料、冷冻饮品、咖啡、果冻，108 植物饮料，109 乳酸菌饮料〕	5		100	13/	13	升/千克	AB/	RS	32.5	4.2/4.2

Chapter 22
Beverages, spirits and vinegar

Notes:

1. This Chapter does not cover:
   (a) Products of this Chapter (other than those of heading No. 22.09) prepared for culinary purposes and thereby rendered unsuitable for consumption as beverages (generally heading No. 21.03);
   (b) Sea water (heading No. 25.01);
   (c) Distilled or conductivity water or water of similar purity (heading No. 28.53);
   (d) Acetic acid of a concentration exceeding 10% by weight of acetic acid (heading No. 29.15);
   (e) Medicaments of heading No. 30.03 or 30.04; or
   (f) Perfumery or toilet preparations (Chapter 33).
2. For the purposes of this Chapter and of Chapter 20 and 21, the "alcoholic strength by volume" shall be determined at a temperature of 20℃.
3. For the purposes of heading No. 22.02, the term "non-alcoholic beverages" means beverages of an alcoholic strength by volume not exceeding 0.5% vol. Alcoholic beverages are classified in headings No. 22.03 to 22.06 or heading No. 22.08 as appropriate.

Subheading Note:

For the purposes of subheading No. 2204.10, the expression "sparkling wine" means wine which, when kept at a temperature of 20℃ in closed containers, has an excess pressure of not less than 3 bars.

协定税率 %								RCEP		特惠税率 %			Article Description
东/冰/格	巴基斯坦	韩国	瑞士上/下	哥/秘/柬	澳/毛	新西/坡/智	中国港/澳/台	东盟及马来/澳/韩	日/新	亚太2国	老/柬/缅	98/97/95	
													Waters, including natural or artificial mineral waters and aerated waters, not containing added sugar or other sweetening matter nor flavoured; ice and snow:
													-Mineral waters and aerated waters:
0/0/0	16	12	2/2	0/0/0	0/0	0/0/0	0/0/	19/19/	/19			0/0/0	---Mineral waters
0/0/0	14	9.3	2/2	0/0/0	0/0	0/0/0	0/0/	18/18/18	18.8/18			0/0/0	---Aerated waters
													-Other:
													---Natural waters:
0/0/0	3.5	2	0/0	0/0/0	0/0	0/0/0	0/0/	0/0/9	9.1/0			0//	----Packaged
0/0/0	3.5	2	0/0	0/0/0	0/0	0/0/0	0/0/	0/0/9	9.1/0			0//	----Other
0/0/0	3.5	2	0/0	0/0/0	0/0	0/0/0	0/0/	0/0/9	9.1/0			0/0/0	---Other
													Waters, including mineral waters and aerated waters, containing added sugar or other sweetening matter or flavoured, and other non-alcoholic beverages, not including fruit or vegetable or nut juices of heading No. 20.09:
													-Waters, including mineral waters and aerated waters, containing added sugar or other sweetening matter or flavoured
0/0/0	0	12	2/2	0/0/0	0/0	0/0/0	0/0/	19/19/	19/19			0/0/0	Waters,containing added sugar or other sweetening matter or flavoured of endangered animals and plant(including mineral waters and aerated water)
0/0/0	0	12	2/2	0/0/0	0/0	0/0/0	0/0/	19/19/	19/19			0/0/0	Other waters, containing added sugan or other sweetening matter or flavoured(including mineral waters and aerated waters)
													-Other:
													--Non-alcoholic beer
0/0/0	29.5	21	5/5	0/0/0	0/21	0/0/0	0/0/	33.3/33.3/	/33.3			0/0/0	Non alcoholic bulk beer containing endangered animal and plant ingredients
0/0/0	29.5	21	5/5	0/0/0	0/21	0/0/0	0/0/	33.3/33.3/	/33.3			0/0/0	Other Non alcoholic bulk beer
0/0/0	29.5	21	5/5	0/0/0	0/21	0/0/0	0/0/	33.3/33.3/	/33.3			0/0/0	Non alcoholic beer containing endangered animal and plant ingredients,in other package
0/0/0	29.5	21	5/5	0/0/0	0/21	0/0/0	0/0/	33.3/33.3/	/33.3			0/0/0	Other non alcoholic bulk beverages containing endangered animal and plant ingredients,excluding the fruit and vebatable juice of heading No.2009
													--Other
0/0/0	29,5	21	5/5	0/0/0	0/21	0/0/0	0/0/	33.3/33.3/	/33.3			0/0/0	Other non — alcoholic beverages in bulk containing endangered animal and plant ingredients (excluding fruit juice, hard juice or vegetable juice of heading 20.09)
0/0/0	29.5	21	5/5	0/0/0	0/21	0/0/0	0/0/	33.3/33.3/	/33.3			0/0/0	Other non — alcoholic beverages in bulk (excluding fruit juice, hard juice or vegetable juice of heading 20.09)

税则号列	货品名称〔CIQ扩展编码及品名—T2表示见附表2〕	最惠(%)	暂定税率	普通	增值/消费	出口退税	计量单位	监管条件/特殊证件	检验检疫	对美关税	亚太上/下
2202.9900 91	其他含濒危动植物成份其他包装无酒精饮料(不包括税目20.09的水果汁、坚果汁或蔬菜汁)〔101碳酸饮料,102含乳饮料,103植物蛋白饮料,104茶饮料,105运动饮料,106其他软饮料,107未列出的其他饮料、冷冻饮品、咖啡、果冻,108具有保健食品批准文号,109植物饮料,110乳酸菌饮料〕	5		100	13/	0	升/千克	ABEF/	RS	32.5	4.2/4.2
2202.9900 99	其他包装无酒精饮料(不包括税目20.09的水果汁、坚果汁或蔬菜汁)〔101碳酸饮料,102含乳饮料,103植物蛋白饮料,104茶饮料,105运动饮料,106其他软饮料,107蛋白型固体饮料,108其他咖啡,109未列出的其他饮料、冷冻饮品、咖啡、果冻,110燕窝制品,以燕窝主要原料制成的饮料,111乳酸菌饮料,112植物饮料〕	5		100	13/	13	升/千克	AB/	RS	32.5	4.2/4.2
22.03	**麦芽酿造的啤酒:**										
2203.0000	麦芽酿造的啤酒〔999〕	T3		T3	13/①	13	升/千克	AB/	RS	T3	
22.04	**鲜葡萄酿造的酒,包括加酒精的;税目20.09以外的酿酒葡萄汁:**										
2204.1000	-汽酒〔999〕	14		180	13/10	13	升/千克	AB/	RS	54/29	
	-其他酒;加酒精抑制发酵的酿酒葡萄汁:										
2204.2100	--装入2升及以下容器的〔999〕	14		180	13/10	13	升/千克	AB/	RS	54/29	
2204.2200	--装入2升以上但不超过10升容器的〔101葡萄酒,102未发酵葡萄酒,103其他原酒〕	20		180	13/10	13	升/千克	AB/	RS	45/35	
2204.2900	--其他〔101葡萄酒,102未发酵葡萄酒,103其他原酒〕	20		180	13/10	13	升/千克	AB/	RS	60/35	
2204.3000	-其他酿酒葡萄汁〔101未发酵葡萄酒,102其他原酒,301需申报仅用于工业用途不用于食品添加剂无检疫要求的化学品〕	30		90	13/10	13	升/千克	AB/	RS	50/45	
22.05	**味美思酒及其他加植物或香料的用鲜葡萄酿造的酒:**										
2205.1000	-装入2升及以下容器的〔101发酵酒配制酒,102未列出的其他酒〕	65	14	180	13/10	13	升/千克	AB/	RS	39	
2205.9000	-其他〔102〕	65		180	13/10	13	升/千克	AB/	RS	75	
22.06	**其他发酵饮料(例如,苹果酒、梨酒、蜂蜜酒、清酒);其他税目未列名的发酵饮料的混合物及发酵饮料与无酒精饮料的混合物:**										
2206.0010	---黄酒〔999〕	40		180	13/0.2495元/升	13	升/千克	AB/	RS	45	
2206.0090	---其他〔101含乳饮料,102未列出的其他饮料、冷冻饮品、咖啡、果冻,103果酒,104清酒,105其他发酵酒,106发酵酒配制酒〕	40		180	13/10	13	升/千克	AB/	RS	65	
22.07	**未改性乙醇,按容量计酒精浓度在80%及以上;任何浓度的改性乙醇及其他酒精:**										
2207.1000	-未改性乙醇,按容量计酒精浓度在80%及以上〔101食用酒精;102其他原酒;301危险化学品,易燃液体〕	40		100	13/	13	升/千克	ABG/3	MRNS	65	
2207.2000	-任何浓度的改性乙醇及其他酒精										
2207.2000 10	任何浓度的改性乙醇〔301危险化学品,易燃液体;302其他化工品〕	30		80	13/	0	升/千克	ABG/3	MRNS	70/45	
2207.2000 90	任何浓度的其他酒精[101食用酒精,102其他原酒,301属于危险化学品的食品添加剂,302无检疫要求食品添加剂,303一般化学品,需申报仅用于工业用途不用于食品添加剂无检疫要求,304易燃液体,需申报仅用于工业用途不用于食品添加剂无检疫要求〕	30		80	13/	0	升/千克	ABG/3	MRNS	70/45	
22.08	**未改性乙醇,按容量计酒精浓度在80%以下;蒸馏酒、利口酒及其他酒精饮料:**										
2208.2000	-蒸馏葡萄酒制得的烈性酒										
2208.2000 10	装入200升及以上容器的蒸馏葡萄酒制得的烈性酒〔101白兰地,102其他蒸馏酒〕	10	5	180	13/②	13	升/千克	AB/	RS	30	
2208.2000 90	其他蒸馏葡萄酒制得的烈性酒〔101白兰地,102其他蒸馏酒〕	10	5	180	13/②	13	升/千克	AB/	RS	30	
2208.3000	-威士忌酒〔999〕	10	5	180	13/②	13	升/千克	AB/	RS	30	
2208.4000	-朗姆酒及蒸馏已发酵甘蔗产品制得的其他烈性酒〔101朗姆酒,102其他蒸馏酒〕	10		180	13/②	13	升/千克	AB/	RS	35	
2208.5000	-杜松子酒〔999〕	10		180	13/②	13	升/千克	AB/	RS	35	
2208.6000	-伏特加酒〔999〕	10		180	13/②	13	升/千克	AB/	RS	35	8.8/8.8

① 进口完税价格≥0.3745美元/升的麦芽酿造啤酒,税率为0.253元/升;进口完税价格<0.3745美元/升的麦芽酿造啤酒,税率为0.2227元/升〕

② 复合消费税:从价20%+从量0.912元每升

协定税率 %								RCEP		特惠税率 %			Article Description
东/冰/格	巴基斯坦	韩国	瑞士上/下	哥/秘/柬	澳/毛	新西/坡/智	中国港/澳/台	东盟及马来/澳/韩	日/新	亚太2国	老/柬/缅	98/97/95	
0/0/0	29.5	21	5/5	0/0/0	0/21	0/0/0	0/0/	33.3/33.3/	/33.3			0/0/0	Other packaged non－alcoholic beverages containing endangered animal and plant ingredients (excluding fruit juice, hard juice or vegetable juice of heading 20.09)
0/0/0	29.5	21	5/5	0/0/0	0/21	0/0/0	0/0/	33.3/33.3/	/33.3			0/0/0	Other packaged non－alcoholic beverages (excluding fruit juice, hard juice or vegetable juice of heading 20.09)
													Beer made from malt:
0/0/0	0	0	0/0	0/0/0	0/0	0//0	0/0/	0/0/0	0/0			0/0/0	Beer made from malt
													Wine of fresh grapes, including fortified wines; grape must other than that of heading No. 20.09:
0/0/0	11.2	2.8	1.4/1.4	0/0/0	0/0	0/0/0	0/0/	0/0/12.6	12.7/0			0/0/0	-Sparkling wine
													-Other wine; grape must with fermentation prevented or arrested by the addition of alcohol:
0/0/0	11.2	2.8	1.4/1.4	0/1.9/0	0/0	0/0/0	0/0/	0/0/12.6	12.7/0			0/0/0	--In containers holding 2L or less
0/0/0		9.3	2/2	0/2.7/0	0/0	0/0/0	0/0/	18.7/19/18.7	18.8/19			0/0/0	--In containers holding more than 2L but not more than 10L
0/0/0		9.3	2/2	0/2.7/0	0/0	0/0/0	0/0/	18.7/19/18.7	18.8/19			0/0/0	--Other
0/0/0		18		0/0/0	0/18	0/0/0	0/0/	29.3/29.3/	/29.3			0//	-Other grape must
													Vermouth and other wine of fresh grapes flavoured with plants or aromatic substances:
0//0		39		0/0/0	0/39	0/0/0	0/0/	63.4/63.4/	/63.4			0//	-In containers holding 2L or less
0//0		39		0/0/0	0/39	0/0/0	0/0/	63.4/63.4/	/63.4			0//	-Other
													Other fermented beverages (for example, cider, perry, mead); mixtures of fermented beverages and mixtures of fermented beverages and non-alcoholic beverages, not elsewhere specified or included:
0/0/0		24		0/0/0	0/24	0/0/0	0/0/	38/38/	/38		//	0/0/0	---Yellow rice wine
0/0/0		24		0/0/0	0/24	0/0/0	0/0/	38/38/	38.1/38			0/0/0	---Other
													Undenatured ethyl alcohol of an alcoholic strength by volume of 80% vol or higher; ethyl alcohol and other spirits, denatured, of any strength:
0/0/0	0	24		0/0/0	0/24	0/0/0	0/0/	38/38/38	/38			0/0/0	-Undenatured ethyl alcohol of an alcoholic strength by volume of 80% vol or higher
													-Ethyl alcohol and other spirits, denatured, of any strength
0/0/0	0	18		0/0/0	0/18	0/0/0	0/0/	28.5/28.5/28.5	/28.5			0/0/0	Ethyl alcohol, denatured of any strength
0/0/0	0	18		0/0/0	0/18	0/0/0	0/0/	28.5/28.5/28.5	/28.5			0/0/0	Other spirits, of any strength
													Undenatured ethyl alcohol of an alcoholic strength by volume of less than 80% vol; spirits, liqueurs and other spirituous beverages:
													-Spirits obtained by distilling grape wine or grape marc
0/0/0	5	2	0/0	0/0/0	0/0	0/0/0	0/0/	0/0/9	9.1/0			0/0/0	In more than 200 litres and containers of alcohol distillation wine
0/0/0	5	2	0/0	0/0/0	0/0	0/0/0	0/0/	0/0/9	9.1/0			0/0/0	Other wine of liquor distillation
0/0/0	5	2	0/0	0/0/0	0/0	0/0/0	0/0/	0/0/	9.1/0			0/0/0	-Whiskies
0/0/0	5	2	0/0	0/0/0	0/0	0/0/0	0/0/	0/0/9	9.1/0			0/0/0	-Rum and other spirit obtained by distilling fermented sugarcane products
0//0	3.5	2	0/0	0/0/0	0/0	0/0/0	0/0/	0/0/9	9.1/0			0/0/0	-Gin and geneva
0//0	3.5	2	0/0	0/0/0	0/0	0/0/0	0/0/	0/0/	9.1/0			0/0/0	-Vodka

税则号列	货品名称〔CIQ 扩展编码及品名－T2 表示见附表 2〕	最惠(%)	暂定税率	普通	增值/消费	出口退税	计量单位	监管条件/特殊证件	检验检疫	对美关税	亚太上/下
2208.7000	-利口酒及柯迪尔酒〔999〕	10		180	13/②	13	升/千克	AB/	RS	35	8.8/8.8
	-其他：										
2208.9010	---龙舌兰酒										
2208.9010 10	濒危龙舌兰酒〔999〕	10		180	13/②	0	升/千克	ABFE/	RS	35	8.8/8.8
2208.9010 90	其他龙兰舌酒〔999〕	10		180	13/②	13	升/千克	AB/	RS	35	8.8/8.8
2208.9020	---白酒〔301 危险化学品，易燃液体；999 中国白酒〕	10		180	13/②	13	升/千克	AB/	RS	35	8.8/8.8
2208.9090	---其他										
2208.9090 01	酒精浓度在 80%以下的未改性乙醇[101 食用酒精，102 其他原酒，301 属于危险化学品的食品添加剂，302 无检疫要求食品添加剂，303 一般化学品，需申报仅用于工业用途不用于食品添加剂无检疫要求，304 易燃液体，需申报仅用于工业用途不用于食品添加剂无检疫要求]	10		180	13/	13	升/千克	AB/	RS	35	8.8/8.8
2208.9090 21	含濒危野生动植物成分的薯类蒸馏酒〔101 中国白酒，102 其他蒸馏酒，103 蒸馏酒配制酒，104 未列出的其他酒，105 具有保健食品批准文号〕	10		180	13/①	0	升/千克	ABEF/	RS	35	8.8/8.8
2208.9090 29	其他薯类蒸馏酒〔101 中国白酒，102 其他蒸馏酒，103 蒸馏酒配制酒，104 未列出的其他酒〕	10		180	13/①	13	升/千克	AB/	RS	35	8.8/8.8
2208.9090 91	含濒危野生动植物成分的其他蒸馏酒及酒精饮料〔101 中药酒，102 其他蒸馏酒，103 蒸馏酒配制酒，104 其他蒸馏配制酒，105 未列出的其他酒，106 具有保健食品批准文号〕	10		180	13/①	0	升/千克	ABEF/	RS	35	8.8/8.8
2208.9090 99	其他蒸馏酒及酒精饮料〔101 其他蒸馏酒，102 蒸馏酒配制酒，103 其他蒸馏配制酒，104 未列出的其他酒，105 按体积比乙醇≥24%，每一容器盛装＞5L 的〕	10		180	13/①	13	升/千克	AB/	MRNS	35	8.8/8.8
22.09	**醋及用醋酸制得的醋代用品：**										
2209.0000	醋及用醋酸制得的醋代用品〔101 配制食醋，102 其他食醋，103 未列出的其他调味品，104 具有保健食品批准文号〕	5		70	13/	13	升/千克	AB/	RS	30	

① 复合消费税：从价 20%＋从量 0.912 元每升

协定税率 %								RCEP		特惠税率 %			Article Description
东/冰/格	巴基斯坦	韩国	瑞士上/下	哥/秘/柬	澳/毛	新西/坡/智	中国港/澳/台	东盟及马来/澳/韩	日/新	亚太2国	老/柬/缅	98/97/95	
0/0/0	3.5	2	0/0	0/0/0	0/0	0/0/0	0/0/	0/0/	9.1/0			0/0/0	-Liqueurs and cordials
													-Other:
													---Tequila, Mezcal
0/0/0	3.5	2	0/0	0/0/0	0/0	0/0/0	0/0/	0/0/9	9.1/0			0/0/0	Endangered Tequila
0/0/0	3.5	2	0/0	0/0/0	0/0	0/0/0	0/0/	0/0/9	9.1/0			0/0/0	Other Tequila
0/0/0	3.5	2	0/0	0/0/0	0/0	0/0/0	0/0/	0/0/9	9.1/0			0/0/0	---Chinese spirits
													---Other
0/0/0	5	6	0/0	0/0/0	0/0	0/0/0	0/0/	9.5/9.5/	9.5/9.5			0/0/0	Undenatured ethyl alcohol of an alcoholic strength by volume of less than 80% vol
0/0/0	5	6	0/0	0/0/0	0/0	0/0/0	0/0/	9.5/9.5/	9.5/9.5			0/0/0	Potato spirits, endangered wild animals and plants
0/0/0	5	6	0/0	0/0/0	0/0	0/0/0	0/0/	9.5/9.5/	9.5/9.5			0/0/0	Other spirits by distilling potatoes
0/0/0	5	6	0/0	0/0/0	0/0	0/0/0	0/0/	9.5/9.5/	9.5/9.5			0/0/0	Spirits and spirituous beverages, containins endangered wild animals and plants
0/0/0	5	6	0/0	0/0/0	0/0	0/0/0	0/0/	9.5/9.5/	9.5/9.5			0/0/0	Other spirits and spirituous beverages
													Vinegar and substitutes for vinegar obtained from acetic acid:
0/0/0		9.3	2/2	0/0/0	0/0	0/0/0	0/0/	18.7/19/18.7	18.8/19			0/0/0	Vinegar and substitutes for vinegar obtained from acetic acid

第二十三章
食品工业的残渣及废料；
配制的动物饲料

注释：

税目 23.09 包括其他税目未列号的配制动物饲料，这些饲料是由动、植物原料加工而成的，并且已改变了原料的基本特性，但加工过程中的植物废料、植物残渣及副产品除外。

子目注释：

子目 2306.41 所称“低芥子酸油菜子”，是指第十二章子目注释一所定义的油菜子。

税则号列	货品名称〔CIQ 扩展编码及品名—T2 表示见附表 2〕	最惠(%)	暂定税率	普通	增值/消费	出口退税	计量单位	监管条件/特殊证件	检验检疫	对美关税	亚太上/下
23.01	**不适于供人食用的肉、杂碎、鱼、甲壳动物、软体动物或其他水生无脊椎动物的渣粉及团粒；油渣：**										
	-肉、杂碎的渣粉及团粒；油渣：										
	---肉骨粉：										
2301.1011	----含牛羊成分的〔101 饲料用牛肉粉(肉成分 67%以上)，102 饲料用牛肉骨粉，103 饲料用牛血粉，104 羊肉粉(饲料用羊肉粉(肉成分 67%以上)，105 饲料用羊肉骨粉，106 饲料用羊血粉，107 饲料用混合型饲养偶蹄动物肉骨粉，108 饲料用野生偶蹄猪、牛、羊肉骨粉，109 饲料用野生偶蹄猪、牛、羊血粉〕	2		11	9/	13	千克	AB/	MPQ	7	
2301.1019	----其他〔T2〕	2		11	9/	13	千克	AB/	MPQ	12	
2301.1020	---油渣〔101 工业用其他动物油脂，102 饲料用动物油渣，103 其他饲用加工植物蛋白〕	5		50	9/	0	千克	AB/	PQ	10	
2301.1090	---其他〔999〕	5		30	9/	0	千克	AB/	PQ	15	
	-鱼、甲壳动物、软体动物或其他水生无脊椎动物的渣粉及团粒：										
2301.2010	---饲料用鱼粉〔101 饲料用红鱼粉，102 饲料用白鱼粉〕	2		11	0/	0	千克	AB/	MPQ		0/0
2301.2090	---其他〔999〕	5		30	0/	0	千克	AB/	PQ		0/0
23.02	**谷物或豆类植物在筛、碾或其他加工过程中所产生的糠、麸及其他残渣，不论是否制成团粒：**										
2302.1000	-玉米的〔999〕	5		30	0/	0	千克	AB/	PQ		
2302.3000	-小麦的〔101 饲用麦麸，102 其他饲用加工植物蛋白〕	3		30	0/	0	千克	AB/	PQ		
2302.4000	-其他谷物的〔101：饲用米糠；102：其他饲用加工植物蛋白；103：米糠粕〕	5		30	0/	0	千克	AB/	PQ		
2302.5000	-豆类植物的〔999〕	5		30	9/	0	千克	AB/	PQ	10	
23.03	**制造淀粉过程中的残渣及类似的残渣，甜菜渣、甘蔗渣及制糖过程中的其他残渣，酿造及蒸馏过程中的糟粕及残渣，不论是否制成团粒：**										
2303.1000	-制造淀粉过程中的残渣及类似的残渣〔101 其他饲用加工植物蛋白，木薯渣除外，102 饲用植物颗粒和植物粉，103 其他植物饲料，104 木薯渣〕	5		30	9/	9,13	千克	AB/	PQ	10	
2303.2000	-甜菜渣、甘蔗渣及制糖过程中的其他残渣〔101 饲用甜菜粕，102 其他饲用加工植物蛋白，103 甘蔗渣(栽培介质)〕	5		30	9/	9，0	千克	AB/	PQ	15	
2303.3000	-酿造及蒸馏过程中的糟粕及残渣										
2303.3000 11	干玉米酒糟〔999〕	5		30	0/	0	千克	7AB/	PQ		
2303.3000 19	其他玉米酒糟〔999〕	5		30	9/	0	千克	7AB/	PQ		
2303.3000 90	其他酿造及蒸馏过程中的糟粕及残渣〔999〕	5		30	9/	0	千克	AB/	PQ		
23.04	**提炼豆油所得的油渣饼及其他固体残渣，不论是否碾磨或制成团粒：**										
2304.0010	---油渣饼〔101 食用，102 饲用，103 其他〕	5		30	9/	0	千克	7AB/	PNQ		0/0
2304.0090	---其他〔101 食用，102 饲用，103 其他〕	5		30	9/	0	千克	7AB/	PNQ	30	0/0
23.05	**提炼花生油所得的油渣饼及其他固体残渣，不论是否碾磨或制成团粒：**										
2305.0000	提炼花生油所得的油渣饼及其他固体残渣，不论是否碾磨或制成团粒〔999〕	5	0	30	0/	0	千克	AB/	PNQ		
23.06	**税目 23.04 或 23.05 以外的提炼植物或微生物油脂所得的油渣饼及其他固体残渣，不论是否碾磨或制成团粒：**										
2306.1000	-棉子的〔999〕	5	0	30	0/	9	千克	AB/	PNQ		
2306.2000	-亚麻子的〔999〕	5	0	30	0/	9	千克	AB/	PNQ		

Chapter 23
Residues and waste from the food industries; prepared animal fodder

Note:

Heading No. 23.09 includes products of a kind used in animal feeding, not elsewhere specified or included, obtained by processing vegetable or animal materials to such an extent that they have lost the essential characteristics of the original material, other than vegetable waste, vegetable residues and by-products of such processing.

Subheading Note:

For the purposes of subheading No. 2306.41, the expression "low erucic acid rape or colza seeds" means seeds as defined in Subheading Note 1 to Chapter 12.

协定税率 %								RCEP		特惠税率 %			Article Description
东/冰/格	巴基斯坦	韩国	瑞士 上/下	哥/秘/柬	澳/毛	新西/坡/智	中国港/澳/台	东盟及马来/澳/韩	日/新	亚太2国	老/柬/缅	98/97/95	
													Flours, meals and pellets, of meat or meat offal, of fish or of crustaceans, molluscs or other aquatic invertebrates, unfit for human consumption; greaves:
													-Flours, meals and pellets, of meat or meat offal; greaves:
													---Flours and meals, of meat bones:
0/0/0	0	0	0/0	0/0/0	0/0	0//0	0/0/	0/0/0	0/0			0/0/0	----Of bovine and sheep
0/0/0	0	0	0/0	0/0/0	0/0	0//0	0/0/	0/0/0	0/0			0/0/0	----Other
0/0/0	0	0	0/0	0/0/0	0/0	0//0	0/0/	0/0/0	0/0			0/0/0	---Greaves
0/0/0	0	0	0/0	0/0/0	0/0	0//0	0/0/	0/0/0	0/0			0/0/0	---Other
													-Flours, meals and pellets, of fish or of crustaceans, molluscs or other aquatic invertebrates:
0/0/0	0	0	0/0	0/0/0	0/0	0//0	0/0/	0/0/0	1.8/0			0/0/0	---Flours and meals of fish, of a kind used in animal feeding
0/0/0	0	0	0/0	0/0/0	0/0	0//0	0/0/	0/0/0	0/0			0/0/0	---Other
													Bran, sharps and other residues, whether or not in the form of pellets, derived from the sifting, milling or other working of cereals or of leguminous plants:
0/0/0	0	0	0/0	0/0/0	0/0	0//0	0/0/	0/0/0	4.5/0			0/0/0	-Of maize (corn)
0/0/0	0	0	0/0	0/0/0	0/0	0//0	0/0/	0/0/0	2.7/0			0/0/0	-Of wheat
0/0/0	0	0	0/0	0/0/0	0/0	0//0	0/0/	0/0/0	4.5/0			0/0/0	-Of other cereals
0/0/0	0	0	0/0	0/0/0	0/0	0//0	0/0/	0/0/0	4.5/0			0/0/0	-Of leguminous plants
													Residues of starch manufacture and similar residues, beet-pulp, bagasses and other waste of sugar manufacture, brewing or distilling dregs and waste, whether or not in the form of pellets:
0/0/0	0	0	0/0	0/0/0	0/0	0//0	0/0/	4.5/4.5/4.5	4.5/4.5			0/0/0	-Residues of starch manufacture and similar residues
0/0/0	0	0	0/0	0/0/0	0/0	0//0	0/0/	0/0/0	4.5/0			0/0/0	-Beet-pulp, bagasses and other waste of sugar manufacture
													-Brewing or distilling dregs and waste
0/0/0	0	0	0/0	0/0/0	0/0	0//0	0/0/	0/0/0	4.5/0			0/0/0	Corn distillers solubles
0/0/0	0	0	0/0	0/0/0	0/0	0//0	0/0/	0/0/0	4.5/0			0/0/0	Corn distillers solubles
0/0/0	0	0	0/0	0/0/0	0/0	0//0	0/0/	0/0/0	4.5/0			0/0/0	Other brewing or distilling dregs and waste
													Oil-cake and other solid residues, whether or not ground or in the form of pellets, resulting from the extraction of soyabean oil:
0/0/0	0	0	0/0	0/0/0	0/0	0//0	0/0/	0/0/0	4.5/0			0/0/0	---Oil-cake
0/0/0	0	0	0/0	0/0/0	0/0	0//0	0/0/	0/0/0	4.5/0			0/0/0	---Other
													Oil-cake and other solid residues, whether or not ground or in the form of pellets, resulting from the extraction of groundnut oil:
0/0/0	0	0	0/0	0/0/0	0/0	0//0	0/0/	0/0/0	4.5/0			0/0/0	Oil-cake and other solid residues, whether or not ground or in the form of pellets, resulting from the extraction of groundnut oil
													Oil-Cake and other solid residues, whether or not ground or in the form of pellets, resulting from the extraction of vegetable or microbial fats or oils, other than those of heading No. 23.04 or 23.05:
0/0/0	0	0	0/0	0/0/0	0/0	0//0	0/0/	0/0/0	4.5/0			0/0/0	-Of cotton seeds
0/0/0	0	0	0/0	0/0/0	0/0	0//0	0/0/	0/0/0	4.5/0		0//	0/0/0	-Of linseed

税则号列	货品名称〔CIQ扩展编码及品名—T2表示见附表2〕	最惠(%)	暂定税率	普通	增值/消费	出口退税	计量单位	监管条件/特殊证件	检验检疫	对美关税	亚太上/下
2306.3000	-葵花子的〔999〕	5	0	30	0/	9	千克	AB/	PNQ		
	-油菜子的：										
2306.4100	--低芥子酸的〔999〕	5	0	30	0/	9	千克	AB/	PNQ		
2306.4900	--其他〔999〕	5	0	30	0/	9	千克	AB/	PNQ		
2306.5000	-椰子或干椰肉的〔999〕	5	0	30	9/	9	千克	AB/	PNQ	5	2.5/2.5
2306.6000	-棕榈果或棕榈仁的										
2306.6000 10	濒危棕榈果或濒危棕榈仁油渣饼及固体残渣(不论是否碾磨或制成团粒)〔999〕	5	0	30	9/	0	千克	ABEF/	PNQ	5	
2306.6000 90	其他棕榈果或其他棕榈仁油渣饼及固体残渣(不论是否碾磨或制成团粒)〔999〕	5	0	30	9/	9	千克	AB/	PNQ	5	
2306.9000	-其他〔101 饲用芝麻饼、粕,102 其他饲用加工植物蛋白〕	5	0	30	9/	0,9,13	千克	AB/	PNQ	25	
23.07	**葡萄酒渣;粗酒石:**										
2307.0000	葡萄酒渣;粗酒石〔301 需申报仅用于工业用途不用于食品添加剂无检疫要求的化学品,999 其他植物饲料〕	5		30	0/	0	千克	AB/	RS		
23.08	**动物饲料用的其他税目未列名的植物原料、废料、残渣及副产品,不论是否制成团粒:**										
2308.0000	动物饲料用的其他税目未列名的植物原料、废料、残渣及副产品,不论是否制成团粒〔101 饲用苜蓿草,102 饲用燕麦草,103 其他饲草,104 饲用其他淀粉,105 饲用青贮,106 饲用植物颗粒和植物粉,107 其他植物饲料,108 辣椒粕,109 橄榄粕,110 榴莲粕,111 扁桃仁粕〕	5	0	35	9/	0,13,9	千克	AB/	PQ	5	
23.09	**配制的动物饲料:**										
	-零售包装的狗食或猫食:										
2309.1010	---罐头〔999〕	15	4	90	9/	9	千克	AB/	PQ	34	
2309.1090	---其他〔101 非罐装宠物食品,102 咀嚼物〕	15	4	90	9/	9	千克	AB/	PQ	29	
	-其他:										
2309.9010	---制成的饲料添加剂〔101 含动物源性饲料添加剂,102 含植物源性饲料添加剂,103 其他饲料添加剂〕	5		14	13/	9,13	千克	AB/	MPQ	15	2.5/2.5
2309.9090	---其他[T2]	6.5	4	14	9/	0,9,13	千克	AB/	MPQ	14	3.3/3.3

协定税率 %								RCEP		特惠税率 %			Article Description
东/冰/格	巴基斯坦	韩国	瑞士上/下	哥/秘/柬	澳/毛	新西/坡/智	中国港/澳/台	东盟及马来/澳/韩	日/新	亚太2国	老/柬/缅	98/97/95	
0/0/0	0	0	0/0	0/0/0	0/0	0//0	0/0/	0/0/0	4.5/0			0/0/0	-Of sunflower seeds
													-Of rape or colza seeds:
0/0/0	0	0	0/0	0/0/0	0/0	0//0	0/0/	0/0/0	4.5/0			0/0/0	--Of low erucic acid rape or colza seeds
0/0/0	0	0	0/0	0/0/0	0/0	0//0	0/0/	0/0/0	4.5/0			0/0/0	--Other
0/0/0	0	0	0/0	0/0/0	0/0	0//0	0/0/	0/4.5/0	0/4.5		/0/	0/0/0	-Of coconut or copra
													-Of palm nuts or kernels
0/0/0	0	0	0/0	0/0/0	0/0	0//0	0/0/	0/0/0	0/0		/0/	0/0/0	Oil residue cake and solid residue of endangered palm fruit or endangered palm kernel (whether or not ground or made into pellets)
0/0/0	0	0	0/0	0/0/0	0/0	0//0	0/0/	0/0/0	0/0		/0/	0/0/0	Other palm fruit or other palm kernel oil cake and solid residue (whether or not ground or made into pellets)
0/0/0	0	0	0/0	0/0/0	0/0	0//0	0/0/	0/0/0	4.5/0		0//	0/0/0	-Other
													Wine lees; argol:
0/0/0	0	0	0/0	0/0/0	0/0	0//0	0/0/	0/0/0	0/0			0/0/0	Wine lees; argol
													Vegetable materials and vegetable waste, vegetable residues and by-products, whether or not in the form of pellets, of a kind used in animal feeding, not elsewhere specified or included:
0/0/0	0	0	0/0	0/0/0	0/0	0//0	0/0/	0/0/0	0/0			0/0/0	Vegetable materials and vegetable waste, vegetable residues and by-products, whether or not in the form of pellets, of a kind used in animal feeding, not elsewhere specified or included
													Preparations of a kind used in animal feeding:
													-Dog or cat food, put up for retail sale:
0/0/0	12	3	1.5/1.5	0/0/0	0/0	0/0/0	0/0/	0/0/13.5	13.6/0			0/0/0	---In airtight containers
0/0/0	12	3	1.5/1.5	0/0/0	0/0	0/0/0	0/0/	0/0/13.5	13.6/0			0/0/0	---Other
													-Other:
0/0/0	0	0	0/0	0/0/0	0/0	0//0	0/0/	0/0/0	0/0			0/0/0	---Preparations for use in making the complete feeds or supplementary feeds
0/0/0	0	1.3	0/0	0/0/0	0/0	0//0	0/0/	5.9/5.9/5.9	5.9/5.9			0/0/0	---Other

第二十四章
烟草及烟草代用品的制品;非经燃烧吸用的产品,不论是否含有尼古丁;其他供人体摄入尼古丁的含尼古丁的产品

注释:

一、本章不包括药用卷烟(第三十章)。

二、既可归入税目 24.04 又可归入本章其他税目的产品,应归入税目 24.04 。

三、税目 24.04 所称"非经燃烧吸用",是指不通过燃烧,而是通过加热或其他方式吸用。"

子目注释:

子目 2403.11 所称"水烟料",是指由烟草和甘油混合而成用水烟筒吸用的烟草,不论是否含有芳香油及提取物、糖蜜或糖,也不论是否用水果调味,但供在水烟筒中吸用的非烟草产品除外。

税则号列	货品名称〔CIQ 扩展编码及品名—T2 表示见附表 2〕	最惠(%)	暂定税率	普通	增值/消费	出口退税	计量单位	监管条件/特殊证件	检验检疫	对美关税	亚太上/下
24.01	**烟草;烟草废料:**										
	-未去梗的烟草:										
2401.1010	---烤烟〔999〕	10		70	13/	9,13	千克	7AB/	PQS	35	9.4/9.4
2401.1090	---其他〔101 香料烟,102 白肋烟〕	10		70	13/	9	千克	7AB/	PQS	35	
	-部分或全部去梗的烟草:										
2401.2010	---烤烟〔999〕	10		70	13/	9,13	千克	7AB/	PQS	35	
2401.2090	---其他〔101 香料烟,102 白肋烟〕	10		70	13/	13	千克	7AB/	PQS	35	
2401.3000	-烟草废料〔999〕	10		70	13/	13, 9	千克	AB7/	PQS	35	
24.02	**烟草或烟草代用品制成的雪茄烟及卷烟:**										
2402.1000	-烟草制的雪茄烟〔999〕	25		180	13/36	0	千克/千支	7/		50	
2402.2000	-烟草制的卷烟〔999〕	25		180	13/0	0	千克/千支	7/		50	
2402.9000	-其他										
2402.9000 01	烟草代用品制的卷烟〔999〕	25		180	13/0	0	千克/千支	7/		50	
2402.9000 09	烟草代用品制的雪茄烟〔999〕	25		180	13/36	0	千克/千支	7/		50	
24.03	**其他烟草及烟草代用品的制品;"均化"或"再造"烟草;烟草精汁:**										
	-供吸用的烟草,不论是否含有任何比例的烟草代用品:										
2403.1100	--本章子目注释所述的水烟料〔999〕	57		180	13/30	13	千克	7AB/	PQS	82	50.2/50.2
2403.1900	--其他〔999〕	57		180	13/30	13	千克	7AB/	PQS	82	50.2/50.2
	-其他:										
2403.9100	--"均化"或"再造"烟草										
2403.9100 10	再造烟草〔999〕	57		180	13/30	13	千克	AB7/	PQ	82	
2403.9100 90	均化烟草〔999〕	57		180	13/30	13	千克	AB7/	PQ	82	
2403.9900	--其他										
2403.9900 10	烟草精汁〔999〕	57		180	13/	13	千克	7AB/	MPNQS	82	
2403.9900 90	其他烟草及烟草代用品的制品〔101 其他烟草及烟草代用品的制品,102 烟用香精〕	57		180	13/30	13	千克	AB/	PQS	82	
24.04	**含烟草、再造烟草、尼古丁、或烟草或尼古丁代用品,非经燃烧吸用的产品;其他供人体摄入尼古丁的 含尼古丁的产品:**										
	-非经燃烧吸用的产品:										
2404.1100	--含烟草或再造烟草的〔999〕	57		180	13/30	13	千克	7AB/	PQ	82	
2404.1200	--其他,含尼古丁的〔999〕	6.5		35	13/	13	千克	7/			4.2/4.2
	--其他:										
2404.1910	---其他,含烟草代用品的〔999〕	57		180	13/30	13	千克	7AB/	PQS	82	
2404.1990	---其他〔999〕	6.5		35	13/	13	千克	7/			4.2/4.2
	-其他:										
2404.9100	--经口腔摄入的										
2404.9100 10	经口腔摄入含濒危动植物成份的供人体摄入尼古丁的产品〔999〕	12		90	13/	0	千克	ABEF/	RS	22	11/11
2404.9100 90	经口腔摄入的其他供人体摄入尼古丁的产品〔999〕	12		90	13/	13	千克	AB/	RS	22	11/11
2404.9200	--经皮肤摄入的〔999〕	6.5		35	13/	13	千克	/			4.2/4.2
2404.9900	--其他〔999〕	6.5		35	13/	13	千克	/			4.2/4.2

Chapter 24

Tobacco and manufactured tobacco substitutes; products, whether or not containing nicotine, intended for inhalation without combustion; other nicotine containing products intended for the intake of nicotine into the human body

Note:

1.This Chapter does not cover medicinal cigarettes (Chapter 30).

2. Any products classifiable in heading 24.04 and any other heading of the Chapter are to be classified in heading 24.04.

3. For the purposes of heading 24.04, the expression "inhalation without combustion" means inhalation through heated delivery or other means, without combustion.

Subheading Note:

For the purposes of Subheading 2403. 11, the expression"water pipe tobacco"means tobacco intended for smoking in a water pipe and which consists of a mixture of tobacco and glycerol, whether or not containing aromatic oils and extracts, molasses or sugar, and whether or not flavoured with fruit. However, tobacco-free products intended for smoking in a water pipe are excluded from this Subheading

协定税率 %								RCEP		特惠税率 %			Article Description
东/冰/格	巴基斯坦	韩国	瑞士上/下	哥/秘/柬	澳/毛	新西/坡/智	中国港/澳/台	东盟及马来/澳/韩	日/新	亚太2国	老/柬/缅	98/97/95	
													Unmanufactured tobacco; tobacco refuse:
													-Tobacco, not stemmed/stripped:
5//	9.4					0//0	0/0/						---Flue-cured
5//						0//0	0/0/						---Other
													-Tobacco, partly or wholly stemmed/stripped:
5//						0//0	0/0/						---Flue-cured
5//						0//0	0/0/						---Other
5//				/0/		0//0	0/0/					0/0/0	-Tobacco refuse
													Cigars, cheroots, cigarillos and cigarettes, of tobacco or of tobacco substitutes:
						0//0	0/0/						-Cigars, cheroots and cigarillos, containing tobacco
						0//0	0/0/						-Cigarettes containing tobacco
													-Other
						0//0	0/0/						Cigarettes containing tobacco substitutes
						0//0	0/0/						Cigars, cheroots and cigarillos, containing tobacco substitutes
													Other manufactured tobacco and manufactured tobacco substitutes; "homogenized" or "reconstituted" tobacco; tobacco extracts and essences:
													-Smoking tobacco, whether or not containing tobacco substitutes in any proportion:
50//	50					0//0	0/0/						--Water pipe tobacco specified in Subheading Note to this Chapter
50//	50					0//0	0/0/						--Other
													-Other:
													--"Homogenized" or "reconstituted" tobacco
50//						0//0	0/0/						Reconstituted tobacco
50//						0//0	0/0/						Homogenized tobacco
													--Other
50//						0//0	0/0/					0//	Tobacco extracts and essences
50//						0//0	0/0/					0//	Other manufactured tobacco and manufactured tobacco substitutes
													Products containing tobacco, reconstituted tobacco, nicotine, or tobacco or nicotine substitutes, intended for inhalation without combustion; other nicotine containing products intended for the intake of nicotine into the human body:
													- Products intended for inhalation without combustion:
50//						0//0	0/0/					0//	-- Containing tobacco or reconstituted tobacco
0/0/0	0	3		0/0/0	0/0	0/0/0	0/0/	5.9/5.9/5.9	6.1/5.9			0/0/0	--Non incendiary smoking products containing nicotine but not tobacco or reconstituted (homogenized) tobacco
													-- Other:
50//						0//0	0/0/						--- Other, containing tobacco substitutes
0/0/0	0	3		0/0/0	0/0	0/0/0	0/0/	5.9/5.9/5.9	6.1/5.9			0/0/0	--- Other
													- Other :
													-- For oral application
0/0/	0	18.4	5/5	0/0/0	0/12	0/0/0	0/0/	19/19/20	19/19			0/0/0	Oral intake of nicotine containing endangered animal and plant ingredients for human consumption
0/0/	0	18.4	5/5	0/0/0	0/12	0/0/0	0/0/	19/19/20	19/19			0/0/0	Other products for human consumption of nicotine taken orally
0/0/0	0	3		0/0/0	0/0	0/0/0	0/0/	5.9/5.9/5.9	6.1/5.9			0/0/0	--For transdermal application
0/0/0	0	3		0/0/0	0/0	0/0/0	0/0/	5.9/5.9/5.9	6.1/5.9			0/0/0	-- Other

第五类
矿　产　品

第二十五章
盐;硫磺;泥土及石料;
石膏料、石灰及水泥

注释:

一、除条文及注释四另有规定的以外,本章各税目只包括原产状态的矿产品,或只经过洗涤(包括用化学物质清除杂质而未改变产品结构的)、破碎、磨碎、研粉、淘洗、筛分以及用浮选、磁选和其他机械物理方法(不包括结晶法)精选过的货品,但不得经过焙烧、煅烧、混合或超过税目所列的加工范围。

本章产品可含有添加的抗尘剂,但所加剂料并不使原产品改变其一般用途而适合于某些特殊用途。

二、本章不包括:

(一)升华硫磺、沉淀硫磺及胶态硫磺(税目 28.02);

(二)土色料,按重量计三氧化二铁含量在70%及以上(税目 28.21);

(三)第三十章的药品及其他产品;

(四)芳香料制品及化妆盥洗品(第三十三章);

(五)夯混白云石(科目 38.16)

(六)长方砌石、路缘石、扁平石(税目 68.01)、镶嵌石或类似石料(税目 68.02)及铺屋顶、饰墙面或防潮用的板石(税目 68.03);

(七)宝石或半宝石(税目 71.02 或 71.03);

(八)每颗重量不低于 2.5 克的氯化钠或氧化镁培养晶体(光学元件除外)(税目 38.24);氯化钠或氧化镁制的光学元件(税目 90.01);

(九)台球用粉块(税目 95.04);

(十)书写或绘画用粉笔及裁缝划粉(税目 96.09)。

三、既可归入税目 25.17 又可归入本章其他税目的产品,应归入税目 25.17。

四、税目 25.30 主要包括:未膨胀的蛭石、珍珠岩及绿泥石;不论是否煅烧或混合的土色料;天然云母氧化铁;海泡石(不论是否磨光成块);琥珀;模制后未经进一步加工的片、条、杆或类似形状的粘聚海泡石及粘聚琥珀;黑玉;菱锶矿(不论是否煅烧),但不包括氧化锶;破碎陶器、砖或混凝土的碎块。

税则号列	货品名称〔CIQ 扩展编码及品名—T2 表示见附表 2〕	最惠(%)	暂定税率	普通	增值/消费	出口退税	计量单位	监管条件/特殊证件	检验检疫	对美关税	亚太上/下
25.01	**盐(包括精制盐及变性盐)及纯氯化钠,不论是否为水溶液,也不论是否添加抗结块剂或松散剂;海水:**										
	---盐:										
2501.0011	----食用盐〔101 饲料用盐,102 食盐〕	0		0	9/	9	千克	AB/	RS	25	
2501.0019	----其他[T2]	0		0	13/	13	千克	AB/	RS	25	
2501.0020	---纯氯化钠〔101 矿物源性饲料添加剂,102 其他盐〕	3		35	13/	13	千克	/		15.5	1.5/1.5
2501.0030	---海水〔999〕	0		0	13/	0	千克	/		10	
25.02	**未焙烧的黄铁矿:**										
2502.0000	未焙烧的黄铁矿〔999〕	3	1	20	13/	0	千克	/		28.5	1.5/1.5
25.03	**各种硫磺,但升华硫磺、沉淀硫磺及胶态硫磺除外:**										
2503.0000	各种硫磺,但升华硫磺、沉淀硫磺及胶态硫磺除外[T2]	3	1	17	13/	0	千克	AB/3	MRNS	28.5	1.5/1.5
25.04	**天然石墨:**										
	-粉末或粉片:										
2504.1010	---粉片〔999〕	3	1	30	13/	0	千克	/		13.5	1.5/1.5
	---其他:										
2504.1091	----球化石墨〔999〕	3		30	13/	13	千克	/		30.5	
2504.1099	----其他〔999〕	3		30	13/	0	千克	/		25.5	1.5/1.5
2504.9000	-其他〔999〕	3		30	13/	0	千克	/		30.5	1.5/1.5
25.05	**各种天然砂,不论是否着色,但第二十六章的含金属矿砂除外:**										
2505.1000	-硅砂及石英砂〔101 栽培介质,102 硅砂〕	3	1	40	13/	0	千克	48xy/		23.5	
2505.9000	-其他										
2505.9000　10	标准砂(不论是否着色,第二十六章的金属矿砂除外)〔101 栽培介质,102 硅砂〕	3	1	40	13/	0	千克	4xy/		28.5	1.5/1.5
2505.9000　90	其他天然砂(不论是否着色,第二十六章的金属矿砂除外)〔101 栽培介质,102 硅砂〕	3	1	40	13/	0	千克	48xy/		28.5	1.5/1.5
25.06	**石英(天然砂除外);石英岩,不论是否粗加修整或仅用锯或其他方法切割成矩形(包括正方形)的板、块:**										

SECTION V
MINERAL PRODUCTS

Chapter 25
Salt; sulphur; earths and stone; plastering materials, lime and cement

Notes:

1. Except where their context or Note 4 to this Chapter otherwise requires, the headings of this Chapter cover only products which are in the crude state or which have been washed (even with chemical substances eliminating the impurities without changing the structure of the product), crushed, ground, powdered, levigated, sifted, screened, concentrated by flotation, magnetic separation or other mechanical or physical processes (except crystallization), but not products which have been roasted, calcined, obtained by mixing or subjected to processing beyond that mentioned in each heading.
   The products of this Chapter may contain an added antidusting agent, provided that such addition does not render the product particularly suitable for specific use rather than for general use.
2. This Chapter does not cover:
   (a) Sublimed sulphur, precipitated sulphur or colloidal sulphur (heading No. 28.02);
   (b) Earth colours containing 70% or more by weight of combined iron evaluated as Fe_2O_3 (heading No. 28.21);
   (c) Medicaments or other products of Chapter 30;
   (d) Perfumery, cosmetic or toilet preparations (Chapter 33);
   (e) Dolomite ramming mix (heding No.38.16);
   (f) Setts, curbstones or flagstones (heading No. 68.01); mosaic cubes or the like (heading No. 68.02); roofing, facing or damp course slates (heading No. 68.03);
   (g) Precious or semi-precious stones (heading No. 71.02 or 71.03);
   (h) Cultured crystals (other than optical elements) weighing not less than 2.5g each, of sodium chloride or of magnesium oxide, of heading No. 38.24; optical elements of sodium chloride or of magnesium oxide (heading No. 90.01);
   (ij) Billiard chalks (heading No. 95.04); or
   (k) Writing or drawing chalks or tailors' chalks (heading No. 96.09).
3. Any products classifiable in heading No. 25.17 and any other heading of this Chapter are to be classified in heading No. 25.17.
4. Heading No. 25.30 applies, *inter alia*, to: vermiculite, perlite and chlorites, unexpanded; earth colours, whether or not calcined or mixed together; natural micaceous iron oxides; meerschaum (whether or not in polished pieces); amber; agglomerated meerschaum and agglomerated amber, in plates, rods, sticks or similar forms, not worked after moulding; jet; strontianite (whether or not calcined), other than strontium oxide; broken pieces of pottery, brick or concrete.

协定税率 %								RCEP		特惠税率 %			Article Description
东/冰/格	巴基斯坦	韩国	瑞士上/下	哥/秘/柬	澳/毛	新西/坡/智	中国港/澳/台	东盟及马来/澳/韩	日/新	亚太2国	老/柬/缅	98/97/95	
													Salt (including table salt and denatured salt) and pure sodium chloride, whether or not in aqueous solution or containing added anticaking or free-flowing agents; sea water:
													---Salt:
0/0/0	0	0	0/0	0/0/0	0/0	0//0	0/0/	0/0/0	0/0			0/0/0	----Edible salt
0/0/0	0	0	0/0	0/0/0	0/0	0//0	0/0/	0/0/0	0/0			0/0/0	Other
0/0/0	0	0	0/0	0/0/0	0/0	0//0	0/0/	0/0/0	0/0		0//	0/0/0	---Pure sodium chloride
0/0/0	0	0	0/0	0/0/0	0/0	0//0	0/0/	0/0/0	0/0			0/0/0	---Sea water
													Unroasted iron pyrites:
0/0/0	0	0	0/0	0/0/0	0/0	0//0	0/0/	0/0/0	0/0			0/0/0	Unroasted iron pyrite
													Sulphur of all kinds, other than sublimed sulphur, precipitated sulphur and colloidal sulphur:
0/0/0	0	0	0/0	0/0/0	0/0	0//0	0/0/	0/0/0	0/0			0/0/0	Sulphur of all kinds, other than sublimed sulphur, precipitated sulphur and colloidal sulphur
													Natural graphite:
													-In powder or in flakes:
0/0/0	0	0	0.3/0.3	0/0/0	0/0	0//0	0/0/	0/0/0	2.7/0			0/0/0	---In flakes
													---Other:
0/0/0	0	0	0/0	0/0/0	0/0	0//0	0/0/	0/0/0	0/0			0/0/0	----Spherical graphite
0/0/0	0	0	0/0	0/0/0	0/0	0//0	0/0/	0/0/0	0/0			0/0/0	----Other
0/0/0	0	0	0/0	0/0/0	0/0	0//0	0/0/	0/0/0	0/0			0/0/0	-Other
													Natural sands of all kinds, whether or not coloured, other than metal-bearing sands of Chapter 26:
0/0/0	0	0	0/0	0/0/0	0/0	0//0	0/0/	0/0/0	0/0			0/0/0	-Silica sands and quartz sands
													-Other
0/0/0	0	0	0/0	0/0/0	0/0	0//0	0/0/	0/0/0	0/0			0/0/0	Standard sands (whether or not coloured, other than metal-bearing sands of Chapter 26)
0/0/0	0	0	0/0	0/0/0	0/0	0//0	0/0/	0/0/0	0/0			0/0/0	Other natural sands of all kinds (whether or not coloured, other than metal-bearing sands of Chapter 26)
													Quartz (other than natural sands); quartzite, whether or not roughly trimed or merely cut, by sawing or otherwise, intoblocks or slabs of a rectangular (including square) shape:

税则号列	货品名称〔CIQ 扩展编码及品名—T2 表示见附表 2〕	最惠(%)	暂定税率	普通	增值/消费	出口退税	计量单位	监管条件/特殊证件	检验检疫	对美关税	亚太上/下
2506.1000	-石英[T2]	3	1	40	13/	0	千克	/		13.5	1.5/1.5
2506.2000	-石英岩〔101 栽培介质,102 石英岩〕	3	1	40	13/	0	千克	/		28.5	1.5/1.5
25.07	**高岭土及类似土,不论是否煅烧:**										
2507.0010	---不论是否煅烧的高岭土〔102〕	3	1	50	13/	0	千克	/			
2507.0090	---其他〔999〕	3	1	50	13/	0	千克	/		28.5	
25.08	**其他黏土(不包括税目 68.06 的膨胀黏土)、红柱石、蓝晶石及硅线石,不论是否煅烧;富铝红柱石;火泥及第纳斯土:**										
2508.1000	-膨润土										
2508.1000 10	钠基膨润土〔101 无检疫要求食品添加剂,102 膨润土〕	3	1	50	13/	0	千克	/		13.5	1.5/1.5
2508.1000 90	其他膨润土,不论是否煅烧〔101 无检疫要求食品添加剂,102 膨润土〕	3		50	13/	0	千克	/		15.5	1.5/1.5
2508.3000	-耐火黏土〔999〕	3	1	20	13/	0	千克	4xy/		23.5	1.5/1.5
2508.4000	-其他黏土〔102〕	3		50	13/	0	千克	/		25.5	
2508.5000	-红柱石、蓝晶石及硅线石〔999〕	3		40	13/	0	千克	/		15.5	1.5/1.5
2508.6000	-富铝红柱石〔999〕	3		40	13/	0	千克	/		15.5	
2508.7000	-火泥及第纳斯土〔998 火泥,999 第纳斯土〕	3		20	13/	0	千克	/		5.5	
25.09	**白垩:**										
2509.0000	白垩〔999〕	3		45	13/	0	千克	/		30.5	
25.10	**天然磷酸钙、天然磷酸铝钙及磷酸盐白垩:**										
	-未碾磨:										
2510.1010	---磷灰石〔999〕	3	0	11	13/	0	千克	4xy/		2.5	
2510.1090	---其他〔999〕	3		20	13/	0	千克	4xy/		5.5	
	-已碾磨:										
2510.2010	---磷灰石〔999〕	3	0	11	13/	0	千克	4xy/		27.5	
2510.2090	---其他〔999〕	3		20	13/	0	千克	4xy/		5.5	
25.11	**天然硫酸钡(重晶石);天然碳酸钡(毒重石),不论是否煅烧,但税目 28.16 的氧化钡除外:**										
2511.1000	-天然硫酸钡(重晶石)〔101 重晶石块,102 重晶石粉〕	3		45	13/	0	千克	/		15.5	1.5/1.5
2511.2000	-天然碳酸钡(毒重石)〔999〕	3		45	13/	0	千克	/		5.5	
25.12	**硅质化石粗粉(例如,各种硅藻土)及类似的硅质土,不论是否煅烧,其表观比重不超过 1:**										
2512.0010	---硅藻土〔101 无检疫要求食品添加剂,102 硅藻土〕	3		40	13/	0	千克	A/	R		1.5/1.5
2512.0090	---其他〔999〕	3		40	13/	0	千克	/		30.5	1.5/1.5
25.13	**浮石;刚玉岩;天然刚玉砂;天然石榴石及其他天然磨料,不论是否热处理:**										
2513.1000	-浮石〔999〕	3		35	13/	0	千克	/		30.5	
2513.2000	-刚玉岩、天然刚玉砂、天然石榴石及其他天然磨料〔101 刚玉岩,102 天然刚玉砂,103 天然石榴石〕	3		17	13/	0	千克	/		15.5	1.5/1.5
25.14	**板岩,不论是否粗加修整或仅用锯或其他方法切割成矩形(包括正方形)的板、块:**										
2514.0000	板岩,不论是否粗加修整或仅用锯或其他方法切割成矩形(包括正方形)的板、块〔999〕	3		50	13/	0	千克	/		5.5	1.5/1.5
25.15	**大理石、石灰华及其他石灰质碑用或建筑用石,表观比重为 2.5 及以上,蜡石,不论是否粗加修整或仅用锯或其他方法切割成矩形(包括正方形)的板、块:**										
	-大理石及石灰华:										
2515.1100	--原状或粗加修整〔999〕	4	0	80	13/	0	千克	/		27.5	2/2
2515.1200	--用锯或其他方法切割成矩形,包括正方形〔999〕	4	0	80	13/	0	千克	/		27.5	2/2
2515.2000	-其他石灰质碑用或建筑用石,蜡石〔999〕	3	0	50	13/	0	千克	/		27.5	
25.16	**花岗石、斑岩、玄武岩、砂岩以及其他碑用或建筑用石,不论是否粗加修整或仅用锯或其他方法切割成矩形(包括正方形)的板、块:**										
	-花岗岩:										
2516.1100	--原状或粗加修整〔999〕	4	0	50	13/	0	千克	A/	M	27.5	2/2
2516.1200	--仅用锯或其他方法切割成矩形,包括正方形〔999〕	4	0	50	13/	0	千克	A/	M	27.5	2/2
2516.2000	-砂岩										

协定税率 %								RCEP		特惠税率 %			Article Description
东/冰/格	巴基斯坦	韩国	瑞士上/下	哥/秘/柬	澳/毛	新西/坡/智	中国港/澳/台	东盟及马来/澳/韩	日/新	亚太2国	老/柬/缅	98/97/95	
0/0/0	0	0	0/0	0/0/0	0/0	0//0	0/0/	0/0/0	0/0			0/0/0	-Quartz
0/0/0	0	0	0/0	0/0/0	0/0	0//0	0/0/	0/0/0	0/0			0/0/0	-Quartzite
													Kaolin and other kaolinic clays, whether or not calcined:
0/0/0	0	0	0/0	0/0/0	0/0	0//0	0/0/	0/0/0	0/0			0/0/0	---whether or not calcined Kaolin
0/0/0	0	0	0/0	0/0/0	0/0	0//0	0/0/	0/0/0	0/0			0/0/0	---Other
													Other clays (not including expanded clays of heading No. 68.06), andalusite, kyanite and sillimanite, whether or not calcined; mullite; chamotte or dinas earths:
													-Bentonite
0/0/0	0	0	0/0	0/0/0	0/0	0//0	0/0/	0/0/0	0/0			0/0/0	Sodium bentonite
0/0/0	0	0	0/0	0/0/0	0/0	0//0	0/0/	0/0/0	0/0			0/0/0	Other bentonite, whether or not calcined
0/0/0	0	0	0/0	0/0/0	0/0	0//0	0/0/	0/0/0	0/0			0/0/0	-Fire-clay
0/0/0	0	0	0/0	0/0/0	0/0	0//0	0/0/	0/0/0	0/0			0/0/0	-Other clays
0/0/0	0	0	0/0	0/0/0	0/0	0//0	0/0/	0/0/0	0/0			0/0/0	-Andalusite, kyanite and sillimanite
0/0/0	0	0	0/0	0/0/0	0/0	0//0	0/0/	0/0/0	0/0			0/0/0	-Mullite
0/0/0	0	0	0.3/0.3	0/0/0	0/0	0//0	0/0/	0/0/0	2.7/0			0/0/0	-Chamotte or dinas earths
													Chalk:
0/0/0	0	0	0/0	0/0/0	0/0	0//0	0/0/	0/0/0	0/0			0/0/0	Chalk
													Natural calcium phosphates, natural aluminium calcium phosphates and phosphatic chalk:
													-Unground:
0/0/0	0	0	0/0	0/0/0	0/0	0//0	0/0/	0/0/0	0/0			0/0/0	---Apatite
0/0/0	0	0	0/0	0/0/0	0/0	0//0	0/0/	0/0/0	0/0			0/0/0	---Other
													-Ground:
0/0/0	0	0	0/0	0/0/0	0/0	0//0	0/0/	0/0/0	0/0			0/0/0	---Apatite
0/0/0	0	0	0/0	0/0/0	0/0	0//0	0/0/	0/0/0	0/0			0/0/0	---Other
													Natural barium sulphate (barytes); natural barium carbonate (witherite), whether or not calcined, other than barium oxide of heading No. 28.16:
0/0/0	0	0	0/0	0/0/0	0/0	0//0	0/0/	0/0/0	0/0			0/0/0	-Natural barium sulphate (barytes)
0/0/0	0	0	0/0	0/0/0	0/0	0//0	0/0/	0/0/0	0/0			0/0/0	-Natural barium carbonate (witherite)
													Siliceous fossil meals (for example, kieselguhr, tripolite and diatomite) and similar siliceous earths, whether or not calcined, of an apparent specific gravity of 1 or less:
0/0/0	0	0	0/0	0/0/0	0/0	0//0	0/0/	0/0/0	0/0			0/0/0	---Kieselguhr
0/0/0	0	0	0/0	0/0/0	0/0	0//0	0/0/	0/0/0	0/0			0/0/0	---Other
													Pumice stone; emery; natural corundum, natural garnet and other natural abrasives, whether or not heat-treated:
0/0/0	0	0	0/0	0/0/0	0/0	0//0	0/0/	0/0/0	0/0			0/0/0	-Pumice stone
0/0/0	0	0	0/0	0/0/0	0/0	0//0	0/0/	0/0/0	0/0			0/0/0	-Emery, natural corundum, narural garnet and other natural abrasives
													Slate, whether or not roughly trimmed or merely cut, by sawing or otherwise, into blocks or slabs of a rectangular (including square) shape:
0/0/0	0	0	0/0	0/0/0	0/0	0//0	0/0/	0/0/0	0/0			0/0/0	Slate, whether or not roughly trimmed or merely cut, by sawing or otherwise, into blocks or slabs of a rectangular (including square) shape
													Marble, travertine, ecaussine and other calcareous monumental or building stone of an apparent specific gravity of 2.5 or more, and alabaster, whether or not roughly trimmed or merely cut, by sawing or otherwise, into blocks or slabs of a rectangular (including square) shape:
													-Marble and travertine:
0/0/0	0	0	0/0	0/0/0	0/0	0//0	0/0/	0/0/0	0/0			0/0/0	--Crude or roughly trimmed
0/0/0	0	0	0/0	0/0/0	0/0	0//0	0/0/	0/3.6/0	0/3.6			0/0/0	--Merely cut, by sawing or otherwise, into blocks or slabs of a rectangular (including square) shape
0/0/0	0	0	0/0	0/0/0	0/0	0//0	0/0/	0/0/0	2.7/0			0/0/0	-Ecaussine and other calcareous monumental or building stone; alabaster
													Granite, porphyry, basalt, sandstone and other monumental or building stone, whether or not building stone whether or not roughly trimmed or merely cut, by sawing or otherwise, into blocks or slabs of a rectangular (including square) shape:
													-Granite:
0/0/0	0	0	0/0	0/0/0	0/0	0//0	0/0/	0/0/0	0/0			0/0/0	--Crude or roughly trimmed
0/0/0	0	0	0/0	0/0/0	0/0	0//0	0/0/	0/3.6/0	0/3.6			0/0/0	--Merely cut, by sawing or otherwise, into blocks or slabs of a rectangular (including square) shape
													-Sandstone

税则号列		货品名称〔CIQ扩展编码及品名—T2表示见附表2〕	最惠(%)	暂定税率	普通	增值/消费	出口退税	计量单位	监管条件/特殊证件	检验检疫	对美关税	亚太上/下
2516.2000	01	原状或粗加修整砂岩〔999〕	3	0	50	13/	0	千克	A/	M	27.5	2.1/2.1
2516.2000	90	矩形(包括正方形)砂岩(用锯或其他方法切割成矩形的板、块)〔999〕	3	0	50	13/	0	千克	/		27.5	2.1/2.1
2516.9000		-其他碑用或建筑用石〔999〕	3	0	50	13/	0	千克	/		27.5	2.1/2.1
25.17		**通常作混凝土粒料、铺路、铁道路基或其他路基用的卵石、砾石及碎石,圆石子及燧石,不论是否热处理;矿渣、浮渣及类似的工业残渣,不论是否混有本税目第一部分所列的材料;沥青碎石;税目25.15、25.16所列各种石料的碎粒、碎屑及粉末,不论是否热处理:**										
2517.1000		-通常作混凝土粒料、铺路、铁道路基或其他路基用的卵石、砾石及碎石,圆石子及燧石,不论是否热处理〔999〕	4		50	13/	0	千克	/		31.5	2/2
2517.2000		-矿渣、浮渣及类似的工业残渣,不论是否混有子目2517.10所列的材料〔999〕	3		50	13/	0	千克	9/			
2517.3000		-沥青碎石〔999〕	3		50	13/	0	千克	9/		5.5	
		-税目25.15及25.16所列各种石料的碎粒、碎屑及粉末,不论是否热处理:										
2517.4100		--大理石的〔999〕	3		50	13/	0	千克	/		15.5	1.5/1.5
2517.4900		--其他〔999〕	3		50	13/	0	千克	/		30.5	
25.18		**白云石,不论是否煅烧或烧结、粗加修整或仅用锯或其他方法切割成矩形(包括正方形)的板、块:**										
2518.1000		-未煅烧或烧结的白云石〔999〕	3	0	40	13/	0	千克	/		27.5	1.5/1.5
2518.2000		-已煅烧或烧结的白云石〔999〕	3	0	40	13/	0	千克	/		2.5	
25.19		**天然碳酸镁(菱镁矿);熔凝镁氧矿;烧结镁氧矿,不论烧结前是否加入少量其他氧化物;其他氧化镁,不论是否纯净:**										
2519.1000		-天然碳酸镁(菱镁矿)〔999〕	3	1	40	13/	0	千克	y4x/			
		-其他:										
2519.9010		---熔凝镁氧矿〔999〕	3	1	40	13/	0	千克	y4x/		28.5	
2519.9020		---烧结镁氧矿(重烧镁)〔999〕	3	1	40	13/	0	千克	y4x/		28.5	
2519.9030		---碱烧镁(轻烧镁)〔999〕	3	1	40	13/	0	千克	y4x/		28.5	
		---其他:										
2519.9091		----化学纯氧化镁[T2]	3		35	13/	0	千克	A/	R		
2519.9099		----其他										
2519.9099	10	其他氧化镁含量在70%及以上的矿产品〔101矿物源性饲料添加剂,102氧化镁〕	3	1	40	13/	0	千克	4xy/		23.5	
2519.9099	90	其他氧化镁〔101矿物源性饲料添加剂,102氧化镁〕	3		40	13/	0	千克	/		25.5	
25.20		**生石膏;硬石膏;熟石膏(由煅烧的生石膏或硫酸钙构成),不论是否着色,也不论是否带有少量促凝剂或缓凝剂:**										
2520.1000		-生石膏;硬石膏〔999〕	5		80	13/	0	千克	/		32.5	2.5/2.5
		-熟石膏:										
2520.2010		---牙科用〔999〕	5		40	13/	0	千克	/		17.5	
2520.2090		---其他〔999〕	5		80	13/	0	千克	/		17.5	
25.21		**石灰石助熔剂;通常用于制造石灰或水泥的石灰石及其他钙质石:**										
2521.0000		石灰石助熔剂;通常用于制造石灰或水泥的石灰石及其他钙质石〔999〕	5		50	13/	0	千克	/		27.5	2.5/2.5
25.22		**生石灰、熟石灰及水硬石灰,但税目28.25的氧化钙及氢氧化钙除外:**										
2522.1000		-生石灰〔999〕	5		80	13/	0	千克	/		32.5	2.5/2.5
2522.2000		-熟石灰〔999〕	5		80	13/	0	千克	/		32.5	2.5/2.5
2522.3000		-水硬石灰〔999〕	5		80	13/	0	千克	/		7.5	
25.23		**硅酸盐水泥、矾土水泥、矿渣水泥、富硫酸盐水泥及类似的水凝水泥,不论是否着色,包括水泥熟料:**										
2523.1000		-水泥熟料〔999〕	5		30	13/	0	千克	/		32.5	2.5/2.5
		-硅酸盐水泥:										
2523.2100		--白水泥,不论是否人工着色〔999〕	5		30	13/	0	千克	/		17.5	3.8/3.8
2523.2900		--其他〔999〕	5		30	13/	0	千克	A/	M	17.5	3.8/3.8
2523.3000		-矾土水泥〔999〕	5		30	13/	0	千克	/		32.5	2.5/2.5

协定税率 %								RCEP		特惠税率 %			Article Description
东/冰/格	巴基斯坦	韩国	瑞士 上/下	哥/秘/柬	澳/毛	新西/坡/智	中国港/澳/台	东盟及马来/澳/韩	日/新	亚太2国	老/柬/缅	98/97/95	
0/0/0	0	0	0/0	0/0/0	0/0	0//0	0/0/	0/0/0	0/0			0/0/0	Crude or roughly trimmed sandstone
0/0/0	0	0	0/0	0/0/0	0/0	0//0	0/0/	0/0/0	0/0			0/0/0	Rectangular(including square) sandstone(cut, by sawing or otherwise, into blocks or slabs of a rectangular)
0/0/0	0	0	0/0	0/0/0	0/0	0//0	0/0/	0/0/0	0/0			0/0/0	-Other monumental or building stone
													Pebbles, gravel, broken or crushed stone, of a kind commonly used for concrete aggregates, for road metalling or for railway or other ballast, shingle and flint, whether or not heat-treated; macadam of slag, dross or similar industrial waste, whether or not incorporating the materials cited in the first part of the heading; tarred macadam; granules, chippings and powder, of stones of heading No. 25.15 or 25.16, whether or not heat-treated:
0/0/0	0	0	0/0	0/0/0	0/0	0//0	0/0/	0/0/0	0/0			0/0/0	-Pebbles, gravel, broken or crushed stone, of a kind commonly used for concrete aggregates, for road metalling or for railway or other ballast, shingle and flint, whether or not heat-treated
0/0/0	0	0	0/0	0/0/0	0/0	0//0	0/0/	0/0/0	0/0			0/0/0	-Macadam of slag, dross or similar industrial waste, whether or not incorporating the materials cited in subheading No. 2517.10
0/0/0	0	0	0/0	0/0/0	0/0	0//0	0/0/	0/0/0	0/0			0/0/0	-Tarred macadam
													-Granules, chippings and powder, stones of heading No. 25.15 or 25.16, whether or not heat-treated:
0/0/0	0	0	0/0	0/0/0	0/0	0//0	0/0/	0/0/0	0/0			0/0/0	--Of marble
0/0/0	0	0	0/0	0/0/0	0/0	0//0	0/0/	0/0/0	0/0			0/0/0	--Other
													Dolomite, whether or not calcined or Sintered, including dolomite roughly trimmed or merely cut, by sawing or otherwise, into blocks or slabs of a rectangular (including square) shape:
0/0/0	0	0	0/0	0/0/0	0/0	0//0	0/0/	0/0/0	0/0			0/0/0	-Dolomite, not calcined or sintered
0/0/0	0	0	0/0	0/0/0	0/0	0//0	0/0/	0/0/0	0/0			0/0/0	-Calcined or sintered dolomite
													Natural magnesium carbonate (magnesite); fused magnesia; dead-burned (sintered) magnesia, whether or not containing small quantities of other oxides added before sintering; other magnesium oxide, whether or not pure:
0/0/0	0	0	0/0	0/0/0	0/0	0//0	0/0/	0/0/0	0/0			0/0/0	-Natural magnesium carbonate (magnesite)
													-Other:
0/0/0	0	0	0/0	0/0/0	0/0	0//0	0/0/	0/0/0	0/0			0/0/0	---Fused magnesia
0/0/0	0	0	0/0	0/0/0	0/0	0//0	0/0/	0/0/0	0/0			0/0/0	---Dead-burned (sintered) magnesia
0/0/0	0	0	0/0	0/0/0	0/0	0//0	0/0/	0/0/0	0/0			0/0/0	---Light-burned magnesia
													---Other:
0/0/0	0	0	0/0	0/0/0	0/0	0//0	0/0/	0/2.7/0	0/2.7			0/0/0	----Magnesium oxide, chemically pure
													----Other
0/0/0	0	0	0/0	0/0/0	0/0	0//0	0/0/	0/0/0	0/0			0/0/0	Other mineral products containing $\geqslant$70% by weight of magnesium oxide
0/0/0	0	0	0/0	0/0/0	0/0	0//0	0/0/	0/0/0	0/0			0/0/0	Other magnesium oxide
													Gypsum; anhydrite; plasters (consisting of calcined gypsum or calcium sulphate) whether or not coloured, with or without small quantities of accelerators or retarders:
0/0/0	0	0	0/0	0/0/0	0/0	0//0	0/0/	0/0/0	4.5/0		0//	0/0/0	-Gypsum; anhydrite
													-Plasters:
0/0/0	0	0	0/0	0/0/0	0/0	0//0	0/0/	0/0/0	0/0		0//	0/0/0	---For dental use
0/0/0	0	1	0/0	0/0/0	0/0	0//0	0/0/	0/0/4.5	4.5/0		0//	0/0/0	---Other
													Limestone flux; limestone and other calcareous stone, of a kind used for the manufacture of lime or cement:
0/0/0	0	0	0/0	0/0/0	0/0	0//0	0/0/	0/0/0	0/0			0/0/0	Limestone flux; limestone and other calcareous stone, of a kind used for the manufacture of lime or cement
													Quicklime, slaked lime and hydraulic lime, other than calcium oxide and hydroxide of heading No. 28.25:
0/0/0	0	0	0/0	0/0/0	0/0	0//0	0/0/	0/0/0	0/0			0/0/0	-Quicklime
0/0/0	0	0	0/0	0/0/0	0/0	0//0	0/0/	0/0/0	0/0			0/0/0	-Slaked lime
0/0/0	0	0	0/0	0/0/0	0/0	0//0	0/0/	0/0/0	0/0			0/0/0	-Hydraulic lime
													Portland cement, aluminous cement, slag cement, supersulphate cement and similar hydraulic cements, whether or not coloured or in the form of clinkers:
0/0/0	2	0	0/0	0/0/0	0/0	0//0	0/0/0	0/0/0	7.3/0			0/0/0	-Cement clinkers
													-Portland cement:
0/0/0	0	0	0/0	0/0/0	0/0	0//0	0/0/0	0/0/0	0/0			0/0/0	--White cement, whether or not artificially coloured
0/0/0	0	0	0/0	0/0/0	0/0	0//0	0/0/0	0/0/0	7.3/0			0/0/0	--Other
0/0/0	4	0	0/0	0/0/0	0/0	0//0	0/0/	0/0/0	0/0			0/0/0	-Aluminous cement

税则号列	货品名称〔CIQ 扩展编码及品名—T2 表示见附表 2〕	最惠(%)	暂定税率	普通	增值/消费	出口退税	计量单位	监管条件/特殊证件	检验检疫	对美关税	亚太上/下
2523.9000	-其他水凝水泥〔101 矿渣水泥,102 其他水泥〕	5		30	13/	0	千克	A/	M	17.5	
25.24	**石棉:**										
2524.1000	-青石棉〔101 栽培介质;301 其他危险化学品〕	5		30	13/	0	千克	89/3		7.5	
	-其他:										
2524.9010	---长纤维的										
2524.9010 10	长纤维阳起石石棉(包括长纤维铁石棉、透闪石石棉及直闪石石棉)[T2]	5		30	13/	0	千克	89/3		7.5	
2524.9010 90	其他长纤维石棉[T2]	5		30	13/	0	千克	/3		7.5	
2524.9090	---其他的										
2524.9090 10	其他阳起石石棉(包括其他铁石棉、透闪石石棉及直闪石石棉)〔101 栽培介质;301 其他危险化学品 〕	5		35	13/	0	千克	89/3		32.5	
2524.9090 90	其他石棉〔101 栽培介质;301 危险化学品;302 其他化工品〕	5		35	13/	0	千克	/3		32.5	
25.25	**云母,包括云母片;云母废料:**										
2525.1000	-原状云母及劈开的云母片〔999〕	5	1	30	13/	0	千克	/		28.5	2.5/2.5
2525.2000	-云母粉〔999〕	5		30	13/	0	千克	/		17.5	2.5/2.5
2525.3000	-云母废料〔101 其他云母,102 废矿〕	5		30	13/	0	千克	9/		7.5	
25.26	**天然冻石,不论是否粗加修整或仅用锯或其他方法切割成矩形(包括正方形)的板、块;滑石:**										
	-未破碎及未研粉:										
2526.1010	---冻石〔999〕	3		50	13/	0	千克	/		5.5	
2526.1020	---滑石〔999〕	3	1	50	13/	0	千克	4xy/		3.5	1.5/1.5
	-已破碎或已研粉:										
2526.2010	---冻石〔999〕	3		50	13/	0	千克	/		5.5	
2526.2020	---滑石										
2526.2020 01	滑石粉(体积百分比 90%及以上的产品颗粒度小于等于 18 微米的)〔999〕	3	1	50	13/	0	千克	4Axy/	R		
2526.2020 90	已破碎或已研粉的其他天然滑石〔999〕	3	1	50	13/	0	千克	4xy/			
25.28	**天然硼酸盐及其精矿(不论是否煅烧),但不包括从天然盐水析离的硼酸盐;天然粗硼酸,含硼酸干重不超过 85%:**										
2528.0010	---天然硼砂及其精矿(不论是否煅烧)〔999〕	3	0	30	13/	0	千克	A/	M	27.5	
2528.0090	---其他〔999〕	5	0	30	13/	0	千克	/		27.5	
25.29	**长石;白榴石;霞石及霞石正长岩;萤石(氟石):**										
2529.1000	-长石〔101 栽培介质,102 长石〕	3	1	50	13/	0	千克	/		28.5	1.5/1.5
	-萤石:										
2529.2100	--按重量计氟化钙含量在 97%及以下〔999〕	3		50	13/	0	千克	4xy/		5.5	1.5/1.5
2529.2200	--按重量计氟化钙含量在 97%以上〔999〕	3		50	13/	0	千克	4xy/		5.5	
2529.3000	-白榴石;霞石及霞石正长岩〔101 栽培介质,102 石材〕	5		50	13/	0	千克	/		32.5	
25.30	**其他税目未列名的矿产品:**										
	-未膨胀的蛭石、珍珠岩及绿泥石:										
2530.1010	---绿泥石〔999〕	5		30	13/	0	千克	/		7.5	
2530.1020	---蛭石及珍珠岩[T2]	5		30	13/	0	千克	/		32.5	2.5/2.5
2530.2000	-硫镁矾矿及泻盐矿(天然硫酸镁)〔999〕	3		30	13/	0	千克	/		15.5	
	-其他:										
2530.9010	---矿物性药材〔999〕	3		30	13/	0	千克	/		5.5	
2530.9020	---稀土金属矿〔999〕	0		0	13/	0	千克	4Bxy/	N		
	---其他:										
2530.9091	----硅灰石〔999〕	3		50	13/	0	千克	/		15.5	1.5/1.5
2530.9099	----其他										
2530.9099 10	废镁砖〔999〕	3	0	50	13/	0	千克	49xy/		27.5	1.5/1.5
2530.9099 20	叶蜡石〔999〕	3	0	50	13/	0	千克	/		27.5	1.5/1.5
2530.9099 30	未煅烧的水镁石〔999〕	3	0	50	13/	0	千克	4xy/		27.5	1.5/1.5
2530.9099 40	钟乳石〔999〕	3	0	50	13/	0	千克	u/		27.5	1.5/1.5
2530.9099 92	其他品目未列名氧化镁含量在 70%及以上的矿产品〔999〕	3	0	50	13/	0	千克	/		27.5	1.5/1.5
2530.9099 99	其他矿产品〔999〕	3	0	50	13/	0	千克	/		27.5	1.5/1.5

协定税率 %								RCEP		特惠税率 %			
东/冰/格	巴基斯坦	韩国	瑞士上/下	哥/秘/柬	澳/毛	新西/坡/智	中国港/澳/台	东盟及马来/澳/韩	日/新	亚太2国	老/柬/缅	98/97/95	Article Description
0/0/0	2	0	0/0	0/0/0	0/0	0//0	0/0/	0/0/0	7.3/0			0/0/0	-Other hydraulic cements
													Asbestos:
0/0/0	0	0	0/0	0/0/0	0/0	0//0	0/0/	0/0/0	0/0			0/0/0	-Grocidlite
													-Other:
													---Of long staple
0/0/0	0	0	0/0	0/0/0	0/0	0//0	0/0/	0/0/0	0/0			0/0/0	Actinolite asbestas of long fibre(including amosite asbestos、tremolite asbestos or anthopylite asbestos)
0/0/0	0	0	0/0	0/0/0	0/0	0//0	0/0/	0/0/0	0/0			0/0/0	Other asbestos of long fibre
													---Other
0/0/0	0	0	0/0	0/0/0	0/0	0//0	0/0/	0/0/0	0/0			0/0/0	Other actinolite asbestas (including other amosa asbestos、tremolite asbestos or anthopylite asbestos)
0/0/0	0	0	0/0	0/0/0	0/0	0//0	0/0/	0/0/0	0/0			0/0/0	Other asbestos
													Mica, including splittings; mica waste:
0/0/0	0	0	0/0	0/0/0	0/0	0//0	0/0/	0/4.5/0	0/4.5			0/0/0	-Crude mica and mica rifted into sheets or splittings
0/0/0	0	0	0/0	0/0/0	0/0	0//0	0/0/	0/0/0	0/0			0/0/0	-Mica powder
0/0/0	0	0	0/0	0/0/0	0/0	0//0	0/0/	0/0/0	0/0			0/0/0	-Mica waste
													Natural steatite, whether or not roughly trimmed or merely cut, by sawing or otherwise, into blocks or slabs or a rectangular (including square) shape; talc:
													-Not crushed, not powdered:
0/0/0	0	0	0/0	0/0/0	0/0	0//0	0/0/	0/0/0	0/0			0/0/0	---Natural steatite
0/0/0	0	0	0/0	0/0/0	0/0	0//0	0/0/	0/0/0	0/0			0/0/0	---Talc
													-Crushed or powdered:
0/0/0	0	0	0/0	0/0/0	0/0	0//0	0/0/	0/0/0	0/0			0/0/0	---Natural steatite
													---Talc
0/0/0	0	0	0/0	0/0/0	0/0	0//0	0/0/	0/0/0	0/0			0/0/0	Talc Powder(volume percent ≥90% , granularity≤18 micron)
0/0/0	0	0	0/0	0/0/0	0/0	0//0	0/0/	0/0/0	0/0			0/0/0	Other natural talc,crushed or powdered
													Natural borates and concentrates thereof (whether or not calcined), but not including borates separated from natural brine; natural boric acid containing not more than 85% of H_3BO_3 calulated on the dry weight:
0/0/0	0	0	0/0	0/0/0	0/0	0//0	0/0/	0/0/0	0/0			0/0/0	---Natural borates and concentrates thereof (whether or not calcined)
0/0/0	0	0	0/0	0/0/0	0/0	0//0	0/0/	0/0/0	0/0			0/0/0	---Other
													Feldspar; leucite; nepheline and nepheline syenite; fluorspar:
0/0/0	0	0	0/0	0/0/0	0/0	0//0	0/0/	0/0/0	0/0			0/0/0	-Feldspar
													-Fluorspar:
0/0/0	0	0	0/0	0/0/0	0/0	0//0	0/0/	0/0/0	0/0			0/0/0	--Containing by weight 97% or less of calcium fluoride
0/0/0	0	0	0/0	0/0/0	0/0	0//0	0/0/	0/0/0	0/0			0/0/0	--Containing by weight more than 97% of calcium fluoride
0/0/0	0	0	0/0	0/0/0	0/0	0//0	0/0/	0/0/0	0/0			0/0/0	-Leucite; nepheline and nepheline syenite
													Mineral substances not elsewhere specified or included:
													-Vermiculite, perlite and chlorites, unexpanded:
0/0/0	0	0	0/0	0/0/0	0/0	0//0	0/0/	0/0/0	0/0			0/0/0	---Chlorites
0/0/0	0	0	0/0	0/0/0	0/0	0//0	0/0/	0/0/0	0/0			0/0/0	---Vermiculite,perlite unexpanded
0/0/0	0	0	0/0	0/0/0	0/0	0//0	0/0/	0/0/0	0/0			0/0/0	-Kieserite, epsomite (natural magnesium sulphates)
													-Other:
0/0/0	0	0	0/0	0/0/0	0/0	0//0	0/0/	0/0/0	0/0			0/0/0	---Mineral medicinal substances
0/0/0	0	0	0/0	0/0/0	0/0	0//0	0/0/	0/0/0	0/0			0/0/0	---Ores of rare earth metals
													---Other:
0/0/0	0	0	0/0	0/0/0	0/0	0//0	0/0/	0/0/0	0/0			0/0/0	----Wollastonite
													----Other
0//0	0	0	0/0	0/0/0	0/0	0//0	0/0/	0/0/0	2.7/0			0/0/0	Waste magnesia brick
0//0	0	0	0/0	0/0/0	0/0	0//0	0/0/	0/0/0	2.7/0			0/0/0	Pyrophyllite
0//0	0	0	0/0	0/0/0	0/0	0//0	0/0/	0/0/0	2.7/0			0/0/0	Brucite
0//0	0	0	0/0	0/0/0	0/0	0//0	0/0/	0/0/0	2.7/0		//	0/0/0	Stalactite
0//0	0	0	0/0	0/0/0	0/0	0//0	0/0/	0/0/0	2.7/0			0/0/0	Mianeral products with 70% or more of magnesia which are not listed in other items
0//0	0	0	0/0	0/0/0	0/0	0//0	0/0/	0/0/0	2.7/0			0/0/0	Other mineral products

第二十六章
矿砂、矿渣及矿灰

注释：

一、本章不包括：

(一)供铺路用的矿渣及类似的工业废渣(税目 25.17)；

(二)天然碳酸镁(菱镁矿)，不论是否煅烧(税目 25.19)；

(三)主要含有石油的石油储罐的淤渣(品目 27.10)

(四)第三十一章的碱性熔渣；

(五)矿物棉(税目 68.06)；

(六)贵金属或包贵金属的废碎料；主要用于回收贵金属的含贵金属或贵金属化合物的其他废碎料(税目 71.12 或 85.49)；

(七)通过熔炼所产生的铜锍、镍锍或钴锍(第十五类)。

二、税目 26.01 至 26.17 所称"矿砂"，是指冶金工业中提炼汞、税目 28.44 的金属以及第十四类、第十五类金属的矿物，即使这些矿物不用于冶金工业，也包括在内。但税目 26.01 至 26.17 不包括不是以冶金工业正常加工方法处理的各种矿物。

三、税目 26.20 只适用于：

(一)在工业上提炼金属或作为生产金属化合物基本原料的矿渣、矿灰及残渣，但焚化城市垃圾所产生的灰、渣除外(税目 26.21)；

(二)含有砷的矿渣、矿灰及残渣，不论其是否含有金属，用于提取或生产砷或金属及其化合物。

子目注释：

一、子目 2620.21 所称 "含铅汽油的淤渣及含铅抗震化合物的淤渣"，是指含铅汽油及含铅抗震化合物(例如，四乙基铅)储罐的淤渣，主要含有铅、铅化合物以及铁的氧化物。

二、含有砷、汞、铊及其混合物的矿渣，矿灰及残渣，用于提取或生产砷、汞、铊及其化合物，归入子目 2620.60。

税则号列	货品名称〔CIQ 扩展编码及品名－T2 表示见附表 2〕	最惠(%)	暂定税率	普通	增值/消费	出口退税	计量单位	监管条件/特殊证件	检验检疫	对美关税	亚太上/下
26.01	**铁矿砂及其精矿，包括焙烧黄铁矿：**										
	-铁矿砂及其精矿，但焙烧黄铁矿除外：										
	--未烧结：										
2601.1110	---平均粒度小于 0.8 毫米的〔999〕	0		0	13/	0	千克	7A/	M		
2601.1120	---平均粒度不小于 0.8 毫米，但不大于 6.3 毫米的〔999〕	0		0	13/	0	千克	7A/	M		
2601.1190	---其他〔999〕	0		0	13/	0	千克	7A/	M		
2601.1200	--已烧结〔999〕	0		0	13/	0	千克	7A/	M	25	
2601.2000	-焙烧黄铁矿〔999〕	0		0	13/	0	千克	7A/	M		
26.02	**锰矿砂及其精矿，包括以干重计含锰量在 20%及以上的锰铁矿及其精矿：**										
2602.0000	锰矿砂及其精矿〔999〕	0		0	13/	0	千克	A/	M	25	
26.03	**铜矿砂及其精矿：**										
2603.0000	铜矿砂及其精矿										
2603.0000 10	铜矿砂及其精矿(黄金价值部分)〔999 铜矿，998 铜精矿〕	0		0	0/	0	千克	7A/	M		
2603.0000 90	铜矿砂及其精矿(非黄金价值部分)〔999 铜矿，998 铜精矿〕	0		0	13/	0	千克	7A/	M	25	
26.04	**镍矿砂及其精矿：**										
2604.0000	镍矿砂及其精矿										
2604.0000 01	镍矿砂及其精矿(黄金价值部分)〔999〕	0		0	0/	0	千克	/			
2604.0000 90	镍矿砂及其精矿(非黄金价值部分)〔999〕	0		0	13/	0	千克	/		25	
26.05	**钴矿砂及其精矿：**										
2605.0000	钴矿砂及其精矿										
2605.0000 01	钴矿砂及其精矿(黄金价值部分)〔999〕	0		0	0/	0	千克	/			
2605.0000 90	钴矿砂及其精矿(非黄金价值部分)〔999〕	0		0	13/	0	千克	/			
26.06	**铝矿砂及其精矿：**										
2606.0000	铝矿砂及其精矿〔999〕	0		0	13/	0	千克	4xy/			
26.07	**铅矿砂及其精矿：**										
2607.0000	铅矿砂及其精矿										
2607.0000 01	铅矿砂及其精矿(黄金价值部分)〔999 铅矿，998 铅精矿〕	0		0	0/	0	千克	A/	M		
2607.0000 90	铅矿砂及其精矿(非黄金价值部分)〔999 铅矿，998 铅精矿〕	0		0	13/	0	千克	A/	M	10	
26.08	**锌矿砂及其精矿：**										
2608.0000	锌矿砂及其精矿										
2608.0000 01	灰色饲料氧化锌(氧化锌 ZnO 含量大于 80%)〔999〕	0	0	0	13/	0	千克	A/	M	25	
2608.0000 90	其他锌矿砂及其精矿〔999 锌矿，998 锌精矿〕	0		0	13/	0	千克	A/	M	25	
26.09	**锡矿砂及其精矿：**										
2609.0000	锡矿砂及其精矿〔999〕	0	0	0	13/	0	千克	4xy/			

Chapter 26
Ores, slag and ash

Notes:

1. This Chapter does not cover:
   (a) Slag or similar industrial waste prepared as macadam (heading No. 25.17);
   (b) Natural magnesium carbonate (magnesite), whether or not calcined (heading No. 25.19);
   (c) Sludges from the storage tanks of petroleum oils, consisting mainly of such oils (heading No. 27.10);
   (d) Basic slag of Chapter 31;
   (e) Slag wool, rock wool or similar mineral wools (heading No. 68.06);
   (f) Waste or scrap of precious metal or of metal clad with precious metal; other waste or scrap containing precious metal or precious metal compounds, of a kind used principally for the recovery of precious metal (heading No. 71.12 or 85.49);
   (g) Copper, nickel or cobalt mattes produced by any process of smelting (Section ⅩⅤ).
2. For the purposes of headings No. 26.01 to 26.17, the term "ores" means minerals of mineralogical species actually used in the metallurgical industry for the extraction of mercury, of the metals of heading No. 28.44 or of the metals of Section ⅩⅣ or ⅩⅤ, even if they are intended for non-metallurgical purposes. Headings No. 26.01 to 26.17 do not, however, include minerals which have been submitted to processes not normal to the metallurgical industry.
3. Heading No. 26.20 applies only to:
   (a) Slag, ash and residues of a kind used in industry either for the extraction of metals or as a basis for the manufacture of chemical compounds of metals, excluding ash and residues from the incineration of municipal waste (heading No. 26.21);
   (b) Slag, ash and residues containing arsenic, whether or not containing metals, of a kind used either for the extraction of arsenic or matals or for the manufacture of their chemical compounds.

Subheading Notes:

1. For the purposes of subheading No. 2620.21, "leaded gasoline sludges and leaded anti-knock compound sludges" mean slud-ges obtained from storage tanks of leaded gasoline and leaded anti-knock compounds(for example, tetraethyl lead), and consisting essentially of lead, lead compounds and iron oxide.
2. Slag ash and residues containing arsenic, mercury, thallium or their mixtures, of a kind used for the extraction of arsenic or those metals or for the manufacture of their chemical compounds, are to be classified in subheading No. 2620.60.

协定税率 %								RCEP		特惠税率 %			Article Description
东/冰/格	巴基斯坦	韩国	瑞士上/下	哥/秘/柬	澳/毛	新西/坡/智	中国港/澳/台	东盟及马来/澳/韩	日/新	亚太2国	老/柬/缅	98/97/95	
													Iron ores and concentrates, including roasted iron pyrites:
													-Iron ores and concentrates, other than roasted iron pyrites:
													--Non-agglomerated:
0/0/0	0	0	0/0	0/0/0	0/0	0//0	0/0/	0/0/0	0/0			0/0/0	---Of a granularity less than 0.8mm
0/0/0	0	0	0/0	0/0/0	0/0	0//0	0/0/	0/0/0	0/0			0/0/0	---Of a granularity 0.8mm or more, but not exceeding 6.3mm
0/0/0	0	0	0/0	0/0/0	0/0	0//0	0/0/	0/0/0	0/0			0/0/0	---Other
0/0/0	0	0	0/0	0/0/0	0/0	0//0	0/0/	0/0/0	0/0			0/0/0	--Agglomerated
0/0/0	0	0	0/0	0/0/0	0/0	0//0	0/0/	0/0/0	0/0			0/0/0	-Roasted iron pyrites
													Manganese ores and concentrates, including ferruginous manganese ores and concentrates with a manganese content of 20% or more, calculated on the dry weight:
0/0/0	0	0	0/0	0/0/0	0/0	0//0	0/0/	0/0/0	0/0			0/0/0	Manganese ores and concentrates, including ferruginous manganese ores and concentrates with a manganese content of 20% or more, calculated on the dry weight
													Copper ores and concentrates:
													Copper ores and concentrates
0/0/0	0	0	0/0	0/0/0	0/0	0//0	0/0/	0/0/0	0/0			0/0/0	Copper ores and concentrates (part of gold value)
0/0/0	0	0	0/0	0/0/0	0/0	0//0	0/0/	0/0/0	0/0			0/0/0	Copper ores and concentrates (part of non-gold value)
													Nickel ores and concentrates:
													Nickel ores and concentrates
0/0/0	0	0	0/0	0/0/0	0/0	0//0	0/0/	0/0/0	0/0			0/0/0	Niclcel ores and concentrates(Part gold value part)
0/0/0	0	0	0/0	0/0/0	0/0	0//0	0/0/	0/0/0	0/0			0/0/0	Nickel ores and concen trates(Part of non-gold Value)
													Cobalt ores and concentrates:
													Cobalt ores and concentrates
0/0/0	0	0	0/0	0/0/0	0/0	0//0	0/0/	0/0/0	0/0			0/0/0	Cobalt ores and concentrates(Part gold value part)
0/0/0	0	0	0/0	0/0/0	0/0	0//0	0/0/	0/0/0	0/0			0/0/0	Cobalt ores and concen trates(Part of non-gold value)
													Aluminium ores and concentrate:
0/0/0	0	0	0/0	0/0/0	0/0	0//0	0/0/	0/0/0	0/0			0/0/0	Aluminium ores and concentrate
													Lead ores and concentrates:
													Lead ores and concentrates
0/0/0	0	0	0/0	0/0/0	0/0	0//0	0/0/	0/0/0	0/0			0/0/0	Lead ores and concentrates(Gold value part)
0/0/0	0	0	0/0	0/0/0	0/0	0//0	0/0/	0/0/0	0/0			0/0/0	Lead ores and con centrates(Non-gold value part)
													Zinc ores and concentrates:
													Zinc ores and concentrates
0/0/0	0	0	0/0	0/0/0	0/0	0//0	0/0/	0/0/0	0/0			0/0/0	Grey feed grade zinc oxide(containing＞80% by weight of ZnO)
0/0/0	0	0	0/0	0/0/0	0/0	0//0	0/0/	0/0/0	0/0			0/0/0	Other zinc ores and concentrates
													Tin ores and concentrates:
0/0/0	0	0	0/0	0/0/0	0/0	0//0	0/0/	0/0/0	0/0			0/0/0	Tin ores and concentrates

税则号列	货品名称〔CIQ 扩展编码及品名—T2 表示见附表 2〕	最惠(%)	暂定税率	普通	增值/消费	出口退税	计量单位	监管条件/特殊证件	检验检疫	对美关税	亚太上/下
26.10	**铬矿砂及其精矿:**										
2610.0000	铬矿砂及其精矿〔999〕	0		0	13/	0	千克	A/	M		
26.11	**钨矿砂及其精矿:**										
2611.0000	钨矿砂及其精矿〔999〕	0		0	13/	0	千克	4xy/			
26.12	**铀或钍矿砂及其精矿:**										
2612.1000	-铀矿砂及其精矿〔999〕	0		0	13/	0	千克	/			
2612.2000	-钍矿砂及其精矿〔999〕	0		0	13/	0	千克	4xy/			
26.13	**钼矿砂及其精矿:**										
2613.1000	-已焙烧〔999〕	0		0	13/	0	千克	4xy/		10	
2613.9000	-其他〔999〕	0		0	13/	0	千克	4xy/		10	
26.14	**钛矿砂及其精矿:**										
2614.0000	钛矿砂及其精矿〔999〕	0		0	13/	0	千克	/		25	
26.15	**铌、钽、钒或锆矿砂及其精矿:**										
2615.1000	-锆矿砂及其精矿〔101 锆悬浮于易燃液体中的,102 锆英砂矿〕	0		0	13/	0	千克	/		25	
	-其他:										
2615.9010	---水合钽铌原料(钽铌矿富集物)〔999〕	0		0	13/	0	千克	/			
2615.9090	---其他										
2615.9090 10	铌,钽精矿及其矿砂〔999〕	0		0	13/	0	千克	/		25	
2615.9090 90	钒矿砂;钒精矿〔999〕	0		0	13/	0	千克	/		25	
26.16	**贵金属矿砂及其精矿:**										
2616.1000	-银矿砂及其精矿〔999〕	0		0	13/	0	千克	/			
2616.9000	-其他										
2616.9000 01	黄金矿砂〔999〕	0		0	0/	0	千克	/			
2616.9000 09	其他贵金属矿砂及其精矿〔999〕	0		0	13/	0	千克	/		25	
26.17	**其他矿砂及其精矿:**										
	-锑矿砂及其精矿:										
2617.1010	---生锑(锑精矿,选矿产品)〔999〕	0		0	13/	0	千克	4xy/			
2617.1090	---其他										
2617.1090 01	其他锑矿砂及其精矿(黄金价值部分)〔999〕	0		0	0/	0	千克	4xy/			
2617.1090 90	其他锑矿砂及其精矿(非黄金价值部分)〔999〕	0		0	13/	0	千克	4xy/			
	-其他:										
2617.9010	---朱砂(辰砂)〔999〕	3		14	13/	0	千克	/3		5.5	
2617.9090	---其他〔999〕	0		0	13/	0	千克	/		25	
26.18	**冶炼钢铁所产生的粒状熔渣(熔渣砂):**										
2618.0010	---主要含锰										
2618.0010 01	主要含锰的冶炼钢铁产生的粒状熔渣,含锰量>25 %(包括熔渣砂)〔999〕	4		35	13/	0	千克	9/		29	
2618.0010 90	其他主要含锰的冶炼钢铁产生的粒状熔渣(包括熔渣砂)〔999〕	4		35	13/	0	千克	9/		29	
2618.0090	---其他〔999〕	4		35	13/	0	千克	9/			3.2/3.2
26.19	**冶炼钢铁所产生的熔渣、浮渣(粒状熔渣除外)、氧化皮及其他废料:**										
2619.0000	冶炼钢铁所产生的熔渣、浮渣(粒状熔渣除外)、氧化皮及其他废料										
2619.0000 10	轧钢产生的氧化皮〔999〕	4		35	13/	0	千克	9/		29	
2619.0000 21	冶炼钢铁所产生的含钒浮渣、熔渣,五氧化二钒含量>20%(冶炼钢铁所产生的粒状熔渣除外)〔999〕	4		35	13/	0	千克	9/		29	
2619.0000 29	其他冶炼钢铁所产生的含钒浮渣、熔渣(冶炼钢铁所产生的粒状熔渣除外)〔999〕	4		35	13/	0	千克	9/		29	
2619.0000 30	含铁大于 80%的冶炼钢铁产生的渣钢铁〔999〕	4		35	13/	0	千克	9/		29	
2619.0000 90	冶炼钢铁产生的其他熔渣、浮渣及其他废料(冶炼钢铁所产生的粒状熔渣除外)〔101 炉渣(栽培介质),102 矿渣(栽培介质)〕	4		35	13/	0	千克	9/		29	
26.20	**含有金属、砷及其化合物的矿渣、矿灰及残渣(冶炼钢铁所产生的灰、渣除外):**										
	-主要含锌:										
2620.1100	--含硬锌〔999〕	4		35	13/	0	千克	9/			
2620.1900	--其他〔999〕	4		35	13/	0	千克	9/			
	-主要含铅:										
2620.2100	--含铅汽油的淤渣及含铅抗震化合物的淤渣〔999〕	4		35	13/	0	千克	9/			

协定税率 %								RCEP		特惠税率 %			Article Description
东/冰/格	巴基斯坦	韩国	瑞士 上/下	哥/秘/柬	澳/毛	新西/坡/智	中国港/澳/台	东盟及马来/澳/韩	日/新	亚太2国	老/柬/缅	98/97/95	
													Chromium ores and concentrates:
0/0/0	0	0	0/0	0/0/0	0/0	0//0	0/0/	0/0/0	0/0			0/0/0	Chromium ores and concentrates
													Tungsten ores and concentrates:
0/0/0	0	0	0/0	0/0/0	0/0	0//0	0/0/	0/0/0	0/0			0/0/0	Tungsten ores and concentrates
													Uranium or thorium ores and concentrates:
0/0/0	0	0	0/0	0/0/0	0/0	0//0	0/0/	0/0/0	0/0			0/0/0	-Uranium ores and concentrates
0/0/0	0	0	0/0	0/0/0	0/0	0//0	0/0/	0/0/0	0/0			0/0/0	-Thorium ores and concentrates
													Molybdenum ores and concentrates:
0/0/0	0	0	0/0	0/0/0	0/0	0//0	0/0/	0/0/0	0/0			0/0/0	-Roasted
0/0/0	0	0	0/0	0/0/0	0/0	0//0	0/0/	0/0/0	0/0			0/0/0	-Other
													Titanium ores and concentrates:
0/0/0	0	0	0/0	0/0/0	0/0	0//0	0/0/	0/0/0	0/0			0/0/0	Titanium ores and concentrates
													Niobium, tantalum, vanadium or zirconium ores and concentrates:
0/0/0	0	0	0/0	0/0/0	0/0	0//0	0/0/	0/0/0	0/0			0/0/0	-Zirconium ores and concentrates
													-Other:
0/0/0	0	0	0/0	0/0/0	0/0	0//0	0/0/	0/0/0	0/0			0/0/0	---Hydrated Tantalum-Niobium materials or enriched materials from Tantalum/Niobium ores
													---Other
0/0/0	0	0	0/0	0/0/0	0/0	0//0	0/0/	0/0/0	0/0			0/0/0	Tantalum and niobium concentrates and ores thereof
0/0/0	0	0	0/0	0/0/0	0/0	0//0	0/0/	0/0/0	0/0			0/0/0	Vanadium ores and concentrates
													Precious metal ores and concentrates:
0/0/0	0	0	0/0	0/0/0	0/0	0//0	0/0/	0/0/0	0/0			0/0/0	-Silver ores and concentrates
													-Other
0/0/0	0	0	0/0	0/0/0	0/0	0//0	0/0/	0/0/0	0/0			0/0/0	Gold ores and concentrates
0/0/0	0	0	0/0	0/0/0	0/0	0//0	0/0/	0/0/0	0/0			0/0/0	Other precious metal ores and concentrates
													Other ores and concentrates:
													-Antimony ores and concentrates:
0/0/0	0	0	0/0	0/0/0	0/0	0//0	0/0/	0/0/0	0/0			0/0/0	---Crude antimony(Antimony concentrates which are mineral products)
													---Other
0/0/0	0	0	0/0	0/0/0	0/0	0//0	0/0/	0/0/0	0/0			0/0/0	Other antimony ores and concentrates(parts of gold value)
0/0/0	0	0	0/0	0/0/0	0/0	0//0	0/0/	0/0/0	0/0			0/0/0	Other antimony ores and concentrates(parts of non-gold value)
													-Other:
0/0/0	0	0	0/0	0/0/0	0/0	0//0	0/0/	0/0/0	0/0			0/0/0	---Cinnabar
0/0/0	0	0	0/0	0/0/0	0/0	0//0	0/0/	0/0/0	0/0			0/0/0	---Other
													Granulated slag (slag sand) from the manufacture of iron or steel:
													---Containing mainly Manganese
0/0/0	0	0	0/0	0/0/0	0/0	0//0	0/0/	0/0/0	0/0			0/0/0	Manganese slag from the manufacture of iron or steel, more than 25% of manganese(including slag sand)
0/0/0	0	0	0/0	0/0/0	0/0	0//0	0/0/	0/0/0	0/0			0/0/0	Other granulated slag(slag sand) from the manufacture of iron or steel, containing mainly Manganese
0/0/0	0	0	0/0	0/0/0	0/0	0//0	0/0/	0/0/0	0/0			0/0/0	---Other
													Slag, dross (other than granulated slag), scalings and other waste from the manufacture of iron or steel:
													Slag, dross (other than granulated slag), scalings and other waste from the manufacture of iron or steel
0/0/0	0	0	0/0	0/0/0	0/0	0//0	0/0/	0/0/0	0/0			0/0/0	Scalings from the manufacture of steel
0/0/0	0	0	0/0	0/0/0	0/0	0//0	0/0/	0/0/0	0/0			0/0/0	Slag, drog, scalings and other waste from the manufacture of iron or steel, more than 20% vanadium pentoxide(other than granulated slag)
0/0/0	0	0	0/0	0/0/0	0/0	0//0	0/0/	0/0/0	0/0			0/0/0	Slap, dross from the manufaceure of iron or steel, containing vanadium(Other than granulated slag)
0/0/0	0	0	0/0	0/0/0	0/0	0//0	0/0/	0/0/0	0/0			0/0/0	Steel slag with more than 80% of steel form the manufaceure of steel and iron
0/0/0	0	0	0/0	0/0/0	0/0	0//0	0/0/	0/0/0	0/0			0/0/0	Slap, dross and other waster from the manufacture of iron or steel(Other than granulated slag)
													Slag, ash and residues (other than from the manufacture of iron or steel), containing metals arsenic, or their compounds:
													-Containing mainly zinc:
0/0/0	0	0	0/0	0/0/0	0/0	0//0	0/0/	0/0/0	0/0			0/0/0	Hard zinc spelter
0/0/0	0	0	0/0	0/0/0	0/0	0//0	0/0/	0/0/0	0/0			0/0/0	--Other
													-Containing mainly lead:
0/0/0	0	0	0/0	0/0/0	0/0	0//0	0/0/	0/0/0	0/0			0/0/0	--Leaded gasoline sludges and leaded anti-knock compound sludges

税则号列	货品名称〔CIQ 扩展编码及品名－T2 表示见附表 2〕	最惠(%)	暂定税率	普通	增值/消费	出口退税	计量单位	监管条件/特殊证件	检验检疫	对美关税	亚太上/下
2620.2900	--其他〔999〕	4		35	13/	0	千克	9/			
2620.3000	-主要含铜〔999〕	4		35	13/	0	千克	9/			
2620.4000	-主要含铝〔999〕	4		35	13/	0	千克	9/			
2620.6000	-含砷、汞、铊及其混合物，用于提取或生产砷、汞、铊及其化合物〔999〕	4		35	13/	0	千克	9/			
	-其他：										
2620.9100	--含锑、铍、镉、铬及其混合物〔999〕	4		35	13/	0	千克	9/			
	--其他：										
2620.9910	---主要含钨〔999〕	4		35	13/	0	千克	y4x9/			
2620.9990	---其他										
2620.9990 11	含其他金属及其化合物的矿渣、矿灰及残渣，五氧化二钒＞20％(冶炼钢铁所产生的及含钒废催化剂除外)〔999〕	4		35	13/	0	千克	9/		29	
2620.9990 19	含其他金属及其化合物的矿渣、矿灰及残渣，10％＜五氧化二钒≤20％的(冶炼钢铁所产生的及含钒废催化剂除外)〔999〕	4		35	13/	0	千克	9/		29	
2620.9990 20	含铜大于 10％的铜冶炼转炉渣及火法精炼渣，其他铜冶炼渣〔101 用作铜冶炼的原料，102 用作除锈磨料的其他铜冶炼渣〕	4		35	13/	0	千克	9/		29	
2620.9990 90	含其他金属及其化合物的矿渣、矿灰及残渣(冶炼钢铁所产生灰、渣的除外)〔999〕	4		35	13/	0	千克	9/		29	
26.21	**其他矿渣及矿灰，包括海藻灰(海草灰)；焚化城市垃圾所产生的灰、渣：**										
2621.1000	-焚化城市垃圾所产生的灰、渣〔999〕	4		35	13/	0	千克	9/			
2621.9000	-其他										
2621.9000 10	海藻灰及其他植物灰(包括稻壳灰)〔999〕	4		35	13/	0	千克	9/		14	
2621.9000 90	其他矿渣及矿灰〔999〕	4		35	13/	0	千克	9/		14	

协定税率 %								RCEP		特惠税率 %			Article Description
东/冰/格	巴基斯坦	韩国	瑞士上/下	哥/秘/柬	澳/毛	新西/坡/智	中国港/澳/台	东盟及马来/澳/韩	日/新	亚太2国	老/柬/缅	98/97/95	
0/0/0	0	0	0/0	0/0/0	0/0	0//0	0/0/	0/0/0	0/0			0/0/0	--Other
0/0/0	0	0	0/0	0/0/0	0/0	0//0	0/0/	0/0/0	0/0			0/0/0	-Containing mainly copper
0/0/0	0	0	0/0	0/0/0	0/0	0//0	0/0/	0/0/0	0/0			0/0/0	-Containing mainly aluminium
0/0/0	0	0	0/0	0/0/0	0/0	0//0	0/0/	0/0/0	0/0			0/0/0	-Containing arsenic, mercury, thallium or their mixtures, of a kind used for the extraction of arsenic or those metals or for the manufacture of their chemical compounds
													-Other:
0/0/0	0	0	0/0	0/0/0	0/0	0//0	0/0/	0/0/0	0/0			0/0/0	--Containing antimony, beryllium, cadmium, chromium or their mixtures
													--Other:
0/0/0	0	0	0/0	0/0/0	0/0	0//0	0/0/	0/0/0	0/0			0/0/0	---Containing mainly tungsten
													---Other
0/0/0	0	0	0/0	0/0/0	0/0	0//0	0/0/	0/0/0	0/0			0/0/0	Slag,ash and residues,containing other metals or their compounds,more than 20% vanadium pentoxide(other than from the manufacture of iron or steel)
0/0/0	0	0	0/0	0/0/0	0/0	0//0	0/0/	0/0/0	0/0			0/0/0	Slag,ash and residues,containing other metals or their compounds,10%< containing vanadium pentoxide≤20%(other than from the manufacture of iron or steel and including vanadium spent catalyst)
0/0/0	0	0	0/0	0/0/0	0/0	0//0	0/0/	0/0/0	0/0			0/0/0	Copper converter slag fire refining slag from copper smelter, containing copper>10%
0/0/0	0	0	0/0	0/0/0	0/0	0//0	0/0/	0/0/0	0/0			0/0/0	Slag, ash and residues, containing other metals or their compounds (other than from the manufacture of iron or steel)
													Other slag and ash, including seaweed ash (kelp); ash and residues from the incineration of municipal waste:
0/0/0	0		0/0	0/0/0	0/0	0//0	0/0/	3.9/3.9/	/3.9			0/0/0	-Ash and residues from the incineration of municipal waste
													-Other
0/0/0	0	0	0/0	0/0/0	0/0	0//0	0/0/	0/0/0	0/0			0/0/0	Algae ash and other plant ash (including rice husk ash)
0/0/0	0	0	0/0	0/0/0	0/0	0//0	0/0/	0/0/0	0/0			0/0/0	Other ore slag and ore ash

第二十七章

矿物燃料、矿物油及其蒸馏产品;沥青物质;矿物蜡

注释:

一、本章不包括:

(一)单独的已有化学定义的有机化合物,但纯甲烷及纯丙烷应归入税目27.11;

(二)税目30.03及30.04的药品;

(三)税目33.01、33.02及38.05的不饱和烃混合物。

二、税目27.10所称"石油及从沥青矿物提取的油类",不仅包括石油、从沥青矿物提取的油及类似油,还包括那些用任何方法提取的主要含有不饱和烃混合物的油,但其非芳族成分的重量必须超过芳族成分。

然而,它不包括采用减压蒸馏法在压力转换为1013毫巴下的温度300℃时,以体积计馏出量小于60%的液体合成聚烯烃(第三十九章)。

三、税目27.10所称"废油",是指主要含石油及从沥青矿物提取的油类(参见本章注释二)的废油,不论其是否与水混合。它们包括:

(一)不再适于作为原产品使用的废油(例如,用过的润滑油、液压油及变压器油);

(二)石油储罐的淤渣油,主要含有废油及高浓度的在生产原产品时使用的添加剂(例如,化学品);

(三)水乳浊液状或与水混合的废油,例如,浮油、清洗油罐所得的油或机械加工中已用过的切削油。

子目注释:

一、子目2701.11所称"无烟煤",是指含挥发物(以干燥、无矿物质计)不超过14%的煤。

二、子目2701.12所称"烟煤",是指含挥发物(以干燥、无矿物质计)超过14%,并且热值(以潮湿、无矿物质计)等于或大于5833大卡/千克的煤。

三、子目2707.10、2707.20、2707.30及2707.40所称"粗苯""粗甲苯""粗二甲苯"及"萘",是分别指按重量计苯、甲苯、二甲苯、萘的含量在50%以上的产品。

四、子目2710.12所称"轻油及其制品",是指根据ISO 3405方法(等同于ASTM D86方法),温度在210℃时以体积计馏出量(包括损耗)在90%及以上的产品。

五、税目27.10的子目所称"生物柴油",是指从动植物油脂或微生物油脂(不论是否使用过)得到的用作燃料的脂肪酸单烷基酯。

税则号列	货品名称〔CIQ扩展编码及品名—T2表示见附表2〕	最惠(%)	暂定税率	普通	增值/消费	出口退税	计量单位	监管条件/特殊证件	检验检疫	对美关税	亚太上/下
27.01	**煤;煤砖、煤球及用煤制成的类似固体燃料:**										
	-煤,不论是否粉化,但未制成型:										
2701.1100	--无烟煤										
2701.1100 10	无烟煤(不论是否粉化,但未制成型)〔999〕	3		20	13/	0	千克	47Axy/1	M	28	
2701.1100 90	无烟煤滤料〔999〕	3		20	13/	0	千克	7A/1	M	28	
	--烟煤:										
2701.1210	---炼焦煤〔999〕	3		20	13/	0	千克	47Axy/1	M	30.5	
2701.1290	---其他〔999〕	6		20	13/	0	千克	47Axy/1	M	31	
2701.1900	--其他煤〔999〕	5		20	13/	0	千克	47Axy/1	M	30	3.5/3.5
2701.2000	-煤砖、煤球及用煤制成的类似固体燃料〔999〕	5		50	13/	0	千克	/1		30	
27.02	**褐煤,不论是否制成型,但不包括黑玉:**										
2702.1000	-褐煤,不论是否粉化,但未制成型〔999〕	3		20	13/	0	千克	4Axy/1	M	28	
2702.2000	-制成型的褐煤〔999〕	3		20	13/	0	千克	A/1	M	28	
27.03	**泥煤(包括肥料用泥煤),不论是否制成型:**										
2703.0000	泥煤(包括肥料用泥煤),不论是否制成型										
2703.0000 10	泥炭(草炭)[沼泽(湿地)中,地上植物枯死、腐烂堆积而成的有机矿体(不论干湿)]〔101 栽培介质,102 化工产品〕	5	3	20	13/	0	千克	8AB/1	PQ	28	2.5/2.5
2703.0000 90	泥煤(包括肥料用泥煤)(不论是否制成型)〔101 栽培介质,102 泥煤〕	5	3	20	13/	0	千克	AB/1	PQ	28	2.5/2.5
27.04	**煤、褐煤或泥煤制成的焦炭及半焦炭,不论是否制成型;甑炭:**										
2704.0010	---焦炭及半焦炭〔999〕	5	0	11	13/	0	千克	4xy/1		25	2.5/2.5
2704.0090	---其他〔999〕	5	0	11	13/	0	千克	/1		25	2.5/2.5
27.05	**煤气、水煤气、炉煤气及类似气体,但石油气及其他烃类气除外**										
2705.0000	煤气、水煤气、炉煤气及类似气体,但石油气及其他烃类气除外										
2705.0000 10	煤气〔301 危险化学品,易燃液体;302 其他化工品〕	5	1	20	9/	0	千克	AB/1	MN	26	
2705.0000 90	水煤气、炉煤气及类似气体(石油气及其他烃类气除外)〔301 危险化学品,易燃液体;302 其他化工产品〕	5	1	20	9/	0	千克	/1		26	

Chapter 27

Mineral fuels, mineral oils and products of their distillation; bituminous substances; mineral waxes

Notes:

1. This Chapter does not cover:
   (a) Separate chemically defined organic compounds, other than pure methane and propane which are to be classified in heading No. 27.11;
   (b) Medicaments of heading No. 30.03 or 30.04; or
   (c) Mixed unsaturated hydrocarbons of heading No. 33.01, 33.02 or 38.05.
2. References in heading No. 27.10 to "petroleum oils and oils obtained from bituminous minerals" include not only petroleum oils and oils obtained from bituminous minerals but also similar oils, as well as those consisting mainly of mixed unsaturated hydrocarbons, obtained by any process, provided that the weight of the non-aromatic constituents exceeds that of the aromatic constituents. However, the references do not include liquid synthetic polyolefins of which less than 60% by volume distils at 300℃, after conversion to 1,013 millibars when a reduced-pressure distillation method is used (Chapter 39).

   (a) Such oils no longer fit for use as primary products (for example, used lubricating oils, used hydraulic oils and used transformer oils);
   (b) Sludge oils from the storage tanks of petroleum oils, mainly containing such oils and a high concentration of additives (for example, chemicals) used in the manufacture of the primary products; and
   (c) Such oils in the form of emulsions in water or mixtures with water, such as those resulting from oil spills or storage tank washings, or from the use of cutting oils for machining operations.

Subheading Notes:

1. For the purposes of subheading No. 2701.11, "anthracite" means coal having a volatile matter limit (on a dry, mineral-matter-free basis) not exceeding 14%.
2. For the purposes of subheading No. 2701.12, "bituminous coal" means coal having a volatile matter limit (on a dry, mineral-matter-free basis) exceeding 14% and a calorific value limit (on a moist, mineral-matter-free basis) equal to or greater than 5,833kcal/kg.

3. For the purposes of subheadings. 2707.10, 2707.20, 2707.30 and 2707.40, the terms "benzole" (benzene), "toluole" (toluene), "xylole" (xylenes) and "naphthalene" apply to products which contain more than 50% by weight of benzene, toluene, xylene, or naphthalene, respectively.
4. For the purposes of subheading No. 2710.11, "light oils and preparations" are those of which according to ISO 3405 method (ASTMD 86 method to identify), 90% or more by volume (including losses) distil at 210℃.
5. For the purposes of the Subheadings of heading 27.10, the term "biodiesel" means mono-alkyl esters of fatty acids of a kind used as a fuel, derived from animal or vegetable or microbial fats and oils, whether or not used.

协定税率 %								RCEP		特惠税率 %			Article Description
东/冰/格	巴基斯坦	韩国	瑞士上/下	哥/秘/柬	澳/毛	新西/坡/智	中国港/澳/台	东盟及马来/澳/韩	日/新	亚太2国	老/柬/缅	98/97/95	
													Coal; briquettes, ovoids and similar solid fuels manufactured from coal:
													-Coal, whether or not pulverized, but not agglomerated:
													--Anthracite
0/0/0	0	0	0/0	0/0/0	0/0	0//0	0/0/	0/0/0	0/0		0//	0/0/0	Anthracite(whether or not pulverized, but not agglomerated)
0/0/0	0	0	0/0	0/0/0	0/0	0//0	0/0/	0/0/0	0/0		0//	0/0/0	Anthracite filter medium
													--Bituminous coal:
0/0/0	0	0	0/0	0/0/0	0/0	0//0	0/0/	0/0/0	0/0		0//	0/0/0	---Coking coal
0/0/0	0	0	0/0	0/0/0	0/0	0//0	0/0/	0/0/0	0/0		0//	0/0/0	---Other
0/0/0	0	0	0/0	0/0/0	0/0	0//0	0/0/	0/0/0	0/0		0//	0/0/0	--Other coal
0/0/0	0	0	0/0	0/0/0	0/0	0//0	0/0/	0/0/0	0/0		0//	0/0/0	-Briquettes, ovoids and similar solid fuels manufactured from coal
													Lignite, whether or not agglomerated, excluding jet:
0/0/0	0	0	0/0	0/0/0	0/0	0//0	0/0/	0/0/0	0/0			0/0/0	-Lignite, whether or not pulverized, but not agglomerated
0/0/0	0	0	0/0	0/0/0	0/0	0//0	0/0/	0/0/0	0/0			0/0/0	-Agglomerated lignite
													Peat (including peat litter), whether or not agglomerated:
													Peat (including peat litter), whether or not agglomerated
0/0/0	0	0	0/0	0/0/0	0/0	0//0	0/0/	0/0/0	0/0			0/0/0	In peat and swamp (wetland), organic ore bodies formed by dried and rotten plants on the ground (whether dry or wet)
0/0/0	0	0	0/0	0/0/0	0/0	0//0	0/0/	0/0/0	0/0			0/0/0	Peat (including peat used as fertilizer), whether shaped or not
													Coke and semi-coke of coal, of lignite or of peat, whether or not agglomerated; retort carbon:
0/0/0	0	0	0/0	0/0/0	0/0	0//0	0/0/	0/0/0	0/0			0/0/0	---Coke and semi-coke
0/0/0	0	0	0/0	0/0/0	0/0	0//0	0/0/	0/0/0	0/0			0/0/0	---Other
													Coal gas, water gas, producer gas and similar gases, other than petroleum gases and other gaseous hydrocarbons:
													Coal gas, water gas, producer gas and similar gases, other than petroleum gases and other gaseous hydrocarbons
0/0/0	0	0	0/0	0/0/0	0/0	0//0	0/0/	0/0/0	0/0			0/0/0	Coal gas
0/0/0	0	0	0/0	0/0/0	0/0	0//0	0/0/	0/0/0	0/0			0/0/0	Water gas, producer gas and similar gases, other than petroleum gases and other gaseous hydrocarbons

税则号列	货品名称〔CIQ 扩展编码及品名—T2 表示见附表 2〕	最惠(%)	暂定税率	普通	增值/消费	出口退税	计量单位	监管条件/特殊证件	检验检疫	对美关税	亚太上/下
27.06	**从煤、褐煤或泥煤蒸馏所得的焦油及其他矿物焦油,不论是否脱水或部分蒸馏,包括再造焦油:**										
2706.0000	从煤、褐煤或泥煤蒸馏所得的焦油及其他矿物焦油,不论是否脱水或部分蒸馏,包括再造焦油										
2706.0000 01	含蒽油≥50%及沥青≥40%的"炭黑油"〔301 危险化学品,易燃液体;302 其他化工产品〕	6	1	30	13/	0	千克	/13		26	
2706.0000 90	其他从煤、褐煤或泥煤蒸馏所得的焦油及矿物焦油(不论是否脱水或部分蒸馏,包括再造焦油)〔301 危险化学品,易燃液体;302 其他化工品〕	6	1	30	13/	0	千克	AB/13	MN	26	
27.07	**蒸馏高温煤焦油所得的油类及其他产品;芳族成分重量超过非芳族成分的类似产品:**										
2707.1000	-粗苯〔999〕	6		20	13/	0	千克	AB/13	MN	31	
2707.2000	-粗甲苯〔999〕	6		30	13/	0	千克	/13		31	
2707.3000	-粗二甲苯〔999〕	6	2	20	13/	0	千克	/13		27	
2707.4000	-萘〔999〕	7		30	13/	0	千克	AB/13	MN	32	6/6
2707.5000	-其他芳烃混合物,根据 ISO 3405 方法(等同于 ASTM D86 方法),温度在 250℃时的馏出量以体积计(包括损耗)在 65%及以上〔999 其他化工产品,998 其他危险化学品〕	7		30	13/	0	千克	/3		32	
2707.5000 10	200 摄氏度以下时蒸馏出的芳烃以体积计小于 95%的其他芳烃混合物(根据 ISO 3405 方法(等同于 ASTM D 86 方法),温度在 250℃时的馏出量以体积计(包括损耗)在 65%及以上)〔301 危险化学品,易燃液体;302 其他化工品〕	7		30	13/1.52元/升	0	千克/升	/13		32	
2707.5000 90	其他芳烃混合物(根据 ISO 3405 方法(等同于 ASTM D 86 方法),温度在 250℃时的馏出量以体积计(包括损耗)在 65%及以上)〔301 危险化学品,易燃液体;302 其他化工产品〕	7		30	13/	0	千克/升	/13		32	
	-其他:										
2707.9100	--杂酚油〔301 其他危险化学品;302 其他化工产品〕	7		30	13/	0	千克	/13		32	
	--其他:										
2707.9910	---酚〔301 其他危险化学品;302 其他化工产品〕	7		30	13/	0	千克	/13		32	
2707.9990	---其他〔301 危险化学品,易燃液体; 302 危险化学品,杂项物质;303 其他危险化学品;304 其他化工品〕	7		30	13/1.52元/升	0	千克/升	/13		32	
27.08	**从煤焦油或其他矿物焦油所得的沥青及沥青焦:**										
2708.1000	-沥青〔301 危险化学品,杂项物质;302 其他化工产品〕	7		35	13/	0	千克	/13		32	
2708.2000	-沥青焦										
2708.2000 01	针状沥青焦〔999〕	6	3	11	13/	0	千克	/1		28	
2708.2000 90	其他沥青焦〔999〕	6		11	13/	0	千克	/1		31	
27.09	**石油原油及从沥青矿物提取的原油:**										
2709.0000	石油原油及从沥青矿物提取的原油〔999〕	T3		T3	13/	0	千克	4x7AByv/13	MN	T3	
27.10	**石油及从沥青矿物提取的油类,但原油除外;以上述油为基本成分(按重量计不低于 70%)的其他税目未列名制品;废油:**										
	-石油及从沥青矿物提取的油类(但原油除外);以及以上述油为基本成分(按重量计不低于 70%)的其他税目未列名制品;不含有生物柴油,但废油除外:										
	--轻油及其制品:										
2710.1210	---车用汽油及航空汽油〔999〕	5	1	14	13/1.52元/升	13	千克/升	47ABvy/123	MN	26	
2710.1220	---石脑油〔999〕	6	0	20	13/1.52元/升	0	千克/升	47ABvy/123	MN	25	5.4/5.4
2710.1230	---橡胶溶剂油、油漆溶剂油、抽提溶剂油〔301 危险化学品,易燃液体;302 其他化工品〕	6		30	13/1.52元/升	0	千克/升	/123		31	
	---其他:										
2710.1291	----壬烯〔999〕										
2710.1291 01	壬烯,不含生物柴油(碳九异构体混合物含量高于 90%)〔999〕	9	4	20	13/	0	千克	4Ay/13	M	29	
2710.1291 90	其他壬烯,不含生物柴油〔301 危险化学品,易燃液体,302 其他化工产品〕	9		20	13/	0	千克	4Ay/13	M	34	

协定税率 %								RCEP		特惠税率 %			Article Description
东/冰/格	巴基斯坦	韩国	瑞士上/下	哥/秘/柬	澳/毛	新西/坡/智	中国港/澳/台	东盟及马来/澳/韩	日/新	亚太2国	老/柬/缅	98/97/95	
													Tar distilled from coal, from lignite or from peat, and other mineral tars, whether or not dehydrated or partially distilled, including reconstituted tars:
													Tar distilled from coal, from lignite or from peat, and other mineral tars, whether or not dehydrated or partially distilled, including reconstituted tars
0/0/0	3.5	0	0/0	0/0/0	0/0	0//0	0/0/	0/0/0	0/0			0/0/0	Containing anthracene oil≥ 50% and asphalt ≥ 40%, carbon "black oil"
0/0/0	3.5	0	0/0	0/0/0	0/0	0//0	0/0/	0/0/0	0/0			0/0/0	Other tars and mineral tars, distelled from coal, lignite or peat, whether or not dehydrated or partially distilled, including reconstituted tars
													Oils and other products of the distillation of high temperature coal tar; similar products in which the weight of the aromatic constituents exceeds that of the non-aromatic constituents:
0/0/0	3.5	2.8	0/0	0/0/0	0/0	0//0	0/0/	0/5.4/5.4	5.5/5.4			0/0/0	-Benzole
0/0/0	3.5	0	0/0	0/0/0	0/0	0//0	0/0/	0/0/0	0/0			0/0/0	-Toluole
0/0/0	3.5	2.8	0/0	0/0/0	0/0	0/0/0	0/0/	0/5.4/5.4	5.6/5.4			0/0/0	-Xylole
0/0/0	2	3.2	0/0	0/0/0	0/0	0/0/0	0/0/	5/5/	/5			0/0/0	-Naphthalene
0/0/0	3	3.7	0	0	0	0/0	0/0/0	0/0/				0/0	-Other aromatic hydrocarbon mixtures of which 65% or more by volume (including losses) distils at 250℃ by the ISO3405 method(equivalent to ASTMD86 method)
0/0/0	2	3.2	0/0	0/0/0	0/0	0/0/0	0/0/	0/6.3/6.3	6.6/6.3			0/0/0	Aromatics distilled below 200°C are less than 95% by volume of other aromatic mixtures (according to ISO 3405 method (equivalent to ASTM D 86 method), and the distillate volume (including loss) at 250 ° C is 65% or more by volume)
0/0/0	2	3.2	0/0	0/0/0	0/0	0/0/0	0/0/	0/6.3/6.3	6.6/6.3			0/0/0	Other aromatic hydrocarbon mixtures of which 65% or more by volume(includinglosses) distils at 250℃ by the ISO3405 method (equivalent to ASTMD86 method)
													-Other:
0/0/0	2	1.4	0/0	0/0/0	0/0	0//0	0/0/	0/0/6.3	6.4/0			0/0/0	--Creosote oils
													--Other:
0/0/0	2	0	0/0	0/0/0	0/0	0/0/0	0/0/	0/0/0	6.4/0			0/0/0	---Phenols
0/0/0	2	3.2	0/0	0/0/0	0/0	0/0/0	0/0/	6.3/6.3/6.3	6.6/6.3			0/0/0	---Other
													Pitch and pitch coke, obtained from coal tar or from other mineral tars:
0/0/0	2	0	0/0	0/0/0	0/0	0//0	0/0/	0/0/0	6.4/0			0/0/0	-Pitch
													-Pitch coke
0/0/0	3.5	1.2	0/0	0/0/0	0/0	0//0	0/0/	5.4/5.4/5.4	5.6/5.4			0/0/0	Needle-shaped pitch coke
0/0/0	3.5	1.2	0/0	0/0/0	0/0	0//0	0/0/	5.4/5.4/5.4	5.6/5.4			0/0/0	Other Needle-shaped pitch coke
													Petroleum oils and oils obtained from bituminous minerals, crude:
0/0/0	0	0	0/0	0/0/0	0/0	0//0	0/0/	0/0/0	0/0			0/0/0	Petroleum oils and oils obtained from bituminous minerals, crude
													Petroleum oils and oils obtained from bituminous minerals, other than crude; preparations not elsewhere specified or included, containing by weight 70% or more of petroleum oils or of oils obtained from bituminous minerals, these oils being the basic constituents of the preparations; waste oils:
													-Petroleum oils and oils obtained from bituminous minerals (other than crude) and preparations not elsewhere specified or included, containing by weight 70% or more of petroleum oils or of oils obtained from bituminous minerals, these oils being the basic constituents of the preparations; other than those containig biodiesel and other than waste oils:
													--Light oils and preparations:
0/0/0	0	2.3	0/0	0//0	0/0	0/0/0	0/0/	0/4.5/4.5	4.7/4.5			0/0/0	---Motor gasoline, aviation gasoline
0/0/0	0	2.8	0/0	0//0	0/0	0/0/0	0/0/	0/5.4/5.4	5.6/5.1			0/0/0	---Naphtha
5/0/0		2.8	0/0	0//0	0/0	0//0	0/0/	5.7/5.7/6	5.7/5.9			0/0/	---Rubber solvent, paint solvent, extractive solvent
													---Other:
													----Nonene
5/0/0		4.2	0/0	0//0	0/0	0//0	0/0/	8.6/8.6/9	8.6/8.8			0/0/	Nonene, excluding biodiesel, excluding biodiesel (Carbon 9 isomer mixtures containing >90%)
5/0/0		4.2	0/0	0//0	0/0	0//0	0/0/	8.6/8.6/9	8.6/8.8			0/0/	Other nonene exctuding biodiesel

税则号列		货品名称〔CIQ扩展编码及品名－T2表示见附表2〕	最惠(%)	暂定税率	普通	增值/消费	出口退税	计量单位	监管条件/特殊证件	检验检疫	对美关税	亚太上/下
2710.1299		----其他										
2710.1299	10	异戊烯同分异构体混合物，不含生物柴油〔999 其他化工产品，301 易燃液体〕	9	5	20	13/1.52元/升	0	千克/升	4Ay/13	M	30	
2710.1299	20	脱模剂（包括按重量计含油≥70%的制品）〔101 其他化工产品 102 易燃液体〕	9		20	13/1.52元/升	0	千克/升	4Ay/13	M		
2710.1299	90	其他轻油及制品，不含生物柴油（包括按重量计含油≥70%的制品）〔301 其他化工产品；999 易燃液体〕	9		20	13/1.52元/升	0	千克/升	4Ay/13	M	34	
		--其他：										
		---煤油馏分：										
2710.1911		----航空煤油〔999〕	9	0	14	13/	13	千克/升	47ABvy/123	MN	25	
2710.1912		----灯用煤油〔301 危险化学品，易燃液体；999 其他化工产品〕	9		14	13/1.2元/升	0	千克/升	47ABvy/13	MN	34	
2710.1919		----其他										
2710.1919	10	正构烷烃（C9～C13），不含生物柴油〔301 危险化学品，易燃液体；302 其他化工产品〕	6		20	13/1.2元/升	0	千克/升	4y/13		31	
2710.1919	20	异构烷烃溶剂，不含生物柴油（初沸点225摄氏度，闪点92摄氏度，密度0.79g/cm³，粘度3.57mm²/s）〔999〕	6		20	13/1.2元/升	0	千克/升	4ABy/13	MN		
2710.1919	90	其他煤油馏分的油及制品，不含生物柴油〔301 危险化学品，易燃液体；302 其他化工品〕	6		20	13/1.2元/升	0	千克/升	4ABy/13	MN	31	
		---柴油及其他燃料油：										
2710.1922		----5～7号燃料油〔301：其他化工产品；302：其他危险化学品〕	6	1	20	13/1.2元/升	0	千克/升	7ABv	MN	2/26	
2710.1922	10	低硫的5－7号燃料油（硫含量不高于0.5% m/m），不含生物柴油〔301：其他化工产品；302：其他危险化学品〕	6	1	20	13/1.2元/升	0，13	千克/升	47ABv/12	MN	26	
2710.1922	90	其他5－7号燃料油，不含生物柴油〔301：其他化工产品；302：其他危险化学品〕	6	1	20	13/1.2元/升	0，13	千克/升	7ABv/12	MN	26	
2710.1923		----柴油〔301 危险化学品，易燃液体；302 其他化工品〕	6	1	11	13/1.2元/升	13	千克/升	47ABvy/13	MN	26	
2710.1929		----其他										
2710.1929	10	蜡油，不含生物柴油（350℃以下馏出物体积＜20%，550℃以下馏出物体积＞80%）〔999 其他化工产品，998 其他危险化学品〕	6	0	20	13/1.2元/升	0	千克/升	7ABv/123	MN	25	
2710.1929	90	其他燃料油，不含生物柴油〔301 危险化学品，易燃液体，302 其他化工产品〕	6		20	13/1.2元/升	0	千克/升	7ABv/123	MN	31	
		---润滑油、润滑脂及其他重油：										
2710.1991		----润滑油〔999 其他化工产品，998 其他危险化学品〕	6		17	13/1.52元/升	0	千克/升	4Axy/1	M		5.4/5.4
2710.1992		----润滑脂〔999 其他化工产品，998 其他危险化学品〕	6		17	13/1.52元/升	0	千克/升	4Axy/12	M		5.4/5.4
2710.1993		----润滑油基础油〔999 其他化工产品，998 其他危险化学品〕	6		17	16/1.52元/升	0	千克/升	4yx		2/31	
2710.1993	10	润滑油基础油，不含生物柴油（产品粘度100℃时37－47，粘度指数80及以上，颜色实测2.0左右，倾点实测－8℃左右）〔999〕	6		17	13/1.52元/升	0	千克/升	4xy/123			
2710.1993	90	其他润滑油基础油，不含生物柴油〔999〕	6		17	13/1.52元/升	0	千克/升	4xy/123		31	
2710.1994		----液体石蜡和重质液体石蜡［301 属于危险化学品的食品添加剂，302 无检疫要求食品添加剂，303 一般化学品，需申报仅用于工业用途不用于食品添加剂无检疫要求，304 易燃液体，需申报仅用于工业用途不用于食品添加剂无检疫要求］	6		20	13/	0	千克	AB/1	MRNS	31	5.4/5.4
2710.1999		----其他	6		20	16/1.2元/升	0	千克/升	B	N	2/31	
2710.1999	10	白油（液体烃类混合物组成的无色透明油状液体，由原油分馏所得）（商品成分为100%白矿油，40℃时该产品粘度为65mm²/s，闪点为225℃，倾点为－10℃，比重（20℃/20℃）为0.885）〔301：易燃液体；302：其他化工产品〕	6		20	13/1.2元/升	0	千克/升	B/123	N		
2710.1999	90	其他重油；其他重油制品，不含生物柴油（包括按重量计含油≥70%的制品）〔999〕	6		20	13/1.2元/升	0	千克/升	B/123	N	31	
2710.2000		-石油及从沥青矿物提取的油类（但原油除外）以及以上述油为基本成分（按重量计不低于70%）的其他税目未列名制品，含有生物柴油，但废油除外〔999 其他化工产品，301 易燃液体〕	6		20	13/1.2元/升	0	千克/升	4Ay/1	M	31	
		-废油：										

协定税率 %								RCEP		特惠税率 %			Article Description
东/冰/格	巴基斯坦	韩国	瑞士上/下	哥/秘/柬	澳/毛	新西/坡/智	中国港/澳/台	东盟及马来/澳/韩	日/新	亚太2国	老/柬/缅	98/97/95	
													----Other
5/0/0		4.2	0/0	0//0	0/0	0//0	0/0/	8.6/8.8/9	8.6/8.8			0/0/	Mixture of isomers of isoamylene, excluding biodiesel
5/0/0		4.2	0/0	0//0	0/0	0//0	0/0/	8.6/8.8/9	8.6/8.8		//	0/0/	Release agent (including products with oil content ≥ 70% by weight)
5/0/0		4.2	0/0	0//0	0/0	0//0	0/0/	8.6/8.8/9	8.6/8.8			0/0/	Other light oils and preparations, excluding biodiesel (containing≥70% by weight of oils)
													--Other:
													---Kerosene distillages:
0/0/0	2	0	0/0	0/0/0	0/0	0/0/0	0/0/0	0/0/0	8.2/0			0/0/0	----Aviation kerosene
5/0/0		4.2	0/0	0/0/0	0/0	0//0	0/0/	5/5/	/5			0/0/	----Lamp-kerosene
													----Other
0/0/0	0	0	0/0	0/0/0	0/0	0/0/0	0/0/0	0/0/0	0/0			0/0/0	Normal paraffin hydrocarbon ($C_9 \sim C_{13}$), excluding biodiesel
0/0/0	0	0	0/0	0/0/0	0/0	0/0/0	0/0/0	0/0/0	0/0		//	0/0/0	Isoalkane solvent, without biodiesel (initial boiling point 225 ℃, flash point 92 ℃, density 0.79g/cm3, viscosity 3.57mm2 / s)
0/0/0	0	0	0/0	0/0/0	0/0	0/0/0	0/0/0	0/0/0	0/0			0/0/0	Other kerosene distillages oils and preparations, excluding biodiesel
													---Diesel oils and other fuel oils:
0/0/0	4.5	0	0	0	0	0	0/0/0	0/0/				0/0/	----Fuel oils No. 5～No. 7
0/0/0	3.5	0	0/0	0/0/0	0/0	0/0/0	0/0/	0/0/0	5.6/0		//	0/0/0	Low sulfur fuel oil No. 5－7 (sulfur content no more than 0.5% m / M), excluding biodiesel
0/0/0	3.5	0	0/0	0/0/0	0/0	0/0/0	0/0/	0/0/0	5.6/0		//	0/0/0	Other fuel oil No. 5－7, excluding biodiesel
5/0/0		2.8	0/0	0/0/5.7	0/0	0//0	0/0/	5.7/5.9/6	5.7/5.9			0//	----Diesel engine
													----Other
0/0/0	3.5	2.8	0/0	0/0/0	0/0	0/0/0	0/0/	5.4/5.4/5.4	5.6/5.4			0/0/	Paraffin oils excluding biodiesel (which<20% by volume distil<350℃, which>80% by volume distil<550℃)
0/0/0	3.5	2.8	0/0	0/0/0	0/0	0/0/0	0/0/	5.4/5.4/5.4	5.6/5.4			0/0/	Other fuel oils, excluding biodiesel
													---Lubricating oils, lubricating greases and other heavy oils:
0/0/0	0	2.8	0/0	0/0/0	0/0	0/0/0	0/0/	0/5.4/5.4	5.6/5.4			0/0/0	----Lubricating grease
0/0/0	0	2.8	0/0	0/0/0	0/0	0/0/0	0/0/	0/5.4/5.4	5.6/5.4			0/0/0	----Lubricating oils
0/0/0	5	4	0	0	0	0	0//0	0/0/0				0/0/	----Basic oils for lubricating oils
0/0/0	2	2.8	0/0	0/0/0	0/0	0/0/0	0/0/0	0/5.4/5.4	5.6/5.4		//	0/0/0	Lubricating oil base oil, excluding biodiesel (product viscosity: 37－47 at 100 ℃, viscosity index: 80 or above, measured color: about 2.0, measured pour point: about － 8 ℃)
0/0/0	2	2.8	0/0	0/0/0	0/0	0/0/0	0/0/0	0/5.4/5.4	5.6/5.4		//	0/0/0	Base oil of other lubricants, excluding biodiesel
0/0/0	0	0	0/0	0/0/0	0/0	0/0/0	0/0/0	0/5.4/0	0/5.4			0/0/0	----Liquid paraffin and heavy liquid paraffin
0/0/0	5	4.5	0	0	0	0	0//0	0/0/				0/0/	----Other
0/0/0	0	3.6	0/0	0/0/0	0/0	0/0/0	0/0/	5.7/5.7/6	5.7/5.7		//	0/0/0	White oil (a colorless and transparent oil like liquid composed of liquid hydrocarbon mixture, obtained from crude oil fractionation) (the commercial component is 100% white mineral oil, the viscosity of the product is 65mm? / s at 40 ℃, the flash point is 225 ℃, the pour point is － 10 ℃, and the specific gravity (20 ℃ / 20 ℃) is 0.885)
0/0/0	0	3.6	0/0	0/0/0	0/0	0/0/0	0/0/	5.7/5.7/6	5.7/5.7		//	0/0/0	Other heavy oil; other heavy oil products, excluding biodiesel (including products with oil content ≥ 70% by weight)
0/0/0	0	2.8	0/0	0//0	0/0	0/0/0	0/0/0	5.4/5.4/5.4	5.6/5.4			0/0/0	-Petroleum oils and oils obtained from bituminous minerals, other than crude; preparations not elsewhere specified or included, containing by weight 70% or more of petroleum oils or of oils obtained from bituminous minerals, these oils being the basic constituents of the preparations, containing biodiesel, other than waste oils
													-Waste oils:

税则号列	货品名称〔CIQ 扩展编码及品名—T2 表示见附表 2〕	最惠(%)	暂定税率	普通	增值/消费	出口退税	计量单位	监管条件/特殊证件	检验检疫	对美关税	亚太上/下
2710.9100	--含多氯联苯(PCBs)、多氯三联苯(PCTs)或多溴联苯(PBBs)的〔999〕	6		20	13/	0	千克	9/13		31	
2710.9900	--其他〔999〕	6		20	13/	0	千克	9/13		31	
27.11	**石油气及其他烃类气:**										
	-液化的:										
2711.1100	--天然气〔999〕	0		20	9/	0	千克	4ABy/13	MN	25	
2711.1200	--丙烷〔301 危险化学品,不用作食品添加剂;302 危险化学品,用作食品添加剂〕	5	1	20	9/	0	千克	AB/13	MN	26	3.5/3.5
	--丁烷:										
2711.1310	---直接灌注香烟打火机及类似打火器用,其包装容器的容积超过 300 立方厘米〔999〕	5		80	13/	0	千克	/13		30	
2711.1390	---其他〔999〕	5	1	20	9/	0	千克	/13		28.5	
2711.1400	--乙烯、丙烯、丁烯及丁二烯										
2711.1400 10	液化的乙烯〔999〕	5		20	13/	0	千克	AB/13	MN	30	
2711.1400 90	液化的丙烯、丁烯及丁二烯〔999〕	5		20	13/	0	千克	/13		30	
	--其他:										
2711.1910	---直接灌注香烟打火机及类似打火器用的燃料,其包装容器的容积超过 300 立方厘米〔101 易燃气体,102 其他化工产品,999〕	5		80	13/	0	千克	/1		30	3.5/3.5
2711.1990	---其他										
2711.1990 10	其他液化石油气〔999〕	3		20	9/	0	千克	AB/13	MN	28	2.1/2.1
2711.1990 90	其他液化烃类气〔999〕	3		20	9/	0	千克	/13		28	2.1/2.1
	-气态的:										
2711.2100	--天然气〔999〕	0		20	9/	0	千克	AB/13	MN	25	
2711.2900	--其他										
2711.2900 10	其他气态石油气〔999〕	5		20	9/	0	千克	AB/13	MN	30	
2711.2900 90	其他气态烃类气〔999〕	5		20	9/	0	千克	/13		30	
27.12	**凡士林;石蜡、微晶石蜡、疏松石蜡、地蜡、褐煤蜡、泥煤蜡、其他矿物蜡及用合成或其他方法制得的类似产品,不论是否着色:**										
2712.1000	-凡士林〔999〕	8		45	13/	0	千克	A/1	R	35.5	
2712.2000	-石蜡,按重量计含油量小于 0.75%〔999 其他化工产品,301 需申报仅用于工业用途不用于食品添加剂无检疫要求的化学品,998 其他危险化学品〕	8		45	13/	0	千克	4Ax/1	R	35.5	
	-其他:										
2712.9010	---微晶石蜡	8		45	13/	0	千克	4Ax	R	/33	
2712.9010 10	食品级微晶石蜡(相应指标符合《食品级微晶石蜡》(GB22160—2008)的要求)〔101 微晶蜡(无检疫要求食品添加剂)102 无检疫要求食品添加剂〕	8		45	13/	0	千克	4Ax/1	R		
2712.9010 90	其他微晶石蜡〔999〕	8		45	13/	0	千克	4Ax/1	R	35.5	
2712.9090	---其他〔999〕	8		45	13/	0	千克	/1		35.5	
27.13	**石油焦、石油沥青及其他石油或从沥青矿物提取的油类的残渣:**										
	-石油焦:										
	--未煅烧:										
2713.1110	---硫的重量百分比小于 3%的〔999〕	3		11	13/	0	千克	/1		28	
2713.1190	---其他〔999〕	3		11	13/	0	千克	/1		30.5	
	--已煅烧:										
2713.1210	---硫的重量百分比小于 0.8%的〔999〕	3		11	13/	0	千克	/1		30.5	
2713.1290	---其他〔999〕	3		11	13/	0	千克	/1		28	
2713.2000	-石油沥青〔999〕	8		35	13/	0	千克	/1		35.5	5.6/5.6
2713.9000	-其他石油或从沥青矿物提取的油类的残渣〔999〕	6		35	13/	0	千克	9/1		33.5	
27.14	**天然沥青(地沥青);沥青页岩、油页岩及焦油砂;沥青岩:**										
2714.1000	-沥青页岩、油页岩及焦油砂〔999〕	6		20	13/	0	千克	/1		33.5	
	-其他:										
2714.9010	---天然沥青(地沥青)〔999〕	8	4	35	13/	0	千克	/1		31.5	
2714.9020	---乳化沥青〔999〕	0		20	13/	0	千克	/1		25	
2714.9090	---其他〔999〕	3		20	13/	0	千克	/1		30.5	
27.15	**以天然沥青(地沥青)、石油沥青、矿物焦油或矿物焦油沥青为基本成分的沥青混合物(例如,沥青胶粘剂、稀释沥青):**										

协定税率 %								RCEP		特惠税率 %			
东/冰/格	巴基斯坦	韩国	瑞士 上/下	哥/秘/柬	澳/毛	新西/坡/智	中国港/澳/台	东盟及马来/澳/韩	日/新	亚太2国	老/柬/缅	98/97/95	Article Description
0/0/0	2		0/0	0/0/0	0/0	0//0	0/0/	5/5/	/5			0/0/0	--Containing polychlorinated biphenyls (PCBs), polychlorinated terphenyls (PCTs) or polybrominated biphenyls (PBBs)
0/0/0	2	0	0/0	0/0/0	0/0	0/0/0	0/0/	0/0/0	0/0			0/0/0	--Other
													Petroleum gases and other gaseous hydrocarbons:
													-Liquefied:
0/0/0	0	0	0/0	0/0/0	0/0	0//0	0/0/	0/0/0	0/0			0/0/0	--Natural gas
0/0/0	0	0	0/0	0/0/0	0/0	0/0/0	0/0/	0/0/0	0/0			0/0/0	--Propane
													--Butanes:
0/0/0	3.5	2.2	1.1/1.1	0/0/0	0/0	0/0/0	0/0/	0/0/9.9	10/0			0/0/0	---Liquid or liquefied-gas fuels in containers of a kind used for filling or refilling cigarette or similar lighters and of a capacity exceeding 300cm³
0/0/0	0	1	0/0	0/0/0	0/0	0/0/0	0/0/	0/0/4.5	4.5/0			0/0/	---Other
													--Ethylene, propylene, butylene and butadiene
0/0/0	0	2.3	0/0	0/0/0	0/0	0/0/0	0/0/	0/4.5/4.5	4.7/4.5			0/0/0	Liquefied ethylene,
0/0/0	0	2.3	0/0	0/0/0	0/0	0/0/0	0/0/	0/4.5/4.5	4.7/4.5			0/0/0	Liquefied propylene, butylene and butadiene,
													--Other:
0/0/0	3.5	2	0/0	0/0/0	0/0	0/0/0	0/0/	0/0/9	9.1/0			0/0/0	---Liquid or liquefied-gas fuels in containers of a kind used for filling or refilling cigarette or similar lighters and of a capacity exceeding 300cm³
													---Other
0/0/0	0	0	0/0	0/0/0	0/0	0/0/0	0/0/	0/0/0	0/0			0/0/	Other liquefied petroleum gases
0/0/0	0	0	0/0	0/0/0	0/0	0/0/0	0/0/	0/0/0	0/0			0/0/	Other liquefied gaseous hydrocar
													-In gaseous state:
0/0/0	0	0	0/0	0/0/0	0/0	0//0	0/0/	0/0/0	0/0			0/0/0	--Natural gas
													--Other
0/0/0	0	0	0/0	0/0/0	0/0	0/0/0	0/0/	0/0/0	0/0			0/0/0	Other petroleum gases, in gaseous state
0/0/0	0	0	0/0	0/0/0	0/0	0/0/0	0/0/	0/0/0	0/0			0/0/0	Other gaseous hydrocar, in gaseous state
													Petroleum jelly; paraffin wax, microcrystalline petroleum wax, slack wax, ozokerite, lignite wax, peat wax, other mineral waxes, and similar products obtained by synthesis or by other processes, whether or not coloured:
0/0/0	2	0	0/0	0/0/0	0/0	0//0	0/0/	0/0/0	7.3/0			0/0/0	-Petroleum jelly
0/0/0	2	1.6	0/0	0/0/0	0/4.8	0//0	0/0/	0/0/7.2	7.3/0			0/0/0	-Paraffin wax containing by weight less than 0.75% of oil
													-Other:
0/0/0	5	4	0	0	0	0	0//0	0/0/				0/0/0	---Microcrystalline petroleum wax
0/0/0	2	1.6	0/0	0/0/0	0/0	0/0/0	0/0/	0/0/7.2	7.3/0		//	0/0/0	Food grade microcrystalline paraffin (corresponding indexes meet the requirements of food grade microcrystalline paraffin (GB22160—2008))
0/0/0	2	1.6	0/0	0/0/0	0/0	0/0/0	0/0/	0/0/7.2	7.3/0		//	0/0/0	Other microcrystalline paraffin
0/0/0	2	1.6	0/0	0/0/0	0/0	0/0/0	0/0/	7.2/7.2/7.2	7.3/7.2			0/0/0	---Other
													Petroleum coke, petroleum bitumen and other residues of petroleum oils or of oils obtained from bituminous minerals:
													-Petroleum coke:
													--Not calcined:
0/0/0	0	1.4	0/0	0/0/0	0/0	0//0	0/0/	2.7/2.7/2.7	2.8/2.7			0/0/0	---Containing by weight less than 3% of Sulphur
0/0/0	0	1.4	0/0	0/0/0	0/0	0//0	0/0/	2.7/2.7/2.7	2.8/2.7			0/0/0	---Other
													--Calcined:
0/0/0	0	1.4	0/0	0/0/0	0/0	0//0	0/0/	2.7/2.7/2.7	2.8/2.7			0/0/0	---Containing by weight less than 0.8% of Sulphur
0/0/0	0	1.4	0/0	0/0/0	0/0	0//0	0/0/	2.7/2.7/2.7	2.8/2.7			0/0/0	---Other
0/0/0	2	3.7	0/0	0/0/0	0/0	0/0/0	0/0/	0/7.2/7.2	7.5/7.2			0/0/0	-Petroleum bitumen
0/0/0	0	0	0/0	0/0/0	0/0	0/0/0	0/0/	0/0/0	0/0			0/0/0	-Other residues of petroleum oils or of oils obtained from bituminous minerals
													Bitumen and asphalt, natural; bituminous or oil shale and tar sands; asphaltites and asphaltic rocks:
0/0/0	3.5	0	0/0	0/0/0	0/0	0/0/0	0/0/	0/0/0	0/0			0/0/0	-Bituminous or oil shale and tar sands
													-Other:
0/0/0	2	3.7	0/0	0/0/0	0/0	0/0/0	0/0/	7.5/7.6/7.5	7.5/7.6			0/0/0	---Natural bitumen and asphalt
0/0/0	0	0	0/0	0/0/0	0/0	0//0	0/0/	0/0/0	0/0			0/0/0	---Emulsified bitumen and asphalt
0/0/0	0	0	0/0	0/0/0	0/0	0/0/0	0/0/	0/0/0	0/0			0/0/0	---Other
													Bituminous mixtures based on natural asphalt, on natural bitumen, on petroleum bitumen, on mineral tar or on mineral tar pitch (for example, bituminous mastics, cut-backs):

税则号列	货品名称〔CIQ 扩展编码及品名—T2 表示见附表 2〕	最惠(%)	暂定税率	普通	增值/消费	出口退税	计量单位	监管条件/特殊证件	检验检疫	对美关税	亚太上/下
2715.0000	以天然沥青(地沥青)、石油沥青、矿物焦油或矿物焦油沥青为基本成分的沥青混合物(例如,沥青胶粘剂、稀释沥青)〔301 易燃固体、自反应物质及固态退敏爆炸品, 302 其他化工产品〕	8		35	13/	0	千克	/		33	
2715.0000 10	440 摄氏度以下时蒸馏出的矿物油以体积计大于 5% 的沥青混合物(例如,沥青胶粘剂、稀释沥青)(以天然沥青(地沥青)、石油沥青、矿物焦油或矿物焦油沥青为基本成分)〔301 易燃固体、自反应物质及固态退敏爆炸品;302 其他化工产品〕	8		35	13/1.2元/升	0	千克/升	/1		33	
2715.0000 90	其他沥青混合物(例如,沥青胶粘剂、稀释沥青)(以天然沥青(地沥青)、石油沥青、矿物焦油或矿物焦油沥青为基本成分)〔301 易燃固体、自反应物质及固态退敏爆炸品;302 其他化工产品〕	8		35	13/	0	千克/升	/1		33	
27.16	电力:										
2716.0000	电力〔999〕	0		8	13/	13	千瓦时	/1			

协定税率 %								RCEP		特惠税率 %			Article Description
东/冰/格	巴基斯坦	韩国	瑞士上/下	哥/秘/柬	澳/毛	新西/坡/智	中国港/澳/台	东盟及马来/澳/韩	日/新	亚太2国	老/柬/缅	98/97/95	
0/0/0	3	2.4	0	0	0	0/0	0/0/0	0/0/				0/0	Bituminous mixtures based on natural asphalt, on natural bitumen, on petroleum bitumen, on mineral tar or on mineral tar pitch (for example, bituminous mastics, cut-backs)
0/0/0	2	1.6	0/0	0/0/0	0/0	0/0/0	0/0/	0/0/7.2	7.3/0			0/0/0	Asphalt mixture (e.g., asphalt adhesive, cutback asphalt) with more than 5% by volume of mineral oil distilled below 440℃ (with natural asphalt (ground asphalt), petroleum asphalt, mineral tar or mineral tar asphalt as the basic component)
0/0/0	2	1.6	0/0	0/0/0	0/0	0/0/0	0/0/	0/0/7.2	7.3/0			0/0/0	Other asphalt mixtures (e.g. asphalt adhesives, cutback asphalt) (based on natural asphalt (ground asphalt), petroleum asphalt, mineral tar or mineral tar asphalt)
													Electrical energy:
0/0/0	0	0	0/0	0/0/0	0/0	0//0	0/0/	0/0/0	0/0			0/0/0	Electrical energy

第六类
化学工业及其相关工业的产品

注释：

一、（一）凡符合税目 28.44 或 28.45 规定的货品（放射性矿砂除外），应分别归入这两个税目而不归入本协调制度的其他税目。

（二）除上述（一）款另有规定的以外，凡符合税目 28.43、28.46 或 28.52 规定的货品，应分别归入这两个税目而不归入本类的其他税目。

二、除上述注释一另有规定的以外，凡由于按一定剂量或作为零售包装而可归入税目 30.04、30.05、30.06、32.12、33.03、33.04、33.05、33.06、33.07、35.06、37.07 或 38.08 的货品，应分别归入以上税目，而不归入本协调制度的其他税目。

三、由两种或两种以上单独成分配套的货品，其部分或全部成分属于本类范围以内，混合后则构成第六类或第七类的货品，应按混合后产品归入相应的税目，但其组成成分必须同时符合下列条件：

（一）其包装形式足以表明这些成分不需经过改装就可一起使用的；

（二）一起报验的；

（三）这些成分的属性及相互比例足以表明是相互配用的。

四、其列名或功能既符合第六类中一个或多个税目的规定，又符合税目 38.27 的规定的产品，应按列名或功能归入相应税目，而不归入税目 38.27。

第二十八章
无机化学品；贵金属、稀土金属、放射性元素及其同位素的有机及无机化合物

注释：

一、除条文另有规定的以外，本章各税目只适用于：

（一）单独的化学元素及单独的已有化学定义的化合物，不论是否含有杂质；

（二）上述（一）款产品的水溶液；

（三）溶于其他溶剂的上述（一）款产品，但该产品处于溶液状态只是为了安全或运输所采取的正常必要方法，其所用溶剂并不使该产品改变其一般用途而适合于某些特殊用途；

（四）为了保存或运输需要，加入稳定剂（包括抗结块剂）的上述（一）、（二）、（三）款产品；

（五）为了便于识别或安全起见，加入抗尘剂或着色剂的上述（一）、（二）、（三）、（四）款产品，但所加剂料并不使原产品改变其一般用途而适合于某些特殊用途。

二、除以有机物质稳定的连二亚硫酸盐及次硫酸盐（税目 28.31），无机碱的碳酸盐及过碳酸盐（税目 28.36），无机碱的氰化物、氧氰化物及氰络合物（税目 28.37），无机碱的雷酸盐、氰酸盐及硫氰酸盐（税目 28.42），税目 28.43 至 28.46 及 28.52 的有机产品，以及碳化物（税目 28.49）之外，本章仅包括下列碳化合物：

（一）碳的氧化物，氰化氢及雷酸、异氰酸、硫氰酸及其他简单或络合氰酸（税目 28.11）；

（二）碳的卤氧化物（税目 28.12）；

（三）二硫化碳（税目 28.13）；

（四）硫代碳酸盐、硒代碳酸盐、碲代碳酸盐、硒代氰酸盐、碲代氰酸盐、四氰硫基二氨基络酸盐及其他无机碱络合氰酸盐（税目 28.42）；

（五）用尿素固化的过氧化氢（税目 28.47）、氧硫化碳、硫代羰基卤化物、氰、卤化氰、氨基氰及其金属衍生物（税目 28.53），不论是否纯净，但氰氨化钙除外（第三十一章）。

三、除第六类注释一另有规定的以外，本章不包括：

（一）氯化钠或氧化镁（不论是否纯净）及第五类的其他产品；

（二）上述注释二所述以外的有机—无机化合物；

（三）第三十一章注释二、三、四或五所述的产品；

（四）税目 32.06 的用作发光剂的无机产品；税目 32.07 的搪瓷玻璃料及其他玻璃，呈粉、粒或粉片状的；

（五）人造石墨（税目 38.01）；税目 38.13 的灭火器的装配药及已装药的灭火弹；税目 38.24 的零售包装的除墨剂；税目 38.24 的每颗重量不少于 2.5 克的碱金属或碱土金属卤化物的培养晶体（光学元件除外）；

（六）宝石或半宝石（天然、合成或再造）及这些宝石、半宝石的粉末（税目 71.02 至 71.05），第七十一章的贵金属及贵金属合金；

（七）第十五类的金属（不论是否纯净）、金属合金或金属陶瓷，包括硬质合金（与金属烧结的金属碳化物）；

（八）光学元件，例如用碱金属或碱土金属卤化物制成的（税目 90.01）。

四、由本章第二分章的非金属酸和第四分章的金属酸所构成的已有化学定义的络酸，应归入税目 28.11。

五、税目 28.26 至 28.42 只适用于金属盐、铵盐及过氧酸盐。除条文另有规定的以外，复盐及络盐应归入税目 28.42。

六、税目 28.44 只适用于：

（一）锝（原子序数 43）、钷（原子序数 61）、钋（原子序数 84）及原子序数大于 84 的所有化学元素；

（二）天然或人造放射性同位素（包括第十四类及第十五类的贵金属和贱金属的放射性同位素），不论是否混合；

（三）上述元素或同位素的无机或有机化合物，不论是否已有化学定义或是否混合；

（四）含有上述元素或同位素及其无机或有机化合物并且具有某种放射性强度超过 74 贝克勒尔/克（0.002 微居里/克）的合金、分散体（包括金属陶瓷）、陶瓷产品及混合物；

SECTION Ⅵ
PRODUCTS OF THE CHEMICAL OR ALLIED INDUSTRIES

Notes:

1. (a) Goods (other than radioactive ores) answering to a description in heading No. 28.44 or 28.45 are to be classified in those headings and in no other heading of the Nomenclature.
   (b) Subject to paragraph (a) above, goods answering to a description in heading No. 28.43, 28.46 or 28.52 are to be classified in those headings and in no other heading of this Seciton.
2. Subject to Note 1 above, goods classifiable in heading No. 30.04, 30.05, 30.06, 32.12, 33.03, 33.04, 33.05, 33.06, 33.07, 35.06, 37.07, or 38.08 by reason of being put up in measured doses or for retail sale are to be classified in those headings and in no other headings of the Nomenclature.
3. Goods put up in sets consisting of two or more separate constituents, some or all of which fall in this Section and are intended to be mixed together to obtain a product of Section Ⅵ or Ⅶ, are to be classified in the heading appropriate to that product, provided that the constituents are:
   (a) having regard to the manner in which they are put up, clearly identifiable as being intended to be used together without first being repacked;
   (b) presented together; and
   (c) identifiable, whether by their nature or by the relative proportions in which they are present, as being complementary one to another.
4. Where a product answers to a description in one or more of the headings in Section VI by virtue of being described by name or function and also to heading No. 38.27, then it is classifiable in a heading that references the product by name or function and not under heading 38.27.

Chapter 28
Inorganic chemicals; organic or inorganic compounds of precious metals, of rare-earth metals of radioactive elements or of isotopes

Notes:

1. Except where the context otherwise requires, the headings of this Chapter apply only to:
   (a) Separate chemical elements and separate chemically defined compounds, whether or not containing impurities;
   (b) The products mentioned in (a) above dissolved in water;
   (c) The products mentioned in (a) above dissolved in other solvents, provided that the solution constitutes a normal and necessary method of putting up these products adopted solely for reasons of safety or for transport, and that the solvent does not render the product particularly suitable for specific use rather than for general use;
   (d) The products mentioned in (a), (b) or (c) above with an added stabilizer (including an anti-caking agent) necessary for their preservation or transport;
   (e) The products mentioned in (a), (b), (c) or (d) above with an added antidusting agent or a colouring substance added to facilitate their identification or for safety reasons, provided that the additions do not render the product particularly suitable for specific use rather than for general use.
2. In addition to dithionites and sulphoxylates, stabilized with organic substances (heading No. 28.31), carbonates and peroxocarbonates of inorganic bases (heading No. 28.36), cyanides, cyanide oxides and complex cyanides of inorganic bases (heading No. 28.37), fulminates, cyanates and thiocyanates, of inorganic bases (heading No. 28.42), organic products included in headings No. 28.43 to 28.46 and 28.52 and carbides (heading No. 28.49), only the following compounds of carbon are to the classified in this Chapter:
   (a) Oxides of carbon, hydrogen cyanide and fulminic, isocyanic, thiocyanic and other simple or complex cyanogen acids (heading No. 28.11);
   (b) Halide oxides of carbon (heading No. 28.12);
   (c) Carbon disulphide (heading No. 28.13);
   (d) Thiocarbonates, selenocarbonates, tellurocarbonates, selenocyanates, tellurocyanates, tetrathiocyanatodiamminochromates (reineckates) and other complex cyanates, of inorganic bases (heading No. 28.42);
   (e) Hydrogen peroxide, solidified with urea (heading No. 28.47), carbon oxysulphide, thiocarbonyl halides, cyanogen, cyanogen halides and cyanamide and its metal derivatives (heading No. 28.53) other than calcium cyanamide, whether or not pure (Chapter 31).
3. Subject to the provisions of Note 1 to Section Ⅵ, this Chapter does not cover:
   (a) Sodium chloride or magnesium oxide, whether or not pure, or other products of Section Ⅴ;
   (b) Organo-inorganic compounds other than those mentioned in Note 2 above;
   (c) Products mentioned in Note 2, 3, 4 or 5 to Chapter 31;
   (d) Inorganic products of a kind used as luminophores, of heading No. 32.06; glass frit and other glass in the form of powder, granules of flakes, of heading No. 32.07;
   (e) Artificial graphite (heading No. 38.01); products put up as charges for fire-extinguishers or put up in fire-extinguishing grenades, of heading No. 38.13; ink removers put up in packings for retail sale, of heading No. 38.24, cultured crystals (other than optical elements) weighing not less than 2.5g each, of the halides of the alkali or alkaline-earth metals, of heading No. 38.24;
   (f) Precious or semi-precious stones (natural, synthetic or reconstructed) or dust or powder of such stones (headings Nos. 71.02 to 71.05), or precious metals or precious metal alloys of Chapter 71;
   (g) The metals, whether or not pure, metal alloys or cermets, including sintered metal carbides (metal carbides sintered with a metal), of Section ⅩⅤ; or
   (h) Optical elements, for example, of the halides of the alkali or alkaline-earth metals (heading No. 90.01).
4. Chemically defined complex acids consisting of a nonmetal acid of sub-Chapter Ⅱ and a metal acid of sub-Chapter Ⅳ are to be classified in heading No. 28.11.
5. Headings Nos. 28.26 to 28.42 apply only to metal or ammonium salts or peroxysalts. Except where the context otherwise requires, double or complex salts are to be classified in heading No. 28.42.
6. Heading No. 28.44 applies only to:
   (a) Technetium (atomic No. 43), promethium (atomic No. 61), polonium (atomic No. 84) and all elements with an atomic number greater than 84;
   (b) Natural or artificial radioactive isotopes (including those of the precious metals or of the base metals of Sections ⅩⅣ and ⅩⅤ), whether or not mixed together;
   (c) Compounds, inorganic or organic, of these elements or isotopes, whether or not chemically defined, whether or not mixed together;
   (d) Alloys, dispersions (including cermets), ceramic products and mixtures containing these elements or isotopes or inorganic or organic compounds thereof and having a specific radioactivity exceeding 74 Bq/g (0.002μ Ci/g);

(五)核反应堆已耗尽(已辐照)的燃料元件(释热元件);

(六)放射性的残渣,不论是否有用。

税目 28.44、28.45 及本注释所称"同位素",是指:

1. 单独的核素,但不包括自然界中以单一同位素状态存在的核素;

2. 同一元素的同位素混合物,其中一种或几种同位素已被浓缩,即人工地改变了该元素同位素的自然构成。

七、税目 28.53 包括按重量计含磷量超过 15%的磷化铜(磷铜)。

八、经掺杂用于电子工业的化学元素(例如,硅、硒),如果拉制后未经加工或呈圆筒形、棒形,应归入本章;如果已切成圆片、薄片或类似形状,则归入税目 38.18。

子目注释:

子目 2812.10 所称"已有化学定义"是指符合第二十八章注释一(一)至(五)或第二十九章注释一(一)至(八)规定的汞的无机或有化合物。

税则号列	货品名称〔CIQ 扩展编码及品名—T2 表示见附表 2〕	最惠(%)	暂定税率	普通	增值/消费	出口退税	计量单位	监管条件/特殊证件	检验检疫	对美关税	亚太上/下
	第一分章　化学元素										
28.01	**氟、氯、溴及碘:**										
2801.1000	-氯〔999〕	5		80	13/	0	千克	AB/13	MN	32.5	
2801.2000	-碘〔999〕	5	1	30	13/	0	千克	G/1		26	
	-氟;溴:										
2801.3010	---氟〔999〕	5		30	13/	0	千克	AB/13	MN		4.5/4.5
2801.3020	---溴〔999〕	5	1	30	13/	0	千克	23AB/13	MN	28.5	
28.02	**升华硫磺、沉淀硫磺;胶态硫磺:**										
2802.0000	升华硫磺、沉淀硫磺;胶态硫磺〔301 危险化学品,不用作食品添加剂;302 危险化学品,用作食品添加剂;303 其他化工产品〕	5	1	17	13/	0	千克	AB/13	MN	23.5	
28.03	**碳(碳黑及其他税目未列名的其他形态的碳):**										
2803.0000	碳(碳黑及其他税号未列名的其他形态的碳)〔301 其他化工品,不用作食品添加剂,302 其他化工品,用作食品添加剂〕	5		35	13/	0	千克	/1		17.5	3.3/3.3
28.04	**氢、稀有气体及其他非金属:**										
2804.1000	-氢〔999〕	5		30	13/	0	千克/立方米	AB/13	MN	27.5	
	-稀有气体:										
2804.2100	--氩〔999〕	5		30	13/	0	千克/立方米	AB/13	MN	32.5	
2804.2900	--其他										
2804.2900 10	氦〔999〕	5	1	30	13/	0	千克/立方米	/13		8.5	
2804.2900 90	其他稀有气体〔999〕	5		30	13/	0	千克/立方米	/13		12.5	
2804.3000	-氮〔999〕	5		30	13/	0	千克/立方米	AB/13	MN	12.5	
2804.4000	-氧〔999〕	5		80	13/	0	千克/立方米	AB/13	MN	12.5	
2804.5000	-硼;碲										
2804.5000 01	碲〔999〕	5	0	17	13/	13	千克	/1		27.5	
2804.5000 10	颗粒<500μm 的硼及其合金(含量≥97%,不论球形、椭球体、雾化、片状、研碎金属燃料)〔999〕	5		17	13/	13	千克	3/1		32.5	
2804.5000 20	能量密度>40MJ/kg 的硼浆(硼溶于溶剂形成的硼浆)〔999〕	5		17	13/	13	千克	3/1		32.5	
2804.5000 90	其他硼〔999〕	5		17	13/	13	千克	/1		32.5	
	-硅:										
	--按重量计含硅量不少于 99.99%:										
	---经掺杂用于电子工业的直径在 7.5 厘米及以上的单晶硅棒:										
2804.6117	----直径在 30 厘米及以上的〔999〕	4		11	13/	13	千克	/1		11.5	
2804.6119	----其他〔999〕	4		11	13/	0	千克	/1		19	
2804.6120	---经掺杂用于电子工业的其他单晶硅棒〔999〕	4		17	13/	0	千克	/1		31.5	3.6/3.6
2804.6190	---其他										
2804.6190 11	含硅量>99.9999999%的多晶硅废碎料(太阳能级多晶硅除外)〔101 多晶硅,102 硅废碎料〕	4		30	13/	0	千克	9/13		26.5	
2804.6190 12	含硅量>99.9999999%的太阳能级多晶硅〔999〕	4		30	13/	0	千克	/13		26.5	
2804.6190 13	含硅量>99.9999999%的太阳能级多晶硅废碎料〔999〕	4		30	13/	0	千克	9/13		26.5	
2804.6190 19	其他含硅量>99.9999999%的多晶硅(太阳能级多晶硅除外)〔999〕	4		30	13/	0	千克	/13			
2804.6190 91	其他含硅量≥99.99%的硅废碎料(太阳能级多晶硅除外)〔101 其他硅,102 硅废碎料〕	4		30	13/	0	千克	9/13		26.5	
2804.6190 92	含硅量≥99.99%的太阳能级多晶硅〔999〕	4		30	13/	0	千克	/13		26.5	
2804.6190 93	含硅量≥99.99%的太阳能级多晶硅废碎料〔999〕	4		30	13/	0	千克	9/13		26.5	

(e) Spent (irradiated) fuel elements (cartridges) of nuclear reactors;

(f) Radioactive residues whether or not usable.

The term "isotopes", for the purposes of this Note and of the wording of headings No. 28.44 and 28.45, refers to:

(i) individual nuclides, excluding, however, those existing in nature in the monoisotopic state;

(ii) mixtures of isotopes of one and the same element, enriched in one or several of the said isotopes, that is, elements of which the natural isotopic composition has been artificially modified.

7. Heading No. 28.53 includes copper phosphide (phosphor copper) containing more than 15% by weight of phosphorus.

8. Chemical elements (for example, silicon and selenium) doped for use in electronics are to be classified in this Chapter, provided that they are in forms unworked as drawn, or in the form of cylinders or rods. When cut in the form of discs, wafers or similar forms, they fall in heading No. 38.18.

Subheading Note:

For the purposes of Subheading 2812.10, the expression "chemically defined" means all organic or inorganic compounds of mercury meeting the requirements of paragraphs (a) to (e) of Note 1 to Chapter 28 or paragraphs (a) to (h) of Note 1 to Chapter 29

协定税率 %								RCEP		特惠税率 %			Article Description
东/冰/格	巴基斯坦	韩国	瑞士上/下	哥/秘/柬	澳/毛	新西/坡/智	中国港/澳/台	东盟及马来/澳/韩	日/新	亚太2国	老/柬/缅	98/97/95	
													Ⅰ. CHEMICAL ELEMENTS
													Fluorine, chlorine, bromine and iodine:
0/0/0	0	0	0/0	0/0/0	0/0	0//0	0/0/	0/0/0	0/0			0/0/0	-Chlorine
0/0/0	0	0	0/0	0//0	0/0	0//	0/0/	0/0/0	5/0			0/0/0	-Iodine
													-Fluorine; bromine:
0/0/0	0	0	0/0	0/0/0	0/0	0//0	0/0/	0/0/0	0/0			0/0/0	---Fluorine
0/0/0	0	0	0/0	0/0/0	0/0	0//0	0/0/	0/0/0	0/0			0/0/0	---Bromine
													Sulphur, sublimed or precipitated; colloidal sulphur:
0/0/0	0	0	0/0	0/0/0	0/0	0//0	0/0/	0/0/0	0/0			0/0/0	Sulphur, sublimed or precipitated; colloidal sulphur
													Carbon (carbon blacks and other forms of carbon not elsewhere specified or included):
0//0	0	2.5	0/0	0/0/0	0/0	0//0	0/0/0	5/5/5	5.2/5			0/0/0	Carbon (carbon blacks and other forms of carbon not elsewhere specified or included)
													Hydrogen, rare gases and other non-metals:
0/0/0	0	1.1	0/0	0/0/0	0/0	0//0	0/0/	0/0/5	5/0			0/0/0	-Hydrogen
													-Rare gases:
0/0/0	0	0	0/0	0/0/0	0/0	0//0	0/0/	0/0/0	0/0			0/0/0	--Argon
													--Other
0/0/0	0	0	0/0	0/0/0	0/0	0//0	0/0/	0/0/0	0/0			0/0/0	helium
0/0/0	0	0	0/0	0/0/0	0/0	0//0	0/0/	0/0/0	0/0			0/0/0	Other rare gases
0/0/0	0	0	0/0	0/0/0	0/0	0//0	0/0/	0/0/0	0/0			0/0/0	-Nitrogen
0/0/0	0	0	0/0	0/0/0	0/0	0//0	0/0/	0/0/0	0/0			0/0/0	-Oxygen
													-Boron; tellurium
0/0/0	0	0	0/0	0/0/0	0/0	0//0	0/0/	0/0/0	0/0			0/0/0	tellurium
0/0/0	0	0	0/0	0/0/0	0/0	0//0	0/0/	0/0/0	0/0			0/0/0	Boron and its alloys, granularity $<500\mu m$ (containing boron $\geqslant 97\%$, whether in the form of spheroid, ellipsoid, flakes, atomized or pulverized metallic fuel)
0/0/0	0	0	0/0	0/0/0	0/0	0//0	0/0/	0/0/0	0/0			0/0/0	Boron paste, energy density >4 Mega J/kg, boron dissolved in solvent
0/0/0	0	0	0/0	0/0/0	0/0	0//0	0/0/	0/0/0	0/0			0/0/0	Other boron
													-Silicon:
													--Containing by weight not less than 99.99% of silicon:
													---Monocrystals doped for use in electronics, in the form of cylinders or rods, 7.5cm or more in diameter:
0/0/0	0	0	0/0	0/0/0	0/0	0//0	0/0/	0/0/0	0/0			0/0/0	----30cm or more in diameter
0/0/0	0		0/0	0/0/0	0/0	0//0	0/0/	3.9/3.9/	/3.9			0/0/0	----Other
0/0/0	0	0	0/0	0/0/0	0/0	0//0	0/0/	0/0/0	0/0			0/0/0	---Other monocrystals doped for use in electronics, in the form of cylinders or rods
													---Other
0/0/0	0	1.8	0/0	0/0/0	0/0	0//0	0/0/	3.6/3.6/3.6	3.8/3.6			0/0/0	Waste and scrape of polycrystalline silicon, containing by weight more than 99.9999999% (excluding solar-grade polysilicon)
0/0/0	0	1.8	0/0	0/0/0	0/0	0//0	0/0/	3.6/3.6/3.6	3.8/3.6			0/0/0	Solar grade polysilicon silicon content $>$99.9999999%
0/0/0	0	1.8	0/0	0/0/0	0/0	0//0	0/0/	3.6/3.6/3.6	3.8/3.6			0/0/0	Solar grade polysilicon silicon content $>$ 99.9999999% of waste and scrap
0/0/0	0	1.8	0/0	0/0/0	0/0	0//0	0/0/	3.6/3.6/3.6	3.8/3.6			0/0/0	Other polycrystalline silicon, containing by weight more than 99.9999999% (excluding solay-grade poly silicon)
0/0/0	0	1.8	0/0	0/0/0	0/0	0//0	0/0/	3.6/3.6/3.6	3.8/3.6			0/0/0	Waste and scrape of silicon, containing by weight not less than 99.99% (excluding solar-grade polysilicon)
0/0/0	0	1.8	0/0	0/0/0	0/0	0//0	0/0/	3.6/3.6/3.6	3.8/3.6			0/0/0	Solar grade polysilicon silicon content $>$ 99.99%
0/0/0	0	1.8	0/0	0/0/0	0/0	0//0	0/0/	3.6/3.6/3.6	3.8/3.6			0/0/0	Solar grade polysilicon silicon content $>$99.99% of waste and scrap

税则号列		货品名称〔CIQ 扩展编码及品名－T2 表示见附表 2〕	最惠(%)	暂定税率	普通	增值/消费	出口退税	计量单位	监管条件/特殊证件	检验检疫	对美关税	亚太上/下
2804.6190	99	其他含硅量≥99.99%的硅(太阳能级多晶硅除外)〔301 危险化学品,易燃固体;302 其他化工品〕	4		30	13/	0	千克	/13		26.5	
2804.6900		--其他〔301 危险化学品,易燃固体;302 其他化工品〕	4		30	13/	0	千克	/13		31.5	
		-磷:										
2804.7010		---黄磷(白磷)〔999〕	5		30	13/	0	千克	AB/13	MN		
2804.7090		---其他										
2804.7090	10	红磷〔999〕	5		30	13/	0	千克	ABG/13	MN	27.5	
2804.7090	90	其他磷〔999〕	5		30	13/	0	千克	/13		27.5	
2804.8000		-砷〔999〕	5		30	13/	0	千克	AB/13	MN	32.5	
		-硒:										
2804.9010		---经掺杂用于电子工业的晶体棒〔999〕	4		17	13/	0	千克	/1			3.2/3.2
2804.9090		---其他〔999〕	5	0	30	13/	13	千克	/13		27.5	
28.05		**碱金属、碱土金属;稀土金属、钪及钇,不论是否相互混合或相互熔合;汞:**										
		-碱金属及碱土金属:										
2805.1100		--钠〔999〕	5		30	13/	0	千克	AB/13	MN	12.5	
2805.1200		--钙										
2805.1200	10	高纯度钙[金属杂质(除镁外)含量<1‰,硼含量小于 $1/10^5$]〔999〕	5	1	30	13/	0	千克	3A/13	M	28.5	
2805.1200	90	其他钙〔999〕	5	1	30	13/	0	千克	/13		28.5	
		--其他:										
2805.1910		---锂〔999〕	5	1	30	13/	0	千克	AB/13	MN	8.5	
2805.1990		---其他[T2]	5	1	30	13/	0	千克	/13		8.5	
		-稀土金属、钪及钇,不论是否相互混合或相互熔合:										
		---稀土金属、钪及钇,未相互混合或相互熔合:										
2805.3011		----钕〔999〕	5	0	30	13/	0	千克	4Bxy/13	N		
2805.3012		----镝〔999〕	5	0	30	13/	0	千克	4Bxy/1	N	7.5	
2805.3013		----铽〔999〕	5	0	30	13/	0	千克	4Bxy/1	N		
2805.3014		----镧〔999〕	5	0	30	13/	0	千克	4Bxy/13	N	7.5	
2805.3015		----铈										
2805.3015	10	颗粒<500μm 的铈及其合金(含量≥97%,不论球形,椭球体,雾化,片状,研碎金属燃料;未相互混合或相互熔合)〔999〕	5	0	30	13/	0	千克	3B/13	N	7.5	
2805.3015	90	其他金属铈(未相互混合或相互熔合)〔999〕	5	0	30	13/	0	千克	4Bxy/13	N	7.5	
2805.3016		----镨〔999〕	5	0	30	13/	0	千克	4Bxy/1	N		
2805.3017		----钇〔999〕	5	0	30	13/	0	千克	4Bxy/1	N	7.5	
2805.3018		----钪〔999〕	5	0	30	13/	0	千克	4Bxy/1	N	7.5	
2805.3019		----其他〔101 金属钐,102 金属铕,103 金属钪,104 稀土金属,105 金属镧(浸在煤油中的),106 金属铈(浸在煤油中的)〕	5	0	30	13/	0	千克	4Bxy/1	N	7.5	
		---稀土金属、钪及钇,相互混合或相互熔合:										
2805.3021		----电池级〔301〕	5	0	30	13/	0	千克	4Bxy/1	N		
2805.3029		----其他〔301 危险化学品,遇水放出易燃气体的物质;302 不属于危险化学品的稀土〕	5	0	30	13/	0	千克	4Bxy/13	N	27.5	
2805.4000		-汞〔999〕	5		17	13/	0	千克	ABX/13	MN		
		第二分章　无机酸及非金属;无机氧化物										
28.06		**氯化氢(盐酸);氯磺酸:**										
2806.1000		-氯化氢(盐酸)[T2]	5		80	13/	0	千克	23AB/13	MRNS	17.5	
2806.2000		-氯磺酸〔999〕	5		40	13/	0	千克	AB/13	MN		
28.07		**硫酸;发烟硫酸:**										
2807.0000		硫酸;发烟硫酸										
2807.0000	10	硫酸〔301 危险化学品,不用作食品添加剂;303 危险化学品,用作食品添加剂〕	5	1	35	13/	0	千克	32/13		28.5	
2807.0000	90	发烟硫酸〔999〕	5	1	35	13/	0	千克	AB/13	MN	28.5	
28.08		**硝酸;磺硝酸:**										
2808.0000		硝酸;磺硝酸										
2808.0000	10	红发烟硝酸〔999〕	5		40	13/	0	千克	3A/13	M	32.5	
2808.0000	90	磺硝酸及其他硝酸〔999〕	5		40	13/	0	千克	/13		32.5	
28.09		**五氧化二磷;磷酸;多磷酸,不论是否已有化学定义:**										
2809.1000		-五氧化二磷〔999〕	1		8	13/	0	千克	AB/13	MN	6	
		-磷酸及多磷酸:										
		---磷酸及偏磷酸、焦磷酸:										
2809.2011		----食品级磷酸〔101 饲料添加剂;301 危险化学品,用作食品添加剂〕	1		8	13/	0	千克	AB/13	RNS		

协定税率 %								RCEP		特惠税率 %			Article Description
东/冰/格	巴基斯坦	韩国	瑞士上/下	哥/秘/柬	澳/毛	新西/坡/智	中国港/澳/台	东盟及马来/澳/韩	日/新	亚太2国	老/柬/缅	98/97/95	
0/0/0	0	1.8	0/0	0/0/0	0/0	0//0	0/0/	3.6/3.6/3.6	3.8/3.6			0/0/0	Other silicon, containing by weight more than 99.99% (excluding solar-grade polysilicon)
0/0/0	0	0	0/0	0/0/0	0/0	0//0	0/0/	0/0/0	0/0			0/0/0	--Other
													-Phosphorus:
0/0/0	0	0	0/0	0/0/0	0/0	0//0	0/0/	0/0/0	0/0			0/0/0	---Yellow phosphorus (white phosphorus)
													---Other
0/0/0	0	1.1	0/0	0/0/0	0/0	0//0	0/0/	0/0/5	5/0			0/0/0	Red phosphorus
0/0/0	0	1.1	0/0	0/0/0	0/0	0//0	0/0/	0/0/5	5/0			0/0/0	Other phosphorus
0/0/0	0	0	0/0	0/0/0	0/0	0//0	0/0/	0/0/0	0/0			0/0/0	-Arsenic
													-Selenium:
0/0/0	0	0	0/0	0/0/0	0/0	0//0	0/0/	0/0/0	0/0			0/0/0	---Crystals doped for use in electronics, in the form of cylinders or rods
0/0/0	0	0	0/0	0/1.2/0	0/0	0//0	0/0/	0/0/0	5/0			0/0/0	---Other
													Alkali or alkaline-earth metals; rare-earth metals, scandium and yttrium, whether or not intermixed or interalloyed; mercury:
													-Alkali or alkaline-earth metals:
0/0/0	0	0	0/0	0/0/0	0/0	0//0	0/0/	0/0/0	0/0			0/0/0	--Sodium
													--Calcium
0/0/0	0	0	0/0	0/0/0	0/0	0//0	0/0/	0/0/0	0/0			0/0/0	Calcium, with a high purity, metallic impurity (other than Magnesium) < 1‰, containing boron < $1/10^5$
0/0/0	0	0	0/0	0/0/0	0/0	0//0	0/0/	0/0/0	0/0			0/0/0	Other Calcium
													--Other:
0/0/0	0	0	0/0	0/0/0	0/0	0//0	0/0/	0/0/0	5/0			0/0/0	---Lithium
0/0/0	0	0	0/0	0/0/0	0/0	0//0	0/0/	0/0/0	5/0			0/0/0	---Other
													-Rare-earth metals, scandium and yttrium, whether or not intermixed or interalloyed:
													---Not intermixed or interalloyed:
0/0/0	0	0	0/0	0/0/0	0/0	0//0	0/0/	0/0/0	0/0			0/0/0	----Neodymium
0/0/0	0	0	0/0	0/0/0	0/0	0//0	0/0/	0/0/0	0/0			0/0/0	----Dysprosium
0/0/0	0	0	0/0	0/0/0	0/0	0//0	0/0/	0/0/0	0/0			0/0/0	----Terbium
0/0/0	0	0	0/0	0/0/0	0/0	0//0	0/0/	0/0/0	0/0			0/0/0	----Lanthanum
													----Cerium
0/0/0	0	0	0/0	0/0/0	0/0	0//0	0/0/	0/0/0	0/0			0/0/0	Cerium and its alloys, granularity < 500μm, containing cerium ≥ 97%, whether in the form of spheroid, ellipsoid, flakes, atomized or pulverized metallic fuel
0/0/0	0	0	0/0	0/0/0	0/0	0//0	0/0/	0/0/0	0/0			0/0/0	Other metalic cerium, not intermixed or interalloyed
0/0/0	0	0	0/0	0/0/0	0/0	0//0	0/0/	0/0/0	0/0			0/0/0	----Praseodymium
0/0/0	0	0	0/0	0/0/0	0/0	0//0	0/0/	0/0/0	0/0			0/0/0	----Yttrium
0/0/0	0	0	0/0	0/0/0	0/0	0//0	0/0/	0/0/0	0/0			0/0/0	Scandium metal (not mixed or fused)
0/0/0	0	0	0/0	0/0/0	0/0	0//0	0/0/	0/0/0	0/0			0/0/0	----Other
													intermixed or interalloyed:
0/0/0	0	0	0/0	0/0/0	0/0	0//0	0/0/	0/0/0	0/0			0/0/0	----Battery grade
0/0/0	0	0	0/0	0/0/0	0/0	0//0	0/0/	0/0/0	0/0			0/0/0	----Other
0/0/0	0	0	0/0	0/0/0	0/0	0//0	0/0/	0/0/0	0/0			0/0/0	-Mercury
													Ⅱ. INORGANIC ACIDS AND INORGANIC OXYGEN COMPOUNDS OF NON-METALS
													Hydrogen chloride (hydrochloric acid); chorosulphuric acid:
0/0/0	0	0	0/0	0/0/0	0/0	0//0	0/0/	0/0/0	0/0			0/0/0	-Hydrogen chloride (hydrochloric acid)
0/0/0	0	0	0/0	0/0/0	0/0	0//0	0/0/	0/0/0	0/0			0/0/0	-Chlorosulphuric acid
													Sulphuric acid; oleum:
													Sulphuric acid; oleum
0/0/0	0	0	0/0	0/0/0	0/0	0//0	0/0/	0/5/0	0/5			0/0/0	Sulphuric acid
0/0/0	0	0	0/0	0/0/0	0/0	0//0	0/0/	0/5/0	0/5			0/0/0	Oleum
													Nitric acid; sulphonitric acids:
													Nitric acid; sulphonitric acids
0/0/0	0	0	0/0	0/0/0	0/0	0//0	0/0/	0/0/0	0/0			0/0/0	Red fuming nitric acid
0/0/0	0	0	0/0	0/0/0	0/0	0//0	0/0/	0/0/0	0/0			0/0/0	Sulphonitric acids, other nitric acids
													Diphosphorus pentaoxide; phosphoric acid; polyphosphoric acids, whether or not chemically defined:
0/0/0	0	0	0/0	0/0/0	0/0	0//0	0/0/	0/0/0	0/0			0/0/0	-Diphosphorus pentaoxide
													-Phosphoric acid and polyphosphoric acids:
													---Phosphoric acid, metaphosphoric acid and pyrophosphoric acid:
0/0/0	0	0	0/0	0/0/0	0/0	0//0	0/0/	0/0/0	0/0			0/0/0	----Phosphoric acid, food grade

税则号列	货品名称〔CIQ 扩展编码及品名—T2 表示见附表 2〕	最惠(%)	暂定税率	普通	增值/消费	出口退税	计量单位	监管条件/特殊证件	检验检疫	对美关税	亚太上/下
2809.2019	----其他〔101 饲料添加剂;301 危险化学品,腐蚀性物质;302 其他化工产品〕	1		8	13/	0	千克	B/13	N	26	
2809.2090	---其他〔101 饲料添加剂;301 危险化学品,腐蚀性物质;302 其他化工品〕	5		35	13/	0	千克	/13		12.5	
28.10	**硼的氧化物;硼酸:**										
2810.0010	---硼的氧化物〔999〕	5		30	13/	0	千克	/1		12.5	4.5/4.5
2810.0020	---硼酸〔999〕	5		30	13/	0	千克	AB/13	MN		
28.11	**其他无机酸及非金属无机氧化物:**										
	-其他无机酸:										
	--氟化氢(氢氟酸):										
2811.1110	---电子级氢氟酸〔301 危险化学品,气体;302 危险化学品,腐蚀性物质〕	5.5		35	13/	0	千克	3AB/13	MN		
2811.1190	---其它〔301:危险化学品,气体;302:危险化学品,腐蚀性物质〕	5		35	13/	0	千克	3AB/13	MN	30	
2811.1200	--氰化氢(氢氰酸)〔301 危险化学品,气体;302 危险化学品,毒性物质〕	5		35	13/	0	千克	23/13			4/4
	--其他:										
2811.1920	---硒化氢〔999〕	5		35	13/	0	千克	AB/13	MN		
2811.1990	---其他										
2811.1990 10	氢碘酸〔999〕	5		35	13/	0	千克	ABG/13	MN	27.5	
2811.1990 20	砷酸、焦砷酸、偏砷酸〔999〕	5		35	13/	0	千克	/13		27.5	
2811.1990 90	其他无机酸[T2]	5		35	13/	0	千克	AB/13	MRNS	27.5	
	-其他非金属无机氧化物:										
2811.2100	--二氧化碳〔301 危险化学品,不用作食品添加剂,302 危险化学品,用作食品添加剂,303 其他化工品,不用作食品添加剂,304 其他化工品,用作食品添加剂〕	5		30	13/	0	千克	AB/13	MRNS	32.5	
	--二氧化硅:										
2811.2210	---硅胶〔999〕	5		30	13/	13	千克	A/1	R	12.5	
2811.2290	---其他〔101 饲料添加剂,301 需申报仅用于工业用途不用于食品添加剂无检疫要求的化学品,302 无检疫要求食品添加剂〕	5		30	13/	13	千克	A/1	R	27.5	
2811.2900	--其他										
2811.2900 10	三氧化二砷、五氧化二砷[亚砷(酸)酐、砒霜、白砒、氧化亚砷、砷(酸)酐、三氧化砷]〔999〕	5		30	13/	0	千克	/13		17.5	
2811.2900 20	四氧化二氮〔999〕	5		30	13/	0	千克	3A/13	M	17.5	
2811.2900 90	其他非金属无机氧化物〔301 危险化学品,气体;302 危险化学品,氧化性物质;303 危险化学品,毒性物质;304 危险化学品,腐蚀性物质;305 其他化工产品〕	5		30	13/	0	千克	/13		17.5	
	第三分章 非金属卤化物及硫化物										
28.12	**非金属卤化物及卤氧化物:**										
	-氯化物及氯氧化物:										
2812.1100	--碳酰二氯(光气)〔999〕	5		30	13/	0	千克	23/13			
2812.1200	--氧氯化磷〔999〕	5		30	13/	0	千克	23/13		12.5	
2812.1300	--三氯化磷〔999〕	5		30	13/	0	千克	23AB/13	MN		
2812.1400	--五氯化磷〔999〕	5		30	13/	0	千克	23AB/13	MN		
2812.1500	--一氯化硫〔999〕	5		30	13/	0	千克	23AB/13	MN		
2812.1600	--二氯化硫〔999〕	5		30	13/	0	千克	23AB/13	MN		
2812.1700	--亚硫酰氯〔999〕	5		30	13/	0	千克	23AB/13	MN		
	--其他:										
2812.1910	----氯化物										
2812.1910 10	三氯化砷〔999〕	5		30	13/	0	千克	23AB/1	MN	32.5	
2812.1910 90	其他非金属氯化物〔301 危险化学品,气体,302 危险化学品,毒性物质,303 危险化学品,腐蚀性物质,304 其他危险化学品,305 其他化工品〕	5		30	13/	0	千克	/1		32.5	
2812.1990	----其他〔301 危险化学品,气体,302 危险化学品,毒性物质,303 危险化学品,腐蚀性物质,304 其他化工品〕	5		30	13/	0	千克	/1		32.5	
	-其他:										
	---氟化物及氟氧化物:										
2812.9011	----三氟化氮〔999〕	5		30	13/	13	千克	AB/13	MN	27.5	
2812.9019	----其他										
2812.9019 10	三氟化氯〔999〕	5		30	13/	0	千克	3A/13	M	12.5	
2812.9019 20	三氟化砷(氟化亚砷)〔999〕	5		30	13/	0	千克	/13		12.5	
2812.9019 30	硫酰氟〔999〕	5		30	13/	0	千克	S/13		12.5	
2812.9019 40	三氟化磷〔999〕	5	3	30	13/	0	千克	/13		10.5	
2812.9019 50	三氟化硼〔999〕	5	3	30	13/	0	千克	/13		10.5	
2812.9019 90	其他氟化物及氟氧化物〔301 危险化学品,气体;302 危险化学品,氧化性物质;303 氧化性物质;304 其他化工产品〕	5		30	13/	0	千克	/13		12.5	

协定税率 %								RCEP		特惠税率 %			Article Description
东/冰/格	巴基斯坦	韩国	瑞士上/下	哥/秘/柬	澳/毛	新西/坡/智	中国港/澳/台	东盟及马来/澳/韩	日/新	亚太2国	老/柬/缅	98/97/95	
0/0/0	0	0.2	0/0	0/0/0	0/0	0//0	0/0/	0/0/0.9	0.9/0			0/0/0	----Other
0/0/0	0	0	0/0	0/0/0	0/0	0//0	0/0/	0/0/0	0/0			0/0/0	---Other
													Oxides of boron; boric acids:
0/0/0	0	0	0/0	0/0/0	0/0	0//0	0/0/	0/0/0	0/0			0/0/0	---Oxides of boron
0/0/0	0	0	0/0	0/0/0	0/0	0//0	0/0/	0/0/0	0/0			0/0/0	---Boric acids
													Other inorganic acids and other inorganic oxygen compounds of non-metals:
													-Other inorganic acids:
													--Hydrofluoric acid,Electronic-grade
0/0/0	0	0	0/0	0/0/0	0/0	0//0	0/0/	0/0/0	5/0			0/0/0	---Other
0/0/0	0	0	0/0	0/0/0	0/0	0//0	0/0/	0/0/0	5/0			0/0/0	---hydrofluoric acid
0/0/0	0	0	0/0	0/0/0	0/0	0//0	0/0/	0/0/0	0/0			0/0/0	--Hydrocyanic acid
													--Other:
0/0/0	0	1.1	0/0	0/0/0	0/0	0//0	0/0/	0/0/5	5/0			0/0/0	---Hydrogen selenide
													---Other
0/0/0	0	1.1	0/0	0/0/0	0/0	0//0	0/0/	0/0/5	5/0			0/0/0	Hydroiodic acid
0/0/0	0	1.1	0/0	0/0/0	0/0	0//0	0/0/	0/0/5	5/0			0/0/0	Arsenic acid, pyroarsenic acid, metaardsenic acid
0/0/0	0	1.1	0/0	0/0/0	0/0	0//0	0/0/	0/0/5	5/0			0/0/0	Other inorganic acids
													-Other inorganic oxygen compounds of non-metals:
0/0/0	0	0	0/0	0/0/0	0/0	0//0	0/0/	0/0/0	0/0			0/0/0	--Carbon dioxide
													--Silicon dioxide:
0/0/0	0	0	0/0	0/0/0	0/0	0//0	0/0/	0/5/0	0/5			0/0/0	---Silica gel
0/0/0	0	0	0/0	0/0/0	0/0	0//0	0/0/	0/5/0	0/5			0/0/0	---Other
													--Other
0/0/0	0	0	0/0	0/0/0	0/0	0//0	0/0/	0/0/0	0/0			0/0/0	Arsenous oxide (*arsenic trioxide*), arsenic pentoxide(including arsenic trioxide, arsenous anhydride, arsenic white)
0/0/0	0	0	0/0	0/0/0	0/0	0//0	0/0/	0/0/0	0/0			0/0/0	Dinitrogen tetroxide
0/0/0	0	0	0/0	0/0/0	0/0	0//0	0/0/	0/0/0	0/0			0/0/0	Other inorganic oxygen compounds of non-metals
													Ⅲ. HALOGEN OR SULPHUR COMPOUNDS OF NON-METALS
													Halides and halide oxides of non-metals:
													-Chlorides and chloride oxides:
0/0/0	0	0	0/0	0/0/0	0/0	0//0	0/0/	0/0/0	0/0			0/0/0	--Carbonyl dichiloride (*phosgene*)
0/0/0	0	0	0/0	0/0/0	0/0	0//0	0/0/	0/0/0	0/0			0/0/0	--Phosphorus oxychloride
0/0/0	0	0	0/0	0/0/0	0/0	0//0	0/0/	0/0/0	0/0			0/0/0	--Phosphorus trichloride
0/0/0	0	0	0/0	0/0/0	0/0	0//0	0/0/	0/0/0	0/0			0/0/0	--Phosphorus pentachloride
0/0/0	0	0	0/0	0/0/0	0/0	0//0	0/0/	0/0/0	0/0			0/0/0	--Sulfur monochloride
0/0/0	0	0	0/0	0/0/0	0/0	0//0	0/0/	0/0/0	0/0			0/0/0	--Sulfur dichloride
0/0/0	0	0	0/0	0/0/0	0/0	0//0	0/0/	0/0/0	5/0			0/0/0	--Thionyl chloride
													--Other:
													----Chlorides
0/0/0	0	0	0/0	0/0/0	0/0	0//0	0/0/	0/0/0	5/0			0/0/0	Arsenic trichloride
0/0/0	0	0	0/0	0/0/0	0/0	0//0	0/0/	0/0/0	5/0			0/0/0	Other non-metallic chlorides
0/0/0	0	0	0/0	0/0/0	0/0	0//0	0/0/	0/0/0	0/0			0/0/0	----Other
													-Other:
													---Fluoride and oxyfluoride:
0/0/0	0	2.5	0/0	0/0/0	0/0	0//0	0/0/	5/5/5	5.2/5			0/0/0	----Nitrogen trifluoride
													----Other
0/0/0	0	0	0/0	0/0/0	0/0	0//0	0/0/	0/0/0	5/0			0/0/0	Chlorine trifluoride
0/0/0	0	0	0/0	0/0/0	0/0	0//0	0/0/	0/0/0	5/0			0/0/0	Arsenic trifluoride
0/0/0	0	0	0/0	0/0/0	0/0	0//0	0/0/	0/0/0	5/0			0/0/0	Sulphurylfluoride
0/0/0	0	0	0/0	0/0/0	0/0	0//0	0/0/	0/0/0	5/0		//	0/0/0	Phosphorus trifluoride
0/0/0	0	0	0/0	0/0/0	0/0	0//0	0/0/	0/0/0	5/0		//	0/0/0	Boron trifluoride
0/0/0	0	0	0/0	0/0/0	0/0	0//0	0/0/	0/0/0	5/0			0/0/0	Other fluoride and oxyfluoride

税则号列	货品名称〔CIQ 扩展编码及品名—T2 表示见附表 2〕	最惠(%)	暂定税率	普通	增值/消费	出口退税	计量单位	监管条件/特殊证件	检验检疫	对美关税	亚太上/下
2812.9090	---其他										
2812.9090 10	三溴化砷,三碘化砷(溴化亚砷,碘化亚砷)〔999〕	5		30	13/	0	千克	/13		12.5	
2812.9090 90	其他非金属卤化物及卤氧化物〔301 危险化学品,气体;302 危险化学品,毒性物质;303 危险化学品,腐蚀性物质;304 其他化工产品〕	5		30	13/	0	千克	/13		12.5	
28.13	**非金属硫化物;商品三硫化二磷:**										
2813.1000	-二硫化碳〔999〕	5		30	13/	0	千克	AB/13	MN		
2813.9000	-其他										
2813.9000 10	五硫化二磷〔999〕	5		30	13/	0	千克	23/13		17.5	
2813.9000 20	三硫化二磷〔999〕	5		30	13/	0	千克	AB/13	MN	17.5	
2813.9000 90	其他非金属硫化物〔301 危险化学品,易燃固体;302 危险化学品,毒性物质;303 其他化工品〕	5		30	13/	0	千克	/13		17.5	
	第四分章　无机碱和金属氧化物、氢氧化物及过氧化物										
28.14	**氨及氨水:**										
2814.1000	-氨〔101 饲料添加剂;301 危险化学品,气体〕	5	0	35	13/	0	千克	AB/13	MN	25	
2814.2000	-氨水										
2814.2000 10	氨水(含量≥10%)〔101 饲料添加剂,301 腐蚀性物质〕	5	0	35	13/	0	千克	AB/13	MN	27.5	
2814.2000 90	其他氨水〔101 饲料添加剂,102 化工产品〕	5	0	35	13/	0	千克	/13		27.5	
28.15	**氢氧化钠(烧碱);氢氧化钾(苛性钾);过氧化钠及过氧化钾:**										
	-氢氧化钠(烧碱):										
2815.1100	--固体〔101 饲料添加剂;301 危险化学品,不用作食品添加剂;302 危险化学品,用作食品添加剂〕	5		35	13/	0	千克	ABG/13	MRNS	32.5	3.3/3.3
2815.1200	--水溶液(氢氧化钠浓溶液及液体烧碱)〔101 饲料添加剂;301 危险化学品,不用作食品添加剂;302 危险化学品,用作食品添加剂;303 其他化工品〕	5		35	13/	0	千克	ABG/13	MN	17.5	3.3/3.3
2815.2000	-氢氧化钾(苛性钾)〔301 危险化学品,不用作食品添加剂;302 危险化学品,用作食品添加剂〕	5		30	13/	13	千克	AB/13	MRNS	12.5	
2815.3000	-过氧化钠及过氧化钾〔999〕	5		30	13/	0	千克	AB/13	MN	32.5	
28.16	**氢氧化镁及过氧化镁;锶或钡的氧化物、氢氧化物及过氧化物:**										
2816.1000	-氢氧化镁及过氧化镁										
2816.1000 10	过氧化镁〔999〕	5		30	13/	0	千克	AB/13	MN	32.5	
2816.1000 90	氢氧化镁〔999〕	5		30	13/	0	千克	/13		32.5	
2816.4000	-锶或钡的氧化物、氢氧化物及过氧化物〔301 危险化学品,氧化性物质;302 危险化学品,腐蚀性物质;303 其他危险化学品;304 其他化工品〕	5	2	30	13/	0	千克	/13		9.5	
28.17	**氧化锌及过氧化锌:**										
2817.0010	---氧化锌〔101 矿物源性饲料添加剂,102 无检疫要求食品添加剂,301 需申报仅用于工业用途不用于食品添加剂无检疫要求的化学品〕	5		40	13/	0	千克	A/1	R	27.5	
2817.0090	---过氧化锌〔999〕	5		30	13/	0	千克	AB/13	MN	17.5	4.5/4.5
28.18	**人造刚玉,不论是否已有化学定义;氧化铝;氢氧化铝:**										
	-人造刚玉,不论是否已有化学定义:										
2818.1010	---棕刚玉〔999〕	5		20	13/	0	千克	/1		32.5	
2818.1090	---其他〔101 化工产品,102 人造刚玉,103 白刚玉,104 黑刚玉,105 锆刚玉〕	5		20	13/	0	千克	/1			
2818.2000	-氧化铝,但人造刚玉除外〔101 饲料添加剂,102 化工产品〕	5	0	30	13/	0	千克	/1		27.5	
2818.3000	-氢氧化铝〔999〕	5		30	13/	0	千克	/1		27.5	
28.19	**铬的氧化物及氢氧化物:**										
2819.1000	-三氧化铬〔999〕	5		20	13/	0	千克	AB/13	MN	10	
2819.9000	-其他〔999〕	5		30	13/	0	千克	/1		17.5	
28.20	**锰的氧化物:**										
2820.1000	-二氧化锰〔101 矿物源性饲料添加剂,102 化工产品〕	5		40	13/	0	千克	/1		12.5	
2820.9000	-其他〔101 矿物源性饲料添加剂,102 化工产品〕	5		30	13/	0	千克	/1		27.5	
28.21	**铁的氧化物及氢氧化物;土色料,按重量计三氧化二铁含量在70%及以上:**										
2821.1000	-铁的氧化物及氢氧化物〔101〕	5		30	13/	0	千克	/1		25	
2821.2000	-土色料〔101 矿物源性饲料添加剂,102 化工产品〕	5		45	13/	0	千克	/1		17.5	
28.22	**钴的氧化物及氢氧化物;商品氧化钴:**										
2822.0010	---四氧化三钴〔999〕	5	2	30	13/	13	千克	4xy/1			
2822.0090	---其他〔999〕	5	2	30	13/	0	千克	4xy/1		29.5	
28.23	**钛的氧化物:**										
2823.0000	钛的氧化物〔999〕	5		30	13/	0	千克	/1		32.5	
28.24	**铅的氧化物;铅丹及铅橙:**										
2824.1000	-一氧化铅(铅黄、黄丹)〔999〕	5		30	13/	0	千克	AB/13	MN		
	-其他:										

协定税率 %								RCEP		特惠税率 %			Article Description
东/冰/格	巴基斯坦	韩国	瑞士 上/下	哥/秘/柬	澳/毛	新西/坡/智	中国港/澳/台	东盟及马来/澳/韩	日/新	亚太2国	老/柬/缅	98/97/95	
													---Other
0/0/0	0	1.1	0/0	0/0/0	0/0	0//0	0/0/	0/0/5	5/0			0/0/0	Arsenic tribromide, arsenic triiodide
0/0/0	0	1.1	0/0	0/0/0	0/0	0//0	0/0/	0/0/5	5/0			0/0/0	Other halides and halide oxides of non-metals
													Sulphides of non-metals; commercial phosphorus trisulphides:
0/0/0	0	0	0/0	0/0/0	0/0	0//0	0/0/	0/0/0	0/0			0/0/0	-Carbon disulphide
													-Other
0/0/0	0	0	0/0	0/0/0	0/0	0//0	0/0/	0/0/0	0/0			0/0/0	Phosphorus pentasulfide
0/0/0	0	0	0/0	0/0/0	0/0	0//0	0/0/	0/0/0	0/0			0/0/0	Phosphorus trisulfide
0/0/0	0	0	0/0	0/0/0	0/0	0//0	0/0/	0/0/0	0/0			0/0/0	Other sulphides of non-metals
													Ⅳ. INORGANIC BASES AND OXIDES, HYDROXIDES AND PEROXIDES OF METALS
													Ammonia, anhydrous or in aqueous solution:
0/0/0	0	0	0/0	0/0/0	0/0	0//0	0/0/	0/0/0	0/0			0/0/0	-Anhydrous ammonia
													-Ammonia in aqueous solution
0/0/0	0	0	0/0	0/0/0	0/0	0//0	0/0/	0/0/0	0/0			0/0/0	Ammonia in aqueous solution
0/0/0	0	0	0/0	0/0/0	0/0	0//0	0/0/	0/0/0	0/0			0/0/0	Other ammonia in aqueous solution
													Sodium hydroxide (caustic soda); potassium hydroxide (caustic potash); peroxides or sodium or potassium:
													-Sodium hydroxide (caustic soda):
5/0/0	7	2	0/0	0/0/0	0/0	0//0	0/0/					0/0/0	--Solid
5/0/0	5.6	1.6	0/0	0/0/0	0/0	0//0	0/0/	5/5/	/5			0/0/0	--In aqueous solution (soda lye or liquid soda)
0/0/0	0	0	0/0	0/0/0	0/0	0//0	0/0/	0/0/0	0/0			0/0/0	-Potassium hydroxide (caustic potash)
0/0/0	0	0	0/0	0/0/0	0/0	0//0	0/0/	0/0/0	0/0			0/0/0	-Peroxides of sodium or potassium
													Hydroxide and peroxide of magnesium; oxides, hydroxides and peroxides, of strontium or barium:
													-Hydroxide and peroxide of magnesium
0/0/0	0	1.1	0/0	0/0/0	0/0	0//0	0/0/	0/0/5	5/0			0/0/0	Peroxide of magnesium
0/0/0	0	1.1	0/0	0/0/0	0/0	0//0	0/0/	0/0/5	5/0			0/0/0	Hydroxide
0/0/0	0	0	0/0	0/0/0	0/0	0//0	0/0/	0/0/0	0/0			0/0/0	-Oxides, hydroxides and peroxides, of strontium or barium
													Zinc oxide; Zinc peroxide:
0/0/0	0	0	0/0	0/0/0	0/0	0//0	0/0/	0/0/0	0/0			0/0/0	---Zinc oxide
0/0/0	0	0	0/0	0/0/0	0/0	0//0	0/0/	0/0/0	0/0			0/0/0	---Zinc peroxide
													Artificial corundum, whether or not chemically defined; aluminium oxide; aluminium hydroxide:
													-Artificial corundum, whether or not chemically defined:
0/0/0	0	1.1	0/0	0/0/0	0/0	0//0	0/0/	0/0/5	5/0			0/0/0	---Brown corundum
0/0/0	0	0	0/0	0/0/0	0/0	0//0	0/0/	0/5/0	0/5			0/0/0	---Other
0/0/0	2	0	0/0	0/0/0	0/0	0/0/0	0/0/	0/0/0	7.3/0			0/0/0	-Aluminium oxide, other than artificial corundum
0/0/0	0	0	0/0	0/0/0	0/0	0//0	0/0/	0/0/0	0/0			0/0/0	-Aluminium hydroxide
													Chromium oxides and hydroxides:
0/0/0	0	1.1	0/0	0/0/0	0/0	0//0	0/0/	0/0/5	5/0			0/0/0	-Chromium trioxide
0/0/0	0	0	0/0	0/0/0	0/0	0//0	0/0/	0/0/0	0/0			0/0/0	-Other
													Manganese oxide:
0/0/0	0	0	0/0	0/0/0	0/0	0//0	0/0/	0/0/0	0/0			0/0/0	-Manganese dioxide
0/0/0	0	0	0/0	0/0/0	0/0	0//0	0/0/	0/0/0	0/0			0/0/0	-Other
													Iron oxides and hydroxides; earth colours containing 70% or more by weight of combined iron evaluated as Fe_2O_3:
0/0/0	0	2.5	0/0	0/0/0	0/0	0//0	0/0/	5/5/5	5.2/5			0/0/0	-Iron oxides and hydroxides
0/0/0	0	1.1	0/0	0/0/0	0/0	0//0	0/0/	0/0/5	5/0			0/0/0	-Earth colours
													Cobalt oxides and hydroxides; commercial cobalt oxides:
0/0/0	0	0	0/0	0/0/0	0/0	0//0	0/0/	0/0/0	0/0			0/0/0	---Cobalt tetroxide
0/0/0	0	0	0/0	0/0/0	0/0	0//0	0/0/	0/0/0	0/0			0/0/0	---Other
													Titanium oxides:
0/0/0	0	0	0/0	0/0/0	0/0	0//0	0/0/	0/0/0	0/0			0/0/0	Titanium oxides
													Lead oxides; red lead and orange lead:
0/0/0	0	0	0/0	0/0/0	0/0	0//0	0/0/	0/0/0	0/0			0/0/0	-Lead monoxide (litharge, massicot)
													-Other:

税则号列	货品名称〔CIQ扩展编码及品名—T2表示见附表2〕	最惠(%)	暂定税率	普通	增值/消费	出口退税	计量单位	监管条件/特殊证件	检验检疫	对美关税	亚太上/下
2824.9010	---铅丹及铅橙〔999〕	5		45	13/	0	千克	AB/13	MN		
2824.9090	---其他〔301 危险化学品,氧化性物质;302 其他化工品〕	5		30	13/	0	千克	/13		12.5	
28.25	**肼(联氨)、胲(羟胺)及其无机盐;其他无机碱;其他金属氧化物、氢氧化物及过氧化物:**										
	-肼(联氨)、胲(羟胺)及其无机盐:										
2825.1010	---水合肼										
2825.1010 10	纯度70%及以上的水合肼〔999〕	5		30	13/	0	千克	3A/13	M	7.5	
2825.1010 90	纯度70%以下的水合肼〔999〕	5		30	13/	0	千克	AB/13	MN	7.5	
2825.1020	---硫酸羟胺〔999〕	5		30	13/	0	千克	AB/13	MN	7.5	
2825.1090	---其他〔301 爆炸品;302 危险化学品,腐蚀性物质;303 其他化工品〕	5		30	13/	0	千克	/13		30	
	-锂的氧化物及氢氧化物:										
2825.2010	---氢氧化锂〔999〕	5		30	13/	0	千克	AB/13	MN	27.5	
2825.2090	---其他〔301 危险化学品,氧化性物质;302 其他化工品〕	5		30	13/	0	千克	/13			
	-钒的氧化物及氢氧化物:										
2825.3010	---五氧化二钒〔999〕	5		30	13/	0	千克	4ABxy/13	MN	32.5	
2825.3090	---其他〔301 其他危险化学品;302 其他化工产品〕	5		30	13/	0	千克	4xy/13		32.5	
2825.4000	-镍的氧化物及氢氧化物〔999〕	5	2	30	13/	13	千克	/1			
2825.5000	-铜的氧化物及氢氧化物〔101 矿物源性饲料添加剂,102 化工产品〕	5		30	13/	0	千克	/1		12.5	
2825.6000	-锗的氧化物及二氧化锆										
2825.6000 01	锗的氧化物〔999〕	5		30	13/	0	千克	4xy/1		12.5	
2825.6000 90	二氧化锆〔999〕	5		30	13/	0	千克	3/1		12.5	
2825.7000	-钼的氧化物及氢氧化物〔999〕	5		30	13/	0	千克	4xy/1		17.5	
2825.8000	-锑的氧化物〔301 危险化学品,杂项物质;302 其他化工产品〕	5		30	13/	0	千克	4xBy/13	N	32.5	
	-其他:										
	---钨的氧化物及氢氧化物:										
2825.9011	----钨酸〔999〕	5		30	13/	0	千克	4xy/1			
2825.9012	----三氧化钨〔999〕	5		30	13/	0	千克	4xy/1		32.5	
2825.9019	----其他										
2825.9019 10	蓝色氧化钨〔999〕	5		30	13/	0	千克	4xy/1			
2825.9019 90	其他钨的氧化物及氢氧化物〔999〕	5		30	13/	0	千克	/1			
	---铋的氧化物及氢氧化物:										
2825.9021	----三氧化二铋〔999〕	5		30	13/	13	千克	4Axy/1	R	27.5	
2825.9029	----其他〔999〕	5		30	13/	0	千克	4Axy/1	R		
	---锡的氧化物及氢氧化物:						千克				
2825.9031	----二氧化锡〔999〕	5		30	13/	0	千克	4Axy/1	R	32.5	
2825.9039	----其他〔999〕	5		30	13/	0	千克	4Axy/1	R		
	---铌的氧化物及氢氧化物:										
2825.9041	----一氧化铌〔999〕	5		30	13/	0	千克	A/1	M		
2825.9049	----其他										
2825.9049 10	五氧化二铌〔999〕	5	2	30	13/	0	千克	AB/1	MRN		
2825.9049 90	其他铌的氧化物及氢氧化物〔999〕	5		30	13/	0	千克	AB/1	MRN		
2825.9090	---其他[T2]	5		30	13/	0	千克	AB/13	MRNS	27.5	
	第五分章 无机酸盐、无机过氧酸盐及金属酸盐、金属过氧酸盐										
28.26	**氟化物;氟硅酸盐、氟铝酸盐及其他氟络盐:**										
	-氟化物:										
	--氟化铝:										
2826.1210	---无水氟化铝〔999〕	5.5		30	13/	0	千克	/1		30.5	
2826.1290	---其他〔999〕	5		30	13/	0	千克	/1			
	--其他:										
2826.1910	---铵的氟化物										
2826.1910 10	氟化氢铵〔999〕	5		30	13/	0	千克	3A/13	M		
2826.1910 90	其他铵的氟化物〔301 其他化工产品;999 毒性物质和感染性物质〕	5		30	13/	0	千克	/13			
2826.1920	---钠的氟化物										
2826.1920 10	氟化钠〔999〕	5		30	13/	0	千克	3AB/13	MRNS	27.5	
2826.1920 20	氟化氢钠〔999〕	5		30	13/	0	千克	3A/13	M	27.5	
2826.1920 90	其他钠的氟化物〔999〕	5		30	13/	0	千克	/13		27.5	
2826.1930	---六氟化钨〔999〕	5		30	13/	0	千克	/1		17.5	
2826.1990	---其他										
2826.1990 10	氟化钾〔999〕	5		30	13/	0	千克	3A/13	M	17.5	
2826.1990 20	氟化氢钾〔999〕	5		30	13/	0	千克	3A/13	M	17.5	
2826.1990 30	氟化铅,四氟化铅,氟化镉〔301 危险化学品,毒性物质;302 危险化学品,杂项物质〕	5		30	13/	0	千克	/13		17.5	

协定税率 %								RCEP		特惠税率 %			Article Description
东/冰/格	巴基斯坦	韩国	瑞士上/下	哥/秘/柬	澳/毛	新西/坡/智	中国港/澳/台	东盟及马来/澳/韩	日/新	亚太2国	老/柬/缅	98/97/95	
0/0/0	0	0	0/0	0/0/0	0/0	0//0	0/0/	0/0/0	0/0			0/0/0	---Red lead and orange lead
0/0/0	0	0	0/0	0/0/0	0/0	0//0	0/0/	0/0/0	0/0			0/0/0	---Other
													Hydrazine and hydroxylamine and their inorganic salts; other inorganic bases; other metal oxides, hydroxides and peroxides:
													-Hydrazine and hydroxylamine and their inorganic salts:
													---Hydrazine hydrate
0/0/0	0	1.1	0/0	0/0/0	0/0	0//0	0/0/	0/0/5	5/0			0/0/0	Hydrazine hydrate, purity≥70%
0/0/0	0	1.1	0/0	0/0/0	0/0	0//0	0/0/	0/0/5	5/0			0/0/0	Hydrazine hydrate, purity<70%
0/0/0	0	1.1	0/0	0/0/0	0/0	0//0	0/0/	0/0/5	5/0			0/0/0	---Hydroxylamine sulfate
0/0/0	0	0	0/0	0/0/0	0/0	0//0	0/0/	0/0/0	0/0			0/0/0	---Other
													-Lithium oxide and hydroxide:
0/0/0	0	0	0/0	0/0/0	0/0	0//0	0/0/	0/0/0	0/0			0/0/0	---Lithium hydroxide
0/0/0	0	0	0/0	0/0/0	0/0	0//0	0/0/	0/0/0	0/0			0/0/0	---Other
													-Vanadium oxides and hydroxides:
0/0/0	0	1.1	0/0	0/0/0	0/0	0//0	0/0/	0/0/5	5/0			0/0/0	---Divanadium pentaoxide
0/0/0	0	0	0/0	0/0/0	0/0	0//0	0/0/	0/0/0	0/0			0/0/0	---Other
0/0/0	0	0	0/0	0/0/0	0/0	0//0	0/0/	0/0/0	0/0			0/0/0	-Nickel oxides and hydroxides
0/0/0	0	0	0/0	0/0/0	0/0	0//0	0/0/	0/0/0	0/0			0/0/0	-Copper oxides and hydroxides
													-Germanium oxides and zirconium dioxide
0/0/0	0	0	0/0	0/0/0	0/0	0//0	0/0/	0/0/0	0/0			0/0/0	Cermaniurn oxides
0/0/0	0	0	0/0	0/0/0	0/0	0//0	0/0/	0/0/0	0/0			0/0/0	Zirconium dioxide
0/0/0	0	0	0/0	0//0	0/0	0//0	0/0/	0/0/0	5/0			0/0/0	-Molybdenum oxides and hydroxides
0/0/0	0	0	0/0	0/0/0	0/0	0//0	0/0/	0/0/0	0/0			0/0/0	-Antimony oxides
													-Other:
													---Tungsten oxides and hydroxides:
0/0/0	0	0	0/0	0/0/0	0/0	0//0	0/0/	0/0/0	0/0			0/0/0	----Tungstic acid
0/0/0	0	0	0/0	0/0/0	0/0	0//0	0/0/	0/0/0	0/0			0/0/0	----Tungstic oxide
													----Other
0/0/0	0	0	0/0	0/0/0	0/0	0//0	0/0/	0/0/0	0/0			0/0/0	Blue tungsten oxides
0/0/0	0	0	0/0	0/0/0	0/0	0//0	0/0/	0/0/0	0/0			0/0/0	Other tungsten oxides and hydroxides
													---Bismuth oxdes and hydroxides:
0/0/0	0	0	0/0	0/0/0	0/0	0//0	0/0/	0/0/0	0/0			0/0/0	----Bismuth trioxide
0/0/0	0	0	0/0	0/0/0	0/0	0//0	0/0/	0/0/0	0/0			0/0/0	----Other
													---Tin oxides and hydroxides:
0/0/0	0	0	0/0	0/0/0	0/0	0//0	0/0/	0/0/0	0/0			0/0/0	----Tin dioxide
0/0/0	0	0	0/0	0/0/0	0/0	0//0	0/0/	0/0/0	0/0			0/0/0	----Other
													---Niobium oxdes and hydroxides:
0/0/0	0	0	0/0	0/0/0	0/0	0//0	0/0/	0/0/0	0/0			0/0/0	----Columbium monoxide
													----Other
0/0/0	0	0	0/0	0/0/0	0/0	0//0	0/0/	0/0/0	0/0			0/0/0	Niobium pentoxide
0/0/0	0	0	0/0	0/0/0	0/0	0//0	0/0/	0/0/0	0/0			0/0/0	Other niobium oxides and hydroxides
0/0/0	0	0	0/0	0/0/0	0/0	0//0	0/0/	0/0/0	0/0			0/0/0	---Other
													Ⅴ. SALTS AND PEROXYSALTS, OF INORGANIC ACIDS AND METALS
													Fluorides; fluorosilicates, fluoroaluminates and other complex fluorine salts:
													-Fluorides:
													--Of aluminium:
0/0/0	0	0	0/0	0/0/0	0/0	0//0	0/0/	0/0/0	0/0			0/0/0	---Anhydrous fluorides of aluminium
0/0/0	0	0	0/0	0/0/0	0/0	0//0	0/0/	0/0/0	0/0			0/0/0	---Other
													--Other:
													---Of ammonium
0/0/0	0	0	0/0	0/0/0	0/0	0//0	0/0/	0/0/0	0/0			0/0/0	Ammonium hydrogen fluoride
0/0/0	0	0	0/0	0/0/0	0/0	0//0	0/0/	0/0/0	0/0			0/0/0	Other ammonium fluorid
													---Of sodium
0/0/0	0	0	0/0	0/0/0	0/0	0//0	0/0/	0/0/0	0/0			0/0/0	Sodium fluoride
0/0/0	0	0	0/0	0/0/0	0/0	0//0	0/0/	0/0/0	0/0			0/0/0	Sodium hydrogen fluoride
0/0/0	0	0	0/0	0/0/0	0/0	0//0	0/0/	0/0/0	0/0			0/0/0	Other sodium fluorid
0/0/0	0	0	0/0	0/0/0	0/0	0//0	0/0/	0/0/0	0/0			0/0/0	---Tungsten hexafluoride
													---Other
0/0/0	0	0	0/0	0/0/0	0/0	0//0	0/0/	0/0/0	0/0			0/0/0	Potassium fluoride
0/0/0	0	0	0/0	0/0/0	0/0	0//0	0/0/	0/0/0	0/0			0/0/0	Potassium hydrogen fluoride
0/0/0	0	0	0/0	0/0/0	0/0	0//0	0/0/	0/0/0	0/0			0/0/0	Lead fluoride,lead tetrafluoried ,cadmium fluoride

税则号列	货品名称〔CIQ 扩展编码及品名—T2 表示见附表 2〕	最惠(%)	暂定税率	普通	增值/消费	出口退税	计量单位	监管条件/特殊证件	检验检疫	对美关税	亚太上/下
2826.1990 90	其他氟化物〔301 危险化学品,气体;302 危险化学品,毒性物质;303 危险化学品,腐蚀性物质;304 危险化学品,杂项物质;305 其他危险化学品;306 其他化工产品〕	5		30	13/	0	千克	/13		17.5	
2826.3000	-六氟铝酸钠(人造冰晶石)〔999〕	5		30	13/	13	千克	/1			
	-其他:										
2826.9010	---氟硅酸盐〔301 危险化学品,毒性物质;302 其他化工品〕	5		30	13/	0	千克	/13		32.5	
2826.9020	---六氟磷酸锂〔999〕	5.5		30	13/	13	千克	/1		30.5	
2826.9090	---其他										
2826.9090 10	氟钽酸钾〔999〕	5		30	13/	0	千克	/13		32.5	
2826.9090 30	氟硼酸铅,氟硼酸镉〔999〕	5		30	13/	0	千克	/13		32.5	
2826.9090 90	氟铝酸盐及其他氟络盐〔301 危险化学品,毒性物质;302 危险化学品,腐蚀性物质;303 其他化工品〕	5		30	13/	0	千克	/13		32.5	
28.27	**氯化物、氯氧化物及氢氧基氯化物;溴化物及溴氧化物;碘化物及碘氧化物:**										
	-氯化铵:										
2827.1010	---肥料用〔999〕	4		11	13/	0	千克	BG/1	N	6.5	
2827.1090	---其他〔999〕	5		30	13/	0	千克	G/1		32.5	
2827.2000	-氯化钙〔101 矿物源性饲料添加剂,102 无检疫要求食品添加剂,103 需申报仅用于工业用途不用于食品添加剂无检疫要求的化学品〕	5		50	13/	13	千克	A/1	R	32.5	
	-其他氯化物:										
2827.3100	--氯化镁〔101 矿物源性饲料添加剂,102 无检疫要求食品添加剂,103 需申报仅用于工业用途不用于食品添加剂无检疫要求的化学品〕	5		30	13/	0	千克	A/1	R	12.5	
2827.3200	--氯化铝〔999〕	5		30	13/	0	千克	/13		17.5	
2827.3500	--氯化镍〔999〕	5		30	13/	0	千克	AB/13	MN	32.5	
	--其他:										
2827.3910	---氯化锂〔999〕	5		30	13/	0	千克	/1		32.5	3.3/3.3
2827.3920	---氯化钡〔999〕	5		30	13/	0	千克	AB/13	MN	27.5	3.3/3.3
2827.3930	---氯化钴〔101 矿物源性饲料添加剂;301 危险化学品,杂项物质〕	5		30	13/	0	千克	4ABxy/13	MRNS	17.5	3.3/3.3
2827.3990	---其他[T2]	5		30	13/	0	千克	AB/13	MRNS	12.5	3.3/3.3
	-氯氧化物及氢氧基氯化物:										
2827.4100	--铜的氯氧化物及氢氧基氯化物〔999〕	5		30	13/	0	千克	/1		12.5	
	--其他:										
2827.4910	---锆的氯氧化物及氢氧基氯化物〔999〕	5		30	13/	0	千克	/1		32.5	
2827.4990	---其他〔301 危险化学品,腐蚀性物质;302 其他化工产品〕	5		30	13/	0	千克	/13		12.5	
	-溴化物及溴氧化物:										
2827.5100	--溴化钠及溴化钾〔999〕	5		30	13/	0	千克	/1		32.5	
2827.5900	--其他〔301 危险化学品,毒性物质;302 危险化学品,腐蚀性物质;303 其他化工品〕	5		30	13/	0	千克	/13		32.5	
2827.6000	-碘化物及碘氧化物[T2]	5		30	13/	0	千克	AB/13	MRNS	32.5	
28.28	**次氯酸盐;商品次氯酸钙;亚氯酸盐;次溴酸盐:**										
2828.1000	-商品次氯酸钙及其他钙的次氯酸盐〔999〕	5		80	13/	13	千克	/13		10	3.3/3.3
2828.9000	-其他[T2]	5		30	13/	0	千克	AB/13	MRNS	32.5	
28.29	**氯酸盐及高氯酸盐;溴酸盐及过溴酸盐;碘酸盐及高碘酸盐:**										
	-氯酸盐:										
2829.1100	--氯酸钠〔999〕	5		30	13/	0	千克	AB/13	MN	10	
	--其他:										
2829.1910	---氯酸钾(洋硝)〔999〕	5		20	13/	0	千克	9B/13	N		
2829.1990	---其他〔301 危险化学品,爆炸品;302 危险化学品,氧化性物质〕	5		30	13/	0	千克	/13			
2829.9000	-其他										
2829.9000 10	颗粒<500μm 的球形高氯酸铵〔301 危险化学品,爆炸品;302 危险化学品,氧化性物质〕	5		30	13/	0	千克	3A/13	M	17.5	
2829.9000 20	高氯酸钾	5		30	13/	0	千克	3/13		17.5	
2829.9000 90	其他高氯酸盐、溴酸盐等(包括过溴酸盐、碘酸盐及高碘酸盐)〔101 矿物源性饲料添加剂;301 危险化学品,氧化性物质;302 其他化工品〕	5		30	13/	0	千克	/13		17.5	
28.30	**硫化物;多硫化物,不论是否已有化学定义:**										
	-钠的硫化物:										
2830.1010	---硫化钠〔301 危险化学品,易于自燃的物质;302 危险化学品,腐蚀性物质〕	5		40	13/	0	千克	3AB/13	MN	12.5	
2830.1090	---其他〔301 危险化学品,易于自燃的物质;302 其他化工品〕	5		30	13/	0	千克	/13		12.5	
	-其他:										

协定税率 %								RCEP		特惠税率 %			Article Description
东/冰/格	巴基斯坦	韩国	瑞士 上/下	哥/秘/柬	澳/毛	新西/坡/智	中国港/澳/台	东盟及马来/澳/韩	日/新	亚太2国	老/柬/缅	98/97/95	
0/0/0	0	0	0/0	0/0/0	0/0	0//0	0/0/	0/0/0	0/0			0/0/0	Other fluorides
0/0/0	0	0	0/0	0/0/0	0/0	0//0	0/0/	0/0/0	0/0			0/0/0	-Sodium hexafluoroaluminate (synthetic cryolite)
													-Other:
0/0/0	0	1.1	0/0	0/0/0	0/0	0//0	0/0/	0/0/5	5/0			0/0/0	---Fluorosilicates
0/0/0	0	2.5	0/0	0/0/0	0/0	0//0	0/0/	5/5/5	5.2/5			0/0/0	---Lithium Hexafluoroarsenate
													---Other
0/0/0	0	2.5	0/0	0/0/0	0/0	0//0	0/0/	5/5/5	5.2/5			0/0/0	Potassium tantalifluoride
0/0/0	0	2.5	0/0	0/0/0	0/0	0//0	0/0/	5/5/5	5.2/5			0/0/0	lead fluoboriate, cadmium fluoboriate
0/0/0	0	2.5	0/0	0/0/0	0/0	0//0	0/0/	5/5/5	5.2/5			0/0/0	Fluoroaluminates and other complex fluorine salts
													Chlorides, chloride oxides and chloride hydroxides; bromides and bromide oxides; iodides and iodide oxides:
													-Ammonium chloride:
0/0/0	0	0	0/0	0/0/0	0/0	0//0	0/0/	0/0/0	3.6/0			0/0/0	---For use as fertilizer
0/0/0	0	0	0/0	0/0/0	0/0	0//0	0/0/	0/0/0	0/0			0/0/0	---Other
0/0/0	0	0	0/0	0/0/0	0/0	0//0	0/0/	0/0/0	0/0			0/0/0	-Calcium chloride
													-Other chlorides:
0/0/0	0	1.1	0/0	0/0/0	0/0	0//0	0/0/	0/0/5	5/0			0/0/0	--Of magnesium
0/0/0	0	0	0/0	0/0/0	0/0	0//0	0/0/	0/0/0	0/0			0/0/0	--Of aluminium
0/0/0	0	0	0/0	0/0/0	0/0	0//0	0/0/	0/0/0	0/0			0/0/0	--Of nickel
													--Other:
0/0/0	0	0	0/0	0//0	0/0	0//0	0/0/	0/0/0	5/0			0/0/0	---Lithium chloride
0/0/0	0	0		0//0	0/0	0//0	0/0/	0/0/0	5/0			0/0/0	---Barium chleride
0/0/0	0	0	0/0	0/0/0	0/0	0//0	0/0/	0/0/0	0/0			0/0/0	---Cobalt chleride
0/0/0	0	0	0/0	0//0	0/0	0//0	0/0/	0/0/0	5/0			0/0/0	---Other
													-Chloride oxides and chloride hydroxides:
0/0/0	0	0	0/0	0/0/0	0/0	0//0	0/0/	0/0/0	0/0			0/0/0	--of copper
													--Other:
0/0/0	0	0	0/0	0/0/0	0/0	0//0	0/0/	0/0/0	0/0			0/0/0	---of zirconium
0/0/0	0	0	0/0	0/0/0	0/0	0//0	0/0/	0/0/0	0/0			0/0/0	---Other
													-Bromides and bromide oxides:
0/0/0	0	0	0/0	0/0/0	0/0	0//0	0/0/	0/0/0	0/0			0/0/0	--Bromides of sodium or of potassium
0/0/0	0	1.1	0/0	0/0/0	0/0	0//0	0/0/	0/0/5	5/0			0/0/0	--Other
0/0/0	0	0	0/0	0//0	0/0	0//0	0/0/	0/0/0	5/0			0/0/0	-Iodides and iodide oxides
													Hypochlorites; commercial calcium hypochlorite; chlorites; hypobromites:
0/0/0	3.5	2.4	1.2/1.2	0/0/0	0/0	0/0/0	0/0/	0/0/10.8	10.9/0			0/0/0	-Commercial calcium hypochlorite and other calcium hypochlorites
0/0/0	0	0	0/0	0/0/0	0/0	0//0	0/0/	0/0/0	0/0			0/0/0	-Other
													Chlorates and perchlorates; bromates and perbromates; iodates and periodates:
													-Chlorates:
0/0/0	6	2.4	1.2/1.2	0/0/0	0/0	0/0/0	0/0/	0/0/10.8	10.9/0			0/0/0	--Of sodium
													--Other:
0/0/0	0	0	0/0	0/0/0	0/0	0//0	0/0/	0/0/0	0/0			0/0/0	---Potassium chlorate
0/0/0	0	0	0/0	0/0/0	0/0	0//0	0/0/	0/0/0	0/0			0/0/0	---Other
													-Other
0/0/0	0	0	0/0	0/0/0	0/0	0//0	0/0/	0/0/0	0/0			0/0/0	Ammonium perchlorate, spheroids. Granularity <500μm
0/0/0	0	0	0/0	0/0/0	0/0	0//0	0/0/	0/0/0	0/0			0/0/0	Potassium perchlorate
0/0/0	0	0	0/0	0/0/0	0/0	0//0	0/0/	0/0/0	0/0			0/0/0	Other perchlorates, bromates (Including perbromates iodates and periodates)
													Sulphides; polysulphides, whether or not chemically defined:
													-Sodium sulphides:
0/0/0	0	0	0/0	0/0/0	0/0	0//0	0/0/	0/0/0	0/0			0/0/0	---Sodium sulphide
0/0/0	0	0	0/0	0/0/0	0/0	0//0	0/0/	0/0/0	0/0			0/0/0	---Other
													-Other:

税则号列	货品名称〔CIQ 扩展编码及品名—T2 表示见附表 2〕	最惠(%)	暂定税率	普通	增值/消费	出口退税	计量单位	监管条件/特殊证件	检验检疫	对美关税	亚太上/下
2830.9020	---硫化锑〔301 危险化学品,杂项物质;302 其他化工品,硫化锑精矿〕	5		45	13/	0	千克	B/13	N		
2830.9030	---硫化钴〔999〕	5		30	13/	0	千克	/1		12.5	
2830.9090	---其他〔301 危险化学品,易于自燃的物质;302 危险化学品,毒性物质;303 危险化学品,腐蚀性物质;304 危险化学品,杂项物质;305 其他危险化学品;306 其他化工产品〕	5		30	13/	0	千克	/13		27.5	
28.31	**连二亚硫酸盐及次硫酸盐:**										
	-钠的连二亚硫酸盐及次硫酸盐:										
2831.1010	---钠的连二亚硫酸盐[T2]	5		30	13/	0	千克	AB/13	MRNS	32.5	
2831.1020	---钠的次硫酸盐〔999〕	5		30	13/	0	千克	/1			
2831.9000	-其他〔301 危险化学品,易于自燃的物质;302 危险化学品,杂项物质;303 其他化工品〕	5		30	13/	0	千克	/13			
28.32	**亚硫酸盐;硫代硫酸盐:**										
2832.1000	-钠的亚硫酸盐〔301 危险化学品,不用作食品添加剂;302 危险化学品,用作食品添加剂;303 其他化工品,不用作食品添加剂;304 其他化工品,用作食品添加剂〕	5		30	13/	0	千克	/13		32.5	
2832.2000	-其他亚硫酸盐[T2]	5		30	13/	0	千克	AB/13	MRNS	27.5	
2832.3000	-硫代硫酸盐〔999〕	5		30	13/	0	千克	/1		27.5	
28.33	**硫酸盐;矾;过硫酸盐:**										
	-钠的硫酸盐:										
2833.1100	--硫酸钠〔101 矿物源性饲料添加剂,102 化工产品〕	5		40	13/	0	千克	4xy/1		32.5	2.5/2.5
2833.1900	--其他〔301 其他危险化学品,302 其他化工产品〕	5		30	13/	0	千克	/13		12.5	
	-其他硫酸盐:										
2833.2100	--硫酸镁〔101 矿物源性饲料添加剂,102 无检疫要求食品添加剂,103 需申报仅用于工业用途不用于食品添加剂无检疫要求的化学品〕	5		30	13/	0	千克	A/1	R	32.5	
2833.2200	--硫酸铝〔999〕	5		30	13/	0	千克	/1		32.5	
2833.2400	--镍的硫酸盐〔999〕	5	2	30	13/	0	千克	/13		24.5	
2833.2500	--铜的硫酸盐〔101 矿物源性饲料添加剂,103 其他化工产品〕,103 硫酸铜(属于危险化学品的食品添加剂)	5		30	13/	0	千克	/1		17.5	
2833.2700	--硫酸钡〔999〕	5		30	13/	0	千克	G/1		32.5	
	--其他:										
2833.2910	---硫酸亚铁〔101 矿物源性饲料添加剂,102 无检疫要求食品添加剂,103 需申报仅用于工业用途不用于食品添加剂无检疫要求的化学品〕	5		45	13/	0	千克	A/1	R	32.5	
2833.2920	---铬的硫酸盐〔999〕	5		30	13/	0	千克	/1		32.5	
2833.2930	---硫酸锌〔101 矿物源性饲料添加剂,102 无检疫要求食品添加剂,103 需申报仅用于工业用途不用于食品添加剂无检疫要求的化学品〕	5		30	13/	13	千克	A/1	R	17.5	
2833.2990	---其他										
2833.2990 10	硫酸钴〔101 矿物源性饲料添加剂,301 其他危险化学品,需申报仅用于工业用途不用于食品添加剂无检疫要求〕	5	2	30	13/	0	千克	4ABxy/13	RS	14.5	
2833.2990 20	其他钴的硫酸盐〔101 矿物源性饲料添加剂,301 其他危险化学品,需申报仅用于工业用途不用于食品添加剂无检疫要求〕	5	2	30	13/	0	千克	AB/13	MRNS	14.5	
2833.2990 90	其他硫酸盐[T2]	5		30	13/	0	千克	AB/13	MRN	17.5	
	-矾:										
2833.3010	---钾铝矾〔999〕	5		45	13/	0	千克	/1			
2833.3090	---其他〔101 其他化工产品,102 硫酸铝铵(铵明矾)(无检疫要求食品添加剂),301 毒性物质和感染性物质〕	5		30	13/	0	千克	/1		12.5	
2833.4000	-过硫酸盐〔301 危险化学品,氧化性物质;302 危险化学品,毒性物质;303 其他化工品〕	5		30	13/	0	千克	/13		17.5	
28.34	**亚硝酸盐;硝酸盐:**										
2834.1000	-亚硝酸盐[T2]	5		30	13/	0	千克	AB/13	MRNS	17.5	
	-硝酸盐:										
	--硝酸钾:										
2834.2110	---肥料用〔301 危险化学品,氧化性物质;302 其他化工品〕	4	1	11	13/	0	千克	AB/1	MN	3.5	
2834.2190	---其他〔301 危险化学品,不用作食品添加剂;302 危险化学品,用作食品添加剂〕	5		30	13/	0	千克	AB/13	MN	32.5	
	--其他:										
2834.2910	---硝酸钴〔999〕	5		30	13/	0	千克	AB/13	MN	12.5	
2834.2990	---其他										
2834.2990 01	硝酸钡〔999〕	5	2	30	13/	0	千克	AB/13	MN	9.5	
2834.2990 90	其他硝酸盐〔301 危险化学品,氧化性物质;302 危险化学品,毒性物质;303 其他化工品,不用作食品添加剂〕	5		30	13/	0	千克	/13		12.5	
28.35	**次磷酸盐、亚磷酸盐及磷酸盐;多磷酸盐,无论是否已有化学定义:**										

协定税率 %								RCEP		特惠税率 %			Article Description
东/冰/格	巴基斯坦	韩国	瑞士上/下	哥/秘/柬	澳/毛	新西/坡/智	中国港/澳/台	东盟及马来/澳/韩	日/新	亚太2国	老/柬/缅	98/97/95	
0/0/0	0	0	0/0	0/0/0	0/0	0//0	0/0/	0/0/0	0/0			0/0/0	---Antimony sulphide
0/0/0	0	1.1	0/0	0/0/0	0/0	0//0	0/0/	0/0/5	5/0			0/0/0	---Cobalt sulphide
0/0/0	0	0	0/0	0/0/0	0/0	0//0	0/0/	0/0/0	0/0			0/0/0	---Other
													Dithionites and sulphoxylates:
													-of sodium:
0/0/0	0	0	0/0	0/0/0	0/0	0//0	0/0/	0/0/0	0/0			0/0/0	---Sodium Dithionites
0/0/0	0	0	0/0	0/0/0	0/0	0//0	0/0/	0/0/0	0/0			0/0/0	---Sodium Sulphoxylates
0/0/0	0	0	0/0	0/0/0	0/0	0//0	0/0/	0/0/0	0/0			0/0/0	-Other
													Sulphites; thiosulphates:
0/0/0	0	0	0/0	0/0/0	0/0	0//0	0/0/	0/0/0	0/0			0/0/0	-Sodium sulphites
0/0/0	0	0	0/0	0/0/0	0/0	0//0	0/0/	0/0/0	0/0			0/0/0	-Other sulphites
0/0/0	0	0	0/0	0/0/0	0/0	0//0	0/0/	0/0/0	0/0			0/0/0	-Thiosulphates
													Sulphates; alums; peroxosulphates (persulphates):
													-Sodium sulphates:
0/0/0	0	0	0.6/0.6	0/0/0	0/0	0//0	0/0/	0/0/0	5/0			0/0/0	--Disodium sulphate
0/0/0	0	0	0/0	0/0/0	0/0	0//0	0/0/	0/0/0	0/0			0/0/0	--Other
													-Other sulphates:
0/0/0	0	0	0/0	0/0/0	0/0	0//0	0/0/	0/0/0	0/0			0/0/0	--Of magnesium
0/0/0	0	0	0/0	0/0/0	0/0	0//0	0/0/	0/0/0	0/0			0/0/0	--Of aluminium
0/0/0	0	0	0/0	0/0/0	0/0	0//0	0/0/	0/0/0	0/0			0/0/0	--Of nickel
0/0/0	0	0	0/0	0/0/0	0/0	0//0	0/0/	0/0/0	0/0			0/0/0	--Of copper
0/0/0	0	1.1	0/0	0/0/0	0/0	0//0	0/0/	0/0/5	5/0			0/0/0	--Of barium
													--Other:
0/0/0	0	0	0/0	0/0/0	0/0	0//0	0/0/	0/0/0	0/0			0/0/0	---Ferrous sulphate
0/0/0	0	0	0/0	0/0/0	0/0	0//0	0/0/	0/0/0	0/0			0/0/0	---Of Chromium
0/0/0	0	1.1	0/0	0/0/0	0/0	0//0	0/0/	0/0/5	5/0			0/0/0	---Of zinc
													---Other
0/0/0	0	0	0.6/0.6	0/0/0	0/0	0//0	0/0/	0/0/0	5/0			0/0/0	Cobalt sulphate
0/0/0	0	0	0.6/0.6	0/0/0	0/0	0//0	0/0/	0/0/0	5/0			0/0/0	Other cobalt sulfate
0/0/0	0	0	0.6/0.6	0/0/0	0/0	0//0	0/0/	0/0/0	5/0			0/0/0	Other sulphates
													-Alums:
0/0/0	0	1.1	0/0	0/0/0	0/0	0//0	0/0/	0/0/5	5/0			0/0/0	---Potassium aluminum sulfate
0/0/0	0	1.1	0/0	0/0/0	0/0	0//0	0/0/	0/0/5	5/0			0/0/0	---Other
0/0/0	0	1.1	0/0	0/0/0	0/0	0//0	0/0/	0/0/5	5/0			0/0/0	-Peroxosulphates (persulphates)
													Nitrites; nitrates:
0/0/0	0	0	0/0	0/0/0	0/0	0//0	0/0/	0/0/0	0/0			0/0/0	-Nitrites
													-Nitrates:
													--Of potassium:
0/0/	0	0	0/0	0/0/0	0/0	0//0	0/0/	0/0/0	3.6/0			0/0/0	---For use as fertilizer
0/0/0	0	0	0/0	0/0/0	0/0	0//0	0/0/	0/0/0	0/0			0/0/0	---Other
													Other:
0/0/0	0	0	0/0	0/0/0	0/0	0//0	0/0/	0/0/0	0/0			0/0/0	---Of cobalt
													---Other
0/0/0	0	0	0/0	0/0/0	0/0	0//0	0/0/	0/0/0	0/0			0/0/0	Barium nitrate
0/0/0	0	0	0/0	0/0/0	0/0	0//0	0/0/	0/0/0	0/0			0/0/0	Other nitrates
													Phosphinates (hypophosphites), phosphonates (phosphites), phosphates and polyphosphates, whether or not chemically defined:

税则号列	货品名称〔CIQ 扩展编码及品名—T2 表示见附表 2〕	最惠(%)	暂定税率	普通	增值/消费	出口退税	计量单位	监管条件/特殊证件	检验检疫	对美关税	亚太上/下
2835.1000	-次磷酸盐及亚磷酸盐〔301 危险化学品，易燃固体；302 其他化工品〕	5		20	13/	0	千克	/13		32.5	
	-磷酸盐：										
2835.2200	--磷酸一钠及磷酸二钠〔101 矿物源性饲料添加剂，102 化工产品〕	5		20	13/	0	千克	/1		27.5	
2835.2400	--钾的磷酸盐〔101〕	5		20	13/	0	千克	/1		27.5	
	--正磷酸氢钙（磷酸二钙）：										
2835.2510	---饲料级的〔101 矿物源性饲料添加剂，102 化工产品〕	5		20	13/	0	千克	AB/1	RS		
2835.2520	---食品级的〔101 矿物源性饲料添加剂，102 食品添加剂（无检疫要求食品添加剂）〕	5		20	13/	13	千克	A/1	R	32.5	
2835.2590	---其他〔999〕	5		20	13/	0	千克	/1		12.5	
2835.2600	--其他磷酸钙〔101 矿物源性饲料添加剂，104 磷酸钙（无检疫要求食品添加剂）〕	5		20	13/	0	千克	/1		12.5	
	--其他：										
2835.2910	---磷酸三钠〔301 需申报仅用于工业用途不用于食品添加剂无检疫要求的化学品，999 其他化工产品〕	5		20	13/	0	千克	A/1	R	32.5	
2835.2990	---其他[T2]	5		20	13/	0	千克	A/13	MR	27.5	
	-多磷酸盐：										
	--三磷酸钠（三聚磷酸钠）：										
2835.3110	---食品级的〔999〕	5		20	13/	13	千克	A/1	R	32.5	
2835.3190	---其他〔999〕	5		20	13/	13	千克	/1		12.5	
	--其他：										
	---六偏磷酸钠：										
2835.3911	----食品级的〔999〕	5		20	13/	13	千克	A/1	R	12.5	
2835.3919	----其他〔999〕	5		20	13/	0	千克	/1		12.5	
2835.3990	---其他〔101〕	5		20	13/	0	千克	/1		17.5	
28.36	**碳酸盐；过碳酸盐；含氨基甲酸铵的商品碳酸铵：**										
2836.2000	-碳酸钠（纯碱）〔101 矿物源性饲料添加剂，102 食品添加剂（无检疫要求食品添加剂），301 需申报仅用于工业用途不用于食品添加剂无检疫要求的化学品〕	5		35	13/	13	千克	AG/1	MR	12.5	
2836.3000	-碳酸氢钠（小苏打）〔101 矿物源性饲料添加剂，301 碳酸氢钠，302 复合膨松剂，303 需申报仅用于工业用途不用于食品添加剂无检疫要求的化学品〕	5		45	13/	13	千克	AG/1	R	15	
2836.4000	-钾的碳酸盐〔101 碳酸氢钾，102 碳酸钾〕	5		30	13/	0	千克	/1		12.5	
2836.5000	-碳酸钙[T2]	5		45	13/	0	千克	A/1	R	27.5	
2836.6000	-碳酸钡〔999〕	5	1	40	13/	0	千克	/1		28.5	
	-其他：										
2836.9100	--锂的碳酸盐〔999〕	5	2	30	13/	0	千克	/1		29.5	
2836.9200	--锶的碳酸盐〔999〕	5	2	30	13/	0	千克	/1		29.5	
	--其他：										
2836.9910	---碳酸镁〔301 无检疫要求食品添加剂，302 需申报仅用于工业用途不用于食品添加剂无检疫要求的化学品〕	5		45	13/	0	千克	A/1	R	32.5	
2836.9930	---碳酸钴〔101 矿物源性饲料添加剂，102 化工产品〕	5	2	30	13/	0	千克	4xy/1			4/4
2836.9940	---商品碳酸铵及其他铵的碳酸盐〔101〕	5		30	13/	0	千克	/1		32.5	
2836.9950	---碳酸锆〔999〕	5		30	13/	0	千克	AB/1	RS		
2836.9990	---其他[T2]	5		30	13/	13	千克	A/13	MR	17.5	
28.37	**氰化物、氧氰化物及氰络合物：**										
	-氰化物及氧氰化物：										
	--氰化钠及氧氰化钠：										
2837.1110	---氰化钠〔999〕	5		20	13/	0	千克	23AB/13	MN		
2837.1120	---氧氰化钠〔999〕	5		30	13/	0	千克	/1			3.3/3.3
	--其他：										
2837.1910	---氰化钾〔999〕	5		20	13/	0	千克	23AB/13	MN	32.5	4/4
2837.1990	---其他										
2837.1990 11	氰化锌、氰化亚铜、氰化铜（氰化高铜）〔999〕	5		30	13/	0	千克	/13		32.5	
2837.1990 12	氰化镍、氰化钙（氰化亚镍）〔999〕	5		30	13/	0	千克	/13		32.5	
2837.1990 13	氰化钡、氰化镉、氰化铅〔999〕	5		30	13/	0	千克	/13		32.5	
2837.1990 14	氰化钴[氰化钴（Ⅱ）、氰化钴（Ⅲ）]〔999〕	5		30	13/	0	千克	/13		32.5	
2837.1990 90	其他氰化物及氧氰化物〔999 其他化工产品，998 其他危险化学品〕	5		30	13/	0	千克	/13		32.5	
2837.2000	-氰络合物										
2837.2000 11	氰化镍钾、氰化钠铜锌（氰化钾镍、镍氰化钾、铜盐）〔999〕	5		30	13/	0	千克	/13		32.5	

协定税率 %								RCEP		特惠税率 %			Article Description
东/冰/格	巴基斯坦	韩国	瑞士上/下	哥/秘/柬	澳/毛	新西/坡/智	中国港/澳/台	东盟及马来/澳/韩	日/新	亚太2国	老/柬/缅	98/97/95	
0/0/0	0	0	0/0	0/0/0	0/0	0//0	0/0/	0/0/0	0/0			0/0/0	-Phosphinates (hypophosphites) and phosphonates (phosphites)
													-Phosphates:
0/0/0	0	1.1	0/0	0/0/0	0/0	0//0	0/0/	0/0/5	5/0			0/0/0	--Of mono- or disodium
0/0/0	0	0	0/0	0/0/0	0/0	0//0	0/0/	0/0/0	0/0			0/0/0	--Of potassium
													--Calcium hydrogenorthophosphate (dicalcium phosphate):
0/0/0	0	0	0/0	0/0/0	0/0	0//0	0/0/	0/0/0	0/0			0/0/0	---Feed grade
0/0/0	0	0	0/0	0/0/0	0/0	0//0	0/0/	0/0/0	0/0			0/0/0	---Food grade
0/0/0	0	0	2.3/2.3	0/0/0	0/0	0//0	0/0/	0/0/0	5/0			0/0/0	---Other
0/0/0	0	1.1	0/0	0/0/0	0/0	0//0	0/0/	0/0/5	5/0			0/0/0	--Other phosphates of calcium
													--Other:
0/0/0	0	0	0/0	0/0/0	0/0	0//0	0/0/	0/0/0	0/0			0/0/0	---Of trisodium
0/0/0	0	1.1	0/0	0/0/0	0/0	0//0	0/0/	0/0/5	5/0			0/0/0	---Other
													-Polyphosphates:
													--Sodium triphosphate (sodium tripolyphosphate):
0/0/0	0	0	0/0	0/0/0	0/0	0//0	0/0/	0/0/0	0/0			0/0/0	---Food grade
0/0/0	0	1.1	0/0	0/0/0	0/0	0//0	0/0/	0/0/5	5/0			0/0/0	---Other
													--Other:
													---Sodium hexametaphosphate:
0/0/0	0	0	0/0	0/0/0	0/0	0//0	0/0/	0/0/0	0/0			0/0/0	----Food grade
0/0/0	0	1.1	0/0	0/0/0	0/0	0//0	0/0/	0/0/5	5/0			0/0/0	----Other
0//0	0	0	0/0	0/0/0	0/0	0//0	0/0/	0/0/0	5/0			0/0/0	---Other
													Carbonates; peroxocarbonates (percarbonates); commercial ammonium carbonate containing ammonium carbamate:
0/0/0	0	0	0/0	0/0/0	0/0	0//0	0/0/	0/0/0	0/0			0/0/0	-Disodium carbonate
0/0/0	0	1.1	0/0	0/0/0	0/0	0//0	0/0/	0/0/5	5/0			0/0/0	-Sodium hydrogencarbonate (sodium bicarbonate)
0/0/0	0	0	0/0	0/0/0	0/0	0//0	0/0/	0/0/0	0/0			0/0/0	-Potassium carbonates
0/0/0	0	0	0/0	0/0/0	0/0	0//0	0/0/	0/0/0	0/0			0/0/0	-Calcium carbonate
0/0/0	0	0	0/0	0/0/0	0/0	0//0	0/0/	0/0/0	0/0			0/0/0	-Barium carbonate
													-Other:
0/0/0	0	0	0/0	0//0	0/0	0//0	0/0/	0/0/0	5/0			0/0/0	--Lithium carbonates
0/0/0	0	0	0/0	0/0/0	0/0	0//0	0/0/	0/0/0	0/0			0/0/0	--Strontium carbonate
													--Other:
0/0/0	0	1.1	0/0	0/0/0	0/0	0//0	0/0/	0/0/5	5/0			0/0/0	---Magnesium carbonate
0/0/0	0	0	0/0	0/0/0	0/0	0//0	0/0/	0/0/0	0/0			0/0/0	---Cobalt carbonate
0/0/0	0	0	0/0	0/0/0	0/0	0//0	0/0/	0/0/0	0/0			0/0/0	---Commericial ammonium carbonate and other ammonium carbonates
0/0/0	0	0	0/0	0/0/0	0/0	0//0	0/0/	0/0/0	0/0			0/0/0	---Zirconium carbonate
0/0/0	0	0	0/0	0/0/0	0/0	0//0	0/0/	0/0/0	0/0			0/0/0	---Other
													Cyanides, cyanide oxides and complex cyanides:
													-Cyanides and cyanide oxides:
													--Of sodium:
0/0/0	0	2.5	0/0	0/0/0	0/0	0//0	0/0/	5/5/5	5.2/5			0/0/0	---Sodium cyanide
0/0/0	0	0	0/0	0/0/0	0/0	0//0	0/0/	0/0/0	0/0			0/0/0	---Sodium cyanide oxide
													--Other:
0/0/0	0	0	0/0	0/0/0	0/0	0//0	0/0/	0/0/0	0/0			0/0/0	---Potassium cyanide
													---Other
0/0/0	0	2.5	0/0	0/0/0	0/0	0//0	0/0/	5/5/5	5.2/5			0/0/0	Znic cyanide, cuprous cyanide, copper cyanide (cupric cyanide)
0/0/0	0	2.5	0/0	0/0/0	0/0	0//0	0/0/	5/5/5	5.2/5			0/0/0	Nickel cyanide, calcium cyanide(Nickelous cygnide)
0/0/0	0	2.5	0/0	0/0/0	0/0	0//0	0/0/	5/5/5	5.2/5			0/0/0	Barium cyanide ,cadmium cyanide ,lead cyanide
0/0/0	0	2.5	0/0	0/0/0	0/0	0//0	0/0/	5/5/5	5.2/5			0/0/0	Cobalt cyanide [Cobalt cyanide (Co(CN)3) , Cobalt cyanide (Co(CN)2)]
0/0/0	0	2.5	0/0	0/0/0	0/0	0//0	0/0/	5/5/5	5.2/5			0/0/0	Other cyanides and cyanide oxides
													-Complex cyanides
0/0/0	0	0	0/0	0/0/0	0/0	0//0	0/0/	0/0/0	0/0			0/0/0	Potassium nickel cyanide, sodium coopper - zinc cyanide (nickel potassium cyanide, nantokite)

税则号列		货品名称〔CIQ 扩展编码及品名—T2 表示见附表 2〕	最惠(%)	暂定税率	普通	增值/消费	出口退税	计量单位	监管条件/特殊证件	检验检疫	对美关税	亚太上/下
2837.2000	12	氰化亚铜(三)钠、氰化亚铜(三)钾(紫铜盐、紫铜矾、氰化铜钠、氰化亚铜钾、亚铜氰化钾)〔999〕	5		30	13/	0	千克	/13		32.5	
2837.2000	90	其他氰络合物〔999 其他化工产品,998 其他危险化学品〕	5		30	13/	0	千克	/13		32.5	
28.39		**硅酸盐;商品碱金属硅酸盐:**										
		-钠盐:										
2839.1100		--偏硅酸钠〔999〕	5		40	13/	0	千克	AB/13	MN	12.5	
		--其他:										
2839.1910		---硅酸钠〔999〕	5		30	13/	0	千克	A/1	M	17.5	
2839.1990		---其他〔999〕	5		30	13/	0	千克	/1		32.5	
2839.9000		-其他										
2839.9000	01	锆的硅酸盐〔999〕	5	2	30	13/	0	千克	/13		9.5	
2839.9000	10	硅酸铅〔999〕	5		30	13/	0	千克	/13		12.5	
2839.9000	90	其他硅酸盐;商品碱金属硅酸盐〔101 硅酸镁,102 硅酸钙铝〕	5		30	13/	0	千克	/13		12.5	
28.40		**硼酸盐及过硼酸盐:**										
		-四硼酸钠(精炼硼砂):										
2840.1100		--无水四硼酸钠〔999〕	5	2	20	13/	0	千克	/1			
2840.1900		--其他〔999〕	5	2	20	13/	0	千克	/1			
2840.2000		-其他硼酸盐〔999〕	5		30	13/	0	千克	/1		12.5	
2840.3000		-过硼酸盐〔301 危险化学品,氧化性物质;302 其他化工品〕	5		30	13/	0	千克	/13		17.5	
28.41		**金属酸盐及过金属酸盐:**										
2841.3000		-重铬酸钠〔999〕	5.5		20	13/	0	千克	AB/13	MN	8	
2841.5000		-其他铬酸盐及重铬酸盐;过铬酸盐〔301 危险化学品,氧化性物质;302 危险化学品,毒性物质;303 危险化学品,杂项物质;304 其他化工品〕	5.5		30	13/	0	千克	/13		33	
		-亚锰酸盐、锰酸盐及高锰酸盐:										
2841.6100		--高锰酸钾〔301 危险化学品,不用作食品添加剂;302 危险化学品,用作食品添加剂〕	5.5		30	13/	0	千克	23AB/13	MRNS	18	
		--其他:										
2841.6910		---锰酸锂〔999〕	5.5		30	13/	13	千克	/1		8	
2841.6990		---其他〔301 危险化学品,氧化性物质;302 其他化工品〕	5.5		30	13/	0	千克	/13		18	
		-钼酸盐:										
2841.7010		---钼酸铵〔999〕	5.5		30	13/	0	千克	4xy/1		13	2.8/2.8
2841.7090		---其他〔101 矿物源性饲料添加剂,102 化工产品〕	5.5		30	13/	0	千克	4xy/1		28	
		-钨酸盐:										
2841.8010		---仲钨酸铵〔999〕	5.5		30	13/	0	千克	4xy/1		8	
2841.8020		---钨酸钠〔999〕	5.5		30	13/	0	千克	4xy/1		13	
2841.8030		---钨酸钙〔999〕	5.5		30	13/	0	千克	4xy/1		8	
2841.8040		---偏钨酸铵〔999〕	5.5		30	13/	0	千克	4xy/1		8	
2841.8090		---其他〔999〕	5.5		30	13/	0	千克	/1		18	2.8/2.8
2841.9000		-其他										
2841.9000	10	钴酸锂〔999〕	5.5	2	30	13/	13	千克	/13		29.5	
2841.9000	20	铼酸盐及高铼酸盐〔999〕	5.5	0	30	13/	0	千克	/13		27.5	
2841.9000	90	其他金属酸盐及过金属酸盐〔301 危险化学品,毒性物质;302 危险化学品,腐蚀性物质;303 其他化工产品〕	5.5		30	13/	0	千克	/13		33	
28.42		**其他无机酸盐或过氧酸盐(包括不论是否已有化学定义的硅铝酸盐),但叠氮化物除外:**										
2842.1000		-硅酸复盐或硅酸络盐,包括不论是否已有化学定义的硅铝酸盐[T2]	5.5		30	13/	0	千克	AB/1	MRNS	28	
		-其他:										
		---雷酸盐、氰酸盐及硫氰酸盐:										
2842.9011		----硫氰酸钠〔301〕	5.5		30	13/	0	千克	/1		8	
2842.9019		----其他										
2842.9019	10	其他硫氰酸盐〔301 其他危险化学品,302 其他化工产品〕	5.5		30	13/	0	千克	AB/13	MN	8	
2842.9019	90	雷酸盐及氰酸盐〔999 其他化工产品,998 其他危险化学品〕	5.5		30	13/	0	千克	/13		8	
2842.9020		---碲化镉〔999〕	5.5		30	13/	0	千克	AB/13	MN	8	
2842.9030		---锂镍钴锰氧化物〔999〕	5.5		30	13/	13	千克	AB/1	RS	33	
2842.9040		---磷酸铁锂〔999〕	5.5		30	13/	0	千克	/1		33	
2842.9050		---硒酸盐及亚硒酸盐[T2]	5.5		30	13/	0	千克	AB/13	MRNS	28	
2842.9060		---锂镍钴铝氧化物〔999〕	5.5		30	13/	13	千克	AB/1	MRNS		
2842.9090		---其他										
2842.9090	13	亚砷酸钠,亚砷酸钾,亚砷酸钙(偏亚砷酸钠)〔999〕	5.5		30	13/	13	千克	/13		28	
2842.9090	14	亚砷酸锶、亚砷酸钡、亚砷酸铁〔999〕	5.5		30	13/	13	千克	/13		28	
2842.9090	15	亚砷酸铜、亚砷酸锌、亚砷酸铅(亚砷酸氢铜)〔999〕	5.5		30	13/	13	千克	/13		28	
2842.9090	16	亚砷酸锑,砷酸铵,砷酸氢二铵〔999〕	5.5		30	13/	13	千克	/13		28	
2842.9090	17	砷酸钠、砷酸氢二钠、砷酸二氢钠(砷酸三钠)〔301〕	5.5		30	13/	13	千克	/13		28	

协定税率 %								RCEP		特惠税率 %			Article Description
东/冰/格	巴基斯坦	韩国	瑞士 上/下	哥/秘/柬	澳/毛	新西/坡/智	中国港/澳/台	东盟及马来/澳/韩	日/新	亚太2国	老/柬/缅	98/97/95	
0/0/0	0	0	0/0	0/0/0	0/0	0//0	0/0/	0/0/0	0/0			0/0/0	Cuprous cyanide (c) sodium, cuprous cyanide (c) potassium (copper salt, copper alum, sodium cyanide copper, cuprous potassium cyanide, cuprous potassium cyanide)
0/0/0	0	0	0/0	0/0/0	0/0	0//0	0/0/	0/0/0	0/0			0/0/0	Other complex cyanide
													Silicates; commercial alkali metal silicates:
													-Of sodium:
0/0/0	0	1.1	0/0	0/0/0	0/0	0//0	0/0/	0/0/5	5/0			0/0/0	--Sodium metasilicates
													--Other:
0/0/0	0	1.1	0/0	0/0/0	0/0	0//0	0/0/	0/0/5	5/0			0/0/0	---Sodium silicate
0/0/0	0	1.1	0/0	0/0/0	0/0	0//0	0/0/	0/0/5	5/0			0/0/0	---Other
													-Other
0/0/0	0	0	0.6/0.6	0/0/0	0/0	0//0	0/0/	0/0/0	5/0			0/0/0	Zirconium silicate
0/0/0	0	0	0.6/0.6	0/0/0	0/0	0//0	0/0/	0/0/0	5/0			0/0/0	Lead silicate
0/0/0	0	0	0.6/0.6	0/0/0	0/0	0//0	0/0/	0/0/0	5/0			0/0/0	Other silicate, commercial alkali metal silicates
													Borates; peroxoborates (perborates):
													-Disodium tetraborate (refined borax):
0/0/0	0	0	0/0	0/0/0	0/0	0//0	0/0/	0/0/0	0/0			0/0/0	--Anhydrous
0/0/0	0	0	0/0	0/0/0	0/0	0//0	0/0/	0/0/0	0/0			0/0/0	--Other
0/0/0	0	1.1	0/0	0/0/0	0/0	0//0	0/0/	0/0/5	5/0			0/0/0	-Other borates
0/0/0	0	0	0/0	0/0/0	0/0	0//0	0/0/	0/0/0	0/0			0/0/0	-Peroxoborates (perborates)
													Salts of oxometallic or peroxometallic acids:
0/0/0	0	0	0/0	0/0/0	0/0	0//0	0/0/	0/0/0	0/0			0/0/0	-Sodium dichromate
0/0/0	0	0	0/0	0/0/0	0/0	0//0	0/0/	0/0/0	0/0			0/0/0	-Other chromates and dichromates; peroxochromates
													-Manganites, manganates and permanganates:
0/0/0	0	0	0/0	0/0/0	0/0	0//0	0/0/	0/0/0	0/0			0/0/0	--Potassium permanganate
													--Other:
0/0/0	0	0	0/0	0/0/0	0/0	0//0	0/0/	0/0/0	0/0			0/0/0	---Lithium manganate
0/0/0	0	0	0/0	0/0/0	0/0	0//0	0/0/	0/0/0	0/0			0/0/0	---Other
													-Molybdates:
0/0/0	0	0	0/0	0/0/0	0/0	0//0	0/0/	0/0/0	0/0			0/0/0	---Ammonium molybdates
0/0/0	0	0	0/0	0/0/0	0/0	0//0	0/0/	0/0/0	0/0			0/0/0	---Other
													-Tungstates (wolframates):
0/0/0	0	0	0/0	0/0/0	0/0	0//0	0/0/	0/0/0	0/0			0/0/0	---Ammonium paratungstate
0/0/0	0	0	0/0	0/0/0	0/0	0//0	0/0/	0/0/0	0/0			0/0/0	---Sodium tungstate
0/0/0	0	0	0/0	0/0/0	0/0	0//0	0/0/	0/0/0	0/0			0/0/0	---Calcium wolframate
0/0/0	0	0	0/0	0/0/0	0/0	0//0	0/0/	0/0/0	0/0			0/0/0	---Ammonium metatungstate
0/0/0	0	0	0/0	0/0/0	0/0	0//0	0/0/	0/0/0	0/0			0/0/0	---Other
													-Other
0/0/0	0	1.1	0/0	0/0/0	0/0	0//0	0/0/	0/0/5	5/0			0/0/0	Lithium cobaltate
0/0/0	0	1.1	0/0	0/0/0	0/0	0//0	0/0/	0/0/5	5/0			0/0/0	Rhenate
0/0/0	0	1.1	0/0	0/0/0	0/0	0//0	0/0/	0/0/5	5/0			0/0/0	Other salts of oxometallic or peroxometallic acids
													Other salts of inorganic acids or peroxoacids (including aluminosilicates whether or not chemically defined), other than azides:
0/0/0	0	0	2.3/2.3	0/0/0	0/0	0//0	0/0/	0/0/0	5/0			0/0/0	-Double or complex silicates, including aluminosilicates whether or not chemically defined
													-Other:
													---Fulminates, cyanates and thiocyanates:
0/0/0	0	0	0/0	0/0/0	0/0	0//0	0/0/	0/0/0	0/0			0/0/0	----Sodium sulfocyanate
													----Other
0/0/0	0	0	0/0	0/0/0	0/0	0//0	0/0/	0/0/0	0/0			0/0/0	Other thiocyanates
0/0/0	0	0	0/0	0/0/0	0/0	0//0	0/0/	0/0/0	0/0			0/0/0	Fulminates and cyanates
0/0/0	0	0	0/0	0/0/0	0/0	0//0	0/0/	0/0/0	0/0			0/0/0	---Cadmium telluride
0/0/0	0	0	0/0	0/0/0	0/0	0//0	0/0/	0/0/0	0/0			0/0/0	---Lithium nickel cobalt manganese oxides
0/0/0	0	1.1	0/0	0/0/0	0/0	0//0	0/0/	0/0/5	5/0			0/0/0	---Lithium iron phosphate
0/0/0	0	0	0/0	0/0/0	0/0	0//0	0/0/	0/0/0	0/0			0/0/0	---Selenium and selenite
0/0/0	0	0	0/0	0/0/0	0/0	0//0	0/0/	0/0/0	0/0			0/0/0	---Lithium nickel cobalt aluminum oxide
													---Other
0/0/0	0	0	0/0	0/0/0	0/0	0//0	0/0/	0/0/0	0/0			0/0/0	Sodium arsenite, potassium arsenite, calcium arsenite
0/0/0	0	0	0/0	0/0/0	0/0	0//0	0/0/	0/0/0	0/0			0/0/0	Strontium arsenite, barium arsenite, Arsenous acid
0/0/0	0	0	0/0	0/0/0	0/0	0//0	0/0/	0/0/0	0/0			0/0/0	Copper arsonate, arsenen ous acrd, lead arsenite
0/0/0	0	0	0/0	0/0/0	0/0	0//0	0/0/	0/0/0	0/0			0/0/0	Antimony arsenite, ammonium arsenate, diammonium hydrogen arsenate
0/0/0	0	0	0/0	0/0/0	0/0	0//0	0/0/	0/0/0	0/0			0/0/0	Sodium arsenate, sodium arsenate dibasic, sodium arsenate monobasic

税则号列	货品名称〔CIQ 扩展编码及品名－T2 表示见附表 2〕	最惠(%)	暂定税率	普通	增值/消费	出口退税	计量单位	监管条件/特殊证件	检验检疫	对美关税	亚太上/下
2842.9090 18	砷酸钾、砷酸二氢钾、砷酸镁〔999〕	5.5		30	13/	13	千克	/13		28	
2842.9090 19	砷酸钙,砷酸钡,砷酸铁(砷酸三钙)〔999〕	5.5		30	13/	13	千克	/13		28	
2842.9090 21	砷酸亚铁、砷酸铜、砷酸锌〔999〕	5.5		30	13/	13	千克	/13		28	
2842.9090 22	砷酸铅、砷酸锑、偏砷酸钠〔999〕	5.5		30	13/	13	千克	/13		28	
2842.9090 23	硒化铅、硒化镉〔301 危险化学品,毒性物质;302 危险化学品,杂项物质〕	5.5		30	13/	13	千克	/13		28	
2842.9090 90	其他无机酸盐及过氧酸盐(迭氮化物除外)[T2]	5.5		30	13/	13	千克	AB/13	MRNS	28	
	第六分章 杂项产品										
28.43	**胶态贵金属;贵金属的无机或有机化合物,不论是否已有化学定义;贵金属汞齐:**										
2843.1000	-胶态贵金属〔999〕	5.5		30	13/	0	克	/1		33	
	-银化合物:										
2843.2100	--硝酸银〔999〕	5.5		30	13/	0	克	AB/13	MN	13	
2843.2900	--其他										
2843.2900 10	氰化银、氰化银钾、亚砷酸银(银氰化钾、砷酸银)〔301〕	5.5		30	13/	0	克	/13		13	
2843.2900 90	其他银化合物(不论是否已有化学定义)〔301 危险化学品,易燃固体;302 危险化学品,氧化性物质;303 危险化学品,毒性物质;304 危险化学品,腐蚀性物质;305 其他化工产品〕	5.5		30	13/	0	克	/13		13	
2843.3000	-金化合物										
2843.3000 10	氰化金、氰化金钾(含金 40%)等[包括氰化亚金(Ⅰ)钾(含金 68.3%)、氰化亚金(Ⅲ)钾(含金 57%)]〔999〕	5.5		30	13/	0	克	J/13		20.5	4.4/4.4
2843.3000 90	其他金化合物(不论是否已有化学定义)〔999〕	5.5		30	13/	0	克	/13		20.5	4.4/4.4
2843.9000	-其他贵金属化合物;贵金属汞齐										
2843.9000 10	氯化钯〔999〕	5.5		30	13/	0	克	G/13		13	
2843.9000 20	氯化铂〔999〕	5.5		30	13/	0	克	4xy/13		13	
2843.9000 31	奥沙利铂、卡铂、奈达铂、顺铂〔999〕	5.5	0	30	3/	0	克	4xy/13		7.5	
2843.9000 39	其他铂化合物〔301 危险化学品,腐蚀性物质,302 其他化工品〕	5.5		30	13/	0	克	4xy/13		13	
2843.9000 91	贵金属汞齐(不论是否已有化学定义)〔101 其他碱金属汞齐,102 硝酸铑,103 硝酸钯〕	5.5		30	13/	0	克	4Xxy/13			
2843.9000 99	其他贵金属化合物(不论是否已有化学定义)〔301 危险化学品,氧化性物质;302 危险化学品,毒性物质;303 其他危险化学品;304 其他化工品〕	5.5		30	13/	0	克	4xy/13			
28.44	**放射性化学元素及放射性同位素(包括可裂变或可转换的化学元素及同位素)及其化合物;含上述产品的混合物及残渣:**										
2844.1000	-天然铀及其化合物;含天然铀或天然铀化合物的合金、分散体(包括金属陶瓷)、陶瓷产品及混合物							23			
2844.1000 10	天然铀及其化合物〔999〕	5	0	30	13/	0	克/百万贝可	23/1		27.5	
2844.1000 90	含天然铀或天然铀化合物的合金、分散体(包括金属陶瓷)、陶瓷产品及混合物〔999〕	5		30	13/	0	克/百万贝可	23/1		32.5	
2844.2000	-铀－235浓缩铀及其化合物;钚及其化合物;含铀－235浓缩铀、钚或它们的化合物的合金、分散体(包括金属陶瓷)、陶瓷产品及混合物										
2844.2000 10	含铀－235 浓度低于 5%的低浓铀及其化合物〔999〕	5	0	30	13/	0	克/百万贝可	23/1		27.5	
2844.2000 90	其他铀－235 浓缩铀,钚及其化合物(包括其合金,分散体,陶瓷产品及混合物)〔999〕	5		30	13/	0	克/百万贝可	23/1		32.5	
2844.3000	-铀－235贫化铀及其化合物;钍及其化合物;含铀－235贫化铀、钍或它们的化合物的合金、分散体(包括金属陶瓷)、陶瓷产品及混合物〔999〕	5		30	13/	0	克/百万贝可	23/1		12.5	

协定税率 %								RCEP		特惠税率 %			Article Description
东/冰/格	巴基斯坦	韩国	瑞士上/下	哥/秘/柬	澳/毛	新西/坡/智	中国港/澳/台	东盟及马来/澳/韩	日/新	亚太2国	老/柬/缅	98/97/95	
0/0/0	0	0	0/0	0/0/0	0/0	0//0	0/0/	0/0/0	0/0			0/0/0	Potassium arsenate, potassium dihyrogwn arsenate, magnesium arsenate
0/0/0	0	0	0/0	0/0/0	0/0	0//0	0/0/	0/0/0	0/0			0/0/0	Calcium arsenate, barium arsenate, ferric arsenate(tricalcium arsenate)
0/0/0	0	0	0/0	0/0/0	0/0	0//0	0/0/	0/0/0	0/0			0/0/0	Ferrous arsenate, cupric arsenate, zinc arsenate
0/0/0	0	0	0/0	0/0/0	0/0	0//0	0/0/	0/0/0	0/0			0/0/0	Lead arsenate, antimony arsenate, sodium metaarsenate
0/0/0	0	0	0/0	0/0/0	0/0	0//0	0/0/	0/0/0	0/0			0/0/0	Lead selenide, cadmium selenide
0/0/0	0	0	0/0	0/0/0	0/0	0//0	0/0/	0/0/0	0/0			0/0/0	Other salts of inorganic acids or peroxoacids
													Ⅵ. MISCELLANEOUS
													Colloidal precious metals; inorganic or organic compounds of precious metals, whether or not chemically defined; amalgams of precious metals:
0/0/0	0	0	0/0	0/0/0	0/0	0//0	0/0/	0/0/0	0/0			0/0/0	-Colloidal precious metals
													-Silver compounds:
0/0/0	0	0	0/0	0/0/0	0/0	0//0	0/0/	0/0/0	0/0			0/0/0	--Silver nitrate
													--Other
0/0/0	0	0	0/0	0/0/0	0/0	0//0	0/0/	0/0/0	0/0			0/0/0	Silver cyanide, potassium arsentocyanide, silverarsenite (potassium silver(I)cyanide, slilver arsenate)
0/0/0	0	0	0/0	0/0/0	0/0	0//0	0/0/	0/0/0	0/0			0/0/0	Other silver compounds (whether or not chemically defined)
													-Gold compounds
0/0/0	0	0	0/0	0/0/0	0/0	0//0	0/0/	0/0/0	0/0			0/0/0	Gold cyanide, potassium cyanide gold (gold content 40%) (containing 40% of gold) (including subcyanide gold (Ⅰ) (gold content 68.3%) postassium subcyanide gold(Ⅲ) (gold content 57%))
0/0/0	0	0	0/0	0/0/0	0/0	0//0	0/0/	0/0/0	0/0			0/0/0	Other gold compounds (whether or not chemically defined)
													-Other compounds; amalgams
0/0/0	0	0		0/0/0	0/0	0//0	0/0/	0/0/0	5/0			0/0/0	Palladium chloride
0/0/0	0	0		0/0/0	0/0	0//0	0/0/	0/0/0	5/0			0/0/0	Platinum chloride
0/0/0	0	0		0/0/0	0/0	0//0	0/0/	0/0/0	5/0			0/0/0	Oxaliplatin, carboplatin, nedaplatin, cisplatin and other platinum—containing anticancer drug preparations and APIs
0/0/0	0	0		0/0/0	0/0	0//0	0/0/	0/0/0	5/0			0/0/0	Other platinum compounds(tax number of Separating anti—cancer pharmaceutical raw materials)
0/0/0	0	0		0/0/0	0/0	0//0	0/0/	0/0/0	5/0		//	0/0/0	Precious metal amalgam (whether or not chemically defined)
0/0/0	0	0		0/0/0	0/0	0//0	0/0/	0/0/0	5/0		//	0/0/0	Other precious metal compounds (whether or not chemically defined)
													Radioactive chemical elements and radioactive isotopes (including the fissile or fertile chemical elements and isotopes) and their compounds; mixtures and residues containing these products:
													-Natural uranium and its compounds; alloys, dispersions (including cermets), ceramic products and mixtures containing natural uranium or natural uranium compouds
0/0/0	0	0	0/0	0/0/0	0/0	0//0	0/0/	0/0/0	0/0			0/0/0	Natural uranium and its compounds
0/0/0	0	0	0/0	0/0/0	0/0	0//0	0/0/	0/0/0	0/0			0/0/0	Contains natural uranium alloy or natural uranium compounds, dispersions (including metal ceramic), ceramic products and mixture
													-Uranium enriched in U235 and its compounds; plutonium and its compounds; alloys dispersion (including cermets), ceramic products and mixtures containing uranium enriched in U235, plutonium or compounds of these products
0/0/0	0	0	0/0	0/0/0	0/0	0//0	0/0/	0/0/0	0/0			0/0/0	Containing U235 concentration less than 5% of low-enriched uranium and its compounds
0/0/0	0	0	0/0	0/0/0	0/0	0//0	0/0/	0/0/0	0/0			0/0/0	Other U235 enriched uranium and plutonium and its compounds (including its alloy, dispersions, ceramic products and mixture)
0/0/0	0	0	0/0	0/0/0	0/0	0//0	0/0/	0/0/0	0/0			0/0/0	-Uranium depleted in U235and its compounds; thorium and its compounds; alloys, dispersions (including cermets), ceramic products and mixtures containing uranium depleted in U235, thorium or compounds of these products

税则号列	货品名称〔CIQ 扩展编码及品名－T2 表示见附表 2〕	最惠(%)	暂定税率	普通	增值/消费	出口退税	计量单位	监管条件/特殊证件	检验检疫	对美关税	亚太上/下
	-除子目 2844.10、2844.20 及 2844.30 以外的放射性元素、同位素及其化合物；含这些元素、同位素及其化合物的合金、分散体(包括金属陶瓷)、陶瓷产品及混合物；放射性残渣：										
2844.4100	--氚及其化合物；含氚及其化合物的合金、分散体（包括金属陶瓷)、陶瓷产品及混合物										
2844.4100 10	氚、氚化物和氚的混合物，以及含有上述任何一种物质的产品(氚－氢原子比超过千分之一的，不包括含氚(任何形态)量小于 1.48×10^{3} GBq 的产品)〔999〕	5		30	13/	0	克/百万贝可	23/1		17.5	
2844.4100 90	其他氚及其化合物；其他含氚及其化合物的合金、分散体(包括金属陶瓷)、陶瓷产品及混合物〔999〕	5		30	13/	0	克/百万贝可	2/1			
	--锕－225、锕－227、锎－253、锔－240、锔－241、锔－242、锔－243、锔－244、锿－253、锿－254、钆－148、钋－208、钋－209、钋－210、镭－223、铀－230 或铀－232 及其化合物；含这些元素及其化合物的合金、分散体（包括金属陶瓷)、陶瓷产品及混合物：										
2844.4210	---镭－223 及镭－223 盐										
2844.4210 10	氯化镭[223Ra]注射液〔999〕	4	0	14	13/	0	克/百万贝可	2/1		22.5	
2844.4210 90	其他镭－223 及镭－223 盐〔999〕	4		14	13/	0	克/百万贝可	2/1		26.5	
2844.4290	---其他										
2844.4290 10	发射α粒子，其α半衰期为 10 天或更长但小于 200 年的放射性核素(1. 单质；2. 含有α总活度为 37GBq/kg 或更大的任何这类放射性核素的化合物；3. 含有α总活度为 37GBq/kg 或更大的任何这类放射性核素的混合物；4. 含有任何上述物质的产品，不包括所含α活度小于 3.7GBq 的产品)〔999〕	5		30	13/	0	克/百万贝可	23/1		17.5	
2844.4290 90	其他锕－225、锕－227、锎－253、锔－240、锔－241、锔－242、锔－243、锔－244、锿－253、锿－254、钆－148、钋－208、钋－209、钋－210、铀－230 或铀－232 及其化合物，其他镭－223 的化合物；含这些元素及其化合物的合金、分散体(包括金属陶瓷)、陶瓷产品及混合物〔999〕	5		30	13/	0	克/百万贝可	2/1			
	--其他放射性元素、同位素及其化合物；其他含这些元素、同位素及其化合物的合金、分散体(包括金属陶瓷)、陶瓷产品及混合物：										
2844.4310	---除镭－223 及镭－223 盐外的镭及镭盐										
2844.4310 10	镭－226 及其盐(两用物项管制商品)〔999〕	4		14	13/	0	克/百万贝可	23/1		26.5	
2844.4310 90	其他除镭－223、镭－226 及它们的盐外的镭及镭盐〔999〕	4		14	13/	0	克/百万贝可	2/1		26.5	
2844.4320	---钴及钴盐〔999〕	4		14	13/	0	克/百万贝可	2/1		31.5	
2844.4390	---其他〔镭－226 的盐除外〕										
2844.4390 10	铀－233 及其化合物(包括呈金属、合金、化合物或浓缩物形态的各种材料)〔999〕	5		30	13/	0	克/百万贝可	23/1		17.5	
2844.4390 21	镭－226 的化合物(镭－226 的盐除外)〔999〕	4		14	13/	0	克/百万贝可	23/1			
2844.4390 29	镭－226 的合金、混合物〔999〕	4		14	13/	0	克/百万贝可	3/1			
2844.4390 30	其他发射α粒子，其α半衰期为 10 天或更长但小于 200 年的放射性核素(1. 单质；2. 含有α总活度为 37GBq/kg 或更大的任何这类放射性核素的化合物；3. 含有α总活度为 37GBq/kg 或更大的任何这类放射性核素的混合物；4. 含有任何上述物质的产品，不包括所含α活度小于 3.7GBq 的产品)〔999〕	5		30	13/	0	克/百万贝可	23/1		17.5	

协定税率 %								RCEP		特惠税率 %			Article Description
东/冰/格	巴基斯坦	韩国	瑞士上/下	哥/秘/柬	澳/毛	新西/坡/智	中国港/澳/台	东盟及马来/澳/韩	日/新	亚太2国	老/柬/缅	98/97/95	
													-Radioactive elements and isotopes and compounds other than those of subheading No. 2844.10,2844.20 or 2844.30; alloys, dispersions (including cermets), ceramic products and mixtures containing these elements, isotopes or compounds; radioactive residues:
													-- Tritium and its compounds; alloys, dispersions (including cermets), ceramic products and mixtures containing tritium or its compounds
0/0/0	0	0	0/0	0/0/0	0/0	0//0	0/0/	0/0/0	0/0			0/0/0	Tritium, tritiated compounds and tritium mixtures, as well as products containing any of the above substances (if the tritium hydrogen atomic ratio exceeds one thousandth, excluding products containing tritium (in any form) less than 1.48 × 1^3gbq products)
0/0/0	0	0	0/0	0/0/0	0/0	0//0	0/0/	0/0/0	0/0			0/0/0	Other tritium and its compounds; Other alloys, dispersions (including cermets), ceramic products and mixtures containing tritium and its compounds
													-- Actinium—225, actinium—227, californium—253, curium—240, curium— 241, curium—242, curium—243, curium—244, einsteinium—253, einsteinium—254, gadolinium—148, polonium—208, polonium—209, polonium—210, radium—223, uranium—230 or uranium—232, and their compounds; alloys, dispersions (including cermets), ceramic products and mixtures containing these elements or compounds
													--Radium—223 and its salts
0/0/0	0	0	0/0	0/0/0	0/0	0//0	0/0/	0/0/0	0/0			0/0/0	Radium chloride [223ra] injection
0/0/0	0	0	0/0	0/0/0	0/0	0//0	0/0/	0/0/0	0/0			0/0/0	Other radium—223 and radium—223 salts
													---Other
0/0/0	0	0	0/0	0/0/0	0/0	0//0	0/0/	0/0/0	0/0			0/0/0	launch α Particle, its α Radionuclides with a half—life of 1 days or more but less than 2 years (1. Simple substance; 2. Containing α Compounds of any such radionuclides with a total activity of 37 GBq / kg or greater; 3. Contains α Mixtures of any such radionuclides with a total activity of 37 GBq / kg or greater; 4. Products containing any of the above substances, excluding α Products with activity less than 3.7gbq)
0/0/0	0	0	0/0	0/0/0	0/0	0//0	0/0/	0/0/0	0/0			0/0/0	Other actinium — 225, actinium — 227, californium — 253, curium— 24, curium — 241, curium — 242, curium — 243, curium—244, 锿 — 253, 锿 — 254, gadolinium—148, polonium—28, polonium—29, polonium—21, uranium—23 or Uranium—232 and their compounds, and other compounds of radium — 223; Alloys, dispersions (including cermets), ceramic products and mixtures containing these elements and their compounds
													-- Other radioactive elements and isotopes and compounds; other alloys, dispersions (including cermets), ceramic products and mixtures containing these elements, isotopes or compounds
													---Radium and its salts, other than Radium—223 and its salts
0/0/0	0	0	0/0	0/0/0	0/0	0//0	0/0/	0/0/0	0/0			0/0/0	Radium—226 and its salts (dual—use controlled commodities)
0/0/0	0	0	0/0	0/0/0	0/0	0//0	0/0/	0/0/0	0/0			0/0/0	Other radium and radium salts other than radium—223, radium—226 and their salts
0/0/0	0	0	0/0	0/0/0	0/0	0//0	0/0/	0/0/0	0/0			0/0/0	---Cobalt and its salts
													---Other
0/0/0	0	0	0/0	0/0/0	0/0	0//0	0/0/	0/0/0	0/0			0/0/0	Uranium—233 and its compounds (including various materials in the form of metals, alloys, compounds or concentrates)
0/0/0	0	0	0/0	0/0/0	0/0	0//0	0/0/	0/0/0	0/0			0/0/0	Compound of radium—226
0/0/0	0	0	0/0	0/0/0	0/0	0//0	0/0/	0/0/0	0/0			0/0/0	Alloys and mixtures of radium—226
0/0/0	0	0	0/0	0/0/0	0/0	0//0	0/0/	0/0/0	0/0			0/0/0	Other launch α Particle, its α Radionuclides with a half—life of 1 days or more but less than 2 years (1. Simple substance; 2. Containing α Compounds of any such radionuclides with a total activity of 37 GBq / kg or greater; 3. Contains α Mixtures of any such radionuclides with a total activity of 37 GBq / kg or greater; 4. Products containing any of the above substances, excluding α Products with activity less than 3.7gbq)

税则号列	货品名称〔CIQ 扩展编码及品名－T2 表示见附表 2〕	最惠(%)	暂定税率	普通	增值/消费	出口退税	计量单位	监管条件/特殊证件	检验检疫	对美关税	亚太上/下
2844.4390 90	其他除子目 2844.10,2844.20 及 2844.30 以外的放射性元素、同位素及其化合物;含这些元素、同位素及其化合物的合金、分散体(包括金属陶瓷)、陶瓷产品及混合物〔999〕	5		30	13/	0	克/百万贝可	2/1			
2844.4400	--放射性残渣〔999〕	5		30	13/	0	克/百万贝可	2/1		17.5	
2844.5000	-核反应堆已耗尽已辐照的燃料元件(释热元件)〔999〕	5		30	13/	0	克	3/1		7.5	
28.45	**税目 28.44 以外的同位素;这些同位素的无机或有机化合物,不论是否已有化学定义:**										
2845.1000	-重水(氧化氘)〔999〕	5		30	13/	0	克	3/1		17.5	
2845.2000	-硼－10 浓缩硼及其化合物										
2845.2000 10	硼－10 浓缩硼及其化合物(硼－10 同位素占硼总量＞20%的硼及其化合物)〔999〕	5		30	13/	0	克/百万贝可	3/13			
2845.2000 90	其他硼－10 浓缩硼及其化合物〔999〕	5		30	13/	0	克/百万贝可	/13			
2845.3000	-锂－6 浓缩锂及其化合物										
2845.3000 10	富集锂－6 同位素及其化合物(富集锂－6 同位素指锂－6 同位素富集度＞7.5%(按原子数计))〔999〕	5		30	13/	0	克	3/13			
2845.3000 90	其他锂－6 浓缩锂及其化合物〔999〕	5		30	13/	0	克	/13			
2845.4000	-氦－3〔999〕	5		30	13/	0	克/百万贝可	3/13			
2845.9000	-其他										
2845.9000 10	除重水外的氘及氘化物〔999〕	5		30	13/	0	克	3/13			
2845.9000 20	其他硼－10 同位素及其化合物、混合物(硼－10 同位素占硼总量＞20%的硼及其化合物、混合物)〔999〕	5		30	13/	0	克	3/13			
2845.9000 30	其他富集锂－6 同位素及其化合物混合物[富集锂－6 同位素指锂－6 同位素富集度＞7.5%(按原子数计)]〔999〕	5		30	13/	0	克	3/13			
2845.9000 40	含有氦－3 的混合物(不包括氦－3 的含量＜1g 的产品)〔999〕	5		30	13/	0	克/百万贝可	3/13			
2845.9000 90	其他同位素及其他化合物(编号 28.44 以外的同位素)〔999〕	5		30	13/	0	克	/13			
28.46	**稀土金属、钇、钪及其混合物的无机或有机化合物:**										
	-铈的化合物:										
2846.1010	---氧化铈〔999〕	5	0	30	13/	0	千克	4Bxy/1	N	22.5	2.5/2.5
2846.1020	---氢氧化铈〔999〕	5	0	30	13/	0	千克	4Bxy/1	N	7.5	2.5/2.5
2846.1030	---碳酸铈〔999〕	5	0	30	13/	0	千克	4Bxy/1	N		2.5/2.5
2846.1090	---其他										
2846.1090 10	氰化铈〔999〕	5	0	30	13/	0	千克	4Bxy/13	N	7.5	2.5/2.5
2846.1090 90	铈的其他化合物〔101 矿物源性饲料添加剂;301 危险化学品,氧化性物质;302 危险化学品,毒性物质;303 其他化工品〕	5	0	30	13/	0	千克	4Bxy/13	N	7.5	2.5/2.5
	-其他:										
	---氧化稀土(氧化铈除外):										
2846.9011	----氧化钇〔999〕	5	0	30	13/	0	千克	4xBy/1	N	27.5	
2846.9012	----氧化镧〔999〕	5	0	30	13/	0	千克	4Bxy/1	N	22.5	
2846.9013	----氧化钕〔999〕	5	0	30	13/	0	千克	4Bxy/1	N		
2846.9014	----氧化铕〔999〕	5	0	30	13/	0	千克	4Bxy/1	N		
2846.9015	----氧化镝〔999〕	5	0	30	13/	0	千克	4Bxy/1	N		
2846.9016	----氧化铽〔999〕	5	0	30	13/	0	千克	4Bxy/1	N		
2846.9017	----氧化镨〔999〕	5	0	30	13/	0	千克	4Bxy/1	N	27.5	
2846.9018	----氧化镥〔999〕	5	0	30	13/	0	千克	4Bxy/1	N	27.5	
2846.9019	----其他										
2846.9019 20	氧化铒〔999〕	5	0	30	13/	0	千克	4Bxy/1	N	27.5	
2846.9019 30	氧化钆〔999〕	5	0	30	13/	0	千克	4Bxy/1	N	27.5	
2846.9019 40	氧化钐〔999〕	5	0	30	13/	0	千克	4Bxy/1	N	27.5	
2846.9019 70	氧化镱〔999〕	5	0	30	13/	0	千克	4Bxy/1	N	27.5	
2846.9019 80	氧化钪〔999〕	5	0	30	13/	0	千克	4Bxy/1	N	27.5	
2846.9019 91	灯用红粉〔999〕	5	0	30	13/	0	千克	4Bxy/1	N	27.5	
2846.9019 92	按重量计中重稀土总含量≥30%的其他氧化稀土(灯用红粉、氧化铈除外)〔999〕	5	0	30	13/	0	千克	4Bxy/1	N	27.5	

协定税率 %								RCEP		特惠税率 %			Article Description
东/冰/格	巴基斯坦	韩国	瑞士上/下	哥/秘/柬	澳/毛	新西/坡/智	中国港/澳/台	东盟及马来/澳/韩	日/新	亚太2国	老/柬/缅	98/97/95	
0/0/0	0	0	0/0	0/0/0	0/0	0//0	0/0/	0/0/0	0/0			0/0/0	Other radioactive elements, isotopes and their compounds other than subheadings 2844.12844.2 and 2844.3; Alloys, dispersions (including cermets), ceramic products and mixtures containing these elements, isotopes and their compounds
0/0/0	0	0	0/0	0/0/0	0/0	0//0	0/0/	0/0/0	0/0			0/0/0	-- Radioactive residues
0/0/0	0	0	0/0	0/0/0	0/0	0//0	0/0/	0/0/0	0/0			0/0/0	-Spent (irradiated) fuel elements (cartridges) of nuclear reactors
													Isotopes other than those of heading No. 28.44; compounds, inorganic or organic, of such isotopes, whether or not chemically defined:
0/0/0	0	0	0/0	0/0/0	0/0	0//0	0/0/	0/0/0	0/0			0/0/0	-Heavy water (deuterium oxide)
													- Boron enriched in boron—10 and its compounds
0/0/0	0	0	0/0	0/0/0	0/0	0//0	0/0/	0/0/0	0/0			0/0/0	Boron—1 concentrated boron and its compounds (boron and its compounds with boron—1 isotopes accounting for more than 2% of the total boron)
0/0/0	0	0	0/0	0/0/0	0/0	0//0	0/0/	0/0/0	0/0			0/0/0	Other boron—1 concentrated boron and its compounds
													- Lithium enriched in lithium—6 and its compounds
0/0/0	0	0	0/0	0/0/0	0/0	0//0	0/0/	0/0/0	0/0			0/0/0	Enrichment of lithium—6 isotopes and their compounds (enrichment of lithium—6 isotopes means that the enrichment degree of lithium—6 isotopes is > 7.5% (calculated by atomic number))
0/0/0	0	0	0/0	0/0/0	0/0	0//0	0/0/	0/0/0	0/0			0/0/0	Other lithium—6 concentrated lithium and its compounds
0/0/0	0	0	0/0	0/0/0	0/0	0//0	0/0/	0/0/0	0/0			0/0/0	- Helium—3
													-Other
0/0/0	0	0	0/0	0/0/0	0/0	0//0	0/0/	0/0/0	0/0			0/0/0	Deuterium and deuterides, other than heavy water
0/0/0	0	0	0/0	0/0/0	0/0	0//0	0/0/	0/0/0	0/0			0/0/0	Boron-10 and its compounds (boron and its compounds and mixtures with a containing of boron-10>20% of the total boron content)
0/0/0	0	0	0/0	0/0/0	0/0	0//0	0/0/	0/0/0	0/0			0/0/0	Lithium enriched in lithium-6 and its compounds and mixtures (lithium enriched in lithium-6 refers to enrichment of lithium-6 isotope>7.5% (atomicity))
0/0/0	0	0	0/0	0/0/0	0/0	0//0	0/0/	0/0/0	0/0			0/0/0	Mixtures containing helium—3 (excluding products with helium—3 content < 1g)
0/0/0	0	0	0/0	0/0/0	0/0	0//0	0/0/	0/0/0	0/0			0/0/0	Other isotopes and other compounds (other than isotopes of heading No. 28.44)
													Compounds, inorganic or organic, of rareearth metals, of yttrium or of scandium or of mixtures of these metals:
													-Ceric compounds:
0/0/0	0	0	0/0	0/0/0	0/0	0//0	0/0/	0/0/0	0/0			0/0/0	---Cerium oxide
0/0/0	0	0	0/0	0/0/0	0/0	0//0	0/0/	0/0/0	0/0			0/0/0	---Cerium hydroxide
0/0/0	0	0	0/0	0/0/0	0/0	0//0	0/0/	0/0/0	0/0			0/0/0	---Cerium carbonate
													---Other
0/0/0	0	0	0/0	0/0/0	0/0	0//0	0/0/	0/0/0	0/0			0/0/0	Cerium cyanide
0/0/0	0	0	0/0	0/0/0	0/0	0//0	0/0/	0/0/0	0/0			0/0/0	Other cerium compounds with
													-Other:
													---Rare-earth oxides (other than cerium oxide):
0/0/0	0	0	0/0	0/0/0	0/0	0//0	0/0/	0/0/0	0/0			0/0/0	----Yttrium oxide
0/0/0	0	0	0/0	0/0/0	0/0	0//0	0/0/	0/0/0	0/0			0/0/0	----Lanthanum oxide
0/0/0	0	0	0/0	0/0/0	0/0	0//0	0/0/	0/0/0	0/0			0/0/0	----Neodymium oxide
0/0/0	0	0	0/0	0/0/0	0/0	0//0	0/0/	0/0/0	0/0			0/0/0	----Europium oxide
0/0/0	0	0	0/0	0/0/0	0/0	0//0	0/0/	0/0/0	0/0			0/0/0	----Dysprosium oxide
0/0/0	0	0	0/0	0/0/0	0/0	0//0	0/0/	0/0/0	0/0			0/0/0	----Terbium oxide
0/0/0	0	0	0/0	0/0/0	0/0	0//0	0/0/	0/0/0	0/0			0/0/0	----Praseodymium oxide
0/0/0	0	0	0/0	0/0/0	0/0	0//0	0/0/	0/0/0	0/0			0/0/0	----Lutetium oxide
													----Other
0/0/0	0	0	0/0	0/0/0	0/0	0//0	0/0/	0/0/0	0/0			0/0/0	Erbium oxide
0/0/0	0	0	0/0	0/0/0	0/0	0//0	0/0/	0/0/0	0/0			0/0/0	Gadolinium oxide
0/0/0	0	0	0/0	0/0/0	0/0	0//0	0/0/	0/0/0	0/0			0/0/0	Samarium oxide
0/0/0	0	0	0/0	0/0/0	0/0	0//0	0/0/	0/0/0	0/0			0/0/0	Ytterbium oxide
0/0/0	0	0	0/0	0/0/0	0/0	0//0	0/0/	0/0/0	0/0			0/0/0	Scandium oxide
0/0/0	0	0	0/0	0/0/0	0/0	0//0	0/0/	0/0/0	0/0			0/0/0	Red powder for lumination
0/0/0	0	0	0/0	0/0/0	0/0	0//0	0/0/	0/0/0	0/0			0/0/0	Other rare-earth oxide, containing by weihgt ≥30% of middle heavy rare-earth (other than red powder for lumination, cerium cyanide)

税则号列	货品名称〔CIQ 扩展编码及品名－T2 表示见附表 2〕	最惠(%)	暂定税率	普通	增值/消费	出口退税	计量单位	监管条件/特殊证件	检验检疫	对美关税	亚太上/下
2846.9019 99	其他氧化稀土(灯用红粉、氧化铈除外)〔999〕	5	0	30	13/	0	千克	4Bxy/1	N	27.5	
	---氯化稀土：										
2846.9021	----氯化铽〔999〕	5	0	30	13/	0	千克	4Bxy/1	N	7.5	
2846.9022	----氯化镝〔999〕	5	0	30	13/	0	千克	4Bxy/1	N		
2846.9023	----氯化镧〔999〕	5	0	30	13/	0	千克	4Bxy/1	N	7.5	
2846.9024	----氯化钕〔999〕	5	0	30	13/	0	千克	4Bxy/1	N		
2846.9025	----氯化镨〔999〕	5	0	30	13/	0	千克	4Bxy/1	N		
2846.9026	----氯化钇〔999〕	5	0	30	13/	0	千克	4Bxy/1	N	7.5	
2846.9028	----混合氯化稀土〔999〕	5	0	30	13/	0	千克	4Bxy/1	N		
2846.9029	----其他〔999〕	5	0	30	13/	0	千克	4Bxy/1	N	12.5	
	---氟化稀土：										
2846.9031	----氟化铽〔999〕	5	0	30	13/	0	千克	4Bxy/1	N		
2846.9032	----氟化镝〔999〕	5	0	30	13/	0	千克	4Bxy/1	N		
2846.9033	----氟化镧〔999〕	5	0	30	13/	0	千克	4ABxy/13	MN		
2846.9034	----氟化钕〔999〕	5	0	30	13/	0	千克	4Bxy/1	N		
2846.9035	----氟化镨〔999〕	5	0	30	13/	0	千克	4Bxy/1	N		
2846.9036	----氟化钇〔999〕	5	0	30	13/	0	千克	4Bxy/1	N		
2846.9039	----其他〔301 不属于危险化学品的稀土，302 属于危险化学品的稀土〕	5	0	30	13/	0	千克	4Bxy/1	N		
	---碳酸稀土：										
2846.9041	----碳酸镧〔999〕	5	0	30	13/	0	千克	4Bxy/1	N		
2846.9042	----碳酸铽〔999〕	5	0	30	13/	0	千克	4Bxy/1	N		
2846.9043	----碳酸镝〔999〕	5	0	30	13/	0	千克	4Bxy/1	N		
2846.9044	----碳酸钕〔999〕	5	0	30	13/	0	千克	4Bxy/1	N		
2846.9045	----碳酸镨〔999〕	5	0	30	13/	0	千克	4Bxy/1	N		
2846.9046	----碳酸钇〔999〕	5	0	30	13/	0	千克	4Bxy/1	N		
2846.9048	----混合碳酸稀土										
2846.9048 10	按重量计中重稀土总含量≥30%的混合碳酸稀土〔999〕	5	0	30	13/	0	千克	4Bxy/1	N	25	
2846.9048 90	其他混合碳酸稀土〔999〕	5	0	30	13/	0	千克	4Bxy/1	N	25	
2846.9049	----其他〔999〕	5	0	30	13/	0	千克	4Bxy/1	N		
	---其他：										
2846.9091	----镧的其他化合物〔301 危险化学品，氧化性物质；302 其他化工品〕	5	0	30	13/	0	千克	4Bxy/13	N	7.5	
2846.9092	----钕的其他化合物〔301 危险化学品，氧化性物质；302 其他化工品〕	5	0	30	13/	0	千克	4Bxy/13	N	7.5	
2846.9093	----铽的其他化合物〔999〕	5	0	30	13/	0	千克	4Bxy/1	N	27.5	
2846.9094	----镝的其他化合物〔301 危险化学品，氧化性物质；302 其他化工品〕	5	0	30	13/	0	千克	4Bxy/13	N		
2846.9095	----镨的其他化合物〔301 危险化学品，氧化性物质；302 其他化工品〕	5	0	30	13/	0	千克	4Bxy/13	N		
2846.9096	----钇的其他化合物										
2846.9096 01	LED 用荧光粉(成分含钇的其他化合物)〔999〕	5	0	30	13/	0	千克	4Bxy B/13	N	27.5	
2846.9096 90	钇的其他化合物(LED 用荧光粉除外)〔301 危险化学品，氧化性物质；302 其他化工品〕	5	0	30	13/	0	千克	4Bxy/13	N	27.5	
2846.9099	----其他										
2846.9099 01	LED 用荧光粉(成分含稀土金属、钪的其他化合物，铈的化合物除外)〔999〕	5	0	30	13/	0	千克	B/13	N	22.5	
2846.9099 10	按重量计中重稀土总含量≥30%的稀土金属、钪的其他化合物(LED 用荧光粉、铈的化合物除外)〔999〕	5	0	30	13/	0	千克	4Bxy/13	N	22.5	
2846.9099 90	其他稀土金属、钪的其他化合物(LED 用荧光粉、铈的化合物除外)〔101 饲料添加剂；301 危险化学品，氧化性物质；302 其他化工品〕	5	0	30	13/	0	千克	4Bxy/13	N	22.5	
28.47	**过氧化氢，不论是否用尿素固化：**										
2847.0000	过氧化氢，不论是否用尿素固化〔301 危险化学品，不用作食品添加剂；302 危险化学品，用作食品添加剂〕	5.5		30	13/	0	千克	AB/13	MRNS	33	
28.49	**碳化物，不论是否已有化学定义：**										
2849.1000	-碳化钙〔999〕	5.5		45	13/	0	千克	AB/13	MN	8	
2849.2000	-碳化硅〔999〕	5.5		30	13/	0	千克	4xy/1		28	
	-其他：										
2849.9010	---碳化硼〔999〕	5.5		30	13/	0	千克	/1		8	
2849.9020	---碳化钨〔999〕	5.5		30	13/	0	千克	4xy/1		13	
2849.9090	---其他〔301 危险化学品，遇水放出易燃气体的物质；302 其他化工品〕	5.5		30	13/	0	千克	/13		28	
28.50	**氢化物、氮化物、叠氮化物、硅化物及硼化物，不论是否已有化学定义，但可归入税目 28.49 的碳化物除外：**										
	---氮化物：										

协定税率 %								RCEP		特惠税率 %			Article Description
东/冰/格	巴基斯坦	韩国	瑞士上/下	哥/秘/柬	澳/毛	新西/坡/智	中国港/澳/台	东盟及马来/澳/韩	日/新	亚太2国	老/柬/缅	98/97/95	
0/0/0	0	0	0/0	0/0/0	0/0	0//0	0/0/	0/0/0	0/0			0/0/0	Other rare-earth oxide(other than red powder for lumination, cerium cyanide)
													---Rare-earth chlorides:
0/0/0	0	0	0/0	0/0/0	0/0	0//0	0/0/	0/0/0	0/0			0/0/0	----Terbium chlorinates
0/0/0	0	0	0/0	0/0/0	0/0	0//0	0/0/	0/0/0	0/0			0/0/0	----Dysprosium chlorinates
0/0/0	0	0	0/0	0/0/0	0/0	0//0	0/0/	0/0/0	0/0			0/0/0	----Lan thanum chloride
0/0/0	0	0	0/0	0/0/0	0/0	0//0	0/0/	0/0/0	0/0			0/0/0	----Neodymium chlorinates
0/0/0	0	0	0/0	0/0/0	0/0	0//0	0/0/	0/0/0	0/0			0/0/0	----Praseodymium chlorinates
0/0/0	0	0	0/0	0/0/0	0/0	0//0	0/0/	0/0/0	0/0			0/0/0	----Yttrium chlorinates
0/0/0	0	0	0/0	0/0/0	0/0	0//0	0/0/	0/0/0	0/0			0/0/0	----Mixture of rareearth chlorides
0/0/0	0	0	0/0	0/0/0	0/0	0//0	0/0/	0/0/0	0/0			0/0/0	----Other
													---Rare-earth fluorides:
0/0/0	0	0	0/0	0/0/0	0/0	0//0	0/0/	0/0/0	0/0			0/0/0	----Terbium fluoride
0/0/0	0	0	0/0	0/0/0	0/0	0//0	0/0/	0/0/0	0/0			0/0/0	----Dysprosium fluoride
0/0/0	0	0	0/0	0/0/0	0/0	0//0	0/0/	0/0/0	0/0			0/0/0	----Lanthanum fluoride
0/0/0	0	0	0/0	0/0/0	0/0	0//0	0/0/	0/0/0	0/0			0/0/0	----Neodymium fluoride
0/0/0	0	0	0/0	0/0/0	0/0	0//0	0/0/	0/0/0	0/0			0/0/0	----Praseodymium fluoride
0/0/0	0	0	0/0	0/0/0	0/0	0//0	0/0/	0/0/0	0/0			0/0/0	----Yttrium fluoride
0/0/0	0	0	0/0	0/0/0	0/0	0//0	0/0/	0/0/0	0/0			0/0/0	----Other
													---Rare-earth carbonate:
0/0/0	0	0	0/0	0/0/0	0/0	0//0	0/0/	0/0/0	0/0			0/0/0	----Lanthanum carbonates
0/0/0	0	0	0/0	0/0/0	0/0	0//0	0/0/	0/0/0	0/0			0/0/0	----Terbium carbonates
0/0/0	0	0	0/0	0/0/0	0/0	0//0	0/0/	0/0/0	0/0			0/0/0	----Dysprosium carbonates
0/0/0	0	0	0/0	0/0/0	0/0	0//0	0/0/	0/0/0	0/0			0/0/0	----Neodymium carbonates
0/0/0	0	0	0/0	0/0/0	0/0	0//0	0/0/	0/0/0	0/0			0/0/0	----Praseodymium carbonates
0/0/0	0	0	0/0	0/0/0	0/0	0//0	0/0/	0/0/0	0/0			0/0/0	----Yttrium carbonates
													----Mixture of rare earth carbonate
0/0/0	0	0	0/0	0/0/0	0/0	0//0	0/0/	0/0/0	0/0			0/0/0	Other mixed rare-earth carbonates, containing by weihgt ≥ 30% of middle heavy rare-earth,
0/0/0	0	0	0/0	0/0/0	0/0	0//0	0/0/	0/0/0	0/0			0/0/0	Other mixed rare-earth carbonates
0/0/0	0	0	0/0	0/0/0	0/0	0//0	0/0/	0/0/0	0/0			0/0/0	----Other
													---Other:
0/0/0	0	0	0/0	0/0/0	0/0	0//0	0/0/	0/0/0	0/0			0/0/0	----Of lanthanum
0/0/0	0	0	0/0	0/0/0	0/0	0//0	0/0/	0/0/0	0/0			0/0/0	----Of neodymium
0/0/0	0	0	0/0	0/0/0	0/0	0//0	0/0/	0/0/0	0/0			0/0/0	----Of terbium
0/0/0	0	0	0/0	0/0/0	0/0	0//0	0/0/	0/0/0	0/0			0/0/0	----Of dysprosium
0/0/0	0	0	0/0	0/0/0	0/0	0//0	0/0/	0/0/0	0/0			0/0/0	----Of praseodymium
													Of yttrium
0/0/0	0	0	0/0	0/0/0	0/0	0//0	0/0/	0/0/0	0/0			0/0/0	LED phosphor(other compounds containing yttrium)
0/0/0	0	0	0/0	0/0/0	0/0	0//0	0/0/	0/0/0	0/0			0/0/0	Other compounds containing yttrium
													----Other
0/0/0	0	0	0/0	0/0/0	0/0	0//0	0/0/	0/0/0	0/0			0/0/0	LED phosphor(other compounds containing rare earth metals, scandium, except for cerium compounds)
0/0/0	0	0	0/0	0/0/0	0/0	0//0	0/0/	0/0/0	0/0			0/0/0	Other rare-earth metals, other compounds of scandium, containing by weihgt ≥30% of middle heavy rare-earth,
0/0/0	0	0	0/0	0/0/0	0/0	0//0	0/0/	0/0/0	0/0			0/0/0	Other rare-earth metals, compounds of scandium
													Hydrogen peroxide, whether or not solidified with urea:
0/0/0	0	2.5	0/0	0/0/0	0/0	0//0	0/0/	5/5/5	5.2/5			0/0/0	Hydrogen peroxide, whether or not solidified with urea
													Carbides, whether or not chemically defined:
0/0/0	0	0	0/0	0/0/0	0/0	0//0	0/0/	0/0/0	0/0			0/0/0	-Of calcium
0/0/0	0	1.1	0/0	0/0/0	0/0	0//0	0/0/	0/0/5	5/0			0/0/0	-Of silicon
													-Other:
0/0/0	0	0	0/0	0/0/0	0/0	0//0	0/0/	0/0/0	0/0			0/0/0	---Of boron
0/0/0	0	0	0/0	0/0/0	0/0	0//0	0/0/	0/0/0	0/0			0/0/0	---Of tungsten
0/0/0	0	0	0/0	0/0/0	0/0	0//0	0/0/	0/0/0	0/0			0/0/0	---Other
													Hydrides, nitrides, azides, silicides and borides, whether or not chemically defined, other than compounds which are also carbides of heading No. 28.49:
													---Nitride:

税则号列		货品名称〔CIQ 扩展编码及品名—T2 表示见附表 2〕	最惠(%)	暂定税率	普通	增值/消费	出口退税	计量单位	监管条件/特殊证件	检验检疫	对美关税	亚太上/下
2850.0011		----氮化锰〔999〕	5.5		30	13/	0	千克	/1		8	3.6/3.6
2850.0012		----氮化硼〔999〕	5.5		30	13/	0	千克	/1			3.6/3.6
2850.0019		----其他〔301 危险化学品，易燃固体；302 危险化学品，遇水放出易燃气体的物质；303 其他化工产品〕	5.5		30	13/	0	千克	/13		28	3.6/3.6
2850.0090		---其他										
2850.0090	10	砷化氢(砷烷、砷化三氢、胂)〔999〕	5.5	3	30	13/	0	千克	/13		10.5	3.6/3.6
2850.0090	90	其他氢化物、硅化物等(包括硼化物，可归入税目 28.49 的碳化物除外)〔301 危险化学品，爆炸品；302 危险化学品，气体；303 危险化学品，易燃固体；304 危险化学品，易于自燃的物质；305 危险化学品，遇水放出易燃气体的物质；306 危险化学品，毒性物质；307 其他化工产品〕	5.5		30	13/	0	千克	/13		13	3.6/3.6
28.52		**汞的无机或有机化合物，不论是否已有化学定义，汞齐除外：**										
2852.1000		-已有化学定义的〔301 危险化学品，爆炸品；302 危险化学品，毒性物质；303 危险化学品，杂项物质；304 其他化工品〕	5.5		30	13/	0	千克	/13		8	
2852.9000		-其他〔301 毒性物质和感染性物质，998 其他危险化学品，999 其他化工产品〕	5.5		30	13/	0	千克	/1		8	
28.53		**磷化物，不论是否已有化学定义，但磷铁除外；其他无机化合物(包括蒸馏水、导电水及类似的纯净水)；液态空气(不论是否除去稀有气体)；压缩空气；汞齐，但贵金属汞齐除外：**										
2853.1000		-氯化氰〔999〕	5.5		30	13/	0	千克	23AB/13	MN	8	
		-其他：										
2853.9010		---饮用蒸馏水〔998 食用，999 实验用〕	5.5		70	13/	0	千克	AB/1	RS	33	
2853.9030		---镍钴锰氢氧化物〔999〕	6.5		30	13/	13	千克	/1		9	
2853.9040		---磷化物，不论是否已有化学定义，但不包括磷铁										
2853.9040	10	磷化铝，磷化锌〔999〕	5.5		20	13/	0	千克	S/13		13	
2853.9040	20	磷烷〔999〕	5.5	3	20	13/	0	千克	/13		10.5	
2853.9040	90	其他磷化物(不论是否已有化学定义，但不包括磷铁)〔301 危险化学品，气体；302 危险化学品，遇水放出易燃气体的物质；303 其他化工产品〕	5.5		20	13/	0	千克	/13		13	
2853.9050		---镍钴铝氢氧化物〔999〕	5.5		30	13/	13	千克	/1		8	
2853.9090		---其他										
2853.9090	10	饮用纯净水〔998 食用，999 实验用〕	5.5		30	13/	0	千克	AB/13	MN	13	
2853.9090	21	氰，氰化碘，氰化溴(包括氰气，碘化氰，溴化氰)〔301 危险化学品，气体；302 危险化学品，毒性物质；999 遇水放出易燃气体的物质〕	5.5		30	13/	0	千克	/13		13	
2853.9090	22	砷化锌，砷化镓〔301 砷化镓；302 砷化锌〕	5.5		30	13/	0	千克	/13		13	
2853.9090	23	铅汞齐〔999〕	5.5		30	13/	0	千克	X/13		13	
2853.9090	24	其他汞齐〔301 遇水放出易燃气体的物质 ，302 毒性物质和感染性物质，303 杂项物质 ，304 其他危险化学品 ，305 其他化工产品〕	5.5		30	13/	0	千克	X/13		13	
2853.9090	25	单氰胺〔999〕	5.5		30	13/	0	千克	S/13		13	
2853.9090	90	其他无机化合物、压缩空气等(包括单导电水、液态空气等)〔301 危险化学品，气体，302 危险化学品，易于自燃的物质，303 危险化学品，遇水放出易燃气体的物质，304 危险化学品，氧化性物质，305 危险化学品，毒性物质，306 危险化学品，腐蚀性物质，307 危险化学品，杂项物质，308 其他化工品〕	5.5		30	13/	0	千克	/13		13	

协定税率 %								RCEP		特惠税率 %			Article Description
东/冰/格	巴基斯坦	韩国	瑞士上/下	哥/秘/柬	澳/毛	新西/坡/智	中国港/澳/台	东盟及马来/澳/韩	日/新	亚太2国	老/柬/缅	98/97/95	
0/0/0	0	0	0/0	0/0/0	0/0	0//0	0/0/	0/0/0	0/0			0/0/0	----Manganese nitride
0/0/0	0	0	0/0	0/0/0	0/0	0//0	0/0/	0/0/0	0/0			0/0/0	----Boron Nitride
0/0/0	0	0	0/0	0/0/0	0/0	0//0	0/0/	0/0/0	0/0			0/0/0	----Other
													---Other
0/0/0	0	2.5	0/0	0/0/0	0/0	0//0	0/0/	5/5/5	5.2/5			0/0/0	Arsenic hydride(arsine,hydride;arsine)
0/0/0	0	2.5	0/0	0/0/0	0/0	0//0	0/0/	5/5/5	5.2/5			0/0/0	Other hydrides, silicides(including borides, other than compounds which qre also carbides of heading No. 28. 49)
													Compounds, inorganic or organic, of mercury, excluding amalgams:
0/0/0	0	0	0/0	0/0/0	0/0	0//0	0/0/	0/0/0	0/0			0/0/0	-Chemically defined
0/0/0	0	0	0/0	0/0/0	0/0	0//0	0/0/	0/0/0	0/0			0/0/0	-Other
													Phosphides, whether or not chemically defined, excluding ferrophosphorus; Other inorganic compounds (including distilled or conductivity water and water of similar purity); liquid air (whether or not rare gases have been removed); compressed air; amalgams, other than amalgams of precious metals:
0/0/0	0	0	0/0	0/0/0	0/0	0//0	0/0/	0/0/0	0/0			0/0/0	-chlorocyanogen, cyanogen chloride
													-Other:
0/0/0	0	0	0/0	0/0/0	0/0	0//0	0/0/	0/0/0	0/0			0/0/0	---Distilled water for human consumption
0/0/0	3.5	0	0/0	0/0/0	0/0	0//0	0/0/	0/0/0	5.9/0			0/0/0	---Nickel cobalt manganese composite hydroxide
													---Phosphides, whether or not chemically defined, excluding ferrophosphorus
0/0/0	0	1.1	0/0	0/0/0	0/0	0//0	0/0/	0/0/5	5/0			0/0/0	Aluminium phosphide, zinc phosphide
0/0/0	0	1.1	0/0	0/0/0	0/0	0//0	0/0/	0/0/5	5/0		//	0/0/0	phosphine
0/0/0	0	1.1	0/0	0/0/0	0/0	0//0	0/0/	0/0/5	5/0			0/0/0	Other phosphides, whether or not chemieally defined, excluding ferrophosphorus
0/0/0	0	0	0/0	0/0/0	0/0	0//0	0/0/	0/0/0	0/0			0/0/0	---Nickel cobalt aluminum hydroxide
													---Other
0/0/0	0	0	0/0	0/0/0	0/0	0//0	0/0/	0/0/0	0/0			0/0/0	Purified water for human consumption
0/0/0	0	0	0/0	0/0/0	0/0	0//0	0/0/	0/0/0	0/0			0/0/0	Mercury Arsenide, Cyanogen, Cyanogen iodide, Bromine cyanide(including Cyanogen Dicyanogen, iodine cyanide, Bromine cyanide)
0/0/0	0	0	0/0	0/0/0	0/0	0//0	0/0/	0/0/0	0/0			0/0/0	Zinc arsenide, gallium arsenide
0/0/0	0	0	0/0	0/0/0	0/0	0//0	0/0/	0/0/0	0/0		//	0/0/0	Lead amalgam
0/0/0	0	0	0/0	0/0/0	0/0	0//0	0/0/	0/0/0	0/0		//	0/0/0	Other amalgam
0/0/0	0	0	0/0	0/0/0	0/0	0//0	0/0/	0/0/0	0/0			0/0/0	cyanamide
0/0/0	0	0	0/0	0/0/0	0/0	0//0	0/0/	0/0/0	0/0			0/0/0	Other inorganic compounds, compressed air, etc. (including single conductive water, liquid air, etc.)

第二十九章
有机化学品

注释：

一、除条文另有规定的以外，本章各税目只适用于：

(一)单独的已有化学定义的有机化合物，不论是否含有杂质；

(二)同一有机化合物的两种或两种以上异构体的混合物(不论是否含有杂质)，但无环烃异构体的混合物(立体异构体除外)，不论是否饱和，应归入第二十七章；

(三)税目 29.36 至 29.39 的产品，税目29.40的糖醚、糖缩醛、糖酯及其盐类和税目 29.41 的产品，不论是否已有化学定义；

(四)上述(一)、(二)、(三)款产品的水溶液；

(五)溶于其他溶剂的上述(一)、(二)、(三)款的产品，但该产品处于溶液状态只是为了安全或运输所采取的正常必要方法，其所用溶剂并不使该产品改变其一般用途而适合于某些特殊用途；

(六)为了保存或运输的需要，加入稳定剂(包括抗结块剂)的上述(一)、(二)、(三)、(四)、(五)各款产品；

(七)为了便于识别或安全起见，加入抗尘剂、着色剂、气味剂或催吐剂的上述(一)、(二)、(三)、(四)、(五)、(六)各款产品，但所加剂料并不使原产品改变其一般用途而适合于某些特殊用途；

(八)为生产偶氮染料而稀释至标准浓度的下列产品：重氮盐，用于重氮盐、可重氮化的胺及其盐类的耦合剂。

二、本章不包括：

(一)税目 15.04 的货品及税目 15.20 的粗甘油；

(二)乙醇(税目 22.07 或 22.08)；

(三)甲烷及丙烷(税目 27.11)；

(四)第二十八章注释二所述的碳化合物；

(五)税目 30.02 的免疫制品。

(六)尿素(税目 31.02 或 31.05)；

(七)植物性或动物性着色料(税目 32.03)、合成有机着色料、用作荧光增白剂或发光体的合成有机产品(税目 32.04)及零售包装的染料或其他着色料(税目 32.12)；

(八)酶(税目 35.07)；

(九)聚乙醛、六亚甲基四胺(乌洛托品)及类似物质，制成片、条或类似形状作为燃料用的，以及包装容器的容积不超过 300 立方厘米的直接灌注香烟打火机及类似打火器用的液体燃料或液化气体燃料(税目 36.06)；

(十)灭火器的装配药及已装药的灭火弹(税目 38.13)；零售包装的除墨剂(税目 38.24)；

(十一)光学元件，例如用酒石酸乙二胺制成的(税目 90.01)。

三、可以归入本章两个或两个以上税目的货品，应归入有关税目中的最后一个税目。

四、税目 29.04 至 29.06、29.08 至 29.11 及29.13至 29.20 的卤化、磺化、硝化或亚硝化衍生物均包括复合衍生物，例如，卤磺化、卤硝化、磺硝化及卤磺硝化衍生物。

硝基及亚硝基不作为税目 29.29 的含氮基官能团。

税目 29.11、29.12、29.14、29.18 及 29.22 所称“含氧基”，仅限于税目 29.05 至 29.20 的各种含氧基(其特征为有机含氧基)。

五、(一)本章第一分章至第七分章的酸基有机化合物与这些分章的有机化合物构成的酯，应归入有关分章的最后一个税目。

(二)乙醇与本章第一分章至第七分章的酸基有机化合物所构成的酯，应按有关酸基化合物归类。

(三)除第六类注释一及第二十八章注释二另有规定的以外：

1. 第一分章至第十分章及税目 29.42 的有机化合物的无机盐，例如，含酸基、酚基或烯醇基的化合物及有机碱的无机盐，应归入相应的有机化合物的税目；
2. 第一分章至第十分章及税目 29.42 的有机化合物之间生成的盐，应按生成该盐的碱或酸(包括酚基或烯醇基化合物)归入本章有关税目中的最后一个税目；以及
3. 除第十一分章或税目 29.41 的产品外，配位化合物应按该化合物所有金属键(金属-碳键除外)“断开”所形成的片段归入第二十九章有关税目中的最后一个税目。

(四)除乙醇外，金属醇化物应按相应的醇归类(税目 29.05)。

(五)羧酸酰卤化物应按相应的酸归类。

六、税目 29.30 及 29.31 的化合物是指有机化合物，其分子中除含氢、氧或氮原子外，还含有与碳原子直接连接的其他非金属或金属原子(例如，硫、砷或铅)。

税目 29.30(有机硫化合物)及税目 29.31(其他有机-无机化合物)不包括某些磺化或卤化衍生物(含复合衍生物)。这些衍生物分子中除氢、氧、氮之外，只有具有磺化或卤化衍生物(或复合衍生物)性质的硫原子或卤素原子与碳原子直接连接。

七、税目 29.32、29.33 及 29.34 不包括三节环环氧化物、过氧化酮、醛或硫醛的环聚合物、多元羧酸酐、多元醇或酚与多元酸构成的环酯及多元酸酰亚胺。

本条规定只适用于由本条所列环化功能形成环内杂原子的化合物。

八、税目 29.37 所称：

(一)“激素”，包括激素释放因子、激素刺激和释放因子、激素抑制剂以及激素抗体；

(二)“主要起激素作用的”，不仅适用于主要起激素作用的激素衍生物及结构类似物，也适用于在本税目所列产品合成过程中主要用作中间体的激素衍生物及结构类似物。

Chapter 29
Organic chemicals

Notes:

1. Except where the context otherwise requires, the headings of this Chapter apply only to:
   (a) Separate chemically defined organic compounds, whether or not containing impurities;
   (b) Mixtures of two or more isomers of the same organic compound (whether or not containing impurities), except mixtures of acyclic hydrocarbon isomers (other than stereoisomers), whether or not saturated (Chapter 27);
   (c) The products of headings No 29.36 to 29.39 or the sugar ethers, sugar acetals and sugar esters, and their salts, of heading No. 29.40, or the products of heading No. 29.41, whether or not chemically defined;
   (d) The products mentioned in (a), (b) or (c) above dissolved in water;
   (e) The products mentioned in (a), (b) or (c) above dissolved in other slovents provided that the solution constitutes a normal and necessary method of putting up these products adopted solely for reasons of safety or for transport and that the solvent does not render the product particularly suitable for specific use rather than for general use;
   (f) The products mentioned in (a), (b), (c), (d) or (e) above with an added stabilizer (including an anti-caking agent) necessary for their preservation or transport;
   (g) The products mentioned in (a), (b), (c), (d), (e) or (f) above with an added anti-dusting agent or a colouring or odoriferous substance or an emetic added to facilitate their identification or for safety reasons, provided that the additions do not render the product particularly suitable for specific use rather than for general use;
   (h) The following products, diluted to standard strengths, for the production of azo dyes: diazonium salts, couplers used for these salts and diazotisable amines and their salts.
2. This Chapter does not cover:
   (a) Goods of heading No. 15.04 or crude glycerol of heading No. 15.20;
   (b) Ethyl alcohol (heading No. 22.07 or 22.08);
   (c) Methane or propane (headng No. 27.11);
   (d) The compounds of carbon mentioned in Note 2 to Chapter 28;
   (e) Immunological products of heading No. 30.02
   (f) Urea (heading No. 31.02 or 31.05);
   (g) Colouring matter of vegetable or animal origin (heading No. 32.03), synthetic organic colouring matter, synthetic organic products of a kind used as fluorescent brightening agents or as luminophores (heading No. 32.04) or dyes or other colouring matter put up in forms or packings for retail sale (heading No. 32.12);
   (h) Enzymes (heading No. 35.07);
   (i) Metaldehyde, hexamethylenetetramine or similar substances, put up in forms (for example, tablets, sticks or similar forms) for use as fuels, or liquid or liquefied-gas fuels in containers of a kind used for filling or refilling cigarette or similar lighters and of a capacity not exceeding 300 cm^3 (heading No. 36.06);
   (j) Products put up as charges for fire-extinguishers or put up in fire-extinguishing grenades, of heading No. 38.13; ink removers put up in packings for retail sale, of heading No. 38.24; or
   (k) Optical elements, for example, of ethylenediamine tartrate (heading No. 90.01)
3. Goods which could be included in two or more of the headings of this Chapter are to be classified in that one of those headings which occurs last in numerical order.
4. In headings No. 29.04 to 29.06, 29.08 to 29.11 and 29.13 to 29.20, any reference to halogenated, sulphonated, nitrated or nitrosated derivatives includes a reference to compound derivatives, such as sulphohalogenated, nitrohalogenated, nitrosulphonated or nitrosulphohalogenated derivatives.
   Nitro or nitroso groups are not to be taken a "nitrogen-functions" for the purpose of heading No. 29.29.
   For the purposes of headings No. 29.11, 29.12, 29.14, 29.18 and 29.22, "oxygen-function" is to be restricted to the functions (the characteristic organic oxygen-containing groups) referred to in headings No. 29.05 to 29.20.
5. (a) The esters of acid-function organic compounds of sub-Chapters Ⅰ to Ⅶ with organic compounds of these sub-Chapters are to be classified with that compound which is classified in the heading which occurs last in numerical order in these sub-Chapters.
   (b) Esters of ethyl alcohol with acid-function organic compounds of sub-Chapters Ⅰ to Ⅶ are to be classified in the same heading as the corresponding acid-function compounds.
   (c) Subject to Note 1 to Section Ⅵ and Note 2 to Chapter 28:
      (i) Inorganic salts of organic compounds such as acid, phenol or enol-function compounds or organic bases, of sub-Chapters Ⅰ to Ⅹ or heading No. 29.42, are to be classified in the heading appropriate to the organic compound;
      (ii) Salts formed between organic compounds of sub-Chapters Ⅰ to Ⅹ or heading No. 29.42 are to be classified in the heading appropriate to the base or to the acid (including phenol or enol-function compounds) from which they are formed, whichever occurs last in numerical order in the Chapter;
      (iii) Co-ordination compounds, other than products classifiable in sub-Chapter Ⅺ or heading 29.41, are to be classified in the heading which occurs last in numberical order in chapter 29. among those appropriate to the fragments formed by "cleaving" of all metal bonds, other than metal carbon bonds.
   (d) Metal alcoholates are to be classified in the same heading as the corresponding alcohols except in the case of ethanol (heading No. 29.05).
   (e) Halides of carboxylic acids are to be classified in the same heading as the corresponding acids.
6. The compounds of headings No. 29.30 and 29.31 are organic compounds the molecules of which contain, in addition to atoms of hydrogen, oxygen or nitrogen, atoms of other non-metals or of metals (such assulphur, arsenic or lead) directly linked to carbon atoms.
   Heading No. 29.30 (organo-sulphur compounds) and heading No. 29.31 (other organo-inorganic compounds) do not include sulphonated or halogenated derivatives (including compound derivatives) which, apart from hydrogen, oxygen and nitrogen, only have directly linked to carbon the atoms of sulphur or of a halogen which give them their nature of sulphonated or halogenated derivatives (or compound derivatives).
7. Headings No. 29.32, 29.33 and 29.34 do not include epoxides with a three-membered ring, ketone peroxides, cyclic polymers of aldehydes or of thioaldehydes, anhydrides of polybasic carboxylic acids, cyclic esters of polyhydric alcohols or phenols with polybasic acids, or imides of polybasic acids.
   These provisions apply only when the ring-position hetero-atoms are those resulting solely form the cyclising function or functions here listed.
8. For the purposes of heading No. 29.37:
   (a) the term "hormones" includes hormone-releasing or hormone-stimulating factors, hormone inhibitors and hormone antagonists (anti-hormones);
   (b) the expression "used primarily as hormones" applies not only to hormone derivatives and structural analogues used primarily for their hormonal effect, but also to those derivatives and structural analogues used primarily as intermediates in the synthesis of products of this heading.

子目注释：

一、属于本章任一税目项下的一种(组)化合物的衍生物，如果该税目其他子目未明确将其包括在内，而且有关的子目中又无列名为“其他”的子目，则应与该种(组)化合物归入同一子目。

二、第二十九章注释三不适用于本章的子目。

税则号列	货品名称〔CIQ 扩展编码及品名－T2 表示见附表 2〕	最惠(%)	暂定税率	普通	增值/消费	出口退税	计量单位	监管条件/特殊证件	检验检疫	对美关税	亚太上/下
	第一分章　烃类及其卤化、磺化、硝化或亚硝化衍生物										
29.01	**无环烃：**										
2901.1000	-饱和〔301 危险化学品，气体；302 危险化学品，易燃液体；303 其他化工产品〕	2		30	13/	13	千克	/13		7	
	-不饱和：										
2901.2100	--乙烯〔999〕	2	1	20	13/	13	千克	AB/13	MN	26	
2901.2200	--丙烯〔999〕	2	1	20	13/	13	千克	AB/13	MN	26	
	--丁烯及其异构体：										
2901.2310	---1-丁烯〔999〕	2		20	13/	13	千克	AB/13	MN		
2901.2320	---2-丁烯〔999〕	2		20	13/	13	千克	AB/13	MN	7	1.6/1.6
2901.2330	---2-甲基丙烯〔999〕	2		20	13/	13	千克	/13		27	
	--1,3-丁二烯及异戊二烯：										
2901.2410	---1.3-丁二烯〔999〕	2		20	13/	13	千克	AB/13	MN	27	
2901.2420	---异戊二烯〔999〕	2		20	13/	13	千克	/13		27	
	--其他：										
2901.2910	---异戊烯〔301〕	2		30	13/	13	千克	AB/13	MN		1.6/1.6
2901.2920	---乙炔〔999〕	2		45	13/	13	千克	AB/13	MN	27	1.6/1.6
2901.2990	---其他										
2901.2990 10	诱虫烯〔999〕	2		30	13/	9,13	千克	S/13		7	
2901.2990 90	其他不饱和无环烃〔301 危险化学品，气体；302 危险化学品，易燃液体；303 其他化工产品〕	2		30	13/	13	千克	/13		7	
29.02	**环烃：**										
	-环烷烃、环烯及环萜烯：										
2902.1100	--环已烷〔999〕	2		30	13/	13	千克	AB/13	MN	27	
	--其他：										
2902.1910	---蒎烯〔301 危险化学品，不用作食品添加剂；302 危险化学品，用作食品添加剂〕	2		30	13/	13	千克	/13		7	
2902.1920	---4-烷基-4’-烷基双环已烷〔999〕	2		30	13/	13	千克	/1			
2902.1990	---其他										
2902.1990 11	1－甲基环丙烯〔999〕	2		30	13/	9,13	千克	S/13		27	
2902.1990 12	d－柠檬烯〔301 危险化学品，不用作食品添加剂，302 危险化学品，用作食品添加剂〕	2		30	13/	9,13	千克	/13		27	
2902.1990 90	其他环烷烃、环烯及环萜稀〔301 危险化学品，气体；302 危险化学品，易燃液体；303 危险化学品，易燃固体；304 其他化工品〕	2		30	13/	13	千克	/13		27	
2902.2000	-苯〔999〕	2	2	20	13/	0	千克	AB/13	MN	27	
2902.3000	-甲苯〔999〕	2		30	13/	13	千克	23AB/13	MN	27	
	-二甲苯：										
2902.4100	--邻二甲苯〔999〕	2		20	13/	13	千克	/13		27	
2902.4200	--间二甲苯〔999〕	2		20	13/	13	千克	/13		27	
2902.4300	--对二甲苯〔999〕	2		20	13/	13	千克	/13		27	
2902.4400	--混合二甲苯异构体〔999〕	2		20	13/	13	千克	/13		27	
2902.5000	-苯乙烯〔999〕	2		30	13/	13	千克	AB/13	MN	27	1.3/1.3
2902.6000	-乙苯〔999〕	2		30	13/	13	千克	AB/13	MN	27	
2902.7000	-异丙基苯〔999〕	2		30	13/	13	千克	AB/13	MN	27	
	-其他：										
2902.9010	---四氢萘〔999〕	2		11	13/	13	千克	/1		12	
2902.9020	---精萘〔999〕	2		35	13/	13	千克	AB/13	MN	22	1.6/1.6
2902.9030	---十二烷基苯〔999〕	2		30	13/	13	千克	/1			
2902.9040	---4-(4’-烷基环已基)环已基乙烯〔999〕	2		30	13/	13	千克	/1			
2902.9050	---1-烷基-4-(4-烷烯基-1,1’-双环已基)苯〔999〕	2		30	13/	9,13	千克	/1			
2902.9090	---其他〔301 危险化学品，易燃液体；302 危险化学品，易燃固体；303 危险化学品，杂项物质；304 其他危险化学品；305 其他化工品〕	2		30	13/	9,13	千克	/13		22	
29.03	**烃的卤化衍生物：**										
	-无环烃的饱和氯化衍生物：										
2903.1100	--一氯甲烷及氯乙烷〔999〕	5.5		30	13/	13	千克	/13		10.5	
2903.1200	--二氯甲烷										
2903.1200 01	纯度在 99％及以上的二氯甲烷〔999〕	8		30	13/	13	千克	/13		18	
2903.1200 90	其他二氯甲烷〔999〕	8		30	13/	13	千克	/13		18	
2903.1300	--氯仿(三氯甲烷)〔999〕	10		30	13/	13	千克	23AB/13	MN		9/9
2903.1400	--四氯化碳										
2903.1400 10	四氯化碳(受控用途)(CTC)〔999〕	8		30	13/	13	千克	89/13			
2903.1400 90	四氯化碳(用于受控用途除外)(CTC)〔999〕	8		30	13/	13	千克	49xy/13			
2903.1500	--1,2-二氯乙烷(ISO)〔301 易燃液体，需申报仅用于工业用途不用于食品添加剂无检疫要求，302 属于危险化学品的食品添加剂〕	5.5	1	30	13/	0	千克	AB/13	MRNS	26	
	--其他：										
2903.1910	---1,1,1-三氯乙烷(甲基氯仿)										

Subheading Notes:

1. Within any one heading of this Chapter, derivatives of a chemical compound (or group of chemical compounds) are to be classified in the same subheading as that compound (or group of compounds) provided that they are not more specifically covered by any other subheading and that there is no residual subheading named "other" in the series of subheadings concerned.
2. Note 3 of Chapter 29 does not apply to the subheading of this Chapter.

协定税率 %								RCEP		特惠税率 %			Article Description
东/冰/格	巴基斯坦	韩国	瑞士上/下	哥/秘/柬	澳/毛	新西/坡/智	中国港/澳/台	东盟及马来/澳/韩	日/新	亚太2国	老/柬/缅	98/97/95	
													Ⅰ. HYDROCARBONS AND THEIR HALOGENATED, SULPHONATED, NITRATED OR NITROSATED DERIVATIVES
													Acyclic hydrocarbons:
0/0/0	0	0	0/0	0/0/0	0/0	0//0	0/0/	0/1.8/0	0/1.8			0/0/0	-Saturated
													-Unsaturated:
0/0/0	0	0.4	0/0	0/0/0	0/0	0/0/0	0/0/	0/0/1.8	1.9/0			0/0/0	--Ethylene
0/0/0	0	0.4	0/0	0/0/0	0/0	0//0	0/0/0	0/0/1.8	1.9/0			0/0/0	--Propene (propylene)
													--Butene (butylene) and isomers thereof:
0/0/0	0	0.4	0/0	0/0/0	0/0	0//0	0/0/	0/0/1.8	1.8/0			0/0/0	---1-butene
0/0/0	0	0	0/0	0/0/0	0/0	0//0	0/0/	0/0/0	0/0			0/0/0	---2-butene
0/0/0	0	0	0/0	0/0/0	0/0	0//0	0/0/	0/1.8/0	0/1.8			0/0/0	---2-methyl-propene
													--Buta-1, 3-diene and isoprene:
0/0/0	0	0.4	0/0	0/0/0	0/0	0//0	0/0/0	0/0/1.8	1.8/0			0/0/0	---Buta-1,3-diene
0/0/0	0	0.9	0/0	0/0/0	0/0	0//0	0/0/0	1.8/1.8/1.8	1.9/1.8			0/0/0	---Isoprene
													--Other:
0/0/0	0	0	0/0	0/0/0	0/0	0//0	0/0/	0/0/0	0/0			0/0/0	---Isopentene
0/0/0	0	0	0/0	0/0/0	0/0	0//0	0/0/	0/0/0	0/0			0/0/0	---Acetylene
													---Other
0/0/0	0	0.4	0/0	0/0/0	0/0	0//0	0/0/	0/0/1.8	1.8/0			0/0/0	Muscalure
0/0/0	0	0.4	0/0	0/0/0	0/0	0//0	0/0/	0/0/1.8	1.8/0			0/0/0	Other unsaturated acyclic hydrocarbon
													Cyclic hydrocarbons:
													-Cyclanes, cyclenes and cycloterpenes:
0/0/0	0	0	0/0	0/0/0	0/0	0//0	0/0/	0/0/0	0/0			0/0/0	--Cyclohexane
													--Other:
0/0/0	0	0	0/0	0/0/0	0/0	0//0	0/0/	0/0/0	0/0			0/0/0	---Pinene
0/0/0	0	0	0/0	0/0/0	0/0	0//0	0/0/	0/0/0	0/0			0/0/0	---4-alkyl-4'-alkyl-bicyclohexane
													---Other
0/0/0	0	0	0/0	0/0/0	0/0	0//0	0/0/	0/1.8/0	0/1.8			0/0/0	1-methyl cyclopropene
0/0/0	0	0	0/0	0/0/0	0/0	0//0	0/0/	0/1.8/0	0/1.8			0/0/0	D-limonene
0/0/0	0	0	0/0	0/0/0	0/0	0//0	0/0/	0/1.8/0	0/1.8			0/0/0	Other cyclanes, cyclenes and cycloterpenes
0/0/0	0	0.9	0/0	0/0/0	0/0	0//0	0/0/	0/1.8/1.8	1.9/1.8			0/0/0	-Benzene
0/0/0	0	0.9	0/0	0/0/0	0/0	0/0/0	0/0/	1.8/1.8/1.8	1.9/1.8			0/0/0	-Toluene
													-Xylenes:
0/0/0	0	0.4	0/0	0/0/0	0/0	0//0	0/0/0	0/0/1.8	1.8/0			0/0/0	--*o*-Xylene
0/0/0	0	0	0/0	0/0/0	0/0	0//0	0/0/0	0/0/0	1.8/0			0/0/0	--*m*-Xylene
0/0/	0		0.2/0.2	0/0/0	0/0	0/0/0	0/0/0	1.9/1.9/	/1.9			0/0/0	--*p*-Xylene
0/0/0	0	0	0/0	0/0/0	0/0	0//0	0/0/0	0/0/0	1.8/0			0/0/0	Mixed xylene isomers
/0/0	0	1.2	0.2/0.2	0/0/1.9	0/0	0//0	0/0/	1.9/1.9/2	1.9/2			0//	-Styrene
0/0/0	0	0.4	0/0	0/0/0	0/0	0//0	0/0/	1.8/1.8/1.8	1.9/1.8			0/0/0	-Ethylbenzene
0/0/0	0	0	0/0	0/0/0	0/0	0/0/0	0/0/	0/0/0	0/0			0/0/0	-Cumene
													-Other:
0/0/0	0	0	0/0	0/0/0	0/0	0//0	0/0/	0/0/0	0/0			0/0/0	---Tetrahydronaphthalene (tetralin)
0/0/0	0	0.9	0/0	0/0/0	0/0	0//0	0/0/	1.8/1.8/1.8	1.9/1.8			0/0/0	---Naphthalene
0/0/0	0		0/0	0/0/0	0/0	0//0	0/0/0	2/2/	/2			0/0/0	---Dodecylbenzene
0/0/0	0	0	0/0	0/0/0	0/0	0//0	0/0/	0/0/0	0/0			0/0/0	---4-(4'-alkyl cyclohexyl) cyclohexyl ethylene
0/0/0	0	0	0/0	0/0/0	0/0	0//0	0/0/	0/1.8/0	0/1.8			0/0/0	---1-Alkyl-N－4(N－4alkeny-1,1'-dicyclohexyl) benzene
0/0/0	0	0	0/0	0/0/0	0/0	0//0	0/0/	0/1.8/0	0/1.8			0/0/0	---Other
													Halogenated derivatives of hydrocarbons:
													-Saturated chlorinated derivatives of acyclic hydrocarbons:
0/0/0	0	0	0/0	0/0/0	0/0	0//0	0/0/	0/0/0	0/0			0/0/0	--Chloromethane (methyl chloride) and chloroethane (ethyl chloride)
													--Dichloromethane (methylene chloride)
0/0/0	2	3.7	0/0	0/0/0	0/0	0//0	0/0/	7.5/7.6/7.5	7.5/7.6			0/0/0	Dichloromethane (methylene chloride) (purity≥99%)
0/0/0	2	3.7	0/0	0/0/0	0/0	0//0	0/0/	7.5/7.6/7.5	7.5/7.6			0/0/0	Other dichloromethane (methylene chloride)
0/0/0	3.5	2	0/0	0/0/0	0/0	0//0	0/0/0	0/0/9	9.1/0			0/0/0	--Chloroform (trichloromethane)
													--Carbon tetrachloride
0/0/0	2	0	0/0	0/0/0	0/0	0//0	0/0/	0/0/0	7.3/0			0/0/0	Carbon tetrachloride, other than for cleaner preparation
0/0/0	2	0	0/0	0/0/0	0/0	0//0	0/0/	0/0/0	7.3/0			0/0/0	Carbon tetrachloride, for cleaner preparation
5/0/0		0	0/0	0//0	0/0	0//0	0/0/	5/5/	/5			0/0/	--1,2-Dichloroethane (ISO) (ethylene dichloride)
													--Other:
													---1,1,1-Trichloroethane (methylchloro form)

税则号列		货品名称〔CIQ 扩展编码及品名—T2 表示见附表 2〕	最惠(%)	暂定税率	普通	增值/消费	出口退税	计量单位	监管条件/特殊证件	检验检疫	对美关税	亚太上/下
2903.1910	10	1,1,1—三氯乙烷/甲基氯仿(受控用途)(TCA)〔999〕	8		30	13/	13	千克	18AB/13	MN		
2903.1910	90	1,1,1—三氯乙烷/甲基氯仿(用于受控用途除外)(TCA)〔999〕	8		30	13/	13	千克	14Axy/13	M		
2903.1990		---其他〔301 危险化学品,易燃液体;302 危险化学品,毒性物质;303 危险化学品,杂项物质;304 其他危险化学品 ;305 其他化工品〕	5.5		30	13/	13	千克	/13		30.5	
		-无环烃的不饱和氯化衍生物:										
2903.2100		--氯乙烯〔999〕	5.5	1	30	13/	13	千克	AB/13	MN		3.6/3.6
2903.2200		--三氯乙烯〔999〕	8		30	13/	13	千克	AB/13	MN	13	
2903.2300		--四氯乙烯(全氯乙烯)〔999〕	5.5		30	13/	13	千克	AB/13	MN	30.5	4.4/4.4
		--其他:										
2903.2910		---3-氯-1-丙烯(氯丙烯)〔999〕	5.5		30	13/	13	千克	/13		10.5	
2903.2990		---其他										
2903.2990	10	1,1-二氯乙烯〔999〕	5.5		30	13/	13	千克	/13			
2903.2990	90	其他无环烃的不饱和氯化衍生物〔301 危险化学品,易燃液体;302 危险化学品,毒性物质;303 危险化学品,腐蚀性物质;304 其他化工产品质〕	5.5		30	13/	13	千克	/13			
		-无环烃的饱和氟化衍生物:										
2903.4100		--三氟甲烷(HFC—23)〔999〕	5.5		30	13/	13	千克	14xy/13			
2903.4200		--二氟甲烷(HFC—32)〔999〕	5.5		30	13/	13	千克	14xy/13			
2903.4300		--一氟甲烷(HFC—41)、1,2—二氟乙烷(HFC—152)及 1,1—二氟乙烷(HFC—152a)〔301 危险化学品,气体,302 其他化工产品〕	5.5		30	13/	13	千克	14xy/13			
2903.4400		--五氟乙烷(HFC—125)、1,1,1—三氟乙烷(HFC— 143a)及 1,1,2—三氟乙烷(HFC—143)〔301 危险化学品,气体,302 其他化工产品〕	5.5		30	13/	13	千克	14xy/13			
2903.4500		--1,1,1,2—四氟乙烷(HFC—134a)及 1,1,2,2— 四氟乙烷(HFC—134)〔999〕	5.5		30	13/	13	千克	14xy/13			
2903.4600		--1,1,1,2,3,3,3—七氟丙烷(HFC—227ea)、1,1,1,2,2,3—六氟丙烷(HFC—236cb)、1,1, 1,2,3,3—六氟丙烷(HFC—236ea)、1,1,1,3, 3,3—六氟丙烷(HFC—236fa)〔999〕	5.5		30	13/	13	千克	14xy/13			
2903.4700		--1,1,1,3,3—五氟丙烷(HFC—245fa)及 1,1, 2,2,3—五氟丙烷(HFC—245ca)〔999〕	5.5		30	13/	13	千克	14xy/13			
2903.4800		--1,1,1,3,3—五氟丁烷(HFC—365mfc)及 1,1, 1,2,2,3,4,5,5,5—十氟戊烷(HFC—43—10mee)〔999〕	5.5		30	13/	13	千克	14xy/13			
2903.4900		--其他〔301 危险化学品,气体,302 其他化工产品〕	5.5		30	13/	13	千克	14xy/13			
		-无环烃的不饱和氟化衍生物:										
2903.5100		--2,3,3,3—四氟丙烯(HFO—1234yf)、1,3,3, 3—四氟丙烯(HFO—1234ze)及(Z)—1,1,1,4,4, 4—六氟—2—丁烯(HFO—1336mzz)〔999〕	5.5		30	13/	13	千克	14xy/13			
		--其他:										
2903.5910		---1,1,3,3,3—五氟—2—三氟甲基—1—丙烯(全氟异丁烯;八氟异丁烯)〔999〕	5.5		30	13/	13	千克	23/13			
2903.5990		---其他〔301 危险化学品,气体,302 其他化工产品〕	5.5		30	13/	13	千克	14xy/13			
		-无环烃的溴化或碘化衍生物:										
2903.6100		--甲基溴(溴甲烷)〔999〕	5.5		30	13/	0	千克	14ABxy/13	MN		
2903.6200		--二溴乙烷(ISO)(1,2—二溴乙烷)〔999〕	5.5		30	13/	0	千克	89/13			
2903.6900		--其他										
2903.6900	10	二溴甲烷、碘甲烷〔301 危险化学品,毒性物质,302 其他危险化学品〕	5.5		30	13/	13	千克	AB/13	MN		
2903.6900	90	其他无环烃的溴化或碘化衍生物〔301 危险化学品,气体,302 危险化学品,易燃液体,303 危险化学品,毒性物质,304 危险化学品,杂项物质,305 其他危险化学品,306 其他化工品〕	5.5		30	13/	13	千克	/13			
		-含有两种或两种以上不同卤素的无环烃卤化衍生物:										
2903.7100		---一氯二氟甲烷(HCFC—22)〔999〕	5.5		30	13/	13	千克	14ABxy/13	MN		
2903.7200		--二氯三氟乙烷(HCFC—123)〔999〕	5.5		30	13/	13	千克	14xy/1			
2903.7300		--二氯一氟乙烷(HCFC—141,141b)〔999〕	5.5		30	13/	13	千克	14xy/1			
2903.7400		---一氯二氟乙烷(HCFC—142,142b)〔301 危险化学品,气体,302 其他化工品〕	5.5		30	13/	13	千克	14xy/13			
2903.7500		--二氯五氟丙烷(HCFC—225,225ca,225cb)〔999〕	5.5		30	13/	13	千克	14xy/1			
2903.7600		--溴氯二氟甲烷(Halon—1211)、一溴三氟甲烷(Halon—1301)及二溴四氟乙烷(Halon—2402)										
2903.7600	10	溴氯二氟甲烷(Halon—1211)〔999〕	5.5		30	13/	13	千克	14xy/13			
2903.7600	20	溴三氟甲烷(Halon—1301)〔999〕	5.5		30	13/	13	千克	14ABxy/13	MN		
2903.7600	30	二溴四氟乙烷(Halon—2402)〔999〕	5.5		30	13/	13	千克	/13			
		--其他,仅含氟和氯的全卤化物:										
2903.7710		---三氯氟甲烷〔999〕	5.5		30	13/	13	千克	14xy/1			
2903.7720		---其他仅含氟和氯的甲烷、乙烷及丙烷的全卤化物										
2903.7720	11	二氯二氟甲烷(CFC-12)〔999〕	5.5		30	13/	13	千克	14ABxy/13	MN		
2903.7720	12	三氯三氟乙烷(用于受控用途除外)(CFC—113)〔999〕	5.5		30	13/	13	千克	14xy/13			
2903.7720	13	三氯三氟乙烷(受控用途)(CFC—113)〔999〕	5.5		30	13/	13	千克	89/13			

协定税率 %								RCEP		特惠税率 %			Article Description
东/冰/格	巴基斯坦	韩国	瑞士上/下	哥/秘/柬	澳/毛	新西/坡/智	中国港/澳/台	东盟及马来/澳/韩	日/新	亚太2国	老/柬/缅	98/97/95	
0/0/0	2	0	0/0	0/0/0	0/0	0/ /0	0/0/	0/0/0	7.3/0			0/0/0	1,1,1—trichloroethane / methyl chloroform (controlled use) (TCA)
0/0/0	2	0	0/0	0/0/0	0/0	0/ /0	0/0/	0/0/0	7.3/0			0/0/0	1,1,1—trichloroethane / methyl chloroform (except for controlled uses) (TCA)
0/0/0	4	1.1	0/0	0/0/0	0/0	0/ /0	0/0/	0/0/5	5/0			0/0/0	---Other
													-Unsaturated chlorinated derivatives of acyclic hydrocarbons:
0/0/0	0	0	0/0	0/0/0	0/0	0/ /0	0/0/0	0/0/0	5.2/0			0/0/0	--Vinyl chloride (chloroethylene)
0/0/0	2	3.7	0/0	0/0/0	0/0	0/ /0	0/0/	7.2/7.2/7.2	7.3/7.2			0/0/0	--Trichloroethylene
0/0/0	0	0	0/0	0/0/0	0/0	0/ /0	0/0/	0/0/0	0/0			0/0/0	--Tetrachloroethylene (perchloroethylene)
													--Other:
0/0/0	0	0	0/0	0/0/0	0/0	0/ /0	0/0/	0/0/0	0/0			0/0/0	---3-Chloro-1-propene (chloropropene)
													---Other
0/0/0	0	0	0/0	0/0/0	0/0	0/ /0	0/0/	0/0/0	0/0			0/0/0	1,1-dichloroethylene
0/0/0	0	0	0/0	0/0/0	0/0	0/ /0	0/0/	0/0/0	0/0			0/0/0	Other unsaturated chlorinated derivatives of acyclic hydrocarbons
													- Saturated fluorinated derivatives of acyclic hydrocarbons:
0/0/0	3.5	0	0/0	0/0/0	0/0	0/ /0	0/0/	0/5/0	0/5			0/0/0	--Trifluoromethane (HFC—23)
0/0/0	3.5	0	0/0	0/0/0	0/0	0/ /0	0/0/	0/5/0	0/5			0/0/0	-- Difluoromethane (HFC—32)
0/0/0	3.5	0	0/0	0/0/0	0/0	0/ /0	0/0/	0/5/0	0/5			0/0/0	-- Fluoromethane (HFC—41), 1,2—difluoroethane (HFC—152) and 1,1— difluoroethane (HFC—152a)
0/0/0	3.5	0	0/0	0/0/0	0/0	0/ /0	0/0/	0/5/0	0/5			0/0/0	-- Pentafluoroethane (HFC—125), 1,1,1—trifluoroethane (HFC—143a) and 1,1,2—trifluoroethane (HFC—143)
0/0/0	3.5	0	0/0	0/0/0	0/0	0/ /0	0/0/	0/5/0	0/5			0/0/0	--1,1,1,2—Tetrafluoroethane (HFC—134a) and 1,1,2,2—tetrafluoroethane (HFC—134)
0/0/0	3.5	0	0/0	0/0/0	0/0	0/ /0	0/0/	0/5/0	0/5			0/0/0	-- 1,1,1,2,3,3,3—Heptafluoropropane (HFC—227ea), 1,1,1,2,2,3— hexafluoropropane (HFC—236cb), 1,1,1,2,3,3—hexafluoropropane (HFC—236ea) and 1,1,1,3,3,3—hexafluoropropane (HFC—236fa)
0/0/0	3.5	0	0/0	0/0/0	0/0	0/ /0	0/0/	0/5/0	0/5			0/0/0	-- 1,1,1,3,3—Pentafluoropropane (HFC—245fa) and 1,1,2,2,3— pentafluoropropane (HFC—245ca)
0/0/0	3.5	0	0/0	0/0/0	0/0	0/ /0	0/0/	0/5/0	0/5			0/0/0	-- 1,1,1,3,3—Pentafluorobutane (HFC—365mfc) and 1,1,1,2,2,3,4,5,5,5—decafluoropentane (HFC—43—10mee)
0/0/0	3.5	0	0/0	0/0/0	0/0	0/ /0	0/0/	0/5/0	0/5			0/0/0	-- Other
													- Unsaturated fluorinated derivatives of acyclic hydrocarbons:
0/0/0	3.5	0	0/0	0/0/0	0/0	0/ /0	0/0/	0/5/0	0/5			0/0/0	-- 2,3,3,3—Tetrafluoropropene (HFO—1234yf), 1,3,3,3 — tetrafluoropropene (HFO—1234ze) and (Z)—1,1,1,4,4,4—hexafluoro— 2—butene (HFO—1336mzz)
													-- Other:
0/0/0	0	0	0/0	0/0/0	0/0	0/ /0	0/0/	0/0/0	0/0			0/0/0	---1,1,3,3,3—Pentafluoro—2 trifluoromethyl—1—propylene (perfluoroisobutylene; octafluoroisobutylene)
0/0/0	3.5	0	0/0	0/0/0	0/0	0/ /0	0/0/	0/5/0	0/5			0/0/0	--- Other
													- Brominated or iodinated derivatives of acyclic hydrocarbons :
0/0/0	3.5	0	0/0	0/0/0	0/0	0/ /0	0/0/	0/5/0	0/5			0/0/0	-- Methyl bromide (bromomethane)
0/0/0	3.5	0	0/0	0/0/0	0/0	0/ /0	0/0/	0/0/0	0/0			0/0/0	-- Ethylene dibromide (ISO) (1,2—dibromoethane)
													-- Other
0/0/0	3.5	0	0/0	0/0/0	0/0	0/ /0	0/0/	0/5/0	0/5			0/0/0	Dibromomethane, iodomethane
0/0/0	3.5	0	0/0	0/0/0	0/0	0/ /0	0/0/	0/5/0	0/5			0/0/0	Brominated or iodized derivatives of other acyclic hydrocarbons
													-Halogenated derivatives of acyclic hydrocarbons containing two or more different halogens:
0/0/0	3.5	0	0/0	0/0/0	0/0	0/ /0	0/0/	0/0/0	0/0			0/0/0	--Chlorodifluoromethane
0/0/0	3.5	0	0/0	0/0/0	0/0	0/ /0	0/0/	0/0/0	0/0			0/0/0	--Dichlorotrifluoroethane
0/0/0	3.5	0	0/0	0/0/0	0/0	0/ /0	0/0/	0/0/0	0/0			0/0/0	--Dichlorofluoroethane
0/0/0	3.5	0	0/0	0/0/0	0/0	0/ /0	0/0/	0/0/0	0/0			0/0/0	--Chlorodifluoroethane
0/0/0	3.5	0	0/0	0/0/0	0/0	0/ /0	0/0/	0/0/0	0/0			0/0/0	--Dichloropentafluoropropane
													--Bromochlorodifluoromethane、bromotrifluoromethane、and dibromotetrafluoroethanes
0/0/0	0	0	0/0	0/0/0	0/0	0/ /0	0/0/	0/0/0	0/0			0/0/0	Bromochlorodifluoromethane(Halon-1211)
0/0/0	0	0	0/0	0/0/0	0/0	0/ /0	0/0/	0/0/0	0/0			0/0/0	Bromotrifluoromethane(Halon-1301)
0/0/0	0	0	0/0	0/0/0	0/0	0/ /0	0/0/	0/0/0	0/0			0/0/0	Dibromotetrafluoroethane
													--Other,perhalogenated,only with fluorine and chlorine:
0/0/0	3.5	0	0/0	0/0/0	0/0	0/ /0	0/0/	0/0/0	0/0			0/0/0	---Trichlorofluoromethane
													---Other,methane,ethane and propane perhalgenated derivatives only with fluorine and chlorine derivatives
0/0/0	0	0	0/0	0/0/0	0/0	0/ /0	0/0/	0/0/0	0/0			0/0/0	Dichlorodifluoromethane(CFC-12)
0/0/0	0	0	0/0	0/0/0	0/0	0/ /0	0/0/	0/0/0	0/0			0/0/0	Trichlorotrifluoroethanes,other than for cleaner preparation (CFC-113)
0/0/0	0	0	0/0	0/0/0	0/0	0/ /0	0/0/	0/0/0	0/0			0/0/0	Trichlorotrifluoroethanes,for cleaner preparation (CFC-113)

税则号列	货品名称〔CIQ 扩展编码及品名—T2 表示见附表 2〕	最惠(%)	暂定税率	普通	增值/消费	出口退税	计量单位	监管条件/特殊证件	检验检疫	对美关税	亚太上/下
2903.7720 14	二氯四氟乙烷(CFC-114)〔999〕	5.5		30	13/	13	千克	14ABxy/13	MN		
2903.7720 15	一氯五氟乙烷(CFC-115)〔999〕	5.5		30	13/	13	千克	14ABxy/13	MN		
2903.7720 16	一氯三氟甲烷(CFC-13)〔999〕	5.5		30	13/	13	千克	14ABxy/13	MN		
2903.7720 17	五氯一氟乙烷、四氯二氟乙烷(CFC—111、CFC—112)〔999〕	5.5		30	13/	13	千克	14xy/13			
2903.7720 18	七氯一氟丙烷、六氯二氟丙烷、五氯三氟丙烷、四氯四氟丙烷、三氯五氟丙烷、二氯六氟丙烷、一氯七氟丙烷(CFC—211、CFC—212、CFC—213、CFC—214、CFC—215、CFC—216、CFC—217)〔999〕	5.5		30	13/	13	千克	14xy/13			
2903.7720 90	其他仅含氟和氯的甲烷、乙烷及丙烷的全卤化物〔301 危险化学品,易燃液体;302 其他化工产品〕	5.5		30	13/	13	千克	14xy/13			
2903.7790	---其他〔301 危险化学品,气体;302 危险化学品,毒性物质;303 其他化工产品〕	5.5		30	13/	13	千克	/13			
2903.7800	--其他全卤化衍生物〔301 危险化学品,气体;302 其他危险化学品;303 其他化工品〕	5.5		30	13/	13	千克	/13		10.5	
	--其他:										
2903.7910	---其他仅含氟和氯的甲烷、乙烷及丙烷的全卤化衍生物										
2903.7910 11	二氯一氟甲烷(HCFC—21)〔999〕	5.5		30	13/	13	千克	14xy/13			
2903.7910 12	2—氯—1,1,1,2—四氟乙烷(HCFC—124)〔999〕	5.5		30	13/	13	千克	14xy/13			
2903.7910 13	一氯三氟乙烷(HCFC—133)〔999〕	5.5		30	13/	13	千克	14xy/13			
2903.7910 14	1-氟-1,1-二氯乙烷〔999〕	5.5		30	13/	13	千克	/13			
2903.7910 15	1,1-二氟-1-氯乙烷〔999〕	5.5		30	13/	13	千克	/13			
2903.7910 90	其他含氢氯氟烃类物质(这里的烃是指甲烷、乙烷及丙烷)〔999〕	5.5		30	13/	13	千克	14xy/13			
2903.7990	---其他										
2903.7990 10	二溴氯丙烷(1,2-二溴-3-氯丙烷)〔999〕	5.5		30	13/	13	千克	89/13		15.5	
2903.7990 21	其他溴氟代甲烷、乙烷和丙烷〔301 危险化学品,易燃液体,302 其他化工产品〕	5.5		30	13/	13	千克	14xy/13		15.5	
2903.7990 22	溴氯甲烷〔999〕	5.5		30	13/	13	千克	14xy/13		15.5	
2903.7990 90	其他无环烃卤化衍生物(含二种或二种以上不同卤素的其他无环烃卤化衍生物)[T2]	5.5		30	13/	13	千克	/13		15.5	
	-环烷烃、环烯烃或环萜烯烃的卤化衍生物:										
2903.8100	--1,2,3,4,5,6-六氯环己烷[六六六(ISO)],包括林丹(ISO,INN)										
2903.8100 10	林丹(ISO,INN)〔999〕	5.5		30	13/	0	千克	89/13			
2903.8100 20	α-六氯环己烷、β-六氯环己烷〔999〕	5.5		30	13/	0	千克	89/13			
2903.8100 90	其他 1,2,3,4,5,6—六氯环己烷{六六六(ISO)}(混合异构体)〔999〕	5.5		30	13/	0	千克	/13			
2903.8200	--艾氏剂(ISO)、氯丹(ISO)及七氯(ISO)										
2903.8200 10	艾氏剂(ISO)及七氯(ISO)[T2]	5.5		30	13/	0	千克	89/13			
2903.8200 90	氯丹(ISO)(别名八氯化甲桥茚)〔999〕	5.5		30	13/	0	千克	89/13			
2903.8300	--灭蚁灵(ISO)〔999〕	5.5		30	13/	0	千克	89/13			
2903.8900	--其他										
2903.8900 10	毒杀芬〔999〕	5.5		30	13/	0	千克	89/13		30.5	
2903.8900 20	六溴环十二烷〔999〕	5.5		30	13/	13	千克	89/13		30.5	
2903.8900 90	其他环烷烃、环烯烃或环萜烯烃的卤化衍生物〔301 危险化学品,气体;302 危险化学品,易燃液体;303 危险化学品,毒性物质;304 其他化工产品〕	5.5		30	13/	13	千克	/13		30.5	
	-芳烃卤化衍生物:										
	--氯苯、邻二氯苯及对二氯苯:										
2903.9110	---邻二氯苯〔999〕	5.5		30	13/	13	千克	/13			
2903.9190	---其他										
2903.9190 10	1,4-二氯苯(对二氯苯)〔999〕	5.5		30	13/	9,13	千克	S/13		30.5	
2903.9190 90	氯苯〔999〕	5.5		30	13/	13	千克	AB/13	MN	30.5	
2903.9200	--六氯苯(ISO)及滴滴涕(ISO,INN)[1,1,1-三氯-2,2-双(4-氯苯基)乙烷]〔301 危险化学品,杂项物质;302 危险化学品,杂项物质〕	5.5		30	13/	0	千克	89/13			
2903.9300	--五氯苯(ISO)〔999〕	5.5		30	13/	13	千克	89/13			
2903.9400	--六溴联苯〔999〕	5.5		30	13/	13	千克	89/13			
	--其他:										
2903.9910	---对氯甲苯〔999〕	5.5		30	13/	13	千克	AB/13	MN		
2903.9920	---3,4-二氯三氟甲苯〔999〕	5.5		30	13/	13	千克	/1			4.4/4.4
2903.9930	---4-(4'-烷基苯基)-1-(4'-烷基苯基)-2-氟苯〔999〕	5.5		30	13/	13	千克	/1			
2903.9990	---其他										
2903.9990 10	多氯联苯,多溴联苯〔301 危险化学品,杂项物质;302 其他危险化学品;303 其他化工品〕	5.5		30	13/	13	千克	89/13		10.5	
2903.9990 30	多氯三联苯(PCT)〔999〕	5.5		30	13/	13	千克	X/13		10.5	
2903.9990 40	稗草烯〔999〕	5.5		30	13/	0	千克	S/13		10.5	
2903.9990 90	其他芳烃卤化衍生物〔301 危险化学品,易燃液体;302 危险化学品,毒性物质;303 危险化学品,腐蚀性物质;304 危险化学品,杂项物质;305 其他危险化学品;306 其他化工产品〕	5.5		30	13/	13	千克	/13		10.5	
29.04	**烃的磺化、硝化或亚硝化衍生物,不论是否卤化:**										
2904.1000	-仅含磺基的衍生物及其盐和乙酯〔301 危险化学品,腐蚀性物质;302 其他化工产品〕	5.5		30	13/	13	千克	/13		15.5	

协定税率 %								RCEP		特惠税率 %			Article Description
东/冰/格	巴基斯坦	韩国	瑞士上/下	哥/秘/柬	澳/毛	新西/坡/智	中国港/澳/台	东盟及马来/澳/韩	日/新	亚太2国	老/柬/缅	98/97/95	
0/0/0	0	0	0/0	0/0/0	0/0	0//0	0/0/	0/0/0	0/0			0/0/0	Dichlorotetrafluoroethane(CFC-114)
0/0/0	0	0	0/0	0/0/0	0/0	0//0	0/0/	0/0/0	0/0			0/0/0	Chloropentafluoroethane(CFC-115)
0/0/0	0	0	0/0	0/0/0	0/0	0//0	0/0/	0/0/0	0/0			0/0/0	Chlorotrifluoromethane(CFC-13)
0/0/0	0	0	0/0	0/0/0	0/0	0//0	0/0/	0/0/0	0/0			0/0/0	Pentachloromonofluoroethane, tetrachlorodifluoroethane (CFC—111, CFC—112)
0/0/0	0	0	0/0	0/0/0	0/0	0//0	0/0/	0/0/0	0/0			0/0/0	Heptachlor monofluoropropane, hexachlorodifluoropropane, pentachlorotrifluoropane, tetrachlorofluoropropane, trichloro pentafluoropropane, dichlorohexafluoropropane, monochloro heptafluoropropane (CFC－211, CFC－212, CFC－213, CFC—214, CFC—215, CFC—216, CFC—217)
0/0/0	0	0	0/0	0/0/0	0/0	0//0	0/0/	0/0/0	0/0			0/0/0	Other methane, ethane and propane halogenated derivatives only with fluorine and bromine
0/0/0	3.5	1.1	0/0	0/0/0	0/0	0//0	0/0/	0/0/5	5/0			0/0/0	---Other
0/0/0	0	0	0/0	0/0/0	0/0	0//0	0/0/	0/0/0	0/0			0/0/0	--Other perhalogenated derivatives
													--Other:
													---Other methane, ethane and propane halogenated derivatives only with fluorine and chlorine
0/0/0	3.5	0	0/0	0/0/0	0/0	0//0	0/0/	0/0/0	0/0			0/0/0	Dichlorofluoromethane
0/0/0	3.5	0	0/0	0/0/0	0/0	0//0	0/0/	0/0/0	0/0			0/0/0	1,1,1,2-Tetrafluoro-2,2-dichloroethane
0/0/0	3.5	0	0/0	0/0/0	0/0	0//0	0/0/	0/0/0	0/0			0/0/0	Trifluoromonochloroethane
0/0/0	3.5	0	0/0	0/0/0	0/0	0//0	0/0/	0/0/0	0/0			0/0/0	1,1-dichloro-1-fluoroethane
0/0/0	3.5	0	0/0	0/0/0	0/0	0//0	0/0/	0/0/0	0/0			0/0/0	1,1-Difluoro--1-chloroethane
0/0/0	3.5	0	0/0	0/0/0	0/0	0//0	0/0/	0/0/0	0/0			0/0/0	Other methane, ethane and propane halogenated derivatives with fluorine and chlorine
													---Other
0/0/0	0	0	0/0	0/0/0	0/0	0//0	0/0/	0/0/0	0/0			0/0/0	Dibromochloropropane(1,2-dibromo-3chloropropane)
0/0/0	0	0	0/0	0/0/0	0/0	0//0	0/0/	0/0/0	0/0			0/0/0	Other methane, ethane and propane only with fluorine and bromine
0/0/0	0	0	0/0	0/0/0	0/0	0//0	0/0/	0/0/0	0/0			0/0/0	Bromochloromethane
0/0/0	0	0	0/0	0/0/0	0/0	0//0	0/0/	0/0/0	0/0			0/0/0	Other Halogenated derivatives of acyclic hydro- carbons containing two or more different halogens
													-Halogenated derivatives of cyclanic, cyclenic or cycloterpenic hydrocarbons:
													--1,2,3,4,5,6-Hexachlorocyclohexane[HCH(ISO)], including lindane(ISO,INN)
0/0/0	0	0	0/0	0/0/0	0/0	0//0	0/0/	0/0/0	0/0			0/0/0	Lindan(ISO,INN)
0/0/0	0	0	0/0	0/0/0	0/0	0//0	0/0/	0/0/0	0/0			0/0/0	α-hexachlorocyclohexane, β-hexachlorocyclohexane
0/0/0	0	0	0/0	0/0/0	0/0	0//0	0/0/	0/0/0	0/0			0/0/0	1,2,3,4,5,6-hexachlorocyclohexane
													--Aldrin(ISO)chlordane(ISO) and heptachlor(ISO)
0/0/0	0	0	0/0	0/0/0	0/0	0//0	0/0/	0/0/0	0/0			0/0/0	Aldrin(ISO), haptachlor(ISO)
0/0/0	0	0	0/0	0/0/0	0/0	0//0	0/0/	0/0/0	0/0			0/0/0	Chlordane(ISO)
0/0/0	0	0	0/0	0/0/0	0/0	0//0	0/0/	0/0/0	0/0			0/0/0	--Mirex(ISO)
													--Other
0/0/0	0	0	0/0	0/0/0	0/0	0//0	0/0/	0/0/0	0/0			0/0/0	Camphechlor
0/0/0	0	0	0/0	0/0/0	0/0	0//0	0/0/	0/0/0	0/0			0/0/0	Hexabromocyclododecane
0/0/0	0	0	0/0	0/0/0	0/0	0//0	0/0/	0/0/0	0/0			0/0/0	Other halogenatives of acycanlic, cyclenic or cycloterpenic hydrocarbons
													-Halogenated derivatives of aromatic hydrocarbons:
													--Chlorobenzene, o-dichlorobenzene and p-dichlorobenzene:
0/0/0	0	1.1	0/0	0/0/0	0/0	0//0	0/0/	0/0/5	5/0			0/0/0	---o-Dichlorobenzene
													---Other
0/0/0	0	0	0/0	0/0/0	0/0	0//0	0/0/	0/0/0	0/0			0/0/0	1,4-dichlorobenzene
0/0/0	0	0	0/0	0/0/0	0/0	0//0	0/0/	0/0/0	0/0			0/0/0	Cldorobenzene
0/0/0	0	0	0/0	0/0/0	0/0	0//0	0/0/	0/0/0	0/0			0/0/0	--Hexachlorobenzene(ISO) and DDT(ISO)clofenotane(INN) [1,1,1-trichloro-2,2-bis(p-chlorophenyl)ethane]
0/0/0	0	0	0/0	0/0/0	0/0	0//0	0/0/	0/0/0	0/0			0/0/0	--Pentachlorobenzene(ISO)
0/0/0	0	0	0/0	0/0/0	0/0	0//0	0/0/	0/0/0	0/0			0/0/0	--Hexabromobiphenyls
													--Other:
0/0/0	0	0	0/0	0/0/0	0/0	0//0	0/0/	0/0/0	0/0			0/0/0	---p-Chlorotoluene
0/0/0	0	0	0/0	0/0/0	0/0	0//0	0/0/	0/0/0	0/0			0/0/0	---3,4-Dichlorotrifluoride toluene
0/0/0	0	0	0/0	0/0/0	0/0	0//0	0/0/	0/0/0	0/0			0/0/0	---4-(4'-alkyl phenyl)-1-(4'-alkyl phenyl)-2-fluorobenzene
													Other
0/0/0	0	0	0/0	0/0/0	0/0	0//0	0/0/	0/0/0	0/0			0/0/0	Polychlorinated biphenyls, polybromobiphenyl
0/0/0	0	0	0/0	0/0/0	0/0	0//0	0/0/	0/0/0	0/0			0/0/0	Polychlorinated terphenyl(pct)
0/0/0	0	0	0/0	0/0/0	0/0	0//0	0/0/	0/0/0	0/0			0/0/0	Tavron
0/0/0	0	0	0/0	0/0/0	0/0	0//0	0/0/	0/0/0	0/0			0/0/0	Other halogen derivatives of aromatic hydrocarbons
													Sulphonated, nitrated or nitrosated derivatives of hydrocarbons, whether or not halogenated:
0/0/0	0	0	0/0	0/0/0	0/0	0//0	0/0/	0/0/0	0/0			0/0/0	-Derivatives containing only sulpho groups, their salts and ethyl esters

税则号列	货品名称〔CIQ扩展编码及品名－T2表示见附表2〕	最惠(%)	暂定税率	普通	增值/消费	出口退税	计量单位	监管条件/特殊证件	检验检疫	对美关税	亚太上/下
	-仅含硝基或亚硝基的衍生物:										
2904.2010	---硝基苯〔999〕	5.5		20	13/	13	千克	AB/13	MN		4.4/4.4
2904.2020	---硝基甲苯〔301 危险化学品,毒性物质;302 危险化学品,杂项物质〕	5.5		30	13/	13	千克	/13			
2904.2030	---二硝基甲苯〔999〕	5.5		20	13/	13	千克	AB/13	MN		4.4/4.4
2904.2040	---三硝基甲苯(TNT)〔999〕	5.5		40	13/	13	千克	ABk/13	MN		4.4/4.4
2904.2090	---其他										
2904.2090 10	六硝基芪〔999〕	5.5		30	13/	13	千克	3/13		10.5	
2904.2090 20	4-硝基联苯〔999〕	5.5		30	13/	13	千克	/13		10.5	
2904.2090 90	其他仅含硝基或亚硝基衍生物〔301 危险化学品,爆炸品;302 危险化学品,易燃液体;303 危险化学品,易燃固体;304 危险化学品,毒性物质;305 危险化学品,杂项物质;306 其他危险化学品;307 其他化工产品〕	5.5		30	13/	13	千克	/13		10.5	
	-全氟辛基磺酸及其盐和全氟辛基磺酰氟:										
2904.3100	--全氟辛基磺酸〔999〕	5.5		30	13/	13	千克	X/13			
2904.3200	--全氟辛基磺酸铵〔999〕	5.5		30	13/	13	千克	X/13			
2904.3300	--全氟辛基磺酸锂〔999〕	5.5		30	13/	13	千克	X/13			
2904.3400	--全氟辛基磺酸钾〔999〕	5.5		30	13/	13	千克	X/13			
2904.3500	--其他全氟辛基磺酸盐〔999〕	5.5		30	13/	13	千克	X/1			
2904.3600	--全氟辛基磺酰氟〔999〕	5.5		30	13/	13	千克	X/13			
	-其他:										
2904.9100	--三氯硝基甲烷(氯化苦)〔999〕	5.5		30	13/	0	千克	23S/13			
2904.9900	--其他										
2904.9900 11	氯硝丙烷〔999〕	5.5		30	13/	0	千克	S/13		25.5	
2904.9900 12	四氯硝基苯〔999〕	5.5		30	13/	0	千克	S/13		25.5	
2904.9900 13	五氯硝基苯〔999〕	5.5		30	13/	0	千克	S/13		25.5	
2904.9900 90	其他烃的磺化、硝化、亚硝化衍生物(不论是否卤化)〔301 危险化学品,爆炸品;302 危险化学品,易燃固体;303 危险化学品,毒性物质;304 危险化学品,腐蚀性物质;305 危险化学品,杂项物质;306 其他危险化学品;307 其他化工产品〕	5.5		30	13/	13	千克	/13		25.5	
	第二分章 醇类及其卤化、磺化、硝化或亚硝化衍生物										
29.05	**无环醇及其卤化、磺化、硝化或亚硝化衍生物:**										
	-饱和一元醇:										
2905.1100	--甲醇〔999〕	5.5		30	13/	13	千克	AB/13	MN	30.5	
	--丙醇及异丙醇:										
2905.1210	---丙醇〔301 危险化学品,不用作食品添加剂;302 危险化学品,用作食品添加剂〕	5.5		30	13/	13	千克	AB/13	MN	10.5	
2905.1220	---异丙醇〔301 危险化学品,不用作食品添加剂;302 危险化学品,用作食品添加剂〕	5.5		30	13/	13	千克	ABG/13	MN	30.5	
2905.1300	--正丁醇〔301 危险化学品,不用作食品添加剂;302 危险化学品,用作食品添加剂〕	5.5		30	13/	13	千克	AB/13	MRNS	15.5	
	--其他丁醇:										
2905.1410	---异丁醇〔301 危险化学品,不用作食品添加剂;302 危险化学品,用作食品添加剂〕	5.5		30	13/	13	千克	/13		15.5	
2905.1420	---仲丁醇〔999〕	5.5		30	13/	13	千克	/13			
2905.1430	---叔丁醇〔999〕	5.5		30	13/	13	千克	/13		25.5	
	--辛醇及其异构体:										
2905.1610	---正辛醇〔101:2－辛醇,102:非工业用无检疫要求食品添加剂〕	5.5		30	13/	13	千克	/1		30.5	
2905.1690	---其他〔999〕	5.5		30	13/	13	千克	/1		30.5	
2905.1700	--十二醇、十六醇及十八醇〔999〕	7		30	13/	13	千克	/1		32	
	--其他:										
2905.1910	---3,3-二甲基丁-2-醇(频哪基醇)〔999〕	5.5		30	13/	13	千克	23/1			4.4/4.4
2905.1990	---其他										
2905.1990 10	三十烷醇〔999〕	5.5		30	13/	9,13	千克	S/13			
2905.1990 90	其他饱和一元醇〔301 危险化学品,易燃液体;302 危险化学品,易于自燃的物质;303 危险化学品,腐蚀性物质;304 危险化学品,食品添加剂;305 其他化工品,不用作食品添加剂;306 其他化工品,用作食品添加剂〕	5.5		30	13/	13	千克	/13			
	-不饱和一元醇:										
	--无环萜烯醇:										
2905.2210	---香叶醇、橙花醇(3,7-二甲基-2,6-辛二烯-1-醇)〔101 反式－3－已烯醇,102 香叶醇,103 橙花醇〕	5.5		30	13/	13	千克	/1		10.5	
2905.2220	---香茅醇(3,7-二甲基-6-辛烯-1-醇)〔999〕	5.5		30	13/	13	千克	/1		10.5	
2905.2230	---芳樟醇〔102 无检疫要求食品添加剂,301 需申报仅用于工业用途不用于食品添加剂无检疫要求的化学品〕	5.5		30	13/	13	千克	A/1	R	10.5	
2905.2290	---其他〔301 危险化学品,易燃液体;302 其他化工品,不用作食品添加剂;303 其他化工品,不用作食品添加剂〕	5.5		30	13/	13	千克	/1		30.5	
2905.2900	--其他[T2]	5.5		30	13/	13	千克	/13		30.5	
	-二元醇:										
2905.3100	--1,2-乙二醇〔999〕	5.5		30	13/	13	千克	/1		30.5	

协定税率 %								RCEP		特惠税率 %			Article Description
东/冰/格	巴基斯坦	韩国	瑞士上/下	哥/秘/柬	澳/毛	新西/坡/智	中国港/澳/台	东盟及马来/澳/韩	日/新	亚太2国	老/柬/缅	98/97/95	
													-Derivatives containing only nitro or only nitroso groups:
0/0/0	0	0	0/0	0/0/0	0/0	0//0	0/0/	0/0/0	0/0			0/0/0	---Nitrobenzene
0/0/0	0	0	0/0	0/0/0	0/0	0//0	0/0/	0/0/0	0/0			0/0/0	---Nitrotoluene and nitrochlorobenzene
0/0/0	0	0	0/0	0/0/0	0/0	0//0	0/0/	0/0/0	0/0			0/0/0	---Dinitrotoluene and dinitrochlorobenzene
0/0/0	0	0	0/0	0/0/0	0/0	0//0	0/0/	0/0/0	0/0			0/0/0	---Trinitrotoluene(TNT)
													---Other
0/0/0	0	0	0/0	0/0/0	0/0	0//0	0/0/	0/0/0	0/0			0/0/0	Hexanitrostilbene
0/0/0	0	0	0/0	0/0/0	0/0	0//0	0/0/	0/0/0	0/0			0/0/0	4-Nitrobiphenyl
0/0/0	0	0	0/0	0/0/0	0/0	0//0	0/0/	0/0/0	0/0			0/0/0	Other derivatives containing only nitro or only nitroso groups
													-Perfluorooctane sulphonic acid, its salts and perfluorooctane sulphonyl fluoride :
0/0/0	0	0	0/0	0/0/0	0/0	0//0	0/0/	0/0/0	0/0			0/0/0	--Perfluorooctane sulphonic acid
0/0/0	0	0	0/0	0/0/0	0/0	0//0	0/0/	0/0/0	0/0			0/0/0	--Ammonium perfluorooctane sulphonate
0/0/0	0	0	0/0	0/0/0	0/0	0//0	0/0/	0/0/0	0/0			0/0/0	--Lithium perfluorooctane sul-phonate
0/0/0	0	0	0/0	0/0/0	0/0	0//0	0/0/	0/0/0	0/0			0/0/0	--Potassium perfluorooctane sul-phonate
0/0/0	0	0	0/0	0/0/0	0/0	0//0	0/0/	0/0/0	0/0			0/0/0	--Other salts of perfluorooctane sulphonic acid
0/0/0	0	0	0/0	0/0/0	0/0	0//0	0/0/	0/0/0	0/0			0/0/0	--Perfluorooctane sulphonyl flu-oride
													-Other:
0/0/0	0	0	0/0	0/0/0	0/0	0//0	0/0/	0/0/0	0/0			0/0/0	--Trichloronitromethane (*chloropicrin*)
													--Other
0/0/0	0	0	0/0	0/0/0	0/0	0//0	0/0/	0/0/0	0/0			0/0/0	Sodium chloride Propane
0/0/0	0	0	0/0	0/0/0	0/0	0//0	0/0/	0/0/0	0/0			0/0/0	Tecnazene
0/0/0	0	0	0/0	0/0/0	0/0	0//0	0/0/	0/0/0	0/0			0/0/0	Quintozene
0/0/0	0	0	0/0	0/0/0	0/0	0//0	0/0/	0/0/0	0/0			0/0/0	Other sulphonated, nitrated,nitrosalted derivatives of hydro-carbons, whether or not halogenated
													Ⅱ. ALCOHOLS AND THEIR HALO-GENATED, SUL-PHONATED, NITRATED OR NITROSATED DERIV-ATIVES
													Acyclic alcohols and their halogenated, sulphonated, nitrated or nitrosated derivatives:
													-Saturated monohydric alcohols:
0/0/0	0		0/0	0//0	0/0	0//0	0/0/	5.2/5.2/	/5.2			0//	--Methanol (methyl alcohol)
													--Propan-1-ol (propyl alcohol) and propan-2-ol (isopropyl al-cohol):
0/0/0	0	2.5	0/0	0/0/0	0/0	0//0	0/0/	0/5/5	5.2/5			0/0/0	---Propan-1-ol (propyl alcohol)
0/0/0	0	2.5	0/0	0/0/0	0/0	0//0	0/0/0	0/5/5	5.2/5			0/0/0	---Propan-2-ol (isopropyl alcohol)
0/0/0	0	2.5	0/0	0/0/0	0/0	0//0	0/0/0	0/5/5	5.2/5			0/0/0	--Butan-1-ol (*n*-butyl alcohol)
													--Other butanols:
0/0/0	0	2.5	0/0	0/0/0	0/0	0//0	0/0/0	0/5/5	5.2/5			0/0/0	---iso-Butyl alcohol
0/0/0	0	2.5	0/0	0/0/0	0/0	0//0	0/0/	0/5/5	5.2/5			0/0/0	---sec-Butyl alcohol
0/0/0	0	2.5	0/0	0/0/0	0/0	0//0	0/0/	0/5/5	5.2/5			0/0/0	---tert-Butgl alcohol
													--Octanol (octyl alcohol) and isomors thereof:
0/0/0	0		0/0	0//0	0/0	0//0	0/0/	5/5/	/5			0//	---N-octyl alchol
0/0/0	0		0/0	0//0	0/0	0//0	0/0/	5.2/5.2/	/5.2			0//	---Other
0/0/0	2	3.2	0/0	0/0/0	0/0	0//0	0/0/	0/6.3/6.3	6.6/6.3			0/0/0	--Dodecan-1-ol (lauryl alcohol), hexadecan-1-ol (cetyl alco-hol) and octadecan-1-ol (stearyl alcohol)
													--Other:
0/0/0	0	0	0/0	0/0/0	0/0	0//0	0/0/	0/0/0	0/0			0/0/0	---3,3-Dimethyl-2-butanol (pinacolyl alcohol)
													---Other
0/0/0	0	0	0.6/0.6	0/0/0	0/0	0//0	0/0/	0/0/0	5/0			0/0/0	Triacontanol
0/0/0	0	0	0.6/0.6	0/0/0	0/0	0//0	0/0/	0/0/0	5/0			0/0/0	Other saturated monohydric alcohols
													-Unsaturated monohydric alcohols:
													--Acyclic terpene alcohols:
0/0/0	0	0	0/0	0/0/0	0/0	0//0	0/0/	0/0/0	0/0			0/0/0	---Geraniol, nerol (cis-3,7-Dimethyl-2,6-octadien-1-ol)
0/0/0	0	0	0/0	0/0/0	0/0	0//0	0/0/	0/0/0	0/0			0/0/0	---Citronellol (3,7-Dimethyl-6-octen-1-ol)
0/0/0	0	0		0/0/0	0/0	0//0	0/0/	0/0/0	5/0			0/0/0	---Linalool
0/0/0	0	0	2.3/2.3	0/0/0	0/0	0//0	0/0/	0/0/0	5/0			0/0/0	---Other
0/0/0	0	0	0/0	0/0/0	0/0	0//0	0/0/	0/5/0	0/5			0/0/0	--Other
													-Diols:
5/0/				0//5	0/0	0//0	0/0/	5/5/	/5			0//	--Ethylene glycol (ethanediol)

税则号列	货品名称〔CIQ 扩展编码及品名－T2 表示见附表 2〕	最惠(%)	暂定税率	普通	增值/消费	出口退税	计量单位	监管条件/特殊证件	检验检疫	对美关税	亚太上/下
2905.3200	--1,2-丙二醇〔101 饲料添加剂;301 无检疫要求食品添加剂;302 其他化工品〕	5.5	3	30	13/	13	千克	/1		13	
	--其他:										
2905.3910	---2,5-二甲基己二醇〔999〕	4		11	13/	13	千克	/1		24	
2905.3990	---其他										
2905.3990 01	1,3-丙二醇〔101 饲料添加剂,102 化工产品〕	5.5	3	30	13/	13	千克	AB/13	RS		
2905.3990 02	1,4-丁二醇〔999〕	5.5		30	13/	13	千克	AB/13	RS	15.5	
2905.3990 10	驱蚊醇〔999〕	5.5		30	13/	9,13	千克	S/13		15.5	
2905.3990 91	白消安〔301 无检疫要求食品添加剂,302 需申报仅用于工业用途不用于食品添加剂无检疫要求的化学品〕	5.5	0	30	3/	13	千克	AB/13	MRNS	10	
2905.3990 99	其他二元醇〔301 危险化学品,毒性物质,302 其他化工品,不用作食品添加剂,303 其他化工品,用作食品添加剂〕	5.5		30	13/	13	千克	AB/13	MRNS	15.5	
	-其他多元醇:										
2905.4100	--2-乙基-2-(羟甲基)丙烷-1,3-二醇(三羟甲基丙烷)〔999〕	5.5		30	13/	13	千克	/1		30.5	
2905.4200	--季戊四醇〔999〕	5.5		30	13/	13	千克	/1		30.5	
2905.4300	--甘露糖醇〔101 饲料添加剂,102 无检疫要求食品添加剂,103 需申报仅用于工业用途不用于食品添加剂无检疫要求的化学品〕	8		30	13/	13	千克	A/1	R	33	
2905.4400	--山梨醇〔101 饲料添加剂,102 非工业用无检疫要求食品添加剂〕	8		40	13/	13	千克	/1			
2905.4500	--丙三醇(甘油)〔101 饲料添加剂,102 无检疫要求食品添加剂,103 需申报仅用于工业用途不用于食品添加剂无检疫要求的化学品〕	8	3	50	13/	13	千克	A/1	R	28	5.2/5.2
	--其他:										
2905.4910	---木糖醇〔999〕	5.5		30	13/	13	千克	A/1	R	10.5	
2905.4990	---其他[T2]	5.5		30	13/	13	千克	/1		10.5	
	-无环醇的卤化、磺化、硝化或亚硝化衍生物:										
2905.5100	--乙氯维诺(INN)〔999〕	5.5		30	13/	13	千克	I/1			
2905.5900	--其他										
2905.5900 10	乙氯维诺的盐〔999〕	5.5		30	13/	13	千克	I/13		25.5	
2905.5900 20	2－氯乙醇〔999〕	5.5		30	13/	13	千克	3A/13	M	25.5	
2905.5900 40	鼠甘伏,溴硝醇〔999〕	5.5		30	13/	9,13	千克	S/13		25.5	
2905.5900 90	其他无环醇的卤化、磺化等衍生物〔301 危险化学品,易燃液体;302 危险化学品,毒性物质;303 其他化工品〕	5.5		30	13/	13	千克	/13		25.5	
29.06	**环醇及其卤化、磺化、硝化或亚硝化衍生物:**										
	-环烷醇、环烯醇及环萜烯醇:										
2906.1100	--薄荷醇〔301〕	5		70	13/	13	千克	/1		30	
2906.1200	--环己醇、甲基环己醇及二甲基环己醇										
2906.1200 10	甲基环己醇〔999〕	5.5		30	13/	13	千克	AB/13	MN	15.5	
2906.1200 90	环己醇,二甲基环己醇〔999〕	5.5		30	13/	13	千克	/13		15.5	
	--固醇及肌醇:										
2906.1310	---固醇〔999〕	5.5	3	30	13/	13	千克	/1		8	
2906.1320	---肌醇〔101 饲料添加剂,102 无检疫要求食品添加剂,103 需申报仅用于工业用途不用于食品添加剂无检疫要求的化学品〕	5.5		30	13/	13	千克	A/1	R	25.5	
	--其他:										
2906.1910	---萜品醇〔101 松油醇,102α-松油醇〕	5.5		30	13/	13	千克	/1		15.5	
2906.1990	---其他										
2906.1990 11	5α－雄烷－3α,17α－二醇(阿法雄烷二醇)(包括 5α－雄烷－3β,17β－二醇(倍他雄烷二醇))〔999〕	5.5		30	13/	13	千克	L/13		25.5	
2906.1990 12	雄甾－4－烯－3α,17α－二醇(4－雄烯二醇(3α,17α))(包括雄甾－4－烯－3α,17β－二醇(4－雄烯二醇(3α,17β)))〔999〕	5.5		30	13/	13	千克	L/13		25.5	
2906.1990 13	雄甾－5－烯－3α,17α－二醇(5－雄烯二醇(3α,17α))(包括雄甾－5－烯－3α,17β－二醇(5－雄烯二醇(3α,17β)))〔999〕	5.5		30	13/	13	千克	L/13		25.5	
2906.1990 14	2－雄烯醇(5α-雄甾-2-烯-17－醇)〔999〕	5.5		30	13/	13	千克	L/13		25.5	
2906.1990 15	3－雄烯醇(5α-雄甾-3-烯-17-醇)〔999〕	5.5		30	13/	13	千克	L/13		25.5	
2906.1990 90	其他环烷醇,环烯醇及环萜烯醇〔301 危险化学品,易燃液体;302 危险化学品,易燃固体;303 其他化工品〕	5.5		30	13/	13	千克	/13		25.5	
	-芳香醇:										
2906.2100	--苄醇〔999〕	5		30	13/	13	千克	/1		30	
	--其他:										
2906.2910	---2-苯基乙醇〔999〕	5.5		30	13/	13	千克	/1		10.5	
2906.2990	---其他										
2906.2990 10	三氯杀螨醇、杀螨醇〔999〕	5.5		30	13/	9,13	千克	S/13		30.5	
2906.2990 90	其他芳香醇〔301 危险化学品,毒性物质〕;302 其他化工品〕	5.5		30	13/	13	千克	/13		30.5	
	第三分章 酚、酚醇及其卤化、磺化、硝化或亚硝化衍生物										
29.07	**酚;酚醇:**										
	--一元酚:										
	--苯酚及其盐:										
2907.1110	---苯酚〔999〕	5.5		30	13/	13	千克	AB/13	MN	15.5	
2907.1190	---其他〔301 危险化学品,腐蚀性物质;302 其他化工品〕	5.5		30	13/	13	千克	/13		10.5	
	--甲酚及其盐:										

协定税率 %								RCEP		特惠税率 %			Article Description
东/冰/格	巴基斯坦	韩国	瑞士上/下	哥/秘/柬	澳/毛	新西/坡/智	中国港/澳/台	东盟及马来/澳/韩	日/新	亚太2国	老/柬/缅	98/97/95	
0/0/0	0	1.1	0/0	0/0/0	0/0	0//0	0/0/	0/5/5	5/5			0/0/0	--Propylene glycol (propane-1,2-diol)
													--Other:
0/0/0	0	0	0/0	0/0/0	0/0	0//0	0/0/	0/0/0	0/0			0/0/0	---2,5-dimethyl hexandiol
													---Other
0/0/0	0		0/0	0/0/0	0/0	0//0	0/0/	5/5/	/5			0/0/0	1,3-Propanediol
0/0/0	0		0/0	0/0/0	0/0	0//0	0/0/	5/5/	/5			0/0/0	1,4-Butanediol
0/0/0	0		0/0	0/0/0	0/0	0//0	0/0/	5/5/	/5			0/0/0	Ethohexadiol
0/0/0	0		0/0	0/0/0	0/0	0//0	0/0/	5/5/	/5			0/0/0	Busulfan and Other Anticancer Drugs
0/0/0	0		0/0	0/0/0	0/0	0//0	0/0/	5/5/	/5			0/0/0	Other diatomic alcohols (tax number of Separating anti－cancer pharmaceutical raw materials)
													-Other polyhydric alcohols:
0/0/0	0	0	0/0	0/0/0	0/0	0//0	0/0/	0/0/0	0/0			0/0/0	--2-Ethyl-2-(hydroxymethyl) propane-1,3-diol (trimethylol-propane)
0/0/0	0	1.1	0/0	0/0/0	0/0	0//0	0/0/	0/0/5	5/0			0/0/0	--Pentaerythritol
0/0/0	2	0	0/0	0/0/0	0/0	0//0	0/0/	0/0/0	7.3/0			0/0/0	--Mannitol
0/0/0	11.2	2.8	1.4/1.4	0/0/0	0/0	0/0/0	0/0/	0/0/12.6	12.7/0			0/0/0	--D-glucitol (sorbitol)
0/0/0	7	2.8	1.4/1.4	0/0/0	0/0	0/0/0	0/0/	0/0/12.6	12.7/0			0/0/0	--Glycerol
													--Other:
0/0/0	0	0	0/0	0/0/0	0/0	0//0	0/0/	0/0/0	0/0			0/0/0	---Xylitol
0/0/0	0	0	0/0	0/0/0	0/0	0//0	0/0/	0/0/0	0/0			0/0/0	---Other
													-Halogenated, sulphonated, nitrated or nitrosated derivatives of acyclic alcohols:
0/0/0	0	0	0/0	0/0/0	0/0	0//0	0/0/	0/0/0	0/0			0/0/0	--Ethchlorvynol (INN)
													--Other
0/0/0	0	1.1	0/0	0/0/0	0/0	0//0	0/0/	0/0/5	5/0			0/0/0	Salts of Ethchlorvynol (INN)
0/0/0	0	1.1	0/0	0/0/0	0/0	0//0	0/0/	0/0/5	5/0			0/0/0	2-Chloroethanol
0/0/0	0	1.1	0/0	0/0/0	0/0	0//0	0/0/	0/0/5	5/0			0/0/0	Geiftor, bromonitrol
0/0/0	0	1.1	0/0	0/0/0	0/0	0//0	0/0/	0/0/5	5/0			0/0/0	Other halogenated, sulphonated derivatives, of acyclic alcohol
													Cyclic alcohols and their halogenated, sulphonated, nitrated or nitrosated derivatives:
													-Cyclanic, cyclenic or cycloterpenic:
0/0/0	0	0	0/0	0/0/0	0/0	0//0	0/0/	0/0/0	0/0			0/0/0	--Menthol
													--Cyclohexanol, methylcyclohexanols and dimethylcyclohexanols
0/0/0	0	0	0/0	0/0/0	0/0	0//0	0/0/	0/0/0	0/0			0/0/0	Methylcyclohexanol
0/0/0	0	0	0/0	0/0/0	0/0	0//0	0/0/	0/0/0	0/0			0/0/0	Cyclohexanol, Dimethylcyclohexanol
													--Sterols and inositols:
0/0/0	0	1.1	0/0	0/0/0	0/0	0//0	0/0/	0/0/5	5/0			0/0/0	---Sterol
0/0/0	0	0	0/0	0/0/0	0/0	0//0	0/0/	0/0/0	0/0			0/0/0	---Inositol
													--Other:
0/0/0	0	0	0/0	0/0/0	0/0	0//0	0/0/	0/0/0	0/0			0/0/0	---Terpineols
													---Other
0/0/0	0	0		0/0/0	0/0	0//0	0/0/	0/0/0	5/0			0/0/0	5 α - androstane -3 α, 17 α - diol (including 5 α - androstane - 3 β, 17 β - estradiol
0/0/0	0	0		0/0/0	0/0	0//0	0/0/	0/0/0	5/0			0/0/0	Androst -4- allyl -3 α, 17 α - diol {including androst -4- allyl - 3 α, 17 β - estrad [4-androstendione(3α,17β)]}
0/0/0	0	0		0/0/0	0/0	0//0	0/0/	0/0/0	5/0			0/0/0	Androst -5- allyl -3α, 17α-diol [5-androstendione(3α, 17α)] {including androst -5 -allyl -3α, 17β-estra}
0/0/0	0	0		0/0/0	0/0	0//0	0/0/	0/0/0	5/0		//	0/0/0	2-androstenol (5a-androsterol-2-ene-17-ol)
0/0/0	0	0		0/0/0	0/0	0//0	0/0/	0/0/0	5/0		//	0/0/0	3－androstenol (5a－androsterol－3－ene－17－ol)
0/0/0	0	0		0/0/0	0/0	0//0	0/0/	0/0/0	5/0			0/0/0	Other cyclanic, cyclenic or cycloterpenic
													-Aromatic:
0/0/0	0	0	0/0	0/0/0	0/0	0//0	0/0/	0/0/0	0/0			0/0/0	--Benzyl alcohol
													--Other:
0/0/0	0	0	0/0	0/0/0	0/0	0//0	0/0/	0/0/0	0/0			0/0/0	---2-Phenyl ethyl alcohol
													---Other
0/0/0	0	1.1	2.3/2.3	0/0/0	0/0	0//0	0/0/	0/0/5	5/0			0/0/0	Dicofol, chlorfenethol
0/0/0	0	1.1	2.3/2.3	0/0/0	0/0	0//0	0/0/	0/0/5	5/0			0/0/0	Other aromatic alcohols
													Ⅲ. PHENOLS, PHENOLALCOHOLS, AND THEIR HALOGENATED, SULPHONATED, NITRATED OR NITROSATED DERIVATIVES
													Phenols; phenol-alcohols:
													Monophenols.
													--Phenol (hydroxybenzene) and its salts:
0/0/0	0		0/0	0/0/0	0/0	0//0	0/0/	5.2/5.2/	/5.2			0/0/0	---Phenol
0/0/0	0		0.6/0.6	0/0/0	0/0	0//0	0/0/	5/5/	/5			0/0/0	---Other
													--Cresol and their salts:

税则号列	货品名称〔CIQ 扩展编码及品名—T2 表示见附表 2〕	最惠(%)	暂定税率	普通	增值/消费	出口退税	计量单位	监管条件/特殊证件	检验检疫	对美关税	亚太上/下
	---甲酚：										
2907.1211	----间甲酚〔301 危险化学品，不用作食品添加剂；302 危险化学品，用作食品添加剂〕	5.5		30	13/	13	千克	/13		10.5	
2907.1212	----邻甲酚〔301 危险化学品，不用作食品添加剂；302 危险化学品，用作食品添加剂〕	5.5	3	30	13/	13	千克	/13		28	
2907.1219	----其他[T2]	5.5		30	13/	13	千克	AB/13	MRNS	30.5	
2907.1290	---其他〔101〕	5.5		30	13/	13	千克	/1			
	--辛基酚、壬基酚及其异构体以及它们的盐：										
2907.1310	---壬基酚〔999〕	5.5		30	13/	13	千克	AB/13	MN		
2907.1390	---其他〔301 危险化学品，腐蚀性物质；302 其他化工品〕	5.5		30	13/	13	千克	/13			
	--萘酚及其盐：										
2907.1510	---2-萘酚(β-萘酚)〔999〕	5.5		30	13/	13	千克	/1			
2907.1590	---其他[T2]	5.5		30	13/	13	千克	AB/1	RS	15.5	
	--其他：										
2907.1910	---邻仲丁基酚、邻异丙基酚										
2907.1910 10	邻异丙基(苯)酚〔999〕	4	2	11	13/	13	千克	AB/13	MN	7	
2907.1910 90	邻仲丁基酚〔999〕	4	2	11	13/	13	千克	/13		7	
2907.1990	---其他										
2907.1990 12	邻烯丙基苯酚及盐〔301 腐蚀性物质，302 其他化工产品〕	5.5		30	13/	0	千克	S/13		15.5	
2907.1990 90	其他一元酚〔301 危险化学品，毒性物质；302 危险化学品，腐蚀性物质；303 危险化学品，杂项物质；304 危险化学品，用作食品添加剂；305 其他危险化学品；306 其他化工品，不用作食品添加剂；307 其他化工品，用作食品添加剂〕	5.5		30	13/	13	千克	/13		15.5	
	-多元酚；酚醇：										
2907.2100	--间苯二酚及其盐										
2907.2100 01	间苯二酚〔301 危险化学品，不用作食品添加剂；302 危险化学品，用作食品添加剂〕	5.5		30	13/	13	千克	/13		25.5	
2907.2100 90	间苯二酚盐〔101 无检疫要求食品添加剂，102 化工产品〕	5.5		30	13/	13	千克	/13		25.5	
	--对苯二酚及其盐：										
2907.2210	---对苯二酚〔999〕	5.5		30	13/	13	千克	/13		10.5	
2907.2290	---其他〔999〕	5.5		30	13/	13	千克	/1		10.5	
2907.2300	--4,4'-异亚丙基联苯酚(双酚 A,二苯基酚丙烷)及其盐										
2907.2300 01	双酚 A(4,4-异亚丙基联苯酚)〔999〕	5.5		30	13/	13	千克	/1		30.5	
2907.2300 90	双酚 A 的盐(4,4-异亚丙基联苯酚的盐)〔999〕	5.5		30	13/	13	千克	/1		30.5	
	--其他：										
2907.2910	---邻苯二酚〔999〕	4		11	13/	13	千克	/13		14	
2907.2990	---其他										
2907.2990 01	特丁基对苯二酚〔999〕	5.5		30	13/	13	千克	AB/13	MRNS	10.5	
2907.2990 10	毒菌酚〔999〕	5.5		30	13/	0	千克	S/13		10.5	
2907.2990 90	其他多元酚；酚醇[T2]	5.5		30	13/	13	千克	AB/13	MRNS	10.5	
29.08	**酚及酚醇的卤化、磺化、硝化或亚硝化衍生物：**										
	-仅含卤素取代基的衍生物及其盐：										
2908.1100	--五氯苯酚(ISO)〔999〕	5.5		30	13/	0	千克	AB/13	MN		
	--其他：										
2908.1910	---对氯苯酚〔999〕	4		11	13/	13	千克	/13			
2908.1990	---其他										
2908.1990 21	格螨酯〔999〕	5.5		30	13/	0	千克	S/13		15.5	
2908.1990 22	双氯酚〔999〕	5.5		30	13/	0	千克	S/13		15.5	
2908.1990 23	五氯酚钠〔999〕	5.5		30	13/	0	千克	S/13		15.5	
2908.1990 90	其他仅含卤素取代基的衍生物及盐〔301 危险化学品，易燃液体；302 危险化学品，毒性物质；303 危险化学品，杂项物质；304 其他危险化学品；305 其他化工产品〕	5.5		30	13/	13	千克	/13		15.5	
	-其他：										
2908.9100	--地乐酚(ISO)及其盐〔301 危险化学品，毒性物质；302 其他化工品〕	5.5		30	13/	0	千克	89/13			
2908.9200	--4,6-二硝基邻甲酚[二硝酚(ISO)]及其盐〔301 危险化学品，爆炸品；302 危险化学品，毒性物质；303 其他化工品〕	5.5		30	13/	13	千克	89/13			
	--其他：										
2908.9910	---对硝基酚、对硝基酚钠										
2908.9910 10	4-硝基苯酚(对硝基苯酚)〔999〕	5.5		30	13/	13	千克	/13			
2908.9910 90	对硝基苯酚钠〔999〕	5.5		30	13/	0	千克	S/13			
2908.9990	---其他										
2908.9990 21	芬螨酯〔999〕	5.5		30	13/	0	千克	S/13		30.5	
2908.9990 22	消螨酚〔999〕	5.5		30	13/	0	千克	S/13		30.5	
2908.9990 23	戊硝酚〔999〕	5.5		30	13/	0	千克	S/13		30.5	
2908.9990 24	特乐酚〔999〕	5.5		30	13/	0	千克	S/13		30.5	
2908.9990 25	壬菌铜〔999〕	5.5		30	13/	0	千克	S/13		30.5	
2908.9990 30	苦味酸(2,4,6—三硝基苯酚)〔999〕	5.5		30	13/	13	千克	k/13		30.5	
2908.9990 90	其他酚及酚醇的卤化等衍生物(包括其磺化、硝化或亚硝化衍生物)〔301 危险化学品，爆炸品；302 危险化学品，易燃固体；303 危险化学品，毒性物质；304 危险化学品，腐蚀性物质；305 危险化学品，杂项物质；306 其他危险化学品；307 其他化工品〕	5.5		30	13/	13	千克	/13		30.5	

协定税率 %								RCEP		特惠税率 %			Article Description
东/冰/格	巴基斯坦	韩国	瑞士 上/下	哥/秘/柬	澳/毛	新西/坡/智	中国港/澳/台	东盟及马来/澳/韩	日/新	亚太2国	老/柬/缅	98/97/95	
													---Cresol:
0/0/0	0	0	0/0	0/0/0	0/0	0//0	0/0/	0/0/0	0/0			0/0/0	----*m*-Cresol
0/0/0	0	0	0/0	0/0/0	0/0	0//0	0/0/	0/0/0	0/0			0/0/0	----*o*-Cresol
0/0/0	0	1.1	0/0	0/0/0	0/0	0//0	0/0/	0/0/5	5/0			0/0/0	----Other
0/0/0	0	0	0/0	0/0/0	0/0	0//0	0/0/	0/0/0	0/0			0/0/0	---Other
													--Octylphenol, nonylphenol and their isomers; salts thereof:
0/0/0	0		0/0	0/0/0	0/0	0//0	0/0/	5/5/	/5			0/0/0	---Nonylphenol
0/0/0	0	2.5	0/0	0/0/0	0/0	0//0	0/0/	5/5/5	5.2/5			0/0/0	---Other
													--Naphthols and their salts:
0/0/0	0	0	0/0	0/0/0	0/0	0//0	0/0/	0/0/0	0/0			0/0/0	---2-Naphthols (β-naphthol)
0/0/0	0	0	0/0	0/0/0	0/0	0//0	0/0/	0/0/0	0/0			0/0/0	---Other
													--Other:
													---*o*-Sec-butyl phenol, *o*-isopropyl phenol
0/0/0	0	0	0.4/0.4	0/0/0	0/0	0//0	0/0/	0/0/0	3.6/0			0/0/0	o-Iisopropyl phenol
0/0/0	0	0	0.4/0.4	0/0/0	0/0	0//0	0/0/	0/0/0	3.6/0			0/0/0	*o*-sec-buyl phenol
													---Other
0/0/0	0	0	0.6/0.6	0/0/0	0/0	0//0	0/0/	5/5/5	5/5			0/0/0	*o*-Allylphenol and its salt
0/0/0	0	0	0.6/0.6	0/0/0	0/0	0//0	0/0/	5/5/5	5/5			0/0/0	Other monophenols
													-Polyphenols; phenol-alcohols:
													--*m*-Dihydroxybenzene (resorcinol) and its salts
0/0/0	0	1.1	0/0	0/0/0	0/0	0//0	0/0/	5/5/5	5.2/5			0/0/0	*m*-Dihydroxybenzene
0/0/0	0	1.1	0/0	0/0/0	0/0	0//0	0/0/	5/5/5	5.2/5			0/0/0	*m*-Dihydroxybenzene salts
													--(hydroquinone)quinol and its salts:
0/0/0	0	0	0/0	0/0/0	0/0	0//0	0/0/	0/0/0	0/0			0/0/0	---Hydroquinone
0/0/0	0	0	0/0	0/0/0	0/0	0//0	0/0/	0/0/0	0/0			0/0/0	---Other
													--4,4′-Isopropylidenediphenol (bisphenol A, diphenylolpropane) and its salts
0/0/0	0		0/0	0/0/0	0/0	0//0	0/0/	5.2/5.2/	/5.2			0/0/0	Bisphenol-A(4,4'-Isopropylidenediphenol)
0/0/0	0		0/0	0/0/0	0/0	0//0	0/0/	5.2/5.2/	/5.2			0/0/0	Salts of bisphenol-A(salts of 4,4'-Isopropylidenediphenol)
													--Other:
0/0/0	0		0/0	0/0/0	0/0	0//0	0/0/	3.9/3.9/	/3.9			0/0/0	---*o*-Dihydroxybenzene (catechol, pyrocatechol)
													---Other
0/0/0	0	2.5	0/0	0/0/0	0/0	0//0	0/0/	5/5/5	5.2/5			0/0/0	tert-Butylhydroquinone
0/0/0	0	2.5	0/0	0/0/0	0/0	0//0	0/0/	5/5/5	5.2/5			0/0/0	Hexachlorophene
0/0/0	0	2.5	0/0	0/0/0	0/0	0//0	0/0/	5/5/5	5.2/5			0/0/0	Other polyphenols, phenol-alcohol
													Halogenated, sulphonated, nitrated or nitrosated derivatives of phenols or phenolalcohols:
													-Derivatives containing only halogen substituents and their salts:
0/0/0	0	0	0/0	0/0/0	0/0	0//0	0/0/	0/0/0	0/0			0/0/0	--Pentachlorophenol(ISO)
													--Other:
0/0/0	0	0	0/0	0/0/0	0/0	0//0	0/0/	0/0/0	0/0			0/0/0	---*p*-Chlorophenol
													---Other
0/0/0	0	0	0/0	0/0/0	0/0	0//0	0/0/	0/0/0	0/0			0/0/0	Genit
0/0/0	0	0	0/0	0/0/0	0/0	0//0	0/0/	0/0/0	0/0			0/0/0	Dichlorophen
0/0/0	0	0	0/0	0/0/0	0/0	0//0	0/0/	0/0/0	0/0			0/0/0	Sodium pentachlorophenate
0/0/0	0	0	0/0	0/0/0	0/0	0//0	0/0/	0/0/0	0/0			0/0/0	Other derivatives containing only halogen substituents and their salts
													-Other:
0/0/0	0	0	0/0	0/0/0	0/0	0//0	0/0/	0/0/0	0/0			0/0/0	--Dinoseb(ISO) and its salts
0/0/0	0	0	0/0	0/0/0	0/0	0//0	0/0/	0/0/0	0/0			0/0/0	--4,6-Dinitro-o-cresol [DNOC(ISO)]and its salts
													--Other:
													---*p*-Nitrophenol, sodium *p*-nitro-phenolate
0/0/0	0	0	0/0	0/0/0	0/0	0//0	0/0/	0/0/0	0/0			0/0/0	4-Ninitrophenol(P-nitrophenol)
0/0/0	0	0	0/0	0/0/0	0/0	0//0	0/0/	0/0/0	0/0			0/0/0	Sodium P-nitro-phenolate
													---Other
0/0/0	0	1.1	0/0	0/0/0	0/0	0//0	0/0/	0/0/5	5/0			0/0/0	Fenson
0/0/0	0	1.1	0/0	0/0/0	0/0	0//0	0/0/	0/0/5	5/0			0/0/0	Dinex
0/0/0	0	1.1	0/0	0/0/0	0/0	0//0	0/0/	0/0/5	5/0			0/0/0	Dinosam
0/0/0	0	1.1	0/0	0/0/0	0/0	0//0	0/0/	0/0/5	5/0			0/0/0	Dinoterb
0/0/0	0	1.1	0/0	0/0/0	0/0	0//0	0/0/	0/0/5	5/0			0/0/0	Nonionic copper
0/0/0	0	1.1	0/0	0/0/0	0/0	0//0	0/0/	0/0/5	5/0		//	0/0/0	Picric acid (2,4,6—trinitrophenol)
0/0/0	0	1.1	0/0	0/0/0	0/0	0//0	0/0/	0/0/5	5/0			0/0/0	Other halogenated, sulphonated, nitrated or nitrosated derivatives of hpenols or phenolalcohols

税则号列	货品名称〔CIQ扩展编码及品名－T2表示见附表2〕	最惠(%)	暂定税率	普通	增值/消费	出口退税	计量单位	监管条件/特殊证件	检验检疫	对美关税	亚太上/下
	第四分章　醚、过氧化醇、过氧化醚、缩醛及半缩醛过氧化物、过氧化酮、三节环环氧化物、缩醛及半缩醛及其卤化、磺化、硝化或亚硝化衍生物										
29.09	**醚、醚醇、醚酚、醚醇酚、过氧化醇、过氧化醚、缩醛及半缩醛过氧化物、过氧化酮(不论是否已有化学定义)及其卤化、磺化、硝化或亚硝化衍生物：**										
	-无环醚及其卤化、磺化、硝化或亚硝化衍生物：										
2909.1100	--乙醚〔999〕	5.5		30	13/	13	千克	23AB/13	MN	10.5	
	--其他：										
2909.1910	---甲醚〔999〕	5.5		30	13/	9	千克	/13		10.5	
2909.1990	---其他										
2909.1990 11	八氯二丙醚〔999〕	5.5		30	13/	9,13	千克	S/13		25.5	
2909.1990 12	二氯异丙醚〔999〕	5.5		30	13/	9,13	千克	S/13		25.5	
2909.1990 90	其他无环醚及其卤化等衍生物(包括其磺化、硝化或亚硝化衍生物)〔301危险化学品，气体；302危险化学品，易燃液体；303危险化学品，易燃液体；304其他化工品〕	5.5		30	13/	9,13	千克	/13		25.5	
2909.2000	-环烷醚、环烯醚或环萜烯醚及其卤化、磺化、硝化或亚硝化衍生物〔101：桉叶油醇，102：1,2－环氧－3－乙氧基丙烷，103：其他化工产品〕	5.5		30	13/	13	千克	/1		25.5	
	-芳香醚及其卤化、磺化、硝化或亚硝化衍生物：										
2909.3010	---1-烷氧基-4-(4-乙烯基环己基)-2,3-二氟苯〔999〕	5.5		30	13/	13	千克	/1			
2909.3020	---4-(4-烷氧基苯基)-4’-烷烯基-1,1’-双环己烷及其氟代衍生物〔999〕	5.5		30	13/	13	千克	/1			
2909.3090	---其他										
2909.3090 11	甲氧滴滴涕、除草醚〔999〕	5.5		30	13/	0	千克	S/13		25.5	
2909.3090 12	醚菊酯、苄螨醚、三氟醚〔999〕	5.5		30	13/	9,13	千克	S/13		25.5	
2909.3090 13	氯苯甲醚、甲氧除草醚〔999〕	5.5		30	13/	9,13	千克	S/13		25.5	
2909.3090 14	三氟硝草醚、草枯醚〔999〕	5.5		30	13/	9,13	千克	S/13		25.5	
2909.3090 15	氟除草醚、乙氧氟草醚〔999〕	5.5		30	13/	9,13	千克	S/13		25.5	
2909.3090 16	四溴二苯醚、五溴二苯醚、六溴二苯醚、七溴二苯醚〔999〕	5.5		30	13/	13	千克	89/13		25.5	
2909.3090 90	其他芳香醚及其卤化、磺化、硝化衍生物(包括其亚硝化衍生物)〔101饲料添加剂；301危险化学品，爆炸品；302危险化学品，易燃液体；303危险化学品，毒性物质；304危险化学品，腐蚀性物质；305危险化学品，杂项物质；306其他危险化学品；307其他化工品〕	5.5		30	13/	13	千克	/13		25.5	
	-醚醇及其卤化、磺化、硝化或亚硝化衍生物：										
2909.4100	--2,2’-氧联二乙醇(二甘醇)〔999〕	5.5	3	30	13/	13	千克	/1		28	
2909.4300	--乙二醇或二甘醇的单丁醚〔301其他危险化学品；302其他化工品〕	5.5		30	13/	13	千克	/13		10.5	
2909.4400	--乙二醇或二甘醇的其他单烷基醚〔301易燃液体，302其他化工产品，303其他危险化学品〕	5.5		30	13/	13	千克	/13		10.5	
2909.4400 10	乙二醇甲醚、二乙二醇甲醚、乙二醇乙醚、二乙二醇乙醚、乙二醇丙醚、二乙二醇丙醚、乙二醇己醚、二乙二醇己醚、乙二醇异辛醚、二乙二醇异辛醚〔301危险化学品，易燃液体；302其他化工品〕	5.5		30	13/	13	千克	/13		10.5	
2909.4400 90	乙二醇或二甘醇的其他单烷基醚〔301危险化学品，易燃液体；302其他化工品〕	5.5		30	13/	13	千克	/13		10.5	
	--其他：										
2909.4910	---间苯氧基苄醇〔999〕	4		11	13/	13	千克	/1			
2909.4990	---其他〔301易燃液体，302毒性物质和感染性物质，303其他化工产品，304其他危险化学品〕	5.5		30	13/	13	千克	/13		15.5	
2909.4990 10	三乙二醇甲醚、四乙二醇甲醚、三乙二醇乙醚、丙二醇乙醚、二丙二醇乙醚、丙二醇丙醚、二丙二醇丙醚、丙二醇丁醚、二丙二醇丁醚、三丙二醇丁醚〔301危险化学品，易燃液体；302其他化工品〕	5.5		30	13/	13	千克	/13		15.5	
2909.4990 90	其他醚醇及其衍生物(包括其卤化、磺化、硝化或亚硝化衍生物)〔301易燃液体；302其他化工产品〕	5.5		30	13/	13	千克	/13		15.5	
2909.5000	-醚酚、醚醇酚及其卤化、磺化、硝化或亚硝化衍生物〔301危险化学品，易燃液体；302其他化工产品〕	5.5		30	13/	13	千克	/13		30.5	
	-过氧化醇、过氧化醚、缩醛及半缩醛过氧化物、过氧化酮及其卤化、磺化、硝化或亚硝化衍生物：	5.5		30	13/	13	千克	/13		10.5	

协定税率 %								RCEP		特惠税率 %			Article Description
东/冰/格	巴基斯坦	韩国	瑞士上/下	哥/秘/柬	澳/毛	新西/坡/智	中国港/澳/台	东盟及马来/澳/韩	日/新	亚太2国	老/柬/缅	98/97/95	
													Ⅳ. ETHERS, ALCOHOL PEROXIDES, ETHER PEROXIDES, ACETAL AND HEMIACETAL PEROXIDES, KETONE PEROXIDES, EPOXIDES WITH A THREE-MEMBERED RING, ACETALS AND HEMIACETALS, AND THEIR HALOGENATED, SULPHONATED, NITRATED OR NITROSATED DERIVATIVES
													Ethers, ether-alcohols, ether-phenols, ether-alcohol-phenols, alcohol peroxides, ether peroxides, acetal and hemiacetal peroxides, ketone peroxides (whether or not chemically defined), and their halogenated, sulphonated, nitrated or nitrosated derivatives:
													-Acyclic ethers and their halogenated, sulphonated, nitrated or nitrosated derivatives:
0/0/0	0	0	0/0	0/0/0	0/0	0//0	0/0/	0/0/0	0/0			0/0/0	--Diethyl ether
													--Other
0/0/0	0	2.5	0/0	0//0	0/0	0//0	0/0/	5/5/5	5.2/5			0/0/	---Methyl ether
													---Other:
0/0/0	0	2.5	0/0	0//0	0/0	0//0	0/0/	5/5/5	5.2/5			0/0/	Octachlorodipropyl ether
0/0/0	0	2.5	0/0	0//0	0/0	0//0	0/0/	5/5/5	5.2/5			0/0/	Nemamort(DCIP)
0/0/0	0	2.5	0/0	0//0	0/0	0//0	0/0/	5/5/5	5.2/5			0/0/	Other acyclic ethers and their halogenated(including sulphonated, nitrated or nitrosated derivatives and their halogenated)
0/0/0	0	0	0/0	0/0/0	0/0	0//0	0/0/	0/0/0	0/0			0/0/0	-Cyclanic, cyclenic or cycloterpenic ethers and their halogenated, sulphonated, nitrated or nitrosated derivatives
													-Aromatic ethers and their halogenated, sulphonated, nitrated or nitrosated derivatives:
0/0/0	0	0	0/0	0/0/0	0/0	0//0	0/0/	0/0/0	0/0			0/0/0	---1-alkoxylate-4-(4-vingl cyclohexyl)-2,3-difluoro benzene
0/0/0	0	0	0/0	0/0/0	0/0	0//0	0/0/	0/0/0	0/0			0/0/0	---4- (4- alkoxy) -4 ′—N—alkenyl -1,1′ -and fluoro derivatives of cyclohexane
													---Other
0/0/0	0	0	0/0	0/0/0	0/0	0//0	0/0/	0/0/0	0/0			0/0/0	Methoxychlor, nitrofen
0/0/0	0	0	0/0	0/0/0	0/0	0//0	0/0/	0/0/0	0/0			0/0/0	Ethofenprox, halfenprox, trifluoro
0/0/0	0	0	0/0	0/0/0	0/0	0//0	0/0/	0/0/0	0/0			0/0/0	Chloroanisole, chlomethoxyfen
0/0/0	0	0	0/0	0/0/0	0/0	0//0	0/0/	0/0/0	0/0			0/0/0	Fluorodifen, chlomitrofen
0/0/0	0	0	0/0	0/0/0	0/0	0//0	0/0/	0/0/0	0/0			0/0/0	Fluoronitrofen, oxyfluorfen
0/0/0	0	0	0/0	0/0/0	0/0	0//0	0/0/	0/0/0	0/0			0/0/0	Tetrabromodiphenyl ether, Pentabromodiphenyl ether, Hexabromodiphenyl ether, Heptabromodiphenyl ether
0/0/0	0	0	0/0	0/0/0	0/0	0//0	0/0/	0/0/0	0/0			0/0/0	Other aromatic ethers and its halogenated, sulphonated, nitrated or nitrosated derivatives
													-Ether-alcohols and their halogenated, sulphonated, nitrated or nitrosated derivatives:
0/0/0	0	0	0/0	0//0	0/0	0//0	0/0/0	0/0/0	5/0			0/0/	--2,2′-Oxydiethanol (diethylene glycol, digol)
0/0/0	0	0	0/0	0/0/0	0/0	0//0	0/0/0	0/0/0	0/0			0/0/0	--Monobutyl ethers of ethylene glycol or of diethylene glycol
0/0/0	0	2.9	0	0	0	0/0	0//0	0/0/				0/0	--Other monoalkylethers of ethylene glycol or of diethylene glycol
0/0/0	0	2.5	0/0	0/0/0	0/0	0//0	0/0/	5/5/5	5.2/5			0/0/0	Ethylene glycol methyl ether, diethylene glycol methyl ether, ethylene glycol ethyl ether, diethylene glycol ethyl ether, ethylene glycol propylene ether, diethylene glycol propylene ether, ethylene glycol hexyl ether, diethylene glycol hexyl ether, ethylene glycol isooctyl ether, diethylene glycol isooctyl ether
0/0/0	0	2.5	0/0	0/0/0	0/0	0//0	0/0/	5/5/5	5.2/5			0/0/0	Other monoalkyl ethers of ethylene glycol or diethylene glycol
													--Other:
0/0/0	0	0	0/0	0/0/0	0/0	0//0	0/0/	0/0/0	0/0			0/0/0	---*m*-Phenoxy benzalcohol
0/0/0	0	2.9	0	0	0	0/0	0//0	0/0/				0/0	---Other
0/0/0	0	2.5	0/0	0/0/0	0/0	0//0	0/0/	5/5/5	5.2/5			0/0/0	Triethylene glycol methyl ether, tetraethylene glycol methyl ether, triethylene glycol ethyl ether, propylene glycol ethyl ether, dipropylene glycol ethyl ether, propylene glycol propylene ether, dipropylene glycol propylene ether, propylene glycol butyl ether, dipropylene glycol butyl ether, tripropylene glycol butyl ether
0/0/0	0	2.5	0/0	0/0/0	0/0	0//0	0/0/	5/5/5	5.2/5			0/0/0	Other ether alcohols and their derivatives (including their halogenated, sulfonated, nitrated or nitrosated derivatives)
0//0	0	2.5	0/0	0/0/0	0/0	0//0	0/0/	5/5/5	5.2/5			0/0/0	Ether-phenols, ether-alcohol-phenols and their halogenated, sulphonated, nitrated or nitrosated derivatives
0/0/0	0	2.9	0	0	0	0/0	0//0	0/0/				0/0	-Alcohol peroxides, ether peroxides, acetal and hemiacetal peroxides, ketone peroxides and their halogenated, sulphonated, nitrated or nitrosated derivatives:

税则号列	货品名称〔CIQ 扩展编码及品名—T2 表示见附表 2〕	最惠(%)	暂定税率	普通	增值/消费	出口退税	计量单位	监管条件/特殊证件	检验检疫	对美关税	亚太上/下
2909.6010	---缩醛及半缩醛过氧化物,及其卤化、磺化、硝化或亚硝化衍生物〔999〕	5.5		30	13/	13	千克	/1		30.5	
2909.6090	---其他〔301 危险化学品,有机过氧化物,302 其他化工品〕	5.5		30	13/	13	千克	/1		10.5	
29.10	**三节环环氧化物、环氧醇、环氧酚、环氧醚及其卤化、磺化、硝化或亚硝化衍生物:**										
2910.1000	-环氧乙烷(氧化乙烯)〔999〕	5.5		30	13/	13	千克	AB/13	MN		
2910.2000	-甲基环氧乙烷(氧化丙烯)〔999〕	5.5		30	13/	0	千克	/13		15.5	
2910.3000	-1-氯-2,3-环氧丙烷(表氯醇)〔999〕	5.5		30	13/	0	千克	AB/13	MN	30.5	
2910.4000	-狄氏剂(ISO,INN)〔999〕	5.5		30	13/	0	千克	89/13			
2910.5000	-异狄氏剂(ISO)〔999〕	5.5		30	13/	0	千克	89/13			
2910.9000	-其他										
2910.9000 20	灭草环〔999〕	5.5		30	13/	9,13	千克	S/13		15.5	
2910.9000 90	三节环环氧化物、环氧醇(酚、醚)(包括其卤化、磺化、硝化或亚硝化的衍生物)〔301 危险化学品,易燃液体;302 危险化学品,毒性物质;303 危险化学品,腐蚀性物质;304 其他危险化学品;305 其他化工品〕	5.5		30	13/	13	千克	/13		15.5	
29.11	**缩醛及半缩醛,不论是否含有其他含氧基,及其卤化、磺化、硝化或亚硝化衍生物:**										
2911.0000	缩醛及半缩醛,不论是否含有其他含氧基,及其卤化、磺化、硝化或亚硝化衍生物〔301 危险化学品,易燃液体;302 其他化工品〕	5.5		30	13/	13	千克	/13		30.5	
	第五分章　醛基化合物										
29.12	**醛,不论是否含有其他含氧基;环聚醛;多聚甲醛:**										
	-不含其他含氧基的无环醛:										
2912.1100	--甲醛〔301 危险化学品,易燃液体;302 危险化学品,腐蚀性物质〕	5.5		30	13/	13	千克	AB/13	MN	10.5	
2912.1200	--乙醛〔999〕	5.5		30	13/	13	千克	AB/13	MN		
2912.1900	--其他										
2912.1900 01	乙二醛〔999〕	5.5	3	30	13/	13	千克	/13		13	
2912.1900 30	丙烯醛〔999〕	5.5		30	13/	13	千克	/13		15.5	
2912.1900 90	其他无环醛(指不含其他含氧基)〔301 危险化学品,易燃液体;302 危险化学品,毒性物质;303 危险化学品,腐蚀性物质;304 危险化学品,用作食品添加剂;305 其他化工品,不用作食品添加剂;306 其他化工品,用作食品添加剂〕	5.5		30	13/	13	千克	/13		15.5	
	-不含其他含氧基的环醛:										
2912.2100	--苯甲醛〔101:2—羰基—4—甲基苯甲醛,102:非工业用无检疫要求食品添加剂〕	5.5		30	13/	13	千克	/1		30.5	
	--其他:										
2912.2910	---铃兰醛(对叔丁基-α-甲基-氧化肉桂醛)〔999〕	5.5		30	13/	13	千克	/1		15.5	4.4/4.4
2912.2990	---其他〔301 危险化学品,易燃液体;302 其他化工产品〕	5.5		30	13/	13	千克	/13		10.5	
	-醛醇、醛酚及含其他含氧基的醛:										
2912.4100	--香草醛(3-甲氧基-4-羟基苯甲醛)〔101 双香兰素,102 香兰素〕	5.5		30	13/	13	千克	/1		25.5	
2912.4200	--乙基香草醛(3-乙氧基-4-羟基苯甲醛)〔999〕	5.5		30	13/	13	千克	/1		10.5	
	--其他:										
2912.4910	---醛醇〔301 危险化学品,毒性物质;302 其他化工品〕	5.5		30	13/	13	千克	/13		30.5	
2912.4990	---其他										
2912.4990 10	间苯氧基苯甲醛〔301〕	5.5		30	13/	13	千克	/13		30.5	
2912.4990 90	其他醛醚、醛酚(包括含其他含氧基的醛)〔301 危险化学品,易燃液体;302 危险化学品,毒性物质;303 其他化工品〕	5.5		30	13/	13	千克	/13		30.5	
2912.5000	-环聚醛										
2912.5000 10	四聚乙醛〔999〕	5.5		30	13/	9,13	千克	S/13			
2912.5000 90	其他环聚醛〔301 危险化学品,易燃液体;302 危险化学品,易燃固体;303 其他化工品〕	5.5		30	13/	13	千克	/13			
2912.6000	-多聚甲醛〔999〕	5.5		30	13/	13	千克	AB/13	MN	15.5	
29.13	**税目 29.12 所列产品的卤化、磺化、硝化或亚硝化衍生物:**										
2913.0000	税目 29.12 所列产品的卤化、磺化、硝化或亚硝化衍生物										
2913.0000 10	三氯乙醛〔999〕	5.5		30	13/	13	千克	ABG/13	MN	30.5	
2913.0000 90	税目 29.12 所列产品的其他衍生物(指卤化、磺化、硝化或亚硝化的衍生物)〔301 危险化学品,毒性物质;302 腐蚀性物质〕	5.5		30	13/	13	千克	/13		30.5	
	第六分章　酮基化合物及醌基化合物										
29.14	**酮及醌,不论是否含有其他含氧基,及其卤化、磺化、硝化或亚硝化衍生物:**										
	-不含其他含氧基的无环酮:										
2914.1100	--丙酮〔999〕	5.5		20	13/	13	千克	23AB/13	MN	30.5	
2914.1200	--丁酮[甲基乙基(甲)酮]〔999〕	5.5		30	13/	13	千克	23/13		30.5	
2914.1300	--4-甲基-2-戊酮[甲基异丁基(甲)酮]〔999〕	5.5		30	13/	13	千克	AB/13	MN	25.5	
2914.1900	--其他										

协定税率 %								RCEP		特惠税率 %			Article Description
东/冰/格	巴基斯坦	韩国	瑞士 上/下	哥/秘/柬	澳/毛	新西/坡/智	中国港/澳/台	东盟及马来/澳/韩	日/新	亚太2国	老/柬/缅	98/97/95	
0/0/0	0	1.1	2.3/2.3	0/0/0	0/0	0//0	0/0/	0/0/5	5/0			0/0/0	--- Acetal and hemiacetal peroxides, and halogenated, sulfonated, nitrated or nitrosated derivatives thereof
0/0/0	0	2.5	0/0	0/0/0	0/0	0//0	0/0/	5/5/5	5.2/5			0/0/0	--- Other
													Epoxides, epoxyalcohols, epoxyphenols and epoxyethers, with a three-membered ring, and their halogenated, sulphonated, nitrated or nitrosated derivatives:
0/0/0	0	2.5	0/0	0/0/0	0/0	0//0	0/0/	5/5/5	5/5			0/0/0	-Oxirane (ethylene oxide)
0/0/0	0	2.5	0/0	0/0/0	0/0	0//0	0/0/	5/5/5	5.2/5			0/0/0	-Methyloxirane (propylene oxide)
0/0/0	0	1.1	0/0	0/0/0	0/0	0//0	0/0/0	5/5/5	5/5			0/0/0	-1-Chloro-2,3-epoxypropane (epichlorohydrin)
0/0/0	0	0	0/0	0/0/0	0/0	0//0	0/0/	0/0/0	0/0			0/0/0	-Dieldrin(ISO,INN)
0/0/0	0	0	2.3/2.3	0/0/0	0/0	0//0	0/0/	0/0/0	5/0			0/0/0	-Endrin(ISO)
													-Other
0/0/0	0	0	2.3/2.3	0/0/0	0/0	0//0	0/0/	0/0/0	5/0			0/0/0	Tridiphane
0/0/0	0	0	2.3/2.3	0/0/0	0/0	0//0	0/0/	0/0/0	5/0			0/0/0	Three-ring epoxide, epoxy alcohol (phenols, ether) (including their halogenated, sulphonated, nitration or nitrosated derivatives)
													Acetals and hemiacetals, whether or not with other oxygen function, and their halogenated, sulphonated, nitrated or nitrosated derivatives:
0/0/0	0	1.1	2.3/2.3	0/0/0	0/0	0//0	0/0/	0/0/5	5/0			0/0/0	Acetals and hemiacetals, whether or not with other oxygen function, and their halogenated, sulphonated, nitrated or nitrosated derivatives
													Ⅴ. ALDEHYDE-FUNCTION COMPOUNDS
													Aldehydes, whether or not with other oxygen function; cyclic polymers of aldehydes; paraformaldehyde:
													-Acyclic aldehydes without other oxygen function:
0/0/0	0	0	0/0	0/0/0	0/0	0//0	0/0/	0/0/0	0/0			0/0/0	--Methanal (formaldehyde)
0/0/0	0	0	0/0	0/0/0	0/0	0//0	0/0/	0/0/0	0/0			0/0/0	--Ethanal (acetaldehyde)
													--Other
0/0/0	0	2.5	0.6/0.6	0/0/0	0/0	0//0	0/0/	5/5/5	5.2/5			0/0/0	Glyoxal (ethanedial)
0/0/0	0	2.5	0.6/0.6	0/0/0	0/0	0//0	0/0/	5/5/5	5.2/5			0/0/0	Acrolein
0/0/0	0	2.5	0.6/0.6	0/0/0	0/0	0//0	0/0/	5/5/5	5.2/5			0/0/0	Other acyclic aldehydes(without other oxygen function)
													-Cyclic aldehydes without other oxygen function:
0/0/0	0	0	0/0	0/0/0	0/0	0//0	0/0/	0/0/0	0/0			0/0/0	--Benzaldehyde
													--Other:
0/0/0	0	0	0/0	0/0/0	0/0	0//0	0/0/	0/0/0	0/0			0/0/0	---Lilial (p-tert-butyl-α-methyl-oxocinn amaldehyde)
0/0/0	0	0	2.3/2.3	0/0/0	0/0	0//0	0/0/	0/0/0	5/0			0/0/0	---Other
													-Aldehyde-alcohols, aldehyde-phenols and aldehydes with other oxygen function:
0/0/0	0	0	0/0	0/0/0	0/0	0//0	0/0/	0/0/0	0/0			0/0/0	--Vanillin (4-hydroxy-3-methoxybenzaldehyde)
0/0/0	0	0	0/0	0/0/0	0/0	0//0	0/0/	0/0/0	0/0			0/0/0	--Ethylvanillin (3-ethoxy-4-hydroxybenzaldehyde)
													--Other:
0/0/0	0	0	0/0	0/0/0	0/0	0//0	0/0/	0/0/0	0/0			0/0/0	---Aldehyde-alcohols
													---Other
0/0/0	0	0	0/0	0/0/0	0/0	0//0	0/0/	0/0/0	0/0			0/0/0	M—phenoxybenzaldehyde
0/0/0	0	0	0/0	0/0/0	0/0	0//0	0/0/	0/0/0	0/0			0/0/0	Other aldehyde ethers, aldehyde phenols (including other oxygen—containing aldehydes)
													-Cyclic polymers of aldehydes
0/0/0	0	2.5		0/0/0	0/0	0//0	0/0/	5/5/5	5.2/5			0/0/0	Metaldehyde
0/0/0	0	2.5		0/0/0	0/0	0//0	0/0/	5/5/5	5.2/5			0/0/0	Other cyclic polymers of aldehydes
0/0/0	0	2.5	0/0	0/0/0	0/0	0//0	0/0/	5/5/5	5.2/5			0/0/0	-Paraformaldehyde
													Halogenated, sulphonated, nitrated or nitrosated derivatives of products of heading No. 29.12:
													Halogenated, sulphonated, nitrated or nitrosated derivatives of products of heading No. 29.12
0/0/0	4	0	0/0	0/0/0	0/0	0//0	0/0/	0/0/0	0/0			0/0/0	Chloral
0/0/0	4	0	0/0	0/0/0	0/0	0//0	0/0/	0/0/0	0/0			0/0/0	Halogenated, sulphonated, nitrated or nitrosated derivatives of products of heading No. 29.12
													Ⅵ.-KETONE-FUNCTION COMPOUNDS AND QUINONE-FUNCTION COMPOUNDS
													Ketones and quinones, whether or not with other oxygen function, and their halogenated, sulphonated, nitrated or nitrosated derivatives:
													-Acyclic ketones without other oxygen function:
0/0/0	0		0/0	0/0/0	0/0	0//0	0/0/	5/5/	/5			0/0/0	--Acetone
0/0/0	0		0/0	0/0/0	0/0	0//0	0/0/	5/5/	/5			0/0/0	--Butanone (methyl ethyl ketone)
0/0/0	0	2.5	0/0	0/0/0	0/0	0//0	0/0/	5/5/5	5.2/5			0/0/0	--4-Methyl-2-pentanone (isobutyl methyl ketone)
													--Other

税则号列	货品名称〔CIQ 扩展编码及品名—T2 表示见附表 2〕	最惠(%)	暂定税率	普通	增值/消费	出口退税	计量单位	监管条件/特殊证件	检验检疫	对美关税	亚太上/下
2914.1900 10	频哪酮〔999〕	5.5		30	13/	13	千克	23/13		10.5	
2914.1900 90	其他不含其他含氧基的无环酮〔301 危险化学品,易燃液体;302 危险化学品,毒性物质;303 其他化工品〕	5.5		30	13/	13	千克	/13		10.5	
	-不含其他含氧基的环烷酮、环烯酮或环萜烯酮:										
2914.2200	--环已酮及甲基环已酮〔999〕	5.5		30	13/	13	千克	AB/13	MN	15.5	
2914.2300	--芷香酮及甲基芷香酮〔999〕	5.5		30	13/	13	千克	/1		30.5	
	--其他:										
2914.2910	---樟脑〔301 属于其他危险化学品 302 其他化工产品〕	5.5		40	13/	9,13	千克	B/1	N	10.5	
2914.2990	---其他										
2914.2990 10	5α-雄烷-2-烯-17-酮〔304〕	5.5		30	13/	13	千克	L/13		15.5	
2914.2990 11	3—雄烯酮(5α-雄甾-3-烯-17-酮)〔999〕	5.5		30	13/	13	千克	L/13		15.5	
2914.2990 90	其他环烷酮.环烯酮或环萜烯酮(指不含其他含氧基的)〔301 危险化学品,易燃液体;302 危险化学品,毒性物质;303 其他化工品〕	5.5		30	13/	13	千克	/13		15.5	
	-不含其他含氧基的芳香酮:										
2914.3100	--苯丙酮(苯基丙-2-酮)〔999〕	5.5		30	13/	13	千克	23/1		10.5	
	--其他:										
2914.3910	---苯乙酮〔1014—甲基苯乙酮,102 非工业用无检疫要求食品添加剂〕	4		11	13/	13	千克	/1		29	
2914.3990	---其他										
2914.3990 11	杀鼠酮〔999〕	5.5		30	13/	9,13	千克	S/13		30.5	
2914.3990 12	鼠完〔999〕	5.5		30	13/	0	千克	S/13		30.5	
2914.3990 13	敌鼠〔101 含量＜2%(毒害品);102 敌鼠乳剂(含量＜2%)(毒害品);301 含量＜2%(毒性物质和感染性物质);302 敌鼠乳剂(含量＜2%)(毒性物质和感染性物质);999 敌鼠〕	5.5		30	13/	9,13	千克	S/13		30.5	
2914.3990 14	邻氯苯基环戊酮〔999〕	5.5		30	13/	9,13	千克	23/13		30.5	
2914.3990 15	1—苯基—1—丙酮〔999〕	5.5		30	13/	13	千克	23/13		30.5	
2914.3990 90	其他不含其他含氧基的芳香酮〔101:2—甲基苯乙酮,102:二苯甲酮〕	5.5		30	13/	13	千克	/13		30.5	
2914.4000	-酮醇及酮醛										
2914.4000 10	敌鼠钠盐〔999〕	5.5		30	13/	0	千克	S/13		30.5	
2914.4000 20	表雄酮(3β—羟基—5α—雄烷—17—酮)、表睾酮〔999〕	5.5		30	13/	13	千克	L/13		30.5	
2914.4000 30	1—表雄酮(3β—羟基—5α—雄甾—1—烯—17—酮),1—雄酮(3α—羟基—5α—雄甾—1—烯—17—酮)〔999〕	5.5		30	13/	13	千克	L/13		30.5	
2914.4000 90	其他酮醇及酮醛〔301 危险化学品,易燃液体;302 危险化学品,毒性物质;303 其他化工产品〕	5.5		30	13/	13	千克	/13		30.5	
	-酮酚及含有其他含氧基的酮:										
	---酮酚:										
2914.5011	----覆盆子酮〔101 覆盆子酮(悬钩子酮),102 复盆子酮?〕	5.5		30	13/	13	千克	/1		15.5	
2914.5019	----其他〔999〕	5.5		30	13/	13	千克	/1		30.5	
2914.5020	---2-羟基-4-甲氧基二苯甲酮〔999〕	5.5		30	13/	13	千克	/1		30.5	
2914.5090	---其他										
2914.5090 11	苯草酮,双炔酰菌胺〔999〕	5.5		30	13/	9,13	千克	S/13		30.5	
2914.5090 12	甲氧虫酰肼〔999〕	5.5		30	13/	9,13	千克	S/13		30.5	
2914.5090 13	苯丙烯菌酮,14—羟基芸苔素甾醇〔999〕	5.5		30	13/	13	千克	S/13		30.5	
2914.5090 90	含其他含氧基的酮〔301 危险化学品,易燃液体;302 危险化学品,有机过氧化物;303 其他化工品〕	5.5		30	13/	13	千克	/13		30.5	
	-醌:										
2914.6100	--蒽醌〔999〕	5.5		30	13/	13	千克	/1		30.5	
2914.6200	--辅酶 Q10[癸烯醌(INN)]〔999〕	5.5		30	13/	13	千克	/1		10.5	
2914.6900	--其他										
2914.6900 10	大黄素甲醚〔999〕	5.5		30	13/	13	千克	S/13		30.5	
2914.6900 90	其他醌〔301 危险化学品,毒性物质;302 其他化工产品〕	5.5		30	13/	13	千克	/13		30.5	
	-卤化、磺化、硝化或亚硝化衍生物:										
2914.7100	--十氯酮(ISO)〔999〕	5.5		30	13/	13	千克	89/13		10.5	
2914.7900	--其他										
2914.7900 11	氯鼠酮、苯菌酮、茚草酮〔301 危险化学品,毒性物质; 302 其他化工产品〕	5.5		30	13/	0	千克	S/13		10.5	
2914.7900 12	二氯萘醌〔999〕	5.5		30	13/	0	千克	S/13		10.5	
2914.7900 13	四氯对醌〔999〕	5.5		30	13/	0	千克	S/13		10.5	
2914.7900 14	六氯丙酮〔999〕	5.5		30	13/	0	千克	S/13		10.5	
2914.7900 15	氯敌鼠钠盐〔999〕	5.5		30	13/	9,13	千克	S/13		10.5	
2914.7900 16	1-苯基-2-溴-1-丙酮〔999〕	5.5		30	13/	13	千克	23/13		10.5	
2914.7900 90	其他酮及醌的卤化、磺化衍生物(包括硝化或亚硝化衍生物)〔301 危险化学品,爆炸品;302 危险化学品,气体;303 危险化学品,易燃液体;304 危险化学品,易燃固体;305 危险化学品,毒性物质;306 危险化学品,腐蚀性物质;307 其他化工产品〕	5.5		30	13/	13	千克	/13		10.5	
	第七分章　羧酸及其酸酐、酰卤化物、过氧化物和过氧酸以及它们的卤化、磺化、硝化或亚硝化衍生物										
29.15	**饱和无环一元羧酸及其酸酐、酰卤化物、过氧化物和过氧酸以及它们的卤化、磺化、硝化或亚硝化衍生物:**										
	-甲酸及其盐和酯:										
2915.1100	--甲酸〔101 饲料添加剂;301 危险化学品,腐蚀性物质〕	5.5		40	13/	13	千克	AB/13	MN	25.5	

协定税率 %								RCEP		特惠税率 %			Article Description
东/冰/格	巴基斯坦	韩国	瑞士上/下	哥/秘/柬	澳/毛	新西/坡/智	中国港/澳/台	东盟及马来/澳/韩	日/新	亚太2国	老/柬/缅	98/97/95	
0/0/0	0	2.5	0/0	0/0/0	0/0	0//0	0/0/	5/5/5	5.2/5			0/0/0	Pinacolone
0/0/0	0	2.5	0/0	0/0/0	0/0	0//0	0/0/	5/5/5	5.2/5			0/0/0	Other acyclic ketones, without other oxygen function
													-Cyclanic, cyclenic or cycloterpenic ketones without other oxygen function:
0/0/0	0	2.5	0/0	0/0/0	0/0	0//0	0/0/	5/5/5	5.2/5			0/0/0	--Cyclohexanone and methylcyclohexanone
0/0/0	0	0		0/0/0	0/0	0//0	0/0/	0/0/0	5/0			0/0/0	--Ionones and methylionones
													--Other:
0/0/0	0	0	0/0	0/0/0	0/0	0//0	0/0/	0/0/0	0/0			0/0/0	---Camphor
													---Other
0/0/0	0	1.1		0/0/0	0/0	0//0	0/0/	0/0/5	5/0			0/0/0	5α-androstane-2-ene-17-ketone
0/0/0	0	1.1		0/0/0	0/0	0//0	0/0/	0/0/5	5/0		//	0/0/0	3—androstenone (5a—androsterone—3—ene—17—one)
0/0/0	0	1.1		0/0/0	0/0	0//0	0/0/	0/0/5	5/0			0/0/0	Other cyclanic, cyclenic or cycloterpenic ketones without other oxygen function
													-Aromatic ketones without other oxygen function:
0/0/0	0	0	0/0	0/0/0	0/0	0//0	0/0/	0/0/0	0/0			0/0/0	--Propiophenone (phenylpropan-2-one)
													--Other:
0/0/0	0	0	0/0	0/0/0	0/0	0//0	0/0/	0/0/0	0/0			0/0/0	---Acetophenone
													---Other
0/0/0	0	0	0.6/0.6	0/0/0	0/0	0//0	0/0/	0/0/0	5/0			0/0/0	Duocide
0/0/0	0	0	0.6/0.6	0/0/0	0/0	0//0	0/0/	0/0/0	5/0			0/0/0	Pindone
0/0/0	0	0	0.6/0.6	0/0/0	0/0	0//0	0/0/	0/0/0	5/0			0/0/0	Diphacinone
0/0/0	0	0	0.6/0.6	0/0/0	0/0	0//0	0/0/	0/0/0	5/0			0/0/0	*o*-Chlorophenyl Cyclopentyl Ketone
0/0/0	0	0	0.6/0.6	0/0/0	0/0	0//0	0/0/	0/0/0	5/0		//	0/0/0	1—phenyl—1—acetone
0/0/0	0	0	0.6/0.6	0/0/0	0/0	0//0	0/0/	0/0/0	5/0			0/0/0	Other aromatic ketones without other oxygen function
													-Ketone-alcohols and ketone-aldehydes
0/0/0	0	0	0.6/0.6	0/0/0	0/0	0//0	0/0/	0/0/0	5/0			0/0/0	Diphacine sodium salt
0/0/0	0	0	0.6/0.6	0/0/0	0/0	0//0	0/0/	0/0/0	5/0			0/0/0	androsterone (3β-Hydroxy-5α-androstane-17-ketone), epitestosterone
0/0/0	0	0	0.6/0.6	0/0/0	0/0	0//0	0/0/	0/0/0	5/0		//	0/0/0	1—epiandrone (3 β — hydroxy—5 α — androsterol—1—ene—17—one)
0/0/0	0	0	0.6/0.6	0/0/0	0/0	0//0	0/0/	0/0/0	5/0			0/0/0	Other ketone-alcohols and ketone-aldehydes
													-Ketone-phenols and ketones with other oxygen function:
													---Ketone-phenols:
0/0/0	0	0	0/0	0/0/0	0/0	0//0	0/0/	0/0/0	0/0			0/0/0	----Raspberry ketone
0/0/0	0	0	0.6/0.6	0/0/0	0/0	0//0	0/0/	0/0/0	5/0			0/0/0	----Other
0/0/0	0	0	0/0	0/0/0	0/0	0//0	0/0/	0/0/0	0/0			0/0/0	---2-Hydroxy-4-methoxybenzophenone
													---Other
0/0/0	0	1.1	0/0	0/0/0	0/0	0//0	0/0/	0/0/5	5/0			0/0/0	Tralkoxydim, mandipropamid
0/0/0	0	1.1	0/0	0/0/0	0/0	0//0	0/0/	0/0/5	5/0			0/0/0	Methoxyfenoxide
0/0/0	0	1.1	0/0	0/0/0	0/0	0//0	0/0/	0/0/5	5/0			0/0/0	Phenylproperone, 14 hydroxybrassinosterol
0/0/0	0	1.1	0/0	0/0/0	0/0	0//0	0/0/	0/0/5	5/0			0/0/0	Other ketone with other oxygen function
													-Quinones:
0/0/0	0	1.1	0/0	0/0/0	0/0	0//0	0/0/	0/0/5	5/0			0/0/0	--Anthraquinone
0/0/0	0	1.1	0/0	0/0/0	0/0	0//0	0/0/	5/5/5	5.2/5			0/0/0	--Coenzyme Q10 (*ubidecarenone* (*INN*))
													--Other
0/0/0	0	1.1	0/0	0/0/0	0/0	0//0	0/0/	5/5/5	5.2/5			0/0/0	Physcione
0/0/0	0	1.1	0/0	0/0/0	0/0	0//0	0/0/	5/5/5	5.2/5			0/0/0	Other quinones
													-halogenated, sulphonated, nitrated or nitrosated derivatives:
0/0/0	0	1.1		0/0/0	0/0	0//0	0/0/	0/0/5	5/0			0/0/0	--Chlordecone (*ISO*)
													--Other
0/0/0	0	1.1		0/0/0	0/0	0//0	0/0/	0/0/5	5/0			0/0/0	Chlorophacinone
0/0/0	0	1.1		0/0/0	0/0	0//0	0/0/	0/0/5	5/0			0/0/0	Dichlone
0/0/0	0	1.1		0/0/0	0/0	0//0	0/0/	0/0/5	5/0			0/0/0	Chloranil
0/0/0	0	1.1		0/0/0	0/0	0//0	0/0/	0/0/5	5/0			0/0/0	Hexachloroacetone
0/0/0	0	1.1		0/0/0	0/0	0//0	0/0/	0/0/5	5/0			0/0/0	Chlorophacinone
0/0/0	0	1.1		0/0/0	0/0	0//0	0/0/	0/0/5	5/0			0/0/0	1-Bromo-1-phenyl-2-propanone?
0/0/0	0	1.1		0/0/0	0/0	0//0	0/0/	0/0/5	5/0			0/0/0	Halogenated, sulphonated, nitrated or nitrosated derivatives of other ketones and quinones
													Ⅷ. CARBOXYLIC ACIDS AND THEIR ANHYDRIDES, HALIDES, PEROXIDES AND PEROXYACIDS AND THEIR HALOGENATED, SULPHONATED, NITRATED OR NITROSATED DERIVATIVES
													Saturated acyclic monocarboxylic acids and their anhydrides, halides, peroxides and peroxyacids; their halogenated, sulphonated, nitrated or nitrosated derivatives:
													-Formic acid, its salts and esters:
0/0/0	4	1.1	0/0	0/0/0	0/0	0//0	0/0/	0/0/5	5/0			0/0/0	--Formic acid

税则号列	货品名称〔CIQ 扩展编码及品名－T2 表示见附表 2〕	最惠(%)	暂定税率	普通	增值/消费	出口退税	计量单位	监管条件/特殊证件	检验检疫	对美关税	亚太上/下
2915.1200	--甲酸盐〔101 饲料添加剂;301 危险化学品,毒性物质;302 其他化工产品〕	5.5		30	13/	13	千克	/13		30.5	
2915.1300	--甲酸酯〔T2〕	5.5		30	13/	13	千克	/13		30.5	
	-乙酸及其盐;乙酸酐:										
	--乙酸:										
	---冰乙酸:										
2915.2111	----食品级的〔101 饲料添加剂,301 属于危险化学品的食品添加剂〕	5.5		30	13/	13	千克	ABG/1	MRNS	10.5	
2915.2119	----其他 101 饲料添加剂;;301 危险化学品,腐蚀性物质〕	5.5		30	13/	13	千克	G/1		30.5	
2915.2190	---其他										
2915.2190 10	乙酸溶液,80≥含量>10%〔101 饲料添加剂,301 腐蚀性物质〕	5.5		50	13/	13	千克	ABG/13	MN	30.5	
2915.2190 20	乙酸,含量>80%〔301〕	5.5		50	13/	13	千克	ABG/13	MN	30.5	
2915.2190 90	其他乙酸〔T2〕	5.5		50	13/	13	千克	ABG/13	MRNS	30.5	
2915.2400	--乙酸酐〔999〕	5.5		50	13/	13	千克	23AB/13	MN	25.5	4.4/4.4
	--其他:										
2915.2910	---乙酸钠〔101 饲料添加剂,301 无检疫要求食品添加剂,302 需申报仅用于工业用途不用于食品添加剂无检疫要求的化学品〕	5.5		50	13/	13	千克	AG/1	R	15.5	
2915.2990	---其他										
2915.2990 11	乙酸铜〔999〕	5.5		50	13/	9,13	千克	/13		15.5	
2915.2990 23	乙酸铅(醋酸铅)〔999〕	5.5		50	13/	13	千克	/13		15.5	
2915.2990 90	其他乙酸盐〔T2〕	5.5		50	13/	13	千克	AB/13	MRNS	15.5	
	-乙酸酯:										
2915.3100	--乙酸乙酯〔301 易燃液体,需申报仅用于工业用途不用于食品添加剂无检疫要求,302 属于危险化学品的食品添加剂〕	5.5		30	13/	13	千克	ABG/13	MRNS	25.5	
2915.3200	--乙酸乙烯酯〔999〕	5.5		30	13/	13	千克	AB/13	MN	30.5	
2915.3300	--乙酸(正)丁酯〔999〕	5.5		30	13/	13	千克	AB/13	MN	15.5	
2915.3600	--地乐酚(ISO)乙酸酯〔999〕	5.5		30	13/	0	千克	S/1		10.5	
2915.3900	--其他										
2915.3900 11	三氯杀虫酯〔999〕	5.5		30	13/	9,13	千克	S/13		10.5	
2915.3900 13	特乐酯〔999〕	5.5		30	13/	9,13	千克	S/13		10.5	
2915.3900 14	灭螨醌〔999〕	5.5		30	13/	0	千克	S/13		10.5	
2915.3900 15	信铃酯〔999〕	5.5		30	13/	9,13	千克	S/13		10.5	
2915.3900 16	种衣酯〔999〕	5.5		30	13/	9,13	千克	S/13		10.5	
2915.3900 90	其他乙酸酯〔T2〕	5.5		30	13/	13	千克	AB/13	MRNS	10.5	
2915.4000	--一氯代乙酸、二氯乙酸或三氯乙酸及其盐和酯										
2915.4000 10	一氯醋酸钠〔999〕	5.5		30	13/	0	千克	/13		30.5	
2915.4000 90	其他一氯代乙酸的盐和酯(包括二氯乙酸或三氯乙酸的盐和酯)〔301 危险化学品,易燃液体;302 危险化学品,毒性物质;303 危险化学品,腐蚀性物质;304 其他危险化学品;305 其他化工产品〕	5.5		30	13/	13	千克	/13		30.5	
	-丙酸及其盐和酯:										
2915.5010	---丙酸〔101 饲料添加剂;301 危险化学品,不用作食品添加剂;302 危险化学品,用作食品添加剂〕	5.5	3	30	13/	13	千克	AB/13	MRNS	8	
2915.5090	---其他〔T2〕	5.5		30	13/	13	千克	AB/13	MRNS	30.5	
2915.6000	-丁酸、戊酸及其盐和酯〔101 饲料添加剂;301 危险化学品,危险化学品,易燃液体;302 危险化学品,腐蚀性物质;303 他化工品,不用作食品添加剂;304 其他化工品,用作食品添加剂;305 有机过氧化物〕	5.5		30	13/	13	千克	/13		10.5	
	-棕榈酸、硬脂酸及其盐和酯:										
2915.7010	---硬脂酸〔101 饲料添加剂,102 化工产品,301 无检疫要求食品添加剂,302 需申报仅用于工业用途不用于食品添加剂无检疫要求的化学品〕	7		50	13/	13	千克	A/1	R	32	
2915.7090	---其他〔101 饲料添加剂,103 其他化工产品〕	5.5		30	13/	13	千克	/1		25.5	
2915.9000	-其他										
2915.9000 11	茅草枯〔999〕	5.5		30	13/	0	千克	S/13		25.5	
2915.9000 12	抑草蓬〔999〕	5.5		30	13/	0	千克	S/13		25.5	
2915.9000 13	四氟丙酸〔999〕	5.5		30	13/	9,13	千克	S/13		25.5	
2915.9000 20	氟乙酸钠〔999〕	5.5		30	13/	13	千克	89/13		25.5	
2915.9000 90	其他饱和无环一元羧酸及其酸酐[(酰卤、过氧)化物,过氧酸及其卤化、硝化、磺化、亚硝化衍生物][T2]	5.5		30	13/	13	千克	AB/13	MRNS		
29.16	**不饱和无环一元羧酸、环一元羧酸及其酸酐、酰卤化物、过氧化物和过氧酸以及它们的卤化、磺化、硝化或亚硝化衍生物:**										
	-不饱和无环一元羧酸及其酸酐、酰卤化物、过氧化物和过氧酸以及它们的衍生物:										
2916.1100	--丙烯酸及其盐〔301 危险化学品,腐蚀性物质;302 其他化工产品〕	6.5		30	13/	13	千克	/13		31.5	
	--丙烯酸酯:										
2916.1210	---丙烯酸甲酯〔999〕	6.5		30	13/	13	千克	AB/13	MN		
2916.1220	---丙烯酸乙酯〔301〕	6.5		30	13/	13	千克	AB/13	MN	16.5	
2916.1230	---丙烯酸丁酯										
2916.1230 01	丙烯酸正丁酯〔999〕	6.5		30	13/	13	千克	AB/13	MN	11.5	
2916.1230 90	丙烯酸异丁酯〔999〕	6.5		30	13/	13	千克	AB/13	MN	11.5	
2916.1240	---丙烯酸异辛酯〔999〕	6.5		30	13/	13	千克	/1		31.5	

协定税率 %								RCEP		特惠税率 %			Article Description
东/冰/格	巴基斯坦	韩国	瑞士 上/下	哥/秘/柬	澳/毛	新西/坡/智	中国港/澳/台	东盟及马来/澳/韩	日/新	亚太2国	老/柬/缅	98/97/95	
0/0/0	4	1.1	0/0	0/0/0	0/0	0//0	0/0/	0/0/5	5/0			0/0/0	--Salts of formic acid
0/0/0	4	0	0/0	0/0/0	0/0	0//0	0/0/	0/0/0	0/0			0/0/0	--Esters of formic acid
													-Acetic acid and its salts; acetic anhydride:
													--Acetic acid:
													---Acetic acid, glacial:
0/0/0	4	0	0/0	0/0/0	0/0	0//0	0/0/0	0/0/0	0/0			0/0/0	----food-grade
0/0/0	4	0	0/0	0/0/0	0/0	0//0	0/0/0	0/0/0	0/0			0/0/0	----Other
													---Other
0/0/0	4	0	0/0	0/0/0	0/0	0//0	0/0/	0/0/0	0/0			0/0/0	Acetic acid solution, 80%≥content>10%
0/0/0	4	0	0/0	0/0/0	0/0	0//0	0/0/	0/0/0	0/0			0/0/0	Acetic acid ,content>80%
0/0/0	4	0	0/0	0/0/0	0/0	0//0	0/0/	0/0/0	0/0			0/0/0	Other acetic acid
0/0/0	0	0	0/0	0/0/0	0/0	0//0	0/0/	0/0/0	0/0			0/0/0	--Acetic anhydride
													--Other:
0/0/0	4	0	0/0	0/0/0	0/0	0//0	0/0/	0/0/0	0/0			0/0/0	---Sodium acetate
													---Other
0/0/0	4	1.1	0/0	0/0/0	0/0	0//0	0/0/	0/0/5	5/0			0/0/0	Copper acetate
0/0/0	4	1.1	0/0	0/0/0	0/0	0//0	0/0/	0/0/5	5/0			0/0/0	Lead acetate
0/0/0	4	1.1	0/0	0/0/0	0/0	0//0	0/0/	0/0/5	5/0			0/0/0	Other Salts of acetate acid
													-Esters of acetic acid:
0/0/0	4	0	0/0	0/0/0	0/0	0//0	0/0/	0/0/0	0/0			0/0/0	--Ethyl acetate
0/0/0	4	0	0/0	0/0/0	0/0	0//0	0/0/0	0/5/0	0/5			0/0/0	--Vinyl acetate
0/0/0	0	2.5	0/0	0/0/0	0/0	0//0	0/0/	5/5/5	5.2/5			0/0/0	--*n*-Butyl acetate
0/0/0	4	0	0/0	0/0/0	0/0	0//0	0/0/	0/0/0	0/0			0/0/0	--Dinoseb (ISO) acetate
													--Other
0/0/0	4	2.5	0.6/0.6	0/0/0	0/0	0//0	0/0/	5/5/5	5.2/5			0/0/0	Acetofenate
0/0/0	4	2.5	0.6/0.6	0/0/0	0/0	0//0	0/0/	5/5/5	5.2/5			0/0/0	Dinoterb acetate
0/0/0	4	2.5	0.6/0.6	0/0/0	0/0	0//0	0/0/	5/5/5	5.2/5			0/0/0	Acequinocy
0/0/0	4	2.5	0.6/0.6	0/0/0	0/0	0//0	0/0/	5/5/5	5.2/5			0/0/0	11-Hexadecadien-l-Yl acetate
0/0/0	4	2.5	0.6/0.6	0/0/0	0/0	0//0	0/0/	5/5/5	5.2/5			0/0/0	Fenitropan
0/0/0	4	2.5	0.6/0.6	0/0/0	0/0	0//0	0/0/	5/5/5	5.2/5			0/0/0	Other esters of acetic acid
													-Mono-, di- or trichloroacetic acids, their salts and esters
0/0/0	4	0	0/0	0/0/0	0/0	0//0	0/0/	0/0/0	0/0			0/0/0	Sodium monochloracetate
0/0/0	4	0	0/0	0/0/0	0/0	0//0	0/0/	0/0/0	0/0			0/0/0	Other mono-, di-or trichloroacetic acids, their salts and esters
													-Propionic acid, its salts and esters:
0/0/0	4	0	0/0	0/0/0	0/0	0//0	0/0/	0/0/0	0/0			0/0/0	---Propionic acid
0/0/0	4	2.5	0/0	0/0/0	0/0	0//0	0/0/	5/5/5	5.2/5			0/0/0	---Other
0/0/0	4	1.1	0/0	0/0/0	0/0	0//0	0/0/	0/0/5	5/0			0/0/0	-Butanoic acids, pentanoic acids, their salts and esters
													-Palmitic acid, stearic acid, their salts and esters:
0/0/0	2	0	0/0	0/0/0	0/0	0//0	0/0/	0/0/0	6.4/0			0/0/0	---Stearic acid
0/0/0	4	2.5	0/0	0/0/0	0/0	0//0	0/0/	5/5/5	5.2/5			0/0/0	---Other
													-Other
0/0/0	0	0	0.6/0.6	0/0/0	0/0	0//0	0/0/	0/0/0	5/0			0/0/0	Dalapon
0/0/0	0	0	0.6/0.6	0/0/0	0/0	0//0	0/0/	0/0/0	5/0			0/0/0	Erbon
0/0/0	0	0	0.6/0.6	0/0/0	0/0	0//0	0/0/	0/0/0	5/0			0/0/0	Flupropanate
0/0/0	0	0	0.6/0.6	0/0/0	0/0	0//0	0/0/	0/0/0	5/0			0/0/0	Sodium fluoroacetate
0/0/0	0	0	0.6/0.6	0/0/0	0/0	0//0	0/0/	0/0/0	5/0			0/0/0	Other saturaed acyclic monocarboxylic acids and their anhydrides, halides, peroxides and peroxyacids; their halogenated, sulphonated, nitrated or nitrosated derivatives
													Unsaturated acyclic monocarboxylic acids, cyclic monocarboxylic acids, their anhydrides, halides, peroxides and peroxyacids; their halogenated, sulphonated, nitrated or nitrosated derivatives:
													-Unsaturated acyclic monocarboxylic acids, their anhydrides, halides, peroxides, peroxyacids and their derivatives:
0/0/0		3	0/0	0/0/0	0/0	0//0	0/0/	0/5.9/5.9	6.1/5.9			0/0/0	--Acrylic acid and its salts
													--Esters of acrylic acid:
0/0/0	4	3	2.7/2.7	0/0/0	0/0	0/0/0	0/0/	5.9/5.9/5.9	6.1/5.9			0/0/0	---Methyl acrylate
0/0/0	4	3	0/0	0/0/0	0/0	0/0/0	0/0/	5.9/5.9/5.9	6.1/5.9			0/0/0	---Ethyl acrylate
													---N—Butyl achylate
0/0/0	4		0/0	0/0/0	0/0	0/0/0	0/0/	5/5/	/5			0/0/0	N-butyl acrylate
0/0/0	4		0/0	0/0/0	0/0	0/0/0	0/0/	5/5/	/5			0/0/0	z—Ethylhexyl acrylate
0/0/0	4	3	0/0	0/0/0	0/0	0/0/0	0/0/	0/5.9/5.9	6.1/5.9			0/0/0	---Isooctyl acrylate

税则号列	货品名称〔CIQ 扩展编码及品名—T2 表示见附表 2〕	最惠(%)	暂定税率	普通	增值/消费	出口退税	计量单位	监管条件/特殊证件	检验检疫	对美关税	亚太上/下
2916.1290	---其他〔301 危险化学品，易燃液体；302 危险化学品，毒性物质；303 危险化学品，杂项物质；304 其他化工产品〕	6.5		30	13/	13	千克	/13		26.5	
2916.1300	--甲基丙烯酸及其盐										
2916.1300 10	甲基丙烯酸〔999〕	6.5		80	13/	13	千克	AB/13	MN	31.5	
2916.1300 90	甲基丙烯酸盐〔999〕	6.5		80	13/	13	千克	/13		31.5	
2916.1400	--甲基丙烯酸酯										
2916.1400 10	甲基丙烯酸甲酯〔999〕	6.5		80	13/	13	千克	/13		31.5	
2916.1400 90	其他甲基丙烯酸酯〔301 危险化学品，易燃液体；302 危险化学品，毒性物质；303 其他化工产品〕	6.5		80	13/	13	千克	/13		31.5	
2916.1500	--油酸、亚油酸或亚麻酸及其盐和酯〔101 亚麻酸，102 亚油酸，103：亚油酸甲酯(48%)、亚麻酸甲酯(52%)混合物，104 亚油酸乙酯，105 油酸乙酯，106 单，双甘油脂肪酸酯〕	6.5		30	13/	13	千克	/1		16.5	
2916.1600	--乐杀螨(ISO)〔999〕	6.5		30	13/	0	千克	S/13			
2916.1900	--其他										
2916.1900 11	烯虫乙酯〔999〕	6.5		30	13/	9,13	千克	S/13		16.5	
2916.1900 12	烯虫炔酯〔999〕	6.5		30	13/	9,13	千克	S/13		16.5	
2916.1900 13	消螨普〔999〕	6.5		30	13/	9,13	千克	S/13		16.5	
2916.1900 90	其他不饱和无环一元羧酸(包括其酸酐、酰卤化物、过氧化物和过氧酸及它们的衍生物)[T2]	6.5		30	13/	13	千克	AB/13	MRNS	16.5	
	-环烷一元羧酸、环烯一元羧酸或环萜烯一元羧酸及其酸酐、酰卤化物、过氧化物和过氧酸以及它们的衍生物：										
2916.2010	---二溴菊酸、DV 菊酸甲酯〔999〕	4		11	13/	13	千克	/1			
2916.2090	---其他										
2916.2090 21	苄菊酯、苯醚菊酯(包括右旋苯醚菊酯、富右旋反式苯醚菊酯)〔999〕	6.5		30	13/	9,13	千克	S/13		31.5	
2916.2090 22	苄烯菊酯、氯菊酯(包括生物氯菊酯)〔301〕	6.5		30	13/	9,13	千克	S/13		31.5	
2916.2090 23	氯烯炔菊酯、联苯菊酯〔999〕	6.5		30	13/	9,13	千克	S/13		31.5	
2916.2090 24	七氟菊酯、四氟苯菊酯、五氟苯菊酯、七氟甲醚酯(包括甲氧苄菊酯、氯氟醚菊酯)〔999〕	6.5		30	13/	9,13	千克	S/13		31.5	
2916.2090 25	戊菊酯、环螨酯〔999〕	6.5		30	13/	9,13	千克	S/13		31.5	
2916.2090 26	四氟甲醚菊酯、烯炔菊酯、四氟醚菊酯(包括右旋烯炔菊酯、富右旋反式烯炔菊酯)〔999〕	6.5		30	13/	9,13	千克	S/13		31.5	
2916.2090 27	炔丙菊酯(包括右旋炔丙菊酯、富右旋反式炔丙菊酯)〔999〕	6.5		30	13/	9,13	千克	S/13		31.5	
2916.2090 28	氯丙炔菊酯(包括右旋反式氯丙炔菊酯、除虫菊素 I、瓜叶菊素 I、茉酮菊素 I)〔999〕	6.5		30	13/	9,13	千克	S/13		31.5	
2916.2090 90	其他(环烷、环烯、环萜烯)一元羧酸(包括酸酐、酰卤化物、过氧化物和过氧酸及其衍生物)〔301 危险化学品，易燃固体；302 其他化工品，不用作食品添加剂；303 其他化工品，用作食品添加剂〕	6.5		30	13/	13	千克	AB/13	MRNS	31.5	
	-芳香一元羧酸及其酸酐、酰卤化物、过氧化物和过氧酸以及它们的衍生物：										
2916.3100	--苯甲酸及其盐和酯[T2]	6.5		30	13/	13	千克	AB/13	MRNS	26.5	
2916.3200	--过氧化苯甲酰及苯甲酰氯〔301 危险化学品，有机过氧化物；302 危险化学品，腐蚀性物质；303 其他化工品〕	6.5		30	13/	13	千克	AB/13	MRNS	31.5	
2916.3400	--苯乙酸及其盐										
2916.3400 10	苯乙酸〔101〕	6.5		30	13/	13	千克	23/1		26.5	
2916.3400 90	苯乙酸盐〔999〕	6.5		30	13/	13	千克	/1		26.5	
	--其他：										
2916.3910	---邻甲基苯甲酸〔999〕	6.5		30	13/	13	千克	/1		11.5	
2916.3920	---布洛芬〔999〕	6.5		30	13/	13	千克	/1		16.5	
2916.3930	---2-(3-碘-4-乙基苯基)-2-甲基丙酸〔999〕	6.5		30	13/	13	千克	/1			
2916.3990	---其他										
2916.3990 12	草芽畏、燕麦酯〔999〕	6.5		30	13/	9,13	千克	S/13		16.5	
2916.3990 13	5-硝基邻甲氧基苯酸钠〔999〕	6.5		30	13/	0	千克	S/13		16.5	
2916.3990 14	对氯苯氧乙酸及其盐〔999〕	6.5		30	13/	9,13	千克	S/13		16.5	
2916.3990 15	三碘苯甲酸〔999〕	6.5		30	13/	0	千克	S/13		16.5	
2916.3990 16	萘乙酸〔999〕	6.5		30	13/	9,13	千克	S/13		16.5	
2916.3990 17	伐草克〔999〕	6.5		30	13/	9,13	千克	S/13		16.5	
2916.3990 18	萘乙酸盐〔999〕	6.5		30	13/	9,13	千克	S/13		16.5	
2916.3990 90	其他芳香一元羧酸[T2]	6.5		30	13/	13	千克	/13		16.5	
29.17	**多元羧酸及其酸酐、酰卤化物、过氧化物和过氧酸以及它们的卤化、磺化、硝化或亚硝化衍生物：**										
	-无环多元羧酸及其酸酐、酰卤化物、过氧化物和过氧酸以及它们的衍生物：										
	--草酸及其盐和酯：										
2917.1110	---草酸〔999〕	6.5		40	13/	13	千克	/1		26.5	
2917.1120	---草酸钴〔999〕	9		30	13/	13	千克	4xy/1			
2917.1190	---其他〔301 其他危险化学品；302 其他化工产品〕	6.5		30	13/	13	千克	/13		11.5	
2917.1200	--己二酸及其盐和酯										
2917.1200 01	己二酸〔999〕	6.5		30	13/	13	千克	A/1	R	31.5	
2917.1200 90	己二酸盐和酯〔999 其他化工产品，301 无检疫要求食品添加剂，302 需申报仅用于工业用途不用于食品添加剂无检疫要求的化学品〕	6.5		30	13/	13	千克	A/1	R	31.5	
	--壬二酸、癸二酸及其盐和酯：										

协定税率 %								RCEP		特惠税率 %			Article Description
东/冰/格	巴基斯坦	韩国	瑞士上/下	哥/秘/柬	澳/毛	新西/坡/智	中国港/澳/台	东盟及马来/澳/韩	日/新	亚太2国	老/柬/缅	98/97/95	
0/0/0	4		0/0	0/0/0	0/0	0/0/0	0/0/	5/5/	/5			0/0/0	---Other
													--Methacrylic acid and its salts
0/0/0	4	0	0/0	0/0/0	0/0	0//0	0/0/0	0/0/0	0/0			0/0/0	Methacrylic acid
0/0/0	4	0	0/0	0/0/0	0/0	0//0	0/0/0	0/0/0	0/0			0/0/0	Salts of methacrylic acid
													--Esters of methacrylic acid
0/0/0	0	0	0/0	0/0/0	0/0	0//0	0/0/0	0/0/0	5.9/0			0/0/0	Methyl methacrylate
0/0/0	0	0	0/0	0/0/0	0/0	0//0	0/0/0	0/0/0	5.9/0			0/0/0	Other esters of methacrylic acid
0/0/0	4	3	0/0	0/0/0	0/0	0//0	0/0/	5.9/5.9/5.9	6.1/5.9			0/0/0	--Oleic, linoleic or linolenic acids, their salts and esters
0/0/0	4	0	0/0	0/0/0	0/0	0//0	0/0/	0/0/0	5.9/0			0/0/0	--Binapacryl(ISO)
													--Other
0/0/0	4	0		0/0/0	0/0	0//0	0/0/	0/0/0	5.9/0			0/0/0	Hydroprene
0/0/0	4	0		0/0/0	0/0	0//0	0/0/	0/0/0	5.9/0			0/0/0	Kinoprene
0/0/0	4	0		0/0/0	0/0	0//0	0/0/	0/0/0	5.9/0			0/0/0	Dinocap
0/0/0	4	0		0/0/0	0/0	0//0	0/0/	0/0/0	5.9/0			0/0/0	Other unsaturated acyclic monocarboxylic acids, their anhydrides, halides, peroxides, peroxyacids and their derivatives
													-Cyclanic, cyclenic or cycloterpenic monocarboxylic acids, their anhydrides, halides, peroxides, peroxyacids and their derivatives:
0/0/0	0	0	0/0	0/0/0	0/0	0//0	0/0/	0/0/0	0/0			0/0/0	---Dibromochrysanthemicacid, DV chrysanthemimono carboxylate
													---Other
0/0/0	4	0	2.7/2.7	0/0/0	0/0	0//0	0/0/	5.9/5.9/5.9	5.9/5.9			0/0/0	Dimethirn , Phenothrin(including d-phenothrin, rich-d-trans-phenothrin)
0/0/0	4	0	2.7/2.7	0/0/0	0/0	0//0	0/0/	5.9/5.9/5.9	5.9/5.9			0/0/0	Butethrin, Permethrin(including biopermethrin)
0/0/0	4	0	2.7/2.7	0/0/0	0/0	0//0	0/0/	5.9/5.9/5.9	5.9/5.9			0/0/0	Chlorempenthrin , Bifenthrin
0/0/0	4	0	2.7/2.7	0/0/0	0/0	0//0	0/0/	5.9/5.9/5.9	5.9/5.9			0/0/0	Tefluthrin, transfluthrin, fenfluthrin, methothrin heptafluoride(including matofluthrin)
0/0/0	4	0	2.7/2.7	0/0/0	0/0	0//0	0/0/	5.9/5.9/5.9	5.9/5.9			0/0/0	Valerate, cyclopropate
0/0/0	4	0	2.7/2.7	0/0/0	0/0	0//0	0/0/	5.9/5.9/5.9	5.9/5.9			0/0/0	Dimefluthrin, empenthrin Four fluorine ethofenprox (including d-empenthrin, rich-d-empenthrin)
0/0/0	4	0	2.7/2.7	0/0/0	0/0	0//0	0/0/	5.9/5.9/5.9	5.9/5.9			0/0/0	Prallethrin(including d-prallethrin、rich-d-t-prallethrin)
0/0/0	4	0	2.7/2.7	0/0/0	0/0	0//0	0/0/	5.9/5.9/5.9	5.9/5.9			0/0/0	Permethrin (including D－trans permethrin, pyrethrin I, chamomile I and jasmine I)
0/0/0	4	0	2.7/2.7	0/0/0	0/0	0//0	0/0/	5.9/5.9/5.9	5.9/5.9			0/0/0	Other cyclanic, cyclenic or cycloterpenic monocarboxylic acids, their anhydrides, halides, peroxides, peroxyacids and their derivatives
													-Aromatic monocarboxylic acids, their anhydrides, halides, peroxides, peroxyacids and their derivatives:
0/0/0	4	1.3		0/0/0	0/0	0//0	0/0/	0/0/5.9	5.9/0			0/0/0	--Benzoic acid, its salts and esters
0/0/0	4	1.3	0/0	0/0/0	0/0	0//0	0/0/	0/0/5.9	5.9/0			0/0/0	--Benzoyl peroxide and benzoyl chloride
													--Phenylacetic acid and its salts
0/0/0	4	0		0/0/0	0/0	0//0	0/0/	0/0/0	5.9/0			0/0/0	Phenylacetic acid
0/0/0	4	0		0/0/0	0/0	0//0	0/0/	0/0/0	5.9/0			0/0/0	Salts of phenylacetic acid
													--Other:
0/0/0	4	0	0/0	0/0/0	0/0	0//0	0/0/	0/0/0	5.9/0			0/0/0	---*m*-Methylbenzoic acid
0/0/0	4	0	0/0	0/0/0	0/0	0//0	0/0/	0/0/0	5.9/0			0/0/0	---Brufen (Ibuprofen)
0/0/0	4	0	2.7/2.7	0/0/0	0/0	0//0	0/0/	0/0/0	5.9/0			0/0/0	---z－(3－iodo－ethylphenyl)－2－methylpropionic acid
													---Other
0/0/0	4	0	2.7/2.7	0/0/0	0/0	0//0	0/0/	0/0/0	5.9/0			0/0/0	2,3,6-TAB, methachlorphenprop
0/0/0	4	0	2.7/2.7	0/0/0	0/0	0//0	0/0/	0/0/0	5.9/0			0/0/0	5-Sodium nitro-o-methoxy-benzene
0/0/0	4	0	2.7/2.7	0/0/0	0/0	0//0	0/0/	0/0/0	5.9/0			0/0/0	p-Chlorophenoxyacetic acid and its salt
0/0/0	4	0	2.7/2.7	0/0/0	0/0	0//0	0/0/	0/0/0	5.9/0			0/0/0	Triiodobenzoic acid
0/0/0	4	0	2.7/2.7	0/0/0	0/0	0//0	0/0/	0/0/0	5.9/0			0/0/0	Naphthylacetic acid
0/0/0	4	0	2.7/2.7	0/0/0	0/0	0//0	0/0/	0/0/0	5.9/0			0/0/0	Chlorfenac
0/0/0	4	0	2.7/2.7	0/0/0	0/0	0//0	0/0/	0/0/0	5.9/0			0/0/0	Naphthylacetate
0/0/0	4	0	2.7/2.7	0/0/0	0/0	0//0	0/0/	0/0/0	5.9/0			0/0/0	Other aromatic monocarboxylic acids
													Polycarboxylic acids, their anhydrides, halides, peroxides and peroxyacids; their halogenated, sulphonated, nitrated or nitrosated derivatives:
													-Acyclic polycarboxylic acids, their anhydrides, halides, peroxides, peroxyacids and their derivatives:
													--Oxalic acid, its salts and esters:
0/0/0	4	1.3	0/0	0/0/0	0/0	0//0	0/0/	0/0/5.9	5.9/0			0/0/0	---Oxalic acid
0/0/0	2	0	0/0	0/0/0	0/0	0//0	0/0/	0/0/0	8.2/0			0/0/0	---Cobalt oxalate
0/0/0	4	1.3	0/0	0/0/0	0/0	0//0	0/0/	0/0/5.9	5.9/0			0/0/0	---Other
													--Adipic acid, its salts and esters
0/0/0	4		0/0	0/0/0	0/0	0//0	0/0/	5/5/	/5			0/0/0	Adipic acid
0/0/0	4		0/0	0/0/0	0/0	0//0	0/0/	5/5/	/5			0/0/0	Adipic acid, its salts and esters
													--Azelaic acid, sebacic acid, their salts and esters:

税则号列		货品名称〔CIQ扩展编码及品名—T2表示见附表2〕	最惠(%)	暂定税率	普通	增值/消费	出口退税	计量单位	监管条件/特殊证件	检验检疫	对美关税	亚太上/下
2917.1310		---癸二酸及其盐和酯〔999〕	6.5		30	13/	13	千克	/1		31.5	
2917.1390		---其他〔999〕	6.5		30	13/	13	千克	/1		11.5	5.2/5.2
2917.1400		--马来酐〔999〕	6.5		30	13/	13	千克	/13		31.5	
2917.1900		--其他										
2917.1900	10	驱虫特、硝苯菌酯〔999〕	6.5		30	13/	0	千克	S/13		16.5	
2917.1900	90	其他无环多元羧酸〔101 饲料添加剂；301 危险化学品，有机过氧化物；302 危险化学品，毒性物质；303 危险化学品，腐蚀性物质；304 其他化工品〕	6.5		30	13/	13	千克	/13		16.5	
		-环烷多元羧酸、环烯多元羧酸、环萜烯多元羧酸及其酸酐、酰卤化物、过氧化物和过氧酸以及它们的衍生物：										
2917.2010		---四氢苯酐〔999〕	4		11	13/	13	千克	/13		29	
2917.2090		---其他										
2917.2090	10	驱蚊灵(包括除虫菊素 II、瓜叶菊素 II、茉酮菊素 II)〔999〕	6.5		30	13/	0	千克	S/1		26.5	
2917.2090	90	其他(环烷、环烯、环萜烯)多元羧酸[T2]	6.5		30	13/	13	千克	AB/1	MRNS	26.5	
		-芳香多元羧酸及其酸酐、酰卤化物、过氧化物和过氧酸以及它们的衍生物：										
2917.3200		--邻苯二甲酸二辛酯〔999〕	6.5		30	13/	13	千克	/1		31.5	
2917.3300		--邻苯二甲酸二壬酯及邻苯二甲酸二癸酯)〔999〕	6.5		30	13/	13	千克	/1		16.5	
		--其他邻苯二甲酸酯：										
2917.3410		---邻苯二甲酸二丁酯										
2917.3410	10	驱蚊叮〔999〕	6.5		30	13/	0	千克	S/1		26.5	
2917.3410	90	其他邻苯二甲酸二丁酯〔301 杂项物质，302 其他化工产品〕	6.5		30	13/	13	千克	/1		26.5	
2917.3490		---其他〔301 危险化学品，杂项物质；302 其他危险化学品；303 其他化工品〕	6.5		30	13/	13	千克	/13		16.5	
2917.3500		--邻苯二甲酸酐〔301 危险化学品，腐蚀性物质；302 其他化工产品〕	6.5		30	13/	13	千克	AB/13	MN		
		--对苯二甲酸及其盐：										
		---对苯二甲酸：										
2917.3611		----精对苯二甲酸〔999〕	6.5		30	13/	13	千克	/1		31.5	6/6
2917.3619		----其他〔999〕	6.5		30	13/	13	千克	/1		31.5	6/6
2917.3690		---其他〔999〕	6.5		30	13/	13	千克	/1		11.5	
2917.3700		--对苯二甲酸二甲酯〔999〕	6.5		30	13/	13	千克	/1		31.5	
		--其他：										
2917.3910		---间苯二甲酸〔999〕	6.5		30	13/	13	千克	/1		31.5	
2917.3990		---其他										
2917.3990	11	酞菌酯〔999〕	6.5		30	13/	9,13	千克	S/13		26.5	
2917.3990	12	氯酞酸甲酯〔999〕	6.5		30	13/	9,13	千克	S/13		26.5	
2917.3990	13	氯酞酸〔999〕	6.5		30	13/	9,13	千克	S/13		26.5	
2917.3990	90	其他芳香多元羧酸〔301 危险化学品，易燃固体；302 危险化学品，有机过氧化物；303 危险化学品，腐蚀性物质；304 危险化学品，杂项物质；305 他危险化学品；306 其他化工产品〕	6.5		30	13/	13	千克	/13		26.5	
29.18		**含附加含氧基的羧酸及其酸酐、酰卤化物、过氧化物和过氧酸以及它们的卤化、磺化、硝化或亚硝化衍生物：**										
		-含醇基但不含其他含氧基的羧酸及其酸酐、酰卤化物、过氧化物和过氧酸以及它们的衍生物：										
2918.1100		--乳酸及其盐和酯[T2]	6.5		30	13/	13	千克	AB/13	MRNS	26.5	
2918.1200		--酒石酸〔101 饲料添加剂，301 无检疫要求食品添加剂，302 需申报仅用于工业用途不用于食品添加剂无检疫要求的化学品〕	6.5		35	13/	13	千克	A/1	R	31.5	
2918.1300		--酒石酸盐及酒石酸酯〔301 危险化学品，毒性物质；302 其他化工品，不用作食品添加剂；303 其他化工品，用作食品添加剂〕	6.5		30	13/	13	千克	AB/13	MRNS	31.5	
2918.1400		--柠檬酸〔101 饲料添加剂，102 无检疫要求食品添加剂，103 需申报仅用于工业用途不用于食品添加剂无检疫要求的化学品〕	6.5		35	13/	13	千克	4Axy/1	R	26.5	
2918.1500		--柠檬酸盐及柠檬酸酯〔101 饲料添加剂，301 无检疫要求食品添加剂，302 需申报仅用于工业用途不用于食品添加剂无检疫要求的化学品〕	6.5		30	13/	13	千克	4Axy/1	R	16.5	
2918.1600		--葡糖酸及其盐和酯〔101 葡萄糖酸钙，102 葡萄糖酸锌，103 葡萄糖酸亚铁，104 葡萄糖酸钠〕	6.5		30	13/	13	千克	/1		16.5	
2918.1700		--2,2-二苯基-2-羟基乙酸(二苯基乙醇酸)〔999〕	6.5		30	13/	13	千克	23/1			
2918.1800		--乙酯杀螨醇(ISO)〔301 危险化学品，杂项物质；302 其他化工产品〕	6.5		30	13/	0	千克	S/13			
2918.1900		--其他										
2918.1900	10	二苯乙醇酸甲酯(包括其酸酐，酰卤化物，过氧化物和过氧酸及其衍生物)〔999〕	6.5		30	13/	13	千克	23/13		16.5	
2918.1900	30	γ-羟基丁酸及其盐〔999〕	6.5		30	13/	13	千克	I/13		16.5	
2918.1900	41	丙酯杀螨醇〔999〕	6.5		30	13/	0	千克	S/13		16.5	
2918.1900	42	溴螨酯〔999〕	6.5		30	13/	9,13	千克	S/13		16.5	
2918.1900	43	芴丁酯〔999〕	6.5		30	13/	9,13	千克	S/13		16.5	
2918.1900	44	整形醇〔999〕	6.5		30	13/	9,13	千克	S/13		16.5	

协定税率 %								RCEP		特惠税率 %			Article Description
东/冰/格	巴基斯坦	韩国	瑞士上/下	哥/秘/柬	澳/毛	新西/坡/智	中国港/澳/台	东盟及马来/澳/韩	日/新	亚太2国	老/柬/缅	98/97/95	
0/0/0	4	3	0/0	0/0/0	0/0	0//0	0/0/	5.9/5.9/5.9	6.1/5.9			0/0/0	---Sebacic acid, its salts and esters
0/0/0	4	0	0/0	0/0/0	0/0	0//0	0/0/	0/0/0	5.9/0			0/0/0	---Other
0/0/0	4	1.3	0/0	0/0/0	0/0	0//0	0/0/	0/0/5.9	5.9/0			0/0/0	--Maleic anhydride
													--Other
0/0/0	4	0	0/0	0/0/0	0/0	0//0	0/0/	0/0/0	5.9/0			0/0/0	Dibutyl succinate, nifedipinestrobin
0/0/0	4	0	0/0	0/0/0	0/0	0//0	0/0/	0/0/0	5.9/0			0/0/0	Other acyclic pohycarboxylic acid
													-Cyclanic, cyclenic or cycloterpenic polycarboxylic acids, their anhydrides, halides, peroxides, peroxyacids and their derivatives:
0/0/0	0	1.8	0/0	0/0/0	0/0	0//0	0/0/	3.6/3.6/3.6	3.8/3.6			0/0/0	---Tetrahydro benzoic anhydride
													---Other
0/0/0	4	3	0/0	0/0/0	0/0	0//0	0/0/	5.9/5.9/5.9	6.1/5.9			0/0/0	Mosquito repellent (including pyrethrin II, chamomile II and jasmine II)
0/0/0	4	3	0/0	0/0/0	0/0	0//0	0/0/	5.9/5.9/5.9	6.1/5.9			0/0/0	Other cyclanic, cyclenic or cycloterpenic) polycarboxylic acids
													-Aromatic polycarboxylic acids, their anhydrides, halides, peroxides, peroxyacids and their derivatives:
0/0/0	0		0/0	0/0/0	0/0	0//0	0/0/0	5/5/	/5			0/0/0	--Dioctyl orthophthalates
0/0/0	4	0	0/0	0/0/0	0/0	0//0	0/0/0	0/0/0	0/0			0/0/0	--Dinonyl or didecyl orthophthalates
													--Other esters of orthaphthalic acid:
													---Dibutyl orthophthalates
0/0/0	4	1.3	0/0	0/0/0	0/0	0//0	0/0/	0/0/5.9	5.9/0			0/0/0	Dinbutyl phthalate
0/0/0	4	1.3	0/0	0/0/0	0/0	0//0	0/0/	0/0/5.9	5.9/0			0/0/0	Other phthalic acid dibutyl ester
0/0/0	4	0	0/0	0/0/0	0/0	0//0	0/0/0	0/0/0	0/0			0/0/0	---Other
0/0/0	0		0/0	0/0/0	0/0	0//0	0/0/	5/5/	/5			0/0/0	--Phthalic anhydride
													--Terephthalic acid and its salts:
													---Tere phthalic acid:
0/0/	0		2.7/2.7	0//0	0/0	0/0/0	0/0/	6.2/6.2/	/6.2			0/0/0	----Purified terephthalic acid
0/0/0	0		2.7/2.7	0/0/0	0/0	0/0/0	0/0/	6.2/6.2/	/6.2			0/0/0	----Other
0/0/0	4		0/0	0/0/0	0/0	0//0	0/0/	5/5/	/5			0/0/0	---Other
0/0/0	4	3	0/0	0/0/0	0/0	0//0	0/0/	5.9/5.9/5.9	6.1/5.9			0/0/0	--Dimethyl terephthalate
													--Other:
0/0/0	0		0/0	0/0/0	0/0	0//0	0/0/	5/5/	/5			0/0/0	---Isophthalic acid
													---Other
0/0/0	0	3	0/0	0/0/0	0/0	0//0	0/0/	0/5.9/5.9	6.1/5.9			0/0/0	Nitrotalisopropyl
0/0/0	0	3	0/0	0/0/0	0/0	0//0	0/0/	0/5.9/5.9	6.1/5.9			0/0/0	Chlorthal-dimethyl
0/0/0	0	3	0/0	0/0/0	0/0	0//0	0/0/	0/5.9/5.9	6.1/5.9			0/0/0	Chlorthal
0/0/0	0	3	0/0	0/0/0	0/0	0//0	0/0/	0/5.9/5.9	6.1/5.9			0/0/0	Other aromatic polycarboxylic acid
													Carboxylic acids with additional oxygen function and their anhydrides, halides, peroxides and peroxyacids; their halogenated, sulphonated, nitrated or nitrosated derivatives:
													-Carboxylic acids with alcohol function but without other oxygen function, their anhydrides, halides, peroxides, peroxyacids and their derivatives:
0/0/0	4	1.3	0/0	0/0/0	0/0	0//0	0/0/	0/0/5.9	5.9/0			0/0/0	--Lactic acid, its salts and esters
0/0/0	4	0	0/0	0/0/0	0/0	0//0	0/0/	0/0/0	5.9/0			0/0/0	--Tartaric acid
0/0/0	4	0	0/0	0/0/0	0/0	0//0	0/0/	0/0/0	5.9/0			0/0/0	--Salts and esters of tartaric acid
0/0/0	4	1.3	0/0	0/0/0	0/0	0//0	0/0/	0/0/5.9	5.9/0			0/0/0	--Citric acid
0/0/0	4	0	0/0	0/0/0	0/0	0//0	0/0/	0/0/0	5.9/0			0/0/0	--Salts and esters of citric acid
0/0/0	4	0	0/0	0/0/0	0/0	0//0	0/0/	0/0/0	5.9/0			0/0/0	--Gluconic acid, its salts and esters
0/0/0	4	0	0/0	0/0/0	0/0	0//0	0/0/	0/0/0	5.9/0			0/0/0	--2, 2-Diphenyl-2-hydroxyacetic acid (*benzilic acid*)
0/0/0	4	0	0/0	0/0/0	0/0	0//0	0/0/	0/0/0	5.9/0			0/0/0	--Chlorobenzilate(ISO)
													--Other
0/0/0	4	0	0/0	0/0/0	0/0	0//0	0/0/	0/0/0	5.9/0			0/0/0	Methyl benzilate(including their anhydrides, halides, peroxides, peroxyacids and their derivatives)
0/0/0	4	0	0/0	0/0/0	0/0	0//0	0/0/	0/0/0	5.9/0			0/0/0	γ-hydroxybutyric acid and its salts
0/0/0	4	0	0/0	0/0/0	0/0	0//0	0/0/	0/0/0	5.9/0			0/0/0	Acaralate
0/0/0	4	0	0/0	0/0/0	0/0	0//0	0/0/	0/0/0	5.9/0			0/0/0	Bromopropylate
0/0/0	4	0	0/0	0/0/0	0/0	0//0	0/0/	0/0/0	5.9/0			0/0/0	Fluorenol butyl ester
0/0/0	4	0	0/0	0/0/0	0/0	0//0	0/0/	0/0/0	5.9/0			0/0/0	Chlorflurenol

税则号列	货品名称〔CIQ 扩展编码及品名—T2 表示见附表 2〕	最惠(%)	暂定税率	普通	增值/消费	出口退税	计量单位	监管条件/特殊证件	检验检疫	对美关税	亚太上/下
2918.1900　90	其他含醇基但不含其他含氧基羧酸(包括其酸酐,酰卤化物,过氧化物和过氧酸及其衍生物)〔101 饲料添加剂;301 危险化学品,易燃液体;302 危险化学品,有机过氧化物;303 其他化工品〕	6.5		30	13/	13	千克	/13		16.5	
	-含酚基但不含其他含氧基的羧酸及其酸酐、酰卤化物、过氧化物和过氧酸以及它们的衍生物:										
	--水杨酸及其盐:										
2918.2110	---水杨酸、水杨酸钠〔999〕	6.5		20	13/	13	千克	/1		26.5	
2918.2190	---其他〔999〕	6.5		30	13/	13	千克	/1		16.5	
	--邻乙酰水杨酸及其盐和酯:										
2918.2210	---邻乙酰水杨酸(阿司匹林)〔999〕	6		20	13/	13	千克	/1		11	
2918.2290	---其他〔999〕	6.5		30	13/	13	千克	/1			
2918.2300	--水杨酸的其他酯及其盐〔101 水杨酸苯乙酯,102 水杨酸苯酯,103 水杨酸苄酯(柳酸苄酯),104 水杨酸甲酯(柳酸甲酯),105 水杨酸乙酯(柳酸乙酯),106 水杨酸异丁酯,107 水杨酸异戊酯(柳酸异戊酯),108 柳酸丁酯(水杨酸丁酯)〕	6.5		30	13/	13	千克	/1		11.5	
2918.2900	--其他〔301 无检疫要求食品添加剂,302 对羟基苯甲酸乙酯需申报仅用于工业用途不用于食品添加剂无检疫要求的化学品〕	6.5		30	13/	13	千克	A/1	R		
2918.3000	-含醛基或酮基但不含其他含氧基的羧酸及其酸酐、酰卤化物、过氧化物和过氧酸以及它们的衍生物										
2918.3000　14	环戊烯丙菊酯〔999〕	6.5		30	13/	9,13	千克	S/13		16.5	
2918.3000　15	调环酸、抗倒酯、环虫菊酯〔999〕	6.5		30	13/	9,13	千克	S/13		16.5	
2918.3000　16	烯丙菊酯等(包括右旋烯丙菊酯、富右旋反式烯丙菊酯,右旋反式烯丙菊酯)〔999〕	6.5		30	13/	9,13	千克	S/13		16.5	
2918.3000　17	Es-生物烯丙菊酯、生物烯丙菊酯等(包括 S-生物烯丙菊酯)〔999〕	6.5		30	13/	9,13	千克	S/13		16.5	
2918.3000　18	乙酰氟菊酯〔999〕	6.5		30	13/	9,13	千克	S/13		16.5	
2918.3000　21	3—氧—2—苯基丁酸甲酯(CAS 号 16648—44—5)〔999〕	6.5		30	13/	13	千克	23/13		16.5	
2918.3000　90	其他含醛基或酮基不含其他含氧基羧酸(包括酸酐、酰卤化物、过氧化物和过氧酸及其衍生物)[T2]	6.5		30	13/	13	千克	/13		16.5	
	-其他:										
2918.9100	--2,4,5-涕(ISO)(2,4,5-三氯苯氧基乙酸)及其盐或酯〔301 危险化学品,杂项物质;302 其他化工产品〕	6.5		30	13/	0	千克	89/13			
2918.9900	--其他										
2918.9900　21	2,4—滴及其盐和酯、2,4—滴丙酸、2,4—滴丁酸等(包括精2,4—滴丙酸、苯醚菌酯)〔301 危险化学品,杂项物质,302 其他化工产品〕	6.5		30	13/	9,13	千克	S/13		16.5	
2918.9900　22	2 甲 4 氯及其盐和酯、2 甲 4 氯丙酸等(包括精 2 甲 4 氯丙酸)〔999〕	6.5		30	13/	9,13	千克	S/13		16.5	
2918.9900　23	2 甲 4 氯丁酸〔999〕	6.5		30	13/	9,13	千克	S/13		16.5	
2918.9900　24	麦草畏及其盐、杀草畏〔999〕	6.5		30	13/	9,13	千克	S/13		16.5	
2918.9900　25	禾草灵、乳氟禾草灵〔999〕	6.5		30	13/	9,13	千克	S/13		16.5	
2918.9900　26	氟萘禾草灵、甲羧除草醚〔999〕	6.5		30	13/	9,13	千克	S/13		16.5	
2918.9900　27	三氟羧草醚、乙羧氟草醚〔999〕	6.5		30	13/	9,13	千克	S/13		16.5	
2918.9900　28	氟乳醚、调果酸、座果酸〔999〕	6.5		30	13/	9,13	千克	S/13		16.5	
2918.9900　29	增糖酯、S—诱抗素(包括烯虫酯)〔999〕	6.5		30	13/	9,13	千克	S/13		16.5	
2918.9900　30	调环酸钙〔999〕	6.5		30	13/	13	千克	S/13		16.5	
2918.9900　41	2 甲 4 氯异辛酯〔999〕	6.5		30	13/	9,13	千克	S/13		16.5	
2918.9900　90	其他含其他附加含氧基羧酸(包括其酸酐、酰卤化物、过氧化物和过氧酸及其衍生物)〔301 危险化学品,易燃液体;302 危险化学品,有机过氧化物;303 危险化学品,腐蚀性物质;304 危险化学品,杂项物质;305 其他危险化学品;306 其他化工产品〕	6.5		30	13/	13	千克	/13		16.5	
	第八分章　非金属无机酸酯及其盐以及它们的卤化、磺化、硝化或亚硝化衍生物										
29.19	**磷酸酯及其盐,包括乳磷酸盐,以及它们的卤化、磺化、硝化或亚硝化衍生物:**										
2919.1000	-三(2,3-二溴丙基)磷酸酯〔999〕	6.5		30	13/	13	千克	89/13			
2919.9000	-其他										
2919.9000　20	磷酸三丁酯〔999〕	6.5		30	13/	13	千克	3/13		26.5	
2919.9000　31	敌敌钙,敌敌畏〔999〕	6.5		30	13/	9,13	千克	S/13		26.5	
2919.9000　32	速灭磷、二溴磷〔301 危险化学品,毒性物质;302 危险化学品,杂项物质〕	6.5		30	13/	9,13	千克	S/13		26.5	
2919.9000　33	巴毒磷、杀虫畏〔999〕	6.5		30	13/	0	千克	S/13		26.5	
2919.9000　34	毒虫畏、甲基毒虫畏〔999〕	6.5		30	13/	0	千克	S/13		26.5	
2919.9000　35	庚烯磷、特普〔999〕	6.5		30	13/	0	千克	S/13		26.5	
2919.9000　36	三乙膦酸铝、乙膦酸〔999〕	6.5		30	13/	9,13	千克	S/13		26.5	

协定税率 %								RCEP		特惠税率 %			Article Description
东/冰/格	巴基斯坦	韩国	瑞士 上/下	哥/秘/柬	澳/毛	新西/坡/智	中国港/澳/台	东盟及马来/澳/韩	日/新	亚太2国	老/柬/缅	98/97/95	
0/0/0	4	0	0/0	0/0/0	0/0	0//0	0/0/	0/0/0	5.9/0			0/0/0	Other carboxylic acids with alcohol function but without other oxygen function(including their anhydrides, etheride, peroxides, peroxyacids and their derivatives
													-Carboxylic acids with phenol function but without other oxygen function, their anhydrides, halides, peroxides, peroxyacids and their derivatives:
													--Salicylic acid and its salts:
0/0/0	4	1.3	2.7/2.7	0/0/0	0/0	0//0	0/0/	0/0/5.9	5.9/0			0/0/0	---Salicylic acid and sodium salicylate
0/0/0	4	0	0/0	0/0/0	0/0	0//0	0/0/	0/0/0	5.9/0			0/0/0	---Other
													--*o*-Acetylsalicylic acid, its salts and esters:
0/0/0	5	0	0/0	0/0/0	0/0	0//0	0/0/	0/0/0	0/0			0/0/0	---Acetylsalicylic acid
0/0/0	5	0	0/0	0/0/0	0/0	0//0	0/0/	0/0/0	5.9/0			0/0/0	---Other
0/0/0	3.5	0		0/0/0	0/0	0//0	0/0/	0/0/0	5.9/0			0/0/0	--Other esters of salicylic acid and their salts
0/0/0	5	3	0/0	0/0/0	0/0	0//0	0/0/	5.9/5.9/5.9	6.1/5.9			0/0/0	--Other
													-Carboxylic acids with aldehyde or ketone function but without other oxygen function, their anhydrides, halides, peroxides, peroxyacids and their derivatives
0/0/0	5	0	2.7/2.7	0/0/0	0/0	0//0	0/0/	0/0/0	5.9/0			0/0/0	Terallethrin
0/0/0	5	0	2.7/2.7	0/0/0	0/0	0//0	0/0/	0/0/0	5.9/0			0/0/0	Prohexadione, trinexapac-ethyl, cyclethrin
0/0/0	5	0	2.7/2.7	0/0/0	0/0	0//0	0/0/	0/0/0	5.9/0			0/0/0	Allethrin (including d-allethrin、rich-d-t-allethrin、d-t-allethrin)
0/0/0	5	0	2.7/2.7	0/0/0	0/0	0//0	0/0/	0/0/0	5.9/0			0/0/0	Es-bioallethrin, bioallethrin(including S-bioallethrin)
0/0/0	5	0	2.7/2.7	0/0/0	0/0	0//0	0/0/	0/0/0	5.9/0			0/0/0	acetyl-fluthrinate
0/0/0	5	0	2.7/2.7	0/0/0	0/0	0//0	0/0/	0/0/0	5.9/0			0/0/0	Methyl 3－oxy－2－phenylbutyrate (CAS NO.16648－44－5)
0/0/0	5	0	2.7/2.7	0/0/0	0/0	0//0	0/0/	0/0/0	5.9/0			0/0/0	Other carboxylic acid with aldehyde or ketone function but without other oxygen function, their anhydrides, halides, peroxides, peroxyacids and their derivatives
													-Other:
0/0/0	5	0	0/0	0/0/0	0/0	0//0	0/0/	0/0/0	5.9/0			0/0/0	--2,4,5-T(ISO) (2,4,5-trichlorophenoxy acetic acid), ist salts and esters
													--Other
0/0/0	5	0	2.7/2.7	0/0/0	0/0	0//0	0/0/	0/0/0	5.9/0			0/0/0	2,4－d and its salts and esters, 2,4－d propionic acid, 2,4－d butyric acid, etc. (including refined 2,4－d propionic acid and phenyl ether ester)
0/0/0	5	0	2.7/2.7	0/0/0	0/0	0//0	0/0/	0/0/0	5.9/0			0/0/0	2 methyl 4 chloride and its salts and esters, 2 methyl 4 Chloropropionic acid, etc. (including refined 2 methyl 4 Chloropropionic acid)
0/0/0	5	0	2.7/2.7	0/0/0	0/0	0//0	0/0/	0/0/0	5.9/0			0/0/0	MCPA butyric acid
0/0/0	5	0	2.7/2.7	0/0/0	0/0	0//0	0/0/	0/0/0	5.9/0			0/0/0	Dicamba, its salt and dicoform
0/0/0	5	0	2.7/2.7	0/0/0	0/0	0//0	0/0/	0/0/0	5.9/0			0/0/0	Diclofop, lactofen
0/0/0	5	0	2.7/2.7	0/0/0	0/0	0//0	0/0/	0/0/0	5.9/0			0/0/0	Fluoro-naphthalene diclofop, bifenox
0/0/0	5	0	2.7/2.7	0/0/0	0/0	0//0	0/0/	0/0/0	5.9/0			0/0/0	Acifluorfen, benzofluorfen
0/0/0	5	0	2.7/2.7	0/0/0	0/0	0//0	0/0/	0/0/0	5.9/0			0/0/0	Ethoxycarbofen, cloprop, cloxyfonac
0/0/0	5	0	2.7/2.7	0/0/0	0/0	0//0	0/0/	0/0/0	5.9/0			0/0/0	Dlcamba-methyl-ester, abscisic acid, ethoxyfen-ethyl (including methoprene)
0/0/0	5	0	2.7/2.7	0/0/0	0/0	0//0	0/0/	0/0/0	5.9/0			0/0/0	Adjustable calcium sulfonate
0/0/0	5	0	2.7/2.7	0/0/0	0/0	0//0	0/0/	0/0/0	5.9/0			0/0/0	2 a 4 chloride isooctyl
0/0/0	5	0	2.7/2.7	0/0/0	0/0	0//0	0/0/	0/0/0	5.9/0			0/0/0	Other carboxylic acids with other additional oxygen function and their anhydrides, halides, peroxides and peroxyacids; their derivatives
													Ⅷ. ESTERS OF INORGANIC ACIDS OF NON-METALS AND THEIR SALTS, AND THEIR HALOGENATED, SULPHONATED, NITRATED OR NITROSATED DERIVATIVES
													Phosphoric esters and their salts, including lactophosphates; their halogenated, sulphonated, nitrated or nitrosated derivatives:
0/0/0	5	0	0/0	0/0/0	0/0	0//0	0/0/	0/0/0	5.9/0			0/0/0	-Tris(2,3-dibromopropyl)phosphate
													-Other
0/0/0	5	0	0/0	0/0/0	0/0	0//0	0/0/	5.9/5.9/5.9	5.9/5.9			0/0/0	Tributyl phosphate
0/0/0	5	0	0/0	0/0/0	0/0	0//0	0/0/	5.9/5.9/5.9	5.9/5.9			0/0/0	Calvinphos, dichlorvos
0/0/0	5	0	0/0	0/0/0	0/0	0//0	0/0/	5.9/5.9/5.9	5.9/5.9			0/0/0	Mevinphos, dibron
0/0/0	5	0	0/0	0/0/0	0/0	0//0	0/0/	5.9/5.9/5.9	5.9/5.9			0/0/0	Crotoxyphos, tetrachlorvinphos
0/0/0	5	0	0/0	0/0/0	0/0	0//0	0/0/	5.9/5.9/5.9	5.9/5.9			0/0/0	Chlorfenvinphos, dimethylvinphos
0/0/0	5	0	0/0	0/0/0	0/0	0//0	0/0/	5.9/5.9/5.9	5.9/5.9			0/0/0	Heptenophos, tepp
0/0/0	5	0	0/0	0/0/0	0/0	0//0	0/0/	5.9/5.9/5.9	5.9/5.9			0/0/0	Fosetyl-aluminium, phosphonoacetic acid

税则号列	货品名称〔CIQ 扩展编码及品名—T2 表示见附表 2〕	最惠(%)	暂定税率	普通	增值/消费	出口退税	计量单位	监管条件/特殊证件	检验检疫	对美关税	亚太 上/下
2919.9000 37	氯瘟磷、伐草磷〔999〕	6.5		30	13/	0	千克	S/13		26.5	
2919.9000 90	其他磷酸酯及其盐(包括乳磷酸盐)(包括它们的卤化、磺化、硝化或亚硝化衍生物)[T2]	6.5		30	13/	9,13	千克	AB/13	MRNS	26.5	
29.20	**其他非金属无机酸酯(不包括卤化氢的酯)及其盐以及它们的卤化、磺化、硝化或亚硝化衍生物:**										
	-硫代磷酸酯及其盐以及它们的卤化、磺化、硝化或亚硝化衍生物:										
2920.1100	--对硫磷(ISO)及甲基对硫磷(ISO)〔999〕	6.5		30	13/	0	千克	/13			
2920.1900	--其他										
2920.1900 12	氯氧磷、虫螨畏〔999〕	6.5		30	13/	0	千克	S/13		26.5	
2920.1900 13	杀螟硫磷、除线磷〔301〕	6.5		30	13/	9,13	千克	S/13		26.5	
2920.1900 14	异氯磷、皮蝇磷〔301〕	6.5		30	13/	9,13	千克	S/13		26.5	
2920.1900 15	溴硫磷、乙基溴硫磷、硝虫硫磷〔301 危险化学品,毒性物质;302 其他化工产品〕	6.5		30	13/	9,13	千克	S/13		26.5	
2920.1900 17	碘硫磷、苯稻瘟净〔999〕	6.5		30	13/	0	千克	S/13		26.5	
2920.1900 18	甲基立枯磷、克菌磷〔999〕	6.5		30	13/	9,13	千克	S/13		26.5	
2920.1900 19	速杀硫磷、丰丙磷〔999〕	6.5		30	13/	9,13	千克	S/13		26.5	
2920.1900 90	其他硫代磷酸酯及其盐(包括它们的卤化、磺化、硝化或亚硝化衍生物)〔301 危险化学品,杂项物质;302 其他化工产品〕	6.5		30	13/	13	千克	/13		26.5	
	-亚磷酸酯及其盐以及它们的卤化、磺化、硝化或亚硝化衍生物:										
2920.2100	--亚磷酸二甲酯〔999〕	6.5		30	13/	13	千克	23/1			5.2/5.2
2920.2200	--亚磷酸二乙酯〔999〕	6.5		30	13/	13	千克	23/1			5.2/5.2
2920.2300	--亚磷酸三甲酯〔999〕	6.5		30	13/	13	千克	23AB/13	MN	11.5	5.2/5.2
2920.2400	--亚磷酸三乙酯〔999〕	6.5		30	13/	13	千克	23AB/13	MN		5.2/5.2
	--其他:										
2920.2910	---其他亚磷酸酯〔301 危险化学品,易燃液体;302 危险化学品,杂项物质;303 其他化工产品〕	6.5		30	13/	9,13	千克	/13		16.5	
2920.2990	---其他										
2920.2990 10	浸种磷〔999〕	6.5		30	13/	0	千克	S/1		11.5	
2920.2990 90	其他亚磷酸酯及其盐以及它们的卤化、磺化、硝化或亚硝化衍生物〔302〕	6.5		30	13/	13	千克	/1		11.5	
2920.3000	-硫丹(ISO)〔999〕	6.5		30	13/	0	千克	89/13			
2920.9000	-其他										
2920.9000 11	碳酸二苯酯〔999〕	6.5	2	30	13/	13	千克	/13		12	
2920.9000 12	治螟磷〔999〕	6.5		30	13/	0	千克	S/13		16.5	
2920.9000 13	消螨通〔999〕	6.5		30	13/	0	千克	S/13		16.5	
2920.9000 14	炔螨特〔999〕	6.5		30	13/	9,13	千克	S/13		16.5	
2920.9000 15	赛松〔999〕	6.5		30	13/	0	千克	S/13		16.5	
2920.9000 16	三乙基砷酸酯〔999〕	6.5		30	13/	13	千克	/13		16.5	
2920.9000 20	太安(PETN)(季戊四醇四硝酸酯)〔999〕	6.5		30	13/	13	千克	k/13		16.5	
2920.9000 90	其他无机酸酯(不包括卤化氢的酯)(包括其盐以及它们的卤化,磺化,硝化或亚硝化衍生物)[T2]	6.5		30	13/	13	千克	/13		16.5	
	第九分章　含氮基化合物										
29.21	**氨基化合物:**										
	-无环单胺及其衍生物以及它们的盐:										
2921.1100	--甲胺、二甲胺或三甲胺及其盐										
2921.1100 10	二甲胺〔301 危险化学品,气体;302 危险化学品,易燃液体〕	6.5		30	13/	13	千克	23/13		26.5	
2921.1100 20	二甲胺盐酸盐〔999〕	6.5		30	13/	13	千克	23/13		26.5	
2921.1100 30	甲胺盐〔301 危险化学品,腐蚀性物质;302 其他化工产品〕	6.5		30	13/	13	千克	/13		26.5	
2921.1100 90	甲胺,三甲胺及其盐,其他二甲胺盐〔301 危险化学品,气体;302 危险化学品,其他化工品〕	6.5		30	13/	13	千克	AB/13	MN	26.5	
2921.1200	--2-(N,N-二甲基氨基)氯乙烷盐酸盐〔999〕	6.5		30	13/	13	千克	/1		11.5	
2921.1300	--2-(N,N-二乙基氨基)氯乙烷盐酸盐〔999〕	6.5		30	13/	13	千克	/1			
2921.1400	--2-(N,N-二异丙基氨基)氯乙烷盐酸盐〔999〕	6.5		30	13/	13	千克	/1			
	--其他:										
2921.1910	---二正丙胺〔999〕	4		11	13/	13	千克	AB/13	MN		3.6/3.6
2921.1920	---异丙胺〔999〕	6.5		30	13/	13	千克	/13			
2921.1930	---N,N-二(2-氯乙基)乙胺〔999〕	6.5		30	13/	13	千克	32/1			5.2/5.2
2921.1940	---N,N-二(2-氯乙基)甲胺〔999〕	6.5		30	13/	13	千克	32/13			5.2/5.2
2921.1950	---三(2-氯乙基)胺〔999〕	6.5		30	13/	13	千克	32/1			5.2/5.2
2921.1960	---二烷(甲、乙、正丙或异丙)氨基乙基-2-氯及其质子化盐〔999〕	6.5		30	13/	13	千克	23/1			5.2/5.2
2921.1990	---其他										
2921.1990 11	三乙胺(单一成分,用做点火剂)〔999〕	6.5		30	13/	13	千克	3A/13	M	16.5	
2921.1990 20	二异丙胺〔999〕	6.5		30	13/	13	千克	3/13		16.5	
2921.1990 31	2-氨基丁烷〔999〕	6.5		30	13/	0	千克	S/13		16.5	
2921.1990 33	胺鲜酯〔999〕	6.5		30	13/	9,13	千克	S/13		16.5	
2921.1990 90	其他无环单胺及其衍生物及其盐〔301 危险化学品,气体;302 危险化学品,易燃液体;303 险化学品,毒性物质;304 危险化学品,腐蚀性物质;305 其他化工产品〕	6.5		30	13/	13	千克	/13		16.5	
	-无环多胺及其衍生物以及它们的盐:										

协定税率 %								RCEP		特惠税率 %			Article Description
东/冰/格	巴基斯坦	韩国	瑞士 上/下	哥/秘/柬	澳/毛	新西/坡/智	中国港/澳/台	东盟及马来/澳/韩	日/新	亚太2国	老/柬/缅	98/97/95	
0/0/0	5	0	0/0	0/0/0	0/0	0//0	0/0/	5.9/5.9/5.9	5.9/5.9			0/0/0	Phosdiphen, grass-killing phosphate
0/0/0	5	0	0/0	0/0/0	0/0	0//0	0/0/	5.9/5.9/5.9	5.9/5.9			0/0/0	Other phosphoric esters and their salts, including lactophosphates; their halogenated, sulphonated, nitrated or nitrosated derivatives
													Esters of other inorganic acids of non-metals (excluding esters of hydrogen halides) and their salts; their halogenated, sulphonated, nitrated or nitrosated derivatives:
													-Thiophosphoric esters (phosphorothioates) and their salts; their halogenated, sulphonated, nitrated or nitrosated derivatives:
0/0/0	5	0	0/0	0/0/0	0/0	0//0	0/0/	0/0/0	5.9/0			0/0/0	--Parathion(ISO) and parathion-metlyl(ISO)(methyl-parathion)
													--Other
0/0/0	5	0	0/0	0/0/0	0/0	0//0	0/0/	0/0/0	5.9/0			0/0/0	Chlorethoxyfos, methacrifos
0/0/0	5	0	0/0	0/0/0	0/0	0//0	0/0/	0/0/0	5.9/0			0/0/0	Fenitrothion, dichlofention
0/0/0	5	0	0/0	0/0/0	0/0	0//0	0/0/	0/0/0	5.9/0			0/0/0	Isochlorthion, fenchlorphos
0/0/0	5	0	0/0	0/0/0	0/0	0//0	0/0/	0/0/0	5.9/0			0/0/0	Bromophos, bromofos-ethyl, xiaochongthion
0/0/0	5	0	0/0	0/0/0	0/0	0//0	0/0/	0/0/0	5.9/0			0/0/0	Idofenphos, Benzene rice blast net
0/0/0	5	0	0/0	0/0/0	0/0	0//0	0/0/	0/0/0	5.9/0			0/0/0	Tolclofos-methyl, pyrazophos
0/0/0	5	0	0/0	0/0/0	0/0	0//0	0/0/	0/0/0	5.9/0			0/0/0	Heterophos, apidan
0/0/0	5	0	0/0	0/0/0	0/0	0//0	0/0/	0/0/0	5.9/0			0/0/0	Other thiophosphoric esters (phosphorothioates) and their salts; their halogenated, sulphonated, nitrated or nitrosated derivatives
													-Phosphite esters and their salts; their halogenated, sulphonated, nitrated or nitrosated derivatives:
0/0/0	5	0	0/0	0/0/0	0/0	0//0	0/0/	0/0/0	5.9/0			0/0/0	--Dimethyl phosphite
0/0/0	5	0	0/0	0/0/0	0/0	0//0	0/0/	0/0/0	5.9/0			0/0/0	--Diethyl phosphite
0/0/0	5	0	0/0	0/0/0	0/0	0//0	0/0/	0/0/0	5.9/0			0/0/0	--Trimethyl phosphite
0/0/0	5	0	0/0	0/0/0	0/0	0//0	0/0/	0/0/0	5.9/0			0/0/0	--Triethyl phosphite
													--Other:
0/0/0	5	0	0/0	0/0/0	0/0	0//0	0/0/	0/0/0	5.9/0			0/0/0	---Other Phosphite esters
													---Other
0/0/0	5	0	0/0	0/0/0	0/0	0//0	0/0/	5.9/5.9/5.9	5.9/5.9			0/0/0	Izopamfos
0/0/0	5	0	0/0	0/0/0	0/0	0//0	0/0/	5.9/5.9/5.9	5.9/5.9			0/0/0	Phosphite esters and their salts; their halogenated, sulphonated, nitrated or nitrosated derivatives
0/0/0	5	0	0/0	0/0/0	0/0	0//0	0/0/	5.9/5.9/5.9	5.9/5.9			0/0/0	-Endosulfan (*ISO*)
													-Other
0/0/0	5	0	0/0	0/0/0	0/0	0//0	0/0/	5.9/5.9/5.9	5.9/5.9			0/0/0	Diphenyl carbonate
0/0/0	5	0	0/0	0/0/0	0/0	0//0	0/0/	5.9/5.9/5.9	5.9/5.9			0/0/0	Sulfotepp
0/0/0	5	0	0/0	0/0/0	0/0	0//0	0/0/	5.9/5.9/5.9	5.9/5.9			0/0/0	Dinobuton
0/0/0	5	0	0/0	0/0/0	0/0	0//0	0/0/	5.9/5.9/5.9	5.9/5.9			0/0/0	Propargite
0/0/0	5	0	0/0	0/0/0	0/0	0//0	0/0/	5.9/5.9/5.9	5.9/5.9			0/0/0	Sesone
0/0/0	5	0	0/0	0/0/0	0/0	0//0	0/0/	5.9/5.9/5.9	5.9/5.9			0/0/0	Thiethyl arsenate
0/0/0	5	0	0/0	0/0/0	0/0	0//0	0/0/	5.9/5.9/5.9	5.9/5.9		//	0/0/0	PETN (Pentaerythritol Tetranitrate)
0/0/0	5	0	0/0	0/0/0	0/0	0//0	0/0/	5.9/5.9/5.9	5.9/5.9			0/0/0	Other Esters of other inorganic acids(excluding esters of hydrogen halides(and their salts; their halogenated, ulphonated, nitrated or nitrosated derivatives
													Ⅸ. NITROGEN-FUNCTION COMPOUNDS
													Amine-function compounds:
													-Acyclic monoamines and their derivatives; salts thereof:
													--Methylamine, di- or trimethylamine and their salts
0/0/0	5	0	0/0	0/0/0	0/0	0//0	0/0/	0/0/0	5.9/0			0/0/0	Dimethylamine
0/0/0	5	0	0/0	0/0/0	0/0	0//0	0/0/	0/0/0	5.9/0			0/0/0	Dimethylamine hydrochloride
0/0/0	5	0	0/0	0/0/0	0/0	0//0	0/0/	0/0/0	5.9/0			0/0/0	Salts of methylamine
0/0/0	5	0	0/0	0/0/0	0/0	0//0	0/0/	0/0/0	5.9/0			0/0/0	Methylamine, trimethylamine and their salts
0/0/0	5	0	0/0	0/0/0	0/0	0//0	0/0/	0/0/0	5.9/0			0/0/0	--2-(*N,N-Dimethylamino*)ethylchloride hydrochloride
0/0/0	5	0	0/0	0/0/0	0/0	0//0	0/0/	0/0/0	5.9/0			0/0/0	--2-(*N,N-Diethylamino*)ethylchloride hydrochloride
0/0/0	5	0	0/0	0/0/0	0/0	0//0	0/0/	0/0/0	5.9/0			0/0/0	--2-(*N,N-Diisopropylamino*)ehylchloride hydrochloride
													--Other:
0/0/0	0	0	0/0	0/0/0	0/0	0//0	0/0/	0/0/0	0/0			0/0/0	---Di-*n*-propylamine
0/0/0	5	0	0/0	0/0/0	0/0	0//0	0/0/	0/0/0	0/0			0/0/0	---Isopropyl amine
0/0/0	5	0	0/0	0/0/0	0/0	0//0	0/0/	0/0/0	5.9/0			0/0/0	---N,N-Bis(2-chloroethyl) ethylamine
0/0/0	5	0	0/0	0/0/0	0/0	0//0	0/0/	0/0/0	5.9/0			0/0/0	---N,N-Bis(2-chloroethyl) methylamine
0/0/0	5	0	0/0	0/0/0	0/0	0//0	0/0/	0/0/0	5.9/0			0/0/0	---Tri-(2-chloroethyl) amine
0/0/0	5	0	0/0	0/0/0	0/0	0//0	0/0/	0/0/0	5.9/0			0/0/0	---N,N-Dialkyl (Me, Et, n-Pr or i-Pr) aminoethyl-2-chlorides and corresponking protonated salts
													---Other
0/0/0	5	0	0/0	0/0/0	0/0	0//0	0/0/	0/0/0	5.9/0			0/0/0	Triethylamine(Single component, used for igniter)
0/0/0	5	0	0/0	0/0/0	0/0	0//0	0/0/	0/0/0	5.9/0			0/0/0	Diisopropylamine
0/0/0	5	0	0/0	0/0/0	0/0	0//0	0/0/	0/0/0	5.9/0			0/0/0	2-Amidobutane
0/0/0	5	0	0/0	0/0/0	0/0	0//0	0/0/	0/0/0	5.9/0			0/0/0	Diethyl aminoethyl hexanoate
0/0/0	5	0	0/0	0/0/0	0/0	0//0	0/0/	0/0/0	5.9/0			0/0/0	Other acyclic monoamines and their derivatives; salts thereof
													-Acyclic polyamines and their derivatives; salts thereof:

税则号列		货品名称〔CIQ 扩展编码及品名—T2 表示见附表 2〕	最惠(%)	暂定税率	普通	增值/消费	出口退税	计量单位	监管条件/特殊证件	检验检疫	对美关税	亚太上/下
		--乙二胺及其盐:										
2921.2110		---乙二胺〔999〕	6.5		30	13/	13	千克	/13		11.5	
2921.2190		---其他〔301 危险化学品,腐蚀性物质;302 其他化工产品〕	6.5		30	13/	13	千克	/13		16.5	
		--六亚甲基二胺及其盐:										
2921.2210		---己二酸己二胺盐(尼龙-6,6 盐)〔999〕	6.5		20	13/	13	千克	/1			5.2/5.2
2921.2290		---其他〔301 危险化学品,腐蚀性物质;302 其他化工产品〕	6.5		30	13/	13	千克	/13		11.5	
2921.2900		--其他										
2921.2900	10	辛菌胺〔101:饲料添加剂;304:其他化工产品〕	6.5		30	13/	13	千克	S/13		16.5	
2921.2900	90	其他无环多胺及其衍生物(包括它们的盐)〔301 危险化学品,易燃液体;302 危险化学品,易燃固体;303 危险化学品,毒性物质;304 危险化学品,腐蚀性物质;305 其他化工产品〕	6.5		30	13/	13	千克	/13		16.5	
2921.3000		-环烷单胺或多胺、环烯单胺或多胺、环萜烯单胺或多胺及其衍生物以及它们的盐										
2921.3000	10	丙己君及其盐〔999〕	6.5		30	13/	13	千克	I/13		26.5	
2921.3000	30	氨基羧酸环丙烷〔999〕	6.5		30	13/	9,13	千克	S/13		26.5	
2921.3000	40	乙撑亚胺〔999〕	6.5		30	13/	13	千克	AB/13	MN	26.5	
2921.3000	90	其他环(烷、烯、萜烯)单胺或多胺(包括其衍生物及它们的盐)〔301 易燃液体,302 易燃固体、自反应物质及固态退敏爆炸品,303 毒性物质和感染性物质,304 腐蚀性物质,305 其他化工产品〕	6.5		30	13/	13	千克	/13		26.5	
		-芳香单胺及其衍生物以及它们的盐:										
		--苯胺及其盐:										
2921.4110		---苯胺〔999〕	6.5		20	13/	13	千克	AB/13	MN		5.2/5.2
2921.4190		---其他〔301 危险化学品,毒性物质;302 危险化学品,杂项物质;303 其他化工产品〕	6.5		30	13/	13	千克	/13			
2921.4200		--苯胺衍生物及其盐										
2921.4200	12	敌锈钠〔999〕	6.5		30	13/	9,13	千克	S/13		31.5	
2921.4200	13	苯草醚〔999〕	6.5		30	13/	9,13	千克	S/13		31.5	
2921.4200	20	邻氯对硝基苯胺〔999〕	6.5		30	13/	13	千克	/13		31.5	
2921.4200	90	其他苯胺衍生物及其盐〔301 危险化学品,爆炸品;302 危险化学品,易于自燃的物质;303 危险化学品,毒性物质;304 危险化学品,杂项物质;305 其他危险化学品;306 其他化工产品〕	6.5		30	13/	13	千克	/13		31.5	
2921.4300		--甲苯胺及其衍生物以及它们的盐										
2921.4300	01	间甲苯胺或对甲苯胺〔999〕	6.5		30	13/	13	千克	/13		26.5	
2921.4300	10	氟乐灵〔999〕	6.5		30	13/	9,13	千克	S/13		26.5	
2921.4300	20	邻甲苯胺〔999〕	6.5		30	13/	13	千克	/13		26.5	
2921.4300	31	溴鼠胺〔999〕	6.5		30	13/	0	千克	S/13		26.5	
2921.4300	32	乙丁氟灵〔999〕	6.5		30	13/	9,13	千克	S/13		26.5	
2921.4300	33	氯乙氟灵〔999〕	6.5		30	13/	9,13	千克	S/13		26.5	
2921.4300	34	环丙氟灵〔999〕	6.5		30	13/	9,13	千克	S/13		26.5	
2921.4300	35	乙丁烯氟灵〔999〕	6.5		30	13/	9,13	千克	S/13		26.5	
2921.4300	36	地乐灵〔999〕	6.5		30	13/	9,13	千克	S/13		26.5	
2921.4300	37	氯乙灵〔999〕	6.5		30	13/	9,13	千克	S/13		26.5	
2921.4300	38	氟节胺〔999〕	6.5		30	13/	9,13	千克	S/13		26.5	
2921.4300	90	甲苯胺盐、甲苯胺衍生物及其盐〔301 危险化学品,毒性物质;302 其他危险化学品;303 其他化工产品〕	6.5		30	13/	13	千克	/13		26.5	
2921.4400		--二苯胺及其衍生物以及它们的盐〔301 危险化学品,爆炸品;302 危险化学品,毒性物质;303 其他危险化学品;304 其他化工产品〕	6.5		30	13/	13	千克	/13		31.5	
2921.4500		--1-萘胺(α-萘胺)、2-萘胺(β-萘胺)及其衍生物以及它们的盐										
2921.4500	10	2-萘胺〔999〕	6.5		30	13/	13	千克	/13		31.5	
2921.4500	90	1-萘胺和 2-萘胺的衍生物及盐(包括 1-萘胺)〔301 危险化学品,爆炸品;302 危险化学品,毒性物质;303 危险化学品,杂项物质;304 其他化工产品〕	6.5		30	13/	13	千克	/13		31.5	
2921.4600		--安非他明(INN)、苄非他明(INN)、右苯丙胺(INN)、乙非他明、芬坎法明(INN)、利非他明(INN)、左苯丙胺(INN)、美芬雷司(INN)、苯丁胺(INN)以及它们的盐										
2921.4600	11	安非他明、苄非他明、右苯丙胺(包括它们的盐)〔999〕	6.5		30	13/	13	千克	I/1		11.5	
2921.4600	12	乙非他明、芬坎法明、利非他明(包括它们的盐)〔999〕	6.5		30	13/	13	千克	I/1		11.5	
2921.4600	13	左苯丙胺、美芬雷司、芬特明(包括它们的盐)〔999〕	6.5		30	13/	13	千克	I/1		11.5	
		--其他:										
2921.4910		---对异丙基苯胺〔999〕	4		11	13/	13	千克	/1			
2921.4920		---二甲基苯胺〔999〕	6.5		20	13/	13	千克	/13		26.5	
2921.4930		---2,6-甲基乙基苯胺〔999〕	4		11	13/	13	千克	/1		9	3.2/3.2
2921.4940		---2,6-二乙基苯胺〔999〕	6.5		20	13/	13	千克	/1			
2921.4990		---其他										
2921.4990	11	异丙乐灵〔999〕	6.5		30	13/	9,13	千克	S/13		26.5	
2921.4990	12	仲丁灵〔999〕	6.5		30	13/	9,13	千克	S/13		26.5	
2921.4990	13	二甲戊灵〔999〕	6.5		30	13/	9,13	千克	S/13		26.5	
2921.4990	20	4-氨基联苯〔999〕	6.5		30	13/	13	千克	/13		26.5	
2921.4990	31	乙环利定,二甲基安非他明(以及它们的盐)〔999〕	6.5		30	13/	13	千克	I/13		26.5	
2921.4990	32	芬氟拉明、右旋芬氟拉明(以及它们的盐)〔999〕	6.5		30	13/	13	千克	I/13		26.5	

协定税率 %								RCEP		特惠税率 %			Article Description
东/冰/格	巴基斯坦	韩国	瑞士 上/下	哥/秘/柬	澳/毛	新西/坡/智	中国港/澳/台	东盟及马来/澳/韩	日/新	亚太2国	老/柬/缅	98/97/95	
													--Ethylenediamine and its salts:
0/0/0	5	3	0/0	0/0/0	0/0	0//0	0/0/	5.9/5.9/5.9	6.1/5.9			0/0/0	---Ethylenediamine
0/0/0	5	1.3	2.7/2.7	0/0/0	0/0	0//0	0/0/	0/0/5.9	5.9/0			0/0/0	---Other
													--Hexamethylenediamine and its salts:
0/0/0	5	0	0/0	0/0/0	0/0	0//0	0/0/	0/0/0	5.9/0			0/0/0	---Hexamethylene adipamide(nylon-6,6 salt)
0/0/0	5	1.3	0/0	0/0/0	0/0	0//0	0/0/	0/0/5.9	5.9/0			0/0/0	---Other
													--Other
0/0/0	0	1.3	0/0	0/0/0	0/0	0//0	0/0/	5.9/5.9/5.9	5.9/5.9			0/0/0	N-octyl-N'-[2-(octylamino) Jethyl (lnendiamine)]
0/0/0	0	1.3	0/0	0/0/0	0/0	0//0	0/0/	5.9/5.9/5.9	5.9/5.9			0/0/0	Other acyclic polyamines and their derivatives (including salts thereof)
													-Cyclanic, cyclenic or cycloterpenic monoor polyamines, and their derivatives; salts thereof
0/0/0	5	0	0/0	0/0/0	0/0	0//0	0/0/	5.9/5.9/5.9	5.9/5.9			0/0/0	Propylhexedrine and its salts
0/0/0	5	0	0/0	0/0/0	0/0	0//0	0/0/	5.9/5.9/5.9	5.9/5.9			0/0/0	1-Aminocy-clopropane-1-carboxylic acid(ACC)
0/0/0	5	0	0/0	0/0/0	0/0	0//0	0/0/	5.9/5.9/5.9	5.9/5.9			0/0/0	Ethylenimine
0/0/0	5	0	0/0	0/0/0	0/0	0//0	0/0/	5.9/5.9/5.9	5.9/5.9			0/0/0	Other cyclanic, cyclenic or cycloterpenic monoor polyamines, and their derivatives; salts thereof
													-Aromatic monoamines and their derivatives; salts thereof:
													--Aniline and its salts:
0/0/0	5	0	0/0	0/0/0	0/0	0//0	0/0/	0/0/0	5.9/0			0/0/0	---Aniline
0/0/0	5	0		0/0/0	0/0	0//0	0/0/	0/0/0	5.9/0			0/0/0	---Other
													--Aniline derivatives and their salts
0/0/0	0	1.3		0/0/0	0/0	0//0	0/0/	5.9/5.9/5.9	5.9/5.9			0/0/0	Sodium-p-aminbenzene sulfonate
0/0/0	0	1.3		0/0/0	0/0	0//0	0/0/	5.9/5.9/5.9	5.9/5.9			0/0/0	Dicloran
0/0/0	0	1.3		0/0/0	0/0	0//0	0/0/	5.9/5.9/5.9	5.9/5.9			0/0/0	OrthoChloro? Para? Nitro? Aniline
0/0/0	0	1.3		0/0/0	0/0	0//0	0/0/	5.9/5.9/5.9	5.9/5.9			0/0/0	Other aniline derivatives and their salts
													--Toluidines and their derivatives; salts thereof
0/0/0	5	3	0/0	0/0/0	0/0	0//0	0/0/	5.9/5.9/5.9	6.1/5.9			0/0/0	M-toluidine or p-toluidine
0/0/0	5	3	0/0	0/0/0	0/0	0//0	0/0/	5.9/5.9/5.9	6.1/5.9			0/0/0	Trifluralin (TC)
0/0/0	5	3	0/0	0/0/0	0/0	0//0	0/0/	5.9/5.9/5.9	6.1/5.9			0/0/0	*O*-Toluidine
0/0/0	5	3	0/0	0/0/0	0/0	0//0	0/0/	5.9/5.9/5.9	6.1/5.9			0/0/0	Bromethalin
0/0/0	5	3	0/0	0/0/0	0/0	0//0	0/0/	5.9/5.9/5.9	6.1/5.9			0/0/0	Benfluralin
0/0/0	5	3	0/0	0/0/0	0/0	0//0	0/0/	5.9/5.9/5.9	6.1/5.9			0/0/0	Fluchloraline
0/0/0	5	3	0/0	0/0/0	0/0	0//0	0/0/	5.9/5.9/5.9	6.1/5.9			0/0/0	Profluralin
0/0/0	5	3	0/0	0/0/0	0/0	0//0	0/0/	5.9/5.9/5.9	6.1/5.9			0/0/0	Ethalfluralin
0/0/0	5	3	0/0	0/0/0	0/0	0//0	0/0/	5.9/5.9/5.9	6.1/5.9			0/0/0	Dipropalin
0/0/0	5	3	0/0	0/0/0	0/0	0//0	0/0/	5.9/5.9/5.9	6.1/5.9			0/0/0	Chlornidine
0/0/0	5	3	0/0	0/0/0	0/0	0//0	0/0/	5.9/5.9/5.9	6.1/5.9			0/0/0	Flumetralin
0/0/0	5	3	0/0	0/0/0	0/0	0//0	0/0/	5.9/5.9/5.9	6.1/5.9			0/0/0	Toluidines,toluidine derivatives and salts thereof
0/0/0	5	1.3		0/0/0	0/0	0//0	0/0/	0/0/5.9	5.9/0			0/0/0	--Diphenylamine and its derivatives; salts thereof
													--1-Naphthylamine (α-naphthylamine), 2-naphthylamine (β-naphthylamine) and their derivatives; salts thereof
0/0/0	5	0		0/0/0	0/0	0//0	0/0/	0/0/0	5.9/0			0/0/0	2-Naphthylamine
0/0/0	5	0		0/0/0	0/0	0//0	0/0/	0/0/0	5.9/0			0/0/0	1-Naphthylamine and 2-Naphthylamine and its derivatires salis thereof
													--Amfetamine(INN), benzfetamine(INN), dexamfetamine (INN), etilamfetamine(INN), fencamfamin(INN), lefetamine(INN), levamfetamine(INN), mefenorex(INN) and phentermine(INN); salts thereof
0/0/0	5	0	0/0	0/0/0	0/0	0//0	0/0/	0/0/0	5.9/0			0/0/0	Amfetamine(INN), benzfetamine(INN), dexamfetamine (INN)(salts thereof)
0/0/0	5	0	0/0	0/0/0	0/0	0//0	0/0/	0/0/0	5.9/0			0/0/0	Etilamfetamine (INN), fencamfamin (INN), lefetamine (INN)(salts thereof)
0/0/0	5	0	0/0	0/0/0	0/0	0//0	0/0/	0/0/0	5.9/0			0/0/0	levamfetamine(INN), mefenorex(INN) and phentermine (INN)(salts thereof)
													--Other:
0/0/0	0	0	0/0	0/0/0	0/0	0//0	0/0/	0/0/0	0/0			0/0/0	---*p*-Isopropyl-aniline
0/0/0	5	1.3	0/0	0/0/0	0/0	0//0	0/0/	0/0/5.9	5.9/0			0/0/0	---Dimethylanilines
0/0/0	0	0	0/0	0/0/0	0/0	0//0	0/0/	0/0/0	0/0			0/0/0	---2,6-Methyl ethyl aniline
0/0/0	5	0		0/0/0	0/0	0//0	0/0/	0/0/0	5.9/0			0/0/0	---2,6-Diethylaniline
													---Other
0/0/0	5	0		0/0/0	0/0	0//0	0/0/	0/0/0	5.9/0			0/0/0	Isopropalin
0/0/0	5	0		0/0/0	0/0	0//0	0/0/	0/0/0	5.9/0			0/0/0	Butralin
0/0/0	5	0		0/0/0	0/0	0//0	0/0/	0/0/0	5.9/0			0/0/0	Pendimethalin
0/0/0	5	0		0/0/0	0/0	0//0	0/0/	0/0/0	5.9/0			0/0/0	4-Aminobiphenyl
0/0/0	5	0		0/0/0	0/0	0//0	0/0/	0/0/0	5.9/0			0/0/0	Eticyclidine, dimethylamphetamine (and their salt)
0/0/0	5	0		0/0/0	0/0	0//0	0/0/	0/0/0	5.9/0			0/0/0	Fenfluramine, d-fenfluramine (and their salt)

税则号列	货品名称〔CIQ 扩展编码及品名—T2 表示见附表 2〕	最惠(%)	暂定税率	普通	增值/消费	出口退税	计量单位	监管条件/特殊证件	检验检疫	对美关税	亚太上/下
2921.4990 90	其他芳香单胺及衍生物及它们的盐〔301 危险化学品，毒性物质；302 危险化学品，腐蚀性物质；303 危险化学品，杂项物质；304 其他危险化学品；305 其他化工产品〕	6.5		30	13/	13	千克	/13		26.5	
	-芳香多胺及其衍生物以及它们的盐：										
	--邻-、间-、对-苯二胺、二氨基甲苯及其衍生物以及它们的盐：										
2921.5110	---邻苯二胺〔999〕	4		11	13/	13	千克	/13		9	3.2/3.2
2921.5190	---其他										
2921.5190 11	氨氟灵〔999〕	6.5		30	13/	9,13	千克	S/13		31.5	
2921.5190 12	氨氟乐灵〔999〕	6.5		30	13/	9,13	千克	S/13		31.5	
2921.5190 20	2,4-二氨基甲苯〔999〕	6.5		30	13/	13	千克	/13		31.5	
2921.5190 90	间-、对-苯二胺、二氨基甲苯等(包括衍生物及它们的盐)〔301 危险化学品，毒性物质；302 危险化学品，杂项物质；303 其他危险化学品；304 其他化工产品〕	6.5		30	13/	13	千克	/13		31.5	
2921.5900	--其他										
2921.5900 10	三氨基三硝基苯〔999〕	6.5		30	13/	13	千克	3/13		31.5	
2921.5900 20	联苯胺(4,4'-二氨基联苯)〔999〕	6.5		30	13/	13	千克	89/13		31.5	
2921.5900 31	4,4'-二氨基-3,3'-二氯二苯基甲烷〔999〕	6.5		30	13/	13	千克	/13		31.5	
2921.5900 32	3,3'-二氯联苯胺〔999〕	6.5		30	13/	13	千克	/13		31.5	
2921.5900 33	4,4'-二氨基二苯基甲烷〔999〕	6.5		30	13/	13	千克	/13		31.5	
2921.5900 90	其他芳香多胺及衍生物及它们的盐〔301 危险化学品，杂项物质；302 其他危险化学品；303 其他化工产品〕	6.5		30	13/	13	千克	/13		31.5	
29.22	**含氧基氨基化合物：**										
	-氨基醇(但含有一种以上含氧基的除外)及其醚和酯，以及它们的盐：										
2922.1100	--单乙醇胺及其盐										
2922.1100 01	单乙醇胺[T2]	6.5		30	13/	13	千克	AB/13	MRNS	11.5	
2922.1100 90	单乙醇胺盐〔999〕	6.5		30	13/	13	千克	/13		11.5	
2922.1200	--二乙醇胺及其盐										
2922.1200 01	二乙醇胺〔999〕	6.5		30	13/	13	千克	/13		16.5	
2922.1200 90	二乙醇胺盐〔999〕	6.5		30	13/	13	千克	/13		16.5	
2922.1400	--右丙氧吩(INN)及其盐〔999〕	6.5		30	13/	13	千克	I/1			
2922.1500	--三乙醇胺〔999〕	6.5		30	13/	13	千克	23A/1	R	11.5	
2922.1600	--全氟辛基磺酸二乙醇铵〔999〕	6.5		30	13/	13	千克	X/13			
2922.1700	--甲基二乙醇胺和乙基二乙醇胺〔999〕	6.5		30	13/	13	千克	23/1		11.5	
2922.1800	--2-(N,N-二异丙基氨基)乙醇〔999〕	6.5		30	13/	13	千克	/13			
	--其他：										
2922.1910	---乙胺丁醇〔999〕	6.5		30	13/	13	千克	/1			
	---二烷(甲、乙、正丙或异丙)氨基乙-2-醇及其质子化盐：										
2922.1921	----二甲氨基乙醇及其质子化盐〔301 危险化学品，腐蚀性物质；302 其他化工产品〕	6.5		30	13/	13	千克	/13		11.5	
2922.1922	----二乙氨基乙醇及其质子化盐										
2922.1922 10	2-二乙氨基乙醇(或称 N,N-二乙基乙醇胺)〔999〕	6.5		30	13/	13	千克	3/13		16.5	
2922.1922 90	二乙氨基乙醇的质子化盐〔999〕	6.5		30	13/	13	千克	/13		16.5	
2922.1929	----其他〔302〕	6.5		30	13/	13	千克	23/1			5.2/5.2
2922.1930	---乙基二乙醇胺的盐〔999〕	6.5		30	13/	13	千克	/1			5.2/5.2
2922.1940	---甲基二乙醇胺的盐〔999〕	6.5		30	13/	13	千克	/1		11.5	5.2/5.2
2922.1950	---本芴醇〔999〕	6.5		30	13/	13	千克	/1		26.5	
2922.1990	---其他										
2922.1990 10	增产胺〔999〕	6.5		30	13/	9,13	千克	S/13		11.5	
2922.1990 20	克仑特罗〔999〕	6.5		30	13/	9,13	千克	L/13		11.5	
2922.1990 31	醋美沙朵、阿醋美沙朵、阿法美沙朵(以及它们的盐)〔999〕	6.5		30	13/	9,13	千克	I/13		11.5	
2922.1990 32	倍醋美沙多、倍他美沙朵(以及它们的盐)〔999〕	6.5		30	13/	9,13	千克	I/13		11.5	
2922.1990 33	地美沙多、地美庚醇、诺美沙朵(以及它们的盐)〔999〕	6.5		30	13/	9,13	千克	I/13		11.5	
2922.1990 41	三乙醇胺盐酸盐〔999〕	6.5		30	13/	13	千克	23/13		11.5	
2922.1990 49	其他三乙醇胺的盐〔999〕	6.5		30	13/	13	千克	/13		11.5	
2922.1990 90	其他氨基醇及其醚、酯和它们的盐(但含有一种以上含氧基的除外)〔301 危险化学品，易燃液体；302 危险化学品，毒性物质；303 危险化学品，腐蚀性物质；304 其他危险化学品；305 其他化工产品〕	6.5		30	13/	9,13	千克	/13		11.5	
	-氨基萘酚和其他氨基酚(但含有一种以上含氧基的除外)及其醚和酯，以及它们的盐：										
2922.2100	--氨基羟基萘磺酸及其盐〔302〕	6.5		30	13/	13	千克	/1		16.5	
	--其他：										
2922.2910	---茴香胺、二茴香胺、氨基苯乙醚及其盐〔301 危险化学品，毒性物质；302 其他化工产品〕	6.5		30	13/	13	千克	/13			
2922.2990	---其他										
2922.2990 11	布苯丙胺、二甲氧基乙基安非他明(以及它们的盐)〔999〕	6.5		30	13/	13	千克	I/13		31.5	
2922.2990 12	二甲氧基安非他明、副甲氧基安非他明(以及它们的盐)〔999〕	6.5		30	13/	13	千克	I/13		31.5	

协定税率 %								RCEP		特惠税率 %			Article Description
东/冰/格	巴基斯坦	韩国	瑞士 上/下	哥/秘/柬	澳/毛	新西/坡/智	中国港/澳/台	东盟及马来/澳/韩	日/新	亚太2国	老/柬/缅	98/97/95	
0/0/0	5	0		0/0/0	0/0	0//0	0/0/	0/0/0	5.9/0			0/0/0	Other aromatic monoamine and derivants and their salt
													-Aromatic polyamines and their derivatives; salts thereof:
													--*o*-, *m*-, *p*-Phenylenediamine, diaminotoluenes, and their derivatives; salts thereof:
0/0/0	0	0	0/0	0/0/0	0/0	0//0	0/0/	0/0/0	0/0			0/0/0	---*o*-Phenylenediamine
													---Other
0/0/0	5	0	0/0	0/0/0	0/0	0//0	0/0/	0/0/0	5.9/0			0/0/0	Dinitamine
0/0/0	5	0	0/0	0/0/0	0/0	0//0	0/0/	0/0/0	5.9/0			0/0/0	Prodiamine
0/0/0	5	0	0/0	0/0/0	0/0	0//0	0/0/	0/0/0	5.9/0			0/0/0	2,4-Diaminotoluene
0/0/0	5	0	0/0	0/0/0	0/0	0//0	0/0/	0/0/0	5.9/0			0/0/0	*o*-, *m*-, *p*-Phenylene diamine, diaminotoluene(including and their derivatives;salts thereof)
													--Other
0/0/0	5	1.3		0/0/0	0/0	0//0	0/0/	0/0/5.9	5.9/0			0/0/0	Triamino trinitrobenzene
0/0/0	5	1.3		0/0/0	0/0	0//0	0/0/	0/0/5.9	5.9/0			0/0/0	Benzidine(4,4'-diaminobiphenyl)
0/0/0	5	1.3		0/0/0	0/0	0//0	0/0/	0/0/5.9	5.9/0			0/0/0	4,4'- Diamino-3,3'- dicophane
0/0/0	5	1.3		0/0/0	0/0	0//0	0/0/	0/0/5.9	5.9/0			0/0/0	3,3'- Dichlorobenzidine
0/0/0	5	1.3		0/0/0	0/0	0//0	0/0/	0/0/5.9	5.9/0			0/0/0	4,4'-Methylenedianiline
0/0/0	5	1.3		0/0/0	0/0	0//0	0/0/	0/0/5.9	5.9/0			0/0/0	Other aromatic polyamines and their derivatives; salts thereof
													Oxygen-function amino-compounds:
													-Amino-alcohols, other than those containing more than one kind of oxygen function,their ethers and esters; salts thereof:
													--Monoethanolamine and its salts
0/0/0	5		0/0	0/0/0	0/0	0//0	0/0/	5/5/	/5			0/0/0	Monoethanolamine
0/0/0	5		0/0	0/0/0	0/0	0//0	0/0/	5/5/	/5			0/0/0	Salts of monoethanolamine
													--Diethanolamine and its salts
0/0/0	5		0/0	0/0/0	0/0	0//0	0/0/	5/5/	/5			0/0/0	Diethanolamine
0/0/0	5		0/0	0/0/0	0/0	0//0	0/0/	5/5/	/5			0/0/0	Diethanolamine salt
0/0/0	5	0	0/0	0/0/0	0/0	0//0	0/0/	0/0/0	5.9/0			0/0/0	--Dextropropoxyphene(INN) and its salts
0/0/0	5	3	0/0	0/0/0	0/0	0//0	0/0/	5.9/5.9/5.9	6.1/5.9			0/0/0	--Triethanolamine
0/0/0	5	0	0/0	0/0/0	0/0	0//0	0/0/	0/0/0	5.9/0			0/0/0	--Diethanolammonium perfluorooctane sulphonate
0/0/0	5	0	0/0	0/0/0	0/0	0//0	0/0/	0/0/0	5.9/0			0/0/0	--Methyldiethanolamine and ethyldiethanolamine
0/0/0	5	0	0/0	0/0/0	0/0	0//0	0/0/	0/0/0	5.9/0			0/0/0	--2-(*N*,*N-Diisopropylamino*) ethanol
													--Other:
0/0/0	5	0	0/0	0/0/0	0/0	0//0	0/0/	0/0/0	5.9/0			0/0/0	---Ethylamino butanol (Ethambutol)
													---N, N-Dialkyl-(Me, Et, n-Pr or i-Pr) aminoethane-2-ols and cornesponding protonated salts:
0/0/0	5	0	0/0	0/0/0	0/0	0//0	0/0/	0/0/0	5.9/0			0/0/0	----N, N-Dimethylaminoethanol and corresponding protonated salts
													----N, N-Diethylaminoethanol and corresponding protonated salts
0/0/0	5	0	0/0	0/0/0	0/0	0//0	0/0/	0/0/0	5.9/0			0/0/0	2-Diethylaminoethanol(N, N-Diethylethanolamine)
0/0/0	5	0	0/0	0/0/0	0/0	0//0	0/0/	0/0/0	5.9/0			0/0/0	Protonated salts of 2-Diethylaminoethanol
0/0/0	5	0	0/0	0/0/0	0/0	0//0	0/0/	0/0/0	5.9/0			0/0/0	----Other
0/0/0	5	0	0/0	0/0/0	0/0	0//0	0/0/	0/0/0	5.9/0			0/0/0	---Ethyldiethanolamine
0/0/0	5	0	0/0	0/0/0	0/0	0//0	0/0/	0/0/0	5.9/0			0/0/0	---Methyldiethanolamine
0/0/0	5	0	0/0	0/0/0	0/0	0//0	0/0/	0/0/0	5.9/0			0/0/0	---Benflumelol
													---Other
0/0/0	5	0	0/0	0/0/0	0/0	0//0	0/0/	0/0/0	5.9/0			0/0/0	Ethanamine
0/0/0	5	0	0/0	0/0/0	0/0	0//0	0/0/	0/0/0	5.9/0			0/0/0	Clenbuterol
0/0/0	5	0	0/0	0/0/0	0/0	0//0	0/0/	0/0/0	5.9/0			0/0/0	Acetylmethadol, alphacetylmethadol, alphamethadol(and its salts)
0/0/0	5	0	0/0	0/0/0	0/0	0//0	0/0/	0/0/0	5.9/0			0/0/0	Betacetylmethadol, betamethadol (and their salt)
0/0/0	5	0	0/0	0/0/0	0/0	0//0	0/0/	0/0/0	5.9/0			0/0/0	Dimenoxadol, dimepheptanol, noracymethadol (and their salt)
0/0/0	5	0	0/0	0/0/0	0/0	0//0	0/0/	0/0/0	5.9/0			0/0/0	Triethanolamine hydrochloride
0/0/0	5	0	0/0	0/0/0	0/0	0//0	0/0/	0/0/0	5.9/0			0/0/0	Other salts of triethanolamine
0/0/0	5	0	0/0	0/0/0	0/0	0//0	0/0/	0/0/0	5.9/0			0/0/0	Other alkamine and their ethers, esters and their salt (other than those containing more than one kind of Oxygen function)
													-Amino-naphthols and amino-phenols, other than those containing more than one kind of oxygen function, their ethers and esters; salts thereof:
0/0/0	5	1.3	0/0	0/0/0	0/0	0//0	0/0/	0/0/5.9	5.9/0			0/0/0	--Aminohydroxynaphthal-ene-sulphonic acid and their salts
													--Other:
0/0/0	5	1.3	0/0	0/0/0	0/0	0//0	0/0/	0/0/5.9	5.9/0			0/0/0	---Anisidine, dianisidine, phenetidine and their salts
													---Other
0/0/0	5	0	0/0	0/0/0	0/0	0//0	0/0/	0/0/0	5.9/0			0/0/0	Brolamfetamine, dimethoxy-4-ethyl,amphetamine (and their salt)
0/0/0	5	0	0/0	0/0/0	0/0	0//0	0/0/	0/0/0	5.9/0			0/0/0	12, 5Dimethoxyamfetamine, paramethoxyamfetamine (and their salt)

税则号列		货品名称〔CIQ 扩展编码及品名—T2 表示见附表 2〕	最惠(%)	暂定税率	普通	增值/消费	出口退税	计量单位	监管条件/特殊证件	检验检疫	对美关税	亚太上/下
2922.2990	13	二甲氧基甲苯异丙胺、三甲氧基安非他明(以及它们的盐)〔999〕	6.5		30	13/	13	千克	I/13		31.5	
2922.2990	14	2,5-二甲氧基-4-溴苯乙胺、地佐辛(以及它们的盐)〔999〕	6.5		30	13/	13	千克	I/13		31.5	
2922.2990	15	他喷他多(Tapentadol;CAS 号:175591—23—8)〔999〕	6.5		30	13/	13	千克	I/13		31.5	
2922.2990	16	2,5—二甲氧基—4—碘苯乙胺(2,5—Dimethoxy—4—iodo-phenethylamine;CAS 号:69587—11—7)〔999〕	6.5		30	13/	13	千克	I/13		31.5	
2922.2990	17	2,5—二甲氧基苯乙胺(2,5—Dimethoxy—phenethylamine;CAS 号:3600—86—0)〔999〕	6.5		30	13/	13	千克	I/13		31.5	
2922.2990	90	其他氨基(萘酚、酚)及醚、酯(包括它们的盐,但含有一种以上含氧基的除外)〔301 危险化学品,爆炸品;302 危险化学品,毒性物质;303 危险化学品,腐蚀性物质;304 危险化学品,杂项物质;305 其他危险化学品;306 其他化工品〕	6.5		30	13/	13	千克	/13		31.5	
		-氨基醛、氨基酮和氨基醌,但含有一种以上含氧基的除外,以及它们的盐:										
2922.3100		--安非拉酮(INN)、美沙酮(INN)和去甲美沙酮(INN)以及它们的盐										
2922.3100	10	安非拉酮及其盐〔999〕	6.5		30	13/	13	千克	I/1		11.5	
2922.3100	20	美沙酮、去甲美沙酮及它们的盐〔999〕	6.5		30	13/	13	千克	I/1		11.5	
		--其他:										
2922.3910		---4-甲基甲卡西酮〔999〕	6.5		30	13/	13	千克	I/1			
2922.3920		---安非他酮及其盐〔999〕	6.5		30	13/	9,13	千克	/1			
2922.3990		---其他										
2922.3990	10	氯胺酮及其盐〔999〕	6.5		30	13/	13	千克	I/1		31.5	
2922.3990	20	灭藻醌〔999〕	6.5		30	13/	9,13	千克	S/1		31.5	
2922.3990	30	异美沙酮及其盐〔999〕	6.5		30	13/	13	千克	I/1		31.5	
2922.3990	40	甲卡西酮及其盐〔999〕	6.5		30	13/	13	千克	I/1		31.5	
2922.3990	50	4—甲基乙卡西酮(4—MEC)(4—Methylethcathinone;CAS 号:1225617—18—4)〔999〕	6.5		30	13/	13	千克	I/1		31.5	
2922.3990	90	其他氨基醛、氨基酮及其盐(包括氨基醌及其盐,但含有一种以上含氧基除外)〔101〕	6.5		30	13/	13	千克	/1		31.5	
		-氨基酸(但含有一种以上含氧基的除外)及其酯以及它们的盐:										
		--赖氨酸及其酯以及它们的盐:										
2922.4110		---赖氨酸〔101 饲料添加剂,301:L—赖氨酸(有检疫要求食品添加剂),302:L—盐酸赖氨酸(有检疫要求食品添加剂)〕	5		20	13/	13	千克	AB/1	MPQ	30	
2922.4190		---其他〔101 饲料添加剂,102:L—赖氨酸盐酸盐(有检疫要求食品添加剂)〕	6		30	13/	13	千克	AB/1	MPRQ	11	
		--谷氨酸及其盐:										
2922.4210		---谷氨酸〔101:饲料添加剂,102:L—谷氨酸(有检疫要求食品添加剂)〕	5		90	13/	13	千克	A/1	MP	30	3.3/3.3
2922.4220		---谷氨酸钠〔101 饲料添加剂,102 有检疫要求食品添加剂〕	5		130	13/	13	千克	A/1	MP	30	
2922.4290		---其他〔101 饲料添加剂,102:L—谷氨酰胺(有检疫要求食品添加剂)〕	6.5		30	13/	13	千克	A/1	MP	26.5	
		--邻氨基苯甲酸(氨茴酸)及其盐:										
2922.4310		---邻氨基苯甲酸(氨茴酸)〔101 饲料添加剂,102 化工产品〕	6.5		20	13/	13	千克	23/1			
2922.4390		---其他〔101〕	6.5		30	13/	13	千克	/1		11.5	
2922.4400		--替利定(INN)及其盐〔999〕	6.5		30	13/	13	千克	I/1			
		--其他:										
		---其他氨基酸:										
2922.4911		----氨甲环酸〔101 饲料添加剂,102 化工产品〕	6.5		20	13/	13	千克	AB/1	MRS	31.5	
2922.4919		----其他										
2922.4919	10	安咪奈丁〔101 饲料添加剂,102 化工产品〕	6.5		20	13/	13	千克	I/1		16.5	
2922.4919	90	其他氨基酸[T2]	6.5		20	13/	13	千克	AB/1	MPRQ	16.5	
		---其他:										
2922.4991		----普鲁卡因〔999〕	6		20	13/	13	千克	/1		11	3.6/3.6
2922.4999		----其他										
2922.4999	11	草灭畏〔999〕	6.5		30	13/	9,13	千克	AS/13	MP	11.5	
2922.4999	12	灭杀威、灭除威、混灭威等(害扑威、速灭威、残杀威、猛杀威)〔301 危险化学品,毒性物质;302 其他化工产品〕	6.5		30	13/	9,13	千克	ABS/13	MN	11.5	
2922.4999	13	兹克威、除害威〔301 危险化学品,毒性物质;302 其他化工品〕	6.5		30	13/	0	千克	ABS/13	MN	11.5	
2922.4999	14	异丙威〔301 毒性物质和感染性物质,302 其他化工产品〕	6.5		30	13/	9,13	千克	ABS/13	MN	11.5	
2922.4999	15	仲丁威、畜虫威、合杀威〔301 危险化学品,毒性物质;302 其他化工品〕	6.5		30	13/	9,13	千克	ABS/13	MN	11.5	
2922.4999	16	甲萘威、地麦威、蜱虱威〔301 毒性物质和感染性物质 302 其他化工品〕	6.5		30	13/	9,13	千克	AS/13	MP	11.5	
2922.4999	17	除线威〔999〕	6.5		30	13/	9,13	千克	AS/13	MP	11.5	
2922.4999	18	氨酰丙酸(盐酸盐)〔101 饲料添加剂,102 化工产品〕	6.5		30	13/	9,13	千克	AS/13	MP	11.5	
2922.4999	19	安咪奈丁的盐〔999〕	6.5		20	13/	13	千克	I/13		11.5	
2922.4999	90	其他氨基酸及其酯及它们的盐(含有一种以上含氧基的除外)[T2]	6.5		30	13/	13	千克	AB/13	MRNQ	11.5	
		-氨基醇酚、氨基酸酚及其他含氧基氨基化合物:										
2922.5010		---对羟基苯甘氨酸及其邓钾盐〔999〕	6.5		30	13/	13	千克	A/1	R		
2922.5020		---莱克多巴胺和盐酸莱克多巴胺〔999〕	6.5		30	13/	13	千克	89/1			
2922.5090		---其他										

协定税率 %								RCEP		特惠税率 %			Article Description
东/冰/格	巴基斯坦	韩国	瑞士 上/下	哥/秘/柬	澳/毛	新西/坡/智	中国港/澳/台	东盟及马来/澳/韩	日/新	亚太2国	老/柬/缅	98/97/95	
0/0/0	5	0	0/0	0/0/0	0/0	0/ /0	0/0/	0/0/0	5.9/0			0/0/0	Domdimethoxy-methyl-amphetamine, trimethoxyamfetamine (and their salt)
0/0/0	5	0	0/0	0/0/0	0/0	0/ /0	0/0/	0/0/0	5.9/0			0/0/0	4-bromo-2,5-dimethoxyphenethylamine, dezocine (and their salt)
0/0/0	5	0	0/0	0/0/0	0/0	0/ /0	0/0/	0/0/0	5.9/0			0/0/0	Tapentadol(CAS:175591-23-8)
0/0/0	5	0	0/0	0/0/0	0/0	0/ /0	0/0/	0/0/0	5.9/0			0/0/0	2,5-Dimethoxy-4-iodophenethylamine(CAS:69587-11-7)
0/0/0	5	0	0/0	0/0/0	0/0	0/ /0	0/0/	0/0/0	5.9/0			0/0/0	2,5-Dimethoxy-phenethylamine(CAS:3600-86-0)
0/0/0	5	0	0/0	0/0/0	0/0	0/ /0	0/0/	0/0/0	5.9/0			0/0/0	Other amino (naphthol, hydroxybenzene) and aether, ester (including their salt, but with the exception of those containing one or more oxygen containing groups
													-Amino-aldehydes, amino-ketones and amino-quinones, other than those containing more than one kind of oxygen function; salts thereof:
													--Amfepramone(INN), methadone(INN) and normethadone (INN); salts thereof
0/0/0	5	0	0/0	0/0/0	0/0	0/ /0	0/0/	0/0/0	5.9/0			0/0/0	Amfepramone(INN) and salts thereof
0/0/0	5	0	0/0	0/0/0	0/0	0/ /0	0/0/	0/0/0	5.9/0			0/0/0	Methadone(INN), normethadone(INN) and salts thereof
													--Other:
0/0/0	5	0	0/0	0/0/0	0/0	0/ /0	0/0/	0/0/0	5.9/0			0/0/0	---4-methyl—Methcathinone
0/0/0	5	0	0/0	0/0/0	0/0	0/ /0	0/0/	0/0/0	5.9/0			0/0/0	---Bupropion and its salts
													---Other
0/0/0	5	0	0/0	0/0/0	0/0	0/ /0	0/0/	0/0/0	5.9/0			0/0/0	Ketamine and salts thereof
0/0/0	5	0	0/0	0/0/0	0/0	0/ /0	0/0/	0/0/0	5.9/0			0/0/0	Quinoclamine
0/0/0	5	0	0/0	0/0/0	0/0	0/ /0	0/0/	0/0/0	5.9/0			0/0/0	Isomethadone and salts thereof
0/0/0	5	0	0/0	0/0/0	0/0	0/ /0	0/0/	0/0/0	5.9/0			0/0/0	Methcathinone and salts thereof
0/0/0	5	0	0/0	0/0/0	0/0	0/ /0	0/0/	0/0/0	5.9/0			0/0/0	4-Methylethcathinone(CAS:1225617-18-4)
0/0/0	5	0	0/0	0/0/0	0/0	0/ /0	0/0/	0/0/0	5.9/0			0/0/0	Other amino-aldehydes, amino-ketones and amino-quinones, other than those containing more than one kind of oxygen function and salts thereof
													-Amino-acids, other than those containing more than one kind of oxygen function, and their esters, salts thereof:
													--Lysine and its esters; salts thereof:
0/0/0	0	2.3	0/0	0/0/0	0/0	0/ /0	0/0/	4.5/4.5/4.5	4.7/4.5			0/0/0	---Lysine
0/0/0	5	0	0/0	0/0/0	0/0	0/ /0	0/0/	0/0/0	0/0			0/0/0	---Other
													--Glutamic acid and its salts:
0/0/0	3.5	2	0/0	0/0/0	0/0	0/0/0	0/0/	0/0/9	9.1/0			0/0/0	---Glutamic acid
0/0/0	3.5	2	0/0	0/0/0	0/0	0/0/0	0/0/	0/0/9	9.1/0			0/0/0	---Sodium glutamate
0/0/0	5	0	0/0	0/0/0	0/0	0/ /0	0/0/	0/0/0	5.9/0			0/0/0	---Other
													--Anthranilic acid and its salts:
0/0/0	5	0	0/0	0/0/0	0/0	0/ /0	0/0/	0/0/0	5.9/0			0/0/0	---Anthranilic acids
0/0/0	5	0	0/0	0/0/0	0/0	0/ /0	0/0/	0/0/0	5.9/0			0/0/0	---Other
0/0/0	5	0	0/0	0/0/0	0/0	0/ /0	0/0/	0/0/0	5.9/0			0/0/0	--Tilidine(INN) and its salts
													--Other:
													---Amino acids:
0/0/0	5	3	0/0	0/0/0	0/0	0/ /0	0/0/	5.9/5.9/5.9	6.1/5.9			0/0/0	----Tranexamic acid
													----Other
0/0/0	5	3	0/0	0/0/0	0/0	0/ /0	0/0/	5.9/5.9/5.9	6.1/5.9			0/0/0	Amineptine
0/0/0	5	3	0/0	0/0/0	0/0	0/ /0	0/0/	5.9/5.9/5.9	6.1/5.9			0/0/0	Other amino acids
													---Other:
0/0/0	5	0	0/0	0/0/0	0/0	0/ /0	0/0/	0/0/0	0/0			0/0/0	----Procaine
													----Other
0/0/0	5	0	0/0	0/0/0	0/0	0/ /0	0/0/	0/0/0	5.9/0			0/0/0	Chloramben
0/0/0	5	0	0/0	0/0/0	0/0	0/ /0	0/0/	0/0/0	5.9/0			0/0/0	Meobal, XMC, dimethacarb (etrofol, metolcarb, propoxur, promecarb)
0/0/0	5	0	0/0	0/0/0	0/0	0/ /0	0/0/	0/0/0	5.9/0			0/0/0	Mexacarbate, allyxycarb
0/0/0	5	0	0/0	0/0/0	0/0	0/ /0	0/0/	0/0/0	5.9/0			0/0/0	Isoprocarb
0/0/0	5	0	0/0	0/0/0	0/0	0/ /0	0/0/	0/0/0	5.9/0			0/0/0	Fenobucarb, butacarb, bufencarb
0/0/0	5	0	0/0	0/0/0	0/0	0/ /0	0/0/	0/0/0	5.9/0			0/0/0	Carbaryl, dimetan, promacyl
0/0/0	5	0	0/0	0/0/0	0/0	0/ /0	0/0/	0/0/0	5.9/0			0/0/0	cloethocarb
0/0/0	5	0	0/0	0/0/0	0/0	0/ /0	0/0/	0/0/0	5.9/0			0/0/0	Hydrochlorate
0/0/0	5	0	0/0	0/0/0	0/0	0/ /0	0/0/	0/0/0	5.9/0			0/0/0	Salts of amineptine
0/0/0	5	0	0/0	0/0/0	0/0	0/ /0	0/0/	0/0/0	5.9/0			0/0/0	Other amino-acids and their esters; their salt (Other than those containing more than one kind of oxygen function)
													-Amino-alcohol-phenols, amino-acid-phenols and other amino-compounds with oxygen function:
0/0/0	5	0	0/0	0/0/0	0/0	0/ /0	0/0/	0/0/0	5.9/0			0/0/0	---D-p-hydroxyphenylglycine and its monopotassium salt
0/0/0	5	3	0/0	0/0/0	0/0	0/ /0	0/0/	5.9/5.9/5.9	5.9/5.9			0/0/0	---Ractopamine and ractopamine hydrochloride
													---Other

税则号列	货品名称〔CIQ 扩展编码及品名—T2 表示见附表 2〕	最惠(%)	暂定税率	普通	增值/消费	出口退税	计量单位	监管条件/特殊证件	检验检疫	对美关税	亚太上/下
2922.5090 10	曲马多〔999〕	6.5		30	13/	13	千克	I/1		31.5	
2922.5090 20	苏氨酸〔101 饲用,301 有检疫要求食品添加剂,999 其他化工产品〕	6.5		20	13/	13	千克	A/1	R	31.5	
2922.5090 91	盐酸米托蒽醌〔301 无检疫要求食品添加剂,302 需申报仅用于工业用途不用于食品添加剂无检疫要求的化学品〕	6.5	0	30	3/	13	千克	A/1	R	25	
2922.5090 99	其他氨基醇酚、氨基酸酚(包括其他含氧基氨基化合物)〔301 无检疫要求食品添加剂,302 需申报仅用于工业用途不用于食品添加剂无检疫要求的化学品〕	6.5		30	13/	13	千克	A/1	R	31.5	
29.23	**季铵盐及季铵碱;卵磷脂及其他磷氨基类脂,不论是否已有化学定义:**										
2923.1000	-胆碱及其盐〔101 饲料添加剂,102 胆碱(无检疫要求食品添加剂),103 需申报仅用于工业用途不用于食品添加剂无检疫要求的化学品〕	6.5		30	13/	13	千克	A/1	R	16.5	
2923.2000	-卵磷脂及其他磷氨基类脂[T2]	6.5		30	13/	13	千克	A/1	R	16.5	
2923.3000	-全氟辛基磺酸四乙基铵〔301 危险化学品,毒性物质;302 其他化工品〕	6.5		30	13/	13	千克	X/13			
2923.4000	-全氟辛基磺酸二癸基二甲基铵〔999〕	6.5		30	13/	13	千克	X/13			
2923.9000	-其他										
2923.9000 11	矮壮素〔101 矮壮素水剂(含量＞30%),102 毒害品〕	6.5		30	13/	9,13	千克	S/13		16.5	
2923.9000 12	菊胺酯〔999〕	6.5		30	13/	9,13	千克	S/13		16.5	
2923.9000 90	其他季铵盐及季铵碱〔101 饲料添加剂;301 危险化学品,易燃液体;302 危险化学品,毒性物质;303 危险化学品,腐蚀性物质;304 其他化工品,不用作食品添加剂;305 其他化工品,用作食品添加剂〕	6.5		30	13/	13	千克	/13		16.5	
29.24	**羧基酰胺基化合物;碳酸酰胺基化合物:**										
	-无环酰胺(包括无环氨基甲酸酯)及其衍生物以及它们的盐:										
2924.1100	--甲丙氨酯(INN)〔999〕	6.5		30	13/	13	千克	I/1			
2924.1200	--氟乙酰胺(ISO)、久效磷(ISO)及磷胺(ISO)										
2924.1200 10	氟乙酰胺(ISO)(氟乙酰胺别名敌蚜胺)〔999〕	6.5		30	13/	0	千克	89/13			
2924.1200 90	久效磷(ISO)及磷胺(ISO)〔999〕	6.5		30	13/	0	千克	/13			
	--其他:										
2924.1910	---二甲基甲酰胺〔999〕	6.5		30	13/	13	千克	/13		11.5	
2924.1990	---其他										
2924.1990 12	百治磷〔999〕	6.5		30	13/	0	千克	S/13		26.5	
2924.1990 13	溴乙酰胺〔999〕	6.5		30	13/	0	千克	S/13		26.5	
2924.1990 14	霜霉威及其盐〔999〕	6.5		30	13/	9,13	千克	S/13		26.5	
2924.1990 15	叶枯炔〔999〕	6.5		30	13/	0	千克	S/13		26.5	
2924.1990 16	二丙烯草胺〔101 草毒死颗粒剂(含量＞35%),102 草毒死(含量＞35%)〕	6.5		30	13/	9,13	千克	S/13		26.5	
2924.1990 18	驱蚊酯〔999〕	6.5		30	13/	9,13	千克	S/13		26.5	
2924.1990 30	甲丙氨酯的盐〔999〕	6.5		30	13/	13	千克	I/13		26.5	
2924.1990 40	丙烯酰胺〔999〕	6.5		30	13/	13	千克	/13		26.5	
2924.1990 90	其他无环酰胺(包括无环氨基甲酸酯)(包括其衍生物及其盐)〔101 饲料添加剂,301 危险化学品,爆炸品,302 危险化学品,毒性物质,303 危险化学品,腐蚀性物质,304 其他危险化学品,305 其他化工产品〕	6.5		30	13/	13	千克	/13		26.5	
	-环酰胺(包括环氨基甲酸酯)及其衍生物以及它们的盐:										
2924.2100	--烷基脲及其衍生物以及它们的盐										
2924.2100 10	氟环脲〔999〕	6.5		30	13/	9,13	千克	S/1		31.5	
2924.2100 20	绿麦隆〔999〕	6.5		30	13/	13	千克	S/1		31.5	
2924.2100 90	其他烷基脲及其衍生物以及它们的盐〔101 饲料添加剂;301 杂项物质;302 其他化工产品;303 爆炸品〕	6.5		30	13/	13	千克	/1		31.5	
2924.2300	--2-乙酰氨基苯甲酸(N-乙酰邻氨基苯甲酸)及其盐										
2924.2300 10	2-乙酰氨基苯甲酸、N-乙酰邻氨基苯酸(包括 N-乙酰邻氨基苯甲酸)〔999〕	6.5		30	13/	13	千克	23/1			
2924.2300 90	2-乙酰氨基苯甲酸的盐〔999〕	6.5		30	13/	13	千克	/1			
2924.2400	--炔己蚁胺(INN)〔999〕	6.5		30	13/	13	千克	I/1			
2924.2500	--甲草胺(ISO)〔999〕	6.5		30	13/	9,13	千克	S/13			
	--其他:										
2924.2910	---对乙酰氨基苯乙醚(非那西丁)〔999〕	6		30	13/	13	千克	Q/1			4.8/4.8
2924.2920	---对乙酰氨基酚(扑热息痛)〔999〕	6		30	13/	13	千克	Q/1		26	4.8/4.8
2924.2930	---阿斯巴甜〔999〕	6.5		30	13/	13	千克	/1		31.5	
2924.2990	---其他										
2924.2990 11	避蚊胺、灭锈胺、叶枯酞、水杨菌胺、氟丁酰草胺(包括苯酰菌胺)〔999〕	6.5		30	13/	9,13	千克	S/13		31.5	
2924.2990 12	萘草胺、新燕灵、非草隆、氯炔灵、苄草隆〔301 危险化学品,杂项物质;302 其他化工产品〕	6.5		30	13/	9,13	千克	S/13		31.5	
2924.2990 13	燕麦灵、苄胺灵、特草灵、特胺灵、环丙酰亚胺〔301 危险化学品,杂项物质;302 其他化工产品〕	6.5		30	13/	9,13	千克	S/13		31.5	
2924.2990 14	毒草胺、丁烯草胺、二氯己酰草胺〔301 危险化学品,杂项物质;302 其他化工产品〕	6.5		30	13/	9,13	千克	S/13		31.5	
2924.2990 15	萘丙胺、牧草胺、溴丁酰草胺〔999〕	6.5		30	13/	9,13	千克	S/13		31.5	
2924.2990 16	氯甲酰草胺、麦草伏 M、麦草伏〔999〕	6.5		30	13/	9,13	千克	S/13		31.5	

协定税率 %								RCEP		特惠税率 %			Article Description
东/冰/格	巴基斯坦	韩国	瑞士上/下	哥/秘/柬	澳/毛	新西/坡/智	中国港/澳/台	东盟及马来/澳/韩	日/新	亚太2国	老/柬/缅	98/97/95	
0/0/0	5	1.3	0/0	0/0/0	0/0	0//0	0/0/	0/0/5.9	5.9/0			0/0/0	Tramadol
0/0/0	5	1.3	0/0	0/0/0	0/0	0//0	0/0/	0/0/5.9	5.9/0			0/0/0	threonine
0/0/0	5	1.3	0/0	0/0/0	0/0	0//0	0/0/	0/0/5.9	5.9/0			0/0/0	Mitoxantrone hydrochloride and other anticancer drug substances
0/0/0	5	1.3	0/0	0/0/0	0/0	0//0	0/0/	0/0/5.9	5.9/0			0/0/0	Other amino alcohol phenols, amino acid phenols (including other amino—compounds with oxygen function) (tax number of Separating anti—cancer pharmaceutical raw materials)
													Quaternary ammonium salts and hydroxides; lecithins and other phosphoaminolipids, whether or not chemically defined:
0/0/0	5	0	0/0	0/0/0	0/0	0//0	0/0/	0/0/0	5.9/0			0/0/0	-Choline and its salts
0/0/0	5	1.3	0/0	0/0/0	0/0	0//0	0/0/	0/0/5.9	5.9/0			0/0/0	-Lecithins and other phosphoaminolipids
0/0/0	5	0	0/0	0/0/0	0/0	0//0	0/0/	5.9/5.9/5.9	5.9/5.9			0/0/0	-Tetraethylammonium perfluorooctane sulphonate
0/0/0	5	0	0/0	0/0/0	0/0	0//0	0/0/	5.9/5.9/5.9	5.9/5.9			0/0/0	-Didecyldimethylammonium perfluorooctane sulphonate
													-Other
0/0/0	5	0	0/0	0/0/0	0/0	0//0	0/0/	5.9/5.9/5.9	5.9/5.9			0/0/0	Chlorocholine chloride
0/0/0	5	0	0/0	0/0/0	0/0	0//0	0/0/	5.9/5.9/5.9	5.9/5.9			0/0/0	Tetramethrin
0/0/0	5	0	0/0	0/0/0	0/0	0//0	0/0/	5.9/5.9/5.9	5.9/5.9			0/0/0	Other quaternary ammonium salts and hydroxides
													Carboxyamide-function compounds; amide-function compounds of carbonic acid:
													-Acyclic amides (including acyclic carbamates) and their derivatives; salts thereof:
0/0/0	5	0	0/0	0/0/0	0/0	0//0	0/0/	0/0/0	5.9/0			0/0/0	--Meprobamate(INN)
													--Fluoroacetamide(ISO), monocrotophos(ISO). and phophamidon(ISO)
0/0/0	5	0	0/0	0/0/0	0/0	0//0	0/0/	0/0/0	5.9/0			0/0/0	Fluoroacetamide(ISO)
0/0/0	5	0	0/0	0/0/0	0/0	0//0	0/0/	0/0/0	5.9/0			0/0/0	Monocrotophos(ISO), phosphamidor(ISO)
													--Other:
0/0/0	5	0	0/0	0/0/0	0/0	0//0	0/0/0	0/0/0	0/0			0/0/0	---N, N-dimethylformamide
													---Other
0/0/0	5	3	0/0	0/0/0	0/0	0//0	0/0/	5.9/5.9/5.9	6.1/5.9			0/0/0	Dicrotophos
0/0/0	5	3	0/0	0/0/0	0/0	0//0	0/0/	5.9/5.9/5.9	6.1/5.9			0/0/0	Bromoacetamide
0/0/0	5	3	0/0	0/0/0	0/0	0//0	0/0/	5.9/5.9/5.9	6.1/5.9			0/0/0	Propamocarb and its salts
0/0/0	5	3	0/0	0/0/0	0/0	0//0	0/0/	5.9/5.9/5.9	6.1/5.9			0/0/0	Cellocidin
0/0/0	5	3	0/0	0/0/0	0/0	0//0	0/0/	5.9/5.9/5.9	6.1/5.9			0/0/0	Allidochlor
0/0/0	5	3	0/0	0/0/0	0/0	0//0	0/0/	5.9/5.9/5.9	6.1/5.9			0/0/0	Dimethyl phthalate
0/0/0	5	3	0/0	0/0/0	0/0	0//0	0/0/	5.9/5.9/5.9	6.1/5.9			0/0/0	Salts of meprobamate (INN)
0/0/0	5	3	0/0	0/0/0	0/0	0//0	0/0/	5.9/5.9/5.9	6.1/5.9			0/0/0	Acrylamide
0/0/0	5	3	0/0	0/0/0	0/0	0//0	0/0/	5.9/5.9/5.9	6.1/5.9			0/0/0	Other acyclic amides (including acyclic carbamates) (and their derivatives; salts thereof)
													-Cyclic amides (including cyclic carbamates) and their derivatives; salts thereof:
													--Ureides and their derivatives; salts thereof
0/0/0	5	0	0/0	0/0/0	0/0	0//0	0/0/	0/0/0	5.9/0			0/0/0	Flucycloxuron
0/0/0	5	0	0/0	0/0/0	0/0	0//0	0/0/	0/0/0	5.9/0			0/0/0	chlortoluron
0/0/0	5	0	0/0	0/0/0	0/0	0//0	0/0/	0/0/0	5.9/0			0/0/0	Other ureides and its derivants and their salt
													--2-Acetamidobenzoic acid (N-Acetylanthranilic acid) and its salts
0/0/0	5	0		0/0/0	0/0	0//0	0/0/	0/0/0	5.9/0			0/0/0	2-Acetamidobenzoic acid; N-acetylanthranilicacid (including N-acetamidobenzoic acid)
0/0/0	5	0		0/0/0	0/0	0//0	0/0/	0/0/0	5.9/0			0/0/0	Salts of 2-acetamidobenzoic acid
0/0/0	5	0	0/0	0/0/0	0/0	0//0	0/0/	0/0/0	5.9/0			0/0/0	--Ethinamate(INN)
0/0/0	0	0	0.7/0.7	0/0/0	0/0	0//0	0/0/	0/0/0	5.9/0			0/0/0	--Alachlor(ISO)
													--Other:
0/0/0	0	0	0/0	0/0/0	0/0	0//0	0/0/	0/0/0	0/0			0/0/0	---Phenacetin
0/0/0	0	0	0/0	0/0/0	0/0	0//0	0/0/	0/0/0	0/0			0/0/0	---*p*-Acetaminophenol (paracetanol)
0/0/0	0	0	0.7/0.7	0/0/0	0/0	0//0	0/0/	0/0/0	5.9/0			0/0/0	---Aspartame
													---Other
0/0/0	0	0	0.7/0.7	0/0/0	0/0	0//0	0/0/	0/0/0	5.9/0			0/0/0	Deet, mepronil, tecloftalam, trichlamide, buflubutamid (including zoxamide)
0/0/0	0	0	0.7/0.7	0/0/0	0/0	0//0	0/0/	0/0/0	5.9/0			0/0/0	Naptalam, benzoylprop-ethyl, fenuron, chlorbufam chlorbufam
0/0/0	0	0	0.7/0.7	0/0/0	0/0	0//0	0/0/	0/0/0	5.9/0			0/0/0	Barban dichlormate, terbutol, karbutilate
0/0/0	0	0	0.7/0.7	0/0/0	0/0	0//0	0/0/	0/0/0	5.9/0			0/0/0	Propachlor, butenachlor, dichloro acetyl thenylchlor
0/0/0	0	0	0.7/0.7	0/0/0	0/0	0//0	0/0/	0/0/0	5.9/0			0/0/0	Naproanilide, tebutam, bromobutide
0/0/0	0	0	0.7/0.7	0/0/0	0/0	0//0	0/0/	0/0/0	5.9/0			0/0/0	Clomeprop, flamprop M, flamprop

税则号列	货品名称〔CIQ 扩展编码及品名－T2 表示见附表 2〕	最惠(%)	暂定税率	普通	增值/消费	出口退税	计量单位	监管条件/特殊证件	检验检疫	对美关税	亚太上/下
2924.2990 17	氯虫酰肼、异丙甲草胺、苯肽胺酸等(包括精异丙甲草胺、缬霉威)〔999〕	6.5		30	13/	9,13	千克	S/13		31.5	
2924.2990 18	灭害威〔999〕	6.5		30	13/	9,13	千克	S/13		31.5	
2924.2990 19	苯氧威〔999〕	6.5		30	13/	9,13	千克	S/13		31.5	
2924.2990 20	氟酰脲、环丙酰草胺、烯草胺〔999〕	6.5		30	13/	9,13	千克	S/13		31.5	
2924.2990 31	苯胺灵、苯霜灵、丙草胺、敌稗等(包括丙炔草胺、草不隆、草完隆、除虫脲、除幼脲)〔101 敌稗,102 敌稗乳剂(含量＞25％)〕	6.5		30	13/	9,13	千克	S/13		31.5	
2924.2990 32	敌草胺、敌草隆、二甲苯草胺等(包括丁草胺、丁酰草胺、二甲草胺、氟苯脲、氟草隆)〔999〕	6.5		30	13/	9,13	千克	S/13		31.5	
2924.2990 33	庚酰草胺、环丙草胺、环酰草胺等(包括氟虫脲、氟铃脲、氟酰胺、氟蚁灵、氟幼脲)〔999〕	6.5		30	13/	9,13	千克	S/13		31.5	
2924.2990 34	甲氯酰草胺、甲霜灵、环草隆等(包括环莠隆、甲氧隆、克草胺、枯草隆)〔101 杂项物质,102 其他化工产品〕	6.5		30	13/	9,13	千克	S/13		31.5	
2924.2990 35	甲基杀草隆、枯莠隆、邻酰胺等(包括氯苯胺灵、麦草氟甲酯、麦草氟异丙酯)〔999〕	6.5		30	13/	9,13	千克	S/13		31.5	
2924.2990 36	灭草隆、灭幼脲、炔苯酰草胺等(包括麦锈灵、棉胺宁、灭草灵、炔草隆、杀草胺)〔101 灭草灵,102 灭草灵乳剂〕	6.5		30	13/	9,13	千克	S/13		31.5	
2924.2990 37	虱螨脲、双苯酰草胺、双酰草胺等(包括杀草隆、杀铃脲、杀螺胺及其盐、莎稗磷)〔101 草乃敌(含量＞55％),102 草乃敌乳剂(含量＞10％)〕	6.5		30	13/	9,13	千克	S/13		31.5	
2924.2990 38	甜菜安、特丁草胺、乙氧苯草胺等(包括甜菜宁、戊菌隆、酰草隆、乙草胺、乙霉威)〔301 危险化学品,杂项物质;302 其他化工产品〕	6.5		30	13/	9,13	千克	S/13		31.5	
2924.2990 39	乙酰甲草胺、异丙隆、异草完隆等(包括异丙草胺、异丁草胺)〔999〕	6.5		30	13/	9,13	千克	S/13		31.5	
2924.2990 40	炔己蚁胺的盐〔999〕	6.5		30	13/	13	千克	I/13		31.5	
2924.2990 46	溴虫氟苯双酰胺〔999〕	6.5		30	13/	13	千克	S/13		31.5	
2924.2990 50	地恩丙胺及其盐〔999〕	6.5		30	13/	13	千克	I/13		31.5	
2924.2990 61	3－氧－2－苯基丁酰胺(CAS 号 4433－77－6)〔999〕	6.5		30	13/	13	千克	23/13		31.5	
2924.2990 62	缬菌胺〔999〕	6.5		30	13/	13	千克	S/13		31.5	
2924.2990 91	氟他胺〔999〕	6.5	0	30	3/	13	千克	/13		25	
2924.2990 99	其他环酰胺(包括环氨基甲酸酯)(包括其衍生物以及它们的盐)〔301 危险化学品,易燃固体,302 危险化学品,毒性物质,303 其他危险化学品,304 其他化工产品〕	6.5		30	13/	13	千克	/13		31.5	
29.25	**羧基酰亚胺化合物(包括糖精及其盐)及亚胺基化合物:**										
	-酰亚胺及其衍生物以及它们的盐:										
2925.1100	--糖精及其盐〔101 饲料添加剂,102 糖精钠无检疫要求食品添加剂,103 需申报仅用于工业用途不用于食品添加剂无检疫要求的化学品〕	9		90	13/	13	千克	A/1	R	34	
2925.1200	--格鲁米特(INN)〔999〕	6.5		30	13/	13	千克	I/1			
2925.1900	--其他										
2925.1900 10	格鲁米特的盐〔999〕	6.5		30	13/	13	千克	I/13		11.5	
2925.1900 21	腐霉利〔999〕	6.5		30	13/	9,13	千克	S/13		11.5	
2925.1900 22	菌核净、菌核利、甲菌利、乙菌利〔999〕	6.5		30	13/	9,13	千克	S/13		11.5	
2925.1900 23	氟烯草酸〔999〕	6.5		30	13/	9,13	千克	S/13		11.5	
2925.1900 24	胺菊酯(包括右旋胺菊酯、右旋反式胺菊酯、富右旋反式胺菊酯)〔999〕	6.5		30	13/	9,13	千克	S/13		11.5	
2925.1900 90	其他酰亚胺及其衍生物、盐〔301 其他危险化学品;302 其他化工产品〕	6.5		30	13/	13	千克	/13		11.5	
	-亚胺及其衍生物以及它们的盐:										
2925.2100	--杀虫脒(ISO)〔999〕	6.5		30	13/	0	千克	89/13			
2925.2900	--其他										
2925.2900 11	杀螨特、杀螨脒〔999〕	6.5		30	13/	9,13	千克	S/13		31.5	
2925.2900 12	单甲脒及其盐、伐虫脒、丙烷脒〔301 危险化学品,毒性物质,302 其他化工产品〕	6.5		30	13/	9,13	千克	S/13		31.5	
2925.2900 13	烯肟菌胺、烯肟菌酯、醚菌酯〔999〕	6.5		30	13/	9,13	千克	S/13		31.5	
2925.2900 14	双胍辛胺、多果定、双胍辛胺乙酸盐等(包括双胍三辛烷基苯磺酸盐)〔999〕	6.5		30	13/	9,13	千克	S/13		31.5	
2925.2900 15	禾草灭、氟草醚、增产肟〔999〕	6.5		30	13/	9,13	千克	S/13		31.5	
2925.2900 16	氯代水杨胺、双胍辛乙酸盐、顺己烯醇〔999〕	6.5		30	13/	9,13	千克	S/13		31.5	
2925.2900 20	羟亚胺及其盐〔999〕	6.5		30	13/	13	千克	23/13		31.5	
2925.2900 30	双甲脒〔999〕	6.5		30	13/	9,13	千克	S/13		31.5	
2925.2900 90	其他亚胺及其衍生物以及它们的盐〔301 危险化学品,氧化性物质;302 危险化学品,毒性物质;303 其他化工产品〕	6.5		30	13/	13	千克	/13		31.5	
29.26	**腈基化合物:**										
2926.1000	-丙烯腈〔999〕	6.5	3	30	13/	13	千克	/13		28	
2926.2000	-1-氰基胍(双氰胺)〔999〕	6.5		30	13/	13	千克	/1		16.5	
2926.3000	-芬普雷司(INN)及其盐;美沙酮(INN)中间体(4-氰基-2-二甲氨基-4,4-二苯基丁烷)										
2926.3000 10	美沙酮中间体(4-氰基-2-二甲氨基-4,4-二苯基丁烷)〔999〕	6.5		30	13/	13	千克	I/1			
2926.3000 20	芬普雷司及其盐〔999〕	6.5		30	13/	13	千克	I/1			
2926.4000	-α-苯基乙酰基乙腈〔999〕	6.5		30	13/	13	千克	/1			
	-其他:										
2926.9010	---对氯氰苄〔999〕	4		11	13/	13	千克	/1			
2926.9020	---间苯二甲腈〔999〕	6.5		30	13/	13	千克	/1			5.2/5.2

协定税率 %								RCEP		特惠税率 %			Article Description
东/冰/格	巴基斯坦	韩国	瑞士 上/下	哥/秘/柬	澳/毛	新西/坡/智	中国港/澳/台	东盟及马来/澳/韩	日/新	亚太2国	老/柬/缅	98/97/95	
0/0/0	0	0	0.7/0.7	0/0/0	0/0	0//0	0/0/	0/0/0	5.9/0			0/0/0	Halofenozide, metolachlor, phthalanillic (including s-metolachlor, iprovalicarb)
0/0/0	0	0	0.7/0.7	0/0/0	0/0	0//0	0/0/	0/0/0	5.9/0			0/0/0	aminocarb
0/0/0	0	0	0.7/0.7	0/0/0	0/0	0//0	0/0/	0/0/0	5.9/0			0/0/0	fenoxycarb
0/0/0	0	0	0.7/0.7	0/0/0	0/0	0//0	0/0/	0/0/0	5.9/0			0/0/0	Fluoylureas, cyclanilide, pethoxamid
0/0/0	0	0	0.7/0.7	0/0/0	0/0	0//0	0/0/	0/0/0	5.9/0			0/0/0	Propham, benalaxyl, pretilachlor, propanil (including prynachlor、neburon, noruron diful Benzuron, penfluron, dichlorbenzuron)
0/0/0	0	0	0.7/0.7	0/0/0	0/0	0//0	0/0/	0/0/0	5.9/0			0/0/0	Napropamide, diuron, xylachlor (including Butachlor, chloranocryl dimethachlor, teflubenzuron, fluometuron)
0/0/0	0	0	0.7/0.7	0/0/0	0/0	0//0	0/0/	0/0/0	5.9/0			0/0/0	Monalide, cyclanilide, cypromid, flufenoxuron (including fluorobenzamide, hexaflumuron, flutolanil nifluridide, penfluron)
0/0/0	0	0	0.7/0.7	0/0/0	0/0	0//0	0/0/	0/0/0	5.9/0			0/0/0	Pentanochlor metalaxyl, siduron (including cycluron, alachlor, metoxuron, kecaoan, chloroxuron)
0/0/0	0	0	0.7/0.7	0/0/0	0/0	0//0	0/0/	0/0/0	5.9/0			0/0/0	Methyldymron, difenoxuron, mebenil (including chlortoluron, chlorpropham, flamprop-methyl, flamprop-isopropyl)
0/0/0	0	0	0.7/0.7	0/0/0	0/0	0//0	0/0/	0/0/0	5.9/0			0/0/0	Monuron, chlorbenzuron, propyzamide (including benodanil, phenisopham, swep, buturon, ethaprochlor)
0/0/0	0	0	0.7/0.7	0/0/0	0/0	0//0	0/0/	0/0/0	5.9/0			0/0/0	Liconylurea, dibenzoyl oxalamide, dibenzoyl oxalamide, etc. (including Chlorsulfuron, camphor, spiramine and its salts, and chlorpyrifos)
0/0/0	0	0	0.7/0.7	0/0/0	0/0	0//0	0/0/	0/0/0	5.9/0			0/0/0	Desmedipham, terbuchlor, ethobenzanid (including Phenmedipham, Pencycuron, Acetochlor, Polystyrene resin)
0/0/0	0	0	0.7/0.7	0/0/0	0/0	0//0	0/0/	0/0/0	5.9/0			0/0/0	Diethatyl, isoproturon, isonoruron (including propisochlor, delachlor)
0/0/0	0	0	0.7/0.7	0/0/0	0/0	0//0	0/0/	0/0/0	5.9/0			0/0/0	Salts of ethinamate (INN)
0/0/0	0	0	0.7/0.7	0/0/0	0/0	0//0	0/0/	0/0/0	5.9/0			0/0/0	Bromodifluorobenzene diamide
0/0/0	0	0	0.7/0.7	0/0/0	0/0	0//0	0/0/	0/0/0	5.9/0			0/0/0	Diampromide and its salts
0/0/0	0	0	0.7/0.7	0/0/0	0/0	0//0	0/0/	0/0/0	5.9/0			0/0/0	3—oxo—2—phenylbutylamide (CAS NO.4433—77—6)
0/0/0	0	0	0.7/0.7	0/0/0	0/0	0//0	0/0/	0/0/0	5.9/0			0/0/0	Valitamine
0/0/0	0	0	0.7/0.7	0/0/0	0/0	0//0	0/0/	0/0/0	5.9/0			0/0/0	Flutamide and Other Anticancer Drugs
0/0/0	0	0	0.7/0.7	0/0/0	0/0	0//0	0/0/	0/0/0	5.9/0			0/0/0	Other cyclic amides (including cyclic carbamates) (including their derivatives and their salts) (tax number of Separating anti—cancer pharmaceutical raw materials)
													Carboxyimide-function compounds (including saccharin and its salts) and imine-function compounds:
													-Imides and their derivatives; salts thereof:
0/0/	2	1.8	0/0	0/0/0	0/0	0//0	0/0/	0/0/8.1	8.2/0			0/0/0	--Saccharin and its salts
0/0/0	5	0	0/0	0/0/0	0/0	0//0	0/0/	0/0/0	5.9/0			0/0/0	--Glutethimide (INN)
													--Other
0/0/0	5	0	2.7/2.7	0/0/0	0/0	0//0	0/0/	0/0/0	5.9/0			0/0/0	Salts of glutethimide (INN)
0/0/0	5	0	2.7/2.7	0/0/0	0/0	0//0	0/0/	0/0/0	5.9/0			0/0/0	Procymidone
0/0/0	5	0	2.7/2.7	0/0/0	0/0	0//0	0/0/	0/0/0	5.9/0			0/0/0	Dimetachlone, dichlozoline, myclozolin, chlozolinate
0/0/0	5	0	2.7/2.7	0/0/0	0/0	0//0	0/0/	0/0/0	5.9/0			0/0/0	Flumiclorac-pentyl
0/0/0	5	0	2.7/2.7	0/0/0	0/0	0//0	0/0/	0/0/0	5.9/0			0/0/0	Tetramethrin (including d-tetramethrin, d-t-tetramethrin, rich-d-t-tetramethrin
0/0/0	5	0	2.7/2.7	0/0/0	0/0	0//0	0/0/	0/0/0	5.9/0			0/0/0	Other imides and their derivatives; salts thereof
													-Imines and their derivatives; salts thereof:
0/0/0	5	0	0/0	0/0/0	0/0	0//0	0/0/	0/0/0	5.9/0			0/0/0	--Chlordimeform (ISO)
													--Other
0/0/0	5	0	0/0	0/0/0	0/0	0//0	0/0/	0/0/0	5.9/0			0/0/0	Aramite, semiamitraz
0/0/0	5	0	0/0	0/0/0	0/0	0//0	0/0/	0/0/0	5.9/0			0/0/0	Formamidine and its salts, varamimidine and Propamidine
0/0/0	5	0	0/0	0/0/0	0/0	0//0	0/0/	0/0/0	5.9/0			0/0/0	Trichlamide, enostroburin, kresoxim-methyl
0/0/0	5	0	0/0	0/0/0	0/0	0//0	0/0/	0/0/0	5.9/0			0/0/0	Iminoctadine, dodine, iminoctadine triacetate (including iminoctadinris)
0/0/0	5	0	0/0	0/0/0	0/0	0//0	0/0/	0/0/0	5.9/0			0/0/0	Alloxydim-sodium, ethoxyfen-ethyl, heptopargil
0/0/0	5	0	0/0	0/0/0	0/0	0//0	0/0/	0/0/0	5.9/0			0/0/0	LDS, Iminoctadine triacetate, cis-hexenyl
0/0/0	5	0	0/0	0/0/0	0/0	0//0	0/0/	0/0/0	5.9/0			0/0/0	Oxyamino and its salts
0/0/0	5	0	0/0	0/0/0	0/0	0//0	0/0/	0/0/0	5.9/0			0/0/0	Amitraz
0/0/0	5	0	0/0	0/0/0	0/0	0//0	0/0/	0/0/0	5.9/0			0/0/0	Other imines and their derivatives; salts thereof
													Nitrile-function compounds:
5/0/			0/0	0/0/0	0/0	0//0	0/0/	5/5/	/5			0/0/0	-Acrylonitrile
0/0/0	5	1.3	0/0	0/0/0	0/0	0//0	0/0/	0/0/5.9	5.9/0			0/0/0	-1-Cyanoguanidine (dicyandiamide)
													-Fenproporex (INN) and its salts; methadone (INN) intermediate (4-cyano-2-dimethylamino-4, 4-diphenylbutane)
0/0/0	5	0	0/0	0/0/0	0/0	0//0	0/0/	0/0/0	5.9/0			0/0/0	Methadone (INN) intermediate (4-cyano-2-dimethylamino-4, 4-diphenylbutane)
0/0/0	5	0	0/0	0/0/0	0/0	0//0	0/0/	0/0/0	5.9/0			0/0/0	Fenproporex (INN) and salts thereof
0/0/0	0	0	0.7/0.7	0/0/0	0/0	0//0	0/0/	5.9/5.9/5.9	5.9/5.9			0/0/0	-alpha-Phenylacetoacetonitrile
													-Other:
0/0/0	0	0	0/0	0/0/0	0/0	0//0	0/0/	0/0/0	0/0			0/0/0	---*p*-Chlorobenzyl cyanide
0/0/0	5	0	0/0	0/0/0	0/0	0//0	0/0/	0/0/0	5.9/0			0/0/0	---*m*-Phthalonitrile

税则号列		货品名称〔CIQ扩展编码及品名－T2表示见附表2〕	最惠(%)	暂定税率	普通	增值/消费	出口退税	计量单位	监管条件/特殊证件	检验检疫	对美关税	亚太上/下
2926.9090		---其他										
2926.9090	10	甲氰菊酯、S-氰戊菊酯、氯氟氰菊酯(包括氰氟虫腙)〔999〕	6.5		30	13/	9,13	千克	S/13		11.5	
2926.9090	20	己二腈〔999〕	6.5	1	30	13/	13	千克	/13			
2926.9090	31	氯氰菊酯、氟氯氰菊酯等(包括高效氯氰菊酯、高效反式氯氰菊酯、高效氟氯氰菊酯)〔301 危险化学品,毒性物质;302 其他化工产品〕	6.5		30	13/	9,13	千克	S/13		11.5	
2926.9090	32	杀螟腈、甲基辛硫磷等(包括敌草腈、碘苯腈、辛酰碘苯腈、溴苯腈、辛酰溴苯腈)〔301 危险化学品,毒性物质;302 其他化工产品〕	6.5		30	13/	9,13	千克	S/13		11.5	
2926.9090	33	氯辛硫磷、戊氰威、苯醚氰菊酯等(包括稻瘟酰胺、丙螨氰、右旋苯醚氰菊酯)〔999〕	6.5		30	13/	9,13	千克	S/13		11.5	
2926.9090	34	戊烯氰氯菊酯、溴氯氰菊酯(包括高效氯氟氰菊酯、精高效氯氟氰菊酯)〔999〕	6.5		30	13/	9,13	千克	S/13		11.5	
2926.9090	35	溴氰菊酯、四溴菊酯、氟丙菊酯〔999〕	6.5		30	13/	9,13	千克	S/13		11.5	
2926.9090	36	氟氰苯菊酯、氰戊菊酯、乙氰菊酯〔999〕	6.5		30	13/	9,13	千克	S/13		11.5	
2926.9090	37	氟氰戊菊酯、溴氟菊酯、溴灭菊酯〔999〕	6.5		30	13/	9,13	千克	S/13		11.5	
2926.9090	38	氰菌胺、百菌清、霜脲氰、溴菌腈〔999〕	6.5		30	13/	9,13	千克	S/13		11.5	
2926.9090	39	氟胺氰菊酯、氰氟草酯(包括富右旋反式苯氰菊酯)〔999〕	6.5		30	13/	9,13	千克	S/13		11.5	
2926.9090	41	氰烯菌酯〔999〕	6.5		30	13/	13	千克	S/13		11.5	
2926.9090	50	辛硫磷〔999〕	6.5		30	13/	13	千克	S/13		11.5	
2926.9090	60	丁氟螨酯〔999〕	6.5		30	13/	13	千克	S/13		11.5	
2926.9090	70	3-氧-2-苯基丁腈〔999〕	6.5		30	13/	13	千克	23/13		11.5	
2926.9090	81	苯乙腈(CAS 号 140－29－4)〔999〕	6.5		30	13/	13	千克	23/13		11.5	
2926.9090	90	其他腈基化合物〔301 危险化学品,易燃液体;302 危险化学品,毒性物质;303 危险化学品,腐蚀性物质;304 其他危险化学品;305 其他化工产品〕	6.5		30	13/	13	千克	/13		11.5	
29.27		**重氮化合物、偶氮化合物及氧化偶氮化合物:**										
2927.0000		重氮化合物、偶氮化合物及氧化偶氮化合物										
2927.0000	10	敌磺钠(包括氧化偶氮化合物)〔999〕	6.5		30	13/	9,13	千克	S/13		31.5	
2927.0000	90	其他重氮化合物、偶氮化合物等(包括氧化偶氮化合物)[T2]	6.5		30	13/	13	千克	/13		31.5	
29.28		**肼(联氨)及胲(羟胺)的有机衍生物:**										
2928.0000		肼(联氨)及胲(羟胺)的有机衍生物										
2928.0000	10	偏二甲肼〔999〕	6.5		20	13/	13	千克	3/13		26.5	
2928.0000	20	甲基肼〔999〕	6.5		20	13/	13	千克	3A/13	M	26.5	
2928.0000	31	抑食肼、虫酰肼、丁酰肼、联苯肼酯(包括肟菌酯,苯氧菌胺)〔999〕	6.5		20	13/	9,13	千克	S/13		26.5	
2928.0000	32	绿谷隆、溴谷隆、利谷隆、氯溴隆〔999〕	6.5		20	13/	9,13	千克	S/13		26.5	
2928.0000	33	溴酚肟、乙二肟〔999〕	6.5		20	13/	9,13	千克	S/13		26.5	
2928.0000	34	苯螨特〔999〕	6.5		20	13/	9,13	千克	S/13		26.5	
2928.0000	35	醌肟腙〔999〕	6.5		20	13/	9,13	千克	S/13		26.5	
2928.0000	36	三甲苯草酮〔999〕	6.5		20	13/	9,13	千克	S/13		26.5	
2928.0000	37	环氟菌胺〔999〕	6.5		20	13/	13	千克	S/13		26.5	
2928.0000	90	其他肼(联氨)及胲(羟胺)的有机衍生物[T2]	6.5		20	13/	13	千克	/13		26.5	
29.29		**其他含氮基化合物:**										
		-异氰酸酯:										
2929.1010		---2,4-和2,6-甲苯二异氰酸酯混合物(甲苯二异氰酸酯 TDI)〔999〕	6.5		30	13/	13	千克	AB/13	MN	31.5	
2929.1020		---二甲苯二异氰酸酯(TODI)〔999〕	6.5		30	13/	13	千克	/1			
2929.1030		---二苯基甲烷二异氰酸酯(纯 MDI)〔999〕	6.5		30	13/	13	千克	/13		31.5	
2929.1040		---六亚甲基二异氰酸酯〔999〕	6.5		30	13/	13	千克	/13			
2929.1090		---其他〔301 危险化学品,毒性物质;302 其他危险化学品;303 其他化工产品〕	6.5		30	13/	13	千克	/13		16.5	
		-其他:										
2929.9010		---环己基氨基磺酸钠(甜蜜素)〔301 环己基氨基磺酸钙(无检疫要求食品添加剂),302 环己基氨基磺酸钠,环己基氨基磺酸钙(甜蜜素)(无检疫要求食品添加剂),303 需申报仅用于工业用途不用于食品添加剂无检疫要求的化学品〕	9		90	13/	13	千克	A/1	R		7.2/7.2
2929.9020		---二烷(甲、乙、正丙或异丙)氨基膦酰二卤〔999〕	6.5		30	13/	13	千克	23/1			5.2/5.2
2929.9030		---二烷(甲、乙、正丙或异丙)氨基膦酸二烷(甲、乙、正丙或异丙)酯〔999〕	6.5		30	13/	13	千克	23/1			5.2/5.2
2929.9040		---乙酰甲胺磷〔999〕	6.5		30	13/	9,13	千克	S/1			
2929.9090		---其他										
2929.9090	11	胺丙畏、胺草磷、抑草磷,丁苯草酮等(包括甲基胺草磷)〔999〕	6.5		30	13/	9,13	千克	S/13		26.5	
2929.9090	12	异柳磷、甲基异柳磷、丙胺氟磷等〔301 危险化学品,毒性物质;302 其他危险化学品;303 其他化工产品〕	6.5		30	13/	0	千克	S/13		26.5	
2929.9090	13	八甲磷、育畜磷、甘氨硫磷等(包括甲氟磷、毒鼠磷、水胺硫磷)〔301 危险化学品,毒性物质;302 其他化工产品〕	6.5		30	13/	9,13	千克	S/13		26.5	
2929.9090	14	N－{1－[二烷基(少于或等于 10 个碳原子的碳链,包括环烷)胺基]亚烷基(氢、少于或等于 10 个碳原子的碳链,包括环烷)}－P－氟膦酰胺和相应的烷基化盐或质子化盐〔999〕	6.5		30	13/	13	千克	23/13		26.5	

协定税率 %								RCEP		特惠税率 %			Article Description
东/冰/格	巴基斯坦	韩国	瑞士上/下	哥/秘/柬	澳/毛	新西/坡/智	中国港/澳/台	东盟及马来/澳/韩	日/新	亚太2国	老/柬/缅	98/97/95	
													---Other
0/0/0	0	0	0.7/0.7	0/0/0	0/0	0//0	0/0/	5.9/5.9/5.9	5.9/5.9			0/0/0	Fenpropathrin, s-fenvalerate, cyhalothrin (including insect hydrazone)
0/0/0	0	0	0.7/0.7	0/0/0	0/0	0//0	0/0/	5.9/5.9/5.9	5.9/5.9			0/0/0	Hexanedinitrile
0/0/0	0	0	0.7/0.7	0/0/0	0/0	0//0	0/0/	5.9/5.9/5.9	5.9/5.9			0/0/0	Cypermethrin, cynuthrin (including beta-cypermethrin, theta-cypermethrin, beta-cyfluthrin)
0/0/0	0	0	0.7/0.7	0/0/0	0/0	0//0	0/0/	5.9/5.9/5.9	5.9/5.9			0/0/0	Cyanophos Phoxim-methyl (including dichlobenil, ioxynil, ioxynil octanoate, bromooxynil, bromoxynil octanoate)
0/0/0	0	0	0.7/0.7	0/0/0	0/0	0//0	0/0/	5.9/5.9/5.9	5.9/5.9			0/0/0	Chlorphoxim, nitrilacarb, cyphenothrin (including fenoxanil, malonoben, d-cyphenothrin)
0/0/0	0	0	0.7/0.7	0/0/0	0/0	0//0	0/0/	5.9/5.9/5.9	5.9/5.9			0/0/0	Pentmethrin, tralocythrin (including lambda-cyhalothrin, gamma- cyhalothrin)
0/0/0	0	0	0.7/0.7	0/0/0	0/0	0//0	0/0/	5.9/5.9/5.9	5.9/5.9			0/0/0	Deltamethrin, tralomerhrin, acrinathrin
0/0/0	0	0	0.7/0.7	0/0/0	0/0	0//0	0/0/	5.9/5.9/5.9	5.9/5.9			0/0/0	Flumethrin, fenvalerate, cycloprothrin
0/0/0	0	0	0.7/0.7	0/0/0	0/0	0//0	0/0/	5.9/5.9/5.9	5.9/5.9			0/0/0	Flucythrinate, brofluthrinate, brofenvalerate
0/0/0	0	0	0.7/0.7	0/0/0	0/0	0//0	0/0/	5.9/5.9/5.9	5.9/5.9			0/0/0	Fenoxanil, chlorothalonil, cymoxanil, bromothalonil
0/0/0	0	0	0.7/0.7	0/0/0	0/0	0//0	0/0/	5.9/5.9/5.9	5.9/5.9			0/0/0	Tau-fluralinate cyhalofop-butyl, cyphenothrin (including rich-d-t-cyphenothrin)
0/0/0	0	0	0.7/0.7	0/0/0	0/0	0//0	0/0/	5.9/5.9/5.9	5.9/5.9			0/0/0	js399-19
0/0/0	0	0	0.7/0.7	0/0/0	0/0	0//0	0/0/	5.9/5.9/5.9	5.9/5.9			0/0/0	Phoxim
0/0/0	0	0	0.7/0.7	0/0/0	0/0	0//0	0/0/	5.9/5.9/5.9	5.9/5.9			0/0/0	Cyflumetofen
0/0/0	0	0	0.7/0.7	0/0/0	0/0	0//0	0/0/	5.9/5.9/5.9	5.9/5.9			0/0/0	3-Methyl-2-phenylbutyronitrile
0/0/0	0	0	0.7/0.7	0/0/0	0/0	0//0	0/0/	5.9/5.9/5.9	5.9/5.9			0/0/0	Phenylacetonitrile (CAS NO.140－29－4)
0/0/0	0	0	0.7/0.7	0/0/0	0/0	0//0	0/0/	5.9/5.9/5.9	5.9/5.9			0/0/0	Other nitrile-function compounds
													Diazo-, azo-. or azoxy-compounds:
													Diazo-, azo-. or azoxy-compounds
0/0/0	5	0	0/0	0/0/0	0/0	0//0	0/0/	0/0/0	5.9/0			0/0/0	Dexon(including azoxy-compounds)
0/0/0	5	0	0/0	0/0/0	0/0	0//0	0/0/	0/0/0	5.9/0			0/0/0	Other diazo-azo-compounds(including azoxy compounds)
													Organic derivatives of hydrazine or of hydroxylamine:
													Organic derivatives of hydrazine or of hydroxylamine
0/0/0	5	1.3	0/0	0/0/0	0/0	0//0	0/0/	0/0/5.9	5.9/0			0/0/0	Dimethylhydrazine
0/0/0	5	1.3	0/0	0/0/0	0/0	0//0	0/0/	0/0/5.9	5.9/0			0/0/0	Methylhydrazine
0/0/0	5	1.3	0/0	0/0/0	0/0	0//0	0/0/	0/0/5.9	5.9/0			0/0/0	RH-5849, tebufenozide, daminozide, bifenazate(including, trifloxystrobin, metomiuostrobin)
0/0/0	5	1.3	0/0	0/0/0	0/0	0//0	0/0/	0/0/5.9	5.9/0			0/0/0	Monolinuron, metobromuron, linuron, chlorbromuron
0/0/0	5	1.3	0/0	0/0/0	0/0	0//0	0/0/	0/0/5.9	5.9/0			0/0/0	Bromofenoxim, glyoxime
0/0/0	5	1.3	0/0	0/0/0	0/0	0//0	0/0/	0/0/5.9	5.9/0			0/0/0	Benzoximate
0/0/0	5	1.3	0/0	0/0/0	0/0	0//0	0/0/	0/0/5.9	5.9/0			0/0/0	Benquinox
0/0/0	5	1.3	0/0	0/0/0	0/0	0//0	0/0/	0/0/5.9	5.9/0			0/0/0	Tralkoxydim
0/0/0	5	1.3	0/0	0/0/0	0/0	0//0	0/0/	0/0/5.9	5.9/0			0/0/0	Cyclofluramine
0/0/0	5	1.3	0/0	0/0/0	0/0	0//0	0/0/	0/0/5.9	5.9/0			0/0/0	Organic derivatives of hydrazine or of hydroxylamine
													Compounds with other nitrogen function:
													-Isocyanates:
0/0/0	0	3	0/0	0/0/0	0/0	0//0	0/0/0	5.9/5.9/5.9	6.1/5.9			0/0/0	---Toluene diisocyanate
0/0/0	5	0		0/0/0	0/0	0//0	0/0/	0/0/0	5.9/0			0/0/0	---*o*-Xylene diisocyanate
0/0/0	0		0.7/0.7	0/0/0	0/0	0//0	0/0/	5/5/	/5			0/0/0	---Diphenylmethane diisocyanate
0/0/0	5	1.3	0/0	0/0/0	0/0	0//0	0/0/	5.9/5.9/5.9	6.1/5.9			0/0/0	---Hexamethylene diisocyanate
0/0/0	0	0	0/0	0/0/0	0/0	0//0	0/0/	5.9/5.9/5.9	5.9/5.9			0/0/0	---Other
													-Other:
0/0/0	2	0	0/0	0/0/0	0/0	0//0	0/0/	0/0/0	8.2/0			0/0/0	---Sodium cyclamate
0/0/0	5	0	0/0	0/0/0	0/0	0//0	0/0/	0/0/0	5.9/0			0/0/0	---N,N-Dialkyl (Me, Et, n-Pr or i-Pr) phosphoramidic dihalides
0/0/0	5	0	0/0	0/0/0	0/0	0//0	0/0/	0/0/0	5.9/0			0/0/0	---Dialkyl (Me, Et, n-Pr or i-Pr) N,N-dialkyl(Me, Et, n-Pr or i-Pr)-phosphoramidates
0/0/0	5	0	0/0	0/0/0	0/0	0//0	0/0/	0/0/0	5.9/0			0/0/0	---Acephate
													---Other
0/0/0	5	3	0/0	0/0/0	0/0	0//0	0/0/	5.9/5.9/5.9	6.1/5.9			0/0/0	Propetamaphos, amiprophos, butamifos (including amiprophos-methl)
0/0/0	5	3	0/0	0/0/0	0/0	0//0	0/0/	5.9/5.9/5.9	6.1/5.9			0/0/0	Isofenphos , isofenphos-methy, mipafox
0/0/0	5	3	0/0	0/0/0	0/0	0//0	0/0/	5.9/5.9/5.9	6.1/5.9			0/0/0	Schradan, crufomate, phosglycin (including dimefox, phosazetim, isocarbophos)
0/0/0	5	3	0/0	0/0/0	0/0	0//0	0/0/	5.9/5.9/5.9	6.1/5.9		//	0/0/0	N－{1－[dialkyl (carbon chain with less than or equal to 10 carbon atoms, including naphthene) amino] alkylene (hydrogen, carbon chain with less than or equal to 10 carbon atoms, including naphthene)}－p－fluorophosphonamide and corresponding alkylated or protonated salts

税则号列	货品名称〔CIQ扩展编码及品名—T2表示见附表2〕	最惠(%)	暂定税率	普通	增值/消费	出口退税	计量单位	监管条件/特殊证件	检验检疫	对美关税	亚太上/下
2929.9090 15	N—[1—二烷基(少于或等于10个碳原子的碳链,包括环烷)胺基]亚烷基(氢、少于或等于10个碳原子的碳链,包括环烷)胺基氟磷酸烷(氢、少于或等于10个碳原子的碳链,包括环烷)酯和相应的烷基化盐或质子化盐〔999〕	6.5		30	13/	13	千克	23/13		26.5	
2929.9090 90	其他含氮基化合物〔301危险化学品,爆炸品;302危险化学品,毒性物质;303危险化学品,杂项物质;304其他化工产品〕	6.5		30	13/	13	千克	/13		26.5	
	第十分章　有机—无机化合物、杂环化合物、核酸及其盐以及磺(酰)胺										
29.30	**有机硫化合物:**										
2930.1000	-2—(N,N—二甲基氨基)乙硫醇〔999〕	6.5		30	13/	13	千克	/13		11.5	
2930.2000	-硫代氨基甲酸盐(或酯)及二硫代氨基甲酸盐										
2930.2000 11	禾草丹、杀螟丹〔101巴丹,102杀草丹颗粒剂,103杀草丹〕	6.5		30	13/	9,13	千克	S/13		11.5	
2930.2000 12	威百亩、代森钠、丙森锌、福美铁等(包括福美锌、代森福美锌、安百亩)〔301危险化学品,毒性物质;302危险化学品,杂项物质;303其他化工产品〕	6.5		30	13/	9,13	千克	S/13		11.5	
2930.2000 13	燕麦敌、野麦畏、硫草敌〔301〕	6.5		30	13/	9,13	千克	S/13		11.5	
2930.2000 14	苄草丹、戊草丹、坪草丹、仲草丹〔999〕	6.5		30	13/	9,13	千克	S/13		11.5	
2930.2000 15	丁草敌、克草敌、茵草敌、灭草敌等(包括环草敌)〔999〕	6.5		30	13/	9,13	千克	S/13		11.5	
2930.2000 16	硫菌威、菜草畏〔301危险化学品,杂项物质;302其他化工产品〕	6.5		30	13/	9,13	千克	S/13		11.5	
2930.2000 90	其他硫代氨基甲酸盐(或酯)(包括二硫代氨基甲酸盐)〔101〕	6.5		30	13/	13	千克	/13		11.5	
2930.3000	-一硫化二烃氨基硫羰、二硫化二烃氨基硫羰及四硫化二烃氨基硫羰										
2930.3000 10	福美双〔999〕	6.5		30	13/	9,13	千克	S/13		26.5	
2930.3000 90	其他一硫化二烃氨基硫羰等(包括二硫化二烃氨基硫羰及四硫化二烃氨基硫羰)〔999〕	6.5		30	13/	13	千克	/13		26.5	
2930.4000	-甲硫氨酸(蛋氨酸)〔101〕	6.5	5	30	13/	13	千克	A/1	MP	30	
2930.6000	-2-(N,N-二乙基氨基)乙硫醇〔999〕	6.5		30	13/	13	千克	/1			
2930.7000	-二(2-羟乙基)硫醚[硫二甘醇(INN)]〔999〕	6.5		30	13/	13	千克	23/1			
2930.8000	-涕灭威(ISO)、敌菌丹(ISO)及甲胺磷(ISO)										
2930.8000 10	甲胺磷(ISO)〔999〕	6.5		30	13/	0	千克	/13			
2930.8000 20	敌菌丹(ISO)〔999〕	6.5		30	13/	0	千克	S/13			
2930.8000 30	涕灭威(ISO)〔999〕	6.5		30	13/	0	千克	S/13			
	-其他:										
2930.9010	---双巯丙氨酸(胱氨酸)〔101〕	6.5		30	13/	13	千克	A/1	MP	31.5	
2930.9020	---二硫代碳酸酯(或盐)[黄原酸酯(或盐)]〔301危险化学品,易于自燃的物质;302其他化工产品〕	6.5		30	13/	13	千克	/13		31.5	
2930.9090	---其他										
2930.9090 11	烯禾啶,双环磺草酮,氟虫酰胺,氟苯虫酰胺〔999〕	6.5		30	13/	9,13	千克	S/13		11.5	
2930.9090 13	2-氯乙基氯甲基硫醚〔999〕	6.5		30	13/	13	千克	32/13		11.5	
2930.9090 14	二(2-氯乙基)硫醚(即芥子气)〔999〕	6.5		30	13/	13	千克	32/13		11.5	
2930.9090 15	二(2-氯乙硫基)甲烷〔999〕	6.5		30	13/	13	千克	32/13		11.5	
2930.9090 16	1,2—二(2—氯乙硫基)乙烷(即倍半芥气)〔999〕	6.5		30	13/	13	千克	32/13		11.5	
2930.9090 17	1,3-二(2-氯乙硫基)正丙烷〔999〕	6.5		30	13/	13	千克	32/13		11.5	
2930.9090 18	1,4-二(2-氯乙硫基)正丁烷〔999〕	6.5		30	13/	13	千克	32/13		11.5	
2930.9090 19	1,5-二(2-氯乙硫基)正戊烷〔999〕	6.5		30	13/	13	千克	32/13		11.5	
2930.9090 21	二(2-氯乙硫基甲基)醚〔999〕	6.5		30	13/	13	千克	32/13		11.5	
2930.9090 22	二(2—氯乙硫基乙基)醚(即氧芥气)〔999〕	6.5		30	13/	13	千克	32/13		11.5	
2930.9090 23	胺吸膦(硫代磷酸二乙基-S-2-二乙氨基乙酯及烷基化或质子化盐)〔999〕	6.5		30	13/	13	千克	23/13		11.5	
2930.9090 24	烷基氨基乙-2-硫醇及相应质子盐〔999〕	6.5		30	13/	13	千克	23/13		11.5	
2930.9090 26	烷基硫代膦酸烷S-2-二烷氨基乙酯(包括相应烷基化盐、质子化盐,烷基指甲、乙、正丙、异丙基)〔999〕	6.5		30	13/	13	千克	23/13		11.5	
2930.9090 27	含一磷原子与甲、乙、丙基结合化合物(不包括地虫磷)〔999〕	6.5		30	13/	13	千克	23/13		11.5	
2930.9090 28	内吸磷〔999〕	6.5		30	13/	13	千克	/13		11.5	
2930.9090 31	4-甲基硫基安非他明〔999〕	6.5		30	13/	13	千克	I/13		11.5	
2930.9090 32	莫达非尼〔999〕	6.5		30	13/	13	千克	I/13		11.5	
2930.9090 51	甲基硫菌灵、硫菌灵、苯螨醚等(包括乙蒜素、敌灭生、丁酮威、丁酮砜威、棉铃威)〔301其他危险化学品,302其他化工产品,303毒性物质和感染性物质〕	6.5		30	13/	9,13	千克	S/13		11.5	
2930.9090 52	灭多威、乙硫苯威等(包括杀线威、甲硫威、多杀威、涕灭砜威、硫双威)〔301危险化学品,毒性物质;302其他化工品〕	6.5		30	13/	0	千克	S/13		11.5	
2930.9090 53	丁醚脲、久效威、苯硫威等(包括敌螨特、2甲4氯乙硫酯)〔301危险化学品,毒性物质,302其他化工产品〕	6.5		30	13/	9,13	千克	S/13		11.5	
2930.9090 54	杀虫双、杀虫单、灭虫脲等(包括避虫醇、烯虫硫酯、三氯杀螨砜、杀螨醚、杀螨酯)〔101一氯杀螨砜,102杀螨酯,103一氯杀螨砜乳剂,104杀螨酯乳剂〕	6.5		30	13/	9,13	千克	S/13		11.5	

协定税率 %								RCEP		特惠税率 %			Article Description
东/冰/格	巴基斯坦	韩国	瑞士上/下	哥/秘/柬	澳/毛	新西/坡/智	中国港/澳/台	东盟及马来/澳/韩	日/新	亚太2国	老/柬/缅	98/97/95	
0/0/0	5	3	0/0	0/0/0	0/0	0//0	0/0/	5.9/5.9/5.9	6.1/5.9		//	0/0/0	N — [1—dialkyl (carbon chain with less than or equal to 10 carbon atoms, including naphthene) amino] alkylene (hydrogen, carbon chain with less than or equal to 10 carbon atoms, including naphthene) amino fluorophosphate (hydrogen, carbon chain with less than or equal to 10 carbon atoms, including naphthene) ester and corresponding alkylate or protonated salt
0/0/0	5	3	0/0	0/0/0	0/0	0//0	0/0/	5.9/5.9/5.9	6.1/5.9			0/0/0	Compounds with other nitrogen function
													Ⅹ. ORGANO-INORGANIC COMPOUNDS, HETEROCYCLIC COMPOUNDS, NUCLEIC ACIDS AND THEIR SALTS, AND SULPHONAMIDES
													Organo-sulphur compounds:
0/0/0	5	0	0/0	0/0/0	0/0	0//0	0/0/	0/0/0	5.9/0			0/0/0	- 2 — (n, N—dimethylamino) ethanethiol
													-Thiocarbamates and dithiocarbamates
0/0/0	5	0	0/0	0/0/0	0/0	0//0	0/0/	0/0/0	5.9/0			0/0/0	Thiobencarb, cartap
0/0/0	5	0	0/0	0/0/0	0/0	0//0	0/0/	0/0/0	5.9/0			0/0/0	Metam-sodium, nabam, propineb, ferbam (including ziram, polycarbamate, meta-ammonium
0/0/0	5	0	0/0	0/0/0	0/0	0//0	0/0/	0/0/0	5.9/0			0/0/0	Diallate, triallate, ethiolate
0/0/0	5	0	0/0	0/0/0	0/0	0//0	0/0/	0/0/0	5.9/0			0/0/0	Prosulfocarb, esprocarb, orbencarb, tiocarbazil
0/0/0	5	0	0/0	0/0/0	0/0	0//0	0/0/	0/0/0	5.9/0			0/0/0	Butylate, pebulate, eradicane, vernolate (including cycloate)
0/0/0	5	0	0/0	0/0/0	0/0	0//0	0/0/	0/0/0	5.9/0			0/0/0	Prothiocarb, sulfallate
0/0/0	5	0	0/0	0/0/0	0/0	0//0	0/0/	0/0/0	5.9/0			0/0/0	Other thiocarbamates and dithiocarbamates(or ester) (including salt dithiocarbamate)
													-Thiuram mono— ,di or tetrasulphide
0/0/0	5	0	0/0	0/0/0	0/0	0//0	0/0/	0/0/0	5.9/0			0/0/0	Thiram
0/0/0	5	0	0/0	0/0/0	0/0	0//0	0/0/	0/0/0	5.9/0			0/0/0	Other thiuram mono(including dihydrocarbon-sulfur vulcanization carbonylation and thiuram tetrasulphides)
0/0/0	0	0	0/0	0/0/0	0/0	0//0	0/0/	0/0/0	5.9/0			0/0/0	-Methionine
0/0/0	5	0	0/0	0/0/0	0/0	0//0	0/0/	0/0/0	5.9/0			0/0/0	-2-(*N*,*N-Diethylamino*) ethanethiol
0/0/0	5	0	0/0	0/0/0	0/0	0//0	0/0/	0/0/0	5.9/0			0/0/0	-Bis (2-*hydroxyethyl*) sulfide (*thiodiglycol*(*INN*))
													-Aldicarb(*ISO*), captafol (*ISO*)and methamidophos (*ISO*)
0/0/0	5	0	0/0	0/0/0	0/0	0//0	0/0/	0/0/0	5.9/0			0/0/0	Methamidophos (ISO)
0/0/0	5	0	0/0	0/0/0	0/0	0//0	0/0/	0/0/0	5.9/0			0/0/0	Coptafol(ISO)
0/0/0	5	0	0/0	0/0/0	0/0	0//0	0/0/	0/0/0	5.9/0			0/0/0	Aldicarb(ISO)
													-Other:
0/0/0	5	0	0/0	0/0/0	0/0	0//0	0/0/	0/0/0	5.9/0			0/0/0	---Cystine
0/0/0	5	0	0/0	0/0/0	0/0	0//0	0/0/	0/0/0	5.9/0			0/0/0	---Dithiocarbonates (Xanth-ates)
													---Other
0/0/0	5	0	0/0	0/0/0	0/0	0//0	0/0/	0/0/0	5.9/0			0/0/0	Sethoxydinm, benzobicylon, flubendiamide
0/0/0	5	0	0/0	0/0/0	0/0	0//0	0/0/	0/0/0	5.9/0			0/0/0	2-chloroethyl chloromethyl sulfide
0/0/0	5	0	0/0	0/0/0	0/0	0//0	0/0/	0/0/0	5.9/0			0/0/0	Bis (2-chloroethyl) sulfide
0/0/0	5	0	0/0	0/0/0	0/0	0//0	0/0/	0/0/0	5.9/0			0/0/0	Bis (2-chloroethyl sulfide) methane
0/0/0	5	0	0/0	0/0/0	0/0	0//0	0/0/	0/0/0	5.9/0			0/0/0	1,2-Bis(2-chloroethyl sulfide) ethane
0/0/0	5	0	0/0	0/0/0	0/0	0//0	0/0/	0/0/0	5.9/0			0/0/0	1,3-Bis(2-chloroethyl sulfide) propane
0/0/0	5	0	0/0	0/0/0	0/0	0//0	0/0/	0/0/0	5.9/0			0/0/0	1,4-Bis(2-chloroethyl sulfide) butane
0/0/0	5	0	0/0	0/0/0	0/0	0//0	0/0/	0/0/0	5.9/0			0/0/0	1,5-Bis(2-chloroethyl sulfide) pentane
0/0/0	5	0	0/0	0/0/0	0/0	0//0	0/0/	0/0/0	5.9/0			0/0/0	Bis (2-chloroethyl sulfide methyl) ester
0/0/0	5	0	0/0	0/0/0	0/0	0//0	0/0/	0/0/0	5.9/0			0/0/0	Bis (2-chloroethyl sulfide ethyl) ester
0/0/0	5	0	0/0	0/0/0	0/0	0//0	0/0/	0/0/0	5.9/0			0/0/0	Amiton O,O-Diethyl S-2-(diethy lamino) ethyl phosphorothilolate and corresponding alkylated or protonated salts
0/0/0	5	0	0/0	0/0/0	0/0	0//0	0/0/	0/0/0	5.9/0			0/0/0	N,N-dialkyl aminoethane-2-thiols and corresponding protonated salts
0/0/0	5	0	0/0	0/0/0	0/0	0//0	0/0/	0/0/0	5.9/0			0/0/0	Alkyl alkane thiophosphate-S-2-aminoethyl, including cyclo alkane-S-2-dialkane (Me, Et, n-Pr or i-Pr) aminoethyl and corresponding alkylated or protonated salts
0/0/0	5	0	0/0	0/0/0	0/0	0//0	0/0/	0/0/0	5.9/0			0/0/0	Chemicals, containing a phosphorus atom to which is boned one methyl, ethyl or propyl group
0/0/0	5	0	0/0	0/0/0	0/0	0//0	0/0/	0/0/0	5.9/0			0/0/0	Demeton
0/0/0	5	0	0/0	0/0/0	0/0	0//0	0/0/	0/0/0	5.9/0			0/0/0	4-methylthioamfetamine
0/0/0	5	0	0/0	0/0/0	0/0	0//0	0/0/	0/0/0	5.9/0			0/0/0	Modafinil
0/0/0	5	0	0/0	0/0/0	0/0	0//0	0/0/	0/0/0	5.9/0			0/0/0	Thiophanate-methyl, thiophanate, phenproxide. (including ethylicin, dimexano , butocarboxim, butoxycarboxim, alanycarb)
0/0/0	5	0	0/0	0/0/0	0/0	0//0	0/0/	0/0/0	5.9/0			0/0/0	Methomyl, aldicarb, ethiofencarb, (including oxamyl, methiocarb, toxisamate, aldoxycarb, thiodicarb)
0/0/0	5	0	0/0	0/0/0	0/0	0//0	0/0/	0/0/0	5.9/0			0/0/0	Diafenthiuron, thiofanox, fenothiocarb(including chlorfensulphide, MCPA-thioethyl)
0/0/0	5	0	0/0	0/0/0	0/0	0//0	0/0/	0/0/0	5.9/0			0/0/0	Disosultap, monosultap, chloromethiuron (including (octylthio) ethanol, triprene, tetradifon, chlorbenside, chlorfenson)

税则号列		货品名称〔CIQ扩展编码及品名－T2表示见附表2〕	最惠(%)	暂定税率	普通	增值/消费	出口退税	计量单位	监管条件/特殊证件	检验检疫	对美关税	亚太上/下
2930.9090	55	代森锌、代森锰、代森锰锌等(包括福美胂、福美甲胂、代森铵、代森联)〔301危险化学品,易于自燃的物质;302其他化工产品〕	6.5		30	13/	9,13	千克	S/13		11.5	
2930.9090	56	烯草酮、磺草酮、嗪草酸甲酯、硝磺草酮等(包括苯氟磺胺、甲磺乐灵、氯硫酰草胺、脱叶磷)〔301危险化学品,毒性物质;302危险化学品,杂项物质;303其他化工产品〕	6.5		30	13/	9,13	千克	S/13		11.5	
2930.9090	57	灭菌丹、克菌丹、杀螨硫醚等(包括氟杀螨、硫肟醚、莠不生)〔999〕	6.5		30	13/	9,13	千克	S/13		11.5	
2930.9090	58	稻瘟净、异稻瘟净、稻丰散等(包括敌瘟磷)〔301危险化学品,毒性物质;302其他化工产品〕	6.5		30	13/	9,13	千克	S/13		11.5	
2930.9090	59	安妥、灭鼠特、二硫氰基甲烷等(包括灭鼠肼、氟硫隆)〔301危险化学品,毒性物质;302其他化工产品〕	6.5		30	13/	9,13	千克	S/13		11.5	
2930.9090	61	马拉硫磷、苏硫磷、赛硫磷等(包括丙虫磷、双硫磷、亚砜磷、异亚砜磷)〔301危险化学品,杂项物质;302其他化工产品〕	6.5		30	13/	9,13	千克	S/13		11.5	
2930.9090	62	丙溴磷、田乐磷、特丁硫磷等(包括硫丙磷、地虫硫膦、乙硫磷、丙硫磷、甲基乙拌磷)〔301危险化学品,毒性物质;302其他化工产品〕	6.5		30	13/	9,13	千克	S/13		11.5	
2930.9090	63	乐果、益硫磷、氧乐果等(包括甲拌磷、乙拌磷、虫螨磷、果虫磷)〔301危险化学品,毒性物质;302其他化工产品〕	6.5		30	13/	9,13	千克	S/13		11.5	
2930.9090	64	氯胺磷、家蝇磷、灭蚜磷等(包括安硫磷、四甲磷、丁苯硫磷、苯线磷、蚜灭磷)〔301危险化学品,毒性物质;302其他化工产品〕	6.5		30	13/	9,13	千克	S/13		11.5	
2930.9090	65	硫线磷、氯甲硫磷、杀虫磺等(包括砜吸磷、砜拌磷、异拌磷、三硫磷、芬硫磷)〔301危险化学品,毒性物质;302其他化工产品〕	6.5		30	13/	9,13	千克	S/13		11.5	
2930.9090	66	倍硫磷、甲基内吸磷、乙酯磷等(包括丰索磷、内吸磷、发硫磷)〔301危险化学品,毒性物质;302其他化工产品〕	6.5		30	13/	9,13	千克	S/13		11.5	
2930.9090	67	灭线磷〔999〕	6.5		30	13/	9,13	千克	S/13		11.5	
2930.9090	68	青霉胺〔999〕	6.5	0	30	3/	13	千克	/13		5	
2930.9090	91	DL-羟基蛋氨酸〔101饲料添加剂,102化工产品〕	6.5		30	13/	13	千克	A/13	MP	11.5	
2930.9090	92	比卡鲁胺〔999〕	6.5	0	30	3/	13	千克	/13		5	
2930.9090	99	其他有机硫化合物[T2]	6.5		30	13/	13	千克	/13		11.5	
29.31		**其他有机—无机化合物：**										
2931.1000		-四甲基铅及四乙基铅〔999〕	6.5		30	13/	13	千克	ABX/13	MN		
2931.2000		-三丁基锡化合物〔301危险化学品,毒性物质;302其他化工产品〕	6.5		30	13/	0	千克	X/13			
		-非卤化有机磷衍生物：										
2931.4100		--甲基膦酸二甲酯〔999〕	6.5		30	13/	13	千克	23/1			
2931.4200		--丙基膦酸二甲酯〔999〕	6.5		30	13/	13	千克	AB/1	MRNS		
2931.4300		--乙基膦酸二乙酯〔999〕	6.5		30	13/	13	千克	23/1			
2931.4400		--甲基膦酸〔999〕	6.5		30	13/	9,13	千克	23/13		31.5	
2931.4500		--甲基膦酸和脒基尿素(1:1)生成的盐〔999〕	6.5		30	13/	13	千克	23AB/1	MRNS		
2931.4600		--1－丙基磷酸环酐〔999〕	6.5		30	13/	13	千克	23AB/1	MRNS		
2931.4700		--(5－乙基－2－甲基－2－氧代－1,3,2－二氧磷杂环己－5－基)甲基膦酸二甲酯〔999〕	6.5		30	13/	13	千克	23/1			
2931.4800		--3,9－二甲基－2,4,8,10－四氧杂－3,9－二磷杂螺[5,5]十一烷－3,9二氧化物〔999〕	6.5		30	13/	13	千克	AB/13	MRNS	31.5	
		--其他：										
2931.4910		---双甘膦〔999〕	6.5		30	13/	0	千克	AB/1	RS		
2931.4990		---其他										
2931.4990	10	烷基亚膦酰烷基－2－二烷氨基乙酯(包括相应烷基化盐或质子化盐),二烷氨基氰膦酸烷酯10碳原子以下(烷基指甲,乙,正丙,异丙基,例如塔崩)〔999〕	6.5		30	13/	13	千克	23/13			
2931.4990	20	丙基膦酸,甲基膦酸二聚乙二醇酯(CAS号:294675－51－7),甲基膦酸二[5－(5－乙基－2－甲基－2－氧代－1,3,2－二氧磷杂环己基)甲基]酯(CAS号:42595－45－9)〔999〕	6.5		30	13/	9,13	千克	23/13			
2931.4990	30	草甘膦及其盐,草铵膦,精草铵膦,草硫膦,杀木膦,双丙氨膦,增甘膦,苯硫膦,苯腈膦〔301危险化学品,毒性物质,302其他化工产品〕	6.5		30	13/	0,9,13	千克	S/13			
2931.4990	40	双[(5－乙基－2－甲基－2－氧代－1,3,2－二氧磷杂环己－5－基)甲基]甲基膦酸酯(阻燃剂FRC－1)(CAS号:42595－45－9)〔999〕	6.5		30	13/	13	千克	AB/13	MRNS		
2931.4990	50	3－(三羟基硅烷基)丙基甲基膦酸钠〔999〕	6.5		30	13/	13	千克	AB/13	MRNS		
2931.4990	90	其他非卤化有机磷衍生物〔301危险化学品,易于自燃的物质,302危险化学品,腐蚀性物质,303其他危险化学品,304其他化工品,不用作食品添加剂,305其他化工品,用作食品添加剂〕	6.5		30	13/	9,13	千克	AB/13	MRNS		
		-卤化有机磷衍生物：										
2931.5100		--甲基膦酰二氯〔999〕	6.5		30	13/	9,13	千克	23/13		31.5	
2931.5200		--丙基膦酰二氯〔999〕	6.5		30	13/	13	千克	AB/13	MRNS	31.5	

协定税率 %								RCEP		特惠税率 %			Article Description
东/冰/格	巴基斯坦	韩国	瑞士上/下	哥/秘/柬	澳/毛	新西/坡/智	中国港/澳/台	东盟及马来/澳/韩	日/新	亚太2国	老/柬/缅	98/97/95	
0/0/0	5	0	0/0	0/0/0	0/0	0//0	0/0/	0/0/0	5.9/0			0/0/0	Zineb, maneb, mancozeb, (including asomate , urbacide (JMAP) , amobam, metiram)
0/0/0	5	0	0/0	0/0/0	0/0	0//0	0/0/	0/0/0	5.9/0			0/0/0	Clethodim, sulcotrione, fluthiacet-methyl mesotrione (including dichlofluanid, nitralin, chlorthiamide, tribuphons)
0/0/0	5	0	0/0	0/0/0	0/0	0//0	0/0/	0/0/0	5.9/0			0/0/0	Folpet, captan, tetrasul (including fluorbenside, sulfoxime, EXD)
0/0/0	5	0	0/0	0/0/0	0/0	0//0	0/0/	0/0/0	5.9/0			0/0/0	Kitazine, iprobenfos phenthoate(including edifenphos)
0/0/0	5	0	0/0	0/0/0	0/0	0//0	0/0/	0/0/0	5.9/0			0/0/0	Antu, thiosemicarbazide, dithiocyano-methane(including promurit, flurothiuron)
0/0/0	5	0	0/0	0/0/0	0/0	0//0	0/0/	0/0/0	5.9/0			0/0/0	Malathion, sophamide, amidithion(including propaphos, temephos, oxydemeton-methyl, oxydeprofos)
0/0/0	5	0	0/0	0/0/0	0/0	0//0	0/0/	0/0/0	5.9/0			0/0/0	Profenofos, demephion, terbufos(including sulprofos, fonofos, ethion, prothiofos, thiometon)
0/0/0	5	0	0/0	0/0/0	0/0	0//0	0/0/	0/0/0	5.9/0			0/0/0	Dimethoate, ethoate-methyl, omethoate(including phorate, disulfoton, chlorthiophos, cyanthoate)
0/0/0	5	0	0/0	0/0/0	0/0	0//0	0/0/	0/0/0	5.9/0			0/0/0	Chloramine phosphorus, acethion mecarbam(including formothion, mecarphon, fosmethilan, fenamiphos, vamidothion)
0/0/0	5	0	0/0	0/0/0	0/0	0//0	0/0/	0/0/0	5.9/0			0/0/0	Cadusafos, chlormephos, bensultap (including oxydemeton-methyl, oxydisulfoton, isothioate, carbophenothion, phenkapton)
0/0/0	5	0	0/0	0/0/0	0/0	0//0	0/0/	0/0/0	5.9/0			0/0/0	Fenthion, demeton-s-methyl, acetophos(including fensulfothion, demeton , prothoate, methylacetophos)
0/0/0	5	0	0/0	0/0/0	0/0	0//0	0/0/	0/0/0	5.9/0			0/0/0	Ethoprophos
0/0/0	5	0	0/0	0/0/0	0/0	0//0	0/0/	0/0/0	5.9/0		//	0/0/0	penicillamine
0/0/0	5	0	0/0	0/0/0	0/0	0//0	0/0/	0/0/0	5.9/0			0/0/0	DL- hydroxy methionine
0/0/0	5	0	0/0	0/0/0	0/0	0//0	0/0/	0/0/0	5.9/0			0/0/0	Bicalutamide, Mesna, Sulindac and Other Anticancer Drugs
0/0/0	5	0	0/0	0/0/0	0/0	0//0	0/0/	0/0/0	5.9/0			0/0/0	Other organic sulfur compounds
													Other organo-inorganic compounds:
0/0/0	5	0	0/0	0/0/0	0/0	0//0	0/0/	0/0/0	5.9/0			0/0/0	-Tetramethyl lead and tetraethyl lead
0/0/0	5	0	0/0	0/0/0	0/0	0//0	0/0/	0/0/0	5.9/0			0/0/0	-Tributyltin compounds:
													- Non—halogenated organo—phosphorous derivatives :
0/0/0	5	0	0/0	0/0/0	0/0	0//0	0/0/	0/0/0	5.9/0			0/0/0	-- Dimethyl methylphosphonate
0/0/0	5	0	0/0	0/0/0	0/0	0//0	0/0/	0/0/0	5.9/0			0/0/0	-- Dimethyl propylphosphonate
0/0/0	5	0	0/0	0/0/0	0/0	0//0	0/0/	0/0/0	5.9/0			0/0/0	-- Diethyl ethylphosphonate
0/0/0	5	0	0/0	0/0/0	0/0	0//0	0/0/	0/0/0	5.9/0			0/0/0	-- Methylphosphonic acid
0/0/0	5	0	0/0	0/0/0	0/0	0//0	0/0/	0/0/0	5.9/0			0/0/0	-- Salt of methylphosphonic acid and (aminoiminomethyl) urea (1 : 1)
0/0/0	5	0	0/0	0/0/0	0/0	0//0	0/0/	0/0/0	5.9/0			0/0/0	-- 2,4,6—Tripropyl—1,3,5,2,4,6—trioxatriphosphinane 2,4,6—trioxide
0/0/0	5	0	0/0	0/0/0	0/0	0//0	0/0/	0/0/0	5.9/0			0/0/0	-- (5—Ethyl—2—methyl—2—oxido—1,3,2—dioxaphosphinan—5—yl) methyl methyl methylphosphonate
0/0/0	5	0	0/0	0/0/0	0/0	0//0	0/0/	0/0/0	5.9/0			0/0/0	-- 3,9—Dimethyl—2,4,8,10—tetraoxa—3,9—diphosphaspiro[5.5] undecane 3,9—dioxide
													-- Other:
0/0/0	5	0	0/0	0/0/0	0/0	0//0	0/0/	0/0/0	5.9/0			0/0/0	---N—phosphonomethylglycine
													--- Other
0/0/0	5	0	0/0	0/0/0	0/0	0//0	0/0/	0/0/0	5.9/0			0/0/0	Alkyl phosphinyl alkyl—2—dialkylamino ethyl ester (including corresponding alkylated salt or protonated salt), alkyl dialkylamino cyanophosphosphonate with less than 1 carbon atoms (alkyl, ethyl, n—propyl, isopropyl, such as tabun)
0/0/0	5	0	0/0	0/0/0	0/0	0//0	0/0/	0/0/0	5.9/0			0/0/0	Propylphosphonic acid, methylphosphonic acid di polyethylene glycol ester (CAS No.: 294675—51—7), methylphosphonic acid di[5 — (5—ethyl—2—methyl—2—oxo—1,3,2—dioxophosphazinyl) methyl] ester (CAS No.: 42595—45—9)
0/0/0	5	0	0/0	0/0/0	0/0	0//0	0/0/	0/0/0	5.9/0			0/0/0	Glyphosate and its salts, glyphosate ammonium phosphine, arginine glyphosate, glyphosate, glyphosate, phenylthiophosphine, phenylnitrile phosphine
0/0/0	5	0	0/0	0/0/0	0/0	0//0	0/0/	0/0/0	5.9/0			0/0/0	Bis[(5—ethyl—2—methyl—2—oxo—1,3,2—dioxophosphazine—5—yl) methyl] methyl phosphonate (flame retardant FRC—1) (CAS No.: 42595—45—9)
0/0/0	5	0	0/0	0/0/0	0/0	0//0	0/0/	0/0/0	5.9/0			0/0/0	Sodium 3 — (trihydroxysilyl) propylmethylphosphonate
0/0/0	5	0	0/0	0/0/0	0/0	0//0	0/0/	0/0/0	5.9/0			0/0/0	Other non halogenated organophosphorus derivatives
													Halogenated organo phosphorous derivatives :
0/0/0	5	0	0/0	0/0/0	0/0	0//0	0/0/	0/0/0	5.9/0			0/0/0	-- Methylphosphonic dichloride
0/0/0	5	0	0/0	0/0/0	0/0	0//0	0/0/	0/0/0	5.9/0			0/0/0	-- Propylphosphonic dichloride

税则号列	货品名称〔CIQ 扩展编码及品名－T2 表示见附表 2〕	最惠(%)	暂定税率	普通	增值/消费	出口退税	计量单位	监管条件/特殊证件	检验检疫	对美关税	亚太上/下
2931.5300	--O－(3－氯丙基)O－[4－硝基－3－(三氟甲基)苯基]甲基硫代膦酸酯〔999〕	6.5		30	13/	13	千克	AB/13	MRNS	31.5	
2931.5400	--敌百虫(ISO)〔999〕	6.5		30	13/	9,13	千克	S/13		31.5	
2931.5900	--其他										
2931.5900 10	氯沙林(甲基氯膦酸异丙酯),氯梭曼(甲基氯膦酸频那酯)〔999〕	6.5		30	13/	13	千克	23/13		31.5	
2931.5900 20	烷基氟膦酸烷酯,10 碳原子以下(烷基指甲,乙,正丙,异丙基,例如沙林,梭曼)〔999〕	6.5		30	13/	13	千克	23/13		31.5	
2931.5900 30	烷基膦酰二氟(烷基指甲,乙,正丙,异丙基,例如,DF:甲基膦酰二氟)〔999〕	6.5		30	13/	13	千克	23/13		31.5	
2931.5900 40	三丁氯苄鏻,乙烯利,氟硅菊酯,毒壤膦,溴苯膦,丁酯膦〔301 危险化学品,毒性物质,302 其他化工产品〕	6.5		30	13/	9,13	千克	S/13		31.5	
2931.5900 50	N－{1－[二烷基(少于或等于 10 个碳原子的碳链,包括环烷)胺基]亚烷基(氢、少于或等于 10 个碳原子的碳链,包括环烷)}－P－烷基(少于或等于 10 个碳原子的碳链,包括环烷)氟膦酰胺和相应的烷基化盐或质子化盐〔999〕	6.5		30	13/	9,13	千克	23/13		31.5	
2931.5900 60	[双(二乙胺基)亚甲基]甲氟膦酰胺(CAS:2387496－14－0)〔999〕	6.5		30	13/	9,13	千克	23/13		31.5	
2931.5900 70	壤虫磷〔999〕	6.5		30	13/	9,13	千克	23s/13		31.5	
2931.5900 90	其他卤化有机磷衍生物〔301 危险化学品,毒性物质,302 危险化学品,腐蚀性物质,303 其他危险化学品,304 其他化工品,不用作食品添加剂,305 其他化工品,用作食品添加剂〕	6.5		30	13/	9,13	千克	AB/13	MRNS	31.5	
2931.9000	-其他										
2931.9000 01	六甲基环三硅氧烷(包括八甲基环四硅氧烷,十甲基环五硅氧烷,十二甲基环六硅氧烷)〔999〕	6.5		30	13/	13	千克	/13		11.5	
2931.9000 11	2-氯乙烯基二氯胂〔999〕	6.5		30	13/	0	千克	23/13		11.5	
2931.9000 12	二(2-氯乙烯基)氯胂〔999〕	6.5		30	13/	0	千克	23/13		11.5	
2931.9000 13	三(2-氯乙烯基)胂〔999〕	6.5		30	13/	0	千克	23/13		11.5	
2931.9000 14	锆试剂,二甲胂酸等(包括 4－二甲氨基偶氮苯－4'－胂酸,卡可基酸,二甲基胂酸钠)〔301 危险化学品,毒性物质;302 其他化工产品〕	6.5		30	13/	0	千克	/13		11.5	
2931.9000 15	4-氨基苯胂酸钠,二氯化苯胂(对氨基苯胂酸钠,二氯苯胂,苯胂化二氯)〔999〕	6.5		30	13/	0	千克	/13		11.5	
2931.9000 16	蒽醌-1-胂酸、三环锡(普特丹)等(包括月桂酸三丁基锡、醋酸三丁基锡)〔301 危险化学品,毒性物质;302 其他化工产品〕	6.5		30	13/	0	千克	/13		11.5	
2931.9000 17	硫酸三乙基锡,二丁基氧化锡等(包括氧化二丁基锡,乙酸三乙基锡,三乙基乙酸锡)〔999〕	6.5		30	13/	13	千克	/13			
2931.9000 18	四乙基锡,乙酸三甲基锡(四乙锡,醋酸三甲基锡)〔999〕	6.5		30	13/	13	千克	/13		11.5	
2931.9000 19	毒菌锡(三苯基羟基锡(含量>20%))〔999〕	6.5		30	13/	13	千克	/13		11.5	
2931.9000 21	乙酰亚砷酸铜,二苯(基)胺氯胂(祖母绿;翡翠绿;醋酸亚砷酸铜,吩吡嗪化氯;亚当氏气)〔999〕	6.5		30	13/	0	千克	/13		11.5	
2931.9000 22	3-硝基-4-羟基苯胂酸(4-羟基-3-硝基苯胂酸)〔999〕	6.5		30	13/	0	千克	/13		11.5	
2931.9000 23	乙基二氯胂,二苯(基)氯胂(包括二氯化乙基胂,氯化二苯胂)〔999〕	6.5		30	13/	0	千克	/13		11.5	
2931.9000 24	甲(基)胂酸,丙(基)胂酸,二碘化苯胂(苯基二碘胂)〔999〕	6.5		30	13/	0	千克	/13		11.5	
2931.9000 25	苯胂酸,2-硝基苯胂酸等(包括邻硝基苯胂酸,3-硝基苯胂酸,间硝基苯胂酸等)〔301 危险化学品,毒性物质; 302 其他化工产品〕	6.5		30	13/	0	千克	/13		11.5	
2931.9000 26	4-硝基苯胂酸,2-氨基苯胂酸(对硝基苯胂酸,邻氨基苯胂酸)〔999〕	6.5		30	13/	0	千克	/13		11.5	
2931.9000 27	3－氨基苯胂酸、4－氨基苯胂酸(间氨基苯胂酸、对氨基苯胂酸)〔999〕	6.5		30	13/	0	千克	/13		11.5	
2931.9000 28	三苯锡,三苯基乙酸锡等(包括三苯基氯化锡,三苯基氢氧化锡,苯丁锡,三唑锡)〔301 危险化学品,毒性物质; 302 其他化工产品〕	6.5		30	13/	9,13	千克	S/13		11.5	
2931.9000 29	田安〔999〕	6.5		30	13/	9,13	千克	S/13		11.5	
2931.9000 31	乙烯硅〔999〕	6.5		30	13/	9,13	千克	S/13		11.5	
2931.9000 90	其他有机-无机化合物〔301 危险化学品,气体;302 危险化学品,易燃液体;303 危险化学品,易于自燃的物质;304 危险化学品,遇水放出易燃气体的物质;305 危险化学品,毒性物质;306 危险化学品,腐蚀性物质;307 危险化学品,杂项物质;308 其他化工品,不用作食品添加剂;309 其他化工品,用作食品添加剂〕	6.5		30	13/	13	千克	AB/13	MRNS	11.5	
29.32	**仅含有氧杂原子的杂环化合物:**										
	-结构上含有一个非稠合呋喃环(不论是否氢化)的化合物:										
2932.1100	--四氢呋喃〔301:危险化学品,易燃液体;302:其他化工品,用作食品添加剂〕	6		20	13/	13	千克	AB/13	MN	26	
2932.1200	--2-糠醛〔999〕	6		20	13/	9,13	千克	B/13	N	31	

协定税率 %								RCEP		特惠税率 %			Article Description
东/冰/格	巴基斯坦	韩国	瑞士上/下	哥/秘/柬	澳/毛	新西/坡/智	中国港/澳/台	东盟及马来/澳/韩	日/新	亚太2国	老/柬/缅	98/97/95	
0/0/0	5	0	0/0	0/0/0	0/0	0//0	0/0/	0/0/0	5.9/0			0/0/0	-- O—(3—chloropropyl) O—[4—nitro—3—(trifluoromethyl)phenyl] methylphosphonothionate
0/0/0	5	0	0/0	0/0/0	0/0	0//0	0/0/	0/0/0	5.9/0			0/0/0	-- Trichlorfon (ISO)
													-- Other
0/0/0	5	0	0/0	0/0/0	0/0	0//0	0/0/	0/0/0	5.9/0			0/0/0	Chlorsarin (isopropyl methyl chlorophosphonate), chlorsoman (pinate methyl chlorophosphonate)
0/0/0	5	0	0/0	0/0/0	0/0	0//0	0/0/	0/0/0	5.9/0			0/0/0	Alkyl fluorophosphonate, less than 1 carbon atoms (alkyl, ethyl, n—propyl, isopropyl, such as sarin, soman)
0/0/0	5	0	0/0	0/0/0	0/0	0//0	0/0/	0/0/0	5.9/0			0/0/0	Alkyl phosphinyl difluoride (alkyl, ethyl, n—propyl, isopropyl, e.g., DF: methyl phosphinyl difluoride)
0/0/0	5	0	0/0	0/0/0	0/0	0//0	0/0/	0/0/0	5.9/0			0/0/0	Tributyl Chlorobenzyl phosphonium, ethephon, cyhalothrin, toxic soil phosphine, bromophenylphosphine, butylphosphine
0/0/0	5	0	0/0	0/0/0	0/0	0//0	0/0/	0/0/0	5.9/0			0/0/0	N — {1 — [dialkyl (carbon chain with less than or equal to 1 carbon atoms, including cycloalkyl) amino] alkylene (hydrogen, carbon chain with less than or equal to 1 carbon atoms, including cycloalkyl)} — p — alkyl (carbon chain with less than or equal to 1 carbon atoms, including cycloalkyl) fluorophosphonamide and corresponding alkylated or protonated salts
0/0/0	5	0	0/0	0/0/0	0/0	0//0	0/0/	0/0/0	5.9/0			0/0/0	[bis (diethylamino) methylene] methylfluorophosphinamide (CAS: 2387496—14—)
0/0/0	5	0	0/0	0/0/0	0/0	0//0	0/0/	0/0/0	5.9/0			0/0/0	Soil insect phosphorus
0/0/0	5	0	0/0	0/0/0	0/0	0//0	0/0/	0/0/0	5.9/0			0/0/0	Other halogenated organophosphorus derivatives
													-Other
0/0/0	5	0	0/0	0/0/0	0/0	0//0	0/0/	5.9/5.9/5.9	5.9/5.9			0/0/0	Hexamethylcyclotrisiloxane (including octamethylcyotetrasiloxane, decamethylcyclotrisiloxane, decamethylcyclotrisiloxane)
0/0/0	5	0	0/0	0/0/0	0/0	0//0	0/0/	5.9/5.9/5.9	5.9/5.9			0/0/0	2-chlorovinyl dichloroarsine
0/0/0	5	0	0/0	0/0/0	0/0	0//0	0/0/	5.9/5.9/5.9	5.9/5.9			0/0/0	Di(2-Chlorovinyl)chloroarsine
0/0/0	5	0	0/0	0/0/0	0/0	0//0	0/0/	5.9/5.9/5.9	5.9/5.9			0/0/0	Tri(2-Chlorovinyl)arsine
0/0/0	5	0	0/0	0/0/0	0/0	0//0	0/0/	5.9/5.9/5.9	5.9/5.9			0/0/0	Zirconin, cacodylic acid, etc.(including 4- dimethyl- aminoazobenzene-4'- arsonic acid, cacodylic acid, sodium cacodylate)
0/0/0	5	0	0/0	0/0/0	0/0	0//0	0/0/	5.9/5.9/5.9	5.9/5.9			0/0/0	4-sodium arsanilate, phenyldichloroarsine (sodium rho-aminophenylarsonate, dichlorophenarsine, phenylarsine dichloride)
0/0/0	5	0	0/0	0/0/0	0/0	0//0	0/0/	5.9/5.9/5.9	5.9/5.9			0/0/0	Anthraquinone-1-arsonic acid, cyhexatin etc.(including lauric acid tributyltin, acetic acid tributyltin)
0/0/0	5	0	0/0	0/0/0	0/0	0//0	0/0/	5.9/5.9/5.9	5.9/5.9			0/0/0	Triethyltin sulphate, Dibutyltin oxide etc. (including oxidation dibutyltin? Acetoxytriethylstannane, triethyl ethyl stannic acid)
0/0/0	5	0	0/0	0/0/0	0/0	0//0	0/0/	5.9/5.9/5.9	5.9/5.9			0/0/0	Tetraethyltin, trimethyltin acetate
0/0/0	5	0	0/0	0/0/0	0/0	0//0	0/0/	5.9/5.9/5.9	5.9/5.9			0/0/0	Fentin hydroxide[Triphenyltin hydroxide(content>20%)]
0/0/0	5	0	0/0	0/0/0	0/0	0//0	0/0/	5.9/5.9/5.9	5.9/5.9			0/0/0	Copper acetoarsenite, phenarsazinechloride
0/0/0	5	0	0/0	0/0/0	0/0	0//0	0/0/	5.9/5.9/5.9	5.9/5.9			0/0/0	4-Hydroxy-3-nitro phenylarsonic acid
0/0/0	5	0	0/0	0/0/0	0/0	0//0	0/0/	5.9/5.9/5.9	5.9/5.9			0/0/0	Ethyldichloroarsine diphenylchloroarsine etc. (including dichloroethyl arsenic, diphenylarsine chloride)
0/0/0	5	0	0/0	0/0/0	0/0	0//0	0/0/	5.9/5.9/5.9	5.9/5.9			0/0/0	Methanearsonic acid, propylarsonic acid , phenyl diiodoarsine etc.(including phenylarsine diiondide)
0/0/0	5	0	0/0	0/0/0	0/0	0//0	0/0/	5.9/5.9/5.9	5.9/5.9			0/0/0	Phenylarsonic acid, 2-nitrophenylarsonic acid(including o-nitrophenyl arsonic acid, 3- nitrophenylarsonic acid, m-nitrophenol arsonic acid etc.)
0/0/0	5	0	0/0	0/0/0	0/0	0//0	0/0/	5.9/5.9/5.9	5.9/5.9			0/0/0	4-Nitrophenylarsonic acid, 2-aminophenylarsonic acid(paranitrotoluene arsonic acid, o-phenetidine arsonic acid)
0/0/0	5	0	0/0	0/0/0	0/0	0//0	0/0/	5.9/5.9/5.9	5.9/5.9			0/0/0	3-Aminophenylarsonic acid, Aminophenylars- onic acid(m-aminophenol arsonic acid , pamin- ophenylarsonic acid)
0/0/0	5	0	0/0	0/0/0	0/0	0//0	0/0/	5.9/5.9/5.9	5.9/5.9			0/0/0	Fentin, fentin acetate etc.(including fentinCh- loride, fentin hydroxide, fenbutatin oxide, azocy- clotin)
0/0/0	5	0	0/0	0/0/0	0/0	0//0	0/0/	5.9/5.9/5.9	5.9/5.9			0/0/0	Neoasozin
0/0/0	5	0	0/0	0/0/0	0/0	0//0	0/0/	5.9/5.9/5.9	5.9/5.9			0/0/0	Etacelasil
0/0/0	5	0	0/0	0/0/0	0/0	0//0	0/0/	5.9/5.9/5.9	5.9/5.9			0/0/0	Other organo-inorganic compound
													Heterocyclic compounds with oxygen hetero-atom(s) only:
													-Compounds containing an unfused furan ring (whether or not hydrogenated) in the structure:
0/0/0	5	0	0/0	0/0/0	0/0	0//0	0/0/0	0/5.4/0	0/5.4			0/0/0	--Tetrahydrofuran
0/0/0	5	0	0/0	0/0/0	0/0	0//0	0/0/	0/0/0	0/0			0/0/0	--2-Furaldehyde (furfuraldehyde)

税则号列		货品名称〔CIQ 扩展编码及品名－T2 表示见附表 2〕	最惠(%)	暂定税率	普通	增值/消费	出口退税	计量单位	监管条件/特殊证件	检验检疫	对美关税	亚太上/下
2932.1300		--糠醇及四氢糠醇〔301 危险化学品，不用作食品添加剂；302 危险化学品，用作食品添加剂〕	6		20	13/	13	千克	/13		16	
2932.1400		--三氯蔗糖〔999〕	6.5		20	13/	13	千克	/1		11.5	
2932.1900		--其他										
2932.1900	11	喃烯菊酯、炔呋菊酯等(包括甲呋炔菊酯、溴苄呋菊酯、右旋炔呋菊酯)〔999〕	6.5		20	13/	9,13	千克	S/13		16.5	
2932.1900	12	呋菌胺、酯菌胺、抑霉胺等(包括环菌胺、甲呋酰胺、二甲呋酰胺)〔999〕	6.5		20	13/	9,13	千克	S/13		16.5	
2932.1900	13	呋氧草醚，环庚草醚，呋草酮等(包括茵多酸，莪术醇，呋喃磺草酮)〔999〕	6.5		20	13/	9,13	千克	S/13		16.5	
2932.1900	14	楝素、呋霜灵等(包括呋菌隆、螺螨酯)〔999〕	6.5		20	13/	9,13	千克	S/13		16.5	
2932.1900	15	苄呋菊酯(包括右旋苄呋菊酯、生物苄呋菊酯)〔999〕	6.5		20	13/	9,13	千克	S/13		16.5	
2932.1900	16	呋虫胺〔999〕	6.5		20	13/	9,13	千克	S/13		16.5	
2932.1900	20	呋芬雷司〔999〕	6.5		20	13/	13	千克	I/13		16.5	
2932.1900	30	恩格列净〔999〕	6.5	0	20	13/	13	千克	/13		10	
2932.1900	90	其他结构上有非稠合呋喃环化合物〔301 危险化学品，易燃液体；302 危险化学品，腐蚀性物质；303 其他化工产品〕	6.5		20	13/	13	千克	/13		16.5	
		-内酯：										
2932.2010		--香豆素、甲基香豆素及乙基香豆素〔301 无检疫要求食品添加剂，302 其他化工产品〕	6.5		20	13/	13	千克	/1		26.5	
2932.2090		--其他内酯										
2932.2090	11	杀鼠灵、克鼠灵、敌鼠灵、溴鼠灵等(包括氯灭鼠灵、氟鼠灵、鼠得克、杀鼠醚)〔301 危险化学品，毒性物质；302 其他化工产品〕	6.5		20	13/	0	千克	S/13		26.5	
2932.2090	12	赤霉酸〔999〕	6.5		20	13/	9,13	千克	S/13		26.5	
2932.2090	13	蝇毒磷、茴蒿素、溴敌隆、呋酰胺等(包括四氯苯酞，畜虫磷)〔301 危险化学品，毒性物质；302 其他化工产品〕	6.5		20	13/	0	千克	S/13		26.5	
2932.2090	14	丁香菌酯〔999〕	6.5		20	13/	9,13	千克	S/13		26.5	
2932.2090	15	甲氨基阿维菌素及其盐〔999〕	6.5		20	13/	9,13	千克	S/13		26.5	
2932.2090	16	阿维菌素〔999〕	6.5		20	13/	9,13	千克	S/13		26.5	
2932.2090	17	丙酰芸苔素内酯，螺螨双酯〔999〕	6.5		20	13/	13	千克	S/13		26.5	
2932.2090	20	鬼臼毒素〔999〕	6.5		20	13/	13	千克	EF/13		26.5	
2932.2090	31	γ－丁内酯(CAS 号 96－48－0)〔999〕	6.5		20	13/	13	千克	23/13		26.5	
2932.2090	90	其他内酯〔301 危险化学品，毒性物质；302 其他化工品，不用作食品添加剂；303 其他化工品，用作食品添加剂〕	6.5		20	13/	13	千克	/13		26.5	
		-其他：										
2932.9100		--4-丙烯基-1,2-亚甲二氧基苯(异黄樟脑)〔999〕	6.5		20	13/	13	千克	23/1			
2932.9200		--1-(1,3-苯并二噁茂-5 基)丙烷-2 酮〔999〕	6.5		20	13/	13	千克	23/1			
2932.9300		--3,4-亚甲二氧基苯甲醛(胡椒醛)〔999〕	6.5		20	13/	13	千克	23/1			
2932.9400		--4-烯丙基-1,2-亚甲二氧基苯(黄樟脑)〔999〕	6.5		20	13/	13	千克	23/1			
2932.9500		--四氢大麻酚(所有异构体)〔999〕	6.5		20	13/	13	千克	I/1		11.5	
2932.9600		--克百威(ISO)〔999〕	6.5		20	13/	9,13	千克	S/1		26.5	
		--其他：										
2932.9910		---7-羟基苯并呋喃(呋喃酚)〔999〕	4		11	13/	13	千克	/1			3.6/3.6
2932.9920		---2,2'-双甲氧羰基-4,4'-双甲氧基-5,5',6,6'-双亚甲二氧基联苯(联苯双酯)〔999〕	6.5		20	13/	13	千克	/1			5.2/5.2
2932.9930		---蒿甲醚〔999〕	6.5		20	13/	13	千克	/1		11.5	
2932.9990		---其他										
2932.9990	12	二氧威，噁虫威，丙硫克百威等(包括丁硫克百威，呋线威)〔101 丁硫威粉剂，102 噁虫威粉剂(含量 5%～65%)，103 二氧威乳剂(含量＞3%)，104 丁硫威，105 二氧威粉剂(含量＞10%)〕〔101 丁硫威粉剂，102 恶虫威粉剂(含量 5%～65%)，103 二氧威乳剂(含量＞3%)，104 丁硫威，105 二氧威粉剂(含量＞10%)〕	6.5		20	13/	9,13	千克	S/13		26.5	
2932.9990	13	因毒磷，敌噁磷，碳氯灵〔999〕	6.5		20	13/	9,13	千克	S/13		26.5	
2932.9990	14	增效特、增效砜、增效醚、增效酯等(包括增效环、增效散)〔999〕	6.5		20	13/	9,13	千克	/13		26.5	
2932.9990	15	吡喃灵、吡喃隆、乙氧呋草黄等(包括呋草黄；氟草肟)〔999〕	6.5		20	13/	9,13	千克	S/13		26.5	
2932.9990	16	避蚊酮，苯虫醚，鱼藤酮，环虫酰肼〔999〕	6.5		20	13/	9,13	千克	S/13		26.5	
2932.9990	17	调呋酸、芸苔素内酯〔999〕	6.5		20	13/	9,13	千克	S/13		26.5	
2932.9990	21	紫杉醇〔999〕	6.5	0	20	3/	0	千克	QFE/13		20	
2932.9990	22	三尖杉宁碱〔999〕	6.5		20	13/	13	千克	FE/13		26.5	
2932.9990	23	十去乙酰基巴卡丁三(红豆杉提取物 10-DAB)〔999〕	6.5		20	13/	13	千克	FE/13		26.5	
2932.9990	24	十去乙酰基紫杉醇(红豆杉提取物 10-DAT)〔999〕	6.5		20	13/	0	千克	FE/13		26.5	
2932.9990	25	巴卡丁三〔999〕	6.5		20	13/	13	千克	FE/13		26.5	
2932.9990	26	7-表紫杉醇〔999〕	6.5		20	13/	0	千克	FE/13		26.5	
2932.9990	27	10-去乙酰 7-表紫杉醇〔999〕	6.5		20	13/	0	千克	FE/13		26.5	
2932.9990	28	7,10-双(三氯乙酰基)-10-去乙酰基巴卡丁三类似物〔999〕	6.5		20	13/	13	千克	EF/13		26.5	
2932.9990	29	多烯紫杉醇(多西他赛)〔999〕	6.5	0	20	3/	0	千克	EF/13		20	
2932.9990	31	7,10-双(三氯乙酰基)-多西他赛〔999〕	6.5		20	13/	13	千克	EF/13		26.5	
2932.9990	32	贝前列素钠〔999〕	6.5	0	20	13/	13	千克	/13		20	
2932.9990	40	替苯丙胺及其盐〔999〕	6.5		20	13/	13	千克	I/13		26.5	
2932.9990	51	(1,2-二甲基庚基)羟基四氢甲基二苯吡喃(包括六氢大麻酚)〔999〕	6.5		20	13/	13	千克	I/13		26.5	
2932.9990	52	甲羟芬胺，乙芬胺，羟芬胺〔999〕	6.5		20	13/	13	千克	I/13		26.5	
2932.9990	53	二亚甲基双氧安非他明及其盐(MDMA)〔999〕	6.5		20	13/	13	千克	I/13		26.5	

协定税率 %								RCEP		特惠税率 %			Article Description
东/冰/格	巴基斯坦	韩国	瑞士上/下	哥/秘/柬	澳/毛	新西/坡/智	中国港/澳/台	东盟及马来/澳/韩	日/新	亚太2国	老/柬/缅	98/97/95	
0/0/0	5	0	0/0	0/0/0	0/0	0//0	0/0/	0/0/0	0/0			0/0/0	--Furfuryl alcohol and tetrahydrofurfuryl alcohol
0/0/0	5	0		0/0/0	0/0	0//0	0/0/	0/0/0	5.9/0			0/0/0	--Sucralose
													--Other
0/0/0	5	0		0/0/0	0/0	0//0	0/0/	0/0/0	5.9/0			0/0/0	Japothrins, furamethrin(JMAF)(including proparthrin, bromethrin, d-furamethrin)
0/0/0	5	0		0/0/0	0/0	0//0	0/0/	0/0/0	5.9/0			0/0/0	Metomedan, cyprofuram, vangard (including cyprodinil, fenfuram, furcarbanil)
0/0/0	5	0		0/0/0	0/0	0//0	0/0/	0/0/0	5.9/0			0/0/0	Oxyfuryl ether, cycloheptanyl ether, furazone, etc. (including indolic acid, Curcumol, furanesulfonone)
0/0/0	5	0		0/0/0	0/0	0//0	0/0/	0/0/0	5.9/0			0/0/0	Toosendanin, furalaxyl(including furophanat, spirodiclofen
0/0/0	5	0		0/0/0	0/0	0//0	0/0/	0/0/0	5.9/0			0/0/0	Emamectin and its salts
0/0/0	5	0		0/0/0	0/0	0//0	0/0/	0/0/0	5.9/0			0/0/0	DEET, phenanthroline, rotenone, cyclotebufenozide
0/0/0	5	0		0/0/0	0/0	0//0	0/0/	0/0/0	5.9/0			0/0/0	Furfennorex
0/0/0	5	0		0/0/0	0/0	0//0	0/0/	0/0/0	5.9/0		//	0/0/0	Empagliflozin
0/0/0	5	0		0/0/0	0/0	0//0	0/0/	0/0/0	5.9/0			0/0/0	Other compounds containing an unfused furaning in the structure
													-Lactones:
0/0/0	5	0	0/0	0/0/0	0/0	0//0	0/0/	0/0/0	5.9/0			0/0/0	---Coumarin, methylcoumarins and ethyl-coumarins
													---Other lactones
0/0/0	5	0	0.7/0.7	0/0/0	0/0	0//0	0/0/	5.9/5.9/5.9	5.9/5.9			0/0/0	warfarin, coumafuryl, melitoxin, brodifacoum (including coumachlor, flocoumafen, difenacoum, coumatetralyl)
0/0/0	5	0	0.7/0.7	0/0/0	0/0	0//0	0/0/	5.9/5.9/5.9	5.9/5.9			0/0/0	Gibberellic acid
0/0/0	5	0	0.7/0.7	0/0/0	0/0	0//0	0/0/	5.9/5.9/5.9	5.9/5.9			0/0/0	Coumaphos, saneonin , bromadiolone, ofurace (including phthalide, coumithoate)
0/0/0	5	0	0.7/0.7	0/0/0	0/0	0//0	0/0/	5.9/5.9/5.9	5.9/5.9			0/0/0	Coumoxystrobin
0/0/0	5	0	0.7/0.7	0/0/0	0/0	0//0	0/0/	5.9/5.9/5.9	5.9/5.9			0/0/0	Emamectin benzoate
0/0/0	5	0	0.7/0.7	0/0/0	0/0	0//0	0/0/	5.9/5.9/5.9	5.9/5.9			0/0/0	Avermectin
0/0/0	5	0	0.7/0.7	0/0/0	0/0	0//0	0/0/	5.9/5.9/5.9	5.9/5.9			0/0/0	Propionyl brassinolide, spiro mite diester
0/0/0	5	0	0.7/0.7	0/0/0	0/0	0//0	0/0/	5.9/5.9/5.9	5.9/5.9			0/0/0	Podophyllotoxin
0/0/0	5	0	0.7/0.7	0/0/0	0/0	0//0	0/0/	5.9/5.9/5.9	5.9/5.9			0/0/0	γ— Butyrolactone (CAS NO.96—48—0)
0/0/0	5	0	0.7/0.7	0/0/0	0/0	0//0	0/0/	5.9/5.9/5.9	5.9/5.9			0/0/0	Other lactones
													-Other:
0/0/0	5	0	0/0	0/0/0	0/0	0//0	0/0/	0/0/0	5.9/0			0/0/0	--Isosafrole
0/0/0	5	0	0/0	0/0/0	0/0	0//0	0/0/	0/0/0	5.9/0			0/0/0	--1-(1,3-Benzodioxol-5-Yl)propan-2-one
0/0/0	5	0	0/0	0/0/0	0/0	0//0	0/0/	0/0/0	5.9/0			0/0/0	--Piperonal
0/0/0	5	0	0/0	0/0/0	0/0	0//0	0/0/	0/0/0	5.9/0			0/0/0	--Safrole
0/0/0	5	0	0/0	0/0/0	0/0	0//0	0/0/	0/0/0	5.9/0			0/0/0	--Tetrahydrocannabinols(all is omers)
0/0/0	0	0	0.7/0.7	0/0/0	0/0	0//0	0/0/	5.9/5.9/5.9	5.9/5.9			0/0/0	--Carbofuran (ISO)
													--Other:
0/0/0	0	1.8	0/0	0/0/0	0/0	0//0	0/0/	3.6/3.6/3.6	3.8/3.6			0/0/0	---Furan phenol
0/0/0	5	0	0/0	0/0/0	0/0	0//0	0/0/	0/0/0	5.9/0			0/0/0	---Bifendate
0/0/0	5	0	0.7/0.7	0/0/0	0/0	0//0	0/0/	0/0/0	5.9/0			0/0/0	---Artemether
													---Other
0/0/0	0	0	0.7/0.7	0/0/0	0/0	0//0	0/0/	5.9/5.9/5.9	5.9/5.9			0/0/0	Dioxocarb, bendiocarb, benfuracarb (including carbosulfan , furathiocarb)
0/0/0	0	0	0.7/0.7	0/0/0	0/0	0//0	0/0/	5.9/5.9/5.9	5.9/5.9			0/0/0	Endothion, dioxathion, isobenzan
0/0/0	0	0	0.7/0.7	0/0/0	0/0	0//0	0/0/	5.9/5.9/5.9	5.9/5.9			0/0/0	Bucarpolate, sufoxide, piperonyl butoxide, propylisorne(including piperonyl cyclonene, sesamex)
0/0/0	0	0	0.7/0.7	0/0/0	0/0	0//0	0/0/	5.9/5.9/5.9	5.9/5.9			0/0/0	Pyracarbolin, metobenzuron, ethofumesate(including benfuresate, fluxofenim)
0/0/0	0	0	0.7/0.7	0/0/0	0/0	0//0	0/0/	5.9/5.9/5.9	5.9/5.9			0/0/0	Butopyronoxyl, difenolan, rotenone
0/0/0	0	0	0.7/0.7	0/0/0	0/0	0//0	0/0/	5.9/5.9/5.9	5.9/5.9			0/0/0	Dikegulac, brassinolide
0/0/0	0	0	0.7/0.7	0/0/0	0/0	0//0	0/0/	5.9/5.9/5.9	5.9/5.9			0/0/0	Taxinol
0/0/0	0	0	0.7/0.7	0/0/0	0/0	0//0	0/0/	5.9/5.9/5.9	5.9/5.9			0/0/0	Cephalomanine
0/0/0	0	0	0.7/0.7	0/0/0	0/0	0//0	0/0/	5.9/5.9/5.9	5.9/5.9			0/0/0	10-Deacetyl-baccatin Ⅲ (Extracts of taxus chinensis 10-DAB)
0/0/0	0	0	0.7/0.7	0/0/0	0/0	0//0	0/0/	5.9/5.9/5.9	5.9/5.9			0/0/0	10-Deacetyl-paclitaxel(Extracts of taxus chinensis 10-DAB)
0/0/0	0	0	0.7/0.7	0/0/0	0/0	0//0	0/0/	5.9/5.9/5.9	5.9/5.9			0/0/0	Baccatin Ⅲ
0/0/0	0	0	0.7/0.7	0/0/0	0/0	0//0	0/0/	5.9/5.9/5.9	5.9/5.9			0/0/0	7 Epitaxinol
0/0/0	0	0	0.7/0.7	0/0/0	0/0	0//0	0/0/	5.9/5.9/5.9	5.9/5.9			0/0/0	10-Deacetyl-7-epi-taxinol
0/0/0	0	0	0.7/0.7	0/0/0	0/0	0//0	0/0/	5.9/5.9/5.9	5.9/5.9			0/0/0	Analogues of 7,10-double(3-trichloroacetyl)-10-deacetyl Baccatin
0/0/0	0	0	0.7/0.7	0/0/0	0/0	0//0	0/0/	5.9/5.9/5.9	5.9/5.9			0/0/0	Docetaxel
0/0/0	0	0	0.7/0.7	0/0/0	0/0	0//0	0/0/	5.9/5.9/5.9	5.9/5.9			0/0/0	7,10-double(3-trichloroacetyl)-taxotere
0/0/0	0	0	0.7/0.7	0/0/0	0/0	0//0	0/0/	5.9/5.9/5.9	5.9/5.9		//	0/0/0	Beraprost sodium
0/0/0	0	0	0.7/0.7	0/0/0	0/0	0//0	0/0/	5.9/5.9/5.9	5.9/5.9			0/0/0	Tenamfetamine and its salts
0/0/0	0	0	0.7/0.7	0/0/0	0/0	0//0	0/0/	5.9/5.9/5.9	5.9/5.9			0/0/0	(1,2-Dimetol)hydroxytetrahydrobiopterin(including parahexyl)
0/0/0	0	0	0.7/0.7	0/0/0	0/0	0//0	0/0/	5.9/5.9/5.9	5.9/5.9			0/0/0	MMDA, N-ethyl MDA, N-hydroxy MDA.
0/0/0	0	0	0.7/0.7	0/0/0	0/0	0//0	0/0/	5.9/5.9/5.9	5.9/5.9			0/0/0	2-methylenedioxy-n-methylamphetamine and its salts

税则号列	货品名称〔CIQ 扩展编码及品名－T2 表示见附表 2〕	最惠(%)	暂定税率	普通	增值/消费	出口退税	计量单位	监管条件/特殊证件	检验检疫	对美关税	亚太上/下
2932.9990 54	3,4－亚甲二氧基甲卡西酮(3,4－methylenedioxy－N－methylcathinone;CAS 号:186028－79－5)〔999〕	6.5		20	13/	9,13	千克	I/13		26.5	
2932.9990 60	二噁英,呋喃(多氯二苯并对二噁英,多氯二苯并呋喃)〔999〕	6.5		20	13/	13	千克	89/13		26.5	
2932.9990 70	1,4－二噁烷〔999〕	6.5		20	13/	13	千克	/13		26.5	
2932.9990 80	二氢黄樟素〔999〕	6.5		20	13/	13	千克	G/13		26.5	
2932.9990 91	其他濒危植物提取的仅含氧杂原子的杂环化合物〔999〕	6.5		20	13/	0	千克	EF/13		26.5	
2932.9990 92	阿卡波糖水合物〔999〕	6.5	0	20	13/	13	千克	/13		20	
2932.9990 93	2－甲基－3－[3,4－(亚甲二氧基)苯基]缩水甘油酸、2－甲基－3－[3,4－(亚甲二氧基)苯基]缩水甘油酸甲酯(CAS 号 2167189－50－4、13605－48－6)〔999〕	6.5		20	13/	13	千克	23/13		26.5	
2932.9990 99	其他仅含氧杂原子的杂环化合物〔301 危险化学品,易燃液体;302 危险化学品,有机过氧化物;303 危险化学品,毒性物质;304 其他化工产品〕	6.5		20	13/	9,13	千克	/13		26.5	
29.33	**仅含有氮杂原子的杂环化合物:**										
	-结构上含有一个非稠合吡唑环(不论是否氢化)的化合物:										
2933.1100	--二甲基苯基吡唑酮(安替比林)及其衍生物〔999〕	6.5		20	13/	13	千克	/1		31.5	4.2/4.2
	--其他:										
2933.1920	---安乃近〔999〕	6		20	13/	13	千克	Q/1			4.8/4.8
2933.1990	---其他										
2933.1990 11	吡硫磷、吡唑硫磷、敌蝇威、乙虫腈等(包括异索威、吡唑威)〔301 危险化学品,毒性物质;302 其他化工品〕	6.5		20	13/	9,13	千克	S/13		31.5	
2933.1990 12	氟虫腈、唑螨酯、吡螨胺等(包括吡唑醚菌酯)〔999〕	6.5		20	13/	9,13	千克	S/13		31.5	
2933.1990 13	吡草醚、吡唑草胺、氟氯草胺等(包括野燕枯、苄草唑、吡唑特、吡草酮)〔999〕	6.5		20	13/	9,13	千克	S/13		31.5	
2933.1990 14	吡唑萘菌胺(包括氟唑菌胺、乙唑螨腈、异丙吡草酯、唑虫酰胺、氟唑环菌胺、氟唑菌酰胺、氟唑菌苯胺)〔999〕	6.5		20	13/	9,13	千克	S/13		31.5	
2933.1990 15	苯并烯氟菌唑〔999〕	6.5		20	13/	13	千克	S/13		31.5	
2933.1990 16	丁虫腈、腈吡螨酯、唑菌酯等(包括氟唑菌酰羟胺、嗪虫唑酰胺、三唑磺草酮、苯唑氟草酮、双唑草酮)〔999〕	6.5		20	13/	13	千克	S/13		31.5	
2933.1990 90	其他结构上有非稠合吡唑环化合物〔301 危险化学品,毒性物质;302 其他化工品〕	6.5		20	13/	13	千克	/13		31.5	
	-结构上含有一个非稠合咪唑环(不论是否氢化)的化合物:										
2933.2100	--乙内酰脲及其衍生物〔999〕	6.5		30	13/	13	千克	/1		11.5	
2933.2900	--其他										
2933.2900 11	异菌脲〔999〕	6.5		20	13/	9,13	千克	S/13		26.5	
2933.2900 12	抑霉唑及其盐,咪菌腈,咪鲜胺及其盐等〔999〕	6.5		20	13/	9,13	千克	S/13		26.5	
2933.2900 13	咪草酸、丁咪酰胺〔999〕	6.5		20	13/	9,13	千克	S/13		26.5	
2933.2900 14	果绿啶〔999〕	6.5		20	13/	9,13	千克	S/13		26.5	
2933.2900 15	氰菌唑〔999〕	6.5		20	13/	9,13	千克	S/13		26.5	
2933.2900 90	其他结构上有非稠合咪唑环化合物〔301 危险化学品,毒性物质;302 其他化工产品〕	6.5		20	13/	13	千克	/13		26.5	
	-结构上含有一个非稠合吡啶环(不论是否氢化)的化合物:										
2933.3100	--吡啶及其盐										
2933.3100 10	吡啶〔999〕	6		20	13/	13	千克	AB/13	MN		
2933.3100 90	吡啶盐〔999〕	6		20	13/	13	千克	/13			
	--六氢吡啶(哌啶)及其盐:										
2933.3210	---六氢吡啶(哌啶)〔999〕	4		11	13/	13	千克	23/13		29	
2933.3220	---六氢吡啶(哌啶)盐〔999〕	6.5		20	13/	13	千克	/1			
2933.3300	--阿芬太尼(INN)、阿尼利定(INN)、苯氰米特(INN)、溴西泮(INN)、卡芬太尼(INN)、地芬诺新(INN)、地芬诺酯(INN)、地匹哌酮(INN)、芬太尼(INN)、凯托米酮(INN)、哌醋甲酯(INN)、喷他左辛(INN)、哌替啶(INN)、哌替啶中间体 A(INN)、苯环利定(INN)、苯哌利定(INN)、哌苯甲醇(INN)、哌氰米特(INN)、哌丙吡胺(INN)、瑞芬太尼(INN)和三甲利定(INN)以及它们的盐										
2933.3300 40	阿芬太尼(INN)、阿尼利定(INN)、苯氰米特(INN)、溴西泮(INN)、卡芬太尼(INN)、地芬诺新(INN)、地芬诺酯(INN)、地匹哌酮(INN)、芬太尼(INN)、凯托米酮(INN)、哌醋甲酯(INN)、喷他左辛(INN)(以及它们的盐)〔999〕	6.5		20	13/	13	千克	I/13		11.5	
2933.3300 50	哌替啶(INN)、哌替啶中间体 A(INN)、苯环利定(INN)、苯哌利定(INN)、哌苯甲醇(INN)、哌氰米特(INN)、哌丙吡胺(INN)、瑞芬太尼(INN)和三甲利定(INN)(以及它们的盐)〔999〕	6.5		20	13/	13	千克	I/13		11.5	
2933.3400	--其他芬太尼及它们的衍生物										
2933.3400 10	乙酰阿法甲基芬太尼,阿法甲基芬太尼,倍他羟基芬太尼,倍他羟基－3－甲基芬太尼,对氟芬太尼(以及它们的盐)〔999〕	6.5		20	13/	13	千克	I/1		14	

协定税率 %								RCEP		特惠税率 %			Article Description
东/冰/格	巴基斯坦	韩国	瑞士上/下	哥/秘/柬	澳/毛	新西/坡/智	中国港/澳/台	东盟及马来/澳/韩	日/新	亚太2国	老/柬/缅	98/97/95	
0/0/0	0	0	0.7/0.7	0/0/0	0/0	0//0	0/0/	5.9/5.9/5.9	5.9/5.9			0/0/0	3,4-methylenedioxy-N-methylcathinone(CAS:186028-79-5)
0/0/0	0	0	0.7/0.7	0/0/0	0/0	0//0	0/0/	5.9/5.9/5.9	5.9/5.9			0/0/0	Dioxin, Furan (Polychrorinate. dibenzo-p-dioxins, polychlorinated dibenzofurans)
0/0/0	0	0	0.7/0.7	0/0/0	0/0	0//0	0/0/	5.9/5.9/5.9	5.9/5.9			0/0/0	1,4-Diaxane
0/0/0	0	0	0.7/0.7	0/0/0	0/0	0//0	0/0/	5.9/5.9/5.9	5.9/5.9			0/0/0	Dihydrosafrol
0/0/0	0	0	0.7/0.7	0/0/0	0/0	0//0	0/0/	5.9/5.9/5.9	5.9/5.9			0/0/0	Other heterocyclic compounds with oxygen hetero-atom only, distilled from endangered plants
0/0/0	0	0	0.7/0.7	0/0/0	0/0	0//0	0/0/	5.9/5.9/5.9	5.9/5.9			0/0/0	Acarbose hydrate
0/0/0	0	0	0.7/0.7	0/0/0	0/0	0//0	0/0/	5.9/5.9/5.9	5.9/5.9			0/0/0	2-methyl-3-[3,4-(methylenedioxy) phenyl] glycidylic acid, 2-methyl-3-[3,4-(methylenedioxy) phenyl] glycidyl acid methyl ester (CAS No.2167189-50-4, 13605-48-6)
0/0/0	0	0	0.7/0.7	0/0/0	0/0	0//0	0/0/	5.9/5.9/5.9	5.9/5.9			0/0/0	Other heterocyclic compounds with oxygen hetero-atom(s) only
													Heterocyclic compounds with nitrogen hetero-atom(s) only:
													-Compounds containing an unfused pyrazole ring (whether or not hydrogenated) in the structure:
0/0/0	5	0	0/0	0/0/0	0/0	0//0	0/0/	0/0/0	5.9/0			0/0/0	--Phenazone (antipyrin) and its derivatives
													--Other:
0/0/0	5	0	0/0	0/0/0	0/0	0//0	0/0/	0/0/0	0/0			0/0/0	---Analgin
													---Other
0/0/0	5	0	0/0	0/0/0	0/0	0//0	0/0/	0/0/0	5.9/0			0/0/0	Pyrazothion, pyraclofos, dimetilan(includins isolan, pyrolan)
0/0/0	5	0	0/0	0/0/0	0/0	0//0	0/0/	0/0/0	5.9/0			0/0/0	Fipronil, fenpyroximate, tebufenpyrad(including pyraclost)
0/0/0	5	0	0/0	0/0/0	0/0	0//0	0/0/	0/0/0	5.9/0			0/0/0	Pyraflufen-ethyl, metazachlor, nipyralo fen(indnding difenzoquat, pyrazoxyfen, pyrazolate, benzofenap)
0/0/0	5	0	0/0	0/0/0	0/0	0//0	0/0/	0/0/0	5.9/0			0/0/0	Isopyrazam(penflufen, fluazolate, tolfenpyrad)
0/0/0	5	0	0/0	0/0/0	0/0	0//0	0/0/	0/0/0	5.9/0			0/0/0	Benzene and olefin triflumizole
0/0/0	5	0	0/0	0/0/0	0/0	0//0	0/0/	0/0/0	5.9/0			0/0/0	Butylachlor, acetonide, oxazole ester, etc. (including fluconazole hydroxylamine, imidazole amide, Triadimefon, oxadimefon, oxadimefon)
0/0/0	5	0	0/0	0/0/0	0/0	0//0	0/0/	0/0/0	5.9/0			0/0/0	Other compounds containing an unfused pyrazole ring in the structure
													-Compounds containing an unfused imidazole ring (whether or not hydrogenated) in the structure:
0/0/0	5	0	0/0	0/0/0	0/0	0//0	0/0/	0/0/0	5.9/0			0/0/0	--Hydantoin and its derivatives
													--Other
0/0/0	5	1.3	2.7/2.7	0/0/0	0/0	0//0	0/0/	5.9/5.9/5.9	5.9/5.9			0/0/0	Iprodine
0/0/0	5	1.3	2.7/2.7	0/0/0	0/0	0//0	0/0/	5.9/5.9/5.9	5.9/5.9			0/0/0	Imazalil, micitrile, prochloraz and its salts, etc
0/0/0	5	1.3	2.7/2.7	0/0/0	0/0	0//0	0/0/	5.9/5.9/5.9	5.9/5.9			0/0/0	Imazamethabenz-methyl, isocarbamide
0/0/0	5	1.3	2.7/2.7	0/0/0	0/0	0//0	0/0/	5.9/5.9/5.9	5.9/5.9			0/0/0	Glyodin
0/0/0	5	1.3	2.7/2.7	0/0/0	0/0	0//0	0/0/	5.9/5.9/5.9	5.9/5.9			0/0/0	Triflumizole
0/0/0	5	1.3	2.7/2.7	0/0/0	0/0	0//0	0/0/	5.9/5.9/5.9	5.9/5.9			0/0/0	Other compounds containing an unfused imidazole ring in the structure
													-Compounds containing an unfused pyridine ring (whether or not hydrogenated) in the structure:
													--Pyridine and its salts
0/0/0	5	0	0/0	0/0/0	0/0	0//0	0/0/0	0/5.4/0	0/5.4			0/0/0	Pyridine
0/0/0	5	0	0/0	0/0/0	0/0	0//0	0/0/0	0/5.4/0	0/5.4			0/0/0	Pyridine salt
													--Piperidine and its salts:
0/0/0	0	0	0/0	0/0/0	0/0	0//0	0/0/	0/0/0	0/0			0/0/0	---Hexahydropyridine (piperidine)
0/0/0	5	0	0/0	0/0/0	0/0	0//0	0/0/	0/0/0	5.9/0			0/0/0	---Isoniazidum
													--Alfentanil(INN)、anileridine(INN)、bezitramide(INN)、bromazepam (INN)、difenoxin (INN)、diphenoxylate (INN)、dipipanone(INN)、fentanyl(INN)、ketobemidone (INN)、methylphenidate(INN)、pentazocine(INN)、pethidine(INN)、pethidine(INN) intermediate A、phencyclidine (INN)(PCP)、phenoperidine(INN)、pipradrol(INN)、piritramide(INN)、propiram(INN) and trimeperidine(INN); salts thereof
0/0/0	5	1.5	0.4/0.4	0/0/0	0/0	0//0	0/0/	5.9/5.9/5.9	5.9/5.9			0/0/0	Alfentanil (inn), anilidine (inn), phenylcyanomide (inn), broazepam (inn), carfentanil (inn), difenoxin (inn), difenoxylate (inn), dipiperenone (inn), fentanyl (inn), ketomidone (inn), methylphenidate (inn), pentazocine (inn) (and their salts)
0/0/0	5	1.5	0.4/0.4	0/0/0	0/0	0//0	0/0/	5.9/5.9/5.9	5.9/5.9			0/0/0	Pethidine (inn), pethidine intermediate a (inn), phencyclidine (inn), phencyclidine (inn), piperidine (inn), pipebenzyl alcohol (inn), pecyanomide (inn), piperopipramine (inn), remifentanil (inn) and trimethylidine (inn) (and their salts)
													-- Other fentanyls and their derivatives
0/0/0	0	0	0.7/0.7	0/0/0	0/0	0//0	0/0/	5.9/5.9/5.9	5.9/5.9			0/0/0	Acetyl Alfa methylfentanyl, Alfa methylfentanyl, betahydroxyfentanyl, betahydroxy-3-methylfentanyl, p-fluorofentanyl (and their salts)

税则号列	货品名称〔CIQ 扩展编码及品名—T2 表示见附表 2〕	最惠(%)	暂定税率	普通	增值/消费	出口退税	计量单位	监管条件/特殊证件	检验检疫	对美关税	亚太上/下
2933.3400 90	其他芬太尼及它们的衍生物〔301 危险化学品，毒性物质，302 其他化工产品〕	6.5		20	13/	13	千克	/1		14	
2933.3500	--奎宁环—3—醇(3—奎宁醇)〔999〕	6.5		20	13/	13	千克	23/1			5.2/5.2
2933.3600	--4—苯氨基—N—苯乙基哌啶(ANPP)〔999〕	6.5		20	13/	13	千克	23/1		14	
2933.3700	--N—苯乙基—4—哌啶酮(NPP)〔999〕	6.5		20	13/	13	千克	23/1		14	
	--其他：										
2933.3910	---二苯乙醇酸-3-奎宁环酯〔999〕	6.5		20	13/	13	千克	23/1			5.2/5.2
2933.3990	---其他										
2933.3990 11	烯丙罗定，阿法美罗定，倍他美罗定，阿法罗定，苄替啶，倍他罗定，依托利定，羟哌替啶，美他佐辛，1—甲基—4—苯基—4—哌啶丙酸酯，诺匹哌酮，以及它们的盐〔999〕	6.5		20	13/	13	千克	I/13		14	
2933.3990 12	1—苯乙基—4—苯基—4—哌啶乙酸酯，哌替啶中间体 B，哌替啶中间体 C，非那丙胺，非那佐辛，匹米诺定，丙哌利定，以及它们的盐；瑞马唑仑及其盐和异构体〔999〕	6.5		20	13/	13	千克	I/13		14	
2933.3990 13	氟氯吡啶酯，氟醚菌酰胺，环吡氟草酮，氯氟吡啶酯，哌虫啶，三氟吡啶胺，四唑虫酰胺〔999〕	6.5		20	13/	9,13	千克	/13		14	
2933.3990 21	精吡氟禾草灵及其酯，毒死蜱，二氯氨基吡啶羧酸(包括二氟吡隆，三氟甲吡醚，氯虫苯甲酰胺，啶酰菌胺，羟哌酯)〔999〕	6.5		20	13/	9,13	千克	S/13		14	
2933.3990 22	啶虫脒〔301 危险化学品，毒性物质，302 其他化工品〕	6.5		20	13/	9,13	千克	S/13		14	
2933.3990 23	精喹禾灵〔999〕	6.5		20	13/	9,13	千克	S/13		14	
2933.3990 24	喹禾灵，氟吡禾灵，吡氟禾草灵等(包括炔禾灵，氟吡乙禾灵，氟吡菌胺，卤草啶)〔999〕	6.5		20	13/	9,13	千克	S/13		14	
2933.3990 25	高效氟吡甲禾灵、氟吡甲禾灵等(包括鼠特灵、灭鼠优、灭鼠安、氟鼠啶)〔301 危险化学品，毒性物质；302 其他化工品〕	6.5		20	13/	9,13	千克	S/13		14	
2933.3990 26	甲基毒死蜱、吡虫啉等(包括吡氯氰菊酯、啶蜱脲、氟啶脲、哒幼酮、吡丙醚)〔999〕	6.5		20	13/	9,13	千克	S/13		14	
2933.3990 27	驱蝇啶、烯啶虫胺〔999〕	6.5		20	13/	9,13	千克	S/13		14	
2933.3990 28	咪唑烟酸，甲咪唑烟酸，咪唑乙烟酸等(包括氨氯吡啶酸，三氯吡氧乙酸及其盐和酯，氯氟吡氧乙酸及其盐和酯，二氯吡啶酸)〔999〕	6.5		20	13/	9,13	千克	S/13		14	
2933.3990 29	炔草酯及其酸，哌草磷，哌草丹，稗草丹等(包括吡氟酰草胺，氟吡酰草胺，氟啶草酮，氟硫草定，甲氧咪草烟)〔999〕	6.5		20	13/	9,13	千克	S/13		14	
2933.3990 30	3-羟基-1-甲基哌啶〔999〕	6.5		20	13/	13	千克	23/13		14	
2933.3990 40	3-奎宁环酮〔999〕	6.5		20	13/	13	千克	23/13		14	
2933.3990 51	甲哌鎓，抗倒胺，氯吡脲，吡啶醇〔999〕	6.5		20	13/	9,13	千克	S/13		14	
2933.3990 52	啶菌噁唑、苯锈啶、啶斑肟等(包括啶菌腈)〔999〕	6.5		20	13/	9,13	千克	S/13		14	
2933.3990 53	氟啶胺、氟啶虫酰胺、三氯甲基吡啶〔999〕	6.5		20	13/	9,13	千克	S/13		14	
2933.3990 54	咪唑嗪、丁硫啶、氯苯吡啶、哌丙灵〔999〕	6.5		20	13/	9,13	千克	S/13		14	
2933.3990 55	氟吡菌酰胺〔999〕	6.5		20	13/	9,13	千克	S/13		14	
2933.3990 56	氯啶菌酯〔999〕	6.5		20	13/	13	千克	S/13		14	
2933.3990 57	氯氨吡啶酸〔999〕	6.5		20	13/	13	千克	S/13		14	
2933.3990 58	哌壮素〔999〕	6.5		20	13/	9,13	千克	S/13		14	
2933.3990 60	啶氧菌酯(包括氟啶虫胺腈、环啶菌胺、四氯虫酰胺、溴氰虫酰胺、玉雄杀)〔999〕	6.5		20	13/	9,13	千克	S/13		14	
2933.3990 91	抗癌药原料(吉美嘧啶、甲磺酸阿帕替尼、西达本胺、甲苯磺酸尼拉帕利)〔999〕	6.5	0	20	3/	13	千克	/13		7.5	
2933.3990 95	氨基甲酸酯类(二甲胺基甲酸吡啶酯类季铵盐和双季铵盐)〔999〕	6.5		20	13/	9,13	千克	23/13		14	
2933.3990 99	其他结构上含有一个非稠合吡啶环(不论是否氢化)的化合物〔301 危险化学品，易燃液体，302 危险化学品，易燃固体，303 危险化学品，毒性物质，304 危险化学品，杂项物质，305 其他危险化学品，306 其他化工产品〕	6.5		20	13/	9,13	千克	/13		14	
	-结构上含有一个喹啉或异喹啉环系(不论是否氢化)的化合物，但未经进一步稠合的：										
2933.4100	--左非诺(INN)及其盐〔999〕	6.5		20	13/	13	千克	I/1		11.5	
2933.4900	--其他										
2933.4900 11	丙烯酸喹啉酯，苯氧喹啉〔999〕	6.5		20	13/	9,13	千克	S/13		31.5	
2933.4900 12	咯喹酮〔999〕	6.5		20	13/	9,13	千克	S/13		31.5	
2933.4900 13	氯甲喹啉酸、二氯喹啉草酮、喹啉铜〔101 饲料添加剂，102 化工产品〕	6.5		20	13/	9,13	千克	S/13		31.5	
2933.4900 14	二氯喹啉酸〔999〕	6.5		20	13/	9,13	千克	S/13		31.5	
2933.4900 15	FG-4592(CAS 号:808118-40-3)(一种缺氧诱导因子—脯氨酸羟化酶抑制剂)〔999〕	6.5		20	13/	13	千克	/13		31.5	
2933.4900 21	羟蒂巴酚、左美沙芬、左芬啡烷〔999〕	6.5		20	13/	13	千克	I/13		31.5	
2933.4900 22	去甲左啡诺、非诺啡烷、消旋甲啡烷、消旋啡烷〔999〕	6.5		20	13/	13	千克	I/13		31.5	
2933.4900 30	布托啡诺〔999〕	6.5		20	13/	13	千克	I/13		31.5	
2933.4900 40	抗癌药原料(马来酸吡咯替尼)〔999〕	6.5	0	20	3/	13	千克	/13		25	

协定税率 %								RCEP		特惠税率 %			Article Description
东/冰/格	巴基斯坦	韩国	瑞士上/下	哥/秘/柬	澳/毛	新西/坡/智	中国港/澳/台	东盟及马来/澳/韩	日/新	亚太2国	老/柬/缅	98/97/95	
0/0/0	0	0	0.7/0.7	0/0/0	0/0	0//0	0/0/	5.9/5.9/5.9	5.9/5.9			0/0/0	Other fentanyl and their derivatives
0/0/0	5	0	0/0	0/0/0	0/0	0//0	0/0/	0/0/0	5.9/0			0/0/0	-- 3—Quinuclidinol
0/0/0	0	0	0.7/0.7	0/0/0	0/0	0//0	0/0/	5.9/5.9/5.9	5.9/5.9			0/0/0	-- 4—Anilino—N—phenethylpiperidine (ANPP)
0/0/0	0	0	0.7/0.7	0/0/0	0/0	0//0	0/0/	5.9/5.9/5.9	5.9/5.9			0/0/0	-- N—Phenethyl—4—piperidone (NPP)
													--Other:
0/0/0	5	0	0/0	0/0/0	0/0	0//0	0/0/	0/0/0	5.9/0			0/0/0	---Benzilic acid-3-quinuclidinate
													---Other
0/0/0	0	0	0.7/0.7	0/0/0	0/0	0//0	0/0/	5.9/5.9/5.9	5.9/5.9			0/0/0	Alloprodine, alfamerodine, betamerodine, alfamerodine, benthidine, betalodine, etolidine, hydroxypethidine, metazocine, 1 — methyl — 4 — phenyl — 4 — piperidine propionate, nopiperone, and their salts
0/0/0	0	0	0.7/0.7	0/0/0	0/0	0//0	0/0/	5.9/5.9/5.9	5.9/5.9			0/0/0	1—phenylethyl—4—phenyl—4—piperidine acetate, piperidine intermediate B, piperidine intermediate C, finapromethamine, finazocine, piminodine, properidine, and their salts; Rimazole and its salts and isomers
0/0/0	0	0	0.7/0.7	0/0/0	0/0	0//0	0/0/	5.9/5.9/5.9	5.9/5.9			0/0/0	Fluclopyridyl ester, fluramide, cyclopyrazone, fluclopyridyl ester, piperidine, trifluoropyridine amine, tetrazolium amide
0/0/0	0	0	0.7/0.7	0/0/0	0/0	0//0	0/0/	5.9/5.9/5.9	5.9/5.9			0/0/0	Piperazol and its esters, chlorpyrifos, dichloroaminopyridine carboxylic acid (including difluoropyrone, trifluoromethyl ether, chlorfenoxamide, pyridylamide, hydroxypiperazide)
0/0/0	0	0	0.7/0.7	0/0/0	0/0	0//0	0/0/	5.9/5.9/5.9	5.9/5.9			0/0/0	Acetamiprid
0/0/0	0	0	0.7/0.7	0/0/0	0/0	0//0	0/0/	5.9/5.9/5.9	5.9/5.9			0/0/0	Quizalofop-p-ethyl
0/0/0	0	0	0.7/0.7	0/0/0	0/0	0//0	0/0/	5.9/5.9/5.9	5.9/5.9			0/0/0	Quizalofop-ethyl, heptenophos, fluazifop, (including chloroazifop-propyny, haloxyfop-methyl picolinafen, haloxydin)
0/0/0	0	0	0.7/0.7	0/0/0	0/0	0//0	0/0/	5.9/5.9/5.9	5.9/5.9			0/0/0	Haloxyfop-P-methyl , haloxyfop-methyl (including norbormide, pyrinuron, flupropadine)
0/0/0	0	0	0.7/0.7	0/0/0	0/0	0//0	0/0/	5.9/5.9/5.9	5.9/5.9			0/0/0	Chlorpyrifos-methyl, imidacloprid(including fenpyrithrin, fluazuron, chlorfluazuron, pyridaben, pyriproxyfen)
0/0/0	0	0	0.7/0.7	0/0/0	0/0	0//0	0/0/	5.9/5.9/5.9	5.9/5.9			0/0/0	Dipropyl pyridine, nitenpyram
0/0/0	0	0	0.7/0.7	0/0/0	0/0	0//0	0/0/	5.9/5.9/5.9	5.9/5.9			0/0/0	Imidazole nicotinic acid, methylimidazole nicotinic acid, imidazole ethylnicotinic acid, etc. (including aminochloropyridine acid, trichloropyroxyacetic acid and its salts and esters, chlorofluoropyroxyacetic acid and its salts and esters, dichloropyridinic acid)
0/0/0	0	0	0.7/0.7	0/0/0	0/0	0//0	0/0/	5.9/5.9/5.9	5.9/5.9			0/0/0	Alkynyl ester and its acid, piperazon, piperazin, barnyardgrasan, etc. (including pyruvoyl oxalamide, pyruvoyl oxalamide, Fluridone, fluthionodine, metoclopramide)
0/0/0	0	0	0.7/0.7	0/0/0	0/0	0//0	0/0/	5.9/5.9/5.9	5.9/5.9			0/0/0	3-hydroxy-1-methyl piperidine
0/0/0	0	0	0.7/0.7	0/0/0	0/0	0//0	0/0/	5.9/5.9/5.9	5.9/5.9			0/0/0	3-Quinuclidone
0/0/0	0	0	0.7/0.7	0/0/0	0/0	0//0	0/0/	5.9/5.9/5.9	5.9/5.9			0/0/0	Mepiquate chloride, inabenfide, forchlorfenuron, pyripropanol
0/0/0	0	0	0.7/0.7	0/0/0	0/0	0//0	0/0/	5.9/5.9/5.9	5.9/5.9			0/0/0	SYP-Z048, fenpropidin, pyrifenox(includins pyridintril)
0/0/0	0	0	0.7/0.7	0/0/0	0/0	0//0	0/0/	5.9/5.9/5.9	5.9/5.9			0/0/0	Fluazinam, flonicamid, nitrapyrin
0/0/0	0	0	0.7/0.7	0/0/0	0/0	0//0	0/0/	5.9/5.9/5.9	5.9/5.9			0/0/0	Triazoxide, buthiobate, parinol, piperlin
0/0/0	0	0	0.7/0.7	0/0/0	0/0	0//0	0/0/	5.9/5.9/5.9	5.9/5.9			0/0/0	Fluopyram
0/0/0	0	0	0.7/0.7	0/0/0	0/0	0//0	0/0/	5.9/5.9/5.9	5.9/5.9			0/0/0	Carbamate
0/0/0	0	0	0.7/0.7	0/0/0	0/0	0//0	0/0/	5.9/5.9/5.9	5.9/5.9			0/0/0	Picloram
0/0/0	0	0	0.7/0.7	0/0/0	0/0	0//0	0/0/	5.9/5.9/5.9	5.9/5.9			0/0/0	Piproctanyl
0/0/0	0	0	0.7/0.7	0/0/0	0/0	0//0	0/0/	5.9/5.9/5.9	5.9/5.9			0/0/0	Picoxystrobin(including fluorine organism worm amine nitrile, ring organism bacteria amine, four chlorine worm amide, bromine cyanide worm amide, jade males kill, fluorine bacteria amine)
0/0/0	0	0	0.7/0.7	0/0/0	0/0	0//0	0/0/	5.9/5.9/5.9	5.9/5.9			0/0/0	Gempirim, apatinib mesylate, sirodine, and other anticancer drug substances
0/0/0	0	0	0.7/0.7	0/0/0	0/0	0//0	0/0/	5.9/5.9/5.9	5.9/5.9		//	0/0/0	Carbamates (pyridine dimethylaminoformate quaternary ammonium salt and BIS quaternary ammonium salt)
0/0/0	0	0	0.7/0.7	0/0/0	0/0	0//0	0/0/	5.9/5.9/5.9	5.9/5.9			0/0/0	Other compounds containing a non — fused pyridine ring (whether hydrogenated or not)(tax number of Separating anti—cancer pharmaceutical raw materials)
													-Compounds containing in the structure a quinoline or isoquinoline ringsystem (whether or not hydrogenated), not further fused:
0/0/0	5	0	0/0	0/0/0	0/0	0//0	0/0/	0/0/0	5.9/0			0/0/0	--Levorpharol(INN) and its salts
													--Other
0/0/0	5	0	0/0	0/0/0	0/0	0//0	0/0/	0/0/0	5.9/0			0/0/0	Halacrinate, quinoxyfen
0/0/0	5	0	0/0	0/0/0	0/0	0//0	0/0/	0/0/0	5.9/0			0/0/0	Pyroquilon
0/0/0	5	0	0/0	0/0/0	0/0	0//0	0/0/	0/0/0	5.9/0			0/0/0	Chloromethylquinolinic acid, dichloroquinolinone, quinoline copper
0/0/0	5	0	0/0	0/0/0	0/0	0//0	0/0/	0/0/0	5.9/0			0/0/0	Quinclorac
0/0/0	5	0	0/0	0/0/0	0/0	0//0	0/0/	0/0/0	5.9/0			0/0/0	FG-4592 (CAS: 808118-40-3) (a kind of hypoxia inducible factor - prolinehydroxylase inhibitor)
0/0/0	5	0	0/0	0/0/0	0/0	0//0	0/0/	0/0/0	5.9/0			0/0/0	Drotebanol, levomethorphan, levophenacylmorphan.
0/0/0	5	0	0/0	0/0/0	0/0	0//0	0/0/	0/0/0	5.9/0			0/0/0	Norlevorphanol, phenomorphan, racemethorphan, racemorphan
0/0/0	5	0	0/0	0/0/0	0/0	0//0	0/0/	0/0/0	5.9/0			0/0/0	Butorphanol
0/0/0	5	0	0/0	0/0/0	0/0	0//0	0/0/	0/0/0	5.9/0		//	0/0/0	Pyrrolotinib maleate

税则号列		货品名称〔CIQ 扩展编码及品名—T2 表示见附表 2〕	最惠(%)	暂定税率	普通	增值/消费	出口退税	计量单位	监管条件/特殊证件	检验检疫	对美关税	亚太上/下
2933.4900	90	其他含喹啉或异喹啉环系的化合物(但未进一步稠合的)〔301 危险化学品,易燃液体;302 危险化学品,毒性物质;303 其他危险化学品;304 其他化工产品〕	6.5		20	13/	13	千克	/13		31.5	
		-结构上含有一个嘧啶环(不论是否氢化)或哌嗪环的化合物:										
2933.5200		--丙二酰脲(巴比土酸)及其盐〔999〕	6.5		20	13/	13	千克	/1		11.5	
2933.5300		--阿洛巴比妥(INN)、异戊巴比妥(INN)、巴比妥(INN)、布他比妥(INN)、正丁巴比妥(INN)、环己巴比妥(INN)、甲苯巴比妥(INN)、戊巴比妥(INN)、苯巴比妥(INN)、仲丁巴比妥(INN)、司可巴比妥(INN)和乙烯比妥(INN)以及它们的盐										
2933.5300	11	阿洛巴比妥、仲丁巴比妥(以及它们的盐)〔999〕	6.5		20	13/	13	千克	I/1		26.5	
2933.5300	12	乙烯比妥、布他比妥、丁巴比妥(以及它们的盐)〔999〕	6.5		20	13/	13	千克	I/1		26.5	
2933.5300	13	环己巴比妥、甲苯巴比妥(以及它们的盐)〔999〕	6.5		20	13/	13	千克	I/1		26.5	
2933.5300	14	司可巴比妥、异戊巴比妥(以及它们的盐)〔999〕	6.5		20	13/	13	千克	I/1		26.5	
2933.5300	15	戊巴比妥、苯巴比妥、巴比妥(以及它们的盐)〔999〕	6.5		20	13/	13	千克	I/1		26.5	
2933.5400		--其他丙二酰脲(巴比土酸)的衍生物以及它们的盐〔999〕	6.5		20	13/	13	千克	/1			
2933.5500		--氯普唑仑(INN)、甲氯喹酮(INN)、甲喹酮(INN)和齐培丙醇(INN)以及它们的盐										
2933.5500	11	甲氯喹酮、甲喹酮(以及它们的盐)〔999〕	6.5		20	13/	13	千克	I/1			
2933.5500	12	氯普唑仑、齐培丙醇(以及它们的盐)〔999〕	6.5		20	13/	13	千克	I/1			
		--其他:										
2933.5910		---胞嘧啶〔999〕	6.5		20	13/	13	千克	/1		11.5	4.2/4.2
2933.5920		---环丙氟哌酸〔999〕	6.5		20	13/	13	千克	/1			4.2/4.2
2933.5990		---其他										
2933.5990	11	嘧啶磷、甲基嘧啶磷、二嗪磷、双苯嘧草酮等(包括嘧啶氧磷、乙嘧硫磷)〔101 嘧啶氧磷粉剂,102 嘧啶氧磷〕	6.5		20	13/	9,13	千克	S/13		31.5	4.2/4.2
2933.5990	12	烯腺嘌呤、苄腺嘌呤、丁基嘧啶磷、嘧啶肟草醚等(包括苄氨基嘌呤、羟烯腺嘌呤)〔999〕	6.5		20	13/	9,13	千克	S/13		31.5	4.2/4.2
2933.5990	13	嘧草醚,双草醚,除草定,环草定等(包括异草定,异丙酯草醚,嘧草硫醚,特草定)〔999〕	6.5		20	13/	9,13	千克	S/13		31.5	4.2/4.2
2933.5990	14	吡菌磷、嘧霉胺、嘧菌胺、嘧菌酯等(包括嘧菌环胺、嘧菌腙)〔999〕	6.5		20	13/	9,13	千克	S/13		31.5	4.2/4.2
2933.5990	15	嘧啶威、抗蚜威、环虫腈、嘧螨醚等(包括嘧螨酯)〔101 抗蚜威粉剂(含量>75%),102 嘧啶威可湿性粉剂、颗粒剂,103 嘧啶威〕	6.5		20	13/	9,13	千克	S/13		31.5	4.2/4.2
2933.5990	16	氯苯嘧啶醇、环丙嘧啶醇、呋嘧醇等(包括氟苯嘧啶醇)〔999〕	6.5		20	13/	9,13	千克	S/13		31.5	4.2/4.2
2933.5990	17	氟蚁腙,鼠立死,三氟苯嘧啶〔301 危险化学品,毒性物质,302 其他化工产品〕	6.5		20	13/	9,13	千克	S/13		31.5	4.2/4.2
2933.5990	18	二甲嘧酚、乙嘧酚、乙嘧酚磺酸酯〔999〕	6.5		20	13/	9,13	千克	S/13		31.5	4.2/4.2
2933.5990	19	嗪氨灵、咪唑喹啉酸、丙酯草醚〔999〕	6.5		20	13/	9,13	千克	S/13		31.5	4.2/4.2
2933.5990	20	氟丙嘧草酯、氯丙嘧啶酸〔999〕	6.5		20	13/	9,13	千克	S/13		31.5	4.2/4.2
2933.5990	30	溴嘧草醚〔999〕	6.5		20	13/	9,13	千克	S/13		31.5	4.2/4.2
2933.5990	40	唑嘧菌胺〔999〕	6.5		20	13/	13	千克	S/13		31.5	4.2/4.2
2933.5990	51	依他喹酮(Etaqualone;CAS 号:7432—25—9)〔999〕	6.5		20	13/	13	千克	I/13		31.5	4.2/4.2
2933.5990	52	苄基哌嗪(Benzylpiperazine;CAS 号:2759—28—6)〔999〕	6.5		20	13/	13	千克	I/13		31.5	4.2/4.2
2933.5990	53	恩替卡韦〔999〕	6.5	0	20	13/	13	千克	/13		25	4.2/4.2
2933.5990	60	利格列汀〔999〕	6.5	0	20	13/	13	千克	/13		25	4.2/4.2
2933.5990	91	抗癌药原料(甲磺酸伊马替尼、硫唑嘌呤、培美曲塞二钠、左亚叶酸钙、甲磺酸氟马替尼、甲磺酸阿美替尼、泽布替尼)〔999〕	6.5	0	20	3/	13	千克	/13		25	4.2/4.2
2933.5990	99	其他结构上有嘧啶环等的化合物(包括其他结构上有哌嗪环的化合物)〔301 危险化学品,易燃液体,302 危险化学品,毒性物质,303 危险化学品,腐蚀性物质,304 其他化工品〕	6.5		20	13/	13	千克	/13		31.5	4.2/4.2
		-结构上含有一个非稠合三嗪环(不论是否氢化)的化合物:										
2933.6100		--三聚氰胺(蜜胺)〔999〕	6.5		20	13/	13	千克	/1		31.5	
		--其他:										
2933.6910		---三聚氰氯〔999〕	6		20	13/	13	千克	/13			5.4/5.4
		---异氰脲酸氯化衍生物:										
2933.6921		----二氯异氰脲酸〔999〕	6.5		20	13/	13	千克	/13			5.2/5.2
2933.6922		----三氯异氰脲酸〔999〕	6.5		20	13/	13	千克	AB/13	MN		
2933.6929		----其他										
2933.6929	10	二氯异氰尿酸钠〔999〕	6.5		20	13/	13	千克	A/1	R	31.5	
2933.6929	90	其他异氰脲酸氯化衍生物〔999〕	6.5		20	13/	13	千克	/1		31.5	
2933.6990		---其他										
2933.6990	11	西玛津、莠去津、扑灭津、草达津等(包括特丁津、氰草津、环丙津、甘扑津、甘草津)〔999〕	6.5		20	13/	9,13	千克	S/13			
2933.6990	12	西草净、扑草净、敌草净、莠灭净等(包括特丁净、异丙净、异戊乙净、氰草净、氟草净、甲氧丙净)〔101 扑草灭颗粒剂,102 扑草灭(含量>80%),103 西草净,104 莠灭净,105 敌草净〕	6.5		20	13/	9,13	千克	S/13		16.5	
2933.6990	13	扑灭通、仲丁通〔999〕	6.5		20	13/	9,13	千克	S/13		16.5	

协定税率 %								RCEP		特惠税率 %			Article Description
东/冰/格	巴基斯坦	韩国	瑞士上/下	哥/秘/柬	澳/毛	新西/坡/智	中国港/澳/台	东盟及马来/澳/韩	日/新	亚太2国	老/柬/缅	98/97/95	
0/0/0	5	0	0/0	0/0/0	0/0	0//0	0/0/	0/0/0	5.9/0			0/0/0	Other compounds containingan quinoline or isoquinoline ring-systerm(not further fused)
													-Compounds containing a pyrimidine ring (whether or not hydrogenated) or piperazine ring in the structure:
0/0/0	5	0	0/0	0/0/0	0/0	0//0	0/0/	0/0/0	5.9/0			0/0/0	--Malonylurea (barbituric acid) and its salts
													--Allobarbital(INN), amobarbital(INN), barbital(INN), butalbital(INN), butobarbital(INN), cyclobarbital(INN), methylphenobarbital(INN), pentobarbital(INN), phenobarbital(INN), secbutabarbital(INN), secobarbital(INN) and vinylbital(INN); salts thereof
0/0/0	5	0	0/0	0/0/0	0/0	0//0	0/0/	0/0/0	5.9/0			0/0/0	Allobarbital (INN), secbutabarbital (INN); salts thereof
0/0/0	5	0	0/0	0/0/0	0/0	0//0	0/0/	0/0/0	5.9/0			0/0/0	Vinylbital(INN), butalbital(INN), butobarbital(INN); salts thereof
0/0/0	5	0	0/0	0/0/0	0/0	0//0	0/0/	0/0/0	5.9/0			0/0/0	Cyclobarbital (INN), methylphenobarbital (INN); salts thereof
0/0/0	5	0	0/0	0/0/0	0/0	0//0	0/0/	0/0/0	5.9/0			0/0/0	Secobarbital (INN), amobarbital (INN), salts thereof
0/0/0	5	0	0/0	0/0/0	0/0	0//0	0/0/	0/0/0	5.9/0			0/0/0	Pentobarbital (INN), phenobarbital (INN), barbital (INN); salts thereof
0/0/0	5	0	0/0	0/0/0	0/0	0//0	0/0/	0/0/0	5.9/0			0/0/0	--Other derivatives of malonylurea (barbituric acid); salts thereof
													--Loprazolam (INN), mecloqualone (INN), methaqualone (INN) and zipeprol (INN); salts thereof
0/0/0	5	0	0/0	0/0/0	0/0	0//0	0/0/	0/0/0	5.9/0			0/0/0	Mecloqualone (INN), methaqualone (INN); salts thereof
0/0/0	5	0	0/0	0/0/0	0/0	0//0	0/0/	0/0/0	5.9/0			0/0/0	Loprazolam(INN), zipeprol(INN); salts thereof
													--Other:
0/0/0	0	0	0/0	0/0/0	0/0	0//0	0/0/	0/0/0	5.9/0			0/0/0	---Cytosine
0/0/0	5	0	0/0	0/0/0	0/0	0//0	0/0/	0/0/0	5.9/0			0/0/0	---Ciprofloxacin
													---Other
0/0/0	0	0	0.7/0.7	0/0/0	0/0	0//0	0/0/	0/0/0	5.9/0			0/0/0	Pyrimithate, pirimiphos-methyl, diazinon (including midinyangrin, etrimfos)
0/0/0	0	0	0.7/0.7	0/0/0	0/0	0//0	0/0/	0/0/0	5.9/0			0/0/0	Enadenine, 6-benzylaminopurine tebupirimfos, pyribenzonxim (including benzolaminopurine, oxyenadenine)
0/0/0	0	0	0.7/0.7	0/0/0	0/0	0//0	0/0/	0/0/0	5.9/0			0/0/0	Pyriminobac-methl, bispyribac-sodium, bromacil, lenacil (including isocil, pyribambenz isoprop pyrithiobac-sodium, terbacil)
0/0/0	0	0	0.7/0.7	0/0/0	0/0	0//0	0/0/	0/0/0	5.9/0			0/0/0	Pyrazophos, pyrimethanil, mepampyrim, azoxystrobin (including cyprodinil, ferimzone)
0/0/0	0	0	0.7/0.7	0/0/0	0/0	0//0	0/0/	0/0/0	5.9/0			0/0/0	Pyramat, pirimicarb, dicyclanil, pyrimidifen (including fluacrypyrim)
0/0/0	0	0	0.7/0.7	0/0/0	0/0	0//0	0/0/	0/0/0	5.9/0			0/0/0	Fenarimol, ancymidol, flurprimidol(including nuarimol)
0/0/0	0	0	0.7/0.7	0/0/0	0/0	0//0	0/0/	0/0/0	5.9/0			0/0/0	Fluorine ant hydrazone, rat death, trifluoropyrimidine
0/0/0	0	0	0.7/0.7	0/0/0	0/0	0//0	0/0/	0/0/0	5.9/0			0/0/0	Dimethirimol, ethirmol, bupirimate
0/0/0	0	0	0.7/0.7	0/0/0	0/0	0//0	0/0/	0/0/0	5.9/0			0/0/0	Triforin, imazquin, pyribambenz-propyl
0/0/0	0	0	0.7/0.7	0/0/0	0/0	0//0	0/0/	0/0/0	5.9/0			0/0/0	Butafenacil
0/0/0	0	0	0.7/0.7	0/0/0	0/0	0//0	0/0/	0/0/0	5.9/0			0/0/0	Bromide-pyriminobac-methyl
0/0/0	0	0	0.7/0.7	0/0/0	0/0	0//0	0/0/	0/0/0	5.9/0			0/0/0	Mepanipyrim
0/0/0	0	0	0.7/0.7	0/0/0	0/0	0//0	0/0/	0/0/0	5.9/0			0/0/0	Etaqualone(CAS:7432-25-9)
0/0/0	0	0	0.7/0.7	0/0/0	0/0	0//0	0/0/	0/0/0	5.9/0			0/0/0	Benzylpiperazine(CAS 号:2759-28-6)
0/0/0	0	0	0.7/0.7	0/0/0	0/0	0//0	0/0/	0/0/0	5.9/0		//	0/0/0	entecavir
0/0/0	0	0	0.7/0.7	0/0/0	0/0	0//0	0/0/	0/0/0	5.9/0		//	0/0/0	Trajenta
0/0/0	0	0	0.7/0.7	0/0/0	0/0	0//0	0/0/	0/0/0	5.9/0			0/0/0	Imatinib mesylate, azathioprine, pemetrexed disodium, calcium levalinate and other anticancer drug substances
0/0/0	0	0	0.7/0.7	0/0/0	0/0	0//0	0/0/	0/0/0	5.9/0			0/0/0	Other compounds containing pyrimidine rings in the structre (including other compounds containing piperazine rings in the strcture)(tax number of Separating anti—cancer pharmaceutical raw materials)
													-Compounds containing an unfused triazine ring (whether or not hydrogenated) in the structure:
0/0/0	5	0	0/0	0/0/0	0/0	0//0	0/0/	0/0/0	5.9/0			0/0/0	--Melamine
													--Other:
0/0/0	5	0	0/0	0/0/0	0/0	0//0	0/0/	0/0/0	0/0			0/0/0	---Cyanuric chloride
													---Chloroisocyanurate:
0/0/0	5	0	0/0	0/0/0	0/0	0//0	0/0/	0/0/0	5.9/0			0/0/0	----Dichloroisocyanurate acid
0/0/0	5	0	0/0	0/0/0	0/0	0//0	0/0/	0/0/0	5.9/0			0/0/0	----Trichloroisooyanurate acid
													----Other
0/0/0	5	0	0/0	0/0/0	0/0	0//0	0/0/	0/0/0	5.9/0			0/0/0	Sodium dichloro isocyanurate
0/0/0	5	0	0/0	0/0/0	0/0	0//0	0/0/	0/0/0	5.9/0			0/0/0	Other chloroisocyanuric acid derivatives
													---Other
0/0/0	5	1.3	0/0	0/0/0	0/0	0//0	0/0/	5.9/5.9/5.9	5.9/5.9			0/0/0	Simazine, atrazine, propazine, trietazine(including terbuthylazine, cyanazine, cyprazine, proglinazine, eglinazine)
0/0/0	5	1.3	0/0	0/0/0	0/0	0//0	0/0/	5.9/5.9/5.9	5.9/5.9			0/0/0	Simetryn, prometryn, desmetryn, ametryn (including terbutryn, dipropetryn, dimethametryn, cyanatryn, SSH-108, methoprotryne)
0/0/0	5	1.3	0/0	0/0/0	0/0	0//0	0/0/	5.9/5.9/5.9	5.9/5.9			0/0/0	Prometon, secbumeton

税则号列		货品名称〔CIQ 扩展编码及品名－T2 表示见附表 2〕	最惠(%)	暂定税率	普通	增值/消费	出口退税	计量单位	监管条件/特殊证件	检验检疫	对美关税	亚太上/下
2933.6990	14	丁嗪草酮、环嗪酮、嗪草酮等(包括苯嗪草酮、乙嗪草酮)〔999〕	6.5		20	13/	9,13	千克	S/13		16.5	
2933.6990	15	灭蚜硫磷、灭蝇胺、吡蚜酮等(包括敌菌灵)〔999〕	6.5		20	13/	9,13	千克	S/13		16.5	
2933.6990	16	三嗪氟草胺,茚嗪氟草胺〔999〕	6.5		20	13/	9,13	千克	S/13		16.5	
2933.6990	91	奥替拉西钾〔999〕	6.5	0	20	3/	13	千克	/13		10	
2933.6990	99	其他结构上含非稠合三嗪环化合物〔301 危险化学品,易燃固体,302 危险化学品,毒性物质,303 危险化学品,杂项物质,304 其他化工产品〕	6.5		20	13/	13	千克	/13		16.5	
		-内酰胺:										
2933.7100		--6-己内酰胺〔999〕	9		35	13/	13	千克	/1			
2933.7200		--氯巴占(INN)和甲乙哌酮(INN)〔999〕	9		15	13/	13	千克	I/1			
2933.7900		--其他内酰胺										
2933.7900	10	氯巴占和甲乙哌酮的盐〔999〕	9		20	13/	13	千克	I/13		19	
2933.7900	20	灭菌磷、螺虫乙酯〔999〕	9		20	13/	9,13	千克	S/13		19	
2933.7900	30	佐匹克隆(Zopiclone;CAS 号:43200－80－2)〔999〕	9		20	13/	13	千克	I/13		19	
2933.7900	41	甲氧哌啶乙酯〔999〕	9		20	13/	13	千克	S/13		19	
2933.7900	42	吡非尼酮〔999〕	9	0	20	3/	13	千克	/13		10	
2933.7900	91	来那度胺〔999〕	9	0	20	3/	13	千克	/13		10	
2933.7900	99	其他内酰胺〔301 其他危险化学品;302 其他化工产品〕	9		20	13/	13	千克	/13		19	
		-其他:										
2933.9100		--阿普唑仑(INN)、卡马西泮(INN)、氯氮卓(INN)、氯硝西泮(INN)、氯拉卓酸、地洛西泮(INN)、地西泮(INN)、艾司唑仑(INN)、氯氟卓乙酯(INN)、氟地西泮(INN)、氟硝西泮(INN)、氟西泮(INN)、哈拉西泮(INN)、劳拉西泮(INN)、氯甲西泮(INN)、马吲哚(INN)、美达西泮(INN)、咪达唑仑(INN)、硝甲西泮(INN)、硝西泮(INN)、去甲西泮(INN)、奥沙西泮(INN)、匹那西泮(INN)、普拉西泮(INN)、吡咯戊酮(INN)、替马西泮(INN)、四氢西泮(INN)和三唑仑(INN)以及它们的盐										
2933.9100	11	阿普唑仑、卡马西泮、氯氮卓(以及它们的盐)〔999〕	6.5		20	13/	13	千克	I/1		11.5	
2933.9100	12	氯硝西泮、氯拉卓酸、地洛西泮(以及它们的盐)〔999〕	6.5		20	13/	13	千克	I/1		11.5	
2933.9100	13	地西泮、艾司唑仑、氯氟卓乙酯(以及它们的盐)〔999〕	6.5		20	13/	13	千克	I/1		11.5	
2933.9100	14	氟地西泮、氟硝西泮、氟西泮(以及它们的盐)〔999〕	6.5		20	13/	13	千克	I/1		11.5	
2933.9100	15	哈拉西泮、劳拉西泮、氯甲西泮(以及它们的盐)〔999〕	6.5		20	13/	13	千克	I/1		11.5	
2933.9100	16	马吲哚、咪达唑仑、硝西泮(以及它们的盐)〔999〕	6.5		20	13/	13	千克	I/1		11.5	
2933.9100	17	奥沙西泮、匹那西泮、普拉西泮(以及它们的盐)〔999〕	6.5		20	13/	13	千克	I/1		11.5	
2933.9100	18	去甲西泮、三唑仑(以及它们的盐)〔999〕	6.5		20	13/	13	千克	I/1		11.5	
2933.9100	21	硝甲西泮、美达西泮(以及它们的盐)〔999〕	6.5		20	13/	13	千克	I/1		11.5	
2933.9100	22	吡咯戊酮、替马西泮、四氢西泮(以及它们的盐)〔999〕	6.5		20	13/	13	千克	I/1		11.5	
2933.9200		--甲基谷硫磷(ISO)〔999〕	6.5		20	13/	13	千克	/1			
2933.9900		--其他										
2933.9900	11	抑芽丹、三唑磷、虫线磷、喹硫磷、唑啶草酮等(包括哒嗪硫磷、亚胺硫磷、氯亚胺硫磷、保棉磷、益棉磷、威菌磷)〔301 危险化学品,毒性物质;302 其他化工品〕	6.5		20	13/	9,13	千克	S/13		31.5	
2933.9900	12	氯唑磷、炔咪菊酯、吲哚酮草酯等(包括呋喃虫酰肼、唑蚜威、不育胺、虫螨腈、抗螨唑、四螨嗪)〔999〕	6.5		20	13/	9,13	千克	S/13		31.5	
2933.9900	13	多菌灵,苯菌灵,氰菌灵,麦穗宁,氟哒嗪草酯等(包括咪菌威,丙硫咗,氟氯菌核利,哒菌酮,拌种咯,杀草强)〔301 危险化学品,杂项物质,302 其他化工品〕	6.5		20	13/	9,13	千克	S/13		31.5	
2933.9900	14	三唑酮,醚草敏,三唑醇,唑草酮等(包括四氯喹噁啉,己唑醇,腈苯唑,亚胺唑,四氟醚唑,氟环唑)〔999〕	6.5		20	13/	9,13	千克	S/13		31.5	
2933.9900	15	苄氯三唑醇,戊菌唑,粉唑醇等(包括联苯三唑醇,腈菌唑,环丙唑醇,戊唑醇,氟硅唑)〔999〕	6.5		20	13/	9,13	千克	S/13		31.5	
2933.9900	16	环菌唑、叶菌唑、灭菌唑、种菌唑等(包括申嗪霉素、氟喹唑、哒螨灵、喹螨醚、氟草敏、氟咯草酮)〔999〕	6.5		20	13/	9,13	千克	S/13		31.5	
2933.9900	17	唑草酯,四环唑,噁草酸等(包括喹禾糠酯,哒草特,咯草隆,禾草敌,唑草胺,敌草快及其盐,氯草敏,丙硫菌唑,氯氟醚菌唑,烯唑醇)〔301 危险化学品,杂项物质,302 其他化工品〕	6.5		20	13/	9,13	千克	S/13		31.5	
2933.9900	18	氟胺草唑,氨唑草酮,三氟苯唑等(包括吲哚丁酸,溴莠敏,吲熟酯,三唑磺,四唑酰草胺)〔999〕	6.5		20	13/	9,13	千克	S/13		31.5	

协定税率 %								RCEP		特惠税率 %			Article Description
东/冰/格	巴基斯坦	韩国	瑞士上/下	哥/秘/柬	澳/毛	新西/坡/智	中国港/澳/台	东盟及马来/澳/韩	日/新	亚太2国	老/柬/缅	98/97/95	
0/0/0	5	1.3	0/0	0/0/0	0/0	0//0	0/0/	5.9/5.9/5.9	5.9/5.9			0/0/0	Isomethiozin, hexazinone, metribuzin (including metamitron, ethiozin)
0/0/0	5	1.3	0/0	0/0/0	0/0	0//0	0/0/	5.9/5.9/5.9	5.9/5.9			0/0/0	Memazon, cyromazine, pymetrozime (including anilazine)
0/0/0	5	1.3	0/0	0/0/0	0/0	0//0	0/0/	5.9/5.9/5.9	5.9/5.9			0/0/0	Triazine fluoxamine, ninazine fluoxamine
0/0/0	5	1.3	0/0	0/0/0	0/0	0//0	0/0/	5.9/5.9/5.9	5.9/5.9			0/0/0	Otlasexi Potassium and Other Anticancer Drugs
0/0/0	5	1.3	0/0	0/0/0	0/0	0//0	0/0/	5.9/5.9/5.9	5.9/5.9			0/0/0	Other compounds containing non－fused triazine ring in the structure (tax number of Separating anti－cancer pharmaceutical raw materials)
													-Lactams:
5/0/0			0/0	0//5	0/0	0//0	0/0/	5/5/	/5			0//	--6-Hexanolactam (epsilon-caprolactam)
0/0/0	2	0	0/0	0/0/0	0/0	0//0	0/0/	0/0/0	8.2/0			0/0/0	--Clobazam (INN) and methyprylon (INN)
													--Other lactams
0/0/0	2	0		0/0/0	0/0	0//0	0/0/	0/0/0	8.2/0			0/0/0	Salts of clobazam (INN) and methyprylon (INN)
0/0/0	2	0		0/0/0	0/0	0//0	0/0/	0/0/0	8.2/0			0/0/0	Ditalimfos, spirotetramat
0/0/0	2	0		0/0/0	0/0	0//0	0/0/	0/0/0	8.2/0			0/0/0	Zopiclone (CAS: 43200-80-2)
0/0/0	2	0		0/0/0	0/0	0//0	0/0/	0/0/0	8.2/0			0/0/0	Methoxypiperidine ethyl ester
0/0/0	2	0		0/0/0	0/0	0//0	0/0/	0/0/0	8.2/0		//	0/0/0	pirfenidone
0/0/0	2	0		0/0/0	0/0	0//0	0/0/	0/0/0	8.2/0		//	0/0/0	Lenalidomide
0/0/0	2	0		0/0/0	0/0	0//0	0/0/	0/0/0	8.2/0		//	0/0/0	Other lactams
													-Other:
													--Alprazolam (INN), camazepam (INN), chlordiazepoxide (INN), clonazepam (INN), clorazepate, delorazepam (INN), diazepam (INN), estazolam (INN), ethyl loflazepate (INN), fludiazepam (INN), flunitrazepam (INN), flurazepam (INN), halazepam (INN), lorazepam (INN), lormetazepam (INN), mazindol (INN), medazepam (INN), midazolam (INN), nimetazepam (INN), nitrazepam (INN), nordazepam (INN), oxazepam (INN), pinazepam (INN), prazepam (INN), pyrovalerone (INN), temazepam (INN), tetrazepam (INN) and triazolam (INN); salts thereof
0/0/0	5	0	0/0	0/0/0	0/0	0//0	0/0/	0/0/0	5.9/0			0/0/0	Alprazolam (INN), camazepam (INN), chlordiazepoxide (INN); salts thereof
0/0/0	5	0	0/0	0/0/0	0/0	0//0	0/0/	0/0/0	5.9/0			0/0/0	Clonazepam (INN), clorazepate, delorazepam (INN); salts thereof
0/0/0	5	0	0/0	0/0/0	0/0	0//0	0/0/	0/0/0	5.9/0			0/0/0	Diazepam (INN), estazolam (INN), ethyl loflazepate (INN); salts thereof
0/0/0	5	0	0/0	0/0/0	0/0	0//0	0/0/	0/0/0	5.9/0			0/0/0	Fludiazepam (INN), flunitrazepam (INN), flurazepam (INN); salts thereof
0/0/0	5	0	0/0	0/0/0	0/0	0//0	0/0/	0/0/0	5.9/0			0/0/0	Halazepam (INN), lorazepam (INN), lormetazepam (INN); salts thereof
0/0/0	5	0	0/0	0/0/0	0/0	0//0	0/0/	0/0/0	5.9/0			0/0/0	Mazindol (INN), midazolam (INN), nimetazepam (INN); salts thereof
0/0/0	5	0	0/0	0/0/0	0/0	0//0	0/0/	0/0/0	5.9/0			0/0/0	Oxazepam (INN), pinazepam (INN), prazepam (INN); salts thereof
0/0/0	5	0	0/0	0/0/0	0/0	0//0	0/0/	0/0/0	5.9/0			0/0/0	Nordazepam (INN), triazolam (INN); salts thereof
0/0/0	5	0	0/0	0/0/0	0/0	0//0	0/0/	0/0/0	5.9/0			0/0/0	Nimetazepam (INN), medazepam (INN); salts thereof
0/0/0	5	0	0/0	0/0/0	0/0	0//0	0/0/	0/0/0	5.9/0			0/0/0	Pyrovalerone (INN), temazepam (INN), tetrazepam (INN); salts thereof
0/0/0	0	0	2.7/2.7	0/0/0	0/0	0//0	0/0/	5.9/5.9/5.9	5.9/5.9			0/0/0	--Azinphos methyl (ISO)
													--Other
0/0/0	0	0	2.7/2.7	0/0/0	0/0	0//0	0/0/	5.9/5.9/5.9	5.9/5.9			0/0/0	Maleic hydrazide, triazophos, thionazin, quinalphos, azafenidin (including pyridaphenthione (JMAF), phosmet, dialifos, azinphos-methyl, azinphos-ethyl, triamiphos)
0/0/0	0	0	2.7/2.7	0/0/0	0/0	0//0	0/0/	5.9/5.9/5.9	5.9/5.9			0/0/0	Isazofos, imiprothrin, cinidon-ethyl (including furan-tebufenozide triaamate, metepa, fenazaflor, clofentezine, chlorfenapyr)
0/0/0	0	0	2.7/2.7	0/0/0	0/0	0//0	0/0/	5.9/5.9/5.9	5.9/5.9			0/0/0	Carbendazim, benomyl, cyanomyl, maisuining, fluridazine oxalate, etc. (including imicarb, propylthio, fluchlorosclerolі, pyridazone, seed dressing, herbicide)
0/0/0	0	0	2.7/2.7	0/0/0	0/0	0//0	0/0/	5.9/5.9/5.9	5.9/5.9			0/0/0	Triadimefo, credazine, triadimeno, carfentrazone-ethyl (including 4-chloroquinoxaline, hexaconazole, fenbuconazole, imbenconazole, tetraconazole, epoxiconazole)
0/0/0	0	0	2.7/2.7	0/0/0	0/0	0//0	0/0/	5.9/5.9/5.9	5.9/5.9			0/0/0	Benzyl chlorotriazole alcohol, pentaconazole, fenoxazole, etc. (including biphenyl triazole alcohol, nitrile oxazole, cyclopropazole alcohol, tebuconazole, flusilazole)
0/0/0	0	0	2.7/2.7	0/0/0	0/0	0//0	0/0/	5.9/5.9/5.9	5.9/5.9			0/0/0	Cyproconazole, metconazole, triticonazole, ipconazole (including shenqinmycin, fluquinconazole, pyridaben, fenazaquin, norflurazon, fluorochloridone)
0/0/0	0	0	2.7/2.7	0/0/0	0/0	0//0	0/0/	5.9/5.9/5.9	5.9/5.9			0/0/0	Oxazolyl ester, tetracyclic azole, oxaoxalic acid, etc. (including quinbranyl ester, pyridazole, rocuron, gramido, oxazolamide, diquat and its salts, chlorpyrimin, thiabendazole, chlorofluridazole, diniconazole)
0/0/0	0	0	2.7/2.7	0/0/0	0/0	0//0	0/0/	5.9/5.9/5.9	5.9/5.9			0/0/0	Flupoxam, foramsulfuron, fluotrimazole (including indole-butytic-acid), brompyrazon, piproctanly, ethychlozate (JMAF), fentrazamide)

税则号列	货品名称〔CIQ 扩展编码及品名－T2 表示见附表 2〕	最惠(%)	暂定税率	普通	增值/消费	出口退税	计量单位	监管条件/特殊证件	检验检疫	对美关税	亚太上/下
2933.9900 19	多效唑，烯效唑，抑芽唑等(包括叶枯净，叶锈特，吡喃草酮，吲哚乙酸)〔999〕	6.5		20	13/	9,13	千克	S/13		31.5	
2933.9900 21	氯尼他秦〔999〕	6.5		20	13/	13	千克	I/13		31.5	
2933.9900 22	依托尼秦〔999〕	6.5		20	13/	13	千克	I/13		31.5	
2933.9900 23	普罗庚嗪，布桂嗪〔999〕	6.5		20	13/	13	千克	I/13		31.5	
2933.9900 30	扎莱普隆、唑吡坦(以及它们的盐)〔999〕	6.5		20	13/	13	千克	I/13		31.5	
2933.9900 40	齐帕特罗，2－(三氟甲基)－4－[(2R)－2－[(1R)－2,2,2－三氟－1－羟基乙基]－1－吡咯烷基]苯甲腈，3－甲基－4－[[(1R,2S)－1－[5－(4－氰基苯基)－1,3,4－噁二唑－2－基]－2－羟基丙基]氨基]－2－氯苯甲腈〔999〕	6.5		20	13/	13	千克	L/13		31.5	
2933.9900 51	二甲基色胺、二乙基色胺〔999〕	6.5		20	13/	13	千克	I/13		31.5	
2933.9900 52	乙色胺，咯环利定〔999〕	6.5		20	13/	13	千克	I/13		31.5	
2933.9900 53	[1－(5－氟戊基)－1H－吲哚－3－基](2－碘苯基)甲酮(1－[(5－Fluoropentyl)－1H－indol－3－yl]－(2－iodophenyl)methanone;CAS 号:335161－03－0)〔999〕	6.5		20	13/	13	千克	I/13		31.5	
2933.9900 54	1－(5－氟戊基)－3－(1－萘甲酰基)－1H－吲哚(1－(5－Fluoropentyl)－3－(1－naphthoyl)indole;CAS 号:335161－24－5)〔999〕	6.5		20	13/	13	千克	I/13		31.5	
2933.9900 55	1－戊基－3－(1－萘甲酰基)吲哚(1－Pentyl－3－(1－naphthoyl)indole;CAS 号:209414－07－3)〔999〕	6.5		20	13/	13	千克	I/13		31.5	
2933.9900 56	1－丁基－3－(1－萘甲酰基)吲哚(1－Butyl－3－(1－naphthoyl)indole;CAS 号:208987－48－8)〔999〕	6.5		20	13/	13	千克	I/13		31.5	
2933.9900 57	2－(2－甲氧基苯基)－1－(1－戊基－1H－吲哚－3－基)乙酮(2－(2－Methoxyphenyl)－1－(1－pentyl－1H－indol－3－yl)ethanone;CAS 号:864445－43－2)〔999〕	6.5		20	13/	13	千克	I/13		31.5	
2933.9900 60	(环)四亚甲基四硝胺(俗名奥托金 HMX)〔999〕	6.5		20	13/	13	千克	3k/13		31.5	
2933.9900 70	(环)三亚甲基三硝基胺(俗名黑索金 RDX)〔999〕	6.5		20	13/	13	千克	3k/13		31.5	
2933.9900 80	丁羟咯酮(包括杀雄啉、杀雄嗪酸、双唑草腈、唑酮草酯)〔999〕	6.5		20	13/	13	千克	S/13		31.5	
2933.9900 91	阿托伐他汀钙〔999〕	6.5	0	20	13/	13	千克	/13		25	
2933.9900 92	阿那曲唑、来曲唑、硼替佐米、替莫唑胺〔999〕	6.5	0	20	3/	13	千克	/13		25	
2933.9900 93	维格列汀〔999〕	6.5	0	20	13/	13	千克	/13		25	
2933.9900 99	其他仅含氮杂原子的杂环化合物〔301 危险化学品，爆炸品；302 危险化学品，易燃液体；303 危险化学品，易燃固体；304 危险化学品，毒性物质；305 危险化学品，杂项物质；306 其他化工产品〕	6.5		20	13/	13	千克	/13		31.5	
29.34	**核酸及其盐；无论是否已有化学定义；其他杂环化合物：**										
	-结构上含有一个非稠合噻唑环(不论是否氢化)的化合物：										
2934.1010	---三苯甲基氨噻肟酸〔999〕	6.5		20	13/	9,13	千克	/1			
2934.1090	---其他										
2934.1090 11	噻螨酮〔999〕	6.5		20	13/	9,13	千克	S/1		31.5	
2934.1090 12	噻唑膦，噻唑硫磷〔999〕	6.5		20	13/	9,13	千克	S/1		31.5	
2934.1090 13	噻唑烟酸，噻唑菌胺〔999〕	6.5		20	13/	9,13	千克	S/1		31.5	
2934.1090 14	氯噻啉，氟螨噻〔999〕	6.5		20	13/	9,13	千克	S/1		31.5	
2934.1090 15	噻菌灵，噻菌胺，噻丙腈(包括氟噻唑吡乙酮，氟烯线砜，异噻菌胺)〔999〕	6.5		20	13/	9,13	千克	S/1		31.5	
2934.1090 16	噻呋酰胺、噻虫胺、噻虫嗪、噻虫啉〔999〕	6.5		20	13/	9,13	千克	S/1		31.5	
2934.1090 17	辛噻酮，拌种灵〔999〕	6.5		20	13/	9,13	千克	S/1		31.5	
2934.1090 18	稻瘟灵〔999〕	6.5		20	13/	9,13	千克	S/1		31.5	
2934.1090 19	甲噻诱胺〔999〕	6.5		20	13/	9,13	千克	S/1		31.5	
2934.1090 91	达沙替尼〔999〕	6.5	0	20	3/	13	千克	/1		25	
2934.1090 99	其他结构上含有非稠合噻唑环的化合物(非稠合噻唑环不论是否氢化)〔301 麦草净，3022－氨基噻唑硫酸盐，3032－氨基噻唑盐酸盐〕	6.5		20	13/	13	千克	/1		31.5	
2934.2000	-结构上含有一个苯并噻唑环系(不论是否氢化)的化合物，但未经进一步稠合的										
2934.2000 11	噻螨威，噻霉酮〔999〕	6.5		20	13/	9,13	千克	S/1		26.5	
2934.2000 12	苯噻硫氰〔999〕	6.5		20	13/	9,13	千克	S/1		26.5	
2934.2000 13	烯丙苯噻唑〔999〕	6.5		20	13/	9,13	千克	S/1		26.5	
2934.2000 14	草除灵〔999〕	6.5		20	13/	9,13	千克	S/1		26.5	
2934.2000 15	噻唑禾草灵〔999〕	6.5		20	13/	9,13	千克	S/1		26.5	
2934.2000 16	苯噻隆〔999〕	6.5		20	13/	9,13	千克	S/1		26.5	
2934.2000 17	甲基苯噻隆〔999〕	6.5		20	13/	9,13	千克	S/1		26.5	
2934.2000 18	苯噻酰草胺〔999〕	6.5		20	13/	9,13	千克	S/1		26.5	
2934.2000 19	苯噻菌酯〔999〕	6.5		20	13/	9,13	千克	S/1		26.5	
2934.2000 21	利鲁唑〔999〕	6.5	0	20	3/	13	千克	/1		20	
2934.2000 22	毒氟磷、苯噻菌胺〔999〕	6.5		20	13/	13	千克	S/1		26.5	
2934.2000 90	其他含一个苯并噻唑环系的化合物〔999〕	6.5		20	13/	13	千克	/1		26.5	
2934.3000	-结构上含有一个吩噻嗪环系(不论是否氢化)的化合物，但未经进一步稠合的〔999〕	6.5		20	13/	13	千克	/1		26.5	

协定税率 %								RCEP		特惠税率 %			Article Description
东/冰/格	巴基斯坦	韩国	瑞士 上/下	哥/秘/柬	澳/毛	新西/坡/智	中国港/澳/台	东盟及马来/澳/韩	日/新	亚太2国	老/柬/缅	98/97/95	
0/0/0	0	0	2.7/2.7	0/0/0	0/0	0//0	0/0/	5.9/5.9/5.9	5.9/5.9			0/0/0	Paclobutrazol, uniconazole, triapenthenol, bifenthrin (including phenazineoxide, butrizol, tepraloxydim, heteroauxin)
0/0/0	0	0	2.7/2.7	0/0/0	0/0	0//0	0/0/	5.9/5.9/5.9	5.9/5.9			0/0/0	Clonitazene
0/0/0	0	0	2.7/2.7	0/0/0	0/0	0//0	0/0/	5.9/5.9/5.9	5.9/5.9			0/0/0	Etonitazene
0/0/0	0	0	2.7/2.7	0/0/0	0/0	0//0	0/0/	5.9/5.9/5.9	5.9/5.9			0/0/0	Proheptazine, bucinnazine
0/0/0	0	0	2.7/2.7	0/0/0	0/0	0//0	0/0/	5.9/5.9/5.9	5.9/5.9			0/0/0	Zaleplon zolpidem (salts thereof)
0/0/0	0	0	2.7/2.7	0/0/0	0/0	0//0	0/0/	5.9/5.9/5.9	5.9/5.9			0/0/0	Zilpaterol
0/0/0	0	0	2.7/2.7	0/0/0	0/0	0//0	0/0/	5.9/5.9/5.9	5.9/5.9			0/0/0	Dimethyltryptamine, diethyltryptamine
0/0/0	0	0	2.7/2.7	0/0/0	0/0	0//0	0/0/	5.9/5.9/5.9	5.9/5.9			0/0/0	Etryptamine, rolicyclidine
0/0/0	0	0	2.7/2.7	0/0/0	0/0	0//0	0/0/	5.9/5.9/5.9	5.9/5.9			0/0/0	1-[(5-Fluoropentyl)-1H-indol-3-Yl]-(2-iodophenyl) methanone(CAS:335161-03-0)
0/0/0	0	0	2.7/2.7	0/0/0	0/0	0//0	0/0/	5.9/5.9/5.9	5.9/5.9			0/0/0	1-(5-Fluoropentyl)-3-(1-naphthoyl) indole (CAS: 335161-24-5)
0/0/0	0	0	2.7/2.7	0/0/0	0/0	0//0	0/0/	5.9/5.9/5.9	5.9/5.9			0/0/0	1-Pentyl-3-(1-naphthoyl)indole(CAS:209414-07-3)
0/0/0	0	0	2.7/2.7	0/0/0	0/0	0//0	0/0/	5.9/5.9/5.9	5.9/5.9			0/0/0	1-Butyl-3-(1-naphthoyl)indole(CAS:208987-48-8)
0/0/0	0	0	2.7/2.7	0/0/0	0/0	0//0	0/0/	5.9/5.9/5.9	5.9/5.9			0/0/0	2-(2-Methoxyphenyl)-1-(1-pentyl-1H-indol-3-Yl) ethanone (CAS:864445-43-2)
0/0/0	0	0	2.7/2.7	0/0/0	0/0	0//0	0/0/	5.9/5.9/5.9	5.9/5.9			0/0/0	Cyclotetramethylene tetranitramine(octogen)
0/0/0	0	0	2.7/2.7	0/0/0	0/0	0//0	0/0/	5.9/5.9/5.9	5.9/5.9			0/0/0	Cycltrimethylene-trinitramine(hexogen)
0/0/0	0	0	2.7/2.7	0/0/0	0/0	0//0	0/0/	5.9/5.9/5.9	5.9/5.9			0/0/0	Tepraloxydim (including sintofen, clofencet, pyraclonil, carfentrazone-ethyl)
0/0/0	0	0	2.7/2.7	0/0/0	0/0	0//0	0/0/	5.9/5.9/5.9	5.9/5.9			0/0/0	Atorvastatin calcium
0/0/0	0	0	2.7/2.7	0/0/0	0/0	0//0	0/0/	5.9/5.9/5.9	5.9/5.9			0/0/0	Anastrozole, letrozole, bortezomib, temozolomide and other anticancer drug substances
0/0/0	0	0	2.7/2.7	0/0/0	0/0	0//0	0/0/	5.9/5.9/5.9	5.9/5.9		//	0/0/0	Vegldin
0/0/0	0	0	2.7/2.7	0/0/0	0/0	0//0	0/0/	5.9/5.9/5.9	5.9/5.9			0/0/0	Nitrogen containing heterocyclic compounds other atoms
													Nucleic acids and their salts, whether or not chemically defined; other heterocyclic compounds:
													-Compounds containing an unfused thiazole ring in the structure (whether or not hydrogenated) Three benzothiothiotaxime acid:
0/0/0	5	3	0/0	0/0/0	0/0	0//0	0/0/	5.9/5.9/5.9	6.1/5.9			0/0/0	---Methoxyiminoacetic acid
													---Other
0/0/0	5	3	0/0	0/0/0	0/0	0//0	0/0/	5.9/5.9/5.9	6.1/5.9			0/0/0	Hexythiazox
0/0/0	5	3	0/0	0/0/0	0/0	0//0	0/0/	5.9/5.9/5.9	6.1/5.9			0/0/0	Thiazolidazole
0/0/0	5	3	0/0	0/0/0	0/0	0//0	0/0/	5.9/5.9/5.9	6.1/5.9			0/0/0	Thiazolidic acid, thiazolamide
0/0/0	5	3	0/0	0/0/0	0/0	0//0	0/0/	5.9/5.9/5.9	6.1/5.9			0/0/0	Chlorothiazoline
0/0/0	5	3	0/0	0/0/0	0/0	0//0	0/0/	5.9/5.9/5.9	6.1/5.9			0/0/0	Thiabendazole, thiabendamine, thiapropionitrile (including fluorothiazole, acetophenone, fluoroalkenylsulfone, isothiabendamine)
0/0/0	5	3	0/0	0/0/0	0/0	0//0	0/0/	5.9/5.9/5.9	6.1/5.9			0/0/0	Thioacetamide, thiamide, thiamoxin and thiamidine
0/0/0	5	3	0/0	0/0/0	0/0	0//0	0/0/	5.9/5.9/5.9	6.1/5.9			0/0/0	Essien Thiazone, Seedvax
0/0/0	5	3	0/0	0/0/0	0/0	0//0	0/0/	5.9/5.9/5.9	6.1/5.9			0/0/0	Isoprothiolane
0/0/0	5	3	0/0	0/0/0	0/0	0//0	0/0/	5.9/5.9/5.9	6.1/5.9			0/0/0	Methiadinil
0/0/0	5	3	0/0	0/0/0	0/0	0//0	0/0/	5.9/5.9/5.9	6.1/5.9			0/0/0	Dasatinib and Other Anticancer Drugs
0/0/0	5	3	0/0	0/0/0	0/0	0//0	0/0/	5.9/5.9/5.9	6.1/5.9			0/0/0	Other compounds that contain unfused thiazole rings in their structure (non — condensed thiazole rings, whether or not they are hydrogenated)(tax number of Separating anti—cancer pharmaceutical raw materials)
													-Compounds containing in the structure a benzothiazole ring-system (whether or not hydrogenated), not further fused
0/0/0	5	1.3	0/0	0/0/0	0/0	0//0	0/0/	0/0/5.9	5.9/0			0/0/0	Tazimcarb, benziothiazolinone
0/0/0	5	1.3	0/0	0/0/0	0/0	0//0	0/0/	0/0/5.9	5.9/0			0/0/0	Benthiozole
0/0/0	5	1.3	0/0	0/0/0	0/0	0//0	0/0/	0/0/5.9	5.9/0			0/0/0	Probenazole
0/0/0	5	1.3	0/0	0/0/0	0/0	0//0	0/0/	0/0/5.9	5.9/0			0/0/0	Benazolin ethyl
0/0/0	5	1.3	0/0	0/0/0	0/0	0//0	0/0/	0/0/5.9	5.9/0			0/0/0	Fenthiaprop-ethyl
0/0/0	5	1.3	0/0	0/0/0	0/0	0//0	0/0/	0/0/5.9	5.9/0			0/0/0	Benzthiazuron
0/0/0	5	1.3	0/0	0/0/0	0/0	0//0	0/0/	0/0/5.9	5.9/0			0/0/0	Methabenzthiazuron
0/0/0	5	1.3	0/0	0/0/0	0/0	0//0	0/0/	0/0/5.9	5.9/0			0/0/0	Mefenacet
0/0/0	5	1.3	0/0	0/0/0	0/0	0//0	0/0/	0/0/5.9	5.9/0			0/0/0	Benzothiostrobin
0/0/0	5	1.3	0/0	0/0/0	0/0	0//0	0/0/	0/0/5.9	5.9/0		//	0/0/0	Riluzole
0/0/0	5	1.3	0/0	0/0/0	0/0	0//0	0/0/	0/0/5.9	5.9/0			0/0/0	Toxic fluorophosphorus and phenylthiamine
0/0/0	5	1.3	0/0	0/0/0	0/0	0//0	0/0/	0/0/5.9	5.9/0			0/0/0	Other compounds containing in the structure a benzothiazole ring-system
0/0/0	5	0	0/0	0/0/0	0/0	0//0	0/0/	0/0/0	5.9/0			0/0/0	-Compounds containing in the structure a phenothiazine ring-system (whether or not hydrogenated), not further fused

税则号列	货品名称〔CIQ 扩展编码及品名—T2 表示见附表 2〕	最惠(%)	暂定税率	普通	增值/消费	出口退税	计量单位	监管条件/特殊证件	检验检疫	对美关税	亚太上/下
	-其他：										
2934.9100	--阿米雷司(INN),溴替唑仑(INN)、氯噻西泮(INN)、氯噁唑仑(INN)、右吗拉胺(INN)、卤噁唑仑(INN)、凯他唑仑(INN)、美索卡(INN)、噁唑仑(INN)、匹莫林(INN)、苯巴曲嗪(INN)、芬美曲嗪(INN)和舒芬太尼(INN)以及它们的盐										
2934.9100 11	阿米雷司、溴替唑仑、氯噻西泮(以及它们的盐)〔999〕	6.5		20	13/	13	千克	I/1		11.5	
2934.9100 12	氯恶唑仑、卤沙(恶)唑仑(以及它们的盐)〔999〕	6.5		20	13/	13	千克	I/1		11.5	
2934.9100 13	凯他唑仑、美索卡、奥沙(恶)唑仑(以及它们的盐)〔999〕	6.5		20	13/	13	千克	I/1		11.5	
2934.9100 14	匹莫林、苯甲曲嗪、芬美曲嗪(以及它们的盐)〔999〕	6.5		20	13/	13	千克	I/1		11.5	
2934.9100 20	右吗拉胺、舒芬太尼(以及它们的盐)〔999〕	6.5		20	13/	13	千克	I/1		11.5	
2934.9200	--其他芬太尼以及它们的衍生物										
2934.9200 10	硫代芬太尼、阿法甲基硫代芬太尼、3－甲基硫代芬太尼以及它们的盐〔999〕	6.5		20	13/	13	千克	I/1		34	
2934.9200 90	其他芬太尼以及它们的衍生物〔999〕	6.5		20	13/	13	千克	/1		34	
	--其他：										
2934.9910	---磺内酯及磺内酰胺〔999〕	6.5		30	13/	13	千克	/1		31.5	
2934.9920	---呋喃唑酮〔999〕	6		20	13/	13	千克	A/1	M		4.8/4.8
2934.9930	---核酸及其盐										
2934.9930 10	人类核酸及其盐〔999〕	6.5		35	13/	13	千克	ABV/1		11.5	
2934.9930 90	其他核酸及其盐〔T2〕	6.5		35	13/	13	千克	/1		11.5	
2934.9940	---奈韦拉平、依发韦仑、利托那韦及它们的盐〔999〕	6.5		20	13/	13	千克	/1			
2934.9950	---克拉维酸及其盐〔999〕	6.5		20	13/	13	千克	/1			
2934.9960	---7-苯乙酰氨基-3-氯甲基-4-头孢烷酸对甲氧基苄酯、7-氨基头孢烷酸、7-氨基脱乙酰氧基头孢烷酸〔999〕	6		20	13/	13	千克	/1			5/5
2934.9990	---其他										
2934.9990 01	核苷酸类食品添加剂〔301 无检疫要求食品添加剂,302 需申报仅用于工业用途不用于食品添加剂无检疫要求的化学品〕	6.5		20	13/	13	千克	A/13	R	34	
2934.9990 10	噁草酮,氟噻草胺,活化酯,高效二甲吩草胺(包括吡噻菌胺)〔999〕	6.5		20	13/	9,13	千克	S/13		34	
2934.9990 21	噁唑磷,蔬果磷,茂硫磷,除害磷等(包括甲基吡噁磷,丁硫环磷,硫环磷,杀扑磷,伏杀硫磷,地胺磷)〔301 危险化学品,毒性物质,302 其他化工品〕	6.5		20	13/	9,13	千克	S/13		34	
2934.9990 22	环线威,杀虫环,杀虫钉,多噻烷等(包括甲基硫环磷,噻嗪酮,噁虫酮,茚虫威,砜吡草唑,氟吡呋喃酮,氟嘧菌酯,硅噻菌胺,糠氨基嘌呤,双丙环虫酯)〔999〕	6.5		20	13/	9,13	千克	S/13			
2934.9990 23	噁唑禾草灵,毒鼠硅,噻鼠灵等(包括福拉比,噻节因,糠菌唑,精噁唑禾草灵)〔301 危险化学品,毒性物质,302 其他化工产品〕	6.5		20	13/	9,13	千克	S/13		34	
2934.9990 24	代森硫,代森环,氟吗啉,咯菌腈等(包括稻瘟酯,烯酰吗啉,噻菌腈,土菌灵,噁霜灵,噁霉灵)〔999〕	6.5		20	13/	9,13	千克	S/13		34	
2934.9990 25	噻霉酮、丙环唑、乙环唑等(包括噁唑菌酮、金核霉素、呋菌唑、叶枯唑、呋醚唑、苯醚甲环唑)〔999〕	6.5		20	13/	9,13	千克	S/13		34	
2934.9990 26	嗪草酸,噻氟隆,丁噻隆,异噁隆等(包括噻苯隆,磺噻隆,噁唑隆,异噁草醚,噻吩草胺,二甲吩草胺)〔999〕	6.5		20	13/	9,13	千克	S/13		34	
2934.9990 27	苯草灭,灭草松,灭草唑等(包括异噁草松,噁嗪草酮,环苯草酮,丙炔氟草胺)〔999〕	6.5		20	13/	9,13	千克	S/13		34	
2934.9990 28	丙炔噁草酮,噻草酮等(包括糖氨基嘌呤,苯螨噻,异噁酰草胺,异噁唑草酮)〔999〕	6.5		20	13/	9,13	千克	S/13		34	
2934.9990 29	噻唑锌(包括噻菌茂,硅丰环)〔999〕	6.5		20	13/	9,13	千克	S/13		34	
2934.9990 31	多抗霉素、灰瘟素〔301 危险化学品,毒性物质;302 其他化工品〕	6.5		20	13/	9,13	千克	S/13		34	
2934.9990 32	三环唑、氧环唑〔999〕	6.5		20	13/	9,13	千克	S/13		34	
2934.9990 33	灭螨猛、克杀螨、螨蜱胺〔301 危险化学品,杂项物质;302 其他化工品〕	6.5		20	13/	9,13	千克	S/13		34	
2934.9990 34	二氰蒽醌、吗菌威〔101 二噻农,102 二噻农乳剂(含量＞50%)〕	6.5		20	13/	9,13	千克	S/13		34	
2934.9990 35	十二环吗啉、十三吗啉〔999〕	6.5		20	13/	9,13	千克	S/13		34	
2934.9990 36	杀螺吗啉、丁苯吗啉〔101 蜗螺净粉剂、颗粒剂,102 蜗螺净乳剂〕	6.5		20	13/	9,13	千克	S/13		34	
2934.9990 37	喹菌酮、肼菌酮〔999〕	6.5		20	13/	9,13	千克	S/13		34	
2934.9990 38	萎锈灵、氧化萎锈灵〔999〕	6.5		20	13/	9,13	千克	S/13		34	
2934.9990 39	棉隆、乙烯菌核利〔999〕	6.5		20	13/	9,13	千克	S/13		34	
2934.9990 41	环酯草醚〔999〕	6.5		20	13/	9,13	千克	S/13		34	
2934.9990 42	噻菌铜〔999〕	6.5		20	13/	9,13	千克	S/13		34	
2934.9990 43	苯唑草酮〔999〕	6.5		20	13/	9,13	千克	S/13		34	
2934.9990 44	丁吡吗啉〔999〕	6.5		20	13/	9,13	千克	S/13		34	
2934.9990 45	环戊噁草酮〔999〕	6.5		20	13/	13	千克	S/13		34	

协定税率 %								RCEP		特惠税率 %			Article Description
东/冰/格	巴基斯坦	韩国	瑞士上/下	哥/秘/柬	澳/毛	新西/坡/智	中国港/澳/台	东盟及马来/澳/韩	日/新	亚太2国	老/柬/缅	98/97/95	
													-Other：
													--Aminorex(INN), brotizolam(INN), clotiazepam(INN), cloxazolam(INN), dextromoramide(INN), haloxazolam(INN), ketazolam(INN), mesocarb(INN), oxazolam(INN), pemoline(INN), phendimetrazine(INN), phenmetrazine(INN) and sufentanil(INN); salts thereof
0/0/0	5	0	0/0	0/0/0	0/0	0//0	0/0/	0/0/0	5.9/0			0/0/0	Aminorex(INN), brotizolam(INN), clotiazepam(INN)(salts thereof)
0/0/0	5	0	0/0	0/0/0	0/0	0//0	0/0/	0/0/0	5.9/0			0/0/0	Cloxazolam(INN), haloxazolam(INN); (salts thereof)
0/0/0	5	0	0/0	0/0/0	0/0	0//0	0/0/	0/0/0	5.9/0			0/0/0	Ketazolam(INN), mesocarb(INN), oxazolam(INN)(salts thereof)
0/0/0	5	0	0/0	0/0/0	0/0	0//0	0/0/	0/0/0	5.9/0			0/0/0	Pemoline(INN), phendimetrazine(INN), phenmetrazine(INN)(salts thereof)
0/0/0	5	0	0/0	0/0/0	0/0	0//0	0/0/	0/0/0	5.9/0			0/0/0	Dextromoramide(INN), sufentanil(INN)(salts thereof)
													-- Other fentanyls and their derivatives
0/0/0	0	0	0/0	0/0/0	0/0	0//0	0/0/	5.9/5.9/5.9	5.9/5.9			0/0/0	Thiofentanyl, alpha methylthiofentanyl, 3－methylthiofentanyl and their salts
0/0/0	0	0	0/0	0/0/0	0/0	0//0	0/0/	5.9/5.9/5.9	5.9/5.9			0/0/0	Other fentanyls and their derivatives
													--Other：
0/0/0	5	0	0/0	0/0/0	0/0	0//0	0/0/	0/0/0	5.9/0			0/0/0	---Sultones and sultams
0/0/0	5	0		0/0/0	0/0	0//0	0/0/	0/0/0	5.5/0			0/0/0	---Furazolidone
0/0/0	3.5	0	0/0	0/0/0	0/0	0//0	0/0/	0/0/0	5.9/0		//	0/0/0	Human nucleic acids and their salts
0/0/0	3.5	0	0/0	0/0/0	0/0	0//0	0/0/	0/0/0	5.9/0		//	0/0/0	Other nucleic acids and their salts
0/0/0	5	0	0/0	0/0/0	0/0	0//0	0/0/	0/0/0	5.9/0			0/0/0	---Nevirapine, Efavirenz, Ritonavir and their salts
0/0/0	5	0	0/0	0/0/0	0/0	0//0	0/0/	0/0/0	5.9/0			0/0/0	---Clavulante acid and its salt
0/0/0	0	0	0/0	0/0/0	0/0	0//0	0/0/	0/0/0	0/0			0/0/0	---7-phenylacetamido-3-(chloromethyl)－3－cephem-4-carbonic acid pmethoxybenzyl ester, 7-Aminocephalosporanic acid, 7-amido acetoxy cefanoic acid
													---Other
0/0/0	0	0	0/0	0/0/0	0/0	0//0	0/0/	5.9/5.9/5.9	5.9/5.9			0/0/0	Nucleotides food additives, hgslmof
0/0/0	0	0	0/0	0/0/0	0/0	0//0	0/0/	5.9/5.9/5.9	5.9/5.9			0/0/0	Oxadiazon, flufenacet, acibenzolar, dimethenamid (including penthiopyrad)
0/0/0	0	0	0/0	0/0/0	0/0	0//0	0/0/	5.9/5.9/5.9	5.9/5.9			0/0/0	Isoxathion, salithion dioxabenzofos, morphothion, (including azamethiphos, fosthietan, phosfolan, methidathion, phosalone, mephosfolan)
0/0/0	0	0	0/0	0/0/0	0/0	0//0	0/0/	5.9/5.9/5.9	5.9/5.9			0/0/0	Cycloprocarb, insecticidal ring, insecticidal nail, polythiaxane, etc. (including methyl thiocyclophosphate, thiazinone, oxamethone, indeclovir, sulfonylpyrazol, fluorofuranone, fluoroazoxystrobin, thiamethoxam, furfuramine, dipropyl)
0/0/0	0	0	0/0	0/0/0	0/0	0//0	0/0/	5.9/5.9/5.9	5.9/5.9			0/0/0	Fenoxaprop-ethyl, silatrane, difethialone (including furametpyr, dimethipin, bromuconazole, fenoxaprop-p-ethyl)
0/0/0	0	0	0/0	0/0/0	0/0	0//0	0/0/	5.9/5.9/5.9	5.9/5.9			0/0/0	Etem(BSI), milmeb(BSI), flumorph fludioxonil (including pefurazoate, dimethomoph, thicyofen, etridiazole, oxadixyl, hymexazol)
0/0/0	0	0	0/0	0/0/0	0/0	0//0	0/0/	5.9/5.9/5.9	5.9/5.9			0/0/0	Benziothiazolinone, propiconazole, etaconazole (including famoxadone, aureonuclemycin, furconazole bismerthiazol, furconazole-cis, difenoconazole)
0/0/0	0	0	0/0	0/0/0	0/0	0//0	0/0/	5.9/5.9/5.9	5.9/5.9			0/0/0	Fluthiacet thiazfluron, tebuthiuron, isoproturon (including thidiazuron, ethidimuron, dimefuron, isoxapyrifop, thenychlor, dimethachlor)
0/0/0	0	0	0/0	0/0/0	0/0	0//0	0/0/	5.9/5.9/5.9	5.9/5.9			0/0/0	Bentranil, bentazone, methazole (including, clomazone, oxaziclomefone, cloproxydim, flumioxazin)
0/0/0	0	0	0/0	0/0/0	0/0	0//0	0/0/	5.9/5.9/5.9	5.9/5.9			0/0/0	Fulthiacet-methyl, oxakiargyl, cycloxydim (including kinetin, triarathene, ixoxaben, isoxaflutole)
0/0/0	0	0	0/0	0/0/0	0/0	0//0	0/0/	5.9/5.9/5.9	5.9/5.9			0/0/0	Oxadiargyl, ethaboxam, zinc thiazole (including Saijunmao, silatrane)
0/0/0	0	0	0/0	0/0/0	0/0	0//0	0/0/	5.9/5.9/5.9	5.9/5.9			0/0/0	Polyoxin, blasticidin
0/0/0	0	0	0/0	0/0/0	0/0	0//0	0/0/	5.9/5.9/5.9	5.9/5.9			0/0/0	Tricyclazole, azaconazole
0/0/0	0	0	0/0	0/0/0	0/0	0//0	0/0/	5.9/5.9/5.9	5.9/5.9			0/0/0	Chinomethionate, thioquino, tifatol
0/0/0	0	0	0/0	0/0/0	0/0	0//0	0/0/	5.9/5.9/5.9	5.9/5.9			0/0/0	Dithianon, carbamorph
0/0/0	0	0	0/0	0/0/0	0/0	0//0	0/0/	5.9/5.9/5.9	5.9/5.9			0/0/0	Dodemorph, tridemorph
0/0/0	0	0	0/0	0/0/0	0/0	0//0	0/0/	5.9/5.9/5.9	5.9/5.9			0/0/0	Trifenmorph, fenpropimorph
0/0/0	0	0	0/0	0/0/0	0/0	0//0	0/0/	5.9/5.9/5.9	5.9/5.9			0/0/0	Oxolinic acid, drazoxolon
0/0/0	0	0	0/0	0/0/0	0/0	0//0	0/0/	5.9/5.9/5.9	5.9/5.9			0/0/0	Carboxin, oxycarboxin
0/0/0	0	0	0/0	0/0/0	0/0	0//0	0/0/	5.9/5.9/5.9	5.9/5.9			0/0/0	Dazomet, vinclozolin
0/0/0	0	0	0/0	0/0/0	0/0	0//0	0/0/	5.9/5.9/5.9	5.9/5.9			0/0/0	Pyriftalid
0/0/0	0	0	0/0	0/0/0	0/0	0//0	0/0/	5.9/5.9/5.9	5.9/5.9			0/0/0	Thiodiazole-copper
0/0/0	0	0	0/0	0/0/0	0/0	0//0	0/0/	5.9/5.9/5.9	5.9/5.9			0/0/0	Carfentrazone-ethyl
0/0/0	0	0	0/0	0/0/0	0/0	0//0	0/0/	5.9/5.9/5.9	5.9/5.9			0/0/0	Pyrimorph
0/0/0	0	0	0/0	0/0/0	0/0	0//0	0/0/	5.9/5.9/5.9	5.9/5.9			0/0/0	Pentoxazone

税则号列	货品名称〔CIQ 扩展编码及品名－T2 表示见附表 2〕	最惠(%)	暂定税率	普通	增值/消费	出口退税	计量单位	监管条件/特殊证件	检验检疫	对美关税	亚太上/下
2934.9990 46	异噁唑虫酰胺〔999〕	6.5		20	13/	13	千克	S/13		34	
2934.9990 50	噁唑酰草胺(包括环氧虫啶、噻噁菊酯、双苯噁唑酯、乙螨唑、异噁氯草酮、唑啉草酯)〔999〕	6.5		20	13/	9,13	千克	S/13		34	
2934.9990 63	甲米雷司,替诺环定,二乙噻丁,二甲噻丁,吗苯丁酯,乙甲噻丁,呋替啶,左吗拉胺,吗拉胺中间体,吗哌利定,苯吗庚酮,消旋吗拉胺,以及它们的盐;亚甲基二氧吡咯戊酮(CAS 号:687603－66－3)〔999〕	6.5		20	13/	13	千克	I/13		34	
2934.9990 76	抗癌药原料(呋喹替尼)〔999〕	6.5	0	20	3/	13	千克	/13		27.5	
2934.9990 91	抗癌药原料(地西他滨、氟脲苷、环磷酰胺、吉非替尼、卡培他滨、雷替曲塞、磷酸氟达拉滨、替加氟、盐酸阿糖胞苷、盐酸吉西他滨、盐酸埃克替尼、异环磷酰胺)〔999〕	6.5	0	20	3/	13	千克	/13			
2934.9990 99	其他杂环化合物〔301 危险化学品,易燃液体,302 危险化学品,易燃固体,303 危险化学品,毒性物质,304 危险化学品,腐蚀性物质,305 其他化工产品〕	6.5		20	13/	13	千克	/13		34	
29.35	**磺(酰)胺:**										
2935.1000	-N-甲基全氟辛基磺酰胺〔999〕	6.5		35	13/	9,13	千克	X/13			
2935.2000	-N-乙基全氟辛基磺酰胺〔999〕	6.5		35	13/	9,13	千克	X/13			
2935.3000	-N-乙基-N-(2-羟乙基)全氟辛基磺酰胺〔999〕	6.5		35	13/	9,13	千克	X/13			
2935.4000	-N-(2-羟乙基)-N-甲基全氟辛基磺酰胺〔999〕	6.5		35	13/	9,13	千克	X/13			
2935.5000	-其他全氟辛基磺酰胺〔999〕	6.5		35	13/	13	千克	/1			
2935.9000	-其他										
2935.9000 11	氟唑磺隆,氟吡磺隆,磺酰磺隆,氯酯磺草胺等(包括甲酰氨基嘧磺隆,乙氧磺隆,氯磺隆,甲磺隆,苯磺隆,胺苯磺隆)〔999〕	6.5		35	13/	9,13	千克	S/13		26.5	
2935.9000 12	醚苯磺隆,噻吩磺隆及其酸,醚磺隆,氟啶嘧磺隆等(包括氟胺磺隆,氟磺隆,甲嘧磺隆,氯嘧磺隆,氟嘧磺隆)〔999〕	6.5		35	13/	9,13	千克	S/13		26.5	
2935.9000 13	苄嘧磺隆,吡嘧磺隆,烟嘧磺隆,双氯磺草胺等(包括啶嘧磺隆,砜嘧磺隆,唑嘧磺隆)〔999〕	6.5		35	13/	9,13	千克	S/13		26.5	
2935.9000 14	四唑嘧磺隆,唑吡嘧磺隆,三氟甲磺隆等(包括氯吡嘧磺隆,酰嘧磺隆,环丙嘧磺隆,甲基二磺隆)〔999〕	6.5		35	13/	9,13	千克	S/13		26.5	
2935.9000 15	氟磺酰草胺,甲磺草胺,嘧苯胺磺隆等(包括唑嘧磺草胺,双氟磺草胺,五氟磺草胺)〔999〕	6.5		35	13/	9,13	千克	S/13		26.5	
2935.9000 16	氟磺胺草醚,磺草灵,吲唑磺菌胺等(包括单嘧磺酯,磺草唑胺,三氟啶磺隆钠盐,丙嗪嘧磺隆,单嘧磺隆,氟酮磺草胺,嗪吡嘧磺隆)〔999〕	6.5		35	13/	9,13	千克	S/13		26.5	
2935.9000 17	磺草膦,氨磺乐灵,三氟啶磺隆,啶磺草胺等(包括甲基碘磺隆钠盐)〔999〕	6.5		35	13/	9,13	千克	S/13		26.5	
2935.9000 18	磺菌胺,增糖胺等(包括甲苯氟磺胺,氟虫胺)〔999〕	6.5		35	13/	9,13	千克	S/13		26.5	
2935.9000 19	畜蜱磷,伐灭磷,地散磷等(包括磺菌威,氰霜唑)〔301 危险化学品,毒性物质;302 危险化学品,杂项物质;303 其他化工产品〕	6.5		35	13/	9,13	千克	S/13		26.5	
2935.9000 20	环氧嘧磺隆〔999〕	6.5		35	13/	9,13	千克	S/13		26.5	
2935.9000 31	苯嘧磺草胺〔999〕	6.5		35	13/	9,13	千克	S/13		26.5	
2935.9000 32	噻酮磺隆〔999〕	6.5		35	13/	9,13	千克	S/13		26.5	
2935.9000 33	磺胺嘧啶〔999〕	6.5		35	13/	13	千克	/13		26.5	
2935.9000 34	磺胺双甲基嘧啶〔999〕	6.5		35	13/	13	千克	/13		26.5	
2935.9000 35	磺胺甲噁唑(磺胺甲基异噁唑,新诺明、新明磺)〔999〕	6.5		35	13/	13	千克	/13		26.5	
2935.9000 36	波生坦〔999〕	6.5	0	35	3/	13	千克	/13		20	
2935.9000 90	其他磺(酰)胺〔301 危险化学品,易燃固体;302 危险化学品,毒性物质;303 其他化工产品〕	6.5		35	13/	13	千克	/13		26.5	
	第十一分章　维生素原、维生素及激素										
29.36	**天然或合成再制的维生素原和维生素(包括天然浓缩物)及其主要用作维生素的衍生物,上述产品的混合物,不论是否溶于溶剂:**										
	-未混合的维生素及其衍生物:										
2936.2100	--维生素 A 及其衍生物〔101 饲料添加剂,301 维生素 A(包括视黄醇、醋酸视黄酯、棕榈酸视黄醇)(无检疫要求食品添加剂),302 需申报仅用于工业用途不用于食品添加剂无检疫要求的化学品〕	4		20	13/	13	千克	A/1	R	29	

协定税率 %								RCEP		特惠税率 %			Article Description
东/冰/格	巴基斯坦	韩国	瑞士上/下	哥/秘/柬	澳/毛	新西/坡/智	中国港/澳/台	东盟及马来/澳/韩	日/新	亚太2国	老/柬/缅	98/97/95	
0/0/0	0	0	0/0	0/0/0	0/0	0//0	0/0/	5.9/5.9/5.9	5.9/5.9			0/0/0	Isoxazolamide
0/0/0	0	0	0/0	0/0/0	0/0	0//0	0/0/	5.9/5.9/5.9	5.9/5.9			0/0/0	Metamifop (including kadethrin, isoxadifen ethyletoxazole, clomazone, pinoxaden)
0/0/0	0	0	0/0	0/0/0	0/0	0//0	0/0/	5.9/5.9/5.9	5.9/5.9			0/0/0	Methylmirex, tenocycline, diethylthiazide, dimethylthiazide, butyl paraben, ethylthiazide, furotidine, levomalamine, malalamine intermediate, meperidine, Phenone, racemic malalamine, and their salts; Methylenedioxypyrrolidone (CAS No.: 687603－66－3)
0/0/0	0	0	0/0	0/0/0	0/0	0//0	0/0/	5.9/5.9/5.9	5.9/5.9			0/0/0	Anticancer drug raw materials (furaquinib)
0/0/0	0	0	0/0	0/0/0	0/0	0//0	0/0/	5.9/5.9/5.9	5.9/5.9			0/0/0	Decitabine, fluorouridine, cyclophosphamide, gefitinib, capecitabine, raltitrexed, fludarabine phosphate, tegafur, cytarabine hydrochloride, gemcitabine hydrochloride, acetic acid hydrochloride Tinglitin, Ifosfamide and Other Anticancer Drugs
0/0/0	0	0	0/0	0/0/0	0/0	0//0	0/0/	5.9/5.9/5.9	5.9/5.9			0/0/0	Other heterocyclic compounds(tax number of Separating anti－cancer pharmaceutical raw materials)
													Sulphonamides:
0/0/0	0	0	2.7/2.7	0/0/0	0/0	0//0	0/0/	0/0/0	5.9/0			0/0/0	-N-Methylperfluorooctane sulphonamide
0/0/0	0	0	2.7/2.7	0/0/0	0/0	0//0	0/0/	0/0/0	5.9/0			0/0/0	-N-Ethylperfluorooctane sulphonamide
0/0/0	0	0	2.7/2.7	0/0/0	0/0	0//0	0/0/	0/0/0	5.9/0			0/0/0	-N-Ethyl-N- (2-*hydroxyethyl*) perfluorooctane sulphonamide
0/0/0	0	0	2.7/2.7	0/0/0	0/0	0//0	0/0/	0/0/0	5.9/0			0/0/0	-N-(2-*Hydroxyethyl*) -N-methylperfluorooctane sulphonamide
0/0/0	0	0	2.7/2.7	0/0/0	0/0	0//0	0/0/	0/0/0	5.9/0			0/0/0	-Other perfluorooctane sulphonamides
													-Other
0/0/0	0	0	2.7/2.7	0/0/0	0/0	0//0	0/0/	0/0/0	5.9/0			0/0/0	Flucarbazone, flucetosulfuron, sulfosulfuron, cloransulammethy etc(including formamide-sulfometuron, ethoxysulfuron, chlorsulfuron, metsulfuron-methyl, tribenuronmethyl, ethametsulfuron-methyl)
0/0/0	0	0	2.7/2.7	0/0/0	0/0	0//0	0/0/	0/0/0	5.9/0			0/0/0	Triasulfuron, thifensulfuron-methyl, cinosulfuron, flupyrsulfuron-methyl-sodium etc(including triflusulfuronmethyl, prosulfuron, sulfometuron-methyl, chlorimuron-ethyl, primisulfuron-methy)
0/0/0	0	0	2.7/2.7	0/0/0	0/0	0//0	0/0/	0/0/0	5.9/0			0/0/0	Bensulfuron-methyl, pyrazosulfuron-ethyl, nicosulfuron, diclosulam etc(including flazasulfuron, rimsulfuron, imazosulfuron)
0/0/0	0	0	2.7/2.7	0/0/0	0/0	0//0	0/0/	0/0/0	5.9/0			0/0/0	Azimsulfuron, mazosulfuron, tritosulfuron etc.(including halosulfuron-methyl, amidosulfuron, cyclosulfamuron, esosulfuron-methyl)
0/0/0	0	0	2.7/2.7	0/0/0	0/0	0//0	0/0/	0/0/0	5.9/0			0/0/0	Mefluidide, sulfentrazone, orthosulfamuron etc. (including flumetsulam, florasulam, penoxsulam)
0/0/0	0	0	2.7/2.7	0/0/0	0/0	0//0	0/0/	0/0/0	5.9/0			0/0/0	Flusulfamethoxate, sulforaphane, indazolomide, etc. (including monosulfonate, sulforazolamide, trifluoridine Sulfuron methyl sodium salt, promethazine Sulfuron methyl, Monosulfuron methyl, fluketosulfoxamide, zinpyrazosulfuron methyl)
0/0/0	0	0	2.7/2.7	0/0/0	0/0	0//0	0/0/	0/0/0	5.9/0			0/0/0	Mcsyl (mcthyl) caramoylmcthyla minome thyl phosphonic acid, oryzalin, trifloxysulfuron, pyroxsulam etc. (including iodosulfuron methyl sodium)
0/0/0	0	0	2.7/2.7	0/0/0	0/0	0//0	0/0/	0/0/0	5.9/0			0/0/0	Flusulfamide, fluoridamid etc.(including toly- lfluanid, sulfluramid)
0/0/0	0	0	2.7/2.7	0/0/0	0/0	0//0	0/0/	0/0/0	5.9/0			0/0/0	Cythioate, famphur(ESA), bensulide etc.(including methasulfocarb, cyazofamid)
0/0/0	0	0	2.7/2.7	0/0/0	0/0	0//0	0/0/	0/0/0	5.9/0			0/0/0	Oxasulfuron
0/0/0	0	0	2.7/2.7	0/0/0	0/0	0//0	0/0/	0/0/0	5.9/0			0/0/0	Saflufenacil
0/0/0	0	0	2.7/2.7	0/0/0	0/0	0//0	0/0/	0/0/0	5.9/0			0/0/0	Thiencarbazone-methyl
0/0/0	0	0	2.7/2.7	0/0/0	0/0	0//0	0/0/	0/0/0	5.9/0			0/0/0	Sulphadiazine
0/0/0	0	0	2.7/2.7	0/0/0	0/0	0//0	0/0/	0/0/0	5.9/0			0/0/0	Sulfadimidine
0/0/0	0	0	2.7/2.7	0/0/0	0/0	0//0	0/0/	0/0/0	5.9/0			0/0/0	Sulfamethoxazole
0/0/0	0	0	2.7/2.7	0/0/0	0/0	0//0	0/0/	0/0/0	5.9/0		//	0/0/0	Bosentan
0/0/0	0	0	2.7/2.7	0/0/0	0/0	0//0	0/0/	0/0/0	5.9/0			0/0/0	Other sulphonamides
													Ⅺ. PROVITAMINS, VITAMINS AND HORMONES
													Provitamins and vitamins, natural or reproduced by synthesis (including natural concentrates), derivatives thereof used primarily as vitamins, and intermixtures of the foregoing, whether or not in any solvent:
													-Vitamins and their derivatives, unmixed:
0/0/0	0	0	1.7/1.7	0/0/0	0/0	0//0	0/0/	0/0/0	3.6/0			0/0/0	--Vitamins A and their derivatives

税则号列	货品名称〔CIQ 扩展编码及品名－T2 表示见附表 2〕	最惠(%)	暂定税率	普通	增值/消费	出口退税	计量单位	监管条件/特殊证件	检验检疫	对美关税	亚太上/下
2936.2200	--维生素 B_1 及其衍生物〔101 饲料添加剂,301 维生素 B1,302 盐酸硫胺素,303 需申报仅用于工业用途不用于食品添加剂无检疫要求的化学品〕	4		20	13/	13	千克	A/1	R	29	
2936.2300	--维生素 B_2 及其衍生物〔101 饲料添加剂,301 维生素 B2,302 核黄素 5′—磷酸钠,303 需申报仅用于工业用途不用于食品添加剂无检疫要求的化学品〕	4		20	13/	13	千克	A/1	R	29	
2936.2400	--D 或 DL-泛酸(维生素 B_5)及其衍生物[T2]	4		20	13/	13	千克	A/1	R	29	
2936.2500	--维生素 B_6 及其衍生物〔101 饲料添加剂,301 维生素 B6,302 需申报仅用于工业用途不用于食品添加剂无检疫要求的化学品〕	4		20	13/	13	千克	A/1	R	24	
2936.2600	--维生素 B_{12} 及其衍生物〔101 饲料添加剂,301 维生素 B12(氰钴铵或羟钴铵),302 氰钴胺,303 需申报仅用于工业用途不用于食品添加剂无检疫要求的化学品〕	4		20	13/	13	千克	A/1	R	29	
2936.2700	--维生素 C 及其衍生物										
2936.2700 10	未混合的维生素 C 原粉(不论是否溶于溶剂)〔301 无检疫要求食品添加剂,302 需申报仅用于工业用途不用于食品添加剂无检疫要求的化学品〕	4		20	13/	13	千克	A/1	R	24	
2936.2700 20	未混合的维生素 C 钙、维生素 C 钠(不论是否溶于溶剂)[T2]	4		20	13/	13	千克	A/1	R	24	
2936.2700 30	颗粒或包衣维生素 C(不论是否溶于溶剂)[T2]	4		20	13/	13	千克	A/1	R	24	
2936.2700 90	维生素 C 酯类及其他(不论是否溶于溶剂)[T2]	4		20	13/	13	千克	A/1	R	24	
2936.2800	--维生素 E 及其衍生物[T2]	4		20	13/	13	千克	A/1	R	14	
2936.2900	--其他维生素及其衍生物〔101 饲料添加剂,301 生物素(无检疫要求食品添加剂),302 维生素 D(无检疫要求食品添加剂),303 维生素 B 族(无检疫要求食品添加剂),304 维生素 k(植物甲萘醌)(无检疫要求食品添加剂),305 需申报仅用于工业用途不用于食品添加剂无检疫要求的化学品〕	4		20	13/	13	千克	A/1	R	14	
	-其他,包括天然浓缩物:										
2936.9010	---维生素 AD_3〔101 饲料添加剂,102 保健食品,103 无检疫要求食品添加剂〕	4		20	13/	13	千克	A/1	R		
2936.9090	---其他〔101 饲料添加剂,102 保健食品,301 叶酸(无检疫要求食品添加剂),302 需申报仅用于工业用途不用于食品添加剂无检疫要求的化学品〕	4		20	13/	13	千克	A/1	R	14	
29.37	**天然或合成再制的激素、前列腺素、血栓烷、白细胞三烯及其衍生物和结构类似物,包括主要用作激素的改性链多肽:**										
	-多肽激素、蛋白激素、糖蛋白激素及其衍生物和结构类似物:										
2937.1100	--生长激素及其衍生物和结构类似物										
2937.1100 10	生长激素(GH)〔999〕	4		20	13/	13	千克	L/1			
2937.1100 20	其他《兴奋剂目录》所列商品〔999〕	4		20	13/	13	千克	L/1			
2937.1100 90	生长激素的衍生物和结构类似物〔999〕	4		20	13/	13	千克	L/1			
	--胰岛素及其盐:										
2937.1210	---重组人胰岛素及其盐〔999〕	4	0	20	13/	13	千克	L/1			
2937.1290	---其他〔999〕	4	0	20	13/	13	千克	L/1		25	
2937.1900	--其他										
2937.1900 13	绒促性素、促黄体生成素等(包括生长激素释放肽类(GH-RPs)、普拉莫瑞林(生长激素释放肽－2)、CJC－1295(CAS 号 863288340)、生长激素释放肽－6、生长激素释放激素及其类似物、生长激素促分泌剂)〔999〕	4		20	13/	13	千克	L/1		29	
2937.1900 15	促皮质素类等肽类激素(包括艾瑞莫瑞林、布舍瑞林、可的瑞林、海沙瑞林、伊莫瑞林、舍莫瑞林、替莫瑞林、戈那瑞林、葛瑞林(脑肠肽)及葛瑞林模拟物类)〔999〕	4		20	13/	13	千克	L/1		29	
2937.1900 16	亮丙瑞林〔999〕	4		20	13/	13	千克	L/1		29	
2937.1900 17	其他《兴奋剂目录》所列商品〔999〕	4		20	13/	13	千克	L/1		29	
2937.1900 91	醋酸曲普瑞林〔999〕	4	0	20	3/	13	千克	L/1		25	
2937.1900 93	卵泡抑素〔999〕	4		20	13/	13	千克	L/1		29	
2937.1900 99	其他多肽激素及衍生物和结构类似物(包括蛋白激素、糖蛋白激素及其衍生物和结构类似物)〔301 其他化工产品,401 其他医用生物制品〕	4		20	13/	13	千克	Q/1		29	
	-甾族激素及其衍生物和结构类似物:										
2937.2100	--可的松、氢化可的松、脱氢可的松及脱氢皮质醇〔999〕	4		20	13/	13	千克	Q/1			
	--皮质(甾)类激素的卤化衍生物:										
2937.2210	---地塞米松〔999〕	4		30	13/	13	千克	Q/1			

协定税率 %								RCEP		特惠税率 %			Article Description
东/冰/格	巴基斯坦	韩国	瑞士上/下	哥/秘/柬	澳/毛	新西/坡/智	中国港/澳/台	东盟及马来/澳/韩	日/新	亚太2国	老/柬/缅	98/97/95	
0/0/0	0	0	0/0	0/0/0	0/0	0//0	0/0/	0/0/0	0/0			0/0/0	--Vitamin B_1 and its derivatives
0/0/0	0	0	0/0	0/0/0	0/0	0//0	0/0/	0/0/0	0/0			0/0/0	--Vitamin B_2 and its derivatives
0/0/0	0	0	0/0	0/0/0	0/0	0//0	0/0/	0/0/0	0/0			0/0/0	--D-or DL-Pantothenic acid (Vitamin B_5) and its derivatives
0/0/0	0	0	0/0	0/0/0	0/0	0//0	0/0/	0/0/0	0/0			0/0/0	--Vitamin B_6 and its derivatives
0/0/0	0	0	0.4/0.4	0/0/0	0/0	0//0	0/0/	0/0/0	3.6/0			0/0/0	--Vitamin B_{12} and its derivatives
													--Vitamin C and its derivatives
0/0/0	0	0	0/0	0/0/0	0/0	0//0	0/0/	0/0/0	0/0			0/0/0	Not mixed vitamin C of original powder(whether or not in any solvent)
0/0/0	0	0	0/0	0/0/0	0/0	0//0	0/0/	0/0/0	0/0			0/0/0	Not mixed Calcium ascorbate, odiumascorbate(whether or not in orny solvent)
0/0/0	0	0	0/0	0/0/0	0/0	0//0	0/0/	0/0/0	0/0			0/0/0	Particles or coated vitamin C(whether or not in any solvent)
0/0/0	0	0	0/0	0/0/0	0/0	0//0	0/0/	0/0/0	0/0			0/0/0	vitamin c of ester and other(whether or not in any solvent)
0/0/0	0	0	0.4/0.4	0/0/0	0/0	0//0	0/0/	0/0/0	3.6/0			0/0/0	--Vitamin E and its derivatives
0/0/0	0	0	0.4/0.4	0/0/0	0/0	0//0	0/0/	0/0/0	3.6/0			0/0/0	--Other vitamins and their deriratives
													-Other, including natural concentrates:
0/0/0	0	0	0/0	0/0/0	0/0	0//0	0/0/	0/0/0	3.6/0			0/0/0	---Vitamin AD3
0/0/0	0	0	0/0	0/0/0	0/0	0//0	0/0/	0/0/0	3.6/0			0/0/0	---Other
													Hormones, prostaglandins, thromboxanes and leukotrienes, natural or reproduced by synthesis; derivatives and structural analogues thereof, including chain modified polypeptides, used primarily as hormones:
													-Polypeptide hormones, protein hormones and glycoprotein hormones, their derivatives and structural analogues:
													--Somatotropin, its derivatives and structural analogues
0/0/0	0	0	0/0	0/0/0	0/0	0//0	0/0/	0/0/0	0/0			0/0/0	Growth hormone(GH)
0/0/0	0	0	0/0	0/0/0	0/0	0//0	0/0/	0/0/0	0/0		//	0/0/0	List of other stimulants
0/0/0	0	0	0/0	0/0/0	0/0	0//0	0/0/	0/0/0	0/0			0/0/0	Growth hormone derivatives and structural analogues
													--Insulin and its salts:
0/0/0	0	0	0/0	0/0/0	0/0	0//0	0/0/	0/0/0	0/0			0/0/0	---Recombinant human insulin and its salts
0/0/0	0	0	0/0	0/0/0	0/0	0//0	0/0/	0/0/0	0/0			0/0/0	---Other
													--Other
0/0/0	0	0	0.4/0.4	0/0/0	0/0	0//0	0/0/	0/0/0	3.6/0			0/0/0	HCG and luteinizing hormone[Including growth hormone releasing peptide (GHRPs), Plummer Relin (growth hormone releasing peptide -2), CJC-1295 (CAS No. 863288-34-0), growth hormone releasing peptide -6, growth hormone releasing hormone and its analogues, growth hormone secretagogue]
0/0/0	0	0	0.4/0.4	0/0/0	0/0	0//0	0/0/	0/0/0	3.6/0			0/0/0	Peptide hormones such as corticotropins (including iremorrilin, busereliin, keterellin, hesarellin, imorelin, shererellin, temerellin, gonarellin, grielin (brain gut peptide) and grielin simulants)
0/0/0	0	0	0.4/0.4	0/0/0	0/0	0//0	0/0/	0/0/0	3.6/0			0/0/0	Light c gonadorelin
0/0/0	0	0	0.4/0.4	0/0/0	0/0	0//0	0/0/	0/0/0	3.6/0		//	0/0/0	List of other stimulants
0/0/0	0	0	0.4/0.4	0/0/0	0/0	0//0	0/0/	0/0/0	3.6/0			0/0/0	Trichoretin acetate and other anticancer medicines
0/0/0	0	0	0.4/0.4	0/0/0	0/0	0//0	0/0/	0/0/0	3.6/0		//	0/0/0	follistatin
0/0/0	0	0	0.4/0.4	0/0/0	0/0	0//0	0/0/	0/0/0	3.6/0			0/0/0	Other polypeptide hormones and derivatives and structural analogues (including protein hormones, glycoprotein hormones and their derivatives and structural analogues)(tax number of Separating anti—cancer pharmaceutical raw materials)
													-Steroidal hormones, their derivatives and structural analogues:
0/0/0	0	0	0/0	0/0/0	0/0	0//0	0/0/	0/0/0	0/0			0/0/0	--Cortisone, hydrocortisone, prednisone(dehydrocortisone) and prednisolone(dehydrohydrocortisone)
													--Halogenated derivatives of corticosteroidal hormones:
0/0/0	0	0	0/0	0/0/0	0/0	0//0	0/0/	0/0/0	0/0			0/0/0	---Dexamethasone

税则号列	货品名称〔CIQ 扩展编码及品名－T2 表示见附表 2〕	最惠(%)	暂定税率	普通	增值/消费	出口退税	计量单位	监管条件/特殊证件	检验检疫	对美关税	亚太上/下
2937.2290	---其他〔999〕	4		30	13/	13	千克	Q/1		29	
	--雌(甾)激素和孕激素：										
	---动物源的：										
2937.2311	----孕马结合雌激素〔999〕	4		30	13/	13	千克	Q/1			
2937.2319	----其他										
2937.2319 10	福美坦〔999〕	4	0	30	3/	13	千克	Q/1			
2937.2319 90	其他动物源雌(甾)激素和孕激素〔999〕	4		30	13/	13	千克	Q/1			
2937.2390	---其他										
2937.2390 10	泽仑诺;孕三烯酮;替勃龙(包括四氢孕三烯酮)〔999〕	4		30	13/	13	千克	L/1		29	
2937.2390 90	其他雌(甾)激素及孕激素〔999〕	4		30	13/	13	千克	Q/1		29	
2937.2900	--其他										
2937.2900 11	1－雄烯二醇;1－雄烯二酮(包括雄甾－4－烯－3β, 17α－二醇(4－雄烯二醇(3β, 17α));雄甾－5－烯－3β, 17α－二醇(5－雄烯二醇(3β, 17α))〔999〕	4		30	13/	13	千克	L/1		29	
2937.2900 12	4－雄烯二醇;5－雄烯二酮(包括 5α－雄烷－3α,17β－二醇(雄烷二醇(3α,17β));5α－雄烷－3β,17α－二醇(雄烷二醇(3β,17α));勃拉睾酮;5β－雄烷－3α,17β－二醇(5β－雄烷二醇(3α,17β)))〔999〕	4		30	13/	13	千克	L/1		29	
2937.2900 13	勃地酮;卡芦睾酮(包括氯司替勃;甲基氯司替勃)〔999〕	4		30	13/	13	千克	L/1		29	
2937.2900 14	达那唑;去氢氯甲睾酮(包括普拉睾酮;去氧甲睾酮)〔999〕	4		30	13/	13	千克	L/1		29	
2937.2900 15	双氢睾酮;屈他雄酮(包括表双氢睾酮;乙雌烯醇;氟甲睾酮;甲酰勃龙)〔999〕	4		30	13/	13	千克	L/1		29	
2937.2900 16	夫拉扎勃(包括 4 －羟基睾酮)〔999〕	4		30	13/	13	千克	L/1		29	
2937.2900 17	美雄诺龙;美睾酮;美雄酮(包括甲基屈他雄酮)〔999〕	4		30	13/	13	千克	L/1		29	
2937.2900 18	甲基-1-睾酮;甲睾酮;甲诺睾酮(包括甲二烯诺龙;去甲雄酮)〔999〕	4		30	13/	13	千克	L/1		29	
2937.2900 19	美替诺龙;美雄醇(包括美曲勃龙)〔999〕	4		30	13/	13	千克	L/1		29	
2937.2900 21	米勃酮;诺龙;诺勃酮;诺司替勃(包括 19-去甲雄烯二醇;诺乙雄龙)〔999〕	4		30	13/	13	千克	L/1		29	
2937.2900 22	19－去甲本胆烷醇酮(包括羟勃龙;氧雄龙)	4		30	13/	13	千克	L/1		29	
2937.2900 23	羟甲睾酮;羟甲烯龙(包括前列他唑)〔999〕	4		30	13/	13	千克	L/1		29	
2937.2900 24	奎勃龙;司坦唑醇;司腾勃龙(包括 1-睾酮;睾酮;群勃龙)〔999〕	4		30	13/	13	千克	L/1		29	
2937.2900 25	7α-羟基-普拉睾酮〔999〕	4		30	13/	13	千克	L/1		29	
2937.2900 26	7β-羟基-普拉睾酮〔999〕	4		30	13/	13	千克	L/1		29	
2937.2900 27	7-羰基-普拉睾酮〔999〕	4		30	13/	13	千克	L/1		29	
2937.2900 28	胆烷醇酮〔999〕	4		30	13/	13	千克	L/1		29	
2937.2900 31	雄甾－5－烯－3β,17β－二醇(5－雄烯二醇(3β, 17β))〔999〕	4		30	13/	13	千克	L/1		29	
2937.2900 32	雄甾－4－烯－3,17－二酮(4－雄烯二酮)〔999〕	4		30	13/	13	千克	L/1		29	
2937.2900 34	雄酮〔999〕	4		30	13/	13	千克	L/1		29	
2937.2900 35	1,4－雄烯二酮(雄甾－1,4－二烯－3,17 －二酮)〔999〕	4		30	13/	13	千克	L/1		29	
2937.2900 36	其他《兴奋剂目录》所列商品〔999〕	4		30	13/	13	千克	L/1		29	
2937.2900 91	依西美坦〔999〕	4	0	30	3/	13	千克	Q/1		25	
2937.2900 99	其他甾类激素及其衍生物和结构类似物〔999〕	4		30	13/	13	千克	Q/1		29	
2937.5000	-前列腺素、血栓烷和白细胞三烯及其衍生物和结构类似物〔999〕	4		30	13/	13	千克	/1		29	
2937.9000	-其他										
2937.9000 10	氨基酸衍生物〔999〕	4		30	13/	13	千克	AQ/13	R	9	
2937.9000 11	马昔瑞林	4		30	13/	13	千克	L/13		9	
2937.9000 90	其他激素及其衍生物和结构类似物〔301 危险化学品,毒性物质;302 其他化工品〕	4		30	13/	13	千克	Q/13		9	
	第十二分章　天然或合成再制的苷(配糖物)、生物碱及其盐、醚、酯和其他衍生物										
29.38	**天然或合成再制的苷(配糖物)及其盐、醚、酯和其他衍生物：**										
2938.1000	-芸香苷芦丁及其衍生物〔999〕	6.5		20	13/	13	千克	Q/1			
	-其他：										
2938.9010	---齐多夫定、拉米夫定、司他夫定、地达诺新及它们的盐〔999〕	6.5		20	13/	13	千克	/1			
2938.9090	---其他										

协定税率 %								RCEP		特惠税率 %			Article Description
东/冰/格	巴基斯坦	韩国	瑞士 上/下	哥/秘/柬	澳/毛	新西/坡/智	中国港/澳/台	东盟及马来/澳/韩	日/新	亚太2国	老/柬/缅	98/97/95	
0/0/0	0	0	0/0	0/0/0	0/0	0//0	0/0/	0/0/0	0/0			0/0/0	---Other
													--Oestrogens and progestogens:
													---Of animals:
0/0/0	0	0	0/0	0/0/0	0/0	0//0	0/0/	0/0/0	0/0			0/0/0	----Pregnant mare conjugated estrogens
													----Other
0/0/0	0	0	0/0	0/0/0	0/0	0//0	0/0/	0/0/0	0/0			0/0/0	Formestane and Other Anticancer Drugs
0/0/0	0	0	0/0	0/0/0	0/0	0//0	0/0/	0/0/0	0/0			0/0/0	Other animal sources of estrogen and progesterone(tax number of Separating anti—cancer pharmaceutical raw materials)
													---Other
0/0/0	0	0	0/0	0/0/0	0/0	0//0	0/0/	0/0/0	0/0			0/0/0	Zearalanol, gestrinone, tibolone (including tetrahydrogestrinone)
0/0/0	0	0	0/0	0/0/0	0/0	0//0	0/0/	0/0/0	0/0		//	0/0/0	Other estrogen (steroid) hormones and progesterone
													--Other
0/0/0	0	0	0/0	0/0/0	0/0	0//0	0/0/	0/0/0	0/0			0/0/0	1- androstenediol; 1- androstene two ketone (including androst -4- allyl -3 β, 17 α - glycol; androst -5- allyl -3 β, 17 α - gly
0/0/0	0	0	0/0	0/0/0	0/0	0//0	0/0/	0/0/0	0/0			0/0/0	Including 5 α - androstane -3 α, 17 β - estradiol; 5 α - androstane -3 β, 17 α - glycol; bolas
0/0/0	0	0	0/0	0/0/0	0/0	0//0	0/0/	0/0/0	0/0			0/0/0	Boldenone;calusterone(including clostebol) Boldenone,calusterone(including 1,4-amdrostodiene-3;17-dione;clostebol)
0/0/0	0	0	0/0	0/0/0	0/0	0//0	0/0/	0/0/0	0/0			0/0/0	Danazol; dehydrochloromethy (including prasterone; desoxymethyl-testosterone)
0/0/0	0	0	0/0	0/0/0	0/0	0//0	0/0/	0/0/0	0/0			0/0/0	Dihydrotestosterone;drostanolone (including epi-dihydrotestosterone ;ethylestrenol ;fluoxymesterone ,formebolone)
0/0/0	0	0	0/0	0/0/0	0/0	0//0	0/0/	0/0/0	0/0			0/0/0	Frazab (including 4—hydroxytestosterone)
0/0/0	0	0	0/0	0/0/0	0/0	0//0	0/0/	0/0/0	0/0			0/0/0	Mestanolone; mesterolone; methandienone (including methyl drostanolone)
0/0/0	0	0	0/0	0/0/0	0/0	0//0	0/0/	0/0/0	0/0			0/0/0	Methyl-1-testosterone, methyltestosterone; Kanok testosterone(including diene nandrolone;19-norandrosterone)
0/0/0	0	0	0/0	0/0/0	0/0	0//0	0/0/	0/0/0	0/0			0/0/0	Methenolone; methandriol(including methyltrienolone)
0/0/0	0	0	0/0	0/0/0	0/0	0//0	0/0/	0/0/0	0/0			0/0/0	Mibolerone;nandrolone;norbolethone;norclostebol (including 19-norandrostenediol, norethandrolone)
0/0/0	0	0	0/0	0/0/0	0/0	0//0	0/0/	0/0/0	0/0			0/0/0	19-noretiocholanolone(including oxandrolone;oxymesterone)
0/0/0	0	0	0/0	0/0/0	0/0	0//0	0/0/	0/0/0	0/0			0/0/0	Oxymesterone,oxymetholone(including prostanozol)
0/0/0	0	0	0/0	0/0/0	0/0	0//0	0/0/	0/0/0	0/0			0/0/0	Quinbolone ,stanozolol,stenbolone(including 1-testosterone, testosterone,trenbolone)
0/0/0	0	0	0/0	0/0/0	0/0	0//0	0/0/	0/0/0	0/0			0/0/0	7α-Hydroxy-DHEA
0/0/0	0	0	0/0	0/0/0	0/0	0//0	0/0/	0/0/0	0/0			0/0/0	7β-Hydroxy-DHEA
0/0/0	0	0	0/0	0/0/0	0/0	0//0	0/0/	0/0/0	0/0			0/0/0	7-Keto-prasterone
0/0/0	0	0	0/0	0/0/0	0/0	0//0	0/0/	0/0/0	0/0			0/0/0	Androstane
0/0/0	0	0	0/0	0/0/0	0/0	0//0	0/0/	0/0/0	0/0			0/0/0	Androst -5- allyl -3 β, 17 β - estradi
0/0/0	0	0	0/0	0/0/0	0/0	0//0	0/0/	0/0/0	0/0			0/0/0	Androst -4- allyl -3,17- two ketone
0/0/0	0	0	0/0	0/0/0	0/0	0//0	0/0/	0/0/0	0/0			0/0/0	androsterone
0/0/0	0	0	0/0	0/0/0	0/0	0//0	0/0/	0/0/0	0/0		//	0/0/0	1,4—androstenedione (androsterone—1,4—diene—3,17—dione)
0/0/0	0	0	0/0	0/0/0	0/0	0//0	0/0/	0/0/0	0/0		//	0/0/0	List of other stimulants
0/0/0	0	0	0/0	0/0/0	0/0	0//0	0/0/	0/0/0	0/0			0/0/0	Exemestane and Other Anticancer Drugs
0/0/0	0	0	0/0	0/0/0	0/0	0//0	0/0/	0/0/0	0/0			0/0/0	Other somatotropin and their derivatives and structural analogs(tax number of Separating anti—cancer pharmaceutical raw materials)
0/0/0	0	0	0/0	0/0/0	0/0	0//0	0/0/	0/0/0	0/0			0/0/0	-Prostaglandins, thromboxanes and leukotrienes, their derivatives and structural analogues
													-Other
0/0/0	0	0	0/0	0/0/0	0/0	0//0	0/0/	0/0/0	0/0			0/0/0	Amino-acid dervatives
0/0/0	0	0	0/0	0/0/0	0/0	0//0	0/0/	0/0/0	0/0		//	0/0/0	Ma Xiruilin
0/0/0	0	0	0/0	0/0/0	0/0	0//0	0/0/	0/0/0	0/0			0/0/0	Other hormone its derivatives and structural analogues
													Ⅺ. GLYCOSIDES AND VEGETABLE ALKALOIDS, NATURAL OR REPRODUCED BY SYNTHESIS, AND THEIR SALTS, ETHERS, ESTERS AND OTHER DERIVATIVES
													Glycosides, natural or reproduced by synthesis, and their salts, ethers, esters and other derivatives:
0/0/0	5	0	0/0	0/0/0	0/0	0//0	0/0/	0/0/0	5.9/0			0/0/0	-Rutoside (rutin) and its derivatives
													-Other:
0/0/0	5	0	0/0	0/0/0	0/0	0//0	0/0/	0/0/0	5.9/0			0/0/0	---Zidovudine, lamivudine, Stavudine, didanosine and their salts
													---Other

税则号列		货品名称〔CIQ 扩展编码及品名－T2 表示见附表 2〕	最惠(%)	暂定税率	普通	增值/消费	出口退税	计量单位	监管条件/特殊证件	检验检疫	对美关税	亚太上/下
2938.9090	10	甘草酸粉〔999〕	6.5	3	20	13/	13	千克	y4x/13		28	
2938.9090	20	甘草酸盐类〔301 需申报仅用于工业用途不用于食品添加剂无检疫要求的化学品,302 无检疫要求食品添加剂〕	6.5		20	13/	13	千克	4Axy/13	R	31.5	
2938.9090	30	甘草次酸及其衍生物〔999〕	6.5		20	13/	13	千克	y4x/13		31.5	
2938.9090	40	其他甘草酸〔999〕	6.5	3	20	13/	13	千克	4/13		28	
2938.9090	90	其他天然或合成再制的苷及其盐等(包括醚、酯和其他衍生物)〔301 危险化学品,毒性物质;302 危险化学品,杂项物质;303 其他化工品,不用作食品添加剂;304 其他化工品,用作食品添加剂〕	6.5		20	13/	13	千克	/13		31.5	
29.39		**天然或合成再制的生物碱及其盐、醚、酯和其他衍生物:**										
		-鸦片碱及其衍生物,以及它们的盐:										
2939.1100		--罂粟秆浓缩物、丁丙诺啡(INN)、可待因、双氢可待因(INN)、乙基吗啡、埃托啡(INN)、海洛因、氢可酮(INN)、氢吗啡酮(INN)、吗啡、尼可吗啡(INN)、羟考酮(INN)、羟吗啡酮(INN)、福尔可定(INN)、醋氢可酮(INN)及蒂巴因,以及它们的盐										
2939.1100	11	罂粟秆浓缩物〔999〕	4		50	13/	13	千克	I/1		24	
2939.1100	12	可待因、双氢可待因、乙基吗啡(以及它们的盐)〔999〕	4		50	13/	13	千克	I/1		24	
2939.1100	13	埃托啡、海洛因、氢可酮(以及它们的盐)〔999〕	4		50	13/	13	千克	I/1		24	
2939.1100	14	氢吗啡酮、吗啡、尼可吗啡(以及它们的盐)〔999〕	4		50	13/	13	千克	I/1		24	
2939.1100	15	羟考酮、羟吗啡酮、福尔可定(以及它们的盐)〔999〕	4		50	13/	13	千克	I/1		24	
2939.1100	16	醋氢可酮、蒂巴因(以及它们的盐)〔999〕	4		50	13/	13	千克	I/1		24	
2939.1100	20	丁丙诺啡及其盐〔999〕	4		50	13/	13	千克	I/1		24	
2939.1900		--其他										
2939.1900	10	二氢埃托啡及其盐〔999〕	4		50	13/	13	千克	I/1		29	
2939.1900	21	苄吗啡、可多克辛、地索吗啡、酯托啡(以及它们的盐)〔999〕	4		50	13/	13	千克	I/1		29	
2939.1900	22	双氢吗啡、氢吗啡醇、甲地索啡、甲二氢吗啡(以及它们的盐)〔999〕	4		50	13/	13	千克	I/1		29	
2939.1900	23	美托酮、吗啡-N-氧化物、麦罗啡、去甲吗啡(以及它们的盐)〔999〕	4		50	13/	13	千克	I/1		29	
2939.1900	24	醋氢可待因、尼可待因、尼二氢可待因、去甲可待因(以及它们的盐)〔999〕	4		50	13/	13	千克	I/1		29	
2939.1900	25	吗啡甲溴化物及其盐〔999〕	4		50	13/	13	千克	I/1		29	
2939.1900	30	纳布啡及其盐〔999〕	4		50	13/	13	千克	I/1		29	
2939.1900	40	奥列巴文(Oripavine;CAS 号:467－04－9)〔999〕	4		50	13/	13	千克	I/1		29	
2939.1900	90	其他鸦片碱及其衍生物及它们的盐〔999〕	4		50	13/	13	千克	Q/1		29	
2939.2000		-金鸡纳生物碱及其衍生物以及它们的盐〔999〕	4		20	13/	13	千克	Q/1			
2939.3000		-咖啡因及其盐										
2939.3000	10	咖啡因〔301 无检疫要求食品添加剂,302 需申报仅用于工业用途不用于食品添加剂无检疫要求的化学品〕	4		20	13/	13	千克	AI/1	R	9	
2939.3000	90	咖啡因的盐〔301 需申报仅用于工业用途不用于食品添加剂无检疫要求的化学品,999 其他化工产品〕	4		20	13/	13	千克	AI/1	R	9	
		-麻黄生物碱及其衍生物,以及它们的盐:										
2939.4100		--麻黄碱及其盐										
2939.4100	10	麻黄碱(麻黄素,盐酸麻黄碱)〔999〕	4		20	13/	13	千克	23Q/1			
2939.4100	20	硫酸麻黄碱〔999〕	4		20	13/	13	千克	23Q/1			
2939.4100	30	消旋盐酸麻黄碱〔999〕	4		20	13/	13	千克	23Q/1			
2939.4100	40	草酸麻黄碱〔999〕	4		20	13/	13	千克	23Q/1			
2939.4100	90	麻黄碱盐〔999〕	4		20	13/	13	千克	Q/1			
2939.4200		--假麻黄碱(INN)及其盐										
2939.4200	10	伪麻黄碱(伪麻黄素、盐酸伪麻黄碱)〔999〕	4		20	13/	13	千克	23Q/1		9	
2939.4200	20	硫酸伪麻黄碱〔999〕	4		20	13/	13	千克	23Q/1		9	
2939.4200	90	假麻黄碱盐(D-2-甲胺基-1-苯基丙醇)〔999〕	4		20	13/	13	千克	Q/1		9	
2939.4300		--d-去甲假麻黄碱(INN)及其盐〔999〕	4		20	13/	13	千克	I/1			
2939.4400		--去甲麻黄碱及其盐〔999〕	4		20	13/	13	千克	23/1			
2939.4500		--左甲苯丙胺、去氧麻黄碱(INN)、去氧麻黄碱外消旋体以及它们的盐〔999〕	4		20	13/	13	千克	I/1		9	
2939.4900		--其他										
2939.4900	10	盐酸甲基麻黄碱〔999〕	4		20	13/	13	千克	Q23/1			
2939.4900	20	消旋盐酸甲基麻黄碱〔999〕	4		20	13/	13	千克	Q23/1			

协定税率 %								RCEP		特惠税率 %			Article Description
东/冰/格	巴基斯坦	韩国	瑞士上/下	哥/秘/柬	澳/毛	新西/坡/智	中国港/澳/台	东盟及马来/澳/韩	日/新	亚太2国	老/柬/缅	98/97/95	
0/0/0	5	0	0/0	0/0/0	0/0	0//0	0/0/	0/0/0	5.9/0			0/0/0	Glycyrrhizic acid powder
0/0/0	5	0	0/0	0/0/0	0/0	0//0	0/0/	0/0/0	5.9/0			0/0/0	Salts of glycyrrhizic acid
0/0/0	5	0	0/0	0/0/0	0/0	0//0	0/0/	0/0/0	5.9/0			0/0/0	Glycyrrhetic acid and its derivatives
0/0/0	5	0	0/0	0/0/0	0/0	0//0	0/0/	0/0/0	5.9/0		//	0/0/0	Other glycyrrhizic acid
0/0/0	5	0	0/0	0/0/0	0/0	0//0	0/0/	0/0/0	5.9/0			0/0/0	Other glycosides, natural or reproduced by synthesis, and their salts, ethers, esters and other derivatives
													Vegetable alkaloids, natural or reproduced by synthesis, and their salts, ethers, esters and other derivatives:
													-Alkaloids of opium and their derivatives; salts thereof:
													--Concentrates of poppy straw; buprenorphine(INN), codeine, dihydrocodeine (INN), ethylmorphine, etorphine (INN), heroin, hydrocodone (INN), hydromorphone (INN), morphine, nicomorphine (INN), oxycodone (INN), oxymorphone(INN), pholcodine(INN), thebacon (INN) and thebaine;salts thereof
0/0/0	0	0	0/0	0/0/0	0/0	0//0	0/0/	0/0/0	0/0			0/0/0	Concentrates of poppy straw
0/0/0	0	0	0/0	0/0/0	0/0	0//0	0/0/	0/0/0	0/0			0/0/0	Codeine, dihydrocodeine (INN), ethylmorphine (salts thereof)
0/0/0	0	0	0/0	0/0/0	0/0	0//0	0/0/	0/0/0	0/0			0/0/0	Etorphine(INN), heroin, hydrocodone(INN)(salts thereof)
0/0/0	0	0	0/0	0/0/0	0/0	0//0	0/0/	0/0/0	0/0			0/0/0	Hydromorphone (INN), morphine, nicomorphine (INN) (salts thereof)
0/0/0	0	0	0/0	0/0/0	0/0	0//0	0/0/	0/0/0	0/0			0/0/0	Oxycodone(INN), oxymorphone(INN), pholcodine(INN) (salts thereof)
0/0/0	0	0	0/0	0/0/0	0/0	0//0	0/0/	0/0/0	0/0			0/0/0	Thebacon(INN) and thebaine(salts thereof)
0/0/0	0	0	0/0	0/0/0	0/0	0//0	0/0/	0/0/0	0/0			0/0/0	Buprenorphine and salts thereof
													--Other
0/0/0	0	0	0/0	0/0/0	0/0	0//0	0/0/	0/0/0	0/0			0/0/0	Dihydroetorphine and its salts
0/0/0	0	0	0/0	0/0/0	0/0	0//0	0/0/	0/0/0	0/0			0/0/0	Benzylmorphine, codoxime, desomorphine, acteorphinp (and their salt)
0/0/0	0	0	0/0	0/0/0	0/0	0//0	0/0/	0/0/0	0/0			0/0/0	Dihydromorphine, hydromorphinol, methyldesorphine, methyldihydromorphine (and their salt)
0/0/0	0	0	0/0	0/0/0	0/0	0//0	0/0/	0/0/0	0/0			0/0/0	Metopon, morphine-N-oxide, myrophine, normorphine (and their salt)
0/0/0	0	0	0/0	0/0/0	0/0	0//0	0/0/	0/0/0	0/0			0/0/0	Acetyldihydrocodeine, nicocodine, nicomorphine, norcodeine (and their salt)
0/0/0	0	0	0/0	0/0/0	0/0	0//0	0/0/	0/0/0	0/0			0/0/0	Morphine methobromide and its salt
0/0/0	0	0	0/0	0/0/0	0/0	0//0	0/0/	0/0/0	0/0			0/0/0	Nalbuphine and its salt
0/0/0	0	0	0/0	0/0/0	0/0	0//0	0/0/	0/0/0	0/0			0/0/0	Oripavine(CAS:467-04-9)
0/0/0	0	0	0/0	0/0/0	0/0	0//0	0/0/	0/0/0	0/0			0/0/0	Other alkaloids of opium and their derivatives; salts thereof
0/0/0	0	0	0/0	0/0/0	0/0	0//0	0/0/	0/0/0	0/0			0/0/0	-Alkaloids of cinchona and their derivatives; salts thereof
													Caffeine and its salts
0/0/0	0	0	0/0	0/0/0	0/0	0//0	0/0/	0/0/0	0/0			0/0/0	Caffeine
0/0/0	0	0	0/0	0/0/0	0/0	0//0	0/0/	0/0/0	0/0			0/0/0	Salts of caffeine
													-Ephedrines and their salts:
													--Ephedra alkaloids and their derivatives, and their salts:
0/0/0	0	0	0/0	0/0/0	0/0	0//0	0/0/	0/0/0	0/0			0/0/0	Ephedrine (ephedrine,ephedrine-hydrochloride)
0/0/0	0	0	0/0	0/0/0	0/0	0//0	0/0/	0/0/0	0/0			0/0/0	Ephedrine sulfate
0/0/0	0	0	0/0	0/0/0	0/0	0//0	0/0/	0/0/0	0/0			0/0/0	Racephedrine hydrochloride
0/0/0	0	0	0/0	0/0/0	0/0	0//0	0/0/	0/0/0	0/0			0/0/0	Ephedrine oxalate
0/0/0	0	0	0/0	0/0/0	0/0	0//0	0/0/	0/0/0	0/0			0/0/0	Salts of ephedrine
													--Pseudoephedrine (INN) and its salts
0/0/0	0	0	0/0	0/0/0	0/0	0//0	0/0/	0/0/0	0/0			0/0/0	Pseudoephedrine(pseudoephedrine, pseudoephedrine hydrochloride)
0/0/0	0	0	0/0	0/0/0	0/0	0//0	0/0/	0/0/0	0/0			0/0/0	Pseudoephedrine sulfate
0/0/0	0	0	0/0	0/0/0	0/0	0//0	0/0/	0/0/0	0/0			0/0/0	Salts of pseudoephedrine (D-2-methylamino-1-phenylethyl carbinol)
0/0/0	0	0	0/0	0/0/0	0/0	0//0	0/0/	0/0/0	0/0			0/0/0	--d-Norpseudoephedrine and its salts
0/0/0	0	0	0/0	0/0/0	0/0	0//0	0/0/	0/0/0	0/0			0/0/0	--Norephedrine and its salts2939.4500 ——左甲苯丙胺、去氧麻黄碱(INN)、去氧麻黄碱外消旋体以及它们的盐
0/0/0	0	0	0/0	0/0/0	0/0	0//0	0/0/	0/0/0	0/0			0/0/0	--Levamphetamine, methamphetamine (inn), methamphetamine racemates and their salts
													--Other
0/0/0	0	0	0.1/0.1	0/0/0	0/0	0//0	0/0/	0/0/0	0/0			0/0/0	Methylephedrine hydrochloride
0/0/0	0	0	0.1/0.1	0/0/0	0/0	0//0	0/0/	0/0/0	0/0			0/0/0	DL-methylephedrine hydrochloride

税则号列	货品名称〔CIQ 扩展编码及品名－T2 表示见附表 2〕	最惠(%)	暂定税率	普通	增值/消费	出口退税	计量单位	监管条件/特殊证件	检验检疫	对美关税	亚太上/下
2939.4900 30	左甲苯丙胺、去氧麻黄碱、去氧麻黄碱外消旋体的其他衍生物(包括酯)〔999〕	4		20	13/	13	千克	I/1			
2939.4900 40	氯代麻黄碱〔999〕	4		20	13/	13	千克	23I/1			
2939.4900 91	其他麻黄生物碱及其盐〔999〕	4		20	13/	13	千克	Q/1			
2939.4900 99	其他麻黄生物碱衍生物,以及它们的盐〔999〕	4		20	13/	13	千克	ABQ/1	MRN		
	-茶碱和氨茶碱及其衍生物以及它们的盐:										
2939.5100	--芬乙茶碱(INN)及其盐〔999〕	4		20	13/	13	千克	I/1			
2939.5900	--其他〔999〕	4		20	13/	13	千克	Q/1			
	-麦角生物碱及其衍生物以及它们的盐:										
2939.6100	--麦角新碱(INN)及其盐										
2939.6100 10	麦角新碱(INN)〔999〕	4		20	13/	13	千克	3Q2/1			
2939.6100 90	麦角新碱盐(INN)〔999〕	4		20	13/	13	千克	Q/1			
2939.6200	--麦角胺(INN)及其盐										
2939.6200 10	麦角胺〔999〕	4		20	13/	13	千克	3Q2/1			
2939.6200 90	麦角胺盐〔999〕	4		20	13/	13	千克	Q/1			
2939.6300	--麦角酸及其盐										
2939.6300 10	麦角酸〔999〕	4		20	13/	13	千克	3Q2/1			
2939.6300 90	麦角酸盐〔999〕	4		20	13/	13	千克	Q/1			
2939.6900	--其他										
2939.6900 10	麦角二乙胺及其盐〔999〕	4		20	13/	13	千克	I/1			
2939.6900 90	其他麦角生物碱及其衍生物(包括它们的盐)〔999〕	4		20	13/	13	千克	Q/1			
	-其他,植物来源的:										
	--可卡因、芽子碱,它们的盐、酯及其他衍生物:										
2939.7210	---可卡因及其盐〔999〕	4		20	13/	13	千克	I/1			
2939.7290	---其他〔999〕	4		20	13/	13	千克	I/1		9	
	--其他:										
2939.7910	---烟碱及其盐										
2939.7910 10	烟碱〔999〕	4		20	13/	13	千克	ABQ/13	MN		
2939.7910 90	烟碱盐〔999〕	4		20	13/	13	千克	Q/13			
2939.7920	---番木鳖碱(士的年)及其盐										
2939.7920 10	番木鳖碱〔999〕	4		17	13/	13	千克	ABQ/13	MN		
2939.7920 90	番木鳖碱盐〔999〕	4		17	13/	13	千克	Q/13			
2939.7990	---其他										
2939.7990 11	卡西酮、麦司卡林(以及它们的盐)〔999〕	4		20	13/	13	千克	I/13			
2939.7990 12	赛洛新、赛洛西宾(以及它们的盐)〔999〕	4		20	13/	13	千克	I/13			
2939.7990 91	酒石酸长春瑞滨、硫酸长春新碱、盐酸托泊替康、盐酸伊立替康[T2]	4	0	20	3/	13	千克	ABQ/13	MRN		
2939.7990 99	其他植物碱及其衍生物(包括植物碱的盐、酯及其他衍生物)〔301 危险化学品,毒性物质,302 其他化工产品〕	4		20	13/	13	千克	ABQ/13	MRN		
2939.8000	-其他〔999 毒性物质和感染性物质,301 需申报仅用于工业用途不用于食品添加剂无检疫要求的化学品〕	4		20	13/	13	千克	ABQ/1	MRN	29	
	第十三分章　其他有机化合物										
29.40	**化学纯糖,但蔗糖、乳糖、麦芽糖、葡萄糖及果糖除外;糖醚、糖缩醛、糖酯及其盐,但不包括税目 29.37、29.38 及 29.39 的产品:**										
2940.0010	---木糖[T2]	6		30	13/	13	千克	AQ/1	R		
2940.0090	---其他										
2940.0090 10	氨基寡糖素〔999〕	6		30	13/	13	千克	AQS/13	R	26	
2940.0090 90	其他化学纯糖,糖醚、糖酯及其盐(蔗糖、乳糖、麦芽糖、葡萄糖、品目 29.37－2939 产品除外)〔101 其他饲料添加剂,201 合成糖,301 危险化学品,毒性物质〕	6		30	13/	13	千克	AQ/13	R	26	
29.41	**抗菌素:**										
	-青霉素和具有青霉烷酸结构的青霉素衍生物及其盐:										
	---氨苄青霉素及其盐:										
2941.1011	----氨苄青霉素〔999〕	6		20	13/	13	千克	Q/1			3/3
2941.1012	----氨苄青霉素三水酸〔999〕	6		20	13/	13	千克	Q/1			3/3
2941.1019	----其他〔999〕	6		20	13/	13	千克	Q/1		11	3/3
	---其他:										
2941.1091	----羟氨苄青霉素〔999〕	4		20	13/	13	千克	Q/1			
2941.1092	----羟氨苄青霉素三水酸〔999〕	4		20	13/	13	千克	Q/1			3.2/3.2
2941.1093	----6－氨基青霉烷酸(6APA)〔999〕	4		20	13/	13	千克	/1		29	
2941.1094	----青霉素 V〔999〕	4		20	13/	13	千克	Q/1			

协定税率 %								RCEP		特惠税率 %			Article Description
东/冰/格	巴基斯坦	韩国	瑞士 上/下	哥/秘/柬	澳/毛	新西/坡/智	中国港/澳/台	东盟及马来/澳/韩	日/新	亚太2国	老/柬/缅	98/97/95	
0/0/0	0	0	0.1/0.1	0/0/0	0/0	0//0	0/0/	0/0/0	0/0			0/0/0	L－methylamphetamine, methamphetamine, other derivatives of methamphetamine racemates (including esters)
0/0/0	0	0	0.1/0.1	0/0/0	0/0	0//0	0/0/	0/0/0	0/0			0/0/0	Chloroephedrine
0/0/0	0	0	0.1/0.1	0/0/0	0/0	0//0	0/0/	0/0/0	0/0			0/0/0	Other ephedra alkaloids and their salts
0/0/0	0	0	0.1/0.1	0/0/0	0/0	0//0	0/0/	0/0/0	0/0			0/0/0	Other ephedra alkaloid derivatives and their salts
													-Theophylline and aminophylline (theophylline-ethylenediamine) and their derivatives; salts thereof:
0/0/0	0	0	0/0	0/0/0	0/0	0//0	0/0/	0/0/0	0/0			0/0/0	--Fenetylline(INN) and its salts
0/0/0	0	0	0/0	0/0/0	0/0	0//0	0/0/	0/0/0	0/0			0/0/0	--Other
													-Alkaloids of rye ergot and their derivatives; salts thereof:
													--Ergometrine (INN) and its salts
0/0/0	0	0	0/0	0/0/0	0/0	0//0	0/0/	0/0/0	0/0			0/0/0	Ergometrine (INN)
0/0/0	0	0	0/0	0/0/0	0/0	0//0	0/0/	0/0/0	0/0			0/0/0	Salt of ergometrine (INN)
													--Ergotamine (INN) and its salts
0/0/0	0	0	0/0	0/0/0	0/0	0//0	0/0/	0/0/0	0/0			0/0/0	Ergotamine (INN)
0/0/0	0	0	0/0	0/0/0	0/0	0//0	0/0/	0/0/0	0/0			0/0/0	Salts of ergotamine (INN)
													--Lysergic acid and its salts
0/0/0	0	0	0/0	0/0/0	0/0	0//0	0/0/	0/0/0	0/0			0/0/0	Lysergic acid
0/0/0	0	0	0/0	0/0/0	0/0	0//0	0/0/	0/0/0	0/0			0/0/0	Salts of lysergic acid
													--Other
0/0/0	0	0	0.4/0.4	0/0/0	0/0	0//0	0/0/	0/0/0	3.6/0			0/0/0	Lysergide and its salts
0/0/0	0	0	0.4/0.4	0/0/0	0/0	0//0	0/0/	0/0/0	3.6/0			0/0/0	Other alkaloids of rye ergot and their derivatives(salts thereof)
													-Other,ofvegetalorigin:
													--Cocaine, alkaloids, their salts, esters and other derivatives:
0/0/0	0	0	0/0	0/0/0	0/0	0//0	0/0/	0/0/0	0/0			0/0/0	---Cocaine and its salts
0/0/0	0	0	0/0	0/0/0	0/0	0//0	0/0/	0/0/0	0/0			0/0/0	---Other
													--Other:
													---Nicotine and its salts
0/0/0	0	0	0/0	0/0/0	0/0	0//0	0/0/	0/0/0	0/0			0/0/0	Nicotine
0/0/0	0	0	0/0	0/0/0	0/0	0//0	0/0/	0/0/0	0/0			0/0/0	Salts of nicotine
													---Strychnine and its salts
0/0/0	0	0	0/0	0/0/0	0/0	0//0	0/0/	0/0/0	0/0			0/0/0	Strychnine
0/0/0	0	0	0/0	0/0/0	0/0	0//0	0/0/	0/0/0	0/0			0/0/0	Salts of strychnine
													---Other
0/0/0	0	0	0.4/0.4	0/0/0	0/0	0//0	0/0/	0/0/0	3.6/0			0/0/0	Cathinone, mescaline (and their salts)
0/0/0	0	0	0.4/0.4	0/0/0	0/0	0//0	0/0/	0/0/0	3.6/0			0/0/0	Psilocine, psilocybin (and their salts)
0/0/0	0	0	0.4/0.4	0/0/0	0/0	0//0	0/0/	0/0/0	3.6/0			0/0/0	Vinorelbine tartrate, vincristine sulfate, topotecan hydrochloride, irinotecan hydrochloride, and other anticancer drug substances
0/0/0	0	0	0.4/0.4	0/0/0	0/0	0//0	0/0/	0/0/0	3.6/0			0/0/0	Other vegetable alkaliods and their derivatives (including salts, esters and other derivatives of vegetable alkaliods)(tax number of Separating anti－cancer pharmaceutical raw materials)
0/0/0	0	0	0.4/0.4	0/0/0	0/0	0//0	0/0/	0/0/0	3.6/0			0/0/0	-Other
													ⅩⅢ. OTHER ORGANIC COMPOUNDS
													Sugars, chemically pure, other than sucrose, lactose, maltose, glucose and fructose, sugar ethers, sugar acetals and sugar esters, and their salts, other than products of heading No. 29.37, 29.38 or 29.39:
0/0/	5	1.2	0/0	0/0/0	0/0	0//0	0/0/	0/0/5.4	5.5/0			0/0/0	---Wood sugar
													---Other
0/0/	5	1.2	0/0	0/0/0	0/0	0//0	0/0/	0/0/5.4	5.5/0			0/0/0	Aminooligosaccharide
0/0/	5	1.2	0/0	0/0/0	0/0	0//0	0/0/	0/0/5.4	5.5/0			0/0/0	Other chemically pure sugars, sugar ethers, sugar esters and their salts (except sucrose, lactose, maltose, glucose, products of heading 29.37－2939)
													Antibiotics:
													Penicillins and their derivatives with a penicillanic acid structure; salts thereof:
													---Ampicillin and its salts:
0/0/0	0	0	0/0	0/0/0	0/0	0//0	0/0/	0/0/0	0/0			0/0/0	----Ampicillin
0/0/0	0	0	0/0	0/0/0	0/0	0//0	0/0/	0/0/0	0/0			0/0/0	----Ampicillin trihydrate
0/0/0	0	0	0/0	0/0/0	0/0	0//0	0/0/	0/0/0	0/0			0/0/0	----Other
													---Other:
0/0/0	0	0	0/0	0/0/0	0/0	0//0	0/0/	0/0/0	0/0			0/0/0	----Amoxycillin
0/0/0	0	0	0/0	0/0/0	0/0	0//0	0/0/	0/0/0	0/0			0/0/0	----Amoxycillin trihydrate
0/0/0	0	0	0/0	0/0/0	0/0	0//0	0/0/	0/0/0	0/0			0/0/0	----6-Aminopenicillanic acid
0/0/0	0	0	0/0	0/0/0	0/0	0//0	0/0/	0/0/0	0/0			0/0/0	----Penicillin V

税则号列	货品名称〔CIQ 扩展编码及品名－T2 表示见附表 2〕	最惠(%)	暂定税率	普通	增值/消费	出口退税	计量单位	监管条件/特殊证件	检验检疫	对美关税	亚太上/下
2941.1095	----磺苄青霉素〔999〕	4		20	13/	13	千克	Q/1			
2941.1096	----邻氯青霉素〔999〕	4		20	13/	13	千克	Q/1			
2941.1099	----其他〔999〕	4		20	13/	13	千克	Q/1			
2941.2000	-链霉素及其衍生物以及它们的盐〔999〕	4		20	13/	13	千克	Q/1		9	
	-四环素及其衍生物以及它们的盐：										
	---四环素及其盐：										
2941.3011	----四环素〔999〕	4		20	13/	13	千克	Q/1			
2941.3012	----四环素盐〔999〕	4		20	13/	13	千克	Q/1			
2941.3020	---四环素衍生物及其盐〔999〕	4		20	13/	13	千克	Q/1			
2941.4000	-氯霉素及其衍生物以及它们的盐〔999〕	4		20	13/	13	千克	Q/1			
2941.5000	-红霉素及其衍生物以及它们的盐〔999〕	4		20	13/	13	千克	Q/1			
	-其他：										
2941.9010	---庆大霉素及其衍生物以及它们的盐〔999〕	4		20	13/	13	千克	Q/1		29	
2941.9020	---卡那霉素及其衍生物以及它们的盐〔999〕	4		20	13/	13	千克	Q/1			
2941.9030	---利福平及其衍生物以及它们的盐〔999〕	4		20	13/	13	千克	Q/1			
2941.9040	---林可霉素及其衍生物以及它们的盐〔999〕	4		20	13/	13	千克	Q/1			
	---头孢菌素及其衍生物以及它们的盐：										
2941.9052	----头孢氨苄及其盐〔999〕	6		20	13/	13	千克	Q/1			3.9/3.9
2941.9053	----头孢唑啉及其盐〔999〕	6		20	13/	13	千克	Q/1			3/3
2941.9054	----头孢拉啶及其盐〔999〕	6		20	13/	13	千克	Q/1			3/3
2941.9055	----头孢三嗪(头孢曲松)及其盐〔999〕	6	0	20	13/	13	千克	Q/1			3/3
2941.9056	----头孢哌酮及其盐〔999〕	6		20	13/	13	千克	Q/1			3/3
2941.9057	----头孢噻肟及其盐〔999〕	6		20	13/	13	千克	Q/1			3/3
2941.9058	----头孢克罗及其盐〔999〕	6		20	13/	13	千克	Q/1		8.5	5/5
2941.9059	----其他										
2941.9059 10	放线菌酮〔999〕	6		20	13/	13	千克	QS/13		31	5/5
2941.9059 90	其他头孢菌素及其衍生物(包括它们的盐)〔999〕	6		20	13/	13	千克	Q/13		31	5/5
2941.9060	---麦迪霉素及其衍生物以及它们的盐〔999〕	6		20	13/	13	千克	Q/1		8.5	3/3
2941.9070	---乙酰螺旋霉素及其衍生物以及它们的盐〔999〕	4		20	13/	13	千克	Q/1			
2941.9090	---其他										
2941.9090 11	中生菌素〔101〕	6		20	13/	13	千克	QS/13		11	3.9/3.9
2941.9090 12	春雷霉素〔101〕	6		20	13/	13	千克	QS/13		11	3.9/3.9
2941.9090 13	吗替麦考酚酯〔999〕	6	0	20	13/	13	千克	Q/13		5	3.9/3.9
2941.9090 14	盐酸阿柔比星〔999〕	6	0	20	13/	13	千克	Q/13		5	3.9/3.9
2941.9090 91	吡柔比星、丝裂霉素、盐酸表柔比星、盐酸多柔比星、盐酸平阳霉素、盐酸柔红霉素、盐酸伊达比星〔301 危险化学品，毒性物质；302 其他危险化学品〕	6	0	20	3/	13	千克	Q/13		5	3.9/3.9
2941.9090 99	其他抗菌素〔301 危险化学品，毒性物质，302 其他化工产品〕	6		20	13/	13	千克	Q/13		11	3.9/3.9
29.42	**其他有机化合物：**										
2942.0000	其他有机化合物[T2]	6.5		30	13/	13	千克	/13		11.5	

协定税率 %								RCEP		特惠税率 %			Article Description
东/冰/格	巴基斯坦	韩国	瑞士上/下	哥/秘/柬	澳/毛	新西/坡/智	中国港/澳/台	东盟及马来/澳/韩	日/新	亚太2国	老/柬/缅	98/97/95	
0/0/0	0	0	0/0	0/0/0	0/0	0//0	0/0/	0/0/0	0/0			0/0/0	----Sulfobenzylpenicillin
0/0/0	0	0	0/0	0/0/0	0/0	0//0	0/0/	0/0/0	0/0			0/0/0	----Cloxacillin
0/0/0	0	0	0/0	0/0/0	0/0	0//0	0/0/	0/3.6/0	0/3.6			0/0/0	----Other
0/0/0	0	0	0/0	0/0/0	0/0	0//0	0/0/	0/0/0	0/0			0/0/0	-Streptomycins and their derivatives; salts thereof
													-Tetracyclines and their derivatives; salts thereof:
													---Tetracyclines and their salts:
0/0/0	0	0	0/0	0/0/0	0/0	0//0	0/0/	0/0/0	0/0			0/0/0	----Tetracyclines
0/0/0	0	0	0/0	0/0/0	0/0	0//0	0/0/	0/0/0	0/0			0/0/0	----Salts of tetracyclines
0/0/0	0	0	0/0	0/0/0	0/0	0//0	0/0/	0/0/0	0/0			0/0/0	---Tetracyclines derivatives and their salts:
0/0/0	0	0	0/0	0/0/0	0/0	0//0	0/0/	0/0/0	0/0			0/0/0	-Chloramphenicol and its derivatives; salts thereof
0/0/0	0	0	0/0	0/0/0	0/0	0//0	0/0/	0/0/0	0/0			0/0/0	-Erythromycin and its derivatives; salts thereof
													-Other:
0/0/0	0	0	0/0	0/0/0	0/0	0//0	0/0/	0/0/0	0/0			0/0/0	---Gentamycin and its derivatives; salts thereof
0/0/0	0	0	0/0	0/0/0	0/0	0//0	0/0/	0/0/0	0/0			0/0/0	---Kanamycin and its derivatives; salts thereof
0/0/0	0	0	0/0	0/0/0	0/0	0//0	0/0/	0/0/0	0/0			0/0/0	---Rifampicin (RFP); salts thereof
0/0/0	0	0	0/0	0/0/0	0/0	0//0	0/0/	0/0/0	0/0			0/0/0	---Lincomycin and its derivatives; salts thereof
													---Cephamycin and its derivatives; salts thereof:
0/0/0	0	0	0/0	0/0/0	0/0	0//0	0/0/	0/0/0	0/0			0/0/0	----Cefalexin and its salts
0/0/0	0	0	0/0	0/0/0	0/0	0//0	0/0/	0/0/0	0/0			0/0/0	----Cefazolin and its salts
0/0/0	0	0	0/0	0/0/0	0/0	0//0	0/0/	0/0/0	0/0			0/0/0	----Cefradine and its salts
0/0/0	0	0	2.5/2.5	0/0/0	0/0	0//0	0/0/	0/0/0	5.5/0			0/0/0	----Ceftriaxone and its salts
0/0/0	0	0	0/0	0/0/0	0/0	0//0	0/0/	0/0/0	0/0			0/0/0	----Cefoperazone and its salts
0/0/0	0	0	0/0	0/0/0	0/0	0//0	0/0/	0/0/0	0/0			0/0/0	----Cefotaxime and its salts
0/0/0	0	0	0/0	0/0/0	0/0	0//0	0/0/	0/5.4/0	0/5.4			0/0/0	----Cefaclor and its salts
													----Other
0/0/0	0	1.2	0/0	0/0/0	0/0	0//0	0/0/	5.4/5.4/5.4	5.5/5.4			0/0/0	Actidione
0/0/0	0	1.2	0/0	0/0/0	0/0	0//0	0/0/	5.4/5.4/5.4	5.5/5.4			0/0/0	Other cephamycin and its derivaatives;salts thereof
0/0/0	0	0	0/0	0/0/0	0/0	0//0	0/0/	0/0/0	0/0			0/0/0	---Midecamycin and its derivatives; salts thereof
0/0/0	0	0	0/0	0/0/0	0/0	0//0	0/0/	0/0/0	0/0			0/0/0	---Acetyl-spiramycin and its derivatives; salts thereof
													---Other
0/0/0	0	0	0/0	0/0/0	0/0	0//0	0/0/	0/5.4/0	0/5.4			0/0/0	Zhongshengmycin
0/0/0	0	0	0/0	0/0/0	0/0	0//0	0/0/	0/5.4/0	0/5.4			0/0/0	Kasugamycin
0/0/0	0	0	0/0	0/0/0	0/0	0//0	0/0/	0/5.4/0	0/5.4			0/0/0	Mycophenolate mofetil
0/0/0	0	0	0/0	0/0/0	0/0	0//0	0/0/	0/5.4/0	0/5.4		//	0/0/0	Arubicin Hydrochloride
0/0/0	0	0	0/0	0/0/0	0/0	0//0	0/0/	0/5.4/0	0/5.4			0/0/0	Pirarubicin, Actinomycin D, Mitomycin, Epirubicin Hydrochloride, Doxorubicin Hydrochloride, Pingyangmycin Hydrochloride, Daunorubicin Hydrochloride, Idarubicin Hydrochloride, and Other Anticancer Drug Raw Materials medicine
0/0/0	0	0	0/0	0/0/0	0/0	0//0	0/0/	0/5.4/0	0/5.4			0/0/0	Other antibiotics (tax number of Separating anti — cancer pharmaceutical raw materials)
													Other organic compounds:
0/0/0	5	0	0/0	0/0/0	0/0	0//0	0/0/	0/0/0	5.9/0			0/0/0	Other organic compounds

第三十章
药　品

注释：

一、本章不包括：

(一)食品及饮料（例如，营养品、糖尿病食品、强化食品、保健食品、滋补饮料及矿泉水），但不包括供静脉摄入用的滋养品(第四类)；

(二)含尼古丁并用于帮助吸烟者戒烟的产品，例如，片剂、咀嚼胶或透皮贴片(税目 24.04)；

(三)经特殊煅烧或精细研磨的牙科用熟石膏(税目 25.20)；

(四)适合医药用的精油水馏液及水溶液(税目 33.01)；

(五)税目 33.03 至 33.07 的制品，不论是否具有治疗及预防疾病的作用；

(六)加有药料的肥皂及税目 34.01 的其他产品；

(七)以熟石膏为基本成分的牙科用制品(税目 34.07)；

(八)不作治疗及预防疾病用的血清蛋白(税目 35.02)；

(九)税目 38.22 的诊断试剂。

二、税目 30.02 所称的"免疫制品"是指直接参与免疫过程调节的多肽及蛋白质(税目 29.37 的货品除外)，例如，单克隆抗体(MAB)、抗体片段、抗体偶联物及抗体片段偶联物、白介素、干扰素(IFN)、趋化因子及特定的肿瘤坏死因子(TNF)、生长因子(GF)、促红细胞生成素及集落刺激因子(CSF)。

三、税目 30.03 及 30.04 以及本章注释四(四)所述的非混合产品及混合产品，按下列规定处理：

(一)非混合产品：

1. 溶于水的非混合产品；
2. 第二十八章及第二十九章的所有货品；
3. 税目 13.02 的单一植物浸膏，只经标定或溶于溶剂的。

(二)混合产品：

1. 胶体溶液及悬浮液(胶态硫磺除外)；
2. 从植物性混合物加工所得的植物浸膏；
3. 蒸发天然矿质水所得的盐及浓缩物。

四、税目 30.06 仅适用于下列物品(这些物品只能归入税目 30.06，而不得归入本目录其他税目)：

(一)无菌外科肠线、类似的无菌缝合材料(包括外科或牙科用无菌可吸收缝线)及外伤创口闭合用的无菌粘合胶布；

(二)无菌昆布及无菌昆布塞条；

(三)外科或牙科用无菌吸收性止血材料；外科或牙科用无菌抗粘连阻隔材料，不论是否可吸收；

(四)用于病人的 X 光检查造影剂及其他诊断试剂，这些药剂是由单一产品配定剂量或由两种以上成分混合而成的；

(五)安慰剂和盲法(或双盲法)临床试验试剂盒，用于经许可的临床试验，已配定剂量，即使它们可能含有活性药物。

(六)牙科粘固剂及其他牙科填料；骨骼粘固剂；

(七)急救药箱、药包；

(八)以激素、税目 29.37 的其他产品或杀精子剂为基本成分的化学避孕药物；

(九)专用于人类或作兽药用的凝胶制品，作为外科手术或体检时躯体部位的润滑剂，或者作为躯体和医疗器械之间的耦合剂；

(十)废药物，即那些因超过有效保存期等原因而不适于作原用途的药品；

(十一)可确定用于造口术的用具，即裁切成型的结肠造口术，回肠造口术、尿道造口术用袋及其具有黏性的片或底盘。

子目注释：

一、子目 3002.13 及 3002.14 所述的非混合产品、纯物质及混合产品，按下列规定处理：

(一)非混合产品或纯物质，不论是否含有杂质；

(二)混合产品：

1.上述(一)款所述的产品溶于水或其他溶剂的；
2.为保存或运输需要，上述(一)款及(二)1 项所述的产品加入稳定剂的；
3.上述(一)款、(二)1 项及(二)2 项所述的产品添加其他添加剂的。

二、子目 3003.60 和 3004.60 包括的药品含有与其他药用活性成分配伍的口服用青蒿素(INN)，或者含有下列任何一种活性成分，不论是否与其他药用活性成分配伍：阿莫地喹(INN)、蒿醚林酸及其盐(INN)、双氢青蒿素(INN)、蒿乙醚(INN)、蒿甲醚(INN)、青蒿琥酯(INN)、氯喹(INN)、二氢青蒿素(INN)、苯芴醇(INN)、甲氟喹(INN)、哌喹(INN)、乙胺嘧啶(INN)或磺胺多辛(INN)。

Chapter 30
Pharmaceutical products

Notes:

1. This Chapter does not cover:
   (a) Foods or beverages (such as dietetic, diabetic or fortified foods, food supplements, tonic beverages and mineral waters), other than nutritional preparations for intraverwas administration (Section Ⅳ);
   (b) Products, such as tablets, chewing gum or patches (transdermal systems), containing nicotine and intended to assist tobacco use cessation (heading No. 24.04);
   (c) Plasters specially calcined or finely ground for use in dentistry (heading No. 25.20);
   (d) Aqueous distillates or aqueous solutions of essential oils, suitable for medicinal uses (heading No. 33.01);
   (e) Preparations of headings No. 33.03 to 33.07, even if they have therapeutic or prophylactic properties;
   (f) Soap or other products of heading No. 34.01 containing added medicaments;
   (g) Preparations with a basis of plaster for use in dentistry (heading No. 34.07);
   (h) Blood albumin not prepared for therapeutic or prophylactic uses (heading No. 35.02); or
   (ij) Diagnostic reagents of heading No. 38.22.
2. For the purposes of heading No. 30.02, the expression "immunological products" applies to peptides and proteins (other than goods of heading No. 29.37) which are directly involved in the regulation of immunological processes, such as monoclonal antibodies (MAB), antibody fragments, antibody conjugates and antibody fragment conjugates, interleukins, interferons (IFN), chemodines and certain tumor necrosis factors (TNF), growth factors (GF), hematopoietins and colony stimulating factors (CSF)
3. For the purposes of headings No. 30.03 and 30.04 and of Note 4 (d) to this Chapter, the following are to be treated:
   (a) As unmixed products:
      (1) Unmixed products dissolved in water;
      (2) All goods of Chapter 28 or 29;
      (3) Simple vegetable extracts of heading No. 13.02, merely standardised or dissolved in any solvent;
   (b) As products which have been mixed:
      (1) Colloidal solutions and suspensions (other than colloidal sulphur);
      (2) Vegetable extracts obtained by the treatment of mixtures of vegetable materials;
      (3) Salts and concentrates obtained by evaporating natural mineral waters.
4. Heading No. 30.06 applies only to the following, which are to be classified in that heading and in no other heading of the Nomenclature:
   (a) Sterile surgical catgut, similar sterile suture materials (including sterile absorbable surgical or denfal yams) and sterile tissue adhesives for surgical wound closure;
   (b) Sterile laminaria and sterile laminaria tents;
   (c) Sterile absorbable surgical or dental haemostatics; sterile surgical or dental adhesion barriers, whether or not absorbable
   (d) Opacifying preparations for X-ray examinations and diagnostic reagents designed to be administered to the patient, being unmixed products put up in measured doses or products consisting of two or more ingredients which have been mixed together for such uses;
   (e) Placebos and blinded (or double—blinded) clinical trial kits for use in recognised clinical trials, put up in measured doses, even if they might contain active medicaments.
   (f) Dental cements and other dental fillings; bone reconstruction cements;
   (g) First-aid boxes and kits;
   (h) Chemical contraceptive preparations based on hormones, on other products of heading No. 29.37 or on spermicides;
   (i) Gel preparations designed to be used in human or veterinary medicine as a lubricant for parts of the body for surgical operations or physical examinations or as a coupling agent between the body and medical instruments;
   (j) Waste pharmaceuticals, that is, pharmaceutical products which are unfit for their original intended purpose due to, for example, expiry of shelf life;
   (k) Appliances identifiable for ostomy use, that is, cdostomy, ileostomy and utosto my pouches cut to shape and their adhesive wafers or faceplates.

Subheading Notes:

a. Un-mixed products, pure substances heading and mixed products of No. 3002.13 and heading No.3002.14, according to the following regulations:
   (a) un-mixed products and Pure substances, Whether or not containing impurities;
   (b) Mixed products;
      i. The products mentioned in the preceding
      (a) paragraph are dissolved in water or other solvents;
      (ii) The products referred to in paragraph (a) and (b) above are added to the stabilizer for preservation or transport;
      iii. The products mentioned in i of (a) or ii of (b) add other additives.

a. Subheading No. 3003.60 and Subheading No.3004.60 include medicines containing oral and other medicinal active ingredients combined with artemisinins (INN), or contain any of the following active ingredients, whether or not with other medicinal active ingredient compatibility: amodiaquine (INN), Artelinic acid and its salts (INN), dihydroartemisinine (INN), artemotil (INN), artemether (INN), artesunate (INN), chloroquine (INN), dihydroartemisinin (INN), lumefantrine (INN), mefloquine (INN), piperaquine (INN), pyrimcthaminc(INN) or sulfadoxine (INN)

税则号列	货品名称〔CIQ扩展编码及品名—T2表示见附表2〕	最惠(%)	暂定税率	普通	增值/消费	出口退税	计量单位	监管条件/特殊证件	检验检疫	对美关税	亚太上/下
30.01	**已干燥的器官疗法用腺体及其他器官，不论是否制成粉末；器官疗法用腺体、其他器官及其分泌物的提取物；肝素及其盐；其他供治疗或预防疾病用的其他税目未列名的人体或动物制品：**										
3001.2000	-腺体、其他器官及其分泌物的提取物										
3001.2000 10	其他濒危野生动物腺体、器官(包括分泌物)〔101动物培养器官，102动物培养细胞，103动物微生物培养培养基，104其他动物器官、细胞、培养基，105未列出的其他动物产品，106其他化工产品〕	3		30	13/	0	千克	AQFEB/1	PQ		
3001.2000 21	含有人类遗传资源的人类腺体、器官及其分泌物提取物〔999〕	3		30	13/	13	千克	ABV/1	VW		
3001.2000 29	其他人类的腺体、器官及其分泌物提取物〔999〕	3		30	13/	13	千克	ABV/1	VW		
3001.2000 90	其他腺体、器官及其分泌物提取物〔T2〕	3		30	13/	13	千克	AB/1	PQ		
	-其他：										
3001.9010	---肝素及其盐〔999〕	3		30	13/	13	千克	Q/1			
3001.9090	---其他										
3001.9090 10	蛇毒制品(供治疗或预防疾病用)〔999〕	3		30	13/	13	千克	AQFEB/1	PVQW		
3001.9090 20	含有人类遗传资源的人体制品〔999〕	3		30	13/	13	千克	ABQV/1	VW		
3001.9090 91	其他濒危动物制品(供治疗或预防疾病用)〔101动物性血液制品，102其他化工产品〕	3		30	13/	0	千克	ABFEQ/1	PQ		
3001.9090 92	人类腺体、器官、组织(供治疗或预防疾病用)〔401含《人间传染的病原微生物名录》内一类病原微生物，402含《人间传染的病原微生物名录》内二类病原微生物，403含《人间传染的病原微生物名录》内三类病原微生物，404含《人间传染的病原微生物名录》内四类病原微生物，405含《人间传染的病原微生物名录》内含新发传染病或名录外再现传染病病原微生物，406含寄生虫，407经灭活处理的组织切片，408其他人类腺体、器官、组织〕	3		30	13/	13	千克	AB/1	VW		
3001.9090 99	其他未列名的人体或动物制品(供治疗或预防疾病用)〔101动物性血液产品，102药用血余炭，401人体制品〕	3		30	13/	9,13	千克	ABQ/1	PVQW		
30.02	**人血；治病、防病或诊断用的动物血制品；抗血清、其他血份及免疫制品，不论是否修饰或通过生物工艺加工制得；疫苗、毒素、培养微生物(不包括酵母)及类似产品；细胞培养物，不论是否修饰：**										
	-抗血清、其他血份及免疫制品，不论是否修饰或通过生物工艺加工制得：										
3002.1200	--抗血清及其他血份										
3002.1200 11	唾液酸促红素、氨甲酰促红素、达促红素、培促红素β、促红素(EPO)类等促红素〔401用于人类医学、生命科学相关领域，999其他化工产品〕	3	0	20	13/	13	千克	ABL/1	PVQW		
3002.1200 12	胰岛素样生长因子1(IGF-1)及其类似物〔401用于人类医学、生命科学相关领域，999其他化工产品〕	3	0	20	13/	13	千克	ABL/1	PVQW		
3002.1200 13	机械生长因子类〔401用于人类医学、生命科学相关领域，999其他化工产品〕	3	0	20	13/	13	千克	ABL/1	PVQW		
3002.1200 14	成纤维细胞生长因子类(FGFs)〔401用于人类医学、生命科学相关领域，999其他化工产品〕	3	0	20	13/	13	千克	ABL/1	PVQW		
3002.1200 15	肝细胞生长因子(HGF)〔401用于人类医学、生命科学相关领域，999其他化工产品〕	3	0	20	13/	13	千克	ABL/1	PVQW		
3002.1200 16	血小板衍生生长因子(PDGF)〔401用于人类医学、生命科学相关领域，999其他化工产品〕	3	0	20	13/	13	千克	ABL/1	PVQW		
3002.1200 17	血管内皮生长因子(VEGF)〔401用于人类医学、生命科学相关领域，999其他化工产品〕	3	0	20	13/	13	千克	ABL/1	PVQW		
3002.1200 18	转化生长因子-β(TGF-β)信号传导抑制剂类〔101医用细胞因子，401用于人类医学、生命科学相关领域，999其他化工产品〕	3	0	20	13/	13	千克	ABL/1	PVQW		
3002.1200 19	培尼沙肽、罗特西普〔401用于人类医学、生命科学相关领域，999其他化工产品〕	3	0	20	13/	13	千克	ABL/1	PVQW		
3002.1200 21	缺氧诱导因子(HIF)激活剂类、缺氧诱导因子(HIF)稳定剂类〔401用于人类医学、生命科学相关领域，999其他化工产品〕	3	0	20	13/	13	千克	ABL/1	PVQW		
3002.1200 22	EPO-Fc(IgG4)融合蛋白、EPO-Fc融合蛋白〔401用于人类医学、生命科学相关领域，999其他化工产品〕	3	0	20	13/	13	千克	ABL/1	PVQW		
3002.1200 23	含有人类遗传资源的抗血清及其他血份〔401含《人间传染的病原微生物名录》内一类病原微生物，402含《人间传染的病原微生物名录》内二类病原微生物，403含《人间传染的病原微生物名录》内三类病原微生物，404含《人间传染的病原微生物名录》内四类病原微生物，405含《人间传染的病原微生物名录》内新发传染病或名录外再现传染病病原微生物，406含寄生虫，407其他抗血清，408其他血份〕	3	0	20	13/	13	千克	ABV/1	PVQW		

协定税率 %								RCEP		特惠税率 %			Article Description
东/冰/格	巴基斯坦	韩国	瑞士 上/下	哥/秘/柬	澳/毛	新西/坡/智	中国港/澳/台	东盟及马来/澳/韩	日/新	亚太2国	老/柬/缅	98/97/95	
													Glands and other organs for organo-therapeutic uses, dried, whether or not powdered; extracts of glands or other organs or of their secretions for organo-therapeutic uses; heparin and its salts; other human or animal substances prepared for therapeutic or prophylactic uses, not elsewhere specified or included:
													-Extracts of glands or other organs or of their secretions
0/0/0	0	0	0/0	0/0/0	0/0	0//0	0/0/	0/0/0	0/0			0/0/0	Extracts of glands or other organs or of their secretions of endangered wild animals
0/0/0	0	0	0/0	0/0/0	0/0	0//0	0/0/	0/0/0	0/0		//	0/0/0	Human glands, organs and secretions containing human genetic resources
0/0/0	0	0	0/0	0/0/0	0/0	0//0	0/0/	0/0/0	0/0		//	0/0/0	Extracts from other human glands, organs and secretions
0/0/0	0	0	0/0	0/0/0	0/0	0//0	0/0/	0/0/0	0/0			0/0/0	Other extracts of glands of other organs or of their secretions
													-Other:
0/0/0	0	0	0/0	0/0/0	0/0	0//0	0/0/	0/0/0	0/0			0/0/0	---Heparin and its salts
													---Other
0/0/0	0	0	0/0	0/0/0	0/0	0//0	0/0/	0/0/0	0/0			0/0/0	Venom substances prepared (for therapeutic or prophylactic uses)
0/0/0	0	0	0/0	0/0/0	0/0	0//0	0/0/	0/0/0	0/0		//	0/0/0	Human products containing human genetic resources
0/0/0	0	0	0/0	0/0/0	0/0	0//0	0/0/	0/0/0	0/0			0/0/0	Other substances of endangered animals for therapeutic or prophylactic uses
0/0/0	0	0	0/0	0/0/0	0/0	0//0	0/0/	0/0/0	0/0		//	0/0/0	Human glands, organs, tissues (for the treatment or prevention of diseases)
0/0/0	0	0	0/0	0/0/0	0/0	0//0	0/0/	0/0/0	0/0			0/0/0	Other human or animal substances prepared (for therapeutic or prophylactic uses) not elsewhere specified or included
													Human blood; animal blood prepared for therapeutic, prophylactic or diagnostic uses; antisera, other blood fractions and immunological products, whether or not modified or obtained by means of biotechnological processes; vaccines, toxins, cultures of micro-organisms (excluding yeasts) and similar products; cell cultures, whether or not modified.
													-Antisera and other blood fractions and immunological products, whether or not modified or obtained by means of biotechnological processes::
													--Antisera and other blood fractions
0/0/0	0	0	1.3/1.3	0/0/0	0/0	0//0	0/0/	0/0/0	2.7/0			0/0/0	Sialic acid erythropoietin, carbamoyl erythropoietin, Da erythropoietin, peierythropoietin β、Erythropoietin (EPO) and other erythropoietins
0/0/0	0	0	1.3/1.3	0/0/0	0/0	0//0	0/0/	0/0/0	2.7/0			0/0/0	Type 1 insulin like growth factor
0/0/0	0	0	1.3/1.3	0/0/0	0/0	0//0	0/0/	0/0/0	2.7/0			0/0/0	Mechano Growth Factor
0/0/0	0	0	1.3/1.3	0/0/0	0/0	0//0	0/0/	0/0/0	2.7/0			0/0/0	Fibroblast growth factor
0/0/0	0	0	1.3/1.3	0/0/0	0/0	0//0	0/0/	0/0/0	2.7/0			0/0/0	Hepatocyte growth factor
0/0/0	0	0	1.3/1.3	0/0/0	0/0	0//0	0/0/	0/0/0	2.7/0			0/0/0	Platelet derived growth factor
0/0/0	0	0	1.3/1.3	0/0/0	0/0	0//0	0/0/	0/0/0	2.7/0			0/0/0	Vascular endothelial growth factor
0/0/0	0	0	1.3/1.3	0/0/0	0/0	0//0	0/0/	0/0/0	2.7/0			0/0/0	Transforming growth factor -β (TGF-β) inhibitors
0/0/0	0	0	1.3/1.3	0/0/0	0/0	0//0	0/0/	0/0/0	2.7/0			0/0/0	Peinisha peptide, Roth Heap
0/0/0	0	0	1.3/1.3	0/0/0	0/0	0//0	0/0/	0/0/0	2.7/0			0/0/0	Hypoxia inducible factor (HIF) activator, hypoxia inducible factor (HIF) stabilizer
0/0/0	0	0	1.3/1.3	0/0/0	0/0	0//0	0/0/	0/0/0	2.7/0			0/0/0	EPO-Fc (IgG4) fusion protein, EPO-Fc fusion protein
0/0/0	0	0	1.3/1.3	0/0/0	0/0	0//0	0/0/	0/0/0	2.7/0		//	0/0/0	Antiserum and other blood components containing human genetic resources

税则号列	货品名称〔CIQ 扩展编码及品名—T2 表示见附表 2〕	最惠(%)	暂定税率	普通	增值/消费	出口退税	计量单位	监管条件/特殊证件	检验检疫	对美关税	亚太上/下
3002.1200 24	其他《兴奋剂目录》所列商品〔999〕	3	0	20	13/	13	千克	ABL/1	PVQW		
3002.1200 30	兽用血清制品〔999〕	3	0	20	13/	13	千克	ABR/1	PVQW		
3002.1200 93	罕见病药品制剂(包括罕见病药品清单第一批、第二批相关商品)〔301 其他化工产品,401 其他人血制品〕	3	0	20	3/	13	千克	AB/1	PVQW		
3002.1200 99	其他抗血清及其他血份(因拆分抗癌药产生的兜底税号)〔T2〕	3	0	20	13/	13	千克	AB/1	PVQW		
3002.1300	--非混合的免疫制品,未配定剂量或制成零售包装〔401 纯化抗体,402 细胞因子,403 其他医学免疫实验用试剂,999 其他化工产品〕	3	0	20	13/	13	千克	AB/1	PVQW		
3002.1400	--混合的免疫制品,未配定剂量或制成零售包装〔401 纯化抗体,402 细胞因子,403 其他医学免疫实验用试剂,999 其他化工产品〕	3	0	20	13/	13	千克	AB/1	PVQW		
3002.1500	--免疫制品,已配定剂量或制成零售包装										
3002.1500 10	抗(防)癌药品制剂(不含癌症辅助治疗药品)(包括抗癌药品清单第一批、第二批相关商品)〔301 其他化工产品,401 生物制品〕	3	0	20	3/	13	千克	AB/1	PVQW		
3002.1500 30	罕见病药品制剂(包括罕见病药品清单第一批、第二批相关商品)〔401 治疗人类疾病用,402 医学科研用〕	3	0	20	3/	13	千克	AB/1	PVQW		
3002.1500 40	兽用免疫学体内诊断制品(已配剂量的)〔999〕	3		20	13/	13	千克	ABR/1	PVQW		
3002.1500 90	其他免疫制品,已配定剂量或制成零售包装〔301 其他化工产品,401 治疗人类疾病用新型冠状病毒(COVID—19)抗体药,402 医学科研用新型冠状病毒(COVID—19)抗体药,403 其他治疗人类疾病用,404 其他人类医学、生命科学研究用〕	3	0	20	13/	13	千克	AB/1	PVQW		
	-疫苗、毒素、培养微生物(不包括酵母)及类似产品:										
3002.4100	--人用疫苗										
3002.4100 11	新型冠状病毒(COVID—19)疫苗,已配定剂量或制成零售包装〔401 预防疾病用,402 医学科研用〕	3	0	20	13/	13	千克	QAB/1	VW		
3002.4100 19	新型冠状病毒(COVID—19)疫苗,未配定剂量或制成零售包装〔401 预防疾病用,402 医学科研用〕	3	0	20	13/	13	千克	QAB/1	VW		
3002.4100 90	其他人用疫苗〔401 预防疾病用,402 医学科研用〕	3	0	20	13/	13	千克	QAB/1	VW		
3002.4200	--兽用疫苗〔101 动检灭活疫苗,102 动检强毒疫苗,103 动检弱毒疫苗,104 动检基因疫苗,105 动检菌苗,106 其他动物疫苗〕	3		20	13/	13	千克	R/1			
	--其他:										
3002.4910	---石房蛤毒素〔401 治疗人类疾病用,402 人类医学、生命科学研究用,403 其他〕	3		20	13/	13	千克	23Q/1			
3002.4920	---蓖麻毒素〔401 治疗人类疾病用,402 人类医学、生命科学研究用,403 其他〕	3		20	13/	13	千克	23Q/1			
3002.4930	---细菌及病毒										
3002.4930 10	两用物项管制细菌及病毒〔101 动检细菌,102 动检病毒,103 动检真菌,104 动检放线菌,105 动检螺旋体,106 动检立克次氏体,107 动检支原体,108 动检衣原体,109 动检菌种,110 动检毒种,111 其他动检微生物,112 动检寄生虫,113 植物细菌,114 植物病毒,401 两用物项管制目录内人及人兽共患病病原体〕	3		20	13/	13	千克/株	3AB/1	PVQW		
3002.4930 20	苏云金杆菌、枯草芽孢杆菌〔401 环保微生物菌剂,402 环保微生物菌剂样品,403 人类医学、生命科学研究用,404 其他〕	3		20	13/	13	千克/株	ABS/1	PVQW		
3002.4930 90	其他细菌及病毒〔T2〕	3		20	13/	13	千克/株	AB/1	PVQW		
3002.4990	---其他										
3002.4990 10	噬菌核霉、淡紫拟青霉、哈茨木霉菌、寡雄腐霉菌〔999〕	3	0	20	13/	13	千克	ABS/1	PVQW		
3002.4990 20	其他两用物项管制毒素〔101 动物毒素,102 含有毒素的动物血液制品,103 含有毒素的动物组织或器官,104 含有毒素的其他动物源性材料,401 人类医学、生命科学研究用〕	3	0	20	13/	13	千克	3AB/1	PVQW		
3002.4990 90	其他毒素、培养微生物(不包括酵母)及类似产品〔T2〕	3	0	20	13/	13	千克	AB/1	PVQW		
	-细胞培养物,不论是否修饰:										
3002.5100	--细胞治疗产品〔101 普通动物细胞,102SPF 级动物细胞,103 细胞库的动物细胞系,104 其他动物细胞,401 治疗人类疾病用,402 人类医学、生命科学研究用〕	3	0	20	13/	13	千克	AB/1	PVQW		

协定税率 %								RCEP		特惠税率 %			Article Description
东/冰/格	巴基斯坦	韩国	瑞士上/下	哥/秘/柬	澳/毛	新西/坡/智	中国港/澳/台	东盟及马来/澳/韩	日/新	亚太2国	老/柬/缅	98/97/95	
0/0/0	0	0	1.3/1.3	0/0/0	0/0	0//0	0/0/	0/0/0	2.7/0		//	0/0/0	List of other stimulants
0/0/0	0	0	1.3/1.3	0/0/0	0/0	0//0	0/0/	0/0/0	2.7/0		//	0/0/0	Veterinary serum products
0/0/0	0	0	1.3/1.3	0/0/0	0/0	0//0	0/0/	0/0/0	2.7/0		//	0/0/0	Pharmaceutical preparations for rare diseases (including the first and second batch of related commodities in the list of drugs for rare diseases)
0/0/0	0	0	1.3/1.3	0/0/0	0/0	0//0	0/0/	0/0/0	2.7/0			0/0/0	Other antisera,other blood fractions and immunological products(Tax number due to separation of anticancer drugs)
0/0/0	0	0	1.3/1.3	0/0/0	0/0	0//0	0/0/	0/0/0	2.7/0			0/0/0	--Immunological products, unmixed, not put up in measured doses or in forms or packings for retail sale
0/0/0	0	0	1.3/1.3	0/0/0	0/0	0//0	0/0/	0/0/0	2.7/0			0/0/0	--Immunological products,mixed,not put up in measured doses or in forms or packings for retail sale
													--Immunological products, put up in measured doses or in forms or packings for retail sale
0/0/0	0	0	1.3/1.3	0/0/0	0/0	0//0	0/0/	0/0/0	2.7/0			0/0/0	Anti—cancer drug preparations (excluding cancer adjuncts)
0/0/0	0	0	1.3/1.3	0/0/0	0/0	0//0	0/0/	0/0/0	2.7/0		//	0/0/0	Pharmaceutical preparations for rare diseases (including the first and second batch of related commodities in the list of drugs for rare diseases)
0/0/0	0	0	1.3/1.3	0/0/0	0/0	0//0	0/0/	0/0/0	2.7/0			0/0/0	Veterinary immunological in vivo diagnostic products (prepared dose)
0/0/0	0	0	1.3/1.3	0/0/0	0/0	0//0	0/0/	0/0/0	2.7/0			0/0/0	Other immunological products, put up in measured doses or in forms or packings for retail sale(Tax number due to separation of anticancer drugs)
													-Vaccines, toxins, cultures of micro—organisms (excluding yeasts) and similar products : --Vaccines for human medicine
0/0/0	0	0	0.3/0.3	0/0/0	0/0	0//0	0/0/	0/0/0	2.7/0			0/0/0	New Coronavirus (COVID—19) vaccine has been dosed or made into retail packaging
0/0/0	0	0	0.3/0.3	0/0/0	0/0	0//0	0/0/	0/0/0	2.7/0			0/0/0	New Coronavirus (COVID—19) vaccine is not prepared for dosage or made into retail packaging.
0/0/0	0	0	0.3/0.3	0/0/0	0/0	0//0	0/0/	0/0/0	2.7/0			0/0/0	Vaccines for others
0/0/0	0	0	0/0	0/0/0	0/0	0//0	0/0/	0/0/0	0/0			0/0/0	--Vaccines for veterinary medicine
													--Other:
0/0/0	0	0	0/0	0/0/0	0/0	0//0	0/0/	0/0/0	0/0			0/0/0	---Saxitoxin
0/0/0	0	0	0/0	0/0/0	0/0	0//0	0/0/	0/0/0	0/0			0/0/0	Ricitoxin
													---Bacteria and virus
0/0/0	0	0	0.3/0.3	0/0/0	0/0	0//0	0/0/	0/0/0	2.7/0			0/0/0	Dual purpose items control bacteria and viruses
0/0/0	0	0	0.3/0.3	0/0/0	0/0	0//0	0/0/	0/0/0	2.7/0			0/0/0	Bacillus thuringiensis, Bacillus subtilis
0/0/0	0	0	0.3/0.3	0/0/0	0/0	0//0	0/0/	0/0/0	2.7/0			0/0/0	Other bacteria and viruses
													---Other
0/0/0	0	0	0/0	0/0/0	0/0	0//0	0/0/	0/0/0	0/0			0/0/0	Sclerotinia, Paecilomyces lilacinus, Trichoderma harzianum, oligomale Pythium
0/0/0	0	0	0/0	0/0/0	0/0	0//0	0/0/	0/0/0	0/0			0/0/0	Other dual—use controlled toxins
0/0/0	0	0	0/0	0/0/0	0/0	0//0	0/0/	0/0/0	0/0			0/0/0	Other toxins, cultured microorganisms (excluding yeast) and similar products
													-Cell cultures, whether or not modified
0/0/0	0	0	0/0	0/0/0	0/0	0//0	0/0/	0/0/0	0/0			0/0/0	--Cell therapy products

税则号列	货品名称〔CIQ 扩展编码及品名—T2 表示见附表 2〕	最惠(%)	暂定税率	普通	增值/消费	出口退税	计量单位	监管条件/特殊证件	检验检疫	对美关税	亚太上/下
3002.5900	--其他〔101 普通动物细胞，102SPF 级动物细胞，103 细胞库的动物细胞系，104 其他动物细胞，401 人源血细胞，402 临床用捐献配型的骨髓造血干细胞，403 临床用捐献配型的外周血造血干细胞，404 临床用捐献配型的脐带血造血干细胞，405 其他人源干细胞，406 国际知名保藏机构的人源细胞株(系)，407 其他商品化的人源细胞株(系)，408 经基因编辑的人源细胞(细胞株)，409 其他培养的人源细胞，410 临床采集，含《人间传染的病原微生物名录》内一类病原微生物，411 临床采集，含《人间传染的病原微生物名录》内二类病原微生物，412 临床采集，含《人间传染的病原微生物名录》内三类病原微生物，413 临床采集，含《人间传染的病原微生物名录》内四类病原微生物，414 临床采集，含新发传染病或名录外再现传染病病原微生物，415 临床采集，含寄生虫，416 临床采集，经过血液传播病原体筛查为阴性，417 商品化含《人间传染的病原微生物名录》内一类病原微生物，418 商品化含《人间传染的病原微生物名录》内二类病原微生物，419 商品化含《人间传染的病原微生物名录》内三类病原微生物，420 商品化含《人间传染的病原微生物名录》内四类病原微生物，421 商品化经过血液传播病原体筛查为阴性〕	3	0	20	13/	13	千克	AB/1	PVQW		
	-其他：										
3002.9040	---遗传物质和基因修饰生物体										
3002.9040 10	两用物项管制遗传物质和基因修饰生物体[T2]	3	0	20	13/	13	千克	3AB/1	PVQW		
3002.9040 90	其他遗传物质和基因修饰生物体[T2]	3	0	20	13/	13	千克	AB/1	PVQW		
3002.9090	---其他										
3002.9090 01	人血〔T2〕	3	0	20	13/	13	千克	ABV/13	VW		
3002.9090 10	治病、防病或诊断用的濒危动物血制品〔101 濒危动物血液，102 濒危动物血浆，103 濒危动物血清，104 其他濒危动物血制品〕	3	0	20	13/	0	千克	ABQFE/13	PQ		
3002.9090 90	治病、防病或诊断用的其他动物血制品〔T2〕	3	0	20	13/	13	千克	ABQ/13	PQ		
30.03	**两种或两种以上成分混合而成的治病或防病用药品(不包括税目 30.02、30.05 或 30.06 的货品)，未配定剂量或制成零售包装：**										
	-含有青霉素及具有青霉烷酸结构的青霉素衍生物或链霉素及其衍生物：										
	---青霉素：										
3003.1011	----氨苄青霉素〔101 其他化工产品，999 含有青霉素及链霉素的药品(未配定剂量)〕	0		30	13/	13	千克	Q/1			0/0
3003.1012	----羟氨苄青霉素〔101 其他化工产品，999 含有青霉素及链霉素的药品(未配定剂量)〕	0		30	13/	13	千克	Q/1			0/0
3003.1013	----青霉素 V〔101 其他化工产品，999 含有青霉素及链霉素的药品(未配定剂量)〕	0		30	13/	13	千克	Q/1			0/0
3003.1019	----其他〔101 其他化工产品，999 含有青霉素及链霉素的药品(未配定剂量)〕	0		30	13/	13	千克	Q/1			0/0
3003.1090	---其他〔101 其他化工产品，999 含有青霉素及链霉素的药品(未配定剂量)〕	0		30	13/	13	千克	Q/1			0/0
	-其他，含有抗菌素：										
	---头孢菌素：										
3003.2011	----头孢噻肟〔999〕	0		30	13/	13	千克	Q/1			0/0
3003.2012	----头孢他啶〔999〕	0		30	13/	13	千克	Q/1			0/0
3003.2013	----头孢西丁〔999〕	0		30	13/	13	千克	Q/1			0/0
3003.2014	----头孢替唑〔999〕	0		30	13/	13	千克	Q/1			0/0
3003.2015	----头孢克罗〔999〕	0		30	13/	13	千克	Q/1			0/0
3003.2016	----头孢呋辛〔999〕	0		30	13/	13	千克	Q/1			0/0
3003.2017	----头孢三嗪(头孢曲松)〔999〕	0		30	13/	13	千克	Q/1			0/0
3003.2018	----头孢哌酮〔999〕	0		30	13/	13	千克	Q/1			0/0
3003.2019	----其他〔999〕	0		30	13/	13	千克	Q/1			0/0
3003.2090	---其他〔999〕	0		30	13/	13	千克	Q/1			0/0
	-其他，含有激素或税目 29.37 的其他产品：										
3003.3100	--含有胰岛素〔999〕	0		30	13/	13	千克	Q/1		2.5	0/0
3003.3900	--其他〔101 其他化工产品，999 其他含有激素的药品(未配定剂量)〕	0		30	13/	13	千克	Q/1			0/0
	-其他，含有生物碱及其衍生物：										
3003.4100	--含有麻黄碱及其盐〔998 药品，999 其他化工产品〕	5		35	13/	13	千克	Q/1			
3003.4200	--含有伪麻黄碱(INN)及其盐〔998 药品，999 其他化工产品〕	5		30	13/	13	千克	Q/1			
3003.4300	--含有去甲麻黄碱及其盐〔998 药品，999 其他化工产品〕	5		35	13/	13	千克	Q/1			
3003.4900	--其他										

协定税率 %								RCEP		特惠税率 %			Article Description
东/冰/格	巴基斯坦	韩国	瑞士上/下	哥/秘/柬	澳/毛	新西/坡/智	中国港/澳/台	东盟及马来/澳/韩	日/新	亚太2国	老/柬/缅	98/97/95	
0/0/0	0	0	0/0	0/0/0	0/0	0//0	0/0/	0/0/0	0/0			0/0/0	--Other
													-Other:
													---Genetics material and gene-modified or ganism
0/0/0	0	0	0/0	0/0/0	0/0	0//0	0/0/	0/0/0	0/0			0/0/0	Genetics material and gene-modified or ganism under sensitive items control
0/0/0	0	0	0/0	0/0/0	0/0	0//0	0/0/	0/0/0	0/0			0/0/0	Other genetics material and gene-modified or ganism
													---Other
0/0/0	0	0	0/0	0/0/0	0/0	0//0	0/0/	0/0/0	0/0			0/0/0	Human blood
0/0/0	0	0	0/0	0/0/0	0/0	0//0	0/0/	0/0/0	0/0			0/0/0	Blood products of endangered animals for treatment, prevention or diagnosis
0/0/0	0	0	0/0	0/0/0	0/0	0//0	0/0/	0/0/0	0/0			0/0/0	Other animal blood products for treatment, prevention or diagnosis
													Medicaments (excluding goods of heading No. 30.02, 30.05 or 30.06) consisting of two or more constituents which have been mixed together for therapeutic or prophylactic uses, not put up in measured doses or in forms or packings for retail sale:
													-Containing penicillins or derivatives thereof, with a penicillanic acid structure, or streptomycins or their derivatives:
													---Containing penicillins:
0/0/0	0	0	0/0	0/0/0	0/0	0//0	0/0/	0/0/0	5.5/0			0/0/0	----Ampicillin
0/0/0	0	0	0/0	0/0/0	0/0	0//0	0/0/	0/0/0	5.5/0			0/0/0	----Amoxycillin
0/0/0	0	0	0/0	0/0/0	0/0	0//0	0/0/	0/0/0	5.5/0			0/0/0	----Penicillin V
0/0/0	0	0	0/0	0/0/0	0/0	0//0	0/0/	0/0/0	5.5/0			0/0/0	----Other
0/0/0	0	0	0/0	0/0/0	0/0	0//0	0/0/	0/0/0	5.5/0			0/0/0	---Other
													-Other, containing antibiotics:
													---Containing cephamycins:
0/0/0	0	0	0/0	0/0/0	0/0	0//0	0/0/	0/0/0	5.5/0			0/0/0	----Cefotaxime
0/0/0	0	0	0/0	0/0/0	0/0	0//0	0/0/	0/0/0	5.5/0			0/0/0	----Ceftazidime
0/0/0	0	0	0/0	0/0/0	0/0	0//0	0/0/	0/0/0	5.5/0			0/0/0	----Cefoxitin
0/0/0	0	0	0/0	0/0/0	0/0	0//0	0/0/	0/0/0	5.5/0			0/0/0	----Ceftezole
0/0/0	0	0	0/0	0/0/0	0/0	0//0	0/0/	0/0/0	5.5/0			0/0/0	----Cefaclor
0/0/0	0	0	0/0	0/0/0	0/0	0//0	0/0/	0/0/0	5.5/0			0/0/0	--Cefuroxime
0/0/0	0	0	0/0	0/0/0	0/0	0//0	0/0/	0/0/0	5.5/0			0/0/0	----Ceftriaxone
0/0/0	0	0	0/0	0/0/0	0/0	0//0	0/0/	0/0/0	5.5/0			0/0/0	----Cefoperazone
0/0/0	0	0	0/0	0/0/0	0/0	0//0	0/0/	0/0/0	5.5/0			0/0/0	----Other
0/0/0	0	0	0/0	0/0/0	0/0	0//0	0/0/	0/0/0	5.5/0			0/0/0	---Other
													-Other, containing hormones or other products of heading 29.37:
0/0/0	0	0	0/0	0/0/0	0/0	0//0	0/0/	0/0/0	4.5/0			0/0/0	--Containing insulin
0/0/0	0	0	0/0	0/0/0	0/0	0//0	0/0/	0/0/0	5.5/0			0/0/0	--Other
													-Other, containing alkaloids or derivatives thereof:
0/0/0	0	0	0/0	0/0/0	0/0	0//0	0/0/	0/0/0	0/0			0/0/0	--Containing ephedrine or its salts
0/0/0	0	0	0/0	0/0/0	0/0	0//0	0/0/	0/0/0	0/0			0/0/0	--Containing pseudoephedrine (*INN*) or its salts
0/0/0	0	0	0/0	0/0/0	0/0	0//0	0/0/	0/0/0	0/0			0/0/0	--Containing norephedrine or its salts
													--Other

税则号列	货品名称〔CIQ 扩展编码及品名－T2 表示见附表 2〕	最惠(%)	暂定税率	普通	增值/消费	出口退税	计量单位	监管条件/特殊证件	检验检疫	对美关税	亚太上/下
3003.4900 10	含奎宁或其盐的混合药品(未配定剂量或非零售包装,混合指含两种或两种以上成分)〔998 药品,999 其他化工产品〕	5		35	13/	13	千克	Q/1			
3003.4900 90	含其他生物碱及衍生物的混合药品(未配定剂量或非零售包装,混合指含两种或两种以上成分)〔998 药品,999 其他化工产品〕	5		30	13/	13	千克	Q/1			
	-其他,含有本章子目注释二所列抗疟疾活性成分的:										
3003.6010	---含有青蒿素及其衍生物〔998 药品,999 其他化工产品〕	0		30	13/	13	千克	Q/1		2.5	
3003.6090	---其他										
3003.6090 10	含有磺胺类的混合药品(未配定剂量或非零售包装,混合指含两种或两种以上成分)〔998 药品,999 其他化工产品〕	0		30	13/	13	千克	Q/1		2.5	
3003.6090 20	含濒危动植物的混合药品(未配定剂量或非零售包装,混合指含两种或两种以上成分)〔998 药品,999 其他化工产品〕	0		30	13/	0	千克	EFQ/1		2.5	
3003.6090 90	其他含有本章子目注释二所列抗疟疾活性成分的混合药品(未配定剂量或非零售包装,混合指含两种或两种以上成分)〔998 药品,999 其他化工产品〕	0		30	13/	13	千克	Q/1		2.5	
3003.9000	-其他										
3003.9000 10	含紫杉醇的混合药品(未配定剂量或非零售包装,混合指含两种或两种以上成分)〔998 药品,999 其他化工产品〕	0		30	13/	0	千克	EFQ/1			
3003.9000 20	其他含未列名濒危动植物混合药品(未配定剂量或非零售包装,混合指含两种或两种以上成分)〔998 药品,999 其他化工产品〕	0		30	13/	0	千克	EFQ/1			
3003.9000 30	其他含磺胺类的混合药品(未配定剂量或非零售包装,混合指含两种或两种以上成分)〔998 药品,999 其他化工产品〕	0		30	13/	13	千克	Q/1			
3003.9000 90	其他含未列名成分混合药品(未配定剂量或非零售包装,混合指含两种或两种以上成分)〔998 药品,999 其他化工产品〕	0		30	13/	13	千克	Q/1			
30.04	**由混合或非混合产品构成的治病或防病用药品(不包括税目 30.02、30.05 或 30.06 的货品),已配定剂量(包括制成皮肤摄入形式的)或制成零售包装:**										
	-含有青霉素及具有青霉烷酸结构的青霉素衍生物或链霉素及其衍生物:										
	---青霉素:										
3004.1011	----氨苄青霉素制剂〔101:其他化工产品;999:含有青霉素和链霉素及其衍生物的药品(已配定剂量)〕	0		30	13/	13	千克	Q/1			0/0
3004.1012	----羟氨苄青霉素制剂										
3004.1012 10	已配剂量兽用制剂(包括进口兽药管理目录的商品)(包括零售包装)〔101 含有青霉素和链霉素及其衍生物的药品(已配定剂量),999 其他化工产品〕	0		30	13/	13	千克	R/1			0/0
3004.1012 90	其他羟氨苄青霉素制剂(包括零售包装)〔101 含有青霉素和链霉素及其衍生物的药品(已配定剂量,999 其他化工产品〕	0		30	13/	13	千克	Q/1			0/0
3004.1013	----青霉素 V 制剂〔101 其他化工产品,999 含有青霉素和链霉素及其衍生物的药品(已配定剂量)〕	0		30	13/	13	千克	Q/1			0/0
3004.1019	----其他										
3004.1019 10	已配剂量兽用制剂(包括进口兽药管理目录的商品;包括零售包装)〔999〕	0		30	13/	13	千克	R/1			0/0
3004.1019 90	其他已配剂量青霉素制剂(包括零售包装)〔999〕	0		30	13/	13	千克	Q/1			0/0
3004.1090	---其他〔999〕	0		30	13/	13	千克	Q/1			0/0
	-其他,含有抗菌素:										
	---头孢菌素:										
3004.2011	----头孢噻肟制剂〔999〕	0		30	13/	13	千克	Q/1			0/0
3004.2012	----头孢他啶制剂〔999〕	0		30	13/	13	千克	Q/1			0/0
3004.2013	----头孢西丁制剂〔999〕	0		30	13/	13	千克	Q/1			0/0
3004.2014	----头孢替唑制剂〔999〕	0		30	13/	13	千克	Q/1			0/0

协定税率 %								RCEP		特惠税率 %			Article Description
东/冰/格	巴基斯坦	韩国	瑞士上/下	哥/秘/柬	澳/毛	新西/坡/智	中国港/澳/台	东盟及马来/澳/韩	日/新	亚太2国	老/柬/缅	98/97/95	
0/0/0	0	0	0/0	0/0/0	0/0	0//0	0/0/	0/0/0	0/0			0/0/0	Medicaments containing quinine or its salts(consisting of two or more constituents which have been mixed together, not put up in measured doses or in forms or packings for retail sale)
0/0/0	0	0	0/0	0/0/0	0/0	0//0	0/0/	0/0/0	0/0			0/0/0	Other medicaments containing alkaloids or derivatives thereof (consisting of two or more constituents which have been mixed together, but not containing hormones or other prouducts of heading 29.37 or antibiotics, not put up in measured doses or in forms or packings for retail sale)
													-Other, containing antimalarial active principles described in Subheading Note 2 to this Chapter:
0/0/0	0	0	0/0	0/0/0	0/0	0//0	0/0/	0/0/0	4.5/0			0/0/0	---Containing artemisinins and their derivatives
													---Other
0/0/0	0	0	0/0	0/0/0	0/0	0//0	0/0/	0/0/0	4.5/0			0/0/0	Medicaments containing sulfa drugs (consisting of two or more constituents which have been mixed together, not put up in measured doses or in forms or packings for retail sale)
0/0/0	0	0	0/0	0/0/0	0/0	0//0	0/0/	0/0/0	4.5/0			0/0/0	Medicaments containing endangered animals and plants(consisting of two or more constituents which have been mixed together, not put up in measured doses or in forms or packings for retail sale)
0/0/0	0	0	0/0	0/0/0	0/0	0//0	0/0/	0/0/0	4.5/0			0/0/0	Other, containing antimalarial active principles described in Subheading Note 2 to this Chapter(consisting of two or more constituents which have been mixed together, but not containing hormones or other prouducts of heading 29.37 or antibiotics, not put up in measured doses or in forms or packings for retail sale)
													-Other
0/0/0	0	0	0/0	0/0/0	0/0	0//0	0/0/	0/0/0	4.5/0			0/0/0	Other medicaments containing sulfa drugs(consisting of two or more constituents which have been mixed together, not put up in measured doses or in forms or packings for retail sale)
0/0/0	0	0	0/0	0/0/0	0/0	0//0	0/0/	0/0/0	4.5/0			0/0/0	Other medicaments containing endangered animals and plants (consisting of two or more constituents which have been mixed together, not put up in measured doses or in forms or packings for retail sale)
0/0/0	0	0	0/0	0/0/0	0/0	0//0	0/0/	0/0/0	4.5/0			0/0/0	Other medicaments containing sulfa drugs(consisting of two or more constituents which have been mixed together, not put up in measured doses or in forms or packings for retail sale)
0/0/0	0	0	0/0	0/0/0	0/0	0//0	0/0/	0/0/0	4.5/0			0/0/0	Other medicaments, containing other two or more constituents, not elsewhere specified or included, not put up in measured doses or in forms of packings for retail sale
													Medicaments (excluding goods of heading No. 30.02, 30.05 or 30.06) consisting of mixed or unmixed products for therapeutic or prophylactic uses, put up in measured doses(including those in the form of transdermal administration systems) or in forms or packings for retail sale:
													Containing penicillins or derivatives thereof, with a penicilla nic acid structure, or streptomycins or their derivatives:
													---Containing penicillins:
0/0/0	0	0	0/0	0/0/0	0/0	0//0	0/0/	0/0/0	5.5/0			0/0/0	----Ampicillin
													----Amoxycillin
0/0/0	0	0	0/0	0/0/0	0/0	0//0	0/0/	0/0/0	5.5/0		//	0/0/0	Formulated dosage of veterinary preparations (including commodities in the Management Catalogue of imported veterinary drugs; including retail packaging)
0/0/0	0	0	0/0	0/0/0	0/0	0//0	0/0/	0/0/0	5.5/0		//	0/0/0	Other ampicillin preparations (including retail packaging)
0/0/0	0	0	0/0	0/0/0	0/0	0//0	0/0/	0/0/0	5.5/0			0/0/0	----Penicillin V
													----Other
0/0/0	0	0	0/0	0/0/0	0/0	0//0	0/0/	0/0/0	5.5/0		//	0/0/0	Formulated dosage of veterinary preparations (including commodities in the Management Catalogue of imported veterinary drugs; including retail packaging)
0/0/0	0	0	0/0	0/0/0	0/0	0//0	0/0/	0/0/0	5.5/0		//	0/0/0	Other prescribed doses of penicillin preparations (including retail packaging)
0/0/0	0	0	0/0	0/0/0	0/0	0//0	0/0/	0/0/0	5.5/0			0/0/0	---Other
													-Other, containing antibiotics:
													---Containing cephamycins:
0/0/0	0	0	0/0	0/0/0	0/0	0//0	0/0/	0/0/0	5.5/0			0/0/0	----Cefotaxime
0/0/0	0	0	0/0	0/0/0	0/0	0//0	0/0/	0/0/0	5.5/0			0/0/0	----Ceftazidime
0/0/0	0	0	0/0	0/0/0	0/0	0//0	0/0/	0/0/0	5.5/0			0/0/0	----Cefoxitin
0/0/0	0	0	0/0	0/0/0	0/0	0//0	0/0/	0/0/0	5.5/0			0/0/0	----Ceftezole

税则号列		货品名称〔CIQ扩展编码及品名—T2表示见附表2〕	最惠(%)	暂定税率	普通	增值/消费	出口退税	计量单位	监管条件/特殊证件	检验检疫	对美关税	亚太上/下
3004.2015		----头孢克罗制剂〔999〕	0		30	13/	13	千克	Q/1			0/0
3004.2016		----头孢呋辛制剂〔999〕	0		30	13/	13	千克	Q/1			0/0
3004.2017		----头孢三嗪(头孢曲松)制剂〔999〕	0		30	13/	13	千克	Q/1			0/0
3004.2018		----头孢哌酮制剂〔999〕	0		30	13/	13	千克	Q/1			0/0
3004.2019		----其他										
3004.2019	20	已配剂量兽用制剂(包括进口兽药管理目录的商品;包括零售包装)〔999〕	0		30	13/	13	千克	R/1			0/0
3004.2019	90	其他已配剂量头孢菌素制剂(包括零售包装的制成品)〔999〕	0		30	13/	13	千克	Q/1			0/0
3004.2090		---其他										
3004.2090	20	已配剂量兽用制剂(包括进口兽药管理目录的商品;包括零售包装)〔999〕	0		30	13/	13	千克	R/1			0/0
3004.2090	91	抗(防)癌药品制剂(不含癌症辅助治疗药品)(包括抗癌药品清单第一批相关商品)〔999〕	0		30	3/	13	千克	Q/1			0/0
3004.2090	99	其他已配剂量含有其他抗菌素的药品(包括制成零售包装)(因拆分抗癌药产生的兜底税号)〔999〕	0		30	13/	13	千克	Q/1			0/0
		-其他,含有激素或税目29.37的其他产品:										
		--含有胰岛素:										
3004.3110		---含有重组人胰岛素的										
3004.3110	10	已配剂量含重组人胰岛素的单方制剂(包括零售包装)〔999〕	0		30	13/	13	千克	L/1			0/0
3004.3110	90	已配剂量含重组人胰岛素的其他药品(不含抗菌素,包括零售包装)〔999〕	0		30	13/	13	千克	Q/1			0/0
3004.3190		---其他										
3004.3190	10	其他已配剂量含胰岛素的单方制剂(包括零售包装)〔999〕	0		30	13/	13	千克	L/1			0/0
3004.3190	90	其他已配剂量含胰岛素的其他药品(不含抗菌素,包括零售包装)〔999〕	0		30	13/	13	千克	Q/1			0/0
3004.3200		--含有皮质甾类激素及其衍生物或结构类似物										
3004.3200	11	已配剂量含1-雄烯二醇或1-雄烯二酮的单方制剂(包括其衍生物及结构类似物,包括零售包装)〔999〕	0		30	13/	13	千克	L/1			0/0
3004.3200	12	已配剂量含甲酰勃龙的单方制剂(包括其衍生物及结构类似物,包括零售包装)〔999〕	0		30	13/	13	千克	L/1			0/0
3004.3200	13	已配剂量含雄甾-4-烯-3β,17α-二醇[4-雄烯二醇(3β,17α)]的单方制剂(包括其衍生物及结构类似物,包括零售包装)〔999〕	0		30	13/	13	千克	L/1			0/0
3004.3200	14	已配剂量含雄甾-5-烯-3β,17α-二醇[5-雄烯二醇(3β,17α)]的单方制剂(包括其衍生物及结构类似物,包括零售包装)〔999〕	0		30	13/	13	千克	L/1			0/0
3004.3200	15	已配剂量含4-雄烯二醇或乙雌烯醇的单方制剂(包括其衍生物及结构类似物,包括零售包装)〔999〕	0		30	13/	13	千克	L/1			0/0
3004.3200	16	已配剂量含5-雄烯二酮的单方制剂(包括其衍生物及结构类似物,包括零售包装)〔999〕	0		30	13/	13	千克	L/1			0/0
3004.3200	17	已配剂量含5α—雄烷—3α,17β—二醇(雄烷二醇(3α,17β))或5β—雄烷—3α,17β—二醇(5β—雄烷二醇(3α,17β))的单方制剂(包括其衍生物及其结构类似物,包括零售包装)〔999〕	0		30	13/	13	千克	L/1			0/0
3004.3200	18	已配剂量5α—雄烷—3β,17α—二醇(雄烷二醇(3β,17α))的单方制剂(包括其衍生物及结构类似物,包括零售包装)〔999〕	0		30	13/	13	千克	L/1			0/0
3004.3200	19	已配剂量含勃拉睾酮的单方制剂(包括其衍生物及结构类似物,包括零售包装)〔999〕	0		30	13/	13	千克	L/1			0/0
3004.3200	21	已配剂量含勃地酮的单方制剂(包括其衍生物及结构类似物,包括零售包装)〔999〕	0		30	13/	13	千克	L/1			0/0

协定税率 %								RCEP		特惠税率 %			Article Description
东/冰/格	巴基斯坦	韩国	瑞士上/下	哥/秘/柬	澳/毛	新西/坡/智	中国港/澳/台	东盟及马来/澳/韩	日/新	亚太2国	老/柬/缅	98/97/95	
0/0/0	0	0	0/0	0/0/0	0/0	0//0	0/0/	0/0/0	5.5/0			0/0/0	----Cefaclor
0/0/0	0	0	0/0	0/0/0	0/0	0//0	0/0/	0/0/0	5.5/0			0/0/0	----Cefuroxime
0/0/0	0	0	0/0	0/0/0	0/0	0//0	0/0/	0/0/0	5.5/0			0/0/0	----Ceftriaxone
0/0/0	0	0	0/0	0/0/0	0/0	0//0	0/0/	0/0/0	5.5/0			0/0/0	----Cefoperazone
													----Other
0/0/0	0	1.2	0/0	0/0/0	0/0	0//0	0/0/	5.4/5.4/5.4	5.5/5.4		//	0/0/0	Formulated dosage of veterinary preparations (including commodities in the Management Catalogue of imported veterinary drugs; including retail packaging)
0/0/0	0	1.2	0/0	0/0/0	0/0	0//0	0/0/	5.4/5.4/5.4	5.5/5.4			0/0/0	Other cephalosporin preparations, put up in measured doses (including in forms of packing for retail sale)
													---Other
0/0/0	0	0	0/0	0/0/0	0/0	0//0	0/0/	0/0/0	5.5/0		//	0/0/0	Formulated dosage of veterinary preparations (including commodities in the Management Catalogue of imported veterinary drugs; including retail packaging)
0/0/0	0	0	0/0	0/0/0	0/0	0//0	0/0/	0/0/0	5.5/0			0/0/0	Anti—cancer drug preparations (excluding cancer adjuncts)
0/0/0	0	0	0/0	0/0/0	0/0	0//0	0/0/	0/0/0	5.5/0			0/0/0	Containing other antibiotics of drugs, put up in measured dose (including in forms or packing for retail sale) (Tax number due to separation of anticancer drugs)
													-Other, containing hormones or other products of heading 29.37:
													--Containing insulin:
													---Containing recombinant human insulin
0/0/0	0	0	0/0	0/0/0	0/0	0//0	0/0/	0/0/0	4.5/0			0/0/0	Simple preparation with recombinant human insulin, put up in measured doses (including in forms or packing for retail sale)
0/0/0	0	0	0/0	0/0/0	0/0	0//0	0/0/	0/0/0	4.5/0			0/0/0	Containing recombinant human insulin of other drugs, put up in measured doses (excluding antibiotics, including in forms or packing for retail sale)
													---Other
0/0/0	0	0	0/0	0/0/0	0/0	0//0	0/0/	0/0/0	4.5/0			0/0/0	Other single preparations, containing insulin, put up in measured dose (including in forms or packing for retail sale)
0/0/0	0	0	0/0	0/0/0	0/0	0//0	0/0/	0/0/0	4.5/0			0/0/0	Other medicaments, containing insulin, put up in measured doses (excluding antibiotics, including in forms or packing for retail sale)
													--Containing corticosteroid hormones, their derivatives and structural analogues
0/0/0	0	0	0/0	0/0/0	0/0	0//0	0/0/	0/0/0	4.5/0			0/0/0	Single preparations, containing androstenediol or androstenedione, put up in measured doses (including in forms or packing for retail sale)
0/0/0	0	0	0/0	0/0/0	0/0	0//0	0/0/	0/0/0	4.5/0			0/0/0	Single preparations, containing formebolone, put up in measured dose (including their derivatives and structural analogues, in forms or packing for retail sale)
0/0/0	0	0	0/0	0/0/0	0/0	0//0	0/0/	0/0/0	4.5/0			0/0/0	Single preparations, containing androst-4-ene-3β, 17α-diol[4-androstenediol (3β, 17α)], put up in measured dose (including their derivatives and structural analogues, in forms or packing for retail sale)
0/0/0	0	0	0/0	0/0/0	0/0	0//0	0/0/	0/0/0	4.5/0			0/0/0	Single preparations, containing androst-5-ene-3β, 17α-diol[5-androstenediol (3β, 17α)], put up in measured dose (including their derivatives and structural analogues, in forms or packing for retail sale)
0/0/0	0	0	0/0	0/0/0	0/0	0//0	0/0/	0/0/0	4.5/0			0/0/0	Single preparations, containing 4-androstenediol or ethylestrenol, put up in measured dose (including their derivatives and structural analogues, in froms or packing for retail sale)
0/0/0	0	0	0/0	0/0/0	0/0	0//0	0/0/	0/0/0	4.5/0			0/0/0	Single preparations, containing androstenedione isomer, put up in measured doses (including their derivatives and structural analogues, in forms or packing for retail sale)
0/0/0	0	0	0/0	0/0/0	0/0	0//0	0/0/	0/0/0	4.5/0			0/0/0	Single preparations, containing 5α-androstane-3α, 17β-estrad[dihydroandrosterone (3β, 17α)] or 5β-androstane-3α, 17β-glycol[5β-dihydroandrosterone (3α, 17β)], put up in measured doses (including their derivatives and structural analogues, in forms or packing for retail sale)
0/0/0	0	0	0/0	0/0/0	0/0	0//0	0/0/	0/0/0	4.5/0			0/0/0	Single preparations, containing 5α-androstane-3α, 17β-estrad[dihydroandrosterone (3β, 17α)], put up in measured doses (including their derivatives and structural analogues, in forms or packing for retail sale)
0/0/0	0	0	0/0	0/0/0	0/0	0//0	0/0/	0/0/0	4.5/0			0/0/0	Single preparations, containing bolasterone, put up in measured doses (including their derivatives and structural analogues, in forms or packing for retail sale)
0/0/0	0	0	0/0	0/0/0	0/0	0//0	0/0/	0/0/0	4.5/0			0/0/0	Single preparations, containing boldenone, put up in measured doses (including their derivatives and structural analogues, in forms or packing for retail sale)

税则号列		货品名称〔CIQ扩展编码及品名—T2表示见附表2〕	最惠(%)	暂定税率	普通	增值/消费	出口退税	计量单位	监管条件/特殊证件	检验检疫	对美关税	亚太上/下
3004.3200	22	已配剂量含勃二酮的单方制剂(包括其衍生物及结构类似物,包括零售包装)〔999〕	0		30	13/	13	千克	/1			0/0
3004.3200	23	已配剂量含卡芦睾酮或达那唑的单方制剂(包括其衍生物及结构类似物,包括零售包装)〔999〕	0		30	13/	13	千克	L/1			0/0
3004.3200	24	已配剂量含氯司替勃的单方制剂(包括其衍生物及结构类似物,包括零售包装)〔999〕	0		30	13/	13	千克	L/1			0/0
3004.3200	25	已配剂量含去氢氯甲睾酮的单方制剂(包括其衍生物及结构类似物,包括零售包装)〔999〕	0		30	13/	13	千克	L/1			0/0
3004.3200	26	已配剂量含甲基氯司替勃的单方制剂(包括其衍生物及结构类似物,包括零售包装)	0		30	13/	13	千克	L/1			0/0
3004.3200	28	已配剂量含普拉睾酮或屈他雄酮的单方制剂(包括其衍生物及结构类似物,包括零售包装)〔999〕	0		30	13/	13	千克	L/1			0/0
3004.3200	29	已配剂量含去氧甲睾酮或双氢睾酮的单方制剂(包括其衍生物及结构类似物,包括零售包装)〔999〕	0		30	13/	13	千克	L/1			0/0
3004.3200	31	已配剂量含表双氢睾酮或氟甲睾酮的单方制剂(包括其衍生物及结构类似物,包括零售包装)〔999〕	0		30	13/	13	千克	L/1			0/0
3004.3200	32	已配剂量含夫拉扎勃的单方制剂(包括其衍生物及结构类似物,包括零售包装)〔999〕	0		30	13/	13	千克	L/1			0/0
3004.3200	33	已配剂量含孕三烯酮或4-羟基睾酮的单方制剂(包括其衍生物及结构类似物,包括零售包装)〔999〕	0		30	13/	13	千克	L/1			0/0
3004.3200	34	含3α-羟基-5α-雄烷-17-酮的单方制剂(包括其衍生物及结构类似物,已配剂量或制成零售包装)〔999〕	0		30	13/	13	千克	/1			0/0
3004.3200	35	已配剂量含美睾酮或美雄酮的单方制剂(包括其衍生物及结构类似物,包括零售包装)〔999〕	0		30	13/	13	千克	L/1			0/0
3004.3200	36	已配剂量含甲基屈他雄酮的单方制剂(包括其衍生物及结构类似物,包括零售包装)〔999〕	0		30	13/	13	千克	L/1			0/0
3004.3200	37	已配剂量含甲二烯诺龙的单方制剂(包括其衍生物及结构类似物,包括零售包装)〔999〕	0		30	13/	13	千克	L/1			0/0
3004.3200	38	已配剂量含甲基—1—睾酮或甲诺睾酮的单方制剂(包括其衍生物及结构类似物,包括零售包装)〔999〕	0		30	13/	13	千克	L/1			0/0
3004.3200	39	已配剂量含美曲勃龙的单方制剂(包括其衍生物及结构类似物,包括零售包装)〔999〕	0		30	13/	13	千克	L/1			0/0
3004.3200	41	已配剂量含美雄诺龙或美替诺龙的单方制剂(包括其衍生物及结构类似物,包括零售包装)〔999〕	0		30	13/	13	千克	L/1			0/0
3004.3200	42	已配剂量含美雄醇或甲睾酮或米勃酮的单方制剂(包括其衍生物及结构类似物,包括零售包装)〔999〕	0		30	13/	13	千克	L/1			0/0
3004.3200	43	已配剂量含诺龙或诺勃酮或诺司替勃的单方制剂(包括其衍生物及结构类似物,包括零售包装)〔999〕	0		30	13/	13	千克	L/1			0/0
3004.3200	44	已配剂量含19-去甲雄烯二酮的单方制剂(包括其衍生物及结构类似物,包括零售包装)〔999〕	0		30	13/	13	千克	L/1			0/0

协定税率 %								RCEP		特惠税率 %			Article Description
东/冰/格	巴基斯坦	韩国	瑞士上/下	哥/秘/柬	澳/毛	新西/坡/智	中国港/澳/台	东盟及马来/澳/韩	日/新	亚太2国	老/柬/缅	98/97/95	
0/0/0	0	0	0/0	0/0/0	0/0	0//0	0/0/	0/0/0	4.5/0			0/0/0	Single preparations, containing androstadien-3, 17-dione, put up in measured doses(including their derivatives and structural analogues, in forms or packing for retail sale)
0/0/0	0	0	0/0	0/0/0	0/0	0//0	0/0/	0/0/0	4.5/0			0/0/0	Single preparations, containing calusterone or danazol, put up in measured doses(including their derivatives and structural analogues, in forms or packing for retail sale)
0/0/0	0	0	0/0	0/0/0	0/0	0//0	0/0/	0/0/0	4.5/0			0/0/0	Single preparations, containing clostebol, put up in measured doses (including their derivatives and structural analogues, in forms or packing for retail sale)
0/0/0	0	0	0/0	0/0/0	0/0	0//0	0/0/	0/0/0	4.5/0			0/0/0	Single preparations, containing dehydrochloro-methyltestosterone, put up in measured doses(including their derivatives and structural analogues, in forms or packing for retail sale)
0/0/0	0	0	0/0	0/0/0	0/0	0//0	0/0/	0/0/0	4.5/0		//	0/0/0	Single dose preparations (including derivatives and structural analogues, including retail packaging) with methylchlorostilbestrol
0/0/0	0	0	0/0	0/0/0	0/0	0//0	0/0/	0/0/0	4.5/0			0/0/0	Single preparations, containing prasterone or dormostanolone, put up in measured doses(including their derivatives and structural analogues, in forms or packing for retail sale)
0/0/0	0	0	0/0	0/0/0	0/0	0//0	0/0/	0/0/0	4.5/0			0/0/0	Single preparations, containing deoxymethyltestosterone or dihydrotestosterone, put up in measured doses(including their derivatives and structural analogues, in forms or packing for retail sale)
0/0/0	0	0	0/0	0/0/0	0/0	0//0	0/0/	0/0/0	4.5/0			0/0/0	Single preparations, containing epi-dihydrotestosterone or fluoxymesterone, put up in measured doses(including their derivatives and structural analogues, in forms or packing for retail sale)
0/0/0	0	0	0/0	0/0/0	0/0	0//0	0/0/	0/0/0	4.5/0			0/0/0	Single preparations, containing furazabol, put up in measured doses(including their derivatives and structural analogues, in forms or packing for retail sale)
0/0/0	0	0	0/0	0/0/0	0/0	0//0	0/0/	0/0/0	4.5/0			0/0/0	Single preparations, containing gestrinone or 4-hydroxyltestosterone, put up in measured doses(including their derivatives and structural analogues, in forms or packing for retail sale)
0/0/0	0	0	0/0	0/0/0	0/0	0//0	0/0/	0/0/0	4.5/0			0/0/0	Single preparations, containing 3α-hydroxide-5α-androstane-17-ketone, put up in measured doses(including their derivatives and structural analogues, in forms or packing for retail sale)
0/0/0	0	0	0/0	0/0/0	0/0	0//0	0/0/	0/0/0	4.5/0			0/0/0	Single preparations, containing mesterolone or methandienone, put up in measured doses(including their derivatives and structural analogues, in forms or packing for retail sale)
0/0/0	0	0	0/0	0/0/0	0/0	0//0	0/0/	0/0/0	4.5/0			0/0/0	Single preparations, containing 2α, 17α-dimethyl-5α-androstane-3-ketone-17β-alcohol, put up in measured doses(including their derivatives and structural analogues, in forms or packing for retail sale)
0/0/0	0	0	0/0	0/0/0	0/0	0//0	0/0/	0/0/0	4.5/0			0/0/0	Single preparations, containing 17α-methyl-17β- hydroxy-estr-4,9(10)-di-3-ketone, put up in measured doses(including their derivatives and structural analogues, in forms or packing for retail sale)
0/0/0	0	0	0/0	0/0/0	0/0	0//0	0/0/	0/0/0	4.5/0			0/0/0	Single preparations, containing Methyl-1-testosterone or methylnortestosterone, put up in measured doses(including their derivatives and structural analogues, in forms or packing for retail sale)
0/0/0	0	0	0/0	0/0/0	0/0	0//0	0/0/	0/0/0	4.5/0			0/0/0	Single preparations, containing 17α-methyl-17β- hydroxy-estr-4,9,11triene-3-ketone, put up in measured doses(including their derivatives and structural analogues, in forms or packing for retail sale)
0/0/0	0	0	0/0	0/0/0	0/0	0//0	0/0/	0/0/0	4.5/0			0/0/0	Single preparations, containing mestanolone or methenolone, put up in measured doses(including their derivatives and structural analogues, in forms or packing for retail sale)
0/0/0	0	0	0/0	0/0/0	0/0	0//0	0/0/	0/0/0	4.5/0			0/0/0	Single preparations, containing methandriol or methyltestosterone or mibolerone, put up in measured doses (including their derivatives and structural analogues , in forms or packing for retail sale)
0/0/0	0	0	0/0	0/0/0	0/0	0//0	0/0/	0/0/0	4.5/0			0/0/0	Single preparations, containing nandrolone or norboletone or norclostebol, put up in measured doses (including their derivatives and structural analogues, in forms or packing for retail sale)
0/0/0	0	0	0/0	0/0/0	0/0	0//0	0/0/	0/0/0	4.5/0			0/0/0	Single preparations, containing 19-norandrostenedion or 19-norandrostenedione, put up in measured doses(including their derivatives and structural analogues, in forms or packing for retail sale)

税则号列		货品名称〔CIQ 扩展编码及品名—T2 表示见附表 2〕	最惠(%)	暂定税率	普通	增值/消费	出口退税	计量单位	监管条件/特殊证件	检验检疫	对美关税	亚太上/下
3004.3200	45	已配剂量含去甲雄酮或诺乙雄龙的单方制剂(包括其衍生物及结构类似物,包括零售包装)〔999〕	0		30	13/	13	千克	L/1			0/0
3004.3200	46	已配剂量含 19—去甲本胆烷醇酮的单方制剂(包括其衍生物及结构类似物,包括零售包装)〔999〕	0		30	13/	13	千克	L/1			0/0
3004.3200	47	已配剂量含羟勃龙或氧雄龙的单方制剂(包括其衍生物及结构类似物,包括零售包装)〔999〕	0		30	13/	13	千克	L/1			0/0
3004.3200	48	已配剂量含羟甲睾酮或羟甲烯龙的单方制剂(包括其衍生物及结构类似物,包括零售包装)〔999〕	0		30	13/	13	千克	L/1			0/0
3004.3200	49	已配剂量含前列他唑的单方制剂(包括其衍生物及结构类似物,包括零售包装)〔999〕	0		30	13/	13	千克	L/1			0/0
3004.3200	51	含奎勃龙或替勃龙或群勃龙的单方制剂(包括其衍生物及结构类似物,已配剂量或制成零售包装)〔999〕	0		30	13/	13	千克	L/1			0/0
3004.3200	52	已配剂量含司坦唑醇或司腾勃龙的单方制剂(包括其衍生物及结构类似物,包括零售包装)〔999〕	0		30	13/	13	千克	L/1			0/0
3004.3200	53	已配剂量含 1-睾酮或睾酮的单方制剂(包括其衍生物及结构类似物,包括零售包装)〔999〕	0		30	13/	13	千克	L/1			0/0
3004.3200	54	已配剂量含四氢孕三烯酮或泽仑诺的单方制剂(包括其衍生物及结构类似物,包括零售包装)〔999〕	0		30	13/	13	千克	L/1			0/0
3004.3200	61	已配剂量兽用制剂(包括进口兽药管理目录的商品;包括零售包装)〔999〕	0		30	13/	13	千克	R/1			0/0
3004.3200	71	已配剂量含雄甾-5-烯-3β,17β-二醇[5-雄烯二醇(3β,17β)]的单方制剂(包括其衍生物及结构类似物,不含抗菌素,包括零售包装)〔999〕	0		30	13/	13	千克	L/1			0/0
3004.3200	72	已配剂量含雄甾-4-烯-3,17-二酮(4-雄烯二酮)的单方制剂(包括其衍生物及结构类似物,不含抗菌素,包括零售包装)〔999〕	0		30	13/	13	千克	L/1			0/0
3004.3200	74	已配剂量含 7α-羟基-普拉睾酮的单方制剂(包括其衍生物及结构类似物,不含抗菌素,包括零售包装)〔999〕	0		30	13/	13	千克	L/1			0/0
3004.3200	75	已配剂量含 7β-羟基-普拉睾酮的单方制剂(包括其衍生物及结构类似物,不含抗菌素,包括零售包装)〔999〕	0		30	13/	13	千克	L/1			0/0
3004.3200	76	已配剂量含 7-羰基-普拉睾酮的单方制剂(包括其衍生物及结构类似物,不含抗菌素,包括零售包装)〔999〕	0		30	13/	13	千克	L/1			0/0
3004.3200	77	已配剂量含胆烷醇酮的单方制剂(包括其衍生物及结构类似物,不含抗菌素,包括零售包装)〔999〕	0		30	13/	13	千克	L/1			0/0
3004.3200	78	已配剂量含 1,4—雄烯二酮(雄甾—1,4—二烯—3,17—二酮)的单方制剂(包括其衍生物及结构类似物,不含抗菌素,包括零售包装)〔999〕	0		30	13/	13	千克	L/1			0/0
3004.3200	99	其他已配剂量含其他皮质甾类激素的药品(包括其衍生物及结构类似物,不含抗菌素,包括零售包装)(因拆分抗癌药产生的兜底税号)〔999〕	0		30	13/	13	千克	Q/1			0/0
3004.3900		--其他										
3004.3900	11	已配剂量含克仑特罗的单方制剂(包括零售包装)〔999〕	0		30	13/	13	千克	L/1			0/0
3004.3900	25	已配剂量含绒促性素、促黄体生成素等的单方制剂(包括含生长激素释放肽类(GHRPs)、普拉莫瑞林(生长激素释放肽 2)、CJC1295(CAS 号 863288340)、生长激素释放肽 6、生长激素释放激素及其类似物、生长激素促分泌剂,零售包装)〔999〕	0		30	13/	13	千克	L/1			0/0
3004.3900	26	已配剂量含促皮质素类等肽类激素的单方制剂(包括零售包装,以及已配剂量或零售包装的艾瑞莫瑞林、阿那瑞林、布舍瑞林、可的瑞林、海沙瑞林、伊莫瑞林、舍莫瑞林、替莫瑞林、戈那瑞林、葛瑞林(脑肠肽)及其模拟物类的单方制剂)〔999〕	0		30	13/	13	千克	L/1			0/0

协定税率 %								RCEP		特惠税率 %			Article Description
东/冰/格	巴基斯坦	韩国	瑞士 上/下	哥/秘/柬	澳/毛	新西/坡/智	中国港/澳/台	东盟及马来/澳/韩	日/新	亚太2国	老/柬/缅	98/97/95	
0/0/0	0	0	0/0	0/0/0	0/0	0//0	0/0/	0/0/0	4.5/0			0/0/0	Single preparations, containing norandrosterone or norethandrolone, put up in measured doses(including their derivatives and structural analogues, in forms or packing for retail sale)
0/0/0	0	0	0/0	0/0/0	0/0	0//0	0/0/	0/0/0	4.5/0			0/0/0	Single preparations, containing 19-noretiocholanolone, put up in measured doses(including their derivatives and structural analogues, in forms or packing for retail sale)
0/0/0	0	0	0/0	0/0/0	0/0	0//0	0/0/	0/0/0	4.5/0			0/0/0	Single preparations, containing oxabolone or oxandrolone, put up in measured doses(including their derivatives and structural analogues, in forms or packing for retail sale)
0/0/0	0	0	0/0	0/0/0	0/0	0//0	0/0/	0/0/0	4.5/0			0/0/0	Single preparations, containing Oxymesterone or oxymetholone, put up in measured doses(including their derivatives and structural analogues, in forms or packing for retailsale)
0/0/0	0	0	0/0	0/0/0	0/0	0//0	0/0/	0/0/0	4.5/0			0/0/0	Single preparations, containing 17β-hydroxy-5α-androstane[3, 2-c] pyrazole, put up in measured doses (including their derivatives and structural analogues, in forms or packing for retail sale)
0/0/0	0	0	0/0	0/0/0	0/0	0//0	0/0/	0/0/0	4.5/0			0/0/0	Single preparations, containing quinbolone or tibolone or trenbolone, put up in measured doses(including their derivatives andstructural analogues, in forms or packing for retail sale)
0/0/0	0	0	0/0	0/0/0	0/0	0//0	0/0/	0/0/0	4.5/0			0/0/0	Single preparations, containing stanozolol or stenbolone, put up in measured doses (including their derivatives and structural analogues, in forms or packing for retail sale)
0/0/0	0	0	0/0	0/0/0	0/0	0//0	0/0/	0/0/0	4.5/0			0/0/0	Single preparations, containing 1-testosterone or testosterone, put up in measured doses (including their derivatives and structural analogues, in forms or packing for retail sale)
0/0/0	0	0	0/0	0/0/0	0/0	0//0	0/0/	0/0/0	4.5/0			0/0/0	Single preparations, containing tetrahydrogestrinone or zeranol, put up in measured doses(including their derivatives and structural analogues, in forms or packing for retail sale)
0/0/0	0	0	0/0	0/0/0	0/0	0//0	0/0/	0/0/0	4.5/0		//	0/0/0	Formulated dosage of veterinary preparations (including commodities in the Management Catalogue of imported veterinary drugs; including retail packaging)
0/0/0	0	0	0/0	0/0/0	0/0	0//0	0/0/	0/0/0	4.5/0			0/0/0	Single preparartions, 5-Androstenediol (3β, 17β) [5-androstene-glycol(3β, 17β)], put up in measured doses(including their derivatives and strutural analogues, in forms or packing for retailsale)
0/0/0	0	0	0/0	0/0/0	0/0	0//0	0/0/	0/0/0	4.5/0			0/0/0	Single preparartions, androstenedione (4-androstene-glycol), put up in measured doses(including their derivatives and strutural analogues, in forms or packing for retailsale)
0/0/0	0	0	0/0	0/0/0	0/0	0//0	0/0/	0/0/0	4.5/0			0/0/0	Single preparartions, 7α-hydroxy-DHEA, put up in measured doses(including their derivatives and strutural analogues, in forms or packing for retailsale)
0/0/0	0	0	0/0	0/0/0	0/0	0//0	0/0/	0/0/0	4.5/0			0/0/0	Single preparartions, 7β-hydroxy-DHEA, put up in measured doses(including their derivatives and strutural analogues, in forms or packing for retailsale)
0/0/0	0	0	0/0	0/0/0	0/0	0//0	0/0/	0/0/0	4.5/0			0/0/0	Single preparartions, 7- carbonyl Prasterone(put up in measured doses and in forms or packing for retail sale)
0/0/0	0	0	0/0	0/0/0	0/0	0//0	0/0/	0/0/0	4.5/0			0/0/0	Single preparartions, Androstane, put up in measured doses (including their derivatives and strutural analogues, in forms or packing for retailsale)
0/0/0	0	0	0/0	0/0/0	0/0	0//0	0/0/	0/0/0	4.5/0		//	0/0/0	Formula containing 1,4—androstenedione (androsterone—1, 4—diene—3,17—dione)
0/0/0	0	0	0/0	0/0/0	0/0	0//0	0/0/	0/0/0	4.5/0			0/0/0	Drugs containing corticosteroed hormone, put up in measured dose (excluding antibiotics, including their derivatives and structural analogues, in forms or packing for retail sale)(Tax number due to separation of anticancer drugs)
													--Other
0/0/0	0	0	0/0	0/0/0	0/0	0//0	0/0/	4.5/4.5/4.5	4.5/4.5			0/0/0	Single preparations, containting clenbuterol, put up in measured doses(including packing for retail sale)
0/0/0	0	0	0/0	0/0/0	0/0	0//0	0/0/	4.5/4.5/4.5	4.5/4.5			0/0/0	Single preparartions, HCG and luteinizing hormone put up in measured doses[including Growth hormone releasing peptide (GHRPs), Plummer Relin (growth hormone releasing peptide -2), CJC-1295 (CAS No. 863288-34-0), growth hormone releasing peptide -6, growth hormone releasing hormone and its analogues, growth Ji Sucu secretion agent, packing for retail sale]
0/0/0	0	0	0/0	0/0/0	0/0	0//0	0/0/	4.5/4.5/4.5	4.5/4.5			0/0/0	Single preparations, peptide hormones[including retail packaging, and have dosage or retail packaging Ai Rui Mo Ruilin, A Bernard Relin, Bushrui Lin, Sha Ruilin, sea corticorelin, Iraq Mo Ruilin, Mo Ruilin, Mo Ruilin, Gore Bernard Relin, on behalf of triptorelin, Ge Ruilin (brain gut peptide) and its preparations) analogue.]

税则号列	货品名称〔CIQ扩展编码及品名一T2表示见附表2〕	最惠(%)	暂定税率	普通	增值/消费	出口退税	计量单位	监管条件/特殊证件	检验检疫	对美关税	亚太上/下
3004.3900 27	已配剂量含亮丙瑞林的单方制剂〔999〕	0		30	13/	13	千克	L/1			0/0
3004.3900 28	已配剂量含雄酮的单方制剂〔999〕	0		30	13/	13	千克	L/1			0/0
3004.3900 29	其他《兴奋剂目录》所列商品〔999〕	0		30	13/	13	千克	L/1			0/0
3004.3900 40	已配剂量兽用制剂(包括进口兽药管理目录的商品;包括零售包装)〔999〕	0		30	13/	13	千克	R/1			0/0
3004.3900 91	抗(防)癌药品制剂(不含癌症辅助治疗药品)(包括抗癌药品清单第一批、第二批相关商品)〔999〕	0		30	3/	13	千克	Q/1			0/0
3004.3900 92	其他已配剂量含卵泡抑素的单方制剂	0		30	13/	13	千克	L/1			0/0
3004.3900 93	其他已配剂量含马昔瑞林的单方制剂	0		30	13/	13	千克	L/1			0/0
3004.3900 95	罕见病药品制剂(包括罕见病药品清单第一批、第二批相关商品)〔999〕	0		30	3/	13	千克	Q/1			0/0
3004.3900 99	其他已配剂量含激素或品目2937产品的药品(不含抗菌素,包括零售包装)(因拆分抗癌药产生的兜底税号)〔999〕	0		30	13/	13	千克	Q/1			0/0
	-其他,含有生物碱及其衍生物:							Q			
3004.4100	--含有麻黄碱及其盐										
3004.4100 10	盐酸麻黄碱片、盐酸麻黄碱注射剂、硫酸麻黄碱片〔998药品,999其他化工产品〕	5		30	13/	13	千克	23Q/1			
3004.4100 20	其他含麻黄碱及其盐的单方制剂(已配定剂量或制成零售包装)〔998药品,999其他化工产品〕	5		30	13/	13	千克	I/1			
3004.4100 90	其他含有麻黄碱及其盐的药品(已配定剂量或制成零售包装)〔998药品,999其他化工产品〕	5		30	13/	13	千克	Q/1			
3004.4200	--含有伪麻黄碱(INN)及其盐										
3004.4200 10	盐酸伪麻黄碱片〔998药品,999其他化工产品〕	5		30	13/	13	千克	23Q/1			
3004.4200 20	其他含伪麻黄碱及其盐的单方制剂(已配定剂量或制成零售包装)〔998药品,999其他化工产品〕	5		30	13/	13	千克	I/1			
3004.4200 90	其他含有伪麻黄碱及其盐的药品(已配定剂量或制成零售包装)〔998药品,999其他化工产品〕	5		30	13/	13	千克	Q/1			
3004.4300	--含有去甲麻黄碱及其盐										
3004.4300 10	去甲麻黄碱及其盐的单方制剂(已配定剂量或制成零售包装)〔998药品,999其他化工产品〕	5		30	13/	13	千克	I/1			
3004.4300 90	其他含有去甲麻黄碱及其盐的药品(已配定剂量或制成零售包装)〔998药品,999其他化工产品〕	5		30	13/	13	千克	Q/1			
3004.4900	--其他										
3004.4900 10	含有奎宁或其盐的药品(已配定剂量或制成零售包装)〔998药品,999其他化工产品〕	5		35	13/	13	千克	Q/1			
3004.4900 20	含可待因及衍生物及盐的复方制剂(已配定剂量或制成零售包装)〔998药品,999其他化工产品〕	5		30	13/	13	千克	I/1			
3004.4900 31	丁丙诺啡透皮贴剂(包括其衍生物,已配定剂量或制成零售包装)〔998药品,999其他化工产品〕	5		30	13/	13	千克	I/1			
3004.4900 39	其他含生物碱类精神药品的单方制剂(包括其衍生物,已配定剂量或制成零售包装)〔998药品,999其他化工产品〕	5		30	13/	13	千克	I/1			
3004.4900 40	含生物碱类麻醉药品的单方制剂(包括其衍生物,已配定剂量或制成零售包装)〔998药品,999其他化工产品〕	5		30	13/	13	千克	I/1			
3004.4900 50	吗啡阿托品注射液〔998药品,999其他化工产品〕	5		30	13/	13	千克	I/1			
3004.4900 61	含有氨酚氢可酮片或其盐〔998药品,999其他化工产品〕	5		30	13/	13	千克	I/1			
3004.4900 62	含有麦角胺咖啡因片/安钠咖或其盐〔998药品,999其他化工产品〕	5		30	13/	13	千克	I/1			
3004.4900 63	阿桔片、复方甘草片(含阿片粉,已配定剂量或制成零售包装)〔998药品,999其他化工产品〕	5		30	13/	13	千克	I/1			
3004.4900 70	氨酚双氢可待因片〔998药品,999其他化工产品〕	5		30	13/	13	千克	I/1			
3004.4900 80	已配剂量兽用制剂(包括进口兽药管理目录的商品;包括零售包装)〔999〕	5		30	13/	13	千克	R/1			
3004.4900 91	具有抗癌作用的含有生物碱及其衍生物的药品(包括抗癌药品清单第一批相关商品,混合或非混合,治病或防病用已配定剂量或零售包装)〔999〕	5	0	30	3/	13	千克	Q/1			
3004.4900 92	噻托溴铵粉吸入剂、噻托溴铵喷雾剂、吸入用复方异丙托溴铵溶液、异丙托溴铵气雾剂(已配定剂量或制成零售包装)〔999〕	5	0	30	13/	13	千克	Q/1			
3004.4900 99	其他含有生物碱及其衍生物的药品(已配定剂量或制成零售包装)〔301其他化工产品,999药品〕	5		30	13/	13	千克	Q/1			
3004.5000	-其他,含有维生素或税目29.36所列产品〔999〕	0		40	13/	13	千克	Q/1			0/0

协定税率 %								RCEP		特惠税率 %			Article Description
东/冰/格	巴基斯坦	韩国	瑞士 上/下	哥/秘/柬	澳/毛	新西/坡/智	中国港/澳/台	东盟及马来/澳/韩	日/新	亚太2国	老/柬/缅	98/97/95	
0/0/0	0	0	0/0	0/0/0	0/0	0//0	0/0/	4.5/4.5/4.5	4.5/4.5			0/0/0	Monomer preparation dose containing leuprolide
0/0/0	0	0	0/0	0/0/0	0/0	0//0	0/0/	4.5/4.5/4.5	4.5/4.5			0/0/0	Monomer preparation containing dose of DHEA therapy
0/0/0	0	0	0/0	0/0/0	0/0	0//0	0/0/	4.5/4.5/4.5	4.5/4.5		//	0/0/0	List of other stimulants
0/0/0	0	0	0/0	0/0/0	0/0	0//0	0/0/	4.5/4.5/4.5	4.5/4.5		//	0/0/0	Formulated dosage of veterinary preparations (including commodities in the Management Catalogue of imported veterinary drugs; including retail packaging)
0/0/0	0	0	0/0	0/0/0	0/0	0//0	0/0/	4.5/4.5/4.5	4.5/4.5			0/0/0	Anti—cancer drug preparations (excluding cancer adjuncts)
0/0/0	0	0	0/0	0/0/0	0/0	0//0	0/0/	4.5/4.5/4.5	4.5/4.5		//	0/0/0	Other formulations containing follistatin in prescribed doses
0/0/0	0	0	0/0	0/0/0	0/0	0//0	0/0/	4.5/4.5/4.5	4.5/4.5		//	0/0/0	Other prescribed doses containing maxillin
0/0/0	0	0	0/0	0/0/0	0/0	0//0	0/0/	4.5/4.5/4.5	4.5/4.5		//	0/0/0	Pharmaceutical preparations for rare diseases (including the first and second batch of related commodities in the list of drugs for rare diseases)
0/0/0	0	0	0/0	0/0/0	0/0	0//0	0/0/	4.5/4.5/4.5	4.5/4.5			0/0/0	Other medicines that have been dosed with hormones or products of heading 2937 (without antibiotics, including retail packaging)(Tax number due to separation of anticancer drugs)
													-Other, containing alkaloids or derivatives thereof:
													--Containing ephedrine or its salts
0/0/0	0	0	0/0	0/0/0	0/0	0//0	0/0/	0/4.5/0	0/4.5			0/0/0	Ephedrine Hydrochloride Tablets, ephedrine hydrochloride injection, ephedrine sulfate tablets
0/0/0	0	0	0/0	0/0/0	0/0	0//0	0/0/	0/4.5/0	0/4.5			0/0/0	Other preparations containing ephedrine and its salts, put up in measured doses or in forms or packings for retail sale
0/0/0	0	0	0/0	0/0/0	0/0	0//0	0/0/	0/4.5/0	0/4.5			0/0/0	Other drugs containing ephedrine and its salts, put up in measured doses or in forms or packings for retail sale
													--Containing pseudoephedrine (*INN*) or its salts
0/0/0	0	0	0/0	0/0/0	0/0	0//0	0/0/	0/4.5/0	0/4.5			0/0/0	Pseudoephedrine Hydrochloride Tablets
0/0/0	0	0	0/0	0/0/0	0/0	0//0	0/0/	0/4.5/0	0/4.5			0/0/0	Other preparations containing pseudoephedrine and its salts, put up in measured doses or in forms or packings for retail sale
0/0/0	0	0	0/0	0/0/0	0/0	0//0	0/0/	0/4.5/0	0/4.5			0/0/0	Other drugs containing pseudoephedrine and its salts, put up in measured doses or in forms or packings for retail sale
													--Containing norephedrine or its salts
0/0/0	0	0	0/0	0/0/0	0/0	0//0	0/0/	0/4.5/0	0/4.5			0/0/0	Preparations cathine and its salts, put up in measured doses, packings for retail sale
0/0/0	0	0	0/0	0/0/0	0/0	0//0	0/0/	0/4.5/0	0/4.5			0/0/0	Other drugs containing norephedrine and salts, put up in measured doses, packings for retail sale
													--Other
0/0/0	0	0	0/0	0/0/0	0/0	0//0	0/0/	0/0/0	0/0			0/0/0	Medicaments containing quinine or its salts, put up in measured doses, packings for retail sale
0/0/0	0	0	0/0	0/0/0	0/0	0//0	0/0/	0/0/0	0/0			0/0/0	Compound preparations, containing codeine, its derivatives and salts, put up in measured doses, packings for retail sale
0/0/0	0	0	0/0	0/0/0	0/0	0//0	0/0/	0/0/0	0/0			0/0/0	Buprenorphine Transdermal patch, and its salts, put up in measured doses, packings for retail sale
0/0/0	0	0	0/0	0/0/0	0/0	0//0	0/0/	0/0/0	0/0			0/0/0	Other single preparations, containing alkaloids spirit drug and its derivatives, put up in measured doses, packings for retail
0/0/0	0	0	0/0	0/0/0	0/0	0//0	0/0/	0/0/0	0/0			0/0/0	Single preparations, containing alkaloids narcotic drugs and its derivatives, put up in measured doses, packings for retail sale
0/0/0	0	0	0/0	0/0/0	0/0	0//0	0/0/	0/0/0	0/0			0/0/0	Morphine and atropine sulfate injection
0/0/0	0	0	0/0	0/0/0	0/0	0//0	0/0/	0/0/0	0/0			0/0/0	Medicaments containing paracetamol and hydrocodone bitartrate tablet or its salt
0/0/0	0	0	0/0	0/0/0	0/0	0//0	0/0/	0/0/0	0/0			0/0/0	Medicaments containing ergotamine and caffeine tablet or caffeine and sodium benzoate or its salt
0/0/0	0	0	0/0	0/0/0	0/0	0//0	0/0/	0/0/0	0/0			0/0/0	Compound Platycodon and Liquorice tablets? put up in measured doses or in forms of packings for retail sale
0/0/0	0	0	0/0	0/0/0	0/0	0//0	0/0/	0/0/0	0/0			0/0/0	Paracetamol and Dihydrocodeine Tartrate Tablets
0/0/0	0	0	0/0	0/0/0	0/0	0//0	0/0/	0/0/0	0/0		//	0/0/0	Formulated dosage of veterinary preparations (including commodities in the Management Catalogue of imported veterinary drugs; including retail packaging)
0/0/0	0	0	0/0	0/0/0	0/0	0//0	0/0/	0/0/0	0/0			0/0/0	Drugs containing alkaloids and their derivatives that have an anticancer effect (mixed or non—mixed, administrated dose or retail package for treatment or prevention)
0/0/0	0	0	0/0	0/0/0	0/0	0//0	0/0/	0/0/0	0/0		//	0/0/0	Tiotropium Bromide Powder for Inhalation, Tiotropium Bromide Spray, Compound Ipratropium Bromide Solution for Inhalation, Ipratropium Bromide Aerosol (fixed dose or made retail packaging)
0/0/0	0	0	0/0	0/0/0	0/0	0//0	0/0/	0/0/0	0/0			0/0/0	Other medicines containing alkaloids and their derivatives (in formulated dose or in retail packaging)
0/0/0	0	0	0/0	0/0/0	0/0	0//0	0/0/	0/0/0	5.5/0			0/0/0	-Other, containing vitamins or other products of heading 29.36

税则号列		货品名称〔CIQ扩展编码及品名—T2表示见附表2〕	最惠(%)	暂定税率	普通	增值/消费	出口退税	计量单位	监管条件/特殊证件	检验检疫	对美关税	亚太上/下
		-其他,含有本章子目注释二所列抗疟疾活性成分的:										
3004.6010		---含有青蒿素及其衍生物〔998药品,999其他化工产品〕	0		30	13/	13	千克	Q/1		2.5	
3004.6090		---其他										
3004.6090	10	含有磺胺类的混合药品(已配定剂量或制成零售包装)〔998药品,999其他化工产品〕	0		30	13/	13	千克	Q/1		2.5	0/0
3004.6090	21	含濒危动植物成分的中式成药(已配定剂量或零售包装)〔998药品,999其他化工产品〕	0		30	13/	0	千克	EFQ/1		2.5	0/0
3004.6090	29	含其他成分的中式成药(已配定剂量或零售包装)〔998药品,999其他化工产品〕	0		30	13/	13	千克	Q/1		2.5	0/0
3004.6090	30	其他含濒危野生动植物成分的药品(已配定剂量或零售包装)〔998药品,999其他化工产品〕	0		30	13/	0	千克	EFQ/1		2.5	0/0
3004.6090	90	其他含有本章子目注释二所列抗疟疾活性成分的药品(已配定剂量或零售包装)〔998药品,999其他化工产品〕	0		30	13/	13	千克	Q/1		2.5	0/0
		-其他:										
3004.9010		---含有磺胺类〔999〕	0		40	13/	13	千克	Q/1			
3004.9010	10	已配剂量兽用制剂(包括进口兽药管理目录的商品;包括零售包装)〔999〕	0		40	13/	13	千克	R/1			0/0
3004.9010	20	抗(防)癌药品制剂(不含癌症辅助治疗药品)(包括抗癌药品清单第二批相关商品,包括零售包装)〔999〕	0		40	3/	13	千克	Q/1			0/0
3004.9010	30	罕见病药品制剂(包括罕见病药品清单第二批相关商品,包括零售包装)〔999〕	0		40	3/	13	千克	Q/1			0/0
3004.9010	90	其他已配剂量含有磺胺类的药品(包括零售包装)〔999〕	0		40	13/	13	千克	Q/1			0/0
3004.9020		---含有联苯双酯〔999〕	4		30	13/	13	千克	Q/1			2/2
		---中式成药:										
3004.9051		----中药酒										
3004.9051	10	含濒危动植物成分的中药酒(已配定剂量或零售包装)〔101中药酒,102保健食品,999其他混合或非混合产品构成的药品(已配定剂量)〕	0		30	13/	0	千克	FE/1		2.5	0/0
3004.9051	90	含其他成分的中药酒(已配定剂量或零售包装)〔101中药酒,102保健食品,103其他化工产品,999其他混合或非混合产品构成的药品(已配定剂量)〕	0		30	13/	13	千克	/1		2.5	0/0
3004.9052		----片仔癀〔101其他化工产品,999其他混合或非混合产品构成的药品(已配定剂量)〕	3		30	13/	13	千克	QFE/1			1.5/1.5
3004.9053		----白药										
3004.9053	10	含天然麝香的白药(已配定剂量或零售包装)〔999〕	3		30	13/	13	千克	FEQ/1			1.5/1.5
3004.9053	90	含人工麝香的白药(已配定剂量或零售包装)〔999〕	3		30	13/	13	千克	Q/1			1.5/1.5
3004.9054		----清凉油〔101其他化工产品,999其他混合或非混合产品构成的药品(已配定剂量)〕	0		30	13/	13	千克	Q/1		2.5	0/0
3004.9055		----安宫牛黄丸			0							
3004.9055	10	含天然麝香的安宫牛黄丸(已配定剂量或零售包装)〔999〕	3		30	13/	0	千克	QFE/1			1.5/1.5
3004.9055	90	其他安宫牛黄丸(已配定剂量或零售包装)〔101其他化工产品,999其他混合或非混合产品构成的药品(已配定剂量)〕	3		30	13/	13	千克	Q/1			1.5/1.5
3004.9059		----其他										
3004.9059	10	含濒危动植物成分的中式成药(已配定剂量或零售包装)〔999〕	0		30	13/	0	千克	QFE/1			0/0
3004.9059	90	含其他成分的中式成药(已配定剂量或零售包装)〔101其他化工产品,999其他混合或非混合产品构成的药品(已配定剂量)〕	0		30	13/	13	千克	Q/1			0/0
3004.9090		---其他										
3004.9090	10	含濒危野生动植物成分的药品(已配定剂量或零售包装,不含紫杉醇)〔999〕	0		30	13/	0	千克	FEQ/1			0/0
3004.9090	21	含紫杉醇成分的抗癌药清单药品(已配定剂量或制成零售包装,已批准注册)〔999	0		30	3/	0	千克	EFQ/1			0/0
3004.9090	29	其他含紫杉醇成分的药品(已配定剂量或制成零售包装)〔999〕	0		30	13/	0	千克	EFQ/1			0/0
3004.9090	30	其他含第29章麻醉药品的单方制剂(已配定剂量或制成零售包装)〔101其他化工产品,999其他混合或非混合产品构成的药品(已配定剂量)〕	0		30	13/	13	千克	I/1			0/0

协定税率 %								RCEP		特惠税率 %			Article Description
东/冰/格	巴基斯坦	韩国	瑞士上/下	哥/秘/柬	澳/毛	新西/坡/智	中国港/澳/台	东盟及马来/澳/韩	日/新	亚太2国	老/柬/缅	98/97/95	
													--Other, containing antimalarial active principles described in Subheading Note 2 to this Chapter:
0/0/0	0	0	0/0	0/0/0	0/0	0//0	0/0/	0/0/0	3.6/0			0/0/0	---Containing artemisinins and their derivatives
													---Other
0/0/0	0	0	0/0	0/0/0	0/0	0//0	0/0/	0/0/0	2.7/0			0/0/0	Medicaments containing sulfa drugs, put up in measured doses, packings for retail sale
0/0/0	0	0	0/0	0/0/0	0/0	0//0	0/0/	0/0/0	2.7/0			0/0/0	Medicaments of Chinese style, containing endangered animals or vegetables, put up in measured doses, packings for retail sale
0/0/0	0	0	0/0	0/0/0	0/0	0//0	0/0/	0/0/0	2.7/0			0/0/0	Medicaments of Chinese style, containing other composition, put up in measured doses, packings for retail sale
0/0/0	0	0	0/0	0/0/0	0/0	0//0	0/0/	0/0/0	2.7/0			0/0/0	Other medicaments of Chinese style, containing endangered animals or vegetables, put up in measured doses, packings for retail sale
0/0/0	0	0	0/0	0/0/0	0/0	0//0	0/0/	0/0/0	2.7/0			0/0/0	Other medicaments, containing antimalarial active principles described in Subheading Note 2 to this Chapter, put up in measured doses, packings for retail sale
													-Other:
0//							//	//				0/0/0	---Containing sulfa drugs
0/0/0	0	0	0/0	0/0/0	0/0	0//0	0/0/	0/0/0	5.5/0		//	0/0/0	Formulated dosage of veterinary preparations (including commodities in the Management Catalogue of imported veterinary drugs; including retail packaging)
0/0/0	0	0	0/0	0/0/0	0/0	0//0	0/0/	0/0/0	5.5/0		//	0/0/0	Anti(prevent) cancer drug preparations (excluding cancer adjuvant therapy drugs) (including the second batch of related commodities in the list of anti—cancer drugs, including retail packaging)
0/0/0	0	0	0/0	0/0/0	0/0	0//0	0/0/	0/0/0	5.5/0		//	0/0/0	Pharmaceutical preparations for rare diseases (including the second batch of related commodities in the list of drugs for rare diseases, including retail packaging)
0/0/0	0	0	0/0	0/0/0	0/0	0//0	0/0/	0/0/0	5.5/0		//	0/0/0	Other drugs containing sulfonamides in dosages (including in retail packaging)
0/0/0	0	0	0/0	0/0/0	0/0	0//0	0/0/	0/0/0	0/0			0/0/0	---Containing biphenyl dicarbxybte
													---Medicaments of Chinese type:
													----Medicated liquors or wines
0/0/0	0	0	0/0	0/0/0	0/0	0//0	0/0/	0/0/0	2.7/0			0/0/0	Medicated liquors or wines, containing composition of endangered animals or plants, (put up in measured doses or in forms or packings for retail sale)
0/0/0	0	0	0/0	0/0/0	0/0	0//0	0/0/	0/0/0	2.7/0			0/0/0	Medicated liquors or wines, containing other composition (put up in measured doses or in forms or packings for retail sale)
0/0/0	0	0	0/0	0/0/0	0/0	0//0	0/0/	0/0/0	0/0			0/0/0	----Pien Tzu Huang
													----Bai Yao
0/0/0	0	0	0/0	0/0/0	0/0	0//0	0/0/	0/0/0	0/0			0/0/0	Bai Yao, containing natural musk(put up in measured doses or in form or packing for retail sale)
0/0/0	0	0	0/0	0/0/0	0/0	0//0	0/0/	0/0/0	0/0			0/0/0	Bai Yao, containing artificial musk(put up in measured doses or in form or packing for retail sale)
0/0/0	0	0	0/0	0/0/0	0/0	0//0	0/0/	0/0/0	2.7/0			0/0/0	----Essential balm
													----Angong niuhuang wan
0/0/0	0	0	0/0	0/0/0	0/0	0//0	0/0/	0/0/0	0/0			0/0/0	Angongniuhuang pills, containing natural musk (put up in measured doses or in form or packings for retail sale)
0/0/0	0	0	0/0	0/0/0	0/0	0//0	0/0/	0/0/0	0/0			0/0/0	Other angongniuhuang pills, (put up in measured doses or in form or packings for retail sale)
													----Other
0/0/0	0	0	0/0	0/0/0	0/0	0//0	0/0/	2.7/2.7/2.7	2.7/2.7			0/0/0	Medicaments of Chinese style, containing composition of endangered animals or plants(put up in measured doses or in forms or packings for retail sale)
0/0/0	0	0	0/0	0/0/0	0/0	0//0	0/0/	2.7/2.7/2.7	2.7/2.7			0/0/0	Medicaments of Chinese style, containing other composition (put up in measured doses or in forms or packings for retail sale)
													---Other
0/0/0	0	0	0/0	0/0/0	0/0	0//0	0/0/	0/0/0	3.6/0			0/0/0	Medicaments containing composition of endangered animals or plants(not containing taxinol, put up in measured doses or in forms or packings for retail sale)
0/0/0	0	0	0/0	0/0/0	0/0	0//0	0/0/	0/0/0	3.6/0			0/0/0	List of anticancer drugs containing taxinol (put up in measured doses or in forms or packings for retail sale, approved for registration)
0/0/0	0	0	0/0	0/0/0	0/0	0//0	0/0/	0/0/0	3.6/0			0/0/0	Other medicaments containing taxinol(put up in measured doses or in forms or packings for retail sale)
0/0/0	0	0	0/0	0/0/0	0/0	0//0	0/0/	0/0/0	3.6/0			0/0/0	Other single preparations containing narcotic drngs of Chapter 29 (put up in measured doses or in forms or packings for retail sale)

税则号列		货品名称〔CIQ扩展编码及品名－T2表示见附表2〕	最惠(%)	暂定税率	普通	增值/消费	出口退税	计量单位	监管条件/特殊证件	检验检疫	对美关税	亚太上/下
3004.9090	41	地芬诺酯复方制剂(已配定剂量或制成零售包装)〔101 其他化工产品,999 其他混合或非混合产品构成的药品(已配定剂量)〕	0		30	13/	13	千克	I/1			0/0
3004.9090	49	其他含第29章精神药品的单方制剂(已配定剂量或制成零售包装)〔101 其他化工产品,999 其他混合或非混合产品构成的药品(已配定剂量)〕	0		30	13/	13	千克	I/1			0/0
3004.9090	50	含右丙氧芬及其盐的复方制剂(已配定剂量或制成零售包装)〔999〕	0		30	13/	13	千克	I/1			0/0
3004.9090	60	复方樟脑酊(含阿片酊、樟脑、苯甲酸、八角茴香油等,包括零售包装)〔999〕	0		30	13/	13	千克	I/1			0/0
3004.9090	71	已配剂量含雄甾-4-烯-3α,17β-二醇[4-雄烯二醇(3α,17β)]的单方制剂(包括零售包装)〔999〕	0		30	13/	13	千克	L/1			0/0
3004.9090	72	已配剂量含雄甾-5-烯-3α,17α-二醇[5-雄烯二醇(3α,17α)]的单方制剂(包括零售包装)〔999〕	0		30	13/	13	千克	L/1			0/0
3004.9090	73	已配剂量含雄甾-5-烯-3α,17β-二醇[5-雄烯二醇(3α,17β)]的单方制剂(包括零售包装)〔999〕	0		30	13/	13	千克	L/1			0/0
3004.9090	74	已配剂量含5α-雄烷-3α,17α-二醇(阿法雄烷二醇)或雄甾-4-烯-3α,17α-二醇[4-雄烯二醇(3α,17α)]的单方制剂(包括零售包装)〔999〕	0		30	13/	13	千克	L/1			0/0
3004.9090	75	已配剂量含5α-雄烷-3β,17β-二醇(倍他雄烷二醇)的单方制剂(包括零售包装)〔999〕	0		30	13/	13	千克	L/1			0/0
3004.9090	77	含表雄酮(3β－羟基－5α－雄烷－17－酮)的单方制剂(已配剂量或制成零售包装)〔101 其他化工产品,999 其他混合或非混合产品构成的药品(已配定剂量)〕	0		30	13/	13	千克	L/1			0/0
3004.9090	78	已配剂量含齐帕特罗的单方制剂(包括零售包装)〔999〕	0		30	13/	13	千克	L/1			0/0
3004.9090	79	已配剂量含表睾酮的单方制剂(包括零售包装)〔999〕	0		30	13/	13	千克	L/1			0/0
3004.9090	83	含1－表雄酮(3β－羟基－5α－雄甾－1－烯－17－酮)的单方制剂(包括零售包装)〔999〕	0		30	13/	13	千克	L/1			0/0
3004.9090	84	已配剂量兽用制剂(包括进口兽药管理目录的商品;包括零售包装)〔999〕	0		30	13/	13	千克	R/1			0/0
3004.9090	85	其他《兴奋剂目录》所列商品(包括零售包装)〔999〕	0		30	13/	13	千克	L/1			0/0
3004.9090	91	含FG-4592(CAS号808118-40-3,一种缺氧诱导因子-脯氨酸羟化酶抑制剂)的已配定剂量的制剂(包括零售包装)〔999〕	0		30	13/	13	千克	Q/1			0/0
3004.9090	92	已配剂量含5α-雄烷-2-烯-17-酮的单方制剂(包括零售包装)〔999〕	0		30	13/	13	千克	L/1			0/0
3004.9090	93	抗(防)癌药品制剂(不含癌症辅助治疗药品)(包括抗癌药品清单第一批、第二批相关商品)〔999〕	0		30	3/	13	千克	Q/1			0/0
3004.9090	94	已配剂量含2－雄烯醇(5α－雄甾－2－烯－17－醇)的单方制剂(包括零售包装)〔999〕	0		30	13/	13	千克	L/1			0/0
3004.9090	95	已配剂量含3－雄烯醇(5α－雄甾－3－烯－17－醇)的单方制剂(包括零售包装)〔999〕	0		30	13/	13	千克	L/1			0/0
3004.9090	96	已配剂量含3－雄烯酮(5α－雄甾－3－烯－17－酮)的单方制剂(包括零售包装)〔999〕	0		30	13/	13	千克	L/1			0/0
3004.9090	98	罕见病药品制剂(包括罕见病药品清单第一批、第二批相关商品)〔999〕	0		30	3/	13	千克	Q/1			0/0
3004.9090	99	其他已配定剂量的药品(包括零售包装)〔999〕	0		30	13/	13	千克	Q/1			0/0
30.05		**软填料、纱布、绷带及类似物品(例如,敷料、橡皮膏、泥罨剂),经过药物浸涂或制成零售包装供医疗、外科、牙科或兽医用:**										
		-胶粘敷料及有胶粘涂层的其他物品:										
3005.1010		---橡皮膏〔101 其他化工产品,999 胶粘敷料及其他有胶粘涂层的物品〕	5		70	13/	13	千克	/1		32.5	4/4
3005.1090		---其他〔101 其他化工产品,999 经药物浸涂或制成零售包装,供医疗、外科、牙科或兽医用〕	5		35	13/	13	千克	/1		12.5	
		-其他:										

协定税率 %								RCEP		特惠税率 %			Article Description
东/冰/格	巴基斯坦	韩国	瑞士上/下	哥/秘/柬	澳/毛	新西/坡/智	中国港/澳/台	东盟及马来/澳/韩	日/新	亚太2国	老/柬/缅	98/97/95	
0/0/0	0	0	0/0	0/0/0	0/0	0//0	0/0/	0/0/0	3.6/0			0/0/0	Compound preparations, containing diphenoxylate(put up in measured doses and in forms or packing for retail sale)
0/0/0	0	0	0/0	0/0/0	0/0	0//0	0/0/	0/0/0	3.6/0			0/0/0	Other single preparations , containing psychotropic substances of Chapter 29(put up in measured doses and in forms or packing for retail sale)
0/0/0	0	0	0/0	0/0/0	0/0	0//0	0/0/	0/0/0	3.6/0			0/0/0	Compound preparations, containing propoxyphene and its salts(put up in measured doses or in forms or packings for retail sale)
0/0/0	0	0	0/0	0/0/0	0/0	0//0	0/0/	0/0/0	3.6/0			0/0/0	Compound camphor tineture(containing opium tincture, camphor benzoic acid, star-anise oil, including in forms or packing for retail sale)
0/0/0	0	0	0/0	0/0/0	0/0	0//0	0/0/	0/0/0	3.6/0			0/0/0	Single preparartions, androst-4-allyl-3α, 17β-estradi[4-androstene-glycol(3α, 17β)], put up in measured doses(including in forms or packing for retail sale)
0/0/0	0	0	0/0	0/0/0	0/0	0//0	0/0/	0/0/0	3.6/0			0/0/0	Single preparartions, androst-5-allyl-3α, 17α-estradi[5-androstene-glycol(3α, 17α)], put up in measured doses(including in forms or packing for retail sale)
0/0/0	0	0	0/0	0/0/0	0/0	0//0	0/0/	0/0/0	3.6/0			0/0/0	Single preparartions, androst-5-allyl-3α, 17β-estradi[5-androstene-glycol(3α, 17β)], put up in measured doses(including in forms or packing for retail sale)
0/0/0	0	0	0/0	0/0/0	0/0	0//0	0/0/	0/0/0	3.6/0			0/0/0	Single preparations, containting 5α-androstane-3α, 17α-diol or androst-4-allyl-3α, 17α-estradi [4-androstene-glycol (3α, 17α)], put up in measured doses(including in forms or packing for retail sale)
0/0/0	0	0	0/0	0/0/0	0/0	0//0	0/0/	0/0/0	3.6/0			0/0/0	Single preparations, containting 5α-androstan-3β, 17β-estradi, put up in measured doses(including in forms or packing for retail sale)
0/0/0	0	0	0/0	0/0/0	0/0	0//0	0/0/	0/0/0	3.6/0			0/0/0	Single preparations, containting androsterone(3β-hydroxy-5α-androstane-17-ketone), put up in measured doses(including in forms or packing for retail sale)
0/0/0	0	0	0/0	0/0/0	0/0	0//0	0/0/	0/0/0	3.6/0			0/0/0	Single preparations, containting zilpaterol, put up in measured doses(including in forms or packing for retail sale)
0/0/0	0	0	0/0	0/0/0	0/0	0//0	0/0/	0/0/0	3.6/0			0/0/0	Single preparations, containting epitestosterone, put up in measured doses(including in forms or packing for retail sale)
0/0/0	0	0	0/0	0/0/0	0/0	0//0	0/0/	0/0/0	3.6/0		//	0/0/0	Single formulation containing 1－epiandrone (3 β － hydroxy －5 α － androsterol－1－ene－17－one) (including retail packaging)
0/0/0	0	0	0/0	0/0/0	0/0	0//0	0/0/	0/0/0	3.6/0		//	0/0/0	Formulated dosage of veterinary preparations (including commodities in the Management Catalogue of imported veterinary drugs; including retail packaging)
0/0/0	0	0	0/0	0/0/0	0/0	0//0	0/0/	0/0/0	3.6/0		//	0/0/0	List of other stimulants(including retail packaging)
0/0/0	0	0	0/0	0/0/0	0/0	0//0	0/0/	0/0/0	3.6/0			0/0/0	With FG-4592 (CAS 808118-40-3, a kind of hypoxia inducible factor - prolinehydroxylase inhibitors) have been preparations dosage (including retail wrapping)
0/0/0	0	0	0/0	0/0/0	0/0	0//0	0/0/	0/0/0	3.6/0			0/0/0	Medicaments containing 5α-androstane 2 ene-17-ketone, put up in measured doses(including in forms or packings for retail sale)
0/0/0	0	0	0/0	0/0/0	0/0	0//0	0/0/	0/0/0	3.6/0			0/0/0	Anti－cancer drug preparations (excluding cancer adjuncts)
0/0/0	0	0	0/0	0/0/0	0/0	0//0	0/0/	0/0/0	3.6/0		//	0/0/0	Formula containing 2－androstenol (5alpha－androsterol－2－ene－17－ol) in prescribed dose
0/0/0	0	0	0/0	0/0/0	0/0	0//0	0/0/	0/0/0	3.6/0		//	0/0/0	Formula containing 3－androstenol (5alpha－androsterol－3－ene－17－ol) in prescribed dose
0/0/0	0	0	0/0	0/0/0	0/0	0//0	0/0/	0/0/0	3.6/0		//	0/0/0	Formula containing 3－androstenone (5alpha－androsterone－3－ene－17－one) in prescribed dose
0/0/0	0	0	0/0	0/0/0	0/0	0//0	0/0/	0/0/0	3.6/0		//	0/0/0	Pharmaceutical preparations for rare diseases (including the first and second batch of related commodities in the list of drugs for rare diseases)
0/0/0	0	0	0/0	0/0/0	0/0	0//0	0/0/	0/0/0	3.6/0			0/0/0	Other equipped with fixed dose drug (including retail wrapping)
													Wadding, gauze, bandages and similar articles (for example, dressings, adhesive plasters, poultices), impregnated or coated with pharmaceutical substances or put up in forms or packings for retail sale for medical, surgical, dental or veterinary purposes:
													-Adhesive dressings and other articles having an adhesive layer:
0/0/0	0	0	0/0	0/0/0	0/0	0//0	0/0/	0/0/0	0/0			0/0/0	---Adhesive plasters
0//0	0	0	0/0	0/0/0	0/0	0//0	0/0/	0/0/0	4.5/0			0/0/0	---Other
													-Other:

税则号列	货品名称〔CIQ扩展编码及品名—T2表示见附表2〕	最惠(%)	暂定税率	普通	增值/消费	出口退税	计量单位	监管条件/特殊证件	检验检疫	对美关税	亚太上/下
3005.9010	---药棉、纱布、绷带〔999〕	5		70	13/	13	千克	/1		12.5	3/3
3005.9090	---其他〔101 其他化工产品,999 其他〕	5		35	13/	13	千克	/1		12.5	
30.06	**本章注释四所规定的医药用品:**										
3006.1000	-无菌外科肠线、类似的无菌缝合材料(包括外科或牙科用无菌可吸收缝线)及外伤创口闭合用的无菌粘合胶布;无菌昆布及无菌昆布塞条;外科或牙科用无菌吸收性止血材料;外科或牙科用无菌抗粘连阻隔材料,不论是否可吸收〔101 其他化工产品,999 无菌外科肠线,昆布,止血材料,阻隔材料〕	5		30	13/	13	千克	/1		10	
3006.3000	-X光检查造影剂;用于病人的诊断试剂〔101 其他化工产品,401 医用诊断试剂〕	4		30	13/	13	千克	ABQ/1	VW	31.5	
3006.4000	-牙科粘固剂及其他牙科填料;骨骼粘固剂〔101 其他化工产品,999 牙科粘固剂及其他牙科填料,骨骼粘固剂〕	5		30	13/	13	千克	/1		17.5	
3006.5000	-急救药箱、药包〔101 其他化工产品,999 其他〕	5		30	13/	13	千克	/1		17.5	
	-以激素、税目29.37的其他产品或杀精子剂为基本成分的化学避孕药物:										
3006.6010	---以激素为基本成分的避孕药〔101 其他化工产品,999 以激素、品目29.37产品等为基本成分避孕药〕	0		0	0/	0	千克	Q/1		25	
3006.6090	---其他〔101 其他化工产品,999 以激素、品目29.37产品等为基本成分避孕药〕	0		0	0/	0	千克	Q/1			
3006.7000	-专用于人类或兽药用的凝胶制品,作为外科手术或体检时躯体部位的润滑剂,或者作为躯体和医疗器械之间的耦合剂〔999〕	6.5		30	13/	13	千克	/1		19	
	-其他:										
3006.9100	--可确定用于造口术的用具〔101 其他化工产品,999 其他〕	10	5	80	13/	13	千克	/1		32.5	5/5
3006.9200	--废药物〔101 其他化工产品,999 其他〕	5		30	13/	13	千克	9/1			
3006.9300	--安慰剂和盲法(或双盲法)临床试验试剂盒,用于经许可的临床试验,已配定剂量〔401 含有微生物、人体组织、生物制品、血液及其制品的,402 其他化工产品〕	0		34	13/	13	千克	Q/1			

协定税率 %								RCEP		特惠税率 %			Article Description
东/冰/格	巴基斯坦	韩国	瑞士上/下	哥/秘/柬	澳/毛	新西/坡/智	中国港/澳/台	东盟及马来/澳/韩	日/新	亚太2国	老/柬/缅	98/97/95	
0/0/0	0	0	0/0	0/0/0	0/0	0//0	0/0/	0/0/0	0/0			0/0/0	---Absorbent cotton, gauze, bandages
0//0	0	0	0/0	0/0/0	0/0	0//0	0/0/	0/0/0	4.5/0			0/0/0	---Other
													Pharmaceutical goods specified in Note 4 to this Chapter:
0/0/0	0	0	0/0	0/0/0	0/0	0//0	0/0/	0/4.5/0	0/4.5			0/0/0	-Sterile surgical catgut, similar sterile suture materials(including sterile absorbable surgical or donfal yams) and sterile tissue adhesives for surgical wound closure; sterile laminaria and sterile laminaria tents; sterile absorbable surgical or dental haemostatics; sterile surgical or dontal adhesion borriers, whether or not absorbable
0/0/0	0	0	0/0	0/0/0	0/0	0//0	0/0/	0/0/0	0/0			0/0/0	-Opacifying preparations for X-ray examinations; diagnostic reagents designed to be administered to the patient
0/0/0	0	1	0/0	0/0/0	0/0	0//0	0/0/	0/0/4.5	4.5/0			0/0/0	-Dental cements and other dental fillings; bone reconstruction cements
0/0/0	0	0	0/0	0/0/0	0/0	0//0	0/0/	0/0/0	0/0			0/0/0	-First-aid boxes and kits
													-Chemical contraceptive preparations based on hormones on other products of heading No. 29. 37 or on spermicides:
0/0/0	0	0	0/0	0/0/0	0/0	0//0	0/0/	0/0/0	0/0			0/0/0	---Contraceptive preparations based on hormones
0/0/0	0	0	0/0	0/0/0	0/0	0//0	0/0/	0/0/0	0/0			0/0/0	---Other
0/0/0	3.5	0	0/0	0/0/0	0/0	0//0	0/0/	0/0/0	5.9/0			0/0/0	-Gel preparations designed to be used in human or veterinary medicine as a lubricant for parts of the body for surgical operations or physical examinations or as a coupling agent between the body and medical instruments
													-Other:
0/0/0	9.2	2	0/0	0/0/0	0/0	0/0/0	0/0/	0/0/9	9.1/0			0/0/0	--Appliamces identifiable for ostomy use
0/0/0	0	0	0/0	0/0/0	0/0	0//0	0/0/	0/0/0	0/0			0/0/0	--Waste pharmaceuticals
0/0/0	0	0	0/0	0/0/0	0/0	0/0/0	0/0/	0/0/0	0/0			0/0/0	--Placebos and blinded (or double—blinded) clinical trial kits for a recognised clinical trial, put up in measured doses

第三十一章
肥　料

注释：

一、本章不包括：

(一)税目 05.11 的动物血；

(二)单独的已有化学定义的化合物（符合下列注释二(一)、三(一)、四(一)或五所规定的化合物除外）；

(三)税目 38.24 的每颗重量不低于 2.5 克的氯化钾培养晶体(光学元件除外)；氯化钾光学元件(税目 90.01)。

二、税目 31.02 只适用于下列货品，但未制成税目 31.05 所述形状或包装：

(一)符合下列任何一条规定的货品：

1. 硝酸钠，不论是否纯净；
2. 硝酸铵，不论是否纯净；
3. 硫酸铵及硝酸铵的复盐，不论是否纯净；
4. 硫酸铵，不论是否纯净；
5. 硝酸钙及硝酸铵的复盐(不论是否纯净)或硝酸钙及硝酸铵的混合物；
6. 硝酸钙及硝酸镁的复盐(不论是否纯净)或硝酸钙及硝酸镁的混合物；
7. 氰氨化钙，不论是否纯净或用油处理；
8. 尿素，不论是否纯净。

(二)由上述(一)款任何货品相互混合的肥料。

(三)由氯化铵或上述(一)或(二)款任何货品与白垩、石膏或其他无肥效无机物混合而成的肥料。

(四)由上述(一)2 或 8 项的货品或其混合物溶于水或液氨的液体肥料。

三、税目 31.03 只适用于下列货品，但未制成税目 31.05 所述形状或包装：

(一)符合下列任何一条规定的货品：

1. 碱性熔渣；
2. 税目 25.10 的天然磷酸盐，已焙烧或经过超出清除杂质范围的热处理；
3. 过磷酸钙(一过磷酸钙、二过磷酸钙或三过磷酸钙)；
4. 磷酸氢钙，按干燥无水产品重量计含氟量不低于 0.2%。

(二)由上述(一)款的任何货品互相混合的肥料，不论含氟量多少。

(三)由上述(一)或(二)款的任何货品与白垩、石膏或其他无肥效无机物混合而成的肥料，不论含氟量多少。

四、税目 31.04 只适用于下列货品，但未制成税目 31.05 所述形状或包装：

(一)符合下列任何一条规定的货品：

1. 天然粗钾盐(例如，光卤石、钾盐镁矾及钾盐)；
2. 氯化钾，不论是否纯净，但上述注释一(三)所述的产品除外；
3. 硫酸钾，不论是否纯净；
4. 硫酸镁钾，不论是否纯净。

(二)由上述(一)款任何货品相互混合的肥料。

五、磷酸二氢铵及磷酸氢二铵(不论是否纯净)及其相互之间的混合物应归入税目 31.05。

六、税目 31.05 所称“其他肥料”，仅适用于其基本成分至少含有氮、磷、钾中一种肥效元素的肥料用产品。

税则号列	货品名称〔CIQ 扩展编码及品名一T2 表示见附表 2〕	最惠(%)	暂定税率	普通	增值/消费	出口退税	计量单位	监管条件/特殊证件	检验检疫	对美关税	亚太上/下
31.01	**动物或植物肥料，不论是否相互混合或经化学处理；动植物产品经混合或化学处理制成的肥料：**										
	---未经化学处理：										
3101.0011	----鸟粪〔999〕	3		11	9/	0	千克	AB/1	PQ		
3101.0019	----其他										
3101.0019　10	未经化学处理的森林凋落物(包括腐叶、腐根、树皮、树叶、树根等森林腐殖质)101 树皮栽培介质，102 其他有机栽培介质，103 植物有机肥，104 其他动植物肥料〕	6.5		30	9/	0	千克	8AB/1	PQ	11.5	3.3/3.3
3101.0019　90	未经化学处理的其他动植物肥料〔101 其他动物器官、细胞、培养基，102 猪、牛、羊等偶蹄动物粪便，103 马等奇蹄动物粪，104 其他动物粪便，105 动物性肥料、垃圾，106 其他动物性废弃物，107 植物有机肥，108 其他动物源性肥料，109 禽源性有机肥〕	6.5		30	9/	0	千克	AB/1	PQ	11.5	3.3/3.3
3101.0090	---其他										

Chapter 31
Fertilizers

Notes:

1. This Chapter does not cover:
 (a) Animal blood of heading No. 05. 11;
 (b) Separate chemically defined compounds (other than those answering to the descriptions in Note 2(a), 3(a), 4(a) or 5 below); or
 (c) Cultured potassium chloride crystals (other than optical elements) weighing not less than 2. 5g each, of heading No. 38. 24; optical elements of potassium chloride (heading No. 90. 01).
2. Heading No. 31. 02 applies only to the following goods, provided that they are not put up in the forms or packages described in heading No. 31. 05:
 (a) Goods which answer to one or other of the descriptions given below:
  (i) Sodium nitrate, whether or not pure;
  (ii) Ammonium nitrate, whether or not pure;
  (iii) Double salts, whether or not pure, of ammonium sulphate and ammonium nitrate;
  (iv) Ammonium sulphate, whether or not pure;
  (v) Double salts (whether or not pure) or mixtures of calcium nitrate and ammonium nitrate;
  (vi) Double salts (whether or not pure) or mixtures of calcium nitrate and magnesium nitrate;
  (vii) Calcium cyanamide, whether or not pure or treated with oil;
  (viii) Urea, whether or not pure.
 (b) Fertilizers consisting of any of the goods described in (a) above mixed together.
 (c) Fertilizers consisting of ammonium chloride or of any of the goods described in (a) or (b) above mixed with chalk, gypsum or other inorganic nonfertilizing substances.
 (d) Liquid fertilizers consisting of the goods of subparagraph (a) (ii) or (viii) above, or of mixtures of those goods, in an aqueous or ammoniacal solution.
3. Heading No. 31. 03 applies only to the following goods, provided that they are not put up in the forms or packages described in heading No. 31. 05:
 (a) Goods which answer to one or other of the descriptions given below:
  (i) Basic slag;
  (ii) Natural phosphates of heading No. 25. 10, calcined or further heat-treated than for the removal of impurities;
  (iii) Superphosphates (single, double or triple);
  (iv) Calcium hydrogenorthophosphate containing not less than 0. 2% by weight of flourine calculated on the dry anhydrous product.
 (b) Fertilizers consisting of any of the goods described in (a) above mixed together, but with no account being taken of the fluorine content limit.
 (c) Fertilizers consisting of any of the goods described in (a) or (b) above, but with no account being taken of the fluorine content limit, mixed with chalk, gypsum or other inorganic non-fertilizing substances.
4. Heading No. 31. 04 applies only to the following goods, provided that they are not put up in the forms or packages described in heading No. 31. 05:
 (a) Goods which answer to one or other of the descriptions given below:
  (i) Crude natural potassium salts (for example, carnallite, kainite and sylvite);
  (ii) Potassium chloride, whether or not pure, except as provided in Note 1(c) above;
  (iii) Potassium sulphate, whether or not pure;
  (iv) Magnesium potassium sulphate, whether or not pure.
 (b) Fertilizers consisting of any of the goods described in (a) above mixed together.
5. Ammonium dihydrogenorthophosphate (monoammonium phosphate) and diammonium hydrogenorthophosphate (diammonium phosphate), whether or not pure, and intermixtures thereof, are to be classified in heading No. 31. 05.
6. For the purposes of heading No. 31. 05, the term "other fertilizers" applies only to products of a kind used as fertilizers and containing, as an essential constituent, at least one of the fertilizing elements nitrogen, phosphorus or potassium.

协定税率 %								RCEP		特惠税率 %			Article Description
东/冰/格	巴基斯坦	韩国	瑞士上/下	哥/秘/柬	澳/毛	新西/坡/智	中国港/澳/台	东盟及马来/澳/韩	日/新	亚太2国	老/柬/缅	98/97/95	
													Animal or vegetable fertilizers, whether or not mixed together or chemically treated; fertilizers produced by the mixing or chemical treatment of animal or vegetable products:
													---Not chemically treated:
0/0/0	0	0	0/0	0/0/0	0/0	0//0	0/0/	0/0/0	0/0			0/0/0	----Guano
													----Other
0/0/0	3.5	0	0/0	0/0/0	0/0	0//0	0/0/	0/0/0	5.9/0			0/0/0	Forest litter, not chemically treated (including rotten leaves, rotten roots, bark, leaves, roots and other forest humus)
0/0/0	3.5	0	0/0	0/0/0	0/0	0//0	0/0/	0/0/0	5.9/0			0/0/0	Other animal and vegetable fertilizer not chemically treated
													---Other

税则号列	货品名称〔CIQ 扩展编码及品名—T2 表示见附表 2〕	最惠(%)	暂定税率	普通	增值/消费	出口退税	计量单位	监管条件/特殊证件	检验检疫	对美关税	亚太上/下
3101.0090 10	经化学处理的含动物源性成分(如粪、羽毛等)动植物肥料〔101 其他动物器官、细胞、培养基,102 猪、牛、羊等偶蹄动物粪便,103 马等奇蹄动物粪,104 其他动物粪便,105 动物性肥料、垃圾,106 其他动物性废弃物,107 其他化工产品,108 禽源性有机肥〕	4		11	9/	0	千克	AB/1	PQ	24	
3101.0090 20	经化学处理的森林凋落物(包括腐叶、腐根、树皮、树叶、树根等森林腐殖质)〔101 其他动物器官、细胞、培养基,102 植物有机肥,103 其他化工产品〕	4		11	9/	0	千克	8AB/1	PQ	24	
3101.0090 90	经化学处理的其他动植物肥料〔101 其他动物器官、细胞、培养基,102 猪、牛、羊等偶蹄动物粪便,103 马等奇蹄动物粪,104 其他动物粪便,105 动物性肥料、垃圾,106 其他动物性废弃物,107 植物有机肥,108 其他动植物肥料,109 其他化工产品,110 禽源性有机肥〕	4		11	9/	0	千克	AB/1	PQ	24	
31.02	**矿物氮肥及化学氮肥:**										
3102.1000	-尿素,不论是否水溶液										
3102.1000 10	尿素(配额内,不论是否水溶液)〔101 饲料添加剂;103 车用尿素溶液〕	4	1	150	9/	0	千克	tAB/1	MN	26	40/40
3102.1000 90	尿素(配额外,不论是否水溶液)〔101 饲料添加剂;102 其他化工产品;103 车用尿素溶液〕	50		150	9/	0	千克	AB/1	MN	75	40/40
	-硫酸铵,硫酸铵和硝酸铵的复盐及混合物:										
3102.2100	--硫酸铵〔101 矿物源性饲料添加剂,102 无检疫要求食品添加剂,103 需申报仅用于工业用途不用于食品添加剂无检疫要求的化学品〕	4		11	9/	0	千克	7Av/1	R	16.5	
3102.2900	--其他〔999〕	4		11	9/	0	千克	7v/1		6.5	
3102.3000	-硝酸铵,不论是否水溶液〔301 危险化学品,爆炸品;302 危险化学品,氧化性物质;303 其他化工产品〕	4		11	9/	0	千克	9kAB/13	MN	6.5	
3102.4000	-硝酸铵与碳酸钙或其他无肥效无机物的混合物〔999〕	4		11	9/	0	千克	7vB/1	N	6.5	
3102.5000	-硝酸钠〔301 危险化学品,不用作食品添加剂;302 危险化学品,用作食品添加剂〕	4		11	9/	0	千克	7ABv/13	MNS	31.5	
3102.6000	-硝酸钙和硝酸铵的复盐及混合物〔999〕	4		11	9/	0	千克	7Bv/1	N	6.5	
3102.8000	-尿素及硝酸铵混合物的水溶液或氨水溶液〔301 危险化学品,腐蚀性物质;302 其他化工产品〕	4		11	9/	0	千克	7Bv/13	N	6.5	
	-其他,包括上述子目未列名的混合物:										
3102.9010	---氰氨化钙〔301 危险化学品,遇水放出易燃气体的物质;302 其他化工产品〕	4		11	9/	0	千克	7ABv/13	MN	6.5	
3102.9090	---其他〔301 危险化学品,腐蚀性物质;302 其他化工产品〕	4		11	9/	0	千克	7Bv/13	N	31.5	
31.03	**矿物磷肥及化学磷肥:**										
	-过磷酸钙:										
	--按重量计五氧化二磷(P_2O_5)含量在 35%及以上:										
3103.1110	---重过磷酸钙〔999〕	4	1	11	9/	0	千克	7ABv/1	MN	3.5	
3103.1190	---其他〔999〕	4	1	11	9/	0	千克	7ABv/1	MN	3.5	
3103.1900	--其他〔999〕	4	1	11	9/	0	千克	7ABv/1	MN	8.5	
3103.9000	-其他〔999〕	4	1	11	9/	0	千克	7Bv/1	N	3.5	
31.04	**矿物钾肥及化学钾肥:**										
	-氯化钾:										
3104.2020	---纯氯化钾〔999〕	3	1	11	9/	0	千克	7Bv/1	N	28.5	
3104.2090	---其他〔101 矿物源性饲料添加剂,102 其他化工产品,301 需申报仅用于工业用途不用于食品添加剂无检疫要求的化学品〕	3	1	11	9/	0	千克	7ABv/1	RN	28.5	
3104.3000	-硫酸钾〔101 矿物源性饲料添加剂,102 其他化工产品〕	3	1	11	9/	0	千克	7ABv/1	MN	28.5	
	-其他:										
3104.9010	---光卤石、钾盐及其他天然粗钾盐〔999〕	3	1	11	9/	0	千克	7Bv/1	N	3.5	
3104.9090	---其他〔999〕	3	1	11	9/	0	千克	7Bv/1	N	8.5	
31.05	**含氮、磷、钾中两种或三种肥效元素的矿物肥料或化学肥料;其他肥料;制成片及类似形状或每包毛重不超过 10 千克的本章各项货品:**										
3105.1000	-制成片及类似形状或每包毛重不超过 10 千克的本章各项货品										
3105.1000 10	制成片状及类似形状或零售包装的硝酸铵(零售包装每包毛重不超过 10 千克)〔999〕	4	1	11	9/	0	千克	9B/1	N	26	
3105.1000 90	制成片状及类似形状或零售包装的第 31 章其他货品(零售包装每包毛重不超过 10 千克)〔999〕	4	1	11	9/	0	千克	7Bv/1	N	26	

协定税率 %								RCEP		特惠税率 %			Article Description
东/冰/格	巴基斯坦	韩国	瑞士上/下	哥/秘/柬	澳/毛	新西/坡/智	中国港/澳/台	东盟及马来/澳/韩	日/新	亚太2国	老/柬/缅	98/97/95	
0/0/0	0	1.8	0/0	0/0/0	0/0	0//0	0/0/	3.6/3.6/3.6	3.8/3.6			0/0/0	Animals or vegetable fertilizer, chemically treated, containing, compositions of animals' natural character
0/0/0	0	1.8	0/0	0/0/0	0/0	0//0	0/0/	3.6/3.6/3.6	3.8/3.6			0/0/0	Forest litter, chemically treated (including rotten leaves, rotten roots, bark, leaves, roots and other forest humus)
0/0/0	0	1.8	0/0	0/0/0	0/0	0//0	0/0/	3.6/3.6/3.6	3.8/3.6			0/0/0	Other vegetable fertilizere, chemical treated
													Mineral or chemical fertilizers, nitrogenous:
													-Urea, whether or not in aqueous solution
//	40						0/0/						Urea(whether or not in aqueous solution, in-quota)
//	40						0/0/						Urea(whether or not in aqueous solution, out -quota)
													-Ammonium sulphate; double salts and mixtures of ammonium sulphate and ammonium nitrate:
0/0/0	0	0	0/0	0/0/0	0/0	0//0	0/0/	0/0/0	0/0			0/0/0	--Ammonium sulphate
0/0/0	0	0	0/0	0/0/0	0/0	0//0	0/0/	0/0/0	0/0			0/0/0	--Other
0/0/0	0	0	0/0	0/0/0	0/0	0//0	0/0/	0/0/0	0/0			0/0/0	-Ammonium nitrate, whether or not in aqueous solution
0/0/0	0	0	0/0	0/0/0	0/0	0//0	0/0/	0/0/0	0/0			0/0/0	-Mixtures of ammonium nitrate with calcium carbonate or other inorganic nonfertilizing substances
0/0/0	0	0	0/0	0/0/0	0/0	0//0	0/0/	0/0/0	0/0			0/0/0	-Sodium nitrate
0/0/0	0	0	0/0	0/0/0	0/0	0//0	0/0/	0/0/0	0/0			0/0/0	-Double salts and mixtures of calcium nitrate and ammonium nitrate
0/0/0	0	0	0/0	0/0/0	0/0	0//0	0/0/	0/0/0	3.6/0			0/0/0	-Mixtures of urea and ammonium ni-trate in aqueous or ammoniacal solution
													-Other, including mixtures not specified in the foregoing subheadings:
0/0/0	0	0	0/0	0/0/0	0/0	0//0	0/0/	0/0/0	0/0			0/0/0	---Calcium cyanamide
0/0/0	0	0	0/0	0/0/0	0/0	0//0	0/0/	0/0/0	0/0			0/0/0	---Other
													Mineral or chemical fertilizers, phosphatic:
													-Superphosphates:
													--Phosphorus pentoxide (P205)≥35% by weight
0/0/0	0	0	0/0	0/0/0	0/0	0//0	0/0/	0/0/0	0/0			0/0/0	---Triple superphosphates
0/0/0	0	0	0/0	0/0/0	0/0	0//0	0/0/	0/0/0	0/0			0/0/0	---Other
0/0/0	0	0	0/0	0/0/0	0/0	0//0	0/0/	0/0/0	0/0			0/0/0	--Other
0/0/0	0	0	0/0	0/0/0	0/0	0//0	0/0/	0/0/0	3.6/0			0/0/0	-Other
													Mineral or chemical fertilizers, potassic:
													-Potassium chloride:
0/0/0	0	0	0/0	0/0/0	0/0	0//0	0/0/	0/0/0	0/0			0/0/0	---Pure
0/0/0	0	0	0/0	0/0/0	0/0	0//0	0/0/	0/0/0	0/0			0/0/0	---Other
0/0/0	0	1.4	0/0	0/0/0	0/0	0//0	0/0/	2.7/2.7/2.7	2.8/2.7			0/0/0	-Potassium sulphate
													-Other:
0/0/0	0	0	0/0	0/0/0	0/0	0//0	0/0/	0/0/0	0/0			0/0/0	---Carnallite, sylvite and other crude natural potassium salts
0/0/	0	0	0/0	0/0/0	0/0	0//0	0/0/	0/0/0	2.7/0			0/0/0	---Other
													Mineral or chemical fertilizers containing two or three of the fertilizing elements nitrogen, phosphorus and potassium; other fertilizers; goods of this Chapter in tablets or similar forms or in packages of a gross weight not exceeding 10kg:
													-Goods of this Chapter in tablets or similar forms or in packages of a gross weight not exceeding 10kg
0/0/0	0	0	0/0	0/0/0	0/0	0//0	0/0/	0/0/0	0/0			0/0/0	Ammonium nitrate, goods of this in tablets or similar in forms or packages of a gross weight≤10kg
0/0/0	0	0	0/0	0/0/0	0/0	0//0	0/0/	0/0/0	0/0			0/0/0	Other goods of the chapter 31, in tablets or similar in forms or packages of a gross weight≤10kg

税则号列	货品名称〔CIQ 扩展编码及品名—T2 表示见附表 2〕	最惠(%)	暂定税率	普通	增值/消费	出口退税	计量单位	监管条件/特殊证件	检验检疫	对美关税	亚太上/下
3105.2000	-含氮、磷、钾三种肥效元素的矿物肥料或化学肥料										
3105.2000 10	化学肥料或矿物肥料(配额内,含氮、磷、钾三种肥效元素)〔301 危险化学品,腐蚀性物质;302 其他化工产品〕	4	1	150	9/	0	千克	ABt/13	MN	26	
3105.2000 90	化学肥料或矿物肥料(配额外,含氮、磷、钾三种肥效元素)〔301 危险化学品,腐蚀性物质;302 其他化工产品〕	50		150	9/	0	千克	AB/13	MN	75	
3105.3000	-磷酸氢二铵										
3105.3000 10	磷酸氢二铵(配额内)〔101 饲料添加剂,301 需申报仅用于工业用途不用于食品添加剂无检疫要求的化学品〕	4	1	150	9/	0	千克	ABt/1	RN	11	
3105.3000 90	磷酸氢二铵(配额外)〔101 矿物源性饲料添加剂,102 其他化工产品,301 需申报仅用于工业用途不用于食品添加剂无检疫要求的化学品〕	50		150	9/	0	千克	AB/1	RN	60	
3105.4000	-磷酸二氢铵及磷酸二氢铵与磷酸氢二铵的混合物〔101 矿物源性饲料添加剂,102 其他化工产品〕	4	1	11	9/	0	千克	7ABv/1	MN	28.5	
	-其他含氮、磷两种肥效元素的矿物肥料或化学肥料:										
3105.5100	--含有硝酸盐及磷酸盐〔301 危险化学品,腐蚀性物质;302 其他化工产品〕	4	1	11	9/	0	千克	7ABv/13	MN	3.5	
3105.5900	--其他〔101 矿物源性饲料添加剂;301 危险化学品,腐蚀性物质;302 其他化工产品〕	4	1	11	9/	0	千克	7ABv/13	MN	8.5	
3105.6000	-含磷、钾两种肥效元素的矿物肥料或化学肥料〔999〕	4	1	11	9/	0	千克	7ABv/1	MN	23.5	
	-其他:										
3105.9010	---有机-无机复混肥料〔301 危险化学品,腐蚀性物质;302 其他化工产品〕	4	1	11	9/	0	千克	7ABv/13	MN	8.5	
3105.9090	---其他:〔301 危险化学品,腐蚀性物质;302 其他化工产品〕	4	1	11	9/	0	千克	7ABv/13	MN	23.5	

协定税率 %								RCEP		特惠税率 %			Article Description
东/冰/格	巴基斯坦	韩国	瑞士上/下	哥/秘/柬	澳/毛	新西/坡/智	中国港/澳/台	东盟及马来/澳/韩	日/新	亚太2国	老/柬/缅	98/97/95	
													-Mineral or chemical fertilizers containing the three fertilizing elements nitrogen, phosphorus and potassium
							0/0/						Mineral or chemical fertilizers containing the three fertilizing elemtnts nitrogen, phosphorus and potassium, in-quota
							0/0/						Mineral or chemical fertilizers (containing the three fertilizing elements nitrogen, phosphorus and potassium, out -quota)
													-Diammonium hydrogenorthophosphate (diammonium phosphate)
							0/0/						Diammonium hydrogenorthophosphate (diammonium phosphate), in-quota
							0/0/						Diammonium hydrogenorthophosphate (diammonium phosphate), out -quota
0/0/0	0	0	0/0	0/0/0	0/0	0//0	0/0/	0/0/0	0/0			0/0/0	-Ammonium dihydrogenorthophosphate (monoammonium phosphate) and mixtures thereof with diammonium hydrogenorthophosphate (diammonium phosphate)
													-Other mineral or chemical fertilizers containing the two fertilizing elements nitrogen and phosphorus:
0/0/0	0	0	0/0	0/0/0	0/0	0//0	0/0/	0/0/0	3.6/0			0/0/0	--Containing nitrates and phosphates
0/0/0	0	0	0/0	0/0/0	0/0	0//0	0/0/	0/0/0	3.6/0			0/0/0	--Other
0/0/0	0	0	0/0	0/0/0	0/0	0//0	0/0/	0/0/0	3.6/0			0/0/0	-Mineral or chemical fertilizers containing the two fertilizing elements phosphorus and potassium
													-Other:
0/0/0	0	0	0/0	0/0/0	0/0	0//0	0/0/	0/0/0	3.6/0			0/0/0	---Fertilizers containing the two fertilizing elements organic and inorganic
0/0/0	0	0	0/0	0/0/0	0/0	0//0	0/0/	0/0/0	3.6/0			0/0/0	---Other:

第三十二章

鞣料浸膏及染料浸膏；鞣酸及其衍生物；染料、颜料及其他着色料；油漆及清漆；油灰及其他类似胶粘剂；墨水、油墨

注释：

一、本章不包括：

（一）单独的已有化学定义的化学元素及化合物（税目 32.03 及 32.04 的货品、税目 32.06 的用作发光体的无机产品、税目 32.07 所述形状的熔融石英或其他熔融硅石制成的玻璃及税目 32.12 的零售形状或零售包装的染料及其他着色料除外）；

（二）税目 29.36 至 29.39、29.41 及 35.01 至 35.04 的鞣酸盐及其他鞣酸衍生物；

（三）沥青胶粘剂（税目 27.15）。

二、税目 32.04 包括生产偶氮染料用的稳定重氮盐与耦合物的混合物。

三、税目 32.03、32.04、32.05 及 32.06 也包括以着色料为基本成分的制品（例如，税目 32.06 包括以税目 25.30 或第二十八章的颜料，金属粉片及金属粉末为基本成分的制品）。该制品是用作原材料着色剂的拼料。但以上税目不包括分散在非水介质中呈液状或浆状的制漆用颜料，例如，税目 32.12 的瓷漆及税目 32.07、32.08、32.09、32.10、32.12、32.13 及 32.15 的其他制品。

四、税目 32.08 包括由税目 39.01 至 39.13 所列产品溶于挥发性有机溶剂的溶液（胶棉除外），但溶剂重量必须超过溶液重量的 50%。

五、本章所称“着色料”，不包括作为油漆填料的产品，不论这些产品能否用于水浆涂料的着色。

六、税目 32.12 所称“压印箔”，只包括用以压印诸如书本封面或帽带之类的薄片，这些薄片由以下材料构成：

（一）金属粉（包括贵金属粉）或颜料经胶水、明胶及其他黏合剂凝结而成的；

（二）金属（包括贵金属）或颜料沉积于任何材料衬片上的。

税则号列	货品名称〔CIQ 扩展编码及品名－T2 表示见附表 2〕	最惠(%)	暂定税率	普通	增值/消费	出口退税	计量单位	监管条件/特殊证件	检验检疫	对美关税	亚太上/下
32.01	**植物鞣料浸膏；鞣酸及其盐、醚、酯和其他衍生物：**										
3201.1000	-坚木浸膏〔999〕	5		35	13/	0	千克	/1		30	
3201.2000	-荆树皮浸膏〔999〕	6.5		35	13/	0	千克	/1		9	
	-其他：										
3201.9010	---其他鞣料浸膏										
3201.9010 10	其他濒危植物鞣料浸膏〔999〕	6.5		40	13/	0	千克	FE/1		34	
3201.9010 90	其他植物鞣料浸膏〔999〕	6.5		40	13/	0	千克	/1		34	
3201.9090	---其他〔101 食用单宁，102 单宁酸，103 固化单宁〕	6.5		35	13/	0	千克	/1		34	
32.02	**有机合成鞣料；无机鞣料；鞣料制剂，不论是否含有天然鞣料；预鞣用酶制剂：**										
3202.1000	-有机合成鞣料〔999〕	6.5		35	13/	0	千克	/1		34	
3202.9000	-其他										
3202.9000 10	无铬鞣料（不论是否含有天然鞣料，包括预鞣用酶制剂）〔999〕	6.5	3	35	13/	0	千克	/1		30.5	
3202.9000 90	其他无机鞣料、鞣料制剂等（不论是否含有天然鞣料，包括预鞣用酶制剂）〔999〕	6.5		35	13/	0	千克	/1		34	
32.03	**动植物质着色料（包括染料浸膏，但动物炭黑除外），不论是否已有化学定义；本章注释三所述的以动植物质着色料为基本成分的制品：**										
	---植物质着色料及以其为基本成分的制品：										
3203.0011	----天然靛蓝及以其为基本成分的制品〔301 无检疫要求食品添加剂，302 需申报仅用于工业用途不用于食品添加剂无检疫要求的化学品〕	6.5		80	13/	0	千克	A/1	R	14	
3203.0019	----其他										
3203.0019 10	濒危植物质着色料及制品（制品是指以植物质着色料为基本成分的）〔101 饲料添加剂，301 其他危险化学品，需申报仅用于工业用途不用于食品添加剂无检疫要求，302 无检疫要求食品添加剂，303 一般化学品，需申报仅用于工业用途不用于食品添加剂无检疫要求，304 属于危险化学品的食品添加剂〕	6.5		45	13/	0	千克	ABEF/1	RS	34	
3203.0019 90	其他植物质着色料及制品（制品是指以植物质着色料为基本成分的）〔101 饲料添加剂，301 其他危险化学品，需申报仅用于工业用途不用于食品添加剂无检疫要求，302 无检疫要求食品添加剂，303 一般化学品，需申报仅用于工业用途不用于食品添加剂无检疫要求，304 属于危险化学品的食品添加剂〕	6.5		45	13/	13	千克	AB/1	RS	34	
3203.0020	---动物质着色料及以其为基本成分的制品［T2］	6.5		50	13/	13	千克	A/1	MR	9	

Chapter 32

Tanning or dyeing extracts; tannins and their derivatives; dyes, pigments and other colouring matter; paints and varnishes; putty and other mastics; inks

Notes:

1. This Chapter does not cover:
   (a) Separate chemically defined elements or compounds (except those of heading No. 32. 03 or 32. 04, inorganic products of a kind used as luminophores (heading No. 32. 06), glass obtained from fused quartz or other fused silica in the forms provided for in heading No. 32. 07, and also dyes and other colouring matter put up in forms or packings for retail sale, of heading No. 32. 12);
   (b) Tannates or other tannin derivatives of products of headings No. 29. 36 to 29. 39, 29. 41 or 35. 01 to 35. 04;
   (c) Mastics of asphalt or other bituminous mastics (heading No. 27. 15).
2. Heading No. 32. 04 includes mixtures of stabilized diazonium salts and couplers for the production of azo dyes.
3. Headings No. 32. 03, 32. 04, 32. 05 and 32. 06 apply also to preparations based on colouring matter (including, in the case of heading No. 32. 06, colouring pigments of heading No. 25. 30 or Chapter 28, metal flakes and metal powders), of a kind used for colouring any material or used as ingredi-ents in the manufacture of colouring preparations. The headings do not apply, however, to pigments dispersed in nonaqueous media, in liquid or paste form, of a kind used in the manufacture of paints, including enamels (heading No. 32. 12), or to other preparations of heading No. 32. 07, 32. 08, 32. 09, 32. 10, 32. 12, 32. 13 or 32. 15.
4. Heading No. 32. 08 includes solutions (other than collodions) consisting of any of the products specified in headings No. 39. 01 to 39. 13 in volatile organic solvents when the weight of the solvent exceeds 50% of the weight of the solution.
5. The expression "colouring matter" in this Chapter does not include products of a kind used as extenders in oil paints, whether or not they are also suitable for colouring distempers.
6. The expression "stamping foils" in heading No. 32. 12 applies only to thin sheets of a kind used for printing, for example, book covers or hat bands, and consisting of:
   (a) Metallic powder (including powder of precious metal) or pigment, agglomerated with glue, gelatin or other binder; or
   (b) Metal (including precious metal) or pigment, deposited on a supporting sheet of any material.

协定税率 %								RCEP		特惠税率 %			Article Description
东/冰/格	巴基斯坦	韩国	瑞士上/下	哥/秘/柬	澳/毛	新西/坡/智	中国港/澳/台	东盟及马来/澳/韩	日/新	亚太2国	老/柬/缅	98/97/95	
													Tanning extracts of vegetable origin; tannins and their salts, ethers, esters and other derivatives:
0/0/0	0	0	0/0	0/0/0	0/0	0//0	0/0/	0/0/0	0/0			0/0/0	-Quebracho extract
0/0/0	3.5	0	0/0	0/0/0	0/0	0//0	0/0/	0/0/0	5.9/0			0/0/0	-Wattle extract
													-Other:
													---Other tanning extracts
0/0/0	3.5	0	0/0	0/0/0	0/0	0//0	0/0/	0/0/0	5.9/0			0/0/0	Other tanning extracts of endangered vegetable origin
0/0/0	3.5	0	0/0	0/0/0	0/0	0//0	0/0/	0/0/0	5.9/0			0/0/0	Other tanning extracts of vegetable origin
0/0/0	2	0	0/0	0/0/0	0/0	0//0	0/0/	0/0/0	5.9/0			0/0/0	---Other
													Synthetic organic tanning substances; inorganic tanning substances; tanning preparations, whether or not containing natural tanning substances; enzymatic preparations for pre-tanning:
0/0/0	0	0	0/0	0/0/0	0/0	0//0	0/0/	5.9/5.9/5.9	5.9/5.9			0/0/0	-Synthetic organic tanning substances
													-Other
0/0/0	2	0	0/0	0/0/0	0/0	0//0	0/0/	0/0/0	5.9/0			0/0/0	Chrome free tanning(whether or not containing natural substances, including enzyme preparation for pre tanning)
0/0/0	2	0	0/0	0/0/0	0/0	0//0	0/0/	0/0/0	5.9/0			0/0/0	Other inorganic tanning and tanning agents(whether or not containing natural substances, including enzyme preparation for pre tanning)
													Colouring matter of vegetable or animal origin (including dyeing extracts but excluding animal black), whether or not chemically defined; preparations as specified in Note 3 to this Chapter based on colouring matter of vegetable or animal origin:
													---Colouring matter of vegetable origin and preparations based thereon:
0/0/0	2	0	0/0	0/1.4/0	0/0	0//0	0/0/	0/0/0	5.9/0			0/0/0	----Natural indigo and preparations based thereon
													----Other
0/0/0	4	0	0/0	0/1.4/0	0/0	0//0	0/0/	0/0/0	5.9/0			0/0/0	Colouring matter and preparations based thereon of endangered vegetable origin
0/0/0	4	0	0/0	0/1.4/0	0/0	0//0	0/0/	0/0/0	5.9/0			0/0/0	Other colouring matter of vegetable origin based thereon of vegetable origin
0/0/0	2	0	0/0	0/1.4/0	0/0	0//0	0/0/	0/0/0	5.9/0			0/0/0	---Colouring matter of animal origin and preparations based thereon

税则号列	货品名称〔CIQ 扩展编码及品名—T2 表示见附表 2〕	最惠(%)	暂定税率	普通	增值/消费	出口退税	计量单位	监管条件/特殊证件	检验检疫	对美关税	亚太上/下
32.04	**有机合成着色料，不论是否已有化学定义；本章注释三所述的以有机合成着色料为基本成分的制品；用作荧光增白剂或发光体的有机合成产品，不论是否已有化学定义：**										
	-有机合成着色料及本章注释三所述的以有机合成着色料为基本成分的制品：										
3204.1100	--分散染料及以其为基本成分的制品[T2]	6.5		35	13/	0	千克	AB/1	RS	34	4.2/4.2
3204.1200	--酸性染料(不论是否与金属络合)及以其为基本成分的制品；媒染染料及以其为基本成分的制品[T2]	6.5		35	13/	0	千克	AB/1	RS	34	4.2/4.2
3204.1300	--碱性染料及以其为基本成分的制品[T2]	6.5		35	13/	0	千克	AB/1	RS	34	4.2/4.2
3204.1400	--直接染料及以其为基本成分的制品[T2]	6.5		35	13/	0	千克	AB/1	RS	19	4.2/4.2
	--瓮染料(包括颜料用的)及以其为基本成分的制品：										
3204.1510	---合成靛蓝(还原靛蓝)〔101 靛蓝(无检疫要求食品添加剂)，102 靛蓝铝色淀(无检疫要求食品添加剂)，103 需申报仅用于工业用途不用于食品添加剂无检疫要求的化学品〕	6.5		35	13/	0	千克	A/1	R	14	4.2/4.2
3204.1590	---其他〔999〕	6.5		35	13/	0	千克	/1		29	4.2/4.2
3204.1600	--活性染料及以其为基本成分的制品〔999〕	6.5		35	13/	0	千克	/1		34	4.2/4.2
3204.1700	--颜料及以其为基本成分的制品	6.5		35	13/	0	千克			1/26.5	4.2
3204.1700　10	彩色光刻胶用光刻胶颜料分散液〔999〕	6.5	3	35	13/	13	千克	/1		25.5	4.2/4.2
3204.1700　90	其他颜料及以其为基本成分的制品〔999〕	6.5		35	13/	13	千克	/1		29	4.2/4.2
	--类胡萝卜素着色料及以其为基本成分的制品 ：										
3204.1810	---类胡萝卜素(包括胡萝卜素)〔101 无检疫要求食品添加剂，301 其他化工产品〕	6.5		20	13/	13	千克	/1		34	4.2/4.2
3204.1820	---以类胡萝卜素(包括胡萝卜素)为基本成分的制品〔301 其他化工品，不用作食品添加剂，302 其他化工品，用作食品添加剂〕	6.5		35	13/	0	千克	AB/1	RS	29	4.2/4.2
	--其他，包括由子目号 3204.11 至 3204.19 中两个或多个子目所列着色料组成的混合物：										
	---硫化染料及以其为基本成分的制品：										
3204.1911	----硫化黑(硫化青)及以其为基本成分的制品〔999〕	6.5		35	13/	0	千克	/1		34	4.2/4.2
3204.1919	----其他〔999〕	6.5		35	13/	0	千克	/1		34	4.2/4.2
3204.1990	---其他[T2]	6.5		35	13/	0	千克	AB/1	RS	29	4.2/4.2
3204.2000	-用作荧光增白剂的有机合成产品〔301 其他危险化学品，302 其他化工产品〕	6.5		40	13/	13	千克	A/1	M	14	4.2/4.2
	-其他：										
3204.9010	---生物染色剂及染料指示剂〔999〕	6.5		20	13/	0	千克	/1		29	4.2/4.2
3204.9090	---其他〔301 危险化学品，易燃液体；302 其他化工产品〕	6.5		40	13/	0	千克	/13		29	4.2/4.2
32.05	**色淀；本章注释三所述的以色淀为基本成分的制品：**										
3205.0000	色淀；本章注释三所述的以色淀为基本成分的制品〔301 新红(无检疫要求食品添加剂)，302 新红铝色淀(无检疫要求食品添加剂)，303 需申报仅用于工业用途不用于食品添加剂无检疫要求的化学品〕	6.5		35	13/	0	千克	A/1	R	14	
32.06	**其他着色料；本章注释三所述的制品，但税目 32.03、32.04 及 32.05 的货品除外；用作发光体的无机产品，不论是否已有化学定义：**										
	-以二氧化钛为基本成分的颜料及制品：										
	--以干物质计二氧化钛含量在 80%及以上的：										
3206.1110	---钛白粉〔999〕	6.5		30	13/	0	千克	4xy/1		19	
3206.1190	---其他〔999〕	6.5		30	13/	0	千克	/1		29	
3206.1900	--其他〔999〕	10		30	13/	0	千克	/1		22.5	
3206.2000	-以铬化合物为基本成分的颜料及制品〔301 危险化学品，易燃液体；302 其他化工产品〕	6.5		35	13/	0	千克	/13		19	
	-其他着色料及其他制品：										
3206.4100	--群青及以其为基本成分的制品〔999〕	6.5		35	13/	0	千克	/1		34	
	--锌钡白及以硫化锌为基本成分的其他颜料和制品：										
3206.4210	---锌钡白〔999〕	6.5		30	13/	0	千克	/1		34	
3206.4290	---其他〔999〕	6.5		30	13/	0	千克	/1		29	
	--其他：										
	---以铋化合物为基本成分的颜料及制品：										
3206.4911	----以钒酸铋为基本成基本成分的颜料及制品〔999〕	6.5		35	13/	0	千克	/1		34	3.3/3.3

协定税率 %								RCEP		特惠税率 %			Article Description
东/冰/格	巴基斯坦	韩国	瑞士 上/下	哥/秘/柬	澳/毛	新西/坡/智	中国港/澳/台	东盟及马来/澳/韩	日/新	亚太2国	老/柬/缅	98/97/95	
													Synthetic organic colouring matter, whether or not chemically defined; preparations as specified in Note 3 to this Chapter based on synthetic organic colouring matter; synthetic organic products of a kind used as fluorescent brightening agents or as luminophores, whether or not chemically defined:
													-Synthetic organic colouring matter and preparations based thereon as specified in Note 3 to this Chapter:
0/0/0	0	0		0/0/0	0/0	0//0	0/0/	5.9/5.9/5.9	5.9/5.9			0/0/0	--Disperse dyes and preparations based thereon
0/0/0	0	0	2.7/2.7	0/0/0	0/0	0//0	0/0/0	5.9/5.9/5.9	5.9/5.9			0/0/0	--Acid dyes, whether or not premetallized, and preparations based thereon; mordant dyes and preparations based thereon
0/0/0	0	0	0/0	0/0/0	0/0	0//0	0/0/	0/0/0	5.9/0			0/0/0	--Basic dyes and preparations based thereon
0/0/0	0	0	0.7/0.7	0/0/0	0/0	0//0	0/0/0	0/0/0	5.9/0			0/0/0	--Direct dyes and preparations based thereon
													--Vat dyes (including those usable in that state as pigments) and preparations based thereon:
0/0/0	0	1.3	0/0	0/0/0	0/0	0//0	0/0/	0/0/5.9	5.9/0			0/0/0	---Synthetic indigo(reductive indigo)
0/0/0	0	1.3	0/0	0/0/0	0/0	0//0	0/0/	0/0/5.9	5.9/0			0/0/0	---Other
0/0/0	0	0	2.7/2.7	0/0/0	0/0	0//0	0/0/0	0/0/0	5.9/0			0/0/0	--Reactive dyes and preparations based thereon
0/0/0	0	0	2.6	0	0	0	0//0	0/0/0				0/0/0	--Pigments and preparations based thereon
0/0/0	0	0	0.7/0.7	0/0/0	0/0	0//0	0/0/0	0/0/0	5.9/0		//	0/0/0	Pigment dispersion of photoresist for color photoresist
0/0/0	0	0	0.7/0.7	0/0/0	0/0	0//0	0/0/0	0/0/0	5.9/0		//	0/0/0	Other pigments and products based on them
													--Carotenoid colouring matters and preparations based thereon
0/0/0	0	0	0/0	0/0/0	0/0	0//0	0/0/	0/0/0	5.9/0			0/0/0	---Carotenoid (including carotene)
0/0/0	0	0		0/0/0	0/0	0//0	0/0/0	0/0/0	5.9/0			0/0/0	---Products based on carotenoids (including carotene)
													--Other, including mixtures of colouring matter of two or more of the subheadings No. 3204. 11 to 3204. 19:
													---Sulphur dyes and preparations based thereon:
0/0/0	0	1.3	0/0	0/0/0	0/0	0//0	0/0/	0/0/5.9	5.9/0			0/0/0	----Sulphur black and preparations based thereon
0/0/0	0	1.3	0/0	0/0/0	0/0	0//0	0/0/	0/0/5.9	5.9/0			0/0/0	----Other
0/0/0	0	0		0/0/0	0/0	0//0	0/0/0	0/0/0	5.9/0			0/0/0	---Other
0/0/0	0	0	2.7/2.7	0/0/0	0/0	0//0	0/0/0	0/0/0	5.9/0			0/0/0	-Synthetic organic products of a kind used as flourescent brightening agents
													-Other:
0/0/0	0	0	0.7/0.7	0/0/0	0/0	0//0	0/0/	5.9/5.9/5.9	6.1/5.9			0/0/0	---Biological stains and dye indicators
0/0/0	0	0	0/0	0/0/0	0/0	0//0	0/0/	0/0/0	5.9/0			0/0/0	---Other
													Colour lakes; preparations as specified in Note 3 to this Chapter based on colour lakes:
0/0/0	2	3	0/0	0/0/0	0/0	0//0	0/0/	5.9/5.9/5.9	6.1/5.9			0/0/0	Colour lakes; preparations as specified in Note 3 to this Chapter based on colour lakes
													Other colouring matter; preparations as specified in Note 3 to this Chapter, other than those of heading No. 32. 03, 32. 04 or 32. 05; inorganic products of a kind used as luminophores, whether or not chemically defined:
													-Pigments and preparations based on titanium dioxide:
													--Containing 80% or more by weight of titanium dioxide calculated on the dry matter:
0/0/0	2	0	0/0	0/0/0	0/0	0//0	0/0/0	0/0/0	0/0			0/0/0	---Titanium White
0/0/0	2	0	0/0	0/0/0	0/0	0//0	0/0/	0/0/0	5.9/0			0/0/0	---Other
0/0/0	3.5	2	0/0	0/0/0	0/0	0/0/0	0/0/0	9/9/9	9.1/9			0/0/0	--Other
0/0/0	2	0	0/0	0/0/0	0/0	0//0	0/0/	0/0/0	5.9/0			0/0/0	-Pigments and preparations based on chromium compounds
													-Other colouring matter and other preparations:
0/0/0	2	0	0/0	0/0/0	0/0	0//0	0/0/	0/0/0	5.9/0			0/0/0	--Ultramarine and preparations based thereon
													--Lithopone and other pigments and preparations based on zinc sulphide:
0/0/0	2	0	0/0	0/0/0	0/0	0//0	0/0/	0/0/0	5.9/0			0/0/0	---Lithopone
0/0/0	2	1.3	0/0	0/0/0	0/0	0//0	0/0/	0/0/5.9	5.9/0			0/0/0	---Other
													--Other:
													---Pigmenlts and preparations based on bismuth compound:
0/0/0	0	1.3	0/0	0/0/0	0/0	0//0	0/0/0	5.9/5.9/5.9	5.9/5.9			0/0/0	----Pigmenlts and preparations based on Bismuth vanad ate

税则号列	货品名称〔CIQ 扩展编码及品名—T2 表示见附表 2〕	最惠(%)	暂定税率	普通	增值/消费	出口退税	计量单位	监管条件/特殊证件	检验检疫	对美关税	亚太上/下
3206.4919	----其他〔999〕	6.5		35	13/	0	千克	/1		14	3.3/3.3
3206.4990	---其他〔301 其他化工品,不用作食品添加剂,302 其他化工品,用作食品添加剂〕	6.5		35	13/	0	千克	/1		19	3.3/3.3
3206.5000	-用作发光体的无机产品〔999〕	6.5		35	13/	0	千克	/1		19	4.2/4.2
32.07	**陶瓷、搪瓷及玻璃工业用的调制颜料、遮光剂、着色剂、珐琅和釉料、釉底料(泥釉)、光瓷釉以及类似产品;搪瓷玻璃料及其他玻璃,呈粉、粒或粉片状的:**										
3207.1000	-调制颜料、遮光剂、着色剂及类似制品〔301 危险化学品,易燃液体;302 其他化工产品〕	5		50	13/	0	千克	/13		30	
3207.2000	-珐琅和釉料、釉底料(泥釉)及类似制品〔999〕	5		50	13/	0	千克	/1		30	
3207.3000	-光瓷釉及类似制品〔999〕	5		50	13/	0	千克	/1		30	
3207.4000	-搪瓷玻璃料及其他玻璃,呈粉、粒或粉片状的〔999〕	5		50	13/	0	千克	/1		15	
32.08	**以合成聚合物或化学改性天然聚合物为基本成分的油漆及清漆(包括瓷漆及大漆),分散于或溶于非水介质的;本章注释四所述的溶液:**										
3208.1000	-以聚酯为基本成分										
3208.1000 10	分散于或溶于非水介质的聚酯油漆及清漆,施工状态下挥发性有机物含量大于 420 克/升(以聚酯为基本成分的(包括瓷漆及大漆)〔301:属于危险化学品的涂料;302:不属于危险化学品的涂料〕	10		50	13/4	0	千克	A/13	M	37.5	9/9
3208.1000 90	其他分散于或溶于非水介质的聚酯油漆及清漆;以聚酯为基本成分的本章注释四所述溶液(以聚酯为基本成分的(包括瓷漆及大漆))〔301:属于危险化学品的涂料;302:不属于危险化学品的涂料〕	10		50	13/	0	千克	A/13	M	37.5	9/9
	-以丙烯酸聚合物或乙烯聚合物为基本成分:										
3208.2010	---以丙烯酸聚合物为基本成分										
3208.2010 20	以丙烯酸聚合物为基本成分的油漆、清漆等,施工状态下挥发性有机物含量大于 420 克/升(分散于或溶于非水质的以丙烯酸聚合物为基本成分,包括瓷漆大漆)〔301 属于危险化学品的涂料;302 不属于危险化学品的涂料〕	10		50	13/4	0	千克	A/13	M	32.5	9/9
3208.2010 90	以丙烯酸聚合物为基本成分的油漆、清漆等;以丙烯酸聚合物为基本成分的本章注释四所述溶液(分散于或溶于非水质的以丙烯酸聚合物为基本成分,包括瓷漆大漆)〔301 属于危险化学品的涂料;302 不属于危险化学品的涂料〕	10		50	13/	0	千克	A/13	M	32.5	9/9
3208.2020	---以乙烯聚合物为基本成分										
3208.2020 10	溶于非水介质的聚乙烯油漆及清漆,施工状态下挥发性有机物含量大于 420 克/升,以乙烯聚合物为基本成分(包括瓷漆及大漆)〔301:属于危险化学品的涂料;302:不属于危险化学品的涂料〕	10		50	13/4	0	千克	A/13	M	37.5	9/9
3208.2020 90	其他分散于或溶于非水介质的以乙烯聚合物为基本成分的油漆及清漆;以乙烯聚合物基本成分的本章注释四所述溶液(以乙烯聚合物为基本成分(包括瓷漆及大漆))〔301:属于危险化学品的涂料;302:不属于危险化学品的涂料〕	10		50	13/	0	千克	A/13	M	37.5	9/9
	-其他:										
3208.9010	---以聚胺酯类化合物为基本成分										
3208.9010 11	分散于或溶于非水介质的光导纤维用涂料,施工状态下挥发性有机物含量大于 420 克/升,主要成分为聚胺酯丙烯酸酯类化合物,以聚胺酯类化合物为基本成分〔301 属于危险化学品的涂料 302 不属于危险化学品的涂料〕	10		50	13/4	0	千克	A/13	M	32.5	9/9
3208.9010 19	其他分散于或溶于非水介质的光导纤维用涂料,(主要成分为聚胺酯丙烯酸酯类化合物,以聚胺酯类化合物为基本成分)〔301 属于危险化学品的涂料 302 不属于危险化学品的涂料〕	10		50	13/	0	千克	A/13	M	32.5	9/9
3208.9010 91	其他聚胺酯油漆清漆等,施工状态下挥发性有机物含量大于 420 克/升,溶于非水介质以聚胺酯类化合物为基本成分,含瓷漆大漆〔301 属于危险化学品的涂料,302 不属于危险化学品的涂料〕	10		50	13/4	0	千克	A/13	LM	32.5	9/9

协定税率 %								RCEP		特惠税率 %			Article Description
东/冰/格	巴基斯坦	韩国	瑞士上/下	哥/秘/柬	澳/毛	新西/坡/智	中国港/澳/台	东盟及马来/澳/韩	日/新	亚太2国	老/柬/缅	98/97/95	
0/0/0	0	1.3	0/0	0/0/0	0/0	0//0	0/0/0	5.9/5.9/5.9	5.9/5.9			0/0/0	----Other
0/0/0	0	1.3	0/0	0/0/0	0/0	0//0	0/0/0	5.9/5.9/5.9	5.9/5.9			0/0/0	---Other
0/0/0	4	1.3	0/0	0/0/0	0/0	0//0	0/0/	0/0/5.9	5.9/0			0/0/0	-Inorganic products of a kind used as luminophores
													Prepared pigments, prepared opacifiers and prepared colours, vitrifiable enamels and glazes, engobes (slips), liquid lustres and similar preparations, of a kind used in the ceramic, enamelling or glass industry; glass frit and other glass, in the form of powder, granules or flakes:
0/0/0	0	1	0/0	0/0/0	0/0	0//0	0/0/	0/0/4.5	4.5/0			0/0/0	-Prepared pigments, prepared opacifiers, prepared colours and similar preparations
0/0/0	0	2.3	0/0	0/0/0	0/0	0//0	0/0/	4.5/4.5/4.5	4.7/4.5			0/0/0	-Vitrifiable enamels and glazes, engobes (slips) and similar preparations
0/0/0	0	0	0/0	0/0/0	0/0	0//0	0/0/	0/0/0	0/0			0/0/0	-Liquid lustres and similar preparations
0/0/0	0	0	0/0	0/0/0	0/0	0//0	0/0/	0/0/0	0/0			0/0/0	-Glass frit and other glass, in the form of powder, granules or flakes
													Paints and varnishes (including enamels and lacquers) based on synthetic polymers or chemically modified natural polymers, dispersed or dissolved in a nonaqueous medium; solutions as defined in Note 4 to this Chapter:
													-Based on polyesters
0/0/0	3.5	6	0/0	0/0/0	0/0	0/0/0	0/0/0	9.5/9.5/9.5	9.5/9.5			0/0/0	-Soluble in non-aqueous medium polyester paint and varnish and so on, the construction condition of volatile organic matter content is more than 420 grams/liter, polyester as the basic ingredients (including enamel and Chinese lacquer)
0/0/0	3.5	6	0/0	0/0/0	0/0	0/0/0	0/0/0	9.5/9.5/9.5	9.5/9.5			0/0/0	Other soluble in non-aqueous medium polyester paint and varnish and so on, with polyester as the basic ingredients (including enamel and Chinese lacquer)
													-Based on acrylic or vinyl polymers:
													---Based on acrylic polymers
0/0/0	4	6	0/0	0/0/0	0/0	0/0/0	0/0/0	9.5/9.5/9.5	9.5/9.5		//	0/0/0	For paints and varnishes with acrylic polymer as the basic component, the content of volatile organic compounds is more than 420 g / L (for paints and varnishes with acrylic polymer as the basic component dispersed in or dissolved in non water, including enamel paints)
0/0/0	4	6	0/0	0/0/0	0/0	0/0/0	0/0/0	9.5/9.5/9.5	9.5/9.5		//	0/0/0	Paints and varnishes, water — based pigments for leather, VOC content of more than 420 g / L in working state (including non polymer based enamel, lacquer and slurry coatings)
													---Based on vinyl polymers
0/0/0	3.5	2	0/0	0/0/0	0/0	0//0	0/0/	0/0/9	9.1/0			0/0/0	Soluble in non-aqueous medium PE paint and varnish, construction condition of volatile organic matter content is more than 420 g/l; Vinyl polymer as basic ingredients (including enamel and Chinese lacquer)
0/0/0	3.5	2	0/0	0/0/0	0/0	0//0	0/0/	0/0/9	9.1/0			0/0/0	Other soluble in non-aqueous medium polyethylene paint and varnish; Vinyl polymer as basic ingredients (including enamel and Chinese lacquer)
													-Other:
													---Based on polyurethane polymers
0/0/0	3.5	2	0/0	0/0/0	0/0	0/0/0	0/0/	9/9/9	9.1/9			0/0/0	Dispersion in optical fibre or dissolve in the water medium with coating, construction condition of volatile organic matter content is more than 420 g/l; Main composition of polyurethane and acrylic ester compounds with polyurethane compounds of the basic ingredients
0/0/0	3.5	2	0/0	0/0/0	0/0	0/0/0	0/0/	9/9/9	9.1/9			0/0/0	Other scattered or dissolve in non-aqueous medium of optical fiber coating; Main composition of polyurethane and acrylic ester compounds with polyurethane compounds of the basic ingredients
0/0/0	3.5	2	0/0	0/0/0	0/0	0/0/0	0/0/	9/9/9	9.1/9			0/0/0	Other polyurethane paint varnish, etc, the construction condition of volatile organic matter content is more than 420 g/l; With polyurethane compounds dissolve in the water as the basic composition, containing enamel Chinese lacquer

税则号列		货品名称〔CIQ扩展编码及品名—T2表示见附表2〕	最惠(%)	暂定税率	普通	增值/消费	出口退税	计量单位	监管条件/特殊证件	检验检疫	对美关税	亚太上/下
3208.9010	99	其他聚胺酯油漆清漆等;以聚氨酯类化合物为基本成分的本章注释四所述溶液(分散于或溶于非水介质以聚胺酯类化合物为基本成分,含瓷漆大漆)〔301:属于危险化学品的涂料;302:不属于危险化学品的涂料〕	10		50	13/	0	千克	A/13	LM	32.5	9/9
3208.9090		---其他										
3208.9090	10	分散于或溶于非水介质其他油漆、清漆溶液,施工状态下挥发性有机物含量大于420克/升(包括以聚合物为基本成分的漆,本章注释四所述溶液)[T2]	10		50	13/4	0	千克	A/13	LM	32.5	9/9
3208.9090	90	分散于或溶于非水介质其他油漆、清漆溶液;其他本章注释四所述溶液(包括以聚合物为基本成分的漆,本章注释四所述溶液)〔301:属于危险化学品的涂料;302:不属于危险化学品的涂料〕	10		50	13/	0	千克	A/13	LM	32.5	9/9
32.09		**以合成聚合物或化学改性天然聚合物为基本成分的油漆及清漆(包括瓷漆及大漆),分散于或溶于水介质的:**										
3209.1000		-以丙烯酸聚合物或乙烯聚合物为基本成分										
3209.1000	10	溶于水介质的聚丙烯酸油漆及清漆,施工状态下挥发性有机物含量大于420克/升,〔以聚丙烯酸或聚乙烯为基本成分的(包括瓷漆及大漆)〕〔301不属于危险化学品的涂料,302属于危险化学品的涂料〕	10		50	13/4	0	千克	A/1	M	22.5	6.5/6.5
3209.1000	90	其他溶于水介质的聚丙烯酸油漆及清漆,以聚丙烯酸或聚乙烯为基本成分的(包括瓷漆及大漆)〔301不属于危险化学品的涂料,302属于危险化学品的涂料〕	10		50	13/	0	千克	A/1	M	22.5	6.5/6.5
		-其他:										
3209.9010		---以环氧树脂为基本成分										
3209.9010	10	以环氧树脂为基本成分的油漆及清漆,施工状态下挥发性有机物含量大于420克/升,(包括瓷漆及大漆,分散或溶于水介质)〔301不属于危险化学品的涂料,302属于危险化学品的涂料〕	10		50	13/4	0	千克	A/1	M	32.5	
3209.9010	90	其他以环氧树脂为基本成分的油漆及清漆,(包括瓷漆及大漆,分散或溶于水介质)〔301属于危险化学品的涂料;302不属于危险化学品的涂料〕	10		50	13/	0	千克	A/1	M	32.5	
3209.9020		---以氟树脂为基本成分										
3209.9020	10	以氟树脂为基本成分的油漆及清漆,施工状态下挥发性有机物含量大于420克/升,(包括瓷漆及大漆,分散于或溶于水介质)〔301不属于危险化学品的涂料,302属于危险化学品的涂料〕	10		50	13/4	13	千克	A/1	M	37.5	
3209.9020	90	其他以氟树脂为基本成分的油漆及清漆,(包括瓷漆及大漆,分散于或溶于水介质)〔301不属于危险化学品的涂料,302属于危险化学品的涂料〕	10		50	13/	13	千克	A/1	M	37.5	
3209.9090		---其他										
3209.9090	10	溶于水介质其他聚合物油漆及清漆,施工状态下挥发性有机物含量大于420克/升,(以合成聚合物或化学改性天然聚合物为基本成分的)〔301不属于危险化学品的涂料,302属于危险化学品的涂料〕	10		50	13/4	0	千克	A/1	M	32.5	
3209.9090	90	溶于水介质其他聚合物油漆及清漆,施工状态下挥发性有机物含量不大于420克/升,(以合成聚合物或化学改性天然聚合物为基本成分的)〔301不属于危险化学品的涂料,302属于危险化学品的涂料〕	10		50	13/	0	千克	A/1	M	32.5	
32.10		**其他油漆及清漆(包括瓷漆、大漆及水浆涂料);加工皮革用的水性颜料:**										
3210.0000		其他油漆及清漆(包括瓷漆、大漆及水浆涂料);加工皮革用的水性颜料										
3210.0000	20	油漆及清漆,皮革用水性颜料,施工状态下挥发性有机物含量大于420克/升(包括非聚合物为基料的瓷漆,大漆及水浆涂料)〔301属于危险化学品的涂料;302不属于危险化学品的涂料〕	10		50	13/4	0	千克	/13		32.5	6.5/6.5
3210.0000	90	油漆及清漆,皮革用水性颜料,施工状态下挥发性有机物含量不大于420克/升(包括非聚合物为基料的瓷漆,大漆及水浆涂料)〔301属于危险化学品的涂料;302不属于危险化学品的涂料〕	10		50	13/	0	千克	/13		32.5	6.5/6.5
32.11		**配制的催干剂:**										

协定税率 %								RCEP		特惠税率 %			Article Description
东/冰/格	巴基斯坦	韩国	瑞士上/下	哥/秘/柬	澳/毛	新西/坡/智	中国港/澳/台	东盟及马来/澳/韩	日/新	亚太2国	老/柬/缅	98/97/95	
0/0/0	3.5	2	0/0	0/0/0	0/0	0/0/0	0/0/	9/9/9	9.1/9			0/0/0	Other polyurethane paint varnish, etc, the construction condition of volatile organic matter content is not more than 420 g/l; With polyurethane compounds dissolve in the water as the basic composition, containing enamel Chinese lacquer
													---Other
0/0/0	3.5	6	1/1	0/0/0	0/0	0/0/0	0/0/0	9.5/9.5/9.5	9.5/9.5			0/0/0	Soluble in non-aqueous medium other paint, varnish solution, construction condition of volatile organic matter content is more than 420 g/l; Including the polymer as the basic ingredients of paint, this chapter four mentioned solution comment
0/0/0	3.5	6	1/1	0/0/0	0/0	0/0/0	0/0/0	9.5/9.5/9.5	9.5/9.5			0/0/0	Soluble in non-aqueous medium other paint, varnish solution, construction condition of volatile organic matter content is not more than 420 g/l; Including the polymer as the basic ingredients of paint, this chapter four mentioned solution comment
													Paints and varnishes (including enamels and lacquers) based on synthetic polymers or chemically modified natural polymers, dispersed or dissolved in an aqueous medium:
													-Based on acrylic or vinyl polymers
0/0/0	3.5	2	0/0	0/0/0	0/0	0/0/0	0/0/	0/0/9	9.1/0			0/0/0	Soluble in water medium poly acrylic paint and varnish, construction condition of volatile organic matter content is more than 420 g/l; With polyacrylic acid or polyethylene as basic ingredients (including Chinese lacquer and enamel)
0/0/0	3.5	2	0/0	0/0/0	0/0	0/0/0	0/0/	0/0/9	9.1/0			0/0/0	Other soluble in water medium of poly (acrylic paint and varnish; With polyacrylic acid or polyethylene as basic ingredients (including Chinese lacquer and enamel)
													-Other:
													---Based on epoxy resin
0/0/0	3.5	6	0/0	0/0/0	0/0	0/0/0	0/0/0	9.5/9.5/	/9.5			0/0/0	With epoxy resin as the basic composition of the paint and varnish, construction condition of volatile organic matter content is more than 420 g/l; Including enamel and Chinese lacquer, dispersed or dissolved in water medium
0/0/0	3.5	6	0/0	0/0/0	0/0	0/0/0	0/0/0	9.5/9.5/	/9.5			0/0/0	Other with epoxy resin as the basic composition of the paint and varnish; Including enamel and Chinese lacquer, dispersed or dissolved in water medium
													---Based on fluororesin
0/0/0	3.5	2	0/0	0/0/0	0/0	0/0/0	0/0/	9/9/9	9.1/9			0/0/0	Fluorine resin as the basic ingredients of paint, varnish, construction condition of volatile organic matter content is more than 420 g/l; Including enamel and Chinese lacquer, decentralised or dissolve in water medium
0/0/0	3.5	2	0/0	0/0/0	0/0	0/0/0	0/0/	9/9/9	9.1/9			0/0/0	Other fluorine resin as the basic composition of the paint and varnish; Including enamel and Chinese lacquer, decentralised or dissolve in water medium
													---Other
0/0/0	3.5	6	1/1	0/0/0	0/0	0/0/0	0/0/0	9.5/9.5/	/9.5			0/0/0	Soluble in water medium and other polymer paint varnish, construction condition of volatile organic matter content is more than 420 g/l; Synthetic polymer or chemical modification of natural polymers as basic elements
0/0/0	3.5	6	1/1	0/0/0	0/0	0/0/0	0/0/0	9.5/9.5/	/9.5			0/0/0	Soluble in water medium and other polymer paint varnish, construction condition of volatile organic matter content is not more than 420 g/l; Synthetic polymer or chemical modification of natural polymers as basic elements
													Other paints and varnishes (including enamels, lacquers and distempers); prepared water pigments of a kind used for finishing leather:
													Other paints and varnishes (including enamels, lacquers and distempers); prepared water pigments of a kind used for finishing leather
0/0/0	4	0	0/0	0/0/0	0/0	0/0/0	0/0/0	9/9/9	9.1/9		//	0/0/0	Paints and varnishes, water—based pigments for leather, the content of volatile organic compounds is more than 420 g / L (including non polymer based enamel, lacquer and slurry coatings)
0/0/0	4	0	0/0	0/0/0	0/0	0/0/0	0/0/0	9/9/9	9.1/9		//	0/0/0	Paints and varnishes, water — based pigments for leather, VOC content not more than 420 g / L under construction (including non polymer based enamel, lacquer and slurry coatings)
													Prepared driers:

税则号列		货品名称〔CIQ 扩展编码及品名—T2 表示见附表 2〕	最惠(%)	暂定税率	普通	增值/消费	出口退税	计量单位	监管条件/特殊证件	检验检疫	对美关税	亚太上/下
3211.0000		配制的催干剂〔301 危险化学品，易燃液体；302 其他化工产品〕	10		50	13/	0	千克	/13		32.5	
32.12		**制造油漆(含瓷漆)用的颜料(包括金属粉末或金属粉片)，分散于非水介质中呈液状或浆状的；压印箔；零售形状及零售包装的染料或其他着色料：**										
3212.1000		-压印箔〔999〕	15		80	13/	0	千克	/1		35	
3212.9000		-其他〔301 危险化学品，易燃液体；302 其他化工产品〕	10		50	13/	0	千克	/13		22.5	
32.13		**艺术家、学生和广告美工用的颜料、调色料、文娱颜料及类似品，片状、管装、罐装、瓶装、扁盒装以及类似形状或包装的：**										
3213.1000		-成套的颜料〔301 危险化学品，易燃液体；302 其他化工产品〕	6.5		70	13/	13	千克	/13		16.5	
3213.9000		-其他〔301 危险化学品，易燃液体；302 其他化工产品〕	6.5		70	13/	13	千克	/13		11.5	4.2/4.2
32.14		**安装玻璃用油灰、接缝用油灰、树脂胶泥、嵌缝胶及其他类似胶粘剂；漆工用填料；非耐火涂面制剂，涂门面、内墙、地板、天花板等用：**										
		-安装玻璃用油灰、接缝用油灰、树脂胶泥、嵌缝胶及其他类似胶粘剂；漆工用填料：										
3214.1010		---半导体器件封装材料〔301 危险化学品，易燃液体；302 其他化工产品〕	9		70	13/	13	千克	/1		36.5	
3214.1090		---其他〔301 危险化学品，易燃液体；302 其他化工产品〕	9		70	13/	13	千克	/13		21.5	
3214.9000		-其他										
3214.9000	10	非耐火涂面制剂，施工状态下挥发性有机物含量大于 420 克/升，涂门面、内墙、地板、天花板等用〔301 危险化学品，易燃液体；302 其他化工产品〕	9		70	13/4	0	千克	/13		21.5	
3214.9000	90	其他非耐火涂面制剂；(涂门面、内墙、地板、天花板等用)〔301 危险化学品，易燃液体；302 其他化工产品〕	9		70	13/	0	千克	/13		21.5	
32.15		**印刷油墨、书写或绘图墨水及其他墨类，不论是否固体或浓缩：**										
		-印刷油墨：										
3215.1100		--黑色										
3215.1100	10	黑色，用于装入税号 8443.31、8443.32 或 8443.39 所列设备的工程形态的固体油墨〔998：其他危险化学品；999：其他化工产品〕	0		45	13/	0	千克	AB/13	MN	22.5	4.2/4.2
3215.1100	90	其他黑色印刷油墨(不论是否固体或浓缩)〔301 危险化学品，易燃液体；302 其他化工产品〕	6.5		45	13/	0	千克	AB/13	MN	29	4.2/4.2
3215.1900		--其他										
3215.1900	10	其他用于装入税号 8443.31、8443.32 或 8443.39 所列设备的工程形态的固体油墨〔999〕	0		45	13/	0	千克	/13		22.5	4.6/4.6
3215.1900	90	其他印刷油墨(不论是否固体或浓缩)〔301 危险化学品，易燃液体；302 其他化工产品〕	6.5		45	13/	0	千克	/13		29	4.6/4.6
		-其他：										
3215.9010		---书写墨水〔301 危险化学品，易燃液体；302 其他化工产品〕	5		70	13/	13	千克	/13		30	
3215.9020		---水性喷墨墨水〔999〕	10		70	13/	13	千克	/1		17.5	
3215.9090		---其他〔301 危险化学品，易燃液体；302 其他化工产品〕	10		70	13/	13	千克	/13		22.5	

协定税率 %								RCEP		特惠税率 %			Article Description
东/冰/格	巴基斯坦	韩国	瑞士上/下	哥/秘/柬	澳/毛	新西/坡/智	中国港/澳/台	东盟及马来/澳/韩	日/新	亚太2国	老/柬/缅	98/97/95	
0/0/0	3.5	4.6	1/1	0/0/0	0/0	0/0/0	0/0/	9.3/9.5/9.3	9.4/9.5			0/0/0	Prepared driers
													Pigments (including metallic powders and flakes) dispersed in non-aqueous media, in liquid or paste form, of a kind used in the manufacture of paints (including enamels); stamping foils; dyes and other colouring matter put up in forms or packings for retail sale:
0/0/0	12	3	1.5/1.5	0/0/0	0/0	0/0/0	0/0/	13.5/13.5/13.5	13.6/13.5			0/0/0	-Stamping foils
0/0/0	3.5	2	0/0	0/0/0	0/0	0/0/0	0/0/	9/9/9	9.1/9			0/0/0	-Other
													Artists', students' or signboard painters' colours, modifying tints, amusement colours and the like, in tablets, tubes, jars, bottles, pans or in similar forms or packings:
0/0/0	3.5	2	0/0	0/0/0	0/0	0//0	0/0/	0/0/9	9.1/0			0/0/0	-Colours in sets
0/0/0	3.5	2	0/0	0/0/0	0/6	0//0	0/0/	0/0/9	9.1/0			0/0/0	-Other
													Glaziers' putty, graftig putty, resin cements, caulking compounds and other mastics; painters' fillings; non-refractory surfacing preparations for facades, indoor walls, floors, ceilings or the like:
													-Glaziers' putty, grafting putty, resin cements, caulking compounds and other mastics; painters' fillings:
0/0/0	2		0/0	0/0/0	0/0	0//0	0/0/	5/5/	/5			0/0/0	---Encpackaging materials for semiconductor device
0/0/0	2	0	0.9/0.9	0/0/0	0/0	0//0	0/0/	8.1/8.1/8.1	8.2/8.1			0/0/0	---Other
													-Other
0/0/0	4	4.2	0/0	0/0/0	0/0	0//0	0/0/	8.4/8.6/8.4	8.4/8.6			0/0/0	The refractory coating preparation, the construction condition of volatile organic matter content is more than 420 g/l; Coated facade, interior wall, floor, ceiling, etc
0/0/0	4	4.2	0/0	0/0/0	0/0	0//0	0/0/	8.4/8.6/8.4	8.4/8.6			0/0/0	Other, refractory coating agent; Coated facade, interior wall, floor, ceiling, etc
													Printing ink, writing or drawing ink and other inks, whether or not concentrated or solid:
													-Printing ink:
													--Black
0/0/0	0	0	0/0	0/0/0	0/0	0//0	0/0/	5.9/5.9/5.9	5.9/5.9			0/0/0	Black, solid ink, for the engineering equipment of subheading No.8443.31, 8443.32 or 8443.39
0/0/0	0	0	0/0	0/0/0	0/0	0//0	0/0/	5.9/5.9/5.9	5.9/5.9			0/0/0	Other black printing oil, whether or not concentrated or solid
													--Other
0/0/0	0	1.3	0.7/0.7	0/0/0	0/0	0//0	0/0/0	0/0/5.9	6.1/0			0/0/0	Other solid ink, for the engineering equipment of subheading No.8443.31, 8443.32 or 8443.39
0/0/0	0	1.3	0.7/0.7	0/0/0	0/0	0//0	0/0/0	0/0/5.9	6.1/0			0/0/0	Other printing oil, whether or not concentrated or solid
													-Other:
0/0/0	2	0	0/0	0/0/0	0/0	0//0	0/0/	0/0/0	5.9/0			0/0/0	---Writing or drawing inks
0/0/0	3.5	0	1/1	0/0/0	0/0	0/0/0	0/0/	9/9/9	9.1/9			0/0/0	---Water based inkjet ink
0/0/0	3.5	0	1/1	0/0/0	0/0	0/0/0	0/0/	9/9/9	9.1/9			0/0/0	---Other

第三十三章
精油及香膏;芳香料制品
及化妆盥洗品

注释:

一、本章不包括:

(一)税目 13.01 及 13.02 的天然油树脂及植物浸膏;

(二)税目 34.01 的肥皂及其他产品;

(三)税目 38.05 的脂松节油、木松节油和硫酸盐松节油及其他产品。

二、税目 33.02 所称"香料"仅指税目 33.01 所列的物质,从这些物质离析出来的香料组分以及合成芳香剂。

三、税目 33.03 至 33.07 主要包括适合作这些税目所列用途的零售包装产品,不论其是否混合(精油水馏液及水溶液除外)。

四、税目 33.07 所称"芳香料制品及化妆盥洗品",主要适用于下列产品:香袋;通过燃烧散发香气的制品;香纸及用化妆品浸渍或涂布的纸;隐形眼镜片或假眼用的溶液;用香水或化妆品浸渍、涂布、包覆的絮胎、毡呢及无纺织物;动物用盥洗品。

税则号列	货品名称〔CIQ 扩展编码及品名—T2 表示见附表 2〕	最惠(%)	暂定税率	普通	增值/消费	出口退税	计量单位	监管条件/特殊证件	检验检疫	对美关税	亚太上/下
33.01	**精油(无萜或含萜),包括浸膏及净油;香膏;提取的油树脂;用花香吸取法或浸渍法制成的含浓缩精油的脂肪、固定油、蜡及类似品;精油脱萜时所得的萜烯副产品;精油水馏液及水溶液:**										
	-柑橘属果实的精油:										
3301.1200	--橙油[T2]	20	10	80	13/	13	千克	A/1	R	17.5	
3301.1300	--柠檬油[T2]	20		80	13/	13	千克	A/1	R	27.5	
	--其他:										
3301.1910	---白柠檬油(酸橙油)[T2]	20		80	13/	13	千克	A/1	R	27.5	
3301.1990	---其他〔111 面部香精油,112 发用香精油,113 体用香精油,301 危险化学品,不用作食品添加剂,302 危险化学品,用作食品添加剂,303 其他化工品,不用做食品添加剂,304 其他化工品,用做食品添加剂〕	20		80	13/	13	千克	A/1	R	27.5	
	-非柑橘属果实的精油:										
3301.2400	--胡椒薄荷油〔111 面部香精油,112 发用香精油,113 体用香精油,301 危险化学品,不用作食品添加剂,302 危险化学品,用作食品添加剂,303 其他化工品,不用做食品添加剂,304 其他化工品,用做食品添加剂〕	20	10	90	13/	13	千克	A/1	R	17.5	
3301.2500	--其他薄荷油[T2]	15	5	90	13/	13	千克	A/1	R	15	14/14
	--其他:										
3301.2910	---樟脑油[T2]	20		90	13/	13	千克	ABE/13	MRN	27.5	
3301.2920	---香茅油〔111 面部香精油,112 发用香精精油,113 体用香精精油,301 无检疫要求食品添加剂〕	15		70	13/	13	千克	A/1	R	35	
3301.2930	---茴香油〔111 面部香精油,112 发用香精精油,113 体用香精精油,301 无检疫要求食品添加剂〕	20		80	13/	9	千克	A/1	R	27.5	
3301.2940	---桂油〔111 面部香精油,112 发用香精精油,113 体用香精精油,301 无检疫要求食品添加剂〕	20		80	13/	13	千克	A/1	R	47.5	
3301.2950	---山苍子油〔111 面部香精油,112 发用香精精油,113 体用香精精油,301 无检疫要求食品添加剂〕	20		80	13/	13	千克	A/1	R	27.5	
3301.2960	---桉叶油〔111 面部香精油;112 发用香精精油;113 体用香精精油;301 危险化学品,不用作食品添加剂;302 危险化学品,用作食品添加剂〕	20		80	13/	13	千克	AB/1	MRN	27.5	
	---其他:										
3301.2991	----老鹳草油(香叶油)〔101 面部香精油,102 发用香精精油,103 体用香精精油,301 无检疫要求食品添加剂〕	20		80	13/	13	千克	A/1	R	42.5	
3301.2999	----其他										
3301.2999 10	黄樟油〔101 面部香精油,102 发用香精精油,103 体用香精精油,301 无检疫要求食品添加剂〕	15	7	80	13/	13	千克	23A/13	R	12	
3301.2999 91	其他濒危植物精油(柑桔属果实除外)(包括浸膏及净油)〔111 面部香精油,112 发用香精精油,113 体用香精精油,301 无检疫要求食品添加剂〕	15		80	13/	0	千克	AFE/13	R	20	
3301.2999 99	其他非柑橘属果实的精油(包括浸膏及净油)〔301 危险化学品,易燃液体;302 危险化学品,毒性物质;303 危险化学品,用作食品添加剂;304 其他化工品,不用作食品添加剂;305 其他化工品,用作食品添加剂;401 面部香精油;402 发用香精精油;403 体用香精精油〕	15		80	13/	13	千克	A/13	R	20	
	-香膏:										
3301.3010	---鸢尾凝脂〔101〕	20	10	80	13/	13	千克	/1		37.5	
3301.3090	---其他										
3301.3090 10	其他濒危植物香膏〔999〕	20		80	13/	0	千克	FE/1		42.5	

Chapter 33
Essential oils and resinoids; perfumery, cosmetic or toilet preparations

Notes:

1. This Chapter does not cover:
   (a) Natural oleoresins or vegetable extracts of heading No. 13.01 or 13.02;
   (b) Soap or other products of heading No. 34.01; or
   (c) Gum, wood or sulphate turpentine or other products of heading No. 38.05.
2. The expression "odoriferous substances" in heading No. 33.02 refers only to the substances of heading No. 33.01, to odoriferous constituents isolated from those substances or to synthetic aromatics.
3. Headings No. 33.03 to 33.07 apply, *inter alia*, to products, whether or not mixed (other than aqueous distillates and aqueous solutions of essential oils), suitable for use as goods of these headings and put up in packings of a kind sold by retail for such use.
4. The expression "perfumery, cosmetic or toilet preparations" in heading No. 33.07 applies, *inter alia*, to the following products: scented sachets; odoriferous preparations which operate by burning; perfumed papers and papers impregnated or coated with cosmetics; contact lens or artificial eye solutions; wadding, felt and nonwovens, impregnated, coated or covered with perfume or cosmetics; animal toilet preparations.

协定税率 %								RCEP		特惠税率 %			
东/冰/格	巴基斯坦	韩国	瑞士上/下	哥/秘/柬	澳/毛	新西/坡/智	中国港/澳/台	东盟及马来/澳/韩	日/新	亚太2国	老/柬/缅	98/97/95	Article Description
													Essential oils (terpeneless or not), including concretes and absolutes; resinoids; extracted oleoresins; concentrates of essential oils in fats, in fixed oils, in waxes or the like, obtained by enfleurage or maceration; terpenic byproducts of the deterpenation of essential oils; aqueous distillates and aqueous solutions of essential oils:
													-Essential oils of citrus fruit:
0/0/0		9.3	5/5	0/0/0	0/0	0/0/0	0/0/	18/18/18	18.8/18			0/0/0	--Of orange
0/0/0		9.3	0/0	0/0/0	0/0	0/0/0	0/0/	18.7/19/18.7	18.8/19			0/0/0	--Of lemon
													--Other:
0/0/0		9.3	2/2	0/0/0	0/0	0/0/0	0/0/	18/18/18	18.8/18			0/0/0	---Of lime
0/0/0		9.3	2/2	0/0/0	0/0	0/0/0	0/0/	18.7/19/18.7	18.8/19			0/0/0	---Other
													-Essential oils other than those of citrus fruit:
0/0/0		9.3	2/2	0/0/0	0/0	0/0/0	0/0/	18.7/19/18.7	18.8/19			0/0/0	--Of peppermint (Mentha piperita)
0/0/0	12	3	1.5/1.5	0/0/0	0/0	0/0/0	0/0/	0/0/13.5	13.6/0			0/0/0	--Of other mints
													--Other:
0/0/0		9.3	2/2	0/0/0	0/0	0/0/0	0/0/	18/18/18	18.8/18			0/0/0	---Of camphor
0/0/0	12	3	1.5/1.5	0/0/0	0/0	0/0/0	0/0/	0/0/13.5	13.6/0			0/0/0	---Of citronella
0/0/0		9.3	2/2	0/0/0	0/0	0/0/0	0/0/	18/18/18	18.8/18			0/0/0	---Of aniseed
0/0/0		9.3	2/2	0/0/0	0/0	0/0/0	0/0/	18/18/18	18.8/18			0/0/0	---Of cassia
0/0/0		9.3	2/2	0/0/0	0/0	0/0/0	0/0/	18/18/18	18.8/18			0/0/0	---Of litsea cubeba
0/0/0		9.3	2/2	0/0/0	0/0	0/0/0	0/0/	18/18/18	18.8/18			0/0/0	---Of eucalyptus
													---Other:
0/0/0		9.3	2/2	0/0/0	0/0	0/0/0	0/0/	18/18/18	18.8/18			0/0/0	----Of geranium
													----Other
0/0/0	12	7	1.5/1.5	0/0/0	0/0	0/0/0	0/0/	13.5/14.3/13.5	13.6/14.3			0/0/0	Oil of sassafras
0/0/0	12	7	1.5/1.5	0/0/0	0/0	0/0/0	0/0/	13.5/14.3/13.5	13.6/14.3			0/0/0	Other endangered essential(other than citrus fruit)(including concretes and absolutes)
0/0/0	12	7	1.5/1.5	0/0/0	0/0	0/0/0	0/0/	13.5/14.3/13.5	13.6/14.3			0/0/0	Other essential oils other than those of citrus fruit(including concretes and absolutes)
													-Resinoids:
0/0/0		9.3	2/2	0/0/0	0/0	0/0/0	0/0/	18/18/18	18.8/18			0/0/0	---Balsam of irises
													---Other
0/0/0		9.3	2/2	0/0/0	0/0	0/0/0	0/0/	18/18/18	18.8/18			0/0/0	Other resinoids of endangered vegetable

税则号列	货品名称〔CIQ 扩展编码及品名—T2 表示见附表 2〕	最惠(%)	暂定税率	普通	增值/消费	出口退税	计量单位	监管条件/特殊证件	检验检疫	对美关税	亚太上/下
3301.3090 90	其他香膏[T2]	20		80	13/	13	千克	/1		42.5	
	-其他：										
3301.9010	---提取的油树脂										
3301.9010 10	濒危植物提取的油树脂〔999〕	20		80	13/	0	千克	FE/13		27.5	13/13
3301.9010 90	其他提取的油树脂[T2]	20		80	13/	13	千克	/13		27.5	13/13
3301.9020	---柑橘属果实的精油脱萜的萜烯副产品〔101〕	20		80	13/	13	千克	/1		27.5	13/13
3301.9090	---其他〔101 香精油；301 危险化学品，不用做食品添加剂；302 危险化学品，用作食品添加剂；303 其他化工品，不用作食品添加剂；304 其他化工品，用作食品添加剂〕	20		80	13/	13	千克	/13		42.5	13/13
33.02	**工业原料用的芳香物质的混合物以及以一种或多种芳香物质为基本成分的混合物(包括酒精溶液)；生产饮料用的以芳香物质为基本成分的其他制品：**										
	-食品或饮料工业用：										
3302.1010	---生产饮料用的以香料为基本成分的制品，按容量计酒精浓度不超过 0.5%的〔301 危险化学品，易燃液体；302 其他化工品〕	15		90	13/	13	千克	A/1	R	40	9.8/9.8
3302.1090	---其他										
3302.1090 01	生产食品、饮料用混合香料及制品(含以香料为基本成分的混合物，按容量计酒精浓度＞0.5%)[T2]	15		130	13/5	13	千克	A/1	R	20	
3302.1090 90	其他生产食品用混合香料及制品(含以香料为基本成分的混合物)[T2]	15		130	13/	13	千克	A/1	R	20	
3302.9000	-其他〔301 危险化学品，易燃液体；302 其他化工品〕	10		130	13/	13	千克	/13		30	
33.03	**香水及花露水：**										
3303.0000	香水及花露水										
3303.0000 10	包装标注含量以重量计的香水及花露水[T2]	3		150	13/①	13	千克/件	AB/1	MN	28	2/2
3303.0000 20	包装标注含量以体积计的香水及花露水[T2]	3		150	13/①	13	千克/件	AB/1	MN	28	2/2
33.04	**美容品或化妆品及护肤品(药品除外)，包括防晒油或晒黑油；指(趾)甲化妆品：**										
3304.1000	-唇用化妆品										
3304.1000 11	包装标注含量以重量计的含濒危植物成分唇用化妆品[T2]	5		150	13/①	0	千克/件	ABEF/1	MN	30	
3304.1000 12	包装标注含量以体积计的含濒危植物成分唇用化妆品[T2]	5		150	13/①	0	千克/件	ABEF/1	MN	30	
3304.1000 13	包装标注规格为“片”或“张”的含濒危植物成分唇用化妆品〔101〕	5		150	13/①	0	千克/件	ABEF/1	MN	30	
3304.1000 20	含汞唇用化妆品(含汞量超过百万分之一)〔999〕	5		150	13/①	13	千克/件	89/1		30	
3304.1000 91	包装标注含量以重量计的其他唇用化妆品[T2]	5		150	13/①	13	千克/件	AB/1	MN	30	
3304.1000 92	包装标注含量以体积计的其他唇用化妆品[T2]	5		150	13/①	13	千克/件	AB/1	MN	30	
3304.1000 93	包装标注规格为“片”或“张”的其他唇用化妆品〔101〕	5		150	13/①	13	千克/件	AB/1	MN	30	
3304.2000	-眼用化妆品										
3304.2000 11	包装标注含量以重量计的含濒危植物成分眼用化妆品[T2]	5		150	13/①	0	千克/件	ABEF/1	MN	30	
3304.2000 12	包装标注含量以体积计的含濒危植物成分眼用化妆品[T2]	5		150	13/①	0	千克/件	ABEF/1	MN	30	
3304.2000 13	包装标注规格为“片”或“张”的含濒危植物成分眼用化妆品〔101〕	5		150	13/①	0	千克/件	ABEF/1	MN	30	
3304.2000 20	含汞眼用化妆品(含汞量超过百万分之一)，不包括以汞为防腐剂且无有效安全替代防腐剂的眼部化妆品〔999〕	5		150	13/①	13	千克/件	89/1		30	
3304.2000 91	包装标注含量以重量计的其他眼用化妆品[T2]	5		150	13/①	13	千克/件	AB/1	MN	30	
3304.2000 92	包装标注含量以体积计的其他眼用化妆品[T2]	5		150	13/①	13	千克/件	AB/1	MN	30	
3304.2000 93	包装标注规格为“片”或“张”的其他眼用化妆品〔101〕	5		150	13/①	13	千克/件	AB/1	MN	30	
3304.3000	-指(趾)甲化妆品										
3304.3000 01	包装标注含量以重量计的指(趾)甲化妆品[T2]	5		150	13/①	13	千克/件	AB/1	MN	30	
3304.3000 02	包装标注含量以体积计的指(趾)甲化妆品[T2]	5		150	13/①	13	千克/件	AB/1	MN	30	
3304.3000 03	包装标注规格为“片”或“张”的指(趾)甲化妆品〔101 成人指(趾)甲护理化妆品，102 成人指(趾)甲美容化妆品，103 婴幼儿指(趾)甲化妆品〕	5		150	13/①	13	千克/件	AB/1	MN	30	
3304.3000 04	指(趾)甲化妆品(含汞量超过百万分之一)〔999〕	5		150	13/①	13	千克/件	89/1		30	
	-其他：										

① 进口完税价格在 10 元/毫升(克)或 15 元/片(张)及以上的税率为 15%。

协定税率 %								RCEP		特惠税率 %			Article Description
东/冰/格	巴基斯坦	韩国	瑞士 上/下	哥/秘/柬	澳/毛	新西/坡/智	中国港/澳/台	东盟及马来/澳/韩	日/新	亚太2国	老/柬/缅	98/97/95	
0/0/0		9.3	2/2	0/0/0	0/0	0/0/0	0/0/	18/18/18	18.8/18			0/0/0	Other resinoids
													-Other:
													---Extracted oleoresins
0/0/0	18	9.3	2/2	0/0/0	0/0	0/0/0	0/0/	18.7/19/18.7	18.8/19			0/0/0	Extracted oleoresins of endangered vegetable
0/0/0	18	9.3	2/2	0/0/0	0/0	0/0/0	0/0/	18.7/19/18.7	18.8/19			0/0/0	Other extracted oleoresins
0/0/0	18	9.3	2/2	0/0/0	0/0	0/0/0	0/0/	18/18/18	18.8/18			0/0/0	---Terpenic byproducts of the deterpenation of essential oils of citrus fruit
0/0/0	18	9.3	2/2	0/0/0	0/0	0/0/0	0/0/	18.7/19/18.7	18.8/19			0/0/0	---Other
													Mixtures of odoriferous substances and mixtures (including alcoholic solutions) with a basis of one or more of these substances, of a kind used as raw materials in industry; other preparations based on odoriferous substances, of a kind used for the manufacture of beverages:
													-Of a kind used in the food or drink industry:
0/0/0	0	3	1.5/1.5	0/0/0	0/0	0/0/0	0/0/	0/0/13.5	13.6/0			0/0/0	---Preparations based on odoriferous substances, of a kind used for the manufacture of beverages, alcoholic strength by volume not exceeding 0.5% vol.
													---Other
0/0/0	0	3	1.5/1.5	0/0/0	0/0	0/0/0	0/0/	0/0/13.5	13.6/0			0/0/0	Mixtures of odoriferous substances and products, alcoholic strength by vol>0.5%, of a kind used in the food or drink industry
0/0/0	0	3	1.5/1.5	0/0/0	0/0	0/0/0	0/0/	0/0/13.5	13.6/0			0/0/0	Other mistures of odoriferous substances and preparations, based on oboriferous substances, of a kind used in the food industry
0/0/0	3.5	2	0/0	0/0/0	0/0	0/0/0	0/0/	0/0/9	9.1/0			0/0/0	-Other
													Perfumes and toilet waters:
													Perfumes and toilet waters
0/0/0	3.5		0/0	0/0/0	0/0	0/0/0	0/0/	3/3/	/3			0/0/0	Perfumes and toilet waters
0/0/0	3.5		0/0	0/0/0	0/0	0/0/0	0/0/	3/3/	/3			0/0/0	Perfumes and toilet waters
													Beauty or make-up preparations and preparations for the care of the skin (other than medicaments), including sunscreen or suntan preparations; manicure or pedicure preparations:
													-Lip make-up preparations
0/0/0	3.5		0/0	0/0/0	0/0	0/0/0	0/0/	5/5/	/5			0/0/0	Lip make-up preparations
0/0/0	3.5		0/0	0/0/0	0/0	0/0/0	0/0/	5/5/	/5			0/0/0	Lip make-up preparations
0/0/0	3.5		0/0	0/0/0	0/0	0/0/0	0/0/	5/5/	/5			0/0/0	Lip make-up preparations
0/0/0	3.5		0/0	0/0/0	0/0	0/0/0	0/0/	5/5/	/5		//	0/0/0	Cosmetics containing mercury for lip use (containing more than one millionth of mercury)
0/0/0	3.5		0/0	0/0/0	0/0	0/0/0	0/0/	5/5/	/5			0/0/0	Lip make-up preparations
0/0/0	3.5		0/0	0/0/0	0/0	0/0/0	0/0/	5/5/	/5			0/0/0	Lip make-up preparations
0/0/0	3.5		0/0	0/0/0	0/0	0/0/0	0/0/	5/5/	/5			0/0/0	Lip make-up preparations
													-Eye make-up preparations
0/0/0	3.5		0/0	0/0/0	0/0	0/0/0	0/0/	5/5/	/5			0/0/0	Eye make-up preparations
0/0/0	3.5		0/0	0/0/0	0/0	0/0/0	0/0/	5/5/	/5			0/0/0	Eye make-up preparations
0/0/0	3.5		0/0	0/0/0	0/0	0/0/0	0/0/	5/5/	/5			0/0/0	Eye make-up preparations
0/0/0	3.5		0/0	0/0/0	0/0	0/0/0	0/0/	5/5/	/5		//	0/0/0	Eye cosmetics containing mercury (containing more than one millionth of mercury), excluding eye cosmetics with mercury as preservative and without effective and safe alternative preservatives
0/0/0	3.5		0/0	0/0/0	0/0	0/0/0	0/0/	5/5/	/5			0/0/0	Eye make-up preparations
0/0/0	3.5		0/0	0/0/0	0/0	0/0/0	0/0/	5/5/	/5			0/0/0	Eye make-up preparations
0/0/0	3.5		0/0	0/0/0	0/0	0/0/0	0/0/	5/5/	/5			0/0/0	Eye make-up preparations
													-Manicure or pedicure preparations
0/0/0	0		1.5/1.5	0/0/0	0/0	0/0/0	0/0/	5/5/	/5			0/0/0	Manicture or pedicure preparations
0/0/0	0		1.5/1.5	0/0/0	0/0	0/0/0	0/0/	5/5/	/5			0/0/0	Manicture or pedicure preparations
0/0/0	0		1.5/1.5	0/0/0	0/0	0/0/0	0/0/	5/5/	/5			0/0/0	Manicture or pedicure preparations
0/0/0	0		1.5/1.5	0/0/0	0/0	0/0/0	0/0/	5/5/	/5		//	0/0/0	Finger nail cosmetics (containing more than one millionth of mercury)
													-Other:

税则号列		货品名称〔CIQ 扩展编码及品名－T2 表示见附表 2〕	最惠(%)	暂定税率	普通	增值/消费	出口退税	计量单位	监管条件/特殊证件	检验检疫	对美关税	亚太上/下
3304.9100		--粉，不论是否压紧										
3304.9100	10	粉状含汞化妆品（含汞量超过百万分之一），不论是否压紧〔999〕	5		150	13/①	13	千克/件	89/1		30	
3304.9100	90	其他粉状化妆品，不论是否压紧〔101 成人爽身粉，102 成人面部用美容化妆品，103 成人体用美容化妆品，104 婴幼儿美容化妆品，105 固体香膏（粉），106 美白化妆品，107 防晒化妆品，108 婴幼儿爽身粉，109 婴幼儿驻留类肤用化妆品，110 婴幼儿淋洗类肤用化妆品，111 成人面部驻留类化妆品，112 成人面部淋洗类化妆品，113 婴幼儿淋洗类发用化妆品，114 成人淋洗类毛发用化妆品，115 成人驻留类毛发用化妆品，116 成人眼部美容化妆品，117 成人眉用美容化妆品〕	5		150	13/①	13	千克/件	AB/1	MN	30	
3304.9900		--其他										
3304.9900	10	其他含汞化妆品（含汞量超过百万分之一）〔999〕	1		150	13/①	13	千克/件	89/1		28.5	
3304.9900	21	包装标注含量以重量计含濒危物种成分的美容品或化妆品及护肤品（包括防晒油或晒黑油，但药品除外）[T2]	1		150	13/①	0	千克/件	ABEF/1	MN	28.5	
3304.9900	29	包装标注含量以重量计的其他美容品或化妆品及护肤品（包括防晒油或晒黑油，但药品除外）[T2]	1		150	13/①	13	千克/件	AB/1	MN	28.5	
3304.9900	31	包装标注含量以体积计的含濒危物种成分美容品或化妆品及护肤品（包括防晒油或晒黑油，但药品除外）[T2]	1		150	13/①	0	千克/件	ABFE/1	MN	28.5	
3304.9900	39	包装标注含量以体积计的其他美容品或化妆品及护肤品（包括防晒油或晒黑油，但药品除外）[T2]	1		150	13/①	13	千克/件	AB/1	MN	28.5	
3304.9900	41	包装标注规格为“片”或“张”的含濒危物种成分美容品或化妆品及护肤品（包括防晒油或晒黑油，但药品除外）〔201 成人面部膜类化妆品，202 成人眼部膜类化妆品，203 成人口唇膜类化妆品，204 成人体用膜类化妆品，205 美白化妆品〕	1		150	13/①	0	千克/件	ABFE/1	MN	28.5	
3304.9900	49	包装标注规格为“片”或“张”的其他美容品或化妆品及护肤品（包括防晒油或晒黑油，但药品除外）〔201 成人面部膜类化妆品，202 成人眼部膜类化妆品，203 成人口唇膜类化妆品，204 成人体用膜类化妆品，205 美白化妆品〕	1		150	13/①	13	千克/件	AB/1	MN	28.5	
3304.9900	91	其他包装标注规格的含濒危物种成分美容品或化妆品及护肤品（包括防晒油或晒黑油，但药品除外）[T2]	1		150	13/①	0	千克/件	ABFE/1	MN	28.5	
3304.9900	99	其他包装标注规格的其他美容品或化妆品及护肤品（包括防晒油或晒黑油，但药品除外）[T2]	1		150	13/①	13	千克/件	AB/1	MN	28.5	
33.05		**护发品：**										
3305.1000		-洗发剂（香波）										
3305.1000	10	含濒危植物成分的洗发剂〔102 婴幼儿淋洗类发用化妆品，107 成人淋洗类毛发用化妆品〕	3	2	150	13/	0	千克	ABFE/1	MN	27	2/2
3305.1000	90	其他洗发剂（香波）〔102 婴幼儿淋洗类发用化妆品，107 成人淋洗类毛发用化妆品〕	3	2	150	13/	13	千克	AB/1	MN	27	2/2
3305.2000		-烫发剂〔101〕	3		150	13/	13	千克	AB/1	MN	28	
3305.3000		-定型剂〔107 婴幼儿驻留类发用化妆品，108 成人驻留类毛发用化妆品〕	3		150	13/	13	千克	AB/1	MN	28	
3305.9000		-其他[T2]	3		150	13/	13	千克	AB/1	MN	28	2/2
33.06		**口腔及牙齿清洁剂，包括假牙稳固剂及粉；清洁牙缝用的纱线（牙线），单独零售包装的：**										
		-洁齿品：										
3306.1010		---牙膏										
3306.1010	10	含濒危植物成分牙膏〔104 成人牙膏，105 婴幼儿口腔类产品〕	3		150	13/	0	千克	ABEF/1	RS	28	2/2
3306.1010	90	其他牙膏〔104 成人牙膏，105 婴幼儿口腔类产品〕	3		150	13/	13	千克	AB/1	RS	28	2/2
3306.1090		---其他〔999〕	3		150	13/	13	千克	/1		28	2/2
3306.2000		-清洁牙缝用的纱线（牙线）〔999〕	3		70	13/	13	千克	/1		28	2/2
		-其他：										

① 进口完税价格在 10 元/毫升（克）或 15 元/片（张）及以上的税率为 15%。

协定税率 %								RCEP		特惠税率 %			Article Description
东/冰/格	巴基斯坦	韩国	瑞士上/下	哥/秘/柬	澳/毛	新西/坡/智	中国港/澳/台	东盟及马来/澳/韩	日/新	亚太2国	老/柬/缅	98/97/95	
													--Powders, whether or not compressed
0/0/0	3.5		0/0	0/0/0	0/0	0/0/0	0/0/	5/5/	/5		//	0/0/0	Cosmetics containing mercury in powder form (containing more than one millionth of mercury), whether pressed or not
0/0/0	3.5		0/0	0/0/0	0/0	0/0/0	0/0/	5/5/	/5		//	0/0/0	Other powder cosmetics, whether or not pressed
													--Other
0/0/0	0	5.2	0/0	0/0/0	0/0	0/0/0	0/0/	6.2/6.2/	/6.2		//	0/0/0	Other cosmetics containing mercury (containing more than one millionth of mercury)
0/0/0	0	5.2	0/0	0/0/0	0/0	0/0/0	0/0/	6.2/6.2/	/6.2			0/0/0	Packaging and labeling content containing by weight of endangered species composition of cosmetics or cosmetics and skin care products (including sunscreen or suntan oil, but the drugs except)
0/0/0	0	5.2	0/0	0/0/0	0/0	0/0/0	0/0/	6.2/6.2/	/6.2			0/0/0	Packaging and labeling content by weight of other cosmetics or cosmetics and skin care products (including sunscreen or suntan oil, but the drugs except)
0/0/0	0	5.2	0/0	0/0/0	0/0	0/0/0	0/0/	6.2/6.2/	/6.2			0/0/0	Packaging and labeling content by volume containing the endangered species components of cosmetics or cosmetic and skin care products (including sunscreen or suntan oil, but the drugs except)
0/0/0	0	5.2	0/0	0/0/0	0/0	0/0/0	0/0/	6.2/6.2/	/6.2			0/0/0	Packaging and labeling content by volume of other cosmetics or cosmetics and skin care products (including sunscreen or suntan oil, but the drugs except)
0/0/0	0	5.2	0/0	0/0/0	0/0	0/0/0	0/0/	6.2/6.2/	/6.2			0/0/0	Packaging and labeling specifications for the endangered species composition of cosmetics or cosmetic and skin care products containing "or" a "(including sunscreen or suntan oil, but the drugs except)
0/0/0	0	5.2	0/0	0/0/0	0/0	0/0/0	0/0/	6.2/6.2/	/6.2			0/0/0	Packaging and labeling specifications for the "slice" or "card" or other cosmetics cosmetics and skin care products (including sunscreen or suntan oil, but the drugs except)
0/0/0	0	5.2	0/0	0/0/0	0/0	0/0/0	0/0/	6.2/6.2/	/6.2			0/0/0	Other packaging labeling specifications containing endangered species composition of cosmetics or cosmetic and skin care products (including sunscreen or suntan oil, but the drugs except)
0/0/0	0	5.2	0/0	0/0/0	0/0	0/0/0	0/0/	6.2/6.2/	/6.2			0/0/0	Other packaging labeling specifications of other cosmetics or cosmetics and skin care products (including sunscreen or suntan oil, but the drugs except)
													Preparations for use on the hair:
													-Shampoos
0//0	2	4.2	0/0	0/0/0	0/0	0/0/0	0/0/	3/3/	/3			0/0/0	Shampoos containing composition of endangered vegetable
0//0	2	4.2	0/0	0/0/0	0/0	0/0/0	0/0/	3/3/	/3			0/0/0	Other shampoos
0/0/0	12		1.5/1.5	0/0/0	0/0	0/0/0	0/0/	3/3/	/3			0/0/0	-Preparations for permanent waving or straightening
0/0/0	12		1.5/1.5	0/0/0	0/0	0/0/0	0/0/	3/3/	/3			0/0/0	-Hair lacquers
0//0	4	6.5	0/0	0/0/0	0/0	0/0/0	0/0/	3/3/	/3			0/0/0	-Other
													Preparations for oral or dental hygiene, including denture stabilizer and powders; yarn used to clean between the teeth (dental floss), in individual retail package:
													-Dentifrices:
													---Toothpastes
0/0/0	3.5	2	0/0	0/0/0	0/0	0/0/0	0/0/	0/0/9	9.1/0			0/0/0	Toothpastes containing composition of endangered vegetable
0/0/0	3.5	2	0/0	0/0/0	0/0	0/0/0	0/0/	0/0/9	9.1/0			0/0/0	Other toothpastes
0/0/0	3.5	2	0/0	0/0/0	0/0	0/0/0	0/0/	0/0/9	9.1/0			0/0/0	---Other
0/0/0	3.5	2	0/0	0/0/0	0/0	0//0	0/0/	0/0/9	9.1/0			0/0/0	-Yarn used to clean between the teeth (dental floss)
													-Other:

税则号列	货品名称〔CIQ 扩展编码及品名—T2 表示见附表 2〕	最惠(%)	暂定税率	普通	增值/消费	出口退税	计量单位	监管条件/特殊证件	检验检疫	对美关税	亚太上/下
3306.9010	---漱口剂〔201 成人液体口腔产品(包括漱口水、口腔清新喷雾),202 成人非液体口腔产品(包括牙粉、牙贴、假牙模膏),203 婴幼儿口腔类产品(包括漱口水、口腔清新喷雾)〕	3		70	13/	13	千克	AB/1	RS	28	
3306.9090	---其他〔201 成人非液体口腔产品(包括牙粉、牙贴、假牙模膏),202 婴幼儿口腔类产品,203 婴幼儿口腔类化妆品〕	3		70	13/	13	千克	AB/1	RS	28	
33.07	**剃须用制剂、人体除臭剂、泡澡用制剂、脱毛剂和其他税目未列名的芳香料制品及化妆盥洗品;室内除臭剂,不论是否加香水或消毒剂:**										
3307.1000	-剃须用制剂〔103 成人面部驻留类化妆品,104 成人淋洗类毛发用化妆品〕	3		150	13/	13	千克	AB/1	MN	28	2/2
3307.2000	-人体除臭剂及止汗剂〔106〕	3		150	13/	13	千克	AB/1	MN	28	2/2
3307.3000	-香浴盐及其他泡澡用制剂〔101 婴幼儿淋洗类肤用化妆品;112 成人体用淋洗类化妆品〕	3		150	13/	13	千克	AB/1	MN	28	2/2
	-室内散香或除臭制品,包括宗教仪式用的香:										
3307.4100	--神香及其他通过燃烧散发香气的制品〔999〕	3		150	13/	13	千克	/1		28	
3307.4900	--其他〔301 危险化学品,易燃液体;302 其他化工品〕	3		150	13/	13	千克	/1		28	
3307.9000	-其他〔301 危险化学品,易燃液体;302 其他化工品〕	3		150	13/	13	千克	/1		28	2/2

协定税率 %								RCEP		特惠税率 %			Article Description
东/冰/格	巴基斯坦	韩国	瑞士上/下	哥/秘/柬	澳/毛	新西/坡/智	中国港/澳/台	东盟及马来/澳/韩	日/新	亚太2国	老/柬/缅	98/97/95	
0/0/0	3.5	2	0/0	0/0/0	0/0	0/0/0	0/0/	0/0/9	9.1/0			0/0/0	---Gargle
0/0/0	3.5	2	0/0	0/0/0	0/0	0/0/0	0/0/	0/0/9	9.1/0			0/0/0	---Other
													Pre-shave, shaving or after-shave preparations, personal deodorants, bath preparations, depilatories and other perfumery, cosmetic or toilet preparations, not elsewhere specified or included; prepared room deodorizers, whether or not perfumed or having disinfectant properties:
0/0/0	3.5		0/0	0/0/0	0/0	0/0/0	0/0/	3/3/	/3			0/0/0	-Pre-shave, shaving or after-shave preparations
0/0/0	3.5		0/0	0/0/0	0/0	0/0/0	0/0/	3/3/	/3			0/0/0	-Personal deodorants and antiperspirants
0/0/0	3.5	6.5	0/0	0/0/0	0/0	0/0/0	0/0/	3/3/	/3			0/0/0	-Perfumed bath salts and other bath preparations
													-Preparations for perfuming or deodorizing rooms, including odoriferous preparations used during religious rites:
0/0/0	4	2	0/0	0/0/0	0/0	0/0/0	0/0/	0/0/9	9.1/0			0/0/0	--Agarbatti and other odoriferous preparations which operate by burning
0/0/0	3.5	2	0/0	0/0/0	0/0	0/0/0	0/0/	0/0/9	9.1/0			0/0/0	--Other
0/0/0	4	5.8	0/0	0/0/0	0/0	0//0	0/0/	3/3/	/3			0/0/0	-Other

第三十四章
肥皂、有机表面活性剂、洗涤剂、润滑剂、人造蜡、调制蜡、光洁剂、蜡烛及类似品、塑型用膏、“牙科用蜡”及牙科用熟石膏制剂

注释：

一、本章不包括：

（一）用作脱模剂的食用动植物油或微生物油、脂混合物或制品（税目 15.17）；

（二）单独的已有化学定义的化合物；

（三）含肥皂或其他有机表面活性剂的洗发剂、洁齿品、剃须膏及泡澡用制剂（税目 33.05、33.06 及 33.07）。

二、税目 34.01 所称“肥皂”，只适用于水溶性肥皂。税目 34.01 的肥皂及其他产品可以含有添加料（例如，消毒剂、磨料粉、填料或药料）。含磨料粉的产品，只有条状、块状或模制形状可以归入税目 34.01。其他形状的应作为“去污粉及类似品”归入 税目 34.05。

三、税目 34.02 所称“有机表面活性剂”，是指温度在 20℃时与水混合配成 0.5%浓度的 水溶液，并在同样温度下搁置一小时后与下列规定相符的产品：

（一）成为透明或半透明的液体或稳定的乳浊液而未离析出不溶解物质；

（二）将水的表面张力减低到每厘米 45 达因及以下。

四、税目 34.03 所称“石油及从沥青矿物提取的油类”，适用于第二十七章注释二所规定的产品。

五、税目 34.04 所称“人造蜡及调制蜡”，仅适用于：

（一）用化学方法生产的具有蜡质特性的有机产品，不论是否为水溶性的；

（二）各种蜡混合制成的产品；

（三）以一种或几种蜡为基本原料并含有油脂、树脂、矿物质或其他原料的具有蜡质特性的产品。

本税目不包括：

（一）税目 15.16、34.02 或 38.23 的产品，不论是否具有蜡质特性；

（二）税目 15.21 的未混合的动物蜡或未混合的植物蜡，不论是否精制或着色；

（三）税目 27.12 的矿物蜡或类似产品，不论是否相互混合或仅经着色；

（四）混合、分散或溶解于液体溶剂的蜡（税目 34.05、38.09 等）。

税则号列		货品名称〔CIQ 扩展编码及品名—T2 表示见附表 2〕	最惠(%)	暂定税率	普通	增值/消费	出口退税	计量单位	监管条件/特殊证件	检验检疫	对美关税	亚太上/下
34.01		**肥皂；作肥皂用的有机表面活性产品及制品，条状、块状或模制形状的，不论是否含有肥皂；洁肤用的有机表面活性产品及制品，液状或膏状并制成零售包装的，不论是否含有肥皂；用肥皂或洗涤剂浸渍、涂面或包覆的纸、絮胎、毡呢及无纺织物：**										
		-肥皂及有机表面活性产品及制品，条状、块状或模制形状的，以及用肥皂或洗涤剂浸渍、涂面或包覆的纸、絮胎、毡呢及无纺织物：										
3401.1100		--盥洗用（包括含有药物的产品）										
3401.1100	10	盥洗用含汞亮肤肥皂（包括含有药物的产品），条状、块状或模制形状的，以及用肥皂浸渍、涂面或包覆的纸、絮胎、毡呢及无纺织物（含汞量超过百万分之一）〔101 婴幼儿淋洗类肤用化妆品，102 成人面部淋洗类化妆品，103 成人体用淋洗类化妆品，104 其他产品〕	6.5		130	13/	13	千克	89/1		31.5	4.2/4.2
3401.1100	90	其他盥洗用皂及有机表面活性产品（包括含有药物的产品、呈条状、块状或模制形状）〔101 婴幼儿淋洗类肤用化妆品，102 成人面部淋洗类化妆品，103 成人体用淋洗类化妆品，104 其他产品〕	6.5		130	13/	13	千克	AB/1	MN	31.5	4.2/4.2
		--其他：										
3401.1910		---洗衣皂〔999〕	6.5		80	13/	13	千克	/1		31.5	
3401.1990		---其他										
3401.1990	10	其他含汞亮肤肥皂，条状、块状或模制形状的，以及用肥皂浸渍、涂面或包覆的纸、絮胎、毡呢及无纺织物（含汞量超过百万分之一）〔999〕	6.5		130	13/	13	千克	89/1		26.5	
3401.1990	90	其他有机表面活性产品及制品（包括用肥皂或洗涤剂浸、涂或包覆的纸、絮胎及无纺织物）〔999〕	6.5		130	13/	13	千克	/1		26.5	
3401.2000		-其他形状的肥皂										
3401.2000	10	其他形状的含汞亮肤肥皂（含汞量超过百万分之一）〔999〕	6.5		130	13/	13	千克	89/1		31.5	4.2/4.2
3401.2000	90	其他形状的肥皂（除条状、块状或模制形状以外的）〔999〕	6.5		130	13/	13	千克	/1		31.5	4.2/4.2

Chapter 34

Soap, organic surface-active agents, washing preparations, lubricating preparations, artificial waxes, prepared waxes, polishing or scouring preparations, candles and similar articles, modelling pastes, "dental waxes" and dental preparations with a basis of plaster

Notes:

1. This Chapter does not cover:
   (a) Edible mixtures or preparations of animal, vegetable or microbial fats or oils of a kind used as mould release preparations (heading No. 15.17);
   (b) Separate chemically defined compounds; or
   (c) Shampoos, dentifrices, shaving creams and foams, or bath preparations, containing soap or other organic surface-active agents (heading No. 33.05, 33.06 or 33.07).
2. For the purposes of heading No. 34.01, the expression "soap" applies only to soap soluble in water. Soap and the other products of heading No. 34.01 may contain added substances (for example, disinfectants, abrasive powders, fillers or medicaments). Products containing abrasive powders remain classified in heading No. 34.01 only if in the form of bars, cakes or moulded pieces or shapes. In other forms they are to be classified in heading No. 34.05 as "scouring powders and similar preparations".
3. For the purposes of heading No. 34.02, "organic surface-active agents" are products which when mixed with water at a concentration of 0.5% at 20℃ and left to stand for one hour at the same temperature:
   (a) give a transparent or translucent liquid or stable emulsion without separation of insoluble matter; and
   (b) reduce the surface tension of water to 4.5×10^{-2} N/m (45 dyen/cm) or less.
4. In heading No. 34.03 the expression "petroleum oils and oils obtained from bituminous minerals" applies to the products defined in Note 2 to Chapter 27.
5. In heading No. 34.04, subject to the exclusions provided below, the expression "artificial waxes and prepared waxes" applies only to:
   (a) Chemically produced organic products of a waxy character, whether or not water-soluble;
   (b) Products obtained by mixing different waxes;
   (c) Products of a waxy character with a basis of one or more waxes and containing fats, resins, mineral substances or other materials.
   The heading does not apply to:
   (a) Products of heading No. 15.16, 34.02 or 38.23, even if having a waxy character;
   (b) Unmixed animal waxes or unmixed vegetable waxes, whether or not refined or coloured, of heading No. 15.21;
   (c) Mineral waxes or similar products of heading No. 27.12, whether or not intermixed or merely coloured;
   (d) Waxes mixed with, dispersed in or dissolved in a liquid medium (headings No. 34.05, 38.09, etc.).

协定税率 %								RCEP		特惠税率 %			Article Description
东/冰/格	巴基斯坦	韩国	瑞士上/下	哥/秘/柬	澳/毛	新西/坡/智	中国港/澳/台	东盟及马来/澳/韩	日/新	亚太2国	老/柬/缅	98/97/95	
													Soap; organic surface-active products and preparations for use as soap, in the form of bars, cakes, moulded pieces or shapes, whether or not containing soap; organic surface-active products and preparations for washing the skin, in the form of liquid or cream and put up for retail sale, whether or not containing soap; paper, wadding, felt and nonwovens, impregnated, coated or covered with soap or detergent:
													-Soap and organic surface-active products and preparations, in the form of bars, cakes, moulded pieces or shapes, and paper, wadding, felt and nonwovens, impregnated, coated or covered with soap or detergent:
													--For toilet use (including medicated products)
0/0/0	0	2	0/0	0/0/0	0/0	0/0/0	0/0/	0/0/9	9.1/0	0	//	0/0/0	Skin lightening soaps containing mercury for toilet use (including products containing drugs), strips, blocks or moulded shapes, and paper, wadding, felt and non — woven fabrics impregnated, coated or coated with soap (containing more than one millionth of mercury)
0/0/0	0	2	0/0	0/0/0	0/0	0/0/0	0/0/	0/0/9	9.1/0	0	//	0/0/0	Organic surface active soap and other toilet products (including products containing drugs, in strips, blocks or moulded shapes)
													--Other:
0/0/0	3.5		0/0	0/0/0	0/0	0/0/0	0/0/	6.5/6.5/	/6.5			0/0/0	---Laundry soap
													---Other
0/0/0	0	3	1.5/1.5	0/0/0	0/0	0//0	0/0/	0/0/13.5	13.6/0		//	0/0/0	Other skin lightening soaps containing mercury, in strips, blocks or moulded shapes, and paper, wadding, felt and non — woven fabrics impregnated, coated or coated with soap (containing more than one millionth of mercury)
0/0/0	0	3	1.5/1.5	0/0/0	0/0	0//0	0/0/	0/0/13.5	13.6/0		//	0/0/0	Other organic surface active products and products (including paper, wadding and nonwovens dipped, coated or coated with soap or detergent)
													-Soap in other forms
0/0/0	0	3	1.5/1.5	0/0/0	0/0	0//0	0/0/	13.5/13.5/13.5	13.6/13.5	0	//	0/0/0	Other shapes of mercuric skin lightening soaps (containing more than one millionth of mercury)
0/0/0	0	3	1.5/1.5	0/0/0	0/0	0//0	0/0/	13.5/13.5/13.5	13.6/13.5	0	//	0/0/0	Soap in other shapes (other than bar, block or molded)

税则号列	货品名称〔CIQ 扩展编码及品名一T2 表示见附表 2〕	最惠(%)	暂定税率	普通	增值/消费	出口退税	计量单位	监管条件/特殊证件	检验检疫	对美关税	亚太上/下
3401.3000	-洁肤用的有机表面活性产品及制品,液状或膏状并制成零售包装的,不论是否含有肥皂										
3401.3000 10	洁肤用有机表面活性产品及制品,液状或膏状并制成零售包装的,含有含汞亮肤肥皂(含汞量超过百万分之一)〔101 婴幼儿淋洗类肤用化妆品,102 成人面部淋洗类化妆品,103 成人体用淋洗类化妆品〕	6.5		130	13/	13	千克	89/1		16.5	
3401.3000 90	洁肤用有机表面活性产品及制品(液状或膏状并制成零售包装的,不论是否含有肥皂)〔101 婴幼儿淋洗类肤用化妆品,102 成人面部淋洗类化妆品,103 成人体用淋洗类化妆品〕	6.5		130	13/	13	千克	AB/1	MN	16.5	
34.02	**有机表面活性剂(肥皂除外);表面活性剂制品、洗涤剂(包括助洗剂)及清洁剂,不论是否含有肥皂,但税目 34.01 的产品除外:**										
	-阴离子型有机表面活性剂,不论是否零售包装:										
3402.3100	--直链烷基苯磺酸及其盐〔999〕	6.5		30	13/	13	千克	/1		11.5	4.2/4.2
3402.3900	--其他〔999〕	6.5		30	13/	13	千克	/1		11.5	4.2/4.2
	-其他有机表面活性剂,不论是否零售包装:										
3402.4100	--阳离子型〔301 危险化学品,易燃液体,302 其他化工产品〕	6.5		30	13/	13	千克	/1		11.5	4.2/4.2
3402.4200	--非离子型〔301 危险化学品,易燃液体,302 其他化工产品〕	6.5		30	13/	13	千克	/1			4.2/4.2
3402.4900	--其他〔301 危险化学品,易燃液体,302 其他化工产品〕	6.5		30	13/	13	千克	/1		16.5	4.2/4.2
	-零售包装的制品:										
3402.5010	---合成洗涤粉〔999〕	6.5		80	13/	13	千克	/1		26.5	4.2/4.2
3402.5090	---其他〔301 危险化学品,易燃液体,302 其他化工产品〕	6.5		80	13/	13	千克	/1		16.5	4.2/4.2
3402.9000	-其他										
3402.9000 01	十二烷基苯磺酸钙甲醇溶液(非零售包装,十二烷基苯磺酸钙含量高于 70%)〔999〕	6.5		80	13/	13	千克	/13		16.5	4.2/4.2
3402.9000 90	非零售包装有机表面活性剂制品(包括洗涤剂及清洁剂,不论是否含有肥皂)〔301 危险化学品,易燃液体;302 其他化工产品〕	6.5		80	13/	13	千克	/13		16.5	4.2/4.2
34.03	**润滑剂(包括以润滑剂为基本成分的切削油制剂、螺栓或螺母松开剂、防锈或防腐蚀制剂及脱模剂)及用于纺织材料、皮革、毛皮或其他材料油脂处理的制剂,但不包括以石油或从沥青矿物提取的油类为基本成分(按重量计不低于 70%)的制剂:**										
	-含有石油或从沥青矿物提取的油类:										
3403.1100	--处理纺织材料、皮革、毛皮或其他材料的制剂〔301 危险化学品,易燃液体;302 其他化工产品〕	10		50	13/	13	千克	/13		30	6.5/6.5
3403.1900	--其他〔301 危险化学品,易燃液体;302 其他化工产品〕	10		50	13/	13	千克	/13			
	-其他:										
3403.9100	--处理纺织材料、皮革、毛皮或其他材料的制剂〔999〕	10		50	13/	13	千克	/1		35	
3403.9900	--其他〔301 危险化学品,易燃液体;302 其他化工产品〕	10		50	13/	13	千克	/13			
34.04	**人造蜡及调制蜡:**										
3404.2000	-聚氧乙烯(聚乙二醇)蜡〔999〕	10		70	13/	13	千克	/1		15	
3404.9000	-其他	10		70	13/	0	千克			1/20	
3404.9000 10	短链氯化石蜡(具有人造蜡特性)〔101:其他化工产品;102:无检疫要求食品添加剂〕	10		70	13/	0	千克	X/1		20	
3404.9000 90	其他人造蜡及调制蜡〔301 危险化学品,不用作食品添加剂;302 危险化学品,用作食品添加剂;303 其他化工品,不用作食品添加剂;304 其他化工品,用作食品添加剂〕	10		70	13/	0	千克	/1		20	
34.05	**鞋靴、家具、地板、车身、玻璃或金属用的光洁剂、擦洗膏、去污粉及类似制品(包括用这类制剂浸渍、涂面或包覆的纸、絮胎、毡呢、无纺织物、泡沫塑料或海绵橡胶),但不包括税目 34.04 的蜡:**										
3405.1000	-鞋靴或皮革用的上光剂及类似制品〔101 饲料添加剂;102 变性淀粉;301 硝化淀粉;302 其他化工品,不用作食品添加剂;303 其他化工品,用作食品添加剂〕	6.5		80	13/	13	千克	/13		26.5	
3405.2000	-保养木制家具、地板或其他木制品用的上光剂及类似制品〔301 危险化学品,易燃液体;302 其他化工产品〕	6.5		80	13/	13	千克	/13		16.5	

协定税率 %								RCEP		特惠税率 %			Article Description
东/冰/格	巴基斯坦	韩国	瑞士上/下	哥/秘/柬	澳/毛	新西/坡/智	中国港/澳/台	东盟及马来/澳/韩	日/新	亚太2国	老/柬/缅	98/97/95	
													-Organic surface-active products and preparations for washing the skin, in the form of liquid or cream and put up for retail sale, whether or not containing soap
0/0/0	3.5	2	0/0	0/0/0	0/0	0/0/0	0/0/	0/0/9	9.1/0		//	0/0/0	Organic surface active products and products for skin cleaning, in liquid or paste form and made into retail packaging, containing mercuric skin lightening soap (containing more than one millionth of mercury)
0/0/0	3.5	2	0/0	0/0/0	0/0	0/0/0	0/0/	0/0/9	9.1/0		//	0/0/0	Organic surface active products and products for skin cleansing (in liquid or paste form and in retail packaging, whether or not containing soap)
													Organic surface-active agents (other than soap); surface-active preparations, washing preparations (including auxiliary washing preparations) and cleaning preparations, whether or not containing soap, other than those of heading No. 34. 01:
													-Other organic surface active agents, whether or not put up for retail sale :
0/0/0	4	4.2	0/0	0/0/0	0/0	0//0	0/0/	5/5/	/5			0/0/0	--Linear alkylbenzene sulfonic acid and its salts
0/0/0	4	4.2	0/0	0/0/0	0/0	0//0	0/0/	5/5/	/5			0/0/0	--Other
													-Other organic surface active agents, whether or not put up for retail sale :
0/0/0	2	4.2	0/0	0/0/0	0/0	0//0	0/0/	5/5/	/5			0/0/0	--Cationic
0/0/0	0	3	0.7/0.7	0/0/0	0/0	0/0/0	0/0/0	5.9/5.9/5.9	6.1/5.9			0/0/0	--Non－ionic
0/0/0	2	4.2	0/0	0/0/0	0/0	0//0	0/0/	5/5/	/5			0/0/0	--Other
													-Preparations put up for retail sale:
0/0/0	3.5	6.5	0/0	0/0/0	0/0	0/0/0	0/0/	6.5/6.5/	/6.5			0/0/0	---Synthetic detergents in powder form
0/0/0	3.5	6.5	0/0	0/0/0	0/0	0/0/0	0/0/	6.5/6.5/	/6.5			0/0/0	---Other
													-Other
0/0/0	0	0	0.9/0.9	0/0/0	0/0	0/0/0	0/0/	0/0/0	8.2/0			0/0/0	Calcium dodecyl benzen sulfonate methanol solution (containing more than 70% of calcium dodecyl benzosulfonate, not put up for retail sale)
0/0/0	0	0	0.9/0.9	0/0/0	0/0	0/0/0	0/0/	0/0/0	8.2/0			0/0/0	Organic surface-active agents, including washing preparations and cleaning preparations, whether or not containing soap, not in forms or packing for retail sale
													Lubricating preparations (including cutting-oil preparations, bolt or nut release preparations, anti-rust or anticorrosion preparations and mould release preparations, based on lubricants) and preparations of a kind used for the oil or grease treatment of textile materials, leather, furskins or other materials, but excluding preparations containing, as basic constituents, 70% or more by weight of petroleum oils or of oils obtained from bituminous minerals:
													-Containing petroleum oils or oils obtained from bituminous minerals:
0/0/0	3.5	2	0/0	0/0/0	0/0	0/0/0	0/0/	0/0/9	9.4/0			0/0/0	--Preparations for the treatment of textile materials, leather, furskins or other materials
0/0/0	4	0	0/0	0/0/0	0/0	0/0/0	0/0/	9/9/9	9.1/9			0/0/0	--Other
													-Other:
0/0/0	3.5	0	0/0	0/0/0	0/0	0/0/0	0/0/	0/0/0	9.1/0			0/0/0	--Preparations for the treatment of textile materials, leather, furskins or other materials
0/0/0	3.5	0	1/1	0/0/0	0/0	0/0/0	0/0/	0/0/0	9.4/0			0/0/0	--Other
													Artificial waxes and prepared waxes:
0/0/0	3.5		0/0	0/0/0	0/0	0//0	0/0/	5/5/	/5			0/0/0	-Of poly(oxyethylene) (polyethylene glycol)
0/0/0	0	0	0	0	0	0	0//0	0/0/				0/0/0	-Other
0/0/0	0	0	0/0	0/0/0	0/0	0//0	0/0/	0/0/0	9.1/0		//	0/0/0	SCCPs (with artificial wax properties)
0/0/0	0	0	0/0	0/0/0	0/0	0//0	0/0/	0/0/0	9.1/0		//	0/0/0	Other artificial waxes and formulated waxes
													Polishes and creams, for footwear, furniture, floors, coachwork, glass or metal, scouring pastes and powders and similar preparations (whether or not in the form of paper, wadding, felt, nonwovens, cellular plastics or cellular rubber, impregnated, coated or covered with such preparations), excluding waxes of heading No. 34. 04:
0/0/0	3.5	2	0/0	0/0/0	0/0	0/0/0	0/0/	0/0/9	9.1/0			0/0/0	-Polishes, creams and similar preparations for footwear or leather
0/0/0	3.5	2	0/0	0/0/0	0/0	0/0/0	0/0/	0/0/9	9.1/0			0/0/0	-Polishes, creams and similar preparations for the maintenance of wooden furniture, floors or other woodwork

税则号列	货品名称〔CIQ 扩展编码及品名－T2 表示见附表 2〕	最惠(%)	暂定税率	普通	增值/消费	出口退税	计量单位	监管条件/特殊证件	检验检疫	对美关税	亚太上/下
3405.3000	-车身用的上光剂及类似制品，但金属用的光洁剂除外〔301 危险化学品，易燃液体；302 其他化工产品〕	6.5		80	13/	13	千克	/13		16.5	
3405.4000	-擦洗膏、去污粉及类似制品〔999〕	6.5		80	13/	13	千克	/1		16.5	
3405.9000	-其他〔301：易燃液体；302：其他化工产品〕	6.5		80	13/	13	千克	/1		16.5	4.2/4.2
34.06	**各种蜡烛及类似品：**										
3406.0000	各种蜡烛及类似品										
3406.0000 10	含濒危动物成分的蜡烛及类似品〔101 含木制品，102 不含木制品〕	6.5		130	13/	0	千克	EF/1		14	
3406.0000 90	其他各种蜡烛及类似品〔101 含木制品，102 不含木制品〕	6.5		130	13/	13	千克	/1		14	
34.07	**塑型用膏，包括供儿童娱乐用的在内；通称为“牙科用蜡”或“牙科造形膏”的制品，成套、零售包装或制成片状、马蹄形、条状及类似形状的；以熟石膏（煅烧石膏或硫酸钙）为基本成分的牙科用其他制品：**										
3407.0010	---牙科用蜡及造型膏〔999〕	6.5		30	13/	13	千克	/1		16.5	
3407.0020	---以熟石膏为基本成分的牙科用其他制品〔999〕	6.5		40	13/	13	千克	/1		31.5	
3407.0090	---其他〔999〕	10		100	13/	13	千克	/1		30	

协定税率 %								RCEP		特惠税率 %			Article Description
东/冰/格	巴基斯坦	韩国	瑞士上/下	哥/秘/柬	澳/毛	新西/坡/智	中国港/澳/台	东盟及马来/澳/韩	日/新	亚太2国	老/柬/缅	98/97/95	
0/0/0	3.5	2	0/0	0/0/0	0/0	0/0/0	0/0/	0/0/9	9.1/0			0/0/0	-Polishes and similar preparations for coachwork, other than metal polishes
0/0/0	3.5	2	0/0	0/0/0	0/0	0//0	0/0/	0/0/9	9.1/0			0/0/0	-Scouring pastes and powders and other scouring preparations
0/0/0	3.5	0	0/0	0/0/0	0/0	0/0/0	0/0/	0/0/0	9.1/0			0/0/0	-Other
													Candles, tapers and the like:
													Candles, tapers and the like
0/0/0	3.5	2	0/0	0/0/0	0/0	0/0/0	0/0/	0/0/9	9.1/0			0/0/0	Candle and gimilar products made from on endangered animals
0/0/0	3.5	2	0/0	0/0/0	0/0	0/0/0	0/0/	0/0/9	9.1/0			0/0/0	Other candles, tapers and the like
													Modelling pastes, including those put up for children's amusement; preparations known as "dental wax" or as "dental impression compounds", put up in sets, in packings for retail sale or in plates, horseshoe shapes, sticks or similar forms; other preparations for use in dentistry, with a basis of plaster (of calcined gypsum or calcium sulphate):
0/0/0	2	1.3	0.7/0.7	0/0/0	0/0	0//0	0/0/	0/0/5.9	5.9/0			0/0/0	---Preparations of a kind known as "dental wax" or as "dental impression compounds"
0/0/0	2	0	0/0	0/0/0	0/0	0//0	0/0/	0/0/0	5.9/0			0/0/0	---Other preparations for use in dentistry, with a basis of plaster
0/0/0	3.5	2	0/0	0/0/0	0/0	0//0	0/0/	0/0/9	9.1/0			0/0/0	---Other

第三十五章
蛋白类物质;改性淀粉;胶;酶

注释:

一、本章不包括:

(一)酵母(税目 21.02);

(二)第三十章的血份(非治病、防病用的血清白蛋白除外)、药品及其他产品;

(三)预鞣用酶制剂(税目 32.02);

(四)第三十四章的加酶的浸透剂、洗涤剂及其他产品;

(五)硬化蛋白(税目 39.13);

(六)印刷工业用的明胶产品(第四十九章)。

二、税目 35.05 所称“糊精”,是指淀粉的降解产品,其还原糖含量以右旋糖的干重量计不超过 10%。

如果还原糖含量超过 10%,应归入税目 17.02。

税则号列	货品名称〔CIQ 扩展编码及品名—T2 表示见附表 2〕	最惠(%)	暂定税率	普通	增值/消费	出口退税	计量单位	监管条件/特殊证件	检验检疫	对美关税	亚太上/下
35.01	**酪蛋白、酪蛋白酸盐及其他酪蛋白衍生物;酪蛋白胶:**										
3501.1000	-酪蛋白〔101 食用,301 无检疫要求食品添加剂,302 需申报仅用于工业用途不用于食品添加剂无检疫要求的化学品,999 非食用性乳品〕	10		35	13/	13	千克	AB/1	RS	35	
3501.9000	-其他〔101 非食用性乳品,102 酪蛋白酸钠(酪朊酸钠)(无检疫要求食品添加剂),103 需申报仅用于工业用途不用于食品添加剂无检疫要求的化学品〕	10		35	13/	13	千克	A/1	R	30	
35.02	**白蛋白(包括按重量计干质成分的乳清蛋白含量超过 80%的两种或两种以上的乳清蛋白浓缩物)、白蛋白盐及其他白蛋白衍生物:**										
	-卵清蛋白:										
3502.1100	--干的〔101〕	10		80	13/	13	千克	AB/1	PQ	15	
3502.1900	--其他〔101〕	10		80	13/	13	千克	AB/1	PQ	15	
3502.2000	-乳白蛋白(包括两种或两种以上的乳清蛋白浓缩物)										
3502.2000 10	乳清蛋白粉(按重量计干质成分的乳清蛋白含量超过 80%)〔101 食用乳清蛋白粉,999 食用乳清蛋白粉除外〕	10	5	35	13/	13	千克	AB/1	RS	10	
3502.2000 20	乳铁蛋白〔301 无检疫要求食品添加剂,302 需申报仅用于工业用途不用于食品添加剂无检疫要求的化学品,999 动物白蛋白〕	10	5	35	13/	13	千克	AB/1	RS	10	
3502.2000 90	其他乳白蛋白(包括两种或两种以上乳清蛋白浓缩物)〔301 无检疫要求食品添加剂,302 需申报仅用于工业用途不用于食品添加剂无检疫要求的化学品,999 动物白蛋白〕	10		35	13/	13	千克	AB/1	RS	15	
3502.9000	-其他〔301 无检疫要求食品添加剂,302 需申报仅用于工业用途不用于食品添加剂无检疫要求的化学品,401 用于人类医学、生命科学相关领域,非用于治疗或预防疾病用,999 动物白蛋白〕	10		35	13/	13	千克	A/1	R	30	
35.03	**明胶(包括长方形、正方形明胶薄片,不论是否表面加工或着色)及其衍生物;鱼鳔胶;其他动物胶,但不包括税目 35.01 的酪蛋白胶:**										
3503.0010	---明胶及其衍生物〔101 饲用,102 工业用,103 有检疫要求食品添加剂〕	12		35	13/	13	千克	AB/1	PRQ	19.5	9.6/9.6
3503.0090	---其他〔101 药用龟甲胶,102 药用阿胶,103 药用鹿角胶,104 紫胶(虫胶)(有检疫要求食品添加剂)〕	12		50	13/	13	千克	AB/1	PRQ	14.5	9.6/9.6
35.04	**蛋白胨及其衍生物;其他税目未列名的蛋白质及其衍生物;皮粉,不论是否加入铬矾:**										
3504.0010	---蛋白胨〔101 保健食品,102 无检疫要求食品添加剂,103 工业用动物骨蛋白胨,301 需申报仅用于工业用途不用于食品添加剂无检疫要求的化学品〕	3		11	13/	13	千克	A/1	R	8	
3504.0090	---其他[T2]	8		35	13/	13	千克	A/1	R	18	
35.05	**糊精及其他改性淀粉(例如,预凝化淀粉或酯化淀粉);以淀粉、糊精或其他改性淀粉为基本成分的胶:**										
3505.1000	-糊精及其他改性淀粉〔101 饲料添加剂,102 变性淀粉,301 爆炸品,需申报仅用于工业用途不用于食品添加剂无检疫要求,302 无检疫要求食品添加剂,303 一般化学品,需申报仅用于工业用途不用于食品添加剂无检疫要求,304 属于危险化学品的食品添加剂〕	12	6	50	13/	13	千克	A/13	MR	18.5	

Chapter 35
Albuminoidal substances; modified starches; glues; enzymes

Notes:

1. This Chapter does not cover:
   (a) Yeasts (heading No. 21.02);
   (b) Blood fractions (other than blood albumin not prepared for therapeutic or prophylactic uses), medicaments or other products of Chapter 30;
   (c) Enzymatic preparations for pre-tanning (heading No. 32.02);
   (d) Enzymatic soaking or washing preparations or other products of Chapter 34;
   (e) Hardened proteins (heading No. 39.13); or
   (f) Gelatin products of the printing industry (Chapter 49).
2. For the purposes of heading No. 35.05, the term "dextrins" means starch degradation products with a reducing sugar content, expressed as dextrose on the dry substance, not exceeding 10%.
   Such products with a reducing sugar content exceeding 10% fall in heading No. 17.02.

协定税率 %								RCEP		特惠税率 %			Article Description
东/冰/格	巴基斯坦	韩国	瑞士 上/下	哥/秘/柬	澳/毛	新西/坡/智	中国港/澳/台	东盟及马来/澳/韩	日/新	亚太2国	老/柬/缅	98/97/95	
													Casein, caseinates and other casein derivatives; casein glues:
0/0/0	4	2	0/0	0/0/0	0/0	0/0/0	0/0/	0/0/9	9.1/0			0/0/0	-Casein
0/0/0	3.5	2	0/0	0/0/0	0/0	0//0	0/0/	0/0/9	9.1/0			0/0/0	-Other
													Albumins (including concentrates of two or more whey proteins, containing by weight more than 80% whey proteins, calculated on the dry matter), albuminates and other albumin derivatives:
													-Egg albumin:
0/0/0	3.5	2	0/0	0/0/0	0/0	0//0	0/0/	0/0/9	9.1/0			0/0/0	--Dried
0/0/0	3.5	2	0/0	0/0/0	0/0	0//0	0/0/	0/0/9	9.1/0			0/0/0	--Other
													-Milk albumin, including concentrates of two or more whey proteins
0/0/0	3.5	2	0/0	0/0/0	0/0	0//0	0/0/	9/9/9	9.1/9		//	0/0/0	Whey protein powder (whey protein content of dry components exceeds 80% by weight)
0/0/0	3.5	2	0/0	0/0/0	0/0	0//0	0/0/	9/9/9	9.1/9		//	0/0/0	lactoferrin
0/0/0	3.5	2	0/0	0/0/0	0/0	0//0	0/0/	9/9/9	9.1/9		//	0/0/0	Other whey protein (including two or more whey protein concentrates)
0/0/0	3.5	2	0/0	0/0/0	0/0	0//0	0/0/	0/0/9	9.1/0			0/0/0	-Other
													Gelatin (including gelatin in rectangular (including square) sheets, whether or not surface-worked or coloured) and gelatin derivatives; isinglass; other glues of animal origin, excluding casein glues of heading No. 35.01:
0/0/0	0	2.4	1.2/1.2	0/0/0	0/0	0/0/0	0/0/	0/0/10.8	10.9/0			0/0/0	---Gelatin and gelatin derivatives
0/0/0	6	2.4	1.2/1.2	0/0/0	0/0	0/0/0	0/0/	0/0/10.8	10.9/0			0/0/0	---Other
													Peptones and their derivatives; other protein substances and their derivatives, not elsewhere specified or included; hide powder, whether or not chromed:
0/0/0	0	0	0/0	0/0/0	0/0	0//0	0/0/	0/0/0	0/0			0/0/0	---Peptones
0/0/0	2	0	0/0	0/0/0	0/0	0//0	0/0/	0/0/0	7.3/0			0/0/0	---Other
													Dextrins and other modified starches (for example, pregelatinized or esterified starches); glues based on starches, or on dextrins or other modified starches:
0/0/0	4.8	2.4	1.2/1.2	0/0/0	0/0	0/0/0	0/0/	0/0/10.8	10.9/0			0/0/0	-Dextrins and other modified starches

税则号列	货品名称〔CIQ 扩展编码及品名—T2 表示见附表 2〕	最惠(%)	暂定税率	普通	增值/消费	出口退税	计量单位	监管条件/特殊证件	检验检疫	对美关税	亚太上/下
3505.2000	-胶〔101 变性淀粉,301 其他危险化学品,需申报仅用于工业用途不用于食品添加剂无检疫要求,302 无检疫要求食品添加剂,303 一般化学品,需申报仅用于工业用途不用于食品添加剂无检疫要求,304 属于危险化学品的食品添加剂〕	20		50	13/	13	千克	A/1	MR	30	
35.06	**其他税目未列名的调制胶及其他调制黏合剂;适于作胶或黏合剂用的产品,零售包装每件净重不超过 1 千克:**										
3506.1000	-适于作胶或黏合剂用的产品,零售包装每件净重不超过 1 千克										
3506.1000 10	硅酮结构密封胶(零售包装每件净重不超过 1 千克)〔301 其他危险化学品,302 其他化工产品〕	10		90	13/	13	千克	A/13	M	20	6.5/6.5
3506.1000 90	其他适于作胶或粘合剂的零售产品(零售包装每件净重不超过 1 千克)〔301 危险化学品,易燃液体;302 其他化工品〕	10		90	13/	13	千克	/13		20	6.5/6.5
	-其他:										
	--以橡胶或税目 39.01 至 39.13 的聚合物为基本成分的黏合剂:										
3506.9110	---以聚酰胺为基本成分的〔301 危险化学品,易燃液体;302 其他化工产品〕	10		90	13/	13	千克	/13		20	7/7
3506.9120	---以环氧树脂为基本成分的〔301 危险化学品,易燃液体;302 其他化工产品〕	10		90	13/	13	千克	/13		20	6.5/6.5
3506.9190	---其他										
3506.9190 10	非零售,硅酮结构密封胶〔301 其他危险化学品,302 其他化工产品〕	10		90	13/	13	千克	A/13	M	35	7/7
3506.9190 20	专门或主要用于显示屏或触摸屏制造的光学透明膜黏合剂和光固化液体黏合剂(包括以人造树脂(环氧树脂除外)为基本成分的)〔301 危险化学品,易燃液体;302 其他化工产品〕	0		90	13/	13	千克	/13		25	7/7
3506.9190 90	其他橡胶或塑料为基本成分粘合剂(包括以人造树脂(环氧树脂除外)为基本成分的)[T2]	10		90	13/	13	千克	/13		35	7/7
3506.9900	--其他〔301 危险化学品,易燃液体;302 其他化工产品〕	10		90	13/	13	千克	/13		20	6.5/6.5
35.07	**酶;其他税目未列名的酶制品:**										
3507.1000	-粗制凝乳酶及其浓缩物〔301:无检疫要求食品添加剂;302:需申报仅用于工业用途不用于食品添加剂无检疫要求的化学品;999:饲用酶制剂〕	6		30	13/	13	千克	A/1	R		
	-其他:										
3507.9010	---碱性蛋白酶〔301:无检疫要求食品添加剂;302:需申报仅用于工业用途不用于食品添加剂无检疫要求的化学品;401:用于人类医学、生命科学相关领域;999:饲用酶制剂〕	6		30	13/	13	千克	A/1	R	11	
3507.9020	---碱性脂肪酶〔301 无检疫要求食品添加剂;302 需申报仅用于工业用途不用于食品添加剂无检疫要求的化学品;401 用于人类医学、生命科学相关领域;999 饲用酶制剂〕	6		30	13/	13	千克	A/1	R	16	
3507.9090	---其他										
3507.9090 10	门冬酰胺酶〔301 其他化工产品,401 用于人类医学、生命科学相关领域,非用于治疗或预防疾病用〕	6	0	30	3/	13	千克	AB/1	RVW	10	
3507.9090 90	其他酶及酶制品〔101 饲用酶制剂,301 无检疫要求食品添加剂,302 需申报仅用于工业用途不用于食品添加剂无检疫要求的化学品,401 人类医学、生命科学研究用〕	6		30	13/	13	千克	AB/1	RVW	16	

协定税率 %								RCEP		特惠税率 %			Article Description
东/冰/格	巴基斯坦	韩国	瑞士 上/下	哥/秘/柬	澳/毛	新西/坡/智	中国港/澳/台	东盟及马来/澳/韩	日/新	亚太2国	老/柬/缅	98/97/95	
0/0/0		9.3	2/2	0/0/0	0/0	0/0/0	0/0/	18/18/18	18.8/18			0/0/0	-Glues
													Prepared glues and other prepared adhesives, not elsewhere specified or included; products suitable for use as glues or adhesives, put up for retail sale as glues or adhesives, not exceeding a net weight of 1 kg:
													-Products suitable for use as glues or adhesives, put up for retail sale as glues or adhesives, not exceeding a net weight of 1kg
0//0	3.5	0	1/1	0/0/0	0/0	0/0/0	0/0/0	0/0/0	9.4/0			0/0/0	Structure silicone sealant (in forms or packing for retail sale as glues or adhesives, not exceeding a net weight of 1kg)
0//0	3.5	0	1/1	0/0/0	0/0	0/0/0	0/0/0	0/0/0	9.4/0			0/0/0	Other-products suitable for use as glues or adhesives, in forms or packing for retail sale as glues or adhesives, not exceeding a net weight of 1kg
													-Other:
													--Adhesives based on polymers of headings Nos. 39. 01 to 39. 13 or on rubber:
0/0/0	3.5	4.6	0/0	0/0/0	0/0	0/0/0	0/0/0	9.3/9.5/9.3	9.4/9.5			0/0/0	---Based on polyamide
0/0/0	3.5	6	1/1	0/0/0	0/0	0/0/0	0/0/0	9.5/9.5/9.5	9.5/9.5			0/0/0	---Based on epoxy resin
													---Other
0/0/0	3.5	2	1/1	0/0/0	0/0	0/0/0	0/0/0	0/0/9	9.4/0			0/0/0	Structure silicone sealant, not in forms or packing for retail sale
0/0/0	3.5	2	1/1	0/0/0	0/0	0/0/0	0/0/0	0/0/9	9.4/0			0/0/0	Specially built or is mainly used to display or touch screen optical transparent film adhesive and light curing liquid adhesive (including synthetic resin (epoxy resin except) as the basic component of)
0/0/0	3.5	2	1/1	0/0/0	0/0	0/0/0	0/0/0	0/0/9	9.4/0			0/0/0	Other adhesives based on rubber or plastic including[artificial resin (other than epoxy resin)]
0/0/0	3.5	6	1/1	0/0/0	0/0	0/0/0	0/0/0	9.5/9.5/9.5	9.5/9.5			0/0/0	--Other
													Enzymes; prepared enzymes not elsewhere specified or included:
0/0/0	0	0	0/0	0/0/0	0/0	0//0	0/0/	0/0/0	0/0			0/0/0	-Rennet and concentrates thereof
													-Other:
0/0/0	0	1.2	0/0	0/0/0	0/0	0//0	0/0/	0/0/5.4	5.5/0			0/0/0	---Basic proteinase
0/0/0	0	1.2	0/0	0/0/0	0/0	0//0	0/0/	0/0/5.4	5.5/0			0/0/0	---Basic lipase
0/0/0	0	0	0/0	0/0/0	0/0	0//0	0/0/	5.4/5.4/5.4	5.5/5.4			0/0/0	---Other
0/0/0	0	0	0/0	0/0/0	0/0	0//0	0/0/	5.4/5.4/5.4	5.5/5.4			0/0/0	Other enzymes and enzyme products(tax number of Separating anti—cancer pharmaceutical raw materials)

第三十六章
炸药;烟火制品;火柴;引火合金;易燃材料制品

注释:

一、本章不包括单独的已有化学定义的化合物,但下列注释二(一)、(二)所述物品除外。

二、税目 36.06 所称"易燃材料制品",只适用于:

(一)聚乙醛、六亚甲基四胺(六甲撑四胺)及类似物质,已制成片、棒或类似形状作燃料用的;以酒精为基本成分的固体或半固体燃料及类似的配制燃料;

(二)直接灌注香烟打火机及类似打火器用的液体燃料或液化气体燃料,其包装容器的容积不超过 300 立方厘米;

(三)树脂火炬、引火物及类似品。

税则号列	货品名称〔CIQ 扩展编码及品名—T2 表示见附表 2〕	最惠(%)	暂定税率	普通	增值/消费	出口退税	计量单位	监管条件/特殊证件	检验检疫	对美关税	亚太上/下
36.01	**发射药:**										
3601.0000	发射药										
3601.0000 10	模压的胶质推进剂〔999〕	9		50	13/	0	千克	3/1		16.5	
3601.0000 20	含硝化粘接剂及铝粉＞5%的推进剂〔999〕	9		50	13/	0	千克	3/1		16.5	
3601.0000 30	黑火药〔999〕	9		50	13/	0	千克	k/1		16.5	
3601.0000 91	民用推进剂(限于购买、销售、运输管理)〔999〕	9		50	13/	0	千克	k/1		16.5	
3601.0000 99	其他发射药〔999〕	9		50	13/	0	千克	/1		16.5	
36.02	**配制炸药,但发射药除外:**										
3602.0010	---硝铵炸药										
3602.0010 10	符合特定标准的硝铵炸药(硝胺类物质超过 2% ,或密度＞1.8g/cm³、爆速＞8000m/s)〔999〕	9		50	13/	0	千克	3/13		11.5	
3602.0010 91	其他铵梯类炸药、铵油类炸药、膨化硝铵炸药、胶状乳化炸药、粉状乳化炸药、震源药柱、其他工业炸药〔999〕	9		50	13/	0	千克	k/13		11.5	
3602.0010 99	其他硝铵炸药,但发射药除外〔999〕	9		50	13/	0	千克	/13		11.5	
3602.0090	---其他										
3602.0090 10	符合特定标准的其他配制炸药(含有超过 2%(按重量计)的下述任何一种物质:(环)四亚甲基四硝胺(HMX);(环)三亚甲基三硝基胺(RDX);三氨基三硝基苯(TATB);氨基二硝基苯并氧化呋咱或 7 氨基 4,6 硝基苯并呋咱 1 氧化物;六硝基芪(HNS)等;或晶体密度大于 1.8g/cm3、爆速超过 8000m/s 的各种炸药。)〔999〕	9		50	13/	0	千克	3k/13		11.5	
3602.0090 91	民用的其他配置炸药,但发射药除外〔999〕	9		50	13/	0	千克	k/13		11.5	
3602.0090 99	其他配制炸药,但发射药除外〔999〕	9		50	13/	0	千克	/13		11.5	
36.03	**安全导火索;导爆索;火帽或雷管;引爆器;电雷管:**										
3603.1000	-安全导火索										
3603.1000 10	民用的安全导火索〔999〕	9		50	13/	0	千克	k/1		21.5	
3603.1000 90	其他安全导火索〔999〕	9		50	13/	0	千克	/1		21.5	
3603.2000	-导爆索										
3603.2000 10	民用的导爆索〔999〕	9		50	13/	0	千克	k/1		21.5	
3603.2000 90	其他导爆索〔999〕	9		50	13/	0	千克	/1		21.5	
3603.3000	-火帽										
3603.3000 10	民用的火帽〔999〕	9		50	13/	0	千克	k/1		21.5	
3603.3000 90	其他火帽〔999〕	9		50	13/	0	千克	/1		21.5	
3603.4000	-雷管										
3603.4000 10	使用单个或多个雷管的装置(由单一点火信号同时起爆,不包括仅使用起爆药的雷管)〔999〕	9		50	13/	0	千克	3/1		21.5	
3603.4000 30	民用的其他雷管〔999〕	9		50	13/	0	千克	k/1		21.5	
3603.4000 90	其他雷管〔999〕	9		50	13/	0	千克	/1		21.5	
3603.5000	-引爆器										
3603.5000 10	炸药雷管点火装置(用于引爆商品编码 3603600010 所列雷管的)〔999〕	9		50	13/	0	千克	3/1		21.5	
3603.5000 20	民用的其他引爆器〔999〕	9		50	13/	0	千克	k/1		21.5	
3603.5000 90	其他引爆器〔999〕	9		50	13/	0	千克	/1		21.5	
3603.6000	-电雷管										
3603.6000 10	爆炸桥、爆炸桥丝、冲击片、爆炸箔起爆器〔999〕	9		50	13/	0	千克	3/1		21.5	
3603.6000 20	民用的其他电雷管〔999〕	9		50	13/	0	千克	k/1		21.5	
3603.6000 90	其他电雷管〔999〕	9		50	13/	0	千克	/1		21.5	
36.04	**烟花、爆竹、信号弹、降雨火箭、浓雾信号弹及其他烟火制品:**										
3604.1000	-烟花、爆竹[T2]	6		130	13/15	13	千克	AB/1	MN	13.5	
3604.9000	-其他										

Chapter 36

Explosives; pyrotechnic products; matches; pyrophoric alloys; certain combustible preparations

Notes:

1. This Chapter does not cover separate chemically defined compounds other than those described in Note 2 (a) or (b) below.
2. The expression "articles of combustible materials" in heading No. 36.06 applies only to:
   (a) Metaldehyde, hexamethylenetetramine and similar substances, put up in forms (for example, tablets, sticks or similar forms) for use as fuels; fuels with a basis of alcohol, and similar prepared fuels, in solid or semi-solid form;
   (b) Liquid or liquefied-gas fuels in containers of a kind used for filling or refilling cigarette or similar lighters and of a capacity not exceeding 300 cm^3;
   (c) Resin torches, firelighters and the like.

协定税率 %								RCEP		特惠税率 %			Article Description
东/冰/格	巴基斯坦	韩国	瑞士上/下	哥/秘/柬	澳/毛	新西/坡/智	中国港/澳/台	东盟及马来/澳/韩	日/新	亚太2国	老/柬/缅	98/97/95	
													Propellent powders:
													Propellent powders
0/0/0	2	0	0/0	0/0/0	0/0	0//0	0/0/	0/0/0	8.2/0			0/0/0	Colloidal propellant, molded
0/0/0	2	0	0/0	0/0/0	0/0	0//0	0/0/	0/0/0	8.2/0			0/0/0	Propellant, containing cementing agent and aluminum powder>5%
0/0/0	2	0	0/0	0/0/0	0/0	0//0	0/0/	0/0/0	8.2/0		//	0/0/0	Black powder
0/0/0	2	0	0/0	0/0/0	0/0	0//0	0/0/	0/0/0	8.2/0		//	0/0/0	Other civil propellants
0/0/0	2	0	0/0	0/0/0	0/0	0//0	0/0/	0/0/0	8.2/0		//	0/0/0	Other propellants
													Prepared explosives, other than propellent powders:
													---Based on ammonals nitrate
0/0/0	2	0	0/0	0/0/0	0/0	0//0	0/0/	0/0/0	8.2/0			0/0/0	Meet specific standard of ammonium nitrate exploseives (containing of ammonium nitrate>2%, density>1.8g/cm^3, explodingvelocity>8000m/s)
0/0/0	2	0	0/0	0/0/0	0/0	0//0	0/0/	0/0/0	8.2/0		//	0/0/0	Other ammonium ladder explosives, ammonium oil explosives, expanded ammonium nitrate explosives, gelatinous emulsion explosives, Powdered Emulsion explosives, source explosive columns, other industrial explosives
0/0/0	2	0	0/0	0/0/0	0/0	0//0	0/0/	0/0/0	8.2/0		//	0/0/0	Other ammonium nitrate explosives except propellants
													---Other
0/0/0	2	0	0/0	0/0/0	0/0	0//0	0/0/	0/0/0	8.2/0			0/0/0	Meet specific standard of explosives (containing hexanitrostilbene>2%, density>1.8g/cm^3, exploding velocity>8000m/s)
0/0/0	2	0	0/0	0/0/0	0/0	0//0	0/0/	0/0/0	8.2/0		//	0/0/0	Other configurations of explosives for civil use, except for propellants
0/0/0	2	0	0/0	0/0/0	0/0	0//0	0/0/	0/0/0	8.2/0		//	0/0/0	Other compound explosives, except propellants
													Safety fuses; detonating fuses; percussion or detonating caps; igniters; electric detonators:
													-Safety fuses
0/0/0	2	0	0/0	0/0/0	0/0	0//0	0/0/	8.1/8.1/8.1	8.2/8.1			0/0/0	Civil safety fuse
0/0/0	2	0	0/0	0/0/0	0/0	0//0	0/0/	8.1/8.1/8.1	8.2/8.1			0/0/0	Other safety fuses
													-Detonating cords
0/0/0	2	0	0/0	0/0/0	0/0	0//0	0/0/	8.1/8.1/8.1	8.2/8.1			0/0/0	Civil detonating cord
0/0/0	2	0	0/0	0/0/0	0/0	0//0	0/0/	8.1/8.1/8.1	8.2/8.1			0/0/0	Other detonating cords
													-Percussion caps
0/0/0	2	0	0/0	0/0/0	0/0	0//0	0/0/	8.1/8.1/8.1	8.2/8.1			0/0/0	Civilian fire cap
0/0/0	2	0	0/0	0/0/0	0/0	0//0	0/0/	8.1/8.1/8.1	8.2/8.1			0/0/0	Other fire caps
													-Detonating caps
0/0/0	2	0	0/0	0/0/0	0/0	0//0	0/0/	8.1/8.1/8.1	8.2/8.1			0/0/0	Devices using single or multiple detonators (detonated simultaneously by a single ignition signal, excluding detonators using only primary explosives)
0/0/0	2	0	0/0	0/0/0	0/0	0//0	0/0/	8.1/8.1/8.1	8.2/8.1			0/0/0	Other detonators for civil use
0/0/0	2	0	0/0	0/0/0	0/0	0//0	0/0/	8.1/8.1/8.1	8.2/8.1			0/0/0	Other detonators
													-Igniters
0/0/0	2	0	0/0	0/0/0	0/0	0//0	0/0/	8.1/8.1/8.1	8.2/8.1			0/0/0	Explosive detonator ignition device (for detonating detonators listed in commodity code 36361)
0/0/0	2	0	0/0	0/0/0	0/0	0//0	0/0/	8.1/8.1/8.1	8.2/8.1			0/0/0	Other detonators for civil use
0/0/0	2	0	0/0	0/0/0	0/0	0//0	0/0/	8.1/8.1/8.1	8.2/8.1			0/0/0	Other detonators
													-Electric detonators
0/0/0	2	0	0/0	0/0/0	0/0	0//0	0/0/	8.1/8.1/8.1	8.2/8.1			0/0/0	Explosive bridge, explosive bridge wire, impact sheet, explosive foil detonator
0/0/0	2	0	0/0	0/0/0	0/0	0//0	0/0/	8.1/8.1/8.1	8.2/8.1			0/0/0	Other electric detonators for civil use
0/0/0	2	0	0/0	0/0/0	0/0	0//0	0/0/	8.1/8.1/8.1	8.2/8.1			0/0/0	Other electric detonators
													Fireworks, signalling flares, rain rockets, fog signals and other pyrotechnic articles:
0/0/0	0	0	0/0	0/0/0	0/0	0//0	0/0/	0/0/0	0/0			0/0/0	-Fireworks
													-Other

税则号列	货品名称〔CIQ扩展编码及品名－T2表示见附表2〕	最惠(%)	暂定税率	普通	增值/消费	出口退税	计量单位	监管条件/特殊证件	检验检疫	对美关税	亚太上/下
3604.9000 10	人工影响天气用燃爆器材、海上救生烟火信号及其他特殊用途烟火制品〔999〕	6		100	13/	13	千克	k/1		13.5	
3604.9000 90	其他信号弹,降雨火箭及其他烟火制品〔999〕	6		100	13/	13	千克	/1		13.5	
36.05	**火柴,但税目36.04的烟火制品除外:**										
3605.0000	火柴,但税目36.04的烟火制品除外〔101 含木制品的其他轻工品,102 任何地方可擦燃〕	6		100	13/	0	千克	/1		8.5	
36.06	**各种形状的铈铁及其他引火合金;本章注释二所述的易燃材料制品:**										
3606.1000	-直接灌注香烟打火机及类似打火器用的液体燃料或液化气体燃料,其包装容器的容积不超过300立方厘米〔301 危险化学品,易燃液体;302 其他化工产品〕	6		80	13/	0	千克	/13		11	
	-其他:										
	---铈铁及其他引火合金:										
3606.9011	----已切成形可直接使用〔999〕	6		80	13/	0	千克	/1		11	
3606.9019	----其他〔301 危险化学品,易燃固体;302 危险化学品,遇水放出易燃气体的物质;303 其他化工品〕	6		50	13/	0	千克	/13			
3606.9090	---其他〔301 危险化学品,易燃液体;302 其他化工产品〕	6		80	13/	0	千克	/13			

协定税率 %								RCEP		特惠税率 %			Article Description
东/冰/格	巴基斯坦	韩国	瑞士上/下	哥/秘/柬	澳/毛	新西/坡/智	中国港/澳/台	东盟及马来/澳/韩	日/新	亚太2国	老/柬/缅	98/97/95	
0/0/0	0	0	0/0	0/0/0	0/0	0//0	0/0/	0/0/0	0/0		//	0/0/0	Fire and explosive devices for weather modification, marine life— saving pyrotechnic signals and other special — purpose pyrotechnic products
0/0/0	0	0	0/0	0/0/0	0/0	0//0	0/0/	0/0/0	0/0		//	0/0/0	Other signal bombs, rain rockets and other pyrotechnics
													Matches, other than pyrotechnic articles of heading No. 36. 04:
0/0/0	0	0	0/0	0/0/0	0/0	0//0	0/0/	0/0/0	0/0			0/0/0	Matches, other than pyrotechnic articles of heading No. 36. 04
													Ferro-cerium and other pyrophoric alloys in all forms; articles of combustible materials as specified in Note 2 to this Chapter:
0/0/0	3.5	2	0/0	0/0/0	0/0	0//0	0/0/	0/0/9	9.1/0			0/0/0	-Liquid or liquefied-gas fuels in containers of a kind used for filling or refilling cigarette or similar lighters and of a capacity not exceeding 300 cm^3
													-Other:
													---Ferro-cerium and other pyrophoric alloys:
0/0/0	2	0	0/0	0/0/0	0/0	0//0	0/0/	0/0/0	8.2/0			0/0/0	----Cut to shape, for immediate use
0/0/0	2	0	0/0	0/0/0	0/0	0//0	0/0/	0/0/0	8.2/0			0/0/0	----Other
0/0/0	2	0	0/0	0/0/0	0/0	0//0	0/0/	0/0/0	8.2/0			0/0/0	---Other

第三十七章
照相及电影用品

注释：

一、本章不包括废碎料。

二、本章所称“摄影”，是指光或其他射线作用于感光面(包括热敏面)上直接或间接形成可见影像的过程。

税则号列	货品名称〔CIQ扩展编码及品名—T2表示见附表2〕	最惠(%)	暂定税率	普通	增值/消费	出口退税	计量单位	监管条件/特殊证件	检验检疫	对美关税	亚太上/下
37.01	**未曝光的摄影感光硬片及平面软片，用纸、纸板及纺织物以外任何材料制成；未曝光的一次成像感光平片，不论是否分装：**										
3701.1000	-X光用〔999〕	20	10	40	13/	13	千克/平方米	/1		22.5	16/16
3701.2000	--一次成像平片〔999〕	5		40	13/	13	千克	/1		30	
	-其他硬片及软片，任何一边超过255毫米：										
	---照相制版用：										
3701.3021	----激光照排片〔999〕	0		50	13/	13	千克/平方米	/1		2.5	
3701.3022	----PS版〔999〕	0		50	13/	13	千克/平方米	/1		27.5	0/0
3701.3024	----CTP版〔999〕	0		50	13/	13	千克/平方米	/1		27.5	
3701.3025	----柔性印刷板〔999〕	0		50	13/	13	千克/平方米	/1		7.5	
3701.3029	----其他〔999〕	0		50	13/	13	千克/平方米	/1		12.5	
3701.3090	---其他〔999〕	0		70	13/	13	千克/平方米	/1		22.5	0/0
	-其他：										
3701.9100	--彩色摄影用〔999〕	20		70	13/	13	千克	/1		45	
	--其他：										
3701.9920	---照相制版用										
3701.9920 01	石英玻璃基质的未曝光感光硬片〔999〕	2.5/1.3		40	13/	13	千克/平方米	/1		30	
3701.9920 90	照相制版用其他未曝光软片及硬片(非彩色摄影用，边长≤255mm)〔999〕	2.5/1.3		40	13/	13	千克/平方米	/1		30	
3701.9990	---其他〔999〕	6.3/3.1		70	13/	13	千克/平方米	/1		13.8	
37.02	**成卷的未曝光摄影感光胶片，用纸、纸板及纺织物以外任何材料制成；未曝光的一次成像感光卷片：**										
3702.1000	-X光用〔999〕	10		40	13/	13	千克/平方米	/1		35	8/8
	-无齿孔的其他胶片，宽度不超过105毫米：										
	--彩色摄影用：										
3702.3110	---一次成像卷片〔999〕	5		40	13/	13	千克/平方米	/1			
3702.3190	---其他〔999〕	T3		T3	13/	13	千克/平方米	/1		T3	
	--其他涂卤化银乳液的：										
3702.3210	---一次成像卷片〔999〕	5		40	13/	13	千克/平方米	/1			
3702.3220	---照相制版用〔999〕	T3		T3	13/	13	千克/平方米	/1			
3702.3290	---其他〔999〕	T3		T3	13/	13	千克/平方米	/1		T3	
	--其他：										
3702.3920	---照相制版用〔999〕	T3		T3	13/	13	千克/平方米	/1		T3	
3702.3990	---其他〔999〕	T3		T3	13/	13	千克/平方米	/1		T3	
	-无齿孔的其他胶片，宽度超过105毫米：										

Chapter 37
Photographic or cinematographic goods

Chapter Notes:

1. This Chapter does not cover waste or scrap.
2. In this Chapter the word "photographic" relates to the process by which visible images are formed, directly or indirectly, by the action of light or other forms of radiation on photosensitive, including thermosensitive, surfaces.

协定税率 %								RCEP		特惠税率 %			Article Description
东/冰/格	巴基斯坦	韩国	瑞士上/下	哥/秘/柬	澳/毛	新西/坡/智	中国港/澳/台	东盟及马来/澳/韩	日/新	亚太2国	老/柬/缅	98/97/95	
													Photographic plates and film in the flat, sensitized, unexposed, of any material other than paper, paperboard or textiles; instant print film in the flat, sensitized, unexposed, whether or not in packs:
5/0/0		16	2/2	0/0/0	0/0	0//0	0/0/					0/0/0	-For X-ray
0/0/0	0	1	2.1/2.1	0/0/0	0/0	0//0	0/0/	4.5/4.5/4.5	4.5/4.5			0/0/0	-Instant print film
													-Other plates and film, with any side exceeding 255 mm:
													---For preparing printing plates or cylinders:
5/0/0		0.7元/平方米	0/0	0/0/0	0/0	0//0	0/0/	0/9/9	0/9			0/0/0	----Laser phototypesetting film
5/0/0		1.6元/平方米	0/0	0/0/0	0/0	0//0	0/0/	0/9/9	0/9			0/0/0	----Precoated sensitized plate
0/0/0	2	1.6元/平方米	0/0	0/0/0	0/0	0//0	0/0/	0/0/9	0/0			0/0/0	----CTP plate
0/0/0		3元/平方米	0/0	0/0/0	0/0	0//0	0/0/	0/0/9	0/0			0/0/0	----Flexible printed board
5/0/0		0元/平方米	0/0	0/0/0	0/0	0//0	0/0/	0/9/0	0/9			0/0/0	----Other
0/0/0		9.3	0/0	0/0/0	0/0	0/0/0	0/0/	0/18/18	0/18			0/0/0	---Other
													-Other:
0/0/0			2.2/2.2	0/0/0	0/13.2	0/0/0	0/0/	5/5/	/5			0/0/0	--For colour photography (polychrome)
													--Other:
													---For preparing printing plates or cylinders
0/0/0	3.5	2	0/0	0/0/0	0/0	0//0	0/0/	0/0/9	9.1/0			0/0/0	Quartz glass matrix of photographic film, unexposed
0/0/0	3.5	2	0/0	0/0/0	0/0	0//0	0/0/	0/0/9	9.1/0			0/0/0	Other photographic plates and film in the flat sensitized for preparing printing plates or cylinders, with any side ≤ 255mm, (other than ultrtafine-grain plate, other than for colour photography)
0/0/0			2.5/2.5	0/0/0	0/0	0/0/0	0/0/	0/0/22.5	22.7/0			0/0/0	---Other
													Photographic film in rolls, sensitized, unexposed, of any material other than paper, paperboard or textiles; instant print film in rolls, sensitized, unexposed:
5/0/0		4.6	0/0	0/0/0	0/7.1	0//0	0/0/	9.5/9.5/9.5	9.5/9.8			0/0/0	-For X-ray
													-Other film, without perforations, of a width not exceeding 105 mm:
													--For colour photography (polychrome):
0/0/0	0	0	0/0	0/0/0	0/3.6	0//0	0/0/	0/0/0	0/0			0/0/0	---Instant print film
0/0/0				0/0/0	0/28.6	0/0/0	0/0/	5/5/	/5			0/0/0	---Other
													--Other, with silver halide emulsion:
0/0/0	0	0	0/0	0/0/0	0/3.6	0//0	0/0/	0/0/0	0/0			0/0/0	---Instant print film
0/0/0	0.9元/平方米	0.9元/平方米	0/0	0/0/0	0/7.1	0//0	0/0/	0/0/9	9.1/0			0/0/0	---For preparing printing plates or cylinders
0/0/0		12.6元/平方米	2.2/2.2	0/0/0	0/15.7	0/0/0	0/0/	20.9/20.9/20.9	/20.9			0/0/0	---Other
													--Other:
0/0/0	24元/平方米	2.4元/平方米	0/0	0/0/0	0/7.1	0//0	0/0/	9/9/9	9.4/9			0/0/0	---For preparing printing plates or cylinders
0/0/0		14.4元/平方米	2.2/2.2	0/0/0	0/15.7	0/0/0	0/0/	20.9/20.9/20.9	/20.9			0/0/0	---Other
													-Other film, without perforations, of a width exceeding 105 mm:

税则号列	货品名称〔CIQ 扩展编码及品名－T2 表示见附表 2〕	最惠(%)	暂定税率	普通	增值/消费	出口退税	计量单位	监管条件/特殊证件	检验检疫	对美关税	亚太上/下
3702.4100	--彩色摄影用,宽度超过 610 毫米,长度超过 200 米〔999〕	T3		T3	13/	13	千克/平方米	/1			
	--非彩色摄影用,宽度超过 610 毫米,长度超过 200 米:										
	---照相制版用:										
3702.4221	----印刷电路板制造用光致抗蚀干膜〔999〕	T3		T3	13/	13	千克/平方米	/1		T3	
3702.4229	----其他〔999〕	T3	0	T3	13/	13	千克/平方米	/1		T3	8/8
	---其他:										
3702.4292	----红色或红外激光胶片										
3702.4292 01	未曝光红色或红外激光胶片(宽长胶卷指宽度＞800mm,长度＞1000m)〔999〕	T3	0	T3	13/	13	千克/平方米	/1		T3	12.8/12.8
3702.4292 90	其他未曝光红色或红外激光胶片(610mm＜宽度≤800mm,200m＜长度≤1000m)〔999〕	T3		T3	13/	13	千克/平方米	/1		T3	12.8/12.8
3702.4299	----其他〔999〕	T3		T3	13/	13	千克/平方米	/1		T3	12.8/12.8
	--宽度超过 610 毫米,长度不超过 200 米:										
	---照相制版用:										
3702.4321	----激光照排片〔999〕	T3		T3	13/	13	千克/平方米	/1			8/8
3702.4329	----其他〔999〕	T3		T3	13/	13	千克/平方米	/1		T3	9/9
3702.4390	---其他〔999〕	T3		T3	13/	13	千克/平方米	/1		T3	16/16
	--宽度超过 105 毫米,但不超过 610 毫米:										
	---照相制版用:										
3702.4421	----激光照排片〔999〕	T3		T3	13/	13	千克/平方米	/1			9/9
3702.4422	----印刷电路板制造用光致抗蚀干膜〔999〕	T3		T3	13/	13	千克/平方米	/1		T3	
3702.4429	----其他〔999〕	T3		T3	13/	13	千克/平方米	/1		T3	
3702.4490	---其他〔999〕	T3		T3	13/	13	千克/平方米	/1		T3	16/16
	-彩色摄影用的其他胶片:										
3702.5200	--宽度不超过 16 毫米〔999〕	T3		T3	13/	13	千克/平方米	/1		T3	
3702.5300	--幻灯片用,宽度超过 16 毫米,但不超过 35 毫米,长度不超过 30 米〔999〕	T3		T3	13/	13	千克/平方米	/1		T3	
	--非幻灯片用,宽度超过 16 毫米,但不超过 35 毫米,长度不超过 30 米:										
3702.5410	---宽度为 35 毫米,长度不超过 2 米〔999〕	T3		T3	13/	13	千克/平方米	/1		T3	8/8
3702.5490	---其他〔999〕	T3		T3	13/	13	千克/平方米	/1			14.4/14.4
	--宽度超过 16 毫米,但不超过 35 毫米,长度超过 30 米:										
3702.5520	---电影胶片〔999〕	T3		T3	13/	13	千克/平方米	/1		T3	20/20
3702.5590	---其他〔999〕	T3		T3	13/	13	千克/平方米	/1			32/32
	--宽度超过 35 毫米:										

协定税率 %								RCEP		特惠税率 %			Article Description
东/冰/格	巴基斯坦	韩国	瑞士 上/下	哥/秘/柬	澳/毛	新西/坡/智	中国港/澳/台	东盟及马来/澳/韩	日/新	亚太2国	老/柬/缅	98/97/95	
/0/0			1.6/1.6	0/0/0	0/11.4	0//0	0/0/					0/0/0	--Of a width exceeding 610 mm and of a length exceeding 200 m, for colour photography (polychrome)
													--Of a width exceeding 610 mm and of a length exceeding 200 m, other than for colour photography:
													---For preparing printing plates or cylinders:
0/0/0	0.1元/平方米		0/0	0/0/0	0/7.1	0/0/0	0/0/	5/5/	/5			0/0/0	----Wide anticorrosive photographic plate for printed circuit processing
0/0/0	0.3元/平方米	0.3元/平方米	0/0	0/0/0	0/7.1	0//0	0/0/	9/9/9	9.1/9			0/0/0	----Other
													---Other:
													----Red or infra-red laser film
0/0/0		0.4元/平方米	1.6/1.6	0/0/0	0/11.4	0/0/0	0/0/	14.4/14.4/14.4	14.5/14.4			0/0/0	Red or infra-red laser film, unexposed, of a width＞800mm, of a length＞1000m,
0/0/0		0.4元/平方米	1.6/1.6	0/0/0	0/11.4	0/0/0	0/0/	14.4/14.4/14.4	14.5/14.4			0/0/0	Other red or infra-red laser film, unexposed, 610mm＜ width ≤800mm, 200m＜length≤1001m,
0/0/0		1.4元/平方米	1.6/1.6	0/0/0	0/11.4	0/0/0	0/0/	0/0/14.4	14.5/0			0/0/0	----Other
													--Of a width exceeding 610 mm and of a length not exceeding 200 m:
													---For preparing printing plates or cylinders:
0/0/0	0.4元/平方米	0.3元/平方米	0/0	0/0/0	0/7.1	0//0	0/0/	9.5/9.5/9.5	/9.5			0/0/0	----Laser phototypesetting film
0/0/0	0.7元/平方米	0.7元/平方米	0/0	0/0/0	0/7.1	0//0	0/0/	0/0/9	9.1/0			0/0/0	----Other
0/0/0		7.9元/平方米	2/2	0/0/0	0/14.3	0/0/0	0/0/	18/18/18	18.8/18			0/0/0	---Other
													--Of a width exceeding 105 mm but not exceeding 610 mm:
													---For preparing printing plates or cylinders:
0/0/0	0.4元/平方米	0.4元/平方米	0/0	0/0/0	0/7.1	0//0	0/0/	0/0/9	9.1/0			0/0/0	----Laser phototypesetting film
0/0/0	0.2元/平方米		0/0	0/0/0	0/7.1	0//0	0/0/	5/5/	/5			0/0/0	----Narrow anticorrosive photographic plate for printed circuit processing
0/0/0	0.6元/平方米	0.5元/平方米	0/0	0/0/0	0/7.1	0//0	0/0/	0/0/9	9.1/0			0/0/0	----Other
0/0/0		12.6元/平方米	2/2	0/0/0	0/14.3	0/0/0	0/0/	18/18/18	18.8/18			0/0/0	---Other
													-Other film, for colour photography (polychrome):
0/0/0				0/0/0	0/33.6	0/0/0	0/0/	5/5/	/5			0/0/0	--Of a width not exceeding 16 mm
0/0/0				0/0/0	0/33.6	0/0/0	0/0/	5/5/	/5			0/0/0	--Of a width exceeding 16 mm but not exceeding 35 mm and of a length not exceeding 30 m, for slides
													--Of a width exceeding 16 mm but not exceeding 35 mm and of a length not exceeding 30 m, other than for slides:
5/0/0		10.2元/平方米	1.8/1.8	0/0/0	0/12.9	0//0	0/0/	17.6/17.6/	/17.6			0/0/0	---Of a width 35 mm and of a length not exceeding 2 m
5/0/0		11.2元/平方米	1.8/1.8	0/0/0	0/12.9	0//0	0/0/					0/0/0	---Other
													--Of a width exceeding 16 mm but not exceeding 35 mm and of a length exceeding 30 m:
5/0/0				0/0/0	0/18.6	0//0	0/0/					0/0/0	---Cinematographic film
5/0/0				0//0	0/28.6	0//0	0/0/					0/0/	---Other
													--Of a width exceeding 35 mm:

税则号列	货品名称〔CIQ 扩展编码及品名—T2 表示见附表 2〕	最惠(%)	暂定税率	普通	增值/消费	出口退税	计量单位	监管条件/特殊证件	检验检疫	对美关税	亚太上/下
3702.5620	---电影胶片〔999〕	T3		T3	13/	13	千克/平方米	/1		T3	
3702.5690	---其他〔999〕	T3		T3	13/	13	千克/平方米	/1		T3	
	-其他：										
3702.9600	--宽度不超过 35 毫米，长度不超过 30 米〔999〕	T3		T3	13/	13	千克/平方米	/1		T3	
3702.9700	--宽度不超过 35 毫米，长度超过 30 米〔101 硝化纤维片基，999 其他未曝光的卷片，宽度不超过 35 毫米，长度超过 30 米〕	T3		T3	13/	13	千克/平方米	/1		T3	
3702.9800	--宽度超过 35 毫米〔999〕	T3		T3	13/	13	千克/平方米	/1			
37.03	**未曝光的摄影感光纸、纸板及纺织物：**										
	-成卷，宽度超过 610 毫米：										
3703.1010	---感光纸及纸板〔999〕	18		100	13/	13	千克	/1		23	14.4/14.4
3703.1090	---其他〔999〕	18		70	13/	13	千克	/1		23	14.4/14.4
	-其他，彩色摄影用：										
3703.2010	---感光纸及纸板〔999〕	35		100	13/	13	千克	/1		45	
3703.2090	---其他〔999〕	18		70	13/	13	千克	/1		23	
	-其他：										
3703.9010	---感光纸及纸板〔999〕	35		100	13/	13	千克	/1		45	
3703.9090	---其他〔999〕	18		70	13/	13	千克	/1		23	
37.04	**已曝光未冲洗的摄影硬片、软片、纸、纸板及纺织物：**										
3704.0010	---电影胶片										
3704.0010 10	含有人类遗传资源信息资料的电影胶片(已曝光但未冲洗)〔999〕	6.5		30	13/	13	千克	V/1		9	
3704.0010 20	录有广播电影电视节目的电影胶片(已曝光但未冲洗)〔999〕	6.5		30	13/	13	千克	b/1		9	
3704.0010 90	其他电影胶片(已曝光但未冲洗)〔999〕	6.5		30	13/	13	千克	/1		9	
3704.0090	---其他〔999〕										
3704.0090 10	含有人类遗传资源信息资料的其他已曝光未冲洗的摄影硬、软片(包括已曝光未冲洗的感光纸、纸板及纺织物)〔999〕	18		70	13/	13	千克	V/1		28	
3704.0090 90	其他已曝光未冲洗的摄影硬、软片(包括已曝光未冲洗的感光纸、纸板及纺织物)〔999〕	18		70	13/	13	千克	/1		28	
37.05	**已曝光已冲洗的摄影硬片及软片，但电影胶片除外：**										
3705.0010	---教学专用幻灯片										
3705.0010 10	含有人类遗传资源信息资料的教学专用幻灯片(已曝光已冲洗)〔999〕	0		0	13/	13	千克	V/1		5	
3705.0010 20	录有广播电影电视节目的教学专用幻灯片(已曝光已冲洗)〔999〕	0		0	13/	13	千克	b/1		5	
3705.0010 90	其他教学专用幻灯片(已曝光已冲洗)〔999〕	0		0	13/	13	千克	/1		5	
	---缩微胶片：										
3705.0021	----书籍、报刊的										
3705.0021 10	含有人类遗传资源信息资料的书籍、报刊用缩微胶片(已曝光已冲洗)〔999〕	0		0	13/	13	千克	V/1		5	
3705.0021 90	其他书籍、报刊用缩微胶片(已曝光已冲洗)〔999〕	0		0	13/	13	千克	/1		5	
3705.0029	----其他										
3705.0029 10	含有人类遗传资源信息资料的其他缩微胶片(已曝光已冲洗)〔999〕	0		14	13/	13	千克	V/1		2.5	
3705.0029 90	其他缩微胶片(已曝光已冲洗)〔999〕	0		14	13/	13	千克	/1		2.5	
3705.0090	---其他										
3705.0090 10	含有人类遗传资源信息资料的其他摄影硬、软片(已曝光已冲洗)(电影胶片除外)〔999〕	0		70	13/	13	千克	V/1		7.5	
3705.0090 90	其他摄影硬、软片(已曝光已冲洗)(电影胶片除外)〔999〕	0		70	13/	13	千克	/1		7.5	
37.06	**已曝光已冲洗的电影胶片，不论是否配有声道或仅有声道：**										
	-宽度在 35 毫米及以上：										
3706.1010	---教学专用										
3706.1010 10	录有广播电影电视节目的已冲洗的教学专用中宽电影胶片〔999〕	0		0	13/	13	千克/米	b/1		5	

协定税率 %								RCEP		特惠税率 %			Article Description
东/冰/格	巴基斯坦	韩国	瑞士上/下	哥/秘/柬	澳/毛	新西/坡/智	中国港/澳/台	东盟及马来/澳/韩	日/新	亚太2国	老/柬/缅	98/97/95	
0/0/0		7.8元/平方米	2.4/2.4	0/0/0	0/17.1	0/0/0	0/0/	22.8/22.8/22.8	/22.8			0/0/0	---Cinematographic film
0/0/0				0/0/0	0/28.6	0/0/0	0/0/	5/5/	/5			0/0/0	---Other
													-Other:
5/0/0		9.8元/平方米	2/2	0/0/0	0/14.3	0//0	0/0/					0/0/0	--Of a width not exceeding 35 mm and of a length not exceeding 30 mm
5/0/0		4.2元/平方米	1.8/1.8	0/0/0	0/12.9	0//0	0/0/					0/0/0	--Of a width not exceeding 35 mm and of a length exceeding 30 mm
0/0/0	8元/平方米	2元/平方米	1.8/1.8	0/0/0	0/12.9	0/0/0	0/0/	0/0/16.2	16.4/0			0/0/0	--Of a width exceeding 35 mm
													Photographic paper, paperboard and textiles, sensitized, unexposed:
													-In rolls of a width exceeding 610 mm:
5/0/0		8.4	1.8/1.8	0/0/0	0/12.9	0//0	0/0/	17.6/17.6/	/17.6			0/0/0	---Photographic paper and paperboard
5/0/0		8.4	1.8/1.8	0/0/0	0/12.9	0//0	0/0/					0/0/0	---Other
													-Other, for colour photography (polychrome):
5/0/0				0//0	0/25	0//0	0/0/					0/0/	---Photographic paper and paperboard
5/0/0		8.4	1.8/1.8	0/0/0	0/12.9	0//0	0/0/	17.6/17.6/	/17.6			0/0/0	---Other
													-Other:
5/0/0				0//0	0/25	0//0	0/0/					0/0/	---Photographic paper and paperboard
5/0/0		8.4	1.8/1.8	0/0/0	0/12.9	0//0	0/0/	17.6/17.6/	/17.6			0/0/0	---Other
													Photographic plates, film, paper, paperboard and textiles, exposed but not developed:
													---Cinematographic film
0/0/0	2	0	0/0	0/0/0	0/0	0//0	0/0/	0/0/0	5.9/0		//	0/0/0	Film Films Containing Information on Human Genetic Resources (Exposed but Not Developed)
0/0/0	2	0	0/0	0/0/0	0/0	0//0	0/0/	0/0/0	5.9/0		//	0/0/0	Film recording of radio, film and television programs (exposed but not developed)
0/0/0	2	0	0/0	0/0/0	0/0	0//0	0/0/	0/0/0	5.9/0		//	0/0/0	Other film (exposed but not developed)
													---Other
0/0/0	14.4	3.6	1.8/1.8	0/0/0	0/0	0/0/0	0/0/	0/0/16.2	16.4/0		//	0/0/0	Other exposed and unprocessed hard and soft films containing information on human genetic resources
0/0/0	14.4	3.6	1.8/1.8	0/0/0	0/0	0/0/0	0/0/	0/0/16.2	16.4/0		//	0/0/0	Other hard and soft photographic films that have been exposed and not developed
													Photographic plates and film, exposed and developed, other than cinematographic film:
													---Lantern slides, for education-al use only
0/0/0	0	0	0/0	0/0/0	0/0	0//0	0/0/	0/0/0	0/0			0/0/0	Teaching slides containing information on human genetic resources (exposed and developed)
0/0/0	0	0	0/0	0/0/0	0/0	0//0	0/0/	0/0/0	0/0		//	0/0/0	Special slides for teaching recording radio, film and television programs (exposed and developed)
0/0/0	0	0	0/0	0/0/0	0/0	0//0	0/0/	0/0/0	0/0		//	0/0/0	Other teaching slides (exposed and developed)
													---Microfilms:
													-----For printed books and news-papers
0/0/0	0	0	0/0	0/0/0	0/0	0//0	0/0/	0/0/0	0/0		//	0/0/0	Microfilm for books and newspapers containing information on human genetic resources (exposed and developed)
0/0/0	0	0	0/0	0/0/0	0/0	0//0	0/0/	0/0/0	0/0		//	0/0/0	Microfilm for other books and newspapers (exposed and developed)
													----Other
0/0/0	0	0	0/0	0/0/0	0/0	0//0	0/0/	0/0/0	0/0		//	0/0/0	Other microfilms containing information on human genetic resources (exposed and developed)
0/0/0	0	0	0/0	0/0/0	0/0	0//0	0/0/	0/0/0	0/0		//	0/0/0	Other microfilms (exposed and developed)
													---Other
0/0/0	14.4	3.6	0/0	0/0/0	0/0	0/0/0	0/0/	0/0/16.2	0/0		//	0/0/0	Other photographic hard and soft films containing information on human genetic resources (exposed and developed)
0/0/0	14.4	3.6	0/0	0/0/0	0/0	0/0/0	0/0/	0/0/16.2	0/0		//	0/0/0	Other Photographic Hard and Soft Films (Exposed and Developed)
													Cinematographic film, exposed and developed, whether or not incorporating sound track or consisting only of sound track:
													-Of a width of 35 mm or more:
													---For educational use only
0/0/0	0	0	0/0	0/0/0	0/0	0//0	0/0/	0/0/0	0/0		//	0/0/0	Developed medium—width film for teaching recording radio, film and television programs

税则号列	货品名称〔CIQ 扩展编码及品名—T2 表示见附表 2〕	最惠(%)	暂定税率	普通	增值/消费	出口退税	计量单位	监管条件/特殊证件	检验检疫	对美关税	亚太上/下
3706.1010 90	其他已冲洗的教学专用中宽电影胶片(中宽胶片指宽度≥35毫米,不论是否配有声道或仅有声道)〔999〕	0		0	13/	13	千克/米	/1		5	
3706.1090	---其他										
3706.1090 10	录有广播电影电视节目的已冲洗的其他中宽电影胶片〔999〕	5		14	13/	13	千克/米	b/1		10	
3706.1090 90	其他已冲洗的其他中宽电影胶片(中宽胶片指宽度≥35毫米,不论是否配有声道或仅有声道)〔999〕	5		14	13/	13	千克/米	/1		10	
	-其他:										
3706.9010	---教学专用										
3706.9010 10	录有广播电影电视节目的教学专用其他已冲洗的电影胶片〔999〕	0		0	13/	13	千克/米	b/1			
3706.9010 90	其他教学专用其他已冲洗的电影胶片(宽度＜35毫米)〔999〕	0		0	13/	13	千克/米	/1			
3706.9090	---其他										
3706.9090 10	录有广播电影电视节目的其他已冲洗的电影胶片〔999〕	4		14	13/	13	千克/米	b/1			
3706.9090 90	其他已冲洗的电影胶片(宽度＜35毫米)〔999〕	4		14	13/	13	千克/米	/1			
37.07	**摄影用化学制剂(不包括上光漆、胶水、黏合剂及类似制剂);摄影用未混合产品;定量包装或零售包装可立即使用的:**										
3707.1000	-感光乳液										
3707.1000 01	不含银的感光乳液剂〔301 危险化学品,易燃液体;302 其他化工产品〕	8	4	35	13/	13	千克	/13			
3707.1000 90	其他感光乳液〔301 危险化学品,易燃液体;302 其他化工产品〕	8		35	13/	13	千克	/13			
	-其他:										
3707.9010	---冲洗照相胶卷及相片用〔301 危险化学品,易燃液体;302 其他化工产品〕	4/2		100	13/	13	千克	/13		31.5	
3707.9020	---复印机用〔999〕	2.5/1.3		45	13/	13	千克	/1		25	
3707.9090	---其他〔301 危险化学品,易燃液体;302 其他化工产品〕	2/1		35	13/	13	千克	/13		24.5	

协定税率 %								RCEP		特惠税率 %			Article Description
东/冰/格	巴基斯坦	韩国	瑞士 上/下	哥/秘/柬	澳/毛	新西/坡/智	中国港/澳/台	东盟及马来/澳/韩	日/新	亚太2国	老/柬/缅	98/97/95	
0/0/0	0	0	0/0	0/0/0	0/0	0//0	0/0/	0/0/0	0/0		//	0/0/0	Other Developed Medium－Width Films for Teaching
													---Other
0/0/0	0	2.3	0/0	0/0/0	0/0	0//0	0/0/	4.5/4.5/4.5	4.7/4.5		//	0/0/0	Other medium－width film developed for recording radio, film and television programs
0/0/0	0	2.3	0/0	0/0/0	0/0	0//0	0/0/	4.5/4.5/4.5	4.7/4.5		//	0/0/0	Other developed medium－width film
													-Other:
													---For educational use only
0/0/0	0	0	0/0	0/0/0	0/0	0//0	0/0/	0/0/0	0/0		//	0/0/0	Other Developed Films for Teaching of Radio, Film and Television Programs
0/0/0	0	0	0/0	0/0/0	0/0	0//0	0/0/	0/0/0	0/0		//	0/0/0	Other films developed for other teaching purposes
													---Other
0/0/0	0	0	0/0	0/0/0	0/0	0//0	0/0/	0/0/0	0/0		//	0/0/0	Other Developed Films Recording Radio, Film and Television Programs
0/0/0	0	0	0/0	0/0/0	0/0	0//0	0/0/	0/0/0	0/0		//	0/0/0	Other Developed Films
													Chemical preparations for photographic uses (other than varnishes, glues, adhesives and similar preparations); unmixed products for photographic uses, put up in measured portions or put up for retail sale in a form ready for use:
													-Sensitizing emulsions
0/0/0	2	3.7	0.8/0.8	0/0/0	0/0	0//0	0/0/	7.2/7.2/7.2	7.5/7.2			0/0/0	Sensitizing emulsions agent, not containing silver
0/0/0	2	3.7	0.8/0.8	0/0/0	0/0	0//0	0/0/	7.2/7.2/7.2	7.5/7.2			0/0/0	Other sensitizing emulsions
													-Other:
0/0/0	12.8	7.4	1.6/1.6	0/0/0	0/0	0/0/0	0/0/	0/0/14.4	14.5/0			0/0/0	---For use in developing photographic film and photographs
0/0/0	3.5	2	0/0	0/0/0	0/0	0/0/0	0/0/	0/0/9	9.1/0			0/0/0	---For use in photo-copying apparatus
0/0/0	2	1.6	0.8/0.8	0/0/0	0/0	0//0	0/0/	0/0/7.2	7.3/0			0/0/0	---Other

第三十八章
杂项化学产品

注释：

一、本章不包括：

(一)单独的已有化学定义的元素及化合物，但下列各项除外：

1. 人造石墨(税目 38.01)；

2. 制成税目 38.08 所述的形状或包装的杀虫剂、杀鼠剂、杀菌剂、除草剂、抗萌剂、植物生长调节剂、消毒剂及类似产品；

3. 灭火器的装配药及已装药的灭火弹(税目 38.13)；

4. 下列注释二所规定的有证标准样品；

5. 下列注释三(一)及三(三)所规定的产品。

(二)化学品与食品或其他营养物质的混合物，配制食品用的(一般归入税目 21.06)。

(三)税目 24.04 的产品；

(四)含有金属，砷及其混合物，并符合第二十六章注释三(一)或三(二)的规定的矿渣、矿灰及残渣(包括淤渣，但下水道淤泥除外)(税目 26.20)；

(五)药品(税目 30.03 及 30.04)。

(六)用于提取贱金属或生产贱金属化合物的废催化剂(税目 26.20)，主要用于回收贵金属的废催化剂(税目 71.12)，或某种形状(例如，精细粉末或纱网状)的金属或金属合金催化剂(第十四类或第十五类)。

二、(一)税目 38.22 所称的“有证标准样品”，是指附有证书的参照物，该证书标明了参照物属性的指标、确定这些指标的方法以及与每一指标相关的确定度，这些参照物适用于分析、校准和比较。

(二)除第二十八章和二十九章的产品外，有证标准样品在本目录中应优先归入税目 38.22。

三、税目 38.24 包括不归入本协调制度其他品目的下列货品：

(一)每颗重量不小于 2.5 克的氧化镁、碱金属或碱土金属卤化物制成的培养晶体 (光学元件除外)；

(二)杂醇油；骨焦油；

(三)零售包装的除墨剂；

(四)零售包装的蜡纸改正液、其他改正液及改正带(税目 96.12 的产品除外)；

(五)可熔性陶瓷测温器(例如，塞格测温锥)。

四、本目录所称“城市垃圾”，是指一种从家庭、宾馆、餐馆、医院、商店、办公室等收集来的废物、马路和人行道的垃圾以及建筑垃圾或拆建垃圾。城市垃圾通常含有大量各种各样的材料，例如，塑料、橡胶、木材、纸张、纺织品、玻璃、金属、食物、破碎家具和其他已损坏或被丢弃的物品，但“城市垃圾”不包括：

(一)已从垃圾中分拣出来的单独的材料或物品 ，例如，废的塑料、橡胶 、木材、纸张、纺织品、玻璃、金属和电子电气废弃物及碎料 (包括废电池)，这些材料或物品应归入本目录中适当税目；

(二)工业废物；

(三)在第三十章注释四(十)所规定的废药物；

(四)本章注释六(一)所规定的医疗废物。

五、税目 38.25 所称“下水道淤泥”，是指城市污水处理厂处理的淤泥，包括预处理的废物、刷洗污垢和性质不稳定的淤泥。但适合作为肥料用的性质稳定的淤泥除外(第三十一章)。

六、税目 38.25 所称“其他废物”适用于：

(一)医疗废物，即医学研究、诊断、治疗以及其他内科、外科、牙科或兽医治疗所产生的被污染的废物，通常含有病菌和药物，需作专门处理(例如，脏的敷料、用过的手套及注射器)；

(二)废有机溶剂；

(三)废的金属酸洗液、液压油、制动油及防冻液；

(四)化学工业及相关工业的其他废物。

但不包括主要含有石油及从沥青矿物提取的油类的废油(税目 27.10)。

七、税目 38.26 所称的“生物柴油”是指从动植物或微生物油脂(不论是否使用过)得到的用作燃料的脂肪酸单烷基酯。

子目注释：

一、子目 3808.52 及 3808.59 仅包括税目 38.08 的货品，含有一种或多种下列物质：甲草胺(ISO)、涕灭威(ISO)、艾氏剂(ISO)谷硫磷(ISO)、乐杀螨(ISO)、毒杀芬(ISO)、敌菌丹(ISO)、克百威 (ISO)、氯丹(ISO)、杀虫脒(ISO)、乙酯杀螨醇(ISO)、滴滴涕 (ISO,INN)〔1,1,1－三氯－2,2－双(4－氯苯基)乙烷〕、狄氏剂(ISO, INN)、4,6－二硝基邻甲酚〔二硝酚(ISO)〕及其盐、地乐酚(ISO)及 其盐或酯、硫丹(ISO)、1,2－二溴乙烷(ISO)、1,2－二氯乙烷(ISO)、氟乙酰胺(ISO)、七氯(ISO)、六氯苯 (ISO)、1,2,3,4,5,6－六氯环己烷〔六六六(ISO)〕，包括林丹 (ISO,INN)、汞化合物、甲胺磷(ISO)、久效磷(ISO)、环氧乙烷 (氧化乙烯)、对硫磷(ISO)、甲基对硫磷(ISO)、五氯苯酚(ISO) 及其盐或酯、全氟辛基磺酸及其盐、全氟辛基磺胺、全氟辛基磺酰氯、磷胺(ISO)、2,4,5－涕(ISO)(2,4,5－三氯苯氧基乙酸)及其盐或酯、三丁基锡化合物、敌百虫(ISO)。

二、子目 3808.61 及 3808.69 仅包括品目 38.08 项下含有下列物质的货品：α-氯氰菊酯(ISO)、恶虫威(ISO)、联苯菊酯(ISO)、虫螨腈(ISO)、氟氯氰菊酯(ISO)、溴氰菊酯(INN,ISO)、醚菊酯(INN)、杀螟硫磷(ISO)、高效氯氟氰菊酯(ISO)、马拉硫磷(ISO)、甲基嘧啶磷(ISO)、残杀威(ISO)。

Chapter 38
Miscellaneous chemical products

Notes:

1. This Chapter does not cover:
   (a) Separate chemically defined elements or compounds with the exception of the following:
   (i) Artificial graphite (heading No. 38. 01);
   (ii) Insecticides, rodenticides, fungicides, herbicides, anti-sprouting products and plant-growth regulators, disinfectants and similar products, put up as described in heading No. 38. 08;
   (iii) Products put up as charges for fire-extinguishers or put up in fire-extinguishing grenades (heading No. 38. 13);
   (iv) Certified reference materials specified in Note 2 below;
   (v) Products specified in Note 3(a) or 3(c) below.
   (b) Mixtures of chemicals with foodstuffs or other substances with nutritive value, of a kind used in the preparations of human foodstuffs (generally heading No. 21. 06).
   (c) Products of heading 24.04;
   (d) Slag, ash and residues (including sludges, other than sewage sludge), containing metals, arsenic or their mixtures and meeting the requirements of Note 3(a) or (b) to Chapter 26 (heading No. 26. 20).
   (e) Medicaments (heading No. 30. 03 or 30. 04). or
   (f) Spent catalysts of a kind used for the extraction of base metals or for the manufacture of chemical compounds of base metals (heading No. 26. 20), spent catalysts of a kind used principally for the recovery of precious metal (heading No. 71. 12) or catalysts consisting of metals or metal alloys in the form of, for example, finely divided powder or woven gauze (Section XIV or XV).
2. (a) For the purpose of heading No. 38. 22, the expression "certified reference materials" means reference materials which are accompanied by a certificate which indicates the values of the certified properties, the methods used to detemine these values and the degree of certainty associated with each value and which are suitable for analytical, calibrating or referencing purposes.
   (b) With the exception of the products of Chapter 28 or 29, for the classification of certified reference materials, heading No. 38. 22 shall take precedence over any other heading in the Nomenclature.
3. Heading No. 38. 24 includes the following goods which are not to be classified in any other heading of the Nomenclature:
   (a) Cultured crystals (other than optical elements) weighing not less than 2. 5 g each, of magnesium oxide or of the halides of the alkali or alkaline-earth metals;
   (b) Fusel oil; Dippel's oil;
   (c) Ink removers put up in packings for retail sale;
   (d) Stencil correctors, other correcting fluids and correction tape, put up in packings for retail sale (other than those of heading, 96. 12);
   (e) Ceramic firing testers, fusible (for example, Seger cones).
4. Throughout the Nomenclature, "municipal waste" means waste of a kind collected from households, hotels, restaurants, hospitals, shops, offices, etc. , road and pavement sweepings, as well as construction and demolition waste. Municipal waste generally contains a large variety of materials such as plastics, rubber, wood, paper, textiles, glass, metals, food materials, broken furniture and other damaged or discarded articles. The term "municipal waste", however, does not cover:
   (a) Individual materials or articles segregated from the waste, for example wastes of plastics, rubber, wood, paper, textiles, glass or metals, electrical and electronic waste and scrap (including spent batteries) which fall in their appropriate headings of the Nomenclature;
   (b) Industrial waste;
   (c) Waste pharmaceuticals, as defined in Note 4(k) to Chapter 30; or
   (d) Clinical waste, as defined in Note 6 (a) below.
5. For the purposes of heading 38. 25, "sewage sludge" means sludge arising from urban effluent treatment plant and includes pretreatment waste, scourings and unstabilised sludge. Stabilised sludge when suitable for use as fertiliser is excluded (Chapter 31).
6. For the purposes of heading No. 38. 25, the expression "other wastes" applies to:
   (a) Clinical waste, that is, contaminated waste arising from medical research, diagnosis, treatment or other medical, surgical, dental or veterinary procedures, which often contain pathogens and pharmaceutical substances and require special disposal procedures (for example, soiled dressings, used gloves and used syringes);
   (b) Waste organic solvents;
   (c) Wastes of metal pickling liquors, hydraulic fluids, brake fluids and anti-freezing fluids; and
   (d) Other wastes from chemical or allied industries.
   The expression "other wastes" does not, however, cover wastes which contain mainly petroleum oils or oils obtained from bituminous minerals (heading No. 27. 10).
7. For the purposes of heading 38. 26, the term "biodiesel" means mono-alkyl esters of fatty acids of a kind used as a fuel, derived from animal, vegetable or microbial fats and oils whether or not used.

Subheading Note:

1. - Subheadings No. 3808.52 and 3808.59 cover only goods of heading 38.08, containing one or more of the following substances : alachlor (ISO); aldicarb (ISO); aldrin (ISO); azinphos—methyl (ISO); binapacryl (ISO); camphechlor (ISO) (toxaphene); captafol (ISO); carbofuran (ISO); chlordane (ISO); chlordimeform (ISO); chlorobenzilate (ISO); DDT (ISO) (clofenotane (INN), 1,1,1—trichloro—2,2—bis(p—chlorophenyl)ethane); dieldrin (ISO, INN); 4,6—dinitro—o—cresol (DNOC (ISO)) or its salts; dinoseb (ISO), its salts or its esters; endosulfan (ISO); ethylene dibromide (ISO) (1,2— dibromoethane); ethylene dichloride (ISO) (1,2—dichloroethane); fluoroacetamide (ISO); heptachlor (ISO); hexachlorobenzene (ISO); 1,2,3,4,5,6—hexachlorocyclohexane (HCH (ISO)), including lindane (ISO, INN); mercury compounds; methamidophos (ISO); monocrotophos (ISO); oxirane (ethylene oxide); parathion (ISO); parathion—methyl (ISO) (methyl— parathion); pentachlorophenol (ISO), its salts or its esters; perfluorooctane sulphonic acid and its salts; perfluorooctane sulphonamides; perfluorooctane sulphonyl fluoride; phosphamidon (ISO); 2,4,5—T (ISO) (2,4,5—trichlorophenoxyacetic acid), its salts or its esters; tributyltin compounds; trichlorfon (ISO).
2. The following Subheading No.3808.61 and Subheading No.3808.69 only containing Heading No.38.08 under the goods: α-alpha cypermethrin (ISO), ficam (ISO), bifenthrin (ISO), chlorfenapyr (ISO), cyhalothrin, permethrin bromine (ISO) (INN, ISO), ethofenprox (INN), fenitrothion (ISO), lambda cyhalothrin (ISO), malathion (ISO) and pirimiphos methyl (ISO), or propoxur (ISO).

三、子目 3824.81 至 3824.89 仅包括含有下列一种或多种物质的混合物及制品：环氧乙烷（氧化乙烯）、多溴联苯（PBBs）、多氯联苯（PCBs）、多氯三联苯（PCTs）、三（2,3－二溴丙基）磷酸酯、艾氏剂（ISO）、毒杀芬（ISO）、氯丹（ISO）、十氯酮（ISO）、滴滴涕（ISO,INN）〔1,1,1－三氯－2,2－双（4－氯苯基）乙烷〕、狄氏剂（ISO,INN）、硫丹（ISO）、异狄氏剂（ISO）、七氯（ISO）、灭蚁灵（ISO）、1,2,3,4,5,6－六氯环己烷〔六六六（ISO）〕，包括林丹（ISO,INN）、五氯苯（ISO）、六氯苯（ISO）、全氟辛基磺酸及其盐、全氟辛基磺胺、全氟辛基磺酰氯，四、五、六、七或八溴联苯醚、短链氯化石蜡。短链氯化石蜡是指分子式为 CxH(2x－y＋2)Cly（其中 x＝10－13，y＝1－13），按重量计氯含量大于 48%的化合物的混合物。

四、子目 3825.41 和 3825.49 所称“废有机溶剂”，是指主要含有有机溶剂的废物，不适合再作原产品使用，不论其是否用于回收溶剂。

税则号列	货品名称〔CIQ 扩展编码及品名－T2 表示见附表 2〕	最惠(%)	暂定税率	普通	增值/消费	出口退税	计量单位	监管条件/特殊证件	检验检疫	对美关税	亚太上/下
38.01	**人造石墨；胶态或半胶态石墨；以石墨或其他碳为基本成分的糊状、块状、板状制品或半制品：**										
3801.1000	-人造石墨										
3801.1000 10	核级石墨（纯度高于百万分之五硼当量，密度大于 1.50g/cm^3）〔999〕	6.5	3	30	13/	0	千克	3/1		13	
3801.1000 20	人造细晶粒整体石墨（20℃下的密度、拉伸断裂应变、热膨胀系数符合特殊要求）〔999〕	6.5	3	30	13/	0	千克	3/1		13	
3801.1000 90	其他人造石墨〔999〕	6.5	3	30	13/	0	千克	3/1		13	
3801.2000	-胶态或半胶态石墨〔104〕	6.5		30	13/	0	千克	/1		11.5	
3801.3000	-电极用碳糊及炉衬用的类似糊〔999〕	6.5		35	13/	0	千克	/1		16.5	
	-其他：										
3801.9010	---表面处理的球化石墨〔999〕	6.5		35	13/	13	千克	3/1		31.5	
3801.9090	---其他〔999〕	6.5		35	13/	0	千克	3/1		16.5	
38.02	**活性碳；活性天然矿产品；动物炭黑，包括废动物炭黑：**										
	-活性碳：										
3802.1010	---木质的〔101〕	6.5		20	13/	0	千克	G/1		14	4.2/4.2
3802.1090	---其他〔999〕	6.5		20	13/	0	千克	G/1		29	4.2/4.2
3802.9000	-其他										
3802.9000 10	濒危动物炭黑（包括废动物炭黑）〔999〕	10		45	13/	0	千克	FE/1		15	
3802.9000 90	活性天然矿产品；其他动物炭黑（包括废动物炭黑）〔102〕	10		45	13/	0	千克	/1		15	
38.03	**妥尔油，不论是否精炼：**										
3803.0000	妥尔油，不论是否精炼〔999〕	6.5		35	13/	0	千克	/1			
38.04	**木浆残余碱液，不论是否浓缩、脱糖或经化学处理，包括木素磺酸盐，但不包括税目 38.03 的妥尔油：**										
3804.0000	木浆残余碱液，不论是否浓缩、脱糖或经化学处理，包括木素磺酸盐，但不包括税目 38.03 的妥尔油										
3804.0000 10	未经浓缩、脱糖或经过化学处理的木浆残余碱液（妥尔油除外）〔999〕	6.5		35	13/	0	千克	9/1		16.5	
3804.0000 90	经浓缩、脱糖或经过化学处理的木浆残余碱液，包括木素磺酸盐（妥尔油除外）〔999〕	6.5		35	13/	0	千克	/1		16.5	
38.05	**脂松节油、木松节油和硫酸盐松节油及其他萜烯油，用蒸馏或其他方法从针叶木制得；粗制二聚戊烯；亚硫酸盐松节油及其他粗制对异丙基苯甲烷；以α萜品醇为基本成分的松油：**										
3805.1000	-脂松节油、木松节油和硫酸盐松节油〔301 危险化学品，易燃液体；302 其他化工产品〕	6.5		50	13/	0	千克	AB/13	MN	31.5	
	-其他：										
3805.9010	---松油〔301 危险化学品，易燃液体；302 其他化工产品〕	6.5		50	13/	0	千克	AB/13	MN	31.5	
3805.9090	---其他〔301：易燃液体 ；302：其他化工产品〕	6.5		50	13/	0	千克	/1		31.5	
38.06	**松香和树脂酸及其衍生物；松香精及松香油；再熔胶：**										
	-松香及树脂酸：										
3806.1010	---松香〔301 危险化学品，易燃固体；302 其他化工产品〕	10		70	13/	0	千克	/13		35	
3806.1020	---树脂酸〔999〕	10		70	13/	0	千克	/1			
	-松香盐、树脂酸盐及松香或树脂酸衍生物的盐，但松香加合物的盐除外：										
3806.2010	---松香盐及树脂酸盐〔301 危险化学品，易燃固体；302 其他化工产品〕	6.5		40	13/	13	千克	/13		11.5	
3806.2090	---其他〔999〕	6.5		40	13/	13	千克	/1		11.5	
3806.3000	-酯胶〔301 其他危险化学品；302 无检疫要求的食品添加剂；303 属于危险化学品的食品添加剂；304 需申报仅用于工业用途不用于食品添加剂无检疫要求的化学品〕	6.5		50	13/	0	千克	AB/1	PRQS	11.5	

3.- Subheadings No. 3824.81 to 3824.89 cover only mixtures and preparations containing one or more of the following substances : oxirane (ethylene oxide); polybrominated biphenyls (PBBs); polychlorinated biphenyls (PCBs); polychlorinated terphenyls (PCTs); tris(2,3-dibromopropyl) phosphate; aldrin (ISO); camphechlor (ISO) (toxaphene); chlordane (ISO); chlordecone (ISO); DDT (ISO) (clofenotane (INN); 1,1,1-trichloro-2,2- bis(p-chlorophenyl)ethane); dieldrin (ISO, INN); endosulfan (ISO); endrin (ISO); heptachlor (ISO); mirex (ISO); 1,2,3,4,5,6-hexachlorocyclohexane (HCH (ISO)), including lindane (ISO, INN); pentachlorobenzene (ISO); hexachlorobenzene (ISO); perfluorooctane sulphonic acid, its salts; perfluorooctane sulphonamides; perfluorooctane sulphonyl fluoride; tetra-, penta-, hexa-, hepta- or octabromodiphenyl ethers; short-chain chlorinated paraffins. Short-chain chlorinated paraffins are mixtures of compounds, with a chlorination degree of more than 48 % by weight, with the following molecular formula : CxH(2x-y+2)Cly, where x=10 - 13 and y= 1-13.

4. For the purposes of subheadings No. 3825. 41 and 3825. 49, "waste organic solvents" are wastes containing mainly organic solvents, not fit for further use as presented as primary products, whether or not intended for recovery of the solvents.

协定税率 %								RCEP		特惠税率 %			Article Description
东/冰/格	巴基斯坦	韩国	瑞士 上/下	哥/秘/柬	澳/毛	新西/坡/智	中国港/澳/台	东盟及马来/澳/韩	日/新	亚太2国	老/柬/缅	98/97/95	
													Artificial graphite; colloidal or semi-colloidal graphite; preparations based on graphite or other carbon in the form of pastes, blocks, plates or other semi-manufactures:
													-Artificial graphite
0/0/0	0	1.3	0.7/0.7	0/0/0	0/0	0//0	0/0/	0/0/5.9	5.9/0			0/0/0	Nuclear graphite (purity>5/million boron equivalent, density>1. 50g/cm³)
0/0/0	0	1.3	0.7/0.7	0/0/0	0/0	0//0	0/0/	0/0/5.9	5.9/0			0/0/0	Artificial fine-grainedgraphite (density, temsile fracture strain, coefficient of thermal expansion in line with specific requirements at 20℃ or below)
0/0/0	0	1.3	0.7/0.7	0/0/0	0/0	0//0	0/0/	0/0/5.9	5.9/0			0/0/0	Other artificial graphite
0/0/0	2	3	0/0	0/0/0	0/0	0//0	0/0/	5.9/5.9/5.9	6.1/5.9			0/0/0	-Colloidal or semi-colloidal graphite
0/0/0	2	0	0.7/0.7	0/0/0	0/0	0//0	0/0/	0/0/0	5.9/0			0/0/0	-Carbonaceous pastes for electrodes and similar pastes for furnace linings
													-Other:
0/0/0	2	0	0/0	0/0/0	0/0	0//0	0/0/	0/0/0	5.9/0			0/0/0	---Surface modified of spherical graphite
0/0/0	0	0	0/0	0/0/0	0/0	0//0	0/0/	5.9/5.9/5.9	5.9/5.9			0/0/0	---Other
													Activated carbon; activated natural mineral products; animal black, including spent animal black:
													-Activated carbon:
0/0/0	2	0	0/0	0/0/0	0/0	0//0	0/0/	0/0/0	5.9/0			0/0/0	---Of wood
0/0/0	2	0	0/0	0/0/0	0/0	0//0	0/0/	5.9/5.9/5.9	5.9/5.9			0/0/0	---Other
													-Other
0/0/0	3.5	2	0/0	0/0/0	0/0	0/0/0	0/0/	0/0/9	9.1/0			0/0/0	Endangered animals black(including spent animal black)
0/0/0	3.5	2	0/0	0/0/0	0/0	0/0/0	0/0/	0/0/9	9.1/0			0/0/0	Activated natural mineral products; other animal black(including spent animal black)
													Tall oil, whether or not refined:
0/0/0	2	0	0/0	0/0/0	0/0	0//0	0/0/	0/0/0	5.9/0			0/0/0	Tall oil, whether or not refined
													Residual lyes from the manufacture of wood pulp, whether or not concentrated, desugared or chemically treated, including lignin sulphonates, but excluding tall oil of heading No. 38. 03:
													Residual lyes from the manufacture of wood pulp, whether or not concentrated, desugared or chemically treated, including lignin sulphonates, but excluding tall oil of heading No. 38. 03
0/0/0	2	1.3	0/0	0/0/0	0/0	0//0	0/0/	0/0/5.9	5.9/0			0/0/0	Residual lyes from the manufactare of wood pulp, non-concentrated, non-desugared or non-chemically treated(exincluding tall oil)
0/0/0	2	1.3	0/0	0/0/0	0/0	0//0	0/0/	0/0/5.9	5.9/0			0/0/0	Residual lyes from the manufacture of wood pulp, concentrated, desugared or chemically treated, including lignin Sulp-honates (excluding tall oil)
													Gum, wood or sulphate turpentine and other terpenic oils produced by the distillation or other treatment of coniferous woods; crude dipentene; sulphite turpentine and other crude paracymene; pine oil containing alpha-terpineol as the main constituent:
0/0/0	2	0	0/0	0/0/0	0/0	0//0	0/0/	0/0/0	5.9/0			0/0/0	-Gum, wood or sulphate turpentine oils
													-Other:
0/0/0	2	0	0/0	0/0/0	0/0	0//0	0/0/	0/0/0	5.9/0			0/0/0	---Pine oil
0/0/0	2	0	0/0	0/0/0	0/0	0//0	0/0/	0/0/0	5.9/0			0/0/0	---Other
													Rosin and resin acids, and derivatives thereof; rosin spirit and rosin oils; run gums:
													-Rosin and resin acids:
0/0/0	3.5	2	0/0	0/0/0	0/0	0/0/0	0/0/	9/9/9	9.1/9			0/0/0	---Rosin
0/0/0	3.5	2	0/0	0/0/0	0/0	0//0	0/0/	0/0/9	9.1/0			0/0/0	---Resin acides
													-Salts of rosin, of resin acids or of derivatives of rosin or resin acids, other than salts of rosin adducts:
0/0/0	2	0	0/0	0/0/0	0/0	0//0	0/0/	0/0/0	5.9/0			0/0/0	---Salts of rosin, of resin acids
0/0/0	2	0	0/0	0/0/0	0/0	0//0	0/0/	0/0/0	5.9/0			0/0/0	---Other
0/0/0	2	0	0/0	0/0/0	0/0	0//0	0/0/	0/0/0	5.9/0			0/0/0	-Ester gums

税则号列	货品名称〔CIQ 扩展编码及品名—T2 表示见附表 2〕	最惠(%)	暂定税率	普通	增值/消费	出口退税	计量单位	监管条件/特殊证件	检验检疫	对美关税	亚太上/下
3806.9000	-其他〔301 危险化学品，易燃液体；302 其他化工产品〕	6.5		40	13/	0	千克	/13		16.5	
38.07	**木焦油；精制木焦油；木杂酚油；粗木精；植物沥青；以松香、树脂酸或植物沥青为基本成分的啤酒桶沥青及类似制品：**										
3807.0000	木焦油；精制木焦油；木杂酚油；粗木精；植物沥青；以松香、树脂酸或植物沥青为基本成分的啤酒桶沥青及类似制品〔301 危险化学品，腐蚀性物质；302 其他危险化学品；303 其他化工品〕	6.5		35	13/	0	千克	/13		11.5	
38.08	**杀虫剂、杀鼠剂、杀菌剂、除草剂、抗萌剂、植物生长调节剂、消毒剂及类似产品，零售形状、零售包装或制成制剂及成品(例如，经硫磺处理的带子、杀虫灯芯、蜡烛及捕蝇纸)：**										
	-本章子目注释一所列货品：										
3808.5200	--DDT(ISO)[滴滴涕(INN)]，每包净重不超过 300 克〔999〕	9		35	9/	9,13	千克	89/13			
	--其他：										
3808.5920	---零售包装的										
3808.5920 30	零售包装含艾氏剂、毒杀芬、氯丹、滴滴涕、狄氏剂、硫丹、七氯、六氯苯、α—六氯环己烷、β—六氯环己烷或林丹的货品〔999〕	9		37	9/	9,13	千克	89/1		14	
3808.5920 40	零售包装的含有克百威或敌百虫的含汞杀虫剂〔999〕	9		37	9/	9,13	千克	89/1		14	
3808.5920 50	零售包装的含有克百威或敌百虫，但不含其他第 38 章子目注释一所列物质的杀虫剂成药〔999〕	9		37	9/	9,13	千克	AS/1	M	14	
3808.5920 60	其他零售包装含一种第 38 章子目注释一所列物质的货品〔999〕	9		37	9/	9,13	千克	S/1		14	
3808.5920 90	其他零售包装含多种第 38 章子目注释一所列物质的货品〔999〕	9		37	9/	9,13	千克	/1		14	
3808.5990	---其他										
3808.5990 30	非零售包装含艾氏剂、毒杀芬、氯丹、滴滴涕、狄氏剂、硫丹、七氯、六氯苯、α—六氯环己烷、β—六氯环己烷或林丹的货品〔999〕	6.5		15	9/	9,13	千克	89/1			
3808.5990 40	非零售包装的含有克百威或敌百虫的含汞杀虫剂〔999〕	6.5		15	9/	9	千克	89/1			
3808.5990 50	非零售包装的含有克百威或敌百虫，但不含其他第 38 章子目注释一所列物质的杀虫剂成药〔999〕	6.5		15	9/	9	千克	AS/1	M		
3808.5990 60	其他非零售包装含一种第 38 章子目注释一所列物质的货品〔999〕	6.5		15	9/	9,13	千克	AS/1	M		
3808.5990 90	其他非零售包装含多种第 38 章子目注释一所列物质的货品〔999〕	6.5		15	9/	9,13	千克	/1			
	-本章子目注释二所列货品：										
3808.6100	--每包净重不超过 300 克〔301 其他危险化学品，302 其他化工产品〕	10		35	9/	9,13	千克	AS/1	M		6.5/6.5
3808.6200	--每包净重超过 300 克，但不超过 7.5 千克〔301:其他危险化学品；999:其他化工产品〕	10		35	9/	9,13	千克	AS/1	M		6.5/6.5
3808.6900	--其他〔301:其他危险化学品；999:其他化工产品〕	6		11	9/	9	千克	AS/1	M	31	3.9/3.9
	-其他：										
	--杀虫剂：										
	---零售包装：										
3808.9111	----蚊香〔301 其他危险化学品，302 其他化工产品〕	10		80	13/	9,13	千克	AS/1	M		0/0
3808.9112	----生物杀虫剂										
3808.9112 10	零售包装的含汞生物杀虫剂〔301 其他危险化学品，302 其他化工产品〕	10		35	9/	9,13	千克	89/1			6.5/6.5
3808.9112 90	零售包装的其他生物杀虫剂〔301 其他危险化学品，302 其他化工产品〕	10		35	9/	9,13	千克	AS/1	M		6.5/6.5
3808.9119	----其他										
3808.9119 10	零售包装的含有灭蚁灵或十氯酮的杀虫剂〔301 其他危险化学品，302 其他化工产品，303 毒性气体〕	10		35	9/	9,13	千克	89/13		35	6.5/6.5
3808.9119 20	零售包装的其他含汞杀虫剂〔301 其他危险化学品，302 其他化工产品，303 毒性气体〕	10		35	9/	9,13	千克	89/13		35	6.5/6.5
3808.9119 90	其他零售包装的杀虫剂成药〔301 危险化学品，气体，302 危险化学品，易燃液体，303 其他化工产品〕	10		35	9/	9,13	千克	AS/13	M	35	6.5/6.5
3808.9190	---其他										
3808.9190 10	非零售包装的含有灭蚁灵或十氯酮的杀虫剂〔301 其他危险化学品，302 其他化工产品〕	6		11	9/	9	千克	89/13		11	3.9/3.9
3808.9190 20	非零售包装的含汞杀虫剂〔301 其他危险化学品，302 其他化工产品〕	6		11	9/	9	千克	89/13		11	3.9/3.9
3808.9190 30	多杀霉素，乙基多杀菌素〔999〕	6		11	9/	9	千克	AS/13	M	11	3.9/3.9
3808.9190 90	其他非零售包装杀虫剂成药〔301 危险化学品，气体；302 其他化工产品〕	6		11	9/	9	千克	AS/13	M	11	3.9/3.9
	--杀菌剂：										

协定税率 %								RCEP		特惠税率 %			Article Description
东/冰/格	巴基斯坦	韩国	瑞士 上/下	哥/秘/柬	澳/毛	新西/坡/智	中国港/澳/台	东盟及马来/澳/韩	日/新	亚太2国	老/柬/缅	98/97/95	
0/0/0	2	0	0/0	0/0/0	0/0	0//0	0/0/	0/0/0	5.9/0			0/0/0	-Other
													Wood tar; wood tar oils; wood creosote; wood naphtha; vegetable pitch; brewers pitch and similar preparations based on rosin, resin acids or on vegetable pitch:
0/0/0	2	0	0/0	0/0/0	0/0	0//0	0/0/	0/0/0	5.9/0			0/0/0	Wood tar; wood tar oils; wood creosote; wood naphtha; vegetable pitch; brewers' pitch and similar preparations based on rosin, resin acids or on vegetable pitch
													Insecticides, rodenticides, fungicides, herbicides, anti-sprouting products and plantgrowth regulators, disinfectants and similar products, put up in forms or packings for retail sale or as preparations or articles (for example, sulphur-treated bands, wicks and candles, and fly-papers):
													-Goods specified in Subheading Note 1 to this Chapter:
0/0/0	2	0	0/0	0/0/0	0/0	0//0	0/0/	0/0/0	8.2/0			0/0/0	--DDT (ISO) (clofenotane (INN)), in packings of a net weight content not exceeding 300 g
													--Other:
													---Put up for retail sale
0/0/0	2.3	0.4	0.2/0.2	0/0/0	0/0	0//0	0/0/	0/0/0	8.2/0			0/0/0	Retail packaging contains aldrin, toxaphene, chlordane, DDT, dieldrin, endosulfan, heptachlor, hexachlorobenzene α — Hexachlorocyclohexane β— Goods of hexachlorocyclohexane or lindane
0/0/0	2.3	0.4	0.2/0.2	0/0/0	0/0	0//0	0/0/	0/0/0	8.2/0			0/0/0	Mercury containing pesticides containing carbofuran or trichlorfon in retail packaging
0/0/0	2.3	0.4	0.2/0.2	0/0/0	0/0	0//0	0/0/	0/0/0	8.2/0			0/0/0	Pesticide patent medicines containing carbofuran or trichlorfon but not other substances listed in note 1 of subheading of chapter 38 in retail packaging
0/0/0	2.3	0.4	0.2/0.2	0/0/0	0/0	0//0	0/0/	0/0/0	8.2/0			0/0/0	Other goods in retail packaging containing a substance listed in note 1 to subheading of chapter 38
0/0/0	2.3	0.4	0.2/0.2	0/0/0	0/0	0//0	0/0/	0/0/0	8.2/0			0/0/0	Other goods in retail packaging containing more than one substance listed in note 1 to subheading of chapter 38
													---Other
0/0/0	0.8	0	0.4/0.4	0/0/0	0/0	0//0	0/0/	0/0/0	0/0			0/0/0	Non retail packaging contains aldrin, toxaphene, chlordane, DDT, dieldrin, endosulfan, heptachlor, hexachlorobenzene α — Hexachlorocyclohexane β— Goods of hexachlorocyclohexane or lindane
0/0/0	0.8	0	0.4/0.4	0/0/0	0/0	0//0	0/0/	0/0/0	0/0			0/0/0	Mercury containing pesticides containing carbofuran or trichlorfon in non retail packaging
0/0/0	0.8	0	0.4/0.4	0/0/0	0/0	0//0	0/0/	0/0/0	0/0			0/0/0	Pesticide patent medicines containing carbofuran or trichlorfon, but not other substances listed in note 1 of subheading of chapter 38, not in retail packaging
0/0/0	0.8	0	0.4/0.4	0/0/0	0/0	0//0	0/0/	0/0/0	0/0			0/0/0	Other goods in non retail packaging containing a substance listed in note 1 of subheading of chapter 38
0/0/0	0.8	0	0.4/0.4	0/0/0	0/0	0//0	0/0/	0/0/0	0/0			0/0/0	Goods not put up for retail sale, containing more than one substance specified in Subheading Note 1 to Chapter 38
													--Goods specified in Subheading Note 2 to this Chapter:
0/0/0	0	2	0/0	0/0/0	0/0	0//0	0/0/	0/0/9	9.1/0			0//	--In packings of a net weight content not exceeding 300 g
0/0/0	0	2	0/0	0/0/0	0/0	0//0	0/0/	0/0/9	9.1/0			0/0/0	--In packings of a net weight content not exceeding 300 g but not exceeding 7.5 kg
0/0/0	0	0	0.6/0.6	0/0/0	0/0	0//0	0/0/	5.4/5.4/5.4	5.5/5.4			0/0/0	--Other
													-Other:
													--Insecticides:
													---Put up for retail sale:
0/0/0	0	0	0/0	0/0/0	0/0	0//0	0/0/	0/0/0	9.1/0			0/0/0	----Mosquito smudges
													----Biotic insecticide
0/0/0	3.5	2	0/0	0/0/0	0/0	0//0	0/0/	0/0/9	9.1/0		//	0/0/0	Mercury containing biopesticides in retail packaging
0/0/0	3.5	2	0/0	0/0/0	0/0	0//0	0/0/	0/0/9	9.1/0		//	0/0/0	Other biopesticides in retail packaging
													----Other
0/0/0	3.5	2	0/0	0/0/0	0/0	0//0	0/0/	0/0/9	9.1/0		//	0/0/0	Pesticides containing mirex or chlordecone in retail packaging
0/0/0	3.5	2	0/0	0/0/0	0/0	0//0	0/0/	0/0/9	9.1/0		//	0/0/0	Other mercury pesticides in retail packaging
0/0/0	3.5	2	0/0	0/0/0	0/0	0//0	0/0/	0/0/9	9.1/0		//	0/0/0	Other retail packaged pesticides
													---Other
0/0/0	0	0	0.6/0.6	0/0/0	0/0	0//0	0/0/	5.4/5.4/5.4	5.5/5.4		//	0/0/0	Pesticides containing mirex or chlordecone, not in retail packaging
0/0/0	0	0	0.6/0.6	0/0/0	0/0	0//0	0/0/	5.4/5.4/5.4	5.5/5.4		//	0/0/0	Mercury pesticides in non retail packaging
0/0/0	0	0	0.6/0.6	0/0/0	0/0	0//0	0/0/	5.4/5.4/5.4	5.5/5.4			0/0/0	Polybactericide, ethyl polybactericide
0/0/0	0	0	0.6/0.6	0/0/0	0/0	0//0	0/0/	5.4/5.4/5.4	5.5/5.4		//	0/0/0	Other non retail packaged pesticides
													--Fungicides:

税则号列	货品名称〔CIQ 扩展编码及品名—T2 表示见附表 2〕	最惠(%)	暂定税率	普通	增值/消费	出口退税	计量单位	监管条件/特殊证件	检验检疫	对美关税	亚太上/下
3808.9210	---零售包装										
3808.9210 10	零售包装的含汞杀菌剂〔999〕	9		35	13/	9,13	千克	89/1		34	
3808.9210 90	零售包装的其他杀菌剂成药〔999〕	9		35	13/	9,13	千克	S/1		34	
3808.9290	---其他										
3808.9290 10	非零售包装的医用杀菌剂〔999〕	6		11	13/	9,13	千克	/1		26	
3808.9290 21	经农药杀菌剂浸渍的纸质水果套袋〔999〕	6		11	13/	9,13	千克	S/1		26	
3808.9290 29	非零售包装的其他农用杀菌剂成药〔301 危险化学品，易燃液体，302 其他〕	6		11	9/	9,13	千克	S/1		26	
3808.9290 30	非零售包装的含汞杀菌剂〔999〕	6		35	13/	9,13	千克	89/1		26	
3808.9290 90	非零售包装的非农用杀菌剂成药(包括非医用杀菌剂)〔301 危险化学品，易燃液体；302 其他化工品〕	6		11	9/	9,13	千克	/1		26	
	--除草剂、抗萌剂及植物生长调节剂：										
	---除草剂：										
3808.9311	----零售包装										
3808.9311 10	零售包装的含汞除草剂〔999〕	9		35	9/	9	千克	89/1		34	
3808.9311 90	零售包装的除草剂成药〔301 其他危险化学品，302 其他化工产品〕	9		35	9/	9	千克	AS/1	M	34	
3808.9319	----其他										
3808.9319 10	非零售包装百草枯母液〔301〕	5		11	9/	9	千克	AS/1	M	15	3.3/3.3
3808.9319 20	非零售包装的含汞除草剂〔999〕	5		11	9/	9	千克	89/1		15	3.3/3.3
3808.9319 90	其他非零售包装的除草剂成药〔301 其他危险化学品，302 其他化工产品〕	5		11	9/	9	千克	AS/1	M	15	3.3/3.3
	---其他：										
3808.9391	----零售包装										
3808.9391 10	零售包装含汞抗萌剂及植物生长调节剂〔999〕	9		35	9/	9	千克	89/1		14	5.9/5.9
3808.9391 90	零售包装其他抗萌剂及植物生长调节剂〔999〕	9		35	9/	9	千克	S/1		14	5.9/5.9
3808.9399	----其他										
3808.9399 10	非零售包装的含汞抗萌剂及植物生长调节剂〔999〕	6		14	9/	9	千克	89/1		16	3.9/3.9
3808.9399 90	非零售包装的其他抗萌剂及植物生长调节剂〔999〕	6		14	9/	9	千克	S/1		16	3.9/3.9
3808.9400	--消毒剂										
3808.9400 10	医用消毒剂〔999〕	9		35	13/	13	千克	/13			
3808.9400 30	含汞消毒剂〔999〕	9		35	9/	13	千克	89/13		19	
3808.9400 40	兽用已配剂量消毒剂(进口兽药管理目录的商品)〔999〕	9		35	9/	13	千克	R/13		19	
3808.9400 90	其他非医用消毒剂〔301 危险化学品，易燃液体；302 其他化工产品〕	9		35	9/	13	千克	/13		19	
	--其他：										
3808.9910	---零售包装										
3808.9910 10	零售包装的农业杀螨剂、杀线虫剂〔999〕	9		35	9/	9	千克	S/1			
3808.9910 90	零售包装的杀鼠剂及其他农药(包括类似品)〔999〕	9		35	9/	9,13	千克	S/1			
3808.9990	---其他										
3808.9990 10	非零售包装的农业杀螨剂、杀线虫剂〔999〕	9		14	9/	9	千克	S/1		14	
3808.9990 90	非零售包装的杀鼠剂及其他农药(包括类似品)〔999〕	9		14	9/	9,13	千克	S/1		14	
38.09	**纺织、造纸、制革及类似工业用的其他税目未列名的整理剂、染料加速着色或固色助剂及其他产品和制剂(例如，修整剂及媒染剂)：**										
3809.1000	-以淀粉物质为基本成分〔999〕	10		35	13/	0	千克	/1		35	
	-其他：										
3809.9100	--纺织工业及类似工业用〔301 危险化学品，易燃液体；302 其他化工品〕	6.5		35	13/	0	千克	/1		26.5	6/6
3809.9200	--造纸工业及类似工业用〔999〕	6.5		35	13/	0	千克	/1		11.5	
3809.9300	--制革工业及类似工业用〔301 危险化学品，易燃液体；302 其他化工产品〕	6.5		35	13/	0	千克	/13		26.5	
38.10	**金属表面酸洗剂；焊接用的焊剂及其他辅助剂；金属及其他材料制成的焊粉或焊膏；作焊条芯子或焊条涂料用的制品：**										
3810.1000	-金属表面酸洗剂；金属及其他材料制成的焊粉或焊膏〔301 危险化学品，易燃液体；302 其他化工品〕	6.5		35	13/	13	千克	/1		26.5	6/6
3810.9000	-其他〔301 危险化学品，易燃液体；302 其他化工品〕	6.5		35	13/	0	千克	/1		16.5	
38.11	**抗震剂、抗氧剂、防胶剂、黏度改良剂、防腐蚀制剂及其他配制添加剂，用于矿物油(包括汽油)或与矿物油同样用途的其他液体：**										
	-抗震剂：										

协定税率 %								RCEP		特惠税率 %			Article Description
东/冰/格	巴基斯坦	韩国	瑞士 上/下	哥/秘/柬	澳/毛	新西/坡/智	中国港/澳/台	东盟及马来/澳/韩	日/新	亚太2国	老/柬/缅	98/97/95	
													---Put up for retail sale
0/0/0	2	0	0.9/0.9	0/0/0	0/0	0//0	0/0/	0/0/0	8.2/0		//	0/0/0	Mercury containing bactericides in retail packaging
0/0/0	2	0	0.9/0.9	0/0/0	0/0	0//0	0/0/	0/0/0	8.2/0		//	0/0/0	Other fungicides in retail packaging
													---Other
0/0/0	0	0	0.6/0.6	0/0/0	0/0	0//0	0/0/	5.4/5.4/5.4	5.5/5.4			0/0/0	Medical fungicides, not in forms or packing for retail sale
0/0/0	0	0	0.6/0.6	0/0/0	0/0	0//0	0/0/	5.4/5.4/5.4	5.5/5.4			0/0/0	Paper bags for fruit protecion, agricultural fungicides scaked
0/0/0	0	0	0.6/0.6	0/0/0	0/0	0//0	0/0/	5.4/5.4/5.4	5.5/5.4			0/0/0	Other agricultural fungicides medicine, not in forms or packing for retail sale
0/0/0	0	0	0.6/0.6	0/0/0	0/0	0//0	0/0/	5.4/5.4/5.4	5.5/5.4		//	0/0/0	Mercury containing fungicides in non retail packaging
0/0/0	0	0	0.6/0.6	0/0/0	0/0	0//0	0/0/	5.4/5.4/5.4	5.5/5.4			0/0/0	Non-agricultural fungicides medicine and non-medical fungicides, not in forms packing for retail sale
													--Herbicides anti-sprouting products and plantgrowth regulators:
													---Herbicides:
													----Put up for retail sale
0/0/0	2	0	0/0	0/0/0	0/0	0//0	0/0/	8.1/8.1/8.1	8.2/8.1		//	0/0/0	Packaging of herbicides containing mercury
0/0/0	2	0	0/0	0/0/0	0/0	0//0	0/0/	8.1/8.1/8.1	8.2/8.1		//	0/0/0	Herbicides in retail packaging
													----Other
0/0/0	0	0	0.5/0.5	0/0/0	0/0	0//0	0/0/	0/0/0	4.5/0			0/0/0	Paraquat liquor, not put up for retail sale
0/0/0	0	0	0.5/0.5	0/0/0	0/0	0//0	0/0/	0/0/0	4.5/0		//	0/0/0	Mercury containing herbicides in non retail packaging
0/0/0	0	0	0.5/0.5	0/0/0	0/0	0//0	0/0/	0/0/0	4.5/0			0/0/0	Other herbicides Patent medicine, not put up for retail sale
													---Other:
													----Put up for retail sale
0/0/0	2	0	0/0	0/0/0	0/0	0//0	0/0/	0/0/0	8.2/0		//	0/0/0	Mercury containing anti sprouting agents and plant growth regulators in retail packaging
0/0/0	2	0	0/0	0/0/0	0/0	0//0	0/0/	0/0/0	8.2/0		//	0/0/0	Retail packaging other anti sprouting agents and plant growth regulators
													----Other
0/0/0	0	0	0/0	0/0/0	0/0	0//0	0/0/	0/0/0	0/0		//	0/0/0	Mercury containing anti sprouting agents and plant growth regulators in non retail packaging
0/0/0	0	0	0/0	0/0/0	0/0	0//0	0/0/	0/0/0	0/0		//	0/0/0	Other anti sprouting agents and plant growth regulators in non retail packaging
													--Disinfectants
0/0/0	3.5	0	0.9/0.9	0/0/0	0/0	0//0	0/0/	8.1/8.1/8.1	8.2/8.1			0/0/0	Medical disinfectants
0/0/0	3.5	0	0.9/0.9	0/0/0	0/0	0//0	0/0/	8.1/8.1/8.1	8.2/8.1		//	0/0/0	Mercury containing disinfectant
0/0/0	3.5	0	0.9/0.9	0/0/0	0/0	0//0	0/0/	8.1/8.1/8.1	8.2/8.1		//	0/0/0	Prepared dose disinfectants for veterinary use (including commodities in the Management Catalogue of imported veterinary drugs)
0/0/0	3.5	0	0.9/0.9	0/0/0	0/0	0//0	0/0/	8.1/8.1/8.1	8.2/8.1			0/0/0	Non-medical disinfectants
													--Other:
													---Put up for retail sale
0/0/0	2	0	0/0	0/0/0	0/0	0//0	0/0/	0/0/0	8.2/0			0/0/0	Agricultural acaricides and nematicides in retail packaging
0/0/0	2	0	0/0	0/0/0	0/0	0//0	0/0/	0/0/0	8.2/0			0/0/0	Rodenticides and other pesticides (including analogues) in retail packaging
													---Other
0/0/0	2	0	0/0	0/0/0	0/0	0//0	0/0/	0/0/0	8.2/0			0/0/0	Agricultural acaricides and nematicides in non retail packaging
0/0/0	2	0	0/0	0/0/0	0/0	0//0	0/0/	0/0/0	8.2/0			0/0/0	Rodenticides and other pesticides (including analogues) in non retail packaging
													Finishing agents, dye carriers to accelerate the dyeing or fixing of dye-stuffs and other products and preparations (for example, dressings and mordants), of a kind used in the textile, paper, leather or like industries, not elsewhere specified or included:
0/0/0	0	2	0/0	0/0/0	0/0	0/0/0	0/0/	0/0/9	9.1/0			0/0/0	-With a basis of amylaceous substances
													-Other:
0/0/0	0	0	0.7/0.7	0/0/0	0/0	0//0	0/0/	0/0/0	5.9/0			0/0/0	--Of a kind used in the textile or like industries
0/0/0	0	1.3	0/0	0/0/0	0/0	0//0	0/0/	5.9/5.9/5.9	5.9/5.9			0/0/0	--Of a kind used in the paper or like industries
0/0/0	0	0	0/0	0/0/0	0/0	0//0	0/0/	5.9/5.9/5.9	5.9/5.9			0/0/0	--Of a kind used in the leather or like industries
													Pickling preparations for metal surfaces; fluxes and other auxiliary preparations for soldering, brazing or welding; soldering, brazing or welding powders and pastes consisting of metal and other materials; preparations of a kind used as cores or coatings for welding electrodes or rods:
0/0/0	0	3	0/0	0/0/0	0/0	0//0	0/0/	5.9/5.9/5.9	6.1/5.9			0/0/0	-Pickling preparations for metal surfaces; soldering, brazing or welding powders and pastes consisting of metal and other materials
0/0/0	0	3	0/0	0/0/0	0/0	0//0	0/0/	5.9/5.9/5.9	6.1/5.9			0/0/0	-Other
													Anti-knock preparations, oxidation inhibitors, gum inhibitors, viscosity improvers, anti-corrosive preparations and other prepared additives, for mineral oils (including gasoline) or for other liquids used for the same purposes as mineral oils:
													-Anti-knock preparations:

税则号列	货品名称〔CIQ 扩展编码及品名－T2 表示见附表 2〕	最惠(%)	暂定税率	普通	增值/消费	出口退税	计量单位	监管条件/特殊证件	检验检疫	对美关税	亚太上/下
3811.1100	--以铅化合物为基本成分〔999〕	6.5		35	13/	0	千克	/1			
3811.1900	--其他〔999〕	6.5		35	13/	0	千克	/1		16.5	
	-润滑油添加剂：										
3811.2100	--含有石油或从沥青矿物提取的油类〔999〕	6.5		35	13/	0	千克	/1			
3811.2900	--其他〔999〕	6.5		35	13/	0	千克	/1			5.5/5.5
3811.9000	-其他〔301 危险化学品，易燃液体；302 其他化工品〕	6.5		35	13/	0	千克	/1		11.5	
38.12	**配制的橡胶促进剂；其他品目未列名的橡胶或塑料用复合增塑剂；橡胶或塑料用抗氧制剂及其他复合稳定剂：**										
3812.1000	-配制的橡胶促进剂〔301 危险化学品，杂项物质；302 其他化工品〕	6		20	13/	13	千克	/1		26	
3812.2000	-橡胶或塑料用复合增塑剂〔999〕	6.5		35	13/	13	千克	/1		16.5	
	-橡胶或塑料用抗氧制剂及其他复合稳定剂：										
3812.3100	--2，2，4-三甲基-1，2-二氢化喹啉(TMQ)低聚体混合物〔999〕	6		20	13/	13	千克	/1		31	
	--其他：										
3812.3910	---其他橡胶防老剂〔999〕	6		20	13/	13	千克	/1		16	
3812.3990	---其他〔999〕	6.5		35	13/	13	千克	/1		16.5	4.6/4.6
38.13	**灭火器的装配药；已装药的灭火弹：**										
3813.0010	---灭火器的装配药〔101 灭火器药剂(腐蚀性液体)；102 其他化工品〕	6.5		35	13/	0	千克	/1	L	11.5	
3813.0020	---已装药的灭火弹〔999〕	10		70	13/	0	千克	/1		15	
38.14	**其他税目未列名的有机复合溶剂及稀释剂；除漆剂：**										
3814.0000	其他税目未列名的有机复合溶剂及稀释剂；除漆剂[T2]	10		50	13/	0	千克	/13		20	9/9
38.15	**其他税目未列名的反应引发剂、反应促进剂、催化剂：**										
	-载体催化剂：										
3815.1100	--以镍及其化合物为活性物的〔301 危险化学品，易燃固体；302 危险化学品，易于自燃的物质；303 其他化工品〕	6.5		35	13/	13	千克	/13		11.5	
3815.1200	--以贵金属及其化合物为活性物的										
3815.1200 10	载铂催化剂(为了从重水中回收氚或为了生产重水而专门设计或制备，用于加速氢和水之间的氢同位素交换反应)〔999〕	6.5	4	35	13/	13	千克	3/1			
3815.1200 90	其他以贵金属为活性物的载体催化剂〔999〕	6.5	4	35	13/	13	千克	/1			
3815.1900	--其他〔301 易燃固体、自反应物质及固态退敏爆炸品，302 其他化工产品〕	6.5		35	13/	13	千克	/1			4.6/4.6
3815.9000	-其他〔301 腐蚀性物质，302 易于自燃的物质，999 未列名的反应引发剂、反应促进剂、催化剂〕	6.5		35	13/	13	千克	/1			4.2/4.2
38.16	**耐火的水泥、灰泥、混凝土及类似耐火混合制品，包括夯混白云石，但税目 38.01 的产品除外：**										
3816.0010	---夯混白云石〔999〕	3	0	40	13/	0	千克	/1		2.5	
3816.0020	---其他〔999〕	6.5		35	13/	0	千克	/1		16.5	
38.17	**混合烷基苯及混合烷基萘，但税目 27.07 及 29.02 的货品除外：**										
3817.0000	混合烷基苯及混合烷基萘，但税目 27.07 及 29.02 的货品除外〔301 危险化学品，易燃液体；302 其他化工产品〕	6.5		35	13/	13	千克	/13		31.5	
38.18	**经掺杂用于电子工业的化学元素，已切成圆片、薄片或类似形状；经掺杂用于电子工业的化合物：**										
	---直径在 7.5 厘米及以上的单晶硅切片：										
3818.0011	----直径在 15.24 厘米及以下的〔999〕	0		11	13/	13	千克/片	/1		10	
3818.0019	----其他〔999〕	0		11	13/	13	千克/片	/1			
3818.0090	---其他〔999〕	0		17	13/	13	千克	/1			
38.19	**闸用液压油及其他液压传动用液体，不含石油或从沥青矿物提取的油类，或者按重量计石油或从沥青矿物提取的油类含量低于 70%：**										
3819.0000	闸用液压油及其他液压传动用液体，不含石油或从沥青矿物提取的油类，或者按重量计石油或从沥青矿物提取的油类含量低于 70%〔999〕	6.5		35	13/	0	千克	/1		16.5	
38.20	**防冻剂及解冻剂：**										
3820.0000	防冻剂及解冻剂〔999〕	10		35	13/	13	千克	/1		20	
38.21	**制成的供微生物(包括病毒及类似品)或植物、人体、动物细胞生长或维持用的培养基：**										

协定税率 %								RCEP		特惠税率 %			Article Description
东/冰/格	巴基斯坦	韩国	瑞士上/下	哥/秘/柬	澳/毛	新西/坡/智	中国港/澳/台	东盟及马来/澳/韩	日/新	亚太2国	老/柬/缅	98/97/95	
0/0/0	2	0	0/0	0/0/0	0/0	0//0	0/0/	0/0/0	5.9/0			0/0/0	--Based on lead compounds
0/0/0	2	0	0/0	0/0/0	0/0	0//0	0/0/	0/0/0	5.9/0			0/0/0	--Other
													-Additives for lubricating oils:
0/0/0	0	0	0/0	0/0/0	0/0	0//0	0/0/	0/0/0	5.9/0			0/0/0	--Containing petroleum oils or oils obtained from bituminous minerals
0/0/0	2	1.3	0/0	0/0/0	0/0	0//0	0/0/	5.9/5.9/5.9	5.9/5.9			0/0/0	--Other
0/0/0	2	0	0/0	0/0/0	0/0	0//0	0/0/	5.9/5.9/5.9	5.9/5.9			0/0/0	-Other
													Prepared rubber accelerators; compounds plasticizers for rubber or plastics, not elsewhere specified or included; anti-oxidizing preparations and other compound stabilizers for rubber or plastics:
0/0/0	0	2.8	0/0	0/0/0	0/0	0//0	0/0/	5.4/5.4/5.4	5.6/5.4			0/0/0	-Prepared rubber accelerators
0/0/0	0	3	0/0	0/0/0	0/0	0//0	0/0/	5.9/5.9/5.9	6.1/5.9			0/0/0	-Compound plasticizers for rubber or plastics
													-Anti-oxidizing preparations and other compound stabilizers for rubber or plastics:
0/0/0	0	2.8	0/0	0/0/0	0/0	0//0	0/0/	5.4/5.4/5.4	5.6/5.4			0/0/0	--Mixtures of oligomers of 2,2,4-trimethyl-1, 2-dihydroquino-line (*TMQ*)
													--Other
0/0/0	0	2.8	0/0	0/0/0	0/0	0//0	0/0/	5.4/5.4/5.4	5.6/5.4			0/0/0	---Other rubber antioxidants
0/0/0	0	0	0.7/0.7	0/0/0	0/0	0//0	0/0/	0/0/0	5.9/0			0/0/0	---Other
													Preparations and charges for fire-extinguishers; charged fire-extinguishing grenades:
0/0/0	2	1.3	0/0	0/0/0	0/0	0//0	0/0/	0/0/5.9	5.9/0			0/0/0	---Preparations and charges for fire-extinguishers
0/0/0	3.5	2	0/0	0/0/0	0/0	0//0	0/0/	0/0/9	9.1/0			0/0/0	---Charged fire-extinguishing grenades
													Organic composite solvents and thinners, not elsewhere specified or included; prepared paint or varnish removers:
0/0/0	3.5	6	1/1	0/0/0	0/0	0/0/0	0/0/	9.5/9.5/	9.5/9.5			0/0/0	Organic composite solvents and thinners, not elsewhere specified or included; prepared paint or varnish removers
													Reaction initiators, reaction accelerators and catalytic preparations, not elsewhere specified or included:
													-Supported catalysts:
0/0/0	2	1.3	0/0	0/0/0	0/0	0//0	0/0/	0/0/5.9	5.9/0			0/0/0	--With nickel or nickel compounds as the active substance
													--With precious metal or precious metal compounds as the active substance
0/0/0	0	1.3	0/0	0/0/0	0/0	0//0	0/0/	0/0/5.9	5.9/0			0/0/0	Platinum supported catalyst(in order to reclaim tritium from heavy water or design or prepare for production of heavy water for accelerate exchange reaction of hydrogen isotope between hydrogen and water)
0/0/0	0	1.3	0/0	0/0/0	0/0	0//0	0/0/	0/0/5.9	5.9/0			0/0/0	Other supported catalysts with precious metal compounds as the active substance
0/0/0	0	0	0/0	0/0/0	0/0	0//0	0/0/	0/0/0	5.9/0			0/0/0	--Other
0/0/0	0	0	0.7/0.7	0/0/0	0/0	0//0	0/0/	0/0/0	5.9/0			0/0/0	-Other
													Refractory cements, mortars, concretes and similar compositions, including dolomite ramming mix, other than products of heading 38.01.
0/0/0	0	0	0/0	0/0/0	0/0	0//0	0/0/	0/0/0	0/0			0/0/0	---Dolomite ramming mix
0/0/0	2	0	0/0	0/0/0	0/0	0//0	0/0/	0/0/0	5.9/0			0/0/0	---Other
													Mixed alkylbenzenes and mixed alkylnaphthalenes, other than those of heading No. 27. 07 or 29. 02:
0/0/0	2	3	0/0	0/0/0	0/0	0//0	0/0/0	5.9/5.9/5.9	6.1/5.9			0/0/0	Mixed alkylbenzenes and alkylnaphthalenes, other than those of heading N. 27. 07or 29. 02
													Chemical elements doped for use in electronics, in the form of discs, wafers or similar forms; chemical compouds doped for use in electronics:
													---Monocrystalline sillicon, in the form of discs, wafers or similar form, 7. 5 cm or more in diameter:
0/0/0	0	0	0/0	0/0/0	0/0	0//0	0/0/	0/0/0	0/0			0/0/0	----Diameter not exceeding 15. 24cm
0/0/0	0	0	0/0	0/0/0	0/0	0//0	0/0/	0/0/0	0/0			0/0/0	----Other
0/0/0	0	0	0/0	0/0/0	0/0	0//0	0/0/	0/0/0	0/0			0/0/0	---Other
													Hydraulic brake fluids and other prepared liquids for hydraulic transmission, not containing or containing less than 70% by weight of petroleum oils or oils obtained from bituminous minerals:
0/0/0	4	0	0/0	0/0/0	0/0	0//0	0/0/	0/0/0	5.9/0			0/0/0	Hydraulic brake fluids and other prepared liquids for hydraulic transmission, not containing or containing less than 70% by weight of petroleum oils or oils obtaines from bituminous minerals
													Anti-freezing preparations and prepared de-icing fluids:
0/0/0	3.5	2	0/0	0/0/0	0/0	0/0/0	0/0/	0/0/9	9.1/0			0/0/0	Anti-freezing preparations and prepared de-icing fluids
													Prepared culture media for the development or maintenance of micro-organisms (including virus and the like) or of plant, human or animal cells:

税则号列	货品名称〔CIQ 扩展编码及品名—T2 表示见附表 2〕	最惠(%)	暂定税率	普通	增值/消费	出口退税	计量单位	监管条件/特殊证件	检验检疫	对美关税	亚太上/下
3821.0000	制成的供微生物(包括病毒及类似品)或植物,人体,动物细胞生长或维持用的培养基〔101 动物微生物培养培养基,103 含有牛源性成分的培养基,401 含人血及其成分、人体组织、细胞、体液、分泌物、排泄物,402 含除人血及其成分、人体组织、细胞、体液、分泌物、排泄物外其他特殊物品成分〕	3	2	11	13/	0	千克	/1		7	
38.22	**附于衬背上的诊断或实验用试剂及不论是否附于衬背上的诊断或实验用配制试剂,不论是否制成试剂盒形式,但税目 30.06 的货品除外;有证标准样品:**										
	-附于衬背上的诊断或实验用试剂及不论是否附于衬背上的诊断或实验用配制试剂,不论是否制成试剂盒形式,但税目 30.06 的货品除外:										
3822.1100	--疟疾用										
3822.1100 10	疟疾诊断试剂盒〔101 其他化工产品,401 诊断人类疾病用,402 人类医学、生命科学研究用〕	3	0	20	13/	13	千克	AB/1	PVQW		
3822.1100 90	其他疟疾用的附于衬背上的诊断或实验用试剂及不论是否附于衬背上的诊断或实验用配制试剂,不论是否制成试剂盒形式,但税目 30.06 的货品除外〔401 诊断人类疾病用,402 人类医学、生命科学研究用〕	3	0	20	13/	13	千克	AB/1	PVQW		
3822.1200	--寨卡病毒及由伊蚊属蚊子传播的其他疾病用〔401 诊断人类疾病用,402 人类医学、生命科学研究用〕	3		26	13/	13	千克	AB/1	PVQW		
3822.1300	--血型鉴定用〔401 诊断人类疾病用,402 人类医学、生命科学研究用,403 其他化工产品〕	3		20	13/	13	千克	AB/1	VW	10.5	
3822.1900	--其他										
3822.1900 10	兽用诊断制品(用于一、二、三类动物疫病诊断的诊断试剂盒、试纸条)(包括已配定剂量或零售包装)〔101 体内诊断用,102 非商品化体外诊断用,103 商品化体外诊断用〕	3		26	13/	13	千克	ABR/1	PVQW		
3822.1900 20	新型冠状病毒检测试剂盒〔401 诊断人类疾病用,402 人类医学、生命科学研究用〕	3		26	13/	13	千克	AB/1	PVQW		
3822.1900 90	其他附于衬背上的诊断或实验用试剂及不论是否附于衬背上的诊断或实验用配制试剂,不论是否制成试剂盒形式,但税目 30.06 的货品除外〔101 非商品化动物体外诊断试剂,102 商品化动物体外诊断试剂,401 含有微生物、人体组织、生物制品、血液及其制品,诊断人类疾病用,402 含人血及其成分,人类医学、生命科学研究用,403 含人体组织、细胞、体液、分泌物、排泄物的,人类医学、生命科学研究用,404 含人间传染的病原微生物成分,人类医学、生命科学研究用,405 含除人血及其成分、人体组织、细胞、体液、分泌物、排泄物外、病原微生物外其他特殊物品成分的,人类医学、生命科学研究用,406 其他化工产品〕	3		26	13/	13	千克	AB/1	VW		
3822.9000	-其他〔101 动物源性有证标准样品,401 含有微生物、人体组织、生物制品、血液及其制品,诊断人类疾病用,402 含人血及其成分,人类医学、生命科学研究用,403 含人体组织、细胞、体液、分泌物、排泄物的,人类医学、生命科学研究用,404 含人间传染的病原微生物成分,人类医学、生命科学研究用,405 含除人血及其成分、人体组织、细胞、体液、分泌物、排泄物外、病原微生物外其他特殊物品成分的,人类医学、生命科学研究用,406 其他化工产品〕	4.5		35	13/	13	千克	AB/1	VW		
38.23	**工业用单羧脂肪酸;精炼所得的酸性油;工业用脂肪醇:**										
	-工业用单羧脂肪酸;精炼所得的酸性油:										
3823.1100	--硬脂酸〔101 饲料添加剂,999 其他〕	16		50	13/	13	千克	/1		41	
3823.1200	--油酸〔301 无检疫要求食品添加剂,302 需申报仅用于工业用途不用于食品添加剂无检疫要求的化学品〕	16	8	50	13/	13	千克	A/1	R	33	
3823.1300	--妥尔油脂肪酸〔999〕	16		50	13/	0	千克	/1		21	
3823.1900	--其他										
3823.1900 01	植物酸性油(酸性油仅指精炼所得的)〔999〕	16	5	50	13/	0	千克	/1		30	
3823.1900 90	其他工业用单羧脂肪酸、酸性油(酸性油仅指精炼所得的)〔999〕	16		50	13/	0	千克	/1		41	
3823.7000	-工业用脂肪醇〔999〕	13	9	50	13/	0	千克	/1		34	
38.24	**铸模及铸芯用黏合剂;其他税目未列名的化学工业及其相关工业的化学产品及配制品(包括由天然产品混合组成的):**										
3824.1000	-铸模及铸芯用黏合剂〔301 危险化学品,易燃液体;302 其他化工产品〕	6.5		35	13/	13	千克	/13		16.5	
3824.3000	-自身混合或与金属黏合剂混合的未烧结金属碳化物										
3824.3000 10	混合的未烧结金属碳化钨(包括自身混合或与金属粘合剂混合的)〔999〕	6.5		35	13/	0	千克	4xy/1		11.5	
3824.3000 90	其他混合的未烧结金属碳化物(包括自身混合或与金属粘合剂混合的)〔999〕	6.5		35	13/	0	千克	/1		11.5	
	-水泥、灰泥及混凝土用添加剂:										

协定税率 %								RCEP		特惠税率 %			Article Description
东/冰/格	巴基斯坦	韩国	瑞士 上/下	哥/秘/柬	澳/毛	新西/坡/智	中国港/澳/台	东盟及马来/澳/韩	日/新	亚太2国	老/柬/缅	98/97/95	
0/0/0	0	0	0/0	0/0/0	0/0	0//0	0/0/	0/0/0	0/0			0/0/0	Prepared culture media for the development or maintenance of micro-organisms (including viruses and the like) or of plant, human or animal cells:
													Diagnostic or laboratory reagents on a backing, prepared diagnostic or laboratory reagents whether or not on a backing, whether or not put up in the form of kits, other than those of heading 30.06; certified reference materials.
													-Diagnostic or experimental reagents attached to the backing and diagnostic or experimental preparations, whether or not attached to the backing, whether or not in the form of kits, except for goods of heading 30.06:
													--For malaria
0/0/0	0	0	1.3/1.3	0/0/0	0/0	0//0	0/0/	0/0/0	2.7/0			0/0/0	Malaria diagnostic kit
0/0/0	0	0	1.3/1.3	0/0/0	0/0	0//0	0/0/	0/0/0	2.7/0			0/0/0	Other diagnostic or experimental reagents attached to the backing and diagnostic or experimental preparations, whether or not attached to the backing, for malaria, whether or not in the form of kits, other than goods of heading 3.6
0/0/0	0	0	1.3/1.3	0/0/0	0/0	0//0	0/0/	0/0/0	0/0			0/0/0	--For Zika and other diseases transmitted by mosquitoes of the genus Aedes
0/0/0	0	0	0.3/0.3	0/0/0	0/0	0//0	0/0/	0/0/0	2.7/0			0/0/0	--For blood—grouping
													--Other
0/0/0	0	0	1.3/1.3	0/0/0	0/0	0//0	0/0/	0/0/0	0/0			0/0/0	Veterinary diagnostic products (diagnostic kits and test strips for the diagnosis of class I, II and III animal epidemics) (including prepared doses or retail packaging)
0/0/0	0	0	1.3/1.3	0/0/0	0/0	0//0	0/0/	0/0/0	0/0			0/0/0	New Coronavirus test kit
0/0/0	0	0	1.3/1.3	0/0/0	0/0	0//0	0/0/	0/0/0	0/0			0/0/0	Other diagnostic or experimental reagents attached to the backing and diagnostic or experimental preparations, whether or not attached to the backing, whether or not in the form of kits, other than goods of heading 3.6
0/0/0	0	0	0/0	0/0/0	0/0	0//0	0/0/	0/0/0	0/0			0/0/0	-Other
													Industrial monocarboxylic fatty acids; acid oils from refining; industrial fatty alcohols:
													-Industrial monocarboxylic fatty acids; acid oils from refining:
0//0	12.8	7.4	1.6/1.6	0/0/0	0/0	0//0	0/0/	14.9/15.2/14.9	15/15.2			0/0/0	--Stearic acid
0//0	12.8	7.4	1.6/1.6	0/0/0	0/0	0/0/0	0/0/	14.9/15.2/14.9	15/15.2			0/0/0	--Oleic acid
0/0/0	12.8	7.4	1.6/1.6	0/0/0	0/0	0/0/0	0/0/	14.4/14.4/14.4	15/14.4			0/0/0	--Tall oil fatty acids
													--Other
0/0/0	12.8	7.4	1.6/1.6	0/0/0	0/0	0/0/0	0/0/	14.9/15.2/14.9	15/15.2			0/0/0	Acid oils of plant(acid oils from refining)
0/0/0	12.8	7.4	1.6/1.6	0/0/0	0/0	0/0/0	0/0/	14.9/15.2/14.9	15/15.2			0/0/0	Other industrial monocarboxylic fatty acids, acid oils(acid oils from refining)
0/0/0	6.5	6	1.3/1.3	0/0/0	0/0	0/0/0	0/0/	12.1/12.4/12.1	12.2/12.4			0/0/0	-Industrial fatty alcohols
													Prepared binders for foundry moulds or cores; chemical products and preparations of the chemical or allied industries (including those consisting of mixtures of natural products), not elsewhere specified or included:
0/0/0	2	1.3	0/0	0/0/0	0/0	0//0	0/0/	0/0/5.9	5.9/0			0/0/0	-Prepared binders for foundry moulds or cores
													-Non-agglomerated metal carbides mixed together or with metallic binders
0/0/0	2	0	0/0	0/0/0	0/0	0//0	0/0/	0/0/0	5.9/0			0/0/0	Non-agglomerated metal carbonizded tungsten (containing mixed together or with metallic binders)
0/0/0	2	0	0/0	0/0/0	0/0	0//0	0/0/	0/0/0	5.9/0			0/0/0	Other non-agglomerated metal carbides(containing mixed together or with metallic binders)
													-Prepared additives for cements, mortars or concretes:

税则号列	货品名称〔CIQ扩展编码及品名－T2表示见附表2〕	最惠(%)	暂定税率	普通	增值/消费	出口退税	计量单位	监管条件/特殊证件	检验检疫	对美关税	亚太上/下
3824.4010	---高效减水剂〔999〕	6.5		35	13/	13	千克	/1		31.5	
3824.4090	---其他〔999〕	6.5		35	13/	0	千克	/1	L	16.5	
3824.5000	-非耐火的灰泥及混凝土〔999〕	6.5		35	13/	0	千克	/1		26.5	
3824.6000	-子目号2905.44以外的山梨醇〔999〕	14		40	13/	0	千克	/1		24	
	-本章子目注释三所列货品：										
3824.8100	--含环氧乙烷(氧化乙烯)的〔999〕	6.5		35	13/	0	千克	/1		31.5	4.2/4.2
3824.8200	--含多氯联苯(PCB_S)、多氯三联苯(PCT_S)或多溴联苯(PBB_S)的										
3824.8200 10	含多氯联苯(PCBs)或六溴联苯的混合物〔301危险化学品，杂项物质；302其他化工产品〕	6.5		35	13/	0	千克	89/13			4.2/4.2
3824.8200 90	含多氯三联苯(PCTs)或其他多溴联苯(PBBs)的混合物〔301属于危险化学品杂项物质，302其他化工产品〕	6.5		35	13/	0	千克	/13			4.2/4.2
3824.8300	--含三(2,3-二溴丙基)磷酸酯的〔999〕	6.5		35	13/	0	千克	/1			4.2/4.2
3824.8400	--含艾氏剂(ISO)、毒杀芬(ISO)、氯丹(ISO)、十氯酮(ISO)、DDT(ISO)[滴滴涕(INN)、1,1,1-三氯-2,2-双(4-氯苯基)乙烷]、狄氏剂(ISO,INN)、硫丹(ISO)、异狄氏剂(ISO)、七氯(ISO)或灭蚁灵(ISO)的〔999〕	6.5		35	13/	0	千克	89/1			4.2/4.2
3824.8500	--含1,2,3,4,5,6－六氯环己烷〔六六六(ISO)〕，包括林丹(ISO,INN)〔六六六(ISO)〕，包括林丹(ISO,INN)的〔999〕	6.5		35	13/	0	千克	89/1			4.2/4.2
3824.8600	--含五氯苯(ISO)或六氯苯(ISO)的〔999〕	6.5		35	13/	13	千克	89/1			4.2/4.2
3824.8700	--含全氟辛基磺酸及其盐，全氟辛基磺胺或全氟辛基磺酰氯的〔999〕	6.5		35	13/	13	千克	/1			4.2/4.2
3824.8800	--含四、五、六、七或八溴联苯醚的										
3824.8800 10	含四、五、六或七溴联苯醚的〔301危险化学品，杂项物质；302其他化工产品〕	6.5		35	13/	13	千克	89/13			4.2/4.2
3824.8800 20	含八溴联苯醚的〔301属于危险化学品杂项物质，302其他化工产品〕	6.5		35	13/	13	千克	/13			4.2/4.2
3824.8900	--含短链氯化石蜡的〔999〕	6.5		35	13/	13	千克	/1			4.2/4.2
	-其他：										
3824.9100	--主要由(5-乙基-2-甲基-2氧代-1,3,2-二氧磷杂环己-5-基)甲基膦酸二甲酯和双[(5-乙基-2-甲基-2氧代-1,3,2-二氧磷杂环己-5-基)甲基]甲基膦酸酯(阻燃剂FRC-1)组成的混合物及制品〔999〕	6.5		35	13/	13	千克	/1			4.2/4.2
3824.9200	--甲基膦酸聚乙二醇酯〔999〕	6.5		35	13/	13	千克	/1			4.2/4.2
	--其他：										
3824.9910	---杂醇油〔301危险化学品，易燃液体；302其他化工品〕	6.5		40	13/	0	千克	/13		16.5	4.2/4.2
3824.9920	---除墨剂、蜡纸改正液及类似品〔301危险化学品，易燃液体；302其他化工品〕	9		80	13/	0	千克	/13		29	5.9/5.9
3824.9930	---增炭剂〔999〕	6.5		35	13/	0	千克	/1			5.2/5.2
	---其他：										
3824.9991	----按重量计含滑石50%以上的混合物〔999〕	6.5		35	13/	0	千克	4xy/1		31.5	4.2/4.2
3824.9992	----按重量计含氧化镁70%以上的混合物〔999〕	6.5		35	13/	0	千克	4xy/1			4.2/4.2
3824.9993	----表面包覆钴化物的氢氧化镍(掺杂碳)〔999〕	6.5		35	13/	13	千克	/1			4.2/4.2
3824.9999	----其他										
3824.9999 10	粗制碳化硅(其中碳化硅含量大于15%(按重量计))〔999〕	6.5		35	13/	0	千克	y4x/13			4.2/4.2
3824.9999 20	混胺(二甲胺和三乙胺混合物的水溶液)〔301危险化学品，易燃液体；302其他化工产品〕	6.5		35	13/	0	千克	3/13			4.2/4.2
3824.9999 30	氰化物的混合物〔999〕	6.5		35	13/	0	千克	/13			4.2/4.2
3824.9999 40	膨胀石墨〔999〕	6.5		35	13/	0	千克	3/13			4.2/4.2
3824.9999 50	三乙醇胺混合物、甲基二乙醇胺混合物、环状膦酸酯A和环状膦酸酯B的混合物〔999〕	6.5		35	13/	13	千克	23/13			4.2/4.2
3824.9999 60	高钛渣(二氧化钛质量百分含量>70%的)〔999〕	6.5	0	35	13/	0	千克	/13			4.2/4.2
3824.9999 70	核苷酸类食品添加剂〔999其他化工产品，301有检疫要求食品添加剂，302需申报仅用于工业用途不用于食品添加剂有检疫要求的化学品〕	6.5		35	13/	13	千克	AB/13	RS		4.2/4.2
3824.9999 80	按重量计氧化锌含量在50%及以上的混合物〔999〕	6.5	3	35	13/	0	千克	/13			4.2/4.2
3824.9999 91	短链氯化石蜡(不具有人造蜡特性)〔101：其他危险化学品；102：其他化工产品〕	6.5		35	13/	13	千克	X/13			4.2/4.2
3824.9999 92	用于生产聚酰胺的发酵液(含氨基酸、有机酸、有机胺、有机醇、核苷酸、多糖等)〔101其他危险化学品，102其他化工产品，〕	6.5	0	35	13/	13	千克	/13			4.2/4.2
3824.9999 93	载金炭〔101其他危险化学品；102其他化工产品〕	6.5	0	35	13/	13	千克	/13			4.2/4.2

协定税率 %								RCEP		特惠税率 %			Article Description
东/冰/格	巴基斯坦	韩国	瑞士 上/下	哥/秘/柬	澳/毛	新西/坡/智	中国港/澳/台	东盟及马来/澳/韩	日/新	亚太2国	老/柬/缅	98/97/95	
0/0/0	2	3	0/0	0/0/0	0/0	0//0	0/0/	5.9/5.9/5.9	6.1/5.9			0/0/0	---High efficiency water reducing admixture
0/0/0	2	0	0/0	0/0/0	0/0	0//0	0/0/	0/0/0	5.9/0			0/0/0	---Other
0/0/0	2	0	0/0	0/0/0	0/0	0//0	0/0/	0/0/0	5.9/0			0/0/0	-Non-refraciory mortars and concretes
0/0/0	11.2	2.8	1.4/1.4	0/0/0	0/0	0/0/0	0/0/	0/0/12.6	12.7/0			0/0/0	-Sorbitol other than that of subheading No. 2905. 44
													-Goods specified in Subheading Note 3 to this Chapter:
0/0/0	2	0	0/0	0/0/0	0/0	0//0	0/0/	0/0/0	5.9/0			0/0/0	--Containing oxirane(ethylene oxide)
													--Containing polychlorinated biphenyls(PCBs), polychlorinoted terphenyls(PCTs) or polybrominated biphenyls(PBBs)
0/0/0	2	0	0/0	0/0/0	0/0	0//0	0/0/	0/0/0	5.9/0		//	0/0/0	A compound containing polychlorinated biphenyls (PCBs) or hexabromobiphenyls
0/0/0	2	0	0/0	0/0/0	0/0	0//0	0/0/	0/0/0	5.9/0		//	0/0/0	A compound containing polychlorinated triphenyls (PCTs) or other polybrominated biphenyls (PBBs)
0/0/0	2	0	0/0	0/0/0	0/0	0//0	0/0/	0/0/0	5.9/0			0/0/0	--Contaning tris (2,3-dibromopopyl)phosphate
0/0/0	0	3		0/0/0	0/0	0/0/0	0/0/	5.9/5.9/5.9	6.1/5.9			0/0/0	--Containing aldrin (*ISO*), cam-phechlor (*ISO*) (*toxaphene*), chlordane (*ISO*), chlordecone (*ISO*), DDT (*ISO*) *clofeno-tane* (INN), 1, 1, 1-*trichloro*-2, 2-*bis* (p-chlorophenyl) *ethane*), dieldrin (*ISO*, *INN*), endosulfan (*ISO*), endrin (*ISO*), heptachlor (*ISO*) or mirex (*ISO*)
0/0/0	0	3		0/0/0	0/0	0/0/0	0/0/	5.9/5.9/5.9	6.1/5.9			0/0/0	--Containing 1, 2, 3, 4, 5, 6-hexa-chlorocyclohexane (*HCH* (ISO)), including lindane (*ISO*, *INN*)
0/0/0	0	3		0/0/0	0/0	0/0/0	0/0/	5.9/5.9/5.9	6.1/5.9			0/0/0	--Containing pentachlorobenzene (ISO) *or hexachlorobenzene* (*ISO*)
0/0/0	0	3		0/0/0	0/0	0/0/0	0/0/	5.9/5.9/5.9	6.1/5.9			0/0/0	--Containing perfluorooctane sulphonic acid, its salts, perfluorooctane sulphonamides, or perfluorooctane sulphonyl fluoride
													--Containing tetra-, penta-, hexa-hepta-or octabromodiphenyl ethers
0/0/0	0	3		0/0/0	0/0	0/0/0	0/0/	5.9/5.9/5.9	6.1/5.9		//	0/0/0	Containing diphenyl ether of four, five, six, or heptabde
0/0/0	0	3		0/0/0	0/0	0/0/0	0/0/	5.9/5.9/5.9	6.1/5.9		//	0/0/0	Octabromodiphenyl ether
0/0/0	0	3		0/0/0	0/0	0/0/0	0/0/	5.9/5.9/5.9	6.1/5.9			0/0/0	--Containing short—chain chlorinated paraffins
													-Other:
0/0/0	0	3		0/0/0	0/0	0/0/0	0/0/	5.9/5.9/5.9	6.1/5.9			0/0/0	--Mixtures and preparations consisting mainly of(5-ethyl-2-methyl-2-oxido-1, 3, 2-dioxaphosphinan-5—Yl) menthylmethyl methylphosphonate and bis[(5-ethyl-2-methyl-2-oxido-1, 3, 2-dioxaphosphinan-5—Yl) methyl]methylphosphonate
0/0/0	0	3		0/0/0	0/0	0/0/0	0/0/	5.9/5.9/5.9	6.1/5.9			0/0/0	--Polyglycol esters of methylphosphonic acid
													--Other:
0/0/0	4	1.3	0/0	0/0/0	0/0	0/0/0	0/0/	0/0/5.9	5.9/0			0/0/0	---Fusel oil
0/0/0	2	0	0/0	0/0/0	0/0	0/0/0	0/0/	0/0/0	8.2/0			0/0/0	---Ink-removers, stencil correc-tors and the like
0/0/0	2	0	0/0	0/0/0	0/0	0/0/0	0/0/	0/0/0	5.9/0			0/0/0	---Carburetant
													---Other:
0/0/0	2	0	0/0	0/0/0	0/0	0/0/0	0/0/	0/0/0	5.9/0			0/0/0	----Mixtures containing more than 50% by weight of talc
0/0/0	2	0	0/0	0/0/0	0/0	0/0/0	0/0/	0/0/0	5.9/0			0/0/0	----Mixtures containing more than 70% by weight of mag nesium oxide
0/0/0	2	3		0/0/0	0/0	0/0/0	0/0/	5.9/5.9/5.9	6.1/5.9			0/0/0	----Nickelous hydroxide (*doped carbon*) covered on the face side with cobalt compound
													----Other
0/0/0	0	3		0/0/0	0/0	0/0/0	0/0/	5.9/5.9/5.9	6.1/5.9			0/0/0	Crude silicon carbide, containing more than 15% by weight of silicon carbide
0/0/0	0	3		0/0/0	0/0	0/0/0	0/0/	5.9/5.9/5.9	6.1/5.9			0/0/0	Mixed amine(dimethylamine and triethylamine mixture in aqueous solution)
0/0/0	0	3		0/0/0	0/0	0/0/0	0/0/	5.9/5.9/5.9	6.1/5.9			0/0/0	Mixtures of cyanide
0/0/0	0	3		0/0/0	0/0	0/0/0	0/0/	5.9/5.9/5.9	6.1/5.9			0/0/0	Expanded graphite
0/0/0	0	3		0/0/0	0/0	0/0/0	0/0/	5.9/5.9/5.9	6.1/5.9			0/0/0	A mixture of methyl phosphonic acid (CAS NO. 170836-68-7) {by methyl phosphonic acid, methyl 5-(5-ethyl-2-methyl-2-oxo-1, 3, 2-two oxygen phosphorusheterocyclic hexyl) methyl ester(CAS NO. 41203-81-0) and methyl phosphonic acid two [5-(5-ethyl-2-methyl-2-oxo-1, 3, 2-two oxygen phosphorus heterocyclichexyl) methyl)] ester (CAS NO. 42595-45-9) and mixed}
0/0/0	0	3		0/0/0	0/0	0/0/0	0/0/	5.9/5.9/5.9	6.1/5.9			0/0/0	Titanium slag (containing more than 70% by weight of titanium dioxide)
0/0/0	0	3		0/0/0	0/0	0/0/0	0/0/	5.9/5.9/5.9	6.1/5.9			0/0/0	Nucleotide food additives
0/0/0	0	3		0/0/0	0/0	0/0/0	0/0/	5.9/5.9/5.9	6.1/5.9			0/0/0	Mixture containing more than 50% by weight of zinc oxide
0/0/0	0	3		0/0/0	0/0	0/0/0	0/0/	5.9/5.9/5.9	6.1/5.9		//	0/0/0	SCCPs (no artificial wax properties)
0/0/0	0	3		0/0/0	0/0	0/0/0	0/0/	5.9/5.9/5.9	6.1/5.9		//	0/0/0	Fermentation broth for polyamide production (including amino acids, organic acids, organic amines, organic alcohols, nucleotides, polysaccharides, etc.)
0/0/0	0	3		0/0/0	0/0	0/0/0	0/0/	5.9/5.9/5.9	6.1/5.9		//	0/0/0	Gold loaded carbon

税则号列	货品名称〔CIQ 扩展编码及品名—T2 表示见附表 2〕	最惠(%)	暂定税率	普通	增值/消费	出口退税	计量单位	监管条件/特殊证件	检验检疫	对美关税	亚太 上/下
3824.9999 99	其他编号未列名的化工产品(包括水解物或水解料、DMC(六甲基环三硅氧烷,八甲基环四硅氧烷,十甲基环五硅氧烷,十二甲基环六硅氧烷中任何 2 种,3 种或 4 种组成的混合物))〔301 危险化学品,气体;302 危险化学品,易燃液体;303 危险化学品,易燃固体;304 危险化学品,遇水放出易燃气体的物质;305 危险化学品,有机过氧化物;306 危险化学品,腐蚀性物质;307 危险化学品,杂项物质;308 其他危险化学品;309 其他化工产品〕	6.5		35	13/	13	千克	/13			4.2/4.2
38.25	**其他税目未列名的化学工业及其相关工业的副产品;城市垃圾;下水道淤泥;本章注释六所规定的其他废物:**										
3825.1000	-城市垃圾〔999〕	6.5		35	13/	0	千克	9/1			
3825.2000	-下水道淤泥〔999〕	6.5		35	13/	0	千克	9/1			
3825.3000	-医疗废物〔999〕	6.5		35	13/	0	千克	9/1			
	-废有机溶剂:										
3825.4100	--卤化物的〔999〕	6.5		35	13/	0	千克	9/1			
3825.4900	--其他〔999〕	6.5		35	13/	0	千克	9/1			
3825.5000	-废的金属酸洗液、液压油、制动油及防冻液〔999〕	6.5		35	13/	0	千克	9/1			
	-其他化学工业及相关工业的废物:										
3825.6100	--主要含有有机成分的〔999〕	6.5		35	13/	0	千克	9/1			
3825.6900	--其他〔301 危险化学品,腐蚀性物质;302 其他未列名化学工业及相关工业的废物〕	6.5		35	13/	0	千克	9/13			
3825.9000	-其他										
3825.9000 10	浓缩糖蜜发酵液〔301 无检疫要求食品添加剂,302 需申报仅用于工业用途不用于食品添加剂无检疫要求的化学品〕	6.5		35	13/	0	千克	A/1	R	31.5	
3825.9000 90	其他商品编号未列名化工副产品及废物〔999〕	6.5		35	13/	0	千克	9/1		31.5	
38.26	**生物柴油及其混合物,不含或含有按重量计低于 70%的石油或从沥青矿物提取的油类:**										
3826.0000	生物柴油及其混合物,不含或含有按重量计低于 70%的石油或从沥青矿物提取的油类										
3826.0000 01	纯生物柴油〔999〕	6.5		35	13/	0	千克/升	/1		31.5	4.2/4.2
3826.0000 90	其他生物柴油及其混合物〔999〕	6.5		35	13/1.2元/升	0	千克/升	/1		31.5	4.2/4.2
38.27	**其他税目未列名的,含甲烷、乙烷或丙烷的卤化衍生物的混合物:**										
	-含全氯氟烃(CFCs)的,不论是否含氢氯氟烃(HCFCs)、全氟烃(PFCs)或氢氟烃(HFCs);含氢溴氟烃(HBFCs)的;含四氯化碳的;含 1,1,1—三氯乙烷(甲基氯仿)的:										
3827.1100	--含全氯氟烃(CFCs)的,不论是否含氢氯氟烃(HCFCs)、全氟烃(PFCs)或氢氟烃(HFCs)										
3827.1100 10	二氯二氟甲烷与二氟乙烷的混合物、一氯二氟甲烷与一氯五氟乙烷的混合物、三氟甲烷与一氯三氟甲烷的混合物(R—500、R—502、R—503)〔999〕	6.5		35	13/	0	千克	14ABxy/1	MN	11.5	
3827.1100 20	一氯二氟甲烷与二氯二氟甲烷的混合物、二氟甲烷与一氯五氟乙烷的混合物、二氯二氟甲烷与一氯一氟甲烷的混合物、一氯一氟甲烷与二氯四氟乙烷的混合物、二氯二氟甲烷与二氯四氟乙烷的混合物(R—501、R—504、R—505、R—506、R—400)〔999〕	6.5		35	13/	0	千克	14xy/1		11.5	
3827.1100 90	其他含全氯氟烃(CFCs)的混合物,不论是否含氢氯氟烃(HCFCs)、全氟烃(PFCs)或氢氟烃(HFCs)〔999〕	6.5		35	13/	0	千克	14xy/1		11.5	
3827.1200	--含氢溴氟烃(HBFCs)的〔999〕	6.5		35	13/	0	千克	/1			
3827.1300	--含四氯化碳的〔999〕	6.5		35	13/	0	千克	/1		11.5	4.2/4.2
3827.1400	--含 1,1,1—三氯乙烷(甲基氯仿)的〔301 危险化学品,易燃液体,302 其他化工产品〕	6.5		35	13/	0	千克	/1		31.5	4.2/4.2
3827.2000	-含溴氯二氟甲烷(Halon—1211)、三氟溴甲烷(Halon—1301)或二溴四氟乙烷(Halon—2402)的〔999〕	6.5		35	13/	0	千克	/1			
	-含氢氯氟烃(HCFCs)的,不论是否含全氟烃(PFCs)或氢氟烃(HFCs),但不含全氯氟烃(CFCs):										

协定税率 %								RCEP		特惠税率 %			Article Description
东/冰/格	巴基斯坦	韩国	瑞士上/下	哥/秘/柬	澳/毛	新西/坡/智	中国港/澳/台	东盟及马来/澳/韩	日/新	亚太2国	老/柬/缅	98/97/95	
0/0/0	0	3		0/0/0	0/0	0/0/0	0/0/	5.9/5.9/5.9	6.1/5.9		//	0/0/0	Other chemical products not listed (including hydrolysate or hydrolysate, DMC (any mixture of 2, 3 or 4 kinds of hexamethylcyclotrisiloxane, octamethylcyclotetrasiloxane, decamethylcyclopentasiloxane and dodecylcyclohexasiloxane))
													Residual products of the chemical or allied industries, not elsewhere specified or included; municipal waste; sewage sludge; other wastes specified in Note 6 to this Chapter:
0/0/0	2	0	0/0	0/0/0	0/0	0//0	0/0/	0/0/0	5.9/0			0/0/0	-Municipal waste
0/0/0	2	0	0/0	0/0/0	0/0	0//0	0/0/	0/0/0	5.9/0			0/0/0	-Sewage sludge
0/0/0	2	0	0/0	0/0/0	0/0	0//0	0/0/	0/0/0	5.9/0			0/0/0	-Clinical waste
													-Waste organic solvents:
0/0/0	2	0	0/0	0/0/0	0/0	0//0	0/0/	0/0/0	5.9/0			0/0/0	--Halogenated
0/0/0	2	0	0/0	0/0/0	0/0	0//0	0/0/	0/0/0	5.9/0			0/0/0	--Other
0/0/0	2	0	0/0	0/0/0	0/0	0/0/0	0/0/	0/0/0	5.9/0			0/0/0	-Wastes of metal pickling liquors, hydraulic fluids, brake fluids and anti-freeze fluids
													-Other wastes from chemical or allied industries:
0/0/0	2	0	0/0	0/0/0	0/0	0//0	0/0/	0/0/0	5.9/0			0/0/0	--Mainly containing organic constituents
0/0/0	2	0	0/0	0/0/0	0/0	0//0	0/0/	0/0/0	5.9/0			0/0/0	--Other
													-Other
0/0/0	2	0	0/0	0/0/0	0/0	0//0	0/0/	0/0/0	5.9/0			0/0/0	Condensed molasses fermented solubles
0/0/0	2	0	0/0	0/0/0	0/0	0//0	0/0/	0/0/0	5.9/0			0/0/0	Other chemical by-product or waste, not elsewhere specified or included
													Biodiesel and mixture thereof, not containing or containing less than 70% by weight of petroleum oils or oils obtaines from bituminous minerals:
													Biodiesel and mixture thereof, not containing or containingless than 70% by weight of petroleum oils or oils obtained from bituminous minerals
0/0/0	2	3		0/0/0	0/0	0//0	0/0/	5.9/5.9/5.9	6.1/5.9			0/0/0	Pure biodiesel
0/0/0	2	3		0/0/0	0/0	0//0	0/0/	5.9/5.9/5.9	6.1/5.9			0/0/0	Other biodiesel and mixture thereof
													Mixtures containing halogenated derivatives of methane, ethane or propane, not elsewhere specified or included.
													-Containing chlorofluorocarbons (CFCs), whether or not containing hydrochlorofluorocarbons (HCFCs), perfluorocarbons (PFCs) or hydrofluorocarbons (HFCs); containing hydrobromofluorocarbons (HBFCs); containing carbon tetrachloride; containing 1, 1, 1 — trichloroethane (methyl chloroform):
													--Containing chlorofluorocarbons (CFCs), whether or not containing hydrochlorofluorocarbons (HCFCs), perfluorocarbons (PFCs) or hydrofluorocarbons (HFCs)
0/0/0	2	0	0/0	0/0/0	0/0	0//0	0/0/	0/0/0	5.9/0			0/0/0	Mixture of dichlorodifluoromethane and difluoroethane, mixture of dichlorodifluoromethane and Chloropentafluoroethane, mixture of trifluoromethane and chlorotrifluoromethane (r—5, r—52, r—53)
0/0/0	2	0	0/0	0/0/0	0/0	0//0	0/0/	0/0/0	5.9/0			0/0/0	Mixture of dichlorodifluoromethane and dichlorodifluoromethane, mixture of difluoromethane and Chloropentafluoroethane, mixture of dichlorodifluoromethane and chloromonofluoromethane, mixture of chloromonofluoromethane and dichlorotetrafluoroethane, mixture of dichlorodifluoromethane and dichlorotetrafluoroethane (r—51, r—54, r—55, r—56, R—4)
0/0/0	2	0	0/0	0/0/0	0/0	0//0	0/0/	0/0/0	5.9/0			0/0/0	Other mixtures containing perfluorocarbons (CFCs), whether or not hydrochlorofluorocarbons (HCFCs), perfluorocarbons (PFCs) or hydrofluorocarbons (HFCS)
0/0/0	2	0	0/0	0/0/0	0/0	0//0	0/0/	0/0/0	5.9/0			0/0/0	--Containing hydrobromofluorocarbons (HBFCs)
0/0/0	2	0	0/0	0/0/0	0/0	0//0	0/0/	0/0/0	5.9/0			0/0/0	--Containing carbon tetrachloride
0/0/0	2	0	0/0	0/0/0	0/0	0//0	0/0/	0/0/0	5.9/0			0/0/0	--Containing 1,1,1—trichloroethane (methyl chloroform)
0/0/0	2	0	0/0	0/0/0	0/0	0//0	0/0/	0/0/0	5.9/0			0/0/0	-Containing bromochlorodifluoromethane (Halon — 1211), bromotrifluoromethane (Halon — 1301) or dibromotetrafluoroethanes (Halon—2402)
													-Containing hydrochlorofluorocarbons (HCFCs), whether or not containing perfluorocarbons (PFCs) or hydrofluorocarbons (HFCs), but not containing chlorofluorocarbons (CFCs):

税则号列	货品名称〔CIQ扩展编码及品名—T2表示见附表2〕	最惠(%)	暂定税率	普通	增值/消费	出口退税	计量单位	监管条件/特殊证件	检验检疫	对美关税	亚太上/下
3827.3100	--含子目2903.41至2903.48物质的〔999〕	6.5		35	13/	13	千克	14xy/1			
3827.3200	--其他,含子目2903.71至2903.75物质的〔999〕	6.5		35	13/	13	千克	14xy/1			
3827.3900	--其他〔999〕	6.5		35	13/	13	千克	14xy/1			
3827.4000	-含溴化甲烷(甲基溴)或溴氯甲烷的〔999〕	6.5		35	13/	0	千克	/1			
	-含三氟甲烷(HFC—23)或全氟烃(PFCs),但不含全氯氟烃(CFCs)或氢氯氟烃(HCFCs)的:										
3827.5100	--含三氟甲烷(HFC—23)的〔999〕	6.5		35	13/	13	千克	14xy/1		26.5	4.2/4.2
3827.5900	--其他〔999〕	6.5		35	13/	13	千克	14xy/1		26.5	4.2/4.2
	-含其他氢氟烃(HFCs),但不含全氯氟烃(CFCs)或氢氯氟烃(HCFCs)的:										
3827.6100	--按重量计含15%及以上1,1,1—三氟乙烷(HFC— 143a)的〔999〕	6.5		35	13/	13	千克	14xy/1		26.5	4.2/4.2
3827.6200	--其他,不归入上述子目,按重量计含55%及以上五氟乙烷(HFC—125),但不含无环烃的不饱和氟化衍生物(HFOs)的〔999〕	6.5		35	13/	13	千克	14xy/1		26.5	4.2/4.2
3827.6300	--其他,不归入上述子目,按重量计含40%及以上五氟乙烷(HFC—125)的〔999〕	6.5		35	13/	13	千克	14xy/1		26.5	4.2/4.2
3827.6400	--其他,不归入上述子目,按重量计含30%及以上1,1,1,2—四氟乙烷(HFC—134a)的,但不含无环烃的不饱和氟化衍生物(HFOs)〔999〕	6.5		35	13/	13	千克	14xy/1		26.5	4.2/4.2
3827.6500	--其他,不归入上述子目的,按重量计含20%及以上二氟甲烷(HFC—32)和20%及以上五氟乙烷(HFC—125) 的〔999〕	6.5		35	13/	13	千克	14xy/1		26.5	4.2/4.2
3827.6800	--其他,不归入上述子目,含子目2903.41至2903.48所列物质的〔999〕	6.5		35	13/	13	千克	14xy/1		26.5	4.2/4.2
3827.6900	--其他〔999〕	6.5		35	13/	13	千克	14xy/1		26.5	4.2/4.2
3827.9000	-其他〔301危险化学品,气体,302其他化工产品〕	6.5		35	13/	0	千克	/1		31.5	

协定税率 %								RCEP		特惠税率 %			Article Description
东/冰/格	巴基斯坦	韩国	瑞士上/下	哥/秘/柬	澳/毛	新西/坡/智	中国港/澳/台	东盟及马来/澳/韩	日/新	亚太2国	老/柬/缅	98/97/95	
0/0/0	2	0	0/0	0/0/0	0/0	0//0	0/0/	0/0/0	5.9/0			0/0/0	--Containing substances of subheadings No. 2903.41 to 2903.48
0/0/0	2	0	0/0	0/0/0	0/0	0//0	0/0/	0/0/0	5.9/0			0/0/0	--Other, containing substances of subheadings No. 2903.71 to 2903.75
0/0/0	2	0	0/0	0/0/0	0/0	0//0	0/0/	0/0/0	5.9/0			0/0/0	--Other
0/0/0	2	0	0/0	0/0/0	0/0	0//0	0/0/	0/0/0	5.9/0			0/0/0	-Containing methyl bromide (bromomethane) or bromochloromethane
													-Containing trifluoromethane (HFC－23) or perfluorocarbons (PFCs) but not containing chlorofluorocarbons (CFCs) or hydrochlorofluorocarbons (HCFCs):
0/0/0	2	0	0/0	0/0/0	0/0	0//0	0/0/	0/0/0	5.9/0			0/0/0	--Containing trifluoromethane (HFC－23)
0/0/0	2	0	0/0	0/0/0	0/0	0//0	0/0/	0/0/0	5.9/0			0/0/0	--Other
													-Containing other hydrofluorocarbons (HFCs) but not containing chlorofluorocarbons (CFCs) or hydrochlorofluorocarbons (HCFCs):
0/0/0	2	0	0/0	0/0/0	0/0	0//0	0/0/	0/0/0	5.9/0			0/0/0	--Containing 15 % or more by mass of 1,1,1－trifluoroethane (HFC－ 143a)
0/0/0	2	0	0/0	0/0/0	0/0	0//0	0/0/	0/0/0	5.9/0			0/0/0	--Other, not included in the subheading above, containing 55 % or more by mass of pentafluoroethane (HFC－ 125) but not containing unsaturated fluorinated derivatives of acyclic hydrocarbons (HFOs)
0/0/0	2	0	0/0	0/0/0	0/0	0//0	0/0/	0/0/0	5.9/0			0/0/0	--Other, not included in the subheadings above, containing 40 % or more by mass of pentafluoroethane (HFC－125)
0/0/0	2	0	0/0	0/0/0	0/0	0//0	0/0/	0/0/0	5.9/0			0/0/0	--Other, not included in the subheadings above, containing 30 % or more by mass of 1,1,1,2－tetrafluoroethane (HFC－134a) but not containing unsaturated fluorinated derivatives of acyclic hydrocarbons (HFOs)
0/0/0	2	0	0/0	0/0/0	0/0	0//0	0/0/	0/0/0	5.9/0			0/0/0	--Other, not included in the subheadings above, containing 20 % or more by mass of difluoromethane (HFC－32) and 20 % or more by mass of pentafluoroethane (HFC－125)
0/0/0	2	0	0/0	0/0/0	0/0	0//0	0/0/	0/0/0	5.9/0			0/0/0	--Other, not included in the subheadings above, containing substances of subheadings No. 2903.41 to 2903.48
0/0/0	2	0	0/0	0/0/0	0/0	0//0	0/0/	0/0/0	5.9/0			0/0/0	--Other
0/0/0	2	0	0/0	0/0/0	0/0	0//0	0/0/	0/0/0	5.9/0			0/0/0	-Other

第七类
塑料及其制品;橡胶及其制品

注释:

一、由两种或两种以上单独成分配套的货品,其部分或全部成分属于本类范围以内,混合后则构成第六类或第七类的货品,应按混合后产品归入相应的税目,但其组成成分必须同时符合下列条件:

(一)其包装形式足以表明这些成分不需经过改装就可以一起使用的;

(二)一起报验;
(三)这些成分的属性及相互比例足以表明是相互配用的。

二、除税目 39.18 或 39.19 的货品外,印有花纹、文字、图画的塑料、橡胶及其制品,如果所印花纹、字画作为其主要用途,应归入第四十九章。

第三十九章
塑料及其制品

注释:

一、本协调制度所称"塑料",是指税目 39.01 至 39.14 的材料,这些材料能够在聚合时或聚合后在外力(一般是热力和压力,必要时加入溶剂或增塑剂)作用下通过模制、浇铸、挤压、滚轧或其他工序制成一定的形状,成形后除去外力,其形状仍保持不变。

本协调制度所称"塑料",还应包括钢纸,但不包括第十一类的纺织材料。

二、本章不包括:
(一)税目 27.10 或 34.03 的润滑油;
(二)税目 27.12 或 34.04 的蜡;
(三)单独的已有化学定义的有机化合物(第二十九章);
(四)肝素及其盐(税目 30.01);
(五)税目 39.01 至 39.13 所列的任何产品溶于挥发性有机溶剂的溶液(火胶棉除外),但溶剂的重量必须超过溶液重量的 50%(税目 32.08);税目 32.12 的压印箔;

(六)有机表面活性剂或税目 34.02 的制剂;
(七)再熔胶及酯胶(税目 38.06);
(八)矿物油(包括汽油)或与矿物油用途相同的其他液体用的配制添加剂(税目 38.11);

(九)以第三十九章的聚乙二醇、聚硅氧烷或其他聚合物为基本成分配制的液压用液体(税目 38.19);
(十)附于塑料衬背上的诊断或实验用试剂(税目 38.22);
(十一)第四十章规定的合成橡胶及其制品;
(十二)鞍具及挽具(税目 42.01);税目 42.02 的衣箱、提箱、手提包及其他容器;
(十三)第四十六章的缏条、编结品及其他制品;
(十四)税目 48.14 的壁纸;
(十五)第十一类的货品(纺织原料及纺织制品);
(十六)第十二类的物品(例如,鞋靴、帽类、雨伞、阳伞、手杖、鞭子、马鞭及其零件);

(十七)税目 71.17 的仿首饰;
(十八)第十六类的物品(机器、机械器具或电气器具);
(十九)第十七类的航空器零件及车辆零件;
(二十)第九十章的物品(例如,光学元件、眼镜架及绘图仪器);
(二十一)第九十一章的物品(例如,钟壳及表壳);
(二十二)第九十二章的物品(例如,乐器及其零件);
(二十三)第九十四章的物品(例如,家具、灯具、照明装置、灯箱及活动房屋);
(二十四)第九十五章的物品(例如,玩具、游戏品及运动用品);
(二十五)第九十六章的物品(例如,刷子、纽扣、拉链、梳子、烟斗的嘴及柄、香烟嘴及类似品、保温瓶的零件及类似品、钢笔、活动铅笔、独脚架、双脚架、三脚架及类似品)。

三、税目 39.01 至 39.11 仅适用于化学合成的下列货品:
(一)采用减压蒸馏法,在压力转换为 1013 毫巴下的温度 300℃时,以体积计馏出量小于 60%的液体合成聚烯烃(税目 39.01 及 39.02);

(二)非高度聚合的苯并呋喃-茚式树脂(税目 39.11);
(三)平均至少有五个单体单元的其他合成聚合物;
(四)聚硅氧烷(税目 39.10);
(五)甲阶酚醛树脂(税目 39.09)及其他预聚物。

四、所称"共聚物",包括在整个聚合物中按重量计没有一种单体单元的含量在 95%及以上的各种聚合物。

在本章中,除条文另有规定以外,共聚物(包括共缩聚物、共加聚物、嵌段共聚物及接枝共聚物)及聚合物混合体应按聚合物中重量最大的那种共聚单体单元所构成的聚合物归入相应税目。在本注释中,归入同一税目的聚合物的共聚单体单元应作为一种单体单元对待。

如果没有任何一种共聚单体单元重量为最大,共聚物或聚合物混合体应按号列顺序归入其可归入的最末一个税目。

五、化学改性聚合物,即聚合物主链上的支链通过化学反应发生了变化的聚合物,应按未改性的聚合物的相应税目归类。本规定不适用于接枝共聚物。

六、税目 39.01 至 39.14 所称"初级形状",只限于下列各种形状:

SECTION Ⅶ
PLASTICS AND ARTICLES THEREOF; RUBBER AND ARTICLES THEREOF

Notes:

1. Goods put up in sets consisting of two or more separate constituents, some or all of which fall in this Section and are intended to be mixed together to obtain a product of Section Ⅵ or Ⅶ, are to be classified in the heading appropriate to that product, provided that the constituents are:
   (a) having regard to the manner in which they are put up, clearly identifiable as being intended to be used together without first being repacked;
   (b) presented together;
   (c) identifiable, whether by their nature or by the relative proportions in which they are present, as being complementary one to another.
2. Except for the goods of heading No. 39.18 or 39.19, plastics, rubber, and articles thereof, printed with motifs, characters or pictorial representations, which are not merely incidental to the primary use of the goods, fall in Chapter 49.

Chapter 39
Plastics and articles thereof

Notes:

1. Throughout the Nomenclature the expression "plastics" means those materials of headings No. 39.01 to 39.14 which are or have been capable, either at the moment of polymerization or at some subsequent stage, of being formed under external influence (usually heat and pressure, if necessary with a solvent or plasticizer) by moulding, casting, extruding, rolling or other process into shapes which are retained on the removal of the external influence.
   Throughout the Nomenclature any reference to "plastics" also includes vulcanized fibre. The expression, however, does not apply to materials regarded as textile materials of Section Ⅺ.
2. This Chapter does not cover:
   (a) Lubricating preparations of heading No. 27.10 or 34.03.
   (b) Waxes of heading No. 27.12 or 34.04;
   (c) Separate chemically defined organic compounds (Chapter 29);
   (d) Heparin or its salts (heading No. 30.01);
   (e) Solutions (other than collodions) consisting of any of the products specified in headings No. 39.01 to 39.13 in volatile organic solvents when the weight of the solvent exceeds 50% of the weight of the solution (heading No. 32.08); stamping foils of heading No. 32.12;
   (f) Organic surface-active agents or preparations of heading No. 34.02;
   (g) Run gums or ester gums (heading No. 38.06);
   (h) Prepared additives for mineral oils (including gasoline) or for other liquids used for the same purposes as mineral oils (heading No. 38.11)
   (i) Prepared hydronlic fluids based on polyglycols silianes or other polymers of chapter 39(heading No. 38.19);
   (j) Diagnostic or laboratory reagents on a backing of plastics (heading No. 38.22);
   (k) Synthetic rubber, as defined for the purposes of Chapter 40, or articles thereof;
   (l) Saddlery or harness (heading No. 42.01) or trunks, suitcases, handbags or other containers of heading No. 42.02;
   (m) Plaits, wickerwork or other articles of Chapter 46;
   (n) Wall coverings of heading No. 48.14;
   (o) Goods of Section Ⅺ (textiles and textile articles);
   (p) Articles of Section Ⅻ (for example, footwear, headgear, umbrellas, sun umbrellas, walking-sticks, whips, riding-crops or parts thereof);
   (q) Imitation jewellery of heading No. 71.17;
   (r) Articles of Section XVI (machines and mechanical or electrical appliances);
   (s) Parts of aircraft or vehicles of Section ⅩⅦ;
   (t) Articles of Chapter 90 (for example, optical elements, spectacle frames, drawing instruments);
   (u) Articles of Chapter 91 (for example, clock or watch cases);
   (v) Articles of Chapter 92 (for example, musical instruments or parts thereof);
   (w) Articles of Chapter 94 (for example, furniture, lamps and lighting fittings. illuminated signs, prefabricated buildings);
   (x) Articles of Chapter 95 (for example, toys, games, sports requisites); or
   (y) Articles of Chapter 96 (for example, brushes, buttons, slide fasteners, combs, mouthpieces or stems for smoking pipes, cigarette-holders or the like, parts of vacuum flasks or the like, pens, propelling pencils unipod, bipod, trpod or the Like).
3. Headings No. 39.01 to 39.11 apply only to goods of a kind produced by chemical synthesis, falling in the following categories:
   (a) Liquid synthetic polyolefins of which less than 60% by volume distils at 300℃, after conversion to 1,013 millibars when a reduced-pressure distillation method is used (headings No. 39.01 and 39.02);
   (b) Resins, not highly polymerized, of the coumarone-indene type (heading No. 39.11);
   (c) Other synthetic polymers with an average of at least 5 monomer units;
   (d) Silicones (heading No. 39.10);
   (e) Resols (heading No. 39.09) and other prepolymers.
4. The expression "copolymers" covers all polymers in which no single monomer unit contributes 95% or more by weight to the total polymer content.
   For the purposes of this Chapter, except where the context otherwise requires, copolymers (including copolycondensates, co-polyaddition products, block copolymers and graft copolymers) and polymer blends are to be classified in the heading covering polymers of that comonomer unit which predominates by weight over every other single comonomer unit. For the purposes of this Note, constituent comonomer units of polymers falling in the same heading shall be taken together.
   If no single comonomer unit predominates, copolymers or polymer blends, as the case may be, are to be classified in the heading which occurs last in numerical order among those which equally merit consideration.
5. Chemically modified polymers, that is those in which only appendages to the main polymer chain have been changed by chemical reaction, are to be classified in the heading appropriate to the unmodified polymer. This provision does not apply to graft copolymers.
6. In headings No. 39.01 to 39.14, the expression "primary forms" applies only to the following forms:

(一)液状及糊状,包括分散体(乳浊液及悬浮液)及溶液;
(二)不规则形状的块、团、粉(包括压型粉)、颗粒、粉片及类似的散装形状。

七、税目 39.15 不适用于已制成初级形状的单一的热塑材料废碎料及下脚料(税目 39.01 至 39.14)。

八、税目 39.17 所称"管子",是指通常用于输送或供给气体或液体的空心制品或半制品(例如,肋纹浇花软管、多孔管),还包括香肠用肠衣及其他扁平管。除肠衣及扁平管外,内截面如果不呈圆形、椭圆形、矩形(其长度不超过宽度的 1.5 倍)或正几何形,则不能视为管子,而应作为异型材。

九、税目 39.18 所称"塑料糊墙品",适用于墙壁或天花板装饰用的宽度不小于 45 厘米的成卷产品,这类产品是将塑料牢固地附着在除纸张以外任何材料的衬背上,并且在塑料面起纹、压花、着色、印制图案或用其他方法装饰。

十、税目 39.20 及 39.21 所称"板、片、膜、箔、扁条",只适用于未切割或仅切割成矩形(包括正方形)(含切割后即可供使用的),但未经进一步加工的板、片、膜、箔、扁条(第五十四章的物品除外)及正几何形块,不论是否经过印制或其他表面加工。

十一、税目 39.25 只适用于第二分章以前各税目未包括的下列物品:
(一)容积超过 300 升的囤、柜(包括化粪池)、罐、桶及类似容器;
(二)用于地板、墙壁、隔墙、天花板或屋顶等方面的结构件;
(三)槽管及其附件;
(四)门、窗及其框架和门槛;
(五)阳台、栏杆、栅栏、栅门及类似品;
(六)窗板、百叶窗(包括威尼斯式百叶窗)或类似品及其零件、附件;
(七)商店、工棚、仓库等用的拼装式固定大型货架;
(八)建筑用的特色(例如,凹槽、圆顶及鸽棚式)装饰件;
(九)固定装于门窗、楼梯、墙壁或建筑物其他部位的附件及架座,例如,球形把手、拉手、挂钩、托架、毛巾架、开关板及其他护板。

子目注释:

一、属于本章任一税号项下的聚合物(包括共聚物)及化学改性聚合物应按下列规则归类:

(一)在同级子目中有一个"其他"子目的:

1. 子目所列聚合物名称冠有"聚(多)"的(例如,聚乙烯及聚酰胺-6,6),是指列名的该种聚合物单体单元一种或多种总量在整个聚合物中按重量计必须占 95%及以上。

2. 子目 3901.30、3901.40、3903.20、3903.30 及 3904.30 所列的共聚物,如果该种共聚单体单元含量在整个聚合物中按重量计占 95%及以上,即应归入上述子目。

3. 化学改性聚合物如未在其他子目具体列名,应归入列明为"其他"的子目内。

4. 不符合上述 1、2、3 款规定的聚合物,应按聚合物中重量最大的那种单体单元(与其他各种单一的共聚单体单元相比)所构成的聚合物归入该级其他相应子目。为此,归入同一子目的聚合物单体单元应作为一种单体单元对待。只有在同级子目中的聚合物共聚单体单元才可以进行比较。

(二)在同级子目中没有"其他"子目的:

1. 聚合物应按聚合物中重量最大的那种单体单元(与其他各种单一的共聚单体单元相比)所构成的聚合物归入该级相应子目。为此,归入同一子目的聚合物单体单元应作为一种单体单元对待。只有在同级子目中的聚合物共聚单体单元才可以进行比较。

2. 化学改性聚合物应按相应的未改性聚合物的子目归类。聚合物混合体应按单体单元比例相等、种类相同的聚合物归入相应子目。

二、子目 3920.43 所称"增塑剂",包括"次级增塑剂"。

税则号列	货品名称〔CIQ 扩展编码及品名—T2 表示见附表 2〕	最惠(%)	暂定税率	普通	增值/消费	出口退税	计量单位	监管条件/特殊证件	检验检疫	对美关税	亚太上/下
	第一分章　初级形状										
39.01	**初级形状的乙烯聚合物:**										
3901.1000	-聚乙烯,比重小于 0.94										
3901.1000 01	初级形状比重<0.94 的聚乙烯(进口 CIF 价高于 3800 美元/吨)〔999〕	6.5	3	45	13/	13	千克	/			6/6
3901.1000 90	初级形状比重<0.94 的聚乙烯〔999〕	6.5		45	13/	13	千克	/			6/6
3901.2000	-聚乙烯,比重在 0.94 及以上			45	17	13	千克				
3901.2000 11	茂金属高密度聚乙烯(密度 0.962g/cm³,熔流率 0.85g/10min)(进口 CIF 价高于 3800 美元/吨)〔999〕	6.5	3	45	13/	13	千克	/			6/6
3901.2000 19	茂金属高密度聚乙烯(密度 0.962g/cm³,熔流率 0.85g/10min)〔999〕	6.5		45	13/	13	千克	/			6/6
3901.2000 91	其他初级形状比重≥0.94 的聚乙烯(进口 CIF 价高于 3800 美元/吨)〔999〕	6.5	3	45	13/	13	千克	/		30.5	6/6
3901.2000 99	其他初级形状比重≥0.94 的聚乙烯〔999〕	6.5		45	13/	13	千克	/		34	6/6
3901.3000	-乙烯-乙酸乙烯酯共聚物〔999〕	6.5		45	13/	13	千克	/		34	6/6
	-乙烯-α-烯烃共聚物,比重小于 0.94:										
3901.4010	---乙烯-丙烯共聚物(乙丙橡胶)	6.5		45	13/	10	千克			/31.5	
3901.4010 10	粘指剂,比重小于 0.94(初级形状,乙烯单体单元 65%,丙烯单体单元 35%)〔999〕	6.5		45	13/	13	千克	/			

(a) Liquids and pastes, including dispersions (emulsions and suspensions) and solutions;

(b) Blocks of irregular shape, lumps, powders (including moulding powders), granules, flakes and similar bulk forms.

7. Heading No. 39.15 does not apply to waste, parings and scrap of a single thermoplastic material, transformed into primary forms (headings No. 39.01 to 39.14).

8. For the purposes of heading No. 39.17, the expression "tubes, pipes and hoses" means hollow products, whether semi-manufactures or finished products, of a kind generally used for conveying, conducting or distributing gases or liquids (for example, ribbed garden hose, perforated tubes). This expression also includes sausage casings and other layflat tubing. However, except for the last-mentioned, those having an internal cross-section other than round, oval, rectangular (in which the length does not exceed 1.5 times the width) or in the shape of a regular polygon are not to be regarded as tubes, pipes and hoses but as profile shapes.

9. For the purposes of heading No. 39.18, the expression "wall or ceiling coverings of plastics" applies to products in rolls, of a width not less than 45 cm, suitable for wall or ceiling decoration, consisting of plastics fixed permanently on a backing of any material other than paper, the layer of plastics (on the face side) being grained, embossed, coloured, design-printed or otherwise decorated.

10. In headings No. 39.20 and 39.21, the expression "plates, sheets, film, foil and strip" applies only to plates, sheets, film, foil and strip (other than those of Chapter 54) and to blocks of regular geometric shape, whether or not printed or otherwise surface-woked, uncut or cut into rectangles (including squares) but not further worked (even if when so cut they become articles ready for use).

11. Heading No. 39.25 applies only to the following articles, not being products covered by any of the earlier headings of sub-Chapter Ⅱ:

(a) Reservoirs, tanks (including septic tanks), vats and similar containers, of a capacity exceeding 300 L;

(b) Structural elements used, for example, in floors, walls or partitions, ceilings or roofs;

(c) Gutters and fittings therefor;

(d) Doors, windows and their frames and thresholds for doors;

(e) Balconies, balustrades, fencing, gates and similar barriers;

(f) Shutters, blinds (including Venetian blinds) and similar articles and parts and fittings thereof;

(g) Large-scale shelving for assembly and permanent installation, for example, in shops, workshops, warehouses;

(h) Ornamental architectural features, for example, flutings, cupolas, dovecotes; and

(i) Fittings and mountings intended for permanent installation in or on doors, windows, staircases, walls or other parts of buildings, for example, knobs, handles, hooks, brackets, towel rails, switch-plates and other protective plates.

Subheading Notes:

1. Within any one heading of this Chapter, polymers (including copolymers) and chemically modified polymers are to be classified according to the following provisions:

(a) Where there is a subheading named "Other" in the same series:

(i) The designation in a subheading of a polymer by the prefix "poly" (forexample, polyethylene and polyamide-6,6) means that the constituent monomer unit or monomer units of the named polymer taken together must contribute 95% or more by weight of the total polymer content.

(ii) The copolymers named in subheadings Nos. 3901.30, 3901.40, 3903.20, 3903.30 and 3904.30 are to be classified in those subheadings, provided that the comonomer units of the named copolymers contribute 95% or more by weight of the total polymer content.

(iii) Chemically modified polymers are to be classified in the subheading named "Other", provided that the chemically modified polymers are not more specifically covered by another subheading.

(iv) Polymers not meeting (1), (2) or (3) above, are to be classified in the subheading, among the remaining subheadings in the series, covering polymers of that monomer unit which predominates by weight over every other single comonomer unit. For this purpose, constituent monomer units of polymers falling in the same subheading shall be taken together. Only the constituent comonomer units of the polymers in the series of subheadings under consideration are to be compared.

(b) Where there is no subheading named "Other" in the same series:

(i) Polymers are to be classified in the subheading covering polymers of that monomer unit which predominates by weight over every other single comonomer unit. For this purpose, constituent monomer units of polymers falling in the same subheading shall be taken together. Only the constituent comonomer units of the polymers in the series under consideration are to be compared.

(ii) Chemically modified polymers are to be classified in the subheading appropriate to the unmodified polymer.

Polymer blends are to be classified in the same subheading as polymers of the same monomer units in the same proportions.

2. For the purposes of subheading No. 3920.43, the term "plasticisers" includes "secondary plasticisers."

协定税率 %								RCEP		特惠税率 %			Article Description
东/冰/格	巴基斯坦	韩国	瑞士上/下	哥/秘/柬	澳/毛	新西/坡/智	中国港/澳/台	东盟及马来/澳/韩	日/新	亚太2国	老/柬/缅	98/97/95	
													1.-PRIMARY FORMS
													Polymers of ethylene, in primary forms:
													-Polyethylene having a specific gravity of less than 0.94
/0/	6	5.9	2.7/2.7	0//	0/0	0//0	0/0/					0//	Polyethylene having a sopecific gravity of less than 0.94, in primary forms(CIF>USD3800/ton)
/0/	6	5.9	2.7/2.7	0//	0/0	0//0	0/0/					0//	Polyethylene having a specific gravity of less than 0.94, in primary forms
													-Polyethylene having a specific gravity of 0.94 or more
/0/	6	5.9	2.7/2.7	0//	0/0	0//0	0/0/				//	0//	Metallocene HDPE (density 0.962g/cm 3, melting rate 0.85g/10min) (CIF price of import is higher than 3800 USD / ton)
/0/	6	5.9	2.7/2.7	0//	0/0	0//0	0/0/				//	0//	Metallocene HDPE (density 0.962g/cm ^{3}, melting rate 0.85g/10min)
/0/	6	5.9	2.7/2.7	0//	0/0	0//0	0/0/				//	0//	Other polyethylene with the proportion of primary shape ≥ 0.94 (CIF price of import is higher than 3800 USD / ton)
/0/	6	5.9	2.7/2.7	0//	0/0	0//0	0/0/				//	0//	Polyethylene with other primary shape specific gravity ≥ 0.94
0/0/	4	5.9	0/0	0/0/0	0/0	0/0/0	0/0/	6.2/6.2/	/6.2			0/0/0	-Ethylene-vinyl acetate copolymers
													-Ethylene－alpha－olefin copoly－mers, having a specific gravity of less than 0.94:
0/0/0	5	4.3	0	0	0	0	0/0/0	0/0/				0/0/	---Ethylene-propylene copoly-mers
0/0/0	0	3	0/0	0/0/0	0/0	0/0/0	0/0/	5.9/5.9/5.9	6.1/5.9		//	0/0/0	Adhesive, specific gravity less than 0.94 (primary shape, ethylene monomer unit 65%, propylene monomer unit 35%)

税则号列		货品名称〔CIQ 扩展编码及品名一T2 表示见附表 2〕	最惠(%)	暂定税率	普通	增值/消费	出口退税	计量单位	监管条件/特殊证件	检验检疫	对美关税	亚太上/下
3901.4010	90	乙烯一丙烯共聚物(乙丙橡胶),比重小于 0.94(初级形状,乙烯单体单元的含量大于丙烯单体单元)〔999〕	6.5		45	13/	13	千克	/		34	
3901.4020		---线型低密度聚乙烯	6.5		45	13/	13	千克			/31.5	
3901.4020	10	线型低密度的乙烯与 1一辛烃共聚物,比重小于 0.94(初级形状的)〔999〕	6.5		45	13/	13	千克	/			
3901.4020	90	线型低密度聚乙烯,比重小于 0.94(初级形状的)〔999〕	6.5		45	13/	13	千克	/		34	
3901.4090		---其他〔999〕	6.5		45	13/	13	千克	/			4.2/4.2
		-其他:										
3901.9010		---乙烯-丙烯共聚物(乙丙橡胶)〔999〕	6.5		45	13/	13	千克	/		34	
3901.9090		---其他〔999〕	6.5		45	13/	13	千克	/			4.2/4.2
39.02		**初级形状的丙烯或其他烯烃聚合物:**										
3902.1000		-聚丙烯										
3902.1000	10	电工级初级形状聚丙烯树脂(灰分含量不大于 30ppm)〔999〕	6.5	3	45	13/	13	千克	/		30.5	
3902.1000	20	共聚抗冲等级初级形状聚丙烯(熔融指数 MI<0.5g/10min,UL 认证黄卡中 RTI(相当于长期工作温度)115℃,悬臂梁缺口冲击强度(测量方法 ISO 180):23℃时为 64KJ/m^2,-40℃时为 4.0KJ/m^2)〔999〕	6.5		45	13/	13	千克	/			
3902.1000	90	其他初级形状的聚丙烯〔999〕	6.5		45	13/	13	千克	/		34	
3902.2000		-聚异丁烯〔101 无检疫要求食品添加剂,301 需申报仅用于工业用途不用于食品添加剂无检疫要求的化学品〕	6.5		45	13/	13	千克	A/	R	34	
		-丙烯共聚物:										
3902.3010		---乙烯-丙烯共聚物(乙丙橡胶)〔999〕	6.5		45	13/	13	千克	/		34	6/6
3902.3090		---其他〔999〕	6.5		45	13/	13	千克	/		34	6/6
3902.9000		-其他										
3902.9000	10	端羧基聚丁二烯,CTPB(做粘接剂或燃料)〔999〕	6.5		45	13/	13	千克	3/		19	
3902.9000	20	端羟基聚丁二烯,HTPB(做粘接剂或燃料)〔999〕	6.5		45	13/	13	千克	3/		19	
3902.9000	90	其他初级形状的烯烃聚合物〔999〕	6.5		45	13/	13	千克	/		19	
39.03		**初级形状的苯乙烯聚合物:**										
		-聚苯乙烯:										
3903.1100		--可发性的〔301 危险化学品,杂项物质;302 其他化工产品〕	6.5		45	13/	13	千克	/		14	6/6
		--其他:										
3903.1910		---改性的〔999〕	6.5		45	13/	13	千克	/		34	6/6
3903.1990		---其他〔999〕	6.5		45	13/	13	千克	/		34	6/6
3903.2000		-苯乙烯-丙烯腈(SAN)共聚物〔999〕	12		45	13/	13	千克	/		39.5	
		-丙烯腈-丁二烯-苯乙烯(ABS)共聚物:										
3903.3010		---改性的〔999〕	6.5		45	13/	13	千克	/		34	6/6
3903.3090		---其他〔999〕	6.5		45	13/	13	千克	/		34	6/6
3903.9000		-其他〔999〕	6.5		45	13/	13	千克	/		19	6/6
39.04		**初级形状的氯乙烯或其他卤化烯烃聚合物:**										
		-聚氯乙烯,未掺其他物质:										
3904.1010		---糊树脂〔999〕	6.5		45	13/	13	千克	/		34	4.2/4.2
3904.1090		---其他										
3904.1090	01	聚氯乙烯纯粉(纯指未掺其他物质)〔999〕	6.5		45	13/	13	千克	7/			4.2/4.2
3904.1090	90	其他初级形状的纯聚氯乙烯(纯指未掺其他物质)〔999〕	6.5		45	13/	13	千克	7/			4.2/4.2
		-其他聚氯乙烯:										
3904.2100		--未塑化〔999〕	6.5		45	13/	13	千克	/		14	
3904.2200		--已塑化〔999〕	6.5		45	13/	13	千克	/		19	
3904.3000		-氯乙烯-乙酸乙烯酯共聚物〔999〕	9		45	13/	13	千克	/		31.5	8.6/8.6
3904.4000		-其他氯乙烯共聚物〔999〕	12		45	13/	13	千克	/		37	7.8/7.8
3904.5000		-偏二氯乙烯聚合物										
3904.5000	10	偏二氯乙烯一氯乙烯共聚树脂〔999〕	6.5		45	13/	13	千克	/		29	
3904.5000	90	其他偏二氯乙烯聚合物〔999〕	6.5		45	13/	13	千克	/		29	
		-氟聚合物:										
3904.6100		--聚四氟乙烯〔301 危险化学品,易燃液体;302 其他化工品〕	10		45	13/	13	千克	/		17.5	
3904.6900		--其他〔999〕	6.5		45	13/	13	千克	/		14	
3904.9000		-其他〔999〕	10		45	13/	13	千克	/		17.5	
39.05		**初级形状的乙酸乙烯酯或其他乙烯酯聚合物;初级形状的其他乙烯基聚合物:**										
		-聚乙酸乙烯酯:										
3905.1200		--水分散体〔999〕	10		45	13/	13	千克	/		17.5	
3905.1900		--其他〔999〕	10		45	13/	13	千克	/		37.5	
		-乙酸乙烯酯共聚物:										
3905.2100		--水分散体〔999〕	10		45	13/	13	千克	/		37.5	
3905.2900		--其他〔999〕	10		45	13/	13	千克	/		37.5	
3905.3000		-聚乙烯醇,不论是否含有未水解的乙酸酯基〔101 聚乙烯醇(无检疫要求食品添加剂),301 需申报仅用于工业用途不用于食品添加剂无检疫要求的化学品〕	14		45	13/	13	千克	A/	R	34	
		-其他:										

协定税率 %								RCEP		特惠税率 %			Article Description
东/冰/格	巴基斯坦	韩国	瑞士 上/下	哥/秘/柬	澳/毛	新西/坡/智	中国港/澳/台	东盟及马来/澳/韩	日/新	亚太2国	老/柬/缅	98/97/95	
0/0/0	0	3	0/0	0/0/0	0/0	0/0/0	0/0/	5.9/5.9/5.9	6.1/5.9		//	0/0/0	Ethylene propylene copolymer (ethylene propylene rubber), specific gravity less than 0.94 (primary shape, ethylene monomer unit content greater than propylene monomer unit)
0/0/	5			0		0	0/0/0	0/0/				0/0/0	---Linearity low density polyeth ylene
0/0/	0			0//0	0/0	0/0/0	0/0/	6.2/6.2/	/6.2		//	0/0/0	Linear low density ethylene and 1—octane copolymer, specific gravity less than 0.94 (primary shape)
0/0/	0			0//0	0/0	0/0/0	0/0/	6.2/6.2/	/6.2		//	0/0/0	Linear low density polyethylene, specific gravity less than 0.94 (primary shape)
0/0/0	0	4.2	0/0	0/0/0	0/0	0/0/0	0/0/	6.2/6.2/	/6.2			0/0/0	---Other
													-Other:
0/0/0	0	3	0/0	0/0/0	0/0	0/0/0	0/0/	5.9/5.9/5.9	6.1/5.9			0/0/0	---Ethylene-propylene copolymers
0/0/0	0	4.2	0/0	0/0/0	0/0	0/0/0	0/0/	6.2/6.2/	/6.2			0/0/0	---Other
													Polymers of propylene or of other olefins, in primary forms:
													-Polypropylene
0/0/	4		2.7/2.7	0//0	0/0	0/0/0	0/0/	0/6.2/	/6.2			0//	Polypropylene resin, in primary forms, electrical grade (ash content≤30ppm)
0/0/	4		2.7/2.7	0//0	0/0	0/0/0	0/0/	0/6.2/	/6.2		//	0//	Impact resistance grade of copolymerized polypropylene of primary shape (MI < 0.5g/10min, RTI (equivalent to long—term working temperature) in UL certified yellow card 115 ℃, impact strength of cantilever notch (Measurement Method ISO 180): 64kj / m ^{2} at 23 ℃, 4.0kj/m ^{2} at — 40 ℃)
0/0/	4		2.7/2.7	0//0	0/0	0/0/0	0/0/	0/6.2/	/6.2			0//	Other polypropylene, in primary forms
0/0/0	2		0/0	0/0/0	0/0	0//0	0/0/	5/5/	/5			0/0/0	-Polyisobutylene
													-Propylene copolymers:
0/0/0	0	3	0/0	0/0/0	0/0	0/0/0	0/0/0	0/5.9/5.9	6.1/5.9			0/0/0	---Ethylene-propylene copolymers
0/0/	4	5.9	0/0	0/0/0	0/0	0/0/0	0/0/	0/5/	/5			0/0/0	---Other
													-Other
0/0/0	0		0/0	0/0/0	0/0	0/0/0	0/0/0	5/5/	/5			0/0/0	Carboxyl-terminal polybutadiene, CTPB (used as adhesive or fuel)
0/0/0	0		0/0	0/0/0	0/0	0/0/0	0/0/0	5/5/	/5			0/0/0	Hydroxyl-terminal polybutadiene, HTPB (used as adhesive or fuel)
0/0/0	0		0/0	0/0/0	0/0	0/0/0	0/0/0	5/5/	/5			0/0/0	Other polymers of olefins, in primary forms
													Polymers of styrene, in primary forms:
													-Polystyrene:
0/0/0	0	5.9	0/0	0/0/0	0/0	0/0/0	0/0/	5/5/	/5			0/0/0	--Expansible
													--Other:
0/0/	0	3.9	0/0	0/0/0	0/0	0/0/0	0/0/	6.2/6.2/6.2	6.2/6.2			0/0/0	---Modified
0/0/	0	3.9	0/0	0/0/0	0/0	0/0/0	0/0/	6.2/6.2/6.2	6.2/6.2			0/0/0	---Other
0/0/0	6	9.6	1.2/1.2	0/0/0	0/0	0/0/0	0/0/0	10.8/5/	/5			0/0/0	-Styrene-acrylonitrile (SAN) copolymers
													-Acrylonitrile-butadiene-styrene (ABS) copolymers:
0/0/	4	3.9	2.7/2.7	0/0/0	0/0	0/0/0	0/0/	6.2/6.2/6.2	6.2/6.2			0/0/0	---Modified
0/0/	4	3.9	0.7/0.7	0/0/0	0/0	0/0/0	0/0/	6.2/6.2/6.2	6.2/6.2			0/0/0	---Other
0/0/0	0	3	0/0	0/0/0	0/0	0/0/0	0/0/0	5.9/5.9/5.9	6.1/5.9			0/0/0	-Other
													Polymers of vinyl chloride or of other halogenated olefins, in primary forms:
													-Poly(vinyl chloride), not mixed with any other substances:
0/0/0	0	3.9	0/0	0/0/0	0/0	0/0/0	0/0/	6.2/6.2/6.2	6.2/6.2			0/0/0	---Paste poly cvinyl chloride
													---Other
0/0/	0	4.2	0/0	0/0/0	0/0	0/0/0	0/0/	5.9/5/	/5			0/0/0	Poly (vinyl chloride)(not mixed with any other substances) in powder
0/0/	0	4.2	0/0	0/0/0	0/0	0/0/0	0/0/	5.9/5/	/5			0/0/0	Other poly (vinyl chloride)(not mixed with any other substances)
													-Other poly(vinyl chloride):
0/0/0	2	3.9	0/0	0/0/0	0/0	0/0/0	0/0/	6.2/6.2/	/6.2			0/0/0	--Non-plasticized
0/0/		3.9	0/0	0/0/0	0/0	0/0/0	0/0/	6.2/6.2/	/6.2			0/0/0	--Plasticized
0/0/0	2	4.2	0/0	0/0/0	0/0	0//0	0/0/	8.4/8.6/8.4	8.4/8.6			0/0/0	-Vinyl chloride-vinyl acetate copolymers
0/0/0	6	5.6	1.2/1.2	0/0/0	0/0	0/0/0	0/0/	11.2/11.4/11.2	11.3/11.4			0/0/0	-Other vinyl chloride copolymers
													-Vinylidene chloride polymers
0/0/0	2	0	0/0	0/0/0	0/0	0//0	0/0/	0/5.9/0	0/5.9			0/0/0	Vinylidene Chloride—Vinyl Chloride Copolymer Resin
0/0/0	2	0	0/0	0/0/0	0/0	0//0	0/0/	0/5.9/0	0/5.9			0/0/0	Other vinylidene chloride polymers, in primary forms
													-Fluoro-polymers:
0/0/0	3.5	2	0/0	0/0/0	0/0	0/0/0	0/0/	9/9/9	9.1/9			0/0/0	--Polytetrafluoroethylene
0/0/0	2	0	0/0	0/0/0	0/0	0//0	0/0/	0/0/0	0/0			0/0/0	--Other
0/0/0	3.5	4.6	0/0	0/0/0	0/0	0//0	0/0/	9.3/9.5/9.3	9.4/9.5			0/0/0	-Other
													Polymers of vinyl acetate or of other vinyl esters, in primary forms; other vinyl polymers in primary forms:
													-Poly(vinyl acetate):
0/0/0		4.6	0/0	0/0/0	0/0	0/0/0	0/0/	9.3/9.5/9.3	9.4/9.5			0/0/0	--In aqueous dispersion
0/0/0	3.5	4.6	0/0	0/0/0	0/0	0//0	0/0/	9.3/9.5/9.3	9.4/9.5			0/0/0	--Other
													-Vinyl acetate copolymers:
0/0/0	3.5	4.6	0/0	0/0/0	0/0	0/0/0	0/0/0	9.3/9.5/9.3	9.4/9.5			0/0/0	--In aqueous dispersion
0/0/0	3.5	4.6		0/0/0	0/0	0/0/0	0/0/	9.3/9.5/9.3	9.4/9.5			0/0/0	--Other
0/0/0	11.2	2.8	1.4/1.4	0/0/0	0/0	0/0/0	0/0/0	5/5/	/5			0/0/0	-Poly(vinyl alcohol), whether or not containing unhydrolyzed acetate groups
													-Other:

税则号列	货品名称〔CIQ扩展编码及品名－T2表示见附表2〕	最惠(%)	暂定税率	普通	增值/消费	出口退税	计量单位	监管条件/特殊证件	检验检疫	对美关税	亚太上/下
3905.9100	--共聚物〔301危险化学品,易燃液体;302其他化工品〕	10		45	13/	13	千克	/		17.5	
3905.9900	--其他〔301危险化学品,易燃液体;302其他化工产品〕	10		45	13/	13	千克	/13		17.5	
39.06	**初级形状的丙烯酸聚合物：**										
3906.1000	-聚甲基丙烯酸甲酯〔301危险化学品,易燃液体,302其他化工产品〕	6.5		45	13/	13	千克	/		34	6/6
	-其他：										
3906.9010	---聚丙烯酰胺〔301无检疫要求食品添加剂,302需申报仅用于工业用途不用于食品添加剂无检疫要求的化学品〕	6.5		45	13/	13	千克	A/	R	34	6/6
3906.9020	---丙烯酸－丙烯酸钠交联共聚物〔301无检疫要求食品添加剂;302需申报仅用于工业用途不用于食品添加剂无检疫要求的化学品〕	6.5		45	13/	13	千克	/			6/6
3906.9090	---其他〔301危险化学品,易燃液体;302其他化工产品;999饲料添加剂〕	6.5		45	13/	13	千克	/13			6/6
39.07	**初级形状的聚缩醛、其他聚醚及环氧树脂;初级形状的聚碳酸酯、醇酸树脂、聚烯丙基酯及其他聚酯：**										
	-聚缩醛：										
3907.1010	---聚甲醛										
3907.1010 10	聚甲醛(均聚聚甲醛及改性聚甲醛除外)〔999〕	6.5		45	13/	13	千克	/		29	6.1/6.1
3907.1010 90	其他聚甲醛〔999〕	6.5		45	13/	13	千克	/		29	6.1/6.1
3907.1090	---其他										
3907.1090 10	共聚聚甲醛(改性聚甲醛除外)〔999〕	6.5		45	13/	13	千克	/13		29	4.2/4.2
3907.1090 90	其他聚缩醛〔301危险化学品,易燃固体;302初级形状的聚缩醛〕	6.5		45	13/	13	千克	/13		29	4.2/4.2
	-其他聚醚：										
3907.2100	--双(聚氧乙烯)甲基膦酸酯〔999〕	6.5		45	13/	13	千克	/			6.1/6.1
	--其他：										
3907.2910	---聚四亚甲基醚二醇〔999〕	6.5	3	45	13/	13	千克	/		30.5	6.1/6.1
3907.2990	---其他										
3907.2990 10	初级形状的聚2,6－二甲基－1,4－苯醚(包括化学改性或物理改性的)〔301危险化学品,易燃液体,302其他化工产品〕	6.5		45	13/	13	千克	/			6.1/6.1
3907.2990 90	初级形状的其他聚醚〔301危险化学品,易燃液体,302其他化工产品〕	6.5		45	13/	13	千克	/			6.1/6.1
3907.3000	-环氧树脂										
3907.3000 01	初级形状溴质量≥18%或进口CIF价>3800美元/吨的环氧树脂(如溶于溶剂,以纯环氧树脂折算溴百分比含量)〔301其他危险化学品,999初级形状的环氧树脂〕	6.5	4	45	13/	13	千克	A/	M		6.1/6.1
3907.3000 90	初级形状的环氧树脂(溴重量百分比含量在18%以下)〔301其他危险化学品,999其他〕	6.5		45	13/	13	千克	AB/	MN		6.1/6.1
3907.4000	-聚碳酸酯〔301危险化学品,有机过氧化物;302其他化工产品〕	6.5		45	13/	13	千克	/13			6.1/6.1
3907.5000	-醇酸树脂〔301易燃液体,999其他〕	10		45	13/	13	千克	AB/	MN	37.5	6.5/6.5
	-聚对苯二甲酸乙二酯：										
	--粘数在78毫升/克或以上：										
3907.6110	---切片〔999〕	6.5		45	13/	13	千克	/		34	
3907.6190	---其他〔999〕	6.5		45	13/	13	千克	/		29	
	--其他：										
3907.6910	---切片〔999〕	6.5		45	13/	13	千克	/		19	
3907.6990	---其他〔999〕	6.5		45	13/	13	千克	/		29	
3907.7000	-聚乳酸〔999〕	6.5	3	45	13/	13	千克	/		8	4.2/4.2
	-其他聚酯：										
3907.9100	--不饱和〔301危险化学品,易燃液体;302其他化工产品〕	6.5		45	13/	13	千克	/13		29	
	--其他：										
3907.9910	---聚对苯二甲酸丁二酯										
3907.9910 01	未经增强或改性的初级形状PBT树脂〔999〕	6.5		45	13/	13	千克	/		29	4.2/4.2
3907.9910 90	其他聚对苯二甲酸丁二酯〔999〕	6.5		45	13/	13	千克	/		29	4.2/4.2
	---其他：										
3907.9991	----聚对苯二甲酸-己二醇-丁二醇酯										
3907.9991 10	初级形状的热塑性液晶聚对苯二甲酸－己二酸－丁二醇酯〔999〕	0		45	13/	13	千克	AB/	RS	7.5	4.2/4.2
3907.9991 90	其他初级形状的聚对苯二甲酸－己二酸－丁二醇酯〔999〕	6.5		45	13/	13	千克	AB/	RS	14	4.2/4.2
3907.9999	----其他										
3907.9999 10	初级形状的热塑性液晶其他聚酯〔999〕	0		45	13/	13	千克	AB/	RS		4.2/4.2
3907.9999 90	初级形状的其他聚酯〔301危险化学品,易燃液体;302其他化工产品〕	6.5		45	13/	13	千克	AB/	RS		4.2/4.2
39.08	**初级形状的聚酰胺：**										
	-聚酰胺-6、-11、-12、-6,6、-6,9、-6,10或-6,12：										
	---切片：										
3908.1011	----聚酰胺-6,6切片										
3908.1011 01	聚酰胺-6,6切片〔999〕	6.5		45	13/	13	千克	/			
3908.1011 90	改性聚酰胺-6,6切片(经螺杆二次混炼加入玻璃纤维、矿物质、增韧剂、阻燃剂的改性聚酰胺-6,6切片)〔999〕	6.5		45	13/	13	千克	/			
3908.1012	----聚酰胺-6切片〔999〕	6.5		45	13/	13	千克	/		34	
3908.1019	----其他〔999〕	6.5		45	13/	13	千克	/		19	

协定税率 %								RCEP		特惠税率 %			Article Description
东/冰/格	巴基斯坦	韩国	瑞士上/下	哥/秘/柬	澳/毛	新西/坡/智	中国港/澳/台	东盟及马来/澳/韩	日/新	亚太2国	老/柬/缅	98/97/95	
0/0/0	3.5	4.6	0/0	0/0/0	0/0	0//0	0/0/	9.3/9.5/9.3	9.4/9.5			0/0/0	--Copolymers
0/0/0		4.6	0/0	0/0/0	0/0	0//0	0/0/	9.3/9.5/9.3	9.4/9.5			0/0/0	--Other
													Acrylic polymers in primary forms:
0/0/0	2	5.9	0/0	0/0/0	0/0	0//0	0/0/0	6.2/6.2/	/6.2			0/0/0	-Poly(methyl methacrylate)
													-Other:
0/0/0	0	5.9	0/0	0/0/0	0/0	0//0	0/0/0	5/5/	/5			0/0/0	---Polyacrylamide
0/0/0	0	1.3	0.7/0.7	0/0/0	0/0	0//0	0/0/0	0/0/5.9	6.1/0			0/0/0	---Acrylic acid sodium acrylate crosslinked copolymer
0/0/0	0	1.3	0.7/0.7	0/0/0	0/0	0//0	0/0/0	0/0/5.9	6.1/0			0/0/0	---Other
													Polyacetals, other polyethers and epoxide resins, in primary forms; polycarbonates, alkyd resins, polyallyl esters and other polyesters, in primary forms:
													-Polyacetals:
													---Polyoxymethylene(POM)
0/0/0	0	3	0/0	0/0/0	0/0	0/0/0	0/0/0	5.9/5.9/5.9	6.1/5.9			0/0/0	Polyoxymethylene(POM),other than homoPOM and modification of POM
0/0/0	0	3	0/0	0/0/0	0/0	0/0/0	0/0/0	5.9/5.9/5.9	6.1/5.9			0/0/0	Other polyoxymethylene(POM)
													---Other
0/0/0	2	0	0/0	0/0/0	0/0	0/0/0	0/0/	0/0/0	5.9/0			0/0/0	Polyformaldehyde,other than modification of POM
0/0/0	2	0	0/0	0/0/0	0/0	0/0/0	0/0/	0/0/0	5.9/0			0/0/0	Other polyacetals
													-Other polyethers:
0/0/0	0	3	0.7/0.7	0/0/0	0/0	0/0/0	0/0/	5.9/5.9/5.9	6.1/5.9			0/0/0	--Bis(polyoxyethylene) methylphosphonate
													--Other
0/0/0	0	0	0/0	0/0/0	0/0	0/0/0	0/0/0	0/5.9/0	0/5.9			0/0/0	---Polytetramethylene ether glycol
													---Other
0/0/0	0	3	0.7/0.7	0/0/0	0/0	0/0/0	0/0/	5.9/5.9/5.9	6.1/5.9			0/0/0	Poly (2,6－dimethyl－1,4－phenyl ether) in primary form (including chemically or physically modified)
0/0/0	0	3	0.7/0.7	0/0/0	0/0	0/0/0	0/0/	5.9/5.9/5.9	6.1/5.9			0/0/0	Other polyether in primary shape
													-Epoxide resins
0/0/0	0	3	2.7/2.7	0/0/0	0/0	0/0/0	0/0/0	5.9/5.9/5.9	6.1/5.9			0/0/0	Epoxide resins, in primary forms, containing ≥18% by weight of bromine, or import CIF price ＞3800 USD/ton (If dissolved into solutions, convert the content percentage of bromine by pure epoxy resin)
0/0/0	0	3	2.7/2.7	0/0/0	0/0	0/0/0	0/0/0	5.9/5.9/5.9	6.1/5.9			0/0/0	Epoxide resins, in primary forms, containing ＜ 18% by weight of bromine
0/0/0	0	3	0.7/0.7	0/0/0	0/0	0/0/0	0/0/0	5.9/5.9/5.9	6.1/5.9			0/0/0	-Polycarbonates
0/0/0	3.5	2	0/0	0/0/0	0/0	0/0/0	0/0/0	0/0/9	9.1/0			0/0/0	-Alkyd resins
													-Poly(ethylene terephthalate):
													--Having a viscosity number of 78 ml/ g or higher:
5/0/0		3.9	0/0	0/0/0	0/0	0//0	0/0/	6.2/6.3/	/6.3			0/0/0	--In the form of slices or chips
0/0/0	0	3	0/0	0/0/0	0/0	0/0/0	0/0/	5.9/5.9/5.9	6.1/5.9			0/0/0	---Other
													--Other:
5/0/	0	3.9	0/0	0/0/0	0/0	0//0	0/0/	6.2/6.3/	/6.3			0/0/0	---In the form of slices or chips
0/0/0	0	3	0/0	0/0/0	0/0	0/0/0	0/0/	5.9/5.9/5.9	6.1/5.9			0/0/0	---Other
0/0/0	2	0	0/0	0/0/0	0/0	0//0	0/0/	0/0/0	5.9/0			0/0/0	-Poly(lactic acid)
													-Other polyesters:
0/0/0	0	1.3	0/0	0/0/0	0/0	0/0/0	0/0/0	5.9/5.9/5.9	5.9/5.9			0/0/0	--Unsaturated
													--Other:
													---Poly butylene terephthalate
0/0/	0	3	0/0	0/0/0	0/0	0/0/0	0/0/	0/5.9/5.9	6.1/5.9			0/0/0	Not reinforced or modified PBT resins,in primary forms
0/0/	0	3	0/0	0/0/0	0/0	0/0/0	0/0/	0/5.9/5.9	6.1/5.9			0/0/0	Other Poly butylene terephthalate
													---Other:
													----Poly butylene adipata－co－terephthalate
0/0/0	0	0	0/0	0/0/0	0/0	0/0/0	0/0/0	0/0/0	0/0			0/0/0	Poly terephthalic acid hexylene glycol - butanediol J28, thermoplastic liquid crystal,in primary forms
0/0/0	0	0	0/0	0/0/0	0/0	0/0/0	0/0/0	0/0/0	0/0			0/0/0	Poly terephthalic acid hexylene glycol - butanediol J28,in other forms
													----Other
0/0/0	0	0	0/0	0/0/0	0/0	0/0/0	0/0/0	0/0/0	5.9/0			0/0/0	Polyesters,thermoplastic liquid crystal,in primary forms
0/0/0	0	0	0/0	0/0/0	0/0	0/0/0	0/0/0	0/0/0	5.9/0			0/0/0	Other polyesters, in primary forms
													Polyamides in primary forms:
													-Polyamide-6, -11, -12, -6,6, -6,9, -6,10 or -6,12:
													---In the form of slices or chips:
													----Of polyamide-6,6
0/0/	2		0.7/0.7	0/0/0	0/0	0/0/0	0/0/	6.2/6.2/	/6.2			0/0/0	Polyamide -6,6 slice
0/0/	2		0.7/0.7	0/0/0	0/0	0/0/0	0/0/	6.2/6.2/	/6.2			0/0/0	Modification polyamide -6,6 slice(screw secondary mixing, adding glass fiber,minerals,plasticizer,flame retardant)
0/0/	2		2.7/2.7	0/0/0	0/0	0/0/0	0/0/	6.2/6.2/	/6.2			0/0/0	----Of polyamide-6
0/0/	2		2.7/2.7	0/0/0	0/0	0/0/0	0/0/	5/5/	/5			0/0/0	----Other

税则号列	货品名称〔CIQ 扩展编码及品名—T2 表示见附表 2〕	最惠(%)	暂定税率	普通	增值/消费	出口退税	计量单位	监管条件/特殊证件	检验检疫	对美关税	亚太上/下
3908.1090	---其他〔999〕	6.5		45	13/	13	千克	/		29	
	-其他：										
3908.9010	---芳香族聚酰胺及其共聚物〔301 危险化学品，易燃液体；302 其他化工产品〕	10		45	13/	13	千克	/13			
3908.9020	---半芳香族聚酰胺及其共聚物〔301 危险化学品，易燃液体；302 其他化工产品〕	10		45	13/	13	千克	/13			
3908.9090	---其他〔301 危险化学品，易燃液体；302 其他化工产品〕	10		45	13/	13	千克	/13			
39.09	**初级形状的氨基树脂、酚醛树脂及聚氨酯类：**										
3909.1000	-尿素树脂；硫尿树脂〔301 危险化学品，易燃液体；302 其他化工品〕	6.5		45	13/	13	千克	/		34	4.2/4.2
3909.2000	-蜜胺树脂；〔301 危险化学品，易燃液体；302 其他化工产品〕	6.5		45	13/	13	千克	/13		19	4.2/4.2
	-其他氨基树脂：										
3909.3100	--聚(亚甲基苯基异氰酸酯)(粗 MDI、聚合 MDI)〔301 危险化学品，易燃液体；302 其他化工品〕	6.5		35	13/	13	千克	/		31.5	6.1/6.1
3909.3900	--其他〔301：易燃液体；999：其他化工产品〕	6.5		45	13/	13	千克	AB/	MN	31.5	
3909.4000	-酚醛树脂〔301 危险化学品，易燃液体；302 其他化工品〕	6.5		45	13/	13	千克	AB/	MN	29	6.1/6.1
3909.5000	-聚氨基甲酸酯〔301 危险化学品，易燃液体；302 其他化工产品〕	6.5		45	13/	13	千克	AB/	MN	29	4.2/4.2
39.10	**初级形状的聚硅氧烷：**										
3910.0000	初级形状的聚硅氧烷〔301 危险化学品，易燃液体；302 其他化工品〕	6.5		45	13/	13	千克	/13			6.1/6.1
39.11	**初级形状的石油树脂、苯并呋喃-茚树脂、多萜树脂、多硫化物、聚砜及本章注释三所规定的其他税目未列名产品：**										
3911.1000	-石油树脂、苯并呋喃树脂、茚树脂、苯并呋喃-茚树脂及多萜树脂〔999〕	6.5		45	13/	13	千克	/		19	4.2/4.2
3911.2000	-聚(1,3－亚苯基甲基膦酸酯)〔999〕	6.5		45	13/	13	千克	/			
3911.9000	-其他										
3911.9000 01	芳基酸与芳基胺预缩聚物〔999〕	6.5	3	45	13/	13	千克	/13			
3911.9000 03	改性三羟乙基脲酸酯类预缩聚物〔999〕	6.5	3	45	13/	13	千克	/13			
3911.9000 04	聚苯硫醚〔999〕	6.5		45	13/	13	千克	/13			
3911.9000 05	偏苯三酸酐和异氰酸预缩聚物〔999〕	6.5	3	45	13/	13	千克	/13			
3911.9000 90	其他初级形状的多硫化物、聚砜等(包括本章注释三所规定的其他编号未列名产品)〔301 危险化学品，易燃液体；302 危险化学品，腐蚀性物质；303 其他化工产品〕	6.5		45	13/	13	千克	/13			
39.12	**初级形状的其他税目未列名的纤维素及其化学衍生物：**										
	-乙酸纤维素：										
3912.1100	--未塑化〔999〕	6.5		40	13/	0,13	千克	/			
3912.1200	--已塑化〔999〕	6.5		40	13/	0	千克	/		14	5.9/5.9
3912.2000	-硝酸纤维素(包括胶棉)〔301 危险化学品，爆炸品；302 危险化学品，易燃液体；303 危险化学品，易燃固体〕	6.5		45	13/	0	千克	/13		34	
	-纤维素醚：										
3912.3100	--羧甲基纤维素及其盐〔101 饲料添加剂，999 其他〕	6.5		45	13/	0	千克	/		19	
3912.3900	--其他〔999〕	6.5		45	13/	0	千克	/		14	
3912.9000	-其他〔999〕	6.5		45	13/	0	千克	/		14	
39.13	**初级形状的其他税目未列名的天然聚合物(例如，藻酸)及改性天然聚合物(例如，硬化蛋白、天然橡胶的化学衍生物)：**										
3913.1000	-藻酸及其盐和酯〔101 其他饲料添加剂，301 其他危险化学品，需申报仅用于工业用途不用于食品添加剂无检疫要求，302 无检疫要求食品添加剂，303 一般化学品，需申报仅用于工业用途不用于食品添加剂无检疫要求，304 属于危险化学品的食品添加剂〕	10		45	13/	0	千克	AB/	RS	37.5	
3913.9000	-其他										
3913.9000 11	香菇多糖〔101 饲料添加剂，999 其他初级形状的天然聚合物及改性天然聚合物〕	6.5		50	13/	13	千克	S/		14	
3913.9000 90	其他初级形状的未列名天然聚合物[包括改性天然聚合物(如硬化蛋白)]〔101 饲料添加剂，999 其他初级形状的天然聚合物及改性天然聚合物〕	6.5		50	13/	13	千克	/		14	
39.14	**初级形状的离子交换剂，以税目 39.01 至 39.13 的聚合物为基本成分的：**										
3914.0000	初级形状的离子交换剂，以税目 39.01 至 39.13 的聚合物为基本成分的〔999〕	6.5		45	13/	13	千克	/		19	
	第二分章　废碎料及下脚料；半制品；制成品										
39.15	**塑料的废碎料及下脚料：**										
3915.1000	-乙烯聚合物的〔101 不包括铝塑复合膜，102 铝塑复合膜〕	6.5		50	13/	0	千克	9/		31.5	
3915.2000	-苯乙烯聚合物的〔999〕	6.5		50	13/	0	千克	9/		31.5	
3915.3000	-氯乙烯聚合物的〔999〕	6.5		50	13/	0	千克	9/		31.5	
	-其他塑料的：										

协定税率 %								RCEP		特惠税率 %			Article Description
东/冰/格	巴基斯坦	韩国	瑞士 上/下	哥/秘/柬	澳/毛	新西/坡/智	中国港/澳/台	东盟及马来/澳/韩	日/新	亚太2国	老/柬/缅	98/97/95	
0/0/	2		0.7/0.7	0/0/0	0/0	0/0/0	0/0/	5/5/	/5			0/0/0	---Other
													-Other:
0/0/	3.5			0/0/0	0/0	0/0/0	0/0/	5/5/	/5			0/0/0	---Aromatic polyamide and copolymers thereof
0/0/	3.5			0/0/0	0/0	0/0/0	0/0/	5/5/	/5			0/0/0	---Semi aromatic polyamide and copolymers thereof
0/0/	3.5			0/0/0	0/0	0/0/0	0/0/	5/5/	/5			0/0/0	---Other
													Amino-resins, phenolic resins and polyurethanes, in primary forms:
0/0/0	2	0	0/0	0/0/0	0/0	0//0	0/0/0	0/0/0	0/0			0/0/0	-Urea resins; thiourea resins
0/0/0	2	0	0/0	0/0/0	0/0	0//0	0/0/0	0/5.9/0	0/5.9			0/0/0	-Melamine resins
													-Other amino-resins:
0/0/0	0	3	0/0	0/0/0	0/0	0/0/0	0/0/	5.9/5.9/5.9	6.1/5.9			0/0/0	--Poly (*methylene phenyl isocy-anate*) (*crude MDI*, *polymeric MDI*)
0/0/0	2	0	0/0	0/0/0	0/0	0/0/0	0/0/0	0/0/0	0/0			0/0/0	--Other
0/0/0	0	1.3	0/0	0/0/0	0/0	0//0	0/0/0	0/0/5.9	5.9/0			0/0/0	-Phenolic resins
0/0/0	4	0	0/0	0/0/0	0/0	0/0/0	0/0/0	0/0/0	0/0			0/0/0	-Polyurethanes
													Silicones in primary forms:
0/0/0	4	1.3	0/0	0/0/0	0/0	0//0	0/0/0	0/0/5.9	6.1/0			0/0/0	Silicones in primary forms
													Petroleum resins, coumarone-indene resins, polyterpenes, polysulphides, polysulphones and other products specified in Note 3 to this Chapter, not elsewhere specified or included, in primary forms:
0/0/0	2	3	0/0	0/0/0	0/0	0//0	0/0/0	5.9/5.9/5.9	6.1/5.9			0/0/0	-Petroleum resins, coumarone, indene or coumarone-indene resins and polyterpenes
0/0/0	0	0	0/0	0/0/0	0/0	0//0	0/0/	0/0/0	5.9/0			0/0/0	-Poly(1,3－phenylene methylphosphonate)
													-Other
0/0/0	0	0	0/0	0/0/0	0/0	0//0	0/0/	0/0/0	5.9/0			0/0/0	Precondensed polymer of aromatic acid and aromatic amide
0/0/0	0	0	0/0	0/0/0	0/0	0//0	0/0/	0/0/0	5.9/0			0/0/0	Precondensed polymer of modified trihydroxy acetate
0/0/0	0	0	0/0	0/0/0	0/0	0//0	0/0/	0/0/0	5.9/0			0/0/0	Polyphenylene sulfide
0/0/0	0	0	0/0	0/0/0	0/0	0//0	0/0/	0/0/0	5.9/0			0/0/0	Precondensed polymer of trimelltic anhydride and isocyanic acid
0/0/0	0	0	0/0	0/0/0	0/0	0//0	0/0/	0/0/0	5.9/0			0/0/0	Other polysulphides, polysulphones (including other products specified in Note 3 to this Chapter, not elsewhere specified or included)in primary forms
													Cellulose and its chemical derivatives, not elsewhere specified or included, in primary forms:
													-Cellulose acetates:
0/0/0	2	1.3	0/0	0/0/0	0/0	0//0	0/0/	0/0/5.9	5.9/0			0/0/0	--Non-plasticized
0/0/0	2	0	0/0	0/0/0	0/0	0//0	0/0/	0/0/0	5.9/0			0/0/0	--Plasticized
0/0/0	2	0	0/0	0/0/0	0/0	0//0	0/0/	0/0/0	5.9/0			0/0/0	-Cellulose nitrates (including collodions)
													-Cellulose ethers:
0/0/0	2	0	0/0	0/0/0	0/0	0//0	0/0/	0/0/0	5.9/0			0/0/0	--Carboxymethylcellulose and its salts
0/0/0	2	0	0/0	0/0/0	0/0	0//0	0/0/	0/0/0	5.9/0			0/0/0	--Other
0/0/0	0	0	0/0	0/0/0	0/0	0//0	0/0/	0/0/0	0/0			0/0/0	-Other
													Natural polymers (for example, alginic acid) and modified natural polymers (for example, hardened proteins, chemical derivatives of natural rubber), not elsewhere specified or included, in primary forms:
0/0/0	3.5	2	0/0	0//0	0/0	0/0/0	0/0/	0/0/9	9.1/0			0/0/0	-Alginic acid, its salts and esters
													-Other
0/0/0	2	0	0/0	0/0/0	0/0	0//0	0/0/	0/0/0	5.9/0			0/0/0	Mushrooms polysaccharide
0/0/0	2	0	0/0	0/0/0	0/0	0//0	0/0/	0/0/0	5.9/0			0/0/0	Other primary NES (including natural polymer modified natural polymer (such ashardening protein))
													Ion-exchangers based on polymers of headings No. 39.01 to 39.13, in primary forms:
0//0	2	0	0/0	0/0/0	0/0	0//0	0/0/	5.9/5.9/5.9	5.9/5.9			0/0/0	Ion-exchangers based on polymers of headings Nos. 39.01 to 39.13, in primary forms
													Ⅱ-WASTE, PARINGS AND SCRAP; SEMI-MANUFACTURES; ARTICLES
													Waste, parings and scrap, of plastics:
0/0/0	0	3	0/0	0/0/0	0/0	0/0/0	0/0/	0/5.9/5.9	6.1/5.9			0/0/0	-Of polymers of ethylene
0/0/0	4	3	0/0	0/0/0	0/0	0/0/0	0/0/	0/5.9/5.9	6.1/5.9			0/0/0	-Of polymers of styrene
0/0/0	4	3	0/0	0/0/0	0/0	0/0/0	0/0/	0/5.9/5.9	6.1/5.9			0/0/0	-Of polymers of vinyl chloride
													-Of other plastics:

税则号列	货品名称〔CIQ 扩展编码及品名－T2 表示见附表 2〕	最惠(%)	暂定税率	普通	增值/消费	出口退税	计量单位	监管条件/特殊证件	检验检疫	对美关税	亚太上/下
3915.9010	---聚对苯二甲酸乙二酯的〔101 不包括废 PET 饮料瓶(砖),102 废 PET 饮料瓶(砖)〕	6.5		50	13/	0	千克	9/		31.5	
3915.9090	---其他〔101 不包括废光盘破碎料,102 废光盘破碎料,301 硝化纤维塑料碎屑〕	6.5		50	13/	0	千克	9/		31.5	
39.16	**塑料制的单丝(截面直径超过 1 毫米)、条、杆、型材及异型材,不论是否经表面加工,但未经其他加工:**										
3916.1000	-乙烯聚合物制〔999〕	10		45	13/	13	千克	/		37.5	
	-氯乙烯聚合物制:										
3916.2010	---异型材〔999〕	10		45	13/	13	千克	/		37.5	6.5/6.5
3916.2090	---其他〔999〕	10		45	13/	13	千克	/		37.5	6.5/6.5
	-其他塑料制:										
3916.9010	---聚酰胺制〔999〕	10		45	13/	13	千克	/		37.5	
3916.9090	---其他〔999〕	10		45	13/	13	千克	/		22.5	
39.17	**塑料制的管子及其附件(例如,接头、肘管、法兰):**										
3917.1000	-硬化蛋白或纤维素材料制的人造肠衣(香肠用肠衣)〔999〕	10		50	13/	13	千克	A/	R	37.5	8/8
	-硬管:										
3917.2100	--乙烯聚合物制〔999〕	10		45	13/	13	千克	/		32.5	
3917.2200	--丙烯聚合物制〔999〕	10		45	13/	13	千克	/		37.5	
3917.2300	--氯乙烯聚合物制〔999〕	10		45	13/	13	千克	/		32.5	
3917.2900	--其他塑料制〔301 危险化学品,易燃固体;302 其他化工品〕	10		45	13/	13	千克	/13		22.5	
	-其他管:										
3917.3100	--软管,最小爆破压力为 27.6 兆帕斯卡〔999〕	10		45	13/	13	千克	/		22.5	6.5/6.5
3917.3200	--其他未装有附件的管子,未经加强也未与其他材料合制〔301 危险化学品,易燃固体;302 其他化工品〕	6.5		45	13/	13	千克	/13		19	4.6/4.6
3917.3300	--其他装有附件的管子,未经加强也未与其他材料合制〔301 危险化学品,易燃固体;302 其他化工品〕	6.5		45	13/	13	千克	/13		14	4.2/4.2
3917.3900	--其他〔999〕	6.5		45	13/	13	千克	/		19	4.2/4.2
3917.4000	-管子附件〔999〕	10		45	13/	13	千克	/		22.5	6.5/6.5
39.18	**块状或成卷的塑料铺地制品,不论是否胶粘;本章注释九所规定的塑料糊墙品:**										
	-氯乙烯聚合物制:										
3918.1010	---糊墙品〔999〕	10		45	13/	13	千克	/		17.5	
3918.1090	---其他〔999〕	10		45	13/	13	千克	/		37.5	
	-其他塑料制:										
3918.9010	---糊墙品〔999〕	10		45	13/	13	千克	/		17.5	
3918.9090	---其他〔999〕	10		45	13/	13	千克	/		22.5	
39.19	**自粘的塑料板、片、膜、箔、带、扁条及其他扁平形状材料,不论是否成卷:**										
	-成卷,宽度不超过 20 厘米:										
3919.1010	---丙烯酸树脂类为基本成分〔999〕	6.5		45	13/	13	千克	/		19	
	---其他:										
3919.1091	----胶囊型反光膜〔999〕	6.5		45	13/	13	千克	/		34	
3919.1099	----其他〔999〕	6.5		45	13/	13	千克	/		19	
	-其他:										
3919.9010	---胶囊型反光膜〔999〕	6.5		45	13/	13	千克	/		34	4.2/4.2
3919.9090	---其他										
3919.9090 10	半导体晶圆制造用自粘式圆形抛光垫〔999〕	0		45	13/	13	千克	/			4.6/4.6
3919.9090 90	其他自粘塑料板、片、膜等材料(包括箔,带,扁条及其他扁平形状材料,不论是否成卷)〔101 车身反光标识零部件,999 其他〕	6.5		45	13/	13	千克	/			4.6/4.6
39.20	**其他非泡沫塑料的板、片、膜、箔及扁条,未用其他材料强化、层压、支撑或用类似方法合制:**										
	-乙烯聚合物制:										
3920.1010	---乙烯聚合物制电池隔膜〔999〕	6.5	3	45	13/	13	千克	/		30.5	4.2/4.2
3920.1090	---其他										
3920.1090 10	农用非泡沫聚乙烯薄膜(未用其他材料强化、层压、支撑或用类似方法合制)〔999〕	6.5		45	9/	0	千克	/			4.6/4.6
3920.1090 90	其他非泡沫乙烯聚合物板、片、膜、箔及扁条(未用其他材料强化、层压、支撑或用类似方法合制,非农用)〔999〕	6.5		45	13/	13	千克	/			4.6/4.6
	-丙烯聚合物制:										
3920.2010	---丙烯聚合物制电池隔膜〔999〕	6.5		45	13/	13	千克	/		14	
3920.2090	---其他										
3920.2090 10	农用非泡沫聚丙烯薄膜(未用其他材料强化、层压、支撑或用类似方法合制)〔999〕	6.5		45	9/	0	千克	/		29	
3920.2090 90	非泡沫丙烯聚合物板、片、膜、箔及扁条(未用其他材料强化、层压、支撑或用类似方法合制,非农用)〔999〕	6.5		45	13/	13	千克	/		29	
3920.3000	-苯乙烯聚合物制〔999〕	6.5		45	13/	13	千克	/		34	4.2/4.2
	-氯乙烯聚合物制:										

协定税率 %								RCEP		特惠税率 %			Article Description
东/冰/格	巴基斯坦	韩国	瑞士上/下	哥/秘/柬	澳/毛	新西/坡/智	中国港/澳/台	东盟及马来/澳/韩	日/新	亚太2国	老/柬/缅	98/97/95	
0/0/0	0	3	0.7/0.7	0/0/0	0/0	0/0/0	0/0/	0/5.9/5.9	6.1/5.9			0/0/0	---Of pdyethylene glycol terephthalate
0/0/0	0	3	0.7/0.7	0/0/0	0/0	0/0/0	0/0/	0/5.9/5.9	6.1/5.9			0/0/0	---Other
													Monofilament of which any cross-sectional dimension exceeds 1 mm, rods, sticks and profile shapes, whether or not surface-worked but not otherwise worked, of plastics:
0/0/0	3.5	2	0/0	0/0/0	0/0	0/0/0	0/0/	0/0/9	9.1/0			0/0/0	-Of polymers of ethylene
													-Of polymers of vinyl chloride:
0/0/0	3.5	2	0/0	0/0/0	0/0	0//0	0/0/	0/0/9	9.1/0			0/0/0	---Profile shapes
0/0/0	3.5	2	0/0	0/0/0	0/0	0//0	0/0/	0/0/9	9.1/0			0/0/0	---Other
													-Of other plastics:
0/0/0	3.5	2	0/0	0/0/0	0/0	0/0/0	0/0/	0/0/9	9.1/0			0/0/0	---Of polyamides
0/0/0	3.5	2	0/0	0/0/0	0/0	0/0/0	0/0/	9/9/9	9.1/9			0/0/0	---Other
													Tubes, pipes and hoses, and fittings therefor (for example, joints, elbows, flanges), of plastics:
0/0/0	3.5	2	0/0	0/0/0	0/0	0//0	0/0/	0/0/9	9.1/0			0/0/0	-Artificial guts (sausage casings) of hardened protein or of cellulosic materials
													-Tubes, pipes and hoses, rigid:
0/0/0	3.5	2	0/0	0/0/0	0/0	0/0/0	0/0/	0/0/9	9.1/0			0/0/0	--Of polymers of ethylene
0/0/0	0	2	0/0	0/0/0	0/0	0//0	0/0/	0/0/9	9.1/0			0/0/0	--Of polymers of propylene
0/0/0	3.5	2	0/0	0/0/0	0/0	0/0/0	0/0/	0/0/9	9.1/0			0/0/0	--Of polymers of vinyl chloride
0/0/0	3.5	2	1/1	0/0/0	0/0	0/0/0	0/0/	9/9/9	9.1/9			0/0/0	--Of other plastics
													-Other tubes, pipes and hoses:
0/0/0	3.5	0	0/0	0/0/0	0/0	0/0/0	0/0/	9/9/9	9.1/9			0/0/0	--Flexible tubes, pipes and hoses, having a minimum burst pressure of 27.6 MPa
0/0/0	0	0	0.7/0.7	0/0/0	0/0	0//0	0/0/	0/0/0	5.9/0			0/0/0	--Other, not reinforced or otherwise combined with other materials, without fittings
0/0/0	0	0	0/0	0/0/0	0/0	0//0	0/0/	0/0/0	5.9/0			0/0/0	--Other, not reinforced or otherwise combined with other materials, with fittings
0/0/0	0	3	0/0	0/0/0	0/0	0/0/0	0/0/	5.9/5.9/5.9	6.1/5.9			0/0/0	--Other
0/0/0	3.5	0	1/1	0/0/0	0/0	0/0/0	0/0/	9/9/9	9.1/9			0/0/0	-Fittings
													Floor coverings of plastics, whether or not self-adhesive, in rolls or in the form of tiles; wall or ceiling coverings of plastics, as defined in Note 9 to this Chapter:
													-Of polymers of vinyl chloride:
0/0/0	3.5	2	0/0	0/0/0	0/0	0//0	0/0/	0/0/9	9.1/0			0/0/0	---Wall or ceiling coverings
0/0/0	3.5		1/1	0/0/0	0/0	0//0	0/0/	5/5/	/5			0/0/0	---Other
													-Of other plastics:
0/0/0	3.5	2	0/0	0/0/0	0/0	0//0	0/0/	0/0/9	9.1/0			0/0/0	---Wall or ceiling coverings
0/0/0	3.5	2	0/0	0/0/0	0/0	0//0	0/0/	0/0/9	9.1/0			0/0/0	---Other
													Self-adhesive plates, sheets, film, foil, tape, strip and other flat shapes, of plastics, whether or not in rolls:
													-In rolls of a width not exceeding 20 cm:
0/0/0	0	0	0/0	0/0/0	0/0	0//0	0/0/	5.9/5.9/5.9	5.9/5.9			0/0/0	---Based on acrylic resin
													---Other:
0/0/0	0	0	0/0	0/0/0	0/0	0//0	0/0/	0/0/0	5.9/0			0/0/0	----Encapsulant reflective film
0/0/0	0		0.7/0.7	0/0/0	0/0	0//0	0/0/0	5.9/5/	5.9/5			0/0/0	----Other
													-Other:
0/0/0	0	3	0/0	0/0/0	0/0	0//0	0/0/	5.9/5.9/5.9	6.1/5.9			0/0/0	---Encapsulant reflective film
													Other
0/0/0	0	3	0/0	0/0/0	0/0	0//0	0/0/0	5.9/5.9/5.9	6.1/5.9			0/0/0	Self-adhesive circular polishing pad for manufacturing semiconductor wafer
0/0/0	0	3	0/0	0/0/0	0/0	0//0	0/0/0	5.9/5.9/5.9	6.1/5.9			0/0/0	Other self-adhesive plates, sheets, film, foil, tape, strip and other flat shapes, of plastics, whether or not in rolls
													Other plates, sheets, film, foil and strip, of plastics, non-cellular and not reinforced, laminated, supported or similarly combined with other materials:
													-Of polymers of ethylene:
0/0/0	0	1.3	0/0	0/0/0	0/0	0//0	0/0/	0/0/5.9	6.1/0			0/0/0	---Battery separator, of polymers of ethylene
													---Other
0/0/0	0	3	0.7/0.7	0/0/0	0/0	0//0	0/0/0	5.9/5.9/5.9	6.1/5.9			0/0/0	Agricultural PE film, non-cellular (not reinforced, laminated, supported or similarly combined with other materials)
0/0/0	0	3	0.7/0.7	0/0/0	0/0	0//0	0/0/0	5.9/5.9/5.9	6.1/5.9			0/0/0	Plates, sheets, film, foil and strip, of PE film, non-cellular (not reinforced, laminated, supported or similarly combined with other materials, non-agricultural)
													-Of polymers of propylene:
0/0/0	0		0/0	0/0/0	0/0	0//0	0/0/	5/5/	/5			0/0/0	---Battery separator, of polymers of propylene
													---Other
0/0/0	0	1.3	0.7/0.7	0/0/0	0/0	0//0	0/0/0	0/0/5.9	5.9/0			0/0/0	Agricultural PP film, non-cellular (not reinforced, laminated, supported or similarly combined with other materials)
0/0/0	0	1.3	0.7/0.7	0/0/0	0/0	0//0	0/0/0	0/0/5.9	5.9/0			0/0/0	Plates, sheets, film, foil and strip, of PP film, non cellular (not reinforced, laminated, supported or similarly combined with other materials, non-agricultural)
0/0/0	0	1.3	0/0	0/0/0	0/0	0//0	0/0/0	5.9/5.9/5.9	5.9/5.9			0/0/0	-Of polymers of styrene
													-Of polymers of vinyl chloride:

税则号列	货品名称〔CIQ扩展编码及品名－T2表示见附表2〕	最惠(%)	暂定税率	普通	增值/消费	出口退税	计量单位	监管条件/特殊证件	检验检疫	对美关税	亚太上/下
3920.4300	--按重量计增塑剂含量不小于6%										
3920.4300 10	农用软质聚氯乙烯薄膜(增塑剂含量≥6%,未用其他材料强化、层压、支撑)〔999〕	6.5		45	9/	0	千克	/		29	4.2/4.2
3920.4300 90	氯乙烯聚合物板、片、膜、箔及扁条(增塑剂含量≥6%,未用其他材料强化、层压、支撑)〔999〕	6.5		45	13/	13	千克	/		29	4.2/4.2
3920.4900	--其他										
3920.4900 10	其他农用软质聚氯乙烯薄膜(非泡沫料的,未用其他材料强化、层压、支撑)〔999〕	6.5		45	9/	0	千克	/		19	4.2/4.2
3920.4900 90	其他氯乙烯聚合物板、片、膜、箔及扁条(非泡沫料的,未用其他材料强化、层压、支撑,非农用)〔999〕	6.5		45	13/	13	千克	/		19	4.2/4.2
	-丙烯酸聚合物制:										
3920.5100	--聚甲基丙烯酸甲酯制〔999〕	6.5		45	13/	13	千克	/		29	4.6/4.6
3920.5900	--其他〔999〕	6.5		45	13/	13	千克	/		29	
	-聚碳酸酯、醇酸树脂、聚烯丙酯或其他聚酯制:										
3920.6100	--聚碳酸酯制〔999〕	6.5		45	13/	13	千克	/		29	4.6/4.6
3920.6200	--聚对苯二甲酸乙二酯制〔999〕	6.5		45	13/	13	千克	/			4.6/4.6
3920.6300	--不饱和聚酯制〔999〕	10		45	13/	13	千克	/		37.5	
3920.6900	--其他聚酯制〔999〕	10		45	13/	13	千克	/		22.5	6.5/6.5
	-纤维素及其化学衍生物制:										
3920.7100	--再生纤维素制〔999〕	6.5		45	13/	13	千克	/		19	
3920.7300	--乙酸纤维素制〔999〕	6.5		45	13/	13	千克	/		34	
3920.7900	--其他纤维素衍生物制〔301危险化学品,易燃固体;302其他化工品〕	10		45	13/	13	千克	/13		37.5	
	-其他塑料制:										
3920.9100	--聚乙烯醇缩丁醛制										
3920.9100 01	聚乙烯醇缩丁醛膜(厚度不超过3毫米)(非泡沫料的,未用其他材料强化、层压、支撑)〔999〕	6.5	3	45	13/	13	千克	/		25.5	
3920.9100 90	聚乙烯醇缩丁醛板、片、箔、扁条及厚度超过3毫米的膜(非泡沫料的,未用其他材料强化、层压、支撑)〔999〕	6.5		45	13/	13	千克	/		29	
3920.9200	--聚酰胺制〔999〕	10		45	13/	13	千克	/		32.5	
3920.9300	--氨基树脂制〔999〕	6.5		45	13/	13	千克	/		14	
3920.9400	--酚醛树脂制〔999〕	10		45	13/	13	千克	/		32.5	6.5/6.5
	--其他塑料制:										
3920.9910	---聚四氟乙烯制〔999〕	6.5		45	13/	13	千克	/		14	
3920.9990	---其他塑料制										
3920.9990 01	聚酰亚胺膜,厚度不超过0.03毫米(未用其他材料强化、层压、支撑)〔999〕	6.5	3	45	13/	13	千克	/			
3920.9990 90	其他非泡沫塑料板、片、膜、箔、扁条(未用其他材料强化、层压、支撑)〔999〕	6.5		45	13/	13	千克	/			
39.21	**其他塑料板、片、膜、箔、扁条:**										
	-泡沫塑料的:										
3921.1100	--苯乙烯聚合物制〔999〕	10		45	13/	13	千克	/		17.5	6.5/6.5
	--氯乙烯聚合物制:										
3921.1210	---人造革及合成革〔999〕	9		70	13/	13	千克/米	/		36.5	
3921.1290	---其他〔999〕	6.5		45	13/	13	千克	/		34	
	--氨酯聚合物制:										
3921.1310	---人造革及合成革〔999〕	9		70	13/	13	千克/米	/		36.5	5.9/5.9
3921.1390	---其他〔999〕	6.5		45	13/	13	千克	/		19	4.6/4.6
3921.1400	--再生纤维素制〔999〕	10		45	13/	13	千克	/		17.5	
	--其他塑料制:										
3921.1910	---人造革及合成革〔999〕	9		45	13/	13	千克/米	/		21.5	6.3/6.3
3921.1990	---其他										
3921.1990 10	电池隔膜〔999〕	6.5	3	45	13/	13	千克	/		15.5	4.2/4.2
3921.1990 90	其他泡沫塑料板,片,膜,箔,扁条〔999〕	6.5		45	13/	13	千克	/		19	4.2/4.2
	-其他:										
3921.9020	---聚乙烯嵌有玻璃纤维的板、片〔999〕	6.5		45	13/	13	千克	/		29	4.2/4.2
3921.9030	---聚异丁烯为基本成分的附有人造毛毡的板、片、卷材〔999〕	6.5		45	13/	13	千克	/		29	4.2/4.2
3921.9090	---其他										
3921.9090 01	离子交换膜〔999〕	6.5	5	45	13/	13	千克	/13			4.6/4.6
3921.9090 10	两用物项管制结构复合材料的层压板(用纤维和丝材增强而制成的各种预浸件和预成形件,其中增强材料的比拉伸强度大于7.62× 10^4 m和比模量大于3.18× 10^6 m)〔999〕	6.5		45	13/	13	千克	3/13			4.6/4.6

协定税率 %								RCEP		特惠税率 %			Article Description
东/冰/格	巴基斯坦	韩国	瑞士上/下	哥/秘/柬	澳/毛	新西/坡/智	中国港/澳/台	东盟及马来/澳/韩	日/新	亚太2国	老/柬/缅	98/97/95	
													--Containing by weight not less than 6% of plasticisers
0/0/0	0	1.3	0/0	0/0/0	0/0	0/0/0	0/0/0	5.9/5.9/5.9	5.9/5.9			0/0/0	Agricultural PVC-P film (containing by weight not less than 6% of plasticisers, not reinforced, laminated, supported or similarly combined with other materials)
0/0/0	0	1.3	0/0	0/0/0	0/0	0/0/0	0/0/0	5.9/5.9/5.9	5.9/5.9			0/0/0	Plates, sheets, film (foil and strip, of PVC film containing by weight not less than 6% of plasticisers, not reinforced, laminated, supported or similarly combined with other materials)
													--Other
0/0/0	0	3	0.7/0.7	0/0/0	0/0	0//0	0/0/0	5.9/5.9/5.9	6.1/5.9			0/0/0	Other agricultural PVC-P film (non-cellular, not reinforced, laminated, supported or similarly combined with other materials)
0/0/0	0	3	0.7/0.7	0/0/0	0/0	0//0	0/0/0	5.9/5.9/5.9	6.1/5.9			0/0/0	Other plates, sheets, film, foil and strip, of PVC (non-cellular, not reinforced, laminated, supported or similarly combined with other materials, non-agricultural)
													-Of acrylic polymers:
0/0/0	0	1.3	0/0	0/0/0	0/0	0//0	0/0/0	0/0/5.9	5.9/0			0/0/0	--Of poly(methyl methacrylate)
0/0/0	2	3	0/0	0/0/0	0/0	0//0	0/0/	5.9/5.9/5.9	6.1/5.9			0/0/0	--Other
													-Of polycarbonates, alkyd resins, polyallyl esters or other polyesters:
0/0/0	0	3	0/0	0/0/0	0/0	0//0	0/0/0	5.9/5.9/5.9	6.1/5.9			0/0/0	--Of polycarbonates
0/0/0	0	3	0/0	0/0/0	0/0	0//0	0/0/0	5.9/5.9/5.9	6.1/5.9			0/0/0	--Of poly(ethylene terephthalate)
0/0/0	3.5	2	0/0	0/0/0	0/0	0//0	0/0/	0/0/9	9.1/0			0/0/0	--Of unsaturated polyesters
0/0/0	3.5	6	0/0	0/0/0	0/0	0/0/0	0/0/0	9.5/9.5/	9.5/9.5			0/0/0	--Of other polyesters
													-Of cellulose or its chemical derivatives:
0/0/0	2	1.3	0/0	0/0/0	0/0	0//0	0/0/	0/0/5.9	5.9/0			0/0/0	--Of regenerated cellulose
0/0/0	2	0	0/0	0/0/0	0/0	0//0	0/0/	5.9/5.9/5.9	5.9/5.9			0/0/0	--Of cellulose acetate
0/0/0	3.5	2	0/0	0/0/0	0/0	0//0	0/0/	0/0/9	9.1/0			0/0/0	--Of other cellulose derivatives
													-Of other plastics:
													--Of poly(vinyl butyral)
0/0/0	0	3	0/0	0/0/0	0/0	0//0	0/0/	5.9/5.9/5.9	6.1/5.9			0/0/0	Film of poly vinyl butyral. (thieck ness≤3mm)(non-cellular, not reinforced, laminated, supported or similarly combined with other materials)
0/0/0	0	3	0/0	0/0/0	0/0	0//0	0/0/	5.9/5.9/5.9	6.1/5.9			0/0/0	Plates, sheets, foil and strip, of poly vinyl butyral. (thickness ≤3mm)(non-cellular, not reinforced, laminated, supported or similarly combined with other materials)
0/0/0	3.5	0	0/0	0/0/0	0/0	0/0/0	0/0/	9/9/9	9.1/9			0/0/0	--Of polyamides
0/0/0	2	0	0/0	0/0/0	0/0	0//0	0/0/	0/0/0	5.9/0			0/0/0	--Of amino-resins
0/0/0	3.5	2	0/0	0/0/0	0/0	0/0/0	0/0/	0/0/9	9.1/0			0/0/0	--Of phenolic resins
													--Of other plastics:
0/0/0	0	3	0/0	0/0/0	0/0	0//0	0/0/	5.9/5.9/5.9	6.1/5.9			0/0/0	---Of polytetrafluoroethylene
													---Of other plastics
0/0/0	0	1.3	0/0	0/0/0	0/0	0//0	0/0/0	0/0/5.9	6.1/0			0/0/0	Polyimide(PI)film, thickness≤0.03mm(not reinforced, laminated, supported or similarly combined with other materials)
0/0/0	0	1.3	0/0	0/0/0	0/0	0//0	0/0/0	0/0/5.9	6.1/0			0/0/0	Other plates, sheets, foil and strip, non-cellular (not reinforced, laminated, supported or similarly combined with other materials)
													Other plates, sheets, film, foil and strip, of plastics:
													-Cellular.
0/0/0	3.5	2	0/0	0/0/0	0/0	0//0	0/0/	0/0/9	9.1/0			0/0/0	--Of polymers of styrene
													--Of polymers of vinyl chloride:
0/0/0	2	4.2	0/0	0/0/0	0/0	0/0/0	0/0/0	8.4/8.6/8.4	8.4/8.6			0/0/0	---Combined with textile fabrics
0/0/0	0	0	0.7/0.7	0/0/0	0/0	0//0	0/0/	0/0/0	5.9/0			0/0/0	---Other
													--Of polyurethanes:
0/0/0	2	4.2	0/0	0/0/0	0/0	0/0/0	0/0/0	8.4/8.6/8.4	8.4/8.6			0/0/0	---Combined with textile fabrics
0/0/0	0	1.3	0/0	0/0/0	0/0	0//0	0/0/	0/0/5.9	5.9/0			0/0/0	---Other
0/0/0	3.5	2	0/0	0/0/0	0/0	0//0	0/0/	0/0/9	9.1/0			0/0/0	--Of regenerated cellulose
													--Of other plastics:
0/0/0	2	4.2	0/0	0/0/0	0/0	0//0	0/0/	8.4/8.6/8.4	8.4/8.6			0/0/0	---Combined with textile fabrics
													---Other
0/0/0	0	3	0.7/0.7	0/0/0	0/0	0//0	0/0/0	5.9/5.9/5.9	6.1/5.9		//	0/0/0	Battery separator
0/0/0	0	3	0.7/0.7	0/0/0	0/0	0//0	0/0/0	5.9/5.9/5.9	6.1/5.9		//	0/0/0	Other foam plastic plates, sheets, films, foils, flat strips
													-Other:
0/0/0	0	0	0.7/0.7	0/0/0	0/0	0//0	0/0/	0/0/0	5.9/0			0/0/0	---Plates, sheets of polyethylene with glass fibres
0/0/0	0	1.3	0/0	0/0/0	0/0	0//0	0/0/	0/0/5.9	5.9/0			0/0/0	---Plates, sheets, coils of polyisobutylene with man-made felt
													---Other
0/0/0	0	3	0.7/0.7	0/0/0	0/0	0//0	0/0/0	5.9/5.9/5.9	6.1/5.9			0/0/0	Ion exchange membrane
0/0/0	0	3	0.7/0.7	0/0/0	0/0	0//0	0/0/0	5.9/5.9/5.9	6.1/5.9			0/0/0	Laminated structural board made of composite materials under sensitive items control (various persoaked and fabricated parts reinforced by fibers and threads, therein the specific tensile strength of reinforcing materials is greater than 7.62 $\times 10^{4}$ m and specific modulus greater than 3.18 $\times 10^{6}$ m)

税则号列	货品名称〔CIQ 扩展编码及品名－T2 表示见附表 2〕	最惠(%)	暂定税率	普通	增值/消费	出口退税	计量单位	监管条件/特殊证件	检验检疫	对美关税	亚太上/下
3921.9090 90	未列名塑料板、片、膜、箔、扁条(离子交换膜,两用物项管制结构复合材料的层压板除外)〔301 危险化学品,易燃固体;302 其他化工品〕	6.5		45	13/	13	千克	/13			4.6/4.6
39.22	**塑料浴缸、淋浴盘、洗涤槽、盥洗盆、坐浴盆、便盆、马桶座圈及盖、抽水箱及类似卫生洁具:**										
3922.1000	-浴缸、淋浴盘、洗涤槽及盥洗盆〔999〕	6.5		80	13/	13	千克	/		34	
3922.2000	-马桶座圈及盖〔999〕	6.5		80	13/	13	千克	/		26.5	
3922.9000	-其他〔999〕	6.5		80	13/	13	千克	/		26.5	
39.23	**供运输或包装货物用的塑料制品;塑料制的塞子、盖子及类似品:**										
3923.1000	-盒、箱(包括板条箱)及类似品										
3923.1000 10	具有特定形状或装置,供运输或包装半导体晶圆、掩模或光罩的塑料盒、箱、板条箱及类似物品〔999〕	0		80	13/	13	千克	/		22.5	6.5/6.5
3923.1000 90	其他塑料制盒,箱及类似品(包括塑料制板条箱,供运输或包装货物用的)〔101 食品用其他塑料包装,999:非食品用塑料制品〕	10		80	13/	13	千克	/		32.5	6.5/6.5
	-袋及包(包括锥形的):										
3923.2100	--乙烯聚合物制〔101 食品用其他塑料包装,999 非食品用塑料制品〕	10		80	13/	13	千克	/		22.5	
3923.2900	--其他塑料制〔101 食品用其他塑料包装,999〕	10		80	13/	13	千克	/		22.5	
3923.3000	-坛、瓶及类似品〔101 食品用其他塑料包装,999 非食品用塑料制品〕	6.5		80	13/	13	千克	/		19	
3923.4000	-卷轴、纡子、筒管及类似品〔101 食品接触其他塑料产品,102 食品用其他塑料包装,999 非食品用塑料制品〕	10		35	13/	13	千克	/		37.5	6.5/6.5
3923.5000	-塞子、盖子及类似品〔101 食品用其他塑料包装,999 非食品用塑料制品〕	10		80	13/	13	千克	/		22.5	
3923.9000	-其他〔101 食品用其他塑料包装,999 非食品用塑料制品〕	10		80	13/	13	千克	/		32.5	6.5/6.5
39.24	**塑料制的餐具、厨房用具、其他家庭用具及卫生或盥洗用具:**										
3924.1000	-餐具及厨房用具[T2]	6.5		80	13/	13	千克	A/	R	26.5	
3924.9000	-其他〔999〕	6.5		80	13/	13	千克	A/	M	34	
39.25	**其他税目未列名的建筑用塑料制品:**										
3925.1000	-囤、柜、罐、桶及类似容器,容积超过 300 升〔101 食品用其他塑料包装,999 非食品用塑料制品〕	6.5		80	13/	13	千克	/		34	
3925.2000	-门、窗及其框架、门槛〔999〕	6.5		80	13/	13	千克	/		11.5	4.2/4.2
3925.3000	-窗板、百叶窗(包括威尼斯式百叶窗)或类似制品及其零件〔999〕	6.5		80	13/	13	千克	/		26.5	
3925.9000	-其他〔999〕	6.5		80	13/	13	千克	/		11.5	
39.26	**其他塑料制品及税目 39.01 至 39.14 所列其他材料的制品:**										
3926.1000	-办公室或学校用品〔999〕	10		80	13/	13	千克	/		37.5	
	-衣服及衣着附件(包括分指手套、连指手套及露指手套):										
	---手套(包括分指手套、连指手套及露指手套):										
3926.2011	----聚氯乙烯制〔999〕	6.5		90	13/	13	千克/双	/		21.5	
3926.2019	----其他〔999〕	6.5		90	13/	13	千克/双	/		21.5	
3926.2090	---其他〔999〕	6.5		90	13/	13	千克	/		26.5	
3926.3000	-家具、车厢或类似品的附件〔101 车辆内饰零部件,999 其他〕	10		80	13/	13	千克	/		32.5	
3926.4000	-小雕塑品及其他装饰品〔999〕	6.5		100	13/	13	千克	/		26.5	4.2/4.2
	-其他:										
3926.9010	---机器及仪器用零件〔999〕	10		35	13/	13	千克	/		25	6.5/6.5
3926.9090	---其他										
3926.9090 10	两用物项管制结构复合材料的预成形件和制品(用纤维和丝材增强而制成的各种预浸件和预成形件,其中增强材料的比拉伸强度大于 7.62×10^4m 和比模量大于 3.18×10^6m)〔999〕	10		80	13/	13	千克	3/			6.5/6.5
3926.9090 20	聚氨酯制避孕套〔999〕	10	0	80	0/	0	千克	/			6.5/6.5
3926.9090 90	其他塑料制品(包括税目 39.01 至 39.14 所列材料的制品)〔999〕	10		80	13/	13	千克	/			6.5/6.5

协定税率 %								RCEP		特惠税率 %			Article Description
东/冰/格	巴基斯坦	韩国	瑞士上/下	哥/秘/柬	澳/毛	新西/坡/智	中国港/澳/台	东盟及马来/澳/韩	日/新	亚太2国	老/柬/缅	98/97/95	
0/0/0	0	3	0.7/0.7	0/0/0	0/0	0//0	0/0/0	5.9/5.9/5.9	6.1/5.9			0/0/0	Other plates, sheets, film, foil fiol and strip of plastic not elsewhere specified or in cluded(other than ion exchanging membrane and laminated structural board made of composite materials under sensitive product control)
													Baths, shower-baths, sinks, wash-basins, bidets, lavatory pans, seats and covers, flushing cisterns and similar sanitary ware, of plastics:
0/0/0	3.5	2	0/0	0/0/0	0/0	0//0	0/0/	0/0/9	9.1/0		0//	0/0/0	-Baths, shower-baths, sinks and wash-basins
0/0/0	3.5	2	0/0	0/0/0	0/0	0//0	0/0/	0/0/9	9.1/0		0//	0/0/0	-Lavatory seats and covers
0/0/0	3.5	2	0/0	0/0/0	0/0	0//0	0/0/	0/0/9	9.1/0			0/0/0	-Other
													Articles for the conveyance or packing of goods, of plastics; stoppers, lids, caps and other closures, of plastics:
													-Boxes, cases, crates and similar articles
0/0/0	4	6	0/0	0/0/0	0/0	0/0/0	0/0/0	9.5/9.5/9.5	9.5/9.5			0/0/0	Plastic boxes, boxes, crates and similar items ,with a specific shape or device ,for the conveyance or packing of semiconductor wafer and mask
0/0/0	4	6	0/0	0/0/0	0/0	0/0/0	0/0/0	9.5/9.5/9.5	9.5/9.5			0/0/0	Other plastic boxes, boxes and similar articles, including plastic crates, for transport or packaging of goods
													-Sacks and bags (including cones):
0/0/0	0	0	0/0	0/0/0	0/0	0/0/0	0/0/	9/9/9	9.1/9			0/0/0	--Of polymers of ethylene
0/0/0	3.5	4.6	0/0	0/0/0	0/6	0/0/0	0/0/	9.3/9.5/9.3	9.4/9.5			0/0/0	--Of other plastics
0/0/0	4	3	0/0	0//0	0/0	0/0/0	0/0/	5.9/5.9/5.9	6.1/5.9			0/0/0	-Carboys, bottles, flasks and similar articles
0/0/0	3.5	4.6	0/0	0/0/0	0/0	0/0/0	0/0/	9.3/9.5/9.3	9.4/9.5			0/0/0	-Spools, cops, bobbins and similar supports
0/0/0	3.5	2	1/1	0/0/0	0/0	0/0/0	0/0/0	0/0/9	9.1/0			0/0/0	-Stoppers, lids, caps and other closures
0/0/0	3.5	6	0/0	0/0/0	0/0	0/0/0	0/0/0	9.5/9.5/9.5	9.5/9.5			0/0/0	-Other
													Tableware, kitchenware, other household articles and hygienic or toilet articles, of plastics:
0/0/0	3.5	4.6	0/0	0/0/0	0/6	0/0/0	0/0/	9.3/9.5/9.3	9.4/9.5	0		0/0/0	-Tableware and kitchenware
0/0/0	0	2	0/0	0/0/0	0/6	0/0/0	0/0/	9/9/9	9.1/9			0/0/0	-Other
													Builders' ware of plastics, not elsewhere specified or included:
0/0/0	3.5	2	0/0	0/0/0	0/0	0//0	0/0/	0/0/9	9.1/0			0/0/0	-Reservoirs, tanks, vats and similar containers, of a capacity exceeding 300L
0/0/0	3.5	2	0/0	0/0/0	0/0	0//0	0/0/	0/0/9	9.1/0			0/0/0	-Doors, windows and their frames and thresholds for doors
0/0/0	3.5	2	0/0	0/0/0	0/0	0//0	0/0/	0/0/9	9.1/0			0/0/0	-Shutters, blinds (including Venetian blinds) and similar articles and parts thereof
0/0/0	3.5	2	4.2/4.2	0/0/0	0/0	0//0	0/0/	9/9/9	9.1/9			0/0/0	-Other
													Other articles of plastics and articles of other materials of headings Nos. 39. 01 to 39. 14:
0/0/0	3.5	2	0/0	0/0/0	0/0	0/0/0	0/0/	0/0/9	9.1/0			0/0/0	-Offices or school supplies
													-Articles of apparel and clothing accessories (including gloves, mittens and mitts):
													---Gloves(mittens and mitts):
0/0/0		2	0/0	0/0/0	0/0	0/0/0	0/0/	0/0/9	9.1/0			0/0/0	----Of poly (vinyl chrlrride)
0/0/0		2	0/0	0/0/0	0/0	0/0/0	0/0/	0/0/9	9.1/0			0/0/0	----Other
0/0/0		2	0/0	0/0/0	0/0	0/0/0	0/0/	0/0/9	9.1/0			0/0/0	Other
0/0/0	3.5	4.6	0/0	0/0/0	0/0	0/0/0	0/0/	9.3/9.5/9.3	9.4/9.5			0/0/0	-Fittings for furniture, coachwork or the like
0/0/0	4	2	0/0	0/0/0	0/0	0//0	0/0/	0/0/9	9.1/0			0/0/0	-Statuettes and other ornamental articles
													-Other:
0/0/0	0	2	1/1	0/0/0	0/0	0/0/0	0/0/0	0/0/9	9.4/0			0/0/0	---Of a kind for used in machines or instruments
													---Other
0/0/0	9.2	2	1/1	0/0/0	0/0	0/0/0	0/0/0	0/0/9	9.4/0			0/0/0	Laminated structural board made of composite materials under sensitive items control (various persoaked and fabricated parts reinforced by fibers and threads, therein the specific tensile strength of reinforcing materials is greater than 7. 62 $\times 10^4$ m and specific modulus greater than 3. 18 $\times 10^6$ m)
0/0/0	9.2	2	1/1	0/0/0	0/0	0/0/0	0/0/0	0/0/9	9.4/0			0/0/0	Polyurethane condom
0/0/0	9.2	2	1/1	0/0/0	0/0	0/0/0	0/0/0	0/0/9	9.4/0			0/0/0	Other articles of plastics (including articles of other materials of heading 39. 01 to 39. 14)

第四十章
橡胶及其制品

注释：

一、除条文另有规定的以外，本目录所称“橡胶”，是指不论是否硫化或硬化的下列产品：天然橡胶、巴拉塔胶、古塔波胶、银胶菊胶、糖胶树胶及类似的天然树胶、合成橡胶、从油类中提取的油膏以及上述物品的再生品。

二、本章不包括：

（一）第十一类的货品（纺织原料及纺织制品）；

（二）第六十四章的鞋靴及其零件；

（三）第六十五章的帽类及其零件（包括游泳帽）；

（四）第十六类的硬质橡胶制的机械器具、电气器具及其零件（包括各种电气用品）；

（五）第九十章、第九十二章、第九十四章或第九十六章的物品；

（六）第九十五章的物品（运动用分指手套、连指手套、露指手套及税目 40.11 至 40.13 的制品除外）。

三、税目 40.01 至 40.03 及 40.05 所称“初级形状”，只限于下列形状：

（一）液状及糊状，包括胶乳（不论是否预硫化）及其他分散体和溶液；

（二）不规则形状的块，团、包、粉、粒、碎屑及类似的散装形状。

四、本章注释一和税目 40.02 所称“合成橡胶”，适用于：

（一）不饱和合成物质，即用硫磺硫化能使其不可逆地变为非热塑物质，这种物质能在温度 18℃ 至 29℃ 之间被拉长到其原长度的三倍而不致断裂，拉长到原长度的两倍时，在五分钟内能回复到不超过原长度的一倍半。为了进行上述试验，可以加入交联所需的硫化活化剂或促进剂；也允许含有注释五（二）2 及 3 所述的物质。但不能加入非交联所需的物质，例如，增量剂、增塑剂及填料；

（二）聚硫橡胶（TM）；

（三）与塑料接枝共聚或混合而改性的天然橡胶、解聚天然橡胶以及不饱和合成物质与饱和合成高聚物的混合物，但这些产品必须符合以上（一）款关于硫化、延伸及回复的要求。

五、（一）税目 40.01 及 40.02 不适用于任何凝结前或凝结后与下列物质相混合的橡胶或橡胶混合物：

1. 硫化剂、促进剂、防焦剂或活性剂（为制造预硫胶乳所加入的除外）；
2. 颜料或其他着色料，但仅为易于识别而加入的除外；
3. 增塑剂或增量剂（用油增量的橡胶中所加的矿物油除外）、填料、增强剂、有机溶剂或其他物质，但以下（二）款所述的除外；

（二）含有下列物质的橡胶或橡胶混合物，只要仍具有原料的基本特性，应归入税目 40.01 或 40.02：

1. 乳化剂或防粘剂；
2. 少量的乳化剂分解产品；
3. 微量的下列物质：热敏剂（一般为制造热敏胶乳用）、阳离子表面活性剂（一般为制造阳性胶乳用）、抗氧剂、凝固剂、碎裂剂、抗冻剂、胶溶剂、保存剂、稳定剂、黏度控制剂或类似的特殊用途添加剂。

六、税目 40.04 所称“废碎料及下脚料”，是指在橡胶或橡胶制品生产或加工过程中由于切割、磨损或其他原因所造成没有使用价值的废橡胶及下脚料。

七、全部用硫化橡胶制成的线，其任一截面的尺寸超过 5 毫米的，应作为带、杆或型材及异型材归入税目 40.08。

八、税目 40.10 包括用橡胶浸渍、涂布、包覆或层压的织物制成的或用橡胶浸渍、涂布、包覆或套裹的纱线或绳制成的传动带、输送带。

九、税目 40.01、40.02、40.03、40.05 及 40.08 所称“板”“片”“带”，仅指未切割或只简单切割成矩形（包括正方形）的板、片、带及正几何形块，不论是否具有成品的特征，也不论是否经过印制或其他表面加工，但未切割成其他形状或进一步加工。

税目 40.08 所称“杆”或“型材及异型材”，仅指不论是否切割成一定长度或表面加工，但未经进一步加工的该类产品。

税则号列	货品名称〔CIQ 扩展编码及品名—T2 表示见附表 2〕	最惠(%)	暂定税率	普通	增值/消费	出口退税	计量单位	监管条件/特殊证件	检验检疫	对美关税	亚太上/下
40.01	**天然橡胶、巴拉塔胶、古塔波胶、银胶菊胶、糖胶树胶及类似的天然树胶，初级形状或板、片、带：**										
4001.1000	-天然胶乳，不论是否预硫化〔101 天然橡胶(乳胶固形物)(有检疫要求食品添加剂)，999 其他〕	20	①	40	13/	9	千克	/			
	-其他形状的天然橡胶：										
4001.2100	--烟胶片〔999〕	20	②	40	13/	9	千克	/			17/17
4001.2200	--技术分类天然橡胶(TSNR)〔999〕	20	②	40	13/	9	千克	/			
4001.2900	--其他〔999〕	20		40	13/	9	千克	/		45	17/17

① 10%或 900 元/吨，两 者从低

② 20%或 1500 元/吨，两 者从低

Chapter 40
Rubber and articles thereof

Notes:

1. Except where the context otherwise requires, throughout the Nomenclature the expression "rubber" means the following products, whether or not vulcanized or hard: natural rubber, balata, gutta-percha, guayule, chicle and similar natural gums, synthetic rubber, factice derived from oils, and such substances reclaimed.
2. This Chapter does not cover:
   (a) Goods of Section XI (texitils and textile articles);
   (b) Footwear or parts thereof of Chapter 64;
   (c) Headgear or parts thereof (including bathing caps) of Chapter 65;
   (d) Mechanical or electrical appliances or parts thereof of Section XVI (including electrical goods of all kinds), of hard rubber;
   (e) Articles of Chapter 90,92,94 or 96;
   (f) Articles of Chapter 95 (other than sports gloves, mittens and mitts and articles of headings No. 40. 11 to 40. 13).
3. In headings No. 40. 01 to 40. 03 and 40. 05, the expression "primary forms" applies only to the following forms:
   (a) Liquids and pastes (including latex, whether or not pre-vulcanized, and other dispersions and solutions);
   (b) Blocks of irregular shape, lumps, bales, powders, granules, crumbs and similar bulk forms.
4. In Note I to this Chapter and in heading No. 40. 02, the expression "synthetic rubber" applies to:
   (a) Unsaturated synthetic substances which can be irreversibly transformed by vulcanization with sulphur into non-thermoplastic substances which, at a temperature between 18℃ and 29℃, will not break on being extended to three times their original length and will return, after being extended to twice their original length, within a period of five minutes, to a length not greater than one and a half times their original length. For the purposes of this test, substances necessary for the cross-linking, such as vulcanisng activators or accelerators, may be added; the presence of substances as provided for by Note 5(b) (ii)and (iii) is also permitted. However, the presence of any substances not necessary for the cross-linking, such as extenders, plasticizers and fillers, is not permitted;
   (b) Thioplasts (TM); and
   (c) Natural rubber modified by grafting or mixing with plastics, depolymerized natural rubber, mixtures of unsaturated synthetic substances with saturated synthetic high polymers provided that all the above-mentioned products comply with the requirements concerning vulcanization, elongation and recovery in (a) above.
5. (a) Headings No. 40. 01 and 40. 02 do not apply to any rubber or mixture of rubbers which has been compounded, before or after coagulation, with:
      (i) vulcanizing agents, accelerators, retarders or activators (other than those added for the preparation of pre-vulcanized rubber latex);
      (ii) pigments or other colouring matter, other than those added solely for the purpose of identification;
      (iii) plasticizers or extenders (except mineral oil in the case of oil-extended rubber), fillers, reinforcing agents, organic solvents or any other substances, except those permitted under (b);
   (b) The presence of the following substances in any rubber or mixture of rubbers shall not affect its classification in heading No. 40. 01 or 40. 02, as the case may be, provided that such rubber or mixture of rubbers retains its essential character as a raw material:
      (i) emulsifiers or anti-tack agents;
      (ii) small amounts of breakdown products of emulsifiers;
      (iii) very small amounts of the following: heat-sensitive agents (generally for obtaining thermosensitive rubber latexes), cationic surface-active agents (generally for obtaining electro-positive rubber latexes), antioxidants, coagulants, crumbling agents, freeze-resisting agents, peptizers, preservatives, stabilizers, viscosity-control agents, or similar special-purpose additives.
6. For the purposes of heading No. 40. 04, the expression "waste, parings and scrap" means rubber waste, parings and scrap from the manufacture or working of rubber and rubber goods definitely not usable as such because of cutting-up, wear or other reasons.
7. Thread wholly of vulcanized rubber, of which any cross-sectional dimension exceeds 5 mm, is to be classified as strip, rods or profile shapes, of heading No. 40. 08.
8. Heading No. 40. 10 includes conveyor or transmission belts or belting of textile fabric impregnated, coated, covered or laminated with rubber or made from textile yarn or cord impregnated, coated, covered or sheathed with rubber.
9. In headings No. 40. 01, 40. 02, 40. 03, 40. 05, and 40. 08, the expressions "plates", "sheets" and "strip" apply only to plates, sheets and strip and to blocks of regular geometric shape, uncut or simply cut to rectangular (including square) shape, whether or not having the character of articles and whether or not printed or otherwise surface-worked, but not otherwise cut to shape or further worked.
   In heading No. 40. 08 the expressions "rods" and "profile shapes" apply only to such products, whether or not cut to length or surface-worked but not otherwise worked.

协定税率 %								RCEP		特惠税率 %			Article Description
东/冰/格	巴基斯坦	韩国	瑞士上/下	哥/秘/柬	澳/毛	新西/坡/智	中国港/澳/台	东盟及马来/澳/韩	日/新	亚太2国	老/柬/缅	98/97/95	
													Natural rubber, balata, gutta-percha, guayule, chicle and similar natural gums, in primary forms or in plates, sheets or strip:
/0/		9.3	2/2	0//	0/	0//0	0/0/						-Natural rubber latex, whether or not prevulcanized
													-Natural rubber in other forms:
/0/	17	9.3	2/2	0//	0/	0//0	0/0/						--Smoked sheets
/0/			2/2	0//	0/	0//0	0/0/						--Technically specified natural rubber (TSNR)
/0/	17		2/2	0//	0/	0//0	0/0/						--Other

税则号列	货品名称〔CIQ扩展编码及品名—T2表示见附表2〕	最惠(%)	暂定税率	普通	增值/消费	出口退税	计量单位	监管条件/特殊证件	检验检疫	对美关税	亚太上/下
4001.3000	-巴拉塔胶、古塔波胶、银胶菊胶、糖胶树胶及类似的天然树胶〔999〕	20		40	13/	9	千克	/			
40.02	**合成橡胶及从油类提取的油膏,初级形状或板、片、带;税号40.01所列产品与本税号所列产品的混合物,初级形状或板、片、带:**										
	-丁苯橡胶(SBR);羧基丁苯橡胶(XSBR):										
	--胶乳:										
4002.1110	---羧基丁苯橡胶〔999〕	7.5		14	13/	13	千克	/		32.5	
4002.1190	---其他〔999〕	7.5		14	13/	13	千克	/		17.5	
	--其他:										
	---初级形状的:										
4002.1911	----未经任何加工的丁苯橡胶(溶聚的除外)〔999〕	7.5		14	13/	13	千克	/		17.5	
4002.1912	----充油丁苯橡胶(溶聚的除外)〔999〕	7.5		14	13/	13	千克	/		32.5	
4002.1913	----热塑丁苯橡胶〔999〕	7.5		14	13/	13	千克	/		27.5	
4002.1914	----充油热塑丁苯橡胶〔999〕	7.5		14	13/	13	千克	/		27.5	
4002.1915	----未经任何加工的溶聚丁苯橡胶〔999〕	7.5		14	13/	13	千克	/		27.5	
4002.1916	----充油溶聚丁苯橡胶〔999〕	7.5		14	13/	13	千克	/		32.5	
4002.1919	----其他〔999〕	7.5		14	13/	13	千克	/		32.5	
4002.1990	---其他	7.5		14	13/	13	千克	/		12.5	
4002.1990 01	简单处理的丁苯橡胶,热塑或充油热塑丁苯橡胶除外(指为便于运输,对初级形状进行压缩、挤压等简单成型处理)〔999〕	7.5		35	13/	13	千克	/		27.5	4.9/4.9
4002.1990 90	其他丁苯橡胶及羧基丁苯橡胶板,片,带(4002199001项下的除外)〔999〕	7.5		35	13/	0	千克	/		27.5	4.9/4.9
	-丁二烯橡胶(BR):										
4002.2010	---初级形状的〔999〕	7.5		14	13/	13	千克	/		32.5	
4002.2090	---其他〔999〕	7.5		35	13/	0	千克	/		27.5	7/7
	-异丁烯-异戊二烯(丁基)橡胶(IIR);卤代丁基橡胶(CIIR或BIIR):										
	--异丁烯-异戊二烯(丁基)橡胶(IIR):										
4002.3110	---初级形状的〔999〕	6		14	13/	13	千克	/		26	3.9/3.9
4002.3190	---其他〔999〕	7.5		35	13/	0	千克	/		17.5	4.9/4.9
	--其他:										
4002.3910	---初级形状的〔999〕	7.5		14	13/	13	千克	/		12.5	
4002.3990	---其他〔999〕	7.5		35	13/	0	千克	/		32.5	4.9/4.9
	-氯丁二烯(氯丁)橡胶(CR):										
4002.4100	--胶乳〔999〕	7.5		14	13/	13	千克	/		17.5	4.9/4.9
	--其他:										
4002.4910	---初级形状的〔999〕	7.5		14	13/	13	千克	7/		32.5	
4002.4990	---其他〔999〕	7.5		35	13/	0	千克	7/		32.5	4.9/4.9
	-丁腈橡胶(NBR):										
4002.5100	--胶乳〔999〕	7.5		14	13/	13	千克	/		32.5	4.9/4.9
	--其他:										
4002.5910	---初级形状的〔999〕	7.5		14	13/	13	千克	/		27.5	
4002.5990	---其他〔999〕	7.5		35	13/	0	千克	/		27.5	
	-异戊二烯橡胶(IR):										
4002.6010	---初级形状的〔999〕	3		14	13/	13	千克	/		13	
4002.6090	---其他〔999〕	5		35	13/	0	千克	/		30	3.3/3.3
	-乙丙非共轭二烯橡胶(EPDM):										
4002.7010	---初级形状的〔999〕	7.5		14	13/	13	千克	/		12.5	
4002.7090	---其他〔999〕	7.5		35	13/	0	千克	/		12.5	7.1/7.1
4002.8000	-税目40.01所列产品与本税目所列产品的混合物〔999〕	7.5		35	13/	0	千克	/		32.5	
	-其他:										
4002.9100	--胶乳〔999〕	7.5		14	13/	0	千克	/		27.5	
	--其他:										
	---其他合成橡胶:										
4002.9911	----初级形状的〔999〕	7.5		14	13/	13	千克	/		12.5	
4002.9919	----其他〔999〕	7.5		35	13/	0	千克	/		17.5	
4002.9990	---其他〔999〕	4		14	13/	13	千克	/		29	
40.03	**再生橡胶,初级形状或板、片、带:**										
4003.0000	再生橡胶,初级形状或板、片、带〔999〕	8		30	13/	13	千克	/		28	
40.04	**橡胶(硬质橡胶的除外)的废碎料、下脚料及其粉、粒:**										

协定税率 %								RCEP		特惠税率 %			Article Description
东/冰/格	巴基斯坦	韩国	瑞士 上/下	哥/秘/柬	澳/毛	新西/坡/智	中国港/澳/台	东盟及马来/澳/韩	日/新	亚太2国	老/柬/缅	98/97/95	
0/0/0		9.3	2/2	0/0/0	0/	0/0/0	0/0/	18/18/18	18.8/18			0/0/0	-Balata, gutta-percha, guayule, chicle and similar natural gums
													Synthetic rubber and factice derived from oils, in primary forms or in plates, sheets or strip; mixtures of any products of heading No. 40. 01 with any product of this heading, in primary forms or in plates, sheets or strip:
													-Styrene-butadiene rubber (SBR); carboxylated styrene-butadiene rubber (XSBR):
													--Latex:
0/0/0	2	3.5	0/0	0/0/0	0/0	0//0	0/0/	6.8/6.8/6.8	7/6.8			0/0/0	---Carboxylated styrene-butadiene rubber (XSBR)
0/0/0	2	3.5	0/0	0/0/0	0/0	0//0	0/0/	6.8/6.8/6.8	7/6.8			0/0/0	---Other
													--Other:
													---In primary forms:
0/0/0	2	3.5	0/0	0/0/0	0/0	0/0/0	0/0/	6.8/6.8/6.8	7/6.8			0/0/0	----SBR, except for SSBR, not worked
0/0/0	2	3.5	0/0	0/0/0	0/0	0/0/0	0/0/	6.8/6.8/6.8	7/6.8			0/0/0	----SBR, except for SSBR, oil-filled
0/0/0	2	3.5	0/0	0/0/0	0/0	0/0/0	0/0/	6.8/6.8/6.8	7/6.8			0/0/0	----SBR, thermo-plasticated
0/0/0	2	3.5	0/0	0/0/0	0/0	0/0/0	0/0/	6.8/6.8/6.8	7/6.8			0/0/0	----SBR, oil-filled and thermo-plasticated
0/0/0	2	3.5	0/0	0/0/0	0/0	0/0/0	0/0/	6.8/6.8/6.8	7/6.8			0/0/0	----SBR, not worked
0/0/0	2	3.5	0/0	0/0/0	0/0	0/0/0	0/0/	6.8/6.8/6.8	7/6.8			0/0/0	----SBR, oil-filled
5/0/0		3.5	0/0	0/0/0	0/0	0//0	0/0/	7.1/7.3/	/7.3			0/0/0	----Other
													---Other
0/0/0	2	3.5	0/0	0/0/0	0/0	0/0/0	0/0/	6.8/6.8/6.8	7/6.8			0/0/0	Except simple treatment of styrene-butadiene rubber or styrene-butadiene-styrene block copolymer (referring to compression, extrusion in order to facilitate transportation)
0/0/0	2	3.5	0/0	0/0/0	0/0	0/0/0	0/0/	6.8/6.8/6.8	7/6.8			0/0/0	Other styrene-butadiene rubber and carboxy lated styrene-butadiene rubber, plates, sheets or strip (except those under item 4002199010)
													-Butadiene rubber (BR):
0/0/0	2	3.5	0/0	0/0/0	0/0	0//0	0/0/	6.8/6.8/6.8	7/6.8			0/0/0	---In primary forms
0/0/0	2	3.5	0/0	0/0/0	0/0	0//0	0/0/	6.8/6.8/6.8	7/6.8			0/0/0	---Other
													-Isobutene-isoprene (butyl) rubber (IIR); halo-isobutene-isoprene rubber (CIIR or BIIR):
													--Isobutene-isoprene (butyl) rubber (IIR):
0/0/0	0	2.8	0/0	0/0/0	0/0	0//0	0/0/	5.4/5.4/5.4	5.6/5.4			0/0/0	---In primary forms
0/0/0	2	3.5	0/0	0/0/0	0/0	0//0	0/0/	6.8/6.8/6.8	7/6.8			0/0/0	---Other
													--Other:
0/0/0	2	3.5	0/0	0/0/0	0/0	0//0	0/0/	6.8/6.8/6.8	7/6.8			0/0/0	---In pimary forms
0/0/0	2	3.5	0/0	0/0/0	0/0	0//0	0/0/	6.8/6.8/6.8	7/6.8			0/0/0	---Other
													-Chloroprene (ehlorobutadiene) rubber(CR):
0/0/0	2	0	0/0	0/0/0	0/0	0//0	0/0/	0/0/0	6.8/0			0/0/0	--Latex
													--Other:
0/0/0	2		0/0	0/0/0	0/0	0//0	0/0/	5/5/	/5			0/0/0	---In primary forms
0/0/0	2	3.5	0/0	0/0/0	0/0	0//0	0/0/	6.8/6.8/6.8	7/6.8			0/0/0	---Other
													-Acrylonitrile-butadient rubber(NBR):
0/0/0	2	3.5	0/0	0/0/0	0/0	0//0	0/0/	6.8/6.8/6.8	7/6.8			0/0/0	--Latex
													--Other:
0/0/0	2	3.5	0/0	0/0/0	0/0	0//0	0/0/	6.8/6.8/6.8	7/6.8			0/0/0	---In primary forms
0/0/0	2	3.5	0/0	0/0/0	0/0	0//0	0/0/	6.8/6.8/6.8	7/6.8			0/0/0	---Other
													-Isoprene rubber (IR):
0/0/0	0	1.4	0/0	0/0/0	0/0	0//0	0/0/	2.7/2.7/2.7	2.8/2.7			0/0/0	---In primary forms
0/0/0	0	2.3	0/0	0/0/0	0/0	0//0	0/0/	4.5/4.5/4.5	4.7/4.5			0/0/0	---Other
													-Ethylene-propylene-non-conjugated diene rubber (EPDM):
0/0/0	2	3.5	0/0	0/0/0	0/0	0//0	0/0/	6.8/6.8/6.8	7/6.8			0/0/0	---In primary forms
0/0/0	2	3.5	0/0	0/0/0	0/0	0//0	0/0/	6.8/6.8/6.8	7/6.8			0/0/0	---Other
0/0/0	2	3.5	0/0	0/0/0	0/0	0//0	0/0/	6.8/6.8/6.8	7/6.8			0/0/0	-Mixtures of any product of heading No. 40. 01 with any product of this heading
													-Other:
0/0/0	2	3.5	0/0	0/0/0	0/0	0//0	0/0/	6.8/6.8/6.8	7/6.8			0/0/0	--Latex
													--Other:
													---Other synthetic rubber:
0/0/0	2	3.5	0/0	0/0/0	0/0	0//0	0/0/0	6.8/6.8/6.8	7/6.8			0/0/0	----In primary forms
0/0/0	2	3.5	0/0	0/0/0	0/0	0//0	0/0/	6.8/6.8/6.8	7/6.8			0/0/0	----Other
0/0/0	0	0	0/0	0/0/0	0/0	0//0	0/0/	0/0/0	0/0			0/0/0	---Other
													Reclaimed rubber in primary forms or in plates, sheets or strip:
0/0/0	2	3.7	0/0	0/0/0	0/0	0//0	0/0/	7.5/7.6/7.5	7.5/7.6			0/0/0	Reclaimed rubber in primary forms or in plates, sheets or strip
													Waste, parings and scrap of rubber (other than hard rubber) and powders and granules obtained therefrom:

税则号列	货品名称〔CIQ 扩展编码及品名—T2 表示见附表 2〕	最惠(%)	暂定税率	普通	增值/消费	出口退税	计量单位	监管条件/特殊证件	检验检疫	对美关税	亚太上/下
4004.0000	橡胶(硬质橡胶的除外)的废碎料、下脚料及其粉、粒										
4004.0000 10	废轮胎及其切块〔999〕	8		30	13/	0	千克	9/			5.2/5.2
4004.0000 20	硫化橡胶废碎料、下脚料及其粉、粒(硬质橡胶的除外)(不包括符合 GB/T19208 标准的硫化橡胶粉产品)〔999〕	8		30	13/	0	千克	9/			5.2/5.2
4004.0000 90	未硫化橡胶废碎料、下脚料及其粉、粒〔101 橡胶皮革废碎料，999 橡胶(硬质橡胶除外)的废碎料、下脚料及其粉、粒〕	8		30	13/	0	千克	9/			5.2/5.2
40.05	**未硫化的复合橡胶，初级形状或板、片、带：**										
4005.1000	-与炭黑或硅石混合〔999〕	8		35	13/	0	千克	A/	M	28	
4005.2000	-溶液；子目 4005.10 以外的分散体〔999〕	8		35	13/	0	千克	A/	M	33	
	-其他：										
4005.9100	--板、片、带〔999〕	8		35	13/	0	千克	A/	M	18	
4005.9900	--其他〔999〕	8		35	13/	0	千克	A/	M	28	
40.06	**其他形状(例如，杆、管或型材及异型材)的未硫化橡胶及未硫化橡胶制品(例如，盘、环)：**										
4006.1000	-轮胎翻新用胎面补料胎条〔999〕	8		35	13/	0	千克	/		33	
	-其他：										
4006.9010	---其他形状的未硫化橡胶〔999〕	8		35	13/	0	千克	/		18	
4006.9020	---未硫化橡胶制品〔999〕	14		80	13/	0	千克	/		19	
40.07	**硫化橡胶线及绳：**										
4007.0000	硫化橡胶线及绳〔999〕	14		80	13/	13	千克	/		39	
40.08	**硫化橡胶(硬质橡胶除外)制的板、片、带、杆或型材及异型材：**										
	-海绵橡胶制：										
4008.1100	--板、片、带〔999〕	8		35	13/	13	千克	/		28	
4008.1900	--其他〔999〕	8		35	13/	13	千克	/		18	
	-非海绵橡胶制：										
4008.2100	--板、片、带〔999〕	8		35	13/	13	千克	/		18	
4008.2900	--其他〔999〕	8		35	13/	13	千克	/		28	
40.09	**硫化橡胶(硬质橡胶除外)制的管子，不论是否装有附件(例如，接头、肘管、法兰)：**										
	-未经加强或未与其他材料合制：										
4009.1100	--未装有附件〔999〕	10		40	13/	13	千克	/		30	
4009.1200	--装有附件〔999〕	10		40	13/	13	千克	/		30	
	-用金属加强或只与金属合制：										
4009.2100	--未装有附件〔999〕	10		40	13/	13	千克	/		20	
4009.2200	--装有附件〔999〕	10		40	13/	13	千克	/	L	20	
	-用纺织材料加强或只与纺织材料合制：										
4009.3100	--未装有附件〔999〕	10		40	13/	13	千克	/		30	
4009.3200	--装有附件〔999〕	10		40	13/	13	千克	/		35	
	-用其他材料加强或与其他材料合制：										
4009.4100	--未装有附件〔999〕	10		40	13/	13	千克	/		20	
4009.4200	--装有附件〔999〕	10		40	13/	13	千克	/		20	
40.10	**硫化橡胶制的传动带或输送带及带料：**										
	-输送带及带料：										
4010.1100	--仅用金属加强的〔999〕	10		35	13/	13	千克	/		35	
4010.1200	--仅用纺织材料加强的〔999〕	10		35	13/	13	千克	/		20	
4010.1900	--其他〔999〕	10		35	13/	13	千克	/		20	
	-传动带及带料：										
4010.3100	--梯形截面的环形传动带(三角带)，V 形肋状的，外周长超过 60 厘米，但不超过 180 厘米〔999〕	8		35	13/	13	千克	/		33	
4010.3200	--梯形截面的环形传动带(三角带)，外周长超过 60 厘米，但不超过 180 厘米，V 形肋状的除外〔999〕	8		35	13/	13	千克	/		28	
4010.3300	--梯形截面的环形传动带(三角带)，V 形肋状的，外周长超过 180 厘米，但不超过 240 厘米〔999〕	8		35	13/	13	千克	/		28	
4010.3400	--梯形截面的环形传动带(三角带)，外周长超过 180 厘米，但不超过 240 厘米，V 形肋状的除外〔999〕	8		35	13/	13	千克	/		28	

协定税率 %								RCEP		特惠税率 %			Article Description
东/冰/格	巴基斯坦	韩国	瑞士上/下	哥/秘/柬	澳/毛	新西/坡/智	中国港/澳/台	东盟及马来/澳/韩	日/新	亚太2国	老/柬/缅	98/97/95	
													Waste, parings and scrap of rubber (other than hard rubber) and powders and granules obtained therefrom
0/0/0	2	0	0/0	0/0/0	0/0	0//0	0/0/	0/0/0	7.3/0			0/0/0	Waste rubber tyres and their cuts
0/0/0	2	0	0/0	0/0/0	0/0	0//0	0/0/	0/0/0	7.3/0			0/0/0	Waste, parings and scrap of vulcanized rubber (other than hard rubber) and powders and granules obtained therefrom
0/0/0	2	0	0/0	0/0/0	0/0	0//0	0/0/	0/0/0	7.3/0			0/0/0	Other waste, parings and scrap of rubber (other than hard rubber) and powders and granules obtained therefrom
													Compounded rubber, unvulcanized, in primary forms or in plates, sheets or strip:
0/0/	2	3.7	0/0	0/0/0	0/0	0//0	0/0/	7.2/7.2/7.2	7.5/7.2			0/0/0	-Compounded with carbon black or silica
0/0/	2	3.7	0/0	0/0/0	0/0	0//0	0/0/	7.5/7.6/7.5	7.5/7.6			0/0/0	-Solutions; dispersions other than those of subheading No. 4005. 10
													-Other:
0/0/	2	0	0/0	0/0/0	0/0	0//0	0/0/	0/0/0	7.3/0			0/0/0	--Plates, sheets and strip
0/0/	2	3.7	0/0	0/0/0	0/0	0//0	0/0/	7.2/7.2/7.2	7.5/7.2			0/0/0	--Other
													Other forms (for example, rods, tubes and profile shapes) and articles (for example, discs and rings), of unvulcanized rubber:
0/0/0	2	0	0/0	0/0/0	0/0	0//0	0/0/	0/0/0	7.3/0			0/0/0	-"Camel-back" strips for retreading rubber tyres
													-Other:
0/0/0	2	1.6	0/0	0/0/0	0/0	0//0	0/0/	0/0/7.2	7.3/0			0/0/0	---Other forms of unvulcanized rubber
0/0/0	11.2	2.8	1.4/1.4	0/0/0	0/0	0/0/0	0/0/	0/0/12.6	12.7/0			0/0/0	---Articles of unvulcanized rubber
													Vulcanized rubber thread and cord:
0/0/0	11.2	2.8	1.4/1.4	0/0/0	0/0	0/0/0	0/0/	0/0/12.6	12.7/0			0/0/0	Vulcanized rubber thread and cord
													Plates, sheets, strip, rods and profile shapes, of vulcanized rubber other than hard rubber:
													-Of cellular rubber:
0/0/0	2	3.7	0/0	0/0/0	0/0	0//0	0/0/	7.5/7.6/7.5	7.5/7.6			0/0/0	--Plates, sheets and strip
0/0/0	2	0	0/0	0/0/0	0/0	0//0	0/0/	0/0/0	7.3/0			0/0/0	--Other
													-Of non-cellular rubber:
0/0/0	2	0	0/0	0/0/0	0/0	0//0	0/0/	7.2/7.2/7.2	7.3/7.2			0/0/0	--Plates, sheets and strip
0/0/0	2	0	0/0	0/0/0	0/0	0//0	0/0/	0/0/0	7.3/0			0/0/0	--Other
													Tubes, pipes and hoses, of vulcanized rubber other than hard rubber, with or without their fittings (for example, joints, elbows, flanges):
													-Not reinforced or otherwise combined with other materials:
0/0/0	3.5	2.1	1.1/1.1	0/0/0	0/0	0/0/0	0/0/	9.5/9.5/9.5	9.5/9.5			0/0/0	--Without fittings
0/0/0	3.5	2	0/0	0/0/0	0/0	0//0	0/0/	0/0/9	9.1/0			0/0/0	--With fittings
													-Reinforced or otherwise combined only with metal:
0/0/0	3.5	2.1	1.1/1.1	0/0/0	0/0	0/0/0	0/0/	9.5/9.5/9.5	9.5/9.5			0/0/0	--Without fittings
0/0/0	3.5	2	0/0	0/0/0	0/0	0/0/0	0/0/	9/9/9	9.1/9			0/0/0	--With fittings
													-Reinforced or otherwise combined only with textile materials:
0/0/0	3.5	6.3	1.1/1.1	0/0/0	0/0	0/0/0	0/0/	10/10/	10/10			0/0/0	--Without fittings
0/0/0	3.5	2	0/0	0/0/0	0/0	0//0	0/0/	9/9/9	9.1/9			0/0/0	--With fittings
													-Reinforced or otherwise combined with other materials:
0/0/0	3.5	2.1	1.1/1.1	0/0/0	0/0	0/0/0	0/0/	0/0/9.5	9.5/0			0/0/0	--Without fittings
0/0/0	3.5	2	0/0	0/0/0	0/0	0/0/0	0/0/	0/0/9	9.1/0			0/0/0	--With fittings
													Conveyor or transmission belts or belting, of vulcanized rubber:
													-Conveyor belts or belting:
0/0/0	3.5	2	2.5/2.5	0/0/0	0/0	0//0	0/0/	0/0/9	9.1/0			0/0/0	--Reinforced only with metal
0/0/0	3.5	2	0/0	0/0/0	0/0	0//0	0/0/	0/0/9	9.1/0			0/0/0	--Reinforced only with textile materials
0/0/0	3.5	2	0/0	0/0/0	0/0	0//0	0/0/	0/0/9	9.1/0			0/0/0	--Other
													-Transmission belts or belting:
0/0/0	2	0	0/0	0/0/0	0/0	0//0	0/0/	7.2/7.2/7.2	7.3/7.2			0/0/0	--Endless transmission belts of trapezoidal cross-section (V-belts), vribbed of a circumference exceeding 60cm but not exceeding 180cm
0/0/0	2	0	0/0	0/0/0	0/0	0//0	0/0/	0/0/0	7.3/0			0/0/0	--Endless transmission belts of trapezoidal cross-section (V-belts), other than V-ribbed, of an outside circumference exceeding 60cm but not exceeding 180cm
0/0/0	2	0	0/0	0/0/0	0/0	0//0	0/0/	0/0/0	7.3/0			0/0/0	--Endless transmission belts of trapezoidal cross-section (V-belts), other than V-ribbed, of an outside circumference exceeding 180cm but not exceeding 240cm
0/0/0	2	0	0/0	0/0/0	0/0	0//0	0/0/	0/0/0	7.3/0			0/0/0	--Endless transmission belts of trapezoidal cross-section (V-belts), V-ribbed, of an outside circumference exceeding 180cm but not exceeding 240cm

税则号列	货品名称〔CIQ扩展编码及品名－T2表示见附表2〕	最惠(%)	暂定税率	普通	增值/消费	出口退税	计量单位	监管条件/特殊证件	检验检疫	对美关税	亚太上/下
4010.3500	--环形同步带,外周长超过60厘米,但不超过150厘米〔999〕	10		35	13/	13	千克	/		30	
4010.3600	--环形同步带,外周长超过150厘米,但不超过198厘米〔999〕	10		35	13/	13	千克	/		30	
4010.3900	--其他〔999〕	8		35	13/	13	千克	/		28	5.2/5.2
40.11	**新的充气橡胶轮胎:**										
4011.1000	-机动小客车(包括旅行小客车及赛车)用〔101有内胎,102无内胎,999其他车辆零部件〕	10		50	13/	13	千克/条	A/	LM	15	6.5/6.5
4011.2000	-客运机动车辆或货运机动车辆用										
4011.2000 10	断面宽≥30英寸客或货车用新充气橡胶轮胎(指机动车辆用橡胶轮胎,断面宽度≥30英寸)〔101轻型、微型载重汽车轮胎,102其他载重轮胎,999其他车辆零部件〕	10		50	13/	13	千克/条	A/	M	15	6.5/6.5
4011.2000 90	其他客或货车用新充气橡胶轮胎(指机动车辆用橡胶轮胎)〔101轻型、微型载重汽车轮胎,102其他载重轮胎,999其他车辆零部件〕	10		50	13/	13	千克/条	A/	LM	15	6.5/6.5
4011.3000	-航空器用〔999〕	1		11	13/	13	千克/条	/		11	
4011.4000	-摩托车用〔999〕	15		80	13/	13	千克/条	A/	LM	40	
4011.5000	-自行车用〔999〕	20		80	13/	13	千克/条	/		22.5	
	-农业或林业车辆及机器用:										
4011.7010	---人字形胎面或类似胎面〔999〕	17		50	13/	13	千克/条	A/	M	44.5	
4011.7090	---其他〔999〕	25		50	13/	13	千克/条	/		37.5	
	-建筑业、采矿业或工业搬运车辆及机器用:										
	---人字形胎面或类似胎面:										
4011.8011	----辋圈尺寸不超过61厘米										
4011.8011 10	断面宽≥24英寸人字形轮胎(建筑业、采矿业或工业搬运车辆及机器用,辋圈≤61cm,新充气橡胶胎,含类似人字形)〔999〕	17		50	13/	13	千克/条	A/	M	44.5	
4011.8011 90	其他人字形胎面轮胎(建筑业、采矿业或工业搬运车辆及机器用,辋圈≤61cm,新充气橡胶胎,含类似人字形)〔999〕	17		50	13/	13	千克/条	A/	M	44.5	
4011.8012	----辋圈尺寸超过61厘米〔999〕	17		50	13/	13	千克/条	A/	M	44.5	
	---其他:										
4011.8091	----辋圈尺寸不超过61厘米〔999〕	25		50	13/	13	千克/条	/		52.5	
4011.8092	----辋圈尺寸超过61厘米										
4011.8092 10	其他断面宽度≥24英寸轮胎(建筑业、采矿业或工业搬运车辆及机器用,辋圈＞61cm,新充气橡胶胎,非人字形胎面)〔999〕	25	17	50	13/	13	千克/条	/		29.5	
4011.8092 90	其他新的充气橡胶轮胎(建筑业、采矿业或工业搬运车辆及机器用,辋圈＞61cm,新充气橡胶胎,非人字形胎面)〔999〕	25		50	13/	13	千克/条	/		37.5	
	-其他:										
4011.9010	---人字形胎面或类似胎面的〔999〕	17		50	13/	13	千克/条	A/	M	24.5	
4011.9090	---其他										
4011.9090 10	其他断面宽度≥30英寸轮胎(其他用途,新充气橡胶轮胎,非人字形胎面)〔999〕	25	17	50	13/	13	千克/条	/		44.5	
4011.9090 90	其他新的充气橡胶轮胎(其他用途,新充气橡胶轮胎,非人字形胎面)〔999〕	25		50	13/	13	千克/条	/	L	52.5	
40.12	**翻新的或旧的充气橡胶轮胎;实心或半实心橡胶轮胎、橡胶胎面及橡胶轮胎衬带:**										
	-翻新轮胎:										
4012.1100	--机动小客车(包括旅行小客车及赛车)用〔999〕	20		50	13/	13	千克/条	A/	M		
4012.1200	--机动大客车或货运机动车用〔999〕	20		50	13/	13	千克/条	A/	M	25	
4012.1300	--航空器用〔999〕	20	4	50	13/	13	千克/条	/		29	
4012.1900	--其他〔999〕	20		50	13/	13	千克/条	/			
	-旧的充气轮胎:										
4012.2010	---汽车用〔999〕	25		50	13/	13	千克/条	A/	M	50	
4012.2090	---其他〔999〕	25		80	13/	13	千克/条	/		50	
	-其他:										
4012.9010	---航空器用〔999〕	3		11	13/	13	千克	/		8	
4012.9020	---汽车用〔101充气轮胎轮辋实心轮胎,102压配式实心轮胎,999其他车辆零部件〕	22		50	13/	13	千克	A/	M	29.5	
4012.9090	---其他〔999〕	22		50	13/	13	千克	/		49.5	
40.13	**橡胶内胎:**										

协定税率 %								RCEP		特惠税率 %			Article Description
东/冰/格	巴基斯坦	韩国	瑞士 上/下	哥/秘/柬	澳/毛	新西/坡/智	中国港/澳/台	东盟及马来/澳/韩	日/新	亚太2国	老/柬/缅	98/97/95	
0/0/0	3.5	2	0/0	0/0/0	0/0	0/0/0	0/0/	0/0/9	9.1/0			0/0/0	--Endless transmission belts, of trapezodal crossseltionl (V-belts) other tlan V-ibbed, of an outside circumference exceeding 60cm but not exceeding 150cm
0/0/0	3.5	2	0/0	0/0/0	0/0	0//0	0/0/	0/0/9	9.1/0			0/0/0	--Endless synchronous belts, of an outside circumference exceeding 150cm but not exceeding 198cm
0/0/0	2	0	0/0	0/0/0	0/0	0//0	0/0/	0/0/0	7.3/0			0/0/0	--Other
													New pneumatic tyres, of rubber:
0/0/0	4	4.6	0/0	0//0	0/0	0/0/0	0/0/0	9.3/9.5/9.3	9.4/9.5			0/0/0	-Of a kind used on motor cars (including station wagons and racing cars)
													-Of a kind used on buses or corries
0/0/0	3.5	4.6	0/0	0/0/0	0/0	0/0/0	0/0/0	9.3/9.5/9.3	9.4/9.5			0/0/0	The section width is greater than or equal to 30 inches off or a truck with new rubber tyres (of a motor vehicle with rubber tires, section width is more than or equal to 30 inches)
0/0/0	3.5	4.6	0/0	0/0/0	0/0	0/0/0	0/0/0	9.3/9.5/9.3	9.4/9.5			0/0/0	Other passengers or freight cars with new rubber tyres (refers to the rubber tirefor motor vehicles)
0/0/0	0	0	0/0	0/0/0	0/0	0//0	0/0/	0/0.9/0	0/0.9			0/0/0	-Of a kind used on aircraft
0/0/0	12	7	1.5/1.5	0/0/0	0/0	0/0/0	0/0/0	14/14.3/14	14.1/14.3			0/0/0	-Of a kind used on motorcycles
0/0/0		9.3	2/2	0/0/0	0/0	0/0/0	0/0/0	18.7/19/18.7	18.8/19			0/0/0	-Of a kind used on bicycles
													-Of a kind used on agricultural or forestry vehicles and ma— chines:
0/0/0	14	3.5	1.8/1.8	0/0/0	0/0	0/0/0	0/0/0	0/0/15.8	15.9/0			0/0/0	---Having a "herring-bone" or similar tread
0/0/0		15		0//0	0/15	0/0/0	0/0/0	23.8/23.8/23.8	/23.8			0/0/0	---Other
													--Of a kind used on construction, mining or industrial handling:
													---Having a "herring—bone" or similar tread:
													----Rim size not exceeding 61cm
0/0/0	14	3.5	1.8/1.8	0/0/0	0/0	0/0/0	0/0/	0/0/15.8	15.9/0			0/0/0	New pneumatic tyres of rubber, with "herring-bone" tread, of a cross-section width ≥ 24 inches, on construction or industrial uses and having a rim size ≤ 61cm
0/0/0	14	3.5	1.8/1.8	0/0/0	0/0	0/0/0	0/0/	0/0/15.8	15.9/0			0/0/0	Other new pneumatic tyres of rubber, with "herring-bone" tread, on construction or industrial uses and having a rim size not exceeding 61cm
0/0/0	14	3.5	1.8/1.8	0/0/0	0/0	0/0/0	0/0/	0/0/15.8	15.9/0			0/0/0	----Rim size exceeding 61cm
													---Other:
0/0/0		15		0//0	0/15	0/0/0	0/0/	23.8/23.8/	/23.8			0/0/	----Rim size not exceeding 61cm
													----Rim size exceeding 61cm
0/0/0		15		0//0	0/15	0/0/0	0/0/	5/5/	/5			0/0/	Other new pneumatic tyres of rubber, other than "herring-bone" tread, on construction or industrial uses and having a rim size not exceeding 61cm
0/0/0		15		0//0	0/15	0/0/0	0/0/	5/5/	/5			0/0/	Other new pneumatic tyres of rubber, other than "herring-bone" tread, on construction or industrial uses and having a rim size > 61cm
													-Other:
0/0/0	14	3.5	1.8/1.8	0/0/0	0/0	0/0/0	0/0/0	0/0/15.8	15.9/0			0/0/0	---Having a "herring-bone" or similar tread:
													---Other
0/0/0		15		0//0	0/15	0/0/0	0/0/	23.8/23.8/23.8	/23.8			0/0/	Other new pneumatic tyres of rubber, other than "herring-bone" tread, of a cross-section width ≥ 30 inches, for other uses
0/0/0		15		0//0	0/15	0/0/0	0/0/	23.8/23.8/23.8	/23.8			0/0/	Other new pneumatic tyres of rubber, with "herring-bone" tread , for other uses
													Retreaded or used pneumatic tyres of rubber; solid or cushion tyres, tyre treads and tyre flaps, of rubber:
													-Retreaded tyres:
0/0/0		9.3	2/2	0/0/0	0/0	0/0/0	0/0/	18/18/18	18.8/18			0/0/0	--Of a kind used on motor cars (including station wagons and racing cars)
0/0/0		9.3	2/2	0/0/0	0/0	0/0/0	0/0/	18/18/18	18.2/18			0/0/0	--Of a kind used on buses or corries
0/0/0		9.3	2/2	0/0/0	0/0	0/0/0	0/0/	18.7/19/18.7	18.8/19			0/0/0	--Of a kind used on aircraft
0/0/0		9.3	2/2	0/0/0	0/0	0/0/0	0/0/	18/18/18	18.8/18			0/0/0	Other
													-Used pneumatic tyres:
0/0/0		15		0//0	0/15	0/0/0	0/0/	23.8/23.8/23.8	/23.8				---Of a kind used on motor cars, buses or lorries
0/0/0		15		0//0	0/15	0/0/0	0/0/	23.8/23.8/23.8	/23.8				---Other
													-Other:
0/0/0	0	0	0/0	0/0/0	0/0	0//0	0/0/	0/0/0	0/0			0/0/0	---Of a kind used on aircraft
0/0/0		13.2	2.2/2.2	0/0/0	0/13.2	0/0/0	0/0/	20.9/20.9/	/20.9			0/0/0	---Of a kind used on motor cars, buses or lorries
0/0/0		13.2	2.2/2.2	0/0/0	0/13.2	0/0/0	0/0/	20.9/20.9/	/20.9			0/0/0	---Other
													Inner tubes, of rubber:

税则号列	货品名称〔CIQ 扩展编码及品名－T2 表示见附表 2〕	最惠(%)	暂定税率	普通	增值/消费	出口退税	计量单位	监管条件/特殊证件	检验检疫	对美关税	亚太上/下
4013.1000	-机动小客车(包括旅行小客车及赛车)、客运机动车辆或货运机动车辆用〔101 轿车轮胎,102 载重轮胎,999 其他车辆零部件〕	15		50	13/3	13	千克/条	A/	M	20	13.1/13.1
4013.2000	-自行车用〔999〕	15		80	13/	13	千克/条	/			
	-其他:										
4013.9010	---航空器用〔999〕	3		11	13/	13	千克/条	/		8	1.8/1.8
4013.9090	---其他〔999〕	15		50	13/3	13	千克/条	/		40	
40.14	**硫化橡胶(硬质橡胶除外)制的卫生及医疗用品(包括奶嘴),不论是否装有硬质橡胶制的附件:**										
4014.1000	-避孕套〔999〕	0		0	0/	0	千克	/		25	
4014.9000	-其他〔101 其他医疗器具,102 食品接触橡胶产品,103 食品用橡胶包装〕	17		50	13/	13	千克	A/	M	29.5	
40.15	**硫化橡胶(硬质橡胶除外)制的衣着用品及附件(包括分指手套、连指手套及露指手套):**										
	-分指手套、连指手套及露指手套:										
4015.1200	--医疗、外科、牙科或兽医用〔301 其他医疗器具,302 硫化橡胶制品〕	8		55	13/	13	千克/双	/		33	
4015.1900	--其他〔999〕	10		80	13/	13	千克/双	/		35	
	-其他:										
4015.9010	---医疗、外科、牙科或兽医用〔999〕	8		30	13/	13	千克	/		18	
4015.9090	---其他〔999〕	10		90	13/	13	千克	/		35	
40.16	**硫化橡胶(硬质橡胶除外)的其他制品:**										
	-海绵橡胶制:										
4016.1010	---机器及仪器用零件〔999〕	8		30	13/	13	千克	/		18	
4016.1090	---其他〔999〕	15		80	13/	13	千克	/		25	
	-其他:										
4016.9100	--铺地制品及门垫〔999〕	10		80	13/	13	千克	/		35	
4016.9200	--橡皮擦〔999〕	10		80	13/	13	千克	/		35	
	--垫片、垫圈及其他密封垫:										
4016.9310	---机器及仪器用〔999〕	8		30	13/	13	千克	/		18	
4016.9390	---其他〔999〕	15		80	13/	13	千克	/		25	
4016.9400	--船舶或码头的碰垫,不论是否可充气〔999〕	18		80	13/	13	千克	/		45.5	
4016.9500	--其他可充气制品										
4016.9500 10	轨道机车用气囊升弓装置〔999〕	18	9	80	13/	13	千克	/		21.5	
4016.9500 90	硫化橡胶制其他可充气制品〔999〕	18		80	13/	13	千克	/		30.5	
	--其他:										
4016.9910	---机器及仪器用零件										
4016.9910 01	奶衬(硬质橡胶除外)〔999〕	8	4	30	13/	13	千克	/		24	7.6/7.6
4016.9910 90	硫化橡胶制机器及仪器其他零件(硬质橡胶除外)〔999〕	8		30	13/	13	千克	/		28	7.6/7.6
4016.9990	---其他										
4016.9990 01	动车组用胶囊、外风挡板,硬质橡胶除外〔101 硫化橡胶制品,102 食品接触橡胶产品,103 食品用橡胶包装〕	10	5	80	13/	13	千克	/		15	6.5/6.5
4016.9990 90	其他未列名硫化橡胶制品(硬质橡胶除外)〔101 硫化橡胶制品,103 食品接触橡胶产品,104 食品用橡胶包装〕	10		80	13/	13	千克	/		20	6.5/6.5
40.17	**各种形状的硬质橡胶(例如纯硬质胶),包括废碎料;硬质橡胶制品:**										
4017.0010	---各种形状的硬质橡胶,包括废碎料										
4017.0010 10	各种形状的硬质橡胶废碎料〔999〕	8		35	13/	13	千克	9/		33	4.8/4.8
4017.0010 90	各种形状的硬质橡胶〔999〕	8		35	13/	13	千克	/		33	4.8/4.8
4017.0020	---硬质橡胶制品〔999〕	15		90	13/	13	千克	/		25	

协定税率 %								RCEP		特惠税率 %			Article Description
东/冰/格	巴基斯坦	韩国	瑞士 上/下	哥/秘/柬	澳/毛	新西/坡/智	中国港/澳/台	东盟及马来/澳/韩	日/新	亚太2国	老/柬/缅	98/97/95	
0/0/0	7.5	7	1.5/1.5	0/0/0	0/0	0/0/0	0/0/	13.5/13.5/13.5	14.1/13.5			0/0/0	-Of a kind used on motor cars (including station wagons and racing cars), buses or lorries
0/0/0	12	3	1.5/1.5	0/0/0	0/0	0/0/0	0/0/	0/0/13.5	13.6/0			0/0/0	-Of a kind used on bicycles
													-Other:
0/0/0	0	0	0/0	0/0/0	0/0	0//0	0/0/	0/0/0	0/0			0/0/0	---Of a kind used on aircraft
0/0/0	12	3	1.5/1.5	0/0/0	0/0	0/0/0	0/0/	0/0/13.5	13.6/0			0/0/0	---Other
													Hygienic or pharmaceutical articles (including teats), of vulcanized rubber other than hard rubber, with or without fittings of hard rubber:
0/0/0	0	0	0/0	0/0/0	0/0	0//0	0/0/	0/0/0	0/0			0/0/0	-Sheath contraceptives
0/0/0	14	3.5	1.8/1.8	0/0/0	0/0	0/0/0	0/0/	0/0/15.8	15.9/0			0/0/0	-Other
													Articles of apparel and clothing accessories (including gloves) mittens and mitts, for all purposes, of vulcanized rubber other than hard rubber:
													-Gloves, mitens and mias:
0/0/0	2	0	0/0	0/0/0	0/0	0/0/0	0/0/	0/0/0	7.3/0			0/0/0	--Of a kind used for medical, surgical, dental or veterinary purposes
0/0/0		3.6	1.8/1.8	0/0/0	0/0	0/0/0	0/0/	0/0/16.2	16.4/0			0/0/0	--Other
													-Other:
0//0	2	0	0/0	0/0/0	0/0	0//0	0/0/	0/0/0	7.3/0			0/0/0	---Of a kind used for medical, surgical, dental or veterinary purposes
0/0/0		3	1.5/1.5	0/0/0	0/0	0/0/0	0/0/	0/0/13.5	13.6/0			0/0/0	---Other
													Other articles of vulcanized rubber other than hard rubber:
													-Of cellular rubber:
0/0/0	2	3.7	0/0	0/0/0	0/0	0//0	0/0/	7.5/7.6/7.5	7.5/7.6			0/0/0	---of a kind used in machines or instruments
0/0/0	12	3	1.5/1.5	0/0/0	0/0	0/0/0	0/0/	0/0/13.5	13.6/0			0/0/0	---Other
													-Other:
0/0/0		3.6	1.8/1.8	0/0/0	0/0	0/0/0	0/0/	0/0/16.2	16.4/0			0/0/0	--Floor coverings and mats
0/0/0		3.6	1.8/1.8	0/0/0	0/0	0//0	0/0/	0/0/16.2	16.4/0			0/0/0	--Erasers
													--Gaskets, washers and other seals:
0/0/0	4	0	0.8/0.8	0/0/0	0/0	0//0	0/0/	0/0/0	7.5/0			0/0/0	---Of a kind used in machines or instruments
0/0/0		0	1.5/1.5	0/0/0	0/0	0/0/0	0/0/	0/0/0	14.1/0			0/0/0	---Other
0/0/0		3.6	1.8/1.8	0/0/0	0/0	0/0/0	0/0/	0/0/16.2	16.4/0			0/0/0	--Boat or dock fenders, whether or not inflatable
													--Other inflatable articles
0/0/0		3.6	1.8/1.8	0/0/0	0/0	0/0/0	0/0/	0/0/16.2	16.4/0		//	0/0/0	Air bag pantograph lifting device for railway locomotive
0/0/0		3.6	1.8/1.8	0/0/0	0/0	0/0/0	0/0/	0/0/16.2	16.4/0			0/0/0	Other inflatable articles, of vulcanized rubber
													--Other:
													---Of a kind used in machines or instruments
0/0/0	2	3.7	0.8/0.8	0/0/0	0/0	0//0	0/0/	7.2/7.2/7.2	7.5/7.2			0/0/0	Milk lining (other than hard rubber)
0/0/0	2	3.7	0.8/0.8	0/0/0	0/0	0//0	0/0/	7.2/7.2/7.2	7.5/7.2			0/0/0	Other machines or instruments of vulcanized rubbtrother than hard and its articles
													---Other
0/0/0	4	2	1/1	0/0/0	0/0	0/0/0	0/0/	0/0/9	9.4/0			0/0/0	Of a kind used on motor train set, capsule and External wind baffle
0/0/0	4	2	1/1	0/0/0	0/0	0/0/0	0/0/	0/0/9	9.4/0			0/0/0	Other articles of vulcanized rubber other than hard rubber
													Hard rubber (for example, ebonite) in all forms, including waste and scrap; articles of hard rubber:
													---Hard rubber in all forms, including waste and scrap
0/0/0	2	1.6	0/0	0/0/0	0/0	0//0	0/0/	0/0/7.2	7.3/0			0/0/0	Waster and scrap of hard rubber in all forms
0/0/0	2	1.6	0/0	0/0/0	0/0	0//0	0/0/	0/0/7.2	7.3/0			0/0/0	Hard rubber in all forms
0/0/0	12	3	1.5/1.5	0/0/0	0/0	0/0/0	0/0/	0/0/13.5	13.6/0			0/0/0	---Articles of hard rubber

第八类
生皮、皮革、毛皮及其制品;鞍具及挽具;旅行用品、手提包及类似容器;动物肠线(蚕胶丝除外)制品

第四十一章
生皮(毛皮除外)及皮革

注释:

一、本章不包括:

(一)生皮的边角废料(税目 05.11);

(二)税目 05.05 或 67.01 的带羽毛或羽绒的整张或部分鸟皮;

(三)带毛生皮或已鞣的带毛皮张(第四十三章);但下列动物的带毛生皮应归入第四十一章:牛(包括水牛)、马、绵羊及羔羊(不包括阿斯特拉罕、喀拉科尔、波斯羔羊或类似羔羊、印度、中国或蒙古羔羊)、山羊或小山羊(不包括也门或蒙古山羊及小山羊)、猪(包括野猪)、小羚羊、瞪羚、骆驼(包括单峰骆驼)、驯鹿、麋、鹿、狍或狗。

二、(一)税目 41.04 至 41.06 不包括经逆鞣(包括预鞣)加工的皮(酌情归入税目 41.01 至 41.03);

(二)税目 41.04 至 41.06 所称"坯革",包括在干燥前经复鞣、染色或加油(加脂)的皮。

三、本目录所称"再生皮革",仅指税目 41.15 的皮革。

税则号列	货品名称〔CIQ 扩展编码及品名—T2 表示见附表 2〕	最惠(%)	暂定税率	普通	增值/消费	出口退税	计量单位	监管条件/特殊证件	检验检疫	对美关税	亚太上/下
41.01	**生牛皮(包括水牛皮)、生马科动物皮(鲜的、盐腌的、干的、石灰浸渍的、浸酸的或以其他方法保藏,但未鞣制、未经羊皮纸化处理或进一步加工的),不论是否去毛或剖层:**										
	-未剖层的整张皮,简单干燥的每张重量不超过 8 千克,干盐腌的不超过 10 千克,鲜的、湿盐腌的或以其他方法保藏的不超过 16 千克:										
	---牛皮:										
4101.2011	----经退鞣处理的										
4101.2011 10	规定重量退鞣未剖层整张濒危生野牛皮(指每张,简单干燥≤8kg,干盐渍≤10kg,鲜或湿盐≤16kg)〔999〕	8		17	9/	0	千克/张	ABFE/	PQ	13	6/6
4101.2011 90	规定重量未剖层退鞣处理整张生牛皮(包括水牛皮)(指每张,简单干燥≤8kg,干盐渍≤10kg,鲜或湿盐≤16kg)〔101 牛皮,102 水牛皮,103 牦牛皮〕	8		17	9/	0	千克/张	AB/	PQ	13	6/6
4101.2019	----其他										
4101.2019 10	规定重量非退鞣未剖层整张濒危生野牛皮(指每张,简单干燥≤8kg,干盐渍≤10kg,鲜或湿盐≤16kg)〔999〕	5		17	9/	0	千克/张	ABFE/	PQ	30	
4101.2019 90	规定重量非退鞣未剖层处理整张生牛皮(包括水牛皮)(指每张,简单干燥≤8kg,干盐渍≤10kg,鲜或湿盐≤16kg)〔101 牛皮,102 水牛皮,103 牦牛皮〕	5		17	9/	0	千克/张	AB/	PQ	30	
4101.2020	---马科动物皮										
4101.2020 11	规定重量未剖层整张濒危生野驴皮(指每张,简单干燥≤8 千克,干盐渍≤10 千克,鲜或湿盐≤16 千克)〔999〕	5	2	30	9/	0	千克/张	ABFE/	PQ	7	
4101.2020 19	规定重量未剖层整张其他濒危生野马科动物皮(指每张,简单干燥≤8 千克,干盐渍≤10 千克,鲜或湿盐≤16 千克)〔999〕	5		30	9/	0	千克/张	ABFE/	PQ	10	
4101.2020 91	规定重量未剖层整张生驴皮(指每张,简单干燥≤8 千克,干盐渍≤10 千克,鲜或湿盐≤16 千克)〔999〕	5	2	30	9/	0	千克/张	AB/	PQ	7	
4101.2020 99	规定重量未剖层整张其他生马科动物皮(指每张,简单干燥≤8 千克,干盐渍≤10 千克,鲜或湿盐≤16 千克)〔999〕	5		30	9/	0	千克/张	AB/	PQ	10	
	-整张皮,重量超过 16 千克:										
	---牛皮:										

SECTION Ⅷ

RAW HIDES AND SKINS, LEATHER, FURSKINS AND ARTICLES THEREOF; SADDLERY AND HARNESS; TRAVEL GOODS, HANDBAGS AND SIMILAR CONTAINERS; ARTICLES OF ANIMAL GUT (OTHER THAN SILK-WORM GUT)

Chapter 41

Raw hides and skins (other than furskins) and leather

Notes:

1. This Chapter does not cover:
   (a) Parings or similar waste, of raw hides or skins (heading No. 05.11);
   (b) Birdskins or parts of birdskins, with their feathers or down, of heading No. 05.05 or 67.01; or
   (c) Hides or skins, with the hair or wool on, raw, tanned or dressed (Chapter 43); the following are, however, to be classified in Chapter 41, namely, raw hides and skins with the hair or wool on, of bovine animals (including buffalo), of equine animals, of sheep or lambs (except Astrakhan, Broadtail, Caracul, Persian or similar lambs, Indian, Chinese, Mongolian or Tibetan lambs), of goats or kids (except Yemen, Mongolian or Tibetan goats and kids), of swine (including peccary), of chamois, of gazelle, of camels (including dromedaries) of reindeer, of elk, of deer, of roebucks or of dogs.
2. (a) Headings No. 41.04 to 41.06 do not cover hides and skins which have undergone a tanning (including pre-tanning) process which is reversible (headings No. 41.01 to 41.03, as the case may be).
   (b) For the purposes of headings No. 41.04 to 41.06, the term "crust" includes hides and skins that have been retanned, coloured or fat-liquored (stuffed) prior to drying.
3. Throughout the Nomenclature the expression "composition leather" means only substances of the kind referred to in heading No. 41.15.

协定税率 %								RCEP		特惠税率 %			Article Description
东/冰/格	巴基斯坦	韩国	瑞士 上/下	哥/秘/柬	澳/毛	新西/坡/智	中国港/澳/台	东盟及马来/澳/韩	日/新	亚太2国	老/柬/缅	98/97/95	
													Raw hides and skins of bovine (including buffalo) or equine animals (fresh, or salted, dried, limed, pickled or otherwise preserved, but not tanned, parchment-dressed or further prepared), whether or not dehaired or split:
													-Whole hides and skins, unsplit, of a weight per skin not exceeding 8 kg when simply dried, 10 kg when dry-salted, or 16 kg when fresh, wet-salted or otherwise preserved:
													---Of bovine animals:
													----Have undergone a reversible tanning process
0/0/0	2	0	0/0	0/0/0	0/0	0//0	0/0/	0/7.2/0	7.3/0			0/0/0	Whole raw hides and skins of endangered wild bovine animals, not split, have undergone a reversible tanning, w≤8kg when simply dried, w≤10kg when dry-salted, w≤16kg when fresh, wet-salted
0/0/0	2	0	0/0	0/0/0	0/0	0//0	0/0/	0/7.2/0	7.3/0			0/0/0	Whole raw hides and skins of bovine animals, not split, have undergone a reversible tanning, w≤8kg when simply dried, w≤10kg when dry-salted, w≤16kg when fresh, wet-salted (including buffalo hides)
													----Other
0/0/0	0	0	0/0	0/0/0	0/0	0//0	0/0/	0/4.5/0	0/0		0/0/	0/0/0	Whole raw hides and skins of endangered wild bovine animals, not split, not have undergone a reversible tanning, not split, w≤8kg when simply dried, w≤10kg when dry-salted, w≤16kg when fresh, wet-salted
0/0/0	0	0	0/0	0/0/0	0/0	0//0	0/0/	0/4.5/0	0/0		0/0/	0/0/0	Whole raw hides and skins of bovine animals, not split, not have undergone a reversible tanning, w≤8kg when simply dried, w≤10kg when dry-salted, w≤16kg when fresh, wet-salted (including buffalo hides)
													---Of equine animals
0/0/0	0	0	0/0	0/0/0	0/0	0//0	0/0/	0/0/0	4.5/0		0/0/	0/0/0	Provisions did not split the whole weight of endangered wild life (of each simple, dry skin is less than or equal to 8 kg, less than 10 kg of dry saline, fresh or wet salt is less than or equal to 16 kg)
0/0/0	0	0	0/0	0/0/0	0/0	0//0	0/0/	0/0/0	4.5/0		0/0/	0/0/0	Provisions did not split the whole weight of other endangered animal skins, raw Mustang (refers to each, simple drying is less than or equal to 8 kg, less than 10 kg of dry saline, fresh or wet salt is less than or equal to 16 kg)
0/0/0	0	0	0/0	0/0/0	0/0	0//0	0/0/	0/0/0	4.5/0		0/0/	0/0/0	Provisions did not split the whole weight of raw donkey skin (of each simple, less than 8 kg dry, dry saline is less than 10 kg, fresh or wet salt is less than or equal to 16 kg)
0/0/0	0	0	0/0	0/0/0	0/0	0//0	0/0/	0/0/0	4.5/0		0/0/	0/0/0	Provisions did not split the whole weight of other equine animal skin (which is less than or equal to 8 kg each, easy drying, dry salted less than 10 kg, fresh or wet salt is less than or equal to 16 kg)
													-Whole hides and skins, of a weight exceeding 16 kg:
													---Of bovine animals:

税则号列	货品名称〔CIQ 扩展编码及品名—T2 表示见附表 2〕	最惠(%)	暂定税率	普通	增值/消费	出口退税	计量单位	监管条件/特殊证件	检验检疫	对美关税	亚太上/下
4101.5011	----经退鞣处理的										
4101.5011 10	重＞16 千克退鞣整张濒危生野牛皮〔999〕	8		17	9/	0	千克/张	ABFE/	PQ		6.6/6.6
4101.5011 90	重＞16 千克退鞣处理整张生牛皮(包括水牛皮)〔101 牛皮,102 水牛皮,103 牦牛皮〕	8		17	9/	0	千克/张	AB/	PQ		6.6/6.6
4101.5019	----其他										
4101.5019 10	重＞16 千克非退鞣整张濒危生野牛皮〔999〕	5		17	9/	0	千克/张	ABFE/	PQ	10	
4101.5019 90	重＞16 千克非退鞣处理整张生牛皮(包括水牛皮)〔101 牛皮,102 水牛皮,103 牦牛皮〕	5		17	9/	0	千克/张	AB/	PQ	10	
4101.5020	---马科动物皮										
4101.5020 10	重＞16 千克整张濒危生野马科动物皮〔999〕	5		30	9/	0	千克/张	ABFE/	PQ	10	
4101.5020 90	重＞16 千克整张生马科动物皮〔999〕	5		30	9/	0	千克/张	AB/	PQ	10	
	-其他,包括整张或半张的背皮及腹皮:										
	---牛皮:										
4101.9011	----经退鞣处理的										
4101.9011 10	其他退鞣处理濒危生野牛皮(包括整张或半张的背皮及腹皮)〔999〕	8		17	9/	0	千克	FEAB/	PQ		6.6/6.6
4101.9011 90	其他退鞣处理生牛皮(包括整张或半张的背皮及腹皮)〔101 牛皮,102 水牛皮,103 牦牛皮〕	8		17	9/	0	千克	AB/	PQ		6.6/6.6
4101.9019	----其他										
4101.9019 10	其他濒危生野牛皮(包括整张或半张的背皮及腹皮)〔999〕	5		17	9/	0	千克	FEAB/	PQ	25	
4101.9019 90	其他生牛皮(包括整张或半张的背皮及腹皮)〔101 牛皮,102 水牛皮,103 牦牛皮〕	5		17	9/	0	千克	AB/	PQ	25	
4101.9020	---马科动物皮										
4101.9020 10	其他濒危生野马科动物皮(包括整张或半张的背皮及腹皮)〔999〕	5		30	9/	0	千克	FEAB/	PQ	10	
4101.9020 90	其他生马科动物皮(包括整张或半张的背皮及腹皮)〔999〕	5		30	9/	0	千克	AB/	PQ	10	
41.02	**绵羊或羔羊生皮(鲜的、盐腌的、干的、石灰浸渍的、浸酸的或经其他方法保藏,但未鞣制、未经羊皮纸化处理或进一步加工的),不论是否带毛或剖层,但本章注释一(三)所述不包括的生皮除外:**										
4102.1000	-带毛〔999〕	7		30	9/	0	千克/张	AB/	PQ	32	
	-不带毛:										
	--浸酸的:										
4102.2110	---经退鞣处理的〔999〕	14		30	9/	0	千克/张	AB/	PQ	19	
4102.2190	---其他〔999〕	9		30	9/	0	千克/张	AB/	PQ	14	8/8
	--其他:										
4102.2910	---经退鞣处理的〔999〕	14		30	9/	0	千克/张	AB/	PQ	19	
4102.2990	---其他〔999〕	7		30	9/	0	千克/张	AB/	PQ	12	6/6
41.03	**其他生皮(鲜的、盐渍的、干的、石灰浸渍的、浸酸的或以其他方法保藏,但未鞣制、未经羊皮纸化处理或进一步加工的),不论是否去毛或剖层,但本章注释一(二)或(三)所述不包括的生皮除外:**										
4103.2000	-爬行动物皮										
4103.2000 10	濒危爬行动物的生皮〔101 鳄鱼皮,102 蜥蜴皮,103 蛇皮,104 蟒蛇皮,105 未列出的其他动物皮张〕	9		30	9/	0	千克/张	FEAB/	PQ	14	
4103.2000 90	其他爬行动物的生皮〔101 鳄鱼皮,102 蜥蜴皮,103 蛇皮,104 蟒蛇皮,105 未列出的其他动物皮张〕	9		30	9/	0	千克/张	AB/	PQ	14	
4103.3000	-猪皮										
4103.3000 10	生鹿豚、姬猪皮〔999〕	9		30	9/	0	千克/张	ABFE/	PQ	14	
4103.3000 90	生猪皮〔999〕	9		30	9/	0	千克/张	AB/	PQ	14	
	-其他:										
	---山羊板皮:										
4103.9011	----经退鞣处理的〔101 山羊皮,102 野羊皮〕	14		35	9/	0	千克/张	AB/	PQ	19	
4103.9019	-----其他〔101 山羊皮,102 野羊皮〕	9		35	9/	0	千克/张	AB/	PQ	14	
	---其他山羊或小山羊皮:										
4103.9021	----经退鞣处理的〔101 山羊皮,102 野羊皮〕	14		30	9/	0	千克/张	AB/	PQ	19	
4103.9029	----其他〔101 山羊皮,102 野羊皮〕	9		30	9/	0	千克/张	AB/	PQ	14	
4103.9090	---其他										

协定税率 %								RCEP		特惠税率 %			Article Description
东/冰/格	巴基斯坦	韩国	瑞士 上/下	哥/秘/柬	澳/毛	新西/坡/智	中国港/澳/台	东盟及马来/澳/韩	日/新	亚太2国	老/柬/缅	98/97/95	
													----Have undergone a reversible tanning process
0/0/0	2	0	0/0	0/0/0	0/0	0//0	0/0/	0/7.6/0	7.6/0			0/0/0	Whole raw hides and skins of endangered wild equine animals, have undergone a reversible tanning, W>16kg
0/0/0	2	0	0/0	0/0/0	0/0	0//0	0/0/	0/7.6/0	7.6/0			0/0/0	Whole raw hides and skins of equine animals, have undergone a tanning which is reversible, W>16kg
													----Other
0/0/0	0	0	0/0	0/0/0	0/0	0//0	0/0/	0/4.5/0	0/0		0/0/	0/0/0	Whole raw hides and skins of endangered wild equine animals, not have undergone a reversible tanning, W>16kg
0/0/0	0	0	0/0	0/0/0	0/0	0//0	0/0/	0/4.5/0	0/0		0/0/	0/0/0	Whole raw hides and skins of equine animals, not have undergone a reversible tanning, W>16kg(including buffalo hioles)
													---Of equine animals
0/0/0	0	0	0/0	0/0/0	0/0	0//0	0/0/	0/0/0	4.5/0		0/0/	0/0/0	Whole raw hides and skins of endangered wild equine animals, W>16kg
0/0/0	0	0	0/0	0/0/0	0/0	0//0	0/0/	0/0/0	4.5/0		0/0/	0/0/0	Whole raw hides and skins of equine animals, W>16kg
													-Other, including butts, bends and bollies:
													---Of bovine animals:
													----Have undergone a reversible tanning process
0/0/0	2	0	0/0	0/0/0	0/0	0//0	0/0/	0/7.6/0	7.6/0			0/0/0	Other whole raw hides and skins (including butts, bends and bellies), of endangered wild bovine animals, have undergone a reversible tanning
0/0/0	2	0	0/0	0/0/0	0/0	0//0	0/0/	0/7.6/0	7.6/0			0/0/0	Other whole raw hides and skins (including butts, bends and bellies), of bovine animals, have undergone a reversible tanning
													----Other
0/0/0	0	0	0/0	0/0/0	0/0	0//0	0/0/	0/4.5/0	0/0		0/0/	0/0/0	Other whole raw hides and skins (including butts, bends and bellies), of endangered wild bovine animals
0/0/0	0	0	0/0	0/0/0	0/0	0//0	0/0/	0/4.5/0	0/0		0/0/	0/0/0	Other whole raw hides and skins (including butts, bends and bellies), of bovine animals
													---of equine animals
0/0/0	0	0	0/0	0/0/0	0/0	0//0	0/0/	0/0/0	4.5/0		0/0/	0/0/0	Other whole raw hides and skins (including butts, bends and bellies), of endangered wild equine animals
0/0/0	0	0	0/0	0/0/0	0/0	0//0	0/0/	0/0/0	4.5/0		0/0/	0/0/0	Other whole raw hides and skins (including butts, bends and bellies), of equine animals
													Raw skins of sheep or lambs (fresh, or salted, dried, limed, pickled or otherwise preseved, but not tanned, parchment-dressed or further prepared), whether or not with wool on or split, other than those excluded by Note 1 (c) to this Chapter:
0/0/0	2	0	0/0	0//0	0/0	0//0	0/0/	0/0/0	6.4/0			0/0/0	-With wool on
													-Without wool on:
													--Pickled:
0/0/0	11.2	2.8	1.4/1.4	0//0	0/0	0/0/0	0/0/	0/12.6/12.6	12.7/0			0/0/0	---Have undergone a reversible tanning process
0/0/0	2	0	0/0	0/0/0	0/0	0//0	0/0/	8.1/8.1/8.1	8.2/8.1			0/0/0	---Other
													--Other:
0/0/0	7	2.8	1.4/1.4	0/0/0	0/0	0/0/0	0/0/	0/12.6/12.6	12.7/0			0/0/0	---Have undergone a reversible tanning process
0/0/0	2	0	0/0	0/0/0	0/0	0//0	0/0/	0/6.3/0	6.4/0			0/0/0	---Other
													Other raw hides and skins (fresh, or salted, dried, limed, pickled or otherwise preserved, but not tanned, parchment-dressed or further prepared), whether or not dehaired or split, other than those excluded by Note 1 (b) or 1 (c) to this Chapter:
													-Of reptiles
0/0/0	2	0	0/0	0/0/0	0/0	0//0	0/0/	0/8.1/0	8.2/0			0/0/0	Endangered raw hides and skins of reptiles
0/0/0	2	0	0/0	0/0/0	0/0	0//0	0/0/	0/8.1/0	8.2/0			0/0/0	Other raw hides and skins of reptiles
													-Of swine
0/0/0	2	0	0/0	0/0/0	0/0	0//0	0/0/	0/0/0	8.2/0		//0	0/0/0	Raw hides and skins of pig-deer (*Babyrousa*)、pygmy pig (*Porcula*)
0/0/0	2	0	0/0	0/0/0	0/0	0//0	0/0/	0/0/0	8.2/0		//0	0/0/0	Raw hides and skins of swine
													Other:
													---Dried hides and skins of goats:
0/0/0	7	2.8	1.4/1.4	0/0/0	0/0	0/0/0	0/0/	0/12.6/12.6	12.7/0			0/0/0	----Have undergone a reversible tanning process
0/0/0	2	0	0/0	0/0/0	0/0	0//0	0/0/	0/0/0	8.2/0			0/0/0	-----Other
													---Other hides and skins of goats or of kids:
0/0/0	7	2.8	1.4/1.4	0/0/0	0/0	0/0/0	0/0/	0/12.6/12.6	12.7/0			0/0/0	----Have undergone a reversible tanning process
0/0/0	2	0	0/0	0/0/0	0/0	0//0	0/0/	0/0/0	8.2/0			0/0/0	----Other
													---Other

税则号列	货品名称〔CIQ 扩展编码及品名－T2 表示见附表 2〕	最惠(%)	暂定税率	普通	增值/消费	出口退税	计量单位	监管条件/特殊证件	检验检疫	对美关税	亚太上/下
4103.9090 10	其他濒危野生动物生皮[本章注释一(二)或(三)所述不包括的生皮除外]〔101 斑马皮,102 野驴皮,103 其他野生奇蹄动物皮张,104 野骆驼皮,105 野鹿皮,106 其他野生偶蹄动物皮张,107 其他禽鸟皮,108 象皮,109 袋鼠皮,110 海豹皮,111 蛇皮,112 貂皮,113 狐狸皮,114 未列出的其他动物皮张,115 艾鼬皮,116 臭鼬皮,117 短尾猫皮,118 负鼠皮,119 海狸皮,120 旱獭皮,121 貉子皮,122 浣熊皮,123 灰鼠皮,124 狼皮,125 猞猁皮,126 麝鼠皮,127 水獭皮,128 松鼠皮〕	9		30	9/	0	千克/张	ABEF/	PQ	14	
4103.9090 90	其他生皮[本章注释一(二)或(三)所述不包括的生皮除外]〔101 驴皮,102 骡皮,103 其他饲养奇蹄动物皮张,104 骆驼皮,105 鹿皮,106 其他饲养偶蹄动物皮张,107 其他禽鸟皮,108 象皮,109 袋鼠皮,110 海豹皮,111 蛇皮,112 貂皮,113 狐狸皮,114 未列出的其他动物皮张,115 艾鼬皮,116 臭鼬皮,117 短尾猫皮,118 负鼠皮,119 海狸皮,120 旱獭皮,121 貉子皮,122 浣熊皮,123 灰鼠皮,124 狼皮,125 猞猁皮,126 麝鼠皮,127 水獭皮,128 松鼠皮〕	9		30	9/	0	千克/张	AB/	PQ	14	
41.04	**经鞣制的不带毛牛皮(包括水牛皮)、马皮及其坯革,不论是否剖层,但未经进一步加工:**										
	-湿革(包括蓝湿皮):										
	--全粒面未剖层革;粒面剖层革:										
	---牛皮:										
4104.1111	----蓝湿的										
4104.1111 10	蓝湿濒危野牛皮(全粒面未剖或粒面剖层,经鞣制不带毛)〔999〕	6	3	17	13/	0	千克	ABFE/	PQ	8	3/3
4104.1111 90	全粒面未剖层或粒面剖层蓝湿牛皮(经鞣制不带毛)〔999〕	6	3	17	13/	0	千克	AB/	PQ	8	3/3
4104.1119	----其他										
4104.1119 10	湿濒危野牛皮(全粒面未剖或粒面剖层,经鞣制不带毛)〔999〕	6		35	13/	0	千克	EF/		11	3/3
4104.1119 90	全粒面未剖层或粒面剖层湿牛皮(经鞣制不带毛)〔999〕	6		35	13/	0	千克	/		11	3/3
4104.1120	---马皮										
4104.1120 10	湿濒危野马科动物皮(全粒面未剖或粒面剖层,经鞣制不带毛)〔999〕	5		35	13/	0	千克	EF/		10	2.5/2.5
4104.1120 90	全粒面未剖层或粒面剖层湿马科动物皮(经鞣制不带毛)〔999〕	5		35	13/	0	千克	/		10	2.5/2.5
	--其他:										
	---牛皮:										
4104.1911	----蓝湿的										
4104.1911 10	其他蓝湿濒危野牛皮(经鞣制不带毛)〔999〕	6	3	17	13/	0	千克	ABFE/	PQ	28	3/3
4104.1911 90	其他蓝湿牛皮(经鞣制不带毛)〔999〕	6	3	17	13/	0	千克	AB/	PQ	28	3/3
4104.1919	----其他										
4104.1919 10	其他湿濒危野牛皮(经鞣制不带毛)〔999〕	7		35	13/	0	千克	EF/		12	3.5/3.5
4104.1919 90	其他湿牛皮(经鞣制不带毛)〔999〕	7		35	13/	0	千克	/		12	3.5/3.5
4104.1920	---马皮										
4104.1920 10	其他湿濒危野马科动物皮(经鞣制不带毛)〔999〕	5		35	13/	0	千克	EF/			2.5/2.5
4104.1920 90	其他湿马科动物皮(经鞣制不带毛)〔999〕	5		35	13/	0	千克	/			2.5/2.5
	-干革(坯革):										
4104.4100	--全粒面未剖层革;粒面剖层革										
4104.4100 10	濒危野牛马干革(全粒面未剖或粒面剖层,经鞣制不带毛)〔999〕	5	3	35	13/	0	千克	EF/		28	3.5/3.5
4104.4100 90	全粒面未剖层或粒面剖层干革(经鞣制不带毛)〔999〕	5	3	35	13/	0	千克	/		28	3.5/3.5
	--其他:										
4104.4910	---机器带用牛、马皮革										
4104.4910 10	其他机器带用濒危野牛马皮革(经鞣制不带毛)〔999〕	5		20	13/	0	千克	FE/		10	3.5/3.5

协定税率 %								RCEP		特惠税率 %			Article Description
东/冰/格	巴基斯坦	韩国	瑞士 上/下	哥/秘/柬	澳/毛	新西/坡/智	中国港/澳/台	东盟及马来/澳/韩	日/新	亚太2国	老/柬/缅	98/97/95	
0/0/0	2	0	0/0	0/0/0	0/0	0//0	0/0/	0/0/0	8.2/0		//0	0/0/0	Other raw hides and skins of endangered wild animals, other than those excluded by Note 1(b) or 1(c) to this Chapter
0/0/0	2	0	0/0	0/0/0	0/0	0//0	0/0/	0/0/0	8.2/0		//0	0/0/0	Other raw hides and skins of animals, other than those excluded by Note 1 (b) or (c) to this Chapter
													Tanned or crust hides and skins of bovine(including buffalo) or equine animals, without hair on, whether or not split, but not further prepared: -In the wet state(including wet-blue): --Full grains, unsplit; grain splits: ---Of bovine animals: ----Wet-blue
0/0/0	0	0	0/0	0/0/0	0/0	0//0	0/0/	0/0/0	6.4/0	1.2		0/0/0	Tanned or crust hides and skins of endangered wild bovine animals, without hair on, in the wet-blue state, full grains, unsplit or grain splits
0/0/0	0	0	0/0	0/0/0	0/0	0//0	0/0/	0/0/0	6.4/0	1.2		0/0/0	Tanned or crust hides and skins of bovine animals, without hair on, in the wet-blue state, full grains, unsplit, grain splits
													----Other
0/0/0	0	0	0/0	0/0/0	0/0	0//0	0/0/	0/0/0	7.3/0	1.5		0/0/0	Tanned or crust hides and skins of endangered wild bovine animals, without hair on, full grains, unsplit or grain splits, in the wet state
0/0/0	0	0	0/0	0/0/0	0/0	0//0	0/0/	0/0/0	7.3/0	1.5		0/0/0	Tanned or crust hides and skins of bovine animals, without hair on, full grains, unsplit or grain splits, in the wet state
													---Of equine animals
0/0/0	0	0	0/0	0/0/0	0/0	0//0	0/0/	0/0/0	4.5/0	2		0/0/0	Tanned or crust hides and skins of endangered wild equine animals, without hair on, full grains, unsplit or grain splits, in the wet state
0/0/0	0	0	0/0	0/0/0	0/0	0//0	0/0/	0/0/0	4.5/0	2		0/0/0	Tanned or crust hides and skins of equine animals, without hair on, full grains, unsplit or grain splits, in the wet state
													--Other: ---Of bovine animals: ----Wet-blue
0/0/0	3	0	0/0	0/0/0	0/0	0//0	0/0/	5.4/5.4/5.4	5.5/5.4	1.5		0/0/0	Other tanned or crust hides and skins of endangered wild bovine animals, without hair on, in the wet-blue state
0/0/0	3	0	0/0	0/0/0	0/0	0//0	0/0/	5.4/5.4/5.4	5.5/5.4	1.5		0/0/0	Other tanned or crust hides and skins, of bovine animals, without hair on, in the wet-blue state
													----Other
0/0/0	0	0	0/0	0/0/0	0/0	0//0	0/0/	0/0/0	6.4/0	1.8		0/0/0	Other tanned or crust hides and skins of endangered wild bovine animals, without hair on, in the wet state
0/0/0	0	0	0/0	0/0/0	0/0	0//0	0/0/	0/0/0	6.4/0	1.8		0/0/0	Other tanned or crust hides and skins of bovine animals, without hair on, in the wet state
													---Of equine animals
0/0/0	0	0	0/0	0/0/0	0/0	0//0	0/0/	0/0/0	6.4/0	1.5		0/0/0	Other tanned or crust hides and skins of endangered wild equine animals, without hair on, in the wet state
0/0/0	0	0	0/0	0/0/0	0/0	0//0	0/0/	0/0/0	6.4/0	1.5		0/0/0	Other tanned or crust hides and skins of equine animals, without hair on, in the wet state
													-In the dry state(crust): --Full grain, unsplit; grain splits
0/0/0	0	0	0/0	0/0/0	0/0	0//0	0/0/	4.5/4.5/4.5	4.5/4.5	2		0/0/0	Tanned or crust hides and skins of endangered wild bovine or equine animals, without hair on, full grains, unsplit or grain splits, in the dry state (crust)
0/0/0	0	0	0/0	0/0/0	0/0	0//0	0/0/	4.5/4.5/4.5	4.5/4.5	2		0/0/0	Tanned or crust hides and skins, without hair on, full grains, unsplit; grain splits, in the dry state (crust)
													--Other: ---For machinery belting
0/0/0	0	0	0/0	0/0/0	0/0	0//0	0/0/	0/0/0	4.5/0	0		0/0/0	Tanned or crust hides and skins of endangered wild bovine or equine animals, without hair on, for machinery belting

税则号列		货品名称〔CIQ 扩展编码及品名－T2 表示见附表 2〕	最惠(%)	暂定税率	普通	增值/消费	出口退税	计量单位	监管条件/特殊证件	检验检疫	对美关税	亚太上/下
4104.4910	90	其他机器带用牛马皮革(经鞣制不带毛)〔101 马皮革,102 牛皮革〕	5		20	13/	0	千克	/		10	3.5/3.5
4104.4990		---其他										
4104.4990	10	其他濒危野牛马皮革(经鞣制不带毛)〔999〕	7		35	13/	0	千克	EF/		32	4.9/4.9
4104.4990	90	其他牛马皮革(经鞣制不带毛)〔101 马皮革,102 牛皮革〕	7		35	13/	0	千克	/		32	4.9/4.9
41.05		**经鞣制的不带毛绵羊或者羔羊皮及其坯革,不论是否剖层,但未经进一步加工:**										
		-湿革(包括蓝湿皮):										
4105.1010		---蓝湿的〔999〕	14	10	50	13/	0	千克	AB/	PQ	15	7/7
4105.1090		---其他〔999〕	10		50	13/	0	千克	/		15	5/5
4105.3000		-干革(坯革)〔999〕	8		50	13/	0	千克	/		13	5.6/5.6
41.06		**经鞣制的其他不带毛动物皮及其坯革,不论是否剖层,但未经进一步加工:**										
		-山羊或小山羊的:										
4106.2100		--湿革(包括蓝湿皮)										
4106.2100	01	蓝湿山羊皮(经鞣制不带毛)〔999〕	14	10	50	13/	0	千克	/		15	12/12
4106.2100	90	其他山羊或小山羊湿革(经鞣制不带毛)〔101 山羊皮革,102 未列出的其他动物皮革〕	14		50	13/	0	千克	/		19	12/12
4106.2200		--干革(坯革)〔101 山羊皮革,102 未列出的其他动物皮革〕	14		50	13/	0	千克	/		19	9.8/9.8
		-猪的:										
		--湿革(包括蓝湿皮):										
4106.3110		---蓝湿的										
4106.3110	10	蓝湿鹿豚、姬猪皮(经鞣制不带毛)〔999〕	14	10	50	13/	0	千克	FEAB/	PQ	35	
4106.3110	90	其他蓝湿猪皮(经鞣制不带毛)〔999〕	14	10	50	13/	0	千克	AB/	PQ	35	
4106.3190		---其他										
4106.3190	10	鹿豚、姬猪湿革(经鞣制不带毛)〔999〕	14		50	13/	0	千克	EF/		19	
4106.3190	90	其他猪湿革(经鞣制不带毛)〔999〕	14		50	13/	0	千克	/		19	
4106.3200		--干革(坯革)										
4106.3200	10	鹿豚、姬猪干革(经鞣制不带毛,坯革)〔999〕	14		50	13/	0	千克	EF/		19	
4106.3200	90	其他猪干革(经鞣制不带毛,坯革)〔999〕	14		50	13/	0	千克	/		19	
4106.4000		-爬行动物的										
4106.4000	10	濒危爬行动物皮革(经鞣制不带毛)〔101 鳄鱼皮,102 鳄鱼皮革,103 蜥蜴皮,104 蟒蛇皮,105 蛇皮革,106 未列出的其他动物皮革〕	14		50	13/	0	千克	FE/		19	
4106.4000	90	其他爬行动物皮革(经鞣制不带毛)〔101 鳄鱼皮,102 鳄鱼皮革,103 蜥蜴皮,104 蟒蛇皮,105 蛇皮革,106 未列出的其他动物皮革〕	14		50	13/	0	千克	/		19	
		-其他:										
4106.9100		--湿革(包括蓝湿皮)										
4106.9100	10	其他濒危野生动物湿革(经鞣制不带毛)〔999〕	14		50	13/	0	千克	FE/		19	
4106.9100	90	其他动物湿革(经鞣制不带毛)〔999〕	14		50	13/	0	千克	/		19	
4106.9200		--干革(坯革)										
4106.9200	10	其他濒危野生动物干革(经鞣制不带毛)〔999〕	14		50	13/	0	千克	FE/		19	
4106.9200	90	其他动物干革(经鞣制不带毛)〔999〕	14		50	13/	0	千克	/		19	
41.07		**经鞣制或半硝处理后进一步加工的不带毛的牛皮革(包括水牛皮革)及马科动物皮革,包括羊皮纸化处理的皮革,不论是否剖层,但税目 41.14 的皮革除外:**										
		-整张的:										
		--全粒面未剖层革:										
4107.1110		---牛皮										
4107.1110	10	全粒面未剖层整张濒危野牛皮(经鞣制或半硝后进一步加工,羊皮纸化处理)〔999〕	6		50	13/	0	千克/张	FE/		31	
4107.1110	90	全粒面未剖层整张牛皮(经鞣制或半硝后进一步加工,羊皮纸化处理)〔999〕	6		50	13/	0	千克/张	/		31	
4107.1120		---马科动物皮										

协定税率 %								RCEP		特惠税率 %			Article Description
东/冰/格	巴基斯坦	韩国	瑞士上/下	哥/秘/柬	澳/毛	新西/坡/智	中国港/澳/台	东盟及马来/澳/韩	日/新	亚太2国	老/柬/缅	98/97/95	
0/0/0	0	0	0/0	0/0/0	0/0	0//0	0/0/	0/0/0	4.5/0	0		0/0/0	Tanned or crust hides and skins of bovine, equine animals, without hair on, for machinery belting
													---Other
0/0/0	0	3.2	0/0	0/0/0	0/0	0//0	0/0/	6.3/6.3/6.3	6.6/6.3	2.1		0/0/0	Other tanned or crust hides and skins of endangered wild bovine or equine animals, without hair on
0/0/0	0	3.2	0/0	0/0/0	0/0	0//0	0/0/	6.3/6.3/6.3	6.6/6.3	2.1		0/0/0	Other tanned or crust hides and skins of bovine, equine animals, without hair on
													Tanned or crust skins of sheep or lambs, without wool on, whether or not split, but not further prepared:
													-In the wet state(including wet-blue):
0/0/0	4	2.8	1.4/1.4	0//0	0/0	0/0/0	0/0/	0/0/12.6	12.7/0	2.1		0/0/0	---Wet-blue
0/0/0	4	2	0/0	0/0/0	0/0	0//0	0/0/	0/0/9	9.1/0	2		0/0/0	---Other
0/0/0	5.6	1.6	0/0	0/0/0	0/0	0//0	0/0/	0/0/7.2	7.3/0	4.8		0/0/0	-In the dry state(crust)
													Tanned or crust hides and skins of other animals, without wool or hair on, whether or not split, but not further prepared:
													-Of goats or kids:
													--In the wet state (including wet-blue)
0/0/0	12	2.8	1.4/1.4	0/0/0	0/0	0/0/0	0/0/	0/0/12.6	12.7/0	2.1		0/0/0	Tannde or crust hides and skins of goats in wet-blue, without hair on, in the wet state
0/0/0	12	2.8	1.4/1.4	0/0/0	0/0	0/0/0	0/0/	0/0/12.6	12.7/0	2.1		0/0/0	Other tanned or crust skins of goats or kids, in the dry state, without hair on, in the wet state
0/0/0	0	2.8	1.4/1.4	0//0	0/0	0/0/0	0/0/	0/0/12.6	12.7/0	8.4		0/0/0	--In the dry state(crust)
													-Of swine:
													--In the wet state(including wet-blue):
													---Wet-blue
0/0/0	11.2	2.8	1.4/1.4	0/0/0	0/0	0/0/0	0/0/	0/0/12.6	12.7/0	4.2		0/0/0	Tanned or crust hides and skins of pig-deer (*Babyrousa*)、pygmy pig (*Porcula*), without hair on, in the wet-blue state
0/0/0	11.2	2.8	1.4/1.4	0/0/0	0/0	0/0/0	0/0/	0/0/12.6	12.7/0	4.2		0/0/0	Other tanned or crust hides and skins of swine, without hair on, in the wet-blue state
													---Other
0/0/0	7	2.8	1.4/1.4	0/0/0	0/0	0/0/0	0/0/	0/0/12.6	12.7/0	4.2		0/0/0	Tanned or crust hides and skins of pig-deer (*Babyrousa*)、pygmy pig (*Porcula*) , without hair on, in the wet state
0/0/0	7	2.8	1.4/1.4	0/0/0	0/0	0/0/0	0/0/	0/0/12.6	12.7/0	4.2		0/0/0	Other tanned or crust hides and skins of swine, without hair on, in the wet state
													--In the dry state(crust)
0/0/0	11.2	2.8	1.4/1.4	0/0/0	0/0	0/0/0	0/0/	0/0/12.6	12.7/0	4.2		0/0/0	Tanned or crust hides and skins of pig-deer (*Babyrousa*)、pygmy pig (*Porcula*), without hair on, in the dry state
0/0/0	11.2	2.8	1.4/1.4	0/0/0	0/0	0/0/0	0/0/	0/0/12.6	12.7/0	4.2		0/0/0	Other tanned or crust hides and skins of swine, without hair on, in the dry state
													-Of reptiles
0/0/0	7	2.8	1.4/1.4	0/0/0	0/0	0/0/0	0/0/	0/0/12.6	12.7/0	0		0/0/0	Endangered tanned or crust hides and skins of reptiles, without wool or hair on
0/0/0	7	2.8	1.4/1.4	0/0/0	0/0	0/0/0	0/0/	0/0/12.6	12.7/0	0		0/0/0	Other tanned or crust hides and skins of reptiles, without wool or hair on
													-Other:
													--In the wet state(including wet-blue)
0/0/0	11.2	2.8	1.4/1.4	0/0/0	0/0	0/0/0	0/0/	0/0/12.6	12.7/0	0		0/0/0	Tanned or crust hides and skins of other endangered wild animals, without wool or hair on, in the wet state
0/0/0	11.2	2.8	1.4/1.4	0/0/0	0/0	0/0/0	0/0/	0/0/12.6	12.7/0	0		0/0/0	Tanned or crust hides and skins of other animals, without wool or hair on, in the wet state
													--In the dry state(crust)
0/0/0	0	2.8	1.4/1.4	0/0/0	0/0	0/0/0	0/0/	0/0/12.6	12.7/0	0		0/0/0	Tanned or crust hides and skins of other endangered wild animals, without wool or hair on, in the dry state
0/0/0	0	2.8	1.4/1.4	0/0/0	0/0	0/0/0	0/0/	0/0/12.6	12.7/0	0		0/0/0	Tanned or crust hides and skins of other animals, without wool or hair on, in the dry state
													Leather further prepared after tanning or crusting, including parchment-dressed leather, of bovine(including buffalo) or equine animals, without hair on, whether or not split, other than leather of heading 41. 14:
													-Whole hides and skins:
													--Full grains, unsplit:
													---Of bovine animals
0/0/0	0	3.7	0/0	0//0	0/4.8	0//0	0/0/	7.5/7.6/7.5	7.5/7.6			0//	Leather further prepared after tanning or crusting, including parchment-dressed leather, of endangered wild bovine animals, whole hides and skins, full grains, unsplit
0/0/0	0	3.7	0/0	0//0	0/4.8	0//0	0/0/	7.5/7.6/7.5	7.5/7.6			0//	Leather further prepared after tanning or crusting, including parchment-dressed leather, of bovine animals, whole hides and skins, full grains, unsplit
													---Of equine animals

税则号列		货品名称〔CIQ扩展编码及品名－T2表示见附表2〕	最惠(%)	暂定税率	普通	增值/消费	出口退税	计量单位	监管条件/特殊证件	检验检疫	对美关税	亚太上/下
4107.1120	10	全粒面未剖层整张濒危野马科动物皮(经鞣制或半硝后进一步加工,羊皮纸化处理)〔999〕	5		50	13/	0	千克/张	FE/		10	
4107.1120	90	全粒面未剖层整张马科动物皮(经鞣制或半硝后进一步加工,羊皮纸化处理)〔999〕	5		50	13/	0	千克/张	/		10	
		--粒面剖层革:										
4107.1210		---牛皮										
4107.1210	10	粒面剖层整张濒危野牛皮(经鞣制或半硝后进一步加工,羊皮纸化处理)〔999〕	6		50	13/	0	千克/张	FE/		31	
4107.1210	90	粒面剖层整张牛皮(经鞣制或半硝后进一步加工,羊皮纸化处理)〔999〕	6		50	13/	0	千克/张	/		31	
4107.1220		---马科动物皮										
4107.1220	10	粒面剖层整张濒危野马科动物皮(经鞣制或半硝后进一步加工,羊皮纸化处理)〔999〕	5		50	13/	0	千克/张	FE/		10	
4107.1220	90	粒面剖层整张马科动物皮(经鞣制或半硝后进一步加工,羊皮纸化处理)〔999〕	5		50	13/	0	千克/张	/		10	
		--其他:										
4107.1910		---机器带用										
4107.1910	10	其他机器带用整张濒危野牛马皮革(经鞣制或半硝后进一步加工,羊皮纸化处理)〔999〕	5		50	13/	0	千克/张	FE/		10	
4107.1910	90	其他机器带用整张牛马皮革(经鞣制或半硝后进一步加工,羊皮纸化处理)〔101 马皮革,102 牛皮革〕	5		50	13/	0	千克/张	/		10	
4107.1990		---其他										
4107.1990	10	其他整张濒危野牛马皮革(经鞣制或半硝后进一步加工,羊皮纸化处理)〔999〕	7		50	13/	0	千克/张	EF/		32	
4107.1990	90	其他整张牛马皮革(经鞣制或半硝后进一步加工,羊皮纸化处理)〔101 马皮革,102 牛皮革〕	7		50	13/	0	千克/张	/		32	
		-其他,包括半张的:										
4107.9100		--全粒面未剖层革										
4107.9100	10	全粒面未剖层非整张濒危野牛马皮(经鞣制或半硝后进一步加工,羊皮纸化处理)〔999〕	5		50	13/	0	千克	EF/		30	
4107.9100	90	全粒面未剖层非整张革(经鞣制或半硝后进一步加工,羊皮纸化处理)〔101 马皮革,102 牛皮革,103 未列出的其他动物皮革〕	5		50	13/	0	千克	/		30	
4107.9200		--粒面剖层革										
4107.9200	10	粒面剖层非整张濒危野牛马皮革(经鞣制或半硝后进一步加工,羊皮纸化处理)〔999〕	5		50	13/	0	千克	FE/		30	
4107.9200	90	粒面剖层非整张革(经鞣制或半硝后进一步加工,羊皮纸化处理)〔101 马皮革,102 牛皮革,103 未列出的其他动物皮革〕	5		50	13/	0	千克	/		30	
		--其他:										
4107.9910		---机器带用										
4107.9910	10	其他机器带用非整张濒危野牛马皮(经鞣制或半硝后进一步加工,羊皮纸化处理)〔999〕	5		50	13/	0	千克	FE/		10	
4107.9910	90	其他机器带用非整张牛马皮革(经鞣制或半硝后进一步加工,羊皮纸化处理)〔101 马皮革,102 牛皮革〕	5		50	13/	0	千克	/		10	
4107.9990		---其他										
4107.9990	10	其他非整张濒危野牛马皮革(经鞣制或半硝后进一步加工,羊皮纸化处理)〔999〕	7		50	13/	0	千克	EF/		32	

协定税率 %								RCEP		特惠税率 %			
东/冰/格	巴基斯坦	韩国	瑞士 上/下	哥/秘/柬	澳/毛	新西/坡/智	中国港/澳/台	东盟及马来/澳/韩	日/新	亚太2国	老/柬/缅	98/97/95	Article Description
0/0/0	0	0	0/0	0/0/0	0/0	0//0	0/0/	0/0/0	4.5/0			0/0/0	Leather further prepared after tanning or crusting, including parchment-dressed leather, of endangered wild equine animals, whole hides and skins, full grains, unsplit
0/0/0	0	0	0/0	0/0/0	0/0	0//0	0/0/	0/0/0	4.5/0			0/0/0	Leather further prepared after tanning or crusting, including parchment-dressed leather, of equine animals, whole hides and skins, full grains, unsplit
													--Grain splits:
													---Of bovine animals
0/0/0	0	1.6	0/0	0//0	0/0	0//0	0/0/	7.2/7.2/7.2	7.3/7.2			0//	Leather further prepared after tanning or crusting, including parchment-dressed leather, of endangered wild bovine animals, whole hides and skins, grain splits
0/0/0	0	1.6	0/0	0//0	0/0	0//0	0/0/	7.2/7.2/7.2	7.3/7.2			0//	Leather further prepared after tanning or crusting, including parchment-dressed leather, of bovine animals, whole hides and skins, grain splits
													---Of equine animals
0/0/0	0	0	0/0	0/0/0	0/0	0//0	0/0/	0/0/0	4.5/0			0/0/0	Leather further prepared after tanning or crusting, including parchment-dressed leather, of endangered wild equine animals, whole hides and skins, grain splits
0/0/0	0	0	0/0	0/0/0	0/0	0//0	0/0/	0/0/0	4.5/0			0/0/0	Leather further prepared after tanning or crusting, including parchment-dressed leather, of equine animals, whole hides and skins, grain splits
													--Other:
													---For machinery belting
0/0/0	0	1	0/0	0/0/0	0/0	0//0	0/0/	0/0/4.5	4.5/0			0/0/0	Leather further prepared after tanning or crusting, including parchment-dressed leather, of endangered wild bovine or wild equine amimals, whole hides and skins, for machinery belting
0/0/0	0	1	0/0	0/0/0	0/0	0//0	0/0/	0/0/4.5	4.5/0			0/0/0	Leather further prepared after tanning or crusting, including parchment-dressed leather, of bevine or equine animals, whole hides and skins, for machinery belting
													---Other
0/0/0		0	0/0	0//0	0/0	0//0	0/0/	6.3/6.3/6.3	6.4/6.3			0//	Other leather further prepared after tanning or crusting, including parchment-dressed leather of endangered wild bovine or wild equine amimals, whole hides and skins
0/0/0		0	0/0	0//0	0/0	0//0	0/0/	6.3/6.3/6.3	6.4/6.3			0//	Other leather further prepared after tanning or crusting, including parchment-dressed leather of bovine or equine animals, whole hides and skins
													-Other, including sides:
													--Full grains, unsplit
0/0/0	0	1	0/0	0/0/0	0/0	0//0	0/0/	0/0/4.5	4.5/0			0/0/0	Leather further prepared after tanning or crusting, including parchment-dressed leather of endangered wild bovine or wild equine animals, other than whole hides and skins, full grains, unsplit
0/0/0	0	1	0/0	0/0/0	0/0	0//0	0/0/	0/0/4.5	4.5/0			0/0/0	Leather further prepared after tanning or crusting, including parchment-dressed leather, other than whole hides and skins, full grains, unsplit
													--Grain splits
0/0/0	0	2.3	0/0	0/0/0	0/0	0//0	0/0/	4.5/4.5/4.5	4.7/4.5			0/0/0	Leather further prepared after tanning or crusting, including parchment-dressed leather, of endangered wild bovine or wild equine animals, other than whole hides and skins, grain, splits
0/0/0	0	2.3	0/0	0/0/0	0/0	0//0	0/0/	4.5/4.5/4.5	4.7/4.5			0/0/0	Leather further prepared after tanning or crusting, including parchment-dressed leather, other than whole hides and skins, grain, splits
													--Other:
													---For machinery belting
0/0/0	0	0	0/0	0/0/0	0/0	0//0	0/0/	0/0/0	4.5/0			0/0/0	Leather further prepared after tanning or crusting, including parchment-dressed leather of endangered wild bovine or wild equine animals, other than whole hides and skins, for machinery belting
0/0/0	0	0	0/0	0/0/0	0/0	0//0	0/0/	0/0/0	4.5/0			0/0/0	Leather further prepared after tanning or crusting, including parchment-dressed leather, of bovine or equine animals, other than whole hides and skins, for machinery belting
													---Other
0/0/0		3.2	0/0	0/0/0	0/0	0//0	0/0/	6.3/6.3/6.3	6.6/6.3			0/0/0	Other leather further prepared after tanning or crusting, including parchment-dressed leather, of endangered wild bovine or wild equine animals, other than whole hides and skins

税则号列		货品名称〔CIQ扩展编码及品名—T2表示见附表2〕	最惠(%)	暂定税率	普通	增值/消费	出口退税	计量单位	监管条件/特殊证件	检验检疫	对美关税	亚太上/下
4107.9990	90	其他非整张牛马皮革(经鞣制或半硝后进一步加工,羊皮纸化处理)〔101马皮革,102牛皮革〕	7		50	13/	0	千克	/		32	
41.12		**经鞣制或半硝处理后进一步加工的不带毛的绵羊或羔羊皮革,包括羊皮纸化处理的,不论是否剖层,但税目41.14的皮革除外:**										
4112.0000		经鞣制或半硝处理后进一步加工的不带毛的绵羊或羔羊皮革,包括羊皮纸化处理的,不论是否剖层,但税目41.14的皮革除外〔999〕	8		50	13/	0	千克	/		33	5.6/5.6
41.13		**经鞣制或半硝处理后进一步加工的不带毛的其他动物皮革,包括羊皮纸化处理的,不论是否剖层,但税目41.14的皮革除外:**										
4113.1000		-山羊或小山羊皮的〔101山羊皮革,102未列出的其他动物皮革〕	14		50	13/	0	千克	/		39	9.8/9.8
4113.2000		-猪的										
4113.2000	10	加工的鹿豚、姬猪皮革(经鞣制或半硝后进一步加工,不带毛,羊皮纸化处理)〔999〕	14		50	13/	0	千克	EF/		39	
4113.2000	90	加工的猪皮革(经鞣制或半硝后进一步加工,不带毛,羊皮纸化处理)〔999〕	14		50	13/	0	千克	/		39	
4113.3000		-爬行动物的										
4113.3000	10	加工的濒危爬行动物皮革(经鞣制或半硝后进一步加工,不带毛,羊皮纸化处理)〔101鳄鱼皮,102鳄鱼皮革,103蜥蜴皮,104蟒蛇皮,105蛇皮革,106未列出的其他动物皮革〕	14		50	13/	0	千克	FE/		34	
4113.3000	90	加工的其他爬行动物皮革(经鞣制或半硝后进一步加工,不带毛,羊皮纸化处理)〔101鳄鱼皮,102鳄鱼皮革,103蜥蜴皮,104蟒蛇皮,105蛇皮革,106未列出的其他动物皮革〕	14		50	13/	0	千克	/		34	
4113.9000		-其他										
4113.9000	10	加工的其他濒危野生动物皮革(经鞣制或半硝后进一步加工,不带毛,羊皮纸化处理)〔101其他奇蹄动物皮革,102骆驼皮革,103鹿皮革,104其他偶蹄动物皮革,105象皮革,106袋鼠皮革,107兔皮革,108海豹皮革,109未列出的其他动物皮革〕	14		50	13/	0	千克	FE/		39	
4113.9000	90	加工的其他动物皮革(经鞣制或半硝后进一步加工,不带毛,羊皮纸化处理)〔101驴皮革,102骡皮革,103其他奇蹄动物皮革,104骆驼皮革,105鹿皮革,106其他偶蹄动物皮革,107象皮革,108袋鼠皮革,109兔皮革,110未列出的其他动物皮革〕	14		50	13/	0	千克	/		39	
41.14		**油鞣皮革(包括结合鞣制的油鞣皮革);漆皮及层压漆皮;镀金属皮革:**										
4114.1000		-油鞣皮革(包括结合鞣制的油鞣皮革)										
4114.1000	10	油鞣其他濒危野生动物皮革(包括结合鞣制的油鞣皮革)〔999〕	14		50	13/	0	千克	FE/		34	
4114.1000	90	油鞣其他动物皮革(包括结合鞣制的油鞣皮革;野生动物皮革除外)〔999〕	14		50	13/	0	千克	/		34	
4114.2000		-漆皮及层压漆皮;镀金属皮革〔999〕	10		50	13/	0	千克	/		35	9/9
41.15		**以皮革或皮革纤维为基本成分的再生皮革,成块、成张或成条的,不论是否成卷;皮革或再生皮革的边角废料,不适宜作皮革制品用;皮革粉末:**										
4115.1000		-以皮革或皮革纤维为基本成分的再生皮革,成块、成张或成条,不论是否成卷〔999〕	14		50	13/	0	千克	/		39	
4115.2000		-皮革或再生皮革的边角废料,不适宜作皮革制品用;皮革粉末										
4115.2000	10	皮革废渣、灰渣、淤渣及粉末〔999〕	14		50	13/	0	千克	9/		19	
4115.2000	90	成品皮革、皮革制品或再生皮革的边角料〔101未列出的其他动物皮革,102橡胶皮革废碎料〕	14		50	13/	0	千克	9/		19	

协定税率 %								RCEP		特惠税率 %			Article Description
东/冰/格	巴基斯坦	韩国	瑞士 上/下	哥/秘/柬	澳/毛	新西/坡/智	中国港/澳/台	东盟及马来/澳/韩	日/新	亚太2国	老/柬/缅	98/97/95	
0/0/0		3.2	0/0	0/0/0	0/0	0//0	0/0/	6.3/6.3/6.3	6.6/6.3			0/0/0	Other leather further prepared after tanning or crusting, (including parchment-dressed leather, of bovine or equine animals, other than whole hides and skins)
													Leather further prepared after tanning or crusting, including parchment-dressed leather, of sheep or lamb, without wool on, whether or not split, other than leather of heading No. 41. 14:
0/0/0	0	3.7	0/0	0/0/0	0/0	0//0	0/0/	7.5/7.6/7.5	7.5/7.6			0/0/0	Leather further prepared after tanning or crusting, including parchment-dressed leather, of sheep or lamb, without wool on, whether or not split, other than leather of heading No. 41. 14
													Leather further prepared after tanning or crusting, including parchment-dressed leather, of other animals, without wool or hair on, whether or not split, other than leather of heading No. 41. 14:
0//0	0	2.8	1.4/1.4	0//0	0/0	0/0/0	0/0/	0/0/12.6	12.7/0			0/0/0	-Of goats or kids
													-Of swine
0/0/0		2.8	1.4/1.4	0/0/0	0/0	0/0/0	0/0/	0/0/12.6	12.7/0			0/0/0	Leather further prepared after tanning or crusting, including parchment-dressed leather, of pig-deer (*Babyrousa*)、pygmy pig (*Porcula*), without hair on
0/0/0		2.8	1.4/1.4	0/0/0	0/0	0/0/0	0/0/	0/0/12.6	12.7/0			0/0/0	Leather further prepared after tanning or crusting, including parchment-dressed leather, of swine, without hair on
													-Of reptiles
0//0	0	2.8	1.4/1.4	0/0/0	0/0	0/0/0	0/0/	0/0/12.6	12.7/0			0/0/0	Endangered leather further prepared after tanning or crusting, including parchment — dressed leather, of reptiles, without wool or hair on
0//0	0	2.8	1.4/1.4	0/0/0	0/0	0/0/0	0/0/	0/0/12.6	12.7/0			0/0/0	Other leather further prepared after tanning or crusting, including parchment — dressed leather, of reptiles, without wool or hair on
													-Other
0/0/0	0	2.8	1.4/1.4	0/0/0	0/0	0/0/0	0/0/	0/0/12.6	12.7/0			0/0/0	Leather further prepared after tanning or crusting, including parchment-dressed leather, of endangered wild animals, without wool or hair on
0/0/0	0	2.8	1.4/1.4	0/0/0	0/0	0/0/0	0/0/	0/0/12.6	12.7/0			0/0/0	Leather further prepared after tanning or crusting, including parchment-dressed leather, of other animals, without wool or hair on
													Chamois(including combination chamois) leather; patent leather and patent laminated leather; metallised leather:
													-Chamois(including combination chamois) leather
0/0/0		2.8	1.4/1.4	0/0/0	0/0	0/0/0	0/0/	0/0/12.6	12.7/0			0/0/0	Chamois (including combination chamois) leather of endangered wild animals
0/0/0		2.8	1.4/1.4	0/0/0	0/0	0/0/0	0/0/	0/0/12.6	12.7/0			0/0/0	Chamois (including combination chamois) leather of other animals
0/0/0	9	6	0/0	0//0	0/0	0/0/0	0/0/	9.5/9.5/	/9.5			0//	-Patent leather and patent laminated leather; metallised leather
													Composition leather with a basis of leather or leather fibre, in slabs, sheets or strip, whether or not in rolls; parings and other waste of leather or of composition leather, not suitable for the manufacture of leather articles; leather dust, powder and flour:
0/0/0		2.8	1.4/1.4	0//0	0/0	0/0/0	0/0/	0/0/12.6	12.7/0			0//	-Composition leather with a basis of leather or leather fibre, in slabs, sheets or strip, whether or not in rolls
													-Parings and other waste of leather or of composition leather, not suitable for the manufacture of leather articles; leather dust, powder and flour
0/0/0		2.8	1.4/1.4	0/0/0	0/0	0/0/0	0/0/	0/0/12.6	12.7/0	4.2		0/0/0	Waste residue, dust, powder and flour of leather or of composition leather
0/0/0		2.8	1.4/1.4	0/0/0	0/0	0/0/0	0/0/	0/0/12.6	12.7/0	4.2		0/0/0	The leftover bits and pieces of finished leather, leather or recycled leather products (after screening, area is larger than 200 square centimeters of leather scrap, used for processing gloves, accessories, toys, etc.)

第四十二章
皮革制品;鞍具及挽具;旅行用品、手提包及类似容器;动物肠线(蚕胶丝除外)制品

注释:

一、本章所称的"皮革"包括油鞣皮革(含结合鞣制的油鞣皮革)、漆皮、层压漆皮和镀金属皮革。

二、本章不包括:

(一)外科用无菌肠线或类似的无菌缝合材料(税目 30.06);

(二)以毛皮或人造毛皮衬里或作面(仅饰边的除外)的衣服及衣着附件(分指手套、连指手套及露指手套除外)(税目 43.03 或 43.04);

(三)网线袋及类似品(税目 56.08);

(四)第六十四章的物品;

(五)第六十五章的帽类及其零件;

(六)税目 66.02 的鞭子、马鞭或其他物品;

(七)袖扣、手镯或其他仿首饰(税目 71.17);

(八)单独报验的挽具附件或装饰物,例如,马镫、马嚼子、马铃铛及类似品、带扣(一般归入第十五类);

(九)弦线、鼓面皮或类似品及其他乐器零件(税目 92.09);

(十)第九十四章的物品(例如,家具、灯具及照明装置);

(十一)第九十五章的物品(例如,玩具、游戏品及运动用品);

(十二)税目 96.06 的纽扣、揿扣、纽扣芯或这些物品的其他零件、纽扣坯。

三、(一)除上述注释二所规定的以外,税目 42.02 也不包括:

1. 非供长期使用的带把手塑料薄膜袋,不论是否印制(税目 39.23);

2. 编结材料制品(税目 46.02)。

(二)税目 42.02、42.03 的制品,如果装有用贵金属、包贵金属、天然或养殖珍珠、宝石或半宝石(天然、合成或再造)制的零件,即使这些零件不是仅作为小配件或小饰物的,只要其未构成物品的基本特征,仍应归入上述税号。但如果这些零件已构成物品的基本特征,则应归入第七十一章。

四、税目 42.03 所称"衣服及衣着附件",主要包括分指手套、连指手套及露指手套(包括运动及防护手套)、围裙及其他防护用衣着、裤吊带、腰带、子弹带及腕带,但不包括表带(税目 91.13)。

税则号列	货品名称〔CIQ 扩展编码及品名一T2 表示见附表 2〕	最惠(%)	暂定税率	普通	增值/消费	出口退税	计量单位	监管条件/特殊证件	检验检疫	对美关税	亚太上/下
42.01	**各种材料制成的鞍具及挽具(包括缰绳、挽绳、护膝垫、口套、鞍褥、马褡裢、狗外套及类似品),适合各种动物用:**										
4201.0000	各种材料制成的鞍具及挽具(包括缰绳、挽绳、护膝垫、口套、鞍褥、马褡裢、狗外套及类似品),适合各种动物用										
4201.0000 10	濒危野生动物材料制的鞍具及挽具(适合各种动物用)〔101 含木制品,102 不含木制品〕	10		100	13/	0	千克	FE/		35	6/6
4201.0000 90	各种材料制成的鞍具及挽具(野生动物材料制的除外;适合各种动物用)〔101 含木制品,102 不含木制品〕	10		100	13/	13	千克	/		35	6/6
42.02	**衣箱、提箱、小手袋、公文箱、公文包、书包、眼镜盒、望远镜盒、照相机套、乐器盒、枪套及类似容器;旅行包、食品或饮料保温包、化妆包、帆布包、手提包、购物袋、钱夹、钱包、地图盒、烟盒、烟袋、工具包、运动包、瓶盒、首饰盒、粉盒、刀叉餐具盒及类似容器,用皮革或再生皮革、塑料片、纺织材料、钢纸或纸板制成,或者全部或主要用上述材料或纸包覆制成:**										
	-衣箱、提箱、小手袋、公文箱、公文包、书包及类似容器:										
	--以皮革或再生皮革作面:										
4202.1110	---衣箱										
4202.1110 10	以含濒危野生动物皮革或再生皮革作面的衣箱〔999〕	8		100	13/	0	千克/个	FE/		33	
4202.1110 90	其他以皮革或再生皮革作面的衣箱〔999〕	8		100	13/	13	千克/个	/		33	
4202.1190	---其他										

Chapter 42
Articles of leather; saddlery and harness; travel goods, handbags and similar containers; articles of animal gut (other than silk-worm gut)

Notes:

1. For the purposes of this Chapter, the term "leather" includes chamois (including combination chamois) leather, patent leather, patent laminated leather and metallised leather
2. This Chapter does not cover:
   (a) Sterile surgical catgut or similar sterile suture materials (heading No. 30.06);
   (b) Articles of apparel or clothing accessories (except gloves, mittens and mitts), lined with furskin or artificial fur or to which furskin or artificial fur is attached on the outside except as mere trimming (heading No. 43.03 or 43.04);
   (c) Made up articles of netting (heading No. 56.08);
   (d) Articles of Chapter 64;
   (e) Headgear or parts thereof of Chapter 65;
   (f) Whips, riding-crops or other articles of heading No. 66.02;
   (g) Cuff-links, bracelets or other imitation jewellery (heading No. 71.17);
   (h) Fittings or trimmings for harness, such as stirrups, bits, horse brasses and buckles, separately presented (generally Section XV);
   (i) Strings, skins for drums or the like, or other parts of musical instruments (heading No. 92.09);
   (j) Articles of Chapter 94 (for example, furniture, lamps and lighting fittings);
   (k) Articles of Chapter 95 (for example, toys, games, sports requisites);
   (l) Buttons, press-fasteners, snap-fasteners, pres-sstuds, button moulds or other parts of these articles, button blanks, of heading No. 96.06.
3. (a) In addition to the provisions of Note 2 above, heading No. 42.02 does not cover:
   (ⅰ) Bags made of sheeting of plastics, whether or not printed, with handles, not designed for prolonged use (heading No. 39.23);
   (ⅱ) Articles of plaiting materials (heading No. 46.02).
   (b) Articles of headings No. 42.02 and 42.03 which have parts of precious metal or metal clad with precious metal, of natural or cultured pearls, of precious or semi-precious stones (natural, synthetic or reconstructed) remain classified in those headings even if such parts constitute more than minor fittings or minor ornamentation, provided that these parts do not give the articles their essential character. If, on the other hand, the parts give the articles their essential character, the articles are to be classified in Chapter 71.
4. For the purpose of heading No. 42.03, the expression "articles of apparel and clothing accessories" applies, *inter alia*, to gloves, mittens and mitts (including those for sport or for protection), aprons and other protective clothing, braces, belts, bandoliers and wrist straps, but excluding watch straps (heading No. 91.13).

协定税率 %								RCEP		特惠税率 %			Article Description
东/冰/格	巴基斯坦	韩国	瑞士上/下	哥/秘/柬	澳/毛	新西/坡/智	中国港/澳/台	东盟及马来/澳/韩	日/新	亚太2国	老/柬/缅	98/97/95	
													Saddlery and harness for any animal (including traces, leads, knee pads, muzzles, saddle cloths, saddle bags, dog coats and the like), of any material:
													Saddlery and harness for any animal (including traces, leads, knee pads, muzzles, saddle cloths, saddle bags, dog coats and the like), of any material
0/0/0	10	9.3	2/2	0/0/0	0/0	0/0/0	0/0/	18/18/18	18.8/18	4		0/0/0	Saddlery and harness for any animal of material of endangered wild animals
0/0/0	10	9.3	2/2	0/0/0	0/0	0/0/0	0/0/	18/18/18	18.8/18	4		0/0/0	Saddlery and harness for any animal, of any material, other than the material of wild animals
													Trunks, suit-cases, vanity-cases, executive-cases, brief-cases, school satchels, spectacle cases, binocular cases, camera cases, musical instrument cases, gun cases, holsters and similar containers; travelling-bags, insulated food or beverages bags, toilet bags, rucksacks, handbags, shopping-bags, wallets, purses, map-cases, cigarett-cases, tobacco-pouches, tool bags, sports bags, bottle-cases, jewellery boxes, powder-boxes, cutlery cases and similar containers, of leather or of composition leather, of sheeting of plastics, of textile materials, of vulcanized fibre or of paperboard, or wholly or mainly covered with such materials or with paper:
													-Trunks, suit-cases, vanity-cases, executive-cases, brief-cases, school satchels and similar containers:
													--With outer surface of leather or of composition leather:
													---Trunks and suit-cases
0/0/0	12	3	1.5/1.5	0/0/0	0/0	0/0/0	0/0/	0/0/13.5	13.6/0	4.4		0/0/0	Trunks with outer surface of leather, of composition leather or of patent leather, of endangered wild animals
0/0/0	12	3	1.5/1.5	0/0/0	0/0	0/0/0	0/0/	0/0/13.5	13.6/0	4.4		0/0/0	Trunks with outer surface of leather, of composition leather, other than of wild animals
													---Other

税则号列	货品名称〔CIQ 扩展编码及品名—T2 表示见附表 2〕	最惠(%)	暂定税率	普通	增值/消费	出口退税	计量单位	监管条件/特殊证件	检验检疫	对美关税	亚太上/下
4202.1190 10	以含濒危野生动物皮革或再生皮革作面的箱包(包括提箱、小手袋、公文包、书包及类似容器,但不包括衣箱)〔101 皮箱,102 皮包〕	6		100	13/	0	千克/个	FE/		31	
4202.1190 90	其他以皮革或再生皮革作面的箱包(包括提箱、小手袋、公文包、书包及类似容器,但不包括衣箱)〔101 皮箱,102 儿童用皮包,103 非儿童用皮包〕	6		100	13/	13	千克/个	/		31	
	--以塑料或纺织材料作面:										
4202.1210	---衣箱〔101 塑料类,102 纺织材料类〕	10		100	13/	13	千克/个	/		35	6.5/6.5
4202.1290	---其他〔101 塑料箱,102 纺织材料箱,103 儿童用塑料包,104 非儿童用塑料包,105 儿童用纺织材料包,106 非儿童用纺织材料包〕	10		100	13/	13	千克/个	/		35	6.5/6.5
4202.1900	--其他〔101 其他箱,102 其他包〕	10		100	13/	13	千克/个	/		35	
	-手提包,不论是否有背带,包括无把手的:										
4202.2100	--以皮革或再生皮革作面										
4202.2100 10	以含濒危野生动物皮革或再生皮革作面的手提包(不论是否有背带,包括无把手的)〔999〕	6		100	13/	0	千克/个	FE/		31	3.9/3.9
4202.2100 90	其他以皮革或再生皮革作面的手提包(不论是否有背带,包括无把手的)〔999〕	6		100	13/	13	千克/个	/		31	3.9/3.9
4202.2200	--以塑料片或纺织材料作面〔101 塑料包,102 纺织材料包〕	6		100	13/	13	千克/个	/		31	3.9/3.9
4202.2900	--其他〔999〕	10		100	13/	13	千克/个	/			6.5/6.5
	-通常置于口袋或手提包内的物品:										
4202.3100	--以皮革或再生皮革或作面										
4202.3100 10	以含濒危野生动物皮革或再生皮革作面的钱包等物品(指通常置于口袋或手提包内的物品)〔999〕	6		100	13/	0	千克/个	FE/		31	3.9/3.9
4202.3100 90	以皮革或再生皮革作面的钱包等物品(指通常置于口袋或手提包内的物品)〔999〕	6		100	13/	13	千克/个	/		31	3.9/3.9
4202.3200	--以塑料片或纺织材料作面〔101 塑料包,102 纺织材料包〕	10		100	13/	13	千克/个	/		35	6.5/6.5
4202.3900	--其他〔999〕	10		100	13/	13	千克/个	/		35	6.5/6.5
	-其他:										
4202.9100	--以皮革或再生皮革或作面										
4202.9100 10	以含濒危野生动物皮革或再生皮革作面的其他容器〔999〕	6		100	13/	0	千克/个	FE/		31	3.9/3.9
4202.9100 90	其他皮革或再生皮革作面其他容器〔999〕	6		100	13/	13	千克/个	/		31	3.9/3.9
4202.9200	--以塑料片或纺织材料作面〔101 塑料包,102 纺织材料包〕	6		100	13/	13	千克/个	/		31	3.9/3.9
4202.9900	--其他〔999〕	10		100	13/	13	千克/个	/		35	
42.03	**皮革或再生皮革制的衣服及衣着附件:**										
4203.1000	-衣服										
4203.1000 10	含濒危野生动物皮革制的衣服(包括再生野生动物皮革制作的)〔999〕	6		100	13/	0	千克/件	EF/		31	
4203.1000 90	皮革或再生皮革制的衣服(野生动物皮革制作的除外)〔999〕	6		100	13/	13	千克/件	/		31	
	-手套,包括连指或露指的:										
4203.2100	--专供运动用										
4203.2100 10	含濒危野生动物皮革制的运动手套(包括再生野生动物皮革制作的)〔999〕	10		100	13/	0	千克/双	FE/		35	6.5/6.5
4203.2100 90	皮革或再生皮革制专供运动用手套(包括连指或露指的,野生动物皮革制作的除外)〔999〕	10		100	13/	13	千克/双	/		35	6.5/6.5
	--其他:										
4203.2910	---劳保手套										
4203.2910 10	含濒危野生动物皮革制的劳保手套(包括再生野生动物皮革制作的)〔999〕	10		100	13/	0	千克/双	FE/		35	
4203.2910 90	皮革或再生皮革制的劳保手套(野生动物皮革制作的除外)〔999〕	10		100	13/	13	千克/双	/		35	
4203.2990	---其他										
4203.2990 10	含濒危野生动物皮革制的其他手套(包括再生野生动物皮革制作的)〔999〕	10		100	13/	0	千克/双	FE/		35	
4203.2990 90	皮革或再生皮革制的其他手套(包括连指或露指的)〔999〕	10		100	13/	13	千克/双	/		35	
	-腰带及子弹带:										
4203.3010	---腰带										

协定税率 %								RCEP		特惠税率 %			Article Description
东/冰/格	巴基斯坦	韩国	瑞士上/下	哥/秘/柬	澳/毛	新西/坡/智	中国港/澳/台	东盟及马来/澳/韩	日/新	亚太2国	老/柬/缅	98/97/95	
0/0/0	4	2	1/1	0/0/0	0/0	0//0	0/0/	0/0/9	9.1/0	4.8		0/0/0	Cases with outer surface of leather, of composition leather, of wild animals, in imminent dangers(including trunks, suit-cases, vanity-cases, executive-cases, brief-cases, school satchels and similar containers)
0/0/0	4	2	1/1	0/0/0	0/0	0//0	0/0/	0/0/9	9.1/0	4.8		0/0/0	Cases(suit-cases, brief-cases, school satchels and similar containers, other than trunks) with outer surface of leather, of composition leather
													--With outer surface of plastics or of textile materials:
0/0/0	0	9.3	2/2	0/0/0	0/0	0/0/0	0/0/0	18.7/19/	18.8/19			0/0/0	---Trunks and suit-cases
0/0/0	0	4	2/2	0/0/0	0/12	0/0/0	0/0/0	18/18/18	18.2/18			0/0/0	---Other
0/0/0	0	9.3	2/2	0/0/0	0/0	0/0/0	0/0/0	18/18/18	18.8/18	4		0/0/0	--Other
													-Handbags, whether or not with shoulder strap, including those without handle:
													--With outer surface of leather or composition leather
0/0/0	0	2	1/1	0/0/0	0/0	0//0	0/0/	9/9/9	9.1/9			0/0/0	Handbags with outer surface of leather, of composition leather, of endangered wild animals (whether or not with shoulder strap, including those without handle)
0/0/0	0	2	1/1	0/0/0	0/0	0//0	0/0/	9/9/9	9.1/9			0/0/0	Handbags, whether or not with shoulder strap, including those without handle, with outer surface of leather, of composition leather
0/0/0	0	2	1/1	0/0/0	0/6	0/0/0	0/0/0	0/0/9	9.1/0			0/0/0	--With outer surface of plastic sheeting or of textile materials
0/0/0	14	9.3	2/2	0/0/0	0/0	0/0/0	0/0/	18/18/18	18.8/18	4		0/0/0	--Other
													-Articles of a kind normally carried in the pocket or in the handbag:
													--With outer surface of leather or composition leather
0/0/0	4	2	1/1	0/0/0	0/0	0//0	0/0/	0/0/9	9.1/0			0/0/0	Wallets or purses, with outer surface of leather, of composition leather of endangered wild animals
0/0/0	4	2	1/1	0/0/0	0/0	0//0	0/0/	0/0/9	9.1/0			0/0/0	Wallets or purses, with outer surface of leather, of composition leather
0/0/0	14	4	2/2	0/0/0	0/12	0/0/0	0/0/	0/0/18	18.2/0			0/0/0	--With outer surface of plastic sheeting or of textile materials
0/0/0	14	9.3	2/2	0/0/0	0/0	0/0/0	0/0/	18/18/18	18.8/18	4		0/0/0	--Other
													-Other:
													--With outer surface of leather or composition leather
0/0/0	3.5	2	1/1	0/0/0	0/0	0//0	0/0/	0/0/9	9.1/0			0/0/0	Other containers with outer surface of leather, of composition leather, of endangered wild animals
0/0/0	3.5	2	1/1	0/0/0	0/0	0//0	0/0/	0/0/9	9.1/0			0/0/0	Other containers with outer surface of leather, of composition leather
0/0/0	0	2	0/0	0/0/0	0/0	0/0/0	0/0/	9/9/9	9.1/9			0/0/0	--With outer surface of plastic sheeting or of textile materials
0/0/0		9.3	8.4/8.4	0/0/0	0/12	0/0/0	0/0/	18.7/19/18.7	18.8/19			0/0/0	--Other
													Articles of apparel and clothing accessories, of leather or of composition leather:
													-Articles of apparel
0/0/0	0	0	0/0	0/0/0	0/0	0//0	0/0/	9/9/9	9.1/9	4.8		0/0/0	Articles of apparel of leather or of composition leather, of endangered wild animals
0/0/0	0	0	0/0	0/0/0	0/0	0//0	0/0/	9/9/9	9.1/9	4.8		0/0/0	Articles of apparel of leather or of composition leather (other than leather of wild animals)
													-Gloves, mittens and mitts:
													--Specially designed for use in sports
0//0	0	9.3	2/2	0/0/0	0/0	0/0/0	0/0/	18.7/19/18.7	18.8/19			0/0/0	Gloves, specially designed for use in sports, of leather or of composition leather, of endangered wild animals
0//0	0	9.3	2/2	0/0/0	0/0	0/0/0	0/0/	18.7/19/18.7	18.8/19			0/0/0	Gloves, mittens and mitts, specially designed for use in sports, of leather or of composition leather, other than leather of wild animals
													--Other:
													---Working gloves
0//0	0	9.3	2/2	0/0/0	0/0	0/0/0	0/0/	18.7/19/18.7	18.8/19	4		0/0/0	Working gloves, of leather or of composition leather, of endangered wild animals
0//0	0	9.3	2/2	0/0/0	0/0	0/0/0	0/0/	18.7/19/18.7	18.8/19	4		0/0/0	Working gloves, of leather or of composition leather, other than leather of wild animals
													---Other
0//0	0	9.3	2/2	0/0/0	0/0	0/0/0	0/0/	18.7/19/18.7	18.8/19	4		0/0/0	Other gloves, mittens and mitts, of leather or of composition leather of endangered wild animals
0//0	0	9.3	2/2	0/0/0	0/0	0/0/0	0/0/	18.7/19/18.7	18.8/19	4		0/0/0	Other gloves, mittens and mitts, of leather or of composition leather
													-Belts and bandoliers:
													---Belts

税则号列	货品名称〔CIQ 扩展编码及品名－T2 表示见附表 2〕	最惠(%)	暂定税率	普通	增值/消费	出口退税	计量单位	监管条件/特殊证件	检验检疫	对美关税	亚太上/下
4203.3010 10	含濒危野生动物皮革制的腰带(包括再生野生动物皮革制作的)〔999〕	6		100	13/	0	千克	FE/		31	
4203.3010 90	其他动物皮革制的腰带(包括再生动物皮革制作的)〔999〕	6		100	13/	13	千克	/		31	
4203.3020	---子弹带										
4203.3020 10	含濒危野生动物皮革制的子弹带(包括再生野生动物皮革制作的)〔999〕	6		100	13/	0	千克	FE/			5.4/5.4
4203.3020 90	其他动物皮革制的子弹带(包括再生动物皮革制作的)〔999〕	6		100	13/	13	千克	/			5.4/5.4
4203.4000	-其他衣着附件										
4203.4000 10	含濒危野生动物皮革制的衣着附件(包括再生野生动物皮革制作的)〔999〕	10		100	13/	0	千克	FE/		35	
4203.4000 90	皮革或再生皮革制的其他衣着附件〔999〕	10		100	13/	13	千克	/		35	
42.05	**皮革或再生皮革的其他制品:**										
4205.0010	---坐具套										
4205.0010 10	含濒危野生动物皮革制的坐具套(包括再生野生动物皮革制作的)〔999〕	6		100	13/	0	千克	FE/		31	
4205.0010 90	其他动物皮革制的坐具套(包括再生皮革制作的)〔999〕	6		100	13/	13	千克	/		31	
4205.0020	---机器、机械器具或其他专门技术用途的										
4205.0020 10	含濒危野生动物皮革制工业用皮革或再生皮革制品(工业用指机器、机械器具或其他专门技术用途的)〔999〕	6		35	13/	0	千克	FE/		31	
4205.0020 90	其他工业用皮革或再生皮革制品(工业用指机器,机械器具或其他专门技术用途的)〔999〕	6		35	13/	13	千克	/		31	
4205.0090	---其他										
4205.0090 10	含濒危野生动物皮革的其他制品(包括再生野生动物皮革制作的)〔999〕	6		100	13/	0	千克	FE/		31	
4205.0090 20	皮革或再生皮革制宠物用品〔999〕	6		100	13/	13	千克	AB/	PQ	31	
4205.0090 90	皮革或再生皮革的其他制品〔999〕	6		100	13/	13	千克	/		31	
42.06	**肠线(蚕胶丝除外)、肠膜、膀胱或筋腱制品:**										
4206.0000	肠线(蚕胶丝除外)、肠膜、膀胱或筋腱制品(不包括外科用无菌肠线或制成乐器弦的肠线,蚕胶丝除外)〔999〕	10		90	13/	13	千克	/			

协定税率 %								RCEP		特惠税率 %			Article Description
东/冰/格	巴基斯坦	韩国	瑞士上/下	哥/秘/柬	澳/毛	新西/坡/智	中国港/澳/台	东盟及马来/澳/韩	日/新	亚太2国	老/柬/缅	98/97/95	
0/0/0	0	2	0/0	0/0/0	0/0	0//0	0/0/	0/0/9	9.1/0	4.8		0/0/0	Belts of leather or of composition leather of endangered wild animals
0/0/0	0	2	0/0	0/0/0	0/0	0//0	0/0/	0/0/9	9.1/0	4.8		0/0/0	Belts of leather or of composition leather,of other animals
													---Bandoliers
0/0/0	0	2	0/0	0/0/0	0/0	0//0	0/0/	0/0/9	9.1/0	4.8		0/0/0	Bandoliers of leather or of composition leather of endangered wild animals
0/0/0	0	2	0/0	0/0/0	0/0	0//0	0/0/	0/0/9	9.1/0	4.8		0/0/0	Bandoliers of leather or of composition leather of other animals
													-Other clothing accessories
0//0	0	9.3	2/2	0/0/0	0/0	0/0/0	0/0/	18.7/19/	18.8/19	4		0/0/0	Clothing accessories of leather or of composition leather, of endangered wild animals
0//0	0	9.3	2/2	0/0/0	0/0	0/0/0	0/0/	18.7/19/	18.8/19	4		0/0/0	Other clothing accessories, of leather or of composition leather
													-Other articles of leather or of composition leather:
													---Cover of seat
0/0/0	0		1.2/1.2	0/0/0	0/0	0/0/0	0/0/	6/6/	/6	3.9		0/0/0	Covering of seats, of leather or of composition leather,of endangered wild animals
0/0/0	0		1.2/1.2	0/0/0	0/0	0/0/0	0/0/	6/6/	/6	3.9		0/0/0	Covering of seats, of leather or of composition leather, of other animals
													---Of a kind used in machinery or mechanical appilances or for other technical uses
0/0/0	2	1.6	3.4/3.4	0/0/0	0/0	0//0	0/0/	0/0/7.2	7.3/0			0/0/0	Articles of leather or of composition leather of endangered animals,of a kind used in machinery or mechanial appilances or for other technical uses
0/0/0	2	1.6	3.4/3.4	0/0/0	0/0	0//0	0/0/	0/0/7.2	7.3/0			0/0/0	Other articles of leather or of composition leather,of a kind used in machinery or mechanial appilances or for other technical uses
													---Other
0/0/0	0	5.6	1.2/1.2	0/0/0	0/7.2	0/0/0	0/0/	11.2/11.4/11.2	11.3/11.4	3.9		0/0/0	Other articles, of leather or of composition leather,of endangered wild animals
0/0/0	0	5.6	1.2/1.2	0/0/0	0/7.2	0/0/0	0/0/	11.2/11.4/11.2	11.3/11.4	3.9		0/0/0	Articles for pets,of leather or of compostition leather
0/0/0	0	5.6	1.2/1.2	0/0/0	0/7.2	0/0/0	0/0/	11.2/11.4/11.2	11.3/11.4	3.9		0/0/0	Other articles of leather or of composition leather
													Articles of gut (other than silk-worm gut), of goldbeater's skin, of bladders or of tendons:
0/0/0		9.3	2/2	0/0/0	0/0	0/0/0	0/0/	18/18/18	18.8/18			0/0/0	Articles of gut (other than silk-worm gut), of goldbeater's skin, of bladders or of tendons

第四十三章
毛皮、人造毛皮及其制品

注释：

一、本协调制度所称“毛皮”，是指已鞣的各种动物的带毛毛皮，但不包括税目 43.01 的生毛皮。

二、本章不包括：

(一)带羽毛或羽绒的整张或部分鸟皮(税目 05.05 或 67.01)；

(二)第四十一章的带毛生皮[见该章注释一(三)]；

(三)用皮革与毛皮或用皮革与人造毛皮制成的分指手套、连指手套及露指手套(税目 42.03)；

(四)第六十四章的物品；

(五)第六十五章的帽类及其零件；

(六)第九十五章的物品(例如，玩具、游戏品及运动用品)。

三、税目 43.03 包括加有其他材料缝合的毛皮和毛皮部分品，以及缝合成衣服、衣服部分品、衣着附件或其他制品的毛皮和毛皮部分品。

四、以毛皮或人造毛皮衬里或作面(仅饰边的除外)的衣服及衣着附件(不包括注释二所述的货品)，应分别归入税目 43.03 或 43.04，但毛皮或人造毛皮仅作为装饰的除外。

五、本目录所称“人造毛皮”，是指以毛、发或其他纤维粘附或缝合于皮革、织物或其他材料之上而构成的仿毛皮，但不包括以机织或针织方法制得的仿毛皮(一般应归入税目 58.01 或 60.01)。

税则号列	货品名称〔CIQ 扩展编码及品名—T2 表示见附表 2〕	最惠(%)	暂定税率	普通	增值/消费	出口退税	计量单位	监管条件/特殊证件	检验检疫	对美关税	亚太上/下
43.01	**生毛皮(包括适合加工皮货用的头、尾、爪及其他块、片)，但税目 41.01、41.02 或 41.03 的生皮除外：**										
4301.1000	-整张水貂皮，不论是否带头、尾或爪〔999〕	15	10	100	9/	0	千克	AB/	PQ	30	12/12
4301.3000	-下列羔羊的整张毛皮，不论是否带头、尾或爪：阿斯特拉罕、喀拉科尔、波斯羔羊及类似羔羊、印度、中国或蒙古羔羊〔101 绵羊皮，102 山羊皮〕	20		90	9/	0	千克	AB/	PQ	25	
4301.6000	-整张狐皮，不论是否带头、尾或爪										
4301.6000 10	整张濒危生狐皮(不论是否带头、尾或爪)〔999〕	20	10	100	9/	0	千克/张	AFEB/	PQ	15	14/14
4301.6000 90	其他整张生狐皮(不论是否带头、尾或爪)〔999〕	20	10	100	9/	0	千克/张	AB/	PQ	15	14/14
	-整张的其他毛皮，不论是否带头、尾或爪：										
4301.8010	---兔皮										
4301.8010 10	整张生濒危野兔皮(不论是否带头，尾或爪)〔999〕	20		90	9/	0	千克/张	AFEB/	PQ	25	14/14
4301.8010 90	整张生兔皮(不论是否带头，尾或爪)〔999〕	20		90	9/	0	千克/张	AB/	PQ	25	14/14
4301.8090	---其他										
4301.8090 10	整张的其他生濒危野生动物毛皮(不论是否带头，尾或爪，包括整张濒危生海豹皮)[T2]	20	10	90	9/	0	千克/张	ABEF/	PQ	15	14/14
4301.8090 90	整张的其他生毛皮(不论是否带头，尾或爪，包括整张生海豹皮)〔101 驴皮，102 骡皮，103 其他饲养奇蹄动物皮张，104 猪皮，105 绵羊皮，106 山羊皮，107 骆驼皮，108 鹿皮，109 其他饲养偶蹄动物皮张，110 鸡、鸭、鹅皮，111 兔皮，112 未列出的其他动物皮张，113 艾鼬皮，114 臭鼬皮，115 短尾猫皮，116 负鼠皮，117 海狸皮，118 旱獭皮，119 貉子皮，120 浣熊皮，121 灰鼠皮，122 狼皮，123 猞猁皮，124 麝鼠皮，125 水獭皮，126 松鼠皮〕	20	10	90	9/	0	千克/张	AB/	PQ	15	14/14
	-适合加工皮货用的头、尾、爪及其他块、片：										
4301.9010	---黄鼠狼尾〔999〕	20		50	9/	0	千克	ABEF/	PQ	25	
4301.9090	---其他										
4301.9090 10	其他濒危野生动物未鞣头尾(加工皮货用，包括爪及其他块、片)〔101 松鼠尾，999 松鼠尾除外〕	20		90	9/	0	千克	ABFE/	PQ	45	
4301.9090 90	适合加工皮货用的其他未鞣头、尾(包括爪及其他块、片)〔101 松鼠尾，999 松鼠尾除外〕	20		90	9/	0	千克	AB/	PQ	45	
43.02	**未缝制或已缝制(不加其他材料)的已鞣毛皮(包括头、尾、爪及其他块、片)，但税目 43.03 的货品除外：**										
	-未缝制的整张毛皮，不论是否带头、尾或爪：										
4302.1100	--水貂皮〔999〕	12		130	13/	13	千克/张	/		37	8.4/8.4
	--其他：										
4302.1910	---灰鼠皮、白鼬皮、其他貂皮、狐皮、水獭皮、旱獭皮及猞猁皮										
4302.1910 10	已鞣未缝制的濒危狐皮(兰狐皮、银狐皮除外)〔999〕	10		130	13/	0	千克/张	EF/		35	7/7

Chapter 43
Furskins and artificial fur;
manufactures thereof

Notes:

1. Throughout the Nomenclature references to "furskins", other than to raw furskins of heading No. 43.01, apply to hides or skins of all animals which have been tanned or dressed with the hair or wool on.
2. This Chapter does not cover:
   (a) Birdskins or parts of birdskins, with their feathers or down (heading No. 05.05 or 67.01);
   (b) Raw hides or skins, with the hair or wool on, of Chapter 41 (see Note 1 (c) to that Chapter);
   (c) Gloves, mittens and mitts, consisting of leather and furskin or of leather and artificial fur (heading No. 42.03);
   (d) Articles of Chapter 64;
   (e) Headgear or parts thereof of Chapter 65;
   (f) Articles of Chapter 95 (for example, toys, games, sports requisites).
3. Heading No. 43.03 includes furskins and parts thereof, assembled with the addition of other materials, and furskins and parts thereof, sewn together in the form of garments or parts or accessories of garments or in the form of other articles.
4. Articles of apparel and clothing accessories (except those excluded by Note 2) lined with furskin or artificial fur or to which furskin or artificial fur is attached on the outside except as mere trimming are to be classified in heading No. 43.03 or 43.04 as the case may be.
5. Throughout the Nomenclature the expression "artificial fur" means any imitation of furskin consisting of wool, hair or other fibres gummed or sewn on to leather, woven fabric or other materials, but does not include imitation furskins obtained by weaving or knitting (generally, heading No. 58.01 or 60.01).

协定税率 %								RCEP		特惠税率 %			Article Description
东/冰/格	巴基斯坦	韩国	瑞士上/下	哥/秘/柬	澳/毛	新西/坡/智	中国港/澳/台	东盟及马来/澳/韩	日/新	亚太2国	老/柬/缅	98/97/95	
													Raw furskins (including heads, tails, paws and other pieces or cuttings, suitable for furriers' use), other than raw hides and skins of heading No. 41.01, 41.02 or 41.03:
0/0/0	12	3	1.5/1.5	0/0/0	0/0	0/0/0	0/0/	0/0/13.5	13.6/0			0/0/0	-Of mink, whole, with or without head, tail or paws
0/0/0		9.3	2/2	0/0/0	0/0	0/0/0	0/0/	18/18/18	18.8/18			0/0/0	-Of lamb, the following: Astrakhan, Broadtail, Caracul, Persian and similar lamb, Indian, Chinese, Mongolian or Tibetan lamb, whole, with or without head, tail or paws
													-Of fox, whole, with or without head, tail or paws
0/0/0		9.3	2/2	0/0/0	0/0	0/0/0	0/0/	18/18/18	18.8/18			0/0/0	Raw furskins of endangered fox, whole, with or without head, tail or paws
0/0/0		9.3	2/2	0/0/0	0/0	0/0/0	0/0/	18/18/18	18.8/18			0/0/0	Other raw furskins of fox, whole, with or without head, tail or paws
													-Other furskins, whole, with or without head, tail or paws:
													---Of rabbit or hare, whole, with or without head, tail or paws
0/0/0		9.3	2/2	0/0/0	0/0	0/0/0	0/0/	18/18/18	18.8/18			0/0/0	Raw furskins of endangered wild rabbit or hare, whole, with or without head tail or paws
0/0/0		9.3	2/2	0/0/0	0/0	0/0/0	0/0/	18/18/18	18.8/18			0/0/0	Raw furskins of rabbit or hare, whole, with or without head tail or paws
													---Other
0/0/0		9.3	2/2	0/0/0	0/0	0/0/0	0/0/	18/18/18	18.8/18			0/0/0	Raw furskins of other endangered wild animals, whole, with or without head tail or paws including endangered raw sealskin
0/0/0		9.3	2/2	0/0/0	0/0	0/0/0	0/0/	18/18/18	18.8/18			0/0/0	Raw furskins of other animals, whole, with or without head tail or paws including raw sealskin
													-Heads, tails, paws and other pieces or cuttings, suitable for furriers' use:
0/0/0		9.3	2/2	0/0/0	0/0	0/0/0	0/0/	18/18/18	18.8/18			0/0/0	---Weasel tails
													---Other
0/0/0		9.3	2/2	0/0/0	0/0	0/0/0	0/0/	18/18/18	18.8/18			0/0/0	Heads, tails, paws and other pieces or cuttings, of endangered wild animals, not tanned or dressed, suitable for furriers' use
0/0/0		9.3	2/2	0/0/0	0/0	0/0/0	0/0/	18/18/18	18.8/18			0/0/0	Other heads, tails, paws and other pieces or cuttings of animals, not tanned or dressed, suitable for furriers' use
													Tanned or dressed furskins (including heads, tails, paws and other pieces or cuttings), unassembled, or assembled (without the addition of other materials) other than those of heading No. 43.03:
													-Whole skins, with or without head, tail or paws, not assembled:
0/0/0	6	2.4	1.2/1.2	0/0/0	0/0	0/0/0	0/0/	0/0/10.8	10.9/0			0/0/0	--Of mink
													--Other:
													---Of grey squirrel, ermine, other marten, fox, otter, marmot and lynx
0/0/0	3.5	2	0/0	0/0/0	0/0	0//0	0/0/	0/0/9	9.1/0			0/0/0	Tanned or dressed furskins of endangered fox, unassembled (other than furskins of blue fox or silver fox)

税则号列		货品名称〔CIQ 扩展编码及品名－T2 表示见附表 2〕	最惠(%)	暂定税率	普通	增值/消费	出口退税	计量单位	监管条件/特殊证件	检验检疫	对美关税	亚太上/下
4302.1910	20	已鞣未缝制的兰狐皮、银狐皮〔999〕	10		130	13/	13	千克/张	/		35	7/7
4302.1910	90	已鞣未缝制的其他贵重濒危动物毛皮(灰鼠皮、白鼬皮、其他貂皮、水獭皮、旱獭皮、猞猁皮)〔999〕	10		130	13/	0	千克/张	EF/		35	7/7
4302.1920		---兔皮										
4302.1920	10	已鞣未缝制的整张濒危野兔皮(不论是否带头、尾或爪)〔999〕	10		100	13/	0	千克/张	FE/		15	
4302.1920	90	已鞣未缝制的整张兔皮(不论是否带头、尾或爪)〔999〕	10		100	13/	13	千克/张	/		15	
4302.1930		---下列羔羊皮:阿斯特拉罕、喀拉科尔、波斯羔羊及类似羔羊、印度、中国或蒙古羔羊〔999〕	20		100	13/	13	千克/张	/		25	
4302.1990		---其他										
4302.1990	10	已鞣未缝制的其他濒危野生动物毛皮〔999〕	10		100	13/	0	千克/张	EF/		35	
4302.1990	90	已鞣未缝制的其他毛皮〔999〕	10		100	13/	13	千克/张	/		35	
4302.2000		-未缝制的头、尾、爪及其他块、片										
4302.2000	10	已鞣未缝濒危野生动物头、尾、爪等(包括块、片)〔999〕	20		100	13/	0	千克	EF/		45	
4302.2000	90	已鞣未缝制的头、尾、爪及其他块、片〔999〕	20		100	13/	13	千克	/		45	
		-已缝制的整张毛皮及其块、片:										
4302.3010		---灰鼠、白鼬、貂、狐、水獭、旱獭及猞猁的整张毛皮及其块、片										
4302.3010	10	已鞣已缝制貂皮、狐皮及其块、片(兰狐银狐、水貂、艾虎的整张毛皮及块、片除外)〔999〕	20		130	13/	13	千克	EF/		25	
4302.3010	90	已鞣已缝制的贵重濒危动物毛皮及其块、片(灰鼠皮、白鼬皮、其他貂皮、水獭皮、旱獭皮、猞猁皮及块、片)〔999〕	20		130	13/	0	千克	EF/		25	
4302.3090		---其他										
4302.3090	10	已鞣缝的其他整张濒危野生毛皮(包括块、片)〔999〕	20		100	13/	0	千克	EF/		25	
4302.3090	90	已鞣已缝制的其他整张毛皮及块、片〔999〕	20		100	13/	13	千克	/		25	
43.03		**毛皮制的衣服、衣着附件及其他物品:**										
		-衣服及衣着附件:										
4303.1010		---毛皮衣服										
4303.1010	10	含濒危野生动物毛皮衣服〔999〕	10		150	13/	0	千克/件	EF/		35	
4303.1010	90	其他毛皮衣服〔999〕	10		150	13/	13	千克/件	/		35	
4303.1020		---毛皮衣着附件										
4303.1020	10	含濒危野生动物毛皮衣着附件〔999〕	10		150	13/	0	千克	EF/		35	
4303.1020	90	其他毛皮衣着附件〔999〕	10		150	13/	13	千克	/		35	
4303.9000		-其他										
4303.9000	10	含濒危野生动物毛皮制其他物品〔999〕	10		150	13/	0	千克	EF/		35	
4303.9000	90	其他毛皮制物品〔999〕	10		150	13/	13	千克	/		35	
43.04		**人造毛皮及其制品:**										
4304.0010		---人造毛皮〔999〕	10		130	13/	13	千克	/			
4304.0020		---人造毛皮制品〔101 其他装饰用纺织制品,102 其他纺织制品〕	10		150	13/	13	千克	/		35	

协定税率 %								RCEP		特惠税率 %			Article Description
东/冰/格	巴基斯坦	韩国	瑞士上/下	哥/秘/柬	澳/毛	新西/坡/智	中国港/澳/台	东盟及马来/澳/韩	日/新	亚太2国	老/柬/缅	98/97/95	
0/0/0	3.5	2	0/0	0/0/0	0/0	0//0	0/0/	0/0/9	9.1/0			0/0/0	Tanned or dressed furskins of blue fox, silver fox, unassembled
0/0/0	3.5	2	0/0	0/0/0	0/0	0//0	0/0/	0/0/9	9.1/0			0/0/0	Tanned or dressed furskins precious furskins of endangered animals(grey squirrel, ermine, other marten, fox, otter, marmot and lynx)unassembled
													---Of rabbit or hare
0/0/0	3.5	2	0/0	0/0/0	0/0	0//0	0/0/	0/0/9	9.1/0			0/0/0	Tanned or dressed furskins of endangered rabbit or hare, endangered whole, with or without head tail or paws, unassembled
0/0/0	3.5	2	0/0	0/0/0	0/0	0//0	0/0/	0/0/9	9.1/0			0/0/0	Tanned or dressed furskins of rabbit or hare, whole, with or without head tail or paws, unassembled
0//0		9.3	2/2	0/0/0	0/0	0/0/0	0/0/	18/18/18	18.8/18			0/0/0	---Of lamb, the following: Astrakhan, Broadtail, Caracul, Persian and similar lamb, Indian, Chinese (cincluding Tibetan) or Mongolian lamb
													---Other
0/0/0		2	0/0	0/0/0	0/0	0//0	0/0/	0/0/9	9.1/0			0/0/0	Tanned or dressed furskins of other endangered wild animals, unassembled
0/0/0		2	0/0	0/0/0	0/0	0//0	0/0/	0/0/9	9.1/0			0/0/0	Other tanned or dressed furskins of other animals, unassembled
													-Heads, tails, paws and other pieces or cuttings, not assembled
0/0/0		9.3	2/2	0/0/0	0/0	0/0/0	0/0/	18.7/19/	18.8/19			0/0/0	Tanned or dressed heads, tails, paws and other pieces or cuttings, of endangered wild animals,unassembled
0/0/0		9.3	2/2	0/0/0	0/0	0/0/0	0/0/	18.7/19/	18.8/19			0/0/0	Tanned or dressed heads, tails, paws and other pieces or cuttings of other animals, unassembled
													-Whole skins and pieces or cuttings thereof, assembled:
													---Of grey squirrel, ermine, other marten, fox, otter, marmot and lynx
0/0/0		9.3	2/2	0/0/0	0/0	0/0/0	0/0/	18/18/18	18.2/18			0/0/0	Tanned or dressed whole skins and pieces or cuttings thereof, of marten, fox, other than whole skins and pieces or cuttings of blue fox, silver fox, mink, perwitsky (ferret-polecat), assembled
0/0/0		9.3	2/2	0/0/0	0/0	0/0/0	0/0/	18/18/18	18.2/18			0/0/0	Tanned or dressed whole skins and pieces or cuttings thereof, of grey squirrel, ermine, other marten, fox, otter, marmot and lynx, endangered,assembled
													---Other
0//0		9.3	2/2	0/0/0	0/0	0/0/0	0/0/	18/18/18	18.8/18			0/0/0	Tanned or dressed whole skins and pieces or cuttings thereof, of other endangered wild animals, assembled
0//0		9.3	2/2	0/0/0	0/0	0/0/0	0/0/	18/18/18	18.8/18			0/0/0	Tanned or dressed whole skins and pieces or cuttings thereof, of other animals, assembled
													Articles of apparel, clothing accessories and other articles of furskin:
													-Articles of apparel and clothing accessories:
													---Articles of apparel
0//0		13.8	2.3/2.3	0/0/0	0/13.8	0/0/0	0/0/	21.9/21.9/	/21.9	4.5		0/0/0	Articles of apparel of endangered wild animals
0//0		13.8	2.3/2.3	0/0/0	0/13.8	0/0/0	0/0/	21.9/21.9/	/21.9	4.5		0/0/0	Articles of apparel of other animals
													---Clothing accessories
0//0		3.6	1.8/1.8	0/0/0	0/0	0/0/0	0/0/	0/0/16.2	16.4/0	5.5		0/0/0	Clothing accessories of endangered wild animals
0//0		3.6	1.8/1.8	0/0/0	0/0	0/0/0	0/0/	0/0/16.2	16.4/0	5.5		0/0/0	Clothing accessories of other animals
													-Other
0//0	14.4	3.6	1.8/1.8	0/0/0	0/0	0/0/0	0/0/	0/0/16.2	16.4/0	5.5		0/0/0	Other articles of furskin,of endangered wild animals
0//0	14.4	3.6	1.8/1.8	0/0/0	0/0	0/0/0	0/0/	0/0/16.2	16.4/0	5.5		0/0/0	Other articles of furskin,of other animals
													Artificial fur and articles thereof:
0//0		3.6	1.8/1.8	0/0/0	0/0	0/0/0	0/0/	0/0/16.2	16.4/0	6		0/0/0	---Artificial fur
0//0	14.4	3.6	1.8/1.8	0/0/0	0/0	0/0/0	0/0/	0/0/16.2	16.4/0	6		0/0/0	---Articles of artificial fur

第九类
木及木制品；木炭；软木及软木制品；稻草、秸秆、针茅或其他编结材料制品；篮筐及柳条编结品

第四十四章
木及木制品；木炭

注释：

一、本章不包括：

（一）主要作香料、药料、杀虫、杀菌或类似用途的木片、刨花、碎木、木粒或木粉（品目12.11）；

（二）竹或主要作编织用的其他木质材料，呈原木状，不论是否经劈开，纵锯或切段（品目 14.01）；

（三）主要作染料或鞣料用的木片、刨花、木粒或木粉（品目 14.04）；
（四）活性炭（品目 38.02）；
（五）品目 42.02 的物品；
（六）第四十六章的货品；
（七）第六十四章的鞋靴及其零件；
（八）第六十六章的货品（例如，伞、手杖及其零件）；
（九）税目 68.08 的货品；
（十）税目 71.17 的仿首饰；
（十一）第十六类或第十七类的货品（例如，机器零件，机器及器具的箱、罩、壳，车辆部件）；

（十二）第十八类的货品（例如，钟壳、乐器及其零件）；
（十三）火器的零件（税目 93.05）；
（十四）第九十四章的物品（例如，家具、灯具及照明器具、活动房屋）；
（十五）第九十五章的物品（例如，玩具、游戏品及运动用品）；
（十六）第九十六章的物品（例如，烟斗及其零件、纽扣、铅笔、独脚架、双脚架、三脚架及类似品），但税目 96.03 所列物品的木身及木柄除外；或
（十七）第九十七章的物品（例如，艺术品）。

二、本章所称"强化木"，是指经过化学或物理方法处理（对于多层粘合木材，其处理应超出一般粘合需要），从而增加了密度或硬度并改善了机械强度、抗化学或抗电性能的木材。

三、税目 44.14 至 44.21 适用于碎料板或类似木质材料板、纤维板、层压板或强化木的制品。

四、税目 44.10、44.11 或 44.12 的产品，可以加工成税目 44.09 所述的各种形状，也可以加工成弯曲、瓦楞、多孔或其他形状（正方形或矩形除外），以及经其他任何加工，但未具有其他税目所列制品的特性。

五、税目 44.17 不包括装有第八十二章注释一所述材料制成的刀片、工作刃、工作面或其他工作部件的工具。

六、除上述注释一及其他条文另有规定的以外，本章税目中所称"木"，也包括竹及其他木质材料。

子目注释：

一、子目 4401.31 所称"木屑棒"是指由木材加工业、家具制造业及其他木材加工活动中产生的副产品（例如，刨花、锯末及碎木片）直接压制而成或加入按重量计不超过 3%的黏合剂后粘聚而成的产品。此类产品呈圆柱状，其直径不超过 25 毫米，长度不超过 100 毫米。

二、子目 4401.32 所称的"木屑块"是指由木材加工业、家具制造业及其 他木材加工活动中产生的副产品（例如，刨花、锯末及碎木片）直接压制而成或加入按重量计不超过 3%的粘合剂后粘聚而成的产品 。此类产品呈立 方体，多面体或圆柱状，其最小横截面尺寸大于 25 毫米。

三、子目 4407.13 所称"云杉—松木—冷杉"是指来源于云杉、松木、冷杉 混合林的木材，其各树种的比例是未知的且各不相同 。

四、子目 4407.14 所称"铁杉—冷杉"是指来源于西部铁杉、冷杉混合林的 木材，其各树种的比例是未知的且各不相同 。

税则号列	货品名称〔CIQ 扩展编码及品名—T2 表示见附表 2〕	最惠(%)	暂定税率	普通	增值/消费	出口退税	计量单位	监管条件/特殊证件	检验检疫	对美关税	亚太上/下
44.01	薪柴（圆木段、块、枝、成捆或类似形状）；木片或木粒；锯末、木废料及碎片，不论是否粘结成圆木段、块、片或类似形状：										
	-薪柴（圆木段、块、枝、成捆或类似形状）										
4401.1100	--针叶木〔999〕	0		70	13/	0	千克	AB/	PQ		
4401.1200	--非针叶木〔999〕	0		70	13/	0	千克	AB/	PQ	25	
	-木片或木粒：										
4401.2100	--针叶木										
4401.2100　10	濒危针叶木木片或木粒〔999〕	0		8	13/	0	千克	ABFE/	PQ	25	
4401.2100　90	其他针叶木木片或木粒〔999〕	0		8	13/	0	千克	AB/	PQ	25	
4401.2200	--非针叶木										

SECTION Ⅸ
WOOD AND ARTICLES OF WOOD; WOOD CHARCOAL; CORK AND ARTICLES OF CORK; MANUFACTURES OF STRAW, OF ESPARTO OR OF OTHER PLAITING MATERIALS; BASKETWARE AND WICKERWORK

Chapter 44
Wood and articles of wood; wood charcoal

Notes:

1. This Chapter does not cover:
   (a) Wood, in chips, in shavings, crushed, ground or powdered, of a kind used primarily in perfumery, in pharmacy, or for insecticidal, fungicidal or similar purposes (heading No. 12. 11);
   (b) Bamboos or other materials of a woody nature of a kind used primarily for plaiting, in the rough, whether or not split, sawn lengthwise or cut to length (heading No. 14. 01);
   (c) Wood, in chips, in shavings, ground or powdered, of a kind used primarily in dyeing or in tanning (heading No. 14. 04);
   (d) Activated charcoal (heading No. 38. 02);
   (e) Articles of heading No. 42. 02;
   (f) Goods of Chapter 46;
   (g) Footwear or parts thereof of Chapter 64;
   (h) Goods of Chapter 66 (for example, umbrellas and walking-sticks and parts thereof);
   (i) Goods of heading No. 68. 08;
   (j) Imitation jewellery of heading No. 71. 17;
   (k) Goods of Section ⅩⅥ or Section ⅩⅦ (for example, machine parts, cases, covers, cabinets for machines and apparatus and wheel wrights' wares);
   (l) Goods of Section ⅩⅧ (for example, clock cases and musical instruments and parts thereof);
   (m) Parts of firearms (heading No. 93. 05);
   (n) Articles of Chapter 94 (for example, furniture, lamps and lighting fittings, prefabricated buildings);
   (o) Articles of Chapter 95 (for example, toys, games, sports requisites);
   (p) Articles of Chapter 96 (for example, smoking pipes and parts thereof, buttons, pencils unipod, bipod, trpod or the Like) excluding bodies and handles, of wood, for articles of heading No. 96. 03;
   (q) Articles, of Chapter 97 (for example, works of art).

2. In this Chapter, the expression "densified wood" means wood which has been subjected to chemical or physical treatment (being, in the case of layers bonded together, treatment in excess of that needed to ensure a good bond), and which has thereby acquired increased density or hardness together with improved mechanical strength or resistance to chemical or electrical agencies.
3. Headings No. 44. 14 to 44. 21 apply to articles of the respective descriptions of particle board or similar board, fibreboard, laminated wood or densified wood as they apply to such articles of wood.
4. Products of heading No. 44. 10, 44. 11 or 44, 12 may be worked to form the shapes provided for in respect of the goods of heading No. 44. 09, curved, corrugated, perforated, cut or formed to shapes other than square or rectangular or submitted to any other operation provided it does not give them the character of articles of other headings.
5. Heading No. 44. 17 does not apply to tools in which the blade, working edge, working surface or other working part is formed by any of the materials specified in Note 1 to Chapter 82.
6. Subject to Note 1 above and except where the context otherwise requires, any reference to "wood" in a heading of this Chapter applies also to bamboos and other materials of a woody nature.

Subheading Note:

1. For the purposes of Subheading No. 4401. 31, the expression "wood pellets" means by-products such as cutter shavings, sawdust or chips, of the mechanical wood processing industry, furnitrue-mading industry or other wood transformation activities, which have been agglomerated either directly by compression or by the addition of a binder in a proportion not exceeding 3% by weight. Such pellets are cylindrical, with a diameter not exceeding 25mm and a length not exceeding 100mm
2. For the purposes of subheading No. 4401.32, the expression "wood briquettes" means by products such as cutter shavings, saw dust or chips, of the mechanical wood processing industry, furniture making or other wood transformation activities, which have been agglomerated either directly by compression or by addition of a binder in a proportion not exceeding 3 % by weight. Such briquettes are in the form of cubiform, polyhedral or cylindrical units with the minimum cross—sectional dimension greater than 25 mm.
3. For the purposes of subheading No. 4407.13, "S—P—F" refers to wood sourced from mixed stands of spruce, pine and fir where the proportion of each species varies and is unknown.
4. For the purposes of subheading No. 4407.14, "Hem—fir" refers to woodsourced from mixed stands of Western hemlock and fir where the proportion of each species varies and is unknown.

协定税率 %								RCEP		特惠税率 %			Article Description
东/冰/格	巴基斯坦	韩国	瑞士上/下	哥/秘/柬	澳/毛	新西/坡/智	中国港/澳/台	东盟及马来/澳/韩	日/新	亚太2国	老/柬/缅	98/97/95	
													Fuel wood, in logs, in billets, in twigs, in faggots or in similar forms; wood in chips or particles; sawdust and wood waste and scrap, whether or not agglomerated in logs, briquettes, pellets or similar forms:
													-Fuel wood, in logs, in billets, in twigs, in faggots or in similar forms
0/0/0	0	0	0/0	0/0/0	0/0	0//0	0/0/	0/0/0	0/0			0/0/0	--Coniferous
0/0/0	0	0	0/0	0/0/0	0/0	0//0	0/0/	0/0/0	0/0			0/0/0	--Non-coniferous
													-Wood in chips or particles:
													--Coniferous
0/0/0	0	0	0/0	0/0/0	0/0	0//0	0/0/	0/0/0	0/0			0/0/0	Chips or particles of endangered coniferous wood
0/0/0	0	0	0/0	0/0/0	0/0	0//0	0/0/	0/0/0	0/0			0/0/0	Chips or particles of other coniferous wood
													--Non-coniferous

税则号列	货品名称〔CIQ扩展编码及品名—T2表示见附表2〕	最惠(%)	暂定税率	普通	增值/消费	出口退税	计量单位	监管条件/特殊证件	检验检疫	对美关税	亚太上/下
4401.2200 10	濒危非针叶木木片或木粒〔999〕	0		8	13/	0	千克	ABFE/	PQ	25	
4401.2200 90	其他非针叶木木片或木粒〔999〕	0		8	13/	0	千克	AB/	PQ	25	
	-锯末、木废料及碎片,粘结成圆木段、块、片或类似形状:										
4401.3100	--木屑棒〔999〕	0		8	13/	0	千克	9AB/	PQ	25	
4401.3200	--木屑块〔999〕	0		8	13/	0	千克	9AB/	PQ	25	
4401.3900	--其他〔999〕	0		8	13/	0	千克	9AB/	PQ	25	
	-锯末、木废料及碎片,未粘结的:										
4401.4100	--锯末〔999〕	0		8	13/	0	千克	9AB/	MPQ	25	
4401.4900	--其他〔999〕	0		8	13/	0	千克	9AB/	MPQ	25	
44.02	**木炭(包括果壳炭及果核炭),不论是否结块:**										
4402.1000	-竹的〔999〕	6	0	70	13/	0	千克	/			
4402.2000	-果壳的或果核的〔999〕	6	0	70	13/	0	千克	/		25	
4402.9000	-其他										
4402.9000 10	以木材为原料直接烧制的木炭(不论是否结块)〔999〕	6	0	70	13/	0	千克	8/		25	
4402.9000 90	其他木炭(不论是否结块)〔999〕	6	0	70	13/	0	千克	/		25	
44.03	**原木,不论是否去皮、去边材或粗锯成方:**										
	-用油漆、着色剂、杂酚油或其他防腐剂处理:										
4403.1100	--针叶木										
4403.1100 10	油漆,着色剂等处理的红豆杉原木(包括用杂酚油或其他防腐剂处理)〔999〕	0		8	9/	0	千克/立方米	8AF/	PQ	25	
4403.1100 20	油漆,着色剂等处理的其他濒危针叶木原木(包括用杂酚油或其他防腐剂处理)〔101 松木,102 其他针叶木〕	0		8	9/	0	千克/立方米	8AF/	PQ	25	
4403.1100 90	其他油漆,着色剂等处理的针叶木原木(包括用杂酚油或其他防腐剂处理)〔101 松木,102 其他针叶木〕	0		8	9/	0	千克/立方米	8A/	PQ	25	
4403.1200	--非针叶木										
4403.1200 10	油漆,着色剂等处理的濒危非针叶木原木(包括用杂酚油或其他防腐剂处理)〔999〕	0		8	9/	0	千克/立方米	8AF/	PQ	20	
4403.1200 90	其他油漆,着色剂等处理的非针叶木原木(包括用杂酚油或其他防腐剂处理)〔999〕	0		8	9/	0	千克/立方米	8A/	PQ	20	
	-其他,针叶木:										
	--松木(松属),最小截面尺寸在15厘米及以上:										
4403.2110	---红松和樟子松										
4403.2110 10	最小截面尺寸在15厘米及以上的红松原木(用油漆着色剂,杂酚油或其他防腐剂处理的除外)〔999〕	0		8	9/	0	千克/立方米	8AEF/	PQ	25	
4403.2110 90	最小截面尺寸在15厘米及以上的樟子松原木(用油漆着色剂,杂酚油或其他防腐剂处理的除外)〔999〕	0		8	9/	0	千克/立方米	8A/	PQ	25	
4403.2120	---辐射松〔999〕	0		8	9/	0	千克/立方米	8A/	PQ		
4403.2190	---其他										
4403.2190 10	最小截面尺寸在15厘米及以上的濒危松木(松属)原木(用油漆着色剂,杂酚油或其他防腐剂处理的除外)〔999〕	0		8	9/	0	千克/立方米	8AF/	MPQ	25	
4403.2190 90	最小截面尺寸在15厘米及以上的其他松木(松属)原木(用油漆着色剂,杂酚油或其他防腐剂处理的除外)〔999〕	0		8	9/	0	千克/立方米	8A/	MPQ	25	
	--其他松木(松属):										
4403.2210	---红松和樟子松										
4403.2210 10	最小截面尺寸在15厘米以下的红松原木(用油漆着色剂,杂酚油或其他防腐剂处理的除外)〔999〕	0		8	9/	0	千克/立方米	8AEF/	PQ		
4403.2210 90	最小截面尺寸在15厘米以下的樟子松原木(用油漆着色剂,杂酚油或其他防腐剂处理的除外)〔999〕	0		8	9/	0	千克/立方米	8A/	PQ		
4403.2220	---辐射松〔999〕	0		8	9/	0	千克/立方米	8A/	PQ		
4403.2290	---其他										
4403.2290 10	最小截面尺寸在15厘米以下的濒危其他松木(松属)原木(用油漆着色剂,杂酚油或其他防腐剂处理的除外)〔999〕	0		8	9/	0	千克/立方米	8AF/	MPQ	20	
4403.2290 90	最小截面尺寸在15厘米以下的其他松木(松属)原木(用油漆着色剂,杂酚油或其他防腐剂处理的除外)〔999〕	0		8	9/	0	千克/立方米	8A/	MPQ	20	
4403.2300	--冷杉和云杉,截面尺寸在15厘米及以上										

协定税率 %								RCEP		特惠税率 %			Article Description
东/冰/格	巴基斯坦	韩国	瑞士上/下	哥/秘/柬	澳/毛	新西/坡/智	中国港/澳/台	东盟及马来/澳/韩	日/新	亚太2国	老/柬/缅	98/97/95	
0/0/0	0	0	0/0	0/0/0	0/0	0//0	0/0/	0/0/0	0/0			0/0/0	Chips or particles of endangered non-coniferous wood
0/0/0	0	0	0/0	0/0/0	0/0	0//0	0/0/	0/0/0	0/0			0/0/0	Chips or particles of other non-coniferous wood
													-Sawdust and wood waste and scrap, agglomerated in logs, briquettes, pellets or similar forms:
0/0/0	0	0	0/0	0/0/0	0/0	0//0	0/0/	0/0/0	0/0			0/0/0	--Wood pellets
0/0/0	0	0	0/0	0/0/0	0/0	0//0	0/0/	0/0/0	0/0			0/0/0	--Wood briquettes
0/0/0	0	0	0/0	0/0/0	0/0	0//0	0/0/	0/0/0	0/0			0/0/0	--Other
													-Sawdust and wood waste and scrap, not agglomerated :
0/0/0	0	0	0/0	0/0/0	0/0	0//0	0/0/	0/0/0	0/0			0/0/0	-Sawdust
0/0/0	0	0	0/0	0/0/0	0/0	0//0	0/0/	0/0/0	0/0			0/0/0	-Other
													Wood charcoal (including shell or nut charcoal), whether or not agglomerated:
0/0/	3.5	2.1	1.1/1.1	0/0/0	0/0	0/0/0	0/0/	0/0/9.5	9.5/0			0/0/0	-Of bamboo
0/0/	3.5	2.1	1.1/1.1	0/0/0	0/0	0/0/0	0/0/	9.5/9.5/9.5	9.5/9.5			0/0/0	-Of shell or nut
													-Other
0/0/	3.5	2.1	1.1/1.1	0/0/0	0/0	0/0/0	0/0/	9.5/9.5/9.5	9.5/9.5			0/0/0	Wood charcoal, obtained by burning wood
0/0/	3.5	2.1	1.1/1.1	0/0/0	0/0	0/0/0	0/0/	9.5/9.5/9.5	9.5/9.5			0/0/0	Other wood charcoal(whether or not agglomerated)
													Wood in the rough, whether or not stripped of bark or sapwood, or roughly squared:
													-Treated with paint, stains, creosote or other preservatives
													--Coniferous
0/0/0	0	0	0/0	0/0/0	0/0	0//0	0/0/	0/0/0	0/0			0/0/0	Rough wood of Taxaceae , treated with paint, stains, creosote or other preservatives
0/0/0	0	0	0/0	0/0/0	0/0	0//0	0/0/	0/0/0	0/0			0/0/0	Other endangered rough wood of coniferous, treated with paint, stains, creosote or other preservatives
0/0/0	0	0	0/0	0/0/0	0/0	0//0	0/0/	0/0/0	0/0			0/0/0	Other rough wood of coniferous, treated with paint, stains, creosote or other preservatives
													--Non-coniferous
0/0/0	0	0	0/0	0/0/0	0/0	0//0	0/0/	0/0/0	0/0			0/0/0	Endangered rough wood of non-coniferous, treated with paint, stains, creosote or other preservatives
0/0/0	0	0	0/0	0/0/0	0/0	0//0	0/0/	0/0/0	0/0			0/0/0	Rough wood of non-coniferous, treated with paint, stains, creosote or other preservatives
													-Other coniferous:
													--Of pine (Pinus spp.), *of which the smallest cross—sectional di—mension is 15 cm or more:*
													---Korean pine and Mongolian scotch pine
0/0/0	0	0	0/0	0/0/0	0/0	0//0	0/0/	0/0/0	0/0			0/0/0	*Korean pine rough wood (other than that treated with paint, stains, creosote or other preservatives), of which cross-sectional dimension≥15cm*
0/0/0	0	0	0/0	0/0/0	0/0	0//0	0/0/	0/0/0	0/0			0/0/0	*Mongolian scotch pine rough wood (other than that treated with paint, stains, creosote or other preservatives), of which cross-sectional dimension≥15cm*
0/0/0	0	0	0/0	0/0/0	0/0	0//0	0/0/	0/0/0	0/0			0/0/0	*Radiata pine*
													---Other
0/0/0	0	0	0/0	0/0/0	0/0	0//0	0/0/	0/0/0	0/0			0/0/0	*Endangered pine rough wood (other than that treated with paint, stains, creosote or other preservatives), of which cross-sectional dimension≥15cm*
0/0/0	0	0	0/0	0/0/0	0/0	0//0	0/0/	0/0/0	0/0			0/0/0	*Other pine rough wood (other than that treated with paint, stains, creosote or other preservatives), of which cross-sectional dimension≥15cm*
													--Of pine (Pinus spp.*), other:*
													---Korean pine and Mongolian scotch pine
0/0/0	0	0	0/0	0/0/0	0/0	0//0	0/0/	0/0/0	0/0			0/0/0	*Korean pine rough wood (other than that treated with paint, stains, creosote or other preservatives), of which cross-sectional dimension < 15cm*
0/0/0	0	0	0/0	0/0/0	0/0	0//0	0/0/	0/0/0	0/0			0/0/0	*Mongolian scotch pine rough wood (other than that treated with paint, stains, creosote or other preservatives), of which cross-sectional dimension < 15cm*
0/0/0	0	0	0/0	0/0/0	0/0	0//0	0/0/	0/0/0	0/0			0/0/0	*---Radiata pine*
													---Other
0/0/0	0	0	0/0	0/0/0	0/0	0//0	0/0/	0/0/0	0/0			0/0/0	*Other endangered pine rough wood (other than that treated with paint, stains, creosote or other preservatives), of which cross-sectional dimension < 15cm*
0/0/0	0	0	0/0	0/0/0	0/0	0//0	0/0/	0/0/0	0/0			0/0/0	*Other pine rough wood (other than that treated with paint, stains, creosote or other preservatives), of which cross-sectional dimension≥15cm*
													--Of fir (Abies spp.*) and spruce (* Picea spp.*), of which any cross-sectional dimension is 15 cm or more*

税则号列	货品名称〔CIQ 扩展编码及品名－T2 表示见附表 2〕	最惠(%)	暂定税率	普通	增值/消费	出口退税	计量单位	监管条件/特殊证件	检验检疫	对美关税	亚太上/下
4403.2300　10	最小截面尺寸在 15 厘米及以上的濒危云杉和冷杉原木(用油漆着色剂,杂酚油或其他防腐剂处理的除外)〔999〕	0		8	9/	0	千克/立方米	8AF/	PQ	20	
4403.2300　90	最小截面尺寸在 15 厘米及以上的其他云杉和冷杉原木(用油漆着色剂,杂酚油或其他防腐剂处理的除外)〔999〕	0		8	9/	0	千克/立方米	8A/	PQ	20	
4403.2400	--其他冷杉和云杉										
4403.2400　10	最小截面尺寸在 15 厘米以下的濒危云杉和冷杉原木(用油漆着色剂,杂酚油或其他防腐剂处理的除外)〔999〕	0		8	9/	0	千克/立方米	8AF/	PQ	25	
4403.2400　90	最小截面尺寸在 15 厘米以下的其他云杉和冷杉原木(用油漆着色剂,杂酚油或其他防腐剂处理的除外)〔999〕	0		8	9/	0	千克/立方米	8A/	PQ	25	
	--其他,最小截面尺寸在 15 厘米及以上:										
4403.2510	---落叶松〔999〕	0		8	9/	0	千克/立方米	8A/	PQ	25	
4403.2520	---花旗松〔999〕	0		8	9/	0	千克/立方米	8A/	PQ	5	
4403.2590	---其他										
4403.2590　10	最小截面尺寸在 15 厘米及以上的濒危红豆杉原木(用油漆着色剂,杂酚油或其他防腐剂处理的除外)〔999〕	0		8	9/	0	千克/立方米	8AF/	PQ	5	
4403.2590　20	最小截面尺寸在 15 厘米及以上的其他濒危针叶木原木(用油漆着色剂,杂酚油或其他防腐剂处理的除外)〔999〕	0		8	9/	0	千克/立方米	8AF/	PQ	5	
4403.2590　90	最小截面尺寸在 15 厘米及以上的其他针叶木原木(用油漆着色剂,杂酚油或其他防腐剂处理的除外)〔999〕	0		8	9/	0	千克/立方米	8A/	PQ	5	
	--其他:										
4403.2610	---落叶松〔999〕	0		8	9/	0	千克/立方米	8A/	PQ		
4403.2620	---花旗松〔999〕	0		8	9/	0	千克/立方米	8A/	MP	20	
4403.2690	---其他										
4403.2690　10	最小截面尺寸在 15 厘米以下的濒危红豆杉原木(用油漆着色剂,杂酚油或其他防腐剂处理的除外)〔999〕	0		8	9/	0	千克/立方米	8AF/	MP	20	
4403.2690　20	最小截面尺寸在 15 厘米以下的其他濒危针叶木原木(用油漆着色剂,杂酚油或其他防腐剂处理的除外)〔999〕	0		8	9/	0	千克/立方米	8AF/	MP	20	
4403.2690　90	最小截面尺寸在 15 厘米以下的其他针叶木原木(用油漆着色剂,杂酚油或其他防腐剂处理的除外)〔999〕	0		8	9/	0	千克/立方米	8A/	MP	20	
	-其他,热带木:										
4403.4100	--深红色红柳桉木、浅红色红柳桉木及巴栲红柳桉木〔999〕	0		8	9/	0	千克/立方米	8A/	PQ		
4403.4200	--柚木〔999〕	0		35	9/	0	千克/立方米	8A/	PQ		
	--其他:										
4403.4920	---奥克曼(奥克榄)〔999〕	0		35	9/	0	千克/立方米	8A/	PQ		
4403.4930	---龙脑香木(克隆)〔999〕	0		35	9/	0	千克/立方米	8A/	PQ		
4403.4940	---山樟(香木)〔999〕	0		35	9/	0	千克/立方米	8A/	PQ		
4403.4950	---印茄木(波罗格)〔999〕	0		35	9/	0	千克/立方米	8A/	PQ		
4403.4960	---大干巴豆(门格里斯或康派斯)〔999〕	0		35	9/	0	千克/立方米	8A/	PQ		
4403.4970	---异翅香木〔999〕	0		35	9/	0	千克/立方米	8A/	PQ		
4403.4980	---红木										
4403.4980　10	濒危热带红木原木(用油漆着色剂,杂酚油或其他防腐剂处理的除外)〔999〕	0		35	9/	0	千克/立方米	8AEF/	PQ		
4403.4980　90	其他热带红木原木(用油漆着色剂,杂酚油或其他防腐剂处理的除外)〔999〕	0		35	9/	0	千克/立方米	8A/	PQ		
4403.4990	---其他										
4403.4990　10	南美蒺藜木(玉檀木)原木(用油漆,着色剂,杂酚油或其他防腐剂处理的除外)〔101〕	0		8	9/	0	千克/立方米	8AEF/	PQ		
4403.4990　20	其他濒危热带原木(用油漆,着色剂,杂酚油或其他防腐剂处理的除外)〔999〕	0		8	9/	0	千克/立方米	8AF/	PQ		
4403.4990　90	其他热带原木(用油漆,着色剂,杂酚油或其他防腐剂处理的除外)[T2]	0		8	9/	0	千克/立方米	8A/	PQ		
	-其他:										
4403.9100	--栎木(橡木)										
4403.9100　10	蒙古栎原木(用油漆、着色剂、杂酚油或其他防腐剂处理的除外)〔999〕	0		8	9/	0	千克/立方米	8AEF/	PQ	25	

协定税率 %								RCEP		特惠税率 %			
东/冰/格	巴基斯坦	韩国	瑞士上/下	哥/秘/柬	澳/毛	新西/坡/智	中国港/澳/台	东盟及马来/澳/韩	日/新	亚太2国	老/柬/缅	98/97/95	Article Description
0/0/0	0	0	0/0	0/0/0	0/0	0//0	0/0/	0/0/0	0/0			0/0/0	Endangered pine (spruce and fir) rough wood (other than that treated with paint, stains, creosote or other preservatives), of which cross-sectional dimension≥15cm
0/0/0	0	0	0/0	0/0/0	0/0	0//0	0/0/	0/0/0	0/0			0/0/0	Other pine(spruce and fir)rough wood(other than that treated with paint, stains, creosote or other preservatives), of which cross-sectional dimension≥15cm
													--Of fir (Abies spp.) and spruce (Picea spp.), other
0/0/0	0	0	0/0	0/0/0	0/0	0//0	0/0/	0/0/0	0/0			0/0/0	Endangered pine (spruce and fir) rough wood (other than that treated with paint, stains, creosote or other preservatives), of which cross-sectional dimension < 15cm
0/0/0	0	0	0/0	0/0/0	0/0	0//0	0/0/	0/0/0	0/0			0/0/0	Other pine(spruce and fir)rough wood(other than that treated with paint, stains, creosote or other preservatives), of which cross-sectional dimension < 15cm
													--Other, of which the smallest cross－sectional dimension is 15cm or more
0/0/0	0	0	0/0	0/0/0	0/0	0//0	0/0/	0/0/0	0/0			0/0/0	---Larch
0/0/0	0	0	0/0	0/0/0	0/0	0//0	0/0/	0/0/0	0/0			0/0/0	---Douglas fir
													-Other
0/0/0	0	0	0/0	0/0/0	0/0	0//0	0/0/	0/0/0	0/0		//	0/0/0	Yew logs with a section size of 15 cm and above (except those treated with paint colorant, creosote or other preservatives)
0/0/0	0	0	0/0	0/0/0	0/0	0//0	0/0/	0/0/0	0/0		//	0/0/0	Other endangered coniferous logs with a section size of 15 cm or more (except those treated with paint colorants, creosote or other preservatives)
0/0/0	0	0	0/0	0/0/0	0/0	0//0	0/0/	0/0/0	0/0		//	0/0/0	Other coniferous logs with a cross section of 15 cm or more (except those treated with paint colorants, creosote or other preservatives)
													--Other:
0/0/0	0	0	0/0	0/0/0	0/0	0//0	0/0/	0/0/0	0/0			0/0/0	---Larch
0/0/0	0	0	0/0	0/0/0	0/0	0//0	0/0/	0/0/0	0/0			0/0/0	---Douglas fir
													---Other:
0/0/0	0	0	0/0	0/0/0	0/0	0//0	0/0/	0/0/0	0/0		//	0/0/0	Yew logs less than 15 cm in cross section (except those treated with paint colorants, creosote or other preservatives)
0/0/0	0	0	0/0	0/0/0	0/0	0//0	0/0/	0/0/0	0/0		//	0/0/0	Other endangered coniferous logs with section size less than 15 cm(other than paint or other preservatives)
0/0/0	0	0	0/0	0/0/0	0/0	0//0	0/0/	0/0/0	0/0		//	0/0/0	Other coniferous logs with sectional dimensions less than 15 cm (except those treated with paint colorants, creosote or other preservatives)
													-Other, of tropical wood:
0/0/0	0	0	0/0	0/0/0	0/0	0//0	0/0/	0/0/0	0/0			0/0/0	--Dark Red Meranti, Light Red Meranti and Meranti Bakau
0/0/0	0	0	0/0	0/0/0	0/0	0//0	0/0/	0/0/0	0/0			0/0/0	--Teak
													--Other:
0/0/0	0	0	0/0	0/0/0	0/0	0//0	0/0/	0/0/0	0/0			0/0/0	---Okoume(Au koumed)klaineana
0/0/0	0	0	0/0	0/0/0	0/0	0//0	0/0/	0/0/0	0/0			0/0/0	---Dipterocarpus spp. Keruing
0/0/0	0	0	0/0	0/0/0	0/0	0//0	0/0/	0/0/0	0/0			0/0/0	---Kapur (Dryobalanops spp.)
0/0/0	0	0	0/0	0/0/0	0/0	0//0	0/0/	0/0/0	0/0			0/0/0	---Intsia spp. (Mengaris)
0/0/0	0	0	0/0	0/0/0	0/0	0//0	0/0/	0/0/0	0/0			0/0/0	---Koompassiaspp. (Mengaris or Kempas)
0/0/0	0	0	0/0	0/0/0	0/0	0//0	0/0/	0/0/0	0/0			0/0/0	---Anisopter spp.
													---Of rosewood
0/0/0	0	0	0/0	0/0/0	0/0	0//0	0/0/	0/0/0	0/0			0/0/0	Endangered tropic rose wood(other than that treated with paint, stains, creosote or other preservatives)
0/0/0	0	0	0/0	0/0/0	0/0	0//0	0/0/	0/0/0	0/0			0/0/0	Other tropic rose wood(other than that treated with paint, stains, creosote or other preservatives)
													---Other
0/0/0	0	0	0/0	0/0/0	0/0	0//0	0/0/	0/0/0	0/0			0/0/0	Bulnesia sarmientoi log(paint, colorant, creosote or other preservative treatmentexcept)
0/0/0	0	0	0/0	0/0/0	0/0	0//0	0/0/	0/0/0	0/0			0/0/0	Other endangered tropic rough wood(other than that treated with paint, stains, creosote or other preservatives)
0/0/0	0	0	0/0	0/0/0	0/0	0//0	0/0/	0/0/0	0/0			0/0/0	Ohter tropical wood(the wood treated with paint, stains, creosote or other preservatives)
													-Other:
													--Of oak (Quercus spp.)
0/0/0	0	0	0/0	0/0/0	0/0	0//0	0/0/	0/0/0	0/0			0/0/0	Mongolia oak logs (paint, colorant, creosote or other preservative treatmentexcept)

税则号列		货品名称〔CIQ扩展编码及品名—T2表示见附表2〕	最惠(%)	暂定税率	普通	增值/消费	出口退税	计量单位	监管条件/特殊证件	检验检疫	对美关税	亚太上/下
4403.9100	90	其他栎木(橡木)原木(用油漆、着色剂、杂酚油或其他防腐剂处理的除外)〔999〕	0		8	9/	0	千克/立方米	8A/	PQ		
4403.9300		--水青冈木(山毛榉木),截面尺寸在15厘米及以上〔999〕	0		8	9/	0	千克/立方米	8A/	PQ		
4403.9400		--其他水青冈木(山毛榉木)〔999〕	0		8	9/	0	千克/立方米	8A/	PQ		
4403.9500		--桦木,截面尺寸在15厘米及以上										
4403.9500	10	濒危的桦木,最小截面尺寸在15厘米及以上(用油漆,着色剂,杂酚油或其他防腐剂处理的除外)〔999〕	0		8	9/	0	千克/立方米	8AF/	PQ	25	
4403.9500	90	其他桦木,最小截面尺寸在15厘米及以上(用油漆,着色剂,杂酚油或其他防腐剂处理的除外)〔999〕	0		8	9/	0	千克/立方米	8A/	PQ	25	
4403.9600		--其他桦木										
4403.9600	10	濒危的桦木,最小截面尺寸在15厘米及以下(用油漆,着色剂,杂酚油或其他防腐剂处理的除外)〔999〕	0		8	9/	0	千克/立方米	8AF/	PQ		
4403.9600	90	其他桦木,最小截面尺寸在15厘米及以下(用油漆,着色剂,杂酚油或其他防腐剂处理的除外)〔999〕	0		8	9/	0	千克/立方米	8A/	PQ		
4403.9700		--杨木〔999〕	0		8	9/	0	千克/立方米	8A/	PQ	25	
4403.9800		--桉木〔999〕	0		8	9/	0	千克/立方米	8A/	PQ	25	
		--其他:										
4403.9930		---红木,但税号4403.4980所列热带红木除外										
4403.9930	10	濒危红木原木,但税号4403.4980所列热带红木除外(用油漆,着色剂,杂酚油或其他防腐剂处理的除外)〔999〕	0		35	9/	0	千克/立方米	8AEF/	PQ		
4403.9930	90	其他红木原木,但税号4403.4980所列热带红木除外(用油漆,着色剂,杂酚油或其他防腐剂处理的除外)〔999〕	0		35	9/	0	千克/立方米	8A/	PQ		
4403.9940		---泡桐木〔999〕	0		8	9/	0	千克/立方米	8A/	PQ		
4403.9950		---水曲柳〔999〕	0		8	9/	0	千克/立方米	8AF/	PQ		
4403.9960		---北美硬阔叶木〔999〕	0		8	9/	0	千克/立方米	8A/	PQ		
4403.9980		---其他未列名的温带非针叶木										
4403.9980	10	其他未列名温带濒危非针叶木原木(用油漆、着色剂、杂酚油或其他防腐剂处理的除外)〔101加蓬榄木、非洲白梧桐木等原木,102白柳桉原木及其他柳桉原木,103羯布罗香木等原木,104安哥拉香桃花心木等原木,105其他非针叶原木〕	0		8	9/	0	千克/立方米	8AF/	PQ	25	
4403.9980	90	其他未列名温带非针叶木原木(用油漆、着色剂、杂酚油或其他防腐剂处理的除外)〔101加蓬榄木、非洲白梧桐木等原木,102白柳桉原木及其他柳桉原木,103羯布罗香木等原木,104安哥拉香桃花心木等原木,105其他非针叶原木〕	0		8	9/	0	千克/立方米	8A/	PQ	25	
4403.9990		---其他										
4403.9990	12	沉香木及拟沉香木原木(用油漆,着色剂,杂酚油或其他防腐剂处理的除外)〔999〕	0		8	9/	0	千克/立方米	8AEF/	PQ	25	
4403.9990	19	其他未列名濒危非针叶原木(用油漆、着色剂、杂酚油或其他防腐剂处理的除外)〔101加蓬榄木、非洲白梧桐木等原木,102白柳桉原木及其他柳桉原木,103羯布罗香木等原木,104安哥拉香桃花心木等原木,105其他非针叶原木〕	0		8	9/	0	千克/立方米	8AEF/	PQ	25	
4403.9990	90	其他未列名非针叶原木(用油漆、着色剂、杂酚油或其他防腐剂处理的除外)〔101加蓬榄木、非洲白梧桐木等原木,102白柳桉原木及其他柳桉原木,103羯布罗香木等原木,104安哥拉香桃花心木等原木,105其他非针叶原木〕	0		8	9/	0	千克/立方米	8A/	PQ	25	
44.04		**箍木;木劈条;已削尖但未经纵锯的木桩;粗加修整但未经车圆、弯曲或其他方式加工的木棒,适合制手杖、伞柄、工具把柄及类似品;木片条及类似品:**										
4404.1000		-针叶木的										
4404.1000	10	濒危针叶木的箍木等及类似品(包括木劈条、棒及类似品)〔999〕	6	0	50	13/	0	千克	ABFE/	PQ		
4404.1000	90	其他针叶木的箍木等及类似品(包括木劈条、棒及类似品)〔999〕	6	0	50	13/	0	千克	AB/	PQ		
4404.2000		-非针叶木的										
4404.2000	10	濒危非针叶木箍木等(包括木劈条、棒及类似品)〔999〕	6	0	50	13/	0	千克	ABFE/	PQ	20	

协定税率 %								RCEP		特惠税率 %			Article Description
东/冰/格	巴基斯坦	韩国	瑞士上/下	哥/秘/柬	澳/毛	新西/坡/智	中国港/澳/台	东盟及马来/澳/韩	日/新	亚太2国	老/柬/缅	98/97/95	
0/0/0	0	0	0/0	0/0/0	0/0	0//0	0/0/	0/0/0	0/0			0/0/0	Other oak (oak) log (paint, colorant, creosote or other preservative treatmentexcept)
0/0/0	0	0	0/0	0/0/0	0/0	0//0	0/0/	0/0/0	0/0			0/0/0	--Of beech (*Fagus spp.*), of which any cross-sectional dimension is 15cm or more
0/0/0	0	0	0/0	0/0/0	0/0	0//0	0/0/	0/0/0	0/0			0/0/0	--Of beech (*Fagus spp.*), other
													--Of birch (*Betula spp.*), of which any cross-sectional dimension is 15cm or more
0/0/0	0	0	0/0	0/0/0	0/0	0//0	0/0/	0/0/0	0/0			0/0/0	Of endangered birch (*Betula spp.*),(other than that treated with paint, stains, creosote or other preservatives) of which any cross-sectional di-mension is 15cm or more
0/0/0	0	0	0/0	0/0/0	0/0	0//0	0/0/	0/0/0	0/0			0/0/0	Of other birch (*Betula spp.*),(other than that treated with paint, stains, creosote or other preservatives) of which any cross-sectional di-mension is 15cm or more
													--Of birch (*Betula spp.*), other
0/0/0	0	0	0/0	0/0/0	0/0	0//0	0/0/	0/0/0	0/0			0/0/0	Of endangered birch (*Betula spp.*),(other than that treated with paint, stains, creosote or other preservatives) of which any cross-sectional di-mension is 15cm or less
0/0/0	0	0	0/0	0/0/0	0/0	0//0	0/0/	0/0/0	0/0			0/0/0	Of other birch (*Betula spp.*),(other than that treated with paint, stains, creosote or other preservatives) of which any cross-sectional di-mension is 15cm or less
0/0/0	0	0	0/0	0/0/0	0/0	0//0	0/0/	0/0/0	0/0			0/0/0	--Of poplar and aspen (*Populus spp.*)
0/0/0	0	0	0/0	0/0/0	0/0	0//0	0/0/	0/0/0	0/0			0/0/0	--Of eucalyptus (*Eucalyptus spp.*)
													--Other:
													---Of rosewood, other than tropical wood of Subheading 4403.4980
0/0/0	0	0	0/0	0/0/0	0/0	0//0	0/0/	0/0/0	0/0			0/0/0	Endangered rosewood, but excluding tropical rosewood of subheading No.4403.4980
0/0/0	0	0	0/0	0/0/0	0/0	0//0	0/0/	0/0/0	0/0			0/0/0	Ohter rosewood log, excluding tropical rosewood of subheading No.4403.4980(the wood treated with paint, stains, creosote or other preservatives)
0/0/0	0	0	0/0	0/0/0	0/0	0//0	0/0/	0/0/0	0/0			0/0/0	---Of Kiri (*Paulownia*)
0/0/0	0	0	0/0	0/0/0	0/0	0//0	0/0/	0/0/0	0/0			0/0/0	---Ash
0/0/0	0	0	0/0	0/0/0	0/0	0//0	0/0/	0/0/0	0/0			0/0/0	---North American hard wood
													---Other, temperate non-coniferous, not specified
0/0/0	0	0	0/0	0/0/0	0/0	0//0	0/0/	0/0/0	0/0			0/0/0	Other temperate zone endangered non-coniferous wood(other than the wood treated with paint, stains, creosote or other preservatives)not elsewhere specified or included
0/0/0	0	0	0/0	0/0/0	0/0	0//0	0/0/	0/0/0	0/0			0/0/0	Other temperate zone non-coniferous wood(other than the wood treated with paint, stains, creosote or other preservatives)not elsewhere specified or included
													---Other
0/0/0	0	0	0/0	0/0/0	0/0	0//0	0/0/	0/0/0	0/0			0/0/0	Chinese eaglewood and similar chinese eaglewood(other than the wood treated with paint, stains, creosote or other preservatives)
0/0/0	0	0	0/0	0/0/0	0/0	0//0	0/0/	0/0/0	0/0			0/0/0	Other endangered non-coniferous wood in the rough(other than the wood treated with paint, stains, creosote or other preservatives)
0/0/0	0	0	0/0	0/0/0	0/0	0//0	0/0/	0/0/0	0/0			0/0/0	Other non-coniferous wood in the rough(other than the wood treated with paint, stains, creosote or other preservatives) not elsewhere specified or included
													Hoopwood; split poles; piles, pickets and stakes of wood, pointed but not sawn lengthwise; wooden sticks, roughly trimmed but not turned, bent or otherwise worked, suitable for the manufacture of walking-sticks, umbrellas, tool handles or the like; chipwood and the like:
													-Coniferous
0/0/	2	0	0/0	0/0/0	0/0	0/0/0	0/0/	0/0/0	7.3/0			0/0/0	Hoopwood; split poles; wooden sticks or the like; of endangered coniferous wood
0/0/	2	0	0/0	0/0/0	0/0	0/0/0	0/0/	0/0/0	7.3/0			0/0/0	Other hoopwood; split poles; wooden sticks or the like; of coniferous wood
													-Non-coniferous
0/0/	2	0	0/0	0/0/0	0/0	0/0/0	0/0/	0/0/0	7.3/0			0/0/0	Hoopwood; split poles, wooden sticks or the like, of endangered non-coniferous wood

税则号列		货品名称〔CIQ 扩展编码及品名—T2 表示见附表 2〕	最惠(%)	暂定税率	普通	增值/消费	出口退税	计量单位	监管条件/特殊证件	检验检疫	对美关税	亚太上/下
4404.2000	90	其他非针叶木箍木等(包括木劈条、棒及类似品)〔101 其他木制品,102 其他碎木料、锯末、刨花〕	6	0	50	13/	0	千克	AB/	PQ	20	
44.05		**木丝;木粉:**										
4405.0000		木丝;木粉〔999〕	6	0	40	13/	0	千克	AB/	PQ	25	
44.06		**铁道及电车道枕木:**										
		-未浸渍										
4406.1100		--针叶木〔999〕	0		14	13/	0	千克/立方米	4ABxy/	PQ		
4406.1200		--非针叶木〔999〕	0		14	13/	0	千克/立方米	4ABxy/	PQ		
		-其他:										
4406.9100		--针叶木										
4406.9100	10	濒危已浸渍针叶木铁道及电车道枕木〔999〕	0		14	13/	0	千克/立方米	FE/		5	
4406.9100	90	其他已浸渍的针叶木铁道及电车道枕木〔999〕	0		14	13/	0	千克/立方米	/		5	
4406.9200		--非针叶木										
4406.9200	10	濒危已浸渍非针叶木铁道及电车道枕木〔999〕	0		14	13/	0	千克/立方米	FE/			
4406.9200	90	其他已浸渍的非针叶木铁道及电车道枕木〔999〕	0		14	13/	0	千克/立方米	/			
44.07		**经纵锯、纵切、刨切或旋切的木材,不论是否刨平、砂光或端部接合,厚度超过 6 毫米:**										
		-针叶木:										
		--松木(松属):										
4407.1110		---红松和樟子松										
4407.1110	11	端部接合的红松厚板材(经纵锯、纵切、刨切或旋切的,厚度超过 6mm)〔999〕	0		14	13/	0	千克/立方米	ABEF/	PQ	25	
4407.1110	19	端部接合的樟子松厚板材(经纵锯、纵切、刨切或旋切的,厚度超过 6mm)〔999〕	0		14	13/	0	千克/立方米	AB/	PQ	25	
4407.1110	91	非端部接合的红松厚板材(经纵锯、纵切、刨切或旋切的,厚度超过 6mm)〔999〕	0		14	13/	0	千克/立方米	4ABEFxy/	PQ	25	
4407.1110	99	非端部接合的樟子松厚板材(经纵锯、纵切、刨切或旋切的,厚度超过 6mm)〔999〕	0		14	13/	0	千克/立方米	4ABxy/	PQ	25	
4407.1120		---辐射松										
4407.1120	10	端部接合的辐射松厚板材(经纵锯、纵切、刨切或旋切的,厚度超过 6mm)〔999〕	0		14	13/	0	千克/立方米	AB/	PQ	25	
4407.1120	90	非端部接合的辐射松厚板材(经纵锯、纵切、刨切或旋切的,厚度超过 6mm)〔999〕	0		14	13/	0	千克/立方米	4ABxy/	PQ	25	
4407.1190		---其他:										
4407.1190	11	端部接合其他濒危松木厚板材(经纵锯、纵切、刨切或旋切的,厚度超过 6mm)〔999〕	0		14	13/	0	千克/立方米	ABEF/	PQ	25	
4407.1190	19	端部接合其他松木厚板材(经纵锯、纵切、刨切或旋切的,厚度超过 6mm)〔999〕	0		14	13/	0	千克/立方米	AB/	PQ	25	
4407.1190	91	非端部接合其他濒危松木厚板材(经纵锯、纵切、刨切或旋切的,厚度超过 6mm)〔999〕	0		14	13/	0	千克/立方米	4ABEFxy/	PQ	25	
4407.1190	99	非端部接合的其他松木厚板材(经纵锯、纵切、刨切或旋切的,厚度超过 6mm)〔999〕	0		14	13/	0	千克/立方米	4ABxy/	PQ	25	
4407.1200		--冷杉及云杉										
4407.1200	11	端部接合的濒危云杉及冷杉厚板材(经纵锯、纵切、刨切或旋切的,厚度超过 6mm)〔999〕	0		14	13/	0	千克/立方米	ABEF/	PQ	25	
4407.1200	19	端部接合的其他云杉及冷杉厚板材(经纵锯、纵切、刨切或旋切的,厚度超过 6mm)〔999〕	0		14	13/	0	千克/立方米	AB/	PQ	25	
4407.1200	91	非端部接合濒危云杉及冷杉厚板材(经纵锯、纵切、刨切或旋切的,厚度超过 6mm)〔999〕	0		14	13/	0	千克/立方米	4ABEFxy/	PQ	25	
4407.1200	99	非端部接合其他云杉及冷杉厚板材(经纵锯、纵切、刨切或旋切的,厚度超过 6mm)〔999〕	0		14	13/	0	千克/立方米	4ABxy/	PQ	25	
4407.1300		--云杉—松木—冷杉										
4407.1300	11	端部接合的濒危云杉—松木—冷杉厚板材(经纵锯、纵切、刨切或旋切的,厚度超过 6mm)〔999〕	0		14	13/	0	千克/立方米	ABEF/	PQ	20	
4407.1300	19	端部接合其他云杉—松木—冷杉厚板材(经纵锯、纵切、刨切或旋切的,厚度超过 6mm)〔999〕	0		14	13/	0	千克/立方米	AB/	PQ	20	

协定税率 %								RCEP		特惠税率 %			Article Description
东/冰/格	巴基斯坦	韩国	瑞士上/下	哥/秘/柬	澳/毛	新西/坡/智	中国港/澳/台	东盟及马来/澳/韩	日/新	亚太2国	老/柬/缅	98/97/95	
0/0/	2	0	0/0	0/0/0	0/0	0/0/0	0/0/	0/0/0	7.3/0			0/0/0	Other hoopwood; split poles, wooden sticks or the like, of non-coniferous wood
													Wood wool; wood flour:
0/0/	2	0	0/0	0/0/0	0/0	0/0/0	0/0/	0/0/0	7.3/0			0/0/0	Wood wool; wood flour
													Railway or tramway sleepers (cross-ties) of wood:
													-Not impregnated
0/0/0	0	0	0/0	0/0/0	0/0	0//0	0/0/	0/0/0	0/0			0/0/0	--Coniferous
0/0/0	0	0	0/0	0/0/0	0/0	0//0	0/0/	0/0/0	0/0			0/0/0	--Non-coniferous
													-Other:
													--Coniferous
0/0/0	0	0	0/0	0/0/0	0/0	0//0	0/0/	0/0/0	0/0			0/0/0	Railway or tramway sleepers(crossties)of endangered Coniferous wood, impregnated
0/0/0	0	0	0/0	0/0/0	0/0	0//0	0/0/	0/0/0	0/0			0/0/0	Railway or tramway sleepers(crossties) of other Coniferous wood, impregnated
													--Non-coniferous
0/0/0	0	0	0/0	0/0/0	0/0	0//0	0/0/	0/0/0	0/0			0/0/0	Railway or tramway sleepers(crossties) of endangered non-Coniferous wood, impregnated
0/0/0	0	0	0/0	0/0/0	0/0	0//0	0/0/	0/0/0	0/0			0/0/0	Railway or tramway sleepers(crossties)of other non-Coniferous wood, impregnated
													Wood sawn or chipped lengthwise, sliced or peeled, whether or not planed, sanded or end-jointed, of a thickness exceeding 6 mm:
													-Coniferous:
													--Of pine (*Pinus spp.*):
													---Korean pine and Mongolian scotch pine
0/0/0	0	0	0/0	0/0/0	0/0	0//0	0/0/	0/0/0	0/0			0/0/0	Korean pine wood, sawn or chipped lengthwise, sliced or peeled, end-jointed, of a thickness exceeding 6mm
0/0/0	0	0	0/0	0/0/0	0/0	0//0	0/0/	0/0/0	0/0			0/0/0	Mongolian scotch pine wood sawn or chipped lengthwise, sliced or peeled, end-jointed, of a thickness exceeding 6mm
0/0/0	0	0	0/0	0/0/0	0/0	0//0	0/0/	0/0/0	0/0			0/0/0	Korean pine and Mongolian scotch pine wood, sawn or chipped lengthwise, sliced or peeled, not end-jointed, of a thickness exceeding 6mm
0/0/0	0	0	0/0	0/0/0	0/0	0//0	0/0/	0/0/0	0/0			0/0/0	Wood sawn or chipped lengthwise, sliced or peeled, not end jointed, of Mongolian scocth pine, of a thinkness exceeding 6mm
													---Rediata pine
0/0/0	0	0	0/0	0/0/0	0/0	0//0	0/0/	0/0/0	0/0			0/0/0	Radiata pine wood sawn or chipped lengthwise, sliced or peeled, end-jointed, of a thickness exceeding 6mm
0/0/0	0	0	0/0	0/0/0	0/0	0//0	0/0/	0/0/0	0/0			0/0/0	Radiata pine wood sawn or chipped lengthwise, sliced or peeled, end-jointed, of a thickness exceeding 6mm
													---Other:
0/0/0	0	0	0/0	0/0/0	0/0	0//0	0/0/	0/0/0	0/0			0/0/0	Other endangered spine wood of conifer, sawn or chipped lengthwise, sliced or peeled, end-jointed, of a thickness exceeding 6mm
0/0/0	0	0	0/0	0/0/0	0/0	0//0	0/0/	0/0/0	0/0			0/0/0	Other pine wood of conifeo sawn or chipped lengthwise, sliced or peeled, end-jointed, of a thickness exceeding 6mm
0/0/0	0	0	0/0	0/0/0	0/0	0//0	0/0/	0/0/0	0/0			0/0/0	Other endangered pine wood sawn or chipped lengthwise, sliced or peeled, end-jointed, of a thickness exceeding 6mm
0/0/0	0	0	0/0	0/0/0	0/0	0//0	0/0/	0/0/0	0/0			0/0/0	Other pine wood, sawn or chipped lengthwise, sliced or peeled, not end-jointed, of a thickness exceeding 6mm
													--Of fir (*Abies spp.*) and sprue (*Picea spp.*)
0/0/0	0	0	0/0	0/0/0	0/0	0//0	0/0/	0/0/0	0/0			0/0/0	Endangered spruce and fir, sawn or chipped lengthwise, sliced or peeled, end-jointed, of a thickness exceeding 6mm
0/0/0	0	0	0/0	0/0/0	0/0	0//0	0/0/	0/0/0	0/0			0/0/0	Other spruce and fir, sawn or chipped lengthwise, sliced or peeled, end-jointed, of a thickness exceeding 6mm
0/0/0	0	0	0/0	0/0/0	0/0	0//0	0/0/	0/0/0	0/0			0/0/0	Endangered spruce and fir, sawn or chipped lengthwise, sliced or peeled, not end-jointed, of a thickness exceeding 6mm
0/0/0	0	0	0/0	0/0/0	0/0	0//0	0/0/	0/0/0	0/0			0/0/0	Other spruce and fir, sawn or chipped lengthwise, sliced or peeled, not end-jointed, of a thickness exceeding 6mm
													--spruce (Picea spp.), pine (Pinus spp.) and fir (Abies spp.)
0/0/0	0	0	0/0	0/0/0	0/0	0//0	0/0/	0/0/0	0/0			0/0/0	Endangered spruce pine fir thick plate with end joint (more than 6mm thick after longitudinal sawing, longitudinal cutting, planing or rotary cutting)
0/0/0	0	0	0/0	0/0/0	0/0	0//0	0/0/	0/0/0	0/0			0/0/0	Joint other spruce pine fir thick plates at the ends (more than 6mm thick after longitudinal sawing, longitudinal cutting, planing or rotary cutting)

税则号列		货品名称〔CIQ 扩展编码及品名—T2 表示见附表 2〕	最惠(%)	暂定税率	普通	增值/消费	出口退税	计量单位	监管条件/特殊证件	检验检疫	对美关税	亚太上/下
4407.1300	91	非端部接合的濒危云杉—松木—冷杉厚板材(经纵锯、纵切、刨切或旋切的,厚度超过 6mm)〔999〕	0		14	13/	0	千克/立方米	ABEF/	PQ	20	
4407.1300	99	非端部接合的其他云杉—松木—冷杉厚板材(经纵锯、纵切、刨切或旋切的,厚度超过 6mm)〔999〕	0		14	13/	0	千克/立方米	AB/	PQ	20	
4407.1400		--铁杉—冷杉										
4407.1400	11	端部接合的濒危铁杉—冷杉厚板材(经纵锯、纵切、刨切或旋切的,厚度超过 6mm)〔999〕	0		14	13/	0	千克/立方米	ABEF/	PQ	20	
4407.1400	19	端部接合其他铁杉—冷杉厚板材(经纵锯、纵切、刨切或旋切的,厚度超过 6mm)〔999〕	0		14	13/	0	千克/立方米	AB/	PQ	20	
4407.1400	91	非端部接合的濒危铁杉—冷杉厚板材(经纵锯、纵切、刨切或旋切的,厚度超过 6mm)〔999〕	0		14	13/	0	千克/立方米	ABEF/	PQ	20	
4407.1400	99	非端部接合的其他铁杉—冷杉厚板材(经纵锯、纵切、刨切或旋切的,厚度超过 6mm)〔999〕	0		14	13/	0	千克/立方米	AB/	PQ	20	
		--其他:										
4407.1910		---花旗松										
4407.1910	10	端部接合的花旗松厚板材(经纵锯、纵切、刨切或旋切的,厚度超过 6mm)〔999〕	0		14	13/	0	千克/立方米	AB/	PQ	20	
4407.1910	90	非端部接合的花旗松厚板材(经纵锯、纵切、刨切或旋切的,厚度超过 6mm)〔999〕	0		14	13/	0	千克/立方米	4ABxy/	PQ	20	
4407.1990		---其他										
4407.1990	11	端部接合其他濒危针叶木厚板材(经纵锯、纵切、刨切或旋切的,厚度超过 6mm)〔999〕	0		14	13/	0	千克/立方米	ABEF/	PQ	25	
4407.1990	19	端部接合其他针叶木厚板材(经纵锯、纵切、刨切或旋切的,厚度超过 6mm)〔999〕	0		14	13/	0	千克/立方米	AB/	PQ	25	
4407.1990	91	非端部接合其他濒危针叶木厚板材(经纵锯、纵切、刨切或旋切的,厚度超过 6mm)〔999〕	0		14	13/	0	千克/立方米	4ABEFxy/	PQ	25	
4407.1990	99	非端部接合的其他针叶木厚板材(经纵锯、纵切、刨切或旋切的,厚度超过 6mm)〔999〕	0		14	13/	0	千克/立方米	4ABxy/	PQ	25	
		-热带木:										
4407.2100		--美洲桃花心木										
4407.2100	10	端部接合美洲桃花心木(经纵锯、纵切、刨切或旋切的,厚度超过 6mm)〔999〕	0		14	13/	0	千克/立方米	FEAB/	PQ		
4407.2100	90	非端部接合美洲桃花心木(经纵锯、纵切、刨切或旋切的,厚度超过 6mm)〔999〕	0		14	13/	0	千克/立方米	4ABEFxy/	PQ		
4407.2200		--苏里南肉豆蔻木、细孔绿心樟及美洲轻木										
4407.2200	10	端部接合的苏里南肉豆蔻木、细孔绿心樟及美洲轻木(经纵锯、纵切、刨切或旋切的,厚度超过 6mm)〔999〕	0		14	13/	0	千克/立方米	AB/	PQ		
4407.2200	90	非端部接合的苏里南肉豆蔻木、细孔绿心樟及美洲轻木(经纵锯、纵切、刨切或旋切的,厚度超过 6mm)〔999〕	0		14	13/	0	千克/立方米	4ABxy/	PQ		
4407.2300		--柚木										
4407.2300	10	端部接合的柚木板材(经纵锯、纵切、刨切或旋切的,厚度超过 6mm)〔999〕	0		40	13/	0	千克/立方米	AB/	PQ	25	
4407.2300	90	非端部接合的柚木板材(经纵锯、纵切、刨切或旋切的,厚度超过 6mm)〔999〕	0		40	13/	0	千克/立方米	4ABxy/	PQ	25	
4407.2500		--深红色红柳桉木、浅红色红柳桉木及巴梣红柳桉木										
4407.2500	10	端部接合的红柳桉木板材(指深红色、浅红色及巴梣红柳桉木,厚度超过 6mm)〔999〕	0		14	13/	0	千克/立方米	AB/	PQ		
4407.2500	90	非端部接合的红柳桉木板材(指深红色、浅红色及巴梣红柳桉木,经纵锯、纵切、刨切或旋切的,厚度超过 6mm)〔999〕	0		14	13/	0	千克/立方米	y4xAB/	PQ		
4407.2600		--白柳桉木、白色红柳桉木、白色柳桉木、黄色红柳桉木及阿兰木										
4407.2600	10	端部接合的白柳桉,其他柳桉木和阿兰木板材(经纵锯、纵切、刨切或旋切的,厚度超过 6mm)〔999〕	0		14	13/	0	千克/立方米	AB/	PQ		
4407.2600	90	非端部接合的白柳桉,其他柳桉木和阿兰木板材(经纵锯、纵切、刨切或旋切的,厚度超过 6mm)〔999〕	0		14	13/	0	千克/立方米	y4xAB/	PQ		
4407.2700		--沙比利										

协定税率 %								RCEP		特惠税率 %			Article Description
东/冰/格	巴基斯坦	韩国	瑞士 上/下	哥/秘/柬	澳/毛	新西/坡/智	中国港/澳/台	东盟及马来/澳/韩	日/新	亚太2国	老/柬/缅	98/97/95	
0/0/0	0	0	0/0	0/0/0	0/0	0//0	0/0/	0/0/0	0/0			0/0/0	Endangered spruce pine fir thick plate (sawn, sliced, planed or spun, thickness exceeding 6mm) not end jointed
0/0/0	0	0	0/0	0/0/0	0/0	0//0	0/0/	0/0/0	0/0			0/0/0	Other spruce pine fir thick plates (sawn, sliced, planed or peeled, more than 6mm thick) not end jointed
													--Western hemlock (Tsuga heterophylla) and fir (Abies spp.)
0/0/0	0	0	0/0	0/0/0	0/0	0//0	0/0/	0/0/0	0/0			0/0/0	Endangered hemlock fir thick plate with end joint (more than 6mm thick after longitudinal sawing, longitudinal cutting, planing or rotary cutting)
0/0/0	0	0	0/0	0/0/0	0/0	0//0	0/0/	0/0/0	0/0			0/0/0	Join other hemlock fir thick plates at the end (more than 6mm thick after longitudinal sawing, longitudinal cutting, planing or rotary cutting)
0/0/0	0	0	0/0	0/0/0	0/0	0//0	0/0/	0/0/0	0/0			0/0/0	Endangered hemlock fir thick plate (sawn, sliced, planed or rotary cut, thickness exceeding 6mm)
0/0/0	0	0	0/0	0/0/0	0/0	0//0	0/0/	0/0/0	0/0			0/0/0	Other hemlock fir thick plates (sawn, sliced, planed or peeled, more than 6mm thick) not end jointed
													--Other:
													---Douglas fir
0/0/0	0	0	0/0	0/0/0	0/0	0//0	0/0/	0/0/0	0/0		//	0/0/0	End jointed thick board of Douglas fir (sawn, cut, planed or peeled, thickness over 6 mm)
0/0/0	0	0	0/0	0/0/0	0/0	0//0	0/0/	0/0/0	0/0		//	0/0/0	Thick plates of Douglas fir not end jointed (sawn, cut, planed or peeled, thickness over 6 mm)
													---Other
0/0/0	0	0	0/0	0/0/0	0/0	0//0	0/0/	0/0/0	0/0		//	0/0/0	End joining of other endangered softwood thick plates (sawn, sliced, sliced or peeled, thickness over 6 mm)
0/0/0	0	0	0/0	0/0/0	0/0	0//0	0/0/	0/0/0	0/0		//	0/0/0	End joining of other softwood thick plates (sawn, sliced, sliced or peeled, thickness over 6 mm)
0/0/0	0	0	0/0	0/0/0	0/0	0//0	0/0/	0/0/0	0/0		//	0/0/0	Non end joining other endangered softwood thick plates(sawing, slitting, planing or rotary cutting, thickness more than 6 mm)
0/0/0	0	0	0/0	0/0/0	0/0	0//0	0/0/	0/0/0	0/0		//	0/0/0	Other softwood thicknesses not end jointed (sawn, cut, planed or peeled, thickness exceeding 6 mm)
													-Of tropical wood:
													--Mahogany (Swietenia spp.)
0/0/0	0	0	0/0	0/0/0	0/0	0//0	0/0/	0/0/0	0/0			0/0/0	Wood sawn or chipped lengthwise, sliced or peeled, of mashogany (swietenia spp.), end-jointed, thickness>6mm
0/0/0	0	0	0/0	0/0/0	0/0	0//0	0/0/	0/0/0	0/0			0/0/0	Wood sawn or chipped lengthwise, sliced or peeled, of mashogany (swietenia spp.), not-end-jointed, thickness>6mm
													--Virola, Imbuia and Balsa
0/0/0	0	0	0/0	0/0/0	0/0	0//0	0/0/	0/0/0	0/0			0/0/0	Wood sawn or chipped lengthwise, sliced or peeled, of virola, embuia and American light wood, end-jointed, thickness>6mm
0/0/0	0	0	0/0	0/0/0	0/0	0//0	0/0/	0/0/0	0/0			0/0/0	Wood sawn or chipped lengthwise, sliced or peeled, of virola, embuia and American light wood, not end-jointed
													--Teak
0/0/0	0	0	0/0	0/0/0	0/0	0//0	0/0/	0/0/0	0/0			0/0/0	Teak board with end joint (sawn, sliced, planed or rotary cut, thickness exceeding 6mm)
0/0/0	0	0	0/0	0/0/0	0/0	0//0	0/0/	0/0/0	0/0			0/0/0	Teak board not end jointed (sawn, sliced, planed or peeled, thickness exceeding 6mm)
													--Dark Red Meranti, Light Red Meranti and Meranti Bakau
0/0/0	0	0	0/0	0/0/0	0/0	0//0	0/0/	0/0/0	0/0			0/0/0	Wood sawn or chipped lengthwise, sliced or peeled, of Dark Red Meranti, Light Red Meranti and Meranti Bakau, end-jointed, thickness>6mm
0/0/0	0	0	0/0	0/0/0	0/0	0//0	0/0/	0/0/0	0/0			0/0/0	Wood sawn or chipped lengthwise, sliced or peeled, of Dark Red Meranti, Light Red Meranti and Meranti Bakau, not end-jointed, thickness>6mm
													--White Lauan, White Meranti, White Seraya, Yellow Meranti and Alan
0/0/0	0	0	0/0	0/0/0	0/0	0//0	0/0/	0/0/0	0/0			0/0/0	Wood sawn or chipped lengthwise, sliced or peeled, of White Lauan, White Meranti, White Seraya, Yellow Meranti and Alan, end-jointed, thickness>6mm
0/0/0	0	0	0/0	0/0/0	0/0	0//0	0/0/	0/0/0	0/0			0/0/0	Wood sawn or chipped lengthwise, sliced or peeled, of White Lauan, White Meranti, White Seraya, Yellow Meranti and Alan, not end-jointed, thickness>6mm
													--Sapelli

税则号列	货品名称〔CIQ 扩展编码及品名—T2 表示见附表 2〕	最惠(%)	暂定税率	普通	增值/消费	出口退税	计量单位	监管条件/特殊证件	检验检疫	对美关税	亚太上/下
4407.2700 10	端部接合的沙比利木板材(经纵锯、纵切、刨切或旋切的,厚度超过 6mm)〔999〕	0		40	13/	0	千克/立方米	AB/	PQ		
4407.2700 90	非端部接合的沙比利木板材(经纵锯、纵切、刨切或旋切的,厚度超过 6mm)〔999〕	0		40	13/	0	千克/立方米	4ABxy/	PQ		
4407.2800	--伊罗科木										
4407.2800 10	端部接合的伊罗科木板材(经纵锯、纵切、刨切或旋切的,厚度超过 6mm)〔999〕	0		14	13/	0	千克/立方米	AB/	PQ		
4407.2800 90	非端部接合的伊罗科木板材(经纵锯、纵切、刨切或旋切的,厚度超过 6mm)〔999〕	0		14	13/	0	千克/立方米	4ABxy/	PQ		
	--其他:										
4407.2920	---非洲桃花心木										
4407.2920 10	端部接合的非洲桃花心木板材(经纵锯、纵切、刨切或旋切的,厚度超过 6mm)〔999〕	0		40	13/	0	千克/立方米	AB/	PQ		
4407.2920 90	非端部接合的非洲桃花心木板材(经纵锯、纵切、刨切或旋切的,厚度超过 6mm)〔999〕	0		40	13/	0	千克/立方米	AB/	PQ		
4407.2930	---波罗格										
4407.2930 10	端部接合的波罗格Merban板材(经纵锯、纵切、刨切或旋切的,厚度超过 6mm)〔999〕	0		40	13/	0	千克/立方米	AB/	PQ	25	
4407.2930 90	非端部接合的波罗格 Merban 板材(经纵锯、纵切、刨切或旋切的,厚度超过 6mm)〔999〕	0		40	13/	0	千克/立方米	AB/	PQ	25	
4407.2940	---红木										
4407.2940 11	端部接合濒危热带红木厚板材(经纵锯、纵切、刨切或旋切的,厚度超过 6mm)〔999〕	0		40	13/	0	千克/立方米	FEAB/	PQ		
4407.2940 19	端部接合其他热带红木厚板材(经纵锯、纵切、刨切或旋切的,厚度超过 6mm)〔999〕	0		40	13/	0	千克/立方米	AB/	PQ		
4407.2940 91	非端部接合濒危热带红木厚板材(经纵锯、纵切、刨切或旋切的,厚度超过 6mm)〔999〕	0		40	13/	0	千克/立方米	4ABEFxy/	PQ		
4407.2940 99	非端部接合其他热带红木厚板材(经纵锯、纵切、刨切或旋切的,厚度超过 6mm)〔999〕	0		40	13/	0	千克/立方米	4ABxy/	PQ		
4407.2990	---其他										
4407.2990 11	端部接合拉敏木厚板材(经纵锯、纵切、刨切或旋切的,厚度超过 6mm)〔999〕	0		14	13/	0	千克/立方米	FEAB/	PQ	25	
4407.2990 12	端部接合的南美蒺藜木(玉檀木)厚板材(经纵锯、纵切、刨切或旋切的,厚度超过 6mm)〔101〕	0		14	13/	0	千克/立方米	FEAB/	PQ	25	
4407.2990 13	端部接合其他未列名濒危热带木厚板材(经纵锯、纵切、刨切或旋切的,厚度超过 6mm)〔999〕	0		14	13/	0	千克/立方米	FEAB/	PQ	25	
4407.2990 19	端部接合其他未列名热带木厚板材(经纵锯、纵切、刨切或旋切的,厚度超过 6mm)〔101〕	0		14	13/	0	千克/立方米	AB/	PQ	25	
4407.2990 91	非端部接合的南美蒺藜木(玉檀木)厚板材(经纵锯、纵切、刨切或旋切的,厚度超过 6mm)〔101〕	0		14	13/	0	千克/立方米	y4xAFEB/	PQ	25	
4407.2990 92	非端部接合其他未列名濒危热带木板材(经纵锯、纵切、刨切或旋切的,厚度超过 6mm)〔999〕	0		14	13/	0	千克/立方米	y4xAFEB/	PQ	25	
4407.2990 99	非端部接合其他未列名热带木板材(经纵锯、纵切、刨切或旋切的,厚度超过 6mm)[T2]	0		14	13/	0	千克/立方米	y4xAB/	PQ	25	
	-其他:										
4407.9100	--栎木(橡木)										
4407.9100 11	端部接合的蒙古栎厚板材(经纵锯、纵切、刨切或旋切的,厚度>6 毫米)〔999〕	0		14	13/	0	千克/立方米	ABEF/	PQ	25	
4407.9100 19	端部接合的其他栎木(橡木)厚板材(经纵锯、纵切、刨切或旋切的,厚度超过 6mm)〔999〕	0		14	13/	0	千克/立方米	AB/	PQ		
4407.9100 91	非端部接合的蒙古栎厚板材(经纵锯、纵切、刨切或旋切的,厚度>6 毫米)〔999〕	0		14	13/	0	千克/立方米	4ABEFxy/	PQ	25	
4407.9100 99	非端部接合的其他栎木(橡木)厚板材(经纵锯、纵切、刨切或旋切的,厚度超过 6mm)〔999〕	0		14	13/	0	千克/立方米	y4xAB/	PQ		
4407.9200	--水青冈木(山毛榉木)										
4407.9200 10	端部接合的水青冈木(山毛榉木)厚板材(经纵锯、纵切、刨切或旋切的,厚度超过 6mm)〔999〕	0		14	13/	0	千克/立方米	ABE/	PQ	25	
4407.9200 90	非端部接合的水青冈木(山毛榉木)厚板材(经纵锯、纵切、刨切或旋切的,厚度超过 6mm)〔999〕	0		14	13/	0	千克/立方米	4ABExy/	PQ	25	
4407.9300	--槭木(枫木)										
4407.9300 10	端部接合的槭木(枫木)厚板材(经纵锯、纵切、刨切或旋切,厚度超过 6mm)〔999〕	0		14	13/	0	千克/立方米	AB/	PQ	5	
4407.9300 90	非端部接合的槭木(枫木)厚板材(经纵锯、纵切、刨切或旋切,厚度超过 6mm)〔999〕	0		14	13/	0	千克/立方米	4ABxy/	PQ	5	

协定税率 %								RCEP		特惠税率 %			Article Description
东/冰/格	巴基斯坦	韩国	瑞士 上/下	哥/秘/柬	澳/毛	新西/坡/智	中国港/澳/台	东盟及马来/澳/韩	日/新	亚太2国	老/柬/缅	98/97/95	
0/0/0	0	0	0/0	0/0/0	0/0	0//0	0/0/	0/0/0	0/0			0/0/0	Wood sawn or chipped lengihwise,sliced or peeled,of sapelli, end-jointed,thinkness>6mm
0/0/0	0	0	0/0	0/0/0	0/0	0//0	0/0/	0/0/0	0/0			0/0/0	Wood sawn or chipped lengthwise,sliced or peeled,of sapelli, not end-jointed,thinkness>6mm
													--Iroko
0/0/0	0	0	0/0	0/0/0	0/0	0//0	0/0/	0/0/0	0/0			0/0/0	Wood sawn or chipped lengthwise,sliced or peeled,of Iroko, end-jointed,thickness>6mm
0/0/0	0	0	0/0	0/0/0	0/0	0//0	0/0/	0/0/0	0/0			0/0/0	Wood sawn or chipped lengthwise,sliced or peeled,of Iroko, not end-jointed,thickness>6mm
													--Other:
													---Acajou
0/0/0	0	0	0/0	0/0/0	0/0	0//0	0/0/	0/0/0	0/0			0/0/0	Wood sawn or chipped lengthwise, sliced or peeled, of acajou, end-jointed, thickness>6mm
0/0/0	0	0	0/0	0/0/0	0/0	0//0	0/0/	0/0/0	0/0			0/0/0	Wood sawn or chipped lengthwise, sliced or peeled, of acajou, not end-jointed, thickness>6mm
													---Merban
0/0/0	0	0	0/0	0/0/0	0/0	0//0	0/0/	0/0/0	0/0			0/0/0	Wood sawn or chipped lengthwise, sliced or peeled, of merban, end-jointed, thickness>6mm
0/0/0	0	0	0/0	0/0/0	0/0	0//0	0/0/	0/0/0	0/0			0/0/0	Wood sawn or chipped lengthwise, sliced or peeled, of merban, not end-jointed, thickness>6mm
													---Of rosewood
0/0/0	0	0	0/0	0/0/0	0/0	0//0	0/0/	0/0/0	0/0			0/0/0	Endangered tropical rosewood, sawn or chipped lengthwise, sliced or peeled, end-jointed, of a thickness exceeding 6mm
0/0/0	0	0	0/0	0/0/0	0/0	0//0	0/0/	0/0/0	0/0			0/0/0	Other tropical rosewood, sawn or chipped lengthwise, sliced or peeled, end-jointed, of a thickness exceeding 6mm
0/0/0	0	0	0/0	0/0/0	0/0	0//0	0/0/	0/0/0	0/0			0/0/0	Endangered tropical rosewood, sawn or chipped lengthwise, sliced or peeled, not end-jointed, of a thickness exceeding 6mm
0/0/0	0	0	0/0	0/0/0	0/0	0//0	0/0/	0/0/0	0/0			0/0/0	Other tropical rosewood, sawn or chipped lengthwise, sliced or peeled, not end-jointed, of a thickness exceeding 6mm
													---Other
0/0/0	0	0	0/0	0/0/0	0/0	0//0	0/0/	0/0/0	0/0			0/0/0	Wood sawn or chipped lengthwise, sliced or peeled, of Ramin wood, end-jointed, thickness>6mm
0/0/0	0	0	0/0	0/0/0	0/0	0//0	0/0/	0/0/0	0/0			0/0/0	Wood sawn or chipped lengthwise,sliced or peeled,of bulnesia sarmientoi,end-jointed
0/0/0	0	0	0/0	0/0/0	0/0	0//0	0/0/	0/0/0	0/0			0/0/0	Endangered tropical wood, sawn or chipped lengthwise, not elsewhere specified or included,sliced or peeled, end-jointed, of a thickness exceeding 6mm
0/0/0	0	0	0/0	0/0/0	0/0	0//0	0/0/	0/0/0	0/0			0/0/0	wood sawn or chipped lengthwise , sliced or peeled , of other tropical wood,not elsewhere specified, endjointed , thicknese >6mm
0/0/0	0	0	0/0	0/0/0	0/0	0//0	0/0/	0/0/0	0/0			0/0/0	Wood sawn or chipped lengthwise,sliced or peeled,of bulnesia sarmientoi,not end-jointed
0/0/0	0	0	0/0	0/0/0	0/0	0//0	0/0/	0/0/0	0/0			0/0/0	Endangered tropical wood, sawn or chipped lengthwise, not elsewhere specified or included, sliced or peeled, not end-jointed, of a thickness exceeding 6mm
0/0/0	0	0	0/0	0/0/0	0/0	0//0	0/0/	0/0/0	0/0			0/0/0	Wood sawn or chipped lengthwise,sliced or peeled,of other tropical wood,not elsewhere specified,not end-jointed
													-Other:
													--Of oak (*Quercus spp.*)
0/0/0	0	0	0/0	0/0/0	0/0	0//0	0/0/	0/0/0	0/0			0/0/0	Mongolia oak planks end joining (sawn or chipped lengthwise, sliced or peeled,the thickness of >6 mm)
0/0/0	0	0	0/0	0/0/0	0/0	0//0	0/0/	0/0/0	0/0			0/0/0	Wood sawn or chipped lengthwise, sliced or peeled, of oak (*Quercus spp.*), end-jointed, thickness>6mm
0/0/0	0	0	0/0	0/0/0	0/0	0//0	0/0/	0/0/0	0/0			0/0/0	Mongolia oak planks - end joining (sawn or chipped lengthwise, sliced or peeled,the thickness of >6 mm)
0/0/0	0	0	0/0	0/0/0	0/0	0//0	0/0/	0/0/0	0/0			0/0/0	Wood sawn or chipped lengthwise, sliced or peeled, of oak (*Quercus spp.*), not end-jointed, thickness>6mm
													--Of beech (*Fagus spp.*)
0/0/0	0	0	0/0	0/0/0	0/0	0//0	0/0/	0/0/0	0/0			0/0/0	Beech(*Fagus spp.*)wood sawn or chipped lengthwise, sliced or peeled, end-jointed, of a thicknessthicknese >6mm
0/0/0	0	0	0/0	0/0/0	0/0	0//0	0/0/	0/0/0	0/0			0/0/0	Beech(*Fagus spp.*)wood sawn or chipped lengthwise, sliced or peeled, not end-jointed, of a thickness >6mm
													--Of maple(*Acer spp.*)
0/0/0	0	0	0/0	0/0/0	0/0	0//0	0/0/	0/0/0	0/0			0/0/0	Maple wood sawn or chipped lengthwise, sliced or peeled, end-jointed, of a thickness exceeding 6mm
0/0/0	0	0	0/0	0/0/0	0/0	0//0	0/0/	0/0/0	0/0			0/0/0	Maple wood sawn or chipped lengthwise, sliced or peeled, end-jointed, of a thickness >6mm

税则号列		货品名称〔CIQ 扩展编码及品名—T2 表示见附表 2〕	最惠(%)	暂定税率	普通	增值/消费	出口退税	计量单位	监管条件/特殊证件	检验检疫	对美关税	亚太上/下
4407.9400		--樱桃木										
4407.9400	10	端部接合的樱桃木厚板材(经纵锯、纵切、刨切或旋切的,厚度超过 6mm)〔999〕	0		14	13/	0	千克/立方米	AB/	PQ		
4407.9400	90	非端部接合的樱桃木厚板材(经纵锯、纵切、刨切或旋切的,厚度超过 6mm)〔999〕	0		14	13/	0	千克/立方米	4ABxy/	PQ		
4407.9500		--白蜡木										
4407.9500	11	端部接合的水曲柳厚板材(经纵锯、纵切、刨切或旋切的,厚度>6 毫米)〔999〕	0		14	13/	0	千克/立方米	ABEF/	PQ		
4407.9500	19	端部接合的白蜡木厚板材(经纵锯、纵切、刨切或旋切的,厚度超过 6mm)〔999〕	0		14	13/	0	千克/立方米	AB/	PQ		
4407.9500	91	非端部接合的水曲柳厚板材(经纵锯、纵切、刨切或旋切的,厚度>6 毫米)〔999〕	0		14	13/	0	千克/立方米	4ABEFxy/	PQ		
4407.9500	99	非端部接合的白蜡木厚板材(经纵锯、纵切、刨切或旋切的,厚度超过 6mm)〔999〕	0		14	13/	0	千克/立方米	4ABxy/	PQ		
4407.9600		--桦木										
4407.9600	11	端部接合的濒危桦木板材(经纵锯、纵切、刨切或旋切,厚度超过 6mm)〔999〕	0		14	13/	0	千克/立方米	ABEF/	PQ	25	
4407.9600	19	端部接合的其他桦木厚板材(经纵锯、纵切、刨切或旋切,厚度超过 6mm)〔999〕	0		14	13/	0	千克/立方米	AB/	PQ	25	
4407.9600	91	非端部结合的濒危桦木厚板材(经纵锯、纵切、刨切或旋切,厚度超过 6mm)〔999〕	0		14	13/	0	千克/立方米	4ABEFxy/	PQ	25	
4407.9600	99	非端部接合的其他桦木厚板材(经纵锯、纵切、刨切或旋切,厚度超过 6mm)〔999〕	0		14	13/	0	千克/立方米	4ABxy/	PQ	25	
4407.9700		--杨木										
4407.9700	10	端部接合的杨木厚板材(经纵锯、纵切、刨切或旋切,厚度超过 6mm)〔999〕	0		14	13/	0	千克/立方米	AB/	PQ	5	
4407.9700	90	非端部接合的杨木厚板材(经纵锯、纵切、刨切或旋切,厚度超过 6mm)〔999〕	0		14	13/	0	千克/立方米	4ABxy/	PQ	5	
		--其他:										
4407.9910		---红木,但税号 4407.2940 所列热带红木除外										
4407.9910	11	端部接合濒危红木厚板材,但税号 4407.2940 所列热带红木除外(经纵锯、纵切、刨切或旋切的,厚度超过 6mm)〔999〕	0		40	13/	0	千克/立方米	AFEB/	PQ	25	
4407.9910	19	端部接合其他红木厚板材,但税号 4407.2940 所列热带红木除外(经纵锯、纵切、刨切或旋切的,厚度超过 6mm)〔999〕	0		40	13/	0	千克/立方米	AB/	PQ	25	
4407.9910	91	非端部接合濒危红木厚板材,但税号 4407.2940 所列热带红木除外(经纵锯、纵切、刨切或旋切的,厚度超过 6mm)〔999〕	0		40	13/	0	千克/立方米	y4xAFEB/	PQ	25	
4407.9910	99	非端部接合其他红木厚板材,但税号 4407.2940 所列热带红木除外(经纵锯、纵切、刨切或旋切的,厚度超过 6mm)〔999〕	0		40	13/	0	千克/立方米	4ABxy/	PQ	25	
4407.9920		---泡桐木										
4407.9920	10	端部接合的泡桐木厚板材(经纵锯、纵切、刨切或旋切的,厚度超过 6mm)〔999〕	0		14	13/	13	千克/立方米	AB/	PQ		
4407.9920	90	非端部接合的泡桐木厚板材(经纵锯、纵切、刨切或旋切的,厚度超过 6mm)〔999〕	0		14	13/	13	千克/立方米	AB/	PQ		
4407.9930		---北美硬阔叶木										
4407.9930	10	端部接合的北美硬阔叶材厚板材(纵锯、纵切、刨切或旋切,厚度超过 6mm)〔999〕	0		14	13/	0	千克/立方米	AB/	PQ		
4407.9930	90	非端部接合的北美硬阔叶材厚板材(纵锯、纵切、刨切或旋切,厚度超过 6mm)〔999〕	0		14	13/	0	千克/立方米	AB/	PQ		
4407.9980		---其他未列名的温带非针叶木										
4407.9980	11	端部接合其他未列名的温带濒危非针叶板材(纵锯、纵切、刨切或旋切的,厚度超过 6mm)〔999〕	0		14	13/	0	千克/立方米	FEAB/	PQ	25	
4407.9980	19	端部接合的其他未列名的温带非针叶厚板材(纵锯、纵切、刨切或旋切的,厚度超过 6mm)〔999〕	0		14	13/	0	千克/立方米	AB/	PQ	25	
4407.9980	91	非端部结合其他未列名的温带濒危非针叶厚板材(纵锯、纵切、刨切或旋切的,厚度超过 6mm)〔999〕	0		14	13/	0	千克/立方米	4ABEFxy/	PQ	25	

协定税率 %								RCEP		特惠税率 %			Article Description
东/冰/格	巴基斯坦	韩国	瑞士 上/下	哥/秘/柬	澳 /毛	新西/坡/智	中国港/澳/台	东盟及马来 /澳/韩	日/新	亚太 2国	老/柬/缅	98/ 97/95	
													--Of cherry (*Prunus spp.*)
0/0/0	0	0	0/0	0/0/0	0/0	0//0	0/0/	0/0/0	0/0			0/0/0	Wood sawn or chipped lengthwise, sliced or peeled, of cherry, end-jointed, thickness>6mm
0/0/0	0	0	0/0	0/0/0	0/0	0//0	0/0/	0/0/0	0/0			0/0/0	Wood sawn or chipped lengthwise, sliced or peeled, of cherry, not end-jointed, thickness>6mm
													--Of ash(Fraxinus *spp.*)
0/0/0	0	0	0/0	0/0/0	0/0	0//0	0/0/	0/0/0	0/0			0/0/0	Fraxinus mandshurica thick plate end joining (sawn or chipped lengthwise, sliced or peeled, the thickness of >6 mm)
0/0/0	0	0	0/0	0/0/0	0/0	0//0	0/0/	0/0/0	0/0			0/0/0	Wood sawn or chipped lengthwise, sliced or peeled, of ash, end-jointed, thickness>6mm
0/0/0	0	0	0/0	0/0/0	0/0	0//0	0/0/	0/0/0	0/0			0/0/0	Fraxinus mandshurica thick plate non end joining (sawn or chipped lengthwise, sliced or peeled, the thickness of >6 mm)
0/0/0	0	0	0/0	0/0/0	0/0	0//0	0/0/	0/0/0	0/0			0/0/0	Wood sawn or chipped lengthwise, sliced or peeled, of ash, not end-jointed, thickness>6mm
													--Of birch (*Betula spp.*)
0/0/0	0		0/0	0/0/0	0/0	0//0	0/0/	0/0/0	0/0			0/0/0	Endangered birch, sawn or chipped lengthwise, sliced or peeled, end-jointed, of a thickness exceeding 6mm
0/0/0	0		0/0	0/0/0	0/0	0//0	0/0/	0/0/0	0/0			0/0/0	Other birch, sawn or chipped lengthwise, sliced or peeled, end-jointed, of a thickness exceeding 6mm
0/0/0	0		0/0	0/0/0	0/0	0//0	0/0/	0/0/0	0/0			0/0/0	Endangered birch, sawn or chipped lengthwise, sliced or peeled, not end-jointed, of a thickness exceeding 6mm
0/0/0	0		0/0	0/0/0	0/0	0//0	0/0/	0/0/0	0/0			0/0/0	Other birch, sawn or chipped lengthwise, sliced or peeled, not end-jointed, of a thickness exceeding 6mm
													--Of poplar and aspen (*Populus spp.*)
0/0/0	0		0/0	0/0/0	0/0	0//0	0/0/	0/0/0	0/0			0/0/0	Poplar, sawn or chipped lengthwise, sliced or peeled, end-jointed, of a thickness exceeding 6mm
0/0/0	0		0/0	0/0/0	0/0	0//0	0/0/	0/0/0	0/0			0/0/0	Poplar, sawn or chipped lengthwise, sliced or peeled, not end-jointed, of a thickness exceeding 6mm
													--Other:
													---Of rosewood, other than tropical wood of Subheading 4407.2940
0/0/0	0	0	0/0	0/0/0	0/0	0//0	0/0/	0/0/0	0/0			0/0/0	Ohter endangered rosewood sawn or chipped lengthwise, sliced or peeled, end-jointed, of a thickness >6mm, excluding tropical rosewood of subheading No.4403.4980
0/0/0	0	0	0/0	0/0/0	0/0	0//0	0/0/	0/0/0	0/0			0/0/0	Ohter rosewood sawn or chipped lengthwise, sliced or peeled, end-jointed, of a thickness >6mm, excluding tropical rosewood of subheading No.4403.4980
0/0/0	0	0	0/0	0/0/0	0/0	0//0	0/0/	0/0/0	0/0			0/0/0	Ohter endangered rosewood sawn or chipped lengthwise, sliced or peeled, not end-jointed, of a thickness >6mm, excluding tropical rosewood of subheading No.4403.4980
0/0/0	0	0	0/0	0/0/0	0/0	0//0	0/0/	0/0/0	0/0			0/0/0	Ohter other rosewood sawn or chipped lengthwise, sliced or peeled, not end-jointed, of a thickness >6mm, excluding tropical rosewood of subheading No.4403.4980
													---Of paulownia
0/0/0	0	0	0/0	0/0/0	0/0	0//0	0/0/	0/0/0	0/0			0/0/0	Wood sawn or chipped lengthwise, sliced or peeled, of paulownia, end-jointed, thickness>6mm
0/0/0	0	0	0/0	0/0/0	0/0	0//0	0/0/	0/0/0	0/0			0/0/0	Wood sawn or chipped lengthwise, sliced or peeled, of paulownia, not end-jointed, thickness>6mm
													---North American hardwood(including walnut)
0/0/0	0	0	0/0	0/0/0	0/0	0//0	0/0/	0/0/0	0/0			0/0/0	Wood sawn or chipped lengthwise, sliced or peeled, of North American broadleaf hardwood (including walnut), end-jointed, thickness>6mm
0/0/0	0	0	0/0	0/0/0	0/0	0//0	0/0/	0/0/0	0/0			0/0/0	Wood sawn or chipped lengthwise, sliced or peeled, of North American broadleaf hardwood (including walnut), not end-jointed, thickness>6mm
													---Other unlisted temperate, non-coniferous wood
0/0/0	0	0	0/0	0/0/0	0/0	0//0	0/0/	0/0/0	0/0			0/0/0	Wood sawn or chipped lengthwise, sliced or peeled, endangered non-coniferous wood, of temperate, end-jointed, thickness>6mm
0/0/0	0	0	0/0	0/0/0	0/0	0//0	0/0/	0/0/0	0/0			0/0/0	Wood sawn or chipped lengthwise, sliced or peeled, of temperate zone, non-coniferous wood, end-jointed, thickness>6mm
0/0/0	0	0	0/0	0/0/0	0/0	0//0	0/0/	0/0/0	0/0			0/0/0	Wood sawn or chipped lengthwise, sliced or peeled, endangered non-coniferous wood of temperate, not end-jointed, thickness>6mm

税则号列		货品名称〔CIQ 扩展编码及品名－T2 表示见附表 2〕	最惠(%)	暂定税率	普通	增值/消费	出口退税	计量单位	监管条件/特殊证件	检验检疫	对美关税	亚太上/下
4407.9980	99	非端部接合的其他未列名的温带非针叶厚板材(纵锯、纵切、刨切或旋切的,厚度超过 6mm)〔999〕	0		14	13/	0	千克/立方米	4ABxy/	PQ	25	
4407.9990		---其他										
4407.9990	12	端部接合的沉香木及拟沉香木厚板材(经纵锯、纵切、刨切或旋切的,厚度超过 6mm)〔999〕	0		14	13/	0	千克/立方米	AFEB/	PQ	20	
4407.9990	15	端部接合的其他濒危木厚板材(经纵锯、纵切、刨切或旋切的,厚度超过 6mm)〔101 针叶木木材,102 其他非针叶木材〕	0		14	13/	0	千克/立方米	AFEB/	PQ	20	
4407.9990	19	端部接合的其他木厚板材(经纵锯、纵切、刨切或旋切的,厚度超过 6mm)〔101 针叶木木材,102 其他非针叶木材〕	0		14	13/	0	千克/立方米	AB/	PQ	20	
4407.9990	92	非端部接合的沉香木及拟沉香木厚板材(经纵锯、纵切、刨切或旋切的,厚度超过 6mm)〔999〕	0		14	13/	0	千克/立方米	y4xAFEB/	PQ	20	
4407.9990	95	非端部接合的其他濒危木厚板材(经纵锯、纵切、刨切或旋切的,厚度超过 6mm)〔101 针叶木木材,102 其他非针叶木材〕	0		14	13/	0	千克/立方米	y4xAFEB/	PQ	20	
4407.9990	99	非端部接合的其他木厚板材(经纵锯、纵切、刨切或旋切的,厚度超过 6mm)〔101 针叶木木材,102 其他非针叶木材〕	0		14	13/	0	千克/立方米	y4xAB/	PQ	20	
44.08		**饰面用单板(包括刨切积层木获得的单板)、制胶合板或类似多层板用单板以及其他经纵锯、刨切或旋切的木材,不论是否刨平、砂光、拼接或端部结合,厚度不超过 6 毫米:**										
		-针叶木:										
		---饰面用单板:										
4408.1011		----用胶合板等多层板制的										
4408.1011	10	胶合板等多层板制濒危针叶木单板(厚度≤6mm,饰面用)〔999〕	6	0	40	13/	0	千克	ABFE/	MPQ		
4408.1011	90	其他胶合板等多层板制针叶木单板(厚度≤6mm,饰面用)〔999〕	6	0	40	13/	0	千克	AB/	MPQ		
4408.1019		----其他										
4408.1019	10	其他饰面濒危针叶木单板(厚度≤6mm)〔999〕	4	0	40	13/	0	千克	ABFE/	MPQ	20	
4408.1019	90	其他饰面针叶木单板(厚度≤6mm)〔999〕	4	0	40	13/	0	千克	AB/	MPQ	20	
4408.1020		---制胶合板用单板										
4408.1020	10	制胶合板用濒危针叶木单板(厚度≤6mm)〔999〕	4	0	17	13/	0	千克	ABFE/	MPQ		
4408.1020	90	其他制胶合板用针叶木单板(厚度≤6mm)〔999〕	4	0	17	13/	0	千克	AB/	MPQ		
4408.1090		---其他										
4408.1090	10	其他濒危针叶木单板材(经纵锯,刨切或旋切的,厚度≤6mm)〔999〕	4	0	30	13/	0	千克	ABFE/	PQ	25	
4408.1090	90	其他针叶木单板材(经纵锯,刨切或旋切的,厚度≤6mm)〔999〕	4	0	30	13/	0	千克	AB/	PQ	25	
		-热带木:										
		--深红色红柳桉木、浅红色红柳桉木及巴栲红柳桉木:										
		---饰面用单板:										
4408.3111		----用胶合板等多层板制的〔999〕	6	0	40	13/	0	千克	AB/	MPQ		
4408.3119		----其他〔999〕	4	0	40	13/	0	千克	AB/	PQ	25	
4408.3120		---制胶合板用单板〔999〕	4	0	17	13/	0	千克	AB/	MPQ		
4408.3190		---其他〔999〕	4	0	30	13/	0	千克	AB/	PQ		
		--其他:										
		---饰面用单板:										
4408.3911		----用胶合板等多层板制的										
4408.3911	10	胶合板多层板制饰面桃花心木单板(厚度≤6mm)〔999〕	6	0	40	13/	0	千克	ABFE/	MPQ		4.2/4.2
4408.3911	20	胶合板多层板制饰面拉敏木单板(厚度≤6mm)〔999〕	6	0	40	13/	0	千克	ABFE/	MPQ		4.2/4.2
4408.3911	30	厚度≤6mm 胶合板多层板制饰面濒危热带木单板〔101 针叶木薄板,102 非针叶木薄板〕	6	0	40	13/	0	千克	ABFE/	MPQ		4.2/4.2
4408.3911	90	厚度≤6mm 胶合板多层板制饰面热带木单板〔101 针叶木薄板,102 非针叶木薄板〕	6	0	40	13/	0	千克	AB/	MPQ		4.2/4.2
4408.3919		----其他										
4408.3919	10	其他饰面用桃花心木单板(厚度≤6mm)〔999〕	4	0	40	13/	0	千克	ABFE/	PQ	25	
4408.3919	30	厚度≤6mm 其他濒危热带木制饰面用单板〔101 针叶木薄板,102 非针叶木薄板〕	4	0	40	13/	0	千克	ABFE/	PQ	25	

协定税率 %								RCEP		特惠税率 %			Article Description
东/冰/格	巴基斯坦	韩国	瑞士上/下	哥/秘/柬	澳/毛	新西/坡/智	中国港/澳/台	东盟及马来/澳/韩	日/新	亚太2国	老/柬/缅	98/97/95	
0/0/0	0	0	0/0	0/0/0	0/0	0//0	0/0/	0/0/0	0/0			0/0/0	Wood sawn or chipped lengthwise, sliced or peeled, of temperate zone, non-coniferous wood, not end-jointed, thickness >6mm
													---Other
0/0/0	0	0	0/0	0/0/0	0/0	0//0	0/0/	0/0/0	0/0			0/0/0	Wood sawn or chipped lengthwise, sliced or peeled, of Chinese eaglewood and similar chinese eaglewood, end-jointed, thickness>6mm
0/0/0	0	0	0/0	0/0/0	0/0	0//0	0/0/	0/0/0	0/0			0/0/0	Wood sawn or chipped lengthwise, sliced or peeled, of other endangered wood , end-jointed, thickness>6mm
0/0/0	0	0	0/0	0/0/0	0/0	0//0	0/0/	0/0/0	0/0			0/0/0	Other wood sawn or chipped lengthwise, sliced or peeled, end-jointed thickness>6mm
0/0/0	0	0	0/0	0/0/0	0/0	0//0	0/0/	0/0/0	0/0			0/0/0	Wood sawn or chipped lengthwise, sliced or peeled, of Chinese eaglewood and similar chinese eaglewood , not end-jointed, thickness>6mm
0/0/0	0	0	0/0	0/0/0	0/0	0//0	0/0/	0/0/0	0/0			0/0/0	Wood sawn or chipped lengthwise, sliced or peeled, of other endangered wood , not end-jointed, thickness>6mm
0/0/0	0	0	0/0	0/0/0	0/0	0//0	0/0/	0/0/0	0/0			0/0/0	Other wood sawn or chipped lengthwise, sliced or peeled, not end-jointed, thickness>6mm
													Sheets for veneering (including those obtained by slicing laminated wood), for plywood or for other similar laminated wood and other wood, sawn lengthwise, sliced or peeled, whether or not planed, sanded, spliced or end-jointed, of a thickness not exceeding 6mm:
													-Coniferous:
													---Veneer sheets:
													----Of laminated plywood
5/0/		3.7	0/0	0/0/0	0/0	0//0	0/0/	7.8/7.8/	/7.8			0/0/	Veneer sheets of endangered coniferous wood, of laminated wood of plywood, thickness≤6mm
5/0/		3.7	0/0	0/0/0	0/0	0//0	0/0/	7.8/7.8/	/7.8			0/0/	Other veneer sheets of coniferous wood, of laminated wood of plywood, thickness≤6mm
													----Other
0/0/	0	0	0/0	0/0/0	0/0	0/0/0	0/0/	0/0/0	3.6/0			0/0/0	Other veneer sheets of endangered coniferous wood, thickness≤6mm
0/0/	0	0	0/0	0/0/0	0/0	0/0/0	0/0/	0/0/0	3.6/0			0/0/0	Other veneer sheets of coniferous wood, thickness≤6mm
													---Sheets for plywood
0/0/	0	0	0/0	0/0/0	0/0	0/0/0	0/0/	0/0/0	3.6/0			0/0/0	Sheets for plywood of coniferous endangered wood, thickness ≤6mm
0/0/	0	0	0/0	0/0/0	0/0	0/0/0	0/0/	0/0/0	3.6/0			0/0/0	Other sheets for plywood of coniferous wood, thickness≤6mm
													---Other
0/0/	0	0	0/0	0/0/0	0/0	0/0/0	0/0/	0/0/0	3.6/0			0/0/0	Sheets for plywood of endangered coniferous wood, wood sawn or chipped lengthwise, sliced or peeled, thickness≤6mm
0/0/	0	0	0/0	0/0/0	0/0	0/0/0	0/0/	0/0/0	3.6/0			0/0/0	Sheets for plywood of coniferous wood, wood sawn or chipped lengthwise, sliced or peeled, thickness≤6mm
													-Of tropical wood:
													--Dark Red Meranti, Light Red Meranti and Meranti Bakau:
													---Veneer sheets:
5/0/		4.6	0/0	0/0/0	0/0	0//0	0/0/	9.8/9.8/	/9.8			0/0/	----Of laminated plywood
0/0/	0	0	0/0	0/0/0	0/0	0/0/0	0/0/	0/0/0	3.6/0			0/0/0	----Other
0/0/	0	0	0/0	0/0/0	0/0	0/0/0	0/0/	0/0/0	3.6/0			0/0/0	---Sheets for plywood
0/0/	0	0	0/0	0/0/0	0/0	0/0/0	0/0/	0/0/0	3.6/0			0/0/0	---Other
													--Other:
													---Veneer sheets:
													----Of laminated plywood
5/0/		4.6	0/0	0/0/0	0/0	0//0	0/0/	3.9/3.9/	/3.9			0/0/	Veneer sheets, of acajou d'afrique, of laminated wood of plywood, thickness≤6mm
5/0/		4.6	0/0	0/0/0	0/0	0//0	0/0/	3.9/3.9/	/3.9			0/0/	Sheets for veneering, of Ramin wood, of laminated wood of plywood, thickness≤6mm
5/0/		4.6	0/0	0/0/0	0/0	0//0	0/0/	3.9/3.9/	/3.9			0/0/	Veneer sheets, of endangered tropical wood, of laminated plywood, of a thickness not exceeding 6mm
5/0/		4.6	0/0	0/0/0	0/0	0//0	0/0/	3.9/3.9/	/3.9			0/0/	Veneer sheets, of tropical wood, of laminated plywood, of a thickness not exceeding 6mm
													----Other
0/0/	0	0	0/0	0/0/0	0/0	0/0/0	0/0/	0/0/0	2.7/0			0/0/0	Other veneer sheets, of acajou d'afri-que, thickness≤6mm
0/0/	0	0	0/0	0/0/0	0/0	0/0/0	0/0/	0/0/0	2.7/0			0/0/0	Veneer sheets, of endangered tropical wood , of a thickness not exceeding 6mm

税则号列	货品名称〔CIQ扩展编码及品名－T2表示见附表2〕	最惠(%)	暂定税率	普通	增值/消费	出口退税	计量单位	监管条件/特殊证件	检验检疫	对美关税	亚太上/下
4408.3919 90	厚度≤6mm其他热带木饰面用单板[T2]	4	0	40	13/	0	千克	AB/	PQ	25	
4408.3920	---制胶合板用单板										
4408.3920 10	其他桃花心木制的胶合板用单板(厚度≤6mm)〔999〕	4	0	17	13/	0	千克	ABFE/	MPQ		3.6/3.6
4408.3920 20	其他拉敏木制的胶合板用单板(厚度≤6mm)〔999〕	4	0	17	13/	0	千克	ABFE/	MPQ		3.6/3.6
4408.3920 30	其他濒危热带木制的胶合板用单板(厚度≤6mm)〔101针叶木薄板,102非针叶木薄板〕	4	0	17	13/	0	千克	ABFE/	MPQ		3.6/3.6
4408.3920 90	其他列名热带木制的胶合板用单板(厚度≤6mm)〔101针叶木薄板,102非针叶木薄板〕	4	0	17	13/	0	千克	AB/	MPQ		3.6/3.6
4408.3990	---其他										
4408.3990 10	其他桃花心木制的其他单板(厚度≤6mm)〔999〕	4	0	30	13/	0	千克	ABFE/	PQ	25	
4408.3990 30	其他列名濒危热带木制的其他单板(厚度≤6mm)〔101针叶木薄板,102非针叶木薄板〕	4	0	30	13/	0	千克	ABFE/	PQ	25	
4408.3990 90	其他列名的热带木制的其他单板(厚度≤6mm)〔101针叶木薄板,102非针叶木薄板〕	4	0	30	13/	0	千克	AB/	PQ	25	
	-其他:										
	---饰面用单板:										
4408.9011	----用胶合板等多层板制的										
4408.9011 10	胶合板多层板制饰面濒危木单板(厚度≤6mm)〔101针叶木薄板,102非针叶木薄板〕	4	0	40	13/	0	千克	ABFE/	MPQ	20	2.8/2.8
4408.9011 90	胶合板多层板制饰面其他木单板(厚度≤6mm,针叶木、热带木除外)〔101针叶木薄板,102非针叶木薄板〕	4	0	40	13/	0	千克	AB/	MPQ	20	2.8/2.8
4408.9012	----温带非针叶木制										
4408.9012 10	温带濒危非针叶木制饰面用木单板(厚度≤6mm,针叶木、热带木除外)〔999〕	3	0	40	13/	0	千克	ABFE/	PQ	20	
4408.9012 90	其他温带非针叶木制饰面用木单板(厚度≤6mm,针叶木、热带木除外)〔999〕	3	0	40	13/	0	千克	AB/	PQ	20	
4408.9013	----竹制										
4408.9013 10	濒危竹制饰面用单板(厚度≤6mm)〔999〕	4	0	40	13/	0	千克	ABE/	PQ		2.8/2.8
4408.9013 90	其他竹制饰面用单板(厚度≤6mm)〔999〕	4	0	40	13/	0	千克	AB/	PQ		2.8/2.8
4408.9019	----其他										
4408.9019 11	家具饰面用濒危木单板(厚度≤6mm)[T2]	3	0	40	13/	0	千克	ABFE/	MPQ	5	
4408.9019 19	其他家具饰面用单板(厚度≤6mm)[T2]	3	0	40	13/	0	千克	AB/	MPQ	5	
4408.9019 91	其他饰面用濒危木单板(厚度≤6mm)[T2]	3	0	40	13/	0	千克	ABFE/	MPQ	5	
4408.9019 99	其他饰面用单板(厚度≤6mm)[T2]	3	0	40	13/	0	千克	AB/	MPQ	5	
	---制胶合板用单板:										
4408.9021	----温带非针叶木制										
4408.9021 10	温带濒危非针叶木制胶合板用单板(厚度≤6mm)〔999〕	3	0	17	13/	0	千克	ABFE/	MPQ	25	
4408.9021 90	其他温带非针叶木制胶合板用单板(厚度≤6mm)〔999〕	3	0	17	13/	0	千克	AB/	MPQ	25	
4408.9029	----其他										
4408.9029 11	其他濒危木制胶合板用旋切单板(厚度≤6mm)〔101针叶木薄板,102非针叶木薄板〕	3	0	17	13/	0	千克	ABFE/	MPQ		
4408.9029 19	其他濒危木制胶合板用其他单板(厚度≤6mm,旋切单板除外)〔101针叶木薄板,102非针叶木薄板〕	3	0	17	13/	0	千克	ABFE/	MPQ		
4408.9029 91	其他木制胶合板用旋切单板(厚度≤6mm)〔101针叶木薄板,102非针叶木薄板〕	3	0	17	13/	0	千克	AB/	MPQ		
4408.9029 99	其他木制胶合板用其他单板(厚度≤6mm,旋切单板除外)〔101针叶木薄板,102非针叶木薄板〕	3	0	17	13/	0	千克	AB/	MPQ		
	---其他:										
4408.9091	----温带非针叶木制										
4408.9091 10	温带濒危非针叶木制其他单板材(经纵锯、刨切或旋切的,厚度≤6mm)〔999〕	3	0	30	13/	0	千克	ABFE/	PQ	25	
4408.9091 90	温带非针叶木制其他单板材(经纵锯、刨切或旋切的,厚度≤6mm)〔999〕	3	0	30	13/	0	千克	AB/	PQ	25	
4408.9099	----其他										
4408.9099 10	其他濒危木制的其他单板材(经纵锯、刨切或旋切的,厚度≤6mm)〔101针叶木薄板,102非针叶木薄板〕	3	0	30	13/	0	千克	ABFE/	PQ	20	
4408.9099 90	其他木材,但针叶木热带木除外(经纵锯、刨切或旋切的,厚度≤6mm)〔999〕	3	0	30	13/	0	千克	AB/	PQ	20	

协定税率 %								RCEP		特惠税率 %			Article Description
东/冰/格	巴基斯坦	韩国	瑞士上/下	哥/秘/柬	澳/毛	新西/坡/智	中国港/澳/台	东盟及马来/澳/韩	日/新	亚太2国	老/柬/缅	98/97/95	
0/0/	0	0	0/0	0/0/0	0/0	0/0/0	0/0/	0/0/0	2.7/0			0/0/0	Veneer sheets, of tropical wood ,of a thickness not exceeding 6mm
													---Sheets for plywood
0/0/	0	0	0/0	0/0/0	0/0	0/0/0	0/0/	0/0/0	2.7/0			0/0/0	Other sheets for plywood, of acajou d'afrique, thickness≤6mm
0/0/	0	0	0/0	0/0/0	0/0	0/0/0	0/0/	0/0/0	2.7/0			0/0/0	Other sheets for plywood, of ramin wood, thickness≤6mm
0/0/	0	0	0/0	0/0/0	0/0	0/0/0	0/0/	0/0/0	2.7/0			0/0/0	Other sheets for plywood, of endangered tropical wood,of a thickness not exceeding 6mm
0/0/	0	0	0/0	0/0/0	0/0	0/0/0	0/0/	0/0/0	2.7/0			0/0/0	Other sheets for plywood, of tropical wood,of a thickness not exceeding 6mm
													---Other
0/0/	0	0	0/0	0/0/0	0/0	0/0/0	0/0/	0/0/0	2.7/0			0/0/0	Other sheets of other Acajou d'afrique, of tropical wood,of a thickness not exceeding 6mm
0/0/	0	0	0/0	0/0/0	0/0	0/0/0	0/0/	0/0/0	2.7/0			0/0/0	Other sheets of endangered specified tropical wood, of a thickness not exceeding 6mm
0/0/	0	0	0/0	0/0/0	0/0	0/0/0	0/0/	0/0/0	2.7/0			0/0/0	Other sheets of other specified tropical wood,of a thickness not exceeding 6mm
													-Other:
													---Veneer sheets:
													----Of laminated plywood
/0/		1.8	0/0	0/0/0	0/0	0//0	0/0/	3.9/3.9/	/3.9			0/0/	Veneer sheets, of wood, of laminatedr plywood of endangered wood , thickness≤6mm
/0/		1.8	0/0	0/0/0	0/0	0//0	0/0/	3.9/3.9/	/3.9			0/0/	Veneer sheets, of other wood, other than tropical coniferous wood, of laminated ply wood of plywood, thickness≤6mm
													----Of temperate non-coniferous wood
0/0/	0	0	0/0	0/0/0	0/0	0/0/0	0/0/	0/0/0	2.7/0			0/0/0	Venner sheets, of temperate zone non-coniferous endangered wood, other than tropical coniferous wood, thickness≤6mm
0/0/	0	0	0/0	0/0/0	0/0	0/0/0	0/0/	0/0/0	2.7/0			0/0/0	Venner sheets of temperate zone non-coniferous wood(other than tropical coniferous wood, thickness≤6mm)
													----Of bamboo
/0/		1.8	0/0	0/0/0	0/0	0//0	0/0/	3.9/3.9/	/3.9			0/0/	Veneer sheets of endangered bamboo(thickness≤6mm)
/0/		1.8	0/0	0/0/0	0/0	0//0	0/0/	3.9/3.9/	/3.9			0/0/	Veneer sheets of other bamboo(thickness≤6mm)
													----Other
0/0/	0	0	0/0	0/0/0	0/0	0/0/0	0/0/	0/0/0	2.7/0			0/0/0	Venner sheets of endangered wood(thickness≤6mm)
0/0/	0	0	0/0	0/0/0	0/0	0/0/0	0/0/	0/0/0	2.7/0			0/0/0	Other venner sheets of wood (thickness≤6mm)
0/0/	0	0	0/0	0/0/0	0/0	0/0/0	0/0/	0/0/0	2.7/0			0/0/0	Other venner sheets of endangered wood(thickness≤6mm)
0/0/	0	0	0/0	0/0/0	0/0	0/0/0	0/0/	0/0/0	2.7/0			0/0/0	Other veneer sheets(thickness≤6mm)
													---Sheets for plywood:
													----Of temperate non-coniferous wood
0/0/	0	0	0/0	0/0/0	0/0	0/0/0	0/0/	0/0/0	2.7/0			0/0/0	Sheets for plywood of temperate zone non-coniferous endangered wood (thickness≤6mm)
0/0/	0	0	0/0	0/0/0	0/0	0/0/0	0/0/	0/0/0	2.7/0			0/0/0	Other sheets for plywood of temperate zone non-coniferous wood(thickness ≤6mm)
													----Other
0/0/	0	0	0/0	0/0/0	0/0	0/0/0	0/0/	2.7/2.7/2.7	2.7/2.7			0/0/0	Other sheets for plywood of endangered wood,peeled sheets (thickness≤6mm)
0/0/	0	0	0/0	0/0/0	0/0	0/0/0	0/0/	2.7/2.7/2.7	2.7/2.7			0/0/0	Other sheets for plywood of endangered wood(thinckness≤6mm,other than peeled sheets)
0/0/	0	0	0/0	0/0/0	0/0	0/0/0	0/0/	2.7/2.7/2.7	2.7/2.7			0/0/0	Other sheets for plywood of wood,peeled sheets(thickness≤6mm)
0/0/	0	0	0/0	0/0/0	0/0	0/0/0	0/0/	2.7/2.7/2.7	2.7/2.7			0/0/0	Other sheets for plywood of wood (thieknesss≤6mm,other than peeled sheets)
													---Other:
													----Of temperate non-coniferous wood
0/0/	0	0	0/0	0/0/0	0/0	0/0/0	0/0/	0/0/0	2.7/0			0/0/0	Sheets of temperate zone endangered non-coniferous wood (sawn or chipped lengthwise, sliced or peeled, thickness ≤6mm)
0/0/	0	0	0/0	0/0/0	0/0	0/0/0	0/0/	0/0/0	2.7/0			0/0/0	Other sheets of temperate zone non-coniferous wood(sawn or chipped lengthwise, sliced or peeled, thickness ≤6mm)
													----Other
0/0/	0	0	0/0	0/0/0	0/0	0/0/0	0/0/	0/0/0	2.7/0			0/0/0	Other sheets of endangered wood(sawn or chipped lengthwise, sliced or peeled, thickness≤6mm)
0/0/	0	0	0/0	0/0/0	0/0	0/0/0	0/0/	0/0/0	2.7/0			0/0/0	Other wood, other than tropical coniferous wood(sawn or chipped lengthwise, sliced or peeled, thickness≤6mm)

税则号列	货品名称〔CIQ 扩展编码及品名－T2 表示见附表 2〕	最惠(%)	暂定税率	普通	增值/消费	出口退税	计量单位	监管条件/特殊证件	检验检疫	对美关税	亚太上/下
44.09	**任何一边、端或面制成连续形状(舌榫、槽榫、半槽榫、斜角、V形接头、珠榫、缘饰、刨圆及类似形状)的木材(包括未装拼的拼花地板用板条及缘板),不论其任意一边或面是否刨平、砂光或端部接合:**										
	-针叶木:										
4409.1010	---地板条(块)										
4409.1010 10	一边或面制成连续形状的濒危针叶木制地板条、块(包括未装拼的拼花地板用板条及缘板)〔999〕	6	0	50	13/5	0	千克	ABFE/	PQ		
4409.1010 90	一边或面制成连续形状的其他针叶木地板条,块(包括未装拼的拼花地板用板条及缘板)〔999〕	6	0	50	13/5	0	千克	AB/	PQ		
4409.1090	---其他										
4409.1090 10	一边或面制成连续形状濒危针叶木材〔999〕	6	0	50	13/	0	千克	ABFE/	PQ		
4409.1090 90	其他一边或面制成连续形状的针叶木材〔999〕	6	0	50	13/	0	千克	AB/	PQ		
	-非针叶木:										
	--竹的:										
4409.2110	---地板条(块)										
4409.2110 10	一边或面制成连续形状的濒危竹地板条(块)(包括未装拼的拼花竹地板用板条及缘板)〔999〕	4	0	50	13/	0	千克	ABE/	PQ		
4409.2110 90	一边或面制成连续形状的竹地板条(块)(包括未装拼的拼花竹地板用板条及缘板)〔999〕	4	0	50	13/	13	千克	AB/	PQ		
4409.2190	---其他										
4409.2190 10	一边或面制成连续形状的其他濒危竹材〔999〕	4	0	50	13/	0	千克	ABE/	PQ		
4409.2190 90	一边或面制成连续形状的其他竹材〔999〕	4	0	50	13/	13	千克	AB/	PQ		
	--热带木的:										
4409.2210	---地板条(块)										
4409.2210 20	一边或面制成连续形状的桃花心木地板条、块(包括未装拼的桃花心木拼花地板用板条及缘板)〔999〕	4	0	50	13/5	0	千克	ABFE/	PQ		
4409.2210 30	一边或面制成连续形状的其他濒危热带木地板条、块(包括未装栟的其他濒危热带木拼花地板用板条及缘条)〔999〕	4	0	50	13/5	0	千克	ABFE/	PQ		
4409.2210 90	一边或面制成连续形状的其他热带木地板条、块(包括未装拼的其他热带木栟花地板用板条及缘板)〔999〕	4	0	50	13/5	0	千克	AB/	PQ		
4409.2290	---其他										
4409.2290 20	一边或面制成连续形状的桃花心木〔999〕	4	0	50	13/	0	千克	ABFE/	PQ		
4409.2290 30	一边或面制成连续形状的其他濒危热带木〔999〕	4	0	50	13/	0	千克	ABFE/	PQ		
4409.2290 90	一边或面制成连续形状的其他热带木〔999〕	4	0	50	13/	0	千克	AB/	PQ		
	--其他:										
4409.2910	---地板条(块)										
4409.2910 30	一边或面制成连续形状的其他濒危木地板条、块(包括未装拼的其他濒危木拼花地板用板条及缘板)〔999〕	4	0	50	13/5	0	千克	ABFE/	PQ	5	
4409.2910 90	一边或面制成连续形状的其他非针叶木地板条、块(包括未装拼的其他非针叶木拼花地板用板条及缘板)〔999〕	4	0	50	13/5	0	千克	AB/	PQ	5	
4409.2990	---其他										
4409.2990 30	一边或面制成连续形状的其他濒危木〔101 针叶木木材,102 其他非针叶木材〕	4	0	50	13/	0	千克	ABFE/	PQ	25	
4409.2990 90	一边或面制成连续形状的其他非针叶木材〔999〕	4	0	50	13/	0	千克	AB/	PQ	25	
44.10	**碎料板,定向刨花板(OSB)及类似板(例如,华夫板),木或其他木质材料制,不论是否用树脂或其他有机黏合剂黏合:**										
	-木制:										
4410.1100	--碎料板〔101 其它胶合板,102 其他碎木料、锯末、刨花〕	4	0	40	13/	13	千克	AB/	PQ	25	

协定税率 %								RCEP		特惠税率 %			Article Description
东/冰/格	巴基斯坦	韩国	瑞士 上/下	哥/秘/柬	澳/毛	新西/坡/智	中国港/澳/台	东盟及马来/澳/韩	日/新	亚太2国	老/柬/缅	98/97/95	
													Wood (including strips and friezes for parquet flooring, not assembled) continuously shaped (tongues, grooved, rebated, chamfered, V-jointed, beaded, moulded, rounded or the like) along any of its "edges, ends or faces, whether or not planed, sanded or end-jointed":
													-Coniferous:
													---Floor board strips
0/0/	2	1.5	0/0	0/0/0	0/0	0/0/0	0/0/	0/0/6.8	6.8/0			0/0/0	Endangered coniferous wood (including strips and friezes for parquet flooring, not assembled) continuously shaped along any of its edges or faces
0/0/	2	1.5	0/0	0/0/0	0/0	0/0/0	0/0/	0/0/6.8	6.8/0			0/0/0	Other coniferous wood (including strips and friezes for parquet flooring, not assembled) continuously shaped along any of its edges or faces
													---Other
0/0/	2	0	0/0	0/0/0	0/0	0/0/0	0/0/	0/0/0	6.8/0			0/0/0	Endangered coniferous wood, continuously shaped along any of its edges or faces
0/0/	2	0	0/0	0/0/0	0/0	0/0/0	0/0/	0/0/0	6.8/0			0/0/0	Coniferous wood, continuously shaped along any of its edges or faces
													-Non-coniferous:
													--Of bamboo:
													---Floor board strips
0/0/	0	0	0/0	0/0/0	0/0	0/0/0	0/0/	0/0/0	3.6/0			0/0/0	Endangered bamboo (including strips and friezes for parquet flooring, not assembled) continuously shaped along any of its edges or faces
0/0/	0	0	0/0	0/0/0	0/0	0/0/0	0/0/	0/0/0	3.6/0			0/0/0	Bamboo (including strips and friezes for parquet flooring, not assembled) continuously shaped along any of its edges or faces
													---Other
0/0/0	0	0	0/0	0/0/0	0/0	0/0/0	0/0/	0/0/0	0/0			0/0/0	Other endangered bamboo, continuously shaped along any of its edges or faces
0/0/0	0	0	0/0	0/0/0	0/0	0/0/0	0/0/	0/0/0	0/0			0/0/0	Other bamboo, continuously shaped along any of its edges or faces
													--Of tropical wood:
													---Floor board strips
0/0/	0	0	0/0	0/0/0	0/0	0/0/0	0/0/	0/0/0	3.6/0			0/0/0	Floor board strips of mahogany wood (including strips and friezes for parquet flooring, not assembled) continuously shaped along any of its edges or faces
0/0/	0	0	0/0	0/0/0	0/0	0/0/0	0/0/	0/0/0	3.6/0			0/0/0	Floor board strips of other endangered tropical wood (including strips and friezes for parquet flooring, not assembled) continuously shaped along any of its edges or faces
0/0/	0	0	0/0	0/0/0	0/0	0/0/0	0/0/	0/0/0	3.6/0			0/0/0	Floor board strips of other tropical wood (including strips and friezes for parquet flooring, not assembled) continuously shaped along any of its edges or faces
													Other
0/0/	0	0	0/0	0/0/0	0/0	0/0/0	0/0/	0/0/0	3.6/0			0/0/0	mahogany wood, continuously shaped along any of its edges or faces
0/0/	0	0	0/0	0/0/0	0/0	0/0/0	0/0/	0/0/0	3.6/0			0/0/0	Endangered tropical wood, continuously shaped along any of its edges or faces
0/0/	0	0	0/0	0/0/0	0/0	0/0/0	0/0/	0/0/0	3.6/0			0/0/0	Other tropical wood, continuously shaped along any of its edges or faces
													--Other:
													---Floor board strips
0/0/	0	0	0/0	0/0/0	0/0	0/0/0	0/0/	0/0/0	3.6/0			0/0/0	Other endangered wood (including strips and friezes for parquet flooring, not assembled) continuously shaped along any of its edges or faces
0/0/	0	0	0/0	0/0/0	0/0	0/0/0	0/0/	0/0/0	3.6/0			0/0/0	Other non-coniferous wood (including strips and friezes for parquet flooring, not assembled) continuously shaped along anyof its edges or faces
													---Other
0/0/	0	0	0/0	0/0/0	0/0	0/0/0	0/0/	0/0/0	3.6/0			0/0/0	Other endangered wood , continuously shaped along any of its edges or faces
0/0/	0	0	0/0	0/0/0	0/0	0/0/0	0/0/	0/0/0	3.6/0			0/0/0	Other non-coniferous wood, continuously sh-aped along any of its edges or faces
													Particle board and similar board of wood or other ligneous materials (for example, oriented strand board and waferboabd) where or not agglomerated with resins or other organlc binging, substancec
													-Of wood:
			0/0	//0	/0	0//0	0/0/					0//	--Particle board

税则号列	货品名称〔CIQ 扩展编码及品名—T2 表示见附表 2〕	最惠(%)	暂定税率	普通	增值/消费	出口退税	计量单位	监管条件/特殊证件	检验检疫	对美关税	亚太上/下
4410.1200	--定向刨花板(OSB)〔999〕	4	0	40	13/	13	千克	AB/	PQ	25	
4410.1900	--其他〔999〕	4	0	40	13/	13	千克	AB/	PQ	25	
	-其他:										
	--碎料板:										
4410.9011	----麦稻秸秆制〔999〕	6		40	13/	13	千克	AB/	PQ		
4410.9019	----其他〔999〕	6		40	13/	13	千克	AB/	PQ	11	
4410.9090	---其他[T2]	6		40	13/	13	千克	AB/	PQ		
44.11	**木纤维板或其他木质材料纤维板,不论是否用树脂或其他有机黏合剂黏合:**										
	-中密度纤维板(MDF):										
	--厚度不超过 5 毫米:										
	---密度超过每立方厘米 0.8 克:										
4411.1211	----未经机械加工或盖面的〔101 针叶木纤维板,102 非针叶木纤维板,103 其他纤维板〕	4	0	40	13/	13	千克	AB/	PQ	25	
4411.1219	----其他[T2]	6	0	40	13/	13	千克	AB/	PQ	20	
	---密度超过每立方厘米 0.5 克,但未超过每立方厘米 0.8 克:										
4411.1221	----辐射松制的〔999〕	4	0	40	13/	13	千克	AB/	PQ		
4411.1229	----其他[T2]	4	0	40	13/	13	千克	AB/	PQ	20	
	---其他:										
4411.1291	----未经机械加工或盖面的[T2]	6	0	40	13/	13	千克	AB/	PQ		
4411.1299	----其他〔999〕	4	0	40	13/	13	千克	AB/	PQ		
	--厚度超过 5 毫米但未超过 9 毫米:										
	---密度超过每立方厘米 0.8 克:										
4411.1311	----未经机械加工或盖面的[T2]	4	0	40	13/	13	千克	AB/	PQ	20	
4411.1319	----其他[T2]	6	0	40	13/	13	千克	AB/	MPQ	25	
	---密度超过每立方厘米 0.5 克,但未超过每立方厘米 0.8 克:										
4411.1321	----辐射松制的〔999〕	4	0	40	13/	13	千克	AB/	PQ		
4411.1329	----其他[T2]	4	0	40	13/	13	千克	AB/	PQ		
	---其他:										
4411.1391	----未经机械加工或盖面的[T2]	6	0	40	13/	13	千克	AB/	PQ		
4411.1399	----其他[T2]	4	0	40	13/	13	千克	AB/	PQ		
	--厚度超过 9 毫米:										
	---密度超过每立方厘米 0.8 克:										
4411.1411	----未经机械加工或盖面的〔999〕	4	0	40	13/	13	千克	AB/	PQ		
4411.1419	----其他〔999〕	6	0	40	13/	13	千克	AB/	MPQ	25	
	---密度超过每立方厘米 0.5 克,但未超过每立方厘米 0.8 克:										
4411.1421	----辐射松制的〔999〕	4	0	40	13/	13	千克	AB/	PQ	25	
4411.1429	----其他[T2]	4	0	40	13/	13	千克	AB/	PQ	25	
	---其他:										
4411.1491	----未经机械加工或盖面的〔999〕	6	0	40	13/	13	千克	AB/	PQ		
4411.1499	----其他[T2]	4	0	40	13/	13	千克	AB/	PQ	25	
	-其他:										
	--密度超过每立方厘米 0.8 克:										
4411.9210	---未经机械加工或盖面的[T2]	4	0	40	13/	13	千克	AB/	PQ	25	
4411.9290	---其他〔999〕	6	0	40	13/	13	千克	AB/	MPQ	25	
	--密度超过每立方厘米 0.5 克,但未超过每立方厘米 0.8 克:										
4411.9310	---辐射松制的〔999〕	4	0	40	13/	13	千克	AB/	PQ		
4411.9390	---其他[T2]	4	0	40	13/	13	千克	AB/	PQ	25	
	--密度未超过每立方厘米 0.5 克:										
4411.9410	---密度超过每立方厘米 0.35 克,但未超过每立方厘米 0.5 克〔999〕	6	0	40	13/	13	千克	AB/	PQ	25	
	---密度未超过每立方厘米 0.35 克:										
4411.9421	----未经机械加工或盖面的[T2]	6	0	40	13/	13	千克	AB/	PQ		
4411.9429	----其他〔999〕	4	0	40	13/	13	千克	AB/	PQ	5	
44.12	**胶合板、单板饰面板及类似的多层板:**										
	-竹制的:										
	---仅由薄板制的胶合板,每层厚度不超过 6 毫米:										
4412.1011	----至少有一表层是热带木										
4412.1011 11	至少有一表层为濒危热带木薄板制濒危竹胶合板(每层厚度≤6mm)〔999〕	6	0	30	13/	0	千克/立方米	ABFE/	MPQ	5	

协定税率 %								RCEP		特惠税率 %			Article Description
东/冰/格	巴基斯坦	韩国	瑞士上/下	哥/秘/柬	澳/毛	新西/坡/智	中国港/澳/台	东盟及马来/澳/韩	日/新	亚太2国	老/柬/缅	98/97/95	
			0/0	//0	/0	0//0	0/0/					0//	--Oriented standard board (OSB)
			0/0	//0	/0	0//0	0/0/					0//	--Other
													-Other:
													---Particle board:
													----Particle board of wheat /rice straw
													----Other
													---Other
													Fibreboard of wood or other ligneous materials, whether or not bonded with resins or other organic substances:
													-Medium density fibreboard (MDF):
													--Of a thickness not exceeding 5mm:
													---Of a density exceeding 0.8/cm³:
		1.8	0/0	//0	/0	0//0	0/0/	3.9/3.9/	/3.9			0//	----Not mechanically worked or surface covered
		0	0/0	//0	/0	0//0	0/0/					0//	----Other
													---Of a density exceeding 0.5 g/cm³ but not exceeding 0.8 g/cm³:
		1.8	0/0	//0	0/0	0//0	0/0/	3.9/3.9/	/3.9			0/0/	----Of radiata pine
		1.8	0/0	//0	/0	0//0	0/0/	3.9/3.9/	/3.9			0//	----Other
													---Other:
5//		3.5	0/0	//0	/0	0//0	0/0/	7.3/7.3/	/7.3			0//	----Not mechanically worked or surface covered
		1.8	0/0	//0	/0	0//	0/0/	3.9/3.9/	/3.9			0//	----Other
													--Of a thickness exceeding 5mm but not exceeding 9mm:
													---Of a density exceeding 0.8g/cm³:
			0/0	//0	/0	0//	0/0/					0//	----Not mechanically worked or surface covered
			3.2/3.2		/0	0//						0//	----Other
													---Of a density exceeding 0.5g/cm³ but not exceeding 0.8g/cm³:
			0/0	//0	0/0	0//0	0/0/					0/0/	----Of radiata pine
			0/0	//0	/0	0//0	0/0/					0//	----Other
													---Other:
5//			0/0	//0	/0	0//0	0/0/					0//	----Not mechanically worked or surface covered
		1.8	0/0	//0	/0	0//0	0/0/					0//	----Other
													--Of a thickness exceeding 9mm:
													---Of a density exceeding 0.8g/cm³:
		1.8	0/0	//0	/0	0//	0/0/					0//	----Not mechanically worked or surface covered
		3.5	3.2/3.2		/0	0//						0//	----Other
													---Of a density exceeding 0.5g/cm³ but not exceeding 0.8g/cm³:
		1.8	0/0	//0	0/0	0//0	0/0/	3.9/3.9/	/3.9			0/0/	----Of radiata pine
		1.8	0/0	//0	/0	0//0	0/0/	3.9/3.9/	/3.9			0//	----Other
													---Other:
5//		3.5	0/0	//0	/0	0//0	0/0/	7.3/7.3/	/7.3			0//	----Not mechanically worked or surface covered
		1.8	0/0	//0	/0	0//0	0/0/	3.9/3.9/	/3.9			0//	----Other
													-Other:
													--Of a density exceeding 0.8g/cm³:
		1.8	0/0	//0	/0	0//0	0/0/	3.9/3.9/	/3.9			0//	---Not mechanically worked or surface covered
		3.5	0/0	//0	/0	0//0	0/0/					0//	---Other
													--Of a density exceeding 0.5g/cm³ but not exceeding 0.8g/cm³:
			0/0	//0	0/0	0//	0/0/					0/0/	---Of radiata pine
			0/0	//0	/0	0//0	0/0/					0//	---Other
													--Of a density not exceeding 0.5g/cm³:
5//		3.5	0/0	//0	/0	0//0	0/0/					0//	---Of a density exceeding 0.35g/cm³ but not exceeding 0.5g/cm³
													---Of a density not exceeding 0.35g/cm³:
		3.5	0/0	//0	/0	0//	0/0/					0//	----Not mechanically worked or suface covered
		1.8	0/0	//0	/0	0//	0/0/					0//	----Other
													Plywood, veneered panels and similar laminated wood:
													-Of bamboo:
													---Plywood consisting solely of sheets, each ply not exceeding 6 mm
													----With at least one outer ply of tropical wood
5/0/		5.6	1.2/1.2	0/0/0	0/0	0//0	0/0/	4/4/	/4			0/0/	With at least one outer ply of endangered tropical wood, plywood consisting solely of sheets of endangered bamboo, each ply not exceeding 6mm thickness

税则号列		货品名称〔CIQ 扩展编码及品名—T2 表示见附表 2〕	最惠(%)	暂定税率	普通	增值/消费	出口退税	计量单位	监管条件/特殊证件	检验检疫	对美关税	亚太上/下
4412.1011	19	至少有一表层为濒危热带木薄板制其他竹胶合板(每层厚度≤6mm)〔999〕	6	0	30	13/	0	千克/立方米	ABFE/	MPQ	5	
4412.1011	91	至少有一表层是其他热带木薄板制濒危竹胶合板(每层厚度≤6mm)〔999〕	6	0	30	13/	0	千克/立方米	ABEF/	MPQ	5	
4412.1011	99	至少有一表层是其他热带木薄板制其他竹胶合板(每层厚度≤6mm)〔999〕	6	0	30	13/	13	千克/立方米	AB/	MPQ	5	
4412.1019		----其他										
4412.1019	11	至少有一表层为濒危非针叶木薄板胶合板(至少有一表层为温带非针叶木制,每层厚度≤6mm)〔999〕	4	0	30	13/	0	千克/立方米	ABFE/	MPQ	25	
4412.1019	19	其他至少有一表层为非针叶木薄板胶合板(至少有一表层为温带非针叶木制,每层厚度≤6mm)〔999〕	4	0	30	13/	13	千克/立方米	AB/	MPQ	25	
4412.1019	21	濒危竹地板层叠胶合而成的多层板(每层厚度≤6mm)〔999〕	4	0	30	13/	0	千克/立方米	ABE/	MPQ	25	
4412.1019	29	其他竹地板层叠胶合而成的多层板(每层厚度≤6mm)〔999〕	4	0	30	13/	13	千克/立方米	AB/	MPQ	25	
4412.1019	91	其他濒危竹胶合板(每层厚度≤6mm)〔999〕	4	0	30	13/	0	千克/立方米	ABE/	MPQ	25	
4412.1019	99	其他竹胶合板(每层厚度≤6mm)〔999〕	4	0	30	13/	13	千克/立方米	AB/	MPQ	25	
4412.1020		---其他,至少有一表层是非针叶木										
4412.1020	11	至少有一表层是濒危非针叶木的濒危竹制多层板(每层厚度≤6mm)〔999〕	6	0	30	13/	0	千克/立方米	ABFE/	MPQ		
4412.1020	19	至少有一表层是其他非针叶木的其他濒危竹制多层板(每层厚度≤6mm)〔999〕	6	0	30	13/	0	千克/立方米	ABEF/	MPQ		
4412.1020	91	至少有一表层是濒危非针叶木的其他竹制多层板(每层厚度≤6mm)〔999〕	6	0	30	13/	0	千克/立方米	ABEF/	MPQ		
4412.1020	99	至少有一表层是其他非针叶木的其他竹制多层板(每层厚度≤6mm)〔999〕	6	0	30	13/	13	千克/立方米	AB/	MPQ		
		---其他:										
4412.1093		----中间至少有一层是本章本国注释一所列的热带木										
4412.1093	10	其他濒危的竹制多层板,中间至少有一层是本章本国注释一所列的热带木〔999〕	6	0	30	13/	0	千克/立方米	ABEF/	MPQ		
4412.1093	90	其他竹制多层板,中间至少有一层是本章本国注释一所列的热带木〔999〕	6	0	30	13/	13	千克/立方米	AB/	MPQ		
4412.1094		----其他,中间至少有一层是其他热带木										
4412.1094	10	其他濒危的竹制多层板,中间至少有一层是其他热带木〔999〕	6	0	30	13/	0	千克/立方米	ABEF/	MPQ		
4412.1094	90	其他竹制多层板,中间至少有一层是其他热带木〔999〕	6	0	30	13/	13	千克/立方米	AB/	MPQ		
4412.1095		----其他,中间至少含有一层木碎料板										
4412.1095	10	其他中间至少含有一层木碎料板的濒危竹制多层板〔999〕	6	0	30	13/	0	千克/立方米	ABEF/	MPQ		
4412.1095	90	其他中间至少含有一层木碎料板的其他竹制多层板〔999〕	6	0	30	13/	13	千克/立方米	AB/	MPQ		
4412.1099		----其他										
4412.1099	10	其他濒危竹制多层板〔999〕	4	0	30	13/	0	千克/立方米	ABE/	MPQ		
4412.1099	90	其他竹制多层板〔999〕	4	0	30	13/	13	千克/立方米	AB/	MPQ		
		-仅由薄木板制的胶合板(竹制除外),每层厚度不超过 6 毫米:										
4412.3100		--至少有一表层是热带木										
4412.3100	10	至少有一表层为桃花心木薄板制胶合板(每层厚度≤6mm)〔999〕	6	0	30	13/	13	千克/立方米	ABFE/	MPQ	25	
4412.3100	20	至少有一表层为拉敏木薄板制胶合板(每层厚度≤6mm)〔999〕	6	0	30	13/	13	千克/立方米	ABFE/	MPQ	25	
4412.3100	30	至少有一表层为濒危热带木薄板制胶合板(每层厚度≤6mm)〔999〕	6	0	30	13/	0	千克/立方米	ABFE/	MPQ	25	
4412.3100	90	至少有一表层是其他热带木制的胶合板(每层厚度≤6mm,竹制除外)〔999〕	6	0	30	13/	13	千克/立方米	AB/	MPQ	25	

协定税率 %								RCEP		特惠税率 %			Article Description
东/冰/格	巴基斯坦	韩国	瑞士 上/下	哥/秘/柬	澳/毛	新西/坡/智	中国港/澳/台	东盟及马来/澳/韩	日/新	亚太2国	老/柬/缅	98/97/95	
5/0/		5.6	1.2/1.2	0/0/0	0/0	0//0	0/0/	4/4/	/4			0/0/	With at least one outer ply of endangered tropical wood, plywood consisting solely of sheets of other bamboo, each ply not exceeding 6mm thickness
5/0/		5.6	1.2/1.2	0/0/0	0/0	0//0	0/0/	4/4/	/4			0/0/	With at least one outer ply of other tropical wood, plywood consisting solely of sheets of endangered bamboo, each ply not exceeding 6mm thickness
5/0/		5.6	1.2/1.2	0/0/0	0/0	0//0	0/0/	4/4/	/4			0/0/	With at least one outer ply of other tropical wood, plywood consisting solely of sheets of other bamboo, each ply not exceeding 6mm thickness
													----Other
		1.8	0/0	//0	/0	0//	0/0/					0//	Plywood consisting solely of sheets of wood, with at least one outer ply of endangered non-coniferous wood, each ply thickness≤6mm
		1.8	0/0	//0	/0	0//	0/0/					0//	Plywood consisting solely of sheets of wood, with at least one outer ply of non-coniferous wood each ply thickness≤6mm
		1.8	0/0	//0	/0	0//	0/0/					0//	Plywood with two or more plies of endangered bamboo, each ply thickness≤6mm
		1.8	0/0	//0	/0	0//	0/0/					0//	Plywood with two or more plies of bamboo, each ply thickness≤6mm
		1.8	0/0	//0	/0	0//	0/0/					0//	Plywood consisting solely of sheets of endangered bamboo, each ply thickness≤6mm
		1.8	0/0	//0	/0	0//	0/0/					0//	Other plywood consisting solely of sheets of other bamboo , each ply thickness≤6mm
													---Other, with at least one outer ply of non-coniferous wood
5//	3.5	4.6	0/0	0/0/0	0/0	0//	0/0/	9.8/9.8/	/9.8			0/0/	Laminated wood of endangered bamboo, with at least one outer ply of endangered non-coniferous wood, each ply thickness≤6mm
5//	3.5	4.6	0/0	0/0/0	0/0	0//	0/0/	9.8/9.8/	/9.8			0/0/	Laminated wood of endangered bamboo, with at least one outer ply of non-coniferous wood, each ply thickness≤6mm
5//	3.5	4.6	0/0	0/0/0	0/0	0//	0/0/	9.8/9.8/	/9.8			0/0/	Laminated wood of bamboo, with at least one outer ply of endangered non-coniferous wood in imminent dangers, each ply thickness≤6mm
5//	3.5	4.6	0/0	0/0/0	0/0	0//	0/0/	9.8/9.8/	/9.8			0/0/	Laminated wood of bamboo, with at least one outer ply of non-coniferous wood, each ply thickness≤6mm
													---Other:
													----At least one layer in the middle is tropical wood listed in note 1 of this chapter
		3.7	0/0	//0	/0	0//	0/0/					0//	For other endangered bamboo multilayer boards, at least one layer in the middle is tropical wood listed in note 1 of this chapter
		3.7	0/0	//0	/0	0//	0/0/					0//	For other bamboo multilayer boards, at least one layer in the middle is tropical wood listed in note 1 of this chapter
													----Other, at least one layer in the middle is other tropical wood
		3.7	0/0	//0	/0	0//	0/0/	0/0/0	3.6/0			0//	Other endangered bamboo multilayer boards, at least one layer in the middle is other tropical wood
		3.7	0/0	//0	/0	0//	0/0/	0/0/0	3.6/0			0//	Other bamboo multilayer boards, at least one layer in the middle is other tropical wood
													----Other, at least one layer of wood particleboard is contained in the middle
		4.6	0/0	//0	/0	0//	0/0/					0//	Other endangered bamboo multilayer boards containing at least one layer of Wood Particleboard in the middle
		4.6	0/0	//0	/0	0//	0/0/					0//	Other bamboo multilayer boards with at least one layer of Wood Particleboard in the middle
													----Other
0/0/	0	0	0/0	0/0/0	0/0	0/0/0	0/0/	0/0/0	3.6/0			0/0/0	Other laminated wood of endangered bamboo
0/0/	0	0	0/0	0/0/0	0/0	0/0/0	0/0/	0/0/0	3.6/0			0/0/0	Other laminated of bamboo
													-Other plywood consisting solely of sheets of wood (other than bamboo), each ply not exceeding 6mm thickness:
													--With at least one outer ply of tropical wood
5/0/		5.6	1.2/1.2	0/0/0	0/0	0//0	0/0/	4/4/	/4			0/0/	Plywood, with at least one outer ply of Acajou d'afrique, each ply thickness≤6mm
5/0/		5.6	1.2/1.2	0/0/0	0/0	0//0	0/0/	4/4/	/4			0/0/	Plywood, with at least one outer ply of Ramin wood, each ply thickness≤6mm
5/0/		5.6	1.2/1.2	0/0/0	0/0	0//0	0/0/	4/4/	/4			0/0/	Plywood, with at least one outer ply of tropical wood, each ply not exceeding 6mm thickness
5/0/		5.6	1.2/1.2	0/0/0	0/0	0//0	0/0/	4/4/	/4			0/0/	Plywood, with at least one outer ply of other tropical wood, each ply not exceeding 6mm thickness, other than bamboo

税则号列		货品名称〔CIQ扩展编码及品名－T2表示见附表2〕	最惠(%)	暂定税率	普通	增值/消费	出口退税	计量单位	监管条件/特殊证件	检验检疫	对美关税	亚太上/下
4412.3300		--其他，至少有一表层是下列非针叶木：桤木、白蜡木、水青冈木(山毛榉木)、桦木、樱桃木、栗木、榆木、桉木、山核桃、七叶树、椴木、槭木、栎木(橡木)、悬铃木、杨木、刺槐木、鹅掌楸或核桃木										
4412.3300	10	至少有一表层是濒危的下列非针叶木：桤木、白蜡木、水青冈木(山毛榉木)、桦木、樱桃木、栗木、榆木、桉木、山核桃、七叶树、椴木、槭木、栎木(橡木)、悬铃木、杨木、刺槐木、鹅掌楸或核桃木薄板制胶合板(每层厚度≤6mm，竹制除外)〔999〕	4	0	30	13/	0	千克/立方米	ABFE/	MPQ	25	
4412.3300	90	至少有一表层是下列非针叶木：桤木、白蜡木、水青冈木(山毛榉木)、桦木、樱桃木、栗木、榆木、桉木、山核桃、七叶树、椴木、槭木、栎木(橡木)、悬铃木、杨木、刺槐木、鹅掌楸或核桃木薄板制胶合板〔999〕	4	0	30	13/	13	千克/立方米	AB/	MPQ	25	
		--其他，至少有一表层为子目4412.33未具体列名的非针叶木：										
4412.3410		---其他，至少有一表层是温带非针叶木(子目4412.33的非针叶木除外)										
4412.3410	10	至少有一表层是濒危温带非针叶木薄板制胶合板(每层厚度≤6毫米，竹制除外)〔999〕	4	0	30	13/	0	千克/立方米	ABEF/	MPQ	25	
4412.3410	90	至少有一表层是其他温带非针叶木薄板制胶合板(每层厚度≤6毫米，竹制除外)〔999〕	4	0	30	13/	13	千克/立方米	AB/	MPQ	25	
4412.3490		---其他										
4412.3490	10	至少有一表层是濒危其他非针叶胶合板(每层厚度≤6mm，竹制除外)〔999〕	4	0	30	13/	0	千克/立方米	ABEF/	MPQ	25	
4412.3490	90	至少有一表层是其他非针叶胶合板(每层厚度≤6毫米，竹制除外)〔999〕	4	0	30	13/	13	千克/立方米	AB/	MPQ	25	
4412.3900		--其他，上下表层均为针叶木										
4412.3900	10	其他濒危薄板制胶合板，上下表层均为针叶木(每层厚度≤6mm，竹制除外)〔101针叶木胶合板，102非针叶木胶合板，103其它胶合板〕	4	0	30	13/	0	千克/立方米	ABFE/	MPQ	25	
4412.3900	90	其他薄板制胶合板，上下表层均为针叶木(每层厚度≤6mm，竹制除外)〔101针叶木胶合板，102非针叶木胶合板，103其它胶合板〕	4	0	30	13/	13	千克/立方米	AB/	MPQ	25	
		-单板层积材：										
4412.4100		--至少有一表层是热带木										
4412.4100	10	至少有一表层是濒危热带木的单板层积材〔999〕	6	0	30	13/	0	千克/立方米	ABFE/	MPQ	25	
4412.4100	90	其他至少有一表层是热带木的单板层积材〔999〕	6	0	30	13/	0,13	千克/立方米	AB/	MPQ	25	
4412.4200		--其他，至少有一表层是非针叶木										
4412.4200	10	其他至少有一表层是濒危非针叶木的单板层积材〔999〕	6	0	30	13/	0	千克/立方米	ABFE/	MPQ	25	
4412.4200	90	其他至少有一表层是非针叶木的单板层积材〔999〕	6	0	30	13/	0,13	千克/立方米	AB/	MPQ	25	
		--其他，上下表层均为针叶木： ---中间至少有一层是热带木：										
4412.4911		----中间至少有一层是本章本国注释一所列的热带木										
4412.4911	10	其他涉濒危的单板层积材，上下表层均为针叶木，中间至少有一层是本章本国注释一所列热带木〔999〕	6	0	30	13/	0	千克/立方米	ABFE/	MPQ		
4412.4911	90	其他单板层积材，上下表层均为针叶木，中间至少有一层是本章本国注释一所列热带木〔999〕	6	0	30	13/	13	千克/立方米	AB/	MPQ		
4412.4919		----其他，中间至少有一层是其他热带木										

协定税率 %								RCEP		特惠税率 %			Article Description
东/冰/格	巴基斯坦	韩国	瑞士 上/下	哥/秘/柬	澳/毛	新西/坡/智	中国港/澳/台	东盟及马来/澳/韩	日/新	亚太2国	老/柬/缅	98/97/95	
													--Other, with at least one outer ply Of non-coniferous wood Of the species alder (*Alnus spp.*), ash (*Fraxinus spp.*), beech(*Fagus spp.*), birch(*Betula spp.*), *chestnut*(Castanea spp.), elm(*Ulmus spp.*), eucalyptus(*eucalyp-tus spp.*)
		1.8	0/0	//0	/0	0//	0/0/					0//	At least one surface of the following endangered non coniferous wood: alder, Chinese ash, water wood (beech), birch, cherry, chestnut, elm, eucalyptus, hickory, chestnut, basswood, maple, oak (oak), sycamore, poplar, locust, Liriodendron or walnut plywood sheet, of a thickness not exceeding 6mm
		1.8	0/0	//0	/0	0//	0/0/					0//	At least one surface of the following non coniferous wood: alder, Chinese ash, water wood (beech), birch, cherry, chestnut, elm, eucalyptus, hickory, chestnut, basswood, maple, oak (oak), sycamore, poplar, locust, Liriodendron or walnut plywood sheet, of a thickness not exceeding 6mm
													--Other, with at least one outer ply of non—coniferous wood not specified under subheading 4412.33:
													---With at least one outer ply of temperate non-coniferous wood(*other than non-conif-erous wood of subheading* 4412.33)
		1.8	0/0	//0	/0	0//	0/0/					0//	*Plywood, with at least one outer ply of other endangered temperate non-coniferous wood, each ply not exceeding 6mm thickness(other than of bamboo)*
		1.8	0/0	//0	/0	0//	0/0/					0//	*Plywood, with at least one outer ply of other temperate non-coniferous wood, each ply not exceeding 6mm thickness (other than of bamboo)*
													---Other
		1.8	0/0	//0	/0	0//	0/0/					0//	*Plywood, with at least one outer ply of other endangered non-coniferous wood, each ply not exceeding 6mm thickness (other than of bamboo)*
		1.8	0/0	//0	/0	0//	0/0/					0//	*Plywood, with at least one outer ply of other non-coniferous wood, each ply not exceeding 6mm thickness (other than of bamboo)*
													--Other, with both outer plies of coniferous wood
0/0/	0	0	0/0	0/0/0	0/0	0/0/0	0/0/	0/0/0	3.6/0			0/0/0	*Plywood, Plywood consisting solely of sheets of endangered wood, Upper and lower surface are needle leaf wood, each ply not exceeding 6mm thickness (other than of bamboo)*
0/0/	0	0	0/0	0/0/0	0/0	0/0/0	0/0/	0/0/0	3.6/0			0/0/0	*Plywood consisting solely of sheets of other wood, Upper and lower surface are needle leaf wood, each ply not exceeding 6mm thickness (other than of bamboo)*
													-Laminated veneered lumber (LVL):
													--With at least one outer ply of tropical wood
5//	3.5	4.6	0/0	//0	/0	0//0	0/0/					0//	*At least one surface layer is veneer laminated timber of endangered tropical wood*
5//	3.5	4.6	0/0	//0	/0	0//0	0/0/					0//	*Other veneer laminated timber with at least one surface layer of tropical wood*
													--Other, with at least one outer ply of non — coniferous wood
5//	3.5	4.6	0/0	//0	/0	0//0	0/0/					0//	*Other laminated veneer lumber with at least one surface layer of endangered non coniferous wood*
5//	3.5	4.6	0/0	//0	/0	0//0	0/0/					0//	*Other veneer laminated timber with at least one surface layer of non coniferous wood*
													--Other, with both outer plies of coniferous wood
													---At least one layer in the middle is tropical wood:
													----At least one layer in the middle is tropical wood listed in note 1 of this chapter
		3.7	0/0	//0	/0	0//0	0/0/					0//	*For other endangered laminated veneer lumber, the upper and lower surface layers are coniferous wood, and at least one layer in the middle is tropical wood listed in note 1 of this chapter*
		3.7	0/0	//0	/0	0//0	0/0/					0//	*For other veneer laminated timber, the upper and lower surface layers are coniferous wood, and at least one layer in the middle is tropical wood listed in note 1 of this chapter*
													----Other, at least one layer in the middle is other tropical wood

税则号列		货品名称〔CIQ 扩展编码及品名－T2 表示见附表 2〕	最惠(%)	暂定税率	普通	增值/消费	出口退税	计量单位	监管条件/特殊证件	检验检疫	对美关税	亚太上/下
4412.4919	10	其他涉濒危的单板层积材，上下表层均为针叶木，中间至少有一层是其他热带木〔999〕	6	0	30	13/	0	千克/立方米	ABFE/	MPQ		
4412.4919	90	其他单板层积材，上下表层均为针叶木，中间至少有一层是其他热带木〔999〕	6	0	30	13/	13	千克/立方米	AB/	MPQ		
4412.4920		---其他，中间至少含有一层木碎料板										
4412.4920	10	其他涉濒危的单板层积材，上下表层均为针叶木，中间至少含有一层木碎料板〔999〕	6	0	30	13/	0	千克/立方米	ABFE/	MPQ		
4412.4920	90	其他单板层积材，上下表层均为针叶木，中间至少含有一层木碎料板〔999〕	6	0	30	13/	13	千克/立方米	AB/	MPQ		
4412.4990		---其他										
4412.4990	10	其他涉濒危的单板层积材，上下表层均为针叶木〔999〕	4	0	30	13/	0	千克/立方米	ABFE/	MPQ	25	2.8/2.8
4412.4990	90	其他单板层积材，上下表层均为针叶木〔999〕	4	0	30	13/	13	千克/立方米	AB/	MPQ	25	2.8/2.8
		-木块芯胶合板、侧板条芯胶合板及板条芯胶合板：										
4412.5100		--至少有一表层是热带木										
4412.5100	10	至少有一表层是濒危热带木的木块芯胶合板等（还包括侧板条芯胶合板及板条芯胶合板）〔999〕	6	0	30	13/	0	千克/立方米	ABFE/	MPQ	25	
4412.5100	90	至少有一表层是其他热带木的木块芯胶合板等（还包括侧板条芯胶合板及板条芯胶合板）〔999〕	6	0	30	13/	13	千克/立方米	AB/	MPQ	25	
4412.5200		--其他，至少有一表层是非针叶木										
4412.5200	10	至少有一表层是濒危非针叶木的木块芯胶合板等（还包括侧板条芯胶合板及板条芯胶合板）〔999〕	6	0	30	13/	0	千克/立方米	ABFE/	MPQ	25	
4412.5200	90	至少有一表层是其他非针叶木的木块芯胶合板等（还包括侧板条芯胶合板及板条芯胶合板）〔999〕	6	0	30	13/	13	千克/立方米	AB/	MPQ	25	
		--其他，上下表层均为针叶木：										
		---中间至少有一层是热带木：										
4412.5911		----中间至少有一层是本章本国注释一所列的热带木										
4412.5911	10	其他涉濒危的木块芯胶合板，上下表层均为针叶木，中间至少有一层是本章本国注释一所列的热带木（还包括侧板条芯胶合板及板条芯胶合板）〔999〕	6	0	30	13/	0	千克/立方米	ABFE/	MPQ		
4412.5911	90	其他木块芯胶合板，上下表层均为针叶木，中间至少有一层是本章本国注释一所列的热带木（还包括侧板条芯胶合板及板条芯胶合板）〔999〕	6	0	30	13/	13	千克/立方米	AB/	MPQ		
4412.5919		----其他，中间至少有一层是其他热带木										
4412.5919	10	其他涉濒危的木块芯胶合板，上下表层均为针叶木，中间至少有一层是其他热带木（还包括侧板条芯胶合板及板条芯胶合板）〔999〕	6	0	30	13/	0	千克/立方米	ABFE/	MPQ		
4412.5919	90	其他木块芯胶合板，上下表层均为针叶木，中间至少有一层是其他热带木（还包括侧板条芯胶合板及板条芯胶合板）〔999〕	6	0	30	13/	13	千克/立方米	AB/	MPQ		
4412.5920		---其他，中间至少含有一层木碎料板										
4412.5920	10	其他涉濒危的木块芯胶合板，上下表层均为针叶木，中间至少含有一层木碎料板（还包括侧板条芯胶合板及板条芯胶合板）〔999〕	6	0	30	13/	0	千克/立方米	ABFE/	MPQ		

协定税率 %								RCEP		特惠税率 %			Article Description
东/冰/格	巴基斯坦	韩国	瑞士上/下	哥/秘/柬	澳/毛	新西/坡/智	中国港/澳/台	东盟及马来/澳/韩	日/新	亚太2国	老/柬/缅	98/97/95	
		3.7	0/0	//0	/0	0//0	0/0/	0/0/0	3.6/0			0//	*For other endangered laminated veneer lumber, the upper and lower surface layers are coniferous wood, and at least one layer in the middle is other tropical wood*
		3.7	0/0	//0	/0	0//0	0/0/	0/0/0	3.6/0			0//	*For other veneer laminated timber, the upper and lower surface layers are coniferous wood, and at least one layer in the middle is other tropical wood*
													---Other, at least one layer of wood particleboard is contained in the middle
		4.6	0/0	//0	/0	0//0	0/0/					0//	*For other endangered laminated veneer lumber, the upper and lower surface layers are coniferous wood, and at least one layer of wood debris board is contained in the middle*
		4.6	0/0	//0	/0	0//0	0/0/					0//	*For other veneer laminated timber, the upper and lower surface layers are coniferous wood, and at least one layer of wood particleboard is contained in the middle*
													---Other
0/0/	0	0	0/0	0/0/0	0/0	0/0/0	0/0/	0/0/0	3.6/0			0/0/0	*Other endangered veneer laminated timber, the upper and lower surface layers are coniferous wood*
0/0/	0	0	0/0	0/0/0	0/0	0/0/0	0/0/	0/0/0	3.6/0			0/0/0	*Other veneer laminated timber, the upper and lower surface layers are coniferous wood*
													-Blockboard, laminboard and battenboard :
													--With at least one outer ply of tropical wood
5//	3.5	4.6	0/0	//0	/0	0//0	0/0/					0//	*Wood block core plywood with at least one surface layer of endangered tropical wood (also including side panel strip core plywood and strip core plywood)*
5//	3.5	4.6	0/0	//0	/0	0//0	0/0/					0//	*At least one surface layer is wood block core plywood of other tropical wood (also including side panel strip core plywood and strip core plywood)*
													--Other, with at least one outer ply of non — coniferous wood
5//	3.5	4.6	0/0	//0	/0	0//0	0/0/					0//	*Wood block core plywood with at least one surface layer of endangered non coniferous wood (also including side panel strip core plywood and strip core plywood)*
5//	3.5	4.6	0/0	//0	/0	0//0	0/0/					0//	*At least one surface layer is other non coniferous wood block core plywood, etc. (also including side panel strip core plywood and strip core plywood)*
													--Other, with both outer plies of coniferous wood
													---At least one layer in the middle is tropical wood:
													----At least one layer in the middle is tropical wood listed in note 1 of this chapter
		3.7	0/0	//0	/0	0//0	0/0/					0//	*For other endangered wood block core plywood, the upper and lower surface layers are coniferous wood, and at least one layer in the middle is tropical wood listed in note 1 of this chapter (also including side panel strip core plywood and strip core plywood)*
		3.7	0/0	//0	/0	0//0	0/0/					0//	*For other wood block core plywood, the upper and lower surface layers are coniferous wood, and at least one layer in the middle is tropical wood listed in note 1 of this chapter (also including side panel strip core plywood and strip core plywood)*
													----Other, at least one layer in the middle is other tropical wood
		3.7	0/0	//0	/0	0//0	0/0/	0/0/0	3.6/0			0//	*For other endangered wood block core plywood, the upper and lower surface layers are coniferous wood, and at least one layer in the middle is other tropical wood (also including side panel strip core plywood and strip core plywood)*
		3.7	0/0	//0	/0	0//0	0/0/	0/0/0	3.6/0			0//	*For other wood block core plywood, the upper and lower surface layers are coniferous wood, and at least one layer in the middle is other tropical wood (also including side panel strip core plywood and strip core plywood)*
													---Other, at least one layer of wood particleboard is contained in the middle
		4.6	0/0	//0	/0	0//0	0/0/					0//	*For other endangered wood block core plywood, the upper and lower surface layers are coniferous wood, and at least one layer of wood chip board is contained in the middle (also including side panel strip core plywood and strip core plywood)*

税则号列		货品名称〔CIQ扩展编码及品名－T2表示见附表2〕	最惠(%)	暂定税率	普通	增值/消费	出口退税	计量单位	监管条件/特殊证件	检验检疫	对美关税	亚太上/下
4412.5920	90	其他木块芯胶合板,上下表层均为针叶木,中间至少含有一层木碎料板(还包括侧板条芯胶合板及板条芯胶合板)〔999〕	6	0	30	13/	13	千克/立方米	AB/	MPQ		
4412.5990		---其他										
4412.5990	10	其他涉濒危的木块芯胶合板,上下表层均为针叶木(还包括侧板条芯胶合板及板条芯胶合板)〔999〕	4	0	30	13/	0	千克/立方米	ABEF/	MPQ		
4412.5990	90	其他木块芯胶合板,上下表层均为针叶木(还包括侧板条芯胶合板及板条芯胶合板)〔999〕	4	0	30	13/	13	千克/立方米	AB/	MPQ		
		-其他:										
4412.9100		--至少有一表层是热带木										
4412.9100	10	其他至少有一表层是濒危热带木的多层板〔999〕	6	0	30	13/	0	千克/立方米	ABFE/	MPQ	25	
4412.9100	90	其他至少有一表层是热带木的多层板〔999〕	6	0	30	13/	0,13	千克/立方米	AB/	MPQ	25	
4412.9200		--其他,至少有一表层是非针叶木										
4412.9200	10	其他至少有一表层濒危非针叶木的多层板〔999〕	6	0	30	13/	0	千克/立方米	ABFE/	MPQ	25	
4412.9200	90	其他至少有一表层是非针叶木的多层板〔999〕	6	0	30	13/	0,13	千克/立方米	AB/	MPQ	25	
		--其他,上下表层均为针叶木:										
4412.9920		---中间至少有一层是本章本国注释一所列的热带木										
4412.9920	10	其他涉濒危的多层板,上下表层均为针叶木,中间至少有一层是本章本国注释一所列的热带木〔999〕	6	0	30	13/	0	千克/立方米	ABFE/	MPQ		
4412.9920	90	其他多层板,上下表层均为针叶木,中间至少有一层是本章本国注释一所列的热带木〔999〕	6	0	30	13/	13	千克/立方米	AB/	MPQ		
4412.9930		---其他,中间至少有一层是其他热带木										
4412.9930	10	其他涉濒危的多层板,上下表层均为针叶木,中间至少有一层是其他热带木〔999〕	6	0	30	13/	0	千克/立方米	ABFE/	MPQ		
4412.9930	90	其他多层板,上下表层均为针叶木,中间至少有一层是其他热带木〔999〕	6	0	30	13/	13	千克/立方米	AB/	MPQ		
4412.9940		---其他,中间至少含有一层木碎料板										
4412.9940	10	其他涉濒危的多层板,上下表层均为针叶木,中间至少含有一层木碎料板〔999〕	6	0	30	13/	0	千克/立方米	ABFE/	MPQ		
4412.9940	90	其他多层板,上下表层均为针叶木,中间至少含有一层木碎料板〔999〕	6	0	30	13/	13	千克/立方米	AB/	MPQ		
4412.9990		---其他										
4412.9990	10	其他涉濒危的多层板,上下表层均为针叶木〔999〕	4	0	30	13/	0	千克/立方米	ABEF/	MPQ	25	2.8/2.8
4412.9990	90	其他多层板,上下表层均为针叶木〔999〕	4	0	30	13/	13	千克/立方米	AB/	MPQ	25	2.8/2.8
44.13		**强化木,成块、板、条或异型的:**										
4413.0000		强化木,成块、板、条或异型的〔999〕	6	0	20	13/	13	千克	AB/	MPQ	25	
44.14		**木制的画框、相框、镜框及类似品:**										
4414.1000		-热带木的										
4414.1000	10	濒危热带木制画框,相框,镜框及类似品〔999〕	7		100	13/	0	千克	ABFE/	PQ	27	
4414.1000	90	其他热带木制的画框,相框,镜框及类似品〔999〕	7		100	13/	13	千克	AB/	PQ	27	
		-其他:										
4414.9010		---辐射松制的〔999〕	7	0	100	13/	13	千克	AB/	PQ	20	
4414.9090		---其他										
4414.9090	10	濒危木制画框,相框,镜框及类似品〔999〕	7		100	13/	0	千克	ABFE/	PQ	27	

协定税率 %								RCEP		特惠税率 %			Article Description
东/冰/格	巴基斯坦	韩国	瑞士上/下	哥/秘/柬	澳/毛	新西/坡/智	中国港/澳/台	东盟及马来/澳/韩	日/新	亚太2国	老/柬/缅	98/97/95	
		4.6	0/0	//0	/0	0//0	0/0/					0//	*For other wood block core plywood, the upper and lower surface layers are coniferous wood, and at least one layer of wood chip board is contained in the middle (also including side plate strip core plywood and strip core plywood)*
													---Other
0/0/	0	0	0/0	0/0/0	0/0	0/0/0	0/0/	0/0/0	3.6/0			0/0/0	*For other endangered wood block core plywood, the upper and lower surface layers are coniferous wood (including side panel strip core plywood and strip core plywood)*
0/0/	0	0	0/0	0/0/0	0/0	0/0/0	0/0/	0/0/0	3.6/0			0/0/0	*For other wood block core plywood, the upper and lower surface layers are coniferous wood (also including side panel strip core plywood and strip core plywood)*
													- Other:
													-- With at least one outer ply of tropical wood
5//	3.5	4.6	0/0	//0	/0	0//0	0/0/					0//	*Other multilayer boards with at least one surface layer of endangered tropical wood*
5//	3.5	4.6	0/0	//0	/0	0//0	0/0/					0//	*Other multilayer boards with at least one surface layer of tropical wood*
													-- Other, with at least one outer ply of non — coniferous wood
5//	3.5	4.6	0/0	//0	/0	0//0	0/0/					0//	*Other multilayer boards with at least one surface layer of endangered non coniferous wood*
5//	3.5	4.6	0/0	//0	/0	0//0	0/0/					0//	*Other multilayer boards with at least one surface layer of non coniferous wood*
													-- Other, with both outer plies of coniferous wood
													---At least one layer in the middle is tropical wood listed in note 1 of this chapter
		3.7	0/0	//0	/0	0//0	0/0/					0//	*For other endangered multilayer boards, the upper and lower surface layers are coniferous wood, and at least one layer in the middle is tropical wood listed in note 1 of this chapter*
		3.7	0/0	//0	/0	0//0	0/0/					0//	*For other multilayer boards, the upper and lower surface layers are coniferous wood, and at least one layer in the middle is tropical wood listed in note 1 of this chapter*
													---Other, at least one layer in the middle is other tropical wood
		3.7	0/0	//0	/0	0//0	0/0/	0/0/0	3.6/0			0//	*For other endangered multilayer boards, the upper and lower surface layers are coniferous wood, and at least one layer in the middle is other tropical wood*
		3.7	0/0	//0	/0	0//0	0/0/	0/0/0	3.6/0			0//	*For other multilayer boards, the upper and lower surface layers are coniferous wood, and at least one layer in the middle is other tropical wood*
													---Other, at least one layer of wood particleboard is contained in the middle
		4.6	0/0	//0	/0	0//0	0/0/					0//	*For other endangered multilayer boards, the upper and lower surface layers are coniferous wood, and at least one layer of wood debris board is contained in the middle*
		4.6	0/0	//0	/0	0//0	0/0/					0//	*For other multilayer boards, the upper and lower surface layers are coniferous wood, and at least one layer of wood chip board is contained in the middle*
													---Other
0/0/	0	0	0/0	0/0/0	0/0	0/0/0	0/0/	0/0/0	3.6/0			0/0/0	*For other endangered multilayer boards, the upper and lower surface layers are coniferous wood*
0/0/	0	0	0/0	0/0/0	0/0	0/0/0	0/0/	0/0/0	3.6/0			0/0/0	*For other multilayer boards, the upper and lower surface layers are coniferous wood*
													Densified wood, in blocks, plates, strips or profile shapes:
0/0/	0	1.2	0/0	0/0/0	0/0	0/0/0	0/0/	0/0/5.4	5.5/0			0/0/0	Densified wood, in blocks, plates, strips or profile shapes
													Wooden frames for paintings, photographs, mirrors or similar objects:
													- Of tropical wood
													Endangered tropical wooden picture frames, photo frames, picture frames and the like
													Other tropical wooden picture frames, photo frames, picture frames and similar products
													-Other:
				//0	0/0	0//0	0/0/					0/0/	---Of radiata pinc
													---Other
												0//	Endangered wooden picture frames, photo frames, mirror frames and the like

税则号列		货品名称〔CIQ 扩展编码及品名一T2 表示见附表 2〕	最惠(%)	暂定税率	普通	增值/消费	出口退税	计量单位	监管条件/特殊证件	检验检疫	对美关税	亚太上/下
4414.9090	90	其他木制的画框,相框,镜框及类似品〔999〕	7		100	13/	13	千克	AB/	PQ	27	
44.15		**包装木箱、木盒、板条箱、圆桶及类似的包装容器;木制电缆卷筒;木托板、箱形托盘及其他装载用木板;木制的托盘护框:**										
4415.1000		-箱、盒、板条箱、圆桶及类似的包装容器;电缆卷筒										
4415.1000	10	拉敏木制木箱及类似包装容器(电缆卷筒)〔999〕	6	0	80	13/	13	千克/件	ABFE/	PQ	25	
4415.1000	20	濒危木制木箱及类似包装容器(电缆卷筒)[T2]	6	0	80	13/	0	千克/件	ABFE/	PQ	25	
4415.1000	90	木箱及类似的包装容器、电缆卷筒[T2]	6	0	80	13/	13	千克/件	AB/	PQ	25	
		-木托板、箱形托盘及其他装载用木板;木制的托盘护框:										
4415.2010		---辐射松制的〔999〕	6	0	80	13/	13	千克/件	AB/	PQ		
4415.2090		---其他										
4415.2090	10	拉敏木托板、箱形托盘及装载木板(包括拉敏木制托盘护框)〔999〕	6	3	80	13/	13	千克/件	ABFE/	PQ	28	
4415.2090	20	濒危木托板、箱形托盘及装载木板(包括濒危木制托盘护框)〔101 针叶木木质包装,102 非针叶木木质包装,103 其他木质包装〕	6	3	80	13/	0	千克/件	ABFE/	PQ	28	
4415.2090	90	其他木制托板、箱形托盘及其他装载木板(包括其他木制托盘护框)[T2]	6	3	80	13/	13	千克/件	AB/	PQ	28	
44.16		**木制大桶、琵琶桶、盆和其他木制箍桶及其零件,包括桶板:**										
4416.0010		---辐射松制的〔101 其他木制品,102 针叶木木质包装〕	12	0	80	13/	0	千克	AB/	PQ		
4416.0090		---其他										
4416.0090	10	拉敏木制大桶、琵琶桶、盆和其他箍桶及其零件(包括拉敏木制桶板)〔101 其他木制品,102 非针叶木木质包装〕	12		80	13/	0	千克	ABFE/	PQ	32	
4416.0090	20	濒危木制大桶、琵琶桶、盆和其他箍桶及其零件(包括濒危木制桶板)〔101 其他木制品,102 针叶木木质包装,103 非针叶木木质包装,104 其他木质包装〕	12		80	13/	0	千克	ABFE/	PQ	32	
4416.0090	30	橡木制大桶、琵琶桶、盆和其他箍桶及其零件(包括橡木制桶板)〔101 其他木制品,102 针叶木木质包装〕	12	5	80	13/	0	千克	AB/	PQ	25	
4416.0090	90	其他木制大桶、琵琶桶、盆和其他箍桶及其零件(包括其他木制桶板)[T2]	12		80	13/	0	千克	AB/	PQ	32	
44.17		**木制的工具、工具支架、工具柄、扫帚及刷子的身及柄;木制鞋靴楦及楦头:**										
4417.0010		---辐射松制的〔999〕	12	0	80	13/	0	千克	AB/	PQ		
4417.0090		---其他										
4417.0090	10	拉敏木制工具、工具支架、工具柄、扫帚及刷子的身及柄(包括拉敏木制鞋靴楦及楦头)〔999〕	12		80	13/	0	千克	ABFE/	PQ	37	
4417.0090	20	濒危木制工具、工具支架、工具柄、扫帚及刷子的身及柄(包括濒危木制鞋靴楦及楦头)〔999〕	12		80	13/	0	千克	ABFE/	PQ	37	
4417.0090	90	其他木制工具、工具支架、工具柄、扫帚及刷子的身及柄(包括其他木制鞋靴楦及楦头)〔999〕	12		80	13/	0	千克	AB/	PQ	37	
44.18		**建筑用木工制品,包括蜂窝结构木镶板、已装拼的地板、木瓦及盖屋板:**										
		-窗、法兰西式(落地)窗及其框架:										
4418.1100		--热带木的										
4418.1100	10	濒危热带木制木窗,落地窗及其框架〔999〕	4		70	13/	0	千克	ABFE/	PQ	29	
4418.1100	90	其他热带木制木窗,落地窗及其框架〔999〕	4		70	13/	13	千克	AB/	PQ	29	
		--其他:										
4418.1910		---辐射松制的〔999〕	4	0	70	13/	13	千克	AB/	PQ		
4418.1990		---其他										
4418.1990	10	其他濒危木制木窗,落地窗及其框架〔999〕	4		70	13/	0	千克	ABFE/	PQ	29	
4418.1990	90	其他木制木窗,落地窗及其框架〔999〕	4		70	13/	13	千克	AB/	PQ	29	
		-门及其框架和门槛:										
4418.2100		--热带木的										
4418.2100	10	濒危热带木制的木门及其框架和门槛〔999〕	4	0	70	13/	0	千克	ABFE/	PQ	25	
4418.2100	90	其他热带木制的木门及其框架和门槛〔101 木门,102 其他木制品〕	4	0	70	13/	13	千克	AB/	PQ	25	

协定税率 %								RCEP		特惠税率 %			Article Description
东/冰/格	巴基斯坦	韩国	瑞士上/下	哥/秘/柬	澳/毛	新西/坡/智	中国港/澳/台	东盟及马来/澳/韩	日/新	亚太2国	老/柬/缅	98/97/95	
												0//	Other wooden picture frames, photo frames, mirror frames and the like
													Packing cases, boxes, crates, drums and similar packings, of wood; cable-drums of wood; pallets, box pallets and other load boards, of wood; pallet collars of wood:
													-Cases, boxes, crates, drums and similar packing; cable-drums
0/0/	2	1.5	0/0	0/0/0	0/0	0/0/0	0/0/	0/0/6.8	6.8/0			0/0/0	Cases and similar packing; cable-drums, of Ramin wood (*gonystylus. spp.*)
0/0/	2	1.5	0/0	0/0/0	0/0	0/0/0	0/0/	0/0/6.8	6.8/0			0/0/0	Cases and similar packing; cable-drums, of endangered wood
0/0/	2	1.5	0/0	0/0/0	0/0	0/0/0	0/0/	0/0/6.8	6.8/0			0/0/0	Cases and similar packing; cable-drums, of wood
													-Pallets, box pallets and other load boards; pallet collars:
5//				//0	0/0	0//0	0/0/	5/5/	/5			0/0/	---Of radiatat pine
													---Other
5//				//5		5//							Pallets, box pallets and other load boards; pallet collars, of Ramin wood (*gonystylus. spp.*)
5//				//5		5//							Pallets, box pallets and other load boards; pallet collars, of endangered wood
5//				//5		5//							Pallets, box pallets and other load boards; pallet collars, of wood
													Casks, barrels, vats, tubs and other coopers' products and parts thereof, of wood, including staves:
				//0	0/0	0//0	0/0/					0/0/	---Of radiata pine
													---Other
													Coopers' products and parts thereof (including staves), of Ramin wood (*gonystylus. spp.*)
													Coopers' products and parts thereof (including staves), of endangered wood
													Oak barrels, Pipa barrels, pots and other cudgels and their parts (including oak barrel boards)
													Coopers' products and parts thereof (including staves), of other wood
													Tools, tool bodies, tool handles, broom or brush bodies and handles, of wood; boot or shoe lasts and trees, of wood:
				//0	0/0	0//0	0/0/					0/0/	---Of radiata pine
													---Other
													Tools, tool bodies, tool handles, broom or brush bodies and handles, of ramin wood (including boot or shoe lasts and trees, of ramin wood)
													Tools, tool bodies, tool handles, broom or brush bodies and handles, of endangered wood(including boot or shoe lasts and trees, of endangered wood)
													Tools, tool bodies, tool handles, broom or brush bodies and handles, of wood(including boot or shoe lasts and trees, of wood)
													Builders' joinery and carpentry of wood, including cellular wood panels, assembled flooring panels, shingles and shakes:
													-wooden windows, floor to ceiling windows and their frames:
													-- Of tropical wood
				//0	/0		0/0/					0/0/	Endangered tropical wooden windows, floor to ceiling windows and their frames
				//0	/0		0/0/					0/0/	Other tropical wooden windows, floor to ceiling windows and their frames
													--Other:
				//0	0/0	0//	0/0/					0/0/	---Of radiata pine
													---Other
				//0	/0		0/0/					0/0/	Other endangered wooden windows, French windows and their frames
				//0	/0		0/0/					0/0/	Other wooden windows, floor to ceiling windows and their frames
													-Doors and their frames and thresholds :
													-- Of tropical wood
0/0/	0	0	0/0	0/0/0	0/0	0/0/0	0/0/	0/0/0	3.6/0			0/0/0	Wooden doors of endangered tropical wood and their frames and thresholds
0/0/	0	0	0/0	0/0/0	0/0	0/0/0	0/0/	0/0/0	3.6/0			0/0/0	Other tropical wooden doors and their frames and thresholds

税则号列	货品名称〔CIQ扩展编码及品名—T2表示见附表2〕	最惠(%)	暂定税率	普通	增值/消费	出口退税	计量单位	监管条件/特殊证件	检验检疫	对美关税	亚太上/下
4418.2900	--其他										
4418.2900 10	其他濒危木制的木门及其框架和门槛〔999〕	4	0	70	13/	0	千克	ABFE/	PQ	25	
4418.2900 90	其他木门及其框架和门槛〔101木门,102其他木制品〕	4	0	70	13/	13	千克	AB/	PQ	25	
4418.3000	-柱及梁,子目4418.81至4418.89的货品除外										
4418.3000 10	濒危木制柱和梁,但子目4418.81至4418.89的货品除外〔999〕	4	0	70	13/	0	千克	ABEF/	PQ	25	
4418.3000 90	其他木制柱和梁,但子目4418.81至4418.90的货品除外〔999〕	4	0	70	13/	13	千克	AB/	PQ	25	
4418.4000	-水泥构件的模板	4	0	70	13/	13	千克	AB/	PQ		
4418.5000	-木瓦及盖屋板	6	0	70	13/	13	千克	AB/	PQ		
	-已装拼的地板:										
	--竹的或至少顶层(耐磨层)是竹的:										
4418.7310	---马赛克地板用〔999〕	4	0	70	13/	0	千克	AB/	PQ		
4418.7320	---其他,竹制多层的〔999〕	4	0	70	13/	13	千克	AB/	PQ		
4418.7390	---其他〔999〕	4	0	70	13/	13	千克	AB/	PQ		
4418.7400	--其他,马赛克地板用										
4418.7400 10	已装拼的拉敏木制马赛克地板〔999〕	4	0	70	13/	0	千克	ABFE/	PQ		
4418.7400 20	已装拼的其他濒危木制马赛克地板〔999〕	4	0	70	13/	0	千克	ABFE/	PQ		
4418.7400 90	已装拼的其他木制马赛克地板〔999〕	4	0	70	13/	0	千克	AB/	PQ		
4418.7500	--其他,多层的										
4418.7500 10	已装拼的拉敏木制多层地板〔999〕	4	0	70	13/	0	千克	ABFE/	PQ	25	
4418.7500 20	已装拼的其他濒危木制多层地板〔999〕	4	0	70	13/	0	千克	ABFE/	PQ	25	
4418.7500 90	已装拼的其他木制多层地板〔999〕	4	0	70	13/	0	千克	AB/	PQ	25	
4418.7900	--其他										
4418.7900 10	已装拼的拉敏木制其他地板〔999〕	4	0	70	13/	0	千克	ABFE/	PQ	20	
4418.7900 20	已装拼的其他濒危木制地板〔999〕	4	0	70	13/	0	千克	ABFE/	PQ	20	
4418.7900 90	已装拼的木制其他地板〔999〕	4	0	70	13/	0	千克	AB/	PQ	20	
	-工程结构木制品:										
4418.8100	--集成材										
4418.8100 10	濒危竹制的集成材〔999〕	4	0	70	13/	0	千克	ABE/	PQ		
4418.8100 20	濒危木制的集成材〔999〕	4	0	70	13/	0	千克	ABEF/	PQ		
4418.8100 90	其他木制的集成材(包括竹制的)〔101竹制的,102木制的〕	4	0	70	13/	13	千克	AB/	PQ		
4418.8200	--正交胶合木										
4418.8200 10	濒危竹制的正交胶合木〔999〕	4	0	70	13/	0	千克	ABE/	PQ		
4418.8200 20	濒危木制的正交胶合木〔999〕	4	0	70	13/	0	千克	ABEF/	PQ		
4418.8200 90	其他木制的正交胶合木(包括竹制的)〔101竹制的,102木制的〕	4	0	70	13/	13	千克	AB/	PQ		
4418.8300	--工字梁										
4418.8300 10	濒危竹制的工字梁〔999〕	4	0	70	13/	0	千克	ABE/	PQ		
4418.8300 20	濒危木制的工字梁〔999〕	4	0	70	13/	0	千克	ABEF/	PQ		
4418.8300 90	其他木制的工字梁(包括竹制的)〔101竹制的,102木制的〕	4	0	70	13/	13	千克	AB/	PQ		
4418.8900	--其他										
4418.8900 10	其他濒危竹制的工程结构木制品〔999〕	4	0	70	13/	0	千克	ABE/	PQ		
4418.8900 20	其他濒危木制的工程结构木制品〔999〕	4	0	70	13/	0	千克	ABEF/	PQ		
4418.8900 90	其他木制的工程结构木制品(包括竹制的)〔101竹制的,102木制的〕	4	0	70	13/	13	千克	AB/	PQ		
	-其他:										
4418.9100	--竹的										
4418.9100 10	濒危竹制的其他建筑用木工制品〔999〕	4	0	70	13/	0	千克	ABE/	PQ		
4418.9100 90	其他竹制的其他建筑用木工制品〔999〕	4	0	70	13/	13	千克	AB/	PQ		
4418.9200	--蜂窝结构木镶板										
4418.9200 10	濒危木制的蜂窝结构木镶板〔999〕	4	0	70	13/	0	千克	ABEF/	PQ	25	
4418.9200 90	其他蜂窝结构木镶板〔999〕	4	0	70	13/	13	千克	AB/	PQ	25	
4418.9900	--其他										
4418.9900 10	濒危木制的其他建筑用木工制品〔999〕	4	0	70	13/	0	千克	FEAB/	PQ	25	
4418.9900 90	其他建筑用木工制品〔999〕	4	0	70	13/	13	千克	AB/	PQ	25	
44.19	**木制餐具及厨房用具:**										
	-竹的:										
4419.1100	--切面包板、砧板及类似板〔999〕	0		100	13/	13	千克	AB/	PRQ	5	
	--筷子:										
4419.1210	---一次性筷子										
4419.1210 10	酸竹制一次性筷子〔998:竹筷;999:食品接触木制产品〕	0		100	13/	0	千克	ABE/	PRQ	5	

协定税率 %								RCEP		特惠税率 %			
东/冰/格	巴基斯坦	韩国	瑞士上/下	哥/秘/柬	澳/毛	新西/坡/智	中国港/澳/台	东盟及马来/澳/韩	日/新	亚太2国	老/柬/缅	98/97/95	Article Description
													--Other
0/0/	0	0	0/0	0/0/0	0/0	0/0/0	0/0/	0/0/0	3.6/0			0/0/0	Other endangered wooden doors and their frames and thresholds
0/0/	0	0	0/0	0/0/0	0/0	0/0/0	0/0/	0/0/0	3.6/0			0/0/0	Other wooden doors and their frames and thresholds
													-Posts and beams other than products of subheadings No. 4418.81 to 4418.89
0/0/	0	0	0/0	0/0/0	0/0	0/0/0	0/0/	0/0/0	3.6/0			0/0/0	Endangered wooden columns and beams, except those of subheadings 4418.81 to 4418.89
0/0/	0	0	0/0	0/0/0	0/0	0/0/0	0/0/	0/0/0	3.6/0			0/0/0	Other wooden columns and beams, except those of subheadings 4418.81 to 4418.9
0/0/	0	0	0/0	0/0/0	0/0	0//0	0/0/	0/0/0	3.6/0			0/0/0	-Shuttering for concrete constructional work
0/0/	2	0	0/0	0/0/0	0/0	0//0	0/0/	0/0/0	6.8/0			0/0/0	-Shingles and shakes
													-Assembled flooring panels:
													--Of bamboo or with at least the top layer (*wear layer*) of bam-boo:
0/0/	0	0	0/0	0/0/0	0/0	0/0/0	0/0/	0/0/0	3.6/0			0/0/0	---For mosaic floors
0/0/	0	0	0/0	0/0/0	0/0	0/0/0	0/0/	0/0/0	3.6/0			0/0/0	---Other, multilayer of bamboo
0/0/	0	0	0/0	0/0/0	0/0	0/0/0	0/0/	0/0/0	3.6/0			0/0/0	---Other
													---Other, for mosaic floors
0/0/	0	0	0/0	0/0/0	0/0	0/0/0	0/0/	0/0/0	3.6/0			0/0/0	Assembled flooring panels for mosaic floor, of Ramin wood
0/0/	0	0	0/0	0/0/0	0/0	0/0/0	0/0/	0/0/0	3.6/0			0/0/0	Assembled flooring panels for mosaic floor, of other endangered wood
0/0/	0	0	0/0	0/0/0	0/0	0/0/0	0/0/	0/0/0	3.6/0			0/0/0	Assembled flooring panels for mosaic floor, of other wood
													---Other, multilayer
0/0/0	0	0	0/0	0/0/0	0/0	0/0/0	0/0/	0/0/0	3.6/0			0/0/0	Assembled flooring panels,multilayer, of Ramin wood
0/0/0	0	0	0/0	0/0/0	0/0	0/0/0	0/0/	0/0/0	3.6/0			0/0/0	Assembled flooring panels,multilayer, of endangered wood
0/0/0	0	0	0/0	0/0/0	0/0	0/0/0	0/0/	0/0/0	3.6/0			0/0/0	Assembled flooring panels,multilayer, of other wood
													--Other
0/0/	0	0	0/0	0/0/0	0/0	0/0/0	0/0/	0/0/0	3.6/0			0/0/0	Other flooring panels of ramin wood , assembled
0/0/	0	0	0/0	0/0/0	0/0	0/0/0	0/0/	0/0/0	3.6/0			0/0/0	Other flooring panels of endangered wood , assembled
0/0/	0	0	0/0	0/0/0	0/0	0/0/0	0/0/	0/0/0	3.6/0			0/0/0	Other flooring panels of other wood , assembled
													- Engineered structural timber products :
													--Glue-laminated timber (glulam)
0/0/	0	0	0/0	0/0/0	0/0	0/0/0	0/0/	0/0/0	3.6/0			0/0/0	Laminated timber made of endangered bamboo
0/0/	0	0	0/0	0/0/0	0/0	0/0/0	0/0/	0/0/0	3.6/0			0/0/0	Endangered wood laminates
0/0/	0	0	0/0	0/0/0	0/0	0/0/0	0/0/	0/0/0	3.6/0			0/0/0	Other wood laminates (including bamboo)
													-- Cross-laminated timber (CLT or X-lam)
0/0/	0	0	0/0	0/0/0	0/0	0/0/0	0/0/	0/0/0	3.6/0			0/0/0	Orthogonal plywood made of endangered bamboo
0/0/	0	0	0/0	0/0/0	0/0	0/0/0	0/0/	0/0/0	3.6/0			0/0/0	Orthogonal plywood of endangered wood
0/0/	0	0	0/0	0/0/0	0/0	0/0/0	0/0/	0/0/0	3.6/0			0/0/0	Other orthogonal glued wood (including bamboo)
													-- I beams
0/0/	0	0	0/0	0/0/0	0/0	0/0/0	0/0/	0/0/0	3.6/0			0/0/0	I-beam made of endangered bamboo
0/0/	0	0	0/0	0/0/0	0/0	0/0/0	0/0/	0/0/0	3.6/0			0/0/0	Endangered wooden I-beam
0/0/	0	0	0/0	0/0/0	0/0	0/0/0	0/0/	0/0/0	3.6/0			0/0/0	Other wooden I-beams (including bamboo)
													--Other
0/0/	0	0	0/0	0/0/0	0/0	0/0/0	0/0/	0/0/0	3.6/0			0/0/0	Other engineering structural wood products made of endangered bamboo
0/0/	0	0	0/0	0/0/0	0/0	0/0/0	0/0/	0/0/0	3.6/0			0/0/0	Other endangered wooden engineering structural wood products
0/0/	0	0	0/0	0/0/0	0/0	0/0/0	0/0/	0/0/0	3.6/0			0/0/0	Other wooden engineering structure wood products (including bamboo)
													-Other:
													--Of bamboo
0/0/	0	0	0/0	0/0/0	0/0	0/0/0	0/0/	0/0/0	3.6/0			0/0/0	Other builder's joinery and carpentry of endangered bamboo
0/0/	0	0	0/0	0/0/0	0/0	0/0/0	0/0/	0/0/0	3.6/0			0/0/0	Other builder's joinery and carpentry of other bamboo
													-- Cellular wood panels
0/0/	0	0	0/0	0/0/0	0/0	0/0/0	0/0/	0/0/0	3.6/0			0/0/0	Honeycomb structure wood panel of endangered wood
0/0/	0	0	0/0	0/0/0	0/0	0/0/0	0/0/	0/0/0	3.6/0			0/0/0	Other honeycomb structure wood panels
													--Other
0/0/	0	0	0/0	0/0/0	0/0	0/0/0	0/0/	0/0/0	3.6/0			0/0/0	Othe rbuilder' s joinery and carpentry of other endangered wood
0/0/	0	0	0/0	0/0/0	0/0	0/0/0	0/0/	0/0/0	3.6/0			0/0/0	Other builder's joinery and carpentry of other bamboo
													Tableware and kitchenware, of wood:
													-Of bamboo:
0/0/0	0	0	0/0	0/0/0	0/0	0//0	0/0/	0/0/0	0/0			0/0/0	--Bread boards, chopping boards and similar boards
													--Chopsticks:
													---One-time chopsticks
0/0/0	0	0	0/0	0/0/0	0/0	0//0	0/0/	0/0/0	0/0			0/0/0	One-time chopsticks, of acidosasa chinensis

税则号列	货品名称〔CIQ 扩展编码及品名－T2 表示见附表 2〕	最惠(%)	暂定税率	普通	增值/消费	出口退税	计量单位	监管条件/特殊证件	检验检疫	对美关税	亚太上/下
4419.1210 90	其他竹制一次性筷子〔998:竹筷;999:食品接触木制产品〕	0		100	13/	13	千克	AB/	PRQ	5	
4419.1290	---其他〔998:竹筷;999:食品接触木制产品〕	0		100	13/	13	千克	AB/	PRQ	5	
4419.1900	--其他〔999〕	0		100	13/	13	千克	AB/	PRQ	5	
4419.2000	-热带木的										
4419.2000 10	濒危热带木制的餐具及厨房用具〔999〕	0		100	13/	0	千克	ABEF/	PRQ	5	
4419.2000 90	其他热带木制的餐具及厨房用具〔101 木质餐具及厨房用具,102 食品接触木制产品〕	0		100	13/	13	千克	AB/	PRQ	5	
	-其他:										
4419.9010	----次性筷子〔101 木质餐具及厨房用具,102 食品接触木制产品〕	0		100	13/5	0	千克	AB/	PQ	5	
4419.9090	---其他										
4419.9090 30	其他濒危木制的其他餐具及厨房用具〔999〕	0		100	13/	0	千克	ABEF/	PRQ	25	
4419.9090 90	其他木制的其他餐具及厨房用具〔999〕	0		100	13/	13	千克	AB/	PRQ	25	
44.20	**镶嵌木(包括细工镶嵌木);装珠宝或刀具用的木制盒子和小匣子及类似品;木制小雕像及其他装饰品;第九十四章以外的木制家具:**										
	-木制小雕像及其他装饰品:										
	--热带木的:										
4420.1110	---木刻										
4420.1110 10	濒危热带木制的木刻〔999〕	0		100	13/	0	千克	ABEF/	PQ	25	
4420.1110 90	其他热带木制的木刻〔101 木制工艺品,102 其他木制品〕	0		100	13/	13	千克	AB/	PQ	25	
4420.1120	---木扇										
4420.1120 10	濒危热带木制的木扇〔999〕	0		100	13/	0	千克	ABEF/	PQ		
4420.1120 90	其他热带木制的木扇〔999〕	0		100	13/	13	千克	AB/	PQ		
4420.1190	---其他										
4420.1190 10	其他濒危热带木制的小雕像及其他装饰品〔999〕	0		100	13/	0	千克	ABEF/	PQ	25	
4420.1190 90	其他热带木制的小雕像及其他装饰品〔999〕	0		100	13/	13	千克	AB/	PQ	25	
	--其他:										
	---木刻及竹刻:										
4420.1911	----木刻										
4420.1911 10	其他濒危木制的木刻〔999〕	0		100	13/	0	千克	ABEF/	PQ	25	
4420.1911 90	其他木制的木刻〔101 木制工艺品,102 其他木制品〕	0		100	13/	13	千克	AB/	PQ	25	
4420.1912	----竹刻〔999〕	0		100	13/	13	千克	AB/	PQ		
4420.1920	---木扇										
4420.1920 10	其他濒危木制的木扇〔999〕	0		100	13/	0	千克	ABEF/	PQ		
4420.1920 90	其他木制的木扇〔999〕	0		100	13/	13	千克	AB/	PQ		
4420.1990	---其他										
4420.1990 10	其他濒危木制的小雕像及其他装饰品〔999〕	0		100	13/	0	千克	ABEF/	PQ	25	
4420.1990 90	其他木制的小雕像及其他装饰品〔999〕	0		100	13/	13	千克	AB/	PQ	25	
	-其他:										
4420.9010	---镶嵌木										
4420.9010 10	拉敏木制的镶嵌木〔999〕	0		45	13/	13	千克	FEAB/	PQ	5	
4420.9010 20	濒危木制的镶嵌木〔999〕	0		45	13/	0	千克	FEAB/	PQ	5	
4420.9010 90	镶嵌木〔999〕	0		45	13/	13	千克	AB/	PQ	5	
4420.9090	---其他										
4420.9090 10	拉敏木盒及类似品,非落地木家具(前者用于装珠宝或家具;后者不包括第九十四章的家具)〔999〕	0		100	13/	13	千克	FEAB/	PQ	25	
4420.9090 20	濒危木盒及类似品,非落地木家具(前者用于装珠宝或家具;后者不包括第九十四章的家具)〔999〕	0		100	13/	0	千克	FEAB/	PQ	25	
4420.9090 90	木盒子及类似品;非落地式木家具(前者用于装珠宝或家具;后者不包括第九十四章的家具)〔999〕	0		100	13/	13	千克	AB/	PQ	25	
44.21	**其他木制品:**										
4421.1000	-衣架										
4421.1000 10	拉敏木制木衣架〔999〕	0		90	13/	13	千克	ABFE/	PQ	25	
4421.1000 20	濒危木制木衣架〔999〕	0		90	13/	0	千克	FEAB/	PQ	25	
4421.1000 90	木衣架〔999〕	0		90	13/	13	千克	AB/	PQ	25	
4421.2000	-棺材										
4421.2000 10	濒危木制的棺材(包括竹制的)〔101 竹制的,102 木制的〕	0		35	13/	0	千克	ABEF/	PQ	20	
4421.2000 90	其他木制的棺材(包括竹制的)〔101 竹制的,102 木制的〕	0		35	13/	13	千克	AB/	PQ	20	
	-其他:										
	--竹的:										
4421.9110	---圆签、圆棒、冰果棒、压舌片及类似一次性制品										

协定税率 %								RCEP		特惠税率 %			Article Description
东/冰/格	巴基斯坦	韩国	瑞士 上/下	哥/秘/柬	澳 /毛	新西/坡/智	中国港/澳/台	东盟及马来/澳/韩	日/新	亚太2国	老/柬/缅	98/97/95	
0/0/0	0	0	0/0	0/0/0	0/0	0/ /0	0/0/	0/0/0	0/0			0/0/0	One-time chopsticks, of other bamboo
0/0/0	0	0	0/0	0/0/0	0/0	0/ /0	0/0/	0/0/0	0/0			0/0/0	---Other
0/0/0	0	0	0/0	0/0/0	0/0	0/ /0	0/0/	0/0/0	0/0			0/0/0	---Other
													- Of tropicalwood
0/0/0	0	0	0/0	0/0/0	0/0	0/ /0	0/0/	0/0/0	0/0			0/0/0	Endangered tropical wooden tableware and kitchenware
0/0/0	0	0	0/0	0/0/0	0/0	0/ /0	0/0/	0/0/0	0/0			0/0/0	Other tropical wooden tableware and kitchen utensils
													-Other
0/0/0	0	0	0/0	0/0/0	0/0	0/ /0	0/0/	0/0/0	0/0			0/0/0	---One-time chopsticks
													---Other
0/0/0	0	0	0/0	0/0/0	0/0	0/ /0	0/0/	0/0/0	0/0			0/0/0	Other endangered wooden tableware and kitchen utensils
0/0/0	0	0	0/0	0/0/0	0/0	0/ /0	0/0/	0/0/0	0/0			0/0/0	Other tableware and kitchenware, of other wood
													Wood marquetry and inlaid wood; caskets and cases for jewellery or cutlery, and similar articles, of wood; statuettes and other ornaments, of wood; wooden articles or furniture not falling in Chapter 94:
													-Statuettes and other ornaments, of wood:
													--Tropical woody:
													---Wood carvings
0/0/0	0	0	0/0	0/0/0	0/0	0/ /0	0/0/	0/0/0	0/0			0/0/0	Wood carvings of endangered tropical wood
0/0/0	0	0	0/0	0/0/0	0/0	0/ /0	0/0/	0/0/0	0/0			0/0/0	Other tropical wood carvings
													---Wooden fans
0/0/0	0	0	0/0	0/0/0	0/0	0/ /0	0/0/	0/0/0	0/0			0/0/0	Endangered tropical wooden fan
0/0/0	0	0	0/0	0/0/0	0/0	0/ /0	0/0/	0/0/0	0/0			0/0/0	Other tropical wooden fans
													---Other
0/0/0	0	0	0/0	0/0/0	0/0	0/ /0	0/0/	0/0/0	0/0			0/0/0	Other endangered tropical wooden figurines and other decorations
0/0/0	0	0	0/0	0/0/0	0/0	0/ /0	0/0/	0/0/0	0/0			0/0/0	Other tropical wooden figurines and other decorations
													--Other
													---Wood or bamboo carvings:
													----Wood carvings
0/0/0	0	0	0/0	0/0/0	0/0	0/ /0	0/0/	0/0/0	0/0			0/0/0	Other endangered wood carvings
0/0/0	0	0	0/0	0/0/0	0/0	0/ /0	0/0/	0/0/0	0/0			0/0/0	Other wooden carvings
0/0/0	0	0	0/0	0/0/0	0/0	0/ /0	0/0/	0/0/0	0/0			0/0/0	---bamboo carvings
													---Wooden fans
0/0/0	0	0	0/0	0/0/0	0/0	0/ /0	0/0/	0/0/0	0/0			0/0/0	Other endangered wooden fans
0/0/0	0	0	0/0	0/0/0	0/0	0/ /0	0/0/	0/0/0	0/0			0/0/0	Other wooden fans
													---Other
0/0/0	0	0	0/0	0/0/0	0/0	0/ /0	0/0/	0/0/0	0/0			0/0/0	Other endangered wooden figurines and other decorations
0/0/0	0	0	0/0	0/0/0	0/0	0/ /0	0/0/	0/0/0	0/0			0/0/0	Other wooden statuettes and other decorations
													-Other:
													---Wood marquetry and inlaid wood
0/0/0	0	0	0/0	0/0/0	0/0	0/ /0	0/0/	0/0/0	0/0			0/0/0	Wood marquetry and inlaid wood of Ramin wood
0/0/0	0	0	0/0	0/0/0	0/0	0/ /0	0/0/	0/0/0	0/0			0/0/0	Wood marquetry and inlaid wood of endangered wood
0/0/0	0	0	0/0	0/0/0	0/0	0/ /0	0/0/	0/0/0	0/0			0/0/0	Wood marquetry and inlaid wood
													---Other
0/0/0	0	0	0/0	0/0/0	0/0	0/ /0	0/0/	0/0/0	0/0			0/0/0	Caskets and similar articles non-floor type furniture not falling, of Ramin wood (the former used for jewelry or furniture, the latter not including furniture falling in Chapter 94)
0/0/0	0	0	0/0	0/0/0	0/0	0/ /0	0/0/	0/0/0	0/0			0/0/0	Caskets and similar articles or non-floor type furniture of endangered wood in(the former used for jewelry or furniture, the latter not including furniture falling in Chapter 94)
0/0/0	0	0	0/0	0/0/0	0/0	0/ /0	0/0/	0/0/0	0/0			0/0/0	Caskets and similar articles or furniture not falling, of wood (the former used for jewelry or furniture, the latter not including furniture falling in Chapter 94)
													Other articles of wood:
													-Clothes hangers
0/0/0	0	0	0/0	0/0/0	0/0	0/ /0	0/0/	0/0/0	0/0			0/0/0	Clothes hangers of Ramin wood
0/0/0	0	0	0/0	0/0/0	0/0	0/ /0	0/0/	0/0/0	0/0			0/0/0	Clothes hangers of endangered wood
0/0/0	0	0	0/0	0/0/0	0/0	0/ /0	0/0/	0/0/0	0/0			0/0/0	Clothes hangers of wood
													-Coffins
0/0/0	0	0	0/0	0/0/0	0/0	0/ /0	0/0/	0/0/0	0/0			0/0/0	Endangered wooden coffins (including bamboo ones)
0/0/0	0	0	0/0	0/0/0	0/0	0/ /0	0/0/	0/0/0	0/0			0/0/0	Other wooden coffins (including bamboo)
													-Other:
													--Of bamboo:
													---Circle sticks, cricle bars, pop-sicle sticks, spatula and the like

税则号列		货品名称〔CIQ 扩展编码及品名－T2 表示见附表 2〕	最惠(%)	暂定税率	普通	增值/消费	出口退税	计量单位	监管条件/特殊证件	检验检疫	对美关税	亚太上/下
4421.9110	10	酸竹制圆签、圆棒、冰果棒、压舌片及类似一次性制品〔998:其他竹及竹制品;999:食品接触竹制产品〕	0		35	13/	0	千克	ABE/	PQ	25	
4421.9110	90	其他竹制圆签、圆棒、冰果棒、压舌片及类似一次性制品〔998:其他竹及竹制品;999:食品接触竹制产品〕	0		35	13/	13	千克	AB/	PQ	25	
4421.9190		---其他										
4421.9190	10	其他未列名的濒危竹制品〔999〕	0		90	13/	0	千克	FEAB/	PQ	20	
4421.9190	90	其他未列名的竹制品〔999〕	0		35	13/	13	千克	AB/	PQ	20	
		--其他:										
4421.9910		---木制圆签、圆棒、冰果棒、压舌片及类似一次性制品										
4421.9910	10	拉敏木制圆签、圆棒、冰果棒、压舌片及类似一次性制品〔998 其他木制品,999 食品接触木制产品〕	0		35	13/	0	千克	FEAB/	PQ		
4421.9910	20	濒危木制圆签、圆棒、冰果棒、压舌片及类似一次性制品〔998:其他木制品;999:食品接触木制产品〕	0		35	13/	0	千克	FEAB/	PQ		
4421.9910	90	其他木制圆签、圆棒、冰果棒、压舌片及类似一次性制品〔998:其他木制品;999:食品接触木制产品〕	0		35	13/	0	千克	AB/	PQ		
4421.9990		---其他										
4421.9990	30	濒危木制的未列名的木制品〔999〕	0		35	13/	0	千克	ABEF/	PQ	25	
4421.9990	90	未列名的木制品〔999〕	0		35	13/	13	千克	AB/	PQ	25	

协定税率 %								RCEP		特惠税率 %			Article Description
东/冰/格	巴基斯坦	韩国	瑞士上/下	哥/秘/柬	澳/毛	新西/坡/智	中国港/澳/台	东盟及马来/澳/韩	日/新	亚太2国	老/柬/缅	98/97/95	
0/0/0	0	0	0/0	0/0/0	0/0	0//0	0/0/	0/0/0	0/0			0/0/0	Round picks and sticks, sticks for ice-sucker, spatulas and similar one time articles, of acidosasa chinensis
0/0/0	0	0	0/0	0/0/0	0/0	0//0	0/0/	0/0/0	0/0			0/0/0	Round picks and sticks, sticks for ice-sucker, spatulas and similar one time articles, of other bamboo
													---Other
0/0/0	0	0	0/0	0/0/0	0/0	0//0	0/0/	0/0/0	0/0			0/0/0	Other endangered bamboo products,not specified
0/0/0	0	0	0/0	0/0/0	0/0	0//0	0/0/	0/0/0	0/0			0/0/0	Other bamboo products,not specified
													--Other:
													---Of wood, circle sticks, cir-cle bars, popsicle sticks, spatula and the like
0/0/0	0	0	0/0	0/0/0	0/0	0//0	0/0/	0/0/0	0/0			0/0/0	Round picks and sticks, sticks for ice-sucker, spatulas and similar one time articles, of Ramin wood
0/0/0	0	0	0/0	0/0/0	0/0	0//0	0/0/	0/0/0	0/0			0/0/0	Round picks and sticks, sticks for ice-sucker, spatulas and similar one time articles, of endangered wood
0/0/0	0	0	0/0	0/0/0	0/0	0//0	0/0/	0/0/0	0/0			0/0/0	Round picks and sticks, sticks for ice-sucker, spatulas and similar one time articles, of other wood
													---Other
0/0/0	0	0	0/0	0/0/0	0/0	0//0	0/0/	0/0/0	0/0			0/0/0	Endangered unlisted wood products
0/0/0	0	0	0/0	0/0/0	0/0	0//0	0/0/	0/0/0	0/0			0/0/0	Articles of wood, not specified

第四十五章
软木及软木制品

注释：

本章不包括：

一、第六十四章的鞋靴及其零件；

二、第六十五章的帽类及其零件；

三、第九十五章的物品(例如，玩具、游戏品及运动用品)。

税则号列	货品名称〔CIQ扩展编码及品名一T2表示见附表2〕	最惠(%)	暂定税率	普通	增值/消费	出口退税	计量单位	监管条件/特殊证件	检验检疫	对美关税	亚太上/下
45.01	**未加工或简单加工的天然软木；软木废料；碎的、粒状的或粉状的软木：**										
4501.1000	-未加工或简单加工的天然软木〔999〕	6	0	17	13/	0	千克	AB/	PQ		
	-其他：										
4501.9010	---软木废料〔102〕	0		17	13/	0	千克	9AB/	PQ	25	
4501.9020	---碎的、粒状的或粉状的软木(软木碎、软木粒或软木粉)〔999〕	0		17	13/	0	千克	AB/	PQ	25	
45.02	**天然软木，除去表皮或粗切成方形，或成长方块、正方块、板、片或条状(包括作塞子用的方块坯料)：**										
4502.0000	天然软木，除去表皮或粗切成方形，或成长方块、正方块、板、片或条状(包括作塞子用的方块坯料)〔999〕	8	0	30	13/	0	千克	AB/	PQ		
45.03	**天然软木制品：**										
4503.1000	-塞子〔101软木、软木粒及软木制品，102食品接触木制产品〕	8	0	50	13/	0	千克	AB/	PQ	25	
4503.9000	-其他〔999〕	8	0	50	13/	0	千克	AB/	PQ	20	
45.04	**压制软木(不论是否使用黏合剂压成)及其制品：**										
4504.1000	-块、板、片及条；任何形状的砖、瓦；实心圆柱体，包括圆片										
4504.1000 10	压制软木塞(包括任何形状的压制软木的砖、瓦、实心圆柱体、圆片)〔999〕	8	0	30	13/	0	千克	AB/	PQ	25	
4504.1000 90	块，板，片及条状压制软木，压制软木塞除外(包括任何形状的压制软木的砖、瓦、实心圆柱体、圆片)〔999〕	8	0	30	13/	0	千克	AB/	PQ	25	
4504.9000	-其他〔999〕	0		50	13/	0	千克	AB/	PQ	25	

Chapter 45
Cork and articles of cork

Notes:

This Chapter does not cover:

(a) Footwear or parts of footwear of Chapter 64;

(b) Headgear or parts of headgear of Chapter 65;

(c) Articles of Chapter 95 (for example, toys, games, sports requisites).

协定税率 %								RCEP		特惠税率 %			Article Description
东/冰/格	巴基斯坦	韩国	瑞士 上/下	哥/秘/柬	澳/毛	新西/坡/智	中国港/澳/台	东盟及马来/澳/韩	日/新	亚太2国	老/柬/缅	98/97/95	
													Natural cork, raw or simply prepared; waste cork; crushed, granulated or ground cork:
0/0/	0	0	0/0	0/0/0	0/0	0//0	0/0/	0/0/0	5.5/0			0/0/0	-Natrual cork, raw or simply prepared
													-Other:
0/0/0	0	0	0/0	0/0/0	0/0	0//0	0/0/	0/0/0	0/0			0/0/0	---Waste cork
0/0/0	0	0	0/0	0/0/0	0/0	0//0	0/0/	0/0/0	0/0			0/0/0	---Crushed, granulated or ground cork
													Natural cork, debarked or roughly squared, or in rectangular (including square) blocks, plates, sheets or strip, (including sharp-edged blanks for corks or stoppers):
0/0/	2	0	0/0	0/0/0	0/0	0//0	0/0/	0/0/0	7.3/0			0/0/0	Natural cork, debarked or roughly squared, or in rectangular (including square) blocks, plates, sheets or strip, (including sharp-edged blanks for corks or stoppers)
													Articles of natural cork:
0/0/	2	0	0/0	0/0/0	0/0	0//0	0/0/	0/0/0	7.3/0			0/0/0	-Corks and stoppers
0/0/	3.5	2.1	1.1/1.1	0/0/0	0/0	0/0/0	0/0/	0/0/9.5	9.5/0			0/0/0	-Other
													Agglomerated cork (with or without a binding substance) and articles of agglomerated cork:
													-Blocks, plates, sheets and strip; tiles of any shape; solid cylinders, including discs
0/0/	2	1.6	0/0	0/0/0	0/0	0//0	0/0/	0/0/7.6	7.6/0			0/0/0	Suppression of cork (including any shape of agglomerated cork brick and tile, solid cylinder, wafer)
0/0/	2	1.6	0/0	0/0/0	0/0	0//0	0/0/	0/0/7.6	7.6/0			0/0/0	Blocks, plates, sheets and strips, excluding suppression of cork(including any shape of agglomerated cork brick and tile, solid cylinder, wafer)
0/0/0	0	0	0/0	0/0/0	0/0	0//0	0/0/	0/0/0	0/0			0/0/0	-Other

第四十六章
稻草、秸秆、针茅或其他编结材料制品；篮筐及柳条编结品

注释：

一、本章所称"编结材料"，是指其状态或形状适于编结、交织或类似加工的材料，包括稻草、秸秆、柳条、竹、藤灯芯草、芦苇、木片条、其他植物材料扁条（例如，树皮条、狭叶、酒椰叶纤维或其他从阔叶获取的条）、未纺的天然纺织纤维、塑料单丝及扁条、纸带，但不包括皮革、再生皮革、毡呢或无纺织物的扁条、人发、马毛、纺织粗纱或纱线以及第五十四章的单丝和扁条。

二、本章不包括：

（一）税目48.14的壁纸；

（二）不论是否编结而成的线、绳、索、缆（税目56.07）；

（三）第六十四章和第六十五章的鞋靴、帽类及其零件；

（四）编结而成的车辆或车身（第八十七章）；

（五）第九十四章的物品（例如，家具、灯及灯具）。

三、税目46.01所称"平行连结的成片编结材料、缏条或类似的编结材料产品"，是指编结材料、缏条及类似的编结材料产品平行排列连结成片的制品，其连结材料不论是否为纺制的纺织材料。

税则号列	货品名称〔CIQ扩展编码及品名－T2表示见附表2〕	最惠(%)	暂定税率	普通	增值/消费	出口退税	计量单位	监管条件/特殊证件	检验检疫	对美关税	亚太上/下
46.01	**用编结材料编成的缏条及类似产品，不论是否缝合成宽条；平行连结或编结的成片材料、缏条或类似的编结材料产品，不论是否制成品（例如，席子、席料、帘子）：**										
	-植物材料制的席子、席料及帘子：										
4601.2100	--竹制的〔101 竹帘，102 竹席〕	7		90	13/	13	千克/张	AB/	PQ	32	
4601.2200	--藤制的〔999〕	7		100	13/	13	千克/张	AB/	PQ		
	--其他：										
	---草制的：										
4601.2911	----灯心草属材料制的										
4601.2911 11	蔺草制的提花席、双苜席、垫子（单位面积＞1m²，不论是否包边）〔999〕	7		90	13/	13	千克/张	4ABxy/	PQ		
4601.2911 12	蔺草制的其他席子（单位面积＞1m²，不论是否包边）〔999〕	7		90	13/	13	千克/张	4ABxy/	PQ		
4601.2911 19	蔺草制的其他席子、席料及帘子（单位面积≤1m²，不论是否包边）〔999〕	7		90	13/	13	千克/张	AB/	PQ		
4601.2911 90	其他灯芯草属材料制的席子等（包括席子、席料、帘子、垫子）〔999〕	7		90	13/	13	千克/张	AB/	PQ		
4601.2919	----其他〔101 稻草及其制品，102 其他草及草制品〕	7		90	13/	13	千克/张	AB/	PQ		
	---芦苇制的：										
4601.2921	----苇帘〔999〕	7		90	13/	13	千克/张	AB/	PQ		
4601.2929	----其他〔999〕	7		90	13/	13	千克/张	AB/	PQ		
4601.2990	---其他〔101 其他草及草制品，102 棕及棕制品，103 葵及葵制品，104 其他竹藤柳草类〕	7		90	13/	13	千克/张	AB/	PQ		
	-其他：										
	--竹制的：										
4601.9210	---缏条及类似产品，不论是否缝合成宽条〔101 其他竹及竹制品，102 其他竹藤柳草类〕	7		100	13/	13	千克	AB/	PQ		
4601.9290	---其他〔101 其他竹及竹制品，102 其他竹藤柳草类〕	7		90	13/	13	千克	AB/	PQ		
	--藤制的：										
4601.9310	---缏条及类似产品，不论是否缝合成宽条〔999〕	7		100	13/	13	千克	AB/	PQ		
4601.9390	---其他〔999〕	7		90	13/	13	千克	AB/	PQ		
	--其他植物材料制的：										
	---稻草制的：										
4601.9411	----缏条（绳）〔999〕	7		90	13/	13	千克	AB/	PQ		
4601.9419	----其他〔101 稻草及其制品，102 其他草及草制品〕	7		90	13/	13	千克	AB/	PQ		
	---其他：										
4601.9491	----缏条及类似产品，不论是否缝合成宽条〔101 其他竹及竹制品，102 藤及藤制品，103 柳及柳制品，104 其他草及草制品，105 棕及棕制品，106 葵及葵制品，107 其他竹藤柳草类〕	7		100	13/	13	千克	AB/	PQ		
4601.9499	----其他〔101 藤及藤制品，102 柳及柳制品，103 其他草及草制品，104 棕及棕制品，105 葵及葵制品，106 其他竹藤柳草类〕	7		90	13/	13	千克	AB/	PQ		
	--其他：										
4601.9910	---缏条及类似产品，不论是否缝合成宽条〔999〕	7		90	13/	13	千克	/			

Chapter 46
Manufactures of straw, of esparto or of other plaiting materials; basketware and wickerwork

Notes:

1. In this Chapter the expression "plaiting materials" means materials in a state or form suitable for plaiting, interlacing or similar processes; it includes straw, osier or willow, bamboos, rattans rushes, reeds, strips of wood, strips of other vegetable material (for example, strips of bark, narrow leaves and raffia or other strips obtained from broad leaves), unspun natural textile fibres, monofilament and strip and the like of plastics and strips of paper, but not strips of leather or composition leather or of felt or nonwovens, human hair, horsehair, textile rovings or yarns, or monofilament and strip and the like of Chapter 54.
2. This Chapter does not cover:
   (a) Wall coverings of heading No. 48.14;
   (b) Twine, cordage, ropes or cables, plaited or not (heading No. 56.07);
   (c) Footwear or headgear or parts thereof of Chapter 64 or 65;
   (d) Vehicles or bodies for vehicles of basketware (Chapter 87);
   (e) Articles of Chapter 94 (for example, furniture, lamps).
3. For the purposes of heading No. 46.01, the expression "plaiting materials, plaits and similar products of plaiting materials, bound together in parallel strands" means plaiting materials, plaits and similar products of plaiting materials, placed side by side and bound together, in the form of sheets, whether or not the binding materials are of spun textile materials.

协定税率 %								RCEP		特惠税率 %			Article Description
东/冰/格	巴基斯坦	韩国	瑞士上/下	哥/秘/柬	澳/毛	新西/坡/智	中国港/澳/台	东盟及马来/澳/韩	日/新	亚太2国	老/柬/缅	98/97/95	
													Plaits and similar products of plaiting materials, whether or not assembled into strips; plaiting materials, plaits and similar products of plaiting materials, bound together in parallel strands or woven, in sheet form, whether or not being finished articles (for example, mats, matting, screens):
													-Mats, matting and screens of vegetable materials:
0/0/0	2	0	0/0	0/0/0	0/0	0//0	0/0/	0/0/0	8.2/0		0//	0/0/0	--Of bamboo
0/0/0	2	0	0/0	0/0/0	0/0	0//0	0/0/	0/0/0	8.2/0		0//	0/0/0	--Of rattan
													--Other:
													---Of grass or straw:
													----Of rushes
0/0/0	2	0	0/0	0/0/0	0/0	0//0	0/0/	0/0/0	8.2/0		0//	0/0/0	Juncaceae mats, pairs of clover mats, mat(ubit area ＞1m², whether or not edged)
0/0/0	2	0	0/0	0/0/0	0/0	0//0	0/0/	0/0/0	8.2/0		0//	0/0/0	Other mats , matting and screens, of Juncaceae, area＞1m², whether or not edged
0/0/0	2	0	0/0	0/0/0	0/0	0//0	0/0/	0/0/0	8.2/0		0//	0/0/0	Jacquard mats, clover mats and cushion, of rush, of per unit area exceeding 1m², whether or not deged
0/0/0	2	0	0/0	0/0/0	0/0	0//0	0/0/	0/0/0	8.2/0		0//	0/0/0	Other mats, matting, of rushes (including mat, matting screens)
0/0/0	2	0	0/0	0/0/0	0/0	0//0	0/0/	0/0/0	8.2/0		0//	0/0/0	----Other
													---Of reeds:
0/0/0	2	0	0/0	0/0/0	0/0	0//0	0/0/	0/0/0	8.2/0		0//	0/0/0	----Screens of reeds
0/0/0	2	0	0/0	0/0/0	0/0	0//0	0/0/	0/0/0	8.2/0		0//	0/0/0	----Other
0/0/0	2	0	0/0	0/0/0	0/0	0//0	0/0/	0/0/0	8.2/0		0//	0/0/0	---Other
													-Other:
													--Of bamboo:
0/0/0	2	0	0/0	0/0/0	0/0	0//0	0/0/	0/0/0	8.2/0		0//	0/0/0	---Plaits and similar products of plaiting materials, whether or not assembled into strips
0/0/0	2	0	0/0	0/0/0	0/0	0//0	0/0/	0/0/0	8.2/0			0/0/0	---Other
													--Of rattan:
0/0/0	2	0	0/0	0/0/0	0/0	0//0	0/0/	0/0/0	8.2/0		0//	0/0/0	---Plaits and similar products of plaiting materials, whether or not assembled into strips
0/0/0	2	0	0/0	0//0	0/0	0//0	0/0/	0/0/0	8.2/0			0/0/	---Other
													--Of other vegetable materials:
													---Of straw:
0/0/0	3.5	2	0/0	0/0/0	0/0	0//0	0/0/	0/0/9	9.1/0			0/0/0	----Plaits
0/0/0	3.5	2	0/0	0/0/0	0/0	0//0	0/0/	0/0/9	9.1/0			0/0/0	----Other
													---Other:
0/0/0	2	0	0/0	0/0/0	0/0	0//0	0/0/	0/0/0	8.2/0		0//	0/0/0	----Plaits and similar products of plaiting materials, whether or not assembled into strips
0/0/0	2	0	0/0	0/0/0	0/0	0//0	0/0/	0/0/0	8.2/0			0/0/0	----Other
													--Other:
0/0/0	2	0	0/0	0/0/0	0/0	0//0	0/0/	0/0/0	8.2/0		0//	0/0/0	---Plaits and similar products of plaiting materials, whether or not assembled into strips

税则号列	货品名称〔CIQ 扩展编码及品名—T2 表示见附表 2〕	最惠(%)	暂定税率	普通	增值/消费	出口退税	计量单位	监管条件/特殊证件	检验检疫	对美关税	亚太上/下
4601.9990	---其他〔999〕	7		90	13/	13	千克	/		27	
46.02	**用编结材料直接编成或用税目 46.01 所列货品制成的篮筐、柳条编结品及其他制品；丝瓜络制品：**										
	-植物材料制：										
4602.1100	--竹制的〔101 竹片、竹地板，102 竹工艺品，103 竹叶，104 竹帘，105 竹椅，106 竹席，107 竹蒌，108 其他竹及竹制品〕	7		100	13/	13	千克	AB/	PQ		4.2/4.2
4602.1200	--藤制的〔101 藤及藤制品，102 其他竹藤柳草类〕	7		100	13/	13	千克	AB/	PQ		4.2/4.2
	--其他：										
4602.1910	---草制的〔101 蔺草及其制品，102 稻草及其制品，103 其他草及草制品，104 其他竹藤柳草类〕	7		100	13/	13	千克	AB/	PQ	32	
4602.1920	---玉米皮制的〔101 其他草及草制品，102 其他竹藤柳草类〕	7		100	13/	13	千克	AB/	PQ		
4602.1930	---柳条制的〔101 柳及柳制品，102 其他竹藤柳草类〕	7		100	13/	13	千克	AB/	PQ		
4602.1990	---其他〔101 藤及藤制品，102 其他草及草制品，103 棕及棕制品，104 葵及葵制品，105 其他竹藤柳草类〕	7		100	13/	13	千克	AB/	PQ	32	
4602.9000	-其他〔999〕	7		100	13/	13	千克	/		32	4.6/4.6

协定税率 %								RCEP		特惠税率 %			Article Description
东/冰/格	巴基斯坦	韩国	瑞士上/下	哥/秘/柬	澳/毛	新西/坡/智	中国港/澳/台	东盟及马来/澳/韩	日/新	亚太2国	老/柬/缅	98/97/95	
0/0/0	2	1.8	0/0	0/0/0	0/0	0//0	0/0/	0/0/8.1	8.2/0			0/0/0	---Other
													Basketwork, wickerwork and other articles, made directly to shape from plaiting materials or made up from goods of heading No. 46. 01; articles of loofah:
													-Of vegetable materials:
0/0/0	2	0	0/0	0/0/0	0/0	0//0	0/0/	0/0/0	8.2/0		/0/	0/0/0	--Of bamboo
0/0/0	2	0	0/0	0//0	0/0	0//0	0/0/	0/0/0	8.2/0		/0/	0/0/0	--Of rattan
													--Other:
0/0/0	2	0	0/0	0/0/0	0/0	0//0	0/0/	0/0/0	8.2/0		/0/	0/0/0	---Of grass or straw
0/0/0	2	0	0/0	0/0/0	0/0	0//0	0/0/	0/0/0	8.2/0		/0/	0/0/0	---Of maize-shuck
0/0/0	2	0	0/0	0/0/0	0/0	0//0	0/0/	0/0/0	8.2/0		/0/	0/0/0	---Of osier
0/0/0	2	0	0/0	0//0	0/0	0//0	0/0/	0/0/0	8.2/0		/0/	0/0/0	---Other
0/0/0	2	0	0/0	0/0/0	0/0	0//0	0/0/	0/0/0	8.2/0		/0/	0/0/0	-Other

第十类
木浆及其他纤维状纤维素浆；回收(废碎)纸或纸板；纸、纸板及其制品

第四十七章
木浆及其他纤维状纤维素浆；回收(废碎)纸或纸板

注释：

税目 47.02 所称“化学木浆，溶解级”，是指温度在 20℃时浸入含 18%氢氧化钠的苛性碱溶液内，一小时后，按重量计含有 92%及以上的不溶级分的碱木浆或硫酸盐木浆，或者含有 88%及以上的不溶级分的亚硫酸盐木浆。对于亚硫酸盐木浆，按重量计灰分含量不得超过 0.15%。

税则号列	货品名称〔CIQ 扩展编码及品名—T2 表示见附表 2〕	最惠(%)	暂定税率	普通	增值/消费	出口退税	计量单位	监管条件/特殊证件	检验检疫	对美关税	亚太上/下
47.01	**机械木浆：**										
4701.0000	机械木浆〔999〕	0		8	13/	0	千克	/		5	
47.02	**化学木浆，溶解级：**										
4702.0000	化学木浆，溶解级										
4702.0000 01	用于生产粘胶等化学纤维(不含醋酸纤维)的化学木浆，溶解级(浆粕的粘度≧3.7dl/g，且＜6.4dl/g，或者≧350ml/g，且＜700ml/g，α 纤维素含量(R18，硫酸盐法)＜95.5%，或者 α 纤维素含量(R18，亚硫酸盐法)＜94%，灰分≦0.15%)〔999〕	0		8	13/	0	千克	/		5	
4702.0000 90	其他化学木浆，溶解级〔999〕	0		8	13/	0	千克	/		5	
47.03	**碱木浆或硫酸盐木浆，但溶解级的除外：**										
	-未漂白：										
4703.1100	--针叶木的〔999〕	0		8	13/	0	千克	/		5	
4703.1900	--非针叶木的〔999〕	0		8	13/	0	千克	/		5	
	-半漂白或漂白：										
4703.2100	--针叶木的										
4703.2100 01	用于生产粘胶等化学纤维(不含醋酸纤维)的漂白针叶木碱木浆或硫酸盐木浆(包括半漂白的，溶解级的除外)(浆粕的黏度≥3.7dl/g，且＜6.4dl/g，或者≥350ml/g，且＜700ml/g，α 纤维素含量(R18，硫酸盐法)≥88%，且＜95.5%，灰分≤0.15%)〔999〕	0		8	13/	0	千克	/		5	
4703.2100 90	其他漂白针叶木碱木浆或硫酸盐木浆(包括半漂白的，溶解级的除外)〔999〕	0		8	13/	0	千克	/			
4703.2900	--非针叶木的〔999〕	0		8	13/	0	千克	/		5	
47.04	**亚硫酸盐木浆，但溶解级的除外：**										
	-未漂白：										
4704.1100	--针叶木的〔999〕	0		8	13/	0	千克	/		5	
4704.1900	--非针叶木的〔999〕	0		8	13/	0	千克	/		5	
	-半漂白或漂白：										
4704.2100	--针叶木的〔999〕	0		8	13/	0	千克	/		5	
4704.2900	--非针叶木的〔999〕	0		8	13/	0	千克	/		5	
47.05	**用机械与化学联合制浆法制得的木浆：**										
4705.0000	用机械与化学联合制浆法制得的木浆〔999〕	0		8	13/	0	千克	/		5	
47.06	**从回收(废碎)纸或纸板提取的纤维浆或其他纤维状纤维素浆：**										
4706.1000	-棉短绒纸浆										

SECTION Ⅹ
PULP OF WOOD OR OF OTHER FIBROUS CELLULOSIC MATERIAL; ZRCOVERED (WASTE AND SCRAP) PAPER OR PAPERBOARD; PAPER AND PAPERBOARD AND ARTICLES THEREOF

Chapter 47
Pulp of wood or of other fibrous cellulosic material; recovered (waste and scrap) paper or paperboard

Notes:

For the purposes of heading No. 47. 02, the expression "chemical wood pulp, dissolving grades" means chemical wood pulp having by weight an insoluble fraction of 92% or more for soda or sulphate wood pulp or of 88% or more for sulphite wood pulp after one hour in a caustic soda solution containing 18% sodium bydroxide (NaOH) at 20℃, and for sulphite wood pulp an ash content that does not exceed 0. 15% by weight.

协定税率 %								RCEP		特惠税率 %			Article Description
东/冰/格	巴基斯坦	韩国	瑞士上/下	哥/秘/柬	澳/毛	新西/坡/智	中国港/澳/台	东盟及马来/澳/韩	日/新	亚太2国	老/柬/缅	98/97/95	
													Mechanical wood pulp:
0/0/0	0	0	0/0	0/0/0	0/0	0//0	0/0/	0/0/0	0/0			0/0/0	Mechanical wood pulp
													Chemical wood pulp, dissolving grades:
													Chemical wood pulp, dissolving grades
0/0/0	0	0	0/0	0/0/0	0/0	0//0	0/0/	0/0/0	0/0			0/0/0	For the production of viscose chemical fiber (not containing cellulose acetate) of chemical wood pulp, dissolving (content of alpha cellulose pulp viscosity is greater than or equal to 3. 7dl/g, and <6.4dl/g, and ≥ 350ml/g, and (<700ml/g, R18, sulfate) ≥ 88%, and <95.5%, or the content of alpha cellulose (R18, sulfite) ≥ 87%, and <94%, ash ≤ 0. 15%)
0/0/0	0	0	0/0	0/0/0	0/0	0//0	0/0/	0/0/0	0/0			0/0/0	Other chemical wood pulp,dissolving grades
													Chemical wood pulp, soda or sulphate, other than dissolving grades:
													-Unbleached:
0/0/0	0	0	0/0	0/0/0	0/0	0//0	0/0/	0/0/0	0/0			0/0/0	--Coniferous
0/0/0	0	0	0/0	0/0/0	0/0	0//0	0/0/	0/0/0	0/0			0/0/0	--Non-coniferous
													-Semi-bleached or bleached:
													--Coniferous
0/0/0	0	0	0/0	0/0/0	0/0	0//0	0/0/	0/0/0	0/0			0/0/0	For the production of viscose chemical fiber (not containing cellulose acetate) of bleached softwood pulp of wood or kraft pulp (including semi bleached, dissolving except) (content of alpha cellulose pulp viscosity is greater than or equal to 3. 7dl/g, and < 6. 4dl/g, and ≥ 350ml/g, and <700ml/g, (R18, sulfur acid salt) ≥ 88%, and <95.5%, ash ≤ 0. 15%)
0/0/0	0	0	0/0	0/0/0	0/0	0//0	0/0/	0/0/0	0/0			0/0/0	Other chemical wood pulp, soda or sulhate(including semi-bleached or bleached,other than dissolving grades)
0/0/0	0	0	0/0	0/0/0	0/0	0//0	0/0/	0/0/0	0/0			0/0/0	--Non-coniferous
													Chemical wood pulp, sulphite, other than dissolving grades:
													-Unbleached:
0/0/0	0	0	0/0	0/0/0	0/0	0//0	0/0/	0/0/0	0/0			0/0/0	--Coniferous
0/0/0	0	0	0/0	0/0/0	0/0	0//0	0/0/	0/0/0	0/0			0/0/0	--Non-coniferous
													-Semi-bleached or bleached:
0/0/0	0	0	0/0	0/0/0	0/0	0//0	0/0/	0/0/0	0/0			0/0/0	--Coniferous
0/0/0	0	0	0/0	0/0/0	0/0	0//0	0/0/	0/0/0	0/0			0/0/0	--Non-coniferous
													Wood pulp obtained by a combination of mechanical and chemical pulping processes:
0/0/0	0	0	0/0	0/0/0	0/0	0//0	0/0/	0/0/0	0/0			0/0/0	Wood pulp obtained by a combination of mechanical and chemical pulping processes
													Pulps of fibres derived from recovered (waste and scrap) paper or paperboard or of other fibrous cellulosic material:
													-Cotton linters pulp

税则号列	货品名称〔CIQ扩展编码及品名—T2表示见附表2〕	最惠(%)	暂定税率	普通	增值/消费	出口退税	计量单位	监管条件/特殊证件	检验检疫	对美关税	亚太上/下
4706.1000 01	用于生产粘胶等化学纤维(不含醋酸纤维)的棉短绒浆粕(浆粕的粘度≧3.7dl/g,且＜6.4dl/g,或者≧350ml/g,且＜700ml/g,α纤维素含量(R18,硫酸盐法)＜95.5％,或者α纤维素含量(R18,亚硫酸盐法)＜94％,灰分≦0.15％)〔999〕	0		8	13/	13	千克	/		5	
4706.1000 90	其他棉短绒纸浆〔999〕	0		8	13/	13	千克	/		5	
4706.2000	-从回收(废碎)纸或纸板提取的纤维浆〔999〕	0		8	13/	0	千克	/			
4706.3000	-其他,竹浆										
4706.3000 01	用于生产粘胶等化学纤维(不含醋酸纤维)的其他纤维状纤维素竹浆(包括机械浆、化学浆、半化学浆)(浆粕的粘度≧3.7dl/g,且＜6.4dl/g,或者≧350ml/g,且＜700ml/g,α纤维素含量(R18,硫酸盐法)＜95.5％,或者α纤维素含量(R18,亚硫酸盐法)＜94％,灰分≦0.15％)〔999〕	0		8	13/	0	千克	/			
4706.3000 90	其他纤维状纤维素竹浆(包括机械浆、化学浆、半化学浆)〔999〕	0		8	13/	0	千克	/			
	-其他:										
4706.9100	--机械浆〔999〕	0		8	13/	0	千克	/			
4706.9200	--化学浆〔999〕	0		8	13/	0	千克	/		25	
4706.9300	--用机械和化学联合法制得的浆〔999〕	0		8	13/	0	千克	/			
47.07	**回收(废碎)纸或纸板:**										
4707.1000	-未漂白的牛皮纸或纸板及瓦楞纸或纸板〔999〕	0		8	13/	0	千克	9AB/	MPQ	25	
4707.2000	-主要由漂白化学木浆制成未经本体染色的其他纸和纸板〔999〕	0		8	13/	0	千克	9AB/	MPQ	25	
4707.3000	-主要由机械浆制成的纸或纸板(例如,报纸、杂志及类似印刷品)的〔999〕	0		8	13/	0	千克	9AB/	MPQ	25	
4707.9000	-其他,包括未分选的废碎品										
4707.9000 10	回收(废碎)墙(壁)纸、涂蜡纸、浸蜡纸、复写纸(包括未分选的废碎品)〔999〕	0		8	13/	0	千克	9AB/	MPQ	25	
4707.9000 90	其他回收纸或纸板(包括未分选的废碎品)〔999〕	0		8	13/	0	千克	9B/	MPQ	25	

协定税率 %								RCEP		特惠税率 %			Article Description
东/冰/格	巴基斯坦	韩国	瑞士上/下	哥/秘/柬	澳/毛	新西/坡/智	中国港/澳/台	东盟及马来/澳/韩	日/新	亚太2国	老/柬/缅	98/97/95	
0/0/0	0	0	0/0	0/0/0	0/0	0//0	0/0/	0/0/0	0/0			0/0/0	For the production of viscose chemical fiber (not containing cellulose acetate) of cotton linter pulp (content of alpha cellulose pulp viscosity is greater than or equal to 3.7dl/g, and <6.4dl/g, and ≥ 350ml/g, and (<700ml/g, R18, sulfate) ≥ 88%, and <95.5%, or the content of alpha cellulose (R18, sulfurous acid salt) ≥ 87%, and <94%, ash ≤ 0.15%)
0/0/0	0	0	0/0	0/0/0	0/0	0//0	0/0/	0/0/0	0/0			0/0/0	Other cotton linters pulp
0/0/0	0	0	0/0	0/0/0	0/0	0//0	0/0/	0/0/0	0/0			0/0/0	-Pulps of fibres derived from recovered (waste and scrap) paper or paperboard
													-Other, of bamboo
0/0/0	0	0	0/0	0/0/0	0/0	0//0	0/0/	0/0/0	0/0			0/0/0	-For the production of viscose chemical fiber (not containing cellulose acetate) of cellulose pulp (including mechanical pulp, chemical pulp, semi chemical pulp) (content of alpha cellulose pulp viscosity is greater than or equal to 3.7dl/g, and <6.4dl/g, and ≥ 350ml/g, and (<700ml/g, R18, sulfate) ≥ 88%, and <95.5%, or alpha the content of cellulose (R18, sulfite) ≥ 87%, and <94%, ash ≤ 0.15%)
0/0/0	0	0	0/0	0/0/0	0/0	0//0	0/0/	0/0/0	0/0			0/0/0	Other fibrous cellulosic material(including mechanical wood pulp, chemical pulp, semi-chemical)
													-Other:
0/0/0	0	0	0/0	0/0/0	0/0	0//0	0/0/	0/0/0	0/0			0/0/0	--Mechanical
0/0/0	0	0	0/0	0/0/0	0/0	0//0	0/0/	0/0/0	0/0			0/0/0	--Chemical
0/0/0	0	0	0/0	0/0/0	0/0	0//0	0/0/	0/0/0	0/0			0/0/0	--Obtained by a combination of mechanical and chemical processes
													Recovered (waste and scrap) paper or paperboard:
0/0/0	0	0	0/0	0/0/0	0/0	0//0	0/0/	0/0/0	0/0			0/0/0	-Unbleached kraft paper or paperboard or of corrugated paper or paperboard
0/0/0	0	0	0/0	0/0/0	0/0	0//0	0/0/	0/0/0	0/0			0/0/0	-Other paper or paperboard made mainly of bleached chemical pulp, not coloured in the mass
0/0/0	0	0	0/0	0/0/0	0/0	0//0	0/0/	0/0/0	0/0			0/0/0	-Paper or paperboard made mainly of mechanical pulp (for example, newspapers, journals and similar printed matter)
													-Other, including unsorted waste and scrap
0/0/0	0	0	0/0	0/0/0	0/0	0//0	0/0/	0/0/0	0/0			0/0/0	Recoverd(waste and scrap) wallpaper, mimeograph or waxed paper and carbon paper(including unsorted waste and scrap)
0/0/0	0	0	0/0	0/0/0	0/0	0//0	0/0/	0/0/0	0/0			0/0/0	Other recovered paper or paperboard (including unsorted waste and scrap)

第四十八章
纸及纸板；纸浆、纸或纸板制品

注释：

一、除条文另有规定外，本章所称“纸”包括“纸板”（不考虑其厚度或每平方米重量）。

二、本章不包括：
（一）第三十章的物品；
（二）税目32.12的压印箔；
（三）香纸及用化妆品浸渍或涂布的纸（第三十三章）；
（四）用肥皂或洗涤剂浸渍、覆盖或涂布的纸或纤维素絮纸（税号34.01）和用光洁剂、擦光膏及类似制剂浸渍、覆盖或涂布的纸或纤维素絮纸（税目34.05）；
（五）税目37.01至37.04的感光纸或感光纸板；
（六）用诊断或实验用试剂浸渍的纸（税目38.22）；
（七）第三十九章的用纸强化的层压塑料板，用塑料覆盖或涂布的单层纸或纸板（塑料部分占总厚度的一半以上），以及上述材料的制品，但税目48.14的壁纸除外；
（八）税目42.02的物品（例如旅行用品）；
（九）第四十六章的物品（编结材料制品）；
（十）纸纱线或纸纱线纺织物（第十一类）；
（十一）第六十四章或第六十五章的物品；
（十二）税目68.05的砂纸或税目68.14的用纸或纸板衬底的云母（但涂布云母粉的纸及纸板归入本章）；
（十三）用纸或纸板衬底的金属箔（通常为第十四类或第十五类）；
（十四）税目92.09的制品；
（十五）第九十五章的物品（例如，玩具、游戏品及运动用品；
（十六）第九十六章的物品[例如，纽扣、卫生巾（护垫）及卫生棉条、尿布及尿布衬里]。

三、除注释七另有规定的以外，税目48.01至48.05包括经研光、高度研光、釉光或类似处理、仿水印、表面施胶的纸及纸板；同时还包括用各种方法本体着色或染成斑纹的纸、纸板、纤维素絮纸及纤维素纤维网纸。除税目48.03另有规定的以外，上述税目不适用于经过其他方法加工的纸、纸板、纤维素絮纸或纤维素纤维网纸。

四、本章所称“新闻纸”，是指所含用机械或化学一机械方法制得的木纤维不少于全部纤维重量的50%的未经涂布的报刊用纸，未施胶或微施胶，每面粗糙度〔帕克印刷表面粗糙度（1兆帕）〕超过2.5微米，每平方米重量不小于40克，但不超过65克，并且仅适用于下列规格的纸：
（一）成条或成卷，宽度超过28厘米；
（二）成张矩形（包括正方形），一边超过28厘米，另一边超过15厘米（以未折叠计）。

五、税目48.02所称“书写、印刷或类似用途的纸及纸板”及“未打孔的穿孔卡片纸及穿孔纸带纸”，是指主要用漂白纸浆或用机械或化学-机械方法制得的纸浆制成的纸及纸板，并且符合下列任一标准：

（一）每平方米重量不超过150克的纸或纸板：
1.用机械或化学—机械方法制得的纤维含量在10%及以上，并且
　（1）每平方米重量不超过80克；
　（2）本体着色；
2.灰分含量在8%以上，并且
　（1）每平方米重量不超过80克；
　（2）本体着色；
3.灰分含量在3%以上，亮度在60%及以上；
4.灰分含量在3%以上，但不超过8%，亮度低于60%，耐破指数等于或小于2.5千帕斯卡·平方米/克；
5.灰分含量在3%及以下，亮度在60% 及以上，耐破指数等于或小于2.5千帕斯卡·平方米/克。
（二）每平方米重量超过150克的纸或纸板：
1.本体着色；
2.亮度在60%及以上，并且
　（1）厚度在225微米及以下；
　（2）厚度在225微米以上，但不超过508微米，灰分含量在3%以上；
3.亮度低于60%，厚度不超过254微米，灰分含量在8%以上。
税目48.02不包括滤纸及纸板（含茶袋纸）或毡纸及纸板。

六、本章所称“牛皮纸及纸板”，是指所含用硫酸盐法或烧碱法制得的纤维不少于全部纤维重量的80% 的纸及纸板。

七、除税目条文另有规定的以外，符合税目48.01至48.11中两个或两个以上税目所规定的纸、纸板、纤维素絮纸及纤维素纤维网纸，应按号列顺序归入有关税目中的最末一个税目。

八、税目48.03至48.09仅适用于下列规格的纸、纸板、纤维素絮纸及纤维素纤维网纸：
（一）成条或成卷，宽度超过36厘米；
（二）成张矩形（包括正方形），一边超过36厘米，另一边超过15厘米（以未折叠计）。

九、税目48.14所称“壁纸及类似品”，仅限于：
（一）适合作墙壁或天花板装饰用的成卷纸张，宽度不小于45厘米，但不超过160厘米：
　1. 起纹、压花、染面、印有图案或经其他装饰的（例如植绒），不论是否用透明的防护塑料涂布或覆盖；
　2. 表面饰有木粒或草粒而凹凸不平的；
　3. 表面用塑料涂布或覆盖并起纹、压花、染面、印有图案或经其他装饰的；
　4. 表面用不论是否平行连结或编织的编结材料覆盖的；

Chapter 48
Paper and paperboard; articles of paper pulp, of paper or of paperboard

Notes:

1. For the purposes of this Chapter, except where the context otherwise requires, a reference to "paper" includes references to paperboard (irrespective of thickness or weight per m^2).
2. This Chapter does not cover:
   (a) Articles of Chapter 30;
   (b) Stamping foils of heading No. 32.12;
   (c) Perfumed papers or papers impregnated or coated with cosmetics (Chapter 33);
   (d) Paper or cellulose wadding impregnated, coated or covered with soap or detergent (heading No. 34.01), or with polishes, creams or similar preparations (heading No. 34.05);
   (e) Sensitized paper or paperboard of headings No. 37.01 to 37.04;
   (f) Paper impregnated with diagnostic or laboratory reagents (heading No. 38.22);
   (g) Paper-reinforced stratified sheeting of plastics, or one layer of paper or paperboard coated or covered with a layer of plastics, the latter constituting more than half the total thickness, or articles of such materials, other than wall coverings of heading No. 48.14 (Chapter 39);
   (h) Articles of heading No. 42.02 (for example, travel goods);
   (i) Articles of Chapter 46 (manufactures of plaiting material);
   (j) Paper yarn or textile articles of paper yarn (Section XI);
   (k) Articles of Chapter 64 or Chapter 65;
   (l) Abrasive paper or paperboard (heading No. 68.05) or paper backed or paperboard-backed mica (heading No. 68.14) (paper and paperboard coated with mica powder are, however, to be classified in this Chapter);
   (m) Metal foil backed with paper or paperboard (generally to be classified in Section XIV or XV);
   (n) Articles of heading No. 92.09;
   (o) Articles of Chapter 95 (for example, toys, games, sports requisites)
   (p) Articles of Chapter 96 (for example, buttons, sanitary towels (pads) and tampons, napkins (diapers) and napkin liners).
3. Subject to the provisions of Note 7, headings Nos. 48.01 to 48.05 include paper and paperboard which have been subjected to calendering, super-calendering, glazing or similar finishing, false watermarking or surface sizing, and also paper, paperboard, cellulose wading and webs of cellulose fibres, coloured or marbled throughout the mass by any method. Except where heading No. 48.03 otherwise requires, these headings do not apply to paper, paperboard, cellulose wadding or webs of cellulose fibres which have been otherwise processed.
4. In this Chapter the expression "newsprint" means uncoated paper of a kind used for the printing of newspapers, of which not less than 50% by weight of the total fibre content consists of wood fibres obtained by a mechanical or chemi-mechanical process, unsized or very lightly sized, having a surface roughness Parker Print Surf (1 MPa) on each side exceeding 2.5 micrometres (microns), weighing not less than 40 g/m^2 and not more than 65 g/m^2, apply only to paper:
   (a) in strips or rolls of a width exceeding 28cm;
   (b) in rectangular (including square) sheets with one side exceeding 28cm and the other side exceeding 15cm in the unfolded state.
5. For the purposes of heading No. 48.02, the expressions "paper and paperboard, of a kind used for writing, printing or other graphic purposes" and "non perforated punch-cards and punch tape paper" mean paper and paperboard made mainly from bleached pulp or from pulp obtained by a mechanical or chemi-mechanical process and satisfying any of the following criteria:
   (A) For paper or paperboard weighing not more than 150g/m^2:
   (a) containing 10% or more of fibres obtained by a mechanical or chemi-mechanical process, and
      (i) weighing not more than 80 g/m^2,
      (ii) coloured throughout the mass; or
   (b) containing more than 8% ash, and
      (i) weighing not more than 80 g/m^2,
      (ii) coloured throughout the mass; or
   (c) containing more than 3% ash and having a brightness of 60% or more;
   (d) containing more than 3% but not more than 8% ash, having a brightness less than 60%, and a burst index equal to or less than 2.5 $kPa/m^2/g$;
   (e) containing 3% ash or less, having a brightness of 60% or more and a burst index equal to or less than 2.5 $kPa \cdot m^2/g$.
   (B) For paper or paperboard weighing more than 150 g/m^2:
   (a) coloured throughout the mass; or
   (b) having a brightness of 60% or more, and
      (i) a caliper of 225 micrometres (microns) or less, or
      (ii) a caliper more than 225 micrometres (microns) but not more than 508 micrometres (microns) and an ash content more than 3%; or
   (c) having a brightness of less than 60%, a caliper of 254 micrometres (microns) or less and an ash content of more than 8%.
   Heading No. 48.02 does not, however, cover filter paper and paperboard (including tea-bag paper) or felt paper or paperboard.
6. In this Chapter "kraft paper and paperboard" means paper and paperhoard of which not less than 80% by weight of the total fibre content consists of fibres obtained by the chemical sulphate or soda processes.
7. Except where the terms of the headings otherwise require, paper, paperboard, cellulose wadding and webs of cellulose fibres answering to a description in two or more of the headings No. 48.01 to 48.11 are to be classified under that one of such headings which occurs last in numerical order in the Nomenclature.
8. Headings No. 48.01 to 48.09 apply only to paper, paperboard, cellulose wadding and webs of cellulose fibres:
   (a) in strips or rolls of a width exceeding 36 cm;
   (b) in rectangular (including square) sheets with one side exceeding 36 cm and the other side exceeding 15 cm in the unfolded state.
9. For the purposes of heading No. 48.14, the expression "wallpaper and similar wall coverings" applies only to:
   (a) Paper in rolls, of a width of not less than 45 cm and not more than 160 cm, suitable for wall or ceiling decoration:
      (i) Grained, embossed, surface-coloured, designprinted or otherwise surface-decorated (for exanple, with textile flock), whether or not coated or covered with transparent protective plastics;
      (ii) With an uneven surface resulting from the incorporation ofparticles of wood, straw, etc.;
      (iii) Coated or covered on the face side with plastics, the layer of plastics being grained, embossed, coloured, design-printed or otherwise decorated;
      (iv) Covered on the face side with plaiting material, whether or not bound together in parallel strands or woven;

(二)适于装饰墙壁或天花板用的经上述加工的纸边及纸条,不论是否成卷;
(三)由几幅拼成的壁纸,成卷或成张,贴到墙上可组成印制的风景或图案。

既可作铺地制品,也可作壁纸的以纸或纸板为底的产品,应归入税目 48.23。

十、税目 48.20 不包括切成一定尺寸的活页纸张或卡片,不论是否印制、压花、打孔。
十一、税目 48.23 主要适用于提花机或类似机器用的穿孔纸或卡片,以及纸花边。
十二、除税目 48.14 及 48.21 的货品外,印有图案、文字或图画的纸、纸板、纤维素絮纸及其制品,如果所印图案、文字或图画作为其主要用途,应归入第四十九章。

子目注释:

一、子目 4804.11 及 4804.19 所称"牛皮衬纸",是指所含用硫酸盐法或烧碱法制得的木纤维不少于全部纤维重量的 80%的成卷机器整饰或上光纸及纸板,每平方米重量超过 115 克,并且最低缪伦耐破度符合下表所示(其他重量的耐破度可参照下表换算):

重　量 克/平方米	最低耐破度 千帕斯卡
115	393
125	417
200	637
300	824
400	961

二、子目 4804.21 及 4804.29 所称"袋用牛皮纸",是指所含用硫酸盐法或烧碱法制得的木纤维不少于全部纤维重量的 80%的成卷机器上光纸,每平方米重量不小于 60 克,但不超过 115 克,并且符合下列一种规格:

(一)缪伦耐破指数不小于 3.7 千帕斯卡·平方米/克,并且横向伸长率大于 4.5%,纵向伸长率大于 2%;

(二)至少能达到下表所示的最小撕裂度和抗张强度(其他重量的可参照下表换算):

重　量 克/平方米	最小撕裂度 毫牛顿		最小抗张强度 千牛顿/米	
	纵　向	纵向 加横向	横　向	纵向 加横向
60	700	1510	1.9	6
70	830	1790	2.3	7.2
80	965	2070	2.8	8.3
100	1230	2635	3.7	10.6
115	1425	3060	4.4	12.3

三、子目 4805.11 所称"半化学的瓦楞纸",是指所含用机械和化学联合法制得的未漂白硬木纤维不少于全部纤维重量的 65%的成卷纸张,并且在温度为 23℃和相对湿度为 50%时,经过 30 分钟的瓦楞芯纸平压强度测定(CMT30),抗压强度超过 1.8 牛顿/克/平方米。

四、子目 4805.12 包括主要用机械和化学联合法制得的草浆制成的成卷纸张,每平方米重量在 130 克及以上,并且在温度为 23℃和相对湿度为 50%时,经过 30 分钟的瓦楞芯纸平压强度测定(CMT30),抗压强度超过 1.4 牛顿/克/平方米。

五、子目 4805.24 及 4805.25 包括全部或主要用回收(废碎)纸及纸板制得的纸浆制成的纸及纸板。强韧箱纸板也可以有一面用染色纸或由漂白或未漂白的非再生浆制得的纸做表层。这些产品缪伦耐破指数不小于 2 千帕斯卡·平方米/克。

六、子目 4805.30 所称"亚硫酸盐包装纸",是指所含用亚硫酸盐法制得的木纤维超过全部纤维重量的 40%的机器研光纸,灰分含量不超过 8%,并且缪伦耐破指数不小于 1.47 千帕斯卡·平方米/克。

七、子目 4810.22 所称"轻质涂布纸",是指双面涂布纸,其每平方米总重量不超过 72 克,每面每平方米的涂层重量不超过 15 克,原纸中所含用机械方法制得的木纤维不少于全部纤维重量的 50%。

税则号列	货品名称〔CIQ扩展编码及品名－T2 表示见附表 2〕	最惠(%)	暂定税率	普通	增值/消费	出口退税	计量单位	监管条件/特殊证件	检验检疫	对美关税	亚太上/下
48.01	**成卷或成张的新闻纸:**										
4801.0010	---成卷的〔999〕	5		30	13/	0	千克	/		30	
4801.0090	---其他〔999〕	5		30	13/	0	千克	/		30	

(b) Borders and friezes, of paper, treated as above, whether or not in rolls, suitable for wall or ceiling decoration;

(c) Wall coverings of paper made up of several panels, in rolls or sheets, printed so as to make up a scene, design or motif when applied to a wall.

Products on a base of paper or paperboard, suitable for use both as floor coverings and as wall coverings, are to be classified in heading No. 48. 23.

10. Heading No. 48. 20 does not cover loose sheets or cards, cut to size, whether or not printed, embossed or perforated.

11. Heading No. 48. 23 applies, *inter alia*, to perforated paper or paperboard cards for Jacquard or similar machines and paper lace.

12. Except for the goods of heading No. 48. 14 or 48. 21, paper, paperboard, cellulose wadding and articles thereof, printed with motifs, characters or pictorial representations, which are not merely incidental to the primary use of the goods, fall in Chapter 49.

Subheading Notes:

1. For the purposes of subheadings No. 4804. 11 and 4804. 19. "kraftliner" means machine-finished or machine-glazed paper and paperboard, of which not less than 80% by weight of the total fibre content consists of wood fibres obtained by the chemical sulphate or soda processes, in rolls, weighing more than 115 g/m^2 and having a minimum Mullen bursting strength as indicated in the following table or the linearly interpolated or extrapolated equivalent for any other weight.

Weight g/m^2	**Minimum Mullen bursting strength kPa**
115	393
125	417
200	637
300	834
400	961

2. For the puposes of subheadings Nos. 4804. 21 and 4804. 29, "sack kraft paper" means machine-finished paper, of which not less than 80% by weight of the total fibre content consists of fibres obtained by the chemical sulphate or soda processes, in rolls, weighing not less than 60 g/m^2 but not more than 115 g/m^2 and meeting one of the following sets of specifications:

(a) Having a Mullen burst index of not less than 3. 7 kPa • m^2/g and a stretch factor of more than 4. 5% in the cross direction and of more than 2% in the machine direction.

(b) Having minima for tear and tensile as indicated in the following table or the linearly interpolated equivalent for any other weight:

Weight g/m^2	**Minimum tear mN**		**Minimum tensile kN/m**	
	Machine direction	**Machine direction plus cross direction**	**Cross direction**	**Machine direction plus cross direction**
60	700	1,510	1. 9	6
70	830	1,790	2. 3	7. 2
80	2965	2070	2. 8	8. 3
100	1230	2635	3. 7	10. 6
115	1425	3060	4. 4	12. 3

3. For the purposes of subheading No. 4805. 11, "semi-chemical fluting paper" means paper, in rolls, of which not less than 65% by weight of the total fibre content consists of unbleached hardwood fibres obtained by a combination of mechanical and chemical pulping processes, and having a CMT 30 (Corrugated Medium Test with 30 minutes of conditioning) crush resistance exceeding 1. 8 $N/g/m^2$ at 50% relative humidity, at 23℃.

4. Subheading No. 4805. 12 covers paper, in rolls, made mainly of straw pulp obtained by a combination of mechanical and chemical process, weighing 130 g/m^2 or more, and having a CMT 30(Corrugated Medium Test with 30 minutes of conditioning) crush resistance exceeding 1. 4 newtons/g/m^2 at 50% relative humidity, at 23℃.

5. Subheadings 4805. 24 and 4805. 25 cover paper and paperboard made wholly or mainly of pulp of recovered(waste and scrap) paper or paperboard. Testliner may also have a surface layer of dyed paper or of paper made of bleached or unbleached non-recovered pulp. These products have a Mullen burst index of not less than 2 kPa • m^2/g.

6. For the purposes of subheading No. 4805. 30, "sulphite wrapping paper" means machine-glazed paper, of which more than 40% by weight of the total fibre content consists of wood fibres obtained by the chemical sulpohite process, having an ash content not exceeding 8% and having a Mullen burst index of not less than 1. 47 kPa • m^2/g.

7. For the purposes of subheading No. 4810. 22, "lightweight coated paper" means paper, coated on both sides, of a total weight not exceeding 72 g/m^2, with a coating weight not exceeding 15 g/m^2 per side, on a base of which not less than 50% by weight of the total fibre content consists of wood fibres obtained by a mechanical process.

协定税率 %								RCEP		特惠税率 %			Article Description
东/冰/格	巴基斯坦	韩国	瑞士上/下	哥/秘/柬	澳/毛	新西/坡/智	中国港/澳/台	东盟及马来/澳/韩	日/新	亚太2国	老/柬/缅	98/97/95	
													Newsprint, in rolls or sheets: ---In rolls ---Other

税则号列	货品名称〔CIQ扩展编码及品名—T2 表示见附表2〕	最惠(%)	暂定税率	普通	增值/消费	出口退税	计量单位	监管条件/特殊证件	检验检疫	对美关税	亚太上/下
48.02	**书写、印刷或类似用途的未经涂布的纸及纸板、未打孔的穿孔卡片纸及穿孔纸带纸，成卷或成张矩形(包括正方形)，任何尺寸，但税目48.01或48.03的纸除外；手工制纸及纸板：**										
	-手工制纸及纸板：										
4802.1010	---宣纸〔999〕	6	4	70	13/	13	千克	/			
4802.1090	---其他〔999〕	6	5	70	13/	13	千克	/		30	
	-光敏、热敏、电敏纸及纸板的原纸和原纸板：										
4802.2010	---照相原纸〔999〕	6	5	40	13/	0	千克	/		30	
4802.2090	---其他〔999〕	6	5	40	13/	0	千克	/		25	
4802.4000	-壁纸原纸〔999〕	6		40	13/	0	千克	/			
	-其他纸及纸板，不含用机械或化学—机械方法制得的纤维或所含前述纤维不超过全部纤维重量的10%：										
4802.5400	--每平方米重量小于40克〔999〕	6		30	13/	0	千克	/		31	
4802.5500	--每平方米重量在40克及以上，但不超过150克，成卷的										
4802.5500 10	40g<每平方米重≤150g的胶版纸(成卷，机械或化学—机械法制得的纤维含量≤10%)〔999〕	5		30	13/	0	千克	/		30	
4802.5500 90	40g<每平方米重≤150g未涂布中厚纸(书写印刷用，成卷，含机械或化学—机械法制纤维≤10%)〔999〕	5		30	13/	0	千克	/		30	
4802.5600	--每平方米重量在40克及以上，但不超过150克，成张的，一边不超过435毫米，另一边不超过297毫米(以未折叠计)，										
4802.5600 10	成张40g<每平方米重≤150g胶版纸(长≤435mm，宽≤297mm含机械或化学—机械法制纤维≤10%)〔999〕	5		30	13/	0	千克	/		30	
4802.5600 90	40g<每平方米重≤150g未涂布纸，成张(书写印刷，长≤435mm，宽≤297mm含机械或半化学浆≤10%)〔999〕	5		30	13/	0	千克	/		30	
4802.5700	--其他，每平方米重量在40克及以上，但不超过150克										
4802.5700 10	其他40g<每平方米重≤150g的胶版纸(机械或化学—机械法制得的纤维含量≤10%)〔999〕	5		30	13/	0	千克	/		30	
4802.5700 90	其他40g<每平方米重≤150g未涂中厚纸(书写印刷用，含机械或化学—机械法制纤维≤10%)〔999〕	5		30	13/	0	千克	/		30	
4802.5800	--每平方米重量超过150克〔999〕	5		30	13/	0	千克	/		25	
	-其他纸及纸板，所含用机械或化学—机械方法制得的纤维超过全部纤维重量的10%：										
4802.6100	--成卷的〔999〕	5		30	13/	0	千克	/		25	
4802.6200	--成张的，一边不超过435毫米，另一边不超过297毫米(以未折叠计)〔999〕	5		30	13/	0	千克	/		30	
4802.6900	--其他〔999〕	5		30	13/	0	千克	/		30	
48.03	**卫生纸、面巾纸、餐巾纸以及家庭或卫生用的类似纸、纤维素絮纸和纤维素纤维网纸，不论是否起纹、压花、打孔、染面、饰面或印花，成卷或成张的：**										
4803.0000	卫生纸、面巾纸、餐巾纸以及家庭或卫生用的类似纸、纤维素絮纸和纤维素纤维网纸，不论是否起纹、压花、打孔、染面、饰面或印花，成卷或成张的〔101 卫生纸原纸、卫生纸，102 面巾纸、餐巾纸及类似纸，103 擦拭用纸〕	5		40	13/	0	千克	A/	M	30	
48.04	**成卷或成张的未经涂布的牛皮纸及纸板，但不包括税目48.02或48.03的货品：**										
	-牛皮衬纸：										
4804.1100	--未漂白〔999〕	5		30	13/	0	千克	/		10	
4804.1900	--其他〔999〕	5		30	13/	0	千克	/		25	
	-袋用牛皮纸：										
4804.2100	--未漂白〔999〕	5		30	13/	0	千克	/		10	
4804.2900	--其他〔999〕	5		30	13/	0	千克	/		30	
	-其他牛皮纸及纸板，每平方米重量不超过150克：										

协定税率 %								RCEP		特惠税率 %			Article Description
东/冰/格	巴基斯坦	韩国	瑞士上/下	哥/秘/柬	澳/毛	新西/坡/智	中国港/澳/台	东盟及马来/澳/韩	日/新	亚太2国	老/柬/缅	98/97/95	
													Uncoated paper and paperboard, of a kind used for writing, printing or other graphic purposes, and non perforated punch-cards and punch tape paper, in rolls or rectangular (including square) sheets, of any size, other than paper of heading No. 48. 01 or 48. 03; hand-made paper and paperboard:
													-Hand-made paper and paperboard:
5//				//5		5//							---Xuan paper
5//				//5		5//							---Other
													-Paper and paperboard of a kind used as a base for photo-sensitive, heat-sensitive or electro-sensitive paper or paperboard:
				//0	/0		0/0/					0/0/	---Photo paper base
5//				//0	/0	0//	0/0/					0/0/	---Other
				//0	/0		0/0/					0/0/	-Wallpaper base
													-Other paper and paperboard, not containing fibres obtained by a mechanical or chemi-mechanical process or of which not more than 10% by weight of the total fibre content consists of such fibres:
				//0	/0		0/0/					0/0/	--Weighing less than 40 g/m^2
													--Weighing 40 g/m^2 or more but not more than 150 g/m^2, in rolls
				//0	/0		0/0/					0/0/	Offset paper, in rolls, 40g/m^2<w≤150g/m^2, containing fibres≤10%, obtained by a mechanical or chemi-mechanical process
				//0	/0		0/0/					0/0/	Paper, of a kind used for writing, printing or other graphic purposes, in rolls, 40g/m^2<w≤150g/m^2, containing fibres ≤10%, obtained by a mechanical or chemi-mechanical process
													--Weighing 40 g/m^2 or more but not more than 150 g/m^2, in sheets with one side not exceeding 435 mm and the other side not exceeding 297 mm in the unfolded state
				//0	/0		0/0/					0/0/	Offset paper, in sheets, 40g/m^2<w≤150g/m^2 (length≤435mm, width≤297mm, containing fibres≤10%, obtained by a mechanical or chemi-mechanical process)
				//0	/0		0/0/					0/0/	Uncoated paper, 40g/m^2<w≤150g/m^2 (of a kind used for writing, printing or other graphic purposes, in sheets, length ≤435mm, width≤297mm, containing fibres≤10%, obtained by a mechanical or chemi-mechanical process)
													--Other, weighing 40 g/m^2 or more but not more than 150 g/m^2
				//0	/0		0/0/					0/0/	Other offset paper, 40g/m^2<w≤150g/m^2, containing fibres ≤10%, obtained by a mechanical or chemi-mechanical process
				//0	/0		0/0/					0/0/	Other uncoated paper, 40g/m^2<w≤150g/m^2, of a kind used for writing, printing or other graphic purposes, containing fibres≤10%, obtained by a mechanical or chemi-mechanical process
				//0	/0		0/0/					0/0/	--Weighing more than 150 g/m^2
													-Other paper and paperboard, of which more than 10% by weight of the total fibre content consists of fibres obtained by a mechanical or chemi—mechanical process:
					/0		0/0/					0/0/	- -In rolls
				//0	/0		0/0/					0/0/	--In sheets with one side not exceeding 435 mm and the other side not exceeding 297 mm in the unfolded state
					/0		0/0/					0/0/	- -Other
													Toilet or facial tissue stock, towel or napkin stock and similar paper of a kind used for household or sanitary purposes, cellulose wadding and webs of cellulose fibres, whether or not creped, crinkled, embossed, perforated, surface-coloured, surface-decorated or printed, in rolls or sheets:
													Toilet or facial tissue stock, towel or napkin stock and similar paper of a kind used for household or sanitary purposes, cellulose wadding and webs of cellulose fibres, whether or not creped, crinkled, embossed, perforated, surface-coloured, surface-decorated or printed, in rolls or sheets
													Uncoated kraft paper and paperboard, in rolls or sheets, other than that of heading No. 48. 02 or 48. 03:
													-Kraftliner:
													--Unbleached
													--Other
													-Sack kraft paper:
													--Unbleached
													--Other
													-Other kraft paper and paperboard weighing 150 g/m^2 or less:

税则号列	货品名称〔CIQ 扩展编码及品名—T2 表示见附表 2〕	最惠(%)	暂定税率	普通	增值/消费	出口退税	计量单位	监管条件/特殊证件	检验检疫	对美关税	亚太上/下
4804.3100	--未漂白										
4804.3100 20	未漂白的其他薄牛皮纸及纸板(抗张指数(横向+纵向)大于等于 69N.M/,撕裂指数(纵向)大于等于 10Mn2/g,抗张能量吸收指数(横向)大于等于 1.0J/g,抗张能量吸收指数(纵向)大于等于 0.8J/g,透气度大于等于 3.4um/(pa.s),伸长率(纵向)大于等于 2%。定量克重≤115 克㎡(薄纸指每平米重≤150 克,成卷或成张未经涂布的。)〔999〕	2		30	13/	0	千克	/		27	
4804.3100 90	未漂白的其他薄牛皮纸及纸板(薄纸指每平米重≤150 克,成卷或成张未经涂布的)〔999〕	2		30	13/	0	千克	/		27	
4804.3900	--其他〔999〕	2		30	13/	0	千克	/		7	
	-其他牛皮纸及纸板,每平方米重量超过 150 克,但小于 225 克:										
4804.4100	--未漂白〔999〕	2		30	13/	0	千克	/		7	
4804.4200	--本体均匀漂白,所含用化学方法制得的木纤维超过全部纤维重量的 95%〔999〕	5		30	13/	0	千克	/		30	
4804.4900	--其他〔999〕	2		30	13/	0	千克	/		27	
	-其他牛皮纸及纸板,每平方米重量在 225 克及以上:										
4804.5100	--未漂白〔999〕	2		30	13/	0	千克	/		7	
4804.5200	--本体均匀漂白,所含用化学方法制得的木纤维超过全部纤维重量的 95%〔999〕	5		30	13/	0	千克	/		10	
4804.5900	--其他〔999〕	2		30	13/	0	千克	/		7	
48.05	**成卷或成张的其他未经涂布的纸及纸板,加工程度不超过本章注释三所列范围:**										
	-瓦楞原纸:										
4805.1100	--半化学的瓦楞原纸〔999〕	6		30	13/	0	千克	/			
4805.1200	--草浆瓦楞原纸〔999〕	6		30	13/	0	千克	/			
4805.1900	--其他〔999〕	6	5	30	13/	0	千克	/		30	
	-强韧箱纸板(再生挂面纸板):										
4805.2400	--每平方米重量在 150 克及以下〔999〕	6		30	13/	0	千克	/			
4805.2500	--每平方米重量超过 150 克〔999〕	6		30	13/	0	千克	/		31	
4805.3000	-亚硫酸盐包装纸〔999〕	6		30	13/	0	千克	/		31	
4805.4000	-滤纸及纸板〔999〕	6		30	13/	0	千克	/		11	
4805.5000	-毡纸及纸板〔999〕	6		30	13/	0	千克	/			
	-其他:										
	--每平方米重量在 150 克及以下:										
4805.9110	---电解电容器原纸〔999〕	6		30	13/	0	千克	/		26	
4805.9190	---其他〔999〕	6	5	30	13/	0	千克	/		25	
4805.9200	--每平方米重量超过 150 克以上,但小于 225 克〔999〕	6		30	13/	0	千克	/		26	
4805.9300	--每平方米重量在 225 克及以上〔999〕	6		30	13/	0	千克	/		31	
48.06	**成卷或成张的植物羊皮纸、防油纸、描图纸、半透明纸及其他高光泽透明或半透明纸:**										
4806.1000	-植物羊皮纸〔999〕	6	5	40	13/	0	千克	/		30	
4806.2000	-防油纸〔999〕	6	5	40	13/	0	千克	/		30	
4806.3000	-描图纸〔999〕	6	5	40	13/	0	千克	/		10	
4806.4000	-高光泽透明或半透明纸〔999〕	6	5	40	13/	0	千克	/		25	
48.07	**成卷或成张的复合纸及纸板(用黏合剂粘合各层纸或纸板制成),未经表面涂布或未浸渍,不论内层是否有加强材料:**										
4807.0000	成卷或成张的复合纸及纸板(用黏合剂粘合各层纸或纸板制成),未经表面涂布或未浸渍,不论内层是否有加强材料〔999〕	6	5	40	13/	0	千克	/		30	
48.08	**成卷或成张的瓦楞纸及纸板(不论是否与平面纸胶合)、皱纹纸及纸板、压纹纸及纸板、穿孔纸及纸板,但税目 48.03 的纸除外:**										
4808.1000	-瓦楞纸及纸板,不论是否穿孔〔999〕	6	0	30	13/	0	千克	/		25	
4808.4000	-皱纹牛皮纸,不论是否压花或穿孔〔999〕	6		40	13/	0	千克	/		11	
4808.9000	-其他〔999〕	6		40	13/	0	千克	/		26	
48.09	**复写纸、自印复写纸及其他拷贝或转印纸(包括涂布或浸渍的油印蜡纸或胶印版纸),不论是否印制,成卷或成张的:**										
4809.2000	-自印复写纸〔999〕	6		40	13/	0	千克	/		11	
4809.9000	-其他〔999〕	6		40	13/	0	千克	/		26	

协定税率 %								RCEP		特惠税率 %			Article Description
东/冰/格	巴基斯坦	韩国	瑞士 上/下	哥/秘/柬	澳/毛	新西/坡/智	中国港/澳/台	东盟及马来/澳/韩	日/新	亚太2国	老/柬/缅	98/97/95	
													--Unbleached
													Uncoatde krafliner paper and paperboard(tensile index (vertical + lateral) is greater than or equal to 69 N. M/g, tear index (vertical) is greater than or equal to 10 mN2/ g, tensile energy absorption index (horizontal) is greater than or equal to 1.0 J/g, tensile energy absorption index (vertical) is greater than or equal to 0.8 J/g, porosity is greater than or equal to 3.4 um/(Pa. s), elongation (vertical) is greater than or equal to 2%. (tissue paper refers to the per square metre weighs≤150 grams or less, roll or into zhang without coating)
													Other uncoated kraft paper and paperboard, unbleached(w≤ $150g/m^2$, in rolls or sheets)
													--Other
													-Other kraft paper and paperboard weighing more than 150 g/m^2 but less than $225g/m^2$:
													--Unbleached
													--Bleached uniformly throughout the mass and of which more than 95% by weight of the total fibre content consists of wood fibres obtained by a chemical process
													--Other
													-Other kraft paper and paperboard weighing 225 g/m^2 or more:
													--Unbleached
													--Bleached uniformly throughout the mass and of which more than 95% by weight of the total fibre content consists of wood fibres obtained by a chemical process
													--Other
													Other uncoated paper and paperboard, in rolls or sheets, not further worked or processed than as specified in Note 3 to this Chapter:
													-Fluting paper:
				//0	/0		0/0/					0/0/	--Semi-chemical fluting paper
				//0	/0		0/0/					0/0/	--Straw fluting paper
5//				//0	/0		0/0/					0/0/	--Other
													-Testliner(recycled liner board):
				//0	/0		0/0/					0/0/	--Weighing 150 g/m^2 or less
				//0	/0		0/0/					0/0/	--Weighing more than 150 g/m^2
													-Sulphite wrapping paper
													-Filter paper and paperboard
													-Felt paper and paperboard
													-Other:
													--Weighing 150 g/m^2 or less:
5//				//0	/0	0//	0/0/					0/0/	---Paper for electrolytic capacitor
5//				//0	/0	0//	0/0/					0/0/	---Other
													--Weighing more than 150 g/m^2 but less than 225 g/m^2
				//0	/0		0/0/					0/0/	--Weighing 225 g/m^2 or more
													Vegetable parchment, greaseproof papers, tracing papers and glassine and other glazed transparent or translucent papers, in rolls or sheets:
5//				//5		5//							-Vegetable parchment
5//				//5		5//							-Greaseproof papers
5//				//5		5//							-Tracing papers
5//				//5		5//							-Glassine and other glazed transparent or translucent papers
													Composite paper and paperboard (made by sticking flat layers of paper or paperboard together with an adhesive), not surface-coated or impregnated, whether or not internally reinforced, in rolls or sheets:
													Composite paper and paperboard (made by sticking flat layers of paper or paperboard together with an adhesive), not surface-coated or impregnated, whether or not internally reinforced, in rolls or sheets
													Paper and paperboard, corrugated (with or without glued flat surface sheets), creped, crinkled, embossed or perforated, in rolls or sheets, other than paper of the kind described in heading No. 48.03:
			3.2/3.2		/0	0//						0//	-Corrugated paper and paperboard, whether or not perforated
													-Kraft paper, creped or crinkled, whether or not embossed or perforated
													-Other
													Carbon paper, self-copy paper and other copying or transfer papers (including coated or impregnated paper for duplicator stencils or offset plates), whether or not printed, in rolls or sheets:
													-Self-copy paper
													-Other

税则号列	货品名称〔CIQ扩展编码及品名—T2表示见附表2〕	最惠(%)	暂定税率	普通	增值/消费	出口退税	计量单位	监管条件/特殊证件	检验检疫	对美关税	亚太上/下
48.10	**成卷或成张矩形(包括正方形)的任何尺寸的单面或双面涂布高岭土或其他无机物质(不论是否加黏合剂)的纸及纸板,但未涂布其他涂料,不论是否染面、饰面或印花:**										
	-书写、印刷或类似用途的纸及纸板,不含用机械或化学—机械方法制得的纤维或所含前述纤维不超过全部纤维重量的10%:										
4810.1300	--成卷的										
4810.1300 01	成卷的铜版纸(所含用机械或化学-机械法制得的纤维≤10%)〔999〕	5		40	13/	0	千克	/		10	
4810.1300 90	涂无机物的其他书写/印刷或类似用途纸/纸板(成卷的,所含用机械或化学-机械法制得的纤维≤10%)〔999〕	5		40	13/	0	千克	/		10	
4810.1400	--成张的,一边不超过435毫米,另一边不超过297毫米(以未折叠计)〔999〕	5		40	13/	0	千克	/		25	
4810.1900	--其他〔999〕	5		40	13/	0	千克	/		25	
	-书写、印刷或类似用途的纸及纸板,所含用机械或化学—机械方法制得的纤维超过全部纤维重量的10%:										
4810.2200	--轻质涂布纸〔999〕	5		40	13/	0	千克	/		25	
4810.2900	--其他〔999〕	5		40	13/	0	千克	/		30	
	-牛皮纸及纸板,但书写、印刷或类似用途的除外:										
4810.3100	--本体均匀漂白,所含用化学方法制得的木纤维超过全部纤维重量的95%,每平方米重量不超过150克										
4810.3100 10	涂无机物的白板纸、白卡纸(薄纸指每平方米重≤150g,含用化学方法制得木纤维)〔999〕	5		40	13/	0	千克	/		30	
4810.3100 90	涂无机物的薄漂白牛皮纸及纸板(薄纸指每平方米重量≤150克,含用化学方法制得的木纤维)〔999〕	5		40	13/	0	千克	/		30	
4810.3200	--本体均匀漂白,所含用化学方法制得的木纤维超过全部纤维重量的95%,每平方米重量超过150克										
4810.3200 10	涂无机物的白板纸、白卡纸(厚纸指每平方米重量>150克,含用化学方法制得的木纤维)〔999〕	5		40	13/	0	千克	/		10	
4810.3200 90	涂无机物的厚漂白牛皮纸及纸板(厚纸指每平方米重量>150g,含用化学方法制得的木纤维)〔999〕	5		40	13/	0	千克	/		10	
4810.3900	--其他〔999〕	5		40	13/	0	千克	/		10	
	-其他纸及纸板:										
4810.9200	--多层的〔999〕	5		40	13/	0	千克	/		30	
4810.9900	--其他〔999〕	6	5	40	13/	0	千克	/		25	
48.11	**成卷或成张矩形(包括正方形)的任何尺寸的经涂布、浸渍、覆盖、染面、饰面或印花的纸、纸板、纤维素絮纸及纤维素纤维网纸,但税目48.03、48.09或48.10的货品除外:**										
4811.1000	-焦油纸及纸板、沥青纸及纸板〔999〕	6	5	40	13/	0	千克	/			
	-胶粘纸及纸板:										
4811.4100	--自粘的〔999〕	6	5	40	13/	0	千克	/		25	
4811.4900	--其他〔999〕	6	5	40	13/	0	千克	/		10	
	-用塑料(不包括黏合剂)涂布、浸渍或覆盖的纸及纸板:										
	--漂白的,每平方米重量超过150克:										
4811.5110	---彩色相纸用双面涂塑厚纸〔999〕	6	5	40	13/	0	千克	/		30	
	---其他:										
4811.5191	----纸塑铝复合材料〔999〕	6	5	40	13/	13	千克	/			
4811.5199	----其他〔999〕	6		40	13/	0	千克	/		26	
	--其他:										
4811.5910	---绝缘纸及纸板〔999〕	6	5	30	13/	0	千克	/		25	
	---其他:										
4811.5991	----镀铝的〔999〕	6	5	40	13/	13	千克	/		10	
4811.5999	----其他〔999〕	6	5	40	13/	0	千克	/		10	

协定税率 %								RCEP		特惠税率 %			Article Description
东/冰/格	巴基斯坦	韩国	瑞士上/下	哥/秘/柬	澳/毛	新西/坡/智	中国港/澳/台	东盟及马来/澳/韩	日/新	亚太2国	老/柬/缅	98/97/95	
													Paper and paperboard, coated on one or both sides with kaolin (China clay) or other inorganic substances, with or without a binder, and with no other coating, whether or not surface-coloured, surface-decorated or printed, in rolls or rectangular(including square) sheets, of any size:
													-Paper and paperboard of a kind used for writing, printing or other graphic purposes, not containing fibres obtained by a mechanical or chemi-mechanical process or of which not more than 10% by weight of the total fibre content consists of such fibres:
													--In rolls
				//0	/0		0/0/	4.5//				0/0/	Art paper, in rolls (containing fibres≤10%, obtained by a mechanical or chemi-mechanical process)
				//0	/0		0/0/	4.5//				0/0/	Other paper and paperboard, coated with inorganic substances, of a kind used for writing, printing or other graphic purposes (containing fibres≤10%, obtained by a mechanical or chemi-mechanical process, in rolls)
				//0	/0		0/0/	4.5//				0/0/	--In sheets with one side not exceeding 435 mm and the other side not exceeding 297 mm in the unfolded state
				//0	/0		0/0/	4.5//				0/0/	--Other
													-Paper and paperboard of a kind used for writing, printing or other graphic purposes, of which more than 10% by weight of the total fibre content consists of fibres obtained by a mechanical or chemi-mechanical process:
													--Light-weight coated paper
				//0	/0		0/0/					0/0/	--Other
													-Kraft paper and paperboard, other than that of a kind used for writing, printing or other graphic purposes:
													--Bleached uniformly throughout the mass and of which more than 95% by weight of the total fibre content consists of wood fibres obtained by a chemical process, and weighing 150 g/m^2 or less
				//0	/0		0/0/					0/0/	White board and ivory board, bleached, coated with inarganic substances (w≤150g/m^2, consisting of wood fibres obtained by a chemical process)
				//0	/0		0/0/					0/0/	White kraft paper and paperboard, bleached, coated with inorganic substances, (w≤150g/m^2, consisting of wood fibres obtained by a chemical process)
													--Bleached uniformly throughout the mass and of which more than 95% by weight of the total fibre content consists of wood fibres obtained by a chemical process, and weighing more than 150g/m^2
				//0	/0		0/0/					0/0/	White board and ivory board, bleached, coated with inorganic substances(w>150g/m^2 consisting of wood fibres obtained by a chemical process)
				//0	/0		0/0/					0/0/	White kraft paper and paperboard, bleached, coated with inorganic substances(w>150g/m^2, consisting of wood fibres obtained by a chemical process)
				//0	/0		0/0/					0/0/	--Other
													-Other paper and paperboard:
				//0	/0		0/0/					0/0/	--Multiply
5//				//0	/0	0//	0/0/					0/0/	--Other
													Paper, paperboard, cellulose wadding and webs of cellulose fibres, coated, impregnated, covered, surface-coloured, surface-decorated or printed, in rolls or rectangular(including square) sheets, of any size, other than goods of the kind described in heading No. 48. 03, 48. 09or 48. 10:
5//				//0	/0	0//	0/0/					0/0/	-Tarred, bituminised or asphalted paper and paperboard
													-Gummed or adhesive paper and paperboard:
5//				//0	/0	0//	0/0/	6.8//				0/0/	--Self-adhesive
5//				//0	/0	0//	0/0/					0/0/	--Other
													-Paper and paperboard coated, impregnated or covered with plastics (excluding adhesives):
													--Bleached, weighing more than 150g/m^2:
5//				//0	/0	0//	0/0/					0/0/	---Paper coated on both sides with plastics for colour photography
													---Other:
5//				//0	/0	0//	0/0/					0/0/	----Paper aluminum- plastic materials
				//0	/0		0/0/					0/0/	----Other
													--Other:
5//				//0	/0	0//	0/0/					0/0/	---Insulating paper and paperboard
													---Other:
5//				//0	/0	0//	0/0/					0/0/	----Aluminium
5//				//0	/0	0//	0/0/					0/0/	----Other

税则号列	货品名称〔CIQ 扩展编码及品名—T2 表示见附表 2〕	最惠(%)	暂定税率	普通	增值/消费	出口退税	计量单位	监管条件/特殊证件	检验检疫	对美关税	亚太上/下
	-用蜡、石蜡、硬脂精、油或甘油涂布、浸渍、覆盖的纸及纸板：										
4811.6010	---绝缘纸及纸板〔999〕	6	5	30	13/	0	千克	/		10	
4811.6090	---其他〔999〕	6	5	40	13/	0	千克	/		25	
4811.9000	-其他纸、纸板、纤维素絮纸及纤维素纤维网纸〔999〕	6	5	40	13/	0	千克	/		10	
48.12	**纸浆制的滤块、滤板及滤片：**										
4812.0000	纸浆制的滤块、滤板及滤片〔999〕	6		40	13/	0	千克	/		26	
48.13	**卷烟纸，不论是否切成一定尺寸、成小本或管状：**										
4813.1000	-成小本或管状〔999〕	7.5		100	13/	0	千克	7/			
4813.2000	-宽度不超过 5 厘米成卷的〔999〕	7.5		100	13/	0	千克	7/			
4813.9000	-其他〔999〕	7.5		100	13/	0	千克	7/			
48.14	**壁纸及类似品；窗用透明纸：**										
4814.2000	-用塑料涂面或盖面的壁纸及类似品，起纹、压花、着色、印刷图案或经其他装饰〔999〕	6	5	50	13/	13	千克	/		25	
4814.9000	-其他										
4814.9000 10	用木粒或草粒等饰面的壁纸〔999〕	6	5	50	13/	0	千克	/		25	
4814.9000 90	其他壁纸及类似品，窗用透明纸〔999〕	6	5	50	13/	0	千克	/		25	
48.16	**复写纸、自印复写纸及其他拷贝或转印纸(不包括税目 48.09 的纸)、油印蜡纸或胶印版纸，不论是否盒装：**										
4816.2000	-自印复写纸〔999〕	6		70	13/	0	千克	/		31	
	-其他：										
4816.9010	---热敏转印纸〔999〕	6		40	13/	0	千克	/		11	
4816.9090	---其他〔999〕	6		70	13/	0	千克	/		26	
48.17	**纸或纸板制的信封、封缄信片、素色明信片及通信卡片；纸或纸板制的盒子、袋子及夹子，内装各种纸制文具：**										
4817.1000	-信封〔999〕	5		80	13/	13	千克	/		30	
4817.2000	-封缄信片、素色明信片及通信卡片〔999〕	5		80	13/	13	千克	/		30	
4817.3000	-纸或纸板制的盒子、袋子及夹子，内装各种纸制文具〔999〕	5		80	13/	13	千克	/		30	
48.18	**卫生纸及类似纸，家庭或卫生用纤维素絮纸及纤维素纤维网纸，成卷宽度不超过 36 厘米或切成一定尺寸或形状的；纸浆、纸、纤维素絮纸或纤维素纤维网纸制的手帕、面巾、台布、餐巾、床单及类似的家庭、卫生或医院用品、衣服及衣着附件：**										
4818.1000	-卫生纸〔999〕	5		80	13/	13	千克	A/	M	30	
4818.2000	-纸手帕及纸面巾〔101 面巾纸、餐巾纸及类似纸，102 擦拭用纸〕	5		90	13/	13	千克	A/	M	30	
4818.3000	-纸台布及纸餐巾〔101 面巾纸、餐巾纸及类似纸，102 擦拭用纸〕	5		90	13/	13	千克	A/	M	30	
4818.5000	-衣服及衣着附件〔101 服装生产用纸板或衬里，102 一次性生活用纸〕	5	0	90	13/	13	千克	A/	M		
4818.9000	-其他〔999〕	5		90	13/	13	千克	A/	M	10	
48.19	**纸、纸板、纤维素絮纸或纤维素纤维网纸制的箱、盒、匣、袋及其他包装容器；纸或纸板制的卷宗盒、信件盘及类似品，供办公室、商店及类似场所使用的：**										
4819.1000	-瓦楞纸或纸板制的箱、盒、匣〔999〕	5		80	13/	13	千克	/		30	
4819.2000	-非瓦楞纸或纸板制的可折叠箱、盒、匣〔999〕	5		80	13/	13	千克	/		30	
4819.3000	-底宽 40 厘米及以上的纸袋〔999〕	6	0	80	13/	13	千克	/		25	
4819.4000	-其他纸袋，包括锥形袋〔999〕	5		80	13/	13	千克	/		30	
4819.5000	-其他包装容器，包括唱片套〔999〕	5		80	13/	13	千克	A/	R	30	
4819.6000	-办公室、商店及类似场所使用的卷宗盒、信件盘、存储盒及类似品〔999〕	5		80	13/	13	千克	/		30	
48.20	**纸或纸板制的登记本、账本、笔记本、订货本、收据本、信笺本、记事本、日记本及类似品、练习本、吸墨纸本、活动封面(活页及非活页)、文件夹、卷宗皮、多联商业表格纸、页间夹有复写纸的本及其他文具用品；纸或纸板制的样品簿、粘贴簿及书籍封面：**										

协定税率 %								RCEP		特惠税率 %			Article Description
东/冰/格	巴基斯坦	韩国	瑞士 上/下	哥/秘/柬	澳/毛	新西/坡/智	中国港/澳/台	东盟及马来/澳/韩	日/新	亚太2国	老/柬/缅	98/97/95	
													-Paper and paperboard, coated, impregnated or covered with wax, paraffin wax, stearin, oil or glycerol:
5//				//0	/0	0//	0/0/					0/0/	---Insulating paper and paperboard
5//				//0	/0	0//	0/0/					0/0/	---Other
5//				//0	/0	0//	0/0/					0/0/	-Other paper, paperboard, cellulose wadding and webs of cellulose fibres
													Filter blocks, slabs and plates, of paper pulp:
													Filter blocks, slabs and plates, of paper pulp
													Cigarette paper, whether or not cut to size or in the form of booklets or tubes:
													-In the form of booklets or tubes
													-In rolls of a width not exceeding 5 cm
													-Other
													Wallpaper and similar wall coverings; window transparencies of paper:
5//				//5		5//							-Wallpaper and similar wall coverings, consisting of paper coated or covered, on the face side, with a grained, embossed, coloured, design-printed or otherwise decorated layer of plastics
													-Other
5//				//5		5//							"Ingrain" paper
5//				//5		5//							Other wallpaper and similar wall coverings, window transparencies of paper
													Carbon paper, self-copy paper and other copying or transfer papers (other than those of heading No. 48.09), duplicator stencils and offset plates, of paper, whether or not put up in boxes:
													-Self-copy paper
													-Other:
													---Heat transfer paper
													---Other
													Envelopes, letter cards, plain postcards and correspondence cards, of paper or paperboard; boxes, pouches, wallets and writing compendiums, of paper or paperboard, containing an assortment of paper stationery:
5//				//5									-Envelopes
5//				//5									-Letter cards, plain postcards and correspondence cards
5//				//5									-Boxes, pouches, wallets and writing compendiums, of paper or paperboard, containing an assortment of paper stationery
													Toilet paper and similar paper, cellulose wadding or webs of cellulose fibres, of a kind used for household or sanitary purposes, in rolls of a width not exceeding 36 cm, or cut to size or shape; handkerchiefs, cleansing tissues, towels, tablecloths, serviettes, bed sheets and similar household, sanitary or hospital articles, articles of apparel and clothing accessories, of paper pulp, paper, cellulose wadding or webs of cellulose fibres:
													-Toilet paper
													-Handkerchiefs, cleansing or facial tissues and towels
5//				//5									-Tablecloths and serviettes
0/0/	2	0	0/0	0/0/0	0/0	0//0	0/0/	0/0/0	6.8/0			0/0/0	-Articles of apparel and clothing accessories
													-Other
													Cartons, boxes, cases, bags and other packing containers, of paper, paperboard, cellulose wadding or webs of cellulose fibres; box files, letter trays and similar articles, of paper or paperboard of a kind used in offices, shops or the like:
				//0	/0		0/0/					0/0/	-Cartons, boxes and cases, of corrugated paper or paperboard
				//0	/0		0/0/					0/0/	-Folding cartons, boxes and cases, of noncorrugated paper or paperboard
0/0/	2	0	0/0	0/0/0	0/0	0/0/0	0/0/	0/0/0	6.8/0			0/0/0	-Sacks and bags, having a base of a width of 40 cm or more
5//				//5									-Other sacks and bags, including cones
5//				//5									-Other packing containers, including record sleeves
5//				//5									-Box files, letter trays, storage boxes and similar articles, of a kind used in offices, shops or the like
													Registers, account books, note books, order books, receipt books, letter pads, memorandum pads, diaries and similar articles, exercise books, blotting-pads, binders (loose-leaf or other), folders, file covers, manifold business forms, interleaved carbon sets and other articles of stationery, of paper or paperboard; albums for samples or for collections and book covers, of paper or paperboard:

税则号列	货品名称〔CIQ 扩展编码及品名—T2 表示见附表 2〕	最惠(%)	暂定税率	普通	增值/消费	出口退税	计量单位	监管条件/特殊证件	检验检疫	对美关税	亚太上/下
4820.1000	-登记本、账本、笔记本、订货本、收据本、信笺本、记事本、日记本及类似品〔999〕	5		80	13/	13	千克	/		30	
4820.2000	-练习本〔999〕	5		80	13/	13	千克	/		30	
4820.3000	-活动封面(书籍封面除外)、文件夹及卷宗皮〔999〕	5		80	13/	13	千克	/		30	
4820.4000	-多联商业表格纸、页间夹有复写纸的本〔999〕	5	0	80	13/	13	千克	/		25	
4820.5000	-样品簿及粘贴簿〔999〕	5		80	13/	13	千克	/		10	
4820.9000	-其他〔999〕	5		80	13/	13	千克	/		30	
48.21	**纸或纸板制的各种标签,不论是否印制:**										
4821.1000	-印制〔999〕	6	5	50	13/	13	千克	/		25	
4821.9000	-其他〔999〕	6	5	50	13/	13	千克	/		25	
48.22	**纸浆、纸或纸板(不论是否穿孔或硬化)制的筒管、卷轴、纡子及类似品:**										
4822.1000	-纺织纱线用〔999〕	6	5	35	13/	13	千克	/		30	
4822.9000	-其他〔999〕	6	5	70	13/	13	千克	/		25	
48.23	**切成一定尺寸或形状的其他纸、纸板、纤维素絮纸及纤维素纤维网纸;纸浆、纸、纸板、纤维素絮纸及纤维素纤维网纸制的其他物品:**										
4823.2000	-滤纸及纸板〔999〕	6		30	13/	13	千克	/		26	
4823.4000	-已印制的自动记录器用打印纸卷、纸张及纸盘〔999〕	6	5	30	13/	13	千克	/		10	
	-纸或纸板制的盘、碟、盆、杯及类似品:										
4823.6100	--竹浆纸制〔101 食品接触复合纸产品(纸和塑料膜等其他材料复合),102 食品接触上蜡纸产品,103 食品接触其他纸产品,104 食品用复合纸包装(纸和塑料膜等其他材料复合),105 食品用上蜡纸包装,106 食品用其他纸包装〕	5	0	90	13/	13	千克	A/	M		
	--其他:										
4823.6910	---非木植物浆制〔101 食品接触复合纸产品(纸和塑料膜等其他材料复合),102 食品接触上蜡纸产品,103 食品接触其他纸产品,104 食品用复合纸包装(纸和塑料膜等其他材料复合),105 食品用上蜡纸包装,106 食品用其他纸包装〕	5	0	90	13/	13	千克	A/	M	25	
4823.6990	---其他〔101:食品接触原纸产品;102:食品接触复合纸产品(纸和塑料膜等其他材料复合);103:食品接触上蜡纸产品;104:食品接触其他纸产品;105:食品用原纸包装;106:食品用复合纸包装(纸和塑料膜等其他材料复合);107:食品用上蜡纸包装;108:食品用其他纸包装〕	5	0	90	13/	13	千克	A/	M	25	
4823.7000	-压制或模制纸浆制品〔999〕	6	5	90	13/	13	千克	/		30	
	-其他:										
4823.9010	---以纸或纸板为底制的铺地制品〔999〕	6	0	90	13/	0	千克	/		25	
4823.9020	---神纸及类似用品〔999〕	6	0	180	13/	13	千克	/			
4823.9030	---纸扇〔999〕	5	0	90	13/	13	千克	/			
4823.9090	---其他〔T2〕	6		90	13/	13	千克	/		26	

协定税率 %								RCEP		特惠税率 %			Article Description
东/冰/格	巴基斯坦	韩国	瑞士上/下	哥/秘/柬	澳/毛	新西/坡/智	中国港/澳/台	东盟及马来/澳/韩	日/新	亚太2国	老/柬/缅	98/97/95	
5//				//5									-Registers, account books, note books, order books, receipt books, letter pads, memorandum pads, diaries and similar articles
5//				//5									-Exercise books
5//				//5									-Binders (other than book covers), folders and file covers
0/0/	3.5	1.5	0/0	0/0/0	0/0	0//0	0/0/	0/0/6.8	6.8/0			0/0/0	-Manifold business forms and interleaved carbon sets
5//				//5									-Albums for samples or for collections
5//				//5									-Other
													Paper or paperboard labels of all kinds, whether or not printed:
5//				//0	/0	0//	0/0/	6.8//				0/0/	-Printed
5//				//5		5//							-Other
													Bobbins, spools, cops and similar supports of paper pulp, paper or paperboard (whether or not perforated or hardened):
5//				//5		5//							-Of a kind used for winding textile yarn
5//				//5		5//							-Other
													Other paper, paperboard, cellulose wadding and webs of cellulose fibres, cut to size or shape; other articles of paper pulp, paper, paperboard, cellulose wadding or webs of cellulose fibres:
													-Filter paper and paperboard
5//				//5									-Rolls, sheets and dials, printed for sel-frecording apparatus
													-Trays, dishes, plates, cups and the like, of paper or paperboard:
0/0/	2	0	0/0	0/0/0	0/0	0//0	0/0/	0/0/0	6.8/0			0/0/0	--Of bamboo
													--Other:
0/0/	2	1.5	0/0	0/0/0	0/0	0//0	0/0/	0/0/6.8	6.8/0			0/0/0	---Other than those of wood
0/0/	2	1.5	0/0	0/0/0	0/4.5	0//0	0/0/	0/0/6.8	6.8/0			0/0/0	---Other
5//				//5		5//							-Moulded or pressed articles of paper pulp
													-Other:
5//		3.5	0/0	//0	/0	0//	0/0/					0//	---Floor coverings on a base of paper or of paperboard
0/0/	2	0	0/0	0/0/0	0/0	0//0	0/0/	0/0/0	6.8/0			0/0/0	---Joss paper and the like
0/0/	2	0	0/0	0/0/0	0/0	0//0	0/0/	0/0/0	6.8/0			0/0/0	---Paper fans
				//0			0/0/					0/0/	---Other

第四十九章
书籍、报纸、印刷图画及其他印刷品;手稿、打字稿及设计图纸

注释:

一、本章不包括:

(一)透明基的照相负片或正片(第三十七章);

(二)立体地图、设计图表或地球仪、天体仪,不论是否印刷(税目90.23);

(三)第九十五章的游戏纸牌或其他物品;

(四)雕版画、印刷画、石印画的原本(税目97.02),税目97.04的邮票、印花税票、纪念封、首日封、邮政信笺及类似品,以及第九十七章的超过一百年的古物或其他物品。

二、第四十九章所称“印刷”,也包括用胶版复印机、油印机印制,在自动数据处理设备控制下打印绘制,压印、冲印、感光复印、热敏复印或打字。

三、用纸以外材料装订成册的报纸、杂志和期刊,以及一期以上装订在同一封面里的成套报纸、杂志和期刊,应归入税目49.01,不论是否有广告材料。

四、税目49.01还包括:

(一)附有说明文字,每页编有号数以便装订成一册或几册的整集印刷复制品,例如,美术作品、绘画;

(二)随同成册书籍的图画附刊;

(三)供装订书籍或小册子用的散页、集页或书帖形式的印刷品,已构成一部作品的全部或部分。

但没有说明文字的印刷图画或图解,不论是否散页或书帖形式,应归入税目49.11。

五、除本章注释三另有规定的以外,税目49.01不包括主要作广告用的出版物(例如,小册子、散页印刷品、商业目录、同业公会出版的年鉴、旅游宣传品),这类出版物应归入税目49.11。

六、税目49.03所称“儿童图画书”,是指以图画为主、文字为辅,供儿童阅览的书籍。

税则号列	货品名称〔CIQ扩展编码及品名—T2表示见附表2〕	最惠(%)	暂定税率	普通	增值/消费	出口退税	计量单位	监管条件/特殊证件	检验检疫	对美关税	亚太上/下
49.01	**书籍、小册子、散页印刷品及类似印刷品,不论是否单张:**										
4901.1000	-单张的,不论是否折叠〔999〕	0		0	9/	0,9,13	千克	/		25	
	-其他:										
4901.9100	--字典或百科全书及其连续出版的分册〔999〕	0		0	9/	0,9	千克	/		25	
4901.9900	--其他〔999〕	0		0	9/	0,9,13	千克	/			
49.02	**报纸、杂志及期刊,不论有无插图或广告材料:**										
4902.1000	-每周至少出版四次〔999〕	0		0	9/	9,13	千克	/			
4902.9000	-其他〔999〕	0		0	9/	9,13	千克	/			
49.03	**儿童图画书、绘画或涂色书:**										
4903.0000	儿童图画书、绘画或涂色书〔999〕	0		0	9/	0,9,13	千克	/		5	
49.04	**乐谱原稿或印本,不论是否装订或印有插图:**										
4904.0000	乐谱原稿或印本,不论是否装订或印有插图〔999〕	0		0	9/	0,9,13	千克	/		5	
49.05	**各种印刷的地图、水道图及类似图表,包括地图册、挂图、地形图及地球仪、天体仪:**										
4905.2000	-成册的〔999〕	0		0	13/	0,9,13	千克	/		25	
4905.9000	-其他〔999〕	0		0	13/	0,9,13	千克	/		5	
49.06	**手绘的建筑、工程、工业、商业、地形或类似用途的设计图纸原稿;手稿;用感光纸照相复印或用复写纸誊写的上述物品复制件:**										
4906.0000	手绘的建筑、工程、工业、商业、地形或类似用途的设计图纸原稿;手稿;用感光纸照相复印或用复写纸誊写的上述物品复制件										
4906.0000 10	含有人类遗传资源信息的设计图纸原稿或手稿及其复制件(手绘的建筑、工程、工业、商业、地形或类似用途的)〔999〕	0		0	13/	13	千克	V/		25	
4906.0000 90	其他设计图纸原稿或手稿及其复制件(手绘的建筑、工程、工业、商业、地形或类似用途的)〔999〕	0		0	13/	13	千克	/		25	

Chapter 49
Printed books, newspapers, pictures and other products of the printing industry; manuscripts, typescripts and plans

Notes:

1. This Chapter does not cover:
   (a) Photographic negatives or positives on transparent bases (Chapter 37);
   (b) Maps, plans or globes, in relief, whether or not printed (heading No. 90.23);
   (c) Playing cards or other goods of Chapter 95;
   (d) Original engravings, prints or lithographs (heading No. 97.02), postage or revenue stamps, stamp-postmarks, first-day covers, postal stationery or the like of heading No. 97.04, antiques of an age exceeding one hundred years or other articles of Chapter 97.
2. For the purposes of Chapter 49, the term "printed" also means reproduced by means of a duplicating machine, produced under the control of an automatic data processing machine, embossed, photographed, photocopied, thermocopied or typewritten.
3. Newspapers, journals and periodicals which are bound otherwise than in paper, and sets of newspapers, journals or periodicals comprising more than one number under a single cover are to be classified in heading No. 49.01, whether or not containing advertising material.
4. Heading No. 49.01 also covers:
   (a) A collection of printed reproductions of, for example, works of art or drawings, with a relative text, put up with numbered pages in a form suitable for binding into one or more volumes;
   (b) A pictorial supplement accompanying, and subsidiary to, a bound volume;
   (c) Printed parts of books or booklets, in the form of assembled or separate sheets or signatures, constituting the whole or a part of a complete work and designed for binding.
   However, printed pictures or illustrations not bearing a text, whether in the form of signatures or separate sheets, fall in heading No. 49.11.
5. Subject to Note 3 to this Chapter, heading No. 49.01 does not cover publications which are essentially devoted to advertising (for example, brochures, pamphlets, leaflets, trade catalogues, year books published by trade associations, tourist propaganda). Such publications are to be classified in heading No. 49.11.
6. For the purposes of heading No. 49.03, the expression "children's picture books" means books for children in which the pictures form the principal interest and the text is subsidiary

协定税率 %								RCEP		特惠税率 %			Article Description
东/冰/格	巴基斯坦	韩国	瑞士上/下	哥/秘/柬	澳/毛	新西/坡/智	中国港/澳/台	东盟及马来/澳/韩	日/新	亚太2国	老/柬/缅	98/97/95	
													Printed books, brochures, leaflets and similar printed matter, whether or not in single sheets:
0/0/0	0	0	0/0	0/0/0	0/0	0//0	0/0/	0/0/0	0/0			0/0/0	-In single sheets, whether or not folded
													-Other:
0/0/0	0	0	0/0	0/0/0	0/0	0//0	0/0/	0/0/0	0/0			0/0/0	--Dictionaries and encyclopaedias, and serial instalments thereof
0/0/0	0	0	0/0	0/0/0	0/0	0//0	0/0/	0/0/0	0/0			0/0/0	--Other
													Newspapers, journals and periodicals, whether or not illustrated or containing advertising material:
0/0/0	0	0	0/0	0/0/0	0/0	0//0	0/0/	0/0/0	0/0			0/0/0	-Appearing at least four times a week
0/0/0	0	0	0/0	0/0/0	0/0	0//0	0/0/	0/0/0	0/0			0/0/0	-Other
													Children's picture, drawing or colouring books:
0/0/0	0	0	0/0	0/0/0	0/0	0//0	0/0/	0/0/0	0/0			0/0/0	Children's picture, drawing or colouring books
													Music, printed or in manuscript, whether or not bound or illustrated:
0/0/0	0	0	0/0	0/0/0	0/0	0//0	0/0/	0/0/0	0/0			0/0/0	Music, printed or in manuscript, whether or not bound or illustrated
													Maps and hydrographic or similar charts of all kinds, including atlases, wall maps, topographical plans and globes, printed:
0/0/0	0	0	0/0	0/0/0	0/0	0//0	0/0/	0/0/0	0/0			0/0/0	- In book form
0/0/0	0	0	0/0	0/0/0	0/0	0//0	0/0/	0/0/0	0/0			0/0/0	-Other
													Plans and drawings for architectural, engineering, industrial, commercial, topographical or similar purposes, being originals drawn by hand; hand-written text; photographic reproductions on sensitized paper and carbon copies of the foregoing:
													Plans and drawings for architectural, engineering, industrial, commercial, topographical or similar purposes, being originals drawn by hand; hand-written text; photographic reproductions on sensitized paper and carbon copies of the foregoing
0/0/0	0	0	0/0	0/0/0	0/0	0//0	0/0/	0/0/0	0/0		//	0/0/0	Printed pictures, design drawings and photographs containing information on human genetic resources
0/0/0	0	0	0/0	0/0/0	0/0	0//0	0/0/	0/0/0	0/0		//	0/0/0	Other original or manuscript of design drawings and copies thereof

税则号列	货品名称〔CIQ 扩展编码及品名—T2 表示见附表 2〕	最惠(%)	暂定税率	普通	增值/消费	出口退税	计量单位	监管条件/特殊证件	检验检疫	对美关税	亚太上/下
49.07	**在承认或将承认其面值的国家流通或新发行并且未经使用的邮票、印花税票及类似票证;印有邮票或印花税票的纸品;钞票;空白支票;股票、债券及类似所有权凭证:**										
4907.0010	---邮票〔999〕	6	0	50	13/	13	千克	/		5	
4907.0020	---钞票〔999〕	0		50	13/	13	千克	/		20	
4907.0030	---证券凭证〔999〕	0		50	13/	13	千克	/			
4907.0090	---其他										
4907.0090 10	给予存取、安装、复制或使用软件(含游戏)、数据、互联网内容物(含游戏内或应用程序内内容物)、服务或电信服务(含移动服务)权利的印刷品(特许权使用凭证除外)〔999〕	0		50	13/	13	千克	/		5	
4907.0090 90	其他在承认或将承认其面值的国家流通新发行未使用的印花税票及类似票证(包括印有邮票或印花税票的纸品、空白支票)〔999〕	6	0	50	13/	13	千克	/		5	
49.08	**转印贴花纸(移画印花法用图案纸):**										
4908.1000	-釉转印贴花纸(移画印花法用图案纸)〔999〕	6	0	50	13/	13	千克	/		20	
4908.9000	-其他〔999〕	6	0	50	13/	13	千克	/		25	
49.09	**印刷或有图画的明信片;印有个人问候、祝贺、通告的卡片,不论是否有图画、带信封或饰边:**										
4909.0010	---印刷或有图画的明信片〔999〕	6	0	50	13/	13	千克	/		20	
4909.0090	---其他〔999〕	6	0	50	13/	13	千克	/		20	
49.10	**印刷的各种日历,包括日历芯:**										
4910.0000	印刷的各种日历(包括日历芯)〔999〕	6	0	50	13/	13	千克	/		25	
49.11	**其他印刷品,包括印刷的图片及照片:**										
	-商业广告品、商品目录及类似印刷品:										
4911.1010	---无商业价值的〔999〕	0		0	13/	13	千克	/		20	
4911.1090	---其他〔999〕	6	0	50	13/	13	千克	/		20	
	-其他:										
4911.9100	--图片、设计图样及照片										
4911.9100 10	含有人类遗传资源信息的印刷图片、设计图样及照片	6	0	50	13/	13	千克	V/		20	
4911.9100 90	其他印刷的图片、设计图样及照片	6	0	50	13/	13	千克	/		20	
	--其他:										
4911.9910	---纸质的										
4911.9910 10	给予存取、安装、复制或使用软件(含游戏)、数据、互联网内容物(含游戏内或应用程序内内容物)、服务或电信服务(含移动服务)权利的印刷品〔999〕	0		50	13/	13	千克	/		25	
4911.9910 20	含有人类遗传资源信息的纸质印刷品	6	0	50	13/	13	千克	V/		25	
4911.9910 90	其他纸质的印刷品〔999〕	6	0	50	13/	13	千克	/		25	
4911.9990	---其他										
4911.9990 10	给予存取、安装、复制或使用软件(含游戏)、数据、互联网内容物(含游戏内或应用程序内内容物)、服务或电信服务(含移动服务)权利的印刷品〔999〕	0		50	13/	13	千克	/		20	
4911.9990 20	含有人类遗传资源信息的其他印刷品	6	0	50	13/	13	千克	V/		20	
4911.9990 90	其他印刷品〔999〕	6	0	50	13/	13	千克	/		20	

协定税率 %								RCEP		特惠税率 %			Article Description
东/冰/格	巴基斯坦	韩国	瑞士上/下	哥/秘/柬	澳/毛	新西/坡/智	中国港/澳/台	东盟及马来/澳/韩	日/新	亚太2国	老/柬/缅	98/97/95	
													Unused postage, revenue or similar stamps of current or new issue in the country in which they have, or will have, a recognised face value; stamp-impressed paper; banknotes; cheque forms; stock, share or bond certificates and similar documents of title:
5//		3.5	0/0	//0	/0	0//	0/0/	7.3/7.3/	/7.3			0/0/0	---Postage
0/0/0	0	0	0/0	0/0/0	0/0	0//0	0/0/	0/0/0	0/0			0/0/0	---Banknotes
0/0/0	0	0	0/0	0/0/0	0/0	0//0	0/0/	0/0/0	0/0			0/0/0	---Documents of title
													---Other
5//		3.5	0/0	//0	/0	0//	0/0/	7.3/7.3/	/7.3			0/0/0	Printed matter giving access to, install, copy or use of software (including games), data, Internet content (including content in games or applications), services or telecommunications services (including mobile services) (except for royalty certificates)
5//		3.5	0/0	//0	/0	0//	0/0/	7.3/7.3/	/7.3			0/0/0	Other newly issued unused stamp duty tickets and similar certificates (including paper products printed with stamps or stamp duty tickets and blank cheques) circulating in countries that recognize or will recognize their face value
													Transfers (decalcomanias):
5//		3.5	0/0	//0	/0	0//	0/0/	7.3/7.3/	/7.3			0/0/0	-Transfers (decalcomanias), vitrifiable
5//		3.5	0/0	//0	/0	0//	0/0/	7.3/7.3/	/7.3			0/0/0	-Other
													Printed or illustrated postcards; printed cards bearing personal greetings, messages or announcements, whether or not illustrated, with or without envelopes or trimmings:
5//		3.5	0/0	//0	/0	0//	0/0/					0/0/0	---Printed or illustrated postcards
5//		3.5	0/0	//0	/0	0//	0/0/					0/0/0	---Other
													Calendars of any kind, printed, including calendar blocks:
5//		3.5	0.8/0.8	//0	/4.5	0//	0/0/					0/0/0	Calendars of any kind, printed, including calendar blocks
													Other printed matter, including printed pictures and photographs:
													-Trade advertising material, commercial catalogues and the like:
0/0/0	0	0	0/0	0/0/0	0/0	0//0	0/0/	0/0/0	0/0			0/0/0	---No commercial value
5//		3.5	0.8/0.8	//0	/4.5	0//	0/0/					0/0/0	---Other
													-Other:
													--Pictures, designs and photographs
5//		3.5	0/0	//0	/0	0//	0/0/				//	0/0/0	Printed pictures, design drawings and photographs containing information on human genetic resources
5//		3.5	0/0	//0	/0	0//	0/0/				//	0/0/0	Other printed pictures, design drawings and photographs
													--Other:
													---Papery
5/0/		3.5	3.2/3.2	//0	/0	0//	0/0/					0/0/0	Presswork, the given access, install, copy or use the software (including games), data, Internet content (including games or applications within contents) services or telecommunications services (including mobile services) rights
5/0/		3.5	3.2/3.2	//0	/0	0//	0/0/				//	0/0/0	Paper Prints Containing Information on Human Genetic Resources
5/0/		3.5	3.2/3.2	//0	/0	0//	0/0/					0/0/0	Other paper printing
													---Other
5/0/		3.5	3.2/3.2	//0	/4.5	0//	0/0/					0/0/0	Presswork, the given access, install, copy or use the software (including games), data, Internet content (including games or applications within contents) services or telecommunications services (including mobile services) rights
5/0/		3.5	3.2/3.2	//0	/4.5	0//	0/0/				//	0/0/0	Other printed materials containing information on human genetic resources
5/0/		3.5	3.2/3.2	//0	/4.5	0//	0/0/					0/0/0	Other printing

第十一类
纺织原料及纺织制品

注释：

一、本类不包括：

(一)制刷用的动物鬃、毛(税目 05.02)；马毛及废马毛(税目 05.11)；

(二)人发及人发制品(税目 05.01、67.03 或 67.04)，但通常用于榨油机或类似机器的滤布除外(税目 59.11)；

(三)第十四章的棉短绒或其他植物材料；

(四)税目 25.24 的石棉、税目 68.12 或 68.13 的石棉制品或其他产品；

(五)税目 30.05 或 30.06 的物品；税号 33.06 的用于清洁牙缝的纱线(牙线)，单独零售包装的；

(六)税目 37.01 至 37.04 的感光布；

(七)截面尺寸超过 1 毫米的塑料单丝和表面宽度超过 5 毫米的塑料扁条及类似品 (例如，人造草)(第三十九章)，以及上述单丝或扁条的缏条、织物、篮筐或柳条编结品(第四十六章)；

(八)第三十九章的用塑料浸渍、涂布、包覆或层压的机织物、针织物或钩编织物、毡呢或无纺织物及其制品；

(九)第四十章的用橡胶浸渍、涂布、包覆或层压的机织物、针织物或钩编织物、毡呢或无纺织物及其制品；

(十)带毛皮张(第四十一章或第四十三章)、税目 43.03 或 43.04 的毛皮制品、人造毛皮及其制品；

(十一)税目 42.01 或 42.02 的用纺织材料制成的物品；

(十二)第四十八章的产品或物品(例如纤维素絮纸)；

(十三)第六十四章的鞋靴及其零件、护腿、裹腿及类似品；

(十四)第六十五章的发网、其他帽类及其零件；

(十五)第六十七章的货品；

(十六)涂有研磨料的纺织材料(税目 68.05)以及税目 68.15 的碳纤维及其制品；

(十七)玻璃纤维及其制品，但可见底布的玻璃线刺绣品除外(第七十章)；

(十八)第九十四章的物品(例如，家具、寝具、灯具及照明装置)；

(十九)第九十五章的物品(例如，玩具、游戏品、运动用品及网具)；

(二十)第九十六章的物品(例如：刷子、旅行用成套缝纫用具、拉链、打字机色带、卫生巾(护垫)及卫生棉条、尿布及尿布衬里；或

(二十一)第九十七章的物品。

二、(一)可归入第五十章至第五十五章及税目 58.09 或 59.02 的由两种或两种以上纺织材料混合制成的货品，应按其中重量最大的那种纺织材料归类。

当没有一种纺织材料的重量较大时，应按可归入的有关税目中最后一个税目所列的纺织材料归类。

(二)应用上述规定时：

1. 马毛粗松螺旋花线(税目 51.10)和含金属纱线(税目 56.05)均应作为一种单一的纺织材料，其重量应为它们在纱线中的合计重量；在机织物的归类中，金属线应作为一种纺织材料；

2. 在选择合适的税目时，应首先确定章，然后再确定该章的有关税目，至于不归入该章的其他材料可不予考虑；

3. 当归入第五十四章及第五十五章的货品与其他章的货品进行比较时，应将这两章作为一个单一的章对待；

4. 同一章或同一税目所列各种不同的纺织材料应作为单一的纺织材料对待。

(三)上述(一)、(二)两款规定亦适用于以下注释三、四、五或六所述纱线。

三、(一)本类的纱线(单纱、多股纱线或缆线)除下列(二)款另有规定的以外，凡符合以下规格的应作为“线、绳、索、缆”：

1. 丝或绢丝纱线，细度在 20000 分特以上；

2. 化学纤维纱线(包括第五十四章的用两根及以上单丝纺成的纱线)，细度在 10000 分特以上；

3. 大麻或亚麻纱线：

(1)加光或上光的，细度在 1429 分特及以上；

(2)未加光或上光的，细度在 20000 分特以上；

4. 三股或三股以上的椰壳纤维纱线；

5. 其他植物纤维纱线，细度在 20000 分特以上；

6. 用金属线加强的纱线。

(二)下列各项不按上述(一)款规定办理：

1. 羊毛或其他动物毛纱线及纸纱线，但用金属线加强的纱线除外；

2. 第五十五章的化学纤维长丝丝束以及第五十四章的未加捻或捻度每米少于 5 转的复丝纱线；

3. 税目 50.06 的蚕胶丝及第五十四章的单丝；

4. 税目 56.05 的含金属纱线；但用金属线加强的纱线按上述(一)款 6 项规定办理；

SECTION Ⅺ
TEXTILES AND TEXTILE ARTICLES

Notes:

1. This Section does not cover:

(a) Animal brush making bristles or hair (heading No. 05. 02); horsehair orhorsehair waste (heading No. 05. 11);

(b) Human hair or articles of human hair (heading No. 05. 01, 67. 03 or 67. 04), except straining cloth of a kind commonly used in oil presses or the like (heading No. 59. 11);

(c) Cotton linters or other vegetable materials of Chapter 14;

(d) Asbestos of heading No. 25. 24 or articles of asbestos or other products of heading No. 68. 12 or 68. 13;

(e) Articles of heading No. 30. 05 or 30. 06; yarn used to clean between the teeth, in individual, retail packages dental floss, of heading No. 33. 06;

(f) Sensitized textiles of headings No. 37. 01 to 37. 04;

(g) Monofilament of which any cross-sectional dimensionexceeds 1mm or strip or the like (for example, artificial straw) of an apparent width exceeding 5mm, of plastics (Chapter 39), or plaits or fabrics or other basketware or wickerwork of such monofilament or strip (Chapter 46);

(h) Woven, knitted or crocheted fabrics, felt or nonwovens, impregnated, coated, covered or laminated with plastics, or articles thereof, ofChapter 39;

(i) Woven, knitted or crocheted fabrics, felt or nonwovens, impregnated, coated, covered or laminated with rubber, or articles thereof, ofChapter 40;

(j) Hides or skins with their hair or wool on (Chapter 41 or43) or artcles of furskin, artificial fur or articles thereof, of heading No. 43. 03 or 43. 04;

(k) Articles of textile materials of heading No. 42. 01or42. 02;

(l) Products or articles of Chapter 48 (for example, cellulose wadding);

(m) Footwear or parts of footwear, gaiters or leggings or similar articles of Chapter 64;

(n) Hair-nets or other headgear or parts thereof of Chapter65;

(o) Goods of Chapter 67;

(p) Abrasive-coated textile material (Heading No. 68. 05) and also carbon fibres or articles of carbon fibres of heading No. 68. 15;

(q) Glass fibres or articles of glass fibres, other thanembroidery with glass thread on a visible ground of fabric (Chapter 70);

(r) Articles of Chapter 94 (for example, furniture, bedding, lamps and lighting fittings);

(s) Articles of Chapter 95 (for example, toys, games, sports requisites and nets);

(t) Articles of Chapter 96 (for example, brushes, travel sets for sewing, slide fasteners, typewriter ribbons, sanitary towels (pads) and tampons, napkins (diapers) and napkin liners); or

(u) Articles of Chapter 97.

2. (a) Goods classifiable in Chapters 50 to 55 or of headingNo. 58. 09 or 59. 02 and of a mixture of two or more textile materials are to beclassified as if consisting wholly of that one textile material which predominates by weight over any other single textile material. When no one textile material predominates by weight, the goods are to be classified as if consisting wholly of that one textile material which is covered by the heading which occurs last in numerical order among those which equally merit consideration.

(b) For the purposes of the above rule:

(ⅰ) Gimped horsehair yarn (heading No. 51. 10) and metallized yarn (heading No. 56. 05) are to be treated as a single textile material the weight of which is to be taken as the aggregate of the weights of its components; for the classification of woven fabrics, metal thread is to be regarded as a textile material;

(ⅱ) The choice of appropriate heading shall be effected by determining first the Chapter and then the applicable heading within that Chapter, disregarding any materials not classified in that Chapter;

(ⅲ) When both Chapters 54 and 55 are involved with any otherChapter, Chapters 54 and 55 are to be treated as a single Chapter;

(ⅳ) Where a Chapter or a heading refers to goods of different textile materials, such materials are to be treated as a single textile material.

(c) The provisions of paragraphs (A) and (B) above apply also to the yarns referred to in Notes 3, 4, 5 or 6 below.

3. (a) For the purposes of this Section, and subject to the exceptions in paragraph (B) below, yarns (single, multiple (folded) or cabled) of the following descriptions are to be treated as "twine, cordage, ropes and cables":

(ⅰ) Of silk or waste silk, measuring more than 20,000 decitex;

(ⅱ) Of man-made fibres (including yarn of two or more monofilaments of Chapter 54), measuring more than 10,000 decitex;

(ⅲ) Of true hemp or flax:

ⅰ) Polished or glazed, measuring 1,429 decitex or more;

ⅱ) Not polished or glazed, measuring more than 20,000 decitex;

(ⅳ) Of coir, consisting of three or more plies;

(ⅴ) Of other vegetable fibres, measuring more than 20,000 decitex;

(ⅵ) Reinforced with metal thread.

(b) Exceptions:

(ⅰ) Yarn of wool or other animal hair and paper yarn, otherthan yarn reinforced with metal thread;

(ⅱ) Man-made filament tow of Chapter 55 and multifilament yarn without twist or with a twist of less than 5 turns per metre of Chapter 54;

(ⅲ) Silk worm gut of heading No. 50. 06, and monofilamentsofChapter 54;

(ⅳ) Metallized yarn of Heading No. 56. 05; yarn reinforcedwith metal thread is subject to paragraph (A) (f) above; and

5. 税目56.06的绳绒线、粗松螺旋花线及纵行起圈纱线。

四、(一)除下列(二)款另有规定的以外,第五十章、第五十一章、第五十二章、第五十四章和第五十五章所称"供零售用"纱线,是指以下列方式包装的纱线(单纱、股纱线或缆线):

1. 绕于纸板、线轴、纱管或类似芯子上,其重量(含线芯)符合下列规定:

(1)丝、绢丝或化学纤维长丝纱线,不超过85克;

(2)其他纱线,不超过125克。

2. 绕成团、绞或束,其重量符合下列规定:

(1) 细度在3000分特以下的化学纤维长丝纱线,丝或绢丝纱线,不超过85克;

(2)细度在2000分特以下的任何其他纱线,不超过125克;

(3)其他纱线,不超过500克。

3. 绕成绞或束,每绞或每束中有若干用线分开的小绞或小束,每小绞或小束的重量相等,并且符合下列规定:

(1)丝、绢丝或化学纤维长丝纱线,不超过85克;

(2)其他纱线,不超过125克。

(二)下列各项不按上述(一)款规定办理:

1. 各种纺织材料制的单纱,但下列两种除外:

(1)未漂白的羊毛或动物细毛单纱;

(2)漂白、染色或印色的羊毛或动物细毛单纱,细度在5000分特以上。

2. 未漂白的多股纱线或缆线:

(1)丝或绢丝制的,不论何种包装;

(2)除羊毛或动物细毛外其他纺织材料制,成绞或成束的。

3. 漂白、染色或印色丝或绢丝制的多股纱线或缆线,细度在133分特及以下;

4. 任何纺织材料制的单纱、多股纱线或缆线:

(1)交叉绕成绞或束的;

(2)绕于纱芯上或以其他方式卷绕,明显用于纺织工业的(例如,绕于纱管、加捻管、纬纱管、锥形筒管或锭子上的或者绕成蚕茧状以供绣花机使用的纱线)。

五、税目52.04、54.01及55.08所称"缝纫线",是指下列多股纱线或缆线:

(一)绕于芯子(例如,线轴、纱管)上,重量(包括纱芯)不超过1000克;

(二)作为缝纫线上过浆的;

(三)终捻为反手(Z)捻的。

六、本类所称"高强力纱",是指断裂强度大于下列标准的纱线:

尼龙、其他聚酰胺或聚酯制的单纱60厘牛顿/特克斯;

尼龙、其他聚酰胺或聚酯制的多股纱线或缆线53厘牛顿/特克斯;

粘胶纤维制的单纱、多股纱线或缆线27厘牛顿/特克斯。

七、本类所称"制成的",是指:

(一)裁剪成除正方形或长方形以外的其他形状的;

(二)呈制成状态,无需缝纫或其他进一步加工(或仅需剪断分隔联线)即可使用的(例如,某些抹布、毛巾、台布、方披巾、毯子);

(三)裁剪成一定尺寸,至少有一边为带有可见的锥形或压平形的热封边,其余各边经本注释其他各项所述加工,但不包括为防止剪边脱纱而用热切法或其他简单方法处理的织物;

(四)已缝边或滚边,或者在任一边带有结制的流苏,但不包括为防止剪边脱纱而锁边或用其他简单方法处理的织物;

(五)裁剪成一定尺寸并经抽纱加工的;

(六)缝合、胶合或用其他方法拼合而成的(将两段或两段以上同样料子的织物首尾连接而成的匹头,以及由两层或两层以上的织物,不论中间有无胎料,层叠而成的匹头除外);

(七)针织或钩编成一定形状,不论报验时是单件还是以若干件相连成幅的。

八、对于第五十章至第六十章:

(一)第五十章至第五十五章和第六十章,以及除条文另有规定以外的第五十六章至第五十九章,不适用于上述注释七所规定的制成货品;

(二)第五十章至第五十五章及第六十章不包括第五十六章至第五十九章的货品。

九、第五十章至第五十五章的机织物包括由若干层平行纱线以锐角或直角相互层叠,在纱线交叉点用黏合剂或以热粘合法粘合而成的织物。

十、以纺织材料和橡胶线制成的弹性产品归入本类。

十一、本类所称"浸渍",包括"浸泡"。

十二、本类所称"聚酰胺",包括"芳族聚酰胺"。

十三、本类及本目录所称"弹性纱线",是指合成纤维纺织材料制成的长丝纱线(包括单丝),但变形纱线除外。这些纱线可拉伸至原长的三倍而不断裂,并可在拉伸至原长两倍后五分钟内回复到不超过原长度的一倍半。

十四、除条文另有规定的以外,各种服装即使成套包装供零售用,也应按各自税目分别归类。本注释所称"纺织服装",是指税目61.01至61.14及税目62.01至62.11所列的各种服装。

(Ⅴ)Chenille yarn, gimped yarn and loop wale—Yarn of heading 56.06.

4. (a)For the purposes of Chapters 50,51,52,54 and 55, the expression"put up for retail sale" in relation to yarn means, subject to the exceptionsin paragraph (B) below, yarn (single, multiple (folded) or cabled) put up:

(ⅰ)On cards, reels, tubes or similar supports, of a weight (including support) not exceeding:

ⅰ)85g in the case of silk, waste silk or man-made filaments; or

ⅱ)125g in other cases;

(ⅱ)In balls, hanks or skeins of a weight not exceeding:

ⅰ)85g in the case of man-made filament yarn of less than 3,000 decitex, silk or silk waste;

ⅱ)125g in the case of all other yarns of less than 2,000 decitex; or

ⅲ)500g in other cases;

(ⅲ)In hanks or skeins comprising several smaller hanks or skeins separated by dividing threads which render them independent one of the other, each of uniform weight not exceeding:

ⅰ)85g in the case of silk, waste silk or man-made filament yarn; or

ⅱ)125g in other cases.

(b)Exceptions:

(ⅰ)Single yarn of any textile material, except:

ⅰ)Single yarn of wool or fine animal hair, unbleached; and

ⅱ)Single yarn of wool or fine animal hair, bleached, dyed or printed, measuring more than 5,000 decitex;

(ⅱ)Multiple (folded) or cabled yarn, unbleached:

ⅰ)Of silk or waste silk, however put up;

ⅱ)Of other textile material except wool or fineanimal hair, in hanks or skeins;

(ⅲ)Multiple (folded) or cabled yarn of silk or waste silk, bleached, dyed or printed, measuring 133 decitex or less; and

(ⅳ)Single, multiple (folded) or cabled yarn of any textilematerial:

ⅰ)In cross-reeled hanks or skeins;

ⅱ)Put up on supports or in some other manner indicating its use in the textile industry (for example, on cops, twisting mill tubes, pirns, conical bobbins or spindles, or reeled in the form of cocoons for embroidery looms).

5. For the purposes of headings No. 52.04, 54.01 and 55.08the expression "sewing thread" means multiple (folded) or cabled yarn:

(a)Put up on supports (for example, reels, tubes) of aweight (including support) not exceeding 1,000g;

(b)Dressed for use as sewing thread;

(c)With a final "Z" twist.

6. For the purposes of this Section, the expression "high tenacity yarn" means yarn having a tenacity, expressed in cN/tex (centinewton per tex), greater than the following:

Single yarn of nylon or other polyamides, or of polyesters 60 cN/tex

Multiple (folded) or cabled yarn of nylon or other polyamides, or of polyesters 53 cN/tex

Single, multiple (folded) or cabled yarn of viscose rayon 27 cN/tex

7. For the purposes of this Section, the expression "made up" means:

(a)Cut otherwise than into squares or rectangles;

(b)Produced in the finished state, ready for use (or merely needing separation by cutting dividing threads) without sewing or other working (for example, certain dusters, towels, table cloths, scarf squares, blankets);

(c)Cut to size and with at least one heatsealed edge with a visibly tapered or compressed border and the other edges treated as described in any other subparagraph of this Note, but excluding fabrics the cut edges of which have been prevented from unravelling by hot cutting or by other simple means;

(d)Hemmed or with rolled edges, or with a knotted fringe atany of the edges, but excluding fabrics the cut edges of which have been prevented from unravelling by whipping or by other simple means;

(e)Cut to size and having undergone a process of drawnthread work;

(f)Assembled by sewing, gumming or otherwise (other than piece goods consisting of two or more lengths of identical material joined end toend and piece goods composed of two or more textiles assembled in layers, whether or not padded);

(g)Knitted or crocheted to shape, whether presented asseparate items or in the form of a number of items in the length.

8. For the purposes of Chapters 50 to 60:

(a)Chapters 50 to 55 and 60 and, except where the context otherwise requires, Chapters 56 to 59 do not apply to goods made up within the meaning of Note 7 above; and

(b)Chapters 50 to 55 and 60 do not apply to goods of Chapters 56 to 59.

9. The woven fabrics of Chapters 50 to 55 include fabrics consisting of layers of parallel textile yarns superimposed on each other at acute or right angles. These layers are bonded at the intersections of the yarns by an adhesive or by thermal bonding.

10. Elastic products consisting of textile materials combined with rubber threads are classified in this Section.

11. For the purposes of this Section, the expression "impregnated" includes "dipped".

12. For the purposes of this Section, the expression "polyamides" includes "aramides".

13. For the purposes of this section and where applicaple throughout the nomeclature the expression"elastomencyarn"means Filament yarn, including monofilament, of synthetic textile material, other than textured yarn, which does not break on being extended to three times its original length and which returns, after being extended to twice its original length, within a period of five minutes, to a length not greater than one and a half times its original length.

14. Unless the context otherwise requires, textile garments of different headings are to be classified in their own headings even if put up in sets for retail sale. For the purposes of this Note, the expression "textile garments" means garments of headings No. 61.01 to 61.14 and headings No. 62.01 to 62.11.

十五、除本类注释一另有规定的以外，装有用作附加功能的化学、机械或电子组件(无论是作为内置组件还是组合在纤维或织物内)的纺织品、服装和其他纺织物，如果其具有本类货品的基本特征，应归入本类相应税目中。

子目注释：

一、本类及本目录所用有关名词解释如下：

(一)未漂白纱线

1. 带有纤维自然色泽并且未经漂染(不论是否整体染色)或印色的纱线；

2. 从回收纤维制得，色泽未定的纱线(本色纱)。

这种纱线可用无色浆料或易褪色染料(可轻易地用肥皂洗去)处理，如果是化学纤维纱线，则整体用消光剂(例如二氧化钛)进行处理。

(二)漂白纱线

1. 经漂白加工、用漂白纤维制得或经染白(除条文另有规定的以外)(不论是否整体染色)及用白浆料处理的纱线；

2. 用未漂白纤维和漂白纤维混纺制得的纱线；

3. 用未漂白纱和漂白纱纺成多股纱线或缆线。

(三)着色(染色或印色)纱线

1. 染成彩色(不论是否整体染色，但白色或易褪色除外)或印色的纱线，以及用染色或印色纤维纺制的纱线；

2. 用各色染色纤维混合纺制或用未漂白或漂白纤维与着色纤维混合制得的纱线(夹色纱或混色纱)，以及用一种或几种颜色间隔印色而获得点纹印迹的纱线；

3. 用已经印色的纱条或粗纱纺制的纱线；

4. 用未漂白纱和漂白纱与着色纱纺成的多股纱线或缆线。

上述定义作相应调整后适用于第五十四章的单丝、扁条或类似产品。

(四)未漂白机织物

用未漂白纱线织成后未经漂白、染色或印花的机织物。这类织物可用无色浆料或易褪色染料处理。

(五)漂白机织物

1. 经漂白、染白或用白浆料处理(除条文另有规定的以外)的成匹机织物；

2. 用漂白纱线织成的机织物；

3. 用未漂白纱线和漂白纱线织成的机织物；

(六)染色机织物

1. 除条文另有规定的以外，染成白色以外的其他单一颜色或用白色以外的其他有色整理剂处理的成匹机织物；

2. 以单一颜色的着色纱线织成的机织物。

(七)色织机织物

除印花机织物以外的下列机织物：

1. 用各种不同颜色纱线或同一颜色不同深浅(纤维的自然色彩除外)纱线织成的机织物；

2. 用未漂白或漂白与着色纱线织成的机织物；

3. 用夹色纱线或混色纱线织成的机织物。

不论何种情况，布边或布头的纱线均可忽略不计。

(八)印花机织物

成匹印花的机织物，不论是否用各色纱线织成。

用刷子或喷枪，经转印纸转印、植绒或蜡防印花等方法印成花纹图案的机织物亦可视为印花机织物。

上述各类纱线或织物如经丝光工艺处理并不影响其归类。

上述(四)至(八)的定义在作必要修改后适用于针织或钩编织物。

(九)平纹织物

每根纬纱在并排的经纱间上下交错而过，而每根经纱也在并排的纬纱间上下交错而过的织物组织。

二、(一)含有两种或两种以上纺织材料的第五十六章至第六十三章的产品，应根据本类注释二对第五十章至第五十五章或税目58.09的此类纺织材料产品归类的规定来确定归类。

(二)运用本条规定时：

1. 应酌情考虑按归类总规则第三条来确定归类；

2. 对由底布和绒面或毛圈面构成的纺织品，在归类时可不考虑底布的属性；

3. 对税目58.10的刺绣品及其制品，归类时应只考虑底布的属性，但不见底布的刺绣品及其制品应根据绣线的属性确定归类。

15. Subject to Note 1 to Section XI, textiles, garments and other textile articles, incorporating chemical, mechanical or electronic components for additional functionality, whether incorporated as built—in components or within the fibre or fabric, are classified in their respective headings in Section XI provided that they retain the essential character of the goods of this Section.

Subheading Notes:

1. In the Section and, where applicable, throughout the Nomenclature, the following expressions have the meanings hereby assigned to them:

(a) Unbleached yarnYarn which:

(ⅰ) has the natural colour of its constituent fibres and hasnot been bleached, dyed (whether or not in the mass) or printed;

(ⅱ) is of indeterminate colour ("grey yarn"), manufactured from garnetted stock.

Such yarn may have been treated with a colourless dressing or fugitive dye(which disappears after simple washing with soap) and, in the case of man-made fibres, treated in the mass with delustring agent (for example, titanium dioxide).

(b) Bleached yarn Yarn which:

(ⅰ) has undergone a bleaching process, is made of bleached fibres or, unless the context otherwise requires, has been dyed white (whether or not in the mass) or treated with a white dressing;

(ⅱ) consists of a mixture of unbleached and bleachedfibres;

(ⅲ) is multiple (folded) or cabled and consists ofunbleached and bleached yarns.

(c) Coloured (dyed or printed) yarn Yarn which:

(ⅰ) is dyed (whether or not in the mass) other thanwhite or in a fugitive colour, or printed, or made from dyed or printed fibres;

(ⅱ) consists of a mixture of dyed fibres of different colours or of a mixture of unbleached or bleached fibres with coloured fibres (marl or mixture yarns), or is printed in one or more colours at intervals to givethe impression of dots;

(ⅲ) is obtained from slivers or rovings which havebeenprinted; or

(ⅳ) is multiple (folded) or cabled and consists ofunbleached or bleached yarn and coloured yarn.

The above definitions also apply, *mutatis mutandis*, to monofilament and to strip or the like of Chapter 54.

(d) Unbleached woven fabric

Woven fabric made from unbleached yarn and which has not been bleached, dyed or printed. Such fabric may have treated with a colourless dressing or a fugitive dye.

(e) Bleached woven fabricwoven fabric which:

(ⅰ) has been bleached or, unless the context otherwise requires, dyed white or treated with a white dressing, in the piece;

(ⅱ) consists of bleached yarn; or

(ⅲ) consists of unbleached and bleached yarn.

(f) Dyed woven fabricwoven fabric which:

(ⅰ) is dyed a single uniform colour other than white (unless the context otherwise requires) or has been treated with a coloured finishother than white (unless the context otherwise requires), in the piece; or

(ⅱ) consists of coloured yarn of a single uniform colour.

(g) Woven fabric of yarns of different colours

Woven fabric (other than printed woven fabric) which:

(ⅰ) consists of yarns of different colours or yarnsofdifferent shades of the same colour (other than the natural colour of the constituent fibres);

(ⅱ) consists of unbleached or bleached yarn and coloured yarn; or

(ⅲ) consists of marl or mixture yarns.

(In all cases, the yarn used in selvedges and pieceends is not taken into consideration.)

(h) Printed woven fabric

Woven fabric which has been printed in the piece, whether or not made from yarnsof differenent colours. (The following are also regarded as printed woven fabrics: woven fabrics bearing designs made, for example, with a brush or spray gun, by means of transfer paper, by flocking or by the batik process.)

The process of mercerization does not affect the classification of yarns or fabrics within the above categories.

The definitions at(d) to (h) above apply, *mutatis mutandis*, to knitted or crocheted fabrics.

(ij) Plain weave

A fabric construction in which each yarn of the weft passes alternately over andunder successive yarns of the warp and each yarn of the warp passes alternatelyover and under successive yarns of the weft.

2. (a) Products of Chapters 56 to 63 containing two or more textilematerials are to be regarded as consisting wholly of that textile material whichwould be selected under Note 2 to this Section for the classification of the product of Chapters 50 to 55 or of heading No. 58. 09 consisting of the same textile materials.

(b) For the application of this rule:

(ⅰ) where appropriate, only the part which determines the classification under interpretative Rule 3 shall be taken into account;

(ⅱ) in the case of textile products consisting of a ground fabric and a pile or looped surface, no account shall be taken of the ground fabric;

(ⅲ) in the case of embroidery of heading No. 58. 10 and goods thereof, only the ground fabric shall be taken into account. However, embroidery without visible ground, and goods thereof, shall be classified with reference to the embroidering threads alone.

第五十章
蚕　丝

税则号列	货品名称〔CIQ 扩展编码及品名—T2 表示见附表 2〕	最惠(%)	暂定税率	普通	增值/消费	出口退税	计量单位	监管条件/特殊证件	检验检疫	对美关税	亚太上/下
50.01	**适于缫丝的蚕茧:**										
5001.0010	---适于缫丝的桑蚕茧〔101 未经加工的蚕茧,999 未经加工的蚕茧除外〕	6		70	13/	9	千克	AB/	PQ	11	
5001.0090	---其他〔101:未经加工的蚕茧;999:未经加工的蚕茧除外〕	6		70	13/	9	千克	AB/	PQ	11	
50.02	**生丝(未加捻):**										
	---桑蚕丝:										
5002.0011	----厂丝〔101 生丝,102 粗丝,103 初级加工丝〕	9		80	13/	13	千克	AB/	PQ		
5002.0012	----土丝〔999〕	9		80	13/	13	千克	AB/	PQ		
5002.0013	----双宫丝〔999〕	9		80	13/	13	千克	AB/	PQ		
5002.0019	----其他〔999〕	9		80	13/	13	千克	AB/	PQ		
5002.0020	---柞蚕丝〔999〕	9		80	13/	13	千克	AB/	PQ		
5002.0090	---其他〔999〕	9		80	13/	13	千克	AB/	PQ		
50.03	**废丝(包括不适于缫丝的蚕茧、废纱及回收纤维):**										
	---未梳:										
5003.0011	----下茧、茧衣、长吐、滞头〔101 未经加工的蚕茧、削口茧,102 未经加工的长吐,滞头,999 未经加工的蚕茧、削口茧、长吐,滞头除外〕	9		70	13/	13	千克	AB/	PQ		
5003.0012	----回收纤维〔999〕	9		70	13/	13	千克	AB/	PQ		
5003.0019	----其他〔999〕	9		70	13/	13	千克	AB/	PQ		
	---其他:										
5003.0091	----绵球〔999〕	9		70	13/	13	千克	AB/	PQ		
5003.0099	----其他〔999〕	9		70	13/	13	千克	AB/	PQ		
50.04	**丝纱线(绢纺纱线除外),非供零售用:**										
5004.0000	丝纱线(绢纺纱线除外),非供零售用〔101 桑蚕捻线丝,102 双宫捻线丝,103 土丝捻线丝,104 特种加工丝〕	6		90	13/	13	千克	/			
50.05	**绢纺纱线,非供零售用:**										
5005.0010	---䌷丝纱线〔999〕	6		90	13/	13	千克	/			
5005.0090	---其他〔101 桑蚕绢丝,102 柞蚕绢丝,103 木薯绢丝〕	6		90	13/	13	千克	/			
50.06	**丝纱线及绢纺纱线,供零售用;蚕胶丝:**										
5006.0000	零售用丝纱线,绢纺纱线;蚕胶丝(含丝及绢丝)〔999〕	6		100	13/	13	千克	/			
50.07	**丝或绢丝机织物:**										
	-䌷丝机织物:										
5007.1010	---未漂白(包括未练白或练白)或漂白〔999〕	8		130	13/	13	米/千克	/			
5007.1090	---其他〔999〕	8		130	13/	13	米/千克	/			
	-其他机织物,按重量计丝或绢丝(䌷丝除外)含量在 85%及以上:										
	---桑蚕丝机织物:										
5007.2011	----未漂白(包括未练白或练白)或漂白〔999〕	8		130	13/	13	米/千克	/		28	5.2/5.2
5007.2019	----其他〔999〕	8		130	13/	13	米/千克	/		33	5.2/5.2
	---柞蚕丝机织物:										
5007.2021	----未漂白(包括未练白或练白)或漂白〔999〕	8		130	13/	13	米/千克	/			5.2/5.2
5007.2029	----其他〔999〕	8		130	13/	13	米/千克	/			5.2/5.2
	---绢丝机织物:										
5007.2031	----未漂白(包括未练白或练白)或漂白〔999〕	8		130	13/	13	米/千克	/			5.2/5.2
5007.2039	----其他〔999〕	8		130	13/	13	米/千克	/		33	5.2/5.2
5007.2090	---其他〔999〕	8		130	13/	13	米/千克	/		33	5.2/5.2
	-其他机织物:										
5007.9010	---未漂白(包括未练白或练白)或漂白〔999〕	8		130	13/	13	米/千克	/		33	5.2/5.2
5007.9090	---其他〔999〕	8		130	13/	13	米/千克	/		33	5.2/5.2

Chapter 50
Silk

协定税率 %								RCEP		特惠税率 %			Article Description
东/冰/格	巴基斯坦	韩国	瑞士上/下	哥/秘/柬	澳/毛	新西/坡/智	中国港/澳/台	东盟及马来/澳/韩	日/新	亚太2国	老/柬/缅	98/97/95	
													Silk-worm cocoons suitable for reeling:
0/0/0	3.5	0	0/0	0/0/0	0/0	0//0	0/0/	0/0/0	0/0			0/0/0	---Bombyx mori cocoons (Mulberry feeding silk-worm cocoons)
0/0/0	4	0	0/0	0/0/0	0/0	0//0	0/0/	0/0/0	0/0			0/0/0	---Other
													Raw silk (not thrown):
													---Steam filature silk:
0/0/0	2	0	0/0	0/0/0	0/0	0//0	0/0/	0/0/0	8.2/0			0/0/0	----Plant reeled (filature silk)
0/0/0	2	0	0/0	0/0/0	0/0	0//0	0/0/	0/0/0	8.2/0			0/0/0	----Home reeled
0/0/0	2	0	0/0	0/0/0	0/0	0//0	0/0/	0/0/0	8.2/0			0/0/0	----Doupion
0/0/0	2	0	0/0	0/0/0	0/0	0//0	0/0/	0/0/0	8.2/0			0/0/0	----Other
0/0/0	2	0	0/0	0/0/0	0/0	0//0	0/0/	0/0/0	8.2/0			0/0/0	---Tussah silk
0/0/0	2	0	0/0	0/0/0	0/0	0//0	0/0/	0/0/0	8.2/0			0/0/0	---Other
													Silk waste (including cocoons unsuitable for reeling, yarn waste and garnetted stock):
													---Not carded or combed:
0/0/0	2	0	0/0	0/0/0	0/0	0//0	0/0/	0/0/0	8.2/0			0/0/0	----Spoiled cocoon, cocoon outer floss, frison, frigon
0/0/0	2	0	0/0	0/0/0	0/0	0//0	0/0/	0/0/0	8.2/0			0/0/0	----Garnetted stock
0/0/0	2	0	0/0	0/0/0	0/0	0//0	0/0/	0/0/0	8.2/0			0/0/0	----Other
													---Other:
0/0/0	2	0	0/0	0/0/0	0/0	0//0	0/0/	0/0/0	8.2/0			0/0/0	----Silk top
0/0/0	2	0	0/0	0/0/0	0/0	0//0	0/0/	0/0/0	8.2/0			0/0/0	----Other
													Silk yarn (other than yarn spun from spun silk waste) not put up for retail sale:
0/0/0	0	0	0/0	0/0/0	0/0	0//0	0/0/	0/0/0	0/0			0/0/0	Silk yarn (other than yarn spun from spun silk waste) not put up for retail sale
													Yarn spun from silk spum waste, not put up for retail sale:
0/0/0	0	0	0/0	0/0/0	0/0	0//0	0/0/	0/0/0	0/0			0/0/0	---Spun from noil
0/0/0	0	0	0/0	0/0/0	0/0	0//0	0/0/	0/0/0	0/0			0/0/0	---Other
													Silk yarn and yarn spun from silk waste, put up for retail sale; silk-worm gut:
0/0/0	0	0	0/0	0/0/0	0/0	0//0	0/0/	0/0/0	0/0			0/0/0	Silk yarn and yarn spun from silk waste, put up for retail sale; silk-worm gut
													Woven fabrics of silk or of spun silk:
													-Fabrics of noil silk:
0/0/0	3.5	0	0/0	0/0/0	0/0	0//0	0/0/	0/0/0	9.1/0		0//	0/0/0	---Unbleaded (unscoured or scoured) or bleached
0/0/0	3.5	0	0/0	0/0/0	0/0	0//0	0/0/	0/0/0	9.1/0		0//	0/0/0	---Other
													-Other fabrics, containing 85% or more by weight of silk or of spun silk other than noil silk:
													---Of Bombyx mori silk:
0/0/0	3.5	0	0/0	0/0/0	0/0	0//0	0/0/	0/0/0	9.1/0		0//	0/0/0	----Unbleached (unscoured or scoured) or bleached
0/0/0	3.5	4.6	0/0	0/0/0	0/0	0//0	0/0/	9.3/9.5/9.3	9.4/9.5		0//	0/0/0	----Other
													---Of tussah silk:
0/0/0	3.5	0	0/0	0/0/0	0/0	0//0	0/0/	0/0/0	9.1/0		0//	0/0/0	---Unblead (unscoured or scoured) or bleached
0/0/0	3.5	0	0/0	0/0/0	0/0	0//0	0/0/	0/0/0	9.1/0		0//	0/0/0	----Other
													---Of silk waste other than noil silk:
0/0/0	3.5	0	0/0	0/0/0	0/0	0//0	0/0/	0/0/0	9.1/0		0//	0/0/0	----Unbleached (unscoured or scoured) or bleached
0/0/0	3.5	0	0/0	0/0/0	0/0	0//0	0/0/	0/0/0	9.1/0		0//	0/0/0	----Other
0/0/0	3.5	0	0/0	0/0/0	0/0	0//0	0/0/	0/0/0	9.1/0		0//	0/0/0	---Other
													-Other fabrics:
0/0/0	3.5	0	0/0	0/0/0	0/0	0//0	0/0/	0/0/0	9.1/0		0//	0/0/0	---Unbleached (unscoured or scoured) or bleached
0/0/0	3.5	0	0/0	0/0/0	0/0	0//0	0/0/	0/0/0	9.1/0		0//	0/0/0	---Other

第五十一章
羊毛、动物细毛或粗毛;马毛纱线及其机织物

注释:

本协调制度所称:

一、"羊毛",是指绵羊或羔羊身上长的天然纤维;

二、"动物细毛",是指下列动物的毛:羊驼、美洲驼、驼马、骆驼(包括单峰骆驼)、牦牛、安哥拉山羊、西藏山羊、克什米尔山羊及类似山羊(普通山羊除外)、家兔(包括安哥拉兔)、野兔、海狸、河狸鼠或麝鼠;

三、"动物粗毛",是指以上未提及的其他动物的毛,但不包括制刷用鬃、毛(税目 05.02)以及马毛(税目 05.11)。

税则号列	货品名称〔CIQ 扩展编码及品名-T2 表示见附表 2〕	最惠(%)	暂定税率	普通	增值/消费	出口退税	计量单位	监管条件/特殊证件	检验检疫	对美关税	亚太 上/下
51.01	**未梳的羊毛:**										
	-含脂羊毛,包括剪前水洗毛:										
5101.1100	--剪羊毛										
5101.1100 01	未梳的含脂剪羊毛(配额内)〔101 绵羊毛,102 山羊毛〕	1		50	9/	9	千克	tAB/	PQ	26	
5101.1100 90	未梳的含脂剪羊毛(配额外)〔101 绵羊毛,102 山羊毛〕	38		50	9/	9	千克	AB/	PQ	63	
5101.1900	--其他										
5101.1900 01	未梳的其他含脂羊毛(配额内)〔101 绵羊毛,102 山羊毛〕	1		50	9/	9	千克	tAB/	PQ	6	
5101.1900 90	未梳的其他含脂羊毛(配额外)〔101 绵羊毛,102 山羊毛〕	38		50	9/	9	千克	AB/	PQ	43	
	-脱脂羊毛,未碳化:										
5101.2100	--剪羊毛										
5101.2100 01	未梳的脱脂剪羊毛(未碳化)(配额内)〔101 洗净绵羊毛,102 洗净山羊毛〕	1		50	13/	13	千克	tAB/	PQ	6	
5101.2100 90	未梳的脱脂剪羊毛(未碳化)(配额外)〔101 洗净绵羊毛,102 洗净山羊毛〕	38		50	13/	13	千克	AB/	PQ	43	
5101.2900	--其他										
5101.2900 01	未梳的其他脱脂羊毛(未碳化)(配额内)〔101 洗净绵羊毛,102 洗净山羊毛〕	1		50	13/	13	千克	tAB/	PQ	6	
5101.2900 90	未梳的其他脱脂羊毛(未碳化)(配额外)〔101 洗净绵羊毛,102 洗净山羊毛〕	38		50	13/	13	千克	AB/	PQ	43	
5101.3000	-碳化羊毛										
5101.3000 01	未梳碳化羊毛(配额内)〔999〕	1		50	13/	13	千克	tAB/	PQ	6	
5101.3000 90	未梳碳化羊毛(配额外)〔999〕	38		50	13/	13	千克	AB/	PQ	43	
51.02	**未梳的动物细毛或粗毛:**										
	-细毛:										
5102.1100	--喀什米尔山羊的〔101 未洗净山羊毛,102 洗净山羊毛,103 山羊绒〕	9		45	13/	0	千克	AB/	PQ	14	
	--其他:										
5102.1910	---兔毛										
5102.1910 10	未梳濒危兔毛〔101 未洗净兔毛,102 洗净兔毛〕	9		50	13/	0	千克	ABFE/	PQ	14	
5102.1910 90	其他未梳兔毛〔101 未洗净兔毛,102 洗净兔毛〕	9		50	13/	9	千克	AB/	PQ	14	
5102.1920	---其他山羊绒〔101 未洗净山羊绒,102 未洗净野羊毛(绒),103 洗净山羊绒,104 洗净野山羊绒〕	9		45	13/	0	千克	AB/	PQ	14	
5102.1930	---骆驼毛、骆驼绒										
5102.1930 10	未梳濒危野生骆驼科动物毛、绒〔101 未洗净驼毛,102 未洗净驼绒,103 未洗净其他野生偶蹄动物鬃毛,104 洗净驼毛(绒),105 洗净其他野生偶蹄动物鬃毛〕	9		45	13/	0	千克	FEAB/	PQ	14	
5102.1930 90	其他未梳骆驼毛、绒〔101 未洗净驼毛,102 未洗净驼绒,103 洗净驼毛,104 洗净驼绒〕	9		45	13/	9	千克	AB/	PQ	14	
5102.1990	---其他										
5102.1990 10	未梳的其他濒危野生动物细毛[T2]	9		45	13/	0	千克	FEAB/	PQ	14	
5102.1990 90	未梳的其他动物细毛[T2]	9		45	13/	9	千克	AB/	PQ	14	
5102.2000	-粗毛										
5102.2000 10	未梳的濒危野生动物粗毛[T2]	9		50	13/	0	千克	FEAB/	PQ	14	
5102.2000 90	未梳的其他动物粗毛[T2]	9		50	13/	9	千克	AB/	PQ	14	
51.03	**羊毛或动物细毛或粗毛的废料,包括废纱线,但不包括回收纤维:**										
	-羊毛及动物细毛的落毛:										
5103.1010	---羊毛落毛										
5103.1010 01	羊毛落毛(配额内)〔101 未洗净绵羊毛,102 未洗净山羊毛,103 未洗净山羊绒,104 未洗净野羊毛(绒),105 洗净羊毛〕	1		50	13/	9	千克	tAB/	PQ	26	
5103.1010 90	羊毛落毛(配额外)〔101 未洗净绵羊毛,102 未洗净山羊毛,103 未洗净山羊绒,104 未洗净野羊毛(绒),105 洗净羊毛〕	38		50	13/	9	千克	AB/	PQ	63	
5103.1090	---其他										
5103.1090 10	其他濒危野生动物细毛的落毛[T2]	9		50	13/	0	千克	FEAB/	PQ	34	
5103.1090 90	其他动物细毛的落毛〔110〕	9		50	13/	9	千克	9B/	PQ	34	
	-羊毛或动物细毛的其他废料:										
5103.2010	---羊毛废料〔999〕	13.5		20	13/	9	千克	AB/	PQ	18.5	
5103.2090	---其他										

① 国别关税配额税率:0

Chapter 51

Wool, fine or coarse animal hair; horsehair yarn and woven fabric

Notes:

Throughout the Nomenclature:

1. "Wool" means the natural fibre grown by sheep or lambs;
2. "Fine animal hair" means the hair of alpaca, llama, vicuna, camel, (including dromedary) yak, Angora, Tibetan, Kashmir or similar goats (but not common goats), rabbit (including Angora rabbit), hare, beaver, nutria or muskrat;
3. "Coarse animal hair" means the hair of animals not mentioned above, excluding brush-making hair and bristles (heading No. 05.02) and horsehair (heading No. 05.11).

协定税率 %								RCEP		特惠税率 %			Article Description
东/冰/格	巴基斯坦	韩国	瑞士 上/下	哥/秘/柬	澳/毛	新西/坡/智	中国港/澳/台	东盟及马来/澳/韩	日/新	亚太2国	老/柬/缅	98/97/95	
													Wool, not carded or combed:
													-Greasy, including fleece-washed wool:
													--Shorn wool
5//					①/	①//	0/0/						Greasy shorn wool, not carded or combeb, in-quota
5//					①/	①//	0/0/						Greasy shorn wool, not carded or combeb, out-quota
													--Other
5//					①/	①//	0/0/						Other greasy wool, not carded or combed, in-quota
5//					①/	①//	0/0/						Other greasy wool, not carded or combed, out-quota
													-Degreased, not carbonized:
													--Shorn wool
5//					①/	①//	0/0/						Degreased shorn wool, not carded or combed, not carbonized, in-quota
5//					①/	①//	0/0/						Degreased shorn wool, not carded or combed, not carbonized, out-quota
													--Other
5//					①/	①//	0/0/						Other degreased wool, not carded or combeb, not carbonized, in-quota
5//					①/	①//	0/0/						Other degreased wool, not carded or combeb, not carbonized, out-quota
													-Carbonized
5//					①/	①//	0/0/						Carbonized wool, not carded or combed, in-quota
5//					①/	①//	0/0/						Carbonized wool, not carded or combed, out-quota
													Fine or coarse animal hair, not carded or combed:
													-Fine animal hair:
0/0/0	2	0	0/0	0/0/0	0/0	0//0	0/0/	0/0/0	8.2/0			0/0/0	--Of Kashmir(cashmere) goats
													--Other:
													---Of rabbit and hare
0/0/0	2	0	0/0	0/0/0	0/0	0//0	0/0/	0/0/0	8.2/0			0/0/0	Hair of endangered rabbit and hare, not carded or combed
0/0/0	2	0	0/0	0/0/0	0/0	0//0	0/0/	0/0/0	8.2/0			0/0/0	Other hair of rabbit and hare, not carded or combed
0/0/0	4	0	0/0	0/0/0	0/0	0//0	0/0/	0/0/0	8.2/0			0/0/0	---Of other goats
													---Of camel
0/0/0	2	0	0/0	0/0/0	0/0	0//0	0/0/	0/0/0	8.2/0			0/0/0	Hair and down of endangered wild camel, not carded or combed
0/0/0	2	0	0/0	0/0/0	0/0	0//0	0/0/	0/0/0	8.2/0			0/0/0	Other hair and down of camel, not carded or combed
													---Other
0/0/0	2	0	0/0	0/0/0	0/0	0//0	0/0/	0/0/0	8.2/0			0/0/0	Fine hair of other endangered wild animals dangers, not carded or combed
0/0/0	2	0	0/0	0/0/0	0/0	0//0	0/0/	0/0/0	8.2/0			0/0/0	Fine hair of other animals, not carded or combed
													-Coarse animal hair
0/0/0	4	0	0/0	0/0/0	0/0	0//0	0/0/	0/0/0	8.2/0			0/0/0	Coarse hair of endangered wild animals not carded or combed
0/0/0	4	0	0/0	0/0/0	0/0	0//0	0/0/	0/0/0	8.2/0			0/0/0	Coarse hair of other animals, not carded or combed
													Waste of wool or of fine or coarse animal hair, including yarn waste but excluding garnetted stock:
													-Noils of wool or of fine animal hair:
													---Of wool
5//					①/	①//	0/0/						Noils of wool(in-quota)
5//					①/	①//	0/0/						Noils of wool(out-quota)
													---Other
0/0/0	2	0	0/0	0/0/0	0/0	0//0	0/0/	0/0/0	8.2/0			0/0/0	Other noils of fine hair of endangered wild animal
0/0/0	2	0	0/0	0/0/0	0/0	0//0	0/0/	0/0/0	8.2/0			0/0/0	Other noils of fine hair of animal
													-Other waste of wool or of fine animal hair:
0/0/0	6.8	2.7	1.4/1.4	0/0/0	0/0	0/0/0	0/0/	0/0/12.2	12.3/0			0/0/0	Of wool
													---Other

税则号列	货品名称〔CIQ扩展编码及品名—T2表示见附表2〕	最惠(%)	暂定税率	普通	增值/消费	出口退税	计量单位	监管条件/特殊证件	检验检疫	对美关税	亚太上/下
5103.2090 10	其他濒危野生动物细毛废料(包括废纱线,不包括回收纤维)〔999〕	9		50	13/	0	千克	FEAB/	PQ	34	
5103.2090 90	其他动物细毛废料(包括废纱线,不包括回收纤维)〔102〕	9		50	13/	9	千克	9B/	PQ	34	
5103.3000	-动物粗毛废料										
5103.3000 10	濒危野生动物粗毛废料(包括废纱线,不包括回收纤维)〔999〕	9		50	13/	0	千克	FEAB/	PQ	34	
5103.3000 90	其他动物粗毛废料(包括废纱线,不包括回收纤维)〔102〕	9		50	13/	9	千克	9B/	PQ	34	
51.04	**羊毛或动物细毛或粗毛的回收纤维:**										
5104.0010	---羊毛的回收纤维〔999〕	15		20	13/	9	千克	AB/	PQ		
5104.0090	---其他										
5104.0090 10	其他濒危野生动物细毛(包括粗毛回收纤维)〔101 毛回收纤维,102 用于纺织原料的其它动物纤维〕	5		50	13/	0	千克	FEAB/	PQ	30	
5104.0090 90	其他动物细毛或粗毛的回收纤维〔103〕	5		50	13/	13	千克	9B/	PQ	30	
51.05	**已梳的羊毛及动物细毛或粗毛(包括精梳片毛):**										
5105.1000	-粗梳羊毛										
5105.1000 01	粗梳羊毛(配额内)〔999〕	3		50	13/	13	千克	tAB/	PQ		
5105.1000 90	粗梳羊毛(配额外)〔999〕	38		50	13/	13	千克	AB/	PQ		
	-羊毛条及其他精梳羊毛:										
5105.2100	--精梳片毛										
5105.2100 01	精梳羊毛片毛(配额内)〔999〕	3		50	13/	13	千克	tAB/	PQ		
5105.2100 90	精梳羊毛片毛(配额外)〔999〕	38		50	13/	13	千克	AB/	PQ		
5105.2900	--其他										
5105.2900 01	羊毛条及其他精梳羊毛(配额内)〔999〕	3		50	13/	13	千克	tAB/	PQ		
5105.2900 90	羊毛条及其他精梳羊毛(配额外)〔999〕	38		50	13/	13	千克	AB/	PQ		
	-已梳动物细毛:										
5105.3100	--喀什米尔山羊的〔999〕	5		50	13/	0	千克	AB/	PQ		
	--其他:										
5105.3910	---兔毛										
5105.3910 10	已梳濒危兔毛〔999〕	5		70	13/	0	千克	ABFE/	PQ		3.5/3.5
5105.3910 90	其他已梳兔毛〔999〕	5		70	13/	13	千克	AB/	PQ		3.5/3.5
	---其他山羊绒:										
5105.3921	----无毛山羊绒〔999〕	5		50	13/	0	千克	AB/	PQ		3.5/3.5
5105.3929	----其他〔999〕	5		50	13/	0	千克	AB/	PQ		3.5/3.5
5105.3990	---其他										
5105.3990 10	其他已梳濒危野生动物细毛〔999〕	5		50	13/	0	千克	ABEF/	PQ		3.5/3.5
5105.3990 90	其他已梳动物细毛〔999〕	5		50	13/	13	千克	AB/	PQ		3.5/3.5
5105.4000	-已梳动物粗毛										
5105.4000 10	其他已梳濒危野生动物粗毛〔999〕	5		50	13/	0	千克	FEAB/	PQ		
5105.4000 90	其他已梳动物粗毛〔999〕	5		50	13/	13	千克	AB/	PQ		
51.06	**粗梳羊毛纱线,非供零售用:**										
5106.1000	-按重量计羊毛含量在85%及以上〔999〕	5		70	13/	13	千克	/			
5106.2000	-按重量计羊毛含量在85%以下〔999〕	5		70	13/	13	千克	/		30	
51.07	**精梳羊毛纱线,非供零售用:**										
5107.1000	-按重量计羊毛含量在85%及以上〔999〕	5		70	13/	13	千克	/		30	2.5/2.5
5107.2000	-按重量计羊毛含量在85%以下〔999〕	5		70	13/	13	千克	/		30	
51.08	**动物细毛(粗梳或精梳)纱线,非供零售用:**										
	-粗梳:										
	---按重量计动物细毛含量在85%及以上的:										
5108.1011	----山羊绒的〔999〕	5		70	13/	13	千克	/		30	3.3/3.3
5108.1019	----其他										
5108.1019 10	非供零售用粗梳其他濒危动物细毛纱线(按重量计其他动物细毛含量≥85%)〔999〕	5		70	13/	0	千克	FE/			3.3/3.3
5108.1019 90	非供零售用粗梳其他动物细毛纱线(按重量计其他动物细毛含量≥85%)〔999〕	5		70	13/	13	千克	/			3.3/3.3
5108.1090	---其他										
5108.1090 10	非供零售用粗梳其他濒危动物细毛纱线(按重量计其他粗梳动物细毛含量<85%)〔999〕	5		70	13/	0	千克	FE/		30	3.3/3.3
5108.1090 90	非供零售用粗梳其他动物细毛纱线(按重量计其他粗梳动物细毛含量<85%)〔999〕	5		70	13/	13	千克	/		30	3.3/3.3
	-精梳:										

① 国别关税配额税率:0

协定税率 %								RCEP		特惠税率 %			Article Description
东/冰/格	巴基斯坦	韩国	瑞士上/下	哥/秘/柬	澳/毛	新西/坡/智	中国港/澳/台	东盟及马来/澳/韩	日/新	亚太2国	老/柬/缅	98/97/95	
0/0/0	2	0	0/0	0/0/0	0/0	0//0	0/0/	0/0/0	8.2/0			0/0/0	Other waste of fine hair of endangered wild animal (including yarn waste, but excluding garnetted stock)
0/0/0	2	0	0/0	0/0/0	0/0	0//0	0/0/	0/0/0	8.2/0			0/0/0	Other waste of fine hair of other animals (including yarn waste, but excluding garnetted stock)
													-Waste of coarse animal hair
0/0/0	2	0	0/0	0/0/0	0/0	0//0	0/0/	0/0/0	8.2/0			0/0/0	Waste of coarse hair of endangered wild animal (including yarn waste but excluding garnetted stock)
0/0/0	2	0	0/0	0/0/0	0/0	0//0	0/0/	0/0/0	8.2/0			0/0/0	Other waste of coarse hair of animals (including yarn waste but excluding garnetted stock)
													Garnetted stock of wool or of fine or coarse animal hair:
0/0/0	12	3	1.5/1.5	0/0/0	0/0	0/0/0	0/0/	0/0/13.5	13.6/0			0/0/0	---Of wool
													---Other
0/0/0	0	0	0/0	0/0/0	0/0	0//0	0/0/	0/0/0	0/0			0/0/0	Garnetted stock of other fine or coarse hair of endangered wild animal
0/0/0	0	0	0/0	0/0/0	0/0	0//0	0/0/	0/0/0	0/0			0/0/0	Garnetted stock of other of fine or coarse animal hair
													Wool and fine or coarse animal hair, carded or combed (including combed wool in fragments):
													-Carded wool
						①//	0/0/						Carded wool(in-quota)
						①//	0/0/						Carded wool(out-quota)
													-Wool tops and other combed wool:
													--Combed wool in fragments
						①//	0/0/						Combed wool in fragments(in-quota)
						①//	0/0/						Combed wool in fragments(out-quota)
													--Other
						①//	0/0/						Wool tops and other combed wool(in-quota)
						①//	0/0/						Wool tops and other combed wool(out-quota)
													-Fine animal hair, Carded or combed:
0/0/0	0	0	0/0	0/0/0	0/0	0//0	0/0/	0/0/0	0/0			0/0/0	--Of Kashmir(cashmere) goats
													--Other:
													---Of rabbit or hare
0/0/0	0	0	0/0	0//0	0/0	0//0	0/0/	0/0/0	4.5/0			0/0/0	Fine hair of endangered rabbit and hare, carded or combed
0/0/0	0	0	0/0	0//0	0/0	0//0	0/0/	0/0/0	4.5/0			0/0/0	Other fine hair of rabbit and hare, carded or combed
													---Of other goats:
0/0/0	0	0	0/0	0//0	0/0	0//0	0/0/	0/0/0	4.5/0			0/0/0	----Dehaired goats wool
0/0/0	0	0	0/0	0//0	0/0	0//0	0/0/	0/0/0	4.5/0			0/0/0	----Other
													---Other
0/0/0	0	0	0/0	0//0	0/0	0//0	0/0/	0/0/0	4.5/0			0/0/0	Other fine hair of wild animals, carded or combed
0/0/0	0	0	0/0	0//0	0/0	0//0	0/0/	0/0/0	4.5/0			0/0/0	Other fine hair of animals, carded or combed
													-Coarse animal hair, carded or combed
0/0/0	0	0	0/0	0//0	0/0	0//0	0/0/	0/0/0	4.5/0			0/0/0	Other coarse hair of endangered wild animals, carded or combed
0/0/0	0	0	0/0	0//0	0/0	0//0	0/0/	0/0/0	4.5/0			0/0/0	Other coarse hair of animals, carded or combed
													Yarn of carded wool, not put up for retailsale:
0/0/0	0	0	0/0	0/0/0	0/0	0//0	0/0/	0/0/0	0/0			0/0/0	-Containing 85% or more by weight of wool
0/0/0	0	0	0/0	0/0/0	0/0	0//0	0/0/	0/0/0	0/0			0/0/0	-Containing less than 85% by weight of wool
													Yarn of combed wool, not put up for retail sale:
0//0	0	0	0/0	0/0/0	0/0	0//0	0/0/	0/0/0	4.5/0			0/0/0	-Containing 85% or more by weight of wool
0/0/0	0	0	0/0	0/0/0	0/0	0//0	0/0/	0/0/0	0/0			0/0/0	-Containing less than 85% by weight of wool
													Yarn of fine animal hair (carded or combed), not put up for retailsale:
													-Carded:
													---Containing 85% or more by weight of fine animal hair
0/0/0	0	0	0/0	0/0/0	0/0	0//0	0/0/	0/0/0	0/0			0/0/0	----Of goats
													----Other
0/0/0	0	0	0/0	0/0/0	0/0	0//0	0/0/	0/0/0	0/0			0/0/0	Yarn of fine hair of endangered animals, carded, not in forms or packing for retail sale(containing≥85% by weight of other animals hair)
0/0/0	0	0	0/0	0/0/0	0/0	0//0	0/0/	0/0/0	0/0			0/0/0	Yarn of fine hair of animals, carded, not in forms or packing for retailsale(containing≥85% by weight of other fine animals hair)
													---Other
0/0/0	0	0	0/0	0/0/0	0/0	0//0	0/0/	0/0/0	0/0			0/0/0	Yarn of fine hair of endangered animals, carded, not in forms or packingfor retail sale(containing<85% by weight of other fine animals hair)
0/0/0	0	0	0/0	0/0/0	0/0	0//0	0/0/	0/0/0	0/0			0/0/0	Yarn of fine hair of animals, carded, not in forms or packing for retail sale(containing<85% by weight of other fine animals hair)
													-Combed:

税则号列	货品名称〔CIQ 扩展编码及品名－T2 表示见附表 2〕	最惠(%)	暂定税率	普通	增值/消费	出口退税	计量单位	监管条件/特殊证件	检验检疫	对美关税	亚太上/下
	---按重量计动物细毛含量在 85%及以上的：										
5108.2011	----山羊绒的〔999〕	5		70	13/	13	千克	/			
5108.2019	----其他										
5108.2019 10	非供零售用精梳其他濒危动物细毛纱线（按重量计其他动物细毛含量≥85%）〔999〕	5		70	13/	0	千克	FE/			
5108.2019 90	非供零售用精梳其他动物细毛纱线（按重量计其他动物细毛含量≥85%）〔999〕	5		70	13/	13	千克	/			
5108.2090	---其他										
5108.2090 10	非供零售用精梳其他濒危动物细毛纱线（按重量计其他精梳动物细毛含量<85%）〔999〕	5		70	13/	0	千克	FE/		30	
5108.2090 90	非供零售用精梳其他动物细毛纱线（按重量计其他精梳动物细毛含量<85%）〔999〕	5		70	13/	13	千克	/		30	
51.09	**羊毛或动物细毛的纱线，供零售用：**										
	-按重量计羊毛或动物细毛含量在 85%及以上：										
	---动物细毛：										
5109.1011	----山羊绒的〔999〕	6		80	13/	13	千克	/			
5109.1019	----其他〔999〕	6		80	13/	13	千克	/			
5109.1090	---其他〔999〕	6		80	13/	13	千克	/		26	
	-其他：										
	---动物细毛：										
5109.9011	----山羊绒的〔999〕	6		80	13/	13	千克	/			4.2/4.2
5109.9019	----其他〔999〕	6		80	13/	13	千克	/			4.2/4.2
5109.9090	---其他〔999〕	6		80	13/	13	千克	/		31	
51.10	**动物粗毛或马毛的纱线（包括马毛粗松螺旋花线），不论是否供零售用：**										
5110.0000	动物粗毛或马毛的纱线（包括马毛粗松螺旋花线），不论是否供零售用										
5110.0000 10	濒危动物粗毛的纱线（包括马毛粗松螺旋花线，不论是否供零售用）〔999〕	6		70	13/	0	千克	FE/			
5110.0000 90	其他动物粗毛或马毛的纱线（包括马毛粗松螺旋花线，不论是否供零售用）〔999〕	6		70	13/	13	千克	/			
51.11	**粗梳羊毛或粗梳动物细毛的机织物：**										
	-按重量计羊毛或动物细毛含量在 85%及以上：										
	--每平方米重量不超过 300 克：										
	---动物细毛的：										
5111.1111	----山羊绒的〔999〕	10		130	13/	13	米/千克	/			6.5/6.5
5111.1119	----其他〔999〕	10		130	13/	13	米/千克	/		35	6.5/6.5
5111.1190	---其他〔999〕	10		130	13/	13	米/千克	/		35	6.5/6.5
	--其他：										
	---动物细毛的：										
5111.1911	----山羊绒的〔999〕	10		130	13/	13	米/千克	/			6.5/6.5
5111.1919	----其他〔999〕	10		130	13/	13	米/千克	/		35	6.5/6.5
5111.1990	---其他〔999〕	10		130	13/	13	米/千克	/		35	6.5/6.5
5111.2000	-其他，主要或仅与化学纤维长丝混纺〔999〕	8		130	13/	13	米/千克	/		33	
5111.3000	-其他，主要或仅与化学纤维短纤混纺〔999〕	8		130	13/	13	米/千克	/		33	5.2/5.2
5111.9000	-其他〔999〕	8		130	13/	13	米/千克	/		33	
51.12	**精梳羊毛或精梳动物细毛的机织物：**										
	-按重量计羊毛或动物细毛含量在 85%及以上：										
5112.1100	--每平方米重量不超过 200 克〔999〕	8		130	13/	13	米/千克	/		33	4/4
5112.1900	--其他〔999〕	8		130	13/	13	米/千克	/		33	4/4
5112.2000	-其他，主要或仅与化学纤维长丝混纺〔999〕	8		130	13/	13	米/千克	/		33	
5112.3000	-其他，主要或仅与化学纤维短纤混纺〔999〕	8		130	13/	13	米/千克	/		33	
5112.9000	-其他〔999〕	8		130	13/	13	米/千克	/		33	
51.13	**动物粗毛或马毛的机织物：**										
5113.0000	动物粗毛或马毛的机织物〔999〕	8		130	13/	13	米/千克	/			

协定税率 %								RCEP		特惠税率 %			Article Description
东/冰/格	巴基斯坦	韩国	瑞士上/下	哥/秘/柬	澳/毛	新西/坡/智	中国港/澳/台	东盟及马来/澳/韩	日/新	亚太2国	老/柬/缅	98/97/95	
													---Containing 85% or more by weight of fine animal hair:
0/0/0	0	0	0/0	0//0	0/0	0//0	0/0/	0/0/0	4.5/0			0/0/0	----Of goats
													----Other
0/0/0	0	0	0/0	0//0	0/0	0//0	0/0/	0/0/0	4.5/0			0/0/0	Yarn of fine hair of endangered animals, combed, not in formsorpacking for retail sale(containing≥85% by weight of other fine animals hair)
0/0/0	0	0	0/0	0//0	0/0	0//0	0/0/	0/0/0	4.5/0			0/0/0	Yarn of fine hair of other animals, combed, not put up for retail sale(containing ≥85% by weight of other fine animals hair)
													---Other
0/0/0	0	0	0/0	0//0	0/0	0//0	0/0/	0/0/0	4.5/0			0/0/0	Yarn of fine hair of endangered animal,combed, not in forms or packing for retail sale(containing <85% by weight of other fine animals hair)
0/0/0	0	0	0/0	0//0	0/0	0//0	0/0/	0/0/0	4.5/0			0/0/0	Yarn of fine hair of animal;combed,not in forms or packing for retail sale(containing <85% by weight of other animals, hair)
													Yarn of wool or of fine animal hair, put up for retail sale:
													-Containing 85% or more by weight of wool or of fine animal hair:
													---Of fine animal hair:
0/0/0	0	0	0/0	0/0/0	0/0	0//0	0/0/	0/0/0	0/0			0/0/0	----Of goats
0/0/0	0	0	0/0	0/0/0	0/0	0//0	0/0/	0/0/0	0/0			0/0/0	----Other
0/0/0	0	0	0/0	0/0/0	0/0	0//0	0/0/	0/0/0	0/0			0/0/0	---Other
													-Other:
													---Of fine animal hair:
0/0/0	0	0	0/0	0//0	0/0	0//0	0/0/	0/0/0	5.5/0			0/0/0	----Of goats
0/0/0	0	0	0/0	0//0	0/0	0//0	0/0/	0/0/0	5.5/0			0/0/0	----Other
0/0/0	0	0	0/0	0//0	0/0	0//0	0/0/	0/0/0	5.5/0			0/0/0	---Other
													Yarn of coarse animal hair or of horsehair (including gimped horsehair yarn), whether or not put up for retail sale:
													Yarn of coarse animal hair or of horsehair (including gimped horsehair yarn), whether or not put up for retail sale
0/0/0	0	0	0/0	0/0/0	0/0	0//0	0/0/	0/0/0	0/0			0/0/0	Yarn of coarse hair of endangered animals hair (including gimped horsehair yarn, whether or not in forms or packing for retail sale)
0/0/0	0	0	0/0	0/0/0	0/0	0//0	0/0/	0/0/0	0/0			0/0/0	Other yarn of coarse hair of animal or horsehair (including gimped horsehair yarn, whether or not put up for retail sale)
													Woven fabrics of carded wool or of carded fine animal hair:
													-Containing 85% or more by weight of wool or of fine animal hair:
													--Of a weight not exceeding 300 g/m^2:
													---Of fine animal hair:
0/0/0	3.5	0	0/0	0/0/0	0/0	0/0/0	0/0/	0/0/0	9.1/0			0/0/0	----Of goats
0/0/0	3.5	0	0/0	0/0/0	0/0	0/0/0	0/0/	0/0/0	9.1/0			0/0/0	----Other
0/0/0	3.5	0	0/0	0/0/0	0/0	0/0/0	0/0/	0/0/0	9.1/0			0/0/0	---Other
													--Other:
													---Of fine animal hair:
0/0/0	3.5	0	0/0	0/0/0	0/0	0/0/0	0/0/	0/0/0	9.1/0			0/0/0	----Of goats
0/0/0	3.5	0	0/0	0/0/0	0/0	0/0/0	0/0/	0/0/0	9.1/0			0/0/0	----Other
0/0/0	4	0	0/0	0/0/0	0/0	0/0/0	0/0/	0/0/0	9.1/0			0/0/0	---Other
0/0/0	3.5	0	0/0	0/0/0	0/0	0/0/0	0/0/	0/0/0	9.1/0			0/0/0	-Other, mixed mainly or solely with manmade filaments
0/0/0	3.5	0	0/0	0/0/0	0/0	0/0/0	0/0/	0/0/0	9.1/0			0/0/0	-Other, mixed mainly or solely with man-made staple fibres
0//0	3.5	0	0/0	0/0/0	0/0	0/0/0	0/0/	0/0/0	9.1/0			0/0/0	-Other
													Woven fabrics of combed wool or of combed fine animal hair:
													-Containing 85% or more by weight of wool or of fine animal hair:
0/0/0	3.5	0	0/0	0/0/0	0/0	0/0/0	0/0/	9/9/9	9.1/9			0/0/0	--Of a weight not exceeding 200 g/m^2
0/0/0	3.5	0	0/0	0/0/0	0/0	0/0/0	0/0/	0/0/0	9.1/0		0/0/0	0/0/0	--Other
0/0/0	3.5	0	0/0	0/0/0	0/0	0/0/0	0/0/	0/0/0	9.1/0			0/0/0	-Other, mixed mainly or solely with manmade filaments
0/0/0	3.5	0	0/0	0/0/0	0/0	0/0/0	0/0/	9/9/9	9.1/9			0/0/0	-Other, mixed mainly or solely with man-made staple fibres
0/0/0	3.5	0	0/0	0/0/0	0/0	0/0/0	0/0/	0/0/0	9.1/0			0/0/0	-Other
													Woven fabrics of coarse animal hair or of horsehair:
0/0/0	3.5	0	0/0	0/0/0	0/0	0/0/0	0/0/	0/0/0	9.1/0			0/0/0	Woven fabrics of coarse animal hair or of horsehair

第五十二章
棉　花

子目注释：

子目号 5209.42 及 5211.42 所称"粗斜纹布(劳动布)"，是指用不同颜色的纱线织成的三线或四线斜纹织物，包括破斜纹组织的织物，这种织物以经纱为面，经纱染成一种相同的颜色，纬纱未漂白或经漂白、染成灰色或比经纱稍浅的颜色。

税则号列	货品名称〔CIQ 扩展编码及品名—T2 表示见附表 2〕	最惠(%)	暂定税率	普通	增值/消费	出口退税	计量单位	监管条件/特殊证件	检验检疫	对美关税	亚太上/下
52.01	**未梳的棉花：**										
5201.0000	未梳的棉花										
5201.0000 01	未梳的棉花[包括脱脂棉花(配额内)]〔999〕	1		125	9/	9	千克	t4xAB/	MPQ	26	
5201.0000 80	未梳的棉花[包括脱脂棉花(关税配额外暂定)]〔999〕	0		0	9/	9	千克	4ABex/	MPQ	25	
5201.0000 90	未梳的棉花[包括脱脂棉花(配额外)]〔999〕	40		125	9/	9	千克	4xAB/	MPQ	65	
52.02	**废棉(包括废棉纱线及回收纤维)：**										
5202.1000	-废棉纱线(包括废棉线)〔999〕	10		30	13/	13	千克	9/		35	
	-其他：										
5202.9100	--回收纤维〔102〕	10		30	13/	13	千克	9B/	PQ	35	
5202.9900	--其他〔102〕	10		30	13/	9	千克	9B/	PQ	35	
52.03	**已梳的棉花：**										
5203.0000	已梳的棉花										
5203.0000 01	已梳的棉花(配额内)〔999〕	1		125	13/	9	千克	t4xAB/	MPQ	26	
5203.0000 90	已梳的棉花(配额外)〔999〕	40		125	13/	9	千克	4xAB/	MPQ	65	
52.04	**棉制缝纫线，不论是否供零售用：**										
	-非供零售用：										
5204.1100	--按重量计含棉量在 85%及以上〔999〕	5		40	13/	13	千克	/		30	
5204.1900	--其他〔999〕	5		40	13/	13	千克	/		15	
5204.2000	-供零售用〔999〕	5		50	13/	13	千克	/		15	
52.05	**棉纱线(缝纫线除外)，按重量计含棉量在 85%及以上，非供零售用：**										
	-未精梳纤维纺制的单纱：										
5205.1100	--细度在 714.29 分特及以上(不超过 14 公支)〔999〕	5		40	13/	13	千克	/		30	3.5/3.5
5205.1200	--细度在 714.29 分特以下，但不细于 232.56 分特(超过 14 公支，但不超过 43 公支)〔999〕	5		40	13/	13	千克	/		30	3.5/3.5
5205.1300	--细度在 232.56 分特以下，但不细于 192.31 分特(超过 43 公支，但不超过 52 公支)〔999〕	5		40	13/	13	千克	/		25	3.5/3.5
5205.1400	--细度在 192.31 分特以下，但不细于 125 分特(超过 52 公支，但不超过 80 公支)〔999〕	5		40	13/	13	千克	/			3.5/3.5
5205.1500	--细度在 125 分特以下(超过 80 公支)〔999〕	5		40	13/	13	千克	/			3.5/3.5
	-精梳纤维纺制的单纱：										
5205.2100	--细度在 714.29 分特及以上(不超过 14 公支)〔999〕	5		40	13/	13	千克	/			3.5/3.5
5205.2200	--细度在 714.29 分特以下，但不细于 232.56 分特(超过 14 公支，但不超过 43 公支)〔999〕	5		40	13/	13	千克	/		30	3.5/3.5
5205.2300	--细度在 232.56 分特以下，但不细于 192.31 分特(超过 43 公支，但不超过 52 公支)〔999〕	5		40	13/	13	千克	/			3.5/3.5
5205.2400	--细度在 192.31 分特以下，但不细于 125 分特(超过 52 公支，但不超过 80 公支)〔999〕	5		40	13/	13	千克	/		30	3.5/3.5
5205.2600	--细度在 125 分特以下，但不细于 106.38 分特(超过 80 公支，但不超过 94 公支)〔999〕	5		40	13/	13	千克	/			
5205.2700	--细度在 106.38 分特以下，但不细于 83.33 分特(超过 94 公支，但不超过 120 公支)〔999〕	5		40	13/	13	千克	/			
5205.2800	--细度在 83.33 分特以下(超过 120 公支)〔999〕	5		40	13/	13	千克	/			
	-未精梳纤维纺制的多股纱线或缆线：										
5205.3100	--每根单纱细度在 714.29 分特及以上(每根单纱不超过 14 公支)〔999〕	5		40	13/	13	千克	/		25	4.5/4.5
5205.3200	--每根单纱细度在 714.29 分特以下，但不细于 232.56 分特(每根单纱超过 14 公支，但不超过 43 公支)〔999〕	5		40	13/	13	千克	/			3.5/3.5

Chapter 52
Cotton

Subheading Note:

For the purposes of subheadings Nos. 5209. 42 and 5211. 42, the expression "denim" means fabrics of yarns of different colours, of 3-thread or 4-thread twill, including broken twill, warp faced, the warp yarns of which are of one and the same colour and the weft yarns of which are unbleached, bleached, dyed grey or coloured a lighter shade of the colour of the warp yarns.

协定税率 %								RCEP		特惠税率 %			Article Description
东/冰/格	巴基斯坦	韩国	瑞士上/下	哥/秘/柬	澳/毛	新西/坡/智	中国港/澳/台	东盟及马来/澳/韩	日/新	亚太2国	老/柬/缅	98/97/95	
													Cotton, not carded or combed:
													Cotton, not carded or combed
5//							0/0/						Cotton, not carded or combed[including absorbent cotton(in-quota)]
5//							0/0/						Cotton, not carded or combed[including absorben cotton (custom,out-guota,interim)]
5//							0/0/						Cotton, not carded or combed[including absorbent cotton (out-quota)]
													Cotton waste (including yarn waste and garnetted stock):
0/0/	0	2	0/0	0/0/0	0/	0/0/0	0/0/	9/9/	9.1/9			0/0/0	-Yarn waste (including thread waste)
													-Other:
0/0/		0	0/0	0/0/0	0/	0/0/0	0/0/	0/0/0	9.1/0			0/0/0	--Garnetted stock
0/0/	0	2	0/0	0//0	0/	0/0/0	0/0/	9/9/	/9				--Other
													Cotton, carded or combed:
													Cotton, carded or combed
							0/0/						Cotton, carded or combed(in-quota)
							0/0/						Cotton, carded or combed(out-quota)
													Cotton sewing thread, whether or not put up for retail sale:
													-Not put up for retail sale:
0/0/0	0	0	0/0	0/0/0	0/	0//0	0/0/	0/0/0	0/0		0//	0/0/0	--Containing 85% or more by weight of cotton
0/0/0	0	0	0/0	0/0/0	0/	0//0	0/0/	0/0/0	0/0			0/0/0	--Other
0/0/0	0	0	0/0	0/0/0	0/	0//0	0/0/	0/0/0	0/0		0//	0/0/0	-Put up for retail sale
													Cotton yarn (other than sewing thread), containing 85% or more by weight of cotton, not put up for retail sale:
													-Single yarn, of uncombed fibres:
0/0/0	0	2.3	0/0	0/0/0	0.6/	0//0	0/0/0	4.5/4.5/4.5	4.7/4.5		0/0/0	0/0/0	--Measuring 714. 29 decitex or more (not exceeding 14 metric number)
0/0/0	0	2.3	0/0	0/0/0	0.6/	0//0	0/0/0	4.5/4.5/4.5	4.7/4.5		0/0/0	0/0/0	--Measuring less than 714. 29 decitex but not less than 232. 56 decitex (exceeding 14 metric number but not exceeding 43 metric number)
0/0/0	0	2.3	0/0	0/0/0	0.6/	0//0	0/0/	4.5/4.5/4.5	4.7/4.5			0/0/0	--Measuring less than 232. 56 decitex but not less than 192. 31 decitex (exceeding 43 metric number but not exceeding 52 metric number)
0/0/0	0	3.5	0/0	0/0/0	0.6/	0//0	0/0/	4.8/4.8/	/4.8		0//0	0/0/0	--Measuring less than 192. 31 decitex but not less than 125 decitex (exceeding 52 metric number but not exceeding 80 metric number)
0/0/0	3.5	2.3	0/0	0/0/0	0.6/	0//0	0/0/	4.5/4.5/4.5	4.7/4.5			0/0/0	--Measuring less than 125 decitex (exceeding 80 metric number)
													-Single yarn, of combed fibres:
0/0/0	0	2.3	0/0	0/0/0	0.6/	0//0	0/0/	4.5/4.5/4.5	4.7/4.5		//0	0/0/0	--Measuring 714. 29 decitex or more (not exceeding 14 metric number)
0/0/0	0	2.3	0/0	0/0/0	0.6/	0//0	0/0/	4.5/4.5/4.5	4.7/4.5			0/0/0	--Measuring less than 714. 29 decitex but not less than 232. 56 decitex (exceeding 14 metric number but not exceeding 43 metric number)
0/0/0	0	1	0/0	0/0/0	0.6/	0//0	0/0/	0/4.5/	/0			0/0/0	--Measuring less than 232. 56 decitex but not less than 192. 31 decitex (exceeding 43 metric number but not exceeding 52 metric number)
0/0/0	0	1	0/0	0/0/0	0.6/	0//0	0/0/	0/4.5/	/0		0//0	0/0/0	--Measuring less than 192. 31 decitex but not less than 125 decitex (exceeding 52 metric number but not exceeding 80 metric number)
0/0/0	0	2.3	0/0	0/0/0	0.6/	0//0	0/0/	4.5/4.5/4.5	4.7/4.5			0/0/0	--Measuring less than 125 decitex but not less than 106. 38 decitex (exceeding 80 metric number but not exceeding 94 metric number)
0/0/0		2.3	0/0	0/0/0	0.6/	0//0	0/0/	4.5/4.5/4.5	4.7/4.5			0/0/0	--Measuring less than 106. 38 decitex but not less than 83. 33 decitex (exceeding 94 metric number but not exceeding 120 metric number)
0/0/0		2.3	0/0	0/0/0	0.6/	0//0	0/0/	4.5/4.5/4.5	4.7/4.5			0/0/0	--Measuring less than 83. 33 decitex (exceeding 120 metric number)
													-Multiple (folded) or cabled yarn, of uncombed fibres:
0/0/0	0	2.3	0/0	0//0	0.6/	0//0	0/0/	4.5/4.5/4.5	4.7/4.5			0//	--Measuring per single yarn 714. 29 decitex or more (not exceeding 14 metric number per single yarn)
0/0/0	0	2.3	0/0	0/0/0	0.6/	0//0	0/0/	4.5/4.5/4.5	4.7/4.5			0/0/0	--Measuring per single yarn less than 714. 29 decitex but not less than 232. 56 decitex (exceeding 14 metric number but not exceeding 43 metric number per single yarn)

税则号列	货品名称〔CIQ 扩展编码及品名—T2 表示见附表 2〕	最惠(%)	暂定税率	普通	增值/消费	出口退税	计量单位	监管条件/特殊证件	检验检疫	对美关税	亚太上/下
5205.3300	--每根单纱细度在 232.56 分特以下,但不细于 192.31 分特(每根单纱超过 43 公支,但不超过 52 公支)〔999〕	5		40	13/	13	千克	/			
5205.3400	--每根单纱细度在 192.31 分特以下,但不细于 125 分特(每根单纱超过 52 公支,但不超过 80 公支)〔999〕	5		40	13/	13	千克	/			
5205.3500	--每根单纱细度在 125 分特以下(每根单纱超过 80 公支)〔999〕	5		40	13/	13	千克	/			
	-精梳纤维纺制的多股纱线或缆线:										
5205.4100	--每根单纱细度在 714.29 分特及以上(每根单纱不超过 14 公支)〔999〕	5		40	13/	13	千克	/			4.5/4.5
5205.4200	--每根单纱细度在 714.29 分特以下,但不细于 232.56 分特(每根单纱超过 14 公支,但不超过 43 公支)〔999〕	5		40	13/	13	千克	/			3.5/3.5
5205.4300	--每根单纱细度在 232.56 分特以下,但不细于 192.31 分特(每根单纱超过 43 公支,但不超过 52 公支)〔999〕	5		40	13/	13	千克	/		30	
5205.4400	--每根单纱细度在 192.31 分特以下,但不细于 125 分特(每根单纱超过 52 公支,但不超过 80 公支)〔999〕	5		40	13/	13	千克	/			
5205.4600	--每根单纱细度在 125 分特以下,但不细于 106.38 分特(每根单纱超过 80 公支,但不超过 94 公支)〔999〕	5		40	13/	13	千克	/			4.5/4.5
5205.4700	--每根单纱细度在 106.38 分特以下,但不细于 83.33 分特(每根单纱超过 94 公支,但不超过 120 公支)〔999〕	5		40	13/	13	千克	/			4.5/4.5
5205.4800	--每根单纱细度 83.33 分特以下(每根单纱超过 120 公支)〔999〕	5		40	13/	13	千克	/			4.5/4.5
52.06	**棉纱线(缝纫线除外),按重量计含棉量在 85%以下,非供零售用:**										
	-未精梳纤维纺制的单纱:										
5206.1100	--细度在 714.29 分特及以上(不超过 14 公支)〔999〕	5		40	13/	13	千克	/			3.5/3.5
5206.1200	--细度在 714.29 分特以下,但不细于 232.56 分特(超过 14 公支,但不超过 43 公支)〔999〕	5		40	13/	13	千克	/		30	3.5/3.5
5206.1300	--细度在 232.56 分特以下,但不细于 192.31 分特(超过 43 公支,但不超过 52 公支)〔999〕	5		40	13/	13	千克	/		15	
5206.1400	--细度在 192.31 分特以下,但不细于 125 分特(超过 52 公支,但不超过 80 公支)〔999〕	5		40	13/	13	千克	/			
5206.1500	--细度在 125 分特以下(超过 80 公支)〔999〕	5		40	13/	13	千克	/			3.5/3.5
	-精梳纤维纺制的单纱:										
5206.2100	--细度在 714.29 分特及以上(不超过 14 公支)〔999〕	5		40	13/	13	千克	/			4.5/4.5
5206.2200	--细度在 714.29 分特以下,但不细于 232.56 分特(超过 14 公支,但不超过 43 公支)〔999〕	5		40	13/	13	千克	/			
5206.2300	--细度在 232.56 分特以下,但不细于 192.31 分特(超过 43 公支,但不超过 52 公支)〔999〕	5		40	13/	13	千克	/		30	
5206.2400	--细度在 192.31 分特以下,但不细于 125 分特(超过 52 公支,但不超过 80 公支)〔999〕	5		40	13/	13	千克	/			
5206.2500	--细度在 125 分特以下(超过 80 公支)〔999〕	5		40	13/	13	千克	/			
	-未精梳纤维纺制的多股纱线或缆线:										
5206.3100	--每根单纱细度在 714.29 分特及以上(每根单纱不超过 14 公支)〔999〕	5		40	13/	13	千克	/		30	
5206.3200	--每根单纱细度在 714.29 分特以下,但不细于 232.56 分特(每根单纱超过 14 公支,但不超过 43 公支)〔999〕	5		40	13/	13	千克	/			
5206.3300	--每根单纱细度在 232.56 分特以下,但不细于 192.31 分特(每根单纱超过 43 公支,但不超过 52 公支)〔999〕	5		40	13/	13	千克	/			
5206.3400	--每根单纱细度在 192.31 分特以下,但不细于 125 分特(每根单纱超过 52 公支,但不超过 80 公支)〔999〕	5		40	13/	13	千克	/			

协定税率 %								RCEP		特惠税率 %			Article Description
东/冰/格	巴基斯坦	韩国	瑞士 上/下	哥/秘/柬	澳/毛	新西/坡/智	中国港/澳/台	东盟及马来/澳/韩	日/新	亚太2国	老/柬/缅	98/97/95	
0/0/0		2.3	0/0	0/0/0	0.6/	0//0	0/0/	4.5/4.5/4.5	4.7/4.5			0/0/0	--Measuring per single yarn less than 232.56 decitex but not less than 192.31 decitex (exceeding 43 metric number but not exceeding 52 metric number per single yarn)
0/0/0	0	2.3	0/0	0/0/0	0.6/	0//0	0/0/	4.5/4.5/4.5	4.7/4.5			0/0/0	--Measuring per single yarn less than 192.31 decitex but not less than 125 decitex (exceeding 52 metric number but not exceeding 80 metric number per single yarn)
0/0/0		2.3	0/0	0/0/0	0.6/	0//0	0/0/	4.5/4.5/4.5	4.7/4.5			0/0/0	--Measuring per single yarn less than 125 decitex (exceeding 80 metric number per single yarn)
													-Multiple (folded) or cabled yarn, of combed fibres:
0/0/0	4.5	2.3	0/0	0//0	0.6/	0//0	0/0/	4.5/4.5/4.5	4.7/4.5			0/0/0	--Measuring per single yarn 714.29 decitex or more (not exceeding 14 metric number per single yarn)
/0/0	0	3.5	0/0	0/0/0	0.6/	0//0	0/0/					0/0/0	--Measuring per single yarn less than 714.29 decitex but not less than 232.56 decitex (exceeding 14 metric number but not exceeding 43 metric number per single yarn)
0/0/0	4	2.3	0/0	0//0	0.6/	0//0	0/0/	4.5/4.5/4.5	4.7/4.5			0/0/0	--Measuring per single yarn less than 232.56 decitex but not less than 192.31 decitex (exceeding 43 metric number but not exceeding 52 metric number per single yarn)
0/0/0	0	2.3	0/0	0/0/0	0.6/	0//0	0/0/	4.5/4.5/4.5	4.7/4.5			0/0/0	--Measuring per single yarn less than 192.31 decitex but not less than 125 decitex (exceeding 52 metric number but not exceeding 80 metric number per single yarn)
0/0/0	3.6	2.3	0/0	0/0/0	0.6/	0//0	0/0/	4.5/4.5/4.5	4.7/4.5			0/0/0	--Measuring per single yarn less than 125 decitex but not less than 106.38 decitex (exceeding 80 metric number but not exceeding 94 metric number per single yarn)
0/0/0	3.6	2.3	0/0	0/0/0	0.6/	0//0	0/0/	4.5/4.5/4.5	4.7/4.5			0/0/0	--Measuring per single yarn less than 106.38 decitex but not less than 83.33 decitex (exceeding 94 metric number but not exceeding 120 metric number per single yarn)
0/0/0	4.5	2.3	0/0	0/0/0	0.6/	0//0	0/0/	4.5/4.5/4.5	4.7/4.5			0/0/0	--Measuring per single yarn less than 83.33 decitex (exceeding 120 metric number per single yarn)
													Cotton yarn (other than sewing thread), containing less than 85% by weight of cotton, not put up for retail sale:
													-Single yarn, of uncombed fibres:
0/0/0	2.8	2.3	0/0	0//0	0.6/	0//0	0/0/	4.5/4.5/4.5	4.7/4.5			0//	--Measuring 714.29 decitex or more (not exceeding 14 metric number)
0/0/0	0	2.3	0/0	0/0/0	0.6/	0//0	0/0/0	4.5/4.5/4.5	4.7/4.5			0/0/0	--Measuring less than 714.29 decitex but not less than 232.56 decitex (exceeding 14 metric number but not exceeding 43 metric number)
0/0/0		2.3	0/0	0/0/0	0.6/	0//0	0/0/	4.5/4.5/4.5	4.7/4.5			0/0/0	--Measuring less than 232.56 decitex but not less than 192.31 decitex (exceeding 43 metric number but not exceeding 52 metric number)
0/0/0	4	2.3	0/0	0/0/0	0.6/	0//0	0/0/	4.5/4.5/4.5	4.7/4.5			0/0/0	--Measuring less than 192.31 decitex but not less than 125 decitex (exceeding 52 metric number but not exceeding 80 metric number)
0/0/0	3.5	2.3	0/0	0/0/0	0.6/	0//0	0/0/	4.5/4.5/4.5	4.7/4.5			0/0/0	--Measuring less than 125 decitex (exceeding 80 metric number)
													-Single yarn, of combed fibres:
0/0/0	4.5	2.3	0/0	0/0/0	0.6/	0//0	0/0/	4.5/4.5/4.5	4.7/4.5			0/0/0	--Measuring 714.29 decitex or more (not exceeding 14 metric number)
0/0/0	0	2.3	0/0	0/0/0	0.6/	0//0	0/0/0	4.5/4.5/4.5	4.7/4.5			0/0/0	--Measuring less than 714.29 decitex but not less than 232.56 decitex (exceeding 14 metric number but not exceeding 43 metric number)
0/0/0		2.3	0/0	0/0/0	0.6/	0//0	0/0/	4.5/4.5/4.5	4.7/4.5			0/0/0	--Measuring less than 232.56 decitex but not less than 192.31 decitex (exceeding 43 metric number but not exceeding 52 metric number)
0/0/0	4	2.3	0/0	0/0/0	0.6/	0//0	0/0/0	4.5/4.5/4.5	4.7/4.5			0/0/0	--Measuring less than 192.31 decitex but not less than 125 decitex (exceeding 52 metric number but not exceeding 80 metric number)
0/0/0		2.3	0/0	0/0/0	0.6/	0//0	0/0/	4.5/4.5/4.5	4.7/4.5			0/0/0	--Measuring less than 125 decitex (exceeding 80 metric number)
													-Multiple (folded) or cabled yarn, of uncombed fibres:
0/0/0		2.3	0/0	0/0/0	0.6/	0//0	0/0/	4.5/4.5/4.5	4.7/4.5			0/0/0	--Measuring per single yarn 714.29 decitex or more (not exceeding 14 metric number per single yarn)
0/0/0	0	2.3	0/0	0/0/0	0.6/	0//0	0/0/	4.5/4.5/4.5	4.7/4.5			0/0/0	--Measuring per single yarn less than 714.29 decitex but not less than 232.56 decitex (exceeding 14 metric number but not exceeding 43 metric number per single yarn)
0/0/0		2.3	0/0	0/0/0	0.6/	0//0	0/0/	4.5/4.5/4.5	4.7/4.5			0/0/0	--Measuring per single yarn less than 232.56 decitex but not less than 192.31 decitex (exceeding 43 metric number but not exceeding 52 metric number per single yarn)
0/0/0		2.3	0/0	0/0/0	0.6/	0//0	0/0/	4.5/4.5/4.5	4.7/4.5			0/0/0	--Measuring per single yarn less than 192.31 decitex but not less than 125 decitex (exceeding 52 metric number but not exceeding 80 metric number per single yarn)

税则号列	货品名称〔CIQ 扩展编码及品名—T2 表示见附表 2〕	最惠(%)	暂定税率	普通	增值/消费	出口退税	计量单位	监管条件/特殊证件	检验检疫	对美关税	亚太上/下
5206.3500	--每根单纱细度在 125 分特以下(每根单纱超过 80 公支)〔999〕	5		40	13/	13	千克	/			
	-精梳纤维纺制的多股纱线或缆线:										
5206.4100	--每根单纱细度在 714.29 分特及以上(每根单纱不超过 14 公支)〔999〕	5		40	13/	13	千克	/			
5206.4200	--每根单纱细度在 714.29 分特以下,但不细于 232.56 分特(每根单纱超过 14 公支,但不超过 43 公支)〔999〕	5		40	13/	13	千克	/			
5206.4300	--每根单纱细度在 232.56 分特以下,但不细于 192.31 分特(每根单纱超过 43 公支,但不超过 52 公支)〔999〕	5		40	13/	13	千克	/			
5206.4400	--每根单纱细度在 192.31 分特以下,但不细于 125 分特(每根单纱超过 52 公支,但不超过 80 公支)〔999〕	5		40	13/	13	千克	/			
5206.4500	--每根单纱细度在 125 分特以下(每根单纱超过 80 公支)〔999〕	5		40	13/	13	千克	/			
52.07	**棉纱线(缝纫线除外),供零售用:**										
5207.1000	-按重量计含棉量在 85%及以上〔999〕	5		50	13/	13	千克	/		30	4.2/4.2
5207.9000	-其他〔999〕	5		50	13/	13	千克	/			
52.08	**棉机织物,按重量计含棉量在 85%及以上,每平方米重量不超过 200 克:**										
	-未漂白:										
5208.1100	--平纹机织物,每平方米重量不超过 100 克〔999〕	8		70	13/	13	米/千克	/		33	
5208.1200	--平纹机织物,每平方米重量超过 100 克〔999〕	8		70	13/	13	米/千克	/		33	
5208.1300	--三线或四线斜纹机织物,包括双面斜纹机织物〔999〕	8		70	13/	13	米/千克	/			5.2/5.2
5208.1900	--其他机织物〔999〕	8		70	13/	13	米/千克	/		33	
	-漂白:										
5208.2100	--平纹机织物,每平方米重量不超过 100 克										
5208.2100 10	漂白全棉平纹府绸及细平布(每平方米重量≤100g,含棉量≥85%)〔999〕	8		70	13/	13	米/千克	/			
5208.2100 20	漂白全棉平纹机织平布(每平方米重量≤100g,68 号及以下)〔999〕	8		70	13/	13	米/千克	/			
5208.2100 30	漂白全棉平纹奶酪布(每平方米重量≤100g,含棉量≥85%)〔999〕	8		70	13/	13	米/千克	/			
5208.2100 40	漂白全棉平纹印染用布(每平方米重量≤100g,43-68 号)〔999〕	8		70	13/	13	米/千克	/			
5208.2100 50	漂白全棉平纹巴里纱及薄细布(每平方米重量≤100g,69 号及以上)〔999〕	8		70	13/	13	米/千克	/			
5208.2100 60	漂白全棉医用纱布(每平方米重量≤100g,含棉量≥85%)〔999〕	8		70	13/	13	米/千克	/			
5208.2200	--平纹机织物,每平方米重量超过 100 克										
5208.2200 10	漂白全棉平纹府绸及细平布(100g<每平方米重量≤200g,含棉量≥85%)〔999〕	8		70	13/	13	米/千克	/		33	
5208.2200 20	漂白全棉平纹机织平布(100g<每平方米重量≤200g,68 号及以下)〔999〕	8		70	13/	13	米/千克	/		33	
5208.2200 30	漂白全棉平纹奶酪布(100g<每平方米重量≤200g,含棉量≥85%)〔999〕	8		70	13/	13	米/千克	/		33	
5208.2200 40	漂白全棉平纹印染用布(100g<每平方米重量≤200g,43-68 号)〔999〕	8		70	13/	13	米/千克	/		33	
5208.2200 50	漂白全棉巴里纱及薄细布(100g<每平方米重量≤200g,69 号及以上)〔999〕	8		70	13/	13	米/千克	/		33	
5208.2300	--三线或四线斜纹机织物,包括双面斜纹机织物〔999〕	8		70	13/	13	米/千克	/			
5208.2900	--其他机织物										
5208.2900 10	漂白其他全棉机织缎布(每平方米重量≤200g,含棉量≥85%)〔999〕	8		70	13/	13	米/千克	/		33	
5208.2900 20	漂白其他全棉机织斜纹布(每平方米重量≤200g,含棉量≥85%)〔999〕	8		70	13/	13	米/千克	/		33	
5208.2900 30	漂白其他全棉机织牛津布(每平方米重量≤200g,含棉量≥85%)〔999〕	8		70	13/	13	米/千克	/		33	
5208.2900 90	漂白其他全棉机织物(每平方米重量≤200g,含棉量≥85%)〔999〕	8		70	13/	13	米/千克	/		33	
	-染色:										
5208.3100	--平纹机织物,每平方米重量不超过 100 克										
5208.3100 10	染色全棉手工织布(每平方米重量≤100g,含棉量≥85%)〔999〕	8		70	13/	13	米/千克	/		33	
5208.3100 91	染色全棉平纹府绸及细平布(每平方米重量≤100g,含棉量≥85%)〔999〕	8		70	13/	13	米/千克	/		33	
5208.3100 92	染色全棉平纹机织平布(每平方米重量≤100g,68 号及以下)〔999〕	8		70	13/	13	米/千克	/		33	

协定税率 %								RCEP		特惠税率 %			Article Description
东/冰/格	巴基斯坦	韩国	瑞士上/下	哥/秘/柬	澳/毛	新西/坡/智	中国港/澳/台	东盟及马来/澳/韩	日/新	亚太2国	老/柬/缅	98/97/95	
0/0/0		2.3	0/0	0/0/0	0.6/	0//0	0/0/	4.5/4.5/4.5	4.7/4.5			0/0/0	--Measuring per single yarn less than 125 decitex (exceeding 80 metric number per single yarn)
													-Multiple (folded) or cabled yarn, of combed fibres:
0/0/0		2.3	0/0	0/0/0	0.6/	0//0	0/0/	4.5/4.5/4.5	4.7/4.5			0/0/0	--Measuring per single yarn 714. 29 decitex or more (not exceeding 14 metric number per single yarn)
0/0/0		2.3	0/0	0/0/0	0.6/	0//0	0/0/	4.5/4.5/4.5	4.7/4.5			0/0/0	--Measuring per single yarn less than 714. 29 decitex but not less than 232. 56 decitex (exceeding 14 metric number but not exceeding 43 metric number per single yarn)
0/0/0		2.3	0/0	0/0/0	0.6/	0//0	0/0/	4.5/4.5/4.5	4.7/4.5			0/0/0	--Measuring per single yarn less than 232. 56 decitex but not less then 192. 31 decitex (exceeding 43 metric number but not exceeding 52 metric number per single yarn)
0/0/0		2.3	0/0	0/0/0	0.6/	0//0	0/0/	4.5/4.5/4.5	4.7/4.5			0/0/0	--Measuring per single yarn less than 192. 31 decitex but not less than 125 decitex (exceeding 52 metric number but not exceeding 80 metric number per single yarn)
0/0/0		2.3	0/0	0/0/0	0.6/	0//0	0/0/	4.5/4.5/4.5	4.7/4.5			0/0/0	--Measuring per single yarn less than 125 decitex (exceeding 80 metric number per single yarn)
													Cotton yarn (other than sewing thread) put up for retail sale:
0/0/0	4	0	0/0	0/0/0	0/	0//0	0/0/	0/0/0	0/0			0/0/0	-Containing 85% or more by weight of cotton
0/0/0	3.5	0	0/0	0/0/0	0/	0//0	0/0/	0/0/0	0/0			0/0/0	-Other
													Woven fabrics of cotton, containing 85% or more by weight of cotton, weighing not more than 200 g/m²:
													-Unbleached:
0/0/0	0	0	0/0	0/0/0	0/0	0//0	0/0/	0/0/0	9.1/0			0/0/0	--Plain weave, weighing not more than 100 g/m²
0/0/0	0	0	0/0	0/0/0	0/0	0/0/0	0/0/	0/0/0	9.1/0			0/0/0	--Plain weave, weighing more than 100 g/m²
0/0/0	0	2	0/0	0/0/0	0/0	0//0	0/0/	0/0/9	9.1/0			0/0/0	--3-thread or 4-thread twill, including cross twill
0/0/0	0	0	0/0	0/0/0	0/0	0/0/0	0/0/	0/0/0	9.1/0			0/0/0	--Other fabrics
													-Bleached:
													--Plain weave, weighing not more than 100 g/m²
0/0/0	0	0	0/0	0/0/0	0/0	0//0	0/0/	0/0/0	9.1/0			0/0/0	Poplin and fine plain cloth of cotton, w≤100g/m², containing≥85% by weight of cotton, bleached
0/0/0	0	0	0/0	0/0/0	0/0	0//0	0/0/	0/0/0	9.1/0			0/0/0	Woven fabrics of cotton, plain weave, ≤No. 68, w≤100g/m², bleached
0/0/0	0	0	0/0	0/0/0	0/0	0//0	0/0/	0/0/0	9.1/0			0/0/0	Cheese cloth of cotton, plain weave, w≤100g/m², containing≥85% by weight of cotton, bleached
0/0/0	0	0	0/0	0/0/0	0/0	0//0	0/0/	0/0/0	9.1/0			0/0/0	Cloth for printing and dying of cotton, plain weave, No. 43～No. 68, w≤100g/m², bleached
0/0/0	0	0	0/0	0/0/0	0/0	0//0	0/0/	0/0/0	9.1/0			0/0/0	Voiles and swiss muslim of cotton, plain weave, w≤100g/m², containing ≥ 85% by weight of cotton, ≥ No. 69, bleached
0/0/0	0	0	0/0	0/0/0	0/0	0//0	0/0/	0/0/0	9.1/0			0/0/0	Medical gauze of cotton, w≤100g/m², containing≥85% by weight of cotton, bleached
													--Plain weave, weighing more than 100 g/m²
0/0/0	0	0	0/0	0/0/0	0/0	0/0/0	0/0/	0/0/0	9.1/0		0/0/0	0/0/0	Poplin and fine plain cloth of cotton, plain weave, 100g/m²<w≤200g/m², containing≥85% by weight of cotton, bleached
0/0/0	0	0	0/0	0/0/0	0/0	0/0/0	0/0/	0/0/0	9.1/0		0/0/0	0/0/0	Plain cloth of cotton, plain weave, 100g/m²<w≤200g/m², ≤No. 68, bleached
0/0/0	0	0	0/0	0/0/0	0/0	0/0/0	0/0/	0/0/0	9.1/0		0/0/0	0/0/0	Cheese cloth of cotton, plain weave, 100g/m²<w≤200g/m², containing≥85% by weight of cotton, bleached
0/0/0	0	0	0/0	0/0/0	0/0	0/0/0	0/0/	0/0/0	9.1/0		0/0/0	0/0/0	Cloth for printing and dying, of cotton, plain weave, No. 43～No. 68, 100g/m²<w≤200g/m², bleached
0/0/0	0	0	0/0	0/0/0	0/0	0/0/0	0/0/	0/0/0	9.1/0		0/0/0	0/0/0	Voiles and swiss muslin of cotton, 100g/m²<w≤200g/m², ≥No. 69, bleached
0/0/0	0	0	5/5	0/0/0	0/0	0/0/0	0/0/	0/0/0	10.9/0			0/0/0	--3-thread or 4-thread twill, including cross twill
													--Other fabrics
0/0/0	0	0	0/0	0/0/0	0/0	0//0	0/0/	0/0/0	9.1/0			0/0/0	Woven fabrics of cotton, satin weave, w≤200 g/m², containing≥85% by weight of cotton, bleached
0/0/0	0	0	0/0	0/0/0	0/0	0//0	0/0/	0/0/0	9.1/0			0/0/0	Woven fabrics of cotton, twill weave, w≤200 g/m², containing≥85% by weight of cotton, bleached
0/0/0	0	0	0/0	0/0/0	0/0	0//0	0/0/	0/0/0	9.1/0			0/0/0	Woven fabrics of cotton, oxford weave, w≤200 g/m², containing≥85% by weight of cotton, bleached
0/0/0	0	0	0/0	0/0/0	0/0	0//0	0/0/	0/0/0	9.1/0			0/0/0	Other woven fabrics of cotton, w≤200g/m², containing≥85% by weight of cotton, bleached
													-Dyed:
													--Plain weave, weighing not more than 100 g/m²
0/0/0	0	0	0/0	0/0/0	0/0	0//0	0/0/0	0/0/0	9.1/0			0/0/0	Handwoven plain cloth of cotton, w≤100g/m², containing≥85% by weight of cotton, dyed
0/0/0	0	0	0/0	0/0/0	0/0	0//0	0/0/0	0/0/0	9.1/0			0/0/0	Popin and fine plain cloth of cotton, w≤100g/m², containing ≥85% by weight of cotton, dyed
0/0/0	0	0	0/0	0/0/0	0/0	0//0	0/0/0	0/0/0	9.1/0			0/0/0	Plain cloth of cotton, w≤100g/m², ≤No. 68, dyed

税则号列	货品名称〔CIQ 扩展编码及品名－T2 表示见附表 2〕	最惠(%)	暂定税率	普通	增值/消费	出口退税	计量单位	监管条件/特殊证件	检验检疫	对美关税	亚太上/下
5208.3100 93	染色全棉平纹奶酪布(每平方米重量≤100g,含棉量≥85％)〔999〕	8		70	13/	13	米/千克	/		33	
5208.3100 94	染色全棉平纹印染用布(每平方米重量≤100g,43-68 号)〔999〕	8		70	13/	13	米/千克	/		33	
5208.3100 95	染色全棉巴里纱及薄细布(每平方米重量≤100g,69 号及以上)〔999〕	8		70	13/	13	米/千克	/		33	
5208.3200	--平纹机织物,每平方米重量超过 100 克										
5208.3200 10	染色全棉手工织布(100g＜每平方米重量≤200g,含棉量≥85％)〔999〕	8		70	13/	13	米/千克	/		33	5.2/5.2
5208.3200 91	染色全棉平纹府绸及细平布(100g＜每平方米重量≤200g,含棉量≥85％)〔999〕	8		70	13/	13	米/千克	/		33	5.2/5.2
5208.3200 92	染色全棉平纹机织平布(100g＜每平方米重量≤200g,68 号及以下)〔999〕	8		70	13/	13	米/千克	/		33	5.2/5.2
5208.3200 93	染色全棉平纹奶酪布(100g＜每平方米重量≤200g,含棉量≥85％)〔999〕	8		70	13/	13	米/千克	/		33	5.2/5.2
5208.3200 94	染色全棉平纹印染用布(100g＜每平方米重量≤200g,43-68 号)〔999〕	8		70	13/	13	米/千克	/		33	5.2/5.2
5208.3200 95	染色全棉巴里纱及薄细布(100g＜每平方米重量≤200g,69 号及以上)〔999〕	8		70	13/	13	米/千克	/		33	5.2/5.2
5208.3300	--三线或四线斜纹机织物,包括双面斜纹机织物〔999〕	8		70	13/	13	米/千克	/			5.2/5.2
5208.3900	--其他机织物										
5208.3900 10	染色其他全棉机织缎布(每平方米重量≤200g,含棉量≥85％)〔999〕	8		70	13/	13	米/千克	/		33	5.2/5.2
5208.3900 20	染色其他全棉机织斜纹布(每平方米重量≤200g,含棉量≥85％)〔999〕	8		70	13/	13	米/千克	/		33	5.2/5.2
5208.3900 30	染色其他全棉机织牛津布(每平方米重量≤200g,含棉量≥85％)〔999〕	8		70	13/	13	米/千克	/		33	5.2/5.2
5208.3900 90	染色其他全棉机织物(每平方米重量≤200g,含棉量≥85％)〔999〕	8		70	13/	13	米/千克	/		33	5.2/5.2
	-色织:										
5208.4100	--平纹机织物,每平方米重量不超过 100 克										
5208.4100 10	色织的全棉手工织布(每平方米重量≤100g,含棉量≥85％)〔999〕	8		70	13/	13	米/千克	/			
5208.4100 90	色织的全棉平纹机织物(每平方米重量≤100g,含棉量≥85％)〔999〕	8		70	13/	13	米/千克	/			
5208.4200	--平纹机织物,每平方米重量 100 克										
5208.4200 10	色织的全棉手工织布(100g＜每平方米重量≤200g,含棉量≥85％)〔999〕	8		70	13/	13	米/千克	/		33	5.2/5.2
5208.4200 90	色织的全棉平纹机织物(100 克＜每平方米重量≤200g,含棉量≥85％)〔999〕	8		70	13/	13	米/千克	/		33	5.2/5.2
5208.4300	--三线或四线斜纹机织物,包括双面斜纹机织物〔999〕	8		70	13/	13	米/千克	/		33	
5208.4900	--其他机织物										
5208.4900 10	色织的其他全棉提花机织物(每平方米重量≤200g,含棉量≥85％)〔999〕	8		70	13/	13	米/千克	/		33	5.2/5.2
5208.4900 90	色织的其他全棉机织物(每平方米重量≤200g,含棉量≥85％)〔999〕	8		70	13/	13	米/千克	/		33	5.2/5.2
	-印花:										
5208.5100	--平纹机织物,每平方米重量不超过 100 克										
5208.5100 10	印花全棉手工织布(每平方米重量≤100g,含棉量≥85％)〔999〕	8		70	13/	13	米/千克	/		33	
5208.5100 91	印花全棉平纹府绸及细平布(每平方米重量≤100g,含棉量≥85％)〔999〕	8		70	13/	13	米/千克	/		33	
5208.5100 92	印花全棉平纹机织平布(每平方米重量≤100g,68 号及以下)〔999〕	8		70	13/	13	米/千克	/		33	
5208.5100 93	印花全棉平纹奶酪布(每平方米重量≤100g,含棉量≥85％)〔999〕	8		70	13/	13	米/千克	/		33	
5208.5100 94	印花全棉平纹印染用布(每平方米重量≤100g,43-68 号)〔999〕	8		70	13/	13	米/千克	/		33	
5208.5100 95	印花全棉平纹巴里纱及薄细布(每平方米重量≤100g,69 号及以上)〔999〕	8		70	13/	13	米/千克	/		33	
5208.5200	--平纹机织物,每平方米重量超过 100 克										
5208.5200 10	印花的全棉手工织布(100g＜每平方米重量≤200g,含棉量≥85％)〔999〕	8		70	13/	13	米/千克	/		33	5.2/5.2
5208.5200 91	印花的全棉平纹府绸及细平布(100g＜每平方米重量≤200g,含棉量≥85％)〔999〕	8		70	13/	13	米/千克	/		33	5.2/5.2
5208.5200 92	印花的全棉平纹机织平布(100g＜每平方米重量≤200g,68 号及以下)〔999〕	8		70	13/	13	米/千克	/		33	5.2/5.2

协定税率 %								RCEP		特惠税率 %			Article Description
东/冰/格	巴基斯坦	韩国	瑞士上/下	哥/秘/柬	澳/毛	新西/坡/智	中国港/澳/台	东盟及马来/澳/韩	日/新	亚太2国	老/柬/缅	98/97/95	
0/0/0	0	0	0/0	0/0/0	0/0	0/ /0	0/0/0	0/0/0	9.1/0			0/0/0	Cheese cloth of cotton, w≤100 g/m², containing≥85% by weight of cotton, dyed
0/0/0	0	0	0/0	0/0/0	0/0	0/ /0	0/0/0	0/0/0	9.1/0			0/0/0	Cloth for printing and dying, of cotton, plain weave, No. 43～No. 68, w≤100g/m², dyed
0/0/0	0	0	0/0	0/0/0	0/0	0/ /0	0/0/0	0/0/0	9.1/0			0/0/0	Voiles and fine thin cloth of cotton, w≤100g/m², ≥No. 69, dyed
													--Plain weave, weighing more than 100 g/m²
0/0/0	0	0	0/0	0/0/0	0/0	0/0/0	0/0/0	0/0/0	9.1/0			0/0/0	Handwoven plain cloth of cotton, 100g/m²＜w≤200g/m², containing≥85% by weight of cotton, dyed
0/0/0	0	0	0/0	0/0/0	0/0	0/0/0	0/0/0	0/0/0	9.1/0			0/0/0	Poplin and fine plain cloth of cotton, 100g/m²＜w≤200g/m², containing≥85% by weight of cotton, dyed
0/0/0	0	0	0/0	0/0/0	0/0	0/0/0	0/0/0	0/0/0	9.1/0			0/0/0	Plain cloth of cotton, 100g/m²＜w≤200g/m², ≤No. 68, dyed
0/0/0	0	0	0/0	0/0/0	0/0	0/0/0	0/0/0	0/0/0	9.1/0			0/0/0	Cheese cloth of cotton, plain weave, 100g/m²＜w≤200g/m², containing≥85% by weight of cotton, dyed
0/0/0	0	0	0/0	0/0/0	0/0	0/0/0	0/0/0	0/0/0	9.1/0			0/0/0	Cloth for printing and dying of cotton, plain weave, No. 43～No. 68, 100g/m²＜w≤200g/m², dyed
0/0/0	0	0	0/0	0/0/0	0/0	0/0/0	0/0/0	0/0/0	9.1/0			0/0/0	Voiles and swiss muslin of cotton, 100g/m²＜w≤200g/m², ≥No. 69, dyed
0/0/0	0	0	0/0	0/0/0	0/0	0/ /0	0/0/	0/0/0	9.1/0		0/0/0	0/0/0	--3-thread or 4-thread twill, including cross twill
													--Other fabrics
0/0/0	0	0	0/0	0/0/0	0/0	0/0/0	0/0/0	9/9/9	9.1/9			0/0/0	Woven fabrics of cotton, satin weave, w≤200 g/m², containing≥85% by weight of cotton, dyed
0/0/0	0	0	0/0	0/0/0	0/0	0/0/0	0/0/0	9/9/9	9.1/9			0/0/0	Woven fabrics of cotton, twill weave, w≤200 g/m², containing≥85% by weight of cotton, dyed
0/0/0	0	0	0/0	0/0/0	0/0	0/0/0	0/0/0	9/9/9	9.1/9			0/0/0	Woven fabrics of cotton, oxford weave, w≤200 g/m², containing≥85% by weight of cotton, dyed
0/0/0	0	0	0/0	0/0/0	0/0	0/0/0	0/0/0	9/9/9	9.1/9			0/0/0	Other woven fabrics of cotton, w≤200g/m², containing≥85% by weight of cotton, dyed
													-Of yarns of different colours:
													--Plain weave, weighing not more than 100 g/m²
0/0/0	0	0	1/1	0/0/0	0/0	0/0/0	0/0/	0/0/0	9.1/0			0/0/0	Handwoven cloth of cotton, w≤100g/m², containing≥85% by weight of cotton, of yarns of different colours
0/0/0	0	0	1/1	0/0/0	0/0	0/0/0	0/0/	0/0/0	9.1/0			0/0/0	Woven fabrics of cotton, plain weave, w≤100 g/m², containing≥85% by weight of cotton, of yarns of different colours
													--Plain weave, weighing more than 100 g/m²
0/0/0	0	0	1/1	0/0/0	0/6	0/0/0	0/0/0	9/9/9	9.1/9			0/0/0	Handwoven cloth of cotton, 100g/m²＜w≤200 g/m², containing≥85% by weight of cotton, of yarns of different colours
0/0/0	0	0	1/1	0/0/0	0/6	0/0/0	0/0/0	9/9/9	9.1/9			0/0/0	Woven fabrics of cotton, plain weave, 100g/m²＜w≤200g/m², containing≥85% by weight of cotton, of yarns of different colours
0/0/0	0	0	1/1	0/0/0	0/0	0/ /0	0/0/	0/0/0	9.1/0			0/0/0	--3-thread or 4-thread twill, including cross twill
													--Other fabrics
0/0/0	0	0	0/0	0/0/0	0/6	0/0/0	0/0/	0/0/0	9.1/0		0/0/0	0/0/0	Other woven fabrics of cotton, jacquard weave, w≤200g/m², containing≥85% by weight of cotton, of yarns of different colours
0/0/0	0	0	0/0	0/0/0	0/6	0/0/0	0/0/	0/0/0	9.1/0		0/0/0	0/0/0	Other woven fabrics of cotton, w≤200g/m², containing≥85% by weight of cotton, of yarns of different colours
													-Printed:
													--Plain weave, weighing not more than 100 g/m²
0/0/0	0	0	0/0	0/0/0	0/0	0/ /0	0/0/	0/0/0	9.1/0			0/0/0	Handwoven cloth of cotton, w≤100g/m², containing≥85% by weight of cotton, printed
0/0/0	0	0	0/0	0/0/0	0/0	0/ /0	0/0/	0/0/0	9.1/0			0/0/0	Poplin and fine plain cloth of cotton, w≤100g/m², containing≥85% by weight of cotton, printed
0/0/0	0	0	0/0	0/0/0	0/0	0/ /0	0/0/	0/0/0	9.1/0			0/0/0	Plain cloth of cotton, plain weave, w≤100g/m², ≤No. 68, printed
0/0/0	0	0	0/0	0/0/0	0/0	0/ /0	0/0/	0/0/0	9.1/0			0/0/0	Cheese cloth of cotton, plain weave, w≤100 g/m², containing≥85% by weight of cotton, printed
0/0/0	0	0	0/0	0/0/0	0/0	0/ /0	0/0/	0/0/0	9.1/0			0/0/0	Cloth for printing and dying of cotton, plain weave, w≤100g/m², No. 43～No. 68, printed
0/0/0	0	0	0/0	0/0/0	0/0	0/ /0	0/0/	0/0/0	9.1/0			0/0/0	Voiles and swiss muslin of cotton, w≤100g/m², ≥No. 69, printed
													--Plain weave, weighing more than 100 g/m²
0/0/0	0	6	0/0	0/0/0	0/0	0/0/0	0/0/	9.5/9.5/	/9.5			0/0/0	Handwoven cloth of cotton, 100g/m²＜w≤200 g/m², containing≥85% by weight of cotton, printed
0/0/0	0	6	0/0	0/0/0	0/0	0/0/0	0/0/	9.5/9.5/	/9.5			0/0/0	Poplin and fine plain cloth of cotton, 100g/m²＜w≤200g/m², containing≥85% by weight of cotton, printed
0/0/0	0	6	0/0	0/0/0	0/0	0/0/0	0/0/	9.5/9.5/	/9.5			0/0/0	Plain cloth of cotton, 100g/m²＜w≤200g/m², ≤No. 68 printed

税则号列	货品名称〔CIQ扩展编码及品名—T2表示见附表2〕	最惠(%)	暂定税率	普通	增值/消费	出口退税	计量单位	监管条件/特殊证件	检验检疫	对美关税	亚太上/下
5208.5200 93	印花的全棉平纹奶酪布(100g<每平方米重量≤200g,含棉量≥85%)〔999〕	8		70	13/	13	米/千克	/		33	5.2/5.2
5208.5200 94	印花的全棉平纹印染用布(100g<每平方米重量≤200g,43-68号)〔999〕	8		70	13/	13	米/千克	/		33	5.2/5.2
5208.5200 95	印花的全棉巴里纱及薄细布(100g<每平方米重量≤200g,69号及以上)〔999〕	8		70	13/	13	米/千克	/		33	5.2/5.2
	--其他机织物:										
5208.5910	---三线或四线斜纹机织物,包括双面斜纹机织物〔999〕	8		70	13/	13	米/千克	/			
5208.5990	---其他										
5208.5990 10	印花其他全棉机织缎布(每平方米重量≤200g,含棉量≥85%)〔999〕	8		70	13/	13	米/千克	/		33	5.2/5.2
5208.5990 20	印花其他全棉机织斜纹布(每平方米重量≤200g,含棉量≥85%)〔999〕	8		70	13/	13	米/千克	/		33	5.2/5.2
5208.5990 30	印花其他全棉机织牛津布(每平方米重量≤200g,含棉量≥85%)〔999〕	8		70	13/	13	米/千克	/		33	5.2/5.2
5208.5990 90	印花其他全棉机织物(每平方米重量≤200g,含棉量≥85%)〔999〕	8		70	13/	13	米/千克	/		33	5.2/5.2
52.09	**棉机织物,按重量计含棉量在85%及以上,每平方米重量超过200克:**										
	-未漂白:										
5209.1100	--平纹机织物〔999〕	8		70	13/	13	米/千克	/		33	
5209.1200	--三线或四线斜纹机织物,包括双面斜纹机织物〔999〕	8		70	13/	13	米/千克	/		33	5.2/5.2
5209.1900	--其他机织物〔999〕	8		70	13/	13	米/千克	/		33	
	-漂白:										
5209.2100	--平纹机织物〔999〕	8		70	13/	13	米/千克	/		33	
5209.2200	--三线或四线斜纹机织物,包括双面斜纹机织物〔999〕	8		70	13/	13	米/千克	/		33	
5209.2900	--其他机织物〔999〕	8		70	13/	13	米/千克	/		33	
	-染色:										
5209.3100	--平纹机织物										
5209.3100 10	染色全棉手工织布(指每平方米重量>200克,含棉量≥85%)〔999〕	8		70	13/	13	米/千克	/		33	5.2/5.2
5209.3100 91	染色全棉平纹府绸及细平布(指每平方米重量>200克,含棉量≥85%)〔999〕	8		70	13/	13	米/千克	/		33	5.2/5.2
5209.3100 92	染色的全棉平纹机织平布(指每平方米重量>200克,含棉量≥85%)〔999〕	8		70	13/	13	米/千克	/		33	5.2/5.2
5209.3100 93	染色的全棉平纹机织帆布(指每平方米重量>200克,含棉量≥85%)〔999〕	8		70	13/	13	米/千克	/		33	5.2/5.2
5209.3200	--三线或四线斜纹机织物,包括双面斜纹机织物〔999〕	8		70	13/	13	米/千克	/		33	5.2/5.2
5209.3900	--其他机织物										
5209.3900 10	染色的其他全棉机织缎布(指每平方米重量>200克,含棉量≥85%)〔999〕	8		70	13/	13	米/千克	/		33	5.2/5.2
5209.3900 20	染色的其他全棉机织斜纹布(指每平方米重量>200克,含棉量≥85%)〔999〕	8		70	13/	13	米/千克	/		33	5.2/5.2
5209.3900 30	染色的其他全棉机织帆布(指每平方米重量>200克,含棉量≥85%)〔999〕	8		70	13/	13	米/千克	/		33	5.2/5.2
5209.3900 90	染色的其他全棉机织物(指每平方米重量>200克,含棉量≥85%)〔999〕	8		70	13/	13	米/千克	/		33	5.2/5.2
	-色织:										
5209.4100	--平纹机织物										
5209.4100 10	色织的全棉手工织布(指每平方米重量>200克,含棉量≥85%)〔999〕	8		70	13/	13	米/千克	/		33	
5209.4100 90	色织的全棉平纹机织物(指每平方米重量>200克,含棉量≥85%)〔999〕	8		70	13/	13	米/千克	/		33	
5209.4200	--粗斜纹布(劳动布)										
5209.4200 10	色织全棉蓝粗斜纹布(劳动布)(指每平方米重量>200克,含棉量≥85%)〔999〕	8		70	13/	13	米/千克	/		33	5.2/5.2
5209.4200 90	色织其他全棉粗斜纹布(劳动布)(指每平方米重量>200克,含棉量≥85%)〔999〕	8		70	13/	13	米/千克	/		33	5.2/5.2
5209.4300	--其他三线或四线斜纹机织物,包括双面斜纹机织物〔999〕	8		70	13/	13	米/千克	/		33	5.2/5.2
5209.4900	--其他机织物										
5209.4900 10	色织的其他全棉提花机织物(指每平方米重量>200克,含棉量≥85%)〔999〕	8		70	13/	13	米/千克	/		33	
5209.4900 90	色织的其他全棉机织物(指每平方米重量>200克,含棉量≥85%)〔999〕	8		70	13/	13	米/千克	/		33	
	-印花:										
5209.5100	--平纹机织物										
5209.5100 10	印花全棉手工织布(指每平方米重量>200克,含棉量≥85%)〔999〕	8		70	13/	13	米/千克	/		33	5.2/5.2
5209.5100 91	印花全棉平纹府绸及细平布(指每平方米重量>200克,含棉量≥85%)〔999〕	8		70	13/	13	米/千克	/		33	5.2/5.2

协定税率 %								RCEP		特惠税率 %			Article Description
东/冰/格	巴基斯坦	韩国	瑞士上/下	哥/秘/柬	澳/毛	新西/坡/智	中国港/澳/台	东盟及马来/澳/韩	日/新	亚太2国	老/柬/缅	98/97/95	
0/0/0	0	6	0/0	0/0/0	0/0	0/0/0	0/0/	9.5/9.5/	/9.5			0/0/0	Cheese cloth of cotton, plain weave, 100g/m² < w≤200g/m², containing≥85% by weight of cotton, printed
0/0/0	0	6	0/0	0/0/0	0/0	0/0/0	0/0/	9.5/9.5/	/9.5			0/0/0	Cloth for printing and dying of cotton, plain weave, 100g/m² <w≤200g/m², No. 43~No. 68, printed
0/0/0	0	6	0/0	0/0/0	0/0	0/0/0	0/0/	9.5/9.5/	/9.5			0/0/0	Voiles and swiss muslin of cotton 100g/m²<w≤200g/m², ≥No. 69, printed
													--Other fabrics:
0/0/0	0	0	0/0	0/0/0	0/0	0//0	0/0/	0/0/0	9.1/0			0/0/0	---3-thread or 4-thread twill, including cross twill
													---Other
0/0/0	0	0	0/0	0/0/0	0/0	0//0	0/0/0	0/0/0	9.1/0			0/0/0	Woven fabrics of cotton, satin weave, w≤200g/m² containing ≥85% by weight of cotton, printed
0/0/0	0	0	0/0	0/0/0	0/0	0//0	0/0/0	0/0/0	9.1/0			0/0/0	Woven fabrics of cotton, twill weave, w≤200 g/m², containing≥85% by weight of cotton, printed
0/0/0	0	0	0/0	0/0/0	0/0	0//0	0/0/0	0/0/0	9.1/0			0/0/0	Woven fabrics of cotton, oxford weave w≤200 g/m², containing≥85% by weight of cotton, printed
0/0/0	0	0	0/0	0/0/0	0/0	0//0	0/0/0	0/0/0	9.1/0			0/0/0	Other woven fabrics of cotton, w≤200g/m², containing≥ 85% by weight of cotton, printed
													Woven fabrics of cotton, containing 85% or more by weight of cotton, weighing more than 200 g/m²:
													-Unbleached:
5/0/0	0	6	0/0	0//0	0/0	0//0	0/0/	9.8/9.8/	/9.8			0/0/0	--Plain weave
0/0/0	0	0	0/0	0/0/0	0/0	0/0/0	0/0/	0/0/0	9.1/0			0/0/0	--3-thread or 4-thread twill, including cross twill
0/0/0	0	0	0/0	0/0/0	0/0	0/0/0	0/0/	0/0/0	9.1/0			0/0/0	--Other fabrics
													-Bleached:
0/0/0	0	0	1.2/1.2	0/0/0	0/0	0/0/0	0/0/	0/0/0	10.9/0			0/0/0	--Plain weave
0/0/0	0	0	1.2/1.2	0/0/0	0/0	0/0/0	0/0/	0/0/0	10.9/0			0/0/0	--3-thread or 4-thread twill, including cross twill
0/0/0	0	0	1.2/1.2	0/0/0	0/0	0/0/0	0/0/	0/0/0	10.9/0			0/0/0	--Other fabrics
													-Dyed:
													--Plain weave
0/0/0	0	0	0/0	0/0/0	0/0	0/0/0	0/0/0	0/0/0	9.1/0		0/0/0	0/0/0	Handwoven cloth of cotton, w>200g/m², containing≥85% by weight of cotton, dyed
0/0/0	0	0	0/0	0/0/0	0/0	0/0/0	0/0/0	0/0/0	9.1/0		0/0/0	0/0/0	Poplin and fine plain cloth of cotton, w>200g/m², containing ≥85% by weight of cotton, dyed
0/0/0	0	0	0/0	0/0/0	0/0	0/0/0	0/0/0	0/0/0	9.1/0		0/0/0	0/0/0	Plain cloth of cotton, w>200g/m², containing≥85% by weight of cotton, dyed
0/0/0	0	0	0/0	0/0/0	0/0	0/0/0	0/0/0	0/0/0	9.1/0		0/0/0	0/0/0	Woven canvas of cotton, plain weave, w>200 g/m², containing≥85% by weight of cotton, dyed
0/0/0	0	0	0/0	0/0/0	0/0	0/0/0	0/0/0	0/0/0	9.1/0		0/0/0	0/0/0	--3-thread or 4-thread twill, including cross twill
													--Other fabrics
0/0/0	0	0	0/0	0/0/0	0/0	0/0/0	0/0/0	9/9/9	9.1/9		0/0/0	0/0/0	Other woven fabrics of cotton, satin weave, w>200 g/m², containing≥85% by weight of cotton, dyed
0/0/0	0	0	0/0	0/0/0	0/0	0/0/0	0/0/0	9/9/9	9.1/9		0/0/0	0/0/0	Other woven fabrics of cotton, twill weave, w>200 g/m², containing≥85% by weight of cotton, dyed
0/0/0	0	0	0/0	0/0/0	0/0	0/0/0	0/0/0	9/9/9	9.1/9		0/0/0	0/0/0	Other woren canvas of cotton, w>200g/m², containing≥ 85% by weight of cotton, dyed
0/0/0	0	0	0/0	0/0/0	0/0	0/0/0	0/0/0	9/9/9	9.1/9		0/0/0	0/0/0	Other woven fabrics of cotton, w>200g/m², containing≥ 85% by weight of cotton, dyed
													-Of yarns of different colours:
													--Plain weave
0/0/0	0	0	0/0	0/0/0	0/0	0/0/0	0/0/0	0/0/0	9.1/0			0/0/0	Handwoven cloth of cotton, w>200g/m² containing≥85% by weight of cotton, of yarns of different colours
0/0/0	0	0	0/0	0/0/0	0/0	0/0/0	0/0/0	0/0/0	9.1/0			0/0/0	Woven fabrics of cotton, plain weave, w>200g/m², containing≥85% by weight of cotton, of yarns of different colours
													--Denim
0/0/0	0	0	0/0	0/0/0	0/0	0/0/0	0/0/0	9/9/9	9.1/9		0/0/0	0/0/0	Blue denim of cotton, w>200g/m², containing≥85% by weight of cotton, of yarns of different colours
0/0/0	0	0	0/0	0/0/0	0/0	0/0/0	0/0/0	9/9/9	9.1/9		0/0/0	0/0/0	Other denim of cotton, w>200g/m², containing≥85% by weight of cotton, of yarns of different colours
0/0/0	0	0	0/0	0/0/0	0/0	0//0	0/0/	0/0/0	9.1/0			0/0/0	--Other fabrics of 3-thread or 4-thread twill, including cross twill
													--Other fabrics
0/0/0	0	4.6	0/0	0/0/0	0/0	0/0/0	0/0/	9.3/9.5/9.3	9.4/9.5			0/0/0	Other woven fabrics of cotton, jacquad weave, w>200g/m², containing≥85% by weight of cotton, of yarns of different colours
0/0/0	0	4.6	0/0	0/0/0	0/0	0/0/0	0/0/	9.3/9.5/9.3	9.4/9.5			0/0/0	Other woven fabrics of cotton, w>200g/m², containing≥ 85% by weight of cotton, of yarns of different colours
													-Printed:
													--Plain weave
0/0/0	0	0	0/0	0/0/0	0/0	0/0/0	0/0/	0/0/0	9.1/0			0/0/0	Handwoven cloth of cotton, w>200g/m², containing≥85% by weight of cotton, printed
0/0/0	0	0	0/0	0/0/0	0/0	0/0/0	0/0/	0/0/0	9.1/0			0/0/0	Poplin and fine plain cloth of cotton, w>200g/m², containing≥85% by weight of cotton, printed

税则号列	货品名称〔CIQ扩展编码及品名－T2表示见附表2〕	最惠(%)	暂定税率	普通	增值/消费	出口退税	计量单位	监管条件/特殊证件	检验检疫	对美关税	亚太上/下
5209.5100 92	印花全棉平纹机织平布(指每平方米重量＞200克,含棉量≥85%)〔999〕	8		70	13/	13	米/千克	/		33	5.2/5.2
5209.5100 93	印花全棉平纹机织帆布(指每平方米重量＞200克,含棉量≥85%)〔999〕	8		70	13/	13	米/千克	/		33	5.2/5.2
5209.5200	--三线或四线斜纹机织物,包括双面斜纹机织物〔999〕	8		70	13/	13	米/千克	/			
5209.5900	--其他机织物										
5209.5900 10	印花的其他全棉机织缎布(指每平方米重量＞200克,含棉量≥85%)〔999〕	8		70	13/	13	米/千克	/		33	5.2/5.2
5209.5900 20	印花的其他全棉机织斜纹布(指每平方米重量＞200克,含棉量≥85%)〔999〕	8		70	13/	13	米/千克	/		33	5.2/5.2
5209.5900 30	印花的其他全棉机织帆布(指每平方米重量＞200克,含棉量≥85%)〔999〕	8		70	13/	13	米/千克	/		33	5.2/5.2
5209.5900 90	印花的其他全棉机织物(指每平方米重量＞200克,含棉量≥85%)〔999〕	8		70	13/	13	米/千克	/		33	5.2/5.2
52.10	**棉机织物,按重量计含棉量在85%以下,主要或仅与化学纤维混纺,每平方米重量不超过200克:**										
	-未漂白:										
5210.1100	--平纹机织物										
5210.1100 11	未漂白与聚酯短纤混纺的棉制府绸(指每平方米重量≤200克,含棉量＜85%,含平细布)〔999〕	8	6	90	13/	13	米/千克	/		31	5.2/5.2
5210.1100 12	未漂白与聚酯短纤混纺棉机织平布(指每平方米重量≤200克,68号及以下,含棉量＜85%)〔999〕	8	6	90	13/	13	米/千克	/		31	5.2/5.2
5210.1100 13	未漂白与聚酯短纤混纺棉奶酪布(指每平方米重量≤200克,含棉量＜85%)〔999〕	8	6	90	13/	13	米/千克	/		31	5.2/5.2
5210.1100 14	未漂白与聚酯短纤混纺棉印染用布(指每平方米重量≤200克,43－68号,含棉量＜85%)〔999〕	8	6	90	13/	13	米/千克	/		31	5.2/5.2
5210.1100 15	未漂白与聚酯短纤混纺棉巴里纱(指每平方米重量≤200克,69号及以上,含棉量＜85%,含薄细布)〔999〕	8	6	90	13/	13	米/千克	/		31	5.2/5.2
5210.1100 91	未漂白与其他化纤混纺棉府绸(指每平方米重量≤200克,含棉量＜85%,含细平布)〔999〕	8	6	90	13/	13	米/千克	/		31	5.2/5.2
5210.1100 92	未漂白与其他化纤混纺棉机织平布(指每平方米重量≤200克,≤68号,含棉量＜85%)〔999〕	8	6	90	13/	13	米/千克	/		31	5.2/5.2
5210.1100 93	未漂白与其他化纤混纺棉奶酪布(指每平方米重量≤200克,含棉量＜85%)〔999〕	8	6	90	13/	13	米/千克	/		31	5.2/5.2
5210.1100 94	未漂白与其他化纤混纺棉印染用布(指每平方米重量≤200克,43－68号,含棉量＜85%)〔999〕	8	6	90	13/	13	米/千克	/		31	5.2/5.2
5210.1100 95	未漂白与其他化纤混纺棉巴里纱(指每平方米重量≤200克,69号及以上,含棉量＜85%,含薄细布)〔999〕	8	6	90	13/	13	米/千克	/		31	5.2/5.2
	--其他机织物:										
5210.1910	---三线或四线斜纹机织物,包括双面斜纹机织物〔999〕	8		90	13/	13	米/千克	/			4.8/4.8
5210.1990	---其他										
5210.1990 11	其他未漂白与聚酯短纤混纺的缎布(每平方米重量≤200克,含棉量＜85%)〔999〕	8	6	90	13/	13	米/千克	/		31	
5210.1990 12	其他未漂白与聚酯短纤混纺斜纹布(每平方米重量≤200克,含棉量＜85%)〔999〕	8	6	90	13/	13	米/千克	/		31	
5210.1990 13	其他未漂白与聚酯短纤混纺牛津布(每平方米重量≤200克,含棉量＜85%)〔999〕	8	6	90	13/	13	米/千克	/		31	
5210.1990 19	其他未漂白与聚酯短纤混纺棉布(每平方米重量≤200克,含棉量＜85%)〔999〕	8	6	90	13/	13	米/千克	/		31	
5210.1990 91	其他未漂白与其他化纤混纺缎布(每平方米重量≤200克,含棉量＜85%)〔999〕	8	6	90	13/	13	米/千克	/		31	
5210.1990 92	其他未漂白与其他化纤混纺斜纹布(每平方米重量≤200克,含棉量＜85%)〔999〕	8	6	90	13/	13	米/千克	/		31	

协定税率 %								RCEP		特惠税率 %			Article Description
东/冰/格	巴基斯坦	韩国	瑞士 上/下	哥/秘/柬	澳/毛	新西/坡/智	中国港/澳/台	东盟及马来/澳/韩	日/新	亚太2国	老/柬/缅	98/97/95	
0/0/0	0	0	0/0	0/0/0	0/0	0/0/0	0/0/	0/0/0	9.1/0			0/0/0	Plain cloth of cotton, w>200g/m^2, containing≥85% by weight of cotton, printed
0/0/0	0	0	0/0	0/0/0	0/0	0/0/0	0/0/	0/0/0	9.1/0			0/0/0	Woven canvas of cotton, plain weave, w>200g/m^2, containing≥85% by weight of cotton, printed
0/0/0	0	0	0/0	0/0/0	0/0	0//0	0/0/	0/0/0	9.1/0			0/0/0	--3-thread or 4-thread twill, including cross twill
													--Other fabrics
0/0/0	0	0	0/0	0/0/0	0/0	0//0	0/0/	0/0/0	9.1/0			0/0/0	Other woven fabrics of cotton, satin weave, w>200 g/m^2, containing≥85% by weight of cotton, printed
0/0/0	0	0	0/0	0/0/0	0/0	0//0	0/0/	0/0/0	9.1/0			0/0/0	Other woven fabrics of cotton, twill weave, w>200 g/m^2, containing≥85% by weight of cotton, printed
0/0/0	0	0	0/0	0/0/0	0/0	0//0	0/0/	0/0/0	9.1/0			0/0/0	Otver canvas of cotton, w>200g/m^2, containing≥85% by weight of cotton, printed
0/0/0	0	0	0/0	0/0/0	0/0	0//0	0/0/	0/0/0	9.1/0			0/0/0	Other woven fabrics of cotton, w>200g/m^2, containing≥85% by weight of cotton, printed
													Woven fabrics of cotton, containing less than 85% by weight of cotton, mixed mainly or solely with man-made fibres, weighing not more than 200 g/m^2:
													-Unbleached:
													--Plain weave
0/0/0	0	0	1.2/1.2	0/0/0	0/0	0/0/0	0/0/	0/0/0	10.9/0			0/0/0	Poplin and fine plain cloth of cotton, mixed with polyester staple fibres, w≤200g/m^2, containing<85% by weight of cotton, unbleached
0/0/0	0	0	1.2/1.2	0/0/0	0/0	0/0/0	0/0/	0/0/0	10.9/0			0/0/0	Plain cloth of cotton, mixed with polyester staple fibres, w≤200g/m^2, ≤No. 68, containing<85% by weight of cotton, unbleached
0/0/0	0	0	1.2/1.2	0/0/0	0/0	0/0/0	0/0/	0/0/0	10.9/0			0/0/0	Cheese cloth of cotton, plain weave, mixed with polyester staple fibres, w≤200g/m^2, containing<85% by weight of cotton, unbleached
0/0/0	0	0	1.2/1.2	0/0/0	0/0	0/0/0	0/0/	0/0/0	10.9/0			0/0/0	Cloth for printing and dying of cotton, plain weave, mixed with polyester staple fibres, w≤200g/m^2, No. 43～No. 68, containing<85% by weight of cotton, unbleached
0/0/0	0	0	1.2/1.2	0/0/0	0/0	0/0/0	0/0/	0/0/0	10.9/0			0/0/0	Voiles and swiss muslin of cotton, plain weave, mixed with polyester staple fibres, w≤200g/m^2, containing<85% by weight of cotton, unbleached
0/0/0	0	0	1.2/1.2	0/0/0	0/0	0/0/0	0/0/	0/0/0	10.9/0			0/0/0	Poplin and fine plain cloth of cotton, mixed with other man-made fibres, w≤200g/m^2, containing<85% by weight of cotton, unbleached
0/0/0	0	0	1.2/1.2	0/0/0	0/0	0/0/0	0/0/	0/0/0	10.9/0			0/0/0	Plain cloth of cotton, mixed with other man-made fibres, w≤200g/m^2, ≤No. 68, containing<85% by weight of cotton, unbleached
0/0/0	0	0	1.2/1.2	0/0/0	0/0	0/0/0	0/0/	0/0/0	10.9/0			0/0/0	Cheese cloth of cotton, plain weave, mixed with other man-made fibres, w≤200g/m^2, containing<85% by weight of cotton, unbleached
0/0/0	0	0	1.2/1.2	0/0/0	0/0	0/0/0	0/0/	0/0/0	10.9/0			0/0/0	Cloth for printing and dying of cotton, plain weave, mixed with other man-made fibres, w≤200g/m^2, No. 43～No. 68, containing<85% by weight of cotton, unbleached
0/0/0	0	0	1.2/1.2	0/0/0	0/0	0/0/0	0/0/	0/0/0	10.9/0			0/0/0	Voiles and swiss muslin of cotton, mixed with man-made fibres, w≤200g/m^2, containing <85% by weight of cotton, ≥No. 69, unbleached
													--Other fabrics:
0/0/0	0	0	1.2/1.2	0/0/0	0/0	0/0/0	0/0/	0/0/0	10.9/0			0/0/0	---3-thread or 4-thread twill, including cross twill
													---Other
0/0/0	0	0	1.2/1.2	0/0/0	0/0	0/0/0	0/0/	0/0/0	10.9/0			0/0/0	Other woven fabrics of cotton, satin weave, mixed with polyester staple fibres, w≤200g/m^2, containing<85% by weight of cotton, unbleached
0/0/0	0	0	1.2/1.2	0/0/0	0/0	0/0/0	0/0/	0/0/0	10.9/0			0/0/0	Other woven fabrics of cotton, twill weave, mixed with polyester staple fibres, w≤200g/m^2, containing<85% by weight of cotton, unbleached
0/0/0	0	0	1.2/1.2	0/0/0	0/0	0/0/0	0/0/	0/0/0	10.9/0			0/0/0	Other woven fabrics of cotton, oxford weave, mixed with polyester staple fibres, w ≤ 200g/m^2, containing < 85% by weight of cotton, unbleached
0/0/0	0	0	1.2/1.2	0/0/0	0/0	0/0/0	0/0/	0/0/0	10.9/0			0/0/0	Other woven fabrics of cotton, mixed with polyester staple fibres, w≤200g/m^2, containing<85% by weight of cotton, unbleached
0/0/0	0	0	1.2/1.2	0/0/0	0/0	0/0/0	0/0/	0/0/0	10.9/0			0/0/0	Other woven of cotton, stain weave, mixed with other man-made fibres, w ≤ 200g/m^2, containing < 85% by weight of cotton, unbleached
0/0/0	0	0	1.2/1.2	0/0/0	0/0	0/0/0	0/0/	0/0/0	10.9/0			0/0/0	Other woven fabrics of cotton, twill weave, mixed with other man-made fibres, w≤200 g/m^2, containing<85% by weight of cotton, unbleached

税则号列	货品名称〔CIQ 扩展编码及品名－T2 表示见附表 2〕	最惠(%)	暂定税率	普通	增值/消费	出口退税	计量单位	监管条件/特殊证件	检验检疫	对美关税	亚太上/下
5210.1990 93	其他未漂白与其他化纤混纺的牛津布(每平方米重量≤200克,含棉量<85%)〔999〕	8	6	90	13/	13	米/千克	/		31	
5210.1990 99	其他未漂白与其他化纤混纺棉布(每平方米重量≤200克,含棉量<85%)〔999〕	8	6	90	13/	13	米/千克	/		31	
	-漂白:										
5210.2100	--平纹机织物〔999〕	8		90	13/	13	米/千克	/			
	--其他机织物:										
5210.2910	---三线或四线斜纹机织物,包括双面斜纹机织物〔999〕	8		90	13/	13	米/千克	/			
5210.2990	---其他〔999〕	8		90	13/	13	米/千克	/			
	-染色:										
5210.3100	--平纹机织物〔999〕	8		90	13/	13	米/千克	/		33	5.2/5.2
5210.3200	--三线或四线斜纹机织物,包括双面斜纹机织物〔999〕	8		90	13/	13	米/千克	/		33	5.2/5.2
5210.3900	--其他机织物〔999〕	8		90	13/	13	米/千克	/		33	5.2/5.2
	-色织:										
5210.4100	--平纹机织物〔999〕	8		90	13/	13	米/千克	/		33	
	--其他机织物:										
5210.4910	---三线或四线斜纹机织物,包括双面斜纹机织物〔999〕	8		90	13/	13	米/千克	/		33	
5210.4990	---其他〔999〕	8		90	13/	13	米/千克	/		33	
	-印花:										
5210.5100	--平纹机织物〔999〕	8		90	13/	13	米/千克	/		33	
	--其他机织物:										
5210.5910	---三线或四线斜纹机织物,包括双面斜纹机织物〔999〕	8		90	13/	13	米/千克	/			
5210.5990	---其他〔999〕	8		90	13/	13	米/千克	/		33	
52.11	**棉机织物,按重量计含棉量在85%以下,主要或仅与化学纤维混纺,每平方米重量超过200克:**										
	-未漂白:										
5211.1100	--平纹机织物										
5211.1100 11	未漂白与聚酯短纤混纺棉府绸(每平方米重量>200克,含棉量<85%,含细平布)〔999〕	8	6	90	13/	13	米/千克	/		31	
5211.1100 12	未漂白与聚酯短纤混纺棉机织平布(每平方米重量>200克,含棉量<85%)〔999〕	8	6	90	13/	13	米/千克	/		31	
5211.1100 19	未漂白与聚酯短纤混纺棉平纹帆布(每平方米重量>200克,含棉量<85%)〔999〕	8	6	90	13/	13	米/千克	/		31	
5211.1100 91	未漂白与其他化纤混纺棉府绸(每平方米重量>200克,含棉量<85%,含细平布)〔999〕	8	6	90	13/	13	米/千克	/		31	
5211.1100 92	未漂白与其他化纤混纺棉机织平布(每平方米重量>200克,含棉量<85%)〔999〕	8	6	90	13/	13	米/千克	/		31	
5211.1100 99	未漂白与其他化纤混纺棉平纹帆布(每平方米重量>200克,含棉量<85%)〔999〕	8	6	90	13/	13	米/千克	/		31	
5211.1200	--三线或四线斜纹机织物,包括双面斜纹机织物										
5211.1200 10	未漂白聚酯短纤混纺斜纹棉布(每平方米重量>200克,含棉量<85%,三、四线斜纹布,双面斜纹布)〔999〕	8	6	90	13/	13	米/千克	/		31	
5211.1200 90	未漂白其他化纤混纺斜纹棉布(每平方米重量>200克,含棉量<85%,三、四线斜纹布,双面斜纹布)〔999〕	8	6	90	13/	13	米/千克	/		31	
5211.1900	--其他机织物〔999〕	8		90	13/	13	米/千克	/			
5211.2000	-漂白〔999〕	8		90	13/	13	米/千克	/		33	
	-染色:										
5211.3100	--平纹机织物〔999〕	8		90	13/	13	米/千克	/		33	6.8/6.8
5211.3200	--三线或四线斜纹机织物,包括双面斜纹机织物〔999〕	8		90	13/	13	米/千克	/		33	5.2/5.2
5211.3900	--其他机织物〔999〕	8		90	13/	13	米/千克	/		33	5.2/5.2
	-色织:										
5211.4100	--平纹机织物〔999〕	8		90	13/	13	米/千克	/		33	
5211.4200	--粗斜纹布(劳动布)										
5211.4200 10	色织与化纤混纺蓝色粗斜纹棉布(每平方米重量超过200克,含棉量<85%)〔999〕	8		90	13/	13	米/千克	/		33	
5211.4200 90	色织与化学纤维混纺非蓝色粗斜纹棉布(每平方米重量超过200克,含棉量<85%)〔999〕	8		90	13/	13	米/千克	/		33	
5211.4300	--其他三线或四线斜纹机织物,包括双面斜纹机织物〔999〕	8		90	13/	13	米/千克	/		33	
5211.4900	--其他机织物〔999〕	8		90	13/	13	米/千克	/		33	

协定税率 %								RCEP		特惠税率 %			Article Description
东/冰/格	巴基斯坦	韩国	瑞士 上/下	哥/秘/柬	澳/毛	新西/坡/智	中国港/澳/台	东盟及马来/澳/韩	日/新	亚太2国	老/柬/缅	98/97/95	
0/0/0	0	0	1.2/1.2	0/0/0	0/0	0/0/0	0/0/	0/0/0	10.9/0			0/0/0	Other woven fabrics of cotton, oxford weave, mixed with other man-made fibres, w≤200g/m², by weight of cotton, unbleached
0/0/0	0	0	1.2/1.2	0/0/0	0/0	0/0/0	0/0/	0/0/0	10.9/0			0/0/0	Other woven fabrics of cotton, mixed with other man-made fibres. w≤200g/m², containing<85% by weight of cotton, unbleached
													-Bleached:
0/0/0	0	2.8	1.4/1.4	0/0/0	0/0	0/0/0	0/0/	0/0/12.6	12.7/0			0/0/0	--Plain weave
													--Other fabrics:
0/0/0	0	2.8	1.4/1.4	0/0/0	0/0	0/0/0	0/0/	0/0/12.6	12.7/0			0/0/0	---3-thread or 4-thread twill, including cross twill
0/0/0	0	2.8	1.4/1.4	0/0/0	0/0	0/0/0	0/0/	0/0/12.6	12.7/0			0/0/0	---Other
													-Dyed:
0/0/0	0	6	0/0	0/0/0	0/0	0/0/0	0/0/0	9.5/9.5/	/9.5			0/0/0	--Plain weave
0/0/0	0	0	0/0	0/0/0	0/0	0/0/0	0/0/	0/0/0	9.1/0			0/0/0	--3-thread or 4-thread twill, including cross twill
0/0/0	0	4.6	0/0	0/0/0	0/0	0/0/0	0/0/0	9.3/9.5/9.3	9.4/9.5			0/0/0	--Other fabrics
													-Of yarns of different colours:
0/0/0	0	0	0/0	0/0/0	0/0	0/0/0	0/0/0	0/0/0	9.1/0			0/0/0	--Plain weave
													--Other fabrics:
0/0/0	0	0	0/0	0/0/0	0/0	0/0/0	0/0/	0/0/0	9.1/0			0/0/0	---3-thread or 4-thread twill, including cross twill, including double twill
0/0/0	0	0	0/0	0/0/0	0/0	0/0/0	0/0/0	0/0/0	9.1/0			0/0/0	---Other
													-Printed:
0/0/0	0	0	0/0	0/0/0	0/0	0//0	0/0/	0/0/0	9.1/0			0/0/0	--Plain weave
													--Other fabrics:
0/0/0	0	0	0/0	0/0/0	0/0	0//0	0/0/	0/0/0	9.1/0			0/0/0	---3-thread or 4-thread twill, including cross twill
0/0/0	0	0	0/0	0/0/0	0/0	0//0	0/0/	0/0/0	9.1/0			0/0/0	---Other
													Woven fabrics of cotton, containing less than 85% by weight of cotton, mixed mainly or solely with man-made fibres, weighing more than 200 g/m²:
													-Unbleached:
													--Plain weave
0/0/0	0	5.6	1.2/1.2	0/0/0	0/0	0/0/0	0/0/	11.4/11.4/	/11.4			0/0/0	Poplin and fine plain cloth of cotton, mixed with polyester staple fibres, w>200g/m², containing<85% by weight of cotton, unbleached
0/0/0	0	5.6	1.2/1.2	0/0/0	0/0	0/0/0	0/0/	11.4/11.4/	/11.4			0/0/0	Plain cloth of cotton, mixed with polyester staple fibres, w>200g/m², containing<85% by weight of cotton, unbleached
0/0/0	0	5.6	1.2/1.2	0/0/0	0/0	0/0/0	0/0/	11.4/11.4/	/11.4			0/0/0	Canvas of cotton, mixed with polyester staple fibres, plain weave, w>200g/m², containing<85% by weight of cotton, unbleached
0/0/0	0	5.6	1.2/1.2	0/0/0	0/0	0/0/0	0/0/	11.4/11.4/	/11.4			0/0/0	Poplin and fine plain cloth of cotton, mixed with other man-made fibres, w>200g/m², containing<85% by weight of cotton, unbleached
0/0/0	0	5.6	1.2/1.2	0/0/0	0/0	0/0/0	0/0/	11.4/11.4/	/11.4			0/0/0	Plain cloth of cotton, mixed with other man-made fibres, w>200g/m², containing<85% by weight of cotton, unbleached
0/0/0	0	5.6	1.2/1.2	0/0/0	0/0	0/0/0	0/0/	11.4/11.4/	/11.4			0/0/0	Canvas of cotton, mixed with other man made fibres, plain weave, w>200g/m², containing<85% by weight of cotton, unbleached
													--3-thread or 4-thread twill, including cross twill
0/0/0	0	0	1.2/1.2	0/0/0	0/0	0/0/0	0/0/	0/0/0	10.9/0			0/0/0	Woven fabrics of cotton, twill weave (3-or 4-thread), mixed with polyester staple fibres, w>200g/m², containing<85% by weight of cotton, unbleached
0/0/0	0	0	1.2/1.2	0/0/0	0/0	0/0/0	0/0/	0/0/0	10.9/0			0/0/0	Woven fabrics of cotton, twill weave (3-or 4-thread), mixed with other man-made fibres, w>200g/m², containing<85% by weight of cotton, unbleached
0/0/0	0	0	1.2/1.2	0/0/0	0/0	0/0/0	0/0/	0/0/0	10.9/0			0/0/0	--Other fabrics
0/0/0	0	2.8	1.4/1.4	0/0/0	0/0	0/0/0	0/0/	0/0/12.6	12.7/0			0/0/0	-Bleached
													-Dyed:
0/0/0	0	8.5	0/0	0/0/0	0/0	0/0/0	0/0/	9.5/9.5/	/9.5			0/0/0	--Plain weave
0/0/0	0	0	0/0	0/0/0	0/0	0/0/0	0/0/	0/0/0	9.1/0			0/0/0	--3-thread or 4-thread twill, including cross twill
0/0/0	0	4.6	0/0	0/0/0	0/0	0/0/0	0/0/0	9.3/9.5/9.3	9.4/9.5			0/0/0	--Other fabrics
													-Of yarns of different colours:
0/0/0	0	0	0/0	0/0/0	0/0	0//0	0/0/	0/0/0	9.1/0			0/0/0	--Plain weave
													--Denim
0/0/0	0	0	0/0	0/0/0	0/0	0/0/0	0/0/	9/9/9	9.1/9			0/0/0	Blue denim of cotton, mixed with other man-made fibres, w>200g/m², containing<85% by weight of cotton, of yarns of different colours
0/0/0	0	0	0/0	0/0/0	0/0	0/0/0	0/0/	9/9/9	9.1/9			0/0/0	Denim of cotton, other than blue, w>200g/m², containing<85% by weight of cotton, of yarns of different colours
0/0/0	0	0	0/0	0/0/0	0/0	0//0	0/0/	0/0/0	9.1/0			0/0/0	--Other fabrics of 3-thread or 4-thread twill, including cross twill
0/0/0	0	4.6	0/0	0/0/0	0/0	0/0/0	0/0/	9.3/9.5/9.3	9.4/9.5			0/0/0	--Other fabrics

税则号列	货品名称〔CIQ 扩展编码及品名—T2 表示见附表 2〕	最惠(%)	暂定税率	普通	增值/消费	出口退税	计量单位	监管条件/特殊证件	检验检疫	对美关税	亚太上/下
	-印花:										
5211.5100	--平纹机织物〔999〕	8		90	13/	13	米/千克	/		33	
5211.5200	--三线或四线斜纹机织物,包括双面斜纹机织物〔999〕	8		90	13/	13	米/千克	/		28	
5211.5900	--其他机织物〔999〕	8		90	13/	13	米/千克	/		18	5.2/5.2
52.12	**其他棉机织物:**										
	-每平方米重量不超过 200 克:										
5212.1100	--未漂白〔999〕	8		80	13/	13	米/千克	/			
5212.1200	--漂白〔999〕	8		80	13/	13	米/千克	/		13	
5212.1300	--染色〔999〕	8		80	13/	13	米/千克	/		33	
5212.1400	--色织〔999〕	8		80	13/	13	米/千克	/		33	
5212.1500	--印花〔999〕	8		80	13/	13	米/千克	/		33	
	-每平方米重量超过 200 克:										
5212.2100	--未漂白										
5212.2100 11	未漂白其他混纺棉布(每平方米重量>200 克,与 36%及以上精梳羊毛/动物细毛混纺)〔999〕	8	6	80	13/	13	米/千克	/		31	
5212.2100 19	未漂白其他混纺棉布(每平方米重量>200 克,与 36%及以下精梳羊毛/动物细毛混纺)〔999〕	8	6	80	13/	13	米/千克	/		31	
5212.2100 21	未漂白其他混纺棉布(每平方米重量>200 克,与 36%及以上其他羊毛/动物细毛混纺)〔999〕	8	6	80	13/	13	米/千克	/		31	
5212.2100 29	未漂白其他混纺棉布(每平方米重量>200 克,与 36%及以下其他羊毛/动物细毛混纺)〔999〕	8	6	80	13/	13	米/千克	/		31	
5212.2100 30	未漂白其他混纺府绸及平细布(每平方米重量>200 克,与化纤以外其他纤维混纺)〔999〕	8	6	80	13/	13	米/千克	/		31	
5212.2100 40	未漂白其他混纺棉机织平布(每平方米重量>200 克,与化纤以外其他纤维混纺)〔999〕	8	6	80	13/	13	米/千克	/		31	
5212.2100 50	未漂白其他混纺棉帆布(每平方米重量>200 克,与化纤以外其他纤维混纺)〔999〕	8	6	80	13/	13	米/千克	/		31	
5212.2100 60	未漂白其他混纺棉缎布(每平方米重量>200 克,与化纤以外其他纤维混纺)〔999〕	8	6	80	13/	13	米/千克	/		31	
5212.2100 70	未漂白其他混纺斜纹棉布(每平方米重量>200 克,与化纤以外其他纤维混纺)〔999〕	8	6	80	13/	13	米/千克	/		31	
5212.2100 90	未漂白其他混纺棉布(每平方米重量>200 克,与化纤以外其他纤维混纺)〔999〕	8	6	80	13/	13	米/千克	/		31	
5212.2200	--漂白〔999〕	8		80	13/	13	米/千克	/		28	
5212.2300	--染色〔999〕	8		80	13/	13	米/千克	/		33	
5212.2400	--色织〔999〕	8		80	13/	13	米/千克	/		33	
5212.2500	--印花〔999〕	8		80	13/	13	米/千克	/		33	

协定税率 %								RCEP		特惠税率 %			Article Description
东/冰/格	巴基斯坦	韩国	瑞士 上/下	哥/秘/柬	澳/毛	新西/坡/智	中国港/澳/台	东盟及马来/澳/韩	日/新	亚太2国	老/柬/缅	98/97/95	
													-Printed:
0/0/0	0	0	0/0	0/0/0	0/0	0//0	0/0/	0/0/0	9.1/0			0/0/0	--Plain weave
0/0/0	0	0	0/0	0/0/0	0/0	0//0	0/0/	0/0/0	9.1/0			0/0/0	--3-thread or 4-thread twill, including cross twill
0/0/0	0	0	0/0	0/0/0	0/0	0//0	0/0/	0/0/0	9.1/0			0/0/0	--Other fabrics
													Other woven fabrics of cotton:
													-Weighing not more than 200 g/m^2:
0/0/0	0	0	1.2/1.2	0/0/0	0/0	0/0/0	0/0/	0/0/0	10.9/0			0/0/0	--Unbleached
0/0/0	0	2.8	1.4/1.4	0/0/0	0/0	0/0/0	0/0/	0/0/12.6	12.7/0			0/0/0	--Bleached
0/0/0	0	0	0/0	0/0/0	0/0	0//0	0/0/	0/0/0	9.1/0			0/0/0	--Dyed
0/0/0	0	0	0/0	0/0/0	0/0	0//0	0/0/	0/0/0	9.1/0			0/0/0	--Of yarns of different colours
0/0/0	0	0	0/0	0/0/0	0/0	0//0	0/0/	0/0/0	9.1/0			0/0/0	--Printed
													-Weighing more than 200 g/m^2:
													--Unbleached
0/0/0	0	0	1.2/1.2	0/0/0	0/0	0/0/0	0/0/	0/0/0	10.9/0			0/0/0	Other woven fabrics of cotton, mixed, containing≥36% by weight of combed wool or fine animal hair, w>200g/m^2, unbleached
0/0/0	0	0	1.2/1.2	0/0/0	0/0	0/0/0	0/0/	0/0/0	10.9/0			0/0/0	Other woven fabrics of cotton, mixed, containing<36% by weight of combed wool or fine animal hair, w>200g/m^2, unbleached
0/0/0	0	0	1.2/1.2	0/0/0	0/0	0/0/0	0/0/	0/0/0	10.9/0			0/0/0	Other woven fabrics of cotton, mixed, containing≥36% by weight of wool or fine animal hair, w>200g/m^2, unbleached
0/0/0	0	0	1.2/1.2	0/0/0	0/0	0/0/0	0/0/	0/0/0	10.9/0			0/0/0	Other woven fabrics of cotton, mixed, containing<36% by weight of wool or fine animal hair, w>200g/m^2, unbleached
0/0/0	0	0	1.2/1.2	0/0/0	0/0	0/0/0	0/0/	0/0/0	10.9/0			0/0/0	Poplin and fine plain cloth, mixed with other fibres, other than man-made fibres, w>200g/m^2, unbleached
0/0/0	0	0	1.2/1.2	0/0/0	0/0	0/0/0	0/0/	0/0/0	10.9/0			0/0/0	Plain cloth of cotton, mixed with other fibres, other than man-made fibres, w>200g/m^2, unbleached
0/0/0	0	0	1.2/1.2	0/0/0	0/0	0/0/0	0/0/	0/0/0	10.9/0			0/0/0	Canvas of cotton, mixed with other fibres, other than man-made fibres, w>200g/m^2, unbleached
0/0/0	0	0	1.2/1.2	0/0/0	0/0	0/0/0	0/0/	0/0/0	10.9/0			0/0/0	Other woven fabrics of cotton, satin weave, mixed with other fibres, other than man-made fibres, w>200g/m^2, unbleached
0/0/0	0	0	1.2/1.2	0/0/0	0/0	0/0/0	0/0/	0/0/0	10.9/0			0/0/0	Other woven fabrics of cotton, twill weave, mixed with other fibres, other than man-made fibres, w > 200g/m^2, unbleached
0/0/0	0	0	1.2/1.2	0/0/0	0/0	0/0/0	0/0/	0/0/0	10.9/0			0/0/0	Other woven fabrics of cotton, mixed with other fibres, other than man-made fibres, w>200g/m^2, unbleached
0/0/0	0	2.8	1.4/1.4	0/0/0	0/0	0/0/0	0/0/	0/0/12.6	12.7/0			0/0/0	--Bleached
0/0/0	0	0	0/0	0/0/0	0/0	0//0	0/0/	0/0/0	9.1/0			0/0/0	--Dyed
0/0/0	0	0	0/0	0/0/0	0/0	0//0	0/0/	0/0/0	9.1/0			0/0/0	--Of yarns of different colours
0/0/0	0	0	0/0	0/0/0	0/0	0//0	0/0/	0/0/0	9.1/0			0/0/0	--Printed

第五十三章
其他植物纺织纤维;纸纱线及其机织物

税则号列	货品名称〔CIQ 扩展编码及品名－T2 表示见附表 2〕	最惠(%)	暂定税率	普通	增值/消费	出口退税	计量单位	监管条件/特殊证件	检验检疫	对美关税	亚太上/下
53.01	**亚麻,生的或经加工但未纺制的;亚麻短纤及废麻(包括废麻纱线及回收纤维):**										
5301.1000	-生的或经沤制的亚麻〔101 亚麻,102 麻纤维〕	6		30	13/	9	千克	AB/	PQ	11	
	-破开、打成、栉梳或经其他加工但未纺制的亚麻:										
5301.2100	--破开的或打成的〔101 亚麻,102 麻纤维〕	6	1	30	13/	9	千克	AB/	PQ	6	
5301.2900	--其他〔101 亚麻,102 麻纤维〕	6		30	13/	9,13	千克	AB/	PQ	11	
5301.3000	-亚麻短纤及废麻〔999〕	6	1	30	13/	9,13	千克	AB/	PQ	6	
53.02	**大麻,生的或经加工但未纺制的;大麻短纤及废麻(包括废麻纱线及回收纤维):**										
5302.1000	-生的或经沤制的大麻〔101 麻,102 麻纤维〕	6		30	13/	9	千克	AB/	PQ	11	
5302.9000	-其他〔999〕	6		30	13/	9	千克	AB/	PQ	11	
53.03	**黄麻及其他纺织用韧皮纤维(不包括亚麻、大麻及苎麻),生的或经加工但未纺制的;上述纤维的短纤及废麻(包括废纱线及回收纤维):**										
5303.1000	-生的或经沤制的黄麻及其他纺织用韧皮纤维〔101 麻,102 麻纤维〕	5		20	9/	9	千克	AB/	PQ		
5303.9000	-其他〔999〕	5		30	13/	9	千克	AB/	PQ		
53.05	**椰壳纤维、蕉麻(马尼拉麻)、苎麻及其他税目未列名的纺织用植物纤维,生的或经加工但未纺制的;上述纤维的短纤、落麻及废料(包括废纱线及回收纤维):**										
	---苎麻:										
5305.0011	----生的〔101 麻,102 麻纤维〕	5		30	13/	9	千克	AB/	PQ		
5305.0012	----经加工但未纺制的〔101 麻,102 麻纤维〕	5		30	13/	9	千克	AB/	PQ		3/3
5305.0013	----短纤及废麻〔999〕	5		30	13/	9	千克	AB/	PQ		3/3
5305.0019	----其他〔999〕	5		20	13/	9	千克	AB/	PQ		
5305.0020	---蕉麻〔999〕	3		20	13/	9	千克	AB/	PQ		1.8/1.8
	---其他:										
5305.0091	----西沙尔麻及其他纺织用龙舌兰纤维〔999〕	5		30	13/	9	千克	AB/	PQ		3/3
5305.0092	----椰壳纤维〔999〕	5		30	13/	9	千克	AB/	PQ		3.3/3.3
5305.0099	----其他〔999〕	5		30	13/	9	千克	AB/	PQ		3/3
53.06	**亚麻纱线:**										
5306.1000	-单纱〔999〕	5		50	13/	13	千克	/			
5306.2000	-多股纱线或缆线〔101 麻纱线,102 绳、索、缆〕	5		50	13/	13	千克	/		30	
53.07	**黄麻纱线或税目 53.03 的其他纺织用韧皮纤维纱线:**										
5307.1000	-单纱〔999〕	5		35	13/	13	千克	/			
5307.2000	-多股纱线或缆线〔101 麻纱线,102 绳、索、缆〕	5		35	13/	13	千克	/			
53.08	**其他植物纺织纤维纱线;纸纱线:**										
5308.1000	-椰壳纤维纱线〔999〕	5		45	13/	13	千克	/			
5308.2000	-大麻纱线〔999〕	5		45	13/	13	千克	/			
	-其他:										
	---苎麻纱线:										
5308.9011	----按重量计苎麻含量在 85%及以上的未漂白或漂白纱线〔999〕	5		50	13/	13	千克	/			3.5/3.5
5308.9012	----按重量计苎麻含量在 85%及以上的色纱线〔999〕	5		50	13/	13	千克	/			3.5/3.5
5308.9013	----按重量计苎麻含量在 85%以下的未漂白或漂白纱线〔999〕	5		50	13/	13	千克	/			3.5/3.5
5308.9014	----按重量计苎麻含量在 85%以下的色纱线〔999〕	5		50	13/	13	千克	/			3.5/3.5
	---其他:										
5308.9091	----纸纱线〔999〕	5		70	13/	13	千克	/			3.5/3.5
5308.9099	----其他〔999〕	5		45	13/	13	千克	/			
53.09	**亚麻机织物:**										
	-按重量计亚麻含量在 85%及以上:										
	--未漂白或漂白:										
5309.1110	---未漂白〔999〕	8		80	13/	13	米/千克	/		33	
5309.1120	---漂白的纯亚麻机织物〔999〕	8		80	13/	13	米/千克	/			
5309.1900	--其他〔999〕	8		80	13/	13	米/千克	/		33	5.2/5.2
	-按重量计亚麻含量在 85%以下:										
	--未漂白或漂白:										
5309.2110	---未漂白〔101 棉混纺坯布,102 亚麻混纺织物〕	8		80	13/	13	米/千克	/		33	

Chapter 53
Other vegetable textile fibres; paper yarn and woven fabrics of paper yarn

协定税率 %								RCEP		特惠税率 %			Article Description
东/冰/格	巴基斯坦	韩国	瑞士上/下	哥/秘/柬	澳/毛	新西/坡/智	中国港/澳/台	东盟及马来/澳/韩	日/新	亚太2国	老/柬/缅	98/97/95	
													Flax, raw or processed but not spun; flax tow and waste (including yarn waste and garnetted stock):
0/0/0	0	0	0/0	0/0/0	0/0	0//0	0/0/	0/0/0	0/0			0/0/0	-Flax, raw or retted
													-Flax, broken, scutched, hackled or otherwise processed, but not spun:
0/0/0	0	0	0/0	0/0/0	0/0	0//0	0/0/	0/0/0	0/0			0/0/0	--Broken or scutched
0/0/0	0	0	0/0	0/0/0	0/0	0//0	0/0/	0/0/0	0/0			0/0/0	--Other
0/0/0	0	0	0/0	0/0/0	0/0	0//0	0/0/	0/0/0	0/0			0/0/0	-Flax tow and waste
													True hemp (*Cannabis sativa L*), raw or processed but not spun; tow and waste of true hemp (including yarn waste and garnetted stock):
0/0/0	0	0	0/0	0/0/0	0/0	0//0	0/0/	0/0/0	0/0			0/0/0	-True hemp, raw or retted
0/0/0	0	0	0/0	0/0/0	0/0	0//0	0/0/	0/0/0	0/0			0/0/0	-Other
													Jute and other textile bast fibres (excluding flax, true hemp and ramie), raw or processed but not spun; tow and waste of these fibres (including yarn waste and garnetted stock):
0/0/0	0	0	0/0	0/0/0	0/0	0//0	0/0/	0/0/0	0/0	0	0/0/0	0/0/0	-Jute and other textile bast fibres, raw or retted
0/0/0	0	0	0/0	0/0/0	0/0	0//0	0/0/	0/0/0	0/0		0/0/0	0/0/0	-Other
													Coconut, abaca (Manila hemp or *Musatextilis Nee*), ramie and other vegetable textile fibres, not elsewhere specified or included, raw or processed but not spun; tow, noils and waste of these fibres (including yarn waste and garnetted stock):
													---Ramie:
0/0/0	0	0	0/0	0/0/0	0/0	0//0	0/0/	0/0/0	0/0			0/0/0	----Raw
0/0/0	0	0	0/0	0/0/0	0/0	0//0	0/0/	0/0/0	0/0			0/0/0	----Processed but not spun
0/0/0	0	0	0/0	0/0/0	0/0	0//0	0/0/	0/0/0	0/0			0/0/0	----Tow and waste
0/0/0	0	0	0/0	0/0/0	0/0	0//0	0/0/	0/0/0	0/0			0/0/0	----Other
0/0/0	0	0	0/0	0/0/0	0/0	0//0	0/0/	0/0/0	0/0			0/0/0	---Of Abaca
													---Other:
0/0/0	0	0	0/0	0/0/0	0/0	0//0	0/0/	0/0/0	0/0			0/0/0	----Sisal and other textile fabircs of the genus Agave, raw
0/0/0	0	0	0/0	0/0/0	0/0	0//0	0/0/	0/0/0	0/0		0/0/0	0/0/0	----of Coconut(coir)
0/0/0	0	0	0/0	0/0/0	0/0	0//0	0/0/	0/0/0	0/0			0/0/0	----Other
													Flax yarn:
0/0/0	0	0	0/0	0/0/0	0/0	0//0	0/0/	0/0/0	0/0			0/0/0	-Single
0/0/0	3.5	0	0/0	0/0/0	0/0	0//0	0/0/	0/0/0	9.1/0			0/0/0	-Multiple (folded) or cabled
													Yarn of jute or of other textile bast fibres of heading No. 53.03:
0/0/0	0	0	0/0	0/0/0	0/0	0//0	0/0/	0/0/0	0/0	2.5	/0/	0/0/0	-Single
0/0/0	0	0	0/0	0/0/0	0/0	0//0	0/0/	0/0/0	0/0	2.5	/0/	0/0/0	-Multiple (folded) or cabled
													Yarn of other vegetable textile fibres; paper yarn:
0/0/0	0	0	0/0	0/0/0	0/0	0//0	0/0/	0/0/0	0/0			0/0/0	-Coir yarn
0/0/0	0	0	0/0	0/0/0	0/0	0//0	0/0/	0/0/0	0/0			0/0/0	-True hemp yarn
													-Other:
													---Ramie yarn:
0/0/0	0	0	0/0	0/0/0	0/0	0//0	0/0/	0/0/0	0/0			0/0/0	----Containing 85% or more by weight of ramie, unbleached or bleached yarn
0/0/0	0	0	0/0	0/0/0	0/0	0//0	0/0/	0/0/0	0/0			0/0/0	----Containing 85% or more by weight of ramie, coloured yarn
0/0/0	0	0	0/0	0/0/0	0/0	0//0	0/0/	0/0/0	0/0			0/0/0	----Containing less than 85% by weight of ramie, unbleached or bleached yarn
0/0/0	0	0	0/0	0/0/0	0/0	0//0	0/0/	0/0/0	0/0			0/0/0	----Containing less than 85% by weight of coloured yarn
													---Other:
0/0/0	0	0	0/0	0/0/0	0/0	0//0	0/0/	0/0/0	0/0			0/0/0	----Paper yarn
0/0/0	0	0	0/0	0/0/0	0/0	0//0	0/0/	0/0/0	0/0			0/0/0	----Other
													Woven fabrics of flax:
													-Containing 85% or more by weight of flax:
													--Unbleached or bleached:
0/0/0	0	0	0/0	0/0/0	0/0	0//0	0/0/	0/0/0	9.1/0			0/0/0	---Unbleached
0/0/0	0	0	0/0	0/0/0	0/0	0//0	0/0/	0/0/0	9.1/0			0/0/0	---Bleached
0/0/0	0	0	0/0	0/0/0	0/0	0//0	0/0/	0/0/0	9.1/0			0/0/0	--Other
													-Containing less than 85% by weight of flax:
													--Unbleached or bleached:
0/0/0	0	0	0/0	0/0/0	0/0	0//0	0/0/	0/0/0	9.1/0			0/0/0	---Unbleached

税则号列	货品名称〔CIQ 扩展编码及品名—T2 表示见附表 2〕	最惠(%)	暂定税率	普通	增值/消费	出口退税	计量单位	监管条件/特殊证件	检验检疫	对美关税	亚太上/下
5309.2120	---漂白〔101 漂白棉混纺布,102 亚麻混纺织物〕	8		80	13/	13	米/千克	/			
5309.2900	--其他〔999〕	8		80	13/	13	米/千克	/		33	5.2/5.2
53.10	**黄麻或税目 53.03 的其他纺织用韧皮纤维机织物:**										
5310.1000	-未漂白〔999〕	8		40	13/	13	米/千克	/			
5310.9000	-其他〔999〕	8		40	13/	13	米/千克	/			
53.11	**其他纺织用植物纤维机织物;纸纱线机织物:**										
	---苎麻的:										
5311.0012	----按重量计苎麻含量在 85%及以上的未漂白机织物〔999〕	8		80	13/	13	米/千克	/			
5311.0013	----按重量计苎麻含量在 85%及以上的其他机织物〔999〕	8		80	13/	13	米/千克	/			
5311.0014	----按重量计苎麻含量在 85%以下的未漂白机织物〔101 棉混纺坯布,102 苎麻混纺织物,103 其他麻织物〕	8		80	13/	13	米/千克	/			4.8/4.8
5311.0015	----按重量计苎麻含量在 85%以下的其他机织物〔101 苎麻混纺织物,102 其他麻织物〕	8		80	13/	13	米/千克	/			
5311.0020	---纸纱线的〔999〕	8		90	13/	13	米/千克	/			4.8/4.8
5311.0030	---大麻的〔999〕	8		50	13/	13	米/千克	/			5.2/5.2
5311.0090	---其他〔999〕	8		50	13/	13	米/千克	/			5.2/5.2

协定税率 %								RCEP		特惠税率 %			Article Description
东/冰/格	巴基斯坦	韩国	瑞士上/下	哥/秘/柬	澳/毛	新西/坡/智	中国港/澳/台	东盟及马来/澳/韩	日/新	亚太2国	老/柬/缅	98/97/95	
0/0/0	0	0	0/0	0/0/0	0/0	0//0	0/0/	0/0/0	9.1/0			0/0/0	---Bleached
0/0/0	0	0	0/0	0/0/0	0/0	0//0	0/0/	0/0/0	9.1/0			0/0/0	--Other
													Woven fabrics of jute or of other textilebast fibres of heading No. 53. 03:
0/0/0	3.5	0	0/0	0/0/0	0/0	0//0	0/0/	0/0/0	9.1/0	4	/0/	0/0/0	-Unbleached
0/0/0	3.5	0	0/0	0/0/0	0/0	0//0	0/0/	0/0/0	9.1/0	4	/0/	0/0/0	-Other
													Woven fabrics of other vegetable textile fibres; woven fabrics of paper yarn:
													---Of ramie:
0/0/0	3.5	0	0/0	0/0/0	0/0	0//0	0/0/	0/0/0	9.1/0			0/0/0	----Containing 85% or more by weight of ramie, unbleached woven fabrics
0/0/0	6	0	1.2/1.2	0/0/0	0/0	0/0/0	0/0/	0/0/0	10.9/0			0/0/0	----Containing 85% or more by weight of ramie, other woven fabrics
0/0/0	3.5	0	0/0	0/0/0	0/0	0//0	0/0/	0/0/0	9.1/0			0/0/0	----Containing less than 85% by weight of ramie, unbleached woven fabrics
0/0/0	6	0	1.2/1.2	0/0/0	0/0	0/0/0	0/0/	0/0/0	10.9/0			0/0/0	----Containing less than 85% by weight of ramie, other woven fabrics
0/0/0	3.5	0	0/0	0/0/0	0/0	0//0	0/0/	0/0/0	9.1/0			0/0/0	---Of paper yarn
0/0/0	3.5	0	0/0	0/0/0	0/0	0//0	0/0/	0/0/0	9.1/0			0/0/0	---Of true hemp
0/0/0	3.5	0	0/0	0/0/0	0/0	0//0	0/0/	0/0/0	9.1/0			0/0/0	---Other

第五十四章
化学纤维长丝,化学纤维纺织材料制扁条及类似品

注释:

一、本协调制度所称"化学纤维",是指通过下列任一方法加工制得的有机聚合物的短纤或长丝:

(一)将有机单体物质加以聚合而制成聚合物,例如,聚酰胺、聚酯、聚烯烃、聚氨基甲酸酯;或通过上述加工将聚合物经化学改性制得(例如,聚乙酸乙烯酯水解得的聚乙烯醇);

(二)将天然有机聚合物(例如,纤维素)溶解或化学处理制成聚合物,例如,铜铵纤维或粘胶纤维;或将天然有机聚合物(例如,纤维素、酪蛋白及其他蛋白质、或藻酸)经化学改性制成聚合物,例如,醋酸纤维素纤维或藻酸盐纤维。

对于化学纤维,所称"合成",是指(一)款所述的纤维;所称"人造",是指(二)款所述的纤维。税目 54.04 或 54.05 的扁条及类似品不视作化学纤维。

对于纺织材料,所称"化学纤维""合成纤维"及"人造纤维",其含义应与上述解释相同。

二、税目 54.02 及 54.03 不适用于第五十五章的合成纤维或人造纤维的长丝丝束。

税则号列	货品名称〔CIQ 扩展编码及品名—T2 表示见附表 2〕	最惠(%)	暂定税率	普通	增值/消费	出口退税	计量单位	监管条件/特殊证件	检验检疫	对美关税	亚太上/下
54.01	**化学纤维长丝纺制的缝纫线,不论是否供零售用:**										
	-合成纤维长丝纺制:										
5401.1010	---非供零售用〔999〕	5		70	13/	13	千克	/		25	
5401.1020	---供零售用〔999〕	5		90	13/	13	千克	/		30	
	-人造纤维长丝纺制:										
5401.2010	---非供零售用〔999〕	5		35	13/	13	千克	/			
5401.2020	---供零售用〔999〕	5		90	13/	13	千克	/			
54.02	**合成纤维长丝纱线(缝纫线除外),非供零售用,包括细度在67分特以下的合成纤维单丝:**										
	-尼龙或其他聚酰胺纺制的高强力纱,不论是否经变形加工:										
	--芳香族聚酰胺纺制:										
5402.1110	---聚间苯二甲酰间苯二胺纺制〔999〕	5		70	13/	13	千克	/		15	
5402.1120	---聚对苯二甲酰对苯二胺纺制〔999〕	5		70	13/	13	千克	/		15	
5402.1190	---其他〔999〕	5		70	13/	13	千克	/		30	
	--其他:										
5402.1910	---聚酰胺-6(尼龙-6)纺制的〔999〕	5		70	13/	13	千克	/		30	
5402.1920	---聚酰胺-6,6(尼龙-6,6)纺制的〔999〕	5		70	13/	13	千克	/		30	
5402.1990	---其他〔999〕	5		70	13/	13	千克	/		30	
5402.2000	-聚酯高强力纱,不论是否经变形加工										
5402.2000 10	非零售聚酯高强力纱,不论是否经变形加工(单丝/未捻或捻度<5 转/米的复丝单纱)〔999〕	5		70	13/	13	千克	/		30	
5402.2000 20	非零售聚酯高强力纱,不论是否经变形加工(捻度≥5 转/米的复丝单纱)〔999〕	5		70	13/	13	千克	/		30	
5402.2000 90	非零售聚酯高强力多股纱,不论是否经变形加工〔999〕	5		70	13/	13	千克	/		30	
	-变形纱线:										
	--尼龙或其他聚酰胺纺制,每根单纱细度不超过 50 特:										
	---弹力丝:										
5402.3111	----聚酰胺-6(尼龙-6)纺制的〔999〕	5		80	13/	13	千克	/		30	
5402.3112	----聚酰胺-6,6(尼龙-6,6)纺制〔999〕	5		80	13/	13	千克	/		30	
5402.3113	----芳香族聚酰胺纺制〔999〕	5		80	13/	13	千克	/			3/3
5402.3119	----其他〔999〕	5		80	13/	13	千克	/		30	
5402.3190	---其他〔999〕	5		70	13/	13	千克	/		30	
	--尼龙或其他聚酰胺纺制,每根单纱细度超过 50 特:										
	---弹力丝:										
5402.3211	----聚酰胺-6(尼龙-6)纺制〔999〕	5		80	13/	13	千克	/		15	
5402.3212	----聚酰胺-6,6(尼龙-6,6)纺制〔999〕	5		80	13/	13	千克	/		15	
5402.3213	----芳香族聚酰胺纺制〔999〕	5		80	13/	13	千克	/			
5402.3219	----其他〔999〕	5		80	13/	13	千克	/		30	
5402.3290	---其他〔999〕	5		70	13/	13	千克	/		15	3.3/3.3

Chapter 54
Man-made filaments; strip and the like of man made textile materials

Notes:

1. Throughout the Nomenclature, the term"man-made fibres"means stapl fibres and filaments of organic polymers produced by manufacruring processes, either:
   (a) By polymerization of organic monomers to prduce polymers such as polyamides, polyesters, polyolefins or polyurethanes, or by chemical modification of polymers plrduced by this process(for example, poly(vinyl alcohol)prepared by the hydrolysis of poly (vinyl acetate);
   (b) By dissolution or chemical treatment of natural organic polymers(for example, cellulose) to produce polymers such as cuprammonium rayon(cupro) or viscose rayon, or by chemical modification of narural organic polymers(for example, cellulose, casein and other proteins, or alginic acid), to produce polymers such as cellulose acetate or alginates.

   The terms"synthetic"and "artificial", used in relation to fibres, mean: synthetic: fibres as defined at(a); artificial: fibres as defined at (b).Strip and the like of heading 50. 04 or 54. 05are not considered to be man made fibres.

   The tems"man-made", "synthetic"and"artificial"shall have the same meanings when used in relation to"textile materials".
2. Headings 54. 02 and 54. 03 do not apply to synthetic or artificial filament tow of chapter 55.

协定税率 %								RCEP		特惠税率 %			Article Description
东/冰/格	巴基斯坦	韩国	瑞士上/下	哥/秘/東	澳/毛	新西/坡/智	中国港/澳/台	东盟及马来/澳/韩	日/新	亚太2国	老/柬/缅	98/97/95	
													Sewing thread of man-made filaments, whether or not put up for retail sale:
													-Of synthetic filaments:
0/0/0	0	2.3	0/0	0/0/0	0/0	0//0	0/0/0	4.5/4.5/4.5	4.7/4.5			0/0/0	---Not put up for retail sale
0/0/0	0	0	0/0	0/0/0	0/0	0//0	0/0/	0/0/0	0/0			0/0/0	---Put up for retail sale
													-Of artificial filaments:
0/0/0	0	0	0/0	0/0/0	0/0	0//0	0/0/	0/0/0	0/0			0/0/0	---Not put up for retail sale
0/0/0	0	0	0/0	0/0/0	0/0	0//0	0/0/	0/0/0	0/0			0/0/0	---Put up for retail sale
													Synthetic filament yarn (other than sewing thread), not put up for retail sale, including synthetic monofilament of less than 67 decitex:
													-High tenacity yarn of nylon or other polyamides, whether or not through texturing processing:
													--Of aramides:
0/0/0	0	2.3	0/0	0/0/0	0/0	0//0	0/0/	4.9/4.9/	/4.9			0/0/0	---Of poly-isophthaloyl metaphenylene diamide
0/0/0	0	2.3	0/0	0/0/0	0/0	0//0	0/0/	4.8/4.8/	/4.8			0/0/0	---Of poly-p-phenylene terephthalamide
0/0/0	0	2.3	0/0	0/0/0	0/0	0//0	0/0/	4.8/4.8/	/4.8			0/0/0	---Other
													--Other:
0/0/0	0		0/0	0/0/0	0/0	0//0	0/0/	4.8/4.8/	/4.8			0/0/0	---Of nylon-6
0/0/0	0		0/0	0/0/0	0/0	0//0	0/0/	4.8/4.8/	/4.8			0/0/0	---Of nylon-6,6
0/0/0	0	2.3	0/0	0/0/0	0/0	0//0	0/0/	4.5/4.5/4.5	4.7/4.5			0/0/0	---Other
													-High tenacity yarn of polyesters, whether or not through texturing processing:
0/0/0	0	2.3	0/0	0/0/0	0/0	0//0	0/0/0	4.5/4.5/4.5	4.7/4.5			0/0/0	High tenacity yarn of polyesters (single filament/multi-filament single yarn not twisted or with a twist of less than 5 turns per meter) not put up for retail sale, whether or not through texturing processing
0/0/0	0	2.3	0/0	0/0/0	0/0	0//0	0/0/0	4.5/4.5/4.5	4.7/4.5			0/0/0	High tenacity yarn of polyesters, multi-filament single yarn with a twist of 5 or more turns per meter, not put up for retail sale, whether or not through texturing processing
0/0/0	0	2.3	0/0	0/0/0	0/0	0//0	0/0/0	4.5/4.5/4.5	4.7/4.5			0/0/0	High tenacity yarn of polyesters, multiple yarn, not put up for retail sale -Textured yarn, whether or not through texturing processing
													-Textured yarn:
													--Of nylon or other polyamides, measuring per single yarn not more than 50 tex:
													---Elastic filament:
0/0/0	0		0/0	0/0/0	0/0	0//0	0/0/	4.8/4.8/	/4.8			0/0/0	----Of nylon-6
0/0/0	0		0/0	0/0/0	0/0	0//0	0/0/	4.8/4.8/	/4.8			0/0/0	----Of nylon-6,6
0/0/0	0		0/0	0/0/0	0/0	0//0	0/0/	4.9/4.9/	/4.9			0/0/0	----Of aramides
0/0/0	0	2.3	0/0	0/0/0	0/0	0//0	0/0/	4.5/4.5/4.5	4.7/4.5			0/0/0	----Other
0/0/0	0	2.3	0/0	0/0/0	0/0	0//0	0/0/	4.5/4.5/4.5	4.7/4.5			0/0/0	---Other
													--Of nylon or other polyamides, measuring per single yarn more than 50tex:
													---Elastic filament:
0/0/0	0		0/0	0/0/0	0/0	0//0	0/0/	4.8/4.8/	/4.8			0/0/0	----Of nylon-6
0/0/0	0		0/0	0/0/0	0/0	0//0	0/0/	4.8/4.8/	/4.8			0/0/0	----Of nylon-6,6
0/0/0	0	2.3	0/0	0/0/0	0/0	0//0	0/0/	4.9/4.9/	/4.9			0/0/0	----Of aramides
0/0/0	0		0/0	0/0/0	0/0	0//0	0/0/	4.8/4.8/	/4.8			0/0/0	----Other
0/0/0	0	3.2	0/0	0/0/0	0/0	0//0	0/0/	4.8/4.8/	/4.8			0/0/0	---Other

税则号列	货品名称〔CIQ扩展编码及品名—T2表示见附表2〕	最惠(%)	暂定税率	普通	增值/消费	出口退税	计量单位	监管条件/特殊证件	检验检疫	对美关税	亚太上/下
	--聚酯纺制:										
5402.3310	---弹力丝〔999〕	5		90	13/	13	千克	/		30	
5402.3390	---其他〔999〕	5		70	13/	13	千克	/		30	
5402.3400	--聚丙烯纺制〔101 合成纤维纱线,102 绳、索、缆〕	5		70	13/	13	千克	/		30	
5402.3900	--其他〔999〕	5		70	13/	13	千克	/		30	
	-其他单纱,未加捻或捻度每米不超过50转:										
	--弹性纱线:										
5402.4410	---氨纶纱线〔101 合成纤维纱线,102 绳、索、缆〕	5		70	13/	13	千克	/		30	
5402.4490	---其他〔999〕	5		70	13/	13	千克	/			3.3/3.3
	--其他,尼龙或其他聚酰胺纱线:										
5402.4510	---聚酰胺-6(尼龙-6)纺制的〔101 合成纤维纱线,102 绳、索、缆〕	5		70	13/	13	千克	/		30	3.3/3.3
5402.4520	---聚酰胺-6,6(尼龙-6,6)纺制的〔101 合成纤维纱线,102 绳、索、缆〕	5		70	13/	13	千克	/		15	3.3/3.3
5402.4530	---芳香族聚酰胺纺制的〔101 合成纤维纱线,102 绳、索、缆〕	5		70	13/	13	千克	/		15	3.3/3.3
5402.4590	---其他〔101 合成纤维纱线,102 绳、索、缆〕	5		70	13/	13	千克	/		15	3.3/3.3
5402.4600	--其他,部分定向聚酯纱线〔999〕	5		70	13/	13	千克	/		15	
5402.4700	--其他,聚酯纱线〔999〕	5		70	13/	13	千克	/		30	3.3/3.3
5402.4800	--其他,聚丙烯纱线〔101 合成纤维纱线,102 绳、索、缆〕	5		70	13/	13	千克	/		30	
	--其他:										
5402.4910	---断裂强度大于等于22cN/dtex,且初始模量大于等于750cN/dtex的聚乙烯纱线〔999〕	5		70	13/	13	千克	/		15	
5402.4990	---其他										
5402.4990 01	非弹性氨纶单纱(非供零售用,未加捻或捻度每米不超过50转,缝纫线除外)〔999〕	5		70	13/	13	千克	/		15	
5402.4990 90	其他合成纤维长丝单纱(非供零售用,未加捻或捻度每米不超过50转,缝纫线除外)〔999〕	5		70	13/	13	千克	/		15	
	-其他单纱,捻度每米超过50转:										
	--尼龙或其他聚酰胺纱线:										
5402.5110	---聚酰胺-6(尼龙-6)纺制的〔999〕	5		70	13/	13	千克	/		30	
5402.5120	---聚酰胺-6,6(尼龙-6,6)纺制的〔999〕	5		70	13/	13	千克	/			4.5/4.5
5402.5130	---芳香族聚酰胺纺制的〔999〕	5		70	13/	13	千克	/			3.5/3.5
5402.5190	---其他〔999〕	5		70	13/	13	千克	/			
5402.5200	--聚酯纱线〔999〕	5		70	13/	13	千克	/		30	3.3/3.3
5402.5300	--聚丙烯纱线〔999〕	5		70	13/	13	千克	/		30	
	--其他:										
5402.5920	---断裂强度大于等于22cN/dtex,且初始模量大于等于750cN/dtex的聚乙烯纱线〔999〕	5		70	13/	13	千克	/		15	
5402.5990	---其他〔999〕	5		70	13/	13	千克	/		15	
	-其他纱线(多股纱线或缆线):										
	--尼龙或其他聚酰胺纺制:										
5402.6110	---聚酰胺-6(尼龙-6)纺制的〔101 合成纤维纱线,102 绳、索、缆〕	5		70	13/	13	千克	/		30	
5402.6120	---聚酰胺-6,6(尼龙-6,6)纺制的〔101 合成纤维纱线,102 绳、索、缆〕	5		70	13/	13	千克	/		30	
5402.6130	---芳香族聚酰胺纺制的〔101 合成纤维纱线,102 绳、索、缆〕	5		70	13/	13	千克	/		25	
5402.6190	---其他〔101 合成纤维纱线,102 绳、索、缆〕	5		70	13/	13	千克	/		30	
5402.6200	--聚酯纺制〔101 合成纤维纱线,102 绳、索、缆〕	5		70	13/	13	千克	/		30	
5402.6300	--聚丙烯纺制〔999〕	5		70	13/	13	千克	/		30	
	--其他:										
5402.6920	---氨纶纱线〔101 合成纤维纱线,102 绳、索、缆〕	5		70	13/	13	千克	/		30	
5402.6990	---其他〔101 合成纤维纱线,102 绳、索、缆〕	5		70	13/	13	千克	/		25	
54.03	**人造纤维长丝纱线(缝纫线除外),非供零售用,包括细度在67分特以下的人造纤维单丝:**										
5403.1000	-粘胶纤维纺制的高强力纱〔999〕	5		35	13/	13	千克	/		15	
	-其他单纱:										
	--粘胶纤维纺制,未加捻或捻度每米不超过120转:										
5403.3110	---竹制〔999〕	5		35	13/	13	千克	/			
5403.3190	---其他〔999〕	5		35	13/	13	千克	/			
	--粘胶纤维纺制,捻度每米超过120转:										
5403.3210	---竹制〔999〕	5		35	13/	13	千克	/			
5403.3290	---其他〔999〕	5		35	13/	13	千克	/			
	--醋酸纤维纺制:										

协定税率 %								RCEP		特惠税率 %			Article Description
东/冰/格	巴基斯坦	韩国	瑞士上/下	哥/秘/柬	澳/毛	新西/坡/智	中国港/澳/台	东盟及马来/澳/韩	日/新	亚太2国	老/柬/缅	98/97/95	
													--Of polyesters:
0/0/0	0	0	0/0	0/0/0	0/0	0//0	0/0/0	0/4.5/0	0/4.5			0/0/0	---Elastic filament
/0/0	0	1	0/0	0/0/0	0/0	0//0	0/0/	4.9/4.9/	/4.9			0/0/0	---Other
0/0/0	0	1	0/0	0/0/0	0/0	0//0	0/0/	0/0/4.5	4.5/0			0/0/0	--Of polypropylene
0/0/0	0	1	0/0	0/0/0	0/0	0//0	0/0/	0/0/4.5	4.5/0			0/0/0	--Other
													-Other yarn, single, untwisted or with a twist not exceeding 50 turns per metre:
													--Elastomeric:
0/0/0	0		0/0	0/0/0	0/0	0//0	0/0/	4.8/4.8/	/4.8			0/0/0	---Of polyurethane
0/0/0	0	0	0/0	0/0/0	0/0	0//0	0/0/	0/0/0	0/0			0/0/0	---Other
													--Other, of nylon or other polyamides:
0/0/0	0	3.2	0/0	0/0/0	0/0	0//0	0/0/	4.8/4.8/	/4.8			0/0/0	---Of nylon-6
0/0/0	0	3.2	0/0	0/0/0	0/0	0//0	0/0/	4.8/4.8/	/4.8			0/0/0	---Of nylon-6,6
0/0/0	0	2.3	0/0	0/0/0	0/0	0//0	0/0/	4.8/4.8/	/4.8			0/0/0	---Of aramides
0/0/0	0	3.2	0/0	0/0/0	0/0	0//0	0/0/	4.8/4.8/	/4.8			0/0/0	---Other
/0/0	0	1	0/0	0/0/0	0/0	0//0	0/0/	4.9/4.9/	/4.9			0/0/0	--Other, of polyesters, partially oriented
/0/0	0	3.2	0.5/0.5	0/0/0	0/0	0//0	0/0/	4.9/4.9/	/4.9			0/0/0	--Other, of polyesters
0/0/0	0	0	0/0	0/0/0	0/0	0//0	0/0/	0/0/0	0/0			0/0/0	--Other, Of polypropylene
													--Other:
0/0/0	0		0/0	0/0/0	0/0	0//0	0/0/	4.9/4.9/	/4.9			0/0/0	---Polyethylene filament yarn (yarn)
													---Other
0/0/0	0		0/0	0/0/0	0/0	0//0	0/0/	4.8/4.8/	/4.8			0/0/0	Single yarn of polyurethane[untwisted or twist<50turns/m multiple(folded), not in forms or packing for retail sale]
0/0/0	0		0/0	0/0/0	0/0	0//0	0/0/	4.8/4.8/	/4.8			0/0/0	Other single yarn of synthetic filaments [untwisted or twist <50turns/m multiple (folded), not in forms or packing for retail sale]
													-Other yarn, single, with a twist exceeding 50 turns per metre:
													--Of nylon or other polyamides:
/0/0	0		0/0	0/0/0	0/0	0//0	0/0/	4.9/4.9/	/4.9			0/0/0	---Of nylon-6
0/0/0	0		0/0	0/0/0	0/0	0//0	0/0/	4.8/4.8/	/4.8			0/0/0	---Of nylon-6,6
0/0/0	0	2.3	0/0	0/0/0	0/0	0//0	0/0/	4.9/4.9/	/4.9			0/0/0	---Of aramides
0/0/0	0	2.3	0/0	0/0/0	0/0	0//0	0/0/	4.5/4.5/4.5	4.7/4.5			0/0/0	---Other
/0/0	0	1	0/0	0/0/0	0/0	0//0	0/0/	4.9/4.9/	/4.9			0/0/0	--Of polyesters
0/0/0	0	0	0/0	0/0/0	0/0	0//0	0/0/	0/0/0	4.5/0			0/0/0	--Of polypropylene
													--Other:
0/0/0	0	0	0/0	0/0/0	0/0	0//0	0/0/	0/0/0	0/0			0/0/0	---Polyethy lene yarn with break strength ≥22cN/dtex, and initial modulus≥750cN/dtex
0/0/0	0	0	0/0	0/0/0	0/0	0//0	0/0/	0/0/0	0/0			0/0/0	---Other
													-Other yarn, multiple (folded) or cabled:
													--Of nylon or other polyamides:
0/0/0	0	2.3	0/0	0/0/0	0/0	0//0	0/0/	4.5/4.5/4.5	4.7/4.5			0/0/0	---Of nylon-6
0/0/0	0	2.3	0/0	0/0/0	0/0	0//0	0/0/	4.5/4.5/4.5	4.7/4.5			0/0/0	---Of nylon-6,6
0/0/0	0	2.3	0/0	0/0/0	0/0	0//0	0/0/	4.8/4.8/	/4.8			0/0/0	---Of aramides
0/0/0	0	0	0/0	0/0/0	0/0	0//0	0/0/	0/0/0	0/0			0/0/0	---Other
0/0/0	0	0	0/0	0/0/0	0/0	0//0	0/0/0	0/0/0	0/0			0/0/0	--Of polyesters
0/0/0	0	2.3	0/0	0/0/0	0/0	0//0	0/0/	4.5/4.5/4.5	4.7/4.5			0/0/0	--Of polypropylene
													--Other:
0/0/0	0		0/0	0/0/0	0/0	0//0	0/0/	4.9/4.9/	/4.9			0/0/0	---Of polyurethane
0/0/0	0	1	0/0	0/0/0	0/0	0//0	0/0/	0/0/4.5	4.5/0			0/0/0	---Other
													Artificial filament yarn (other than sewing thread), not put up for retail sale, including artificial monofilament of less than 67 decitex:
0/0/0	0	0	0/0	0/0/0	0/0	0//0	0/0/	0/0/0	0/0			0/0/0	-High tenacity yarn of viscose rayon
													-Other yarn, single:
													--Of viscose rayon, untwisted or with a twist not exceeding 120 turns per metre:
0/0/0	0	0	0/0	0/0/0	0/0	0//0	0/0/	0/0/0	0/0			0/0/0	---Of bamboo
0/0/0	0	0	0/0	0/0/0	0/0	0//0	0/0/	0/0/0	0/0			0/0/0	---Other
													--Of viscose rayon, with a twist exceeding 120 turns per metre:
0/0/0	0	0	0/0	0/0/0	0/0	0//0	0/0/	0/0/0	0/0			0/0/0	---Of bomboo
0/0/0	0	0	0/0	0/0/0	0/0	0//0	0/0/	0/0/0	0/0			0/0/0	---Other
													--Of cellulose acetate:

税则号列	货品名称〔CIQ 扩展编码及品名－T2 表示见附表 2〕	最惠(%)	暂定税率	普通	增值/消费	出口退税	计量单位	监管条件/特殊证件	检验检疫	对美关税	亚太上/下
5403.3310	---二醋酸纤维纺制										
5403.3310 10	非零售二醋酸纤维单纱(单丝/未捻或捻度 5 转/米以下的复丝单纱,包括变形纱线)〔999〕	5		40	13/	13	千克	/		15	
5403.3310 20	非零售二醋酸纤维单纱(捻度 5 转/米及以上不超过 250 转,包括变形纱线)〔999〕	5		40	13/	13	千克	/		15	
5403.3310 90	非零售二醋酸纤维单纱(捻度超过 250 转/米)〔999〕	5		40	13/	13	千克	/		15	
5403.3390	---其他〔999〕	5		35	13/	13	千克	/		15	
5403.3900	--其他〔999〕	5		35	13/	13	千克	/			
	-其他纱线(多股纱线或缆线):										
5403.4100	--粘胶纤维纺制〔999〕	5		35	13/	13	千克	/			
5403.4200	--醋酸纤维纺制〔999〕	5		35	13/	13	千克	/			
5403.4900	--其他〔999〕	5		35	13/	13	千克	/		30	
54.04	**截面尺寸不超过 1 毫米,细度在 67 分特及以上的合成纤维单丝;表观宽度不超过 5 毫米的合成纤维纺织材料制扁条及类似品(例如,人造草):**										
	-单丝:										
5404.1100	--弹性单丝										
5404.1100 10	细度≥67 分特的涤纶纤维弹性单丝(截面尺寸≤1mm,细度<67分特的合成纤维单丝归入编号 5402)〔999〕	5		80	13/	13	千克	/		15	
5404.1100 90	细度≥67 分特的其他合成纤维弹性单丝(截面尺寸≤1mm,细度<67 分特的合成纤维单丝归入编号 5402)〔999〕	5		80	13/	13	千克	/		15	
5404.1200	--其他,聚丙烯单丝〔999〕	5		80	13/	13	千克	/			
5404.1900	--其他										
5404.1900 10	细度≥67 分特的涤纶纤维单丝(截面尺寸≤1mm,细度<67 分特的合成纤维单丝归入税目 54.02)〔999〕	5		80	13/	13	千克	/		25	
5404.1900 90	细度≥67 分特的其他合成纤维单丝(截面尺寸≤1mm,细度<67分特的合成纤维单丝归入税目 54.02)〔999〕	5		80	13/	13	千克	/		25	
5404.9000	-其他〔999〕	5		80	13/	13	千克	/		25	
54.05	**截面尺寸不超过 1 毫米,细度在 67 分特及以上的人造纤维单丝;表观宽度不超过 5 毫米的人造纤维纺织材料制扁条及类似品(例如,人造草):**										
5405.0000	截面尺寸不超过 1 毫米,细度在 67 分特及以上的人造纤维单丝;表观宽度不超过 5 毫米的人造纤维纺织材料制扁条及类似品(例如,人造草)〔999〕	5		80	13/	13	千克	/		25	
54.06	**化学纤维长丝纱线(缝纫线除外),供零售用:**										
5406.0010	---合成纤维长丝纱线〔999〕	5		90	13/	13	千克	/		25	
5406.0020	---人造纤维长丝纱线〔999〕	5		90	13/	13	千克	/			
54.07	**合成纤维长丝纱线的机织物,包括税目 54.04 所列材料的机织物:**										
	-尼龙或其他聚酰胺高强力纱、聚酯高强力纱纺制的机织物:										
5407.1010	---尼龙或其他聚酰胺高强力纱纺制〔999〕	8		130	13/	13	米/千克	/		33	
5407.1020	---聚酯高强力纱纺制										
5407.1020 10	聚酯高强力纱纺制机织物(重量≤170 克/平方米)〔999〕	8		130	13/	13	米/千克	/		33	
5407.1020 90	聚酯高强力纱纺制机织物(重量>170 克/平方米)〔999〕	8		130	13/	13	米/千克	/		33	
5407.2000	-扁条及类似品的机织物〔999〕	8		130	13/	13	米/千克	/		28	
5407.3000	-第十一类注释九所列的机织物〔999〕	8		130	13/	13	米/千克	/		23	
	-其他机织物,按重量计尼龙或其他聚酰胺长丝含量在 85%及以上:										
5407.4100	--未漂白或漂白〔999〕	8		130	13/	13	米/千克	/		33	
5407.4200	--染色〔999〕	8		130	13/	13	米/千克	/		33	5.2/5.2
5407.4300	--色织〔999〕	8		130	13/	13	米/千克	/		33	5.2/5.2
5407.4400	--印花〔999〕	8		130	13/	13	米/千克	/		33	
	-其他机织物,按重量计聚酯变形长丝含量在 85%及以上:										

协定税率 %								RCEP		特惠税率 %			Article Description
东/冰/格	巴基斯坦	韩国	瑞士上/下	哥/秘/柬	澳/毛	新西/坡/智	中国港/澳/台	东盟及马来/澳/韩	日/新	亚太2国	老/柬/缅	98/97/95	
													---Of cellulose diacetate
0/0/0	0	0	0/0	0/0/0	0/0	0//0	0/0/	0/0/0	0/0			0/0/0	Single yarn of cellulose diacetate, untwisted or twist ＜ 5 turns/m multiple (folded), not in forms or packing for retail sale, including textured yarn
0/0/0	0	0	0/0	0/0/0	0/0	0//0	0/0/	0/0/0	0/0			0/0/0	Single yarn of cellulose diacetate, 5 turns/m ≤ twist ≤ 250 turns/m, not put up for retail sale, including Deformation yarn
0/0/0	0	0	0/0	0/0/0	0/0	0//0	0/0/	0/0/0	0/0			0/0/0	Single yarn of cellulose diacetate, twist ＞ 250 turns/m, not put up for retail sale
0/0/0	0	0	0/0	0/0/0	0/0	0//0	0/0/	0/0/0	0/0			0/0/0	---Other
0/0/0	0	0	0/0	0/0/0	0/0	0//0	0/0/	0/4.5/0	0/4.5			0/0/0	--Other
													-Other yarn, multiple (folded) or cabled:
0/0/0	0	0	0/0	0/0/0	0/0	0//0	0/0/	0/0/0	0/0			0/0/0	--Of viscose rayon
0/0/0	0	0	0/0	0/0/0	0/0	0//0	0/0/	0/0/0	0/0			0/0/0	--Of cellulose acetate
0/0/0	0	0	0/0	0/0/0	0/0	0//0	0/0/	0/0/0	0/0			0/0/0	--Other
													Synthetic monofilament of 67 decitex or more and of which no cross-sectional dimension exceeds 1 mm; strip and the like (for example, artificial straw) of synthetic textile materials of an apparent width not exceeing 5 mm:
													-Monofilament:
													--Elastomeric
0/0/0	0	2.3	0/0	0/0/0	0/0	0//0	0/0/	4.5/4.5/4.5	4.7/4.5			0/0/0	Elastomeric monofilament of polyester, fineness ≥ 67 decitex (cross-sectional dimension ≤ 1mm, fineness ＜ 67 decitex, should be classified under No. 5402)
0/0/0	0	2.3	0/0	0/0/0	0/0	0//0	0/0/	4.5/4.5/4.5	4.7/4.5			0/0/0	Other synthetic elastomeric monofilament, fineness ≥ 67 decitex (cross-sectional dimension ≤ 1mm, fineness ＜ 67 decitex, should be classified under No. 5402)
0/0/0	0	0	0/0	0/0/0	0/0	0//0	0/0/	0/0/0	0/0			0/0/0	--Other, of polypropylene
													--Other
0/0/0	0	1	0/0	0/0/0	0/0	0//0	0/0/	0/0/4.5	4.5/0			0/0/0	Monofilament of polyester, fineness ≥ 67 decitex (cross-sectional dimension ≤ 1mm, fineness ＜ 67 decitex, should be classified under No. 5402)
0/0/0	0	1	0/0	0/0/0	0/0	0//0	0/0/	0/0/4.5	4.5/0			0/0/0	Other synthetic monofilament, fineness ≥ 67 decitex (cross-sectional dimension ≤ 1mm, fineness ＜ 67 decitex, should be classified under No. 5402)
0/0/0	0	1	0/0	0/0/0	0/0	0//0	0/0/	0/0/4.5	4.5/0			0/0/0	-Other
													Artificial monofilament of 67 decitex or more and of which no cross-sectional dimension exceeds 1 mm; strip and the like (for example, artificial straw) of artificial textile materials of an apparent width not exceeding 5 mm:
0/0/0	0	0	0/0	0/0/0	0/0	0//0	0/0/	0/0/0	0/0			0/0/0	Artificial monofilament of 67 decitex or more of whichno cross sectional dimension exceeds 1 mm, strip and the like (for example, artificial straw) of artificial textile materials of an apparent width not exceeding 5 mm
													Man-made filament yarn (other than sewing thread), put up for retail sale:
0/0/0	0	0	0/0	0/0/0	0/0	0//0	0/0/	0/0/0	0/0			0/0/0	--Synthetic filament yarn
0/0/0	0	0	0/0	0/0/0	0/0	0//0	0/0/	0/0/0	0/0			0/0/0	--Artificial filament yarn
													Woven fabrics of synthetic filamentyarn, including woven fabrics obtained from materials of heading 54. 04:
													-Woven fabrics obtained from high tenacity yarn of nylon or other polyamides or of polyesters:
0/0/0	0	0	0/0	0/0/0	0/0	0/0/0	0/0/0	9/9/9	9.1/9			0/0/0	---Of nylon or other polyamides
													---Of polyesters
0/0/0	0	0	0/0	0/0/0	0/0	0/0/0	0/0/0	0/0/0	9.1/0			0/0/0	Woven fabrics of high tenacity yarn of polyesters, weight ≤ 170g/m^2
0/0/0	0	0	0/0	0/0/0	0/0	0/0/0	0/0/0	0/0/0	9.1/0			0/0/0	Woven fabrics of high tenacity yarn of polyesters, weight ＞ 170g/m^2
0/0/0	0	6	0/0	0/0/0	0/0	0/0/0	0/0/	9.5/9.5/	/9.5			0/0/0	-Woven fabrics obtained from strip or the like
0/0/0	0	0	0/0	0/0/0	0/0	0/0/0	0/0/	0/0/0	9.1/0			0/0/0	-Fabrics specified in Note 9 to Section Ⅺ
													-Other woven fabrics, containing 85% or more by weight of filaments of nylon or other polyamides:
0/0/0	0	0	0/0	0/0/0	0/0	0/0/0	0/0/0	0/0/0	9.1/0			0/0/0	--Unbleached or bleached
0/0/0	0	6	0/0	0/0/0	0/0	0/0/0	0/0/0	9.5/9.5/9.5	9.5/9.5		0/0/0	0/0/0	--Dyed
0/0/0	0	0	0/0	0/0/0	0/0	0/0/0	0/0/0	0/0/0	9.1/0			0/0/0	--Of yarns of different colours
0/0/0	0	6	0/0	0/0/0	0/0	0/0/0	0/0/	9.5/9.5/	/9.5			0/0/0	--Printed
													-Other woven fabrics, containing 85% or more by weight of textured polyester filaments:

税则号列	货品名称〔CIQ 扩展编码及品名－T2 表示见附表 2〕	最惠(%)	暂定税率	普通	增值/消费	出口退税	计量单位	监管条件/特殊证件	检验检疫	对美关税	亚太上/下
5407.5100	--未漂白或漂白〔999〕	8		130	13/	13	米/千克	/		33	5.2/5.2
5407.5200	--染色〔999〕	8		130	13/	13	米/千克	/		33	5.2/5.2
5407.5300	--色织〔999〕	8		130	13/	13	米/千克	/		33	
5407.5400	--印花〔999〕	8		130	13/	13	米/千克	/		33	
	-其他机织物，按重量计聚酯长丝含量在 85%及以上：										
5407.6100	--按重量计聚酯非变形长丝含量在 85%及以上〔999〕	8		130	13/	13	米/千克	/		33	5.2/5.2
5407.6900	--其他〔999〕	8		130	13/	13	米/千克	/		33	5.2/5.2
	-其他机织物，按重量计其他合成纤维长丝含量在 85%及以上：										
5407.7100	--未漂白或漂白〔999〕	8		130	13/	13	米/千克	/		33	5.2/5.2
5407.7200	--染色〔999〕	8		130	13/	13	米/千克	/		33	5.2/5.2
5407.7300	--色织〔999〕	8		130	13/	13	米/千克	/		33	
5407.7400	--印花〔999〕	8		130	13/	13	米/千克	/		33	5.2/5.2
	-其他机织物，按重量计其他合成纤维长丝含量在 85%以下，主要或仅与棉混纺：										
5407.8100	--未漂白或漂白〔101 棉混纺坯布，102 漂白棉混纺布，103 合成纤维混纺机织物〕	8		130	13/	13	米/千克	/		33	
5407.8200	--染色〔101 棉混纺染色布，102 合成纤维混纺机织物〕	8		130	13/	13	米/千克	/		33	
5407.8300	--色织〔101 色织棉混纺布，102 合成纤维混纺机织物〕	8		130	13/	13	米/千克	/		33	
5407.8400	--印花〔101 棉混纺印花布，102 合成纤维混纺机织物〕	8		130	13/	13	米/千克	/		28	
	-其他机织物：										
5407.9100	--未漂白或漂白〔999〕	8		130	13/	13	米/千克	/		33	
5407.9200	--染色〔999〕	8		130	13/	13	米/千克	/		33	
5407.9300	--色织〔999〕	8		130	13/	13	米/千克	/		28	
5407.9400	--印花〔999〕	8		130	13/	13	米/千克	/		33	
54.08	**人造纤维长丝纱线的机织物，包括品目 54.05 所列材料的机织物：**										
5408.1000	-粘胶纤维高强力纱的机织物〔999〕	8		130	13/	13	米/千克	/		18	
	-其他机织物，按重量计人造纤维长丝、扁条或类似品含量在 85%及以上：										
	--未漂白或漂白：										
5408.2110	---粘胶长丝制〔999〕	8		130	13/	13	米/千克	/		33	
5408.2120	---醋纤长丝制〔999〕	8		130	13/	13	米/千克	/			
5408.2190	---其他〔999〕	8		130	13/	13	米/千克	/		33	
	--染色：										
5408.2210	---粘胶长丝制〔999〕	8		130	13/	13	米/千克	/		33	
5408.2220	---醋纤长丝制〔999〕	8		130	13/	13	米/千克	/			
5408.2290	---其他〔999〕	8		130	13/	13	米/千克	/		33	
	--色织：										
5408.2310	---粘胶长丝制〔999〕	8		130	13/	13	米/千克	/		33	
5408.2320	---醋纤长丝制〔999〕	8		130	13/	13	米/千克	/			
5408.2390	---其他〔999〕	8		130	13/	13	米/千克	/		33	
	--印花：										
5408.2410	---粘胶长丝制〔999〕	8		130	13/	13	米/千克	/			
5408.2420	---醋纤长丝制〔999〕	8		130	13/	13	米/千克	/			
5408.2490	---其他〔999〕	8		130	13/	13	米/千克	/			
	-其他机织物：										
5408.3100	--未漂白或漂白〔999〕	8		130	13/	13	米/千克	/			
5408.3200	--染色〔999〕	8		130	13/	13	米/千克	/		33	5.2/5.2
5408.3300	--色织〔999〕	8		130	13/	13	米/千克	/		33	
5408.3400	--印花〔999〕	8		130	13/	13	米/千克	/		33	

协定税率 %								RCEP		特惠税率 %			Article Description
东/冰/格	巴基斯坦	韩国	瑞士上/下	哥/秘/柬	澳/毛	新西/坡/智	中国港/澳/台	东盟及马来/澳/韩	日/新	亚太2国	老/柬/缅	98/97/95	
0/0/0	0	0	0/0	0/0/0	0/0	0/0/0	0/0/0	0/0/0	9.1/0			0/0/0	--Unbleached or bleached
0/0/0	0	6	0/0	0/0/0	0/0	0/0/0	0/0/0	9.5/9.5/9.5	9.5/9.5		0/0/0	0/0/0	--Dyed
0/0/0	0	0	0/0	0/0/0	0/0	0/0/0	0/0/0	0/0/0	9.1/0			0/0/0	--Of yarns of different colours
0/0/0	0	4.6	0/0	0/0/0	0/0	0/0/0	0/0/0	9.3/9.5/9.3	9.4/9.5			0/0/0	--Printed
													-Other woven fabrics, containing 85% or more by weight of polyester filaments:
0/0/0	0	6	0/0	0/0/0	0/0	0/0/0	0/0/0	9.5/9.5/9.5	9.5/9.5			0/0/0	--Containing 85% or more by weight of non-textured polyester filaments
0/0/0	0	6	0/0	0/0/0	0/0	0/0/0	0/0/0	9.5/9.5/	/9.5			0/0/0	--Other
													-Other woven fabrics, containing 85% or more by weight of synthetic filaments:
0/0/0	0	0	0/0	0/0/0	0/0	0/0/0	0/0/0	0/0/0	9.1/0			0/0/0	--Unbleached or bleached
0/0/0	0	6	0/0	0/0/0	0/0	0/0/0	0/0/0	9.5/9.5/10	9.5/9.5		0/0/0	0/0/0	--Dyed
0/0/0	0	6	0/0	0/0/0	0/0	0/0/0	0/0/	9.5/9.5/	/9.5			0/0/0	--Of yarns of different colours
0/0/0	0	0	0/0	0/0/0	0/0	0/0/0	0/0/	0/0/0	9.1/0			0/0/0	--Printed
													-Other woven fabrics, containing less than 85% by weight of synthetic filaments, mixed mainly or solely with cotton:
0/0/0	0	0	0/0	0/0/0	0/0	0/0/0	0/0/	0/0/0	9.1/0			0/0/0	--Unbleached or bleached
0/0/0	0	6	0/0	0/0/0	0/0	0/0/0	0/0/0	9.5/9.5/	9.5/9.5			0/0/0	--Dyed
0/0/0	0	0	0/0	0/0/0	0/0	0/0/0	0/0/0	0/0/0	9.1/0			0/0/0	--Of yarns of different colours
0/0/0	0	0	0/0	0/0/0	0/0	0/0/0	0/0/	0/0/0	9.1/0			0/0/0	--Printed
													-Other woven fabrics:
0/0/0	0	6	0/0	0/0/0	0/0	0/0/0	0/0/	9.5/9.5/	/9.5			0/0/0	--Unbleached or bleached
0/0/0	0	6	0/0	0/0/0	0/0	0/0/0	0/0/0	9.5/9.5/	/9.5		0/0/0	0/0/0	--Dyed
0/0/0	0	0	0/0	0/0/0	0/0	0/0/0	0/0/0	0/0/0	9.1/0			0/0/0	--Of yarns of different colours
0/0/0	0	0	0/0	0/0/0	0/0	0/0/0	0/0/	0/0/0	9.1/0			0/0/0	--Printed
													Woven fabrics of artificial filament yarn, including woven fabrics obtained from materials of heading No. 54.05:
0/0/0	0	0	0/0	0/0/0	0/0	0/0/0	0/0/	0/0/0	9.1/0			0/0/0	-Woven fabrics obtained from high tenacity yarn of viscose rayon
													-Other woven fabrics, containing 85% or more by weight of artificial filament or strip or the like:
													--Unbleached or bleached:
0/0/0	0	0	1.2/1.2	0/0/0	0/0	0/0/0	0/0/	0/0/0	10.9/0			0/0/0	---Of yarns of viscose rayon
0/0/0	0	7.2	1.2/1.2	0/0/0	0/0	0/0/0	0/0/	11.4/11.4/	/11.4			0/0/0	---Of yarns of cellulose acetate
0/0/0	0	0	1.2/1.2	0/0/0	0/0	0/0/0	0/0/	0/0/0	10.9/0			0/0/0	---Other
													--Dyed:
0/0/0	0	0	0/0	0/0/0	0/0	0/0/0	0/0/	0/0/0	9.1/0			0/0/0	---Of yarns of viscose rayon
0/0/0	0	0	0/0	0/0/0	0/0	0/0/0	0/0/0	0/0/0	9.1/0			0/0/0	---Of yarns of cellulose acetate
0/0/0	0	0	0/0	0/0/0	0/0	0/0/0	0/0/0	9/9/9	9.1/9			0/0/0	---Other
													--Of yarns of different colours:
0/0/0	0	0	0/0	0/0/0	0/0	0/0/0	0/0/	0/0/0	9.1/0			0/0/0	---Of yarns of viscose rayon
0/0/0	0	0	0/0	0/0/0	0/0	0/0/0	0/0/	0/0/0	9.1/0			0/0/0	---Of yarns of cellulose acetate
0/0/0	0	0	0/0	0/0/0	0/0	0/0/0	0/0/0	0/0/0	9.1/0			0/0/0	---Other
													--Printed:
0/0/0	0	0	0/0	0/0/0	0/0	0/0/0	0/0/	0/0/0	9.1/0			0/0/0	---Of yarns of viscose rayon
0/0/0	0	0	0/0	0/0/0	0/0	0/0/0	0/0/	0/0/0	9.1/0			0/0/0	---Of yarns of cellulose acetate
0/0/0	0	0	0/0	0/0/0	0/0	0/0/0	0/0/	0/0/0	9.1/0			0/0/0	---Other
													-Other woven fabrics:
0/0/0	0	0	0/0	0/0/0	0/0	0/0/0	0/0/	0/0/0	9.1/0			0/0/0	--Unbleached or bleached
0/0/0	0	4.6	0/0	0/0/0	0/0	0/0/0	0/0/0	9.3/9.5/9.3	9.4/9.5			0/0/0	--Dyed
0/0/0	0	0	0/0	0/0/0	0/0	0/0/0	0/0/	0/0/0	9.1/0			0/0/0	--Of yarns of different colours
0/0/0	0	0	0/0	0/0/0	0/0	0/0/0	0/0/	0/0/0	9.1/0			0/0/0	--Printed

第五十五章
化学纤维短纤

注释：

税目 55.01 和 55.02 仅适用于每根与丝束长度相等的平行化学纤维长丝丝束。前述丝束应同时符合下列规格：

一、丝束长度超过 2 米；
二、捻度每米少于 5 转；
三、每根长丝细度在 67 分特以下；
四、合成纤维长丝丝束，须经拉伸处理，即本身不能被拉伸至超过本身长度的一倍；
五、丝束总细度大于 20000 分特。

丝束长度不超过 2 米的归入税目 55.03 或 55.04。

税则号列	货品名称〔CIQ 扩展编码及品名—T2 表示见附表 2〕	最惠(%)	暂定税率	普通	增值/消费	出口退税	计量单位	监管条件/特殊证件	检验检疫	对美关税	亚太上/下
55.01	**合成纤维长丝丝束：**										
	-尼龙或其他聚酰胺制：										
5501.1100	--芳族聚酰胺制〔999〕	5		70	13/	13	千克	/		30	
5501.1900	--其他〔999〕	5		70	13/	13	千克	/		30	
5501.2000	-聚酯制〔999〕	5		70	13/	13	千克	/		15	
5501.3000	-聚丙烯腈或变性聚丙烯腈制										
5501.3000 10	聚丙烯腈制长丝丝束(不包括变性聚丙烯腈制)〔999〕	5		35	13/	13	千克	/		30	3.3/3.3
5501.3000 90	变性聚丙烯腈长丝丝束〔999〕	5		35	13/	13	千克	/		30	3.3/3.3
5501.4000	-聚丙烯制〔999〕	5		70	13/	13	千克	/			
5501.9000	-其他〔999〕	5		70	13/	13	千克	/		30	
55.02	**人造纤维长丝丝束：**										
	-醋酸纤维丝束：										
5502.1010	---二醋酸纤维丝束〔999〕	3		40	13/	13	千克	7/		13	2/2
5502.1090	---其他〔999〕	5		35	13/	13	千克	/			3.3/3.3
5502.9000	-其他〔999〕	5		35	13/	13	千克	/			3.3/3.3
55.03	**合成纤维短纤，未梳或未经其他纺前加工：**										
	-尼龙或其他聚酰胺制：										
	--芳族聚酰胺纺制：										
5503.1110	---聚间苯二甲酰间苯二胺纺制〔999〕	5		70	13/	13	千克	/		30	
5503.1120	---聚对苯二甲酰对苯二胺纺制〔999〕	5		70	13/	13	千克	/		15	
5503.1190	---其他〔999〕	5		70	13/	13	千克	/		30	
5503.1900	--其他〔999〕	5		70	13/	13	千克	/		15	
5503.2000	-聚酯制〔999〕	5		70	13/	13	千克	/		30	3.3/3.3
5503.3000	-聚丙烯腈或变性聚丙烯腈制										
5503.3000 10	未梳或未经其他纺前加工的聚丙烯腈制短纤维(不包括变性聚丙烯腈制)〔999〕	5		35	13/	13	千克	/		30	3.3/3.3
5503.3000 90	未梳或未经其他纺前加工的变性聚丙烯腈制短纤维〔999〕	5		35	13/	13	千克	/		30	3.3/3.3
5503.4000	-聚丙烯制〔999〕	5		70	13/	13	千克	/		30	
	-其他：										
5503.9010	---聚苯硫醚制〔999〕	5		70	13/	13	千克	/		30	
5503.9090	---其他〔999〕	5		70	13/	13	千克	/		30	
55.04	**人造纤维短纤，未梳或未经其他纺前加工：**										
	-粘胶纤维制：										
5504.1010	---竹制〔999〕	5		35	13/	13	千克	/			4.5/4.5
	---木制：										
5504.1021	----阻燃的〔999〕	5		35	13/	13	千克	/			4/4
5504.1029	----其他〔999〕	5		35	13/	13	千克	/			
5504.1090	---其他〔999〕	5		35	13/	13	千克	/		30	
5504.9000	-其他〔999〕	5		35	13/	13	千克	/		30	
55.05	**化学纤维废料(包括落棉、废纱及回收纤维)：**										
5505.1000	-合成纤维的〔999〕	5		70	13/	13	千克	9/		30	
5505.2000	-人造纤维的〔999〕	5		70	13/	13	千克	9/		30	3.5/3.5
55.06	**合成纤维短纤，已梳或经其他纺前加工：**										
	-尼龙或其他聚酰胺制：										
	---芳族聚酰胺纺制：										
5506.1011	----聚间苯二甲酰间苯二胺纺制〔999〕	5		70	13/	13	千克	/		30	
5506.1012	----聚对苯二甲酰对苯二胺纺制〔999〕	5		70	13/	13	千克	/		15	
5506.1019	----其他〔999〕	5		70	13/	13	千克	/			
5506.1090	---其他〔999〕	5		70	13/	13	千克	/		30	
5506.2000	-聚酯制〔999〕	5		70	13/	13	千克	/		30	3.3/3.3
5506.3000	-聚丙烯腈或变性聚丙烯腈制										
5506.3000 10	已梳或经其他纺前加工的聚丙烯腈制短纤(不包括变性聚丙烯腈制)〔999〕	5		35	13/	13	千克	/		25	3.3/3.3

Chapter 55
Man-made staple fibres

Notes:

Headings 55. 01 and 55. 02 apply only to man-made filament tow, consisting of parallel filaments of a uniform length equal to the length of the tow, meeting the following specifications:

1. Length of tow exceeding 2 m;
2. Twist less than 5 turns per metre;
3. Measuring per filament less than 67 decitex;
4. Synthetic filament tow only: the tow must be drawn, that is to say, be incapable of being stretched by more than 100% of its length;
5. Total measurement of tow more than 20,000 decitex.

Tow of a length not exceeding 2 m is to be classified in heading No.55. 03 or 55. 04.

协定税率 %								RCEP		特惠税率 %			Article Description
东/冰/格	巴基斯坦	韩国	瑞士上/下	哥/秘/柬	澳/毛	新西/坡/智	中国港/澳/台	东盟及马来/澳/韩	日/新	亚太2国	老/柬/缅	98/97/95	
													Synthetic filament tow:
													- Of nylon or other polyamides :
0/0/0	0	0	0/0	0/0/0	0/0	0//0	0/0/	0/0/0	0/0			0/0/0	-- Of aramids
0/0/0	0	0	0/0	0/0/0	0/0	0//0	0/0/	0/0/0	0/0			0/0/0	--Other
/0/0	0	1	0/0	0/0/0	0/0	0//0	0/0/					0/0/0	-Of polyesters
													-Acrylic or modacrylic
/0/0	0	2.3	0/0	0//0	0/0	0//0	0/0/	4.9/4.9/	/4.9			0/0/0	Filament tow of acrylic(other than modacrylic)
/0/0	0	2.3	0/0	0//0	0/0	0//0	0/0/	4.9/4.9/	/4.9			0/0/0	Filament tow of modacrylic
0/0/0	0	0	0/0	0/0/0	0/0	0//0	0/0/	0/0/0	0/0			0/0/0	-Of polypropylene
0/0/0	0	1	0/0	0/0/0	0/0	0//0	0/0/	0/0/4.5	4.5/0			0/0/0	-Other
													Artificial filament tow:
													--Cellulose acetate filament tow:
0/0/0	0	0	0/0	0/0/0	0/0	0//0	0/0/	0/0/0	2.7/0			0/0/0	---Cellulose diacetate filament tow
0/0/0	0	2.3	0/0	0/0/0	0/0	0//0	0/0/	4.5/4.5/4.5	4.7/4.5			0/0/0	---Other
0/0/0	0	2.3	0/0	0/0/0	0/0	0//0	0/0/	4.5/4.5/4.5	4.7/4.5			0/0/0	-Other
													Synthetic staple fibres, not carded, combed or otherwise processed for spinning:
													-Of nylon or other polyamides:
													--Of aramides:
0/0/0	0		0/0	0/0/0	0/0	0//0	0/0/	4.9/4.9/	/4.9			0/0/0	---Of poly-isophthaloyl metaphenylene diamine
0/0/0	0		0/0	0/0/0	0/0	0//0	0/0/	4.9/4.9/	/4.9			0/0/0	---Of poly-p-phenylene terephthalamide
0/0/0	0		0.5/0.5	0/0/0	0/0	0//0	0/0/	4.9/4.9/	/4.9			0/0/0	---Other
0/0/0	0	1	0.5/0.5	0/0/0	0/0	0//0	0/0/	0/0/4.5	4.5/0			0/0/0	--Other
/0/0	0	2.3	0/0	0/0/0	0/0	0//0	0/0/	4.9/4.9/	/4.9			0/0/0	-Of polyesters
													-Acrylic or modacrylic
/0/0	0	1	0/0	0/0/0	0/0	0//0	0/0/					0/0/0	Staple fibres of acrylic, not carded, combed or otherwise processed forspinning(other than modacrylic)
/0/0	0	1	0/0	0/0/0	0/0	0//0	0/0/					0/0/0	Staple fibres of modacrylic, not carded, combed or otherwise processed forspinning
0/0/0	0	1	0/0	0/0/0	0/0	0//0	0/0/	0/0/4.5	4.5/0			0/0/0	-Of polypropylene
													-Other:
0/0/0	0	1	0/0	0/0/0	0/0	0//0	0/0/0	4.5/4.5/4.5	4.5/4.5			0/0/0	---Of polyphenylene sulfide
0/0/0	0	0	0/0	0/0/0	0/0	0//0	0/0/0	0/4.5/0	0/4.5			0/0/0	---Other〔999〕
													Artificial staple fibres, not carded, combed or otherwise processed for spinning:
													-Of viscose rayon:
0/0/0	0	0	0/0	0/0/0	0/0	0//0	0/0/	0/0/0	0/0			0/0/0	---Of bamboo
													---Of wood:
0/0/0	0	1	0/0	0/0/0	0/0	0//0	0/0/	0/0/4.5	4.5/0			0/0/0	----Flame retardancy
0/0/0	0	1	0/0	0/0/0	0/0	0//0	0/0/	4.5/4.5/4.5	4.5/4.5			0/0/0	----Other
0/0/0	0	1	0/0	0/0/0	0/0	0//0	0/0/	0/0/4.5	4.5/0			0/0/0	---Other
0/0/0	0	0	0/0	0/0/0	0/0	0//0	0/0/0	0/0/0	0/0			0/0/0	-Other
													Waste (including noils, yarn waste and garnetted stock) of man-made fibres:
0/0/0	0	1	0/0	0/0/0	0/0	0//0	0/0/	4.5/4.5/4.5	4.5/4.5			0/0/0	-Of synthetic fibres
0/0/0	0	1	0/0	0/0/0	0/0	0//0	0/0/	0/0/4.5	4.5/0			0/0/0	-Of artificial fibres
													Synthetic staple fibres, carded, combed or otherwise processed for spinning:
													-Of nylon or other polyamides:
													---Of aramides:
0/0/0	0		0/0	0/0/0	0/0	0//0	0/0/	4.9/4.9/	/4.9			0/0/0	----Of poly isophthaloy polpamides:l metaphenylene diamine
0/0/0	0		0/0	0/0/0	0/0	0//0	0/0/	4.9/4.9/	/4.9			0/0/0	----Of poly-p-phenylene terephthalamide
0/0/0	0	2.3	0/0	0/0/0	0/0	0//0	0/0/	4.9/4.9/	/4.9			0/0/0	----Other
0/0/0	0	0	0/0	0/0/0	0/0	0//0	0/0/	0/0/0	0/0			0/0/0	---Other
/0/0	4.5	1	0/0	0/0/0	0/0	0//0	0/0/					0/0/0	-Of polyesters
													-Acrylic or modacrylic
/0/0	4.5	1	0/0	0/0/0	0/0	0//0	0/0/					0/0/0	Staple fibres of acrylic, carded, combed or otherwise processed forspinning(other than modacrylic)

税则号列	货品名称〔CIQ 扩展编码及品名－T2 表示见附表 2〕	最惠(%)	暂定税率	普通	增值/消费	出口退税	计量单位	监管条件/特殊证件	检验检疫	对美关税	亚太上/下
5506.3000 90	已梳或经其他纺前加工的变性聚丙烯腈制短纤〔999〕	5		35	13/	13	千克	/		25	3.3/3.3
5506.4000	-聚丙烯制〔999〕	5		70	13/	13	千克	/			
	-其他：										
5506.9010	---聚苯硫醚制〔999〕	5		70	13/	13	千克	/			
5506.9090	---其他〔999〕	5		70	13/	13	千克	/		15	
55.07	**人造纤维短纤，已梳或经其他纺前加工：**										
5507.0000	人造纤维短纤，已梳或经其他纺前加工〔999〕	5		35	13/	13	千克	/		30	
55.08	**化学纤维短纤纺制的缝纫线，不论是否供零售用：**										
5508.1000	-合成纤维短纤纺制〔999〕	5		90	13/	13	千克	/		30	3.3/3.3
5508.2000	-人造纤维短纤纺制〔999〕	5		70	13/	13	千克	/			
55.09	**合成纤维短纤纺制的纱线（缝纫线除外），非供零售用：**										
	-按重量计尼龙或其他聚酰胺短纤含量在 85%及以上：										
5509.1100	--单纱〔999〕	5		90	13/	13	千克	/		15	
5509.1200	--多股纱线或缆线〔999〕	5		90	13/	13	千克	/		30	
	-按重量计聚酯短纤含量在 85%及以上：										
5509.2100	--单纱〔999〕	5		90	13/	13	千克	/		30	
5509.2200	--多股纱线或缆线〔999〕	5		90	13/	13	千克	/		30	
	-按重量计聚丙烯腈或变性聚丙烯腈短纤含量在 85%及以上：										
5509.3100	--单纱〔999〕	5		90	13/	13	千克	/			
5509.3200	--多股纱线或缆线〔999〕	5		90	13/	13	千克	/		30	3.3/3.3
	-其他纱线，按重量计合成纤维短纤含量在 85%及以上：										
5509.4100	--单纱〔999〕	5		90	13/	13	千克	/			
5509.4200	--多股纱线或缆线〔999〕	5		90	13/	13	千克	/		30	
	-其他聚酯短纤纺制的纱线：										
5509.5100	--主要或仅与人造纤维短纤混纺〔999〕	5		90	13/	13	千克	/		30	
5509.5200	--主要或仅与羊毛或动物细毛混纺〔999〕	5		90	13/	13	千克	/		30	
5509.5300	--主要或仅与棉混纺〔999〕	5		90	13/	13	千克	/		30	3.3/3.3
5509.5900	--其他〔999〕	5		90	13/	13	千克	/		15	
	-其他聚丙烯腈或变性聚丙烯腈短纤纺制的纱线：										
5509.6100	--主要或仅与羊毛或动物细毛混纺〔999〕	5		90	13/	13	千克	/		30	
5509.6200	--主要或仅与棉混纺〔999〕	5		90	13/	13	千克	/			3.3/3.3
5509.6900	--其他〔999〕	5		90	13/	13	千克	/			
	-其他纱线：										
5509.9100	--主要或仅与羊毛或动物细毛混纺〔999〕	5		90	13/	13	千克	/			
5509.9200	--主要或仅与棉混纺〔999〕	5		90	13/	13	千克	/			
5509.9900	--其他〔999〕	5		90	13/	13	千克	/		25	
55.10	**人造纤维短纤纺制的纱线（缝纫线除外），非供零售用：**										
	-按重量计人造纤维短纤含量在 85%及以上：										
5510.1100	--单纱〔999〕	5		70	13/	13	千克	/			3.3/3.3
5510.1200	--多股纱线或缆线〔999〕	5		70	13/	13	千克	/		30	
5510.2000	-其他纱线，主要或仅与羊毛或动物细毛混纺〔999〕	5		70	13/	13	千克	/		30	
5510.3000	-其他纱线，主要或仅与棉混纺〔999〕	5		70	13/	13	千克	/			3.3/3.3
5510.9000	-其他〔999〕	5		70	13/	13	千克	/			3.3/3.3
55.11	**化学纤维短纤纺制的纱线（缝纫线除外），供零售用：**										
5511.1000	-按重量计合成纤维短纤含量在 85%及以上〔999〕	5		90	13/	13	千克	/		25	
5511.2000	-按重量计合成纤维短纤含量在 85%以下〔999〕	5		90	13/	13	千克	/		30	
5511.3000	-人造纤维短纤纺制〔999〕	5		90	13/	13	千克	/			
55.12	**合成纤维短纤纺制的机织物，按重量计合成纤维短纤含量在 85%及以上：**										
	-按重量计聚酯短纤含量在 85%及以上：										
5512.1100	--未漂白或漂白〔999〕	8		130	13/	13	米/千克	/		33	5.2/5.2
5512.1900	--其他〔999〕	8		130	13/	13	米/千克	/		33	
	-按重量计聚丙烯腈或变性聚丙烯腈短纤含量在 85%及以上：										
5512.2100	--未漂白或漂白〔999〕	8		130	13/	13	米/千克	/		28	
5512.2900	--其他〔999〕	8		130	13/	13	米/千克	/		18	5.2/5.2
	-其他：										
5512.9100	--未漂白或漂白〔999〕	8		130	13/	13	米/千克	/		33	

协定税率 %								RCEP		特惠税率 %			Article Description
东/冰/格	巴基斯坦	韩国	瑞士 上/下	哥/秘/柬	澳/毛	新西/坡/智	中国港/澳/台	东盟及马来/澳/韩	日/新	亚太2国	老/柬/缅	98/97/95	
/0/0	4.5	1	0/0	0/0/0	0/0	0//0	0/0/					0/0/0	Staple fibres of modacrylic,carded,combed or otherwise processed forspinning
0/0/0	0	2.3	0/0	0/0/0	0/0	0//0	0/0/	4.5/4.5/4.5	4.7/4.5			0/0/0	-Of polyphenylene
													-Other:
0/0/0	0	2.3	0/0	0/0/0	0/0	0//0	0/0/	4.8/4.8/4.8	/4.8			0/0/0	Polyphe-nylenesu sulfide
0/0/0	0	2.3	0/0	0/0/0	0/0	0//0	0/0/	4.5/4.5/4.5	4.7/4.5			0/0/0	---Other
													Artificial staple fibres, carded, combed or otherwise processed for spinning:
0/0/0	0	0	0/0	0/0/0	0/0	0//0	0/0/	0/0/0	0/0			0/0/0	Artificial staple fibres,carded,combed or otherwise processed for spinning
													Sewingthread of man-made staple fibres, whether or not put up for retail sale:
0/0/0	0	0	0/0	0/0/0	0/0	0//0	0/0/	0/0/0	0/0			0/0/0	-Of synthetic staple fibres
0/0/0	0	0	0/0	0/0/0	0/0	0//0	0/0/	0/0/0	0/0			0/0/0	-Of artificial staple fibres
													Yarn (other than sewing thread) of synthetic staple fibres, not put up for retail sale:
													-Containing 85% or more by weight of staple fibres of nylon or other polyamides:
0/0/0	0	0	0/0	0/0/0	0/0	0//0	0/0/	0/0/0	0/0			0/0/0	--Single yarn
0/0/0	0	0	0/0	0/0/0	0/0	0//0	0/0/	0/0/0	0/0			0/0/0	--Multiple (folded) or cabled yarn
													-Containing 85% or more by weight of polyester staple fibres:
0/0/0	0	0	0/0	0/0/0	0/0	0//0	0/0/	0/0/0	0/0			0/0/0	--Single yarn
0/0/0	0	0	0/0	0/0/0	0/0	0//0	0/0/	0/0/0	0/0			0/0/0	--Multiple (folded) or cabled yarn
													-Containing 85% or more by weight of acrylic or modacrylic staple fibres:
0/0/0	0	0	0/0	0/0/0	0/0	0//0	0/0/	0/0/0	0/0			0/0/0	--Single yarn
0/0/0	0	0	0/0	0/0/0	0/0	0//0	0/0/0	0/0/0	0/0			0/0/0	--Multiple (folded) or cabled yarn
													-Other yarn,containing 85% or more by weight of synthetic staple fibres:
0/0/0	0	0	0/0	0/0/0	0/0	0//0	0/0/	0/0/0	0/0			0/0/0	--Single yarn
0/0/0	0	1	0/0	0/0/0	0/0	0//0	0/0/	0/0/4.5	4.5/0			0/0/0	--Multiple (folded) or cabled yarn
													-Other yarn,of polyester staple fibres:
0/0/0	0	1	0/0	0/0/0	0/0	0//0	0/0/	0/0/4.5	4.5/0			0/0/0	--Mixed mainly or solely with artificial staple fibres
0/0/0	0	0	0/0	0/0/0	0/0	0//0	0/0/	0/0/0	0/0			0/0/0	--Mixed mainly or solely with wool or fine animal hair
0/0/0	0	0	0/0	0/0/0	0/0	0//0	0/0/0	0/4.5/0	0/4.5			0/0/0	--Mixed mainly or solely with cotton
0/0/0	0	0	0/0	0/0/0	0/0	0//0	0/0/	0/0/0	0/0			0/0/0	--Other
													-Other yarn,of acrylic or modacrylic staple fibres:
0/0/0	0	0	0/0	0/0/0	0/0	0//0	0/0/	0/0/0	0/0			0/0/0	--Mixed mainly or solely with wool or fine animal hair
0/0/0	0	0	0/0	0/0/0	0/0	0//0	0/0/	0/0/0	0/0			0/0/0	--Mixed mainly or solely with cotton
0/0/0	0	0	0/0	0/0/0	0/0	0//0	0/0/	0/0/0	0/0			0/0/0	--Other
													-Other yarn:
0//0	0	0	0/0	0/0/0	0/0	0//0	0/0/	0/0/0	4.5/0			0/0/0	--Mixed mainly or solely with wool or fine animal hair
0/0/0	0	0	0/0	0/0/0	0/0	0//0	0/0/0	0/0/0	0/0			0/0/0	--Mixed mainly or solely with cotton
0/0/0	0	0	0/0	0/0/0	0/0	0//0	0/0/	0/0/0	0/0			0/0/0	--Other
													Yarn (other than sewing thread) of artificial staple fibres, not put up for retail sale:
													-Containing 85% or more by weight of artificial staple fibres:
0/0/0	0	2.3	0/0	0/0/0	0/0	0//0	0/0/0	4.5/4.5/4.5	4.7/4.5			0/0/0	--Single yarn
0/0/0	0	2.3	0/0	0/0/0	0/0	0//0	0/0/0	4.5/4.5/4.5	4.7/4.5			0/0/0	--Multiple (folded) or cabled yarn
0/0/0	0	0	0/0	0/0/0	0/0	0//0	0/0/	0/0/0	0/0			0/0/0	-Other yarn,mixed mainly or solely with wool or fine animal hair
0/0/0	0	0	0/0	0/0/0	0/0	0//0	0/0/0	0/0/0	0/0			0/0/0	-Other yarn,mixed mainly or solely with cotton
0/0/0	0	1	0/0	0/0/0	0/0	0//0	0/0/	0/0/4.5	4.5/0			0/0/0	-Other yarn
													Yarn (other than sewing thread) of man-made staple fibres, put up for retail sale:
0/0/0	0	0	0/0	0/0/0	0/0	0//0	0/0/	0/0/0	0/0			0/0/0	-Of synthetic staple fibres,containing 85% or more by weight of such fibres
0/0/0	0	0	0/0	0/0/0	0/0	0//0	0/0/	0/0/0	0/0			0/0/0	-Of synthetic staple fibres, containing less than 85% by weight of such fibres
0/0/0	0	0	0/0	0/0/0	0/0	0//0	0/0/	0/0/0	0/0			0/0/0	-Of artificial staple fibres
													Woven fabrics of synthetic staple fibres, containing 85% or more by weight of synthetic staple fibres:
													-Containing 85% or more by weight of polyester staple fibres:
0/0/0	0	3	1.5/1.5	0/0/0	0/0	0/0/0	0/0/0	0/0/13.5	13.6/0			0/0/0	--Unbleached or bleached
0/0/0	0	6	0/0	0/0/0	0/0	0/0/0	0/0/0	9.5/9.5/9.5	9.5/9.5			0/0/0	--Other
													-Containing 85% or more by weight of acrylic or modacrylic staple fibres:
0/0/0	0	2.6	1.3/1.3	0/0/0	0/0	0/0/0	0/0/	0/0/11.7	11.8/0			0/0/0	--Unbleached or bleached
0/0/0	0	0	0/0	0/0/0	0/0	0/0/0	0/0/	0/0/0	9.1/0			0/0/0	--Other
													-Other:
0/0/0	0	3.6	1.8/1.8	0/0/0	0/0	0/0/0	0/0/	0/0/16.2	16.4/0			0/0/0	--Unbleached or bleached

税则号列	货品名称〔CIQ 扩展编码及品名－T2 表示见附表 2〕	最惠(%)	暂定税率	普通	增值/消费	出口退税	计量单位	监管条件/特殊证件	检验检疫	对美关税	亚太上/下
5512.9900	--其他〔999〕	8		130	13/	13	米/千克	/		33	
55.13	**合成纤维短纤纺制的机织物，按重量计合成纤维短纤含量在85%以下，主要或仅与棉混纺，每平方米重量不超过170克：**										
	-未漂白或漂白：										
	--聚酯短纤纺制的平纹机织物：										
5513.1110	---未漂白〔101 棉混纺坯布，102 合成纤维混纺机织物〕	8		130	13/	13	米/千克	/		13	4.8/4.8
5513.1120	---漂白										
5513.1120 10	与棉混纺漂白聚酯短纤平纹府绸(聚酯短纤 85%以下，每平方米重≤170 克，含细平布)〔101 漂白棉混纺布，102 合成纤维混纺机织物〕	8		130	13/	13	米/千克	/		13	4.8/4.8
5513.1120 20	与棉混纺漂白聚酯短纤机织平布(混纺为含聚酯短纤 85%以下，轻质指每平方米重≤170 克)〔101 漂白棉混纺布，102 合成纤维混纺机织物〕	8		130	13/	13	米/千克	/		13	4.8/4.8
5513.1120 30	与棉混纺漂白聚酯平纹印染用布(混纺为含聚酯短纤 85%以下，轻质指每平方米重≤170 克)〔101 漂白棉混纺布，102 合成纤维混纺机织物〕	8		130	13/	13	米/千克	/		13	4.8/4.8
5513.1120 40	与棉混纺漂白聚酯短纤平纹奶酪布等(聚酯短纤＜85%，每平方米重≤170 克，含薄细布、巴里纱)〔101 漂白棉混纺布，102 合成纤维混纺机织物〕	8		130	13/	13	米/千克	/		13	4.8/4.8
	--聚酯短纤纺制的三线或四线斜纹机织物，包括双面斜纹机织物：										
5513.1210	---未漂白〔101 棉混纺坯布，102 漂白棉混纺布，103 合成纤维混纺机织物〕	8		130	13/	13	米/千克	/		13	
5513.1220	---漂白〔101 漂白棉混纺布，102 合成纤维混纺机织物〕	8		130	13/	13	米/千克	/		13	
	--其他聚酯短纤纺制的机织物：										
5513.1310	---未漂白〔101 棉混纺坯布，102 合成纤维混纺机织物〕	8		130	13/	13	米/千克	/		13	7.2/7.2
5513.1320	---漂白〔101 漂白棉混纺布，102 合成纤维混纺机织物〕	8		130	13/	13	米/千克	/		13	
5513.1900	--其他机织物〔101 棉混纺坯布，102 漂白棉混纺布，103 合成纤维混纺机织物〕	8		130	13/	13	米/千克	/		13	4.8/4.8
	-染色：										
5513.2100	--聚酯短纤纺制的平纹机织物〔101 棉混纺染色布，102 合成纤维混纺机织物〕	8		130	13/	13	米/千克	/		33	5.2/5.2
	--其他聚酯短纤纺制的机织物：										
5513.2310	---聚酯短纤纺制的三线或四线斜纹机织物，包括双面斜纹机织物〔101 棉混纺染色布，102 合成纤维混纺机织物〕	8		130	13/	13	米/千克	/			
5513.2390	---其他〔101 棉混纺染色布，102 合成纤维混纺机织物〕	8		130	13/	13	米/千克	/		33	
5513.2900	--其他机织物〔101 棉混纺染色布，102 合成纤维混纺机织物〕	8		130	13/	13	米/千克	/		33	
	-色织：										
5513.3100	--聚酯短纤纺制的平纹机织物〔101 色织棉混纺布，102 合成纤维混纺机织物〕	8		130	13/	13	米/千克	/		33	
	--其他机织物：										
5513.3910	---聚酯短纤纺制的三线或四线斜纹机织物，包括双面斜纹机织物〔101 色织棉混纺布，102 合成纤维混纺机织物〕	8		130	13/	13	米/千克	/			5.2/5.2
5513.3920	---其他聚酯短纤纺制的机织物〔101 色织棉混纺布，102 合成纤维混纺机织物〕	8		130	13/	13	米/千克	/			
5513.3990	---其他〔101 色织棉混纺布，102 合成纤维混纺机织物〕	8		130	13/	13	米/千克	/			
	-印花：										
5513.4100	--聚酯短纤纺制的平纹机织物〔101 棉混纺印花布，102 合成纤维混纺机织物〕	8		130	13/	13	米/千克	/			
	--其他机织物：										
5513.4910	---聚酯短纤纺制的三线或四线斜纹机织物，包括双面斜纹机织物〔101 棉混纺印花布，102 合成纤维混纺机织物〕	8		130	13/	13	米/千克	/			
5513.4920	---其他聚酯短纤纺制的机织物〔101 棉混纺印花布，102 合成纤维混纺机织物〕	8		130	13/	13	米/千克	/			
5513.4990	---其他〔101 棉混纺印花布，102 合成纤维混纺机织物〕	8		130	13/	13	米/千克	/			
55.14	**合成纤维短纤纺制的机织物，按重量计合成纤维短纤含量在85%以下，主要或仅与棉混纺，每平方米重量超过170克：**										
	-未漂白或漂白：										
	--聚酯短纤纺制的平纹机织物：										
5514.1110	---未漂白〔101 棉混纺坯布，102 合成纤维混纺机织物〕	8		130	13/	13	米/千克	/		13	5.2/5.2
5514.1120	---漂白〔101 漂白棉混纺布，102 合成纤维混纺机织物〕	8		130	13/	13	米/千克	/		33	
	--聚酯短纤纺制的三线或四线斜纹机织物，包括双面斜纹机织物：										
5514.1210	---未漂白〔101 棉混纺坯布，102 合成纤维混纺机织物〕	8		130	13/	13	米/千克	/		13	
5514.1220	---漂白〔101 漂白棉混纺布，102 合成纤维混纺机织物〕	8		130	13/	13	米/千克	/		13	
	--其他机织物：										
	---聚酯短纤纺制的机织物：										
5514.1911	----未漂白〔101 棉混纺坯布，102 合成纤维混纺机织物〕	8		130	13/	13	米/千克	/		18	
5514.1912	----漂白〔101 漂白棉混纺布，102 合成纤维混纺机织物〕	8		130	13/	13	米/千克	/		13	

协定税率 %								RCEP		特惠税率 %			Article Description
东/冰/格	巴基斯坦	韩国	瑞士上/下	哥/秘/柬	澳/毛	新西/坡/智	中国港/澳/台	东盟及马来/澳/韩	日/新	亚太2国	老/柬/缅	98/97/95	
0/0/0	0	4.6	0/0	0/0/0	0/0	0/0/0	0/0/0	9.3/9.5/9.3	9.4/9.5		0/0/0	0/0/0	--Other
													Woven fabrics of synthetic staple fibres, containing less than 85% by weight of such fibres, mixed mainly or solely with cotton, of a weight not exceeding 170 g/m²:
													-Unbleached or bleached:
													--Of polyester staple fibres, plain weave:
0/0/0	0	3.2	1.6/1.6	0/0/0	0/0	0/0/0	0/0/	0/0/14.4	14.5/0			0/0/0	---Unbleached
													---Bleached
0/0/0	0	3	1.5/1.5	0/0/0	0/0	0/0/0	0/0/	0/0/13.5	13.6/0			0/0/0	Poplin, plain weave, including fine plain cloth, mixed with cotton, containing＜85% by weight of polyester staple fibres, weight≤170g/m², bleached
0/0/0	0	3	1.5/1.5	0/0/0	0/0	0/0/0	0/0/	0/0/13.5	13.6/0			0/0/0	Plain cloth, mixed with cotton, containing＜85% by weight of polye ster staple fibres, weight≤170g/m², bleached
0/0/0	0	3	1.5/1.5	0/0/0	0/0	0/0/0	0/0/	0/0/13.5	13.6/0			0/0/0	Woven fabrics for printing and dying, plain weave, mixed with cotton, containing＜85% by weight of polyesterstaple fibres, weight≤170g/m², bleached
0/0/0	0	3	1.5/1.5	0/0/0	0/0	0/0/0	0/0/	0/0/13.5	13.6/0			0/0/0	Cheese cloth, plain weave, including voiles and fine thin cloth, mixed with cotton, containing＜85% by weight of polyester staple fibres, weight≤170g/m², bleached
													--3-thread or 4-thread twill, including cross twill, of polyester staple fibres:
0/0/0	0	3.2	1.6/1.6	0/0/0	0/0	0/0/0	0/0/	0/0/14.4	14.5/0			0/0/0	---Unbleached
0/0/0	0	3.6	1.8/1.8	0/0/0	0/0	0/0/0	0/0/	0/0/16.2	16.4/0			0/0/0	---Bleached
													--Other woven fabrics of polyester staple fibres:
0/0/0	0	3.2	1.6/1.6	0/0/0	0/0	0/0/0	0/0/	0/0/14.4	14.5/0			0/0/0	---Unbleached
0/0/0	0	3.6	1.8/1.8	0/0/0	0/0	0/0/0	0/0/	0/0/16.2	16.4/0			0/0/0	---Bleached
0/0/0	0	3.6	1.8/1.8	0/0/0	0/0	0/0/0	0/0/	0/0/16.2	16.4/0			0/0/0	--Other woven fabrics
													-Dyed:
0/0/0	0	0	0/0	0/0/0	0/0	0/0/0	0/0/0	0/0/0	9.1/0			0/0/0	--Of polyester staple fibres, plain weave
													--Other woven fabrics of polyester staple fibres:
0/0/0	0	0	0/0	0/0/0	0/0	0/0/0	0/0/	0/0/0	9.1/0			0/0/0	---3-thread or 4-thread twill, including cross twill, of polyester staple fibres
0/0/0	0	2	0/0	0/0/0	0/0	0/0/0	0/0/	0/0/9	9.1/0			0/0/0	---Other
0/0/0	0	0	0/0	0/0/0	0/0	0/0/0	0/0/	0/0/0	9.1/0			0/0/0	--Other woven fabrics
													-Of yarns of different colours:
0/0/0	0	0	0/0	0/0/0	0/0	0/0/0	0/0/	0/0/0	9.1/0			0/0/0	--Of polyester staple fibres, plain weave
													--Other woven fabrics:
0/0/0	0	0	0/0	0/0/0	0/0	0/0/0	0/0/	0/0/0	9.1/0			0/0/0	---3-thread or 4-thread twill, including cross twill, of polyester staple fibres
0/0/0	0	0	0/0	0/0/0	0/0	0/0/0	0/0/	0/0/0	9.1/0			0/0/0	---Other woven fabrics of polyester staple fibres
0/0/0	0	0	0/0	0/0/0	0/0	0/0/0	0/0/	0/0/0	9.1/0			0/0/0	---Other
													-Printed:
0/0/0	0	0	0/0	0/0/0	0/0	0/0/0	0/0/	0/0/0	9.1/0		0/0/0	0/0/0	--Of polyester staple fibres, plain weave
													--Other woven fabrics:
0/0/0	0	0	0/0	0/0/0	0/0	0/0/0	0/0/	0/0/0	9.1/0			0/0/0	---3-thread or 4-thread twill, including cross twill, of polyeste staple fibres
0/0/0	0	0	0/0	0/0/0	0/0	0/0/0	0/0/	0/0/0	9.1/0			0/0/0	---Other woven fabrics of polyester staple fibres
0/0/0	0	0	0/0	0/0/0	0/0	0/0/0	0/0/	0/0/0	9.1/0			0/0/0	---Other
													Woven fabrics of synthetic staple fibres, containing less than 85% by weight of such fibres, mixed mainly or solely with cotton, of a weight exceeding 170 g/m²:
													-Unbleached or bleached:
													Of polyester staple fibres, plain weave:
0/0/0	0	3.2	1.6/1.6	0/0/0	0/0	0/0/0	0/0/	0/0/14.4	14.5/0			0/0/0	---Unbleached
0/0/0	0	3.6	1.8/1.8	0/0/0	0/0	0/0/0	0/0/	0/0/16.2	16.4/0			0/0/0	---Bleached
													--3-thread or 4-thread twill, including cross twill, of polyester staple fibres:
0/0/0	0	3.2	1.6/1.6	0/0/0	0/0	0/0/0	0/0/	0/0/14.4	14.5/0			0/0/0	---Unbleached
0/0/0	0	3.6	1.8/1.8	0/0/0	0/0	0/0/0	0/0/	0/0/16.2	16.4/0			0/0/0	---Bleached
													--Other woven fabrics:
													---Other woven fabrics of polyester staple fibres:
0/0/0	0	3.2	1.6/1.6	0/0/0	0/0	0/0/0	0/0/	0/0/14.4	14.5/0			0/0/0	----Unbleached
0/0/0	0	3.6	1.8/1.8	0/0/0	0/0	0/0/0	0/0/	0/0/16.2	16.4/0			0/0/0	----Bleached

税则号列	货品名称〔CIQ 扩展编码及品名—T2 表示见附表 2〕	最惠(%)	暂定税率	普通	增值/消费	出口退税	计量单位	监管条件/特殊证件	检验检疫	对美关税	亚太上/下
5514.1990	---其他〔101 棉混纺坯布,102 漂白棉混纺布,103 合成纤维混纺机织物〕	8		130	13/	13	米/千克	/		33	5.2/5.2
	-染色：										
5514.2100	--聚酯短纤纺制的平纹机织物〔101 棉混纺染色布,102 合成纤维混纺机织物〕	8		130	13/	13	米/千克	/		33	
5514.2200	--聚酯短纤纺制的三线或四线斜纹机织物,包括双面斜纹机织物〔101 棉混纺染色布,102 合成纤维混纺机织物〕	8		130	13/	13	米/千克	/		33	
5514.2300	--其他聚酯短纤纺制的机织物〔101 棉混纺染色布,102 合成纤维混纺机织物〕	8		130	13/	13	米/千克	/		33	
5514.2900	--其他机织物〔101 棉混纺染色布,102 合成纤维混纺机织物〕	8		130	13/	13	米/千克	/		33	
	-色织：										
5514.3010	---聚酯短纤纺制的平纹机织物〔101 色织棉混纺布,102 合成纤维混纺机织物〕	8		130	13/	13	米/千克	/		33	
5514.3020	---聚酯短纤纺制的三线或四线斜纹机织物,包括双面斜纹机织物〔101 色织棉混纺布,102 合成纤维混纺机织物〕	8		130	13/	13	米/千克	/			
5514.3030	---其他聚酯短纤纺制的机织物〔101 色织棉混纺布,102 合成纤维混纺机织物〕	8		130	13/	13	米/千克	/		28	
5514.3090	---其他机织物〔101 色织棉混纺布,102 合成纤维混纺机织物〕	8		130	13/	13	米/千克	/		33	
	-印花：										
5514.4100	--聚酯短纤纺制的平纹机织物〔101 棉混纺印花布,102 合成纤维混纺机织物〕	8		130	13/	13	米/千克	/		18	
5514.4200	--聚酯短纤纺制的三线或四线斜纹机织物,包括双面斜纹机织物〔101 棉混纺印花布,102 合成纤维混纺机织物〕	8		130	13/	13	米/千克	/			
5514.4300	--其他聚酯短纤纺制的机织物〔101 棉混纺印花布,102 合成纤维混纺机织物〕	8		130	13/	13	米/千克	/		18	
5514.4900	--其他机织物〔101 棉混纺印花布,102 合成纤维混纺机织物〕	8		130	13/	13	米/千克	/			
55.15	**合成纤维短纤纺制的其他机织物：**										
	-聚酯短纤纺制：										
5515.1100	--主要或仅与粘胶纤维短纤混纺〔999〕	8		130	13/	13	米/千克	/		33	5.2/5.2
5515.1200	--主要或仅与化学纤维长丝混纺〔999〕	8		130	13/	13	米/千克	/		33	5.2/5.2
5515.1300	--主要或仅与羊毛或动物细毛混纺〔999〕	8		130	13/	13	米/千克	/		33	
5515.1900	--其他〔999〕	8		130	13/	13	米/千克	/		33	5.2/5.2
	-聚丙烯腈或变性聚丙烯腈短纤纺制：										
5515.2100	--主要或仅与化学纤维长丝混纺〔999〕	8		130	13/	13	米/千克	/		18	
5515.2200	--主要或仅与羊毛或动物细毛混纺〔999〕	8		130	13/	13	米/千克	/			
5515.2900	--其他〔999〕	8		130	13/	13	米/千克	/		33	
	-其他机织物：										
5515.9100	--主要或仅与化学纤维长丝混纺〔999〕	8		130	13/	13	米/千克	/		33	
5515.9900	--其他〔999〕	8		130	13/	13	米/千克	/		28	5.2/5.2
55.16	**人造纤维短纤纺制的机织物：**										
	-按重量计人造纤维短纤含量在85%及以上：										
5516.1100	--未漂白或漂白〔999〕	8		130	13/	13	米/千克	/		33	
5516.1200	--染色〔999〕	8		130	13/	13	米/千克	/		28	
5516.1300	--色织〔999〕	8		130	13/	13	米/千克	/		33	
5516.1400	--印花〔999〕	8		130	13/	13	米/千克	/		33	
	-按重量计人造纤维短纤含量在85%以下,主要或仅与化学纤维长丝混纺：										
5516.2100	--未漂白或漂白〔999〕	8		130	13/	13	米/千克	/		28	
5516.2200	--染色〔999〕	8		130	13/	13	米/千克	/		33	5.2/5.2
5516.2300	--色织〔999〕	8		130	13/	13	米/千克	/		28	
5516.2400	--印花〔999〕	8		130	13/	13	米/千克	/			
	-按重量计人造纤维短纤含量在85%以下,主要或仅与羊毛或动物细毛混纺：										
5516.3100	--未漂白或漂白〔999〕	8		130	13/	13	米/千克	/			
5516.3200	--染色〔999〕	8		130	13/	13	米/千克	/			
5516.3300	--色织〔999〕	8		130	13/	13	米/千克	/		33	
5516.3400	--印花〔999〕	8		130	13/	13	米/千克	/			
	-按重量计人造纤维短纤含量在85%以下,主要或仅与棉混纺：										
5516.4100	--未漂白或漂白〔101 棉混纺坯布,102 漂白棉混纺布,103 人造纤维混纺机织物〕	8		130	13/	13	米/千克	/		33	
5516.4200	--染色〔101 棉混纺染色布,102 人造纤维混纺机织物〕	8		130	13/	13	米/千克	/		33	
5516.4300	--色织〔101 色织棉混纺布,102 人造纤维混纺机织物〕	8		130	13/	13	米/千克	/		28	
5516.4400	--印花〔101 棉混纺印花布,102 人造纤维混纺机织物〕	8		130	13/	13	米/千克	/			
	-其他：										
5516.9100	--未漂白或漂白〔999〕	8		130	13/	13	米/千克	/			
5516.9200	--染色〔999〕	8		130	13/	13	米/千克	/		33	
5516.9300	--色织〔999〕	8		130	13/	13	米/千克	/		33	
5516.9400	--印花〔999〕	8		130	13/	13	米/千克	/		33	5.2/5.2

协定税率 %								RCEP		特惠税率 %			Article Description
东/冰/格	巴基斯坦	韩国	瑞士上/下	哥/秘/柬	澳/毛	新西/坡/智	中国港/澳/台	东盟及马来/澳/韩	日/新	亚太2国	老/柬/缅	98/97/95	
0/0/0	0	3.2	1.6/1.6	0/0/0	0/0	0/0/0	0/0/	0/0/14.4	14.5/0			0/0/0	---Other
													-Dyed:
0/0/0	0	0	0/0	0/0/0	0/0	0/0/0	0/0/	0/0/0	9.1/0			0/0/0	--Of polyester staple fibres, plain weave
0/0/0	0	0	0/0	0/0/0	0/0	0/0/0	0/0/	9/9.5/9	9.1/9.5			0/0/0	--3-thread or 4-thread twill, including cross twill, of polyester staple fibres
0/0/0	0	0	0/0	0/0/0	0/0	0/0/0	0/0/	0/0/0	9.1/0		0/0/0	0/0/0	--Other woven fabrics of polyester staple fibres
0/0/0	0	0	0/0	0/0/0	0/0	0/0/0	0/0/	0/0/0	9.1/0			0/0/0	--Other woven fabrics
													-Of yarns of different colours:
0/0/0	0	0	0/0	0/0/0	0/0	0/0/0	0/0/	0/0/0	9.1/0			0/0/0	---Of polyester staple fibres, plain weave
0/0/0	0	0	0/0	0/0/0	0/0	0/0/0	0/0/	0/0/0	9.1/0			0/0/0	---3-thread or 4-thread twill, including cross twill, of polyester staple fibres
0/0/0	0	0	0/0	0/0/0	0/0	0/0/0	0/0/	0/0/0	9.1/0			0/0/0	---Other woven fabrics of polyester staple fibres
0/0/0	0	0	0/0	0/0/0	0/0	0/0/0	0/0/	0/0/0	9.1/0			0/0/0	---Other woven fabrics
													-Printed:
0/0/0	0	0	0/0	0/0/0	0/0	0/0/0	0/0/	0/0/0	9.1/0			0/0/0	--Of polyester staple fibres, plain weave
0/0/0	0	0	0/0	0/0/0	0/0	0/0/0	0/0/	0/0/0	9.1/0			0/0/0	--3-thread or 4-thread twill, including cross twill, of polyester staple fibres
0/0/0	0	0	0/0	0/0/0	0/0	0/0/0	0/0/	0/0/0	9.1/0			0/0/0	--Other woven fabrics of polyester staple fibres
0/0/0	0	0	0/0	0/0/0	0/0	0/0/0	0/0/	0/0/0	9.1/0			0/0/0	--Other woven fabrics
													Other woven fabrics of synthetic staple fibres:
													-Of polyester staple fibres:
0/0/0	0	0	0/0	0/0/0	0/0	0/0/0	0/0/0	0/0/0	9.1/0			0/0/0	--Mixed mainly or solely with viscose rayon staple fibres
0/0/0	0	0	0/0	0/0/0	0/0	0/0/0	0/0/0	0/0/0	9.1/0			0/0/0	--Mixed mainly or solely with man-made filaments
0/0/0	0	0	0/0	0/0/0	0/0	0/0/0	0/0/	9/9/9	9.1/9			0/0/0	--Mixed mainly or solely with wool or fine animal hair
0/0/0	0	0	0/0	0/0/0	0/0	0/0/0	0/0/	0/0/0	9.1/0			0/0/0	--Other
													-Of acrylic or modacrylic staple fibres:
0/0/0	0	0	0/0	0/0/0	0/0	0/0/0	0/0/	0/0/0	9.1/0			0/0/0	--Mixed mainly or solely with man-made filaments
0/0/0	0	0	1.2/1.2	0/0/0	0/0	0/0/0	0/0/	0/0/0	10.9/0			0/0/0	--Mixed mainly or solely with wool or fine animal hair
0/0/0	0	0	0/0	0/0/0	0/0	0/0/0	0/0/	0/0/0	9.1/0			0/0/0	--Other
													-Other woven fabrics:
0/0/0	0	0	0/0	0/0/0	0/0	0/0/0	0/0/	0/0/0	9.1/0			0/0/0	--Mixed mainly or solely with man-made filaments
0/0/0	0	0	0/0	0/0/0	0/0	0/0/0	0/0/	0/0/0	9.1/0			0/0/0	--Other
													Woven fabrics of artificial staple fibres:
													-Containing 85% or more by weight of artificial staple fibres:
0/0/0	0	0	1.2/1.2	0/0/0	0/0	0/0/0	0/0/	0/0/0	10.9/0			0/0/0	--Unbleached or bleached
0/0/0	0	0	0/0	0/0/0	0/0	0/0/0	0/0/0	0/0/0	9.1/0			0/0/0	--Dyed
0/0/0	0	0	0/0	0/0/0	0/0	0/0/0	0/0/	0/0/0	9.1/0			0/0/0	--Of yarns of different colours
0/0/0	0	0	0/0	0/0/0	0/0	0/0/0	0/0/	0/0/0	9.1/0			0/0/0	--Printed
													-Containing less than 85% by weight of artificial staple fibres, mixed mainly or solely with man-made filaments:
0/0/0	0	0	1.2/1.2	0/0/0	0/0	0/0/0	0/0/	0/0/0	10.9/0			0/0/0	--Unbleached or bleached
0/0/0	0	4.6	0/0	0/0/0	0/0	0/0/0	0/0/0	9.3/9.5/9.3	9.4/9.5			0/0/0	--Dyed
0/0/0	0	0	0/0	0/0/0	0/0	0/0/0	0/0/	0/0/0	9.1/0			0/0/0	--Of yarns of different colours
0/0/0	0	0	0/0	0/0/0	0/0	0/0/0	0/0/	0/0/0	9.1/0			0/0/0	--Printed
													-Containing less than 85% by weight of artficial staple fibres, mixed mainly or solely with wool or fine animal hair:
0/0/0	0	0	1.2/1.2	0/0/0	0/0	0/0/0	0/0/	0/0/0	10.9/0			0/0/0	--Unbleached or bleached
0/0/0	0	0	0/0	0/0/0	0/0	0/0/0	0/0/	0/0/0	9.1/0			0/0/0	--Dyed
0/0/0	0	0	0/0	0/0/0	0/0	0/0/0	0/0/	0/0/0	9.1/0			0/0/0	--Of yarns of different colours
0/0/0	0	0	0/0	0/0/0	0/0	0/0/0	0/0/	0/0/0	9.1/0			0/0/0	--Printed
													-Containing less than 85% by weight of artificial staple fibres, mixed mainly or solely with cotton:
0/0/0	0	0	1.2/1.2	0/0/0	0/0	0/0/0	0/0/	0/0/0	10.9/0			0/0/0	--Unbleached or bleached
0/0/0	0	0	1.2/1.2	0/0/0	0/0	0/0/0	0/0/	0/0/0	10.9/0			0/0/0	--Dyed
0/0/0	0	0	0/0	0/0/0	0/0	0/0/0	0/0/	0/0/0	9.1/0			0/0/0	--Of yarns of different colours
0/0/0	0	0	0/0	0/0/0	0/0	0/0/0	0/0/	0/0/0	9.1/0			0/0/0	--Printed
													-Other:
0/0/0	0	0	1.2/1.2	0/0/0	0/0	0/0/0	0/0/	0/0/0	10.9/0			0/0/0	--Unbleached or bleached
0/0/0	0	4.6	0/0	0/0/0	0/0	0/0/0	0/0/	9.3/9.5/9.3	9.4/9.5			0/0/0	--Dyed
0/0/0	0	0	0/0	0/0/0	0/0	0/0/0	0/0/	0/0/0	9.1/0			0/0/0	--Of yarns of different colours
0/0/0	0	0	0/0	0/0/0	0/0	0/0/0	0/0/	0/0/0	9.1/0			0/0/0	--Printed

第五十六章
絮胎、毡呢及无纺织物；特种纱线；线、绳、索、缆及其制品

注释：

一、本章不包括：

(一)用各种物质或制剂(例如，第三十三章的香水或化妆品、税目34.01的肥皂或洗涤剂、税目34.05的光洁剂及类似制剂、税目38.09的织物柔软剂)浸渍、涂布、包覆的絮胎、毡呢或无纺织物，其中的纺织材料仅作为承载介质；

(二)税目58.11的纺织产品；

(三)以毡呢或无纺织物为底的砂布及类似品(税目68.05)；

(四)以毡呢或无纺织物为底的粘聚或复制云母(税目68.14)；

(五)以毡呢或无纺织物为底的金属箔(通常归入第十四类或第十五类)。

(六)税目96.19的卫生巾(护垫)及卫生棉条、尿布及尿布衬里和类似品。

二、所称“毡呢”，包括针刺机制毡呢以及纤维本身通过缝编工序增强了抱合力的纺织纤维网状织物。

三、税目56.02及56.03分别包括用各种性质(紧密结构或泡沫状)的塑料或橡胶浸渍、涂布、包覆或层压的毡呢及无纺织物。税目56.03还包括用塑料或橡胶作粘合材料的无纺织物。

但税目56.02及56.03不包括：

(一)用塑料或橡胶浸渍、涂布、包覆或层压，按重量计纺织材料含量在50%及以下的毡呢或者完全嵌入塑料或橡胶之内的毡呢(第三十九章或第四十章)；

(二)完全嵌入塑料或橡胶之内的无纺织物，以及用肉眼可辨别出两面都用塑料或橡胶涂布、包覆的无纺织物，涂布或包覆所引起的颜色变化可不予考虑(第三十九章或第四十章)；

(三)与毡呢或无纺织物混制的泡沫塑料或海绵橡胶板、片或扁条，纺织材料仅在其中起增强作用(第三十九章或第四十章)。

四、税目56.04不包括用肉眼无法辨别出是否经过浸渍、涂布或包覆的纺织纱线或税目54.04或54.05的扁条及类似品(通常归入第五十章至第五十五章)；运用本条规定，可不考虑浸渍、涂布或包覆所引起的颜色变化。

税则号列		货品名称〔CIQ扩展编码及品名—T2表示见附表2〕	最惠(%)	暂定税率	普通	增值/消费	出口退税	计量单位	监管条件/特殊证件	检验检疫	对美关税	亚太上/下
56.01		**纺织材料絮胎及其制品；长度不超过5毫米的纺织纤维(纤维屑)、纤维粉末及球结：**										
		-纺织材料制的絮胎及其制品：										
5601.2100		--棉制〔999〕	8		50	13/	13	千克	/		33	
		--化学纤维制：										
5601.2210		---卷烟滤嘴〔999〕	8		100	13/	13	千克	7/			
5601.2290		---其他〔999〕	8		100	13/	13	千克	/		18	
5601.2900		--其他〔999〕	8		90	13/	13	千克	/		33	
5601.3000		-纤维屑、纤维粉末及球结										
5601.3000	10	由两种或以上有机聚合物纺制的纤维(横截面为皮芯结构或并列结构或海岛结构，长度不超过5mm)〔999〕	8	5	100	13/	13	千克	/		15	
5601.3000	90	纺织纤维屑，纤维粉末及球结(纺织纤维长度不超过5mm)〔999〕	8		100	13/	13	千克	/		18	
56.02		**毡呢，不论是否浸渍、涂布、包覆或层压：**										
5602.1000		-针刺机制毡呢及纤维缝编织物〔999〕	8		100	13/	13	千克	/		18	
		-其他毡呢，未浸渍、涂布、包覆或层压：										
5602.2100		--羊毛或动物细毛制〔999〕	8		100	13/	13	千克	/		33	
5602.2900		--其他纺织材料制〔999〕	8		100	13/	13	千克	/		28	
5602.9000		-其他〔999〕	8		100	13/	13	千克	/		28	
56.03		**无纺织物，不论是否浸渍、涂布、包覆或层压：**										
		-化学纤维长丝制：										
		--每平方米重量不超过25克：										
5603.1110		---经浸渍、涂布、包覆或层压〔999〕	8		70	13/	13	千克	/		33	5.2/5.2
5603.1190		---其他〔999〕	8		130	13/	13	千克	/		33	6.8/6.8
		--每平方米重量超过25克，但不超过70克：										
5603.1210		---经浸渍、涂布、包覆或层压〔999〕	8		70	13/	13	千克	/		18	5.2/5.2
5603.1290		---其他〔999〕	8		130	13/	13	千克	/			
		--每平方米重量超过70克，但不超过150克：										
5603.1310		---经浸渍、涂布、包覆或层压〔999〕	8		70	13/	13	千克	/			5.2/5.2
5603.1390		---其他〔999〕	8		130	13/	13	千克	/			
		--每平方米重量超过150克：										
5603.1410		---经浸渍、涂布、包覆或层压〔999〕	8		70	13/	13	千克	/		28	5.2/5.2
5603.1490		---其他〔999〕	8		130	13/	13	千克	/		28	5.2/5.2
		-其他：										
		--每平方米重量不超过25克：										
5603.9110		---经浸渍、涂布、包覆或层压										
5603.9110	10	每平方米重量≤25克经浸渍的乙烯聚合物制电池隔膜基布(浸渍包括涂布、包覆或层压)〔999〕	8	5	70	13/	13	千克	/		25	5.2/5.2

Chapter 56
Wadding, felt and nonwovens; special yarns; twine, cordage, ropes and cables and articles thereof

Notes:

1. This Chapter does not cover:
   (a) Wadding, felt or nonwovens, impregnated, coated or covered with substances or preparations (for example, pefumes or cosmetics of Chapter 33, soaps or detergents of heading No.34.01, polishes, creams or similar preparations of heading No.34.05, fabric softeners of heading No.38.09) where the textile material is present merely as a carrying medium;
   (b) Textile products of heading No.58.11;
   (c) Natural or artificial abrasive powder or grain, on a backing of felt or nonwovens (heading No.68.05);
   (d) Agglomerated or reconstituted mica, on a backing of felt or nonwovens (heading No.68.14);
   (e) Metal foil on a backing of felt or nonwovens (Generelly section ⅩⅣ orsectionⅩⅤ).

   (f) Sanitary towels (pads) and tampons, napkins (diapers) and napkin liners and similar articles of heading 96.19.
2. The term "felt" includes needleloom felt and fabrics consisting of a web of textile fibres the cohesion of which has been enhanced by a stitch-bonding process using fibres from the web itself.
3. Headings No.56.02 and 56.03 cover respectively felt and nonwovens, impregnated, coated, covered or laminated with plastics or rubber whatever the nature of these materials (compact or cellular).
   Heading No.56.03 also includes nonwovens in which plastics or rubber forms the bonding substance.
   Headings No.56.02 and 56.03 do not, however, cover:
   (a) Felt impregnated, coated, covered or laminated with plastics or rubber, containing 50% or less by weight of textile material or felt completely embedded in plastics or rubber (Chapter 39 or 40);
   (b) Nonwovens, either completely embedded in plastics or rubber, or entirely coated or covered on both sides with such materials, provided that such coating or covering can be seen with the naked eye with no account being taken of any resulting change of colour (Chapter 39 or 40); or
   (c) Plates, sheets or strips of cellular plastics or cellular rubber combined with felt or nonwovens, where the textile material is present merely for reinforcing purposes (Chapter 39 or 40).
4. Heading No.56.04 does not cover textile yarn, or strip or the like of heading No.54.04 or 54.05, in which the impregnation, coating or covering cannot be seen with the naked eye (usually Chapters 50 to 55); for the purpose of this provision, no account should be taken of any resulting change of colour.

协定税率 %								RCEP		特惠税率 %			Article Description
东/冰/格	巴基斯坦	韩国	瑞士上/下	哥/秘/柬	澳/毛	新西/坡/智	中国港/澳/台	东盟及马来/澳/韩	日/新	亚太2国	老/柬/缅	98/97/95	
													Wadding of textile materials and articles thereof; textile fibres, not exceeding 5 mm in length (flock), textile dust and mill neps:
													-wadding of textile materials and articles thereof:
0/0/0	3.5	0	0/0	0/0/0	0/0	0/0/0	0/0/	0/0/0	9.1/0			0/0/0	--Of cotton
													--Of man-made fibres:
0/0/	4.8		1.2/1.2	0/0/0	/0	0/0/0	0/0/					0/0/0	---Cigarette filter tips
0/0/0		5.6	1.2/1.2	0/0/0	0/0	0/0/0	0/0/0	11.2/11.4/11.2	11.3/11.4			0/0/0	---Other
0/0/0	3.5	0	0/0	0/0/0	0/0	0/0/0	0/0/	0/0/0	9.1/0			0/0/0	--Other
													-Textile flock and dust and mill neps
0/0/0	3.5	0	0/0	0/0/0	0/0	0/0/0	0/0/	0/0/0	9.1/0			0/0/0	Textile fibres of two or more organic polymers (skin/core, side-by-side or island-in-the-sea type cross-section, length ≤ 5mm)
0/0/0	3.5	0	0/0	0/0/0	0/0	0/0/0	0/0/	0/0/0	9.1/0			0/0/0	Textile flock and dust and mill neps, length≤5mm
													Felt, whether or not impregnated, coated, covered or laminated:
0/0/0	3.5	0	0/0	0/0/0	0/0	0/0/0	0/0/	0/0/0	9.1/0			0/0/0	-Needleloom felt and stitch-bonded fibre fabrics
													-Other felt, not impregnated, coated, covered or laminated:
0/0/0	3.5	0	0/0	0/0/0	0/0	0/0/0	0/0/	0/0/0	9.1/0			0/0/0	--Of wool or fine animal hair
0/0/0	3.5	0	0/0	0/0/0	0/0	0/0/0	0/0/	0/0/0	9.1/0			0/0/0	--Of other textile materials
0/0/0	3.5	0	0/0	0/0/0	0/0	0/0/0	0/0/	0/0/0	9.1/0			0/0/0	-Other
													Nonwovens, whether or not impregnated, coated, covered or laminated:
													-Of man-made filaments:
													--Weighing not more than 25 g/m²
0/0/0	0	0	0/0	0/0/0	0/0	0/0/0	0/0/0	0/0/0	9.1/0		0/0/0	0/0/0	---Impregnated, coated, covered or laminated
0/0/0	0	2	0/0	0/0/0	0/0	0/0/0	0/0/	9/9/9	9.1/9			0/0/0	---Other
													--Weighing more than 25 g/m² but not more than 70 g/m²:
0/0/0	0	4.6	0/0	0/0/0	0/0	0/0/0	0/0/	9.3/9.5/9.3	9.4/9.5		0/0/0	0/0/0	---Impregnated, coated, covered or laminated
0/0/0	0	0	0/0	0/0/0	0/0	0/0/0	0/0/0	0/0/0	9.1/0			0/0/0	---Other
													--Weighing more than 70 g/m² but not more than 150 g/m²:
0/0/0	0	0	0/0	0/0/0	0/0	0/0/0	0/0/0	0/0/0	9.1/0			0/0/0	---Impregnated, coated, covered or laminated
0/0/0	0	0	0/0	0/0/0	0/0	0/0/0	0/0/0	9/9/9	9.1/9			0/0/0	---Other
													--Weighing more than 150 g/m²:
0/0/0	0	4.6	0/0	0/0/0	0/0	0/0/0	0/0/0	9.3/9.5/9.3	9.4/9.5			0/0/0	---Impregnated, coated, covered or laminated
0/0/0	0	0	0/0	0/0/0	0/0	0/0/0	0/0/0	9/9/9	9.1/9			0/0/0	---Other
													-Other:
													--Weighing not more than 25 g/m²:
													---Impregnated, coated, covered or laminated
0/0/0	0	2	0/0	0/0/0	0/0	0/0/0	0/0/	0/0/9	9.1/0			0/0/0	The weight per square meter is less than or equal to 25 grams of the impregnated polymers of ethylene (including battery diaphragm base fabricimpregnated, coated or laminated coating)

税则号列	货品名称〔CIQ 扩展编码及品名—T2 表示见附表 2〕	最惠(%)	暂定税率	普通	增值/消费	出口退税	计量单位	监管条件/特殊证件	检验检疫	对美关税	亚太上/下
5603.9110 90	每平方米重量≤25 克经浸渍其他无纺布(浸渍包括涂布、包覆或层压)〔999〕	8		70	13/	13	千克	/		28	5.2/5.2
5603.9190	---其他〔999〕	8		85	13/	13	千克	/		33	6.8/6.8
	--每平方米重量超过 25 克,但不超过 70 克:										
5603.9210	---经浸渍、涂布、包覆或层压										
5603.9210 10	25 克<每平方米重量≤70 克浸渍的乙烯聚合物制电池隔膜基布(浸渍包括涂布、包覆或层压)〔999〕	8	5	70	13/	13	千克	/		15	5.2/5.2
5603.9210 90	25 克<每平方米重量≤70 克经浸渍其他无纺布(浸渍包括涂布、包覆或层压)〔999〕	8		70	13/	13	千克	/		18	5.2/5.2
5603.9290	---其他〔999〕	8		85	13/	13	千克	/		18	5.2/5.2
	--每平方米重量超过 70 克,但不超过 150 克:										
5603.9310	---经浸渍、涂布、包覆或层压										
5603.9310 10	70<每平方米重≤150 克浸渍的乙烯聚合物制电池隔膜基布(浸渍包括涂布、包覆或压层)〔999〕	8	5	70	13/	13	千克	/		25	5.2/5.2
5603.9310 90	70<每平方米重≤150 克浸渍其他无纺布(浸渍包括涂布、包覆或压层)〔999〕	8		70	13/	13	千克	/		28	5.2/5.2
5603.9390	---其他〔999〕	8		85	13/	13	千克	/		28	5.2/5.2
	--每平方米重量超过 150 克:										
5603.9410	---经浸渍、涂布、包覆或层压〔999〕	8		70	13/	13	千克	/		28	5.2/5.2
5603.9490	---其他〔999〕	8		85	13/	13	千克	/		28	5.2/5.2
56.04	**用纺织材料包覆的橡胶线及绳;用橡胶或塑料浸渍、涂布、包覆或套裹的纺织纱线及税目 54.04 或 54.05 的扁条及类似品:**										
5604.1000	-用纺织材料包覆的橡胶线及绳〔999〕	5		80	13/	13	千克	/		15	
5604.9000	-其他〔999〕	5		80	13/	13	千克	/		15	
56.05	**含金属纱线,不论是否螺旋花线,由纺织纱线或税目 54.04 或 54.05 的扁条及类似品与金属线、扁条或粉末混合制得或用金属包覆制得:**										
5605.0000	含金属纱线,不论是否螺旋花线,由纺织纱线或税目 54.04 或 54.05 的扁条及类似品与金属线、扁条或粉末混合制得或用金属包覆制得〔999〕	5		70	13/	13	千克	/		30	
56.06	**粗松螺旋花线,税目 54.04 或 54.05 的扁条及类似品制的螺旋花线(税目 56.05 的货品及马毛粗松螺旋花线除外);绳绒线(包括植绒绳绒线);纵行起圈纱线:**										
5606.0000	粗松螺旋花线,税目 54.04 或 54.05 的扁条及类似品制的螺旋花线(税目 56.05 的货品及马毛粗松螺旋花线除外);绳绒线(包括植绒绳绒线);纵行起圈纱线〔999〕	5		70	13/	13	千克	/		30	
56.07	**线、绳、索、缆,不论是否编织或编结而成,也不论是否用橡胶或塑料浸渍、涂布、包覆或套裹:**										
	-西沙尔麻或其他纺织用龙舌兰类纤维纺制:										
5607.2100	--包扎用绳〔999〕	5		50	13/	13	千克	/			
5607.2900	--其他〔999〕	5		50	13/	13	千克	/			
	-聚乙烯或聚丙烯纺制:										
5607.4100	--包扎用绳〔999〕	5		100	13/	13	千克	/		15	
5607.4900	--其他〔999〕	5		100	13/	13	千克	/		15	
5607.5000	-其他合成纤维纺制〔999〕	5		100	13/	13	千克	/		15	
	-其他:										
5607.9010	---蕉麻(马尼拉麻)或其他硬质(叶)纤维纺制〔999〕	5		50	13/	13	千克	/			
5607.9090	---其他〔999〕	5		100	13/	13	千克	/		25	
56.08	**线、绳或索结制的网料;纺织材料制成的渔网及其他网:**										
	-化学纤维材料制:										
5608.1100	--制成的渔网〔999〕	8		50	13/	13	千克	/			
5608.1900	--其他〔999〕	8		100	13/	13	千克	/		28	
5608.9000	-其他〔999〕	8		100	13/	13	千克	/		28	
56.09	**用纱线、税目 54.04 或 54.05 的扁条及类似品或线、绳、索、缆制成的其他税目未列名物品:**										
5609.0000	用纱线、税目 54.04 或 54.05 的扁条及类似品或线、绳、索、缆制成的其他税目未列名物品〔999〕	8		100	13/	13	千克	/		33	

协定税率 %								RCEP		特惠税率 %			Article Description
东/冰/格	巴基斯坦	韩国	瑞士上/下	哥/秘/柬	澳/毛	新西/坡/智	中国港/澳/台	东盟及马来/澳/韩	日/新	亚太2国	老/柬/缅	98/97/95	
0/0/0	0	2	0/0	0/0/0	0/0	0/0/0	0/0/	0/0/9	9.1/0			0/0/0	The weight per square meter is less than or equal to 25 grams of impregnatedother non-woven (impregnated, coated or laminated including coating)
0/0/0	0	2	0/0	0/0/0	0/0	0/0/0	0/0/	0/0/9	9.1/0			0/0/0	---Other
													--Weighing more than 25 g/m² but not more than 70 g/m²:
													---Impregnated, coated, covered or laminated
0/0/0	0	2	0/0	0/0/0	0/0	0/0/0	0/0/	0/0/9	9.1/0			0/0/0	25 g < the weight per square meter is less than or equal to 70 grams ofimpregnated polymers of ethylene (including battery diaphragm base fabricimpregnated, coated or laminated coating)
0/0/0	0	2	0/0	0/0/0	0/0	0/0/0	0/0/	0/0/9	9.1/0			0/0/0	25 g < the weight per square meter is less than or equal to 70 grams ofimpregnated other non-woven (impregnated, coated or laminated including coating)
0/0/0	0	0	0/0	0/0/0	0/0	0//0	0/0/0	9/9/9	9.1/9		0/0/0	0/0/0	---Other
													--Weighing more than 70 g/m² but not more than 150 g/m²:
													---Impregnated, coated, covered or laminated
0/0/0	0	2	0/0	0/0/0	0/0	0/0/0	0/0/	9/9/9	9.1/9			0/0/0	70<per square metre weighs≤150 grams or less system of impregnation of the vinyl polymer battery diaphragm base cloth (dip coating, coating or laminating)
0/0/0	0	2	0/0	0/0/0	0/0	0/0/0	0/0/	9/9/9	9.1/9			0/0/0	70<per square metre weighs≤150 grams or less other non-woven impregnated (dip coating, coating or laminating)
0/0/0	0	0	0/0	0/0/0	0/0	0/0/0	0/0/0	0/0/0	9.1/0			0/0/0	---Other
													--Weighing more than 150 g/m²:
0/0/0	0	0	0/0	0/0/0	0/0	0/0/0	0/0/0	9/9/9	9.1/9			0/0/0	---Impregnated, coated, covered or laminated
0/0/0	0	4.6	0/0	0/0/0	0/0	0/0/0	0/0/0	9.3/9.5/9.3	9.4/9.5		0/0/0	0/0/0	---Other
													Rubber thread and cord, textile covered; textile yarn, and strip and the like of heading No.54. 04 or 54. 05, impregnated, coated, covered or sheathed with rubber or plastics:
0/0/0	0	0	0/0	0/0/0	0/0	0//0	0/0/	0/0/0	0/0		0/0/0	0/0/0	-Rubber thread and cord, textile covered
0/0/0	0	1	0/0	0/0/0	0/0	0//0	0/0/	4.5/4.5/4.5	4.7/4.5			0/0/0	-Other
													Metallized yarn, whether or not gimped, being textile yarn, or strip or the like of heading No. 54. 04 or 54. 05, combined with metal in the form of thread, strip or powder or covered with metal:
0/0/0	0	0	0/0	0/0/0	0/0	0//0	0/0/	0/0/0	0/0			0/0/0	Metallzied yarn, whether or not gimped, being textile yarn, or strip or the like of heading No. 54. 04 or 54. 05, combined with metal in the form of thread, strip or powder or covered with metal
													Gimped yarn, and strip and the like of heading No. 54. 04 or 54. 05, gimped (other than those of heading No. 56, 05 and gimped horsehair yarn); chenille yarn (including flock chenille yarn); loop wale —Yarn:
0/0/0	0	0	0/0	0/0/0	0/0	0//0	0/0/	0/0/0	0/0			0/0/0	Gimped yarn, and strip and the like of heading No. 54. 04 or 54. 05, gimped (other than those of heading No. 56. 05 and gimped horsehair yarn); chenille yarn (including flock chenille yarn); loopwale—Yarn
													Twine, cordage, ropes and cables, whether or not plaited or braided and whether or not impregnated, coated, covered or sheathed with rubber or plastics:
													-Of sisal or other textile fibres of the genus Agave:
0/0/0	0	0	0/0	0/0/0	0/0	0//0	0/0/	0/0/0	0/0			0/0/0	--Binder or baler twine
0/0/0	0	0	0/0	0/0/0	0/0	0//0	0/0/	0/0/0	0/0			0/0/0	--Other
													-Of polyethylene or polypropylene:
0/0/0	0	0	0/0	0/0/0	0/0	0//0	0/0/	0/0/0	0/0			0/0/0	--Binder or baler twine
0/0/0	0	0	0/0	0/0/0	0/0	0//0	0/0/	0/0/0	0/0			0/0/0	--Other
0/0/0	0	0	0/0	0/0/0	0/0	0//0	0/0/0	0/0/0	0/0			0/0/0	-Of other synthetic fibres
													-Other:
0/0/0	0	0	0/0	0/0/0	0/0	0//0	0/0/	0/0/0	0/0			0/0/0	---Of abaca(Manila hemp or *Musa textilis Nee*) or other hard (leaf) fibres
0/0/0	0	0	0/0	0/0/0	0/0	0//0	0/0/	0/0/0	0/0	2.5	0/0/0	0/0/0	---Other
													Knotted netting of twine, cordage or rope; made up fishing nets and other made up nets, of textile materials:
													-Of man-made textile materials:
0/0/0	3.5	0	0/0	0/0/0	0/0	0//0	0/0/	0/0/0	9.1/0			0/0/0	--Made up fishing nets
0/0/0	0	0	1.2/1.2	0/0/0	0/0	0/0/0	0/0/0	0/0/0	10.9/0			0/0/0	--Other
0/0/0	3.5	0	0/0	0/0/0	0/0	0//0	0/0/	0/0/0	9.1/0			0/0/0	-Other
													Articles of yarn, strip or the like of heading No. 54. 04 or 54. 05, twine, cordage, rope or cables, not elsewhere specified or included:
0/0/0	4	0	0/0	0/0/0	0/6	0//0	0/0/	0/0/0	9.1/0	0		0/0/0	Articles of yarn, strip or the like of heading No. 54. 04 or 54. 05, twine, cordage, rope or cables, not elsewhere specified or included

第五十七章
地毯及纺织材料的其他铺地制品

注释：

一、本章所称"地毯及纺织材料的其他铺地制品"，是指使用时以纺织材料作面的铺地制品，也包括具有纺织材料铺地制品特征但作其他用途的物品。

二、本章不包括铺地制品衬垫。

税则号列	货品名称〔CIQ扩展编码及品名一T2表示见附表2〕	最惠(%)	暂定税率	普通	增值/消费	出口退税	计量单位	监管条件/特殊证件	检验检疫	对美关税	亚太上/下
57.01	**结织栽绒地毯及纺织材料的其他结织栽绒铺地制品，不论是否制成的：**										
5701.1000	-羊毛或动物细毛制〔999〕	6		130	13/	13	千克/平方米	/		31	
	-其他纺织材料制：										
5701.9010	---化学纤维制〔999〕	6		130	13/	13	千克/平方米	/		31	
5701.9020	---丝制〔999〕	6		100	13/	13	千克/平方米	/		31	
5701.9090	---其他〔999〕	6		100	13/	13	千克/平方米	/		31	
57.02	**机织地毯及纺织材料的其他机织铺地制品，未簇绒或未植绒，不论是否制成的，包括"开来姆""苏麦克""卡拉马尼"及类似的手织地毯：**										
5702.1000	-"开来姆""苏麦克""卡拉马尼"及类似的手织地毯〔999〕	6		130	13/	13	千克/平方米	/		31	
5702.2000	-椰壳纤维制的铺地制品〔999〕	6		100	13/	13	千克/平方米	/			
	-其他起绒结构的铺地制品，未制成的：										
5702.3100	--羊毛或动物细毛制〔999〕	4		130	13/	13	千克/平方米	/		29	
5702.3200	--化学纤维制〔999〕	6		130	13/	13	千克/平方米	/		31	
5702.3900	--其他纺织材料制〔999〕	6		100	13/	13	千克/平方米	/			
	-其他起绒结构的铺地制品，制成的：										
5702.4100	--羊毛或动物细毛制〔999〕	4		130	13/	13	千克/平方米	/		29	
5702.4200	--化学纤维制〔999〕	4		130	13/	13	千克/平方米	/		29	
5702.4900	--其他纺织材料制〔999〕	6		100	13/	13	千克/平方米	/			4/4
	-其他非起绒结构的铺地制品，未制成的：										
5702.5010	---羊毛或动物细毛制〔999〕	6		130	13/	13	千克/平方米	/			
5702.5020	---化学纤维制〔999〕	6		130	13/	13	千克/平方米	/			
5702.5090	---其他纺织材料制〔999〕	6		100	13/	13	千克/平方米	/			
	-其他非起绒结构的铺地制品，制成的：										
5702.9100	--羊毛或动物细毛制〔999〕	6		130	13/	13	千克/平方米	/		31	
5702.9200	--化学纤维制〔999〕	6		130	13/	13	千克/平方米	/		31	
5702.9900	--其他纺织材料制〔999〕	6		100	13/	13	千克/平方米	/		31	
57.03	**簇绒地毯及纺织材料的其他簇绒铺地制品（包括人造草皮），不论是否制成的：**										
5703.1000	-羊毛或动物细毛制	6		130	13/	13	千克/平方米	/		16	
	-尼龙或其他聚酰胺制：										
5703.2100	--人造草皮〔999〕	4		130	13/	13	千克/平方米	/		14	
5703.2900	--其他〔999〕	4		130	13/	13	千克/平方米	/		14	
	-其他化学纤维制：										
5703.3100	--人造草皮〔999〕	4		130	13/	13	千克/平方米	/		29	
5703.3900	--其他〔999〕	4		130	13/	13	千克/平方米	/		29	
5703.9000	-其他纺织材料制〔999〕	6		100	13/	13	千克/平方米	/		16	
57.04	**毡呢地毯及纺织材料的其他毡呢铺地制品，未簇绒或未植绒，不论是否制成的：**										
5704.1000	-最大表面面积不超过0.3平方米〔999〕	6		130	13/	13	千克/平方米	/			
5704.2000	-最大表面面积超过0.3平方米但不超过1平方米〔999〕	4		130	13/	13	千克/平方米	/		29	
5704.9000	-其他〔999〕	4		130	13/	13	千克/平方米	/		29	
57.05	**其他地毯及纺织材料的其他铺地制品，不论是否制成的：**										
5705.0010	---羊毛或动物细毛制〔999〕	6		130	13/	13	千克/平方米	/		31	
5705.0020	---化学纤维制〔999〕	4		130	13/	13	千克/平方米	/		14	
5705.0090	---其他纺织材料制〔999〕	6		100	13/	13	千克/平方米	/		31	

Chapter 57
Carpets and other textile floor coverings

Notes:

1. For the purposes of this Chapter, the term "carpets and other textilefloor coverings" means floor coverings in which textile materials serve as the exposed surface of the article when in use and includes articles having the characteristics of textile floor coverings but intended for use for other purposes.
2. This Chapter does not cover floor covering underlays.

协定税率 %								RCEP		特惠税率 %			Article Description
东/冰/格	巴基斯坦	韩国	瑞士上/下	哥/秘/柬	澳/毛	新西/坡/智	中国港/澳/台	东盟及马来/澳/韩	日/新	亚太2国	老/柬/缅	98/97/95	
													Carpets and other textile floor coverings, knotted, whether or not made up:
0/0/0	0	2.8	1.4/1.4	0/0/0	0/0	0/0/0	0/0/	0/0/12.6	12.7/0			0/0/0	-Of wool or fine animal hair
													-Of other textile materials:
0/0/0	12.8	3.2	1.6/1.6	0/0/0	0/0	0/0/0	0/0/	0/0/14.4	14.5/0			0/0/0	---Of man-made textile materials
0/0/0	7	2.8	1.4/1.4	0/0/0	0/0	0/0/0	0/0/	0/0/12.6	12.7/0			0/0/0	---Of silk
0/0/0	7	2.8	1.4/1.4	0/0/0	0/0	0/0/0	0/0/	0/0/12.6	12.7/0			0/0/0	---Other
													Carpets and other textile floor coverings, woven, not tufted or flocked, whether or not made up, including "Kelem", "Schumacks", "Karamanie" and similar handwoven rugs:
0/0/0	0	2.8	1.4/1.4	0/0/0	0/0	0/0/0	0/0/	0/0/12.6	12.7/0	0		0/0/0	-"Kelem", "Schumacks", "Karamanie" and similar handwoven rugs
0/0/0	0	2.8	1.4/1.4	0/0/0	0/0	0/0/0	0/0/	0/0/12.6	12.7/0			0/0/0	-Floor coverings of coconut fibres (coir)
													-Other, of pile construction, not made up:
0/0/0	0	0	1/1	0/0/0	0/0	0/0/0	0/0/	0/0/0	9.1/0			0/0/0	--Of wool or fine animal hair
0/0/0	0	3.2	1.6/1.6	0/0/0	0/0	0/0/0	0/0/	0/0/14.4	14.5/0			0/0/0	--Of man-made textile materials
0/0/0	0	2.8	1.4/1.4	0/0/0	0/0	0/0/0	0/0/	0/0/12.6	12.7/0	0		0/0/0	--Of other textile materials
													-Other, of pile construction, made up:
0/0/0	0	0	0/0	0/0/0	0/0	0/0/0	0/0/	0/0/0	9.1/0			0/0/0	--Of wool or fine animal hair
0/0/0	0	0	0/0	0/0/0	0/0	0/0/0	0/0/	0/0/0	9.1/0			0/0/0	--Of man-made textile materials
0/0/0	0	2.8	1.4/1.4	0/0/0	0/0	0/0/0	0/0/	0/0/12.6	12.7/0			0/0/0	--Of other textile materials
													-Other, not of pile construction, not made up:
0/0/0	0	2.8	1.4/1.4	0/0/0	0/0	0/0/0	0/0/	0/0/12.6	12.7/0			0/0/0	---Of wool or fine animal hair
0/0/0	0	3.2	1.6/1.6	0/0/0	0/0	0/0/0	0/0/	0/0/14.4	14.5/0			0/0/0	---Of man made textile materials
0/0/0	0	2.8	1.4/1.4	0/0/0	0/0	0/0/0	0/0/	0/0/12.6	12.7/0			0/0/0	---Of other textile materials
													-Other, not of pile construction, made up:
0/0/0	0	2.8	1.4/1.4	0/0/0	0/0	0/0/0	0/0/	0/0/12.6	12.7/0			0/0/0	--Of wool or fine animal hair
0/0/0	0	3.2	1.6/1.6	0/0/0	0/0	0/0/0	0/0/	0/0/14.4	14.5/0			0/0/0	--Of man-made textile materials
0/0/0	0	2.8	1.4/1.4	0/0/0	0/0	0/0/0	0/0/	0/0/12.6	12.7/0			0/0/0	--Of other textile materials
													Carpets and other textile floor coverings (including turf), tufted, whether or not madeup.
0/0/0		2.8	1.4/1.4	0/0/0	0/0	0/0/0	0/0/	0/0/12.6	12.7/0			0/0/0	- Of wool or fine animal hair
													- Of nylon or other polyamides :
0/0/0	3.5	6	0/0	0/0/0	0/0	0/0/0	0/0/	9.5/9.5/	/9.5			0/0/0	--Turf
0/0/0	3.5	6	0/0	0/0/0	0/0	0/0/0	0/0/	9.5/9.5/	/9.5			0/0/0	--Other
													-Of other man—made textile materials:
0/0/0		0	0/0	0/0/0	0/0	0/0/0	0/0/	0/0/0	9.1/0			0/0/0	--Artificial turf
0/0/0		0	0/0	0/0/0	0/0	0/0/0	0/0/	0/0/0	9.1/0			0/0/0	--Other
0/0/0	11.2	2.8	1.4/1.4	0/0/0	0/0	0/0/0	0/0/	0/0/12.6	12.7/0	0		0/0/0	-Of other textile materials
													Carpets and other textile floor coverings, of felt, not tufted or flocked, whether or not made up:
0/0/0	7	2.8	1.4/1.4	0/0/0	0/0	0/0/0	0/0/	0/0/12.6	12.7/0			0/0/0	-Tiles, having a maximum surface area of 0.3 m^2
0/0/0	2	0	0/0	0/0/0	0/0	0/0/0	0/0/	0/0/0	9.1/0			0/0/0	-Tiles, having a maximum sur-face area more then 0.3m2 but not more than 1 m^2
0/0/0	2	0	0/0	0/0/0	0/0	0/0/0	0/0/	0/0/0	9.1/0			0/0/0	-Other
													Other carpets and other textile floor coverings, whether or not made up:
0/0/0	11.2	2.8	1.4/1.4	0/0/0	0/0	0/0/0	0/0/	0/0/12.6	12.7/0	0		0/0/0	---Of wool or fine animal hair
0/0/0	4	0	0/0	0/0/0	0/0	0/0/0	0/0/	0/0/0	9.1/0	0		0/0/0	---Of man-made textile materials
0/0/0	11.2	2.8	1.4/1.4	0/0/0	0/0	0/0/0	0/0/	0/0/12.6	12.7/0	0		0/0/0	---Of other textile materialar

第五十八章
特种机织物;簇绒织物;花边;装饰毯;装饰带;刺绣品

注释:

一、本章不适用于经浸渍、涂布、包覆或层压的第五十九章注释一所述的纺织物或第五十九章的其他货品。

二、税目 58.01 也包括因未将浮纱割断而使表面无竖绒的纬起绒织物。

三、税目 58.03 所称"纱罗",是指经线全部或部分由地经纱和绞经纱构成的织物,其中绞经纱绕地经纱半圈、一圈或几圈而形成圈状,纬纱从圈中穿过。

四、税目 58.04 不适用于税目 56.08 的线、绳、索结制的网状织物。

五、税目 58.06 所称"狭幅机织物",是指:

(一)幅宽不超过 30 厘米的机织物,不论是否织成或从宽幅料剪成,但两侧必须有织成的、胶粘的或用其他方法制成的布边;

(二)压平宽度不超过 30 厘米的圆筒机织物;

(三)折边的斜裁滚条布,其未折边时的宽度不超过 30 厘米。

流苏状的狭幅织物归入税目 58.08。

六、税目 58.10 所称"刺绣品",除了一般纺织材料绣线绣制的刺绣品外,还包括在可见底布上用金属线或玻璃线刺绣的刺绣品,也包括用珠片、饰珠或纺织材料或其他材料制的装饰用花纹图案所缝绣的贴花织物。该税目不包括手工针绣嵌花装饰毯(税目 58.05)。

七、除税目号 58.09 的产品外,本章还包括金属线制的用于衣着、装饰及类似用途的物品。

税则号列	货品名称〔CIQ 扩展编码及品名—T2 表示见附表 2〕	最惠(%)	暂定税率	普通	增值/消费	出口退税	计量单位	监管条件/特殊证件	检验检疫	对美关税	亚太上/下
58.01	**起绒机织物及绳绒织物,但税号 58.02 或 58.06 的织物除外:**										
5801.1000	-羊毛或动物细毛制〔999〕	8		130	13/	13	米/千克	/		33	
	-棉制:										
5801.2100	--不割绒的纬起绒织物〔101 棉混纺坯布,102 其他特种机织物〕	8		70	13/	13	米/千克	/			
5801.2200	--割绒的灯芯绒〔999〕	8		70	13/	13	米/千克	/		33	
5801.2300	--其他纬起绒织物〔101 棉混纺坯布,102 其他特种机织物〕	8		70	13/	13	米/千克	/			
5801.2600	--绳绒织物〔101 棉混纺坯布,102 其他特种机织物〕	8		70	13/	13	米/千克	/		18	
	--经起绒织物:										
5801.2710	---不割绒的(棱纹绸)〔999〕	8		70	13/	13	米/千克	/		33	
5801.2720	---割绒的〔101 棉混纺坯布,102 其他特种机织物〕	8		70	13/	13	米/千克	/		33	
	-化学纤维制:										
5801.3100	--不割绒的纬起绒织物〔999〕	8		130	13/	13	米/千克	/		33	
5801.3200	--割绒的灯芯绒〔999〕	8		130	13/	13	米/千克	/		33	
5801.3300	--其他纬起绒织物〔999〕	8		130	13/	13	米/千克	/		33	
5801.3600	--绳绒织物〔999〕	8		130	13/	13	米/千克	/		28	
	--经起绒织物:										
5801.3710	---不割绒的(棱纹绸)〔999〕	8		130	13/	13	米/千克	/		28	
5801.3720	---割绒的〔999〕	8		130	13/	13	米/千克	/		28	
	-其他纺织材料制:										
5801.9010	---丝及绢丝制〔999〕	8		130	13/	13	米/千克	/		33	
5801.9090	---其他〔101 亚麻混纺织物,102 其他特种机织物〕	8		80	13/	13	米/千克	/		33	
58.02	**毛巾织物及类似的毛圈机织物,但税目 58.06 的狭幅织物除外;簇绒织物,但税目 57.03 的产品除外:**										
	-棉制毛巾织物及类似毛圈机织物:										
5802.1010	---未漂白〔999〕	8		70	13/	13	米/千克	/			
5802.1090	---其他〔999〕	8		70	13/	13	米/千克	/			
	-其他纺织材料制的毛巾织物及类似的毛圈机织物:										
5802.2010	---丝及绢丝制〔999〕	8		130	13/	13	米/千克	/			
5802.2020	---羊毛或动物细毛制〔999〕	8		130	13/	13	米/千克	/			
5802.2030	---化学纤维制〔999〕	8		130	13/	13	米/千克	/		13	
5802.2090	---其他〔999〕	8		80	13/	13	米/千克	/			
	-簇绒织物:										
5802.3010	---丝及绢丝制〔999〕	8		130	13/	13	米/千克	/			
5802.3020	---羊毛或动物细毛制〔999〕	8		130	13/	13	米/千克	/			
5802.3030	---棉或麻制〔999〕	8		70	13/	13	米/千克	/			
5802.3040	---化学纤维制〔999〕	8		130	13/	13	米/千克	/		33	
5802.3090	---其他纺织材料制〔999〕	8		80	13/	13	米/千克	/			
58.03	**纱罗,但税目 58.06 的狭幅织物除外:**										
5803.0010	---棉制〔999〕	8		70	13/	13	米/千克	/			
5803.0020	---丝及绢丝制〔999〕	8		130	13/	13	米/千克	/			
5803.0030	---化学纤维制〔999〕	8		130	13/	13	米/千克	/			
5803.0090	---其他纺织材料制〔999〕	8		80	13/	13	米/千克	/		18	

Chapter 58
Special woven fabrics; tufted textile fabrics; lace; tapestries; trimmings; embroidery

Notes:

1. This Chapter does not apply to textile fabrics referred to in Note 1 to Chapter 59, impregnated, coated, covered or laminated, or to other goods of Chapter 59.
2. Heading No. 58.01 also includes woven weft pile fabrics which have not yet had the floats cut, at which stage they have no pile standing up.
3. For the purpose of heading No. 58.03, "gauze" means a fabric with a warp composed wholly or in part of standing or ground threads and crossing or doup threads which cross the standing or ground threads making a half turn, a complete turn or more to form loops through which weft threads pass.
4. Heading No. 58.04 does not apply to knotted net fabrics of twine, cordage or rope, of heading No. 56.08.
5. For the purposes of heading No. 58.06, the expression "narrow woven fabrics" means:
   (a) Woven fabrics of a width not exceeding 30 cm, whether woven as such or cut from wider pieces, provided with selvedges (woven, gummed or otherwise made) on both edges;
   (b) Tubular woven fabrics of a flattened width not exceeding 30 cm;
   (c) Bias binding with folded edges, of a width when unfolded not exceeding 30 cm.
   Narrow woven fabrics with woven fringes are to be classified in heading No. 58.08.
6. In heading No.58.10, the expression "embroidery" means, *inter alia*, embroidery with metal or glass thread on a visible ground of textile fabric, and sewn appliquè work of sequins, beads or ornamental motifs of textile or other materials. The heading does not apply to needlework tapestry (heading No. 58.05).
7. In addition to the products of heading No. 58.09, this Chapter also includes articles made of metal thread and of a kind used in apparel, as furnishing fabrics or for similar purposes.

协定税率 %								RCEP		特惠税率 %			Article Description
东/冰/格	巴基斯坦	韩国	瑞士上/下	哥/秘/柬	澳/毛	新西/坡/智	中国港/澳/台	东盟及马来/澳/韩	日/新	亚太2国	老/柬/缅	98/97/95	
													Woven pile fabrics and chenille fabrics, other than fabrics of heading No. 58.02 or 58.06:
0/0/0	0	0	0/0	0/0/0	0/0	0/0/0	0/0/	0/0/0	9.1/0			0/0/0	-Of wool or fine animal hair
													-Of cotton:
0/0/0	0	0	1.2/1.2	0/0/0	0/0	0/0/0	0/0/	0/0/0	10.9/0			0/0/0	--Uncut weft pile fabrics
0/0/0	0	0	0/0	0/0/0	0/0	0//0	0/0/0	0/0/0	9.1/0			0/0/0	--Cut corduroy
0/0/0	0	2	0/0	0/0/0	0/0	0//0	0/0/	0/0/9	9.1/0			0/0/0	--Other weft pile fabrics
0/0/0	0	0	0/0	0/0/0	0/0	0//0	0/0/	0/0/0	9.1/0			0/0/0	--Chenille fabrics
													--Warp pile fabrics:
0/0/0	0	0	0/0	0/0/0	0/0	0//0	0/0/	0/0/0	9.1/0			0/0/0	---Warp pile fabrics(epingle)(nucut)
0/0/0	0	0	0/0	0/0/0	0/0	0//0	0/0/	0/0/0	9.1/0			0/0/0	---Warp pile fabrics(epingle)(cut)
													-Of man-made fibres:
0/0/0	0	4.6	0/0	0/0/0	0/0	0/0/0	0/0/	9.3/9.5/9.3	9.4/9.5			0/0/0	--Uncut weft pile fabrics
0/0/0	0	0	0/0	0/0/0	0/0	0/0/0	0/0/	0/0/0	9.1/0			0/0/0	--Cut corduroy
0/0/0	0	0	0/0	0/0/0	0/0	0/0/0	0/0/0	0/0/0	9.1/0		0/0/0	0/0/0	--Other weft pile fabrics
0/0/0	0	0	0/0	0/0/0	0/0	0/0/0	0/0/	0/0/0	9.1/0			0/0/0	--Chenille fabrics
													--Warp pile fabrics:
0/0/0	0	0	0/0	0/0/0	0/0	0/0/0	0/0/	0/0/0	9.1/0			0/0/0	---Warp pile fabrics(epingle)(nucut)
0/0/0	0	0	0/0	0/0/0	0/0	0/0/0	0/0/	0/0/0	9.1/0			0/0/0	---Warp pile fabrics(epingle)(cut)
													-Of other textile materials:
0/0/0	0	0	0/0	0/0/0	0/0	0/0/0	0/0/	0/0/0	9.1/0			0/0/0	---Of silk or silk waste
0/0/0	0	0	0/0	0/0/0	0/0	0/0/0	0/0/	0/0/0	9.1/0			0/0/0	---Other
													Terry towelling and similar woven terry fabrics, other than narrow fabricsof heading No. 58.06; tufted textile fabrics, other than products of heading No. 57.03:
													-Terry towelling and similar woven terry fabrics, of cotton:
0/0/0	0	0	1.2/1.2	0/0/0	0/0	0/0/0	0/0/	0/0/0	10.9/0	0		0/0/0	---Unbleached
0/0/0	0	0	0/0	0/0/0	0/0	0//0	0/0/	0/0/0	9.1/0			0/0/0	---Other
													-Terry towelling and similar woven terry fabrics, of other textile materials:
0/0/0	0	0	1.2/1.2	0/0/0	0/0	0/0/0	0/0/	0/0/0	10.9/0	0		0/0/0	---Of silk or silk waste
0/0/0	0	0	1.2/1.2	0/0/0	0/0	0/0/0	0/0/	0/0/0	10.9/0	0		0/0/0	---Of wool or fine animal hair
0/0/0	0	2.8	1.4/1.4	0/0/0	0/0	0/0/0	0/0/	0/0/12.6	12.7/0	0		0/0/0	---Of man-made fibres
0/0/0	0	0	1.2/1.2	0/0/0	0/0	0/0/0	0/0/	0/0/0	10.9/0	0		0/0/0	---Other
													-Tufted textile fabrics:
0/0/0	0	0	0/0	0/0/0	0/0	0/0/0	0/0/	0/0/0	9.1/0			0/0/0	---Of silk or silk waste
0/0/0	0	0	0/0	0/0/0	0/0	0/0/0	0/0/	0/0/0	9.1/0			0/0/0	---Of wool or fine animal hair
0/0/0	0	0	0/0	0/0/0	0/0	0//0	0/0/	0/0/0	9.1/0			0/0/0	---Of cotton or bast fibres
0/0/0	0	0	0/0	0/0/0	0/0	0/0/0	0/0/	0/0/0	9.1/0			0/0/0	---Of man-made fibres
0/0/0	0	0	0/0	0/0/0	0/0	0/0/0	0/0/	0/0/0	9.1/0			0/0/0	---Of other textile materials
													Gauze, other than narrow fabrics of heading No. 58.06:
0/0/0	2	0	0/0	0/0/0	0/0	0//0	0/0/	0/0/0	9.1/0			0/0/0	---Of cotton
0/0/0	2	0	0/0	0/0/0	0/0	0/0/0	0/0/	0/0/0	9.1/0			0/0/0	---Of silk or silk waste
0/0/0	5	0	0/0	0/0/0	0/0	0/0/0	0/0/	0/0/0	9.1/0			0/0/0	---Of man-made fibres
0/0/0	2	0	0/0	0/0/0	0/0	0/0/0	0/0/	0/0/0	9.1/0			0/0/0	---Of other textile materials

税则号列	货品名称〔CIQ 扩展编码及品名－T2 表示见附表 2〕	最惠(%)	暂定税率	普通	增值/消费	出口退税	计量单位	监管条件/特殊证件	检验检疫	对美关税	亚太上/下
58.04	**网眼薄纱及其他网眼织物，但不包括机织物、针织物或钩编织物；成卷、成条或成小块图案的花边，但税目 60.02 的织物除外：**										
	-网眼薄纱及其他网眼织物：										
5804.1010	---丝及绢丝制〔999〕	8		130	13/	13	千克	/			5.2/5.2
5804.1020	---棉制〔999〕	8		70	13/	13	千克	/		33	5.2/5.2
5804.1030	---化学纤维制〔999〕	8		130	13/	13	千克	/		33	5.2/5.2
5804.1090	---其他纺织材料制〔999〕	8		90	13/	13	千克	/		18	5.2/5.2
	-机制花边：										
5804.2100	--化学纤维制〔999〕	8		130	13/	13	千克	/		33	
	--其他纺织材料制：										
5804.2910	---丝及绢丝制〔999〕	8		130	13/	13	千克	/			
5804.2920	---棉制〔999〕	8		70	13/	13	千克	/		33	
5804.2990	---其他〔999〕	8		90	13/	13	千克	/			
5804.3000	-手工制花边〔999〕	8		100	13/	13	千克	/			
58.05	**"哥白林""弗朗德""奥步生""波威"及类似式样的手织装饰毯，以及手工针绣嵌花装饰毯(例如，小针脚或十字绣)，不论是否制成的：**										
5805.0010	---手工针绣嵌花装饰毯〔999〕	6		130	13/	13	平方米/千克	/			
5805.0090	---其他〔999〕	6		130	13/	13	平方米/千克	/			
58.06	**狭幅机织物，但税目 58.07 的货品除外；用黏合剂粘合制成的有经纱而无纬纱的狭幅织物(包扎匹头用带)：**										
	-起绒机织物(包括毛巾织物及类似的毛圈织物)及绳绒织物：										
5806.1010	---棉或麻制〔999〕	8		70	13/	13	千克	/		33	6.4/6.4
5806.1090	---其他纺织材料制〔999〕	8		80	13/	13	千克	/		18	5.2/5.2
5806.2000	-按重量计弹性纱线或橡胶线含量在 5%及以上的其他机织物〔999〕	8		100	13/	13	千克	/		33	
	-其他机织物：										
5806.3100	--棉制〔999〕	8		70	13/	13	千克	/		33	
5806.3200	--化学纤维制〔999〕	8		130	13/	13	千克	/		28	5.2/5.2
	--其他纺织材料制：										
5806.3910	---丝及绢丝制〔999〕	8		130	13/	13	千克	/		18	
5806.3920	---羊毛或动物细毛制〔999〕	8		130	13/	13	千克	/			
5806.3990	---其他〔999〕	8		80	13/	13	千克	/		33	
	-用黏合剂粘合制成的有经纱而无纬纱的织物(包扎匹头用带)：										
5806.4010	---棉或麻制〔999〕	8		70	13/	13	千克	/			4.8/4.8
5806.4090	---其他纺织材料制〔999〕	8		80	13/	13	千克	/		28	
58.07	**非绣制的纺织材料制标签、徽章及类似品，成匹、成条或裁成一定形状或尺寸：**										
5807.1000	-机织〔999〕	8		100	13/	13	千克	/		33	5.2/5.2
5807.9000	-其他〔999〕	8		100	13/	13	千克	/		28	
58.08	**成匹的编带；非绣制的成匹装饰带，但针织或钩编的除外；流苏、绒球及类似品：**										
5808.1000	-成匹的编带										
5808.1000 20	蕉麻或苎麻制成匹的编带(适合制造或装饰帽类用)〔999〕	8		100	13/	13	千克	/		33	
5808.1000 90	其他纺织材料制成匹的编带〔999〕	8		100	13/	13	千克	/		33	
5808.9000	-其他〔999〕	8		100	13/	13	千克	/		33	
58.09	**其他税目未列名的金属线机织物及税目 56.05 所列含金属纱线的机织物，用于衣着、装饰及类似用途：**										
5809.0010	---与棉混制〔999〕	8		90	13/	13	米/千克	/			
5809.0020	---与化学纤维混制〔999〕	8		130	13/	13	米/千克	/		18	
5809.0090	---其他〔999〕	8		100	13/	13	米/千克	/		18	
58.10	**成匹、成条或成小块图案的刺绣品：**										
5810.1000	-不见底布的刺绣品〔999〕	8		130	13/	13	千克	/		33	
	-其他刺绣品：										
5810.9100	--棉制〔999〕	8		130	13/	13	千克	/			
5810.9200	--化学纤维制〔999〕	8		130	13/	13	千克	/		33	
5810.9900	--其他纺织材料制〔999〕	8		130	13/	13	千克	/		33	
58.11	**用一层或几层纺织材料与胎料经绗缝或其他方法组合制成的被褥状纺织品，但税目 58.10 的刺绣品除外：**										
5811.0010	---丝及绢丝制〔101 被子，102 褥垫〕	8		130	13/	13	千克	/			5.6/5.6
5811.0020	---羊毛或动物细毛制〔101 被子，102 褥垫〕	8		130	13/	13	千克	/			
5811.0030	---棉制〔101 被子，102 褥垫〕	8		80	13/	13	千克	/		28	
5811.0040	---化学纤维制〔101 被子，102 褥垫，103 毯子〕	8		130	13/	13	千克	/		28	
5811.0090	---其他纺织材料制〔101 被子，102 褥垫〕	8		90	13/	13	千克	/			

协定税率 %								RCEP		特惠税率 %			Article Description
东/冰/格	巴基斯坦	韩国	瑞士上/下	哥/秘/柬	澳/毛	新西/坡/智	中国港/澳/台	东盟及马来/澳/韩	日/新	亚太2国	老/柬/缅	98/97/95	
													Tulles and other net fabrics, not including woven, knitted or crocheted fabrics; lace in the piece, in strips or in motifs, other than fabrics of headings No. 60.02:
													-Tulles and other net fabrics:
0/0/0	2	0	0/0	0/0/0	0/0	0/0/0	0/0/	0/0/0	9.1/0			0/0/0	---Of silk or silk waste
0/0/0	2	0	4.2/4.2	0/0/0	0/0	0//0	0/0/	0/0/0	9.1/0			0/0/0	---Of cotton
0/0/0	3.5	7.2	1.2/1.2	0/0/0	0/0	0/0/0	0/0/0	11.4/11.4/	/11.4		0/0/0	0/0/0	---Of man-made fibres
0/0/0	2	0	0/0	0/0/0	0/0	0/0/0	0/0/0	0/0/0	9.1/0			0/0/0	---Of other textile materials
													-Mechanically made lace:
0/0/0	4	0	0/0	0/0/0	0/0	0/0/0	0/0/0	9/9/9	9.1/9			0/0/0	--Of man-made fibres
													--Of other textile materials:
0/0/0	2	0	0/0	0/0/0	0/0	0/0/0	0/0/	0/0/0	9.1/0			0/0/0	---Of silk or silk waste
0/0/0	2	0	0/0	0/0/0	0/0	0//0	0/0/	0/0/0	9.1/0		0/0/0	0/0/0	---Of cotton
0/0/0	2	0	0/0	0/0/0	0/0	0/0/0	0/0/	0/0/0	9.1/0			0/0/0	---Other
0/0/0	2	0	0/0	0/0/0	0/0	0/0/0	0/0/	0/0/0	9.1/0			0/0/0	-Hand-made lace
													Hand-woven tapestries of the type Gobelins, Flanders, Aubusson, Beauvais and the like, and needle-worked tapestries (for example, petit point, cross stitch), whether or not made up:
0/0/0	6	0	1.2/1.2	0/0/0	0/0	0/0/0	0/0/	0/0/0	10.9/0			0/0/0	---Needle-worked tapestries
0/0/0	6	0	1.2/1.2	0/0/0	0/0	0/0/0	0/0/	0/0/0	10.9/0			0/0/0	---Other
													Narrow woven fabrics, other than goods of heading No. 58.07; narrow fabrics consisting of warp without weft assembled by means of an adhesive (bolducs):
													-Woven pile fabrics (including terry towelling and similar terry fabris) and chenille fabrics:
0/0/0	2	0	0/0	0/0/0	0/0	0//0	0/0/	0/0/0	9.1/0			0/0/0	---Of cotton or bast fibres
0/0/0	2	0	0/0	0/0/0	0/0	0/0/0	0/0/0	0/0/0	9.1/0		0/0/0	0/0/0	---Of other textile materials
0/0/0	2	0	0/0	0/0/0	0/0	0/0/0	0/0/0	0/0/0	9.1/0		0/0/0	0/0/0	-Other woven fabrics, containing by weight 5% or more of elastomeric yarn or rubber thread
													-Other woven fabrics:
0/0/0	4	0	0/0	0/0/0	0/0	0//0	0/0/	0/0/0	9.1/0		0/0/0	0/0/0	--Of cotton
0/0/0	4	0	0/0	0/0/0	0/0	0/0/0	0/0/0	0/0/0	9.1/0		0/0/0	0/0/0	--Of man-made fibres
													--Of other textile materials:
0/0/0	2	0	0/0	0/0/0	0/0	0/0/0	0/0/	0/0/0	9.1/0			0/0/0	---Of silk or silk waste
0/0/0	2	0	0/0	0/0/0	0/0	0/0/0	0/0/	0/0/0	9.1/0			0/0/0	---Of wool or fine animal hair
0/0/0	2	0	0/0	0/0/0	0/0	0/0/0	0/0/	0/0/0	9.1/0			0/0/0	---Other
													-Fabrics consisting of warp without weft assembled by means of an adhesive (bolducs):
0/0/0	2	0	0/0	0/0/0	0/0	0//0	0/0/	0/0/0	9.1/0			0/0/0	---Of cotton or bast fibres
0/0/0	2	0	0/0	0/0/0	0/0	0/0/0	0/0/	0/0/0	9.1/0			0/0/0	---Of other textile materials
													Labels, badges and similar articles of textile materials, in the piece, in strips or cut to shape or size, not embroidered:
0/0/0	0	0	0/0	0/0/0	0/0	0/0/0	0/0/0	9/9/9	9.1/9		0/0/0	0/0/0	-Woven
0/0/0	2	0	0/0	0/0/0	0/0	0/0/0	0/0/	0/0/0	9.1/0			0/0/0	-Other
													Braids in the piece; ornamental trimmings in the piece, without embroidery, other than knitted or crocheted; tassels, pompons and similar articles:
													-Braids in the piece
0/0/0		0	0/0	0/0/0	0/0	0/0/0	0/0/	0/0/0	9.1/0			0/0/0	Braids in the piece, of abaca or ramie (suitable for manufacturing or decoration of head gear)
0/0/0		0	0/0	0/0/0	0/0	0/0/0	0/0/	0/0/0	9.1/0			0/0/0	Braids in the piece, of other textile materials
0/0/0	4	0	0/0	0/0/0	0/0	0/0/0	0/0/	0/0/0	9.1/0		0/0/0	0/0/0	-Other
													Woven fabrics of metal thread and woven fabrics of metallized yarn of heading No. 56.05, of a kind used in apparel, as furnishing fabrics or for similar purposes, not elsewhere specified or included:
0/0/0	2	0	0/0	0/0/0	0/0	0/0/0	0/0/	0/0/0	9.1/0			0/0/0	---Combined with cotton
0/0/0	2	0	0/0	0/0/0	0/0	0/0/0	0/0/	0/0/0	9.1/0			0/0/0	---Combined with man-made fibres
0/0/0	2	0	0/0	0/0/0	0/0	0/0/0	0/0/	0/0/0	9.1/0			0/0/0	---Other
													Embroidery in the piece, in strips or in motifs:
0/0/0	2	0	0/0	0/0/0	0/0	0/0/0	0/0/	0/0/0	9.1/0			0/0/0	-Embroidery without visible ground
													-Other embroidery:
0/0/0		0	0/0	0/0/0	0/0	0/0/0	0/0/	0/0/0	9.1/0			0/0/0	--Of cotton
0/0/0	4	4.6	0/0	0/0/0	0/0	0/0/0	0/0/0	9.3/9.5/9.3	9.4/9.5			0/0/0	--Of man-made fibres
0/0/0	4	0	0/0	0/0/0	0/0	0/0/0	0/0/	0/0/0	9.1/0			0/0/0	--Of other textile materials
													Quilted textile products in the piece, composed of one or more layers of textile materials assembled with padding by stitching or otherwise, other than embroidery of heading No. 58.10:
0/0/0	0	0	0/0	0/0/0	0/0	0/0/0	0/0/	0/0/0	9.1/0			0/0/0	---Of silk or silk waste
0/0/0	0	0	0/0	0/0/0	0/0	0/0/0	0/0/	0/0/0	9.1/0			0/0/0	---Of wool or fine animal hair
0/0/0	0	0	0/0	0/0/0	0/0	0//0	0/0/	0/0/0	9.1/0			0/0/0	---Of cotton
0/0/0	0	7.2	1.2/1.2	0/0/0	0/0	0/0/0	0/0/	11.4/11.4/	/11.4			0/0/0	---Of man-made fibres
0/0/0	0	0	0/0	0/0/0	0/0	0/0/0	0/0/	0/0/0	9.1/0			0/0/0	---Of other textile materials

第五十九章
浸渍、涂布、包覆或层压的纺织物;工业用纺织制品

注释:

一、除条文另有规定的以外,本章所称"纺织物",仅适用于第五十章至第五十五章、税目58.03及58.06的机织物、税目58.08的成匹编带和装饰带及税目60.02至60.06的针织物或钩编织物。

二、税目59.03适用于:

(一)用塑料浸渍、涂布、包覆或层压的纺织物,不论每平方米重量多少以及塑料的性质如何(紧密结构或泡沫状的),但下列各项除外:

1. 用肉眼无法辨别出是否经过浸渍、涂布、包覆或层压的织物(通常归入第五十章至第五十五章、第五十八章或第六十章);但由于浸渍、涂布、包覆或层压所引起的颜色变化可不予考虑;
2. 温度在15℃至30℃时,用手工将其绕于直径7毫米的圆柱体上会发生断裂的产品(通常归入第三十九章);
3. 纺织物完全嵌入塑料内或在其两面均用塑料完全包覆或涂布,而这种包覆或涂布用肉眼是能够辨别出的产品(但由于包覆或涂布所引起的颜色变化可不予考虑)(第三十九章);
4. 用塑料部分涂布或包覆并由此而形成图案的织物(通常归入第五十章至第五十五章、第五十八章或第六十章);
5. 与纺织物混制而其中纺织物仅起增强作用的泡沫塑料板、片或带(第三十九章);
6. 税目58.11的纺织品;

(二)由税目56.04的用塑料浸渍、涂布、包覆或套裹的纱线、扁条或类似品制成的织物。

三、税目59.03所称"用塑料层压的纺织物"是指由一层或多层纺织物与一层或多层塑料片或膜以任何方式结合在一起的产品,不论其塑料片或膜从横截面上是否肉眼可见。

四、税目59.05所称"糊墙织物",是指以纺织材料作面,固定在一衬背上或在背面进行处理(浸渍或涂布以便于裱糊),适于装饰墙壁或天花板,且宽度不小于45厘米的成卷产品。

但本税目不适用于以纺织纤维屑或粉末直接粘于纸上(税目48.14)或布底上(通常归入税目59.07)的糊墙物品。

五、税目59.06所称"用橡胶处理的纺织物"是指:

(一)用橡胶浸渍、涂布、包覆或层压的纺织物:

1. 每平方米重量不超过1 500克;
2. 每平方米重量超过1 500克,按重量计纺织材料含量在50%以上。

(二)由税目56.04的用橡胶浸渍、涂布、包覆或套裹的纱线、扁条或类似品制成的织物;以及

(三)平行纺织纱线经橡胶粘合的织物,不论每平方米重量多少。

但本税目不包括与纺织物混制而其中纺织物仅起增强作用的海绵橡胶板、片或带(第四十章),也不包括税目58.11的纺织品。

六、税目59.07不适用于:

(一)用肉眼无法辨别出是否经过浸渍、涂布或包覆的织物(通常归入第五十章至第五十五章、第五十八章或第六十章),但由于浸渍、涂布或包覆所引起的颜色变化可不予考虑;

(二)绘有图画的织物(作为舞台、摄影布景或类似品的已绘制的画布除外);

(三)用短绒、粉末、软木粉或类似品部分覆面并由此而形成图案的织物,但仿绒织物仍归入本税目;

(四)以淀粉或类似物质为基本成分的普通浆料上浆整理的织物;

(五)以纺织物为底的木饰面板(税目44.08);

(六)以纺织物为底的砂布及类似品(税号68.05);

(七)以纺织物为底的粘聚或复制云母片(税号68.14);

(八)以纺织物为底的金属箔(通常为第十四类或第十五类)。

七、税目59.10不适用于:

(一)厚度小于3毫米的纺织材料制传动带料或输送带料;

(二)用橡胶浸渍、涂布、包覆或层压的织物制成的或用橡胶浸渍、涂布、包覆或套裹的纱线或绳制成的传动带料及运输带料(税目40.10)。

八、税目59.11适用于下列不能归入第十一类其他税目的货品:

(一)下列成匹的、裁成一定长度或仅裁成矩形(包括正方形)的纺织产品(具有税目59.08至59.10所列产品特征的产品除外):

1. 用橡胶、皮革或其他材料涂布、包覆或层压的作针布用的纺织物、毡呢及毡呢衬里机织物,以及其他专门技术用途的类似织物,包括用橡胶浸渍的用于包覆纺锤(织轴)的狭幅丝绒织物。
2. 筛布;
3. 用于榨油机器或类似机器的纺织材料制或人发制滤布;
4. 用多股经纱或纬纱平织而成的纺织物,不论是否毡化、浸渍或涂布,通常用于机械或其他专门技术用途;
5. 专门技术用途的增强纺织物;
6. 工业上作填塞或润滑材料的线绳、编带及类似品,不论是否涂布、浸渍或用金属加强。

(二)专门技术用途的纺织制品(税目59.08至59.10的货品除外),例如,造纸机器或类似机器(如制浆机或制石棉水泥的机器)用的环状或装有连接装置的纺织物或毡呢、密封垫、垫圈、抛光盘及其他机器零件。

税则号列	货品名称〔CIQ扩展编码及品名—T2表示见附表2〕	最惠(%)	暂定税率	普通	增值/消费	出口退税	计量单位	监管条件/特殊证件	检验检疫	对美关税	亚太上/下
59.01	用胶或淀粉物质涂布的纺织物,作书籍封面及类似用途的;描图布;制成的油画布;作帽里的硬衬布及类似硬挺纺织物:										
	-用胶或淀粉物质涂布的纺织物,作书籍封面及类似用途的:										
5901.1010	---棉或麻制										

Chapter 59
Impregnated, coated, covered or laminated textile fabrics; textile articles of a kind suitable for industrial use

Notes:

1. Except where the context otherwise requires, for the purposes of this Chapter the expression "textile fabrics" applies only to the woven fabrics of Chapters 50 to 55 and headings No.58. 03 and 58. 06, the braids and ornamental trimmings in the piece of heading No.58. 08 and the knitted or crocheted fabrics of headings No.60. 02 to 60. 06.
2. Heading No. 59. 03 applies to:
   (a) Textile fabrics, impregnated, coated, covered or laminated with plastics, whatever the weight per square metre and whatever the nature of the plastic material (compact or cellular), other than:
      (ⅰ) Fabrics in which the impregnation, coating, or covering cannot be seen with the naked eye (usually Chapters 50 to 55, 58 or 60); for the purpose of this provision, no account should be taken of any resulting change of colour;
      (ⅱ) Products which cannot, without fracturing, be bent manually around a cylinder of a diameter of 7 mm, at a temperature between 15℃ and 30℃ (usually Chapter 39);
      (ⅲ) Products in which the textile fabric is either completely embedded in plastics or entirely coated or covered on both sides with such material, provided that such coating or covering can be seen with the naked eye with no account being taken of any resulting change of colour (Chapter 39);
      (ⅳ) Fabrics partially coated or partially covered with plastics and bearing designs resulting from these treatments (usually Chapters 50 to 55, 58 or 60);
      (ⅴ) Plates, sheets or strip of cellular plastics, combined with textile fabric, where the textile fabric is present merely for reinforcing purposes (Chapter 39);
      (ⅵ) Textile products of heading No. 58. 11;
   (b) Fabrics made from yarn, strip or the like, impregnated, coated, covered or sheathed with plastics, of heading No. 56. 04.
3. For the purposes of heading No. 59.03, "textile fabrics laminated withplastics" means products made by the assembly of one or more layers of fabrics with one or more sheets or film of plastics which are combined by any process that bonds the layers together, whether or not the sheets or film of plastics are visible to the naked eye in the cross—section.
4. For the purposes of heading No. 59. 05, the expression "textile wall coverings" applies to products in rolls, of a width of not less than 45 cm, suitable for wall or ceiling decoration, consisting of a textile surface which has been fixed on a backing or has been treated on the back (impregnated or coated to permit pasting).
   This heading does not, however, apply to wall coverings consisting of textile flock or dust fixed directly on a backing of paper (heading No. 48. 14) or on a textile backing (generally heading No. 59. 07).
5. For the purposes of heading No. 59. 06, the expression "rubberized textile fabrics" means:
   (a) Textile fabrics impregnated, coated, covered or laminated with rubber:
      (ⅰ) Weighing not more than 1,500 g/m^2; or
      (ⅱ) Weighing more than 1,500 g/m^2 and containing more than 50% by weight of textile material。
   (b) Fabrics made from yarn, strip or the like, impregnated, coated, covered or sheathed with rubber, of heading No. 56. 04; and
   (c) Fabrics composed of parallel textile yarns agglomerated with rubber, irrespective of their weight per square metre.
   This heading does not, however, apply to plates, sheets or strip of cellular rubber, combined with textile fabric, where the textile fabric is present merely for reinforcing purposes (Chapter 40), or textile products of heading No. 58. 11.
6. Heading No. 59. 07 does not apply to:
   (a) Fabrics in which the impregnation, coating or covering cannot be seen with the naked eye (usually Chapters 50 to 55, 58 or 60); for the purpose of this provision, no account should be taken of any resulting change of colour;
   (b) Fabrics painted with designs (other than painted canvas being theatrical scenery, studio back-cloths or the like);
   (c) Fabrics partially covered with flock, dust, powdered cork or the like and bearing designs resulting from these treatments; however, imitation pile fabrics remain classified in this heading;
   (d) Fabrics finished with normal dressings having a basis of amylaceous or similar substances;
   (e) Wood veneered on a backing of textile fabrics (heading No. 44. 08);
   (f) Natural or artificial abrasive powder or grain, on a backing of textile fabrics (heading No. 68. 05);
   (g) Agglomerated or reconstituted mica, on a backing of textile fabrics (heading No. 68. 14); or
   (h) Metal foil on a backing of textile fabrics (Generauy section XIV or XV).
7. Heading No. 59. 10 does not apply to:
   (a) Transmission or conveyor belting, of textile material, of a thickness of less than 3 mm; or
   (b) Transmission or conveyor belts or belting of textile fabric impregnated, coated, covered or laminated with rubber or made from textile yarn or cord impregnated, coated, covered or sheathed with rubber (heading No. 40. 10).
8. Heading No. 59. 11 applies to the following goods, which do not fall in any other heading of Section XI.
   (a) Textile products in the piece, cut to length or simply cut to rectangular (including square) shape (other than those having the character of the products of headings No. 59. 08 to 59. 10), the following only:
      (ⅰ) Textile fabrics, felt and felt-lined woven fabrics, coated, covered or laminated with rubber, leather or other material, of a kind used for card clothing, and similar fabrics of a kind used for other technical purposes, including narrow fabrics made of velvet impregnated with rubber, for covering weaving spindles (weaving beams);
      (ⅱ) Bolting cloth;
      (ⅲ) Straining cloth of a kind used in oil presses or the like, of textile material or of human hair;
      (ⅳ) Flat woven textile fabrics with multiple warp or weft, whether or not felted, impregnated or coated, of a kind used in machinery or for other technical purposes;
      (ⅴ) Textile fabrics reinforced with metal, of a kind used for technical purposes;
      (ⅵ) Cords, braids and the like, whether or not coated, impregnated or reinforced with metal, of a kind used in industry as packing or lubricating materials;
   (b) Textile articles (other than those of headings No. 59. 08 to 59. 10) of a kind used for technical purposes, for example, textile fabrics and felts, endless or fitted with linking devicse, of a kind used in paper-making or similar machines (for example, for pulp or asbestos-cement), gaskets, washers, polishing discs and other machinery parts.

协定税率 %								RCEP		特惠税率 %			Article Description
东/冰/格	巴基斯坦	韩国	瑞士上/下	哥/秘/柬	澳/毛	新西/坡/智	中国港/澳/台	东盟及马来/澳/韩	日/新	亚太2国	老/柬/缅	98/97/95	
													Textile fabrics coated with gum or amylaceous substances, of a kind used for the outer covers of books or the like; tracing cloth; prepared painting canvas, buckram and similar stiffened textile fabrics of a kind used for hat foundations: -Textile fabrics coated with gum or amylaceous substances, of a kind used for the outer covers of books or the like: ---Of cotton or bast fibres

税则号列		货品名称〔CIQ 扩展编码及品名－T2 表示见附表 2〕	最惠(%)	暂定税率	普通	增值/消费	出口退税	计量单位	监管条件/特殊证件	检验检疫	对美关税	亚太上/下
5901.1010	10	胶或淀粉涂布的棉纺织物(作书籍封面,棉织物重≥50%,经漂染印花)〔101 棉混纺印花布,999 用胶或淀粉涂布的纺织物,作书籍封面等用途〕	8		80	13/	13	千克	/		18	
5901.1010	90	胶或淀粉涂布的麻及其他棉纺织(作书籍封面及类似用途的)〔999〕	8		80	13/	13	千克	/		18	
5901.1020		---化学纤维制										
5901.1020	10	胶或淀粉涂布的涤棉短纤混纺织品(书籍封面及类似用途,聚酯短纤棉混纺漂染织物重>50%)〔999〕	8		130	13/	13	千克	/		33	
5901.1020	90	胶或淀粉涂布的其他化学纤维纺织物(作书籍封面及类似用途的)〔999〕	8		130	13/	13	千克	/		33	
5901.1090		---其他										
5901.1090	10	用胶或淀粉涂布的精梳毛纺织物(书籍封面及类似用途,精梳羊毛或动物细毛织物重≥50%)〔999〕	8		100	13/	13	千克	/		28	
5901.1090	90	用胶或淀粉涂布的其他纺织物(作书籍封面及类似用途的)〔999〕	8		100	13/	13	千克	/		28	
		-其他:										
5901.9010		---制成的油画布〔999〕	8		50	13/	13	千克	/		33	
		---其他:										
5901.9091		----棉或麻制										
5901.9091	10	棉制描图布、帽里硬衬布等(包括类似硬挺纺织物,棉织物重≥50%经漂染印花)〔101 棉混纺印花布,102 服装衬布 999 油画布、描图布、作帽里硬衬布等硬挺纺织物〕	8		80	13/	13	千克	/		33	
5901.9091	90	麻及其他棉制描图布、帽里硬衬布(包括类似硬挺纺织物)〔101 服装衬布,999 油画布、描图布、作帽里硬衬布等硬挺纺织物〕	8		80	13/	13	千克	/		33	
5901.9092		----化学纤维制										
5901.9092	10	聚酯短纤与棉混纺织物制描图布(含帽里硬衬类似硬挺纺织物,织物重≥50%,经漂染印)〔101 服装衬布,999 油画布、描图布、作帽里硬衬布等硬挺纺织物〕	8		130	13/	13	千克	/			
5901.9092	90	其他化学纤维制描图布,帽里硬衬布等(包括类似硬挺纺织物)〔101 服装衬布,999 油画布、描图布、作帽里硬衬布等硬挺纺织物〕	8		130	13/	13	千克	/			
5901.9099		----其他										
5901.9099	10	精梳毛纺织物制描图布,帽里硬衬(包括类似硬挺纺织物,精梳羊毛或动物细毛织物重≥50%)〔101 服装衬布,999 油画布、描图布、作帽里硬衬布等硬挺纺织物〕	8		100	13/	13	千克	/		33	
5901.9099	90	其他纺织物制描图布,帽里硬衬布(包括类似硬挺纺织物)〔101 服装衬布,999 油画布、描图布、作帽里硬衬布等硬挺纺织物〕	8		100	13/	13	千克	/		33	
59.02		**尼龙或其他聚酰胺,聚酯或粘胶纤维高强力纱制的帘子布:**										
		-尼龙或其他聚酰胺制:										
5902.1010		---聚酰胺-6(尼龙-6)制〔999〕	8		40	13/	13	千克	/		33	5.2/5.2
5902.1020		---聚酰胺-6,6(尼龙-6,6)制〔999〕	8		40	13/	13	千克	/		33	5.2/5.2
5902.1090		---其他〔999〕	8		40	13/	13	千克	/		33	5.2/5.2
5902.2000		-聚酯制〔999〕	8		40	13/	13	千克	/			5.2/5.2
5902.9000		-其他〔999〕	8		40	13/	13	千克	/		33	
59.03		**用塑料浸渍、涂布、包覆或层压的纺织物,但税目 59.02 的货品除外:**										
		-用聚氯乙烯浸渍、涂布、包覆或层压的:										
5903.1010		---绝缘布或带〔999〕	8		40	13/	13	千克	/		18	5.2/5.2
5903.1020		---人造革〔101 棉混纺印花布,999 聚氯乙烯浸涂、包覆或层压的纺织物〕	8		70	13/	13	千克/米	/		33	5.2/5.2
5903.1090		---其他〔101 棉混纺印花布,999 聚氯乙烯浸涂、包覆或层压的纺织物〕	8		90	13/	13	千克	/		28	5.2/5.2
		-用聚氨基甲酸酯浸渍、涂布、包覆或层压的:										
5903.2010		---绝缘布或带〔999〕	8		40	13/	13	千克	/		18	5.2/5.2
5903.2020		---人造革〔999〕	8		70	13/	13	千克/米	/		33	5.2/5.2
5903.2090		---其他〔999〕	8		90	13/	13	千克	/		33	5.2/5.2
		-其他:										
5903.9010		---绝缘布或带〔999〕	8		40	13/	13	千克	/		18	5.2/5.2
5903.9020		---人造革〔101 棉混纺印花布,999 其他塑料浸涂、包覆或层压的纺织物〕	8		70	13/	13	千克/米	/		28	5.2/5.2
5903.9090		---其他〔101 棉混纺印花布,999 其他塑料浸涂、包覆或层压的纺织物〕	8		90	13/	13	千克	/		28	5.2/5.2

协定税率 %								RCEP		特惠税率 %			Article Description
东/冰/格	巴基斯坦	韩国	瑞士上/下	哥/秘/柬	澳/毛	新西/坡/智	中国港/澳/台	东盟及马来/澳/韩	日/新	亚太2国	老/柬/缅	98/97/95	
0/0/0	2	2	0/0	0/0/0	0/0	0/0/0	0/0/	0/0/9	9.1/0			0/0/0	Textile fabrics coated with gum or amylaceous substances, of a kind used for the outer covers of books or the like, containing≥50% by weight of cotton, bleached, dyed, printed
0/0/0	2	2	0/0	0/0/0	0/0	0/0/0	0/0/	0/0/9	9.1/0			0/0/0	Textile fabrics coated with gum or amylaceous substances, of a kind used for the outer covers of books or the like, of bast fibres and other cotton
													---Of man-made fibres
0/0/0	2	0	0/0	0/0/0	0/0	0/0/0	0/0/	0/0/0	9.1/0			0/0/0	Textile fabrics coated with gum or amylaceous substances, of a kind used for the outer covers of books or the like, containing≥50% by weight of polyester staple fibres and cotton, bleached, dyed
0/0/0	2	0	0/0	0/0/0	0/0	0/0/0	0/0/	0/0/0	9.1/0			0/0/0	Other man-made textile fabrics coated with gum or amylaceous substances, of a kind used for the outer covers of books or the like, of other textile fabrics
													---Other
0/0/0	2	0	0/0	0/0/0	0/0	0/0/0	0/0/	0/0/0	9.1/0			0/0/0	Woollen textile fabrics coated with gum or amylaceous substances, of a kind used for the outer covers of books or the like, containing≥50% by weight of combed wool or fine animal hair
0/0/0	2	0	0/0	0/0/0	0/0	0/0/0	0/0/	0/0/0	9.1/0			0/0/0	Other textile fabrics coated with gum or amylaceous substances, of a kind used for the outer covers of books or the like, of other textile fabrics
													-Other:
0/0/0	3.5	0	0/0	0/0/0	0/0	0//0	0/0/	0/0/0	9.1/0			0/0/0	---Prepared painting canvas
													---Other:
													----Of cotton or bast fibres
0/0/0	3.5	0	0/0	0/0/0	0/0	0//0	0/0/	0/0/0	9.1/0		0/0/0	0/0/0	Tracing cloth, buckram and similar stiffened textile fabrics, of a kind used for hat foundations, of cotton, containing≥50% by weight of cotton, bleached dyed printed
0/0/0	3.5	0	0/0	0/0/0	0/0	0//0	0/0/	0/0/0	9.1/0		0/0/0	0/0/0	Tracing cloth, buckram and similar stiffened textile fabrics, of a kind used for hat foundations, of bast fibres and other cotton
													----Of man-made fibres
0/0/0	3.5	0	0/0	0/0/0	0/0	0//0	0/0/	0/0/0	9.1/0			0/0/0	Tracing cloth, buckram and similar stiffened textile fabrics, of a kind used for hat foundations, mixed, containing≥50% by weight of polyester staple fibres and cotton, bleached, dyed, printed
0/0/0	3.5	0	0/0	0/0/0	0/0	0//0	0/0/	0/0/0	9.1/0			0/0/0	Tracing cloth, buckram and similar stiffened textile fabrics, of a kind used for hat foundations, of other man-made fibres
													----Other
0/0/0	3.5	0	0/0	0/0/0	0/0	0//0	0/0/	0/0/0	9.1/0			0/0/0	Tracing cloth, buckram and similar stiffened textile fabrics, of a kind used for hat foundations, containing≥50% by weight, of combed wool or combed fine animals hair
0/0/0	3.5	0	0/0	0/0/0	0/0	0//0	0/0/	0/0/0	9.1/0			0/0/0	Tracing cloth, buckram and similar stiffened textile fabrics, of a kind used for hat foundations, of other textile fabrics
													Tyre cord fabric of high tenacity yarn of nylon or other polyamides, polyesters or viscose rayon:
													-Of nylon or other polyamides:
0/0/0	2	6.5	0/0	0/0/0	0/0	0/0/0	0/0/	5/5/	/5			0/0/0	---Of polyamides(nylon-6)
0/0/0	2	6.5	0/0	0/0/0	0/0	0/0/0	0/0/	5/5/	/5			0/0/0	---Of polyamides(nylon-6,6)
0/0/0	2	2	0/0	0/0/0	0/0	0/0/0	0/0/	0/0/9	9.1/0			0/0/0	---Other
0/0/0	2	6	0/0	0/0/0	0/0	0/0/0	0/0/	9.5/9.5/	/9.5			0/0/0	-Of polyesters
0/0/0	2	0	1/1	0/0/0	0/0	0//0	0/0/	0/0/0	9.1/0			0/0/0	-Other
													Textile fabrics impregnated, coated, covered or laminated with plastics, other than those of heading No. 59.02:
													-With poly(vinyl chloride):
0/0/0	2	0	0/0	0/0/0	0/0	0//0	0/0/	0/0/0	9.1/0			0/0/0	---Insulating cloth or tape
0/0/0	4	6	0/0	0/0/0	0/0	0/0/0	0/0/0	9.5/9.5/	9.5/9.5			0/0/0	---Imitation leather
0/0/0	4	6	0/0	0/0/0	0/0	0/0/0	0/0/0	9.5/9.5/	/9.5			0/0/0	---Other
													-With polyurethane:
0/0/0	3.5	0	0/0	0/0/0	0/0	0//0	0/0/	0/0/0	9.1/0			0/0/0	---Insulating cloth or tape
0/0/0	0	6	0/0	0/0/0	0/0	0/0/0	0/0/0	9.5/9.5/9.5	9.5/9.5			0/0/0	---Imitation leather
0/0/0	0	6	0/0	0/0/0	0/0	0/0/0	0/0/0	9.5/9.5/9.5	9.5/9.5			0/0/0	---Other
													-Other:
0/0/0	2	0	1/1	0/0/0	0/0	0//0	0/0/	0/0/0	9.1/0			0/0/0	---Insulating cloth or tape
0/0/0	3.5	4.6	0/0	0/0/0	0/0	0/0/0	0/0/0	9.3/9.5/9.3	9.4/9.5			0/0/0	---Imitation leather
0/0/0	8.5	6	0/0	0/0/0	0/0	0/0/0	0/0/0	9.5/9.5/9.5	9.5/9.5		0/0/0	0/0/0	---Other

税则号列	货品名称〔CIQ 扩展编码及品名—T2 表示见附表 2〕	最惠(%)	暂定税率	普通	增值/消费	出口退税	计量单位	监管条件/特殊证件	检验检疫	对美关税	亚太上/下
59.04	**列诺伦(亚麻油地毡),不论是否剪切成形;以织物为底布经涂布或覆面的铺地制品,不论是否剪切成形:**										
5904.1000	-列诺伦(亚麻油地毡)〔999〕	6		90	13/	13	千克/平方米	/			
5904.9000	-其他〔999〕	6		90	13/	13	千克/平方米	/			
59.05	**糊墙织物:**										
5905.0000	糊墙织物〔999〕	8		80	13/	13	千克/平方米	/		28	
59.06	**用橡胶处理的纺织物,但税目 59.02 的货品除外:**										
	-宽度不超过 20 厘米的胶粘带:										
5906.1010	---绝缘带〔999〕	8		40	13/	13	千克	/		33	
5906.1090	---其他〔999〕	8		100	13/	13	千克	/		28	
	-其他:										
5906.9100	--针织或钩编的〔999〕	8		130	13/	13	千克	/		33	
	--其他:										
5906.9910	---绝缘布或带〔101 棉混纺印花布,999 用橡胶处理的非针织或钩编织物,宽度＞20cm〕	8		40	13/	13	千克	/		33	
5906.9990	---其他〔101 棉混纺印花布,999 用橡胶处理的非针织或钩编织物,宽度＞20cm〕	8		100	13/	13	千克	/		18	
59.07	**用其他材料浸渍、涂布或包覆的纺织物;作舞台、摄影布景或类似用途的已绘制画布:**										
5907.0010	---绝缘布或带〔999〕	8		40	13/	13	千克	/		33	5.2/5.2
5907.0020	---已绘制画布〔999〕	8		50	13/	13	千克	/		28	5.2/5.2
5907.0090	---其他〔999〕	8		100	13/	13	千克	/		18	5.2/5.2
59.08	**用纺织材料机织、编结或针织而成的灯芯、炉芯、打火机芯、烛芯或类似品;煤气灯纱筒及纱罩,不论是否浸渍:**										
5908.0000	用纺织材料机织、编结或针织而成的灯芯、炉芯、打火机芯、烛芯或类似品;煤气灯纱筒及纱罩,不论是否浸渍〔999〕	8		70	13/	13	千克	/		18	
59.09	**纺织材料制的水龙软管及类似的管子,不论有无其他材料作衬里、护套或附件:**										
5909.0000	纺织材料制的水龙软管及类似的管子,不论有无其他材料作衬里、护套或附件〔999〕	8		35	13/	13	千克	/		18	
59.10	**纺织材料制的传动带或输送带及带料,不论是否用塑料浸渍、涂布、包覆或压层,也不论是否用金属或其他材料加强:**										
5910.0000	纺织材料制的传动带或输送带及带料,不论是否用塑料浸渍、涂布、包覆或压层,也不论是否用金属或其他材料加强〔999〕	8		35	13/	13	千克	/		28	
59.11	**本章注释八所规定的作专门技术用途的纺织产品及制品:**										
	-用橡胶、皮革或其他材料涂布、包覆或层压的作针布用的纺织物、毡呢及毡呢衬里机织物,以及作专门技术用途的类似织物,包括用橡胶浸渍的、用于包覆纺锤(织轴)的狭幅丝绒织物:										
5911.1010	---用橡胶浸渍的、用于包覆纺锤(织轴)的狭幅丝绒织物〔999〕	8		75	13/	13	千克	/		28	5.2/5.2
5911.1090	---其他〔999〕	8		35	13/	13	千克	/		33	
5911.2000	-筛布,不论是否制成的										
5911.2000 10	丝制筛布(不论是否制成的)〔101 网料与筛布,999 其他〕	8		35	13/	13	千克	/		28	
5911.2000 90	其他纺织材料制筛布(不论是否制成的,刻版筛网印布除外)〔101 网料与筛布,999 不论是否制成的,刻版筛网印布除外〕	8		35	13/	13	千克	/		28	
	-环状或装有连接装置的纺织物及毡呢,用于造纸机器或类似机器(例如,制浆机或制石棉水泥的机器):										
5911.3100	--每平方米重量在 650 克以下〔101 毡呢,999 造纸机等用环状或有联接物织物,平米＜650g〕	8		35	13/	13	千克	/		28	
5911.3200	--每平方米重量在 650 克及以上〔101 毡呢,999 造纸机等用环状或有联接物织物,平米≥650g〕	8		35	13/	13	千克	/		28	
5911.4000	-用于榨油机器或类似机器的滤布,包括人发制滤布〔101 网料与筛布,999 榨油机器或类似机器的滤布,包括人发制滤布〕	8		35	13/	13	千克	/		28	
5911.9000	-其他										
5911.9000 10	半导体晶圆制造用自粘式圆形抛光垫(见第 59 章注释八)〔999〕	0		35	13/	13	千克	/			
5911.9000 90	其他专门技术用途纺织产品及制品(见第 59 章注释八)〔101 网料与筛布,102 其他产业用纺织制品〕	8		35	13/	13	千克	/		18	

协定税率 %								RCEP		特惠税率 %			Article Description
东/冰/格	巴基斯坦	韩国	瑞士上/下	哥/秘/柬	澳/毛	新西/坡/智	中国港/澳/台	东盟及马来/澳/韩	日/新	亚太2国	老/柬/缅	98/97/95	
													Linoleum, whether or not cut to shape; floor coverings consisting of a coating or covering applied on a textile backing, whether or not cut to shape:
0/0/0	11.2	2.8	1.4/1.4	0/0/0	0/0	0/0/0	0/0/	0/0/12.6	12.7/0			0/0/0	-Linoleum
0/0/0	7	2.8	1.4/1.4	0/0/0	0/0	0/0/0	0/0/	0/0/12.6	12.7/0			0/0/0	-Other
													Textile wall coverings:
0/0/0	2	0	0/0	0/0/0	0/0	0/0/0	0/0/	0/0/0	9.1/0			0/0/0	Textile wall coverings
													Rubberized textile fabrics, other than those of heading No. 59.02:
													-Adhesive tape of a width not exceeding 20 cm:
0/0/0	2	0	0/0	0/0/0	0/0	0//0	0/0/	0/0/0	9.1/0			0/0/0	---Insulating tape
0//0	2	0	0/0	0/0/0	0/0	0/0/0	0/0/	0/0/0	9.1/0			0/0/0	---Other
													-Other:
0/0/0	2	0	0/0	0/0/0	0/0	0/0/0	0/0/0	0/0/0	9.1/0			0/0/0	--Knitted or crocheted
													--Other:
0/0/0	2	0	0/0	0/0/0	0/0	0//0	0/0/	0/0/0	9.1/0			0/0/0	---Insulating cloth or tape
0/0/0	2	0	0/0	0/0/0	0/0	0/0/0	0/0/0	0/0/0	9.1/0			0/0/0	---Other
													Textile fabrics otherwise impregnated, coated or covered; painted canvas being theatrical scenery, studio back-cloths or the like:
0/0/0	3.5	0	1/1	0/0/0	0/0	0//0	0/0/	0/0/0	9.1/0			0/0/0	---Insulating cloth or tape
0/0/0	3.5	0	0/0	0/0/0	0/0	0//0	0/0/	0/0/0	9.1/0			0/0/0	---Painted canvas
0/0/0	3.5	6	0/0	0/0/0	0/6	0/0/0	0/0/	9.5/9.5/	/9.5			0/0/0	---Other
													Textile wicks, woven, plaited or knitted, for lamps, stoves, lighters, candles or the like; incandescent gas mantles and tubular knitted gas mantle fabric therefor, whether or not impregnated:
0/0/0	2	0	0/0	0/0/0	0/0	0//0	0/0/	0/0/0	9.1/0			0/0/0	Textile wicks, woven, plaited or knitted, for lamps, stoves, lighters, candles or the like; incandescent gas mantles and tubular knitted gas mantle fabric therefor, whether or not impregnated
													Textile hosepiping and similar textile tubing, with or without lining, armour or accessories of other materials:
0/0/0	2	0	0/0	0/0/0	0/0	0//0	0/0/	0/0/0	7.3/0			0/0/0	Textile hosepiping and similar textile tubing, with or without lining, armour or accessories of other materials
													Transmission or conveyor belts or belting, of textile material, whether or not impregnated, coated, covered or laminated with plastics, or reinforced with metal or other material:
0/0/0	2	0	0/0	0/0/0	0/0	0//0	0/0/0	0/0/0	7.3/0			0/0/0	Transmission or conveyor belts or belting, of textile material, whether or not impregnated, coated, covered or laminated with plastics, or reinforced with metal or other material
													Textile products and articles, for technical uses, specified in Note 8 to this Chapter:
													-Textile fabrics, felt and felt-lined woven fabrics, coated, covered or laminated with rubber, leather or other material, of a kind used for card clothing, and similar fabrics of a kind used for other technical purposes, including narrow fabrics made of velvet impregnated with rubber, for covering weaving spindles (weaving beams):
0/0/0	2	0	0/0	0/0/0	0/0	0//0	0/0/	0/0/0	7.3/0			0/0/0	---Narrow fabrics made of velvet impregnated with rubber, for covering weaving spindles (weaving beams)
0/0/0	2	0	0/0	0/0/0	0/0	0//0	0/0/	0/0/0	7.3/0			0/0/0	---Other
													-Bolting cloth, whether or not made up
0/0/0	2	0	0/0	0/0/0	0/0	0//0	0/0/	7.2/7.2/7.2	7.3/7.2			0/0/0	Bolting cloth of silk, whether or not made up
0/0/0	2	0	0/0	0/0/0	0/0	0//0	0/0/	7.2/7.2/7.2	7.3/7.2			0/0/0	Bolting cloth of other textile materials, whether or not made up, other than stencil screen
													-Textile fabrics and felts, endless or fitted with linking devices, of a kind used in paper-making or similar machines (for example, for pulp or asbestos-cement):
0/0/0	2	0	0/0	0/0/0	0/0	0//0	0/0/	0/0/0	7.3/0			0/0/0	--Weighing less than 650 g/m^2
0/0/0	2	0	0.8/0.8	0/0/0	0/0	0//0	0/0/	7.2/7.2/7.2	7.3/7.2			0/0/0	--Weighing 650 g/m^2 or more
0/0/0	2	0	0/0	0/0/0	0/0	0//0	0/0/	0/0/0	7.3/0			0/0/0	-Straining cloth of a kind used in oil presses or the like, including that of human hair
													-Other
0/0/0	2		0/0	0/0/0	0/0	0//0	0/0/	7.2/5/7.6	7.3/5			0/0/0	With self — adhesive circular polishing pad manufacturing semi—conductor wafer (Notes 8 of Chapter 59)
0/0/0	2		0/0	0/0/0	0/0	0//0	0/0/	7.2/5/7.6	7.3/5			0/0/0	Other specialized technical purposes for textile productsand products(Notes 8 of Chapter 59)

第六十章
针织物及钩编织物

注释：

一、本章不包括：

(一)税目58.04的钩编花边；

(二)税目58.07的针织或钩编的标签、徽章及类似品；或

(三)第五十九章的经浸渍、涂布、包覆或层压的针织物及钩编织物。但经浸渍、涂布、包覆或层压的起绒针织物及起绒钩编织物仍归入税目60.01。

二、本章还包括用金属线制的用于衣着、装饰或类似用途的织物。

三、本协调制度所称"针织物"，包括由纺织纱线用链式针法构成的缝编织物。

子目注释：

一、子目6005.35包括由聚乙烯单丝或涤纶复丝制成的织物，重量不小于30克/平方米，但不超过55克/平方米，网眼尺寸不小于20孔/平方厘米，但不超过100孔/平方厘米，并且用α-氯氰菊酯(ISO)、虫螨腈(ISO)、溴氰菊酯(INN,ISO)、高效氯氟氰菊酯(ISO)、除虫菊酯(ISO)或甲基嘧啶磷(ISO)浸渍或涂层。

税则号列	货品名称〔CIQ扩展编码及品名—T2表示见附表2〕	最惠(%)	暂定税率	普通	增值/消费	出口退税	计量单位	监管条件/特殊证件	检验检疫	对美关税	亚太上/下
60.01	**针织或钩编的起绒织物，包括"长毛绒"织物及毛圈织物：**										
6001.1000	-"长毛绒"织物〔999〕	8		130	13/	13	米/千克	/		33	5.2/5.2
	-毛圈绒头织物：										
6001.2100	--棉制〔999〕	8		70	13/	13	米/千克	/		33	5.2/5.2
6001.2200	--化学纤维制〔999〕	8		130	13/	13	米/千克	/		28	5.2/5.2
6001.2900	--其他纺织材料制〔999〕	8		130	13/	13	米/千克	/			
	-其他：										
6001.9100	--棉制〔999〕	8		70	13/	13	米/千克	/		33	5.2/5.2
6001.9200	--化学纤维制〔999〕	8		130	13/	13	米/千克	/		33	5.2/5.2
6001.9900	--其他纺织材料制〔999〕	8		130	13/	13	米/千克	/		33	
60.02	**宽度不超过30厘米，按重量计弹性纱线或橡胶线含量在5%及以上的针织物或钩编织物，但税目60.01的货品除外：**										
	-按重量计弹性纱线含量在5%及以上，但不含橡胶线：										
6002.4010	---棉制〔999〕	8		70	13/	13	米/千克	/			5.2/5.2
6002.4020	---丝及绢丝制〔999〕	8		130	13/	13	米/千克	/			5.2/5.2
6002.4030	---合成纤维制〔999〕	8		130	13/	13	米/千克	/			
6002.4040	---人造纤维制〔999〕	8		130	13/	13	米/千克	/			
6002.4090	---其他〔999〕	8		130	13/	13	米/千克	/			5.2/5.2
	-其他：										
6002.9010	---棉制〔999〕	8		70	13/	13	米/千克	/		18	5.2/5.2
6002.9020	---丝及绢丝制〔999〕	8		130	13/	13	米/千克	/			5.2/5.2
6002.9030	---合成纤维制〔999〕	8		130	13/	13	米/千克	/		33	4/4
6002.9040	---人造纤维制〔999〕	8		130	13/	13	米/千克	/		18	4/4
6002.9090	---其他〔999〕	8		130	13/	13	米/千克	/		33	5.2/5.2
60.03	**宽度不超过30厘米的针织或钩编织物，但税目60.01或60.02的货品除外：**										
6003.1000	-羊毛或动物细毛制〔999〕	8		130	13/	13	米/千克	/			
6003.2000	-棉制〔999〕	8		70	13/	13	米/千克	/		33	
6003.3000	-合成纤维制〔999〕	8		130	13/	13	米/千克	/		33	5.2/5.2
6003.4000	-人造纤维制〔999〕	8		130	13/	13	米/千克	/			5.2/5.2
6003.9000	-其他〔999〕	8		130	13/	13	米/千克	/		18	
60.04	**宽度超过30厘米，按重量计弹性纱线或橡胶线含量在5%及以上的针织物或钩编织物，但税目60.01的货品除外：**										
	-按重量计弹性纱线含量在5%及以上，但不含橡胶线										
6004.1010	---棉制〔999〕	8		70	13/	13	米/千克	/		33	5.2/5.2
6004.1020	---丝及绢丝制〔999〕	8		130	13/	13	米/千克	/			5.2/5.2
6004.1030	---合成纤维制〔999〕	8		130	13/	13	米/千克	/		33	
6004.1040	---人造纤维制〔999〕	8		130	13/	13	米/千克	/		33	
6004.1090	---其他〔999〕	8		130	13/	13	米/千克	/		33	5.2/5.2
	-其他：										
6004.9010	---棉制〔999〕	8		70	13/	13	米/千克	/		33	5.2/5.2
6004.9020	---丝及绢丝制〔999〕	8		130	13/	13	米/千克	/			5.2/5.2
6004.9030	---合成纤维制〔999〕	8		130	13/	13	米/千克	/		33	
6004.9040	---人造纤维制〔999〕	8		130	13/	13	米/千克	/		33	
6004.9090	---其他〔999〕	8		130	13/	13	米/千克	/		33	5.2/5.2
60.05	**经编针织物(包括由镶边针织机织成的)，但税目60.01至60.04的货品除外：**										

Chapter 60
Knitted or crocheted fabrics

Notes:

1. This Chapter does not cover:
   (a) Crochet lace of heading No. 58.04;
   (b) Labels, badges or similar articles, knitted or crocheted, of heading No. 58.07; or
   (c) Knitted or crocheted fabrics, impregnated, coated, covered or laminated, of Chapter 59. However, knitted or crocheted pile fabrics, impregnated, coated, covered or laminated, remain classified in heading No. 60.01.
2. This Chapter also includes fabrics made of metal thread and of a kind used in apparel, as furnishing fabrics or for similar purposes.
3. Throughout the Nomenclature any reference to "knitted" goods includes a reference to stitch-bonded goods in which the chain stitches are formed of textile yarn.

Subheading Notes:

1. Subheading No. 6005.35 includes made of polyethylene monofilament or multifilament polyester fabric, the weight of not less than 30 g/m2, but not more than 55 g/m2, mesh size of not less than 20 holes per square centimeter, but not more than 100 holes per square centimeter, and alpha cypermethrin (ISO), insects and mites nitrile (ISO) and deltamethrin (INN, ISO), lambda cyhalothrin (ISO), pyrethrins (ISO) or pirimiphos methyl (ISO), impregnated or coated.

协定税率 %								RCEP		特惠税率 %			Article Description
东/冰/格	巴基斯坦	韩国	瑞士上/下	哥/秘/柬	澳/毛	新西/坡/智	中国港/澳/台	东盟及马来/澳/韩	日/新	亚太2国	老/柬/缅	98/97/95	
													Pile fabrics, including "long pile" fabrics and terry fabrics, knitted or crocheted:
0/0/0	0	4.6	0/0	0/0/0	0/0	0/0/0	0/0/	9.3/9.5/9.3	9.4/9.5			0/0/0	-"Long pile" fabrics
													-Looped pile fabrics:
0/0/0	0	0	0/0	0/0/0	0/0	0//0	0/0/	0/0/0	9.1/0			0/0/0	--Of cotton
0/0/0	0	0	0/0	0/0/0	0/0	0/0/0	0/0/	0/0/0	9.1/0			0/0/0	--Of man-made fibres
0/0/0	0	0	1.2/1.2	0/0/0	0/0	0/0/0	0/0/	0/0/0	10.9/0			0/0/0	--Of other textile materials
													-Other:
0/0/0	0	0	0/0	0/0/0	0/0	0//0	0/0/	0/0/0	9.1/0			0/0/0	--Of cotton
0/0/0	0	6	0/0	0/0/0	0/0	0/0/0	0/0/0	9.5/9.5/	/9.5			0/0/0	--Of man-made fibres
0/0/0	0	0	1.2/1.2	0/0/0	0/0	0/0/0	0/0/	0/0/0	10.9/0			0/0/0	--Of other textile materials
													Knitted or crocheted fabrics of a width not exceeding 30 cm, containing by weight 5% or more of elastomeric yarn or rubber thread, other than those of heading No. 60.01:
													-Containing by weight 5% or more of elastomeric yarn but not containing rubber thread:
0/0/0	0	0	0/0	0/0/0	0/0	0//0	0/0/	0/0/0	9.1/0			0/0/0	---Of cotton
0/0/0	0	0	0/0	0/0/0	0/0	0/0/0	0/0/	0/0/0	9.1/0			0/0/0	---Of silk or silk waste
0/0/0	0	0	0/0	0/0/0	0/0	0/0/0	0/0/	0/0/0	9.1/0			0/0/0	---Of synthetic fibres
0/0/0	0	0	0/0	0/0/0	0/0	0/0/0	0/0/	0/0/0	9.1/0			0/0/0	---Of artificial fibres
0/0/0	0	0	0/0	0/0/0	0/0	0/0/0	0/0/	0/0/0	9.1/0			0/0/0	---Other
													-Other:
0/0/0	0	0	0/0	0/0/0	0/0	0//0	0/0/	0/0/0	9.1/0		0/0/0	0/0/0	---Of cotton
0/0/0	0	0	0/0	0/0/0	0/0	0/0/0	0/0/	0/0/0	9.1/0			0/0/0	---Of silk or silk waste
0/0/0	0	4.6	0/0	0/0/0	0/0	0/0/0	0/0/	9.3/9.5/9.3	9.4/9.5		0/0/0	0/0/0	---Of synthetic fibres
0/0/0	0	0	0/0	0/0/0	0/0	0/0/0	0/0/	0/0/0	9.1/0			0/0/0	---Of artificial fibres
0/0/0	0	0	0/0	0/0/0	0/0	0/0/0	0/0/	0/0/0	9.1/0			0/0/0	---Other
													Knitted or crocheted fabrics of a width not exceeding 30 cm, other than those of heading No. 60.01 or 60.02:
0/0/0	0	0	0/0	0/0/0	0/0	0/0/0	0/0/	0/0/0	9.1/0			0/0/0	-Of wool or fine animal hair
0/0/0	0	0	0/0	0/0/0	0/0	0//0	0/0/	0/0/0	9.1/0			0/0/0	-Of cotton
0/0/0	0	0	0/0	0/0/0	0/0	0/0/0	0/0/	0/0/0	9.1/0			0/0/0	-Of synthetic fibres
0/0/0	0	0	0/0	0/0/0	0/0	0/0/0	0/0/	0/0/0	9.1/0			0/0/0	-Of artificial fibres
0/0/0	0	0	0/0	0/0/0	0/0	0/0/0	0/0/	0/0/0	9.1/0			0/0/0	-Other
													Knitted or crocheted fabrics of a width exceeding 30 cm, containing by weight 5% or more of elastomeric yarn or rubber thread, other than those of heading No. 60.01:
													-Containing by weight 5% or more of elastomeric yarn but not containing rubber thread:
0/0/0	0	0	0/0	0/0/0	0/0	0/0/0	0/0/	0/0/0	9.1/0		0/0/0	0/0/0	---Of cotton
0/0/0	0	0	0/0	0/0/0	0/0	0/0/0	0/0/	0/0/0	9.1/0			0/0/0	---Of silk or silk waste
0/0/0	0	6	0/0	0/0/0	0/0	0/0/0	0/0/0	9.5/9.5/9.5	9.5/9.5			0/0/0	---Of synthetic fibres
0/0/0	0	4.6	0/0	0/0/0	0/0	0/0/0	0/0/	9.3/9.5/9.3	9.4/9.5			0/0/0	Of artificial fibres
0/0/0	0	0	0/0	0/0/0	0/0	0/0/0	0/0/0	0/0/0	9.1/0			0/0/0	---Other
													-Other:
0/0/0	0	0	0/0	0/0/0	0/0	0//0	0/0/	0/0/0	9.1/0			0/0/0	---Of cotton
0/0/0	0	0	0/0	0/0/0	0/0	0/0/0	0/0/	0/0/0	9.1/0			0/0/0	---Of silk or silk waste
0/0/0	0	6	0/0	0/0/0	0/0	0/0/0	0/0/0	9.5/9.5/	/9.5			0/0/0	---Of synthetic fibres
0/0/0	0	0	0/0	0/0/0	0/0	0/0/0	0/0/	0/0/0	9.1/0			0/0/0	---Of artificial fibres
0/0/0	0	0	0/0	0/0/0	0/0	0/0/0	0/0/0	0/0/0	9.1/0			0/0/0	---Other
													Warp knit fabrics (including those made on galloon knitting machines), other than those of headings Nos. 60.01 to 60.04:

税则号列	货品名称〔CIQ 扩展编码及品名—T2 表示见附表 2〕	最惠(%)	暂定税率	普通	增值/消费	出口退税	计量单位	监管条件/特殊证件	检验检疫	对美关税	亚太上/下
	-棉制：										
6005.2100	--未漂白或漂白〔999〕	8		70	13/	13	米/千克	/			
6005.2200	--染色〔999〕	8		70	13/	13	米/千克	/			
6005.2300	--色织〔999〕	8		70	13/	13	米/千克	/			
6005.2400	--印花〔999〕	8		70	13/	13	米/千克	/			
	-合成纤维制：										
6005.3500	--本章子目注释一所列织物〔999〕	8		130	13/	13	米/千克	/		33	5.2/5.2
6005.3600	--其他，未漂白或漂白〔999〕	8		130	13/	13	米/千克	/		28	5.2/5.2
6005.3700	--其他，染色〔999〕	8		130	13/	13	米/千克	/		33	5.2/5.2
6005.3800	--其他，色织〔999〕	8		130	13/	13	米/千克	/		33	5.2/5.2
6005.3900	--其他，印花〔999〕	8		130	13/	13	米/千克	/			5.2/5.2
	-人造纤维制：										
6005.4100	--未漂白或漂白〔999〕	8		130	13/	13	米/千克	/			5.2/5.2
6005.4200	--染色〔999〕	8		130	13/	13	米/千克	/		33	5.2/5.2
6005.4300	--色织〔999〕	8		130	13/	13	米/千克	/		33	5.2/5.2
6005.4400	--印花〔999〕	8		130	13/	13	米/千克	/			5.2/5.2
	-其他：										
6005.9010	---羊毛或动物细毛制〔999〕	8		130	13/	13	米/千克	/			
6005.9090	---其他〔999〕	8		130	13/	13	米/千克	/		33	
60.06	**其他针织或钩编织物：**										
6006.1000	-羊毛或动物细毛制〔999〕	8		130	13/	13	米/千克	/		33	
	-棉制：										
6006.2100	--未漂白或漂白〔999〕	8		70	13/	13	米/千克	/		33	5.2/5.2
6006.2200	--染色〔999〕	8		70	13/	13	米/千克	/		33	5.2/5.2
6006.2300	--色织〔999〕	8		70	13/	13	米/千克	/		33	5.2/5.2
6006.2400	--印花〔999〕	8		70	13/	13	米/千克	/		33	5.2/5.2
	-合成纤维制：										
6006.3100	--未漂白或漂白〔999〕	8		130	13/	13	米/千克	/		33	5.2/5.2
6006.3200	--染色〔999〕	8		130	13/	13	米/千克	/		33	5.2/5.2
6006.3300	--色织〔999〕	8		130	13/	13	米/千克	/		33	5.2/5.2
6006.3400	--印花〔999〕	8		130	13/	13	米/千克	/		33	5.2/5.2
	-人造纤维制：										
6006.4100	--未漂白或漂白〔999〕	8		130	13/	13	米/千克	/			5.2/5.2
6006.4200	--染色〔999〕	8		130	13/	13	米/千克	/		33	5.2/5.2
6006.4300	--色织〔999〕	8		130	13/	13	米/千克	/		33	5.2/5.2
6006.4400	--印花〔999〕	8		130	13/	13	米/千克	/			5.2/5.2
6006.9000	-其他〔999〕	8		130	13/	13	米/千克	/		33	5.2/5.2

协定税率 %								RCEP		特惠税率 %			Article Description
东/冰/格	巴基斯坦	韩国	瑞士上/下	哥/秘/柬	澳/毛	新西/坡/智	中国港/澳/台	东盟及马来/澳/韩	日/新	亚太2国	老/柬/缅	98/97/95	
													-Of cotton:
0/0/0	0	0	0/0	0/0/0	0/0	0//0	0/0/	0/0/0	9.1/0			0/0/0	--Unbleached or bleached
0/0/0	0	0	0/0	0/0/0	0/0	0//0	0/0/	0/0/0	9.1/0			0/0/0	--Dyed
0/0/0	0	0	0/0	0/0/0	0/0	0//0	0/0/	0/0/0	9.1/0			0/0/0	--Of yarns of different colours
0/0/0	0	0	0/0	0/0/0	0/0	0//0	0/0/	0/0/0	9.1/0			0/0/0	--Printed
													-Of synthetic fibres:
0/0/0	0	0	0/0	0/0/0	0/0	0/0/0	0/0/0	0/0/0	9.1/0			0/0/0	--Fabrics specified in Subheading Note 1 to this Chapter
0/0/0	0	0	0/0	0/0/0	0/0	0/0/0	0/0/0	0/0/0	9.1/0			0/0/0	--Other, unbleached or bleached
0/0/0	0	6	0/0	0/0/0	0/0	0/0/0	0/0/0	9.5/9.5/	/9.5		0/0/0	0/0/0	--Other, dyed
0/0/0	0	0	0/0	0/0/0	0/0	0/0/0	0/0/	0/0/0	9.1/0			0/0/0	--Other, of yarns of different colours
0/0/0	0	0	0/0	0/0/0	0/0	0/0/0	0/0/	0/0/0	9.1/0			0/0/0	--Other, printed
													-Of artificial fibres:
0/0/0	0	0	0/0	0/0/0	0/0	0/0/0	0/0/	0/0/0	9.1/0			0/0/0	--Unbleached or bleached
0/0/0	0	0	0/0	0/0/0	0/0	0/0/0	0/0/	0/0/0	9.1/0			0/0/0	--Dyed
0/0/0	0	0	0/0	0/0/0	0/0	0/0/0	0/0/	0/0/0	9.1/0			0/0/0	--Of yarns of different colours
0/0/0	0	0	0/0	0/0/0	0/0	0/0/0	0/0/	0/0/0	9.1/0			0/0/0	--Printed
													-Other:
0/0/0	0	0	1.2/1.2	0/0/0	0/0	0/0/0	0/0/	0/0/0	10.9/0			0/0/0	---Of wool or fine animal hair
0/0/0	0	0	1.2/1.2	0/0/0	0/0	0/0/0	0/0/	0/0/0	10.9/0			0/0/0	---Other
													Other knitted or crocheted fabrics:
0/0/0	0	0	1.2/1.2	0/0/0	0/0	0/0/0	0/0/	10.8/10.8/10.8	10.9/10.8			0/0/0	-Of wool or fine animal hair
													-Of cotton:
0/0/0	0	4.6	0/0	0/0/0	0/0	0//0	0/0/	9.3/9.5/9.3	9.4/9.5			0/0/0	--Unbleached or bleached
0/0/0	0	0	0/0	0/0/0	0/6	0/0/0	0/0/	9/9/9	9.1/9		0/0/0	0/0/0	--Dyed
0/0/0	0	0	0/0	0/0/0	0/0	0/0/0	0/0/	0/0/0	9.1/0		0/0/0	0/0/0	--Of yarns of different colours
0/0/0	0	0	0/0	0/0/0	0/0	0//0	0/0/0	0/0/0	9.1/0			0/0/0	--Printed
													-Of synthetic fibres:
0/0/0	0	0	0/0	0/0/0	0/0	0/0/0	0/0/0	0/0/0	9.1/0			0/0/0	--Unbleached or bleached
0/0/0	0	6	0/0	0/0/0	0/0	0/0/0	0/0/0	9.5/9.5/9.5	9.5/9.5			0/0/0	--Dyed
0/0/0	0	6	0/0	0/0/0	0/0	0/0/0	0/0/0	9.5/9.5/	/9.5			0/0/0	--Of yarns of different colours
0/0/0	0	6	0/0	0/0/0	0/0	0/0/0	0/0/0	9.5/9.5/	/9.5			0/0/0	--Printed
													-Of artificial fibres:
0/0/0	0	0	0/0	0/0/0	0/0	0/0/0	0/0/	0/0/0	9.1/0			0/0/0	--Unbleached or bleached
0/0/0	0	4.6	0/0	0/0/0	0/0	0/0/0	0/0/0	9.3/9.5/9.3	9.4/9.5			0/0/0	--Dyed
0/0/0	0	0	0/0	0/0/0	0/0	0/0/0	0/0/	0/0/0	9.1/0			0/0/0	--Of yarns of different colours
0/0/0	0	0	0/0	0/0/0	0/0	0/0/0	0/0/	0/0/0	9.1/0			0/0/0	--Printed
0/0/0	0	0	1.2/1.2	0/0/0	0/0	0/0/0	0/0/	0/0/0	10.9/0			0/0/0	-Other

第六十一章
针织或钩编的服装及衣着附件

注释：

一、本章仅适用于制成的针织品或钩编织品。

二、本章不包括：

（一）税目 62.12 的货品；

（二）税目 63.09 的旧衣着或其他旧物品；

（三）矫形器具、外科手术带、疝气带及类似品（税目 90.21）。

三、税目 61.03 及 61.04 所称：

（一）“西服套装”，是指面料用相同的织物制成的两件套或三件套的下列成套服装：

一件人体上半身穿着的外套或短上衣，除袖子外，其面料数为四片或四片以上；也可附带一件马甲（西服背心），这件马甲（西服背心）的前片面料应与套装其他各件的面料相同，后片面料则应与外套或短上衣的衬里料相同；

以及一件人体下半身穿着的服装，即不带背带或护胸的长裤、马裤、短裤（游泳裤除外）、裙子或裙裤。

西服套装各件面料质地、颜色及构成必须相同，其款式也必须相同，尺寸大小还须相互般配，但可以用不同织物滚边（缝口上缝入长条织物）。

如果数件人体下半身穿着的服装同时报验或出口（例如，两条长裤、长裤与短裤、裙 子或裙裤与长裤），构成西服套装下装的应是一条长裤，而对于女式西服套装，则应是一条裙子或裙裤，其他服装应分别归类。
所称“西服套装”，包括不论是否完全符合上述条件的下列配套服装：
1.常礼服，由一件后襟下垂并下端开圆弧形叉的素色短上衣和一条条纹长裤组成；
2.晚礼服（燕尾服），一般用黑色织物制成，上衣前襟较短且不闭合，背后有燕尾；

3.无燕尾套装夜礼服，其中上衣款式与普通上衣相似（可以更为显露衬衣前胸），但有光滑丝质或仿丝质的翻领。

（二）“便服套装”，是指面料相同并作零售包装的下列成套服装（西服套装及税目 61.07、61.08或 61.09 的物品除外）：

一件人体上半身穿着的服装，但套衫及背心除外，因为套衫可在两件套服装中作为内衣，背心也可作为内衣；以及一件或两件不同的人体下半身穿着的服装，即长裤、护胸背带工装裤、马裤、短裤（游泳裤除外）、裙子或裙裤。

便服套装各件面料质地、款式、颜色及构成必须相同；尺寸大小也须相互般配。所称“便服套装”，不包括税目 61.12 的运动服及滑雪服。

四、税目 61.05 及 61.06 不包括在腰围以下有口袋的服装、带有罗纹腰带及以其他方式收紧下摆的服装或其织物至少在 10 厘米×10 厘米的面积内沿各方向的直线长度上平均每厘米少于 10 针的服装。税目 61.05 不包括无袖服装。

衬衫及仿男式女衬衫是指人体上身穿着并从领口处全开襟或半开襟的长袖或短袖衣服；罩衫也是上半身穿着的宽松服装，但可以无袖，领口处也可以不开襟。衬衫、仿男式女衬衫及罩衫可有衣领。

五、税目 61.09 不包括带有束带、罗纹腰带或其他方式收紧下摆的服装。

六、对于税目 61.11：

（一）所称“婴儿服装及衣着附件”，是指用于身高不超过 86 厘米幼儿的服装；

（二）既可归入税目 61.11，也可归入本章其他税目的物品，应归入税目 61.11。

七、税目 61.12 所称“滑雪服”，是指从整个外观和织物质地来看，主要在滑雪（速度滑雪或高山滑雪）时穿着的下列服装或成套服装：

（一）“滑雪连身服”，即上下身连在一起的单件服装；除袖子和领子外，滑雪连身服可有口袋或脚带；

（二）“滑雪套装”，即由两件或三件构成一套并作零售包装的下列服装：
一件用一条拉链扣合的带风帽的厚夹克、防风衣、防风短上衣或类似的服装，可以附带一件背心（滑雪背心）；以及一条不论是否过腰的长裤、一条马裤或一条护胸背带工装裤。

“滑雪套装”也可由一件类似以上（一）款所述的连身服和一件可套在连身服外面的有胎料背心组成。

“滑雪套装”各件颜色可以不同，但面料质地、款式及构成必须相同；尺寸大小也须相互般配。

八、既可归入税目 61.13，也可归入本章其他税号的服装，除税目 61.11 所列的仍归入该税号外，其余的应一律归入税目 61.13。

九、本章的服装，凡门襟为左压右的，应视为男式；右压左的，应视为女式。但本规定不适用于其式样已明显为男式或女式的服装。无法区别是男式还是女式的服装，应按女式服装归入有关税目。

十、本章物品可用金属线制成。

税则号列	货品名称〔CIQ 扩展编码及品名－T2 表示见附表 2〕	最惠(%)	暂定税率	普通	增值/消费	出口退税	计量单位	监管条件/特殊证件	检验检疫	对美关税	亚太上/下
61.01	**针织或钩编的男式大衣、短大衣、斗篷、短斗篷、带风帽的防寒短上衣（包括滑雪短上衣）、防风衣、防风短上衣及类似品，但税目 61.03 的货品除外：**										
6101.2000	-棉制〔999〕	8		90	13/	13	件/千克	/		33	5.2/5.2

Chapter 61
Articles of apparel and clothing accessories, knitted or crocheted

Notes:

1. This Chapter applies only to made up knitted or crocheted articles.
2. This Chapter does not cover:
   (a) Goods of heading No.62. 12;
   (b) Worn clothing or other worn articles of heading No.63. 09; or
   (c) Orthopaedic appliances, surgical belts, trusses or the like (heaing No.90. 21).
3. For the purposes of headings Nos.61. 03 and 61. 04:

(a) The term "suit" means a set of garments composed of two or three pieces made up, in respect of their outer surface, in identical fabric and comprising:

One suit coat or jacket the outer shell of which, exclusive of sleeves, consists of four or more panels, designed to cover the upper part of the body, possibly with a tailored waistcoat in addition whose front is made from the same fabric as the outer sulrace of the other components of the set and whose back is made from the same fabric as the lining of the suit coat or jacket, and

one garment designed to cover the lower part of the body and consisting of trousers, breeches or shorts (other than swimwear), a skirt or a divided skirt, having neither braces nor bibs.

All of the components of a suit must be of the same fabric construction, style, colour and composition; they must also be of corresponding or compatible size. However, these components may have bindings of different fabric (the narrow fabric stitched to finish raw edges).

If several separate components to cover the lower part of the body are presented together (for example, trousers and shorts, or a skirt or divided skirt and trousers), the constituent lower part shall be one pair of trousers, or, in the case of women's or girls' suits, the skirt or divided skirt, the other garments being considered separately.

The term "suit" includes the following sets of garments, whether or not they fulfill all the above conditions:

(ⅰ) morning dress, comprising a plain jacket (cutaway) with rounded tails hanging well down at the back and striped trousers;

(ⅱ) evening dress (tailcoat), generally made of black fabric, the jacket of which is relatively short at the front, does not close and has narrow skirts cut in at the hips and hanging down behind;

(ⅲ) dinner jacket suits, in which the jacket is similar in style to an ordinary jacket (though perhaps revealing more of the shirt front), but has shiny silk or imitation silk lapels.

(b) The term "ensemble" means a set of garments (other than suits and articles of heading No.61. 07, 61. 08 or 61. 09), composed of several pieces made up in identical fabric, put up for retail sale, and comprising:

One garment designed to cover the upper part of the body, with the exception of pullovers which may form a second upper garment in the sole context of twin sets, and of waistcoats which may also form a second upper garment, and

One or two different garments, designed to cover the lower part of the body and consisting of trousers, bib and brace overalls, breeches, shorts (other than swimwear), a skirt or a divided skirt.

All of the components of an ensemble must be of the same fabric construction, style, colour and composition; they also must be of corresponding or compatible size. The term "ensemble" does not apply to track suits or ski suits, of heading No.61. 12.

4. Headings Nos.61. 05 and 61. 06 do not cover garments with pockets below the waist, with a ribbed waistband or other means of tightening at the bottom of the garment, or garments having an average of less than 10 stitches per linear centimetre in each direction counted on an area measuring at least 10cm×10cm. Heading No.61. 05 does not cover sleeveless garments.
   "Shirts" and "shirt－blouses" are garments designed to cover the upper part of the body, having long or short sleeves and a full or partial opening starting at the neckline. "Blouses" are loose－fitting garments also designed to cover the upper part of the body but may be sleeveless and with or without an opening at the neckline. "Shirts", "shirt－blouses" and "blouses" may also have a collar.
5. Heading No.61. 09 does not cover garments with a drawstring, a ribbed waistband or other means of tightening at the bottom of the garment.
6. For the purposes of heading No.61. 11:
   (a) The expression "babies' garments and clothing accessories" means articles for young children of a body height not exceeding 86cm;
   (b) Articles which are, *prima facie*, classifiable both in heading No.61. 11 and in other headings of this Chapter are to be classified in heading No.61. 11.
7. For the purposes of heading No.61. 12, "ski suits" means garments or sets of garments which, by their general appearance and texture, are identifiable as intended to be worn principally for skiing (cross-country or alpine). They consist either of:
   (a) a "ski overall", that is, a one-piece garment designed to cover the upper and the lower parts of the body; in addition to sleeves and a collar the ski overall may have pockets or footstraps; or
   (b) a "ski ensemble", that is, a set of garments composed of two or three pieces, put up for retail sale and comprising:
   -One garment such as an anorak, wind-cheater, windjacket or similar article, closed by a slide fastener (zipper), possibly with a waistcoat in addition, and-one pair of trousers whether or not extending above waist-level, one pair of breeches or one bib and brace overall.
   The "ski ensemble" may also consist of an overall similar to the one mentioned in paragraph (a) above and a type of padded, sleeveless jacket worn over the overall.
   All the components of a "ski ensemble" must be made up in a fabric of the same texture, style and composition whether or not of the same colour; they also must be of corresponding or compatible size.
8. Garments which are, *prima facie*, classifiable both in heading No.61. 13 and in other headings of this Chapter, excluding heading No. 61. 11, are to be classified in heading No.61. 13.
9. Garments of this Chapter desinged for left over right closure at the front shall be regarded as men's or boys' garments, and those designed for right over left closure at the front as women's or girls' garments. These provisions do not apply where the cut of the garment clearly indicates that it is designed for one or other of the sexes. Garments which cannot be identified as either men's or boys' garments or as women's or girls' garments are to be classified in the headings covering women's or girls' garments.
10. Articles of this Chapter may be made of metal thread.

协定税率 %								RCEP		特惠税率 %			Article Description
东/冰/格	巴基斯坦	韩国	瑞士上/下	哥/秘/柬	澳/毛	新西/坡/智	中国港/澳/台	东盟及马来/澳/韩	日/新	亚太2国	老/柬/缅	98/97/95	
													Men's or boys' overcoats, car-coats, capes, cloaks, anoraks (including ski-jackets), wind-cheaters, wind-jackets and similar articles, knitted or crocheted, other than those of heading No. 61. 03:
0/0/0	14	3.5	1.8/1.8	0/0/0	0/0	0/0/0	0/0/	0/0/15.8	15.9/0			0/0/0	-Of cotton

税则号列	货品名称〔CIQ 扩展编码及品名－T2 表示见附表 2〕	最惠(%)	暂定税率	普通	增值/消费	出口退税	计量单位	监管条件/特殊证件	检验检疫	对美关税	亚太上/下
6101.3000	-化学纤维制〔999〕	8		130	13/	13	件/千克	/		33	5.2/5.2
	-其他纺织材料制：										
6101.9010	---羊毛或动物细毛制										
6101.9010 10	毛制针织或钩编非手工制男式防风衣(包括防寒短上衣、防风短上衣及类似品)〔999〕	10		130	13/	13	件/千克	/			6.5/6.5
6101.9010 90	毛制针织或钩编其他男大衣、斗篷、防风衣等(包括防寒短上衣,防风短上衣、短大衣,短斗篷及类似品)〔999〕	10		130	13/	13	件/千克	/			6.5/6.5
6101.9090	---其他纺织材料制〔999〕	8		130	13/	13	件/千克	/		33	5.2/5.2
61.02	**针织或钩编的女式大衣、短大衣、斗篷、短斗篷、带风帽的防寒短上衣(包括滑雪短上衣)、防风衣、防风短上衣及类似品,但税目 61.04 的货品除外：**										
6102.1000	-羊毛或动物细毛制										
6102.1000 10	毛制针织或钩编女式大衣等(包括短大衣、斗篷、短斗篷及类似品,雨衣除外)〔999〕	10		130	13/	13	件/千克	/		35	6.5/6.5
6102.1000 21	毛制针织或钩编手工制女式防风衣(包括防寒短上衣、防风短上衣及类似品)〔999〕	10		130	13/	13	件/千克	/		35	6.5/6.5
6102.1000 29	毛制针织或钩编女式防风衣(包括防寒短上衣,防风短上衣及类似品)〔999〕	10		130	13/	13	件/千克	/		35	6.5/6.5
6102.1000 30	毛制针织或钩编女式雨衣〔999〕	10		130	13/	13	件/千克	/		35	6.5/6.5
6102.2000	-棉制〔999〕	8		90	13/	13	件/千克	/		33	5.2/5.2
6102.3000	-化学纤维制〔999〕	8		130	13/	13	件/千克	/		33	5.2/5.2
6102.9000	-其他纺织材料制〔999〕	10		130	13/	13	件/千克	/			6.5/6.5
61.03	**针织或钩编的男式西服套装、便服套装、上衣、长裤、护胸背带工装裤、马裤及短裤(游泳裤除外)：**										
	-西服套装：										
6103.1010	---羊毛或动物细毛制〔999〕	10		130	13/	13	套/千克	/			6.5/6.5
6103.1020	---合成纤维制〔999〕	10		130	13/	13	套/千克	/			6.5/6.5
6103.1090	---其他纺织材料制〔999〕	8		130	13/	13	套/千克	/			5.2/5.2
	-便服套装：										
6103.2200	--棉制〔999〕	10		90	13/	13	套/千克	/		35	6.5/6.5
6103.2300	--合成纤维制〔999〕	10		130	13/	13	套/千克	/			6.5/6.5
	--其他纺织材料制：										
6103.2910	---羊毛或动物细毛制〔999〕	10		130	13/	13	套/千克	/			6.5/6.5
6103.2990	---其他纺织材料制〔999〕	10		130	13/	13	套/千克	/		35	6.5/6.5
	-上衣：										
6103.3100	--羊毛或动物细毛制〔999〕	6		130	13/	13	件/千克	/		31	3.9/3.9
6103.3200	--棉制〔999〕	6		90	13/	13	件/千克	/		31	3.9/3.9
6103.3300	--合成纤维制〔999〕	8		130	13/	13	件/千克	/		33	5.2/5.2
6103.3900	--其他纺织材料制〔999〕	6		130	13/	13	件/千克	/		31	3.9/3.9
	-长裤、护胸背带工装裤、马裤及短裤：										
6103.4100	--羊毛或动物细毛制〔101：针织外衣；102：针织童装；999：针织裤子〕	6		130	13/	13	条/千克	/		31	3.9/3.9
6103.4200	--棉制										
6103.4200 12	棉制针织钩编男童非保暖背带工装裤(2－7 号男童护胸背带工装裤)〔999〕	6		90	13/	13	条/千克	A/	M	31	3.9/3.9
6103.4200 21	棉制针织或钩编男童游戏套装长裤(指男童 8－18 号)〔999〕	6		90	13/	13	条/千克	A/	M	31	3.9/3.9
6103.4200 29	棉制针织或钩编其他男童游戏套装裤(包括长裤、马裤、短裤)〔999〕	6		90	13/	13	条/千克	A/	M	31	3.9/3.9
6103.4200 90	棉制针织或钩编其他男裤等(包括马裤、短裤及其他长裤)〔999〕	6		90	13/	13	条/千克	/		31	3.9/3.9
6103.4300	--合成纤维制										
6103.4300 90	其他合纤制针织或钩编其他男裤(包括马裤、短裤及其他长裤)〔101 针织童装；999 针织裤子〕	8		130	13/	13	条/千克	/		33	5.2/5.2
6103.4300 92	其他合成纤维制男童游戏套装长裤(针织或钩编,指男童 8－18 号)〔999〕	8		130	13/	13	条/千克	A/	M	33	5.2/5.2
6103.4300 93	其他合成纤维制男童游戏套装长裤(针织或钩编,包括马裤、短裤及其他长裤)〔999〕	8		130	13/	13	条/千克	A/	M	33	5.2/5.2
6103.4900	--其他纺织材料制										
6103.4900 13	丝制针织或钩编其他男童长裤、马裤(丝及绢丝含量在 70%及以上)〔999〕	6		130	13/	13	条/千克	A/	M	31	3.9/3.9
6103.4900 23	人造纤维制针织或钩编其他男童长裤、马裤(含毛 23%及以上)〔999〕	6		130	13/	13	条/千克	A/	M	31	3.9/3.9

协定税率 %								RCEP		特惠税率 %			Article Description
东/冰/格	巴基斯坦	韩国	瑞士上/下	哥/秘/柬	澳/毛	新西/坡/智	中国港/澳/台	东盟及马来/澳/韩	日/新	亚太2国	老/柬/缅	98/97/95	
0/0/0	0	3.5	1.8/1.8	0/0/0	0/10.5	0/0/0	0/0/	0/0/15.8	15.9/0			0/0/0	-Of man-made fibres
													-Of other textile materials:
													---Of wool or fine animal hair
0/0/0	0	15	2.5/2.5	0/0/0	0/15	0/0/0	0/0/	23.8/23.8/23.8	/23.8			0/0/0	Men's or boys' wind-cheaters, anoraks, wind-jackets and similar articles, not hand-worked, knitted or crocheted, of wool or fine animal hair
0/0/0	0	15	2.5/2.5	0/0/0	0/15	0/0/0	0/0/	23.8/23.8/23.8	/23.8			0/0/0	Men's or boys' overcoats, capes, wind-cheaters, anoraks, wind-jackets, car-coats, cloak and similar articles, knitted or crocheted, of wool or fine animal hair
0/0/0	8.8	3.5	1.8/1.8	0/0/0	0/0	0/0/0	0/0/	0/0/15.8	15.9/0			0/0/0	---Of other textile materials
													Women's or girls' overcoats, car-coats, capes, cloaks, anoraks (including ski-jackets), wind-cheaters, wind-jackets and similar articles, knitted or crocheted, other than those of heading No. 61.04:
													-Of wool or fine animal hair
0/0/0	18	15	2.5/2.5	0/0/0	0/15	0/0/0	0/0/	23.8/23.8/	/23.8			0/0/0	Women's or girls' overcoats, car-coats, capes, cloak and similar articles, other than raincoats, knitted or crocheted, of wool or fine animal hair
0/0/0	18	15	2.5/2.5	0/0/0	0/15	0/0/0	0/0/	23.8/23.8/	/23.8			0/0/0	Women's or girls' wind-cheaters, anoraks, wind-jackets and similar articles, hand-worked, knitted or crocheted, of wool or fine animal hair
0/0/0	18	15	2.5/2.5	0/0/0	0/15	0/0/0	0/0/	23.8/23.8/	/23.8			0/0/0	Other women's or girls' wind-cheaters, anoraks, wind-jackets and similar articles, knitted or crocheted, of wool or fine animal hair
0/0/0	18	15	2.5/2.5	0/0/0	0/15	0/0/0	0/0/	23.8/23.8/	/23.8			0/0/0	Women's or girls' raincoats, knitted or crocheted, of wool or fine animal hair
0/0/0	14	3.5	1.8/1.8	0//0	0/10.5	0/0/0	0/0/	0/0/15.8	15.9/0			0/0/0	-Of cotton
0/0/0	0	3.5	1.8/1.8	0/0/0	0/0	0/0/0	0/0/	0/0/15.8	15.9/0			0/0/0	-Of man-made fibres
0/0/0	10	9.3	2/2	0/0/0	0/0	0/0/0	0/0/	18/18/18	18.8/18			0/0/0	-Of other textile materials
													Men's or boys' suits, ensembles, jackets, blazers, trousers, bib and brace overalls, breeches and shorts (other than swimwear), knitted or crocheted:
													-Suits:
0/0/0	18	15	2.5/2.5	0/0/0	0/15	0/0/0	0/0/	23.8/23.8/23.8	/23.8			0/0/0	---Of wool or fine animal hair
0/0/0	18	15	2.5/2.5	0/0/0	0/15	0/0/0	0/0/	23.8/23.8/23.8	/23.8			0/0/0	---Of synthetic fibres
0/0/0	8.8	3.5	1.8/1.8	0/0/0	0/0	0/0/0	0/0/	0/0/15.8	15.9/0		0//	0/0/0	---Of other textile materials
													-Ensembles:
0/0/0	14.8	9.3	2/2	0/0/0	0/0	0/0/0	0/0/	19/19/	/19		0//	0/0/0	--Of cotton
0/0/0	18	15	2.5/2.5	0/0/0	0/15	0/0/0	0/0/	23.8/23.8/23.8	/23.8			0/0/0	--Of synthetic fibres
													--Of other textile materials:
0/0/0	18	15	2.5/2.5	0/0/0	0/15	0/0/0	0/0/	23.8/23.8/23.8	/23.8			0/0/0	---Of wool or fine animal hair
0/0/0	18	15	2.5/2.5	0/0/0	0/15	0/0/0	0/0/	23.8/23.8/23.8	/23.8		0//	0/0/0	---Of other textile materials
													-Jackets and blazers:
0/0/0	8	3.2	1.6/1.6	0/0/0	0/9.6	0/0/0	0/0/	0/0/14.4	14.5/0			0/0/0	--Of wool or fine animal hair
0/0/0	0	3.2	1.6/1.6	0/0/0	0/0	0/0/0	0/0/	0/0/14.4	14.5/0		0/0/0	0/0/0	--Of cotton
0/0/0	0	3.8	1.9/1.9	0/0/0	0/11.4	0/0/0	0/0/	0/0/17.1	17.3/0		/0/	0/0/0	--Of synthetic fibres
0/0/0	0	3.2	1.6/1.6	0/0/0	0/0	0/0/0	0/0/	0/0/14.4	14.5/0		0/0/	0/0/0	--Of other textile materials
													-Trousers, bib and brace overalls, breeches and shorts:
0/0/0	8	3.2	1.6/1.6	0/0/0	0/9.6	0/0/0	0/0/	0/0/14.4	14.5/0	0		0/0/0	--Of wool or fine animal hair
													--Of cotton
0/0/0	0	3.2	1.6/1.6	0/0/0	0/0	0/0/0	0/0/	0/0/14.4	14.5/0	2.4	0/0/0	0/0/0	Boys' bib and brace overalls(not keep warm), No. 2～No. 7, knitted or crocheted, of cotton
0/0/0	0	3.2	1.6/1.6	0/0/0	0/0	0/0/0	0/0/	0/0/14.4	14.5/0	2.4	0/0/0	0/0/0	Boys' playsuit trousers No.8～No.18, knitted or crocheted, of cotton
0/0/0	0	3.2	1.6/1.6	0/0/0	0/0	0/0/0	0/0/	0/0/14.4	14.5/0	2.4	0/0/0	0/0/0	Other boys' playsuit, including trousers, breeches and shorts, knitted or crocheted, of cotton
0/0/0	0	3.2	1.6/1.6	0/0/0	0/0	0/0/0	0/0/	0/0/14.4	14.5/0	2.4	0/0/0	0/0/0	Other men's or boys' trousers, breeches and shorts, knitted or crocheted, of cotton
													--Of synthetic fibres
0/0/0	0	3.5	1.8/1.8	0/0/0	0/0	0/0/0	0/0/	0/0/15.8	15.9/0	0	/0/	0/0/0	Other men's or boys' trousers, breeches and shorts, of synthetic fibres, knitted or crocheted
0/0/0	0	3.5	1.8/1.8	0/0/0	0/0	0/0/0	0/0/	0/0/15.8	15.9/0	0	/0/	0/0/0	Other boys' playsuit trousers No. 8～No. 18, knitted or crocheted, of synthe3tic fibres
0/0/0	0	3.5	1.8/1.8	0/0/0	0/0	0/0/0	0/0/	0/0/15.8	15.9/0	0	/0/	0/0/0	Other boys' playsuit trousers, including breeches, shorts and other trousers, knitted or crocheted, of synthetic fibres
													--Of other textile materials
0/0/0	0	3.2	1.6/1.6	0/0/0	0/0	0/0/0	0/0/	0/0/14.4	14.5/0	0	0/0/	0/0/0	Boys' trousers and breeches, containing≥70% by weight of silk or spun silk knitted or crocheted
0/0/0	0	3.2	1.6/1.6	0/0/0	0/0	0/0/0	0/0/	0/0/14.4	14.5/0	0	0/0/	0/0/0	Other boys' trousers, breeches, of artificial fibres, containing ≥23% by weight of wool or fine animal hair, knitted or crocheted

税则号列	货品名称〔CIQ扩展编码及品名—T2表示见附表2〕	最惠(%)	暂定税率	普通	增值/消费	出口退税	计量单位	监管条件/特殊证件	检验检疫	对美关税	亚太上/下
6103.4900 26	其他人造纤维制针织或钩编其他男童长裤(包括马裤)〔999〕	6		130	13/	13	条/千克	A/	M	31	3.9/3.9
6103.4900 51	其他纺织材料制其他男童长裤、马裤(针织或钩编,棉限内)〔999〕	6		130	13/	13	条/千克	A/	M	31	3.9/3.9
6103.4900 52	其他纺织材料制其他男童长裤、马裤(针织或钩编,羊毛限内)〔999〕	6		130	13/	13	条/千克	A/	M	31	3.9/3.9
6103.4900 53	其他纺织材料制其他男童长裤、马裤(针织或钩编,化学纤维限内)〔999〕	6		130	13/	13	条/千克	A/	M	31	3.9/3.9
6103.4900 59	其他纺织材料制其他男童长裤、马裤(针织或钩编)〔999〕	6		130	13/	13	条/千克	A/	M	31	3.9/3.9
6103.4900 90	其他纺材制针织或钩编其他男式长裤、护胸背带工装裤、马裤及短裤〔101针织童装,999针织裤子〕	6		130	13/	13	条/千克	/		31	3.9/3.9
61.04	**针织或钩编的女式西服套装、便服套装、上衣、连衣裙、裙子、裙裤、长裤、护胸背带工装裤、马裤及短裤(游泳服除外):**										
	-西服套装:										
6104.1300	--合成纤维制〔999〕	10		130	13/	13	套/千克	/			6.5/6.5
	--其他纺织材料制:										
6104.1910	---羊毛或动物细毛制〔999〕	8		130	13/	13	套/千克	/			5.2/5.2
6104.1920	---棉制〔999〕	8		90	13/	13	套/千克	/			5.2/5.2
6104.1990	---其他〔999〕	8		130	13/	13	套/千克	/			5.2/5.2
	-便服套装:										
6104.2200	--棉制〔999〕	8		90	13/	13	套/千克	/		33	5.2/5.2
6104.2300	--合成纤维制〔999〕	10		130	13/	13	套/千克	/			6.5/6.5
	--其他纺织材料制:										
6104.2910	---羊毛或动物细毛制〔999〕	8		130	13/	13	套/千克	/			5.2/5.2
6104.2990	---其他〔999〕	6		130	13/	13	套/千克	/			3.9/3.9
	-上衣:										
6104.3100	--羊毛或动物细毛制〔999〕	6		130	13/	13	件/千克	/		31	3.9/3.9
6104.3200	--棉制〔999〕	6		90	13/	13	件/千克	/		31	3.9/3.9
6104.3300	--合成纤维制〔999〕	10		130	13/	13	件/千克	/		35	6.5/6.5
6104.3900	--其他纺织材料制〔999〕	6		130	13/	13	件/千克	/		31	3.9/3.9
	-连衣裙:										
6104.4100	--羊毛或动物细毛制〔999〕	6		130	13/	13	件/千克	/		31	3.9/3.9
6104.4200	--棉制〔999〕	6		90	13/	13	件/千克	/		31	3.9/3.9
6104.4300	--合成纤维制〔999〕	8		130	13/	13	件/千克	/		33	5.2/5.2
6104.4400	--人造纤维制〔999〕	6		130	13/	13	件/千克	/		31	3.9/3.9
6104.4900	--其他纺织材料制〔999〕	6		130	13/	13	件/千克	/		31	3.9/3.9
	-裙子及裙裤:										
6104.5100	--羊毛或动物细毛制〔999〕	6		130	13/	13	件/千克	/		31	3.9/3.9
6104.5200	--棉制〔999〕	6		90	13/	13	件/千克	/		31	3.9/3.9
6104.5300	--合成纤维制〔999〕	6		130	13/	13	件/千克	/		31	3.9/3.9
6104.5900	--其他纺织材料制〔999〕	6		130	13/	13	件/千克	/		31	3.9/3.9
	-长裤、护胸背带工装裤、马裤及短裤:										
6104.6100	--羊毛或动物细毛制〔101针织童装,999针织裤子〕	6		130	13/	13	条/千克	/		31	3.9/3.9
6104.6200	--棉制										
6104.6200 30	棉制针织或钩编女童游戏套装长裤(指女童7—16号,包括马裤)〔999〕	6		90	13/	13	条/千克	A/	M	31	3.9/3.9
6104.6200 40	棉针织或钩编其他女童游戏套装裤(包括马裤、短裤、非保暖护胸背带工装裤及其他长裤)〔999〕	6		90	13/	13	条/千克	A/	M	31	3.9/3.9
6104.6200 90	棉制针织或钩编其他女裤〔101针织裤子,102针织童装〕	6		90	13/	13	条/千克	/		31	3.9/3.9
6104.6300	--合成纤维制										
6104.6300 90	其他合成纤维制针织或钩编女裤〔101针织裤子,102针织童装〕	8		130	13/	13	条/千克	/		33	5.2/5.2
6104.6300 91	其他合成纤维制女童游戏套装长裤、马裤(针织或钩编,指女童7—16号)〔999〕	8		130	13/	13	条/千克	A/	M	33	5.2/5.2
6104.6300 92	其他合成纤维制女童游戏套装裤(针织或钩编,包括短裤及其他长裤)〔999〕	8		130	13/	13	条/千克	A/	M	33	5.2/5.2
6104.6900	--其他纺织材料制〔101针织童装,999针织裤子〕	6		130	13/	13	条/千克	/		31	3.9/3.9
61.05	**针织或钩编的男衬衫:**										
6105.1000	-棉制										
6105.1000 11	棉制针织或钩编男童游戏套装衬衫(不带缝制领,指男童8—18号)〔999〕	6		90	13/	13	件/千克	A/	M	31	3.9/3.9
6105.1000 19	棉制其他男童游戏套装衬衫(针织或钩编)〔999〕	6		90	13/	13	件/千克	A/	M	31	3.9/3.9
6105.1000 90	其他棉制针织或钩编其他男衬衫〔101针织童装,999针织衬衫〕	6		90	13/	13	件/千克	/		31	3.9/3.9
6105.2000	-化学纤维制										
6105.2000 21	化学纤维制针织或钩编男童游戏套装衬衫(不带缝制领,指男童8—18号)〔999〕	8		130	13/	13	件/千克	A/	M	33	5.2/5.2
6105.2000 29	化学纤维制其他男童游戏套装衬衫(针织或钩编)〔999〕	8		130	13/	13	件/千克	A/	M	33	5.2/5.2
6105.2000 90	其他化纤制针织或钩编其他男衬衫〔101针织童装,999针织衬衫〕	8		130	13/	13	件/千克	/		33	5.2/5.2

协定税率 %								RCEP		特惠税率 %			Article Description
东/冰/格	巴基斯坦	韩国	瑞士 上/下	哥/秘/柬	澳/毛	新西/坡/智	中国港/澳/台	东盟及马来/澳/韩	日/新	亚太2国	老/柬/缅	98/97/95	
0/0/0	0	3.2	1.6/1.6	0/0/0	0/0	0/0/0	0/0/	0/0/14.4	14.5/0	0	0/0/	0/0/0	Other boys' trousers and breeches, of artificial fibres, knitted or crocheted
0/0/0	0	3.2	1.6/1.6	0/0/0	0/0	0/0/0	0/0/	0/0/14.4	14.5/0	0	0/0/	0/0/0	Other boys' trousers and breeches, cotton within limitations, knitted or crocheted, of other textile materials
0/0/0	0	3.2	1.6/1.6	0/0/0	0/0	0/0/0	0/0/	0/0/14.4	14.5/0	0	0/0/	0/0/0	Other boys' trousers and breeches, wool within limitations, knitted or crocheted, of other textile materials
0/0/0	0	3.2	1.6/1.6	0/0/0	0/0	0/0/0	0/0/	0/0/14.4	14.5/0	0	0/0/	0/0/0	Other boys' trousers and breeches, man-made fibres within limitations, knitted or crocheted, of other textile materials
0/0/0	0	3.2	1.6/1.6	0/0/0	0/0	0/0/0	0/0/	0/0/14.4	14.5/0	0	0/0/	0/0/0	Other boys' trousers and breeches, knitted or crocheted, of other textile materials
0/0/0	0	3.2	1.6/1.6	0/0/0	0/0	0/0/0	0/0/	0/0/14.4	14.5/0	0	0/0/	0/0/0	Men's knitted or crocheted trousers breeches, bib and brace overalls of other textile materials,
													Women's or girls' suits, ensembles, jackets, blazers, dresses, skirts, divided skirts, trousers, bib and brace overalls, breeches and shorts (otherthan swimwear), knitted or crocheted:
													-Suits:
0/0/0	18	15	2.5/2.5	0/0/0	0/15	0/0/0	0/0/	23.8/23.8/23.8	/23.8			0/0/0	--Of synthetic fibres
													--Of other textile materials:
0/0/0	8.8	3.5	1.8/1.8	0/0/0	0/0	0/0/0	0/0/	0/0/15.8	15.9/0			0/0/0	---Of wool or fine animal hair
0/0/0	14	3.5	1.8/1.8	0/0/0	0/0	0/0/0	0/0/	0/0/15.8	15.9/0		0//	0/0/0	---Of cotton
0/0/0	8.8	3.5	1.8/1.8	0/0/0	0/0	0/0/0	0/0/	0/0/15.8	15.9/0		0//	0/0/0	---Other
													-Ensembles:
0/0/0	14	3.5	1.8/1.8	0/0/0	0/0	0/0/0	0/0/	0/0/15.8	15.9/0		0//	0/0/0	--Of cotton
0/0/0	18	15	2.5/2.5	0/0/0	0/15	0/0/0	0/0/	23.8/23.8/23.8	/23.8			0/0/0	--Of synthetic fibres
													--Of other textile materials:
0/0/0	8.8	3.5	1.8/1.8	0/0/0	0/0	0/0/0	0/0/	0/0/15.8	15.9/0			0/0/0	---Of wool or fine animal hair
0/0/0	7.5	3	1.5/1.5	0/0/0	0/0	0/0/0	0/0/	0/0/13.5	13.6/0			0/0/0	---Other
													-Jackets and blazers:
0/0/0	8	3.2	1.6/1.6	0/0/0	0/9.6	0/0/0	0/0/	0/0/14.4	14.5/0			0/0/0	--Of wool or fine animal hair
0/0/0	0	3.2	1.6/1.6	0/0/0	0/0	0/0/0	0/0/	0/0/14.4	14.5/0		0/0/0	0/0/0	--Of cotton
0/0/0	7.6	3.8	1.9/1.9	0/0/0	0/0	0/0/0	0/0/	0/0/17.1	17.3/0		/0/	0/0/0	--Of synthetic fibres
0/0/0	0	3.2	1.6/1.6	0/0/0	0/0	0/0/0	0/0/	0/0/14.4	14.5/0		/0/	0/0/0	--Of other textile materials
													-Dresses:
0/0/0	8	3.2	1.6/1.6	0/0/0	0/9.6	0/0/0	0/0/	0/0/14.4	14.5/0			0/0/0	--Of wool or fine animal hair
0/0/0	0	3.2	1.6/1.6	0/0/0	0/0	0/0/0	0/0/	0/0/14.4	14.5/0			0/0/0	--Of cotton
0/0/0	7	3.5	1.8/1.8	0/0/0	0/0	0/0/0	0/0/	0/0/15.8	15.9/0		/0/	0/0/0	--Of synthetic fibres
0/0/0	8	3.2	1.6/1.6	0/0/0	0/0	0/0/0	0/0/	0/0/14.4	14.5/0		/0/	0/0/0	--Of artificial fibres
0/0/0	0	3.2	1.6/1.6	0/0/0	0/0	0/0/0	0/0/	0/0/14.4	14.5/0		/0/	0/0/0	--Of other textile materials
													-Skirts and divided skirts:
0/0/0	7	2.8	1.4/1.4	0/0/0	0/10	0/0/0	0/0/	0/0/12.6	12.7/0			0/0/0	--Of wool or fine animal hair
0/0/0	5.6	2.8	1.4/1.4	0/0/0	0/8.4	0/0/0	0/0/	0/0/12.6	12.7/0			0/0/0	--Of cotton
0/0/0	8	3.2	1.6/1.6	0/0/0	0/0	0/0/0	0/0/	0/0/14.4	14.5/0		/0/	0/0/0	--Of synthetic fibres
0/0/0	7	2.8	1.4/1.4	0/0/0	0/8.4	0/0/0	0/0/	0/0/12.6	12.7/0		0/0/0	0/0/0	--Of other textile materials
													-Trousers, bib and brace overalls, breeches and shorts:
0/0/0	8	3.2	1.6/1.6	0/0/0	0/9.6	0/0/0	0/0/	0/0/14.4	14.5/0			0/0/0	--Of wool or fine animal hair
													--Of cotton
0/0/0	0	3.2	1.6/1.6	0/0/0	0/0	0/0/0	0/0/	14.4/14.4/14.4	14.5/14.4	2.4		0/0/0	Girls' playsuit trousers No. 7～No. 16, including breeches, knitted or crocheted, of cotton
0/0/0	0	3.2	1.6/1.6	0/0/0	0/0	0/0/0	0/0/	14.4/14.4/14.4	14.5/14.4	2.4		0/0/0	Other girls' playsuit, including breeches, shorts, bib and brace overalls and other trousers, knitted or crocheted, of cotton
0/0/0	0	3.2	1.6/1.6	0/0/0	0/0	0/0/0	0/0/	14.4/14.4/14.4	14.5/14.4	2.4		0/0/0	Other knitted or crocheted women's and girls's trousers, of cotton
													--Of synthetic fibres
0/0/0	0	3.5	1.8/1.8	0/0/0	0/0	0/0/0	0/0/	0/0/15.8	15.9/0			0/0/0	Other women's or girl' trousers, breeches and shorts, of synthetic fibres, knitted or crocheted
0/0/0	0	3.5	1.8/1.8	0/0/0	0/0	0/0/0	0/0/	0/0/15.8	15.9/0			0/0/0	Girls' playsuit trousers or breeches No.7～No.16, knitted or crocheted, of synthetic fibres
0/0/0	0	3.5	1.8/1.8	0/0/0	0/0	0/0/0	0/0/	0/0/15.8	15.9/0			0/0/0	Other girls' playsuit, shorts and other trousers, knitted or crocheted, of synthetic fibres
0/0/0	0	3.2	1.6/1.6	0/0/0	0/9.6	0/0/0	0/0/	0/0/14.4	14.5/0	0		0/0/0	--Of other textile materials
													Men's or boys' shirts, knitted or crocheted:
													-Of cotton
0/0/0	0	3.2	1.6/1.6	0//0	0/0	0/0/0	0/0/0	14.4/14.4/14.4	14.5/14.4	4.2	0/0/0	0/0/0	Boys' playsuit shirts No. 8～No. 18, having no made-to-order collar, knitted or crocheted, of cotton
0/0/0	0	3.2	1.6/1.6	0//0	0/0	0/0/0	0/0/0	14.4/14.4/14.4	14.5/14.4	4.2	0/0/0	0/0/0	Other boys' playsuit shirts, knitted or crocheted, of cotton
0/0/0	0	3.2	1.6/1.6	0//0	0/0	0/0/0	0/0/0	14.4/14.4/14.4	14.5/14.4	4.2	0/0/0	0/0/0	Other knitted or crocheted men's or boys' shirts, of cotton
													-Of man-made fibres
0/0/0	0	3.5	1.8/1.8	0/0/0	0/0	0/0/0	0/0/	0/0/15.8	15.9/0	0		0/0/0	Boys' playsuit shirts No. 8～No. 18, having no made-to-order collar, knitted or crocheted, of man-made fibres
0/0/0	0	3.5	1.8/1.8	0/0/0	0/0	0/0/0	0/0/	0/0/15.8	15.9/0	0		0/0/0	Other boys' playsuit shirts, knitted or crocheted, of man-made fibres
0/0/0	0	3.5	1.8/1.8	0/0/0	0/0	0/0/0	0/0/	0/0/15.8	15.9/0	0		0/0/0	Other knitted or crocheted men's or boys' shirts, of man-made fibres

税则号列	货品名称〔CIQ 扩展编码及品名—T2 表示见附表 2〕	最惠(%)	暂定税率	普通	增值/消费	出口退税	计量单位	监管条件/特殊证件	检验检疫	对美关税	亚太上/下
6105.9000	-其他纺织材料制〔101 针织童装,102 针织或钩编,999 针织衬衫〕	6		130	13/	13	件/千克	/		31	3.9/3.9
61.06	**针织或钩编的女衬衫:**										
6106.1000	-棉制										
6106.1000 10	棉制针织或钩编女童游戏套装衬衫〔999〕	6		90	13/	13	件/千克	A/	M	31	3.9/3.9
6106.1000 90	棉制针织或钩编其他女衬衫〔999〕	6		90	13/	13	件/千克	/		31	3.9/3.9
6106.2000	-化学纤维制										
6106.2000 20	其他化学纤维制女童游戏套装衬衫(针织或钩编)〔999〕	8		130	13/	13	件/千克	A/	M	33	5.2/5.2
6106.2000 90	其他化学纤维制针织或钩编未列名女衬衫(针织或钩编)〔999〕	8		130	13/	13	件/千克	/		33	5.2/5.2
6106.9000	-其他纺织材料制〔101 毛衫,999 针织衬衫〕	6		130	13/	13	件/千克	/		31	3.9/3.9
61.07	**针织或钩编的男式内裤、三角裤、长睡衣、睡衣裤、浴衣、晨衣及类似品:**										
	-内裤及三角裤:										
6107.1100	--棉制〔999〕	6		90	13/	13	件/千克	A/	M	31	
6107.1200	--化学纤维制〔999〕	6		130	13/	13	件/千克	A/	M		3.9/3.9
	--其他纺织材料制:										
6107.1910	---丝及绢丝制										
6107.1910 10	丝及绢丝制男内裤及三角裤(含丝 70%及以上,针织或钩编)〔999〕	6		130	13/	13	件/千克	A/	M		3.9/3.9
6107.1910 90	其他丝及绢丝制男内裤及三角裤(含丝 70%以下,针织或钩编)〔999〕	6		130	13/	13	件/千克	A/	M		3.9/3.9
6107.1990	---其他										
6107.1990 10	羊毛或动物细毛制男内裤及三角裤(针织或钩编)〔999〕	6		130	13/	13	件/千克	A/	M	31	3.9/3.9
6107.1990 90	其他纺织材料制男内裤及三角裤(针织或钩编)〔999〕	6		130	13/	13	件/千克	A/	M	31	3.9/3.9
	-长睡衣及睡衣裤:										
6107.2100	--棉制〔999〕	6		90	13/	13	件/千克	A/	M		
6107.2200	--化学纤维制〔999〕	6		130	13/	13	件/千克	A/	M		3.9/3.9
	--其他纺织材料制:										
6107.2910	---丝及绢丝制										
6107.2910 10	丝及绢丝制针织或钩编男睡衣裤(含丝 70%及以上,包括长睡衣)〔999〕	6		130	13/	13	件/千克	A/	M		3.9/3.9
6107.2910 90	其他丝及绢丝制针织或钩编男睡衣裤(含丝 70%以下,包括长睡衣)〔999〕	6		130	13/	13	件/千克	A/	M		3.9/3.9
6107.2990	---其他〔999〕	6		130	13/	13	件/千克	A/	M		3.9/3.9
	-其他:										
6107.9100	--棉制										
6107.9100 10	棉制针织或钩编其他睡衣裤〔999〕	6		90	13/	13	件/千克	A/	M		
6107.9100 90	棉制针织或钩编男浴衣、晨衣等(包括类似品)〔999〕	6		90	13/	13	件/千克	A/	M		
	--其他纺织材料制:										
6107.9910	---化学纤维制〔999〕	6		130	13/	13	件/千克	A/	M	31	3.9/3.9
6107.9990	---其他〔999〕	6		130	13/	13	件/千克	A/	M	31	3.9/3.9
61.08	**针织或钩编的女式长衬裙、衬裙、三角裤、短衬裤、睡衣、睡衣裤、浴衣、晨衣及类似品:**										
	-长衬裙及衬裙:										
6108.1100	--化学纤维制〔999〕	6		130	13/	13	件/千克	/			3.9/3.9
	--其他纺织材料制:										
6108.1910	---棉制〔999〕	6		90	13/	13	件/千克	/			
6108.1920	---丝及绢丝制〔999〕	6		130	13/	13	件/千克	/			
6108.1990	---其他〔999〕	6		130	13/	13	件/千克	/			3.9/3.9
	-三角裤及短衬裤:										
6108.2100	--棉制〔999〕	6		90	13/	13	件/千克	A/	M	31	
6108.2200	--化学纤维制										
6108.2200 10	化学纤维制一次性女三角裤及短衬裤(针织或钩编)〔999〕	6		130	13/	13	件/千克	A/	M	31	3.9/3.9
6108.2200 90	化学纤维制其他女三角裤及短衬裤(针织或钩编)〔999〕	6		130	13/	13	件/千克	A/	M	31	3.9/3.9
	--其他纺织材料制:										
6108.2910	---丝及绢丝制										
6108.2910 10	丝及绢丝制女三角裤及短衬裤(针织或钩编,含丝 70%及以上)〔999〕	6		130	13/	13	件/千克	A/	M		3.9/3.9
6108.2910 90	其他丝及绢丝制女三角裤及短衬裤(针织或钩编,含丝 70%以下)〔999〕	6		130	13/	13	件/千克	A/	M		3.9/3.9
6108.2990	---其他										
6108.2990 10	羊毛制女三角裤及短衬裤(针织或钩编)〔999〕	6		130	13/	13	件/千克	A/	M		3.9/3.9

协定税率 %								RCEP		特惠税率 %			Article Description
东/冰/格	巴基斯坦	韩国	瑞士上/下	哥/秘/柬	澳/毛	新西/坡/智	中国港/澳/台	东盟及马来/澳/韩	日/新	亚太2国	老/柬/缅	98/97/95	
0/0/0	0	3.2	1.6/1.6	0/0/0	0/0	0/0/0	0/0/	0/0/14.4	14.5/0	0		0/0/0	-Of other textile materials
													Women's or girls' blouses, shirts and shirt-blouses, knitted or crocheted:
													-Of cotton
0/0/0	0	3.2	1.6/1.6	0/0/0	0/9.6	0/0/0	0/0/	0/0/14.4	14.5/0	2.4	0/0/0	0/0/0	Girls'playsuit shirts, knittedor crocheted, knitted or crocheted, of cotton
0/0/0	0	3.2	1.6/1.6	0/0/0	0/9.6	0/0/0	0/0/	0/0/14.4	14.5/0	2.4	0/0/0	0/0/0	Other women's or girls' shirts, knitted or crocheted, of cotton
													-Of man-made fibres
0/0/0	8.8	3.5	1.8/1.8	0/0/0	0/10.5	0/0/0	0/0/	0/0/15.8	15.9/0	0		0/0/0	Girls' playsuit shirts, knitted or crocheted, of man-made fibres
0/0/0	8.8	3.5	1.8/1.8	0/0/0	0/10.5	0/0/0	0/0/	0/0/15.8	15.9/0	0		0/0/0	Other women's or girls' shirts, knitted or crocheted, not elsewhere specified or included, of man-made fibres
0/0/0	0	3.2	1.6/1.6	0/0/0	0/9.6	0/0/0	0/0/0	0/0/14.4	14.5/0	0		0/0/0	-Of other textile materials
													Men's or boys' underpants, briefs, nightshirts, pyjamas, bathrobes, dressing gowns and similar articles, knitted or crocheted:
													-Underpants and briefs:
0/0/0	0	2.8	1.4/1.4	0/0/0	0/8.4	0/0/0	0/0/	0/0/12.6	12.7/0	2.4	0/0/0	0/0/0	--Of cotton
0/0/0	6.4	3.2	1.6/1.6	0/0/0	0/9.6	0/0/0	0/0/	0/0/14.4	14.5/0			0/0/0	--Of man-made fibres
													--Of other textile materials:
													---Of silk or silk waste
0/0/0	7	2.8	1.4/1.4	0/0/0	0/0	0/0/0	0/0/	0/0/12.6	12.7/0			0/0/0	Men's or boys' underpants and briefs, knitted or crocheted, containing≥70% by weight of silk or spun silk
0/0/0	7	2.8	1.4/1.4	0/0/0	0/0	0/0/0	0/0/	0/0/12.6	12.7/0			0/0/0	Men's or boys' underpants and briefs, knitted or crocheted, other, containing<70% by weight of silk or spun silk
													---Other
0/0/0	7	2.8	1.4/1.4	0/0/0	0/0	0/0/0	0/0/	0/0/12.6	12.7/0			0/0/0	Men's or boys' underpants and briefs, knitted or crocheted, of wool or fine animal hair
0/0/0	7	2.8	1.4/1.4	0/0/0	0/0	0/0/0	0/0/	0/0/12.6	12.7/0			0/0/0	Men's or boys' underpants and briefs, knitted or crocheted, of other textile fibres
													-Nightshirts and pyjamas:
0/0/0	0	2.8	1.4/1.4	0//0	0/0	0/0/0	0/0/	0/0/12.6	12.7/0	2.4	0/0/0	0/0/0	--Of cotton
0/0/0	8	3.2	1.6/1.6	0/0/0	0/0	0/0/0	0/0/	0/0/14.4	14.5/0	0		0/0/0	--Of man-made fibres
													--Of other textile materials:
													---Of silk or silk waste
0/0/0	7	2.8	1.4/1.4	0/0/0	0/0	0/0/0	0/0/	0/0/12.6	12.7/0	0		0/0/0	Men's or boys' nightshirts, pyjamas, knitted or crocheted, containing≥70% by weight of silk or spun silk
0/0/0	7	2.8	1.4/1.4	0/0/0	0/0	0/0/0	0/0/	0/0/12.6	12.7/0	0		0/0/0	Men's or boys' nightshirts, pyjamas, knitted or crocheted, containing<70% by weight of silk or spun silk
0/0/0	7	2.8	1.4/1.4	0/0/0	0/0	0/0/0	0/0/	0/0/12.6	12.7/0	0	0/0/0	0/0/0	---Other
													-Other:
													--Of cotton
0/0/0	5.6	2.8	1.4/1.4	0/0/0	0/0	0/0/0	0/0/	0/0/12.6	12.7/0			0/0/0	Other men's or boys' pyjamas, knitted or crocheted, of cotton
0/0/0	5.6	2.8	1.4/1.4	0/0/0	0/0	0/0/0	0/0/	0/0/12.6	12.7/0			0/0/0	Men's or boys' bathrobes, dressing gowns and similar articles, knitted or crocheted, of cotton
													--Of other textile materials:
0/0/0	8	3.2	1.6/1.6	0/0/0	0/0	0/0/0	0/0/	0/0/14.4	14.5/0			0/0/0	---Of man-made fibres
0/0/0	7	2.8	1.4/1.4	0/0/0	0/0	0/0/0	0/0/	0/0/12.6	12.7/0			0/0/0	---Of other
													Women's or girls' slips, petticoats, briefs, panties, nightdresses, pyjamas, nègligès, bathrobes, dressing gowns and similar articles, knitted or crocheted:
													-Slips and petticoats:
0/0/0	8	3.2	1.6/1.6	0/0/0	0/0	0/0/0	0/0/	0/0/14.4	14.5/0			0/0/0	--Of man-made fibres
													--Of other textile materials:
0/0/0	7	2.8	1.4/1.4	0/0/0	0/0	0/0/0	0/0/	0/0/12.6	12.7/0			0/0/0	---Of cotton
0/0/0	7	2.8	1.4/1.4	0/0/0	0/0	0/0/0	0/0/	0/0/12.6	12.7/0			0/0/0	---Of silk or silk waste
0/0/0	7	2.8	1.4/1.4	0/0/0	0/0	0/0/0	0/0/	0/0/12.6	12.7/0			0/0/0	---Other
													-Briefs and panties:
0/0/0	0	2.8	1.4/1.4	0/0/0	0/0	0/0/0	0/0/	0/0/12.6	12.7/0		0/0/0	0/0/0	--Of cotton
													--Of man-made fibres
0/0/0	8	3.2	1.6/1.6	0/0/0	0/9.6	0/0/0	0/0/	0/0/14.4	14.5/0			0/0/0	Women's or girls' briefs and panties, knitted or crocheted, throw away, of man-made fibres
0/0/0	8	3.2	1.6/1.6	0/0/0	0/9.6	0/0/0	0/0/	0/0/14.4	14.5/0			0/0/0	Other women's or girls' briefs and panties, knitted or crocheted, of man-made fibres
													--Of other textile materials:
													---Of silk or silk waste
0/0/0	7	2.8	1.4/1.4	0/0/0	0/0	0/0/0	0/0/	0/0/12.6	12.7/0			0/0/0	Women's or girls' briefs and panties, knitted or crocheted containing≥70% by weight of silk or spun silk
0/0/0	7	2.8	1.4/1.4	0/0/0	0/0	0/0/0	0/0/	0/0/12.6	12.7/0			0/0/0	Other women's or girls' briefs and panties, knitted or crocheted, containing<70% by weight of silk or spun silk
													---Other
0/0/0	7	2.8	1.4/1.4	0/0/0	0/0	0/0/0	0/0/	0/0/12.6	12.7/0			0/0/0	Women's or girls' briefs and panties, knitted or crocheted, of wool

税则号列		货品名称〔CIQ扩展编码及品名－T2表示见附表2〕	最惠(%)	暂定税率	普通	增值/消费	出口退税	计量单位	监管条件/特殊证件	检验检疫	对美关税	亚太上/下
6108.2990	90	其他纺织材料制女三角裤及短衬裤(针织或钩编)〔999〕	6		130	13/	13	件/千克	A/	M		3.9/3.9
		-睡衣及睡衣裤:										
6108.3100		--棉制〔999〕	6		90	13/	13	件/千克	A/	M	31	
6108.3200		--化学纤维制〔999〕	6		130	13/	13	件/千克	A/	M	31	3.9/3.9
		--其他纺织材料制:										
6108.3910		---丝及绢丝制										
6108.3910	10	丝及绢丝制女睡衣及睡衣裤(针织或钩编,含丝70%及以上)〔999〕	6		130	13/	13	件/千克	A/	M		3.9/3.9
6108.3910	90	其他丝及绢丝制女睡衣及睡衣裤(针织或钩编,含丝70%以下)〔999〕	6		130	13/	13	件/千克	A/	M		3.9/3.9
6108.3990		---其他										
6108.3990	10	羊毛或动物细毛制女睡衣及睡衣裤(针织或钩编)〔999〕	6		130	13/	13	件/千克	A/	M		3.9/3.9
6108.3990	90	其他纺织材料制女睡衣及睡衣裤(针织或钩编)〔999〕	6		130	13/	13	件/千克	A/	M		3.9/3.9
		-其他:										
6108.9100		--棉制										
6108.9100	10	棉制针织或钩编女内裤,内衣〔999〕	6		90	13/	13	件/千克	A/	M	31	
6108.9100	90	其他棉制针织或钩编女浴衣、晨衣等(包括类似品)〔999〕	6		90	13/	13	件/千克	A/	M	31	
6108.9200		--化学纤维制										
6108.9200	10	化学纤维制针织或钩编女内裤,内衣〔999〕	6		130	13/	13	件/千克	A/	M	31	3.9/3.9
6108.9200	90	其他化学纤维针织或钩编女浴衣、晨衣等(包括类似品)〔999〕	6		130	13/	13	件/千克	A/	M	31	3.9/3.9
6108.9900		--其他纺织材料制										
6108.9900	10	丝及绢丝制女浴衣、晨衣等(针织或钩编,包括类似品,含丝70%及以上)〔999〕	6		130	13/	13	件/千克	A/	M		3.9/3.9
6108.9900	20	羊毛或动物细毛制女浴衣、晨衣等(针织或钩编,包括类似品)〔999〕	6		130	13/	13	件/千克	A/	M		3.9/3.9
6108.9900	90	其他纺织材料制女浴衣、晨衣等(针织或钩编,包括类似品)〔999〕	6		130	13/	13	件/千克	A/	M		3.9/3.9
61.09		**针织或钩编的T恤衫、汗衫及其他背心:**										
6109.1000		-棉制										
6109.1000	10	棉制针织或钩编T恤衫、汗衫等(内衣式,包括其他背心)〔999〕	6		90	13/	13	件/千克	A/	M	31	3.9/3.9
6109.1000	21	其他棉制针织或钩编男式T恤衫(内衣除外)〔999〕	6		90	13/	13	件/千克	A/	M	31	3.9/3.9
6109.1000	22	其他棉制针织或钩编女式T恤衫(内衣除外)〔999〕	6		90	13/	13	件/千克	A/	M	31	3.9/3.9
6109.1000	91	其他棉制男式汗衫及其他背心(针织或钩编,内衣除外,包括男童8－18号)〔101针织外衣,102针织童装〕	6		90	13/	13	件/千克	A/	M	31	3.9/3.9
6109.1000	92	其他棉制男式汗衫及其他背心(针织或钩编,内衣除外)〔999〕	6		90	13/	13	件/千克	A/	M	31	3.9/3.9
6109.1000	99	其他棉制女式汗衫及其他背心(针织或钩编,内衣除外)〔999〕	6		90	13/	13	件/千克	A/	M	31	3.9/3.9
		-其他纺织材料制:										
6109.9010		---丝及绢丝制										
6109.9010	11	丝及绢丝针织钩编T恤衫、汗衫、背心(内衣式,含丝≥70%)〔999〕	6		130	13/	13	件/千克	A/	M	31	3.9/3.9
6109.9010	19	其他丝及绢丝针织钩编T恤衫、背心(包括汗衫,内衣式,含丝70%以下)〔999〕	6		130	13/	13	件/千克	A/	M	31	3.9/3.9
6109.9010	21	丝及绢丝针织钩编汗衫、背心(内衣除外,含丝≥70%,男童8－18号,女童7－16号)〔101针织外衣,102针织童装〕	6		130	13/	13	件/千克	A/	M	31	3.9/3.9
6109.9010	29	其他丝及绢丝针织或钩编汗衫、背心(内衣除外,含丝<70%,男童8－18号,女童7－16号)〔101针织外衣,102针织童装〕	6		130	13/	13	件/千克	A/	M	31	3.9/3.9
6109.9010	91	其他丝及绢丝针织或钩编T恤衫、汗衫(含丝≥70%,包括其他背心)〔999〕	6		130	13/	13	件/千克	A/	M	31	3.9/3.9
6109.9010	99	其他丝及绢丝针织或钩编T恤衫、汗衫(含丝<70%,包括其他背心)〔999〕	6		130	13/	13	件/千克	A/	M	31	3.9/3.9
6109.9090		---其他										
6109.9090	11	毛制针织或钩编T恤衫、汗衫等(内衣式,长袖衫)〔999〕	6		130	13/	13	件/千克	A/	M	31	3.9/3.9
6109.9090	12	毛制针织或钩编男式T恤衫、汗衫(内衣式,长袖衫除外)〔999〕	6		130	13/	13	件/千克	A/	M	31	3.9/3.9

协定税率 %								RCEP		特惠税率 %			Article Description
东/冰/格	巴基斯坦	韩国	瑞士 上/下	哥/秘/柬	澳/毛	新西/坡/智	中国港/澳/台	东盟及马来/澳/韩	日/新	亚太2国	老/柬/缅	98/97/95	
0/0/0	7	2.8	1.4/1.4	0/0/0	0/0	0/0/0	0/0/	0/0/12.6	12.7/0			0/0/0	Women's or girls' briefs and panties, knitted or crocheted, of other textile materials
													-Nightdresses and pyjamas:
0/0/0	0	2.8	1.4/1.4	0/0/0	0/8.4	0/0/0	0/0/	0/0/12.6	12.7/0	2.4	0/0/0	0/0/0	--Of cotton
0/0/0	8	3.2	1.6/1.6	0/0/0	0/9.6	0/0/0	0/0/	0/0/14.4	14.5/0	0		0/0/0	--Of man-made fibres
													--Of other textile materials:
													---Of silk or silk waste
0/0/0	7	2.8	1.4/1.4	0/0/0	0/0	0/0/0	0/0/	0/0/12.6	12.7/0	0		0/0/0	Women's or girls' nightshirts and pyjamas, knitted or crocheted, containing≥70% by weight of silk or spun silk
0/0/0	7	2.8	1.4/1.4	0/0/0	0/0	0/0/0	0/0/	0/0/12.6	12.7/0	0		0/0/0	Other women's or girls' nightshirts and pyjamas, knitted or crocheted, containing<70% by weight of silk or spun silk
													---Other
0/0/0	7	2.8	1.4/1.4	0/0/0	0/0	0/0/0	0/0/	0/0/12.6	12.7/0	0		0/0/0	Women's or girls' nightshirts and pyjamas, knitted or crocheted, of wool or fine animal hair
0/0/0	7	2.8	1.4/1.4	0/0/0	0/0	0/0/0	0/0/	0/0/12.6	12.7/0	0		0/0/0	Women's or girls' nightshirts and pyjamas, knitted or crocheted, of other textile materials
													-Other:
													--Of cotton
0/0/0	11.2	2.8	1.4/1.4	0/0/0	0/8.4	0/0/0	0/0/	0/0/12.6	12.7/0		0/0/0	0/0/0	Women's or girls' briefs, panties and underwear, knitted or crocheted, of cotton
0/0/0	11.2	2.8	1.4/1.4	0/0/0	0/8.4	0/0/0	0/0/	0/0/12.6	12.7/0		0/0/0	0/0/0	Women's or girls' bathrobes, dressing gowns and similar articles, knitted or crocheted, of cotton
													--Of man-made fibres
0/0/0	8	3.2	1.6/1.6	0/0/0	0/9.6	0/0/0	0/0/	0/0/14.4	14.5/0			0/0/0	Women's or girls' briefs, panties and underwear, of man-made fibres
0/0/0	8	3.2	1.6/1.6	0/0/0	0/9.6	0/0/0	0/0/	0/0/14.4	14.5/0			0/0/0	Women's or girls' bathrobes, dressing gowns and similar articles, knitted or crocheted, of man-made fibres
													--Of other textile materials
0/0/0	7	2.8	1.4/1.4	0/0/0	0/0	0/0/0	0/0/	0/0/12.6	12.7/0			0/0/0	Women's or girls' bathrobes, dressing gowns and similar articles, containing≥70% by weight of silk or spun silk, knitted or crocheted
0/0/0	7	2.8	1.4/1.4	0/0/0	0/0	0/0/0	0/0/	0/0/12.6	12.7/0			0/0/0	Women's or girls' bathrobes, dressing gowns and similar articles, of wool or fine animal hair, knitted or crocheted
0/0/0	7	2.8	1.4/1.4	0/0/0	0/0	0/0/0	0/0/	0/0/12.6	12.7/0			0/0/0	Women's or girls' bathrobes, dressing gowns and similar articles, of other textile materials, knitted or crocheted
													T-shirts, singlets and other vests, knitted or crocheted:
													-Of cotton
0/0/0	0	0	1.4/1.4	0/0/0	0/0	0/0/0	0/0/	12.6/12.6/12.6	12.7/12.6		0/0/0	0/0/0	T-shirts, singlets, underwear style, including other vests, of cotton, knitted or crocheted
0/0/0	0	0	1.4/1.4	0/0/0	0/0	0/0/0	0/0/	12.6/12.6/12.6	12.7/12.6		0/0/0	0/0/0	Other men's or boys' T-shirts, other than underwear, of cotton, knitted or crocheted
0/0/0	0	0	1.4/1.4	0/0/0	0/0	0/0/0	0/0/	12.6/12.6/12.6	12.7/12.6		0/0/0	0/0/0	Other women's or girls' T-shirts other than underwear, of cotton, knitted or crocheted
0/0/0	0	0	1.4/1.4	0/0/0	0/0	0/0/0	0/0/	12.6/12.6/12.6	12.7/12.6		0/0/0	0/0/0	Other men's singlets and other vests, including boys' No. 8～No. 18, other than underwear, of cotton, knitted or crocheted
0/0/0	0	0	1.4/1.4	0/0/0	0/0	0/0/0	0/0/	12.6/12.6/12.6	12.7/12.6		0/0/0	0/0/0	Other men's or boys' singlets and other vests, other than underwear, of cotton, knitted or crocheted
0/0/0	0	0	1.4/1.4	0/0/0	0/0	0/0/0	0/0/	12.6/12.6/12.6	12.7/12.6		0/0/0	0/0/0	Other women's or girls' singlets and other vests, other than underwear, of cotton, knitted or crocheted
													-Of other textile materials:
													---Of silk or silk waste
0/0/0	0	2.8	1.4/1.4	0/0/0	0/0	0/0/0	0/0/	0/0/12.6	12.7/0	0		0/0/0	T-shirts, singlets and other vests, underwear, containing ≥70% by weightof silk or spun silk, knitted or crocheted
0/0/0	0	2.8	1.4/1.4	0/0/0	0/0	0/0/0	0/0/	0/0/12.6	12.7/0	0		0/0/0	Other T-shirts, singlets and other vests, underwear, containing<70% by weight of silk or spun silk, knitted or crocheted
0/0/0	0	2.8	1.4/1.4	0/0/0	0/0	0/0/0	0/0/	0/0/12.6	12.7/0	0		0/0/0	Singlets, vests, including boys' No. 8～No. 18, girls' No. 7～No. 16, other than underwear, containing≥70% by weightof silk or spun silk, knitted or crocheted
0/0/0	0	2.8	1.4/1.4	0/0/0	0/0	0/0/0	0/0/	0/0/12.6	12.7/0	0		0/0/0	Other singlets, vests, including boys' No. 8～No. 18, girls' No. 7～No. 16, other than underwear, containing<70% by weight of silk or spun silk, knitted or crocheted
0/0/0	0	2.8	1.4/1.4	0/0/0	0/0	0/0/0	0/0/	0/0/12.6	12.7/0	0		0/0/0	Other T-shirts, singlets and other vests, including other vests, containing≥70% by weight of silk or spun silk, knitted or crocheted
0/0/0	0	2.8	1.4/1.4	0/0/0	0/0	0/0/0	0/0/	0/0/12.6	12.7/0	0		0/0/0	Other of other textile materials, including other vests, containing<70% by weight of silk or spun silk, knitted or crocheted
													---Other
0/0/0	0	2.8	1.4/1.4	0/0/0	0/0	0/0/0	0/0/	12.6/12.6/12.6	12.7/12.6	0	0/0/0	0/0/0	T-shirts, singlets and other vests, underwear style, long sleeve, of wool or fine animal hair, knitted or crocheted
0/0/0	0	2.8	1.4/1.4	0/0/0	0/0	0/0/0	0/0/	12.6/12.6/12.6	12.7/12.6	0	0/0/0	0/0/0	Men's or boys' T-shirts, singlets, underwear style, other than long sleeve, of wool or fine animal hair, knitted or crocheted

税则号列	货品名称〔CIQ 扩展编码及品名－T2 表示见附表 2〕	最惠(%)	暂定税率	普通	增值/消费	出口退税	计量单位	监管条件/特殊证件	检验检疫	对美关税	亚太上/下
6109.9090 13	毛制针织或钩编女式 T 恤衫、汗衫（内衣式，长袖衫除外）〔999〕	6		130	13/	13	件/千克	A/	M	31	3.9/3.9
6109.9090 21	毛制针织或钩编男式其他 T 恤衫（内衣除外）〔999〕	6		130	13/	13	件/千克	A/	M	31	3.9/3.9
6109.9090 22	毛制针织或钩编女式其他 T 恤衫（内衣除外）〔999〕	6		130	13/	13	件/千克	A/	M	31	3.9/3.9
6109.9090 31	毛制男式汗衫及其他背心（针织或钩编，内衣除外，含男童 8－18 号）〔101 毛衫，102 针织童装〕	6		130	13/	13	件/千克	A/	M	31	3.9/3.9
6109.9090 32	其他毛制男式汗衫及其他背心（针织或钩编，内衣除外）〔999〕	6		130	13/	13	件/千克	A/	M	31	3.9/3.9
6109.9090 33	其他毛制女式汗衫及其他背心（针织或钩编，内衣除外）〔999〕	6		130	13/	13	件/千克	A/	M	31	3.9/3.9
6109.9090 40	化学纤维制针织或钩编内衣〔999〕	6		130	13/	13	件/千克	A/	M	31	3.9/3.9
6109.9090 50	化纤制针织或钩编 T 恤衫（内衣除外）〔999〕	6		130	13/	13	件/千克	A/	M	31	3.9/3.9
6109.9090 60	化纤针织或钩编汗衫及其他背心（内衣除外）〔101 针织外衣，102 针织童装〕	6		130	13/	13	件/千克	A/	M	31	3.9/3.9
6109.9090 91	其他纺织材料制 T 恤衫.汗衫等（针织或钩编，内衣式，包括其他背心）〔999〕	6		130	13/	13	件/千克	A/	M	31	3.9/3.9
6109.9090 92	其他纺材针织钩编汗衫及其他背心（内衣除外，包括男童 8－18 号，女童7－16 号）〔101 针织外衣，102 针织童装〕	6		130	13/	13	件/千克	A/	M	31	3.9/3.9
6109.9090 93	其他纺材制针织钩编 T 恤衫、汗衫（内衣除外，包括其他背心）〔999〕	6		130	13/	13	件/千克	A/	M	31	3.9/3.9
61.10	**针织或钩编的套头衫、开襟衫、马甲（背心）及类似品：**										
	-羊毛或动物细毛制：										
6110.1100	--羊毛制〔999〕	6		130	13/	13	件/千克	/		31	3.9/3.9
6110.1200	--喀什米尔山羊细毛制										
6110.1200 11	喀什米尔山羊细毛手工起绒男套头衫（针织或钩编，包括开襟衫、外穿背心及类似品）〔999〕	6	5	130	13/	13	件/千克	/		30	3.9/3.9
6110.1200 19	喀什米尔山羊细毛制起绒男套头衫（针织或钩编，包括开襟衫、外穿背心及类似品）〔999〕	6	5	130	13/	13	件/千克	/		30	3.9/3.9
6110.1200 21	喀什米尔山羊细毛手工起绒女套头衫（针织或钩编，包括开襟衫、外穿背心及类似品）〔999〕	6	5	130	13/	13	件/千克	/		30	3.9/3.9
6110.1200 29	喀什米尔山羊细毛制起绒女套头衫（针织或钩编，包括开襟衫、外穿背心及类似品）〔999〕	6	5	130	13/	13	件/千克	/		30	3.9/3.9
6110.1200 31	喀什米尔山羊细毛手工非起绒男套头衫（针织或钩编，包括开襟衫、外穿背心及类似品）〔999〕	6	5	130	13/	13	件/千克	/		30	3.9/3.9
6110.1200 39	喀什米尔山羊细毛非起绒男套头衫（针织或钩编，包括开襟衫、外穿背心及类似品）〔999〕	6	5	130	13/	13	件/千克	/		30	3.9/3.9
6110.1200 41	喀什米尔山羊细毛手工非起绒女套头衫（针织或钩编，包括开襟衫、外穿背心及类似品）〔999〕	6	5	130	13/	13	件/千克	/		30	3.9/3.9
6110.1200 49	喀什米尔山羊细毛非起绒女套头衫（针织或钩编，包括开襟衫、外穿背心及类似品）〔999〕	6	5	130	13/	13	件/千克	/		30	3.9/3.9
	--其他：										
6110.1910	---其他山羊细毛制〔999〕	6		130	13/	13	件/千克	/		31	3.9/3.9
6110.1920	---兔毛制〔999〕	6		130	13/	13	件/千克	/			3.9/3.9
6110.1990	---其他〔999〕	6		130	13/	13	件/千克	/		31	3.9/3.9
6110.2000	-棉制										
6110.2000 11	棉制儿童游戏套装紧身衫及套头衫（针织起绒，轻薄细针翻领、开领、高领，含亚麻 36％以下）〔999〕	6		90	13/	13	件/千克	A/	M	31	3.9/3.9
6110.2000 12	棉制其他起绒儿童游戏套头衫等（针织或钩编，包括开襟衫、背心及类似品，含亚麻 36％以下）〔999〕	6		90	13/	13	件/千克	A/	M	31	3.9/3.9
6110.2000 51	其他棉制儿童游戏套装紧身及套头衫（针织、非起绒、轻薄细针翻领、开领、高领）〔999〕	6		90	13/	13	件/千克	A/	M	31	3.9/3.9
6110.2000 52	其他棉制儿童游戏套装套头衫等（针织或钩编、非起绒、包括开襟衫、背心及类似品）〔999〕	6		90	13/	13	件/千克	A/	M	31	3.9/3.9
6110.2000 90	其他棉制针织或钩编的套头衫、开襟衫、马甲（背心）及类似品〔999〕	6		90	13/	13	件/千克	/		31	3.9/3.9

协定税率 %								RCEP		特惠税率 %			Article Description
东/冰/格	巴基斯坦	韩国	瑞士上/下	哥/秘/柬	澳/毛	新西/坡/智	中国港/澳/台	东盟及马来/澳/韩	日/新	亚太2国	老/柬/缅	98/97/95	
0/0/0	0	2.8	1.4/1.4	0/0/0	0/0	0/0/0	0/0/	12.6/12.6/12.6	12.7/12.6	0	0/0/0	0/0/0	Women's or grils' T-shirts, singlets, underwear style, other than long sleeve, of wool or fine animal hair, knitted or crocheted
0/0/0	0	2.8	1.4/1.4	0/0/0	0/0	0/0/0	0/0/	12.6/12.6/12.6	12.7/12.6	0	0/0/0	0/0/0	Men's or boys' T-shirts, other than underwear, of wool or fine animal hair, knitted or crocheted
0/0/0	0	2.8	1.4/1.4	0/0/0	0/0	0/0/0	0/0/	12.6/12.6/12.6	12.7/12.6	0	0/0/0	0/0/0	Women's or girls' T-shirts, other than underwear, of wool or fine animal hair, knitted or crocheted
0/0/0	0	2.8	1.4/1.4	0/0/0	0/0	0/0/0	0/0/	12.6/12.6/12.6	12.7/12.6	0	0/0/0	0/0/0	Men's singlets, vests, and boys' No. 8～No. 18, other than underwear, knitted or crocheted, of wool or fine animal hair
0/0/0	0	2.8	1.4/1.4	0/0/0	0/0	0/0/0	0/0/	12.6/12.6/12.6	12.7/12.6	0	0/0/0	0/0/0	Men's or boys' singlets, vests, other than underwear, of wool or fine animal hair, knitted or crocheted
0/0/0	0	2.8	1.4/1.4	0/0/0	0/0	0/0/0	0/0/	12.6/12.6/12.6	12.7/12.6	0	0/0/0	0/0/0	Women's or girls singlets vests, other than underwear, of wool or fine animal hair, knitted or crocheted
0/0/0	0	2.8	1.4/1.4	0/0/0	0/0	0/0/0	0/0/	12.6/12.6/12.6	12.7/12.6	0	0/0/0	0/0/0	Underwear, of man-made fibres, knitted or crocheted
0/0/0	0	2.8	1.4/1.4	0/0/0	0/0	0/0/0	0/0/	12.6/12.6/12.6	12.7/12.6	0	0/0/0	0/0/0	T-shirts, of man-made fibres, knitted or crocheted
0/0/0	0	2.8	1.4/1.4	0/0/0	0/0	0/0/0	0/0/	12.6/12.6/12.6	12.7/12.6	0	0/0/0	0/0/0	Other singlets, vests, of man-made fibres, knitted or crocheted
0/0/0	0	2.8	1.4/1.4	0/0/0	0/0	0/0/0	0/0/	12.6/12.6/12.6	12.7/12.6	0	0/0/0	0/0/0	Other T-shirts, singlets and other vests underwear style, of other textile materials, knitted or crocheted
0/0/0	0	2.8	1.4/1.4	0/0/0	0/0	0/0/0	0/0/	12.6/12.6/12.6	12.7/12.6	0	0/0/0	0/0/0	Other singlets, and other vests, other than underwear, of other textile materials, including boys' No. 8～No. 18 or girls' No. 7～No. 16, knitted or crocheted
0/0/0	0	2.8	1.4/1.4	0/0/0	0/0	0/0/0	0/0/	12.6/12.6/12.6	12.7/12.6	0	0/0/0	0/0/0	Other T-shirts, singlets and other vests, other than underwear, of other textile materials, knitted or crocheted
													Jerseys, pullovers, cardigans, waistcoats and similar articles, knitted or crocheted:
													-Of wool or fine animal hair:
0/0/0	0	0	1.4/1.4	0/0/0	0/8.4	0/0/0	0/0/0	0/0/0	12.7/0	0	0/0/0	0/0/0	--Of wool
													--Of Kashmir(cashmere) goats
0/0/0	0	2.8	1.4/1.4	0/0/0	0/8.4	0/0/0	0/0/	0/0/12.6	12.7/0			0/0/0	Men's or boys' pullovers, cardigans, waistcoats and similar articles, of fine hair of Kashmir (cashmere) goats, knitted or crocheted, piled, hand-worked
0/0/0	0	2.8	1.4/1.4	0/0/0	0/8.4	0/0/0	0/0/	0/0/12.6	12.7/0			0/0/0	Men's or boys' pullovers, cardigans, waistcoats and similar articles of fine hair of Kashmir (cashmere) goats, knitted or crocheted, piled
0/0/0	0	2.8	1.4/1.4	0/0/0	0/8.4	0/0/0	0/0/	0/0/12.6	12.7/0			0/0/0	Women's or girls' pullovers, cardigans, waistcoats and similar articles, of fine hair of Kashmir (cashmere) goats, knitted or crocheted, piled, hand-worked
0/0/0	0	2.8	1.4/1.4	0/0/0	0/8.4	0/0/0	0/0/	0/0/12.6	12.7/0			0/0/0	Women's or girls' pullovers, cardigans, waistcoats and similar articles, of fine hair of Kashmir (cashmere) goats, knitted or crocheted, piled
0/0/0	0	2.8	1.4/1.4	0/0/0	0/8.4	0/0/0	0/0/	0/0/12.6	12.7/0			0/0/0	Men's or boys' pullovers, cardigans, waistcoats and similar articles, of fine hair of Kashmir (cashmere) goats, knitted or crocheted, not piled, hand worked
0/0/0	0	2.8	1.4/1.4	0/0/0	0/8.4	0/0/0	0/0/	0/0/12.6	12.7/0			0/0/0	Men's or boys' pullovers, cardigans, waistcoats and similar articles, of fine hair of Kashmir (cashmere) goats, knitted or crocheted, not piled
0/0/0	0	2.8	1.4/1.4	0/0/0	0/8.4	0/0/0	0/0/	0/0/12.6	12.7/0			0/0/0	Women's or girls' pullovers, cardigans, waistcoats and similar articles, of fine hair of Kashmir (cashmere) goats, knitted or crocheted, not piled, hand-worked
0/0/0	0	2.8	1.4/1.4	0/0/0	0/8.4	0/0/0	0/0/	0/0/12.6	12.7/0			0/0/0	Women's or girls' pullovers, cardigans, waistcoats and similar articles, of fine hair of Kashmir (cashmere) goats, knitted or crocheted, not piled
													--Other:
0/0/0	0	2.8	1.4/1.4	0/0/0	0/0	0/0/0	0/0/	0/0/12.6	12.7/0			0/0/0	---Of other goats
0/0/0	0	2.8	1.4/1.4	0/0/0	0/0	0/0/0	0/0/	0/0/12.6	12.7/0			0/0/0	---Of rabbit and hare
0/0/0	0	2.8	1.4/1.4	0/0/0	0/10	0/0/0	0/0/	0/0/12.6	12.7/0			0/0/0	---Other
													-Of cotton
0/0/0	0	2.8	1.4/1.4	0/0/0	0/0	0/0/0	0/0/0	12.6/12.6/12.6	12.7/12.6	2.4	0/0/0	0/0/0	Boys' or girls' playsuit, jerseys, pullovers, tricolette turn-down collar, open-necked collar, high-necked collar, containing<36% by weight of flax, of cotton knitted, piled
0/0/0	0	2.8	1.4/1.4	0/0/0	0/0	0/0/0	0/0/0	12.6/12.6/12.6	12.7/12.6	2.4	0/0/0	0/0/0	Other boys' or girls' playsuit, pullovers, cardigans, waistcoats and similar articles, containing<36% by weight of flax, of cotton, knitted or crocheted
0/0/0	0	2.8	1.4/1.4	0/0/0	0/0	0/0/0	0/0/0	12.6/12.6/12.6	12.7/12.6	2.4	0/0/0	0/0/0	Other boys' or girls' playsuit, jerseys, pullovers, tricolette turn-down collar, open-necked collar, high-necked collar, not piled, of cotton, knitted
0/0/0	0	2.8	1.4/1.4	0/0/0	0/0	0/0/0	0/0/0	12.6/12.6/12.6	12.7/12.6	2.4	0/0/0	0/0/0	Other boys' or girls' playsuit pullovers, cardigans, waistcoats and similar articles, of cotton, knitted or crocheted not piled
0/0/0	0	2.8	1.4/1.4	0/0/0	0/0	0/0/0	0/0/0	12.6/12.6/12.6	12.7/12.6	2.4	0/0/0	0/0/0	Pullovers, cardigans, waistcoats and similar articles of cotton, knitted or crocheted

税则号列	货品名称〔CIQ 扩展编码及品名－T2 表示见附表 2〕	最惠(%)	暂定税率	普通	增值/消费	出口退税	计量单位	监管条件/特殊证件	检验检疫	对美关税	亚太上/下
6110.3000	-化学纤维制										
6110.3000 11	化学纤维儿童游戏套装紧身衫及套头衫(针织起绒,轻薄细针翻领、开领、高领毛＜23%,丝＜30%)〔999〕	6		130	13/	13	件/千克	A/	M	31	3.9/3.9
6110.3000 12	化学纤维起绒儿童游戏套装及套头衫等(针织或钩编包括开襟衫、背心及类似品含毛＜23%,含丝＜30%)〔999〕	6		130	13/	13	件/千克	A/	M	31	3.9/3.9
6110.3000 41	化学纤维其他儿童游戏套装紧身及套头衫(针织非起绒,轻薄细针翻领、开领、高领)〔999〕	6		130	13/	13	件/千克	A/	M	31	3.9/3.9
6110.3000 42	化学纤维制其他儿童游戏套装套头衫等(针织或钩编,非起绒,包括开襟衫、背心及类似品)〔999〕	6		130	13/	13	件/千克	A/	M	31	3.9/3.9
6110.3000 90	其他化纤制针织或钩编的套头衫、开襟衫、马甲(背心)及类似品〔999〕	6		130	13/	13	件/千克	/		31	3.9/3.9
	-其他纺织材料制:										
6110.9010	---丝及绢丝制〔999〕	6		130	13/	13	件/千克	/		31	3.9/3.9
6110.9090	---其他〔999〕	6		130	13/	13	件/千克	/		31	3.9/3.9
61.11	**针织或钩编的婴儿服装及衣着附件:**										
6111.2000	-棉制										
6111.2000 10	棉制针织或钩编婴儿袜〔999〕	10	6	90	13/	13	千克	A/	M	31	
6111.2000 20	棉制婴儿分指、连指、露指手套(针制或钩编)〔999〕	10	6	90	13/	13	千克	A/	M	31	
6111.2000 40	棉制针织婴儿外衣、雨衣、滑雪装(针制或钩编,包括夹克类似品)〔999〕	10	6	90	13/	13	千克	A/	M	31	
6111.2000 50	棉制针织钩编婴儿其他服装〔999〕	10	6	90	13/	13	千克	A/	M	31	
6111.2000 90	棉制针织钩编婴儿衣着附件〔999〕	10	6	90	13/	13	千克	A/	M	31	
6111.3000	-合成纤维制										
6111.3000 10	合成纤维制针织或钩编婴儿袜〔999〕	10	6	130	13/	13	千克	A/	M	31	6.5/6.5
6111.3000 20	合成纤维婴儿分指、连指及露指手套(针制或钩编)〔999〕	10	6	130	13/	13	千克	A/	M	31	6.5/6.5
6111.3000 40	合成纤维婴儿外衣、雨衣、滑雪装(针制或钩编,包括夹克类似服装)〔999〕	10	6	130	13/	13	千克	A/	M	31	6.5/6.5
6111.3000 50	合成纤维针织或钩编婴儿其他服装(包括衣着附件)〔999〕	10	6	130	13/	13	千克	A/	M	31	6.5/6.5
6111.3000 90	合成纤维针织或钩编婴儿衣着附件〔999〕	10	6	130	13/	13	千克	A/	M	31	6.5/6.5
	-其他纺织材料制:										
6111.9010	---羊毛或动物细毛制〔999〕	10	6	130	13/	13	千克	A/	M		6.5/6.5
6111.9090	---其他										
6111.9090 10	人造纤维针织或钩编婴儿袜〔999〕	10	6	130	13/	13	千克	A/	M		6.5/6.5
6111.9090 90	其他纺织材料制婴儿服装及衣着附件(针织或钩编)〔999〕	10	6	130	13/	13	千克	A/	M		6.5/6.5
61.12	**针织或钩编的运动服、滑雪服及游泳服:**										
	-运动服:										
6112.1100	--棉制〔999〕	6		90	13/	13	套/千克	/		31	3.9/3.9
6112.1200	--合成纤维制〔999〕	8		130	13/	13	套/千克	/		33	5.2/5.2
6112.1900	--其他纺织材料制〔999〕	6		130	13/	13	套/千克	/		31	3.9/3.9
	-滑雪服:										
6112.2010	---棉制〔999〕	6		90	13/	13	套/千克	/			3.9/3.9
6112.2090	---其他〔999〕	10		130	13/	13	套/千克	/			6.5/6.5
	-男式游泳服:										
6112.3100	--合成纤维制〔999〕	8		130	13/	13	件/千克	/			5.2/5.2
6112.3900	--其他纺织材料制〔999〕	6		130	13/	13	件/千克	/			3.9/3.9
	-女式游泳服:										
6112.4100	--合成纤维制〔999〕	8		130	13/	13	件/千克	/		33	5.2/5.2
6112.4900	--其他纺织材料制〔999〕	6		130	13/	13	件/千克	/		31	3.9/3.9
61.13	**用税目 59.03、59.06 或 59.07 的针织物或钩编织物制成的服装:**										
6113.0000	用税目 59.03、59.06 或 59.07 的针织物或钩编织物制成的服装〔999〕	6		130	13/	13	件/千克	/		31	3.9/3.9
61.14	**针织或钩编的其他服装:**										
6114.2000	-棉制										
6114.2000 11	棉制针织或钩编儿童非保暖连身裤〔999〕	6		90	13/	13	件/千克	A/	M	31	
6114.2000 21	棉制针织或钩编男成人及男童 TOPS(指 8－18 号男童 TOPS)〔101 针织童装,102 其他针织服装〕	6		90	13/	13	件/千克	A/	M	31	
6114.2000 22	棉制针织或钩编其他男童 TOPS〔101 针织童装,102 其他针织服装〕	6		90	13/	13	件/千克	A/	M	31	

协定税率 %								RCEP		特惠税率 %			
东/冰/格	巴基斯坦	韩国	瑞士上/下	哥/秘/柬	澳/毛	新西/坡/智	中国港/澳/台	东盟及马来/澳/韩	日/新	亚太2国	老/柬/缅	98/97/95	Article Description
													-Of man-made fibres
0/0/0	0	7.4	1.6/1.6	0/0/0	0/0	0/0/0	0/0/0	14.9/15.2/14.9	15/15.2	0		0/0/0	Boys' or girls' playsuit, jerseys, pullovers, tricolette turn-down collar, open-necked collar, high-necked collar, containing<23% by weight of wool or fine animal hair, containing <30% by weight of silk or silk waste, of man-made fibres, knitted, piled
0/0/0	0	7.4	1.6/1.6	0/0/0	0/0	0/0/0	0/0/0	14.9/15.2/14.9	15/15.2	0		0/0/0	Boys' or girls' playsuit, jerseys, pullovers, tricolette turn-down collar, open-necked collar, high-necked collar, containing<23% by weight of wool or fine animal hair, containing <30% by weight of silk or silk waste, of man-made fibres knitted, piled
0/0/0	0	7.4	1.6/1.6	0/0/0	0/0	0/0/0	0/0/0	14.9/15.2/14.9	15/15.2	0		0/0/0	Other boys' or girls' playsuit, jerseys, pullovers, knitted, tricolette turn-down collar, open-necked collar, high-necked collar, not piled, of man-made fibres, knitted
0/0/0	0	7.4	1.6/1.6	0/0/0	0/0	0/0/0	0/0/0	14.9/15.2/14.9	15/15.2	0		0/0/0	Other boys' or girls' playsuit, including cardigans, waistcoats and similar articles, not piled, of man-made fibres, knitted or crocheted
0/0/0	0	7.4	1.6/1.6	0/0/0	0/0	0/0/0	0/0/0	14.9/15.2/14.9	15/15.2	0		0/0/0	Pullovers, cardigans, waistcoats and similar articles of synthetic fibres, knitted or crocheted
													-Of other textile materials:
0/0/0	0	2.8	1.4/1.4	0/0/0	0/0	0/0/0	0/0/	0/0/12.6	12.7/0	0		0/0/0	---Of silk or silk waste
0/0/0	0	2.8	1.4/1.4	0/0/0	0/0	0/0/0	0/0/	0/0/12.6	12.7/0	0		0/0/0	---Other
													Babies' garments and clothing accessories, knitted or crocheted:
													-Of cotton
0/0/0	0	2.8	1.4/1.4	0/0/0	0/0	0/0/0	0/0/	12.6/12.6/12.6	12.7/12.6			0/0/0	Babies' hosiery of cotton, knitted or crocheted
0/0/0	0	2.8	1.4/1.4	0/0/0	0/0	0/0/0	0/0/	12.6/12.6/12.6	12.7/12.6			0/0/0	Babies' gloves, mittens and mitts of cotton, knitted or crocheted
0/0/0	0	2.8	1.4/1.4	0/0/0	0/0	0/0/0	0/0/	12.6/12.6/12.6	12.7/12.6			0/0/0	Babies' coat, raincoat, ski suit, including jacked and similar articles, of cotton, knitted or crocheted
0/0/0	0	2.8	1.4/1.4	0/0/0	0/0	0/0/0	0/0/	12.6/12.6/12.6	12.7/12.6			0/0/0	Other babies' garments of cotton, knitted or crocheted
0/0/0	0	2.8	1.4/1.4	0/0/0	0/0	0/0/0	0/0/	12.6/12.6/12.6	12.7/12.6			0/0/0	Babies' clothing accessories of cotton, knitted or crocheted
													-Of synthetic fibres
0/0/0	6.4	3.2	1.6/1.6	0/0/0	0/9.6	0/0/0	0/0/	0/0/14.4	14.5/0			0/0/0	Babies' hosiery of synthetic fibres, knitted or crocheted
0/0/0	6.4	3.2	1.6/1.6	0/0/0	0/9.6	0/0/0	0/0/	0/0/14.4	14.5/0			0/0/0	Babies' gloves, mittens and mitts of synthetic fibres, knitted or crocheted
0/0/0	6.4	3.2	1.6/1.6	0/0/0	0/9.6	0/0/0	0/0/	0/0/14.4	14.5/0			0/0/0	Babies' coat, raincoat, ski suit, jacked and similar articles, of synthetic fibres, knitted or crocheted
0/0/0	6.4	3.2	1.6/1.6	0/0/0	0/9.6	0/0/0	0/0/	0/0/14.4	14.5/0			0/0/0	Other babies' garments of synthetic fibres, knitted or crocheted
0/0/0	6.4	3.2	1.6/1.6	0/0/0	0/9.6	0/0/0	0/0/	0/0/14.4	14.5/0			0/0/0	Babies' clothing accessories of synthetic fibres, knitted or crocheted
													-Of other textile materials:
0/0/0	7	2.8	1.4/1.4	0/0/0	0/10	0/0/0	0/0/	0/0/12.6	12.7/0			0/0/0	---Of wool or fine animal hair
													---Other
0/0/0	7	2.8	1.4/1.4	0/0/0	0/0	0/0/0	0/0/	0/0/12.6	12.7/0			0/0/0	Babies' hosiery of artificial fibres, knitted or crocheted
0/0/0	7	2.8	1.4/1.4	0/0/0	0/0	0/0/0	0/0/	0/0/12.6	12.7/0			0/0/0	Babies' garments and clothing accessories, of other textile materials, knitted or crocheted
													Track suits, ski suits and swimwear, knitted or crocheted:
													-Track suits:
0/0/0	6.4	3.2	1.6/1.6	0/0/0	0/0	0/0/0	0/0/	0/0/14.4	14.5/0			0/0/0	--Of cotton
0/0/0	0	3.5	1.8/1.8	0/0/0	0/0	0/0/0	0/0/	0/0/15.8	15.9/0			0/0/0	--Of synthetic fibres
0/0/0	8	3.2	1.6/1.6	0/0/0	0/0	0/0/0	0/0/	0/0/14.4	14.5/0			0/0/0	--Of other textile materials
													-Ski suits:
0/0/0	8	3.2	1.6/1.6	0/0/0	0/0	0/0/0	0/0/	0/0/14.4	14.5/0			0/0/0	---Of cotton
0/0/0	9.5	3.8	1.9/1.9	0/0/0	0/0	0/0/0	0/0/	0/0/17.1	17.3/0			0/0/0	---Other
													-Men's or boys' swimwear:
0/0/0	8.8	3.5	1.8/1.8	0/0/0	0/0	0/0/0	0/0/	0/0/15.8	15.9/0			0/0/0	--Of synthetic fibres
0/0/0	8	3.2	1.6/1.6	0/0/0	0/0	0/0/0	0/0/	0/0/14.4	14.5/0			0/0/0	--Of other textile materials
													-Women's or girls' swimwear:
0/0/0	8.8	3.5	1.8/1.8	0/0/0	0/0	0/0/0	0/0/0	0/0/15.8	15.9/0			0/0/0	--Of Synthetic fibres
0/0/0	8	3.2	1.6/1.6	0/0/0	0/0	0/0/0	0/0/	0/0/14.4	14.5/0			0/0/0	--Of other textile materials
													Garments, made up of knitted or crocheted fabrics of heading No.59.03, 59.06 or 59.07:
0/0/0	8	3.2	1.6/1.6	0/0/0	0/0	0/0/0	0/0/	0/0/14.4	14.5/0	0		0/0/0	Carments, made up of knitted or crocheted fabrics of heading No. 59.03, 59.06 or 59.07
													Other garments, knitted or crocheted:
													-Of cotton
0/0/0	0	3.2	1.6/1.6	0//0	0/0	0/0/0	0/0/	0/0/14.4	14.5/0	2.4		0/0/0	Boys' or girls' overall, not thermal, knitted or crocheted, of cotton
0/0/0	0	3.2	1.6/1.6	0//0	0/0	0/0/0	0/0/	0/0/14.4	14.5/0	2.4		0/0/0	Men's TOPS or boys' TOPS No.8~No.18, knitted or crocheted, of cotton
0/0/0	0	3.2	1.6/1.6	0//0	0/0	0/0/0	0/0/	0/0/14.4	14.5/0	2.4		0/0/0	Other boys' TOPS, knitted or crocheted, of cotton

税则号列	货品名称〔CIQ扩展编码及品名－T2表示见附表2〕	最惠(%)	暂定税率	普通	增值/消费	出口退税	计量单位	监管条件/特殊证件	检验检疫	对美关税	亚太上/下
6114.2000 40	棉制针织或钩编夏服、水洗服(包括女成人、女童及男童)〔101针织外衣,102针织童装〕	6		90	13/	13	件/千克	A/	M	31	
6114.2000 90	棉制针织或钩编其他服装〔999〕	6		90	13/	13	件/千克	/		31	
6114.3000	-化学纤维制										
6114.3000 21	化纤针织或钩编男成人及男TOPS(指8－18号男童TOPS)〔101针织童装,102其他针织服装〕	8		130	13/	13	件/千克	A/	M	33	
6114.3000 22	化学纤维针织或钩编其他男童TOPS〔999〕	8		130	13/	13	件/千克	A/	M	33	
6114.3000 90	化学纤维针织或钩编其他服装〔101针织外衣,102针织衬衫,103针织运动服,104针织童装,999其他针织服装〕	8		130	13/	13	件/千克	/		33	
	-其他纺织材料制:										
6114.9010	---羊毛或动物细毛制〔999〕	6		130	13/	13	件/千克	/		31	
6114.9090	---其他〔999〕	6		130	13/	13	件/千克	/		31	
61.15	**针织或钩编的连裤袜、紧身裤袜、长筒袜、短袜及其他袜类,包括渐紧压袜类(例如,用以治疗静脉曲张的长筒袜)和无外绱鞋底的鞋类:**										
6115.1000	-渐紧压袜类(例如,用以治疗静脉曲张的长筒袜)〔999〕	6		130	13/	13	双/千克	/		31	3.5/3.5
	-其他连裤袜及紧身裤袜:										
6115.2100	--每根单丝细度在67分特以下的合成纤维制〔999〕	6		130	13/	13	双/千克	/		31	3.9/3.9
6115.2200	--每根单丝细度在67分特及以上的合成纤维制〔999〕	6		130	13/	13	双/千克	/		31	3.9/3.9
	--其他纺织材料制:										
6115.2910	---棉制〔999〕	6		90	13/	13	双/千克	/			
6115.2990	---其他〔999〕	6		130	13/	13	双/千克	/		31	3.9/3.9
6115.3000	-其他女式长筒袜及中筒袜,每根单丝细度在67分特以下〔999〕	6		130	13/	13	双/千克	/		31	3.9/3.9
	-其他:										
6115.9400	--羊毛或动物细毛制〔999〕	6		130	13/	13	双/千克	/		16	
6115.9500	--棉制										
6115.9500 11	棉制针织或钩编矫正袜(外科用带压缩刻度)〔999〕	6		90	13/	13	双/千克	/		31	
6115.9500 19	棉制针织或钩编短袜及其他袜类〔999〕	6		90	13/	13	双/千克	/		31	
6115.9600	--合成纤维制〔999〕	6		130	13/	13	双/千克	/		31	3.9/3.9
6115.9900	--其他纺织材料制〔999〕	6		130	13/	13	双/千克	/			3.9/3.9
61.16	**针织或钩编的分指手套、连指手套及露指手套:**										
6116.1000	-用塑料或橡胶浸渍、涂布、包覆或层压的〔999〕	6		122	13/	13	双/千克	/		31	
	-其他:										
6116.9100	--羊毛或动物细毛制〔999〕	6		130	13/	13	双/千克	/			
6116.9200	--棉制〔999〕	6		90	13/	13	双/千克	/		16	
6116.9300	--合成纤维制										
6116.9300 10	合成纤维制其他针织或钩编手套(含羊毛或动物细毛23%及以上)〔999〕	6		130	13/	13	双/千克	/		31	3.9/3.9
6116.9300 90	合成纤维制其他针织或钩编手套(含羊毛或动物细毛23%以下)〔999〕	6		130	13/	13	双/千克	/		31	3.9/3.9
6116.9900	--其他纺织材料制〔999〕	6		130	13/	13	双/千克	/		31	3.9/3.9
61.17	**其他制成的针织或钩编的衣着附件;服装或衣着附件的针织或钩编的零件:**										
	-披巾、头巾、围巾、披纱、面纱及类似品:										
	---动物细毛制:										
6117.1011	----山羊绒制〔999〕	6		130	13/	13	条/千克	/		31	3.9/3.9
6117.1019	----其他〔999〕	6		130	13/	13	条/千克	/		31	3.9/3.9
6117.1020	---羊毛制〔999〕	6		130	13/	13	条/千克	/		31	3.9/3.9
6117.1090	---其他〔999〕	6		130	13/	13	条/千克	/		31	3.9/3.9
	-其他附件:										
6117.8010	---领带及领结〔999〕	6		130	13/	13	千克/条	/		31	3.9/3.9
6117.8090	---其他〔999〕	6		130	13/	13	千克	/		31	3.9/3.9
6117.9000	-零件〔999〕	6		130	13/	13	千克	/		31	3/3

协定税率 %								RCEP		特惠税率 %			
东/冰/格	巴基斯坦	韩国	瑞士 上/下	哥/秘/柬	澳/毛	新西/坡/智	中国港/澳/台	东盟及马来/澳/韩	日/新	亚太2国	老/柬/缅	98/97/95	Article Description
0/0/0	0	3.2	1.6/1.6	0//0	0/0	0/0/0	0/0/	0/0/14.4	14.5/0	2.4		0/0/0	Women's or girls' and boys' summer wear, wash wear, knitted or crocheted, of cotton
0/0/0	0	3.2	1.6/1.6	0//0	0/0	0/0/0	0/0/	0/0/14.4	14.5/0	2.4		0/0/0	Other garments, knitted or crocheted, of cotton
													-Of man-made fibres
0/0/0	0	3.5	1.8/1.8	0/0/0	0/0	0/0/0	0/0/	0/0/15.8	15.9/0			0/0/0	Men's TOPS or boys' TOPS No.8～No.18, knitted or crocheted, of man-made fibres
0/0/0	0	3.5	1.8/1.8	0/0/0	0/0	0/0/0	0/0/	0/0/15.8	15.9/0			0/0/0	Other boys' TOPS, knitted or crocheted, of man-made fibres
0/0/0	0	3.5	1.8/1.8	0/0/0	0/0	0/0/0	0/0/	0/0/15.8	15.9/0			0/0/0	Other garments, knitted or crocheted, of man-made fibres
													-Of other textile materials:
0/0/0	0	3.2	1.6/1.6	0/0/0	0/0	0/0/0	0/0/	0/0/14.4	14.5/0			0/0/0	---Of wool or fine animal hair
0/0/0	0	3.2	1.6/1.6	0/0/0	0/9.6	0/0/0	0/0/	0/0/14.4	14.5/0			0/0/0	---Other
													Panty hose, tights, stockings, socks and other hosiery, including graduate compression hosiery (for example, stockings for varicose veins) and footwear without applied soles, knitted or crocheted:
0/0/0	0	3.2	6/6	0/0/0	0/0	0/0/0	0/0/	0/0/14.4	14.5/0			0/0/0	-Graduated compression hosiery (for example, stockings for varicose veins)
													-Other panty hose and tights:
0/0/0	12.8	3.2	1.6/1.6	0/0/0	0/0	0/0/0	0/0/	0/0/14.4	14.5/0			0/0/0	--Of synthetic fibres, measuring per single yarn less than 67 decitex
0/0/0	8	3.2	1.6/1.6	0/0/0	0/0	0/0/0	0/0/0	0/0/14.4	14.5/0			0/0/0	--Of synthetic fibres, measuring per single yarn 67 decitex or more
													--Of other textile materials:
0/0/0	11.2	2.8	1.4/1.4	0/0/0	0/0	0/0/0	0/0/	0/0/12.6	12.7/0			0/0/0	---Of cotton
0/0/0	7	2.8	1.4/1.4	0/0/0	0/0	0/0/0	0/0/0	0/0/12.6	12.7/0			0/0/0	---Other
0/0/0	0	2.8	1.4/1.4	0/0/0	0/0	0/0/0	0/0/	0/0/12.6	12.7/0	0		0/0/0	-Women's full-length or knee-length hosiery, measuring per single yarn less than 67 decitex
													-Other:
0/0/0	11.2	2.8	1.4/1.4	0/0/0	0/0	0/0/0	0/0/	0/0/12.6	12.7/0			0/0/0	--Of wool or fine animal hair
													--Of cotton
0/0/0	0	2.8	1.4/1.4	0/0/0	0/0	0/0/0	0/0/	0/0/12.6	12.7/0			0/0/0	Orthopedic stockings, with surgical restriction scale, of cotton, knitted or crocheted
0/0/0	0	2.8	1.4/1.4	0/0/0	0/0	0/0/0	0/0/	0/0/12.6	12.7/0			0/0/0	Socks and other hosiery of cotton, knitted or crocheted
0/0/0	0	3.2	1.6/1.6	0/0/0	0/0	0/0/0	0/0/	0/0/14.4	14.5/0			0/0/0	--Of synthetic fibres
0/0/0	0	2.8	1.4/1.4	0/0/0	0/0	0/0/0	0/0/0	0/0/12.6	12.7/0			0/0/0	--Of other textile materials
													Gloves, mittens and mitts, knitted or crocheted:
0/0/0	0	2.9	1.4/1.4	0/0/0	0/0	0/0/0	0/0/	0/0/12.6	12.7/0			0/0/0	-Impregnated, coated, covered or laminated with plastics or rubber
													-Other:
0/0/0	0	2.8	1.4/1.4	0/0/0	0/0	0/0/0	0/0/	0/0/12.6	12.7/0			0/0/0	--Of wool of fine animal hair
0/0/0	0	2.8	1.4/1.4	0/0/0	0/0	0/0/0	0/0/	0/0/12.6	12.7/0			0/0/0	--Of cotton
													--Of synthetic fibres
0/0/0	0	3.2	1.6/1.6	0/0/0	0/0	0/0/0	0/0/	0/0/14.4	14.5/0			0/0/0	Mittens and mitts, containing≥23% by weight of wool or fine animal hair, knitted or crocheted, of synthetic fibres
0/0/0	0	3.2	1.6/1.6	0/0/0	0/0	0/0/0	0/0/	0/0/14.4	14.5/0			0/0/0	Mittens and mitts, containing<23% by weight of wool or fine animal hair, knitted or crocheted, of synthetic fibres
0/0/0	0	2.8	1.4/1.4	0/0/0	0/0	0/0/0	0/0/	0/0/12.6	12.7/0			0/0/0	--Of other textile materials
													Other made up clothing accessories, knitted or crocheted; knitted or crocheted parts of garments or of clothing accessories:
													-Shawls, scarves, mufflers, mantillas, veils and the like:
													---Of fine animal hair:
0/0/0	0	2.8	1.4/1.4	0/0/0	0/0	0/0/0	0/0/	0/0/12.6	12.7/0			0/0/0	----Of goats
0/0/0	0	2.8	1.4/1.4	0/0/0	0/10	0/0/0	0/0/	0/0/12.6	12.7/0			0/0/0	----Other
0/0/0	0	2.8	1.4/1.4	0/0/0	0/10	0/0/0	0/0/	0/0/12.6	12.7/0			0/0/0	---Of wool
0/0/0	0	2.8	1.4/1.4	0/0/0	0/8.4	0/0/0	0/0/	0/0/12.6	12.7/0			0/0/0	---Other
													-Other accessories:
0/0/0	0	2.8	1.4/1.4	0/0/0	0/0	0/0/0	0/0/0	0/0/12.6	12.7/0			0/0/0	---Ties, bow ties and cravats
0/0/0	0	2.8	1.4/1.4	0/0/0	0/0	0/0/0	0/0/0	0/0/12.6	12.7/0			0/0/0	---Other
0/0/0	0	2.8	1.4/1.4	0/0/0	0/0	0/0/0	0/0/0	0/0/12.6	12.7/0			0/0/0	-Parts

第六十二章
非针织或非钩编的服装及衣着附件

注释：

一、本章仅适用于除絮胎以外任何纺织物的制成品，但不适用于针织品或钩编织品（税目62.12的除外）。

二、本章不包括：

（一）税目63.09的旧衣服及其他旧物品；

（二）矫形器具、外科手术带、疝气带及类似品（税目90.21）。

三、税目62.03及62.04所称：

（一）“西服套装”，是指面料用相同的织物制成的两件套或三件套的下列成套服装：

一件人体上半身穿着的外套或短上衣，除袖子外，应由四片或四片以上面料组成；也可附带一件马甲（西服背心），这件马甲（西服背心）的前片面料应与套装其他各件的面料相同，后片料则应与外套或短上衣的衬里料相同；

以及一件人体下半身穿着的服装，即不带背带或护胸的长裤、马裤、短裤（游泳裤除外）、裙子或裙裤。

西服套装各件面料质地、颜色及构成必须完全相同，其款式、尺寸大小也须相互般配，但套装的各件可以用不同织物滚边（缝入夹缝中的长条织物）。

如果数件人体下半身穿着的服装同时报验（例如，两条长裤、长裤与短裤、裙子或裙裤与长裤），构成西服套装下装的应是一条长裤，而对于女式西服套装，则应是一条裙子或裙裤，其他服装应分别归类。

所称“西服套装”，包括不论是否完全符合上述条件的下列配套服装：

1.常礼服，由一件后襟下垂并下端开圆弧形叉的素色短上衣和一条条纹长裤组成；

2.晚礼服（燕尾服），一般用黑色织物制成，上衣前襟较短且不闭合，背后有燕尾；

3.无燕尾套装夜礼服，其中上衣款式与普通上衣相似（可以更为显露衬衣前胸），但有光滑丝质或仿丝质的翻领。

（二）“便服套装”，是指面料相同并作零售包装的下列成套服装（西服套装及税目62.07或62.08的物品除外）；

一件人体上半身穿着的服装，但背心除外，因为背心可作为内衣；以及一件或两件不同的人体下半身穿着的服装，即长裤、护胸背带工装裤、马裤、短裤（游泳裤除外）、裙子或裙裤。

便服套装各件面料质地、款式、颜色及构成必须相同；尺寸大小也须相互般配。所称“便服套装”，不包括税目62.11的运动服及滑雪服。

四、税目62.05及62.06不包括在腰围以下有口袋的服装、带有罗纹腰带及以其他方式收紧下摆的服装。税目62.05不包括无袖服装。衬衫及仿男式女衬衫是指人体上身穿着并从领口处全开襟或半开襟的长袖或短袖衣服；罩衫也是上半身穿着的宽松服装，但可以无袖，领口处也可以不开襟。衬衫、仿男式女衬衫及罩衫可有衣领。

五、对于税目62.09：

（一）所称“婴儿服装及衣着附件”，是指用于身高不超过86厘米幼儿的服装；

（二）既可归入税目62.09，也可归入本章其他税目的物品，应归入税目62.09；

六、既可归入税目62.10，也可归入本章其他税目的服装，除税目62.09所列的仍归入该税目外，其余的应一律归入税目62.10。

七、税目62.11所称“滑雪服”，是指从整个外观和织物质地来看，主要在滑雪（速度滑雪和高山滑雪）时穿着的下列服装或成套服装：

（一）“滑雪连身服”，即上下身连在一起的单件服装；除袖子和领子外，滑雪连身服可有口袋或脚带；

（二）“滑雪套装”，即由两件或三件构成一套并作零售包装的下列服装：

一件用一条拉链扣合的带风帽的厚夹克、防风衣、防风短上衣或类似的服装，可以附带一件背心；以及一条不论是否过腰的长裤、一条马裤或一条护胸背带工装裤。

“滑雪套装”也可由一件类似以上（一）款所述的类似连身服和一件可套在连身服外面的有胎料背心组成。

“滑雪套装”各件颜色可以不同，但面料质地、款式及构成必须相同；尺寸大小也须相互般配。

八、正方形或近似正方形的围巾及围巾式样的物品，如果每边均不超过60厘米，应作为手帕归类（税目62.13）。任何一边超过60厘米的手帕，应归入税目62.14。

九、本章的服装，凡门襟为左压右的，应视为男式；右压左的，应视为女式。但本规定不适用于其式样已明显为男式或女式的服装。无法区别是男式还是女式的服装，应按女式服装归入有关税目。

十、本章物品可用金属线制成。

税则号列	货品名称〔CIQ扩展编码及品名－T2表示见附表2〕	最惠(%)	暂定税率	普通	增值/消费	出口退税	计量单位	监管条件/特殊证件	检验检疫	对美关税	亚太上/下
62.01	**男式大衣、短大衣、斗篷、短斗篷、带风帽的防寒短上衣（包括滑雪短上衣）、防风衣、防风短上衣及类似品，但税号62.03的货品除外：**										
6201.2000	-羊毛或动物细毛制										
6201.2000　10	毛制男式大衣、斗篷〔999〕	6	5	130	13/	13	件/千克	/		30	3.9/3.9

Chapter 62
Articles of apparel and clothing accessories, not knitted or crocheted

Notes:

1. This Chapter applies only to made up articles of any textile fabric other than wadding, excluding knitted or crocheted articles (other than those of heading No.62.12).
2. This Chapter does not cover:
   (a) Worn clothing or other worn articles of heading No.63.09; or
   (b) Orthopaedic appliances, surgical belts, trusses or the like (heading No.90.21).
3. For the purposes of headings Nos.62.03 and 62.04:
   (a) The term "suit" means a set of garments composed of two or three pieces made up in hespect of their outer surface, in identical fabric and comprising:
   One suit coat or jacket the outer shell of which, exclusive of sleeves, consists of four or more panels, designed to cover the upper part of the body, possibly with a tailored waistcoat in addition whose front is made from the same fabric as the outer shell of the other components of the set and whose back is made from the same fabric as the lining of the suit coat or jacket, and
   One garment designed to cover the lower part of the body and consisting of trousers, breeches or shorts (other than swimwear), a skirt or a divided skirt, having neither braces nor bibs.
   All of the components of a suit must be of the same fabric construction, colour and composition; they must also be of the same style and of corresponding or compatible size. However, these components may have piping (a strip of fabric sewn into the seam) in a different fabric.
   If several separate components to cover the lower part of the body are presented together (for example two palls of trousers or, trousers and shorts, or a skirt or divided skirt and trousers), the constituent lower part shall be one pair of trousers, or, in the case of women's or girls' suits, the skirt or divided skirt, the other garments being considered separately.
   The term "suit" includes the following sets of garments, whether or not they fulfil all the above conditions:
   (i) Morning dress, comprising a plain jacket (cutaway) with rounded tails hanging well down at the back and striped trousers;
   (ii) Evening dress (tailcoat), generally made of black cloth, the jacket of which is relatively short at the front, does not close and has narrow skirts cut in at the hips and hanging down behind;
   (iii) Dinner jacket suits, in which the jacket is similar in style to an ordinary jacket (though perhaps revealing more of the shirt front), but has shiny silk or imitation silk lapels.
   (b) The term "ensemble" means a set of garments (other than suits and articles of heading No.62.07 or 62.08) composed of several pieces made up in identical fabric, put up for retail sale, and comprising:
   One garment designed to cover the upper part of the body, with the exception of waistcoats which may also form a second upper garment, and one or two different garments, designed to cover the lower part of the body and consisting of trousers, bib and brace overalls, breeches, shorts (other than swimwear), a skirt or a divided skirt.
   All of the components of an ensemble must be of the same fabric construction, style, colour and composition; they also must be of corresponding or compatible size. The term "ensemble" does not apply to track suits or ski suits, of heading No.62.11.
4. Headings 62.05 and 62.06 do not cover garments with pockets below the waist, with a ribbed waistband or other means of tightening at the bottom of the garment. Heading 62.05 does not cover sleeveless garments. "Shirts" and "shirt—blouses" are garments designed to cover the upper part of the body, having long or short sleeves and a full or partial opening starting at the neckline. "Blouses" are loose—fitting garments also designed to cover the upper part of the body but may be sleeveless and with or without an opening at the neckline. "Shirts", "shirt—blouses" and "blouses" may also have a collar.
5. For the purposes of heading No.62.09:
   (a) The expression "babies' garments and clothing accessories" means articles for young children of a body height not exceeding 86cm;
   (b) Articles which are, *prima facie*, classifiable both in heading 62.09 and in other headings of this Chapter are to be classified in heading No.62.09.
6. Garments which are, *prima facie*, classifiable both in heading No.62.10 and in other headings of this Chapter, excluding heading No. 62.09, are to be classified in heading No.62.10.
7. For the purposes of heading No.62.11, "ski suits" means garments or sets of garments which, by their general appearance and texture, are identifiable as intended to be worn principally for skiing (cross-country or alpine).
   They consist either of:
   (a) A "ski overall", that is, a one-piece garment designed to cover the upper and the lower parts of the body; in addition to sleeves and a collar the ski overall may have pockets or footstraps; or
   (b) A "ski ensemble", that is, a set of garments composed of two or three pieces, put up for retail sale and comprising:
   One garment such as an anorak, wind-cheater, wind-jacket or similar article, closed by a slide fastener (zipper), possibly with a waistcoat in addition, and one pair of trousers whether or not extending above waist-level, one pair of breeches or one bib and brace overall.
   The "ski ensemble" may also consist of an overall similar to the one mentioned in paragraph (a) above and a type of padded, sleeveless jacket worn over the overall.
   All the components of a "ski ensemble" must be made up in a fabric of the same texture, style and composition whether or not of the same colour; they also must be of corresponding or compatible size.
8. Scarves and articles of the scarf type, square or approximately square, of which no side exceeds 60cm, are to be classified as handkerchiefs (heading No.62.13). Handkerchiefs of which any side exceeds 60cm are to be classified in heading No.62.14.
9. Garments of this Chapter designed for left over right closure at the front shall be regarded as men's or boys' garments, and those designed for right over left closure at the front as women's or girls' garments. these provisions do not apply where the cut of the garment clearly indicates that it is designed for one or other of the sexes. Garments which cannot be identified as either men's or boys' garments or as women's or girls' garments are to be classified in the headings covering women's or girls' garments.
10. Articles of this Chapter may be made of metal thread.

协定税率 %								RCEP		特惠税率 %			Article Description
东/冰/格	巴基斯坦	韩国	瑞士上/下	哥/秘/柬	澳/毛	新西/坡/智	中国港/澳/台	东盟及马来/澳/韩	日/新	亚太2国	老/柬/缅	98/97/95	
													Men's or boys' overcoats, car-coats, capes, cloaks, anoraks (including ski-jackets), wind-cheaters, wind-jackets and similar articles, other than those of heading No. 62.03:
													Of wool or fine animal hair
0/0/0	8	3.2	1.6/1.6	0/0/0	0/4.8	0/0/0	0/0/	0/0/14.4	14.5/0			0/0/0	Men's coat and cloak made of wool

税则号列	货品名称〔CIQ扩展编码及品名—T2表示见附表2〕	最惠(%)	暂定税率	普通	增值/消费	出口退税	计量单位	监管条件/特殊证件	检验检疫	对美关税	亚太上/下
6201.2000 90	毛制男式短大衣、短斗篷(含带风帽的防寒短上衣(包括滑雪短上衣)、防风衣、防风短上衣及类似品,但税目62.03的货品除外)〔101大衣、短大衣,102上衣〕	6		130	13/	13	件/千克	/		31	3.9/3.9
	-棉制:										
6201.3010	---羽绒服〔999〕	6		90	13/	13	件/千克	/			
6201.3090	---其他										
6201.3090 10	棉制男式大衣、斗篷〔999〕	6	5	90	13/	13	件/千克	/		30	
6201.3090 90	棉制男式短大衣、短斗篷(含带风帽的防寒短上衣(包括滑雪短上衣)、防风衣、防风短上衣及类似品,但税目62.03的货品除外)〔101大衣、短大衣,102上衣〕	6		90	13/	13	件/千克	/		31	
	-化学纤维制:										
6201.4010	---羽绒服〔999〕	8		130	13/	13	件/千克	/		33	5.2/5.2
6201.4090	---其他〔101大衣、短大衣,102上衣〕	8		130	13/	13	件/千克	/		33	5.2/5.2
6201.9000	-其他纺织材料制〔999〕	6		100	13/	13	件/千克	/		31	3.9/3.9
62.02	**女式大衣、短大衣、斗篷、短斗篷、带风帽的防寒短上衣(包括滑雪短上衣)、防风衣、防风短上衣及类似品,但税目62.04的货品除外:**										
6202.2000	-羊毛或动物细毛制										
6202.2000 10	毛制女式大衣、斗篷〔999〕	6	5	130	13/	13	件/千克	/		30	3.9/3.9
6202.2000 90	毛制女式短大衣、短斗篷(含带风帽的防寒短上衣(包括滑雪短上衣)、防风衣、防风短上衣及类似品,但税目62.03的货品除外)〔999〕	6		130	13/	13	件/千克	/		31	3.9/3.9
	-棉制:										
6202.3010	---羽绒服〔999〕	6		90	13/	13	件/千克	/			
6202.3090	---其他										
6202.3090 10	棉制女式大衣、斗篷〔999〕	6	5	90	13/	13	件/千克	/		30	
6202.3090 90	棉制女式短大衣、短斗篷(含带风帽的防寒短上衣(包括滑雪短上衣)、防风衣、防风短上衣及类似品,但税目62.03的货品除外)〔999〕	6		90	13/	13	件/千克	/		31	
	-化学纤维制:										
6202.4010	---羽绒服〔999〕	9		130	13/	13	件/千克	/		34	5.9/5.9
6202.4090	---其他〔999〕	9		130	13/	13	件/千克	/		34	5.9/5.9
6202.9000	-其他纺织材料制〔999〕	6		100	13/	13	件/千克	/		31	3.9/3.9
62.03	**男式西服套装、便服套装、上衣、长裤、护胸背带工装裤、马裤及短裤(游泳裤除外):**										
	-西服套装:										
6203.1100	--羊毛或动物细毛制〔999〕	8	5	130	13/	13	套/千克	/		25	5.2/5.2
6203.1200	--合成纤维制										
6203.1200 10	合成纤维制男式西服套装(含羊毛或动物细毛36%及以上)〔999〕	8		130	13/	13	套/千克	/			5.2/5.2
6203.1200 90	其他合成纤维制男式西服套装〔999〕	8		130	13/	13	套/千克	/			5.2/5.2
	--其他纺织材料制:										
6203.1910	---丝及绢丝制〔999〕	8		100	13/	13	套/千克	/			5.2/5.2
6203.1990	---其他〔999〕	8		100	13/	13	套/千克	/		33	5.2/5.2
	-便服套装:										
6203.2200	--棉制〔999〕	8		90	13/	13	套/千克	/		33	
6203.2300	--合成纤维制〔999〕	8		130	13/	13	套/千克	/		33	5.2/5.2
	--其他纺织材料制:										
6203.2910	---丝及绢丝制〔999〕	8		130	13/	13	套/千克	/			5.2/5.2
6203.2920	---羊毛或动物细毛制〔999〕	8		130	13/	13	套/千克	/			5.2/5.2
6203.2990	---其他〔999〕	8		100	13/	13	套/千克	/			5.2/5.2
	-上衣:										
6203.3100	--羊毛或动物细毛制										
6203.3100 10	毛制男式西服式上衣(羊毛或动物细毛制)〔999〕	6	5	130	13/	13	件/千克	/		30	3.9/3.9
6203.3100 90	毛制男式其他上衣(羊毛或动物细毛制)〔999〕	6	5	130	13/	13	件/千克	/		30	3.9/3.9
6203.3200	--棉制										
6203.3200 10	棉制工业及职业用男式上衣〔999〕	6		90	13/	13	件/千克	/		31	3.9/3.9
6203.3200 90	棉制其他男式上衣〔999〕	6		90	13/	13	件/千克	/		31	3.9/3.9
6203.3300	--合成纤维制〔999〕	12		130	13/	13	件/千克	/		37	7.8/7.8
	--其他纺织材料制:										
6203.3910	---丝及绢丝制										
6203.3910 10	丝制男式上衣(含丝70%及以上)〔999〕	6		130	13/	13	件/千克	/		31	3.9/3.9
6203.3910 90	丝制男式上衣(含丝70%以下)〔999〕	6		130	13/	13	件/千克	/		31	3.9/3.9
6203.3990	---其他〔999〕	6		100	13/	13	件/千克	/		31	3.9/3.9
	-长裤、护胸背带工装裤、马裤及短裤:										
6203.4100	--羊毛或动物细毛制										
6203.4100 22	毛制男式长裤、马裤(羊毛或动物细毛制,含8—18号男童)〔101裤子,102童装〕	6		130	13/	13	条/千克	A/	M	31	3.9/3.9
6203.4100 29	毛制其他男童长裤、马裤(羊毛或动物细毛制)〔999〕	6		130	13/	13	条/千克	A/	M	31	3.9/3.9

协定税率 %								RCEP		特惠税率 %			Article Description
东/冰/格	巴基斯坦	韩国	瑞士上/下	哥/秘/柬	澳/毛	新西/坡/智	中国港/澳/台	东盟及马来/澳/韩	日/新	亚太2国	老/柬/缅	98/97/95	
0/0/0	8	3.2	1.6/1.6	0/0/0	0/4.8	0/0/0	0/0/	0/0/14.4	14.5/0			0/0/0	Men's overcoats, cloaks (including hooded winter jackets (including ski jackets), windbreakers, wind jackets and similar articles, except those of heading 62.3)
													-Of cotton
0/0/0	12.8	3.2	1.6/1.6	0/0/0	0/0	0/0/0	0/0/	0/0/14.4	14.5/0			0/0/0	---Padded with feathers or down
													---Other
0/0/0	12.8	3.2	1.6/1.6	0/0/0	0/0	0/0/0	0/0/	0/0/14.4	14.5/0		0/0/0	0/0/0	Men's coat and cloak made of cotton
0/0/0	12.8	3.2	1.6/1.6	0/0/0	0/0	0/0/0	0/0/	0/0/14.4	14.5/0		0/0/0	0/0/0	Men's overcoats, cloaks (including hooded winter jackets (including ski jackets), windbreakers, wind jackets and similar articles, except those of heading 62.3)
													-Of man—made fibres
0/0/	4.4	3.5	1.8/1.8	0/0/0	0/0	0/0/0	0/0/	0/0/15.8	15.9/0			0/0/0	---Padded with feathers or down
0/0/0	4.4	3.5	1.8/1.8	0/0/0	0/0	0/0/0	0/0/	0/0/15.8	15.9/0			0/0/0	---Other
0/0/0	8	3.2	1.6/1.6	0/0/0	0/0	0/0/0	0/0/	0/0/14.4	14.5/0		//0	0/0/0	-Of other textile materials
													Women's or girls' overcoats, car-coats, capes, cloaks, anoraks (including ski-jackets), wind-cheaters, wind-jackets and similar articles, other than those of heading No.62.04:
													-Of wool or fine animal hair
0/0/0	8	3.2	1.6/1.6	0/0/0	0/0	0/0/0	0/0/	0/0/14.4	14.5/0			0/0/0	Wool Women's coat and cloak
0/0/0	8	3.2	1.6/1.6	0/0/0	0/0	0/0/0	0/0/	0/0/14.4	14.5/0			0/0/0	Women's overcoats, cloaks (including hooded winter jackets (including ski jackets), windbreakers, wind jackets and similar articles, except those of heading 62.3)
													-Of cotton:
0/0/	12.8	3.2	1.6/1.6	0/0/0	0/0	0/0/0	0/0/	0/0/14.4	14.5/0			0/0/0	---Padded with feathers or down
													---Other
0/0/0	12.8	3.2	1.6/1.6	0/0/0	0/0	0/0/0	0/0/	0/0/14.4	14.5/0			0/0/0	Cotton women's coat and cloak
0/0/0	12.8	3.2	1.6/1.6	0/0/0	0/0	0/0/0	0/0/	0/0/14.4	14.5/0			0/0/0	Cotton women′s overcoats, cloaks (including hooded cold proof jackets (including ski jackets), windproof jackets, windproof jackets and similar articles, except those of heading 62.3)
													-Of man—made fibres:
0/0/	9.2	3.7	1.9/1.9	0/0/0	0/0	0/0/0	0/0/	0/0/15.8	15.9/0			0/0/0	---Padded with feathers or down
0/0/0	8.3	3.7	1.9/1.9	0/0/0	0/0	0/0/0	0/0/	0/0/15.8	15.9/0			0/0/0	---Other
0/0/0	8	3.2	1.6/1.6	0/0/0	0/0	0/0/0	0/0/	0/0/14.4	14.5/0			0/0/0	-Other
													Men's or boys' suits, ensembles, jackets, blazers, trousers, bib and brace overalls, breeches and shorts (other than swim wear):
													-Suits:
0/0/0	8.8	3.5	0/0	0/0/0	0/10.5	0/0/0	0/0/	0/0/15.8	15.9/0			0/0/0	--Of wool or fine animal hair
													--Of synthetic fibres
0/0/0	8.8	3.5	1.8/1.8	0/0/0	0/0	0/0/0	0/0/	0/0/15.8	15.9/0			0/0/0	Men's or boys' suits, containing≥36% by weight of wool or fine animal hair, of synthetic fibres
0/0/0	8.8	3.5	1.8/1.8	0/0/0	0/0	0/0/0	0/0/	0/0/15.8	15.9/0			0/0/0	Other men's or boys' suits of synthetic fibres
													--Of other textile materials:
0/0/0	0	3.5	1.8/1.8	0/0/0	0/0	0/0/0	0/0/	0/0/15.8	15.9/0			0/0/0	---Of silk or silk waste
0/0/0	0	3.5	7.4/7.4	0/0/0	0/10.5	0/0/0	0/0/	0/0/15.8	15.9/0			0/0/0	---Other
													-Ensembles:
0/0/0	0	3.5	1.8/1.8	0/0/0	0/0	0/0/0	0/0/	0/0/15.8	15.9/0			0/0/0	Of cotton
0/0/0	8.8	3.5	1.8/1.8	0/0/0	0/0	0/0/0	0/0/	0/0/15.8	15.9/0			0/0/0	--Of synthetic fibres
													--Of other textile materials:
0/0/0	8.8	3.5	1.8/1.8	0/0/0	0/0	0/0/0	0/0/	0/0/15.8	15.9/0			0/0/0	---Of silk or silk waste
0/0/0	8.8	3.5	1.8/1.8	0/0/0	0/0	0/0/0	0/0/	0/0/15.8	15.9/0			0/0/0	---Of wool or fine animal hair
0/0/0	8.8	3.5	1.8/1.8	0/0/0	0/0	0/0/0	0/0/	0/0/15.8	15.9/0			0/0/0	---Other
													-Jackets and blazers:
													--Of wool or fine animal hair
0/0/0	8	3.2	1.6/1.6	0/0/0	0/9.6	0/0/0	0/0/	0/0/14.4	14.5/0	3.6	0/0/0	0/0/0	Men's or boys' suit jackets and blazers, of wool or fine animal hair
0/0/0	8	3.2	1.6/1.6	0/0/0	0/9.6	0/0/0	0/0/	0/0/14.4	14.5/0	3.6	0/0/0	0/0/0	Other men's or boys' jackets and blazers, of wool or fine animal hair
													--Of cotton
0/0/0	0	3.2	1.6/1.6	0/0/0	0/0	0/0/0	0/0/	0/0/14.4	14.5/0	4.2	0/0/0	0/0/0	Men's or boys' jackets and blazers of cotton, industrial and career apparel
0/0/0	0	3.2	1.6/1.6	0/0/0	0/0	0/0/0	0/0/	0/0/14.4	14.5/0	4.2	0/0/0	0/0/0	Men's or boys' jackets and blazers of cotton
0/0/0	0	0	1.8/1.8	0/0/0	0/0	0/0/0	0/0/	0/0/0	15.9/0			0/0/0	--Of synthetic fibres
													Of other textile materials:
													---Of silk or silk waste
0/0/0	0	3.2	1.6/1.6	0/0/0	0/0	0/0/0	0/0/	0/0/14.4	14.5/0	3.6		0/0/0	Men's or boys' jackets and blazers of silk, containing≥70% by weight of silk
0/0/0	0	3.2	1.6/1.6	0/0/0	0/0	0/0/0	0/0/	0/0/14.4	14.5/0	3.6		0/0/0	Men's or boys' jackets and blazers of silk, containing<70% by weight of silk
0/0/0	0	3.2	1.6/1.6	0/0/0	0/9.6	0/0/0	0/0/	0/0/14.4	14.5/0	3.6		0/0/0	---Other
													-Trousers, bib and brace overalls, breeches and shorts:
													--Of wool or fine animal hair
0/0/0	0	3.2	0/0	0/0/0	0/9.6	0/0/0	0/0/	0/0/14.4	14.5/0	0		0/0/0	Men's trousers, breeches, including boys' No.8～No.18, of wool or fine animal hair
0/0/0	0	3.2	0/0	0/0/0	0/9.6	0/0/0	0/0/	0/0/14.4	14.5/0	0		0/0/0	Other boys' trousers, breeches, of wool or fine animal hair

税则号列		货品名称〔CIQ 扩展编码及品名－T2 表示见附表 2〕	最惠(%)	暂定税率	普通	增值/消费	出口退税	计量单位	监管条件/特殊证件	检验检疫	对美关税	亚太上/下
6203.4100	90	毛制其他男式长裤、护胸背带工装裤、马裤及短裤〔999〕	6		130	13/	13	条/千克	/		31	3.9/3.9
		--棉制：										
6203.4210		---阿拉伯裤〔999〕	6		90	13/	13	条/千克	/			3.9/3.9
6203.4290		---其他										
6203.4290	15	棉制其他男童护胸背带工装裤(带防寒衬里)〔999〕	6		90	13/	13	条/千克	A/	M	31	3.9/3.9
6203.4290	19	棉制其他男童护胸背带工装裤〔999〕	6		90	13/	13	条/千克	A/	M	31	3.9/3.9
6203.4290	49	棉制其他男童长裤、马裤(游戏装,不带防寒衬里)〔999〕	6		90	13/	13	条/千克	A/	M	31	3.9/3.9
6203.4290	62	棉制男式长裤、马裤(非游戏装,不带防寒衬里,含 8－18 号男童)〔101 裤子,102 童装〕	6		90	13/	13	条/千克	A/	M	31	3.9/3.9
6203.4290	69	棉制其他男童长裤、马裤(非游戏装,不带防寒衬里)〔999〕	6		90	13/	13	条/千克	A/	M	31	3.9/3.9
6203.4290	90	棉制其他男式长裤、护胸背带工装裤、马裤及短裤〔101 裤子,102 童装〕	6		90	13/	13	条/千克	/		31	3.9/3.9
		--合成纤维制：										
6203.4310		---阿拉伯裤〔999〕	8		130	13/	13	条/千克	/			5.2/5.2
6203.4390		---其他										
6203.4390	15	其他合成纤维制男童护胸背带工装裤(带防寒衬里)〔999〕	12		130	13/	13	条/千克	A/	M	37	7.8/7.8
6203.4390	19	其他合成纤维制男童护胸背带工装裤〔999〕	12		130	13/	13	条/千克	A/	M	37	7.8/7.8
6203.4390	49	其他合成纤维制男童长裤、马裤(不带防寒衬里,含羊毛或动物细毛 36%及以上)〔999〕	12		130	13/	13	条/千克	A/	M	37	7.8/7.8
6203.4390	61	其他合成纤维制男式长裤、马裤(不带防寒衬里,游戏装,含 8－18 号男童)〔101 裤子,102 童装〕	12		130	13/	13	条/千克	A/	M	37	7.8/7.8
6203.4390	69	其他合成纤维制其他男童长裤、马裤(不带防寒衬里,游戏装)〔999〕	12		130	13/	13	条/千克	A/	M	37	7.8/7.8
6203.4390	82	其他合成纤维制男童长裤、马裤(不带防寒衬里,非游戏装和滑雪裤,指 8-18 号男童)〔999〕	12		130	13/	13	条/千克	A/	M	37	7.8/7.8
6203.4390	89	其他合成纤维制其他男童长裤、马裤(不带防寒衬里,非游戏装和滑雪裤)〔999〕	12		130	13/	13	条/千克	A/	M	37	7.8/7.8
6203.4390	90	合纤制其他男式长裤、护胸背带工装裤、马裤及短裤〔101 裤子,102 童装〕	12		130	13/	13	条/千克	/		37	7.8/7.8
		--其他纺织材料制：										
6203.4910		---阿拉伯裤〔999〕	6		100	13/	13	条/千克	/			3.9/3.9
6203.4990		---其他										
6203.4990	12	人造纤维制男童护胸背带工装裤(带防寒衬里)〔999〕	6		100	13/	13	条/千克	A/	M	31	3.9/3.9
6203.4990	19	人造纤维制男童护胸背带工装裤〔999〕	6		100	13/	13	条/千克	A/	M	31	3.9/3.9
6203.4990	90	其他材料制其他男式长裤、护胸背带工装裤、马裤及短裤〔999〕	6		100	13/	13	条/千克	/		31	3.9/3.9
62.04		**女式西服套装、便服套装、上衣、连衣裙、裙子、裙裤、长裤、护胸背带工装裤、马裤及短裤(游泳服除外)：**										
		-西服套装：										
6204.1100		--羊毛或动物细毛制〔999〕	8	5	130	13/	13	套/千克	/			5.2/5.2
6204.1200		--棉制										
6204.1200	10	含裤子的棉制女式西服套装〔999〕	8		90	13/	13	套/千克	/			
6204.1200	90	不含裤子的棉制女式西服套装〔999〕	8		90	13/	13	套/千克	/			
6204.1300		--合成纤维制										
6204.1300	10	合成纤维制女式西服套装(含羊毛或动物细毛 36%及以上)〔999〕	8		130	13/	13	套/千克	/			5.2/5.2
6204.1300	90	其他合成纤维制女式西服套装〔999〕	8		130	13/	13	套/千克	/			5.2/5.2
		--其他纺织材料制：										
6204.1910		---丝及绢丝制〔999〕	8		100	13/	13	套/千克	/			5.2/5.2
6204.1990		---其他〔999〕	8		100	13/	13	套/千克	/			5.2/5.2
		-便服套装：										
6204.2100		--羊毛或动物细毛制〔999〕	8		130	13/	13	套/千克	/			5.2/5.2
6204.2200		--棉制〔999〕	8		90	13/	13	套/千克	/			
6204.2300		--合成纤维制〔999〕	10		130	13/	13	套/千克	/		35	6.5/6.5
		--其他纺织材料制：										
6204.2910		---丝及绢丝制										
6204.2910	10	丝制女式便服套装(含丝及绢丝≥70%)〔999〕	10		130	13/	13	套/千克	/			6.5/6.5
6204.2910	90	丝制其他女式便服套装(含丝及绢丝＜70%)〔999〕	10		130	13/	13	套/千克	/			6.5/6.5
6204.2990		---其他〔999〕	6		100	13/	13	套/千克	/			3.9/3.9
		-上衣：										
6204.3100		--羊毛或动物细毛制〔999〕	6	5	130	13/	13	件/千克	/		30	3.9/3.9
6204.3200		--棉制										
6204.3200	10	棉制女式上衣(工业及职业用)〔999〕	6		90	13/	13	件/千克	/		31	

协定税率 %								RCEP		特惠税率 %			
东/冰/格	巴基斯坦	韩国	瑞士上/下	哥/秘/柬	澳/毛	新西/坡/智	中国港/澳/台	东盟及马来/澳/韩	日/新	亚太2国	老/柬/缅	98/97/95	Article Description
0/0/0	0	3.2	0/0	0/0/0	0/9.6	0/0/0	0/0/	0/0/14.4	14.5/0	0		0/0/0	Wool other men's trousers, bib and brace overalls, breeches and shorts
													--Of cotton:
0/0/0	0	3.2	1.6/1.6	0/0/0	0/0	0/0/0	0/0/	0/0/14.4	14.5/0	4.2		0/0/0	---Arabian trousers
													---Other
0/0/0	0	3.2	1.6/1.6	0/0/0	0/0	0/0/0	0/0/	14.4/14.4/14.4	14.5/14.4	4.2	0/0/0	0/0/0	Other boys' bib and brace overalls, with thermal lining, of cotton
0/0/0	0	3.2	1.6/1.6	0/0/0	0/0	0/0/0	0/0/	14.4/14.4/14.4	14.5/14.4	4.2	0/0/0	0/0/0	Other boys' bib and brace overalls of cotton
0/0/0	0	3.2	1.6/1.6	0/0/0	0/0	0/0/0	0/0/	14.4/14.4/14.4	14.5/14.4	4.2	0/0/0	0/0/0	Other boys' trousers, breeches, of cotton, playsuit, without thermal lining
0/0/0	0	3.2	1.6/1.6	0/0/0	0/0	0/0/0	0/0/	14.4/14.4/14.4	14.5/14.4	4.2	0/0/0	0/0/0	Men's trousers, breeches, including boys' No. 8～No. 18, of cotton, other than playsuit, without thermal lining
0/0/0	0	3.2	1.6/1.6	0/0/0	0/0	0/0/0	0/0/	14.4/14.4/14.4	14.5/14.4	4.2	0/0/0	0/0/0	Other boys' trousers, breeches, of cotton, other than playsuit, without thermal lining
0/0/0	0	3.2	1.6/1.6	0/0/0	0/0	0/0/0	0/0/	14.4/14.4/14.4	14.5/14.4	4.2	0/0/0	0/0/0	Other men's or boys' trousers, breeches and shorts, of cotton, knitted or crocheted
													--Of synthetic fibres:
0/0/0	8.8	3.5	1.8/1.8	0/0/0	0/0	0/0/0	0/0/	0/0/15.8	15.9/0			0/0/0	---Arabian trousers
													---Other
0/0/0	0	3.5	1.8/1.8	0/0/0	0/10.5	0/0/0	0/0/	15.8/15.8/15.8	15.9/15.8			0/0/0	Other boys' bib and brace overalls, with thermal lining of synthetic fibres
0/0/0	0	3.5	1.8/1.8	0/0/0	0/10.5	0/0/0	0/0/	15.8/15.8/15.8	15.9/15.8			0/0/0	Other boys' bib and brace overalls of synthetic fibres
0/0/0	0	3.5	1.8/1.8	0/0/0	0/10.5	0/0/0	0/0/	15.8/15.8/15.8	15.9/15.8			0/0/0	Boys' trousers, breeches, containing≥36% by weight of wool or fine animal hair, without thermal lining, of synthetic fibres
0/0/0	0	3.5	1.8/1.8	0/0/0	0/10.5	0/0/0	0/0/	15.8/15.8/15.8	15.9/15.8			0/0/0	Other men's trousers, breeches, of synthetic fibres, without thermal lining, including boys' No.8～No.18, playsuit
0/0/0	0	3.5	1.8/1.8	0/0/0	0/10.5	0/0/0	0/0/	15.8/15.8/15.8	15.9/15.8			0/0/0	Other boys' trousers, breeches, playsuit, of synthetic fibres, without thermal lining
0/0/0	0	3.5	1.8/1.8	0/0/0	0/10.5	0/0/0	0/0/	15.8/15.8/15.8	15.9/15.8			0/0/0	Other men's trousers, breeches, including boys' No.8～No.18, of synthetic fibres, other than playsuit or ski trousers without thermal lining
0/0/0	0	3.5	1.8/1.8	0/0/0	0/10.5	0/0/0	0/0/	15.8/15.8/15.8	15.9/15.8			0/0/0	Other boys' trousers, breeches of synthetic fibres, other than playsuit or ski trousers without thermal lining
0/0/0	0	3.5	1.8/1.8	0/0/0	0/10.5	0/0/0	0/0/	15.8/15.8/15.8	15.9/15.8			0/0/0	Men's knitted or crocheted trousers breeches, bib and brace overalls of woven fabrics
													--Of other textile materials:
0/0/0	8	3.2	1.6/1.6	0/0/0	0/0	0/0/0	0/0/	0/0/14.4	14.5/0	0		0/0/0	---Arabian trousers
													---Other
0/0/0	0	3.2	1.6/1.6	0/0/0	0/0	0/0/0	0/0/	0/0/14.4	14.5/0	0		0/0/0	Boys' bib and brace overalls, with thermal lining, of artificial fibres
0/0/0	0	3.2	1.6/1.6	0/0/0	0/0	0/0/0	0/0/	0/0/14.4	14.5/0	0		0/0/0	Boys' bib and brace overalls, of artificial fibres
0/0/0	0	3.2	1.6/1.6	0/0/0	0/0	0/0/0	0/0/	0/0/14.4	14.5/0	0		0/0/0	Other men's or boys' trousers, breeches and shorts, of other textile materials
													Women's or girls' suits, ensembles, jackets, blazers, dresses, skirts, divided skirts, trousers, bib and brace overalls, breeches and shorts (other than swimwear):
													-Suits:
0/0/0	8.8	3.5	1.8/1.8	0/0/0	0/0	0/0/0	0/0/	0/0/15.8	15.9/0			0/0/0	--Of wool or fine animal hair
													--Of cotton
0/0/0	14	3.5	1.8/1.8	0/0/0	0/0	0/0/0	0/0/	0/0/15.8	15.9/0			0/0/0	Women's or girls' suits, including trousers, of cotton
0/0/0	14	3.5	1.8/1.8	0/0/0	0/0	0/0/0	0/0/	0/0/15.8	15.9/0			0/0/0	Women's or girls' suits, not including trousers, of cotton
													--Of synthetic fibres
0/0/0	8.8	3.5	1.8/1.8	0/0/0	0/0	0/0/0	0/0/	0/0/15.8	15.9/0			0/0/0	Women's or girls' suits, containing≥36% by weight of wool or fine animal hair, of synthetic fibres
0/0/0	8.8	3.5	1.8/1.8	0/0/0	0/0	0/0/0	0/0/	0/0/15.8	15.9/0			0/0/0	Other women's or girls' suits of synthetic fibres
													--Of other textile materials:
0/0/0	8.8	3.5	1.8/1.8	0/0/0	0/0	0/0/0	0/0/	0/0/15.8	15.9/0			0/0/0	---Of silk or silk waste
0/0/0	8.8	3.5	1.8/1.8	0/0/0	0/0	0/0/0	0/0/	0/0/15.8	15.9/0			0/0/0	---Other
													-Ensembles:
0/0/0	8.8	3.5	1.8/1.8	0/0/0	0/0	0/0/0	0/0/	0/0/15.8	15.9/0			0/0/0	--Of wool or fine animal hair
0/0/0	0	3.5	1.8/1.8	0/0/0	0/0	0/0/0	0/0/	0/0/15.8	15.9/0			0/0/0	--Of cotton
0/0/0	10	9.3	2/2	0/0/0	0/0	0/0/0	0/0/	18/18/18	18.8/18			0/0/0	--Of synthetic fibres
													--Of other textile materials:
													---Of silk or silk waste
0/0/0	10	9.3	2/2	0/0/0	0/0	0/0/0	0/0/	18/18/18	18.8/18			0/0/0	Women's or girls' ensembles, containing≥70% by weight of silk or spun silk
0/0/0	10	9.3	2/2	0/0/0	0/0	0/0/0	0/0/	18/18/18	18.8/18			0/0/0	Women's or girls' ensembles, containing<70% by weight of silk or spun silk
0/0/0	7	2.8	1.4/1.4	0/0/0	0/0	0/0/0	0/0/	0/0/12.6	12.7/0			0/0/0	---Other
													-Jackets and blazers:
0/0/0	8	3.2	1.6/1.6	0/0/0	0/9.6	0/0/0	0/0/	0/0/14.4	14.5/0			0/0/0	--Of wool or fine animal hair
													--Of cotton
0/0/0	0	3.2	1.6/1.6	0/0/0	0/9.6	0/0/0	0/0/	0/0/14.4	14.5/0	2.4	0/0/0	0/0/0	Women's or girls' jackets and blazers of cotton, industrial and career apparel

税则号列	货品名称〔CIQ 扩展编码及品名－T2 表示见附表 2〕	最惠(%)	暂定税率	普通	增值/消费	出口退税	计量单位	监管条件/特殊证件	检验检疫	对美关税	亚太上/下
6204.3200 90	棉制其他女式上衣〔999〕	6		90	13/	13	件/千克	/		31	
6204.3300	--合成纤维制〔999〕	12		130	13/	13	件/千克	/		37	7.8/7.8
	--其他纺织材料制：										
6204.3910	---丝及绢丝制										
6204.3910 10	丝制女式上衣(含丝及绢丝 70%及以上)〔999〕	6		130	13/	13	件/千克	/		31	3.9/3.9
6204.3910 90	丝制其他女式上衣(含丝及绢丝 70%以下)〔999〕	6		130	13/	13	件/千克	/		31	3.9/3.9
6204.3990	---其他〔999〕	6		100	13/	13	件/千克	/		31	3.9/3.9
	-连衣裙：										
6204.4100	--羊毛或动物细毛制〔999〕	6		130	13/	13	件/千克	/		31	3.9/3.9
6204.4200	--棉制〔999〕	6		90	13/	13	件/千克	/		31	
6204.4300	--合成纤维制										
6204.4300 10	合成纤维制女式连衣裙(含羊毛或动物细毛≥36%)〔999〕	8		130	13/	13	件/千克	/		33	5.2/5.2
6204.4300 90	合成纤维制其他女式连衣裙〔999〕	8		130	13/	13	件/千克	/		33	5.2/5.2
6204.4400	--人造纤维制										
6204.4400 10	人造纤维制女式连衣裙(含羊毛或动物细毛≥36%)〔999〕	6		130	13/	13	件/千克	/		31	3.9/3.9
6204.4400 90	人造纤维制其他女式连衣裙〔999〕	6		130	13/	13	件/千克	/		31	3.9/3.9
	--其他纺织材料制：										
6204.4910	---丝及绢丝制										
6204.4910 10	丝制女式连衣裙(含丝及绢丝 70%及以上)〔999〕	6		130	13/	13	件/千克	/		31	3.9/3.9
6204.4910 90	丝制其他女式连衣裙(含丝及绢丝 70%以下)〔999〕	6		130	13/	13	件/千克	/		31	3.9/3.9
6204.4990	---其他〔999〕	6		100	13/	13	件/千克	/		31	3.9/3.9
	-裙子及裙裤：										
6204.5100	--羊毛或动物细毛制〔999〕	6		130	13/	13	件/千克	/		31	3.9/3.9
6204.5200	--棉制〔999〕	6		90	13/	13	件/千克	/		31	
6204.5300	--合成纤维制										
6204.5300 10	合成纤维制女式裙子及裙裤(含羊毛或动物细毛≥36%)〔999〕	6		130	13/	13	件/千克	/		31	3.9/3.9
6204.5300 90	合成纤维制其他女式裙子及裙裤〔999〕	6		130	13/	13	件/千克	/		31	3.9/3.9
	--其他纺织材料制：										
6204.5910	---丝及绢丝制										
6204.5910 10	丝制女式裙子及裙裤(含丝 70%及以上)〔999〕	6		130	13/	13	件/千克	/		31	3.9/3.9
6204.5910 90	其他丝制女式裙子及裙裤(含丝 70%以下)〔999〕	6		130	13/	13	件/千克	/		31	3.9/3.9
6204.5990	---其他〔999〕	6		100	13/	13	件/千克	/		31	3.9/3.9
	-长裤、护胸背带工装裤、马裤及短裤：										
6204.6100	--羊毛或动物细毛制〔999〕	6		130	13/	13	条/千克	/		31	3.9/3.9
6204.6200	--棉制〔999〕	6		90	13/	13	条/千克	/		31	3.9/3.9
6204.6300	--合成纤维制〔999〕	12		130	13/	13	条/千克	/		37	7.8/7.8
6204.6900	--其他纺织材料制〔999〕	6		100	13/	13	条/千克	/		31	3.9/3.9
62.05	男衬衫：										
6205.2000	-棉制										
6205.2000 10	不带特制领的棉制男成人衬衫(含男童 8－18 号衬衫)〔101 衬衫,102 童装〕	6		90	13/	13	件/千克	A/	M	31	3/3
6205.2000 91	其他棉制男童游戏套装衬衫(不包括长衬衫)〔999〕	6		90	13/	13	件/千克	A/	M	31	3/3
6205.2000 99	其他棉制男式衬衫〔999〕	6		90	13/	13	件/千克	/		31	3/3
6205.3000	-化学纤维制										
6205.3000 11	不带特制领的化学纤维制男式衬衫(含羊毛或动物细毛 36%及以上,含男童8－18 号衬衫)〔101 衬衫,102 童装〕	6		130	13/	13	件/千克	A/	M	31	3.9/3.9
6205.3000 19	不带特制领的化学纤维制其他男童衬衫(含羊毛或动物细毛 36%及以上)〔999〕	6		130	13/	13	件/千克	A/	M	31	3.9/3.9
6205.3000 91	化学纤维制其他男成人及男童衬衫(不带特制领,男童衬衫指 8－18 号)〔101 衬衫,102 童装〕	6		130	13/	13	件/千克	A/	M	31	3.9/3.9
6205.3000 92	化学纤维制其他男童游戏套装衬衫〔999〕	6		130	13/	13	件/千克	A/	M	31	3.9/3.9
6205.3000 99	化学纤维制其他男成人衬衫〔999〕	6		130	13/	13	件/千克	/		31	3.9/3.9
	-其他纺织材料制：										
6205.9010	---丝及绢丝制										
6205.9010 11	不带特制领的丝制非针织男式衬衫(含丝 70%及以上,含男童 8－18 号衬衫)〔101 衬衫,102 童装〕	6		130	13/	13	件/千克	A/	M	31	3.9/3.9
6205.9010 19	丝制非针织其他男式衬衫(含丝 70%及以上)〔999〕	6		130	13/	13	件/千克	A/	M	31	3.9/3.9
6205.9010 21	丝制其他非针织男式衬衫(棉限内,不带特制领的,含男童 8－18 号衬衫)〔101 衬衫,102 童装〕	6		130	13/	13	件/千克	A/	M	31	3.9/3.9
6205.9010 29	丝制其他非针织其他男式衬衫(棉限内)〔999〕	6		130	13/	13	件/千克	A/	M	31	3.9/3.9

协定税率 %								RCEP		特惠税率 %			Article Description
东/冰/格	巴基斯坦	韩国	瑞士上/下	哥/秘/柬	澳/毛	新西/坡/智	中国港/澳/台	东盟及马来/澳/韩	日/新	亚太2国	老/柬/缅	98/97/95	
0/0/0	0	3.2	1.6/1.6	0/0/0	0/9.6	0/0/0	0/0/	0/0/14.4	14.5/0	2.4	0/0/0	0/0/0	Women's or girls' jackets and blazers of cotton
0/0/0	7	8.1	1.8/1.8	0/0/0	0/10.5	0/0/0	0/0/	16.3/16.6/16.3	16.4/16.6	0		0/0/0	--Of synthetic fibres
													--Of other textile materials:
													---Of silk or silk waste
0/0/0	0	3.2	1.6/1.6	0/0/0	0/0	0/0/0	0/0/	0/0/14.4	14.5/0	0		0/0/0	Women's or girls' jackets and blazers of silk, containing≥70% by weight of silk or spun silk
0/0/0	0	3.2	1.6/1.6	0/0/0	0/0	0/0/0	0/0/	0/0/14.4	14.5/0	0		0/0/0	Women's or girls' jackets and blazers of silk, containing<70% by weight of silk or spun silk
0/0/0	0	3.2	1.6/1.6	0/0/0	0/0	0/0/0	0/0/	0/0/14.4	14.5/0	0		0/0/0	---Other
													-Dresses:
0/0/0	8	3.2	1.6/1.6	0/0/0	0/0	0/0/0	0/0/	0/0/14.4	14.5/0			0/0/0	--Of wool or fine animal hair
0/0/0	0	3.2	1.6/1.6	0/0/0	0/9.6	0/0/0	0/0/	0/0/14.4	14.5/0		0/0/0	0/0/0	--Of cotton
													--Of synthetic fibres
0/0/0	0	8.1	1.8/1.8	0/0/0	0/0	0/0/0	0/0/	16.3/16.6/16.3	16.4/16.6			0/0/0	Women's or girls' dresses of synthetic fibres, containing≥36% by weight of wool or fine animal hair
0/0/0	0	8.1	1.8/1.8	0/0/0	0/0	0/0/0	0/0/	16.3/16.6/16.3	16.4/16.6			0/0/0	Other women's or girls' dresses of synthetic fibres
													--Of artificial fibres
0/0/0	6.4	3.2	1.6/1.6	0/0/0	0/0	0/0/0	0/0/	0/0/14.4	14.5/0			0/0/0	Women's or girls' dresses of artificial fibres, containing≥36% by weight of wool or fine animal hair
0/0/0	6.4	3.2	1.6/1.6	0/0/0	0/0	0/0/0	0/0/	0/0/14.4	14.5/0			0/0/0	Other women's or girls' dresses of artificial fibres
													--Of other textile materials:
													---Of silk or silk waste
0/0/0	0	3.2	1.6/1.6	0/0/0	0/0	0/0/0	0/0/	0/0/14.4	14.5/0			0/0/0	Women's or girls' dresses of silk, containing≥70% by weight of silk or spun silk
0/0/0	0	3.2	1.6/1.6	0/0/0	0/0	0/0/0	0/0/	0/0/14.4	14.5/0			0/0/0	Other women's or girls' dresses of silk, containing<70% by weight of silk or spun silk
0/0/0	8	3.2	1.6/1.6	0/0/0	0/0	0/0/0	0/0/	0/0/14.4	14.5/0			0/0/0	---Other
													-Skirts and divided skirts:
0/0/0	7	2.8	1.4/1.4	0/0/0	0/0	0/0/0	0/0/	0/0/12.6	12.7/0			0/0/0	--Of wool or fine animal hair
0/0/0	0	2.8	1.4/1.4	0/0/0	0/8.4	0/0/0	0/0/	0/0/12.6	12.7/0			0/0/0	--Of cotton
													--Of synthetic fibres
0/0/0	6.4	3.2	1.6/1.6	0/0/0	0/0	0/0/0	0/0/	0/0/14.4	14.5/0			0/0/0	Women's or girls' skirts and divided skirts, of synthetic fibres, containing≥36% by weight of wool or fine animal hair
0/0/0	6.4	3.2	1.6/1.6	0/0/0	0/0	0/0/0	0/0/	0/0/14.4	14.5/0			0/0/0	Women's or girls' skirts and divided skirts, of synthetic fibres
													--Of other textile materials:
													---Of silk or silk waste
0/0/0	0	2.8	1.4/1.4	0/0/0	0/0	0/0/0	0/0/	0/0/12.6	12.7/0			0/0/0	Women's or girls' skirts and divided skirts, containing≥70% by weight of silk
0/0/0	0	2.8	1.4/1.4	0/0/0	0/0	0/0/0	0/0/	0/0/12.6	12.7/0			0/0/0	Women's or girls' skirts and divided skirts, containing<70% by weight of silk
0/0/0	0	2.8	1.4/1.4	0/0/0	0/0	0/0/0	0/0/	0/0/12.6	12.7/0			0/0/0	---Other
													-Trousers, bib and brace overalls, breeches and shorts:
0/0/0	8	3.2	1.6/1.6	0/0/0	0/9.6	0/0/0	0/0/	0/0/14.4	14.5/0			0/0/0	--Of wool or fine animal hair
0/0/0	0	0	1.6/1.6	0/0/0	0/0	0/0/0	0/0/	14.4/14.4/14.4	14.5/14.4	4.2	0/0/0	0/0/0	--Of cotton
0/0/0	0	3.5	1.8/1.8	0/0/0	0/10.5	0/0/0	0/0/	0/0/15.8	15.9/0			0/0/0	--Of synthetic fibres
0/0/0	0	3.2	1.6/1.6	0/0/0	0/9.6	0/0/0	0/0/	0/0/14.4	14.5/0			0/0/0	Of other textile materials
													Men's or boys' shirts:
													-Of cotton
0/0/0	0	3.2	1.6/1.6	0/0/0	0/0	0/0/0	0/0/	14.4/14.4/14.4	14.5/14.4	2.4	0/0/0	0/0/0	Men's shirts and boys' No.8~No.18, without specially made collar, of cotton
0/0/0	0	3.2	1.6/1.6	0/0/0	0/0	0/0/0	0/0/	14.4/14.4/14.4	14.5/14.4	2.4	0/0/0	0/0/0	Boy's shirts, playsuit, other than long shirts, of cotton
0/0/0	0	3.2	1.6/1.6	0/0/0	0/0	0/0/0	0/0/	14.4/14.4/14.4	14.5/14.4	2.4	0/0/0	0/0/0	Other men's or boys' shirts, of cotton
													-Of man-made fibres
0/0/0	6.4	3.2	1.6/1.6	0/0/0	0/0	0/0/0	0/0/	0/0/14.4	14.5/0	0		0/0/0	Men's or boys' shirts, without specially made collar, containing≥36% by weight of wool or fine animal hair, including boys' No.8~No.18, of man-made fibres
0/0/0	6.4	3.2	1.6/1.6	0/0/0	0/0	0/0/0	0/0/	0/0/14.4	14.5/0	0		0/0/0	Boys' shirts, without specially made collar, containing≥36% by weight of wool or fine animal hair, of man-made fibres
0/0/0	6.4	3.2	1.6/1.6	0/0/0	0/0	0/0/0	0/0/	0/0/14.4	14.5/0	0		0/0/0	Men's or boys' shirts without specially made collar, including boys' No.8~No.18, of man-made fibres
0/0/0	6.4	3.2	1.6/1.6	0/0/0	0/0	0/0/0	0/0/	0/0/14.4	14.5/0	0		0/0/0	Other boy's shirts of playsuit, of man-made fibres
0/0/0	6.4	3.2	1.6/1.6	0/0/0	0/0	0/0/0	0/0/	0/0/14.4	14.5/0	0		0/0/0	Other men's shirts of man-made fibres
													-Of other textile materials:
													---Of silk or silk waste
0/0/0	0	3.2	1.6/1.6	0/0/0	0/0	0/0/0	0/0/	0/0/14.4	14.5/0	0		0/0/0	Men's or boys' shirts of silk, without specially made collar, not knitted, containing≥70% by weight of silk, including boys' No.8~No.18
0/0/0	0	3.2	1.6/1.6	0/0/0	0/0	0/0/0	0/0/	0/0/14.4	14.5/0	0		0/0/0	Men's or boys' shirts of silk, not knitted, containing≥70% by weight of silk
0/0/0	0	3.2	1.6/1.6	0/0/0	0/0	0/0/0	0/0/	0/0/14.4	14.5/0	0		0/0/0	Men's or boys' shirts of silk, not knitted, without specially made collar, including boys' No.8~No.18, cotton within limitations
0/0/0	0	3.2	1.6/1.6	0/0/0	0/0	0/0/0	0/0/	0/0/14.4	14.5/0	0		0/0/0	Men's or boys' shirts of silk, not knitted, cotton within limitations

税则号列	货品名称〔CIQ扩展编码及品名－T2表示见附表2〕	最惠(%)	暂定税率	普通	增值/消费	出口退税	计量单位	监管条件/特殊证件	检验检疫	对美关税	亚太上/下
6205.9010 31	丝制其他非针织男式衬衫(羊毛限内,不带特制领的,含男童8－18号衬衫)〔101衬衫,102童装〕	6		130	13/	13	件/千克	A/	M	31	3.9/3.9
6205.9010 39	丝制其他非针织其他男式衬衫(羊毛限内)〔999〕	6		130	13/	13	件/千克	A/	M	31	3.9/3.9
6205.9010 41	丝制非针织男式衬衫(化学纤维限内,不带特制领的,含男童8－18号衬衫)〔101衬衫,102童装〕	6		130	13/	13	件/千克	A/	M	31	3.9/3.9
6205.9010 49	丝制其他非针织其他男式衬衫(化学纤维限内)〔999〕	6		130	13/	13	件/千克	A/	M	31	3.9/3.9
6205.9010 91	未列名丝制非针织男式衬衫(含丝70%以下,不带特制领的,含男童8－18号衬衫)〔101衬衫,102童装〕	6		130	13/	13	件/千克	A/	M	31	3.9/3.9
6205.9010 99	未列名丝制非针织其他男式衬衫(含丝70%以下)〔999〕	6		130	13/	13	件/千克	A/	M	31	3.9/3.9
6205.9020	---羊毛或动物细毛制〔101衬衫,102童装〕	6		100	13/	13	件/千克	A/	M	31	3.9/3.9
6205.9090	---其他										
6205.9090 11	其他纺织材料制男式衬衫(棉限内,不带特制领的,含男童8－18号衬衫)〔101衬衫,102童装〕	6		100	13/	13	件/千克	A/	M	31	3.9/3.9
6205.9090 19	其他纺织材料制其他男式衬衫(棉纤限内)〔999〕	6		100	13/	13	件/千克	A/	M	31	3.9/3.9
6205.9090 21	其他纺织材料制男式衬衫(羊毛限内,不带特制领的,含男童8－18号衬衫)〔101衬衫,102童装〕	6		100	13/	13	件/千克	A/	M	31	3.9/3.9
6205.9090 29	其他纺织材料制其他男式衬衫(羊毛限内)〔999〕	6		100	13/	13	件/千克	A/	M	31	3.9/3.9
6205.9090 31	其他纺织材料制男式衬衫(化学纤维限内,不带制特领的,含男童8－18号衬衫)〔101衬衫,102童装〕	6		100	13/	13	件/千克	A/	M	31	3.9/3.9
6205.9090 39	其他纺织材料制其他男式衬衫(化学纤维限内)〔999〕	6		100	13/	13	件/千克	A/	M	31	3.9/3.9
6205.9090 91	未列名纺织材料制男式衬衫(不带特制领的,含男童8－18号衬衫)〔101衬衫,102童装〕	6		100	13/	13	件/千克	A/	M	31	3.9/3.9
6205.9090 99	未列名纺织材料制其他男式衬衫〔999〕	6		100	13/	13	件/千克	A/	M	31	3.9/3.9
62.06	女衬衫:										
6206.1000	-丝及绢丝制										
6206.1000 11	丝及绢丝制女式衬衫(棉限内,成人及7－16号女童衬衫)〔101衬衫,102童装〕	6		130	13/	13	件/千克	A/	M	31	3.9/3.9
6206.1000 19	丝及绢丝制其他女童衬衫(棉限内)〔999〕	6		130	13/	13	件/千克	A/	M	31	3.9/3.9
6206.1000 21	丝及绢丝制女式衬衫(羊毛限内,成人及7－16号女童衬衫)〔101衬衫,102童装〕	6		130	13/	13	件/千克	A/	M	31	3.9/3.9
6206.1000 29	丝及绢丝制其他女童衬衫(羊毛限内)〔999〕	6		130	13/	13	件/千克	A/	M	31	3.9/3.9
6206.1000 31	丝及绢丝制女式衬衫(化学纤维限内,成人及7－16号女童衬衫)〔101衬衫,102童装〕	6		130	13/	13	件/千克	A/	M	31	3.9/3.9
6206.1000 39	丝及绢丝制其他女童衬衫(化学纤维限内)〔999〕	6		130	13/	13	件/千克	A/	M	31	3.9/3.9
6206.1000 41	丝制女成人及7－16号女童衬衫(含丝70%及以上)〔101衬衫,102童装〕	6		130	13/	13	件/千克	A/	M	31	3.9/3.9
6206.1000 49	其他丝及绢丝制女童衬衫(含丝70%及以上)〔999〕	6		130	13/	13	件/千克	A/	M	31	3.9/3.9
6206.1000 91	丝制女成人及7－16号女童衬衫(含丝70%以下)〔101衬衫,102童装〕	6		130	13/	13	件/千克	A/	M	31	3.9/3.9
6206.1000 99	其他丝及绢丝制女童衬衫(含丝70%以下)〔999〕	6		130	13/	13	件/千克	A/	M	31	3.9/3.9
6206.2000	-羊毛或动物细毛制										
6206.2000 10	毛制女成人及7－16号女童衬衫〔101衬衫,102童装〕	6		130	13/	13	件/千克	A/	M	31	3.9/3.9
6206.2000 90	其他羊毛或动物细毛制女童衬衫〔999〕	6		130	13/	13	件/千克	A/	M	31	3.9/3.9
6206.3000	-棉制										
6206.3000 10	棉制女成人及7－16号女童衬衫〔101衬衫,102童装〕	6		90	13/	13	件/千克	A/	M	31	3.9/3.9
6206.3000 20	棉制女童游戏套装衫(含游戏套装衬衫)〔999〕	6		90	13/	13	件/千克	A/	M	31	3.9/3.9
6206.3000 90	其他棉制女式衬衫〔999〕	6		90	13/	13	件/千克	A/	M	31	3.9/3.9
6206.4000	-化学纤维制										
6206.4000 11	化学纤维制女成人及女童衬衫(含羊毛或动物细毛36%及以上,成人及7－16号女童衬衫)〔101衬衫,102童装〕	8		130	13/	13	件/千克	A/	M	33	5.2/5.2
6206.4000 19	化学纤维制女成人及女童衬衫(含羊毛或动物细毛36%及以上)〔101衬衫,102童装〕	8		130	13/	13	件/千克	A/	M	33	5.2/5.2

协定税率 %								RCEP		特惠税率 %			Article Description
东/冰/格	巴基斯坦	韩国	瑞士 上/下	哥/秘/柬	澳/毛	新西/坡/智	中国港/澳/台	东盟及马来/澳/韩	日/新	亚太2国	老/柬/缅	98/97/95	
0/0/0	0	3.2	1.6/1.6	0/0/0	0/0	0/0/0	0/0/	0/0/14.4	14.5/0	0		0/0/0	Men's or boys' shirts of silk, not knitted, without specially made collar, including boys' No.8～No.18, wool within limitations
0/0/0	0	3.2	1.6/1.6	0/0/0	0/0	0/0/0	0/0/	0/0/14.4	14.5/0	0		0/0/0	Men's or boys' shirts of silk, not knitted, wool within limitations
0/0/0	0	3.2	1.6/1.6	0/0/0	0/0	0/0/0	0/0/	0/0/14.4	14.5/0	0		0/0/0	Men's or boys' shirts of silk, not knitted, without specially made collar, including boys' No.8～No.18, man-made fibres within limitations
0/0/0	0	3.2	1.6/1.6	0/0/0	0/0	0/0/0	0/0/	0/0/14.4	14.5/0	0		0/0/0	Men's or boys' shirts of silk, not knitted, man-made fibres within limitations
0/0/0	0	3.2	1.6/1.6	0/0/0	0/0	0/0/0	0/0/	0/0/14.4	14.5/0	0		0/0/0	Men's or boys' shirts of silk, not knitted, containing＜70% by weight of silk, without specially made collar, including boys' No.8～No.18, not elsewhere specified or included
0/0/0	0	3.2	1.6/1.6	0/0/0	0/0	0/0/0	0/0/	0/0/14.4	14.5/0	0		0/0/0	Other men's or boys' shirts of silk, not knitted, containing＜70% by weight of silk, not elsewhere specified or included
0/0/0	8	3.2	1.6/1.6	0/0/0	0/0	0/0/0	0/0/	0/0/14.4	14.5/0	0		0/0/0	---Of wool or fine animal hair
													---Other
0/0/0	0	3.2	1.6/1.6	0/0/0	0/9.6	0/0/0	0/0/	0/0/14.4	14.5/0	0		0/0/0	Men's or boys' shirts of other textile materials, without specially made collar, including boys' No.8～No.18, cotton within limitations
0/0/0	0	3.2	1.6/1.6	0/0/0	0/9.6	0/0/0	0/0/	0/0/14.4	14.5/0	0		0/0/0	Men's or boys' shirts of other textile materials, cotton or man-made fibres within limitations
0/0/0	0	3.2	1.6/1.6	0/0/0	0/9.6	0/0/0	0/0/	0/0/14.4	14.5/0	0		0/0/0	Men's or boys' shirts of other textile materials, without specially made collar, including boys' No.8～No.18, wool within limitations
0/0/0	0	3.2	1.6/1.6	0/0/0	0/9.6	0/0/0	0/0/	0/0/14.4	14.5/0	0		0/0/0	Men's or boys' shirts of other textile materials, wool or man-made fibres within limitations
0/0/0	0	3.2	1.6/1.6	0/0/0	0/9.6	0/0/0	0/0/	0/0/14.4	14.5/0	0		0/0/0	Men's or boys' shirts of other textile materials, without specially made collar, including boys' No.8～No.18, man-made fibres within limitations
0/0/0	0	3.2	1.6/1.6	0/0/0	0/9.6	0/0/0	0/0/	0/0/14.4	14.5/0	0		0/0/0	Men's or boys' shirts of other textile materials, man-made fibres within limitations
0/0/0	0	3.2	1.6/1.6	0/0/0	0/9.6	0/0/0	0/0/	0/0/14.4	14.5/0	0		0/0/0	Men's or boys' shirts of other textile materials, without speciallymade collar, including boys' No.8～No.18, not elsewhere specified or included
0/0/0	0	3.2	1.6/1.6	0/0/0	0/9.6	0/0/0	0/0/	0/0/14.4	14.5/0	0		0/0/0	Other men's or boys' shirts of other textile materials, not elsewhere specified or included
													Women's or girls' blouses, shirts and shirt-blouses:
													-Of silk or silk waste
0/0/0	8	3.2	1.6/1.6	0/0/0	0/0	0/0/0	0/0/	0/0/14.4	14.5/0			0/0/0	Women's or girls' shirts of silk or spun silk, cotton within limitations, including girls' No.7～No.16
0/0/0	8	3.2	1.6/1.6	0/0/0	0/0	0/0/0	0/0/	0/0/14.4	14.5/0			0/0/0	Other girls' shirts of silk or spun silk, cotton within limitations
0/0/0	8	3.2	1.6/1.6	0/0/0	0/0	0/0/0	0/0/	0/0/14.4	14.5/0			0/0/0	Women's or girls' shirts of silk or spun silk, wool within limitations, including girls' No.7～No.16
0/0/0	8	3.2	1.6/1.6	0/0/0	0/0	0/0/0	0/0/	0/0/14.4	14.5/0			0/0/0	Other girls' shirts of silk and spun silk, wool within limitations
0/0/0	8	3.2	1.6/1.6	0/0/0	0/0	0/0/0	0/0/	0/0/14.4	14.5/0			0/0/0	Women's or girls' shirts of silk and spun silk, including girls' No.7～No.16, man-made fibres within limitations
0/0/0	8	3.2	1.6/1.6	0/0/0	0/0	0/0/0	0/0/	0/0/14.4	14.5/0			0/0/0	Other girls' shirts of silk and spun silk, man-made fibres within limitations
0/0/0	8	3.2	1.6/1.6	0/0/0	0/0	0/0/0	0/0/	0/0/14.4	14.5/0			0/0/0	Women's shirts of silk, containing≥70% by weight of silk, including girls' No.7～No.16
0/0/0	8	3.2	1.6/1.6	0/0/0	0/0	0/0/0	0/0/	0/0/14.4	14.5/0			0/0/0	Other girls' shirts of silk and spun silk, containing≥70% by weight of silk
0/0/0	8	3.2	1.6/1.6	0/0/0	0/0	0/0/0	0/0/	0/0/14.4	14.5/0			0/0/0	Women's shirts of silk, containing＜70% by weight of silk, including girls' No.7～No.16
0/0/0	8	3.2	1.6/1.6	0/0/0	0/0	0/0/0	0/0/	0/0/14.4	14.5/0			0/0/0	Other girls' shirts of silk and spun silk, containing＜70% by weight of silk
													-Of wool or fine animal hair
0/0/0	8	3.2	1.6/1.6	0/0/0	0/0	0/0/0	0/0/	0/0/14.4	14.5/0			0/0/0	Women's and girls No.7～No.16 shirts, of wool or fine animal hair
0/0/0	8	3.2	1.6/1.6	0/0/0	0/0	0/0/0	0/0/	0/0/14.4	14.5/0			0/0/0	Other girls' shirts of wool or fine animal hair
													-Of cotton
0/0/0	0	3.2	1.6/1.6	0/0/0	0/9.6	0/0/0	0/0/	14.4/14.4/14.4	14.5/14.4	2.4	0/0/0	0/0/0	Women's and girls' No.7～No.16 shirts, of cotton
0/0/0	0	3.2	1.6/1.6	0/0/0	0/9.6	0/0/0	0/0/	14.4/14.4/14.4	14.5/14.4	2.4	0/0/0	0/0/0	Girls' shirt of playsuit, of cotton
0/0/0	0	3.2	1.6/1.6	0/0/0	0/9.6	0/0/0	0/0/	14.4/14.4/14.4	14.5/14.4	2.4	0/0/0	0/0/0	Other women's or girls' shirts of cotton
													-Of man-made fibres
0/0/0	8.8	3.5	1.8/1.8	0/0/0	0/10.5	0/0/0	0/0/	0/0/15.8	15.9/0			0/0/0	Women's and girls' No.7～No.16 shirts, containing≥36% by weight of wool or fine animal hair, of man-made fibres
0/0/0	8.8	3.5	1.8/1.8	0/0/0	0/10.5	0/0/0	0/0/	0/0/15.8	15.9/0			0/0/0	Other women's or girls' shirts, containing≥36% by weight of wool or fine animal hair, of man-made fibres

税则号列	货品名称〔CIQ扩展编码及品名－T2表示见附表2〕	最惠(%)	暂定税率	普通	增值/消费	出口退税	计量单位	监管条件/特殊证件	检验检疫	对美关税	亚太上/下
6206.4000　20	化学纤维制女成人及7－16号女童衬衫〔101衬衫,102童装〕	8		130	13/	13	件/千克	A/	M	33	5.2/5.2
6206.4000　30	化学纤维制女童游戏套装衫〔999〕	8		130	13/	13	件/千克	A/	M	33	5.2/5.2
6206.4000　90	其他化学纤维制女式衬衫〔999〕	8		130	13/	13	件/千克	A/	M	33	5.2/5.2
6206.9000	-其他纺织材料制										
6206.9000　10	其他纺织材料制女式衬衫(棉限内)〔999〕	6		100	13/	13	件/千克	A/	M		3.9/3.9
6206.9000　20	其他纺织材料制女式衬衫(羊毛限内)〔999〕	6		100	13/	13	件/千克	A/	M		3.9/3.9
6206.9000　30	其他纺织材料制女式衬衫(化学纤维限内)〔999〕	6		100	13/	13	件/千克	/			3.9/3.9
6206.9000　91	其他纺织材料制女成人及女童衬衫(女童衬衫指7－16号)〔101衬衫,102童装〕	6		100	13/	13	件/千克	A/	M		3.9/3.9
6206.9000　99	其他纺织材料制女成人及女童衬衫〔101衬衫,102童装〕	6		100	13/	13	件/千克	A/	M		3.9/3.9
62.07	**男式汗衫及其他内衣背心、内裤、三角裤、长睡衣、睡衣裤、浴衣、晨衣及类似品：**										
	-内裤及三角裤：										
6207.1100	--棉制〔999〕	6		90	13/	13	件/千克	A/	M	31	3.9/3.9
	--其他纺织材料制：										
6207.1910	---丝及绢丝制										
6207.1910　10	含丝70%及以上男式内裤及三角裤〔999〕	6		130	13/	13	件/千克	A/	M		
6207.1910　90	含丝70%以下男式内裤及三角裤〔999〕	6		130	13/	13	件/千克	A/	M		
6207.1920	---化学纤维制〔999〕	6		130	13/	13	件/千克	A/	M		
6207.1990	---其他										
6207.1990　10	毛制男式内裤及三角裤〔999〕	6		100	13/	13	件/千克	A/	M		
6207.1990　90	其他材料制男式内裤及三角裤〔999〕	6		100	13/	13	件/千克	A/	M		
	-长睡衣及睡衣裤：										
6207.2100	--棉制〔101内衣,102内裤〕	6		90	13/	13	件/千克	A/	M	31	
6207.2200	--化学纤维制〔101内衣,102内裤〕	6		130	13/	13	件/千克	A/	M		
	--其他纺织材料制：										
6207.2910	---丝及绢丝制										
6207.2910　11	含丝70%及以上男式长睡衣、睡衣裤(含8－18号男童长睡衣、睡衣裤)〔101内衣,102内裤,103童装〕	6		130	13/	13	件/千克	A/	M		
6207.2910　19	含丝70%以下男式长睡衣、睡衣裤(含8－18号男童长睡衣、睡衣裤)〔101内衣,102内裤,103童装〕	6		130	13/	13	件/千克	A/	M		
6207.2910　91	其他含丝≥70%男童长睡衣、睡衣裤〔999〕	6		130	13/	13	件/千克	A/	M		
6207.2910　99	其他含丝＜70%男童长睡衣、睡衣裤〔999〕	6		130	13/	13	件/千克	A/	M		
6207.2990	---其他										
6207.2990　10	毛制男式长睡衣及睡衣裤〔101内衣,102内裤〕	6		100	13/	13	件/千克	A/	M		
6207.2990　91	其他材料制男式长睡衣及睡衣裤(含8－18号男童长睡衣及睡衣裤)〔101内衣,102内裤,103童装〕	6		100	13/	13	件/千克	A/	M		
6207.2990　99	其他材料制男童长睡衣及睡衣裤〔999〕	6		100	13/	13	件/千克	A/	M		
	-其他：										
6207.9100	--棉制										
6207.9100　11	棉制男式内衣式背心〔999〕	6		90	13/	13	件/千克	A/	M	31	
6207.9100　12	棉制男式非内衣式背心(男成人及8－18号男童背心)〔101内衣,102童装〕	6		90	13/	13	件/千克	A/	M	31	
6207.9100　19	棉制其他男童非内衣式背心〔999〕	6		90	13/	13	件/千克	A/	M	31	
6207.9100　91	棉制男式浴衣、晨衣及类似品〔999〕	6		90	13/	13	件/千克	A/	M	31	
6207.9100　92	棉制男式睡衣、睡裤(男成人及8－18号男童背心)〔101内衣,102内裤,103童装〕	6		90	13/	13	件/千克	A/	M	31	
6207.9100　99	棉制男式其他内衣(男成人及8－18号男童背心)〔101内衣,102童装〕	6		90	13/	13	件/千克	A/	M	31	
	--其他纺织材料制：										
6207.9910	---丝及绢丝制										
6207.9910　11	丝制男式内衣式背心(含丝70%及以上)〔999〕	6		130	13/	13	件/千克	A/	M		3.9/3.9
6207.9910　19	丝制其他男式内衣式背心〔999〕	6		130	13/	13	件/千克	A/	M		3.9/3.9
6207.9910　21	丝制男式非内衣式背心(含丝70%及以上)〔999〕	6		130	13/	13	件/千克	A/	M		3.9/3.9
6207.9910　29	丝制其他男式非内衣式背心〔999〕	6		130	13/	13	件/千克	A/	M		3.9/3.9
6207.9910　91	丝制男睡衣,浴衣,晨衣及类似品(含丝70%及以上)〔999〕	6		130	13/	13	件/千克	A/	M		3.9/3.9
6207.9910　99	丝制其他男睡衣,浴衣,晨衣(含类似品)〔999〕	6		130	13/	13	件/千克	A/	M		3.9/3.9

协定税率 %								RCEP		特惠税率 %			Article Description
东/冰/格	巴基斯坦	韩国	瑞士上/下	哥/秘/柬	澳/毛	新西/坡/智	中国港/澳/台	东盟及马来/澳/韩	日/新	亚太2国	老/柬/缅	98/97/95	
0/0/0	8.8	3.5	1.8/1.8	0/0/0	0/10.5	0/0/0	0/0/	0/0/15.8	15.9/0			0/0/0	Women's shirts and girls' No.7～No.16, of man-made fibres
0/0/0	8.8	3.5	1.8/1.8	0/0/0	0/10.5	0/0/0	0/0/	0/0/15.8	15.9/0			0/0/0	Girls' shirts, playsuit, of man-made fibres
0/0/0	8.8	3.5	1.8/1.8	0/0/0	0/10.5	0/0/0	0/0/	0/0/15.8	15.9/0			0/0/0	Other women's or girls' shirts of man-made fibres
													-Of other textile materials
0/0/0	0	3.2	1.6/1.6	0/0/0	0/0	0/0/0	0/0/	0/0/14.4	14.5/0	0		0/0/0	Women's or girls' shirts of other textile materials, cotton within limitations
0/0/0	0	3.2	1.6/1.6	0/0/0	0/0	0/0/0	0/0/	0/0/14.4	14.5/0	0		0/0/0	Women's or girls' shirts of other textile materials, wool within limitations
0/0/0	0	3.2	1.6/1.6	0/0/0	0/0	0/0/0	0/0/	0/0/14.4	14.5/0	0		0/0/0	Women's or girls' shirts of other textile materials, man-made fibres within limitations
0/0/0	0	3.2	1.6/1.6	0/0/0	0/0	0/0/0	0/0/	0/0/14.4	14.5/0	0		0/0/0	Women's and girls' No.7～No.16, shirts of other textile materials
0/0/0	0	3.2	1.6/1.6	0/0/0	0/0	0/0/0	0/0/	0/0/14.4	14.5/0	0		0/0/0	Other women's or girls' shirts of other textile materials
													Men's or boys' singlets and other vests, underpants, briefs, nightshirts, pyjamas, bathrobes, dressing gowns and similar articles:
													-Underpants and briefs:
0/0/0	7	2.8	1.4/1.4	0/0/0	0/0	0/0/0	0/0/	0/0/12.6	12.7/0			0/0/0	--Of cotton
													--Of other textile materials:
													---Of silk or silk waste
0/0/0	7	2.8	1.4/1.4	0/0/0	0/0	0/0/0	0/0/	0/0/12.6	12.7/0			0/0/0	Men's or boys' underpants and briefs, containing≥70% by weight of silk
0/0/0	7	2.8	1.4/1.4	0/0/0	0/0	0/0/0	0/0/	0/0/12.6	12.7/0			0/0/0	Men's or boys' underpants and briefs, containing<70% by weight of silk
0/0/0	12.8	3.2	1.6/1.6	0/0/0	0/0	0/0/0	0/0/	0/0/14.4	14.5/0			0/0/0	---Of man-made fibres
													---Other
0/0/0	7	2.8	1.4/1.4	0/0/0	0/0	0/0/0	0/0/	0/0/12.6	12.7/0			0/0/0	Men's or boys' underpants and briefs of wool or fine animal hair
0/0/0	7	2.8	1.4/1.4	0/0/0	0/0	0/0/0	0/0/	0/0/12.6	12.7/0			0/0/0	Men's or boys' underpants and briefs of other textile materials
													-Nightshirts and pyjamas:
0/0/0	11.2	2.8	1.4/1.4	0/0/0	0/0	0/0/0	0/0/	0/0/12.6	12.7/0		0/0/0	0/0/0	--Of cotton
0/0/0	12.8	3.2	1.6/1.6	0/0/0	0/0	0/0/0	0/0/	0/0/14.4	14.5/0			0/0/0	--Of man-made fibres
													--Of other textile materials:
													---Of silk or silk waste
0/0/0	7	2.8	1.4/1.4	0/0/0	0/0	0/0/0	0/0/	0/0/12.6	12.7/0			0/0/0	Men's nightshirts and pyjamas containing≥70% by weight of silk, including boys' No.8～No.18
0/0/0	7	2.8	1.4/1.4	0/0/0	0/0	0/0/0	0/0/	0/0/12.6	12.7/0			0/0/0	Men's or boys' nightshirts and pyjamas, containing<70% by weight of silk, including boys' No.8～No.18
0/0/0	7	2.8	1.4/1.4	0/0/0	0/0	0/0/0	0/0/	0/0/12.6	12.7/0			0/0/0	Other boys' nightshirts and pyjamas, containing≥70% by weight of silk
0/0/0	7	2.8	1.4/1.4	0/0/0	0/0	0/0/0	0/0/	0/0/12.6	12.7/0			0/0/0	Other boys' nightshirts and pyjamas, containing<70% by weight of silk
													---Other
0/0/0	7	2.8	1.4/1.4	0/0/0	0/0	0/0/0	0/0/	0/0/12.6	12.7/0		0/0/0	0/0/0	Men's or boys' nightshirts and pyjamas, of wool or fine animal hair
0/0/0	7	2.8	1.4/1.4	0/0/0	0/0	0/0/0	0/0/	0/0/12.6	12.7/0		0/0/0	0/0/0	Men's or boys' nightshirts and pyjamas, of other textile materials, including boys' No.8～No.18
0/0/0	7	2.8	1.4/1.4	0/0/0	0/0	0/0/0	0/0/	0/0/12.6	12.7/0		0/0/0	0/0/0	Boys' nightshirts and pyjamas of other textile materials
													-Other:
													--Of cotton
0/0/0	0	2.8	1.4/1.4	0/0/0	0/0	0/0/0	0/0/	0/0/12.6	12.7/0			0/0/0	Men's or boys' singlets, vest style, of cotton
0/0/0	0	2.8	1.4/1.4	0/0/0	0/0	0/0/0	0/0/	0/0/12.6	12.7/0			0/0/0	Men's and boys' No.8～No.18 singlets, of cotton, non-vest style
0/0/0	0	2.8	1.4/1.4	0/0/0	0/0	0/0/0	0/0/	0/0/12.6	12.7/0			0/0/0	Other boy's singlets of cotton, non-vests style
0/0/0	0	2.8	1.4/1.4	0/0/0	0/0	0/0/0	0/0/	0/0/12.6	12.7/0			0/0/0	Men's or boys' bathrobes, dressing gowns and similar articles of cotton
0/0/0	0	2.8	1.4/1.4	0/0/0	0/0	0/0/0	0/0/	0/0/12.6	12.7/0			0/0/0	Men's or boys' nightshirts and pyjamas, men's and boy's No.8～No.18 singlets, of cotton
0/0/0	0	2.8	1.4/1.4	0/0/0	0/0	0/0/0	0/0/	0/0/12.6	12.7/0			0/0/0	Other men's or boys' vests, men's and boys' No.8～No.18 singlets, of cotton
													--Of other textile materials:
													---Of silk or silk waste
0/0/0	7	2.8	1.4/1.4	0/0/0	0/0	0/0/0	0/0/	0/0/12.6	12.7/0			0/0/0	Men's or boys' singlets of silk, vest style, containing≥70% by weight of silk
0/0/0	7	2.8	1.4/1.4	0/0/0	0/0	0/0/0	0/0/	0/0/12.6	12.7/0			0/0/0	Other men's or boys' singlets of sil, vest style
0/0/0	7	2.8	1.4/1.4	0/0/0	0/0	0/0/0	0/0/	0/0/12.6	12.7/0			0/0/0	Men's or boys' singlets of silk, non-vest style, containing≥70% by weight of silk
0/0/0	7	2.8	1.4/1.4	0/0/0	0/0	0/0/0	0/0/	0/0/12.6	12.7/0			0/0/0	Other men's or boys' singlets of silk, non-vests style
0/0/0	7	2.8	1.4/1.4	0/0/0	0/0	0/0/0	0/0/	0/0/12.6	12.7/0			0/0/0	Men's or boys' bathrobes, dressing gowns and similar articles, of silk, containing≥70% by weight of silk
0/0/0	7	2.8	1.4/1.4	0/0/0	0/0	0/0/0	0/0/	0/0/12.6	12.7/0			0/0/0	Other men's or boys' pyjamas, bathrobes, dressing gowns and similar articles, of silk

税则号列	货品名称〔CIQ 扩展编码及品名－T2 表示见附表 2〕	最惠(%)	暂定税率	普通	增值/消费	出口退税	计量单位	监管条件/特殊证件	检验检疫	对美关税	亚太上/下
6207.9920	---化学纤维制										
6207.9920 11	化学纤维制男式内衣式背心〔999〕	6		130	13/	13	件/千克	A/	M	31	
6207.9920 12	化学纤维制男式非内衣式背心（男成人及 8－18 号男童背心）〔101 童装，102 其他服装〕	6		130	13/	13	件/千克	A/	M	31	
6207.9920 19	化学纤维制其他男式非内衣式背心〔999〕	6		130	13/	13	件/千克	A/	M	31	
6207.9920 21	化学纤维制男式浴衣、晨衣（含羊毛或动物细毛 36％及以上，含类似品）〔999〕	6		130	13/	13	件/千克	A/	M	31	
6207.9920 29	其他化学纤维制男浴衣、晨衣（含类似品）〔999〕	6		130	13/	13	件/千克	A/	M	31	
6207.9920 91	化学纤维制男睡衣、睡裤（含类似品）〔101 内衣，102 内裤〕	6		130	13/	13	件/千克	A/	M	31	
6207.9920 99	化学纤维制男式其他内衣（含类似品）〔999〕	6		130	13/	13	件/千克	A/	M	31	
6207.9990	---其他										
6207.9990 11	毛制男式内衣式背心〔999〕	6		100	13/	13	件/千克	A/	M		3.9/3.9
6207.9990 12	毛制男式非内衣式背心（男成人及 8－18 号男童背心）〔101 内衣，102 童装〕	6		100	13/	13	件/千克	A/	M		3.9/3.9
6207.9990 13	毛制其他男式非内衣式背心〔999〕	6		100	13/	13	件/千克	A/	M		3.9/3.9
6207.9990 19	毛制男睡衣，浴衣，晨衣及类似品〔999〕	6		100	13/	13	件/千克	A/	M		3.9/3.9
6207.9990 91	其他材料制男式内衣式背心〔999〕	6		100	13/	13	件/千克	A/	M		3.9/3.9
6207.9990 92	其他材料制男式非内衣式背心〔999〕	6		100	13/	13	件/千克	A/	M		3.9/3.9
6207.9990 99	其他材料制男睡衣、浴衣、晨衣（含类似品）〔999〕	6		100	13/	13	件/千克	A/	M		3.9/3.9
62.08	**女式汗衫及其他内衣背心、长衬裙、衬裙、三角裤、短衬裤、睡衣、睡衣裤、浴衣、晨衣及类似品：**										
	-长衬裙及衬裙：										
6208.1100	--化学纤维制〔999〕	6		130	13/	13	件/千克	/		31	
	--其他纺织材料制：										
6208.1910	---丝及绢丝制〔101 裙子，102 童装〕	6		130	13/	13	件/千克	/			4.2/4.2
6208.1920	---棉制〔999〕	6		90	13/	13	件/千克	/			
6208.1990	---其他										
6208.1990 10	毛制女式长衬裙及衬裙〔999〕	6		100	13/	13	件/千克	/			
6208.1990 90	其他材料制女式长衬裙及衬裙〔999〕	6		100	13/	13	件/千克	/			
	-睡衣及睡衣裤：										
6208.2100	--棉制〔101 内衣，102 内裤〕	6		90	13/	13	件/千克	A/	M	31	3.9/3.9
6208.2200	--化学纤维制〔101 内衣，102 内裤〕	6		130	13/	13	件/千克	A/	M	31	
	--其他纺织材料制：										
6208.2910	---丝及绢丝制										
6208.2910 10	丝及绢丝≥70％女式睡衣及睡衣裤〔101 内衣，102 内裤〕	6		130	13/	13	件/千克	A/	M	31	
6208.2910 90	丝及绢丝＜70％女式睡衣及睡衣裤〔101 内衣，102 内裤〕	6		130	13/	13	件/千克	A/	M	31	
6208.2990	---其他										
6208.2990 10	毛制女式睡衣及睡衣裤〔101 内衣，102 内裤〕	6		100	13/	13	件/千克	A/	M		
6208.2990 90	其他材料制女式睡衣及睡衣裤〔101 内衣，102 内裤〕	6		100	13/	13	件/千克	A/	M		
	-其他：										
6208.9100	--棉制										
6208.9100 10	棉制女式内衣式背心、三角裤等（包括短衬裤）〔101 内衣，102 内裤〕	6		90	13/	13	件/千克	A/	M	31	
6208.9100 21	棉制女式非内衣式背心（女成人及 7－16 号女童背心）〔101 内衣，102 童装〕	6		90	13/	13	件/千克	A/	M	31	
6208.9100 29	棉制其他女式非内衣式背心〔999〕	6		90	13/	13	件/千克	A/	M	31	
6208.9100 90	棉制女式浴衣、晨衣及类似品〔999〕	6		90	13/	13	件/千克	A/	M	31	
6208.9200	--化学纤维制										
6208.9200 10	化学纤维制女式内衣式背心、三角裤（含短衬裤）〔101 内衣，102 内裤〕	6		130	13/	13	件/千克	A/	M	31	
6208.9200 21	化学纤维制女式非内衣式背心（女成人及 7－16 号女童背心）〔101 内衣，102 童装〕	6		130	13/	13	件/千克	A/	M	31	
6208.9200 29	化学纤维制其他女式非内衣式背心〔999〕	6		130	13/	13	件/千克	A/	M	31	

协定税率 %								RCEP		特惠税率 %			Article Description
东/冰/格	巴基斯坦	韩国	瑞士上/下	哥/秘/柬	澳/毛	新西/坡/智	中国港/澳/台	东盟及马来/澳/韩	日/新	亚太2国	老/柬/缅	98/97/95	
													---Of man-made fibres
0/0/0	12.8	3.2	1.6/1.6	0/0/0	0/0	0/0/0	0/0/	0/0/14.4	14.5/0			0/0/0	Men's or boys' singlets, vest style, of man-made fibres
0/0/0	12.8	3.2	1.6/1.6	0/0/0	0/0	0/0/0	0/0/	0/0/14.4	14.5/0			0/0/0	Men's or boys' singlets, non-vests style, men's and boys' No. 8～No.18 singlets, of man-made fibres
0/0/0	12.8	3.2	1.6/1.6	0/0/0	0/0	0/0/0	0/0/	0/0/14.4	14.5/0			0/0/0	Other men's or boys' singlets, non-vests style, of man-made fibres
0/0/0	12.8	3.2	1.6/1.6	0/0/0	0/0	0/0/0	0/0/	0/0/14.4	14.5/0			0/0/0	Men's or boys' bathrobes, dressing gowns and similar articles, containing≥36% by weight of wool or fine animal hair, of man-made fibres
0/0/0	12.8	3.2	1.6/1.6	0/0/0	0/0	0/0/0	0/0/	0/0/14.4	14.5/0			0/0/0	Other men's or boys' bathrobes, dressing gowns and similar articles, of man-made fibres
0/0/0	12.8	3.2	1.6/1.6	0/0/0	0/0	0/0/0	0/0/	0/0/14.4	14.5/0			0/0/0	Men's or boys' nightshirts, pyjamas and similar articles, of man-made fibres
0/0/0	12.8	3.2	1.6/1.6	0/0/0	0/0	0/0/0	0/0/	0/0/14.4	14.5/0			0/0/0	Other men's or boys' vest and similar articles of man-made fibres
													---Other
0/0/0	7	2.8	1.4/1.4	0/0/0	0/0	0/0/0	0/0/	0/0/12.6	12.7/0			0/0/0	Men's or boys' singlets, vests style, of wool or fine animal hair
0/0/0	7	2.8	1.4/1.4	0/0/0	0/0	0/0/0	0/0/	0/0/12.6	12.7/0			0/0/0	Men's or boys' singlets, non-vests style(men's and boys' No. 8～No.18), of wool or fine animal hair
0/0/0	7	2.8	1.4/1.4	0/0/0	0/0	0/0/0	0/0/	0/0/12.6	12.7/0			0/0/0	Other men's or boys' singlets, non-vests style, of wool or fine animal hair
0/0/0	7	2.8	1.4/1.4	0/0/0	0/0	0/0/0	0/0/	0/0/12.6	12.7/0			0/0/0	Men's or boys' bathrobes, dressing gowns and similar articles, of wool or fine animal hair
0/0/0	7	2.8	1.4/1.4	0/0/0	0/0	0/0/0	0/0/	0/0/12.6	12.7/0			0/0/0	Men's or boys' singlets, vests style, of other textile materials
0/0/0	7	2.8	1.4/1.4	0/0/0	0/0	0/0/0	0/0/	0/0/12.6	12.7/0			0/0/0	Men's or boys' singlets, non-vests style, of other textile materials
0/0/0	7	2.8	1.4/1.4	0/0/0	0/0	0/0/0	0/0/	0/0/12.6	12.7/0			0/0/0	Other men's or boys' bathrobes, dressing gowns and similar articles, of other textile materials
													Women's or girls' singlets and other vests, slips, petticoats, briefs, panties, night-dresses, pyjamas, nègligès, bathrobes, dressing gowns and similar articles:
													-Slips and petticoats:
0/0/0	12.8	3.2	1.6/1.6	0/0/0	0/0	0/0/0	0/0/	0/0/14.4	14.5/0			0/0/0	--Of man-made fibres
													--Of other textile materials:
0/0/0	7	2.8	1.4/1.4	0/0/0	0/0	0/0/0	0/0/	0/0/12.6	12.7/0			0/0/0	---Of silk or silk waste
0/0/0	7	2.8	1.4/1.4	0/0/0	0/0	0/0/0	0/0/	0/0/12.6	12.7/0			0/0/0	---Of cotton
													---Other
0/0/0	7	2.8	1.4/1.4	0/0/0	0/0	0/0/0	0/0/	0/0/12.6	12.7/0			0/0/0	Women's or girls' slips and petticoats of wool or fine animal hair
0/0/0	7	2.8	1.4/1.4	0/0/0	0/0	0/0/0	0/0/	0/0/12.6	12.7/0			0/0/0	Women's or girls' slips and petticoats of other textile materials
													-Nightdresses and pyjamas:
0/0/0	5.6	2.8	1.4/1.4	0/0/0	0/0	0/0/0	0/0/	0/0/12.6	12.7/0		0/0/0	0/0/0	--Of cotton
0/0/0	12.8	3.2	1.6/1.6	0/0/0	0/0	0/0/0	0/0/	0/0/14.4	14.5/0		0/0/0	0/0/0	--Of man-made fibres
													--Of other textile materials:
													---Of silk or silk waste
0/0/0	7	2.8	1.4/1.4	0/0/0	0/0	0/0/0	0/0/	0/0/12.6	12.7/0			0/0/0	Women's or girls' night-dresses and pyjamas, containing≥70% by weight of silk or silk waste
0/0/0	7	2.8	1.4/1.4	0/0/0	0/0	0/0/0	0/0/	0/0/12.6	12.7/0			0/0/0	Women's or girls' night-dresses and pyjamas, containing<70% by weight of silk or silk waste
													---Other
0/0/0	7	2.8	1.4/1.4	0/0/0	0/0	0/0/0	0/0/	0/0/12.6	12.7/0			0/0/0	Women's or girls' night-dresses and pyjamas, of wool or fine animal hair
0/0/0	7	2.8	1.4/1.4	0/0/0	0/0	0/0/0	0/0/	0/0/12.6	12.7/0			0/0/0	Women's or girls' nightdresses and pyjamas of other textile materials
													-Other:
													--Of cotton
0/0/0	0	2.8	1.4/1.4	0/0/0	0/0	0/0/0	0/0/	0/0/12.6	12.7/0		0/0/0	0/0/0	Women's or girls' singlets, briefs, panties, vest style, of cotton
0/0/0	0	2.8	1.4/1.4	0/0/0	0/0	0/0/0	0/0/	0/0/12.6	12.7/0		0/0/0	0/0/0	Women's or girls' singlets, non-vest style, (women's and girls No.7～No.16) of cotton
0/0/0	0	2.8	1.4/1.4	0/0/0	0/0	0/0/0	0/0/	0/0/12.6	12.7/0		0/0/0	0/0/0	Other women's or girls' singlets, non-vest style, of cotton
0/0/0	0	2.8	1.4/1.4	0/0/0	0/0	0/0/0	0/0/	0/0/12.6	12.7/0		0/0/0	0/0/0	Women's or girls' bathrobes, dressing gowns and similar articles, of cotton
													--Of man-made fibres
0/0/0	12.8	3.2	1.6/1.6	0/0/0	0/9.6	0/0/0	0/0/0	0/0/14.4	14.5/0		0/0/0	0/0/0	Women's or girls' singlets, vest style, briefs, panties, of man-made fibres
0/0/0	12.8	3.2	1.6/1.6	0/0/0	0/9.6	0/0/0	0/0/0	0/0/14.4	14.5/0		0/0/0	0/0/0	Women's or girls' singlets, non-vest style (women's and girls No.7～No.16), of man-made fibres
0/0/0	12.8	3.2	1.6/1.6	0/0/0	0/9.6	0/0/0	0/0/0	0/0/14.4	14.5/0		0/0/0	0/0/0	Other women's or girls' singlets, non-vest style, of man-made fibres

税则号列		货品名称〔CIQ 扩展编码及品名－T2 表示见附表 2〕	最惠(%)	暂定税率	普通	增值/消费	出口退税	计量单位	监管条件/特殊证件	检验检疫	对美关税	亚太上/下
6208.9200	90	化学纤维制女式浴衣、晨衣及类似品〔999〕	6		130	13/	13	件/千克	A/	M	31	
		--其他纺织材料制：										
6208.9910		---丝及绢丝制										
6208.9910	11	丝制女内衣式背心、三角裤等(含丝及绢丝≥70%,包括短衬裤)〔101 内衣,102 内裤〕	6		130	13/	13	件/千克	A/	M		3.9/3.9
6208.9910	19	丝制女内衣式背心、三角裤等(含丝及绢丝＜70%,包括短衬裤)〔101 内衣,102 内裤〕	6		130	13/	13	件/千克	A/	M		3.9/3.9
6208.9910	21	丝制女式非内衣式背心(含丝及绢丝 70%及以上)〔999〕	6		130	13/	13	件/千克	A/	M		3.9/3.9
6208.9910	29	丝制女式非内衣式背心(含丝 70%以下)〔999〕	6		130	13/	13	件/千克	A/	M		3.9/3.9
6208.9910	91	丝制女式浴衣、晨衣及类似品(含丝及绢丝 70%及以上)〔999〕	6		130	13/	13	件/千克	A/	M		3.9/3.9
6208.9910	99	丝制女式浴衣、晨衣及类似品(含丝及绢丝 70%以下)〔999〕	6		130	13/	13	件/千克	A/	M		3.9/3.9
6208.9990		---其他										
6208.9990	11	毛制女式内衣式背心、三角裤等(包括短衬裤)〔101 内衣,102 内裤〕	6		100	13/	13	件/千克	A/	M	31	3.9/3.9
6208.9990	12	毛制女式非内衣式背心(女成人及 7－16 号女童背心)〔101 内衣,102 童装〕	6		100	13/	13	件/千克	A/	M	31	3.9/3.9
6208.9990	13	毛制其他女式非内衣式背心〔999〕	6		100	13/	13	件/千克	A/	M	31	3.9/3.9
6208.9990	19	毛制女式浴衣、晨衣及类似品〔999〕	6		100	13/	13	件/千克	A/	M	31	3.9/3.9
6208.9990	90	其他材料制女式背心、三角裤、短衬裤、浴衣、晨衣及类似品〔101 内衣,102 内裤〕	6		100	13/	13	件/千克	A/	M	31	3.9/3.9
62.09		**婴儿服装及衣着附件：**										
6209.2000		-棉制〔999〕	10	6	90	13/	13	千克	A/	M	31	
6209.3000		-合成纤维制										
6209.3000	10	合成纤维制婴儿手套、袜子(含分指、连指及露指手套,长袜、短袜及其他袜)〔999〕	10	6	130	13/	13	千克	A/	M	31	
6209.3000	20	合成纤维婴儿外衣、雨衣、滑雪装(包括夹克类似服装)〔999〕	10	6	130	13/	13	千克	A/	M	31	
6209.3000	30	合成纤维制婴儿其他服装(含裤子、衬衫、裙子、睡衣、内衣等)〔999〕	10	6	130	13/	13	千克	A/	M	31	
6209.3000	90	合成纤维制婴儿衣着附件〔999〕	10	6	130	13/	13	千克	A/	M	31	
		-其他纺织材料制：										
6209.9010		---羊毛或动物细毛制〔999〕	10	6	130	13/	13	千克	A/	M		
6209.9090		---其他纺织材料制〔999〕	10	6	100	13/	13	千克	A/	M		
62.10		**用税目 56.02、56.03、59.03、59.06 或 59.07 的织物制成的服装：**										
		-用税目 56.02 或 56.03 的织物制成的服装：										
6210.1010		---羊毛或动物细毛制〔999〕	6		130	13/	13	件/千克	/			3.9/3.9
6210.1020		---棉或麻制〔999〕	6		90	13/	13	件/千克	/		31	
6210.1030		---化学纤维制	8		130	13/	13	件/千克			/38	5.2
6210.1030	10	化纤制防护服〔999〕	8		130	13/	13	件/千克	/		33	5.2/5.2
6210.1030	90	其他化纤制用税目 56.02 或 56.03 的织物制成的服装〔999〕	8		130	13/	13	件/千克	/		33	5.2/5.2
6210.1090		---其他纺织材料制〔999〕	6		100	13/	13	件/千克	/		16	
6210.2000		-税目 62.01 所列类型的其他服装〔999〕	6		100	13/	13	件/千克	/		31	3.9/3.9
6210.3000		-税目 62.02 所列类型的其他服装〔999〕	6		100	13/	13	件/千克	/			3.9/3.9
6210.4000		-其他男式服装〔999〕	6		100	13/	13	件/千克	/		31	3.9/3.9
6210.5000		-其他女式服装〔999〕	6		100	13/	13	件/千克	/		31	3.9/3.9
62.11		**运动服、滑雪服及游泳服；其他服装：**										
		-游泳服：										
6211.1100		--男式										
6211.1100	10	羊毛或动物细毛制男式游泳服〔999〕	6		130	13/	13	件/千克	/		31	3.9/3.9
6211.1100	41	丝制男式游泳服(含丝 70%及以上)〔999〕	6		130	13/	13	件/千克	/		31	3.9/3.9
6211.1100	49	丝制男式游泳服(含丝 70%以下)〔999〕	6		130	13/	13	件/千克	/		31	3.9/3.9
6211.1100	90	其他纺织材料制男式游泳服〔999〕	6		130	13/	13	件/千克	/		31	3.9/3.9
6211.1200		--女式										
6211.1200	10	羊毛或动物细毛制女式游泳服〔999〕	6		130	13/	13	件/千克	/		31	3.9/3.9
6211.1200	41	丝制女式游泳服(含丝 70%及以上)〔999〕	6		130	13/	13	件/千克	/		31	3.9/3.9
6211.1200	49	丝制女式游泳服(含丝 70%以下)〔999〕	6		130	13/	13	件/千克	/		31	3.9/3.9
6211.1200	90	其他纺织材料制女式游泳服〔999〕	6		130	13/	13	件/千克	/		31	3.9/3.9
		-滑雪服：										
6211.2010		---棉制〔999〕	6		90	13/	13	套/千克	/			

协定税率 %								RCEP		特惠税率 %			Article Description
东/冰/格	巴基斯坦	韩国	瑞士上/下	哥/秘/柬	澳/毛	新西/坡/智	中国港/澳/台	东盟及马来/澳/韩	日/新	亚太2国	老/柬/缅	98/97/95	
0/0/0	12.8	3.2	1.6/1.6	0/0/0	0/9.6	0/0/0	0/0/0	0/0/14.4	14.5/0		0/0/0	0/0/0	Women's or girls' bathrobes, dressing gowns and similar articles, of man-made fibres
													--Of other textile materials:
													---Of silk or silk waste
0/0/0	7	2.8	1.4/1.4	0/0/0	0/0	0/0/0	0/0/	0/0/12.6	12.7/0			0/0/0	Women's or girls' singlets, vest style briefs, panties of silk, containing≥70% by weight of silk or silk waste
0/0/0	7	2.8	1.4/1.4	0/0/0	0/0	0/0/0	0/0/	0/0/12.6	12.7/0			0/0/0	Women's or girls' singlets, vest style briefs, panties of silk, containing<70% by weight of silk or silk waste
0/0/0	7	2.8	1.4/1.4	0/0/0	0/0	0/0/0	0/0/	0/0/12.6	12.7/0			0/0/0	Women's or girls' singlets of silk, non-vest style, containing≥70% by weight of silk or silk waste
0/0/0	7	2.8	1.4/1.4	0/0/0	0/0	0/0/0	0/0/	0/0/12.6	12.7/0			0/0/0	Women's or girls' singlets of silk, non-vest style, containing<70% by weight of silk or silk waste
0/0/0	7	2.8	1.4/1.4	0/0/0	0/0	0/0/0	0/0/	0/0/12.6	12.7/0			0/0/0	Women's or girls' bathrobes, dressing gowns and similar articles of silk, containing≥70% by weight of silk or silk waste
0/0/0	7	2.8	1.4/1.4	0/0/0	0/0	0/0/0	0/0/	0/0/12.6	12.7/0			0/0/0	Women's or girls' bathrobes, dressing gowns and similar articles, of silk, containing<70% by weight of silk or silk waste
													---Other
0/0/0	7	2.8	1.4/1.4	0/0/0	0/8.4	0/0/0	0/0/	0/0/12.6	12.7/0			0/0/0	Women's or girls' singlets, vest style briefs, panties, of wool or fine animal hair
0/0/0	7	2.8	1.4/1.4	0/0/0	0/8.4	0/0/0	0/0/	0/0/12.6	12.7/0			0/0/0	Women's and girls' No. 7－No. 16 singlets, non-vest style, of wool or fine animal hair
0/0/0	7	2.8	1.4/1.4	0/0/0	0/8.4	0/0/0	0/0/	0/0/12.6	12.7/0			0/0/0	Other women's or girls' singlets, non-vest style, of wool or fine animal hair
0/0/0	7	2.8	1.4/1.4	0/0/0	0/8.4	0/0/0	0/0/	0/0/12.6	12.7/0			0/0/0	Women's or girls' bathrobes, dressing gowns and similar articles, of wool or fine animal hair
0/0/0	7	2.8	1.4/1.4	0/0/0	0/8.4	0/0/0	0/0/	0/0/12.6	12.7/0			0/0/0	Women's or girls' singlets, vest style briefs, panties, other textile materials
													Babies' garments and clothing accessories:
0/0/0	0	2.8	1.4/1.4	0/0/0	0/0	0/0/0	0/0/	0/0/12.6	12.7/0			0/0/0	-Of cotton
													-Of synthetic fibres
0/0/0	0	3.2	1.6/1.6	0/0/0	0/0	0/0/0	0/0/	0/0/14.4	14.5/0			0/0/0	Babies' gloves, mittens, mitts, stockings, socks and similar articles, of synthetic fibres
0/0/0	0	3.2	1.6/1.6	0/0/0	0/0	0/0/0	0/0/	0/0/14.4	14.5/0			0/0/0	Babies' coats, raincoats, ski-suits, jackets and similar articles, of synthetic fibres
0/0/0	0	3.2	1.6/1.6	0/0/0	0/0	0/0/0	0/0/	0/0/14.4	14.5/0			0/0/0	Babies' other garments, including trousers, shirt, skirt, night clothes, underwear, of synthetic fibres
0/0/0	0	3.2	1.6/1.6	0/0/0	0/0	0/0/0	0/0/	0/0/14.4	14.5/0			0/0/0	Babies' clothing accessories, of synthetic fibres
													-Of other textile materials:
0/0/0	7	2.8	1.4/1.4	0/0/0	0/0	0/0/0	0/0/	0/0/12.6	12.7/0			0/0/0	---Of wool or fine animal hair
0/0/0	5.6	2.8	1.4/1.4	0/0/0	0/0	0/0/0	0/0/	0/0/12.6	12.7/0			0/0/0	---Other textile materials
													Garments, made up of fabrics of heading No. 56.02, 56.03, 59.03, 59.06 or 59.07:
													-Of fabrics of heading No.56.02 or 56.03:
0/0/0	8	3.2	1.6/1.6	0/0/0	0/0	0/0/0	0/0/	0/0/14.4	14.5/0	0		0/0/0	---Of wool or fine animal hair
0/0/0	12.8	3.2	1.6/1.6	0/0/0	0/0	0/0/0	0/0/	0/0/14.4	14.5/0	2.4		0/0/0	---Of cotton or bast fibres
0/0/0	8.8	7	5.3	0	0	0	0/0/0	0/0/		0		0/0/0	---Of man-made fibres
0/0/0	8.8	3.5	1.8/1.8	0/0/0	0/0	0/0/0	0/0/	0/0/15.8	15.9/0	0	//	0/0/0	Chemical fiber protective clothing
0/0/0	8.8	3.5	1.8/1.8	0/0/0	0/0	0/0/0	0/0/	0/0/15.8	15.9/0	0	//	0/0/0	Clothing made of fabrics of heading 56.02 or 56.03 of other chemical fibres
0/0/0	12.8	3.2	1.6/1.6	0/0/0	0/0	0/0/0	0/0/	0/0/14.4	14.5/0	0		0/0/0	---Of other textile materials
0/0/0	8	3.2	1.6/1.6	0/0/0	0/0	0/0/0	0/0/	0/0/14.4	14.5/0	0		0/0/0	--Other garments, made up of the type described in subheadings No.6201
0/0/0	8	3.2	1.6/1.6	0/0/0	0/0	0/0/0	0/0/	0/0/14.4	14.5/0			0/0/0	-Other garments, of the type described in subheadings No. 6202
0/0/0	0	3.2	1.6/1.6	0/0/0	0/0	0/0/0	0/0/	14.4/14.4/14.4	14.5/14.4	0		0/0/0	-Other men's or boys' garments
0/0/0	6.4	3.2	1.6/1.6	0/0/0	0/0	0/0/0	0/0/	0/0/14.4	14.5/0	0		0/0/0	-Other women's or girls' garments
													Track suits, ski suits and swimwear; other garments:
													-Swimwear:
													--Men's or boys'
0/0/0	8	3.2	1.6/1.6	0/0/0	0/9.6	0/0/0	0/0/	0/0/14.4	14.5/0			0/0/0	Men's or boys' swimwear of wool or fine animal hair
0/0/0	8	3.2	1.6/1.6	0/0/0	0/9.6	0/0/0	0/0/	0/0/14.4	14.5/0			0/0/0	Men's or boys' swimwear of silk, containing≥70% by weight of silk
0/0/0	8	3.2	1.6/1.6	0/0/0	0/9.6	0/0/0	0/0/	0/0/14.4	14.5/0			0/0/0	Men's or boys' swimwear of silk, containing<70% by weight of silk
0/0/0	8	3.2	1.6/1.6	0/0/0	0/9.6	0/0/0	0/0/	0/0/14.4	14.5/0			0/0/0	Men's or boys' swimwear of other textile materials
													--Women's or girls'
0/0/0	8	3.2	1.6/1.6	0/0/0	0/9.6	0/0/0	0/0/	0/0/14.4	14.5/0			0/0/0	Women's or girls' swimwear of wool or fine animal hair
0/0/0	8	3.2	1.6/1.6	0/0/0	0/9.6	0/0/0	0/0/	0/0/14.4	14.5/0			0/0/0	Women's or girls' swimwear of silk, containing ≥70% by weight of silk
0/0/0	8	3.2	1.6/1.6	0/0/0	0/9.6	0/0/0	0/0/	0/0/14.4	14.5/0			0/0/0	Women's or girls' swimwear of silk, containing <70% by weight of silk
0/0/0	8	3.2	1.6/1.6	0/0/0	0/9.6	0/0/0	0/0/	0/0/14.4	14.5/0			0/0/0	Women's or girls' swimwear of other textile materials
													-Ski suits:
0/0/0	12.8	3.2	1.6/1.6	0/0/0	0/0	0/0/0	0/0/	0/0/14.4	14.5/0			0/0/0	---Of cotton

税则号列	货品名称〔CIQ 扩展编码及品名一T2 表示见附表 2〕	最惠(%)	暂定税率	普通	增值/消费	出口退税	计量单位	监管条件/特殊证件	检验检疫	对美关税	亚太上/下
6211.2090	---其他纺织材料制〔999〕	10		130	13/	13	套/千克	/		35	6.5/6.5
	-其他男式服装：										
	--棉制：										
6211.3210	---阿拉伯袍〔999〕	6		90	13/	13	件/千克	/			
6211.3220	---运动服〔999〕	6		90	13/	13	套/千克	/		31	
6211.3290	---其他〔101 大衣、短大衣，102 上衣，103 裤子，104 衬衫，105 童装，999 其他梭织服装〕	6		90	13/	13	件/千克	/		31	
	--化学纤维制：										
6211.3310	---阿拉伯袍〔999〕	8		130	13/	13	件/千克	/		33	5.2/5.2
6211.3320	---运动服〔999〕	8		130	13/	13	套/千克	/		33	5.2/5.2
6211.3390	---其他〔101 大衣、短大衣，102 上衣，103 衬衫，104 童装，999 其他梭织服装〕	8		130	13/	13	件/千克	/		33	5.2/5.2
	--其他纺织材料制：										
6211.3910	---丝及绢丝制〔101 大衣、短大衣，102 上衣，103 裤子，104 运动服，999 其他梭织服装〕	6		130	13/	13	件/千克	/			3.9/3.9
6211.3920	---羊毛或动物细毛制〔999〕	6		130	13/	13	件/千克	/		31	3.9/3.9
6211.3990	---其他〔101 大衣、短大衣，102 上衣，103 裤子，104 运动服，999 其他梭织服装〕	6		100	13/	13	件/千克	/		31	3.9/3.9
	-其他女式服装：										
	--棉制：										
6211.4210	---运动服〔999〕	6		90	13/	13	套/千克	/		31	
6211.4290	---其他〔999〕	6		90	13/	13	件/千克	/		31	
	--化学纤维制：										
6211.4310	---运动服〔999〕	8		130	13/	13	套/千克	/		33	5.2/5.2
6211.4390	---其他〔999〕	8		130	13/	13	件/千克	/		33	5.2/5.2
	--其他纺织材料制：										
6211.4910	---丝及绢丝制〔101 大衣、短大衣，102 上衣，103，裤子，104 运动服，999 其他梭织服装〕	6		130	13/	13	件/千克	/		31	3.9/3.9
6211.4990	---其他〔101 运动服，998 其他梭织服装，999 其他服装〕	6		100	13/	13	件/千克	/		31	3.9/3.9
62.12	**胸罩、束腰带、紧身胸衣、吊裤带、吊袜带、束袜带和类似品及其零件，不论是否针织或钩编的：**										
	-胸罩：										
6212.1010	---化学纤维制〔999〕	6		130	13/	13	件/千克	A/	M	31	3.9/3.9
6212.1090	---其他纺织材料制										
6212.1090 10	毛制其他胸罩(不论是否针织或钩编)〔999〕	6		100	13/	13	件/千克	A/	M	31	3.9/3.9
6212.1090 20	棉制其他胸罩(不论是否针织或钩编)〔999〕	6		100	13/	13	件/千克	A/	M	31	3.9/3.9
6212.1090 31	丝制胸罩(不论是否针织或钩编，含丝 70%及以上)〔999〕	6		100	13/	13	件/千克	A/	M	31	3.9/3.9
6212.1090 39	丝制其他胸罩(不论是否针织或钩编，含丝 70%以下)〔999〕	6		100	13/	13	件/千克	A/	M	31	3.9/3.9
6212.1090 90	其他纺织材料制其他胸罩(不论是否针织或钩编)〔999〕	6		100	13/	13	件/千克	A/	M	31	3.9/3.9
	-束腰带及腹带：										
6212.2010	---化学纤维制〔999〕	6		130	13/	13	件/千克	A/	M	31	
6212.2090	---其他纺织材料制										
6212.2090 10	毛制束胸带及腹带(不论是否针织或钩编)〔999〕	6		100	13/	13	件/千克	A/	M	31	
6212.2090 20	棉制束腰带及腹带(不论是否针织或钩编)〔999〕	6		100	13/	13	件/千克	A/	M	31	
6212.2090 31	丝制束腰带及腹带(不论是否针织或钩编，含丝 70%及以上)〔999〕	6		100	13/	13	件/千克	A/	M	31	
6212.2090 39	丝制束腰带及腹带(不论是否针织或钩编，含丝 70%以下)〔999〕	6		100	13/	13	件/千克	A/	M	31	
6212.2090 90	其他材料制束胸带及腹带(不论是否针织或钩编)〔999〕	6		100	13/	13	件/千克	A/	M	31	
	-束腰胸衣：										
6212.3010	---化学纤维制〔999〕	6		130	13/	13	件/千克	A/	M	31	
6212.3090	---其他纺织材料制										
6212.3090 10	毛制紧身胸衣(不论是否针织或钩编)〔999〕	6		100	13/	13	件/千克	A/	M	31	
6212.3090 20	棉制紧身胸衣(不论是否针织或钩编)〔999〕	6		100	13/	13	件/千克	A/	M	31	
6212.3090 31	丝制紧身胸衣(不论是否针织或钩编，含丝 70%及以上)〔999〕	6		100	13/	13	件/千克	A/	M	31	
6212.3090 39	丝制其他紧身胸衣(不论是否针织或钩编，含丝 70%以下)〔999〕	6		100	13/	13	件/千克	A/	M	31	
6212.3090 90	其他材料制紧身胸衣(不论是否针织或钩编)〔999〕	6		100	13/	13	件/千克	A/	M	31	
	-其他：										
6212.9010	---化学纤维制〔999〕	6		130	13/	13	件/千克	/		31	3.9/3.9
6212.9090	---其他纺织材料制〔999〕	6		100	13/	13	件/千克	/			3.9/3.9
62.13	**手帕：**										
	-棉制：										
6213.2010	---刺绣的〔999〕	6		90	13/	13	条/千克	/			

协定税率 %								RCEP		特惠税率 %			Article Description
东/冰/格	巴基斯坦	韩国	瑞士上/下	哥/秘/柬	澳/毛	新西/坡/智	中国港/澳/台	东盟及马来/澳/韩	日/新	亚太2国	老/柬/缅	98/97/95	
0/0/0	9.5	3.8	1.9/1.9	0/0/0	0/0	0/0/0	0/0/	0/0/17.1	17.3/0			0/0/0	---Of other textile materials
													-Other garments, men's or boys':
													--Of cotton:
0/0/0	12.8	3.2	1.6/1.6	0/0/0	0/0	0/0/0	0/0/	0/0/14.4	14.5/0			0/0/0	---Arabian robes
0/0/0	0	3.2	1.6/1.6	0/0/0	0/9.6	0/0/0	0/0/	0/0/14.4	14.5/0			0/0/0	--- Track suits
0/0/0	0	3.2	1.6/1.6	0/0/0	0/0	0/0/0	0/0/	0/0/14.4	14.5/0			0/0/0	---Other
													--Of man-made fibres:
0/0/0	8.8	3.5	1.8/1.8	0/0/0	0/0	0/0/0	0/0/	0/0/15.8	15.9/0			0/0/0	---Arabian robes
0/0/0	0	3.6	1.8/1.8	0/0/0	0/0	0/0/0	0/0/	0/0/16.2	16.4/0			0/0/0	---Track suits
0/0/0	0	3.5	1.8/1.8	0/0/0	0/0	0/0/0	0/0/	0/0/15.8	15.9/0			0/0/0	---Other
													--Of other textile materials:
0/0/0	8	3.2	1.6/1.6	0/0/0	0/0	0/0/0	0/0/	0/0/14.4	14.5/0			0/0/0	---Of silk or silk waste
0/0/0	8	3.2	1.6/1.6	0/0/0	0/11.4	0/0/0	0/0/	0/0/14.4	14.5/0			0/0/0	--Of wool or fine animal hair
0/0/0	6.4	3.2	1.6/1.6	0/0/0	0/0	0/0/0	0/0/	0/0/14.4	14.5/0			0/0/0	---Other
													-Other garments, women's or girls':
													--Of cotton:
0/0/0	12.8	3.2	1.6/1.6	0/0/0	0/0	0/0/0	0/0/	0/0/14.4	14.5/0			0/0/0	--- Track suits
0/0/0	12.8	3.2	1.6/1.6	0/0/0	0/9.6	0/0/0	0/0/	0/0/14.4	14.5/0			0/0/0	---Other
													--Of man-made fibres:
0/0/0	8.8	3.5	1.8/1.8	0/0/0	0/0	0/0/0	0/0/	0/0/15.8	15.9/0			0/0/0	---Track suits
0/0/0	7	3.5	1.8/1.8	0/0/0	0/10.5	0/0/0	0/0/	0/0/15.8	15.9/0			0/0/0	---Other
													--Of other textile materials:
0/0/0	0	3.2	1.6/1.6	0/0/0	0/0	0/0/0	0/0/	0/0/14.4	14.5/0			0/0/0	---Of silk or silk waste
0/0/0	0	3.2	1.6/1.6	0/0/0	0/0	0/0/0	0/0/	0/0/14.4	14.5/0			0/0/0	---Other
													Brassières, girdles, corsets, braces, suspenders, garters and similar articles and parts thereof, whether or not knitted or crocheted:
													-Brassières:
0/0/0	12.8	3.2	1.6/1.6	0/0/0	0/9.6	0/0/0	0/0/0	14.4/14.4/14.4	14.5/14.4		0/0/0	0/0/0	---Of man-made fibres
													---Of other textile materials
0/0/0	7	2.8	1.4/1.4	0/0/0	0/8.4	0/0/0	0/0/0	0/0/12.6	12.7/0			0/0/0	Brassieres of wool or fine animal hair(whether or not knitted or crocheted)
0/0/0	7	2.8	1.4/1.4	0/0/0	0/8.4	0/0/0	0/0/0	0/0/12.6	12.7/0			0/0/0	Brassières, whether or not knitted or crocheted, of cotton
0/0/0	7	2.8	1.4/1.4	0/0/0	0/8.4	0/0/0	0/0/0	0/0/12.6	12.7/0			0/0/0	Brassieres of silk, whether or not knitted or crocheted, containing≥70% by weight of silk
0/0/0	7	2.8	1.4/1.4	0/0/0	0/8.4	0/0/0	0/0/0	0/0/12.6	12.7/0			0/0/0	Brassières of silk, whether or not knitted or crocheted, containing<70% by weight of silk
0/0/0	7	2.8	1.4/1.4	0/0/0	0/8.4	0/0/0	0/0/0	0/0/12.6	12.7/0			0/0/0	Brassières, whether or not knitted or crocheted, of other textile materials
													-Girdles and panty-girdles:
0/0/0	12.8	3.2	1.6/1.6	0/0/0	0/0	0/0/0	0/0/0	0/0/14.4	14.5/0			0/0/0	---Of man-made fibres
													---Of other textile materials
0/0/0	11.2	2.8	1.4/1.4	0/0/0	0/0	0/0/0	0/0/0	0/0/12.6	12.7/0			0/0/0	Girdles and panty-girdles, whether or not knitted or crocheted, of wool or fine animal hair
0/0/0	11.2	2.8	1.4/1.4	0/0/0	0/0	0/0/0	0/0/0	0/0/12.6	12.7/0			0/0/0	Girdles and panty-girdles of cotton, whether or not knitted or crocheted
0/0/0	11.2	2.8	1.4/1.4	0/0/0	0/0	0/0/0	0/0/0	0/0/12.6	12.7/0			0/0/0	Girdles and panty-girdles of silk, whether or not knitted or crocheted, containing≥70% by weight of silk
0/0/0	11.2	2.8	1.4/1.4	0/0/0	0/0	0/0/0	0/0/0	0/0/12.6	12.7/0			0/0/0	Girdles and panty-girdles of silk, whether or not knitted or crocheted, containing<70% by weight of silk
0/0/0	11.2	2.8	1.4/1.4	0/0/0	0/0	0/0/0	0/0/0	0/0/12.6	12.7/0			0/0/0	Girdles and panty-girdles, whether or not knitted or crocheted, of other textile materials
													-Corselettes:
0/0/0	12.8	3.2	1.6/1.6	0/0/0	0/9.6	0/0/0	0/0/	0/0/14.4	14.5/0			0/0/0	---Of man-made fibres
													---Of other textile materials
0/0/0	7	2.8	1.4/1.4	0/0/0	0/0	0/0/0	0/0/	0/0/12.6	12.7/0			0/0/0	Croselettes, of wool or fine animal hair
0/0/0	7	2.8	1.4/1.4	0/0/0	0/0	0/0/0	0/0/	0/0/12.6	12.7/0			0/0/0	Croselettes, whether or not knitted or crocheted, of cotton
0/0/0	7	2.8	1.4/1.4	0/0/0	0/0	0/0/0	0/0/	0/0/12.6	12.7/0			0/0/0	Croselettes of silk, whether or not knitted or crocheted, containing≥70% by weight of silk
0/0/0	7	2.8	1.4/1.4	0/0/0	0/0	0/0/0	0/0/	0/0/12.6	12.7/0			0/0/0	Croselettes of silk, whether or not knitted or crocheted, containing<70% by weight of silk
0/0/0	7	2.8	1.4/1.4	0/0/0	0/0	0/0/0	0/0/	0/0/12.6	12.7/0			0/0/0	Croselettes of other textile materials, whether or not knitted or crocheted
													-Other:
0/0/0	12.8	3.2	1.6/1.6	0/0/0	0/9.6	0/0/0	0/0/0	0/0/14.4	14.5/0			0/0/0	---Of man-made fibres
0/0/0	7	2.8	1.4/1.4	0/0/0	0/8.4	0/0/0	0/0/0	0/0/12.6	12.7/0			0/0/0	---Of other textile materials
													Handkerchiefs:
													-Of cotton:
0/0/0	7	2.8	1.4/1.4	0/0/0	0/0	0/0/0	0/0/	0/0/12.6	12.7/0		0//	0/0/0	---Embroidered

税则号列	货品名称〔CIQ 扩展编码及品名一T2 表示见附表 2〕	最惠(%)	暂定税率	普通	增值/消费	出口退税	计量单位	监管条件/特殊证件	检验检疫	对美关税	亚太上/下
6213.2090	---其他〔999〕	6		90	13/	13	条/千克	/		31	
	-其他纺织材料制：										
6213.9020	---刺绣的〔999〕	6		100	13/	13	条/千克	/			
6213.9090	---其他〔999〕	6		100	13/	13	条/千克	/		31	
62.14	**披巾、领巾、围巾、披纱、面纱及类似品：**										
6214.1000	-丝或绢丝制										
6214.1000 10	含丝 70%及以上的披巾、头巾、围巾(包括披纱、面纱等及类似品)〔999〕	6	5	130	13/	13	条/千克	/		30	
6214.1000 90	含丝 70%以下的披巾、头巾、围巾(包括披纱、面纱等及类似品)〔999〕	6	5	130	13/	13	条/千克	/		30	
	-羊毛或动物细毛制：										
6214.2010	---羊毛制〔999〕	6	5	130	13/	13	条/千克	/		30	
6214.2020	---山羊绒制〔999〕	6	5	130	13/	13	条/千克	/		30	
6214.2090	---其他〔999〕	6		130	13/	13	条/千克	/			
6214.3000	-合成纤维制〔999〕	6		130	13/	13	条/千克	/		31	
6214.4000	-人造纤维制〔999〕	6		130	13/	13	条/千克	/			
6214.9000	-其他纺织材料制										
6214.9000 10	棉制披巾、头巾及类似品(包括围巾、披纱、面纱)〔999〕	6		100	13/	13	条/千克	/		31	
6214.9000 90	其他材料制披巾、头巾及类似品(包括围巾、披纱、面纱及类似品)〔999〕	6		100	13/	13	条/千克	/		31	
62.15	**领带及领结：**										
6215.1000	-丝或绢丝制〔999〕	6		130	13/	13	条/千克	/		31	
6215.2000	-化学纤维制〔999〕	6		130	13/	13	条/千克	/		31	3.9/3.9
6215.9000	-其他纺织材料制〔999〕	6		100	13/	13	条/千克	/		31	
62.16	**分指手套、连指手套及露指手套：**										
6216.0000	分指手套、连指手套及露指手套〔999〕	6		100	13/	13	双/千克	/		31	
62.17	**其他制成的衣着附件；服装或衣着附件的零件，但税目 62.12 的货品除外：**										
	-附件：										
6217.1010	---袜子及袜套〔999〕	6		130	13/	13	千克/双	/		31	3.9/3.9
6217.1020	---和服腰带〔999〕	6		100	13/	13	千克/条	/			3.9/3.9
6217.1090	---其他〔999〕	6		100	13/	13	千克	/		31	3.9/3.9
6217.9000	-零件〔999〕	6		100	13/	13	千克	/		31	3.9/3.9

协定税率 %								RCEP		特惠税率 %			Article Description
东/冰/格	巴基斯坦	韩国	瑞士上/下	哥/秘/柬	澳/毛	新西/坡/智	中国港/澳/台	东盟及马来/澳/韩	日/新	亚太2国	老/柬/缅	98/97/95	
0/0/0	11.2	2.8	1.4/1.4	0/0/0	0/0	0/0/0	0/0/	0/0/12.6	12.7/0		0//	0/0/0	---Other
													-Of other textile materials:
0/0/0	7	2.8	1.4/1.4	0/0/0	0/0	0/0/0	0/0/	0/0/12.6	12.7/0		0//	0/0/0	---Embroidered
0/0/0	7	2.8	1.4/1.4	0/0/0	0/0	0/0/0	0/0/	0/0/12.6	12.7/0		0//	0/0/0	---Other
													Shawls, scarves, mufflers, mantillas, veils and the like:
													-Of silk or silk waste
0/0/0	11.2	2.8	1.4/1.4	0/0/0	0/0	0/0/0	0/0/	0/0/12.6	12.7/0			0/0/0	Shawls, scarves, mufflers, mantillas, veils and the like, containing≥70% by weight of silk
0/0/0	11.2	2.8	1.4/1.4	0/0/0	0/0	0/0/0	0/0/	0/0/12.6	12.7/0			0/0/0	Shawls, scarves, mufflers, mantillas, veils and the like, containing<70% by weight of silk
													-Of wool or fine animal hair:
0/0/0	11.2	2.8	1.4/1.4	0/0/0	0/0	0/0/0	0/0/	0/0/12.6	12.7/0			0/0/0	---Of wool
0/0/0	11.2	2.8	1.4/1.4	0/0/0	0/0	0/0/0	0/0/	0/0/12.6	12.7/0			0/0/0	---Of goats
0/0/0	11.2	2.8	1.4/1.4	0/0/0	0/0	0/0/0	0/0/	0/0/12.6	12.7/0			0/0/0	---Other
0/0/0	12.8	3.2	1.6/1.6	0/0/0	0/0	0/0/0	0/0/	0/0/14.4	14.5/0			0/0/0	-Of synthetic fibres
0/0/0	11.2	2.8	1.4/1.4	0/0/0	0/0	0/0/0	0/0/	0/0/12.6	12.7/0			0/0/0	-Of artificial fibres
													-Of other textile materials
0/0/0	0	2.8	1.4/1.4	0/0/0	0/0	0/0/0	0/0/	0/0/12.6	12.7/0			0/0/0	Shawls, scarves, mufflers, mantillas, veils and the like, of cotton
0/0/0	0	2.8	1.4/1.4	0/0/0	0/0	0/0/0	0/0/	0/0/12.6	12.7/0			0/0/0	Shawls, scarves, mufflers, mantillas, veils and the like, of other textile materials
													Ties, bow ties and cravats:
0/0/0	11.2	2.8	1.4/1.4	0/0/0	0/0	0/0/0	0/0/	0/0/12.6	12.7/0			0/0/0	-Of silk or silk waste
0/0/0	12.8	3.2	1.6/1.6	0/0/0	0/0	0/0/0	0/0/	0/0/14.4	14.5/0			0/0/0	-Of man-made fibres
0/0/0	7	2.8	1.4/1.4	0/0/0	0/0	0/0/0	0/0/	0/0/12.6	12.7/0			0/0/0	-Of other textile materials
													Gloves, mittens and mitts:
0/0/0	0	2.8	1.4/1.4	0/0/0	0/0	0/0/0	0/0/	0/0/12.6	12.7/0			0/0/0	Gloves, mittens and mitts
													Other made up clothing accessories; parts of garments or of clothing accessories, other than those of heading No. 62.12:
													-Accessories:
0/0/0	7	2.8	1.4/1.4	0/0/0	0/0	0/0/0	0/0/0	0/0/12.6	12.7/0			0/0/0	---Stocking, socks and sockettes
0/0/0	5.6	2.8	1.4/1.4	0/0/0	0/0	0/0/0	0/0/0	0/0/12.6	12.7/0			0/0/0	---Kimono belts
0/0/0	0	2.8	1.4/1.4	0/0/0	0/0	0/0/0	0/0/0	0/0/12.6	12.7/0		0/0/0	0/0/0	---Other
0/0/0	0	6.5	1.4/1.4	0/0/0	0/0	0/0/0	0/0/0	13.1/13.3/13.1	13.1/13.3		0/0/0	0/0/0	-Parts

第六十三章
其他纺织制成品；成套物品；旧衣着及旧纺织品；碎织物

注释：

一、第一分章仅适用于各种纺织物制成的物品。

二、第一分章不包括：

(一)第五十六章至第六十二章的货品；

(二)税目 63.09 的旧衣着或其他旧物品。

三、税目 63.09 仅适用于下列货品：

(一)纺织材料制品：

1.衣着和衣着附件及其零件；

2.毯子及旅行毯；

3.床上、餐桌、盥洗及厨房用的织物制品；

4.装饰用织物制品，但税目 57.01 至 57.05 的地毯及税目 58.05 的装饰毯除外。

(二)用石棉以外其他任何材料制成的鞋帽类。

上述物品只有同时符合下列两个条件才能归入本税目：

1.必须明显看得出穿用过；

2.必须以散装、捆装、袋装或类似的大包装形式报验。

子目注释：

一、子目 6304.20 包括用 α-氯氰菊酯(ISO)、虫螨腈(ISO)、溴氰菊酯(INN，ISO)、高效氯氟氰菊酯(ISO)、除虫菊酯(ISO)或甲基嘧啶磷(ISO)浸渍或涂层的经编针织物制品。

税则号列	货品名称〔CIQ 扩展编码及品名－T2 表示见附表 2〕	最惠(%)	暂定税率	普通	增值/消费	出口退税	计量单位	监管条件/特殊证件	检验检疫	对美关税	亚太上/下
	第一分章 其他纺织制成品										
63.01	**毯子及旅行毯：**										
6301.1000	-电暖毯〔101 其它电热器具及其零件，102 毯子〕	6		100	13/	13	条/千克	A/	ML	16	
6301.2000	-羊毛或动物细毛制的毯子(电暖毯除外)及旅行毯										
6301.2000 10	毛制毯子及旅行毯(羊毛或动物细毛制，非电暖的，长度不超过 3 米)〔999〕	6	5	130	13/	13	条/千克	/		30	
6301.2000 20	其他毛制毯子及旅行毯(羊毛或动物细毛制，非电暖的，长度超过 3 米)〔999〕	6	5	130	13/	13	条/千克	/		30	
6301.3000	-棉制的毯子(电暖毯除外)及旅行毯〔999〕	6		90	13/	13	条/千克	/		31	
6301.4000	-合成纤维制的毯子(电暖毯除外)及旅行毯〔999〕	8		130	13/	13	条/千克	/		33	
6301.9000	-其他毯子及旅行毯〔999〕	6		90	13/	13	条/千克	/		31	
63.02	**床上、餐桌、盥洗及厨房用的织物制品：**										
	-针织或钩编的床上用织物制品：										
6302.1010	---棉制〔999〕	6		90	13/	13	条/千克	/			
6302.1090	---其他纺织材料制〔999〕	6		130	13/	13	条/千克	/			
	-其他印花的床上用织物制品：										
	--棉制：										
6302.2110	---床单〔999〕	6		90	13/	13	条/千克	/		31	
6302.2190	---其他〔101 枕芯、枕套，999 其他日用纺织制品〕	6		90	13/	13	条/千克	/		31	
	--化学纤维制：										
6302.2210	---床单〔999〕	6		130	13/	13	条/千克	/		31	
6302.2290	---其他〔101 枕芯、枕套，999 其他日用纺织制品〕	6		130	13/	13	条/千克	/		31	
	--其他纺织材料制：										
6302.2910	---丝及绢丝制〔999〕	6		130	13/	13	条/千克	/		31	
6302.2920	---麻制〔999〕	6		90	13/	13	条/千克	/		16	
6302.2990	---其他〔101 床单、床罩，102 其他日用纺织制品〕	6		100	13/	13	条/千克	/			
	-其他床上用织物制品：										
	--棉制：										
6302.3110	---刺绣的〔999〕	6		90	13/	13	条/千克	/		31	
	---其他：										
6302.3191	----床单〔999〕	6		90	13/	13	条/千克	/		31	
6302.3192	----毛巾被〔999〕	6		90	13/	13	条/千克	/			
6302.3199	----其他〔101 被子，102 枕芯、枕套，999 其他日用纺织制品〕	6		90	13/	13	条/千克	/		31	
	--化学纤维制：										
6302.3210	---刺绣的〔999〕	6		130	13/	13	条/千克	/			
6302.3290	---其他〔101 床单、床罩，102 被子，103 枕芯、枕套，999 其他日用纺织制品〕	6		130	13/	13	条/千克	/		31	
	--其他纺织材料制：										
6302.3910	---丝及绢丝材料										
6302.3910 10	丝及绢丝制其他床上用织物制品(含丝 85%及以上)〔999〕	6		130	13/	13	条/千克	/			
6302.3910 90	丝及绢丝制其他床上用织物制品(含丝 85%以下)〔999〕	6		130	13/	13	条/千克	/			
	---麻制：										
6302.3921	----刺绣的										
6302.3921 10	亚麻或苎麻制其他床上用织物制品(刺绣的)〔999〕	6		90	13/	13	条/千克	/		31	
6302.3921 90	其他麻制其他床上用织物制品(刺绣的)〔999〕	6		90	13/	13	条/千克	/		31	
6302.3929	----其他										
6302.3929 10	亚麻或苎麻制其他床上用织物制品〔999〕	6		90	13/	13	条/千克	/		16	
6302.3929 90	其他麻制其他床上用织物制品〔999〕	6		90	13/	13	条/千克	/		16	
	---其他：										
6302.3991	----刺绣的										
6302.3991 10	毛制刺绣床上用织物制品〔999〕	6		100	13/	13	条/千克	/			

Chapter 63
Other made up textile articles; sets; worn clothing and worn textile articles; rags

Notes:

1. Sub-Chapter 1 applies only to made uparticles,of any textile fabric.
2. Sub-Chapter 1 does not cover:
   (a) Goods of Chapters 56 to 62; or
   (b) Worn clothing or other worn articles of heading No.63. 09.
3. Heading No.63. 09 applies only to the following goods:
   (a) Articles of textile materials:
   (ⅰ) Clothing and clothing accessories,and parts thereof;
   (ⅱ) Blankets and travelling rugs;
   (ⅲ) Bed linen,table linen,toilet lined and kitchen linen;
   (ⅳ) Furnishing articles,other than carpets of headings No.57. 01 to 57. 05 and tapestries of heading No.58. 05;
   (b) Footwear and headgear of any material other than asbestos.
   In order to be classified in this heading,the articles mentioned above must comply with both of the following requirements:
   (ⅰ) They must show signs of appreciable wear,and
   (ⅱ) They must be presented in bulk or in bales,sacks or similar packings.

Subheading Notes:

1. Subheading No. 6304.20 including the use of alpha cypermethrin (ISO), chlorfenapyr (ISO) and deltamethrin (INN, ISO), lambda cyhalothrin (ISO), pyrethrins (ISO) or pirimiphos methyl (ISO) warp knitted fabric impregnated or coated products.

协定税率 %								RCEP		特惠税率 %			Article Description
东/冰/格	巴基斯坦	韩国	瑞士 上/下	哥/秘/柬	澳/毛	新西/坡/智	中国港/澳/台	东盟及马来/澳/韩	日/新	亚太2国	老/柬/缅	98/97/95	
													Ⅰ.-OTHER MADE UP TEXTILE ARTICLES
													Blankets and travelling rugs:
0/0/0	12.8	3.2	1.6/1.6	0/0/0	0/0	0/0/0	0/0/	0/0/14.4	14.5/0			0/0/0	-Electric blankets
													-Blankets(other than electric blankets)and travelling rugs,of wool or of fine animal hair
0/0/0	12.8	3.2	1.6/1.6	0/0/0	0/11.4	0/0/0	0/0/	0/0/14.4	14.5/0			0/0/0	Blankets (other than electric blankets) and travelling rugs,of wool or fine animal hair,length≤3m
0/0/0	12.8	3.2	1.6/1.6	0/0/0	0/11.4	0/0/0	0/0/	0/0/14.4	14.5/0			0/0/0	Other blankets (other than electric blankets) and travelling rugs,of wool or of fine animal hair,length>3m
0/0/0	12.8	3.2	1.6/1.6	0/0/0	0/0	0/0/0	0/0/	0/0/14.4	14.5/0			0/0/0	-Blankets (other than electric blankets) and travelling rugs, of cotton
0/0/0	0	3.5	1.8/1.8	0/0/0	0/0	0/0/0	0/0/	0/0/15.8	15.9/0			0/0/0	-Blankets (other than electric blankets) and travelling rugs, of synthetic fibres
0/0/0	12.8	3.2	1.6/1.6	0/0/0	0/0	0/0/0	0/0/0	0/0/14.4	14.5/0			0/0/0	-Other blankets and travelling rugs
													Bed linen,table linen,toilet linen and kitchen linen:
													-Bed linen,knitted or crocheted:
0/0/0	0	2.8	1.4/1.4	0/0/0	0/0	0/0/0	0/0/	0/0/12.6	12.7/0			0/0/0	---Of cotton
0/0/0	0	2.8	1.4/1.4	0/0/0	0/0	0/0/0	0/0/	0/0/12.6	12.7/0			0/0/0	---Other
													-Other bed linen,printed:
													--Of cotton:
0/0/0	0	2.8	5.9/5.9	0/0/0	0/0	0/0/0	0/0/	0/0/12.6	12.7/0			0/0/0	---Bed sheets
0/0/0	0	2.8	1.4/1.4	0/0/0	0/0	0/0/0	0/0/	0/0/12.6	12.7/0			0/0/0	---Other
													--Of man-made fibres:
0/0/0	0	3.2	1.6/1.6	0/0/0	0/0	0/0/0	0/0/	0/0/14.4	14.5/0			0/0/0	Bed sheets
0/0/0	0	3.2	1.6/1.6	0/0/0	0/0	0/0/0	0/0/	0/0/14.4	14.5/0			0/0/0	---Other
													--Of other textile materials:
0/0/0	0	2.8	1.4/1.4	0/0/0	0/0	0/0/0	0/0/	0/0/12.6	12.7/0			0/0/0	---Of silk or silk waste
0/0/0	0	2.8	1.4/1.4	0/0/0	0/0	0/0/0	0/0/	0/0/12.6	12.7/0			0/0/0	---Of bast fibres
0/0/0	0	2.8	1.4/1.4	0/0/0	0/0	0/0/0	0/0/	0/0/12.6	12.7/0			0/0/0	---Other
													-Other bed linen:
													--Of cotton:
0/0/0	0	2.8	1.4/1.4	0/0/0	0/0	0/0/0	0/0/	0/0/12.6	12.7/0			0/0/0	---Embroidered
													---Other:
0/0/0	0	2.8	1.4/1.4	0/0/0	0/0	0/0/0	0/0/	0/0/12.6	12.7/0			0/0/0	----Bed sheets
0/0/0	0	2.8	1.4/1.4	0/0/0	0/0	0/0/0	0/0/	0/0/12.6	12.7/0			0/0/0	----Towelling coverlets
0/0/0	0	2.8	1.4/1.4	0/0/0	0/0	0/0/0	0/0/	0/0/12.6	12.7/0			0/0/0	----Other
													--Of man-made fibres:
0/0/0	0	3.2	1.6/1.6	0/0/0	0/0	0/0/0	0/0/	0/0/14.4	14.5/0			0/0/0	---Embroidered
0/0/0	0	3.2	1.6/1.6	0/0/0	0/0	0/0/0	0/0/	0/0/14.4	14.5/0			0/0/0	---Other
													--Of other textile materials:
													---Of silk or silk waste
0/0/0	0	2.8	1.4/1.4	0/0/0	0/0	0/0/0	0/0/	0/0/12.6	12.7/0			0/0/0	Other bed linen of silk and silk waste,containing silk≥85%
0/0/0	0	2.8	1.4/1.4	0/0/0	0/0	0/0/0	0/0/	0/0/12.6	12.7/0			0/0/0	Other bed linen of silk and silk waste,containing silk<85%
													---Of bast fibres:
													----Embroidered
0/0/0	0	2.8	1.4/1.4	0/0/0	0/0	0/0/0	0/0/	0/0/12.6	12.7/0			0/0/0	Other bed linen of flax or ramie,embroidered
0/0/0	0	2.8	1.4/1.4	0/0/0	0/0	0/0/0	0/0/	0/0/12.6	12.7/0			0/0/0	Other bed linen of other bast fibres,embroidered
													----Other
0/0/0	0	2.8	1.4/1.4	0/0/0	0/0	0/0/0	0/0/	0/0/12.6	12.7/0			0/0/0	Other bed linen of flax or ramie
0/0/0	0	2.8	1.4/1.4	0/0/0	0/0	0/0/0	0/0/	0/0/12.6	12.7/0			0/0/0	Other bed linen of other bast fibres
													---Other:
													----Embroidered
0/0/0	0	2.8	1.4/1.4	0/0/0	0/0	0/0/0	0/0/	0/0/12.6	12.7/0			0/0/0	Other bed linen of wool or fine animal hair,embroidered

税则号列	货品名称〔CIQ扩展编码及品名—T2表示见附表2〕	最惠(%)	暂定税率	普通	增值/消费	出口退税	计量单位	监管条件/特殊证件	检验检疫	对美关税	亚太上/下
6302.3991 90	其他材料制刺绣床上用织物制品〔999〕	6		100	13/	13	条/千克	/			
6302.3999	----其他										
6302.3999 10	毛制非刺绣床上用织物制品〔999〕	6		100	13/	13	条/千克	/			
6302.3999 90	其他材料制其他床上用织物制品〔999〕	6		100	13/	13	条/千克	/			
	-针织或钩编的餐桌用织物制品：										
6302.4010	---手工制〔999〕	6		100	13/	13	件/千克	/			
6302.4090	---其他〔999〕	6		100	13/	13	件/千克	/			
	-其他餐桌用织物制品：										
	--棉制：										
6302.5110	---刺绣的〔999〕	6		90	13/	13	件/千克	/			
6302.5190	---其他〔999〕	6		90	13/	13	件/千克	/		31	
	--化学纤维制：										
6302.5310	---刺绣的〔999〕	6		130	13/	13	件/千克	/			
6302.5390	---其他										
6302.5390 10	化学纤维无纺织物制餐桌用织物制品〔999〕	6		130	13/	13	件/千克	/		31	
6302.5390 90	化学纤维制其他餐桌用织物制品〔999〕	6		130	13/	13	件/千克	/		31	
	--其他纺织材料制：										
	---亚麻制：										
6302.5911	----刺绣的〔999〕	6		90	13/	13	件/千克	/			
6302.5919	----其他〔999〕	6		90	13/	13	件/千克	/			
6302.5990	---其他										
6302.5990 10	羊毛或动物细毛制餐桌用织物制品〔999〕	6		100	13/	13	件/千克	/			
6302.5990 90	其他纺织材料制餐桌用织物制品〔999〕	6		100	13/	13	件/千克	/			
	-盥洗及厨房用棉制毛巾织物或类似的毛圈织物的制品：										
6302.6010	---浴巾										
6302.6010 10	棉制针织或钩编毛巾织物浴巾(含类似毛圈织物的制品)〔999〕	6		90	13/	13	条/千克	/		31	
6302.6010 90	棉制非针织或非钩编毛巾织物浴巾(含类似毛圈织物的制品)〔999〕	6		90	13/	13	条/千克	/		31	
6302.6090	---其他〔999〕	6		90	13/	13	条/千克	/		31	
	-其他：										
6302.9100	--棉制〔999〕	6		90	13/	13	条/千克	/		31	
6302.9300	--化学纤维制										
6302.9300 10	化学纤维无纺织物制盥洗及厨房制品〔999〕	6		130	13/	13	条/千克	/		31	
6302.9300 90	化学纤维制其他盥洗及厨房织物制品〔999〕	6		130	13/	13	条/千克	/		31	
	--其他纺织材料制：										
6302.9910	---亚麻制〔999〕	6		90	13/	13	条/千克	/			
6302.9990	---其他										
6302.9990 10	毛制盥洗及厨房用织物制品〔999〕	6		100	13/	13	条/千克	/			
6302.9990 90	其他材料制盥洗及厨房织物制品〔999〕	6		100	13/	13	条/千克	/			
63.03	**窗帘(包括帷帘)及帐幔；帘帷或床帷：**										
	-针织或钩编的：										
	--合成纤维制：										
6303.1210	---针织的										
6303.1210 10	合成纤维制针织百叶窗、卷帘和窗幔〔999〕	6		130	13/	13	千克	/		31	
6303.1210 90	其他合成纤维制针织窗帘等(包括帷帘、帐幔、帘帷及床帷)〔999〕	6		130	13/	13	千克	/		31	
6303.1220	---钩编的										
6303.1220 10	合成纤维制钩编百叶窗、卷帘和窗幔〔999〕	6		130	13/	13	千克	/			
6303.1220 90	其他合成纤维制钩编的窗帘等(包括帷帘、帐幔、帘帷及床帷)〔999〕	6		130	13/	13	千克	/			
	--其他纺织材料制：										
	---棉制：										
6303.1931	----针织的〔999〕	6		90	13/	13	千克	/		16	
6303.1932	----钩编的〔999〕	6		90	13/	13	千克	/			
	---其他纺织材料制：										
6303.1991	----针织的〔999〕	6		130	13/	13	千克	/		16	
6303.1992	----钩编的〔999〕	6		130	13/	13	千克	/			
	-其他：										
6303.9100	--棉制										
6303.9100 10	棉制非针织网眼窗帘(包括帷帘、帐幔、帘帷及床帷)〔999〕	6		90	13/	13	千克	/		31	
6303.9100 90	棉制非针织非钩编窗帘(包括帷帘、帐幔、帘帷及床帷)〔999〕	6		90	13/	13	千克	/		31	
6303.9200	--合成纤维制										
6303.9200 10	合成纤维百叶窗、卷帘和窗幔(非针织非钩编)〔999〕	6		130	13/	13	千克	/		31	
6303.9200 90	其他合成纤维制非针织非钩编窗帘等(包括帷帘、帐幔、帘帷及床帷)〔999〕	6		130	13/	13	千克	/		31	
6303.9900	--其他纺织材料制〔999〕	6		100	13/	13	千克	/		31	
63.04	**其他装饰用织物制品，但税目94.04的货品除外：**										
	-床罩：										

协定税率 %								RCEP		特惠税率 %			Article Description
东/冰/格	巴基斯坦	韩国	瑞士 上/下	哥/秘/柬	澳/毛	新西/坡/智	中国港/澳/台	东盟及马来/澳/韩	日/新	亚太2国	老/柬/缅	98/97/95	
0/0/0	0	2.8	1.4/1.4	0/0/0	0/0	0/0/0	0/0/	0/0/12.6	12.7/0			0/0/0	Other bed linen of other textile materials, embroidered
													----Other
0/0/0	0	2.8	1.4/1.4	0/0/0	0/8.4	0/0/0	0/0/	0/0/12.6	12.7/0			0/0/0	Other bed linen of wool or fine animal hair, embroidered
0/0/0	0	2.8	1.4/1.4	0/0/0	0/8.4	0/0/0	0/0/	0/0/12.6	12.7/0			0/0/0	Other bed linen of other textile materials
													-Table linen, knitted or crocheted:
0/0/0	0	2.8	1.4/1.4	0/0/0	0/0	0/0/0	0/0/	0/0/12.6	12.7/0			0/0/0	---Hand-worked
0/0/0	0	2.8	1.4/1.4	0/0/0	0/0	0/0/0	0/0/	0/0/12.6	12.7/0			0/0/0	---Other
													-Other table linen:
													--Of cotton:
0/0/0	0	2.8	1.4/1.4	0/0/0	0/0	0/0/0	0/0/	0/0/12.6	12.7/0			0/0/0	---Embroidered
0/0/0	0	2.8	1.4/1.4	0/0/0	0/0	0/0/0	0/0/	0/0/12.6	12.7/0			0/0/0	---Other
													--Of man-made fibres:
0/0/0	0	2.8	1.4/1.4	0/0/0	0/0	0/0/0	0/0/	0/0/12.6	12.7/0			0/0/0	---Embroidered
													---Other
0/0/0	0	3.2	1.6/1.6	0/0/0	0/0	0/0/0	0/0/	0/0/14.4	14.5/0			0/0/0	Table linen made up of nonwoven fabrics of man-made fibres
0/0/0	0	3.2	1.6/1.6	0/0/0	0/0	0/0/0	0/0/	0/0/14.4	14.5/0			0/0/0	Other table linen of man-made fibres
													--Of other textile materials:
													---Of flax:
0/0/0	0	2.8	1.4/1.4	0/0/0	0/0	0/0/0	0/0/	0/0/12.6	12.7/0			0/0/0	----Embroidered
0/0/0	0	2.8	1.4/1.4	0/0/0	0/0	0/0/0	0/0/	0/0/12.6	12.7/0			0/0/0	----Other
													---Other
0/0/0	0	2.8	1.4/1.4	0/0/0	0/0	0/0/0	0/0/	0/0/12.6	12.7/0			0/0/0	Table linen of wool or other fine animal hair
0/0/0	0	2.8	1.4/1.4	0/0/0	0/0	0/0/0	0/0/	0/0/12.6	12.7/0			0/0/0	Table linen of other textile materials
													-Toilet linen and kitchen linen, of terry towelling or similar terry fabrics, of cotton:
													---Bath towels
0/0/0	0	2.8	1.4/1.4	0/0/0	0/0	0/0/0	0/0/0	0/0/12.6	12.7/0			0/0/0	Bath towels, of terry towelling or similar terry fabrics, of cotton, knitted or crocheted
0/0/0	0	2.8	1.4/1.4	0/0/0	0/0	0/0/0	0/0/0	0/0/12.6	12.7/0			0/0/0	Bath towels, of terry towelling or similar terry fabrics, of cotton, not knitted or crocheted
0/0/0	0	2.8	1.4/1.4	0/0/0	0/0	0/0/0	0/0/0	0/0/12.6	12.7/0			0/0/0	---Other
													-Other:
0/0/0	0	2.8	1.4/1.4	0/0/0	0/0	0/0/0	0/0/	0/0/12.6	12.7/0			0/0/0	--Of cotton
													--Of man-made fibres
0/0/0	0	3.2	1.6/1.6	0/0/0	0/0	0/0/0	0/0/	0/0/14.4	14.5/0			0/0/0	Toilet linen and kitchen linen of nonwoven fabrics of man-made fibres
0/0/0	0	3.2	1.6/1.6	0/0/0	0/0	0/0/0	0/0/	0/0/14.4	14.5/0			0/0/0	Other toilet linen and kitchen linen of man-made fibres
													--Of other textile materials:
0/0/0	0	2.8	1.4/1.4	0/0/0	0/0	0/0/0	0/0/	0/0/12.6	12.7/0			0/0/0	---Of flax
													---Other
0/0/0	0	2.8	1.4/1.4	0/0/0	0/0	0/0/0	0/0/	0/0/12.6	12.7/0			0/0/0	Other toilet linen and kitchen linen, of wool or fine animal hair
0/0/0	0	2.8	1.4/1.4	0/0/0	0/0	0/0/0	0/0/	0/0/12.6	12.7/0			0/0/0	Other toilet linen and kitchen linen of other textile materials
													Curtains (including drapes) and interior blinds; curtain or bed valances:
													-Knitted or crocheted:
													--Of synthetic fibres:
													---Knitted
0/0/0	0	3.2	1.6/1.6	0/0/0	0/0	0/0/0	0/0/	0/0/14.4	14.5/0			0/0/0	Shutter, valance, roller shutter, of knitted, of synthetic fibres
0/0/0	0	3.2	1.6/1.6	0/0/0	0/0	0/0/0	0/0/	0/0/14.4	14.5/0			0/0/0	Curtains, of knitted, of synthetic fibres (including drapes, interior blinds, curtain and bed valances)
													---Crocheted
0/0/0	0	3.2	1.6/1.6	0/0/0	0/0	0/0/0	0/0/	0/0/14.4	14.5/0			0/0/0	Shutter, valance, roller shutter, of crocheted, of synthetic fibres
0/0/0	0	3.2	1.6/1.6	0/0/0	0/0	0/0/0	0/0/	0/0/14.4	14.5/0			0/0/0	Other curtains of crocheted, of synthetic fibres etc (including drapes, inter, or blinds, curtain and bed valances)
													--Of other textile materials:
													---Of cotton:
0/0/0	0	2.8	1.4/1.4	0/0/0	0/0	0/0/0	0/0/	0/0/12.6	12.7/0			0/0/0	----Knitted
0/0/0	0	2.8	1.4/1.4	0/0/0	0/0	0/0/0	0/0/	0/0/12.6	12.7/0			0/0/0	----Crocheted
													---Of other textile materials:
0/0/0	0	2.8	1.4/1.4	0/0/0	0/0	0/0/0	0/0/	0/0/12.6	12.7/0			0/0/0	----Knitted
0/0/0	0	2.8	1.4/1.4	0/0/0	0/0	0/0/0	0/0/	0/0/12.6	12.7/0			0/0/0	----Crocheted
													-Other:
													--Of cotton
0/0/0	0	2.8	1.4/1.4	0/0/0	0/0	0/0/0	0/0/	0/0/12.6	12.7/0			0/0/0	Curtains(including drapes, interior blinds, curtain or bed valances) of cotton, nets, not knitted
0/0/0	0	2.8	1.4/1.4	0/0/0	0/0	0/0/0	0/0/	0/0/12.6	12.7/0			0/0/0	Curtains (including drapes, interior blinds, curtain or bed valances) of cotton, nets, not knitted or crocheted
													--Of synthetic fibres
0/0/0	0	3.2	1.6/1.6	0/0/0	0/0	0/0/0	0/0/	0/0/14.4	14.5/0			0/0/0	Shutter, valance, roller shutter, of synthetic fibres, not knittedor crocheted
0/0/0	0	3.2	1.6/1.6	0/0/0	0/0	0/0/0	0/0/	0/0/14.4	14.5/0			0/0/0	Curtains (including drapes) and interior blinds; curtain or bed valances, of synthetic fibres, not knitted or crocheted
0/0/0	0	2.8	1.4/1.4	0/0/0	0/0	0/0/0	0/0/	0/0/12.6	12.7/0			0/0/0	--Of other textile materials
													Other furnishing articles, excluding those of heading No.94.04:
													-Bedspreads:

税则号列		货品名称〔CIQ扩展编码及品名－T2表示见附表2〕	最惠(%)	暂定税率	普通	增值/消费	出口退税	计量单位	监管条件/特殊证件	检验检疫	对美关税	亚太上/下
		--针织或钩编的：										
		---针织的：										
6304.1121		----手工制〔999〕	6		100	13/	13	件/千克	/			
6304.1129		----其他〔999〕	6		100	13/	13	件/千克	/		31	
		---钩编的：										
6304.1131		----手工制〔999〕	6		100	13/	13	件/千克	/			
6304.1139		----其他〔999〕	6		100	13/	13	件/千克	/		31	
		--其他：										
6304.1910		---丝及绢丝制										
6304.1910	10	丝及绢丝制非针织非钩编床罩(含丝85%及以上)〔999〕	6		130	13/	13	件/千克	/			
6304.1910	90	丝及绢丝制非针织非钩编床罩(含丝85%以下)〔999〕	6		130	13/	13	件/千克	/			
		---棉或麻制：										
6304.1921		----刺绣的〔999〕	6		90	13/	13	件/千克	/			
6304.1929		----其他〔999〕	6		90	13/	13	件/千克	/		31	
		---化学纤维制：										
6304.1931		----刺绣的〔999〕	6		130	13/	13	件/千克	/			
6304.1939		----其他〔999〕	6		130	13/	13	件/千克	/			
		---其他纺织材料制：										
6304.1991		----刺绣的										
6304.1991	10	毛制非针织非钩编刺绣床罩(羊毛或动物细毛制)〔999〕	6		100	13/	13	件/千克	/			
6304.1991	90	其他纺织材料制非针织刺绣床罩(含非钩编的)〔999〕	6		100	13/	13	件/千克	/			
6304.1999		----其他										
6304.1999	10	毛制其他非针织非钩编床罩(羊毛或动物细毛制)〔999〕	6		100	13/	13	件/千克	/			
6304.1999	90	其他材料制非针织非钩编其他床罩〔999〕	6		100	13/	13	件/千克	/			
		-本章子目注释一所列的蚊帐：										
6304.2010		---手工制〔999〕	6		100	13/	13	件/千克	S/			
6304.2090		---其他〔999〕	6		100	13/	13	件/千克	S/			
		-其他：										
		--针织或钩编的：										
		---针织的：										
6304.9121		----手工制〔999〕	6		100	13/	13	千克	/			
6304.9129		----其他〔999〕	6		100	13/	13	千克	/		31	
		---钩编的：										
6304.9131		----手工制〔999〕	6		100	13/	13	千克	/			
6304.9139		----其他〔999〕	6		100	13/	13	千克	/			
		--非针织或非钩编的，棉制：										
6304.9210		---刺绣的〔999〕	6		90	13/	13	千克	/		31	
6304.9290		---其他〔999〕	6		90	13/	13	千克	/		31	
		--非针织或非钩编的，合成纤维制：										
6304.9310		---刺绣的〔999〕	6		130	13/	13	千克	/			
6304.9390		---其他〔999〕	6		130	13/	13	千克	/		16	
		--非针织或非钩编的，其他纺织材料制：										
6304.9910		---丝及绢丝制										
6304.9910	10	丝制非针织非钩编的装饰制品(含绢丝制品，含丝85%及以上)〔999〕	6		130	13/	13	千克	/			
6304.9910	90	丝制非针织非钩编的装饰制品(含绢丝制品，含丝85%以下)〔999〕	6		130	13/	13	千克	/			
		---麻制：										
6304.9921		----刺绣的										
6304.9921	10	亚麻或苎麻非针织其他刺绣装饰品(含非钩编制品)〔999〕	6		90	13/	13	千克	/			
6304.9921	90	其他麻制非针织其他刺绣装饰品(包括非钩编的)〔999〕	6		90	13/	13	千克	/			
6304.9929		----其他										
6304.9929	10	亚麻或苎麻制其他非针织的装饰品(含非钩编制品)〔999〕	6		90	13/	13	千克	/		16	
6304.9929	90	其他麻制其他非针织的装饰制品(含非钩编制品)〔999〕	6		90	13/	13	千克	/		16	
6304.9990		---其他〔999〕	6		100	13/	13	千克	/		16	
63.05		**货物包装用袋：**										
6305.1000		-黄麻或税目53.03的其他韧皮纺织纤维制										
6305.1000	10	黄麻制旧的货物包装袋(含税目53.03的其他韧皮纤维制)〔999〕	4		40	13/	13	条/千克	/			
6305.1000	90	黄麻制其他货物包装袋(含税目53.03的其他韧皮纤维制)〔999〕	4		40	13/	13	条/千克	/			
6305.2000		-棉制〔999〕	6		90	13/	13	条/千克	/		31	
		-化学纤维材料制：										
6305.3200		--散装货物储运软袋〔999〕	6		100	13/	13	条/千克	/		31	
6305.3300		--其他，聚乙烯、聚丙烯扁条或类似材料制										

协定税率 %								RCEP		特惠税率 %			Article Description
东/冰/格	巴基斯坦	韩国	瑞士上/下	哥/秘/柬	澳/毛	新西/坡/智	中国港/澳/台	东盟及马来/澳/韩	日/新	亚太2国	老/柬/缅	98/97/95	
													--Knitted or crocheted:
													---Knitted:
0/0/0	7	2.8	1.4/1.4	0/0/0	0/0	0/0/0	0/0/	0/0/12.6	12.7/0			0/0/0	----Hand-worked
0/0/0	5.6	2.8	1.4/1.4	0/0/0	0/0	0/0/0	0/0/	0/0/12.6	12.7/0			0/0/0	----Other
													---Crocheted:
0/0/0	7	2.8	1.4/1.4	0/0/0	0/0	0/0/0	0/0/	0/0/12.6	12.7/0			0/0/0	----Hand-worked
0/0/0	7	2.8	1.4/1.4	0/0/0	0/0	0/0/0	0/0/	0/0/12.6	12.7/0			0/0/0	----Other
													--Other:
													---Of silk or silk waste
0/0/0	0	2.8	1.4/1.4	0/0/0	0/0	0/0/0	0/0/	0/0/12.6	12.7/0			0/0/0	Bedspreads of silk or silk waste, containing silk≥85%, not knitted or crocheted
0/0/0	0	2.8	1.4/1.4	0/0/0	0/0	0/0/0	0/0/	0/0/12.6	12.7/0			0/0/0	Bedspreads of silk or silk waste, containing silk<85%, not knitted or crocheted
													---Of cotton or bast fibres:
0/0/0	0	2.8	1.4/1.4	0/0/0	0/0	0/0/0	0/0/	0/0/12.6	12.7/0			0/0/0	----Embroidered
0/0/0	0	2.8	1.4/1.4	0/0/0	0/0	0/0/0	0/0/	0/0/12.6	12.7/0			0/0/0	----Other
													---Of man-made fibres:
0/0/0	12.8	3.2	1.6/1.6	0/0/0	0/0	0/0/0	0/0/	0/0/14.4	14.5/0			0/0/0	----Embroidered
0/0/0	12.8	3.2	1.6/1.6	0/0/0	0/0	0/0/0	0/0/	0/0/14.4	14.5/0			0/0/0	----Other
													---Of other textile materials:
													----Embroidered
0/0/0	7	2.8	1.4/1.4	0/0/0	0/0	0/0/0	0/0/	0/0/12.6	12.7/0			0/0/0	Bedspreads, not knitted or crocheted, embroidered, of wool or fine animal hair
0/0/0	7	2.8	1.4/1.4	0/0/0	0/0	0/0/0	0/0/	0/0/12.6	12.7/0			0/0/0	Bedspreads, not knitted or crocheted, embroidered, of other textile materials
													----Other
0/0/0	7	2.8	1.4/1.4	0/0/0	0/0	0/0/0	0/0/	0/0/12.6	12.7/0			0/0/0	Bedspreads, not knitted or crocheted, embroidered, of wool or fine animal hair
0/0/0	7	2.8	1.4/1.4	0/0/0	0/0	0/0/0	0/0/	0/0/12.6	12.7/0			0/0/0	Bedspreads, not knitted or crocheted, embroidered, of other textile materials
													-Mosquito net in Subheading Note 1 to this chapter
0/0/0	7	2.8	1.4/1.4	0/0/0	0/0	0/0/0	0/0/	0/0/12.6	12.7/0			0/0/0	---Hand-worked
0/0/0	7	2.8	1.4/1.4	0/0/0	0/0	0/0/0	0/0/	0/0/12.6	12.7/0			0/0/0	---Other
													-Other:
													--Knitted or crocheted:
													---Knitted:
0/0/0	7	2.8	1.4/1.4	0/0/0	0/0	0/0/0	0/0/	0/0/12.6	12.7/0			0/0/0	----Hand-worked
0/0/0	7	2.8	1.4/1.4	0/0/0	0/0	0/0/0	0/0/	0/0/12.6	12.7/0			0/0/0	----Other
													---Crocheted:
0/0/0	11.2	2.8	1.4/1.4	0/0/0	0/0	0/0/0	0/0/	0/0/12.6	12.7/0			0/0/0	----Hand-worked
0/0/0	5.6	2.8	1.4/1.4	0/0/0	0/0	0/0/0	0/0/	0/0/12.6	12.7/0			0/0/0	----Other
													--Not knitted or crocheted, of cotton:
0/0/0	7	2.8	1.4/1.4	0/0/0	0/0	0/0/0	0/0/	0/0/12.6	12.7/0			0/0/0	---Embroidered
0/0/0	0	2.8	1.4/1.4	0/0/0	0/0	0/0/0	0/0/	0/0/12.6	12.7/0			0/0/0	---Other
													--Not knitted or crocheted, of synthetic fibres:
0/0/0	12.8	3.2	1.6/1.6	0/0/0	0/0	0/0/0	0/0/	0/0/14.4	14.5/0			0/0/0	---Embroidered
0/0/0	12.8	3.2	1.6/1.6	0/0/0	0/0	0/0/0	0/0/	0/0/14.4	14.5/0			0/0/0	---Other
													--Not knitted or crocheted, of other textile materials:
													---Of silk or silk waste
0/0/0	7	2.8	1.4/1.4	0/0/0	0/0	0/0/0	0/0/	0/0/12.6	12.7/0			0/0/0	Other furnishing articles of silk or silk waste, not knitted or crocheted, containing silk≥85%
0/0/0	7	2.8	1.4/1.4	0/0/0	0/0	0/0/0	0/0/	0/0/12.6	12.7/0			0/0/0	Other furnishing articles of silk or silk waste, not knitted or crocheted, containing silk<85%
													---Of bast fibres:
													----Embroidered
0/0/0	7	2.8	1.4/1.4	0/0/0	0/0	0/0/0	0/0/	0/0/12.6	12.7/0			0/0/0	Other furnishing articles, not knitted or crocheted, embroidered, of flax or ramie
0/0/0	7	2.8	1.4/1.4	0/0/0	0/0	0/0/0	0/0/	0/0/12.6	12.7/0			0/0/0	Other furnishing articles, not knitted or crocheted, embroidered, of other bast fibres
													----Other
0/0/0	7	2.8	1.4/1.4	0/0/0	0/0	0/0/0	0/0/	0/0/12.6	12.7/0			0/0/0	Other furnishing articles, not knitted or crocheted, of flax or ramie
0/0/0	7	2.8	1.4/1.4	0/0/0	0/0	0/0/0	0/0/	0/0/12.6	12.7/0			0/0/0	Other furnishing articles not knitted or crocheted, of other bast fibres
0/0/0	0	2.8	1.4/1.4	0/0/0	0/0	0/0/0	0/0/	0/0/12.6	12.7/0			0/0/0	---Other
													Sacks and bags, of a kind used for the packing of goods:
													-Of jute or of other textile bast fibres of heading No.53.03
0/0/0	3.5	0	0/0	0/0/0	0/0	0//0	0/0/	0/0/0	9.1/0	0		0/0/0	Sacks and bags, of a kind used for the packing of goods, of jute or of other textile bast fibres of heading No.53.03
0/0/0	3.5	0	0/0	0/0/0	0/0	0//0	0/0/	0/0/0	9.1/0	0		0/0/0	Other sacks and bags, of a kind used for the packing of goods, of jute or of other textile bast fibres of heading No.53.03
0/0/0	0	3.2	1.6/1.6	0/0/0	0/0	0/0/0	0/0/	0/0/14.4	14.5/0			0/0/0	-Of cotton
													-Of man-made textile materials:
0/0/0	12.8	3.2	1.6/1.6	0/0/0	0/0	0/0/0	0/0/	0/0/14.4	14.5/0			0/0/0	--Flexible intermediate bulk containers
													--Other, of polyethylene or polypropylene strip or the like

税则号列	货品名称〔CIQ 扩展编码及品名—T2 表示见附表 2〕	最惠(%)	暂定税率	普通	增值/消费	出口退税	计量单位	监管条件/特殊证件	检验检疫	对美关税	亚太上/下
6305.3300 10	聚乙烯或聚丙烯制其他货物包装袋(针织或钩编的,用扁条及类似材料制成)〔999〕	6		100	13/	13	条/千克	/		31	3.9/3.9
6305.3300 90	聚乙烯或聚丙烯制其他货物包装袋(非针织或钩编的,用扁条及类似材料制成)〔999〕	6		100	13/	13	条/千克	/		31	3.9/3.9
6305.3900	--其他〔999〕	6		100	13/	13	条/千克	/		31	
6305.9000	-其他纺织材料制〔999〕	6		90	13/	13	条/千克	/		31	
63.06	**油苫布、天篷及遮阳篷;帐篷(包括临时顶篷及类似品);风帆;野营用品:**										
	-油苫布、天篷及遮阳篷:										
6306.1200	--合成纤维制〔999〕	6		130	13/	13	件/千克	/		31	
	--其他纺织材料制:										
6306.1910	---麻制〔999〕	6		80	13/	13	件/千克	/		16	
6306.1920	---棉制〔999〕	6		80	13/	13	件/千克	/			
6306.1990	---其他										
6306.1990 10	人造纤维制油苫布、天篷及遮阳篷〔999〕	6		100	13/	13	件/千克	/		16	
6306.1990 90	其他材料制油苫布、天篷及遮阳篷〔999〕	6		100	13/	13	件/千克	/		16	
	-帐篷(包括临时顶篷及类似品):										
6306.2200	--合成纤维制										
6306.2200 10	合纤制移动帐篷(包括临时顶篷及类似品)〔999〕	6		130	13/	13	件/千克	/		31	
6306.2200 90	其他合纤制帐篷(包括临时顶篷及类似品)〔999〕	6		130	13/	13	件/千克	/		31	
	--其他纺织材料制:										
6306.2910	---棉制〔999〕	6		80	13/	13	件/千克	/		31	
6306.2990	---其他〔999〕	6		100	13/	13	件/千克	/		31	
	-风帆:										
6306.3010	---合成纤维制〔999〕	6		130	13/	13	件/千克	/		16	
6306.3090	---其他纺织材料制〔999〕	6		100	13/	13	件/千克	/			
	-充气褥垫:										
6306.4010	---棉制〔999〕	6		80	13/	13	件/千克	/			
6306.4020	---化学纤维制〔999〕	6		130	13/	13	件/千克	/		31	
6306.4090	---其他〔999〕	6		100	13/	13	件/千克	/		16	
	-其他:										
6306.9010	---棉制〔999〕	6		80	13/	13	件/千克	/			
6306.9020	---麻制〔999〕	6		80	13/	13	件/千克	/			
6306.9030	---化学纤维制〔999〕	6		130	13/	13	件/千克	/		31	
6306.9090	---其他〔999〕	6		100	13/	13	件/千克	/			
63.07	**其他制成品,包括服装裁剪样:**										
6307.1000	-擦地布、擦碗布、抹布及类似擦拭用布〔999〕	6		130	13/	13	千克	/		31	3.9/3.9
6307.2000	-救生衣及安全带〔999〕	6		70	13/	13	千克/件	/		16	
	-其他:										
6307.9010	---口罩										
6307.9010 10	医疗或外科口罩((C))〔999〕	6		100	13/	13	千克/个	/		31	
6307.9010 90	其他口罩((C))〔999〕	6		100	13/	13	千克/个	/		31	
6307.9090	---其它〔999〕	6		100	13/	13	千克/个	/		31	
	第二分章　成套物品										
63.08	**由机织物及纱线构成的零售包装成套物品,不论是否带附件,用以制作小地毯、装饰毯、绣花台布、餐巾或类似的纺织物品:**										
6308.0000	由机织物及纱线构成的零售包装成套物品,不论是否带附件,用以制作小地毯、装饰毯、绣花台布、餐巾或类似的纺织物品〔998 其他装饰用纺织制品,999 其他纺织制品〕	6		130	13/	13	千克	/		31	
	第三分章　旧衣着及旧纺织品;碎织物										
63.09	旧衣物:										
6309.0000	旧衣物〔999〕	6		130	13/	0	千克	9/			
63.10	**新或旧的破、碎织物,线、绳、索、缆的废、碎料以及线、绳、索、缆或纺织材料的破旧制品:**										
6310.1000	-经分拣的										
6310.1000 10	新的或未使用过的纺织材料制经分拣的碎织物等(新的或未使用过的,包括废线、绳、索、缆及其制品)〔999〕	6		50	13/	13	千克	9/		31	
6310.1000 90	其他纺织材料制经分拣的碎织物等(包括废线、绳、索、缆及其制品)〔999〕	6		50	13/	13	千克	9/		31	
6310.9000	-其他										
6310.9000 10	新的或未使用过的纺织材料制其他碎织物等(新的或未使用过的,包括废线、绳、索、缆及其制品)〔999〕	6		50	13/	13	千克	9/		31	
6310.9000 90	其他纺织材料制碎织物等(包括废线、绳、索、缆及其制品)〔999〕	6		50	13/	13	千克	9/		31	

协定税率 %								RCEP		特惠税率 %			Article Description
东/冰/格	巴基斯坦	韩国	瑞士上/下	哥/秘/柬	澳/毛	新西/坡/智	中国港/澳/台	东盟及马来/澳/韩	日/新	亚太2国	老/柬/缅	98/97/95	
0/0/0	0	3.2	1.6/1.6	0/0/0	0/0	0/0/0	0/0/	0/0/14.4	14.5/0			0/0/0	Sacks and bags, of a kind used for the packing of goods, of PE or PP strip or the like, knitted or crocheted
0/0/0	0	3.2	1.6/1.6	0/0/0	0/0	0/0/0	0/0/	0/0/14.4	14.5/0			0/0/0	Sacks and bags, of a kind used for the packing of goods, of PE or PP strip or the like, not knitted or crocheted
0/0/0	0	3.2	1.6/1.6	0/0/0	0/0	0/0/0	0/0/	0/0/14.4	14.5/0			0/0/0	--Other
0/0/0	0	2.8	1.4/1.4	0/0/0	0/0	0/0/0	0/0/	0/0/12.6	12.7/0			0/0/0	-Of other textile materials
													Tarpaulins, awnings and sunblinds; tents (including temporary canopies and similar articles); sails for boats, sailboards or landcraft; camping goods:
													-Tarpaulins, awnings and sunblinds:
0/0/0	0	3.2	1.6/1.6	0/0/0	0/0	0/0/0	0/0/	0/0/14.4	14.5/0			0/0/0	--Of synthetic fibres
													--Of other textile materials:
0/0/0	0	2.8	1.4/1.4	0/0/0	0/0	0/0/0	0/0/	0/0/12.6	12.7/0			0/0/0	---Of bast fibres
0/0/0	0	2.8	1.4/1.4	0/0/0	0/0	0/0/0	0/0/	0/0/12.6	12.7/0			0/0/0	---Of cotton
													---Other
0/0/0	0	2.8	1.4/1.4	0/0/0	0/0	0/0/0	0/0/	0/0/12.6	12.7/0			0/0/0	Tarpaulins, awnings and sunblinds, of artificial fibres
0/0/0	0	2.8	1.4/1.4	0/0/0	0/0	0/0/0	0/0/	0/0/12.6	12.7/0			0/0/0	Tarpaulins, awnings and sunblinds, of other textile materials
													-Tents (including temporary canopies and similar articles):
													--Of synthetic fibres
0/0/0	0	3.2	1.6/1.6	0/0/0	0/0	0/0/0	0/0/	0/0/14.4	14.5/0			0/0/0	Moveable, of synthetic fibres
0/0/0	0	3.2	1.6/1.6	0/0/0	0/0	0/0/0	0/0/	0/0/14.4	14.5/0			0/0/0	Other synthetic fiber tents
													--Of other textile materials:
0/0/0	0	2.8	1.4/1.4	0/0/0	0/0	0/0/0	0/0/	0/0/12.6	12.7/0			0/0/0	---Of cotton
0/0/0	0	2.8	1.4/1.4	0/0/0	0/0	0/0/0	0/0/	0/0/12.6	12.7/0			0/0/0	---Other
													-Sails:
0/0/0	0	3.2	1.6/1.6	0/0/0	0/0	0/0/0	0/0/	0/0/14.4	14.5/0			0/0/0	---Of synthetic fibres
0/0/0	0	2.8	1.4/1.4	0/0/0	0/0	0/0/0	0/0/	0/0/12.6	12.7/0			0/0/0	---Of other textile materials
													-Pneumatic mattresses:
0/0/0	0	2.8	1.4/1.4	0/0/0	0/0	0/0/0	0/0/	0/0/12.6	12.7/0			0/0/0	--Of cotton
0/0/0	0	3.2	1.6/1.6	0/0/0	0/0	0/0/0	0/0/	0/0/14.4	14.5/0			0/0/0	---Of man-made fibres
0/0/0	0	2.8	1.4/1.4	0/0/0	0/0	0/0/0	0/0/	0/0/12.6	12.7/0			0/0/0	---Of other textile materials
													-Other:
0/0/0	0	2.8	1.4/1.4	0/0/0	0/0	0/0/0	0/0/	0/0/12.6	12.7/0			0/0/0	---Of cotton
0/0/0	0	2.8	1.4/1.4	0/0/0	0/0	0/0/0	0/0/	0/0/12.6	12.7/0			0/0/0	---Of bast fibres
0/0/0	0	3.2	1.6/1.6	0/0/0	0/0	0/0/0	0/0/	0/0/14.4	14.5/0			0/0/0	---Of man-made fibres
0/0/0	0	2.8	1.4/1.4	0/0/0	0/0	0/0/0	0/0/	0/0/12.6	12.7/0			0/0/0	---Other
													Other made up articles, including dress patterns:
0/0/0	0	2.8	1.4/1.4	0/0/0	0/0	0/0/0	0/0/0	0/0/12.6	12.7/0			0/0/0	-Floor-cloths, dish-cloths, dusters and similar cleaning cloths
0/0/0	11.2	2.8	1.4/1.4	0/0/0	0/0	0/0/0	0/0/	0/0/12.6	12.7/0			0/0/0	-Life-jackets and life-belts
													-Other:
													---Mask
0/0/0	0	6.5	1.4/1.4	0/0/0	0/0	0/0/0	0/0/	13.1/13.3/13.1	13.1/13.3		0/0/0	0/0/0	Medical or surgical masks ((c))
0/0/0	0	6.5	1.4/1.4	0/0/0	0/0	0/0/0	0/0/	13.1/13.3/13.1	13.1/13.3		0/0/0	0/0/0	Other masks ((c))
0/0/0	0	6.5	1.4/1.4	0/0/0	0/0	0/0/0	0/0/	13.1/13.3/13.1	13.1/13.3		0/0/0	0/0/0	---Other
													Ⅱ. SETS
													Sets consisting of woven fabric and yarn, whether or not with accessories, for making up into rugs, tapestries, embroidered table cloths or serviettes, or similar textile articles, put up in packings for retail sale:
0/0/0	7	2.8	1.4/1.4	0/0/0	0/0	0/0/0	0/0/	0/0/12.6	12.7/0			0/0/0	Sets consisting of woven fabric and yarn, whether or not with accessories, for making up into rugs, tapestries, embroidered table cloths or serviettes, or similar textile articles, put up in packings for retail sale
													Ⅲ. WORN CLOTHING AND WORN TEXTILE ARTICLES; RAGS
													Worn clothing and other worn articles:
0/0/0	7	2.8	1.4/1.4	0/0/0	0/0	0/0/0	0/0/	0/0/12.6	12.7/0			0/0/0	Worn clothing and other worn articles
													Used or new rags, scrap twine, cordage, rope and cables and worn out articles of twine, cordage, rope or cables, of textile materials:
													-Sorted
0/0/0	0	2.8	1.4/1.4	0/0/0	0/8.4	0/0/0	0/0/	12.6/12.6/12.6	12.7/12.6			0/0/0	Not used or new rags, scrap twine, cordage, rope and cables and worn out articles of twine, cordage, rope or cables, of textile materials, sorted
0/0/0	0	2.8	1.4/1.4	0/0/0	0/8.4	0/0/0	0/0/	12.6/12.6/12.6	12.7/12.6			0/0/0	Other sorted rags, including scrap twine, cordage, rope and cables and worn out articles of twine, of textile materials
													-Other
0/0/0	0	2.8	1.4/1.4	0/0/0	0/0	0/0/0	0/0/	12.6/12.6/12.6	12.7/12.6		0/0/0	0/0/0	Not used or new rags, scrap twine, cordage, rope and cables and worn out articles of twine, cordage, rope or cables, of textile materials
0/0/0	0	2.8	1.4/1.4	0/0/0	0/0	0/0/0	0/0/	12.6/12.6/12.6	12.7/12.6		0/0/0	0/0/0	Other rags, scrap twine, cordage, rope and cables and worn out articles of twine, cordage, rope or cables, of textile materials

第十二类
鞋、帽、伞、杖、鞭及其零件；已加工的羽毛及其制品；人造花；人发制品

第六十四章
鞋靴、护腿和类似品及其零件

注释：

一、本章不包括：

(一)易损材料(例如，纸、塑料薄膜)制的无外绱鞋底的一次性鞋靴罩或套，这些产品应按其构成材料归类；

(二)纺织材料制的鞋靴，没有用粘、缝或其他方法将外底固定或安装在鞋面上的(第十一类)；

(三)税目 63.09 的旧鞋靴；

(四)石棉制品(税目 68.12)；

(五)矫形鞋靴或其他矫形器具及其零件(税目 90.21)；

(六)玩具鞋及装有冰刀或轮子的滑冰鞋；护胫或类似的运动防护服装(第九十五章)。

二、税目 64.06 所称"零件"，不包括鞋钉、护鞋铁掌、鞋眼、鞋钩、鞋扣、饰物、编带、鞋带、绒球或其他装饰带(应分别归入相应税目)及税目 96.06 的纽扣或其他货品。

三、本章所称：

(一)"橡胶"及"塑料"，包括能用肉眼辨出其外表有一层橡胶或塑料的机织物或其他纺织产品，运用本款时，橡胶或塑料仅引起颜色变化的不计在内；

(二)"皮革"，是指税目 41.07 及 41.12 至 41.14 的货品。

四、除本章注释三另有规定的以外：

(一)鞋面的材料应以占表面面积最大的那种材料为准，计算表面面积可不考虑附件及加固件，例如，护踝、裹边、饰物、扣子、拉襻、鞋眼或类似附属件。

(二)外底的主要材料应以与地面接触最广的那种材料为准，计算接触面时可不考虑鞋底钉、铁掌或类似附属件。

子目注释：

子目 6402.12、6402.19、6403.12、6403.19 及 6404.11 所称"运动鞋靴"，仅适用于：

一、带有或可装鞋底钉、止滑柱、夹钳、马蹄掌或类似品的体育专用鞋靴。

二、滑冰靴，滑雪靴及越野滑雪用鞋靴、滑雪板靴、角力靴、拳击靴及赛车鞋。

税则号列	货品名称〔CIQ 扩展编码及品名－T2 表示见附表 2〕	最惠(%)	暂定税率	普通	增值/消费	出口退税	计量单位	监管条件/特殊证件	检验检疫	对美关税	亚太上/下
64.01	**橡胶或塑料制外底及鞋面的防水鞋靴，其鞋面不是用缝、铆、钉、旋、塞或类似方法固定在鞋底上的：**										
	-装有金属防护鞋头的鞋靴：										
6401.1010	---橡胶制鞋面的〔999〕	10		100	13/	13	千克/双	/			5/5
6401.1090	---塑料制鞋面的〔999〕	10		100	13/	13	千克/双	/		35	5/5
	-其他鞋靴：										
	--鞋靴(过踝但未到膝)：										
6401.9210	---橡胶制鞋面的过踝但未到膝防水鞋靴(鞋面与鞋非用缝铆钉旋塞等类似方法连结的)〔999〕	10		100	13/	13	千克/双	/		35	5/5
6401.9290	---塑料制鞋面的过踝但未到膝防水鞋靴(鞋面与鞋非用缝铆钉旋塞等类似方法连结的)〔999〕	10		100	13/	13	千克/双	/			5/5
6401.9900	--其他〔999〕	10		100	13/	13	千克/双	/		35	5/5
64.02	**橡胶或塑料制外底及鞋面的其他鞋靴：**										
	-运动鞋靴：										
6402.1200	--滑雪靴、越野滑雪鞋靴及滑雪板靴										
6402.1200 10	含濒危动物毛皮橡胶、塑料底及面滑雪靴(包括越野滑雪鞋靴及滑雪板靴)〔999〕	4		100	13/	0	千克/双	EF/		29	2/2
6402.1200 90	其他橡胶、塑料底及面滑雪靴(包括越野滑雪鞋靴及滑雪板靴)〔101 非婴童用橡塑类鞋靴，102 运动类鞋靴〕	4		100	13/	13	千克/双	/		29	2/2
6402.1900	--其他										
6402.1900 10	含濒危动物毛皮其他运动鞋靴(橡胶、塑料制底及面)〔999〕	10		100	13/	0	千克/双	EF/		35	5/5
6402.1900 90	橡胶、塑料制底及面的其他运动鞋靴〔999〕	10		100	13/	13	千克/双	/		35	5/5
6402.2000	-用栓塞方法将鞋面条带装配在鞋底上的鞋〔101 内底长度小于等于 17cm，102 内底长度大于 17cm〕	10		100	13/	13	千克/双	/		35	5/5
	-其他鞋靴：										

SECTION XII
FOOTWEAR, HEADGEAR, UMBRELLAS, SUN UMBRELLAS, WALKING-STICKS, SEAT-STICKS, WHIPS, RIDING-CROPS AND PARTS THEREOF; PREPARED FEATHERS AND ARTICLES MADE THEREWITH; ARTIFICIAL FLOWERS; ARTICLES OF HUMAN HAIR

Chapter 64
Footwear, gaiters and the like; parts of such articles

Notes:

1. This Chapter does not cover:
   (a) Disposable foot or shoe coverings of flimsy material (for example, paper, sheeting of plastics) without applied soles. These products are classified according to their constituent material;
   (b) Footwear of textile material, without an outer sole glued, sewn or otherwise affixed or applied to the upper (Section XI);
   (c) Worn footwear of heading No.63.09;
   (d) Articles of asbestos (heading No.68.12);
   (e) Orthopaedic footwear or other orthopaedic appliances, or parts thereof (heading No.90.21) or;
   (f) Toy footwear or skating boots with ice or roller skates attached; shin-guards or similar protective sportswear (Chapter 95).
2. For the purposes of heading No.64.06, the term "parts" does not include pegs, protectors, eyelets, hooks, buckles, ornaments, braid, laces, pompons or other trimmings (which are to be classified in their appropriate headings) or buttons or other goods of heading No.96.06.
3. For the purposes of this Chapter:
   (a) The terms "rubber" and "plastics" include woven fabrics or other textile products with an external layer of rubber or plastics being visible to the naked eye; for the purpose of this provision, no account should be taken of any resulting change of colour;
   (b) The term "leather" refers to the goods of headings No.41.07 and 41.12 to 41.14.
4. Subject to Note 3 to this Chapter:
   (a) The material of the upper shall be taken to be the constituent material having the greatest external surface area, no account being taken of accessories or reinforcements such as ankle patches, edging, ornamentation, buckles, tabs, eyelet stays or similar attachments;
   (b) The constituent material of the outer sole shall be taken to be the material having the greatest surface area in contact with the ground, no account being taken of accessories or reinforcements such as spikes, bars, nails, protectors or similar attachments.

Subheading Notes:

For the purposes of subheadings No.6402.12, 6402.19, 6403.12, 6403.19 and 6404.11, the expression "sports footwear" applies only to:

1. Footwear which is designed for a sporting activity and has, or has provsion for the attachment of, spikes, sprigs, stops, clips, bars or the like;
2. Skating boots, ski-boots and cross-country ski footwear, snowboard boots, wrestling boots, boxing boots and cycling shoes.

协定税率 %								RCEP		特惠税率 %			Article Description
东/冰/格	巴基斯坦	韩国	瑞士上/下	哥/秘/柬	澳/毛	新西/坡/智	中国港/澳/台	东盟及马来/澳/韩	日/新	亚太2国	老/柬/缅	98/97/95	
													Waterproof footwear with outer soles and uppers of rubber or of plastics, the uppers of which are neither fixed to the sole nor assembled by stitching, riveting, nailing, screwing, plugging or similar processes:
													-Footwear incorporating a protective metal toe-cap:
0/0/0	12	14.4	2.4/2.4	0/0/0	0/14.4	0/0/0	0/0/	22.8/22.8/22.8	22.9/22.8			0/0/0	---With uppers of rubber
0/0/0	12	14.4	2.4/2.4	0/0/0	0/14.4	0/0/0	0/0/	22.8/22.8/22.8	22.9/22.8			0/0/0	---With uppers of plastics
													-Other footwear:
													Covering the ankle but not covering the knee:
0/0/0	12	14.4	2.4/2.4	0/0/0	0/14.4	0/0/0	0/0/	22.8/22.8/22.8	22.9/22.8			0/0/0	---With uppers of rubber
0/0/0	12	14.4	2.4/2.4	0/0/0	0/14.4	0/0/0	0/0/	22.8/22.8/22.8	22.9/22.8			0/0/0	---With uppers of plastics
0/0/0	12	14.4	2.4/2.4	0/0/0	0/14.4	0/0/0	0/0/	22.8/22.8/22.8	22.9/22.8			0/0/0	--Other
													Other footwear with outer soles and uppers of rubber or plastics:
													-Sports footwear:
													--Ski-boots, cross-country ski footwear and snowboard boots
0/0/0	2	2	0/0	0/0/0	0/0	0//0	0/0/	0/0/9	9.1/0			0/0/0	Inverted skiing boot with rubber、plastic sole and hair of endangered animals (including cross-counory skiing boots and boots for skin)
0/0/0	2	2	0/0	0/0/0	0/0	0//0	0/0/	0/0/9	9.1/0			0/0/0	Other ski-boots cross-country ski footwear and snoroboard boots, with outer soles and upper of rubber or plastics
													--Other
0/0/0	12	14.4	2.4/2.4	0/0/0	0/14.4	0/0/0	0/0/	22.8/22.8/	/22.8			0/0/0	Other sports shoes and boots containing endangered animal hair and hide (rubbor and plastic shoes and inverced)
0/0/0	12	14.4	2.4/2.4	0/0/0	0/14.4	0/0/0	0/0/	22.8/22.8/	/22.8			0/0/0	Other sport footwear, with outer soles and uppers of rubber or plastics (rubber and plastic shoes and inverted)
0/0/0	12	14.4	2.4/2.4	0/0/0	0/14.4	0/0/0	0/0/	22.8/22.8/22.8	/22.8			0/0/0	-Footwear with upper straps or thongs assembled to the sole by means of plugs
													-Other footwear:

税则号列	货品名称〔CIQ 扩展编码及品名—T2 表示见附表 2〕	最惠(%)	暂定税率	普通	增值/消费	出口退税	计量单位	监管条件/特殊证件	检验检疫	对美关税	亚太上/下
6402.9100	--鞋靴(过踝)〔101 内底长度小于等于 17cm;102 内底长度大于 17cm 的橡塑类鞋靴〕	10		100	13/	13	千克/双	/		35	5/5
	--其他:										
6402.9910	---橡胶制鞋面的〔101 内底长度小于等于 17cm,102 内底长度大于 17cm〕	10		100	13/	13	千克/双	/		35	5/5
	---塑料制鞋面的:										
6402.9921	----以机织物或其他纺织材料做衬底的〔101 内底长度小于等于 17cm,102 内底长度大于 17cm〕	10		100	13/	13	千克/双	/			5/5
6402.9929	----其他〔101 内底长度小于等于 17cm,102 内底长度大于 17cm〕	10		100	13/	13	千克/双	/		35	5/5
64.03	**橡胶、塑料、皮革或再生皮革制外底,皮革制鞋面的鞋靴:**										
	-运动鞋靴:										
6403.1200	--滑雪靴、越野滑雪鞋靴及滑雪板靴										
6403.1200 10	含濒危野生动物皮革制鞋面的滑雪靴〔999〕	14	4	100	13/	0	千克/双	EF/			
6403.1200 90	其他皮革制鞋面的滑雪靴(包括橡胶、塑料、皮革制外底和越野滑雪鞋靴及板靴)〔999〕	14	4	100	13/	13	千克/双	/			
6403.1900	--其他										
6403.1900 10	含濒危野生动物皮革制鞋面其他运动鞋靴〔999〕	10		100	13/	0	千克/双	EF/		35	
6403.1900 90	皮革制鞋面的其他运动鞋靴(橡胶、塑料、皮革或再生皮革制外底)〔999〕	10		100	13/	13	千克/双	/		35	
6403.2000	-皮革制外底,由交叉于脚背并绕大脚趾的皮革条带构成鞋面的鞋										
6403.2000 10	含濒危野生动物皮革条带为鞋面的皮底鞋〔101:内底长度小于等于 17cm;102:内底长度大于 17cm〕	14		100	13/	0	千克/双	EF/			
6403.2000 90	其他皮革条带为鞋面的皮底鞋(皮革条带交叉于脚背并绕大脚趾的)〔999〕	14		100	13/	13	千克/双	/			
6403.4000	-装有金属防护鞋头的其他鞋靴										
6403.4000 10	其他含濒危野生动物皮革面鞋靴(装有金属护鞋头的)〔999〕	14		100	13/	0	千克/双	FE/		24	
6403.4000 90	装有金属护鞋头的其他皮革面鞋靴(橡胶、塑料、皮革或再生皮革制外底)〔999〕	14		100	13/	13	千克/双	/		24	
	-皮革制外底的其他鞋靴:										
	--鞋靴(过踝):										
	---过脚踝但低于小腿的鞋靴,按内底长度分类:										
6403.5111	----小于 24cm 的										
6403.5111 10	含濒危野生动物皮革制外底皮革面过脚踝但低于小腿的短筒靴(内底长度小于 24cm,运动用靴除外)〔101 内底长度小于等于 17cm,102 内底长度大于 17cm〕	8		100	13/	0	千克/双	FE/		33	
6403.5111 90	皮革制外底皮革面过脚踝但低于小腿的短筒靴(内底长度小于 24cm,运动用靴除外)〔101 内底长度小于等于 17cm,102 内底长度大于 17cm,适用于 14 周岁及以下儿童穿用,103 内底长度大于 17cm,不适用于 14 周岁及以下儿童穿用〕	8		100	13/	13	千克/双	A/	M	33	
6403.5119	----其他										
6403.5119 10	其他含濒危野生动物皮革制外底皮革面过脚踝但低于小腿的鞋靴(运动用靴除外)〔101 内底长度小于等于 17cm,102 内底长度大于 17cm〕	8		100	13/	0	千克/双	EF/		33	
6403.5119 90	其他皮革制外底皮革面过脚踝但低于小腿的鞋靴(运动用靴除外)〔101 内底长度小于等于 17cm,102 内底长度大于 17cm〕	8		100	13/	13	千克/双	/		33	
	---其他,按内底长度分类:										
6403.5191	----小于 24cm 的										
6403.5191 10	含濒危野生动物皮革制外底皮革面的鞋靴(过踝)(内底长度小于 24cm,运动用靴除外)〔101 内底长度小于等于 17cm,102 内底长度大于 17cm〕	8		100	13/	0	千克/双	EF/			
6403.5191 90	皮革制外底的皮革面的鞋靴(过踝)(内底长度小于 24cm,运动用靴除外)〔101 内底长度小于等于 17cm,102 内底长度大于 17cm,适用于 14 周岁及以下儿童穿用,103 内底长度大于 17cm,不适用于 14 周岁及以下儿童穿用〕	8		100	13/	13	千克/双	A/	M		
6403.5199	----其他										
6403.5199 10	含濒危野生动物皮革制外底皮革面的鞋靴(过踝)(运动用靴除外)〔101 内底长度小于等于 17cm,102 内底长度大于 17cm〕	8		100	13/	0	千克/双	FE/		33	

协定税率 %								RCEP		特惠税率 %			Article Description
东/冰/格	巴基斯坦	韩国	瑞士上/下	哥/秘/柬	澳/毛	新西/坡/智	中国港/澳/台	东盟及马来/澳/韩	日/新	亚太2国	老/柬/缅	98/97/95	
0/0/0	12	14.4	2.4/2.4	0/0/0	0/14.4	0/0/0	0/0/	22.8/22.8/	/22.8			0/0/0	--Footwear(covering the ankle)
													--Other:
0/0/0	12	14.4	2.4/2.4	0/0/0	0/14.4	0/0/0	0/0/	22.8/22.8/22.8	22.9/22.8			0/0/0	---With uppers of rubber
													---With uppers of plastics:
0/0/0	0	14.4	2.4/2.4	0/0/0	0/14.4	0/0/0	0/0/	22.8/22.8/22.8	/22.8			0/0/0	----With substrate of woven fabrics or other textile materials
0/0/0	0	14.4	2.4/2.4	0/0/0	0/14.4	0/0/0	0/0/	22.8/22.8/22.8	22.9/22.8			0/0/0	----Other
													Footwear with outer soles of rubber, plastics, leather or composition leather and upers of leather:
													-Sports footwear:
													--Ski-boots, cross-country ski footwear and snowboard boots
0/0/0		14.4	2.4/2.4	0/0/0	0/14.4	0/0/0	0/0/	22.8/22.8/22.8	22.9/22.8		/0/	0/0/0	Ski-boots, with uppers of leather of wild animals
0/0/0		14.4	2.4/2.4	0/0/0	0/14.4	0/0/0	0/0/	22.8/22.8/22.8	22.9/22.8		/0/	0/0/0	Ski-boots, cross-country sik footwear and snowboard boots, with outer soles of rubber, plastics, leather or composition leather and upers of leather
													--Other
0/0/0	12	3	1.5/1.5	0/0/0	0/0	0/0/0	0/0/	0/0/13.5	13.6/0		/0/	0/0/0	Other sports footwear with uppers of leather of wild animals
0/0/0	12	3	1.5/1.5	0/0/0	0/0	0/0/0	0/0/	0/0/13.5	13.6/0		/0/	0/0/0	Other sports footwear with outer soles of rubber, plastics, leather or composition leather and uppers of leather
													-Footwear with outer soles of leather, and uppers which consist of leather straps across the instep and around the big toe
0/0/0	0	14.4	2.4/2.4	0/0/0	0/14.4	0/0/0	0/0/	22.8/22.8/22.8	22.9/22.8		/0/	0/0/0	Footwear with outer soles of leather and with uppers of leather straps of wild animals
0/0/0	0	14.4	2.4/2.4	0/0/0	0/14.4	0/0/0	0/0/	22.8/22.8/22.8	22.9/22.8		/0/	0/0/0	Footwear with outer soles of leather and with uppers which consist of leather straps across the instep and around the big toe
													-Other footwear, incorporating a protective metal toe-cap
0/0/0		14.4	2.4/2.4	0/0/0	0/14.4	0/0/0	0/0/	22.8/22.8/	/22.8		/0/	0/0/0	Other footwear, incorporating a protective metal toe-cap with uppers of leather of wild animals
0/0/0		14.4	2.4/2.4	0/0/0	0/14.4	0/0/0	0/0/	22.8/22.8/	/22.8		/0/	0/0/0	Other footwear, incorporating a protective metal toe-cap, with outer soles of rubber, plastics, leather or composition leather and uppers of leather
													-Other footwear with outer soles of leather:
													--Footwear(covering the ankle)
													---Covering the ankle but not covering the calf, by length of inner soles:
													----Less than 24cm
0/0/0	2	2	0/0	0/0/0	0/0	0//0	0/0/	0/0/9	9.1/0		/0/	0/0/0	Other footwear with outer soles of leather and uppers of leather, covering the ankle but lower than crus, with uppers of leather of wild animals(inner sole length<24cm, other than sports boots)
0/0/0	2	2	0/0	0/0/0	0/0	0//0	0/0/	0/0/9	9.1/0		/0/	0/0/0	Footwear, with outer soles of leather and uppers of leather, covering the ankle but lower than crus, with uppers of leather (inner sole length<24cm, other than sports boots)
													----Other
0/0/0	2	2	0/0	0/0/0	0/0	0//0	0/0/	0/0/9	9.1/0		/0/	0/0/0	Other footwear with outer soles of leather and uppers of leather, covering the ankle but lower than crus, with uppers of leather of wild animals, other than sports footwear
0/0/0	2	2	0/0	0/0/0	0/0	0//0	0/0/	0/0/9	9.1/0		/0/	0/0/0	Other footwear with outer soles of leather and uppers of leather, covering the ankle but lower than crus, other than sports footwear
													---Other, by length of inner soles:
													----Less than 24cm
0/0/0	2	2	0/0	0/0/0	0/0	0//0	0/0/	0/0/9	9.1/0		/0/	0/0/0	Footwear with outer soles of leather and uppers of leather, covering the ankle, with uppers of leather of wild animals(inner soles<24cm, other than sports footwear)
0/0/0	2	2	0/0	0/0/0	0/0	0//0	0/0/	0/0/9	9.1/0		/0/	0/0/0	Footwear with outer soles of leather and uppers of leather, covering the ankle(inner soles<24cm other than sports footwear)
													----Other
0/0/0	2	2	0/0	0/0/0	0/0	0//0	0/0/	0/0/9	9.1/0		/0/	0/0/0	Footwear with outer soles of leather and uppers of leather, covering the ankle, with uppers of leather of wild animals (other than sports footwear)

税则号列	货品名称〔CIQ 扩展编码及品名－T2 表示见附表 2〕	最惠(%)	暂定税率	普通	增值/消费	出口退税	计量单位	监管条件/特殊证件	检验检疫	对美关税	亚太上/下
6403.5199 90	皮革制外底的皮革面短筒靴(过踝)(运动用靴除外)〔101 内底长度小于等于 17cm,102 内底长度大于 17cm〕	8		100	13/	13	千克/双	/		33	
6403.5900	--其他										
6403.5900 10	含濒危野生动物皮革制外底皮革面其他鞋(包括靴,运动用鞋靴除外)〔101 内底长度小于等于 17cm,102 内底长度大于 17cm〕	8		100	13/	0	千克/双	EF/		33	
6403.5900 90	皮革制外底的皮革面其他鞋靴(运动用鞋靴除外)〔101 内底长度小于等于 17cm,102 内底长度大于 17cm〕	8		100	13/	13	千克/双	/		33	
	-其他鞋靴:										
	--鞋靴(过踝):										
	---过脚踝但低于小腿的鞋靴,按内底长度分类:										
6403.9111	----小于 24cm 的										
6403.9111 10	其他含濒危野生动物皮革制面过脚踝但低于小腿的鞋靴(内底＜24cm,橡胶、塑料、再生皮革制外底,运动用靴除外)〔101 内底长度小于等于 17cm,102 内底长度大于 17cm〕	8		100	13/	0	千克/双	EF/		33	
6403.9111 90	其他皮革制面过脚踝但低于小腿的鞋靴(内底＜24cm,橡胶、塑料、再生皮革制外底,运动用靴除外)〔101 内底长度小于等于 17cm,102 内底长度大于 17cm,适用于 14 周岁及以下儿童穿用,103 内底长度大于 17cm,不适用于 14 周岁及以下儿童穿用〕	8		100	13/	13	千克/双	A/	M	33	
6403.9119	----其他										
6403.9119 10	其他含濒危野生动物皮革制面过脚踝但低于小腿的鞋靴(橡胶、塑料、再生皮革制外底,运动用靴除外)〔101 内底长度小于等于 17cm,102 内底长度大于 17cm〕	8		100	13/	0	千克/双	EF/		33	
6403.9119 90	其他皮革制面过脚踝但低于小腿的鞋靴(橡胶、塑料、再生皮革制外底,运动用靴除外)〔101 内底长度小于等于 17cm,102 内底长度大于 17cm〕	8		100	13/	13	千克/双	/		33	
	---其他,按内底长度分类:										
6403.9191	----小于 24cm 的										
6403.9191 10	其他含濒危野生皮革制面的鞋靴(过踝)(内底＜24cm,橡胶、塑料、再生皮革制外底,运动用靴除外)〔101 内底长度小于等于 17cm,102 内底长度大于 17cm〕	8		100	13/	0	千克/双	EF/		33	
6403.9191 90	其他皮革制面的鞋靴(过踝)(内底＜24cm,橡胶、塑料、再生皮革制外底,运动用靴除外)〔101 内底长度小于等于 17cm,102 内底长度大于 17cm,适用于 14 周岁及以下儿童穿用,103 内底长度大于 17cm,不适用于 14 周岁及以下儿童穿用〕	8		100	13/	13	千克/双	A/	M	33	
6403.9199	----其他										
6403.9199 10	其他含濒危野生皮革制面的鞋靴(过踝)(橡胶、塑料、再生皮革制外底,运动用靴除外)〔101 内底长度小于等于 17cm,102 内底长度大于 17cm〕	8		100	13/	0	千克/双	EF/		33	
6403.9199 90	其他皮革制面的鞋靴(过踝)(橡胶、塑料、再生皮革制外底,运动用靴除外)〔101 内底长度小于等于 17cm,102 内底长度大于 17cm〕	8		100	13/	13	千克/双	/		33	
6403.9900	--其他										
6403.9900 10	含濒危野生动物皮革制面的其他鞋靴(橡胶、塑料、再生皮革制外底,运动用鞋靴除外)〔101 内底长度小于等于 17cm,102 内底长度大于 17cm〕	8		100	13/	0	千克/双	EF/		33	5.2/5.2
6403.9900 90	其他皮革制面的其他鞋靴(橡胶、塑料、再生皮革制外底,运动用鞋靴除外)〔101 内底长度小于等于 17cm,102 内底长度小于等于 17cm〕	8		100	13/	13	千克/双	/		33	5.2/5.2
64.04	**橡胶、塑料、皮革或再生皮革制外底,用纺织材料制鞋面的鞋靴:**										
	-橡胶或塑料制外底的鞋靴:										
6404.1100	--运动鞋靴;网球鞋、篮球鞋、体操鞋、训练鞋及类似鞋〔999〕	10		100	13/	13	千克/双	/		35	5/5
	--其他:										
6404.1910	---拖鞋〔101 内底长度小于等于 17cm,102 内底长度大于 17cm〕	10		100	13/	13	千克/双	/		35	5/5
6404.1990	---其他〔101 内底长度小于等于 17cm,102 内底长度大于 17cm〕	10		100	13/	13	千克/双	/		35	5/5
	-皮革或再生皮革制外底的鞋靴:										
6404.2010	---拖鞋〔101 内底长度小于等于 17cm,102 内底长度大于 17cm,非运动鞋,103 运动类鞋靴〕	10		100	13/	13	千克/双	/			5/5
6404.2090	---其他〔101 内底长度小于等于 17cm,102 内底长度大于 17cm,非运动鞋,103 运动类鞋靴〕	10		100	13/	13	千克/双	/		35	5/5

协定税率 %								RCEP		特惠税率 %			Article Description
东/冰/格	巴基斯坦	韩国	瑞士上/下	哥/秘/柬	澳/毛	新西/坡/智	中国港/澳/台	东盟及马来/澳/韩	日/新	亚太2国	老/柬/缅	98/97/95	
0/0/0	2	2	0/0	0/0/0	0/0	0//0	0/0/	0/0/9	9.1/0		/0/	0/0/0	Footwear with outer soles of leather and uppers of leather, covering the ankle, with uppers of leather(other than sports footwear)
													--Other
0/0/0	2	2	1/1	0/0/0	0/0	0//0	0/0/	0/0/9	9.1/0		/0/	0/0/0	Other footwear with outer soles of leather and upers of leather of wild animals(other than sports footwear)
0/0/0	2	2	1/1	0/0/0	0/0	0//0	0/0/	0/0/9	9.1/0		/0/	0/0/0	Other footwear with outer soles of leather and upers of leather of other animals(other than sports footwear)
													-Other footwear:
													--Covering the ankle:
													---Covering the ankle but not covering the calf, by length of inner soles
													----Less than 24cm
0/0/0	3.5	2	1/1	0/0/0	0/0	0/0/0	0/0/	0/0/9	9.1/0		/0/	0/0/0	Footwear with outer uper of feather, covering the ankle but lower than crus, with upers of wild animal leather, inner soles of rubber or plastic and the length<24cm, outer soles of composition leather, other than sports footwear
0/0/0	3.5	2	1/1	0/0/0	0/0	0/0/0	0/0/	0/0/9	9.1/0		/0/	0/0/0	Footwear with outer uper of feather, lovering the ankle but lower than crus, with inner soles of rubber or plastic and the length<24cm, outer soles of composition leather, other than sports footwear
													----Other
0/0/0	0	2	0/0	0/0/0	0/0	0/0/0	0/0/	9/9/9	9.1/9		/0/	0/0/0	Footwear covering the ankle but lower than crus, with outer soles of rubber, plastics, leather of composition leather and upers of wild animal feather, other than sports footwear
0/0/0	0	2	0/0	0/0/0	0/0	0/0/0	0/0/	9/9/9	9.1/9		/0/	0/0/0	Footwear covering the ankle but lower than crus, with outer soles of rubber, plastics, leather of composition leather and upers of leather, other than sports footwear
													---Other, by length of inner soles:
													----Less than 24cm
0/0/0	0	2	0/0	0/0/0	0/0	0/0/0	0/0/	0/0/9	9.1/0		/0/	0/0/0	Footwear covering ankle, with outer upers of leather of wild animal, inner soles of rubber, plastic and the length<24cm, outer soles of composition leather, other than sports footwear
0/0/0	0	2	0/0	0/0/0	0/0	0/0/0	0/0/	0/0/9	9.1/0		/0/	0/0/0	Footwear covering ankle, with outer upers of leather, inner soles of rubber, plastic and the length<24cm, outer soles of composition leather, other than sports footwear
													----Other
0/0/0	0	2	0/0	0/0/0	0/0	0/0/0	0/0/	0/0/9	9.1/0		/0/	0/0/0	Footwear covering the ankle with outer soles of rubber, plastics, leather or composition leather and upers of leather, of wild animals, other than sports footwear
0/0/0	0	2	0/0	0/0/0	0/0	0/0/0	0/0/	0/0/9	9.1/0		/0/	0/0/0	Footwear covering the ankle with outer soles of rubber, plastics, leather or composition leather and upers of leather, of other animals, other than sports footwear
													--Other
0/0/0	0	2	1/1	0/0/0	0/6	0/0/0	0/0/	0/0/9	9.1/0		/0/	0/0/0	Other footwear with outer soles of rubber, plastics, leather or composition leather and upers of leather of wild animals, other than sports footwear
0/0/0	0	2	1/1	0/0/0	0/6	0/0/0	0/0/	0/0/9	9.1/0		/0/	0/0/0	Other footwear with outer soles of rubber, plastics, leather or composition leather and upers of leather of other animals, other than sports footwear
													Footwear with outer soles of rubber, plastics, leather or composition leather and uppers of textile materials:
													-Footwear with outer soles of rubber or plastics:
0/0/0	0	14.4	2.4/2.4	0/0/0	0/14.4	0/0/0	0/0/	22.8/22.8/	/22.8			0/0/0	--Sports footwear, tennis shoes, basketball shoes, gym shoes, training shoes and the like
													--Other:
0/0/0	9.6	14.4	2.4/2.4	0/0/0	0/14.4	0/0/0	0/0/	22.8/22.8/22.8	22.9/22.8			0//	---Slippers
0/0/0	9.6	14.4	2.4/2.4	0/0/0	0/14.4	0/0/0	0/0/	22.8/22.8/22.8	22.9/22.8			0//	---Other
													-Footwear with outer soles of leather or composition leather:
0/0/0	12	14.4	2.4/2.4	0/0/0	0/14.4	0/0/0	0/0/	22.8/22.8/22.8	22.9/22.8			0//	---Slippers
0/0/0	12	14.4	2.4/2.4	0/0/0	0/14.4	0/0/0	0/0/	22.8/22.8/22.8	22.9/22.8			0//	---Other

税则号列	货品名称〔CIQ扩展编码及品名－T2表示见附表2〕	最惠(%)	暂定税率	普通	增值/消费	出口退税	计量单位	监管条件/特殊证件	检验检疫	对美关税	亚太上/下
64.05	**其他鞋靴：**										
	-皮革或再生皮革制鞋面的：										
6405.1010	---橡胶、塑料、皮革及再生皮革制外底的〔101 内底长度小于等于17cm,102 内底长度大于17cm〕	12		100	13/	13	千克/双	/			6/6
6405.1090	---其他材料制外底的										
6405.1090 10	含濒危野生动物皮革制面的其他鞋靴(外底用橡胶、塑料、皮革及再生皮革以外材料制成)〔101 内底长度小于等于17cm,102 内底长度大于17cm〕	12		100	13/	0	千克/双	EF/			6/6
6405.1090 90	其他皮革或再生皮革制面的其他鞋靴(外底用橡胶,塑料,皮革及再生皮革以外材料制成)〔101 内底长度小于等于17cm,102 内底长度大于17cm〕	12		100	13/	13	千克/双	/			6/6
6405.2000	-纺织材料制鞋面的										
6405.2000 10	羊毛毡呢制内底及鞋面的鞋靴(外底用橡胶,塑料,皮革或再生皮革制以外材料制成)〔101 内底长度小于等于17cm,102 内底长度大于17cm〕	10		100	13/	13	千克/双	/		35	5/5
6405.2000 90	纺织材料制鞋面的其他鞋靴(外底用橡胶,塑料,皮革或再生皮革制以外材料制成)〔101 内底长度小于等于17cm,102 内底长度大于17cm〕	10		100	13/	13	千克/双	/		35	5/5
	-其他：										
6405.9010	---橡胶、塑料、皮革及再生皮革制外底的〔101 日常穿着用,102 非日常穿着用〕	6		100	13/	13	千克/双	/		31	3.9/3.9
6405.9090	---其他材料制外底的〔101 日常穿着用,102 非日常穿着用〕	6		100	13/	13	千克/双	/		31	3.9/3.9
64.06	**鞋靴零件(包括鞋面,不论是否带有除外底以外的其他鞋底);活动式鞋内底、跟垫及类似品;护腿、裹腿和类似品及其零件：**										
6406.1000	-鞋面及其零件,但硬衬除外										
6406.1000 10	含濒危野生动物皮的鞋面及其零件〔999〕	6		90	13/	0	千克/个	FE/		31	3.9/3.9
6406.1000 90	其他鞋面及其零件(不包括硬衬及毡呢制品)〔999〕	6		90	13/	13	千克/个	/		31	3.9/3.9
	-橡胶或塑料制的外底及鞋跟：										
6406.2010	---橡胶制的〔999〕	6		90	13/	13	千克/个	/		31	
6406.2020	---塑料制的〔999〕	6		90	13/	13	千克/个	/		31	
	-其他：										
6406.9010	---木制〔999〕	6		90	13/	13	千克/个	/			3.9/3.9
	--其他材料制：										
6406.9091	----活动式鞋内底、跟垫及类似品〔999〕	6		90	13/	13	千克/个	/		31	3.9/3.9
6406.9092	----护腿、裹脚和类似品及其零件〔999〕	6		90	13/	13	千克/个	/		31	3.9/3.9
6406.9099	----其他〔999〕	6		90	13/	13	千克/个	/		16	3.9/3.9

协定税率 %								RCEP		特惠税率 %			Article Description
东/冰/格	巴基斯坦	韩国	瑞士 上/下	哥/秘/柬	澳/毛	新西/坡/智	中国港/澳/台	东盟及马来/澳/韩	日/新	亚太2国	老/柬/缅	98/97/95	
													Other footwear:
													-With uppers of leather or composition leather:
0/0/0	12	14.4	2.4/2.4	0/0/0	0/14.4	0/0/0	0/0/	22.8/22.8/	22.9/22.8			0/0/0	---With outer soles of rubber, plastics, leather or composition leather
													---With outer soles of other materials
0/0/0	12	14.4	2.4/2.4	0/0/0	0/14.4	0/0/0	0/0/	22.8/22.8/22.8	22.9/22.8			0/0/0	Other footwear with uppers of leather or composition leather of wid andimds(with outer soles of materials other than rubber, plastics ,leather or composition leather)
0/0/0	12	14.4	2.4/2.4	0/0/0	0/14.4	0/0/0	0/0/	22.8/22.8/22.8	22.9/22.8			0/0/0	Other footwear eieh uppers of leather or composition leather (with outer soles of materials other than rubber, plastics, leather or composition leather)
													-With uppers of textile materials
0/0/0	11	13.2	2.2/2.2	0/0/0	0/13.2	0/0/0	0/0/	20.9/20.9/	21/20.9			0/0/0	Footwear with inner soles and uppers of wool felt, outer soled of materials other than rubber, plastics, leather or composition leather
0/0/0	11	13.2	2.2/2.2	0/0/0	0/13.2	0/0/0	0/0/	20.9/20.9/	21/20.9			0/0/0	Other footwear with uppers of textile materials, outer soles of materials other than rubber, plastics, leather or composition leather
													-Other:
0/0/0	0	3	1.5/1.5	0/0/0	0/0	0/0/0	0/0/	0/0/13.5	13.6/0			0/0/0	---With outer soles of rubber, plastics, leather or composition leather
0/0/0	7.5	3	1.5/1.5	0/0/0	0/0	0/0/0	0/0/	0/0/13.5	13.6/0			0/0/0	---With outer soles of other materials
													Parts of footwear (including uppers whether or not attached to soles other than outer soles); removable in-soles, heel cushions and similar articles; gaiters, leggings and similar articles, and parts thereof:
													-Uppers and parts thereof, other than stiffeners
0/0/0	7.5	9	1.5/1.5	0/0/0	0/0	0/0/0	0/0/0	14.3/14.3/	/14.3			0/0/0	Uppers and parts thereof, consist of leather of wild animals
0/0/0	7.5	9	1.5/1.5	0/0/0	0/0	0/0/0	0/0/0	14.3/14.3/	/14.3			0/0/0	Other uppers and parts thereof(other than stiffeners and articles of felt)
													-Outer soles and heels, of rubber or plastics:
0/0/0	12	3	1.5/1.5	0/0/0	0/0	0/0/0	0/0/0	13.5/13.5/13.5	13.6/13.5			0/0/0	---Of rubber
0/0/0	12	3	1.5/1.5	0/0/0	0/0	0/0/0	0/0/	0/0/13.5	13.6/0			0/0/0	---Of plastics
													-Other:
0/0/0	7.5	3	1.5/1.5	0/0/0	0/0	0/0/0	0/0/	0/0/13.5	13.6/0			0/0/0	---Of wood
													--Of other materials:
0/0/0	7.5	9	1.5/1.5	0/0/0	0/0	0/0/0	0/0/0	14.3/14.3/	/14.3			0/0/0	----Removable in-soles, heel cushions and similar articles
0/0/0	6	9	1.5/1.5	0/0/0	0/0	0/0/0	0/0/0	14.3/14.3/	/14.3			0/0/0	----Gaiters, leggings and similar articles, and parts thereof
0/0/0	6	9	1.5/1.5	0/0/0	0/0	0/0/0	0/0/0	14.3/14.3/	/14.3			0/0/0	----Other

第六十五章
帽类及其零件

注释：

一、本章不包括：

（一）税目 63.09 的旧帽类；

（二）石棉制帽类（税目 68.12）；

（三）第九十五章的玩偶帽、其他玩具帽或狂欢节用品。

二、税目 65.02 不包括缝制的帽坯，但仅将条带缝成螺旋形的除外。

税则号列		货品名称〔CIQ 扩展编码及品名—T2 表示见附表 2〕	最惠(%)	暂定税率	普通	增值/消费	出口退税	计量单位	监管条件/特殊证件	检验检疫	对美关税	亚太上/下
65.01		**毡呢制的帽坯、帽身及帽兜，未楦制成形，也未加帽边；毡呢制的圆帽片及制帽用的毡呢筒（包括裁开的毡呢筒）：**										
6501.0000		毡呢制的帽坯、帽身及帽兜，未楦制成形，也未加帽边；毡呢制的圆帽片及制帽用的毡呢筒（包括裁开的毡呢筒）〔101 纤维素纤维制生活帽，102 动物纤维制生活帽，103 化学纤维制生活帽〕	10		100	13/	13	千克	/		30	
65.02		**编结的帽坯或用任何材料的条带拼制而成的帽坯，未楦制成形，也未加帽边、衬里或装饰物：**										
6502.0000		编结的帽坯或用任何材料的条带拼制成而的帽坯，未楦制成形，也未加帽边、衬里或装饰物〔101 皮革制生活帽，102 纤维素纤维制生活帽，103 动物纤维制生活帽，104 化学纤维制生活帽〕	8		100	13/	13	千克	/			
65.04		**编结帽或用任何材料的条带拼制而成的帽类，不论有无衬里或装饰物：**										
6504.0000		编结帽或用任何材料的条带拼制而成的帽类，不论有无衬里或装饰物〔101 皮革制生活帽，102 纤维素纤维制生活帽，103 动物纤维制生活帽，104 化学纤维制生活帽〕	8		130	13/	13	个/千克	/		28	
65.05		**针织或钩编的帽类，用成匹的花边、毡呢或其他纺织物（条带除外）制成的帽类，不论有无衬里或装饰物；任何材料制的发网，不论有无衬里或装饰物：**										
6505.0010		---发网〔999〕	4		130	13/	13	个/千克	/		29	
6505.0020		---钩编的帽类〔101 纤维素纤维制生活帽，102 动物纤维制生活帽，103 化学纤维制生活帽〕	8		130	13/	13	个/千克	/		33	5.2/5.2
		---其他：										
6505.0091		----用税目 65.01 的帽身、帽兜或圆帽片制成的毡呢帽类，无论有无衬里或装饰物〔101 纤维素纤维制生活帽，102 动物纤维制生活帽，103 化学纤维制生活帽〕	8		130	13/	13	个/千克	/		18	4.8/4.8
6505.0099		----其他〔101 纤维素纤维制生活帽，102 动物纤维制生活帽，103 化学纤维制生活帽〕	8		130	13/	13	个/千克	/		33	5.2/5.2
65.06		**其他帽类，不论有无衬里或装饰物：**										
6506.1000		-安全帽										
6506.1000	10	防护面罩（带有能够滤除生物因子滤器的面罩）〔999〕	4		100	13/	13	个/千克	3/		29	
6506.1000	90	其他安全帽（不论有无衬里或饰物）〔101 工业用安全帽，102 非工业用安全帽〕	4		100	13/	13	个/千克	/	L	29	
		-其他：										
6506.9100		--橡胶或塑料制〔999〕	4		100	13/	13	个/千克	/		14	
		--其他材料制：										
6506.9910		---皮革制										
6506.9910	10	含濒危野生动物皮革制帽类〔999〕	8		130	13/	0	个/千克	EF/		28	
6506.9910	90	其他皮革制帽类〔999〕	8		130	13/	13	个/千克	/		28	
6506.9920		---毛皮制										
6506.9920	10	含濒危野生动物毛皮制的帽类（无论有无衬里或饰物）〔999〕	4		130	13/	0	个/千克	EF/		14	
6506.9920	90	其他毛皮制的帽类（无论有无衬里或饰物）〔999〕	4		130	13/	13	个/千克	/		14	
6506.9990		---其他〔999〕	10		100	13/	13	个/千克	/		35	
65.07		**帽圈、帽衬、帽套、帽帮、帽骨架、帽舌及帽颏带：**										
6507.0000		帽圈、帽衬、帽套、帽帮、帽骨架、帽舌及帽颏带	24		100	17	15	千克				
6507.0000	10	含濒危野生动物成分的帽类附件（指帽圈、衬、套、帮、骨架、舌及颏带）〔999〕	10		100	13/	0	千克	FE/		20	
6507.0000	90	其他帽类附件（指帽圈、衬、套、帮、骨架、舌及颏带）〔999〕	10		100	13/	13	千克	/		20	

Chapter 65
Headgear and parts thereof

Notes:

1. This Chapter does not cover:
   (a) Worn headgear of heading No.63.09;
   (b) Asbestos headgear (Heading No.68.12) or;
   (c) Dolls' hats, other toy hats or carnival articles of Chapter 95.
2. Heading No.65.02 does not cover hat-shapes made by sewing, other than those obtained simply by sewing strips in spirals.

协定税率 %								RCEP		特惠税率 %			Article Description
东/冰/格	巴基斯坦	韩国	瑞士上/下	哥/秘/柬	澳/毛	新西/坡/智	中国港/澳/台	东盟及马来/澳/韩	日/新	亚太2国	老/柬/缅	98/97/95	
													Hat-forms, hat bodies and hoods of felt, neither blocked to shape nor with made brims; plateaux and manchons (including slit manchons), of felt:
0/0/0		13.2	2.2/2.2	0/0/0	0/13.2	0/0/0	0/0/	20.9/20.9/20.9	21/20.9			0/0/0	Hat-forms, hat bodies and hoods of felt, neither blocked to shape nor with made brims; plateaux and manchons (including slit manchons), of felt
													Hat-shapes, plaited or made by assembling strips of any material, neither blocked to shape, nor with made brims, nor lined, nor trimmed:
0/0/0		9.3	2/2	0/0/0	0/0	0/0/0	0/0/	18/18/18	18.8/18			0/0/0	Hat-shapes, plaited or made by assembling strips of any material, neither blocked to shape, nor with made brims, nor lined, nor trimmed
													Hats and other headgear, plaited or made by assembling strips of any material, whether or not lined or trimmed:
0/0/0		9.3	2/2	0/0/0	0/0	0/0/0	0/0/	18/18/18	18.8/18			0/0/0	Hats and other headgear, plaited or made by assembling strips of any material, whether or not lined or trimmed
													Hats and other headgear, knitted or crocheted, or made up from lace, felt or other textile fabric, in the piece (but not in strips), whether or not lined or trimmed; hair-nets of any material, whether or not lined or trimmed:
0/0/0	2	2	0/0	0/0/0	0/0	0//0	0/0/	0/0/9	9.1/0			0/0/0	---Hair-nets
0/0/0	19	9.3	2/2	0/0/0	0/12	0/0/0	0/0/	18/18/18	18.8/18			0/0/0	---Hats and other headgear, knitted or crocheted
													---Other:
0/0/0		13.2	2.2/2.2	0/0/0	0/13.2	0/0/0	0/0/	20.9/20.9/20.9	21/20.9			0/0/0	----Felt hats and other felt headgear, made from the hat bodies, hoods or plateaux of heading No.65.01, whether or not lined or trimmed
0/0/0	19	4	2/2	0/0/0	0/12	0/0/0	0/0/	0/0/18	18.2/0			0/0/0	----Other
													Other headgear, whether or not lined or trimmed:
													-Safety headgear
0/0/0	4	2	0/0	0/0/0	0/0	0//0	0/0/	0/0/9	9.1/0			0/0/0	Protecting cover (with veil and colander that can screen biological elements)
0/0/0	4	2	0/0	0/0/0	0/0	0//0	0/0/	0/0/9	9.1/0			0/0/0	Other safety caps (whether or not lined or trimmed)
													-Other:
0/0/0	2	2	0/0	0/0/0	0/0	0//0	0/0/	0/0/9	9.1/0			0/0/0	--Of rubber or of plastics
													--Of other materials:
													---Of leather
0/0/0	4	2	0/0	0/0/0	0/0	0//0	0/0/	0/0/9	9.1/0			0/0/0	Other headgear, of leather of wild animals
0/0/0	4	2	0/0	0/0/0	0/0	0//0	0/0/	0/0/9	9.1/0			0/0/0	Other headgear, of leather of other animals
													---Of furskin
0/0/0	2	2	0/0	0/0/0	0/0	0//0	0/0/	0/0/9	9.1/0			0/0/0	Other headgear, of leather of wild animals (whether or not lined or trimmed)
0/0/0	2	2	0/0	0/0/0	0/0	0//0	0/0/	0/0/9	9.1/0			0/0/0	Other headgear, of leather of other animals (whether or not lined or trimmed)
0/0/0		14.4	2.4/2.4	0/0/0	0/14.4	0/0/0	0/0/	22.8/22.8/	/22.8			0/0/0	---Other
													Head-bands, linings, covers, hat foundations, hat frames, peaks and chinstraps, for headgear:
													Head-bands, linings, covers, hat foundations, hat frames, peaks and chinstraps, for headgear
0/0/0		14.4	2.4/2.4	0/0/0	0/14.4	0/0/0	0/0/	22.8/22.8/	/22.8			0/0/0	Headwear accessories (including head bands, linings, covers, hat foundations, hat frames, peaks and chinstraps) containing materials of wild animals
0/0/0		14.4	2.4/2.4	0/0/0	0/14.4	0/0/0	0/0/	22.8/22.8/	/22.8			0/0/0	Other headwear accessories (including head-bands, linings, covers, hat foundations, hat frames, peaks and chinstraps)

第六十六章
雨伞、阳伞、手杖、鞭子、马鞭及其零件

注释：

一、本章不包括：

(一)丈量用杖及类似品(税目 90.17)；

(二)火器手杖、刀剑手杖、灌铅手杖及类似品(第九十三章)；

(三)第九十五章的货品(例如，玩具雨伞、玩具阳伞)。

二、税目 66.03 不包括纺织材料制的零件、附件及装饰品或者任何材料制的罩套、流苏、鞭梢、伞套及类似品。此类货品即使与税目 66.01 或 66.02 的物品一同报验，只要未装配在一起，则不应视为上述税目所列物品的组成零件，而应分别归入各有关税目。

税则号列	货品名称〔CIQ 扩展编码及品名－T2 表示见附表 2〕	最惠(%)	暂定税率	普通	增值/消费	出口退税	计量单位	监管条件/特殊证件	检验检疫	对美关税	亚太上/下
66.01	**雨伞及阳伞(包括手杖伞、庭园用伞及类似伞)：**										
6601.1000	-庭院用伞及类似伞〔101 含木制品，102 不含木制品〕	6		130	13/	13	千克/把	/		16	
	-其他：										
6601.9100	--折叠伞〔101 含木制品，102 不含木制品〕	4		130	13/	13	千克/把	/		29	
6601.9900	--其他〔101 含木制品，102 不含木制品〕	4		130	13/	13	千克/把	/		29	
66.02	**手杖、带座手杖、鞭子、马鞭及类似品：**										
6602.0000	手杖、带座手杖、鞭子、马鞭及类似品										
6602.0000 11	含濒危野生动物成分的手杖、带座手杖(包括马鞭、鞭子及类似品)〔101 含木制品，102 不含木制品〕	4		130	13/	0	千克/把	EF/		29	
6602.0000 19	动植物材料制手杖、鞭子及类似品(包括带座手杖)〔101 含木制品，102 不含木制品〕	4		130	13/	13	千克/把	/		29	
6602.0000 90	其他手杖、带座手杖、鞭子及类似品〔101 含木制品，102 不含木制品〕	4		130	13/	13	千克/把	/		29	
66.03	**税目 66.01 或 66.02 所列物品的零件及装饰品：**										
6603.2000	-伞骨，包括装在伞柄上的伞骨〔101 含木制品，102 不含木制品〕	6		130	13/	13	千克	/		31	
6603.9000	-其他										
6603.9000 10	含濒危野生动物成分的伞、手杖的零件及装饰品(包括鞭子的其他零件及饰品)〔101 含木制品，102 不含木制品〕	6		130	13/	0	千克	EF/		31	
6603.9000 90	伞、手杖及鞭子的其他零件及饰品(罩套、流苏、鞭梢及纺织材料制品除外)〔101 含木制品，102 不含木制品〕	6		130	13/	13	千克	/		31	

Chapter 66
Umbrellas, sun umbrellas, walking-sticks, seat-sticks, whips, riding-crops and parts thereof

Notes:

1. This Chapter does not cover:
   (a) Measure walking-sticks or the like (heading No.90. 17);
   (b) Firearm-sticks, sword-sticks, loaded walking-sticks or the like (Chapter 93) or;
   (c) Goods of Chapter 95 (for example, toy umbrellas, toy sun umbrellas).
2. Heading No.66. 03 does not cover parts, trimmings or accessories of textile material, or covers, tassels, thongs, umbrella cases or the like, of any material. Such goods presented with, but not fitted to, articles of heading No.66. 01 or 66. 02 are to be classified separately and not to be treated as forming part of those articles.

协定税率 %								RCEP		特惠税率 %			Article Description
东/冰/格	巴基斯坦	韩国	瑞士上/下	哥/秘/柬	澳/毛	新西/坡/智	中国港/澳/台	东盟及马来/澳/韩	日/新	亚太2国	老/柬/缅	98/97/95	
													Umbrellas and sun umbrellas (including walking-stick umbrellas, garden umbrellas and similar umbrellas):
0/0/0	7	2.8	1.4/1.4	0/0/0	0/0	0/0/0	0/0/	0/0/12.6	12.7/0			0/0/0	-Garden or similar umbrellas
													-Other:
0/0/0	2	2	0/0	0/0/0	0/0	0/ /0	0/0/	0/0/9	9.1/0			0/0/0	--Having a telescopic shaft
0/0/0	2	2	0/0	0/0/0	0/0	0/ /0	0/0/	0/0/9	9.1/0			0/0/0	--Other
													Walking-sticks, seat-sticks, whips, riding-crops and the like:
													Walking-sticks, seat-sticks, whips, riding-crops and the like
0/0/0	2	2	0/0	0/0/0	0/0	0/ /0	0/0/	0/0/9	9.1/0			0/0/0	Walking-sticks, seat-sticks, whips, riding-crops and the like, containing materials of wild animals
0/0/0	2	2	0/0	0/0/0	0/0	0/ /0	0/0/	0/0/9	9.1/0			0/0/0	Walking-sticks, seat-sticks, whips, riding-crops and the like, of plant materials or animal materials
0/0/0	2	2	0/0	0/0/0	0/0	0/ /0	0/0/	0/0/9	9.1/0			0/0/0	Other walking-sticks, seat-sticks, whips, riding-crops and the like
													Parts, trimmings and accessories of articles of heading No. 66. 01 or 66. 02:
0/0/0	11.2	2.8	1.4/1.4	0/0/0	0/0	0/0/0	0/0/	0/0/12.6	12.7/0			0/0/0	-Umbrella frames, including frames mounted on shafts (sticks)
													-Other
0/0/0	11.2	2.8	1.4/1.4	0/0/0	0/0	0/0/0	0/0/	0/0/12.6	12.7/0			0/0/0	Parts, trimmings and accessories of articles, containing materials of wild animals
0/0/0	11.2	2.8	1.4/1.4	0/0/0	0/0	0/0/0	0/0/	0/0/12.6	12.7/0			0/0/0	Other parts, trimmings and accessories of articles, other than covers, tassels, thongs and other articles of textile material

第六十七章
已加工羽毛、羽绒及其制品；人造花；人发制品

注释：

一、本章不包括：

（一）人发制滤布（税目59.11）；

（二）花边、刺绣品或其他纺织物制成的花卉图案（第十一类）；

（三）鞋靴（第六十四章）；

（四）帽类及发网（第六十五章）；

（五）玩具、运动用品或狂欢节用品（第九十五章）；

（六）羽毛掸帚、粉扑及人发制的筛子（第九十六章）。

二、税目67.01不包括：

（一）羽毛或羽绒仅在其中作为填充料的物品（例如税目94.04的寝具）；

（二）羽毛或羽绒仅作为饰物或填充料的衣服或衣着附件；

（三）税目67.02的人造花、叶及其部分品，以及它们的制成品。

三、税目67.02不包括：

（一）玻璃制品（第七十章）；

（二）用陶器、石料、金属、木料或其他材料经模铸、锻造、雕刻、冲压或用其他方法整件制成形的人造花、叶或果实；用捆扎、胶粘及类似方法以外的其他方法将部分品组合而成的上述制品。

税则号列	货品名称〔CIQ扩展编码及品名—T2表示见附表2〕	最惠(%)	暂定税率	普通	增值/消费	出口退税	计量单位	监管条件/特殊证件	检验检疫	对美关税	亚太上/下
67.01	**带羽毛或羽绒的鸟皮及鸟体其他部分、羽毛、部分羽毛、羽绒及其制品（税目05.05的货品和经加工的羽管及羽轴除外）：**										
6701.0000	带羽毛或羽绒的鸟皮及鸟体其他部分、羽毛、部分羽毛、羽绒及其制品（税目05.05的货品和经加工的羽管及羽轴除外）										
6701.0000 10	已加工野禽羽毛、羽绒及其制品〔999〕	8		130	13/	13	千克	AFEB/	PQ	18	
6701.0000 90	其他已加工羽毛、羽绒及其制品（税目05.05的货品及经加工的羽管及羽轴除外）〔999〕	8		130	13/	13	千克	AB/	PQ	18	
67.02	**人造花、叶、果实及其零件；用人造花、叶或果实制成的物品：**										
6702.1000	-塑料制〔101含木制品，102不含木制品〕	8		130	13/	13	千克	/		18	
	-其他材料制：										
6702.9010	---羽毛制										
6702.9010 10	野禽羽毛制花、叶、果实及其制品〔101含木制品，102不含木制品〕	8		130	13/	13	千克	AFEB/	PQ		4.8/4.8
6702.9010 90	其他羽毛制花、叶、果实及其制品（包括花、叶、果实的零件）〔101含木制品，102不含木制品〕	8		130	13/	13	千克	AB/	PQ		4.8/4.8
6702.9020	---丝及绢丝制〔101含木制品，102不含木制品〕	8		130	13/	13	千克	/		33	
6702.9030	---化学纤维制〔101含木制品，102不含木制品〕	8		130	13/	13	千克	/		23	
6702.9090	---其他〔101含木制品，102不含木制品〕	8		130	13/	13	千克	/		33	
67.03	**经梳理、稀疏、脱色或其他方法加工的人发；作假发及类似品用的羊毛、其他动物毛或其他纺织材料：**										
6703.0000	经梳理、稀疏、脱色或其他方法加工的人发；作假发及类似品用的羊毛、其他动物毛或其他纺织材料〔101含木制品，102不含木制品〕	8		100	13/	13	千克	/		33	5.2/5.2
67.04	**人发、动物毛或纺织材料制的假发、假胡须、假眉毛、假睫毛及类似品；其他税目未列名的人发制品：**										
	-合成纤维纺织材料制：										
6704.1100	--整头假发〔101含木制品，102不含木制品〕	8		130	13/	13	千克	/		28	
6704.1900	--其他〔101含木制品，102不含木制品〕	8		130	13/	13	千克	/		33	
6704.2000	-人发制〔101含木制品，102不含木制品〕	6		130	13/	13	千克	/		16	
6704.9000	-其他材料制〔101含木制品，102不含木制品〕	8		130	13/	13	千克	/		33	

Chapter 67
Prepared feathers and down and articles made of feathers or of down; artificial flowers; articles of human hair

Notes:

1. This Chapter does not cover:
   (a) Straining cloth of human hair (heading No.59.11);
   (b) Floral motifs of lace, of embroidery or other textile fabric (Section XI);
   (c) Footwear (Chapter 64);
   (d) Headgear or hair-nets (Chapter 65);
   (e) Toys, sports requisites or carnival articles (Chapter 95); or
   (f) Feather dusters, powder-puffs or hair sieves (Chapter 96).
2. Heading No.67.01 does not cover:
   (a) Articles in which feathers or down constitute only filling or padding (for example, bedding of heading No.94.04);
   (b) Articles of apparel or clothing accessories in which feathers or down constitute no more than mere trimming or padding; or
   (c) Artificial flowers or foliage or parts thereof or made up articles of heading No.67.02.
3. Heading No.67.02 does not cover:
   (a) Articles of glass (Chapter 70); or
   (b) Artificial flowers, foliage or fruit of pottery, stone, metal, wood or other materials, obtained in one piece by moulding, forging, carving, stamping or other process, or consisting of parts assembled otherwise than by binding, glueing, fitting into one another or similar methods.

协定税率 %								RCEP		特惠税率 %			Article Description
东/冰/格	巴基斯坦	韩国	瑞士 上/下	哥/秘/柬	澳/毛	新西/坡/智	中国港/澳/台	东盟及马来/澳/韩	日/新	亚太2国	老/柬/缅	98/97/95	
													Skins and other parts of birds with their feathers or down, feathers, parts of feathers, down and articles thereof (other than goods of heading No. 05. 05 and worked quills and scapes):
													Skins and other parts of birds with their feathers or down, feathers, parts of feathers, down and articles thereof (other than goods of heading No. 05. 05 and worked quills and scapes)
0/0/0		9.3	2/2	0/0/0	0/0	0/0/0	0/0/	18.7/19/	18.8/19			0/0/0	Worked feathers, down and articles thereof, of wild birds
0/0/0		9.3	2/2	0/0/0	0/0	0/0/0	0/0/	18.7/19/	18.8/19			0/0/0	Other worked feathers, down and articles thereof (other than goods of heading No.0505 and worked quills and scapes)
													Artificial flowers, foliage and fruit and parts thereof; articles made of artificial flowers, foliage or fruit:
0/0/0		9.3	2/2	0/0/0	0/0	0/0/0	0/0/	18/18/18	18.8/18			0/0/0	-Of plastics
													-Of other materials:
													---Of feathers or down
0/0/0		9.3	2/2	0/0/0	0/0	0/0/0	0/0/	18/18/18	18.8/18			0/0/0	Flowers, foliage and fruit and articles thereof, of feathers or down of wild birds
0/0/0		9.3	2/2	0/0/0	0/0	0/0/0	0/0/	18/18/18	18.8/18			0/0/0	Flowers, foliage and fruit and parts thereof; articles made of artificial flowers, foliage or fruit, of other feathers or down
0/0/0		14.4	2.4/2.4	0/0/0	0/14.4	0/0/0	0/0/	22.8/22.8/22.8	22.9/22.8			0/0/0	---Of silk or silk waste
0/0/0		14.4	2.4/2.4	0/0/0	0/14.4	0/0/0	0/0/	22.8/22.8/22.8	22.9/22.8			0/0/0	---Of man-made fibres
0/0/0		9.3	2/2	0/0/0	0/0	0/0/0	0/0/	18/18/18	18.8/18			0/0/0	---Other
													Human hair, dressed, thinned, bleached or otherwise worked; wool or other animal hair or other textile materials, prepared for use in making wigs or the like:
0/0/0	18	4	2/2	0/0/0	0/0	0/0/0	0/0/	0/0/18	18.2/0			0/0/0	Human hair, dressed, thinned, bleached or otherwise worked; wool or other animal hair or other textile materials, prepared for use in making wigs or the like
													Wigs, false beards, eyebrows and eyelashes, switches and the like, of human or animal hair or of textile materials; articles of human hair not elsewhere specified or included:
													-Of synthetic textile materials:
0/0/0		15	8/8	0/0/0	0/15	0/0/0	0/0/	23.8/23.8/23.8	23.8/23.8			0/0/0	--Complete wigs
0/0/0		15	8/8	0/0/0	0/15	0/0/0	0/0/	23.8/23.8/	/23.8			0/0/0	--Other
0/0/0	12	3	1.5/1.5	0/0/0	0/0	0/0/0	0/0/	0/0/13.5	13.6/0			0/0/0	Of human hair
0/0/0		15	8/8	0/0/0	0/15	0/0/0	0/0/	23.8/23.8/	/23.8			0/0/0	-Of other materials

第十三类

石料、石膏、水泥、石棉、云母及类似材料的制品；陶瓷产品；玻璃及其制品

第六十八章

石料、石膏、水泥、石棉、云母及类似材料的制品

注释：

一、本章不包括：

(一)第二十五章的货品；

(二)税目48.10或48.11的经涂布、浸渍或覆盖的纸及纸板(例如，用云母粉或石墨涂布的纸及纸板、沥青纸及纸板)；

(三)第五十六章或第五十九章的经涂布、浸渍或包覆的纺织物(例如，用云母粉、沥青涂布或包覆的织物)；

(四)第七十一章的物品；

(五)第八十二章的工具及其零件；

(六)税目84.42的印刷用石板；

(七)绝缘子(税目85.46)或绝缘材料制的零件(税目85.47)；

(八)牙科用磨锉(税目90.18)；

(九)第九十一章的物品(例如，钟及钟壳)；

(十)第九十四章的物品(例如，家具、灯具及照明装置、活动房屋)；

(十一)第九十五章的物品(例如，玩具、游戏品及运动用品)；

(十二)用第九十六章注释二(二)所述材料制成的税目96.02的物品或税目96.06的物品(例如，纽扣)、税目96.09的物品(例如，石笔)、税目96.10的物品(例如，绘画石板)或税目96.20的物品(独脚架、双脚架、三脚架及类似品)；

(十三)第九十七章的物品(例如，艺术品)。

二、税目68.02所称"已加工的碑石或建筑用石"，不仅适用于已加工的税目25.15、25.16的各种石料，也适用于所有经类似加工的其他天然石料(例如，石英岩、燧石、白云石及冻石)，但不适用于板岩。

税则号列	货品名称〔CIQ扩展编码及品名－T2表示见附表2〕	最惠(%)	暂定税率	普通	增值/消费	出口退税	计量单位	监管条件/特殊证件	检验检疫	对美关税	亚太上/下
68.01	**天然石料(不包括板岩)制的长方砌石、路缘石、扁平石：**										
6801.0000	天然石料(不包括板岩)制的长方砌石、路缘石、扁平石〔999〕	12		70	13/	0	千克	/			
68.02	**已加工的碑石或建筑用石(不包括板岩)及其制品，但税目68.01的货品除外；天然石料(包括板岩)制的镶嵌石(马赛克)及类似品，不论是否有衬背；天然石料(包括板岩)制的人工染色石粒、石片及石粉：**										
	-砖、瓦、方块及类似品，不论是否为矩形(包括正方形)，其最大面以可置入边长小于7厘米的方格为限；人工染色的石粒、石片及石粉：										
6802.1010	---大理石〔999〕	15		90	13/	0	千克	/			9.8/9.8
6802.1090	---其他〔999〕	15		90	13/	0	千克	/			9.8/9.8
	-简单切削或锯开并具有一个平面的其他碑石或建筑用石及其制品：										
	--大理石、石灰华及蜡石：										
6802.2110	---大理石〔999〕	10		90	13/	0	千克	/		35	
6802.2120	---石灰华〔999〕	15		90	13/	13	千克	/			10.5/10.5
6802.2190	---其他〔999〕	15		90	13/	0	千克	/			10.5/10.5
6802.2300	--花岗岩〔999〕	10		90	13/	0	千克	A/	M		6.5/6.5
	--其他石：										
6802.2910	---其他石灰石〔999〕	15		90	13/	0	千克	/			
6802.2990	---其他〔999〕	15		90	13/	0	千克	/			
	-其他：										
	--大理石、石灰华及蜡石：										
6802.9110	---石刻〔999〕	15		90	13/	13	千克	/		40	
6802.9190	---其他〔999〕	10		90	13/	13	千克	/		35	
	--其他石灰质石：										
6802.9210	---石刻〔999〕	15		90	13/	13	千克	/		25	
6802.9290	---其他〔999〕	10		90	13/	13	千克	/		30	
	--花岗岩：										
	---石刻：										
6802.9311	----墓碑石〔999〕	15		90	13/	13	千克	A/	M		
6802.9319	----其他〔999〕	15		90	13/	13	千克	A/	M		10.5/10.5
6802.9390	---其他〔999〕	10		90	13/	13	千克	A/	M	35	6.5/6.5
	--其他石：										
6802.9910	---石刻〔101含木制品的工艺品，102不含木制品的工艺品，103其他石材、石料〕	15		90	13/	13	千克	/		40	
6802.9990	---其他〔999〕	15		90	13/	13	千克	/		40	
68.03	**已加工的板岩及板岩或粘聚板岩的制品：**										
6803.0010	---板岩制〔999〕	15		80	13/	13	千克	/			
6803.0090	---其他〔999〕	15		80	13/	13	千克	/			

SECTION Ⅻ

ARTICLES OF STONE, PLASTER, CEMENT, ASBESTOS, MICA OR SIMILAR MATERIALS; CERAMIC PRODUCTS; GLASS AND GLASSWARE

Chapter 68

Articles of stone, plaster, cement, asbestos, mica or similar materials

Notes:

1. This Chapter does not cover:
   (a) Goods of Chapter 25;
   (b) Coated, impregnated or covered paper and paperboard of heading No.48.10 or 48.11 (for example, paper and paperboard coated with mica powder or graphite, bituminized or asphalted paper and paperboard);
   (c) Coated, impregnated or covered textile fabric of Chapter 56 or 59 (for example, fabric coated or covered with mica powder, bituminized or asphalted fabric);
   (d) Articles of Chapter 71;
   (e) Tools or parts of tools, of Chapter 82;
   (f) Lithographic stones of heading No.84.42;
   (g) Electrical insulators (heading No.85.46) or fittings of insulating material of heading No.85.47;
   (h) Dental burrs (heading No.90.18);
   (ij) Articles of Chapter 91 (for example, clocks and clock cases);
   (k) Articles of Chapter 94 (for example, furniture, lamps and lighting fittings, prefabricated buildings);
   (l) Articles of Chapter 95 (for example, toys, games and sports requisites);
   (m) Articles of heading No.96.02, if made of materials specified in Note 2 (b) to Chapter 96, or of heading No.96.06 (for example, buttons), No.96.09 (for example, slate pencils) or No.96.10 (for example, drawing slates); or of heading No.96.20 (unipod, bipod, tripod or the like)
   (n) Articles of Chapter 97 (for example, works of art).
2. In heading No.68.02, the expression "worked monumental or building stone" applies not only to the varieties of stone referred to in heading No.25.15 or 25.16, but also to all other natural stone (for example, quartzite, flint, dolomite and steatite) similarly worked; it does not, however, apply to slate.

协定税率 %								RCEP		特惠税率 %			Article Description
东/冰/格	巴基斯坦	韩国	瑞士 上/下	哥/秘/柬	澳/毛	新西/坡/智	中国港/澳/台	东盟及马来/澳/韩	日/新	亚太2国	老/柬/缅	98/97/95	
													Setts, curbstones and flagstones, of natural stone (except slate):
0/0/0	6	2.4	1.2/1.2	0/0/0	0/0	0/0/0	0/0/	0/0/10.8	10.9/0			0/0/0	Setts, curbstones and flagstones, of natural stone (except slate)
													Worked monumental or building stone (except slate) and articles thereof, other than goods of heading No. 68.01; mosaic cubes and the like, of natural stone (including slate), whether or not on a backing; artificially coloured granules, chippings and powder, of natural stone (including slate):
													-Tiles, cubes and similar articles, whether or not rectangular (including square), the largest surface area of which is capable of being enclosed in a square the side of which is less than 7cm; artificially coloured granules, chippings and powder:
0/0/0	0	14.4	2.4/2.4	0/0/0	0/14.4	0/0/0	0/0/	22.8/22.8/22.8	22.9/22.8			0/0/0	---Marble
0/0/0	0	9.3	2/2	0/0/0	0/0	0/0/0	0/0/	18/18/18	18.8/18			0/0/0	---Other
													-Other monumental or building stone and articles thereof, simply cut or sawn, with a flat or even surface:
													--Marble, travertine and alabaster:
0/0/0	0	2	0/0	0/0/0	0/0	0//0	0/0/	0/0/9	9.1/0			0/0/0	---Marble
0/0/0	0	14.4	2.4/2.4	0/0/0	0/14.4	0/0/0	0/0/	22.8/22.8/22.8	22.9/22.8			0/0/0	---Travertine
0/0/0	0	14.4	2.4/2.4	0/0/0	0/14.4	0/0/0	0/0/	22.8/22.8/22.8	22.9/22.8			0/0/0	---Other
0/0/0	0	2	0/0	0/0/0	0/0	0//0	0/0/	0/0/9	9.1/0			0/0/0	--Granite
													--Other stone:
0/0/0	0	14.4	2.4/2.4	0/0/0	0/14.4	0/0/0	0/0/	22.8/22.8/22.8	22.9/22.8			0/0/0	---Other calcareous stone
0/0/0	0	3	1.5/1.5	0/0/0	0/0	0/0/0	0/0/	0/0/13.5	13.6/0			0/0/0	---Other
													-Other:
													--Marble, travertine and alabaster:
0/0/0	0	14.4	2.4/2.4	0/0/0	0/14.4	0/0/0	0/0/	22.8/22.8/22.8	22.9/22.8			0/0/0	---Carvings
0/0/0	0	2	0/0	0/0/0	0/0	0//0	0/0/	0/0/9	9.1/0			0/0/0	---Other
													--Other calcareous stone:
0/0/0	0	14.4	2.4/2.4	0/0/0	0/14.4	0/0/0	0/0/	22.8/22.8/22.8	22.9/22.8			0/0/0	---Carvings
0/0/0	0	2	0/0	0/0/0	0/0	0//0	0/0/	0/0/9	9.1/0			0/0/0	---Other
													--Granite:
													---Carvings:
0/0/0	0	14.4	2.4/2.4	0/0/0	0/14.4	0/0/0	0/0/	22.8/22.8/22.8	/22.8			0/0/0	----Tombstone(gravestone)
0/0/0	0	14.4	2.4/2.4	0/0/0	0/14.4	0/0/0	0/0/	22.8/22.8/22.8	/22.8			0/0/0	----Other
0/0/0	0	2	0/0	0/0/0	0/0	0//0	0/0/	0/0/9	9.1/0			0/0/0	---Other
													--Other stone:
0/0/0	0	14.4	2.4/2.4	0/0/0	0/14.4	0/0/0	0/0/	22.8/22.8/22.8	/22.8			0/0/0	---Carvings
0/0/0	0	14.4	2.4/2.4	0/0/0	0/14.4	0/0/0	0/0/	22.8/22.8/22.8	/22.8			0/0/0	---Other
													Worked slate and articles of slate or of agglomerated slate:
0/0/0		9.3	2/2	0/0/0	0/0	0/0/0	0/0/	18/18/18	18.8/18			0/0/0	---Of slate
0/0/0		9.3	2/2	0/0/0	0/0	0/0/0	0/0/	18/18/18	18.8/18			0/0/0	---Other

税则号列	货品名称〔CIQ 扩展编码及品名—T2 表示见附表 2〕	最惠(%)	暂定税率	普通	增值/消费	出口退税	计量单位	监管条件/特殊证件	检验检疫	对美关税	亚太上/下
68.04	**未装支架的石磨、石碾、砂轮和类似品及其零件，用于研磨、磨刃、抛光、整形或切割，以及手用磨石、抛光石及其零件，用天然石料、粘聚的天然磨料、人造磨料或陶瓷制成，不论是否装有其他材料制成的零件：**										
6804.1000	-碾磨或磨浆用石磨、石碾〔999〕	8		40	13/	13	千克	/		18	
	-其他石磨、石碾、砂轮及类似品：										
	--粘聚合成或天然金刚石制：	8		17	17	5	千克				
6804.2110	---砂轮〔999〕	8		17	13/	13	千克	/			
6804.2190	---其他〔101 石磨或石碾，102 其它磨具，103 其他石材、石料〕	8		17	13/	13	千克	/			
	--其他粘聚磨料制或陶瓷制：										
6804.2210	---砂轮〔999〕	8		17	13/	13	千克	/		28	
6804.2290	---其他〔999〕	8		40	13/	13	千克	/		33	
	--天然石料制：										
6804.2310	---砂轮〔999〕	8		17	13/	13	千克	/		28	
6804.2390	---其他〔999〕	8		40	13/	13	千克	/		28	
	-手用磨石及抛光石：										
6804.3010	---琢磨油石〔999〕	8		17	13/	13	千克	/		18	5.2/5.2
6804.3090	---其他〔999〕	8		40	13/	13	千克	/		28	6.4/6.4
68.05	**砂布、砂纸及以其他材料为底的类似品，不论是否裁切、缝合或用其他方法加工成形：**										
6805.1000	-砂布〔999〕	8		40	13/	13	千克	/		18	
6805.2000	-砂纸〔999〕	8		40	13/	13	千克	/		18	
6805.3000	-其他〔999〕	8		40	13/	13	千克	/		18	
68.06	**矿渣棉、岩石棉及类似的矿质棉；页状蛭石、膨胀黏土、泡沫矿渣及类似的膨胀矿物材料；具有隔热、隔音或吸音性能的矿物材料的混合物及制品，但税目 68.11、68.12 或第六十九章的货品除外：**										
	-矿渣棉、岩石棉及类似的矿质棉(包括其相互混合物)，块状、成片或成卷：										
6806.1010	---硅酸铝纤维及其制品〔999〕	10		40	13/	13	千克	/		20	
6806.1090	---其他										
6806.1090 01	其他矿物纤维，渣球含量小于 5%〔999〕	10	5	40	13/	13	千克	/		25	
6806.1090 90	其他矿渣棉，岩石棉及类似矿质棉(包括相互混合物，块状、成片或成卷)〔999〕	10		40	13/	13	千克	/		30	
6806.2000	-页状硅石、膨胀黏土、泡沫矿渣及类似的膨胀矿物材料(包括其相互混合物)〔999〕	10		40	13/	0	千克	/		20	
6806.9000	-其他〔999〕	10		50	13/	0	千克	/		20	
68.07	**沥青或类似原料(例如，石油沥青或煤焦油沥青)的制品：**										
6807.1000	-成卷〔999〕	10		50	13/	0	千克	/		35	
6807.9000	-其他〔999〕	10		50	13/	0	千克	/		35	8/8
68.08	**镶板、平板、瓦、砖及类似品，用水泥、石膏及其他矿物粘合材料粘合植物纤维、稻草、刨花、木片屑、木粉、锯末或木废料制成：**										
6808.0000	镶板、平板、瓦、砖及类似品，用水泥、石膏及其他矿物粘合材料粘合植物纤维、稻草、刨花、木片屑、木粉、锯末或木废料制成〔999〕	8		40	13/	13	千克	/		33	
68.09	**石膏制品及以石膏为基本成分的混合材料制品：**										
	-未经装饰的板、片、砖、瓦及类似品：										
6809.1100	--仅用纸、纸板贴面或加强的〔999〕	15		100	13/	13	千克	/		40	
6809.1900	--其他〔999〕	15		100	13/	13	千克	/		35	
6809.9000	-其他制品〔999〕	15		100	13/	13	千克	/		40	
68.10	**水泥、混凝土或人造石制品，不论是否加强：**										
	-砖、瓦、扁平石及类似品：										
6810.1100	--建筑用砖及石砌块〔999〕	10		40	13/	13	千克	/		20	6.5/6.5
	--其他：										
6810.1910	---人造石制〔999〕	10		70	13/	13	千克	/		35	6.5/6.5
6810.1990	---其他〔999〕	10		70	13/	13	千克	/		35	6.5/6.5
	-其他制品：										
	--建筑或土木工程用的预制结构件：										
6810.9110	---钢筋混凝土和预应力混凝土管、杆、板、桩等〔999〕	10		40	13/	13	千克	/			
6810.9190	---其他〔999〕	10		40	13/	13	千克	/		20	
	--其他：										
6810.9910	---铁道用水泥枕〔999〕	8		14	13/	13	千克	/			

协定税率 %								RCEP		特惠税率 %			Article Description
东/冰/格	巴基斯坦	韩国	瑞士 上/下	哥/秘/柬	澳/毛	新西/坡/智	中国港/澳/台	东盟及马来/澳/韩	日/新	亚太2国	老/柬/缅	98/97/95	
													Millstones, grindstones, grinding wheels and the like, without frameworks, for grinding, sharpening, polishing, trueing or cutting, hand sharpening or polishing stones, and parts thereof, of natural stone, of agglomerated natural or artificial abrasives, or of ceramics, with or without parts of other materials:
0/0/0	2	0	0/0	0/0/0	0/0	0//0	0/0/	0/0/0	7.3/0			0/0/0	-Millstones and grindstones for milling, grinding or pulping
													-Other millstones, grindstones, grinding wheels and the like:
													--Of agglomerated synthetic or natural diamond:
0/0/0	2	1.6	0.8/0.8	0/0/0	0/0	0//0	0/0/	7.2/7.2/7.2	7.3/7.2			0/0/0	---Grinding wheels
0/0/0	2	1.6	0.8/0.8	0/0/0	0/0	0//0	0/0/	7.2/7.2/7.2	7.3/7.2			0/0/0	---Other
													--Of other agglomerated abrasives or of ceramics:
0/0/0	2	0	0.8/0.8	0/0/0	0/0	0//0	0/0/	7.2/7.2/7.2	7.3/7.2			0/0/0	---Grinding wheels
0/0/0	2	0	0/0	0/0/0	0/0	0//0	0/0/	0/0/0	7.3/0			0/0/0	---Other
													--Of natural stone:
0/0/0	2	0	0/0	0/0/0	0/0	0//0	0/0/	0/0/0	7.3/0			0/0/0	---Grinding wheels
0/0/0	2	1.6	0/0	0/0/0	0/0	0//0	0/0/	0/0/7.2	7.3/0			0/0/0	---Other
													-Hand sharpening or polishing stones:
0/0/0	2	0	0/0	0/0/0	0/0	0//0	0/0/	0/0/0	7.3/0			0/0/0	---Oilstones
0/0/0	2	1.6	0/0	0/0/0	0/0	0//0	0/0/	0/0/7.2	7.3/0			0/0/0	---Other
													Natural or artificial abrasive powder or grain, on a base of textile material, of paper, of paperboard or of other materials, whether or not cut to shape or sewn or otherwise made up:
0/0/0	2	3.7	0.8/0.8	0/0/0	0/0	0//0	0/0/	7.5/7.6/7.5	7.5/7.6			0/0/0	-On a base of woven textile fabric only
0/0/0	2	1.6	0.8/0.8	0/0/0	0/0	0//0	0/0/	7.2/7.2/7.2	7.3/7.2			0/0/0	-On a base of paper or paperboard only
0/0/0	2	1.6	0/0	0/0/0	0/0	0//0	0/0/	7.2/7.2/7.2	7.3/7.2			0/0/0	-On a base of other materials
													Slag wool, rock wool and similar mineral wools; exfoliated vermiculite, expanded clays, foamed slag and similar expanded mineral materials; mixtures and articles of heat-insulating, sound-insulating or sound-absorbing mineral materials, other than those of heading No.68. 11 or 68. 12 or of Chapter 69:
													-Slag wool, rock wool and similar mineral wools (including intermixtures thereof), in bulk, sheets or rolls:
0/0/0	3.5	2.1	1.1/1.1	0/0/0	0/0	0/0/0	0/0/	0/0/9.5	9.5/0			0/0/0	---Aluminum silicate fiber and its products
													---Other
0/0/0	3.5	2.1	1.1/1.1	0/0/0	0/0	0/0/0	0/0/	9.5/9.5/9.5	9.5/9.5			0/0/0	Other mineral fibre, containing slag, <5%
0/0/0	3.5	2.1	1.1/1.1	0/0/0	0/0	0/0/0	0/0/	9.5/9.5/9.5	9.5/9.5			0/0/0	Slag wool, rock wool and similar mineral wools(including intermixtures thereof, inbulk, sheets or rolls)
0/0/0	3.5	2.1	1.1/1.1	0/0/0	0/0	0/0/0	0/0/	0/0/9.5	9.5/0			0/0/0	-Exfoliated vermiculite, expanded clays, foamed slag and similar expanded mineral materials (including intermixtures thereof)
0/0/0	2	4.6	0/0	0/0/0	0/0	0//0	0/0/	9.3/9.5/9.3	9.4/9.5			0/0/0	-Other
													Articles of asphalt or of similar material (for example, petroleum bitumen or coal tar pitch):
0/0/0	6	2.4	1.2/1.2	0/0/0	0/0	0/0/0	0/0/	0/0/10.8	10.9/0			0/0/0	-In rolls
0/0/0	3.5	2.4	1.2/1.2	0/0/0	0/0	0/0/0	0/0/	0/0/10.8	10.9/0			0/0/0	-Other
													Panels, boards, tiles, blocks and similar articles of vegetable fibre, of straw or of shavings, chips, particles, sawdust or other waste, of wood, agglomerated with cement, plaster or other mineral binders:
0/0/0	3.5	2.1	1.1/1.1	0/0/0	0/0	0/0/0	0/0/	0/0/9.5	9.5/0			0/0/0	Panels, boards, tiles, blocks and similar articles of vegetable fibre, of straw or of shavings, chips, particles, sawdust or other waste, of wood, agglomerated with cement, plaster or other mineral binders
													Articles of plaster or of compositions based on plaster:
													-Boards, sheets, panels, tiles and similar articles, not ornamented:
0/0/0			2.8/2.8	0/0/0	0/16.8	0/0/0	0/0/	5/5/	/5			0/0/0	--Faced or reinforced with paper or paper-board only
0/0/0		15		0/0/0	0/15	0/0/0	0/0/	23.8/23.8/	/23.8			0/0/0	--Other
0/0/0		15		0/0/0	0/15	0/0/0	0/0/	23.8/23.8/23.8	23.8/23.8			0/0/0	-Other articles
													Articles of cement, of concrete or of artificial stone, whether or not reinforced:
													-Tiles, flagstones, bricks and similar articles:
0/0/0	3.5	2.1	1.1/1.1	0/0/0	0/0	0/0/0	0/0/	0/0/9.5	9.5/0			0/0/0	--Building blocks and bricks
													--Other:
0/0/0	3.5	2.1	1.1/1.1	0/0/0	0/0	0/0/0	0/0/	0/0/9.5	9.5/0			0/0/0	---Of artificial stone
0/0/0	3.5	2.1	1.1/1.1	0/0/0	0/0	0/0/0	0/0/	0/0/9.5	9.5/0			0/0/0	---Other
													-Other articles:
													--Prefabricated structural components for building or civil engineering:
0/0/0	3.5	2.1	1.1/1.1	0/0/0	0/0	0/0/0	0/0/	0/0/9.5	9.5/0			0/0/0	---Reinforced concrete and prestressed concrete tubes, pipes, rods, plates, piles and similar articles
0/0/0	3.5	2.1	1.1/1.1	0/0/0	0/0	0/0/0	0/0/	0/0/9.5	9.5/0			0/0/0	---Other
													--Other:
0/0/0	2	0	0/0	0/0/0	0/0	0//0	0/0/	0/0/0	7.3/0			0/0/0	---Railway sleepers of concrete

税则号列	货品名称〔CIQ扩展编码及品名—T2表示见附表2〕	最惠(%)	暂定税率	普通	增值/消费	出口退税	计量单位	监管条件/特殊证件	检验检疫	对美关税	亚太上/下
6810.9990	---其他〔999〕	10		70	13/	13	千克	/		35	
68.11	**石棉水泥、纤维素水泥或类似材料的制品：**										
	-含石棉的：										
6811.4010	---瓦楞板〔999〕	5		40	13/	13	千克	/			
6811.4020	---其他片、板、砖、瓦及类似制品〔999〕	8		40	13/	13	千克	/		33	
6811.4030	---管子及管子附件〔999〕	8		40	13/	13	千克	/			
6811.4090	---其他制品〔999〕	8		40	13/	13	千克	/		18	
	-不含石棉的：										
6811.8100	--瓦楞板〔999〕	5		40	13/	13	千克	/			
6811.8200	--其他片、板、砖、瓦及类似制品〔999〕	8		40	13/	13	千克	/		33	
	--其他制品：										
6811.8910	---管子及管子附件〔999〕	8		40	13/	13	千克	/			
6811.8990	---其他〔999〕	8		40	13/	13	千克	/		33	
68.12	**已加工的石棉纤维；以石棉为基本成分或以石棉和碳酸镁为基本成分的混合物；上述混合物或石棉的制品(例如，纱线、机织物、服装、帽类、鞋靴、衬垫)，不论是否加强，但税号68.11或68.13的货品除外：**										
6812.8000	-青石棉的〔999〕	10		40	13/	13	千克	/			
	-其他：										
6812.9100	--服装、衣着附件、帽类及鞋靴〔999〕	10		40	13/	13	千克	/		35	
	--其他：										
6812.9910	---纸、麻丝板及毡子〔999〕	10		40	13/	13	千克	/		20	
6812.9920	---成片或成卷的压缩石棉纤维接合材料〔999〕	10		40	13/	13	千克	/		20	
6812.9990	---其他〔999〕	10		40	13/	13	千克	/		20	
68.13	**以石棉、其他矿物质或纤维素为基本成分的未装配摩擦材料及其制品(例如，片、卷、带、盘、圈、垫及扇形)，适于作制动器、离合器及类似品，不论是否与织物或其他材料结合而成：**										
	-含石棉的：										
6813.2010	---闸衬、闸垫〔999〕	10		40	13/	13	千克	/		20	
6813.2090	---其他〔999〕	10		40	13/	13	千克	/		20	
	-不含石棉的：										
6813.8100	--闸衬、闸垫〔999〕	10		40	13/	13	千克	/		35	
6813.8900	--其他〔999〕	10		40	13/	13	千克	/		20	
68.14	**已加工的云母及其制品，包括粘聚或复制的云母，不论是否附于纸、纸板或其他材料上：**										
6814.1000	-粘聚或复制云母制的板、片、带，不论是否附于其他材料上〔999〕	8		35	13/	13	千克	/		33	
6814.9000	-其他〔999〕	8		35	13/	13	千克	/		33	
68.15	**其他税号未列名的石制品及其他矿物制品(包括碳纤维及其制品和泥煤制品)：**										
	-碳纤维；非电气用的碳纤维制品；其他非电气用的石墨或其他碳精制品：										
6815.1100	--碳纤维										
6815.1100 10	两用物项管制的碳纤维(比模量≥12.7×10⁶ m，或比抗拉强度≥23.5×10⁴ m)〔999〕	17		70	13/	13	千克	3/			
6815.1100 90	其他碳纤维〔999〕	17		70	13/	13	千克	/			
6815.1200	--碳纤维织物〔999〕	17		70	13/	13	千克	/		27	
	--其他碳纤维制品：										
6815.1310	---碳纤维预浸料										
6815.1310 10	两用物项管制的碳纤维预浸料(制品)〔999〕	17		70	13/	13	千克	3/		27	
6815.1310 90	其他碳纤维预浸料(制品)〔999〕	17		70	13/	13	千克	/		27	
6815.1390	---其他〔999〕	17		70	13/	13	千克	/		37	
6815.1900	--其他										
6815.1900 10	碳化硅外延生产设备用石墨配件(金属含量≤5ppm)〔999〕	10	5	70	13/	0	千克	3/			
6815.1900 90	其他非电器用的石墨或其他碳精制品〔999〕	10		70	13/	0	千克	3/			
6815.2000	-泥煤制品〔999〕	10		70	13/	0	千克	/			
	-其他制品：										
6815.9100	--含有菱镁矿、方镁石形态的氧化镁、白云石(包括煅烧形态)或铬铁矿的〔999〕	10		70	13/	0	千克	/		35	
	--其他：										
6815.9940	---玄武岩纤维及其制品〔999〕	17		70	13/	13	千克	/		42	
6815.9990	---其他〔999〕	10		70	13/	0	千克	/		30	

协定税率 %								RCEP		特惠税率 %			Article Description
东/冰/格	巴基斯坦	韩国	瑞士 上/下	哥/秘/柬	澳/毛	新西/坡/智	中国港/澳/台	东盟及马来/澳/韩	日/新	亚太2国	老/柬/缅	98/97/95	
0/0/0	3.5	2.1	1.1/1.1	0/0/0	0/0	0/0/0	0/0/	0/0/9.5	9.5/0			0/0/0	---Other
													Articles of asbestos-cement, of cellulose fibre-cement or the like:
													-Containing aspestos:
0/0/0	0	0	0/0	0/0/0	0/0	0//0	0/0/	0/0/0	0/0			0/0/0	---Corrugated sheets
0/0/0	3.5	2.1	1.1/1.1	0/0/0	0/0	0/0/0	0/0/	0/0/9.5	9.5/0			0/0/0	---Other sheets, panels, tiles and similar articles
0/0/0	2	0	0/0	0/0/0	0/0	0//0	0/0/	0/0/0	7.3/0			0/0/0	---Tubes, pipes and tube or pipe fittings
0/0/0	2	1.6	0/0	0/0/0	0/0	0//0	0/0/	0/0/7.6	7.6/0			0/0/0	---Other articles
													-Not containing asbestos:
0/0/0	0	0	0/0	0/0/0	0/0	0//0	0/0/	0/0/0	0/0			0/0/0	--Corrugated sheets
0/0/0	3.5	2.1	4.4/4.4	0/0/0	0/0	0/0/0	0/0/	0/0/9.5	9.5/0			0/0/0	--Other sheets, panels, tiles and similar articles
													--Other articles:
0/0/0	2	0	0/0	0/0/0	0/0	0//0	0/0/	0/0/0	7.3/0			0/0/0	---Tubes, pipes and tube or pipe fittings
0/0/0	2	0	0/0	0/0/0	0/0	0//0	0/0/	0/0/0	7.6/0			0/0/0	---Other
													Fabricated asbestos fibres; mixtures with a basis of asbestos or with a basis of asbestos and magnesium carbonate; articles of such mixtures or of asbestos (for example, thread, woven fabric, clothing, headgear, footwear, gaskets), whether or not reinforced, other than goods of heading No.68. 11 or 68. 13:
0/0/0	3.5	2.1	1.1/1.1	0/0/0	0/0	0/0/0	0/0/	0/0/9.5	9.5/0			0/0/0	-Of crocidolite
													-Other:
0/0/0	3.5	2.1	1.1/1.1	0/0/0	0/0	0/0/0	0/0/	0/0/9.5	9.5/0			0/0/0	--Clothing, clothing accessories, footwear and headgear
													--Other:
0/0/0	3.5	2.1	1.1/1.1	0/0/0	0/0	0/0/0	0/0/	0/0/9.5	9.5/0			0/0/0	---Paper, millboard and felt
0/0/0	3.5	2.1	1.1/1.1	0/0/0	0/0	0/0/0	0/0/	0/0/9.5	9.5/0			0/0/0	---Compressed asbestos fibre jointing, in sheets or rolls
0/0/0	2	2	0/0	0/0/0	0/0	0//0	0/0/	0/0/9	9.1/0			0/0/0	---Other
													Friction material and articles thereof (for example, sheets, rolls, strips, segments, discs, washers, pads), not mounted, for brakes, for clutches or the like, with a basis of asbestos, of other mineral substances or of cellulose, whether or not combined with textile or other materials:
													-Containing asbestos:
0/0/0	2	2	0/0	0/0/0	0/0	0//0	0/0/	0/0/9	9.1/0			0/0/0	---Brake linings and pads
0/0/0	6	2.4	1.2/1.2	0/0/0	0/0	0/0/0	0/0/	0/0/10.8	10.9/0			0/0/0	---Other
													-Not containing asbestos:
0/0/0	2	2	0/0	0/0/0	0/0	0//0	0/0/	0/0/9	9.1/0			0/0/0	--Brake linings and pads
0/0/0	6	2.4	1.2/1.2	0/0/0	0/0	0/0/0	0/0/	10.8/10.8/10.8	10.9/10.8			0/0/0	--Other
													Worked mica and articles of mica, including agglomerated or reconstituted mica, whether or not on a support of paper, paperboard or other meterials:
0/0/0	3.5	2.1	0/0	0/0/0	0/0	0/0/0	0/0/	0/0/9.5	9.5/0			0/0/0	-Plates, sheets and strips of agglomerated or reconstituted mica, whether or not on a support
0/0/0	3.5	2.1	1.1/1.1	0/0/0	0/0	0/0/0	0/0/	0/0/9.5	9.5/0			0/0/0	-Other
													Articles of stone or of other mineral substances (including carbon fibres, articles of carbon fibres and articles of peat), not elsewhere specified or included:
													- Carbon fibres; articles of carbon fibres for nonelectrical uses; other articles of graphite or other carbon for nonelectrical uses
													--Carbon fibres
0/0/0			1.8/1.8	0/0/0	0/0	0/0/0	0/0/	5/5/	/5			0/0/0	Carbon fiber under dual—use item control (specific modulus $\geqslant$ 12.7) $\times$ 1^{6} m, or specific tensile strength $\geqslant$ 23.5 $\times$ 1^{4} m)
0/0/0			1.8/1.8	0/0/0	0/0	0/0/0	0/0/	5/5/	/5			0/0/0	Other carbon fibers
0/0/0			1.8/1.8	0/0/0	0/0	0/0/0	0/0/	5/5/	/5			0/0/0	--Fabrics of carbon fibres
													--Other articles of carbon fibres:
													---Carbon fiber prepreg
0/0/0			1.8/1.8	0/0/0	0/0	0/0/0	0/0/	5/5/	/5			0/0/0	Carbon fiber prepreg (product) for dual—use item control
0/0/0			1.8/1.8	0/0/0	0/0	0/0/0	0/0/	5/5/	/5			0/0/0	Other carbon fiber prepregs (products)
0/0/0			1.8/1.8	0/0/0	0/0	0/0/0	0/0/	5/5/	/5			0/0/0	---Other
													--Other
0/0/0	12		1.5/1.5	0/0/0	0/0	0/0/0	0/0/	5/5/	/5			0/0/0	Graphite accessories for silicon carbide epitaxial production equipment (metal content $\leqslant$ 5ppm)
0/0/0	12		1.5/1.5	0/0/0	0/0	0/0/0	0/0/	5/5/	/5			0/0/0	Other non electrical graphite or other carbon products
0/0/0	12	3	1.5/1.5	0/0/0	0/0	0/0/0	0/0/	0/0/13.5	13.6/0			0/0/0	-Articles of peat
													-Other articles:
0/0/0	12	3.3	1.7/1.7	0/0/0	0/0	0/0/0	0/0/	0/0/13.5	13.6/0			0/0/0	--Containing magnesite, magnesia in the form of periclase, dolomite (including calcined form) or chromite
													--Other:
0/0/0	0	3.5	1.8/1.8	0/0/0	0/0	0/0/0	0/0/	0/0/15.8	15.9/0			0/0/0	---Basalt fiber and its products
0/0/0	0	3.5	1.8/1.8	0/0/0	0/0	0/0/0	0/0/	0/0/15.8	15.9/0			0/0/0	---Other

第六十九章
陶瓷产品

注释：

一、本章仅适用于成形后经过烧制的陶瓷产品：

(一)税目 69.04 至 69.14 仅适用于不能归入税目 69.01 至 69.03 的产品；

(二)为树脂固化、加速水合作用、除去水分或其他挥发成分等目的而将其加热至低于 800℃的物品，不应视为经过烧制。这些物品不应归入第六十九章；

(三)陶瓷制品是用通常在室温下预先调制成形的无机非金属材料烧制而成的。原料主要包括：粘土、含硅材料(包括熔融硅石)、高熔点的材料(例如，氧化物、碳化物、氮化物、石墨或其他碳)，有时还有诸如耐火粘土或磷酸盐的粘合剂。

二、本章不包括：

(一)税目 28.44 的产品；

(二)税目 68.04 的物品；

(三)第七十一章的物品(例如，仿首饰)；

(四)税目 81.13 的金属陶瓷；

(五)第八十二章的物品；

(六)绝缘子(税目 85.46)或绝缘材料制的零件(税目 85.47)；

(七)假牙(税目 90.21)；

(八)第九十一章的物品(例如，钟及钟壳)；

(九)第九十四章的物品(例如，家具、灯具及照明装置、活动房屋)；

(十)第九十五章的物品(例如，玩具、游戏品及运动用品)；

(十一)税目 96.06 的物品(例如，纽扣)或税目 96.14 的物品(例如，烟斗)；

(十二)第九十七章的物品(例如，艺术品)。

税则号列	货品名称〔CIQ 扩展编码及品名－T2 表示见附表 2〕	最惠(%)	暂定税率	普通	增值/消费	出口退税	计量单位	监管条件/特殊证件	检验检疫	对美关税	亚太上/下
	第一分章　硅化石粉或类似硅土及耐火材料制品										
69.01	**硅质化石粉(例如，各种硅藻土)或类似硅土制的砖、块、瓦及其他陶瓷制品：**										
6901.0000	硅质化石粉(例如，各种硅藻土)或类似硅土制的砖、瓦、块及其他陶瓷制品〔999〕	8		50	13/	0	千克	/		33	5.2/5.2
69.02	**耐火砖、块、瓦及类似耐火陶瓷建材制品，但硅质化石粉及类似硅土制的除外：**										
6902.1000	-单独或同时含有按重量计超过 50%的镁、钙或铬(分别以氧化镁、氧化钙及三氧化二铬的含量计)〔999〕	8		30	13/	0	千克	/		18	
6902.2000	-含有按重量计超过 50%的三氧化二铝、二氧化硅或其混合物或化合物〔999〕	8		30	13/	0	千克	/		18	
6902.9000	-其他〔999〕	8		30	13/	0	千克	/		33	
69.03	**其他耐火陶瓷制品(例如，甑、坩埚、马弗罩、喷管、栓塞、支架、烤钵、管子、护套、棒条及滑阀式水口)，但硅质化石粉及类似硅土制的除外：**										
6903.1000	-含有按重量计超过 50%的单体碳〔999〕	8		20	13/	0	千克	/		18	
6903.2000	-含有按重量计超过 50%的三氧化二铝或三氧化二铝和二氧化硅的混合物或化合物〔999〕	8		20	13/	0	千克	/		28	
6903.9000	-其他〔999〕	8		20	13/	13	千克	/		18	
	第二分章　其他陶瓷产品										
69.04	**陶瓷制建筑用砖、铺地砖、支撑或填充用砖及类似品：**										
6904.1000	-建筑用砖〔999〕	15		90	13/	13	千克/千块	/	L		
6904.9000	-其他〔999〕	15		90	13/	13	千克	/	L	35	
69.05	**屋顶瓦、烟囱罩、通风帽、烟囱衬壁、建筑装饰物及其他建筑用陶瓷制品：**										
6905.1000	-屋顶瓦〔999〕	15		90	13/	13	千克	/		20	
6905.9000	-其他〔999〕	15		90	13/	13	千克	/	L	30	
69.06	**陶瓷套管、导管、槽管及管子附件：**										
6906.0000	陶瓷套管、导管、槽管及管子附件〔999〕	15	10	90	13/	13	千克	/		30	
69.07	**陶瓷贴面砖、铺面砖，包括炉面砖及墙面砖；陶瓷镶嵌砖(马赛克)及其类似品，不论是否有衬背；饰面陶瓷：**										
	-贴面砖、铺面砖，包括炉面砖及墙面砖，但子目 6907.30 和 6907.40 所列商品除外：										
	--按重量计吸水率不超过 0.5%：										

Chapter 69
Ceramic products

Notes:

1. This Chapter applies only to ceramic products which have been fired after shaping:
   (a) Headings 69.04 to 69.14 apply only to such products other than those classifiable in headings 69.01 to 69.03;
   (b) Articles heated to temperatures less than 800 °C for purposes such as curing of resins, accelerating hydration reactions, or for the removal of water or other volatile components, are not considered to be fired. Such articles are excluded from Chapter 69; and
   (c) Ceramic articles are obtained by firing inorganic, non—metallic materials which have been prepared and shaped previously at, in general, room temperature. Raw materials comprise, inter alia, clays, siliceous materials including fused silica, materials with a high melting point, such as oxides, carbides, nitrides, graphite or other carbon, and in some cases binders such as refractory clays or phosphates.
2. This Chapter does not cover:
   (a) Products of heading No.28. 44;
   (b) Articles of heading No.68. 04;
   (c) Articles of Chapter 71 (for example, imitation jewellery);
   (d) Cermets of heading No.81. 13;
   (e) Articles of Chapter 82;
   (f) Electrical insulators (heading No.85. 46) or fittings of insulating material of heading No.85. 47;
   (g) Artificial teeth (heading No.90. 21);
   (h) Articles of Chapter 91 (for example, clocks and clock cases);
   (ij) Articles of Chapter 94 (for example, furniture, lamps and lighting fittings, prefabricated buildings);
   (k) Articles of Chapter 95 (for example, toys, games and sports requisites);
   (m) Articles of heading No.96. 06 (for example, buttons) or of heading No.96. 14 (for example, smoking pipes); or
   (l) Articles of Chapter 97 (for example, works of art).

协定税率 %								RCEP		特惠税率 %			Article Description
东/冰/格	巴基斯坦	韩国	瑞士上/下	哥/秘/柬	澳/毛	新西/坡/智	中国港/澳/台	东盟及马来/澳/韩	日/新	亚太2国	老/柬/缅	98/97/95	
													Ⅰ. GOODS OF SILICEOUS FOSSIL MEALS OR OF SIMILAR SILICEOUS EARTHS, AND REFRACTORY GOODS
													Bricks, blocks, tiles and other ceramic goods of siliceous fossil meals (for example, kieselguhr, tripolite or diatomite) or of similar siliceous earths:
0/0/0	2	0	0/0	0/0/0	0/0	0//0	0/0/	0/0/0	7.3/0			0/0/0	Bricks, blocks, tiles and other ceramic goods of siliceous fossil meals (for example, kieselguhr, tripolite or diatomite) or of similar siliceous earths
													Refractory bricks, blocks, tiles and similar refractory ceramic constructional goods, other than those of siliceous fossil meals or similar siliceous earths:
0/0/0	2	0	0/0	0/0/0	0/0	0//0	0/0/	0/0/0	7.3/0			0/0/0	-Containing by weight, singly or together, more than 50% of the elements Mg, Ca or Cr, expressed as MgO, CaO or Cr_2O_3
0/0/0	2	0	0.8/0.8	0/0/0	0/0	0//0	0/0/	0/0/0	7.3/0			0/0/0	-Containing by weight more than 50% of alumina (Al_2O_3), of silica (SiO_2) or of a mixture or compound of these products
0/0/0	2	1.6	0/0	0/0/0	0/0	0//0	0/0/	0/0/7.2	7.3/0			0/0/0	-Other
													Other refractory ceramic goods (for example, retorts, crucibles, muffles, nozzles, plugs, supports, cupels, tubes, pipes, sheaths, rods and slide gates), other than those of siliceous fossil meals or of similar siliceous earths:
0/0/0	2	1.6	0/0	0/0/0	0/0	0//0	0/0/	0/0/7.2	7.3/0		0//	0/0/0	-Containing by weight more than 50% of Monmer carbon
0/0/0	2	0	0/0	0/0/0	0/0	0//0	0/0/	0/0/0	7.3/0		0//	0/0/0	-Containing by weight more than 50% of alumina (AL_2O_3) or of a mixture of compound of alumina and of silica (SiO_2)
0/0/0	2	0	0/0	0/0/0	0/0	0//0	0/0/	0/0/0	7.3/0		0//	0/0/0	-Other
													Ⅱ. -OTHER CERAMIC PRODUCTS
													Ceramic building bricks, flooring blocks, support or filler tiles and the like:
0/0/0	12	3	1.5/1.5	0/0/0	0/0	0/0/0	0/0/	0/0/13.5	13.6/0			0/0/0	-Building bricks
0/0/0		14.7	2.5/2.5	0/0/0	0/14.7	0/0/0	0/0/	23.3/23.3/23.3	23.3/23.3			0/0/0	-Other
													Roofing tiles, chimney-pots, cowls, chimney liners, architectural ornaments and other ceramic constructional goods:
0/0/0		14.7	2.5/2.5	0/0/0	0/14.7	0/0/0	0/0/	23.3/23.3/23.3	/23.3			0/0/0	-Roofing tiles
0/0/0		14.7	2.5/2.5	0/0/0	0/14.7	0/0/0	0/0/	23.3/23.3/23.3	23.3/23.3			0/0/0	-Other
													Ceramic pipes, conduits, guttering and pipe fittings:
0/0/0	12	3	1.5/1.5	0/0/0	0/0	0/0/0	0/0/	0/0/13.5	13.6/0			0/0/0	Ceramic pipes, conduits, guttering and pipe fittings
													Ceramic flags and paving, hearth or wall tiles; ceramic mosaic cubes and the like, whether or not on a backing; finished ceramic:
													-Ceramic flags and paving, hearth or wall tiles, other than that of subheading No.6907.30 or 6907.40:
													--Of water absorption coefficient by weight not exceeding 0.5%

税则号列	货品名称〔CIQ 扩展编码及品名－T2 表示见附表 2〕	最惠(%)	暂定税率	普通	增值/消费	出口退税	计量单位	监管条件/特殊证件	检验检疫	对美关税	亚太上/下
6907.2110	---不论是否矩形，其最大表面积以可置入边长小于 7 厘米的方格为限〔999〕	7		100	13/	13	千克/平方米	/	L	22	4.6/4.6
6907.2190	---其他〔999〕	7		100	13/	13	千克/平方米	/	L	32	
	--按重量计吸水率超过 0.5%，但不超过 10%：										
6907.2210	---不论是否矩形，其最大表面积以可置入边长小于 7 厘米的方格为限〔999〕	7		100	13/	13	千克/平方米	/		32	4.6/4.6
6907.2290	---其他〔999〕	7		100	13/	13	千克/平方米	/		32	
	--按重量计吸水率超过 10%：										
6907.2310	---不论是否矩形，其最大表面积以可置入边长小于 7 厘米的方格为限〔999〕	7		100	13/	13	千克/平方米	/			4.6/4.6
6907.2390	---其他〔999〕	7		100	13/	13	千克/平方米	/		32	
	-镶嵌砖（马赛克）及其类似品，但子目 6907.40 的货品除外：										
6907.3010	---不论是否矩形，其最大表面积以可置入边长小于 7 厘米的方格为限〔999〕	7		100	13/	13	千克/平方米	/	L		4.6/4.6
6907.3090	---其他〔999〕	7		100	13/	13	千克/平方米	/	L		
	-饰面陶瓷：										
6907.4010	---不论是否矩形，其最大表面积以可置入边长小于 7 厘米的方格为限〔999〕	7		100	13/	13	千克/平方米	/	L		4.6/4.6
6907.4090	---其他〔999〕	7		100	13/	13	千克/平方米	/	L	32	
69.09	**实验室、化学或其他专门技术用途的陶瓷器；农业用陶瓷槽、缸及类似容器；通常供运输及盛装货物用的陶瓷罐、坛及类似品：**										
	-实验室、化学或其他专门技术用途的陶瓷器：										
6909.1100	--瓷制〔999〕	8		30	13/	13	千克	/			
6909.1200	--莫氏硬度为 9 或以上的物品〔999〕	8		30	13/	13	千克	/			
6909.1900	--其他〔999〕	8		30	13/	13	千克	/		18	
6909.9000	-其他〔999〕	15		90	13/	13	千克	/		25	
69.10	**陶瓷洗涤槽、脸盆、脸盆座、浴缸、坐浴盆、抽水马桶、水箱、小便池及类似的固定卫生设备：**										
6910.1000	-瓷制〔101 洗涤槽，102 面盆，103 浴缸，104 座便器，105 小便器，106 其他卫生瓷〕	7		100	13/	13	千克/件	/		32	4.6/4.6
6910.9000	-其他〔101 洗涤槽，102 面盆，103 浴缸，104 座便器，105 小便器，106 其他卫生陶〕	7		100	13/	13	千克/件	A/	M	32	
69.11	**瓷餐具、厨房器具及其他家用或盥洗用瓷器：**										
	-餐具及厨房器具：										
	---餐具：										
6911.1011	----骨瓷〔101 食品接触陶瓷产品，102 食品用陶瓷包装〕	7		100	13/	13	千克	A/	R	32	4.6/4.6
6911.1019	----其他〔101 食品接触陶瓷产品，102 食品用陶瓷包装〕	7		100	13/	13	千克	A/	R	32	4.6/4.6
	---厨房器具：										
6911.1021	----刀具〔101 食品接触陶瓷产品，102 食品用陶瓷包装〕	7		100	13/	13	千克	A/	R		4.6/4.6
6911.1029	----其他〔101 食品接触陶瓷产品，102 食品用陶瓷包装〕	7		100	13/	13	千克	A/	R	32	4.6/4.6
6911.9000	-其他〔999〕	7		100	13/	13	千克	/		32	4.6/4.6
69.12	**陶餐具、厨房器具及其他家用或盥洗用陶器：**										
6912.0010	---餐具〔101 食品接触陶瓷产品，102 食品用陶瓷包装〕	7		100	13/	13	千克	A/	R	32	
6912.0090	---其他〔101 食品接触陶瓷产品，102 食品用陶瓷包装〕	7		100	13/	13	千克	A/	R	32	
69.13	**塑像及其他装饰用陶瓷制品：**										
6913.1000	-瓷制〔999〕	7		100	13/	13	千克	/		32	
6913.9000	-其他〔999〕	7		100	13/	13	千克	/		32	
69.14	**其他陶瓷制品：**										
6914.1000	-瓷制〔101 其他陶瓷及制品，102 食品接触陶瓷产品，103 食品用陶瓷包装〕	15		100	13/	13	千克	/		35	
6914.9000	-其他〔101 其他陶瓷及制品，102 食品接触陶瓷产品，103 食品用陶瓷包装〕	10		100	13/	13	千克	/		20	

协定税率 %								RCEP		特惠税率 %			Article Description
东/冰/格	巴基斯坦	韩国	瑞士 上/下	哥/秘/柬	澳/毛	新西/坡/智	中国港/澳/台	东盟及马来/澳/韩	日/新	亚太2国	老/柬/缅	98/97/95	
0/0/0	3.5	2.4	1.2/1.2	0/0/0	0/0	0/0/0	0/0/	0/0/10.8	10.9/0			0/0/0	--Tiles, cubes and similar arti-cles, whether or not rectan-gular, the largest surface area of which is capable of being enclosed in a square the side of which is less than 7 cm
0/0/0	6	2.4	1.2/1.2	0/0/0	0/0	0/0/0	0/0/	0/0/10.8	10.9/0			0/0/0	---Other
													--Of water absorption coefficient by weight exceeding 0.5% but not exceeding 10%
0/0/0	3.5	2.4	1.2/1.2	0/0/0	0/0	0/0/0	0/0/	0/0/10.8	10.9/0			0/0/0	--Tiles, cubes and similar articles, whether or not rectan-gu-lar, the largest surface area of which is capable of being en-closed in a square the side of which is less than 7 cm
0/0/0	6	2.4	1.2/1.2	0/0/0	0/0	0/0/0	0/0/	0/0/10.8	10.9/0			0/0/0	---Other
													--Of water absorption coefficient by weight exceeding 10%
0/0/0	3.5	2.4	1.2/1.2	0/0/0	0/0	0/0/0	0/0/	0/0/10.8	10.9/0			0/0/0	--Tiles, cubes and similar arti-cles, whether or not rectan-gular, the largest surface area of which is capable of being enclosed in a square the side of which is less than 7 cm
0/0/0	6	2.4	1.2/1.2	0/0/0	0/0	0/0/0	0/0/	0/0/10.8	10.9/0			0/0/0	---Other
													-Mosaic cubes and the like, other than those of subheading No.6907.40:
0/0/0	3.5	2.4	1.2/1.2	0/0/0	0/0	0/0/0	0/0/	0/0/10.8	10.9/0			0/0/0	---Tiles, cubes and similar articles, whether or not rectan-gular, the largest surface area of which is capable of being encolsed in a square the side of which is less than 7 cm
0/0/0	6	2.4	1.2/1.2	0/0/0	0/0	0/0/0	0/0/	0/0/10.8	10.9/0			0/0/0	---Other
													-Finishing ceramic:
0/0/0	3.5	2.4	1.2/1.2	0/0/0	0/0	0/0/0	0/0/	0/0/10.8	10.9/0			0/0/0	---Tiles, cubes and similar arti-cles, whether or not rectan-gular, the largest surface area of which is capable of being encolsed in a square the side of which is less than 7 cm
0/0/0	6	2.4	1.2/1.2	0/0/0	0/0	0/0/0	0/0/	0/0/10.8	10.9/0			0/0/0	---Other
													Ceramic wares for laboratory, chemical or other technical uses; ceramic troughs, tubs and similar receptacles of a kind used in agriculture; ceramic pots, jars and similar articles of a kind used for the conveyance or packing of goods:
													-Ceramic wares for laboratory, chemical or other technical u-ses:
0/0/0	2	0	0/0	0/0/0	0/0	0//0	0/0/	0/0/0	7.3/0			0/0/0	--Of porcelain or china
0/0/0	2	0	0/0	0/0/0	0/0	0//0	0/0/	0/0/0	7.3/0			0/0/0	--Articles having a hardness equivalent to 9 or more on the Mohs scale
0/0/0	2	0	0/0	0/0/0	0/0	0//0	0/0/	7.2/7.2/7.2	7.3/7.2			0/0/0	--Other
0/0/0		12.6	2.1/2.1	0/0/0	0/0	0/0/0	0/0/	20/20/20	/20			0/0/0	-Other
													Ceramic sinks, wash basins, wash basin pedestals, baths, bidets, water closet pans, flushing cisterns, urinals and similar sanitary fixtures:
0/0/0	2	2	0/0	0/0/0	0/0	0/0/0	0/0/	0/0/9	9.1/0			0/0/0	-Of porcelain or china
0/0/0	2	2	0/0	0/0/0	0/0	0/0/0	0/0/	0/0/9	9.1/0			0/0/0	-Other
													Tableware, kitchenware, other houschold articles and toilet arti-cles, of porcelain or china:
													-Tableware and kitchenware:
													---Tableware:
0/0/0	3.5	2.4	1.2/1.2	0/0/0	0/0	0/0/0	0/0/	0/0/10.8	10.9/0			0/0/0	----Bone china
0/0/0	3.5	2.4	1.2/1.2	0/0/0	0/0	0/0/0	0/0/	0/0/10.8	10.9/0			0/0/0	----Other
													---Kitchenware:
0/0/0	7.5	3	1.5/1.5	0/0/0	0/0	0/0/0	0/0/	0/0/13.5	13.6/0			0/0/0	----Knife tool
0/0/0	7.5	3	1.5/1.5	0/0/0	0/0	0/0/0	0/0/	0/0/13.5	13.6/0			0/0/0	----Other
0/0/0	20	14.7	2.5/2.5	0/0/0	0/14.7	0/0/0	0/0/	23.3/23.3/23.3	23.3/23.3			0/0/0	-Other
													Ceramic tableware, kitchenware, other household articles and toilet articles, other than of procelain or china:
0/0/0	12	3	1.5/1.5	0/0/0	0/0	0/0/0	0/0/	0/0/13.5	13.6/0			0/0/0	---Tableware
0/0/0	12	3	1.5/1.5	0/0/0	0/0	0/0/0	0/0/	0/0/13.5	13.6/0			0/0/0	---Other
													Statuettes and other ornamental ceramic articles:
0/0/0	12	3	1.5/1.5	0/0/0	0/0	0/0/0	0/0/	0/0/13.5	13.6/0			0/0/0	-Of porcelain or china
0/0/0	12	3	1.5/1.5	0/0/0	0/0	0/0/0	0/0/	0/0/13.5	13.6/0			0/0/0	-Other
													Other ceramic articles:
0/0/0		14.7	2.5/2.5	0/0/0	0/14.7	0/0/0	0/0/	23.3/23.3/	/23.3			0/0/0	Of porcelain or china
0/0/0	3.5	4.6	1/1	0/0/0	0/0	0/0/0	0/0/	9.3/9.5/9.3	9.4/9.5			0/0/0	-Other

第七十章
玻璃及其制品

注释：

一、本章不包括：

(一)税目 32.07 的货品(例如，珐琅和釉料、搪瓷玻璃料及其他玻璃粉、粒或粉片)；

(二)第七十一章的物品(例如，仿首饰)；

(三)税目 85.44 的光缆、税目 85.46 的绝缘子或税目 85.47 所列绝缘材料制的零件；

(四)第八十六章至第八十八章的运输工具用的带框的前挡风玻璃、后窗或其他窗；

(五)第八十六章至第八十八章的运输工具用的前挡风玻璃、后窗或其他窗，装有加热装置或其他电气或电子装置的，不论是否带框；

(六)光导纤维、经光学加工的光学元件、注射用针管、假眼、温度计、气压计、液体比重计或第九十章的其他物品；

(七)有永久固定电光源的灯具及照明装置、灯箱标志或铭牌和类似品及其零件(税目94.05)；

(八)玩具、游戏品、运动用品、圣诞树装饰品及第九十五章的其他物品（供玩偶或第九十五章其他物品用的无机械装置的玻璃假眼除外)；

(九)纽扣、保温瓶、香水喷雾器和类似的喷雾器及第九十六章的其他物品。

二、对于税目 70.03、70.04 及 70.05：

(一)玻璃在退火前的各种处理都不视为“已加工”；

(二)玻璃切割成一定形状并不影响其作为板片归类；

(三)所称“吸收、反射或非反射层”，是指极薄的金属或化合物(例如，金属氧化物)镀层，该镀层可以吸收红外线等光线或可以提高玻璃的反射性能，同时仍然使玻璃具有一定程度的透明性或半透明性；或者该镀层可以防止光线在玻璃表面的反射。

三、税目 70.06 所述产品，不论是否具有制成品的特性仍归入该税目。

四、税目 70.19 所称“玻璃棉”，是指：

(一)按重量计二氧化硅的含量在 60%及以上的矿质棉；

(二)按重量计二氧化硅的含量在 60%以下，但碱性氧化物(氧化钾或氧化钠)的含量在 5%以上或氧化硼的含量在 2%以上的矿质棉。

不符合上述规定的矿质棉归入税目 68.06。

五、本协调制度所称“玻璃”，包括熔融石英及其他熔融硅石。

子目注释：

子目号 7013.22、7013.33 及 7013.41 及 7013.91 所称“铅晶质玻璃”，仅指按重量计氧化铅含量不低于 24%的玻璃。

税则号列	货品名称〔CIQ 扩展编码及品名－T2 表示见附表 2〕	最惠(%)	暂定税率	普通	增值/消费	出口退税	计量单位	监管条件/特殊证件	检验检疫	对美关税	亚太上/下
70.01	**碎玻璃及废玻璃，来源于阴极射线管或税目 85.49 的其他活化玻璃除外；玻璃块料：**										
7001.0010	---无色光学玻璃块料〔999〕	12		50	13/	13	千克	/		22	
7001.0090	---其他										
7001.0090 10	废碎玻璃(来源于阴极射线管或税目 85.49 的其他活化玻璃除外)〔999〕	12		50	13/	13	千克	9/		22	
7001.0090 90	其他玻璃块料〔999〕	12		50	13/	13	千克	/		22	
70.02	**未加工的玻璃球、棒及管(税目 70.18 的微型玻璃球除外)：**										
7002.1000	-玻璃球〔999〕	12		50	13/	0	千克	/		37	
	-玻璃棒：										
7002.2010	---光导纤维预制棒										
7002.2010 10	直径≥60 毫米的光导纤维预制棒〔999〕	6		50	13/	13	千克	/		31	
7002.2010 90	其他光导纤维预制棒〔999〕	6		50	13/	13	千克	/		31	
7002.2090	---其他〔999〕	12		50	13/	0	千克	/		22	
	-玻璃管：										
	--熔融石英或其他熔融硅石制：										
7002.3110	---光导纤维用波导级石英玻璃管〔999〕	5	1	17	13/	13	千克	/		26	
7002.3190	---其他〔999〕	12		50	13/	0	千克	/		22	
7002.3200	--温度在 0℃至 300℃时线膨胀系数不超过 5×10^{-6}/开尔文的其他玻璃制										
7002.3200 10	药用硼硅玻璃管(三氧化二硼含量≥8%)(0－300℃时线膨胀系数不超过 5×10－6/开尔文的玻璃制)〔999〕	12	7	50	13/	13	千克	/		27	
7002.3200 90	其他未加工的玻璃管(0－300℃时线膨胀系数不超过 5×10－6/开尔文的玻璃制)〔999〕	12		50	13/	13	千克	/		32	
7002.3900	--其他〔999〕	12		50	13/	13	千克	/		32	
70.03	**铸制或轧制玻璃板、片或型材及异型材，不论是否有吸收、反射或非反射层，但未经其他加工：**										
	-非夹丝玻璃板、片：										
7003.1200	--整块着色、不透明、镶色或具有吸收、反射或非反射层的〔999〕	15		50	13/	0	千克/平方米	/		40	
7003.1900	--其他										

Chapter 70
Glass and glassware

Notes:

1. This Chapter does not cover:
   (a) Goods of heading No.32.07 (for example, vitrifiable enamels and glazes, glass frit, other glass in the form of powder, granules or flakes);
   (b) Articles of Chapter 71 (for example, imitation jewellery);
   (c) Optical fibre cables (heading No.85.44), electrical insulators (heading 85.46) or fitting of insulating material of heading No.85.47;
   (d) Front windscreens (windshields), rear windows and other windows, framed, for vehicles of Chapters 86 to 88;
   (e) Front windscreens (windshields), rear windows and other windows, whether or not framed, incorporating heating devices or other electrical or electronic devices, for vehicles of Chapters 86 to 88;
   (f) Optical fibres, optically worked optical elements, hypodermic syringes, artificial eyes, thermometers, barometers, hydrometers or other articles of Chapter 90;
   (g) Lamps or lighting fittings, illuminated signs, illuminated nameplates or the like, having a permanently fixed light source, or parts thereof of heading No.94.05;
   (h) Toys, games, sports requisites, Christmas tree ornaments or other articles of Chapter 95 (excluding glass eyes without mechanisms for dolls or for other articles of Chapter 95); or
   (i) Buttons, fitted vacuum flasks, scent or similar sprays or other articles of Chapter 96.
2. For the purposes of headings Nos.70.03, 70.04 and 70.05:
   (a) glass is not regarded as "worked" by reason of any process it has undergone before annealing;
   (b) cutting to shape does not affect the classification of glass in sheets;
   (c) the expression "absorbent, reflecting or non-reflecting layer" means a microscopically thin coating of metal or of a chemical compound (for example, metal oxide) which absorbs, for example, infra-red light or improves the reflecting qualities of the glass while still allowing it to retain a degree of transparency or translucency; or which prevents light from being reflected on the surface of the glass.
3. The products referred to in heading No.70.06 remain classified in that heading whether or not they have the character of articles.
4. For the purposes of heading No.70.19, the expression "glass wool" means:
   (a) Mineral wools with a silica (SiO_2) content not less than 60% by weight;
   (b) Mineral wools with a silica (SiO_2) content less than 60% but with an alkaline oxide (K_2O or Na_2O) content exceeding 5% by weight or a boric oxide (B_2O_3) content exceeding 2% by weight.
   Mineral wools which do not comply with the above specifications fall in heading No.68.06.
5. Throughout the Nomenclature, the expression "glass" includes fused quartz and other fused silica.

Subheading Note:

For the purposes of subheadings Nos.7013.22, 7013.33, 7013.41 and 7013.91, the expression "lead crystal" means only glass having a minimum lead monoxide (PbO) content by weight of 24%.

协定税率 %								RCEP		特惠税率 %			Article Description
东/冰/格	巴基斯坦	韩国	瑞士上/下	哥/秘/柬	澳/毛	新西/坡/智	中国港/澳/台	东盟及马来/澳/韩	日/新	亚太2国	老/柬/缅	98/97/95	
													Cullet and other waste and scrap of glass, excluding glass from cathode ray tubes or other activated glass of heading 85.49; glass in the mass.
0/0/0	6	2.4	1.2/1.2	0/0/0	0/0	0/0/0	0/0/	10.8/10.8/10.8	10.9/10.8			0/0/0	---Colorless optical glass in the mass
													---Other
0/0/0	6	2.4	1.2/1.2	0/0/0	0/0	0/0/0	0/0/	10.8/10.8/10.8	10.9/10.8		//	0/0/0	Broken glass
0/0/0	6	2.4	1.2/1.2	0/0/0	0/0	0/0/0	0/0/	10.8/10.8/10.8	10.9/10.8		//	0/0/0	Other glass blocks
													Glass in balls (other than microspheres of heading No.70.18), rods or tubes, unworked:
0/0/0	6	2.4	1.2/1.2	0/0/0	0/0	0/0/0	0/0/	0/0/10.8	10.9/0			0/0/0	-Balls
													-Rods:
													---Preformed bars for drawing optical fibre
0/0/0	0	0	0/0	0/0/0	0/0	0//0	0/0/	0/0/0	5.5/0		//	0/0/0	Preformed bars for drawing optical fibre, with diameter ≥ 60 mm
0/0/0	0	0	0/0	0/0/0	0/0	0//0	0/0/	0/0/0	5.5/0		//	0/0/0	Other preformed bars for drawing optical fibre, with diameter ≥ 60 mm
0/0/0	6	2.4	1.2/1.2	0/0/0	0/0	0/0/0	0/0/	0/0/10.8	10.9/0			0/0/0	---Other
													-Tubes:
													--Of fused quartz or other fused silica:
0/0/0	0	0	0/0	0/0/0	0/0	0//0	0/0/	0/0/0	0/0			0/0/0	---Waveguide quartz tubes for optical fibres use
0/0/0	11.2	2.8	1.4/1.4	0/0/0	0/0	0/0/0	0/0/	0/0/12.6	12.7/0			0/0/0	---Other
													--Of other glass having a linear coefficient of expansion not exceeding 5×10^{-6} per Kelvin within a temperature range of 0℃ to 300℃
0/0/0	6	2.4	1.2/1.2	0/0/0	0/0	0/0/0	0/0/	0/0/10.8	10.9/0		//	0/0/0	Pharmaceutical borosilicate glass tube (boron trioxide content ≥ 8%) (made of glass with coefficient of linear expansion less than 5 × 10−6 / Kelvin at 0−300 ℃)
0/0/0	6	2.4	1.2/1.2	0/0/0	0/0	0/0/0	0/0/	0/0/10.8	10.9/0		//	0/0/0	Other raw glass tubes (made of glass with coefficient of linear expansion less than 5 × 10−6 / Kelvin at 0−300 ℃)
0/0/0	6	2.4	1.2/1.2	0/0/0	0/0	0/0/0	0/0/	0/0/10.8	10.9/0			0/0/0	--Other
													Cast glass and rolled glass, in sheets or profiles, whether or not having an absorbent, reflecting or non-reflecting layer, but not otherwise worked:
													-Non-wired sheets:
0/0/0	12	3	1.5/1.5	0/0/0	0/0	0/0/0	0/0/	0/0/13.5	13.6/0			0/0/0	--Coloured throughout the mass (body tinted), opacified, flashed or having an absorbent, or non-reflecting reflecting layer
													--Other

税则号列	货品名称〔CIQ 扩展编码及品名－T2 表示见附表 2〕	最惠(%)	暂定税率	普通	增值/消费	出口退税	计量单位	监管条件/特殊证件	检验检疫	对美关税	亚太上/下
7003.1900 01	液晶或有机发光二极管(OLED)显示屏基板用原板玻璃,包括保护屏用含碱玻璃(铸、轧制的非夹丝玻璃板、片,未着色,透明及不具吸收层的,未经其他加工)〔999〕	15	3	50	13/	13	千克/平方米	/		13	
7003.1900 02	手机或平板电脑盖板(包括前盖、后盖)用原板玻璃(未着色,透明及不具吸收层的,未经其他加工)〔999〕	15	5	50	13/	0	千克/平方米	/		15	
7003.1900 90	铸、轧制的其他非夹丝玻璃板、片(未着色,透明及不具吸收层的,未经其他加工)〔999〕	15		50	13/	0	千克/平方米	/		25	
7003.2000	-夹丝玻璃板、片〔999〕	15		50	13/	0	千克/平方米	/			
7003.3000	-型材及异型材〔999〕	15		50	13/	0	千克/平方米	/		25	
70.04	**拉制或吹制玻璃板、片,不论是否有吸收、反射或非反射层,但未经其他加工:**										
7004.2000	-整块着色、不透明、镶色或具有吸收、反射或非反射层的〔999〕	15		50	13/	0	千克/平方米	/		40	
7004.9000	-其他玻璃										
7004.9000 01	光学平板玻璃,厚度 0.7mm 以下(未着色,透明及不具吸收层的,未经其他加工)〔999〕	15	9	50	13/	0	千克/平方米	/		19	
7004.9000 90	拉、吹制的其他玻璃板、片(未着色,透明及不具吸收层的,未经其他加工)〔999〕	15		50	13/	0	千克/平方米	/		25	
70.05	**浮法玻璃板、片及表面研磨或抛光玻璃板、片,不论是否有吸收、反射或非反射层,但未经其他加工:**										
7005.1000	-具有吸收、反射或非反射层的非夹丝玻璃〔999〕	15		50	13/	0	千克/平方米	/		25	
	-其他非夹丝玻璃:										
7005.2100	--整块着色、不透明、镶色或仅表面研磨的〔999〕	15		50	13/	0	千克/平方米	/		35	
7005.2900	--其他										
7005.2900 02	液晶或有机发光二极管(OLED)显示屏基板用原板玻璃(非夹丝浮法玻璃板、片)〔999〕	10	3	50	13/	13	千克/平方米	/		23	
7005.2900 03	手机或平板电脑盖板(包括前盖、后盖)用原板玻璃〔999〕	10	5	50	13/	0	千克/平方米	/		25	
7005.2900 90	其他非夹丝浮法玻璃板、片〔999〕	10		50	13/	0	千克/平方米	/		30	
7005.3000	-夹丝玻璃〔999〕	15		50	13/	0	千克/平方米	/		40	
70.06	**经弯曲、磨边、镂刻、钻孔、涂珐琅或其他加工的税目 70.03、70.04 或 70.05 的玻璃,但未用其他材料镶框或装配:**										
7006.0000	经弯曲、磨边、镂刻、钻孔、涂珐琅或其他加工的税目 70.03、70.04 或 70.05 的玻璃,但未用其他材料镶框或装配										
7006.0000 01	液晶玻璃基板,6 代(1850mm×1500mm)以上,不含 6 代(经弯曲、磨边、镂刻、钻孔、涂珐琅等加工,款镶框或装配)〔999〕	10	4	50	13/	13	千克	/		29	
7006.0000 02	液晶玻璃基板,6 代(1850mm×1500mm)及以下(经弯曲、磨边、镂刻、钻孔、涂珐琅等加工,款镶框或装配)〔999〕	10	6	50	13/	13	千克	/		31	
7006.0000 90	经其他加工税目 70.03-70.05 的玻璃(经弯曲、磨边、镂刻、钻孔、涂珐琅等加工、未镶框或装配)〔999〕	10		50	13/	13	千克	/		35	
70.07	**钢化或层压玻璃制的安全玻璃:**										
	-钢化安全玻璃: --规格及形状适于安装在车辆、航空器、航天器及船舶上:										
7007.1110	---航空器、航天器及船舶用										
7007.1110 01	空载重量≥25 吨飞机的挡风玻璃〔999〕	2	1	11	13/	13	千克	/			
7007.1110 90	航空航天器及船舶用钢化安全玻璃(其他规格及形状适于安装在航空航天器及船上的)〔999〕	2		11	13/	13	千克	/			
7007.1190	---其他〔101 其他车辆零部件,102 钢化玻璃〕	10		50	13/	13	千克	A/	L	20	
7007.1900	--其他〔999〕	14		50	13/	13	千克/平方米	/	L	39	
	-层压安全玻璃: --规格及形状适于安装在车辆、航空器、航天器及船舶上:										
7007.2110	---航空器、航天器及船舶用〔999〕	2		11	13/	13	千克	/		12	
7007.2190	---其他〔101 其他车辆零部件,102 钢化玻璃〕	14		50	13/	13	千克	A/	L	24	
7007.2900	--其他〔999〕	14		50	13/	13	千克/平方米	/	L	39	

协定税率 %								RCEP		特惠税率 %			Article Description
东/冰/格	巴基斯坦	韩国	瑞士上/下	哥/秘/柬	澳/毛	新西/坡/智	中国港/澳/台	东盟及马来/澳/韩	日/新	亚太2国	老/柬/缅	98/97/95	
0/0/0	14	3.5	1.8/1.8	0/0/0	0/0	0/0/0	0/0/0	0/0/15.8	16.4/0			0/0/0	Original plate glass using for liquid crystal or an organic light-emitting diode (OLED) displayincluding the protection screen containing alkali glass(cast and rolled other non-wired glass,in sheets or parcel,not colored,transparent and without absorbing layer,not processed in other way)
0/0/0	14	3.5	1.8/1.8	0/0/0	0/0	0/0/0	0/0/0	0/0/15.8	16.4/0		//	0/0/0	Original glass for mobile phone or tablet cover (including front cover and back cover) (uncolored, transparent and without absorbing layer, without other processing)
0/0/0	14	3.5	1.8/1.8	0/0/0	0/0	0/0/0	0/0/0	0/0/15.8	16.4/0			0/0/0	Cast and rolled other non-wired glass,in sheets or parcel (not colored, transparent and without absorbing layer, not processed in other way)
0/0/0	12	3	1.5/1.5	0/0/0	0/0	0/0/0	0/0/	0/0/13.5	13.6/0			0/0/0	-Wired sheets
0/0/0	12	3	1.5/1.5	0/0/0	0/0	0/0/0	0/0/	0/0/13.5	13.6/0			0/0/0	-Profiles
													Drawn glass and blown glass, in sheets, whether or not having an absorbent, reflecting or non-reflecting layer, but not otherwise worked:
0/0/0	14	3.5	1.8/1.8	0/0/0	0/0	0/0/0	0/0/	0/0/15.8	15.9/0			0/0/0	-Glass, coloured throughout the mass (body tinted), opacified, flashed or having an absorbent, reflecting or non-reflecting layer
													-Other glass
0/0/0	14	10.5	1.8/1.8	0/0/0	0/0	0/0/0	0/0/	16.6/16.6/16.6	16.7/16.6			0/0/0	Optic plane glass, thickness<0.7mm (not coloured, transparent and not having an absorbent, not otherwise worked)
0/0/0	14	10.5	1.8/1.8	0/0/0	0/0	0/0/0	0/0/	16.6/16.6/16.6	16.7/16.6			0/0/0	Other glass plate and piece made by blowing and pulling (not colonred, transparent and not having an absorbent not othermie worked)
													Float glass and surface ground or polished glass, in sheets, whether or not having an absorbent, reflecting or non-reflecting layer, but not otherwise worked:
0/0/0	12	3	1.5/1.5	0/0/0	0/0	0/0/0	0/0/	0/0/13.5	13.6/0			0/0/0	-Non-wired glass, having an absorbent, reflecting or non-reflecting layer
													-Other non-wired glass:
0/0/0	12	3	1.5/1.5	0/0/0	0/0	0/0/0	0/0/	0/0/13.5	13.6/0			0/0/0	--Coloured throughout the mass (body tinted), opacified, flashed or merely surface ground
													--Other
0/0/0	0	3	1.5/1.5	0/0/0	0/0	0/0/0	0/0/	0/0/13.5	14.1/0			0/0/0	Lidquid cry stal or organic luminous diode (OLED) original plate glass used for display including the protection screen containing alkali glass(Non-wired float slass and piece
0/0/0	0	3	1.5/1.5	0/0/0	0/0	0/0/0	0/0/	0/0/13.5	14.1/0		//	0/0/0	Original glass for mobile phone or tablet cover (including front cover and back cover) (uncolored, transparent and without absorbing layer, without other processing)
0/0/0	0	3	1.5/1.5	0/0/0	0/0	0/0/0	0/0/	0/0/13.5	14.1/0			0/0/0	Other float non-wired glass, in sheets
0/0/0	14	3.5	1.8/1.8	0/0/0	0/0	0/0/0	0/0/	15.8/15.8/15.8	16.4/15.8			0/0/0	-Wired glass
													Glass of heading No.70.03, 70.04 or 70.05, bent, edge-worked, engraved, drilled, enamelled or otherwise worked, but not framed or fitted with other materials:
													Glass of heading No. 70.03, 70.04 or 70.05, bent, edge-worked, engraved, drilled, enamelled or otherwise worked, but not framed or fitted with other materials
0/0/0	12	7	1.5/1.5	0/0/0	0/0	0/0/0	0/0/0	14/14.3/14	14.1/14.3			0/0/0	LCD glass base plate, more than 6 generation, (1850mm × 1500mm), other than 6 generation (bent, edge-worked, engraved, drilled, enamelled or otherwise worked, but not framed or fitted)
0/0/0	12	7	1.5/1.5	0/0/0	0/0	0/0/0	0/0/0	14/14.3/14	14.1/14.3			0/0/0	LCD glass base plate, 6 generation and less than, (1850mm × 1500mm), other than 6 generation(bent, edge-worked, engraved, drilled, enamelled or otherwise worked, but not framed or fitted)
0/0/0	12	7	1.5/1.5	0/0/0	0/0	0/0/0	0/0/0	14/14.3/14	14.1/14.3			0/0/0	Glass in other process Nos.from 70.03 to 70.05 (after being bent, edged, carved, holed and painted with enamel, not mounted in cabinet or fixed)
													Safety glass, consisting of toughened (tempered) or laminated glass:
													-Toughened (tempered) safety glass:
													--Of size and shape suitable for incorporation in vehicles, aircraft, spacecraft or vessels:
													---For aircraft, spacecraft or vessels
0/0/0	0	0	0/0	0/0/0	0/0	0//0	0/0/	0/0/0	0/0			0/0/0	Toughened (tempered) safety glass, of size and shape suitable for incorporation in aircraft, W≥25 tons
0/0/0	0	0	0/0	0/0/0	0/0	0//0	0/0/	0/0/0	0/0			0/0/0	Toughened safety glass for aircraft, spacecraft and ships (other specs and forms suitable for installation in aircraft, spacecraft and ships)
0/0/0	2	4.6	0/0	0/0/0	0/0	0//0	0/0/	9.3/9.5/9.3	9.4/9.5			0/0/0	---Other
0/0/0	11.2	2.8	1.4/1.4	0/0/0	0/0	0/0/0	0/0/	0/0/12.6	12.7/0			0/0/0	--Other
													-Laminated safety glass:
													--Of size and shape suitable for incorporation in vehicles, aircraft, spacecraft or vessels:
0/0/0	0	0	0/0	0/0/0	0/0	0//0	0/0/	0/0/0	0/0			0/0/0	---for aircraft, spacecraft or vessels
0/0/0	16	12	2/2	0/0/0	0/0	0/0/0	0/0/	19/19/	/19			0/0/0	---Other
0/0/0	9	2.8	1.4/1.4	0/0/0	0/0	0/0/0	0/0/	0/0/12.6	12.7/0			0/0/0	--Other

税则号列	货品名称〔CIQ扩展编码及品名—T2表示见附表2〕	最惠(%)	暂定税率	普通	增值/消费	出口退税	计量单位	监管条件/特殊证件	检验检疫	对美关税	亚太上/下
70.08	**多层隔温、隔音玻璃组件:**										
7008.0010	---中空或真空隔温、隔音玻璃〔101其他车辆零部件,102钢化玻璃,103其他玻璃及制品〕	14		50	13/	13	千克	/	L	24	
7008.0090	---其他〔101其他车辆零部件,102钢化玻璃,103其他玻璃及制品〕	14		50	13/	13	千克	/	L	39	
70.09	**玻璃镜(包括后视镜),不论是否镶框:**										
7009.1000	-车辆后视镜〔101其他车辆零部件,102玻璃镜〕	10		100	13/	13	千克	/	L	20	
	-其他:										
7009.9100	--未镶框〔999〕	14		70	13/	13	千克	/	L	24	
7009.9200	--已镶框〔999〕	12		100	13/	13	千克	/		37	7.8/7.8
70.10	**玻璃制的坛、瓶、缸、罐、安瓿及其他容器,用于运输或盛装货物;玻璃制保藏罐;玻璃塞、盖及类似的封口器:**										
7010.1000	-安瓿〔999〕	14		50	13/	13	千克	/		39	
7010.2000	-塞、盖及类似的封口器〔101非食品用玻璃器皿,102食品用玻璃包装〕	14		50	13/	13	千克	/		39	
	-其他:										
7010.9010	---超过1升〔101非食品用玻璃器皿,102食品用玻璃包装〕	14		50	13/	13	千克	/		39	
7010.9020	---超过0.33升,但不超过1升〔101非食品用玻璃器皿,102食品用玻璃包装〕	14		50	13/	13	千克	/		24	
7010.9030	---超过0.15升,但不超过0.33升〔101非食品用玻璃器皿,102食品用玻璃包装〕	14		50	13/	13	千克	/		39	
7010.9090	---不超过0.15升〔101非食品用玻璃器皿,102食品用玻璃包装〕	14		50	13/	13	千克	/		39	
70.11	**制灯泡和光源、阴极射线管及类似品用的未封口玻璃外壳(包括玻璃泡及管)及其玻璃零件,但未装有配件:**										
7011.1000	-电灯用〔999〕	12		80	13/	0	千克	/		37	
	-阴极射线管用:										
7011.2010	---显像管玻壳及其零件〔101其它电光源及其零件,102其它显像管及其零件〕	10		35	13/	13	千克	6/			6.5/6.5
7011.2090	---其他〔101其它电光源及其零件;102其它显像管及其零件〕	10		35	13/	13	千克	6/		20	6.5/6.5
	-其他:										
7011.9010	---电子管用(阴极射线管用的除外)〔999〕	8		35	13/	13	千克	/		28	
7011.9090	---其他〔999〕	14		80	13/	0	千克	/		24	
70.13	**玻璃器,供餐桌、厨房、盥洗室、办公室、室内装饰或类似用途(税号70.10或70.18的货品除外):**										
7013.1000	-玻璃陶瓷制〔999〕	7		100	13/	13	千克	/		32	
	-高脚杯,但玻璃陶瓷制的除外:										
7013.2200	--铅晶质玻璃制〔101非食品用玻璃器皿,102食品接触玻璃产品〕	7		100	13/	13	千克	/		32	
7013.2800	--其他〔101非食品用玻璃器皿,102食品接触玻璃产品〕	7		100	13/	13	千克	A/	R	32	
	-其他杯子,但玻璃陶瓷制的除外:										
7013.3300	--铅晶质玻璃制〔101非食品用玻璃器皿,102食品接触玻璃产品,103食品用玻璃包装〕	7		100	13/	13	千克	/		32	
7013.3700	--其他〔101非食品用玻璃器皿,102食品接触玻璃产品,103食品用玻璃包装〕	7		100	13/	13	千克	A/	R	32	
	-餐桌或厨房用玻璃器皿(不包括杯子),但玻璃陶瓷制的除外:										
7013.4100	--铅晶质玻璃剂〔101非食品用玻璃器皿,102食品接触玻璃产品,103食品用玻璃包装〕	7		100	13/	13	千克	A/	R	32	
7013.4200	--温度在0℃至300℃时线膨胀系数不超过5×10^{-6}/开尔文的其他玻璃制〔101非食品用玻璃器皿,102食品接触玻璃产品,103食品用玻璃包装〕	7		100	13/	13	千克	A/	R	22	
7013.4900	--其他〔101非食品用玻璃器皿,102食品接触玻璃产品,103食品用玻璃包装〕	7		100	13/	13	千克	A/	R	32	
	-其他玻璃器:										
7013.9100	--铅晶质玻璃制〔101非食品用玻璃器皿,102食品接触玻璃产品,103食品用玻璃包装〕	7		100	13/	13	千克	/		32	
7013.9900	--其他〔101非食品用玻璃器皿,102食品接触玻璃产品,103食品用玻璃包装〕	7		100	13/	13	千克	/		32	
70.14	**未经光学加工的信号玻璃器及玻璃制光学元件(税目70.15的货品除外):**										
7014.0010	---光学仪器用光学元件毛坯〔999〕	10		40	13/	13	千克	/		35	
7014.0090	---其他										
7014.0090 01	滤波玻璃(带有抗红外和防反射薄膜的)〔999〕	15	9	80	13/	13	千克	/		34	
7014.0090 90	其他未经光学加工的信号玻璃器(包括玻璃制光学元件,编号7015的物品除外)〔999〕	15		80	13/	13	千克	/		40	
70.15	**钟表玻璃及类似玻璃、视力矫正或非视力矫正眼镜用玻璃,呈弧面、弯曲、凹形或类似形状但未经光学加工的;制造上述玻璃用的凹面圆形及扇形玻璃:**										
	-视力矫正眼镜用玻璃:										

协定税率 %								RCEP		特惠税率 %			Article Description
东/冰/格	巴基斯坦	韩国	瑞士 上/下	哥/秘/柬	澳/毛	新西/坡/智	中国港/澳/台	东盟及马来/澳/韩	日/新	亚太2国	老/柬/缅	98/97/95	
													Multiple-walled insulating units of glass:
0/0/0	7.8	2.8	1.4/1.4	0/0/0	0/0	0/0/0	0/0/	0/0/12.6	12.7/0			0/0/0	---Sealed or vacuum insulating glass
0/0/0	7.8	2.8	1.4/1.4	0/0/0	0/0	0/0/0	0/0/	0/0/12.6	12.7/0			0/0/0	---Other
													Glass mirrors, whether or not framed, including rear-view mirrors:
0/0/0	4	6	0/0	0/0/0	0/0	0/0/0	0/0/0	9.5/9.5/	/9.5			0/0/0	-Rear-view mirrors for vehicles
													-Other:
0/0/0	16.8	12.6	2.1/2.1	0/0/0	0/0	0/0/0	0/0/	20/20/	/20			0/0/0	--Unframed
0/0/0	4	2.4	1.2/1.2	0/0/0	0/0	0/0/0	0/0/	0/0/10.8	10.9/0			0/0/0	--Framed
													Carboys, bottles, flasks, jars, pots, phials, ampoules and other containers, of glass, of a kind used for the conveyance or packing of goods; preserving jars of glass; stoppers, lids and other closures, of glass:
0/0/0	9	2.8	1.4/1.4	0/0/0	0/0	0/0/0	0/0/	0/0/12.6	12.7/0			0/0/0	-Ampoules
0/0/0	7.8	2.8	1.4/1.4	0/0/0	0/0	0/0/0	0/0/	0/0/12.6	12.7/0			0/0/0	-Stoppers, lids and other closures
													-Other:
0/0/0	7.8	2.8	1.4/1.4	0/0/0	0/0	0/0/0	0/0/	0/0/12.6	12.7/0			0/0/0	---Exceeding 1L
0/0/0	7.8	2.8	1.4/1.4	0/0/0	0/0	0/0/0	0/0/	0/0/12.6	12.7/0			0/0/0	---Exceeding 0.33L but not exceeding 1L
0/0/0	9	2.8	1.4/1.4	0/0/0	0/0	0/0/0	0/0/	0/0/12.6	12.7/0			0/0/0	---Exceeding 0. 15L but not exceeding 0. 33L
0/0/0	9	2.8	1.4/1.4	0/0/0	0/0	0/0/0	0/0/	0/0/12.6	12.7/0			0/0/0	---Not exceeding 0. 15L
													Glass envelopes (including bulbs and tubes), open, and glass parts thereof, without fittings, for electric lamps and light sources, cathode-ray tubes or the like:
0/0/0		12.6	2.1/2.1	0/0/0	0/0	0/0/0	0/0/	20/20/	/20			0/0/0	-For electric lighting
													-For cathode-ray tubes:
0/0/0	3.5	2	0/0	0/0/0	0/0	0//0	0/0/	9/9/9	9.1/9			0/0/0	---Glass envelopes for kinescope and glass parts thereof
0/0/0	3.5		0/0	0/0/0	0/0	0//0	0/0/	5/5/	/5			0/0/0	---Other
													-Other:
0/0/0	2	0	0/0	0/0/0	0/0	0//0	0/0/	0/0/0	7.3/0			0/0/0	---For electronic tubes and valves (other than cathode-ray tubes)
0/0/0		12.6	2.1/2.1	0/0/0	0/0	0/0/0	0/0/	20/20/	/20			0/0/0	---Other
													Glassware of a kind used for table, kitchen, toilet, office, indoor decoration or similar purposes (other than that of heading No. 70. 10 or 70. 18):
0/0/0		14.7	2.5/2.5	0/0/0	0/14.7	0/0/0	0/0/	23.3/23.3/23.3	23.3/23.3			0/0/0	-Of glass-ceramics
													-Stemware drinking glasses, other than of glass-ceramics:
0/0/0		14.7	2.5/2.5	0/0/0	0/14.7	0/0/0	0/0/	23.3/23.3/23.3	23.3/23.3			0/0/0	--Of lead crystal
0/0/0	2	0	0/0	0/0/0	0/0	0/0/0	0/0/	0/0/0	7.3/0			0/0/0	--Other
													-Other drinking glasses, other than of glass-ceramics:
0/0/0		14.7	2.5/2.5	0/0/0	0/14.7	0/0/0	0/0/	23.3/23.3/23.3	/23.3			0/0/0	--Of lead crystal
0/0/0	2	0	0/0	0/0/0	0/0	0/0/0	0/0/	0/0/0	7.3/0			0/0/0	--Other
													Glassware of a kind used for table (other than drinkings glasses) or kitchen purposes other than of glass-ceramics:
0/0/0		14.7	2.5/2.5	0/0/0	0/14.7	0/0/0	0/0/	23.3/23.3/23.3	/23.3			0/0/0	--Of lead crystal
0/0/0	2	2	0/0	0/0/0	0/0	0/0/0	0/0/	0/0/9	9.1/0			0/0/0	--Of glasc having a linear coefficient of expansion not exceeding 5×10^{-6} perkelvin within a temperature range of 0℃ to 300℃
0/0/0	2	2	0/0	0/0/0	0/0	0/0/0	0/0/	9/9/9	9.1/9			0/0/0	--Other
													-Other glassware:
0/0/0	2	2	0/0	0/0/0	0/0	0/0/0	0/0/	0/0/9	9.1/0			0/0/0	--Of lead crystal
0/0/0	2	2	0/0	0/0/0	0/6	0/0/0	0/0/	0/0/9	9.1/0			0/0/0	--Other
													Signalling glassware and optical elements of glass (other than thoseof heading No.70. 15), not optically worked:
0/0/0	2	0	0/0	0/0/0	0/0	0/0/0	0/0/	0/0/0	9.1/0			0/0/0	---Blanks of optical elements, for optical instruments
													---Other
0/0/0	14	3.5	1.8/1.8	0/0/0	0/0	0/0/0	0/0/	15.8/15.8/15.8	15.9/15.8			0/0/0	Wave filtering glass (with anti-infrared and anti-radiation film)
0/0/0	14	3.5	1.8/1.8	0/0/0	0/0	0/0/0	0/0/	15.8/15.8/15.8	15.9/15.8			0/0/0	Other signaling glassware and optical elements of glass (including glass optical elements, other than thoseof heading No. 70. 15)
													Clock or watch glasses and similar glasses, glasses for non-corrective or corrective spectacles, curved, bent, hollowed or the like, not optically worked; hollow glass spheres and their segments, for the manufacture of such glasses:
													-Glasses for corrective spectacles:

税则号列	货品名称〔CIQ扩展编码及品名－T2表示见附表2〕	最惠(%)	暂定税率	普通	增值/消费	出口退税	计量单位	监管条件/特殊证件	检验检疫	对美关税	亚太上/下
7015.1010	---变色镜片坯件〔999〕	15		80	13/	13	千克	/		25	
7015.1090	---其他〔999〕	15		70	13/	13	千克	/			
	-其他：										
7015.9010	---钟表玻璃〔999〕	15		70	13/	0	千克	/		40	
7015.9020	---平光变色镜片坯件〔999〕	15		80	13/	13	千克	/			10.5/10.5
7015.9090	---其他〔999〕	12		80	13/	0	千克	/		37	10.8/10.8
70.16	**建筑用压制或模制的铺面用玻璃块、砖、片、瓦及其他制品，不论是否夹丝；供镶嵌或类似装饰用的玻璃马赛克及其他小件玻璃品，不论是否有衬背；花饰铅条窗玻璃及类似品；多孔或泡沫玻璃块、板、片及类似品：**										
7016.1000	-供镶嵌或类似装饰用的玻璃马赛克及其他小件玻璃品，不论是否有衬背〔999〕	15		100	13/	13	千克	/		40	
	-其他：										
7016.9010	---花饰铅条窗玻璃及类似品〔999〕	15		90	13/	13	千克	/		40	10.5/10.5
7016.9090	---其他〔999〕	15		90	13/	13	千克	/		25	10.5/10.5
70.17	**实验室、卫生及配药用的玻璃器，不论有无刻度或标量：**										
7017.1000	-熔融石英或其他熔融硅石制〔999〕	0		30	13/	13	千克	/		10	
7017.2000	-温度在0℃至300℃时线膨胀系数不超过5×10^{-6}/开尔文的其他玻璃制〔999〕	8		30	13/	13	千克	/		18	
7017.9000	-其他〔999〕	8		30	13/	13	千克	/		18	
70.18	**玻璃珠、仿珍珠、仿宝石或仿半宝石和类似小件玻璃品及其制品，但仿首饰除外；玻璃假眼，但医用假眼除外；灯工方法制作的玻璃塑像及其他玻璃装饰品，但仿首饰除外；直径不超过1毫米的微型玻璃球：**										
7018.1000	-玻璃珠、仿珍珠、仿宝石或仿半宝石及类似小件玻璃品〔999〕	10		100	13/	13	千克	/		35	
7018.2000	-直径不超过1毫米的微型玻璃球										
7018.2000 01	熔融球形二氧化硅微粉，直径≤100um〔999〕	15	5.5	100	13/	13	千克	/		30.5	
7018.2000 90	其他直径≤1毫米的微型玻璃珠〔999〕	15		100	13/	13	千克	/		40	
7018.9000	-其他〔999〕	15	10	100	13/	13	千克	/		30	
70.19	**玻璃纤维（包括玻璃棉）及其制品（例如，纱线、无捻粗纱及机织物）：**										
	-定长纤维纱条、无捻粗纱、纱线、短切原丝及其毡：										
7019.1100	--长度不超过50毫米的短切原丝										
7019.1100 10	两用物项管制的长度不超过50mm的短切原丝（比模量≥3.18×10^{-6}m，以及比抗拉强度≥7.62×10^{-4}m）〔999〕	10		50	13/	13	千克	3/		30	
7019.1100 90	其他长度不超过50mm的短切原丝〔999〕	10		50	13/	13	千克	/		30	
7019.1200	--无捻粗纱										
7019.1200 20	两用物项管制的玻璃纤维无捻粗纱（比模量≥3.18×10^{-6}m，以及比抗拉强度≥7.62×10^{-4}m）〔999〕	10		50	13/	13	千克	3/		35	
7019.1200 90	其他玻璃纤维无捻粗纱〔999〕	10		50	13/	13	千克	/		35	
7019.1300	--其他纱线，定长纤维纱条										
7019.1300 10	其他玻璃纤维或纤丝材料（其"比模量"为3.18×10^{6}米或更大和"比抗拉强度"为7.62×10^{4}米或更大的玻璃纤维或纤丝材料）〔999〕	8		50	13/	13	千克	3/		18	
7019.1300 90	其他纱线、定长纤维纱条〔999〕	8		50	13/	13	千克	/		18	
7019.1400	--机械结合毡										
7019.1400 10	两用物项管制的玻璃纤维制的机械结合毡（比模量≥3.18×10^{6} m，以及比抗拉强度≥7.62×10^{4} m）〔999〕	5		40	13/	13	千克	3/		15	
7019.1400 90	其他玻璃纤维制的机械结合毡〔999〕	5		40	13/	13	千克	/		15	
7019.1500	--化学粘合毡										
7019.1500 10	两用物项管制的玻璃纤维制的化学粘合毡（比模量≥3.18×10^{6} m，以及比抗拉强度≥7.62×10^{4} m）〔999〕	5		40	13/	13	千克	3/		15	
7019.1500 90	其他玻璃纤维制的化学粘合毡〔999〕	5		40	13/	13	千克	/		15	
7019.1900	--其他										
7019.1900 12	两用物项管制的其他短切原丝（比模量≥3.18×10^{-6}m，以及比抗拉强度≥7.62×10^{-4}m）〔999〕	8		50	13/	13	千克	3/		18	
7019.1900 90	其他短切原丝〔999〕	8		50	13/	13	千克	/		18	
	-机械结合织物：										
7019.6100	--紧密粗纱机织物										
7019.6100 10	两用物项管制的紧密粗纱机织物（比模量≥3.18×10^{6} m，以及比抗拉强度≥7.62×10^{4} m，机械结合的）〔999〕	10		40	13/	13	千克	3/		20	
7019.6100 90	其他紧密粗纱机织物（机械结合的）〔999〕	10		40	13/	13	千克	/		20	
7019.6200	--其他紧密粗纱织物										

协定税率 %								RCEP		特惠税率 %			Article Description
东/冰/格	巴基斯坦	韩国	瑞士上/下	哥/秘/柬	澳/毛	新西/坡/智	中国港/澳/台	东盟及马来/澳/韩	日/新	亚太2国	老/柬/缅	98/97/95	
0/0/0		9.8	2.1/2.1	0/0/0	0/0	0/0/0	0/0/	18.9/18.9/18.9	19.7/18.9			0/0/0	---Blanks for photochromic spectacles
0/0/0	14	3.5	1.8/1.8	0/0/0	0/0	0/0/0	0/0/	0/0/15.8	15.9/0			0/0/0	---Other
													-Other:
0/0/0	14	3.5	1.8/1.8	0/0/0	0/10.5	0/0/0	0/0/	0/0/15.8	15.9/0			0/0/0	---Clock and watch glasses
0/0/0	14.4	3.6	1.8/1.8	0/0/0	0/0	0/0/0	0/0/	0/0/16.2	16.4/0			0/0/0	---Blanks for plane photochromic spectacles
0/0/0	4.2	2.4	5/5	0/0/0	0/0	0/0/0	0/0/	0/0/10.8	10.9/0			0/0/0	---Other
													Paving blocks, slabs, bricks, squares, tiles and other articles of pressed or moulded glass, whether or not wired, of a kind used for building or construction purposes; glass cubes and other glass smallwares, whether or not on a backing, for mosaics or similar decorative purposes; leaded lights and the like; multicellular or foam glass in blocks, panels, plates, shells or similar forms:
0/0/0		13.2	2.2/2.2	0/0/0	0/13.2	0/0/0	0/0/	20.9/20.9/20.9	/20.9			0/0/0	-Glass cubes and other glass smallwares, whether or not on a backing, for mosaics or similar decorative purposes
													-Other:
0/0/0		14.4	2.4/2.4	0/0/0	0/14.4	0/0/0	0/0/	22.8/22.8/22.8	22.9/22.8			0/0/0	---Leaded lights and the like
0/0/0		3.6	1.8/1.8	0/0/0	0/0	0/0/0	0/0/	0/0/16.2	16.4/0			0/0/0	---Other
													Laboratory, hygienic or pharmaceutical glassware, whether or not graduated or calibrated:
0/0/0	0	0	0/0	0/0/0	0/0	0//0	0/0/	0/0/0	0/0			0/0/0	-Of fused quartz or other fused silica
0/0/0	2	0	3.4/3.4	0/0/0	0/0	0//0	0/0/	0/0/0	7.3/0			0/0/0	-Of other glass having a linear coefficient of expansion not exceeding 5×10^{-6} per Kelvin within a temperature range of 0℃ to 300℃
0/0/0	2	1.6	0/0	0/0/0	0/0	0//0	0/0/	0/0/7.2	7.3/0			0/0/0	-Other
													Glass beads, imitation pearls, imitation precious or semi-precious stones and similar glass smallwares, and articles thereof other than imitation jewellery; glass eyes other than prosthetic articles; statuettes and other ornaments of lampworked glass, other than imitation jewellery; glass microspheres not exceeding 1mm in diameter:
0/0/0	4	0	0/0	0/0/0	0/0	0/0/0	0/0/	0/0/0	9.1/0			0/0/0	-Glass beads, imitation pearls, imitation precious or semi-precious stones and similar glass smallwares
													-Glass microspheres, diameter≤1mm
0/0/0		9.3	2/2	0/0/0	0/0	0/0/0	0/0/	18.7/19/18.7	18.8/19			0/0/0	Molten spherical silica powder, diameter ≤ 100um
0/0/0		9.3	2/2	0/0/0	0/0	0/0/0	0/0/	18.7/19/18.7	18.8/19			0/0/0	Other glass microspheres not exceeding lmm in diameler
0/0/0		9.3	2/2	0/0/0	0/0	0/0/0	0/0/	18/18/18	18.8/18			0/0/0	-Other
													Glass fibres (including glass wool) and articles thereof (for example, yarn, roving, woven fabrics):
													-Fixed length fiber yarn, roving, yarn, chopped strands and felt:
													--Chopped strands, of a length of not more than 50mm
0/0/0	4.2	2.4	1.2/1.2	0/0/0	0/0	0/0/0	0/0/0	0/0/10.8	10.9/0			0/0/0	Chopped precursor with length not exceeding 50mm for dual—purpose item control (specific modulus ≥ 3.18) × 10^{6} m, and specific tensile strength ≥ 7.62 × 10^{4} m)
0/0/0	4.2	2.4	1.2/1.2	0/0/0	0/0	0/0/0	0/0/0	0/0/10.8	10.9/0			0/0/0	Other chopped filaments not exceeding 50mm in length
													--Rovings
0/0/0	4.2		1.2/1.2	0/0/0	0/0	0/0/0	0/0/	5/5/	/5			0/0/0	Glass fibres rovings, fual-use items control, modulus atio≥3.18×10^{6} m, specific ultimate tensile strength≥7.62×10^{4} m
0/0/0	4.2		1.2/1.2	0/0/0	0/0	0/0/0	0/0/	5/5/	/5			0/0/0	Other glass fibres rovings
													--Other yarn, slivers
0/0/0	3.5	2	0/0	0/0/0	0/0	0//0	0/0/0	9/9/9	9.1/9			0/0/0	Other glass fiber or filament materials with a "specific modulus" of 3.18 × 1^{6} m or more and "specific tensile strength" is 7.62 × 1^{4} meters or larger glass fiber or filament material)
0/0/0	3.5	2	0/0	0/0/0	0/0	0//0	0/0/0	9/9/9	9.1/9			0/0/0	Other yarn, fixed length fiber yarn
													--Mechanically bonded mats
0/0/0	0	0	0/0	0/0/0	0/0	0//0	0/0/	0/0/0	0/0			0/0/0	Mechanical bonded felt of glass fiber for dual—purpose item control(Specific modulus ≥ 3.18 × 10^{6} m and specific tensile strength ≥ 7.62 × 10^{4} m)
0/0/0	0	0	0/0	0/0/0	0/0	0//0	0/0/	0/0/0	0/0			0/0/0	Other mechanically bonded felts of glass fibres
													--Chemically bonded mats
0/0/0	0	0	0/0	0/0/0	0/0	0//0	0/0/	0/0/0	0/0			0/0/0	Chemical bonded felt of glass fiber for dual—purpose item control(Specific modulus ≥ 3.18 × 10^{6} m and specific tensile strength ≥ 7.62 × 10^{4} m)
0/0/0	0	0	0/0	0/0/0	0/0	0//0	0/0/	0/0/0	0/0			0/0/0	Other chemically bonded felts of glass fibres
													--Other
0/0/0	3.5	2	0/0	0/0/0	0/0	0//0	0/0/0	9/9/9	9.1/9			0/0/0	Other chopped precursor under dual use item control (its "specific modulus" is 3.18 × 10^{6} m or more and "specific tensile strength" is 7.62 × 10^{4} meters or larger glass fiber or filament material)
0/0/0	3.5	2	0/0	0/0/0	0/0	0//0	0/0/0	9/9/9	9.1/9			0/0/0	Other chopped precursor
													-Mechanically bonded fabrics:
													--Closed woven fabrics of rovings
0/0/0	4.2	2.4	1.2/1.2	0/0/0	0/0	0/0/0	0/0/	0/0/10.8	10.9/0			0/0/0	Compact roving woven fabric with dual purpose item control(Specific modulus ≥ 3.18× 10^{6} m and specific tensile strength ≥ 7.62 × 10^{4} m, mechanically bonded)
0/0/0	4.2	2.4	1.2/1.2	0/0/0	0/0	0/0/0	0/0/	0/0/10.8	10.9/0			0/0/0	Other compact roving woven fabrics(Mechanically combined)
													--Other closed fabrics of rovings

税则号列	货品名称〔CIQ 扩展编码及品名－T2 表示见附表 2〕	最惠(%)	暂定税率	普通	增值/消费	出口退税	计量单位	监管条件/特殊证件	检验检疫	对美关税	亚太上/下
7019.6200 10	两用物项管制的其他紧密粗纱织物(比模量≥3.18×10^{6} m,以及比抗拉强度≥7.62×10^{4} m,机械结合的,机织物除外)〔999〕	10		40	13/	13	千克	3/		20	
7019.6200 90	其他紧密粗纱织物(机械结合的,机织物除外)〔999〕	10		40	13/	13	千克	/		20	
	--纱线制紧密平纹机织物,未经涂布或层压:										
7019.6310	---宽度不超过 30 厘米的										
7019.6310 10	两用物项管制的宽度≤15mm 的玻璃纤维纱线制紧密平纹机织物,未经涂布或层压(机械结合的)〔999〕	10		40	13/	13	千克	3/		20	
7019.6310 90	其他宽度≤30cm 的玻璃纤维纱线制紧密平纹机织物,未经涂布或层压(机械结合的)〔999〕	10		40	13/	13	千克	/		20	
7019.6320	---宽度超过 30 厘米的长丝平纹织物,每平方米重量不超过 110 克,单根纱线细度不超过 22 特克斯										
7019.6320 10	两用物项管制的玻璃纤维制宽度超过 30 厘米的长丝平纹织物,每平方米重量不超过 110 克,单根纱线细度不超过 22 特克斯(比模量≥3.18×10^{6} m,以及比抗拉强度≥7.62×10^{4} m,机械结合的)〔999〕	10		40	13/	13	千克	3/		35	
7019.6320 90	玻璃纤维制宽度超过 30 厘米的长丝平纹织物,每平方米重量不超过 110 克,单根纱线细度不超过 22 特克斯(机械结合的)〔999〕	10		40	13/	13	千克	/		35	
7019.6390	---其他										
7019.6390 10	两用物项管制的其他玻璃纤维纱线制紧密平纹机织物,未经涂布或层压(比模量≥3.18×10^{6} m,以及比抗拉强度≥7.62×10^{4} m,机械结合的)〔999〕	10		40	13/	13	千克	3/		20	
7019.6390 90	其他玻璃纤维纱线制紧密平纹机织物,未经涂布或层压(机械结合的)〔999〕	10		40	13/	13	千克	/		20	
	--纱线制紧密平纹机织物,经涂布或层压:										
7019.6410	---宽度不超过 30 厘米的										
7019.6410 10	两用物项管制的宽度≤15mm 的玻璃纤维纱线制紧密平纹机织物,经涂布或层压(机械结合的)〔999〕	10		40	13/	13	千克	3/		20	
7019.6410 90	其他宽度≤30cm 的玻璃纤维纱线制紧密平纹机织物,经涂布或层压(机械结合的)〔999〕	10		40	13/	13	千克	/		20	
7019.6490	---其他										
7019.6490 10	两用物项管制的其他玻璃纤维纱线制紧密平纹机织物,经涂布或层压(比模量≥3.18×10^{6} m,以及比抗拉强度≥7.62×10^{4} m,机械结合的)〔999〕	10		40	13/	13	千克	3/		20	
7019.6490 90	其他玻璃纤维纱线制紧密平纹机织物,经涂布或层压(机械结合的)〔999〕	10		40	13/	13	千克	/		20	
	--宽度不超过 30 厘米的网孔机织物:										
7019.6510	---粗纱机织物										
7019.6510 10	两用物项管制的宽度≤30cm 的玻璃纤维粗纱制网孔机织物(比模量≥3.18×10^{6} m,以及比抗拉强度≥7.62×10^{4} m,机械结合的)〔999〕	10		40	13/	13	千克	3/		20	
7019.6510 90	宽度≤30cm 的玻璃纤维粗纱制网孔机织物(机械结合的)〔999〕	10		40	13/	13	千克	/		20	
7019.6590	---其他										
7019.6590 10	两用物项管制的宽度≤15mm 的玻璃纤维网孔机织物(机械结合的,但粗纱制的除外)〔999〕	10		40	13/	13	千克	3/		20	
7019.6590 90	其他宽度≤30cm 的玻璃纤维网孔机织物(机械结合的,但粗纱制的除外)〔999〕	10		40	13/	13	千克	/		20	
	--宽度超过 30 厘米的网孔机织物:										
7019.6610	---粗纱机织物										
7019.6610 10	两用物项管制的宽度＞30cm 的玻璃纤维粗纱制网孔机织物(比模量≥3.18×10^{6} m,以及比抗拉强度≥7.62×10^{4} m,机械结合的)〔999〕	10		40	13/	13	千克	3/		20	
7019.6610 90	宽度＞30cm 的玻璃纤维粗纱制网孔机织物(机械结合的)〔999〕	10		40	13/	13	千克	/		20	
7019.6690	---其他										
7019.6690 10	两用物项管制的宽度＞30cm 的其他玻璃纤维纱线制网孔机织物(比模量≥3.18×10^{6} m,以及比抗拉强度≥7.62×10^{4} m,机械结合的)〔999〕	10		40	13/	13	千克	3/		20	
7019.6690 90	其他玻璃纤维纱线制网孔机织物(机械结合的)〔999〕	10		40	13/	13	千克	/		20	
	--其他:										

协定税率 %								RCEP		特惠税率 %			Article Description
东/冰/格	巴基斯坦	韩国	瑞士上/下	哥/秘/柬	澳/毛	新西/坡/智	中国港/澳/台	东盟及马来/澳/韩	日/新	亚太2国	老/柬/缅	98/97/95	
0/0/0	3.5	2.1	1.1/1.1	0/0/0	0/0	0/0/0	0/0/0	0/0/9.5	9.5/0			0/0/0	Other compact roving fabrics under dual－use item control (Specific modulus ≥ 3.18 × 10^6 m and specific tensile strength ≥ 7.62 × 10^4 m, mechanically bonded, except woven)
0/0/0	3.5	2.1	1.1/1.1	0/0/0	0/0	0/0/0	0/0/0	0/0/9.5	9.5/0			0/0/0	Other compact roving fabrics (Mechanically bonded, except woven fabrics)
													--Closed woven fabrics, plain weave, of yarns, not coated or laminated:
													---Open woven fabrics of a width not exceeding 30cm
0/0/0	4.2	2.4	1.2/1.2	0/0/0	0/0	0/0/0	0/0/	0/0/10.8	10.9/0			0/0/0	Compact plain woven fabric of glass fiber yarn with width ≤ 15mm, uncoated or laminated (mechanically bonded)
0/0/0	4.2	2.4	1.2/1.2	0/0/0	0/0	0/0/0	0/0/	0/0/10.8	10.9/0			0/0/0	Other compact plain woven fabrics of glass fiber yarn with width ≤ 3cm, uncoated or laminated (mechanically bonded)
													---Open woven fabrics of a width exceeding 30cm, weighing less than 110g/m2, of filaments meaningsuring per single yarn not more than 22tex
0/0/0	4.2		1.2/1.2	0/0/0	0/0	0/0/0	0/0/	5/5/	/5			0/0/0	Filament plain fabric of glass fiber with a width of more than 30 cm under dual－use item control, with a weight of no more than 110 grams per square meter and a single yarn fineness of no more than 22 tex (Specific modulus ≥ 3.18 × 10^6 m and specific tensile strength ≥ 7.62 × 10^4 m, mechanically bonded)
0/0/0	4.2		1.2/1.2	0/0/0	0/0	0/0/0	0/0/	5/5/	/5			0/0/0	Filament plain fabric of glass fiber with a width of more than 30 cm, weighing no more than 110 grams per square meter and a single yarn fineness of no more than 22 tex (Mechanically combined)
													---Other
0/0/0	3.9		1.2/1.2	0/0/0	0/0	0/0/0	0/0/	5/5/	/5			0/0/0	Compact plain woven fabrics of other glass fibre yarns, uncoated or laminated, of dual－use item control (Specific modulus ≥ 3.18 × 10^6 m and specific tensile strength ≥ 7.62 × 10^4 m, mechanically bonded)
0/0/0	3.9		1.2/1.2	0/0/0	0/0	0/0/0	0/0/	5/5/	/5			0/0/0	Other compact plain woven fabrics of glass fibre yarn, uncoated or laminated (Mechanically combined)
													--Closed woven fabrics, plain weave, of yarns, coated or laminated:
													---Open woven fabrics of a width not exceeding 30cm
0/0/0	4.2	2.4	1.2/1.2	0/0/0	0/0	0/0/0	0/0/	0/0/10.8	10.9/0			0/0/0	Compact plain woven fabric of glass fiber yarn with width ≤ 15mm of dual－purpose item control, coated or laminated (mechanically bonded)
0/0/0	4.2	2.4	1.2/1.2	0/0/0	0/0	0/0/0	0/0/	0/0/10.8	10.9/0			0/0/0	Other compact plain woven fabrics of glass fiber yarn with width ≤ 3cm, coated or laminated (mechanically bonded)
													---Other
0/0/0	3.9		1.2/1.2	0/0/0	0/0	0/0/0	0/0/	5/5/	/5			0/0/0	Compact plain woven fabrics, coated or laminated, of other glass fibre yarns under dual－use item control (Specific modulus ≥ 3.18 × 10^6 m and specific tensile strength ≥ 7.62 × 10^4 m, mechanically bonded)
0/0/0	3.9		1.2/1.2	0/0/0	0/0	0/0/0	0/0/	5/5/	/5			0/0/0	Other compact plain woven fabrics of glass fibre yarn, coated or laminated (Mechanically combined)
													--Mesh woven fabric with width not exceeding 30cm:
													---Roving woven fabric
0/0/0	4.2	2.4	1.2/1.2	0/0/0	0/0	0/0/0	0/0/	0/0/10.8	10.9/0			0/0/0	Mesh woven fabric of glass fiber roving with width ≤ 30cm of dual－purpose item control (Specific modulus ≥ 3.18 × 10^6 m and specific tensile strength ≥ 7.62 × 10^4 m, mechanically bonded)
0/0/0	4.2	2.4	1.2/1.2	0/0/0	0/0	0/0/0	0/0/	0/0/10.8	10.9/0			0/0/0	Mesh woven fabric of glass fiber roving with width ≤ 30cm (Mechanically combined)
													---Other
0/0/0	4.2	2.4	1.2/1.2	0/0/0	0/0	0/0/0	0/0/	0/0/10.8	10.9/0			0/0/0	Glass fiber mesh woven fabric with width ≤ 15mm of dual－purpose item control (mechanically bonded, except roving)
0/0/0	4.2	2.4	1.2/1.2	0/0/0	0/0	0/0/0	0/0/	0/0/10.8	10.9/0			0/0/0	Other glass fiber mesh woven fabrics with width ≤ 3cm (mechanically bonded, except roving)
													--Open woven fabrics of a width exceeding 30cm:
													---Roving woven fabric
0/0/0	4.2	2.4	1.2/1.2	0/0/0	0/0	0/0/0	0/0/	0/0/10.8	10.9/0			0/0/0	Mesh woven fabric of glass fiber roving with width > 30cm of dual－purpose item control (Specific modulus ≥ 3.18 × 10^6 m and specific tensile strength ≥ 7.62 × 10^4 m, mechanically bonded)
0/0/0	4.2	2.4	1.2/1.2	0/0/0	0/0	0/0/0	0/0/	0/0/10.8	10.9/0			0/0/0	Mesh woven fabric of glass fiber roving with width > 30cm (Mechanically combined)
													---Other
0/0/0	3.9		1.2/1.2	0/0/0	0/0	0/0/0	0/0/	5/5/	/5			0/0/0	Mesh woven fabrics of other glass fiber yarns with width > 30cm of dual－purpose item control (Specific modulus ≥ 3.18 × 10^6 m and specific tensile strength ≥ 7.62 × 10^4 m, mechanically bonded)
0/0/0	3.9		1.2/1.2	0/0/0	0/0	0/0/0	0/0/	5/5/	/5			0/0/0	Other cellular woven fabrics of glass fibre yarn (Mechanically combined)
													--Other:

税则号列	货品名称〔CIQ 扩展编码及品名—T2 表示见附表 2〕	最惠(%)	暂定税率	普通	增值/消费	出口退税	计量单位	监管条件/特殊证件	检验检疫	对美关税	亚太上/下
7019.6910	---垫										
7019.6910　10	两用物项管制的其他玻璃纤维制的垫(比模量≥3.18×10^6 m,以及比抗拉强度≥7.62×10^4 m,机械结合的)〔999〕	10		40	13/	13	千克	3/		20	
7019.6910　90	其他玻璃纤维制的垫(机械结合的)〔999〕	10		40	13/	13	千克	/		20	
7019.6920	---纤维网、板及类似无纺产品										
7019.6920　10	两用物项管制的其他玻璃纤维制的网、板及类似无纺产品(比模量≥3.18×10^6 m,以及比抗拉强度≥7.62×10^4 m,机械结合的)〔999〕	10		40	13/	13	千克	3/		20	
7019.6920　90	其他玻璃纤维制的网、板及类似无纺产品(机械结合的)〔999〕	10		40	13/	13	千克	/		20	
7019.6930	---宽度不超过 30 厘米的机织物										
7019.6930　10	两用物项管制的宽度≤15mm 的其他玻璃纤维机织物(机械结合的)〔999〕	10		40	13/	13	千克	3/		20	
7019.6930　90	其他宽度≤30cm 的玻璃纤维机织物(机械结合的)〔999〕	10		40	13/	13	千克	/		20	
7019.6990	---其他										
7019.6990　10	两用物项管制的其他玻璃纤维织物(比模量≥3.18×10^6 m,以及比抗拉强度≥7.62×10^4 m,机械结合的)〔999〕	10		40	13/	13	千克	3/		20	6.5/6.5
7019.6990　90	其他玻璃纤维织物(机械结合的)〔999〕	10		40	13/	13	千克	/		20	6.5/6.5
	-化学粘合的织物:										
7019.7100	--覆面毡(薄毡)										
7019.7100　10	两用物项管制的玻璃纤维制的覆面毡(薄毡)(比模量≥3.18×10^6 m,以及比抗拉强度≥7.62×10^4 m,化学粘合的)〔999〕	10		40	13/	13	千克	3/		20	
7019.7100　90	玻璃纤维制的覆面毡(薄毡)(化学粘合的)〔999〕	10		40	13/	13	千克	/		20	
	--其他紧密织物:										
7019.7210	---垫										
7019.7210　10	两用物项管制的紧密玻璃纤维垫(比模量≥3.18×10^6 m,以及比抗拉强度≥7.62×10^4 m,化学粘合的)〔999〕	10		40	13/	13	千克	3/		20	
7019.7210　90	紧密玻璃纤维垫(化学粘合的)〔999〕	10		40	13/	13	千克	/		20	
7019.7290	---其他										
7019.7290　10	两用物项管制的其他玻璃纤维制紧密织物(比模量≥3.18×10^6 m,以及比抗拉强度≥7.62×10^4 m,化学粘合的,不包括垫)〔999〕	10		40	13/	13	千克	3/		20	
7019.7290　90	其他玻璃纤维制紧密织物(化学粘合的,不包括垫)〔999〕	10		40	13/	13	千克	/		20	
	--其他网孔织物:										
7019.7310	---垫										
7019.7310　10	两用物项管制的网孔玻璃纤维垫(比模量≥3.18×10^6 m,以及比抗拉强度≥7.62×10^4 m,化学粘合的)〔999〕	10		40	13/	13	千克	3/		20	
7019.7310　90	网孔玻璃纤维垫(化学粘合的)〔999〕	10		40	13/	13	千克	/		20	
7019.7390	---其他										
7019.7390　10	两用物项管制的其他玻璃纤维制网孔织物(比模量≥3.18×10^6 m,以及比抗拉强度≥7.62×10^4 m,化学粘合的,不包括垫)〔999〕	10		40	13/	13	千克	3/		20	
7019.7390　90	其他玻璃纤维制网孔织物(化学粘合的,不包括垫)〔999〕	10		40	13/	13	千克	/		20	
	-玻璃棉及其制品:										
7019.8010	---垫〔999〕	10		40	13/	13	千克	/		20	
7019.8020	---纤维网、板及类似无纺产品〔999〕	10		40	13/	13	千克	/		20	
7019.8090	---其他〔999〕	7		40	13/	13	千克	/		17	
	-其他:						千克				
	--- 玻璃纤维布浸胶制品:										
7019.9021	----每平方米重量<450 克										
7019.9021　10	两用物项管制的玻璃纤维布浸胶的宽度不超过 15mm 的带(预浸料坯)(用比模量≥3.18×10^6 m 以及比抗拉强度≥7.62×10^4 m 的玻璃纤维制成并浸渍了热固性树脂,每平方米重量<450 克)〔999〕	7		40	13/	13	千克	3/		17	
7019.9021　90	玻璃纤维布浸胶制品(每平方米重量<450 克)〔999〕	7		40	13/	13	千克	/		17	
7019.9029	----其他										
7019.9029　10	两用物项管制的其他玻璃纤维布浸胶的宽度不超过 15mm 的带(预浸料坯)(用比模量≥3.18×10^6 m 以及比抗拉强度≥7.62×10^4 m 的玻璃纤维制成并浸渍了热固性树脂,每平方米重量≥450 克)〔999〕	7		40	13/	13	千克	3/		17	
7019.9029　90	其他玻璃纤维布浸胶制品(每平方米重量≥450 克)〔999〕	7		40	13/	13	千克	/		17	
	---其他:						千克				
7019.9091	----垫										

协定税率 %								RCEP		特惠税率 %			Article Description
东/冰/格	巴基斯坦	韩国	瑞士 上/下	哥/秘/柬	澳/毛	新西/坡/智	中国港/澳/台	东盟及马来/澳/韩	日/新	亚太2国	老/柬/缅	98/97/95	
													---Mattresses
0/0/0	3.5	2.1	1.1/1.1	0/0/0	0/0	0/0/0	0/0/0	0/0/9.5	9.5/0			0/0/0	Other mats of fiberglass for dual－use item control(Specific modulus ≥ 3.18× 10^6 m and specific tensile strength ≥ 7.62 × 10^4 m, mechanically bonded)
0/0/0	3.5	2.1	1.1/1.1	0/0/0	0/0	0/0/0	0/0/0	0/0/9.5	9.5/0			0/0/0	Other mats of fiberglass(Mechanically combined)
													---Web、boards and similar nonwoven products
0/0/0	3.5	2.1	1.1/1.1	0/0/0	0/0	0/0/0	0/0/0	0/0/9.5	9.5/0			0/0/0	Other glass fiber nets, plates and similar non－woven products under dual－use item control(Specific modulus ≥ 3.18 × 10^6 m and specific tensile strength ≥ 7.62 × 10^4 m, mechanically bonded)
0/0/0	3.5	2.1	1.1/1.1	0/0/0	0/0	0/0/0	0/0/0	0/0/9.5	9.5/0			0/0/0	Other glass fiber mesh, board and similar non－woven products(Mechanically combined)
													---Woven fabric not exceeding 30cm in width
0/0/0	4.2	2.4	1.2/1.2	0/0/0	0/0	0/0/0	0/0/	0/0/10.8	10.9/0			0/0/0	Other glass fiber woven fabrics (mechanically bonded) with width ≤ 15mm of dual－purpose item control
0/0/0	4.2	2.4	1.2/1.2	0/0/0	0/0	0/0/0	0/0/	0/0/10.8	10.9/0			0/0/0	Other glass fiber woven fabrics with width ≤ 3cm (mechanically bonded)
													---Other
0/0/0	3.5	7.8	1.2/1.2	0/0/0	0/0	0/0/0	0/0/	5/5/	/5			0/0/0	Other glass fiber fabrics under dual－use item control(Specific modulus ≥ 3.18× 10^6 m and specific tensile strength ≥ 7.62 × 10^4 m, mechanically bonded)
0/0/0	3.5	7.8	1.2/1.2	0/0/0	0/0	0/0/0	0/0/	5/5/	/5			0/0/0	Other fiberglass fabrics(Mechanically combined)
													-Chemically bonded fabrics:
													--Veils (thin sheets)
0/0/0	7.8	2.8	1.4/1.4	0/0/0	0/0	0/0/0	0/0/	0/0/12.6	12.7/0			0/0/0	Coated felt (felt) of glass fiber for dual－purpose item control(Specific modulus ≥ 3.18× 10^6 m and specific tensile strength ≥ 7.62 × 10^4 m, chemically bonded)
0/0/0	7.8	2.8	1.4/1.4	0/0/0	0/0	0/0/0	0/0/	0/0/12.6	12.7/0			0/0/0	Covered felt (felt) of glass fiber(Chemically bonded)
													--Other closed fabrics:
													---Mattresses
0/0/0	3.5	2.1	1.1/1.1	0/0/0	0/0	0/0/0	0/0/0	0/0/9.5	9.5/0			0/0/0	Tight fiberglass mat for dual－purpose item control(Specific modulus ≥ 3.18× 10^6 m and specific tensile strength ≥ 7.62 × 10^4 m, chemically bonded)
0/0/0	3.5	2.1	1.1/1.1	0/0/0	0/0	0/0/0	0/0/0	0/0/9.5	9.5/0			0/0/0	Compact fiberglass mat(Chemically bonded)
													---Other
0/0/0	3.5	2.1	1.1/1.1	0/0/0	0/0	0/0/0	0/0/0	0/0/9.5	9.5/0			0/0/0	Other compact fabrics of glass fibre under dual－use item control(Specific modulus ≥ 3.18× 10^6 m and specific tensile strength ≥ 7.62 × 10^4 m, chemically bonded, excluding pads)
0/0/0	3.5	2.1	1.1/1.1	0/0/0	0/0	0/0/0	0/0/0	0/0/9.5	9.5/0			0/0/0	Other compact fabrics of glass fibres(Chemically bonded, excluding pads)
													--Other open fabrics:
													---Mattresses
0/0/0	3.5	2.1	1.1/1.1	0/0/0	0/0	0/0/0	0/0/0	0/0/9.5	9.5/0			0/0/0	Mesh fiberglass mat for dual－purpose item control(Specific modulus ≥ 3.18× 10^6 m and specific tensile strength ≥ 7.62 × 10^4 m, chemically bonded)
0/0/0	3.5	2.1	1.1/1.1	0/0/0	0/0	0/0/0	0/0/0	0/0/9.5	9.5/0			0/0/0	Mesh fiberglass mat(Chemically bonded)
													---Other
0/0/0	3.5	2.1	1.1/1.1	0/0/0	0/0	0/0/0	0/0/0	0/0/9.5	9.5/0			0/0/0	Other mesh fabrics of glass fibre under dual－use item control(Specific modulus ≥ 3.18× 10^6 m and specific tensile strength ≥ 7.62 × 10^4 m, chemically bonded, excluding pads)
0/0/0	3.5	2.1	1.1/1.1	0/0/0	0/0	0/0/0	0/0/0	0/0/9.5	9.5/0			0/0/0	Other perforated fabrics of glass fibre(Chemically bonded, excluding pads)
													-Glass wool and articles of glass wool:
0/0/0	3.5	2.1	1.1/1.1	0/0/0	0/0	0/0/0	0/0/0	0/0/9.5	9.5/0			0/0/0	---mattresses
0/0/0	3.5	2.1	1.1/1.1	0/0/0	0/0	0/0/0	0/0/0	0/0/9.5	9.5/0			0/0/0	---Web、boards and similar nonwoven products
0/0/0	2	3.2	0/0	0/0/0	0/0	0//0	0/0/	6.3/6.3/6.3	6.6/6.3			0/0/0	---Other
													-Other:
													---Glass fiber cloth impregnated products:
													----Weighing<450g/m^2
0/0/0	2	3.2	0/0	0/0/0	0/0	0//0	0/0/	6.3/6.3/6.3	6.6/6.3			0/0/0	A strip (prepreg blank) of glass fiber cloth impregnated with glue with a width not exceeding 15mm under dual－purpose item control(Specific modulus ≥ 3.18 × 10^6 m and specific tensile strength ≥ 7.62 × 10^4 m glass fiber and impregnated with thermosetting resin, weight per square meter < 450g)
0/0/0	2	3.2	0/0	0/0/0	0/0	0//0	0/0/	6.3/6.3/6.3	6.6/6.3			0/0/0	Glass fiber cloth impregnated products(Weight per square meter < 450g)
													----Other
0/0/0	2	3.2	0/0	0/0/0	0/0	0//0	0/0/	6.3/6.3/6.3	6.6/6.3			0/0/0	Other glass fiber cloth impregnated with glue with width not exceeding 15mm under dual－purpose item control (prepreg blank)(Specific modulus ≥ 3.18× 10^6 m and specific tensile strength ≥ 7.62 × 10^4 m glass fiber and impregnated with thermosetting resin, weight per square meter ≥ 450g)
0/0/0	2	3.2	0/0	0/0/0	0/0	0//0	0/0/	6.3/6.3/6.3	6.6/6.3			0/0/0	Other glass fiber cloth impregnated products(Weight per square meter ≥ 450g)
													---Other:
													----Mattresses

税则号列	货品名称〔CIQ 扩展编码及品名—T2 表示见附表 2〕	最惠(%)	暂定税率	普通	增值/消费	出口退税	计量单位	监管条件/特殊证件	检验检疫	对美关税	亚太上/下
7019.9091 10	两用物项管制的其他玻璃纤维制的垫(比模量≥3.18×10^6 m,以及比抗拉强度≥7.62×10^4 m)〔999〕	10		40	13/	13	千克	3/		20	
7019.9091 90	其他玻璃纤维制的垫〔999〕	10		40	13/	13	千克	/		20	
7019.9092	----其他纤维网、板及类似无纺织产品										
7019.9092 10	两用物项管制的其他玻璃纤维制的网、板及类似无纺产品(比模量≥3.18×10^6 m,以及比抗拉强度≥7.62×10^4 m)〔999〕	10		40	13/	13	千克	3/		20	
7019.9092 90	其他玻璃纤维制的网、板及类似无纺产品〔999〕	10		40	13/	13	千克	/		20	
7019.9099	----其他										
7019.9099 10	两用物项管制的其他玻璃纤维及其制品(比模量≥3.18×10^6 m,以及比抗拉强度≥7.62×10^4 m)〔999〕	7		40	13/	13	千克	3/		17	
7019.9099 20	两用物项管制的其他玻璃纤维及其制品(用比模量≥3.18×10^6 m以及比抗拉强度≥7.62×10^4 m的玻璃纤维制成并浸渍了热固性树脂的连续的细线、粗纱、纱或宽度不超过15mm的带(预浸料坯))〔999〕	7		40	13/	13	千克	3/		17	
7019.9099 90	其他玻璃纤维及其制品〔999〕	7		40	13/	13	千克	/			
70.20	**其他玻璃制品:**										
	---工业用:										
7020.0011	----导电玻璃〔999〕	10	7	40	13/	13	千克	/		32	
7020.0012	----绝缘子用玻璃伞盘〔999〕	10		40	13/	0	千克	/			6.5/6.5
7020.0013	----熔融石英或其他熔融硅石制										
7020.0013 01	半导体晶片生产用石英反应管及夹持器(熔融石英或其他熔融硅石制)(用于插入熔化和氧化炉内)〔999〕	0		40	13/	13	千克	/		10	6.5/6.5
7020.0013 90	熔融石英或其他熔融硅石制工业用其他玻璃制品(导电玻璃及绝缘子用玻璃伞盘除外)〔999〕	10		40	13/	13	千克	/		20	6.5/6.5
7020.0019	----其他										
7020.0019 01	半导体晶片生产用石英反应管及夹持器(用于插入熔化和氧化炉内)〔999〕	0		40	13/	0	千克	/		10	6.5/6.5
7020.0019 90	其他工业用玻璃制品〔999〕	10		40	13/	0	千克	/		20	6.5/6.5
	---其他:										
7020.0091	----保温瓶或其他保温容器用的玻璃胆〔999〕	20		100	13/	13	千克/个	A/	R	25	
7020.0099	----其他										
7020.0099 01	石英玻璃,平整度小于等于1微米〔999〕	10	4	100	13/	0	千克	/		14	6.5/6.5
7020.0099 90	其他非工业用玻璃制品〔999〕	10		100	13/	0	千克	/		20	6.5/6.5

协定税率 %								RCEP		特惠税率 %			Article Description
东/冰/格	巴基斯坦	韩国	瑞士上/下	哥/秘/柬	澳/毛	新西/坡/智	中国港/澳/台	东盟及马来/澳/韩	日/新	亚太2国	老/柬/缅	98/97/95	
0/0/0	3.5	2.1	1.1/1.1	0/0/0	0/0	0/0/0	0/0/0	0/0/9.5	9.5/0			0/0/0	Other mats of fiberglass for dual－use item control(Specific modulus $\geq 3.18 \times 10^6$ m and specific tensile strength $\geq 7.62 \times 10^4$ m)
0/0/0	3.5	2.1	1.1/1.1	0/0/0	0/0	0/0/0	0/0/0	0/0/9.5	9.5/0			0/0/0	Other mats of fiberglass
													----Other web、boards and similar nonwoven products
0/0/0	3.5	2.1	1.1/1.1	0/0/0	0/0	0/0/0	0/0/0	0/0/9.5	9.5/0			0/0/0	Other glass fiber nets, plates and similar non－woven products under dual－use item control (Specific modulus $\geq 3.18 \times 10^6$ m and specific tensile strength $\geq 7.62 \times 10^4$ m)
0/0/0	3.5	2.1	1.1/1.1	0/0/0	0/0	0/0/0	0/0/0	0/0/9.5	9.5/0			0/0/0	Other glass fiber mesh, board and similar non－woven products
													----Other
0/0/0	2	3.2	0/0	0/0/0	0/0	0//0	0/0/	6.3/6.3/6.3	6.6/6.3			0/0/0	Other glass fibers and their products under dual－use item control(Specific modulus $\geq 3.18 \times 10^6$ m and specific tensile strength $\geq 7.62 \times 10^4$ m)
0/0/0	2	3.2	0/0	0/0/0	0/0	0//0	0/0/	6.3/6.3/6.3	6.6/6.3			0/0/0	Other glass fibers and their products under dual－use item control(Specific modulus $\geq 3.18 \times 10^6$ m and specific tensile strength $\geq 7.62 \times 10^4$ m made of glass fiber and impregnated with thermosetting resin continuous yarn, roving, yarn or tape (prepreg blank) with a width not exceeding 15mm)
0/0/0	2	3.2	0/0	0/0/0	0/0	0//0	0/0/	6.3/6.3/6.3	6.6/6.3			0/0/0	Other glass fibers and their products
													Other articles of glass:
													---For technical use:
0/0/0	3.5		1.1/1.1	0/0/0	0/0	0/0/0	0/0/	5/5/	/5			0/0/0	----Conductivity glass
0/0/0	3.5	2.1	1.1/1.1	0/0/0	0/0	0/0/0	0/0/	0/0/9.5	9.5/0			0/0/0	----Glass umbrella for insulator
													----Of fused quartz or other fused silica
0/0/0	3.5	0	1.1/1.1	0/0/0	0/0	0/0/0	0/0/	9.5/9.5/9.5	9.5/9.5			0/0/0	Quartz reactor tubes and holders for production of semiconductor wafers,of fused quartz or other fused silica(for inserting in melting and oxidation)
0/0/0	3.5	0	1.1/1.1	0/0/0	0/0	0/0/0	0/0/	9.5/9.5/9.5	9.5/9.5			0/0/0	Other articles of fused quartz or other fused silica(other than glass umbrella for insulator)
													----Other
0/0/0	3.5	0	1.1/1.1	0/0/0	0/0	0/0/0	0/0/	0/0/0	9.5/0			0/0/0	Quartz reactor tubes and holders for production of semiconductor wafers (for inserting in melting and oxidation)
0/0/0	3.5	0	1.1/1.1	0/0/0	0/0	0/0/0	0/0/	0/0/0	9.5/0			0/0/0	Other galss articles for other technical use
													---Other:
0/0/0		9.8	2.1/2.1	0/0/0	0/0	0/0/0	0/0/	19.6/20/19.6	19.7/20			0/0/0	----Glass inners for vacuum flasks or for other vacuum vessels
													----Other
0/0/0	5.3	3	1.5/1.5	0/0/0	0/0	0/0/0	0/0/	13.5/13.5/13.5	13.6/13.5			0/0/0	Quartz glass,levelling degree ≤ 1 μm
0/0/0	5.3	3	1.5/1.5	0/0/0	0/0	0/0/0	0/0/	13.5/13.5/13.5	13.6/13.5			0/0/0	Other glass articles not for other technical use

第十四类
天然或养殖珍珠、宝石或半宝石、贵金属、包贵金属及其制品;仿首饰;硬币

第七十一章
天然或养殖珍珠、宝石或半宝石、贵金属、包贵金属及其制品;仿首饰;硬币

注释:

一、除第六类注释一(一)及下列各款另有规定的以外,凡制品的全部或部分由下列物品构成,均应归入本章:
(一)天然或养殖珍珠、宝石或半宝石(天然、合成或再造);
(二)贵金属或包贵金属。

二、(一)税目71.13、71.14及71.15不包括带有贵金属或包贵金属制的小附件或小装饰品(例如,交织字母、套、圈、套环)的制品,上述注释一(二)也不适用于这类制品;

(二)税目71.16不包括含有贵金属或包贵金属(仅作为小零件或小装饰品的除外)的制品。

三、本章不包括:
(一)贵金属汞齐及胶态贵金属(税目28.43);
(二)第三十章的外科用无菌缝合材料、牙科填料或其他货品;
(三)第三十二章的货品(例如,光瓷釉);
(四)载体催化剂(税目38.15);
(五)第四十二章注释三(二)所述的税目42.02或42.03的物品;
(六)税目43.03或43.04的物品;
(七)第十一类的货品(纺织原料及纺织制品);
(八)第六十四章或第六十五章的鞋靴、帽类及其他物品;
(九)第六十六章的伞、手杖及其他物品;
(十)税目68.04或68.05及第八十二章含有宝石或半宝石(天然或合成)粉末的研磨材料制品;第八十二章装有宝石或半宝石(天然、合成或再造)工作部件的器具;第十六类的机器、机械器具、电气设备及其零件。然而,完全以宝石或半宝石(天然、合成或再造)制成的物品及其零件,除未安装的唱针用已加工蓝宝石或钻石外(税目85.22),其余仍应归入本章;

(十一)第九十章、第九十一章或第九十二章的物品(科学仪器、钟表及乐器);
(十二)武器及其零件(第九十三章);
(十三)第九十五章注释二所述物品;
(十四)根据第九十六章注释四应归入该章的物品;
(十五)雕塑品原件(税目97.03)、收藏品(税目97.05)或超过一百年的古物(税目97.06),但天然或养殖珍珠、宝石及半宝石除外。

四、(一)所称"贵金属",是指银、金及铂;
(二)所称"铂",是指铂、铱、锇、钯、铑及钌;
(三)所称"宝石或半宝石",不包括第九十六章注释二(二)所述任何物质。

五、含有贵金属的合金(包括烧结及化合的),只要其中任何一种贵金属的含量达到合金重量的2%,即应视为本章的贵金属合金。贵金属合金应按下列规则归类:

(一)按重量计含铂量在2%及以上的合金,应视为铂合金;
(二)按重量计含金量在2%及以上,但不含铂或按重量计含铂量在2%以下的合金,应视为金合金;

(三)按重量计含银量在2%及以上的其他合金,应视为银合金。

六、除条文另有规定的以外,本协调制度所称贵金属应包括上述注释五所规定的贵金属合金,但不包括包贵金属或表面镀以贵金属的贱金属及非金属。

七、本协调制度所称"包贵金属",是指以贱金属为底料,在其一面或多面用焊接、熔接、热轧或类似机械方法覆盖一层贵金属的材料。除条文另有规定的以外,也包括镶嵌贵金属的贱金属。

八、除第六类注释一(一)另有规定的以外,凡符合税目71.12规定的货品,应归入该税目而不归入本协调制度的其他税目。

九、税目71.13所称"首饰",是指:
(一)个人用小饰物(例如,戒指、手镯、项圈、饰针、耳环、表链、表链饰物、垂饰、领带别针、袖扣、饰扣、宗教性或其他勋章及徽章);

(二)通常放置在衣袋、手提包或佩戴在身上的个人用品(例如,雪茄盒或烟盒、鼻烟盒、口香糖或药丸盒、粉盒、链袋、念珠)。
这些物品可以和下列物品组合或镶嵌。例如,天然或养殖珍珠、宝石或半宝石、合成或再造的宝石或半宝石、玳瑁壳、珍珠母、兽牙、天然或再生琥珀、黑玉或珊瑚。

十、税目71.14所称"金银器",包括装饰品、餐具、梳妆用具、吸烟用具及类似的家庭、办公室或宗教用的其他物品。

十一、税目71.17所称"仿首饰",是指不含天然或养殖珍珠、宝石或半宝石(天然、合成或再造)及贵金属或包贵金属(仅作为镀层或小零件、小装饰品的除外)的上述注释九(一)所述的首饰(不包括税目96.06的纽扣及其他物品或税目96.15的梳子、发夹及类似品)。

子目注释:

一、子目7106.10、7108.11、7110.11、7110.21、7110.31及7110.41所称"粉末",是指按重量计90%及以上可从网眼孔径为0.5毫米的筛子通过的产品;

二、子目7110.11及7110.19所称"铂",可不受本章注释四(二)的规定约束,不包括铱、锇、钯、铑及钌。

三、对于税目71.10项下的子目所列合金的归类,按其所含铂、钯、铑、铱、锇或钌中重量最大的一种金属归类。

SECTION XIV
NATURAL OR CULTURED PEARLS, PRECIOUS OR SEMI-PRECIOUS STONES, PRECIOUS METALS, METALS CLAD WITH PRECIOUS METAL, AND ARTICLES THEREOF; IMITATION JEWELLERY; COIN

Chapter 71

Natural or cultured pearls, precious or semi-precious stones, precious metals, metals clad with precious metal, and articles thereof; imitation jewellery; coin

Notes:

1. Subject to Note 1 (a) to Section VI and except as provided below, all articles consisting wholly or partly:
   (a) Of natural or cultured pearls or of precious or semi-precious stones (natural, synthetic or reconstructed), or
   (b) Of precious metal or of metal clad with precious metal, are to be classified in this Chapter.
2. (a) Headings Nos.71.13, 71.14 and 71.15 do not cover articles in which precious metal or metal clad with precious metal is present as minor constituents only, such as minor fittings or minor ornamentation (for example, monograms, ferrules and rims), and paragraph Note 1(b) of the foregoing Note does not apply to such articles;
   (b) Heading No.71.16 does not cover articles containing precious metal or metal clad with precious metal (other than as minor constituents).
3. This Chapter does not cover:
   (a) Amalgams of precious metal, or colloidal precious metal (heading No.28.43);
   (b) Sterile surgical suture materials, dental fillings or other goods of Chapter 30;
   (c) Goods of Chapter 32 (for example, lustres);
   (d) Supported catalysts (heading No.38.15);
   (e) Articles of heading No.42.02 or 42.03 referred to in Note 3(B) to Chapter 42;
   (f) Articles of heading No.43.03 or 43.04;
   (g) Goods of Section XI (textiles and textile articles);
   (h) Footwear, headgear or other articles of Chapter 64 or 65;
   (ij) Umbrellas, walking-sticks or other articles of Chapter 66;
   (k) Abrasive goods of heading 68.04 or 68.05 or Chapter 82, containing dust or powder of precious or semi-precious stones (natural or synthetic); articles of Chapter 82 with a working part of precious or semi-precious stones (natural, synthetic or reconsturcted); machinery, mechanical appliances or electrical goods, or parts thereof, of Section XVI. However, articles and parts thereof, wholly of precious or semi-precious stones (natural, synthetic or reconstructed) remain classified in this Chapter, except unmounted worked sapphires and diamonds for styli (heading No.85.22);
   (l) Articles of Chapter 90, 91 or 92 (scientific instruments, clocks and watches, musical instruments);
   (m) Arms or parts thereof (Chapter 93);
   (n) Articles covered by Note 2 to Chapter 95;
   (o) Articles classified in Chapter 96 by virtue of Note 4 to that Chapter;
   (p) Original sculptures or statuary (heading No.97.03), collectors' pieces (heading No.97.05) or antiques of an age exceeding one hundred years (heading No.97.06), other than natural or cultured pearls or precious or semi-precious stones.
4. (a) The expression "precious metal" means silver, gold and platinum.
   (b) The expression "platinum" means platinum, iridium, osmium, palladium, rhodium and ruthenium.
   (c) The expression "precious or semi-precious stones" does not include any of the substances specified in Note 2 (b) to Chapter 96.
5. For the purposes of this Chapter, any alloy (including a sintered mixture and an inter-metallic compound) containing precious metal is to be treated as an alloy of precious metal if any one precious metal constitutes as much as 2%, by weight, of the alloy. Alloys of precious metal are to be classified according to the following rules:
   (a) An alloy containing 2% or more, by weight, of platinum is to be treated as an alloy of platinum;
   (b) An alloy containing 2% or more, by weight, of gold but no platinum, or less than 2%, by weight, of platinum, is to be treated as an alloy of gold;
   (c) Other alloys containing 2% or more, by weight, of silver are to be treated as alloys of silver.
6. Except where the context otherwise requires, any reference in the Nomenclature to precious metal or to any particular precious metal includes a reference to alloys treated as alloys of precious metal or of the particular metal in accordance with the rules in Note 5 above, but not to metal clad with precious metal or to base metal or nonmetals plated with precious metal.
7. Throughout the Nomenclature the expression "metal clad with precious metal" means material made with a base of metal upon one or more surfaces of which there is affixed by soldering, brazing, welding, hot-rolling or similar mechanical means a covering of precious metal. Except where the context otherwise requires, the expression also covers base metal inlaid with precious metal.
8. Subject to Note 1 (a) to Section VI, goods answering to a description in heading No.71.12 are to be classified in that heading and in no otherheading of the Nomenclature.
9. For the purposes of heading No.71.13, the expression "articles of jewellery" means:
   (a) Any small objects of personal adornment (for example, rings, bracelets, necklaces, brooches, ear-rings, watch-chains, fobs, pendants, tie-pins, cuff-links, dress-studs, religious or other medals and insignia); and
   (b) Articles of personal use of a kind normally carried in the pocket, in the handbag or on the person (for example) cigar or cigarette cases snuffboxes cachou or pill boxes, powder boxes chain purses or prayer beads.
   These articles may be combined or set, for example, with natural or cultured pearls, precious or semiprecious stone, synthetic or reconstructed precious or semi-precious stones, tortoise shell, mother-of-pearl, ivory, natural or reconstituted amber, jet or coral.
10. For the purposes of heading No.71.14, the expression "articles of goldsmiths' or silversmiths' wares" includes such articles as ornaments, tableware, toilet-ware, smokers' requisites and other articles of household, office or religious use.
11. For the purposes of heading No.71.17, the expression "imitation jewellery" means articles of jewellery within the meaning of Note 9(a) above (but not including buttons or other articles of heading 96.06, or dress-combs, hair-slides or the like, or hairpins, of heading No. 96.15), not incorporating natural or cultured pearls, precious or semi-precious stones (natural synthetic, or reconstructed) nor (except as plating or as minor constituents) precious metal or metal clad with precious metal.

Subheading Notes:

1. For the purposes of subheadings Nos.7106.10, 7108.11, 7110.11, 7110.21, 7110.31 and 7110.41, the expressions "powder" and "in powder form" mean products of which 90% or more by weight passes through a sieve having a mesh aperture of 0.5mm.
2. Notwithstanding the provisions of Chapter Note 4 (b), for the purposes of subheadings Nos.7110.11 and 7110.19, the expression "platinum" does not include iridium, osmium, palladium, rhodium or ruthenium.
3. For the classification of alloys in the subheadings of heading No.71.10, each alloy is to be classified with that metal, platinum, palladium, rhodium, iridium, osmium or ruthenium which predominates by weight over each other of these metals.

税则号列	货品名称〔CIQ 扩展编码及品名－T2 表示见附表 2〕	最惠(%)	暂定税率	普通	增值/消费	出口退税	计量单位	监管条件/特殊证件	检验检疫	对美关税	亚太上/下
	第一分章 天然或养殖珍珠、宝石或半宝石										
71.01	**天然或养殖珍珠，不论是否加工或分级，但未成串或镶嵌；天然或养殖珍珠，为便于运输而暂穿成串：**										
	-天然珍珠：										
	---未分级：										
7101.1011	----黑珍珠〔999〕	21	0	100	13/10	9,13	克	AB/	PQ		
7101.1019	----其他〔999〕	21		100	13/10	9,13	克	AB/	PQ		
	---其他：										
7101.1091	----黑珍珠〔999〕	21	0	130	13/10	9,13	克	AB/	PQ		
7101.1099	----其他〔101 药用天然珍珠，999 天然珍珠〕	21		130	13/10	9,13	克	AB/	PQ		
	-养殖珍珠：										
	--未加工：										
7101.2110	---未分级										
7101.2110 01	未分级、未加工的养殖黑珍珠(未制成制品)〔999〕	21	0	100	13/10	9	千克	AB/	PQ		
7101.2110 90	其他未分级、未加工的养殖珍珠(未制成制品)〔999〕	21		100	13/10	9	千克	AB/	PQ		
7101.2190	---其他										
7101.2190 01	其他未加工的养殖黑珍珠(未制成制品)〔999〕	21	0	130	13/10	9	千克	AB/	PQ		
7101.2190 90	其他未加工的养殖珍珠(未制成制品)〔101 药用未加工珍珠，999 未加工养殖珍珠〕	21		130	13/10	9	千克	AB/	PQ		
	--已加工：										
7101.2210	---未分级										
7101.2210 01	未分级、已加工的养殖黑珍珠(未制成制品)〔999〕	21	0	100	13/10	13	千克	/			
7101.2210 90	其他未分级、已加工的养殖珍珠(未制成制品)〔999〕	21		100	13/10	13	千克	/			
7101.2290	---其他										
7101.2290 01	其他已加工的养殖黑珍珠(未制成制品)〔999〕	21	0	130	13/10	13	千克	/		25	
7101.2290 90	其他已加工的养殖珍珠(未制成制品)〔101 药用未加工珍珠，999 未加工养殖珍珠〕	21		130	13/10	13	千克	/		46	
71.02	**钻石，不论是否加工，但未镶嵌：**										
7102.1000	-未分级〔999〕	3		14	13/	0	克拉	D/			
	-工业用：										
7102.2100	--未加工或经简单锯开、劈开或粗磨〔999〕	0		14	13/	9,13	克拉	D/		25	
7102.2900	--其他〔999〕	0		14	13/	9,13	克拉	/		25	
	-非工业用：										
7102.3100	--未加工或经简单锯开、劈开或粗磨〔999〕	3		14	13/	0	克拉	D/		28	
7102.3900	--其他〔999〕	4		35	13/	0	克拉	/		29	0/0
71.03	**宝石(钻石除外)或半宝石，不论是否加工或分级，但未成串或镶嵌；未分级的宝石(钻石除外)或半宝石，为便于运输而暂穿成串：**										
7103.1000	-未加工或经简单锯开或粗制成形〔999〕	3		14	13/10	9,13	千克	/		28	2/2
	-经其他加工：										
7103.9100	--红宝石、蓝宝石、祖母绿〔999〕	4		35	13/10	13	克拉	/		29	2/2
	--其他：										
7103.9910	---翡翠〔999〕	4		35	13/10	13	克拉	/			2/2
7103.9920	---水晶〔999〕	4		35	13/10	13	克拉	/		29	2/2
7103.9930	---碧玺〔999〕	4		35	13/10	13	克拉	/			2/2
7103.9940	---软玉〔999〕	4		35	13/10	13	克拉	/			2/2
7103.9990	---其他〔999〕	4		35	13/10	13	克拉	/		29	2/2
71.04	**合成或再造的宝石或半宝石，不论是否加工或分级，但未成串或镶嵌的；未分级的合成或再造的宝石或半宝石，为便于运输而暂穿成串：**										
7104.1000	-压电石英〔999〕	4		14	13/	13	克	/		29	
	-其他，未加工或经简单锯开或粗制成形：										
7104.2100	--钻石〔999〕	0		14	13/	0	克	/		10	
7104.2900	--其他〔999〕	0		14	13/10	13	克	/		25	
	-其他：	0		14	13/10	13	克	/		25	
	--钻石：										
7104.9110	---工业用〔999〕	4		14	13/	13	克	/		19	
7104.9190	---其他〔999〕	4		35	13/	0	克	/			2.8/2.8
	--其他：										
	---工业用：										
7104.9911	----蓝宝石〔999〕	4		14	13/10	13	克	/		29	
7104.9919	----其他〔999〕	4		14	13/10	13	克	/		14	
7104.9990	---其他〔999〕	4		35	13/10	13	克	/		29	3.6/3.6

协定税率 %								RCEP		特惠税率 %			Article Description
东/冰/格	巴基斯坦	韩国	瑞士上/下	哥/秘/柬	澳/毛	新西/坡/智	中国港/澳/台	东盟及马来/澳/韩	日/新	亚太2国	老/柬/缅	98/97/95	
													Ⅰ. NATURAL OR CULTURED PEARLS AND PRECIOUS OR SEMI-PRECIOUS STONES
													Pearls, natural or cultured, whether or not worked or graded but not strung, mounted or set; ungraded pearls, natural or cultured, temporarily strung for convenience of transport:
													-Natural pearls:
													---Ungraded:
0/0/0		9.8	2.1/2.1	0/0/0	0/0	0/0/0	0/0/	18.9/18.9/18.9	19.7/18.9			0/0/0	----Tahitian pearls
0/0/0		9.8	2.1/2.1	0/0/0	0/0	0/0/0	0/0/	18.9/18.9/18.9	19.7/18.9			0/0/0	----Other
													---Other:
0/0/0		9.8	2.1/2.1	0/0/0	0/0	0/0/0	0/0/	18.9/18.9/18.9	19.7/18.9			0/0/0	----Tahitan pearls
0/0/0		9.8	2.1/2.1	0/0/0	0/0	0/0/0	0/0/	18.9/18.9/18.9	19.7/18.9			0/0/0	----Other
													-Cultured pearls:
													--Unworked:
													---Ungraded
0/0/0		9.8	2.1/2.1	0/0/0	0/0	0/0/0	0/0/	18.9/18.9/18.9	19.7/18.9			0/0/0	Ungraded and unworked cultured tahitan pearls(semi-manufactured)
0/0/0		9.8	2.1/2.1	0/0/0	0/0	0/0/0	0/0/	18.9/18.9/18.9	19.7/18.9			0/0/0	Other uagraded and unworked cultured pearls(semi-manufactured)
													---Other
0/0/0		9.8	2.1/2.1	0/0/0	0/0	0/0/0	0/0/	18.9/18.9/18.9	19.7/18.9			0/0/0	Other unworked cultured tahitan pearls(semi-manufactured)
0/0/0		9.8	2.1/2.1	0/0/0	0/0	0/0/0	0/0/	18.9/18.9/18.9	19.7/18.9			0/0/0	Other unworked cultured pearls(semi-manufactured)
													--Worked:
													---Ungraded
0/0/0		12.6	2.1/2.1	0/0/0	0/0	0/0/0	0/0/	20/20/20	/20			0/0/0	Cultured Tahitan pearls, ungraded, worlced (semi-manufactured)
0/0/0		12.6	2.1/2.1	0/0/0	0/0	0/0/0	0/0/	20/20/20	/20			0/0/0	Other cultured pearls, ungraded, worked (semi-manufactured)
													---Other
0/0/0		12.6	2.1/2.1	0/0/0	0/0	0/0/0	0/0/	20/20/20	/20			0/0/0	Other worked cultured tahitan pearls(semi-manufactured)
0/0/0		12.6	2.1/2.1	0/0/0	0/0	0/0/0	0/0/	20/20/20	/20			0/0/0	Other worked cultured pearls(semi-manufactured)
													Diamonds, whether or not worked, but not mounted or set:
0/0/0	0	0	0/0	0/0/0	0/0	0//0	0/0/	0/0/0	0/0			0/0/0	-Unsorted
													-Industrial:
0/0/0	0	0	0/0	0/0/0	0/0	0//0	0/0/	0/0/0	0/0			0/0/0	--Unworked or simply sawn, cleaved or bruted
0/0/0	0	0	0/0	0/0/0	0/0	0//0	0/0/	0/0/0	0/0			0/0/0	--Other
													-Non-industrial:
0/0/0	0	0	0.3/0.3	0/0/0	0/0	0//0	0/0/	0/0/0	2.7/0			0/0/0	--Unworked or simply sawn, cleaved or bruted
0/0/0	0	0	0.8/0.8	0/0/0	0/0	0//0	0/0/	0/0/0	7.3/0			0/0/0	--Other
													Precious stones (other than diamonds) and semi-precious stones, whether or not worked or graded but not strung, mounted or set; ungraded precious stones (other than diamonds) and semi-precious stones, temporarily strung for covenience of transport:
0/0/0	0	0	0/0	0/0/0	0/0	0//0	0/0/	0/0/0	2.7/0		0//	0/0/0	-Unworked or simply sawn or roughly shaped
													-Otherwise worked:
0/0/0	0	0	0.8/0.8	0/0/0	0/0	0//0	0/0/	0/0/0	7.3/0		0//	0/0/0	--Rubies, sapphires and emeralds
													--Other:
0/0/0	0	0	0/0	0/0/0	0/0	0//0	0/0/	7.2/7.2/7.2	7.3/7.2			0/0/0	---Jadeite
0/0/0	0	1.6	0.8/0.8	0/0/0	0/0	0//0	0/0/	0/0/7.2	7.3/0			0/0/0	---Crystal
0/0/0	0	1.6	0.8/0.8	0/0/0	0/0	0//0	0/0/	0/0/7.2	7.3/0			0/0/0	---Tourmaline
0/0/0	0	1.6	0.8/0.8	0/0/0	0/0	0//0	0/0/	0/0/7.2	7.3/0			0/0/0	---Nephrite
0/0/0	0	1.6	0.8/0.8	0/0/0	0/0	0//0	0/0/	0/0/7.2	7.3/0			0/0/0	---Other
													Synthetic or reconstructed precious or semi-precious stones, whether or not worked or graded but not strung, mounted or set; ungraded synthetic or reconstructed precious or semi-precious stones, temporarily strung for convenience of transport:
0/0/0	0		0/0	0/0/0	0/0	0//0	0/0/	5/5/	/5			0/0/0	-Piezo-electric quartz
													-Other, unworked or simply sawn or roughly shaped:
0/0/0	0	0	0/0	0/0/0	0/0	0//0	0/0/	0/0/0	0/0			0/0/0	--Diamonds
0/0/0	0	0	0/0	0/0/0	0/0	0//0	0/0/	0/0/0	0/0			0/0/0	--Other
0/0/0	0	0	0/0	0/0/0	0/0	0//0	0/0/	0/0	0/0			0/0/0	-Other:
													--Diamonds:
0/0/0	0	0	0/0	0/0/0	0/0	0//0	0/0/	0/0/0	0/0			0/0/0	---For technical use
0/0/0	2	0	0/0	0/0/0	0/0	0//0	0/0/	0/0/0	7.3/0			0/0/0	---Other
													--Other:
													---For technical use:
0/0/0	0	0	0/0	0/0/0	0/0	0//0	0/0/	0/5.4/0	0/5.4			0/0/0	----Sapphires
0/0/0	0	1.2	0/0	0/0/0	0/0	0//0	0/0/	0/0/5.4	5.5/0			0/0/0	----Other
0/0/0	2	0	0/0	0/0/0	0/0	0//0	0/0/	0/0/0	7.3/0			0/0/0	---Other

税则号列	货品名称〔CIQ 扩展编码及品名—T2 表示见附表 2〕	最惠(%)	暂定税率	普通	增值/消费	出口退税	计量单位	监管条件/特殊证件	检验检疫	对美关税	亚太上/下
71.05	**天然或合成的宝石或半宝石的粉末：**										
	-钻石的：										
7105.1010	---天然的〔999〕	0		17	13/	0	克拉	/			
7105.1020	---人工合成的〔999〕	0		17	13/	13	克拉	/		10	
7105.9000	-其他〔999〕	0		17	13/10	13	克	/		25	
	第二分章　贵金属及包贵金属										
71.06	**银(包括镀金、镀铂的银),未锻造、半制成或粉末状：**										
	-银粉：										
	---非片状粉末：										
7106.1011	----平均粒径小于 3 微米〔999〕	0		0	13/	0	克	4xy/		25	
7106.1019	----其他〔101 银粉浆,102 银粉〕	0		0	13/	0	克	4xy/		20	
	---片状粉末：										
7106.1021	----平均粒径小于 10 微米〔999〕	0		0	13/	0	克	4xy/		10	
7106.1029	----其他〔999〕	0		0	13/	0	克	4xy/		10	
	-其他：										
	--未锻造：										
7106.9110	---纯度达 99.99%及以上〔999〕	0		0	13/	0	克	4xy/		25	
7106.9190	---其他〔999〕	0		0	13/	0	克	4xy/		25	
	--半制成：										
7106.9210	---纯度达 99.99%及以上〔999〕	0		50	13/	0	克	4xy/		25	
7106.9290	---其他〔999〕	0		50	13/	0	克	4xy/		20	
71.07	**以贱金属为底的包银材料：**										
7107.0000	以贱金属为底的包银材料〔999〕	8		50	13/	13	千克	/		23	
71.08	**金(包括镀铂的金),未锻造、半制成或粉末状：**										
	-非货币用：										
7108.1100	--金粉〔999〕	0		0	0/	0	克	J/			
7108.1200	--其他未锻造形状〔999〕	0		0	0/	0	克	J/			
7108.1300	--其他半制成形状〔999〕	0		50	0/	0	克	J/			
7108.2000	-货币用〔999〕	0		0	0/	0	克	J/			
71.09	**以贱金属或银为底的包金材料：**										
7109.0000	以贱金属或银为底的包金材料〔999〕	8		50	13/	13	克	/		33	
71.10	**铂,未锻造、半制成或粉末状：**										
	-铂：										
7110.1100	--未锻造或粉末状〔999〕	0		0	0/	0	克	8x/			
	--其他：										
7110.1910	---板、片〔999〕	0		0	0/	0	克	8x/			
7110.1990	---其他〔999〕	3		11	0/	0	克	4xy/			
	-钯：										
7110.2100	--未锻造或粉末状〔999〕	0		10	13/	0	克	4xy/		25	
	--其他：										
7110.2910	---板、片〔999〕	0		0	13/	0	克	4xy/		10	
7110.2990	---其他〔999〕	3		11	13/	0	克	4xy/		23	
	-铑：										
7110.3100	--未锻造或粉末状〔999〕	0		0	13/	0	克	4xy/		25	
	--其他：										
7110.3910	---板、片〔999〕	0		0	13/	0	克	4xy/		25	
7110.3990	---其他〔999〕	3		11	13/	0	克	4xy/		13	
	-铱、锇及钌：										
7110.4100	--未锻造或粉末状〔999〕	0		0	13/	0	克	4xy/		25	
	--其他：										
7110.4910	---板、片〔999〕	0		0	13/	0	克	4xy/		25	
7110.4990	---其他〔999〕	3		11	13/	0	克	4xy/		28	
71.11	**以贱金属、银或金为底的包铂材料：**										
7111.0000	以贱金属、银或金为底的包铂材料〔999〕	3		11	13/	0,13	克	4xy/		28	
71.12	**贵金属或包贵金属的废碎料;含有贵金属或贵金属化合物的其他废碎料,主要用于回收贵金属,税目 85.49 的货品除外：**										
	-含有贵金属或贵金属化合物的灰：										
7112.3010	---含有银或银化合物的〔999〕	8		50	13/	13	克	9/			
7112.3090	---其他〔999〕	6		50	13/	0	克	9/			

协定税率 %								RCEP		特惠税率 %			Article Description
东/冰/格	巴基斯坦	韩国	瑞士上/下	哥/秘/柬	澳/毛	新西/坡/智	中国港/澳/台	东盟及马来/澳/韩	日/新	亚太2国	老/柬/缅	98/97/95	
													Dust and powder of natural orsynthetic precious or semi-precious stones:
													-Of diamonds:
0/0/0	0	0	0/0	0/0/0	0/0	0//0	0/0/	0/0/0	0/0			0/0/0	---Natural
0/0/0	0	0	0/0	0/0/0	0/0	0//0	0/0/	0/0/0	0/0			0/0/0	---Synthetic
0/0/0	0	0	0/0	0/0/0	0/0	0//0	0/0/	0/0/0	0/0			0/0/0	-Other
													Ⅱ. PRECIOUS METALS AND METALS CLAD WITH PRECIOUS METAL
													Silver (including silver plated with gold or platinum), unwrought or in semi-manufactured forms, or in powder form:
													-Powder:
													---Not Flake:
0/0/0	0	0	0/0	0/0/0	0/0	0//0	0/0/	0/0/0	0/0			0/0/0	----Average diameter less than 3 micron
0/0/0	0	0	0/0	0/0/0	0/0	0//0	0/0/	0/0/0	0/0			0/0/0	----Other
													---Flake:
0/0/0	0	0	0/0	0/0/0	0/0	0//0	0/0/	0/0/0	0/0			0/0/0	----Average diameter less than 10 micron
0/0/0	0	0	0/0	0/0/0	0/0	0//0	0/0/	0/0/0	0/0			0/0/0	----Other
													-Other:
													--Unwrought:
0/0/0	0	0	0/0	0/0/0	0/0	0//0	0/0/	0/0/0	0/0			0/0/0	---of a purity of 99.99 or more
0/0/0	0	0	0/0	0/0/0	0/0	0//0	0/0/	0/0/0	0/0			0/0/0	---Other
													--Semi-manufactured:
0/0/0	0	0	0/0	0/0/0	0/0	0//0	0/0/	0/0/0	0/0			0/0/0	---of a purity of 99.99 or more
0/0/0	0	0	0/0	0/0/0	0/0	0//0	0/0/	0/0/0	0/0			0/0/0	---Other
													Base metals clad with silver, not further worked than semi-manufactured:
0/0/0	3.5	2.1	1.1/1.1	0/0/0	0/0	0/0/0	0/0/	0/0/9.5	9.5/0		0//	0/0/0	Base metals clad with silver, not further worked than semi-manufactured
													Gold (including gold plated with platinum) unwrought or in semi-manufactured forms, or in powder form:
													-Non-monetary:
0/0/0	0	0	0/0	0/0/0	0/0	0//0	0/0/	0/0/0	0/0			0/0/0	--Powder
0/0/0	0	0	0/0	0/0/0	0/0	0//0	0/0/	0/0/0	0/0			0/0/0	--Other unwrought forms
0/0/0	0	0	0/0	0/0/0	0/0	0//0	0/0/	0/0/0	0/0		0//	0/0/0	--Other semi-manufactured forms
0/0/0	0	0	0/0	0/0/0	0/0	0//0	0/0/	0/0/0	0/0			0/0/0	-Monetary
													Base metals or silver, clad with gold, not further worked than semi-manufactured:
0/0/0	3.5	2.1	1.1/1.1	0/0/0	0/0	0/0/0	0/0/	0/0/9.5	9.5/0			0/0/0	Base metals or silver, clad with gold, not further worked than semi-manufactured
													Platinum, unwrought or in semi-manufactured forms, or in powder form:
													-Platinum:
0/0/0	0	0	0/0	0/0/0	0/0	0//0	0/0/	0/0/0	0/0			0/0/0	--Unwrought or in powder form
													--Other:
0/0/0	0	0	0/0	0/0/0	0/0	0//0	0/0/	0/0/0	0/0			0/0/0	---Plates and sheets
0/0/0	0	0	0/0	0/0/0	0/0	0//0	0/0/	0/0/0	0/0			0/0/0	---Other
													-Palladium:
0/0/0	0	0	0/0	0/0/0	0/0	0//0	0/0/	0/0/0	0/0			0/0/0	--Unwrought or in powder form
													--Other:
0/0/0	0	0	0/0	0/0/0	0/0	0//0	0/0/	0/0/0	0/0			0/0/0	---Plates and sheets
0/0/0	0	0	0/0	0/0/0	0/0	0//0	0/0/	0/0/0	0/0			0/0/0	---Other
													-Rhodium:
0/0/0	0	0	0/0	0/0/0	0/0	0//0	0/0/	0/0/0	0/0			0/0/0	--Unwrought or in powder form
													--Other:
0/0/0	0	0	0/0	0/0/0	0/0	0//0	0/0/	0/0/0	0/0			0/0/0	---Plates and sheets
0/0/0	0	0	0/0	0/0/0	0/0	0//0	0/0/	0/0/0	0/0			0/0/0	---Other
													-Iridium, osmium and ruthenium:
0/0/0	0	0	0/0	0/0/0	0/0	0//0	0/0/	0/0/0	0/0			0/0/0	--Unwrought or in powder form
													--Other:
0/0/0	0	0	0/0	0/0/0	0/0	0//0	0/0/	0/0/0	0/0			0/0/0	---Plates and sheets
0/0/0	0	0	0/0	0/0/0	0/0	0//0	0/0/	0/0/0	0/0			0/0/0	---Other
													Base metals, silver or gold, clad with platinum, not further worked than semi-manufactured:
0/0/0	0	0	0/0	0/0/0	0/0	0//0	0/0/	0/0/0	0/0			0/0/0	Base metals, silver or gold, clad with platinum, not further worked than semi-manufactured
													Waste and scrap of precious metal or of metal clad with precious metal; other waste and scrap containing precious metal or precious metal compounds, of a kind used principally for the recovery of precious metal other than goods of heading 85.49:
													-Ash containing precious metal or precious metal compounds:
0/0/0	2	0	0/0	0/0/0	0/0	0//0	0/0/	0/0/0	7.3/0			0/0/0	---Of silver or silver compounds
0/0/0	0	0	0/0	0/0/0	0/0	0//0	0/0/	0/0/0	0/0			0/0/0	---Other

税则号列	货品名称〔CIQ 扩展编码及品名－T2 表示见附表 2〕	最惠(%)	暂定税率	普通	增值/消费	出口退税	计量单位	监管条件/特殊证件	检验检疫	对美关税	亚太上/下
	-其他:										
	--金及包金的废碎料,但含有其他贵金属的地脚料除外:										
7112.9110	---金及包金的废碎料〔999〕	0		0	13/	0	克	9/		25	
7112.9120	---含有金或金化合物的废碎料〔999〕	6		35	13/	0	克	9/			
	--铂及包铂的废碎料,但含有其他贵金属的地脚料除外:										
7112.9210	---铂及包铂的废碎料〔999〕	0		0	13/	0	克	49xy/		25	
7112.9220	---含有铂或铂化合物的废碎料										
7112.9220 01	铂含量在3%以上的其他含有铂或铂化合物的废碎料(但税目85.49的货品及含有其他贵金属的地脚料除外,主要用于回收铂)〔999〕	6	0	35	13/	0	克	4xy/		10	
7112.9220 90	其他含有铂及铂化合物的废碎料(但税目85.49的货品及含有其他贵金属的地脚料除外,主要用于回收铂)〔999〕	6		35	13/	0	克	4xy/		16	
	--其他:										
7112.9910	---含有银或银化合物的废碎料〔999〕	8		35	13/	13	克	9/			
7112.9920	---含有其他贵金属或贵金属化合物的矿灰及矿渣〔999〕	6		35	13/	0	克	9/			
7112.9990	---其他〔999〕	0		50	13/	0	克	/			
	第三分章　珠宝首饰、金银器及其他制品										
71.13	**贵金属或包贵金属制的首饰及其零件:**										
	-贵金属制,不论是否包、镀贵金属:										
	--银制,不论是否包、镀其他贵金属:										
7113.1110	---镶嵌钻石的〔999〕	8		130	13/	0	克	/		18	5.2/5.2
7113.1190	---其他										
7113.1190 10	镶嵌濒危物种制品的银首饰及零件(不论是否包、镀其他贵金属)〔999〕	8		130	13/	0	克	FE/		33	5.2/5.2
7113.1190 90	其他银首饰及其零件(不论是否包、镀其他贵金属)〔999〕	8		130	13/	13	克	/		33	5.2/5.2
	--其他贵金属制,不论是否包、镀贵金属:										
	---黄金制:										
7113.1911	----镶嵌钻石的〔999〕	8		130	13/	0	克	/		28	5.2/5.2
7113.1919	----其他										
7113.1919 10	镶嵌濒危物种制品的金首饰及零件(不论是否包、镀其他贵金属)〔999〕	8		130	13/	0	克	EF/		28	5.2/5.2
7113.1919 90	其他黄金制首饰及其零件(不论是否包、镀其他贵金属)〔999〕	8		130	13/	0	克	J/		28	5.2/5.2
	---铂制:										
7113.1921	----镶嵌钻石的〔999〕	10		130	13/	0	克	/		20	6.5/6.5
7113.1929	----其他										
7113.1929 10	镶嵌濒危物种制品的铂金首饰及零件(不论是否包、镀其他贵金属)〔999〕	10		130	13/	0	克	EF/		20	6.5/6.5
7113.1929 90	其他铂金制首饰及其零件(不论是否包、镀其他贵金属)〔999〕	10		130	13/	0	克	/		20	6.5/6.5
	-以贱金属为底的包贵金属制:										
7113.2010	---镶嵌钻石的〔999〕	10		130	13/	0	克	/		35	6.5/6.5
7113.2090	---其他										
7113.2090 10	镶嵌濒危物种制品以贱金属为底的包贵金属制首饰(包括零件)〔999〕	10		130	13/10	0	克	FE/		35	6.5/6.5
7113.2090 90	其他以贱金属为底的包贵金属制首饰(包括零件)〔999〕	10		130	13/10	13	克	/		35	6.5/6.5
71.14	**贵金属或包贵金属制的金银器及其零件:**										
	-贵金属制,不论是否包、镀贵金属:										
7114.1100	--银制,不论是否包、镀其他贵金属										
7114.1100 10	镶嵌濒危物种制品的银器及零件(不论是否包、镀贵金属)〔999〕	10		100	13/	0	克	FE/		20	
7114.1100 90	其他银器及零件(不论是否包、镀贵金属)〔999〕	10		100	13/	13	克	/		20	

协定税率 %								RCEP		特惠税率 %			Article Description
东/冰/格	巴基斯坦	韩国	瑞士 上/下	哥/秘/柬	澳/毛	新西/坡/智	中国港/澳/台	东盟及马来/澳/韩	日/新	亚太2国	老/柬/缅	98/97/95	
													-Other:
													--Of gold, including metal clad with gold but excluding sweepings containing other precious metals:
0/0/0	0	0	0/0	0/0/0	0/0	0//0	0/0/	0/0/0	0/0			0/0/0	---Of gold,or gold compounds
0/0/0	0	0	0/0	0/0/0	0/0	0//0	0/0/	0/0/0	0/0			0/0/0	---Waste and scrap with gold or gold compounds
													--Of platinum,including metal clad with platinum but excluding sweepings containing other precious metals:
0/0/0	0	0	0/0	0/0/0	0/0	0//0	0/0/	0/0/0	0/0			0/0/0	---Of platinum
													---Wastes and scrap with platinum
0/0/0	0	0	0/0	0/0/0	0/0	0//0	0/0/	0/0/0	0/0			0/0/0	Other waste and scraps with platinum and its compounds, containing>3% of platinum(but excluding sweeping contcaining other precious metals,used for recycling platinum)
0/0/0	0	0	0/0	0/0/0	0/0	0//0	0/0/	0/0/0	0/0			0/0/0	Other waste and scraps containing platinum(but excluding sweepings containing other precious metals,used for recycling platinum)
													--Other:
0/0/0	2	0	0/0	0/0/0	0/0	0//0	0/0/	0/0/0	7.3/0			0/0/0	---Waste and scrap with silver or silver compounds
0/0/0	0	0	0/0	0/0/0	0/0	0//0	0/0/	0/0/0	0/0			0/0/0	---Waste and scrap with other precious metals
0/0/0	0	0	0/0	0/0/0	0/0	0//0	0/0/	0/0/0	0/0			0/0/0	---Other
													Ⅲ. JEWELLERY, GOLDSMITHS' AND SILVERSMITHS' WARES AND OTHER ARTICLES
													Articles of jewellery and parts thereof, of precious metal or of metal chad with precious metal:
													-Of precious metal whether or not plated or clad with precious metal:
													--Of silver,whether or not plated or clad with other precious metal:
0/0/0	0	9.3	8/8	0/0/0	0/0	0/0/0	0/0/	18/18/18	18.8/18			0/0/0	---Diamond mounted of set
													---Other
0/0/0	0	9.3	0/0	0/0/0	0/0	0/0/0	0/0/	18.7/19/18.7	18.8/19			0/0/0	Silver jewellery and parts thereof,inlaid with articles of endangered species(whether or not plated or clad with other precious metal)
0/0/0	0	9.3	0/0	0/0/0	0/0	0/0/0	0/0/	18.7/19/18.7	18.8/19			0/0/0	Other silver jewellery and parts thereof(whether or not plated or clad with other precious metal)
													--Of other precious metal,whether or not plated or clad with predious metal:
													---Of gold:
0/0/0	0	9.3	5/5	0/0/0	0/0	0/0/0	0/0/	18.7/19/18.7	18.8/19			0/0/0	----Diomond mounted
													----Other
0/0/0	0	4	0/0	0/0/0	0/0	0/0/0	0/0/	0/0/18	18.2/0			0/0/0	Gold jewellery and parts thereof,inlaid with articles of endangered species (whether or not plated or clad with other precious metal)
0/0/0	0	4	0/0	0/0/0	0/0	0/0/0	0/0/	0/0/18	18.2/0			0/0/0	Other gold jewellery and parts thereof(whether or not plated or clad with other precious metal)
													---Of platinum
0/0/0	0			0/0/0	0/21	0/0/0	0/0/	33.3/33.3/	/33.3			0/0/0	----Diamond mounted
													----Other
0/0/0	0		0/0	0/0/0	0/21	0/0/0	0/0/	33.3/33.3/	/33.3			0/0/0	Platinum jewellery and parts thereof, inlaid with articles of endangered species,whether or not plated or clad with other precious metal
0/0/0	0		0/0	0/0/0	0/21	0/0/0	0/0/	33.3/33.3/	/33.3			0/0/0	Other platinum jewellery and parts thereof, whether or not plated or clad with other precious metal
													-Of base metal clad with precious metal:
0//0	30		10/10	0/0/0	0/21	0/0/0	0/0/	34.1/34.1/	/34.1			0/0/0	---Diamond mounted or set
													---Other
0/0/0	30			0/0/0	0/21	0/0/0	0/0/	34.1/34.1/	/34.1			0/0/0	Jewellery and parts thereof,of base metal clad with precious metal,inlaid with articles of endangered species
0/0/0	30			0/0/0	0/21	0/0/0	0/0/	34.1/34.1/	/34.1			0/0/0	Other jewellery and parts thereof, of base metal clad with precious metal
													Articles of goldsmiths' or silversmiths' wares and parts thereof, of precious metal or of metal clad with precious metal:
													-Of precious metal whether or not plated or clad with precious metal:
													--Of silver,whether or not plated or clad with other precious metal
0/0/0			0/0	0/0/0	0/21	0/0/0	0/0/	34.1/34.1/	/34.1			0/0/0	Silversmiths' wares and parts thereof,inlaid with articles of endangered species(whether or not plated or clad with other precious metal)
0/0/0			0/0	0/0/0	0/21	0/0/0	0/0/	34.1/34.1/	/34.1			0/0/0	Other silversmiths' wares and parts thereof(whether or not plated or clad with other precious metal)

税则号列	货品名称〔CIQ 扩展编码及品名－T2 表示见附表 2〕	最惠(%)	暂定税率	普通	增值/消费	出口退税	计量单位	监管条件/特殊证件	检验检疫	对美关税	亚太上/下
7114.1900	--其他贵金属制，不论是否包、镀贵金属										
7114.1900 10	镶嵌濒危物种制品的金银器及零件（不论是否包、镀贵金属）〔999〕	10		100	13/	0	克	FE/		35	
7114.1900 20	其他贵金属制金器及零件（工艺金章，摆件等，不论是否包，镀贵金属）〔999〕	10		100	13/	0	克	J/		35	
7114.1900 90	其他贵金属制银器及零件（不论是否包，镀贵金属）〔999〕	10		100	13/	0	克	/		35	
7114.2000	-以贱金属为底的包贵金属制										
7114.2000 10	以贱金属为底的包贵金属制金银器（镶嵌濒危物种制品，包括零件）〔999〕	10		100	13/	0	克	FE/			8/8
7114.2000 90	其他贱金属为底包贵金属制金银器（包括零件）〔999〕	10		100	13/	0,13	克	/			8/8
71.15	**贵金属或包贵金属的其他制品：**										
7115.1000	-金属丝布或格栅形状的铂催化剂〔999〕	3		11	13/	0	克	4xy/		13	
	-其他：										
7115.9010	---工业或实验室用										
7115.9010 10	银制工业、实验室用制品〔999〕	3	0	11	13/	13	克	/		10	
7115.9010 20	金制工业、实验室用制品〔999〕	3	0	11	13/	0	克	/		10	
7115.9010 90	其他工业、实验室用贵或包贵金制品〔999〕	3	0	11	13/	0,13	克	/		10	
7115.9090	---其他〔999〕	10		100	13/	0,13	克	/		30	
71.16	**用天然或养殖珍珠、宝石或半宝石（天然、合成或再造）制成的物品：**										
7116.1000	-天然或养殖珍珠制〔101 保健食品，102 珍珠宝石制品〕	10		130	13/10	13	千克	/		35	
7116.2000	-宝石或半宝石（天然、合成或再造）制〔999〕	10		130	13/10	0,13	千克	/		35	
71.17	**仿首饰：**										
	-贱金属制，不论是否镀贵金属：										
7117.1100	--袖扣、饰扣[101 锌合金制儿童用仿真首饰，102 铜合金制儿童用仿真首饰，103 不锈钢制儿童用仿真首饰，104 其他材料制儿童用仿真首饰，105 接触皮肤的成人用仿真首饰，106 非接触皮肤的成人用仿真首饰]	10		130	13/	13	千克	/		35	
7117.1900	--其他[101 锌合金制儿童用仿真首饰，102 铜合金制儿童用仿真首饰，103 不锈钢制儿童用仿真首饰，104 其他材料制儿童用仿真首饰，105 接触皮肤的成人用仿真首饰，106 非接触皮肤的成人用仿真首饰]	8		130	13/	13	千克	/		33	5.2/5.2
7117.9000	-其他〔101 其他材料制儿童用仿真首饰，102 接触皮肤的成人用仿真首饰，103 非接触皮肤的成人用仿真首饰〕	18		130	13/	13	千克	/		43	11.7/11.7
71.18	**硬币：**										
7118.1000	-非法定货币的硬币（金币除外）〔999〕	0		0	13/	13	千克	/		20	
7118.9000	-其他										
7118.9000 10	金质铸币（金质贵金属纪念币）〔999〕	0		0	13/	0	千克	J/			
7118.9000 90	其他硬币〔999〕	0		0	13/	0	千克	/			

协定税率 %								RCEP		特惠税率 %			Article Description
东/冰/格	巴基斯坦	韩国	瑞士上/下	哥/秘/柬	澳/毛	新西/坡/智	中国港/澳/台	东盟及马来/澳/韩	日/新	亚太2国	老/柬/缅	98/97/95	
													--Of other precious metal, whether or not plated or clad with precious metal
0/0/0			8.8/8.8	0/0/0	0/21	0/0/0	0/0/	34.1/34.1/	/34.1			0/0/0	Goldsmiths' or silversmiths' wares and parts thereof, inlaid with articles of endangered species(whether or not plated or clad with other precious metal)
0/0/0			8.8/8.8	0/0/0	0/21	0/0/0	0/0/	34.1/34.1/	/34.1			0/0/0	Of other precious metal gold and parts (regardless of whether the packet, plated with precious metal)
0/0/0			8.8/8.8	0/0/0	0/21	0/0/0	0/0/	34.1/34.1/	/34.1			0/0/0	Other goldsmiths' or silversmiths' wares and parts thereof, of precious metal(whether or not plated or clad with other precious metal)
													-Of base metal clad with precious metal
0/0/0			10/10	0/0/0	0/21	0/0/0	0/0/	34.1/34.1/	/34.1			0/0/0	Goldsmiths' or silversmiths' wares and parts thereof, inlaid with articles of endangered species, of base metal cald with precious metal
0/0/0			10/10	0/0/0	0/21	0/0/0	0/0/	34.1/34.1/	/34.1			0/0/0	Other goldsmiths' or silversmiths' wares and parts thereof, of base metal cald with precious metal
													Other articles of precious metal or of metal clad with precious metal:
0/0/0	0	0	0/0	0/0/0	0/0	0//0	0/0/	0/0/0	0/0			0/0/0	-Catalysts in the form of wire cloth or grill, of platinum
													-Other:
													---For technical or laboratory use
0/0/0	0	0	0/0	0/0/0	0/0	0//0	0/0/	0/0/0	0/0			0/0/0	Articles of silver for industrial or laboratory use
0/0/0	0	0	0/0	0/0/0	0/0	0//0	0/0/	0/0/0	0/0			0/0/0	Articles of gold for industrial or laboratory use
0/0/0	0	0	0/0	0/0/0	0/0	0//0	0/0/	0/0/0	0/0			0/0/0	Articles of precious metal or of metal clad with precious metal for industrial or laboratory use
0/0/0				0/0/0	0/21	0/0/0	0/0/	33.3/33.3/	/33.3			0/0/0	---Other
													Articles of natural or cultured pearls, precious or semi-precious stones (natural, synthetic or reconstructed):
0/0/0			3.5/3.5	0/0/0	0/21	0/0/0	0/0/	34.1/34.1/	/34.1			0/0/0	-Of natural or cultured pearls
0/0/0	0		0/0	0/0/0	0/21	0/0/0	0/0/	33.3/33.3/	/33.3			0/0/0	-Of precious or semi-precious stones (natural, synthetic or reconstructed)
													Imitation jewellery:
													-Of base metal, whether or not plated with precious metal:
0/0/0			10/10	0/0/0	0/21	0/0/0	0/0/	34.1/34.1/	/34.1			0/0/0	--Cuff-links and studs
0/0/0	13.6	3.4	1.7/1.7	0/0/0	0/10.2	0/0/0	0/0/	15.3/15.3/15.3	15.5/15.3			0/0/0	--Other
0//0	30	22.7		0/0/0	0/21	0/0/0	0/0/	33.3/33.3/	/33.3			0/0/0	-Other
													Coin:
0/0/0	0	0	0/0	0/0/0	0/0	0//0	0/0/	0/0/0	0/0			0/0/0	-Coin (other than gold coin), not being legal tender
													-Other
0/0/0	0	0	0/0	0/0/0	0/0	0//0	0/0/	0/0/0	0/0			0/0/0	Gold coins (gold precious metal commemorative coins)
0/0/0	0	0	0/0	0/0/0	0/0	0//0	0/0/	0/0/0	0/0			0/0/0	Other coins

第十五类
贱金属及其制品

注释：

一、本类不包括：

(一)以金属粉末为基本成分的调制油漆、油墨或其他产品(税目 32.07 至 32.10、32.12、32.13 或 32.15)；

(二)铈铁或其他引火合金(税目 36.06)；

(三)税目 65.06 或 65.07 的帽类及其零件；

(四)税目 66.03 的伞骨及其他物品；

(五)第七十一章的货品(例如，贵金属合金、以贱金属为底的包贵金属、仿首饰)；

(六)第十六类的物品(机器、机械器具及电气设备)；

(七)已装配的铁道或电车轨道(税目 86.08)或第十七类的其他物品(车辆、船舶、航空器)；

(八)第十八类的仪器及器具，包括钟表发条；

(九)做弹药用的铅弹(税目 93.06)或第十九类的其他物品(武器、弹药)；

(十)第九十四章的物品(例如，家具、弹簧床垫，灯具及照明装置、发光标志、活动房屋)；

(十一)第九十五章的物品(例如，玩具、游戏品及运动用品)；

(十二)手用筛子、纽扣、钢笔、铅笔套、钢笔尖、独脚架、双脚架、三脚架及类似品或第九十六章的其他物品(杂项制品)；

(十三)第九十七章的物品(例如，艺术品)。

二、本协调制度所称“通用零件”，是指：

(一)税目 73.07、73.12、73.15、73.17 或 73.18 的物品及其他贱金属制的类似品，不包括专用医疗、外科、牙科或兽医的植入物(税目 90.21)；

(二)贱金属制的弹簧及弹簧片，但钟表发条(税目 91.14)除外；

(三)税目 83.01、83.02、83.08、83.10 的物品及税目 83.06 的贱金属制的框架及镜子。

第七十三章至第七十六章(税目 73.15 除外)及第七十八章至第八十二章所列货品的零件，不包括上述的通用零件。

除上段及第八十三章注释一另有规定的以外，第七十二章至第七十六章及第七十八章至第八十一章不包括第八十二章、第八十三章的物品。

三、本协调制度所称“贱金属”是指：铁及钢、铜、镍、铝、铅、锌、锡、钨、钼、钽、镁、钴、铋、镉、钛、锆、锑、锰、铍、铬、锗、钒、镓、铪、铟、铌(钶)、铼及铊。

四、本协调制度所称“金属陶瓷”，是指金属与陶瓷成分的极细微粒不均匀结合而成的产品。“金属陶瓷”包括硬质合金(金属碳化物与金属烧结而成)。

五、合金的归类规则(第七十二章、第七十四章所规定的铁合金及母合金除外)：

(一)贱金属的合金按其所含重量最大的金属归类；

(二)由本类的贱金属和非本类的元素构成的合金，如果所含贱金属的总重量等于或超过所含其他元素的总重量，应作为本类贱金属合金归类；

(三)本类所称“合金”，包括金属粉末的烧结混合物、熔化而得的不均匀紧密混合物(金属陶瓷除外)及金属间化合物。

六、除条文另有规定的以外，本协调制度所称的贱金属包括贱金属合金，这类合金应按上述注释五的规则进行归类。

七、复合材料制品的归类规则：

除各税目另有规定的以外，贱金属制品(包括根据“归类总规则”作为贱金属制品的混合材料制品)如果含有两种或两种以上贱金属的，按其所含重量最大的贱金属的制品归类。为此：

(一)钢、铁或不同种类的钢铁，均视为一种金属；

(二)按照注释五的规定作为某一种金属归类的合金，应视为一种金属；

(三)税目 81.13 的金属陶瓷，应视为一种贱金属。

八、本类所用有关名词解释如下：

(一)废碎料

(1)所有金属废碎料；

(2)因破裂、切断、磨损及其他原因而明显不能作为原物使用的金属货品。

(二)粉末

按重量计 90%及以上可从网眼孔径为 1 毫米的筛子通过的产品。

九、第七十四章至第七十六章以及第七十八章至第八十一章所述有关名词解释如下：

(一)条、杆

轧、挤、拔或锻制的实心产品，非成卷的，其全长截面均为圆形、椭圆形、矩形(包括正方形)、等边三角形或规则外凸多边形(包括相对两边为弧拱形，另外两边为等长平行直线的“扁圆形”及“变形矩形”)。对于矩形(包括正方形)、三角形或多边形截面的产品，其全长边角可经磨圆。矩形(包括“变形矩形”)截面的产品，其厚度应大于宽度的十分之一。所述条、杆也包括同样形状及尺寸的铸造或烧结产品。该产品在铸造或烧结后再经加工(简单剪修或去氧化皮的除外)，但不具有其他税目所列制品或产品的特征。第七十四章的线锭及坯段，已具锥形尾端或经其他简单加工以便送入机器制成盘条或管子等的，仍应作为未锻轧铜归入税目 74.03。此条注释在必要的地方稍加修改后，适用于第八十一章的产品。

(二)型材及异型材

轧、挤、拔、锻制的产品或其他成型产品，不论是否成卷，其全长截面相同，但与条、杆、丝、板、片、带、箔、管的定义不相符合。同时也包括同样形状的铸造或烧结产品。该产品在铸造或烧结后再经加工(简单剪修或去氧化皮的除外)，但不具有其他税目所列制品或产品的特征。

(三)丝

盘卷的轧、挤或拔制实心产品，其全长截面均为圆形、椭圆形、矩形(包括正方形)、等边三角形或规则外凸多边形(包括相对两边为弧拱形，另外两边为等长平行直线的“扁圆形”及“变形矩形”)。对于矩形(包括正方形)、三角形或多边形截面的产品，其全长边角可经磨圆。矩形(包括“变形矩形”)截面的产品，其厚度应大于宽度的十分之一。

SECTION XV
BASE METALS AND
ARTICLES OF BASE METAL

Notes:

1. This Section does not cover:
   (a) Prepared paints, inks or other products with a basis of metallic flakes or powder (headings Nos.32.07 to 32.10, 32.12, 32.13 or 32.15);
   (b) Ferro-cerium or other pyrophoric alloys (heading No.36.06);
   (c) Headgear or parts thereof of heading No.65.06 or 65.07;
   (d) Umbrella frames or other articles of heading No.66.03;
   (e) Goods of Chapter 71 (for example, precious metal alloys, base metal clad with precious metal, imitation Jewelry);
   (f) Articles of Section XVI (machinery, mechanical appliances and electrical goods);
   (g) Assembled railway or tramway track (heading No.86.08) or other articles of Section XVII (vehicles, ships and boats, aircraft);
   (h) Instruments or apparatus of Section XVIII, including clock or watch springs;
   (ij) Lead shot prepared for anmmunition (heading No.93.06) or other articles of Section XIX (arms and ammunition);
   (k) Articles of Chapter 94 (for example, furniture, mattress supports, lamps and lighting fittings, illuminated signs, prefabricated buildings);
   (l) Articles of Chapter 95 (for example, toys, games, sports requisites);
   (m) Hand sieves, buttons, pens, pencil-holders, pen nibs or other articles of Chapter 96 (miscellaneous manufactured articles); unipod, bipod, trpod or the Like
   (n) Articles of Chapter 97 (for example, works of art).
2. Throughout the Nomenclature, the expression "parts of general use" means:
   (a) Articles of heading 73.07, 73.12, 73.15, 73.17 or 73.18 and similar articles of other base metal, other than articles specially designed for use exclusively in implants in medical, surgical, dental or veterinary sciences (heading 90.21);
   (b) Springs and leaves for springs, of base metal, other than clock or watch springs (heading No.91.14); and
   (c) Articles of headings Nos.83.01, 83.02, 83.08, 83.10 and frames and mirrors, of base metal, of heading No.83.06.

   In Chapters 73 to 76 and 78 to 82 (but not in heading No.73.15) references to parts of goods do not include references to parts of general use as defined above.

   Subject to the preceding paragraph and to Note 1 to Chapter 83, the articles of Chapter 82 or 83 are excluded from Chapters 72 to 76 and 78 to 81.
3. Throughout the Nomenclature, the expression "base metals" means: iron and steel, copper, nickel, aluminium, lead, zinc, tin, tungsten (wolfram), molybdenum, tantalum, magnesium, cobalt, bismuth, cadmium, titanium, zirconium, antimony, manganese, beryllium, chromium, germanium, vanadium, gallium, hafnium, indium, niobium (columbium), rhenium and thallium.
4. Throughout the Nomenclature, the term "cermets" means products containing a microscopic heterogeneous combination of a metallic component and a ceramic component. The term "cermets" includes sintered metal carbides (metal carbides sintered with a metal).
5. Classification of alloys (other than ferro-alloys and master alloys as defined in Chapters 72 and 74):
   (a) An alloy of base metals is to be classified as an alloy of the metal which predominates by weight over each of the other metals;
   (b) An alloy composed of base metals of this Section and of elements not falling within this Section is to be treated as an alloy of base metals of this Section if the total weight of such metals equals or exceeds the total weight of the other elements present;
   (c) In this Section the term "alloys" includes sintered mixtures of metal powders, heterogeneous intimate mixtures obtained by melting (other than cermets) and intermetallic compounds.
6. Unless the context otherwise requires, any reference in the Nomenclature to a base metal includes a reference to alloys which, by virtue of Note 5 above, are to be classified as alloys of that metal.
7. Classification of composite articles:

   Except where the headings otherwise require, articles of base metal (including articles of mixed materials treated as articles of base metal under the Interpretative Rules) containing two or more base metals are to be treated as articles of the base metal predominating by weight over each of the other metals. For this purpose:
   (a) Iron and steel, or different kinds of iron or steel, are regarded as one and the same metal;
   (b) An alloy is regarded as being entirely composed of that metal as an alloy of which, by virtue of Note 5, it is classified; and
   (c) A cermet of heading No.81.13 is regarded as a single base metal.
8. In this Section, the following expressions have the meanings hereby assigned to them:
   (a) Waste and scrap
      (i) All metal waste and scrap;
      (ii) and metal goods definitely not usable as such because of breakage, cutting-up, wear or other reasons.
   (b) Powders
      Products of which 90% or more by weight passes through a sieve having a mesh aperture of 1mm.

9. For the purposes of Chapters 74 to 76 and 78 to 81, the following expressions have the meanings hereby assigned to them :
   (a) Bars and rods Rolled, extruded, drawn or forged products, not in coils, which have a uniform solid cross—section along their whole length in the shape of circles, ovals, rectangles (including squares), equilateral triangles or regular convex polygons (including "flattened circles" and "modified rectangles", of which two opposite sides are convex arcs, the other two sides being straight, of equal length and parallel). Products with a rectangular (including square), triangular or polygonal cross—section may have corners rounded along their whole length. The thickness of such products which have a rectangular (including "modified rectangular") cross—section exceeds one—tenth of the width. The expression also covers cast or sintered products, of the same forms and dimensions, which have been subsequently worked after production (otherwise than by simple trimming or de—scaling), provided that they have not thereby assumed the character of articles or products of other headings. Wire—bars and billets of Chapter 74 with their ends tapered or otherwise worked simply to facilitate their entry into machines for converting them into, for example, drawing stock (wire—rod) or tubes, are however to be taken to be unwrought copper of heading 74.03. This provision applies mutatis mutandis to the products of Chapter 81.
   (b) Profiles Rolled, extruded, drawn, forged or formed products, coiled or not, of a uniform cross—section along their whole length, which do not conform to any of the definitions of bars, rods, wire, plates, sheets, strip, foil, tubes or pipes. The expression also covers cast or sintered products, of the same forms, which have been subsequently worked after production (otherwise than by simple trimming or de—scaling), provided that they have not thereby assumed the character of articles or products of other headings.
   (c) Wire Rolled, extruded or drawn products, in coils, which have a uniform solid cross—section along their whole length in the shape of circles, ovals, rectangles (including squares), equilateral triangles or regularconvex polygons (including "flattened circles" and "modified rectangles", of which two opposite sides are convex arcs, the other two sides being straight, of equal length and parallel). Products with a rectangular (including square), triangular or polygonal cross—section may have corners rounded along their whole length. The thickness of such products which have a rectangular (including "modified rectangular") cross—section exceeds one—tenth of thewidth.

（四）板、片、带、箔

成卷或非成卷的平面产品（未锻轧产品除外），截面均为厚度相同的实心矩形（不包括正方形），不论边角是否磨圆（包括相对两边为弧拱形，另外两边为等长平行直线的"变形矩形"），并且符合以下规格：

1.矩形（包括正方形）的，厚度不超过宽度的十分之一；

2.矩形或正方形以外形状的，任何尺寸，但不具有其他税目所列制品或产品的特征。这些税目还适用于具有花样（例如，凹槽、肋条形、格槽、珠粒及菱形）的板、片、带、箔以及穿孔、抛光、涂层或制成瓦楞形的这类产品，但不具有其他税目所列制品或产品的特征。

（五）管

全长截面及管壁厚度相同并只有一个闭合空间的空心产品，成卷或非成卷的，其截面为圆形、椭圆形、矩形（包括正方形）、等边三角形或规则外凸多边形。对于截面为矩形（包括正方形）、等边三角形或规则外凸多边形的产品，不论全长边角是否磨圆，只要其内外截面为同一圆心并为同样形状及同一轴向，也可视为管子。上述截面的管子可经抛光、涂层、弯曲、攻丝、钻孔、缩腰、胀口、成锥形或装法兰、颈圈或套环。

第七十二章
钢　铁

注释：

一、本章所述有关名词解释如下（本条注释（四）、（五）、（六）适用于本协调制度其他各章）：

（一）生铁

无实用可锻性的铁碳合金，按重量计含碳量在2％以上并可含有一种或几种下列含量范围的其他元素：

铬不超过10％；
锰不超过6％；
磷不超过3％；
硅不超过8％；
其他元素合计不超过10％。

（二）镜铁

按重量计含锰量在6％以上，但不超过30％的铁碳合金，其他方面符合上述（一）款所列标准。

（三）铁合金

锭、块、团或类似初级形状、连续铸造而形成的各种形状及颗粒、粉末状的合金，不论是否烧结，通常用于其他合金生产过程中的添加剂或在黑色金属冶炼中作除氧剂、脱硫剂及类似用途，一般无实用可锻性，按重量计铁元素含量在4％及以上并含有下列一种或几种元素：

铬超过10％；
锰超过30％；
磷超过3％；
硅超过8％；
除碳以外的其他元素，合计超过10％，但最高含铜量不得超过10％。

（四）钢

除税目72.03以外的黑色金属材料（某些铸造而成的种类除外），具有实用可锻性，按重量计含碳量在2％及以下，但铬钢可具有较高的含碳量。

（五）不锈钢

按重量计含碳量在1.2％及以下，含铬量在10.5％及以上的合金钢，不论是否含有其他元素。

（六）其他合金钢

不符合以上不锈钢定义的钢，含有一种或几种按重量计符合下列含量比例的元素：

铝0.3％及以上；
硼0.0008％及以上；
铬0.3％及以上；
钴0.3％及以上；
铜0.4％及以上；
铅0.4％及以上；
锰1.65％及以上；
钼0.08％及以上；
镍0.3％及以上；
铌0.06％及以上；
硅0.6％及以上；
钛0.05％及以上；
钨0.3％及以上；
钒0.1％及以上；
锆0.05％及以上；

其他元素（硫、磷、碳及氮除外）单项含量在0.1％及以上。

（七）供再熔的碎料钢铁锭

粗铸成形无缩孔或冒口的锭块产品，表面有明显瑕疵，化学成分不同于生铁、镜铁及铁合金。

（八）颗粒

按重量计不到90％可从网眼孔径为1毫米的筛子通过，而90％及以上可从网眼孔径为5毫米的筛子通过的产品。

（九）半制成品

连续铸造的实心产品，不论是否初步热轧；其他实心产品，除经初步热轧或锻造粗制成形以外未经进一步加工，包括角材、型材及异型材的坯件。

本类产品不包括成卷的产品。

（十）平板轧材

截面为矩形（正方形除外）并且不符合以上第（九）款所述定义的下列形状实心轧制产品：

1. 层叠的卷材；
2. 平直形状，其厚度如果在4.75毫米以下，则宽度至少是厚度的十倍；其厚度如果在4.75毫米及以上，其宽度应超过150毫米，并且至少应为厚度的两倍。

(d) Plates, sheets, strip and foil Flat—surfaced products (other than the unwrought products of heading 80.01), coiled or not, of solid rectangular (other than square) cross—section with or without rounded corners (including "modified rectangles" of which two opposite sides are convex arcs, the other two sides being straight, of equal length and parallel) of a uniform thickness, which are : — of rectangular (including square) shape with a thickness not exceeding one—tenth of the width; — of a shape other than rectangular or square, of any size, provided that they do not assume the character of articles or products of other headings. Headings for plates, sheets, strip, and foil apply, inter alia, to plates, sheets, strip, and foil with patterns (for example, grooves, ribs, chequers, tears, buttons, lozenges) and to such products which have been perforated, corrugated, polished or coated, provided that they do not thereby assume the character of articles or products of other headings.

(e) Tubes and pipes Hollow products, coiled or not, which have a uniform cross—section with only one enclosed void along their whole length in the shape of circles, ovals, rectangles (including squares), equilateral triangles or regular convex polygons, and which have a uniform wall thickness. Products with a rectangular (including square), equilateral triangularor regular convex polygonal cross—section, which may have corners rounded along their whole length, are also to be considered as tubes and pipes provided the inner and outer cross—sections are concentric and have the same form and orientation. Tubes and pipes of the foregoing cross—sections may be polished, coated, bent, threaded, drilled, waisted, expanded, cone—shaped or fitted with flanges, collars or rings.

Chapter 72
Iron and steel

Notes:

1. In this Chapter and, in the case of Notes (d), (e) and (f) throughout the Nomenclature, the following expressions have the meanings hereby assigned to them:

(a) Pig iron

Iron-carbon alloys not usefully malleable, containing more than 2% by weight ofcarbon and which may contain by weight one or more other elements within the following limits:

Not more than 10% of chromium,
Not more than 6% of manganese,
Not more than 3% of phosphorus,
Not more than 8% of silicon,
A total of not more than 10% of other elements.

(b) Spiegeleisen

Iron-carbon alloys containing by weight more than 6% but not more than 30% of manganese and otherwise conforming to the specification at (a) above.

(c) Ferro-alloys

Alloys in pigs, blocks, lumps or similar primary forms, in forms obtained by continuous casting and also in granular or powder forms, whether or not agglomerated, commonly used as an additive in the manufacture of other alloys or as de-oxidants, de-sulphurizing agents or for similar uses in ferrous metal-lurgy and generally not usefully malleable, containing by weight 4% or more of the elementiron and one or more of the following:

More than 10% of chromium,
More than 30% of manganese,
More than 3% of phosphorus,
More than 8% of silicon,
A total of more than 10% of other elements, excluding carbon, subject to a maximum content of 10% in the case of copper.

(d) Steel

Ferrous materials other than those of heading 72. 03 which (with the exception of certain types produced in the form of castings) are usefully malleable andwhich contain by weight 2% or less of carbon. However, chromium steels may contain higher proportions of carbon.

(e) Stainlesssteel

Alloy steels containing, by weight, 1. 2% or less of carbon and 10. 5% ormore of chromium, with or without other elements.

(f) Other alloy steel

Steels not complying with the definition of stainless steel and containing by weight one or more of the following elements in the proportion shown:

0. 3% or more of aluminium,
0. 0008% or more of boron,
0. 3% or more of chromium,
0. 3% or more of cobalt,
0. 4% or more of copper,
0. 4% or more of lead,
1. 65% or more of manganese,
0. 08% or more of molybdenum,
0. 3% or more of nickel,
0. 06% or more of niobium,
0. 6% or more of silicon,
0. 05% or more of titanium,
0. 3% or more of tungsten (wolfram),
0. 1% or more of vanadium,
0. 05% or more of zirconium,

0. 1% or more of other elements (except sulphur, phosphorus, carbon andnitrogen), taken separately.

(g) Remelting scrap ingots of iron or steel

Products roughly cast in the form of ingots without feeder-heads or hot tops, or of pigs, having obvious surface faults and not complying with the chemical composition of pig iron, spiegeleisen or ferro-alloys.

(h) Granules

Products of which less than 90% by weight passes through a sieve with a mesh aperture of 1mm and of which 90% or more by weight passes through a sieve with a mesh aperture of 5mm.

(ij) Semi-finished products

Continuous cast products of solid section, whether or not subjected to primary hot-rolling; and other products of solid section, which have not been further worked than subjected to primary hot-rolling or roughly shaped by forging, including blanks for angles, shapes or sections.

These products are not presented in coils.

(k) Flat-rolled products

Rolled products of solid rectangular (other than square) cross-section, which do not conform to the definition at (ij) above in the form of:

(i) Coils of successively superimposed layers; or

(ii) Straight lenghths, which if of athickness less than 4. 75mm are of a width measuring at least ten times the thickness or if of a thickness of 4. 75mm or more are of a width which exceeds 150mm and measures at least twice the thickness.

平板轧材包括直接轧制而成并有凸起式样(例如,凹槽、肋条形、格槽、珠粒、菱形)的产品以及穿孔、抛光或制成瓦楞形的产品,但不具有其他税目所列制品或产品的特征。

各种规格的平板轧材(矩形或正方形除外),但不具有其他税目所列制品或产品的特征,都应作为宽度为600毫米及以上的产品归类。

(十一)不规则盘绕的热轧条、杆

经热轧不规则盘绕的实心产品,其截面为圆形、扇形、椭圆形、矩形(包括正方形)、三角形及其他外凸多边形(包括“扁圆形”及“变形矩形”,即相对两边为弧拱形,另外两边为等长平行直线形)。这类产品可带有在轧制过程中产生的凹痕、凸缘、槽沟或其他变形(钢筋)。

(十二)其他条、杆

不符合上述(九)、(十)、(十一)款或“丝”定义的实心产品,其全长截面均为圆形、扇形、椭圆形、矩形(包括正方形)三角形或其他外凸多边形(包括“扁圆形”及“变形矩形”,即相对两边为弧拱形,另外两边为等长平行直线形)。这些产品可以:

1. 带有在轧制过程中产生的凹痕、凸缘、槽沟或其他变形(钢筋);
2. 轧制后扭曲的。

(十三)角材、型材及异型材

不符合上述(九)、(十)、(十一)、(十二)款或“丝”定义,但其全长截面均为同样形状的实心产品。

第七十二章不包括税目73.01或73.02的产品。

(十四)丝

不符合平板轧材定义但全长截面均为同样形状的盘卷冷成形实心产品。

(十五)空心钻钢

适合钻探用的各种截面的空心条、杆,其最大外形尺寸超过15毫米但不超过52毫米,最大内孔尺寸不超过最大外形尺寸的二分之一。不符合本定义的钢铁空心条、杆应归入税目73.04。

二、用一种黑色金属包覆不同种类的黑色金属,应按其中重量最大的材料归类。

三、用电解沉积法、压铸法或烧结法所得的钢铁产品,应按其形状、成分及外观归入本章类似热轧产品的相应税目。

子目注释:

一、本章所用有关名词解释如下:

(一)合金生铁

按重量计含有一种或几种下列比例的元素的生铁:
铬0.2%以上;
铜0.3%以上;
镍0.3%以上;
0.1%以上的任何下列元素:
铝、钼、钛、钨、钒。

(二)非合金易切削钢

按重量计含有一种或几种下列比例的元素的非合金钢:
硫0.08%及以上;
铅0.1%及以上;
硒0.05%以上;
碲0.01%以上;
铋0.05%以上。

(三)硅电钢

按重量计含硅量至少为0.6%但不超过6%,含碳量不超过0.08%的合金钢。这类钢还可含有按重量计不超过1%的铝,但所含其他元素的比例并不使其具有其他合金钢的特性。

(四)高速钢

不论是否含有其他元素,但至少含有按重量计合计含量在7%及以上的钼、钨、钒中两种元素的合金钢,按重量计其含碳量在0.6%及以上,含铬量在3%~6%。

(五)硅锰钢

按重量计同时含有下列元素的合金钢:
碳不超过0.7%;
锰0.5%及以上,但不超过1.9%;
硅0.6%及以上,但不超过2.3%。但所含其他元素的比例并不使其具有其他合金钢的特性。

二、税目72.02项下的子目所列铁合金,应按照下列规则归类:

对于只有一种元素超出本章注释一(三)规定的最低百分比的铁合金,应作为二元合金归入相应的子目号。以此类推,如果有两种或三种合金元素超出了最低百分比的,则可分别作为三元或四元合金。

在运用本规定时,本章注释一(三)所述的未列名的“其他元素”,按重量计单项含量必须超过10%。

税则号列	货品名称〔CIQ扩展编码及品名—T2表示见附表2〕	最惠(%)	暂定税率	普通	增值/消费	出口退税	计量单位	监管条件/特殊证件	检验检疫	对美关税	亚太上/下
	第一分章 原料;粒状及粉状产品										
72.01	**生铁及镜铁,锭、块或其他初级形状:**										
7201.1000	-非合金生铁,按重量计含磷量在0.5%及以下〔999〕	1	0	8	13/	0	千克	B/	N		
7201.2000	-非合金生铁,按重量计含磷量在0.5%以上〔999〕	1	0	8	13/	0	千克	B/	N		
7201.5000	-合金生铁;镜铁										
7201.5000 10	合金生铁〔999〕	1	0	8	13/	0	千克	B/	N	25	
7201.5000 90	镜铁〔999〕	1	0	8	13/	0	千克	B/	N	25	
72.02	铁合金:										
	-锰铁:										
7202.1100	--按重量计含碳量在2%以上〔999〕	2		11	13/	0	千克	4xy/			
7202.1900	--其他〔999〕	2		11	13/	0	千克	4xy/		27	
	-硅铁:										

Flat-rolled products include those with patterns in relief derived directly from rolling (for example, grooves, ribs, chequers, tears, buttons, lozenges) and those which have been perforated, corrugated or polished, provided that they do not thereby assume the character of articles or products of other headings.

Flat-rolled products of a shape other than rectangular or square, of any size, are to be classified as products of a width of 600mm or more, provided that theydo not assume the character of articles or products of other headings.

(l) Bars and rods, hot-rolled, in irregularly wound coils

Hot-rolled products in irregularly wound coils, which have a solid cross-section in the shape of circles, segments of circles, ovals, rectangles (including squares), triangles or other convex polygons (including "flattened circles" and modified rectangles of which two opposite sides are convex arcs, the other two sides being straight, of equal length and paralled). These products may have indentations, ribs, grooves or other deformations produced during the rolling process(reinforcing bars and rods).

(m) Other bars and rods

Products which do not conform to any of the definitions at (ij), (k) or (l) above or to the definition of wire, which have a uni-form solid cross-section alongtheir whole length in the shape of circles, segments of circles, ovals, rectangles (including squares), triangles or other convex polygons (including "flattened circles" and "modified rectangles", of which two opposite sides are convexarcs, the other two sides being straight, of equal length and parallel). Theseproducts may:

(ⅰ) Have indentations, ribs, grooves or other deformations produced during the rolling process (reinforcing bars and rods);

(ⅱ) Be twisted after rolling.

(n) Angles, shapes and sections

Products having a uniform solid cross-section along their whole length which donot conform to any of the definitions at (ij), (k), (l) or (m) above or to thedefinition of wire.

Chapter 72 does not include products of heading No.73.01 or 73.02.

(o) Wire

Cold-formed products in coils, of any uniform solid cross-section along theirwhole length, which do not conform to the definition of flat-rolled products.

(p) Hollow drill bars and rods

Hollow bars and rods of any cross-section, suitable for drills, of which the greatest external dimension of the cross-section exceeds 15mm but does not exceed 52mm, and of which the greatest internal dimension does not exceed one half of the greatest external dimension. Hollow bars and rods of iron or steel not conforming to this definition are to be classified in heading No.73.04.

2. Ferrous metals clad with another ferrous metal are to be classified as products of the ferrous metal predominating by weight.

3. Iron or steel products obtained by electrolytic deposition, by pressure casting or by sintering are to be classified, according to their form, their composition and their appearance, in the headings of this Chapter appropriate to similar hot-rolled products.

Subheading Notes:

1. In this Chapter the followingexpressions have the meanings hereby assigned to them:

(a) Alloy pig iron

Pig iron containing, by weight, one or more of the following elements in the specified proportions:

More than 0.2% of chromium,

More than 0.3% of copper,

More than 0.3% of nickel,

More than 0.1% of any of the following elements:

Aluminium, molybdenum, titanium, tungsten (wolfram), vanadium.

(b) Non-alloy free-cutting steel

Non-alloy steel containing, by weight, one or more of the following elements inthe specified proportions:

0.08% or more of sulphur,

0.1% or more of lead,

More than 0.05% of selenium,

More than 0.01% of tellur,ium

More than 0.05% of bismuth.

(c) Silicon-electrical steel

Alloy steels containing by weight at least 0.6% but not more than 6% of siliconand not more than 0.08% of carbon. They may also contain by weight not more than 1% of aluminium but no other element in a proportion that would give the steel the characteristics of another alloy steel.

(d) High speed steel

Alloy steels containing, with or without other elements, at least two of the three elements molybdenum, tungsten and vanadium with a combined content by weight of 7% or more, 0.6% or more of carbon and 3% to 6% of chromium.

(e) Silico-manganese steel

Alloy steels containing by weight:

Not more than 0.7% of carbon,

0.5% or more but not more than 1.9% of manganese, and

0.6% or more but not more than 2.3% of silicon, but no other elementina proportion that would give the steel the characteristics of another alloy steel.

2. For the classification of ferro-alloys in the subheadings of heading 72.02 the following rule should be observed: A ferro-alloy is considered as binary and classified under the relevant subheading (if it exists) if only one of the alloy elements exceeds the minimum percentage laid down in Chapter Note 1 (c); by analogy, it is considered respectively as ternary or quaternary if two or three alloy elements exceed the minimum percentage.

For the application of this rule the unspecified "other elements" referred to in Chapter Note 1 (c) must each exceed 10% by weight.

协定税率 %								RCEP		特惠税率 %			Article Description
东/冰/格	巴基斯坦	韩国	瑞士上/下	哥/秘/柬	澳/毛	新西/坡/智	中国港/澳/台	东盟及马来/澳/韩	日/新	亚太2国	老/柬/缅	98/97/95	
													Ⅰ. PRIMARY MATERIALS; PRODUCTS IN GRANULAR OR POWDER FORM
													Pig iron and spiegeleisen in pigs, blocks or other primary forms:
0/0/0	0	0	0/0	0/0/0	0/0	0//0	0/0/	0/0.9/0	0/0.9			0/0/0	-Non alloy pig iron containing by weight 0.5% or less of phosphorus
0/0/0	0	0	0/0	0/0/0	0/0	0//0	0/0/	0/0/0	0/0			0/0/0	-Non-alloy pig iron containing by weight more than 0.5% of phosphorus
													-Alloy pig iron; spiegeleisen
0/0/0	0	0	0/0	0/0/0	0/0	0//0	0/0/	0/0/0	0/0			0/0/0	Alloy pig iron
0/0/0	0	0	0/0	0/0/0	0/0	0//0	0/0/	0/0/0	0/0			0/0/0	Spiegeleisen
													Ferro-alloys:
													-Ferro-manganese:
0/0/0	0	0	0/0	0/0/0	0/0	0//0	0/0/	0/0/0	0/0			0/0/0	--Containing by weight more than 2% of carbon
0/0/0	0	0	0/0	0/0/0	0/0	0//0	0/0/	0/0/0	0/0			0/0/0	--Other
													-Ferro-silicon:

税则号列		货品名称〔CIQ 扩展编码及品名—T2 表示见附表 2〕	最惠(%)	暂定税率	普通	增值/消费	出口退税	计量单位	监管条件/特殊证件	检验检疫	对美关税	亚太上/下
7202.2100		--按重量计含硅量在 55%以上										
7202.2100	10	硅铁,含硅量大于 55%,小于 90%〔999〕	2		11	13/	0	千克	4xy/		27	
7202.2100	90	硅铁,含硅量大于 90%〔999〕	2		11	13/	0	千克	4xy/		27	
7202.2900		--其他										
7202.2900	10	硅铁,含硅量大于等于 30%且不超过 55%〔999〕	2		11	13/	0	千克	4xy/		22	
7202.2900	90	硅铁,含硅量小于 30%〔999〕	2		11	13/	0	千克	4xy/		22	
7202.3000		-硅锰铁〔999〕	2		11	13/	0	千克	4xy/			
		-铬铁:										
7202.4100		--按重量计含碳量在 4%以上〔999〕	2	0	8	13/	0	千克	4xy/			
7202.4900		--其他〔999〕	2	0	8	13/	0	千克	4xy/		25	
7202.5000		-硅铬铁〔999〕	2		11	13/	0	千克	4xy/			
7202.6000		-镍铁〔999〕	2	0	11	13/	0	千克	4xy/		25	
7202.7000		-钼铁〔999〕	2	1	11	13/	0	千克	4xy/			
		-钨铁及硅钨铁:										
7202.8010		---钨铁〔999〕	2	1	11	13/	0	千克	4xy/			
7202.8020		---硅钨铁〔999〕	2		11	13/	0	千克	4xy/			
		-其他:										
7202.9100		--钛铁及硅钛铁〔101 硅钛铁,102 钛铁〕	2		11	13/	0	千克	4xy/		27	
		--钒铁:										
7202.9210		---按重量计含钒量在 75%及以上〔999〕	5		30	13/	0	千克	4xy/		30	
7202.9290		---其他〔999〕	5		30	13/	0	千克	4xy/			
7202.9300		--铌铁										
7202.9300	10	铁钽铌合金(钽含量<10%)〔999〕	2	0	11	13/	0	千克	4xy/			
7202.9300	90	其他铌铁〔101 铌铁,102 其他铁合金〕	2	0	11	13/	0	千克	4xy/			
		--其他:										
		---钕铁硼合金:										
7202.9911		----速凝永磁片〔999〕	2		11	13/	0	千克	4xy/		12	
7202.9912		----磁粉〔999〕	2		11	13/	0	千克	4xy/		27	
7202.9919		----其他〔999〕	2		11	13/	0	千克	4xy/			
		---其他:										
7202.9991		----按重量计稀土元素总含量在 10%以上的										
7202.9991	10	按重量计中重稀土总含量≥ 30%的铁合金(按重量计稀土元素总含量在 10%以上)〔104〕	2		11	13/	0	千克	4xy/			
7202.9991	91	稀土硅铁合金(按重量计稀土元素总含量在 10%以上)〔104〕	2		11	13/	0	千克	4xy/			
7202.9991	99	其他按重量计稀土元素总含量在 10%以上的铁合金〔104〕	2		11	13/	0	千克	4xy/			
7202.9999		----其他〔301〕	2		11	13/	0	千克	4xy/		12	
72.03		**直接从铁矿还原所得的铁产品及其他海绵铁产品,块、团、团粒及类似形状;按重量计纯度在 99.94%及以上的铁,块、团、团粒及类似形状:**										
7203.1000		-直接从铁矿还原所得的铁产品〔999〕	2	0	8	13/	0	千克	/		25	
7203.9000		-其他〔999〕	2	0	8	13/	0	千克	/		20	
72.04		**钢铁废碎料;供再熔的碎料钢铁锭:**										
7204.1000		-铸铁废碎料										
7204.1000	10	符合 GB/T 39733—2020 标准要求的再生钢铁原料	2	0	8	13/	0	千克	A/	M	25	
7204.1000	90	其他铸铁废碎料	2		8	13/	0	千克	9A/	M	27	
		-合金钢废碎料:										
7204.2100		--不锈钢废碎料										
7204.2100	10	其他符合 GB/T 39733—2020 标准要求的再生钢铁原料	0		8	13/	0	千克	A/	M	25	
7204.2100	90	其他不锈钢废碎料	0		8	13/	0	千克	9A/	M	25	
7204.2900		--其他										
7204.2900	10	其他符合 GB/T 39733—2020 标准要求的再生钢铁原料	0		8	13/	0	千克	A/	M	25	
7204.2900	90	其他合金钢废碎料	0		8	13/	0	千克	9A/	M	25	
7204.3000		-镀锡钢铁废碎料〔999〕	2		8	13/	0	千克	9/		27	
		-其他废碎料:										
7204.4100		--车、刨、铣、磨、锯、锉、剪、冲加工过程中产生的废料,不论是否成捆										
7204.4100	10	符合 GB/T 39733—2020 标准要求的机械加工中产生的再生钢铁原料(机械加工指车,刨,铣,磨,锯,锉,剪,冲加工)	2	0	8	13/	0	千克	A/	M	25	
7204.4100	90	其他机械加工中产生的钢铁废料(机械加工指车,刨,铣,磨,锯,锉,剪,冲加工)	2		8	13/	0	千克	9A/	M	27	
7204.4900		--其他										
7204.4900	10	废汽车压件〔999〕	0		8	13/	0	千克	9/		25	
7204.4900	20	以回收钢铁为主的废五金电器〔999〕	0		8	13/	0	千克	9/		25	
7204.4900	30	符合 GB/T 39733—2020 标准要求的未列名再生钢铁原料	0		8	13/	0	千克	A/	M	25	

协定税率 %								RCEP		特惠税率 %			Article Description
东/冰/格	巴基斯坦	韩国	瑞士上/下	哥/秘/柬	澳/毛	新西/坡/智	中国港/澳/台	东盟及马来/澳/韩	日/新	亚太2国	老/柬/缅	98/97/95	
													--Containing by weight more than 55% of silicon
0/0/0	0	0	0/0	0/0/0	0/0	0//0	0/0/	0/0/0	0/0			0/0/0	Ferro-silicon, containing more than 55% but less than 90% of silicon
0/0/0	0	0	0/0	0/0/0	0/0	0//0	0/0/	0/0/0	0/0			0/0/0	Ferro-silicon, containing more than 90% of silicon
													--Other
0/0/0	0	0	0/0	0/0/0	0/0	0//0	0/0/	0/0/0	0/0			0/0/0	Ferro-silicon, containing more than 30% but less than 55% of silicon
0/0/0	0	0	0/0	0/0/0	0/0	0//0	0/0/	0/0/0	0/0			0/0/0	Ferro-silicon, containing less than 30% of silicon
0/0/0	0	0	0/0	0/0/0	0/0	0//0	0/0/	0/0/0	0/0			0/0/0	-Ferro-silico-manganese
													-Ferro-chromium:
0/0/0	0	0	0/0	0/0/0	0/0	0//0	0/0/	0/0/0	0/0			0/0/0	--Containing by weight more than 4% of carbon
0/0/0	0	0	0/0	0/0/0	0/0	0//0	0/0/	0/0/0	0/0			0/0/0	--Other
0/0/0	0	0	0/0	0/0/0	0/0	0//0	0/0/	0/0/0	0/0			0/0/0	-Ferro-silico-chromium
0/0/0	0	0	0/0	0/0/0	0/0	0//0	0/0/	0/0/0	0/0			0/0/0	-Ferro-nickel
0/0/0	0	0	0/0	0/0/0	0/0	0//0	0/0/	0/0/0	0/0			0/0/0	-Ferro-molybdenum
													-Ferro-tungsten and ferro-silico-tungsten:
0/0/0	0	0	0/0	0/0/0	0/0	0//0	0/0/	0/0/0	0/0			0/0/0	---Ferro-tungsten
0/0/0	0	0	0/0	0/0/0	0/0	0//0	0/0/	0/0/0	0/0			0/0/0	---Ferro-silico-tungsten
													-Other:
0/0/0	0	0	0/0	0/0/0	0/0	0//0	0/0/	0/0/0	0/0			0/0/0	--Ferro-titanium and ferro-silico-titanium
													--Ferro-vanadium:
0/0/0	2	0	0/0	0/0/0	0/0	0//0	0/0/	0/0/0	8.2/0			0/0/0	---Containing by weight more than 75% of ranadium
0/0/0	2	0	0/0	0/0/0	0/0	0//0	0/0/	0/0/0	8.2/0			0/0/0	---Other
													--Ferro-niobium
0/0/0	0	0	0/0	0/0/0	0/0	0//0	0/0/	0/0/0	0/0			0/0/0	Ferro-tantalum-niobium alloy(containing<10% by weight of tantalum)
0/0/0	0	0	0/0	0/0/0	0/0	0//0	0/0/	0/0/0	0/0			0/0/0	Other ferro-niobium
													--Other:
													---Na-Fe-B alloy:
0/0/0	0	0	0/0	0/0/0	0/0	0//0	0/0/	0/0/0	0/0			0/0/0	----Rapidly sdidified permanent magnetic sheet
0/0/0	0	0	0/0	0/0/0	0/0	0//0	0/0/	0/0/0	0/0			0/0/0	----Magnetic powder
0/0/0	0	0	0/0	0/0/0	0/0	0//0	0/0/	0/0/0	0/0			0/0/0	----Other
													---Other:
													----Containing by weight more than 10% of rate eath elements
0/0/0	0	0	0/0	0/0/0	0/0	0//0	0/0/	0/0/0	0/0			0/0/0	Containing by weight more than 30% of middle heavy rare-earth, alloy iron (containing by weight more than 10% of rare-earth element)
0/0/0	0	0	0/0	0/0/0	0/0	0//0	0/0/	0/0/0	0/0			0/0/0	Rare earth ferrosilicon alloy (containing by weight more than 10% of rare-earth element)
0/0/0	0	0	0/0	0/0/0	0/0	0//0	0/0/	0/0/0	0/0			0/0/0	Containing weight by more than 10% of rare-earth element, alloy iron
0/0/0	0	0	0/0	0/0/0	0/0	0//0	0/0/	0/0/0	0/0			0/0/0	----Other
													Ferrous products obtained by direct reduction of iron ore and other spongy ferrous products, in lumps, pellets or similar forms; iron having a minimum purity by weight of 99.94%, in lumps, pellets or similar forms:
0/0/0	0	0	0/0	0/0/0	0/0	0//0	0/0/	0/1.8/0	0/1.8			0/0/0	-Ferrous products obtained by direct reduction of iron ore
0/0/0	0	0	0/0	0/0/0	0/0	0//0	0/0/	0/0/0	0/0			0/0/0	-Other
													Ferrous waste and scrap; remelting scrap ingots of iron steel:
													Waste and scrap of cast iron
0/0/0	0	0	0/0	0/0/0	0/0	0//0	0/0/	0/0/0	0/0		//	0/0/0	Recycled iron and steel raw materials meeting the requirements of GB / T 39733—2020
0/0/0	0	0	0/0	0/0/0	0/0	0//0	0/0/	0/0/0	0/0		//	0/0/0	Other cast iron scrap
													-Waste and scrap of alloy steel:
													--Of stainless steel
0/0/0	0	0	0/0	0/0/0	0/0	0//0	0/0/	0/0/0	0/0		//	0/0/0	Other recycled iron and steel raw materials meeting the requirements of GB / T 39733—2020
0/0/0	0	0	0/0	0/0/0	0/0	0//0	0/0/	0/0/0	0/0		//	0/0/0	Other stainless steel scrap
													--Other
0/0/0	0	0	0/0	0/0/0	0/0	0//0	0/0/	0/0/0	0/0		//	0/0/0	Other recycled iron and steel raw materials meeting the requirements of GB / T 39733—2020
0/0/0	0	0	0/0	0/0/0	0/0	0//0	0/0/	0/0/0	0/0		//	0/0/0	Other alloy steel scrap
0/0/0	0	0	0/0	0/0/0	0/0	0//0	0/0/	0/0/0	0/0			0/0/0	-Waste and scrap of tinned iron or steel
													-Other waste and scrap:
													--Turnings, shavings, chips, milling waste, sawdust, filings, trimmings and stampings, whether or not in bundles
0/0/0	0	0.4	0/0	0/0/0	0/0	0//0	0/0/	1.8/1.8/1.8	1.8/1.8		//	0/0/0	Recycled iron and steel raw materials produced in mechanical processing meeting the requirements of GB / T 39733—2020 standard (mechanical processing refers to turning, planing, milling, grinding, sawing, filing, shearing and punching)
0/0/0	0	0.4	0/0	0/0/0	0/0	0//0	0/0/	1.8/1.8/1.8	1.8/1.8		//	0/0/0	Iron and steel scrap produced in other machining (machining refers to turning, planing, milling, grinding, sawing, filing, shearing and punching)
													--Other
0/0/0	0	0	0/0	0/0/0	0/0	0//0	0/0/	0/0/0	0/0			0/0/0	Compressed piece of scrap automobile
0/0/0	0	0	0/0	0/0/0	0/0	0//0	0/0/	0/0/0	0/0			0/0/0	Waste hardware and electric appliance mainly for recoverying steel and iron
0/0/0	0	0	0/0	0/0/0	0/0	0//0	0/0/	0/0/0	0/0		//	0/0/0	Unlisted recycled iron and steel raw materials meeting the requirements of GB / T 39733—2020

税则号列	货品名称〔CIQ 扩展编码及品名—T2 表示见附表 2〕	最惠(%)	暂定税率	普通	增值/消费	出口退税	计量单位	监管条件/特殊证件	检验检疫	对美关税	亚太上/下
7204.4900 90	未列名钢铁废碎料〔999〕	0		8	13/	0	千克	9A/		25	
7204.5000	-供再熔的碎料钢铁锭〔999〕	0		8	13/	0	千克	9/		25	
72.05	**生铁、镜铁及钢铁的颗粒和粉末：**										
7205.1000	-颗粒〔101 非合金生铁，102 合金生铁，103 其他铁合金〕	2		30	13/	0	千克	B/	N	27	
	-粉末：										
7205.2100	--合金钢的〔999〕	2		17	13/	0	千克	B/	N	12	
	--其他：										
7205.2910	---铁粉，平均粒径小于 10 微米〔999〕	2		17	13/	0	千克	B/	N	22	
7205.2990	---其他〔999〕	2		17	13/	0	千克	B/	N	22	
	第二分章　铁及非合金钢										
72.06	**铁及非合金钢，锭状或其他初级形状（税目 72.03 的铁除外）：**										
7206.1000	-锭状〔999〕	2	0	11	13/	0	千克	B/	N	25	
7206.9000	-其他〔101 板坯，102 其他钢坯（锭）〕	2	0	11	13/	0	千克	B/	N	10	
72.07	**铁及非合金钢的半制成品：**										
	-按重量计含碳量在 0.25%以下：										
7207.1100	--矩形（包括正方形）截面，宽度小于厚度的两倍〔999〕	2	0	11	13/	0	千克	B/	N	25	
7207.1200	--其他矩形（正方形除外）截面的										
7207.1200 10	其他矩形截面的厚度大于 400MM 的连铸板坯（含碳量小于 0.25%（正方形截面除外））〔999〕	2	0	11	13/	0	千克	B/	N		
7207.1200 90	其他矩形截面钢坯（含碳量小于 0.25%（正方形截面除外））〔999〕	2	0	11	13/	0	千克	B/	N		
7207.1900	--其他										
7207.1900 10	其他含碳量小于 0.25%的厚度大于 400MM 的连铸板坯〔999〕	2	0	11	13/	0	千克	B/	N	25	
7207.1900 90	其他含碳量小于 0.25%的钢坯〔999〕	2	0	11	13/	0	千克	B/	N	25	
7207.2000	-按重量计含碳量在 0.25%及以上										
7207.2000 10	车轮用连铸圆坯（直径为 380MM 和 450MM，公差±1.2%，含碳量：0.38%－0.85%，含锰量：0.68%－1.2%，含磷量≤0.012%，总氧化物含量≤0.0012%）〔999〕	2	0	11	13/	0	千克	B/	N		
7207.2000 90	其他含碳量不小于 0.25%的钢坯〔999〕	2	0	11	13/	0	千克	B/	N		
72.08	**宽度在 600 毫米及以上的铁或非合金钢平板轧材，经热轧，但未经包覆、镀层或涂层：**										
7208.1000	-已轧压花纹的卷材，除热轧外未经进一步加工〔999〕	5		14	13/	0	千克	/		30	
	-其他经酸洗的卷材，除热轧外未经进一步加工：										
7208.2500	--厚度在 4.75 毫米及以上〔999〕	5		14	13/	0	千克	/		30	
	--厚度在 3 毫米及以上，但小于 4.75 毫米：										
7208.2610	---屈服强度大于 355 牛顿/平方毫米〔999〕	5		14	13/	0	千克	/		10	
7208.2690	---其他〔999〕	5		14	13/	0	千克	/		30	
	--厚度小于 3 毫米：										
7208.2710	---厚度小于 1.5 毫米〔999〕	5		14	13/	0	千克	/		30	
7208.2790	---其他〔999〕	5		14	13/	0	千克	/		30	
	-其他卷材，除热轧外未经进一步加工：										
7208.3600	--厚度超过 10 毫米〔999〕	6		14	13/	0	千克	/			
7208.3700	--厚度在 4.75 毫米及以上，但不超过 10 毫米〔999〕	5		14	13/	0	千克	/		10	
	--厚度在 3 毫米及以上，但小于 4.75 毫米：										
7208.3810	---屈服强度大于 355 牛顿/平方毫米〔999〕	5		14	13/	0	千克	/		10	
7208.3890	---其他〔999〕	5		14	13/	0	千克	/		10	
	--厚度小于 3 毫米：										
7208.3910	---厚度小于 1.5 毫米〔999〕	3		14	13/	0	千克	/		28	
7208.3990	---其他〔999〕	3		14	13/	0	千克	/		28	
7208.4000	-已轧压花纹的非卷材，除热轧外未经进一步加工〔999〕	6		17	13/	0	千克	/		26	
	-其他非卷材，除热轧外未经进一步加工：										
	--厚度超过 10 毫米：										
7208.5110	---厚度超过 50 毫米〔999〕	6		17	13/	0	千克	/		31	
7208.5120	---厚度在 20 毫米以上，但不超过 50 毫米〔999〕	6		17	13/	0	千克	/		31	
7208.5190	---其他〔999〕	6		17	13/	0	千克	/		31	
7208.5200	--厚度在 4.75 毫米及以上，但不超过 10 毫米〔999〕	6		17	13/	0	千克	/		31	
	--厚度在 3 毫米及以上，但小于 4.75 毫米：										
7208.5310	---屈服强度大于 355 牛顿/平方毫米〔999〕	6		17	13/	0	千克	/			5.1/5.1
7208.5390	---其他〔999〕	6		17	13/	0	千克	/		16	5.1/5.1
	--厚度小于 3 毫米：										
7208.5410	---厚度小于 1.5 毫米〔999〕	6		17	13/	0	千克	/		31	5.1/5.1
7208.5490	---其他〔999〕	6		17	13/	0	千克	/		31	5.1/5.1
7208.9000	-其他〔999〕	6		17	13/	0	千克	/		31	
72.09	**宽度在 600 毫米及以上的铁或非合金钢平板轧材，经冷轧，但未经包覆、镀层或涂层：**										
	-卷材，除冷轧外未经进一步加工：										
	--厚度在 3 毫米及以上：										
7209.1510	---屈服强度大于 355 牛顿/平方毫米〔999〕	6		17	13/	0	千克	/			
7209.1590	---其他〔999〕	6		17	13/	0	千克	/		31	
	--厚度超过 1 毫米，但小于 3 毫米：										
7209.1610	---屈服强度大于 275 牛顿/平方毫米〔999〕	6		17	13/	0	千克	/		31	4.2/4.2
7209.1690	---其他〔999〕	6		17	13/	0	千克	/		31	4.2/4.2

协定税率 %								RCEP		特惠税率 %			Article Description
东/冰/格	巴基斯坦	韩国	瑞士上/下	哥/秘/柬	澳/毛	新西/坡/智	中国港/澳/台	东盟及马来/澳/韩	日/新	亚太2国	老/柬/缅	98/97/95	
0/0/0	0	0	0/0	0/0/0	0/0	0//0	0/0/	0/0/0	0/0			0/0/0	Other ferrous waste and scrap, not elsewhere specifiled or included
0/0/0	0	0	0/0	0/0/0	0/0	0//0	0/0/	0/0/0	0/0			0/0/0	-Remelting scrap ingots
													Granules and powders, of pig iron, spiegeleiseniron or steel:
0/0/0	0	0	0/0	0/0/0	0/0	0//0	0/0/	0/0/0	0/0			0/0/0	-Granules
													-Powders:
0/0/0	0	0	0/0	0/0/0	0/0	0//0	0/0/	0/1.8/0	0/1.8			0/0/0	--Of alloy steel
													--Other:
0/0/0	0	0.4	0/0	0/0/0	0/0	0//0	0/0/	1.8/1.8/1.8	1.8/1.8			0/0/0	---Iron powders , of average particle size less than 10 μm
0/0/0	0	0.4	0/0	0/0/0	0/0	0//0	0/0/	1.8/1.8/1.8	1.8/1.8			0/0/0	---Other
													Ⅱ. IRON AND NON-ALLOY STEEL
													Iron and non-alloy steel in ingots or other primary forms (excluding iron of heading No. 72. 03):
0/0/0	0	0	0/0	0/0/0	0/0	0//0	0/0/	0/0/0	0/0			0/0/0	-Ingots
0/0/0	0	0	0/0	0/0/0	0/0	0//0	0/0/	0/0/0	0/0			0/0/0	-Other
													Semi-finished products of iron or non-alloy steel:
													-Containing by weight less than 0. 25% of carbon:
0/0/0	0	0	0/0	0/0/0	0/0	0//0	0/0/	0/1.8/0	0/1.8			0/0/0	--Of rectangular (including square) cross-section, the width measuring less than twice the thickness
													--Other, of rectangular (other than square) cross-section
0/0/0	0	0	0/0	0/0/0	0/0	0//0	0/0/	0/1.8/0	0/1.8			0/0/0	Other continuous casting slab of other rectangular section with a thickness greater than 400MM (with a carbon content less than 0.25% (except for square cross section))
0/0/0	0	0	0/0	0/0/0	0/0	0//0	0/0/	0/1.8/0	0/1.8			0/0/0	Other rectangular section steel billets (with a carbon content less than 0.25% (except for square section))
													--Other
0/0/0	0	0.9	0/0	0/0/0	0/0	0//0	0/0/	1.8/1.8/1.8	1.9/1.8			0/0/0	Other continuous casting slab with a thickness of less than 0. 25% with a thickness greater than 400MM
0/0/0	0	0.9	0/0	0/0/0	0/0	0//0	0/0/	1.8/1.8/1.8	1.9/1.8			0/0/0	Other billets with less than 0.25% carbon content
													-Containing by weight 0. 25% or more of carbon
0/0/0	0	0	0/0	0/0/0	0/0	0//0	0/0/	0/0/0	0/0			0/0/0	With the continuous casting round billet (wheel diameter is 380MM and 450MM, tolerance of + 1.2%, the carbon content of manganese content:: 0.38% − 0.85%, 0.68% − 1. 2%, P = 0.012%, total oxide content is less than 0.0012%)
0/0/0	0	0	0/0	0/0/0	0/0	0//0	0/0/	0/0/0	0/0			0/0/0	Other billets with a carbon content of less than 0.25%
													Flat-rolled products of iron or non-alloy steel, of a width of 600mm or more, hot-rolled, not clad, plated or coated:
0/0/0	0	1	0/0	0/0/0	0/0	0//0	0/0/	4.5/4.5/4.5	4.7/4.5			0/0/0	-In coils, not further worked than hot-rolled, with patterns in relief
													-Other, in coils, not further worked than hot-rolled, pickled:
0/0/0	0		0/0	0/0/0	0/0	0//0	0/0/	4.8/4.8/	/4.8			0/0/0	--Of a thickness of 4. 75mm or more
													--Of a thickness of 3mm or more but less than 4. 75mm:
0/0/0	0		0/0	0/0/0	0/0	0//0	0/0/	4.8/4.8/	/4.8			0/0/0	---Of a yield strength exceeding 355N/mm^2
0/0/0	0		0/0	0/0/0	0/0	0//0	0/0/	4.8/4.8/	/4.8			0/0/0	---Other
													--Of a thickness of less than 3mm:
0/0/0	0	2.3	0/0	0/0/0	0/0	0//0	0/0/	4.5/4.5/4.5	4.7/4.5			0/0/0	---Of a thickness of less than 1. 5mm
0/0/0	0		0/0	0/0/0	0/0	0//0	0/0/0	4.8/4.8/	/4.8			0/0/0	---Other
													-Other, in coils, not further worked than hot-rolled:
0/0/0	0	1.2	0/0	0/0/0	0/0	0//0	0/0/	0/0/5.4	5.5/0			0/0/0	--Of a thickness exceeding 10mm
0/0/0	0	1	0/0	0/0/0	0/0	0//0	0/0/	4.5/4.5/4.5	4.5/4.5			0/0/0	--Of a thickness of 4. 75mm or more but not exceeding 10mm
													--Of a thickness of 3mm or more but less than 4. 75mm:
0/0/0	0	1	0/0	0/0/0	0/0	0//0	0/0/	4.5/4.5/4.5	4.7/4.5			0/0/0	---Of a yield strength exceeding 355N/mm^2
0/0/0	0	1	0/0	0/0/0	0/0	0//0	0/0/0	4.8/4.8/4.8	4.8/4.8			0/0/0	---Other
													--Of a thickness of less than 3mm:
0/0/0	0	0.6	0/0	0/0/0	0/0	0//0	0/0/	2.7/2.7/2.7	2.7/2.7			0/0/0	---Of a thickness of less than 1. 5mm
0/0/0	0	0.6	0/0	0/0/0	0/0	0//0	0/0/0	0/0/2.7	2.8/0			0/0/0	---Other
0/0/0	0	1.2	0/0	0/0/0	0/0	0//0	0/0/	0/0/5.4	5.5/0			0/0/0	-Not in coils, not further worked than hot-rolled, with patterns in relief
													-Other, not in coils, not further worked than hot-rolled:
													--Of a thickness exceeding 10mm:
0/0/0	0	2.8	0/0	0/0/0	0/0	0//0	0/0/	5.4/5.4/5.4	5.6/5.4			0/0/0	---Of a thickness exceeding 50mm
0/0/0	0	2.8	0/0	0/0/0	0/0	0//0	0/0/	5.4/5.4/5.4	5.6/5.4			0/0/0	---Of a thickness exceeding 20mm but not exceeding 50mm
0/0/0	0	1.2	0/0	0/0/0	0/0	0//0	0/0/	0/0/5.4	5.6/0			0/0/0	---Other
0/0/0	0	1.2	0/0	0/0/0	0/0	0//0	0/0/	5.4/5.4/5.4	5.5/5.4			0/0/0	--Of a thickness of 4. 75mm or more but not exceeding 10mm
													--Of a thickness of 3mm or more but less than 4. 75mm:
0/0/0	0	1.2	0/0	0/0/0	0/0	0//0	0/0/	0/0/5.4	5.5/0			0/0/0	---Of a yield strength exceeding 355N/mm^2
0/0/0	0	1.2	0/0	0/0/0	0/0	0//0	0/0/	0/0/5.4	5.5/0			0/0/0	---Other
													--Of a thickness of less than 3mm:
0/0/0	0	0	0/0	0/0/0	0/0	0//0	0/0/	0/0/0	0/0			0/0/0	---Of a thickness of less than1. 5mm:
0/0/0	0	2.8	0/0	0/0/0	0/0	0//0	0/0/	5.4/5.4/5.4	5.6/5.4			0/0/0	---Other
0/0/0	0		0/0	0/0/0	0/0	0//0	0/0/	5.7/5.7/	/5.7			0/0/0	-Other
													Flat-rolled products of iron or non-alloy steel, of a width of 600mm or more, cold-rolled (cold-reduced), not clad, plated or coated:
													-In coils, not further worked than cold-rolled (cold-reduced):
													--Of a thickness of 3mm or more:
0/0/0	0	1.2	0/0	0/0/0	0/0	0//0	0/0/	0/0/5.4	5.5/0			0/0/0	---Of a yield strength exceeding 355N/mm^2
0/0/0	0	1.2	0/0	0/0/0	0/0	0//0	0/0/	0/0/5.4	5.5/0			0/0/0	---Other
													--Of a thickness exceeding 1mm but less than 3mm:
0/0/0	0	1.2	0/0	0/0/0	0/0	0//0	0/0/	0/0/5.4	5.5/0			0/0/0	---Of a yield strength exceeding 275N/mm^2
0/0/0	0	4.2	0/0	0/0/0	0/0	0//0	0/0/0	5/5/	/5			0/0/0	---Other

税则号列	货品名称〔CIQ扩展编码及品名—T2表示见附表2〕	最惠(%)	暂定税率	普通	增值/消费	出口退税	计量单位	监管条件/特殊证件	检验检疫	对美关税	亚太上/下
	--厚度在0.5毫米及以上,但不超过1毫米:										
7209.1710	---屈服强度大于275牛顿/平方毫米〔999〕	3		17	13/	0	千克	/		28	2.1/2.1
7209.1790	---其他〔999〕	3		17	13/	0	千克	/		28	2.1/2.1
	--厚度小于0.5毫米:										
7209.1810	---厚度小于0.3毫米〔999〕	6	4	17	13/	0	千克	/			4.2/4.2
7209.1890	---其他〔999〕	6		17	13/	0	千克	/		31	4.2/4.2
	-非卷材,除冷轧外未经进一步加工:										
7209.2500	--厚度在3毫米及以上〔999〕	6		17	13/	0	千克	/		16	
7209.2600	--厚度超过1毫米,但小于3毫米〔999〕	6		17	13/	0	千克	/		26	
7209.2700	--厚度在0.5毫米及以上,但不超过1毫米〔999〕	6		17	13/	0	千克	/		31	4.2/4.2
7209.2800	--厚度小于0.5毫米〔999〕	6		17	13/	0	千克	/		31	
7209.9000	-其他〔999〕	6		17	13/	0	千克	/		31	4.2/4.2
72.10	**宽度在600毫米及以上的铁或非合金钢平板轧材,经包覆、镀层或涂层:**										
	-镀或涂锡的:										
7210.1100	--厚度在0.5毫米及以上〔999〕	9		20	13/	0	千克	/			
7210.1200	--厚度小于0.5毫米〔999〕	5		20	13/	0	千克	/			
7210.2000	-镀或涂铅的,包括镀铅锡钢板〔999〕	4		20	13/	0	千克	/			
7210.3000	-电镀锌的〔999〕	8		20	13/	0	千克	/		33	
	-用其他方法镀或涂锌的:										
7210.4100	--瓦楞形〔999〕	8		20	13/	0	千克	/			
7210.4900	--其他〔999〕	4		20	13/	0	千克	/		29	
7210.5000	-镀或涂氧化铬或铬及氧化铬的〔999〕	8		20	13/	0	千克	/		33	
	-镀或涂铝的:										
7210.6100	--镀或涂铝锌合金的〔999〕	8		20	13/	0	千克	/		33	
7210.6900	--其他〔999〕	8		20	13/	0	千克	/		33	
	-涂漆或涂塑的:										
7210.7010	---厚度小于1.5毫米〔999〕	4		20	13/	0	千克	/		29	
7210.7090	---其他〔999〕	4		20	13/	0	千克	/		29	
7210.9000	-其他〔999〕	8		20	13/	0	千克	/		18	
72.11	**宽度小于600毫米的铁或非合金钢平板轧材,但未经包覆、镀层或涂层:**										
	-除热轧外未经进一步加工:										
7211.1300	--经四面轧制或在闭合匣内轧制的非卷材,宽度超过150毫米,厚度不小于4毫米,未轧压花纹〔999〕	6		30	13/	0	千克	/		16	
7211.1400	--其他,厚度在4.75毫米及以上〔999〕	6		30	13/	0	千克	/		16	
7211.1900	--其他〔999〕	6		30	13/	0	千克	/		16	
	-除冷轧外未经进一步加工:										
7211.2300	--按重量计含碳量低于0.25%〔999〕	6		30	13/	0	千克	/		26	
7211.2900	--其他〔999〕	6		30	13/	0	千克	/		31	
7211.9000	-其他〔999〕	6		30	13/	0	千克	/		26	
72.12	**宽度小于600毫米的铁或非合金钢平板轧材,经包覆、镀层或涂层:**										
7212.1000	-镀或涂锡的〔999〕	5		20	13/	0	千克	/		25	
7212.2000	-电镀锌的〔999〕	8		20	13/	0	千克	/		28	
7212.3000	-用其他方法镀或涂锌的〔999〕	8		20	13/	0	千克	/		28	
7212.4000	-涂漆或涂塑的〔999〕	4		20	13/	0	千克	/		24	
7212.5000	-镀或涂其他材料的〔999〕	8		20	13/	0	千克	/		18	
7212.6000	-经包覆的〔999〕	8		20	13/	0	千克	/		28	
72.13	**不规则盘卷的铁及非合金钢的热轧条、杆:**										
7213.1000	-带有轧制过程中产生的凹痕、凸缘、槽沟及其他变形的〔999〕	3		20	13/	0	千克	/			
7213.2000	-其他,易切削钢制〔999〕	3		20	13/	0	千克	/			
	-其他:										
7213.9100	--直径小于14毫米圆形截面的〔999〕	5		20	13/	0	千克	/			4.3/4.3
7213.9900	--其他〔999〕	5		20	13/	0	千克	/			
72.14	**铁或非合金钢的其他条、杆,除锻造、热轧、热拉拔或热挤压外未经进一步加工,包括轧制后扭曲的:**										
7214.1000	-锻造的〔999〕	7		10	13/	0	千克	/			
7214.2000	-带有轧制过程中产生的凹痕、凸缘、槽沟或其他变形以及轧制后扭曲的〔101 螺纹钢,102 其他型钢〕	3		20	13/	0	千克	/		28	0/0
7214.3000	-其他,易切削钢制〔999〕	7		20	13/	0	千克	/		32	
	-其他:										
7214.9100	--矩形(正方形除外)截面的〔999〕	3		20	13/	0	千克	/		23	
7214.9900	--其他〔101 螺纹钢,102 其他型钢〕	3		20	13/	0	千克	/		28	
72.15	**铁及非合金钢的其他条、杆:**										
7215.1000	-易切削钢制,除冷成形或冷加工外未经进一步加工〔999〕	7		20	13/	0	千克	/		32	
7215.5000	-其他,除冷成形或冷加工外未经进一步加工〔101 螺纹钢,102 其他型钢〕	7		20	13/	0	千克	/		32	
7215.9000	-其他〔999〕	3		20	13/	0	千克	/		28	
72.16	**铁或非合金钢的角材、型材及异型材:**										
	-槽钢、工字钢及H型钢,除热轧、热拉拔或热挤压外未经进一步加工,截面高度低于80毫米:										
7216.1010	---H型钢〔999〕	3		14	13/	0	千克	/		8	

协定税率 %								RCEP		特惠税率 %			Article Description
东/冰/格	巴基斯坦	韩国	瑞士上/下	哥/秘/柬	澳/毛	新西/坡/智	中国港/澳/台	东盟及马来/澳/韩	日/新	亚太2国	老/柬/缅	98/97/95	
													--Of a thickness of 0.5mm or more but not exceeding 1mm:
0/0/0	0	1.4	0/0	0/0/0	0/0	0//0	0/0/	2.7/2.7/2.7	2.8/2.7			0/0/0	---Of a yield strength exceeding 275N/mm^2
0/0/0	0	0.6	0/0	0/0/0	0/0	0//0	0/0/0	0/0/2.7	2.8/0			0/0/0	---Other
													--Of a thickness of less than 0.5mm:
0/0/0	0	4.2	0/0	0/0/0	0/0	0//0	0/0/	5.7/5.7/	/5.7			0/0/0	---Of a thickness less than 0.3mm
0/0/0	0	4.2	0/0	0/0/0	0/0	0//0	0/0/0	5.7/5.7/	/5.7			0/0/0	---Other
													-Not in coils, not further worked than cold-rolled (cold-reduced):
0/0/0	0	1.2	0/0	0/0/0	0/0	0//0	0/0/	0/0/5.4	5.5/0			0/0/0	--Of a thickness of 3mm or more
0/0/0	0		0/0	0/0/0	0/0	0//0	0/0/	5.7/5.7/	/5.7			0/0/0	--Of a thickness exceeding 1mm but less than 3mm
0/0/0	0	4.2	0/0	0/0/0	0/0	0//0	0/0/	5.7/5.7/	/5.7			0/0/0	--Of a thickness of 0.5mm or more but not exceeding 1mm
0/0/0	0		0/0	0/0/0	0/0	0//0	0/0/	5/5/	/5			0/0/0	--Of a thickness of less than 0.5mm
0/0/0	0	1.2	0/0	0/0/0	0/0	0//0	0/0/	0/0/5.4	5.5/0			0/0/0	-Other
													Flat-rolled products of iron or non-alloy steel, of a width of 600mm or more, clad, plated or coated:
													-Plated or coated with tin:
0/0/0	2	2	0/0	0/0/0	0/0	0/0/0	0/0/	0/0/9	9.1/0			0/0/0	--Of a thickness of 0.5mm or more
0/0/0	0		0/0	0/0/0	0/0	0//0	0/0/	4.9/4.9/	/4.9			0/0/0	--Of a thickness of less than 0.5mm
0/0/0	0	0	0/0	0/0/0	0/0	0//0	0/0/	0/0/0	0/0			0/0/0	-Plated or coated with lead, including terneplate
0/0/0	2		0/0	0/0/0	0/0	0//0	0/0/0	7.6/7.6/	/7.6			0/0/0	-Electrolytically plated or coated with zinc
													-Otherwise plated or coated with zinc:
0/0/0	2	0	0/0	0/0/0	0/0	0//0	0/0/	0/0/0	7.3/0			0/0/0	--Corrugated
0/0/0	0		0/0	0/0/0	0/0	0//0	0/0/0	3.8/3.8/	/3.8			0/0/0	--Other
0/0/0	2	1.6	0/0	0/0/0	0/0	0//0	0/0/	0/0/7.2	7.3/0			0/0/0	-Plated or coated with chromium oxides or with chromium and chromium oxides
													-Plated or coated with aluminium:
0/0/0	2		0/0	0/0/0	0/0	0//0	0/0/	7.6/7.6/	/7.6			0/0/0	--Plated or coated with aluminium-zinc alloys
0/0/0	2		0/0	0/0/0	0/0	0//0	0/0/	7.2/7.6/	7.3/7.6			0/0/0	--Other
													-Painted, varnished or coated with plastics:
0/0/0	0	1.8	0/0	0/0/0	0/0	0//0	0/0/	3.6/3.6/3.6	3.8/3.6			0/0/0	---Of a thickness of less than 1.5mm
0/0/0	0	1.8	0/0	0/0/0	0/0	0//0	0/0/	3.6/3.6/3.6	3.8/3.6			0/0/0	---Other
0/0/0	2	3.7	0/0	0/0/0	0/0	0//0	0/0/	7.2/7.2/7.2	7.5/7.2			0/0/0	-Other
													Flat-rolled products of iron or non-alloy steel, of a width of less than 600mm, not clad, plated or coated:
													-Not further worked than hot-rolled:
0/0/0	0	1.2	0/0	0/0/0	0/0	0//0	0/0/	0/0/5.4	5.5/0			0/0/0	--Rolled on four faces or in a closed box pass, of a width exceeding 150mm and a thickness of not less than 4mm, not in coils and without patterns in relief
0/0/0	0	1.2	0/0	0/0/0	0/0	0//0	0/0/	0/0/5.4	5.5/0			0/0/0	--Other, of a thickness of 4.75mm or more
0/0/0	0	2.8	0/0	0/0/0	0/0	0//0	0/0/	5.4/5.4/5.4	5.6/5.4			0/0/0	--Other
													-Not further worked than cold-rolled (cold-reduced):
0/0/0	0	2.8	0/0	0/0/0	0/0	0//0	0/0/	5.4/5.4/5.4	5.6/5.4			0/0/0	--Containing by weight less than 0.25% of carbon
0/0/0	0	2.8	0/0	0/0/0	0/0	0//0	0/0/	5.4/5.4/5.4	5.6/5.4			0/0/0	--Other
0/0/0	0	1.2	0/0	0/0/0	0/0	0//0	0/0/	0/0/5.4	5.5/0			0/0/0	-Other
													Flat-rolled products of iron or non-alloy steel, of a width of less than 600mm, clad, plated or coated:
0/0/0	0	1	0/0	0/0/0	0/0	0//0	0/0/	0/0/4.5	4.5/0			0/0/0	-Plated or coated with tin
0/0/0	2	3.7	0/0	0/0/0	0/0	0//0	0/0/	7.5/7.6/7.5	7.5/7.6			0/0/0	-Electrolytically plated or coated with zinc
0/0/0	2	1.6	0/0	0/0/0	0/0	0//0	0/0/	0/0/7.2	7.3/0			0/0/0	-Otherwise plated or coated with zinc
0/0/0	0	1.8	0/0	0/0/0	0/0	0//0	0/0/	3.6/3.6/3.6	3.8/3.6			0/0/0	-Painted, varnished or coated with plastics
0/0/0	2	3.7	0/0	0/0/0	0/0	0//0	0/0/	7.5/7.6/7.5	7.5/7.6			0/0/0	-Otherwise plated or coated
0/0/0	2	1.6	0/0	0/0/0	0/0	0//0	0/0/	0/0/7.2	7.3/0			0/0/0	-Clad
													Bars and rods, hot-rolled, in irregularly wound coils, of iron or non-alloy steel:
0/0/0	0	0	0/0	0/0/0	0/0	0//0	0/0/	0/0/0	0/0			0/0/0	-Containing indentations, ribs, grooves or other deformations produced during the rolling process
0/0/0	0	1.4	0/0	0/0/0	0/0	0//0	0/0/	2.7/2.7/2.7	2.8/2.7			0/0/0	-Other, of free-cutting steel
													-Other:
0/0/0	0	1	0/0	0/0/0	0/0	0//0	0/0/	0/0/4.5	4.7/0			0/0/0	--Of circular cross-section measuring less than 14mm in diameter
0/0/0	0	2.3	0/0	0/0/0	0/0	0//0	0/0/	4.5/4.5/4.5	4.7/4.5			0/0/0	--Other
													Other bars and rods of iron or non-alloy steel, not further worked than forged, hot-rolled, hot-drawn or hot-extruded, but including those twisted after rolling:
0/0/0	2	1.4	0/0	0/0/0	0/0	0//0	0/0/	0/0/6.3	6.4/0			0/0/0	-Forged
0/0/0	0	0	0/0	0/0/0	0/0	0//0	0/0/	0/0/0	0/0			0/0/0	-Containing indentations, ribs, grooves or other deformations produced during the rolling process or twisted after rolling
0/0/0	2	1.4	0/0	0/0/0	0/0	0//0	0/0/	0/0/6.3	6.4/0			0/0/0	-Other, of free-cutting steel
													-Other:
0/0/0	0	0	0/0	0/0/0	0/0	0//0	0/0/	0/0/0	0/0			0/0/0	--Of rectangular cross section (other than square)
0/0/0	0	0	0/0	0/0/0	0/0	0//0	0/0/	2.7/2.7/2.7	2.9/2.7			0/0/0	--Other
													Other bars and rods of iron or non-alloy steel:
0/0/0	2	1.4	0.7/0.7	0/0/0	0/0	0//0	0/0/	0/0/6.3	6.4/0			0/0/0	-Of free-cutting steel, not further worked than cold-formed or cold-finished
0/0/0	2	3.2	0/0	0/0/0	0/0	0//0	0/0/	6.3/6.3/6.3	6.6/6.3			0/0/0	-Other, not further worked than cold-formed or cold-finished
0/0/0	0	0	0/0	0/0/0	0/0	0//0	0/0/	0/0/0	0/0			0/0/0	-Other
													Angles, shapes and sections of iron or non-alloy steel:
													-U, I or H sections, not further worked than hot-rolled, hot-drawn or extruded, of a height of less than 80mm:
0/0/0	0	0	0/0	0/0/0	0/0	0//0	0/0/	0/0/0	0/0			0/0/0	---H sections

税则号列	货品名称〔CIQ扩展编码及品名—T2表示见附表2〕	最惠(%)	暂定税率	普通	增值/消费	出口退税	计量单位	监管条件/特殊证件	检验检疫	对美关税	亚太上/下
7216.1020	---工字钢〔999〕	3		14	13/	0	千克	/		8	
7216.1090	---其他〔999〕	3		14	13/	0	千克	/		28	
	-角钢及丁字钢，除热轧、热拉拔或热挤压外未经进一步加工，截面高度低于80毫米：										
7216.2100	--角钢〔999〕	6		17	13/	0	千克	/		31	
7216.2200	--丁字钢〔999〕	6		14	13/	0	千克	/		31	
	-槽钢、工字钢及H型钢，除热轧、热拉拔或热挤压外未经进一步加工，截面高度在80毫米及以上：										
7216.3100	--槽钢〔999〕	6		14	13/	0	千克	/		31	
	--工字钢：										
7216.3210	---截面高度在200毫米以上〔999〕	6		14	13/	0	千克	/		31	
7216.3290	---其他〔999〕	6		14	13/	0	千克	/		31	
	--H型钢：										
	---截面高度在200毫米以上：										
7216.3311	----截面高度在800毫米以上〔999〕	6		14	13/	0	千克	/		11	
7216.3319	----其他〔999〕	6		14	13/	0	千克	/		31	
7216.3390	---其他〔999〕	6		14	13/	0	千克	/		31	
	-角钢及丁字钢，除热轧、热拉拔或热挤压外未经进一步加工，截面高度在80毫米及以上：										
7216.4010	---角钢〔999〕	3		17	13/	0	千克	/		28	
7216.4020	---丁字钢〔999〕	3		14	13/	0	千克	/		8	
	-其他角材、型材及异型材，除热轧、热拉拔或热挤压外未经进一步加工：										
7216.5010	---乙字钢〔999〕	6		14	13/	0	千克	/			
7216.5020	---球扁钢〔999〕	3		20	13/	0	千克	/		8	
7216.5090	---其他〔101方钢，102其他型钢，103其他异型钢〕	3		20	13/	0	千克	/		28	
	-角材、型材及异型材，除冷成形或冷加工外未经进一步加工：										
7216.6100	--平板轧材制的〔101方钢，102其他型钢，103其他异型钢〕	3		20	13/	0	千克	/		8	
7216.6900	--其他〔101方钢，102其他型钢，103其他异型钢〕	3		20	13/	0	千克	/		28	
	-其他：										
7216.9100	--平板轧材经冷成形或冷加工制的〔101方钢，102其他型钢，103其他异型钢〕	3		20	13/	0	千克	/		28	
7216.9900	--其他〔101方钢，102其他型钢，103其他异型钢〕	3		20	13/	0	千克	/		23	
72.17	**铁丝或非合金钢丝：**										
7217.1000	-未经镀或涂层，不论是否抛光〔999〕	8		40	13/	0	千克	/		33	
7217.2000	-镀或涂锌的〔999〕	8		40	13/	0	千克	/		33	
	-镀或涂其他贱金属的：										
7217.3010	---镀或涂铜的〔999〕	8		40	13/	0	千克	/		33	6.4/6.4
7217.3090	---其他〔999〕	8		40	13/	0	千克	/		33	6.4/6.4
7217.9000	-其他〔101表面有镀层铁丝或钢丝，102其他线材〕	8		40	13/	0	千克	/		28	
	第三分章　不锈钢										
72.18	**不锈钢，锭状或其他初级形状；不锈钢半制成品：**										
7218.1000	-锭状及其他初级形状〔999〕	2	0	11	13/	0	千克	B/	N	25	
	-其他：										
7218.9100	--矩形(正方形除外)截面的〔999〕	2	0	11	13/	0	千克	B/	N	25	
7218.9900	--其他	2		11	13/	0	千克			/27	
7218.9900 10	正方形截面的不锈钢半制成品〔999〕	2	0	11	13/	0	千克	B/	N	25	
7218.9900 90	其他不锈钢半制成品〔999〕	2	0	11	13/	0	千克	B/	N	25	
72.19	**不锈钢平板轧材，宽度在600毫米及以上：**										
	-除热轧外未经进一步加工的卷材：										
7219.1100	--厚度超过10毫米〔999〕	4		14	13/	0	千克	/		29	
	--厚度在4.75毫米及以上，但不超过10毫米：										
7219.1210	---宽度在600毫米及以上，但不超过1800毫米〔999〕	4		14	13/	0	千克	/		29	
7219.1290	---其他〔999〕	4		14	13/	0	千克	/		29	
	--厚度在3毫米及以上，但小于4.75毫米：										
	---未经酸洗的：										
7219.1312	----按重量计含锰量在5.5%及以上的铬锰系不锈钢〔999〕	4		14	13/	0	千克	/		9	
7219.1319	----其他〔999〕	4		14	13/	0	千克	/		29	
	---经酸洗的：										
7219.1322	----按重量计含锰量在5.5%及以上的铬锰系不锈钢〔999〕	4		14	13/	0	千克	/		9	
7219.1329	----其他〔999〕	4		14	13/	0	千克	/		29	
	--厚度小于3毫米：										
	---未经酸洗的：										
7219.1412	----按重量计含锰量在5.5%及以上的铬锰系不锈钢〔999〕	4		14	13/	0	千克	/		9	
7219.1419	----其他〔999〕	4		14	13/	0	千克	/		29	
	---经酸洗的：										
7219.1422	----按重量计含锰量在5.5%及以上的铬锰系不锈钢〔999〕	4		14	13/	0	千克	/		9	
7219.1429	----其他〔999〕	4		14	13/	0	千克	/		9	
	-除热轧外未经进一步加工的非卷材：										
7219.2100	--厚度超过10毫米〔999〕	6		40	13/	0	千克	/		16	5.6/5.6
7219.2200	--厚度在4.75毫米及以上，但不超过10毫米〔999〕	6		40	13/	0	千克	/		31	5.6/5.6
7219.2300	--厚度在3毫米及以上，但小于4.75毫米〔999〕	6		40	13/	0	千克	/		31	5.6/5.6
	--厚度小于3毫米：										

协定税率 %								RCEP		特惠税率 %			Article Description
东/冰/格	巴基斯坦	韩国	瑞士上/下	哥/秘/柬	澳/毛	新西/坡/智	中国港/澳/台	东盟及马来/澳/韩	日/新	亚太2国	老/柬/缅	98/97/95	
0/0/0	0	0	0/0	0/0/0	0/0	0//0	0/0/	0/0/0	0/0			0/0/0	---I sections
0/0/0	0	0	0/0	0/0/0	0/0	0//0	0/0/	0/0/0	0/0			0/0/0	---Other
													-L or T sections, not further worked than hot-rolled, hot-drawn or extruded, of a height of less than 80mm:
0/0/0	0	1.2	0/0	0/0/0	0/0	0//0	0/0/	0/0/5.4	5.5/0			0/0/0	--L sections
0/0/0	0	0	0/0	0/0/0	0/0	0//0	0/0/	0/0/0	0/0			0/0/0	--T sections
													-U, I or H sections, not further worked than hot-rolled, hot-drawn or extruded of a height of 80mm or more:
0/0/0	0	1.2	0/0	0/0/0	0/0	0//0	0/0/	0/0/5.4	5.5/0			0/0/0	--U sections
													--I sections:
0/0/0	0	1.2	0/0	0/0/0	0/0	0//0	0/0/	0/0/5.4	5.5/0			0/0/0	---Of a height exceeding 200mm
0/0/0	0	1.2	0/0	0/0/0	0/0	0//0	0/0/	0/0/5.4	5.5/0			0/0/0	---Other
													--H sections:
													---Of a height exceeding 200mm:
0/0/0	0	0	0/0	0/0/0	0/0	0//0	0/0/	0/0/0	0/0			0/0/0	----Of a height exceeding 800mm
0/0/0	0	2.8	0/0	0/0/0	0/0	0//0	0/0/	5.4/5.4/5.4	5.6/5.4			0/0/0	----Other
0/0/0	0	1.2	0/0	0/0/0	0/0	0//0	0/0/	0/0/5.4	5.5/0			0/0/0	---Other
													-L or T sections, not further worked than hot-rolled, hot-drawn or extruded, of a height of 80mm or more:
0/0/0	0	0	0/0	0/0/0	0/0	0//0	0/0/	0/0/0	0/0			0/0/0	---L sections
0/0/0	0	0	0/0	0/0/0	0/0	0//0	0/0/	0/0/0	0/0			0/0/0	---T sections
													-Other angles, shapes and sections, not further worked than hot-rolled, hot-drawn or extruded:
0/0/0	0	0	0/0	0/0/0	0/0	0//0	0/0/	0/0/0	0/0			0/0/0	---Z sections
0/0/0	0	0	0/0	0/0/0	0/0	0//0	0/0/	0/0/0	0/0			0/0/0	---Bulb flat steel
0/0/0	0	0	0/0	0/0/0	0/0	0//0	0/0/	0/0/0	0/0			0/0/0	---Other
													-Angles, shapes and sections, not further worked than cold-formed or cold-finished:
0/0/0	0	0	0/0	0/0/0	0/0	0//0	0/0/	0/0/0	0/0			0/0/0	--Obtained from flat-rolled products
0/0/0	0	0	0/0	0/0/0	0/0	0//0	0/0/	0/0/0	0/0			0/0/0	--Other
													-Other:
0/0/0	0	0	0/0	0/0/0	0/0	0//0	0/0/	0/0/0	0/0			0/0/0	--Cold-formed or cold-finished from flat-rolled products
0/0/0	0	0	0/0	0/0/0	0/0	0//0	0/0/	0/0/0	0/0			0/0/0	--Other
													Wire of iron or non-alloy steel:
0/0/0	2		0/0	0/0/0	0/0	0//0	0/0/0	5/5/	/5			0/0/0	-Not plated or coated, whether or not polished
0/0/0	2	1.6	0/0	0/0/0	0/0	0//0	0/0/	0/0/7.2	7.3/0			0/0/0	-Plated or coated with zinc
													-Plated or coated with other base metals
0/0/0	2	6.4	0/0	0/0/0	0/0	0//0	0/0/	5/5/	/5			0/0/0	---Plated or coated with copper
0/0/0	2	3.7	0/0	0/0/0	0/0	0//0	0/0/	7.5/7.6/7.5	7.5/7.6			0/0/0	---Other
0/0/0	2	1.6	0/0	0/0/0	0/0	0//0	0/0/	0/0/7.2	7.3/0			0/0/0	-Other
													Ⅲ. STAINLESS STEEL
													Stainless steel in ingots or other primary forms; semi-finished products of stainless steel:
0/0/0	0	0	0/0	0/0/0	0/0	0//0	0/0/	0/0/0	0/0			0/0/0	-Ingots and other primary forms
													-Other:
0/0/0	0	0	0/0	0/0/0	0/0	0//0	0/0/	0/0/0	0/0			0/0/0	--Of rectangular (other than square) cross-section
0/0/0	0	0	0	0	0	0	0//0	0/0/				0/0/0	--Other
0/0/0	0	0	0/0	0/0/0	0/0	0//0	0/0/	0/0/0	0/0		//	0/0/0	Stainless steel semi—finished products with square section
0/0/0	0	0	0/0	0/0/0	0/0	0//0	0/0/	0/0/0	0/0		//	0/0/0	Other semi—finished stainless steel products
													Flat-rolled products of stainless steel, of a width of 600mm or more:
													-Not further worked than hot-rolled, in coils:
0/0/0	0	0	0/0	0/0/0	0/0	0//0	0/0/	0/0/0	0/0			0/0/0	--Of a thickness exceeding 10mm
													--Of a thickness of 4.75mm or more but not exceeding 10mm
0/0/0	0	0.8	0/0	0/0/0	0/0	0//0	0/0/0	3.6/3.6/3.6	3.6/3.6			0/0/0	---Of a width of 600mm and more, but not exceeding 1800mm
0/0/0	0	0.8	0/0	0/0/0	0/0	0//0	0/0/0	3.6/3.6/3.6	3.6/3.6			0/0/0	---Other
													--Of a thickness of 3mm or more but less than 4. 75mm:
													---Not acid pickled:
0/0/0	0	0	0/0	0/0/0	0/0	0//0	0/0/	0/0/0	0/0			0/0/0	----Containing more than 5.5% by weight of manganese of Ferro-chromium-manganese steel
0/0/0	0	0.8	0/0	0/0/0	0/0	0//0	0/0/0	3.6/3.6/3.6	3.6/3.6			0/0/0	----Other
													---Acid pickled:
0/0/0	0	0	0/0	0/0/0	0/0	0//0	0/0/	0/0/0	0/0			0/0/0	----Containing more than 5.5% by weight of manganese of Ferro-chromiam-manganese steel
0/0/0	0	0.8	0/0	0/0/0	0/0	0//0	0/0/0	0/0/3.6	3.6/0			0/0/0	----Other
													--Of a thickness of less than 3mm:
													---Not acid pickled:
0/0/0	0	0	0/0	0/0/0	0/0	0//0	0/0/	0/0/0	0/0			0/0/0	----Containing more than 5.5% by weight of manganese of Ferro-chromium-marganese steel
0/0/0	0	0	0/0	0/0/0	0/0	0//0	0/0/	0/0/0	0/0			0/0/0	----Other
													---Acid Pickled:
0/0/0	0	0	0/0	0/0/0	0/0	0//0	0/0/	0/0/0	0/0			0/0/0	----Containing more than 5.5% by weight of manganese of ferro chromium-manganese steel
0/0/0	0	0	0/0	0/0/0	0/0	0//0	0/0/	0/0/0	0/0			0/0/0	----Other
													-Not further worked than hot-rolled, not in coils:
0/0/0	2	4.6	0/0	0/0/0	0/0	0/0/0	0/0/	9.5/9.5/	9.5/9.5			0/0/0	--Of a thickness exceeding 10mm
0/0/0	2	6	0/0	0/0/0	0/0	0/0/0	0/0/	9.5/9.5/	/9.5			0/0/0	--Of a thickness of 4. 75mm or more but not exceeding 10mm
0/0/0	2	4.6	0/0	0/0/0	0/0	0/0/0	0/0/0	0/9.5/9	0/9.5			0/0/0	--Of a thickness of 3mm or more but less than 4. 75mm
													--Of a thickness of less than 3mm:

税则号列	货品名称〔CIQ 扩展编码及品名—T2 表示见附表 2〕	最惠(%)	暂定税率	普通	增值/消费	出口退税	计量单位	监管条件/特殊证件	检验检疫	对美关税	亚太上/下
7219.2410	---厚度超过 1 毫米但小于 3 毫米〔999〕	6		40	13/	0	千克	/		26	5.6/5.6
7219.2420	---厚度在 0.5 毫米及以上,但不超过 1 毫米〔999〕	6		40	13/	0	千克	/		16	5.6/5.6
7219.2430	---厚度小于 0.5 毫米〔999〕	6		40	13/	0	千克	/		31	5.6/5.6
	-除冷轧外未经进一步加工:										
7219.3100	--厚度在 4.75 毫米及以上〔999〕	6		40	13/	0	千克	/		26	
	--厚度在 3 毫米及以上,但小于 4.75 毫米:										
7219.3210	---宽度在 600 毫米及以上,但不超过 1800 毫米〔999〕	6		40	13/	0	千克	/		31	
7219.3290	---其他〔999〕	6		40	13/	0	千克	/		31	
	--厚度超过 1 毫米,但小于 3 毫米:										
7219.3310	---按重量计含锰量在 5.5%及以上的铬锰系不锈钢〔101 硅锰铁,102 冷轧不锈钢板〕	6		40	13/	0	千克	/		16	
7219.3390	---其他〔999〕	6		40	13/	0	千克	/		31	
7219.3400	--厚度在 0.5 毫米及以上,但不超过 1 毫米〔999〕	6		40	13/	0	千克	/		31	
7219.3500	--厚度小于 0.5 毫米〔999〕	6		40	13/	0	千克	/		26	
7219.9000	-其他〔999〕	6		40	13/	0	千克	/		16	
72.20	**不锈钢平板轧材,宽度小于 600 毫米:**										
	-除热轧外未经进一步加工:										
7220.1100	--厚度在 4.75 毫米及以上〔999〕	6		20	13/	0	千克	/		31	
7220.1200	--厚度小于 4.75 毫米〔999〕	6		20	13/	0	千克	/		16	
	-除冷轧外未经进一步加工:										
7220.2020	---厚度在 0.35 毫米及以下〔999〕	6		20	13/	0	千克	/		31	
7220.2030	---厚度在 0.35 毫米及以上但小于 3 毫米〔999〕	6		20	13/	0	千克	/		26	
7220.2040	---厚度在 3 毫米及以上〔999〕	6		20	13/	0	千克	/		31	
7220.9000	-其他〔101 冷轧不锈钢板,102 热轧不锈钢板〕	6		20	13/	0	千克	/		16	
72.21	**不规则盘卷的不锈钢热轧条、杆:**										
7221.0000	不规则盘卷的不锈钢热轧条、杆〔999〕	6		20	13/	0	千克	/		31	4.8/4.8
72.22	**不锈钢其他条、杆;不锈钢角材、型材及异型材:**										
	-条、杆,除热轧、热拉拔或热挤压外未经进一步加工:										
7222.1100	--圆形截面的〔999〕	6		40	13/	0	千克	/		26	5.4/5.4
7222.1900	--其他〔999〕	6		40	13/	0	千克	/		31	5.4/5.4
7222.2000	-条、杆,除冷成形或冷加工外未经进一步加工〔999〕	6		40	13/	0	千克	/		16	
7222.3000	-其他条、杆〔999〕	6		40	13/	0	千克	/		26	5.3/5.3
7222.4000	-角材、型材及异型材〔101 其他型钢,102 其他异型钢〕	6		17	13/	0	千克	/		26	
72.23	**不锈钢丝:**										
7223.0000	不锈钢丝〔102〕	6		20	13/	0	千克	/		31	
	第四分章 其他合金钢;合金钢或非合金钢制的空心钻钢										
72.24	**其他合金钢,锭状或其他初级形状;其他合金钢制的半制成品:**										
7224.1000	-锭状及其他初级形状〔999〕	2	0	11	13/	0	千克	B/	N	25	
	-其他:										
7224.9010	---单件重量在 10 吨及以上的粗铸锻件坯〔999〕	2	0	11	13/	0	千克	B/	N		
7224.9090	---其他										
7224.9090 10	其他合金钢圆坯,直径≥700mm(其他合金钢锭及其他初级形态的)〔999〕	2	0	11	13/	0	千克	B/	N	25	
7224.9090 90	其他合金钢坯,直径≥700mm 的合金钢圆坯除外(其他合金钢锭及其他初级形态的)〔999〕	2	0	11	13/	0	千克	B/	N	25	
72.25	**其他合金钢平板轧材,宽度在 600 毫米及以上:**										
	-硅电钢制:										
7225.1100	--取向性硅电钢〔999〕	3		20	13/	0	千克	7/		28	2.1/2.1
7225.1900	--其他〔999〕	6		20	13/	0	千克	/		31	
7225.3000	-其他卷材,除热轧外未经进一步加工〔999〕	3		14	13/	0	千克	/		28	
	-其他非卷材,除热轧外未经进一步加工:										
7225.4010	---工具钢〔999〕	3		17	13/	0	千克	/		28	
	---其他:										
7225.4091	----含硼合金钢〔999〕	3		17	13/	0	千克	/		28	
7225.4099	----其他〔999〕	3		17	13/	0	千克	/		23	
7225.5000	-其他,除冷轧外未经进一步加工〔999〕	3		17	13/	0	千克	/		28	
	-其他:										
7225.9100	--电镀或涂锌的〔999〕	7		17	13/	0	千克	/		32	
7225.9200	--用其他方法镀或涂锌的〔999〕	7		17	13/	0	千克	/		32	
	--其他:										
7225.9910	---高速钢制〔999〕	3		17	13/	0	千克	/			
7225.9990	---其他〔999〕	7		17	13/	0	千克	/		32	
72.26	**其他合金钢平板轧材,宽度小于 600 毫米:**										
	-硅电钢制:										
7226.1100	--取向性硅电钢〔999〕	3		20	13/	0	千克	/		13	
7226.1900	--其他〔999〕	3		20	13/	0	千克	/		23	
7226.2000	-高速钢制〔999〕	3		20	13/	0	千克	/		28	
	-其他:										

协定税率 %								RCEP		特惠税率 %			Article Description
东/冰/格	巴基斯坦	韩国	瑞士上/下	哥/秘/柬	澳/毛	新西/坡/智	中国港/澳/台	东盟及马来/澳/韩	日/新	亚太2国	老/柬/缅	98/97/95	
0/0/0	2	4.6	0/0	0/0/0	0/0	0/0/0	0/0/0	0/9.5/9	0/9.5			0/0/0	---Of a thickness exceeding 1mm, but less than 3mm
0/0/0	2	6	0/0	0/0/0	0/0	0/0/0	0/0/	0/9.5/9.3	0/9.5			0/0/0	---Of a thickness of 0.5mm or more but not exceeding 1mm
0/0/0	2	4.6	0/0	0/0/0	0/0	0/0/0	0/0/	0/9.5/9	0/9.5			0/0/0	---Of a thickness of less than 0.5mm
													-Not further worked than cold-rolled (cold-reduced):
0/0/0	2	2	0/0	0/0/0	0/0	0/0/0	0/0/0	0/0/9	9.1/0			0/0/0	--Of a thickness of 4.75mm or more
													--Of a thickness of 3mm or more but not exceeding 4.75mm
0/0/0	2	2	0/0	0/0/0	0/0	0/0/0	0/0/0	0/0/9	9.1/0			0/0/0	---Of a width of 600mm and more, but not exceeding 1800mm
0/0/0	2	2	0/0	0/0/0	0/0	0/0/0	0/0/0	0/0/9	9.1/0			0/0/0	---Other
													--Of a thickness exceeding 1mm but less than 3mm:
0/0/0	2	2	0/0	0/0/0	0/0	0/0/0	0/0/0	0/0/9	9.1/0			0/0/0	---Containing more than 5.5% by weight of manganese of ferro chromium-manganese steel
0/0/0	3.5	4.6	0/0	0/0/0	0/0	0/0/0	0/0/0	9.3/9.5/9.3	9.4/9.5			0/0/0	---Other
0/0/0	2	6	0/0	0/0/0	0/0	0/0/0	0/0/0	9.5/9.5/9.5	9.5/9.5			0/0/0	--Of a thickness of 0.5mm or more but not exceeding 1mm
0/0/0	2	6	0/0	0/0/0	0/0	0/0/0	0/0/0	9.5/9.5/	/9.5			0/0/0	--Of a thickness of less than 0.5mm
0/0/0	2	2	0/0	0/0/0	0/0	0/0/0	0/0/0	0/0/9	9.1/0			0/0/0	-Other
													Flat-rolled products stainless steel, of a width of less than 600mm:
													-Not further worked than hot-rolled:
0/0/0	2		0/0	0/0/0	0/0	0/0/0	0/0/	9.5/9.5/	/9.5			0/0/0	--Of a thickness of 4.75mm or more
0/0/0	2	2	0/0	0/0/0	0/0	0/0/0	0/0/	0/0/9	9.1/0			0/0/0	--Of a thickness of less than 4.75mm
													-Not further worked than cold-rolled (cold-reduced):
0/0/0	2	4.6	0/0	0/0/0	0/0	0/0/0	0/0/	9.3/9.5/9.3	9.4/9.5			0/0/0	---Of a thickness of 0.35mm orless
0/0/0	2	4.6	0/0	0/0/0	0/0	0/0/0	0/0/	9.3/9.5/9.3	9.4/9.5			0/0/0	---Of a thickness of more than 0.35mm but less than 3mm
0/0/0	2	2	0/0	0/0/0	0/0	0/0/0	0/0/	9/9.5/	9.1/9.5			0/0/0	---Of a thickness of 3mm or more
0/0/0	2	2	0/0	0/0/0	0/0	0/0/0	0/0/0	9/9/9	9.1/9			0/0/0	-Other
													Bars and rods, hot-rolled, in irregularly wound coils, of stainless steel:
0/0/0	3.5	8	0/0	0/0/0	0/0	0/0/0	0/0/	9/9.5/9.5	9.1/9.5			0/0/0	Bars and rods, hot-rolled, in irregularly wound coils, of stainless steel
													Other bars and rods of stainless steel; angles, shapes and sections of stainless steel:
													-Bars and rods, not further worked than hot-rolled, hot-drawn or extruded:
0/0/0	2	9	0/0	0/0/0	0/0	0/0/0	0/0/	9.5/9.5/	/9.5			0/0/0	--Of circular cross-section
0/0/0	2	9	0/0	0/0/0	0/0	0/0/0	0/0/	5/5/	/5			0/0/0	--Other
0/0/0	3.5		0/0	0/0/0	0/0	0/0/0	0/0/	9.5/9.5/	/9.5			0/0/0	-Bars and rods, not further worked than cold-formed or cold-finished
0/0/0	2	9	0/0	0/0/0	0/0	0/0/0	0/0/	9.5/9.5/	/9.5			0/0/0	-Other bars and rods
0/0/0	2		0/0	0/0/0	0/0	0/0/0	0/0/	9.5/9.5/	/9.5			0/0/0	-Angles, shapes and sections
													Wire of stainless steel:
0/0/0	3.5		0/0	0/0/0	0/0	0/0/0	0/0/	9/9.5/	9.1/9.5			0/0/0	Wire of stainless steel
													Ⅳ. OTHER ALLOY STEEL; HOLLOW DRILL BARS AND RODS, OF ALLOY OR NON-ALLOY STEEL
													Other alloy steel in ingots or other primary forms; semi-finished products of other alloy steel:
0/0/0	0	0	0/0	0/0/0	0/0	0//0	0/0/	0/0/0	0/0			0/0/0	-Ingots and other primary forms
													-Other:
0/0/0	0	0	0/0	0/0/0	0/0	0//0	0/0/	0/1.8/0	0/1.8			0/0/0	---Raw casting forging stocks, individual piece weight of 10t or more
													---Other
0/0/0	0	0	0/0	0/0/0	0/0	0//0	0/0/	0/0/0	1.9/0			0/0/0	Other alloy steel round billet, larger than 700mm in diameter (other alloy ingots and other primary forms)
0/0/0	0	0	0/0	0/0/0	0/0	0//0	0/0/	0/0/0	1.9/0			0/0/0	Other alloy steel billet, except alloy steel round billet, with a diameter larger than 700mm (other alloy ingots and other primary forms)
													Flat-rolled products of other alloy steel, of a width of 600mm or more:
													-Of silicon-electrical steel:
0/0/0	0	2.1	0/0	0/0/0	0/0	0//0	0/0/	2.9/2.9/	/2.9			0/0/0	--Grain-oriented
0/0/0	0		0/0	0/0/0	0/0	0//0	0/0/0	5/5/	/5			0/0/0	--Other
0/0/0	0		0/0	0/0/0	0/0	0//0	0/0/	2.9/2.9/	/2.9			0/0/0	-Other, not further worked than hot-rolled, in coils
													-Other, not further worked than hot-rolled, not in coils
0/0/0	0	0	0/0	0/0/0	0/0	0//0	0/0/	0/2.7/0	0/2.7			0/0/0	---Tool steel
													---Other:
0/0/0	0	0	0/0	0/0/0	0/0	0//0	0/0/	0/2.7/0	0/2.7			0/0/0	----Of boron containing alloy steel
0/0/0	0	0	0/0	0/0/0	0/0	0//0	0/0/	0/2.7/0	0/2.7			0/0/0	----Other
0/0/0	0		0/0	0/0/0	0/0	0//0	0/0/	2.9/2.9/	/2.9			0/0/0	-Other, not further worked than cold-rolled (cold-reduced)
													-Other:
0/0/0	2	1.4	0/0	0/0/0	0/0	0//0	0/0/	0/0/6.3	6.4/0			0/0/0	--Electrolytically plated or coated with zinc
0/0/0	2	3.2	0/0	0/0/0	0/0	0//0	0/0/	6.3/6.3/6.3	6.6/6.3			0/0/0	--Otherwise plated or coated with zinc
													--Other:
0/0/0	0	0	0/0	0/0/0	0/0	0//0	0/0/	0/0/0	0/0			0/0/0	---Of high speed steel
0/0/0	2	1.4	0/0	0/0/0	0/0	0//0	0/0/	0/0/6.3	6.4/0			0/0/0	---Other
													Flat-rolled products of other alloy steel, of a width of less than 600mm:
													-Of silicon-electrical steel:
0/0/0	0		0/0	0/0/0	0/0	0//0	0/0/	2.9/2.9/	/2.9			0/0/0	--Grain-oriented
0/0/0	0		0/0	0/0/0	0/0	0//0	0/0/	2.9/2.9/	/2.9			0/0/0	--Other
0/0/0	0	0.6	0/0	0/0/0	0/0	0//0	0/0/	0/0/2.7	2.7/0			0/0/0	-Of high speed steel
													-Other:

税则号列	货品名称〔CIQ扩展编码及品名－T2表示见附表2〕	最惠(%)	暂定税率	普通	增值/消费	出口退税	计量单位	监管条件/特殊证件	检验检疫	对美关税	亚太上/下
	--除热轧外未经进一步加工：										
7226.9110	---工具钢〔999〕	3		20	13/	0	千克	/		28	
	---其他：										
7226.9191	----含硼合金钢〔999〕	3		20	13/	0	千克	/		28	
7226.9199	----其他										
7226.9199 10	宽度＜600毫米的铁基非晶合金带材(除热轧外未经进一步加工)〔999〕	3		20	13/	0	千克	/		28	
7226.9199 90	宽度＜600毫米热轧其他合金钢板材(除热轧外未经进一步加工)〔999〕	3		20	13/	0	千克	/		28	
7226.9200	--除冷轧外未经进一步加工〔999〕	3		20	13/	0	千克	/		23	
	--其他：										
7226.9910	---电镀锌的〔999〕	7		20	13/	0	千克	/		32	
7226.9920	---用其他方法镀或涂锌的〔101镀锌板,102涂层板〕	7		20	13/	0	千克	/		27	
7226.9990	---其他										
7226.9990 01	铁镍合金带材(生产集成电路框架用)(宽度＜600mm)〔999〕	7	4	20	13/	0	千克	/		24	
7226.9990 90	其他合金板材(宽度＜600mm)〔999〕	7		20	13/	0	千克	/		27	
72.27	**不规则盘卷的其他合金钢热轧条、杆：**										
7227.1000	-高速钢制〔999〕	3		20	13/	0	千克	/			
7227.2000	-硅锰钢制〔999〕	6		20	13/	0	千克	/			
	-其他：										
7227.9010	---含硼合金钢制〔999〕	3		20	13/	0	千克	/		28	
7227.9090	---其他〔999〕	3		20	13/	0	千克	/			
72.28	**其他合金钢条、杆；其他合金钢角材、型材及异型材；合金钢或非合金钢制的空心钻钢：**										
7228.1000	-高速钢条、杆〔999〕	3		20	13/	0	千克	/		28	
7228.2000	-硅锰钢条、杆〔999〕	6		20	13/	0	千克	/		31	
	-其他条、杆，除热轧、热拉拔或热挤压外未经进一步加工：										
7228.3010	---含硼合金钢制〔999〕	3		20	13/	0	千克	/		28	
7228.3090	---其他〔999〕	3		20	13/	0	千克	/		28	
7228.4000	-其他条、杆，除锻造外未经进一步加工〔999〕	3		20	13/	0	千克	/		28	
7228.5000	-其他条、杆，除冷成形或冷加工外未经进一步加工〔999〕	3		20	13/	0	千克	/		28	
7228.6000	-其他条、杆〔999〕	3		20	13/	0	千克	/		28	
	-角材、型材及异型材：										
7228.7010	---履带板型钢〔999〕	6		17	13/	0	千克	/			
7228.7090	---其他〔999〕	5		17	13/	0	千克	/		30	
7228.8000	-空心钻钢〔999〕	7		35	13/	0	千克	/			
72.29	**其他合金钢丝：**										
7229.2000	-硅锰钢丝〔999〕	7		20	13/	0	千克	/		32	
	-其他：										
7229.9010	---高速钢丝〔999〕	3		20	13/	0	千克	/			
7229.9090	---其他〔999〕	7		20	13/	0	千克	/		32	

协定税率 %								RCEP		特惠税率 %			Article Description
东/冰/格	巴基斯坦	韩国	瑞士上/下	哥/秘/柬	澳/毛	新西/坡/智	中国港/澳/台	东盟及马来/澳/韩	日/新	亚太2国	老/柬/缅	98/97/95	
													--Not further worked than hot-rolled:
0/0/0	0	0.6	0/0	0/0/0	0/0	0//0	0/0/	0/0/2.7	2.7/0			0/0/0	---Tool steel
													---Other:
0/0/0	0	0.6	0/0	0/0/0	0/0	0//0	0/0/	0/0/2.7	2.7/0			0/0/0	----Of boron containing alloy steel
													----Other
0/0/0	0	0.6	0/0	0/0/0	0/0	0//0	0/0/	0/0/2.7	2.7/0			0/0/0	Amorphous alloy strip, with a width less than 600 mm (in hot rolled without further processing)
0/0/0	0	0.6	0/0	0/0/0	0/0	0//0	0/0/	0/0/2.7	2.7/0			0/0/0	Other alloy steel plates , with a width of 600 mm (other than hot rolling without further processing)
0/0/0	0	1.4	0/0	0/0/0	0/0	0//0	0/0/	2.7/2.7/2.7	2.8/2.7			0/0/0	--Not further worked than cold-rolled (cold-reduced)
													--Other:
0/0/0	2	1.4	0/0	0/0/0	0/0	0//0	0/0/	0/0/6.3	6.4/0			0/0/0	---Electrolytically plated or coated with zinc
0/0/0	2	1.4	0/0	0/0/0	0/0	0//0	0/0/	0/0/6.3	6.4/0			0/0/0	---Otherwise plated or coated with zinc
													---Other
0/0/0	2	1.4	0/0	0/0/0	0/0	0//0	0/0/	6.3/6.3/6.3	6.4/6.3			0/0/0	Other flat-rolled products of other alloy steel, Fe-Ni alloys strip, width<600mm (production of the frame for electronic integrated circuits)
0/0/0	2	1.4	0/0	0/0/0	0/0	0//0	0/0/	6.3/6.3/6.3	6.4/6.3			0/0/0	Other flat-rolled products of other alloy steel, width<600mm
													Bars and rods, hot-rolled, in irregularly wound coils, of other alloy steel:
0/0/0	0	0	0/0	0/0/0	0/0	0//0	0/0/	0/0/0	0/0			0/0/0	-Of high speed steel
0/0/0	0	2.8	0/0	0/0/0	0/0	0//0	0/0/	5.4/5.4/5.4	5.6/5.4			0/0/0	-Of silico-manganese steel
													-Other:
0/0/0	0	0	0/0	0/0/0	0/0	0//0	0/0/	0/2.7/0	0/2.7			0/0/0	---Of boron containing alloy steel
0/0/0	0	0	0/0	0/0/0	0/0	0//0	0/0/	0/2.7/0	0/2.7			0/0/0	---Other
													Other bars and rods of other alloy steel; angles, shapes and sections, of other alloy steel; hollow drill bars and rods, of alloy or non-alloy steel:
0/0/0	0	0.6	0/0	0/0/0	0/0	0//0	0/0/	0/0/2.7	2.7/0			0/0/0	-Bars and rods, of high speed steel
0/0/0	0	1.2	0/0	0/0/0	0/0	0//0	0/0/	0/0/5.4	5.5/0			0/0/0	-Bars and rods, of silico-manganese steel
													-Other bars and rods, not further worked than hot-crolled, hot-drawn or extruded:
0/0/0	0	0.6	0/0	0/0/0	0/0	0//0	0/0/	2.9/2.9/	/2.9			0/0/0	---Of boron containing alloy steel
0/0/0	0	0.6	0/0	0/0/0	0/0	0//0	0/0/	2.9/2.9/2.9	2.9/2.9			0/0/0	---Other
0/0/0	0	0.6	0/0	0/0/0	0/0	0//0	0/0/	2.7/2.7/2.7	2.8/2.7			0/0/0	-Other bars and rods, not further worked than forged
0/0/0	0	0.6	0/0	0/0/0	0/0	0//0	0/0/	2.7/2.7/2.7	2.7/2.7			0/0/0	-Other bars and rods, not further worked than cold-formed of cold-finished
0/0/0	0	0.6	0/0	0/0/0	0/0	0//0	0/0/	0/0/2.7	2.7/0			0/0/0	-Other bars and rods
													-Angles, shapes and sections:
0/0/0	0	0	0/0	0/0/0	0/0	0//0	0/0/	0/0/0	0/0			0/0/0	---Shapes of crawler tread
0/0/0	0	1.2	0/0	0/0/0	0/0	0//0	0/0/	5.4/5.4/5.4	5.6/5.4			0/0/0	---Other
0/0/0	2	0	0/0	0/0/0	0/0	0//0	0/0/	0/0/0	6.4/0			0/0/0	-Hollow drill bars and rods
													Wire of other alloy steel:
0/0/0	2	3.2	0/0	0/0/0	0/0	0//0	0/0/	6.3/6.3/6.3	6.6/6.3			0/0/0	-Of silico-manganese steel
													-Other:
0/0/0	0	0.6	0/0	0/0/0	0/0	0//0	0/0/	0/0/2.7	2.7/0			0/0/0	---Of high speed steel
0/0/0	2		0/0	0/0/0	0/0	0//0	0/0/	6.7/6.7/	/6.7			0/0/0	---Other

第七十三章
钢 铁 制 品

注释：

一、本章所称“铸铁”，适用于经铸造而得的产品，按重量计其铁元素含量超过其他元素单项含量并与第七十二章注释一(四)所述的钢的化学成分不同。

二、本章所称“丝”，是指热或冷成形的任何截面形状的产品，但其截面尺寸均不超过16毫米。

税则号列	货品名称〔CIQ扩展编码及品名－T2表示见附表2〕	最惠(%)	暂定税率	普通	增值/消费	出口退税	计量单位	监管条件/特殊证件	检验检疫	对美关税	亚太上/下
73.01	**钢铁板桩，不论是否钻孔、打眼或组装；焊接的钢铁角材、型材及异型材：**										
7301.1000	-钢铁板桩〔999〕	7		20	13/	0	千克	/		32	6.3/6.3
7301.2000	-角材、型材及异型材〔999〕	7		30	13/	0	千克	/		32	
73.02	**铁道及电车道铺轨用钢铁材料(钢轨、护轨、齿轨、道岔尖轨、辙叉、尖轨拉杆及其他岔道段体、轨枕、鱼尾板、轨座、轨座楔、钢轨垫板、钢轨夹、底板、固定板及其他专门用于连接或加固路轨的材料)：**										
7302.1000	-钢轨〔999〕	6		14	13/	0	千克	/		31	
7302.3000	-道岔尖轨、辙叉、尖轨拉杆及其他岔道段体〔999〕	8		17	13/	0	千克	/			
7302.4000	-鱼尾板及钢轨垫板〔999〕	7		17	13/	0	千克	/			
	-其他：										
7302.9010	---轨枕〔999〕	6		14	13/	0	千克	/			5.1/5.1
7302.9090	---其他〔999〕	7		17	13/	0	千克	/		32	6/6
73.03	**铸铁管及空心异型材：**										
7303.0010	---内径在500毫米及以上的圆形截面管〔101〕	4		40	13/	0	千克	/			
7303.0090	---其他〔101〕	4		40	13/	0	千克	/		29	
73.04	**无缝钢铁管及空心异型材(铸铁的除外)：**										
	-石油或天然气管道管：										
	--不锈钢制：										
7304.1110	---外径大于等于215.9毫米，但不超过406.4毫米〔101无缝钢管压力管道，102无缝钢管〕	5		17	13/	0	千克	A/	M	30/20	
7304.1120	---外径超过114.3毫米，但小于215.9毫米〔101无缝钢管压力管道，102无缝钢管〕	5		17	13/	0	千克	A/	M	30/20	
7304.1130	---外径不超过114.3毫米〔101无缝钢管压力管道，102无缝钢管〕	5		17	13/	0	千克	A/	M	30/20	
7304.1190	---其他〔101无缝钢管压力管道，102无缝钢管〕	5		17	13/	0	千克	A/	M	30/20	
	--其他：										
7304.1910	---外径大于等于215.9毫米，但不超过406.4毫米〔101无缝钢管压力管道，102无缝钢管〕	5		17	13/	0	千克	A/	M	45/20	
7304.1920	---外径超过114.3毫米，但小于215.9毫米〔101无缝钢管压力管道，102无缝钢管〕	5		17	13/	0	千克	A/	M	20/20	
7304.1930	---外径不超过114.3毫米〔101无缝钢管压力管道，102无缝钢管〕	5		17	13/	0	千克	A/	M	45/20	
7304.1990	---其他〔101无缝钢管压力管道，102无缝钢管〕	5		17	13/	0	千克	A/	M	45/20	
	-钻探石油及天然气用的套管、导管及钻管：										
	--不锈钢钻管：										
7304.2210	---外径不超过168.3毫米〔101无缝钢管压力管道，102无缝钢管〕	4		17	13/	0	千克	A/	M	19/19	
7304.2290	---其他〔101无缝钢管压力管道，102无缝钢管〕	4		17	13/	0	千克	A/	M	19/19	
	--其他钻管：										
7304.2310	---外径不超过168.3毫米〔101无缝钢管压力管道，102无缝钢管〕	4		17	13/	0	千克	A/	M	29/19	
7304.2390	---其他〔101无缝钢管压力管道，102无缝钢管〕	4		17	13/	0	千克	A/	M	19/19	
7304.2400	--其他不锈钢管〔101无缝钢管压力管道，102无缝钢管〕	4		17	13/	0	千克	A/	M	44/19	2/2
	--其他：										
7304.2910	---屈服强度小于552兆帕的〔101无缝钢管压力管道，102无缝钢管〕	4		17	13/	0	千克	A/	M	44/19	2/2
7304.2920	---屈服强度大于等于552兆帕，但小于758兆帕的〔101无缝钢管压力管道，102无缝钢管〕	4		17	13/	0	千克	A/	M	19/19	2/2
7304.2930	---屈服强度大于等于758兆帕的〔101无缝钢管压力管道，102无缝钢管〕	4		17	13/	0	千克	A/	M	19/19	2/2
	-铁或非合金钢的其他圆形截面管：										
	--冷拔或冷轧的：										
7304.3110	---锅炉管〔101无缝钢管压力管道，102无缝钢管〕	4		17	13/	0	千克	A/	M	44/19	
7304.3120	---地质钻管、套管〔101无缝钢管压力管道，102无缝钢管〕	8		17	13/	0	千克	A/	M	23/23	

Chapter 73
Articles of iron or steel

Notes:

1. In this Chapter the expression "cast iron" applies to products obtained by casting in which iron predominates by weight over each of the other elements and which do not comply with the chemical composition of steel as defined in Note 1 (d) to Chapter 72.
2. In this Chapter the word "wire" means hot or cold-formed products of any cross-sectional shape, of which no cross-sectional dimension exceeds 16mm.

协定税率 %								RCEP		特惠税率 %			Article Description
东/冰/格	巴基斯坦	韩国	瑞士上/下	哥/秘/柬	澳/毛	新西/坡/智	中国港/澳/台	东盟及马来/澳/韩	日/新	亚太2国	老/柬/缅	98/97/95	
													Sheet piling of iron or steel, whether or not drilled, punched or made from assembled elements; welded angles, shapes and sections, of iron or steel:
0/0/0	2	1.4	0/0	0/0/0	0/0	0//0	0/0/	6.3/6.3/6.3	6.4/6.3			0/0/0	-Sheet piling
0/0/0	2	1.4	0/0	0/0/0	0/0	0//0	0/0/	6.3/6.3/6.3	6.4/6.3			0/0/0	-Angles, shapes and sections
													Railway or tramway track construction material of iron or steel, the following: rails, check-rails and rack rails, switch blades, crossing frogs, point rods and other crossing pieces, sleepers (cross-ties), fish-plates, chairs, chair wedges, sole plates (base plates), rail clips, bedplates, ties and other material specialized for jointing or fixing rails:
0/0/0	0	1.2	0/0	0/0/0	0/0	0//0	0/0/	0/0/5.4	5.5/0			0/0/0	-Rails
0/0/0	2	0	0/0	0/0/0	0/0	0//0	0/0/	0/0/0	7.3/0			0/0/0	-Switch blades, crossing frogs, point rods and other crossing pieces
0/0/0	2	1.4	0/0	0/0/0	0/0	0//0	0/0/	0/0/6.3	6.4/0			0/0/0	-Fish-plates and sole plates
													-Other:
0/0/0	0	0	0/0	0/0/0	0/0	0//0	0/0/	0/0/0	0/0			0/0/0	---Sleepers(cross-ties)
0/0/0	2	0	0.7/0.7	0/0/0	0/0	0//0	0/0/	0/0/0	6.4/0			0/0/0	---Other
													Tubes, pipes and hollow profiles, of cast iron:
0/0/0	0	0	0/0	0/0/0	0/0	0//0	0/0/	0/0/0	0/0			0/0/0	---Tubes and pipes of circular cross-section, of the internal diameter of 500mm or more
0/0/0	0	0	0/0	0/0/0	0/0	0//0	0/0/	0/0/0	0/0			0/0/0	---Other
													Tubes, pipes and hollow profiles, seamless, of iron (other than cast iron) or steel:
													-Line pipe of a kind used for oil or gas pipelines:
													--Of stainless steel:
0/0/0	0	1	0/0	0/0/0	0/0	0//0	0/0/	0/0/4.5	4.5/0			0/0/0	---Having an outside diameter of 215.9mm or more but not exceeding 406.4mm
0/0/0	0	1	0/0	0/0/0	0/0	0//0	0/0/	0/0/4.5	4.5/0			0/0/0	---Having an outside diameter exceeding 114.3mm but less than 215.9mm
0/0/0	0	1	0/0	0/0/0	0/0	0//0	0/0/	0/0/4.5	4.5/0			0/0/0	---Having an outside diameter≤114.3mm
0/0/0	0	0	0/0	0/0/0	0/0	0//0	0/0/	0/0/0	0/0			0/0/0	---Other
													--Other:
0/0/0	0	1	0/0	0/0/0	0/0	0//0	0/0/	0/0/4.5	4.5/0			0/0/0	---Having an outside diameter of 215.9mm or more but not exceeding 406.4mm
0/0/0	0	1	0/0	0/0/0	0/0	0//0	0/0/	0/0/4.5	4.5/0			0/0/0	---Having an outside diameter exceeding 114.3mm but less than 215.9mm
0/0/0	0	1	0/0	0/0/0	0/0	0//0	0/0/	0/0/4.5	4.5/0			0/0/0	---Having an outside diameter not exceeding 114.3mm
0/0/0	0	0	0/0	0/0/0	0/0	0//0	0/0/	0/0/0	0/0			0/0/0	---Other
													-Casing, tubing and drill pipe, of a kind used in drilling for oil or gas:
													--Drill pipe, of stainless steel:
0/0/0	0	0	0/0	0/0/0	0/0	0//0	0/0/	0/0/0	0/0			0/0/0	---Having an outside diameter≤168.3mm
0/0/0	0	0	0/0	0/0/0	0/0	0//0	0/0/	0/0/0	0/0			0/0/0	---Other
													--Other drill pipe:
0/0/0	0	0	0/0	0/0/0	0/0	0//0	0/0/	0/0/0	0/0			0/0/0	---Having an outside diameter ≤168.3mm
0/0/0	0	0	0/0	0/0/0	0/0	0//0	0/0/	0/0/0	0/0			0/0/0	---Other
0/0/0	0	0	0/0	0/0/0	0/0	0//0	0/0/	0/0/0	3.8/0			0/0/0	--Other pipe, of stainless steel
													--Other:
0/0/0	0	0	0/0	0/0/0	0/0	0//0	0/0/	0/3.6/0	0/3.6			0/0/0	---Having an yield strength<552MPa
0/0/0	0	0	0/0	0/0/0	0/0	0//0	0/0/	0/3.6/0	0/3.6			0/0/0	---552MPa≤Having an yield strength<758MPa
0/0/0	0	0	0/0	0/0/0	0/0	0//0	0/0/	0/3.6/0	0/3.6			0/0/0	---Having an yield strength>758MPa
													-Other, of circular cross-section, of iron or non-alloy steel:
													--Cold-drawn or cold-rolled (cold-reduced):
0/0/0	0	0	0/0	0/0/0	0/0	0//0	0/0/	0/0/0	0/0			0/0/0	---Boiler tubes and pipes
0/0/0	2	0	0/0	0/0/0	0/0	0//0	0/0/	0/0/0	7.3/0			0/0/0	---Geological casing and drill pipes

税则号列	货品名称〔CIQ 扩展编码及品名—T2 表示见附表 2〕	最惠(%)	暂定税率	普通	增值/消费	出口退税	计量单位	监管条件/特殊证件	检验检疫	对美关税	亚太上/下
7304.3190	---其他〔101 无缝钢管压力管道,102 无缝钢管〕	4		17	13/	0	千克	A/	M	29/19	
	--其他:										
7304.3910	---锅炉管〔101 无缝钢管压力管道,102 无缝钢管〕	4		17	13/	0	千克	A/	M	44/19	
7304.3920	---地质钻管、套管〔101 无缝钢管压力管道,102 无缝钢管〕	5		17	13/	0	千克	A/	M	20/20	
7304.3990	---其他〔101 无缝钢管压力管道,102 无缝钢管〕	4		17	13/	0	千克	A/	M	29/19	
	-不锈钢的其他圆形截面管:										
	--冷拔或冷轧的:										
7304.4110	---锅炉管〔101 无缝钢管压力管道,102 无缝钢管〕	8		17	13/	0	千克	A/	M	48/23	
7304.4190	---其他〔101 无缝钢管压力管道,102 无缝钢管〕	8		40	13/	0	千克	A/	M	43/23	
	--其他:										
7304.4910	---锅炉管〔101 无缝钢管压力管道,102 无缝钢管〕	8		17	13/	0	千克	A/	M	43/23	
7304.4990	---其他〔101 无缝钢管压力管道,102 无缝钢管〕	8		40	13/	0	千克	A/	M	48/23	
	-其他合金钢的其他圆形截面管:										
	--冷拔或冷轧的:										
7304.5110	---锅炉管										
7304.5110 01	高温承压用合金钢无缝钢管(抗拉强度≥620MPa、屈服强度≥440MPa)(外径在 127mm 以上(含 127mm),化学成分(wt%)中碳(C)的含量≥0.07 且≤0.13、铬(Cr)的含量≥8.5 且≤9.5、钼(Mo)的含量≥0.3 且≤0.6、钨(W)的含量≥1.5 且≤2.0、抗拉强度≥620Mpa、屈服强度≥440Mpa)〔101 无缝钢管压力管道,102 无缝钢管〕	4		17	13/	0	千克	A/	M	19/19	
7304.5110 90	冷轧的其他合金钢无缝锅炉管(冷拔或冷轧的,包括内螺纹)〔101 无缝钢管压力管道,102 无缝钢管〕	4		17	13/	0	千克	A/	M	19/19	
7304.5120	---地质钻管、套管〔101 无缝钢管压力管道,102 无缝钢管〕	4		17	13/	0	千克	A/	M	19/19	
7304.5190	---其他										
7304.5190 01	高温承压用合金钢无缝钢管(抗拉强度≥620MPa、屈服强度≥440MPa)(外径在 127mm 以上(含 127mm),化学成分(wt%)中碳(C)的含量≥0.07 且≤0.13、铬(Cr)的含量≥8.5 且≤9.5、钼(Mo)的含量≥0.3 且≤0.6、钨(W)的含量≥1.5 且≤2.0、抗拉强度≥620Mpa、屈服强度≥440Mpa)〔101 无缝钢管压力管道,102 无缝钢管〕	4		17	13/	0	千克	A/	M	44/19	
7304.5190 90	冷轧的其他合金钢制其他无缝管(冷拔或冷轧的)〔101 无缝钢管压力管道,102 无缝钢管〕	4		17	13/	0	千克	A/	M	44/19	
	--其他:										
7304.5910	---锅炉管										
7304.5910 01	高温承压用合金钢无缝钢管(抗拉强度≥620MPa、屈服强度≥440MPa)(外径在 127mm 以上(含 127mm),化学成分(wt%)中碳(C)的含量≥0.07 且≤0.13、铬(Cr)的含量≥8.5 且≤9.5、钼(Mo)的含量≥0.3 且≤0.6、钨(W)的含量≥1.5 且≤2.0、抗拉强度≥620Mpa、屈服强度≥440Mpa)〔101 无缝钢管压力管道,102 无缝钢管〕	4		17	13/	0	千克	A/	M	29/19	
7304.5910 90	非冷轧其他合金钢无缝锅炉管(非冷拔或冷轧的)〔101 无缝钢管压力管道,102 无缝钢管〕	4		17	13/	0	千克	A/	M	29/19	
7304.5920	---地质钻管、套管〔101 无缝钢管压力管道,102 无缝钢管〕	4		17	13/	0	千克	A/	M	19/19	
7304.5990	---其他										
7304.5990 01	高温承压用合金钢无缝钢管(抗拉强度≥620MPa、屈服强度≥440MPa)(外径在 127mm 以上(含 127mm),化学成分(wt%)中碳(C)的含量≥0.07 且≤0.13、铬(Cr)的含量≥8.5 且≤9.5、钼(Mo)的含量≥0.3 且≤0.6、钨(W)的含量≥1.5 且≤2.0、抗拉强度≥620Mpa、屈服强度≥440Mpa)〔101 无缝钢管压力管道,102 无缝钢管〕	4		17	13/	0	千克	A/	M	44/19	
7304.5990 90	非冷轧其他合金钢制无缝圆形截面管(非冷拔或冷轧的)〔101 无缝钢管压力管道,102 无缝钢管〕	4		17	13/	0	千克	A/	M	44/19	
7304.9000	-其他〔101 无缝钢管压力管道,102 无缝钢管〕	4		17	13/	0	千克	A/	M	39/19	
73.05	**其他圆形截面钢铁管(例如,焊、铆及用类似方法接合的管),外径超过 406.4 毫米:**										
	-石油或天然气管道管:										
7305.1100	--纵向埋弧焊接的〔101 焊接钢管压力管道,102 焊接钢管〕	7		17	13/	0	千克	A/	M	32	
7305.1200	--其他纵向焊接的〔101 焊接钢管压力管道,102 焊接钢管〕	3		17	13/	0	千克	A/	M		
7305.1900	--其他〔101 焊接钢管压力管道,102 焊接钢管〕	7		17	13/	0	千克	A/	M		
7305.2000	-钻探石油或天然气用套管〔101 焊接钢管压力管道,102 焊接钢管〕	7		17	13/	0	千克	A/	M		
	-其他焊接的:										
7305.3100	--纵向焊接的〔101 焊接钢管压力管道,102 焊接钢管〕	6		30	13/	0	千克	A/	M	31	
7305.3900	--其他〔101 焊接钢管压力管道,102 焊接钢管〕	6		30	13/	0	千克	A/	M	26	
7305.9000	-其他〔101 焊接钢管压力管道,102 焊接钢管〕	6		30	13/	0	千克	A/	M		
73.06	**其他钢铁管及空心异型材(例如,辊缝、焊、铆及类似方法接合的):**										
	-石油及天然气管道管:										
7306.1100	--不锈钢焊缝管〔101 焊接钢管压力管道,102 焊接钢管〕	7		17	13/	0	千克	A/	M		
7306.1900	--其他〔101 焊接钢管压力管道,102 焊接钢管〕	7		17	13/	0	千克	A/	M	32	
	-钻探石油或天然气用的套管及导管:										

协定税率 %								RCEP		特惠税率 %			Article Description
东/冰/格	巴基斯坦	韩国	瑞士上/下	哥/秘/柬	澳/毛	新西/坡/智	中国港/澳/台	东盟及马来/澳/韩	日/新	亚太2国	老/柬/缅	98/97/95	
0/0/0	0	0	0/0	0/0/0	0/0	0//0	0/0/	0/0/0	3.8/0			0/0/0	---Other
													--Other:
0/0/0	0	0	0/0	0/0/0	0/0	0//0	0/0/	0/0/0	0/0			0/0/0	---Boiler tubes and pipes
0/0/0	0	0	0/0	0/0/0	0/0	0//0	0/0/	0/0/0	0/0			0/0/0	---Geological casing and drill pipes
0/0/0	0	0.8	0/0	0/0/0	0/0	0//0	0/0/	0/0/3.6	3.6/0			0/0/0	---Other
													-Other, of circular cross-section, of stainless steel:
													--Cold-drawn or cold-rolled (cold-reduced):
0/0/0	2	2	0/0	0/0/0	0/0	0/0/0	0/0/	9.5/9.5/9.5	9.5/9.5			0/0/0	---Boiler tubes and pipes
0/0/0	2	6	0/0	0/0/0	0/0	0/0/0	0/0/	9.5/9.5/	/9.5			0/0/0	---Other
													--Other:
0/0/0	2	2	0/0	0/0/0	0/0	0/0/0	0/0/	0/0/9	9.1/0			0/0/0	---Boiler tubes and pipes
0/0/0	2	2	0/0	0/0/0	0/0	0/0/0	0/0/	9/9/9	9.1/9			0/0/0	---Other
													-Other, of circular cross-section, of other alloy steel:
													--Cold-drawn or cold-rolled (cold-reduced):
													---Boiler tubes and pipes
0/0/0	0	0	0/0	0/0/0	0/0	0//0	0/0/	0/0/0	0/0			0/0/0	Alloy steel seamless steel tubes for pressure and high temperature (tensile strength, yield strength ≥ 620MPa ≥ 440MPa ≥ 127mm) (boiler tube, the chemical composition (wt%) 0.07 ≤ C ≤ 0.13, 8.5 ≤ Cr ≤ 9.5, 0.3 ≤ Mo ≤ 0.6, 1.5 ≤ W ≤ 2, cold drawn or cold rolled, whether or not after further processing, including the internal thread)
0/0/0	0	0	0/0	0/0/0	0/0	0//0	0/0/	0/0/0	0/0			0/0/0	Other alloy steel seamless boiler tubes (cold cold drawn or cold rolled, including internal thread)
0/0/0	0	0	0/0	0/0/0	0/0	0//0	0/0/	0/0/0	0/0			0/0/0	---Geological casing and drill pipes
													---Other
0/0/0	0	0	0/0	0/0/0	0/0	0//0	0/0/	0/0/0	0/0			0/0/0	Alloy steel seamless steel tubes for pressure and high temperature (≥ 620MPa, tensile strength, yield strength ≥ 440MPa) (chemical composition diameter ≥ 127mm, (wt%) 0.07 ≤ C ≤ 0.13, 8.5 ≤ Cr ≤ 9.5, 0.3 ≤ Mo ≤ 0.6, 1.5 ≤ W ≤ 2, cold drawn or cold rolled, whether or not after further processing)
0/0/0	0	0	0/0	0/0/0	0/0	0//0	0/0/	0/0/0	0/0			0/0/0	Other alloy steel cold rolling for other seamless tubes (cold drawn or cold-rolled)
													--Other:
													---Boiler tubes and pipes
0/0/0	0	0	0/0	0/0/0	0/0	0//0	0/0/	0/3.6/0	0/3.6			0/0/0	Alloy steel seamless steel tubes for pressure and high temperature (tensile strength, yield strength ≥ 620MPa ≥ 440MPa ≥ 127mm) (boiler tube, the chemical composition (wt%) 0.07 ≤ C ≤ 0.13, 8.5 ≤ Cr ≤ 9.5, 0.3 ≤ Mo ≤ 0.6, 1.5 ≤ W ≤ 2, non cold drawn or cold rolled, whether or not the further engineering)
0/0/0	0	0	0/0	0/0/0	0/0	0//0	0/0/	0/3.6/0	0/3.6			0/0/0	Other non rolled alloy steel seamless boiler tubes (non cold drawn or cold)
0/0/0	0	0	0/0	0/0/0	0/0	0//0	0/0/	0/0/0	0/0			0/0/0	---Geological casing and drill pipes
													---Other
0/0/0	0	0	0/0	0/0/0	0/0	0//0	0/0/	0/3.6/0	0/3.6			0/0/0	Alloy steel seamless steel tubes for pressure and high temperature (≥ 620MPa, tensile strength, yield strength ≥ 440MPa) (chemical composition diameter ≥ 127mm, (wt%) 0.07 ≤ C ≤ 0.13, 8.5 ≤ Cr ≤ 9.5, 0.3 ≤ Mo ≤ 0.6, 1.5 ≤ W ≤ 2, non cold drawn or cold-rolled, whether or not after further processing)
0/0/0	0	0	0/0	0/0/0	0/0	0//0	0/0/	0/3.6/0	0/3.6			0/0/0	Other non rolled alloy steel seamless pipe (non circular cross section of cold drawn or cold rolled)
0/0/0	0	0	0/0	0/0/0	0/0	0//0	0/0/	0/0/0	0/0			0/0/0	-Other
													Other tubes and pipes (for example, welded, riveted or similarly closed), having circular cross-sections, the external diameter of which exceeds 406.4mm, of iron or steel:
													-Line pipe of a kind used for oil or gas pipelines:
0/0/0	2	3.2	0/0	0/0/0	0/0	0//0	0/0/	6.3/6.3/6.3	6.6/6.3			0/0/0	--Longitudinally submerged arc welded
0/0/0	0	0	0/0	0/0/0	0/0	0//0	0/0/	0/0/0	0/0			0/0/0	--Other, longitudinally welded
0/0/0	2	0	0/0	0/0/0	0/0	0//0	0/0/	0/0/0	6.4/0			0/0/0	--Other
0/0/0	2	0	0/0	0/0/0	0/0	0//0	0/0/	0/0/0	6.4/0			0/0/0	-Casing of a kind used in drilling for oil or gas
													-Other, welded:
0/0/0	0	2.8	0/0	0/0/0	0/0	0//0	0/0/	5.4/5.4/5.4	5.6/5.4			0/0/0	--Longitudinally welded
0/0/0	0	2.8	0/0	0/0/0	0/0	0//0	0/0/	5.4/5.4/5.4	5.6/5.4			0/0/0	--Other
0/0/0	0	0	0/0	0/0/0	0/0	0//0	0/0/	0/0/0	0/0			0/0/0	-Other
													Other tubes, pipes and hollow profiles (for example, open seam or welded, riveted or similarly closed), of iron or steel:
													-Line pipe of a kind used for oil or gas pipelines:
0/0/0	2	1.4	0/0	0/0/0	0/0	0//0	0/0/	0/0/6.3	6.4/0			0/0/0	--Welded, of stainless steel
0/0/0	2	3.2	0/0	0/0/0	0/0	0//0	0/0/	6.3/6.3/6.3	6.6/6.3			0/0/0	--other
													-Casing and tubing of a kind used in drilling for oil or gas:

税则号列	货品名称〔CIQ 扩展编码及品名—T2 表示见附表 2〕	最惠(%)	暂定税率	普通	增值/消费	出口退税	计量单位	监管条件/特殊证件	检验检疫	对美关税	亚太上/下
7306.2100	--不锈钢焊缝管〔101 焊接钢管压力管道,102 焊接钢管〕	3		17	13/	0	千克	A/	M	23	
7306.2900	--其他〔101 无缝钢管压力管道,102 焊接钢管压力管道,103 无缝钢管,104 焊接钢管〕	3		17	13/	0	千克	A/	M	23	
	-铁或非合金钢的其他圆形截面焊缝管:										
	---外径不超过 10 毫米的:										
7306.3011	----壁厚在 0.7 毫米及以下〔101〕	3		30	13/	0	千克	/		28	
7306.3019	----其他〔101〕	3		30	13/	0	千克	/		23	
7306.3090	---其他〔101〕	3		30	13/	0	千克	/		28	
7306.4000	-不锈钢的其他圆形截面焊缝管〔101〕	6		30	13/	0	千克	/		16	
7306.5000	-其他合金钢的圆形截面焊缝管〔101〕	3		30	13/	0	千克	/		28	
	-非圆形截面的其他焊缝管:										
7306.6100	--矩形或正方形截面的〔101 焊接钢管压力管道,102 铸铁管压力管道,103 其它铸铁管压力管道〕	3		30	13/	0	千克	/		23	
7306.6900	--其他非圆形截面的〔101 焊接钢管压力管道,102 铸铁管压力管道〕	3		30	13/	0	千克	/		23	
7306.9000	-其他										
7306.9000 10	多壁式管道(直接与化学品接触表面由特殊耐腐蚀材料制成)〔101 无缝钢管压力管道,102 焊接钢管压力管道,103 铸铁管压力管道,104 无缝钢管,105 焊接钢管,106 铸铁管,107 其他钢铁及制品〕	6		30	13/	0	千克/个	3A/	M	26	
7306.9000 90	未列名其他钢铁管及空心异型材〔101 无缝钢管压力管道,102 焊接钢管压力管道,103 铸铁管压力管道,104 无缝钢管,105 焊接钢管,106 铸铁管,107 其他钢铁及制品〕	6		30	13/	0	千克/个	A/	M	26	
73.07	**钢铁管子附件(例如,接头、肘管、管套):**										
	-铸件:										
7307.1100	--无可锻性铸铁制〔101 其它金属制法兰及管件压力管件,102 其它金属制法兰及管件〕	5		20	13/	0	千克	/		15	
7307.1900	--其他〔101 其它金属制法兰及管件压力管件,102 其它金属制法兰及管件,103 其他金属及制品〕	8		20	13/	0	千克	/		18	
	-其他,不锈钢制:										
7307.2100	--法兰〔999〕	8		20	13/	0	千克	/		18	6.4/6.4
7307.2200	--螺纹肘管、弯管及管套〔101 不锈钢制螺纹管子附件压力管件,102 不锈钢制其它管子附件〕	8		20	13/	0	千克	/		18	
7307.2300	--对焊件〔101 不锈钢制对焊件管子附件压力管件,102 不锈钢制其它管子附件〕	8		20	13/	0	千克	/		18	
7307.2900	--其他〔101 不锈钢制对焊件管子附件压力管件,102 不锈钢制其它管子附件〕	8		20	13/	0	千克	/		18	
	-其他:										
7307.9100	--法兰〔101 其它金属制法兰及管件压力管件,102 其它金属制法兰及管件〕	7		20	13/	0	千克	/		27	
7307.9200	--螺纹肘管、弯管及管套〔101 其它金属制法兰及管件压力管件,102 其它金属制法兰及管件,103 其他金属及制品〕	4		20	13/	0	千克	/		24	
7307.9300	--对焊件〔101 其它金属制法兰及管件压力管件,102 其它金属制法兰及管件〕	7		20	13/	0	千克	/		32	
7307.9900	--其他〔101 其它金属制法兰及管件压力管件,102 其它金属制法兰及管件〕	4		20	13/	0	千克	/		14	
73.08	**钢铁结构体(税目 94.06 的活动房屋除外)及其部件(例如,桥梁及桥梁体段、闸门、塔楼、格构杆、屋顶、屋顶框架、门窗及其框架、门槛、百叶窗、栏杆、支柱及立柱);上述结构体用的已加工钢铁板、杆、角材、型材、异型材、管子及类似品:**										
7308.1000	-桥梁及桥梁体段〔999〕	8		30	13/	13	千克	/			
7308.2000	-塔楼及格构杆〔999〕	8		30	13/	13	千克	/		28	
7308.3000	-门窗及其框架、门槛〔999〕	8		50	13/	13	千克	/		33	
7308.4000	-脚手架、模板或坑道支撑用的支柱及类似设备〔999〕	8		30	13/	13	千克	/		28	
7308.9000	-其他〔999〕	4		30	13/	13	千克	/		29	
73.09	**盛装物料用的钢铁囤、柜、罐、桶及类似容器(装压缩气体或液化气体的除外),容积超过 300 升,不论是否衬里或隔热,但无机械或热力装置:**										
7309.0000	盛装物料用的钢铁囤、柜、罐、桶及类似容器(装压缩气体或液化气体的除外),容积超过 300 升,不论是否衬里或隔热,但无机械或热力装置〔999〕	8		35	13/	13	千克/个	/		28	

协定税率 %								RCEP		特惠税率 %			Article Description
东/冰/格	巴基斯坦	韩国	瑞士上/下	哥/秘/柬	澳/毛	新西/坡/智	中国港/澳/台	东盟及马来/澳/韩	日/新	亚太2国	老/柬/缅	98/97/95	
0/0/0	0	0	0/0	0/0/0	0/0	0/ /0	0/0/	0/0/0	0/0			0/0/0	--Welded of stainless steel
0/0/0	0	0	0/0	0/0/0	0/0	0/ /0	0/0/	0/0/0	0/0			0/0/0	--Welded other
													-Other, welded, of circular cross-section, of iron or non-alloy steel:
													---Having an Outeside diameter not exceedins 10mm:
0/0/0	0	0	0/0	0/0/0	0/0	0/ /0	0/0/	0/2.7/0	0/2.7			0/0/0	----Having a wall thickness of 0. 7mm or less
0/0/0	0	1.4	0/0	0/0/0	0/0	0/ /0	0/0/	2.7/2.7/2.7	2.8/2.7			0/0/0	----Other
0/0/0	0	1.4	0/0	0/0/0	0/0	0/ /0	0/0/	2.7/2.7/2.7	2.8/2.7			0/0/0	---Other
0/0/0	0		0/0	0/0/0	0/0	0/ /0	0/0/	5/5/	/5			0/0/0	-Other, welded, of circular cross-section, of stainless steel
0/0/0	0	1.4	0/0	0/0/0	0/0	0/ /0	0/0/	2.7/2.7/2.7	2.8/2.7			0/0/0	-Other, welded, of circular cross-section, of other alloy steel
													-Other, welded, of non-circular cross-section:
0/0/0	0	0	0/0	0/0/0	0/0	0/ /0	0/0/	0/0/0	0/0			0/0/0	--Of square or rectangular cross-section
0/0/0	0	1.4	0/0	0/0/0	0/0	0/ /0	0/0/	2.7/2.7/2.7	2.8/2.7			0/0/0	--Of other non-circular cross section
													-Other
0/0/0	0		0/0	0/0/0	0/0	0/ /0	0/0/	5/5/	/5			0/0/0	Multiple-wall channel (produced by special erosionproof materials)
0/0/0	0		0/0	0/0/0	0/0	0/ /0	0/0/	5/5/	/5			0/0/0	Other tubes, pipes and hollow profiles, not elsewhere specified or included
													Tube or pipe fittings (for example, couplings, elbows, sleeves), of iron or steel:
													-Cast fittings:
0/0/0	0	0	0/0	0/0/0	0/0	0/ /0	0/0/	0/0/0	0/0			0/0/0	--Of non-malleable cast iron
0/0/0	2	0	0.8/0.8	0/0/0	0/0	0/ /0	0/0/	0/0/0	7.3/0			0/0/0	--Other
													-Other, of stainless steel:
0/0/0	4	0	0/0	0/0/0	0/0	0/ /0	0/0/	0/0/0	7.6/0			0/0/0	--Flanges
0/0/0	2	0	0/0	0/0/0	0/0	0/ /0	0/0/	0/0/0	7.6/0			0/0/0	--Threaded elbows, bends and sleeves
0/0/0	2	0	0/0	0/0/0	0/0	0/ /0	0/0/	0/0/0	7.6/0			0/0/0	--Butt welding fittings
0/0/0	2		0.8/0.8	0/0/0	0/0	0/ /0	0/0/	5/5/	/5			0/0/0	--Other
													-Other:
0/0/0	4	3.2	0/0	0/0/0	0/0	0/ /0	0/0/	6.3/6.3/6.3	6.6/6.3			0/0/0	--Flanges
0/0/0	0	0	0/0	0/0/0	0/0	0/ /0	0/0/	0/3.6/0	0/3.6			0/0/0	--Threaded elbows, bends and sleeves
0/0/0	2	0	0/0	0/0/0	0/0	0/ /0	0/0/	0/0/0	6.4/0			0/0/0	--Butt welding fittings
0/0/0	0	0	0/0	0/0/0	0/0	0/ /0	0/0/	0/0/0	0/0			0/0/0	--Other
													Structures (excluding prefabricated buildings of heading No. 94.06) and parts of structures (for example, bridges and bridge-sections, lockgates, towers, lattice masts, roofs, roofing frameworks, doors and windows and their frames and thresholds for doors, shutters, balustrades, pillars and columns), of iron or steel; plates, rods, angles, shapes, sections, tubes and the like, prepared for use in structures, of iron or steel:
0/0/0	0	0	0/0	0/0/0	0/0	0/ /0	0/0/	0/0/0	7.3/0			0/0/0	-Bridges and bridge-sections
0/0/0	0	1.6	0/0	0/0/0	0/0	0/ /0	0/0/	0/0/7.6	7.6/0			0/0/0	-Towers and lattice masts
0/0/0	0	2	0/0	0/0/0	0/0	0/0/0	0/0/	0/0/9	9.1/0			0/0/0	-Doors, windows and their frames and thresholds for doors
0/0/0	0	0	0/0	0/0/0	0/0	0/ /0	0/0/	0/0/0	7.6/0			0/0/0	-Equipment for scaffolding, shuttering, propping or pit-propping
0/0/0	0	0	0/0	0/0/0	0/0	0/ /0	0/0/	0/0/0	0/0			0/0/0	-Other
													Reservoirs, tanks, vats and similar containers for any material (other than compressed or liquefied gas), of iron or steel, of a capacity exceeding 300 L, whether or not lined or heat-insulated, but not fitted with mechanical or thermal equipment:
0/0/0	3.5	2.1	1.1/1.1	0/0/0	0/0	0/0/0	0/0/	9.5/9.5/9.5	9.5/9.5			0/0/0	Reservoirs, tanks, vats and similar containers for any material (other than compressed or liquefied gas), of iron or steel, of a capacity exceeding 300L whether or not lined or heat-insulated, but not fitted with mechanical or thermal equipment

税则号列	货品名称〔CIQ扩展编码及品名—T2表示见附表2〕	最惠(%)	暂定税率	普通	增值/消费	出口退税	计量单位	监管条件/特殊证件	检验检疫	对美关税	亚太上/下
73.10	**盛装物料用的钢铁柜、桶、罐、听、盒及类似容器(装压缩气体或液化气体的除外),容积不超过300升,不论是否衬里或隔热,但无机械或热力装置:**										
7310.1000	-容积在50升及以上										
7310.1000 10	总容积大于100升不超过300升的容器(与所处理或盛放的化学品接触表面由特殊耐腐蚀材料制成)〔999〕	8		40	13/	13	千克/个	3/		33	
7310.1000 90	50L≤容积≤300L的其他钢铁制盛物容器(钢铁柜、桶、罐、听及类似容器)〔999〕	8		40	13/	13	千克/个	/		33	
	-容积在50升以下:										
	--焊边或卷边接合的罐:										
7310.2110	---易拉罐及罐体〔999〕	8		70	13/	13	千克	A/	R	33	
7310.2190	---其他〔999〕	8		70	13/	13	千克	/		18	
	--其他:										
7310.2910	---易拉罐及罐体〔999〕	8		70	13/	13	千克	A/	R	28	
7310.2990	---其他〔999〕	8		70	13/	13	千克	A/	R	18	
73.11	**装压缩气体或液化气体用的钢铁容器:**										
7311.0010	---零售包装用〔999〕	8		70	13/	13	千克	6A/	M	18	
7311.0090	---其他〔999〕	8		17	13/	13	千克	6A/	M	18	
73.12	**非绝缘的钢铁绞股线、绳、缆、编带、吊索及类似品:**										
7312.1000	-绞股线、绳、缆〔101其他深加工金属制品,102钢丝绳,103其他钢铁及制品〕	4		20	13/	13	千克	A/	M	29	
7312.9000	-其他〔101〕	4		20	13/	13	千克	/		14	
73.13	**带刺钢铁丝;围篱用的钢铁绞带或单股扁丝(不论是否带刺)及松绞的双股丝:**										
7313.0000	带刺钢铁丝;围篱用的钢铁绞带或单股扁丝(不论是否带刺)及松绞的双股丝〔101〕	7		70	13/	13	千克	/		17	6.3/6.3
73.14	**钢铁丝制的布(包括环形带)、网、篱、格栅;网眼钢铁板:**										
	-机织品:										
7314.1200	--不锈钢制的机器用环形带〔101〕	8		20	13/	13	千克	/		28	
7314.1400	--不锈钢制的其他机织品〔101〕	8		20	13/	13	千克	/		33	
7314.1900	--其他〔101〕	7		20	13/	13	千克	/		27	
7314.2000	-交点焊接的网、篱及格栅,其丝的最大截面尺寸在3毫米及以上,网眼尺寸在100平方厘米及以上〔101〕	7		70	13/	13	千克	/		27	
	-其他交点焊接的网、篱及格栅:										
7314.3100	--镀或涂锌的〔101〕	7		70	13/	13	千克	/		32	
7314.3900	--其他〔101〕	7		70	13/	13	千克	/		17	
	-其他网、篱及格栅:										
7314.4100	--镀或涂锌的〔101〕	8		20	13/	13	千克	/		18	6/6
7314.4200	--涂塑的〔101〕	8		20	13/	13	千克	/		18	
7314.4900	--其他〔101〕	8		20	13/	13	千克	/		33	
7314.5000	-网眼钢铁板〔101〕	8		70	13/	13	千克	/		33	
73.15	**钢铁链及其零件:**										
	-铰接链及其零件:										
	--滚子链:										
7315.1110	---自行车用〔999〕	8		80	13/	13	千克	/			
7315.1120	---摩托车用〔101其他车辆零部件,102滚子链〕	8		80	13/	13	千克	/			
7315.1190	---其他〔999〕	8		80	13/	13	千克	/		33	
7315.1200	--其他链〔999〕	8		80	13/	13	千克	/		18	
7315.1900	--零件〔999〕	8		80	13/	13	千克	/		28	
7315.2000	-防滑链〔999〕	8		80	13/	13	千克	/		28	
	-其他链:										
7315.8100	--日字环节链〔999〕	8		80	13/	13	千克	/		33	
7315.8200	--其他焊接链〔999〕	8		80	13/	13	千克	/		33	
7315.8900	--其他〔999〕	8		80	13/	13	千克	/		33	
7315.9000	-其他零件〔999〕	8		80	13/	13	千克	/		33	
73.16	**钢铁锚、多爪锚及其零件:**										
7316.0000	钢铁锚、多爪锚及其零件〔999〕	8		40	13/	13	千克	/		28	
73.17	**钢铁制的钉、平头钉、图钉、波纹钉、U形钉(税目83.05的货品除外)及类似品,不论钉头是否用其他材料制成,但不包括铜头钉:**										
7317.0000	钢铁制的钉、平头钉、图钉、波纹钉、U形钉(税目83.05的货品除外)及类似品,不论钉头是否用其他材料制成,但不包括铜头钉〔999〕	8		80	13/	13	千克	/		18	

协定税率 %								RCEP		特惠税率 %			Article Description
东/冰/格	巴基斯坦	韩国	瑞士上/下	哥/秘/柬	澳/毛	新西/坡/智	中国港/澳/台	东盟及马来/澳/韩	日/新	亚太2国	老/柬/缅	98/97/95	
													Tanks, casks, drums, cans, boxes and similar containers, for any material (other than compressed or liquefied gas), of iron or steel, of a capacity not exceeding 300L whether or not lined or heat-insulated, but not fitted with mechanical or thermal equipment:
													-Of a capacity of 50L or more
0/0/0	3.5	6.3	1.1/1.1	0/0/0	0/0	0/0/0	0/0/	10/10/	/10			0/0/0	Containers, 100L＜capacity≤300L (surface in contact with chemicals treated or contained is made of special corrosion-resistant materials)
0/0/0	3.5	6.3	1.1/1.1	0/0/0	0/0	0/0/0	0/0/	10/10/	/10			0/0/0	Tanks, casks, drums, cans, boxes and similar containers, 50L ≤capacity≤300L, of iron or steel
													-Of a capacity of less than 50L:
													--Cans which are to be closed by soldering or crimping:
0/0/0	14	3.5	1.8/1.8	0/0/0	0/0	0/0/0	0/0/	0/0/15.8	15.9/0			0/0/0	---Tear tab ends and bodies
0/0/0	14	3.5	1.8/1.8	0/0/0	0/0	0/0/0	0/0/	0/0/15.8	15.9/0			0/0/0	---Other
													--Other:
0/0/0	14	3.5	4.4/4.4	0/0/0	0/0	0/0/0	0/0/	0/0/15.8	15.9/0			0/0/0	---Tear tab ends and bodies
0/0/0	14	3.5	4.4/4.4	0/0/0	0/0	0/0/0	0/0/	0/0/15.8	15.9/0			0/0/0	---Other
													Containers for compressed or liquefied gas, of iron or steel:
0/0/0	14	3.5	1.8/1.8	0/0/0	0/0	0/0/0	0/0/	0/0/15.8	15.9/0			0/0/0	---For retail packing
0/0/0	2	3.7	0/0	0/0/0	0/0	0//0	0/0/	7.5/7.6/7.5	7.5/7.6			0/0/0	---Other
													Stranded wire, ropes, cables, plaited bands, slings and the like, of iron or steel, not electrically insulated:
0/0/0	0	0	0/0	0/0/0	0/0	0//0	0/0/	0/0/0	0/0			0/0/0	-Stranded wire, ropes and cables
0/0/0	0	0	0/0	0/0/0	0/0	0//0	0/0/	0/3.6/0	0/3.6			0/0/0	-Other
													Barbed wire of iron or steel; twisted hoop or single flat wire, barbed or not, and loosely twisted double wire, of a kind used for fencing, of iron or steel:
0/0/0	2	0	0/0	0/0/0	0/0	0//0	0/0/	0/0/0	6.4/0			0/0/0	Barbed wire of iron or steel; twisted hoop or single flat wire, barbed or not, and loosely twisted double wire, of a kind used for fencing, of iron or steel
													Cloth (including endless bands), grill, netting and fencing, of iron or steel wire; expanded metal of iron or steel:
													-Woven cloth:
0/0/0	4.2	2.4	5/5	0/0/0	0/0	0/0/0	0/0/	0/0/10.8	10.9/0			0/0/0	--Endless bands for machinery, of stainless steel
0/0/0	4.2	2.4	0/0	0/0/0	0/0	0/0/0	0/0/	10.8/10.8/10.8	10.9/10.8			0/0/0	--Other woven cloth, of stainless steel
0/0/0	2.5	0		0/0/0	0/0	0//0	0/0/	0/0/0	6.4/0			0/0/0	--Other
0/0/0	2	0	0/0	0/0/0	0/0	0//0	0/0/	0/0/0	6.4/0			0/0/0	-Grill, netting and fencing, welded at the intersection, of wire with a maximum cross-sectional dimension of 3mm or more and having a mesh size of 100cm^2 or more
													-Other grill, netting and fencing, welded at the intersection:
0/0/0	2	0	0/0	0/0/0	0/0	0//0	0/0/	0/0/0	6.4/0			0/0/0	--Plated or coated with zinc
0/0/0	2	1.4	0/0	0/0/0	0/0	0//0	0/0/	0/0/6.3	6.4/0			0/0/0	--Other
													-Other grill, netting and fencing:
0/0/0	2	0	0/0	0/0/0	0/0	0//0	0/0/	0/0/0	7.3/0			0/0/0	--Plated or coated with zinc
0/0/0	2	1.6	0.8/0.8	0/0/0	0/0	0//0	0/0/	0/0/7.2	7.3/0			0/0/0	--Coated whith plastics
0/0/0	2	0	0.8/0.8	0/0/0	0/0	0//0	0/0/	7.2/7.2/7.2	7.3/7.2			0/0/0	--Other
0/0/0	2	0	0/0	0/0/0	0/0	0//0	0/0/	0/0/0	7.3/0			0/0/0	-Expanded metal
													Chain and parts thereof, of iron or steel:
													-Articulated link chain and parts thereof:
													--Roller chain:
0/0/0	4.8	2.4	1.2/1.2	0/0/0	0/0	0/0/0	0/0/	0/0/10.8	10.9/0			0/0/0	---For bicycles
0/0/0	4.2	5.6	1.2/1.2	0/0/0	0/0	0/0/0	0/0/	11.2/11.4/11.2	11.3/11.4			0/0/0	---For motorcycles
0/0/0	4.2	2.4	1.2/1.2	0/0/0	0/0	0/0/0	0/0/	10.8/10.8/10.8	10.9/10.8			0/0/0	---Other
0/0/0	4.2	7.2	1.2/1.2	0/0/0	0/0	0/0/0	0/0/	11.4/11.4/	11.4/11.4			0/0/0	--Other chain
0/0/0	4.2	2.4	1.2/1.2	0/0/0	0/0	0/0/0	0/0/	10.8/10.8/10.8	10.9/10.8			0/0/0	--Parts
0/0/0	4.2	2.4	1.2/1.2	0/0/0	0/0	0/0/0	0/0/	0/0/10.8	10.9/0			0/0/0	-Skid chain
													-Other chain:
0/0/0	4.2	2.4	1.2/1.2	0/0/0	0/0	0/0/0	0/0/	0/0/10.8	10.9/0			0/0/0	--Stud-link
0/0/0	4.2	2.4	1.2/1.2	0/0/0	0/0	0/0/0	0/0/	0/0/10.8	10.9/0			0/0/0	--Other, welded link
0/0/0	4.2	2.4	1.2/1.2	0/0/0	0/0	0/0/0	0/0/	0/0/10.8	10.9/0			0/0/0	--Other
0/0/0	2	2	0/0	0/0/0	0/0	0//0	0/0/	0/0/9	9.1/0			0/0/0	-Other parts
													Anchors, grapnels and parts thereof, of iron or steel:
0/0/0	2	2	0/0	0/0/0	0/0	0//0	0/0/	0/0/9	9.1/0			0/0/0	Anchors, grapnels and parts thereof, of iron or steel
													Nails, tacks, drawing pins, corrugated nails, staples (other than those of heading No. 83.05) and similar articles, of iron or steel, whether or not with heads of other material, but excluding such articles with heads of copper:
0/0/0	3.5	2	0/0	0/0/0	0/0	0//0	0/0/	0/0/9	9.1/0			0/0/0	Nails, tacks, drawing pins, corrugated nails, staples (other than those of heading No. 83.05) and similar articles, of iron or steel, whether or not with heads of other material, but excluding such articles with heads of copper

税则号列	货品名称〔CIQ扩展编码及品名—T2表示见附表2〕	最惠(%)	暂定税率	普通	增值/消费	出口退税	计量单位	监管条件/特殊证件	检验检疫	对美关税	亚太上/下
73.18	**钢铁制的螺钉、螺栓、螺母、方头螺钉、钩头螺钉、铆钉、销、开尾销、垫圈(包括弹簧垫圈)及类似品:**										
	-螺纹制品:										
7318.1100	--方头螺钉〔999〕	8		80	13/	13	千克	/		18	
7318.1200	--其他木螺钉										
7318.1200 01	非用于民用航空器维护和修理的其他木螺钉(不包括不锈钢紧固件)〔999〕	8		80	13/	13	千克	/		33	
7318.1200 90	其他木螺钉〔999〕	8		80	13/	13	千克	/		33	
7318.1300	--钩头螺钉及环头螺钉〔999〕	8		80	13/	13	千克	/		18	
7318.1400	--自攻螺钉										
7318.1400 01	非用于民用航空器维护和修理的自攻螺钉(不包括不锈钢紧固件)〔999〕	8		80	13/	13	千克	/		28	
7318.1400 90	其他自攻螺钉〔999〕	8		80	13/	13	千克	/		28	
	--其他螺钉及螺栓,不论是否带有螺母或垫圈:										
7318.1510	---抗拉强度≥800兆帕的										
7318.1510 01	抗拉强度≥800兆帕,杆径>6mm的其他螺钉及螺栓(不包括不锈钢紧固件)(不论是否带有螺母或垫圈,非用于民用航空器维护和修理的)〔999〕	8		80	13/	13	千克	/			4/4
7318.1510 90	其他抗拉强度≥800兆帕的螺钉及螺栓(不论是否带有螺母或垫圈)〔999〕	8		80	13/	13	千克	/			4/4
7318.1590	---其他										
7318.1590 01	杆径>6mm的其他螺钉及螺栓(不包括不锈钢紧固件)(不论是否带有螺母或垫圈,非用于民用航空器维护和修理的)〔101螺钉,102螺栓〕	8		80	13/	13	千克	/		28	4/4
7318.1590 90	其他螺钉及螺栓(不论是否带有螺母或垫圈)〔101螺钉,102螺栓〕	8		80	13/	13	千克	/		28	4/4
7318.1600	--螺母〔999〕	8		80	13/	13	千克	/		18	
7318.1900	--其他〔999〕	5		80	13/	13	千克	/		15	
	-无螺纹制品:										
7318.2100	--弹簧垫圈及其他防松垫圈										
7318.2100 01	弹簧垫圈及其他防松垫圈(不包括不锈钢紧固件)(非用于民用航空器维护和修理的)〔999〕	8		80	13/	13	千克	/		28	
7318.2100 90	其他弹簧垫圈及其他防松垫圈〔999〕	8		80	13/	13	千克	/		28	
7318.2200	--其他垫圈										
7318.2200 01	其他垫圈(不包括不锈钢紧固件)(非用于民用航空器维护和修理的)〔999〕	8		80	13/	13	千克	/		18	
7318.2200 90	其他垫圈〔999〕	8		80	13/	13	千克	/		18	
7318.2300	--铆钉〔999〕	8		80	13/	13	千克	/		28	
7318.2400	--销及开尾销〔999〕	8		80	13/	13	千克	/		18	
7318.2900	--其他〔999〕	8		80	13/	13	千克	/		18	
73.19	**钢铁制的手工缝针、编织针、引针、钩针、刺绣穿孔锥及类似制品;其他税目未列名的钢铁制安全别针及其他别针:**										
	-安全别针及其他别针:										
7319.4010	---安全别针〔999〕	7		90	13/	13	千克	/		22	
7319.4090	---其他〔999〕	7		90	13/	13	千克	/		32	
7319.9000	-其他〔999〕	7		80	13/	13	千克	/		22	
73.20	**钢铁制弹簧及弹簧片:**										
	-片簧及簧片:										
7320.1010	---铁道车辆用〔999〕	6		14	13/	13	千克	/		31	
7320.1020	---汽车用〔999〕	8		14	13/	13	千克	/			
7320.1090	---其他〔999〕	8		50	13/	13	千克	/		28	
	-螺旋弹簧:										
7320.2010	---铁道车辆用〔999〕	6		14	13/	13	千克	/		26	
7320.2090	---其他〔999〕	8		50	13/	13	千克	/		18	6.8/6.8
	-其他:										
7320.9010	---铁道车辆用〔999〕	6		14	13/	13	千克	/		31	
7320.9090	---其他〔999〕	8		50	13/	13	千克	/		28	
73.21	**非电热的钢铁制家用炉、灶(包括附有集中供暖用的热水锅的炉)、烤肉架、烤炉、煤气灶、加热板和类似非电热的家用器具及其零件:**										
	-炊事器具及加热板:										
7321.1100	--使用气体燃料或可使用气体燃料及其他燃料的〔999〕	7		80	13/	13	千克/个	6/	L	32	
	--使用液体燃料的:										
7321.1210	---煤油炉〔999〕	7		80	13/	13	千克/个	/			
7321.1290	---其他〔999〕	7		80	13/	13	千克/个	/			
7321.1900	--其他,包括使用固体燃料的〔999〕	7		80	13/	13	千克/个	/		17	
	-其他器具:										

协定税率 %								RCEP		特惠税率 %			
东/冰/格	巴基斯坦	韩国	瑞士上/下	哥/秘/柬	澳/毛	新西/坡/智	中国港/澳/台	东盟及马来/澳/韩	日/新	亚太2国	老/柬/缅	98/97/95	Article Description
													Screws, bolts, nuts, coach screws, screw hooks, rivets, cotters, cotter-pins, washers (including spring washers) and similar articles, of iron of steel:
													-Threaded articles:
0/0/0	2		0/0	0/0/0	0/0	0//0	0/0/	5/5/	/5			0/0/0	--Coach screws
													--Other wood screws
0/0/0	2	2	0/0	0/0/0	0/0	0//0	0/0/	0/0/9	9.1/0			0/0/0	Other wood screws, not used for the maintenance and repair of Civil Aircraft(excluding stainless steel fasteners)
0/0/0	2	2	0/0	0/0/0	0/0	0//0	0/0/	0/0/9	9.1/0			0/0/0	Other screws of wood
0/0/0	2		0/0	0/0/0	0/0	0//0	0/0/	5/5/	/5			0/0/0	--Screw hooks and screw rings
													--Self-tapping screws
0/0/0	2		1/1	0/0/0	0/0	0/0/0	0/0/	9/5/	9.1/5			0/0/0	Self-tapping screws, not used for the maintenance and repair of Civil Aircraft(excluding stainless steel fasteners)
0/0/0	2		1/1	0/0/0	0/0	0/0/0	0/0/	9/5/	9.1/5			0/0/0	Other self-tapping screws
													--Other screws and bolts, whether or not with their nuts or washers:
													---Tensile strength≥800MPa
0/0/0	0	3.7	0.8/0.8	0/0/0	0/0	0//0	0/0/	7.2/7.2/7.2	7.5/7.2			0/0/0	Other screws and bolts, with tensile strength 800MPa or more, stem diameters exceeding 6mm (whether or not with their nuts or washers, not used for the maintenance and repair of Civil Aircraft)(excluding stainless steel fasteners)
0/0/0	0	3.7	0.8/0.8	0/0/0	0/0	0//0	0/0/	7.2/7.2/7.2	7.5/7.2			0/0/0	Other screws and bolts, tensile strength≥800MPa(whether or not with their nuts or washers)
													---Other
0/0/0	0	3.7	0.8/0.8	0/0/0	0/0	0//0	0/0/	7.2/7.2/7.2	7.5/7.2			0/0/0	Other screws and bolts, stem diameter more than 6mm(whether or not with their nuts or washers, not used for the maintenance and repair of Civil Aircraft)(excluding stainless steel fasteners)
0/0/0	0	3.7	0.8/0.8	0/0/0	0/0	0//0	0/0/	7.2/7.2/7.2	7.5/7.2			0/0/0	Other screws and bolts,(whether or not with their nuts or washers)
0/0/0	4		0.8/0.8	0/0/0	0/0	0//0	0/0/	5/5/	/5			0/0/0	--Nuts
0/0/0	0	0	0/0	0/0/0	0/0	0//0	0/0/	0/4.5/0	0/4.5			0/0/0	--Other
													-Non-threaded articles:
													--Spring washers and other lock washers
0/0/0	2		0/0	0/0/0	0/0	0/0/0	0/0/	9/5/	9.1/5			0/0/0	Spring washers and other lock washers (not used for the maintenance and repair of Civil Aircraft) (excluding stainless steel fasteners)
0/0/0	2		0/0	0/0/0	0/0	0/0/0	0/0/	9/5/	9.1/5			0/0/0	Other spring washers and other lock washers
													--Other washers
0/0/0	3.5		0/0	0/0/0	0/0	0/0/0	0/0/	5/5/	/5			0/0/0	Other washers(not used for the maintenance and repair of Civil Aircraft)(excluding stainless steel fasteners)
0/0/0	3.5		0/0	0/0/0	0/0	0/0/0	0/0/	5/5/	/5			0/0/0	Other washers
0/0/0	2		0/0	0/0/0	0/0	0/0/0	0/0/	9/5/	9.1/5			0/0/0	--Rivets
0/0/0	3.5	6	1/1	0/0/0	0/0	0/0/0	0/0/	9.5/9.5/9.5	9.5/9.5			0/0/0	--Cotters and cotter-pins
0/0/0	3.5		0/0	0/0/0	0/0	0/0/0	0/0/	5/5/	/5			0/0/0	--Other
													Sewing needles, knitting needles, bodkins, crochet hooks, embroidery stilettos and similar articles, for use in the hand, of iron or steel; safety pins and other pins of iron or steel, not elsewhere specified or included:
													-Safety pins and other pins:
0/0/0	2	2	0/0	0/0/0	0/0	0//0	0/0/	0/0/9	9.1/0			0/0/0	---Safety pins
0/0/0	2	2	0/0	0/0/0	0/0	0//0	0/0/	0/0/9	9.1/0			0/0/0	---Other
0/0/0	2		1/1	0/0/0	0/0	0//0	0/0/	7/7/	/7			0/0/0	-Other
													Springs and leaves for springs, of iron or steel:
													-Leaf-springs and leaves thereof:
0/0/0	0	0	0/0	0/0/0	0/0	0//0	0/0/	0/0/0	0/0			0/0/0	---For railway locomotives and rollingstock
0/0/0	2	6	0/0	0/0/0	0/0	0//0	0/0/	9.5/9.5/	9.5/9.5			0/0/0	---For motor vehicles
0/0/0	2		1/1	0/0/0	0/0	0/0/0	0/0/	9/5/	9.1/5			0/0/0	---Other
													-Helical springs:
0/0/0	0	0	0/0	0/0/0	0/0	0//0	0/0/	0/0/0	0/0			0/0/0	---For railway locomotives and rollingstock
0/0/0	4	6	1/1	0/0/0	0/0	0/0/0	0/0/	9.5/9.5/9.5	9.5/9.5			0/0/0	---Other
													-Other:
0/0/0	0	0	0/0	0/0/0	0/0	0//0	0/0/	0/0/0	0/0			0/0/0	---For railway locomotives and rollingstock
0/0/0	4.8		1.2/1.2	0/0/0	0/0	0/0/0	0/0/	5/5/	/5			0/0/0	---Other
													Stoves, ranges, grates, cookers (including those with subsidiary boilers for central heating), barbecues, braziers, gas-rings, plate warmers and similar non-electric domestic appliances, and parts thereof, of iron or steel:
													-Cooking appliances and plate warmers:
0/0/0	8.4	3	1.5/1.5	0/0/0	0/0	0/0/0	0/0/	0/0/13.5	13.6/0			0/0/0	--For gas fuel or for both gas and other fuels
													--For liquid fuel:
0/0/0		12.6	2.1/2.1	0/0/0	0/0	0/0/0	0/0/	20/20/20	/20			0/0/0	---Kerosene cooking stoves
0/0/0		12.6	2.1/2.1	0/0/0	0/0	0/0/0	0/0/	20/20/20	/20			0/0/0	---Other
0/0/0		12.6	2.1/2.1	0/0/0	0/0	0/0/0	0/0/	20/20/	/20			0/0/0	--Other including appliances for solid fuel
													-Other appliances:

税则号列	货品名称〔CIQ扩展编码及品名—T2表示见附表2〕	最惠(%)	暂定税率	普通	增值/消费	出口退税	计量单位	监管条件/特殊证件	检验检疫	对美关税	亚太上/下
7321.8100	--使用气体燃料或可使用气体燃料及其他燃料的〔999〕	7		80	13/	13	千克/个	6/		27	4.2/4.2
7321.8200	--使用液体燃料的〔999〕	7		80	13/	13	千克/个	/		17	
7321.8900	--其他，包括使用固体燃料的〔999〕	7		80	13/	13	千克/个	/		32	
7321.9000	-零件〔999〕	8		80	13/	13	千克	/		33	6.4/6.4
73.22	**非电热的钢铁制集中供暖用散热器及其零件；非电热的钢铁制空气加热器、暖气分布器(包括可分布新鲜空气或调节空气的)及其零件，装有电动风扇或鼓风机：**										
	-散热器及其零件：										
7322.1100	--铸铁制〔999〕	8		80	13/	13	千克	/			
7322.1900	--其他〔999〕	8		80	13/	13	千克	/		33	
7322.9000	-其他〔999〕	8		80	13/	13	千克	/		18	
73.23	**餐桌、厨房或其他家用钢铁器具及其零件；钢铁丝绒；钢铁制擦锅器、洗刷擦光用的块垫、手套及类似品：**										
7323.1000	-钢铁丝绒；擦锅器及洗刷擦光用的块垫、手套及类似品〔999〕	7		80	13/	13	千克	A/	R	27	
	-其他：										
7323.9100	--铸铁制，未搪瓷〔101食品接触铸铁产品，102食品用铸铁包装〕	7		80	13/	13	千克	A/	R	27	
7323.9200	--铸铁制，已搪瓷〔101食品接触铸铁产品，102食品用铸铁包装〕	7		100	13/	13	千克	A/	R	32	
7323.9300	--不锈钢制〔101食品接触不锈钢产品，102食品用不锈钢包装〕	7		80	13/	13	千克	A/	R	32	4.9/4.9
	--钢铁(铸铁除外)制，已搪瓷：										
7323.9410	---面盆〔101食品接触搪瓷产品，102食品用搪瓷包装〕	7		100	13/	13	千克	A/	R		
7323.9420	---烧锅〔999〕	7		100	13/	13	千克	A/	R		
7323.9490	---其他〔101食品接触搪瓷产品，102食品用搪瓷包装〕	7		100	13/	13	千克	A/	R	32	
7323.9900	--其他〔101食品接触铁产品，102食品用铁包装〕	7		80	13/	13	千克	A/	R	32	
73.24	**钢铁制卫生器具及其零件：**										
7324.1000	-不锈钢制洗涤槽及脸盆〔999〕	7		80	13/	13	千克	/		27	
	-浴缸：										
7324.2100	--铸铁制，不论是否搪瓷〔999〕	7		100	13/	13	千克	/		32	
7324.2900	--其他〔999〕	7		100	13/	13	千克	/		32	
7324.9000	-其他，包括零件〔999〕	7		100	13/	13	千克	/		17	
73.25	**其他钢铁铸造制品：**										
	-无可锻性铸铁制：										
7325.1010	---工业用〔999〕	7		40	13/	13	千克	/		27	
7325.1090	---其他〔999〕	8		90	13/	13	千克	/		33	
	-其他：										
7325.9100	--研磨机用的研磨球及类似品〔999〕	8		40	13/	13	千克	/			
	--其他：										
7325.9910	---工业用〔999〕	8		40	13/	13	千克	/		18	6.8/6.8
7325.9990	---其他〔999〕	8		90	13/	13	千克	/		33	4.8/4.8
73.26	**其他钢铁制品：**										
	-经锻造或冲压，但未经进一步加工：										
7326.1100	--研磨机用的研磨球及类似品〔999〕	8		40	13/	13	千克	/		18	
	--其他：										
7326.1910	---工业用〔999〕	8		40	13/	13	千克	/		18	
7326.1990	---其他〔999〕	8		90	13/	13	千克	/		28	
	-钢铁丝制品：										
7326.2010	---工业用〔999〕	8		40	13/	13	千克	/		18	4/4
7326.2090	---其他〔999〕	8		90	13/	13	千克	/		28	5.6/5.6
	-其他：										
	---工业用：										
7326.9011	----钢铁纤维及其制品〔999〕	8		40	13/	13	千克	/		18	6.8/6.8
7326.9019	----其他〔999〕	8		40	13/	13	千克	/		33	6.8/6.8
7326.9090	---其他〔999〕	8		90	13/	13	千克	/		33	6.8/6.8

协定税率 %								RCEP		特惠税率 %			Article Description
东/冰/格	巴基斯坦	韩国	瑞士上/下	哥/秘/柬	澳/毛	新西/坡/智	中国港/澳/台	东盟及马来/澳/韩	日/新	亚太2国	老/柬/缅	98/97/95	
0/0/0	8.1	13.8	2.3/2.3	0/0/0	0/13.8	0/0/0	0/0/	21.9/21.9/	/21.9			0/0/0	--For gas fuel or for both gas and other fuels
0/0/0		12.6	2.1/2.1	0/0/0	0/0	0/0/0	0/0/	20/20/20	/20			0/0/0	--For liquid fuel
0/0/0		12.6	2.1/2.1	0/0/0	0/0	0/0/0	0/0/	20/20/20	/20			0/0/0	--Other induding appliances for solid fuel
0/0/0	3.5	2.4	1.2/1.2	0/0/0	0/0	0/0/0	0/0/	0/0/10.8	10.9/0			0/0/0	-Parts
													Radiators for central heating, not electrically heated, and parts thereof, of iron or steel; air heaters and hot air distributors (including distributors which can also distribute fresh or conditioned air), not electrically heated, incorporating a motor-dirven fan or blower, and parts thereof, of iron or steel:
													-Radiators and parts thereof:
0/0/0		12.6	2.1/2.1	0/0/0	0/0	0/0/0	0/0/	20/20/20	/20			0/0/0	--Of cast iron
0/0/0		12.6	2.1/2.1	0/0/0	0/0	0/0/0	0/0/	20/20/	/20			0/0/0	--Other
0/0/0		9.3	2/2	0/0/0	0/0	0/0/0	0/0/	18.7/19/18.7	18.8/19			0/0/0	-Other
													Table, kitchen or other household articles and parts thereof, of iron or steel; iron or steel wool; pot scourers and scouring or polishing pads, gloves and the like, of iron or steel:
0/0/0	7.8	2.8	1.4/1.4	0/0/0	0/0	0/0/0	0/0/	0/0/12.6	12.7/0			0/0/0	-Iron or steel wool; pot scourers and scouring or polishing pads, gloves and the like
													-Other:
0/0/0		9.3	2/2	0/0/0	0/0	0/0/0	0/0/	19/19/	/19			0/0/0	--Of cast iron, not enamelled
0/0/0		9.3	2/2	0/0/0	0/0	0/0/0	0/0/	18/18/18	18.8/18			0/0/0	--Of cast iron, enamelled
0/0/0	3.5	2.4	1.2/1.2	0/0/0	0/0	0/0/0	0/0/	10.8/10.8/10.8	10.9/10.8			0/0/0	--Of stainless steel
													--Of iron (other than cast iron) or steel, enamelled:
0/0/0		9.3	2/2	0/0/0	0/0	0/0/0	0/0/	18/18/18	18.8/18			0/0/0	---Basin
0/0/0		9.3	2/2	0/0/0	0/0	0/0/0	0/0/	19/19/19	/19			0/0/0	---Casserole
0/0/0		9.3	2/2	0/0/0	0/0	0/0/0	0/0/	19/19/19	/19			0/0/0	---Other
0/0/0		9.3	2/2	0/0/0	0/0	0/0/0	0/0/	18.7/19/18.7	18.8/19			0/0/0	--Other
													Sanitary ware and parts thereof, of iron or steel:
0/0/0		3.6	1.8/1.8	0/0/0	0/0	0/0/0	0/0/	0/0/16.2	16.4/0			0/0/0	-Sinks and wash basins, of stainless steel
													-Baths:
0/0/0	2	2	0/0	0/0/0	0/0	0/0/0	0/0/	0/0/9	9.1/0			0/0/0	--Of cast iron, whether or not enamelled
0/0/0		18	3/3	0/0/0	0/18	0/0/0	0/0/	28.5/28.5/28.5	/28.5			0/0/0	--Other
0/0/0		15	2.5/2.5	0/0/0	0/15	0/0/0	0/0/	23.8/23.8/23.8	/23.8			0/0/0	-Other, including parts
													Other cast articles of iron or steel:
													-Of non-malleable cast iron:
0//0	2	3.2	0/0	0/0/0	0/0	0//0	0/0/	6.3/6.3/6.3	6.6/6.3			0/0/0	---For technical use
0/0/0		9.3	2/2	0/0/0	0/0	0/0/0	0/0/	18.7/19/18.7	18.8/19			0/0/0	---Other
													-Other:
0/0/0	3.5	2.1	1.1/1.1	0/0/0	0/0	0/0/0	0/0/	0/0/9.5	9.5/0			0/0/0	--Grinding balls and similar articles for mills
													--Other:
0/0/0	3.5	2.1	1.1/1.1	0/0/0	0/0	0/0/0	0/0/	0/0/9.5	9.5/0			0/0/0	---For technical use
0/0/0	7	9.3	2/2	0/0/0	0/0	0/0/0	0/0/	19/19/	/19			0/0/0	---Other
													Other articles of iron or steel:
													-Forged or stamped, but not further worked:
0/0/0	3.5	2.1	1.1/1.1	0/0/0	0/0	0/0/0	0/0/	0/0/9.5	9.5/0			0/0/0	--Grinding balls and similar articles for mills
													--Other:
0/0/0	0		1.1/1.1	0/0/0	0/0	0/0/0	0/0/	5/5/	/5			0/0/0	---For technical use
0/0/0	0	4	2/2	0/0/0	0/0	0/0/0	0/0/	0/0/18	18.2/0			0/0/0	---Other
													-Articles of iron or steel wire:
0/0/0	4	2	0/0	0/0/0	0/0	0//0	0/0/	0/0/9	9.1/0			0/0/0	---For technical use
0/0/0	6.3	3.6	1.8/1.8	0/0/0	0/0	0/0/0	0/0/	0/0/16.2	16.4/0			0/0/0	---Other
													-Other:
													---For technical use:
0/0/0	0	2.1	1.1/1.1	0/0/0	0/0	0/0/0	0/0/	0/0/9.5	9.8/0			0/0/0	----Steel fiber and its products
0/0/0	0	2.1	1.1/1.1	0/0/0	0/0	0/0/0	0/0/	0/0/9.5	9.8/0			0/0/0	----Other
0/0/0	0	0	0.8/0.8	0/0/0	0/4.8	0/0/0	0/0/	0/0/0	7.6/0			0/0/0	---Other

第七十四章
铜及其制品

注释：

本章所用有关名词解释如下：

一、精炼铜

按重量计含铜量至少为 99.85% 的金属；或按重量计含铜量至少为 97.5%，但其他各种元素的含量不超过下表中规定的限量的金属：

其他元素表

元　　素		所含重量百分比
Ag	银	0.25
As	砷	0.5
Cd	镉	1.3
Cr	铬	1.4
Mg	镁	0.8
Pb	铅	1.5
S	硫	0.7
Sn	锡	0.8
Te	碲	0.8
Zn	锌	1
Zr	锆	0.3
其他元素*，每种		0.3

*其他元素，例如，铝、铍、钴、铁、锰、镍、硅。

二、铜合金

除未精炼铜以外的金属物质，按重量计含铜量大于其他元素单项含量，但：

（一）按重量计至少有一种其他元素的含量超过上表中规定的限量；

（二）按重量计其他元素的总含量超过 2.5%。

三、铜母合金

含有其他元素，但按重量计含铜量超过 10% 的合金，该合金无实用可锻性，通常用作生产其他合金的添加剂或冶炼有色金属的脱氧剂、脱硫剂及类似用途。但按重量计含磷量超过 15% 的磷化铜（磷铜）归入税目 28.53。

子目注释：

本章所用有关名词解释如下：

一、铜锌合金（黄铜）

铜与锌的合金，不论是否含有其他元素。含有其他元素时：

（一）按重量计含锌量应大于其他各种元素的单项含量；

（二）按重量计含镍量应低于 5%［参见铜镍锌合金（德银）］；

（三）按重量计含锡量应低于 3%［参见铜锡合金（青铜）］。

二、铜锡合金（青铜）

铜与锡的合金，不论是否含有其他元素。含有其他元素时，按重量计含锡量应大于其他各种元素的单项含量。当按重量计含锡量在 3% 及以上时，锌的含量可大于锡的含量，但必须小于 10%。

三、铜镍锌合金（德银）

铜、镍、锌的合金，不论是否含有其他元素，按重量计含镍量在 5% 及以上［参见铜锌合金（黄铜）］。

四、铜镍合金

铜与镍的合金，不论是否含有其他元素，但按重量计含锌量不得大于 1%。含有其他元素时，按重量计含镍量应大于其他各种元素的单项含量。

税则号列	货品名称〔CIQ 扩展编码及品名—T2 表示见附表 2〕	最惠(%)	暂定税率	普通	增值/消费	出口退税	计量单位	监管条件/特殊证件	检验检疫	对美关税	亚太上/下
74.01	**铜锍；沉积铜（泥铜）：**										
7401.0000	铜锍，沉积铜（泥铜）										
7401.0000 10	沉积铜（泥铜）〔999〕	2		11	13/	0	千克	9/			
7401.0000 90	铜锍〔999〕	2	0	11	13/	0	千克	/			
74.02	**未精炼铜；电解精炼用的铜阳极：**										
7402.0000	未精炼铜；电解精炼用的铜阳极										
7402.0000 01	锭状未精炼铜（含黄金价值部分）〔101 粗铜，102 电解铜〕	2	0	11	0/	0	千克	/			
7402.0000 90	其他未精炼铜、电解精炼用铜阳极〔101 粗铜，102 电解铜〕	2	0	11	13/	0	千克	/		25	
74.03	**未锻轧的精炼铜及铜合金：**										
	-精炼铜：										
	--阴极及阴极型材：										
	---阴极：										
7403.1111	----按重量计铜含量超过 99.9935% 的										
7403.1111 01	高纯阴极铜（99.9999%＞铜含量＞99.9935%）（未锻轧的）〔999〕	2	0	11	13/	0	千克	/		25	1/1
7403.1111 90	高纯阴极铜（铜含量≥99.9999%）未锻轧的〔999〕	2	0	11	13/	0	千克	/		25	1/1

Chapter 74
Copper and articles thereof

Notes:

In this Chapter the following expressions have the meanings hereby assigned to them:

1. Refined copper

   Metal containing at least 99.85% by weight of copper; or metal containing at least 97.5% by weight of copper, provided that the content by weight of any other element does not exceed the limit specified in the following table:

TABLE - Other elements

Element		Limiting content % by weight
Ag	Silver	0.25
As	Arsenic	0.5
Cd	Cadmium	1.3
Cr	Chromium	1.4
Mg	Magnesium	0.8
Pb	Lead	1.5
S	Sulphur	0.7
Sn	Tin	0.8
Te	Tellurium	0.8
Zn	Zinc	1
Zr	Zirconium	0.3
Other elements*, each		0.3

* Other elements are, for example, Al, Be, Co, Fe, Mn, Ni, Si.

2. Copper alloys

   Metallic substances other than unrefined copper in which copper predominates by weight over each of the other elements, provided that:

   (a) the content by weight of at least one of the other elements is greater than the limit specified in the foregoing table; or

   (b) the total content by weight of such other elements exceeds 2.5%.

3. Master alloys

   Alloys containing with other elements more than 10% by weight of copper, not usefully malleable and commonly used as an additive in the manufacture of other alloys or as de-oxidants, de-sulphurizing agents or for similar uses in the metallurgy of non-ferrous metals. However, copper phosphide (phosphor copper) containing more than 15% by weight of phosphorus falls in heading No.28.53.

Subheading Note:

In this Chapter the following expressions have the meanings hereby assigned to them:

1. Copper-zinc base alloys (brasses)

   Alloys of copper and zinc, with or without other elements. When other elments are present:

   (a) zinc predominates by weight over each of such other elements;

   (b) any nickel content by weight is less than 5% (see copper-nickel-zinc alloys (nickel silvers)); and

   (c) any tin content by weight is less than 3% (see copper-tin alloys (bronzes)).

2. Copper-tin base alloys (bronzes)

   Alloys of copper and tin, with or without other elements. When other elements are present, tin predominates by weight over each of such other elements, except that when the tin content is 3% or more the zinc content by weight may exceed that of tin but must be less than 10%.

3. Copper-nickel-zinc base alloys (nickel silvers)

   Alloys of copper, nickel and zinc, with or without other elements. The nickel content is 5% or more by weight (see copper-zinc alloys (brasses)).

4. Copper-nickel base alloys

   Alloys of copper and nickel, with or without other elements but in any case containing by weight not more than 1% of zinc. When other elements are present, nickel predominates by weight over each of such other elements.

协定税率 %								RCEP		特惠税率 %			Article Description
东/冰/格	巴基斯坦	韩国	瑞士上/下	哥/秘/柬	澳/毛	新西/坡/智	中国港/澳/台	东盟及马来/澳/韩	日/新	亚太2国	老/柬/缅	98/97/95	
													Copper mattes; cement copper (precipitated copper):
													Copper mattes; cement copper (precipitated copped)
0/0/0	0	0	0/0	0/0/0	0/0	0//0	0/0/	0/1.8/0	0/1.8		0//	0/0/0	cement copper (precipitated copped)
0/0/0	0	0	0/0	0/0/0	0/0	0//0	0/0/	0/1.8/0	0/1.8		0//	0/0/0	Copper mattes
													Unrefined copper; copper anodes for electrolytic refining:
													Unrefined copper; copper anodes for electrolytic refining
0/0/0	0	0	0/0	0//0	0/1.4	0//0	0/0/	1.8/1.8/1.8	1.8/1.8			0/0/0	Unrefined copper, copper anodes for electrolytic refining(containing gold value part)
0/0/0	0	0	0/0	0//0	0/1.4	0//0	0/0/	1.8/1.8/1.8	1.8/1.8			0/0/0	Unrefined copper, copper anodes for electrolytic refining(not containing gold value part)
													Refined copper and copper alloys, unwrought:
													-Refined copper:
													--Cathodes and sections of cathodes:
													---Cathodes:
													----Containing at least 99.9935% by weight of copper
0/0/0	0	0	0/0	0/0/0	0/0	0//0	0/0/	0/0/0	0/0			0/0/0	Higher purity copper cathode(99.9999%>copper content>99.9935%)
0/0/0	0	0	0/0	0/0/0	0/0	0//0	0/0/	0/0/0	0/0			0/0/0	Higher purity copper cathode(copper content≥99.9999%), unwrought

税则号列		货品名称〔CIQ 扩展编码及品名—T2 表示见附表 2〕	最惠(%)	暂定税率	普通	增值/消费	出口退税	计量单位	监管条件/特殊证件	检验检疫	对美关税	亚太上/下
7403.1119		----其他〔999〕	2	0	11	13/	0	千克	/		25	
7403.1190		---阴极型材〔999〕	2	0	11	13/	0	千克	/			
7403.1200		--线锭〔999〕	2	0	11	13/	0	千克	/			
7403.1300		--坯段〔999〕	2	0	11	13/	0	千克	/		25	
7403.1900		--其他〔999〕	2	0	11	13/	0	千克	/		25	
		-铜合金：										
7403.2100		--铜锌合金(黄铜)〔999〕	1	1	14	13/	0	千克	/		26	0.5/0.5
7403.2200		--铜锡合金(青铜)〔999〕	1	1	17	13/	0	千克	/		26	
7403.2900		--其他铜合金(税目 74.05 的铜母合金除外)〔301 危险化学品，遇水放出易燃气体的物质;302 其他化工产品〕	1	1	17	13/	0	千克	/13		26	
74.04		**铜废碎料：**										
7404.0000		铜废碎料										
7404.0000	10	以回收铜为主的废电机等(包括废电机、电线、电缆、五金电器)〔999〕	1.5	1.5	11	13/	0	千克	9/		26.5	0.8/0.8
7404.0000	20	符合标准 GB/T 38470—2019 规定的再生黄铜原料〔999〕	1.5	0	11	13/	0	千克	A/	M	25	0.8/0.8
7404.0000	30	符合标准 GB/T 38471—2019 规定的再生铜原料〔999〕	1.5	0	11	13/	0	千克	A/	M	25	0.8/0.8
7404.0000	90	其他铜废碎料〔999〕	1.5	1.5	11	13/	0	千克	9/		26.5	0.8/0.8
74.05		**铜母合金：**										
7405.0000		铜母合金〔999〕	4		17	13/	0	千克	/		29	
74.06		**铜粉及片状粉末：**										
		-非片状粉末：										
7406.1010		---精炼铜制〔999〕	3		14	13/	0	千克	/		13	
7406.1020		---铜镍合金(白铜)或铜镍锌合金(德银)制〔999〕	6		40	13/	0	千克	/		16	4.2/4.2
7406.1030		---铜锌合金(黄铜)制〔999〕	6		30	13/	0	千克	/		16	
7406.1040		---铜锡合金(青铜)制〔999〕	6		30	13/	0	千克	/		16	
7406.1090		---其他铜合金制〔999〕	6		30	13/	0	千克	/		16	
		-片状粉末：										
7406.2010		---精炼铜制〔999〕	4		14	13/	0	千克	/		14	
7406.2020		---铜镍合金(白铜)或铜镍锌合金(德银)制〔999〕	6		40	13/	0	千克	/			4.2/4.2
7406.2090		---其他铜合金制〔999〕	6		30	13/	0	千克	/		31	4.2/4.2
74.07		**铜条、杆、型材及异型材：**										
		-精炼铜制：										
7407.1010		---铬锆铜制〔999〕	4	4	14	13/	13	千克	/			
7407.1090		---其他〔999〕	4	4	14	13/	0	千克	/		29	
		-铜合金制：										
		--铜锌合金(黄铜)										
		---铜条、杆：										
7407.2111		----直线度≤0.5 毫米/米〔999〕	7	7	20	13/	13	千克	/		32	
7407.2119		----其他〔999〕	7	7	20	13/	13	千克	/		32	
7407.2190		---其他〔999〕	7	7	20	13/	13	千克	/		32	
7407.2900		--其他〔999〕	7	7	20	13/	13	千克	/		17	
74.08		**铜丝：**										
		-精炼铜制：										
7408.1100		--最大截面尺寸超过 6 毫米〔999〕	4	4	14	13/	13	千克	/		29	2.6/2.6
7408.1900		--其他										
7408.1900	01	其他含氧量＜5PPM 的精炼铜丝(截面尺寸≤6mm)〔999〕	4	2	14	13/	13	千克	/		27	2.6/2.6
7408.1900	90	其他截面尺寸≤6mm 的精炼铜丝〔999〕	4	4	14	13/	13	千克	/		29	2.6/2.6
		-铜合金制：										
7408.2100		--铜锌合金(黄铜)〔999〕	7	7	20	13/	13	千克	/		27	
		--铜镍合金(白铜)或铜镍锌合金(德银)：										
7408.2210		---铜镍锌铅合金(加铅德银)〔999〕	8	8	40	13/	13	千克	/		33	
7408.2290		---其他〔999〕	8	8	40	13/	0	千克	/		18	
7408.2900		--其他〔999〕	7	7	20	13/	13	千克	/		17	
74.09		**铜板、片及带，厚度超过 0.15 毫米：**										
		-精炼铜制：										
		--盘卷的：										
7409.1110		---含氧量不超过 10PPM 的〔999〕	4	4	14	13/	13	千克	/		14	
7409.1190		---其他〔999〕	4	4	14	13/	13	千克	/		29	
7409.1900		--其他〔999〕	4	4	14	13/	13	千克	/		29	
		-铜锌合金(黄铜)制：										
7409.2100		--盘卷的〔999〕	7	7	20	13/	13	千克	/		32	

协定税率 %								RCEP		特惠税率 %			Article Description
东/冰/格	巴基斯坦	韩国	瑞士上/下	哥/秘/柬	澳/毛	新西/坡/智	中国港/澳/台	东盟及马来/澳/韩	日/新	亚太2国	老/柬/缅	98/97/95	
0/0/0	0	0	0/0	0/0/0	0/0	0//0	0/0/	0/0/0	0/0			0/0/0	----Other
0/0/0	0	0	0/0	0/0/0	0/0	0//0	0/0/	0/1.8/0	0/1.8			0/0/0	---Sections of cathodes
0/0/0	0	0	0.2/0.2	0/0/0	0/0	0//0	0/0/	0/0/0	1.8/0			0/0/0	--Wire-bars
0/0/0	0	0	0/0	0/0/0	0/0	0//0	0/0/	0/0/0	1.8/0			0/0/0	--Billets
0/0/0	0	0	0/0	0/0/0	0/0	0//0	0/0/	0/0/0	1.8/0			0/0/0	--Other
													-Copper alloys:
0/0/0	0	0	0/0	0/0/0	0/0	0//0	0/0/	0.9/0.9/0.9	0.9/0.9			0/0/0	--Copper-zinc base alloys (brass)
0/0/0	0	0	0/0	0/0/0	0/0	0//0	0/0/	0/0.9/0	0/0.9			0/0/0	--Copper-tin base alloys (bronze)
0/0/0	0	0	0/0	0/0/0	0/0	0//0	0/0/	0/0/0	0/0			0/0/0	--Other copper alloys (other than master alloys of heading No.74. 05)
													Copper waste and scrap:
													Copper waste and scrap
0/0/0	0	0	0/0	0//0	0/0	0//0	0/0/	0/0/0	1.4/0		0//	0/0/0	Waste electric machines, waste wires, cables, mainly for re-coverying copper
0/0/0	0	0	0/0	0//0	0/0	0//0	0/0/	0/0/0	1.4/0		0//	0/0/0	Recycled brass materials conforming to GB / T 38470—2019
0/0/0	0	0	0/0	0//0	0/0	0//0	0/0/	0/0/0	1.4/0		0//	0/0/0	Recycled copper raw materials conforming to GB / T 38471—2019
0/0/0	0	0	0/0	0//0	0/0	0//0	0/0/	0/0/0	1.4/0		0//	0/0/0	Other copper waste and scrap
													Master alloys of copper:
0/0/0	0	0	0/0	0/0/0	0/0	0//0	0/0/	0/0/0	0/0			0/0/0	Master alloys of copper
													Copper powders and flakes:
													-Powders of non-lamellar structure:
0/0/0	0	0	0/0	0/0/0	0/0	0//0	0/0/	0/0/0	0/0			0/0/0	---Of refined copper
0/0/0	0	0	0/0	0/0/0	0/0	0//0	0/0/	0/0/0	0/0			0/0/0	---Of copper-nickel base alloys (cupronickel) or copper-nick-el-zinc base alloys (nickel silver)
0/0/0	0	1.2	0/0	0/0/0	0/0	0//0	0/0/	0/0/5.4	5.5/0			0/0/0	---Of copper-zinc base alloys (brass)
0/0/0	0	0	0/0	0/0/0	0/0	0//0	0/0/	0/0/0	0/0			0/0/0	---Of copper-tin base alloys (bronze)
0/0/0	0	0	0/0	0/0/0	0/0	0//0	0/0/	0/0/0	0/0			0/0/0	---Other
													-Powders of lamellar structure; flakes:
0/0/0	0	0	0/0	0/0/0	0/0	0//0	0/0/	0/0/0	0/0			0/0/0	---Of refined copper
0/0/0	0	0	0/0	0/0/0	0/0	0//0	0/0/	0/0/0	0/0			0/0/0	---Of copper-nickel base alloys (cupronick el) or copper-nick-el-zinc base alloys (nickel silver)
0/0/0	0	0	0/0	0/0/0	0/0	0//0	0/0/	0/0/0	0/0			0/0/0	---Other
													Copper bars, rods and profiles:
													-Of refined copper:
0/0/0	0	0	0/0	0/0/0	0/0	0//0	0/0/0	0/0/0	0/0			0/0/0	---Of Chrome-zircorium-copper
0/0/0	0	0	0/0	0/0/0	0/0	0//0	0/0/0	0/3.6/0	0/3.6			0/0/0	---Other
													-Of copper alloys:
													--Of copper-zinc base alloys (brass):
													---Copper bars, rods:
0/0/0	2		0.7/0.7	0/0/0	0/0	0//0	0/0/0	5/5/	/5			0/0/0	----Straightness≤0.5mm/m
0/0/0	2		0.7/0.7	0/0/0	0/0	0//0	0/0/0	5/5/	/5			0/0/0	----Other
0/0/0	2		0.7/0.7	0/0/0	0/0	0//0	0/0/0	5/5/	/5			0/0/0	---Other
0/0/0	2	0	0.7/0.7	0/0/0	0/0	0//0	0/0/0	0/0/0	6.4/0			0/0/0	--Other
													Copper wire:
													-Of refined copper:
0/0/0	0	0	0/0	0/0/0	0/0	0//0	0/0/0	0/0/0	0/0			0/0/0	--Of which the maximum cross-sectional dimension exceeds 6mm
													--Other
0/0/0	0	0	0/0	0/0/0	0/0	0//0	0/0/0	0/0/0	0/0			0/0/0	Other refined copper wire, containing oxygen less than 5PPM (cross-sectional dimension≤6mmm)
0/0/0	0	0	0/0	0/0/0	0/0	0//0	0/0/0	0/0/0	0/0			0/0/0	Other refined copper wire, cross-sectional dimension ≤6mm
													-Of copper alloys:
0/0/0	2	3.2	0/0	0/0/0	0/0	0//0	0/0/0	6.3/6.3/6.3	6.6/6.3			0/0/0	--Of copper-zinc base alloys (brass)
													--Of copper-nickel base alloys (cupronickel) or copper-nickel-zinc base alloys (nickel silver):
0/0/0	2	0	0/0	0/0/0	0/0	0//0	0/0/	0/0/0	7.3/0			0/0/0	---Of copper—nickel—zinc—lead base alloys (lead nickel sil-ver)
0/0/0	2	0	0/0	0/0/0	0/0	0//0	0/0/	0/0/0	7.3/0			0/0/0	---Other
0/0/0	2	1.4	0/0	0/0/0	0/0	0//0	0/0/	0/0/6.3	6.4/0			0/0/0	--Other
													Copper plates, sheets and strip, of a thickness exceeding 0. 15mm:
													-Of refined copper:
													--In coils:
0/0/0	0	0	0/0	0/0/0	0/0	0//0	0/0/	0/3.6/0	0/3.6			0/0/0	---Containing oxygen not exceeding 10ppm
0/0/0	0	0	0/0	0/0/0	0/0	0//0	0/0/	0/0/0	0/0			0/0/0	---Other
0/0/0	0	0	0/0	0/0/0	0/0	0//0	0/0/0	0/0/0	0/0			0/0/0	--Other
													-Of copper-zinc base alloys (brass):
0/0/0	2	3.2	0.7/0.7	0/0/0	0/0	0//0	0/0/0	6.3/6.3/6.3	6.6/6.3			0/0/0	--In coils

税则号列	货品名称〔CIQ 扩展编码及品名—T2 表示见附表 2〕	最惠(%)	暂定税率	普通	增值/消费	出口退税	计量单位	监管条件/特殊证件	检验检疫	对美关税	亚太上/下
7409.2900	--其他〔999〕	7	7	20	13/	13	千克	/		32	
	-铜锡合金(青铜)制:										
7409.3100	--盘卷的〔999〕	7	7	20	13/	13	千克	/		32	
7409.3900	--其他〔999〕	7	7	20	13/	13	千克	/		32	
7409.4000	-铜镍合金(白铜)或铜镍锌合金(德银)制〔999〕	7	7	40	13/	13	千克	/		32	
7409.9000	-其他铜合金制〔999〕	7	7	20	13/	13	千克	/		27	
74.10	**铜箔(不论是否印花或用纸、纸板、塑料或类似材料衬背),厚度(衬背除外)不超过 0.15 毫米:**										
	-无衬背:										
7410.1100	--精炼铜制〔999〕	4		14	13/	13	千克	/			2.6/2.6
	--铜合金制:										
7410.1210	---铜镍合金(白铜)或铜镍锌合金(德银)〔999〕	7		40	13/	13	千克	/			
7410.1290	---其他〔999〕	7		20	13/	13	千克	/		27	
	-有衬背:										
	--精炼铜制:										
7410.2110	---印制电路用覆铜板〔999〕	4		14	13/	13	千克	/			2.6/2.6
7410.2190	---其他〔999〕	4		14	13/	13	千克	/		29	2.6/2.6
	--铜合金制:										
7410.2210	---铜镍合金(白铜)或铜镍锌合金(德银)〔999〕	7		40	13/	13	千克	/		32	
7410.2290	---其他〔999〕	7		20	13/	13	千克	/		32	
74.11	**铜管:**										
	-精炼铜制:										
	---外径不超过 25 毫米的:										
7411.1011	----带有螺纹或翅片的〔101〕	4		14	13/	13	千克	/		29	2.6/2.6
7411.1019	----其他										
7411.1019 01	其他含氧量＜5PPM,外径≤25mm 的精炼铜管〔101〕	4	2	14	13/	13	千克	/		27	2.6/2.6
7411.1019 90	外径≤25mm 的其他精炼铜管〔101〕	4		14	13/	13	千克	/		29	2.6/2.6
7411.1020	---外径超过 70 毫米的〔101〕	4		14	13/	13	千克	/		29	2.6/2.6
7411.1090	---其他〔101〕	4		14	13/	13	千克	/		24	2.6/2.6
	-铜合金制:										
	--铜锌合金(黄铜):										
7411.2110	---盘卷的〔101〕	7		20	13/	13	千克	/		32	6.3/6.3
7411.2190	---其他〔101〕	7		20	13/	13	千克	/		32	
7411.2200	--铜镍合金(白铜)或铜镍锌合金(德银)〔101〕	7		40	13/	13	千克	/		17	
7411.2900	--其他〔101〕	7		20	13/	13	千克	/		27	
74.12	**铜制管子附件(例如,接头、肘管、管套):**										
7412.1000	-精炼铜制〔101 其它金属制法兰及管件压力管件,102 其它金属制法兰及管件〕	4		14	13/	0	千克	/		24	
	-铜合金制:										
7412.2010	---铜镍合金(白铜)或铜镍锌合金(德银)〔101 其它金属制法兰及管件压力管件,102 其它金属制法兰及管件〕	7		40	13/	0	千克	/		32	4.6/4.6
7412.2090	---其他〔101 其它金属制法兰及管件压力管件,102 其它金属制法兰及管件〕	7		20	13/	0	千克	/		27	4.6/4.6
74.13	**非绝缘的铜丝绞股线、缆、编带及类似品:**										
7413.0000	非绝缘的铜丝绞股线、缆、编带及类似品〔999〕	5		14	13/	0	千克	/		30	
74.15	**铜制或钢铁制带铜头的钉、平头钉、图钉、U 形钉(税目 83.05 的货品除外)及类似品;铜制螺钉、螺栓、螺母、钩头螺钉、铆钉、销、开尾销、垫圈(包括弹簧垫圈)及类似品:**										
7415.1000	-钉、平头钉、图钉、U 形钉及类似品〔999〕	8		80	13/	0	千克	/		18	
	-其他无螺纹制品:										
7415.2100	--垫圈(包括弹簧垫圈)〔999〕	8		80	13/	0	千克	/		28	
7415.2900	--其他〔999〕	8		80	13/	0	千克	/		28	
	-其他螺纹制品:										
	--螺钉;螺栓及螺母:										
7415.3310	---木螺钉〔999〕	8		80	13/	0	千克	/			6.4/6.4
7415.3390	---其他〔101 螺钉,102 螺栓,103 螺母〕	8		80	13/	0	千克	/		28	
7415.3900	--其他〔999〕	8		80	13/	0	千克	/		18	

协定税率 %								RCEP		特惠税率 %			Article Description
东/冰/格	巴基斯坦	韩国	瑞士上/下	哥/秘/柬	澳/毛	新西/坡/智	中国港/澳/台	东盟及马来/澳/韩	日/新	亚太2国	老/柬/缅	98/97/95	
0/0/0	2	3.2	0/0	0/0/0	0/0	0//0	0/0/0	6.3/6.3/6.3	6.6/6.3			0/0/0	--Other
													-Of copper-tin base alloys (bronze):
0/0/0	2	1.4	0/0	0/0/0	0/0	0//0	0/0/0	0/0/6.3	6.4/0			0/0/0	--In coils
0/0/0	2	0	0/0	0/0/0	0/0	0//0	0/0/0	0/0/0	0/0			0/0/0	--Other
0/0/0	2	0	0/0	0/0/0	0/0	0//0	0/0/0	0/6.3/0	0/6.3			0/0/0	-Of copper-nickel base alloys (cupro-nickel) or copper-nickel-zinc base alloys (nickel silver)
0/0/0	2	1.4	0/0	0/0/0	0/0	0//0	0/0/0	0/0/6.3	6.4/0			0/0/0	-Of other copper alloys
													Copper foil (whether or not printed or backed with paper, paperboard, plastics or similar backing materials) of a thickness (excluding any backing) not exceeding 0.15mm:
													-Not backed:
0/0/0	0	0	0/0	0/0/0	0/0	0//0	0/0/0	0/0/0	0/0			0/0/0	--Of refined copper
													--Of copper alloys:
0/0/0	2	0	0/0	0/0/0	0/0	0//0	0/0/0	0/6.3/0	0/6.3			0/0/0	---Of copper-nickel base alloys (cupronickel) or copper-nickel-zinc base alloys (nickel silver)
0/0/0	2	0	0/0	0/0/0	0/0	0//0	0/0/0	0/0/0	0/0			0/0/0	---Other
													-Backed:
													--Of refined copper:
0/0/0	0	0	0/0	0/0/0	0/0	0//0	0/0/0	0/0/0	3.8/0			0/0/0	---Copper-clad board used to print circuit
0/0/0	0	0	0/0	0/0/0	0/0	0//0	0/0/0	0/3.6/0	0/3.6			0/0/0	---Other
													--Of copper alloys:
0/0/0	2	0	0/0	0/0/0	0/0	0//0	0/0/	0/0/0	6.4/0			0/0/0	---Of copper-nickel base alloys (cupronickel) or copper-nickel-zinc base alloys (nickel silver)
0/0/0	2	0	0/0	0/0/0	0/0	0//0	0/0/	0/0/0	6.4/0			0/0/0	---Other
													Copper tubes and pipes:
													-Of refined copper:
													---Having an outside diameter not exceeding 25mm:
0/0/0	0	0	0/0	0/0/0	0/0	0//0	0/0/	0/0/0	0/0			0/0/0	----Threaded or with fins
													----Other
0/0/0	0	0	0/0	0/0/0	0/0	0//0	0/0/	0/3.6/0	0/3.6			0/0/0	Other refined copper wire, containing oxygen less than 5PPM, having an outside diameter not exceeding 25mm
0/0/0	0	0	0/0	0/0/0	0/0	0//0	0/0/	0/3.6/0	0/3.6			0/0/0	Refined copper tubing, outer diameter≤25mm
0/0/0	0	0	0/0	0/0/0	0/0	0//0	0/0/	0/0/0	0/0			0/0/0	---Having an outside diameter exceeding 70mm
0/0/0	0	0	0.4/0.4	0/0/0	0/2.4	0//0	0/0/	3.6/3.6/3.6	3.6/3.6			0/0/0	---Other
													-Of copper alloys:
													--Of copper-zinc base alloys(brass):
0/0/0	2	0	0/0	0/0/0	0/0	0//0	0/0/	0/0/0	6.4/0			0/0/0	---In coils
0/0/0	2	3.2	0/0	0/0/0	0/0	0//0	0/0/	6.3/6.3/6.3	6.6/6.3			0/0/0	---Other
0/0/0	2	0	0/0	0/0/0	0/0	0//0	0/0/	0/0/0	6.4/0			0/0/0	--Of copper-nickel base alloys (cupronickel) or copper-nickel-zinc base alloys (nickel silver)
0/0/0	2	0	0/0	0/0/0	0/0	0//0	0/0/	0/0/0	6.4/0			0/0/0	--Other
													Copper tube or pipe fittings (for example, couplings, elbows, sleeves):
0/0/0	0	0	0.4/0.4	0/0/0	0/0	0//0	0/0/	0/0/0	3.6/0			0/0/0	-Of refined copper
													-Of copper alloys:
0/0/0	2	0	0.7/0.7	0/0/0	0/0	0//0	0/0/	0/0/0	6.4/0			0/0/0	---Of copper-nickel base alloys (cupronickel) or copper-nickel-zinc base alloys (nickel silver)
0/0/0	2	0	0/0	0/0/0	0/0	0//0	0/0/	6.3/6.3/6.3	6.4/6.3			0/0/0	---Other
													Stranded wire, cables, plaited bands and the like, of copper, not electrically insulated:
0/0/0	0	2.3	0/0	0/0/0	0/0	0//0	0/0/	4.5/4.5/4.5	4.7/4.5			0/0/0	Stranded wire, cables, plaited bands and the like, of copper, not electrically insulated
													Nails, tacks, drawing pins, staples (other than those of heading No.83.05) and similar articles, of copper or of iron or steel with heads of copper; screws, bolts, nuts, screw hooks, rivets, cotters, cotter-pins, washers (including spring washers) and similar articles, of copper:
0/0/0	2	0	0/0	0/0/0	0/0	0//0	0/0/	0/0/0	7.3/0			0/0/0	-Nails and tacks, drawing pins, staples and similar articles
													-Other articles, not threaded:
0/0/0	2	2	0/0	0/0/0	0/0	0/0/0	0/0/	0/0/9	9.1/0			0/0/0	--Washers (including spring washers)
0/0/0	2	2	0/0	0/0/0	0/0	0/0/0	0/0/	0/0/9	9.1/0			0/0/0	--Other
													-Other threaded articles:
													--Screws; bolts and nuts:
0/0/0	2	0	0/0	0/0/0	0/0	0//0	0/0/	0/0/0	7.3/0			0/0/0	---Screws for wood
0/0/0	4	0	0/0	0/0/0	0/0	0//0	0/0/	7.2/7.2/7.2	7.3/7.2			0/0/0	---Other
0/0/0	2	2	0/0	0/0/0	0/0	0//0	0/0/	0/0/9	9.1/0			0/0/0	--Other

税则号列	货品名称〔CIQ 扩展编码及品名—T2 表示见附表 2〕	最惠(%)	暂定税率	普通	增值/消费	出口退税	计量单位	监管条件/特殊证件	检验检疫	对美关税	亚太上/下
74.18	**餐桌、厨房或其他家用铜制器具及其零件；铜制擦锅器、洗刷擦光用的块垫、手套及类似品；铜制卫生器具及其零件：**										
	-餐桌、厨房或其他家用器具及其零件；擦锅器及洗刷擦光用的块垫、手套及类似品：										
7418.1010	---擦锅器及洗刷擦光用的块垫、手套及类似品〔999〕	7		80	13/	13	千克	A/	R	17	
7418.1020	---非电热的铜制家用烹饪器具及其他零件〔101 食品接触铜产品，102 食品用铜包装〕	7		80	13/	13	千克	A/	R		
7418.1090	---其他〔101 食品接触铜产品，102 食品用铜包装〕	7		80	13/	13	千克	A/	R	32	
7418.2000	-卫生器具及其零件〔999〕	9		80	13/	13	千克	/		34	
74.19	**其他铜制品：**										
	-铸造、模压、冲压或锻造，但未经进一步加工的：										
7419.2010	---链条及其零件〔999〕	9		80	13/	0	千克	/		34	
7419.2020	---其他，工业用〔999〕	9		40	13/	0	千克	/		29	
7419.2090	---其他〔999〕	9		80	13/	13	千克	/		19	
	-其他：										
7419.8010	---链条及其零件〔999〕	9		80	13/	0	千克	/		34	
7419.8020	---铜弹簧〔999〕	9		40	13/	13	千克	/		34	
7419.8030	---铜丝制的布(包括环形带)〔999〕	7		20	13/	13	千克	/		32	
7419.8040	---铜丝制的网、格栅，网眼铜板〔999〕	8		20	13/	13	千克	/		18	
7419.8050	---非电热的铜制家用供暖器具及其零件〔101 其它装压缩或液化气的容器及其零件，102 深加工铜制品〕	9		80	13/	13	千克	/			6.3/6.3
	---其他：										
7419.8091	----工业用〔101 其它装压缩或液化气的容器及其零件，102 深加工铜制品〕	9		40	13/	0	千克	/		29	5.9/5.9
7419.8099	----其他〔101 其它装压缩或液化气的容器及其零件，102 深加工铜制品〕	9		80	13/	13	千克	/		29	5.9/5.9

协定税率 %								RCEP		特惠税率 %			Article Description
东/冰/格	巴基斯坦	韩国	瑞士上/下	哥/秘/柬	澳/毛	新西/坡/智	中国港/澳/台	东盟及马来/澳/韩	日/新	亚太2国	老/柬/缅	98/97/95	
													Table, kitchen or other household articles and parts thereof, of copper; pot scourers and scouring or polishing pads, gloves and the like, of copper; sanitary ware and parts thereof, of copper:
													-Table, kitchen or other household articles and parts thereof; pot scourers and scouring or polishing pads, gloves and the like:
0/0/0	10.1	3.6	1.8/1.8	0/0/0	0/0	0/0/0	0/0/	0/0/16.2	16.4/0			0/0/0	---Pot scourers and scouring or polishing pads, gloves and the like
0/0/0		9.3	2/2	0/0/0	0/0	0/0/0	0/0/	18/18/18	18.8/18			0/0/0	---Cooking apparatus of a kind used for domestic purposes, non-electric, and parts thereof, of copper
0/0/0	10.1	3.6	1.8/1.8	0/0/0	0/0	0/0/0	0/0/	0/0/16.2	16.4/0			0/0/0	---Other
0/0/0	0	3.6	1.8/1.8	0/0/0	0/0	0/0/0	0/0/	0/0/16.2	16.4/0			0/0/0	-Sanitary ware and parts thereof
													Other articles of copper:
													-Cast, moulded, stamped or forged, but not further worded:
0/0/0	7.8	2.8	1.4/1.4	0/0/0	0/0	0/0/0	0/0/	0/0/12.6	12.7/0			0/0/0	---Chain and parts thereof
0/0/0	2	0	0/0	0/0/0	0/0	0/0/0	0/0/	9/9/9	9.1/9			0/0/0	---Other, for technical use
0/0/0	16	9.3	2/2	0/0/0	0/0	0/0/0	0/0/	18.7/19/	18.8/19			0/0/0	---Other
													-Other:
0/0/0	7.8	2.8	1.4/1.4	0/0/0	0/0	0/0/0	0/0/	0/0/12.6	12.7/0			0/0/0	---Chain and parts thereof
0/0/0	3.5	2	1/1	0/0/0	0/0	0//0	0/0/	0/0/9	9.1/0			0/0/0	---Copper springs
0/0/0	3.9	0	0/0	0/0/0	0/0	0//0	0/0/	0/0/0	6.4/0			0/0/0	---Cloth(cincluding endless bands), of copper wire
0/0/0	4.5	1.6	0/0	0/0/0	0/0	0//0	0/0/	0/0/7.2	7.3/0			0/0/0	---Grill and netting、of copper wire expanded metal of copper
0/0/0	16	9.3	2/2	0/0/0	0/0	0/0/0	0/0/	18/18/18	18.2/18			0/0/0	---Heating apparatus of a kind used for dimestic purposes, nonelectric, and parts thereof, of copper
													---Other:
0//0	3.5	0	1/1	0/0/0	0/0	0/0/0	0/0/	0/0/0	9.1/0			0/0/0	----For technical use
0/0/0	16	12	2/2	0/0/0	0/0	0/0/0	0/0/	19/19/	/19			0/0/0	----Other

第七十五章
镍及其制品

子目注释：

一、本章所用有关名词解释如下：

（一）非合金镍

按重量计镍及钴的含量至少为99%的金属，但：

1. 按重量计含钴量不超过1.5%；
2. 按重量计其他各种元素的含量不超过下表中规定的限量：

其他元素表

元　　素	所含重量百分比
Fe　　铁	0.5
O　　氧	0.4
其他元素，每种	0.3

（二）镍合金

按重量计含镍量大于其他元素单项含量的金属物质，但：

1. 按重量计含钴量超过1.5%；
2. 按重量计至少有一种其他元素的含量超过上表中规定的限量；
3. 除镍及钴以外，按重量计其他元素的总含量超过1%。

二、子目7508.10所称“丝”，不受第十五类注释九（三）的限制，仅适用于截面尺寸不超过6毫米的任何截面形状的产品，不论是否盘卷。

税则号列	货品名称〔CIQ扩展编码及品名－T2表示见附表2〕	最惠(%)	暂定税率	普通	增值/消费	出口退税	计量单位	监管条件/特殊证件	检验检疫	对美关税	亚太上/下
75.01	**镍锍、氧化镍烧结物及镍冶炼的其他中间产品：**										
7501.1000	-镍锍〔999〕	3	0	11	13/	0	千克	4xy/			
	-氧化镍烧结物及镍冶炼的其他中间产品：										
7501.2010	---镍湿法冶炼中间品〔999〕	3	0	11	13/	0	千克	4xy/			
7501.2090	---其他〔999〕	3	0	11	13/	0	千克	4xy/		25	
75.02	**未锻轧镍：**										
	-非合金镍：										
7502.1010	---按重量计镍、钴总量在99.99%及以上的，但钴含量不超过0.005%〔999〕	3	1	11	13/	0	千克	4xy/		26	
7502.1090	---其他〔999〕	3	1	11	13/	0	千克	4xy/		26	
7502.2000	-镍合金〔999〕	3	3	11	13/	0	千克	4xy/			
75.03	**镍废碎料：**										
7503.0000	镍废碎料〔999〕	1.5		11	13/	0	千克	49xy/		26.5	
75.04	**镍粉及片状粉末：**										
7504.0010	---非合金镍粉及片状粉末〔999〕	4	1	17	13/	13	千克	3/		26	
7504.0020	---合金镍粉及片状粉末〔999〕	4		17	13/	13	千克	/		14	
75.05	**镍条、杆、型材及异型材或丝：**										
	-条、杆、型材及异型材：										
7505.1100	--非合金镍制〔999〕	6		14	13/	13	千克	/		16	
7505.1200	--镍合金制〔999〕	6		14	13/	13	千克	/		16	
	-丝：										
7505.2100	--非合金镍制〔999〕	6		17	13/	13	千克	/		26	
7505.2200	--镍合金制〔999〕	6		17	13/	13	千克	/			
75.06	**镍板、片、带、箔：**										
7506.1000	-非合金镍制〔999〕	6		14	13/	13	千克	/		26	
7506.2000	-镍合金制〔999〕	6		14	13/	0	千克	/			
75.07	**镍管及管子附件（例如，接头、肘管、管套）：**										
	-镍管：										
7507.1100	--非合金镍制〔101〕	6		17	13/	0	千克	/			
7507.1200	--镍合金制〔101〕	6		17	13/	13	千克	/			
7507.2000	-管子附件〔101镍管压力管道，102其它金属制法兰及管件〕	6		17	13/	0	千克	/		16	
75.08	**其他镍制品：**										
	-镍丝布、网及格栅：										
7508.1010	---镍丝布〔101〕	6		20	13/	0	千克	/		31	
7508.1080	---其他工业用镍制品〔101〕	6		40	13/	0	千克	/		31	
7508.1090	---其他〔101〕	6		70	13/	0	千克	/		16	
	-其他：										
7508.9010	---电镀用镍阳极〔101〕	4	4	14	13/	0	千克	/		29	
7508.9080	---其他工业用镍制品〔101〕	6		40	13/	0	千克	/		16	
7508.9090	---其他〔101〕	6		70	13/	0	千克	/		16	

Chapter 75
Nickel and articles thereof

Subheading Notes:

1. In this Chapter the following expressions have the meanings hereby assigned to them:

(a) Nickel, not alloyed

Metal containing by weight at least 99% of nickel plus cobalt, provided that:

(ⅰ) the cobalt content by weight does not exceed 1.5%, and

(ⅱ) the content by weight of any other element does not exceed the limit specified in the following table:

TABLE - Other elements

Element	Limiting content % by weight
Fe　　Iron	0.5
O　　Oxygen	0.4
Other elements, each	0.3

(b) Nickel alloys

Metallic substances in which nickel predominates by weight over each of the other elements provided that:

(ⅰ) the content by weight of cobalt exceeds 1.5%,

(ⅱ) the content by weight of at least one of the other elements is greater than the limit specified in the foregoing table, or

(ⅲ) the total content by weight of elements other than nickel plus cobalt exceeds 1%.

2. Notwithstanding the provisions of Note 9(c) to Section XV, for the purposes of subheading No.7508.10 the term "wire" applies only to products, whether or not in coils, of any cross-sectional shape, of which no cross-sectional dimension exceeds 6mm.

协定税率 %								RCEP		特惠税率 %			Article Description
东/冰/格	巴基斯坦	韩国	瑞士上/下	哥/秘/柬	澳/毛	新西/坡/智	中国港/澳/台	东盟及马来/澳/韩	日/新	亚太2国	老/柬/缅	98/97/95	
													Nickel mattes, nickel oxide sinters and other intermediate products of nickel metallurgy
0/0/0	0	0	0/0	0/0/0	0/0	0//0	0/0/	0/0/0	0/0			0/0/0	-Nickel mattes
													-Nickel oxide sinters and other intermediate products of nickel metallurgy:
0/0/0	0	0	0/0	0/0/0	0/0	0//0	0/0/	0/0/0	0/0			0/0/0	---Intermediate products of nickel metallurgy by wet process
0/0/0	0	0	0/0	0/0/0	0/0	0//0	0/0/	0/0/0	0/0			0/0/0	---Other
													Unwrought nickel:
													-Nickel, not alloyed:
0/0/0	0	0	0/0	0/0/0	0/0	0//0	0/0/	0/0/0	0/0			0/0/0	---Containing 99.99% or more than by total weight of nickel and cobalt, but containing cobalt not exceeding 0.005%
0/0/0	0	0	0/0	0/0/0	0/0	0//0	0/0/	0/0/0	0/0			0/0/0	---Other
0/0/0	0	0	0/0	0/0/0	0/0	0//0	0/0/	0/0/0	0/0			0/0/0	-Nickel, alloys
													Nickel waste and scrap:
0/0/0	0	0	0/0	0/0/0	0/0	0//0	0/0/	0/0/0	0/0			0/0/0	Nickel waste and scrap
													Nickel powders and flakes:
0/0/0	0	0	0/0	0/0/0	0/0	0//0	0/0/	0/0/0	0/0			0/0/0	---Nickel powders and flakes, not alloyed
0/0/0	0	0	0/0	0/0/0	0/0	0//0	0/0/	0/0/0	0/0			0/0/0	---Nickel powders and flakes, alloys
													Nickel bars, rods, profiles and wire:
													-Bars, rods and profiles:
0/0/0	0	1.2	0/0	0/0/0	0/0	0//0	0/0/	0/0/5.4	5.5/0			0/0/0	--Of nickel, not alloyed
0/0/0	0	1.2	0/0	0/0/0	0/0	0//0	0/0/	0/0/5.4	5.5/0			0/0/0	--Of nickel alloys
													-Wire:
0/0/0	0	0	0.6/0.6	0/0/0	0/0	0//0	0/0/	0/0/0	5.5/0			0/0/0	--Of nickel, not alloyed
0/0/0	0	0	0/0	0/0/0	0/0	0//0	0/0/	0/0/0	0/0			0/0/0	--Of nickel alloys
													Nickel plates, sheets, strip and foil:
0/0/0	0	1.2	0/0	0/0/0	0/0	0//0	0/0/	5.4/5.4/5.4	5.5/5.4			0/0/0	-Of nickel, not alloyed
0/0/0	0	0	0/0	0/0/0	0/0	0//0	0/0/	0/5.4/0	0/5.4			0/0/0	-Of nickel alloys
													Nickel tubes, pipes and tube or pipe fittings (for example, couplings, elbows, sleeves):
													-Tubes and pipes:
0/0/0	0	0	2.5/2.5	0/0/0	0/0	0//0	0/0/	0/0/0	5.5/0			0/0/0	--Of nickel, not alloyed
0/0/0	0	1.2	0/0	0/0/0	0/0	0//0	0/0/	5.4/5.4/5.4	5.5/5.4			0/0/0	--Of nickel alloys
0/0/0	0	0	0/0	0/0/0	0/0	0//0	0/0/	0/0/0	0/0			0/0/0	-Tube or pipe fittings
													Other articles of nickel:
													-Cloth, grill and netting, of nickel wire:
0/0/0	0	0	0/0	0/0/0	0/0	0//0	0/0/	0/0/0	0/0			0/0/0	---Wire cloth
0/0/0	0	0	0/0	0/0/0	0/0	0//0	0/0/	0/0/0	0/0			0/0/0	---Other articles of nickel, for technical use
0/0/0	0	0	0/0	0/0/0	0/0	0//0	0/0/	0/0/0	0/0			0/0/0	---Other
													-Other:
0/0/0	0	0	0/0	0/0/0	0/0	0//0	0/0/	0/0/0	0/0			0/0/0	---Electroplating anodes
0/0/0	0	0	0/0	0/0/0	0/0	0//0	0/0/	0/5.4/0	0/5.4			0/0/0	---Other articles of nickel, for technical use
0/0/0	4	0	0/0	0/0/0	0/0	0//0	0/0/	0/0/0	0/0			0/0/0	---Other

第七十六章
铝及其制品

子目注释：

一、本章所用有关名词解释如下：

（一）非合金铝

按重量计含铝量至少为 99%的金属，但其他各种元素的含量不超过下表中规定的限量：

其他元素表

元　　素	所含重量百分比
Fe+Si(铁+硅)	1
其他元素[①]，每种	0.1[②]
①其他元素，例如，铬、铜、镁、锰、镍、锌。 ②含铜成分可大于 0.1%，但不得大于 0.2%，且铬和锰的含量均不得超过 0.05%。	

（二）铝合金

按重量计含铝量大于其他元素单项含量的金属物质，但：

1. 按重量计至少有一种其他元素或铁加硅的含量大于上表中规定的限量；

2. 按重量计其他元素的总含量超过 1%。

二、子目 7616.91 所称"丝"，不受第十五类注释九(三)的限制，仅适用于截面尺寸不超过 6 毫米的任何截面形状的产品，不论是否盘卷。

税则号列	货品名称〔CIQ 扩展编码及品名－T2 表示见附表 2〕	最惠(%)	暂定税率	普通	增值/消费	出口退税	计量单位	监管条件/特殊证件	检验检疫	对美关税	亚太上/下
76.01	**未锻轧铝：**										
	-非合金铝：										
7601.1010	---按重量计含铝量在 99.95%及以上〔999〕	5	5	14	13/	0	千克	/		30	
7601.1090	---其他〔999〕	5	0	14	13/	0	千克	/		25	2.5/2.5
7601.2000	-铝合金										
7601.2000　10	碱金属含量(钠+钾+钙)＜10ppm，氢含量＜0.12 毫升/100 克铝的低碱精炼铝合金〔999〕	7	7	14	13/	0	千克	/		32	4.6/4.6
7601.2000　90	其他未锻轧铝合金〔999〕	7	7	14	13/	0	千克	/		32	4.6/4.6
76.02	**铝废碎料：**										
7602.0000	铝废碎料										
7602.0000　10	以回收铝为主的废电线等(包括废电线、电缆、五金电器)〔999〕	1.5	1.5	14	13/	0	千克	9/		51.5/26.5	
7602.0000　20	符合标准 GB/T 38472－2019 规定的再生铸造铝合金原料〔999〕	1.5	0	14	13/	0	千克	A/	M	50/25	
7602.0000　90	其他铝废碎料〔999〕	1.5	1.5	14	13/	0	千克	9/		51.5/26.5	
76.03	**铝粉及片状粉末：**										
7603.1000	-非片状粉末										
7603.1000　10	颗粒＜500μm 的微细球形铝粉(颗粒均匀，铝含量≥97%)〔301 危险化学品，易燃固体；302 危险化学品，遇水放出易燃气体的物质；303 其他〕	6		30	13/	0	千克	3A/13	M	16	
7603.1000　90	其他非片状铝粉〔301 危险化学品，易燃固体；302 其他〕	6		30	13/	0	千克	AB/13	MN	16	
7603.2000	-片状粉末〔999〕	7		30	13/	0	千克	/		32	
76.04	**铝条、杆、型材及异型材：**										
	-非合金铝制：										
7604.1010	---铝条、杆〔999〕	5	5	30	13/	0	千克	/		25	
7604.1090	---其他〔999〕	5	5	30	13/	0	千克	/		30	
	-铝合金制：										
7604.2100	--空心异型材〔999〕	5	5	30	13/	13	千克	A/	M	15	
	--其他：										
7604.2910	---铝合金条、杆										
7604.2910　10	柱形实心体铝合金(在 293K(20 摄氏度)时的极限抗拉强度能达到 460 兆帕(0.46×10^9 牛顿/平方米)或更大)〔999〕	5	5	30	13/	13	千克	3/		15	3.3/3.3
7604.2910　90	其他铝合金制条、杆〔101 铝条，102 其他铝及制品〕	5	5	30	13/	0	千克	/		15	3.3/3.3
7604.2990	---其他〔999〕	5	5	30	13/	13	千克	A/	M	25	3.3/3.3
76.05	**铝丝：**										
	-非合金铝制：										

Chapter 76
Aluminium and articles thereof

Subheading Notes:

1. In this Chapter the following expressions have the meanings hereby assigned to them:

(a) Aluminium, not alloyed

Metal containing by weight at least 99% of aluminium, provided that the content by weight of any other element does not exceed the limit specified in the following table:

TABLE - Other elements

Element	Limiting content % by weight
Fe+Si(iron plus silicon)	1
Other elements [①], each	0.1[②]

①Other elements are, for example, Cr, Cu, Mg, Mn, Ni, Zn.

②Copper is permitted in a proportion greater than 0.1% but not more than 0.2%, provided that neither the chromium nor manganese content exceeds 0.05%.

(b) Aluminium alloys

Metallic substances in which aluminium predominates by weight over each of the other elements, provided that:

(ⅰ) the content by weight of at least one of the other elements or of iron plus silicon taken together is greater than the limit specified in the foregoing table;

(ⅱ) the total content by weight of such other elements exceeds 1%.

2. Notwithstanding the provisions of Note 9(c) to Section XV, for the purposes of subheading No.7616.91 the term "wire" applies only to products, whether or not in coils, of any cross-sectional shape, of which no cross-sectional dimension exceeds 6mm.

协定税率 %								RCEP		特惠税率 %			Article Description
东/冰/格	巴基斯坦	韩国	瑞士上/下	哥/秘/柬	澳/毛	新西/坡/智	中国港/澳/台	东盟及马来/澳/韩	日/新	亚太2国	老/柬/缅	98/97/95	
													Unwrought aluminium:
													-Aluminium, not alloyed:
0/0/0	0	1	0/0	0/0/0	0/0	0//0	0/0/	0/0/4.5	4.5/0			0/0/0	---Containing by weight 99.95% or more of aluminium
0/0/0	0	0	0/0	0/0/0	0/0	0//0	0/0/	0/0/0	0/0			0/0/0	---Other
													-Aluminium alloys
0/0/0	0	0	0/0	0/0/0	0/0	0//0	0/0/	6.3/6.3/6.3	6.4/6.3			0/0/0	The content of alkali metals (Na + K + calcium) < 10ppm, low alkali hydrogen content of < 0.12 ml/100 grams of aluminum in the refining process of aluminum alloy
0/0/0	0	0	0/0	0/0/0	0/0	0//0	0/0/	6.3/6.3/6.3	6.4/6.3			0/0/0	Other unwrought aluminum alloy
													Aluminium waste and scrap:
													Aluminium waste and scrap
0/0/0	0	0	0/0	0//0	0/0	0//0	0/0/	0/0/0	1.4/0			0/0/0	Aluminium waste wires, cables, hardware and electric appliance, mainly for recoverying aluminium
0/0/0	0	0	0/0	0//0	0/0	0//0	0/0/	0/0/0	1.4/0		//	0/0/0	Recycled cast aluminum alloy raw materials conforming to GB / T 38472—2019
0/0/0	0	0	0/0	0//0	0/0	0//0	0/0/	0/0/0	1.4/0			0/0/0	Aluminium waste and scrap
													Aluminium powders and flakes:
													-Powders of non-lamellar structure
0/0/0	0	0	0/0	0/0/0	0/0	0//0	0/0/	0/0/0	0/0			0/0/0	Microspherical aluminum powder, granularity < 500μm, containing ≥ 97% by weight of aluminium
0/0/0	0	0	0/0	0/0/0	0/0	0//0	0/0/	0/0/0	0/0			0/0/0	Other powders of non-lamellar structure, of aluminium
0/0/0	2	0	0/0	0/0/0	0/0	0//0	0/0/	0/0/0	6.4/0			0/0/0	-Powders of lamellar structure; flakes
													Aluminium bars, rods and profiles:
													-Of aluminium, not alloyed:
0/0/0	0	0	0/0	0/0/0	0/0	0//0	0/0/	0/0/0	0/0			0/0/0	---Bars and rods
0/0/0	0	2.3	0/0	0/0/0	0/0	0//0	0/0/	4.5/4.5/4.5	4.7/4.5			0/0/0	---Other
													-Of aluminium alloys:
0/0/0	0	2.3	0/0	0/0/0	0/0	0//0	0/0/	4.5/4.5/4.5	4.7/4.5			0/0/0	--Hollow profiles
													--Other:
													---Bars and rods
0/0/0	0	2.3	0/0	0/0/0	0/0	0//0	0/0/	4.5/4.5/4.5	4.7/4.5			0/0/0	Aluminum alloy bar and rod〔tensile strength reaches at least 460 Mpa(0.46×10⁹N/m²) at 293k(20℃)〕
0/0/0	0	2.3	0/0	0/0/0	0/0	0//0	0/0/	4.5/4.5/4.5	4.7/4.5			0/0/0	Other aluminum alloy bar and rod, cross-section perimeter ≤ 210mm
0/0/0	0	0	0/0	0/0/0	0/0	0//0	0/0/	0/4.5/0	0/4.5			0/0/0	---Other
													Aluminium wire:
													-Of aluminium, not alloyed:

税则号列	货品名称〔CIQ扩展编码及品名－T2表示见附表2〕	最惠(%)	暂定税率	普通	增值/消费	出口退税	计量单位	监管条件/特殊证件	检验检疫	对美关税	亚太上/下
7605.1100	--最大截面尺寸超过7毫米〔999〕	8	8	17	13/	0	千克	/		33	
7605.1900	--其他〔999〕	8	8	17	13/	0	千克	/		33	5.2/5.2
	-铝合金制：										
7605.2100	--最大截面尺寸超过7毫米〔999〕	8	8	17	13/	0	千克	/		18	
7605.2900	--其他〔999〕	8	8	17	13/	0	千克	/		18	
76.06	**铝板、片及带，厚度超过0.2毫米：**										
	-矩形(包括正方形)：										
	--非合金铝制：										
	---厚度在0.30毫米及以上，但不超过0.36毫米：										
7606.1121	----铝塑复合的〔101铝板，102其他铝及制品〕	6	6	50	13/	13	千克	/		31	4.2/4.2
7606.1129	----其他〔999〕	6	6	50	13/	13	千克	/		31	4.2/4.2
	---其他：										
7606.1191	----铝塑复合的〔101铝板，102其他铝及制品〕	6	6	30	13/	13	千克	/		16	3.9/3.9
7606.1199	----其他〔999〕	6	6	30	13/	13	千克	/		31	3.9/3.9
	--铝合金制：										
7606.1220	---厚度小于0.28毫米〔999〕	6	6	30	13/	13	千克	/		31	4.2/4.2
7606.1230	---厚度在0.28毫米及以上，但不超过0.35毫米〔999〕	6	6	30	13/	13	千克	/		26	4.2/4.2
	---厚度在超过0.35毫米以上，但不超过4毫米：										
7606.1251	----铝塑复合的〔101铝板，102其他铝及制品〕	6	6	50	13/	13	千克	/		31	3.9/3.9
7606.1259	----其他〔999〕	6	6	50	13/	13	千克	/		31	3.9/3.9
7606.1290	---其他〔999〕	6	6	50	13/	13	千克	/		16	3.9/3.9
	-其他：										
7606.9100	--非合金铝制〔999〕	6	6	30	13/	13	千克	/		31	
7606.9200	--铝合金制〔999〕	8	8	30	13/	13	千克	/		28	
76.07	**铝箔(不论是否印花或用纸、纸板、塑料或类似材料衬背)，厚度(衬背除外)不超过0.2毫米：**										
	-无衬背：										
	--轧制后未经进一步加工的：										
7607.1110	---厚度不超过0.007毫米〔999〕	6		35	13/	13	千克	/		31	3.9/3.9
7607.1120	---厚度大于0.007毫米，但不超过0.01毫米〔999〕	6		35	13/	13	千克	/		16	3.9/3.9
7607.1190	---其他〔999〕	6		35	13/	13	千克	/		31	3.9/3.9
7607.1900	--其他〔999〕	6		35	13/	13	千克	/		31	3.9/3.9
7607.2000	-有衬背〔999〕	6		35	13/	13	千克	/		26	
76.08	**铝管：**										
7608.1000	-非合金铝制〔101〕	8		30	13/	13	千克	/		33	
	-铝合金制：										
7608.2010	---外径不超过10厘米的										
7608.2010 10	外径≤10厘米的管状铝合金[在293K(20摄氏度)时的极限抗拉强度能达到460兆帕(0.46×10^9牛顿/平方米)或更大]〔101铝管压力管道，102铝管〕	8		30	13/	13	千克	3A/	M		
7608.2010 90	外径≤10厘米的其他合金制铝管〔101铝管压力管道，102铝管〕	8		30	13/	13	千克	A/	M		
	---其他：										
7608.2091	----壁厚不超过25毫米										
7608.2091 10	外径>10厘米，壁厚≤25毫米的管状铝合金[在293K(20摄氏度)时的极限抗拉强度能达到460兆帕(0.46×10^9牛顿/平方米)或更大]〔101铝管压力管道，102铝管〕	8		30	13/	13	千克	3A/	M	33	
7608.2091 90	外径>10厘米，壁厚≤25毫米的其他合金制铝管〔101铝管压力管道，102铝管〕	8		30	13/	13	千克	A/	M	33	
7608.2099	----其他										
7608.2099 10	外径>10厘米，其他管状铝合金[在293K(20摄氏度)时的极限抗拉强度能达到460兆帕(0.46×10^9牛顿/平方米)或更大]〔101铝管压力管道，102铝管〕	8		30	13/	13	千克	3A/	M	18	
7608.2099 90	外径>10厘米，其他合金制铝管〔101铝管压力管道，102铝管〕	8		30	13/	13	千克	A/	M	18	
76.09	**铝制管子附件(例如，接头、肘管、管套)：**										
7609.0000	铝制管子附件(例如，接头、肘管、管套)〔101其它金属制法兰及管件压力管件，102深加工铝制品压力管件，103其它金属制法兰及管件，104深加工铝制品〕	8		35	13/	13	千克	/		18	

协定税率 %								RCEP		特惠税率 %			Article Description
东/冰/格	巴基斯坦	韩国	瑞士上/下	哥/秘/柬	澳/毛	新西/坡/智	中国港/澳/台	东盟及马来/澳/韩	日/新	亚太2国	老/柬/缅	98/97/95	
0/0/0	2	0	0/0	0/0/0	0/0	0//0	0/0/	0/0/0	7.3/0			0/0/0	--Of which the maximum cross-sectional dimension exceeding 7mm
0/0/0	2	0	0/0	0/0/0	0/0	0//0	0/0/	0/0/0	7.3/0			0/0/0	--Other
													-Of aluminium alloys:
0/0/0	2	0	0/0	0/0/0	0/0	0//0	0/0/	0/0/0	7.3/0			0/0/0	--Of which the maximum cross-sectional dimension exceeding 7mm
0/0/0	2	0	0/0	0/0/0	0/0	0//0	0/0/	0/0/0	7.3/0			0/0/0	--Other
													Aluminium plates, sheets and strip, of a thickness exceeding 0.2mm:
													-Rectangular (including square):
													--Of aluminium, not alloyed:
													---Of a thickness of 0.30mm or more but not exceeding 0.36mm:
0/0/0	0	0	0/0	0/0/0	0/0	0//0	0/0/	0/0/0	0/0			0/0/0	----Aluminum-plastic composite
0/0/0	0	2.8	0/0	0/0/0	0/0	0//0	0/0/	5.4/5.4/5.4	5.6/5.4			0/0/0	----Other
													---Other:
0/0/0	0	0	0/0	0/0/0	0/0	0//0	0/0/0	0/0/0	0/0			0/0/0	----Aluminum-plastic composite
0/0/0	0	1.2	0/0	0/0/0	0/0	0//0	0/0/0	5.4/5.4/5.4	5.5/5.4			0/0/0	----Other
													--Of aluminium alloys:
0/0/0	0	2.8	0/0	0/0/0	0/0	0//0	0/0/0	5.4/5.4/5.4	5.6/5.4			0/0/0	---Of a thickness less than 0.28mm
0/0/0	0	2.8	0/0	0/0/0	0/0	0//0	0/0/0	5.4/5.4/5.4	5.6/5.4			0/0/0	---Of a thickness of 0.28mm or more but not exceeding 0.35mm
													---Of a thickness more than 0.35mm but not exceeding 4mm:
0/0/0	0	1.2	0.6/0.6	0/0/0	0/0	0//0	0/0/	0/0/5.4	5.5/0			0/0/0	----Aluminum-plastic composite
0/0/0	0	2.8	0.6/0.6	0/0/0	0/0	0//0	0/0/	5.4/5.4/5.4	5.6/5.4			0/0/0	----Other
0/0/0	0	0	0.6/0.6	0/0/0	0/0	0//0	0/0/	5.4/5.4/5.4	5.5/5.4			0/0/0	---Other
													-Other:
0/0/0	0	2.8	0/0	0/0/0	0/0	0//0	0/0/0	5.4/5.4/5.4	5.6/5.4			0/0/0	--Of aluminium, not alloyed
0/0/0	2	4.6	0/0	0/0/0	0/0	0/0/0	0/0/0	9.3/9.5/9.3	9.4/9.5			0/0/0	--Of aluminium alloys
													Aluminium foil (whether or not printed or backed with paper, paperboard, plastics or similar backing materials) of a thickness (excluding any backing) not exceeding 0.2mm:
													-Not backed:
													--Rolled but not further worked:
0/0/0	0	2.8	0.6/0.6	0/0/0	0/0	0//0	0/0/	5.4/5.4/5.4	5.6/5.4			0/0/0	---Of a thickness not exceeding 0.007mm
0/0/0	0	0	0/0	0/0/0	0/0	0//0	0/0/	0/0/0	0/0			0/0/0	---Of a thickness exceeding 0.007mm, but not exceeding 0.01mm
0//0	0	0	0/0	0/0/0	0/0	0//0	0/0/0	5.4/5.4/5.4	5.5/5.4			0/0/0	---Other
0//0	0	1.2	0/0	0/0/0	0/0	0//0	0/0/0	0/0/5.4	5.6/0			0/0/0	--Other
0//0	0	2.8	0.6/0.6	0/0/0	0/0	0//0	0/0/0	5.4/5.4/5.4	5.6/5.4			0/0/0	-Backed
													Aluminium tubes and pipes:
0/0/0	2	3.7	0/0	0/0/0	0/0	0//0	0/0/	7.5/7.6/7.5	7.5/7.6			0/0/0	-Of aluminium, not alloyed
													-Of aluminium alloys:
													---Having an outside diameter not exceeding locm
0/0/0	2	3.7	0/0	0/0/0	0/0	0//0	0/0/	7.5/7.6/7.5	7.5/7.6			0/0/0	Tube aluminum alloy, outer diameter≤10cm, can reach at least 460 MPa-Pa(0.46×10^9 N/m^2) at 293K(20℃)
0/0/0	2	3.7	0/0	0/0/0	0/0	0//0	0/0/	7.5/7.6/7.5	7.5/7.6			0/0/0	Other alloy aluminum pipes, outer diameter≤10 cm
													---Other:
													----Having a wall thickness not exceeding 25mm
0/0/0	2	0	0/0	0/0/0	0/0	0//0	0/0/	0/0/0	7.3/0			0/0/0	Tubular aluminum alloy, outer diameter>10 cm, wall thickness ≤25mm, can reach at least 460 MPa(0.46×10^9 N/m^2) at 293K (20℃)
0/0/0	2	0	0/0	0/0/0	0/0	0//0	0/0/	0/0/0	7.3/0			0/0/0	Other alloy aluminum pipes, outer diameter> 10 cm, wall thickness ≤25mm
													----Ohter
0/0/0	2	0	0/0	0/0/0	0/0	0//0	0/0/	0/0/0	7.3/0			0/0/0	The tensile strength of tube aluminum alloy can reach at least 460 MPa(0.46×10^9 N/m^2) at 293K (20℃)
0/0/0	2	0	0/0	0/0/0	0/0	0//0	0/0/	0/0/0	7.3/0			0/0/0	Other aluminium tubes and pipes, alloys
													Aluminium tube or pipe fittings (for example, couplings, elbows, sleeves):
0/0/0	2	1.6	0/0	0/0/0	0/0	0//0	0/0/	7.2/7.2/7.2	7.3/7.2			0/0/0	Aluminium tube or pipe fittings (for example, couplings, elbows, sleeves)

税则号列	货品名称〔CIQ扩展编码及品名－T2表示见附表2〕	最惠(%)	暂定税率	普通	增值/消费	出口退税	计量单位	监管条件/特殊证件	检验检疫	对美关税	亚太上/下
76.10	**铝制结构体(税目94.06的活动房屋除外)及其部件(例如,桥梁及桥梁体段、塔、格构杆、屋顶、屋顶框架、门窗及其框架、门槛、栏杆、支柱及立柱);上述结构体用的已加工铝板、杆、型材、异型材、管子及类似品:**										
7610.1000	-门窗及其框架、门槛〔999〕	9		80	13/	13	千克	/		29	
7610.9000	-其他〔999〕	6		50	13/	13	千克	/		26	
76.11	**盛装物料用的铝制囤、柜、罐、桶及类似容器(装压缩气体或液化气体的除外),容积超过300升,不论是否衬里或隔热,但无机械或热力装置:**										
7611.0000	盛装物料用的铝制囤、柜、罐、桶及类似容器(装压缩气体或液化气体的除外),容积超过300升,不论是否衬里或隔热,但无机械或热力装置〔999〕	9		35	13/	13	千克	/		19	
76.12	**盛装物料用的铝制桶、罐、听、盒及类似容器,包括软管容器及硬管容器(装压缩气体或液化气体的除外),容积不超过300升,不论是否衬里或隔热,但无机械或热力装置:**										
7612.1000	-软管容器〔999〕	9		50	13/	13	千克	/		34	
	-其他:										
7612.9010	---易拉罐及罐体〔101 深加工铝制品,102 食品用铝包装〕	9		100	13/	13	千克	A/	R	34	
7612.9090	---其他〔999〕	9		70	13/	13	千克	/		19	
76.13	**装压缩气体或液化气体用的铝制容器:**										
7613.0010	---零售包装用〔101 装压缩或液化气的铝容器,102 深加工铝制品〕	9		70	13/	13	千克	/		19	7.2/7.2
7613.0090	---其他〔101 装压缩或液化气的铝容器,102 深加工铝制品〕	6		17	13/	13	千克	6/		16	
76.14	**非绝缘的铝制绞股线、缆、编带及类似品:**										
7614.1000	-带钢芯的〔999〕	6		20	13/	13	千克	A/	M	16	
7614.9000	-其他〔999〕	6		20	13/	13	千克	/		26	4.8/4.8
76.15	**餐桌、厨房或其他家用铝制器具及其零件;铝制擦锅器、洗刷擦光用的块垫、手套及类似品;铝制卫生器具及其零件:**										
	-餐桌、厨房或其他家用器具及其零件;擦锅器及洗刷擦光用的块垫、手套及类似品:										
7615.1010	---擦锅器、洗刷、擦光用的块垫、手套及类似品〔999〕	7		90	13/	13	千克	A/	R		
7615.1090	---其他										
7615.1090 10	铝制高压锅〔101 深加工铝制品,102 食品接触铝产品〕	7		90	13/	13	千克	A/	R	32	
7615.1090 90	其他餐桌厨房等家用铝制器具及其零件〔101 深加工铝制品,102 食品接触铝产品,103 食品用铝包装〕	7		90	13/	13	千克	A/	R	32	
7615.2000	-卫生器具及其零件〔101 深加工铝制品,102 食品接触铝产品,103 食品用铝包装〕	8		90	13/	13	千克	/		18	
76.16	**其他铝制品:**										
7616.1000	-钉、平头钉、U形钉(税目83.05的货品除外)、螺钉、螺栓、螺母、钩头螺钉、铆钉、销、开尾销、垫圈及类似品〔101 螺钉,102 螺栓,103 螺母,104 垫圈,105 其它紧固件,106 深加工铝制品〕	8		40	13/	13	千克	/		18	5.2/5.2
	-其他:										
7616.9100	--铝丝制的布、网、篱及格栅〔101〕	8		40	13/	13	千克	/		18	
	--其他:										
7616.9910	---工业用										
7616.9910 10	高度小于直径的柱形实心体铝合金[在293K(20摄氏度)时的极限抗拉强度能达到460兆帕(0.46×10^9牛顿/平方米)或更大]〔101〕	8		40	13/	13	千克	3/		18	5.2/5.2
7616.9910 90	其他工业用铝制品(不包括铝丝布、网、格栅及栅栏)〔101〕	8		40	13/	13	千克	/		18	5.2/5.2
7616.9990	---其他〔101〕	8		80	13/	13	千克	/		18	5.2/5.2

协定税率 %								RCEP		特惠税率 %			Article Description
东/冰/格	巴基斯坦	韩国	瑞士上/下	哥/秘/柬	澳/毛	新西/坡/智	中国港/澳/台	东盟及马来/澳/韩	日/新	亚太2国	老/柬/缅	98/97/95	
													Aluminium structures (excluding prefabricated buildings of heading 94. 06) and parts of structures (for example, bridges and bridge-sections, towers, lattice masts, roofs, roofing frame-works, doors and windows and their frames and thresholds for doors, balustrades, pillars and columns); aluminium plates, rods, profiles, tubes and the like, prepared for use in structures:
0/0/0	20	15	2.5/2.5	0/0/0	0/15	0/0/0	0/0/	23.8/23.8/	/23.8			0/0/0	-Doors, windows and their frames and thresholds for doors
0/0/0	0	0	0/0	0/0/0	0/0	0//0	0/0/	0/5.4/0	0/5.4			0/0/0	-Other
													Aluminium reservoirs, tanks, vats and similar containers, for any material (other than compressed or liquefied gas), of a capacity exceeding 300L, whether or not lined or heat-insulated, but not fitted with mechanical or thermal equipment:
0/0/0	4.2	2.4	1.2/1.2	0/0/0	0/0	0/0/0	0/0/	0/0/10.8	10.9/0			0/0/0	Aluminium reservoirs, tanks, vats and similar containers, for any material (other than compressed or liquefied gas), of a capacity exceeding 300L whether or not lined or heat-insulated, but not fitted with mechanical or thermal equipment
													Aluminium casks, drums, cans, boxes and similar containers (including rigid or collapsible tubular containers), for any material (other than compressed or liquefied gas), of a capacity not exceeding 300 l, whether or not lined or heat-insulated, but not fitted with mechanical or thermal equipment:
0/0/0	4.8	2.4	1.2/1.2	0/0/0	0/0	0/0/0	0/0/	0/0/10.8	10.9/0			0/0/0	-Collapsible tubular containers
													-Other:
0/0/0	24		3/3	0/0/0	0/18	0/0/0	0/0/	5/5/	/5			0/0/0	---Tear tab ends and bodies thereof
0/0/0	4.2	2.4	1.2/1.2	0/0/0	0/0	0/0/0	0/0/	0/0/10.8	10.9/0			0/0/0	---Other
													Aluminium containers for compressed or liquefied gas:
0/0/0	4.2	2.4	5/5	0/0/0	0/0	0/0/0	0/0/	0/0/10.8	10.9/0			0/0/0	---For retail packing
0/0/0	0	0	0/0	0/0/0	0/0	0//0	0/0/	0/0/0	0/0			0/0/0	---Other
													Stranded wire, cables, plaited bands and the like, of aluminium, not electrically insulated:
0/0/0	0	0	0/0	0/0/0	0/0	0//0	0/0/	0/0/0	0/0			0/0/0	-With steel core
0/0/0	0	0	0/0	0/0/0	0/0	0//0	0/0/	0/0/0	0/0			0/0/0	-Other
													Table, kitchen or other household articles and parts thereof, of aluminium; pot scourers and scouring or polishing pads, gloves and the like, of aluminium; sanitary ware and parts thereof, of aluminium:
													-Table, kitchen or other household articles and parts thereof; pot scourers and scouring or polishing pads, gloves and the like:
0/0/0	10.1	3.6	1.8/1.8	0/0/0	0/0	0/0/0	0/0/	0/0/16.2	16.4/0			0/0/0	---Pot scourers and scouring or polishing pads, gloves and the like
													---Other
0/0/0	8.4	9	1.5/1.5	0/0/0	0/9	0/0/0	0/0/	14.3/14.3/	/14.3			0/0/0	Aluminum pressure cooker
0/0/0	8.4	9	1.5/1.5	0/0/0	0/9	0/0/0	0/0/	14.3/14.3/	/14.3			0/0/0	Other household aluminum utensils used on dining tables and in kitchens and parts thereof
0/0/0	10.1	3.6	1.8/1.8	0/0/0	0/0	0/0/0	0/0/	0/0/16.2	16.4/0			0/0/0	-Sanitary ware and parts thereof
													Other articles of aluminium:
0/0/0	2	2	0/0	0/0/0	0/0	0/0/0	0/0/	9/9/9	9.1/9			0/0/0	-Nails, tacks, staples (other than those of heading 83.05), screws, bolts, nuts, screw hooks, rivets, cotters, cotter-pins, washers and similar articles
													-Other:
0/0/0	8	2	0/0	0/0/0	0/0	0/0/0	0/0/	0/0/9	9.1/0			0/0/0	--Cloth, grill, netting and fencing, of aluminium wire
													--Other:
													---For technical use
0/0/0	3.5	6	1/1	0/0/0	0/0	0/0/0	0/0/	9.5/9.5/9.5	9.5/9.5			0/0/0	Aluminum of cylinder shape with height less than diameter [tensile strengh can reach 460 MPa ($0.46 \times 10^9 N/m^2$) or more at 293k (20℃)]
0/0/0	3.5	6	1/1	0/0/0	0/0	0/0/0	0/0/	9.5/9.5/9.5	9.5/9.5			0/0/0	Other articles of alumnum for thechnical use (other than cloth, grill, netting and fencing, of aluminum wire)
0/0/0	6	3	1.5/1.5	0/0/0	0/0	0/0/0	0/0/	13.5/13.5/13.5	13.6/13.5			0/0/0	---Other

第七十八章
铅及其制品

子目注释：

本章所称“精炼铅”，是指：

按重量计含铅量至少为99.9%的金属，但其他各种元素的含量不超过下表中规定的限量：

其他元素表

元　　素		所含重量百分比
Ag	银	0.02
As	砷	0.005
Bi	铋	0.05
Ca	钙	0.002
Cd	镉	0.002
Cu	铜	0.08
Fe	铁	0.002
S	硫	0.002
Sb	锑	0.005
Sn	锡	0.005
Zn	锌	0.002
其他（例如碲），每种		0.001

税则号列	货品名称〔CIQ扩展编码及品名－T2表示见附表2〕	最惠(%)	暂定税率	普通	增值/消费	出口退税	计量单位	监管条件/特殊证件	检验检疫	对美关税	亚太上/下
78.01	**未锻轧铅：**										
7801.1000	-精炼铅〔999〕	3		20	13/	0	千克	/			
	-其他：										
7801.9100	--按重量计所含其他元素是以锑为主的〔999〕	3		20	13/	0	千克	/		28	
7801.9900	--其他〔999〕	3		20	13/	0	千克	/		28	2.7/2.7
78.02	**铅废碎料：**										
7802.0000	铅废碎料〔999〕	1.5		10	13/	0	千克	9/			
78.04	**铅板、片、带、箔；铅粉及片状粉末：**										
	-板、片、带、箔：										
7804.1100	--片、带及厚度（衬背除外）不超过0.2毫米的箔〔999〕	6		30	13/	13	千克	/		16	
7804.1900	--其他〔999〕	6		30	13/	0	千克	/		31	
7804.2000	-粉末及片状粉末〔999〕	6		35	13/	0	千克	/		16	
78.06	**其他铅制品：**										
7806.0010	---铅条、杆、型材及异型材或丝〔101〕	6		30	13/	0	千克	/		16	
7806.0090	---其他〔101其它装压缩或液化气的容器及其零件，102深加工铅制品〕	6		40	13/	0	千克	/		16	

Chapter 78
Lead and articles thereof

Subheading Note:

In this Chapter the expression "refined lead" means:

Metal containing by weight at least 99. 9% of lead, provided that the content by weight of any other element does not exceed the limit specified in the following table:

TABLE — Other elements

Element		Limiting centen% by weight
Ag	Silver	0.02
As	Arsenic	0.005
Bi	Bismuth	0.05
Ca	Calcium	0.002
Cd	Cadmium	0.002
Cu	Copper	0.08
Fe	Iron	0.002
S	Sulphur	0.002
Sb	Antimony	0.005
Sn	Tin	0.005
Zn	Zinc	0.002
Other(for example Te), each		0.001

协定税率 %								RCEP		特惠税率 %			Article Description
东/冰/格	巴基斯坦	韩国	瑞士上/下	哥/秘/柬	澳/毛	新西/坡/智	中国港/澳/台	东盟及马来/澳/韩	日/新	亚太2国	老/柬/缅	98/97/95	
													Unwrought lead:
0/0/0	0	0	0/0	0/0/0	0/0	0//0	0/0/	0/0/0	0/0			0/0/0	-Refined lead
													-Other:
0/0/0	0	0	0/0	0/0/0	0/0	0//0	0/0/	0/0/0	2.7/0			0/0/0	--Containing by weight antimony as the principal other element
0/0/0	0	0	0/0	0/0/0	0/0	0//0	0/0/	0/0/0	0/0			0/0/0	--Other
													Lead waste and scrap:
0/0/0	0	0	0/0	0/0/0	0/0	0//0	0/0/	0/0/0	0/0			0/0/0	Lead waste and scrap
													Lead plates sheets, strip and foil; lead powders and flakes:
													-Plates, sheets, strip and foil:
0/0/0	0	0	0/0	0/0/0	0/0	0//0	0/0/	0/0/0	0/0			0/0/0	--Sheets, strip and foil of a thickness (excluding any backing) not exceeding 0. 2mm
0/0/0	0	0	0/0	0/0/0	0/0	0//0	0/0/	0/0/0	0/0			0/0/0	--Other
0/0/0	0	0	0/0	0/0/0	0/0	0//0	0/0/	0/0/0	0/0			0/0/0	-Powders and flakes
													Other articles of lead:
0/0/0	0	1.2	0/0	0/0/0	0/0	0//0	0/0/	0/0/5.4	5.5/0			0/0/0	---Lead bars, rods, profiles and wire
0/0/0	3.5	0	0/0	0/0/0	0/0	0//0	0/0/	0/0/0	0/0			0/0/0	---Other

第七十九章
锌及其制品

子目注释：

本章所用有关名词解释如下：

一、非合金锌

按重量计含锌量至少为97.5%的金属。

二、锌合金

按重量计含锌量大于其他元素单项含量的金属物质，但按重量计其他元素的总含量超过2.5%。

三、锌末

冷凝锌雾所得的锌末。该产品由球形微粒组成，比锌粉更为精细，按重量计至少80%的微粒可以通过孔径为63微米的筛子，而且必须含有按重量计至少为85%的金属锌。

税则号列	货品名称〔CIQ扩展编码及品名—T2表示见附表2〕	最惠(%)	暂定税率	普通	增值/消费	出口退税	计量单位	监管条件/特殊证件	检验检疫	对美关税	亚太上/下
79.01	**未锻轧锌：**										
	-非合金锌：										
	--按重量计含锌量在99.99%及以上：										
7901.1110	---按重量计含锌量在99.995%及以上〔999〕	3	1	20	13/	0	千克	/		26	
7901.1190	---其他〔999〕	3	1	20	13/	0	千克	/			
7901.1200	--按重量计含锌量低于99.99%〔999〕	3	1	20	13/	0	千克	/		21	
7901.2000	-锌合金〔999〕	3	1	20	13/	0	千克	/		26	
79.02	**锌废碎料：**										
7902.0000	锌废碎料〔999〕	1.5		20	13/	0	千克	9/		26.5	
79.03	**锌末、锌粉及片状粉末：**										
7903.1000	-锌末〔301危险化学品，遇水放出易燃气体的物质；302其他〕	6		20	13/	0	千克	A/13	M	31	
7903.9000	-其他										
7903.9000 10	颗粒＜500μm的锌及其合金(含量≥97%，不论球形、椭球体、雾化、片状、研碎金属燃料)〔301危险化学品，遇水放出易燃气体的物质；302其他〕	6		20	13/	0	千克	3A/13	M	16	
7903.9000 90	其他锌粉及片状粉末〔301危险化学品，遇水放出易燃气体的物质；302其他〕	6		20	13/	0	千克	AB/13	MN	16	
79.04	**锌条、杆、型材及异型材或丝：**										
7904.0000	锌条、杆、型材及异型材或丝〔999〕	6		30	13/	0	千克	/		31	
79.05	**锌板、片、带、箔：**										
7905.0000	锌板、片、带、箔〔999〕	6		30	13/	0	千克	/		16	
79.07	**其他锌制品：**										
7907.0020	---锌管及锌制管子附件(例如，接头、肘管、管套)〔101其它装压缩或液化气的容器及其零件，102深加工锌制品〕	6		30	13/	0	千克	/		16	
7907.0030	---电池壳体坯料(锌饼)〔101〕	6		40	13/	0	千克	/			4.2/4.2
7907.0090	---其他〔101其它装压缩或液化气的容器及其零件，102深加工锌制品〕	6		40	13/	0	千克	/		31	

Chapter 79
Zinc and articles thereof

Subheading Note:

In this Chapter the following expressions have the meanings hereby assigned to them:

1. Zinc, not alloyed
   Metal containing by weight at least 97.5% of zinc.
2. Zinc alloys
   Metallic substances in which zinc predominates by weight over each of the other elements, provided that the total content by weight of such other elements exceeds 2.5%.
3. Zinc dust
   Dust obtained by condensation of zinc vapour, consisting of spherical particles which are finer than zinc powders. At least 80% by weight of the particles pass through a sieve with 63 micrometres (microns) mesh. It must contain at least 85% by weight of metallic zinc.

协定税率 %								RCEP		特惠税率 %			Article Description
东/冰/格	巴基斯坦	韩国	瑞士上/下	哥/秘/柬	澳/毛	新西/坡/智	中国港/澳/台	东盟及马来/澳/韩	日/新	亚太2国	老/柬/缅	98/97/95	
													Unwrought zinc:
													-Zinc, not alloyed:
													--Containing by weight 99.99% or more of zinc:
0/0/0	0	0	0/0	0/0/0	0/0	0//0	0/0/	0/0/0	0/0			0/0/0	---Containing by weight 99.995% or more of zinc
0/0/0	0	0	0/0	0/0/0	0/0	0//0	0/0/	0/0/0	0/0			0/0/0	---Other
0/0/0	0	0	0/0	0/0/0	0/0	0//0	0/0/	0/0/0	0/0			0/0/0	--Containing by weight less than 99.99% of zinc
0/0/0	0	0	0/0	0/0/0	0/0	0//0	0/0/	0/0/0	0/0			0/0/0	-Zinc alloys
													Zinc waste and scrap:
0/0/0	0	0	0/0	0/0/0	0/0	0//0	0/0/	0/0/0	0/0			0/0/0	Zinc waste and scrap
													Zinc dust, powders and flakes:
0/0/0	0	1.2	0/0	0/0/0	0/0	0//0	0/0/	0/0/5.4	5.5/0			0/0/0	-Zinc dust
													-Other
0/0/0	0	1.2	0.6/0.6	0/0/0	0/0	0//0	0/0/	0/0/5.4	5.5/0			0/0/0	Zinc and its alloys, granularity<500μm (containing zinc≥97%, whether spheroid, ellipsoid, atomized, flake formed, ground metallic fuels)
0/0/0	0	1.2	0.6/0.6	0/0/0	0/0	0//0	0/0/	0/0/5.4	5.5/0			0/0/0	Other zine powders and flakes
													Zinc bars, rods, profiles and wire:
0/0/0	0	2.8	0/0	0/0/0	0/0	0//0	0/0/	5.4/5.4/5.4	5.6/5.4			0/0/0	Zinc bars, rods, profiles and wire
													Zinc plates, sheets, strip and foil:
0/0/0	0	0	0/0	0/0/0	0/0	0//0	0/0/	0/0/0	0/0			0/0/0	Zinc plates, sheets, strip and foil
													Other articles of zinc:
0/0/0	0	0	0/0	0/0/0	0/0	0//0	0/0/	0/0/0	0/0			0/0/0	---Zinc tubes pipes and tube or pipe fittings (for example, couplings, elbows, sleeves)
0/0/0	0	0	0/0	0/1.3/0	0/0	0//0	0/0/	0/0/0	5.5/0			0/0/0	---Cellpacking blanks(zinc biscuits)
0/0/0	0	0	0/0	0/0/0	0/0	0//0	0/0/	0/0/0	0/0			0/0/0	---Other

第八十章
锡及其制品

子目注释：

本章所用有关名词解释如下：

一、非合金锡

按重量计含锡量至少为99%的金属，但含铋量或含铜量不超过下表中规定的限量：

其他元素表

元　　素	所含重量百分比
Bi　　铋	0.1
Cu　　铜	0.4

二、锡合金

按重量计含锡量大于其他元素单项含量的金属物质，但：

(一)按重量计其他元素的总含量超过1%；

(二)按重量计含铋量或含铜量应等于或大于上表中规定的限量。

税则号列	货品名称〔CIQ扩展编码及品名－T2表示见附表2〕	最惠(%)	暂定税率	普通	增值/消费	出口退税	计量单位	监管条件/特殊证件	检验检疫	对美关税	亚太上/下
80.01	**未锻轧锡：**										
8001.1000	-非合金锡〔999〕	3		20	13/	0	千克	4xy/		28	
	-锡合金：										
8001.2010	---锡基巴毕脱合金〔999〕	3		20	13/	0	千克	4xy/		13	2.4/2.4
	---焊锡：										
8001.2021	----按重量计含铅量在0.1%以下的〔101 焊锡，102 锡合金〕	3		30	13/	0	千克	4xy/		28	
8001.2029	----其他〔101 焊锡，102 锡合金〕	3		30	13/	0	千克	4xy/		28	
8001.2090	---其他〔999〕	3		30	13/	0	千克	4xy/		28	
80.02	**锡废碎料：**										
8002.0000	锡废碎料〔999〕	1.5		30	13/	0	千克	49xy/		26.5	
80.03	**锡条、杆、型材及异型材或丝：**										
8003.0000	锡条、杆、型材及异型材或丝〔999〕	8		40	13/	0	千克	4xy/		33	
80.07	**其他锡制品：**										
8007.0020	---锡板、片及带，厚度超过0.2毫米〔101〕	8		40	13/	0	千克	4xy/		33	
8007.0030	---锡箔(不论是否印花或用纸、纸板、塑料或类似材料衬背)，厚度(衬背除外)不超过0.2毫米；锡粉及片状粉末〔101〕	8		40	13/	13	千克	/		28	
8007.0040	---锡管及管子附件(例如，接头、肘管、管套)〔101 其它装压缩或液化气的容器及其零件，102 深加工锡制品〕	8		45	13/	0	千克	4xy/		18	6.4/6.4
8007.0090	---其他〔101 其它装压缩或液化气的容器及其零件，102 深加工锡制品〕	8		80	13/	0	千克	/		33	

Chapter 80
Tin and articles thereof

Subheading Note:

In this Chapter the following expressions have the meanings hereby assigned to them:

1. Tin, not alloyed.

Metal containing by weight at least 99% of tin, provided that the content by weight of any bismuth or copper is less than the limit specified in the following table:

TABLE — Other elements

Element		Limiting content % by weight
Bi	Bismuth	0.1
Cu	Copper	0.4

2. **Tin alloys**

Metallic substances in which tin predominates by weight over each of the other elements, provided that:

(a) the total content by weight of such other elements exceeds 1%; or

(b) the content by weight of either bismuth or copper is equal to or greater than the limit specified in the foregoing table.

协定税率 %									RCEP		特惠税率 %			Article Description
东/冰/格	巴基斯坦	韩国	瑞士上/下	哥/秘/柬	澳/毛	新西/坡/智	中国港/澳/台	东盟及马来/澳/韩	日/新	亚太2国	老/柬/缅	98/97/95	
													Unwrought tin:
0/0/0	0	0	0/0	0/0/0	0/0	0//0	0/0/	0/0/0	0/0			0/0/0	-Tin, not alloyed
													-Tin alloys:
0/0/0	0	0	0/0	0/0/0	0/0	0//0	0/0/	0/0/0	0/0			0/0/0	---Babbitt metal
													---solder:
0/0/0	0	0	0/0	0/0/0	0/0	0//0	0/0/	0/0/0	0/0			0/0/0	----Containing by weight less than 0.1% of lead
0/0/0	0	0	0/0	0/0/0	0/0	0//0	0/0/	0/0/0	0/0			0/0/0	----Other
0/0/0	0	0	0/0	0/0/0	0/0	0//0	0/0/	0/0/0	0/0			0/0/0	---Other
													Tin waste and scrap:
0/0/0	0	0	0/0	0/0/0	0/0	0//0	0/0/	0/0/0	0/0			0/0/0	Tin waste and scrap
													Tin bars, rods, profiles and wire:
0/0/0	2	1.6	0/0	0/0/0	0/0	0//0	0/0/	0/0/7.2	7.3/0			0/0/0	Tin bars, rods, profiles and wire
													Other articles of tin:
0/0/0	2	0	0/0	0/0/0	0/0	0//0	0/0/	0/0/0	7.3/0			0/0/0	---Tin plates, sheets and strip, of a thickness exceeding 0.2mm
0/0/0	2	0	0/0	0/0/0	0/0	0//0	0/0/	0/0/0	7.3/0			0/0/0	---Tin foil (whether or not printed or backed with paper, paperboard, plastics or similar backing materials), of a thickness (excluding and backing) not exceeding 0.2mm; tin powders and flakes
0/0/0	2	0	0.8/0.8	0/0/0	0/0	0//0	0/0/	0/0/0	7.3/0			0/0/0	---Tin tubes, pipes and tube or pipe fittings (for example, couplings, elbows, sleeves)
0/0/0	5.1	3.7	0/0	0/0/0	0/0	0//0	0/0/	7.5/7.6/7.5	7.5/7.6			0/0/0	---Other

第八十一章
其他贱金属、金属陶瓷及其制品

税则号列	货品名称〔CIQ 扩展编码及品名－T2 表示见附表 2〕	最惠(%)	暂定税率	普通	增值/消费	出口退税	计量单位	监管条件/特殊证件	检验检疫	对美关税	亚太上/下
81.01	**钨及其制品，包括废碎料：**										
8101.1000	-粉末										
8101.1000 10	颗粒＜500μm 的钨及其合金(含量≥97%，不论球形、椭球体、雾化、片状、研碎金属燃料)〔999〕	6		20	13/	0	千克	3/		26	
8101.1000 90	其他钨粉末〔999〕	6		20	13/	0	千克	4xy/		26	
	-其他：										
8101.9400	--未锻轧钨，包括简单烧结而成的条、杆〔999〕	3		20	13/	0	千克	4xy/		23	
8101.9600	--丝〔999〕	8		20	13/	13	千克	/		28	
8101.9700	--废碎料〔999〕	3		20	13/	0	千克	49xy/		28	
	--其他：										
8101.9910	---条、杆，但简单烧结而成的除外；型材及异型材，板、片、带、箔〔999〕	5		30	13/	0	千克	/		15	
8101.9990	---其他〔999〕	8		70	13/	0	千克	/		18	
81.02	**钼及其制品，包括废碎料：**										
8102.1000	-粉末〔999〕	6		20	13/	0	千克	4xy/		16	
	-其他：										
8102.9400	--未锻轧钼，包括简单烧结而成的条、杆〔999〕	3		20	13/	0	千克	4xy/		28	
8102.9500	--条、杆，但简单烧结而成的除外；型材及异型材，板、片、带、箔〔101〕	8		30	13/	0	千克	/		33	
8102.9600	--丝〔101〕	8		20	13/	13	千克	/		33	
8102.9700	--废碎料〔999〕	3		20	13/	0	千克	49xy/			
8102.9900	--其他〔101 其他深加工金属制品〕	8		70	13/	0	千克	4xy/		18	
81.03	**钽及其制品，包括废碎料：**										
	-未锻轧钽，包括简单烧结而成的条、杆；粉末：										
	---钽粉：										
8103.2011	----松装密度小于 2.2g/cm³ 的〔999〕	6		14	13/	13	千克	4xy/		31	4.2/4.2
8103.2019	----其他〔999〕	6		14	13/	0	千克	4xy/		16	
8103.2090	---其他〔999〕	6		14	13/	0	千克	4xy/		26	
8103.3000	-废碎料〔999〕	6		14	13/	0	千克	49xy/		31	
	-其他：										
8103.9100	--坩埚										
8103.9100 10	钽坩埚(容积在 50ml 至 2L 之间)(用纯度为 99.9%或更高的钽制造或作衬里，或用纯度 98%或更高的钽制造或作衬里并用碳化钽、氮化钽或硼化钽(或其任何组合)涂层)〔999〕	8		30	13/	0	千克	3/		18	7.2/7.2
8103.9100 90	其他钽坩埚〔999〕	8		30	13/	13	千克	/		18	7.2/7.2
	--其他：										
	---钽丝：										
8103.9911	----直径小于 0.5mm〔101 其他深加工金属制品〕〔999〕	8		30	13/	13	千克	4xy/			5.6/5.6
8103.9919	----其他〔101 其他深加工金属制品〕〔999〕	8		30	13/	13	千克	4xy/		18	5.6/5.6
8103.9990	---其他〔999〕	8		30	13/	13	千克	4xy/		18	7.2/7.2
81.04	**镁及其制品，包括废碎料：**										
	-未锻轧镁：										
8104.1100	--按重量计含镁量至少为 99.8%〔301 危险化学品，易燃固体；302 不属于危险化学品的金属〕	6		20	13/	0	千克	/13		31	3/3
8104.1900	--其他〔301 属于危险化学品的金属，302 不属于危险化学品的金属〕	6		20	13/	0	千克	/		16	
8104.2000	-废碎料〔999〕	1.5		20	13/	0	千克	9/		26.5	
8104.3000	-锉屑、车屑及颗粒，已按规格分级的；粉末										
8104.3000 10	颗粒＜500μm 的镁及其合金(含量≥97%，不论球形、椭球体、雾化、片状、研碎金属燃料)〔301 危险化学品，遇水放出易燃气体的物质；302 不属于危险化学品的金属〕	8		30	13/	0	千克	3/13		33	
8104.3000 90	其他已分级的镁锉屑，车屑，颗粒；粉末〔301 属于危险化学品的金属，302 不属于危险化学品的金属〕	8		30	13/	0	千克	/13		33	
	-其他：										
8104.9010	---锻轧镁〔301 危险化学品，易燃固体；302 其他深加工金属制品〕	8		30	13/	0	千克	/13		18	
8104.9020	---镁制品										
8104.9020 10	镁金属基复合材料(包括各种结构件和制品、各种预成形件，其中增强材料的比拉伸强度大于 7.62×10^4 m 和比模量大于 3.18×10^6 m)〔101〕	8		70	13/	13	千克	3/		33	
8104.9020 90	其他镁制品〔101〕	8		70	13/	0	千克	/		33	

Chapter 81
Other base metals; cermets; artiles thereof

协定税率 %								RCEP		特惠税率 %			Article Description
东/冰/格	巴基斯坦	韩国	瑞士上/下	哥/秘/柬	澳/毛	新西/坡/智	中国港/澳/台	东盟及马来/澳/韩	日/新	亚太2国	老/柬/缅	98/97/95	
													Tungsten (wolfram) and articles thereof, including waste and scrap:
													-Powders
0/0/0	0	0	0/0	0/0/0	0/0	0//0	0/0/	0/0/0	0/0			0/0/0	Tungesten and tungsten alloys, granularity＜500μm, (containing tungsten≥97%, whether in the form of spheroid, elipsoid, flakes, atomized or pulverized metallic fuel)
0/0/0	0	0	0/0	0/0/0	0/0	0//0	0/0/	0/0/0	0/0			0/0/0	Other tungsten powders
													-Other:
0/0/0	0	0	0.3/0.3	0/0/0	0/0	0//0	0/0/	0/0/0	2.7/0			0/0/0	--Unwrought tungsten, including bars and rods obtained simply by sintering
0/0/0	2	0	0/0	0/0/0	0/0	0//0	0/0/	0/0/0	7.3/0			0/0/0	--Wire
0/0/0	0	0	0/0	0/0/0	0/0	0//0	0/0/	0/0/0	0/0			0/0/0	--Waste and scrap
													--Other:
0/0/0	0	0	0/0	0/0/0	0/0	0//0	0/0/	0/0/0	0/0			0/0/0	---Bars and rods, other than those obtained simply by sintering, profiles, plates, sheets, strip and foil
0/0/0	2	0	0/0	0/0/0	0/0	0//0	0/0/	0/0/0	7.3/0			0/0/0	---Other
													Molybdenum and articles thereof, including waste and scrap:
0/0/0	0	0	0/0	0/0/0	0/0	0//0	0/0/	0/0/0	0/0			0/0/0	-Powders
													-Other:
0/0/0	0	0	0/0	0/0/0	0/0	0//0	0/0/	0/0/0	0/0			0/0/0	--Unwrought molybdenum, including bars and rods obtained simply by sintering
0/0/0	2	1.6	0/0	0/0/0	0/0	0//0	0/0/	0/0/7.2	7.3/0			0/0/0	--Bars and rods, other than those obtained simply by sintering, profiles, plates, sheets, strip and foil
0/0/0	2	0	0/0	0/0/0	0/0	0//0	0/0/	0/0/0	7.3/0			0/0/0	--Wire
0/0/0	0	0	0/0	0/0/0	0/0	0//0	0/0/	0/0/0	0/0			0/0/0	--Waste and scrap
0/0/0	2	0	0/0	0/0/0	0/0	0//0	0/0/	0/0/0	7.3/0			0/0/0	--Other
													Tantalum and articles thereof, including waste and scrap:
													-Unwrought tantalum, including bars and rods obtained simply by sinteing; powders:
													---Powders:
0/0/0	0	0	0/0	0/0/0	0/0	0//0	0/0/	5.4/5.4/5.4	5.5/5.4			0/0/0	----Loose density less than 2.2g/cm³
0/0/0	0	0	0/0	0/0/0	0/0	0//0	0/0/	0/0/0	0/0			0/0/0	----Other
0/0/0	0	0	0/0	0/0/0	0/0	0//0	0/0/	0/0/0	0/0			0/0/0	---Other
0/0/0	0	0	0/0	0/0/0	0/0	0//0	0/0/	0/0/0	0/0			0/0/0	-Waste and scrap
													-Other:
													--Crucible
0/0/0	2	0	0/0	0/0/0	0/0	0//0	0/0/	0/0/0	7.3/0			0/0/0	Tantalum crucible (volume between 5ml and 2L) (made or lined with tantalum with purity of 99.9% or higher, or made or lined with tantalum with purity of 98% or higher and coated with tantalum carbide, tantalum nitride or tantalum boride (or any combination thereof))
0/0/0	2	0	0/0	0/0/0	0/0	0//0	0/0/	0/0/0	7.3/0			0/0/0	Other tantalum crucibles
													--Other:
													---Wire of tantalum:
0/0/0	2	0	0/0	0/0/0	0/0	0//0	0/0/	0/0/0	7.3/0			0/0/0	----Diameter less than 0.5mm
0/0/0	2	0	0/0	0/0/0	0/0	0//0	0/0/	0/0/0	7.3/0			0/0/0	----Other
0/0/0	2	0	0/0	0/0/0	0/0	0//0	0/0/	0/0/0	7.3/0			0/0/0	---Other
													Magnesium and articles thereof, including waste and scrap:
													-Unwrought magnesium:
0/0/0	0	0	0/0	0/0/0	0/0	0//0	0/0/	0/0/0	0/0			0/0/0	--Containing at least 99.8% by weight of magnesium
0/0/0	0	0	0/0	0/0/0	0/0	0//0	0/0/	0/0/0	0/0			0/0/0	--Other
0/0/0	0	0	0/0	0/0/0	0/0	0//0	0/0/	0/0/0	0/0			0/0/0	-Waste and scrap
													-Raspings, turnings and granules, graded according to size; powders
0/0/0	2	0	0/0	0/0/0	0/0	0//0	0/0/	0/0/0	7.3/0			0/0/0	Magnesium and magnesium alloys, granularity＜500μm (containing magnesium≥97%, whether spheroid, ellipsoid, atomized, flake formed, ground metallic fuels)
0/0/0	2	0	0/0	0/0/0	0/0	0//0	0/0/	0/0/0	7.3/0			0/0/0	Other magnesium raspings, turnings and granules, graded according to size; powders
													-Other:
0/0/0	2	0	0/0	0/0/0	0/0	0//0	0/0/	0/0/0	7.3/0			0/0/0	---Wrought magnesium
													---Magnesium articles
0/0/0	2	0	0/0	0/0/0	0/0	0//0	0/0/	0/0/0	7.6/0			0/0/0	Masnesium composite materials (including various structural parts and products, various prefabricated parts and their specific tensile strength is bigger than 7.62×10^4 m and specific modulus bigger than 3.18×10^6 m)
0/0/0	2	0	0/0	0/0/0	0/0	0//0	0/0/	0/0/0	7.6/0			0/0/0	Other magnesium articlec

税则号列	货品名称〔CIQ扩展编码及品名－T2表示见附表2〕	最惠(%)	暂定税率	普通	增值/消费	出口退税	计量单位	监管条件/特殊证件	检验检疫	对美关税	亚太上/下
81.05	**钴锍及其他冶炼钴时所得的中间产品；钴及其制品，包括废碎料：**										
	-钴锍及其他冶炼钴时所得的中间产品；未锻轧钴；粉末：										
8105.2010	---钴湿法冶炼中间品〔999〕	4	0	14	13/	0	千克	4xy/			
8105.2020	---未锻轧钴〔999〕	4	2	14	13/	0	千克	4xy/			
8105.2090	---其他										
8105.2090 01	钴锍及其他冶炼钴时所得中间产品〔999〕	4	0	14	13/	0	千克	4xy/		25	
8105.2090 10	钴≥99.5%的超细钴粉(费氏粒度0.8-1.5μm，松装密度0.4-0.8g/cm³)〔999〕	4		14	13/	0	千克	/		29	
8105.2090 90	其他钴锍、粉末〔999〕	4		14	13/	0	千克	4xy/		29	
8105.3000	-废碎料〔999〕	4		14	13/	0	千克	49xy/			
8105.9000	-其他										
8105.9000 10	外科植入用钴铬钼合金棒(钴≥55%，铬26%－30%，钼5%－7%)〔999〕	8	4	30	13/	0	千克	4xy/		14	
8105.9000 90	其他钴及制品〔999〕	8		30	13/	0	千克	4xy/		18	
81.06	**铋及其制品，包括废碎料：**										
	-按重量计铋含量在99.99%以上：										
8106.1010	---未锻轧铋；废碎料；粉末										
8106.1010 11	高纯度未锻轧的铋(纯度≥99.99%，含银量低于1/10⁵)〔999〕	3	1	20	13/	0	千克	3/		26	
8106.1010 19	高纯度未锻轧的铋废料、粉末(纯度≥99.99%，含银量低于1/10⁵)〔999〕	3		20	13/	0	千克	3/		28	
8106.1010 91	其他未锻轧铋(纯度≥99.99%)〔999〕	3	1	20	13/	0	千克	4xy/		26	
8106.1010 92	其他未锻轧铋废碎料(纯度≥99.99%)〔999〕	3		20	13/	0	千克	49xy/		28	
8106.1010 99	其他未锻轧铋粉末(纯度≥99.99%)〔999〕	3		20	13/	0	千克	4xy/		28	
8106.1090	---其他										
8106.1090 10	其他高纯度铋及其制品(纯度≥99.99%，含银量低于1/10⁵)〔999〕	8		30	13/	13	千克	3/		18	
8106.1090 90	其他铋及铋制品(纯度≥99.99%)〔999〕	8		30	13/	0	千克	4xy/		18	
	-其他：										
8106.9010	---未锻轧铋；废碎料；粉末										
8106.9010 11	其他未锻轧铋(纯度为99.99%，含银量低于1/10⁵)〔999〕	3		20	13/	0	千克	3/		26	
8106.9010 19	其他未锻轧铋〔999〕	3		20	13/	0	千克	4xy/		26	
8106.9010 21	其他未锻轧铋废碎料(纯度为99.99%，含银量低于1/10⁵)〔999〕	3		20	13/	0	千克	39/		28	
8106.9010 29	其他未锻轧铋废碎料〔999〕	3		20	13/	0	千克	49xy/		28	
8106.9010 91	其他未锻轧铋粉末(纯度为99.99%，含银量低于1/10⁵)〔999〕	3		20	13/	0	千克	3/		28	
8106.9010 99	其他未锻轧铋粉末〔999〕	3		20	13/	0	千克	4xy/		28	
8106.9090	---其他										
8106.9090 10	其他铋及铋制品(纯度为99.99%，含银量低于1/10⁵)〔999〕	8		30	13/	0	千克	3/		18	
8106.9090 90	其他铋及铋制品〔999〕	8		30	13/	0	千克	4xy/		18	
81.08	**钛及其制品，包括废碎料：**										
	-未锻轧钛；粉末：										
	---未锻轧钛：										
8108.2021	----海绵钛〔301〕	3		14	13/	0	千克	4xy/		28	
8108.2029	----其他										
8108.2029 10	颗粒＜500μm的钛及其合金(含量≥97%，不论球形、椭球体、雾化、片状、研碎金属燃料)〔301 属于危险化学品的金属，999 低风险金属材料〕	3		14	13/	0	千克	3A/	M	13	
8108.2029 90	其他未锻轧钛〔999〕	3		14	13/	0	千克	4xy/		13	
8108.2030	---粉末〔301 危险化学品，易于自燃的物质；302 其他〕	3		14	13/	0	千克	4Axy/13	M	28	
8108.3000	-废碎料〔999〕	3		14	13/	0	千克	49xy/		28	
	-其他：										
8108.9010	---条、杆、型材及异型材										
8108.9010 10	钛合金，实心圆柱体，包括锻件(20℃下极限抗拉强度≥900兆帕，外径超过75mm)〔999〕	8		30	13/	13	千克	3/		18	
8108.9010 20	钛金属基复合材料的条、杆、型材及异型材(其中增强材料的比拉伸强度大于7.62×10⁶米和比模量大于3.18×10⁷米)〔999〕	8		30	13/	13	千克	3/		18	
8108.9010 30	外科植入用钛合金条、杆、型材及异型材(钛≥88%，5.5%≤铝≤6.75%，3.5%≤钒≤4.5%)，复合材料除外〔999〕	8	4	30	13/	13	千克	/		14	
8108.9010 90	其他钛条、杆、型材及异型材〔999〕	8		30	13/	13	千克	/		18	
8108.9020	---丝〔101〕	8		30	13/	13	千克	/		18	6.4/6.4
	---板、片、带、箔：										
8108.9031	----厚度不超过0.8毫米〔101〕	8	4	30	13/	13	千克	/		24	
8108.9032	----厚度超过0.8毫米										

协定税率 %								RCEP		特惠税率 %			Article Description
东/冰/格	巴基斯坦	韩国	瑞士上/下	哥/秘/柬	澳/毛	新西/坡/智	中国港/澳/台	东盟及马来/澳/韩	日/新	亚太2国	老/柬/缅	98/97/95	
													Cobalt mattes and other intermediate products of cobalt matallurgy; cobalt and articles thereof, including waste and scrap:
													-Cobalt mattes and other intermediate products of cobalt matallurgy; unwrought cobalt; powders:
0/0/0	0	0	0/0	0/0/0	0/0	0//0	0/0/	0/0/0	0/0			0/0/0	---Intermediate products of cobalt metallurgy by wet process
0/0/0	0	0	0/0	0/0/0	0/0	0//0	0/0/	0/0/0	0/0			0/0/0	---Unwrought cobalt
													---Other
0/0/0	0	0	0/0	0/0/0	0/0	0//0	0/0/	0/3.6/0	0/3.6			0/0/0	Mid-product smelted with cobalt and sulfur and others
0/0/0	0	0	0/0	0/0/0	0/0	0//0	0/0/	0/3.6/0	0/3.6			0/0/0	Supper-fine cobalt powders, containing ≥99.5% by weight of cobalt (fischer granularinty 0.8～1.5μm. bulk package density 0.4～0.8g/cm³)
0/0/0	0	0	0/0	0/0/0	0/0	0//0	0/0/	0/3.6/0	0/3.6			0/0/0	Other cobalt mattes;powders
0/0/0	0	0	0/0	0/0/0	0/0	0//0	0/0/	0/0/0	0/0			0/0/0	-Waste and scrap
													-Other
0/0/0	2	1.6	0/0	0/0/0	0/0	0//0	0/0/	0/0/7.2	7.3/0			0/0/0	Cobalt chromium molybdenum alloy rod for surgical implantation (cobalt ≥ 55%, chromium 26% － 3%, molybdenum 5% － 7%)
0/0/0	2	1.6	0/0	0/0/0	0/0	0//0	0/0/	0/0/7.2	7.3/0			0/0/0	Other cobalt and products
													Bismuth and articles thereof, including waste and scrap:
													-Containing more than 99.99 % of bismuth, by weight:
													---Unwrought cadmium;waste and scrap powders
0/0/0	0	0	0/0	0/0/0	0/0	0//0	0/0/	0/0/0	0/0			0/0/0	High purity unwrought bismuth (purity ≥ 99.99%, silver content less than 1/10⁵)
0/0/0	0	0	0/0	0/0/0	0/0	0//0	0/0/	0/0/0	0/0			0/0/0	High purity unwrought bismuth scrap and powder (purity ≥ 99.99%, silver content less than 1/10⁵)
0/0/0	0	0	0/0	0/0/0	0/0	0//0	0/0/	0/0/0	0/0			0/0/0	Other unwrought bismuth (purity ≥ 99.99%)
0/0/0	0	0	0/0	0/0/0	0/0	0//0	0/0/	0/0/0	0/0			0/0/0	Other unwrought bismuth scrap (purity ≥ 99.99%)
0/0/0	0	0	0/0	0/0/0	0/0	0//0	0/0/	0/0/0	0/0			0/0/0	Other unwrought bismuth powder (purity ≥ 99.99%)
													---Other
0/0/0	2	1.6	0/0	0/0/0	0/0	0//0	0/0/	0/0/7.2	7.3/0			0/0/0	Other high purity bismuth and its products (purity ≥ 99.99%, silver content less than1/10⁵)
0/0/0	2	1.6	0/0	0/0/0	0/0	0//0	0/0/	0/0/7.2	7.3/0			0/0/0	Other bismuth and bismuth products (purity ≥ 99.99%)
													-Other:
													---Unwrought cadmium;waste and scrap powders
0/0/0	0	0	0/0	0/0/0	0/0	0//0	0/0/	0/0/0	0/0			0/0/0	Other unwrought bismuth(The purity is 99.99%, and the silver content is less than 1/10⁵)
0/0/0	0	0	0/0	0/0/0	0/0	0//0	0/0/	0/0/0	0/0			0/0/0	Other unwrought bismuth
0/0/0	0	0	0/0	0/0/0	0/0	0//0	0/0/	0/0/0	0/0			0/0/0	Other unwrought bismuth scrap(The purity is 99.99%, and the silver content is less than 1/10⁵)
0/0/0	0	0	0/0	0/0/0	0/0	0//0	0/0/	0/0/0	0/0			0/0/0	Other unwrought bismuth scrap
0/0/0	0	0	0/0	0/0/0	0/0	0//0	0/0/	0/0/0	0/0			0/0/0	Other unwrought bismuth powders(The purity is 99.99%, and the silver content is less than 1/10⁵)
0/0/0	0	0	0/0	0/0/0	0/0	0//0	0/0/	0/0/0	0/0			0/0/0	Other unwrought bismuth powders
													---Other
0/0/0	2	1.6	0/0	0/0/0	0/0	0//0	0/0/	0/0/7.2	7.3/0			0/0/0	Other bismuth and bismuth products(The purity is 99.99%, and the silver content is less than 1/10⁵)
0/0/0	2	1.6	0/0	0/0/0	0/0	0//0	0/0/	0/0/7.2	7.3/0			0/0/0	Other bismuth and bismuth products
													Titanium and articles thereof, including waste and scrap:
													-Unwrought titanium; powders:
													---Unwrousht titanium:
0/0/0	0	0	0/0	0/0/0	0/0	0//0	0/0/	0/0/0	0/0			0/0/0	----Sponge titanium
													----Other
0/0/0	0	0	0/0	0/0/0	0/0	0//0	0/0/	0/0/0	0/0			0/0/0	Titanium and its alloy with the particles ＜500μm (containing ≥97%,whether in balls, atomized, in sheet or in pulverized metal fuel)
0/0/0	0	0	0/0	0/0/0	0/0	0//0	0/0/	0/0/0	0/0			0/0/0	Other unwrought titanium;powders
0/0/0	0	0	0/0	0/0/0	0/0	0//0	0/0/	0/0/0	0/0			0/0/0	---Powders
0/0/0	0	0	0/0	0/0/0	0/0	0//0	0/0/	0/0/0	0/0			0/0/0	-Waste and scrap
													-Other:
													---Bars, rods, shapes and sections
0/0/0	2	1.6	0/0	0/0/0	0/0	0//0	0/0/	0/0/7.2	7.3/0			0/0/0	Titanium alloys, solid cylinder, including castings (ultimate tensile strength≥900MPa at 20℃, outer diameter＞75mm)
0/0/0	2	1.6	0/0	0/0/0	0/0	0//0	0/0/	0/0/7.2	7.3/0			0/0/0	Bars, rods, shaps and sections, made of composite material with titanium metal (the degree of streangth of intensity waterial ＞7.62×10⁶ m,and specific modulus ＞3.18×10⁷ m)
0/0/0	2	1.6	0/0	0/0/0	0/0	0//0	0/0/	0/0/7.2	7.3/0			0/0/0	Titanium alloy bars, rods, profiles and profiles for surgical implantation (titanium ≥ 88%, 5.5% ≤ aluminum ≤ 6.75%, 3.5% ≤ vanadium ≤ 4.5%), except composite materials
0/0/0	2	1.6	0/0	0/0/0	0/0	0//0	0/0/	0/0/7.2	7.3/0			0/0/0	Other bars, rods, shapes and sections,of titanium
0/0/0	2	0	0/0	0/0/0	0/0	0//0	0/0/	0/0/0	7.3/0			0/0/0	---Wire
													---Plates, sheets, strap, foil:
0/0/0	2	0	0/0	0/0/0	0/0	0//0	0/0/	7.2/7.2/7.2	7.3/7.2			0/0/0	----Of a thickness not more than 0.8mm
													----Of a thickness more than 0.8mm

税则号列	货品名称〔CIQ 扩展编码及品名－T2 表示见附表 2〕	最惠(%)	暂定税率	普通	增值/消费	出口退税	计量单位	监管条件/特殊证件	检验检疫	对美关税	亚太上/下
8108.9032 10	钛金属基复合材料的板、片、带、箔(其中增强材料的比拉伸强度大于 7.62×10⁴m 和比模量大于 3.18×10⁷m,厚度大于 0.8mm)〔999〕	8	4	30	13/	13	千克	3/		14	
8108.9032 90	其他厚度＞0.8 毫米的钛板、片、带、箔〔101〕	8	4	30	13/	13	千克	/		14	
8108.9040	---管										
8108.9040 10	钛合金管(20℃下极限抗拉强度≥900MPa,外径＞75mm)〔999〕	8		30	13/	13	千克	3/			
8108.9040 90	其他钛管〔999〕	8		30	13/	13	千克	/			
8108.9090	---其他〔101〕	8		30	13/	13	千克	/		18	
81.09	**锆及其制品,包括废碎料:**										
	-未锻轧锆;粉末:										
8109.2100	--按重量计铪与锆之比低于 1:500										
8109.2100 10	颗粒＜500μm 的锆及其合金,按重量计铪与锆之比低于 1:500(含量≥97%,不论球形,椭球体,雾化,片状,研碎金属燃料)〔301 危险化学品,易燃固体,302 不属于危险化学品的金属〕	3		20	13/	0	千克	3A/	M	28	
8109.2100 90	其他未锻轧锆及粉末,按重量计铪与锆之比低于 1:500〔301 危险化学品,易燃固体,302 不属于危险化学品的金属〕	3		20	13/	0	千克	3A/	M	28	
8109.2900	--其他										
8109.2900 10	其他颗粒＜500μm 的锆及其合金(含量≥97%,不论球形,椭球体,雾化,片状,研碎金属燃料)〔301 危险化学品,易燃固体,302 不属于危险化学品的金属〕	3		20	13/	0	千克	3A/	M	28	
8109.2900 90	其他未锻轧锆及粉末〔301 危险化学品,易燃固体,302 不属于危险化学品的金属〕	3		20	13/	0	千克	3A/	M	28	
	-废碎料:										
8109.3100	--按重量计铪与锆之比低于 1:500〔999〕	3		20	13/	0	千克	39/		28	
8109.3900	--其他〔999〕	3		20	13/	0	千克	39/		28	
	-其他:										
8109.9100	--按重量计铪与锆之比低于 1:500										
8109.9100 10	锆管(铪与锆重量比低于 1:500 的锆金属和合金的管或组件)〔999〕	8		20	13/	13	千克	3/		18	
8109.9100 90	其他锻轧锆及锆制品,按重量计铪与锆之比低于 1:500〔999〕	8		20	13/	0	千克	3/		18	
8109.9900	--其他〔999〕	8		20	13/	0	千克	3/		18	
81.10	**锑及其制品,包括废碎料:**										
	-未锻轧锑;粉末:										
8110.1010	---未锻轧锑〔101 高铅锑,102 锑合金,103 其他锑及其制品〕	3	1	30	13/	0	千克	4xy/		26	
8110.1020	---粉末〔301 其他危险化学品;302 不属于危险化学品的金属〕	3		30	13/	0	千克	4Axy/13	M	28	
8110.2000	-废碎料〔999〕	3		30	13/	0	千克	49xy/			
8110.9000	-其他〔101 锑合金,102 其他锑及其制品〕	8		40	13/	0	千克	4xy/		18	
81.11	**锰及其制品,包括废碎料:**										
8111.0010	---未锻轧锰;废碎料;粉末										
8111.0010 10	锰废碎料〔999〕	3		20	13/	0	千克	49xy/13		28	
8111.0010 90	未锻轧锰;粉末〔301 危险化学品,易燃固体;302 不属于危险化学品的金属〕	3		20	13/	0	千克	4Axy/13	M	28	
8111.0090	---其他〔101〕	8		30	13/	0	千克	4xy/		18	
81.12	**铍、铬、铪、铼、铊、镉、锗、钒、镓、铟、铌及其制品,包括废碎料:**										
	-铍:										
8112.1200	--未锻轧铍;粉末〔301 危险化学品,毒性物质;302 不属于危险化学品的金属〕	3		30	13/	0	千克	3A/13	M	28	
8112.1300	--废碎料〔999〕	3		30	13/	0	千克	39/			
8112.1900	--其他〔101〕	8		30	13/	0	千克	3/		18	
	-铬:										
8112.2100	--未锻轧铬;粉末〔999〕	3		20	13/	0	千克	4xy/		13	
8112.2200	--废碎料〔999〕	3		20	13/	0	千克	49xy/			
8112.2900	--其他〔999〕	3		20	13/	0	千克	4xy/		23	
	-铪:										
8112.3100	--未锻轧铪;废碎料;粉末										
8112.3100 11	铪废碎料,按重量计铪含量超过 60%〔999〕	3		20	13/	0	千克	39/		28	2.7/2.7
8112.3100 19	其他铪废碎料〔999〕	3		20	13/	0	千克	9/		28	2.7/2.7
8112.3100 91	未锻轧的铪或粉末,按重量计铪含量超过 60%〔301 危险化学品,易于自燃的物质,302 不属于危险化学品的金属〕	3		20	13/	0	千克	3A/	M	28	2.7/2.7
8112.3100 99	其他未锻轧的铪或粉末〔301 危险化学品,易于自燃的物质,302 不属于危险化学品的金属〕	3		20	13/	0	千克	A/	M	28	2.7/2.7
8112.3900	--其他										

协定税率 %								RCEP		特惠税率 %			Article Description
东/冰/格	巴基斯坦	韩国	瑞士上/下	哥/秘/柬	澳/毛	新西/坡/智	中国港/澳/台	东盟及马来/澳/韩	日/新	亚太2国	老/柬/缅	98/97/95	
0/0/0	2	0	0/0	0/0/0	0/0	0//0	0/0/	0/0/0	7.3/0			0/0/0	Plates.sheets, strip and foil made of conyosite material with titanium metal (the degree of strength of intensity material > 7.62×10⁴ m, and specific mondulus > 3.18×10⁷ mm, thickness > 0.8mm)
0/0/0	2	0	0/0	0/0/0	0/0	0//0	0/0/	0/0/0	7.3/0			0/0/0	Other plates, sheets, strap, foil of titanium thickness > 0.8mm
													---Tubes or pipes
0/0/0	2	1.6	0/0	0/0/0	0/0	0//0	0/0/	7.5/7.6/7.5	7.5/7.6			0/0/0	Tubes or pipes of titanium (ultimate tensile strength ≥ 900MPa at 20℃, outer diameter > 75mm)
0/0/0	2	1.6	0/0	0/0/0	0/0	0//0	0/0/	7.5/7.6/7.5	7.5/7.6			0/0/0	Other titanium tubes or pipes
0/0/0	4	0	0/0	0/0/0	0/0	0//0	0/0/	0/0/0	7.3/0			0/0/0	---Other
													Zirconium and articles thereof, including waste and scrap:
													-Unwrought zirconium; powders:
													--Containing less than 1 part hafnium to 500 parts zirconium by weight
0/0/0	0	0	0/0	0/0/0	0/0	0//0	0/0/	0/0/0	0/0			0/0/0	Particles < 5 μM zirconium and its alloys, the ratio of hafnium to zirconium by weight is less than 1:5 (content ≥ 97%, whether spherical, ellipsoid, atomized, flake, ground metal fuel)
0/0/0	0	0	0/0	0/0/0	0/0	0//0	0/0/	0/0/0	0/0			0/0/0	Other unwrought zirconium and powders, the ratio of hafnium to zirconium by weight is less than 1:5
													--Other
0/0/0	0	0	0/0	0/0/0	0/0	0//0	0/0/	0/0/0	0/0			0/0/0	Other particles < 5 μM zirconium and its alloys (content ≥ 97%, whether spherical, ellipsoid, atomized, flake, ground metal fuel)
0/0/0	0	0	0/0	0/0/0	0/0	0//0	0/0/	0/0/0	0/0			0/0/0	Other unwrought zirconium and powder
													-Waste and scrap:
0/0/0	0	0	0/0	0/0/0	0/0	0//0	0/0/	0/0/0	0/0			0/0/0	--Containing less than 1 part hafnium to 500 parts zirconium by weight
0/0/0	0	0	0/0	0/0/0	0/0	0//0	0/0/	0/0/0	0/0			0/0/0	--Other
													-Other:
													--Containing less than 1 part hafnium to 500 parts zirconium by weight
0/0/0	2	1.6	0/0	0/0/0	0/0	0//0	0/0/	0/0/7.2	7.3/0			0/0/0	Zirconium tube (tube or component of zirconium metal and alloy with weight ratio of hafnium to zirconium less than 1:5)
0/0/0	2	1.6	0/0	0/0/0	0/0	0//0	0/0/	0/0/7.2	7.3/0			0/0/0	Other forged zirconium and zirconium products, the ratio of hafnium to zirconium is less than 1:5 by weight
0/0/0	2	1.6	0/0	0/0/0	0/0	0//0	0/0/	0/0/7.2	7.3/0			0/0/0	--Other
													Antimony and articles thereof, including waste and scrap:
													-Unwrought antimony; powders:
0/0/0	0	0	0/0	0/0/0	0/0	0//0	0/0/	0/0/0	0/0			0/0/0	---Unwrought antimony
0/0/0	0	0	0/0	0/0/0	0/0	0//0	0/0/	0/0/0	0/0			0/0/0	---Powders
0/0/0	0	0	0/0	0/0/0	0/0	0//0	0/0/	0/0/0	0/0			0/0/0	-Antimony waste and scrap
0/0/0	2	0	0/0	0/0/0	0/0	0//0	0/0/	0/0/0	7.3/0			0/0/0	-Other
													Manganese and articles thereof, including waste and scrap:
													---Unwrought manganese; waste and scrap; powders
0/0/0	0	0	0/0	0/0/0	0/0	0//0	0/0/	0/0/0	0/0			0/0/0	Unwrought manganese waste and scraps
0/0/0	0	0	0/0	0/0/0	0/0	0//0	0/0/	0/0/0	0/0			0/0/0	Unwrought manganese powders
0/0/0	2	0	0/0	0/0/0	0/0	0//0	0/0/	0/0/0	7.3/0			0/0/0	---Other
													Beryllium, chromium, hafnium, rhenium, thallium, cadmium, germanium, vanadium, gallium, indium and niobium (columbium), articles of these metals, including waste and scrap:
													-Beryllium:
0/0/0	0	0	0/0	0/0/0	0/0	0//0	0/0/	0/0/0	0/0			0/0/0	--Unwrought; powders
0/0/0	0	0	0/0	0/0/0	0/0	0//0	0/0/	0/0/0	0/0			0/0/0	--Waste and scrap
0/0/0	2	0	0/0	0/0/0	0/0	0//0	0/0/	0/0/0	7.3/0			0/0/0	--Other
													-Chromium:
0/0/0	0	0	0/0	0/0/0	0/0	0//0	0/0/	0/0/0	0/0			0/0/0	--Unwrought; powders
0/0/0	0	0	0/0	0/0/0	0/0	0//0	0/0/	0/0/0	0/0			0/0/0	--Waste and scrap
0/0/0	0	0	0/0	0/0/0	0/0	0//0	0/0/	0/0/0	2.7/0			0/0/0	--Other
													-Hafnium:
0/0/0	0	0	0/0	0/0/0	0/0	0//0	0/0/	0/0/0	0/0			0/0/0	Hafnium scrap, with hafnium content exceeding 60% by weight
0/0/0	0	0	0/0	0/0/0	0/0	0//0	0/0/	0/0/0	0/0			0/0/0	Other hafnium scrap
0/0/0	0	0	0/0	0/0/0	0/0	0//0	0/0/	0/0/0	0/0			0/0/0	Hafnium or powder, unwrought, containing more than 60% hafnium by weight
0/0/0	0	0	0/0	0/0/0	0/0	0//0	0/0/	0/0/0	0/0			0/0/0	Other unwrought hafnium or powder
													--Other

税则号列	货品名称〔CIQ 扩展编码及品名—T2 表示见附表 2〕	最惠(%)	暂定税率	普通	增值/消费	出口退税	计量单位	监管条件/特殊证件	检验检疫	对美关税	亚太上/下
8112.3900 10	锻轧的铪及铪制品，按重量计铪含量超过 60%〔999〕	8		30	13/	0	千克	3/		18	5.6/5.6
8112.3900 90	其他锻轧的铪及铪制品〔999〕	8		30	13/	0	千克	/		18	5.6/5.6
	-铼：										
8112.4100	--未锻轧铼；废碎料；粉末										
8112.4100 10	未锻轧的铼废碎料〔999〕	3		20	13/	0	千克	49Axy/	M	28	2.7/2.7
8112.4100 90	未锻轧的铼；粉末〔999〕	3		20	13/	0	千克	4Axy/	M	28	2.7/2.7
8112.4900	--其他〔999〕	8		30	13/	0	千克	4xy/		18	5.6/5.6
	-铊：										
8112.5100	--未锻轧铊；粉末〔301 危险化学品，毒性物质；302 不属于危险化学品的金属〕	3		20	13/	0	千克	AB/13	MN		
8112.5200	--废碎料〔999〕	3		20	13/	0	千克	9/			
8112.5900	--其他〔999〕	8		30	13/	0	千克	/		18	
	-镉：										
8112.6100	--废碎料〔999〕	3		14	13/	0	千克	9/			
	--其他：										
8112.6910	---未锻轧镉；粉末〔301 危险化学品，毒性物质，302 不属于危险化学品的金属〕	3		14	13/	0	千克	/		28	
8112.6990	---其他〔999〕	8		30	13/	0	千克	/		18	5.6/5.6
	-其他：										
	--未锻轧；废碎料；粉末：										
8112.9210	---锗										
8112.9210 10	未锻轧锗废碎料〔999〕	3		20	13/	0	千克	49Axy/		28	
8112.9210 90	未锻轧的锗；锗粉末〔999〕	3		20	13/	0	千克	4xy/		28	
8112.9220	---钒										
8112.9220 01	未锻轧、废碎料或粉末状的钒氮合金〔102〕	3	0	20	13/	0	千克	4xy/		25	
8112.9220 10	未锻轧的钒废碎料〔999〕	3		20	13/	0	千克	49Axy/		28	
8112.9220 90	未锻轧的钒；钒粉末〔999〕	3		20	13/	0	千克	4xy/		28	
8112.9230	---铟										
8112.9230 10	未锻轧的铟及铟粉末〔999〕	3		20	13/	0	千克	4xy/		28	
8112.9230 90	未锻轧的铟废碎料〔999〕	3		20	13/	0	千克	49xy/		28	
8112.9240	---铌										
8112.9240 10	铌废碎料〔999〕	3		20	13/	0	千克	49xy/		28	
8112.9240 90	未锻轧的铌；铌粉末〔999〕	3	0	20	13/	0	千克	4xy/		25	
8112.9290	---其他										
8112.9290 10	未锻轧的镓废碎料〔999〕	3		20	13/	0	千克	49Axy/13	M	28	2.7/2.7
8112.9290 90	未锻轧的镓；粉末〔301 危险化学品，腐蚀性物质，302 不属于危险化学品的金属〕	3		20	13/	0	千克	4Axy/13	M	28	2.7/2.7
	--其他：										
8112.9910	---锗〔101〕	3		20	13/	13	千克	4xy/		28	
8112.9920	---钒										
8112.9920 01	其他钒氮合金〔101〕	3	0	20	13/	0	千克	4xy/		25	
8112.9920 90	其他钒及其制品〔101〕	3		20	13/	0	千克	4xy/		28	
8112.9930	---铟〔101〕	8		20	13/	0	千克	4xy/		18	
8112.9940	---铌〔101〕	8		20	13/	0	千克	4xy/		18	
8112.9990	---其他〔301 危险化学品，腐蚀性物质，302 其他〕	8		30	13/	0	千克	4xy/13		18	5.6/5.6
81.13	**金属陶瓷及其制品，包括废碎料：**										
8113.0010	---颗粒；粉末										
8113.0010 10	颗粒或粉末状碳化钨废碎料〔999〕	8		30	13/	0	千克	9/		33	
8113.0010 90	颗粒或粉末状其他金属陶瓷及其制品〔999〕	8		30	13/	0	千克	/		33	
8113.0090	---其他										
8113.0090 10	其他碳化钨废碎料，颗粒或粉末除外〔999〕	8		30	13/	0	千克	9/		33	
8113.0090 20	铝碳化硅（AlSiC）基板（包括废料）〔999〕	8	4	30	13/	0	千克	/		29	
8113.0090 90	其他金属陶瓷及其制品，颗粒或粉末除外（包括废料）〔999〕	8		30	13/	0	千克	/		33	

协定税率 %								RCEP		特惠税率 %			Article Description
东/冰/格	巴基斯坦	韩国	瑞士上/下	哥/秘/柬	澳/毛	新西/坡/智	中国港/澳/台	东盟及马来/澳/韩	日/新	亚太2国	老/柬/缅	98/97/95	
0/0/0	0	0	0/0	0/0/0	0/0	0//0	0/0/	0/0/0	7.3/0			0/0/0	Hafnium and hafnium products forged and rolled, with hafnium content exceeding 60% by weight
0/0/0	0	0	0/0	0/0/0	0/0	0//0	0/0/	0/0/0	7.3/0			0/0/0	Forged and rolled hafnium and hafnium products with hafnium content exceeding 60% by weight other forged and rolled hafnium and hafnium products
													-Rhenium :
													--Unwrought rhenium; waste and scrap powders
0/0/0	0	0	0/0	0/0/0	0/0	0//0	0/0/	0/0/0	0/0			0/0/0	Rhenium scrap not forged and rolled
0/0/0	0	0	0/0	0/0/0	0/0	0//0	0/0/	0/0/0	0/0			0/0/0	Unwrought rhenium; powder
0/0/0	0	0	0/0	0/0/0	0/0	0//0	0/0/	0/0/0	7.3/0			0/0/0	--Other
													-Thallium:
0/0/0	0	0	0/0	0/0/0	0/0	0//0	0/0/	0/0/0	0/0			0/0/0	--Unwrought; powders
0/0/0	0	0	0/0	0/0/0	0/0	0//0	0/0/	0/0/0	0/0			0/0/0	--Waste and scrap
0/0/0	2	0	0/0	0/0/0	0/0	0//0	0/0/	0/0/0	7.3/0			0/0/0	--Other
													-Cadmium:
0/0/0	0	0	0/0	0/0/0	0/0	0//0	0/0/	0/0/0	0/0			0/0/0	--Waste and scrap
													--Other:
0/0/0	0	0	0/0	0//0	0/0	0//0	0/0/	0/0/0	2.7/0			0/0/0	---Unwrought cadmium; waste and scrap powders
0/0/0	2	0	0/0	0/0/0	0/0	0//0	0/0/	0/0/0	7.3/0			0/0/0	---Other
													-Other:
													--Unwrought; waste and scrap; powders:
													---Germanium
0/0/0	0	0	0/0	0/0/0	0/0	0//0	0/0/	0/0/0	0/0			0/0/0	Unwrought germanium waste and scraps
0/0/0	0	0	0/0	0/0/0	0/0	0//0	0/0/	0/0/0	0/0			0/0/0	Unwrought germanium; powders
													---Vanadium
0/0/0	0	0	0/0	0/0/0	0/0	0//0	0/0/	0/0/0	0/0			0/0/0	Unwrought, waste and scrap, powders, vanadium-nitrogen alloys
0/0/0	0	0	0/0	0/0/0	0/0	0//0	0/0/	0/0/0	0/0			0/0/0	Unwrought, vanadium waste and scraps
0/0/0	0	0	0/0	0/0/0	0/0	0//0	0/0/	0/0/0	0/0			0/0/0	Unwrought vanadium; Powders
													---Indium
0/0/0	0	0	0/0	0/0/0	0/0	0//0	0/0/	0/0/0	0/0			0/0/0	Indium and indium powder not forged
0/0/0	0	0	0/0	0/0/0	0/0	0//0	0/0/	0/0/0	0/0			0/0/0	Unwrought indium waste and scrap
													---Niobium
0/0/0	0	0	0/0	0/0/0	0/0	0//0	0/0/	0/0/0	0/0			0/0/0	Unwrought niobium waste and scrap
0/0/0	0	0	0/0	0/0/0	0/0	0//0	0/0/	0/0/0	0/0			0/0/0	Unwrought niobium; powders
													---Other
0/0/0	0	0	0/0	0/0/0	0/0	0//0	0/0/	0/0/0	0/0			0/0/0	Unwrought gallium scrap
0/0/0	0	0	0/0	0/0/0	0/0	0//0	0/0/	0/0/0	0/0			0/0/0	Unwrought gallium; powder
													--Other:
0/0/0	0	0	0/0	0/0/0	0/0	0//0	0/0/	0/0/0	0/0			0/0/0	---Germanium
													---Vanadiurn
0/0/0	0	0	0/0	0/0/0	0/0	0//0	0/0/	0/0/0	0/0			0/0/0	Other vanadium-nitrogen alloys
0/0/0	0	0	0/0	0/0/0	0/0	0//0	0/0/	0/0/0	0/0			0/0/0	Other vanadium and articles thereof
0/0/0	2	0	0/0	0/0/0	0/0	0//0	0/0/	0/0/0	7.3/0			0/0/0	---Indium
0/0/0	2	0	0/0	0/0/0	0/0	0//0	0/0/	0/0/0	7.3/0			0/0/0	---Niobium
0/0/0	0	0	0/0	0/0/0	0/0	0//0	0/0/	0/0/0	7.3/0			0/0/0	---Other
													Cermets and articles thereof, including waste and scrap:
													Cermets and articles thereof, including waste and scrap:
													---Granules, powder
0/0/0	2		0/0	0/0/0	0/0	0//0	0/0/0	5/5/	/5			0/0/0	Waster and scrap of tungsten carbide, granules or powders
0/0/0	2		0/0	0/0/0	0/0	0//0	0/0/0	5/5/	/5			0/0/0	Other metal cermets and articles thereof, granules or powders
													---Other
0/0/0	2		0/0	0/0/0	0/0	0//0	0/0/0	5/5/	/5			0/0/0	Other tungsten carbide waste and scrap, other than granules or powders
0/0/0	2		0/0	0/0/0	0/0	0//0	0/0/0	5/5/	/5		//	0/0/0	Aluminum silicon carbide (AlSiC) substrate (including scrap)
0/0/0	2		0/0	0/0/0	0/0	0//0	0/0/0	5/5/	/5			0/0/0	Other metal cermets and articles thereof, other than grainor powders(including waster and scrap)

第八十二章
贱金属工具、器具、利口器、餐匙、餐叉及其零件

注释：

一、除喷灯、轻便锻炉、带支架的砂轮、修指甲和修脚用器具及税目 82.09 的货品外，本章仅包括带有用下列材料制成的刀片、工作刃、工作面或其他工作部件的物品：

(一)贱金属；

(二)硬质合金或金属陶瓷；

(三)装于贱金属、硬质合金或金属陶瓷底座上的宝石或半宝石(天然、合成或再造)；

(四)附于贱金属底座上的磨料，当附上磨料后，所具有的切齿、沟、槽或类似结构仍保持其特性及功能。

二、本章所列物品的贱金属零件，应与该制品归入同一税目，但具体列名的零件及手工工具的工具夹具(税目 84.66)除外。第十五类注释二所述的通用零件，均不归入本章。电动剃须刀及电动毛发推剪的刀头、刀片应归入税目 85.10。

三、由税目 82.11 的一把或多把刀具与税目 82.15 至少数量相同的物品构成的成套货品应归入税目 82.15。

税则号列		货品名称〔CIQ 扩展编码及品名－T2 表示见附表 2〕	最惠(%)	暂定税率	普通	增值/消费	出口退税	计量单位	监管条件/特殊证件	检验检疫	对美关税	亚太上/下
82.01		**锹、铲、镐、锄、叉及耙；斧子、钩刀及类似砍伐工具；各种修枝用剪刀；镰刀、秣刀、树篱剪、伐木楔子及其他农业、园艺或林业用手工工具：**										
8201.1000		-锹及铲										
8201.1000	10	含植物性材料的锹及铲〔101 其他木制品，102 农用手工具〕	8		50	9/	9,13	千克/把	AB/	PQ	28	
8201.1000	90	其他锹及铲〔999〕	8		50	9/	9,13	千克/把	/		28	
8201.3000		-镐、锄及耙										
8201.3000	10	含植物性材料的镐、锄、耙〔101 其他木制品，102 农用手工具〕	8		50	9/	9,13	千克/把	AB/	PQ	33	
8201.3000	90	其他镐、锄、耙〔999〕	8		50	9/	9,13	千克/把	/		33	
8201.4000		-斧子、钩刀及类似砍伐工具										
8201.4000	10	含植物性材料的砍伐工具(包括斧子、钩刀及类似砍伐工具)〔101 其他木制品，102 农用手工具〕	8		50	9/	9,13	千克/把	AB/	PQ	18	
8201.4000	90	其他斧子、钩刀及类似砍伐工具〔999〕	8		50	9/	9,13	千克/把	/		18	
8201.5000		-修枝剪及类似的单手操作剪刀(包括家禽剪)										
8201.5000	10	含植物性材料的单手操作农用剪(包括家禽剪)〔101 其他木制品，102 农用手工具〕	8		50	9/	9,13	千克/把	AB/	PQ	33	
8201.5000	90	其他修枝剪等单手操作农用剪(包括家禽剪)〔999〕	8		50	9/	9,13	千克/把	/		33	
8201.6000		-树篱剪、双手修枝剪及类似的双手操作剪刀										
8201.6000	10	含植物性材料的双手操作农用剪〔101 其他木制品，102 农用手工具〕	8		50	9/	9	千克/把	AB/	PQ	33	
8201.6000	90	其他修枝等双手操作农用剪〔999〕	8		50	9/	9,13	千克/把	/		33	
		-用于农业、园艺或林业的其他手工工具：										
8201.9010		---叉										
8201.9010	10	含植物性材料的农业、园艺、林业用叉〔101 其他木制品，102 农用手工具〕	8		50	9/	9	千克/把	AB/	PQ	18	
8201.9010	90	其他农业、园艺、林业用叉〔999〕	8		50	9/	9,13	千克/把	/		18	
8201.9090		---其他										
8201.9090	10	含植物性材料的农林、园艺、林业用手工工具〔101 其他木制品，102 农用手工具〕	8		50	9/	9,13	千克/把	AB/	PQ	18	
8201.9090	90	其他农业、园艺、林业用手工工具〔999〕	8		50	9/	9,13	千克/把	/		18	
82.02		**手工锯；各种锯的锯片(包括切条、切槽或无齿锯片)：**										
8202.1000		-手工锯〔999〕	8		50	13/	9,13	千克/把	/		33	
		-带锯片：										
8202.2010		---双金属带锯条〔999〕	8		20	13/	13	千克	/		28	
8202.2090		---其他〔999〕	8		20	13/	13	千克	/		28	

Chapter 82
Tools, implements, cutlery, spoons and forks, parts thereof of base metal

Notes:

1. Apart from blow lamps, portable forges, grinding wheels with frameworks, manicure or pedicure sets, and goods of heading No.82. 09, this Chapter covers only articles with a blade, working No. edge, working surface or other working part of :
   (a) Base metal;
   (b) Metal carbides or cermets;
   (c) Precious or semi-precious stones (natural, synthetic or reconstructed) on a support of base metal, metal carbide or cermet; or
   (d) Abrasive materials on a support of base metal, provided that the articles have cutting teeth, flutes, grooves, or the like, of base metal, which retain their identity and function after the application of the abrasive.
2. Parts of base metal of the articles of this Chapter are to be classified with the articles of which they are parts, except parts separately specified as such and tool-holders for hand tools (heading No.84. 66). However, parts of general use as defined in Note 2 to Section XV are in all cases excluded from this Chapter. Heads, blades and cutting plates for electric shavers and electric hair clippers are to be classified in heading No.85. 10.
3. Sets consisting of one or more knives of heading No.82. 11 and at least an equal number of articles of heading No.82. 15 are to be classified in heading No.82. 15.

协定税率 %								RCEP		特惠税率 %			
东/冰/格	巴基斯坦	韩国	瑞士 上/下	哥/秘/柬	澳/毛	新西/坡/智	中国港/澳/台	东盟及马来/澳/韩	日/新	亚太2国	老/柬/缅	98/97/95	Article Description
													Hand tools, the following: spades, shovels, mattocks, picks, hoes, forks and rakes; axes, bill hooks and similar hewing tools; secateurs and prundrs of any kind; scythes, hay knives, hedge shears, timber wedges and other tools of a kind used in agriculture, horticulture or forestry:
													-Spades and shovels
0/0/0	4	0	0/0	0/0/0	0/0	0//0	0/0/	0/0/0	7.3/0			0/0/0	Spades and shovels with vegetable materials
0/0/0	4	0	0/0	0/0/0	0/0	0//0	0/0/	0/0/0	7.3/0			0/0/0	Other spades and shovels
													-Mattocks, picks, hoes and rakes
0/0/0	2	0	0/0	0/0/0	0/0	0//0	0/0/	0/0/0	7.3/0			0/0/0	Mattocks, picks, hoes and rakes with vegetable materials
0/0/0	2	0	0/0	0/0/0	0/0	0//0	0/0/	0/0/0	7.3/0			0/0/0	Other mattocks, picks, hoes and rakes
													-Axes, bill hooks and similar hewing tools
0/0/0	4	0	0/0	0/0/0	0/0	0//0	0/0/	0/0/0	7.3/0			0/0/0	Hewing tools with vegetable materials (including axes, bill hooks and similar hewing tools)
0/0/0	4	0	0/0	0/0/0	0/0	0//0	0/0/	0/0/0	7.3/0			0/0/0	Other axes, bill hooks and similar hewing tools
													-Secateurs and similar one-handed pruners and shears (including poultry shears)
0/0/0	2	0	0/0	0/0/0	0/0	0//0	0/0/	0/0/0	7.3/0			0/0/0	Secateurs and similar one-handed pruners and shears (including poultry shears), with vegetable materials, of a kind used in agriculture
0/0/0	2	0	0/0	0/0/0	0/0	0//0	0/0/	0/0/0	7.3/0			0/0/0	Other secateurs and similar one-handed pruners and shears (including poultry shears), of a kind used in agriculture
													-Hedge shears, two handed pruning shears and similar two-handed shears
0/0/0	2	0	0/0	0/0/0	0/0	0//0	0/0/	0/0/0	7.3/0			0/0/0	Hedge shears, two-handed pruning shears and similar two-handed shears, with vegetable materials, of a kind used in agriculture
0/0/0	2	0	0/0	0/0/0	0/0	0//0	0/0/	0/0/0	7.3/0			0/0/0	Other hedge shears, two-handed pruning shears and similar two-handed shears, of a kind used in agriculture
													-Other hand tools of a kind used in agriculture, horticulture or forestry:
													---Forks
0/0/0	2	0	0/0	0/0/0	0/0	0//0	0/0/	0/0/0	7.3/0			0/0/0	Forks of a kind used in argiculture, horticulture or forestry, with vegetable materials
0/0/0	2	0	0/0	0/0/0	0/0	0//0	0/0/	0/0/0	7.3/0			0/0/0	Other forks of a kind used in argiculture, horticulture or forestry
													---Other
0/0/0	2	1.6	0/0	0/0/0	0/0	0//0	0/0/	0/0/7.2	7.3/0			0/0/0	Hand tools of a kind used in agriculture, horticulture or forestry, with vegetable materials
0/0/0	2	1.6	0/0	0/0/0	0/0	0//0	0/0/	0/0/7.2	7.3/0			0/0/0	Other hand tools of a kind used in agriculture, horticulture or forestry
													Hand saws; blades for saws of all kinds (including slitting, slotting or toothless saw blades):
0/0/0	2	1.6	0/0	0/0/0	0/0	0//0	0/0/	0/0/7.6	7.6/0			0/0/0	-Hand saws
													-Band saw blades:
0/0/0	2	1.6	0.8/0.8	0/0/0	0/0	0//0	0/0/	0/0/7.2	7.3/0			0/0/0	---Bimetal band saw blades
0/0/0	2	1.6	0.8/0.8	0/0/0	0/0	0//0	0/0/	0/0/7.2	7.3/0			0/0/0	---Other

税则号列	货品名称〔CIQ扩展编码及品名—T2表示见附表2〕	最惠(%)	暂定税率	普通	增值/消费	出口退税	计量单位	监管条件/特殊证件	检验检疫	对美关税	亚太上/下
	-圆锯片(包括切条或切槽锯片):										
8202.3100	--带有钢制工作部件〔999〕	8		20	13/	13	千克	/		33	
	--其他,包括部件:										
8202.3910	---带有天然或合成金刚石、立方氮化硼制的工作部件〔999〕	8		20	13/	13	千克	/		33	
8202.3990	---其他〔999〕	8		20	13/	13	千克	/		33	
8202.4000	-链锯片〔999〕	8		20	13/	13	千克	/		18	
	-其他锯片:										
	--直锯片,加工金属用:										
8202.9110	---机械锯用〔999〕	8		20	13/	13	千克	/		18	5.2/5.2
8202.9190	---其他〔999〕	8		50	13/	13	千克	/		18	
	--其他:										
8202.9910	---机械锯用〔999〕	8		20	13/	13	千克	/		28	
8202.9990	---其他〔999〕	8		50	13/	13	千克	/		18	
82.03	**钢锉、木锉、钳子(包括剪钳)、镊子、白铁剪、切管器、螺栓切头器、打孔冲子及类似手工工具:**										
8203.1000	-钢锉、木锉及类似工具〔999〕	8		50	13/	13	千克/把	/		33	
8203.2000	-钳子(包括剪钳)、镊子及类似工具〔999〕	8		50	13/	13	千克/把	/		28	
8203.3000	-白铁剪及类似工具〔999〕	8		50	13/	13	千克/把	/		28	
8203.4000	-切管器、螺栓切头器、打孔冲子及类似工具〔999〕	8		50	13/	13	千克/把	/		18	
82.04	**手动扳手及扳钳(包括转矩扳手,但不包括丝锥扳手);可互换的扳手套筒,不论是否带手柄:**										
	-手动扳手及扳钳:										
8204.1100	--固定的〔999〕	8		50	13/	13	千克/把	/		28	
8204.1200	--可调的〔999〕	8		50	13/	13	千克/把	/		18	
8204.2000	-可互换的扳手套筒,不论是否带手柄〔999〕	8		50	13/	13	千克/套	/		33	
82.05	**其他税号未列名的手工工具(包括玻璃刀);喷灯;台钳、夹钳及类似品,但作为机床或水射流切割机附件或零件的除外;砧;轻便锻炉;带支架的手摇或脚踏砂轮:**										
8205.1000	-钻孔或攻丝工具〔999〕	8		50	13/	13	千克/个	/		18	
8205.2000	-锤子〔999〕	8		50	13/	13	千克/个	/		28	
8205.3000	-木工用刨子、凿子及类似切削工具〔999〕	8		50	13/	13	千克/个	/		28	
8205.4000	-螺丝刀〔999〕	8		50	13/	13	千克/个	/		28	
	-其他手工工具(包括玻璃刀):										
8205.5100	--家用工具〔999〕	7		50	13/	13	千克/个	/		22	
8205.5900	--其他〔999〕	8		50	13/	13	千克/个	/		18	5.2/5.2
8205.6000	-喷灯〔999〕	8		50	13/	13	千克/个	/		28	
8205.7000	-台钳、夹钳及类似品〔101台钳、夹钳及类似品,102其它五金工具〕	8		50	13/	13	千克/个	/		28	
8205.9000	-其他,包括由本税目项下两个或多个子目所列物品组成的成套货品〔999〕	8		50	13/	13	千克	/		18	
82.06	**由税目82.02至82.05中两个或多个税目所列工具组成的零售包装成套货品:**										
8206.0000	由税目82.02至82.05中两个或多个税目所列工具组成的零售包装成套货品〔999〕	8		50	13/	13	千克	/		18	
82.07	**手工工具(不论是否有动力装置)及机床(例如,锻压、冲压、攻丝、钻孔、镗孔、铰孔及铣削、车削或上螺丝用的机器)的可互换工具,包括金属拉拔或挤压用模以及凿岩或钻探工具:**										
	-凿岩或钻探工具:										
8207.1300	--带有金属陶瓷制的工作部件〔999〕	8		20	13/	13	千克	/		28	
	--其他,包括部件:										
8207.1910	---带有天然或合成金钢石、立方氮化硼制的工作部件〔999〕	8		20	13/	13	千克	/		18	
8207.1990	---其他〔999〕	8		20	13/	13	千克	/		18	
	-金属拉拔或挤压用模:										
8207.2010	---带有天然或合成金刚石、立方氮化硼制的工作部件〔999〕	8		20	13/	13	千克/套	/		33	

协定税率 %								RCEP		特惠税率 %			Article Description
东/冰/格	巴基斯坦	韩国	瑞士上/下	哥/秘/柬	澳/毛	新西/坡/智	中国港/澳/台	东盟及马来/澳/韩	日/新	亚太2国	老/柬/缅	98/97/95	
													-Circular saw blades (including slitting or slotting saw blades):
0/0/0	2	1.6	0/0	0/0/0	0/0	0//0	0/0/	0/0/7.2	7.3/0			0/0/0	--With working part of steel
													--Other, including parts:
0/0/0	2	0	0/0	0/0/0	0/0	0//0	0/0/	0/0/0	7.3/0			0/0/0	---with working part of natural or synthetic diamond, cubic boron nitride
0/0/0	2	0	0/0	0/0/0	0/0	0//0	0/0/	0/0/0	7.3/0			0/0/0	---Other
0/0/0	2	0	0.8/0.8	0/0/0	0/0	0//0	0/0/	0/0/0	7.3/0			0/0/0	-Chain saw blades
													-Other saw blades:
													--Straight saw blades, for working metal:
0/0/0	2	1.6	0.8/0.8	0/0/0	0/0	0//0	0/0/	0/0/7.2	7.3/0			0/0/0	---For sawing machines
0/0/0	2	0	0.8/0.8	0/0/0	0/0	0//0	0/0/	0/0/0	7.3/0			0/0/0	---Other
													--Other:
0/0/0	2	1.6	0.8/0.8	0/0/0	0/0	0//0	0/0/	0/0/7.6	7.6/0			0/0/0	---For sawing machines
0/0/0	3.5	2.1	1.1/1.1	0/0/0	0/0	0/0/0	0/0/	0/0/9.5	9.5/0			0/0/0	---Other
													Files, rasps, pliers (including cutting pliers), pincers, tweezers, metal cutting shears, pipe-cutters, bolt croppers, perforating punches and similar hand tools:
0/0/0	4	2.1	1.1/1.1	0/0/0	0/0	0/0/0	0/0/	0/0/9.5	9.5/0			0/0/0	-Files, rasps and similar tools
0/0/0		2.1	1.1/1.1	0/0/0	0/0	0/0/0	0/0/0	0/0/9.5	9.5/0			0/0/0	-Pliers (including cutting pliers), pincers, tweezers and similar tools
0/0/0	4	2.1	1.1/1.1	0/0/0	0/0	0/0/0	0/0/	0/0/9.5	9.5/0			0/0/0	-Metal cutting shears and similar tools
0/0/0	3.5	2.1	1.1/1.1	0/0/0	0/0	0/0/0	0/0/	0/0/9.5	9.5/0			0/0/0	-Pipe-cutters, bolt croppers, perforating punches and similar tools
													Hand-operated spanners and wrenches (including torque meter wrenches but not including tap wrenches); interchangeable spanner sockets, with or without handles:
													-Hand-operated spanners and wrenches:
0/0/0	3.5	2.1	1.1/1.1	0/0/0	0/0	0/0/0	0/0/	0/0/9.5	9.5/0			0/0/0	--Non-adjustable
0/0/0	2	2	0/0	0/0/0	0/0	0//0	0/0/0	0/0/9	9.1/0			0/0/0	--Adjustable
0/0/0	2	2	0/0	0/0/0	0/0	0//0	0/0/	0/0/9	9.1/0			0/0/0	-Interchangeable spanner sockets, with or without handles
													Hand tools (including glaziers' diamonds), not elsewhere specified or included; blow lamps; vices, clamps and the like, other than accessories for and parts of, machine tools or water jet cutting machine; anvils; portable forges; hand or pedal operated grinding wheels with frame works:
0/0/0	2	2	0/0	0/0/0	0/0	0//0	0/0/	0/0/9	9.1/0			0/0/0	-Drilling, threading or tapping tools
0/0/0	3.5	2	0/0	0/0/0	0/0	0//0	0/0/0	0/0/9	9.1/0			0/0/0	-Hammers and sledge hammers
0/0/0	4	2.1	1.1/1.1	0/0/0	0/0	0/0/0	0/0/	0/0/9.5	9.5/0			0/0/0	-Planes, chisels, gouges and similar cutting tools for working wood
0/0/0	3.5	2.1	1.1/1.1	0/0/0	0/0	0/0/0	0/0/0	0/0/9.5	9.5/0			0/0/0	-Screwdrivers
													-Other hand tools (including glaziers' diamonds):
0/0/0	4	2.1	1.1/1.1	0/0/0	0/0	0/0/0	0/0/	0/0/9.5	9.5/0			0/0/0	--Household tools
0/0/0	0	2	1/1	0/0/0	0/0	0//0	0/0/0	0/0/9	9.1/0			0/0/0	--Other
0/0/0	2	2	1/1	0/0/0	0/0	0//0	0/0/	0/0/9	9.1/0			0/0/0	-Blow lamps
0/0/0	4	2.1	4.4/4.4	0/0/0	0/0	0/0/0	0/0/	0/0/9.5	9.5/0			0/0/0	-Vices, clamps and the like
0/0/0	4	2.1	1.1/1.1	0/0/0	0/0	0/0/0	0/0/	0/0/9.5	9.5/0			0/0/0	-Other, including sets of articles of two or more the foregoing subheadings
													Tools of two or more of the headings Nos.82.02 to 82.05, put up in sets for retail sale:
0/0/0	4	2.1	2.6/2.6	0/0/0	0/0	0/0/0	0/0/	0/0/9.5	9.5/0			0/0/0	Tools of two or more of the headings Nos.82.02 to 82.05, put up in sets for retail sale
													Interchangeable tools for hand tools, whether or not power-operated, or for machine-tools (for example, for pressing, stamping, punching, tapping, threading, drilling, boring, broaching, milling, turning or screw driving), including dies for drawing or extruding metal, and rock drilling or earth boring tools:
													-Rock drilling or earth boring tools:
0/0/0	2	0	0/0	0/0/0	0/0	0//0	0/0/	0/0/0	7.3/0			0/0/0	--With working part of cermets
													--Other, including parts:
0/0/0	2	0	0/0	0/0/0	0/0	0//0	0/0/	0/0/0	7.3/0			0/0/0	---With working part of natural or synthetic diamonds or cubic boronnitride
0/0/0	2	1.6	0/0	0/0/0	0/0	0//0	0/0/	0/0/7.2	7.3/0			0/0/0	---Other
													-Dies for drawing or extruding metal:
0/0/0	2	0	0/0	0/0/0	0/0	0//0	0/0/0	0/0/0	7.3/0			0/0/0	---With working part of natural or synthetic diamonds or cubic boronnitride

税则号列	货品名称〔CIQ扩展编码及品名一T2表示见附表2〕	最惠(%)	暂定税率	普通	增值/消费	出口退税	计量单位	监管条件/特殊证件	检验检疫	对美关税	亚太上/下
8207.2090	---其他〔999〕	8		20	13/	13	千克/套	/		33	
8207.3000	-锻压或冲压工具										
8207.3000 10	加工税号87.03所列车辆车身冲压件用的4种关键模具(侧围外板、翼子板、拼接整体侧围内板、拼焊整体侧围加强板用模具)〔999〕	8	6	20	13/	13	千克	/		31	6.8/6.8
8207.3000 20	加工税号87.03所列车辆车身冲压件用的4种特种模具($\sigma b \geq 980N/mm^2$的冷冲压、热成型、内高压成型和铝板用模具)〔999〕	8	6	20	13/	13	千克	/		31	6.8/6.8
8207.3000 90	其他锻压或冲压工具〔999〕	8		20	13/	13	千克	/		33	6.8/6.8
8207.4000	-攻丝工具〔999〕	8		20	13/	13	千克/件	/		33	
	-钻孔工具，但凿岩及钻探用的除外：										
8207.5010	---带有天然或合成金刚石、立方氮化硼制的工作部件〔999〕	8		20	13/	13	千克/件	/		28	
8207.5090	---其他〔999〕	8		20	13/	13	千克/件	/		33	
	-镗孔或铰孔工具：										
8207.6010	---带有天然或合成金刚石、立方氮化硼制的工作部件〔999〕	8		20	13/	13	千克/件	/		33	
8207.6090	---其他〔999〕	8		20	13/	13	千克/件	/		33	
	-铣削工具：										
8207.7010	---带有天然或合成金刚石、立方氮化硼制的工作部件〔999〕	8		20	13/	13	千克/件	/		33	
8207.7090	---其他〔999〕	8		20	13/	13	千克/件	/		33	
	-车削工具：										
8207.8010	---带有天然或合成金刚石、立方氮化硼制的工作部件〔999〕	8		20	13/	13	千克/件	/		18	5.2/5.2
8207.8090	---其他〔999〕	8		20	13/	13	千克/件	/		28	5.2/5.2
	-其他可互换工具：										
8207.9010	---带有天然或合成金刚石、立方氮化硼制的工作部件〔999〕	8		20	13/	13	千克/件	/		18	5.2/5.2
8207.9090	---其他〔999〕	8		20	13/	13	千克/件	/		28	5.2/5.2
82.08	**机器或机械器具的刀及刀片：**										
	-金属加工用：										
	---硬质合金制的：										
8208.1011	----经镀或涂层的〔999〕	8		20	13/	13	千克	/		28	
8208.1019	----其他〔999〕	8		20	13/	13	千克	/		33	
8208.1090	---其他〔999〕	8		20	13/	13	千克	/		28	
8208.2000	-木器(材)加工用〔999〕	8		20	13/	13	千克	/		33	
8208.3000	-厨房器具或食品工业机器用〔999〕	8		20	13/	13	千克	A/	R	18	
8208.4000	-农业、园艺或林业机器用〔999〕	8		20	9/	9,13	千克	/		18	
8208.9000	-其他〔999〕	8		20	13/	13	千克	/		33	5.2/5.2
82.09	**未装配的工具用金属陶瓷板、杆、刀头及类似品：**										
8209.0010	---板〔999〕	8		20	13/	13	千克	/		33	5.2/5.2
	---条、杆：										
8209.0021	----晶粒度<0.8微米的〔999〕	8		20	13/	13	千克	/		33	5.2/5.2
8209.0029	----其他〔999〕	8		20	13/	13	千克	/		33	5.2/5.2
8209.0030	---刀头〔999〕	8		20	13/	13	千克	/		33	5.2/5.2
8209.0090	---其他〔999〕	8		20	13/	13	千克	/		18	5.2/5.2
82.10	**用于加工或调制食品或饮料的手动机械器具，重量不超过10千克：**										
8210.0000	用于加工或调制食品或饮料的手动机械器具，重量不超过10千克〔999〕	8		80	13/	13	千克/台	A/	R	28	5.2/5.2
82.11	**有刃口的刀及其刀片，不论是否有锯齿(包括整枝刀)，但税目82.08的刀除外：**										
8211.1000	-成套货品〔999〕	8		80	13/	13	千克/套	/		33	
	-其他：										
8211.9100	--刃面固定的餐刀〔101餐桌用具，102食品接触不锈钢产品，103食品接触铁产品，104食品接触铝产品，105食品接触其他金属产品〕	7		80	13/	13	千克/把	A/	R	32	

协定税率 %								RCEP		特惠税率 %			Article Description
东/冰/格	巴基斯坦	韩国	瑞士 上/下	哥/秘/柬	澳/毛	新西/坡/智	中国港/澳/台	东盟及马来/澳/韩	日/新	亚太2国	老/柬/缅	98/97/95	
0/0/0	2	0	0.8/0.8	0/0/0	0/0	0//0	0/0/0	7.2/7.2/7.2	7.3/7.2			0/0/0	---Other
													-Tools for pressing, stamping or punching
0/0/0	2	3.7	0/0	0/0/0	0/0	0//0	0/0/0	7.2/7.2/7.2	7.5/7.2			0/0/0	Processing of car body stamping parts with four key mold (side wall outer panel, fender, integral joint side wall inner plate, fight the whole welding of side wall reinforcing plate mold)
0/0/0	2	3.7	0/0	0/0/0	0/0	0//0	0/0/0	7.2/7.2/7.2	7.5/7.2			0/0/0	Processing of car body stamping parts with four special mould(cold stamping of sigma B is more than or equal to 980N/mm^2, thermoforming, in high-pressure molding and aluminum plate with mold)
0/0/0	2	3.7	0/0	0/0/0	0/0	0//0	0/0/0	7.2/7.2/7.2	7.5/7.2			0/0/0	Other tools for pressing, stamping or punching
0/0/0	2		0/0	0/0/0	0/0	0//0	0/0/0	5/5/	/5			0/0/0	-Tools for tapping or threading
													-Tools for drilling, other than for rock drilling:
0/0/0	2		0/0	0/0/0	0/0	0//0	0/0/0	5/5/	/5			0/0/0	---With working part of natural or synthetic diamonds or cubic boronnitride
0/0/0	2		0/0	0/0/0	0/0	0//0	0/0/0	5/5/	/5			0/0/0	---Other
													-Tools for boring or broaching:
0/0/0	2		0/0	0/0/0	0/0	0//0	0/0/0	5/5/	/5			0/0/0	---With working part of natural or synthetic diamonds or cubic boronnitride
0/0/0	2	3.7	0/0	0/0/0	0/0	0//0	0/0/	7.5/7.6/7.5	7.5/7.6			0/0/0	---Other
													-Tools for milling:
0/0/0	2		0/0	0/0/0	0/0	0//0	0/0/0	5/5/	/5			0/0/0	---With working part of natural or synthetic diamonds or cubic boronnitride
0/0/0	2		0/0	0/0/0	0/0	0//0	0/0/0	5/5/	/5			0/0/0	---Other
													-Tools for turning:
0/0/0	2	5.2	0/0	0/0/0	0/0	0//0	0/0/0	5/5/	/5			0/0/0	---With working part of natural or synthetic diamonds or cubic boronnitride
0/0/0	2	5.2	0/0	0/0/0	0/0	0//0	0/0/0	5/5/	/5			0/0/0	---Other
													-Other interchangeable tools:
0/0/0	2	5.2	0/0	0/0/0	0/0	0//0	0/0/0	5/5/	/5			0/0/0	---With working part of natural or synthetic diamonds or cubic boronnitride
0/0/0	2	5.2	0.8/0.8	0/0/0	0/0	0//0	0/0/0	5/5/	/5			0/0/0	---Other
													Knives and cutting blades, for machines or for mechanical appliances:
													-For metal working:
													---Of metal carbides:
0/0/0	2	3.7	0.8/0.8	0/0/0	0/0	0//0	0/0/	7.5/7.6/7.5	7.5/7.6			0/0/0	----Plated or coated
0/0/0	2	3.7	0.8/0.8	0/0/0	0/0	0//0	0/0/	7.2/7.2/7.2	7.5/7.2			0/0/0	----Other
0/0/0	2	3.7	0.8/0.8	0/0/0	0/0	0//0	0/0/	7.5/7.6/7.5	7.5/7.6			0/0/0	---Other
0/0/0	2	0	0/0	0/0/0	0/0	0//0	0/0/0	0/0/0	7.3/0			0/0/0	-For wood working
0/0/0	2	1.6	0/0	0/0/0	0/0	0//0	0/0/	0/0/7.2	7.3/0			0/0/0	-For kitchen appliances or for machines used by the food industry
0/0/0	2	0	0.8/0.8	0/0/0	0/0	0//0	0/0/0	0/0/0	7.3/0			0/0/0	-For agricultural, horticultural or forestry machines
0/0/0	0	0	0.8/0.8	0/0/0	0/0	0//0	0/0/0	0/0/0	7.3/0			0/0/0	-Other
													Plates, sticks, tips and the like for tools, unmounted, of cermets:
0/0/0	2	1.6	0/0	0/0/0	0/0	0//0	0/0/	0/0/7.2	7.3/0			0/0/0	---plates
													---Bar, sticks:
0/0/0	2	0	0.8/0.8	0/0/0	0/0	0//0	0/0/	0/0/0	7.3/0			0/0/0	----Grain size <0.8μm
0/0/0	2	0	0.8/0.8	0/0/0	0/0	0//0	0/0/	0/0/0	7.3/0			0/0/0	----Other
0/0/0	2	3.7	0/0	0/0/0	0/0	0//0	0/0/	7.5/7.6/7.5	7.5/7.6			0/0/0	---Tips
0/0/0	2	0	0/0	0/0/0	0/0	0//0	0/0/	0/0/0	7.3/0			0/0/0	---Other
													Hand-operated mechanical appliances, weighing 10g or less, used in the preparation, conditioning or serving of food or drink:
0/0/0	10.1	3.6	1.8/1.8	0/0/0	0/0	0/0/0	0/0/	0/0/16.2	16.4/0			0/0/0	Hand-operated mechanical appliances, weighing 10kg or less, used in the preparation, conditioning or serving of food or drink
													Knives with cutting blades, serrated or not (including pruning knives), other than knives of heading No. 82.08, and blades therefor:
0/0/0	0	3.6	1.8/1.8	0/0/0	0/0	0/0/0	0/0/	0/0/16.2	16.4/0			0/0/0	-Sets of assorted articles
													-Other:
0/0/0	0	3.6	1.8/1.8	0/0/0	0/0	0/0/0	0/0/	0/0/16.2	16.4/0			0/0/0	--Table knives having fixed blades

税则号列	货品名称〔CIQ 扩展编码及品名—T2 表示见附表 2〕	最惠(%)	暂定税率	普通	增值/消费	出口退税	计量单位	监管条件/特殊证件	检验检疫	对美关税	亚太上/下
8211.9200	--刃面固定的其他刀〔101 其它食品加工机器及其零件,102 食品接触不锈钢产品,103 食品接触铁产品,104 食品接触铝产品,105 食品接触其他金属产品〕	7		80	13/	13	千克/把	/		22	
8211.9300	--可换刃面的刀〔101 其它食品加工机器及其零件,102 食品接触不锈钢产品,103 食品接触铝产品,104 食品接触其他金属产品,105 食品接触铁产品〕	7		80	13/	13	千克/把	/		32	
8211.9400	--刀片〔101 其它食品加工机器及其零件,102 食品接触不锈钢产品,103 食品接触铁产品,104 食品接触铝产品,105 食品接触其他金属产品〕	7		80	13/	13	千克	/		27	
8211.9500	--贱金属制的刀柄〔101 其它食品加工机器及其零件,102 食品接触其他金属产品〕	7		80	13/	13	千克	/		32	
82.12	**剃刀及其刀片(包括未分开的刀片条):**										
8212.1000	-剃刀〔999〕	7		80	13/	13	千克/把	/		22	
8212.2000	-安全刀片,包括未分开的刀片条〔999〕	7		80	13/	13	千克/片	/		17	
8212.9000	-其他零件〔999〕	7		80	13/	13	千克	/		22	
82.13	**剪刀、裁缝剪刀及类似品、剪刀片:**										
8213.0000	剪刀、裁缝剪刀及类似品、剪刀片〔101 其它机电产品及其零件,103 其他金属及制品〕	7		80	13/	13	千克	/		32	4.6/4.6
82.14	**其他利口器(例如,理发推剪、屠刀、砍骨刀、切肉刀、切菜刀、裁纸刀);修指甲及修脚用具(包括指甲锉):**										
8214.1000	-裁纸刀、开信刀、改错刀、铅笔刀及其刀片〔999〕	7		80	13/	13	千克	/		27	4.6/4.6
8214.2000	-修指甲及修脚用具(包括指甲锉)〔999〕	7		90	13/	13	千克	/		32	4.6/4.6
8214.9000	-其他										
8214.9000 10	切菜刀等厨房用利口器〔101 厨房用具,102 食品接触不锈钢产品,103 食品接触铁产品,104 食品接触铝产品,105 食品接触其他金属产品〕	7		80	13/	13	千克	A/	R	32	
8214.9000 90	理发推子等其他利口器〔999〕	7		80	13/	13	千克	/		32	
82.15	**餐匙、餐叉、长柄勺、漏勺、糕点夹、鱼刀、黄油刀、糖块夹及类似的厨房或餐桌用具:**										
8215.1000	-成套货品,至少其中一件物品是镀贵金属的〔101 厨房用具,102 餐桌用具,103 食品接触其他金属产品,104 食品用其他金属包装〕	7		80	13/	13	千克	A/	R	32	
8215.2000	-其他成套货品〔101 厨房用具,102 餐桌用具,103 食品接触其他金属产品,104 食品用其他金属包装〕	7		80	13/	13	千克	A/	R	27	
	-其他:										
8215.9100	--镀贵金属的〔101 厨房用具,102 餐桌用具,103 食品接触其他金属产品,104 食品用其他金属包装〕	7		80	13/	13	千克	A/	R	32	
8215.9900	--其他〔101 厨房用具,102 餐桌用具,103 食品接触其他金属产品,104 食品用其他金属包装〕	7		80	13/	13	千克	A/	R	32	

协定税率 %								RCEP		特惠税率 %			Article Description
东/冰/格	巴基斯坦	韩国	瑞士上/下	哥/秘/柬	澳/毛	新西/坡/智	中国港/澳/台	东盟及马来/澳/韩	日/新	亚太2国	老/柬/缅	98/97/95	
0/0/0	0	2.4	3/3	0/0/0	0/0	0/0/0	0/0/	0/0/10.8	10.9/0			0/0/0	--Other knives having fixed blades
0/0/0	0	3.6	0/0	0/0/0	0/0	0/0/0	0/0/	0/0/16.2	16.4/0			0/0/0	--Knives having other than fixed blades
0/0/0	0	2.8	1.4/1.4	0/0/0	0/0	0/0/0	0/0/	0/0/12.6	12.7/0			0/0/0	--Blades
0/0/0	0	2.4	5/5	0/0/0	0/0	0/0/0	0/0/	0/0/10.8	10.9/0			0/0/0	--Handles of base metal
													Razors and razor blades (including razor blade blanks in strips):
0/0/0	0	2.4	1.2/1.2	0/0/0	0/0	0/0/0	0/0/	0/0/10.8	10.9/0			0/0/0	-Razors
0/0/0	0	2.8	1.4/1.4	0/0/0	0/0	0/0/0	0/0/	0/0/12.6	12.7/0			0/0/0	-Safety razor blades, including razor blade blanks in strips
0/0/0	0	2.4	1.2/1.2	0/0/0	0/0	0/0/0	0/0/	0/0/10.8	10.9/0			0/0/0	-Other parts
													Scissors, tailors' shears and similar shears, and blades therefor:
0/0/0	0	2.4	1.2/1.2	0/0/0	0/0	0/0/0	0/0/	0/0/10.8	10.9/0			0/0/0	Scissors, tailors' shears and similar shears, and blades therefor
													Other articles of cutlery (for example, hair clippers, butchers' or kitchen cleavers, choppers and mincing knives, paper knives); manicure or pedicure sets and instruments (including nail files):
0/0/0	3.5	2.4	1.2/1.2	0/0/0	0/0	0/0/0	0/0/	0/0/10.8	10.9/0			0/0/0	-Paper knives, letter openers, erasing knives, pencil sharpeners and blades therefor
0/0/0	0	3.6	1.8/1.8	0/0/0	0/0	0/0/0	0/0/	0/0/16.2	16.4/0			0/0/0	-Manicure or pedicure sets and instruments (including nail files)
													-Other
0/0/0		3.6	1.8/1.8	0/0/0	0/0	0/0/0	0/0/	0/0/16.2	16.4/0			0/0/0	Kitchen cleavers, choppers mincing knives and other articles of cutlery
0/0/0		3.6	1.8/1.8	0/0/0	0/0	0/0/0	0/0/	0/0/16.2	16.4/0			0/0/0	Hair clippers and other articles of cutlery
													Spoons, forks, ladles, skimmers, cakeservers, fish-knives, butter-knives, sugar tongs and similar kitchen or tableware:
0/0/0	0	3.6	1.8/1.8	0/0/0	0/0	0/0/0	0/0/	0/0/16.2	16.4/0			0/0/0	-Sets of assorted articles containing at least one article plated with precious metal
0/0/0	0	3.6	1.8/1.8	0/0/0	0/0	0/0/0	0/0/	0/0/16.2	16.4/0			0/0/0	-Other sets of assorted articles
													-Other:
0/0/0	0	3.6	1.8/1.8	0/0/0	0/0	0/0/0	0/0/	0/0/16.2	16.4/0			0/0/0	--Plated with precious metal
0/0/0	0	3.6	1.8/1.8	0/0/0	0/0	0/0/0	0/0/	0/0/16.2	16.4/0			0/0/0	--Other

第八十三章
贱金属杂项制品

注释：

一、在本章，贱金属零件应与制品一同归类。但税目73.12、73.15、73.17、73.18及73.20的钢铁制品或其他贱金属（第七十四章至第七十六章及第七十八章至第八十一章）制的类似物品不应视为本章制品的零件。

二、税目83.02所称"脚轮"，是指直径（对于有胎的，连胎计算在内，下同）不超过75毫米的或直径虽超过75毫米，但所装轮或胎的宽度必须小于30毫米的脚轮。

税则号列	货品名称〔CIQ扩展编码及品名－T2表示见附表2〕	最惠(%)	暂定税率	普通	增值/消费	出口退税	计量单位	监管条件/特殊证件	检验检疫	对美关税	亚太上/下
83.01	**贱金属制的锁（钥匙锁、数码锁及电动锁）；贱金属制带锁的扣环及扣环框架；上述锁的贱金属制钥匙：**										
8301.1000	-挂锁〔999〕	7		80	13/	13	千克/把	/		22	
	-机动车用锁：										
8301.2010	---中央控制门锁〔101其他车辆零部件，102机动车锁〕	9		80	13/	13	千克/套	/		19	
8301.2090	---其他〔101其他车辆零部件，102机动车锁〕	9		80	13/	13	千克/套	/		19	
8301.3000	-家具用锁〔999〕	7		80	13/	13	千克/个	/		27	
8301.4000	-其他锁〔999〕	9		80	13/	13	千克/个	/		19	
8301.5000	-带锁的扣环及扣环框架〔999〕	9		80	13/	13	千克	/		19	
8301.6000	-零件〔999〕	9		80	13/	13	千克	/		29	
8301.7000	-钥匙〔999〕	7		80	13/	13	千克	/		32	
83.02	**用于家具、门窗、楼梯、百叶窗、车厢、鞍具、衣箱、盒子及类似品的贱金属附件及架座；贱金属制帽架、帽钩、托架及类似品；用贱金属做支架的小脚轮；贱金属制的自动闭门器：**										
8302.1000	-铰链（折叶）〔101其他车辆零部件，102其他深加工金属制品〕	9		80	13/	13	千克	/		34	
8302.2000	-小脚轮〔999〕	9		80	13/	13	千克	/		34	
8302.3000	-机动车辆用的其他附件及架座〔101其他车辆零部件，102其他深加工金属制品〕	9		80	13/	13	千克	/		19	
	-其他附件及架座：										
8302.4100	--建筑用〔999〕	9		80	13/	13	千克	/		34	
8302.4200	--其他，家具用〔999〕	9		80	13/	13	千克	/		34	
8302.4900	--其他〔999〕	9		80	13/	13	千克	/		19	
8302.5000	-帽架、帽钩、托架及类似品〔999〕	7		80	13/	13	千克	/		27	
8302.6000	-自动闭门器〔999〕	9		80	13/	13	千克/个	/		34	
83.03	**装甲或加强的贱金属制保险箱、保险柜及保险库的门和带锁保险储存橱、钱箱、契约箱及类似品：**										
8303.0000	装甲或加强的贱金属制保险箱、保险柜及保险库的门和带锁保险储存橱、钱箱、契约箱及类似品〔999〕	9		50	13/	13	千克/个	/		34	
83.04	**贱金属制的档案柜、卡片索引柜、文件盘、文件篮、笔盘、公章架及类似的办公用具，但税目94.03的办公室家具除外：**										
8304.0000	贱金属制的档案柜、卡片索引柜、文件盘、文件篮、笔盘、公章架及类似的办公用具，但税目94.03的办公室家具除外〔999〕	9		80	13/	13	千克	/		29	
83.05	**活页夹、卷宗夹的贱金属附件，贱金属制的信夹、信角、文件夹、索引标签及类似的办公用品；贱金属制的成条订书钉（例如，供办公室、室内装饰或包装用）：**										
8305.1000	-活页夹或宗卷夹的附件〔999〕	9		80	13/	13	千克	/			
8305.2000	-成条订书钉〔999〕	7		80	13/	13	千克	/		32	
8305.9000	-其他，包括零件〔999〕	7		80	13/	13	千克	/		27	
83.06	**非电动的贱金属铃、钟、锣及类似品；贱金属雕塑像及其他装饰品；贱金属相框或画框及类似框架；贱金属镜子：**										
8306.1000	-铃、钟、锣及类似品〔999〕	8		80	13/	13	千克	/			
	-雕塑像及其他装饰品：										
8306.2100	--镀贵金属的〔999〕	7		100	13/	13	千克	/		32	
	--其他：										

Chapter 83
Miscellaneous articles of base metal

Notes:

1. For the purposes of this Chapter, parts of base metal are to be classified with their parent artcles. However, articles of iron or steel of heading Nos.73. 12, 73. 15, 73. 17, 73. 18 or 73. 20, or similar articles of other base metal (Chapters 74 to 76 and 78 to 81) are not to be taken as parts of articles of this Chapter.
2. For the purposes of heading No.83. 02, the word "castors" means those having a diameter (including, where appropriate, tyres) not exceeding 75mm, or those having a diameter (including, where appropriate, tyres) exceeding 75mm provided that the width of the wheel or tyre fitted thereto is less than 30mm.

协定税率 %								RCEP		特惠税率 %			Article Description
东/冰/格	巴基斯坦	韩国	瑞士 上/下	哥/秘/柬	澳/毛	新西/坡/智	中国港/澳/台	东盟及马来/澳/韩	日/新	亚太2国	老/柬/缅	98/97/95	
													Padlocks and locks (key, combination or electrically operated), of base metal; clasps and frames with clasps, incorporating locks, of base metal; keys for any of the foregoing articles, of base metal:
0/0/0	7.8	2.8	1.4/1.4	0/0/0	0/0	0/0/0	0/0/	0/0/12.6	12.7/0			0/0/0	-Padlocks
													-Locks of a kind used for motor vehicles:
5/0/0	8	6	0/0	0/0/0	0/0	0//0	0/0/	9.8/9.8/	/9.8			0/0/0	---Central controll door lock
5/0/0	8	6	0/0	0/0/0	0/0	0//0	0/0/	9.8/9.8/	/9.8			0/0/0	---Other
0/0/0	7.8	2.8	1.4/1.4	0/0/0	0/0	0/0/0	0/0/	0/0/12.6	12.7/0			0/0/0	-Locks of a kind used for furniture
0/0/0	9	2.8	1.4/1.4	0/0/0	0/0	0/0/0	0/0/	12.6/12.6/12.6	12.7/12.6			0/0/0	-Other locks
0/0/0	7.8	2.8	1.4/1.4	0/0/0	0/0	0/0/0	0/0/	0/0/12.6	12.7/0			0/0/0	-Clasps and frames with clasps, incorporating locks
0/0/0	4.2	2.4	1.2/1.2	0/0/0	0/0	0/0/0	0/0/	0/0/10.8	10.9/0			0/0/0	-Parts
0/0/0	2	4.6	0/0	0/0/0	0/0	0//0	0/0/	9.3/9.5/9.3	9.4/9.5			0/0/0	-Keys presented separately
													Base metal mountings, fittings and similar articles suitable for furniture, doors, staircases, windows, blinds, coachwork, saddlery, trunks, chests, caskets, or the like; base metal hat-racks, hat-pegs, brackets and similar fixtures; castors with mountings of base metal; automatic door closers of base metal:
0/0/0	3.5	0	0/0	0/0/0	0/0	0//0	0/0/	0/9/0	0/9			0/0/0	-Hinges
0/0/0	4.2	2.4	1.2/1.2	0/0/0	0/0	0/0/0	0/0/	0/0/10.8	10.9/0			0/0/0	-Castors
0/0/0	2	4.6	0/0	0/0/0	0/0	0//0	0/0/	9.3/9.5/9.3	9.4/9.5			0/0/0	-Other mountings, fittings and similar articles suitable for motor vehicles
													-Other mountings, fittings and similar articles:
0/0/0	7.8	2.8	1.4/1.4	0/0/0	0/0	0/0/0	0/0/	0/0/12.6	12.7/0			0/0/0	--Suitable for buildings
0/0/0	4.2	2.4	1.2/1.2	0/0/0	0/0	0/0/0	0/0/	0/0/10.8	10.9/0			0/0/0	--Other, suitable for furniture
0/0/0	4.2	2.4	1.2/1.2	0/0/0	0/0	0/0/0	0/0/	0/0/10.8	10.9/0			0/0/0	--Other
0/0/0	7.8	2.8	1.4/1.4	0/0/0	0/8.4	0/0/0	0/0/	0/0/12.6	12.7/0			0/0/0	-Hat-racks, hat-pegs, brackets and similar fixtures
0/0/0	4.2	2.4	1.2/1.2	0/0/0	0/0	0/0/0	0/0/	0/0/10.8	10.9/0			0/0/0	-Automatic door closers
													Armoured or reinforced safes, strong-boxes and doors and safe deposit lockers for strong-rooms, cash or deed boxes and the like, of base metal:
0/0/0	7.8	2.8	1.4/1.4	0/0/0	0/0	0/0/0	0/0/	0/0/12.6	12.7/0			0/0/0	Armoured or reinforced safes, strong-boxes and doors and safe deposit lockers for strong-rooms, cash or deed boxes and the like, of base metal
													Filing cabinets, card-index cabinets, paper trays, paper rests, pen trays, office-stamp stands and similar office or desk equipment, of base metal, other than office furniture of heading No. 94. 03:
0/0/0	3.5	2.1	1.1/1.1	0/0/0	0/0	0/0/0	0/0/	0/0/9.5	9.5/0			0/0/0	Filing cabinets, card-index cabinets, paper trays, paper rests, pen trays, office-stamp stands and similar office or desk equipment, of base metal, other than office furniture of heading No.94. 03
													Fittings for loose-leaf binders or files, letter clips, letter corners, paper clips, indexing tags and similar office articles, of base metal; staples in strips (for example, for offices, upholstery, packaging), of base metal:
0/0/0	3.5	2.1	1.1/1.1	0/0/0	0/0	0/0/0	0/0/	0/0/9.5	9.5/0			0/0/0	-Fittings for loose-leaf binders or files
0/0/0	3.5	2.1	1.1/1.1	0/0/0	0/0	0/0/0	0/0/	9.8/10/9.8	9.8/10			0/0/0	-Staples in strips
0/0/0	3.5	2.1	1.1/1.1	0/0/0	0/6.3	0/0/0	0/0/	0/0/9.5	9.5/0			0/0/0	-Other, including parts
													Bells, gongs and the like, non-electric, of base metal; statuettes and other ornaments, of base metal; photograph, picture or similar frames, of base metal; mirrors of base metal:
0/0/0	4	1.6	0/0	0/0/0	0/0	0//0	0/0/	0/0/7.2	7.3/0			0/0/0	-Bells, gongs and the like
													-Statuettes and other ornaments:
0/0/0	2	0	0/0	0/0/0	0/0	0//0	0/0/	0/0/0	7.3/0			0/0/0	--Plated with precious metal
													--Other:

税则号列	货品名称〔CIQ 扩展编码及品名—T2 表示见附表 2〕	最惠(%)	暂定税率	普通	增值/消费	出口退税	计量单位	监管条件/特殊证件	检验检疫	对美关税	亚太上/下
8306.2910	---景泰蓝的〔999〕	7		100	13/	13	千克	/			
8306.2990	---其他〔999〕	7		100	13/	13	千克	/		22	
8306.3000	-相框、画框及类似框架;镜子〔999〕	7		100	13/	13	千克	/		32	
83.07	**贱金属软管,不论是否有附件:**										
8307.1000	-钢铁制〔999〕	8		35	13/	13	千克	/		18	
8307.9000	-其他贱金属制〔999〕	8		35	13/	13	千克	/		18	
83.08	**贱金属制的扣、钩、环、眼及类似品,用于衣着或衣着附件、鞋靴、珠宝首饰、手表、书籍、天篷、皮革制品、旅行用品或马具或其他制成品;贱金属制的管形铆钉及开口铆钉;贱金属制的珠子及亮晶片:**										
8308.1000	-钩、环及眼〔999〕	9		80	13/	13	千克	/		29	
8308.2000	-管形铆钉及开口铆钉〔999〕	9		80	13/	13	千克	/		19	
8308.9000	-其他,包括零件〔999〕	9		80	13/	13	千克	/		29	
83.09	**贱金属制的塞子、盖子(包括冠形瓶塞、螺口盖及倒水塞)、瓶帽、螺口塞、塞子帽、封志及其他包装用附件:**										
8309.1000	-冠形瓶塞〔999〕	9		90	13/	13	千克	/		29	
8309.9000	-其他〔999〕	9		80	13/	13	千克	/		19	
83.10	**贱金属制的标志牌、铭牌、地名牌及类似品、号码、字母及类似标志,但税目 94.05 的货品除外:**										
8310.0000	贱金属制的标志牌、铭牌、地名牌及类似品、号码、字母及类似标志,但税目 94.05 的货品除外〔999〕	9		80	13/	13	千克	/		29	
83.11	**贱金属或硬质合金制的丝、条、管、板、电极及类似品,以焊剂涂面或以焊剂为芯,用于焊接或沉积金属、硬质合金;贱金属粉粘聚而成的丝或条,供金属喷镀用:**										
8311.1000	-以焊剂涂面的贱金属制电极,电弧焊用〔999〕	8		30	13/	13	千克	/		18	
8311.2000	-以焊剂为芯的贱金属制焊丝,电弧焊用〔999〕	8		30	13/	13	千克	/		28	
8311.3000	-以焊剂涂面或以焊剂为芯的贱金属条或丝,钎焊或气焊用〔999〕	8		30	13/	13	千克	/		18	
8311.9000	-其他〔999〕	8		30	13/	13	千克	/		18	5.2/5.2

协定税率 %								RCEP		特惠税率 %			Article Description
东/冰/格	巴基斯坦	韩国	瑞士上/下	哥/秘/柬	澳/毛	新西/坡/智	中国港/澳/台	东盟及马来/澳/韩	日/新	亚太2国	老/柬/缅	98/97/95	
0/0/0	2	0	0/0	0/0/0	0/0	0//0	0/0/	0/0/0	7.3/0			0/0/0	---Cloisonne
0/0/0	4	1.6	0/0	0/0/0	0/0	0/0/0	0/0/	0/0/7.2	7.3/0			0/0/0	---Other
0/0/0	2	1.6	0/0	0/0/0	0/0	0//0	0/0/	0/0/7.2	7.3/0			0/0/0	-Photograph, picture or similar frames; mirrors
													Flexible tubing of base metal, with or without fittings:
0/0/0	2	1.6	0.8/0.8	0/0/0	0/0	0//0	0/0/	7.6/7.6/7.6	7.6/7.6			0/0/0	-Of iron or steel
0/0/0	2	1.6	0/0	0/0/0	0/0	0//0	0/0/	0/0/7.6	7.6/0			0/0/0	-Of other base metal
													Clasps, frames with clasps, buckles, buckle-clasps, hooks, eyes, eyelets and the like, of base metal, of a kind used for clothing, clothing allessories footwear, jewelry, watches, books, awnings, leather, travel goods or harness or other made up articles; tubular or bifurcated rivets, of base metal; beads and spangles, of base metal:
0/0/0	0	6.3	1.1/1.1	0/0/0	0/6.3	0/0/0	0/0/	10/10/	/10			0/0/0	-Hooks, eyes and eyelets
0/0/0	3.5	2.1	1.1/1.1	0/0/0	0/0	0/0/0	0/0/	0/0/9.5	9.5/0			0/0/0	-Tubular or bifurcated rivets
0/0/0	3.5	6.3	1.1/1.1	0/0/0	0/0	0/0/0	0/0/	10/10/	/10			0/0/0	-Other, including parts
													Stoppers, caps and lids (including crown corks, screw caps and pouring stoppers), capsules for bottles, threaded bungs, bung covers, seals and other packing accessories, of base metal:
0/0/0	11.5	3.6	1.8/1.8	0/0/0	0/0	0/0/0	0/0/	0/0/16.2	16.4/0			0/0/0	-Crown corks
0/0/0	4.8	2.4	1.2/1.2	0/0/0	0/0	0/0/0	0/0/	10.8/10.8/10.8	10.9/10.8			0/0/0	-Other
													Sign-plates, name-plates, address-plates and similar plates, numbers, letters and other symbols, of base metal, excluding those of heading No.94. 05:
0/0/0		3.6	1.8/1.8	0/0/0	0/0	0/0/0	0/0/	16.2/16.2/16.2	16.4/16.2			0/0/0	Sign-plates, name-plates, address-plates and similar plates, numbers, letters and other symbols, of base metal, excluding those of heading No.94. 05
													Wire, rods, tubes, plates, electrodes and similar products, of base metal or of metal carbides, coated or cored with flux material, of a kind used for soldering, brazing, welding or deposition of metal or of metal carbides; wire and rods, of agglomerated base metal powder, used for metal spraying:
0/0/0	2	0	0/0	0/0/0	0/0	0//0	0/0/	0/0/0	7.3/0			0/0/0	-Coated electrodes of base metal, for electric arc-welding
0/0/0	2	3.7	0/0	0/0/0	0/0	0//0	0/0/	7.5/7.6/7.5	7.5/7.6			0/0/0	-Cored wire of base metal, for electric arc-welding
0/0/0	2		0/0	0/0/0	0/0	0//0	0/0/	5/5/	/5			0/0/0	-Coated rods and cored wire, of base metal, for soldering, brazing or welding by flame
0/0/0	2	0	0/0	0/0/0	0/0	0//0	0/0/	0/0/0	7.3/0			0/0/0	-Other

第十六类
机器、机械器具、电气设备及其零件；录音机及放声机、电视图像、声音的录制和重放设备及其零件、附件

注释：

一、本类不包括：

(一)第三十九章的塑料或税目40.10的硫化橡胶制的传动带、输送带；除硬质橡胶以外的硫化橡胶制的机器、机械器具、电气器具或其他专门技术用途的物品(税目40.16)；

(二)机器、机械器具或其他专门技术用途的皮革、再生皮革(税目42.05)或毛皮（税目43.03)的制品；

(三)各种材料（例如，第三十九章、第四十章、第四十四章、第四十八章及第十五类的材料)制的筒管、卷轴、纡子、锥形筒管、芯子、线轴及类似品；

(四)提花机及类似机器用的穿孔卡片（例如，归入第三十九章、第四十八章或第十五类的)；

(五)纺织材料制的传动带、输送带及其带料(税目59.10)或专门技术用途的其他纺织材料制品(税目59.11)；

(六)税目71.02至71.04的宝石或半宝石(天然、合成或再造)或税目71.16的完全以宝石或半宝石制成的物品，但已加工未装配的唱针用蓝宝石和钻石除外（税目85.22)；

(七)第十五类注释二所规定的贱金属制通用零件(第十五类)及塑料制的类似品(第三十九章)；

(八)钻管(税目73.04)；

(九)金属丝、带制的环形带(第十五类)；

(十)第八十二章或第八十三章的物品；

(十一)第十七类的物品；

(十二)第九十章的物品；

(十三)第九十一章的钟、表及其他物品；

(十四)税目82.07的可互换工具及作为机器零件的刷子(税目96.03)；类似的可互换工具应按其构成工作部件的材料归类(例如，归入第四十章、第四十二章、第四十三章、第四十五章、第五十九章或税目68.04、69.09)；

(十五)第九十五章的物品；

(十六)打字机色带或类似色带，不论是否装轴或装盒(应按其材料属性归类；如已上油或经其他方法处理能着色的，应归入税目96.12)，或税号96.20的独脚架、双脚架、三脚架及类似品。

二、除本类注释一、第八十四章注释一及第八十五章注释一另有规定的以外，机器零件(不属于税目84.84、85.44、85.45、85.46或85.47所列物品的零件）应按下列规定归类：

(一)凡在第八十四章、第八十五章的税目(税目84.09、84.31、84.48、84.66、84.73、84.87、85.03、85.22、85.29、85.38及85.48除外)列名的货品，均应归入该两章的相应税目；

(二)专用于或主要用于某一种机器或同一税目的多种机器（包括税目84.79或85.43的机器)的其他零件，应与该种机器一并归类，或酌情归入税目84.09、84.31、84.48、84.66、84.73、85.03、85.22、85.29或85.38。但能同时主要用于税目85.17和85.25至85.28所列货品的零件应归入税目85.17，专用于或主要用于税目85.24所列货品的零件应归入税目85.29；

(三)所有其他零件应酌情归入税目84.09、84.31、84.48、84.66、84.73、85.03、85.22、85.29或85.38，如不能归入上述税目，则应归入税目84.87或85.48。

三、由两部及两部以上机器装配在一起形成的组合式机器，或具有两种及两种以上互补或交替功能的机器，除条文另有规定的以外，应按具有主要功能的机器归类。

四、由不同独立部件(不论是否分开或由管道、传动装置、电缆或其他装置连接)组成的机器(包括机组)，如果组合后明显具有一种第八十四章或第八十五章某个税号所列功能，则全部机器应按其功能归入有关税目。

五、上述各注释所称“机器”，是指第八十四章或第八十五章各税目所列的各种机器、设备、装置及器具。

六、(一)本协调制度所称“电子电气废弃物及碎料”，是指下列电气和电子组件、印刷电路板以及电气或电子产品：

1.因破损、拆解或其他处理而无法用于其原用途，或通过维修、翻新或修理以使其仍用作原用途是不经济的；以及

2.其包装或运输方式不是为了保护单件物品在运输、装卸过程中不受损坏的。

(二)“电子电气废弃物及碎料”与其他废物、废料的混合物归入税目85.49。

(三)本类不包括第三十八章注释四所规定的城市垃圾。

第八十四章
核反应堆、锅炉、机器、机械器具及其零件

注释：

一、本章不包括：

(一)第六十八章的石磨、石碾及其他物品；

(二)陶瓷材料制的机器或器具(例如，泵)及供任何材料制的机器或器具用的陶瓷零件(第六十九章)；

(三)实验室用玻璃器(税目70.17)；玻璃制的机器、器具或其他专门技术用途的物品及其零件(税目70.19或70.20)；

(四)税目73.21或73.22的物品或其他贱金属制的类似物品（第七十四章至第七十六章或第七十八章至第八十一章)；

(五)税目85.08的真空吸尘器；

(六)税目85.09的家用电动器具；税目85.25的数字照相机；

(七)第十七类物品用的散热器；或

SECTION XVI
MACHINERY AND MECHANICAL APPLIANCES; ELECTRICAL EQUIPMENT; PARTS THEREOF; SOUND RECORDERS AND REPRODUCERS, TELEVISION IMAGE AND SOUND RECORDERS AND REPRODUCERS, AND PARTS AND ACCESSORIES OF SUCH ARTICLES

Notes:

1. This Section does not cover:
   (a) Transmission or conveyor belts or belting, of plastics of Chapter 39, or of vulcanized rubber (heading No.40.10); or other articles of a kind used in machinery or mechanical or electrical appliances or for other technical uses, of vulcanized rubber other than hard rubber (heading No.40.16);
   (b) Articles of leather or of composition leather (heading No.42.05) or of furskin (heading No.43.03), of a kind used in machinery or mechanical appliances or for other technical uses;
   (c) Bobbins, spools, cops, cones, cores, reels or similar supports of any material (for example, Chapter 39, 40, 44 or 48 or Section XV);
   (d) Perforated cards for Jacquard or similar machines (for example, Chapter 39 or 48 Section XV);
   (e) Transmission or conveyor belts or belting of textile material (heading No.59.10) or other articles of textile material for technical uses (heading No.59.11);
   (f) Precious or semi-precious stones (natural, synthetic or reconstructed) of headings Nos.71.02 to 71.04, or articles wholly of such stones of heading 71.16, except unmounted worked sapphires and diamonds for styli (heading No.85.22);
   (g) Parts of general use, as defined in Note 2 to Section XV, of base metal (Section XV), or similar goods of plastics (Chapter 39);
   (h) Drill pipe (heading No.73.04);
   (ij) Endless belts of metal wire or strip (Section XV);
   (k) Articles of Chapter 82 or 83;
   (l) Articles of Section XVII;
   (m) Articles of Chapter 90;
   (n) Clocks, watches or other articles of Chapter 91;
   (o) Interchangeable tools of headingNo.82.07 or brushes of a kind used as parts of machines (heading No.96.03), similar interchangable tools are to be classified according to constituent material of their working part (for example in Chapter 40, 42, 43, 45, 59 or heading No.68.04, or 69.09);
   (p) Articles of Chapter 95; or
   (q) Typewriter or similar ribbons, whether or not on spools or in cartridges (classified according to their constituent material, or in heading No.96.12 if inked or otherwise prepared for giving impressions) or unipod, bipod, tripod or the like of heading No.96.20.
2. Subject to Note 1 to this Section, Note 1 to Chapter 84 and Note 1 to Chapter 85, parts of machines (not being parts of the articles of heading No.84.84, 85.44, 85.45, 85.46 or 85.47) are to be classified according to the following rules:
   (a) Parts which are goods included in any of the headings of Chapter 84 or 85 (other than headingsNo.84.09, 84.31, 84.48, 84.66, 84.73, 84.87, 85.03, 85.22, 85.29, 85.38, and 85.48) are in all cases to be classified in their respective headings;
   (b) Other parts, if suitable for use solely or principally with a particular kind of machine, or with a number of machines of the same heading (including a machine of heading No.84.79 or 85.43) are to be classified with the machines of that kind or in heading No.84.09, 84.31, 84.48, 84.66, 84.73, 85.03, 85.22, 85.29 or 85.38 as appropriate. However, parts which are equally suitable for use principally with the goods of headings No.85.17 and 85.25 to 85.28 are to be classified in headingNo.85.17, and parts which are suitable for use solely or principally with the goods of heading 85.24 are to be classified in heading 85.29;
   (c) All other parts are to be classified in heading No.84.09, 84.31, 84.48, 84.66, 84.73, 85.03, 85.22, 85.29 or 85.38 as appropriate or, failing that, in heading No.84.87 or 85.48.
3. Unless the context otherwise requires, composite machines consisting of two or more machines fitted together to form a whole and other machines adapted for the purpose of performing two or more complementary or alternative functions are to be classified as if consisting only of that component or as being that machine which performs the principal function.
4. Where a machine (including a combination of machines) consists of individual components (whether separate or interconnected by piping, by transmission devices, by electric cables or by other devices) intended to contribute together to a clearly defined function covered by one of the headings in Chapter 84 or Chapter 85, then the whole falls to be classified in the heading appropriate to that function.
5. For the purposes of these Notes, the expression "machine" means any machine, machinery, plant, equipment, apparatus or appliance cited in the headings of Chapter 84 or 85.
6. (a) Throughout the Nomenclature, the expression "electrical and electronic waste and scrap" means electrical and electronic assemblies, printed circuit boards, and electrical or electronic articles that :
   (i) have been rendered unusable for their original purposes by breakage, cutting—up or other processes or are economically unsuitable for repair, refurbishment or renovation to render them fit for their original purposes; and
   (ii) are packaged or shipped in a manner not intended to protect individual articles from damage during transportation, loading and unloading operations.
   (c) Mixed consignments of "electrical and electronic waste and scrap" and other waste and scrap are to be classified in heading 85.49.
   (d) This Section does not cover municipal waste, as defined in Note 4 to Chapter 38.

Chapter 84
Nuclear reactors, boilers, machinery and mechanical appliances; parts thereof

Notes:

1. This Chapter does not cover:
   (a) Millstones, grindstones and other articles of Chapter 68;
   (b) Machinery or appliances (for example, pumps) of ceramic material and ceramic parts of machinery or appliances of any material (Chapter 69);
   (c) Laboratory glassware (heading No.70.17); machinery, appliances or other articles for technical uses or parts thereof, of glass (heading No.70.19 or 70.20);
   (d) Articles of heading No.73.21 or 73.22 or similar articles of other base metals (Chapters 74 to 76 or 78 to 81);
   (e) Vacuum cleaners of heading No.85.08
   (f) Electro-mechanical domestic appliances of heading No.85.09; digital cameras of heading No.85.25; or
   (g) Seltion XVII items with radiator;

(八)非机动的手工操作地板清扫器(税目96.03)。

二、除第十六类注释三及本章注释十一另有规定以外,如果某种机器或器具既符合税目84.01至84.24中一个或几个税目的规定,或符合税目84.86的规定,又符合税目84.25至84.80中一个或几个税目的规定,则应酌情归入税目84.01至84.24中的相应税目或税目84.86,而不归入税目84.25至84.80中的有税目。

(一)但税目84.19不包括:

1.催芽装置、孵卵器或育雏器(税目84.36);
2.谷物调湿机(税目84.37);
3.萃取糖汁的浸提装置(税目84.38);
4.纱线、织物及纺织制品的热处理机器(税目84.51);
5.温度变化(即使必不可少)仅作为辅助功能的机器、设备或实验室设备。

(二)税目84.22不包括:

1.缝合袋子或类似品用的缝纫机(税目84.52);
2.税目84.72的办公室用机器。

(三)税目84.24不包括:

1.喷墨印刷(打印)机器(税目84.43);
2.水射流切割机(税目84.56)。

三、如果用于加工各种材料的某种机床既符合税目84.56的规定,又符合税目84.57、84.58、84.59、84.60、84.61、84.64或84.65的规定,则应归入税目84.56。

四、税目84.57仅适用于可以完成下列不同形式机械操作的金属加工机床,但车床(包括车削中心)除外:

(一)按照机械加工程序从刀具库中自动更换刀具(加工中心);

(二)同时或顺序地自动使用不同的动力头对固定不动的工件进行加工(单工位组合机床);

(三)自动将工件送向不同的动力头(多工位组合机床)。

五、税目84.62用于板材的"纵剪线"是由开卷机、矫平机、纵剪机和收卷机组成的生产线。用于板材的"定尺剪切线"是由开卷机、矫平机和剪切机组成的生产线。

六、(一)税目84.71所称"自动数据处理设备",是指具有以下功能的机器:

1. 存储处理程序和执行程序直接需要的起码的数据;
2. 按照用户的要求随意编辑程序;
3. 按照用户指令进行算术计算;以及
4. 在运行过程中,可不需人为干预而通过逻辑判断,执行一个处理程序,这个处理程序可改变计算机指令的执行。

(二)自动数据处理设备可以是一套由若干单独部件所组成的系统。

(三)除本条注释(四)及(五)另有规定以外,一个部件如果符合下列所有规定,即可视为自动数据处理系统的一部分:

1. 专用于或主要用于自动数据处理系统;
2. 可以直接或通过一个或几个其他部件同中央处理机相连接;
3. 能够以本系统所使用的方式(代码或信号)接收或传送数据。

自动数据处理设备的部件如果单独报验,应归入税目84.71。

但是,键盘、X-Y坐标输入装置及盘(片)式存储部件,只要符合上述注释(三)2及(三)3所列的规定,应一律作为税目84.71的部件归类。

(四)税目84.71不包括单独报验的下述设备,即使它们符合上述注释六(三)的所有规定:

1. 打印机、复印机、传真机,不论是否组合式;
2. 发送或接收声音、图像或其他数据的设备,包括有线或无线网络(例如局域网或广域网)通信设备;
3. 扬声器及传声器(麦克风);
4. 电视摄相机、数字照相机及视频摄录一体机;
5. 监视器及投影机,未装有电视接收装置。

(五)装有自动数据处理设备或与自动数据处理设备连接使用,但却从事数据处理以外的某项专门功能的机器,应按其功能归入相应的税目,对于无法按功能归类的,应归入未列名税目。

七、税目84.82还包括最大直径及最小直径与标称直径相差均不超过1%或0.05毫米(以相差数值较小的为准)的抛光钢珠,其他钢珠归入税目73.26。

八、具有一种以上用途的机器在归类时,其主要用途可作为唯一的用途对待。除本章注释二、第十六类注释三另有规定的以外,凡任何税目都未列明其主要用途的机器,以及没有哪一种用途是主要用途的机器,均应归入税目84.79。税目84.79还包括将金属丝、纺织纱线或其他各种材料以及它们的混合材料制成绳、缆的机器(例如,捻股机、绞扭机、制缆机)。

九、税目84.70所称"袖珍式",仅适用于外形尺寸不超过170毫米×100毫米×45毫米的机器。

十、税目84.85所称"增材制造"(也称3D打印)指以数字模型为基础,将介质材料(例如,金属、塑料或陶瓷)通过连续添加、堆叠、凝结和固化形成物体。

除第十六类注释一及第八十四章注释一另有规定的以外,符合税目84.85规定的设备,应归入该税目而不归入本协调制度的其他税目。

十一、(一)第八十五章注释十一(一)及(二)也同样适用于本条注释及品目84.86中所称的"半导体器件"及"集成电器"。但本条注释及品目84.86所称"半导体器件",也包括光敏半导体器件及发光二极管(LED)。

(二)本条注释和税目84.86所称"平板显示器的制造",包括将各层基片制造成一层平板,但不包括玻璃的制造或将印刷电路板或其他电子元件装配在平板上。所称"平板显示"不包括阴极射线管技术。

(三)税目84.86也包括专用于或主要用于下列用途的机器及装置:

1. 制造或修补掩膜版及投影掩膜版;
2. 组装半导体器件或集成电路;
3. 升降、搬运、装卸单晶柱、晶圆、半导体器件、集成电路及平板显示器。

(h) Hand-operated mechanical floor sweepers, not motorized (heading No. 96.03).

2. Subject to the operation of Note 3 to Section XVI and subject to Note11 to this chapter, a machine or appliance which answers to a description in one or more of the headings No.84.01 to 84.24 or heading 84.86 and at the same time to a description in one or other of the headings Nos.84.25 to 84.80 is to be classified under the appropriate headings of the former group or under heading 84.86, as the case may be, and not the latter.
   (a) HeadingNo.84.19 does not, however, cover:
      (i) Germination plant, incubators or brooders (headingNo.84.36);
      (ii) Grain dampening machines (heading No.84.37);
      (iii) Diffusing apparatus for sugar juice extraction (headingNo.84.38);
      (iv) Machinery for the heat-treatment of textile yarns, fabrics or made up textile articles (heading No.84.51); or
      (v) Machinery or plant, designed for mechanical operation or la boratorg equipment, in which a change of temperature, even if necessary, is subsidiary.
   (b) Heading No.84.22 does not cover:
      (i) Sewing machines for closing bags or similar containers ;
      (ii) Office machinery of heading No.84.72.
   (c) Heading No.84.24 does not cover:
      (i) Ink-jet printing machines (heading No.84.43).
      (ii) Water-jet cutting machines(heading No.84.56).
3. A machine-tool for working any material which answers to a description in heading No.84.56 and at the same time to a description in heading Nos.84.57, 84.58, 84.59, 84.60, 84.61, 84.64 or 84.65 is to be classified in heading No.84.56.
4. Heading No.84.57 applies only to machine-tools for working metal other than lathes (including turning centres), which can carry out different types of machining operations either:
   (a) by automatic tool change from a magazine or the like in conformity with a machining programme (machining centres),
   (b) by the automatic use, simultaneously or sequentially, of different unit heads working on a fixed position workpiece (unit construction machines, single station), or
   (c) by the automatic transfer of the workpiece to different unit heads (multi-station transfer machines).
5. For the purposes of heading 84.62, a "slitting line" for flat products is a processing line composed of an uncoiler, a coil flattener, a slitter and a recoiler. A "cut—to—length line" for flat products is a processing line composed of an uncoiler, a coil flattener, and a shear.
6. (a) For the purposes of heading No.84.71, the expression "automatic data processing machines" means machines capable of:
      (i) Storing the processing program or programs and at least the data immediately necessary for the execution of the program;
      (ii) being freely programmed in accordance with the requirements of the user;
      (iii) performing arthmetical computations specified by the user; and,
      (iv) executing, without human intervention, a processing program which requires them to modify their execution, by logical decision during the processing run;
   (b) Automatic data processing machines may be in the form of systems consisting of a variable number of separate units.
   (c) Subject to paragraph(d) and(e) below, a unit is to be rgearded as being a part of an automatic data processing system if it meets all of the following condition
      (i) It is of a kind solehy or praincipally used in an automatic data processing system;
      (ii) It is connectable to the central processing unit either directly or through one or more other units; and
      (iii) It is able to accept or delirer data in afrom(codes or signals), which can be used by the system.
      Separatly presented units of an automatic data processing malhine are to be classified heading 84.71.
      However keybards X—Y co-ordinate input devices and disk storage units which satisfy the cond it ions of paragraphs (c)(ii) and(c)(iii) above are in all cases to be dassified as anits of heading No.84.71.
   (d) Heading 84.71 does not cover the following when prestented separateby eren if they meet all of conditions set sixth in Notes(c) above:
      (i) printers copying machines facsimile machines whether or not combined.
      (ii) Apparats for the transmission or reception of voice images or other data including apparatus for communication in a wired or wireless network (Such as alocal or wide area netaork)
      (iii) Loud speakers and microphones
      (iv) Television camera, digital cemera and video camera recorders
      (v) Monitors and projectors not incorp orating television reception apparatus recezvers.
   (e) Machines performing a specific function other than data processing and incorporating or working in conjunction with an automatic data processing machine are to be classified in the headings appropriate to their respective functions or, failing that, in residual headings.
7. Heading No.84.82 applies, *inter alia*, to polished steel balls, the maximum and minimum diameters of which do not differ from the nominal diameter by more than 1% or by more than 0.05mm, whichever is less. Other steel balls are to be classified in heading No.73.26.
8. A machine which is used for more than one purpose is, for the purposes of classification, to be treated as if its principal purpose were its sole purpose. Subject to Note 2 to this Chapter and Note 3 to Section XVI, a machine, the principal purpose of which is not described in any heading or for which no one purpose is the principal purpose, unless the context otherwise requires, is to be classified in heading No.84.79. Heading No.84.79 also covers machines for making rope or cable (for example, stranding, twisting or cabling machines) from metal wire, textile yarn or any other material or from a combination of such materials.
9. For the purposes of headingNo.84.70, the term "pocket-size" applies only to machines the dimensions of which do not exceed 170mm×100mm×45mm.
10. For the purposes of heading 84.85, the expression "additive manufacturing" (also referred to as 3D printing) means the formation of physical objects, based on a digital model, by the successive addition and layering, andconsolidation and solidification, of material (for example, metal, plastics or ceramics). Subject to Note 1 to Section XVI and Note 1 to Chapter 84, machines answering to the description in heading 84.85 are to be classified in that heading and in no other heading of the Nomenclature.
11. (a) Notes 11(a) and 11(b) to chapter 85 also apply with respect to the expressions "semicoiductor devices and electonic integrated circuits" respectively, as used in this Note and in heading 84.86. However for the parposes of this Note and of heading 84.86. the expression semicondutor devices also covers photo sensitive semicondactor devices and light emitting diodes(LED).
   (b) For the purposes of this Note and of heading 84.86 the expression "manufacture of flat pane displays" covers the fabrication of substrtes into aftat panel. It does not cover the manufacture of glass or the assembly of plinted circuit boards or other electronie components onto the flat panel The expression "flat panel display" does not cover calhoderay tube technology.
   (c) Heading No.84.86 also includesmachines apparatus solely or principally of a kind used for
      (i) The manafactre or rapair of masks and retides
      (ii) Assemb semiconductordevices or electronic; integrated circuits; and
      (iii) Lifting handing loadingor unlading of boules, wafers, semicondu ctor devices electonic integrated circuits and flat panel displays.

（四）除十六类注释一及第八十四章注释一另有规定的以外，符合税目 84.86 规定的设备及装置，应归入该税目而不归入本协调制度的其他税目。

子目注释：

一、子目 8465.20 所称"加工中心"，仅适用于加工木材、软木、骨、硬质橡胶、硬质塑料或类似硬质材料的加工机床。这些设备可根据机械加工程序，从刀具库或类似装置中自动更换刀具，以完成不同形式的机械加工。

二、子目 8471.49 所称"系统"，是指各部件符合第八十四章注释六（三）所列条件，并且至少由一个中央处理部件、一个输入部件（例如，键盘或扫描仪）及一个输出部件（例如，视频显示器或打印机）组成的自动数据处理设备。

三、子目 8481.20 所称"油压或气压传动阀"，是指在液压或气压系统中专用于传递"流体动力"的阀门，其能源以加压流体（液体或气体）的形式供给。这些阀门可以具有各种形式（例如，减压阀、止回阀）。子目 8481.20 优先于税目 84.81 的所有其他子目。

四、子目 8482.40 仅包括滚柱直径相同，最大不超过 5 毫米，且长度至少是直径三倍的圆滚柱轴承，滚柱的两端可以磨圆。

税则号列	货品名称〔CIQ 扩展编码及品名－T2 表示见附表 2〕	最惠(%)	暂定税率	普通	增值/消费	出口退税	计量单位	监管条件/特殊证件	检验检疫	对美关税	亚太上/下
84.01	**核反应堆；核反应堆的未辐照燃料元件（释热元件）；同位素分离机器及装置：**										
8401.1000	-核反应堆〔999〕	2		8	13/	13	千克/台	3/			
8401.2000	-同位素分离机器、装置及其零件〔999〕	1		8	13/	13	个/千克	3/			
	-未辐照燃料元件（释热元件）：										
8401.3010	---未辐照燃料元件〔999〕	2	1	8	13/	13	千克	3/			
8401.3090	---未辐照燃料元件的零件〔999〕	1		8	13/	13	千克	/			
	-核反应堆零件：										
8401.4010	---未辐照相关组件〔999〕	1		8	13/	13	千克/台	/			
8401.4020	---堆内构件〔999〕	1		8	13/	13	千克/台	3/			
8401.4090	---其他										
8401.4090 10	核反应堆压力容器（包括其顶板）（专门设计或制造来用于容纳核反应堆的堆芯）〔999〕	1		8	13/	13	千克/台	3/			
8401.4090 20	核反应堆控制棒和设备（专用于核反应堆裂变控制棒、支承结构或悬吊结构等）〔999〕	1		8	13/	13	千克/台	3/			
8401.4090 30	核反应堆压力管（专用于容纳核燃料元件和一次冷却剂的，压力＞5.1MPa）〔999〕	1		8	13/	13	千克/台	3/			
8401.4090 90	其他核反应堆零件〔999〕	1		8	13/	13	千克/台	/			
84.02	**蒸汽锅炉（能产生低压水蒸气的集中供暖用的热水锅炉除外）；过热水锅炉：**										
	-蒸汽锅炉：										
	--蒸发量超过 45 吨/时的水管锅炉：										
8402.1110	---蒸发量在 900 吨/时及以上的发电用锅炉〔999〕	3		11	13/	13	台/千克	6A/	M		2/2
8402.1190	---其他〔999〕	10		35	13/	13	台/千克	6A/	M		6.5/6.5
8402.1200	--蒸发量不超过 45 吨/时的水管锅炉										
8402.1200 10	纸浆厂废料锅炉（蒸发量≤45 吨/时蒸汽水管锅炉）〔999〕	5		35	13/	13	台/千克	6A/	M		3.3/3.3
8402.1200 90	其他蒸发量未超 45 吨/时水管锅炉〔999〕	5		35	13/	13	台/千克	6A/	M		3.3/3.3
8402.1900	--其他蒸汽锅炉，包括混合式锅炉〔999〕	5		35	13/	13	台/千克	6A/	M	30	
8402.2000	-过热水锅炉〔999〕	10		35	13/	13	台/千克	6A/	M	15	
8402.9000	-零件〔999〕	2		11	13/	13	千克	/		27	
84.03	**集中供暖用的热水锅炉，但税目 84.02 的货品除外：**										
	-锅炉：										
8403.1010	---家用型〔999〕	8		80	13/	13	台/千克	6A/	ML	33	5.2/5.2
8403.1090	---其他〔101 承压热水锅炉，102 沼气锅炉〕	8		80	13/	13	台/千克	6A/	M	18	5.2/5.2
8403.9000	-零件〔999〕	6		80	13/	13	千克	/		16	
84.04	**税目 84.02 或 84.03 所列锅炉的辅助设备（例如，节热器、过热器、除灰器、气体回收器）；水蒸气或其他蒸汽动力装置的冷凝器：**										
	-税目 84.02 或 84.03 所列锅炉的辅助设备：										
8404.1010	---税目 84.02 所列锅炉的辅助设备										
8404.1010 10	使用（可再生）生物质燃料的非水管蒸汽锅炉的辅助设备（例如，节热器、过热器、除灰器、气体回收器）〔999〕	7	5	35	13/	13	千克	6/			3.5/3.5
8404.1010 90	其他蒸汽锅炉、过热水锅炉的辅助设备（例如，节热器、过热器、除灰器、气体回收器）〔999〕	7		35	13/	13	千克	6/			3.5/3.5
8404.1020	---税目 84.03 所列锅炉的辅助设备〔999〕	8	5	80	13/	13	千克	6/			4/4
8404.2000	-水蒸气或其他蒸汽动力装置的冷凝器〔999〕	8	5	35	13/	13	千克	6/		30	
	-零件：										
8404.9010	---子目 8404.1020 所列设备的零件〔999〕	7	5	80	13/	13	千克	/		30	0/0
8404.9090	---其他										

(d) Subject to Notel to section XVI and Note 1 to chapter 84.machines and apparatus answring to the description in heading 84.86 are to be classfied in that heading and in no other heading of the Nomenclature.

Subheading Notes:

1.Subheading No. 8465.20 called "machining center", processing machine is only suitable for the processing of wood, cork, bone, hard rubber, hard plastics or similar hard materials. These devices can automatically replace the tool from the tool library or similar device according to the machining procedure to complete different forms of machining.

2. For the purposes of subheading No.8471. 49, the term "systems" means automatic data processing machines whose units satisfy the conditions laid down in Note 6 (c) to Chapter 84 and which comprise at least a central processing unit, one input unit (for example: a keyboard or a scanner), and one output unit (for example: a visual display unit or a printer).

3.Subheading No.8481.20 called "hydraulic or pneumatic valve" refers to the transfer of "fluid power valve in hydraulic or pneumatic system secondary energy in a pressurized fluid (liquid or gas) in the form of supply. These valves can have various forms (e.g., pressure relief valves, check valves).Subheading No. 8481.20 priority to all other Subheading of Heading No. 84.81

4. Subheading No.8482. 40 applies only to bearings with cylindrical rollers of a uniform diameter not exceeding 5mm and having a length which is at least three times the diameter. The ends of the rollers may be rounded.

协定税率 %								RCEP		特惠税率 %			
东/冰/格	巴基斯坦	韩国	瑞士上/下	哥/秘/柬	澳/毛	新西/坡/智	中国港/澳/台	东盟及马来/澳/韩	日/新	亚太2国	老/柬/缅	98/97/95	Article Description
													Nuclear reactors; fuel elements (cartridges), non-irradiated, for nuclear reactors; machinery and apparatus for isotopic separation:
0/0/0	0	0	0/0	0/0/0	0/0	0//0	0/0/	0/0/0	0/0			0/0/0	-Nuclear reactors
0/0/0	0	0	0/0	0/0/0	0/0	0//0	0/0/	0/0/0	0/0			0/0/0	-Machinery and apparatus for isotopic separation, and parts thereof
													-Fuel elements (cartridges), non-irradiated:
0/0/0	0	0	0/0	0/0/0	0/0	0//0	0/0/	0/0/0	0/0			0/0/0	---Fuel elements, non-irrdadiated
0/0/0	0	0	0/0	0/0/0	0/0	0//0	0/0/	0/0/0	0/0			0/0/0	---Parts for fuel elements non-irradiated
													-Parts of nuclear reactors:
0/0/0	0	0	0/0	0/0/0	0/0	0//0	0/0/	0/0/0	0/0			0/0/0	---Non-irradiated Associated Assembly
0/0/0	0	0	0/0	0/0/0	0/0	0//0	0/0/	0/0/0	0/0			0/0/0	---Reactor internals
													---Other
0/0/0	0	0	0/0	0/0/0	0/0	0//0	0/0/	0/0/0	0/0			0/0/0	Pressure vessels for nuclear reactors(including top slabs) specially designed or produced to hold the reactor core of the nuclear reactors
0/0/0	0	0	0/0	0/0/0	0/0	0//0	0/0/	0/0/0	0/0			0/0/0	Control rods and devices of nuclear reactors (fission control rod and support and suspension structures thereof, specified for nuclear reactors)
0/0/0	0	0	0/0	0/0/0	0/0	0//0	0/0/	0/0/0	0/0			0/0/0	Pressure tubes of nuclear reactors (specified for holding fuel elements or primary coolants, pressure>5.1MPa)
0/0/0	0	0	0/0	0/0/0	0/0	0//0	0/0/	0/0/0	0/0			0/0/0	Other parts of nuclear reactors
													Steam or other vapour generating boilers (other than central heating hot water boilers capable also of producting low pressure steam); super-heated water boilers:
													-Steam or other vapour generating boilers:
													--Watertube boilers with a steam production exceeding 45t per hour:
0/0/0	0	0	0/0	0/0/0	0/0	0//0	0/0/	0/0/0	0/0			0/0/0	---Boilers for generating electricity with a steam production 900t or more per hour
0/0/0	4.9	2.8	1.4/1.4	0/0/0	0/0	0/0/0	0/0/	0/0/12.6	12.7/0			0/0/0	---Other
													--Watertube boilers with a steam production not exceeding 45t per hour
0/0/0	0	2.3	0/0	0/0/0	0/0	0//0	0/0/	4.5/4.5/4.5	4.7/4.5			0/0/0	Waster material boiler of pulp mill(steam water tube boilers with their evaporation≤45tons/hour)
0/0/0	0	2.3	0/0	0/0/0	0/0	0//0	0/0/	4.5/4.5/4.5	4.7/4.5			0/0/0	Other wate tube boilers with the evaporation ≤45tons/hour
0/0/0	0	2.3	0/0	0/0/0	0/0	0//0	0/0/	4.5/4.5/4.5	4.7/4.5			0/0/0	--Other vapour generating boilers, including hybrid boilers
0/0/0	9	3.2	1.6/1.6	0/0/0	0/0	0/0/0	0/0/	0/0/14.4	14.5/0			0/0/0	-Super-heated water boilers
0/0/0	0	0	0/0	0/0/0	0/0	0//0	0/0/	0/0/0	0/0			0/0/0	-Parts
													Central heating boilers other than those of headingNo.84. 02:
													-Boilers:
0/0/0	3.5	2	0/0	0/0/0	0/0	0//0	0/0/	0/0/9	9.1/0			0/0/0	---Household type
0/0/0	2	2	0/0	0/0/0	0/0	0//0	0/0/	0/0/9	9.1/0			0/0/0	---Other
0/0/0	0	1.2	0/0	0/0/0	0/0	0//0	0/0/	0/0/5.4	5.5/0			0/0/0	-Parts
													Auxiliary plant for use with boilers of headingNo. 84. 02 or 84. 03 (for example, economizers, super-heaters, soot removers, gas recoverers); condensers for steam or other vapour power units:
													-Auxiliary plant for use with boilers of headingNo. 84. 02 or 84. 03:
													---For use with boilers of headingNo.84. 02
0/0/0	0	0	0.7/0.7	0/0/0	0/0	0//0	0/0/	0/0/0	6.4/0			0/0/0	Use (renewable) of biomass fuel pipe steam boiler auxiliary equipment (for example, heat exchanger, superheater, ash separator and gas collector)
0/0/0	0	0	0.7/0.7	0/0/0	0/0	0//0	0/0/	0/0/0	6.4/0			0/0/0	Other steam boiler, hot water boiler auxiliary equipment(e.g., economizer, superheater, soot removers, gas recovery device)
0/0/0	2	2	0/0	0/0/0	0/0	0//0	0/0/	0/0/9	9.1/0			0/0/0	---For use with boilers of headingNo.84. 03
0/0/0	7.8	2.8	1.4/1.4	0/0/0	0/0	0/0/0	0/0/	0/0/12.6	12.7/0			0/0/0	-Condensers for steam or other vapour power units
													-Parts:
0/0/0	0	0	0/0	0/0/0	0/0	0//0	0/0/	0/0/0	9.1/0			0/0/0	---Of the auxiliary plant of subheading No. 8404. 1020
													---Other

税则号列	货品名称〔CIQ扩展编码及品名—T2 表示见附表 2〕	最惠(%)	暂定税率	普通	增值/消费	出口退税	计量单位	监管条件/特殊证件	检验检疫	对美关税	亚太上/下
8404.9090　10	使用(可再生)生物质燃料的非水管蒸汽锅炉的辅助设备的零件;水蒸气或其他蒸汽动力装置的冷凝器的零件(编号84041010、84042000 所列辅助设备的)〔999〕	7	5	35	13/	13	千克	/		30	0/0
8404.9090　90	其他辅助设备用零件(编号 84041010、84042000 所列辅助设备的)〔999〕	7		35	13/	13	千克	/		32	0/0
84.05	**煤气发生器,不论有无净化器;乙炔发生器及类似的水解气体发生器,不论有无净化器:**										
8405.1000	-煤气发生器,不论有无净化器;乙炔发生器及类似的水解气体发生器,不论有无净化器〔999〕	10		30	13/	13	千克	A/	M	20	
8405.9000	-零件〔999〕	6		30	13/	13	千克	/		26	
84.06	**汽轮机:**										
8406.1000	-船舶动力用汽轮机〔999〕	5		35	13/	13	台/千克	/			3.5/3.5
	-其他汽轮机:										
	--输出功率超过 40 兆瓦的:										
8406.8110	---输出功率不超过 100 兆瓦的〔999〕	5		35	13/	13	台/千克	/		30	
8406.8120	---输出功率超过 100 兆瓦,但不超过 350 兆瓦的〔999〕	5		35	13/	13	台/千克	/			3.5/3.5
8406.8130	---输出功率超过 350 兆瓦的〔999〕	6		11	13/	13	台/千克	/			4.2/4.2
8406.8200	--输出功率不超过 40 兆瓦的〔999〕	5		35	13/	13	台/千克	/		15	3.5/3.5
8406.9000	-零件〔999〕	2		11	13/	13	千克	/		27	
84.07	**点燃往复式或旋转式活塞内燃发动机:**										
	-航空器发动机:										
8407.1010	---输出功率不超过 298 千瓦〔999〕	2		11	13/	13	台/千克	/		12	
8407.1020	---输出功率超过 298 千瓦							6			
8407.1020　10	输出功率>298kw 的无人驾驶航空飞行器、无人驾驶飞艇用高效率内燃引擎(设计或改型后用于在 15420 米以上高空飞行的吸气活塞式或转子式内燃发动机)〔999〕	2		11	13/	13	台/千克	3/			
8407.1020　90	其他输出功率>298kw 航空器内燃引擎(指点燃往复式或旋转式)〔999〕	2		11	13/	13	台/千克	/			
	-船舶发动机:										
8407.2100	--舷外发动机〔999〕	8		35	13/	13	台/千克	/		18	
8407.2900	--其他〔999〕	8		20	13/	13	台/千克	/		13	
	-用于第八十七章所列车辆的往复式活塞发动机:										
8407.3100	--气缸容量(排气量)不超过 50 毫升〔101 其他车辆零部件,102 汽油发动机〕	10		35	13/	13	台/千克	y4xA6/	M		
8407.3200	--气缸容量(排气量)超过 50 毫升,但不超过 250 毫升〔101 其他车辆零部件,102 汽油发动机〕	10		35	13/	13	台/千克	y4xA6/	M		
8407.3300	--气缸容量(排气量)超过 250 毫升,但不超过 1000 毫升〔101 其他车辆零部件,102 汽油发动机〕	10		70	13/	13	台/千克	A6/	M		
	--气缸容量(排气量)超过 1000 毫升:										
8407.3410	---气缸容量(排气量)超过 1000 毫升,但不超过 3000 毫升〔101 其他车辆零部件,102 汽油发动机〕	10		70	13/	13	台/千克	A6/	M		6.5/6.5
8407.3420	---气缸容量(排气量)超过 3000 毫升										
8407.3420　10	排气量≥5.9 升的天然气发动机(第 87 章所列车辆用的点燃往复式活塞发动机)〔101 其他车辆零部件,102 汽油发动机〕	10		35	13/	13	台/千克	6/			6.5/6.5
8407.3420　90	其他超 3000cc 车用往复式活塞引擎(第 87 章所列车辆用的点燃往复式活塞发动机)〔101 其他车辆零部件,102 汽油发动机〕	10		35	13/	13	台/千克	6/			6.5/6.5
	-其他发动机:										
8407.9010	---沼气发动机〔999〕	10		35	13/	13	台/千克	/			7/7
8407.9090	---其他										
8407.9090　10	转速<3600r/min 汽油发动机(发电机用,立式输出轴汽油发动机除外)〔999〕	18		35	13/	13	台/千克	/		23	
8407.9090　20	转速<4650r/min 汽油发动机(品目 8426、8428－8430 所列机械用,立式输出轴汽油发动机除外)〔999〕	18		35	13/	13	台/千克	/		23	
8407.9090　31	叉车用汽油发动机(800 转/分≤转速≤3400 转/分)(立式输出轴汽油发动机除外)〔999〕	18	9	35	13/	13	台/千克	/		14	
8407.9090　39	其他转速<4650 转/分汽油发动机(税目 84.27 所列机械用,立式输出轴汽油发动机除外)〔999〕	18		35	13/	13	台/千克	/		23	
8407.9090　40	立式输出轴汽油发动机(非第 87 章所列车辆用其他往复式活塞发动机)〔999〕	18	9	35	13/	13	台/千克	/		14	
8407.9090　90	其他往复或旋转式活塞内燃引擎(非第 87 章所列车辆用其他点燃往复式或旋转式活塞发动机)〔999〕	18		35	13/	13	台/千克	/		23	

协定税率 %								RCEP		特惠税率 %			
东/冰/格	巴基斯坦	韩国	瑞士 上/下	哥/秘/柬	澳/毛	新西/坡/智	中国港/澳/台	东盟及马来/澳/韩	日/新	亚太2国	老/柬/缅	98/97/95	Article Description
0/0/0	0	0	0/0	0/0/0	0/0	0//0	0/0/	0/0/0	0/0			0/0/0	Use (renewable) of biomass fuel pipe steam boiler auxiliary equipment parts; Water vapor or other steam condenser of power plant parts (no. 84041010, 84042000, auxiliary equipment listed)
0/0/0	0	0	0/0	0/0/0	0/0	0//0	0/0/	0/0/0	0/0			0/0/0	Other auxiliary equipment with parts listed (no. 84041010, 84042000, auxiliary equipment)
													Producer gas or water gas generators, with or without their purifiers; acetylene gas generators and similar water process gas generators, with or without their purifiers:
0/0/0	7.8	8.4	1.4/1.4	0/0/0	0/0	0/0/0	0/0/	13.3/13.3/14	/13.3			0/0/0	-Producer gas or water gas generators, with or without their purifiers; acetylene gas generators and similar water process gas generators, with or without their purifiers
0/0/0	2	0	0/0	0/0/0	0/0	0//0	0/0/	0/0/0	7.3/0			0/0/0	-Parts
													Steam turbines and other vapour turbines:
0/0/0	0	1	0/0	0/0/0	0/0	0//0	0/0/	0/0/4.5	4.5/0			0/0/0	-Turbines for marine propulsion
													-Other turbines:
													--Of an output exceeding 40 MW:
0/0/0	0	0	0/0	0/0/0	0/0	0//0	0/0/	0/0/0	4.7/0			0/0/0	---Of an output not exceeding 100 MW
0/0/0	0	0	0/0	0/0/0	0/0	0//0	0/0/	0/0/0	4.8/0			0/0/0	---Of an output exceeding 100 MW but not exceeding 350 MW
0/0/0	0	0	0/0	0/0/0	0/0	0//0	0/0/	0/0/0	0/0			0/0/0	---Of an output exceeding 350 MW
0/0/0	0	0	2.1/2.1	0/0/0	0/0	0//0	0/0/	0/0/0	4.5/0			0/0/0	--Of an output not exceeding 40 MW
0/0/0	0	0	0.2/0.2	0/0/0	0/0	0//0	0/0/	0/0/0	1.8/0			0/0/0	-Parts
													Spark-ignition reciprocating or rotary internal combustion piston engines:
													-Aircraft engines:
0/0/0	0	0	0/0	0/0/0	0/0	0//0	0/0/	0/0/0	0/0			0/0/0	---Of an output not exceeding 298kW
													---Of an output exceeding 298kW
0/0/0	0	0	0/0	0/0/0	0/0	0//0	0/0/	0/0/0	0/0			0/0/0	Spark-ignition reciprocating or rotary internal combustion piston aircraft engines , of an output exceeding 298kW
0/0/0	0	0	0/0	0/0/0	0/0	0//0	0/0/	0/0/0	0/0			0/0/0	Spark-ignition reciprocating or rotary internal combustion piston aircraft engines , of an output exceeding 298kW
													-Marine propulsion engines:
0/0/0	2		0/0	0/0/0	0/0	0//0	0/0/	7.6/7.6/	/7.6			0/0/0	--Outboard motors
0/0/0	2		0/0	0/0/0	0/0	0//0	0/0/	7.6/7.6/	/7.6			0/0/0	--Other
													-Reciprocating piston engines of a kind used for the propulsion of vehicles of Chapter 87:
0/0/0	2	6	0/0	0/0/0	0/0	0//0	0/0/	9.5/9.5/10	9.5/9.5			0/0/0	--Of a cylinder capacity not exceeding 50cc
0/0/0	2	6	0/0	0/0/0	0/0	0//0	0/0/	0/9.5/10	0/9.5			0/0/0	--Of a cylinder capacity exceeding 50cc but not exceeding 250cc
0/0/0	5.6	6	0/0	0/0/0	0/0	0/0/0	0/0/	9.5/9.5/10	9.5/9.5			0/0/0	--Of a cylinder capacity exceeding 250cc but not exceeding 1000cc
													--Of a cylinder capacity exceeding 1000cc:
5/0/0	7	6	0/0	0//5	0/0	0//0	0/0/	9.8/9.8/10	/9.8			0//	---Of a cylinder capacity exceeding 1000cc but not exceeding 3000cc
													---Of a cylinder capacity exceeding 3000cc
5/0/0	7	6	0/0	0//0	0/0	0//0	0/0/					0/0/	Natural gas engines with displacement≥5.9L (spark-ignition reciprocating piston engines for the vehicles listed in Chapter 87)
5/0/0	7	6	0/0	0//0	0/0	0//0	0/0/					0/0/	Other vehicle use reciprocating piston engines with displacement>3000cc (spark-ignition reciprocating piston engines for the vehicles listed in Chapter 87)
													-Other engines:
0/0/0	4.2	2.4	1.2/1.2	0/0/0	0/0	0/0/0	0/0/	0/0/10.8	10.9/0			0/0/0	---Friedamp engines
													---Other
0/0/0		8.4	1.8/1.8	0/0/0	0/0	0/0/0	0/0/	16.8/17.1/16.8	16.9/17.1			0/0/0	Speed < 3600r/min gasoline engine (generator)
0/0/0		8.4	1.8/1.8	0/0/0	0/0	0/0/0	0/0/	16.8/17.1/16.8	16.9/17.1			0/0/0	Speed < 4650r/min gasoline engine (heading 84.26, 84.28-84.30 listed machinery)
0/0/0		8.4	1.8/1.8	0/0/0	0/0	0/0/0	0/0/	16.8/17.1/16.8	16.9/17.1			0/0/0	Gasoline engine forklift (800 rpm is less than or equal to the speed below 3400r/min) (except for vertical output shaft of the gasoline engine)
0/0/0		8.4	1.8/1.8	0/0/0	0/0	0/0/0	0/0/	16.8/17.1/16.8	16.9/17.1			0/0/0	Other speed <4650 r/min gasoline engine (heading 84.27 column machinery, vertical output shaft of the gasoline engine except)
0/0/0		8.4	1.8/1.8	0/0/0	0/0	0/0/0	0/0/	16.8/17.1/16.8	16.9/17.1			0/0/0	Vertical output shaft of the gasoline engine (the eighty-seventh chapter car trainnon other reciprocating piston engines)
0/0/0		8.4	1.8/1.8	0/0/0	0/0	0/0/0	0/0/	16.8/17.1/16.8	16.9/17.1			0/0/0	Other reciprocating or rotary internal combustion piston engines (spark-ignition reciprocating or rotary piston engines for the vehicles not listed in Chapter 87)

税则号列	货品名称〔CIQ扩展编码及品名－T2表示见附表2〕	最惠(%)	暂定税率	普通	增值/消费	出口退税	计量单位	监管条件/特殊证件	检验检疫	对美关税	亚太上/下
84.08	压燃式活塞内燃发动机(柴油或半柴油发动机):										
8408.1000	-船舶发动机〔999〕	5		11	13/	13	台/千克	/		30	2.5/2.5
	-用于第八十七章所列车辆的发动机:										
8408.2010	---输出功率在132.39千瓦(180马力)及以上										
8408.2010 01	输出功率在441千瓦及以上的柴油发动机(600马力)〔101其他车辆零部件,102柴油发动机〕	9	4	14	13/	13	台/千克	6/			6.3/6.3
8408.2010 10	功率≥132.39kW拖拉机用柴油机〔101其他车辆零部件,102柴油发动机〕	9		14	9/	13	台/千克	6/			6.3/6.3
8408.2010 90	功率≥132.39kW其他用柴油机[指87章车辆用压燃式活塞内燃发动机(132.39kW=180马力)]〔101其他车辆零部件,102柴油发动机〕	9		14	13/	13	台/千克	6/			6.3/6.3
8408.2090	---其他										
8408.2090 10	功率<132.39千瓦拖拉机用柴油机〔101其他车辆零部件,102柴油发动机〕	25		35	9/	9,13	台/千克	6/			17.5/17.5
8408.2090 20	升功率≥50kw的输出功率<132.39kw的轿车用柴油发动机〔101其他车辆零部件,102柴油发动机〕	25	20	35	13/	13	台/千克	6/			17.5/17.5
8408.2090 90	功率<132.39千瓦其他用柴油机(指第87章车辆用压燃式活塞内燃发动机)〔101其他车辆零部件,102柴油发动机〕	25		35	13/	13	台/千克	6/			17.5/17.5
	-其他发动机:										
8408.9010	---机车发动机〔101其他车辆零部件,102柴油发动机〕	6		11	13/	13	台/千克	/		11	3.9/3.9
	---其他:										
8408.9091	----输出功率不超过14千瓦										
8408.9091 11	功率≤14千瓦农业用单缸柴油机[非87章车辆用压燃式活塞内燃发动机(14kW=19.05马力)]〔999〕	5		35	9/	9	台/千克	/		10	3.3/3.3
8408.9091 19	功率≤14千瓦农业用柴油发动机[非87章车辆用压燃式活塞内燃发动机(14千瓦=19.05马力)]〔999〕	5		35	9/	9	台/千克	/		10	3.3/3.3
8408.9091 91	功率≤14千瓦其他用单缸柴油机[非87章车辆用压燃式活塞内燃发动机(14千瓦=19.05马力)]〔999〕	5		35	13/	9	台/千克	/		10	3.3/3.3
8408.9091 99	功率≤14千瓦其他用柴油发动机[非87章车辆用压燃式活塞内燃发动机(14千瓦=19.05马力)]〔999〕	5		35	13/	9	台/千克	/		10	3.3/3.3
8408.9092	----输出功率超过14千瓦,但小于132.39千瓦(180马力)										
8408.9092 10	转速<4650r/min柴油发动机,14<功率<132.39kw(品目8426－8430所列工程机械用)〔999〕	8		35	13/	13	台/千克	/		33	7.2/7.2
8408.9092 20	14千瓦<功率<132.39千瓦的农业用柴油机[非87章车辆用压燃式活塞内燃发动机(1千瓦=1.36马力)]〔999〕	8		35	9/	9,13	台/千克	/		33	7.2/7.2
8408.9092 90	14千瓦<功率<132.39千瓦的其他用柴油机[非87章车辆用压燃式活塞内燃发动机(1千瓦=1.36马力)]〔999〕	8		35	13/	13	台/千克	/		33	7.2/7.2
8408.9093	----输出功率在132.39千瓦(180马力)及以上										
8408.9093 10	功率≥132.39千瓦的农业用柴油机[非87章用压燃式活塞内燃发动机(132.39千瓦=180马力)]〔999〕	5		14	9/	13	台/千克	/		10	3.3/3.3
8408.9093 90	功率≥132.39千瓦其他用柴油发动机[非87章用压燃式活塞内燃发动机(132.39千瓦=180马力)]〔999〕	5		14	13/	13	台/千克	/		10	3.3/3.3
84.09	**专用于或主要用于税目84.07或84.08所列发动机的零件:**										
8409.1000	-航空器发动机用〔999〕	2		11	13/	13	千克	/			
	-其他:										
	--专用于或主要用于点燃式活塞内燃发动机的:										
8409.9110	---船舶发动机用〔999〕	6		17	13/	13	千克	/		16	3.9/3.9
	---其他:										
8409.9191	----电控燃油喷射装置〔101其他车辆零部件,102其它动力设备及其零部件〕	5		35	13/	13	千克/套	/			3.3/3.3
8409.9199	----其他										
8409.9199 10	汽车用电子节气门〔301其他车辆零部件,302其它动力设备及其零部件〕	5	3	35	13/	13	千克	/			3.3/3.3
8409.9199 20	废气再循环(EGR)装置(专用或主要用于内燃发动机)〔101其他车辆零部件,102其它动力设备及其零部件〕	5		35	13/	13	千克	/			3.3/3.3
8409.9199 30	连杆(专用或主要用于内燃发动机)〔101其他车辆零部件,102其它动力设备及其零部件〕	5		35	13/	13	千克	/			3.3/3.3

协定税率 %								RCEP		特惠税率 %			Article Description
东/冰/格	巴基斯坦	韩国	瑞士上/下	哥/秘/柬	澳/毛	新西/坡/智	中国港/澳/台	东盟及马来/澳/韩	日/新	亚太2国	老/柬/缅	98/97/95	
													Compression-ignition internal combustion piston engines (diesel or semi-diesel engines):
0/0/0	0	2.5	0/0	0/0/0	0/0	0/0/0	0/0/	4.8/4.8/	/4.8			0/0/0	-Marine propulsion engines
													-Engines of a kind used for the propulsion of vehicles of Chapter 87:
													---Of an output of 132.39kW (180HP) or more
5/0/0	6.3	4.2	0/0	0/0/0	0/0	0//0	0/0/	8.6/8.6/9	8.6/8.8			0/0/0	Diesel genines, output power≥441kW(600HP)
5/0/0	6.3	4.2	0/0	0/0/0	0/0	0//0	0/0/	8.6/8.6/9	8.6/8.8			0/0/0	Diesel engines for tractors, output power≥132.39kW
5/0/0	6.3	4.2	0/0	0/0/0	0/0	0//0	0/0/	8.6/8.6/9	8.6/8.8			0/0/0	Other diesel engines, output power≥132.39kW (refers to compression-ignition internal combustion piston engines for the vehicles listed in Chaper 87)
													---Other
5/0/0	17.5	15		0//0	0/15	0//0	0/0/					0/0/	Diesel engines for tractors, output power<132.39kW
5/0/0	17.5	15		0//0	0/15	0//0	0/0/					0/0/	L power more than 50 kilowatts, diesel engine power output of132.39 kilowatts of car "
5/0/0	17.5	15		0//0	0/15	0//0	0/0/					0/0/	Other diesel engines, output power<132.39kw (refers to compression-ignition internal combustion piston engines for the vehicles listed in Chapter 87)
													-Other engines:
0/0/0	0	0	0/0	0/0/0	0/0	0//0	0/0/	0/0/0	0/0			0/0/0	---Locomotive engines
													---Other:
													----Of an output not exceeding 14kW
0/0/0	0	2.3	0/0	0/0/0	0/0	0//0	0/0/	4.8/4.8/5	/4.8			0/0/0	Single-cylinder diesel engines for agricultural use, output power≤14kW (19.05HP) (other than compression-ignition internal combustion piston engines for the vehicles of chapter 87)
0/0/0	0	2.3	0/0	0/0/0	0/0	0//0	0/0/	4.8/4.8/5	/4.8			0/0/0	Diesel engines for agricultural use, output power≤14kW (19.05HP) (other than compression-ignition internal combustion piston engines for the vehicles of chapter 87)
0/0/0	0	2.3	0/0	0/0/0	0/0	0//0	0/0/	4.8/4.8/5	/4.8			0/0/0	Single-cyclinder diesel engines for other use, output power≤14kW (19.05HP), (other than compression-ignition internal combustion piston engines for the vehicles of chapter 87)
0/0/0	0	2.3	0/0	0/0/0	0/0	0//0	0/0/	4.8/4.8/5	/4.8			0/0/0	Other diesel engines, output power≤14kW (19.05HP) (other than compression-ignition internal combustion piston engines for the vehicles of chapter 87)
													----Of an output exceeding 14kW but not exceeding 132.39kW(180HP)
0/0/0	2	3.9	0/0	0/0/0	0/0	0//0	0/0/	7.8/8/7.8	7.9/8			0/0/0	Diesel engines, rotational speed<4650 r/min, 14kW<output power<132.39 kW(for engineering machinery listed in heading No. 8426 to 8430)
0/0/0	2	3.9	0/0	0/0/0	0/0	0//0	0/0/	7.8/8/7.8	7.9/8			0/0/0	Diesel engines for agricutural use, 14kW<output powder<132.39kW (compression-ignition internal combustion piston engines for the vehicles not listed in Chapter87) (1kW=1.36HP)
0/0/0	2	3.9	0/0	0/0/0	0/0	0//0	0/0/	7.8/8/7.8	7.9/8			0/0/0	Diesel engine for other use, 14kW<output powder<132.39kW (compression-ignition internal combustion piston engines for the vehicles not listed in Chapter87) (1kW=1.36HP)
													----Of an output of 132.39KW (180HP) or more
0/0/0	0	2.3	0/0	0/0/0	0/0	0//0	0/0/	4.5/4.5/4.5	4.7/4.5			0/0/0	Diesel engines for agricutural use, output powder≥132.39kW (180HP) (compression-ignition internal combustion piston engines for the vehicles not listed in Chapter 87)
0/0/0	0	2.3	0/0	0/0/0	0/0	0//0	0/0/	4.5/4.5/4.5	4.7/4.5			0/0/0	Diesel engine for other use, output powder≥132.39kW (180HP) (compression-ignition internal combustion piston engines for the vehicles not listed in Chapter 87)
													Parts suitable for use solely or principally with the engines of headingNo.84.07 or 84.08:
0/0/0	0	0	0/0	0/0/0	0/0	0//0	0/0/	0/0/0	0/0			0/0/0	-For aircraft engines
													-Other:
													--Suitable for use solely or principally with spark-ignition internal combustion piston engines:
0/0/0	0	3.9	0/0	0/0/0	0/0	0//0	0/0/	5.7/5.7/	/5.7			0/0/0	---For marine propulsion engines
													---Other:
0/0/0	0	2.3	0/0	0/0/0	0/0	0/0/0	0/0/	4.5/4.5/4.5	4.7/4.5			0/0/0	----Electric fuel injection devices
													----Other
0/0/0	0	1	0.5/0.5	0/0/0	0/0	0/0/0	0/0/	0/0/4.5	4.7/0			0/0/0	Electronic throttle for automobile
0/0/0	0	1	0.5/0.5	0/0/0	0/0	0/0/0	0/0/	0/0/4.5	4.7/0			0/0/0	Exhaust gas recycling apparatuses (EGR) (suitable for use solely or principally with combustion piston engines)
0/0/0	0	1	0.5/0.5	0/0/0	0/0	0/0/0	0/0/	0/0/4.5	4.7/0			0/0/0	Links (connecting rods) (suitable for use solely or principally with combustion piston engines)

税则号列	货品名称〔CIQ 扩展编码及品名－T2 表示见附表 2〕	最惠(%)	暂定税率	普通	增值/消费	出口退税	计量单位	监管条件/特殊证件	检验检疫	对美关税	亚太上/下
8409.9199 40	喷嘴(专用或主要用于内燃发动机)〔101 其他车辆零部件,102 其它动力设备及其零部件〕	5		35	13/	13	千克	/			3.3/3.3
8409.9199 50	气门摇臂(专用或主要用于内燃发动机)〔101 其他车辆零部件,102 其它动力设备及其零部件〕	5		35	13/	13	千克	/			3.3/3.3
8409.9199 90	其他点燃式活塞内燃发动机用零件〔101 其他车辆零部件,102 其它动力设备及其零部件〕	5		35	13/	13	千克	/			3.3/3.3
	--其他:										
8409.9910	---船舶发动机用〔999〕	5		11	13/	13	千克	/		30	3.3/3.3
8409.9920	---机车发动机用〔101 其他车辆零部件,102 其它动力设备及其零部件〕	2		11	13/	13	千克	/		7	1.3/1.3
	---其他:										
8409.9991	----输出功率在 132.39 千瓦(180 马力)及以上的发动机用〔101 其他车辆零部件,102 其它动力设备及其零部件〕	2		11	13/	13	千克	/			1.3/1.3
8409.9999	----其他										
8409.9999 10	电控柴油喷射装置及其零件(指品目 8408 所列的其他发动机用)〔101 其他车辆零部件,102 其它动力设备及其零部件〕	8	5	35	13/	13	千克	/			5.2/5.2
8409.9999 90	其他发动机的专用零件(指税目 84.07 或 84.08 所列的其他发动机)〔101 其他车辆零部件,102 其它动力设备及其零部件〕	8		35	13/	13	千克	/			5.2/5.2
84.10	**水轮机、水轮及其调节器:**										
	-水轮机及水轮:										
8410.1100	--功率不超过 1000 千瓦〔999〕	8		35	13/	13	台/千克	/		33	
8410.1200	--功率超过 1000 千瓦,但不超过 10000 千瓦〔999〕	8		35	13/	13	台/千克	/			
	--功率超过 10000 千瓦:										
8410.1310	---功率超过 30000 千瓦的冲击式水轮机及水轮〔999〕	8		35	13/	13	台/千克	/			5.6/5.6
8410.1320	---功率超过 35000 千瓦的贯流式水轮机及水轮〔999〕	8		35	13/	13	台/千克	/			5.6/5.6
8410.1330	---功率超过 200000 千瓦的水泵水轮机及水轮〔999〕	8		35	13/	13	台/千克	/			5.6/5.6
8410.1390	---其他〔999〕	8		35	13/	13	台/千克	/			5.6/5.6
	-零件,包括调节器:										
8410.9010	---调节器〔999〕	6		35	13/	13	千克/套	/			4.2/4.2
8410.9090	---其他〔999〕	6		35	13/	13	千克	/			
84.11	**涡轮喷气发动机、涡轮螺桨发动机及其他燃气轮机:**										
	-涡轮喷气发动机:										
	--推力不超过 25 千牛顿:										
8411.1110	---涡轮风扇发动机〔999〕	1		11	13/	13	台/千克	3/			
8411.1190	---其他〔999〕	1		11	13/	13	台/千克	/			
	--推力超过 25 千牛顿:										
8411.1210	---涡轮风扇发动机〔999〕	1		11	13/	13	台/千克	3/			0/0
8411.1290	---其他										
8411.1290 10	小型燃烧率高轻型涡轮喷气发动机(推力大于或等于 90 千牛顿的涡轮喷气发动机)〔999〕	1		11	13/	13	台/千克	3/			0.5/0.5
8411.1290 90	其他涡轮喷气发动机(推力超过 25kN)〔999〕	1		11	13/	13	台/千克	/			0.5/0.5
	-涡轮螺桨发动机:										
8411.2100	--功率不超过 1100 千瓦〔999〕	2		11	13/	13	台/千克	/			
	--功率超过 1100 千瓦:										
8411.2210	---功率超过 1100 千瓦,但不超过 2238 千瓦〔999〕	2		11	13/	13	台/千克	/			1.4/1.4
8411.2220	---功率超过 2238 千瓦,但不超过 3730 千瓦〔999〕	2		11	13/	13	台/千克	/			1.4/1.4
8411.2230	---功率超过 3730 千瓦〔999〕	2		11	13/	13	台/千克	/			1.4/1.4
	-其他燃气轮机:										
8411.8100	--功率不超过 5000 千瓦										
8411.8100 01	涡轮轴航空发动机(功率≤5000kW)〔999〕	15	1	35	13/	13	台/千克	/			
8411.8100 10	功率≥3500kw 的涡轮轴发动机(航空发动机除外)〔999〕	15	3	35	13/	13	台/千克	/			
8411.8100 90	功率≤5000kW 的其他燃气轮机〔999〕	15		35	13/	13	台/千克	/			
8411.8200	--功率超过 5000 千瓦〔999〕	3		35	13/	13	台/千克	/			2.1/2.1
	-零件:										
8411.9100	--涡轮喷气发动机或涡轮螺桨发动机用〔999〕	1		11	13/	13	千克	/			
	--其他:										
8411.9910	---涡轮轴发动机用										
8411.9910 10	涡轮轴航空发动机用零件〔999〕	5	1	35	13/	13	千克	/			3.5/3.5
8411.9910 90	其他涡轮轴发动机用零件〔999〕	5		35	13/	13	千克	/			3.5/3.5
8411.9990	---其他〔999〕	5		35	13/	13	千克	/			
84.12	**其他发动机及动力装置:**										
	-喷气发动机,但涡轮喷气发动机除外:										
8412.1010	---航空器及航天器用										
8412.1010 10	冲压喷气发动机(包括超燃冲压喷气发动机)〔999〕	3		11	13/	13	台/千克	3/			
8412.1010 20	脉冲喷气发动机〔999〕	3		11	13/	13	台/千克	3/			
8412.1010 30	组合循环发动机〔999〕	3		11	13/	13	台/千克	3/			
8412.1010 90	其他航空、航天器用喷气发动机(涡轮喷气发动机除外)〔999〕	3		11	13/	13	台/千克	/			
8412.1090	---其他〔999〕	10		35	13/	13	台/千克	/		15	
	-液压动力装置:										
8412.2100	--直线作用(液压缸)的										
8412.2100 10	飞机发动机用作动筒〔999〕	12	1	35	13/	13	台/千克	/			

协定税率 %								RCEP		特惠税率 %			Article Description
东/冰/格	巴基斯坦	韩国	瑞士上/下	哥/秘/柬	澳/毛	新西/坡/智	中国港/澳/台	东盟及马来/澳/韩	日/新	亚太2国	老/柬/缅	98/97/95	
0/0/0	0	1	0.5/0.5	0/0/0	0/0	0/0/0	0/0/	0/0/4.5	4.7/0			0/0/0	Nozzles(suitable for use solely or principally with combustion piston engines)
0/0/0	0	1	0.5/0.5	0/0/0	0/0	0/0/0	0/0/	0/0/4.5	4.7/0			0/0/0	Valve rockers arms(suitable for use solely or principally with combustion piston engines)
0/0/0	0	1	0.5/0.5	0/0/0	0/0	0/0/0	0/0/	0/0/4.5	4.7/0			0/0/0	Other parts of spark-ignition internal combustion piston engines
													--Other:
0/0/0	0	2.3	0.5/0.5	0/0/0	0/0	0/0/0	0/0/	4.5/4.5/4.5	4.7/4.5			0/0/0	---For marine propulsion engines
0/0/0	0	0	0/0	0/0/0	0/0	0//0	0/0/	0/0/0	1.8/0			0/0/0	---For locomotive engines
													---Other:
0/0/0	0	0.4	0/0	0/0/0	0/1.2	0//0	0/0/	0/0/1.8	1.8/0			0/0/0	----For engines with an output of 132.39kW (180HP) or more
													----Other
0/0/0	4	3.9	0/0	0/0/0	0/0	0/0/0	0/0/	7.8/8/7.8	7.9/8			0/0/0	Electronically controlled diesel fuel injection device and its parts(refer to other items listed in the 8408 engine use)
0/0/0	4	3.9	0/0	0/0/0	0/0	0/0/0	0/0/	7.8/8/7.8	7.9/8			0/0/0	Special parts for other engines(other engines listed in Heding No.84.07 or 84.08)
													Hydraulic turbines, water wheels, and regulators therefor:
													-Hydraulic turbines and water wheels:
0/0/0	2	2	0/0	0/0/0	0/0	0//0	0/0/	0/0/9	9.1/0			0/0/0	--Of a power not exceeding 1000kW
0/0/0	2	2	0/0	0/0/0	0/0	0/0/0	0/0/	0/0/9	9.1/0			0/0/0	--Of a power exceeding 1000KW but not exceeding 10000kW
													--Of a power exceeding 10000kW:
0/0/0	2	2	0/0	0/0/0	0/0	0/0/0	0/0/	0/0/9	9.1/0			0/0/0	---Impulse hydraulic turbines and water wheels of a power exceeding 30000 kW
0/0/0	2	2	0/0	0/0/0	0/0	0/0/0	0/0/	0/0/9	9.1/0			0/0/0	---Radial hydraulic turbines and water wheels of a power exceeding 35000 kW
0/0/0	2	2	0/0	0/0/0	0/0	0//0	0/0/	0/0/9	9.1/0			0/0/0	---Pumping hydraulic turbines and water wheels of a power exceeding 200000kW
0/0/0	2	2	0/0	0/0/0	0/0	0//0	0/0/	0/0/9	9.1/0			0/0/0	---Other
													-Parts, including regulators:
0/0/0	0	0	0/0	0/0/0	0/0	0//0	0/0/	0/0/0	0/0			0/0/0	---Regulators
0/0/0	0	1.2	0/0	0/0/0	0/0	0//0	0/0/	0/0/5.4	5.5/0			0/0/0	---Other
													Turbo-jets, turbo-propellers and other gas turbines:
													-Turbo-jets:
													--Of a thrust not exceeding 25kN:
0/0/0	0	0	0/0	0/0/0	0/0	0//0	0/0/	0/0/0	0/0			0/0/0	---Turbofan engines
0/0/0	0	0	0/0	0/0/0	0/0	0//0	0/0/	0/0/0	0/0			0/0/0	---Other
													--Of a thrust exceeding 25kN:
0/0/0	0	0	0/0	0/0/0	0/0	0//0	0/0/	0/0/0	0/0			0/0/0	---Turbofan engines
													---Other
0/0/0	0	0	0/0	0/0/0	0/0	0//0	0/0/	0/0/0	0/0			0/0/0	Minitype turbo-jets with high combustion rate(turo-jets with propulsive force≥90kN)
0/0/0	0	0	0/0	0/0/0	0/0	0//0	0/0/	0/0/0	0/0			0/0/0	Other turbo-jets(propulsive force>25kN)
													-Turbo-propellers:
0/0/0	0	0	0/0	0/0/0	0/0	0//0	0/0/	0/0/0	0/0			0/0/0	--Of a power not exceeding 1100kW
													--Of a power exceeding 1100kW:
0/0/0	0	0	0/0	0/0/0	0/0	0//0	0/0/	0/0/0	0/0			0/0/0	---Of a power exceeding 1100kW but not cxcccding 2238kW
0/0/0	0	0	0/0	0/0/0	0/0	0//0	0/0/	0/0/0	0/0			0/0/0	---Of a power exceeding 2238kW but not exceeding 3730kW
0/0/0	0	0	0/0	0/0/0	0/0	0//0	0/0/	0/0/0	0/0			0/0/0	---Of a power exceeding 3730kW
													-Other gas turbines:
													--Of a power not exceeding 5000kW
0/0/0	8.4	3	1.5/1.5	0/0/0	0/0	0/0/0	0/0/	0/0/13.5	13.6/0			0/0/0	Turbine shaft aeroengine(power≤5000kW)
0/0/0	8.4	3	1.5/1.5	0/0/0	0/0	0/0/0	0/0/	0/0/13.5	13.6/0		//	0/0/0	Turboshaft engines with power ≥ 3500kW (except aero-engines)
0/0/0	8.4	3	1.5/1.5	0/0/0	0/0	0/0/0	0/0/	0/0/13.5	13.6/0			0/0/0	Other gas turbines, Power≤5000kW
0/0/0	0	0	0/0	0/0/0	0/0	0//0	0/0/	0/0/0	0/0			0/0/0	--Of a power exceeding 5000kW
													-Parts:
0/0/0	0	0	0/0	0/0/0	0/0	0//0	0/0/	0/0/0	0/0			0/0/0	--Of turbo-jets or turbo-propellers
													--Other:
													---Of turbine shaft engines
0/0/0	0	0	0/0	0/0/0	0/0	0//0	0/0/	0/0/0	0/0			0/0/0	The turbine shaft Aeroengine Parts
0/0/0	0	0	0/0	0/0/0	0/0	0//0	0/0/	0/0/0	0/0			0/0/0	Other part of turbine shaft engines
0/0/0	0	1	0/0	0/0/0	0/0	0//0	0/0/	0/0/4.5	4.7/0			0/0/0	---Other
													Other engines and motors:
													-Jet engines other than turbo-jets:
													---For aircraft or spacecraft
0/0/0	0	0	0/0	0/0/0	0/0	0//0	0/0/	0/0/0	0/0			0/0/0	Ramjet engines(including scramjet engines)
0/0/0	0	0	0/0	0/0/0	0/0	0//0	0/0/	0/0/0	0/0			0/0/0	Pulse jet engines
0/0/0	0	0	0/0	0/0/0	0/0	0//0	0/0/	0/0/0	0/0			0/0/0	Combined cycle engines
0/0/0	0	0	0/0	0/0/0	0/0	0//0	0/0/	0/0/0	0/0			0/0/0	Other jet engines (other than turbo-jets) for aircraft or spacecraft
0/0/0	2	2	0/0	0/0/0	0/0	0//0	0/0/	0/0/9	9.1/0			0/0/0	---Other
													-Hydraulic power engines and motors:
													--Linear acting (cylinders)
0/0/0	4.2	7.2	1.2/1.2	0/0/0	0/0	0/0/0	0/0/0	11.4/11.4/11.4	11.4/11.4		//	0/0/0	Aircraft engines are used as moving cylinders

税则号列		货品名称〔CIQ 扩展编码及品名－T2 表示见附表 2〕	最惠(%)	暂定税率	普通	增值/消费	出口退税	计量单位	监管条件/特殊证件	检验检疫	对美关税	亚太上/下
8412.2100	90	其他直线作用的液压动力装置(液压缸)〔999〕	12		35	13/	13	台/千克	/			
		--其他：										
8412.2910		---液压马达〔999〕	10		35	13/	13	台/千克	/			
8412.2990		---其他										
8412.2990	10	抓桩器(抱桩器)〔999〕	14	7	35	13/	13	台/千克	/		17	
8412.2990	20	飞机发动机用液压作动器〔999〕	14	1	35	13/	13	台/千克	/		11	
8412.2990	90	其他液压动力装置〔999〕	14		35	13/	13	台/千克	/		24	
		-气压动力装置：										
8412.3100		--直线作用(气压缸)的										
8412.3100	01	三坐标测量机用平衡气缸〔999〕	14	7	35	13/	13	台/千克	/			9.1/9.1
8412.3100	10	飞机舱门气动作动筒〔999〕	14	1	35	13/	13	台/千克	/			9.1/9.1
8412.3100	90	其他直线作用的气压动力装置(气压缸)〔999〕	14		35	13/	13	台/千克	/			9.1/9.1
8412.3900		--其他										
8412.3900	10	飞机发动机用气压作动器〔999〕	14	1	35	13/	13	台/千克	/		11	
8412.3900	90	其他气压动力装置〔999〕	14		35	13/	13	台/千克	/		24	
8412.8000		-其他										
8412.8000	10	液体火箭发动机(推力大于或等于 90 千牛顿可贮存推进剂的)〔999〕	10		35	13/	13	台/千克	3/		20	
8412.8000	20	固体火箭发动机(总冲大于或等于 1100 千牛顿每秒的)〔999〕	10		35	13/	13	台/千克	3/		20	
8412.8000	90	其他发动机及动力装置〔999〕	10		35	13/	13	台/千克	/		20	
		-零件：										
8412.9010		---税目 8412.1010 所列机器的零件										
8412.9010	10	燃烧调节装置(冲压或脉冲喷气发动机的)〔999〕	2		11	13/	13	千克	3/			
8412.9010	20	火箭发动机的壳体〔999〕	2		11	13/	13	千克	3/			
8412.9010	90	航空、航天器用喷气发动机的零件(涡轮喷气发动机的零件，编号 8412901010 除外)〔999〕	2		11	13/	13	千克	/			
8412.9090		---其他										
8412.9090	10	风力发动机零件〔999〕	8	5	35	13/	13	千克	/			
8412.9090	20	飞机发动机用作动筒壳体〔999〕	8	1	35	13/	13	千克	/			
8412.9090	90	其他发动机及动力装置的零件〔999〕	8		35	13/	13	千克	/			
84.13		**液体泵，不论是否装有计量装置；液体提升机：**										
		-装有或可装计量装置的泵：										
8413.1100		--分装燃料或润滑油的泵，用于加油站或车库〔999〕	10	6	30	13/	13	台/千克	/		26	
8413.1900		--其他〔999〕	10	6	30	13/	13	台/千克	/		16	
8413.2000		-手泵，但子目 8413.11 或 8413.19 的货品除外〔999〕	10		30	13/	13	台/千克	/		30	
		-活塞式内燃发动机用的燃油泵、润滑油泵或冷却剂泵：										
		---燃油泵：										
8413.3021		----输出功率在 132.39 千瓦(180 马力)及以上的发动机用燃油泵〔101 其他车辆零部件，102 燃油泵〕	3		30	13/	13	台/千克	/		23	2/2
8413.3029		----其他〔101 其他车辆零部件，102 燃油泵〕	3		30	13/	13	台/千克	/		23	
8413.3030		---润滑油泵〔101 其他车辆零部件，102 燃油泵〕	3		30	13/	13	台/千克	/		23	
8413.3090		---其他〔101 其他车辆零部件，102 燃油泵〕	3		30	13/	13	台/千克	/		23	2/2
8413.4000		-混凝土泵〔999〕	8		30	13/	13	台/千克	/		33	
		-其他往复式排液泵：										
8413.5010		---气动式										
8413.5010	10	农业用气动往复式排液泵〔999〕	10		40	9/	9	台/千克	/		15	
8413.5010	20	气动式耐腐蚀波纹或隔膜泵(流量大于 $0.6m^3/h$，接触表面由特殊耐腐蚀材料制成)〔999〕	10		40	13/	13	台/千克	3/			
8413.5010	90	其他非农业用气动往复式排液泵〔999〕	10		40	13/	13	台/千克	/		15	
8413.5020		---电动式										
8413.5020	10	农业用电动往复式排液泵〔999〕	10		40	9/	9	台/千克	/		30	
8413.5020	20	电动式耐腐蚀波纹或隔膜泵(流量大于 $0.6m^3/h$，接触表面由特殊耐腐蚀材料制成)〔999〕	10		40	13/	13	台/千克	3/			
8413.5020	30	电动往复式排液多重密封泵(两用物项管制)〔999〕	10		40	13/	13	台/千克	3/		30	
8413.5020	90	其他非农业用电动往复式排液泵〔999〕	10		40	13/	13	台/千克	/		30	
		---液压式：										
8413.5031		----柱塞泵										
8413.5031	01	农业用柱塞泵〔999〕	10	6	40	9/	9	台/千克	/		16	
8413.5031	10	飞机用液压柱塞泵〔999〕	10	1	40	13/	13	台/千克	/		11	
8413.5031	90	其他非农业用柱塞泵〔999〕	10	6	40	13/	13	台/千克	/			
8413.5039		----其他										

协定税率 %								RCEP		特惠税率 %			Article Description
东/冰/格	巴基斯坦	韩国	瑞士 上/下	哥/秘/柬	澳/毛	新西/坡/智	中国港/澳/台	东盟及马来/澳/韩	日/新	亚太2国	老/柬/缅	98/97/95	
0/0/0	4.2	7.2	1.2/1.2	0/0/0	0/0	0/0/0	0/0/0	11.4/11.4/11.4	11.4/11.4		//	0/0/0	Other linear acting hydraulic power unit (hydraulic cylinder)
													--Other:
0/0/0	3.5	6	1/1	0/0/0	0/0	0/0/0	0/0/	9.5/9.5/9.5	9.5/9.5			0/0/0	---Hydraulic motors
													---Other
0/0/0	7.8	6.5	1.4/1.4	0/0/0	0/0	0/0/0	0/0/	13.1/13.3/13.1	13.1/13.3			0/0/0	Pile gripper
0/0/0	7.8	6.5	1.4/1.4	0/0/0	0/0	0/0/0	0/0/	13.1/13.3/13.1	13.1/13.3			0/0/0	Hydraulic actuator for aircraft,with pressure above 20MPa
0/0/0	7.8	6.5	1.4/1.4	0/0/0	0/0	0/0/0	0/0/	13.1/13.3/13.1	13.1/13.3			0/0/0	Other hydrulic power engines and motors
													-Pneumatic power engines and motors:
													--Linear acting (cylinders)
0/0/0	4.9	0	0/0	0/0/0	0/0	0/0/0	0/0/0	0/0/0	12.7/0			0/0/0	Balance cylinder for three-dimensional measuring machine
0/0/0	4.9	0	0/0	0/0/0	0/0	0/0/0	0/0/0	0/0/0	12.7/0		//	0/0/0	Aircraft door pneumatic actuator
0/0/0	4.9	0	0/0	0/0/0	0/0	0/0/0	0/0/0	0/0/0	12.7/0			0/0/0	Other pneumatic power engines and motors of straightening (cylinders)
													--Other
0/0/0	7.8	2.8	0/0	0/0/0	0/0	0/0/0	0/0/	0/0/12.6	12.7/0		//	0/0/0	Pneumatic actuators for aircraft engines
0/0/0	7.8	2.8	0/0	0/0/0	0/0	0/0/0	0/0/	0/0/12.6	12.7/0		//	0/0/0	Other pneumatic power plants
													-Other
0/0/0	2	2	0/0	0/0/0	0/0	0//0	0/0/	0/0/9	9.1/0			0/0/0	Liquid-propellant rocket engines (thrust≥90kN, capable of storing propellant)
0/0/0	2	2	0/0	0/0/0	0/0	0//0	0/0/	0/0/9	9.1/0			0/0/0	Solid-propellant rocket engine (of a total impulse≥1100kN)
0/0/0	2	2	0/0	0/0/0	0/0	0//0	0/0/	0/0/9	9.1/0			0/0/0	Other engines and motors
													-Parts:
													---For machines of subheading No.8412. 1010
0/0/0	0	0	0/0	0/0/0	0/0	0//0	0/0/	0/0/0	0/0			0/0/0	Combustion control devices (for ramjet engine or pulse jet engines)
0/0/0	0	0	0/0	0/0/0	0/0	0//0	0/0/	0/0/0	0/0			0/0/0	Shells of rocket engines
0/0/0	0	0	0/0	0/0/0	0/0	0//0	0/0/	0/0/0	0/0			0/0/0	Parts of jet engines for aircraft or spacecraft, (other than parts of turbo-jets engines and parts of subheading No. 8412. 9010 10)
													---Other
0/0/0	2	3.7	0/0	0/0/0	0/0	0//0	0/0/	7.2/7.2/7.2	7.5/7.2			0/0/0	Wind power engine parts
0/0/0	2	3.7	0/0	0/0/0	0/0	0//0	0/0/	7.2/7.2/7.2	7.5/7.2		//	0/0/0	The aircraft engine is used as the rotor shell
0/0/0	2	3.7	0/0	0/0/0	0/0	0//0	0/0/	7.2/7.2/7.2	7.5/7.2			0/0/0	Other parts for engines and motors
													Pumps for liquids, whether or not fitted with a measuring device; liquid elevators:
													-Pumps fitted or designed to be fitted with a measuring device:
0/0/0	2	2	0/0	0/0/0	0/0	0/0/0	0/0/	0/0/9	9.1/0			0/0/0	--Pumps for dispensing fuel or lubricants, of the type used in filling-stations or in garages
0/0/0	3.5	6	1/1	0/0/0	0/0	0/0/0	0/0/	9.5/9.5/10	9.5/9.5			0/0/0	--Other
0/0/0	4	2	0/0	0/0/0	0/0	0/0/0	0/0/	0/0/9	9.1/0			0/0/0	-Hand pumps, other than those of subheadingNo.8413. 11 or 8413. 19
													-Fuel, lubricating or cooling medium pumps for internal combustion piston engines:
													---Fuel pumps:
0/0/0	0	0	0/0	0/0/0	0/0	0//0	0/0/	0/2.7/0	0/2.7			0/0/0	----Fuel pumps for engines of an output of 132. 39kW (180HP) or more
0/0/0	0	0	0/0	0/0/0	0/0	0//0	0/0/	0/0/0	2.9/0			0/0/0	----Other
0/0/0	0	0	0/0	0/0/0	0/1.8	0//0	0/0/	0/2.7/0	0/2.7			0/0/0	---Lubricating oil pumps
0/0/0	0	0	0/0	0/0/0	0/1.8	0//0	0/0/	0/2.7/0	0/2.7			0/0/0	---Other
0/0/0	2	1.6	0/0	0/0/0	0/0	0//0	0/0/	0/0/7.2	7.3/0			0/0/0	Concrete pumps
													-Other reciprocating positive displacement pumps:
													---Pneumatic
0/0/0	2	4.6	0/0	0/0/0	0/0	0/0/0	0/0/	9.3/9.5/9.3	9.4/9.5			0/0/0	Pneumatic reciprocating positive displacement pumps for agricultural use
0/0/0	2	4.6	0/0	0/0/0	0/0	0/0/0	0/0/	9.3/9.5/9.3	9.4/9.5			0/0/0	Pneumatic corrosion-resisting bellows or diaphragm pumps (flow capacity>0. 6m³/h, with a contact surface of special corrosion-resisting material)
0/0/0	2	4.6	0/0	0/0/0	0/0	0/0/0	0/0/	9.3/9.5/9.3	9.4/9.5			0/0/0	Pneumatic reciprocating positive displacement pumps for nonargricultural use
													---Electric
0/0/0	3.5	2	2.5/2.5	0/0/0	0/0	0/0/0	0/0/	9/9/9	9.1/9			0/0/0	Electric reciprocating positive displacement pumps for agricutlural use
0/0/0	3.5	2	2.5/2.5	0/0/0	0/0	0/0/0	0/0/	9/9/9	9.1/9			0/0/0	Electric corrosion-resisting bellows diaphragm pumps (flow capacity>0. 6m³/h with a contact-surface of special corrosion-resisting materials)
0/0/0	3.5	2	2.5/2.5	0/0/0	0/0	0/0/0	0/0/	9/9/9	9.1/9			0/0/0	Electric reciprocating multiple-sealed positive displacement pumps for non-argricultural use
0/0/0	3.5	2	2.5/2.5	0/0/0	0/0	0/0/0	0/0/	9/9/9	9.1/9			0/0/0	Other electric reciprocating positive displacement pumps for non-argricultlral use
													---Hydraulic:
													----Plunger pumps
0/0/0	3.5	6	0/0	0/0/0	0/0	0/0/0	0/0/	9.5/9.5/10	9.5/9.5			0/0/0	Plunger pumps for agriculture use
0/0/0	3.5	6	0/0	0/0/0	0/0	0/0/0	0/0/	9.5/9.5/10	9.5/9.5		//	0/0/0	Hydraulic piston pump for aircraft
0/0/0	3.5	6	0/0	0/0/0	0/0	0/0/0	0/0/	9.5/9.5/10	9.5/9.5			0/0/0	Other plunger pumps for non-agriculture use
													----Other

税则号列	货品名称〔CIQ 扩展编码及品名—T2 表示见附表 2〕	最惠(%)	暂定税率	普通	增值/消费	出口退税	计量单位	监管条件/特殊证件	检验检疫	对美关税	亚太上/下
8413.5039 01	其他农业用液压往复统排液泵〔999〕	10		40	9/	9	台/千克	/		30	
8413.5039 20	液压式耐腐蚀波纹或隔膜泵(流量大于 0.6m³/h,接触表面由特殊耐腐蚀材料制成)〔999〕	10		40	13/	13	台/千克	3/		30	
8413.5039 90	其他非农业用液压往复式排液泵〔999〕	10		40	13/	13	台/千克	/		30	
8413.5090	---其他										
8413.5090 10	其他农用往复式排液泵〔999〕	10		40	9/	9	台/千克	/		35	
8413.5090 20	其他耐腐蚀波纹或隔膜泵(流量大于 0.6m³/h,接触表面由特殊耐腐蚀材料制成)〔999〕	10		40	13/	13	台/千克	3/		35	
8413.5090 90	其他非农用往复式排液泵〔999〕	10		40	13/	13	台/千克	/		35	
	-其他回转式排液泵:										
	---齿轮泵										
8413.6021	----电动式										
8413.6021 01	农业用电动齿轮泵(回转式排液泵)〔999〕	10	6	40	9/	9	台/千克	/		11	
8413.6021 10	电动齿轮多重密封泵(非农业用回转式排液泵)〔999〕	10	6	40	13/	13	台/千克	3/		11	
8413.6021 90	其他非农业用电动齿轮泵(回转式排液泵,多重密封泵除外)〔999〕	10	6	40	13/	13	台/千克	/			
8413.6022	----液压式										
8413.6022 01	农业用回转式液压油泵(输入转速＞2000r/min,输入功率＞190kW,最大流量＞2×280L/min)〔999〕	10	3	40	9/	9	台/千克	/		23	
8413.6022 02	非农业用回转式液压油泵(输入转速＞2000r/min,输入功率＞190kW,最大流量＞2×280L/min)〔999〕	10	3	40	13/	13	台/千克	/		23	
8413.6022 10	其他农业用液压齿轮泵(回转式排液泵)〔999〕	10	6	40	9/	9	台/千克	/		26	
8413.6022 20	液压齿轮多重密封泵(非农业用回转式排液泵)〔999〕	10	6	40	13/	13	台/千克	3/		26	
8413.6022 90	其他非农业用液压齿轮泵(回转式排液泵,多重密封泵除外)〔999〕	10	6	40	13/	13	台/千克	/			
8413.6029	----其他										
8413.6029 01	其他农业用齿轮泵(回转式排液泵)〔999〕	10		40	9/	9	台/千克	/		35	
8413.6029 90	其他非农业用齿轮泵(回转式排液泵)〔999〕	10		40	13/	13	台/千克	/		35	
	---叶片泵:										
8413.6031	----电动式										
8413.6031 01	农业用电动叶片泵(回转式排液泵)〔999〕	10		40	9/	9	台/千克	/			
8413.6031 10	电动叶片多重密封泵(非农业用回转式排液泵)〔999〕	10		40	13/	13	台/千克	3/			
8413.6031 90	其他非农业用电动叶片泵(回转式排液泵,多重密封泵除外)〔999〕	10		40	13/	13	台/千克	/			
8413.6032	----液压式										
8413.6032 01	农业用液压叶片泵(回转式排液泵)〔999〕	10	6	40	9/	9	台/千克	/		26	
8413.6032 10	液压叶片多重密封泵(非农业用回转式排液泵)〔999〕	10	6	40	13/	13	台/千克	3/		26	
8413.6032 90	其他非农业用液压叶片泵(回转式排液泵,多重密封泵除外)〔999〕	10	6	40	13/	13	台/千克	/		26	
8413.6039	----其他										
8413.6039 01	其他农业用叶片泵(回转式排液泵)〔999〕	10	6	40	9/	9	台/千克	/		31	
8413.6039 90	其他非农业用叶片泵(回转式排液泵)〔999〕	10	6	40	13/	13	台/千克	/		31	
8413.6040	---螺杆泵										
8413.6040 01	农业用螺杆泵(回转式排液泵)〔999〕	10	6	40	9/	9	台/千克	/		16	
8413.6040 10	螺杆多重密封泵(非农业用回转式排液泵)〔999〕	10	6	40	13/	13	台/千克	3/		16	
8413.6040 90	其他非农业用螺杆泵(回转式排液泵,多重密封泵除外)〔999〕	10	6	40	13/	13	台/千克	/			
8413.6050	---径向柱塞泵										
8413.6050 01	农业用径向柱塞泵(回转式排液泵)〔999〕	10	6	40	9/	9	台/千克	/		31	
8413.6050 90	其他非农业用径向柱塞泵(回转式排液泵)〔999〕	10	6	40	13/	13	台/千克	/		31	
8413.6060	---轴向柱塞泵										
8413.6060 01	农业用轴向柱塞泵(回转式排液泵)〔999〕	10	6	40	9/	9	台/千克	/		31	

协定税率 %								RCEP		特惠税率 %			Article Description
东/冰/格	巴基斯坦	韩国	瑞士 上/下	哥/秘/柬	澳/毛	新西/坡/智	中国港/澳/台	东盟及马来/澳/韩	日/新	亚太2国	老/柬/缅	98/97/95	
0/0/0	0	4.6	0/0	0/0/0	0/0	0/0/0	0/0/	9.3/9.5/9.3	9.4/9.5			0/0/0	Other hydraulic reciprocating positive displacement pumps for agricultural use
0/0/0	0	4.6	0/0	0/0/0	0/0	0/0/0	0/0/	9.3/9.5/9.3	9.4/9.5			0/0/0	Hydraulic corrosion-resisting bellows or diaphragm pumps (flow capacity＞0. 6m^3/h with a contact-surface of special corrosion-resisting materials)
0/0/0	0	4.6	0/0	0/0/0	0/0	0/0/0	0/0/	9.3/9.5/9.3	9.4/9.5			0/0/0	Other hydraulic reciprocating positive displacement pumps for non-argricultural use
													---Other
0/0/0	3.5	6	0/0	0/0/0	0/0	0/0/0	0/0/	9.5/9.5/10	9.5/9.5			0/0/0	Other reciprocating positive displacement pumps for agricutural use
0/0/0	3.5	6	0/0	0/0/0	0/0	0/0/0	0/0/	9.5/9.5/10	9.5/9.5			0/0/0	Other corrosion-resisting bellows or diaphragm pumps(flow capacity＞0. 6m^3/h with a contact-surface of special corrosion-resisting materials)
0/0/0	3.5	6	0/0	0/0/0	0/0	0/0/0	0/0/	9.5/9.5/10	9.5/9.5			0/0/0	Other reciprocating positive displacement pumps for non-argricultural use
													-Other rotary positive displacement pumps:
													---Gear pumps
													----Electric
0//0	3.5	6	0/0	0/0/0	0/0	0/0/0	0/0/	9.5/9.5/10	9.5/9.5			0/0/0	Electric gear pumps for agricultural use(rotary positive displacement pumps)
0//0	3.5	6	0/0	0/0/0	0/0	0/0/0	0/0/	9.5/9.5/10	9.5/9.5			0/0/0	Electric multiple-sealed gear pumps(rotary positive displacement pumps for non-agricultural use)
0//0	3.5	6	0/0	0/0/0	0/0	0/0/0	0/0/	9.5/9.5/10	9.5/9.5			0/0/0	Other electric gear pumps for non-agricultural use (rotary positive displacement pumps for non-agricultural use)
													----Hydraulic
0/0/0	2	4.6	0/0	0/0/0	0/0	0//0	0/0/	9.3/9.5/9.3	9.4/9.5			0/0/0	Rotary hydraulic oil pumps for agricultural use (input speed ＞2000 r/min, input power＞190 kW, maximum flow quantity＞2×280L/min)
0/0/0	2	4.6	0/0	0/0/0	0/0	0//0	0/0/	9.3/9.5/9.3	9.4/9.5			0/0/0	Rotary hydraulic oil pumps for non-agricultural use (input speed＞2000 r/min, input power＞190 kW, maximum flow quantity＞2×280L/min)
0/0/0	2	4.6	0/0	0/0/0	0/0	0//0	0/0/	9.3/9.5/9.3	9.4/9.5			0/0/0	Other hydraulic gear pumps for agricultural use (rotary positive displacement pumps)
0/0/0	2	4.6	0/0	0/0/0	0/0	0//0	0/0/	9.3/9.5/9.3	9.4/9.5			0/0/0	Hydraulic gear multiple-sealed pumps (rotary positive discharging hydraulic pump for non-agricultural use)
0/0/0	2	4.6	0/0	0/0/0	0/0	0//0	0/0/	9.3/9.5/9.3	9.4/9.5			0/0/0	Other hydraulic gear pumps for non-agricultural use(except rotary positive displacement pumps, multiple-sealed pumps)
													----Other
0/0/0	3.5	2	0/0	0/0/0	0/0	0//0	0/0/	9/9/9	9.1/9			0/0/0	Other gear pumps for agricultural use(rotary positive displacement pumps)
0/0/0	3.5	2	0/0	0/0/0	0/0	0//0	0/0/	9/9/9	9.1/9			0/0/0	Other gear pumps for non-agricultural use (rotary positive displacement pumps)
													---Vane pumps:
													----Electric
0/0/0	2	2	0/0	0/0/0	0/0	0//0	0/0/	0/0/9	9.1/0			0/0/0	Electric vane pumps for agricultural use(rotary positive displacement pumps)
0/0/0	2	2	0/0	0/0/0	0/0	0//0	0/0/	0/0/9	9.1/0			0/0/0	Electric multiple-sealed vane pumps (rotary positive displacement pumps for non-agricultural use)
0/0/0	2	2	0/0	0/0/0	0/0	0//0	0/0/	0/0/9	9.1/0			0/0/0	Other electric vane pumps for non-agricultural use(except rotary positive displacement pumps, multiple-sealed pumps)
													----Hydraulic
0/0/0	2	6	0/0	0/0/0	0/0	0//0	0/0/	9.5/9.5/10	9.5/9.5			0/0/0	Hydraulic vane pumps for agricultural use (rotary positive displacement pumps)
0/0/0	2	6	0/0	0/0/0	0/0	0//0	0/0/	9.5/9.5/10	9.5/9.5			0/0/0	Hydraulic vane multiple-sealed pumps (rotary positive displacement pumps for non-agricultural use)
0/0/0	2	6	0/0	0/0/0	0/0	0//0	0/0/	9.5/9.5/10	9.5/9.5			0/0/0	Other hydraulic vane pumps for non-agricultural use(except rotary positive displacement pumps, multiple-sealed pumps)
													----Other
0/0/0	2	6	0/0	0/0/0	0/0	0//0	0/0/	9.5/9.5/10	9.5/9.5			0/0/0	Other vane pumps for agricultural use (rotary positive displacement pumps)
0/0/0	2	6	0/0	0/0/0	0/0	0//0	0/0/	9.5/9.5/10	9.5/9.5			0/0/0	Other vane pumps for non-agricultural use (rotary positive displacement pumps)
													---Screw pumps
0/0/0	2	6	0/0	0/0/0	0/0	0//0	0/0/	9.5/9.5/10	9.5/9.5			0/0/0	Screw pumps for agricultural use (rotary positive displacement pumps)
0/0/0	2	6	0/0	0/0/0	0/0	0//0	0/0/	9.5/9.5/10	9.5/9.5			0/0/0	Screw pumps (rotary positive multiple sealed displacement pumps for non-agricultural use.)
0/0/0	2	6	0/0	0/0/0	0/0	0//0	0/0/	9.5/9.5/10	9.5/9.5			0/0/0	Other screw pumps for non-agricultural use(except rotary positive displacement pumps, multiple-sealed pumps)
													---Radial plunger pumps
0/0/0	2	6	0/0	0/0/0	/0/0	0//0	0/0/	9.5/9.5/10	9.5/9.5			0/0/0	Radial plunger pumps for agricultural use(rotary positive displacement pumps)
0/0/0	2	6	0/0	0/0/0	0/0	0//0	0/0/	9.5/9.5/10	9.5/9.5			0/0/0	Other radial plunger pumps for non-agricultural use (rotary positive displacement pumps)
													---Axial plunger pumps
0/0/0	3.5	4.6	0/0	0/0/0	0/0	0//0	0/0/	9.3/9.5/9.3	9.4/9.5			0/0/0	Axial plunger pumps for agricultural use(rotary positive displacement pumps)

税则号列	货品名称〔CIQ 扩展编码及品名—T2 表示见附表 2〕	最惠(%)	暂定税率	普通	增值/消费	出口退税	计量单位	监管条件/特殊证件	检验检疫	对美关税	亚太上/下
8413.6060 90	其他非农业用轴向柱塞泵(回转式排液泵)〔999〕	10	6	40	13/	13	台/千克	/		31	
8413.6090	---其他										
8413.6090 10	农业用其他回转式排液泵〔999〕	10		40	9/	9	台/千克	/		15	
8413.6090 90	其他回转式排液泵〔999〕	10		40	13/	13	台/千克	/		15	
	-其他离心泵:										
8413.7010	---转速在 10000 转/分及以上										
8413.7010 10	农业用其他离心泵(转速在 10000 转/分及以上)〔999〕	8		40	9/	9	台/千克	/		13	5.2/5.2
8413.7010 20	液体推进剂用泵(转速≥10000 转/分,出口压力≥7000 千帕的)〔999〕	8		40	13/	13	台/千克	3/		13	5.2/5.2
8413.7010 30	离心泵多重密封泵(两用物项管制)〔999〕	8		40	13/	13	台/千克	3/		13	5.2/5.2
8413.7010 90	其他非农用离心泵(转速在 10000 转/分及以上)〔999〕	8		40	13/	13	台/千克	/		13	5.2/5.2
	---其他:										
8413.7091	----电动潜油泵及潜水电泵										
8413.7091 10	农业用电动潜油泵及潜水电泵(转速在 10000 转/分以下)〔999〕	8		40	9/	9	台/千克	/		23	
8413.7091 90	其他非农业用电动潜油泵及潜水电泵(转速在 10000 转/分以下)〔999〕	8		40	13/	13	台/千克	/		23	
8413.7099	----其他										
8413.7099 10	其他农业用离心泵(转速在 10000 转/分以下)〔999〕	8		40	9/	9	台/千克	/		13	5.2/5.2
8413.7099 20	一次冷却剂泵(全密封驱动泵,有惯性质量系统的泵,及鉴定为 NC—1 泵等)〔999〕	8		40	13/	13	台/千克	3/		13	5.2/5.2
8413.7099 30	转速小于 10000 转/分的离心式屏蔽泵(流量大于 0.6m^3/h,接触表面由特殊耐腐蚀材料制成)〔999〕	8		40	13/	13	台/千克	3/		13	5.2/5.2
8413.7099 40	转速小于 10000 转/分的离心式磁力泵(流量大于 0.6m^3/h,接触表面由特殊耐腐蚀材料制成)〔999〕	8		40	13/	13	台/千克	3/		13	5.2/5.2
8413.7099 50	液体推进剂用泵(8000 转/分＜转速＜10000 转/分,出口压力≥7000kPa 的)〔999〕	8		40	13/	13	台/千克	3/		13	5.2/5.2
8413.7099 60	其他离心泵多重密封泵(两用物项管制)〔999〕	8		40	13/	13	台/千克	3/		13	5.2/5.2
8413.7099 70	飞机发动机用燃油泵〔999〕	8	1	40	13/	13	台/千克	/		6	5.2/5.2
8413.7099 90	其他非农业用离心泵(转速在 10000 转/分以下)〔999〕	8		40	13/	13	台/千克	/		13	5.2/5.2
	-其他泵;液体提升机:										
8413.8100	--泵										
8413.8100 10	农业用其他液体泵〔999〕	8		40	9/	9	台/千克	/		28	4/4
8413.8100 20	生产重水用多级泵(专门为利用氨—氢交换法生产重水而设计或制造的多级泵)〔999〕	8		40	13/	13	台/千克	3/		28	4/4
8413.8100 90	其他非农用液体泵〔999〕	8		40	13/	13	台/千克	/		28	4/4
8413.8200	--液体提升机〔999〕	8		30	13/	13	台/千克	/		28	
	-零件:										
8413.9100	--泵用〔999〕	5		30	13/	13	千克	/		15	2.5/2.5
8413.9200	--液体提升机用〔999〕	6		30	13/	13	千克	/		26	
84.14	**空气泵或真空泵、空气及其他气体压缩机、风机、风扇;装有风扇的通风罩或循环气罩,不论是否装有过滤器;气密生物安全柜,不论是否装有过滤器;**										
8414.1000	-真空泵										
8414.1000 10	耐腐蚀真空泵(流量大于 5m^3/h,接触表面由特殊耐腐蚀材料制成)〔101 其它空气压缩机(站)及零件 I 类器具,102 其它空气压缩机(站)及零件 II 类器具,103 其它空气压缩机(站)及零件 III 类器具,104 其它空气压缩机(站)及零件 0I 类器具,105 其它空气压缩机(站)及零件 0 类器具〕	8	5	30	13/	13	台/千克	3/		30	
8414.1000 20	真空泵(抽气口≥38 厘米,速度≥15m^3/秒,产生＜10^{-4}托极限真空度〔999〕	8	5	30	13/	13	台/千克	3/		30	
8414.1000 30	能在含 UF6 气氛中使用的真空泵(用耐 UF6 腐蚀的材料制成或保护。这些泵可以是旋转式或正压式,可有排代式密封和碳氟化合物密封并且可以有特殊工作流体存在)〔999〕	8	5	30	13/	13	台/千克	3/		30	
8414.1000 40	专门设计或制造的抽气能力≥5m^3/min 的真空泵(专用于同位素气体扩散浓缩)〔999〕	8	5	30	13/	13	台/千克	3/		30	
8414.1000 50	能在含 UF6 气氛中使用的真空泵(耐 UF6 腐蚀的,也可用氟碳密封和特殊工作流体)〔999〕	8	5	30	13/	13	台/千克	3/		30	
8414.1000 60	专门或主要用于半导体或平板显示屏制造的真空泵((P))〔999〕	0		30	13/	13	台/千克	/			
8414.1000 90	其他真空泵〔999〕	8	5	30	13/	13	台/千克	/		30	
8414.2000	-手动或脚踏式空气泵〔999〕	8		30	13/	13	台/千克	/		28	

协定税率 %								RCEP		特惠税率 %			Article Description
东/冰/格	巴基斯坦	韩国	瑞士上/下	哥/秘/柬	澳/毛	新西/坡/智	中国港/澳/台	东盟及马来/澳/韩	日/新	亚太2国	老/柬/缅	98/97/95	
0/0/0	3.5	4.6	0/0	0/0/0	0/0	0//0	0/0/	9.3/9.5/9.3	9.4/9.5			0/0/0	Other axial plunger pumps for non-agricultural use (rotary positive displacement pumps)
													---Other
0/0/0	3.5	4.6	1/1	0/0/0	0/0	0/0/0	0/0/	9.3/9.5/9.3	9.4/9.5			0/0/0	Other rotary positive displacement pumps for agricutural use
0/0/0	3.5	4.6	1/1	0/0/0	0/0	0/0/0	0/0/	9.3/9.5/9.3	9.4/9.5			0/0/0	Other rotary positive displacement pumps
													-Other centrifugal pumps:
													---Rotational speed no less than 10000r/min
0/0/0	2	0	0/0	0/0/0	0/0	0//0	0/0/	0/0/0	7.3/0			0/0/0	Other centrifugal pumps for agricutural use, rotational speed ⩾10000r/min
0/0/0	2	0	0/0	0/0/0	0/0	0//0	0/0/	0/0/0	7.3/0			0/0/0	Liquid-propellant pumps, rotational speed ⩾ 10000r/min, outlet pressure⩾7000kPa
0/0/0	2	0	0/0	0/0/0	0/0	0//0	0/0/	0/0/0	7.3/0			0/0/0	centrifugal Multiple sealedg pumps (subject to regulation of sensitive items)
0/0/0	2	0	0/0	0/0/0	0/0	0//0	0/0/	0/0/0	7.3/0			0/0/0	Other centrifugal pumps, for non-argricultural use rotational speed⩾10000r/min,
													---Other:
													----Electric submersible oil pumps and electric submrsible pumps
0/0/0	2	2	0/0	0/0/0	0/0	0/0/0	0/0/	0/0/9	9.1/0			0/0/0	Electric submersible oil pumps and electric submrsible pumps for agricultural use (rotational speed⩾10000r/min)
0/0/0	2	2	0/0	0/0/0	0/0	0/0/0	0/0/	0/0/9	9.1/0			0/0/0	Other electric submersible oil pumps and electric submrsible pumps for non-agricultural use (rotational speed⩾10000r/min)
													----Other
0/0/0	2	0	0.8/0.8	0/0/0	0/0	0//0	0/0/	0/0/0	7.5/0			0/0/0	Other centrifugal pumps for agricultural use (rotational speed <10000r/min)
0/0/0	2	0	0.8/0.8	0/0/0	0/0	0//0	0/0/	0/0/0	7.5/0			0/0/0	Primary coolant pumps (completely-sealed driving pumps, pumps with inertia mass system, approved NC-1pumps)
0/0/0	2	0	0.8/0.8	0/0/0	0/0	0//0	0/0/	0/0/0	7.5/0			0/0/0	Canned centrifugal pumps, rotational speed < 10000r/min (flow capacity > 0.6m^3/h with a contact-surface of special corrosion-resisting materials)
0/0/0	2	0	0.8/0.8	0/0/0	0/0	0//0	0/0/	0/0/0	7.5/0			0/0/0	Magnetically-driven centrifugal pumps, rotational speed < 10000r/min (flow capacity>0.6m^3/h with a contact-surface of special corrosion-resisting materials)
0/0/0	2	0	0.8/0.8	0/0/0	0/0	0//0	0/0/	0/0/0	7.5/0			0/0/0	Liquid-propellant pumps (8000r/min < rotational speed < 10000r/min, outlet pressure⩾7000kPa)
0/0/0	2	0	0.8/0.8	0/0/0	0/0	0//0	0/0/	0/0/0	7.5/0			0/0/0	Other centrifugal pumps and multiple-sealed pumps (subject to regulation of sensitive items)
0/0/0	2	0	0.8/0.8	0/0/0	0/0	0//0	0/0/	0/0/0	7.5/0		//	0/0/0	Fuel pump for aircraft engine
0/0/0	2	0	0.8/0.8	0/0/0	0/0	0//0	0/0/	0/0/0	7.5/0			0/0/0	Other centrifugal pumps for non-agricultural use, rotational speed<10000r/min
													-Other pumps; liquid elevators:
													--Pumps
0/0/0	0	0	0.8/0.8	0/0/0	0/0	0//0	0/0/0	0/0/0	7.3/0			0/0/0	Other liquid pumps for agricultural use
0/0/0	0	0	0.8/0.8	0/0/0	0/0	0//0	0/0/0	0/0/0	7.3/0			0/0/0	Multiple-staged pumps specified for heavy water (specially designed or manufactured for heavy water production with ammonia-hydrogen exchange)
0/0/0	0	0	0.8/0.8	0/0/0	0/0	0//0	0/0/0	0/0/0	7.3/0			0/0/0	Other liquid pump for non-agricultural use
0/0/0	2	1.6	3.4/3.4	0/0/0	0/0	0//0	0/0/	0/0/7.2	7.3/0			0/0/0	--Liquid elevators
													-Parts:
0/0/0	0	0	0.5/0.5	0/0/0	0/0	0//0	0/0/0	0/0/0	4.7/0			0/0/0	--Of pumps
0/0/0	0	0	0/0	0/0/0	0/0	0//0	0/0/	0/0/0	0/0			0/0/0	--Of liquid elevators
													Air or vacuum pumps, air or other gas compressors and fans; ventilating or recycling hoods incorporating a fan, whether or not fitted with filters; gas－tight biological safety cabinets, whether or not fitted with filters.
													-Vacuum pumps
0/0/0	2	1.6	0.8/0.8	0/0/0	0/0	0//0	0/0/0	0/0/7.2	7.6/0			0/0/0	Corrosion-resisting vacuum pumps (flow capacity>5m^3/h, with a contact-surface of special corrosion-resisting materials)
0/0/0	2	1.6	0.8/0.8	0/0/0	0/0	0//0	0/0/0	0/0/7.2	7.6/0			0/0/0	Vacucm pumps (aspirating hole⩾38cm, speed⩾15kl/s, capacity<10^{-4} absolute vaccum degree
0/0/0	2	1.6	0.8/0.8	0/0/0	0/0	0//0	0/0/0	0/0/7.2	7.6/0			0/0/0	Vacuum pumps, suitable to be used in UF6 atmosphere (made of or lined with aluminum, nickel or alloys containing more than 60% nickel)
0/0/0	2	1.6	0.8/0.8	0/0/0	0/0	0//0	0/0/0	0/0/7.2	7.6/0			0/0/0	Vacuum pump whose specially designed or produced air-exhausting capacity⩾5m^3/min (especially used for the diffusion and concentration of isotope gas)
0/0/0	2	1.6	0.8/0.8	0/0/0	0/0	0//0	0/0/0	0/0/7.2	7.6/0			0/0/0	Vacuum pumps, suitable to be used in UF6 atmosphere (can be sealed with fluorine-carbon or can be used with other special working fluid)
0/0/0	2	1.6	0.8/0.8	0/0/0	0/0	0//0	0/0/0	0/0/7.2	7.6/0			0/0/0	Vacuum pump, specially or primary semiconductor wafer or flat panel display
0/0/0	2	1.6	0.8/0.8	0/0/0	0/0	0//0	0/0/0	0/0/7.2	7.6/0			0/0/0	Other vacuum pumps
0/0/0	2	0	0/0	0/0/0	0/0	0//0	0/0/	0/0/0	7.3/0			0/0/0	-Handor footoperated pumps

税则号列	货品名称〔CIQ 扩展编码及品名－T2 表示见附表 2〕	最惠(%)	暂定税率	普通	增值/消费	出口退税	计量单位	监管条件/特殊证件	检验检疫	对美关税	亚太上/下
	-用于制冷设备的压缩机：										
	---电动机驱动的压缩机：										
8414.3011	----冷藏箱或冷冻箱用，电动机额定功率不超过 0.4 千瓦〔999〕	8		80	13/	13	台/千克	A/	LM	33	5.2/5.2
8414.3012	----冷藏箱或冷冻箱用，电动机额定功率超过 0.4 千瓦，但不超过 5 千瓦〔999〕	8		80	13/	13	台/千克	A/	LM	33	5.2/5.2
8414.3013	----空气调节器用，电动机额定功率超过 0.4 千瓦，但不超过 5 千瓦〔999〕	8		80	13/	13	台/千克	A/	LM	33	5.2/5.2
8414.3014	----空气调节器用，电动机额定功率超过 5 千瓦〔999〕	8		80	13/	13	台/千克	/		18	5.2/5.2
8414.3015	----冷冻或冷藏设备用，电动机额定功率超过 5 千瓦〔999〕	8		30	13/	13	台/千克	/		28	5.2/5.2
8414.3019	----其他〔999〕	8		30	13/	13	台/千克	A/	LM	23	5.2/5.2
8414.3090	---非电动机驱动的压缩机〔102 其他车辆零部件，101 其它制冷设备用压缩机及其零件〕	8		80	13/	13	台/千克	/		33	5.2/5.2
8414.4000	-装在拖车底盘上的空气压缩机〔999〕	8		30	13/	13	台/千克	/		28	
	-风机、风扇：										
	--台扇、落地扇、壁扇、换气扇或吊扇，包括风机，本身装有一个输出功率不超过 125 瓦的电动机：										
8414.5110	---吊扇〔101 吊扇 I 类器具，102 吊扇 II 类器具，103 吊扇 III 类器具，104 吊扇 0I 类器具，105 吊扇 0 类器具〕	6		130	13/	13	台/千克	A/	LM	11	4.2/4.2
8414.5120	---换气扇[T2]	6		130	13/	13	台/千克	A/	LM	31	4.8/4.8
8414.5130	---具有旋转导风轮的风扇[T2]	6		130	13/	13	台/千克	/	L	31	
	---其他：										
8414.5191	----台扇〔101 台扇 I 类器具，102 台扇 II 类器具，103 台扇 III 类器具，104 台扇 0I 类器具，105 台扇 0 类器具〕	6		130	13/	13	台/千克	A/	LM		4.2/4.2
8414.5192	----落地扇〔101 落地扇 I 类器具，102 落地扇 II 类器具，103 落地扇 III 类器具，104 落地扇 0I 类器具，105 落地扇 0 类器具〕	6		130	13/	13	台/千克	A/	LM		4.2/4.2
8414.5193	----壁扇〔101 壁扇 I 类器具，102 壁扇 II 类器具，103 壁扇 III 类器具，104 壁扇 0I 类器具，105 壁扇 0 类器具〕	6		130	13/	13	台/千克	A/	LM	31	4.8/4.8
8414.5199	----其他[T2]	6		130	13/	13	台/千克	/	L	31	
	--其他：										
8414.5910	---吊扇[T2]	8		30	13/	13	台/千克	A/	LM	33	5.2/5.2
8414.5920	---换气扇[T2]	8		30	13/	13	台/千克	A/	LM	33	5.2/5.2
8414.5930	---离心通风机〔999〕	8		30	13/	13	台/千克	/		33	5.2/5.2
8414.5990	---其他										
8414.5990 10	罗茨式鼓风机〔999〕	8		30	13/	13	台/千克	A/	M	33	5.2/5.2
8414.5990 20	吸气≥$1m^3$/min 的耐 UF6 腐蚀的鼓风机（出口压力高达 500 千帕，设计成在 UF6 环境中长期运行。这种鼓风机的压力比为 10:1 或更低，用耐 UF6 的材料制成或用这种材料进行保护）〔999〕	8		30	13/	13	台/千克	3A/	M	33	5.2/5.2
8414.5990 30	吸气≥$2m^3$/min 的耐 UF_6 腐蚀鼓风机（轴向离心式或正排量鼓风机，压力比在 1.2:1 和 6:1 之间）〔999〕	8		30	13/	13	台/千克	3A/	M	33	5.2/5.2
8414.5990 40	吸气≥$56m^3$/s 的鼓风机（用于循环硫化氢气体的单级、低压头离心式鼓风机）〔999〕	8		30	13/	13	台/千克	3A/	M	33	5.2/5.2
8414.5990 50	电子产品散热用轴流风扇〔101 换气扇 I 类器具，102 换气扇 II 类器具，103 换气扇 III 类器具，104 换气扇 0I 类器具，105 换气扇 0 类器具〕	8		30	13/	13	台/千克	/		33	5.2/5.2
8414.5990 60	专门或主要用于微处理器、电信设备、自动数据处理设备或装置的散热扇〔101 换气扇 I 类器具，102 换气扇 II 类器具，103 换气扇 III 类器具，104 换气扇 0I 类器具，105 换气扇 0 类器具〕	0		30	13/	13	台/千克	/		25	5.2/5.2
8414.5990 91	其他台扇、落地扇、壁扇（电动机输出功率超过 125 瓦的）[T2]	8		30	13/	13	台/千克	A/	ML	33	5.2/5.2
8414.5990 99	其他风机、风扇[T2]	8		30	13/	13	台/千克	/	L	33	5.2/5.2
	-罩的平面最大边长不超过 120 厘米的通风罩或循环气罩：										
8414.6010	---抽油烟机〔999〕	8	6	130	13/	13	台/千克	/	L	31	
8414.6090	---其他										
8414.6090 12	活动（柔软的）隔离装置（具有与三级生物安全柜类似标准，罩的最大边长≤120 厘米）〔101 非家用过滤及净化装置，102 气体纯化过滤、净化机器及装置〕	8		130	13/	13	台/千克	3/		33	
8414.6090 14	吸收塔（两用物项管制，罩的最大边长≤120 厘米）〔101 非家用过滤及净化装置，102 气体纯化过滤、净化机器及装置〕	8		130	13/	13	台/千克	3/		33	
8414.6090 15	带有风扇的高效空气粒子过滤单元的封闭洁净设备（高效空气粒子过滤单元（HEPA），罩的最大边长≤120 厘米）〔101 非家用过滤及净化装置，102 气体纯化过滤、净化机器及装置〕	8		130	13/	13	台/千克	3/		33	
8414.6090 90	其他≤120 厘米的通风罩或循环气罩（指罩的平面最大边长不超过 120 厘米，装有风扇的）〔999〕	8		130	13/	13	台/千克	/		33	
	-气密生物安全柜：										
8414.7010	---罩的平面最大边长不超过 120 厘米的										
8414.7010 10	三级生物安全柜（具有与三级生物安全柜类似标准，罩的最大边长≤120 厘米）〔101 非家用过滤及净化装置，102 气体纯化过滤、净化机器及装置〕	8		130	13/	13	台/千克	3/		33	

协定税率 %								RCEP		特惠税率 %			Article Description
东/冰/格	巴基斯坦	韩国	瑞士上/下	哥/秘/柬	澳/毛	新西/坡/智	中国港/澳/台	东盟及马来/澳/韩	日/新	亚太2国	老/柬/缅	98/97/95	
													-Compressors of a kind used in refrigerating equipment:
													---Driven by a motor:
0/0/0	2	3.7	0/0	0/0/0	0/0	0/0/0	0/0/	7.5/7.6/7.5	7.5/7.6			0/0/0	----For refrigerators or freezers, of a motor power not exceeding 0.4kW
0/0/0	2	6	0/0	0/0/0	0/0	0/0/0	0/0/	9/9.5/10	9.1/9.5			0/0/0	----For refrigerators or freezers, of a motor power exceeding 0.4kW but not exceeding 5kW
0/0/0	2	0	0/0	0/0/0	0/0	0/0/0	0/0/0	0/0/0	9.1/0			0/0/0	----For air conditioning machines, of a motor power exceeding, 0.4kW but not exceeding 5kW
0/0/0	2	2	0/0	0/0/0	0/0	0/0/0	0/0/0	0/0/9	9.1/0			0/0/0	----For air conditioning machines, of a motor power>5kW
0/0/0	2	2	0/0	0/0/0	0/0	0//0	0/0/	9/9/9	9.1/9			0/0/0	----For refrigerators or freezers, of a motor power>5kW
0/0/0	2	6	0/0	0/0/0	0/0	0/0/0	0/0/	9.5/9.5/10	9.5/9.5			0/0/0	----Other
0/0/0	2	4.2	0/0	0/0/0	0/0	0/0/0	0/0/	8.4/8.6/8.4	8.4/8.6			0/0/0	---Drive by a non-motor
0/0/0	2	1.6	0/0	0/0/0	0/0	0//0	0/0/	0/0/7.2	7.3/0			0/0/0	-Air compressors mounted on a wheeled chassis for towing
													-Fans:
													--Table, floor, wall, window, ceiling or roof fans, with a self-contained electric motor of an output not exceeding 125W:
0/0/0	16	9.3	2/2	0/0/0	0/0	0/0/0	0/0/	18/18/18	18.2/18		0//	0/0/0	---Ceiling or roof fans
0/0/0	0	9.3	2/2	0/0/0	0/0	0/0/0	0/0/0	18.7/19/18.7	18.8/19		0//	0/0/0	---Window fans
0/0/0	4.2	2.4	1.2/1.2	0/0/0	0/0	0/0/0	0/0/	0/0/10.8	10.9/0		0//	0/0/0	---Repeating front louver fan
													---Other:
0/0/0	2	2	0/0	0/0/0	0/0	0//0	0/0/	0/0/9	9.1/0		0//	0/0/0	----Table fans
0/0/0	2	2	0/0	0/0/0	0/0	0//0	0/0/	0/0/9	9.1/0		0//	0/0/0	----Floor fans
0/0/0	2	2	0/0	0/0/0	0/0	0//0	0/0/	0/0/9	9.1/0		0//	0/0/0	----Wall fans
0/0/0	0	2	0/0	0/0/0	0/0	0/0/0	0/0/0	9/9/9	9.1/9		0//	0/0/0	----Other
													--Other:
0/0/0	2	0	0/0	0/0/0	0/0	0//0	0/0/	0/0/0	7.3/0			0/0/0	---Ceiling or roof fans
0/0/0	2	0	0/0	0/0/0	0/0	0//0	0/0/	0/0/0	7.3/0			0/0/0	---Window fans
0/0/0	3.5	0	0/0	0/0/0	0/0	0/0/0	0/0/	9/9/9	9.1/9			0/0/0	---Centrifugal ventilation fans
													---Other
0/0/0	2	0	0.8/0.8	0/0/0	0/0	0//0	0/0/0	0/0/0	7.3/0			0/0/0	Root's blower
0/0/0	2	0	0.8/0.8	0/0/0	0/0	0//0	0/0/0	0/0/0	7.3/0			0/0/0	Blower, suitable to be used in UF6 atmosphere, extraction capability≥1m³/min (axial centrifugal fans or positive-discharge fans, pressure ratio between 2∶1～6∶1)
0/0/0	2	0	0.8/0.8	0/0/0	0/0	0//0	0/0/0	0/0/0	7.3/0			0/0/0	Blower, suitable to be used in UF6 atmosphere, extraction capability≥2m³/min (axial centrifugal fans or positive-discharge fans, pressure ratio between 1.2∶1 and 6∶1)
0/0/0	2	0	0.8/0.8	0/0/0	0/0	0//0	0/0/0	0/0/0	7.3/0			0/0/0	Blower, extraction capability≥56m³/s (one-stage, low-pressure centrifugal blowers used for cycling hydrogen sulphide gas)
0/0/0	2	0	0.8/0.8	0/0/0	0/0	0//0	0/0/0	0/0/0	7.3/0			0/0/0	Axial flow fans for heat elimination of electronic products
0/0/0	2	0	0.8/0.8	0/0/0	0/0	0//0	0/0/0	0/0/0	7.3/0			0/0/0	Radiating fan, specially or primary for microprocessor, telecommunication equipment, automatic data processing equipment or device
0/0/0	2	0	0.8/0.8	0/0/0	0/0	0//0	0/0/0	0/0/0	7.3/0			0/0/0	Other desk fans, floor-standing fans and wall-mounted fans (electric output power>125W)
0/0/0	2	0	0.8/0.8	0/0/0	0/0	0//0	0/0/0	0/0/0	7.3/0			0/0/0	Other fans
													-Hoods having a maximum horizontal side not exceeding 120cm:
0/0/0	2	2	0/0	0/0/0	0/0	0//0	0/0/	0/0/9	9.1/0		0//	0/0/0	---Range hoods
													---Other
0/0/0	2	2	0/0	0/0/0	0/0	0/0/0	0/0/	0/0/9	9.1/0		0//	0/0/0	Movable (soft) isolation device (with standards similar to level III biosafety cabinet, and the maximum side length of the cover is ≤ 120cm)
0/0/0	2	2	0/0	0/0/0	0/0	0/0/0	0/0/	0/0/9	9.1/0		0//	0/0/0	Absorbing tower(subject to regulation of sensitive items, the longest sides covered ≤120 cm)
0/0/0	2	2	0/0	0/0/0	0/0	0/0/0	0/0/	0/0/9	9.1/0		0//	0/0/0	HEPA closed cleaning equipment with fans (HEPA referring high efficiency particulate air filter, the longest sides covered ≤120cm)
0/0/0	2	2	0/0	0/0/0	0/0	0/0/0	0/0/	0/0/9	9.1/0		0//	0/0/0	Other ventilating or recycling hoods with the side length≤120cm(meaning the maximum side length≤120cm, fitted with a fan)
													-Gastight biological safety cabinets
													---The maximum side length of the plane ≤120 cm
0/0/0	2	2	0/0	0/0/0	0/0	0/0/0	0/0/	0/0/9	9.1/0		0//	0/0/0	Class III biosafety cabinet (with standards similar to class III biosafety cabinet, with the maximum side length of the cover ≤ 12cm)

税则号列		货品名称〔CIQ 扩展编码及品名—T2 表示见附表 2〕	最惠(%)	暂定税率	普通	增值/消费	出口退税	计量单位	监管条件/特殊证件	检验检疫	对美关税	亚太上/下
8414.7010	90	其他气密生物安全柜(符合世界卫生组织规定的生物安全水平三级标准,罩的最大边长≤120 厘米)〔101 非家用过滤及净化装置,102 气体纯化过滤、净化机器及装置,999 其它风机及其零件〕	8		130	13/	13	台/千克	/		33	
8414.7090		---其他										
8414.7090	10	三级生物安全柜(具有与三级生物安全柜类似标准,平面边长>120cm)〔101 非家用过滤及净化装置,102 气体纯化过滤、净化机器及装置〕	7		30	13/	13	台/千克	3/		22	4.6/4.6
8414.7090	90	其他气密生物安全柜(符合世界卫生组织规定的生物安全水平三级标准,平面边长>120cm)〔101 非家用过滤及净化装置,102 气体纯化过滤、净化机器及装置〕	7		30	13/	13	台/千克	/		22	4.6/4.6
		-其他:										
8414.8010		---燃气轮机用的自由活塞式发生器〔999〕	8		50	13/	13	台/千克	/			5.2/5.2
8414.8020		---二氧化碳压缩机〔999〕	7		30	13/	13	台/千克	/		27	4.6/4.6
8414.8030		---发动机用增压器										
8414.8030	01	乘用车机械增压器〔999〕	7	5	30	13/	13	台/千克	/		30	4.6/4.6
8414.8030	90	发动机用增压器〔101 其他车辆零部件,102 其它风机及其零件,103 其它空气压缩机(站)及零件〕	7		30	13/	13	台/千克	/		32	4.6/4.6
		---空气及其他气体压缩机:										
8414.8041		----螺杆空压机〔999〕	7		30	13/	13	台/千克	/		12	4.6/4.6
8414.8049		----其他										
8414.8049	10	吸气≥1m3UF6/min 的耐 UF6 腐蚀压缩机(出口压力高达 500 千帕,设计成在 UF6 环境中长期运行。这种压缩机的压力比为 10:1 或更低,用耐 UF6 的材料制成或用这种材料进行保护)〔999〕	7		30	13/	13	台/千克	3/		12	4.6/4.6
8414.8049	20	MLIS 用 UF6/载气压缩机(能在 UF6 环境中长期操作 UF6/载气混合气压缩机)〔999〕	7		30	13/	13	台/千克	3/		12	4.6/4.6
8414.8049	30	吸气≥56m3/s 的压缩机(用于循环硫化氢气体的单级、低压头离心式压缩机)〔999〕	7		30	13/	13	台/千克	3/		12	4.6/4.6
8414.8049	40	吸气≥2m3/min 的耐 UF6 腐蚀压缩机(轴向离心式或正排量压缩机,压力比在 1.2:1 和 6:1 之间)〔999〕	7		30	13/	13	台/千克	3/		12	4.6/4.6
8414.8049	50	燃料电池增压器〔999〕	7	5	30	13/	13	台/千克	/		10	4.6/4.6
8414.8049	60	飞机用离心式氮气系统压缩机〔999〕	7	1	30	13/	13	台/千克	/		6	4.6/4.6
8414.8049	90	其他空气及气体压缩机〔999〕	7		30	13/	13	台/千克	/		12	4.6/4.6
8414.8090		---其他										
8414.8090	52	其他活动(柔软的)隔离装置(具有与三级生物安全柜类似标准)〔101 非家用过滤及净化装置,102 气体纯化过滤、净化机器及装置〕	7		30	13/	13	台/千克	3/		22	4.6/4.6
8414.8090	54	其他吸收塔(两用物项管制)〔999〕	7		30	13/	13	台/千克	3/		22	4.6/4.6
8414.8090	55	其他带有风扇的高效空气粒子过滤单元的封闭洁净设备[高效空气粒子过滤单元(HEPA)]〔101 非家用过滤及净化装置,102 气体纯化过滤、净化机器及装置〕	7		30	13/	13	台/千克	3/		22	4.6/4.6
8414.8090	57	燃料电池循环泵〔999〕	7	2	30	13/	13	台/千克	/		17	4.6/4.6
8414.8090	90	其他空气泵及通风罩(通风罩指装有风扇的通风罩或循环气罩,平面边长>120cm)〔101 其它风机及其零件,102 站及零件〕	7		30	13/	13	台/千克	/		22	4.6/4.6
		-零件:										
		---税号 8414.3011 至 8414.3014 及 8414.3090 所列机器的零件:										
8414.9011		----压缩机进、排气阀片〔999〕	8	5	80	13/	13	千克	/		25	5.6/5.6
8414.9019		----其他〔999〕	8	5	80	13/	13	千克	/		15	5.6/5.6
8414.9020		---税号 8414.5110 至 8414.5199 及 8414.6000 所列机器的零件〔101 其它风机及其零件,102 其它电扇及其零件〕	7	6	130	13/	13	千克	/		26	4.6/4.6
8414.9090		---其他										
8414.9090	10	分子泵(气体离心机的静态部件,专门设计或制造的内部有已加工或挤压的螺纹槽和已加工的腔的泵体)[T2]	7	4	30	13/	13	千克	3/		24	4.6/4.6
8414.9090	90	税目 84.14 其他未列名零件〔101 其它风机及其零件,102 其它电扇及其零件,103 其它空气压缩机(站)及零件〕	7	4	30	13/	13	千克	/		24	4.6/4.6
84.15		**空气调节器,装有电扇及调温、调湿装置,包括不能单独调湿的空调器:**										
		-窗式、壁式、置于天花板或地板上的,独立的或分体的:										
8415.1010		---独立式〔999〕	8		130	13/	13	台/千克	A/	LM	28	5.2/5.2
		---分体式:										
8415.1021		----制冷量不超过 4000 大卡/时〔999〕	8		130	13/	13	台/千克	A/	LM	28	5.2/5.2
8415.1022		----制冷量超过 4000 大卡/时										

协定税率 %								RCEP		特惠税率 %			Article Description
东/冰/格	巴基斯坦	韩国	瑞士上/下	哥/秘/柬	澳/毛	新西/坡/智	中国港/澳/台	东盟及马来/澳/韩	日/新	亚太2国	老/柬/缅	98/97/95	
0/0/0	2	2	0/0	0/0/0	0/0	0/0/0	0/0/	0/0/9	9.1/0		0//	0/0/0	Other gas tight biosafety cabinets (meet the biosafety level III standard stipulated by the World Health Organization, and the maximum side length of the cover is ≤ 12cm)
													---Other
0/0/0	0	0	2.9/2.9	0/0/0	0/0	0//0	0/0/0	0/0/0	6.6/0			0/0/0	Class III biosafety cabinet (with standards similar to class III biosafety cabinet, plane side length > 12cm)
0/0/0	0	0	2.9/2.9	0/0/0	0/0	0//0	0/0/0	0/0/0	6.6/0			0/0/0	Other gas tight biosafety cabinets (meet the biosafety level III standard stipulated by the World Health Organization, and the plane side length is > 12cm)
													-Other:
0/0/0	2	0	0/0	0/0/0	0/0	0//0	0/0/	0/0/0	7.3/0			0/0/0	---Free piston generators for gas turbines
0/0/0	0	1.4	0/0	0/0/0	0/0	0//0	0/0/	0/0/6.3	6.4/0			0/0/0	---CO_2 compressors
													---Supercharger for engines
0/0/0	0	3.2		0//0	0/0	0//0	0/0/	6.3/6.3/6.3	6.6/6.3			0/0/	Passenger car mechanical supercharger
0/0/0	0	3.2		0//0	0/0	0//0	0/0/	6.3/6.3/6.3	6.6/6.3			0/0/	Supercharger for engine
													---Air or other gas compressors:
0/0/0	0	0	2.9/2.9	0/0/0	0/0	0//0	0/0/0	0/0/0	6.6/0			0/0/0	----Screw air compressor
													----Other
0/0/0	0	0	2.9/2.9	0/0/0	0/0	0//0	0/0/0	0/0/0	6.6/0		//	0/0/0	When the suction pressure of the compressor is more than 6 kPa (UF3 / UF500) for a long time, it is designed as high as 6 kPa. The pressure ratio of the compressor is 10:1 or lower, and it is made of or protected by UF6 resistant material)
0/0/0	0	0	2.9/2.9	0/0/0	0/0	0//0	0/0/0	0/0/0	6.6/0		//	0/0/0	UF6 / carrier gas compressor for MLIS
0/0/0	0	0	2.9/2.9	0/0/0	0/0	0//0	0/0/0	0/0/0	6.6/0		//	0/0/0	Compressor with suction ≥ 56m3 / S (single stage, low pressure head centrifugal compressor for circulating hydrogen sulfide gas)
0/0/0	0	0	2.9/2.9	0/0/0	0/0	0//0	0/0/0	0/0/0	6.6/0		//	0/0/0	UF6 corrosion resistant compressor with suction ≥ 2m3 / min (axial centrifugal or positive displacement compressor, pressure ratio between 1.2:1 and 6:1)
0/0/0	0	0	2.9/2.9	0/0/0	0/0	0//0	0/0/0	0/0/0	6.6/0		//	0/0/0	Fuel cell supercharger
0/0/0	0	0	2.9/2.9	0/0/0	0/0	0//0	0/0/0	0/0/0	6.6/0		//	0/0/0	Centrifugal nitrogen compressor for aircraft
0/0/0	0	0	2.9/2.9	0/0/0	0/0	0//0	0/0/0	0/0/0	6.6/0		//	0/0/0	Other air and gas compressors
													---Other
0/0/0	0	0	2.9/2.9	0/0/0	0/0	0//0	0/0/0	0/0/0	6.6/0			0/0/0	Other movable (soft) isolation devices (with standards similar to level III biosafety cabinets)
0/0/0	0	0	2.9/2.9	0/0/0	0/0	0//0	0/0/0	0/0/0	6.6/0			0/0/0	Absorbing tower (subject to regulation of sensitive items)
0/0/0	0	0	2.9/2.9	0/0/0	0/0	0//0	0/0/0	0/0/0	6.6/0			0/0/0	Other HEPA closed cleaning equipment with fans (HEPA referring high efficiency particulate air filter.)
0/0/0	0	0	2.9/2.9	0/0/0	0/0	0//0	0/0/0	0/0/0	6.6/0		//	0/0/0	Fuel cell circulating pump
0/0/0	0	0	2.9/2.9	0/0/0	0/0	0//0	0/0/0	0/0/0	6.6/0			0/0/0	Other air pumps, air compressors and ventilating hoods(ventilating or recycling hoods incorporating fan, having a maximum horizontal side>120cm)
													-Parts:
													---Of the machines of subheadings No. 8414.3011 to 8414.3014 and 8414.3090:
0/0/0	2	0	0/0	0/0/0	0/0	0//0	0/0/	0/0/0	7.3/0		0//	0/0/0	----In take valve leaf or discharge valve leaf
0/0/0	2	0	0.8/0.8	0/0/0	0/0	0//0	0/0/0	0/0/0	7.5/0			0/0/0	----Other
0/0/0	4.2	2.4	1.2/1.2	0/0/0	0/0	0/0/0	0/0/0	0/0/10.8	10.9/0			0/0/0	---Of the machines of subheadings No. 8414.5110 to 8414.5199 and 8414.6000
													---Other
0/0/0	3.5	0	2.9/2.9	0/0/0	0/0	0//0	0/0/0	0/0/0	6.6/0			0/0/0	Molec ular pumpcstatic component of gas centrifuge, Specialized design and manufacture, interior has been processing extrusion screw groove and processing chamber of the pump body
0/0/0	3.5	0	2.9/2.9	0/0/0	0/0	0//0	0/0/0	0/0/0	6.6/0			0/0/0	Other parts ont listed in Heading No.84. 14
													Air conditioning machines, comprising a motor-driven fan and elements for changing the temperature and humidity, including those machines in which the humidity cannot be separately regulated:
													-Window, wall types, on the ceiling or floor, self-contained or "split-system":
0/0/0	0	3	1.5/1.5	0/0/0	0/0	0/0/0	0/0/	0/0/13.5	13.6/0			0/0/0	---Self-contained
													---Split-system:
0/0/0	0	3	1.5/1.5	0/0/0	0/0	0/0/0	0/0/	0/0/13.5	13.6/0			0/0/0	----Of a refrigerating effect not exceeding 4000 Cal per hour
													----Of a refrigerating effect exceeding 4000 Cal per hour

税则号列	货品名称〔CIQ扩展编码及品名－T2表示见附表2〕	最惠(%)	暂定税率	普通	增值/消费	出口退税	计量单位	监管条件/特殊证件	检验检疫	对美关税	亚太上/下
8415.1022 10	4000大卡/时＜制冷量≤12046大卡/时(14000W)分体式空调,窗式、壁式、置于天花板或地板上的(装有电扇及调温、调湿装置,包括不能单独调湿的空调器)〔999〕	8		90	13/	13	台/千克	A/	LM	28	5.2/5.2
8415.1022 90	其他制冷量＞12046大卡/时(14000W)分体式空调,窗式、壁式、置于天花板或地板上的(装有电扇及调温、调湿装置,包括不能单独调湿的空调器)〔999〕	8		90	13/	13	台/千克	A/	LM	28	5.2/5.2
8415.2000	-机动车辆上供人使用的[T2]	10		110	13/	13	台/千克	/		30	
	-其他:										
	--装有制冷装置及冷热循环换向阀(可逆式热泵)的:										
8415.8110	---制冷量不超过4000大卡/时[T2]	8		130	13/	13	台/千克	A/	LM	28	
8415.8120	---制冷量超过4000大卡/时										
8415.8120 01	4000大卡/时＜制冷量≤12046大卡/时(14000W)热泵式空调器(装有制冷装置及一个冷热循环换向阀的)[T2]	10		90	13/	13	台/千克	A/	LM	30	
8415.8120 90	其他制冷量＞12046大卡/时(14000W)热泵式空调器(装有制冷装置及一个冷热循环换向阀的)[T2]	10		90	13/	13	台/千克	A/	LM	30	
	--其他,装有制冷装置的:										
8415.8210	---制冷量不超过4000大卡/时[T2]	8		130	13/	13	台/千克	A/	LM	28	
8415.8220	---制冷量超过4000大卡/时										
8415.8220 01	4000大卡/时＜制冷量≤12046大卡/时(14000W)的其他空调(仅装有制冷装置,而无冷热循环装置的)[T2]	10		90	13/	13	台/千克	A/	LM	30	
8415.8220 90	其他制冷量＞12046大卡/时(14000W)的其他空调(仅装有制冷装置,而无冷热循环装置的)[T2]	10		90	13/	13	台/千克	A/	LM	30	
8415.8300	--未装有制冷装置的[T2]	8		90	13/	13	台/千克	/		28	
	-零件:										
8415.9010	---税号8415.1010、8415.1021、8415.8110及8415.8210所列设备的零件〔999〕	8	6	130	13/	13	千克	/		31	5.2/5.2
8415.9090	---其他〔999〕	8	6	90	13/	13	千克	/		26	5.2/5.2
84.16	**使用液体燃料、粉状固体燃料或气体燃料的炉用燃烧器;机械加煤机,包括其机械炉箅、机械出灰器及类似装置:**										
8416.1000	-使用液体燃料的炉用燃烧器〔999〕	10		35	13/	13	千克/台	6/		30	6.5/6.5
	-其他炉用燃烧器,包括复式燃烧器:										
	---气体的:										
8416.2011	----使用天然气的										
8416.2011 01	溴化锂空调用天然气燃烧机〔999〕	10	5	35	13/	13	千克/台	6/		25	
8416.2011 90	其他使用天然气的炉用燃烧器〔999〕	10		35	13/	13	千克/台	6/		30	
8416.2019	----其他〔999〕	10		35	13/	13	千克/台	6/		35	
8416.2090	---其他							6			
8416.2090 01	溴化锂空调用复式燃烧机〔999〕	10	5	35	13/	13	千克/台	6/		30	
8416.2090 90	其他使用粉状固体燃料炉用燃烧器(包括其他复式燃烧器)〔999〕	10		35	13/	13	千克/台	6/		35	
8416.3000	-机械加煤机,包括其机械炉箅、机械出灰器及类似装置〔101煤炭行业成套设备,102其他行业成套设备〕	8		35	13/	13	千克/台	6/			
8416.9000	-零件〔999〕	6		35	13/	13	千克	/		16	
84.17	**非电热的工业或实验室用炉及烘箱,包括焚烧炉:**										
8417.1000	-矿砂、黄铁矿或金属的焙烧、熔化或其他热处理用炉及烘箱〔999〕	10		35	13/	13	台/千克	6/		30	
8417.2000	-面包房用烤炉及烘箱,包括做饼干用的〔999〕	10		35	13/	13	台/千克	A/	R	20	
	-其他:										
8417.8010	---炼焦炉〔999〕	10		35	13/	13	台/千克	6/			
8417.8020	---放射性废物焚烧炉〔999〕	5		35	13/	13	台/千克	6/			3.5/3.5
8417.8030	---水泥回转窑〔999〕	10		35	13/	13	台/千克	/			7/7
8417.8040	---石灰石分解炉〔999〕	10		35	13/	13	台/千克	/			
8417.8050	---垃圾焚烧炉〔999〕	10	5	35	13/	13	台/千克	6/			
8417.8090	---其他										
8417.8090 10	平均温度＞1000℃的耐腐蚀焚烧炉(为销毁管制化学品或化学弹药用)〔999〕	10		35	13/	13	台/千克	36/		35	
8417.8090 20	热裂解炉〔999〕	10	5	35	13/	13	台/千克	6/		30	
8417.8090 90	其他非电热的工业用炉及烘箱(包括实验室用炉、烘箱和焚烧炉)〔999〕	10		35	13/	13	台/千克	6/		35	
	-零件:										
8417.9010	---海绵铁回转窑用〔999〕	7		35	13/	13	千克	/			4.9/4.9
8417.9020	---炼焦炉用〔999〕	7		35	13/	13	千克	/			4.9/4.9
8417.9090	---其他										
8417.9090 10	垃圾焚烧炉和放射性废物焚烧炉的零件〔999〕	7	5	35	13/	13	千克	/		25	

协定税率 %								RCEP		特惠税率 %			Article Description
东/冰/格	巴基斯坦	韩国	瑞士上/下	哥/秘/柬	澳/毛	新西/坡/智	中国港/澳/台	东盟及马来/澳/韩	日/新	亚太2国	老/柬/缅	98/97/95	
0/0/0	0	3	1.5/1.5	0/0/0	0/0	0/0/0	0/0/	0/0/13.5	13.6/0			0/0/0	Air conditioning machines, comprising a motor-driven fan and elements for changing the temperature and humidity, including those machines in which the humidity cannot be separately regulated , split-system , window or wall types, of a refrigerating effect exceeding 4000 Cal per hour, but not exceeding 12046 Cal(14000W) per hour
0/0/0	0	3	1.5/1.5	0/0/0	0/0	0/0/0	0/0/	0/0/13.5	13.6/0			0/0/0	Other air conditioning machines, including those machines in which the humidity cannot be separately regulated , split-system , window, wall types and On the ceiling or floor, of a refrigerating effect exceeding 12046 Cal per hour
5/0/0		12	2/2	0//0	0/0	0//0	0/0/	10/19.5/20	10/19.5			0/0/	-Of a kind used for persons, in motor vehicles
													-Other:
													--Incorporating a refrigerating unit and a valve for reversal of the cooling/heat cycle(reversible heat pumps):
0/0/0	8.4	3	1.5/1.5	0/0/0	0/0	0/0/0	0/0/	0/0/13.5	13.6/0			0/0/0	---Of a refirigerating effect not exceeding 4000 Cal per hour
													---Of a refrigerating effect exceeding 4000 Cal per hour
0/0/0		12	2/2	0/0/0	0/0	0/0/0	0/0/	19/19/20	/19			0/0/0	Heat pump type air conditioner, 4000Cal/hour<refirigerating effect≤12046Cal/hour(incorporating a refrigerating unit and a valve for reversal of the cooling/beat cycle)
0/0/0		12	2/2	0/0/0	0/0	0/0/0	0/0/	19/19/20	/19			0/0/0	Other heat pump type air conditioner, refirigerating effect>12046Cal/hour(incorporating a refrigerating unit and a valve for reversal of the cooling/beat cycle)
													--Other, incorporating a refrigerating unit:
0/0/0	8.4		1.5/1.5	0/0/0	0/0	0/0/0	0/0/	8/8/	/8			0/0/0	---Of a refrigerating effect not exceeding 4000 Cal per hour
													---Of a refrigerating effect exceeding 4000 Cal per hour
0/0/0			2/2	0/0/0	0/0	0/0/0	0/0/	5/5/	/5			0/0/0	Other air conditioner, 4000Cal/hour<refirigerating effect≤12046Cal/hour, incorporating a refrigerating unit, No thermal cycling device
0/0/0			2/2	0/0/0	0/0	0/0/0	0/0/	5/5/	/5			0/0/0	Other air conditioner, refirigerating effect>12046Cal/hour, incorporating a refrigerating unit, No thermal cycling device
0/0/0	2	2	0/0	0/0/0	0/0	0/0/0	0/0/	0/0/9	9.1/0			0/0/0	--Not incorporating a refrigerating unit
													-Parts:
0/0/0	4	2	0/0	0/0/0	0/0	0/0/0	0/0/	9/9/9	9.1/9			0/0/0	---Of the machines of subheading No.8415. 1010, 8415. 1021, 8415. 8110 and 8415. 8210
0/0/0	2	2	0/0	0/0/0	0/0	0/0/0	0/0/0	0/0/9	9.4/0			0/0/0	---Other
													Furnace burners for liquid fuel, for pulverzied solid fuel or for gas; mechanical stokers, including their mechanical grates, mechanical ash dischargers and similar appliances:
0/0/0	2	2	0/0	0/0/0	0/0	0/0/0	0/0/	0/0/9	9.1/0			0/0/0	-Furnace burners for liquid fuel
													-Other furnace burners, including combination burners:
													---For gas:
													----Of using natural gas
0/0/0	3.5	2.1	1.1/1.1	0/0/0	0/0	0/0/0	0/0/	0/0/9.5	9.5/0			0/0/0	Natural gas burners for lithium bromide air conditioners
0/0/0	3.5	2.1	1.1/1.1	0/0/0	0/0	0/0/0	0/0/	0/0/9.5	9.5/0			0/0/0	Other natural gas furnace burners
0/0/0	3.5	2.1	1.1/1.1	0/0/0	0/0	0/0/0	0/0/	0/0/9.5	9.5/0			0/0/0	----Other
													---Other
0/0/0	3.5	2.1	0/0	0/0/0	0/0	0/0/0	0/0/	0/0/9.5	9.5/0			0/0/0	Combination burners for lithium bromide air conditioner
0/0/0	3.5	2.1	0/0	0/0/0	0/0	0/0/0	0/0/	0/0/9.5	9.5/0			0/0/0	Other furnace burners for pulverzied solid fuel(including other combination burners)
0/0/0	2	0	0/0	0/0/0	0/0	0//0	0/0/	0/0/0	7.6/0			0/0/0	-Mechanical stokers, including their mechanical grates, mechanical ash dischargers and similar appliances
0/0/0	0	0	0/0	0/0/0	0/0	0//0	0/0/	0/0/0	0/0			0/0/0	-Parts
													Industrial or laboratory furnaces and ovens, including incinerators, non-electric:
0/0/0	2	2	0/0	0/0/0	0/0	0/0/0	0/0/	9/9/9	9.1/9			0/0/0	-Furnaces and ovens for the roasting, melting or other heat-treatment of ores, pyrites or of metals
0/0/0	2	2	0/0	0/0/0	0/0	0//0	0/0/	0/0/9	9.1/0			0/0/0	-Bakery ovens, including biscuit ovens
													-Other:
0/0/0	2	2	0/0	0/0/0	0/0	0//0	0/0/	0/0/9	9.1/0			0/0/0	---Coke ovens
0/0/0	0	0	0/0	0/0/0	0/0	0//0	0/0/	0/0/0	0/0			0/0/0	---Burn furnaces for radioactive waste
0/0/0	2	2	0/0	0/0/0	0/0	0/0/0	0/0/	0/0/9	9.1/0			0/0/0	---Cement rotary kilns
0/0/0	2	2	0/0	0/0/0	0/0	0//0	0/0/	0/0/9	9.1/0			0/0/0	---Limestone decomposition furnace
0/0/0	2	6	2.5/2.5	0/0/0	0/0	0/0/0	0/0/0	0/0/9.3	9.1/0			0/0/0	---Refuse incinerator
													---Other
0/0/0	3.5	6	2.5/2.5	0/0/0	0/0	0/0/0	0/0/0	9.5/9.5/10	9.5/9.5			0/0/0	Corrosion-resisting incinerators, average temperature > 1000℃ (for incinerating controlled chemicals or chemical ammunitions)
0/0/0	3.5	6	2.5/2.5	0/0/0	0/0	0/0/0	0/0/0	9.5/9.5/10	9.5/9.5			0/0/0	Thermal cracking furnace
0/0/0	3.5	6	2.5/2.5	0/0/0	0/0	0/0/0	0/0/0	9.5/9.5/10	9.5/9.5			0/0/0	Other non-electric industrial furnaces and ovens(including laboratory furnaces, ovens and incinerators)
													-Parts:
0/0/0	2	0	0/0	0/0/0	0/0	0//0	0/0/	0/0/0	6.4/0			0/0/0	---For sponge iron rotary kiln
0/0/0	2	0	0/0	0/0/0	0/0	0//0	0/0/	0/0/0	6.4/0			0/0/0	For coke ovens
													---Other
0/0/0	2	0	0.7/0.7	0/0/0	0/0	0//0	0/0/	0/0/0	6.4/0			0/0/0	Furnace and radioactive waste incinerator waste incineration parts

税则号列	货品名称〔CIQ扩展编码及品名－T2表示见附表2〕	最惠(%)	暂定税率	普通	增值/消费	出口退税	计量单位	监管条件/特殊证件	检验检疫	对美关税	亚太上/下
8417.9090 90	其他非电热工业用炉及烘箱的零件(包括实验室用炉及烘箱的零件和焚烧炉零件)〔999〕	7		35	13/	13	千克	/		27	
84.18	**电气或非电气的冷藏箱、冷冻箱及其他制冷设备;热泵,但税目84.15的空气调节器除外:**										
	-冷藏-冷冻组合机,各自装有单独外门或抽屉,或其组合的:										
8418.1010	---容积超过500升[T2]	9		100	13/	13	台/千克	A/	LM	34	
8418.1020	---容积超过200升,但不超过500升[T2]	8		130	13/	13	台/千克	A/	LM	33	
8418.1030	---容积不超过200升[T2]	8		130	13/	13	台/千克	A/	LM	18	
	-家用型冷藏箱:										
	--压缩式:										
8418.2110	---容积超过150升[T2]	8		130	13/	13	台/千克	A/	LMR	33	
8418.2120	---容积超过50升,但不超过150升[T2]	8		130	13/	13	台/千克	A/	LMR	33	5.2/5.2
8418.2130	---容积不超过50升[T2]	8		130	13/	13	台/千克	A/	LMR	18	5.2/5.2
	--其他:										
8418.2910	---半导体制冷式〔999〕	8		130	13/	13	台/千克	A/	LMR		
8418.2920	---电气吸收式[T2]	8		130	13/	13	台/千克	A/	LR	13	
8418.2990	---其他〔999〕	8		130	13/	13	台/千克	A/	LMR		
	-柜式冷冻箱,容积不超过800升:										
8418.3010	---制冷温度在-40℃及以下〔999〕	9		50	13/	13	台/千克	A/	ML	14	
	---制冷温度在-40℃以上:										
8418.3021	----容积超过500升〔999〕	9		100	13/	13	台/千克	A/	L	29	
8418.3029	----其他〔999〕	8		130	13/	13	台/千克	A/	LM	28	
	-立式冷冻箱,容积不超过900升:										
8418.4010	---制冷温度在-40℃及以下〔999〕	9		50	13/	13	台/千克	A/	ML	14	
	---制冷温度在-40℃以上:										
8418.4021	----容积超过500升〔999〕	9		100	13/	13	台/千克	A/	L	14	6.3/6.3
8418.4029	----其他〔999〕	8		130	13/	13	台/千克	A/	LM	28	
8418.5000	-装有冷藏或冷冻装置的其他设备(柜、箱、展示台、陈列箱及类似品)用于存储及展示[T2]	9		100	13/	13	台/千克	A/	LM	19	
	-其他制冷设备;热泵:										
	--热泵,税目84.15的空气调节器除外:										
8418.6120	---压缩式										
8418.6120 10	压缩式制冷机组的热泵(介质为氢、氦的可冷却到≤23K且排热>150W)〔999〕	9		90	13/	13	台/千克	3/		34	5.9/5.9
8418.6120 90	其他压缩式热泵,税目84.15的空气调节器除外〔999〕	9		90	13/	13	台/千克	/		34	5.9/5.9
8418.6190	---其他〔999〕	9		130	13/	13	台/千克	/		34	4.5/4.5
	--其他:										
8418.6920	---制冷机组										
8418.6920 10	其他压缩式制冷设备(介质为氢或氦,可冷却到≤23K且排热>150W)〔999〕	9		90	13/	13	台/千克	3/		34	5.9/5.9
8418.6920 90	其他制冷机组〔999〕	9		90	13/	13	台/千克	/		34	5.9/5.9
8418.6990	---其他										
8418.6990 10	带制冷装置的发酵罐(不发散气溶胶,且容积大于20升)〔999〕	9		130	13/	13	台/千克	3/		14	5.9/5.9
8418.6990 20	制冰机、冰激凌机[T2]	9		130	13/	13	台/千克	/		14	5.9/5.9
8418.6990 90	其他制冷设备〔999〕	9		130	13/	13	台/千克	/		14	5.9/5.9
	-零件:										
8418.9100	--冷藏或冷冻设备专用的特制家具〔999〕	9		130	13/	13	千克	/		34	5.9/5.9
	--其他:										
8418.9910	---制冷机组及热泵用〔999〕	9	6	90	13/	13	千克	/		16	
	---其他:										
8418.9991	----制冷温度在-40℃及以下的冷冻设备用〔999〕	9	6	50	13/	13	千克	/		11	
8418.9992	----制冷温度在-40℃以上,但容积超过500升的冷藏或冷冻设备用〔999〕	9	6	100	13/	13	千克	/		31	
8418.9999	----其他										
8418.9999 10	耐腐蚀冷凝器(20平方米>换热面积>0.15平方米)〔999〕	9	6	130	13/	13	千克	3/		11	
8418.9999 90	税目84.18其他制冷设备用零件〔999〕	9	6	130	13/	13	千克	/		11	
84.19	**利用温度变化处理材料的机器、装置及类似的实验室设备,例如,加热、烹煮、烘炒、蒸馏、精馏、消毒、灭菌、汽蒸、干燥、蒸发、气化、冷凝、冷却的机器设备,不论是否电热的(不包括税目85.14的炉、烘箱及其他设备),但家用的除外;非电热的快速热水器或贮备式热水器:**										

协定税率 %								RCEP		特惠税率 %			Article Description
东/冰/格	巴基斯坦	韩国	瑞士上/下	哥/秘/柬	澳/毛	新西/坡/智	中国港/澳/台	东盟及马来/澳/韩	日/新	亚太2国	老/柬/缅	98/97/95	
0/0/0	2	0	0.7/0.7	0/0/0	0/0	0//0	0/0/	0/0/0	6.4/0			0/0/0	Other electric industrial stove and oven parts (including laboratory parts and incinerator parts) from the stove and oven
													Refrigerators, freezers and other refrigerating or freezing equipment, electric or other; heat pumps other than air conditioning machines of headingNo.84. 15:
													-Combined refrigerator—freezers, fitted with separate external doors or drawers, or combinations thereof:
0/0/0	0	6	0/0	0/0/0	0/0	0/0/0	0/0/	9/9.5/10	9.1/9.5			0/0/0	---Of a capacity exceeding 500 L
0/0/0	0	3	1.5/1.5	0/0/0	0/0	0/0/0	0/0/	13.5/13.5/13.5	13.6/13.5			0/0/0	---Of a capacity exceeding 200 L,not exceeding 500 L
0/0/0	0		1.5/1.5	0/0/0	0/0	0/0/0	0/0/	8/8/	/8			0/0/0	---Of a capacity not exceeding 200 L
													-Refrigerators, household type:
													--Compression-type:
0/0/0	0	2	0/0	0/0/0	0/0	0/0/0	0/0/	0/0/9	9.1/0			0/0/0	---Of a capacity exceeding 150 L
0/0/0	0	2	0/0	0/0/0	0/0	0/0/0	0/0/	0/0/9	9.1/0			0/0/0	---Of a capacity exceeding 50 L,not exceeding 150 L
0/0/0	0	2	0/0	0/0/0	0/0	0/0/0	0/0/	0/0/9	9.1/0			0/0/0	---Of a capacity not exceeding 50 L
													--Other:
0/0/0			3/3	0/0/0	0/18	0/0/0	0/0/	5/5/	/5			0/0/0	---Semiconductor freezing type
0/0/0	8.4	3	1.5/1.5	0/0/0	0/0	0/0/0	0/0/	0/0/13.5	13.6/0			0/0/0	---Absorption-type, electrical
0/0/0			3/3	0/0/0	0/18	0/0/0	0/0/	8/8/	/8			0/0/0	---Other
													-Freezers of the chest type, not exceeding 800L capacity:
0/0/0	2		0/0	0/0/0	0/0	0//0	0/0/	5/5/	/5			0/0/0	---Of a refrigerating temperature of -40℃ or lower
													---Of a refrigerating temperature higher than -40℃:
0/0/0	18.4	13.8	2.3/2.3	0/0/0	0/13.8	0/0/0	0/0/	0/21.9/23	0/21.9			0/0/0	----Of a capacity exceeding 500 L
0/0/0			8/8	0/0/0	0/18	0/0/0	0/0/	8/8/	/8			0/0/0	----Other
													-Freezers of the upright type, not exceeding 900L capacity:
0/0/0	2		0/0	0/0/0	0/0	0//0	0/0/	5/5/	/5			0/0/0	---Of a refrigerating temperature of -40℃ or lower
													---Of a refrigerating temperature higher than -40℃:
0/0/0	8.4		1.5/1.5	0/0/0	0/0	0/0/0	0/0/	5/5/	/5			0/0/0	----Of a capacity exceeding 500 L
0/0/0	0			0/0/0	0/18	0/0/0	0/0/	8/8/	/8			0/0/0	----Other
0/0/0	2	2	0/0	0/0/0	0/0	0/0/0	0/0/	0/0/9	9.1/0			0/0/0	-Other furniture (chests,cabinets,display counters,show cases and the like)for storage and display,incorporating refrigerating or freeezing equipment
													-Other refrigerating or freezing equipment;heat pumps:
													--Heat pumps other than air conditioning madimes of heading 84. 15:
													---Compression-type
0/0/0	2	2	0/0	0/0/0	0/0	0/0/0	0/0/	0/0/9	9.1/0			0/0/0	Hot pump for compression-type refrigerating units(medium being hydrogen or helium, and can be cooled to temperature ≤23K, and remove heat >150W)
0/0/0	2	2	0/0	0/0/0	0/0	0/0/0	0/0/	0/0/9	9.1/0			0/0/0	Other compression-type hot pumps,excluding air conditioning machines listed in heading No. 84. 15
0/0/0	4.9	3	1.5/1.5	0/0/0	0/0	0/0/0	0/0/	0/0/13.5	13.6/0			0/0/0	---Other
													--Other:
													---Refigerating units
0/0/0	3.5	2	0/0	0/0/0	0/0	0/0/0	0/0/	0/0/9	9.1/0			0/0/0	Other compression-type refrigerating equipment(medium being hydrogen or helium, and can be cooled to temperature ≤ 23K, and remove heat >150W)
0/0/0	3.5	2	0/0	0/0/0	0/0	0/0/0	0/0/	0/0/9	9.1/0			0/0/0	Other refrigerating units
													---Other
0/0/0	2	2	1/1	0/0/0	0/0	0/0/0	0/0/	9/9/9	9.1/9			0/0/0	Fermenters with refrigeration appliances(not divergent aerosol,capacity> 20L)
0/0/0	2	2	1/1	0/0/0	0/0	0/0/0	0/0/	9/9/9	9.1/9			0/0/0	Ice-making machine,ice cream machine
0/0/0	2	2	1/1	0/0/0	0/0	0/0/0	0/0/	9/9/9	9.1/9			0/0/0	Other refrigrating equipments
													-Parts:
0/0/0	14.4	3.6	1.8/1.8	0/0/0	0/0	0/0/0	0/0/	0/0/16.2	16.4/0			0/0/0	--Furniture designed to receive refrigerating or freezing equipment
													--Other:
0/0/0	2	2	0/0	0/0/0	0/0	0/0/0	0/0/	0/0/9	9.1/0			0/0/0	---Of refrigerating units and heat pumps
													---Other:
0/0/0	2	0	0/0	0/0/0	0/0	0//0	0/0/	0/0/0	8.6/0			0/0/0	----Of freezing equipment of a refrigerating temperature of -40℃ or lower
0/0/0	2	2	0/0	0/0/0	0/0	0//0	0/0/	0/0/9	9.1/0			0/0/0	----Of refrigerating or freezing equipment of a refrigerating temperature higher than-40℃ and a capacity exceeding 500 L
													----Other
0/0/0	4	2	0/0	0/0/0	0/0	0/0/0	0/0/	9/9/9	9.1/9			0/0/0	Corrosion-resisting condensers ($20m^2$>area of heat-exchange >$0.15m^2$)
0/0/0	4	2	0/0	0/0/0	0/0	0/0/0	0/0/	9/9/9	9.1/9			0/0/0	Parts of other refrigerating equipment of heading No.84. 18
													Machinery, plant or laboratory equipment, whether or not electrically heated(excluding furnaces, ovens and other equipment of headingNo.85. 14), for the treatment of materials by a process involving a change of temperature such as heating, cooking, roasting, distilling, rectifying, sterilizing, pasteurizing, steaming, drying, evaporating, vaporizing, condensing or cooling, other than machinery or plant of a kind used for domestic purposes; instantaneous or storage water heaters, non-electric:

税则号列	货品名称〔CIQ扩展编码及品名－T2表示见附表2〕	最惠(%)	暂定税率	普通	增值/消费	出口退税	计量单位	监管条件/特殊证件	检验检疫	对美关税	亚太上/下
	-非电热的快速热水器或贮备式热水器：										
8419.1100	--燃气快速热水器〔999〕	8		100	13/	13	台/千克	A/	ML	33	
8419.1200	--太阳能热水器〔999〕	8	5	100	13/	13	台/千克	A/	LM	10	6.4/6.4
8419.1900	--其他〔101 燃气热水器，102 其他非电热热水器及其零件〕	8		100	13/	13	台/千克	A/	M	13	
8419.2000	-医用或实验室用消毒器具〔999〕	4		30	13/	13	台/千克	A/	M	24	
	-干燥器：										
	--冷冻干燥装置、冷冻干燥单元和喷雾式干燥器：										
8419.3310	---农产品干燥用〔999〕	8		30	9/	9,13	台/千克	A/	M	33	
8419.3320	---木材、纸浆、纸或纸板干燥用〔999〕	9		30	13/	13	台/千克	A/	M	34	
8419.3390	---其他										
8419.3390 10	其他冻干设备(10≤24小时凝冰量≤1000千克，并可蒸汽消毒)〔999〕	9		30	13/	13	台/千克	3A/	M	29	4.5/4.5
8419.3390 20	冷冻或喷雾式烟丝烘干机〔999〕	9		30	13/	13	台/千克	O/		29	4.5/4.5
8419.3390 30	其他冷冻或喷雾式干燥箱(具有与三级生物安全柜类似标准)〔999〕	9		30	13/	13	台/千克	3/		29	4.5/4.5
8419.3390 50	冷冻或喷雾式污泥干燥机〔999〕	9	5	30	13/	13	台/千克	/		25	4.5/4.5
8419.3390 90	其他冷冻干燥装置、冷冻干燥单元和喷雾式干燥器〔999〕	9		30	13/	13	台/千克	/		29	4.5/4.5
8419.3400	--其他，农产品干燥用〔999〕	8		30	9/	9,13	台/千克	A/	M	33	
8419.3500	--其他，木材、纸浆、纸或纸板干燥用〔999〕	9		30	13/	13	台/千克	A/	M	34	
	--其他：										
8419.3910	---微空气流动陶瓷坯件干燥器〔999〕	9		30	13/	13	台/千克	/			4.5/4.5
8419.3990	---其他										
8419.3990 20	其他烟丝烘干机〔999〕	9		30	13/	13	台/千克	O/		29	4.5/4.5
8419.3990 30	其他干燥箱(具有与三级生物安全柜类似标准)〔999〕	9		30	13/	13	台/千克	3/		29	4.5/4.5
8419.3990 40	生产奶粉用其他干燥器〔999〕	9	4	30	13/	13	台/千克	A/	M	24	4.5/4.5
8419.3990 50	其他污泥干燥机(冷冻式、喷雾式除外)〔999〕	9	5	30	13/	13	台/千克	/		25	4.5/4.5
8419.3990 90	其他用途的干燥器〔999〕	9		30	13/	13	台/千克	/		29	4.5/4.5
	-蒸馏或精馏设备：										
8419.4010	---提净塔〔999〕	10		30	13/	13	台/千克	A/	R	35	
8419.4020	---精馏塔〔999〕	10		30	13/	13	台/千克	A/	R	35	
8419.4090	---其他										
8419.4090 10	氢－低温蒸馏塔(温度≤－238℃，压力为0.5-5兆帕，内径≥1米等条件)〔999〕	10		30	13/	13	台/千克	3/		35	
8419.4090 20	耐腐蚀蒸馏塔(内径大于0.1米，接触表面由特殊耐腐蚀材料制成)〔999〕	10		30	13/	13	台/千克	3/		35	
8419.4090 90	其他蒸馏或精馏设备〔999〕	10		30	13/	13	台/千克	/		35	
8419.5000	-热交换装置										
8419.5000 10	热交换器(专用于核反应堆的一次冷却剂回路的)〔101 螺旋板式交换器，102 其它热交换装置〕	10		30	13/	13	台/千克	3/		20	6.5/6.5
8419.5000 20	蒸汽发生器(专用于核反应堆内生成的热量输送到进水以产生蒸汽的)〔999〕	10		30	13/	13	台/千克	3/		20	6.5/6.5
8419.5000 30	冷却UF6的热交换器(专门设计或制造的用耐UF6材料制成或保护的热交换器，在压差为100kPa下渗透压力变化率小于10Pa/h)〔999〕	10		30	13/	13	台/千克	3/		20	6.5/6.5
8419.5000 40	冷却气体用热交换器(用耐 UF_6 腐蚀材料制成或加以保护的)〔999〕	10		30	13/	13	台/千克	3/		20	6.5/6.5
8419.5000 50	耐腐蚀热交换器(0.15平方米<换热面积<20平方米)〔999〕	10		30	13/	13	台/千克	3A/	M	20	6.5/6.5
8419.5000 60	用氟聚合物制造的、入口管和出口管内径不超过3厘米的热交换装置〔999〕	0		30	13/	13	台/千克	A/	M	10	6.5/6.5
8419.5000 90	其他热交换装置〔101 废热锅炉，102 螺旋板式交换器，103 其它热交换装置〕	10		30	13/	13	台/千克	A/	M	20	6.5/6.5
	-液化空气或其他气体的机器：										
	---制氧机：										
8419.6011	----制氧量在15000立方米/小时及以上〔999〕	12		30	13/	13	台/千克	A/	M		
8419.6019	----其他〔999〕	13		30	13/	13	台/千克	A/	M	18	
8419.6090	---其他										
8419.6090 10	液化器(将来自级联的UF6气体压缩并冷凝成液态UF6)〔999〕	10		30	13/	13	台/千克	3/		15	
8419.6090 20	通过冷凝分离和去除污染物的气体液化设备〔101 其它液化空气或其它气体用的机器，102 其它液化空气或气体用的机器及其零件〕	10	5	30	13/	13	台/千克	A/	M	10	
8419.6090 90	其他液化空气或其他气体用的机器〔101 其它液化空气或其它气体用的机器，102 其它液化空气或气体用的机器及其零件〕	10		30	13/	13	台/千克	A/	M	15	
	-其他机器设备：										
8419.8100	--加工热饮料或烹调、加热食品用〔999〕	10	6	30	13/	13	台/千克	A/	LMR	16	
	--其他：										
8419.8910	---加氢反应器〔999〕	0		30	13/	13	台/千克	/		5	
8419.8990	---其他										
8419.8990 10	带加热装置的发酵罐(不发散气溶胶，且容积大于20升)〔999〕	0		30	13/	13	台/千克	3A/	M	20	

协定税率 %								RCEP		特惠税率 %			Article Description
东/冰/格	巴基斯坦	韩国	瑞士上/下	哥/秘/柬	澳/毛	新西/坡/智	中国港/澳/台	东盟及马来/澳/韩	日/新	亚太2国	老/柬/缅	98/97/95	
													-Instantaneous or storage water heaters, non-electric:
0/0/0	28	21	8/8	0/0/0	0/21	0/0/0	0/0/	33.3/33.3/35	/33.3			0/0/0	--Instantaneous gas water heaters
0/0/0	28		3.5/3.5	0/0/0	0/21	0/0/0	0/0/0	0/0/31.5	31.8/0			0/0/0	--Solar water heaters
0/0/0			8/8	0/0/0	0/21	0/0/0	0/0/0	5/5/	/5			0/0/0	--Other
0/0/0	0	0	0/0	0/0/0	0/0	0//0	0/0/	0/0/0	0/0			0/0/0	-Medical, surgical or laboratory sterilizers
													-Dryers:
													--Lyophilisation apparatus, freeze drying units and spray dryers:
0/0/0	2	1.6	0/0	0/0/0	0/0	0//0	0/0/	0/0/7.2	7.3/0		0//	0/0/0	---For agricultural products
0/0/0	2	0	0/0	0/0/0	0/0	0//0	0/0/0	0/0/0	8.2/0		0//	0/0/0	---For wood, paper pulp, paper or paperboard
													---Other
0/0/0	1.8	1.8	0/0	0/0/0	0/0	0//0	0/0/0	0/0/8.1	8.2/0			0/0/0	Other freeze－drying equipment (1 ≤ 24h ice coagulation ≤ 1kg, and steam disinfection)
0/0/0	1.8	1.8	0/0	0/0/0	0/0	0//0	0/0/0	0/0/8.1	8.2/0			0/0/0	Freezing or spray tobacco drying machine
0/0/0	1.8	1.8	0/0	0/0/0	0/0	0//0	0/0/0	0/0/8.1	8.2/0			0/0/0	Other refrigerated or spray drying boxes (similar to those of grade three biosafety cabinets)
0/0/0	1.8	1.8	0/0	0/0/0	0/0	0//0	0/0/0	0/0/8.1	8.2/0			0/0/0	Freeze or spray dryer for sludge
0/0/0	1.8	1.8	0/0	0/0/0	0/0	0//0	0/0/0	0/0/8.1	8.2/0			0/0/0	Other freeze－drying equipment, freeze drying unit and spray dryer.
0/0/0	2	1.6	0/0	0/0/0	0/0	0//0	0/0/	0/0/7.2	7.3/0		0//	0/0/0	--Other,or agricultural products
0/0/0	2	0	0/0	0/0/0	0/0	0//0	0/0/0	0/0/0	8.2/0		0//	0/0/0	--Other, for wood, paper pulp, paper or paperboard
													--Other:
0/0/0	1.8	0	0/0	0/0/0	0/0	0//0	0/0/	0/0/0	8.2/0			0/0/0	---Breeze pottery blanks dryers
													---Other
0/0/0	1.8	1.8	0/0	0/0/0	0/0	0//0	0/0/0	0/0/8.1	8.2/0			0/0/0	Other cut tobacco dryer
0/0/0	1.8	1.8	0/0	0/0/0	0/0	0//0	0/0/0	0/0/8.1	8.2/0			0/0/0	Other drying ovens (with standards similar to level III biosafety cabinet)
0/0/0	1.8	1.8	0/0	0/0/0	0/0	0//0	0/0/0	0/0/8.1	8.2/0			0/0/0	Other dryers for milk powder production
0/0/0	1.8	1.8	0/0	0/0/0	0/0	0//0	0/0/0	0/0/8.1	8.2/0			0/0/0	Other sludge driers (except refrigerated and spray type)
0/0/0	1.8	1.8	0/0	0/0/0	0/0	0//0	0/0/0	0/0/8.1	8.2/0			0/0/0	Dryers for other use
													-Distilling or rectifying plant:
0/0/0	2	2	0/0	0/0/0	0/0	0/0/0	0/0/	0/0/9	9.1/0			0/0/0	---Stripping towers
0/0/0	2	2	0/0	0/0/0	0/0	0/0/0	0/0/	0/0/9	9.1/0			0/0/0	---Rectifying towers
													---Other
0/0/0	2	2	0/0	0/0/0	0/0	0/0/0	0/0/	0/0/9	9.1/0			0/0/0	Hydrogen-low temperature distilling towers (temperature≤-238℃, pressure=0.5MPa～5MPa, inside diameter≥1m)
0/0/0	2	2	0/0	0/0/0	0/0	0/0/0	0/0/	0/0/9	9.1/0			0/0/0	Corrosion-resisten distilling towers (inside diameter>0.1m, with a contact surface of special corrosion-resisten materials)
0/0/0	2	2	0/0	0/0/0	0/0	0/0/0	0/0/	0/0/9	9.1/0			0/0/0	Other distillation or rectification equipment
													-Heat exchange units
0/0/0	0	0	2.5/2.5	0/0/0	0/0	0/0/0	0/0/0	0/0/0	9.4/0		0//	0/0/0	Heat exchanger(used exclusively for nuclear reactor primary coolant loop)
0/0/0	0	0	2.5/2.5	0/0/0	0/0	0/0/0	0/0/0	0/0/0	9.4/0		0//	0/0/0	Steam generators(used exclusively to transmit the heat generated within nuclear reactors to the inlet to produce vapors)
0/0/0	0	0	2.5/2.5	0/0/0	0/0	0/0/0	0/0/0	0/0/0	9.4/0		0//	0/0/0	Heat exchangers for cooling UF_6 (rate of change of osmotic pressure change rate <10Pa/h under differential pressure of less than 100kPa)
0/0/0	0	0	2.5/2.5	0/0/0	0/0	0/0/0	0/0/0	0/0/0	9.4/0		0//	0/0/0	Heat exchangers for cooling gases (made of or protected with UF_6-resistant materials)
0/0/0	0	0	2.5/2.5	0/0/0	0/0	0/0/0	0/0/0	0/0/0	9.4/0		0//	0/0/0	Corrosion-resisting heat exchangers ($20m^2$ >area of heat-exchange area>$0.15m^2$)
0/0/0	0	0	2.5/2.5	0/0/0	0/0	0/0/0	0/0/0	0/0/0	9.4/0		0//	0/0/0	Heat exchange device,made of fluoropolymer, inlet pipe and outlet pipe inner diameter not exceeding 3 cm
0/0/0	0	0	2.5/2.5	0/0/0	0/0	0/0/0	0/0/0	0/0/0	9.4/0		0//	0/0/0	Other heat exchange devices
													-Machinery for liquefying air or other gases:
													---Oxygen producers:
0/0/0	4.2	2.4	1.2/1.2	0/0/0	0/0	0/0/0	0/0/	0/0/10.8	10.9/0			0/0/0	----Oxygen preparation volume no less than $15000m^3/h$
0/0/0	4.6	2.6	1.3/1.3	0/0/0	0/0	0/0/0	0/0/	0/0/11.7	11.8/0			0/0/0	----Other
													---Other
0/0/0	2	2	0/0	0/0/0	0/0	0/0/0	0/0/	9/9/9	9.1/9			0/0/0	Liquefiers (to compress and condense gaseous UF_6 from cascade into liquefied UF_6)
0/0/0	2	2	0/0	0/0/0	0/0	0/0/0	0/0/	9/9/9	9.1/9			0/0/0	Through the gas condensate separation and pollutants removal of liquefaction equipment
0/0/0	2	2	0/0	0/0/0	0/0	0/0/0	0/0/	9/9/9	9.1/9			0/0/0	Other machinery for liquefying air or other gases
													-Other machinery, plant and equipment:
0/0/0	3.5	2	0/0	0/0/0	0/0	0/0/0	0/0/	9/9/9	9.1/9		0//	0/0/0	--For making hot drinks of for cooking or heating food
													--Other:
0/0/0	0	0	0/0	0/0/0	0/0	0//0	0/0/	0/0/0	0/0		0//	0/0/0	---Hydroformer vessels
													---Other
0/0/0	0	0	0/0	0/0/0	0/0	0//0	0/0/	0/0/0	0/0		0//	0/0/0	Fermenter fitted with heat devices (not diverging aerosol, volume>20L)

税则号列	货品名称〔CIQ 扩展编码及品名—T2 表示见附表 2〕	最惠(%)	暂定税率	普通	增值/消费	出口退税	计量单位	监管条件/特殊证件	检验检疫	对美关税	亚太上/下
8419.8990 21	凝华器(或冷阱)(从扩散级联中取出 UF6 并可再蒸发转移)〔101 氨气提法二氧化碳气提塔等,102 其它利用温度变化处理材料的机器〕	0		30	13/	13	台/千克	3/		20	
8419.8990 22	低温制冷设备(能承受-120℃或更低的温度)〔101 氨气提法二氧化碳气提塔等,102 其它利用温度变化处理材料的机器〕	0		30	13/	13	台/千克	3A/	M	20	
8419.8990 23	UF6 冷阱(能冻结分离出 UF6 的冷阱)〔101 氨气提法二氧化碳气提塔等,102 其它利用温度变化处理材料的机器〕	0		30	13/	13	台/千克	3/		20	
8419.8990 90	其他利用温度变化处理材料的机器(包括类似的实验室设备)〔101 氨气提法二氧化碳气提塔等,102 其它利用温度变化处理材料的机器,103 非压力容器产品〕	0		30	13/	13	台/千克	A/	M	20	
	-零件:										
8419.9010	---热水器用〔999〕	0		100	13/	13	千克	/		25	
8419.9090	---其他〔999〕	4		30	13/	13	千克	/		24	
84.20	**研光机或其他滚压机器及其滚筒,但加工金属或玻璃用的除外:**										
8420.1000	-研光机或其他滚压机器										
8420.1000 01	织物轧光机〔999〕	8	6	30	13/	13	台/千克	/		31	
8420.1000 20	专门或主要用于印刷电路板基板或印刷电路制造的滚压机(加工金属或玻璃用的除外)〔999〕	0		30	13/	13	台/千克	/		25	
8420.1000 90	其他研光机或滚压机器(加工金属或玻璃用的除外)〔101 纺织行业成套设备,102 轻工行业成套设备,103 印刷行业成套设备,104 其他行业成套设备〕	8		30	13/	13	台/千克	/		33	
	-零件:										
8420.9100	--滚筒〔101 纺织行业成套设备,102 轻工行业成套设备,103 印刷行业成套设备,104 其他行业成套设备〕	8		30	13/	13	个/千克	/		33	
8420.9900	--其他〔999〕	8		30	13/	13	千克	/		28	
84.21	**离心机,包括离心干燥机;液体或气体的过滤、净化机器及装置:**										
	-离心机,包括离心干燥机:										
8421.1100	--奶油分离器〔999〕	8		30	13/	13	台/千克	A/	R		
	--干衣机:										
8421.1210	---干衣量不超过 10 千克〔101 干衣机 I 类器具,102 干衣机 II 类器具,103 干衣机 III 类器具,104 干衣机 0I 类器具,105 干衣机 0 类器具〕	7		70	13/	13	台/千克	/	L	32	
8421.1290	---其他〔101 干衣机 I 类器具,102 干衣机 II 类器具,103 干衣机 III 类器具,104 干衣机 0I 类器具,105 干衣机 0 类器具〕	8		30	13/	13	台/千克	/		28	
	--其他:										
8421.1910	---脱水机〔999〕	10	6	30	13/	13	台/千克	/	L	31	
8421.1920	---固液分离机〔999〕	10		30	13/	13	台/千克	/		35	
8421.1990	---其他										
8421.1990 20	液-液离心接触器(为化学交换过程的铀浓缩而专门设计或制造的)〔999〕	10		30	13/	13	台/千克	3/		20	
8421.1990 30	离心分离器,包括倾析器(不发散气溶胶、可对致病性微生物进行连续分离的)〔999〕	10		30	13/	13	台/千克	3/		20	
8421.1990 90	其他离心机及离心干燥机〔101 其它干燥器及其零件,102 其他离心机及类似装置及其零件〕	10		30	13/	13	台/千克	/		20	
	-液体的过滤、净化机器及装置:										
	--过滤或净化水用:										
8421.2110	---家用型[T2]	7	5	63	13/	13	台/千克	A/	R	20	4.6/4.6
	---其他:										
8421.2191	----船舶压载水处理设备〔999〕	5		50	13/	13	台/千克	/		30	3.3/3.3
8421.2199	----其他										
8421.2199 10	喷灌设备用叠式净水过滤器〔999〕	5	1	50	13/	13	台/千克	/		21	3.3/3.3
8421.2199 20	船舶压载水处理设备用过滤器〔999〕	5	2	50	13/	13	台/千克	/		22	3.3/3.3
8421.2199 90	其他非家用型过滤或净化水的装置〔999〕	5		50	13/	13	台/千克	/		25	3.3/3.3
8421.2200	--过滤或净化饮料(水除外)用[T2]	8		40	13/	13	台/千克	A/	R	28	
8421.2300	--内燃发动机的滤油器〔101 其他车辆零部件,102 动力设备零部件,103 非家用过滤及净化装置〕	8		40	13/	13	个/千克	/			
	--其他:										
8421.2910	---压滤机							O			
8421.2910 10	用氟聚合物制造的厚度不超过 140 微米的过滤膜或净化膜的压滤机〔999〕	0		40	13/	13	个/千克	/		25	3.3/3.3
8421.2910 90	其他压滤机〔999〕	5		40	13/	13	个/千克	/		30	3.3/3.3
8421.2990	---其他										
8421.2990 10	用氟聚合物制造的厚度不超过 140 微米的过滤膜或净化膜的其他液体过滤或净化机器及装置〔999〕	0		40	13/	13	个/千克	/			3.3/3.3
8421.2990 40	液体截流过滤设备(可连续分离致病性微生物、毒素和细胞培养物)〔999〕	5		40	13/	13	个/千克	3/			3.3/3.3
8421.2990 90	其他液体的过滤、净化机器及装置[T2]	5		40	13/	13	个/千克	/		15	3.3/3.3
	-气体的过滤、净化机器及装置:										

协定税率 %								RCEP		特惠税率 %			
东/冰/格	巴基斯坦	韩国	瑞士上/下	哥/秘/柬	澳/毛	新西/坡/智	中国港/澳/台	东盟及马来/澳/韩	日/新	亚太2国	老/柬/缅	98/97/95	Article Description
0/0/0	0	0	0/0	0/0/0	0/0	0//0	0/0/	0/0/0	0/0		0//	0/0/0	Sublimator (or cold trap) (take out UF_6 diffusion cascade and can transfer by evaporation)
0/0/0	0	0	0/0	0/0/0	0/0	0//0	0/0/	0/0/0	0/0		0//	0/0/0	Low-temperature refrigeration equipment (bearing -120℃ or evem lower temperature)
0/0/0	0	0	0/0	0/0/0	0/0	0//0	0/0/	0/0/0	0/0		0//	0/0/0	UF_6 cold traps(bearing-120℃ or even lower tem perature)
0/0/0	0	0	0/0	0/0/0	0/0	0//0	0/0/	0/0/0	0/0		0//	0/0/0	Other machinery for the treatment of materials by a process involving a change of temperature(including similar laboratory equipment)
													-Parts:
0/0/0	0	0	0/0	0/0/0	0/0	0//0	0/0/	0/0/0	0/0			0/0/0	---Of water heaters
0/0/0	0	0	0/0	0/0/0	0/0	0//0	0/0/0	0/0/0	0/0			0/0/0	---Other
													Calendering or other rolling machines, other than for metals or glass, and cylinders therefor:
													-Calendering or other rolling machines
0/0/0	2	0	0/0	0/0/0	0/0	0//0	0/0/0	0/0/0	8/0			0/0/0	Textile calenders
0/0/0	2	0	0/0	0/0/0	0/0	0//0	0/0/0	0/0/0	8/0			0/0/0	Rolling machine, especially for the manufacture of printed circuit board or printed circuit (except for processing metal or glass)
0/0/0	2	0	0/0	0/0/0	0/0	0//0	0/0/0	0/0/0	8/0			0/0/0	Other calendar or rolling machines (excluding those for processing metals or glass)
													-Parts:
0/0/0	4	0	0/0	0/0/0	0/0	0//0	0/0/	0/0/0	7.3/0			0/0/0	--Cylinders
0/0/0	2	0	0/0	0/0/0	0/0	0//0	0/0/	0/0/0	7.3/0			0/0/0	--Other
													Centrifuges, including centrifugal dryers; filtering or purifying machinery and apparatus, for liquids or gases:
													-Centrifuges, including centrifugal dryers:
0/0/0	2	0	0/0	0/0/0	0/0	0//0	0/0/	0/0/0	7.6/0			0/0/0	--Cream separators
													--Clothes-dryers:
0/0/0	9.8	3.5	1.8/1.8	0/0/0	0/0	0/0/0	0/0/	0/0/15.8	15.9/0			0/0/0	---Of a dry linen capacity not exceeding 10kg
0/0/0	2	1.6	0/0	0/0/0	0/0	0//0	0/0/	0/0/7.2	7.3/0			0/0/0	---Other
													--Other:
0/0/0	4	2	0/0	0/0/0	0/0	0//0	0/0/	0/0/9	9.1/0			0/0/0	---Dewaterers
0/0/0	3.5	2	0/0	0/0/0	0/0	0/0/0	0/0/	9/9/9	9.1/9			0/0/0	---Solid-liquor separators
													---Other
0/0/0	3.5	2	1/1	0/0/0	0/0	0/0/0	0/0/	9/9/9	9.1/9			0/0/0	Liquid-liquid centrifugal contactors (specially designed or manufactured for uranium concentration in chemical exchange process)
0/0/0	3.5	2	1/1	0/0/0	0/0	0/0/0	0/0/	9/9/9	9.1/9			0/0/0	Centrifugal separator including decanters (not diverging aerosol, capable of continuously separating disease microorganism)
0/0/0	3.5	2	1/1	0/0/0	0/0	0/0/0	0/0/	9/9/9	9.1/9			0/0/0	Other centrifuges and centrifugal dryers
													-Filtering or purifying machinery and apparatus for liquids:
													--For filtering or purifying water:
0/0/0	14	15	7/7	0/0/0	0/15	0/0/0	0/0/	0/0/23.3	22.7/0			0/0/0	---Of the household type
													---Other:
0/0/0	0	2.3	0/0	0/0/0	0/0	0//0	0/0/0	4.5/4.5/4.5	4.5/4.5			0/0/0	----Ship ballast water treatment equipment
													----Other
0/0/0	0	2.3	0/0	0/0/0	0/0	0//0	0/0/0	4.5/4.5/4.5	4.5/4.5			0/0/0	Stack type water purifying filter for irrigation equipment
0/0/0	0	2.3	0/0	0/0/0	0/0	0//0	0/0/0	4.5/4.5/4.5	4.5/4.5			0/0/0	Ballast water treatment equipment with a filter
0/0/0	0	2.3	0/0	0/0/0	0/0	0//0	0/0/0	4.5/4.5/4.5	4.5/4.5			0/0/0	Other non-household filtering or purifying water equipment
0/0/0	4.2	2.4	0/0	0/0/0	0/0	0/0/0	0/0/	0/0/10.8	10.9/0			0/0/0	--For filtering or purifying beverages other than water
0/0/0	3.5	2	0/0	0/0/0	0/0	0/0/0	0/0/	0/0/9	9.1/0			0/0/0	--Oil or petrol-filters for internal combustion engines
													--Other:
													---Press filters
0/0/0	0	1	0/0	0/0/0	0/0	0//0	0/0/	0/0/4.5	4.5/0			0/0/0	Press filters, with a filter membrane or purification film with a thickness of not more than 140 microns, made of a fluoropolymer
0/0/0	0	1	0/0	0/0/0	0/0	0//0	0/0/	0/0/4.5	4.5/0			0/0/0	Other press filters
													---Other
0/0/0	0	0	0.5/0.5	0/0/0	0/0	0//0	0/0/0	0/0/0	4.7/0			0/0/0	Other liquid filtration or purification machines and devices made of fluoropolymer films with a thickness of not more than 140 microns
0/0/0	0	0	0.5/0.5	0/0/0	0/0	0//0	0/0/0	0/0/0	4.7/0			0/0/0	Liquid closure filtration equipment (which can continuously separate pathogenic microorganisms, toxins and cell culture)
0/0/0	0	0	0.5/0.5	0/0/0	0/0	0//0	0/0/0	0/0/0	4.7/0			0/0/0	Other filtering, purifying machinery and apparatuses for other liquids
													-Filtering or purifying machinery and apparatus for gases:

税则号列	货品名称〔CIQ 扩展编码及品名－T2 表示见附表 2〕	最惠(%)	暂定税率	普通	增值/消费	出口退税	计量单位	监管条件/特殊证件	检验检疫	对美关税	亚太上/下
8421.3100	--内燃发动机的进气过滤器〔101 其他车辆零部件，102 动力设备零部件，103 非家用过滤及净化装置，104 其他离心机及类似装置及其零件〕	10		40	13/	13	个/千克	/		15	
8421.3200	--用于净化或过滤内燃机所排出废气的催化转化器或微粒过滤器，不论是否组合										
8421.3200 10	摩托车发动机排气过滤及净化装置(装备不锈钢外壳、入口管和出口管内径不超过 1.3 厘米的气体过滤或净化机器及装置除外)〔101 其他车辆零部件，102 非家用过滤及净化装置，103 气体纯化过滤、净化机器及装置〕	5	3	40	13/	13	个/千克	/		13	3.3/3.3
8421.3200 20	装备不锈钢外壳、入口管和出口管内径不超过 1.3 厘米的其他内燃发动机排气过滤及净化装置〔999〕	0		40	13/	13	个/千克	/		10	3.3/3.3
8421.3200 30	柴油发动机排气过滤及净化装置(装备不锈钢外壳、入口管和出口管内径不超过 1.3 厘米的气体过滤或净化机器及装置除外)〔101 其他车辆零部件，102 非家用过滤及净化装置，103 气体纯化过滤、净化机器及装置〕	5	3	40	13/	13	个/千克	/		13	3.3/3.3
8421.3200 40	汽油机颗粒捕集器(装备不锈钢外壳、入口管和出口管内径不超过 1.3 厘米的气体过滤或净化机器及装置除外)〔999〕	5	3	40	13/	13	个/千克	/		13	3.3/3.3
8421.3200 90	其他用于净化或过滤内燃机所排出废气的催化转化器或微粒过滤器(不论是否组合式)〔101 其他车辆零部件，102 非家用过滤及净化装置，103 气体纯化过滤、净化机器及装置〕	5		40	13/	13	个/千克	/		15	3.3/3.3
	--其他：										
8421.3910	---家用型[T2]	7	5	100	13/	13	个/千克	/		30	4.6/4.6
	---工业用除尘器：										
8421.3921	----静电除尘器										
8421.3921 10	装备不锈钢外壳、入口管和出口管内径不超过 1.3 厘米的工业用静电除尘器〔999〕	0		40	13/	13	个/千克	/		20	3.3/3.3
8421.3921 90	其他工业用静电除尘器〔999〕	5		40	13/	13	个/千克	/		25	3.3/3.3
8421.3922	----袋式除尘器										
8421.3922 10	装备不锈钢外壳、入口管和出口管内径不超过 1.3 厘米的工业用袋式除尘器〔999〕	0		40	13/	13	个/千克	/		20	3.3/3.3
8421.3922 90	其他工业用袋式除尘器〔999〕	5		40	13/	13	个/千克	/		25	3.3/3.3
8421.3923	----旋风式除尘器										
8421.3923 10	装备不锈钢外壳、入口管和出口管内径不超过 1.3 厘米的工业用旋风式除尘器〔999〕	0		40	13/	13	个/千克	/		10	3.3/3.3
8421.3923 90	其他工业用旋风式除尘器〔999〕	5		40	13/	13	个/千克	/		15	3.3/3.3
8421.3924	----电袋复合除尘器										
8421.3924 10	装备不锈钢外壳、入口管和出口管内径不超过 1.3 厘米的电袋复合除尘器〔999〕	0		40	13/	13	个/千克	/		25	3.3/3.3
8421.3924 90	其他电袋复合除尘器〔999〕	5		40	13/	13	个/千克	/		30	3.3/3.3
8421.3929	----其他										
8421.3929 10	装备不锈钢外壳、入口管和出口管内径不超过 1.3 厘米的其他工业用除尘器〔999〕	0		40	13/	13	个/千克	/		25	3.3/3.3
8421.3929 90	其他工业用除尘器〔999〕	5		40	13/	13	个/千克	/		30	3.3/3.3
8421.3940	---烟气脱硫装置										
8421.3940 10	装备不锈钢外壳、入口管和出口管内径不超过 1.3 厘米的烟气脱硫装置〔999〕	0		40	13/	13	个/千克	/		25	3.3/3.3
8421.3940 90	其他烟气脱硫装置〔101 非家用过滤及净化装置，102 气体纯化过滤、净化机器及装置〕	5		40	13/	13	个/千克	/		30	3.3/3.3
8421.3950	---烟气脱硝装置										
8421.3950 10	装备不锈钢外壳、入口管和出口管内径不超过 1.3 厘米的烟气脱硝装置〔999〕	0		40	13/	13	个/千克	/		10	3.3/3.3
8421.3950 90	其他烟气脱硝装置〔101 非家用过滤及净化装置，102 气体纯化过滤、净化机器及装置〕	5		40	13/	13	个/千克	/		15	3.3/3.3
8421.3990	---其他										
8421.3990 10	装备不锈钢外壳、入口管和出口管内径不超过 1.3 厘米的其他气体过滤或净化机器及装置〔999〕	0		40	13/	13	个/千克	/		10	3.3/3.3
8421.3990 90	其他气体过滤、净化机器及装置〔101 非家用过滤及净化装置，102 气体纯化过滤、净化机器及装置〕	5		40	13/	13	个/千克	/		15	3.3/3.3
	-零件：										
	--离心机用，包括离心干燥机用：										
8421.9110	---干衣量不超过 10 千克的干衣机用〔999〕	0		70	13/	13	千克	/		5	
8421.9190	---其他										
8421.9190 11	离心机壳/收集器(容纳气体离心机的转筒组件的耐 UF6 部件)〔999〕	0		30	13/	13	千克	3/		20	
8421.9190 12	收集器(由内径不同的同心管组成用于供取 UF6 气体的管件)〔999〕	0		30	13/	13	千克	3/		20	
8421.9190 13	气体扩散膜(由耐 UF6 材料制成的多细孔过滤薄膜)〔999〕	0		30	13/	13	千克	3/		20	

协定税率 %								RCEP		特惠税率 %			Article Description
东/冰/格	巴基斯坦	韩国	瑞士上/下	哥/秘/柬	澳/毛	新西/坡/智	中国港/澳/台	东盟及马来/澳/韩	日/新	亚太2国	老/柬/缅	98/97/95	
0/0/0	2	6	0/0	0/0/0	0/0	0//0	0/0/	9.5/9.5/10	9.5/9.5			0/0/0	--Intake air filters for internal combustion engines
													--Catalytic converters or particulate filters, whether or not combined, for purifying or filtering exhaust gases from internal combustion engines
0/0/0	0	2.3	0/0	0/0/0	0/0	0//0	0/0/	4.5/4.5/4.5	4.7/4.5			0/0/0	Exhaust filtration and purification device for motorcycle engine (except for gas filtration or purification machines and devices equipped with stainless steel shell, inlet pipe and outlet pipe with inner diameter not exceeding 1.3 cm)
0/0/0	0	2.3	0/0	0/0/0	0/0	0//0	0/0/	4.5/4.5/4.5	4.7/4.5			0/0/0	Other internal combustion engine exhaust filtration and purification devices equipped with stainless steel shell, inlet pipe and outlet pipe with inner diameter not exceeding 1.3 cm
0/0/0	0	2.3	0/0	0/0/0	0/0	0//0	0/0/	4.5/4.5/4.5	4.7/4.5			0/0/0	Diesel engine exhaust filtration and purification device
0/0/0	0	2.3	0/0	0/0/0	0/0	0//0	0/0/	4.5/4.5/4.5	4.7/4.5			0/0/0	Particle trap for gasoline engine (except for gas filtration or purification machines and devices equipped with stainless steel shell, inlet pipe and outlet pipe with inner diameter not exceeding 1.3 cm)
0/0/0	0	2.3	0/0	0/0/0	0/0	0//0	0/0/	4.5/4.5/4.5	4.7/4.5			0/0/0	Other catalytic converters or particulate filters (whether combined or not) for purifying or filtering exhaust gases from internal combustion engines
													--Other:
0/0/0	5.3	9.7	1.5/1.5	0/0/0	0/0	0/0/0	0/0/0	13.5/13.5/14.3	13.6/13.5			0/0/0	---Of the household type
													---Dust collectors for industry uses:
													----Electrostatic
0/0/0	0	0	0/0	0/0/0	0/0	0//0	0/0/0	0/0/0	0/0			0/0/0	Industrial electrostatic precipitator with stainless steel casing, inlet pipe and outlet pipe inner diameter not exceeding 1.3 cm
0/0/0	0	0	0/0	0/0/0	0/0	0//0	0/0/0	0/0/0	0/0			0/0/0	Other industrial electrostatic precipitators
													----Baghoused
0/0/0	0	0	0/0	0/0/0	0/0	0//0	0/0/	0/0/0	0/0			0/0/0	Industrial bag type dust collector equipped with stainless steel shell, inlet pipe and outlet pipe inner diameter not exceeding 1.3 cm
0/0/0	0	0	0/0	0/0/0	0/0	0//0	0/0/	0/0/0	0/0			0/0/0	Other industrial bag type dust collector
													----Cyclone
0/0/0	0	0	0/0	0/0/0	0/0	0//0	0/0/0	0/0/0	0/0			0/0/0	Industrial cyclone dust collector with stainless steel casing, inlet pipe and outlet pipe inner diameter not exceeding 1.3 cm
0/0/0	0	0	0/0	0/0/0	0/0	0//0	0/0/0	0/0/0	0/0			0/0/0	Other industrial cyclone dust collector
													----Electric bag composite dust collector
0/0/0	0	2.3	0/0	0/0/0	0/0	0//0	0/0/0	0/0/4.5	4.5/0			0/0/0	Electric bag composite dust remover with stainless steel casing, inlet pipe and outlet pipe inner diameter less than 1.3 cm
0/0/0	0	2.3	0/0	0/0/0	0/0	0//0	0/0/0	0/0/4.5	4.5/0			0/0/0	Other electric bag composite dust collector
													----Other
0/0/0	0	2.3	0/0	0/0/0	0/0	0//0	0/0/0	0/0/4.5	4.5/0			0/0/0	Other industrial dust remover with stainless steel casing, inlet pipe and outlet pipe diameter not exceeding 1.3 cm
0/0/0	0	2.3	0/0	0/0/0	0/0	0//0	0/0/0	0/0/4.5	4.5/0			0/0/0	Other industrial dust collector
													Flue gas desulpharisation apparatus
0/0/0	0	0	0/0	0/0/0	0/0	0//0	0/0/0	0/0/0	0/0			0/0/0	Flue gas desulfurization device equipped with stainless steel casing, inlet pipe and outlet pipe diameter less than 1.3 cm
0/0/0	0	0	0/0	0/0/0	0/0	0//0	0/0/0	0/0/0	0/0			0/0/0	Other flue gas desulfurization device
													---Flue gas denitration apparatus
0/0/0	0	0	0/0	0/0/0	0/0	0//0	0/0/0	0/4.5/0	0/4.5			0/0/0	Flue gas denitration device equipped with stainless steel casing, inlet pipe and outlet pipe diameter less than 1.3 cm
0/0/0	0	0	0/0	0/0/0	0/0	0//0	0/0/0	0/4.5/0	0/4.5			0/0/0	Other flue gas denitrification device
													---Other
0/0/0	0	1	0/0	0/0/0	0/0	0//0	0/0/0	0/0/4.5	4.8/0			0/0/0	Other gas filtration or purification equipment and devices equipped with stainless steel casing, inlet pipe and outlet pipe inner diameter not exceeding 1.3 cm
0/0/0	0	1	0/0	0/0/0	0/0	0//0	0/0/0	0/0/4.5	4.8/0			0/0/0	Other filtering or purifying machinery and apparatus, for gases
													-Parts:
													--Of centrifuges, including centrifugal dryers:
0/0/0	0	0	0/0	0/0/0	0/0	0//0	0/0/	0/0/0	0/0			0/0/0	---Of clothes-dryers of a dry linen capacity not exceeding 10kg
													---Other
0/0/0	0	0	0/0	0/0/0	0/0	0//0	0/0/	0/0/0	0/0			0/0/0	Centrifugal cover/collectors (accommodate gas centrifuge rotor components to UF_6 resistance)
0/0/0	0	0	0/0	0/0/0	0/0	0//0	0/0/	0/0/0	0/0			0/0/0	Collectors (parts of tube used for providing air of UF_6, made up of concentric tubes with different radiuses)
0/0/0	0	0	0/0	0/0/0	0/0	0//0	0/0/	0/0/0	0/0			0/0/0	Air diffusion membrances (multiple stoma filtration membrane made of UF_6 resistance materials)

税则号列	货品名称〔CIQ 扩展编码及品名－T2 表示见附表 2〕	最惠(%)	暂定税率	普通	增值/消费	出口退税	计量单位	监管条件/特殊证件	检验检疫	对美关税	亚太上/下
8421.9190 14	扩散室(专门设计或制造的密闭式容器,用于容纳气体扩散膜,由耐 UF6 的材料制成或用这种材料进行保护)〔999〕	0		30	13/	13	千克	3/		20	
8421.9190 90	其他离心机用零件〔999〕	0		30	13/	13	千克	/		20	
	--其他:										
8421.9910	---家用型过滤、净化装置用〔999〕	7	5	100	13/	13	千克	/		10	4.6/4.6
8421.9990	---其他										
8421.9990 10	用氟聚合物制造的厚度不超过 140 微米的过滤膜或净化膜的液体过滤或净化机器及装置的零件;装备不锈钢外壳、入口管和出口管内径不超过 1.3 厘米的气体过滤或净化机器及装置的零件〔999〕	0		40	13/	13	千克	/			3.3/3.3
8421.9990 90	其他过滤、净化装置用零件〔101 其它工业用旋除尘器及其零件,102 非家用过滤及净化装置,103 气体纯化过滤、净化机器及装置,104 其它过滤及其喷射装置及其零件〕	5		40	13/	13	千克	/		10	3.3/3.3
84.22	**洗碟机;瓶子及其他容器的洗涤或干燥机器;瓶、罐、箱、袋或其他容器装填、封口、密封、贴标签的机器;瓶、罐、管、筒或类似容器的包封机器;其他包装或打包机器(包括热缩包装机器);饮料充气机:**										
	-洗碟机:										
8422.1100	--家用型[T2]	8	4	90	13/	13	台/千克	/		29	
8422.1900	--其他[T2]	8		90	13/	13	台/千克	/		33	
8422.2000	-瓶子或其他容器的洗涤或干燥机器[T2]	8		35	13/	13	台/千克	/		28	
	-瓶、罐、箱、袋或其他容器的装填、封口、密封、贴标签的机器;瓶、罐、管、筒或类似容器的包封机器;饮料充气机:										
8422.3010	---饮料及液体食品灌装设备										
8422.3010 10	乳品加工用自动化灌装设备〔999〕	12	8	45	13/	13	台/千克	A/	R	33	7.8/7.8
8422.3010 90	其他饮料及液体食品灌装设备〔999〕	12		45	13/	13	台/千克	A/	R	37	7.8/7.8
	---水泥包装机:										
8422.3021	----全自动灌包机〔999〕	8		45	13/	13	台/千克	/			5.2/5.2
8422.3029	----其他〔999〕	8		45	13/	13	台/千克	/		13	5.2/5.2
8422.3030	---其他包装机										
8422.3030 01	全自动无菌灌装生产线用包装机(加工速度≥20000 只/小时)〔999〕	8	6	35	13/	13	台/千克	A/	R	31	5.2/5.2
8422.3030 90	其他包装机〔999〕	8		35	13/	13	台/千克	A/	R	33	5.2/5.2
8422.3090	---其他										
8422.3090 01	全自动无菌灌装生产线用贴吸管机(加工速度≥22000 只/小时)〔999〕	8	6	35	13/	13	台/千克	A/	R	31	5.2/5.2
8422.3090 10	充装设备(两用物项管制)〔999〕	8		35	13/	13	台/千克	3/		33	5.2/5.2
8422.3090 90	其他瓶、罐、箱、袋或其他容器的封口、密封、贴标签的机器;其他瓶、罐、管、筒或类似容器的包封机器;饮料充气机〔999〕	8		35	13/	13	台/千克	A/	R	33	5.2/5.2
8422.4000	-其他包装或打包机器(包括热缩包装机器)〔999〕	8		35	13/	13,9	台/千克			/33	5.2
8422.4000 10	半导体检测分选编带机〔999〕	8	5	35	13/	13	台/千克	/		30	5.2/5.2
8422.4000 90	其他包装或打包机器(包括热缩包装机器)	8		35	13/	9,13	台/千克	/		33	5.2/5.2
	-零件:										
8422.9010	---洗碟机用〔999〕	8	4	90	13/	13	千克	/		29	
8422.9020	---饮料及液体食品灌装设备用										
8422.9020 10	乳品加工用自动化灌装设备用零件〔999〕	8.5	4	45	13/	13	千克	/		29	
8422.9020 90	其他饮料及液体食品灌装设备用零件〔999〕	8.5		45	13/	13	千克	/		33.5	
8422.9090	---其他										
8422.9090 10	全自动无菌灌装生产线用包装机(加工速度≥20000 只/小时)、贴吸管机(加工速度≥22000 只/小时)用零件〔101 建材行业成套设备,102 包装行业成套设备,103 其它餐具清洗机及其零件〕	8.5	4	35	13/	13	千克	/		29	
8422.9090 90	税目 8422 其他未列名机器零件〔101 建材行业成套设备,102 包装行业成套设备,103 其它餐具清洗机及其零件〕	8.5		35	13/	13	千克	/		33.5	
84.23	**衡器(感量为 50 毫克或更精密的天平除外),包括计数或检验用的衡器;衡器用的各种砝码、秤砣:**										
8423.1000	-体重计,包括婴儿秤;家用秤〔101 电子衡器,102 机械衡器〕	6		80	13/	13	台/千克	/		31	
	-输送带上连续称货的秤:										
8423.2010	---电子皮带秤〔999〕	0		80	13/	13	台/千克	/		25	
8423.2090	---其他〔999〕	10		80	13/	13	台/千克	/		35	
	-恒定秤、物料定量装袋或装容器用的秤,包括库秤:										

协定税率 %								RCEP		特惠税率 %			Article Description
东/冰/格	巴基斯坦	韩国	瑞士上/下	哥/秘/柬	澳/毛	新西/坡/智	中国港/澳/台	东盟及马来/澳/韩	日/新	亚太2国	老/柬/缅	98/97/95	
0/0/0	0	0	0/0	0/0/0	0/0	0//0	0/0/	0/0/0	0/0			0/0/0	Diffusion rooms (a closed spectacle that accommodate other diffusion membrances, with one inlet pipe and two outlet pipes)
0/0/0	0	0	0/0	0/0/0	0/0	0//0	0/0/	0/0/0	0/0			0/0/0	Other parts of centrifuge machines
													-Other:
0/0/0	0	2	0/0	0/0/0	0/0	0/0/0	0/0/	9/9/9	9.1/9			0/0/0	---Of household-type filtering or purifying machines
													---Other
0/0/0	0	0	0/0	0/0/0	0/0	0//0	0/0/0	0/0/0	0/0			0/0/0	Parts of liquid membrane filtration or purification device and machine, made of fluorine polymer thickness less than 140 microns filtration or purification ; gas filter equipment stainless steel shell, entrance pipe and the outlet pipe diameter not exceeding 1.3 cm or purification machines and apparatus parts
0/0/0	0	0	0/0	0/0/0	0/0	0//0	0/0/0	0/0/0	0/0			0/0/0	Other parts of filtering and purifying machines and apparatuses
													Dish washing machines; machinery for cleaning or drying bottles or other containers; machinery for filling, closing, sealing or labelling bottles, cans, boxes, bags or other containers; machinery for capsuling bottles, jars, tubes and similar containers other packing or wrapping machinery (including heat-shrink wrapping machinery); machinery for aerating beverages:
													-Dish washing machines:
0/0/0	2		0/0	0/0/0	0/0	0//0	0/0/	5/5/	/5			0/0/0	--Of the household type
0/0/0	7.8	2.8	0/0	0/0/0	0/0	0/0/0	0/0/	0/0/12.6	12.7/0			0/0/0	--Other
0/0/0	2	2	0/0	0/0/0	0/0	0/0/0	0/0/	0/0/9	9.1/0			0/0/0	-Machinery for cleaning or drying bottles or other containers
													-Machinery for filling, closing, sealing, or labelling bottles, cans, boxes, bags or other containers; machinery for capsuling bottles, jars, tubes and similar containers; machinery for aerating beverages:
													---Bottling or canning machinery for beverages or liquid food
0/0/0	3.5	2.4	1.2/1.2	0/0/0	0/0	0/0/0	0/0/	0/0/10.8	10.9/0			0/0/0	With the automatic filling equipment in dairy processing
0/0/0	3.5	2.4	1.2/1.2	0/0/0	0/0	0/0/0	0/0/	0/0/10.8	10.9/0			0/0/0	Other botting or canning machinery for beverages or liquid food
													---Machinery for packing cement:
0/0/0	3.5	2.4	1.2/1.2	0/0/0	0/0	0/0/0	0/0/	0/0/10.8	10.9/0			0/0/0	----Automatic filling and sacking machines
0/0/0	3.5	2.4	1.2/1.2	0/0/0	0/0	0/0/0	0/0/	0/0/10.8	10.9/0			0/0/0	----Other
													---Other packing machines
0/0/0	3.5	0	0/0	0/0/0	0/0	0/0/0	0/0/	9/9/9	9.1/9			0/0/0	Packing machines for fully automatic aseptic filling production lines (processing speed≥2000 bottles/hour)
0/0/0	3.5	0	0/0	0/0/0	0/0	0/0/0	0/0/	9/9/9	9.1/9			0/0/0	Other packing machines
													---Other
0/0/0	3.5	0	0/0	0/0/0	0/0	0/0/0	0/0/	9/9/9	9.1/9			0/0/0	Pipette machines for fully automatic filling production lines (processing speed ≥2000 bottles/hour)
0/0/0	3.5	0	0/0	0/0/0	0/0	0/0/0	0/0/	9/9/9	9.1/9			0/0/0	Filling equipment(Subject to regulation of sensitive items)
0/0/0	3.5	0	0/0	0/0/0	0/0	0/0/0	0/0/	9/9/9	9.1/9			0/0/0	Machines for the filling, sealing, sealing, labeling of other bottles, cans, boxes, bags or other containers, and other packaging machines for bottles, cans, tubes, tubes, or similar containers; machinery for aerating beverages
0/0/0	5	5	0	0	0	0	0/0/0	0/0/				0/0/0	-Other packing or wrapping machinery (including heat-shrink wrapping machinery)
0/0/0	2	2	0/0	0/0/0	0/0	0/0/0	0/0/	0/0/9	9.4/0		//	0/0/0	Semiconductor testing, sorting and taping machine
0/0/0	2	2	0/0	0/0/0	0/0	0/0/0	0/0/	0/0/9	9.4/0		//	0/0/0	Other packaging or packaging machines (including heat shrinkable packaging machines)
													-Parts:
0/0/0	3.5	2.1	1.1/1.1	0/0/0	0/0	0/0/0	0/0/	0/0/9.5	9.5/0			0/0/0	---Of dish washing machines
													---Of bottling or canning machinery for beverages or liquid food
0/0/0	2	1.7	0/0	0/0/0	0/0	0//0	0/0/	0/0/7.7	7.7/0		//	0/0/0	Parts of automatic filling equipment for dairy processing
0/0/0	2	1.7	0/0	0/0/0	0/0	0//0	0/0/	0/0/7.7	7.7/0		//	0/0/0	Other parts for beverage and liquid food filling equipment
													---Other
0//0	2	0	0.9/0.9	0/0/0	0/0	0//0	0/0/	7.7/7.7/7.7	7.7/7.7		//	0/0/0	Packaging machine for automatic aseptic filling production line (processing speed ≥ 20000 pieces / h) and parts for pipette sticking machine (processing speed ≥ 22000 pieces / h)
0//0	2	0	0.9/0.9	0/0/0	0/0	0//0	0/0/	7.7/7.7/7.7	7.7/7.7		//	0/0/0	Other machine parts not listed in heading 8422
													Weighing machinery (excluding balances of a sensitivity of 50 mg or better), including weight operated counting or checking machines; weighing machine weights of all kinds:
0/0/0	3.5	2.1	1.1/1.1	0/0/0	0/0	0/0/0	0/0/	0/0/9.5	9.5/0			0/0/0	-Personal weighing machines, including baby scales; household scales
													-Scales for continuous weighing of goods on conveyors:
0/0/0	2	2	0/0	0/0/0	0/0	0//0	0/0/	0/0/9	0/0			0/0/0	---Electronic belt weighing machines
0/0/0	2	2	0/0	0/0/0	0/0	0//0	0/0/	0/0/9	9.1/0			0/0/0	---Other
													-Constant weight scales and scales for discharging a predetermined weight of material into a bag or container, including hopper scales:

税则号列	货品名称〔CIQ 扩展编码及品名－T2 表示见附表 2〕	最惠(%)	暂定税率	普通	增值/消费	出口退税	计量单位	监管条件/特殊证件	检验检疫	对美关税	亚太上/下
8423.3010	---定量包装秤										
8423.3010 10	以电子方式称重的定量包装秤〔999〕	0		80	13/	13	台/千克	/		25	
8423.3010 90	其他定量包装秤〔999〕	10		80	13/	13	台/千克	/		35	
8423.3020	---定量分选秤〔101 电子衡器,102 机械衡器〕	10		80	13/	13	台/千克	/		35	
8423.3030	---配料秤										
8423.3030 10	以电子方式称重的配料秤〔999〕	0		80	13/	13	台/千克	/		25	
8423.3030 90	其他配料秤〔999〕	10		80	13/	13	台/千克	/		35	
8423.3090	---其他										
8423.3090 10	以电子方式称重的恒定秤,库秤及其他包装秤,分选秤〔999〕	0		80	13/	13	台/千克	/		25	
8423.3090 90	其他恒定秤,库秤及其他包装秤,分选秤〔999〕	10		80	13/	13	台/千克	/		35	
	-其他衡器:										
	--最大称量不超过 30 千克:										
8423.8110	---计价秤〔101 电子衡器,102 机械衡器〕	0		80	13/	13	台/千克	/		25	
8423.8120	---弹簧秤〔999〕	10		80	13/	13	台/千克	/		35	
8423.8190	---其他										
8423.8190 10	其他以电子方式称重的衡器,最大称量不超过 30 千克〔999〕	0		80	13/	13	台/千克	/		20	
8423.8190 90	最大称量≤30 千克的其他衡器〔999〕	10		80	13/	13	台/千克	/		30	
	--最大称量超过 30 千克,但不超过 5000 千克:										
8423.8210	---地中衡										
8423.8210 10	其他以电子方式称重的地中衡,最大称量大于 30 千克但不超过 5000 千克,但对车辆称重的衡器除外〔999〕	0		80	13/	13	台/千克	/		20	
8423.8210 90	30＜最大称量≤5000kg 的其他地中衡〔999〕	10		80	13/	13	台/千克	/		30	
8423.8290	---其他										
8423.8290 10	其他以电子方式称重的衡器,最大称量大于 30 千克但不超过 5000 千克,但对车辆称重的衡器除外〔999〕	0		80	13/	13	台/千克	/		20	
8423.8290 90	30＜最大称量≤5000kg 的其他衡器〔999〕	10		80	13/	13	台/千克	/		30	
	--其他:										
8423.8910	---地中衡										
8423.8910 10	其他以电子方式称重的地中衡,最大称量超过 5000 千克,但对车辆称重的衡器除外〔999〕	0		80	13/	13	台/千克	/		25	
8423.8910 90	最大秤量＞5000KG 的其他地中衡〔999〕	10		80	13/	13	台/千克	/		35	
8423.8920	---轨道衡										
8423.8920 10	其他以电子方式称重的轨道衡,最大称量超过 5000 千克,但对车辆称重的衡器除外〔999〕	0		80	13/	13	台/千克	/		25	
8423.8920 90	最大秤量＞5000KG 的其他轨道衡〔999〕	10		80	13/	13	台/千克	/		35	
8423.8930	---吊秤										
8423.8930 10	其他以电子方式称重的吊秤,最大称量超过 5000 千克,但对车辆称重的衡器除外〔999〕	0		80	13/	13	台/千克	/		10	
8423.8930 90	最大秤量＞5000KG 的其他吊秤〔999〕	10		80	13/	13	台/千克	/		20	
8423.8990	---其他										
8423.8990 10	其他以电子方式称重的衡器,最大称量超过 5000 千克,但对车辆称重的衡器除外〔999〕	0		80	13/	13	台/千克	/		10	
8423.8990 90	最大秤量＞5000KG 的其他衡器〔999〕	10		80	13/	13	台/千克	/		20	
8423.9000	-衡器用的各种砝码、秤砣;衡器的零件										
8423.9000 10	以电子方式称重的衡器的零件,但对车辆称重的衡器零件除外〔999〕	0		80	13/	13	千克/台	/		20	
8423.9000 90	其他衡器用的各种砝码、秤砣及其零件〔999〕	8		80	13/	13	千克/台	/		28	
84.24	**液体或粉末的喷射、散布或喷雾的机械器具(不论是否手工操作);灭火器,不论是否装药;喷枪及类似器具;喷汽机、喷砂机及类似的喷射机器:**										
8424.1000	-灭火器,不论是否装药										
8424.1000 10	飞机用灭火器(不论是否装药)〔999〕	8	1	70	13/	13	个/千克	A/	M	11	
8424.1000 90	其他灭火器(不论是否装药)〔999〕	8		70	13/	13	个/千克	A/	LM	18	
8424.2000	-喷枪及类似器具〔999〕	8		40	13/	13	个/千克	/		13	5.2/5.2
8424.3000	-喷气机、喷砂机及类似的喷射机器〔999〕	8		40	13/	13	台/千克	/		28	
	-农业或园艺用喷雾器:										

协定税率 %								RCEP		特惠税率 %			
东/冰/格	巴基斯坦	韩国	瑞士 上/下	哥/秘/柬	澳/毛	新西/坡/智	中国港/澳/台	东盟及马来/澳/韩	日/新	亚太2国	老/柬/缅	98/97/95	Article Description
													---Rationed packing scales
0/0/0	3.5	2.1	1.1/1.1	0/0/0	0/0	0/0/0	0/0/	9.8/10/9.8	9.8/10			0/0/0	Electronic rationed packing scales
0/0/0	3.5	2.1	1.1/1.1	0/0/0	0/0	0/0/0	0/0/	9.8/10/9.8	9.8/10			0/0/0	Other rationed packing scales
0/0/0	3.5	2.1	1.1/1.1	0/0/0	0/0	0/0/0	0/0/	0/0/9.5	9.5/0			0/0/0	---Rationed sorting scales
													---Proporating scales
0/0/0	3.5	2.1	1.1/1.1	0/0/0	0/0	0/0/0	0/0/	0/0/9.5	9.5/0			0/0/0	Ecletronic proporating scales
0/0/0	3.5	2.1	1.1/1.1	0/0/0	0/0	0/0/0	0/0/	0/0/9.5	9.5/0			0/0/0	Other proporating scales
													---Other
0/0/0	3.5	2.1	1.1/1.1	0/0/0	0/0	0/0/0	0/0/	0/0/9.5	9.5/0			0/0/0	Constant weight scales , hopper scales and other packing scales ,soting scales,in ecletronic
0/0/0	3.5	2.1	1.1/1.1	0/0/0	0/0	0/0/0	0/0/	0/0/9.5	9.5/0			0/0/0	Other constant weight scales , hopper scales and other packing scales ,soting scales
													-Other weighing machinery:
													--Having a maximum weighing capacity not exceeding 30kg:
0/0/0	3.5	2.1	0/0	0/0/0	0/0	0/0/0	0/0/	0/0/9.5	0/0			0/0/0	---Account balances
0/0/0	3.5	2.1	1.1/1.1	0/0/0	0/0	0/0/0	0/0/	0/0/9.5	9.5/0			0/0/0	---Spring balances
													---Other
0/0/0	3.5	2.1	4.8/4.8	0/0/0	0/0	0/0/0	0/0/	0/0/9.5	9.5/0			0/0/0	Other electronic weighing scales, having a maximum weighing capacity not exceeding 30KG
0/0/0	3.5	2.1	4.8/4.8	0/0/0	0/0	0/0/0	0/0/	0/0/9.5	9.5/0			0/0/0	Other weighing scales, having a maximum weighing capacity not exceeding 30KG
													--Having a maximum weighing capacity exceeding 30kg but not exceeding 5000kg:
													---Weighbridges
0/0/0	3.5	2.1	1.1/1.1	0/0/0	0/0	0/0/0	0/0/	0/0/9.5	9.5/0			0/0/0	Other electronic weighbridges, having a maximum weighing capacity exceeding 30KG but not exceeding 5000KG, but the vehicle weighing scales except
0/0/0	3.5	2.1	1.1/1.1	0/0/0	0/0	0/0/0	0/0/	0/0/9.5	9.5/0			0/0/0	Other weighbridges , having a maximum weighing capacity exceeding 30KG but not exceeding 5000KG
													---Other
0/0/0	3.5	2.1	0/0	0/0/0	0/0	0/0/0	0/0/	0/0/9.5	9.5/0			0/0/0	Other electronic weighing machinery, aving a maximum weighing capacity exceeding 30KG but not exceeding 5000KG, but the vehicle weighing scales except
0/0/0	3.5	2.1	0/0	0/0/0	0/0	0/0/0	0/0/	0/0/9.5	9.5/0			0/0/0	Other weighing machinery ,having a maximum weighing capacity exceeding 30KG but not exceeding 5000KG
													--Other:
													---Weighbridges
0/0/0	2	2	0/0	0/0/0	0/0	0//0	0/0/	0/0/9	9.1/0			0/0/0	Other electronic weighbridges, having a maximum weighing capacity exceeding 5000KG, but the vehicle weighing scales except
0/0/0	2	2	0/0	0/0/0	0/0	0//0	0/0/	0/0/9	9.1/0			0/0/0	Other weighbridges , having a maximum weighing capacity exceeding 5000KG
													---Track scales
0/0/0	2	2	0/0	0/0/0	0/0	0//0	0/0/	0/0/9	9.1/0			0/0/0	Other electronic track scales , having a maximum weighing capacity exceeding 5000KG
0/0/0	2	2	0/0	0/0/0	0/0	0//0	0/0/	0/0/9	9.1/0			0/0/0	Other track scales , having a maximum weighing capacity exceeding 5000KG
													Hanging scales
0/0/0	2	2	0/0	0/0/0	0/0	0//0	0/0/	0/0/9	9.1/0			0/0/0	Other electronic Hanging scales, having a maximum weighing capacity exceeding 5000KG
0/0/0	2	2	0/0	0/0/0	0/0	0//0	0/0/	0/0/9	9.1/0			0/0/0	Hanging scales, having a maximum weighing capacity exceeding 5000KG
													---Other
0/0/0	2	2	0/0	0/0/0	0/0	0//0	0/0/	0/0/9	9.1/0			0/0/0	Other electronic weighing machinery , having a maximum weighing capacity exceeding 5000KG, but the vehicle weighing scales except
0/0/0	2	2	0/0	0/0/0	0/0	0//0	0/0/	0/0/9	9.1/0			0/0/0	Other weighing machinery ,having a maximum weighing capacity exceeding 5000KG, but the vehicle weighing scales except
													-Weighing machine weights of all kinds; parts of weighing machinery
0/0/0	2	2	1/1	0/0/0	0/0	0/0/0	0/0/	0/0/9	9.1/0			0/0/0	Electronic weighing instrument parts, but the parts of vehicle weighing scales except
0/0/0	2	2	1/1	0/0/0	0/0	0/0/0	0/0/	0/0/9	9.1/0			0/0/0	kinds of weight, weight and other parts of the weighing machine
													Mechanical appliances (whether or not hand-operated) for projecting, dispersing or spraying liquids or powders; fire extinguishers, whether or not charged; spray guns and similar appliances; steam or sand blasting machines and similar jet projecting machines:
													-Fire extinguishers, whether or not charged
0/0/0	2	3.9	0/0	0/0/0	0/0	0//0	0/0/	7.8/8/7.8	7.9/8		//	0/0/0	Aircraft fire extinguisher (whether or not charged)
0/0/0	2	3.9	0/0	0/0/0	0/0	0//0	0/0/	7.8/8/7.8	7.9/8		//	0/0/0	Other fire extinguishers (whether charged or not)
0/0/0	2	0	0/0	0/0/0	0/0	0//0	0/0/	7.6/7.6/7.6	7.6/7.6			0/0/0	-Spray guns and similar appliances
0/0/0	2	1.6	0.8/0.8	0/0/0	0/0	0//0	0/0/0	0/0/7.6	7.6/0			0/0/0	-Steam or sand blasting machines and similar jet projecting machines
													-Agricultural or horticultural sprayers:

税则号列	货品名称〔CIQ 扩展编码及品名－T2 表示见附表 2〕	最惠(%)	暂定税率	普通	增值/消费	出口退税	计量单位	监管条件/特殊证件	检验检疫	对美关税	亚太上/下
8424.4100	--便携式喷雾器〔999〕	8		30	9/	9,13	台/千克	/	L	33	5.2/5.2
8424.4900	--其他〔999〕	8		30	9/	9,13	台/千克	/	L	13	5.2/5.2
	-其他器具：										
8424.8200	--农业或园艺用〔999〕	8		30	9/	9,13	台/千克	/	L	28	5.2/5.2
	--其他：										
8424.8910	---家用型[T2]	0		80	13/	13	台/千克	/		10	
8424.8920	---喷涂机器人〔999〕	0		80	13/	13	台/千克	/		10	
	---其他：										
8424.8991	----船用洗舱机〔999〕	0		30	13/	13	台/千克	/		25	
8424.8999	----其他										
8424.8999 10	分离喷嘴(由狭缝状、曲率半径极小的弯曲通道组成，内有分离楔尖)[T2]	0		30	13/	13	台/千克	3/		10	
8424.8999 90	其他用途的喷射、喷雾机械器具[T2]	0		30	13/	13	台/千克	/	L	10	
	-零件：										
8424.9010	---税号 8424.1000 所列器具的零件〔999〕	0		70	13/	13	千克	/		5	
8424.9020	---税号 8424.8910 所列器具的零件〔101 蒸脸器，102 家用型喷射、喷雾机械器具〕	0		80	13/	13	千克	/		5	
8424.9090	---其他〔999〕	0		30	13/	9,13	千克	/		10	
84.25	**滑车及提升机，但倒卸式提升机除外；卷扬机及绞盘；千斤顶：**										
	-滑车及提升机，但倒卸式提升机及提升车辆用的提升机除外：										
8425.1100	--电动的〔999〕	6		30	13/	13	台/千克	/		16	
8425.1900	--其他〔999〕	5		30	13/	13	台/千克	/		15	
	-其他卷扬机；绞盘：										
	--电动的：										
8425.3110	---矿井口卷扬装置；专为井下使用设计的卷扬机〔999〕	10		30	13/	13	台/千克	/			7/7
8425.3190	---其他〔999〕	5		30	13/	13	台/千克	/		25	
	--其他：										
8425.3910	---矿井口卷扬装置；专为井下使用设计的卷扬机〔999〕	10		30	13/	13	台/千克	/		30	7/7
8425.3990	---其他〔999〕	5		30	13/	13	台/千克	/		30	
	-千斤顶；提升车辆用的提升机：										
8425.4100	--车库中使用的固定千斤顶系统〔999〕	3		30	13/	13	台/千克	/		23	2/2
	--其他液压千斤顶及提升机：										
8425.4210	---液压千斤顶〔999〕	3		30	13/	13	台/千克	/			
8425.4290	---其他〔999〕	5		30	13/	13	台/千克	/		30	
	--其他：										
8425.4910	---其他千斤顶〔999〕	5		30	13/	13	台/千克	/		15	
8425.4990	---其他〔999〕	10		30	13/	13	台/千克	/		30	
84.26	**船用桅杆式起重机；起重机，包括缆式起重机；移动式吊运架、跨运车及装有起重机的工作车：**										
	-高架移动式起重机、桁架桥式起重机、龙门起重机、桥式起重机、移动式吊运架及跨运车：										
	--固定支架的高架移动式起重机：										
8426.1120	---通用桥式起重机〔999〕	8		30	13/	13	台/千克	/		33	
8426.1190	---其他〔999〕	8		30	13/	13	台/千克	/		28	
8426.1200	--带胶轮的移动式吊运架及跨运车〔999〕	6		30	13/	13	台/千克	/		26	
	--其他：										
8426.1910	---装船机〔999〕	5		30	13/	13	台/千克	/			2.5/2.5
	---卸船机：										
8426.1921	----抓斗式〔999〕	5		30	13/	13	台/千克	/			3.3/3.3
8426.1929	----其他〔999〕	5		30	13/	13	台/千克	O/			3.3/3.3
8426.1930	---龙门式起重机〔999〕	10		30	13/	13	台/千克	/		35	6.5/6.5
	---装卸桥：										
8426.1941	----门式装卸桥〔999〕	10		30	13/	13	台/千克	/			6.5/6.5
8426.1942	----集装箱装卸桥〔999〕	10		30	13/	13	台/千克	/			6.5/6.5
8426.1943	----其他动臂式装卸桥〔999〕	10		30	13/	13	台/千克	/			6.5/6.5
8426.1949	----其他〔999〕	10		30	13/	13	台/千克	/			6.5/6.5
8426.1990	---其他〔999〕	10		30	13/	13	台/千克	/			6.5/6.5
8426.2000	-塔式起重机〔999〕	10		30	13/	13	台/千克	O/			
8426.3000	-门座式起重机及座式旋臂起重机〔999〕	6		30	13/	13	台/千克	/		31	
	-其他自推进机械：										
	--带胶轮的：										
8426.4110	---轮胎式起重机〔999〕	5		30	13/	13	台/千克	O/	L		3.5/3.5
8426.4190	---其他〔999〕	5		30	13/	13	台/千克	/		30	
	--其他：										
8426.4910	---履带式起重机〔999〕	8		30	13/	13	台/千克	O/		33	5.6/5.6
8426.4990	---其他〔999〕	8		30	13/	13	台/千克	/			5.6/5.6
	-其他机械：										
8426.9100	--供装于公路车辆的〔999〕	8		30	13/	13	台/千克	/			
8426.9900	--其他〔999〕	6		30	13/	13	台/千克	/		31	
84.27	**叉车；其他装有升降或搬运装置的工作车：**										
	-电动机推进的机动车：										
8427.1010	---有轨巷道堆垛机〔999〕	9		30	13/	13	台/千克	A/	M		

协定税率 %								RCEP		特惠税率 %			Article Description
东/冰/格	巴基斯坦	韩国	瑞士上/下	哥/秘/柬	澳/毛	新西/坡/智	中国港/澳/台	东盟及马来/澳/韩	日/新	亚太2国	老/柬/缅	98/97/95	
0/0/0	2	0	0/0	0/0/0	0/0	0//0	0/0/	0/0/0	7.3/0			0/0/0	-Portable sprayers
0/0/0	2	0	0/0	0/0/0	0/0	0//0	0/0/	0/0/0	7.3/0			0/0/0	--Other
													-Other appliances:
0/0/0	2	0	0/0	0/0/0	0/0	0//0	0/0/	0/0/0	7.3/0			0/0/0	-Agricultural or horticultural
													--Other:
0/0/0	0	0	0/0	0/0/0	0/0	0//0	0/0/	0/0/0	0/0			0/0/0	---Of the household type
0/0/0	0	0	0/0	0/0/0	0/0	0//0	0/0/	0/0/0	0/0			0/0/0	---Spraying robot
													---Other:
0/0/0	0	0	0/0	0/0/0	0/0	0//0	0/0/	0/0/0	0/0			0/0/0	----Marine cabinet washer
													----Other
0/0/0	0	0	0/0	0/0/0	0/0	0//0	0/0/	0/0/0	0/0			0/0/0	Separating nozzles(composed of slik-like curved and channels of very small curvature radius,with separation of wedge tip)
0/0/0	0	0	0/0	0/0/0	0/0	0//0	0/0/	0/0/0	0/0			0/0/0	Mechanical appliances for projecting,or spraying for other use
													-Parts:
0/0/0	0	0	0/0	0/0/0	0/0	0//0	0/0/	0/0/0	0/0			0/0/0	---Of the apparatus of subheading No.8424. 1000
0/0/0	0	0	0/0	0/0/0	0/0	0//0	0/0/	0/0/0	0/0			0/0/0	---Of the apparatus of subheading No.8424. 8910
0/0/0	0	0	0/0	0/0/0	0/0	0//0	0/0/	0/0/0	0/0			0/0/0	---Other
													Pulley tackle and hoists other than skip hoists; winches and capstans; jacks:
													-Pulley tackle and hoists other than skip hoists or hoists of a kind used for raising vehicles:
0/0/0	0	2.8	0/0	0/0/0	0/0	0//0	0/0/	5.4/5.4/5.4	5.6/5.4			0/0/0	--Powered by electric motor
0/0/0	0	1	0/0	0/0/0	0/0	0//0	0/0/	0/0/4.5	4.5/0			0/0/0	--Other
													-Winches; capstans:
													--Powered by electric motor:
0/0/0	2	2	0/0	0/0/0	0/0	0//0	0/0/	0/0/9	9.1/0			0/0/0	---Pit-head winding gear; winches specially designed for use underground
0/0/0	0	2.3	0/0	0/0/0	0/0	0//0	0/0/	4.5/4.5/4.5	4.7/4.5			0/0/0	---Other
													--Other:
0/0/0	2	2	0/0	0/0/0	0/0	0//0	0/0/	0/0/9	9.1/0			0/0/0	---Pit-head winding gear; winches specially designed for use underground
0/0/0	0	2.3	0/0	0/0/0	0/0	0//0	0/0/	4.5/4.5/4.5	4.7/4.5			0/0/0	---Other
													-Jacks; hoists of a kind used for raising vehicles:
0/0/0	0	0	0/0	0/0/0	0/0	0//0	0/0/	0/0/0	0/0			0/0/0	--Built-in jacking systems of a type used in garages
													--Other jacks and hoists, hydraulic:
0/0/0	0	0	0/0	0/0/0	0/0	0//0	0/0/	0/0/0	0/0			0/0/0	---Hydraulic jacks
0/0/0	0	2.3	0/0	0/0/0	0/0	0//0	0/0/	4.5/4.5/4.5	4.7/4.5			0/0/0	---Other
													--Other:
0/0/0	0	1	0/0	0/0/0	0/0	0//0	0/0/	0/0/4.5	4.5/0			0/0/0	---Other jacks
0/0/0	2	2	0/0	0/0/0	0/0	0//0	0/0/	0/0/9	9.1/0			0/0/0	---Other
													Ships derricks; cranes, including cable cranes; mobile lifting frames, straddle carriers and works trucks fitted with a crane:
													-Overhead travelling cranes, transporter cranes, gantry cranes, bridge cranes, mobile lifting frames and straddle carriers:
													--Overhead travelling cranes on fixed support:
0/0/0	2	3.7	0/0	0/0/0	0/0	0//0	0/0/	7.5/7.6/7.5	7.5/7.6			0/0/0	---Bridge cranes, all-purpose
0/0/0	2	3.7	0/0	0/0/0	0/0	0//0	0/0/	7.5/7.6/7.5	7.5/7.6			0/0/0	---Other
0/0/0	0	2.8	0/0	0/0/0	0/0	0//0	0/0/	5.4/5.4/5.4	5.6/5.4			0/0/0	--Mobile lifting frames on tyres and straddle carriers
													--Other:
0/0/0	0	2.3	0/0	0/0/0	0/0	0//0	0/0/	4.5/4.5/4.5	4.7/4.5			0/0/0	---Ship loading cranes
													---Ship unloading cranes:
0/0/0	0	2.3	0/0	0/0/0	0/0	0//0	0/0/	4.5/4.5/4.5	4.5/4.5			0/0/0	----Grab ship unloading cranes
0/0/0	0	2.3	0/0	0/0/0	0/0	0//0	0/0/	4.5/4.5/4.5	4.5/4.5			0/0/0	----Other
0/0/0	2	4.6	0/0	0/0/0	0/0	0//0	0/0/	9/9/9	9.4/9			0/0/0	---Gantry cranes
													---Loading and unlcading bridges:
0/0/0	2	4.6	0/0	0/0/0	0/0	0//0	0/0/	9/9/9	9.1/9			0/0/0	----Frame loading and unloading bridges
0/0/0	2	4.6	0/0	0/0/0	0/0	0//0	0/0/	9/9/9	9.1/9			0/0/0	----Container loading and unloading bridges
0/0/0	2	6	0/0	0/0/0	0/0	0//0	0/0/	0/9.5/10	0/9.5			0/0/0	----Derrick loading and unloading bridges
0/0/0	2	4.6	0/0	0/0/0	0/0	0//0	0/0/	9/9/9	9.1/9			0/0/0	----Other
0/0/0	2	6	0/0	0/0/0	0/0	0/0/0	0/0/	0/9.5/10	0/9.5			0/0/0	---Other
0/0/0	2	6	0/0	0/0/0	0/0	0//0	0/0/	0/9.5/10	0/9.5			0/0/0	-Tower cranes
0/0/0	0	2.8	0/0	0/0/0	0/0	0//0	0/0/	5.4/5.4/5.4	5.6/5.4			0/0/0	-Portal or pedestal jib cranes
													-Other machinery, self-propelled:
													--On tyres:
0/0/0	0	2.3	0/0	0/0/0	0/0	0//0	0/0/	4.5/4.5/4.5	4.7/4.5			0/0/0	---Wheel-mounted cranes
0/0/0	0	2.3	0/0	0/0/0	0/0	0//0	0/0/	4.5/4.5/4.5	4.7/4.5			0/0/0	---Other
													--Other:
0/0/0	2	3.7	0/0	0/0/0	0/0	0//0	0/0/	7.2/7.2/7.2	7.5/7.2			0/0/0	---Crawler cranes
0/0/0	4.6	6	1.3/1.3	0/0/0	0/0	0/0/0	0/0/	11.7/11.7/11.7	12.2/11.7			0/0/0	---Other
													-Other machinery:
0/0/0	2	6	0/0	0/0/0	0/0	0//0	0/0/	0/9.5/10	0/9.5			0/0/0	--Designed for mounting on road vehicles
0/0/0	0	2.8	0/0	0/0/0	0/0	0//0	0/0/	5.4/5.4/5.4	5.6/5.4			0/0/0	--Other
													Fork-lift trucks; other works trucks fitted with lifting or handling equipment:
													-Self-propelled trucks powered by an electric motor:
0/0/0	2	0	0/0	0/0/0	0/0	0//0	0/0/	0/0/0	8.2/0			0/0/0	---Track alleyway stackers

税则号列	货品名称〔CIQ 扩展编码及品名－T2 表示见附表 2〕	最惠(%)	暂定税率	普通	增值/消费	出口退税	计量单位	监管条件/特殊证件	检验检疫	对美关税	亚太上/下
8427.1020	---无轨巷道堆垛机〔999〕	9		30	13/	13	台/千克	A/	M	29	
8427.1090	---其他〔999〕	9		30	13/	13	台/千克	A/	M	19	
	-其他机动车：										
8427.2010	---集装箱叉车〔999〕	9		30	13/	13	台/千克	A/	M		5.9/5.9
8427.2090	---其他〔999〕	9		30	13/	13	台/千克	A/	M	19	5.9/5.9
8427.9000	-其他车〔999〕	9		30	13/	13	台/千克	A/	M	19	
84.28	**其他升降、搬运、装卸机械(例如，升降机、自动梯、输送机、缆车)：**										
	-升降机及倒卸式起重机：										
8428.1010	---载客电梯										
8428.1010 01	无障碍升降机〔999〕	8	4	30	13/	13	台/千克	A/	M		5.2/5.2
8428.1010 90	其他载客电梯〔999〕	8		30	13/	13	台/千克	A/	M		5.2/5.2
8428.1090	---其他〔101 载货电梯、升降机，102 起重机，103 机械式停车设备及其它装卸、储运设备及其零件，104 集装箱装卸桥，105 其他装卸桥、提升、起重设备及零件〕	6		30	13/	13	台/千克	A/	M	31	3.9/3.9
8428.2000	-气压升降机及输送机〔101 载货电梯、升降机，102 其他装卸桥、提升、起重设备及零件〕	5		30	13/	9,13	台/千克	/		15	
	-其他用于连续运送货物或材料的升降机及输送机：										
8428.3100	--地下专用的〔101 载货电梯、升降机，102 其他装卸桥、提升、起重设备及零件〕	5		30	13/	13	台/千克	/			
8428.3200	--其他，斗式〔101 载货电梯、升降机，102 其他装卸桥、提升、起重设备及零件〕	5		30	13/	13	台/千克	/		15	
8428.3300	--其他，带式〔101 载货电梯、升降机，102 其他装卸桥、提升、起重设备及零件〕	5		30	13/	13	台/千克	/		30	3.3/3.3
	--其他：										
8428.3910	---链式〔101 载货电梯、升降机，102 其他装卸桥、提升、起重设备及零件〕	5		30	13/	13	台/千克	/		25	3.3/3.3
8428.3920	---辊式〔101 载货电梯、升降机，102 其他装卸桥、提升、起重设备及零件〕	5		30	13/	13	台/千克	/		30	3.3/3.3
8428.3990	---其他[T2]	5		30	13/	13	台/千克	/		25	3.3/3.3
8428.4000	-自动梯及自动人行道〔999〕	5		30	13/	13	台/千克	A/	M		
	-缆车、座式升降机、滑雪拉索；索道用牵引装置：										
8428.6010	---货运架空索道〔999〕	8		30	13/	13	台/千克	/			5.6/5.6
	---客运架空索道：										
8428.6021	----单线循环式〔999〕	8		30	13/	13	台/千克	/			5.6/5.6
8428.6029	----其他〔999〕	8		30	13/	13	台/千克	/			5.6/5.6
8428.6090	---其他〔101 载货电梯、升降机，102 客货运缆车〕	8		30	13/	13	台/千克	/			
8428.7000	-工业机器人〔999〕	5		30	13/	13	台/千克	/		30	
	-其他机械：										
8428.9010	---矿车推动机、铁道机车或货车的转车台、货车倾卸装置及类似的铁道货车搬运装置〔999〕	10		30	13/	13	台/千克	/			
8428.9020	---机械式停车设备〔999〕	5		30	13/	13	台/千克	/			
	---其他装卸机械：										
8428.9031	----堆取料机械〔999〕	5		30	13/	13	台/千克	/		30	
8428.9039	----其他〔999〕	5		30	13/	13	台/千克	/		30	
8428.9090	---其他										
8428.9090 10	放化分离作业和热室用遥控机械手(能贯穿 0.6 米以上热室壁或壁厚为 0.6 米以上热室顶)〔999〕	5		30	13/	13	台/千克	3/		25	
8428.9090 20	核反应堆燃料装卸机(用于在核反应堆中插入或取出燃料的操作设备)〔999〕	5		30	13/	13	台/千克	3/		25	
8428.9090 90	其他升降、搬运、装卸机械〔999〕	5		30	13/	13	台/千克	/		25	
84.29	**机动推土机、侧铲推土机、筑路机、平地机、铲运机、机械铲、挖掘机、机铲装载机、捣固机械及压路机：**										
	-推土机及侧铲推土机：										
	--履带式：										
8429.1110	---发动机输出功率超过 235.36 千瓦(320 马力)的〔999〕	7		17	13/	13	台/千克	A/	M	27	4.9/4.9
8429.1190	---其他〔999〕	7		30	13/	13	台/千克	A/	M	32	4.9/4.9
	--其他：										
8429.1910	---发动机输出功率超过 235.36 千瓦(320 马力)的〔999〕	7		17	13/	13	台/千克	A/	M		
8429.1990	---其他〔999〕	7		30	13/	13	台/千克	A/	M		
	-筑路机及平地机：										
8429.2010	---发动机输出功率超过 235.36 千瓦(320 马力)的〔999〕	5		17	13/	9,13	台/千克	A/	M		3.5/3.5
8429.2090	---其他〔999〕	5		30	13/	9,13	台/千克	A/	M	15	3.5/3.5
	-铲运机：										
8429.3010	---斗容量超过 10 立方米的〔999〕	3		17	13/	13	台/千克	A/	M		2.1/2.1
8429.3090	---其他〔999〕	5		30	13/	13	台/千克	A/	M		3.5/3.5
	-捣固机械及压路机：										
	---机动压路机：										
8429.4011	----机重 18 吨及以上的振动压路机〔999〕	7		20	13/	13	台/千克	OA/	M		4.9/4.9
8429.4019	----其他〔999〕	8		40	13/	13	台/千克	OA/	M	33	5.6/5.6
8429.4090	---其他〔101 压路机，102 捣固机〕	6		30	13/	13	台/千克	A/	M		4.2/4.2
	-机械铲、挖掘机及机铲装载机：										

协定税率 %								RCEP		特惠税率 %			Article Description
东/冰/格	巴基斯坦	韩国	瑞士上/下	哥/秘/柬	澳/毛	新西/坡/智	中国港/澳/台	东盟及马来/澳/韩	日/新	亚太2国	老/柬/缅	98/97/95	
0/0/0	2	4.2	0/0	0/0/0	0/0	0//0	0/0/	8.1/8.1/8.1	8.4/8.1			0/0/0	---Trackless alleyway stackers
0/0/0	2	0	0/0	0/0/0	0/0	0//0	0/0/	8.1/8.1/8.1	8.2/8.1			0/0/0	---Other
													-Other self-propelled trucks:
0/0/0	2	0	0/0	0/0/0	0/0	0//0	0/0/	0/0/0	8.2/0			0/0/0	---Fork-lift trucks cranes
0/0/0	2	0	0/0	0/0/0	0/0	0//0	0/0/	0/0/0	8.2/0			0/0/0	---Other
0/0/0	2	0	0/0	0/0/0	0/0	0//0	0/0/	0/0/0	8.2/0			0/0/0	-Other trucks
													Other lifting, handling, loading or unloading machinery (for example, lifts, escalators, conveyors, teleferics):
													-Lifts and skip hoists:
													---Designed for the transport of persons
0/0/0	2	1.6	0.8/0.8	0/0/0	0/0	0/0/0	0/0/	7.6/7.6/7.6	7.6/7.6			0/0/0	Accessibility lifts
0/0/0	2	1.6	0.8/0.8	0/0/0	0/0	0/0/0	0/0/	7.6/7.6/7.6	7.6/7.6			0/0/0	Other passenger elevators
0/0/0	0	0	0/0	0/0/0	0/0	0//0	0/0/0	0/0/0	0/0			0/0/0	---Other
0/0/0	0	2.3	0/0	0/0/0	0/0	0//0	0/0/	4.5/4.5/4.5	4.7/4.5			0/0/0	-Pneumatic elevators and conveyors
													-Other continuous-action elevators and conveyors, for goods or materials:
0/0/0	0	0	0/0	0/0/0	0/0	0//0	0/0/	0/0/0	0/0			0/0/0	--Specially designed for underground use
0/0/0	0	1		0/0/0	0/0	0//0	0/0/	0/0/4.5	4.5/0			0/0/0	--Other, bucket type
0/0/0	0	2.3	0/0	0/0/0	0/0	0//0	0/0/0	4.5/4.5/4.5	4.7/4.5			0/0/0	--Other, belt type
													--Other:
0/0/0	0	2.3	0/0	0/0/0	0/0	0//0	0/0/0	4.5/4.5/4.5	4.7/4.5			0/0/0	---Chain type
0/0/0	0	1	0/0	0/0/0	0/0	0//0	0/0/0	0/0/4.5	4.5/0			0/0/0	---Roller type
0/0/0	0	0	2.1/2.1	0/0/0	0/0	0//0	0/0/0	0/0/0	4.5/0			0/0/0	---Other
0/0/0	0	0	0/0	0/0/0	0/0	0//0	0/0/	0/0/0	0/0			0/0/0	-Escalators and moving walkways
													-Teleferics, chair-lifts, ski-draglines; traction mechanisms for funiculars:
0/0/0	2	0	0/0	0/0/0	0/0	0//0	0/0/	0/0/0	7.3/0			0/0/0	---Cargo aerial cableways
													---Passanger aerial cableways:
0/0/0	2	0	0/0	0/0/0	0/0	0//0	0/0/	0/0/0	7.3/0			0/0/0	----Monocable endless
0/0/0	2	0	0/0	0/0/0	0/0	0//0	0/0/	0/0/0	7.3/0			0/0/0	----Other
0/0/0	2	1.6	0/0	0/0/0	0/0	0//0	0/0/	0/0/7.2	7.3/0			0/0/0	---Other
0/0/0	0	2.3	0.5/0.5	0/0/0	0/0	0//0	0/0/0	4.5/4.5/4.5	4.7/4.5			0/0/0	-Industrial robots
													-Other machinery:
0/0/0	3.5	2	0/0	0/0/0	0/0	0//0	0/0/	0/0/9	9.1/0			0/0/0	---Mine wagon pushers, locmotive or wagon traversers, wagon tippers and similar railway wagon handling equipment
0/0/0	0	1	0/0	0/0/0	0/0	0//0	0/0/	0/0/4.5	4.5/0			0/0/0	---Machinery parking equipment
													---Unloading machinery:
0/0/0	0	2.3	0.5/0.5	0/0/0	0/0	0//0	0/0/0	4.5/4.5/4.5	4.7/4.5			0/0/0	----Stacker reclaimers machinery
0/0/0	0	2.3	0.5/0.5	0/0/0	0/0	0//0	0/0/0	4.5/4.5/4.5	4.7/4.5			0/0/0	----Other
													---Other
0/0/0	0	2.3	0.5/0.5	0/0/0	0/0	0//0	0/0/0	4.5/4.5/4.5	4.7/4.5			0/0/0	Remote manipulators for radioactive chemical separating operation and hot cell (capable of penetrating wall of hot cell thickness>0.6m or top of hot cell thickness>0.6m)
0/0/0	0	2.3	0.5/0.5	0/0/0	0/0	0//0	0/0/0	4.5/4.5/4.5	4.7/4.5			0/0/0	nuclear reactor fuel loader and unloader (operational appliances used for putting inor taking out the fuels in nuclear reactor)
0/0/0	0	2.3	0.5/0.5	0/0/0	0/0	0//0	0/0/0	4.5/4.5/4.5	4.7/4.5			0/0/0	Other lifting, carrying, loading or unloading machinery
													Self-propelled bulldozers, angledozers, graders, levellers, scrapers, mechanical shovels, excavators, shovel loaders, tamping machines and road rollers:
													-Bulldozers and angledozers:
													--Track laying:
0/0/0	2	0	0/0	0/0/0	0/0	0//0	0/0/	6.3/6.3/6.3	6.4/6.3			0/0/0	---With an engine of an output exceeding 235.36kW (320HP)
0/0/0	2	0	0/0	0/0/0	0/0	0//0	0/0/	0/0/0	6.4/0			0/0/0	---Other
													--Other:
0/0/0	2	0	0/0	0/0/0	0/0	0//0	0/0/	0/0/0	6.4/0			0/0/0	---With an engine of an output exceeding 235.36kW (320HP)
0/0/0	2	0	0/0	0/0/0	0/0	0//0	0/0/	0/0/0	6.4/0			0/0/0	---Other
													-Graders and levellers:
0/0/0	0	0	0/0	0/0/0	0/0	0//0	0/0/	0/0/0	0/0			0/0/0	---With an engine of an output exceeding 235.36kW (320HP)
0/0/0	0	0	0/0	0/0/0	0/0	0//0	0/0/	0/0/0	0/0			0/0/0	---Other
													-Scrapers:
0/0/0	0	0	0/0	0/0/0	0/0	0//0	0/0/	0/0/0	0/0			0/0/0	---Having a capacity of shovel exceeding $10m^3$
0/0/0	0	0	0/0	0/0/0	0/0	0//0	0/0/	0/0/0	0/0			0/0/0	---Other
													-Tamping machines and road rollers:
													---Self-propelled road rollers:
0/0/0	2	0	0/0	0/0/0	0/0	0//0	0/0/	0/0/0	6.4/0			0/0/0	----Vibration type, of a deadweight of 18t or more
0/0/0	2	0	0/0	0/0/0	0/0	0//0	0/0/	0/0/0	7.3/0			0/0/0	----Other
0/0/0	0	0	0/0	0/0/0	0/0	0//0	0/0/	0/0/0	0/0			0/0/0	---Other
													-Mechanical shovels, excavators and shovel loaders:

税则号列	货品名称〔CIQ扩展编码及品名－T2表示见附表2〕	最惠(%)	暂定税率	普通	增值/消费	出口退税	计量单位	监管条件/特殊证件	检验检疫	对美关税	亚太上/下
8429.5100	--前铲装载机〔999〕	5		30	13/	13	台/千克	A/	M	10	
	--上部结构可旋转360度的机械:										
	---挖掘机:										
8429.5211	----轮胎式〔999〕	8		30	13/	13	台/千克	OA/	M		7.2/7.2
8429.5212	----履带式〔999〕	8		30	13/	13	台/千克	OA/	M	33	
8429.5219	----其他〔999〕	8		30	13/	13	台/千克	OA/	M		5.2/5.2
8429.5290	---其他〔999〕	8		30	13/	13	台/千克	OA/	M		5.2/5.2
8429.5900	--其他〔999〕	8		30	13/	13	台/千克	OA/	M	28	
84.30	**泥土、矿物或矿石的运送、平整、铲运、挖掘、捣固、压实、开采或钻探机械;打桩机及拔桩机;扫雪机及吹雪机:**										
8430.1000	-打桩机及拔桩机〔999〕	10		30	13/	13	台/千克	/		15	
8430.2000	-扫雪机及吹雪机〔999〕	10		30	13/	13	台/千克	/		15	
	-截煤机、凿岩机及隧道掘进机:										
	--自推进的:										
8430.3110	---采(截)煤机〔999〕	10		30	13/	13	台/千克	O/		30	
8430.3120	---凿岩机〔999〕	10		30	13/	13	台/千克	O/			
8430.3130	---隧道掘进机〔999〕	10		30	13/	13	台/千克	O/			
8430.3900	--其他〔999〕	6		30	13/	13	台/千克	/		26	
	-其他钻探或凿井机械:										
	--自推进的:										
	---石油及天然气钻探机:										
8430.4111	----钻探深度在6000米及以上的〔999〕	5		11	13/	13	台/千克	/		10	3.5/3.5
8430.4119	----其他〔999〕	5		17	13/	13	台/千克	/		25	3.5/3.5
	---其他钻探机:										
8430.4121	----钻探深度在6000米及以上的〔999〕	5		11	13/	13	台/千克	/		10	3.5/3.5
8430.4122	----钻探深度在6000米以下的履带式自推进钻机〔999〕	5		17	13/	13	台/千克	/		15	
8430.4129	----钻探深度在6000米以下的其他钻探机〔999〕	5		17	13/	13	台/千克	/		25	
8430.4190	---其他〔999〕	5		30	13/	13	台/千克	/		10	
8430.4900	--其他〔999〕	5		30	13/	13	台/千克	/		30	
	-其他自推进机械:										
8430.5010	---其他采油机械〔999〕	3		17	13/	13	台/千克	/		8	2.1/2.1
8430.5020	---矿用电铲〔999〕	7		30	13/	13	台/千克	/			
	---采矿钻机:										
8430.5031	----牙轮直径380毫米及以上〔999〕	5		30	13/	13	台/千克	/		10	3.5/3.5
8430.5039	----其他〔999〕	5		30	13/	13	台/千克	/		10	3.5/3.5
8430.5090	---其他〔999〕	5		30	13/	13	台/千克	/		30	
	-其他非自推进机械:										
8430.6100	--捣固或压实机械〔999〕	6		30	13/	13	台/千克	/			
	--其他:										
	---工程钻机:										
8430.6911	----钻筒直径在3米及以上〔999〕	6		30	13/	13	台/千克	/			4.2/4.2
8430.6919	----其他〔999〕	6		30	13/	13	台/千克	/		31	
8430.6920	---铲运机〔101铲运机,102其它工程机械及其零件,103建筑工业行业成套设备〕	6		30	13/	13	台/千克	/		26	4.2/4.2
8430.6990	---其他〔999〕	6		30	13/	13	台/千克	/		26	
84.31	**专用于或主要用于税目84.25至84.30所列机械的零件:**										
8431.1000	-税目84.25所列机械的零件〔999〕	3		30	13/	13	千克	/		13	
	-税目84.27所列机械的零件:										
8431.2010	---装有差速器的驱动桥及其零件,不论是否装有传动部件〔999〕	6		30	13/	13	千克/个	/		31	3.9/3.9
8431.2090	---其他〔999〕	6	3	30	13/	13	千克	/		23	3.9/3.9
	-税目84.28所列机械的零件:										
8431.3100	--升降机、倒卸式起重机或自动梯的零件										
8431.3100　01	无障碍升降机的零件〔999〕	3	1	30	13/	13	千克	/		21	
8431.3100　90	其他升降机、倒卸式起重机零件(包括自动梯零件)〔999〕	3		30	13/	13	千克	/		23	
8431.3900	--其他〔999〕	5		30	13/	13	千克	/		25	2.5/2.5
	-税目84.26、84.29或84.30所列机械的零件:										
8431.4100	--戽斗、铲斗、抓斗及夹斗〔101其它工程机械及其零件,102其他装卸桥、提升、起重设备及零件〕	6		17	13/	13	千克/个	/		31	3.9/3.9
8431.4200	--推土机或侧铲推土机用铲〔999〕	6		17	13/	13	千克/个	/		26	
	--子目8430.41或8430.49所列钻探或凿井机械的零件:										
8431.4310	---石油或天然气钻探机用〔999〕	4		11	13/	13	千克	/		9	2.6/2.6
8431.4320	---其他钻探机用〔999〕	4		11	13/	13	千克	/		14	2.6/2.6
8431.4390	---其他〔999〕	5		17	13/	13	千克	/		30	3.3/3.3
	--其他:										
8431.4920	---装有差速器的驱动桥及其零件,不论是否装有传动部件〔999〕	5		17	13/	13	千克/个	/		30	3.3/3.3
	---其他:										
8431.4991	----矿用电铲用〔101其它工程机械及其零件,102其他装卸桥、提升、起重设备及零件〕	5		17	13/	13	千克	/		25	3.3/3.3

协定税率 %								RCEP		特惠税率 %			
东/冰/格	巴基斯坦	韩国	瑞士上/下	哥/秘/柬	澳/毛	新西/坡/智	中国港/澳/台	东盟及马来/澳/韩	日/新	亚太2国	老/柬/缅	98/97/95	Article Description
0/0/0	0	1	0/0	0/0/0	0/0	0//0	0/0/	0/0/4.5	4.5/0			0/0/0	--Front-end shovel loaders
													--Machinery with a 360° revolving super-structure:
													---Excavators:
0/0/0	2	7.2	0/0	0/0/0	0/0	0//0	0/0/	7.6/7.6/	/7.6			0/0/0	----Tyre-mounted
0/0/0	2		0/0	0/0/0	0/0	0//0	0/0/	7.6/7.6/	/7.6			0/0/0	----Track-mounted
0/0/0	2	5.2	0/0	0/0/0	0/0	0//0	0/0/	7.6/7.6/	/7.6			0/0/0	----Other
0/0/0	2	5.2	0/0	0/0/0	0/0	0//0	0/0/	7.6/7.6/	/7.6			0/0/0	---Other
0/0/0	2	0	0/0	0/0/0	0/0	0//0	0/0/	0/0/0	7.3/0			0/0/0	--Other
													Other moving, grading, levelling, scraping, excavating, tamping, compacting, extracting or boring machinery, for earth, minerals or ores; pile-drivers and pile-extractors; snow-ploughs and snow-blowers:
0/0/0	2	2	0/0	0/0/0	0/0	0//0	0/0/	0/0/9	9.1/0			0/0/0	-Pile-drivers and pile-extranctors
0/0/0	2	2	0/0	0/0/0	0/0	0//0	0/0/	0/0/9	9.1/0			0/0/0	-Snow-ploughs and snow-blowers
													-Coal or rock cutters and tunnelling machinery:
													--Self-propelle:
0/0/0	2	2	0/0	0/0/0	0/0	0/0/0	0/0/	0/0/9	9.1/0			0/0/0	---Coal cutters
0/0/0	2	2	0/0	0/0/0	0/0	0/0/0	0/0/	0/0/9	9.1/0			0/0/0	---Rock drilling machine
0/0/0	2	2	0/0	0/0/0	0/0	0/0/0	0/0/	0/0/9	9.1/0			0/0/0	---Tunnel boring machine
0/0/0	0	1.2	0/0	0/0/0	0/0	0//0	0/0/	0/0/5.4	5.5/0			0/0/0	--Other
													-Other boring or sinking machinery:
													--Self-propelled:
													---Oil and natural gas drilling machinery:
0/0/0	0	0	0/0	0/0/0	0/0	0//0	0/0/	0/0/0	0/0			0/0/0	----Of drilling depth of 6000m or more
0/0/0	0	0	0/0	0/0/0	0/0	0//0	0/0/	0/0/0	0/0			0/0/0	----Other
													---Other drilling machinery:
0/0/0	0	0	0/0	0/0/0	0/0	0//0	0/0/	0/0/0	0/0			0/0/0	----Of drilling depth of 6000m or more
0/0/0	0	1	0/0	0/0/0	0/0	0//0	0/0/	0/0/4.5	4.5/0			0/0/0	----Crawler boring machinery of drilling depth not exceeding 6000 m
0/0/0	0	0	0/0	0/0/0	0/0	0//0	0/0/	0/0/0	0/0			0/0/0	----Other boring machinery of drilling depth exceeding 6000 m
0/0/0	0	0	0/0	0/0/0	0/0	0//0	0/0/	0/0/0	0/0			0/0/0	---Other
0/0/0	0	1	0/0	0/0/0	0/0	0//0	0/0/	0/0/4.5	4.5/0			0/0/0	--Other
													-Other machinery, self-propelled:
0/0/0	0	0	0/0	0/0/0	0/0	0//0	0/0/	0/0/0	0/0			0/0/0	---For oil production
0/0/0	2	0	0/0	0/0/0	0/0	0//0	0/0/	0/0/0	6.4/0			0/0/0	---Mining power shovels
													---Mining drills:
0/0/0	0	0	0/0	0/0/0	0/0	0//0	0/0/	0/0/0	0/0			0/0/0	----Gear wheel diameter more than 380mm
0/0/0	0	0	0/0	0/0/0	0/0	0//0	0/0/	0/0/0	0/0			0/0/0	----Other
0/0/0	0	2.3	0/0	0/0/0	0/0	0//0	0/0/	4.5/4.5/4.5	4.7/4.5			0/0/0	---Other
													-Other machinery, not self-propelled:
0/0/0	0	0	0/0	0/0/0	0/0	0//0	0/0/	0/0/0	0/0			0/0/0	--Tamping or compacting machinery
													--Other:
													---Engineering drills:
0/0/0	0	0	0/0	0/0/0	0/0	0//0	0/0/	0/0/0	0/0			0/0/0	----Boring casing diameter more than 3m
0/0/0	0	1.2	0/0	0/0/0	0/0	0//0	0/0/	0/0/5.4	5.5/0			0/0/0	----Other
0/0/0	0	0	0/0	0/0/0	0/0	0//0	0/0/	0/0/0	0/0			0/0/0	---Serapers
0/0/0	0	0	0/0	0/0/0	0/0	0//0	0/0/	0/0/0	0/0			0/0/0	---Other
													Parts suitable for use solely or principally with the machinery of headings No.84. 25 to 84. 30:
0/0/0	0	0	0/0	0/0/0	0/0	0//0	0/0/	0/0/0	0/0			0/0/0	-Of machinery of heading No. 84. 25
													-Of machinery of heading No. 84. 27:
0/0/0	0	2.8	0/0	0/0/0	0/0	0//0	0/0/	5.4/5.4/5.4	5.6/5.4			0/0/0	---Drive-axle with differential and parts thereof, whether or not provided transmussion components
0/0/0	0	2.8	0/0	0/0/0	0/0	0//0	0/0/	5.4/5.4/5.4	5.6/5.4			0/0/0	---Other
													-Of machinery of heading No. 84. 28:
													--Of lifts, skip hoists or escalators
0/0/0	0	0	0/0	0/0/0	0/0	0//0	0/0/	0/2.7/0	0/2.7			0/0/0	Parts of accessibility lifts
0/0/0	0	0	0/0	0/0/0	0/0	0//0	0/0/	0/2.7/0	0/2.7			0/0/0	Other lifters, unloading crane parts (including automatic elevator parts)
0/0/0	0	2.3	0/0	0/0/0	0/0	0//0	0/0/	4.5/4.5/4.5	4.7/4.5			0/0/0	--Other
													-Of machinery of headingNo.84. 26, 84. 29 or 84. 30:
0/0/0	0	1.2	0/0	0/0/0	0/0	0//0	0/0/	0/0/5.4	5.5/0			0/0/0	--Buckets, shovels, grabs and grips
0/0/0	0	0	0/0	0/0/0	0/0	0//0	0/0/	0/0/0	0/0			0/0/0	--Bulldozer or angledozer blades
													--Parts of boring or sinking machinery of subheading No. 8430. 41 or 8430. 49:
0/0/0	0	0	0/0	0/0/0	0/0	0//0	0/0/	0/0/0	0/0			0/0/0	---Of oil and natural gas drilling machinery
0/0/0	0	0	0/0	0/0/0	0/0	0//0	0/0/	0/0/0	0/0			0/0/0	---Of other drilling machinery
0/0/0	0	1	0/0	0/0/0	0/0	0//0	0/0/	0/0/4.5	4.5/0			0/0/0	---Other
													--Other
0/0/0	0	2.3	0/0	0/0/0	0/0	0//0	0/0/	4.5/4.5/4.5	4.7/4.5			0/0/0	---Drive-axle with differential and parts thereof, whether or not provided transmussion components
													---Other:
0/0/0	0	1	0/0	0/0/0	0/0	0//0	0/0/	0/0/4.5	4.5/0			0/0/0	----For electrical shovels for mining

税则号列	货品名称〔CIQ 扩展编码及品名—T2 表示见附表 2〕	最惠(%)	暂定税率	普通	增值/消费	出口退税	计量单位	监管条件/特殊证件	检验检疫	对美关税	亚太上/下
8431.4999	----其他〔101 其它工程机械及其零件,102 其他装卸桥、提升、起重设备及零件〕	5		17	13/	13	千克	/		25	3.3/3.3
84.32	**农业、园艺及林业用整地或耕作机械;草坪及运动场地滚压机:**										
8432.1000	-犁〔999〕	5		30	9/	9	台/千克	/			
	-耙、松土机、中耕机、除草机及耕耘机:										
8432.2100	--圆盘耙〔999〕	5		30	9/	9	台/千克	/		25	
8432.2900	--其他〔101 耕作机,102 其它农牧业机械及其零件〕	4		30	9/	9	台/千克	/		24	
	-播种机、种植机及移植机:										
	--免耕直接播种机、种植机及移植机:										
	---免耕直接播种机:										
8432.3111	----谷物播种机〔999〕	4		30	9/	9	台/千克	/		24	2.6/2.6
8432.3119	----其他〔999〕	4		30	9/	9	台/千克	/		24	2.6/2.6
	---免耕直接种植机:										
8432.3121	----马铃薯种植机〔999〕	4		30	9/	9	台/千克	/			2.6/2.6
8432.3129	----其他〔999〕	4		30	9/	9	台/千克	/		29	2.6/2.6
	---免耕直接移植机(栽植机):										
8432.3131	----水稻插秧机〔999〕	4		30	9/	9	台/千克	/			2.6/2.6
8432.3139	----其他〔999〕	4		30	9/	9	台/千克	/		29	2.6/2.6
	--其他:										
	---播种机:										
8432.3911	----谷物播种机〔999〕	4		30	9/	9	台/千克	/		24	2.6/2.6
8432.3919	----其他〔999〕	4		30	9/	9,13	台/千克	/		24	2.6/2.6
	---种植机:										
8432.3921	----马铃薯种植机〔999〕	4		30	9/	9	台/千克	/			2.6/2.6
8432.3929	----其他〔999〕	4		30	9/	9	台/千克	/			2.6/2.6
	---移植机(栽植机):										
8432.3931	----水稻插秧机〔999〕	4		30	9/	9	台/千克	/			2.6/2.6
8432.3939	----其他〔999〕	4		30	9/	9	台/千克	/			2.6/2.6
	-施肥机:										
8432.4100	--粪肥施肥机〔999〕	4		30	9/	9	台/千克	/		14	
8432.4200	--化肥施肥机〔999〕	4		30	9/	9	台/千克	/		29	
	-其他机械:										
8432.8010	---草坪及运动场地滚压机〔999〕	7		40	13/	13	台/千克	/		27	5.6/5.6
8432.8090	---其他〔999〕	4		30	9/	9,13	台/千克	/		14	
8432.9000	-零件〔999〕	4		17	13/	13	千克	/		29	
84.33	**收割机、脱粒机,包括草料打包机;割草机;蛋类、水果或其他农产品的清洁、分选、分级机器,但税目 84.37 的机器除外:**										
	-草坪、公园或运动场地用的割草机:										
8433.1100	--机动的,切割装置在同一水平面上旋转的〔999〕	6		30	9/	9,13	台/千克	/		11	
8433.1900	--其他〔999〕	6		30	13/	13	台/千克	/		11	
8433.2000	-其他割草机,包括牵引装置用的刀具杆〔999〕	4		30	9/	9	台/千克	/		14	
8433.3000	-其他干草切割、翻晒机器〔999〕	5		30	9/	9	台/千克	/		25	
8433.4000	-草料打包机,包括收集打包机〔999〕	5		30	9/	9	台/千克	/		15	
	-其他收割机;脱粒机:										
8433.5100	--联合收割机										
8433.5100 01	功率≥160 马力的联合收割机〔999〕	8	6	17	9/	9	台/千克	/		26	5.2/5.2
8433.5100 90	功率<160 马力的联合收割机〔999〕	8		17	9/	9	台/千克	/		28	5.2/5.2
8433.5200	--其他脱粒机〔999〕	8		30	9/	9	台/千克	/			
8433.5300	--根茎或块茎收获机										
8433.5300 01	功率≥160 马力的土豆、甜菜收获机〔999〕	8	6	30	9/	9	台/千克	/		26	
8433.5300 90	其他根茎或块茎收获机〔999〕	8		30	9/	9	台/千克	/		28	
	--其他:										
8433.5910	---甘蔗收获机										
8433.5910 01	功率≥160 马力的甘蔗收获机〔999〕	8	6	30	9/	9	台/千克	/		11	5.6/5.6
8433.5910 90	其他甘蔗收获机〔999〕	8		30	9/	9	台/千克	/		13	5.6/5.6
8433.5920	---棉花采摘机〔999〕	8	5	30	9/	9	台/千克	A/	M		5.6/5.6
8433.5990	---其他										
8433.5990 01	自走式青储饲料收获机〔999〕	8	6	30	9/	9	台/千克	/		31	
8433.5990 02	茶叶采摘机〔999〕	8	6	30	9/	9	台/千克	/		31	
8433.5990 90	其他收割机及脱粒机〔101 收割机,102 脱粒机〕	8		30	9/	9	台/千克	/		33	
	-蛋类、水果或其他农产品的清洁、分选、分级机器:										
8433.6010	---蛋类清洁、分级、分选机器〔999〕	5		30	9/	9	台/千克	/			
8433.6090	---其他〔999〕	5		30	9/	9,13	台/千克	/		25	
	-零件:										
8433.9010	---联合收割机用〔999〕	5		11	13/	13	千克	/		25	
8433.9090	---其他〔999〕	3		17	13/	13	千克	/		8	
84.34	**挤奶机及乳品加工机器:**										
8434.1000	-挤奶机〔999〕	8	4	20	9/	9	台/千克	/		9	
8434.2000	-乳品加工机器〔999〕	6	2	30	13/	13	台/千克	A/	R	27	4.2/4.2
8434.9000	-零件〔999〕	5	2	17	13/	13	千克	/		7	
84.35	**制酒、制果汁或制类似饮料用的压榨机、轧碎机及类似机器:**										
8435.1000	-机器〔999〕	8		30	13/	13	台/千克	A/	R	28	

协定税率 %								RCEP		特惠税率 %			Article Description
东/冰/格	巴基斯坦	韩国	瑞士上/下	哥/秘/柬	澳/毛	新西/坡/智	中国港/澳/台	东盟及马来/澳/韩	日/新	亚太2国	老/柬/缅	98/97/95	
0/0/0	0	2.3	0/0	0/0/0	0/0	0//0	0/0/	4.5/4.5/4.5	4.7/4.5			0/0/0	----Other
													Agricultural, horticultural or forestry machinery for soil preparation or cultivation; lawn or sports-ground rollers:
0/0/0	0	1	0/0	0/0/0	0/0	0//0	0/0/	0/0/4.5	4.5/0			0/0/0	-Ploughs
													-Harrows, scarifiers, cultivators, weeders and hoes:
0/0/0	0	0	0/0	0/0/0	0/0	0//0	0/0/	0/0/0	0/0			0/0/0	--Disc harrows
0/0/0	0	0	0/0	0/0/0	0/0	0//0	0/0/	0/0/0	0/0			0/0/0	--Other
													-Seeders, planters and transplanters:
													--No—till direct seeders, planters and transplanters:
													---No—till direct seeders:
0/0/0	0	0	0/0	0/0/0	0/0	0//0	0/0/	0/0/0	3.6/0			0/0/0	----Seeders for grain
0/0/0	0	0.8	0/0	0/0/0	0/0	0//0	0/0/	0/0/3.6	3.6/0			0/0/0	----Other
													---No—till direct seeders
0/0/0	0	0	0/0	0/0/0	0/0	0//0	0/0/	0/0/0	3.6/0			0/0/0	----Planters for potato
0/0/0	0	0	0/0	0/0/0	0/0	0//0	0/0/	0/0/0	3.6/0			0/0/0	----Other
													--No—till direct transplanters:
0/0/0	0	0	0/0	0/0/0	0/0	0//0	0/0/	3.6/3.6/3.6	3.6/3.6			0/0/0	---Tansplanters for rice
0/0/0	0	1.8	0/0	0/0/0	0/0	0//0	0/0/	3.8/3.8/4	3.8/3.8			0/0/0	----other
													--Other:
													---Seeders:
0/0/0	0	0	0/0	0/0/0	0/0	0//0	0/0/	0/0/0	3.6/0			0/0/0	---Seeders for grain
0/0/0	0	0.8	0/0	0/0/0	0/0	0//0	0/0/	0/0/3.6	3.6/0			0/0/0	---other
													---planters:
0/0/0	0	0	0/0	0/0/0	0/0	0//0	0/0/	0/0/0	3.6/0			0/0/0	----Planters for potato
0/0/0	0	0	0/0	0/0/0	0/0	0//0	0/0/	0/0/0	3.6/0			0/0/0	----Other
													---transplanters:
0/0/0	0	0	0/0	0/0/0	0/0	0//0	0/0/	3.6/3.6/3.6	3.6/3.6			0/0/0	----Tansplanters for rice
0/0/0	0	1.8	0/0	0/0/0	0/0	0//0	0/0/	3.8/3.8/4	3.8/3.8			0/0/0	----Other
													-Manure spreaders and fertilizer distributors
0/0/0	0	0	0/0	0/0/0	0/0	0//0	0/0/	0/0/0	3.6/0			0/0/0	--Manure spreaders
0/0/0	0	0	0/0	0/0/0	0/0	0//0	0/0/	0/0/0	3.6/0			0/0/0	--Fertfllzer dmtrl butors
													-Other machinery:
0/0/0	2	3.2	0/0	0/0/0	0/0	0//0	0/0/	6.3/6.3/6.3	6.6/6.3			0/0/0	---Lawn or sports-ground rollers
0/0/0	0	0	0/0	0/0/0	0/0	0//0	0/0/	0/0/0	0/0			0/0/0	---Other
0/0/0	0	0	0/0	0/0/0	0/0	0//0	0/0/	0/3.6/0	0/3.6			0/0/0	-Parts
													Harvesting or threshing machinery, including straw or fodder balers; grass or hay mowers; machines for cleaning, sorting or grading eggs, fruit or other agricultural produce, other than machinery of heading No.84.37:
													-Mowers for lawns, parks or sports grounds:
0/0/0	0	0	0/0	0/0/0	0/0	0//0	0/0/	0/0/0	0/0			0/0/0	--Powered, with the cutting device rotating in a horizontal plane
0/0/0	0	0	0/0	0/0/0	0/0	0//0	0/0/	0/0/0	0/0			0/0/0	--Other
0/0/0	0	0	0/0	0/0/0	0/0	0//0	0/0/	0/0/0	0/0			0/0/0	-Other mowers, including cutter bars for tractor mounting
0/0/0	0	0	0/0	0/0/0	0/0	0//0	0/0/	0/0/0	0/0			0/0/0	-Other haymaking machinery
0/0/0	0	2.3	0/0	0/0/0	0/0	0//0	0/0/	4.5/4.5/4.5	4.7/4.5			0/0/0	-Straw or fodder balers, including pick-up balers
													-Other harvesting machinery; threshing machinery:
													--Combine harvester-threshers
0/0/0	2	3.7	0/0	0/0/0	0/0	0//0	0/0/	7.5/7.6/7.5	7.5/7.6			0/0/0	Combine harvester-threshers, power≥160HP
0/0/0	2	3.7	0/0	0/0/0	0/0	0//0	0/0/	7.5/7.6/7.5	7.5/7.6			0/0/0	Combine harvester-threshers, power<160HP
0/0/0	2	0	0/0	0/0/0	0/0	0//0	0/0/	0/0/0	7.3/0			0/0/0	--Other threshing machinery
													--Root or tuber harvesting machines
0/0/0	2	1.6	0/0	0/0/0	0/0	0//0	0/0/	0/0/7.2	7.3/0			0/0/0	Potatoes, beets harvesting machines, power ≥160HP
0/0/0	2	1.6	0/0	0/0/0	0/0	0//0	0/0/	0/0/7.2	7.3/0			0/0/0	Other root or tuber harvesting machines
													--Other:
													---Sugarcane harvesters
0/0/0	2	0	0/0	0/0/0	0/0	0//0	0/0/	0/0/0	7.3/0			0/0/0	Sugarcane harvesting machines, power ≥160HP
0/0/0	2	0	0/0	0/0/0	0/0	0//0	0/0/	0/0/0	7.3/0			0/0/0	Other sugarcane harvesters
0/0/0	2	0	0/0	0/0/0	0/0	0//0	0/0/	0/0/0	7.3/0			0/0/0	---Cotton picker
													---Other
0/0/0	2	0	0/0	0/0/0	0/0	0//0	0/0/	0/0/0	7.3/0			0/0/0	Self-propelled silage harvester
0/0/0	2	0	0/0	0/0/0	0/0	0//0	0/0/	0/0/0	7.3/0			0/0/0	Tea picker
0/0/0	2	0	0/0	0/0/0	0/0	0//0	0/0/	0/0/0	7.3/0			0/0/0	Other harvesers and threshers
													-Machines for cleaning, sorting or grading eggs, fruit or other agricultural produce:
0/0/0	0	1	0/0	0/0/0	0/0	0//0	0/0/	0/0/4.5	4.5/0			0//	---Machine for cleaning, Sorting or grading eggs
0/0/0	0	1	0/0	0/0/0	0/0	0//0	0/0/	0/0/4.5	4.5/0			0//	---Other
													-Parts:
0/0/0	0	2.3	0/0	0/0/0	0/0	0//0	0/0/	4.5/4.5/4.5	4.7/4.5			0/0/0	---Of combine harvester-threshers
0/0/0	0	0	0/0	0/0/0	0/0	0//0	0/0/	0/0/0	0/0			0/0/0	---Other
													Milking machines and dairy machinery:
0/0/0	2	2	0/0	0//0	0/0	0//0	0/0/	0/0/9	9.1/0			0/0/0	-Milking machines
0/0/0	0	0	0/0	0/0/0	0/0	0//0	0/0/	0/0/0	0/0			0/0/0	-Dairy machinery
0/0/0	0	0	0/0	0/0/0	0/0	0//0	0/0/	0/0/0	0/0			0/0/0	-Parts
													Presses, crushers and similar machinery used in the manufacture of wine, cider, fruit juices or similar beverages:
0/0/0	2	2	0/0	0/0/0	0/0	0//0	0/0/	0/0/9	9.1/0			0/0/0	-Machinery

税则号列	货品名称〔CIQ扩展编码及品名—T2表示见附表2〕	最惠(%)	暂定税率	普通	增值/消费	出口退税	计量单位	监管条件/特殊证件	检验检疫	对美关税	亚太上/下
8435.9000	-零件〔999〕	6		30	13/	13	千克	/		26	
84.36	**农业、园艺、林业、家禽饲养业或养蜂业用的其他机器，包括装有机械或热力装置的催芽设备；家禽孵卵器及育雏器：**										
8436.1000	-动物饲料配制机〔999〕	7		30	9/	9	台/千克	/		27	
	-家禽饲养用的机器；家禽孵卵器及育雏器：										
8436.2100	--家禽孵卵器及育雏器〔999〕	5		30	9/	9	台/千克	/		15	
8436.2900	--其他〔999〕	8		30	9/	9	台/千克	/		28	
8436.8000	-其他机器										
8436.8000 01	青储饲料切割上料机〔999〕	8	5	30	9/	9,13	台/千克	/		10	
8436.8000 02	自走式饲料搅拌投喂车〔999〕	8	6	30	9/	9,13	台/千克	/		11	
8436.8000 90	农、林业、园艺等用的其他机器（包括装有机械或热力装置的催芽设备）〔999〕	8		30	9/	9,13	台/千克	/		13	
	-零件：										
8436.9100	--家禽饲养用机器的零件或家禽孵卵器及育雏器的零件〔999〕	6		17	13/	13	千克	/		16	
8436.9900	--其他〔999〕	6		17	13/	13	千克	/		16	
84.37	**种子、谷物或干豆的清洁、分选或分级机器；谷物磨粉业加工机器或谷物、干豆加工机器，但农业用机器除外：**										
	-种子、谷物或干豆的清洁、分选或分级机器：										
8437.1010	---光学色差颗粒选别机（色选机）〔999〕	8		30	9/	9,13	台/千克	/			
8437.1090	---其他〔999〕	8		30	9/	9	台/千克	/		13	
8437.8000	-其他机器〔999〕	8		30	13/	9	台/千克	A/	R	28	5.2/5.2
8437.9000	-零件〔999〕	6		30	13/	13	千克	/		26	
84.38	**本章其他税目未列名的食品、饮料工业用的生产或加工机器，但提取、加工动物油脂、植物固定油脂或微生物油脂的机器除外：**										
8438.1000	-糕点加工机器及生产通心粉、面条或类似产品的机器										
8438.1000 10	糕点生产线〔999〕	7		30	13/	13	台/千克	A/	R	27	
8438.1000 90	通心粉，面条的生产加工机器（包括类似产品的加工机）〔999〕	7		30	13/	13	台/千克	A/	R	27	
8438.2000	-生产糖果、可可粉、巧克力的机器〔999〕	8		30	13/	13	台/千克	A/	R	33	
8438.3000	-制糖机器〔999〕	8		30	13/	13	台/千克	A/	R	33	
8438.4000	-酿酒机器〔999〕	7		30	13/	13	台/千克	A/	R	32	
8438.5000	-肉类或家禽加工机器〔999〕	7		30	13/	13	台/千克	A/	R	27	
8438.6000	-水果、坚果或蔬菜加工机器〔999〕	8		30	13/	13	台/千克	A/	R	18	
8438.8000	-其他机器〔999〕	8		30	13/	9,13	台/千克	A/	R	28	5.2/5.2
8438.9000	-零件〔999〕	5		30	13/	13	千克	/		25	
84.39	**纤维素纸浆、纸及纸板的制造或整理机器：**										
8439.1000	-制造纤维素纸浆的机器〔999〕	8		30	13/	13	台/千克	/		33	
8439.2000	-纸或纸板的抄造机器〔999〕	8		30	13/	13	台/千克	/			5.6/5.6
8439.3000	-纸或纸板的整理机器〔999〕	8		30	13/	13	台/千克	/		33	
	-零件：										
8439.9100	--制造纤维素纸浆的机器用〔999〕	6		30	13/	13	千克	/		11	
8439.9900	--其他〔999〕	6		30	13/	13	千克	/		31	3/3
84.40	**书本装订机器，包括锁线订书机：**										
	-机器：										
8440.1010	---锁线装订机〔999〕	10		35	13/	13	台/千克	/		35	7/7
8440.1020	---胶订机〔999〕	12		35	13/	13	台/千克	/			
8440.1090	---其他〔999〕	12		35	13/	13	台/千克	/		37	
8440.9000	-零件〔999〕	8		35	13/	13	千克	/		33	
84.41	**其他制造纸浆制品、纸制品或纸板制品的机器，包括各种切纸机：**										
8441.1000	-切纸机〔999〕	12		50	13/	13	台/千克	/		37	
8441.2000	-制造包、袋或信封的机器〔999〕	12		30	13/	13	台/千克	/			7.8/7.8
	-制造箱、盒、管、桶或类似容器的机器，但模制成型机器除外：										
8441.3010	---制造纸塑铝复合罐的生产设备〔999〕	12		30	13/	13	台/千克	/			7.8/7.8
8441.3090	---其他〔999〕	12		30	13/	13	台/千克	/		17	7.8/7.8
8441.4000	-纸浆、纸或纸板制品模制成型机器〔999〕	12		30	13/	13	台/千克	/		37	
	-其他机器：										
8441.8010	---制造纸塑铝软包装的生产设备〔999〕	12		30	13/	13	台/千克	/		22	7.8/7.8
8441.8090	---其他〔999〕	12		30	13/	13	台/千克	/		37	7.8/7.8
	-零件：										

协定税率 %								RCEP		特惠税率 %			Article Description
东/冰/格	巴基斯坦	韩国	瑞士上/下	哥/秘/柬	澳/毛	新西/坡/智	中国港/澳/台	东盟及马来/澳/韩	日/新	亚太2国	老/柬/缅	98/97/95	
0/0/0	0	0	0/0	0/0/0	0/0	0//0	0/0/	0/0/0	0/0			0/0/0	-Parts
													Other agricultural, horticultural, forestry, poultry-keeping or bee-keeping machinery, including germination plant fitted with mechanical or thermal equipment; poultry incubators and brooders:
0/0/0	2	3.2	2.9/2.9	0/0/0	0/0	0//0	0/0/	6.3/6.3/6.3	6.6/6.3			0/0/0	-Machinery for preparing animal feeding stuffs
													-Poultry-keeping machinery; poultry incubators and brooders:
0/0/0	0	2.3	0/0	0/0/0	0/0	0//0	0/0/	4.5/4.5/4.5	4.7/4.5			0/0/0	--Poultry incubators and brooders
0/0/0	2	6	0/0	0/0/0	0/0	0//0	0/0/	0/9.5/10	0/9.5			0/0/0	--Other
													-Other machinery
0/0/0	2	2	0/0	0/0/0	0/0	0//0	0/0/	0/0/9	9.1/0			0/0/0	Silage cutting feeders
0/0/0	2	2	0/0	0/0/0	0/0	0//0	0/0/	0/0/9	9.1/0			0/0/0	self-propelled type feed mixing and feeding vehicle
0/0/0	2	2	0/0	0/0/0	0/0	0//0	0/0/	0/0/9	9.1/0			0/0/0	Other machines for agricultural, horticultural, forestry (lincluding germination equipments fitted with mechanical or thermal equipment)
													-Parts:
0/0/0	0	2.8	0/0	0/0/0	0/0	0//0	0/0/	5.4/5.4/5.4	5.6/5.4			0/0/0	--Of poultry-keeping machinery or poultry incubators and brooders
0/0/0	0	1.2	2.5/2.5	0/0/0	0/0	0//0	0/0/	0/0/5.4	5.5/0			0/0/0	--Other
													Machines for cleaning, sorting or grading seed, grain or dried leguminous vegetables; machinery used in the milling industry or for the working of cereals or dried leguminous vegetables, other than farm-type machi-nery:
													-Machines for cleaning, sorting or grading seed, grain or dried leguminous vegetables:
0/0/0	2	2	0/0	0/0/0	0/0	0//0	0/0/	0/0/9	9.1/0			0/0/0	---Optical color granule sorter(color sorter)
0/0/0	2	6	0/0	0/0/0	0/0	0//0	0/0/	9.5/9.5/10	9.5/9.5			0/0/0	---Other
0/0/0	4	6	0/0	0/0/0	0/0	0//0	0/0/	0/9.5/10	0/9.5			0/0/0	-Other machinery
0/0/0	0	1.2	0.6/0.6	0/0/0	0/0	0//0	0/0/	0/0/5.4	5.5/0			0/0/0	-Parts
													Machinery, not specified or included else-where in this Chapter, for the industrial preparation or manufacture of food or drink, other than machinery for the extraction or preparation of animal or fixed vegetable or microbial fats or oils
													-Bakery machinery and machinery for the manufacture of macaroni, spaghetti or similar products
0/0/0	2	3.2	0.7/0.7	0/0/0	0/0	0//0	0/0/	6.3/6.3/6.3	6.6/6.3			0/0/0	Bakery production lines
0/0/0	2	3.2	0.7/0.7	0/0/0	0/0	0//0	0/0/	6.3/6.3/6.3	6.6/6.3			0/0/0	Machines for producing and processing macaroni and noodles (including processing machine of similar products)
0/0/0	2	0	0/0	0/0/0	0/0	0//0	0/0/	0/0/0	7.3/0			0/0/0	-Machinery for the manufacture of confectionery, cocoa or chocolate
0/0/0	2	2		0/0/0	0/0	0//0	0/0/	0/0/9	9.1/0			0/0/0	-Machinery for sugar manufacture
0/0/0	2	1.4	0/0	0/0/0	0/0	0//0	0/0/	0/0/6.3	6.4/0			0/0/0	-Brewery machinery
0/0/0	2	1.4	0/0	0/0/0	0/0	0//0	0/0/	0/0/6.3	6.4/0			0/0/0	-Machinery for the preparation of meat or poultry
0/0/0	2	2	0/0	0/0/0	0/0	0/0/0	0/0/	0/0/9	9.1/0			0/0/0	-Machinery for the preparation of fruits, nuts or vegetables
0/0/0	2	0	0.9/0.9	0/0/0	0/0	0//0	0/0/0	7.7/7.7/7.7	7.7/7.7			0/0/0	-Other machinery
0/0/0	0	0	0/0	0/0/0	0/0	0//0	0/0/	0/0/0	0/0			0/0/0	-Parts
													Machinery for making pulp of fibrous cellulosic material or for making or finishing paper or paperboard:
0/0/0	2	1.6	0/0	0/0/0	0/0	0//0	0/0/	0/0/7.6	7.6/0			0/0/0	-Machinery for making pulp of fibrous cellulosic material
0/0/0	2	0	0.8/0.8	0/0/0	0/0	0//0	0/0/0	0/0/0	7.6/0			0/0/0	Machinery for making paper or paper board
0/0/0	2	0	0/0	0/0/0	0/0	0//0	0/0/0	0/0/0	7.6/0			0/0/0	-Machinery for finishing paper or paper board
													-Parts:
0/0/0	0	2.8	0/0	0/0/0	0/0	0//0	0/0/	5.4/5.4/5.4	5.6/5.4			0/0/0	--Of machinery for making pulp of fibrous cellulosic material
0/0/0	0	2.8	0.6/0.6	0/0/0	0/0	0//0	0/0/	5.4/5.4/5.4	5.6/5.4			0/0/0	--Other
													Book-binding machinery, including book-sewing machines:
													-Machinery:
0/0/0	2	2	0/0	0/0/0	0/0	0//0	0/0/	0/0/9	9.1/0			0/0/0	---Sewing bookbinders
0/0/0	4.2	2.4	0/0	0/0/0	0/0	0/0/0	0/0/	0/0/10.8	10.9/0			0/0/0	---Glueing bookbinders
0/0/0	4.2	2.4	0/0	0/0/0	0/0	0/0/0	0/0/	0/0/10.8	10.9/0			0/0/0	---Other
0/0/0	2	0	0.8/0.8	0/0/0	0/0	0//0	0/0/	0/0/0	7.3/0			0/0/0	-Parts
													Other machinery for making up paper pulp, paper or paperboard, including cutting machines of all kinds:
0/0/0	4.2	2.4		0/0/0	0/0	0/0/0	0/0/0	0/0/10.8	10.9/0			0/0/0	-Cutting machines
0/0/0	4.2	2.4	1.2/1.2	0/0/0	0/0	0/0/0	0/0/	0/0/10.8	10.9/0			0/0/0	-Machines for making bags, sacks or envelopes
													-Machines for making cartons, boxes, cases, tubes, drums or similar containers, other than by moulding:
0/0/0	4.8	2.7	1.4/1.4	0/0/0	0/0	0/0/0	0/0/	0/0/12.2	12.3/0			0/0/0	---Machines for paper, plastic and aluminium composite can manufacture
0/0/0	4.8	8.1	1.4/1.4	0/0/0	0/0	0/0/0	0/0/	12.8/12.8/13.5	/12.8			0/0/0	---Other
0/0/0	4.2	7.2	1.2/1.2	0/0/0	0/0	0/0/0	0/0/	11.4/11.4/12	/11.4			0/0/0	-Machines for moulding articles in paper pulp, paper or paperboard
													-Other machinery:
0/0/0	4.2	2.4	1.2/1.2	0/0/0	0/0	0/0/0	0/0/	0/0/10.8	10.9/0			0/0/0	---Machines for paper plastic and aluminium flexible packaging manufacture
0/0/0	4.2	2.4	1.2/1.2	0/0/0	0/0	0/0/0	0/0/0	0/0/10.8	10.9/0			0/0/0	---Other
													-Parts:

税则号列	货品名称〔CIQ 扩展编码及品名—T2 表示见附表 2〕	最惠(%)	暂定税率	普通	增值/消费	出口退税	计量单位	监管条件/特殊证件	检验检疫	对美关税	亚太上/下
8441.9010	---切纸机用										
8441.9010 01	切纸机用弧形辊〔999〕	8	4	50	13/	13	千克	/		24	
8441.9010 02	切纸机用横切刀单元〔999〕	8	3	50	13/	13	千克	/		23	
8441.9010 90	其他切纸机零件〔999〕	8		50	13/	13	千克	/		28	
8441.9090	---其他〔999〕	8		30	13/	13	千克	/		28	
84.42	**制印刷版(片)、滚筒及其他印刷部件用的机器、器具及设备(税目 84.56 至 84.65 的机器除外);印刷用版(片)、滚筒及其他印刷部件;制成供印刷用(例如,刨平、压纹或抛光)的板(片)、滚筒及石板:**										
	-机器、器具及设备:										
8442.3010	---铸字机〔999〕	0		35	13/	13	台/千克	/		20	
	---制版机器、器具及设备:										
8442.3021	----计算机直接制版设备										
8442.3021 10	凹版式计算机直接制版设备(CTP)〔999〕	0		35	13/	13	台/千克	/		25	
8442.3021 90	除凹版式以外的其他计算机直接制版设备(CTP)〔999〕	0		35	13/	13	台/千克	/		25	
8442.3029	----其他〔999〕	0		35	13/	13	台/千克	/		25	
8442.3090	---其他〔999〕	0		35	13/	13	台/千克	/		25	
8442.4000	-上述机器、器具及设备的零件										
8442.4000 10	计算机直接制版机器用零件〔999〕	0		20	13/	13	千克	/		25	
8442.4000 90	其他铸字、排字、制版机器的零件〔999〕	0		20	13/	13	千克	/		25	
8442.5000	-印刷用版(片)、滚筒及其他印刷部件;制成供印刷用(例如,刨平、压纹或抛光)的板(片)、滚筒及石板〔999〕	0		35	13/	13	千克	/		25	
84.43	**用税目 84.42 的印刷用版(片)、滚筒及其他印刷部件进行印刷的机器;其他印刷(打印)机、复印机及传真机,不论是否组合式;上述机器的零件及附件:**										
	-用税目 84.42 的印刷用版(片)、滚筒及其他印刷部件进行印刷的机器:										
8443.1100	--卷取进料式胶印机〔999〕	10		35	13/	13	台/千克	/			7/7
8443.1200	--办公室用片取进料式胶印机(以未折叠计,片尺寸一边长不超过 22cm,另一边长不超过 36cm)〔999〕	10		35	13/	13	台/千克	/			
	--其他胶印机:										
	---平张纸进料式:										
8443.1311	----单色机〔999〕	10		35	13/	13	台/千克	/			7/7
8443.1312	----双色机〔999〕	10		35	13/	13	台/千克	/			7/7
8443.1313	----四色机										
8443.1313 01	四色平张纸胶印机(对开单张单面印刷速度≥17000 张/小时)〔999〕	10	7	35	13/	13	台/千克	/			7/7
8443.1313 02	四色平张纸胶印机(对开单张双面印刷速度≥13000 张/小时)〔999〕	10	7	35	13/	13	台/千克	/			7/7
8443.1313 03	四色平张纸胶印机(全张或超全张单张单面印刷速度≥13000 张/小时)〔999〕	10	7	35	13/	13	台/千克	/			7/7
8443.1313 90	其他四色平张纸胶印机(用税目 84.42 项下商品进行印刷的机器)〔999〕	10		35	13/	13	台/千克	/			7/7
8443.1319	----其他										
8443.1319 01	五色及以上平张纸胶印机(对开单张单面印刷速度≥17000 张/小时)〔999〕	10	7	35	13/	13	台/千克	/			7/7
8443.1319 02	五色及以上平张纸胶印机(对开单张双面印刷速度≥13000 张/小时)〔999〕	10	7	35	13/	13	台/千克	/			7/7
8443.1319 03	五色及以上平张纸胶印机(全张或超全张单张单面印刷速度≥13000 张/小时)〔999〕	10	7	35	13/	13	台/千克	/			7/7
8443.1319 90	其他平张纸进料式胶印机(用税目 84.42 项下商品进行印刷的机器)〔999〕	10		35	13/	13	台/千克	/			7/7
8443.1390	---其他〔999〕	10		35	13/	13	台/千克	/		15	7/7
8443.1400	--卷取进料式凸版印刷机,但不包括苯胺印刷机〔999〕	10		35	13/	13	台/千克	/		15	
8443.1500	--除卷取进料式以外的凸版印刷机,但不包括苯胺印刷机〔999〕	10		35	13/	13	台/千克	/		15	
8443.1600	--苯胺印刷机										
8443.1600 01	苯胺印刷机,线速度≥350 米/分钟,幅宽≥800 毫米(柔性版印刷机,用税目 84.42 项下商品进行印刷的机器)〔999〕	10	3	35	13/	13	台/千克	/		23	
8443.1600 02	机组式柔性版印刷机,线速度≥160m/min,250mm≤幅宽<800mm(具有烫印或全息或丝网印刷功能单元的)〔999〕	10	5	35	13/	13	台/千克	/		25	

协定税率 %								RCEP		特惠税率 %			Article Description
东/冰/格	巴基斯坦	韩国	瑞士上/下	哥/秘/柬	澳/毛	新西/坡/智	中国港/澳/台	东盟及马来/澳/韩	日/新	亚太2国	老/柬/缅	98/97/95	
													---Of cutting machines
0/0/0	2	1.6	0/0	0/0/0	0/0	0//0	0/0/	0/0/7.2	7.3/0			0/0/0	Bowed roll,of a kind used in paper cutter
0/0/0	2	1.6	0/0	0/0/0	0/0	0//0	0/0/	0/0/7.2	7.3/0			0/0/0	Crosscut knife unit,of a kind used in paper cutter
0/0/0	2	1.6	0/0	0/0/0	0/0	0//0	0/0/	0/0/7.2	7.3/0			0/0/0	Other parts of paper cutter
0/0/0	2	0		0/0/0	0/0	0//0	0/0/	0/0/0	7.6/0			0/0/0	---Other
													Machinery, apparatus and equipment (other than the machine-tools of headings 84.56 to 84.65) for preparing or making platescylinders or other printing components; plates, cylinders andother printing components; plates, cylinders and lithographicstones, prepared for printing purposes (for example, planed, grained or polished):
													-Machinery, apparatus and equipment:
0/0/0	2	0	0/0	0/0/0	0/0	0//0	0/0/	0/0/0	0/0			0/0/0	---Type casters
													---Other machinery, apparatus and equipment for typesetting:
													----Machines for preparing CTP plates
0/0/0	2	0	0/0	0/0/0	0/0	0//0	0/0/	0/0/0	0/0			0/0/0	Concave layout of computer direct plate making equipment (CTP)
0/0/0	2	0	0/0	0/0/0	0/0	0//0	0/0/	0/0/0	0/0			0/0/0	Other computer direct plate making equipment in addition to outside the concaveformat (CTP)
0/0/0	2	4.2	0/0	0/0/0	0/0	0//0	0/0/	0/0/8.1	0/0			0/0/0	----Other
0/0/0	2	4.2	0/0	0/0/0	0/0	0//0	0/0/	0/0/8.1	0/0			0/0/0	---Other
													-Parts of the foregoing machinery, apparatus or equipment
0/0/0	2	0	0/0	0/0/0	0/0	0//0	0/0/	0/0/0	0/0			0/0/0	Computer to plate machine parts
0/0/0	2	0	0/0	0/0/0	0/0	0//0	0/0/	0/0/0	0/0			0/0/0	Other components of typecasting, typesetting and platemaking machines
0/0/0	2	0	0/0	0/0/0	0/0	0//0	0/0/	0/0/0	0/0			0/0/0	-Plates, cylinders and other printing components; plates, cylinders and lithographic stones, prepared for printing purposes (for example, planed, grained or polished)
													Printing machinery used for printing, cylinders and other printing components of heading84.42; other printers Copying mechines and facsimile machines, whether or not combined; Part and accessories there of:
													-Printing machinery used for printing by means of plates, cylinders and other printing components of heading No. 84.42:
0/0/0	2	2	0/0	0/0/0	0/0	0//0	0/0/	0/0/9	9.1/0			0/0/0	--Offset printing machinery reel-fed
0/0/0	4.2	2.4	1.2/1.2	0/0/0	0/0	0/0/0	0/0/	0/0/10.8	10.9/0			0/0/0	--Offset printhg machinery sheet-fed, office type(using sheets with one side not exceeding 22cm and the other side not exceedig 36cm in the unfoldool state)
													--Other offset printing machinery:
													---Sheet fed:
0/0/0	2	2	0/0	0/0/0	0/0	0//0	0/0/	9/9/9	9.4/9			0/0/0	----Single color
0/0/0	2	2	0/0	0/0/0	0/0	0//0	0/0/	0/0/9	9.1/0			0/0/0	----Double colors
													----Four colors
0/0/0	3.5	2	0/0	0/0/0	0/0	0//0	0/0/	0/0/9	9.4/0			0/0/0	Four-color sheet fed offset printing presses(single folio double side printing speed≥17000pcs/hr)
0/0/0	3.5	2	0/0	0/0/0	0/0	0//0	0/0/	0/0/9	9.4/0			0/0/0	Four-color sheet fed offset printing press(single folio double sides printing speed≥13000pcs/hr)
0/0/0	3.5	2	0/0	0/0/0	0/0	0//0	0/0/	0/0/9	9.4/0			0/0/0	Four-color sheet fed offset printing press(sheetwise or full-sheet one piece single side printing speed≥13000pcs/hr)
0/0/0	3.5	2	0/0	0/0/0	0/0	0//0	0/0/	0/0/9	9.4/0			0/0/0	Other four-color sheet fed offset printing press (machines printing with commodities in Duty item 84.42)
													----Other
0/0/0	3.5	2	0/0	0/0/0	0/0	0//0	0/0/	9/9/9	9.1/9			0/0/0	Five(or higher)-color sheet fed offset printing press(speed≥16000pcs/hr)
0/0/0	3.5	2	0/0	0/0/0	0/0	0//0	0/0/	9/9/9	9.1/9			0/0/0	Five(or higher)-color sheet fed offset printing press(single folio double sides printing speed≥13000pcs/hr)
0/0/0	3.5	2	0/0	0/0/0	0/0	0//0	0/0/	9/9/9	9.1/9			0/0/0	Five(or higher)-color sheet fed offset printins press(sheetwise or full-sheet one piece single side printing speed ≥ 13000pcs/hr)
0/0/0	3.5	2	0/0	0/0/0	0/0	0//0	0/0/	9/9/9	9.1/9			0/0/0	Other sheet fed offset printing press (machines printing with commodities under heading No. 84. 42)
0/0/0	2	2	0/0	0/0/0	0/0	0//0	0/0/	9/9/9	9.1/9			0/0/0	---Other
0/0/0	4.2		1.2/1.2	0/0/0	0/0	0/0/0	0/0/	5/5/	/5			0/0/0	--Letterpress printing machinery, reelfed, excluding flexographic printing
0/0/0	4.2		1.2/1.2	0/0/0	0/0	0/0/0	0/0/	5/5/	/5			0/0/0	--Letterpress printing machinery other than reelfed, excluding flexographic printing
													--Flexographic printing machinery
0/0/0	2		0/0	0/0/0	0/0	0//0	0/0/	5/5/	/5			0/0/0	Flexographic pringting machinery, linear speed ≥350m/min, Wide≥800mm flexographic persses, using good in heading No. 84.42 to printing
0/0/0	2		0/0	0/0/0	0/0	0//0	0/0/	5/5/	/5			0/0/0	Flexographic press, unit-Type, linear speed ≥ 160m/min, 250mm≤width<800mm(with function of stamping or holography or screen printing)

税则号列	货品名称〔CIQ 扩展编码及品名－T2 表示见附表 2〕	最惠(%)	暂定税率	普通	增值/消费	出口退税	计量单位	监管条件/特殊证件	检验检疫	对美关税	亚太上/下
8443.1600 90	其他苯胺印刷机(柔性版印刷机,用税目 84.42 项下商品进行印刷的机器)〔999〕	10		35	13/	13	台/千克	/		30	
8443.1700	--凹版印刷机										
8443.1700 01	凹版印刷机,印刷速度≥350 米/分钟(用税目 84.42 项下商品进行印刷的机器)〔999〕	10	9	35	13/	13	台/千克	/		34	6.5/6.5
8443.1700 90	其他凹版印刷机(用税目 84.42 项下商品进行印刷的机器)〔999〕	10		35	13/	13	台/千克	/		35	6.5/6.5
	--其他:										
	---网式印刷机:										
8443.1921	----圆网印刷机										
8443.1921 01	纺织用圆网印花机〔999〕	10	6	35	13/	13	台/千克	/		31	6.5/6.5
8443.1921 90	其他圆网印刷机(用税目84.42项下商品进行印刷的机器)〔999〕	10		35	13/	13	台/千克	/		35	6.5/6.5
8443.1922	----平网印刷机										
8443.1922 01	纺织用平网印花机〔999〕	10	6	35	13/	13	台/千克	/		31	9/9
8443.1922 10	用于光盘生产的盘面印刷机(用税目 84.42 项下商品进行印刷的机器)〔999〕	10		35	13/	13	台/千克	/		35	9/9
8443.1922 90	其他平网印刷机(用税目 84.42 项下商品进行印刷的机器)〔999〕	10		35	13/	13	台/千克	/		35	9/9
8443.1929	----其他〔999〕	10		35	13/	13	台/千克	/			6.5/6.5
8443.1980	---其他〔999〕	8		35	13/	13	台/千克	O/		18	5.2/5.2
	-其他印刷(打印)机、复印机及传真机,不论是否组合式:										
	--具有印刷(打印)、复印或传真中两种及以上功能的机器,可与自动数据处理设备或网络连接:										
8443.3110	---静电感光式										
8443.3110 10	静电感光式多功能一体加密传真机(可与自动数据处理设备或网络连接)〔101 多功能一体打印机,102 打印机,103 复印机,104 电话机,105 传真机,106 电传打字机〕	0		70	13/	13	台/千克	2/	L	25	
8443.3110 90	其他静电感光式多功能一体机(可与自动数据处理设备或网络连接)〔101 多功能一体打印机,102 打印机,103 复印机,104 电话机,105 传真机,106 电传打字机〕	0		70	13/	13	台/千克	/	L	25	
8443.3190	---其他								L		
8443.3190 10	其他具有打印和复印两种功能的机器(可与自动数据处理设备或网络连接)〔101 多功能一体打印机,102 打印机,103 复印机,104 电话机,105 传真机,106 电传打字机〕	0		17	13/	13	台/千克	A/	L	25	
8443.3190 20	其他多功能一体加密传真机(兼有打印、复印中一种及以上功能的机器)〔101 多功能一体打印机,102 打印机,103 复印机,104 电话机,105 传真机,106 电传打字机〕	0		17	13/	13	台/千克	2A/	LM	25	
8443.3190 90	其他具有打印、复印或传真中两种及以上功能的机器(具有打印和复印两种功能的机器除外,可与自动数据处理设备或网络连接)〔101 打印机,102 复印机,103 电话机,104 传真机,105 电传打字机〕	0		17	13/	13	台/千克	A/	LM	25	
	--其他,可与自动数据处理设备或网络连接:										
	---专用于税目 84.71 所列设备的打印机:										
8443.3211	----针式打印机〔999〕	0		14	13/	13	台/千克	A/	L	25	
8443.3212	----激光打印机〔999〕	0		14	13/	13	台/千克	A/	L	25	
8443.3213	----喷墨打印机〔999〕	0		14	13/	13	台/千克	A/	L	25	
8443.3214	----热敏打印机〔999〕	0		14	13/	13	台/千克	A/	L	20	
8443.3219	----其他〔999〕	0		14	13/	13	台/千克	A/	L	20	
	---数字式印刷设备:										
8443.3221	----喷墨印刷机〔999〕	0		30	13/	13	台/千克	/		20	
8443.3222	----静电照相印刷机(激光印刷机)〔999〕	0		35	13/	13	台/千克	/		20	0/0
8443.3229	----其他〔999〕	0		30	13/	13	台/千克	/		20	0/0
8443.3290	---其他										
8443.3290 10	其他加密传真机(可与自动数据处理设备或网络连接)〔999〕	0		17	13/	13	台/千克	2A/	LM	25	
8443.3290 90	其他印刷(打印)机、复印机、传真机和电传打字机(可与自动数据处理设备或网络连接)〔101 打印机,102 油印机,103 复印机,104 电话机,105 电传打字机〕	0		17	13/	13	台/千克	A/	LM	25	
	--其他:										
	---静电感光复印设备:										
8443.3911	----将原件直接复印的(直接法)〔101 印刷行业成套设备,102 打印机,103 复印机〕	0		70	13/	13	台/千克	/			
8443.3912	----将原件通过中间体转印的(间接法)〔101 印刷行业成套设备,102 打印机,103 复印机〕	2.5/1.3		70	13/	13	台/千克	/			
	---其他感光复印设备:										
8443.3921	----带有光学系统的〔101 印刷行业成套设备,102 打印机,103 复印机〕	0		70	13/	13	台/千克	/			

协定税率 %								RCEP		特惠税率 %			Article Description
东/冰/格	巴基斯坦	韩国	瑞士 上/下	哥/秘/柬	澳/毛	新西/坡/智	中国港/澳/台	东盟及马来/澳/韩	日/新	亚太2国	老/柬/缅	98/97/95	
0/0/0	2		0/0	0/0/0	0/0	0//0	0/0/	5/5/	/5			0/0/0	Other flexographic printing machinery(flexographic press and machines printing with commodities under heading No. 84. 42)
													--Gravure printing machinery
0/0/0	11.5	11.7	1.8/1.8	0/0/0	0/0	0/0/0	0/0/	5/5/	/5			0/0/0	Gravure printing machinery, linear speed≥350m/min, using goods in heading No. 84. 42 to printing
0/0/0	11.5	11.7	1.8/1.8	0/0/0	0/0	0/0/0	0/0/	5/5/	/5			0/0/0	Other gravure printing machinery, using goods in heading No. 84. 42 to printing
													--Other:
													---Screen printing machinery:
													----Cylinder screen press
0/0/0	2	2	0/0	0/0/0	0/0	0//0	0/0/	9/9.5/10	9.1/9.5			0/0/0	Rotary screen printing machines for textile
0/0/0	2	2	0/0	0/0/0	0/0	0//0	0/0/	9/9.5/10	9.1/9.5			0/0/0	Other rotary screen printing machines(printing machinery using the commodities under heading No.84.42)
													----Platen screen press
0/0/0	3.5	4.6	1/1	0/0/0	0/0	0//0	0/0/0	9.3/9.5/9.3	9.4/9.5			0/0/0	Flat screen printing machines for textile
0/0/0	3.5	4.6	1/1	0/0/0	0/0	0//0	0/0/0	9.3/9.5/9.3	9.4/9.5			0/0/0	Disk presser for producing compact disks(machines using the commodities under heading No. 84. 42 for printing)
0/0/0	3.5	4.6	1/1	0/0/0	0/0	0//0	0/0/0	9.3/9.5/9.3	9.4/9.5			0/0/0	Other platen screen presses (printing machinery using the commodities under heading No. 84. 42)
0/0/0	2	2	0/0	0/0/0	0/0	0/0/0	0/0/0	0/0/9	9.1/0			0/0/0	----Other
0/0/0	2	0	0/0	0/0/0	0/0	0//0	0/0/0	0/0/0	7.3/0			0/0/0	---Other
													-Other printers, copying machines and facsimile machines, whether or not combined:
													--Machines which perform two or more of the functions of printing, copying or facsimile transmission, capable of connecting to an automatic data processing machine or to a network:
													---Electrostatic photosensitive-type
0/0/0	3.5		0/0	0/0/0	0/0	0/0/0	0/0/	0/0/9	9.1/0			0/0/0	Electrostatic-sensitive multifunctional integrated encrypting facsimile machines (capable of connecting to an automatic data processing machine or to a network)
0/0/0	3.5		0/0	0/0/0	0/0	0/0/0	0/0/	0/0/9	9.1/0			0/0/0	Other electrostatic-sensitive multifunctional integrated machines (capable of cconnecting to an automatic data processing machine or to a network)
													---Other
0/0/0	0	0	0/0	0/0/0	0/0	0//0	0/0/	0/0/0	0/0			0/0/0	Other machines which perform two of the function of printing, copying(capable of connecting to an automatic data processing machine or to a network)
0/0/0	0	0	0/0	0/0/0	0/0	0//0	0/0/	0/0/0	0/0			0/0/0	Other multifunctional integrated encrypting facsimile machines (machines with the function of printing, copying or both)
0/0/0	0	0	0/0	0/0/0	0/0	0//0	0/0/	0/0/0	0/0			0/0/0	Other machines which perform two or more of the function of printing, copying, facsimile transmission(other than machines which perform two of the function of printing, copying, capable of connecting to an automatic data processing machine or to a network)
													--Other, capable of connecting to an automatic data processing machine or to a net work:
													---Printer of a kind solely used in the machines of heading No. 84. 71:
0/0/0	0	0	0/0	0/0/0	0/0	0//0	0/0/	0/0/0	0/0			0/0/0	----Stylus printers
0/0/0	0	0	0/0	0/0/0	0/0	0//0	0/0/	0/0/0	0/0			0/0/0	----Laser printers
0/0/0	0	0	0/0	0/0/0	0/0	0//0	0/0/	0/0/0	0/0			0/0/0	----Ink-jet-printers
0/0/0	0	0	0/0	0/0/0	0/0	0//0	0/0/	0/0/0	0/0			0/0/0	----Thermal printers
0/0/0	0	0	0/0	0/0/0	0/0	0//0	0/0/	0/0/0	0/0			0/0/0	----Other
													---Digital printing machines:
0/0/0	2	1.6	0/0	0/0/0	0/0	0/0/0	0/0/	0/0/7.2	7.3/0			0/0/0	----Ink-jet printing machines
0/0/0	2	3.7	0/0	0/0/0	0/0	0//0	0/0/	7.2/7.2/7.2	7.3/7.2			0/0/0	----Electrostatic photographic printing machines (laser printing machines)
0/0/0	2	1.6	0/0	0/0/0	0/0	0//0	0/0/	0/0/7.2	7.3/0			0/0/0	----Other
													---Other
0/0/0	0	0	0/0	0/0/0	0/0	0//0	0/0/	0/0/0	0/0			0/0/0	Other encryption facsimile machine (capable commecting to an automatic data processing machine or to a network)
0/0/0	0	0	0/0	0/0/0	0/0	0//0	0/0/	0/0/0	0/0			0/0/0	Other presses(pinters), copying machine, facsimile machine, and teleprinters (capable of connecting to an automatic data processing machine or to a network)
													--Other:
													---Electrostatic photo-copying appcocrtus:
0/0/0	0	0	0/0	0/0/0	0/0	0//0	0/0/	0/0/0	0/0			0/0/0	----Operating by reproducing the original image directly onto the capy(direct process)
0/0/0	2		0/0	0/0/0	0/0	0/0/0	0/0/	0/0/9	9.1/0			0/0/0	----Operating by reproducing the original image via an intermediate onto the copy (indirect process)
													---Other photocopying apparatus:
0/0/0	0	0	0/0	0/0/0	0/0	0//0	0/0/	0/0/0	0/0			0/0/0	----Incorporoting an optical system

税则号列	货品名称〔CIQ 扩展编码及品名－T2 表示见附表 2〕	最惠(%)	暂定税率	普通	增值/消费	出口退税	计量单位	监管条件/特殊证件	检验检疫	对美关税	亚太上/下
8443.3922	----接触式的〔101 印刷行业成套设备，102 打印机，103 复印机〕	5.5/2.8		70	13/	13	台/千克	/			
8443.3923	----热敏复印设备〔999〕	5.5/2.8		70	13/	13	台/千克	/		15.5	
8443.3924	----热升华复印设备〔101 印刷行业成套设备，102 打印机，103 复印机〕	5.5/2.8		70	13/	13	台/千克	/			
	---数字式印刷设备：										
8443.3931	----喷墨印刷机〔999〕	2/1		30	13/	13	台/千克	/		12	
8443.3932	----静电照相印刷机(激光印刷机)〔999〕	2/1		35	13/	13	台/千克	/			1.3/0.7
8443.3939	----其他〔999〕	2/1		30	13/	13	台/千克	/		22	1.3/0.7
8443.3990	---其他〔999〕	0		30	13/	13	台/千克	/		25	
	-零件及附件：										
	--用税目 84.42 的印刷版(片)、滚筒及其他印刷部件进行印刷的机器零件及附件：										
	---印刷用辅助机器：										
8443.9111	----卷筒料给料机								L		
8443.9111 10	卷筒料自动给料机，给料线速度≥12m/s〔999〕	0		35	13/	13	千克/台	O/		5	
8443.9111 90	其他卷筒料给料机〔999〕	0		35	13/	13	千克/台	O/		5	
8443.9119	----其他〔999〕	0		35	13/	13	千克/台	O/		20	
8443.9190	---其他										
8443.9190 10	胶印机用墨量遥控装置(包括墨色控制装置，墨量调节装置、墨斗体等组成部分)〔999〕	0		20	13/	13	千克/个	O/		25	
8443.9190 90	传统印刷机用零件及附件(胶印机用墨量遥控装置除外)〔999〕	0		20	13/	13	千克/个	/		25	
	--其他：										
8443.9910	---数字印刷设备用辅助机器〔999〕	0		35	13/	13	千克/台	O/		25	0/0
	---数字印刷设备的零件：										
8443.9921	----热敏打印头〔999〕	0		20	13/	13	千克/个	/		25	
8443.9929	----其他										
8443.9929 10	压电式喷墨头(非用品目 84.42 项下商品进行印刷的机器零件)〔999〕	0		20	13/	13	千克	/		5	
8443.9929 90	其他数字印刷设备的零件(非用税目 84.42 项下商品进行印刷的机器零件)〔999〕	0		20	13/	13	千克	/		5	
8443.9990	---其他										
8443.9990 10	其他印刷(打印)机、复印机及传真机的感光鼓和含感光鼓的碳粉盒〔999〕	0		35	13/	13	千克	/		25	
8443.9990 90	其他印刷(打印)机、复印机及传真机的零件和附件〔999〕	0		35	13/	13	千克	/		25	
84.44	**化学纺织纤维挤压、拉伸、变形或切割机器：**										
8444.0010	---合成纤维长丝纺丝机〔999〕	8		30	13/	13	台/千克	/			5.6/5.6
8444.0020	---合成纤维短丝纺丝机〔999〕	8		30	13/	13	台/千克	/			5.2/5.2
8444.0030	---人造纤维纺丝机〔999〕	8		30	13/	13	台/千克	/			5.2/5.2
8444.0040	---化学纤维变形机〔999〕	8		30	13/	13	台/千克	/		33	5.2/5.2
8444.0050	---化学纤维切断机〔999〕	8		30	13/	13	台/千克	/		33	5.2/5.2
8444.0090	---其他〔999〕	8		30	13/	13	台/千克	/		33	5.2/5.2
84.45	**纺织纤维的预处理机器；纺纱机、并线机、加捻机及其他生产纺织纱线的机器；摇纱机、络纱机(包括卷纬机)及处理税目 84.46 或 84.47 所列机器用的纺织纱线的机器：**										
	-纺织纤维的预处理机器：										
	--梳理机：										
	---棉纤维型：										
8445.1111	----清梳联合机〔999〕	8		30	13/	13	台/千克	/			5.2/5.2
8445.1112	----自动抓棉机〔999〕	8		30	13/	13	台/千克	/			5.2/5.2
8445.1113	----梳棉机〔999〕	8		30	13/	13	台/千克	/			5.2/5.2
8445.1119	----其他〔999〕	8		30	13/	13	台/千克	/			5.2/5.2
8445.1120	---毛纤维型〔999〕	8		30	13/	13	台/千克	/		28	5.2/5.2
8445.1190	---其他										
8445.1190 01	宽幅非织造布梳理机(工作幅宽＞3.5 米，工作速度＞120 米/分钟)〔999〕	8	6	30	13/	13	台/千克	/		31	5.2/5.2
8445.1190 90	其他纺织纤维梳理机〔999〕	8		30	13/	13	台/千克	/		33	5.2/5.2
	--精梳机：										
8445.1210	---棉精梳机〔999〕	8		30	13/	13	台/千克	/			5.6/5.6
8445.1220	---毛精梳机〔999〕	8		30	13/	13	台/千克	/			5.6/5.6
8445.1290	---其他〔999〕	8		30	13/	13	台/千克	/			5.6/5.6
	--拉伸机或粗纱机：										
8445.1310	---拉伸机〔999〕	8		30	13/	13	台/千克	/			
	---粗纱机：										
8445.1321	----棉纺粗纱机〔999〕	8		30	13/	13	台/千克	/			5.6/5.6
8445.1322	----毛纺粗纱机〔999〕	8		30	13/	13	台/千克	/			5.6/5.6
8445.1329	----其他〔999〕	8		30	13/	13	台/千克	/			5.6/5.6
8445.1900	--其他〔999〕	8		30	13/	13	台/千克	/		28	5.2/5.2

协定税率 %								RCEP		特惠税率 %			Article Description
东/冰/格	巴基斯坦	韩国	瑞士上/下	哥/秘/柬	澳/毛	新西/坡/智	中国港/澳/台	东盟及马来/澳/韩	日/新	亚太2国	老/柬/缅	98/97/95	
0/0/0		0	2/2	0/0/0	0/0	0/0/0	0/0/	0/0/0	18.2/0			0/0/0	----Of the contact type
0/0/0		0	2/2	0/0/0	0/0	0/0/0	0/0/	0/0/0	18.2/0			0/0/0	----Thermo copying apparatus
0/0/0		0	2/2	0/0/0	0/0	0/0/0	0/0/	0/0/0	18.2/0			0/0/0	----Thermo-sublime copying apparatus
													---Digital printing machines:
0/0/0	2	0	0/0	0/0/0	0/0	0/0/0	0/0/	0/0/0	7.3/0			0/0/0	----Ink-jet printing machines
0/0/0	2	0	0/0	0/0/0	0/0	0//0	0/0/	0/0/0	7.3/0			0/0/0	----Electrostatic photographic printing machine (Laser printing machines)
0/0/0	2	1.6	0/0	0/0/0	0/0	0/0/0	0/0/	0/0/7.2	7.3/0			0/0/0	----Other
0/0/0	0	0	0/0	0/0/0	0/0	0//0	0/0/	0/0/0	0/0			0/0/0	---Other
													-Parts and accessories:
													--Parts and accessories of printing machinery used for printing by means of plates, cylinders and other printing components of heading 84.42:
													---Machines for uses ancillary to printing:
													----Web feeder
0/0/0	4.2	2.4	0/0	0/0/0	0/0	0/0/0	0/0/	0/0/10.8	10.9/0			0/0/0	Automatic rolling materials feeder, Feeding linear velocity≥12m/s
0/0/0	4.2	2.4	0/0	0/0/0	0/0	0/0/0	0/0/	0/0/10.8	10.9/0			0/0/0	Other roll material feeder
0/0/0	4.2	2.4	0/0	0/0/0	0/0	0/0/0	0/0/	0/0/10.8	10.9/0			0/0/0	----Other
													---Other
0/0/0	0	1.2	0/0	0/0/0	0/0	0//0	0/0/	5.4/5.4/5.4	5.5/5.4			0/0/0	Ink remote control device for offset printing machine(including ink ink quantity control device, adjusting device, etc. the ink fountain body part)
0/0/0	0	1.2	0/0	0/0/0	0/0	0//0	0/0/	5.4/5.4/5.4	5.5/5.4			0/0/0	Traditional printing machine with spare parts and accessories (except for offset printing ink quantity remote control device)
													--Other:
0/0/0	4.2	2.4	0/0	0/0/0	0/0	0/0/0	0/0/	0/0/10.8	10.9/0			0/0/0	---Machines for uses ancillary to digital printing machines
													---Parts of digital printing machines:
0/0/0	0	1.2	0/0	0/0/0	0/0	0//0	0/0/	5.4/5.4/5.4	5.5/5.4			0/0/0	----Thermal print heads
													----Other
0/0/0	0	3	0/0	0/0/0	0/0	0//0	0/0/	0/0/5.4	5.5/0			0/0/0	Piezoelectric ink gun (printing machine parts unlisted under item 84.42)
0/0/0	0	3	0/0	0/0/0	0/0	0//0	0/0/	0/0/5.4	5.5/0			0/0/0	Other parts of digital printing machine(other than parts and accessories of machinery using the commodities under heading No.84.22 for printing)
													---Other
0/0/0	0	0	0/0	0/0/0	0/0	0//0	0/0/	0/0/0	0/0			0/0/0	Silicon drum? of other presses (printers), copying machines and facsimile machines
0/0/0	0	0	0/0	0/0/0	0/0	0//0	0/0/	0/0/0	0/0			0/0/0	Spare parts and accessories of other presses (printers), copying machines and facsimile machines
													Machines for extruding, drawing, texturing or cutting man-made textile materials:
0/0/0	3.5	0		0/0/0	0/0	0//0	0/0/0	0/0/0	9.4/0			0/0/0	---Synthetic filaments spinning jets
0/0/0	3.5	2	0/0	0/0/0	0/0	0//0	0/0/	0/0/9	9.1/0			0/0/0	---Synthetic staple fibres spinning jets
0/0/0	3.5	2	0/0	0/0/0	0/0	0//0	0/0/	0/0/9	9.1/0			0/0/0	---Artificial fibres spinning jets
0/0/0	3.5	2	1/1	0/0/0	0/0	0//0	0/0/	9.5/9.5/10	9.5/9.5			0/0/0	---Man-made filaments crimping machinery
0/0/0	3.5	2	1/1	0/0/0	0/0	0//0	0/0/	0/0/9	9.1/0			0/0/0	Man-made filaments cutting machinery
0/0/0	3.5	2	1/1	0/0/0	0/0	0//0	0/0/	0/0/9	9.4/0			0/0/0	---Other
													Machines for preparing textile fibres; spinning, doubling or twisting machines and other machinery for producing textile yarns; textile reeling or winding (including weft-winding) machines and machines for preparing textile yarns for use on the machines of headingNo.84.46 or 84.47:
													-Machines for preparing textile fibres:
													--Carding machines:
													---For cotton type fibres:
0/0/0	2	2	0/0	0/0/0	0/0	0//0	0/0/	0/0/9	9.1/0			0/0/0	----Blowing-carding-Machinery
0/0/0	2	2		0/0/0	0/0	0//0	0/0/	0/0/9	9.1/0			0/0/0	----Bale Pucker
0/0/0	3.5	2	1/1	0/0/0	0/0	0//0	0/0/	0/0/9	9.1/0			0/0/0	----Card or carding Machine
0/0/0	2	2	0/0	0/0/0	0/0	0//0	0/0/	0/0/9	9.1/0			0/0/0	----Other
0/0/0	3.5	2	0/0	0/0/0	0/0	0//0	0/0/	0/0/9	9.1/0			0/0/0	---For wool type fibres
													---Other
0/0/0	3.5		0/0	0/0/0	0/0	0//0	0/0/	5/5/	/5			0/0/0	Extra-width non-woven cloth carding machine (working width >3.5m, working speed >120m/min)
0/0/0	3.5		0/0	0/0/0	0/0	0//0	0/0/	5/5/	/5			0/0/0	Other carding machines for textile fibres
													--Combing Machines:
0/0/0	2	2		0/0/0	0/0	0//0	0/0/	0/0/9	9.1/0			0/0/0	---Cotton Comber
0/0/0	2	2	0/0	0/0/0	0/0	0//0	0/0/	0/0/9	9.1/0			0/0/0	---Worsted Comber
0/0/0	2	2	0/0	0/0/0	0/0	0//0	0/0/	0/0/9	9.1/0			0/0/0	---Other
													--Drawing or roving machines:
0/0/0	2	2	0/0	0/0/0	0/0	0//0	0/0/	0/0/9	9.1/0			0/0/0	---Drawing machines
													---Roving machines:
0/0/0	2	2		0/0/0	0/0	0//0	0/0/	0/0/9	9.1/0			0/0/0	----Cotton Roving Frames
0/0/0	2	2	0/0	0/0/0	0/0	0//0	0/0/	0/0/9	9.1/0			0/0/0	----Worsted Roving Machines
0/0/0	2	2	0/0	0/0/0	0/0	0//0	0/0/	0/0/9	9.1/0			0/0/0	----Other
0/0/0	2			0/0/0	0/0	0//0	0/0/	5/5/	/5			0/0/0	--Other

税则号列	货品名称〔CIQ 扩展编码及品名－T2 表示见附表 2〕	最惠(%)	暂定税率	普通	增值/消费	出口退税	计量单位	监管条件/特殊证件	检验检疫	对美关税	亚太上/下
	-纺纱机：										
	---自由端纺纱机：										
8445.2031	----转杯纺纱机										
8445.2031 01	全自动转杯纺纱机〔999〕	8	5	30	13/	13	台/千克	/			5.2/5.2
8445.2031 90	其他自由端转杯纺纱机〔999〕	8		30	13/	13	台/千克	/			5.2/5.2
8445.2032	----喷气纺纱机〔999〕	8	5	30	13/	13	台/千克	/			5.6/5.6
8445.2039	----其他〔999〕	8		30	13/	13	台/千克	/			5.6/5.6
	---环锭细纱机：										
8445.2041	----棉细纱机〔999〕	8		40	13/	13	台/千克	/			7.2/7.2
8445.2042	----毛细纱机〔999〕	8		40	13/	13	台/千克	/			
8445.2049	----其他〔999〕	8		40	13/	13	台/千克	/			
8445.2090	---其他〔999〕	8		30	13/	13	台/千克	/			5.2/5.2
8445.3000	-并线机或加捻机〔999〕	8		30	13/	13	台/千克	/		33	5.2/5.2
	-络纱机(包括卷纬机)或摇纱机：										
8445.4010	---自动络筒机〔999〕	8		30	13/	13	台/千克	O/		33	7.2/7.2
8445.4090	---其他〔101 自动络筒机，102 卷纬机及遥纱机，103 其它纺织机械及其零件〕	8		30	13/	13	台/千克	/		33	5.2/5.2
	-其他：										
8445.9010	---整经机〔999〕	8		30	13/	13	台/千克	/			5.2/5.2
8445.9020	---浆纱机〔999〕	8		30	13/	13	台/千克	/			5.2/5.2
8445.9090	---其他〔999〕	8		30	13/	13	台/千克	/			5.2/5.2
84.46	**织机：**										
8446.1000	-所织织物宽度不超过 30 厘米的织机〔999〕	8		30	13/	13	台/千克	/		33	5.2/5.2
	-所织织物宽度超过 30 厘米的梭织机：										
	--动力织机：										
8446.2110	---地毯织机〔999〕	8		35	13/	13	台/千克	/			5.2/5.2
8446.2190	---其他〔999〕	8		30	13/	13	台/千克	/			5.2/5.2
8446.2900	--其他〔999〕	8		30	13/	13	台/千克	/			
	-所织织物宽度超过 30 厘米的无梭织机：										
8446.3020	---剑杆织机〔999〕	8		30	13/	13	台/千克	/			5.2/5.2
8446.3030	---片梭织机〔999〕	8		30	13/	13	台/千克	/			5.2/5.2
8446.3040	---喷水织机〔999〕	8		30	13/	13	台/千克	O/			5.2/5.2
8446.3050	---喷气织机〔999〕	8		30	13/	13	台/千克	O/		33	6.8/6.8
8446.3090	---其他〔999〕	8		30	13/	13	台/千克	/			5.2/5.2
84.47	**针织机、缝编机及制粗松螺旋花线、网眼薄纱、花边、刺绣品、装饰带、编织带或网的机器及簇绒机：**										
	-圆型针织机：										
8447.1100	--圆筒直径不超过 165 毫米〔999〕	8		30	13/	13	台/千克	/		33	7/7
8447.1200	--圆筒直径超过 165 毫米〔999〕	8		30	13/	13	台/千克	/		33	
	-平型针织机；缝编机：										
	---经编机：										
8447.2011	----特里科经编机〔999〕	8		30	13/	13	台/千克	/			5.2/5.2
8447.2012	----拉舍尔经编机〔999〕	8		30	13/	13	台/千克	/			5.2/5.2
8447.2019	----其他〔999〕	8		30	13/	13	台/千克	/			5.2/5.2
8447.2020	---平型纬编机〔999〕	8		30	13/	13	台/千克	/		33	5.2/5.2
8447.2030	---缝编机〔999〕	8		30	13/	13	台/千克	/		18	5.2/5.2
	-其他：										
	---簇绒机：										
8447.9011	----地毯织机〔999〕	7		35	13/	13	台/千克	/		12	4.6/4.6
8447.9019	----其他〔999〕	8		30	13/	13	台/千克	/		13	5.2/5.2
8447.9020	---绣花机〔999〕	8		30	13/	13	台/千克	/			5.2/5.2
8447.9090	---其他〔101 采棉机，102 清花机，103 其它纺织机械及其零件〕	8		30	13/	13	台/千克	/		28	4/4
84.48	**税目 84.44、84.45、84.46 或 84.47 所列机器的辅助机器(例如，多臂机、提花机、自停装置及换梭装置)；专用于或主要用于税目 84.44、84.45、84.46 或 84.47 所列机器的零件、附件(例如，锭子、锭壳、钢丝针布、梳、喷丝头、梭子、综丝、综框、针织机用针)：**										
	-税目 84.44、84.45、84.46 或 84.47 所列机器的辅助机器：										
8448.1100	--多臂机或提花机及其所用的卡片缩小、复制、穿孔或汇编机器										
8448.1100 01	多臂机或提花机(转速指标 500 转/分以上)〔999〕	8	3	20	13/	13	千克	/			
8448.1100 90	多臂机或提花机所用卡片缩小、复制、穿孔或汇编机器(包括其所用的卡片缩小、复制、穿孔或汇编机器)〔999〕	8		20	13/	13	千克	/			
8448.1900	--其他〔999〕	8		20	13/	13	千克	/		33	
	-税目 84.44 所列机器及其辅助机器的零件、附件：										
8448.2020	---喷丝头或喷丝板〔999〕	6		14	13/	13	个/千克	/		31	
8448.2090	---其他〔999〕	6		17	13/	13	千克	/		31	

协定税率 %								RCEP		特惠税率 %			Article Description
东/冰/格	巴基斯坦	韩国	瑞士上/下	哥/秘/柬	澳/毛	新西/坡/智	中国港/澳/台	东盟及马来/澳/韩	日/新	亚太2国	老/柬/缅	98/97/95	
													-Textile spinning machines:
													---Open-end spinner:
													----Rotor spinning machine
0/0/0	2	2	0/0	0/0/0	0/0	0//0	0/0/	0/0/9	9.1/0			0/0/0	Fully automatic rotor spinning machines
0/0/0	2	2	0/0	0/0/0	0/0	0//0	0/0/	0/0/9	9.1/0			0/0/0	Other open-end spinner machine
0/0/0	2	2		0/0/0	0/0	0//0	0/0/	9.5/9.5/10	9.5/9.5			0/0/0	----Jet spinner
0/0/0	2	2	0/0	0/0/0	0/0	0//0	0/0/	9.5/9.5/10	9.5/9.5			0/0/0	----Other
													---Ring spining frames:
0/0/0	3.5	2.1	1.1/1.1	0/0/0	0/0	0/0/0	0/0/	0/0/9.5	9.5/0			0/0/0	----Cotton Ring Spinning Frame
0/0/0	2	2	0/0	0/0/0	0/0	0//0	0/0/	0/0/9	9.1/0			0/0/0	----Worsted Ring Spinning Frame
0/0/0	2	2	0/0	0/0/0	0/0	0//0	0/0/	0/0/9	9.1/0			0/0/0	----Other
0/0/0	2	2		0/0/0	0/0	0//0	0/0/	0/0/9	9.1/0			0/0/0	---Other
0/0/0	2	2	0/0	0/0/0	0/0	0//0	0/0/	0/0/9	9.1/0			0/0/0	-Textile doubling or twisting machines
													-Textile winding (including weft-winding) or reeling machines:
0/0/0	3.5	6	0/0	0/0/0	0/0	0//0	0/0/	9.5/9.5/9.5	9.5/9.5			0/0/0	---Automatic bobbin winders
0/0/0	2	6.5	0/0	0/0/0	0/0	0//0	0/0/	5/5/	/5			0/0/0	---Other
													-Other:
0/0/0	2	2		0/0/0	0/0	0//0	0/0/	0/0/9	9.1/0			0/0/0	---Warping machines
0/0/0	2	2		0/0/0	0/0	0//0	0/0/	0/0/9	9.1/0			0/0/0	---Sizing machines
0/0/0	2	6.5	1/1	0/0/0	0/0	0//0	0/0/	5/5/	/5			0/0/0	---Other
													Weaving machines(looms):
0/0/0	2	1.6	0.8/0.8	0/0/0	0/0	0//0	0/0/	0/0/7.2	7.3/0			0/0/0	-For weaving fabrics of a width not exceeding 30cm
													-For weaving fabrics of width exceeding 30cm, shuttle type:
													--Power looms:
0/0/0	3.5	2.4	1.2/1.2	0/0/0	0/0	0/0/0	0/0/	0/0/10.8	10.9/0			0/0/0	---For making carpets or rugs
0/0/0	2	2		0/0/0	0/0	0/0/0	0/0/	0/0/9	9.1/0			0/0/0	---Other
0/0/0	2	2	0/0	0/0/0	0/0	0//0	0/0/	0/0/9	9.1/0			0/0/0	--Other
													-For weaving fabrics of a width exceeding 30cm, shuttleless type:
0/0/0	2	1.6	0.8/0.8	0/0/0	0/0	0//0	0/0/	0/0/7.2	7.3/0			0/0/0	---Rapier looms
0/0/0	2	0		0/0/0	0/0	0//0	0/0/	0/0/0	7.3/0			0/0/0	---Carrier looms
0/0/0	2	0	0/0	0/0/0	0/0	0//0	0/0/0	7.2/7.6/7.2	7.3/7.6			0/0/0	---Water jet looms
0/0/0	2	3.7	0/0	0/0/0	0/0	0//0	0/0/	7.2/7.2/7.2	7.5/7.2			0/0/0	---Air jet looms
0/0/0	2	0	0/0	0/0/0	0/0	0//0	0/0/	0/0/0	7.3/0			0/0/0	---Other
													Knitting machines, stitch-bonding machines and machines for making gimped yarn, tulle lace, embroidery, trimmings, braid or net and machines for tufting:
													-Circular knitting machines:
0/0/0	2	0	0/0	0/0/0	0/0	0//0	0/0/0	0/0/0	7.3/0			0/0/0	--With cylinder diameter not exceeding 165mm
0/0/0	2	0	0/0	0/0/0	0/0	0//0	0/0/0	0/0/0	7.3/0			0/0/0	--With cylinder diameter exceeding 165mm
													-Flat knitting machines; stitch-bonding machines:
													---Warp knitting machines:
0/0/0	2	0	0/0	0/0/0	0/0	0//0	0/0/	0/0/0	7.3/0			0/0/0	----Tricot machines
0/0/0	2	1.6	0/0	0/0/0	0/0	0//0	0/0/	0/0/7.2	7.3/0			0/0/0	----Raschel machines
0/0/0	2	1.6	0/0	0/0/0	0/0	0//0	0/0/	0/0/7.2	7.3/0			0/0/0	----Other
0/0/0	2	0	0.8/0.8	0/0/0	0/0	0//0	0/0/0	0/0/0	7.3/0			0/0/0	---Flat weft rnitting machimes
0/0/0	2	0	0/0	0/0/0	0/0	0//0	0/0/	0/0/0	7.3/0			0/0/0	Stitch-bonding machines
													-Other:
													---Tufting machines:
0/0/0	0	0	0/0	0/0/0	0/0	0//0	0/0/	0/0/0	6.4/0			0/0/0	----For making carpets or rugs
0/0/0	2	0	0/0	0/0/0	0/0	0//0	0/0/	0/0/0	7.3/0			0/0/0	----Other
0/0/0	2	1.6		0/0/0	0/0	0//0	0/0/	0/0/7.2	7.3/0			0/0/0	---Embroidery machines
0/0/0	2	5		0/0/0	0/0	0//0	0/0/	5/5/	/5			0/0/0	---Other
													Auxiliary machinery for use with machines of headingNos. 84.44, 84.45, 84.46 or 84.47 (for example, dobbies, Jacquards, automatic stop motions, shuttle changing mechanisms); parts and accessories suitable for use solely or principally with the machines of this heading or of headingNos. 84.44, 84.45, 84.46 or 84.47 (for example, spindles and spindle flyers, card clothing, combs, extruding nipples, shuttles, healds and heald-frames, hosiery needles):
													-Auxiliary machinery for machines of heading No. 84.44, 84.45, 84.46 or 84.47:
													--Dobbies and Jacquards; card reducing, copying, punching or assembling machines for use there with
0/0/0	2	1.6	0/0	0/0/0	0/0	0//0	0/0/	0/0/7.2	7.3/0			0/0/0	Dobbies or jacquards (index of revolution speed>500r/min)
0/0/0	2	1.6	0/0	0/0/0	0/0	0//0	0/0/	0/0/7.2	7.3/0			0/0/0	Card narrowing , copying, perforation, or compilation machines used by dobbies or jacquards (including the use of card narrowing, copying, perforation or compilation machines)
0/0/0	4	1.6	0.8/0.8	0/0/0	0/0	0//0	0/0/	0/0/7.2	7.3/0			0/0/0	--Other
													-Parts and accessories of machines of heading No. 84.44 or of their auxiliary machinery:
0/0/0	0	1.2	0.6/0.6	0/0/0	0/0	0//0	0/0/	0/0/5.4	5.5/0			0/0/0	---Extruding nipples or spinnerets
0/0/0	0	2.8	0.6/0.6	0/0/0	0/0	0//0	0/0/	5.4/5.4/5.4	5.6/5.4			0/0/0	---Other

税则号列	货品名称〔CIQ 扩展编码及品名－T2 表示见附表 2〕	最惠(%)	暂定税率	普通	增值/消费	出口退税	计量单位	监管条件/特殊证件	检验检疫	对美关税	亚太上/下
	-税目 84.45 所列机器及其辅助机器的零件、附件：										
8448.3100	--钢丝针布〔999〕	6		17	13/	13	千克	/		31	
8448.3200	--纺织纤维预处理机器的零件、附件，但钢丝针布除外〔999〕	6		17	13/	13	千克	/		31	
	--锭子、锭壳、纺丝环、钢丝圈：										
8448.3310	---络筒锭〔999〕	6		17	13/	13	个/千克	/			4.8/4.8
8448.3390	---其他〔999〕	6		17	13/	13	千克	/		26	
	--其他：										
8448.3910	---气流杯〔999〕	6		14	13/	13	个/千克	/			4.2/4.2
8448.3920	---电子清纱器〔999〕	6	3	17	13/	13	个/千克	/			
8448.3930	---空气捻接器〔999〕	6	3	17	13/	13	个/千克	/		28	
8448.3940	---环锭细纱机紧密纺装置〔101 细纱机，102 其它纺织机械及其零件〕	6		17	13/	13	个/千克	/			4.8/4.8
8448.3990	---其他〔999〕	6	3	17	13/	13	千克	/		28	
	-织机及其辅助机器的零件、附件：										
8448.4200	--织机用筘、综丝及综框〔999〕	6		50	13/	13	千克	/		31	
	--其他：										
8448.4910	---接、投梭箱〔999〕	6		17	13/	13	个/千克	/			4.2/4.2
8448.4920	---引纬、送经装置〔999〕	6	3	17	13/	13	个/千克	/			
8448.4930	---梭子〔999〕	6		50	13/	13	个/千克	/		26	
8448.4990	---其他〔999〕	6	3	17	13/	13	千克	/		28	
	-税目 84.47 所列机器及其辅助机器的零件、附件：										
	--沉降片、织针及其他成圈机件：										
8448.5120	---针织机用 28 号以下的弹簧针、钩针及复合针〔999〕	6		50	13/	13	千克	/		31	
8448.5190	---其他〔999〕	6		17	13/	13	千克	/		31	
8448.5900	--其他〔999〕	6	3	17	13/	13	千克	/		28	
84.49	**成匹、成形的毡呢或无纺织物制造或整理机器，包括制毡呢帽机器；帽模：**										
8449.0010	---针刺机										
8449.0010 01	高速针刺机，针刺频率＞2000 次/分钟〔999〕	8	6	30	13/	13	台/千克	/		31	
8449.0010 90	其他针刺机〔999〕	8		30	13/	13	台/千克	/		33	
8449.0020	---水刺设备										
8449.0020 01	高速宽幅水刺设备(工作幅宽＞3.5 米，工作速度＞250 米/分钟，水刺压力≥400 帕)〔999〕	8	6	30	13/	13	台/千克	/			
8449.0020 90	其他水刺设备〔999〕	8		30	13/	13	台/千克	/			
8449.0090	---其他〔999〕	8		30	13/	13	千克	/		28	
84.50	**家用型或洗衣房用洗衣机，包括洗涤干燥两用机：**										
	-干衣量不超过 10 千克的洗衣机：										
	--全自动的：										
8450.1110	---波轮式〔101 洗衣机 I 类器具，102 洗衣机 II 类器具，103 洗衣机 III 类器具，104 洗衣机 0I 类器具，105 洗衣机 0 类器具〕	7		130	13/	13	台/千克	A/	LM	32	4.6/4.6
8450.1120	---滚筒式〔101 洗衣机 I 类器具，102 洗衣机 II 类器具，103 洗衣机 III 类器具，104 洗衣机 0I 类器具，105 洗衣机 0 类器具〕	7		130	13/	13	台/千克	A/	LM	32	4.6/4.6
8450.1190	---其他〔101 洗衣机 I 类器具，102 洗衣机 II 类器具，103 洗衣机 III 类器具，104 洗衣机 0I 类器具，105 洗衣机 0 类器具〕	7		130	13/	13	台/千克	A/	LM	32	4.6/4.6
8450.1200	--其他机器，装有离心甩干机〔101 洗衣机 I 类器具，102 洗衣机 II 类器具，103 洗衣机 III 类器具，104 洗衣机 0I 类器具，105 洗衣机 0 类器具〕	7		130	13/	13	台/千克	A/	LM		4.6/4.6
8450.1900	--其他〔101 洗衣机 I 类器具，102 洗衣机 II 类器具，103 洗衣机 III 类器具，104 洗衣机 0I 类器具，105 洗衣机 0 类器具〕	7		130	13/	13	台/千克	A/	LM		
	-干衣量超过 10 千克的洗衣机：						台				
	---全自动的：										
8450.2011	----波轮式[T2]	10		80	13/	13	台/千克	/		20	
8450.2012	----滚筒式[T2]	10		80	13/	13	台/千克	/		30	
8450.2019	----其他〔101 洗衣机 I 类器具，102 洗衣机 II 类器具，103 洗衣机 III 类器具，104 洗衣机 0I 类器具，105 洗衣机 0 类器具〕	10		80	13/	13	台/千克	/		15	
8450.2090	---其他〔101 洗衣机 I 类器具，102 洗衣机 II 类器具，103 洗衣机 III 类器具，104 洗衣机 0I 类器具，105 洗衣机 0 类器具〕	10		80	13/	13	台/千克	/		30	
	-零件：										
8450.9010	---干衣量不超过 10 千克的洗衣机用〔999〕	5		130	13/	13	千克	/		30	3.3/3.3
8450.9090	---其他〔999〕	8	5	80	13/	13	千克	/		15	5.2/5.2
84.51	**纱线、织物及纺织制品的洗涤、清洁、绞拧、干燥、熨烫、挤压、(包括熔压)、漂白、染色、上浆、整理、涂布或浸渍机器(税目 84.50 的机器除外)；列诺伦(亚麻油地毡)及类似铺地制品的布基或其他底布的浆料涂布机器；纺织物的卷绕、退绕、折叠、剪切或剪齿边机器：**										

协定税率 %								RCEP		特惠税率 %			Article Description
东/冰/格	巴基斯坦	韩国	瑞士上/下	哥/秘/柬	澳/毛	新西/坡/智	中国港/澳/台	东盟及马来/澳/韩	日/新	亚太2国	老/柬/缅	98/97/95	
													-Parts and accessories of machines of headingNo.84.45 or of their auxiliary machinery:
0/0/0	0	1.2	2.4/2.4	0/0/0	0/0	0//0	0/0/	0/0/5.4	5.5/0			0/0/0	--Card clothing
0/0/0	0	2.8	0.6/0.6	0/0/0	0/0	0//0	0/0/	5.4/5.4/5.4	5.6/5.4			0/0/0	--Of machines for preparing textile fibres, other than card clothing
													--Spindles, spindle flyers, spinning rings and ring travellers:
0/0/0	0	0	0/0	0/0/0	0/0	0//0	0/0/	0/0/0	0/0			0/0/0	---Winding spindle
0/0/0	0	1.2	0.6/0.6	0/0/0	0/0	0//0	0/0/	0/0/5.4	5.5/0			0/0/0	---Other
													--Other:
0/0/0	0	0	0/0	0/0/0	0/0	0//0	0/0/	0/0/0	0/0			0/0/0	---Open-end rotors
0/0/0	0	0	2.4/2.4	0/0/0	0/0	0//0	0/0/	0/0/0	5.5/0			0/0/0	---Electronic yarn clearers
0/0/0	0	0	0/0	0/0/0	0/0	0//0	0/0/	0/0/0	0/0			0/0/0	---Air twisting devices
0/0/0	0	0	2.5/2.5	0/0/0	0/0	0//0	0/0/	0/0/0	5.5/0			0/0/0	---Compact set of ring spinning frames
0/0/0	0	2.8	2.4/2.4	0/0/0	0/0	0//0	0/0/	5.4/5.4/5.4	5.6/5.4			0/0/0	---Other
													-Parts and accessories of weaving machines (looms) or of their auxiliary machinery:
0/0/0	0	2.8	0.6/0.6	0/0/0	0/0	0//0	0/0/	5.4/5.4/5.4	5.6/5.4			0/0/0	--Reeds for looms, healds and heald-frames
													--Other:
0/0/0	0	0	0.6/0.6	0/0/0	0/0	0//0	0/0/	0/0/0	5.5/0			0/0/0	---Catching and throwing shuttle boxes
0/0/0	0	1.2	0.6/0.6	0/0/0	0/0	0//0	0/0/	0/0/5.4	5.5/0			0/0/0	---Weft insertion and let-off motions
0/0/0	0	0	0/0	0/0/0	0/0	0//0	0/0/	0/0/0	0/0			0/0/0	---Shuttles
0/0/0	0	2.8	0.6/0.6	0/0/0	0/0	0//0	0/0/	5.4/5.4/5.4	5.6/5.4			0/0/0	---Other
													-Parts and accessories of machines of heading No.84.47 or of their auxiliary machinery:
													--Sinkers, needles and other articles used in forming stitches:
0/0/0	0	1.2	0/0	0/0/0	0/0	0//0	0/0/	0/0/5.4	5.5/0			0/0/0	---Barbered needles, crotchet hooks and complex needles for knitting machines, smaler than gauge No. 28
0/0/0	0	2.8	0/0	0/0/0	0/0	0//0	0/0/	5.4/5.4/5.4	5.6/5.4			0/0/0	---Other
0/0/0	4	0	0.6/0.6	0/0/0	0/0	0//0	0/0/0	5.4/5.4/5.4	5.5/5.4			0/0/0	--Other
													Machinery for the manufacture or finishing of felt or nonwovens in the piece or in shapes, including machinery for making felt hats; blocks for making hats:
													---Machinery for stitch
0/0/0	2	1.6	0/0	0/0/0	0/0	0//0	0/0/	0/0/7.2	7.3/0			0/0/0	High-speed needle-punching machines, stroke frequency ＞ 2000time/min
0/0/0	2	1.6	0/0	0/0/0	0/0	0//0	0/0/	0/0/7.2	7.3/0			0/0/0	Other needle-punching machines
													---Spunlaced Equipment
0/0/0	2	0	0/0	0/0/0	0/0	0//0	0/0/	0/0/0	7.3/0			0/0/0	High-speed width spun-laced equipment (working width ＞ 3.5m, working speed ＞250m/min, spun-laced pressure ≥ 400 Pa)
0/0/0	2	0	0/0	0/0/0	0/0	0//0	0/0/	0/0/0	7.3/0			0/0/0	Other spun-laced equipment
0/0/0	2	3.7	0/0	0/0/0	0/0	0//0	0/0/	7.5/7.6/7.5	7.5/7.6			0/0/0	---Other
													Household or laundry-type washing machines, including machines which both wash and dry:
													-Machines, each of a dry linen capacity not exceeding 10kg:
													--Fully-automatic machines:
0/0/0	2	2	0/0	0/0/0	0/0	0/0/0	0/0/	0/0/9	9.1/0			0/0/0	---Of the continuously rotating impeller
0/0/0	2	6.5	0/0	0/0/0	0/0	0/0/0	0/0/	7/7/	/7			0/0/0	---Of the drum type
0/0/0	2		0/0	0/0/0	0/0	0/0/0	0/0/	7/7/	/7			0/0/0	---Other
0/0/0	0		7/7	0/0/0	0/18	0/0/0	0/0/	7/7/	/7			0/0/0	--Other machines, with built-in centrifugal drier
0/0/0	0		7/7	0/0/0	0/18	0/0/0	0/0/	7/7/	/7			0/0/0	--Other
													-Machines, each of a dry linen capacity exceeding 10kg:
													---Full automatic :
0/0/0	2		0/0	0/0/0	0/0	0//0	0/0/	5/5/	/5			0/0/0	----Of the continuously rotating impeller
0/0/0	2		0/0	0/0/0	0/0	0//0	0/0/	5/5/	/5			0/0/0	----of the Drum-type
0/0/0	2		0/0	0/0/0	0/0	0//0	0/0/	5/5/	/5			0/0/0	----Other
0/0/0	2		0/0	0/0/0	0/0	0//0	0/0/	5/5/	/5			0/0/0	---Other
													-Parts:
0/0/0	0	2.3	0/0	0/0/0	0/0	0//0	0/0/	4.5/4.5/4.5	4.7/4.5			0/0/0	---Of the machines of subheadings 8540.1110 to 8450.1900
0/0/0	9	3.2	1.6/1.6	0/0/0	0/0	0/0/0	0/0/	0/0/14.4	14.5/0			0/0/0	---Other
													Machinery (other than machines of headingNo. 84.50) for washing, cleaning, wringing, drying, ironing, pressing (including fusing presses), bleaching, dyeing, dressing, finishing, coating or impregnating textile yarns, fabrics or made up textile articles and machines for applying the paste to the base fabric or other support used in the manufacture of floor coverings such as linoleum; machines for reeling, unreeling, folding, cutting or pinking textile fabrics:

税则号列	货品名称〔CIQ 扩展编码及品名—T2 表示见附表 2〕	最惠(%)	暂定税率	普通	增值/消费	出口退税	计量单位	监管条件/特殊证件	检验检疫	对美关税	亚太上/下
8451.1000	-干洗机〔101 干洗机 I 类器具,102 干洗机 II 类器具,103 干洗机 III 类器具,104 干洗机 0I 类器具,105 干洗机 0 类器具〕	10		80	13/	13	台/千克	/		35	6.5/6.5
	-干燥机:										
8451.2100	--干衣量不超过 10 千克〔101 干衣机 I 类器具,102 干衣机 II 类器具,103 干衣机 III 类器具,104 干衣机 0I 类器具,105 干衣机 0 类器具〕	8		80	13/	13	台/千克	/		33	5.2/5.2
8451.2900	--其他〔101 干衣机 I 类器具,102 干衣机 II 类器具,103 干衣机 III 类器具,104 干衣机 0I 类器具,105 干衣机 0 类器具〕	8		30	13/	13	台/千克	/		18	5.2/5.2
8451.3000	-熨烫机及挤压机(包括熔压机)[T2]	8		30	13/	13	台/千克	/		33	5.2/5.2
8451.4000	-洗涤、漂白或染色机器〔101 染色机,102 其它印染机械及其零件,103 纺织行业成套设备〕	8		20	13/	13	台/千克	/		33	5.2/5.2
8451.5000	-纺织物的卷绕、退绕、折叠、剪切或剪齿边机器〔999〕	8		20	13/	13	台/千克	/		18	5.2/5.2
8451.8000	-其他机器										
8451.8000 01	服装定型焙烘炉;服装液氨整理机;预缩机;罐蒸机[T2]	8		30	13/	13	台/千克	/		28	7.2/7.2
8451.8000 02	剪绒,洗缩联合机;剪毛联合机;柔软整理机[T2]	8		30	13/	13	台/千克	/		28	7.2/7.2
8451.8000 03	定型机;精练机;丝光机;磨毛机[T2]	8		30	13/	13	台/千克	/		28	7.2/7.2
8451.8000 04	涂层机〔999〕	8		30	13/	13	台/千克	/		28	7.2/7.2
8451.8000 90	税目 84.51 未列名的其他机器[T2]	8		30	13/	13	台/千克	/		28	7.2/7.2
8451.9000	-零件〔101 其它印染机械及其零件,102 纺织行业成套设备,103 其它衣物处理设备及其零件〕	8		20	13/	13	千克	/		28	5.2/5.2
84.52	**缝纫机,但税目 84.40 的锁线订书机除外;缝纫机专用的特制家具、底座及罩盖;缝纫机针:**										
	-家用型缝纫机:										
8452.1010	---多功能型〔999〕	9		80	13/	13	台/千克	/		34	5.9/5.9
	---其他:										
8452.1091	----手动式〔999〕	9		80	13/	13	台/千克	/		34	5.9/5.9
8452.1099	----其他〔101 电动家用缝纫机,102 机械家用缝纫机〕	9		80	13/	13	台/千克	/			5.9/5.9
	-其他缝纫机:										
	--自动的:										
8452.2110	---平缝机〔101 电动工业用缝纫机,102 机械工业用缝纫机〕	9		40	13/	13	台/千克	/		34	5.9/5.9
8452.2120	---包缝机〔101 电动工业用缝纫机,102 机械工业用缝纫机〕	9		40	13/	13	台/千克	/		34	5.9/5.9
8452.2130	---绷缝机〔101 电动工业用缝纫机,102 机械工业用缝纫机〕	9		40	13/	13	台/千克	/		34	5.9/5.9
8452.2190	---其他〔101 电动工业用缝纫机,102 机械工业用缝纫机,103 其它缝纫机〕	9		40	13/	13	台/千克	/		34	5.9/5.9
8452.2900	--其他〔101 电动工业用缝纫机,102 机械工业用缝纫机,103 其它缝纫机〕	9		40	13/	13	台/千克	/		34	5.9/5.9
8452.3000	-缝纫机针〔999〕	9		100	13/	13	千克	/		34	5.9/5.9
	-缝纫机专用的特制家具、底座和罩盖及其零件;缝纫机的其他零件:										
	---家用型缝纫机用:										
8452.9011	----旋梭〔999〕	8		80	13/	13	千克	/			5.2/5.2
8452.9019	----其他〔999〕	8		80	13/	13	千克	/		33	5.2/5.2
	---其他:										
8452.9091	----旋梭〔999〕	8		80	13/	13	千克	/			5.6/5.6
8452.9092	----缝纫机专用的特制家具、底座和罩盖及其零件〔999〕	8		100	13/	13	千克	/		13	
8452.9099	----其他〔999〕	8		80	13/	13	千克	/		33	5.2/5.2
84.53	**生皮、皮革的处理、鞣制或加工机器,鞋靴、毛皮及其他皮革制品的制作或修理机器,但缝纫机除外:**										
8453.1000	-生皮、皮革的处理、鞣制或加工机器〔999〕	8		30	13/	13	台/千克	/		33	5.2/5.2
8453.2000	-鞋靴制作或修理机器〔999〕	8		30	13/	13	台/千克	/		33	5.2/5.2
8453.8000	-其他机器〔999〕	8		30	13/	13	台/千克	/			
8453.9000	-零件〔999〕	8		30	13/	13	千克	/		33	
84.54	**金属冶炼及铸造用的转炉、浇包、锭模及铸造机:**										
8454.1000	-转炉〔999〕	8		35	13/	13	台/千克	/		28	
	-锭模及浇包:										
8454.2010	---炉外精炼设备										
8454.2010 10	VOD 炉(真空脱气炉)〔999〕	8		35	13/	13	台/千克	O/		28	
8454.2010 90	其他炉外精炼设备〔999〕	8		35	13/	13	台/千克	O/		28	
8454.2090	---其他〔999〕	8		35	13/	13	台/千克	/		33	
	-铸造机:										
8454.3010	---冷室压铸机〔999〕	12		35	13/	13	台/千克	O/			7.8/7.8
	---钢坯连铸机:										
8454.3021	----方坯连铸机〔999〕	10		35	13/	13	台/千克	/			6.5/6.5
8454.3022	----板坯连铸机〔999〕	12		35	13/	13	台/千克	O/			7.8/7.8
8454.3029	----其他〔999〕	12		35	13/	13	台/千克	O/			7.8/7.8
8454.3090	---其他〔999〕	12		35	13/	13	台/千克	/		17	7.8/7.8

协定税率 %								RCEP		特惠税率 %			Article Description
东/冰/格	巴基斯坦	韩国	瑞士 上/下	哥/秘/柬	澳/毛	新西/坡/智	中国港/澳/台	东盟及马来/澳/韩	日/新	亚太2国	老/柬/缅	98/97/95	
0/0/0	11.2	9.8	2.1/2.1	0/0/0	0/0	0/0/0	0/0/	18.9/18.9/18.9	19.7/18.9			0/0/0	-Dry-cleaning machines
													-Drying machines:
0/0/0	5.3	3	1.5/1.5	0/0/0	0/0	0/0/0	0/0/	0/0/13.5	13.6/0			0/0/0	--Each of a dry linen capacity not exceeding 10kg
0/0/0	2	1.6	0/0	0/0/0	0/0	0//0	0/0/	0/0/7.2	7.3/0			0/0/0	--Other
0/0/0	2	1.6	0/0	0/0/0	0/0	0/0/0	0/0/	0/0/7.2	7.3/0			0/0/0	-Ironing machines and presses (including fusing presses)
0/0/0	2	0	0/0	0/0/0	0/0	0//0	0/0/0	7.6/7.6/7.6	7.6/7.6			0/0/0	-Washing, bleaching or dyeing machines
0/0/0	2	0	0/0	0/0/0	0/0	0//0	0/0/0	0/0/0	7.3/0			0/0/0	-Machines for reeling, unreeling, folding, cutting or pinking textile fabrics
													-Other machinery
0/0/0	3.5	7.2		0/0/0	0/0	0/0/0	0/0/0	11.4/11.4/12	/11.4			0/0/0	Baking furnaces for finalizing the design of clothes; machine with liquid ammonia for finishing clothes; pre-shrinkage machine; tank vapor
0/0/0	3.5	7.2		0/0/0	0/0	0/0/0	0/0/0	11.4/11.4/12	/11.4			0/0/0	Pile shearing and shrinking combine, potting steamer, sheepshearing combination machine, supple finishing machine
0/0/0	3.5	7.2		0/0/0	0/0	0/0/0	0/0/0	11.4/11.4/12	/11.4			0/0/0	Boarding machine; refining machine; mercerizing range; napping grinder
0/0/0	3.5	7.2		0/0/0	0/0	0/0/0	0/0/0	11.4/11.4/12	/11.4			0/0/0	Coating machine
0/0/0	3.5	7.2		0/0/0	0/0	0/0/0	0/0/0	11.4/11.4/12	/11.4			0/0/0	Other machinery of heading No.8451, not elsewhere specified or included
0/0/0	2	1.6	0/0	0/0/0	0/0	0//0	0/0/	0/0/7.2	7.3/0			0/0/0	-Parts
													Sewing machines, other than book-sewing machines of heading No.84.40; furniture, bases and covers specially designed for sewing machines; sewing machine needles:
													-Sewing machines of household type:
0/0/0	13.4	9.8	2.1/2.1	0/0/0	0/0	0/0/0	0/0/	19.6/20/19.6	19.7/20			0/0/0	---Multifuncitonal
													---Other:
0/0/0	13.4	9.8	2.1/2.1	0/0/0	0/0	0/0/0	0/0/	18.9/18.9/18.9	19.1/18.9			0/0/0	----Hand ooperated
0/0/0	13.4	9.8	2.1/2.1	0/0/0	0/0	0/0/0	0/0/	18.9/18.9/18.9	19.7/18.9			0/0/0	----Other
													-Other sewing machines:
													--Automatic units:
0/0/0	3.5	2.4	1.2/1.2	0/0/0	0/0	0/0/0	0/0/	11.2/11.4/11.2	11.3/11.4			0/0/0	---Flatseam
0/0/0	3.5	2.4	1.2/1.2	0/0/0	0/0	0/0/0	0/0/0	0/0/10.8	10.9/0			0/0/0	---Overlock machine
0/0/0	3.5	2.4	1.2/1.2	0/0/0	0/0	0/0/0	0/0/0	0/0/10.8	10.9/0			0/0/0	---Interlock machine
0/0/0	3.5	2.4	1.2/1.2	0/0/0	0/0	0/0/0	0/0/0	10.8/10.8/10.8	10.9/10.8			0/0/0	---Other
0/0/0	3.5	2.4	1.2/1.2	0/0/0	0/0	0/0/0	0/0/	0/0/10.8	10.9/0			0/0/0	--Other
0/0/0	4.9	2.8	1.4/1.4	0/0/0	0/0	0/0/0	0/0/	0/0/12.6	12.7/0			0/0/0	-Sewing machine needles
													-Furniture, bases and covers for sewing machines and parts thereof; other parts of sewing machines:
													---Of sewing machines of the household type:
0/0/0	4.9	2.8	1.4/1.4	0/0/0	0/0	0/0/0	0/0/	0/0/12.6	12.7/0			0/0/0	----Rotating shuttles
0/0/0	5.6	2.8	1.4/1.4	0/0/0	0/0	0/0/0	0/0/	0/0/12.6	12.7/0			0/0/0	----Other
													---Other:
0/0/0	4.9	2.8	1.4/1.4	0/0/0	0/0	0/0/0	0/0/	5/5/	/5			0/0/0	----Rotating shuttles
0/0/0	7.8	2.8	1.4/1.4	0/0/0	0/0	0/0/0	0/0/	0/0/12.6	12.7/0			0/0/0	----Furniture, bases and covers for sewing machines and parts thereof
0/0/0	4.9	2.8	1.4/1.4	0/0/0	0/0	0/0/0	0/0/0	12.6/12.6/12.6	12.7/12.6			0/0/0	----Other
													Machinery for preparing, tanning or working hides, skins or leather or for making or repairing footwear or other articles of hides, skins or leather, other than sewing machines:
0/0/0	2	1.6	0/0	0/0/0	0/0	0//0	0/0/	0/0/7.6	7.6/0			0/0/0	-Machinery for preparing, tanning or working hides, skins or leather
0/0/0	2	1.6	0/0	0/0/0	0/0	0//0	0/0/	0/0/7.6	7.6/0			0/0/0	-Machinery for making or repairing footwear
0/0/0	2	1.6	0/0	0/0/0	0/0	0//0	0/0/	0/0/7.6	7.6/0			0/0/0	-Other machinery
0/0/0	3.5	1.6	0/0	0/0/0	0/0	0//0	0/0/	0/0/7.2	7.3/0			0/0/0	-Parts
													Converters, ladles, ingot moulds and casting machines, of a kind used in metallurgy or in metal foundries:
0/0/0	2	0	0/0	0/0/0	0/0	0//0	0/0/	0/0/0	7.6/0			0/0/0	-Converters
													-Ingot moulds and ladles:
													---Fining equipments, outside of converters
0/0/0	2	0	0/0	0/0/0	0/0	0//0	0/0/	0/0/0	7.6/0			0/0/0	VOD furnaces(vacuum degassing furnaces)
0/0/0	2	0	0/0	0/0/0	0/0	0//0	0/0/	0/0/0	7.6/0			0/0/0	Other secondary refining equipments
0/0/0	2	1.6		0/0/0	0/0	0//0	0/0/	0/0/7.6	7.6/0			0/0/0	---Other
													-Casting machines:
0/0/0	4.2	2.4	1.2/1.2	0/0/0	0/0	0/0/0	0/0/	5/5/	/5			0/0/0	---Cold chamber die-casting machines
													---Ingot continuous casting machines:
0/0/0	2	2	1/1	0/0/0	0/0	0//0	0/0/	0/0/9	9.1/0			0/0/0	----Ingot block
0/0/0	4.2	2.4	1.2/1.2	0/0/0	0/0	0/0/0	0/0/	0/0/10.8	10.9/0			0/0/0	----Ingot slab
0/0/0	4.2	2.4	1.2/1.2	0/0/0	0/0	0/0/0	0/0/	0/0/10.8	10.9/0			0/0/0	----Other
0/0/0	4.2	7.2	1.2/1.2	0/0/0	0/0	0/0/0	0/0/	11.4/11.4/12	11.4/11.4			0/0/0	---Other

税则号列	货品名称〔CIQ 扩展编码及品名—T2 表示见附表 2〕	最惠(%)	暂定税率	普通	增值/消费	出口退税	计量单位	监管条件/特殊证件	检验检疫	对美关税	亚太上/下
	-零件:										
8454.9010	---炉外精炼设备用〔999〕	8		20	13/	13	千克	/		28	
	---钢坯连铸机用:										
8454.9021	----结晶器〔999〕	8		20	13/	13	千克	/			
8454.9022	----振动装置〔999〕	8		20	13/	13	千克	/			
8454.9029	----其他〔999〕	8		20	13/	13	千克	/		33	
8454.9090	---其他〔999〕	8		20	13/	13	千克	/		28	
84.55	**金属轧机及其轧辊:**										
	-轧管机:										
8455.1010	---热轧管机〔999〕	12		35	13/	13	台/千克	/			7.8/7.8
8455.1020	---冷轧管机〔999〕	12		35	13/	13	台/千克	O/		32	7.8/7.8
8455.1030	---定减径轧管机〔999〕	12		35	13/	13	台/千克	O/			7.8/7.8
8455.1090	---其他〔999〕	12		35	13/	13	台/千克	O/			7.8/7.8
	-其他轧机:										
	--热轧机或冷热联合轧机:										
8455.2110	---板材热轧机〔999〕	15		35	13/	13	台/千克	/			9.8/9.8
8455.2120	---型钢轧机〔999〕	15		35	13/	13	台/千克	O/			9.8/9.8
8455.2130	---线材轧机〔999〕	15		35	13/	13	台/千克	O/		20	9.8/9.8
8455.2190	---其他〔999〕	15		35	13/	13	台/千克	O/			10.5/10.5
	--冷轧机:										
8455.2210	---板材冷轧机〔999〕	10		35	13/	13	台/千克	O/		30	
8455.2290	---其他										
8455.2290 10	铝箔粗轧机〔999〕	15		35	13/	13	台/千克	/		35	
8455.2290 90	其他金属冷轧机〔999〕	15		35	13/	13	台/千克	/		35	
8455.3000	-轧机用轧辊〔999〕	8		20	13/	13	个/千克	/		18	
8455.9000	-其他零件〔999〕	8		20	13/	13	千克	/		28	4/4
84.56	**用激光、其他光、光子束、超声波、放电、电化学法、电子束、离子束或等离子弧处理各种材料的加工机床;水射流切割机:**										
	-用激光、其他光或光子束处理的:										
8456.1100	--用激光处理的										
8456.1100 10	辐照元件激光切割机(切割燃料包壳以使辐照核材料能溶解,含遥控设备)〔999〕	0		30	13/	13	台/千克	3A/	M		
8456.1100 90	其他用激光处理的机床〔999〕	0		30	13/	13	台/千克	/			
8456.1200	--用其他光或光子束处理的〔999〕	0		30	13/	13	台/千克	/			
8456.2000	-用超声波处理的〔999〕	10		30	13/	13	台/千克	/		35	
	-用放电处理的:										
8456.3010	---数控的										
8456.3010 10	数控放电加工机床(2 轴或多轴成形控制的无线型放电加工机床)〔999〕	9		30	13/	13	台/千克	3O/		34	
8456.3010 90	其他数控的放电处理加工机床〔999〕	9		30	13/	13	台/千克	O/		34	
8456.3090	---其他										
8456.3090 10	非数控放电加工机床(2 轴或多轴成形控制的无线型放电加工机床)〔999〕	10		30	13/	13	台/千克	3/		20	
8456.3090 90	其他非数控的放电处理加工机床〔999〕	10		30	13/	13	台/千克	/		20	
	-用等离子弧处理的:										
8456.4010	---等离子切割机〔999〕	0		30	13/	13	台/千克	A/	L		
8456.4090	---其他〔999〕	0		30	13/	13	台/千克	/			
8456.5000	-水射流切割机〔999〕	0		30	13/	13	台/千克	/		5	
8456.9000	-其他〔T2〕	0		30	13/	13	台/千克	/		20	
84.57	**加工金属的加工中心、单工位组合机床及多工位组合机床:**										
	-加工中心:										
8457.1010	---立式〔999〕	9		20	13/	13	台/千克	O/		34	6.3/6.3
8457.1020	---卧式〔999〕	9		20	13/	13	台/千克	O/		34	6.3/6.3
8457.1030	---龙门式〔999〕	9		20	13/	13	台/千克	O/		34	6.3/6.3
	---其他:										
8457.1091	----铣车复合〔999〕	9		20	13/	13	台/千克	O/		34	6.3/6.3
8457.1099	----其他〔999〕	9		20	13/	13	台/千克	O/			6.3/6.3
8457.2000	-单工位组合机床〔999〕	8		20	13/	13	台/千克	O/		33	
8457.3000	-多工位组合机床〔999〕	5		20	13/	13	台/千克	O/		30	
84.58	**切削金属的车床(包括车削中心):**										
	-卧式车床:										
8458.1100	--数控的										
8458.1100 10	两用物项管制的切削金属的卧式数控车床(包括车削中心)〔999〕	9		20	13/	13	台/千克	3O/		34	
8458.1100 90	其他切削金属的卧式数控车床(包括车削中心)〔999〕	9		20	13/	13	台/千克	O/		34	
8458.1900	--其他〔999〕	9		50	13/	13	台/千克	/		29	
	-其他车床:										
	--数控的:										
8458.9110	---立式										
8458.9110 10	两用物项管制的切削金属立式数控车床(包括车削中心)〔999〕	5		20	13/	13	台/千克	3O/		30	
8458.9110 90	其他切削金属的立式数控车床(包括车削中心)〔999〕	5		20	13/	13	台/千克	O/		30	

协定税率 %								RCEP		特惠税率 %			Article Description
东/冰/格	巴基斯坦	韩国	瑞士 上/下	哥/秘/柬	澳/毛	新西/坡/智	中国港/澳/台	东盟及马来/澳/韩	日/新	亚太2国	老/柬/缅	98/97/95	
													-Parts:
0/0/0	2	1.6	0/0	0/0/0	0/0	0//0	0/0/	0/0/7.2	7.3/0			0/0/0	---For the fining equipments outside of converters
													---For ingot continuous casting machines:
0/0/0	2	0	0/0	0/0/0	0/0	0//0	0/0/	0/0/0	7.3/0			0/0/0	----Crystallizers
0/0/0	2	0	0/0	0/0/0	0/0	0//0	0/0/	0/0/0	7.3/0			0/0/0	----Vibrating devices
0/0/0	2	1.6	0.8/0.8	0/0/0	0/0	0//0	0/0/	0/0/7.2	7.3/0			0/0/0	----Other
0/0/0	2	0	0.8/0.8	0/0/0	0/0	0//0	0/0/	0/0/0	7.3/0			0/0/0	---Other
													Metal-rolling mills and rolls therefof:
													-Tube mills:
0/0/0	3.5	2.4	1.2/1.2	0/0/0	0/0	0/0/0	0/0/	0/0/10.8	10.9/0			0/0/0	---Tube mills, for hot-rolled
0/0/0	3.5	2.4	1.2/1.2	0/0/0	0/0	0/0/0	0/0/	5/5/	/5			0/0/0	---Tube mills for cold-rolled
0/0/0	3.5	2.4	1.2/1.2	0/0/0	0/0	0/0/0	0/0/	0/0/10.8	10.9/0			0/0/0	---Fixed and reduced tube mills
0/0/0	3.5	2.4	1.2/1.2	0/0/0	0/0	0/0/0	0/0/	0/0/10.8	10.9/0			0/0/0	---Other
													-Other rolling mills:
													--Hot or combination hot and cold:
0/0/0	5.3	3	1.5/1.5	0/0/0	0/0	0/0/0	0/0/	0/0/13.5	13.6/0			0/0/0	---Sheet mills, hot-rolled
0/0/0	5.3	3	1.5/1.5	0/0/0	0/0	0/0/0	0/0/	0/0/13.5	13.6/0			0/0/0	---Rolled-steel section mills
0/0/0	5.3	3	1.5/1.5	0/0/0	0/0	0/0/0	0/0/	0/0/13.5	13.6/0			0/0/0	---Wire mills
0/0/0	5.3	3	1.5/1.5	0/0/0	0/0	0/0/0	0/0/	0/0/13.5	13.6/0			0/0/0	---Other
													--Cold mills:
0/0/0	2	2	0/0	0/0/0	0/0	0//0	0/0/	0/0/9	9.1/0			0/0/0	---Sheet mills
													---Other
0/0/0	8.4	3	1.5/1.5	0/0/0	0/0	0/0/0	0/0/	0/0/13.5	13.6/0			0/0/0	Aluminium foil roughing mills
0/0/0	8.4	3	1.5/1.5	0/0/0	0/0	0/0/0	0/0/	0/0/13.5	13.6/0			0/0/0	Other cold rolling mills of metal
0/0/0	2	0	0/0	0/0/0	0/0	0//0	0/0/	7.6/7.6/7.6	7.6/7.6			0/0/0	-Rolls for rolling mills
0/0/0	0	0	0/0	0/0/0	0/0	0//0	0/0/	7.2/7.2/7.2	7.3/7.2			0/0/0	-Other parts
													Machine-tools for working any material by removal of material, by laser or other light or photon beam, ultrasonic, electro-discharge, electro-chemical, electron beam, ionic-beam or plasma arc processes; water-jet cutting machines
													-Operated by laser or other light or photon beam processes
													--Operated by laser processes
0/0/0	0	0	0/0	0/0/0	0/0	0//0	0/0/	0/0/0	0/0			0/0/0	Irradiated-component laser cutting machines (cutting the fuel claddings to make the irradiated nuclear materials to melt down, with a remote control)
0/0/0	0	0	0/0	0/0/0	0/0	0//0	0/0/	0/0/0	0/0			0/0/0	Other laser processing machine tools
0/0/0	0	0	0/0	0/0/0	0/0	0//0	0/0/	0/0/0	0/0			0/0/0	--Operated by other light or photon beam processes
0/0/0	2			0/0/0	0/0	0/0/0	0/0/	5/5/	/5			0/0/0	-Operated by ultrasonic processes
													-Operated by electro-discharge processes:
													---Numerically controlled
0/0/	4			0/0/0	0/0	0//0	0/0/	5/5/	/5			0/0/0	CNC EDM machne tools (wireless-type EDM machine tools controlled by 2-axis or multi-axis contours)
0/0/	4			0/0/0	0/0	0//0	0/0/	5/5/	/5			0/0/0	Other CNC processing machine tools
													---Other
0/0/0	2		0/0	0/0/0	0/0	0/0/0	0/0/	5/5/	/5			0/0/0	Non-CNC EDM machine tools (wireless-type EDM machine tools controlled by 2-axis or multi-axis contours)
0/0/0	2		0/0	0/0/0	0/0	0/0/0	0/0/	5/5/	/5			0/0/0	Other non-CNC EDM machine Tools
													-Operated by plasma arc processes:
0/0/0	0	0	0/0	0/0/0	0/0	0//0	0/0/	0/0/0	0/0			0/0/0	---Cutting machines of plasmaarc
0/0/0	0	0	0/0	0/0/0	0/0	0//0	0/0/	0/0/0	0/0			0/0/0	---Other
0/0/0	0	0	0/0	0/0/0	0/0	0//0	0/0/	0/0/0	0/0			0/0/0	-Water-jet cutting machines
0/0/0	0	0	0/0	0/0/0	0/0	0//0	0/0/	0/0/0	0/0			0/0/0	-Other
													Machining centres, unit construction machines (single station) and multi-station transfer machines, for working metal:
													-Machining centres:
0/0/	4	6.7		0/0/0	0/	0//0	0/0/	9.2/9.2/	/9.2			0/0/0	---Vertical
0/0/	4	6.7		0/0/0	0/	0//0	0/0/	9.2/9.2/	/9.2			0/0/0	---Horizontal
0/0/	4	6.7	0/0	0/0/0	0/	0//0	0/0/	5/5/	/5			0/0/0	---Plano
													---Other:
0/0/	4	6.7		0/0/0	0/	0//0	0/0/	5/5/	/5			0/0/0	----Mill—Turn centres
0/0/	4	6.7		0/0/0	0/	0//0	0/0/	5/5/	/5			0/0/0	----Other
0/0/	2	4.8	0/0	0/0/0	0/	0//0	0/0/	7.6/7.6/8	7.6/7.6			0/0/0	-Unit construction machines (single station)
0/0/	0			0/0/0	0/	0//0	0/0/	4.9/4.9/	/4.9			0/0/0	-Multi-station transfer machines
													Lathes (including turning centres) for removing metal:
													-Horizontal lathes:
													--Numerically controlled
0/0/0	2		4.1/4.1	0/0/0	0/	0//0	0/0/0	5/5/	/5			0/0/0	Lathes for removing metal, fual use items control, horizontal lathes, numerically controlled(including turning centres)
0/0/0	2		4.1/4.1	0/0/0	0/	0//0	0/0/0	5/5/	/5			0/0/0	Other lathes for removing metal, horizontal lathes, numerically controlled(including turning centres)
0/0/0	4.2	7.2	1.2/1.2	0/0/0	0/	0/0/0	0/0/	11.4/11.4/12	/11.4			0/0/0	--Other
													-Other lathes:
													--Numerically controlled:
													---Vertical
0/0/0	0		0/0	0/0/0	0/	0//0	0/0/0	4.9/4.9/	/4.9			0/0/0	Lathes for removing metal, fual-use items control, vertical, numerically controlled(including turning centres)
0/0/0	0		0/0	0/0/0	0/	0//0	0/0/0	4.9/4.9/	/4.9			0/0/0	Lathes for removing metal, numerically controlled(including turning centres)

税则号列	货品名称〔CIQ扩展编码及品名—T2表示见附表2〕	最惠(%)	暂定税率	普通	增值/消费	出口退税	计量单位	监管条件/特殊证件	检验检疫	对美关税	亚太上/下
8458.9120	---其他										
8458.9120 10	其他两用物项管制的切削金属数控车床(包括车削中心)〔999〕	5		20	13/	13	台/千克	3O/		30	
8458.9120 90	其他切削金属的数控车床(包括车削中心)〔999〕	5		20	13/	13	台/千克	O/		30	
8458.9900	--其他〔999〕	9		50	13/	13	台/千克	/		34	
84.59	**切削金属的钻床、镗床、铣床、攻丝机床(包括直线移动式动力头机床),但税目84.58的车床(包括车削中心)除外:**										
8459.1000	-直线移动式动力头机床〔999〕	9		50	13/	13	台/千克	/		14	
	-其他钻床:										
8459.2100	--数控的〔999〕	9		20	13/	13	台/千克	O/		34	
8459.2900	--其他〔999〕	9		50	13/	13	台/千克	/		34	
	-其他镗铣机床:										
8459.3100	--数控的〔999〕	9		20	13/	13	台/千克	O/			
8459.3900	--其他〔999〕	9		50	13/	13	台/千克	/			
	-其他镗床:										
8459.4100	--数控的〔999〕	9		20	13/	13	台/千克	O/		34	
8459.4900	--其他〔999〕	9		50	13/	13	台/千克	/		34	
	-升降台式铣床:										
8459.5100	--数控的〔999〕	9		20	13/	13	台/千克	O/			
8459.5900	--其他〔999〕	9		50	13/	13	台/千克	/		14	
	-其他铣床:										
	--数控的:										
8459.6110	---龙门铣床〔999〕	5		20	13/	13	台/千克	O/			
8459.6190	---其他〔999〕	5		20	13/	13	台/千克	O/		30	
	--其他:										
8459.6910	---龙门铣床〔999〕	9		50	13/	13	台/千克	/			7.5/7.5
8459.6990	---其他〔999〕	9		50	13/	13	台/千克	/		29	8.3/8.3
8459.7000	-其他攻丝机床〔999〕	9		50	13/	13	台/千克	/		29	
84.60	**用磨石、磨料或抛光材料对金属或金属陶瓷进行去毛刺、刃磨、磨削、珩磨、研磨、抛光或其他精加工的机床,但税目84.61的切齿机、齿轮磨床或齿轮精加工机床除外:**										
	-平面磨床:										
	--数控的:										
8460.1210	---在任一坐标的定位精度至少是0.01毫米〔999〕	9		20	13/	13	台/千克	O/		34	
8460.1290	---其他〔999〕	9		50	13/	13	台/千克	/			
	--其他:										
8460.1910	---在任一坐标的定位精度至少是0.01毫米〔999〕	9		50	13/	13	台/千克	/		34	
8460.1990	---其他〔999〕	9		50	13/	13	台/千克	/		14	
	-其他磨床:										
	--数控无心磨床:										
8460.2210	---在任一坐标的定位精度至少是0.01毫米〔999〕	9		20	13/	13	台/千克	O/		34	
8460.2290	---其他〔999〕	9		50	13/	13	台/千克	/		19	
	--数控外圆磨床:										
	---在任一坐标的定位精度至少是0.01毫米:										
8460.2311	----曲轴磨床〔999〕	9		20	13/	13	台/千克	O/		34	
8460.2319	----其他〔999〕	9		20	13/	13	台/千克	O/		34	
8460.2390	---其他〔999〕	9		50	13/	13	台/千克	/			
	--其他,数控的:										
	---在任一坐标的定位精度至少是0.01毫米:										
8460.2411	----内圆磨床〔999〕	9		20	13/	13	台/千克	O/		34	
8460.2419	----其他〔999〕	9		20	13/	13	台/千克	O/		34	
8460.2490	---其他〔999〕	9		50	13/	13	台/千克	/			
	--其他:										
	---在任一坐标的定位精度至少是0.01毫米:										
8460.2911	----外圆磨床〔999〕	12		50	13/	13	台/千克	/			
8460.2912	----内圆磨床〔999〕	9		50	13/	13	台/千克	/			
8460.2913	----轧辊磨床〔999〕	9		50	13/	13	台/千克	/		19	
8460.2919	----其他〔999〕	12		50	13/	13	台/千克	/			
8460.2990	---其他〔999〕	9		50	13/	13	台/千克	/			
	-刃磨(工具或刀具)机床:										
8460.3100	--数控的〔999〕	9		20	13/	13	台/千克	/		34	
8460.3900	--其他〔999〕	12		50	13/	13	台/千克	/		37	
	-珩磨或研磨机床:										
8460.4010	---珩磨〔999〕	12	6	50	13/	13	台/千克	/		16	
8460.4020	---研磨〔999〕	12		50	13/	13	台/千克	/		37	
	-其他:										
8460.9010	---砂轮机〔101磨床,102砂磨工具〕	12		50	13/	13	台/千克	/		37	
8460.9020	---抛光机床〔999〕	12		50	13/	13	台/千克	/		22	

协定税率 %								RCEP		特惠税率 %			Article Description
东/冰/格	巴基斯坦	韩国	瑞士上/下	哥/秘/柬	澳/毛	新西/坡/智	中国港/澳/台	东盟及马来/澳/韩	日/新	亚太2国	老/柬/缅	98/97/95	
													---Other
0/0/0	0		0/0	0/0/0	0/	0//0	0/0/0	4.9/4.9/	/4.9			0/0/0	Other lathes for removing metal，fual-use items control，(including turning centres)
0/0/0	0		0/0	0/0/0	0/	0//0	0/0/0	4.9/4.9/	/4.9			0/0/0	Other lathes for removing metal(including turning centres)
0/0/0	4.2	7.2	1.2/1.2	0/0/0	0/	0/0/0	0/0/	11.4/11.4/12	/11.4			0/0/0	--Other
													Machine-tools (including way-type unit head machines) for drilling, boring, milling, threading or tapping by removing metal, other than lathes (including turning centres) of heading No.84. 58:
0/0/0	8.4	9	1.5/1.5	0/0/0	0/	0/0/0	0/0/	14.3/14.3/15	/14.3			0/0/0	-Way-type unit head machines
													-Other drilling machines:
0/0/0	2		0/0	0/0/0	0/	0//0	0/0/0	5/5/	/5			0/0/0	--Numerically controlled
0/0/0	8.4	9	1.5/1.5	0/0/0	0/	0/0/0	0/0/	14.3/14.3/15	/14.3			0/0/0	--Other
													-Other boring-milling machines:
0/0/	4		1/1	0/0/0	0/	0//0	0/0/	5/5/	/5			0/0/0	--Numerically controlled
0/0/	2		0/0	0/0/0	0/	0//0	0/0/	5/5/	/5			0/0/0	--Other
													-Other boring machines:
0/0/	2		0/0	0/0/0	0/	0//0	0/0/	5/5/	/5			0/0/0	--Numerically xontrolled
0/0/0	8.4		1.5/1.5	0/0/0	0/	0/0/0	0/0/	5/5/	/5			0/0/0	-- Other
													-Milling machines, knee-type:
0/0/	2			0/0/0	0/	0//0	0/0/	5/5/	/5			0/0/0	--Numerically controlled
0/0/0	8.4		1.5/1.5	0/0/0	0/	0/0/0	0/0/	5/5/	/5			0/0/0	--Other
													-Other milling machines:
													--Numerically controlled:
0/0/	0		0/0	0/0/0	0/	0//0	0/0/	4.9/4.9/	/4.9			0/0/0	---Planomilling machines
0/0/	0		0/0	0/0/0	0/	0//0	0/0/	4.9/4.9/	/4.9			0/0/0	---Other
													--Other:
0/0/0	3.5		1.2/1.2	0/0/0	0/	0/0/0	0/0/	5/5/	/5			0/0/0	---Planomilling machines
0/0/0	4.2	11	1.2/1.2	0/0/0	0/	0/0/0	0/0/	5/5/	/5			0/0/0	---Other
0/0/0	4.2			0/0/0	0/	0/0/0	0/0/	5/5/	/5			0/0/0	-Other threading or tapping machines
													Machine-tools for deburring, sharpening, grinding, honing, lapping, polishing or otherwise finishing metal or cermets by means of grinding stones, abrasives or polishing products, other than gear cutting, gear grinding or gear finishing machines of heading No.84. 61:
													-Flat-surface grinding machines:
													--Numerically controlled:
0/0/	2		0/0	0/0/0	0/	0//0	0/0/0	5/5/	/5			0/0/0	--The positioning in any one axis can be set up to an accuracy of at least 0.01mm
0/0/0	8.4	9	1.5/1.5	0/0/0	0/	0/0/0	0/0/	14.3/14.3/15	/14.3			0/0/0	---Other
													--Other
0/0/0	8.4		1.5/1.5	0/0/0	0/	0/0/0	0/0/	5/5/	/5			0/0/0	--The positioning in anY 0ne axis can be set up to an accuracy of at least 0.01mm
0/0/0	8.4	9	1.5/1.5	0/0/0	0/	0/0/0	0/0/	14.3/14.3/15	/14.3			0/0/0	---Other
													-Other grinding machines:
													--Centreless grinding machines，numerically controlled:
0/0/	2		4.1/4.1	0/0/0	0/	0//0	0/0/	5/5/	/5			0/0/0	--The positioning in any one axis can be set up to an accuracy of at least 0.01mm:
0/0/0	8.4	9	1.5/1.5	0/0/0	0/	0/0/0	0/0/	14.3/14.3/15	/14.3			0/0/0	---Other
													--Other cylindrical grinding Inachines，numerically controlled:
													The Positioning in any one axis can be set up to an accuracy of at least 0.01mm:
0/0/	2			0/0/0	0/	0//0	0/0/	5/5/	/5			0/0/0	---Crank shaft grinding machines
0/0/	2			0/0/0	0/	0//0	0/0/	5/5/	/5			0/0/0	----Other
0/0/0	8.4	9	1.5/1.5	0/0/0	0/	0/0/0	0/0/	14.3/14.3/15	/14.3			0/0/0	---Other
													--Other，numerically controlled:
													---The posltlomng in any one axis can be set up to an accuracy of at least 0.01mm:
0/0/	2			0/0/0	0/	0//0	0/0/	5/5/	/5			0/0/0	---Internal grinding machines
0/0/	2		4.1/4.1	0/0/0	0/	0//0	0/0/	5/5/	/5			0/0/0	----Other
0/0/0	8.4	9	1.5/1.5	0/0/0	0/	0/0/0	0/0/	14.3/14.3/15	/14.3			0/0/0	---Other
													--Other:
													--The posmomng in anY 0ne axis can be set up to an accuracy of at least 0.01mm:
0/0/	8.4		1.5/1.5	0/0/0	0/	0/0/0	0/0/	5/5/	/5			0/0/0	----Cylindrical grinding mflchines
0/0/	8.4		1.5/1.5	0/0/0	0/	0/0/0	0/0/	5/5/	/5			0/0/0	----Internal grinding machrues
0/0/0	4.6		1.3/1.3	0/0/0	0/	0/0/0	0/0/	5/5/	/5			0/0/0	----Grinding machines of roll
0/0/	4.6			0/0/0	0/	0/0/0	0/0/	5/5/	/5			0/0/0	----Other
0/0/0	8.4	9		0/0/0	0/	0/0/0	0/0/	14.3/14.3/15	/14.3			0/0/0	---Other
													-Sharpening (tool or cutter grinding) machines:
0/0/	4			0/0/0	0/	0//0	0/0/	5/5/	/5			0/0/0	--Numerically controlled
0/0/0	8.4			0/0/0	0/	0/0/0	0/0/	5/5/	/5			0/0/0	--Other
													-Honing or lapping machines:
0/0/0	4.6		1.3/1.3	0/0/0	0/	0/0/0	0/0/	5/5/	/5			0/0/0	---Honing
0/0/0	4.6		1.3/1.3	0/0/0	0/	0/0/0	0/0/0	5/5/	/5			0/0/0	---Lapping
													-Other:
0/0/0	8.4	3	1.5/1.5	0/0/0	0/	0/0/0	0/0/0	0/0/13.5	13.6/0			0/0/0	---Grinding wheel machines
0/0/0	8.4	0	1.5/1.5	0/0/0	0/	0/0/0	0/0/0	13.5/13.5/13.5	13.6/13.5			0/0/0	---Polishing machines

税则号列	货品名称〔CIQ 扩展编码及品名－T2 表示见附表 2〕	最惠(%)	暂定税率	普通	增值/消费	出口退税	计量单位	监管条件/特殊证件	检验检疫	对美关税	亚太上/下
8460.9090	---其他〔999〕	12		50	13/	13	台/千克	/		37	
84.61	**切削金属或金属陶瓷的刨床、牛头刨床、插床、拉床、切齿机、齿轮磨床或齿轮精加工机床、锯床、切断机及其他税目未列名的切削机床：**										
	-牛头刨床或插床：										
8461.2010	---牛头刨床〔999〕	12		50	13/	13	台/千克	/			
8461.2020	---插床〔999〕	12		50	13/	13	台/千克	/			
8461.3000	-拉床〔999〕	12		50	13/	13	台/千克	/		37	
	-切齿机、齿轮磨床或齿轮精加工机床：										
	---数控的：										
8461.4011	----齿轮磨床〔999〕	9		20	13/	13	台/千克	O/		34	
8461.4019	----其他〔999〕	9		20	13/	13	台/千克	O/		34	
8461.4090	---其他〔999〕	9		50	13/	13	台/千克	/		34	
8461.5000	-锯床或切断机										
8461.5000 10	辐照元件刀具切割机[切割燃料包壳以使辐照核材料能溶解(含遥控设备)]〔999〕	12		50	13/	13	台/千克	3/			
8461.5000 90	其他锯床或切断机〔999〕	12		50	13/	13	台/千克	/			
	-其他：										
	---刨床：										
8461.9011	----龙门刨床〔999〕	12		50	13/	13	台/千克	/			
8461.9019	----其他〔999〕	12		50	13/	13	台/千克	/			
8461.9090	---其他〔999〕	12		50	13/	13	台/千克	/		37	
84.62	**加工金属的锻造、锻锤或模锻(但轧机除外)机床（包括压力机）;加工金属的弯曲、折叠、矫直、矫平、剪切、冲孔、开槽或步冲机床(包括压力机、纵剪线及定尺剪切线,但拉拔机除外);其他加工金属或硬质合金的压力机：**										
	-热锻设备,热模锻设备(包括压力机)及热锻锻锤：										
	--闭式锻造机(模锻机)：										
8462.1110	---数控的〔999〕	9		20	13/	13	台/千克	/			6.3/6.3
8462.1190	---其他〔999〕	9		50	13/	13	台/千克	/			6.3/6.3
	--其他：										
8462.1910	---数控的〔101 锻造机床,102 冲压机床〕	9		20	13/	13	台/千克	/			6.3/6.3
8462.1990	---其他〔101 锻造机床,102 冲压机床〕	9		50	13/	13	台/千克	/			6.3/6.3
	-用于板材的弯曲、折叠、矫直或矫平机床(包括折弯机)：										
	--型材成型机：										
8462.2210	---数控的〔101 折叠机,102 矫直机或矫平机,103 折弯机〕	9		20	13/	13	台/千克	/		34	
8462.2290	---其他〔101 折叠机,102 矫直机或矫平机,103 折弯机〕	9		50	13/	13	台/千克	/		34	
8462.2300	--数控折弯机〔999〕	9		20	13/	13	台/千克	/		34	
8462.2400	--数控多边折弯机〔999〕	9		20	13/	13	台/千克	/		34	
8462.2500	--数控卷板机〔999〕	9		20	13/	13	台/千克	/		34	
	--其他数控弯曲、折叠、矫直或矫平机床：										
8462.2610	---矫直机〔999〕	9		20	13/	13	台/千克	/		34	
8462.2690	---其他〔101 折叠机,102 矫直机或矫平机,103 折弯机〕	9		20	13/	13	台/千克	/		34	
	--其他：										
8462.2910	---矫直机〔999〕	9		50	13/	13	台/千克	/		29	
8462.2990	---其他〔101 折叠机,102 矫直机或矫平机,103 折弯机〕	9		50	13/	13	台/千克	/		34	
	-板材用纵剪线、定尺剪切线和其他剪切机床（不包括压力机),但冲剪两用机除外：										
	--纵剪线和定尺剪切线：										
8462.3210	---数控的〔999〕	7		20	13/	13	台/千克	/			
8462.3290	---其他〔999〕	9		50	13/	13	台/千克	/			8.6/8.6
8462.3300	--数控剪切机床〔999〕	7		20	13/	13	台/千克	/			
8462.3900	--其他〔999〕	9		50	13/	13	台/千克	/			8.6/8.6
	-板材用冲孔、开槽或步冲机床(不包括压力机),包括冲剪两用机：										
	--数控的：										
	---冲床：										
8462.4211	----自动模式数控步冲压力机〔101 冲压机床,102 开槽机,103 冲孔机,104 组合机床〕	9		20	13/	13	台/千克	/		34	
8462.4212	----其他〔101 冲压机床,102 组合机床〕	9		20	13/	13	台/千克	/		34	
8462.4290	---其他〔999〕	9		20	13/	13	台/千克	/		34	
8462.4900	--其他〔101 开槽机,102 冲孔机,103 组合机床〕	9		50	13/	13	台/千克	/		34	
	-金属管道、管材、型材、空心型材和棒材的加工机床（非压力机)：										
8462.5100	---数控的										

协定税率 %								RCEP		特惠税率 %			Article Description
东/冰/格	巴基斯坦	韩国	瑞士上/下	哥/秘/柬	澳/毛	新西/坡/智	中国港/澳/台	东盟及马来/澳/韩	日/新	亚太2国	老/柬/缅	98/97/95	
0/0/0	8.4	9	1.5/1.5	0/0/0	0/	0/0/0	0/0/	14.3/14.3/15	/14.3			0/0/0	---Other
													Machine-tools for planing, shaping, slotting, broaching, gear cutting, gear grinding or gear finishing, sawing, cutting-off and other machine-tools working by removing metal or cermets, not elsewhere specified or included:
													-Shaping or slotting machines:
0/0/0	8.4	3	1.5/1.5	0/0/0	0/	0/0/0	0/0/	0/0/13.5	13.6/0			0/0/0	---Shaping machines
0/0/0	8.4	3	1.5/1.5	0/0/0	0/	0/0/0	0/0/0	0/0/13.5	13.6/0			0/0/0	---Slotting machines
0/0/0	4.2	2.4	1.2/1.2	0/0/0	0/	0/0/0	0/0/0	10.8/10.8/10.8	10.9/10.8			0/0/0	-Broaching machines
													-Gear cutting, gear grinding or gear finishing machines:
													---Numerically controlled:
0/0/	4			0/0/0	0/	0//0	0/0/	5/5/	/5			0/0/0	----Gear grinder
0/0/	4			0/0/0	0/	0//0	0/0/	5/5/	/5			0/0/0	----Other
0/0/0	8.4			0/0/0	0/	0/0/0	0/0/	5/5/	/5			0/0/0	---Other
													-Sawing or cutting-off machines
0/0/0	4.2		1.2/1.2	0/0/0	0/	0/0/0	0/0/0	5/5/	/5			0/0/0	Irradiated-component cutting machine toole[cutting the fuel claddings to make the irradiated nuclear materials to melt down(including remote control)]
0/0/0	4.2		1.2/1.2	0/0/0	0/	0/0/0	0/0/0	5/5/	/5			0/0/0	Other sawing or cutting-off
													-Other:
													---Planing machines:
0/0/0	8.4	3	1.5/1.5	0/0/0	0/	0/0/0	0/0/0	0/0/13.5	13.6/0			0/0/0	----Double-column (open-side) planing machines
0/0/0	8.4	3	0/0	0/0/0	0/	0/0/0	0/0/0	0/0/13.5	13.6/0			0/0/0	----Other
0/0/0	4.2	7.2	1.2/1.2	0/0/0	0/	0/0/0	0/0/	11.4/11.4/12	/11.4			0/0/0	---Other
													Machine—tools (including presses) for working metal by forging, hammering or die forging (excluding rolling mills); machine—tools (including presses, slitting lines and cut—to—length lines) for working metal by bending, folding, straightening, flattening, shearing, punching, notching or nibbling (excluding draw— benches); presses for working metal or metal carbides, not specified above
													-Hot forming machines for forging, die forging (including presses) and hot hammers :
													--Closed die forging machines:
0/0/	2	6.7	1/1	0/0/0	0/	0//0	0/0/0	5/5/	/5			0/0/0	---Numerically controlled
0/0/0	3.5	8.4	1.2/1.2	0/0/0	0/	0/0/0	0/0/0	5/5/	/5			0/0/0	---Other
													--Other:
0/0/	2	6.7	1/1	0/0/0	0/	0//0	0/0/0	5/5/	/5			0/0/0	---Numerically controlled
0/0/0	3.5	8.4	1.2/1.2	0/0/0	0/	0/0/0	0/0/0	5/5/	/5			0/0/0	---Other
													-Bending, folding, straightening or flattening machines (including press brakes) for flat products:
													--Profile forming machines:
0/0/	4		1/1	0/0/0	0/	0//0	0/0/	5/5/	/5			0/0/0	---Numerically controlled
0/0/0	2		0/0	0/0/0	0/	0/0/0	0/0/	5/5/	/5			0/0/0	---Other
0/0/	4		1/1	0/0/0	0/	0//0	0/0/	5/5/	/5			0/0/0	--Numerically bending machine
0/0/	4		1/1	0/0/0	0/	0//0	0/0/	5/5/	/5			0/0/0	--Numerically multilateral bending machine
0/0/	4		1/1	0/0/0	0/	0//0	0/0/	5/5/	/5			0/0/0	--Numerically rolling machine
													--Other numerically controlled bending, folding, straightening or flattening machines:
0/0/	4		1/1	0/0/0	0/	0//0	0/0/	5/5/	/5			0/0/0	---Straightening machines
0/0/	4		1/1	0/0/0	0/	0//0	0/0/	5/5/	/5			0/0/0	---Other
													--Other:
0/0/0	2		4.2/4.2	0/0/0	0/	0//0	0/0/	5/5/	/5			0/0/0	---Straightening machines
0/0/0	2		0/0	0/0/0	0/	0/0/0	0/0/	5/5/	/5			0/0/0	---Other
													-Longitudinal shear lines, fixed length shear lines and other shear machines (excluding presses) for plates, except for punching and shearing machines:
													--Slitting lines and cut—to—length lines
0/0/	4		0/0	0/0/0	0/	0//0	0/0/	5/5/	/5			0/0/0	---Numerically controlled
0/0/0	2		0/0	0/0/0	0/	0//0	0/0/	5/5/	/5			0/0/0	---Other
0/0/	3.3		0/0	0/0/0	0/	0//0	0/0/	5/5/	/5			0/0/0	--Numerically controlled shearing machines
0/0/0	2		0/0	0/0/0	0/	0//0	0/0/	5/5/	/5			0/0/0	--Other
													-Punching, slotting or step punching machine tools for plates (excluding presses), including punching and shearing machines:
													--Numerically controlled:
													---Punch press:
0/0/	2		1/1	0/0/0	0/	0//0	0/0/	5/5/	/5			0/0/0	----CNC automatic tool change punch press
0/0/	4		0/0	0/0/0	0/	0//0	0/0/	5/5/	/5			0/0/0	----Other
0/0/	2		0/0	0/0/0	0/	0/0/0	0/0/	5/5/	/5			0/0/0	---Other
0/0/0	2		0/0	0/0/0	0/	0/0/0	0/0/0	5/5/	/5			0/0/0	--Other
													-Machine tools for processing metal pipes, pipes, profiles, hollow profiles and bars (non Press):
													--Numerically controlled shearing machines

税则号列		货品名称〔CIQ 扩展编码及品名－T2 表示见附表 2〕	最惠(%)	暂定税率	普通	增值/消费	出口退税	计量单位	监管条件/特殊证件	检验检疫	对美关税	亚太上/下
8462.5100	10	数控金属管道、管材、型材、空心型材和棒材的锻造或冲压机床及锻锤(压力机除外(P))〔101 锻造机床,102 冲压机床,103 挤压机〕	8.5		20	13/	13	台/千克	/			
8462.5100	90	其他金属管道、管材、型材、空心型材和棒材的数控加工机床(压力机除外)〔999〕	8.5		20	13/	13	台/千克	/		33.5	
8462.5900		--其他										
8462.5900	10	非数控金属管道、管材、型材、空心型材和棒材的锻造或冲压机床及锻锤(压力机除外(P))〔101 锻造机床,102 冲压机床,103 挤压机〕	9		50	13/	13	台/千克	/			
8462.5900	90	其他金属管道、管材、型材、空心型材和棒材的非数控加工机床(压力机除外)〔999〕	9		50	13/	13	台/千克	/		19	
		-金属冷加工压力机:										
		--液压压力机										
8462.6110		---数控的										
8462.6110	10	数控液压式锻造或冲压机床及锻锤(加工金属或硬质合金(P))〔101 锻造机床,102 冲压机床,103 挤压机〕	9		40	13/	13	台/千克	/			8.3/8.3
8462.6110	90	其他数控液压压力机(加工金属或硬质合金)〔101 冲压机床,102 锻造机床,103 挤压机〕	9		40	13/	13	台/千克	/		34	8.3/8.3
8462.6190		---其他										
8462.6190	10	非数控液压式锻造或冲压机床及锻锤(加工金属或硬质合金(P))〔101 锻造机床,102 冲压机床,103 挤压机〕	9		50	13/	13	台/千克	/			8.3/8.3
8462.6190	90	其他非数控液压压力机(加工金属或硬质合金)〔101 冲压机床,102 锻造机床,103 挤压机〕	9		50	13/	13	台/千克	/		34	8.3/8.3
		--机械压力机:										
8462.6210		---数控的										
8462.6210	10	数控机械式锻造或冲压机床及锻锤(加工金属或硬质合金(P))〔101 锻造机床,102 冲压机床,103 挤压机〕	9		35	13/	13	台/千克	/			8.6/8.6
8462.6210	90	其他数控机械压力机(加工金属或硬质合金)〔101 冲压机床,102 锻造机床,103 挤压机〕	9		35	13/	13	台/千克	/		34	8.6/8.6
8462.6290		---其他										
8462.6290	10	非数控机械式锻造或冲压机床及锻锤(加工金属或硬质合金(P))〔101 锻造机床,102 冲压机床,103 挤压机〕	9		50	13/	13	台/千克	/			8.6/8.6
8462.6290	90	其他非数控机械压力机(加工金属或硬质合金)〔101 冲压机床,102 锻造机床,103 挤压机〕	9		50	13/	13	台/千克	/		34	8.6/8.6
8462.6300		--伺服压力机										
8462.6300	10	伺服锻造或冲压机床及锻锤(加工金属或硬质合金(P))〔101 锻造机床,102 冲压机床,103 挤压机〕	9		35	13/	13	台/千克	/			8.6/8.6
8462.6300	90	其他伺服压力机(加工金属或硬质合金)〔101 冲压机床,102 锻造机床,103 挤压机〕	9		35	13/	13	台/千克	/		34	8.6/8.6
		--其他:										
8462.6910		---数控的										
8462.6910	10	其他锻造或冲压机床及锻锤(加工金属或硬质合金(P))〔101 锻造机床,102 冲压机床,103 挤压机〕	9		35	13/	13	台/千克	/			8.6/8.6
8462.6910	90	其他数控压力机(加工金属或硬质合金)〔101 冲压机床,102 锻造机床,103 挤压机〕	9		35	13/	13	台/千克	/		34	8.6/8.6
8462.6990		---其他										
8462.6990	10	其他非数控锻造或冲压机床及锻锤(加工金属或硬质合金(P))〔101 锻造机床,102 冲压机床〕	9		50	13/	13	台/千克	/			8.6/8.6
8462.6990	90	其他非数控压力机(加工金属或硬质合金)〔101 冲压机床,102 锻造机床,103 挤压机〕	9		50	13/	13	台/千克	/		34	8.6/8.6
		-其他:										
8462.9010		---数控的										
8462.9010	10	税目 84.62 的其他数控的金属管道、管材、型材、空心型材和棒材的数控锻造或冲压机床及锻锤((P))〔101 锻造机床,102 冲压机床,103 挤压机〕	9		35	13/	13	台/千克	/			8.6/8.6
8462.9010	90	税目 84.62 的其他数控机床〔999〕	9		35	13/	13	台/千克	/		34	8.6/8.6
8462.9090		---其他										
8462.9090	10	税目 84.62 的其他非数控的金属管道、管材、型材、空心型材和棒材的数控锻造或冲压机床及锻锤((P))〔101 锻造机床,102 冲压机床,103 挤压机〕	9		50	13/	13	台/千克	/			8.6/8.6
8462.9090	90	税目 84.62 的其他非数控机床〔999〕	9		50	13/	13	台/千克	/		34	8.6/8.6
84.63		**金属或金属陶瓷的其他非切削加工机床:**										
		-杆、管、型材、异型材、丝及类似品的拉拔机:										
		---冷拔管机:										
8463.1011		----拉拔力为 300 吨及以下〔999〕	9		50	13/	13	台/千克	/			
8463.1019		----其他〔999〕	9		50	13/	13	台/千克	/			
8463.1020		---拔丝机〔999〕	9		50	13/	13	台/千克	/		34	
8463.1090		---其他〔999〕	9		50	13/	13	台/千克	/		19	
8463.2000		-螺纹滚轧机〔999〕	9		50	13/	13	台/千克	/		34	
8463.3000		-金属丝加工机〔999〕	9		50	13/	13	台/千克	/		34	
8463.9000		-其他										
8463.9000	10	滚压成形机床(数控,装 3 个以上压辊)〔999〕	9		50	13/	13	台/千克	3/		29	
8463.9000	20	具有滚压功能的旋压成形机床(数控,装 3 个以上压辊)〔999〕	9		50	13/	13	台/千克	3/		29	
8463.9000	90	其他非切削加工机床(是指加工金属或金属陶瓷的)〔999〕	9		50	13/	13	台/千克	/		29	

协定税率 %								RCEP		特惠税率 %			
东/冰/格	巴基斯坦	韩国	瑞士上/下	哥/秘/柬	澳/毛	新西/坡/智	中国港/澳/台	东盟及马来/澳/韩	日/新	亚太2国	老/柬/缅	98/97/95	Article Description
0/0/	2.9		0.5/0.5	0/0/0	0/	0//0	0/0/	5/5/	/5			0/0/0	CNC forging or stamping machines and hammers for metal pipes, pipes, profiles, hollow profiles and bars (except presses (P))
0/0/	2.9		0.5/0.5	0/0/0	0/	0//0	0/0/	5/5/	/5			0/0/0	CNC machine tools for other metal pipes, pipes, profiles, hollow profiles and bars (except presses)
													--Other
0/0/0	2.3		1.1/1.1	0/0/0	0/	0/0/0	0/0/0	5/5/	/5			0/0/0	Forging or stamping machines and hammers for non CNC metal pipes, pipes, profiles, hollow profiles and bars (except presses (P))
0/0/0	2.3		1.1/1.1	0/0/0	0/	0/0/0	0/0/0	5/5/	/5			0/0/0	Non CNC machine tools for processing other metal pipes, pipes, profiles, hollow profiles and bars (except presses)
													-Cold metal working presses
													--Hydraulic press
													---Numerically controlled shearing machines
0/0/3.2	3.3	8.4	0.7/0.7	0/0/0	0/	0/0/0	0/0/	5/5/	/5			0/0/0	CNC hydraulic forging or stamping machine tools and forging hammers (machining metal or cemented carbide (P))
0/0/3.2	3.3	8.4	0.7/0.7	0/0/0	0/	0/0/0	0/0/	5/5/	/5			0/0/0	Other CNC hydraulic presses (machining metal or cemented carbide)
													---Other
0/0/0	3.8	8.9	0.7/0.7	0/0/0	0/	0/0/0	0/0/	5/5/	/5			0/0/0	Non NC hydraulic forging or stamping machine tools and forging hammers (machining metal or cemented carbide (P))
0/0/0	3.8	8.9	0.7/0.7	0/0/0	0/	0/0/0	0/0/	5/5/	/5			0/0/0	Other non CNC hydraulic presses (processing metal or cemented carbide)
													--Mechanical presses:
													---Numerically controlled shearing machines
0/0/	2	8	0.5/0.5	0/0/0	0/	0/0/0	0/0/0	5/5/	/5			0/0/0	CNC mechanical forging or stamping machine tools and forging hammers (machining metal or cemented carbide (P))
0/0/	2	8	0.5/0.5	0/0/0	0/	0/0/0	0/0/0	5/5/	/5			0/0/0	Other CNC Mechanical Presses (processing metal or cemented carbide)
													---Other
0/0/0	2.8	8.8	0.6/0.6	0/0/0	0/	0/0/0	0/0/0	5/5/	/5			0/0/0	Non NC mechanical forging or stamping machine tools and forging hammers (machining metal or cemented carbide (P))
0/0/0	2.8	8.8	0.6/0.6	0/0/0	0/	0/0/0	0/0/0	5/5/	/5			0/0/0	Other non CNC Mechanical Presses (processing metal or cemented carbide)
													--Servo—presses
0/0/	2	8	0.5/0.5	0/0/0	0/	0/0/0	0/0/0	5/5/	/5			0/0/0	Servo forging or stamping machine tools and forging hammers (machining metal or cemented carbide (P))
0/0/	2	8	0.5/0.5	0/0/0	0/	0/0/0	0/0/0	5/5/	/5			0/0/0	Other Servo Presses (machining metal or cemented carbide)
													--Other:
													---Numerically controlled shearing machines
0/0/	2	8	0.5/0.5	0/0/0	0/	0/0/0	0/0/	5/5/	/5			0/0/0	Other forging or stamping machines and hammers (machining metal or cemented carbide (P))
0/0/	2	8	0.5/0.5	0/0/0	0/	0/0/0	0/0/	5/5/	/5			0/0/0	Other CNC presses (machining metal or cemented carbide)
													---Other
0/0/0	2.8	8.8	0.6/0.6	0/0/0	0/	0/0/0	0/0/	5/5/	/5			0/0/0	Other non NC forging or stamping machine tools and forging hammers (processing metal or cemented carbide (P))
0/0/0	2.8	8.8	0.6/0.6	0/0/0	0/	0/0/0	0/0/	5/5/	/5			0/0/0	Other non CNC presses (processing metal or cemented carbide)
													-Other:
													---Numerically controlled shearing machines
0/0/	2	8	0.5/0.5	0/0/0	0/	0/0/0	0/0/	5/5/	/5			0/0/0	CNC forging or stamping machines and hammers for other CNC metal pipes, pipes, sections, hollow sections and bars of heading 84.62 ((P))
0/0/	2	8	0.5/0.5	0/0/0	0/	0/0/0	0/0/	5/5/	/5			0/0/0	Other CNC machine tools under heading 84.62
													---Other
0/0/0	2.8	8.8	0.6/0.6	0/0/0	0/	0/0/0	0/0/	5/5/	/5			0/0/0	CNC forging or stamping machines and hammers for other non CNC metal pipes, pipes, sections, hollow sections and bars of heading 84.62 ((P))
0/0/0	2.8	8.8	0.6/0.6	0/0/0	0/	0/0/0	0/0/	5/5/	/5			0/0/0	Other non CNC machine tools under heading 84.62
													Other machine-tools for working metal or cermets, without removing material:
													-Draw-benches for bars, tubes, profiles, wire or the like:
													---Cold-drawing tube benches:
0/0/0	2	6	0/0	0/0/0	0/0	0//0	0/0/	9/9.5/10	9.1/9.5			0/0/0	----With drawing force≤300t
0/0/0	2		0/0	0/0/0	0/0	0/0/0	0/0/0	5/5/	/5			0/0/0	----Other
0/0/0	2		0/0	0/0/0	0/0	0//0	0/0/	5/5/	/5			0/0/0	---Wiredrawing machines
0/0/0	2		0/0	0/0/0	0/0	0//0	0/0/	5/5/	/5			0/0/0	---Other
0/0/0	8.4		1.5/1.5	0/0/0	0/0	0/0/0	0/0/	5/5/	/5			0/0/0	-Thread rolling machines
0/0/0	2		0/0	0/0/0	0/0	0//0	0/0/	5/5/	/5			0/0/0	-Machines for working wire
													-Other
0/0/0	4		1/1	0/0/0	0/0	0//0	0/0/	5/5/	/5			0/0/0	Roll forming machine tools(CNC with three or more rollers)
0/0/0	4		1/1	0/0/0	0/0	0//0	0/0/	5/5/	/5			0/0/0	Spin forming machines with roll forming function(CNC with three or more rollers)
0/0/0	4		1/1	0/0/0	0/0	0//0	0/0/	5/5/	/5			0/0/0	Other non-cutting machine tools (for processing metals or metal ceramics)

税则号列	货品名称〔CIQ 扩展编码及品名－T2 表示见附表 2〕	最惠(%)	暂定税率	普通	增值/消费	出口退税	计量单位	监管条件/特殊证件	检验检疫	对美关税	亚太上/下
84.64	**石料、陶瓷、混凝土、石棉水泥或类似矿物材料的加工机床、玻璃冷加工机床：**										
	-锯床：										
8464.1010	---圆盘锯〔999〕	0		30	13/	13	台/千克	/		10	
8464.1020	---钢丝锯〔999〕	0		30	13/	13	台/千克	/		25	
8464.1090	---其他〔999〕	0		30	13/	13	台/千克	/		25	
	-研磨或抛光机床：										
8464.2010	---玻璃研磨或抛光机床〔999〕	0		30	13/	13	台/千克	/		25	
8464.2090	---其他〔999〕	0		30	13/	13	台/千克	/		25	
	-其他：										
	---玻璃的其他冷加工机床：										
8464.9011	----切割机〔999〕	0		30	13/	13	台/千克	/		25	
8464.9012	----刻花机〔999〕	0		30	13/	13	台/千克	/		25	
8464.9019	----其他〔999〕	0		30	13/	13	台/千克	/		25	
8464.9090	---其他〔999〕	0		30	13/	13	台/千克	/		25	
84.65	**木材、软木、骨、硬质橡胶、硬质塑料或类似硬质材料的加工机床(包括用打钉或打 U 形钉、胶粘或其他方法组合前述材料的机器)：**										
8465.1000	-不需更换工具即可进行不同机械加工的机器〔999〕	9		30	13/	13	台/千克	/		34	
	-加工中心：										
8465.2010	--以刨、铣、钻孔、研磨、抛光、凿榫及其他切削为主的加工中心,加工木材及类似硬质材料的〔999〕	9		30	13/	13	台/千克	/			
8465.2090	--其他〔999〕	9		30	13/	13	台/千克	/			
	-其他：										
8465.9100	--锯床〔999〕	9		30	13/	13	台/千克	/		34	
8465.9200	--刨、铣或切削成形机器〔999〕	9		30	13/	13	台/千克	/		34	
8465.9300	--研磨、砂磨或抛光机器〔101 研磨或抛光机器,102 加工木材等材料的其它机床〕	9		30	13/	13	台/千克	/		19	
8465.9400	--弯曲或装配机器〔999〕	9		30	13/	13	台/千克	/		34	
8465.9500	--钻孔或凿榫机器〔999〕	9		30	13/	13	台/千克	/		34	
8465.9600	--剖开、切片或刮削机器〔999〕	9		30	13/	13	台/千克	/		34	
8465.9900	--其他〔999〕	9		30	13/	13	台/千克	/		34	
84.66	**专用于或主要用于税目 84.56 至 84.65 所列机器的零件、附件,包括工件或工具的夹具、自启板牙切头、分度头及其他专用于机器的附件;各种手提工具的工具夹具：**										
8466.1000	-工具夹具及自启板牙切头〔999〕	7		17	13/	13	千克	/		32	
8466.2000	-工件夹具〔999〕	7		17	13/	13	千克	/		32	4.9/4.9
8466.3000	-分度头及其他专用于机器的附件〔999〕	7		17	13/	13	千克	/		32	
	-其他：										
8466.9100	--税目 84.64 所列机器用〔101 机床附件,102 机床零件〕	0		17	13/	13	千克	/		20	
8466.9200	--税目 84.65 所列机器用〔101 机床附件,102 机床零件〕	6		17	13/	13	千克	/		31	
	--税目 84.56 至 84.61 所列机器用：										
8466.9310	---刀库及自动换刀装置〔101 机床附件,102 机床零件〕	0		17	13/	13	千克	/		25	
8466.9390	---其他〔101 机床附件,102 机床零件〕	0		17	13/	13	千克	/		20	
8466.9400	--税目 84.62 或 84.63 所列机器用										
8466.9400 10	滚压成形机床用芯轴(转筒成形用的芯轴,内径在 75 毫米至 400 毫米之间)〔999〕	6		17	13/	13	千克	3/		26	
8466.9400 20	有滚压功能的旋压成形机用芯轴(转筒成形用的芯轴,内径在 75 毫米至 400 毫米之间)〔999〕	6		17	13/	13	千克	3/		26	
8466.9400 90	税目 84.62－84.63 机器用其他零件〔101 机床附件,102 机床零件〕	6		17	13/	13	千克	/		26	
84.67	**手提式风动或液压工具及本身装有电动或非电动动力装置的手提式工具：**										
	-风动的：										
8467.1100	--旋转式(包括旋转冲击式的)〔999〕	8		30	13/	13	台/千克	/		18	
8467.1900	--其他〔999〕	8		30	13/	13	台/千克	/		18	
	-本身装有电动动力装置的：										
8467.2100	--各种钻〔999〕	8		30	13/	13	台/千克	A/	L	33	5.2/5.2
	--锯：										
8467.2210	---链锯〔999〕	8		30	13/	13	台/千克	/		13	5.2/5.2
8467.2290	---其他〔999〕	8		30	13/	13	台/千克	/		33	5.2/5.2
	--其他：										
8467.2910	---砂磨工具(包括磨光机、砂光机、砂轮机等)〔999〕	8		30	13/	13	台/千克	A/	L	33	5.2/5.2
8467.2920	---电刨〔999〕	8		30	13/	13	台/千克	/			5.2/5.2
8467.2990	---其他〔999〕	8		30	13/	13	台/千克	A/	L	28	5.2/5.2
	-其他工具：										
8467.8100	--链锯〔999〕	8		30	13/	13	台/千克	/		28	
8467.8900	--其他〔101 手提式液压工具,102 其他手提式动力工具及其零件〕	8		30	13/	13	台/千克	/		13	
	-零件：										
	--链锯用：										

协定税率 %								RCEP		特惠税率 %			Article Description
东/冰/格	巴基斯坦	韩国	瑞士上/下	哥/秘/柬	澳/毛	新西/坡/智	中国港/澳/台	东盟及马来/澳/韩	日/新	亚太2国	老/柬/缅	98/97/95	
													Machine-tools for working stone, ceramics, concrete, asbestos-cement or like mineral materials or for cold working glass:
													-Sawing machines:
0/0/0	0	0	0/0	0/0/0	0/0	0//0	0/0/	0/0/0	0/0			0/0/0	---Of disk saw
0/0/0	0	0	0/0	0/0/0	0/0	0//0	0/0/	0/0/0	0/0			0/0/0	---Of scroll saw
0/0/0	0	0	0/0	0/0/0	0/0	0//0	0/0/	0/0/0	0/0			0/0/0	---Other
													-Grinding or polishing machines:
0/0/0	0	0	0/0	0/0/0	0/0	0//0	0/0/	0/0/0	0/0			0/0/0	---Machines for grinding or polishing glass or glassware
0/0/0	0	0	0/0	0/0/0	0/0	0//0	0/0/	0/0/0	0/0			0/0/0	---Other
													-Other:
													---Other machines for cold-working glass or glassware:
0/0/0	0	0	0/0	0/0/0	0/0	0//0	0/0/	0/0/0	0/0			0/0/0	----Cutting-off machines
0/0/0	0	0	0/0	0/0/0	0/0	0//0	0/0/	0/0/0	0/0			0/0/0	----Carving machines
0/0/0	0	0	0/0	0/0/0	0/0	0//0	0/0/	0/0/0	0/0			0/0/0	----Other
0/0/0	0	0	0/0	0/0/0	0/0	0//0	0/0/	0/0/0	0/0			0/0/0	---Other
													Machine-tools (including machines for nailing, stapling, glueing or otherwise assembling) for working wood, cork, bone, hard rubber, hard plastics or similar hard materials:
0/0/0	2	6	0/0	0/0/0	0/0	0/0/0	0/0/	0/9.5/10	0/9.5			0/0/0	-Machines which can carry out different types of machining operations without tool change between such operations
													-Machining centres:
0/0/0	2	6	0/0	0/0/0	0/0	0/0/0	0/0/	9.5/9.5/10	9.5/9.5			0/0/0	--A machining center mainly engaged in planing, milling, drilling, grinding, polishing, tenon chiseling and other cutting to process wood and similar hard materials
0/0/0	2	6	0/0	0/0/0	0/0	0/0/0	0/0/	9.5/9.5/10	/9.5			0/0/0	--Other
													-Other:
0/0/0	2	6	0/0	0/0/0	0/0	0//0	0/0/	9/9.5/10	9.1/9.5			0/0/0	--Sawing machines
0/0/0	2	6	0/0	0/0/0	0/0	0/0/0	0/0/	9.5/9.5/10	9.5/9.5			0/0/0	--Planing, milling or moulding (by cutting) machines
0/0/0	2	6	0/0	0/0/0	0/0	0//0	0/0/	9.5/9.5/10	9.5/9.5			0/0/0	--Grinding, sanding or polishing machines
0/0/0	2	6	0/0	0/0/0	0/0	0/0/0	0/0/	9.5/9.5/10	9.5/9.5			0/0/0	--Bending or assembling machines
0/0/0	2	6	1/1	0/0/0	0/0	0/0/0	0/0/	9.5/9.5/10	9.5/9.5			0/0/0	--Drilling or mortising machines
0/0/0	2	6	0/0	0/0/0	0/0	0/0/0	0/0/	9.5/9.5/10	/9.5			0/0/0	--Splitting, slicing or paring machines
0/0/0	2	6	0/0	0/0/0	0/0	0/0/0	0/0/	9.5/9.5/10	/9.5			0/0/0	--Other
													Parts and accessories suitable for use solely or principally with the machines of headings No.84.56 to 84.65, including work or tool holders, self-opening dieheads, dividing heads and other special attachments for machine-tools; tool holders for any type of tool for working in the hand:
0/0/0	2	3.2	0.7/0.7	0/0/0	0/0	0//0	0/0/	6.3/6.3/6.3	6.6/6.3			0/0/0	-Tool holders and self-opening dieheads
0/0/0	0	1.4	0.7/0.7	0/0/0	0/0	0//0	0/0/0	0/0/6.3	6.4/0			0/0/0	-Work holders
0/0/0	2	3.2	0.7/0.7	0/0/0	0/0	0//0	0/0/	6.3/6.3/6.3	6.6/6.3			0/0/0	-Dividing heads and other special attachments for machine-tools
													-Other:
0/0/0	0	0	0/0	0/0/0	0/0	0//0	0/0/	0/0/0	0/0			0/0/0	--For machines of heading No.84.64
0/0/0	0	2.8	0/0	0/0/0	0/0	0//0	0/0/	5.4/5.4/5.4	5.6/5.4			0/0/0	--For machines of heading No.84.65
													--For machines of headings No.84.56 to 84.61:
0/0/0	0	0	0/0	0/0/0	0/0	0//0	0/0/	0/0/0	0/0			0/0/0	---Tool storage and automatic tool change machine
0/0/0	0	0	0/0	0/0/0	0/0	0//0	0/0/	0/0/0	0/0			0/0/0	---Other
													--For machines of heading No.84.62 or 84.63
0/0/0	0	0	0.6/0.6	0/0/0	0/0	0//0	0/0/0	0/0/0	5.5/0			0/0/0	Mandrels for roll forming machines tools(mandrel for forming of revolving drum, inner diameter 75mm~400mm)
0/0/0	0	0	0.6/0.6	0/0/0	0/0	0//0	0/0/0	0/0/0	5.5/0			0/0/0	Mandrels for spin forming machines with roll forming functions(spindles for forming of revolving drum, inner diameter 75mm~400mm)
0/0/0	0	0	0.6/0.6	0/0/0	0/0	0//0	0/0/0	0/0/0	5.5/0			0/0/0	Other parts for machines of heading No.84.62 ~ 84.63
													Tools for working in the hand, pneumatic and hydraulic and with self-contained electric or non-electric motor:
													-Pneumatic:
0/0/0	2	3.7	0/0	0/0/0	0/0	0//0	0/0/	7.5/7.6/7.5	7.5/7.6			0/0/0	--Rotary type (including combined rotary-percussion)
0/0/0	2	0	0/0	0/0/0	0/0	0//0	0/0/	0/0/0	7.3/0			0/0/0	--Other
													-With self-contained electric motor:
0/0/0	2	2	0/0	0/0/0	0/0	0/0/0	0/0/	9/9/9	9.1/9			0/0/0	--Drills of all kinds
													--Saws:
0/0/0	2	2	0/0	0/0/0	0/0	0//0	0/0/	0/0/9	9.1/0			0/0/0	---Chain saws
0/0/0	2	2	0/0	0/0/0	0/0	0/0/0	0/0/	0/0/9	9.1/0			0/0/0	---Other
													--Other:
0/0/0	2	2	4.2/4.2	0/0/0	0/0	0/0/0	0/0/	0/0/9	9.1/0			0/0/0	---Grinding tools (including burnisher, belt sander, wheel-sander)
0/0/0	2	2	0/0	0/0/0	0/0	0//0	0/0/	0/0/9	9.1/0			0/0/0	---Planings
0/0/0	2	2	0/0	0/0/0	0/0	0/0/0	0/0/	0/0/9	9.1/0			0/0/0	---Other
													-Other tools:
0/0/0	2	0	0/0	0/0/0	0/0	0//0	0/0/	0/0/0	7.3/0			0/0/0	--Chain saws
0/0/0	2	3.7	0/0	0/0/0	0/0	0//0	0/0/	7.5/7.6/7.5	7.5/7.6			0/0/0	--Other
													-Parts:
													--Of chain saws:

税则号列	货品名称〔CIQ 扩展编码及品名－T2 表示见附表 2〕	最惠(%)	暂定税率	普通	增值/消费	出口退税	计量单位	监管条件/特殊证件	检验检疫	对美关税	亚太上/下
8467.9110	---电动的〔999〕	6		30	13/	13	千克	/		16	3.9/3.9
8467.9190	---其他〔999〕	6		30	13/	13	千克	/		16	4.2/4.2
8467.9200	--风动工具用〔999〕	6		30	13/	13	千克	/		16	
	--其他：										
8467.9910	---电动工具用〔999〕	8		30	13/	13	千克	/		33	5.2/5.2
8467.9990	---其他〔999〕	6		30	13/	13	千克	/		16	
84.68	**焊接机器及装置，不论是否兼有切割功能，但税目 85.15 的货品除外；气体加温表面回火机器及装置：**										
8468.1000	-手提喷焊器〔999〕	9		30	13/	13	台/千克	/		29	
8468.2000	-其他气体焊接或表面回火机器及装置										
8468.2000 10	自动焊接机［将端塞焊接于燃料细棒（或棒）的自动焊接机］〔999〕	9		30	13/	13	台/千克	3/		29	
8468.2000 90	其他气体焊接或表面回火机器及装置〔999〕	9		30	13/	13	台/千克	/		29	
8468.8000	-其他机器及装置〔101 波峰焊设备，102 其它焊接设备及其零件〕	9		30	13/	13	台/千克	/		34	
8468.9000	-零件〔999〕	7	3	30	13/	13	千克	/		23	
84.70	**计算机器及具有计算功能的袖珍式数据记录、重现及显示机器；装有计算装置的会计计算机、邮资盖戳机、售票机及类似机器；现金出纳机：**										
8470.1000	-不需外接电源的电子计算器及具有计算功能的袖珍式数据记录、重现及显示机器〔999〕	0		80	13/	13	台/千克	/		25	
	-其他电子计算器：										
8470.2100	--装有打印装置的〔999〕	0		80	13/	13	台/千克	/			
8470.2900	--其他〔999〕	0		80	13/	13	台/千克	/		25	
8470.3000	-其他计算机器〔999〕	0		40	13/	13	台/千克	/		5	
	-现金出纳机：										
8470.5010	---销售点终端出纳机〔999〕	0		40	13/	13	台/千克	/	L	25	
8470.5090	---其他〔999〕	0		40	13/	13	台/千克	/	L	10	
8470.9000	-其他〔999〕	0		40	13/	13	台/千克	/		25	
84.71	**自动数据处理设备及其部件；其他税目未列名的磁性或光学阅读机、将数据以代码形式转录到数据记录媒体的机器及处理这些数据的机器：**										
	-重量不超过 10 千克的便携自动数据处理设备，至少由一个中央处理部件、一个键盘及一个显示器组成：										
8471.3010	---平板电脑〔101 便携数字自动数据处理机，102 掌上电脑〕	0		70	13/	13	台/千克	A/	L	25	
8471.3090	---其他〔101 便携数字自动数据处理机，102 掌上电脑〕	0		70	13/	13	台/千克	A/	L	25	
	-其他自动数据处理设备：										
	--同一机壳内至少有一个中央处理部件及一个输入和输出部件，不论是否组合式：										
8471.4110	---巨型机、大型机及中型机										
8471.4110 10	高性能数字计算机（高性能数字计算机是指调整后峰值性能（APP）大于 8.0 加权每秒万亿次浮点运算的数字计算机）〔999〕	0		14	13/	13	台/千克	3/		20	
8471.4110 90	其他巨、大、中型自动数据处理设备〔999〕	0		14	13/	13	台/千克	/		20	
8471.4120	---小型机〔999〕	0		14	13/	13	台/千克	/	L	5	
8471.4140	---微型机〔999〕	0		70	13/	13	台/千克	A/	L	5	
8471.4190	---其他〔999〕	0		70	13/	13	台/千克	/	L	10	
	--其他，以系统形式进口或出口的：										
8471.4910	---巨型机、大型机及中型机										
8471.4910 10	系统形式报验的高性能数字计算机（计算机指自动数据处理设备，高性能数字计算机是指调整后峰值性能（APP）大于 8.0 加权每秒万亿次浮点运算的数字计算机）〔999〕	0		29	13/	13	台/千克	3/		5	
8471.4910 90	其他系统形式报验的巨、大、中型机，计算机指自动数据处理设备〔999〕	0		29	13/	13	台/千克	/		5	
8471.4920	---小型机〔999〕	0		29	13/	13	台/千克	/	L	20	
8471.4940	---微型机〔999〕	0		70	13/	13	台/千克	/	L	20	
	---其他：										
8471.4991	----分散型工业过程控制设备〔999〕	0		70	13/	13	台/千克	/		20	
8471.4999	----其他〔999〕	0		70	13/	13	台/千克	/	L	10	
	-子目 8471.41 或 8471.49 所列以外的处理部件，不论是否在同一机壳内有一个或两个下列部件：存储部件、输入部件、输出部件：										
8471.5010	---巨型机、大型机及中型机的										

协定税率 %								RCEP		特惠税率 %			Article Description
东/冰/格	巴基斯坦	韩国	瑞士上/下	哥/秘/柬	澳/毛	新西/坡/智	中国港/澳/台	东盟及马来/澳/韩	日/新	亚太2国	老/柬/缅	98/97/95	
0/0/0	0	0	0/0	0/0/0	0/0	0//0	0/0/	0/0/0	0/0			0/0/0	---With self-contained electric motor
0/0/0	0	0	0.6/0.6	0/0/0	0/0	0//0	0/0/	0/0/0	5.5/0			0/0/0	---Other
0//0	0	0	0/0	0/0/0	0/0	0//0	0/0/	0/0/0	5.5/0			0/0/0	--Of pneumatic tools
													--Other:
0/0/0	3.5	2	1/1	0/0/0	0/0	0/0/0	0/0/	9/9/9	9.1/9			0/0/0	---With self-contained elecric motor
0/0/0	0	1.2	0/0	0/0/0	0/0	0//0	0/0/	0/0/5.4	5.5/0			0/0/0	---Other
													Machinery and apparatus for soldering, brazing or welding, whether or not capable of cutting, other than those of heading No.85. 15; gas-operated surface tempering machines and appliances:
0/0/0	4.2	2.4	1.2/1.2	0/0/0	0/0	0/0/0	0/0/	0/0/10.8	10.9/0			0/0/0	-Hand-held blow pipes
													-Other gas-operated machinery and apparatus
0/0/0	4.2	2.4	0/0	0/0/0	0/0	0/0/0	0/0/	0/0/10.8	10.9/0			0/0/0	Automatic welding machine [the automatic welder machine that joint the end plug with the fuel thin-stick (or stick)]
0/0/0	4.2	2.4	0/0	0/0/0	0/0	0/0/0	0/0/	0/0/10.8	10.9/0			0/0/0	Other gas welding or surface tempering machines and equipments
0/0/0	4.2		1.2/1.2	0/0/0	0/0	0/0/0	0/0/	5/5/	/5			0/0/0	-Other machinery and apparatus
0/0/0	2	0	0/0	0/0/0	0/0	0//0	0/0/	0/0/0	6.4/0			0/0/0	-Parts
													Calculating machines and pocket-size data recording, reproducing and displaying machines with calculating functions; accounting machines, postage-franking machines, ticket-issuing machines and similar machines, incorporating a calculating device; cash registers:
0/0/0	0	0	0/0	0/0/0	0/0	0//0	0/0/	0/0/0	0/0			0/0/0	-Electronic calculators capable of operation without an external source of electric power and pocket-size data recording, reproducing and displaying machines with caluclating functions
													-Other electronic calculating machines:
0/0/0	0	0	0/0	0/0/0	0/0	0//0	0/0/	0/0/0	0/0			0/0/0	--Incorporating a printing device
0/0/0	0	0	0/0	0/0/0	0/0	0//0	0/0/	0/0/0	0/0			0/0/0	--Other
0/0/0	0	0	0/0	0/0/0	0/0	0//0	0/0/	0/0/0	0/0			0/0/0	-Other calculating machines
													-Cash registers:
0/0/0	0	0	0/0	0/0/0	0/0	0//0	0/0/	0/0/0	0/0			0/0/0	---Terminal registers for market
0/0/0	0	0	0/0	0/0/0	0/0	0//0	0/0/	0/0/0	0/0			0/0/0	---Other
0/0/0	0	0	0/0	0/0/0	0/0	0//0	0/0/	0/0/0	0/0			0/0/0	-Other
													Automatic data processing machines and units thereof; magnetic or optical readers, machines for transcribing data onto data media in coded form and machines for processing such data, not elsewhere specified or included:
													-Portable automatic data processing machines, weighing not more than 10kg, consisting of at least a central processing unit, a keyboard and a display:
0/0/0	0	0	0/0	0/0/0	0/0	0//0	0/0/	0/0/0	0/0			0/0/0	---Tablet computer
0/0/0	0	0	0/0	0/0/0	0/0	0//0	0/0/	0/0/0	0/0			0/0/0	---Other
													-Other automatic data processing machines:
													--Comprising in the same housing at least a central processing unit and an input and output unit, whether or not combined:
													---mainframes
0/0/0	0	0	0/0	0/0/0	0/0	0//0	0/0/	0/0/0	0/0			0/0/0	Automatic data processing machines, mainframes
0/0/0	0	0	0/0	0/0/0	0/0	0//0	0/0/	0/0/0	0/0			0/0/0	Other automatic data processing machines, mainframes
0/0/0	0	0	0/0	0/0/0	0/0	0//0	0/0/	0/0/0	0/0			0/0/0	---Mini-computers
0/0/0	0	0	0/0	0/0/0	0/0	0//0	0/0/	0/0/0	0/0			0/0/0	---Microprocessings
0/0/0	0	0	0/0	0/0/0	0/0	0//0	0/0/	0/0/0	0/0			0/0/0	---Other
													--Other, presented in the form of systems:
													---Mainframes
0/0/0	0	0	0/0	0/0/0	0/0	0//0	0/0/	0/0/0	0/0			0/0/0	Mainframes(automatic data processing machines) presented in the form of systems
0/0/0	0	0	0/0	0/0/0	0/0	0//0	0/0/	0/0/0	0/0			0/0/0	Mainframes(automatic data processing machines) presented in the form of systems
0/0/0	0	0	0/0	0/0/0	0/0	0//0	0/0/	0/0/0	0/0			0/0/0	---Mini-computers
0/0/0	0	0	0/0	0/0/0	0/0	0//0	0/0/	0/0/0	0/0			0/0/0	---Microprocessings
													---Other:
0/0/0	0	0	0/0	0/0/0	0/0	0//0	0/0/	0/0/0	0/0			0/0/0	----Processing machines for the distributed control system
0/0/0	0	0	0/0	0/0/0	0/0	0//0	0/0/	0/0/0	0/0			0/0/0	----Other
													-Processing units other than those of subheading No.8471. 41 or 8471. 49, whether or not containing in the same housing one or two of the following types of unit: storage units, input units, output units:
													---Mainframes

税则号列	货品名称〔CIQ 扩展编码及品名－T2 表示见附表 2〕	最惠(%)	暂定税率	普通	增值/消费	出口退税	计量单位	监管条件/特殊证件	检验检疫	对美关税	亚太上/下
8471.5010 10	高性能数字计算机处理部件(不论是否在同一机壳内有一或两个存储,输入或输出部件,高性能数字计算机是指调整后峰值性能(APP)大于 8.0 加权每秒万亿次浮点运算的数字计算机)〔999〕	0		14	13/	13	台/千克	3/		10	
8471.5010 90	其他巨,大,中型机处理部件(不论是否在同一机壳内有一或两个存储,输入或输出部件)〔999〕	0		14	13/	13	台/千克	/		10	
8471.5020	---小型机的〔999〕	0		14	13/	13	台/千克	/		10	
8471.5040	---微型机的										
8471.5040 01	含显示器和主机的微型机(不论是否在同一机壳内有一或两个存储,输入或输出部件)〔999〕	0		70	13/	13	台/千克	/	L	20	
8471.5040 90	其他的微型机的处理部件(不论是否在同一机壳内有一或两个存储,输入或输出部件)〔999〕	0		70	13/	13	台/千克	/		20	
8471.5090	---其他〔999〕	0		70	13/	13	台/千克	/		10	
	-输入或输出部件,不论是否在同一机壳内有存储部件:										
8471.6040	---巨型机、大型机、中型机及小型机用终端〔999〕	0		14	13/	13	台/千克	/		25	
8471.6050	---扫描仪〔999〕	0		14	13/	13	台/千克	/	L	25	
8471.6060	---数字化仪〔999〕	0		14	13/	13	台/千克	/		10	
	---键盘、鼠标器:										
8471.6071	----键盘〔999〕	0		40	13/	13	个/千克	/		25	
8471.6072	----鼠标器〔999〕	0		40	13/	13	个/千克	/		25	
8471.6090	---其他〔999〕	0		14	13/	13	台/千克	/		25	
	-存储部件:										
	---硬盘驱动器:										
8471.7011	----固态硬盘(SSD)〔999〕	0		14	13/	13	台/千克	/		25	
8471.7019	----其他〔999〕	0		14	13/	13	台/千克	/		25	
8471.7020	---软盘驱动器〔999〕	0		14	13/	13	台/千克	/		5	
8471.7030	---光盘驱动器〔999〕	0		14	13/	13	台/千克	/		25	
8471.7090	---其他〔999〕	0		14	13/	13	台/千克	/		20	
8471.8000	-自动数据处理设备的其他部件〔999〕	0		40	13/	13	台/千克	/		25	
8471.9000	-其他										
8471.9000 10	专用于复制的光盘刻录机(也称光盘复读机)〔999〕	0		40	13/	13	台/千克	/		20	
8471.9000 90	未列名的磁性或光学阅读器(包括将数据以代码形式转录的机器及处理这些数据的机器)〔999〕	0		40	13/	13	台/千克	/	L	20	
84.72	**其他办公室用机器(例如,胶版复印机、油印机、地址印写机、自动付钞机、硬币分类、计数及包装机、削铅笔机、打洞机或订书机):**										
8472.1000	-胶版复印机、油印机〔999〕	0		40	13/	13	台/千克	/	L		
	-信件分类或折叠机或信件装封机、信件开封或闭封机、粘贴或盖销邮票机:										
8472.3010	---邮政信件分拣及封装设备〔999〕	8		40	13/	13	台/千克	/		28	
8472.3090	---其他〔999〕	8		40	13/	13	台/千克	/			
	-其他:										
8472.9010	---自动柜员机〔999〕	0		40	13/	13	台/千克	/	L	25	
	---装订用机器:										
8472.9021	----打洞机〔999〕	0		40	13/	13	台/千克	/		25	
8472.9022	----订书机〔999〕	0		40	13/	13	台/千克	/		25	
8472.9029	----其他〔999〕	0		40	13/	13	台/千克	/		5	
8472.9030	---碎纸机〔999〕	0		40	13/	13	台/千克	/		20	
8472.9040	---地址印写机及地址铭牌压印机〔999〕	0		40	13/	13	台/千克	/			
8472.9050	---文字处理机〔101 打印机,102 打字机〕	0		40	13/	13	台/千克	/		5	
8472.9060	----打字机,但税目 84.43 的打印机除外〔101 打印机,102 打字机〕	8		40	13/	13	台/千克	/		13	
8472.9090	---其他〔999〕	0		40	13/	13	台/千克	/		25	
84.73	**专用于或主要用于税目 84.70 至 84.72 所列机器的零件、附件(罩套、提箱及类似品除外):**										
	-税目 84.70 所列机器的零件、附件:										
8473.2100	--子目 8470.10、8470.21 或 8470.29 所列电子计算器的零件、附件〔999〕	0		50	13/	13	千克	/		25	
8473.2900	--其他〔999〕	0		35	13/	13	千克	/		25	
	-税目 84.71 所列机器的零件、附件:										

协定税率 %								RCEP		特惠税率 %			Article Description
东/冰/格	巴基斯坦	韩国	瑞士上/下	哥/秘/柬	澳/毛	新西/坡/智	中国港/澳/台	东盟及马来/澳/韩	日/新	亚太2国	老/柬/缅	98/97/95	
0/0/0	0	0	0/0	0/0/0	0/0	0//0	0/0/	0/0/0	0/0			0/0/0	High-performance digital computer parts, whether or not in the same case with one or two storage, input or output component, the processor after polymerization way can make aggregation "adjusted peak performance (APP) is greater than 8.0 Weighted one trillion floating point operations per second (Weighted TeraFLOPS) specially designed or modified electronic components
0/0/0	0	0	0/0	0/0/0	0/0	0//0	0/0/	0/0/0	0/0			0/0/0	processing units of Mainframes (whether or not containing in the same housing one or two storage units, input units, output units)
0/0/0	0	0	0/0	0/0/0	0/0	0//0	0/0/	0/0/0	0/0			0/0/0	---Mini-computers
													---Microprocessings
0/0/0	0	0	0/0	0/0/0	0/0	0//0	0/0/	0/0/0	0/0			0/0/0	Microprocessings, with display and host(whether or not containing in the same housing one or two ofstorage nuits, input or output units)
0/0/0	0	0	0/0	0/0/0	0/0	0//0	0/0/	0/0/0	0/0			0/0/0	Other processing unit of microprocessings (whether or not containing in the same housing one or two ofstorage nuits, input or output units)
0/0/0	0	0	0/0	0/0/0	0/0	0//0	0/0/	0/0/0	0/0			0/0/0	---Other
													-Input or output units, whether or not containing storage units in the same housing:
0/0/0	0	0	0/0	0/0/0	0/0	0//0	0/0/	0/0/0	0/0			0/0/0	---Terminating machines for the huge computers, mainframes and mini-computers
0/0/0	0	0	0/0	0/0/0	0/0	0//0	0/0/	0/0/0	0/0			0/0/0	---Scanner
0/0/0	0	0	0/0	0/0/0	0/0	0//0	0/0/	0/0/0	0/0			0/0/0	---Digitizer
													---Keyboards, mouses:
0/0/0	0	0	0/0	0/0/0	0/0	0//0	0/0/	0/0/0	0/0			0/0/0	----Keyboards
0/0/0	0	0	0/0	0/0/0	0/0	0//0	0/0/	0/0/0	0/0			0/0/0	----Mouses
0/0/0	0	0	0/0	0/0/0	0/0	0//0	0/0/	0/0/0	0/0			0/0/0	---Other
													-Storage units:
													---Rigid disk drivers:
0/0/0	0	0	0/0	0/0/0	0/0	0//0	0/0/	0/0/0	0/0			0/0/0	----Solid state disk (SSD)
0/0/0	0	0	0/0	0/0/0	0/0	0//0	0/0/	0/0/0	0/0			0/0/0	----Other
0/0/0	0	0	0/0	0/0/0	0/0	0//0	0/0/	0/0/0	0/0			0/0/0	---Floppy disk drivers
0/0/0	0	0	0/0	0/0/0	0/0	0//0	0/0/	0/0/0	0/0			0/0/0	---CD drivers
0/0/0	0	0	0/0	0/0/0	0/0	0//0	0/0/	0/0/0	0/0			0/0/0	---Other
0/0/0	0	0	0/0	0/0/0	0/0	0//0	0/0/	0/0/0	0/0			0/0/0	-Other units of automatic data processing machines
													-Other
0/0/0	0	0	0/0	0/0/0	0/0	0//0	0/0/	0/0/0	0/0			0/0/0	CD-R machines used exclusively for copying(also called CD repeaters)
0/0/0	0	0	0/0	0/0/0	0/0	0//0	0/0/	0/0/0	0/0			0/0/0	Magnetic or optical readers, not elsewhere specified or included(including machines for transcribing data onto data media in coded form and machines for processing such data)
													Other office machines (for example, hectograph or stencil duplicating machines, addressing machines, automatic banknote dispensers, coin-sorting machines, coin-counting or wrapping machines, pencil-sharpening machines, perforating or stapling machines):
0/0/0	7.8	2.8	0/0	0/0/0	0/0	0/0/0	0/0/	0/0/12.6	0/0			0/0/0	-Duplicating machines
													-Machines for sorting or folding mail or for inserting mail in envelopes or bands, machines for opening, closing or sealing mail and machines for affixing or cancelling postage stamps:
0/0/0	2	2		0/0/0	0/0	0//0	0/0/	0/0/9	9.1/0			0/0/0	---Machines for sorting or banding mail
0/0/0	4.9	2.8	0/0	0/0/0	0/0	0/0/0	0/0/	0/0/12.6	12.7/0			0/0/0	---Other
													-Other:
0/0/0	0	0	0/0	0/0/0	0/0	0//0	0/0/	0/0/0	0/0			0/0/0	---Automated teller
													---Stapling machines:
0/0/0	0	0	0/0	0/0/0	0/0	0//0	0/0/	0/0/0	0/0			0/0/0	----Perforator
0/0/0	0	0	0/0	0/0/0	0/0	0//0	0/0/	0/0/0	0/0			0/0/0	----Stapler
0/0/0	0	0	0/0	0/0/0	0/0	0//0	0/0/	0/0/0	0/0			0/0/0	----Other
0/0/0	0	0	0/0	0/0/0	0/0	0//0	0/0/	0/0/0	0/0			0/0/0	---Paper shrudders
0/0/0	7.8	2.8	0/0	0/0/0	0/0	0/0/0	0/0/	0/0/12.6	0/0			0/0/0	---Addressing machines and address plate embossing machines
0/0/0	0	0	0/0	0/0/0	0/0	0//0	0/0/	0/0/0	0/0			0/0/0	---Word—processing machines
0/0/0	4.2		1.2/1.2	0/0/0	0/0	0/0/0	0/0/	0/0/10.8	10.9/0			0/0/0	---Typewnters other than priners of heading No.84.43
0/0/0	0	0	0/0	0/0/0	0/0	0//0	0/0/	0/0/0	0/0			0/0/0	---Other
													Parts and accessories (other than covers, carrying cases and the like) suitable for use solely or principally with machines of headings No.84.70 to 84.72:
													-Parts and accessories of the machines of heading No.84.70:
0/0/0	0	0	0/0	0/0/0	0/0	0//0	0/0/	0/0/0	0/0			0/0/0	--Of the electronic calculating machines of subheading No 8470.10, 8470.21 or 8470.29
0/0/0	0	0	0/0	0/0/0	0/0	0//0	0/0/	0/0/0	0/0			0/0/0	--Other
													-Parts and accessories of the machines of heading No.84.71:

税则号列	货品名称〔CIQ 扩展编码及品名－T2 表示见附表 2〕	最惠(%)	暂定税率	普通	增值/消费	出口退税	计量单位	监管条件/特殊证件	检验检疫	对美关税	亚太上/下
8473.3010	---子目号 8471.4110、8471.4120、8471.4910、8471. 4920、8471.5010、8471.5020、8471.6090、8471.7010、8471.7020、8471.7030 及 8471.7090 所列机器及装置的零件、附件〔999〕	0		14	13/	13	千克	/		25	
8473.3090	---其他〔999〕	0		40	13/	13	千克	/		25	
	-税目 84.72 所列机器的零件、附件:										
8473.4010	---自动柜员机用出钞器和循环出钞器〔999〕	0		35	13/	13	千克	/		25	
8473.4020	---税目 8472.9050、8472.9060 所列机器的零件、附件〔999〕	0		35	13/	13	千克	/		25	
8473.4090	---其他										
8473.4090 10	钞票清分机零附件〔999〕	0		35	13/	13	千克	/		25	
8473.4090 90	其他办公室用机器零件附件〔999〕	0		35	13/	13	千克	/		25	
8473.5000	-同样适用于税目 84.70 至 84.72 中两个或两个以上税目所列机器的零件、附件〔101 其它计算机、辅助设备及其零件，102 其它办公机器及其零件〕	0		35	13/	13	千克	/		25	
84.74	**泥土、石料、矿石或其他固体(包括粉状、浆状)矿物质的分类、筛选、分离、洗涤、破碎、磨粉、混合或搅拌机器；固体矿物燃料、陶瓷坯泥、未硬化水泥、石膏材料或其他粉状、浆状矿产品的粘聚或成型机器；铸造用砂模的成形机器:**										
8474.1000	-分类、筛选、分离或洗涤机器〔101 其它工程机械及其零件，102 建筑工业行业成套设备〕	5		30	13/	13	台/千克	/		25	
	-破碎或磨粉机器:										
8474.2010	---齿辊式[T2]	5		30	13/	13	台/千克	/		25	
8474.2020	---球磨式[T2]	5		30	13/	13	台/千克	/		30	
8474.2090	---其他[T2]	5		30	13/	13	台/千克	/		30	
	-混合或搅拌机器:										
8474.3100	--混凝土或砂浆混合机器〔101 其它工程机械及其零件，102 建筑工业行业成套设备〕	7		30	13/	13	台/千克	/		32	
8474.3200	--矿物与沥青的混合机器〔101 其它工程机械及其零件，102 建筑工业行业成套设备〕	7		30	13/	13	台/千克	/		12	
8474.3900	--其他〔101 其它工程机械及其零件，102 建筑工业行业成套设备〕	5		30	13/	13	台/千克	/		25	
	-其他机器:										
8474.8010	---辊压成型机〔101 其它工程机械及其零件，102 建筑工业行业成套设备〕	5		30	13/	13	台/千克	/		30	3.3/3.3
8474.8020	---模压成型机[T2]	5		30	13/	13	台/千克	/		25	3.3/3.3
8474.8090	---其他										
8474.8090 10	纸面角线石膏板搅拌成型机〔101 其它工程机械及其零件，102 建筑工业行业成套设备〕	5		30	13/	13	台/千克	/		25	3.3/3.3
8474.8090 90	税目 84.74 未列名的其他机器(如矿产品的粘聚或成型机器及铸造用砂模的成型机器)〔101 其它工程机械及其零件，102 建材行业成套设备，103 建筑工业行业成套设备，104 其他行业成套设备〕	5		30	13/	13	台/千克	/		25	3.3/3.3
8474.9000	-零件〔101 其它工程机械及其零件，102 建筑工业行业成套设备〕	5		30	13/	13	千克	/		25	
84.75	**白炽灯泡、灯管、放电灯管、电子管、闪光灯泡及类似品的封装机器；玻璃或玻璃制品的制造或热加工机器:**										
8475.1000	-白炽灯泡、灯管、放电灯管、电子管、闪光灯泡及类似品的封装机器〔999〕	8		30	13/	13	台/千克	/			
	-玻璃或玻璃制品的制造或热加工机器:										
8475.2100	--制造光导纤维及其预制棒的机器〔999〕	2.5/1.3		30	13/	13	台/千克	/		27.5	
	--其他:										
	---玻璃的热加工设备:										
8475.2911	----连续式玻璃热弯炉〔999〕	8		30	13/	13	台/千克	/		33	5.2/5.2
8475.2912	----玻璃纤维拉丝机(光纤拉丝机除外)〔999〕	8		30	13/	13	台/千克	/		33	5.2/5.2
8475.2919	----其他〔999〕	8		30	13/	13	台/千克	/		33	
8475.2990	---其他〔999〕	8		30	13/	13	台/千克	/		33	
8475.9000	-零件										
8475.9000 10	税号 8475.21 所列机器的零件〔999〕	0		30	13/	13	千克	/		10	
8475.9000 90	其他税目 84.75 所列机器的零件(灯泡等封装机及玻璃等制造机器的零件)〔999〕	8		30	13/	13	千克	/		18	
84.76	**自动售货机(例如，出售邮票、香烟、食品或饮料的机器)，包括钱币兑换机:**										
	-饮料自动销售机:										
8476.2100	--装有加热或制冷装置的〔999〕	11		50	13/	13	台/千克	A/	R	36	
8476.2900	--其他〔999〕	12		50	13/	13	台/千克	A/	R		
	-其他机器:										
8476.8100	--装有加热或制冷装置的〔999〕	11		50	13/	13	台/千克	/		16	
8476.8900	--其他										

协定税率 %								RCEP		特惠税率 %			Article Description
东/冰/格	巴基斯坦	韩国	瑞士上/下	哥/秘/柬	澳/毛	新西/坡/智	中国港/澳/台	东盟及马来/澳/韩	日/新	亚太2国	老/柬/缅	98/97/95	
0/0/0	0	0	0/0	0/0/0	0/0	0//0	0/0/	0/0/0	0/0			0/0/0	---Of the machines of subheading 8471.4110, 8471.4120, 8471.4910, 8471.4920, 8471.5010, 8471.5020, 8471.6090, 8471.7010, 8471.7020, 8471.7030 and 8471.7090
0/0/0	0	0	0/0	0/0/0	0/0	0//0	0/0/	0/0/0	0/0			0/0/0	---Other
													-Parts and accessories of the machines of heading No.84.72:
0/0/0	3.5	6.3	0/0	0/0/0	0/0	0/0/0	0/0/	0/9.5/9.8	0/9.5			0/0/0	---Banknote dispenser of automated teller and recycle banknote
0/0/0	2	3.7	0/0	0/0/0	0/0	0//0	0/0/	0/0/7.2	0/0			0/0/0	---Parts and accessories of the subheadings No. 8472.9050、8472.9060
													---Other
0/0/0	3.5	2.1	0/0	0/0/0	0/0	0/0/0	0/0/	0/0/0	0/0			0/0/0	Parts and accessories of banknote sorters
0/0/0	3.5	2.1	0/0	0/0/0	0/0	0/0/0	0/0/	0/0/0	0/0			0/0/0	Parts and accessories of other office machines
0/0/0	0	0	0/0	0/0/0	0/0	0//0	0/0/	0/0/0	0/0			0/0/0	-Parts and accessories equally suitable for use with machines of two or more of the heading No.84.70 to 84.72
													Machinery for sorting, screening, separating, washing, crushing, grinding, mixing or kneading earth, stone, ores or other mineral substances, in solid (including powder or paste) form; machinery for agglomerating, shaping or moulding solid mineral fuels, ceramic paste unhardned cements plastering materials or other mineral products in powder or paste form, machines for forming foundry moulds of sand
0/0/0	0	1	0/0	0/0/0	0/0	0//0	0/0/	4.5/4.5/4.5	4.5/4.5			0/0/0	-Sorting, screening, separating or washing machines
													-Crushing or grinding machines:
0/0/0	0	1	0/0	0/0/0	0/0	0//0	0/0/	0/0/4.5	4.5/0			0/0/0	---Toothing roller type
0/0/0	0	2.3	0/0	0/0/0	0/0	0//0	0/0/	4.5/4.5/4.5	4.7/4.5			0/0/0	---Em-Peters type
0/0/0	0	1	0/0	0/0/0	0/0	0//0	0/0/	0/0/4.5	4.5/0			0/0/0	---Other
													-Mixing or kneading machines:
0/0/0	2	1.4	0/0	0/0/0	0/0	0//0	0/0/	0/0/6.3	6.4/0			0/0/0	--Concrete or mortar mixers
0/0/0	2	1.4		0/0/0	0/0	0//0	0/0/	0/0/6.3	6.4/0			0/0/0	--Machines for mixing mineral substances with bitumen
0/0/0	0	1	2.1/2.1	0/0/0	0/0	0//0	0/0/	0/0/4.5	4.5/0			0/0/0	--Other
													-Other machinery:
0/0/0	0	1	0/0	0/0/0	0/0	0//0	0/0/	0/0/4.5	4.5/0			0/0/0	---Rolling forming machines
0/0/0	0	2.3	0/0	0/0/0	0/0	0//0	0/0/	4.5/4.5/4.5	4.7/4.5			0/0/0	---Molud pressing machines
													---Other
0/0/0	0	1	0/0	0/0/0	0/0	0//0	0/0/	4.5/4.5/4.5	4.5/4.5			0/0/0	Paper faced angle line gypsum board mixing machines
0/0/0	0	1	0/0	0/0/0	0/0	0//0	0/0/	4.5/4.5/4.5	4.5/4.5			0/0/0	Other machines, not elsewhere specified or included of heading No.84.74 (for example, machinery for agglomerating, shaping or moulding or machines for forming foundry moulds of sand)
0/0/0	0	1	0.5/0.5	0/0/0	0/0	0//0	0/0/	4.5/4.5/4.5	4.5/4.5			0/0/0	-Parts
													Machines for assembling electric or electronic lamps, tubes or valves or flash-bulbs, in glass envelopes; machines for manufacturing or hot working glass or glassware:
0/0/0	2	1.6	0/0	0/0/0	0/0	0//0	0/0/	0/0/7.2	7.3/0			0/0/0	-Machines for assembling electric or electronic lamps, tubes or valves or flashbulbs, in glass envelopes
													-Machines for manufacturing or hot working glass or glassware:
0/0/0	2	2	0/0	0/0/0	0/0	0/0/0	0/0/	9/9/9	9.1/9			0/0/0	--Machines for making optical fibres and preforms thereof
													--Other:
													---Equipments for hot working glass or glasswares:
0/0/0	2	2	0/0	0/0/0	0/0	0//0	0/0/	0/0/9	9.1/0			0/0/0	----Continuous hot bending furnaces
0/0/0	2	2	0/0	0/0/0	0/0	0//0	0/0/	0/0/9	9.1/0			0/0/0	----Fiber glass winder(excluding opticae fiber winder)
0/0/0	2	2	0/0	0/0/0	0/0	0/0/0	0/0/	0/0/9	9.1/0			0/0/0	----Other
0/0/0	2	2	0/0	0/0/0	0/0	0//0	0/0/	0/0/9	9.1/0			0/0/0	---Other
													-Parts
0/0/0	4	1.6	0/0	0/0/0	0/0	0//0	0/0/	0/0/7.2	7.3/0			0/0/0	Parts of machines of heading No.8475.21
0/0/0	4	1.6	0/0	0/0/0	0/0	0//0	0/0/	0/0/7.2	7.3/0			0/0/0	Parts of machines of heading No.84.75(parts of machines for assembling lamps in glass envelopes or; parts of machines for manufacturing or hot working glass or glassware)
													Automatic goods-vending machines (for example, postage stamp, cigarette, food or beverage machines), including money-changing machines:
													-Automatic beverage-vending machines:
0/0/0	7.8	2.8	1.4/1.4	0/0/0	0/0	0/0/0	0/0/	0/0/12.6	12.7/0			0/0/0	--Incorporating heating or refrigerating devices
0/0/0	8.4	3	1.5/1.5	0/0/0	0/0	0/0/0	0/0/	0/0/13.5	13.6/0			0/0/0	--Other
													-Other machines:
0/0/0	4.9	2.8	1.4/1.4	0/0/0	0/0	0/0/0	0/0/	0/0/12.6	12.7/0			0/0/0	--Incorporating heating or refrigerating devices
													--Other

税则号列	货品名称〔CIQ 扩展编码及品名－T2 表示见附表 2〕	最惠(%)	暂定税率	普通	增值/消费	出口退税	计量单位	监管条件/特殊证件	检验检疫	对美关税	亚太上/下
8476.8900　10	钱币兑换机〔999〕	0		50	13/	13	台/千克	/		5	
8476.8900　90	其他无加热或制冷装置的自动售货机〔999〕	12		50	13/	13	台/千克	/		17	
8476.9000	-零件										
8476.9000　10	钱币兑换机的零件〔999〕	0		50	13/	13	千克	/		25	
8476.9000　90	其他品目 84.76 所列机器的零件〔999〕	8		50	13/	13	千克	/		33	
84.77	**本章其他税目未列名的橡胶或塑料及其产品的加工机器：**										
	-注射机：										
8477.1010	---注塑机										
8477.1010　10	用于光盘生产的精密注塑机(加工塑料的)〔999〕	0		45	13/	13	台/千克	/		25	
8477.1010　90	其他注塑机〔101 电子行业成套设备，102 化工行业成套设备，103 轻工行业成套设备〕	0		45	13/	13	台/千克	/		25	
8477.1090	---其他〔101 电子行业成套设备，102 化工行业成套设备，103 轻工行业成套设备〕	0		30	13/	13	台/千克	/		25	
	-挤出机：										
8477.2010	---塑料造粒机〔101 电子行业成套设备，102 化工行业成套设备，103 轻工行业成套设备〕	5		30	13/	13	台/千克	/		30	3.3/3.3
8477.2090	---其他〔101 电子行业成套设备，102 化工行业成套设备，103 轻工行业成套设备〕	5		30	13/	13	台/千克	/		25	3.3/3.3
	-吹塑机：										
8477.3010	---挤出吹塑机〔101 电子行业成套设备，102 化工行业成套设备，103 轻工行业成套设备〕	5		30	13/	13	台/千克	/		25	
8477.3020	---注射吹塑机〔101 电子行业成套设备，102 化工行业成套设备，103 轻工行业成套设备〕	5		30	13/	13	台/千克	/			
8477.3090	---其他〔101 电子行业成套设备，102 化工行业成套设备，103 轻工行业成套设备〕	5		30	13/	13	台/千克	/		25	
	-真空模塑机器及其他热成型机器：										
8477.4010	---塑料中空成型机〔101 电子行业成套设备，102 化工行业成套设备，103 轻工行业成套设备〕	5		30	13/	13	台/千克	/		30	3.3/3.3
8477.4020	---塑料压延成型机〔101 电子行业成套设备，102 化工行业成套设备，103 轻工行业成套设备〕	5		30	13/	13	台/千克	/		30	3.3/3.3
8477.4090	---其他〔101 电子行业成套设备，102 化工行业成套设备，103 轻工行业成套设备〕	5		30	13/	13	台/千克	/		30	3.3/3.3
	-其他模塑或成型机器：										
8477.5100	--用于充气轮胎模塑或翻新的机器及内胎模塑或用其他方法成型的机器〔999〕	5		30	13/	13	台/千克	/		30	
8477.5900	--其他〔101 电子行业成套设备，102 化工行业成套设备，103 轻工行业成套设备〕	5		30	13/	13	台/千克	/		30	3.3/3.3
8477.8000	-其他机器〔101 电子行业成套设备，102 化工行业成套设备，103 轻工行业成套设备〕	5		30	13/	13	台/千克	/		30	3.3/3.3
8477.9000	-零件〔101 电子行业成套设备，102 化工行业成套设备，103 轻工行业成套设备〕	0		30	13/	13	千克	/		20	
84.78	**本章其他税目未列名的烟草加工及制作机器：**										
8478.1000	-机器〔999〕	5		30	13/	13	台/千克	O/		25	2.5/2.5
8478.9000	-零件〔999〕	8	5	30	13/	13	千克	O/			
84.79	**本章其他税目未列名的具有独立功能的机器及机械器具：**										
	-公共工程用机器：										
	---摊铺机：										
8479.1021	----沥青混凝土摊铺机〔999〕	8		30	13/	13	台/千克	O/		33	5.2/5.2
8479.1022	----稳定土摊铺机〔999〕	8		30	13/	13	台/千克	/			5.2/5.2
8479.1029	----其他〔999〕	8		30	13/	13	台/千克	O/			5.2/5.2
8479.1090	---其他〔999〕	8		30	13/	13	台/千克	/		18	5.2/5.2
8479.2000	-提取、加工动物油脂、植物固定油脂或微生物油脂的机器〔999〕〔101 食品加工机器，102 其他行业成套设备〕	8		30	13/	13	台/千克	A/	R	33	
8479.3000	-木碎料板或木纤维板的挤压机及其他木材或软木处理机〔999〕	8		30	13/	13	台/千克	/			
8479.4000	-绳或缆的制造机器〔999〕	7		30	13/	13	台/千克	/		32	
	-未列名工业机器人：										
8479.5010	---多功能工业机器人〔101 电子行业成套设备，102 其他行业成套设备〕	0		20	13/	13	台/千克	/		25	
8479.5090	---其他										
8479.5090　10	机器人，末端操纵装置[能处理高能炸药或能抗大于 5×10^4 戈瑞(硅)辐射的]〔999〕	0		30	13/	13	台/千克	3/		20	
8479.5090　90	其他工业机器人(多功能工业机器人除外)〔101 电子行业成套设备，102 其他行业成套设备〕	0		30	13/	13	台/千克	/		20	
8479.6000	-蒸发式空气冷却器[T2]	8		30	13/	13	台/千克	/		28	5.2/5.2
	-旅客登机(船)桥：										
8479.7100	--用于机场的〔999〕	0		30	13/	13	台/千克	/			
8479.7900	--其他〔999〕	0		30	13/	13	台/千克	A/	M	25	
	-其他机器及机械器具：										

协定税率 %								RCEP		特惠税率 %			Article Description
东/冰/格	巴基斯坦	韩国	瑞士 上/下	哥/秘/柬	澳/毛	新西/坡/智	中国港/澳/台	东盟及马来/澳/韩	日/新	亚太2国	老/柬/缅	98/97/95	
0/0/0	8.4	3	0/0	0/0/0	0/0	0/0/0	0/0/	0/0/13.5	13.6/0			0/0/0	Money-changing machines
0/0/0	8.4	3	0/0	0/0/0	0/0	0/0/0	0/0/	0/0/13.5	13.6/0			0/0/0	Other automatic goods-vending machines not incorporating heating or refrigerating devices
													-Parts
0/0/0	2	2	0/0	0/0/0	0/0	0//0	0/0/	0/0/9	9.1/0			0/0/0	parts of money-changing machines
0/0/0	2	2	0/0	0/0/0	0/0	0//0	0/0/	0/0/9	9.1/0			0/0/0	Parts of machines of heading No.84.76
													Machinery for working rubber or plastics or for the manufacture of products from these materials, not specified or included elsewhere in this Chapter:
													-Injection-moulding machines:
													---For working plastics
0/0/0	0	0	0/0	0/0/0	0/0	0//0	0/0/	0/0/0	0/0			0/0/0	Precision injection-moulders for disks production (for working plastics)
0/0/0	0	0	0/0	0/0/0	0/0	0//0	0/0/	0/0/0	0/0			0/0/0	Other working plastics machines
0/0/0	0	0	0/0	0/0/0	0/0	0//0	0/0/	0/0/0	0/0			0/0/0	---Other
													-Extruders:
0/0/0	0	0	0/0	0/0/0	0/0	0//0	0/0/0	0/4.5/0	0/4.5			0/0/0	---Plastic pelletizers
0/0/0	0	0	2.1/2.1	0/0/0	0/0	0//0	0/0/0	0/0/0	4.5/0			0/0/0	---Other
													-Blow moulding machines:
0/0/0	0	1	0/0	0/0/0	0/0	0//0	0/0/	0/0/4.5	4.5/0			0/0/0	---Extruders blow moulding machines
0/0/0	0	0	0/0	0/0/0	0/0	0//0	0/0/	0/0/0	0/0			0/0/0	---Injection blow moulding machines
0/0/0	0	1	0/0	0/0/0	0/0	0//0	0/0/	0/0/4.5	4.5/0			0/0/0	---Other
													-Vacuum moulding machines and other thermoforming machines:
0/0/0	0	0		0/0/0	0/0	0//0	0/0/0	0/0/0	4.5/0			0/0/0	---Plastics brideg-die-forming machines
0/0/0	0	0	0.5/0.5	0/0/0	0/0	0//0	0/0/0	0/0/0	4.5/0			0/0/0	---Plastics calender-forming machines
0/0/0	0	0	2.1/2.1	0/0/0	0/0	0//0	0/0/0	4.5/4.5/4.5	4.5/4.5			0/0/0	---Other
													-Other machinery for moulding or otherwise forming:
0/0/0	0	1	0/0	0/0/0	0/0	0//0	0/0/	4.5/4.5/4.5	4.5/4.5			0/0/0	--For moulding or retreading pneumatic tyres or for moulding or otherwise forming inner tubes
0/0/0	0	2.3	0/0	0/0/0	0/0	0//0	0/0/0	4.5/4.5/4.5	4.7/4.5			0/0/0	--Other
0/0/0	0	0	2.1/2.1	0/0/0	0/0	0//0	0/0/0	0/0/0	4.7/0			0/0/0	-Other machinery
0/0/0	0	0	0/0	0/0/0	0/0	0//0	0/0/	0/0/0	0/0			0/0/0	-Parts
													Machinery for preparing or making up tobacco, not specified or included elsewhere in this Chapter:
0/0/	0		0/0	0/0/0	/0	0//0	0/0/					0/0/0	-Machinery
0/0/	4		0/0	0/0/0	/0	0//0	0/0/					0/0/0	-Parts
													Machines and mechanical appliances having individual functions, not specified or included elsewhere in this Chapter:
													-Machinery for public works, building or the like:
													---Spreading machines:
0/0/0	2	0	0/0	0/0/0	0/0	0//0	0/0/	0/0/0	7.3/0			0/0/0	----Machines for spreading bituminous concrete
0/0/0	2	0	0/0	0/0/0	0/0	0//0	0/0/	0/0/0	7.3/0			0/0/0	----Stabilizer spreading machines
0/0/0	2	0	0/0	0/0/0	0/0	0//0	0/0/	0/0/0	7.3/0			0/0/0	----Other
0/0/0	2	1.6	0/0	0/0/0	0/0	0//0	0/0/	0/0/7.2	7.3/0			0/0/0	---Other
0/0/0	2	1	0.5/0.5	0/0/0	0/0	0/0/0	0/0/	0/0/7.7	7.7/0			0/0/0	-Machinery for the extraction or preparation of animal or fixed vegetable fats or oils
0/0/0	2	2	0/0	0/0/0	0/0	0//0	0/0/	0/0/9	9.1/0			0/0/0	-Presses for the manufacture of particle board or fibre building board or wood or other ligneous materials and other machinery for treating wood or cork
0/0/0	2	0	0/0	0/0/0	0/0	0//0	0/0/	0/0/0	6.4/0			0/0/0	-Rope or cable-making machines
													-Industrial robots, not elsewhere specified or included:
0/0/0	0	0	0/0	0/0/0	0/0	0//0	0/0/	0/0/0	0/0			0/0/0	---Industrial robots for multiple uses
													---Other
0/0/0	0	0	0/0	0/0/0	0/0	0//0	0/0/	0/0/0	0/0			0/0/0	Robots, end-control devices (capable of handling high-energy explosives or resisting radiance $>5\times10^4$ Gy (Si))
0/0/0	0	0	0/0	0/0/0	0/0	0//0	0/0/	0/0/0	0/0			0/0/0	Other industrial robots (other than multiple-functional industrial robots)
0/0/0	2	2	0/0	0/0/0	0/0	0//0	0/0/	0/0/9	9.1/0			0/0/0	-Evaporative air coolers
													-Passenger boarding (boats) bridge use at airport:
0/0/0	0	0	0/0	0/0/0	0/0	0//0	0/0/	0/0/0	0/0			0/0/0	--Of a kind used in airports
0/0/0	0	0	0/0	0/0/0	0/0	0//0	0/0/	0/0/0	0/0			0/0/0	--Other
													-Other machines and mechanical appliances:

税则号列	货品名称〔CIQ 扩展编码及品名－T2 表示见附表 2〕	最惠(%)	暂定税率	普通	增值/消费	出口退税	计量单位	监管条件/特殊证件	检验检疫	对美关税	亚太上/下
	--处理金属的机械，包括线圈绕线机：										
8479.8110	---绕线机〔101 机械行业成套设备，102 电子行业成套设备〕	9		30	13/	13	台/千克	/		34	6.3/6.3
8479.8190	---其他〔101 机械行业成套设备，102 电子行业成套设备〕	9		30	13/	13	台/千克	/		29	5.9/5.9
8479.8200	--混合、搅拌、轧碎、研磨、筛选、均化或乳化机器										
8479.8200 10	两用物项管制搅拌器(耐腐蚀热交换器、搅拌器用，带搅拌的发酵罐)〔101 轻工行业成套设备，102 其他行业成套设备〕	7		30	13/	13	台/千克	3/		17	4.6/4.6
8479.8200 20	用于废物和废水处理的混合、搅拌、轧碎、研磨、筛选、均化或乳化机器〔101 轻工行业成套设备，102 其他行业成套设备〕	7	5	30	13/	13	台/千克	/		15	4.6/4.6
8479.8200 90	其他混合、搅拌、轧碎、研磨机器(包括筛选、均化、乳化机器)〔101 轻工行业成套设备，102 其他行业成套设备〕	7		30	13/	13	台/千克	/		17	4.6/4.6
	--冷等静压机：										
8479.8310	---处理金属的										
8479.8310 10	处理金属的冷等静压机(两用物项管制机器及机械器具)〔101 机械行业成套设备，102 电子行业成套设备〕	9		30	13/	13	台/千克	3/		29	5.9/5.9
8479.8310 90	处理金属的冷等静压机〔101 机械行业成套设备，102 电子行业成套设备〕	9		30	13/	13	台/千克	/		29	5.9/5.9
8479.8390	---其他										
8479.8390 10	其他冷等静压压力机(两用物项管制机器及机械器具)〔999〕	0		30	13/	13	台/千克	3/		20	
8479.8390 90	其他冷等静压压力机〔999〕	0		30	13/	13	台/千克	/		20	
	--其他：										
8479.8910	---船舶用舵机及陀螺稳定器〔101 船舶用零部件，102 船舶行业成套设备〕	0		14	13/	13	台/千克	/		25	
8479.8920	---空气增湿器及减湿器[T2]	0		70	13/	13	台/千克	/	L	10	
8479.8940	---邮政用包裹、印刷品分拣设备〔999〕	0		30	13/	13	台/千克	/		10	
8479.8950	---放射性废物压实机〔999〕	0		30	13/	13	台/千克	/			
	---在印刷电路电路板上装配元器件的机器：										
8479.8961	----自动插件机〔999〕	0		30	13/	13	台/千克	A/	M	25	
8479.8962	----自动贴片机〔999〕	0		30	13/	13	台/千克	A/	M	25	
8479.8969	----其他〔999〕	0		30	13/	13	台/千克	A/	M	20	
	---其他：										
8479.8992	----自动化立体仓储设备[T2]	0		30	13/	13	台/千克	A/	M	25	
8479.8999	----其他										
8479.8999 10	用于光盘生产的金属母盘生产设备(具有独立功能的)〔999〕	0		30	13/	13	台/千克	A/	M	20	
8479.8999 20	用于光盘生产的粘合机(具有独立功能的)〔999〕	0		30	13/	13	台/千克	A/	M	20	
8479.8999 30	用于光盘生产的真空金属溅镀机(具有独立功能的)〔999〕	0		30	13/	13	台/千克	A/	M	20	
8479.8999 40	保护胶涂覆机及染料层旋涂机(光盘生产用，具有独立功能的)〔999〕	0		30	13/	13	台/千克	A/	M	20	
8479.8999 52	生物反应器(两用物项管制机器及机械器具)〔999〕	0		30	13/	13	台/千克	3/			
8479.8999 53	恒化器(两用物项管制机器及机械器具)〔999〕	0		30	13/	13	台/千克	3/		20	
8479.8999 54	连续灌流系统(两用物项管制机器及机械器具)〔999〕	0		30	13/	13	台/千克	3/		20	
8479.8999 55	三坐标或多坐标联动和程控的纤维缠绕机(两用物项管制机器及机械器具)〔999〕	0		30	13/	13	台/千克	3/		20	
8479.8999 59	其他两用物项管制机器及机械器具〔999〕	0		30	13/	13	台/千克	3/		20	
8479.8999 60	绕线机(能卷绕直径在 75mm 至 400mm、长度为 600mm 或更长的)〔999〕	0		30	13/	13	台/千克	3A/	M	20	
8479.8999 90	本章其他未列名机器及机械器具(具有独立功能的)[T2]	0		30	13/	13	台/千克	A/	M	20	
	-零件：										
8479.9010	---船舶用舵机及陀螺稳定器用[T2]	0		14	13/	13	千克	/		20	
8479.9020	---空气增湿器及减湿器用〔999〕	0		70	13/	13	千克	/		5	
8479.9090	---其他										
8479.9090 10	绕线机的精密芯轴(专用于编号 8479899060 绕线机的精密芯轴)[T2]	0		20	13/	13	千克	3/		20	
8479.9090 90	税目 84.79 所列机器的其他零件〔101 船舶用零部件，102 机械行业成套设备，103 电子行业成套设备，104 船舶行业成套设备，105 其他行业成套设备，106 其它过滤及其喷射装置及其零件〕	0		20	13/	13	千克	/		20	
84.80	**金属铸造用型箱；型模底板；阳模；金属用型模(锭模除外)、硬质合金、玻璃、矿物材料、橡胶或塑料用型模：**										
8480.1000	-金属铸造用型箱〔999〕	8		20	13/	13	千克	/		33	
8480.2000	-型模底板〔999〕	8		20	13/	13	千克	/		33	
8480.3000	-阳模〔999〕	8		20	13/	13	千克	/		28	
	-金属、硬质合金用型模：										
	--注模或压模：										

协定税率 %								RCEP		特惠税率 %			Article Description
东/冰/格	巴基斯坦	韩国	瑞士上/下	哥/秘/柬	澳/毛	新西/坡/智	中国港/澳/台	东盟及马来/澳/韩	日/新	亚太2国	老/柬/缅	98/97/95	
													--For treating metal, including electric wire coil-winders:
0/0/0	2	1.9	1/1	0/0/0	0/0	0//0	0/0/0	0/0/8.6	8.9/0			0/0/0	---Filament winding machines
0/0/0	2	1.9	1/1	0/0/0	0/0	0//0	0/0/0	0/0/8.6	8.9/0			0/0/0	---Other
													--Mixing, kneading, crushing, grinding, screening, sifting, homogenizing, emulsifying or stirring machines
0/0/0	0	0		0/0/0	0/0	0//0	0/0/0	0/0/0	6.4/0			0/0/0	Beaters subject to regulations of sensitive item (Rotproof heat exchanger and ferment jar for use of beater)
0/0/0	0	0		0/0/0	0/0	0//0	0/0/0	0/0/0	6.4/0			0/0/0	For mixed waste and wastewater treatment, mixing, crushing, grinding, screening, homogenizing or emulsifying machine
0/0/0	0	0		0/0/0	0/0	0//0	0/0/0	0/0/0	6.4/0			0/0/0	Other mixing, kneading, crushing, grinding, screening, sifting, homogenizing, emulsifying or stirring machines
													---—Without driver or control circuit:
													---For metal handling
0/0/0	2	1.9	1/1	0/0/0	0/0	0//0	0/0/0	0/0/8.6	8.9/0			0/0/0	Cold isostatic press for processing metal (dual—purpose item control machines and mechanical appliances)
0/0/0	2	1.9	1/1	0/0/0	0/0	0//0	0/0/0	0/0/8.6	8.9/0			0/0/0	Cold isostatic press for processing metal
													---Other
0/0/0	0	0	0/0	0/0/0	0/0	0//0	0/0/	0/0/0	0/0			0/0/0	Other cold isostatic pressing machines (dual—purpose item control machines and mechanical appliances)
0/0/0	0	0	0/0	0/0/0	0/0	0//0	0/0/	0/0/0	0/0			0/0/0	Other cold isostatic press
													--Other:
0/0/0	0	0	0/0	0/0/0	0/0	0//0	0/0/	0/0/0	0/0			0/0/0	---Steering and rudder equipment or gyroscopic stabilizers for ships
0/0/0	0	0	0/0	0/0/0	0/0	0//0	0/0/	0/0/0	0/0			0/0/0	---Air humidifiers or dehumidifiers
0/0/0	0	0	0/0	0/0/0	0/0	0//0	0/0/	0/0/0	0/0			0/0/0	---Bundle and printed matter sorting machines used in post offices
0/0/0	0	0	0/0	0/0/0	0/0	0//0	0/0/	0/0/0	0/0			0/0/0	---Presses for radioactive waste material
													---Machines for assemblying elements on printed circuit boards:
0/0/0	0	0	0/0	0/0/0	0/0	0//0	0/0/	0/0/0	0/0			0/0/0	----Automatic plug-in machines
0/0/0	0	0	0/0	0/0/0	0/0	0//0	0/0/	0/0/0	0/0			0/0/0	----Automatic coreslice adhering machines
0/0/0	0	0	0/0	0/0/0	0/0	0//0	0/0/	0/0/0	0/0			0/0/0	----Other
													---Other:
0/0/0	0	0	0/0	0/0/0	0/0	0//0	0/0/	0/0/0	0/0			0/0/0	----Three-dimensional automatic warehouse equipmentt
													----Other
0/0/0	0	0	0/0	0/0/0	0/0	0//0	0/0/	0/0/0	0/0			0/0/0	Metal master production equipment for CD production(having independent functions)
0/0/0	0	0	0/0	0/0/0	0/0	0//0	0/0/	0/0/0	0/0			0/0/0	Fusing machine for CD production(having independent functions)
0/0/0	0	0	0/0	0/0/0	0/0	0//0	0/0/	0/0/0	0/0			0/0/0	Vacuum metal-splashers for CD production(having independent functions)
0/0/0	0	0	0/0	0/0/0	0/0	0//0	0/0/	0/0/0	0/0			0/0/0	Protective rubber-coating machine and dye-layer spin-coating machine(for CD production, having independent functions)
0/0/0	0	0	0/0	0/0/0	0/0	0//0	0/0/	0/0/0	0/0			0/0/0	Biological reactor(Dual-use items control machines and mechanical appliances)
0/0/0	0	0	0/0	0/0/0	0/0	0//0	0/0/	0/0/0	0/0			0/0/0	Chemostat(Dual-use items control machines and mechanical appliances)
0/0/0	0	0	0/0	0/0/0	0/0	0//0	0/0/	0/0/0	0/0			0/0/0	Continuous langendorff (Dual-use items control machines and mechanical appliances)
0/0/0	0	0	0/0	0/0/0	0/0	0//0	0/0/	0/0/0	0/0			0/0/0	Filament winding Machines coordinated and programmed in three or more axes, (Dual-use items control machines and mechanical appliances)
0/0/0	0	0	0/0	0/0/0	0/0	0//0	0/0/	0/0/0	0/0			0/0/0	Other dual-use items control machines and mechanical appliances
0/0/0	0	0	0/0	0/0/0	0/0	0//0	0/0/	0/0/0	0/0			0/0/0	winding machines(capable of winding wire diameter 75mm～400mm, length≥600mm)
0/0/0	0	0	0/0	0/0/0	0/0	0//0	0/0/	0/0/0	0/0			0/0/0	Machines and mechanical appliances having independent functions, not specified or included elsewhere in this Chapter
													-Parts:
0/0/0	0	0	0/0	0/0/0	0/0	0//0	0/0/	0/0/0	0/0			0/0/0	---Of the machines of subheading No.8479.8910
0/0/0	0	0	0/0	0/0/0	0/0	0//0	0/0/	0/0/0	0/0			0/0/0	---Of the machines of subheading No.8479.8920
													---Other
0/0/0	0	0	0/0	0/0/0	0/0	0//0	0/0/	0/0/0	0/0			0/0/0	Precision mandrels for winding machines(precision mandrels used exclusively for No.84798990.60 winding machines)
0/0/0	0	0	0/0	0/0/0	0/0	0//0	0/0/	0/0/0	0/0			0/0/0	Other parts of machiners of heading No.84.79
													Moulding boxes for metal foundry; mould bases; moulding patterns; moulds for metal (other than ingot moulds), metal carbides, glass, mineral materials, rubber or plastics:
0/0/0	2	2	0/0	0/0/0	0/0	0//0	0/0/	0/0/9	9.1/0			0/0/0	-Moulding boxes for metal foundry
0/0/0	2	1.6	0/0	0/0/0	0/0	0//0	0/0/	0/0/7.2	7.3/0			0/0/0	-Mould bases
0/0/0	2	2	0/0	0/0/0	0/0	0/0/0	0/0/	0/0/9	9.1/0			0/0/0	-Moulding patterns
													-Moulds for metal or metal carbides:
													--Injection or compression types:

税则号列	货品名称〔CIQ 扩展编码及品名－T2 表示见附表 2〕	最惠(%)	暂定税率	普通	增值/消费	出口退税	计量单位	监管条件/特殊证件	检验检疫	对美关税	亚太上/下
8480.4110	---压铸模[T2]	8		20	13/	13	千克	/		33	5.2/5.2
8480.4120	---粉末冶金用压模[T2]	8		20	13/	13	千克	/		33	5.2/5.2
8480.4190	---其他[T2]	8		20	13/	13	千克	/		28	5.2/5.2
8480.4900	--其他[T2]	8		20	13/	13	千克	/		18	5.2/5.2
8480.5000	-玻璃用型模[T2]	8		20	13/	13	套/千克	/			
8480.6000	-矿物材料用型模〔999〕	8		20	13/	13	套/千克	/		13	
	-塑料或橡胶用型模：										
	--注模或压模：										
8480.7110	---硫化轮胎用囊式型模〔999〕	0		20	13/	13	套/千克	/		25	
8480.7190	---其他										
8480.7190 10	用于光盘生产的专用模具(注模或压模)〔999〕	0		20	13/	13	套/千克	/		25	
8480.7190 90	其他塑料或橡胶用注模或压模〔101 机械行业成套设备，102 电子行业成套设备，103 轻工行业成套设备〕	0		20	13/	13	套/千克	/		25	
8480.7900	--其他										
8480.7900 10	农用双壁波纹管生产线用其他模具〔999〕	5		20	13/	13	套/千克	/		30	3.3/3.3
8480.7900 90	塑料或橡胶用其他型模[T2]	5		20	13/	13	套/千克	/		30	3.3/3.3
84.81	**用于管道、锅炉、罐、桶或类似品的龙头、旋塞、阀门及类似装置，包括减压阀及恒温控制阀：**										
8481.1000	-减压阀										
8481.1000 01	喷灌设备用减压阀(用于管道、锅炉、罐、桶或类似品的)〔101：减压阀(安全附件)；102：减压阀〕	5	2	30	13/	13	套/千克	/		12	
8481.1000 90	其他减压阀(用于管道、锅炉、罐、桶或类似品的)〔101 减压阀(安全附件)，102 减压阀〕	5		30	13/	13	套/千克	/		15	
	-油压或气压传动阀：										
8481.2010	---油压的										
8481.2010 10	飞机发动机用液压传动阀(用于管道、锅炉、罐、桶或类似品的)〔101 安全附件，102 传动阀〕	5	1	30	13/	13	套/千克	/			
8481.2010 90	其他油压传动阀(用于管道、锅炉、罐、桶或类似品的)〔101 安全附件，102 传动阀〕	5		30	13/	13	套/千克	/			
8481.2020	---气压的										
8481.2020 10	飞机发动机用气压传动阀(用于管道、锅炉、罐、桶或类似品的)〔101 安全附件，102 传动阀〕	5	1	30	13/	13	套/千克	/		21	
8481.2020 90	其他气压传动阀(用于管道、锅炉、罐、桶或类似品的)〔101 安全附件，102 传动阀〕	5		30	13/	13	套/千克	/		25	
8481.3000	-止回阀〔101 止回阀(安全附件)，102 止回阀〕	5		30	13/	13	套/千克	/		15	
8481.4000	-安全阀或溢流阀〔101 安全阀或溢流阀(安全附件)，102 安全阀或溢流阀〕	5		30	13/	13	套/千克	/		10	
	-其他器具：										
	---换向阀：										
8481.8021	----电磁式										
8481.8021 10	两用物项管制的电磁式换向阀[T2]	7		30	13/	13	套/千克	3/		27	4.6/4.6
8481.8021 90	其他电磁式换向阀(用于管道、锅炉、罐、桶或类似品的)〔101 其它阀门及类似品(安全附件)，102 其它阀门及类似品〕	7		30	13/	13	套/千克	/		27	4.6/4.6
8481.8029	----其他										
8481.8029 10	两用物项管制的其他换向阀[T2]	7		30	13/	13	套/千克	3/		17	4.6/4.6
8481.8029 90	其他换向阀(用于管道、锅炉、罐、桶或类似品的)〔101 其它阀门及类似品(安全附件)，102 其它阀门及类似品〕	7		30	13/	13	套/千克	/		17	4.6/4.6
	---流量阀：										
8481.8031	----电子膨胀阀										
8481.8031 10	两用物项管制的电子膨胀流量阀〔101 其它阀门及类似品(安全附件)，102 其它阀门及类似品〕	7		30	13/	13	套/千克	3/		32	4.6/4.6
8481.8031 90	其他电子膨胀流量阀(用于管道、锅炉、罐、桶或类似品的)〔101 其它阀门及类似品(安全附件)，102 其它阀门及类似品〕	7		30	13/	13	套/千克	/		32	4.6/4.6
8481.8039	----其他										
8481.8039 10	两用物项管制的其他流量阀〔101 其它阀门及类似品(安全附件)，102 其它阀门及类似品〕	7		30	13/	13	套/千克	3/		17	4.6/4.6
8481.8039 20	飞机发动机用流量阀(用于管道、锅炉、罐、桶或类似品的)〔101 安全附件，102 其它阀门及类似品〕	7	1	30	13/	13	套/千克	/		11	4.6/4.6
8481.8039 90	其他流量阀(用于管道、锅炉、罐、桶或类似品的)〔101 其它阀门及类似品(安全附件)，102 其它阀门及类似品〕	7		30	13/	13	套/千克	/		17	4.6/4.6
8481.8040	---其他阀门										
8481.8040 10	两用物项管制的其他阀门[T2]	7	5	30	13/	13	套/千克	3/		15	4.6/4.6
8481.8040 20	高压涡轮间隙控制阀门(用于管道、锅炉、罐、桶或类似品的)〔101 安全附件，102 非安全附件〕	7	1	30	13/	13	套/千克	/		11	4.6/4.6
8481.8040 30	废气再循环阀(用于管道、锅炉、罐、桶或类似品的)〔101 安全附件，102 其它阀门及类似品〕	7	5	30	13/	13	套/千克	/		15	4.6/4.6
8481.8040 40	飞机发动机用预冷控制阀门(用于管道、锅炉、罐、桶或类似品的)〔101 安全附件，102 其它阀门及类似品〕	7	1	30	13/	13	套/千克	/		11	4.6/4.6
8481.8040 90	其他阀门(用于管道、锅炉、罐、桶或类似品的)[T2]	7	5	30	13/	13	套/千克	/		15	4.6/4.6
8481.8090	---其他〔101 其它阀门及类似品(安全附件)，102 其它阀门及类似品〕	5		50	13/	13	套/千克	/		15	
	-零件：										

协定税率 %								RCEP		特惠税率 %			Article Description
东/冰/格	巴基斯坦	韩国	瑞士上/下	哥/秘/柬	澳/毛	新西/坡/智	中国港/澳/台	东盟及马来/澳/韩	日/新	亚太2国	老/柬/缅	98/97/95	
0/0/0	2	3.7	0/0	0/0/0	0/0	0//0	0/0/0	7.5/7.6/7.5	7.5/7.6			0/0/0	---Die-casting mould
0/0/0	2	3.7	0/0	0/0/0	0/0	0//0	0/0/0	7.5/7.6/7.5	7.5/7.6			0/0/0	---Moulds for powder metallurgy
0/0/0	2	3.7	0/0	0/0/0	0/0	0//0	0/0/0	7.5/7.6/7.5	7.5/7.6			0/0/0	---Other
0/0/0	2	3.7	0/0	0/0/0	0/0	0//0	0/0/	7.5/7.6/7.5	7.5/7.6			0/0/0	--Other
0/0/0	4	3.9	0/0	0/0/0	0/0	0//0	0/0/	7.8/8/7.8	7.9/8			0/0/0	-Moulds for glass
0/0/0	4	1.6	0/0	0/0/0	0/0	0//0	0/0/	0/0/7.6	7.6/0			0/0/0	-Moulds for mineral materials
													-Moulds for rubber or plastics:
													--Other:
0/0/0	0	0	0/0	0/0/0	0/0	0//0	0/0/	0/0/0	0/0			0/0/0	---Tyre vulcanizing mould for capsule type(injection or compression types)
													---Other
0/0/0	0	0	0/0	0/0/0	0/0	0//0	0/0/	0/0/0	0/0			0/0/0	Injection molds for CD production(injection or compression types)
0/0/0	0	0	0/0	0/0/0	0/0	0//0	0/0/	0/0/0	0/0			0/0/0	Other injection or compression types for rubber or plastics
													--Other
0//0	0	0	0/0	0/0/0	0/0	0//0	0/0/0	4.5/4.5/4.5	4.5/4.5			0/0/0	Other molds for agricultural double-wall corrugated pipe production lines
0//0	0	0	0/0	0/0/0	0/0	0//0	0/0/0	4.5/4.5/4.5	4.5/4.5			0/0/0	Other moulds for rubber plastics
													Taps, cocks, valves and similar appliances for pipes, boiler shells, tanks, vats or the like, including pressure-reducing valves and thermostatically controlled valves:
													-Pressure-reducing valves
0/0/0	0	2.3	0.5/0.5	0/0/0	0/0	0//0	0/0/	4.5/4.5/4.5	4.7/4.5			0/0/0	Pressure-reducing valves for spray irrigation equipment(used in pipes, boiler shells, tanks, vats or similar products)
0/0/0	0	2.3	0.5/0.5	0/0/0	0/0	0//0	0/0/	4.5/4.5/4.5	4.7/4.5			0/0/0	Other pressure-reducing valves(used in pipes, boiler shells, thanks, vats or similar products)
													-Valves for oleohydraulic or pneumatic transmissions:
													---For oleohydraulic transmissions
0/0/0	0	2.3	0.5/0.5	0/0/0	0/0	0//0	0/0/0	4.5/4.5/4.5	4.7/4.5		//	0/0/0	Hydraulic transmission valve for aircraft engine(used for tubing, boilers, Cans, barrels or similar products)
0/0/0	0	2.3	0.5/0.5	0/0/0	0/0	0//0	0/0/0	4.5/4.5/4.5	4.7/4.5		//	0/0/0	Other hydraulic transmission valves(used for tubing, boilers, Cans, barrels or similar products)
													---For pneumatic transmissions
0/0/0	0	2.3	0.5/0.5	0/0/0	0/0	0//0	0/0/	4.5/4.5/4.5	4.7/4.5		//	0/0/0	Pneumatic transmission valve for aircraft engine(used for tubing, boilers, Cans, barrels or similar products)
0/0/0	0	2.3	0.5/0.5	0/0/0	0/0	0//0	0/0/	4.5/4.5/4.5	4.7/4.5		//	0/0/0	Other pneumatic transmission valves(used for tubing, boilers, Cans, barrels or similar products)
0/0/0	0	2.3	0.5/0.5	0/0/0	0/0	0//0	0/0/0	4.5/4.5/4.5	4.7/4.5			0/0/0	-Check (nonreturn) valves
0/0/0	0	2.3	0/0	0/0/0	0/0	0//0	0/0/0	4.5/4.5/4.5	4.7/4.5			0/0/0	-Safety or relief valves
													-Other appliances:
													---Directional valve:
													----Electromagnetic
0/0/0	0	3.2	0.7/0.7	0/0/0	0/0	0//0	0/0/0	6.3/6.3/6.3	6.6/6.3			0/0/0	Electromagnetic directional valve of dual-use items control
0/0/0	0	3.2	0.7/0.7	0/0/0	0/0	0//0	0/0/0	6.3/6.3/6.3	6.6/6.3			0/0/0	Other electromagnetic selector valve(used for tubing, boilers, Cans, barrels or similar products)
													----Other
0/0/0	0	3.2	0.7/0.7	0/0/0	0/0	0//0	0/0/0	6.3/6.3/6.3	6.6/6.3			0/0/0	Other selector valve of dual-use items control
0/0/0	0	3.2	0.7/0.7	0/0/0	0/0	0//0	0/0/0	6.3/6.3/6.3	6.6/6.3			0/0/0	Other selector valve(used for tubing, boilers, Cans, barrels or similar products)
													---Flow control valves:
													----Electronic expansion valves
0/0/0	0	3.2	0/0	0/0/0	0/0	0//0	0/0/0	6.3/6.3/6.3	6.6/6.3			0/0/0	Electronic expansion flow valve of dual-use items control
0/0/0	0	3.2	0/0	0/0/0	0/0	0//0	0/0/0	6.3/6.3/6.3	6.6/6.3			0/0/0	Other electronic expansion flow valve(used for tubing, boilers, Cans, barrels or similar products)
													----Other
0/0/0	0	3.2	0.7/0.7	0/0/0	0/0	0//0	0/0/0	6.3/6.3/6.3	6.6/6.3			0/0/0	Other flow control valve of sensitive items control
0/0/0	0	3.2	0.7/0.7	0/0/0	0/0	0//0	0/0/0	6.3/6.3/6.3	6.6/6.3		//	0/0/0	Flow valve for aircraft engine (used for tubing, boilers, Cans, barrels or similar products)
0/0/0	0	3.2	0.7/0.7	0/0/0	0/0	0//0	0/0/0	6.3/6.3/6.3	6.6/6.3			0/0/0	Other flow control valve(used for tubing, boilers, Cans, barrels or similar products)
													---Other valve
0/0/0	0	0	0.7/0.7	0/0/0	0/0	0//0	0/0/0	0/0/0	6.6/0			0/0/0	Other valve of sensitive items control
0/0/0	0	0	0.7/0.7	0/0/0	0/0	0//0	0/0/0	0/0/0	6.6/0		//	0/0/0	HP Turbine clearance control valve (for pipes, boilers, tanks, barrels or similar)
0/0/0	0	0	0.7/0.7	0/0/0	0/0	0//0	0/0/0	0/0/0	6.6/0		//	0/0/0	EGR valve(used for tubing, boilers, Cans, barrels or similar products)
0/0/0	0	0	0.7/0.7	0/0/0	0/0	0//0	0/0/0	0/0/0	6.6/0		//	0/0/0	Precooling control valves for aircraft engines(used for tubing, boilers, Cans, barrels or similar products)
0/0/0	0	0	0.7/0.7	0/0/0	0/0	0//0	0/0/0	0/0/0	6.6/0			0/0/0	Other valve(used for tubing, boilers, Cans, barrels or similar products)
0/0/0	0	0	0/0	0/0/0	0/0	0//0	0/0/	4.5/4.5/4.5	4.8/4.5			0/0/0	---Other
													-Parts:

税则号列	货品名称〔CIQ 扩展编码及品名－T2 表示见附表 2〕	最惠(%)	暂定税率	普通	增值/消费	出口退税	计量单位	监管条件/特殊证件	检验检疫	对美关税	亚太上/下
8481.9010	---阀门用〔101 其它阀门及类似品(安全附件),102 其它阀门及类似品零件〕	8	4	30	13/	13	千克	/		14	
8481.9090	---其他〔101 其它阀门及类似品(安全附件),102 其它阀门及类似品零件〕	8		50	13/	13	千克	/		28	
84.82	**滚动轴承:**										
	-滚珠轴承:										
8482.1010	---调心球轴承〔999〕	8		20	13/	13	套/千克	/			5.2/5.2
8482.1020	---深沟球轴承〔999〕	8		20	13/	13	套/千克	/		33	5.2/5.2
8482.1030	---角接触轴承〔999〕	8		20	13/	13	套/千克	/		33	5.2/5.2
8482.1040	---推力球轴承										
8482.1040 11	飞机发动机用外径 30CM 的推力球轴承(滚珠轴承)〔999〕	8	1	20	13/	13	套/千克	/			5.2/5.2
8482.1040 19	飞机发动机用其他推力球轴承(滚珠轴承)〔999〕	8	1	20	13/	13	套/千克	/		21	5.2/5.2
8482.1040 90	其他推力球轴承(滚珠轴承)〔999〕	8		20	13/	13	套/千克	/		28	5.2/5.2
8482.1090	---其他〔999〕	8		20	13/	13	套/千克	/		28	5.2/5.2
8482.2000	-锥形滚子轴承,包括锥形滚子组件〔999〕	8		20	13/	13	套/千克	/		28	
8482.3000	-鼓形滚子轴承〔999〕	8	6	20	13/	13	套/千克	/		26	
8482.4000	-滚针轴承,包括保持架和滚针组件										
8482.4000 10	飞机发动机用滚针轴承(包括保持架和滚针组件)〔999〕	8	1	20	13/	13	套/千克	/		11	
8482.4000 90	其他滚针轴承(包括保持架和滚针组件)〔999〕	8	6	20	13/	13	套/千克	/		16	
8482.5000	-其他圆柱形滚子轴承,包括保持架和滚子组件										
8482.5000 10	三环、二环偏心滚动轴承,飞机发动机主推进轴用滚子轴承除外(包括保持架和滚子组件)〔999〕	8	4	20	13/	13	套/千克	/		24	
8482.5000 20	飞机发动机主推进轴用滚子轴承(包括保持架和滚子组件)〔999〕	8	1	20	13/	13	套/千克	/		21	
8482.5000 90	其他圆柱形滚子轴承(包括保持架和滚子组件)〔999〕	8		20	13/	13	套/千克	/		28	
8482.8000	-其他,包括球、柱混合轴承〔999〕	8		20	13/	13	套/千克	/		28	5.2/5.2
	-零件:										
8482.9100	--滚珠、滚针及滚柱〔999〕	8	6	20	13/	13	千克	/		26	
8482.9900	--其他〔999〕	6	3	20	13/	13	千克	/		23	
84.83	**传动轴(包括凸轮轴及曲柄轴)及曲柄;轴承座及滑动轴承;齿轮及齿轮传动装置;滚珠或滚子螺杆传动装置;齿轮箱及其他变速装置,包括扭矩变换器;飞轮及滑轮,包括滑轮组;离合器及联轴器(包括万向节):**										
	-传动轴(包括凸轮轴及曲柄轴)及曲柄:										
	---船舶用传动轴:										
8483.1011	----柴油机曲轴〔999〕	6		14	13/	13	个/千克	/		31	3.9/3.9
8483.1019	----其他〔999〕	6		14	13/	13	个/千克	/		16	3.9/3.9
8483.1090	---其他										
8483.1090 10	飞机发动机用传动轴〔999〕	6	1	30	13/	13	个/千克	/		21	3.9/3.9
8483.1090 90	其他传动轴及曲柄(包括凸轮轴及曲柄轴)〔999〕	6		30	13/	13	个/千克	/		26	3.9/3.9
8483.2000	-装有滚珠或滚子轴承的轴承座〔999〕	6		30	13/	13	个/千克	/		16	
8483.3000	-未装滚珠或滚子轴承的轴承座;滑动轴承										
8483.3000 10	磁悬浮轴承(轴承组合件,由悬浮在充满阻尼介质的环形磁铁组成)〔999〕	6	4	30	13/	13	个/千克	3/		24	
8483.3000 20	轴承/阻尼器(安装在阻尼器上的具有枢轴/盖的轴承)〔999〕	6	4	30	13/	13	个/千克	3/		24	
8483.3000 90	其他未装有滚珠或滚子轴承的轴承座;其他滑动轴承〔999〕	6	4	30	13/	13	个/千克	/		24	
	-齿轮及齿轮传动装置,但单独进口或出口的带齿的轮、链轮及其他传动元件除外;滚珠或滚子螺杆传动装置;齿轮箱及其他变速装置,包括扭矩变换器:										
8483.4010	---滚子螺杆传动装置										
8483.4010 10	飞机水平尾翼螺旋杆〔999〕	8	1	30	13/	13	个/千克	/		21	5.2/5.2
8483.4010 90	其他滚子螺杆传动装置〔999〕	8		30	13/	13	个/千克	/		28	5.2/5.2
8483.4020	---行星齿轮减速器〔999〕	8		30	13/	13	个/千克	/		33	5.2/5.2
8483.4090	---其他										
8483.4090 10	飞机发动机用齿轮传动装置(齿轮箱)〔999〕	8	1	30	13/	13	个/千克	/		21	5.2/5.2
8483.4090 90	其他传动装置及变速装置(指齿轮及齿轮传动装置,齿轮箱和扭矩变换器)〔999〕	8		30	13/	13	个/千克	/		28	5.2/5.2
8483.5000	-飞轮及滑轮,包括滑轮组〔999〕	8		30	13/	13	个/千克	/		33	
8483.6000	-离合器及联轴器(包括万向节)										
8483.6000 01	压力机用组合式湿式离合/制动器(离合扭矩为 60kNM-300kNM,制动扭矩为 30kNM-100kNM)〔999〕	8	4	30	13/	13	个/千克	/		24	
8483.6000 20	高速轴联轴器(风力发电机组用),扭矩保护值为 160KNM－1000KNM〔999〕	8	4	30	13/	13	个/千克	/		24	

协定税率 %								RCEP		特惠税率 %			Article Description
东/冰/格	巴基斯坦	韩国	瑞士上/下	哥/秘/柬	澳/毛	新西/坡/智	中国港/澳/台	东盟及马来/澳/韩	日/新	亚太2国	老/柬/缅	98/97/95	
0/0/0	4	0	0.8/0.8	0/0/0	0/0	0//0	0/0/0	0/0/0	7.5/0			0/0/0	---Of valves
0/0/0	2	0	0/0	0/0/0	0/0	0//0	0/0/0	7.2/7.2/7.2	7.3/7.2			0/0/0	---Other
													Ball or roller bearings:
													-Ball bearings:
0/0/0	2	0	0/0	0/0/0	0/0	0/0/0	0/0/	7.2/7.2/7.2	7.3/7.2			0/0/0	---Self-aliging ball bearing
0/0/0	2	0	0/0	0/0/0	0/0	0/0/0	0/0/	0/0/0	7.6/0			0/0/0	---Deep groove ball bearing
0/0/0	2	0	0/0	0/0/0	0/0	0/0/0	0/0/	0/0/0	7.3/0			0/0/0	---Angular contact ball bearing
													---Thrust ball bearing
0/0/0	2	0	0/0	0/0/0	0/0	0/0/0	0/0/	7.2/7.2/7.2	7.3/7.2			0/0/0	Thrust ball bearing (ball bearing) with outer diameter of 30cm for aircraft engine
0/0/0	2	0	0/0	0/0/0	0/0	0/0/0	0/0/	7.2/7.2/7.2	7.3/7.2			0/0/0	Other thrust ball bearings (ball bearings) for aircraft engines
0/0/0	2	0	0/0	0/0/0	0/0	0/0/0	0/0/	7.2/7.2/7.2	7.3/7.2			0/0/0	Other thrust ball bearing
0/0/0	4	0	0.8/0.8	0/0/0	0/0	0/0/0	0/0/	0/0/0	7.6/0			0/0/0	---Other
0/0/0	2	0	0/0	0/0/0	0/0	0//0	0/0/	0/0/0	7.6/0			0/0/0	-Tapered roller bearings, including cone and tapered roller assemblies
0/0/0	2	0	0/0	0/0/0	0/0	0//0	0/0/	7.2/7.2/7.2	7.3/7.2			0/0/0	-Spherical roller bearings
													-Needle roller bearings, including cage and needle roller assemblies
0//0	2	0	0/0	0/0/0	0/0	0//0	0/0/0	7.2/7.2/7.2	7.3/7.2		//	0/0/0	Needle roller bearings for aircraft engines
0//0	2	0	0/0	0/0/0	0/0	0//0	0/0/0	7.2/7.2/7.2	7.3/7.2		//	0/0/0	Other needle roller bearings
													-Other cylindrical roller bearings, including cage and needle roller assemblies
0/0/0	2	3.7	0.8/0.8	0/0/0	0/0	0/0/0	0/0/	7.2/7.2/7.2	7.5/7.2			0/0/0	Tricyclic or bicyclic eccentric rolling bearing
0/0/0	2	3.7	0.8/0.8	0/0/0	0/0	0/0/0	0/0/	7.2/7.2/7.2	7.5/7.2		//	0/0/0	Roller bearing for main propulsion shaft of aircraft engine
0/0/0	2	3.7	0.8/0.8	0/0/0	0/0	0/0/0	0/0/	7.2/7.2/7.2	7.5/7.2			0/0/0	Other cylindrical roller bearings
0/0/0	2	3.7	0.8/0.8	0/0/0	0/0	0//0	0/0/	7.5/7.6/7.5	7.5/7.6			0/0/0	-Other, including combined ball/roller bearings
													-Parts:
0/0/0	2	0	0/0	0/0/0	0/0	0//0	0/0/	0/0/0	7.3/0			0/0/0	--Balls, needles and rollers
0/0/0	0	0	0.6/0.6	0/0/0	0/0	0//0	0/0/0	5.4/5.4/5.4	5.6/5.4			0/0/0	--Other
													Transmission shafts (including cam shafts and crank shafts) and cranks; bearing housings and plain shaft bearings; gears and gearing ball or roller screws; gear boxes and other speed changers, including torque converters; flywheels and pulleys, including pulley blocks; clutches and shaft couplings (including universal joints):
													-Transmission shafts (including cam shafts and crank shafts) and cranks:
													---Transmission shafts for ships:
0/0/0	0	3.9	0/0	0/0/0	0/0	0//0	0/0/	5/5/	/5			0/0/0	----Crank shaft for diesel engine
0/0/0	4	2.8	0/0	0/0/0	0/0	0//0	0/0/	5.4/5.4/5.4	5.6/5.4			0/0/0	----Other
													---Other
0/0/0	4	2.8	0.6/0.6	0/0/0	0/0	0//0	0/0/	5.4/5.4/5.4	5.6/5.4		//	0/0/0	Transmission shaft for aircraft engine
0/0/0	4	2.8	0.6/0.6	0/0/0	0/0	0//0	0/0/	5.4/5.4/5.4	5.6/5.4		//	0/0/0	Other transmission shafts and cranks (including camshaft and crankshaft)
0/0/0	0	0	0.6/0.6	0/0/0	0/0	0//0	0/0/	5.4/5.4/5.4	5.5/5.4			0/0/0	-Bearing housings, incorporating ball or roller bearings
													-Bearing housings, not incorporating ball or roller bearings; plain shaft bearings
0/0/0	0	0	0.6/0.6	0/0/0	0/0	0//0	0/0/	0/0/0	5.6/0			0/0/0	Magnetic suspension bearing (assembly of bearing, compased of circular magnets of supending in filled with damping medi-un)
0/0/0	0	0	0.6/0.6	0/0/0	0/0	0//0	0/0/	0/0/0	5.6/0			0/0/0	Bearings dampers (installed on the bearing with a pivot lid on the damper)
0/0/0	0	0	0.6/0.6	0/0/0	0/0	0//0	0/0/	0/0/0	5.6/0			0/0/0	Other bearing housing not incorporalins ball or rouer bear-ings; other plain shaft bearins
													-Gears and gearing, other than toothed wheels, chain sprockets and other transmission elements presented separately; ball or roller screws; gear boxes and other speed changers, including torque converters:
													---Roller Screws
0/0/0	2	0	0.8/0.8	0/0/0	0/0	0//0	0/0/0	7.2/7.2/7.2	7.3/7.2		//	0/0/0	Plane horizontal tail screw rod
0/0/0	2	0	0.8/0.8	0/0/0	0/0	0//0	0/0/0	7.2/7.2/7.2	7.3/7.2		//	0/0/0	Other roller screw drives
0/0/0	2	5.2	0.8/0.8	0/0/0	0/0	0//0	0/0/	5/5/	/5			0/0/0	---Planet decelerators
													---Other
0/0/0	2	3.7	0.8/0.8	0/0/0	0/0	0//0	0/0/0	7.2/7.2/7.2	7.5/7.2		//	0/0/0	Gearing (Gearbox) for aircraft engines
0/0/0	2	3.7	0.8/0.8	0/0/0	0/0	0//0	0/0/0	7.2/7.2/7.2	7.5/7.2		//	0/0/0	Other gears gearing (gears and gearing, gearboxes and torque converters)
0/0/0	2	1.6	0.8/0.8	0/0/0	0/0	0//0	0/0/	7.2/7.2/7.2	7.3/7.2			0/0/0	-Flywheels and pulleys, including pulley blocks
													-Clutches and shaft couplings (including universal joints)
0/0/0	4	3.7	0.8/0.8	0/0/0	0/0	0//0	0/0/	7.5/7.6/7.5	7.5/7.6			0/0/0	Combined wet clutches/ brakes for presses (the on-off torque is 60KNM～300KNM and the braking torque is 30KNM～100KNM)
0/0/0	4	3.7	0.8/0.8	0/0/0	0/0	0//0	0/0/	7.5/7.6/7.5	7.5/7.6			0/0/0	High speed shaft coupling (for wind turbine generator set), torque protection value is 16knm－1knm

税则号列		货品名称〔CIQ 扩展编码及品名－T2 表示见附表 2〕	最惠(%)	暂定税率	普通	增值/消费	出口退税	计量单位	监管条件/特殊证件	检验检疫	对美关税	亚太上/下
8483.6000	90	离合器及联轴器(包括万向节)〔999〕	8		30	13/	13	个/千克	/		28	
8483.9000		-单独进口或出口的带齿的轮、链轮及其他传动元件;零件										
8483.9000	10	车用凸轮轴相位调节器(汽车发动机用)〔999〕	8	4	30	13/	13	千克	/		24	
8483.9000	20	飞机发动机用齿轮箱用单个齿轮〔999〕	8	1	30	13/	13	千克	/		21	
8483.9000	90	税目 84.83 所列货品用其他零件(包括单独报验的带齿的轮、链轮及其他传动元件)〔999〕	8		30	13/	13	千克	/		28	
84.84		**密封垫或类似接合衬垫,用金属片与其他材料制成或用双层或多层金属片制成;成套或各种不同材料的密封垫或类似接合衬垫,装于袋、套或类似包装内;机械密封件:**										
8484.1000		-密封垫或类似接合衬垫,用金属片与其他材料制成或用双层或多层金属片制成〔999〕	8	5	30	13/	13	千克	/		15	
8484.2000		-机械密封件										
8484.2000	10	耐 UF6 腐蚀的转动轴封(专门设计的真空密封装置,缓冲气体泄漏率 1000cm³/min)〔999〕	8	5	30	13/	13	千克	3/		25	
8484.2000	20	转动轴封(专门设计的带有密封式进气口和出气口的转动轴封)〔999〕	8	5	30	13/	13	千克	3/		25	
8484.2000	30	MLIS 用转动轴封(专门设计的带密封进气口和出气口的转动轴封)〔999〕	8	5	30	13/	13	千克	3/		25	
8484.2000	90	其他机械密封件〔999〕	8	5	30	13/	13	千克	/		25	
8484.9000		-其他〔999〕	8	5	30	13/	13	千克	/		10	
84.85		**增材制造设备:**										
8485.1000		-用金属材料的〔999〕	9		50	13/	13	台/千克	/		29	
8485.2000		-用塑料或橡胶材料的〔999〕	5		30	13/	13	台/千克	/		10	3.3/3.3
		-用石膏、水泥、陶瓷或玻璃材料的:										
8485.3010		---用玻璃材料的〔999〕	8		30	13/	13	台/千克	/		33	
8485.3020		---用石膏、水泥、陶瓷材料的〔999〕	5		30	13/	13	台/千克	/		25	3.3/3.3
		-其他:										
8485.8010		---用纸或纸浆的〔999〕	12		30	13/	13	台/千克	/		37	7.8/7.8
8485.8020		---用木材、软木的〔999〕	9		30	13/	13	台/千克	/		34	
8485.8090		---其他〔999〕	0		30	13/	13	台/千克	A/	M	20	
		-零件:										
8485.9010		---用金属材料的〔101 机床附件,102 机床零件〕	6		17	13/	13	千克	/		26	
8485.9020		---用玻璃材料的〔999〕	8		30	13/	13	千克	/		18	
8485.9030		---用橡胶或塑料材料的〔101 电子行业成套设备,102 化工行业成套设备,103 轻工行业成套设备〕	0		30	13/	13	千克	/		20	
8485.9040		---用石膏、水泥、陶瓷材料的〔999〕	5		30	13/	13	千克	/		25	
8485.9050		---用纸或纸浆的〔999〕	8		30	13/	13	千克	/		28	
8485.9060		---用木材、软木的〔101 机床附件,102 机床零件〕	6		17	13/	13	千克	/		31	
8485.9090		---其他〔999〕	0		20	13/	13	千克	/		20	
84.86		**专用于或主要用于制造半导体单晶柱或晶圆、半导体器件、集成电路或平板显示器的机器及装置;本章注释十一(三)规定的机器及装置,零件及附件:**										
		-制造单晶柱或晶圆用的机器及装置:										
8486.1010		---利用温度变化处理单晶硅的机器及装置〔999〕	0		30	13/	13	台/千克	/			
8486.1020		---研磨设备〔999〕	0		30	13/	13	台/千克	/			
8486.1030		---切割设备〔999〕	0		30	13/	13	台/千克	/			
8486.1040		---化学机械抛光设备(CMP)〔999〕	0		30	13/	13	台/千克	/			
8486.1090		---其他〔999〕	0		30	13/	13	台/千克	/			
		-制造半导体器件或集成电路用的机器及装置:										
8486.2010		---氧化、扩散、退火及其他热处理设备〔999〕	0		30	13/	13	台/千克	/			
		---薄膜沉积设备:										
8486.2021		----化学气相沉积装置(CVD)〔999〕	0		30	13/	13	台/千克	/			
8486.2022		----物理气相沉积装置(PVD)〔999〕	0		30	13/	13	台/千克	/			
8486.2029		----其他〔999〕	0		30	13/	13	台/千克	/			
		---将电路图投影或绘制到感光半导体材料上的装置:										
8486.2031		----分步重复光刻机(步进光刻机)〔999〕	0		100	13/	13	台/千克	/			
8486.2039		----其他〔101 其它机床,102 电子行业成套设备〕	0		100	13/	13	台/千克	/			
		---刻蚀及剥离设备:										
8486.2041		----等离子体干法刻蚀机[T2]	0		30	13/	13	台/千克	/			
8486.2049		----其他〔101 其它机床,102 电子行业成套设备〕	0		30	13/	13	台/千克	/			
8486.2050		---离子注入机〔999〕	0		11	13/	13	台/千克	/			
8486.2090		---其他〔101 其它机床,102 电子行业成套设备〕	0		30	13/	13	台/千克	/			
		-制造平板显示器用的机器及装置:										
8486.3010		---扩散、氧化、退火及其他热处理设备〔999〕	0		30	13/	13	台/千克	/			

协定税率 %								RCEP		特惠税率 %			
东/冰/格	巴基斯坦	韩国	瑞士上/下	哥/秘/柬	澳/毛	新西/坡/智	中国港/澳/台	东盟及马来/澳/韩	日/新	亚太2国	老/柬/缅	98/97/95	Article Description
0/0/0	4	3.7	0.8/0.8	0/0/0	0/0	0//0	0/0/	7.5/7.6/7.5	7.5/7.6			0/0/0	Clutches and shaft couplings(including universal joints)
													-Toothed wheels, chain sprockets and other transmission elements presented separately; parts
0/0/0	4	0	0.8/0.8	0/0/0	0/0	0//0	0/0/0	0/0/0	7.5/0			0/0/0	Car camshaft phase regulator (car engine)
0/0/0	4	0	0.8/0.8	0/0/0	0/0	0//0	0/0/0	0/0/0	7.5/0		//	0/0/0	Single gear for gearbox of aircraft engine
0/0/0	4	0	0.8/0.8	0/0/0	0/0	0//0	0/0/0	0/0/0	7.5/0			0/0/0	Other components for goods of heading 84.83 goods (toothed wheels, chain sprockets and other transmission components including separately presented)
													Gaskets and similar joints of metal sheeting combined with other material or of two or more layers of metal; sets or assortments of gaskets and similar joints, dissimilar in composition, put up in pouches, envelopes or similar packings mechanical seals:
0/0/0	2	3.7	0.8/0.8	0/0/0	0/0	0//0	0/0/0	7.5/7.6/7.5	7.5/7.6			0/0/0	-Gaskets and similar joints of metal sheeting combined with other material or of two or more layers of metal
													-Mechanical seals
0/0/0	2	3.7	0.8/0.8	0/0/0	0/0	0//0	0/0/	7.5/7.6/7.5	7.5/7.6			0/0/0	UF_6 resisting rotary shaft seals(specially designed vacuum airtight devices, rate of leakage of buffer gas $1000cm^3/min$)
0/0/0	2	3.7	0.8/0.8	0/0/0	0/0	0//0	0/0/	7.5/7.6/7.5	7.5/7.6			0/0/0	Rotary shalt seals (specially designed shaft seals with an airtight inlet and outlet)
0/0/0	2	3.7	0.8/0.8	0/0/0	0/0	0//0	0/0/	7.5/7.6/7.5	7.5/7.6			0/0/0	Rotary shalt seals for MLIS(specially designed, shaft seals an airtight inlet and outlet)
0/0/0	2	3.7	0.8/0.8	0/0/0	0/0	0//0	0/0/	7.5/7.6/7.5	7.5/7.6			0/0/0	Other mechanical seals
0/0/0	2	3.7	0/0	0/0/0	0/0	0//0	0/0/	7.5/7.6/7.5	7.5/7.6			0/0/0	-Other
													Additive manufacturing equipment:
0/0/0	4		1/1	0/0/0	0/0	0//0	0/0/	5/5/	/5			0/0/0	-By made of metal
0/0/0	0	2.3	0/0	0/0/0	0/0	0//0	0/0/0	4.5/4.5/4.5	4.7/4.5			0/0/0	-By plastics or rubber deposit
													-By plaster, cement, ceramics or glass deposit:
0/0/0	2	2	0/0	0/0/0	0/0	0/0/0	0/0/	0/0/9	9.1/0			0/0/0	---By made of glass
0/0/0	0	1	0/0	0/0/0	0/0	0//0	0/0/	4.5/4.5/4.5	4.5/4.5			0/0/0	---By plaster, cement, ceramics deposit
													-Other:
0/0/0	4.2	2.4	1.2/1.2	0/0/0	0/0	0/0/0	0/0/0	0/0/10.8	10.9/0			0/0/0	---By made of paper or pulp
0/0/0	2	6	0/0	0/0/0	0/0	0/0/0	0/0/	9.5/9.5/10	/9.5			0/0/0	---By made of wood or cork
0/0/0	0	0	0/0	0/0/0	0/0	0//0	0/0/	0/0/0	0/0			0/0/0	---Other
													-spare parts:
0/0/0	0	0	0.6/0.6	0/0/0	0/0	0//0	0/0/0	0/0/0	5.5/0			0/0/0	---By made of metal
0/0/0	4	1.6	0/0	0/0/0	0/0	0//0	0/0/	0/0/7.2	7.3/0			0/0/0	---By made of glass
0/0/0	0	0	0/0	0/0/0	0/0	0//0	0/0/	0/0/0	0/0			0/0/0	---By rubber or plastics deposit
0/0/0	0	1	0.5/0.5	0/0/0	0/0	0//0	0/0/	4.5/4.5/4.5	4.5/4.5			0/0/0	---By plaster, cement, ceramics deposit
0/0/0	2	0		0/0/0	0/0	0//0	0/0/	0/0/0	7.6/0			0/0/0	---By made of paper or pulp
0/0/0	0	2.8	0/0	0/0/0	0/0	0//0	0/0/	5.4/5.4/5.4	5.6/5.4			0/0/0	---By made of wood or cork
0/0/0	0	0	0/0	0/0/0	0/0	0//0	0/0/	0/0/0	0/0			0/0/0	---Other
													Machines and apparatus of a kind used soldy or principally for the manufacture of semiconduc tor boules or wafors, semiconductor devices, electronic integrated circuits or flat panel displays; machines and apparatus specified in Note 11(C) to this chaptcr; Parts and accessories
													-Machines and apparatus for the manvifacture of boules or wafers:
0/0/0	0	0	0/0	0/0/0	0/0	0//0	0/0/	0/0/0	0/0		0//	0/0/0	---Machines and apparatus for the treatment of monocrystalline sillicon by aprocess involving a change of temperature
0/0/0	0	0	0/0	0/0/0	0/0	0//0	0/0/	0/0/0	0/0			0/0/0	---Grinding machines
0/0/0	0	0	0/0	0/0/0	0/0	0//0	0/0/	0/0/0	0/0			0/0/0	---Sawing machines
0/0/0	0	0	0/0	0/0/0	0/0	0//0	0/0/	0/0/0	0/0			0/0/0	---Chemical mechanical polishers (CMP)
0/0/0	0	0	0/0	0/0/0	0/0	0//0	0/0/	0/0/0	0/0			0/0/0	---other
													-Machines and apparatus for the manufacture of semiconductor devices or of electronic integrated circuis:
0/0/0	0	0	0/0	0/0/0	0/0	0//0	0/0/	0/0/0	0/0		0//	0/0/0	---Diffusion, oxidatation annealing and other heat treatment equipment
													---Film deposition oquipment:
0/0/0	0	0	0/0	0/0/0	0/0	0//0	0/0/	0/0/0	0/0			0/0/0	----Chemical Vapor Deposition (CVD) equipment
0/0/0	0	0	0/0	0/0/0	0/0	0//0	0/0/	0/0/0	0/0			0/0/0	----Physical Vapour Deposition (PVD) equipment
0/0/0	0	0	0/0	0/0/0	0/0	0//0	0/0/	0/0/0	0/0			0/0/0	----Other
													---Apparatus for the projection or drawing of circuit patterns on sensitized semiconductor materials:
0/0/0	0	0	0/0	0/0/0	0/0	0//0	0/0/	0/0/0	0/0			0/0/0	----step and repeat alignersw
0/0/0	0	0	0/0	0/0/0	0/0	0//0	0/0/	0/0/0	0/0			0/0/0	----Other
													---Etching and stripoing equipment:
0/0/0	0	0	0/0	0/0/0	0/0	0//0	0/0/	0/0/0	0/0			0/0/0	----Dry plasma etching
0/0/0	0	0	0/0	0/0/0	0/0	0//0	0/0/	0/0/0	0/0			0/0/0	----Other
0/0/0	0	0	0/0	0/0/0	0/0	0//0	0/0/	0/0/0	0/0			0/0/0	---Ion Implanters
0/0/0	0	0	0/0	0/0/0	0/0	0//0	0/0/	0/0/0	0/0			0/0/0	---Other
													-Machines and apparatus for the manufacture of flat panel displays:
0/0/0	0	0	0/0	0/0/0	0/0	0//0	0/0/	0/0/0	0/0		0//	0/0/0	---Oxidatation diffusinon annealing and other heat treatment equipment

税则号列	货品名称〔CIQ 扩展编码及品名—T2 表示见附表 2〕	最惠(%)	暂定税率	普通	增值/消费	出口退税	计量单位	监管条件/特殊证件	检验检疫	对美关税	亚太上/下
	---薄膜沉积设备：										
8486.3021	----化学气相沉积设备(CVD)〔999〕	0		30	13/	13	台/千克	/			
8486.3022	----物理气相沉积设备(PVD)〔999〕	0		30	13/	13	台/千克	/			
8486.3029	----其他〔999〕	0		30	13/	13	台/千克	/			
	---将电路图投影或绘制到感光半导体材料上的装置：										
8486.3031	----分布重复光刻机〔999〕	0		100	13/	13	台/千克	/			
8486.3039	----其他〔101 其它机床，102 电子行业成套设备〕	0		100	13/	13	台/千克	/			
	---湿法蚀刻、显影、剥离、清洗装置：										
8486.3041	----超声波清洗装置[T2]	0		30	13/	13	台/千克	/			
8486.3049	----其他[T2]	0		30	13/	13	台/千克	/			
8486.3090	---其他〔101 其它机床，102 电子行业成套设备〕	0		30	13/	13	台/千克	/			
	-本章注释十一(三)规定的机器及装置：										
8486.4010	---主要用于或专用于制作和修复掩膜版(mask)或投影掩膜版(reticle)的装置〔999〕	0		70	13/	13	台/千克	/			
	---主要用于或专用于装配与封装半导体器件或集成电路的设备：										
8486.4021	----塑封机〔999〕	0		30	13/	13	台/千克	/			0/0
8486.4022	----引线键合装置〔999〕	0		30	13/	13	台/千克	/			0/0
8486.4029	----其他〔999〕	0		17	13/	13	台/千克	/			
	---主要用于或专用于升降、装卸、搬运单晶柱、晶圆、半导体器件、集成电路或平板显示器的装置：										
8486.4031	----集成电路工厂专用的自动搬运机器人[T2]	0		20	13/	13	台/千克	/			
8486.4039	----其他[T2]	0		30	13/	13	台/千克	/			0/0
	-零件及附件：										
8486.9010	---升降、搬运、装卸机器用(自动搬运设备用除外)[T2]	0		30	13/	13	千克	/			0/0
8486.9020	---引线键合装置用〔999〕	0		30	13/	13	千克	/			0/0
	---其他：										
8486.9091	----带背板的溅射靶材组件〔999〕	0		17	13/	13	千克	/			
8486.9099	----其他〔999〕	0		17	13/	13	千克	/			
84.87	**本章其他税目未列名的机器零件，不具有电气接插件、绝缘体，线圈、触点或其他电气器材特征的：**										
8487.1000	-船用推进器及桨叶〔999〕	6		14	13/	13	千克	/		26	
8487.9000	-其他〔999〕	8		30	13/	13	千克	/		28	

协定税率 %								RCEP		特惠税率 %			Article Description
东/冰/格	巴基斯坦	韩国	瑞士上/下	哥/秘/柬	澳/毛	新西/坡/智	中国港/澳/台	东盟及马来/澳/韩	日/新	亚太2国	老/柬/缅	98/97/95	
													---Film deposition equipment:
0/0/0	0	0	0/0	0/0/0	0/0	0//0	0/0/	0/0/0	0/0			0/0/0	---- Chemical vapour deposition (CVD) equipment
0/0/0	0	0	0/0	0/0/0	0/0	0//0	0/0/	0/0/0	0/0			0/0/0	----Physical Vapour Deposition (PVD) equipment
0/0/0	0	0	0/0	0/0/0	0/0	0//0	0/0/	0/0/0	0/0			0/0/0	----Other
													---Apparatus for the projection or drawing of circuit patterns on sensitized stmiconductor materials:
0/0/0	0	0	0/0	0/0/0	0/0	0//0	0/0/	0/0/0	0/0			0/0/0	----Step and repeat alignersw
0/0/0	0	0	0/0	0/0/0	0/0	0//0	0/0/	0/0/0	0/0			0/0/0	----Other
													---Apparatus for wet-etching developing stripping or cleaning:
0/0/0	2		0/0	0/0/0	0/0	0/0/0	0/0/	0/0/9	9.1/0			0/0/0	----Ultrasonic apparatus for cleaning
0/0/0	0	0	0/0	0/0/0	0/0	0//0	0/0/	0/0/0	0/0			0/0/0	----Other
0/0/0	0	0	0/0	0/0/0	0/0	0//0	0/0/	0/0/0	0/0			0/0/0	---Other
													-Machines and apparatus specified in Note 11 (c) to this chapter:
0/0/0	0	0	0/0	0/0/0	0/0	0//0	0/0/	0/0/0	0/0			0/0/0	---Apparatus solely or principally of a kind used for the manufacture or repair of masks and reticles
													---Machines solely or principally of a kind used for assembling or encapsulating semiconductor devices or electronic integrated circuits:
0/0/0	0	4.5	0/0	0/0/0	0/0	0//0	0/0/	4.5/4.5/4.8	4.5/4.5			0/0/0	----Plastics encapsulating machines
0/0/0	2		0/0	0/0/0	0/0	0//0	0/0/	0/0/7.2	7.3/0			0/0/0	----Wire bonders
0/0/0	0	0	0/0	0/0/0	0/0	0//0	0/0/	0/0/0	0/0			0/0/0	----Other
													---Apparatus solely or principally of a kind used for lifting, handling, loading or unloading of boules, wafers, semiconductor devices, electronic integrated circuits and flat panel displays:
0/0/0	0	0	0/0	0/0/0	0/0	0//0	0/0/	0/0/0	0/0			0/0/0	----Automated material handling machines solely or principally of a kind used in the electronic integrated circuits factories
0/0/0	0	3.5	0/0	0/0/0	0/0	0//0	0/0/	0/0/4.5	4.5/0			0/0/0	----Other
													-Parts and accessories:
0/0/0	0	0	0/0	0/0/0	0/0	0//0	0/0/	0/0/0	4.8/0			0/0/0	---Of machines for lifting, handling, loading or unloading (other than automated material handling machines)
0/0/0	0	0	0/0	0/0/0	0/0	0//0	0/0/	0/5.4/0	0/5.4			0/0/0	---Of wire bonders
													---Other:
0/0/0	0	0	0/0	0/0/0	0/0	0//0	0/0/	0/0/0	0/0			0/0/0	Componets of sputtering target material with backing
0/0/0	0	0	0/0	0/0/0	0/0	0//0	0/0/	0/0/0	0/0			0/0/0	----Other〔999〕
													Machinery parts, not containing electrical connectors insulators, coils, contacts or other eledrical features, not specified or included cleswhere in this chopter:
0/0/0	0	2.8	0/0	0/0/0	0/0	0//0	0/0/	5.4/5.4/5.4	5.6/5.4			0/0/0	-Ships'or boats'propellers and blades therefor
0/0/0	2	1.6	0.8/0.8	0/0/0	0/0	0//0	0/0/0	0/0/7.2	7.3/0			0/0/0	-other

第八十五章
电机、电气设备及其零件；录音机及放声机、电视图像、声音的录制和重放设备及其零件、附件

注释：

一、本章不包括：

(一)电暖的毯子、褥子、足套及类似品，电暖的衣服、靴、鞋、耳套或其他供人穿戴的电暖物品；

(二)税目70.11的玻璃制品；

(三)税目84.86的机器及装置；

(四)用于医疗、外科、牙科或兽医的真空设备(税目90.18)

(五)第九十四章的电热家具。

二、税目85.01至85.04不适用于税目85.11、85.12、85.40、85.41或85.42的货品。但金属槽汞弧整流器仍归入税目85.04。

三、税号85.07所称"蓄电池"，包括与其一同报验的辅助元件，这些辅助元件具有储电、供电功能，或保护蓄电池免遭损坏，例如，电路连接器、温控装置(例如，热敏电阻)及电路保护装置，也可包括蓄电池的部分保护外壳。

四、税目85.09仅包括通常供家用的下列电动器具：

(一)任何重量的地板打蜡机、食品研磨机及食品搅拌器、水果或蔬菜的榨汁机；

(二)重量不超过20千克的其他机器。

但该税目不适用于风机、风扇或装有风扇的通风罩及循环气罩(不论是否装有过滤器)(税目84.14)、离心干衣机(税目84.21)、洗碟机(税目84.22)、家用洗衣机(税目84.50)、滚筒式或其他形式的熨烫机器(税目84.20或84.51)、缝纫机(税目84.52)、电剪子(税目84.67)或电热器具(税目85.16)。

五、税目85.17所称"智能手机"是指使用蜂窝网络的电话机，其安装有移动操作系统，设计用于实现自动数据处理设备功能，例如，可下载并同时执行多个应用程序(包括第三方应用程序)，并且不论是否集成了如数字照相机、辅助导航系统等其他特征。

六、税目85.23所称：

(一)"固态、非易决性存储器件"(例如，"闪存卡"或"电子闪存卡")，是指带有接口的存储器件，其在同一壳体内包含一个或多个闪存(FLASH E^2 PROM)，以集成电路的形式装配在一块印刷电路板上。它们可以包括一个集成电路形式的控制器及多个分立无源元件，例如，电容器及电阻器；

(二)所称"智能卡"是指装有一个或多个集成电路[微处理器、随机存取存储器(RAM)或只读存储器(ROM)]芯片的卡。这些卡可带有触点、磁条或嵌入式天线，但不包含任何其他有源或无源电路元件。

七、税目85.24所称"平板显示模组"，是指用于显示信息的装置或器具，至少有一个显示屏，设计为在使用前安装于其他税目所列货品中。平板显示模组的显示屏包括但不限于平面、曲面、柔性、可折叠或可拉伸等类型。平板显示模组可装有附加元件，包括接收视频信号所需并将这些信号分配给显示器像素的元件。但是，税目85.24不包括装有转换视频信号的组件(例如，图像缩放集成电路，解码集成电路或程序处理器)的显示模组，或具有其他税目所列货品特征的显示模组。本注释所述平板显示模组在归类时，税目85.24优先于其他税目。

八、税目85.34所称"印刷电路"，是指采用各种印制方法(例如，压印、覆镀、腐蚀)或采用"膜电路"工艺，将导线、接点或其他印制元件(例如，电感器、电阻器、电容器)按预定的图形单独或互相连接地印制在绝缘基片上的电路，但能够产生、整流、调制或放大电信号的元件(例如，半导体元件)除外。

所称"印刷电路"，不包括装有非印制元件的电路，也不包括单个的分立式电阻器、电容器及电感器，但印刷电路可配有非经印刷的连接元件。

用同样工艺制得的无源元件及有源元件组成的薄膜电路或厚膜电路应归入税目85.42。

九、税目85.36所称"光导纤维、光导纤维束或光缆用连接器"，是指在有线数字通讯设备中，简单机械地把光纤端部相连成一线的连接器。它们不具备诸如对信号进行放大、再生或修正等其他功能。

十、税目85.37不包括电视接收机或其他电气设备用的无绳红外遥控器(税目85.43)

十一、税目85.39所称"发光二极管(LED)光源"包括：(一)"发光二极管(LED)模块"，是基于发光二极管的电路构成的电光源，模块中包含电气、机械、热力或者光学等其他元件。模块还装有分立的有源或无源元件，或用于提供或控制电源的税目85.36、85.42的物品。发光二极管(LED)模块没有便于在灯具中安装或更换并确保机械和电气连接的灯头设计。(二)"发光二极管(LED)灯泡(管)"，是由一个或多个带有电气、机械、热力或者光学元件的LED模块组成的电光源。发光二极管(LED)模块与发光二极管(LED)灯泡(管)的区别在于后者有便于在灯具中安装或更换并确保机械和电气连接的灯头设计。

Chapter 85
Electrical machinery and equipment and parts thereof; sound recorders and reproducers, television image and sound recorders and reproducers, and parts and accessories of such articles

Notes:

1. This Chapter does not cover:
   (a) Electrically warmed blankets, bed pads, foot-muffs or the like; electrically warmed clothing, footwear or ear pads or other electrically warmed articles worn on or about the person;
   (b) Articles of glass of heading No. 70. 11.
   (c) Machines and apparaatus of heading 84. 86;
   (d) Vacuum apparatus of a kind used in medical, surgical, dencal or veterinary purposes (Heading No. 90. 18);
   (e) Electrically heated furniture of Chapter 94.
2. HeadingsNo. 85. 01 to 85. 04 do not apply to goods described in headingNo. 85. 11, 85. 12, 85. 40, 85. 41 or 85. 42. However, metal tank mercury arc rectifiers remain classified in headingNo. 85. 04.
3. Heading 85.07 called "battery", including auxiliary components together with its inspection, the auxiliary components has a power storage and power supply function, or protect the battery from damage, for example, circuit connector, temperature control device (e.g., thermistor) and circuit protection device, May also include a battery partial protection housing.
4. HeadingNo. 85. 09 covers only the following electro-mechanical machines of the kind commonly used for domestic purposes:
   (a) Floor polishers, food grinders and mixers, and fruit or vegetable juice extractors, of any weight;
   (b) Other machines provided the weight of such machines does not exceed 20 kg.
   The heading does not, however, apply to fans or ventilating or recycling hoods incorporating a fan, whether or not fitted with filters (headingNo. 84. 14), centrifugal clothes-dryers (headingNo. 84. 21), dish washing machines (headingNo. 84. 22), household washing machines (headingNo. 84. 50), roller or other ironing machines (headingNo. 84. 20 or 84. 51), sewing machines (headingNo. 84. 52), electric scissors (headingNo. 84. 67) or to electro-thermic appliances (headingNo. 85. 16).
5. For the purposes of heading 85.17, the term "smartphones" means telephones for cellular networks, equipped with a mobile operating system designed to perform the functions of an automatic data processing machine such as downloading and running multiple applications simultaneously, including third—party applications, and whether or not integrating other features such as digital cameras and navigational aid systems.
6. For the purposes of heading 85. 23:
   (a) "Solid-state non-volatile storage devices" (for example, "flash memory cards" or "flash electronic storage cards") are storage devices with a connecting socket, comprising in the same housing one or more flash memories (for example, "FLASH E^2PROM") in the form of integrated circuits mounted on a printed circuit board. They may include a controller in the form of an integrated circuit and discrete passive components, such as capacitors and resistors;
   (b) The term "smart cards" means cards which have embedded in them one or more electronic integrated circuits (a microprocessor, random access memory (RAM) or readonly memory (ROM)) in the form of chips. These cards may contain contacts, a magnetic stripe or an embedded antenna but do not contain any other active or passive circuit elements.
7. For the purposes of heading 85.24, "flat panel display modules" refer to devices or apparatus for the display of information, equipped at a minimum with a display screen, which are designed to be incorporated into articles of other headings prior to use. Display screens for flat panel display modules include, but are not limited to, those which are flat, curved, flexible, foldable or stretchable in form. Flat panel display modules may incorporate additional elements, including those necessary for receiving video signals and the allocation of those signals to pixels on the display. However, heading 85.24 does not include display modules which are equipped with components for converting video signals (e.g., a scaler IC, decoder IC or application processer) or have otherwise assumed the character of goods of other headings.
   For the classification of flat panel display modules defined in this Note, heading 85.24 shall take precedence over any other heading in the Nomenclature.
8. For the purposes of headingNo. 85. 34 "printed circuits" are circuits obtained by forming on an insulating base, by any printing process (for example, embossing, plating-up, etching) or by the "film circuit" technique, conductor elements, contacts or other printed components (for example, inductances, resistors, capacitors) alone or interconnected according to a pre-established pattern, other than elements which can produce, rectify, modulate or amplify an electrical signal (for example, semiconductor elements).
   The expression "printed circuits" does not cover circuits combined with elements other than those obtained during the printing process, nor does it cover individual, discrete resistors, capacitors or inductances.
   Thinor thick-film circuits comprising passive and active elements obtained during the same technological process are to be classified in heading No. 85. 42.
9. For the purpose of heading 85. 36. "connectors for opticalfl bres, optical fibre bundles or cables" means connectors that simply mechanically align optical fibres end to end in a ligital line system. They perform on other function, such as the am plification, regeneration or modification of a signal.
10. Heading 85. 37 does not include cordless infrared devices for the remote control of television receivers or other electrical quipment (heading 85. 43).
11. For the purposes of heading 85.39, the expression "light—emitting diode (LED) light sources" covers : (a) "Light—emitting diode (LED) modules" which are electrical light sources based on light—emitting diodes (LED) arranged in electrical circuits and containing further elements like electrical, mechanical, thermal or optical elements. They also contain discrete active elements, discrete passive elements, or articles of heading 85.36 or 85.42 for the purposes of providing power supply or power control. Light—emitting diode (LED) modules do not have a cap designed to allow easy installation or replacement in a luminaire and ensure mechanical and electrical contact. (b) "Light—emitting diode (LED) lamps" which are electrical light sources containing one or more LED modules containing further elements like electrical, mechanical, thermal or optical elements. The distinction between light—emitting diode (LED) modules and light— emitting diode (LED) lamps is that lamps have a cap designed to allow easy installation or replacement in a luminaire and ensure mechanical and electrical contact."

十二、税目 85.41 及 85.42 所称：

(一)1."半导体器件"是指那些依靠外加电场引起电阻率的变化而进行工作的半导体器件，或半导体基换能器。半导体器件也可以包括由多个元件组装在一起的组件，无论是否有起辅助功能的有源和无源元件。本定义所称"半导体基换能器"是指半导体基传感器、半导体基执行器、半导体基谐振器和半导体基振荡器。这些是不同类型的半导体基分立器件，能实现固有的功能，即可以将任何物理、化学现象或活动转换为电信号，或者将电信号转换为任何物理现象或活动。半导体基换能器内的所有元件都不可分割地组合在一起，它们也包括为实现其结构或功能而不可分割地连接在一起的必要材料。下列名词的含义是：

(1)"半导体基"是指用半导体技术，在半导体基片上构建、制造或由半导体材料制造。半导体基片或材料在换能器的作用和性能中起到不可替代的关键作用，其工作是基于半导体的物理、电气、化学和光学等特性。

(2)"物理或化学现象"是指诸如压力、声波、加速度、振动、运动、方向、张力、磁场强度、电场强度、光、放射性、湿度、流量和化学浓度等。

(3)半导体基传感器是一种半导体器件，其由在半导体材料内部或表面制作的微电子或机械结构组成，具有探测物理量和化学量并将其转换成电信号(因电特性变化或机械结构位移而产生)的功能。

(4)半导体基执行器是一种半导体器件，其由在半导体材料内部或表面制作的微电子或机械结构组成，具有将电信号转换成物理运动的功能。

(5)半导体基谐振器是一种半导体器件，其由在半导体材料内部或表面制作的微电子或机械结构组成，具有按预先设定的频率产生机械或电振荡的功能，频率取决于响应外部输入的结构的物理参数。

(6)半导体基振荡器是一种半导体器件，其由在半导体材料内部或表面制作的微电子或机械结构组成，具有按预先设定的频率产生机械或电振荡的功能，频率取决于这些结构的物理参数。

2."发光二极管(LED)"是半导体器件，基于可将电能变成可见光、红外线或紫外线的半导体材料，不论这些器件之间是否通过电路连接以及不论是否带有保护二极管。税目 85.41 的发光二极管(LED)不装有以提供或控制电源为目的的元件。

(二)"集成电路"，是指：

1.单片集成电路，即电路元件(二极管、晶体管、电阻器、电容器、电感器等)主要整体制作在一片半导体材料或化合物半导体材料(例如，掺杂硅、砷化镓、硅锗或磷化铟)基片的表面，并不可分割地连接在一起的电路。

2.混合集成电路，即通过薄膜或厚膜工艺制得的无源元件(电阻器、电容器、电感器等)和通过半导体工艺制得的有源元件(二极管、晶体管、单片集成电路等)用互连或连接线实际上不可分割地组合在同一绝缘基片(玻璃、陶瓷等)上的电路。这种电路也可包括分立元件。

3.多芯片集成电路是由两个或多个单片集成电路实际上不可分割地组合在一片或多片绝缘基片上构成的电路，不论是否带有引线框架，但不带有其他有源或无源的电路元件。

4.多元件集成电路(MCOs)：由一个或多个单片、混合或多芯片集成电路以及下列至少一个元件组成：硅基传感器、执行器、振荡器、谐振器或其组件所构成的组合体，或者具有税目 85.32、85.33、85.41 所列货品功能的元件，或税目 85.04 的电感器。其像集成电路一样实际上不可分割地组合成一体，作为一种元件，通过引脚、引线、焊球、底面触点、凸点或导电压点进行连接，组装到印刷电路板(PCB)或其他载体上。

在本定义中：

(1)元件可以是分立的，独立制造后组装到多元件(MCO)的其余部分上，或者集成到其他元件内。

(2)"硅基"是指在硅基片上制造，或由硅材料制造而成，或者制造在集成电路裸片上。

(3)①硅基传感器是由在半导体材料内部或表面制作的微电子或机械结构组成，具有探测物理或化学现象并将其转换成电信号(因电特性变化或机械结构位移而产生)的功能。"物理或化学现象"是指诸如压力、声波、加速度、振动、运动、方向、张力、磁场强度、电场强度、光、放射性、湿度、流量和化学浓度等现象。

②硅基执行器是由在半导体材料内部或表面制作的微电子或机械结构组成，具有将电信号转换成物理运动的功能。

③硅基谐振器是由在半导体材料内部或表面制作的微电子或机械结构组成，具有按预先设定的频率产生机械或电振荡的功能，频率取决于响应外部输入的结构的物理参数。

④硅基振荡器是由在半导体材料内部或表面制作的微电子或机械结构组成，具有按预先设定的频率产生机械或电振荡的功能，频率取决于这些结构的物理参数。本注释所述物品在归类时，即使本协调制度其他税目涉及到上述物品，尤其是物品的功能，仍应优先考虑归入税目 85.41 及 85.42，但涉及税目 85.23 的情况除外。

12. For the classification of the articles defined in this Note, headings 85.41 and 85.42 shall thke precedence over any other headings in the Nomenclature, except in the case of heading 85.23, which might cover them by reference to, in paricular, their function.

(a)(i)"Semiconductor devices" are semiconductor devices the operation of which depends on variations in resistivity on the application of an electric field or semiconductor—based transducers. Semiconductor devices may also include assembly of plural elements, whether or not equipped with active and passive device ancillary functions."Semiconductor—based transducers" are, for the purposes of this definition, semiconductor—based sensors, semiconductor—based actuators, semiconductor—based resonators and semiconductor—based oscillators, which are types of discrete semiconductor—based devices, which perform an intrinsic function, which are able to convert any kind of physical or chemical phenomena or an action into an electrical signal or an electrical signal into any type of physical phenomenon or an action. All the elements in semiconductor—based transducers are indivisibly combined, and may also include necessary materials indivisibly attached, that enable their construction or function. The following expressions mean :

(1)"Semiconductor—based" means built or manufactured on a semiconductor substrate or made of semiconductor materials, manufactured by semiconductor technology, in which the semiconductor substrate or material plays a critical and unreplaceable role of transducer function and performance, and the operation of which is based on semiconductor properties including physical, electrical, chemical and optical properties.

(2)"Physical or chemical phenomena" relate to phenomena, suchas pressure, acoustic waves, acceleration, vibration, movement, orientation, strain, magnetic field strength, electric field strength, light, radioactivity, humidity, flow, chemicals concentration, etc.

(3)"Semiconductor—based sensor" is a type of semiconductor device, which consists of microelectronic or mechanical structures that are created in the mass or on the surface of a semiconductor and that have the function of detecting physical or chemical quantities and converting these into electric signals caused by resulting variations in electric properties or displacement of a mechanical structure.

(4)"Semiconductor—based actuator" is a type of semiconductordevice, which consists of microelectronic or mechanical structures that are created in the mass or on the surface of a semiconductor and that have the function of converting electric signals into physical movement.

(5)"Semiconductor—based resonator" is a type of semiconductordevice, which consists of microelectronic or mechanical structures that are created in the mass or on the surface of a semiconductor and that have the function of generating a mechanical or electrical oscillation of a predefined frequency that depends on the physical geometry of these structures in response to an external input.

(6) "Semiconductor—based oscillator" is a type of semiconductor device, which consists of microelectronic or mechanical structures that are created in the mass or on the surface of a semiconductor and that have the function of generating a mechanical or electrical oscillation of a predefined frequency that depends on the physical geometry of these structures.

(ii)"Light—emitting diodes (LED)" are semiconductor devices based on semiconductor materials which convert electrical energy into visible, infra—red or ultra—violet rays, whether or not electrically connected among each other and whether or not combined with protective diodes. Light—emitting diodes (LED) of heading 85.41 do not incorporate elements for the purposes of providing power supply or power control;".

(b)"Electronic integrated circuits" are:

(i) Monolithic integrated circuits in which the circuit elements(diodes, transistors resistors capacitors, interconnections, etc) are created in the mass (essentially) and on the surface of a semiconductor or compound semiconductor materical (for example, doped silicon, gallium arsenide silicon, gemanium indium phospide) and are inseparably associated;

(ii) Hybrid integrated circuits in which passive elements (resistors, capacitors, inductances, etc), obtained by thin-or thick-film technology, and active elements (diodes, transistors, monolithic integrated circuits, etc.), obtained by semiconductor technology, are combined to all intents and purposes indivisibly, by interconne cltions or interconnecting cables on a single insulating substrate (glass, ceramic, etc.). These circuits may also include discrete components;

(iii) Multichip integrated circuits consisting of two or more interconnected monolithic integrated circuits combined to all intents and purposes indivisibly, whether or not on one or more insulating substrates, with or without leadframes, but with no other active or passive circuit elements.

(iv) Multi element integrated circuit (MCOs) is composed of one or more single, mixed or multi chip integrated circuit and at least containing one of the following components: the combination of silicon sensor, actuator, oscillator, resonator or its components, or with heading No.85.32, 85.33, 85.41 items of commodities listed in the function components. Inductor of heading 85.04. In fact, the same is inseparably integrated like integrated circuits, as an components, through the pin, lead wire, solder ball, bottom contact, bump or conductive pressure points are connected to the printed circuit board assembly (PCB) or other carrier, through the connecting of pins, leads, balls, lands, bumps, or pads.

For the purpose ot this definition:

(i)"Components" may be discrete, manu factured independently then assembled onto the rest of the MCO, or integrated into other components.

(ii)"Silicon based" means built on a silicon substrate, or made of silicon materials, or manufactured onto integrated circuit die.

(iii) a)"Silicon based sensors" consist of microelectronic or meehanical strue tures that are created in the nlass or on the surface of a semiconductor and that have the function of detecting physical or chemical quantities and transducing these into electric signals, caused by resulting variations in electric properties or displacement 0f a mechanical structure. "Physical or chemical quantities" relates tO real world phenomena, such as pressure, acoustic waves, acceleration, vibration, movement, orientation, strain, magnetic field strength, electric field strength, light, radioaclivity, humidity, flow, ehemi eals concentration, etc.

b)"Silicon based actuators" consist of microelectronic and mechanical structures that are created in the mass or on the surface of a semiconductor and that have the function of converting e lectrical signals into physical movement.

c)"Silicon based resonators" are components that consist of microelec tronic or mechanical structures that are created in the mass or on the surface of a semiconductor and have the function of generating a mechanical or electrical oscillation of a predefined frequency that depends on the physical geometry of these structures in re sponse to an external input.

d)"Silicon based oscillators" are active components that consist of micro electronic or mechanical structures that are created in the mass or on the surface of a semieond uctor and that have the function of generating a mechanical or electrical oscillation of a predefined frequency that depends on the physical geometry of these structures.

子目注释：

一、子目 8525.81 仅包括具有以下一项或多项特征的高速电视摄像机、数字照相机及视频摄录一体机：写入速度超过 0.5 毫米/微秒；时间分辨率 50 纳秒或更短；帧速率超过 225,000 帧/秒。

二、子目 8525.82 所称抗辐射或耐辐射电视摄像机、数字照相机及视频摄录一体机，是指经设计或防护以能在高辐射环境中工作。这些设备可承受至少 50×10^3 Gy(Si)〔5×10^6 RAD(Si)〕的总辐射剂量而不会使其操作性能退化。

三、子目 8525.83 包括夜视电视摄像机、数字照相机及视频摄录一体机，这些设备通过光阴极将捕获的光转换为电子，再将其放大和转换以形成可见图像。本子目不包括热成像的摄像机或照相机（通常归入子目 8525.89）。

四、子目号 8527.12 仅包括有内置放大器但无内置扬声器的盒式磁带放声机，它不需外接电源即能工作，且外形尺寸不超过 170 毫米×100 毫米×45 毫米。

五、子目 8549.11 至 8549.19 所称“废原电池、废原电池组及废蓄电池”是指因破损、拆解、耗尽或其他原因而不能再使用或不能再充电的电池。

税则号列	货品名称〔CIQ 扩展编码及品名－T2 表示见附表 2〕	最惠(%)	暂定税率	普通	增值/消费	出口退税	计量单位	监管条件/特殊证件	检验检疫	对美关税	亚太上/下
85.01	电动机及发电机（不包括发电机组）：										
	-输出功率不超过 37.5 瓦的电动机：										
8501.1010	---玩具用〔999〕	12		80	13/	13	台/千克	/			7.8/7.8
	---其他：										
8501.1091	----微电机，机座尺寸在 20 毫米及以上，但不超过 39 毫米										
8501.1091 01	激光视盘机机芯精密微型电机（1 瓦≤功率＜18 瓦，20mm≤直径≤30mm）〔999〕	9	5	70	13/	13	台/千克	/		30	5.9/5.9
8501.1091 02	摄像机、摄录一体机用精密微型电机（0.5 瓦≤功率≤10 瓦），20mm≤直径≤39mm）〔999〕	9	5	70	13/	13	台/千克	/		30	5.9/5.9
8501.1091 90	其他机座最大尺寸在 20mm 至 39mm 微电机（输出功率不超过 37.5 瓦）〔999〕	9		70	13/	13	台/千克	/		34	5.9/5.9
8501.1099	----其他										
8501.1099 01	功率≤0.5W 非用于激光视盘机机芯的微型电机（圆柱形直径≤6mm，高≤25mm；扁圆型直径≤15mm，厚≤5mm）〔999〕	9	5	35	13/	13	台/千克	/		30	5.9/5.9
8501.1099 02	激光视盘机机芯用精密微型电机（0.5 瓦≤功率≤2 瓦），5mm≤直径≤20mm〔999〕	9	5	35	13/	13	台/千克	/		30	5.9/5.9
8501.1099 03	摄像机、摄录一体机用精密微型电机（0.5 瓦≤功率≤10 瓦，5mm≤直径＜20mm 或 39mm＜直径≤40mm）〔999〕	9	5	35	13/	13	台/千克	/		30	5.9/5.9
8501.1099 90	其他微电机（输出功率不超过 37.5 瓦）〔101 玩具电机，102 微电机〕	9		35	13/	13	台/千克	/		34	5.9/5.9
8501.2000	-交直流两用电动机，输出功率超过 37.5 瓦〔999〕	12		35	13/	13	台/千克	/	L	32	
	-其他直流电动机；直流发电机；不包括光伏发电机：										
8501.3100	--输出功率不超过 750 瓦〔101 微电机，102 直流电动机，103 其它发电机（组）及其零件〕	12		35	13/	13	台/千克	/	L		7.8/7.8
8501.3200	--输出功率超过 750 瓦，但不超过 75 千瓦〔101 直流电动机，102 其它发电机（组）及其零件〕	10		35	13/	13	台/千克	/	L	25	
8501.3300	--输出功率超过 75 千瓦，但不超过 375 千瓦〔101 直流电动机，102 其它发电机（组）及其零件〕	5		35	13/	13	台/千克	/		25	
8501.3400	--输出功率超过 375 千瓦〔101 直流电动机，102 其它发电机（组）及其零件〕	10		35	13/	13	台/千克	/		30	
8501.4000	-其他单相交流电动机〔999〕	10		35	13/	13	台/千克	/	L	30	
	-其他多相交流电动机：										
8501.5100	--输出功率不超过 750 瓦										
8501.5100 10	发电机（功率≥40 瓦特，频率 600 至 2000 赫兹，谐波畸变低于 10%等）〔999〕	5		35	13/	13	台/千克	3/		30	
8501.5100 90	其他输出功率≤750W 多相交流电动机〔999〕	5		35	13/	13	台/千克	/	L	30	
8501.5200	--输出功率超过 750 瓦，但不超过 75 千瓦〔999〕	10		35	13/	13	台/千克	/	L		
8501.5300	--输出功率超过 75 千瓦〔999〕	10		35	13/	13	台/千克	/		30	6.5/6.5
	-交流发电机，不包括光伏发电机：										
8501.6100	--输出功率不超过 75 千伏安〔999〕	5		30	13/	13	台/千克	/		25	
8501.6200	--输出功率超过 75 千伏安，但不超过 375 千伏安〔999〕	10		30	13/	13	台/千克	/		15	
8501.6300	--输出功率超过 375 千伏安，但不超过 750 千伏安〔999〕	10		30	13/	13	台/千克	/		30	
	--输出功率超过 750 千伏安：										
8501.6410	---输出功率超过 750 千伏安，但不超过 350 兆伏安										
8501.6410 10	由使用可再生燃料锅炉和涡轮机组驱动的交流发电机，750KVA＜输出功率≤350MVA〔999〕	10	5	30	13/	13	台/千克	O/		25	
8501.6410 90	其他 750KVA＜输出功率≤350MVA 的交流发电机（不包括光伏发电机）〔999〕	10		30	13/	13	台/千克	O/		30	
8501.6420	---输出功率超过 350 兆伏安，但不超过 665 兆伏安										

Subheading Notes:

1. Subheading 8525.81 covers only high—speed television cameras, digital cameras and video camera recorders having one or more of the following characteristics : — writing speed exceeding 0.5 mm per microsecond; — time resolution 50 nanoseconds or less; — frame rate exceeding 225,000 frames per second.
2. In respect of subheading 8525.82, radiation—hardened or radiation—tolerant television cameras, digital cameras and video camera recorders are designed or shielded to enable operation in a high—radiation environment. These cameras are designed to withstand a total radiation dose of at least 50 × 103 Gy(silicon) (5 × 106 RAD (silicon)), without operational degradation.
3. Subheading 8525.83 covers night vision television cameras, digital cameras and video camera recorders which use a photocathode to convert available light to electrons, which can be amplified and converted to yield a visible image. This subheading excludes thermal imaging cameras(generally subheading 8525.89)."
4. Subheadings 8527. 12 cover only cassetteplayers with built-in amplifier, without built-in loudspeaker, capable of operating without an external source of electric power and the dimensions of which do not exceed 170mm×100mm×45mm.
5. For the purposes of subheadings 8549.11 to 8549.19, "spent primary cells, spent primary batteries and spent electric accumulators" are those which are neither usable as such because of breakage, cutting—up, wear or other reasons, nor capable of being recharged."

协定税率 %								RCEP		特惠税率 %			Article Description
东/冰/格	巴基斯坦	韩国	瑞士上/下	哥/秘/柬	澳/毛	新西/坡/智	中国港/澳/台	东盟及马来/澳/韩	日/新	亚太2国	老/柬/缅	98/97/95	
													Electric motors and generators (excluding generating sets):
													-Motors of an output not exceeding 37. 5W:
0/0/0	18.6	14.7	2.5/2.5	0/0/0	0/14.7	0/0/0	0/0/0	23.3/23.3/	23.3/23.3			0/0/0	---For use in toys
													---Other:
													----Micromotors with a housing size of 20mm or more but not exceeding 39mm
0/0/0	2	4.2	0.9/0.9	0/0/0	0/0	0/0/0	0/0/	8.4/8.6/8.4	8.4/8.6			0/0/0	Precision micromotors for the movement of laser disc players (1W≤power≤18W,20mm≤diameter≤30mm)
0/0/0	2	4.2	0.9/0.9	0/0/0	0/0	0/0/0	0/0/	8.4/8.6/8.4	8.4/8.6			0/0/0	Micro motor with a video camera, camcorder (0.5W≤ power ≤ 10W), 20mm ≤ diameter ≤ 39mm)
0/0/0	2	4.2	0.9/0.9	0/0/0	0/0	0/0/0	0/0/	8.4/8.6/8.4	8.4/8.6			0/0/0	Other micromotors with a housing size of 20mm or more but not exceeding 39mm (output≤37. 5W)
													----Other
0/0/0	3.5	4.2	0.9/0.9	0/0/0	0/0	0/0/0	0/0/0	8.4/8.6/8.4	8.4/8.6			0/0/0	Micromotors,power≤0. 5W, not for movements of laser disc players(cylindricd diameter≤6mm, high≤25mm; oblate diameter≤15mm, thick≤5mm)
0/0/0	3.5	4.2	0.9/0.9	0/0/0	0/0	0/0/0	0/0/0	8.4/8.6/8.4	8.4/8.6			0/0/0	Precision micro motor with laser videodisc (0.5≤power ≤ 2W), 5mm ≤ diameter ≤ 20mm
0/0/0	3.5	4.2	0.9/0.9	0/0/0	0/0	0/0/0	0/0/0	8.4/8.6/8.4	8.4/8.6			0/0/0	Precision micromotors for video camera, camcorder, movement of laser discplayers(0.5W≤power≤2W,5mm≤Diameter<20mm Or 39 mm< diameter≤ 40 mm)
0/0/0	3.5	4.2	0.9/0.9	0/0/0	0/0	0/0/0	0/0/0	8.4/8.6/8.4	8.4/8.6			0/0/0	Other micromotors(output power≤37. 5W)
0/0/0	4.2	2.4	1.2/1.2	0/0/0	0/0	0/0/0	0/0/	0/0/10.8	10.9/0			0/0/0	-Universal AC/DC motors of an output exceeding 37. 5 W
													-Other DC motors; DC generators; excluding photovoltaic generator
0/0/0	4.8	7.8	0/0	0/0/0	0/0	0/0/0	0/0/0	5/5/6	6/5			0/0/0	--Of an output not exceeding 750 W
0/0/0	2	2	0/0	0/0/0	0/0	0/0/0	0/0/	0/0/9	9.1/0			0/0/0	--Of an output exceeding 750 W but not exceeding 75 kW
0/0/0	0	0	0/0	0/0/0	0/0	0//0	0/0/	0/0/0	0/0			0/0/0	--Of an output exceeding 75 kW but not exceeding 375 kW
0/0/0	4.2	7.2	1.2/1.2	0/0/0	0/0	0/0/0	0/0/	11.4/11.4/	/11.4			0/0/0	--Of an output exceeding 375 kW
0/0/0	4.2	5.6	1.2/1.2	0/0/0	0/0	0/0/0	0/0/	11.2/11.4/11.2	11.3/11.4			0/0/0	-Other AC motors, single-phase
													-Other AC motors, multi-phase:
													--Of an output not exceeding 750 W
0/0/0	0		0/0	0/0/0	0/0	0//0	0/0/	4.9/4.9/	/4.9			0/0/0	Generators(power≥40W, frequency = 600 ~ 2000Hz, harmonic distortion<10%)
0/0/0	0		0/0	0/0/0	0/0	0//0	0/0/	4.9/4.9/	/4.9			0/0/0	Other AC motors, multi-phase, output power≤750W
0/0/0	3.5	6	1/1	0/0/0	0/0	0/0/0	0/0/	9.5/9.5/9.5	9.5/9.5			0/0/0	--Of an output exceeding 750 W but not exceeding 75 kW
0/0/0	4.2	5.6	1.2/1.2	0/0/0	0/0	0/0/0	0/0/	11.2/11.4/11.2	11.3/11.4			0/0/0	--Of an output exceeding 75 kW
													-AC generators (alternators); excluding photovoltaic generator
0/0/0	0	1	0/0	0/0/0	0/0	0//0	0/0/	0/0/4.5	4.5/0			0/0/0	--Of an output not exceeding 75 kVA
0/0/0	4.2	7.2	1.2/1.2	0/0/0	0/0	0/0/0	0/0/	11.4/11.4/	/11.4			0/0/0	--Of an output exceeding 75 KVA but not exceeding 375 kVA
0/0/0	4.2	7.2	1.2/1.2	0/0/0	0/0	0/0/0	0/0/	11.4/11.4/	/11.4			0/0/0	--Of an output exceeding 375 KVA but not exceeding 750 kVA
													--Of an output exceeding 750 kVA:
													---Of an output exceeding 750 kVA but not exceeding 350 MVA
0/0/0	2	6	0/0	0/0/0	0/0	0/0/0	0/0/	9.5/9.5/	9.5/9.5			0/0/0	By the use of renewable fuel boiler and turbine drive the alternator, <750 kva power output of 350 mva or less
0/0/0	2	6	0/0	0/0/0	0/0	0/0/0	0/0/	9.5/9.5/	9.5/9.5			0/0/0	Other 750kva < output power ≤ 350MVA alternator (excluding photovoltaic generator)
													---Of an output exceeding 350 MVA but not exceeding 665 MVA

税则号列		货品名称〔CIQ 扩展编码及品名—T2 表示见附表 2〕	最惠(%)	暂定税率	普通	增值/消费	出口退税	计量单位	监管条件/特殊证件	检验检疫	对美关税	亚太上/下
8501.6420	10	由使用可再生燃料锅炉和涡轮机组驱动的交流发电机，350MVA＜输出功率≤665MVA〔999〕	5.5	5	14	13/	13	台/千克	/			3.6/3.6
8501.6420	90	其他 350MVA＜输出功率≤665MVA 交流发电机(不包括光伏发电机)〔999〕	5.5		14	13/	13	台/千克	O/			3.6/3.6
8501.6430		---输出功率超过 665 兆伏安										
8501.6430	10	由使用可再生燃料锅炉和涡轮机组驱动的交流发电机，输出功率＞665MVA〔999〕	6	5	11	13/	13	台/千克	/		10	3.9/3.9
8501.6430	90	其他输出功率＞665MVA 交流发电机(不包括光伏发电机)〔999〕	6		11	13/	13	台/千克	/		11	3.9/3.9
		-光伏直流发电机：										
8501.7100		--输出功率不超过 50 瓦〔101 微电机，102 直流电动机，103 其它发电机(组)及其零件〕	12		35	13/	13	台/千克	/	L		7.8/7.8
		--输出功率超过 50 瓦：										
8501.7210		---输出功率超过 50 瓦，但不超过 750 瓦〔101 微电机，102 直流电动机，103 其它发电机(组)及其零件〕	12		35	13/	13	台/千克	/	L		7.8/7.8
8501.7220		---输出功率超过 750 瓦，但不超过 75 千瓦〔101 直流电动机，102 其它发电机(组)及其零件〕	10		35	13/	13	台/千克	/	L	25	
8501.7230		---输出功率超过 75 千瓦，但不超过 375 千瓦〔101 直流电动机，102 其它发电机(组)及其零件〕	5		35	13/	13	台/千克	/		25	
8501.7240		---输出功率超过 375 千瓦〔101 直流电动机，102 其它发电机(组)及其零件〕	10		35	13/	13	台/千克	/		30	
		-光伏交流发电机：										
8501.8010		---输出功率不超过 75 千伏安〔999〕	5		30	13/	13	台/千克	/		25	
8501.8020		---输出功率超过 75 千伏安，但不超过 375 千伏安〔999〕	10		30	13/	13	台/千克	/		15	
8501.8030		---输出功率超过 375 千伏安，但不超过 750 千伏安〔999〕	10		30	13/	13	台/千克	/		30	
		---输出功率超过 750 千伏安：										
8501.8041		----输出功率超过 750 千伏安，但不超过 350 兆伏安〔999〕	10		30	13/	13	台/千克	O/		30	
8501.8042		----输出功率超过 350 兆伏安，但不超过 665 兆伏安〔999〕	5.5		14	13/	13	台/千克	O/			3.6/3.6
8501.8043		----输出功率超过 665 兆伏安〔999〕	6		11	13/	13	台/千克	/		11	3.9/3.9
85.02		**发电机组及旋转式变流机：**										
		-装有压燃式活塞内燃发动机(柴油或半柴油发动机)的发电机组：										
8502.1100		--输出功率不超过 75 千伏安〔999〕	10		45	13/	13	台/千克	/		15	
8502.1200		--输出功率超过 75 千伏安，但不超过 375 千伏安〔999〕	10		45	13/	13	台/千克	O/		30	
		--输出功率超过 375 千伏安：										
8502.1310		---输出功率超过 375 千伏安，但不超过 2 兆伏安〔999〕	10		45	13/	13	台/千克	O/		25	6.5/6.5
8502.1320		---输出功率超过 2 兆伏安〔999〕	10		30	13/	13	台/千克	O/		30	7/7
8502.2000		-装有点燃式活塞内燃发动机的发电机组〔999〕	10		45	13/	13	台/千克	/		35	
		-其他发电机组：										
8502.3100		--风力驱动的〔999〕	8	5	30	13/	13	台/千克	/		30	
8502.3900		--其他										
8502.3900	10	依靠可再生能源(太阳能、小水电、潮汐、沼气、地热能、生物质/余热驱动的汽轮机)生产电力的发电机组〔999〕	10	5	30	13/	13	台/千克	/		10	
8502.3900	90	其他发电机组(风力驱动除外)〔999〕	10		30	13/	13	台/千克	/		15	
8502.4000		-旋转式变流机〔999〕	10		30	13/	13	台/千克	/			
85.03		**专用于或主要用于税目 85.01 或 85.02 所列机器的零件：**										
8503.0010		---税号 8501.1010 及 8501.1091 所列电动机用〔999〕	8		70	13/	13	千克	/		33	5.2/5.2
8503.0020		---税号 8501.6420 及 8501.6430 所列发电机用〔999〕	3		11	13/	13	千克	/		28	2/2
8503.0030		---税号 8502.3100 所列发电机组用〔999〕	3	1	30	13/	13	千克	/		26	2.5/2.5
8503.0090		---其他										
8503.0090	10	电动机定子(用于真空中频率 600－2000Hz、功率 50－1000VA 条件下)〔999〕	8		30	13/	13	千克	3/		33	5.2/5.2
8503.0090	20	由使用可再生燃料锅炉和涡轮机组驱动的输出功率超过 750 千伏安不超过 350 兆伏安的交流发电机的零件〔999〕	8	5	30	13/	13	千克	/		30	5.2/5.2
8503.0090	30	靠可再生能源(太阳能、小水电、潮汐、沼气、地热能、生物质/余热驱动的汽轮机)生产电力发电机组的零件〔999〕	8	5	30	13/	13	千克	/		30	5.2/5.2
8503.0090	40	飞机发动机用交流发电机定子〔999〕	8	1	30	13/	13	千克	/		26	5.2/5.2
8503.0090	50	燃料电池用膜电极组件(主要由质子交换膜、催化剂和气体扩散层构成)〔999〕	8	4	30	13/	13	千克	/		29	5.2/5.2
8503.0090	60	燃料电池用双极板〔999〕	8	4	30	13/	13	千克	/		29	5.2/5.2
8503.0090	90	其他电动机、发电机(组)零件〔999〕	8		30	13/	13	千克	/		33	5.2/5.2

协定税率 %								RCEP		特惠税率 %			Article Description
东/冰/格	巴基斯坦	韩国	瑞士上/下	哥/秘/柬	澳/毛	新西/坡/智	中国港/澳/台	东盟及马来/澳/韩	日/新	亚太2国	老/柬/缅	98/97/95	
0/0/0	0	0	0/0	0/0/0	0/0	0//0	0/0/	0/5.2/0	0/5.2			0/0/0	By the use of renewable fuel boiler and turbine drive the alternator, 350 mva power output of 665 mva or less
0/0/0	0	0	0/0	0/0/0	0/0	0//0	0/0/	0/5.2/0	0/5.2			0/0/0	Other 350MVA < output power ≤ 665mva alternator (excluding photovoltaic generator)
													---Of an output exceeding 665 MVA
0/0/0	0	0	0/0	0/0/0	0/0	0//0	0/0/	5.4/5.4/5.4	5.6/5.4			0/0/0	By the use of renewable fuel boiler and turbine drive the alternator, output>665 mva
0/0/0	0	0	0/0	0/0/0	0/0	0//0	0/0/	5.4/5.4/5.4	5.6/5.4			0/0/0	Other alternator with output power > 665mva (excluding photovoltaic generator)
													-photovoltaic DC generator:
0/0/0	4.8	7.8	0/0	0/0/0	0/0	0/0/0	0/0/0	5/5/6	6/5			0/0/0	--Of an output not exceeding 50 W
													--Of an output exceeding 50 W
0/0/0	4.8	7.8	0/0	0/0/0	0/0	0/0/0	0/0/0	5/5/6	6/5			0/0/0	---Of an output exceeding 50 W but not exceeding 750 W
0/0/0	2	2	0/0	0/0/0	0/0	0/0/0	0/0/	0/0/9	9.1/0			0/0/0	---Of an output exceeding 750 W but not exceeding 75 kW
0/0/0	0	0	0/0	0/0/0	0/0	0//0	0/0/	0/0/0	0/0			0/0/0	---Of an output exceeding 75 kW but not exceeding 375 kW
0/0/0	4.2	7.2	1.2/1.2	0/0/0	0/0	0/0/0	0/0/	11.4/11.4/	/11.4			0/0/0	---Of an output exceeding 375 kW
													-Photovoltaic DC generator
0/0/0	0	1	0/0	0/0/0	0/0	0//0	0/0/	0/0/4.5	4.5/0			0/0/0	---Of an output not exceeding 75 kVA
0/0/0	4.2	7.2	1.2/1.2	0/0/0	0/0	0/0/0	0/0/	11.4/11.4/	/11.4			0/0/0	---Of an output exceeding 75 kVA but not exceeding 375 kVA
0/0/0	4.2	7.2	1.2/1.2	0/0/0	0/0	0/0/0	0/0/	11.4/11.4/	/11.4			0/0/0	---Of an output exceeding 375 kVA but not exceeding 750 kVA
													---Of an output exceeding 750 kVA
0/0/0	2	6	0/0	0/0/0	0/0	0/0/0	0/0/	9.5/9.5/	9.5/9.5			0/0/0	----Of an output exceeding 750 kVA but not exceeding 350 MVA
0/0/0	0	0	0/0	0/0/0	0/0	0//0	0/0/	0/5.2/0	0/5.2			0/0/0	----Of an output exceeding 350 MVA but not exceeding 665 MVA
0/0/0	0	0	0/0	0/0/0	0/0	0//0	0/0/	5.4/5.4/5.4	5.6/5.4			0/0/0	----Of an output exceeding 665 MVA
													Electric generating sets and rotary converters:
													-Generating sets with compression-ignition internal combustion piston engines (diesel or semi-diesel engines):
0/0/0	2	2	0/0	0/0/0	0/0	0/0/0	0/0/	0/0/9	9.1/0			0/0/0	--Of an output not exceeding 75 kVA
0/0/0	2	4.6	0/0	0/0/0	0/0	0/0/0	0/0/	9.3/9.5/9.3	9.4/9.5			0/0/0	--Of an output exceeding 75 kVA but not exceeding 375 kVA
													--Of an output exceeding 375 kVA:
0/0/0	2	6	0/0	0/0/0	0/0	0/0/0	0/0/	9.5/9.5/9.5	9.5/9.5			0/0/0	---Of an output exceeding 375 kVA but not exceeding 2 MVA
0/0/0	2	6	0/0	0/0/0	0/0	0/0/0	0/0/	9.5/9.5/9.5	9.5/9.5			0/0/0	---Of an output exceeding 2 MVA
0/0/0	3.5	2	0/0	0/0/0	0/0	0/0/0	0/0/	0/0/9	9.1/0			0/0/0	-Generating sets with spark-ignition internal combustion piston engines
													-Other generating sets:
0/0/0	2	3.7	0/0	0/0/0	0/0	0//0	0/0/	0/0/7.2	7.3/0			0/0/0	--Wind-powered
													Other
0/0/0	2	4.6	0/0	0/0/0	0/0	0//0	0/0/	9.3/9.5/9.3	9.4/9.5			0/0/0	Rely on renewable energy (solar, small hydropower, tidal, methane gas, geothermal energy, biomass/waste heat driven turbine) in the production of electric power generating set
0/0/0	2	4.6	0/0	0/0/0	0/0	0//0	0/0/	9.3/9.5/9.3	9.4/9.5			0/0/0	Other units(except wind driven)
0/0/0	2	2	0/0	0/0/0	0/0	0//0	0/0/	0/0/9	9.1/0			0/0/0	-Electric rotary converters
													Parts suitable for use solely or principally with the machines of headingNo. 85. 01 or 85. 02:
0/0/0	4.2	7.8	1.2/1.2	0/0/0	0/0	0/0/0	0/0/0	5/5/	/5			0/0/0	---Of the motors of subheading No. 8501. 1010 and 8501. 1091
0/0/0	0	0	0.3/0.3	0/0/0	0/0	0//0	0/0/	2.7/2.7/2.7	2.7/2.7			0/0/0	---Of the generators of subheading No. 8501. 6420 and 8501. 6430
0/0/0	0	0	0/0	0/0/0	0/0	0//0	0/0/	0/0/0	0/0			0/0/0	---Of the generating sets of subheading No. 8502. 3100
													---Other
0//0	3.5	0	0.8/0.8	0/0/0	0/0	0//0	0/0/0	0/0/0	7.5/0			0/0/0	Motor stator(used under vacuum conditions, frequency range =600Hz~2000Hz, power=50VA~1000VA)
0//0	3.5	0	0.8/0.8	0/0/0	0/0	0//0	0/0/0	0/0/0	7.5/0			0/0/0	The alternator output power is driven by the use of renewable fuel boiler and turbine unit more than 750 thousand ampere of not more than 350 MVA parts
0//0	3.5	0	0.8/0.8	0/0/0	0/0	0//0	0/0/0	0/0/0	7.5/0			0/0/0	Rely on renewable energy (solar, small hydropower, tidal, methane gas, geothermal energy, biomass/waste heat driven turbine) production power generating sets of parts
0//0	3.5	0	0.8/0.8	0/0/0	0/0	0//0	0/0/0	0/0/0	7.5/0		//	0/0/0	Alternator stator for aircraft engine
0//0	3.5	0	0.8/0.8	0/0/0	0/0	0//0	0/0/0	0/0/0	7.5/0			0/0/0	Membrane electrode assembly for fuel cell (mainly composed of proton exchange membrane, catalyst and gas diffusion layer)
0//0	3.5	0	0.8/0.8	0/0/0	0/0	0//0	0/0/0	0/0/0	7.5/0			0/0/0	Bipolar plate for fuel cell
0//0	3.5	0	0.8/0.8	0/0/0	0/0	0//0	0/0/0	0/0/0	7.5/0			0/0/0	Other parts of electric motors, generators and generating sets

税则号列	货品名称〔CIQ 扩展编码及品名—T2 表示见附表 2〕	最惠(%)	暂定税率	普通	增值/消费	出口退税	计量单位	监管条件/特殊证件	检验检疫	对美关税	亚太上/下
85.04	**变压器、静止式变流器(例如,整流器)及电感器:**										
	-放电灯或放电管用镇流器:										
8504.1010	---电子镇流器〔999〕	10		35	13/	13	个/千克	/	L	30	
8504.1090	---其他〔101 电子镇流器,102 其它镇流器及其零件〕	10		35	13/	13	个/千克	/	L	30	
	-液体介质变压器:										
8504.2100	--额定容量不超过 650 千伏安〔999〕	10		50	13/	13	个/千克	/		30	
8504.2200	--额定容量超过 650 千伏安,但不超过 10 兆伏安〔999〕	10		50	13/	13	个/千克	/		35	
	--额定容量超过 10 兆伏安:										
	---额定容量超过 10 兆伏安,但小于 400 兆伏安:										
8504.2311	----额定容量超过 10 兆伏安,但小于 220 兆伏安〔999〕	10		50	13/	13	个/千克	/		35	6.5/6.5
8504.2312	----额定容量在 220 兆伏安及以上,但小于 330 兆伏安〔999〕	10		50	13/	13	个/千克	/			6.5/6.5
8504.2313	----额定容量在 330 兆伏安及以上,但小于 400 兆伏安〔999〕	10		50	13/	13	个/千克	/			6.5/6.5
	---额定容量在 400 兆伏安及以上:										
8504.2321	----额定容量在 400 兆伏安及以上,但小于 500 兆伏安〔999〕	6		11	13/	13	个/千克	/			3.9/3.9
8504.2329	----其他〔999〕	6		11	13/	13	个/千克	/		31	3.9/3.9
	-其他变压器:										
	--额定容量不超过 1 千伏安:										
8504.3110	---互感器〔999〕	5		50	13/	13	个/千克	/		25	3.3/3.3
8504.3190	---其他〔999〕	5		50	13/	13	个/千克	/		30	3.3/3.3
	--额定容量超过 1 千伏安,但不超过 16 千伏安:										
8504.3210	---互感器〔999〕	5		50	13/	13	个/千克	/		25	
8504.3290	---其他〔999〕	5		50	13/	13	个/千克	/		30	
	--额定容量超过 16 千伏安,但不超过 500 千伏安:										
8504.3310	---互感器〔999〕	5		50	13/	13	个/千克	/		25	
8504.3390	---其他〔999〕	5		50	13/	13	个/千克	/		15	
	--额定容量超过 500 千伏安:										
8504.3410	---互感器〔999〕	10		50	13/	13	个/千克	/			
8504.3490	---其他〔999〕	10		50	13/	13	个/千克	/		30	
	-静止式变流器:										
	---稳压电源:										
8504.4013	----税目 84.71 所列机器用[T2]	0		40	13/	13	个/千克	A/	L	25	
8504.4014	----其他直流稳压电源,功率小于 1 千瓦,精度低于万分之一[T2]	0		80	13/	13	个/千克	/	L		0/0
8504.4015	----其他交流稳压电源,功率小于 10 千瓦,精度低于千分之一[T2]	0		80	13/	13	个/千克	/		10	
8504.4019	----其他										
8504.4019 10	同位素电磁分离器离子源磁体电源(高功率直流型)〔101:Ⅰ类稳压电源,102:Ⅱ类稳压电源,103:Ⅲ类稳压电源〕	0		50	13/	13	个/千克	3/		20	
8504.4019 20	直流高功率电源(能 8 小时连续产生 100V,500A 电流,稳定度优于 0.1%)[T2]	0		50	13/	13	个/千克	3/		20	
8504.4019 30	高压直流电源(能 8 小时连续产生 20kV,1A 电流,稳定度优于 0.2%)[T2]	0		50	13/	13	个/千克	3/		20	
8504.4019 40	同位素电磁分离器离子源高压电源[T2]	0		50	13/	13	个/千克	3/		20	
8504.4019 90	其他稳压电源[T2]	0		50	13/	13	个/千克	/	L	20	
8504.4020	---不间断供电电源〔999〕	0		50	13/	13	个/千克	/		20	0/0
8504.4030	---逆变器										
8504.4030 10	两用物项管制的逆变器(功率≥40 瓦特,频率 600 至 2000 赫兹,谐波畸变低于 10%等)〔999〕	0		30	13/	13	个/千克	3/		25	
8504.4030 20	纯电动或混合动力汽车用逆变器模块,功率密度≥8 千瓦/升〔999〕	0		30	13/	13	个/千克	/		25	
8504.4030 90	其他逆变器〔999〕	0		30	13/	13	个/千克	/		25	
	---其他:										
8504.4091	----具有变流功能的半导体模块										
8504.4091 10	具有变流功能的半导体模块(自动数据处理设备机器及组件、电讯设备用的)〔999〕	0		30	13/	13	个/千克	/			
8504.4091 90	其他具有变流功能的半导体模块〔999〕	0		30	13/	13	个/千克	/			
8504.4099	----其他										
8504.4099 10	静止式变流器(自动数据处理设备机器及组件、电讯设备用)〔999〕	0		30	13/	13	个/千克	/		20	

协定税率 %								RCEP		特惠税率 %			Article Description
东/冰/格	巴基斯坦	韩国	瑞士 上/下	哥/秘/柬	澳/毛	新西/坡/智	中国港/澳/台	东盟及马来/澳/韩	日/新	亚太2国	老/柬/缅	98/97/95	
													Electrical transformers, static converters (for example, rectifiers) and inductors:
													-Ballasts for discharge lamps or tubes:
0/0/0	2	2	0/0	0/0/0	0/0	0/0/0	0/0/	9/9/9	9.1/9			0/0/0	---Electronic ballats
0/0/0	2	2	0/0	0/0/0	0/0	0//0	0/0/	0/0/9	9.1/0			0/0/0	---Other
													-Liquid dielectric transformers:
0/0/0	3.5	2.1	1.1/1.1	0/0/0	0/0	0/0/0	0/0/	0/0/9.5	9.5/0			0/0/0	--Having a power handling capacity not exceeding 650 kVA
0/0/0	4.4	2.5	1.3/1.3	0/0/0	0/0	0/0/0	0/0/	0/0/11.3	11.5/0			0/0/0	--Having a power handling capacity exceeding 650 kVA but not exceeding 10 MVA
													--Having a power handling capacity exceeding 10 MVA:
													---Having a power handling capacity exceeding 10MVA but less than 400MVA:
0/0/0	2	4.6		0/0/0	0/0	0//0	0/0/	9.3/9.5/9.3	9.4/9.5			0/0/0	----Having a power handling capacity exceding 10MVA but less than 220MVA
0/0/0	2	2	0/0	0/0/0	0/0	0//0	0/0/	0/0/9	9.1/0			0/0/0	----Having a power handling capacity exceding 220MVA but less than 330MVA
0/0/0	2	2	0/0	0/0/0	0/0	0//0	0/0/	9.5/9.5/9.5	/9.5			0/0/0	----Having a power handling capacity exceding 330MVA but less than 400MVA
													---Having a power handling capacity of 400 MVA or more:
0/0/0	0	0	0/0	0/0/0	0/0	0//0	0/0/	0/0/0	0/0			0/0/0	----Having a power handling capacity exceding 400MVA but less than 500MVA
0/0/0	0	0	0/0	0/0/0	0/0	0//0	0/0/	0/0/0	0/0			0/0/0	----Other
													-Other transformers:
													--Having a power handling capacity not exceeding 1 kVA:
0/0/0	0	0	0/0	0/0/0	0/0	0//0	0/0/0	0/0/0	0/0			0/0/0	---Mutual inductor
0/0/0	0	0	0/0	0/0/0	0/0	0/0/0	0/0/0	0/0/0	0/0			0/0/0	---Other
													--Having a power handling capacity exceeding 1kVA but not exceeding 16kVA:
0/0/0	0	2.3	0/0	0/0/0	0/0	0//0	0/0/	4.5/4.5/4.5	4.7/4.5			0/0/0	---Mutual inductor
0/0/0	0	0	0/0	0/0/0	0/0	0//0	0/0/	0/0/0	0/0			0/0/0	---Other
													--Having a power handling capacity exceeding 16 kVA but not exceeding 500 kVA:
0/0/0	0	2.3	0/0	0/0/0	0/0	0//0	0/0/	4.5/4.5/4.5	4.7/4.5			0/0/0	---Mutual inductor
0/0/0	0	2.3	0/0	0/0/0	0/0	0//0	0/0/	4.5/4.5/4.5	4.7/4.5			0/0/0	---Other
													--Having a power handling capacity exceeding 500 kVA:
0/0/0	11.2	6.5	0/0	0/0/0	0/0	0/0/0	0/0/	13.1/13.3/13.1	13.1/13.3			0/0/0	---Mutual inductor
0/0/0	7.8	6.5	0/0	0/0/0	0/0	0/0/0	0/0/	13.1/13.3/13.1	13.1/13.3			0/0/0	---Other
													-Static converters:
													---Voltage-stabilized suppliers:
0/0/0	0	0	0/0	0/0/0	0/0	0//0	0/0/	0/0/0	0/0			0/0/0	----Of the machines of heading No. 84. 71
0/0/0	2	3.2	0/0	0/0/0	0/0	0//0	0/0/	0/0/6.3	6.4/0			0/0/0	----Other DC voltage-stabilized suppliers, of a power of less than 1 kW and an accuracy of not better than 0. 0001
0/0/0	0	0	0/0	0/0/0	0/0	0//0	0/0/	0/0/0	0/0			0/0/0	----Other AC voltage-stabilized suppliers, of a power of less than 10 kW and an accuracy of not better than 0. 001
													----Other
0/0/0	0	0	0/0	0/0/0	0/0	0//0	0/0/	0/0/0	0/0			0/0/0	Ion source magnetic power suppliers of isotopioes electromagnetic separators (high-power, DC type)
0/0/0	0	0	0/0	0/0/0	0/0	0//0	0/0/	0/0/0	0/0			0/0/0	High-power DC power suppliers (capable of generating 100V, 500A current uninterrupted in 8 hours, stability better than 0. 1%)
0/0/0	0	0	0/0	0/0/0	0/0	0//0	0/0/	0/0/0	0/0			0/0/0	High-voltage DC power suppliers (capable of generating 20KV, 1A current uninterrupted in 8 hours, stability better than 0. 2%)
0/0/0	0	0	0/0	0/0/0	0/0	0//0	0/0/	0/0/0	0/0			0/0/0	Ion source high-voltage power suppliers of isotopies electromagnetic separators
0/0/0	0	0	0/0	0/0/0	0/0	0//0	0/0/	0/0/0	0/0			0/0/0	Other voltage-stabilized suppliers
0/0/0	3.5	4.6		0/0/0	0/0	0/0/0	0/0/	9/9/9	9.1/9			0/0/0	---Uninterrupted power suppliers
													---Inverter
0/0/0	3.5	4.6	0/0	0/0/0	0/0	0/0/0	0/0/	0/0/9	9.1/0			0/0/0	Inverter of sensitive items control(power≥40W, frequency=600Hz~2000Hz, harmonic distortion<10%)
0/0/0	3.5	4.6	0/0	0/0/0	0/0	0/0/0	0/0/	0/0/9	9.1/0			0/0/0	Pure electric or hybrid cars use inverter module, power density or 8kw/l
0/0/0	3.5	4.6	0/0	0/0/0	0/0	0/0/0	0/0/	0/0/9	9.1/0			0/0/0	Other inverter
													---Other:
													----Semiconductor modules with a converting function
0/0/0	3.5	0	0/0	0/0/0	0/0	0/0/0	0/0/	0/0/0	9.1/0			0/0/0	Semi-conductor modules with converting function (for automatic data-processing machines and units as well as telecommunication equipments)
0/0/0	3.5	0	0/0	0/0/0	0/0	0/0/0	0/0/	0/0/0	9.1/0			0/0/0	Other Semi-conductor modules with converting function
													----Other
0/0/0	3.5	4.6	0/0	0/0/0	0/5.9	0/0/0	0/0/	0/0/9	9.1/0			0/0/0	Static converters(for automatic data processing machines and units thereof and telecommunication apparatus)

税则号列		货品名称〔CIQ扩展编码及品名－T2表示见附表2〕	最惠(%)	暂定税率	普通	增值/消费	出口退税	计量单位	监管条件/特殊证件	检验检疫	对美关税	亚太上/下
8504.4099	20	ITA产品用的印刷电路组件(包括外接组件,如符合PCM-CIA标准的卡)〔999〕	0		30	13/	13	个/千克	/		20	
8504.4099	30	专用85030090.10电动机定子的频率变换器(1.多相输出600Hz或更高;2.高稳定性(频率控制优于0.2%))〔999〕	0		30	13/	13	个/千克	3/		20	
8504.4099	40	两用物项管制的频率变换器(功率≥40瓦特,频率600至2000赫兹,谐波畸变低于10%等)〔999〕	0		30	13/	13	个/千克	3/		20	
8504.4099	50	电源(真空或受控环境感应炉用电源,额定输出功率≥5千瓦)〔999〕	0		30	13/	13	个/千克	3/		20	
8504.4099	60	模块式电脉冲发生器(在15ms内输出电流＞100A,密封在防尘罩内,温宽范围大)〔999〕	0		30	13/	13	个/千克	3/		20	
8504.4099	70	高速(200km/h及以上)电力机车的牵引变流器〔999〕	0		30	13/	13	个/千克	/		20	
8504.4099	80	汽车冲压线用压力机变频调速装置〔999〕	0		30	13/	13	个/千克	/		20	
8504.4099	92	纯电动汽车或插电式混合动力汽车用车载充电机〔999〕	0		30	13/	13	个/千克	/		20	
8504.4099	99	其他未列名静止式变流器〔999〕	0		30	13/	13	个/千克	/		20	
8504.5000		-其他电感器〔999〕	0		35	13/	13	个/千克	/		25	
		-零件:										
		---变压器用:										
8504.9011		----税号8504.2321和8504.2329所列变压器用〔999〕	0		11	13/	13	千克	/		25	0/0
8504.9019		----其他〔999〕	0		50	13/	13	千克	/		25	0/0
8504.9020		---稳压电源及不间断供电电源用〔999〕	0		50	13/	13	千克	/		20	0/0
8504.9090		---其他										
8504.9090	10	用于将可再生能源发电机组输出的直流电转换成交流电的逆变器的零件〔999〕	0		30	13/	13	千克	/		25	0/0
8504.9090	90	其他静止式变流器及电感器零件〔999〕	0		30	13/	13	千克	/		25	0/0
85.05		**电磁铁;永磁铁及磁化后准备制永磁铁的物品;电磁铁或永磁铁卡盘、夹具及类似的工件夹具;电磁联轴节、离合器及制动器;电磁起重吸盘:**										
		-永磁铁及磁化后准备制永磁铁的物品:										
		--金属的:										
8505.1110		---稀土的〔999〕	7		20	13/	13	千克	/		32	
8505.1190		---其他〔999〕	7		20	13/	13	千克	/		27	
8505.1900		--其他										
8505.1900	10	磁极块(直径大于2m,用在同位素电磁分离器内)〔999〕	7		20	13/	13	千克	3/		32	4.6/4.6
8505.1900	90	其他非金属永磁铁及永磁体〔999〕	7		20	13/	13	千克	/		32	4.6/4.6
8505.2000		-电磁联轴节、离合器及制动器〔999〕	8		20	13/	13	千克	/			5.2/5.2
		-其他,包括零件:										
8505.9010		---电磁起重吸盘〔999〕	8		20	13/	13	个/千克	/		28	
8505.9090		---其他										
8505.9090	10	超导螺线电磁体(产生超过2个泰斯拉磁场,长径比≥2mm,内径≥300mm等)〔999〕	8		20	13/	13	个/千克	3/		33	5.6/5.6
8505.9090	20	专门或主要用于核磁共振成像装置的电磁体,但税号90.18所列其他电磁铁除外〔999〕	0		20	13/	13	个/千克	/		25	5.6/5.6
8505.9090	90	其他电磁铁;电磁铁或永磁铁卡盘、夹具及类似的工件夹具;编号8505的零件〔999〕	8		20	13/	13	个/千克	/		33	5.6/5.6
85.06		**原电池及原电池组:**										
		-二氧化锰的:										
		---碱性锌锰的:										
8506.1011		----扣式										
8506.1011	10	扣式无汞碱性锌锰的原电池及原电池组(汞含量＜电池重量的0.0005%)[T2]	8		80	13/	13	个/千克	/		28	
8506.1011	90	扣式含汞碱性锌锰的原电池及原电池组(汞含量≥电池重量的0.0005%)[T2]	8		80	13/4	0	个/千克	89/		28	
8506.1012		----圆柱形										
8506.1012	10	圆柱形无汞碱性锌锰的原电池及原电池组,汞含量＜电池重量的0.0001%[T2]	8		80	13/	13	个/千克	/		28	

协定税率 %								RCEP		特惠税率 %			Article Description
东/冰/格	巴基斯坦	韩国	瑞士上/下	哥/秘/柬	澳/毛	新西/坡/智	中国港/澳/台	东盟及马来/澳/韩	日/新	亚太2国	老/柬/缅	98/97/95	
0/0/0	3.5	4.6	0/0	0/0/0	0/5.9	0/0/0	0/0/	0/0/9	9.1/0			0/0/0	Printed circuit assemblies for products falling within the ITA (including external assemblies, for example, cards in accordance with PCMCIA)
0/0/0	3.5	4.6	0/0	0/0/0	0/5.9	0/0/0	0/0/	0/0/9	9.1/0			0/0/0	Frequency converters, specially, for stators of heading 8503.009010
0/0/0	3.5	4.6	0/0	0/0/0	0/5.9	0/0/0	0/0/	0/0/9	9.1/0			0/0/0	Frequency converters (power≥40W, frequency=600Hz～2000Hz, harmonic distortion<10%)
0/0/0	3.5	4.6	0/0	0/0/0	0/5.9	0/0/0	0/0/	0/0/9	9.1/0			0/0/0	Power suppliers (for vacuum or atmosphere-controlled induction furnace, rated output power≥5kW)
0/0/0	3.5	4.6	0/0	0/0/0	0/5.9	0/0/0	0/0/	0/0/9	9.1/0			0/0/0	Module-type electric pulse generator (output electric current >100A in 15ms and greater in temperature span when sealed in dustproof cover)
0/0/0	3.5	4.6	0/0	0/0/0	0/5.9	0/0/0	0/0/	0/0/9	9.1/0			0/0/0	High speed electric locomotive traction converter (for (200 km/ h) electric locomotive)
0/0/0	3.5	4.6	0/0	0/0/0	0/5.9	0/0/0	0/0/	0/0/9	9.1/0			0/0/0	Press of variable frequency speed regulating device in automobile press line
0/0/0	3.5	4.6	0/0	0/0/0	0/5.9	0/0/0	0/0/	0/0/9	9.1/0			0/0/0	Pure electric vehicle or a plug in hybrid electric vehicle onboard charger
0/0/0	3.5	4.6	0/0	0/0/0	0/5.9	0/0/0	0/0/	0/0/9	9.1/0			0/0/0	Other static converters, not elsewhere specified or included
0/0/0	0	0	0/0	0/0/0	0/0	0//0	0/0/	0/0/0	0/0			0/0/0	-Other inductors
													-Parts:
													---Of transformers:
0/0/0	0	2.3	0/0	0/0/0	0/0	0//0	0/0/	0/0/4.5	4.5/0			0/0/0	----Of the transformers of subheading No. 8504. 2321, 8504. 2329
0/0/0	1.8	3.7	0/0	0/0/0	0/0	0//0	0/0/0	0/0/7.2	7.3/0			0/0/0	----Other
0/0/0	2	3.7	0/0	0/0/0	0/0	0//0	0/0/0	7.2/7.2/7.2	7.3/7.2			0/0/0	---Of voltage-stabilized suppliers and uninterrupted power suppliers
													---Other
0/0/0	2	3.7	0/0	0/0/0	0/0	0//0	0/0/0	0/0/7.2	7.3/0			0/0/0	For the output of renewable energy power generation unit of DC to AC inverter components
0/0/0	2	3.7	0/0	0/0/0	0/0	0//0	0/0/0	0/0/7.2	7.3/0			0/0/0	Static converters and other parts of the inductor
													Electro-magnets; permanent magnets and articles intended to become permanent magnets after magnetization; electro-magnetic or permanent magnet chucks, clamps and similar holding devices; electro-magnetic couplings, clutches and brakes; electro-magnetic lifting heads:
													-Permanent magnets and articles intended to become permanent magnets after magnetization:
													--Of metal:
0/0/0	2	0	0/0	0/0/0	0/0	0//0	0/0/0	0/0/0	6.4/0			0/0/0	---Of rare-earth
0/0/0	2	0	0/0	0/0/0	0/0	0//0	0/0/0	0/0/0	6.7/0			0/0/0	---Other
													--Other
0/0/0	2	1.4	0/0	0/0/0	0/0	0//0	0/0/	0/0/6.3	6.4/0			0/0/0	Magnet pole pieces (diameter>2m, used for electromagnetic isotope separator)
0/0/0	2	1.4	0/0	0/0/0	0/0	0//0	0/0/	0/0/6.3	6.4/0			0/0/0	Non metal permanent magnets
0/0/0	2	3.7	0/0	0/0/0	0/0	0//0	0/0/	7.5/7.6/7.5	7.5/7.6			0/0/0	-Electro-magnetic couplings, clutches and brakes
													-Other, including parts:
0/0/0	2	0	0/0	0/0/0	0/0	0//0	0/0/	0/0/0	7.3/0			0/0/0	---Electro-magnetic lifting heads
													---Other
0/0/0	2	0	0.8/0.8	0/0/0	0/0	0//0	0/0/	0/0/0	7.3/0			0/0/0	Superconduction spiral electro magnets (capable of generating more than two Tesla magnetic fields, L/D≥2, inside diameter≥300mm)
0/0/0	2	0	0.8/0.8	0/0/0	0/0	0//0	0/0/	0/0/0	7.3/0			0/0/0	Solely or primarily for the electromagnet magnetic resonance imaging device, but excludingelectromagnet of heading No. 90.18
0/0/0	2	0	0.8/0.8	0/0/0	0/0	0//0	0/0/	0/0/0	7.3/0			0/0/0	Other electromagnets; electromagnet or permanent magnet chuck, fixture and similar workpiece fixture; parts of heading No.85.05
													Primary cells and primary batteries:
													-Manganese dioxide:
													---Alkaline zinc-manganese dioxide:
													----Button shape
0/0/0	16	12	2/2	0/0/0	0/0	0/0/0	0/0/	19/19/	/19			0/0/0	Button type alkaline zinc manganese battery and battery pack, mercury content < 0.0005% by weight of the battery
0/0/0	16	12	2/2	0/0/0	0/0	0/0/0	0/0/	19/19/	/19			0/0/0	Button type alkaline zinc manganese battery and battery pack, mercury content of 0.0005% by weight of the battery or higher
													----Cycinder shape
0/0/0	16	12	2/2	0/0/0	0/0	0/0/0	0/0/	19/19/	/19			0/0/0	Cylindrical mercury-free alkaline zinc manganese battery and original battery mercury content < 0.0001% by weight of the battery

税则号列	货品名称〔CIQ 扩展编码及品名－T2 表示见附表 2〕	最惠(%)	暂定税率	普通	增值/消费	出口退税	计量单位	监管条件/特殊证件	检验检疫	对美关税	亚太上/下
8506.1012 90	圆柱形含汞碱性锌锰的原电池及原电池组,汞含量≥电池重量的 0.0001%[T2]	8		80	13/4	0	个/千克	89/		28	
8506.1019	----其他										
8506.1019 10	其他无汞碱性锌锰的原电池及原电池组,汞含量＜电池重量的 0.0001%[T2]	8		80	13/	13	个/千克	/		33	
8506.1019 90	其他碱性锌锰的原电池及原电池组,汞含量≥电池重量的 0.0001%[T2]	8		80	13/4	13	个/千克	89/		33	
8506.1090	---其他										
8506.1090 10	其他无汞二氧化锰的原电池及原电池组(汞含量＜电池重量的 0.0001%,扣式电池的汞含量＜电池重量的 0.0005%)〔101 锌－锰原电池及原电池组,102 碱性锌－锰原电池及原电池组,103 其他二氧化锰的原电池及原电池组〕	8		80	13/	13	个/千克	/		33	
8506.1090 90	其他含汞二氧化锰的原电池及原电池组(汞含量≥电池重量的 0.0001%,扣式电池的汞含量≥电池重量的 0.0005%)〔101 锌－锰原电池及原电池组,102 碱性锌－锰原电池及原电池组,103 其他二氧化锰的原电池及原电池组〕	8		80	13/4	13	个/千克	89/		33	
8506.3000	-氧化汞的〔999〕	8		40	13/4	0	个/千克	89/			
8506.4000	-氧化银的										
8506.4000 10	氧化银的原电池及原电池组(无汞),汞含量＜电池重量的 0.0001%,扣式电池的汞含量＜电池重量的 0.0005%〔101 锌银扣式电池,102 锌银其他电池,103 其他氧化银的原电池及原电池组〕	8		40	13/	13	个/千克	/		33	5.2/5.2
8506.4000 90	氧化银的原电池及原电池组(含汞),汞含量≥电池重量的 0.0001%,扣式电池的汞含量≥电池重量的 0.0005%〔101 锌银扣式电池,102 锌银其他电池,103 其他氧化银的原电池及原电池组〕	8		40	13/4	13	个/千克	89/		33	5.2/5.2
8506.5000	-锂的〔101 锂－二氧化锰扣式电池,102 锂－二氧化锰其他电池,103 其他锂的原电池及原电池组〕	8		40	13/	13	个/千克	A/	M	33	
8506.6000	-锌空气的										
8506.6000 10	锌空气的原电池及原电池组(无汞),汞含量＜电池重量的 0.0001%,扣式电池的汞含量＜电池重量的 0.0005%〔999〕	8		40	13/	13	个/千克	/		33	
8506.6000 90	锌空气的原电池及原电池组(含汞),汞含量≥电池重量的 0.0001%,扣式电池的汞含量≥电池重量的 0.0005%〔999〕	8		40	13/4	13	个/千克	89/		33	
8506.8000	-其他原电池及原电池组										
8506.8000 11	无汞燃料电池,汞含量＜电池重量的 0.0001%,扣式电池的汞含量＜电池重量的 0.0005%〔999〕	8		40	13/	13	个/千克	/		28	
8506.8000 19	其他无汞原电池及原电池组,汞含量＜电池重量的 0.0001%,扣式电池的汞含量＜电池重量的 0.0005%〔999〕	8		40	13/	13	个/千克	/		28	
8506.8000 91	含汞燃料电池,汞含量≥电池重量的 0.0001%,扣式电池的汞含量≥电池重量的 0.0005%〔999〕	8		40	13/4	13	个/千克	89/		28	
8506.8000 99	其他含汞原电池及原电池组(汞含量≥电池重量的 0.0001%,扣式电池的汞含量≥电池重量的 0.0005%)〔999〕	8		40	13/4	13	个/千克	89/		28	
	-零件:										
8506.9010	---子目 8506.10 所列电池用〔999〕	8		80	13/	13	千克	/		28	5.2/5.2
8506.9090	---其他〔301 属于危险化学品的金属;302 其它原电池及原电池组及其零件〕	8		40	13/	13	千克	/		28	
85.07	**蓄电池,包括隔板,不论是否矩形(包括正方形):**										
8507.1000	-铅酸蓄电池,用于启动活塞式发动机[T2]	10		90	13/4	0	个/千克	/		35	6.5/6.5
8507.2000	-其他铅酸蓄电池[T2]	10		90	13/4	0	个/千克	/		30	6.5/6.5
8507.3000	-镍镉蓄电池										
8507.3000 10	飞机用镍镉蓄电池〔101 圆柱镍镉电池,102 形开口镉镍单体蓄电池,103 其他镍镉电池〕	10	1	40	13/4	0	个/千克	/			6.5/6.5
8507.3000 90	其他镍镉蓄电池〔101 圆柱镍镉电池,102 方形开口镉镍单体蓄电池,103 其他镍镉电池〕	10		40	13/4	0	个/千克	/			6.5/6.5
8507.5000	-镍氢蓄电池[T2]	10		40	13/	13	个/千克	/		35	6.5/6.5
8507.6000	-锂离子蓄电池										
8507.6000 10	纯电动汽车或插电式混合动力汽车用锂离子蓄电池单体(容量≥10Ah,比能量≥110Wh/kg)〔999〕	10		40	13/	13	个/千克	A/	M	35	8/8

协定税率 %								RCEP		特惠税率 %			Article Description
东/冰/格	巴基斯坦	韩国	瑞士 上/下	哥/秘/柬	澳/毛	新西/坡/智	中国港/澳/台	东盟及马来/澳/韩	日/新	亚太2国	老/柬/缅	98/97/95	
0/0/0	16	12	2/2	0/0/0	0/0	0/0/0	0/0/	19/19/	/19			0/0/0	Cylindrical mercury alkaline zinc manganese battery and the mercury content of 0.0001% by weight of the battery or the battery pack
													----Other
0/0/0	16		2/2	0/0/0	0/0	0/0/0	0/0/	8/8/	/8			0/0/0	Other mercury-free alkaline zinc manganese battery and battery pack, mercury content < 0.0001% by weight of the battery
0/0/0	16		2/2	0/0/0	0/0	0/0/0	0/0/	8/8/	/8			0/0/0	Other alkaline zinc manganese battery and battery pack, mercury content of 0.0001% by weight of the battery or higher
													---Other
0/0/0	16	12	2/2	0/0/0	0/0	0/0/0	0/0/	19/19/19	/19			0/0/0	Other manganese dioxide, primary cells and primary batteries, mercury content < 0.0001% by weight of the battery, button cell of mercury content < 0.0005% by weight of the battery
0/0/0	16	12	2/2	0/0/0	0/0	0/0/0	0/0/	19/19/19	/19			0/0/0	Other manganese dioxide, primary cells and primary batteries, the mercury content of 0.0001% by weight of the battery, or the mercury content of the button cell battery or 0.0005% of the weight
0/0/0	7.8	2.8	1.4/1.4	0/0/0	0/0	0/0/0	0/0/	0/0/12.6	12.7/0			0/0/0	-Mercuric oxide
													-Silver oxide
0/0/0	7.8	2.8	1.4/1.4	0/0/0	0/0	0/0/0	0/0/	8/8/	/8			0/0/0	Silver oxide battery and the battery pack (mercury), mercury content < 0.0001% by weight of the battery, button cell of mercury content < 0.0005% by weight of the battery
0/0/0	7.8	2.8	1.4/1.4	0/0/0	0/0	0/0/0	0/0/	8/8/	/8			0/0/0	Primary cells and primary batteries, silver oxide(mercury), mercury content of 0.0001% by weight of the battery, or the mercury content of the button cell battery weight of 0.0005% or higher
0/0/0	7.8		1.4/1.4	0/0/0	0/0	0/0/0	0/0/	13.3/13.3/	/13.3			0/0/0	-Lithium
													-Air-zinc
0/0/0	7.8	2.8		0/0/0	0/0	0/0/0	0/0/	0/0/12.6	12.7/0			0/0/0	Primary cells and primary batteries, air-zinc(No mercury), mercury content < 0.0001% by weight of the battery, button cell of mercury content < 0.0005% by weight of the battery
0/0/0	7.8	2.8		0/0/0	0/0	0/0/0	0/0/	0/0/12.6	12.7/0			0/0/0	Primary cells and primary batteries, air-zinc(mercury), mercury content of 0.0001% by weight of the battery, or the mercury content of the button cell battery weight of 0.0005% or higher
													-Other primary cells and primary batteries
0/0/0	7.8	2.8	1.4/1.4	0/0/0	0/0	0/0/0	0/0/	0/0/12.6	12.7/0			0/0/0	Mercury-free fuel cell, mercury content < 0.0001% by weight of the battery, button cell mercury content < 0.0005% by weight of the battery
0/0/0	7.8	2.8	1.4/1.4	0/0/0	0/0	0/0/0	0/0/	0/0/12.6	12.7/0			0/0/0	mercury content < 0.0001% by weight of the battery, button cell of mercury content < 0.0005% by weight of the battery
0/0/0	7.8	2.8	1.4/1.4	0/0/0	0/0	0/0/0	0/0/	0/0/12.6	12.7/0			0/0/0	Mercury fuel cell, a mercury content of 0.0001% by weight of the battery, or the mercury content of the button cell battery or 0.0005% of the weight
0/0/0	7.8	2.8	1.4/1.4	0/0/0	0/0	0/0/0	0/0/	0/0/12.6	12.7/0			0/0/0	the mercury content of 0.0001% by weight of the battery, or the mercury content of the button cell battery or 0.0005% of the weight
													-Parts:
0/0/0	7.8		1.4/1.4	0/0/0	0/0	0/0/0	0/0/	5/5/	/5			0/0/0	---Of the cells of subheading No. 8506. 1000
0/0/0	2	6	0/0	0/0/0	0/0	0/0/0	0/0/	9.5/9.5/9.5	/9.5			0/0/0	---Other
													Electric accumulators, including separators therefor, whether or not rectangular(including square):
0/0/0	0	6	0/0	0/0/0	0/0	0/0/0	0/0/	9.5/9.5/	9.5/9.5			0/0/0	-Lead-acid, of a kind used for starting piston engines
0/0/0	0	2	0/0	0/0/0	0/0	0/0/0	0/0/	9/9/9	9.1/9			0/0/0	-Other lead-acid accumulators
													-Nickel-cadmium
0/0/0	2	2	0/0	0/0/0	0/0	0/0/0	0/0/	0/0/9	9.1/0		//	0/0/0	Nickel cadmium batteries for aircraft
0/0/0	2	2	0/0	0/0/0	0/0	0/0/0	0/0/	0/0/9	9.1/0		//	0/0/0	Other nickel cadmium batteries
0/0/0	3.5	2.4	1.2/1.2	0/0/0	0/0	0/0/0	0/0/	10.8/10.8/10.8	10.9/10.8			0/0/0	-Nickel-metal hydride
													-Lithium ion
0/0/0	5	9.6	1.2/1.2	0/0/0	0/0	0/0/0	0/0/0	11.4/11.4/	/11.4			0/0/0	Pure electric vehicle or a plug in hybrid electric vehicle lithium ion batterymonomer (capacity is greater than or equal to 10Ah, ratio of energy is higher than or equal to 110Wh/kg)

税则号列	货品名称〔CIQ 扩展编码及品名—T2 表示见附表 2〕	最惠(%)	暂定税率	普通	增值/消费	出口退税	计量单位	监管条件/特殊证件	检验检疫	对美关税	亚太上/下
8507.6000 20	纯电动汽车或插电式混合动力汽车用锂离子蓄电池系统(包含蓄电池模块、容器、盖、冷却系统、管理系统等,比能量≥80Wh/kg)〔999〕	10		40	13/	13	个/千克	A/	M		8/8
8507.6000 30	飞机用锂离子蓄电池〔999〕	10	1	40	13/	13	个/千克	/		26	8/8
8507.6000 90	其他锂离子蓄电池[T2]	10		40	13/	13	个/千克	A/	M	35	8/8
	-其他蓄电池:										
8507.8030	---全钒液流电池〔999〕	10		40	13/	13	个/千克	/			6.5/6.5
8507.8090	---其他										
8507.8090 10	燃料电池[T2]	10		40	13/	13	个/千克	/		30	6.5/6.5
8507.8090 90	其他蓄电池[T2]	10		40	13/4	13	个/千克	/		30	6.5/6.5
	-零件:										
8507.9010	---铅酸蓄电池用〔999〕	10		90	13/	0	千克	/		30	
8507.9090	---其他〔999〕	8	5	40	13/	13	千克	/		30	
85.08	**真空吸尘器:**										
	-电动的:										
8508.1100	--功率不超过 1500 瓦,且带有容积不超过 20 升的集尘袋或其他集尘容积器[T2]	8		130	13/	13	台/千克	/	L	33	5.2/5.2
8508.1900	--其他[T2]	0		30	13/	13	台/千克	/	L	25	
8508.6000	-其他真空吸尘器[T2]	0		30	13/	13	台/千克	/		25	
	-零件:										
8508.7010	---税号 8508.1100 所列吸尘器用〔999〕	6		100	13/	13	千克	/		31	
8508.7090	---其他〔999〕	0		20	13/	13	千克	/		5	
85.09	**家用电动器具,税目 85.08 的真空吸尘器除外:**										
	-食品研磨机及搅拌器;水果或蔬菜的榨汁机:										
8509.4010	---水果或蔬菜的榨汁机[T2]	7	6	100	13/	13	台/千克	A/	LR	31	
8509.4090	---其他[T2]	7	6	100	13/	13	台/千克	A/	LR	11	
	-其他器具:										
8509.8010	---地板打蜡机[T2]	8		100	13/	13	台/千克	/			
8509.8020	---厨房废物处理器[T2]	8		100	13/	13	台/千克	/		33	
8509.8090	---其他〔101:其它电动器具及其零件 I 类器具;102:其它电动器具及其零件 II 类器具;103:其它电动器具及其零件 III 类器具;104:其它电动器具及其零件 0I 类器具;105:其它电动器具及其零件 0 类器具;106:其它小型家用及类似用途电器及其零件 I 类器具;107:其它小型家用及类似用途电器及其零件 II 类器具;108:其它小型家用及类似用途电器及其零件 III 类器具;109:其它小型家用及类似用途电器及其零件 0I 类器具;110:其它小型家用及类似用途电器及其零件 0 类器具〕	8		100	13/	13	台/千克	A/	L	33	
8509.9000	-零件[T2]	6		100	13/	13	千克	/		31	
85.10	**电动剃须刀、电动毛发推剪及电动脱毛器:**										
8510.1000	-剃须刀[T2]	8		100	13/	13	个/千克	/		33	
8510.2000	-毛发推剪[T2]	8		100	13/	13	个/千克	/		33	
8510.3000	-脱毛器[T2]	8		100	13/	13	个/千克	/		33	
8510.9000	-零件〔999〕	8		100	13/	13	千克	/		33	
85.11	**点燃式或压燃式内燃发动机用的电点火及电启动装置(例如,点火磁电机、永磁直流发电机、点火线圈、火花塞、电热塞及启动电机);附属于上述内燃发动机的发电机(例如,直流发电机、交流发电机)及断流器:**										
8511.1000	-火花塞〔101 其他车辆零部件,102 动力设备零部件〕	8		30	13/	13	个/千克	/		18	
	-点火磁电机;永磁直流发电机;磁飞轮:										
8511.2010	---机车、航空器及船舶用[T2]	5		11	13/	13	个/千克	/			
8511.2090	---其他〔999〕	8		30	13/	13	个/千克	/		33	
	-分电器;点火线圈:										
8511.3010	---机车、航空器及船舶用[T2]	5		11	13/	13	个/千克	/			
8511.3090	---其他〔101 其他车辆零部件,102 其它发电机(组)及其零件〕	8		30	13/	13	个/千克	/		13	
	-启动电机及两用启动发电机:										
8511.4010	---机车、航空器及船舶用										
8511.4010 10	飞机辅助动力装置电源启动马达〔101 其它电动机及其零件,102 其它发电机(组)及其零件〕	5	1	11	13/	13	个/千克	/		6	
8511.4010 90	其他启动电机及两用启动发电机(指机车,航空器,船舶用)〔101 其它电动机及其零件,102 其它发电机(组)及其零件〕	5		11	13/	13	个/千克	/		10	
	---其他:										
8511.4091	----输出功率在 132.39 千瓦(180 马力)及以上的发动机用启动电机〔999〕	8		30	13/	13	个/千克	/		33	
8511.4099	----其他〔999〕	8		30	13/	13	个/千克	/		33	
	-其他发电机:										
8511.5010	---机车、航空器及船舶用〔999〕	5		11	13/	13	个/千克	/		10	
8511.5090	---其他〔999〕	8		30	13/	13	个/千克	/		33	

协定税率 %								RCEP		特惠税率 %			Article Description
东/冰/格	巴基斯坦	韩国	瑞士 上/下	哥/秘/柬	澳/毛	新西/坡/智	中国港/澳/台	东盟及马来/澳/韩	日/新	亚太2国	老/柬/缅	98/97/95	
0/0/0	5	9.6	1.2/1.2	0/0/0	0/0	0/0/0	0/0/0	11.4/11.4/	/11.4			0/0/0	Pure electric vehicles and plug-in hybrid vehicle lithium ion battery (includedbattery module, container, cover, cooling system, management system, specific energy is greater than or equal to 80Wh/kg)
0/0/0	5	9.6	1.2/1.2	0/0/0	0/0	0/0/0	0/0/0	11.4/11.4/	/11.4		//	0/0/0	Lithium ion batteries for aircraft
0/0/0	5	9.6	1.2/1.2	0/0/0	0/0	0/0/0	0/0/0	11.4/11.4/	/11.4			0/0/0	Other lithium ion
													-Other accumulators
0/0/0	3.5	2.4	1.2/1.2	0/0/0	0/0	0/0/0	0/0/	0/0/10.8	10.9/0			0/0/0	---Vanadium redox flow battery
													---Other
0/0/0	3.5	2.4	1.2/1.2	0/0/0	0/0	0/0/0	0/0/	0/0/10.8	10.9/0			0/0/0	fuel cell
0/0/0	3.5	2.4	1.2/1.2	0/0/0	0/0	0/0/0	0/0/	0/0/10.8	10.9/0			0/0/0	Other accumulators
													-Parts:
0/0/0	2	2	0/0	0/0/0	0/0	0//0	0/0/	0/0/9	9.1/0	5		0/0/0	---Of lead-acid accumulators
0/0/0	2	3.7	0/0	0/0/0	0/0	0//0	0/0/	7.2/7.2/7.2	7.5/7.2	4		0/0/0	---Other
													Vacuum cleaners:
													-With self-contained electric-motor:
0/0/0	2	2	0/0	0/0/0	0/0	0/0/0	0/0/0	0/0/9	9.1/0			0/0/0	--Of a power not exceeding 1500W and hawing a dust bag or other receptade capaeity not excecding 20L
0/0/0	0	0	0/0	0/0/0	0/0	0//0	0/0/	0/0/0	0/0			0/0/0	--Other
0/0/0	0	0	0/0	0/0/0	0/0	0//0	0/0/	0/0/0	0/0			0/0/0	-Other vacuum cleaners
													-Parts:
0/0/0	4.2	2.4	1.2/1.2	0/0/0	0/0	0/0/0	0/0/	0/0/10.8	10.9/0			0/0/0	---Of the cleamers of subheading No. 8508. 1100
0/0/0	0	0	0/0	0/0/0	0/0	0//0	0/0/	0/0/0	0/0			0/0/0	---Other
													Electro-mechanical domestic appliances, with self-contained electric motor, other than vacuum cleaners of heading No. 85. 08:
													-Food grinders and mixers; fruit or vegetable juice extractors:
0/0/0	2	6	0/0	0/0/0	0/0	0/0/0	0/0/	9.5/9.5/	/9.5			0/0/0	---Fruit or vegetable juice extractors
0/0/0	2	2	0/0	0/0/0	0/0	0/0/0	0/0/0	0/0/9	9.1/0			0/0/0	---Other
													-Other appliances:
0/0/0	24		8/8	0/0/0	0/18	0/0/0	0/0/	8/8/	/8			0/0/0	---Floor polishers
0/0/0	16	12	2/2	0/0/0	0/0	0/0/0	0/0/	19/19/	/19			0/0/0	---Kitchen waste disposers
0/0/0	24			0/0/0	0/18	0/0/0	0/0/	8/8/	/8			0/0/0	---Other
0/0/0	4.2	2.4	1.2/1.2	0/0/0	0/0	0/0/0	0/0/	10.8/10.8/10.8	10.9/10.8			0/0/0	-Parts
													Shavers, hair clippers and hair-removing appliances, with self-contained electric motor:
0//0	24		8/8	0/0/0	0/18	0/0/0	0/0/	8/8/	/8			0/0/0	-Shavers
0/0/0	24		8/8	0/0/0	0/18	0/0/0	0/0/	8/8/	/8			0/0/0	-Hair clippers
0/0/0	16	9.3	2/2	0/0/0	0/0	0/0/0	0/0/	18/18/18	18.8/18			0/0/0	-Hair-removing appliances
0/0/0	19.6	14.7	2.5/2.5	0/0/0	0/14.7	0/0/0	0/0/	23.3/23.3/	23.3/23.3			0/0/0	-Parts
													Electrical ignition or starting equipment of a kind used for spark-ignition or compression-ignition internal combustion engines (for example, ignition magnetos, magneto-dynamos, ignition coils, sparking plugs and glow plugs, starter motors); generators (for example, dynamos, alternators) and cut-outs of a kind used in conjunction with such engines:
0/0/0	3.5	2	0/0	0/0/0	0/0	0/0/0	0/0/	0/0/9	9.1/0			0/0/0	-Sparking plugs
													-Ignition magnetos; magneto-dynamos; magnetic flywheels:
0/0/0	0	0	0/0	0/0/0	0/0	0//0	0/0/	0/0/0	0/0			0/0/0	---For locomotives, aircraft or ships
0/0/0	2	2	0/0	0/0/0	0/0	0//0	0/0/	0/0/9	9.1/0			0/0/0	---Other
													-Distributors; ignition coils:
0/0/0	0	0	0/0	0/0/0	0/0	0//0	0/0/	0/0/0	0/0			0/0/0	---For locomotives, aircraft or ships
0/0/0	2	3.9	0/0	0/0/0	0/0	0//0	0/0/	7.8/8/7.8	7.9/8			0/0/0	---Other
													-Starter motors and dual purpose starter-generators:
													---For locomotives, aircraft or ships
0/0/0	0	1	0/0	0/0/0	0/0	0//0	0/0/	0/0/4.5	4.5/0		//	0/0/0	Power starting motor of aircraft auxiliary power unit
0/0/0	0	1	0/0	0/0/0	0/0	0//0	0/0/	0/0/4.5	4.5/0		//	0/0/0	Other starter motors and dual－purpose start－generators (for locomotives, aircraft and ships)
													---Other:
0/0/0	2	1.6	0/0	0/0/0	0/0	0//0	0/0/	0/0/7.6	7.6/0			0/0/0	----Starter motors for engines of an output of 132. 39kW (180HP) or more
0/0/0	4	3.9	0/0	0/0/0	0/0	0//0	0/0/	7.8/8/7.8	7.9/8			0/0/0	----Other
													-Other generators:
0/0/0	0	1	0/0	0/0/0	0/0	0//0	0/0/	0/0/4.5	4.5/0			0/0/0	---For locomotives, aircraft or ships
0/0/0	2		0/0	0/0/0	0/0	0//0	0/0/	5/5/	/5			0/0/0	---Other

税则号列	货品名称〔CIQ 扩展编码及品名－T2 表示见附表 2〕	最惠(%)	暂定税率	普通	增值/消费	出口退税	计量单位	监管条件/特殊证件	检验检疫	对美关税	亚太上/下
8511.8000	-其他装置〔999〕	8		30	13/	13	个/千克	/		13	
	-零件：										
8511.9010	---本税目所列供机车、航空器及船舶用的各种装置的零件										
8511.9010　10	飞机发动机用三相交流发电机用壳体〔999〕	4.5	1	11	13/	13	千克	/		6	
8511.9010　90	车船飞机用其他电点火，启动装置零件（指品目 8511 所列供机车、航空器及船舶用各种装置的零件）〔101 航空器用零部件，102 船舶用零部件，103 铁道机车用零部件〕	4.5		11	13/	13	千克	/		9.5	
8511.9090	---其他〔999〕	5		30	13/	13	千克	/		30	
85.12	**自行车或机动车辆用的电气照明或信号装置（税目 85.39 的物品除外）、风挡刮水器、除霜器及去雾器：**										
8512.1000	-自行车用照明或视觉信号装置〔999〕	10		45	13/	13	个/千克	/		35	
	-其他照明或视觉信号装置：										
8512.2010	---机动车辆用照明装置〔999〕	10		45	13/	13	个/千克	/	L	15	
8512.2090	---其他〔999〕	10		45	13/	13	个/千克	/	L	15	
	-音响信号装置：										
	---机动车辆用：										
8512.3011	----喇叭、蜂鸣器〔999〕	10		45	13/	13	个/千克	/		15	6.5/6.5
8512.3012	----防盗报警器〔999〕	10		40	13/	13	个/千克	/		15	6.5/6.5
8512.3019	----其他〔999〕	10		45	13/	13	个/千克	/		15	6.5/6.5
8512.3090	---其他〔999〕	10		45	13/	13	个/千克	/		20	6.5/6.5
8512.4000	-风挡刮水器、除霜器及去雾器〔999〕	10		45	13/	13	个/千克	/		15	
8512.9000	-零件〔999〕	8		45	13/	13	千克	/		13	
85.13	**自供能源（例如，使用干电池、蓄电池、永磁发电机）的手提式电灯，但税目 85.12 的照明装置除外：**										
	-灯：										
8513.1010	---手电筒〔999〕	5		100	13/	13	个/千克	/		15	3.3/3.3
8513.1090	---其他〔999〕	6		70	13/	13	个/千克	/		31	
	-零件：										
8513.9010	---手电筒用〔999〕	5		100	13/	13	千克	/		30	
8513.9090	---其他〔999〕	5		70	13/	13	千克	/		30	
85.14	**工业或实验室用电炉及电烘箱（包括通过感应或介质损耗工作的）；工业或实验室用其他通过感应或介质损耗对材料进行热处理的设备：**										
	-电阻加热的炉及烘箱：										
8514.1100	--热等静压机										
8514.1100　10	热等静压机（两用物项管制机器及机械器具）〔999〕	0		30	13/	13	台/千克	3/		10	
8514.1100　90	热等静压机〔999〕	0		30	13/	13	台/千克	/		10	
	--其他：										
8514.1910	---可控气氛热处理炉（8514.1010）〔999〕	0		30	13/	13	台/千克	/		25	
8514.1990	---其他〔999〕	0		30	13/	13	台/千克	/		10	
8514.2000	-通过感应或介质损耗工作的炉及烘箱										
8514.2000　10	真空感应炉或受控环境感应炉（工作温度＞850℃，感应线圈直径≤600mm，功率≥5 千瓦）〔999〕	0		30	13/	13	台/千克	3/		10	
8514.2000　90	其他感应或介质损耗工作炉及烘箱（包括实验室用）〔999〕	0		30	13/	13	台/千克	/		10	
	-其他炉及烘箱：										
8514.3100	--电子束炉										
8514.3100　10	电子束熔化炉（功率≥50 千瓦，能在＞1200℃的熔化温度工作）〔999〕	0		30	13/	13	台/千克	3/		10	
8514.3100　90	其他电子束炉（包括实验室用）〔999〕	0		30	13/	13	台/千克	/		10	
8514.3200	--等离子及真空电弧炉										
8514.3200　10	真空电弧重熔炉、真空电弧熔炉和真空电弧融化铸造炉（容量 1 千－2 万立方厘米，使用自耗电极，工作温度 1700℃以上）〔999〕	0		30	13/	13	台/千克	3/			
8514.3200　20	等离子体雾化炉和等离子体熔化炉（功率≥50 千瓦，能在＞1200℃的熔化温度工作）〔999〕	0		30	13/	13	台/千克	3/		10	
8514.3200　90	其他等离子及真空电弧炉（包括实验室用）〔999〕	0		30	13/	13	台/千克	/		10	
8514.3900	--其他										
8514.3900　10	其他电弧重熔炉、电弧熔炉和电弧融化铸造炉（容量 1 千－2 万立方厘米，使用自耗电极，工作温度 1700℃以上）〔999〕	0		30	13/	13	台/千克	3/			

协定税率 %								RCEP		特惠税率 %			Article Description
东/冰/格	巴基斯坦	韩国	瑞士上/下	哥/秘/柬	澳/毛	新西/坡/智	中国港/澳/台	东盟及马来/澳/韩	日/新	亚太2国	老/柬/缅	98/97/95	
0/0/0	2	1.6	0/0	0/0/0	0/0	0//0	0/0/	0/0/7.6	7.6/0			0/0/0	-Other equipment
													-Parts:
													---Of the equipment of headingNo. 85. 11 used for locomotives, aircraft or ships
0/0/0	0		0/0	0/0/0	0/0	0//0	0/0/	4.4/4.4/	/4.4		//	0/0/0	Case of three phase alternator for aircraft engine
0/0/0	0		0/0	0/0/0	0/0	0//0	0/0/	4.4/4.4/	/4.4		//	0/0/0	Parts of other electric ignition and starting devices for vehicles, ships and aircraft (parts of various devices for locomotives, aircraft and ships listed in heading 8511)
0/0/0	0	1	0/0	0/0/0	0/0	0//0	0/0/	0/0/4.5	4.7/0			0/0/0	---Other
													Electrical lighting or signalling equipment (excluding articles of headingNo.85. 39), windscreen wipers, defrosters and demisters, of a kind used for cycles or motor vehicles:
0/0/0	3.5	2.1	1.1/1.1	0/0/0	0/0	0/0/0	0/0/	0/0/9.5	9.5/0			0/0/0	-Lighting or visual signalling equipment of a kind used on bicycles
													-Other lighting or visual signalling equipment:
5/0/0	8	6	0/0	0/0/0	0/0	0//0	0/0/0	9/9.8/10	9.1/9.8			0/0/0	---Lighting equipment of a kind used for motor vehicles
5/0/0	8	6	0/0	0/0/0	0/0	0//0	0/0/	9.5/9.8/	9.5/9.8			0/0/0	---Other
													-Sound signalling equipment:
													---For motor vehicles:
5/0/0	6	4.6	0/0	0/0/0	0/0	0//0	0/0/	9/9.5/	9.1/9.8			0/0/0	----Loudspeaker, buzzers
0/0/0	2	4.6	0/0	0/0/0	0/0	0//0	0/0/	9/9/9	9.4/9			0/0/0	----Burglay alarm
5/0/0	6	4.6	0/0	0/0/0	0/0	0//0	0/0/	9/9.5/10	9.1/9.8			0/0/0	----Other
5/0/0	6		0/0	0/0/0	0/0	0//0	0/0/	9//	9.1/			0/0/0	---Other
5/0/0	8		0/0	0/0/0	0/0	0//0	0/0/					0/0/0	-Windscreen wipers, defrosters and demisters
0/0/0	4	1.6	0/0	0/0/0	0/0	0//0	0/0/0	0/0/7.2	7.5/0			0/0/0	-Parts
													Portable electric lamps designed to function by their own source of energy (for example, dry batteries, accumulators, magnetos), other than lighting equipment of headingNo. 85. 12:
													-Lamps:
0/0/0	6	3	1.5/1.5	0/0/0	0/0	0/0/0	0/0/	0/0/13.5	13.6/0			0/0/0	---Portable electric torches designed to function by dry batteries
0/0/0	9.8	3.5	1.8/1.8	0/0/0	0/0	0/0/0	0/0/	0/0/15.8	15.9/0			0/0/0	---Other
													-Parts:
0/0/0	7.8	2.8	1.4/1.4	0/0/0	0/0	0/0/0	0/0/	0/0/12.6	12.7/0			0/0/0	---Of the torches of subheading No. 8513. 1010
0/0/0	7.8	2.8	1.4/1.4	0/0/0	0/0	0/0/0	0/0/	0/0/12.6	12.7/0			0/0/0	---Other
													Industrial or laboratory electric furnaces and ovens (including those functioning by induction or dielectric loss); other industrial or laboratory equipment for the heat treatment of materials by induction or dielectric loss:
													-Resistance heated furnaces and ovens:
													--Hot isostatic press
0/0/0	0	0	0/0	0/0/0	0/0	0//0	0/0/	0/0/0	0/0			0/0/0	Hot isostatic press (dual purpose item control machines and mechanical appliances)
0/0/0	0	0	0/0	0/0/0	0/0	0//0	0/0/	0/0/0	0/0			0/0/0	Hot isostatic press
													--Other
0/0/0	0	0	0/0	0/0/0	0/0	0//0	0/0/	0/0/0	0/0			0/0/0	---Controllable atmosphere heat treatment furnace (8514. 1010)
0/0/0	0	0	0/0	0/0/0	0/0	0//0	0/0/	0/0/0	0/0			0/0/0	---Other
													-Furnaces and ovens functioning by induction or dielectric loss
0/0/0	0	0	0/0	0/0/0	0/0	0//0	0/0/	0/0/0	0/0			0/0/0	Vacuum induction furnaces or controlled atmosphere induction furnaces (rated output power≥5kW, diameter of induction coil≤600mm, working temperature>850℃)
0/0/0	0	0	0/0	0/0/0	0/0	0//0	0/0/	0/0/0	0/0			0/0/0	Other furnaces and ovens functioning by induction or dielectric loss(including laboratory)
													-Other furnaces and ovens
													--Electron beam furnace
0/0/0	0	0	0/0	0/0/0	0/0	0//0	0/0/	0/0/0	0/0			0/0/0	Electron beam melting furnace (power ≥ 5 kW, capable of working at melting temperature > 12 ℃)
0/0/0	0	0	0/0	0/0/0	0/0	0//0	0/0/	0/0/0	0/0			0/0/0	Other electron beam furnaces (including laboratory)
													--Plasma and vacuum arc furnace
0/0/0	0	0	0/0	0/0/0	0/0	0//0	0/0/	0/0/0	0/0			0/0/0	Vacuum arc remelting furnace, vacuum arc melting furnace and vacuum arc melting casting furnace (capacity of 1－2 cubic centimeters, use consumable electrode, working temperature above 17 ℃)
0/0/0	0	0	0/0	0/0/0	0/0	0//0	0/0/	0/0/0	0/0			0/0/0	Plasma atomizing furnace and plasma melting furnace (power ≥ 5 kW, capable of working at melting temperature > 12 ℃)
0/0/0	0	0	0/0	0/0/0	0/0	0//0	0/0/	0/0/0	0/0			0/0/0	Other plasma and vacuum arc furnaces (including laboratory)
													--Other
0/0/0	0	0	0/0	0/0/0	0/0	0//0	0/0/	0/0/0	0/0			0/0/0	Other electric arc remelting furnaces, electric arc melting furnaces and electric arc melting casting furnaces (with a capacity of 1 － 2 cubic centimeters, using consumable electrodes, and working temperature above 17 ℃)

税则号列	货品名称〔CIQ扩展编码及品名—T2表示见附表2〕	最惠(%)	暂定税率	普通	增值/消费	出口退税	计量单位	监管条件/特殊证件	检验检疫	对美关税	亚太上/下
8514.3900 90	工业用其他电炉及电烘箱(包括实验室用)〔999〕	0		30	13/	13	台/千克	/		10	
8514.4000	-其他通过感应或介质损耗对材料进行热处理的设备										
8514.4000 01	焊缝中频退火装置〔999〕	10	7	30	13/	13	台/千克	/		27	
8514.4000 90	其他感应或介质损耗的加热设备(包括实验室用)〔999〕	10		30	13/	13	台/千克	/		30	
	-零件:										
8514.9010	---炼钢电炉用〔999〕	8		30	13/	13	千克	/		33	
8514.9090	---其他〔999〕	0		30	13/	13	千克	/		10	
85.15	**电气(包括电热气体)、激光、其他光、光子束、超声波、电子束、磁脉冲或等离子弧焊接机器及装置,不论是否兼有切割功能;用于热喷金属或金属陶瓷的电气机器及装置:**										
	-钎焊机器及装置:										
8515.1100	--烙铁及焊枪〔101 钎焊机器及装置,102 钎焊烙铁及焊枪〕	10		30	13/	13	个/千克	/		30	
8515.1900	--其他										
8515.1900 10	专门或主要用于印刷电路组件制造的其他波峰焊接机器〔999〕	0		30	13/	13	台/千克	/		25	
8515.1900 90	其他钎焊机器及装置〔999〕	10		30	13/	13	台/千克	/		35	
	-电阻焊接机器及装置:										
	--全自动或半自动的:										
8515.2120	---机器人										
8515.2120 01	汽车生产线电阻焊接机器人〔999〕	10	5	30	13/	13	台/千克	O/		30	
8515.2120 90	其他电阻焊接机器人〔999〕	10		30	13/	13	台/千克	O/		35	
	---其他:										
8515.2191	----直缝焊管机〔999〕	10		30	13/	13	台/千克	/		30	
8515.2199	----其他〔999〕	10		30	13/	13	台/千克	O/		30	
8515.2900	--其他〔999〕	10		30	13/	13	台/千克	/		35	6.5/6.5
	-用于金属加工的电弧(包括等离子弧)焊接机器及装置:										
	--全自动或半自动的:										
8515.3120	---机器人〔999〕	10		30	13/	13	台/千克	AO/	L	35	
	---其他:										
8515.3191	----螺旋焊管机〔999〕	10		30	13/	13	台/千克	/	L	35	
8515.3199	----其他〔999〕	10		30	13/	13	台/千克	AO/	L	30	
8515.3900	--其他〔999〕	10		30	13/	13	台/千克	A/	L	30	
	-其他机器及装置:										
8515.8010	---激光焊接机器人										
8515.8010 01	汽车生产线激光焊接机器人〔999〕	8	5	30	13/	13	台/千克	/		30	5.2/5.2
8515.8010 90	其他激光焊接机器人〔999〕	8		30	13/	13	台/千克	/		33	5.2/5.2
8515.8090	---其他										
8515.8090 10	电子束、激光自动焊接机(将端塞焊接于燃料细棒(或棒)的自动焊接机)〔101 波峰焊设备,102 其它焊接设备及其零件〕	8		30	13/	13	台/千克	3/		28	5.2/5.2
8515.8090 90	其他焊接机器及装置[T2]	8		30	13/	13	台/千克	/	L	28	5.2/5.2
8515.9000	-零件										
8515.9000 10	专门或主要用于印刷电路组件制造的其他波峰焊接机器的零件〔999〕	0		30	13/	13	千克	/		20	3.9/3.9
8515.9000 90	其他电气等焊接机器及装置零件(包括激光,其他光,光子束,超声波,电子束磁脉冲等)〔999〕	6	3	30	13/	13	千克	/		23	3.9/3.9
85.16	**电热的快速热水器、储存式热水器、浸入式液体加热器;电气空间加热器及土壤加热器;电热的理发器具(例如,电吹风机、电卷发器、电热发钳)及干手器;电熨斗;其他家用电热器具;加热电阻器,但税目85.45的货品除外:**										
	-电热的快速热水器、储存式热水器、浸入式液体加热器:										
8516.1010	---储存式电热水器[T2]	7		100	13/	13	个/千克	A/	L	22	
8516.1020	---即热式电热水器[T2]	7		100	13/	13	个/千克	A/	L	12	
8516.1090	---其他[T2]	7		100	13/	13	个/千克	A/	L	12	
	-电气空间加热器及土壤加热器:										
8516.2100	--储存式散热器[T2]	7		100	13/	13	个/千克	/		32	
	--其他:										
8516.2910	---土壤加热器[T2]	7		40	13/	13	个/千克	/		17	5.6/5.6
8516.2920	---辐射式空间加热器[T2]	7		100	13/	13	个/千克	/	L	32	
	---对流式空间加热器:										
8516.2931	----风扇式[T2]	7		100	13/	13	个/千克	/	L	32	
8516.2932	----充液式[T2]	7		100	13/	13	个/千克	/	L	32	
8516.2939	----其他[T2]	7		100	13/	13	个/千克	/	L	22	

协定税率 %								RCEP		特惠税率 %			
东/冰/格	巴基斯坦	韩国	瑞士 上/下	哥/秘/柬	澳/毛	新西/坡/智	中国港/澳/台	东盟及马来/澳/韩	日/新	亚太2国	老/柬/缅	98/97/95	Article Description
0/0/0	0	0	0/0	0/0/0	0/0	0//0	0/0/	0/0/0	0/0			0/0/0	Other electric furnaces and ovens for industrial use (including laboratory use)
													-Other equipment for the heat treatment of materials by induction or dielectric loss
0/0/0	3.5	0	0/0	0/0/0	0/0	0/0/0	0/0/	9/9/9	9.1/9			0/0/0	Welding seam intermediate frequency annealing device
0/0/0	3.5	0	0/0	0/0/0	0/0	0/0/0	0/0/	9/9/9	9.1/9			0/0/0	Other equipment for the heat treatment of materials by induction or dielectric loss
													-Parts:
0/0/0	2	0	0/0	0/0/0	0/0	0//0	0/0/	0/0/0	7.3/0			0/0/0	---Of steel making electric furnaces
0/0/0	0	0	0/0	0/0/0	0/0	0//0	0/0/	0/0/0	0/0			0/0/0	---Other
													Electric (including electrically heated gas), laser or other light or photon beam, ultrasonic, electron beam, magnetic pulse or plasma arc soldering, brazing or welding machines and apparatus, whether or not capable of cutting; electric machines and apparatus for hot spraying of metals or cermets:
													-Brazing or soldering machines and apparatus:
0/0/0	2	2	0/0	0/0/0	0/0	0/0/0	0/0/	0/0/9	9.1/0			0/0/0	--Soldering irons and guns
													--Other
0/0/0	2		4/4	0/0/0	0/0	0/0/0	0/0/	5/5/	/5			0/0/0	Other wave soldering machines, especially for the manufacture of printed circuit assemblies
0/0/0	2		4/4	0/0/0	0/0	0/0/0	0/0/	5/5/	/5			0/0/0	Other soldering machines and devices
													-Machines and apparatus for resistance welding of metals:
													--Fully or partly automatic:
													---Robot
0/0/0	3.5	6		0/0/0	0/0	0/0/0	0/0/	9.5/9.5/	/9.5			0/0/0	Resistance of automotive production line welding robot
0/0/0	3.5	6		0/0/0	0/0	0/0/0	0/0/	9.5/9.5/	/9.5			0/0/0	Other resistance welding robot
													---Other:
0/0/0	2	6	0/0	0/0/0	0/0	0//0	0/0/	9.5/9.5/	/9.5			0/0/0	----Aligning tube welding machines
0/0/0	3.5	6		0/0/0	0/0	0/0/0	0/0/	9.5/9.5/	/9.5			0/0/0	----Other:
0/0/0	2	6	0/0	0/0/0	0/0	0/0/0	0/0/	9.5/9.5/	/9.5			0/0/0	--Other
													-Machines and apparatus for arc (including plasma arc) welding of metals:
													--Fully or partly automatic:
5/0/0	8	6	0/0	0/0/0	0/0	0//0	0/0/					0/0/0	---Robot
													---Other:
0/0/0	2	2	0/0	0/0/0	0/0	0//0	0/0/	0/0/9	9.1/0			0/0/0	----Spiralling tube welding machines
/0/0	8	6	0/0	0/0/0	0/0	0//0	0/0/					0/0/0	----Other
0/0/0	2	2	0/0	0/0/0	0/0	0//0	0/0/	0/0/9	9.1/0			0/0/0	--Other
													-Other machines and apparatus:
													---Laser welding robot
0/0/0	2	0	3.2/3.2	0/0/0	0/0	0//0	0/0/0	0/0/0	7.6/0			0/0/0	Laser welding robot used for auto production line
0/0/0	2	0	3.2/3.2	0/0/0	0/0	0//0	0/0/0	0/0/0	7.6/0			0/0/0	Other laser wdlding robot
													---Other
0/0/0	2	0	3.2/3.2	0/0/0	0/0	0//0	0/0/0	0/0/0	7.3/0			0/0/0	Automatic electron beam, laser wdlding machine (automatic welding machine for welding end plug onto fuelpins or rods)
0/0/0	2	0	3.2/3.2	0/0/0	0/0	0//0	0/0/0	0/0/0	7.3/0			0/0/0	Other welding machines and devices
													-Parts
0/0/0	0	0	0.6/0.6	0/0/0	0/0	0//0	0/0/	5.4/5.4/5.4	5.5/5.4			0/0/0	Parts of other wave soldering machines, especially for the manufacture of printed circuit assemblies
0/0/0	0	0	0.6/0.6	0/0/0	0/0	0//0	0/0/	5.4/5.4/5.4	5.5/5.4			0/0/0	Parts of other electric brazing or welding machines and apparatus (including laser or other light or photon beam, ultrasonic, electron beam, magnetic pulse)
													Electric instantaneous or storage water heaters and immersion heaters; electric space heating apparatus and soil heating apparatus; electro-thermic hair-dressing apparatus (for example, hair dryers, hair curlers, curling tong heaters) and hand dryers; electric smoothing irons; other electro-thermic appliances of a kind used for domestic purposes; electric heating resistors, other than those of headingNo. 85.45:
													-Electric instantaneous or storage water heaters and immersion heaters:
0/0/0	2	2	0/0	0/0/0	0/0	0/0/0	0/0/	0/0/9	9.1/0			0/0/0	---Electric storage water heaters
0/0/0	2	2	0/0	0/0/0	0/0	0/0/0	0/0/	0/0/9	9.1/0			0/0/0	---Electric instantaneous water heaters
0/0/0	2		0/0	0/0/0	0/0	0/0/0	0/0/	7/7/	/7			0/0/0	---Other
													-Electric space heating apparatus and electric soil heating apparatus:
0/0/0			7/7	0/0/0	0/21	0/0/0	0/0/0	7/7/	/7			0/0/0	--Storage heating radiators
													--Other:
0/0/0	2	2	0/0	0/0/0	0/0	0//0	0/0/	0/0/9	9.1/0			0/0/0	---Electric soil heating apparatus
0/0/0	2	2	0/0	0/0/0	0/0	0/0/0	0/0/	0/0/9	9.1/0			0/0/0	---Radiat space heating apparatus
													---Convectiom space heating apparatus:
0/0/0	2	2	0/0	0/0/0	0/0	0/0/0	0/0/	0/0/9	9.1/0			0/0/0	---Fan type
0/0/0	2	2	0/0	0/0/0	0/0	0/0/0	0/0/	0/0/9	9.1/0			0/0/0	---Oil-filled type
0/0/0	2	2	0/0	0/0/0	0/0	0/0/0	0/0/	0/0/9	9.1/0			0/0/0	---Other

税则号列	货品名称〔CIQ 扩展编码及品名—T2 表示见附表 2〕	最惠(%)	暂定税率	普通	增值/消费	出口退税	计量单位	监管条件/特殊证件	检验检疫	对美关税	亚太上/下
8516.2990	---其他[T2]	7		100	13/	13	个/千克	/	L	32	
	-电热的理发器具及干手器：										
8516.3100	--吹风机[T2]	7		100	13/	13	个/千克	A/	LM	32	
8516.3200	--其他理发器具[T2]	7		100	13/	13	个/千克	A/	LM		
8516.3300	--干手器[T2]	7		100	13/	13	个/千克	A/	LM		
8516.4000	-电熨斗[T2]	7		100	13/	13	个/千克	A/	LM		
8516.5000	-微波炉[T2]	7		130	13/	13	个/千克	A/	LMR	32	4.6/4.6
	-其他炉；电锅、电热板、加热环、烧烤炉及烘烤器：										
8516.6010	---电磁炉[T2]	7		130	13/	13	个/千克	A/	L	32	5.6/5.6
8516.6030	---电饭锅[T2]	7		130	13/	13	个/千克	A/	LR		
8516.6040	---电炒锅[T2]	7		130	13/	13	个/千克	A/	R		
8516.6050	---电烤箱[T2]	7		130	13/	13	个/千克	A/	LM	32	
8516.6090	---其他[T2]	7		130	13/	13	个/千克	A/	LM	32	
	-其他电热器具：										
	--咖啡壶或茶壶：										
8516.7110	---滴液式咖啡机[T2]	7		130	13/	13	个/千克	A/	LR	32	
8516.7120	---蒸馏渗滤式咖啡机[T2]	7		130	13/	13	个/千克	A/	LR	32	
8516.7130	---泵压式咖啡机[T2]	7		130	13/	13	个/千克	A/	LR	32	
8516.7190	---其他[T2]	7		130	13/	13	个/千克	A/	LR	17	
	--烤面包器：										
8516.7210	---家用自动面包机[T2]	7		130	13/	13	个/千克	A/	LMR		
8516.7220	---片式烤面包机(多士炉)[T2]	7		130	13/	13	个/千克	A/	LMR	32	
8516.7290	---其他[T2]	7		130	13/	13	个/千克	A/	LMR	32	
	--其他：										
8516.7910	---电热饮水机[T2]	7		100	13/	13	台/千克	A/	L	32	
8516.7990	---其他	7		100	13/	13	个/千克	A/	L	32	
8516.8000	-加热电阻器[T2]	7		40	13/	13	个/千克	/			
	-零件：										
8516.9010	---土壤加热器及加热电阻器用〔999〕	6		40	13/	13	千克	/		16	
8516.9090	---其他〔999〕	6		100	13/	13	千克	/		31	
85.17	**电话机，包括用于蜂窝网络或其他无线网络的智能手机及其他电话机；其他发送或接收声音、图像或其他数据用的设备，包括有线或无线网络(例如，局域网或广域网)的通信设备，但税目 84.43、85.25、85.27 或 85.28 的发送或接收设备除外：**										
	-电话机，包括蜂窝网络或其他无线网络用智能手机及其他电话机：										
8517.1100	--无绳电话机										
8517.1100 10	无绳加密电话机〔999〕	0		30	13/	13	台/千克	2A/	L	25	
8517.1100 90	其他无绳电话机〔999〕	0		30	13/	13	台/千克	A/	L	25	
8517.1300	--智能手机〔101 不带附件及包装，102 包含附件及包装〕	0		20	13/	13	台/千克	A/	L	25	
	--其他用于蜂窝网络或其他无线网络的电话机 ：										
8517.1410	---手持(包括车载)式无线电话机										
8517.1410 11	GSM 数字式手持无线电话整套散件〔101 不带附件及包装，102 包含附件及包装〕	0		20	13/	13	台/千克	/		25	
8517.1410 19	其他 GSM 数字式手持无线电话机〔101 不带附件及包装，102 包含附件及包装〕	0		20	13/	13	台/千克	A/	L	25	
8517.1410 21	CDMA 数字式手持无线电话整套散件〔101 不带附件及包装，102 包含附件及包装〕	0		20	13/	13	台/千克	/		25	
8517.1410 29	其他 CDMA 数字式手持无线电话机〔101 不带附件及包装，102 包含附件及包装〕	0		20	13/	13	台/千克	A/	L	25	
8517.1410 90	其他手持式无线电话机(包括车载式无线电话机)〔101 不带附件及包装，102 包含附件及包装〕	0		20	13/	13	台/千克	A/	L	25	
8517.1420	---对讲机〔101 对讲机，102 其它通讯设备及其零件〕	0		17	13/	13	台/千克	/		25	
8517.1490	---其他〔101 不带附件及包装，102 包含附件及包装，103 其它通讯设备及其零件〕	0		14	13/	13	台/千克	/	L	25	
8517.1800	--其他										
8517.1800 10	其他加密电话机〔999〕	0		30	13/	13	台/千克	2/		25	
8517.1800 90	其他电话机〔999〕	0		30	13/	13	台/千克	/		25	
	-其他发送或接收声音、图像或其他数据用的设备，包括有线或无线网络(例如，局域网或广域网)的通信设备：										
	--基站：										
8517.6110	---移动通信基站										
8517.6110 10	GSM 式移动通信基地站〔999〕	0		14	13/	13	台/千克	O/		25	
8517.6110 20	CDMA 式移动通信基地站〔999〕	0		14	13/	13	台/千克	O/		25	
8517.6110 30	TACS 式移动通信基地站〔999〕	0		14	13/	13	台/千克	/		25	
8517.6110 90	其他移动通信基地站〔999〕	0		14	13/	13	台/千克	O/		25	
8517.6190	---其他[T2]	0		14	13/	13	台/千克	O/		20	

协定税率 %								RCEP		特惠税率 %			Article Description
东/冰/格	巴基斯坦	韩国	瑞士上/下	哥/秘/柬	澳/毛	新西/坡/智	中国港/澳/台	东盟及马来/澳/韩	日/新	亚太2国	老/柬/缅	98/97/95	
0/0/0	4	2	0/0	0/0/0	0/0	0/0/0	0/0/	0/0/9	9.1/0			0/0/0	---Other
													-Electro-thermic hair-dressing or hand-drying apparatus:
0/0/0	2	2	1/1	0/0/0	0/0	0/0/0	0/0/	0/0/9	9.1/0			0/0/0	--Hair dryers
0/0/0	28	21	7/7	0/0/0	0/21	0/0/0	0/0/	33.3/33.3/33.3	/33.3			0/0/0	--Other hair-dressing apparatus
0/0/0	28		7/7	0/0/0	0/21	0/0/0	0/0/	5/5/	/5			0/0/0	--Hand-drying apparatus
0/0/0	28		3.5/3.5	0/0/0	0/21	0/0/0	0/0/0	7/7/	/7			0/0/0	-Electric smoothing irons
0/0/0	5.3	3	1.5/1.5	0/0/0	0/0	0/0/0	0/0/	0/0/13.5	13.6/0			0/0/0	-Microwave ovens
													-Other ovens; cookers, cooking plates, boiling rings, grillers and roasters:
0/0/0	8.4	3	1.5/1.5	0/0/0	0/0	0/0/0	0/0/	0/0/13.5	13.6/0			0/0/0	---Electromagnetic ovens
0/0/0	8.4	3	1.5/1.5	0/0/0	0/0	0/0/0	0/0/0	13.5/13.5/13.5	13.6/13.5			0/0/0	---Electric rice cookers
0/0/0	8.4	3	1.5/1.5	0/0/0	0/0	0/0/0	0/0/	0/0/13.5	13.6/0			0/0/0	---Electric frying pans
0/0/0	8.4	3	1.5/1.5	0/0/0	0/0	0//0	0/0/0	0/0/13.5	13.6/0			0/0/0	---Roaster oven
0/0/0	8.4	3	1.5/1.5	0/0/0	0/0	0/0/0	0/0/	0/0/13.5	13.6/0			0/0/0	---Other
													-Other electro-thermic appliances:
													--Coffee or tea makers:
0//0	25.6		0/0	0/0/0	0/19.2	0/0/0	0/0/	7/7/	/7			0/0/0	---Drip coffee maker
0//0	25.6		0/0	0/0/0	0/19.2	0/0/0	0/0/	7/7/	/7			0/0/0	---Steam espresso makers
0/0/0	25.6		0/0	0/0/0	0/19.2	0/0/0	0/0/	7/7/	/7			0/0/0	---Pump-espresso makers
0/0/0	25.6		0/0	0/0/0	0/19.2	0/0/0	0/0/	7/7/	/7			0/0/0	---Other
													--Toasters:
0//0	25.6		7/7	0/0/0	0/19.2	0/0/0	0/0/0	7/7/	/7			0/0/0	---Household automated bread makers
0//0	25.6		7/7	0/0/0	0/19.2	0/0/0	0/0/	7/7/	/7			0/0/0	---Slice pop-up toasters
0//0	25.6		7/7	0/0/0	0/19.2	0/0/0	0/0/	7/7/	/7			0/0/0	---Other
													--Other:
0//0	25.6		3.2/3.2	0/0/0	0/19.2	0/0/0	0/0/	7/7/	/7			0/0/0	---Electro-thermic water dispensers
0//0				0/0/0	0/19.2	0/0/0	0/0/	7/7/	/7			0/0/0	---Other
0/0/0	2	2	1/1	0/0/0	0/0	0/0/0	0/0/	0/0/9	9.1/0			0/0/0	-Electric heating resistors
													-Parts:
0/0/0	2	1.6	0/0	0/0/0	0/0	0//0	0/0/	0/0/7.2	7.3/0			0/0/0	---Of apparatus of subheading 8516.2910 or 8516.8000
0/0/0	4.2	2.4	0/0	0/0/0	0/0	0/0/0	0/0/	10.8/10.8/10.8	10.9/10.8			0/0/0	---Other
													Telephone sets, including telephones for cellular networks or for other wireless networks; other apparatus for the transmission or reception of voice, images or other data, including apparatus for communication in a wired or wireless network(such as a local or wide are network), other than transmission or reception apparatus of heading 84.43, 85.25, 85.27 or 85.28:
													-Telephone sets, including telephones for cellular networks or for other wireless networks:
													--Line telephone sets with cordless handsets
0/0/0	0	0	0/0	0/0/0	0/0	0//0	0/0/	0/0/0	0/0			0/0/0	Cordless encrypting telephones
0/0/0	0	0	0/0	0/0/0	0/0	0//0	0/0/	0/0/0	0/0			0/0/0	Other cordless telephones
0/0/0	0	0	0/0	0/0/0	0/0	0//0	0/0/	0/0/0	0/0			0/0/0	--Intelligent mobile phone
													--other telephones for cellular net works or for other wireless networks:
													---Wirelrss telephones handsets(including vehicle installed)
0/0/0	0	0	0/0	0/0/0	0/0	0//0	0/0/	0/0/0	0/0			0/0/0	GSM digital handheld radiotelephone complete set of parts
0/0/0	0	0	0/0	0/0/0	0/0	0//0	0/0/	0/0/0	0/0			0/0/0	Other GSM digital handheld radiotelephones
0/0/0	0	0	0/0	0/0/0	0/0	0//0	0/0/	0/0/0	0/0			0/0/0	CDMA digital handheld wireless telephone complete set of parts
0/0/0	0	0	0/0	0/0/0	0/0	0//0	0/0/	0/0/0	0/0			0/0/0	Other CDMA digital handheld radiotelephones
0/0/0	0	0	0/0	0/0/0	0/0	0//0	0/0/	0/0/0	0/0			0/0/0	Other handheld radiotelephones (including vehicle mounted radiotelephones)
0/0/0	0	0	0/0	0/0/0	0/0	0//0	0/0/	0/0/0	0/0			0/0/0	---Walkie—talkie(8517.1220)
0/0/0	0	0	0/0	0/0/0	0/0	0//0	0/0/	0/0/0	0/0			0/0/0	---Other (8517.1290)
													--Other
0/0/0	0	0	0/0	0/0/0	0/0	0//0	0/0/	0/0/0	0/0			0/0/0	Other encrypting telephones
0/0/0	0	0	0/0	0/0/0	0/0	0//0	0/0/	0/0/0	0/0			0/0/0	Other telephones
													-Other apparatus for tromsmission or reception of voice, images or other data including apparatus for communication in a wired or wireless network (such as a local or wide area network):
													--Base stations:
													---Mobile communication base station
0/0/0	0	0	0/0	0/0/0	0/0	0//0	0/0/	0/0/0	0/0			0/0/0	GSM mobile communication base station
0/0/0	0	0	0/0	0/0/0	0/0	0//0	0/0/	0/0/0	0/0			0/0/0	CDMA mobile communication base station
0/0/0	0	0	0/0	0/0/0	0/0	0//0	0/0/	0/0/0	0/0			0/0/0	TACS mobile communication base station
0/0/0	0	0	0/0	0/0/0	0/0	0//0	0/0/	0/0/0	0/0			0/0/0	Other mobile communication base station
0/0/0	0	0	0/0	0/0/0	0/0	0//0	0/0/	0/0/0	0/0			0/0/0	---Other

税则号列	货品名称〔CIQ 扩展编码及品名－T2 表示见附表 2〕	最惠(%)	暂定税率	普通	增值/消费	出口退税	计量单位	监管条件/特殊证件	检验检疫	对美关税	亚太上/下
	--接收、转换并且发送或再生声音、图像或其他数据用的设备，包括交换及路由设备：										
	---数字式程控电话或电报交换机：										
8517.6211	----局用电话交换机；长途电话交换机；电报交换机〔101 电话交换机，102 网络交换机，103 其它通讯设备及其零件〕	0		17	13/	13	台/千克	/		10	
8517.6212	----移动通信交换机[T2]	0		40	13/	13	台/千克	O/		5	
8517.6219	----其他电话交换机〔999〕	0		40	13/	13	台/千克	/		20	
	---光通讯设备：										
8517.6221	----光端机及脉冲编码调制设备(PCM)〔101 调制解调器，102 光通信数字同步设备，103 其它通讯设备及其零件〕	0		17	13/	13	台/千克	O/	L	20	
8517.6222	----波分复用光传输设备〔999〕	0		30	13/	13	台/千克	O/	L	25	
8517.6229	----其他										
8517.6229 10	光通讯加密路由器、加密 VPN 设备[T2]	0		30	13/	13	台/千克	AO/	L	5	
8517.6229 20	光通讯加密 VPN 设备〔101：光通信数字同步设备；102：其它通讯设备及其零件〕	0		30	13/	13	台/千克	23A/	LM	5	
8517.6229 90	其他光通讯设备[T2]	0		30	13/	13	台/千克	A/	L	5	
	---其他有线数字通信设备：										
8517.6231	----通信网络时钟同步设备〔999〕	0		30	13/	13	台/千克	/	L	5	
8517.6232	----以太网络交换机	0		30	13/	13	台/千克	/		20	
8517.6233	----IP 电话信号转换设备〔999〕	0		30	13/	13	台/千克	/		25	
8517.6234	----调制解调器〔999〕	0		30	13/	13	台/千克	/		5	
8517.6235	----集线器〔999〕	0		40	13/	13	台/千克	A/	L	20	
8517.6236	----路由器	0		40	13/	13	台/千克	/		25	
8517.6237	----有线网络接口卡										
8517.6237 10	为聚合高性能数字计算机性能而专门设计的有线网络接口卡，单链路单向通信速率超过 2.0GB/s，高性能数字计算机是指调整后峰值性能(APP)大于 8.0 加权每秒万亿次浮点运算的数字计算机〔999〕	0		30	13/	13	台/千克	3/		25	
8517.6237 90	其他有线网络接口卡〔999〕	0		30	13/	13	台/千克	/	L	25	
8517.6239	----其他										
8517.6239 10	为聚合高性能数字计算机性能而专门设计的交换机，单链路单向通信速率超过 2.0GB/s，自定义通信协议。高性能数字计算机是指调整后峰值性能(APP)大于 8.0 加权每秒万亿次浮点运算的数字计算机〔999〕	0		30	13/	13	台/千克	3O/		10	
8517.6239 20	其他加密 VPN 设备	0		30	13/	13	台/千克	23/		10	
8517.6239 90	其他有线数字通信设备〔999〕	0		30	13/	13	台/千克	/	L	10	
	---其他：										
8517.6292	----无线网络接口卡〔999〕	0		14	13/	13	台/千克	/	L	25	
8517.6293	----无线接入固定台〔999〕	0		14	13/	13	台/千克	/	L	25	
8517.6294	----无线耳机[T2]	0		14	13/	13	个/千克	/		25	
8517.6299	----其他〔999〕	0		14	13/	13	台/千克	/	L	25	
	--其他：										
8517.6910	---其他无线设备										
8517.6910 01	用于呼叫、提示和寻呼的便携式接收器[T2]	0		14	13/	13	台/千克	/		10	
8517.6910 91	卫星地球站(含终端地球站)无线电发射设备[T2]	0		14	13/	13	台/千克	O/		10	
8517.6910 99	其他无线通信设备〔101 不带附件及包装，102 包含附件及包装〕	0		14	13/	13	台/千克	A/	L	10	
8517.6990	---其他有线设备[T2]	0		30	13/	13	台/千克	/	L	10	
	-零件：										
8517.7100	--各种天线和天线反射器及其零件〔999〕	0		20	13/	13	千克	/		25	
	--其他：										
8517.7910	---数字式程控电话或电报交换机用〔999〕	0		14	13/	13	千克	/		25	

协定税率 %								RCEP		特惠税率 %			Article Description
东/冰/格	巴基斯坦	韩国	瑞士上/下	哥/秘/柬	澳/毛	新西/坡/智	中国港/澳/台	东盟及马来/澳/韩	日/新	亚太2国	老/柬/缅	98/97/95	
													--Machines for the reception, conversion and transmission or regeneration of voice images or other data, induding switchig and routing apparatus:
													---Digital program-controlled telephonic or telephooic switching apparatus:
0/0/0	0	0	0/0	0/0/0	0/0	0//0	0/0/	0/0/0	0/0			0/0/0	----Public telephonic switching apparatus, toll telephonic switching apparatus telegrapbic switching apparatus
0/0/0	0	0	0/0	0/0/0	0/0	0//0	0/0/	0/0/0	0/0			0/0/0	----Mobile communication switching system
0/0/0	0	0	0/0	0/0/0	0/0	0//0	0/0/	0/0/0	0/0			0/0/0	----Other telephonic switching appatatus
													---Optical communication equipments:
0/0/0	0	0	0/0	0/0/0	0/0	0//0	0/0/	0/0/0	0/0			0/0/0	----Optical line terminal equipments and pulse code modulation equipments
0/0/0	0	0	0/0	0/0/0	0/0	0//0	0/0/	0/0/0	0/0			0/0/0	----Optical transmission equipments for wave-division multlplexing
													----Other
0/0/0	0	0	0/0	0/0/0	0/0	0//0	0/0/	0/0/0	0/0			0/0/0	Optical communication encrypting routers
0/0/0	0	0	0/0	0/0/0	0/0	0//0	0/0/	0/0/0	0/0		//	0/0/0	Optical communication encryption VPN equipment
0/0/0	0	0	0/0	0/0/0	0/0	0//0	0/0/	0/0/0	0/0			0/0/0	Other optical communication equipment
													---Other telecommunication apparatus for digit line system:
0/0/0	0	0	0/0	0/0/0	0/0	0//0	0/0/	0/0/0	0/0			0/0/0	----Communication network synchronization equipments
0/0/0	0	0	0/0	0/0/0	0/0	0//0	0/0/	0/0/0	0/0			0/0/0	----Ethernet exchangers
0/0/0	0	0	0/0	0/0/0	0/0	0//0	0/0/	0/0/0	0/0			0/0/0	----IP telephone signal converters
0/0/0	0	0	0/0	0/0/0	0/0	0//0	0/0/	0/0/0	0/0			0/0/0	----Modem
0/0/0	0	0	0/0	0/0/0	0/0	0//0	0/0/	0/0/0	0/0			0/0/0	----Hubs
0/0/0	0	0	0/0	0/0/0	0/0	0//0	0/0/	0/0/0	0/0			0/0/0	----Routers
													----Wired network interface card
0/0/0	0	0	0/0	0/0/0	0/0	0//0	0/0/	0/0/0	0/0			0/0/0	Specially designed for the polymerization of high-performance digital computer performance cable network interface card, single link one-way communication rate of more than 2.0 GB/s, high-performance digital computer is adjusted peak performance (APP) is greater than 8.0 digital computer weighted one trillion floating point operations per second
0/0/0	0	0	0/0	0/0/0	0/0	0//0	0/0/	0/0/0	0/0			0/0/0	Wired network interface cards
													----Other
0/0/0	0	0	0/0	0/0/0	0/0	0//0	0/0/	0/0/0	0/0			0/0/0	Specially designed for the polymerization of high-performance digital computer performance switches, one-way communication rate of more than 2.0 GB/s single link, the custom communication protocol. High performance digital computer is adjusted peak performance (APP) is greater than 8.0 weighted one trillion floating point operations per second, a digital computer
0/0/0	0	0	0/0	0/0/0	0/0	0//0	0/0/	0/0/0	0/0		//	0/0/0	Other encrypted VPN devices
0/0/0	0	0	0/0	0/0/0	0/0	0//0	0/0/	0/0/0	0/0			0/0/0	Other telecommunication apparatus for digital line system
													---Other:
0/0/0	0	0	0/0	0/0/0	0/0	0//0	0/0/	0/0/0	0/0			0/0/0	----Wireless network interface cards
0/0/0	0	0	0/0	0/0/0	0/0	0//0	0/0/	0/0/0	0/0			0/0/0	----Fixed wireless access station
0/0/0	0	0	0/0	0/0/0	0/0	0//0	0/0/	0/0/0	0/0			0/0/0	----Wireless headset
0/0/0	0	0	0/0	0/0/0	0/0	0//0	0/0/	0/0/0	0/0			0/0/0	----Other
													--Other:
													---Other equipments in a wireless network
0/0/0	0	0	0/0	0/0/0	0/0	0//0	0/0/	0/0/0	8.2/0			0/0/0	Portable receivers for calling ,promoting and paging
0/0/0	0	0	0/0	0/0/0	0/0	0//0	0/0/	0/0/0	8.2/0		//	0/0/0	Radio transmitting equipment of satellite earth station (including terminal earth station)
0/0/0	0	0	0/0	0/0/0	0/0	0//0	0/0/	0/0/0	8.2/0		//	0/0/0	Other wireless communication equipment
0/0/0	0	0	0/0	0/0/0	0/0	0//0	0/0/	0/0/0	0/0			0/0/0	---Other equipments in a wired network
													-Parts:
0/0/0	0	0	0/0	0/0/0	0/0	0//0	0/0/	0/0/0	0/0			0/0/0	--Various antennas and antenna reflectors and their parts
													--Other
0/0/0	0	0	0/0	0/0/0	0/0	0//0	0/0/	0/0/0	0/0			0/0/0	---For digital program controlled telephone or telegraph exchange

税则号列		货品名称〔CIQ 扩展编码及品名—T2 表示见附表 2〕	最惠(%)	暂定税率	普通	增值/消费	出口退税	计量单位	监管条件/特殊证件	检验检疫	对美关税	亚太上/下
8517.7920		---光端机及脉冲编码调制设备 (PCM)用〔999〕	0		14	13/	13	千克	/		25	
8517.7930		---手持式无线电话机用(天线除外)〔999〕	0		17	13/	13	千克	/		25	
8517.7940		---对讲机用(天线除外)〔101 移动通讯设备,102 其它通讯设备及其零件〕	0		20	13/	13	千克	/		25	0/0
8517.7950		---光通信设备的激光收发模块〔999〕	0		30	13/	13	千克	/			
8517.7990		---其他〔999〕	0		20	13/	13	千克	/		25	
85.18		**传声器(麦克风)及其座架;扬声器,不论是否装成音箱;耳机及耳塞机,不论是否装有传声器,以及由传声器及一个或多个扬声器组成的组合机,音频扩大器;电气扩音机组:**										
8518.1000		-传声器(麦克风)及其座架										
8518.1000	01	电讯用频率在 300～3400Hz 麦克风(直径不超过 10mm,高不超过 3mm)[T2]	0		40	13/	13	个/千克	/		25	
8518.1000	90	其他传声器(麦克风)及其座架[T2]	0		40	13/	13	个/千克	/		25	
		-扬声器,不论是否装成音箱:										
8518.2100		--单喇叭音箱[T2]	0		40	13/	13	个/千克	/	L	25	
8518.2200		--多喇叭音箱[T2]	0		40	13/	13	个/千克	/	L	20	
8518.2900		--其他[T2]	0		40	13/	13	个/千克	/		25	
8518.3000		-耳机、耳塞机,不论是否装有传声器,以及由传声器及一个或多个扬声器组成的组合机[T2]	0		40	13/	13	个/千克	/		25	
8518.4000		-音频扩大器										
8518.4000	01	电器扩音器(列入 ITA 的有线电话重复器用的)[T2]	0		40	13/	13	台/千克	/		20	
8518.4000	90	其他音频扩大器[T2]	0		40	13/	13	台/千克	/	L	20	
8518.5000		-电气扩音机组[T2]	0		40	13/	13	套/千克	/	L	20	
8518.9000		-零件										
8518.9000	01	税目 8518.400001 所列货品的零件(列入 ITA 的有线电话重复器用的)[T2]	0		40	13/	13	千克	/		25	
8518.9000	90	税目 85.18 所列货品的其他零件[T2]	0		40	13/	13	千克	/		25	
85.19		**声音录制或重放设备:**										
8519.2000		-用硬币、钞票、银行卡、代币或其他支付方式使其工作的设备										
8519.2000	10	以特定支付方式使其工作的激光唱机(用硬币、钞票、银行卡、代币或其他支付方式使其工作)〔101:Ⅰ类激光唱机,102:Ⅱ类激光唱机,103:Ⅲ类激光唱机〕	12		80	13/	13	台/千克	/	L	17	7.8/7.8
8519.2000	90	其他以特定支付方式使其工作的声音录制或重放设备(用硬币、钞票、银行卡、代币或其他支付方式使其工作)[T2]	12		80	13/	13	台/千克	/	L	17	7.8/7.8
8519.3000		-转盘(唱机唱盘)[T2]	7		130	13/	13	台/千克	/		32	
		-其他设备:										
		--使用磁性、光学或半导体媒体的:										
		---使用磁性媒体的:										
8519.8111		----未装有声音录制装置的盒式磁带型声音重放装置,编辑节目用放声机除外[T2]	0		130	13/	13	台/千克	A/	L	5	
8519.8112		----装有声音重放装置的盒式磁带录音机[T2]	0		130	13/	13	台/千克	A/	L	25	
8519.8119		----其他 [T2]	0		80	13/	13	台/千克	6A/	L		0/0
		---使用光学媒体的:										
8519.8121		----激光唱机,未装有声音录制装置[T2]	0		80	13/	13	台/千克	A/	L	25	0/0
8519.8129		----其他										
8519.8129	10	具有录音功能的激光唱机[T2]	0		80	13/	13	台/千克	6A/	L	15	0/0
8519.8129	90	其他使用光学媒体的声音录制或重放设备[T2]	0		80	13/	13	台/千克	A/	L	15	0/0
		---使用半导体媒体:										

协定税率 %								RCEP		特惠税率 %			Article Description
东/冰/格	巴基斯坦	韩国	瑞士上/下	哥/秘/柬	澳/毛	新西/坡/智	中国港/澳/台	东盟及马来/澳/韩	日/新	亚太2国	老/柬/缅	98/97/95	
0/0/0	0	0	0/0	0/0/0	0/0	0//0	0/0/	0/0/0	0/0			0/0/0	---For optical transceiver and pulse code modulation equipment (PCM)
0/0/0	0	0	0/0	0/0/0	0/0	0//0	0/0/	0/0/0	0/0			0/0/0	---For handheld radiotelephone (except antenna)
0/0/0	2	1.6	0/0	0/0/0	0/0	0//0	0/0/	0/0/7.2	0/0			0/0/0	---For interphone (except antenna)
0/0/0	0	0	0/0	0/0/0	0/0	0//0	0/0/	0/0/0	0/0			0/0/0	---Laser transceiver module of optical communication equipment
0/0/0	0	0	0/0	0/0/0	0/0	0//0	0/0/	0/0/0	0/0			0/0/0	---Other
													Microphones and stands therefor; loudspeakers, whether or not mounted in their enclosures; headphones earphones, whether or not combined with a microphone, and sets consisting of a microphone and one or more loudspeakers; audio-frequency electric amplifiers; electric sound amplifier sets:
													-Microphones and stands therefor
0/0/0	3.5	0	0/0	0/0/0	0/0	0/0/0	0/0/0	0/0/0	9.1/0			0/0/0	Microphones, telecommunication use, frequency between 300Hz~3400Hz (with a diameter≤10mm and a height≤3mm)
0/0/0	3.5	0	0/0	0/0/0	0/0	0/0/0	0/0/0	0/0/0	9.1/0			0/0/0	Other microphones and stands therefor
													-Loudspeakers, whether or not mounted in their enclosures:
0/0/0	2	2	0/0	0/0/0	0/0	0/0/0	0/0/	0/0/9	0/0			0/0/0	--Single loudspeakers, mounted in their enclosures
0/0/0	2	2	0/0	0/0/0	0/0	0/0/0	0/0/	0/0/9	0/0			0/0/0	--Multiple loudspeakers, mounted in the same enclosure
0/0/0	0	0	0/0	0/0/0	0/0	0//0	0/0/	0/0/0	0/0			0/0/0	--Other
0/0/0	0	0	0/0	0/0/0	0/0	0//0	0/0/	0/0/0	0/0			0/0/0	-Headphones and earphones, whether or not combined with a microphone, and sets consisting of a microphone and one or more loudspeakers
													-Audio-frequency electric amplifiers
0/0/0	4.2	2.4	0/0	0/0/0	0/0	0/0/0	0/0/0	0/0/10.8	10.9/0			0/0/0	Amplifiers for electric equipment(on ITA cable phone repeatedly used)
0/0/0	4.2	2.4	0/0	0/0/0	0/0	0/0/0	0/0/0	0/0/10.8	10.9/0			0/0/0	Other audio-frequency electric amplifiers
0/0/0	2	6	0/0	0/0/0	0/0	0/0/0	0/0/	0/0/9.3	0/0			0/0/0	-Electric sound amplifier sets
													-Parts
0/0/0	4	8.4	0/0	0/0/0	0/0	0/0/0	0/0/0	0/0/9.5	9.5/0			0/0/0	Parts for goods of heading No. 8518. 400001(for telephone repeaters falling within ITA)
0/0/0	4	8.4	0/0	0/0/0	0/0	0/0/0	0/0/0	0/0/9.5	9.5/0			0/0/0	Other parts of goods of heading No. 85. 18
													Sound recording or reproducing apparatus:
													-Apparatus oporated by coins barknotes, bank cards tokens or by other means of payment
0/0/0	11.5	9.3	2/2	0/0/0	0/0	0/0/0	0/0/	18/18/18	18.8/18			0/0/0	Laser phonographs that work by special means of payment (coins, notes, bank card, token coins or other mcans of pay ment are used to make it work)
0/0/0	11.5	9.3	2/2	0/0/0	0/0	0/0/0	0/0/	18/18/18	18.8/18			0/0/0	Other sound recording or reproducing apparatus that work by special means of payment (coins, notes, bank card, token coins or other means of payment are used to make it work)
0/0/0	24		7/7	0/0/0	0/18	0/0/0	0/0/	7/7/	/7			0/0/0	-Tuntables(record-decks)
													-Other equipment:
													--Using magnetic, optical or semiconductor media:
													---Using magnetic media:
0/0/0	9.5	3.4	0/0	0/0/0	0/0	0/0/0	0/0/	0/0/15.3	0/0			0/0/0	----Cassette-type sound reproducing apparatus not incorporating a sound recording device, other than transchibing machines
0/0/0	24	18	0/0	0/0/0	0/13.5	0/0/0	0/0/	0/0/28	0/0			0/0/0	----Cassette-type magnetic tape recorders in corporating sound reproducing apparatus
0/0/0	11.5	9.3	0/0	0/0/0	0/0	0/0/0	0/0/	0/0/0	0/0			0/0/0	----Other
													---Using optical media:
0/0/0	20.8	18	0/0	0/0/0	0/13.5	0/0/0	0/0/	0/0/28	0/0			0/0/0	----Compact disc players, not in corporating a sound recondig devices
													----Other
0/0/0	11.2	9.3	0/0	0/0/0	0/0	0/0/0	0/0/	0/0/0	0/0			0/0/0	Recordable laser phonographs
0/0/0	11.2	9.3	0/0	0/0/0	0/0	0/0/0	0/0/	0/0/0	0/0			0/0/0	Other sound recording or reproducing apparontus using optics media
													---Using semiconductor media:

税则号列	货品名称〔CIQ 扩展编码及品名—T2 表示见附表 2〕	最惠(%)	暂定税率	普通	增值/消费	出口退税	计量单位	监管条件/特殊证件	检验检疫	对美关税	亚太上/下
8519.8131	----装有声音重放装置的闪速存储器型声音录制设备〔101 电子行业成套设备,102 Ⅰ类录音机,103 Ⅱ类录音机,104 Ⅲ类录音机〕	0		80	13/	13	台/千克	6A/	L	25	
8519.8139	----其他[T2]	0		80	13/	13	台/千克	6A/	L	5	0/0
	--其他:										
8519.8910	---不带录制装置的其他唱机,不论是否带有扬声器[T2]	0		130	13/	13	台/千克	A/	L	25	
8519.8990	---其他声音录制或重放设备[T2]	0		80	13/	13	台/千克	6A/	L	20	0/0
85.21	**视频信号录制或重放设备,不论是否装有高频调谐器:**										
	-磁带型:										
	---录像机:										
8521.1011	----广播级[T2]	0		0	13/	13	台/千克	/			0/0
8521.1019	----其他[T2]	0		0	13/	13	台/千克	/	L		0/0
8521.1020	---放像机[T2]	0		0	13/	13	台/千克	/	L	5	0/0
	-其他:										
	---激光视盘机:										
8521.9011	----视频高密光盘(VCD)播放机										
8521.9011 10	具有录制功能的视频高密光盘(VCD)播放机(不论是否装有高频调谐放大器)[T2]	0		130	13/	13	台/千克	A/	L		0/0
8521.9011 90	其他视频高密光盘(VCD)播放机(不论是否装有高频调谐放大器)[T2]	0		130	13/	13	台/千克	A/	L		0/0
8521.9012	----数字化视频光盘(DVD)播放机										
8521.9012 10	具有录制功能的数字化视频光盘(DVD)播放机(不论是否装有高频调谐放大器)[T2]	0		130	13/	13	台/千克	A/	L	25	0/0
8521.9012 90	其他数字化视频光盘(DVD)播放机(不论是否装有高频调谐放大器)[T2]	0		130	13/	13	台/千克	A/	L	25	0/0
8521.9019	----其他										
8521.9019 10	具有录制功能的其他激光视盘播放机(不论是否装有高频调谐放大器)[T2]	0		130	13/	13	台/千克	A/	L	25	0/0
8521.9019 90	其他激光视盘播放机(不论是否装有高频调谐放大器)[T2]	0		130	13/	13	台/千克	A/	L	25	0/0
8521.9090	---其他										
8521.9090 10	用于光盘生产的金属母盘生产设备(不论是否装有高频调谐放大器)〔999〕	0		130	13/	13	台/千克	/		20	0/0
8521.9090 20	光盘型广播级录像机〔999〕	0		130	13/	13	台/千克	6/		20	0/0
8521.9090 90	其他视频信号录制或重放设备(不论是否装有高频调谐放大器)[T2]	0		130	13/	13	台/千克	6A/	L	20	0/0
85.22	**专用于或主要用于税目 85.19 或 85.21 所列设备的零件、附件:**										
8522.1000	-拾音头[T2]	12		130	13/	13	个/千克	/			
	-其他:										
8522.9010	---转盘或唱机用[T2]	6.3/3.1		130	13/	13	千克	/		31.3	4.1/2
	---盒式磁带录音机或放声机用:										
8522.9021	----走带机构(机芯),不论是否装有磁头[T2]	6.3/3.1		100	13/	13	千克	/			4.1/2
8522.9022	----磁头[T2]	6.3/3.1		100	13/	13	个/千克	/		31.3	4.1/2

① 完税价格不高于 2000 美元/台:11.2%;完税价格高于 2000 美元/台:3.0%+1326.5 元/台
② 完税价格≤2000 美元/台:18%;完税价格>2000 美元/台:1.8%+2624.4 元/台
③ 完税价格不高于 2000 美元/台:17.2%;完税价格高于 2000 美元/台:3.0%+2300.4 元/台
④ 完税价格不高于 2000 美元/台:12.6%;完税价格高于 2000 美元/台:3.0%+1555.2 元/台

协定税率 %								RCEP		特惠税率 %			Article Description
东/冰/格	巴基斯坦	韩国	瑞士 上/下	哥/秘/柬	澳/毛	新西/坡/智	中国港/澳/台	东盟及马来/澳/韩	日/新	亚太2国	老/柬/缅	98/97/95	
0/0/0	16	12	0/0	0/0/0	0/0	0/0/0	0/0/	0/0/18.7	0/0			0/0/0	----Flash memory type recorders incorporating sound reproducing apparatus
0/0/0	11.5	9.3	0/0	0/0/0	0/0	0/0/0	0/0/	0/0/0	0/0			0/0/0	----Other
													--Other:
0/0/0	24	18	0/0	0/0/0	0/13.5	0/0/0	0/0/	0/0/28	0/0			0/0/0	---Other record-players, not incorporating a sound recording device with or without loudspeaker
0/0/0	11.2	9.3	0/0	0/0/0	0/0	0/0/0	0/0/	0/0/18	0/0			0/0/0	---Other sound recording or reproducing apparatus
													Video recording or reproducing apparatus, whether or not incorporating a video tuner:
													-Magnetic tape-type:
													---Video tape recorders:
0/0/0	①	②	0/0	0/0/0	0/13.5	0/0/0	0/0/	0/0/28	0/0			0/0/0	----Broadcast quality
0/0/0	③	②	0/0	0/0/0	0/13.5	0/0/0	0/0/	0/0/28	0/0		//	0/0/0	----Other
0/0/0	④	②	0/0	0/0/0	0/13.5	0/0/0	0/0/	0/0/28	0/0		//	0/0/0	---Video tape reproducers
													-Other:
													---Laser video compact disk player:
													----Video Compact Disc player
0/0/0	11.2	9.3	0/0	0/0/0	0/0	0/0/0	0/0/	0/0/18	0/0			0/0/0	Recordable video compact Disc(VCD) player(whether or not incorporating with a high-frequency amplifier tuner)
0/0/0	11.2	9.3	0/0	0/0/0	0/0	0/0/0	0/0/	0/0/18	0/0			0/0/0	Other video compact disc(VCD) player(whether or not incorporating with ahigh-frequency ammelifer tuner)
													----Digital Video Disc player
0/0/0	11.2	12	0/0	0/0/0	0/0	0/0/0	0/0/	0/0/18.7	0/0			0/0/0	Recordable Digital video Disc(DVD)player(whether or not in corporating with a high-frequency tuner)
0/0/0	11.2	12	0/0	0/0/0	0/0	0/0/0	0/0/	0/0/18.7	0/0			0/0/0	Other Digital video Disc(DVD) player(whether or not incorporating with a high-frequency tuned amplifier)
													----Other
0/0/0	11.2	9.3	0/0	0/0/0	0/0	0/0/0	0/0/	0/0/18	0/0			0/0/0	Laser video compact disk (VCD) player with CD-R drivers (whether or not incorporating with a high - frequency tuned amplifier)
0/0/0	11.2	9.3	0/0	0/0/0	0/0	0/0/0	0/0/	0/0/18	0/0			0/0/0	Other laser video compact disk (VCD) player(whether or not incorporating with a high - frequency tuned amplifier)
													---Other
0/0/0	11.2	12	0/0	0/0/0	0/0	0/0/0	0/0/	0/0/18.7	0/0			0/0/0	Metal master disc production equipments for CD production (whether or not incorporating with a high - frequency tuned amplifier)
0/0/0	11.2	12	0/0	0/0/0	0/0	0/0/0	0/0/	0/0/18.7	0/0			0/0/0	Disc-type broadcast-quality video recorders
0/0/0	11.2	12	0/0	0/0/0	0/0	0/0/0	0/0/	0/0/18.7	0/0			0/0/0	Other video recording or reproducing apparatus, whether or not incorporating with a high-frequency tuner amlifier
													Parts and accessories suitable for use solely or principally with the apparatus of headings No. 85. 19 or 85. 21:
0/0/0	28		12/12	0/0/0	0/21	0/0/0	0/0/	5/5/	/5			0/0/0	-Pick-up cartridges
													-Other:
0/0/0	14	11.6	6.3/3.1	0/0/0	0/0	0/0/0	0/0/	0/0/22.5	22.7/0			0/0/0	---Of turntables (record decks) or record-players
													---Of cassette magnetic tape recorders or reproducers:
0/0/0	18	11.6	6.3/3.1	0/0/0	0/0	0/0/0	0/0/	0/0/22.5	22.7/0			0/0/0	Transport mechanisms, whether or not incorporating a magnetic head
0/0/0	18	16.2	6.3/3.1	0/0/0	0/0	0/0/0	0/0/	0/0/22.5	22.7/0			0/0/0	----Magnetic heads

税则号列	货品名称〔CIQ 扩展编码及品名－T2 表示见附表 2〕	最惠(%)	暂定税率	普通	增值/消费	出口退税	计量单位	监管条件/特殊证件	检验检疫	对美关税	亚太上/下
8522.9023	----磁头零件[T2]	5/2.5		100	13/	13	千克	/		15	3.3/1.6
8522.9029	----其他[T2]	7.5/3.8		100	13/	13	千克	/			4.9/2.5
	---视频信号录制或重放设备用：										
8522.9031	----激光视盘机的机芯										
8522.9031 10	车载导航仪视频播放机机芯〔999〕	7.5/3.8		100	13/	13	千克	/		32.5	4.9/2.5
8522.9031 90	其他激光视盘机的机芯[T2]	7.5/3.8		100	13/	13	千克	/		32.5	4.9/2.5
8522.9039	----其他〔999〕	7.5/3.8		100	13/	13	千克	/		32.5	4.9/2.5
	---其他：										
8522.9091	----车载音频转播器或发射器[T2]	5/2.5		80	13/	13	台/千克	/		10	3.3/1.6
8522.9099	----其他[T2]	5/2.5		80	13/	13	千克	/		30	3.3/1.6
85.23	**录制声音或其他信息用的圆盘、磁带、固态非易失性数据存储器件、"智能卡"及其他媒体，不论是否已录制，包括供复制圆盘用的母片及母带，但不包括第三十七章的产品：**										
	-磁性媒体：										
	--磁条卡：										
8523.2110	---未录制〔999〕	0		70	13/	13	个/千克	/		20	
8523.2120	---已录制〔999〕	0		130	9/	9,13	个/千克	/		15	
	--其他：										
	---磁盘：										
8523.2911	----未录制〔999〕	0		14	13/	13	个/千克	/		25	
8523.2919	----其他〔999〕	0		14	9/	9,13	个/千克	/		5	
	---磁带：										
8523.2921	----未录制的宽度不超过 4 毫米磁带〔999〕	0		130	13/	13	盘/千克	/			
8523.2922	----未录制的宽度超过 4 毫米，但不超过 6.5 毫米的磁带〔999〕	0		130	13/	13	盘/千克	/			
8523.2923	----未录制的宽度超过 6.5 毫米的磁带〔999〕	0		20	13/	13	盘/千克	/		25	
8523.2928	----重放声音或图像信息的磁带										
8523.2928 10	含人类遗传资源信息资料的重放声音或图像信息的磁带〔999〕	0		130	9/	9,13	盘/千克	V/		15	
8523.2928 20	录有广播电影电视节目的重放声音或图像信息的磁带〔999〕	0		130	9/	9,13	盘/千克	b/		15	
8523.2928 90	其他重放声音或图像信息的磁带〔999〕	0		130	9/	9,13	盘/千克	f/		15	
8523.2929	----已录制的其他磁带										
8523.2929 10	其他含人类遗传资源信息资料的磁带〔999〕	0		14	13/	9,13	盘/千克	V/			
8523.2929 20	录有广播电影电视节目的其他磁带〔999〕	0		14	13/	9,13	盘/千克	b/			
8523.2929 90	已录制的其他磁带〔999〕	0		14	13/	9,13	盘/千克	f/			
8523.2990	---其他										
8523.2990 10	其他含人类遗传资源信息资料的磁性媒体〔999〕	0		14	13/	9,13	盘/千克	V/		25	
8523.2990 20	其他录有广播电影电视节目的磁性媒体〔999〕	0		14	13/	9,13	盘/千克	b/		25	
8523.2990 90	其他磁性媒体〔999〕	0		14	13/	9,13	盘/千克	f/		25	
	-光学媒体：										
8523.4100	--未录制〔999〕	0		14	13/	13	张/千克	/		25	
	--其他：										
8523.4910	---仅用于重放声音信息的已录制光盘〔999〕										

协定税率 %								RCEP		特惠税率 %			Article Description
东/冰/格	巴基斯坦	韩国	瑞士 上/下	哥/秘/柬	澳/毛	新西/坡/智	中国港/澳/台	东盟及马来/澳/韩	日/新	亚太2国	老/柬/缅	98/97/95	
0/0/0	12.6	9.3	2/2	0/0/0	0/0	0/0/0	0/0/	0/0/18	18.2/0			0/0/0	----Parts of magnetic heads
0/0/0	21.6	19.5	7.5/3.8	0/0/0	0/15.8	0/0/0	0/0/	0/0/27	27.3/0			0/0/0	----Other
													---Of video recording or reproducing apparatus:
													----Movements for laser video compact disk player
0/0/0	14.7	19.5	7.5/3.8	0/0/0	0/15.8	0/0/0	0/0/	27/27/28.5	27.3/27			0/0/0	Car navigator video player core
0/0/0	14.7	19.5	7.5/3.8	0/0/0	0/15.8	0/0/0	0/0/	27/27/28.5	27.3/27			0/0/0	Other movements for laser video compact disk player
0/0/0	14.7	19.5		0/0/0	0/15.8	0/0/0	0/0/	0/0/27	27.3/0			0/0/0	----Other
													---Other:
0/0/0	11.2	9.3	2/2	0/0/0	0/0	0/0/0	0/0/	0/0/18	18.2/0			0/0/0	----Tone converters or transmission apparatus of a kind used for vehides
0/0/0	11.2	9.3	2/2	0/0/0	0/0	0/0/0	0/0/	0/0/18	18.2/0			0/0/0	----Other
													Discs, tapes, solid-state nonvolatile storage devices, "smart cards" and other media for the recording of sound or of other phenomena whether or not recorded including matrices and masters for the production of discs, but excluding products of chapter 37:
													-Magnetic media:
													--Cads incorporating a magnetic stripe:
0/0/0	9.8	3.5	0/0	0/0/0	0/0	0/0/0	0/0/	0/0/15.8	0/0			0/0/0	---Unrecorded
0/0/0	8.4	3	0/0	0/0/0	0/0	0/0/0	0/0/	0/0/13.5	0/0			0/0/0	---Recorded
													--Other:
													---Magnetic discs:
0/0/0	0	0	0/0	0/0/0	0/0	0//0	0/0/	0/0/0	0/0			0/0/0	----Unrecorded
0/0/0	0	0	0/0	0/0/0	0/0	0//0	0/0/	0/0/0	0/0			0/0/0	----Other
													---Magnetic tapes:
0/0/0	0	0	0/0	0/0/0	0/0	0//0	0/0/	0/0/0	0/0			0/0/0	----Of a width not exceedig 4mm unrecorded
0/0/0	0	0	0/0	0/0/0	0/0	0//0	0/0/	0/0/0	0/0			0/0/0	----Of a width excecdig 4mm, but not exceedig 6.5mm unrecorded
0/0/0	0	0	0/0	0/0/0	0/0	0//0	0/0/	0/0/0	0/0			0/0/0	----Of a width exceeding 6.5mm unrecorded
													----For reproducing sound or image phencomena
0/0/0	2	4.6	0/0	0/0/0	0/0	0/0/0	0/0/	0/0/9	0/0		//	0/0/0	Tape containing information about human genetic resources that reproduces sound or image information
0/0/0	2	4.6	0/0	0/0/0	0/0	0/0/0	0/0/	0/0/9	0/0		//	0/0/0	Tape recording sound or image information reproduced from radio, film and television programs
0/0/0	2	4.6	0/0	0/0/0	0/0	0/0/0	0/0/	0/0/9	0/0		//	0/0/0	Other tapes that reproduce sound or image information
													----Other recorded magnetic tapes
0/0/0	0	0	0/0	0/0/0	0/0	0//0	0/0/	0/0/0	0/0		//	0/0/0	Other tapes containing information on human genetic resources
0/0/0	0	0	0/0	0/0/0	0/0	0//0	0/0/	0/0/0	0/0		//	0/0/0	Other tapes recording radio, film and television programs
0/0/0	0	0	0/0	0/0/0	0/0	0//0	0/0/	0/0/0	0/0		//	0/0/0	Other tapes recorded
													---Other
0/0/0	0	0	0/0	0/0/0	0/0	0//0	0/0/	0/0/0	0/0		//	0/0/0	Other magnetic media containing information on human genetic resources
0/0/0	0	0	0/0	0/0/0	0/0	0//0	0/0/	0/0/0	0/0		//	0/0/0	Other magnetic media recording radio, film and television programs
0/0/0	0	0	0/0	0/0/0	0/0	0//0	0/0/	0/0/0	0/0		//	0/0/0	Other magnetic media
													-Optical media:
0/0/0	0	0	0/0	0/0/0	0/0	0//0	0/0/	0/0/0	0/0			0/0/0	--Unrecorded
													--Other
													---For reproducing sound

税则号列		货品名称〔CIQ 扩展编码及品名－T2 表示见附表 2〕	最惠(%)	暂定税率	普通	增值/消费	出口退税	计量单位	监管条件/特殊证件	检验检疫	对美关税	亚太上/下
8523.4910	10	含人类遗传资源信息资料的仅用于重放声音信息的光学媒体〔999〕	0		130	9/	9,13	张/千克	V/		20	
8523.4910	20	录有广播电影电视节目的仅用于重放声音信息的光学媒体〔999〕	0		130	9/	9,13	张/千克	b/		20	
8523.4910	90	其他仅用于重放声音信息的已录制光学媒体〔999〕	0		130	9/	9,13	张/千克	f/		20	
8523.4920		---用于重放声音、图像以外信息的，税目 84.71 所列机器用										
8523.4920	10	含人类遗传资源信息资料的用于重放声音、图像以外信息的光学媒体〔999〕	0		14	9/	9,13	张/千克	V/		5	
8523.4920	90	其他用于重放声音、图像以外信息的光学媒体(品目 8471 所列机器用，已录制)〔999〕	0		14	9/	9,13	张/千克	/		5	
8523.4990		---其他										
8523.4990	10	其他含人类遗传资源信息资料的光学媒体〔999〕	0		14	13/	9,13	张/千克	V/		5	
8523.4990	20	其他录有广播电影电视节目的光学媒体〔999〕	0		14	13/	9,13	张/千克	b/		5	
8523.4990	30	其他赴境外加工并返回境内的已录制光盘〔999〕	0		14	13/	9,13	张/千克	Z/		5	
8523.4990	90	其他已录制光学媒体〔999〕	0		14	13/	9,13	张/千克	f/		5	
		-半导体媒体：										
		--固态非易失性存储器件(闪速存储器)：										
8523.5110		---未录制[T2]	0		70	13/	13	个/千克	/		25	
8523.5120		---已录制	0		14	10/	10,16	个/千克				
8523.5120	10	含人类遗传资源信息资料的固态非易失性存储器件(闪速存储器)〔999〕	0		14	9/	9,13	个/千克	V/		10	
8523.5120	20	录有广播电影电视节目的固态非易失性存储器件(闪速存储器)〔999〕	0		14	9/	9,13	个/千克	b/		10	
8523.5120	30	赴境外加工并返回境内的已录制的固态非易失性存储器件(闪速存储器)〔999〕	0		14	9/	9,13	个/千克	Z/		10	
8523.5120	90	其他已录制的固态非易失性存储器件(闪速存储器)〔999〕	0		14	9/	9,13	个/千克	/		10	
		--“智能卡”：										
8523.5210		---未录制[T2]	0		21	9/	13	个/千克	/		25	
8523.5290		---其他[T2]	0		21	9/	9,13	个/千克	/		20	
		--其他：										
8523.5910		---未录制〔999〕	0		70	13/	13	个/千克	/		25	
8523.5920		---已录制										
8523.5920	10	其他含人类遗传资源信息资料的半导体媒体〔999〕	0		14	9/	9,13	个/千克	V/		10	
8523.5920	20	其他录有广播电影电视节目的半导体媒体〔999〕	0		14	9/	9,13	个/千克	b/		10	
8523.5920	30	其他赴境外加工并返回境内的已录制的半导体媒体〔999〕	0		14	9/	9,13	个/千克	Z/		10	
8523.5920	90	其他已录制的半导体媒体〔999〕	0		14	9/	9,13	个/千克	/		10	
		-其他：										
		---唱片：										
8523.8011		----已录制										
8523.8011	10	录有广播电影电视节目的唱片〔101：磁带、磁盘；102：其它视听设备及其零件〕	0		130	9/	9,13	张/千克	b/		20	
8523.8011	20	赴境外加工并返回境内的已录制唱片〔101：磁带、磁盘；102：其它视听设备及其零件〕	0		130	9/	9,13	张/千克	Z/		20	
8523.8011	90	其他已录制唱片〔101：磁带、磁盘；102：其它视听设备及其零件〕	0		130	9/	9,13	张/千克	f/		20	
8523.8019		----其他〔101 磁带、磁盘，102 其它视听设备及其零件〕	0		70	13/	9,13	张/千克	/		5	
		---税目 84.71 所列机器用：										

协定税率 %								RCEP		特惠税率 %			Article Description
东/冰/格	巴基斯坦	韩国	瑞士上/下	哥/秘/柬	澳/毛	新西/坡/智	中国港/澳/台	东盟及马来/澳/韩	日/新	亚太2国	老/柬/缅	98/97/95	
0/0/0	3.5	2	0/0	0/0/0	0/0	0//0	0/0/	0/0/9	0/0		//	0/0/0	Optical media containing information about human genetic resources for reproducing sound information only
0/0/0	3.5	2	0/0	0/0/0	0/0	0//0	0/0/	0/0/9	0/0		//	0/0/0	Optical media recording radio, film and television programs for reproducing sound information only
0/0/0	3.5	2	0/0	0/0/0	0/0	0//0	0/0/	0/0/9	0/0		//	0/0/0	Other recorded optical media for reproducing sound information only
													---Forreproducing phenomena other than sound or image for the machines of heading 84.71
0/0/0	0	0	0/0	0/0/0	0/0	0//0	0/0/	0/0/0	0/0		//	0/0/0	Optical media containing information of human genetic resources for reproducing information other than sound and image
0/0/0	0	0	0/0	0/0/0	0/0	0//0	0/0/	0/0/0	0/0		//	0/0/0	Other optical media for reproducing information other than sound and image
													---Other
0/0/0	0	0	0/0	0/0/0	0/0	0//0	0/0/	0/0/0	0/0		//	0/0/0	Other Optical Media Containing Information on Human Genetic Resources
0/0/0	0	0	0/0	0/0/0	0/0	0//0	0/0/	0/0/0	0/0		//	0/0/0	Other Optical Media Containing Radio, Film and Television Programs
0/0/0	0	0	0/0	0/0/0	0/0	0//0	0/0/	0/0/0	0/0		//	0/0/0	Other recorded CD—ROMs processed abroad and returned to China
0/0/0	0	0	0/0	0/0/0	0/0	0//0	0/0/	0/0/0	0/0		//	0/0/0	Other recorded optical media
													-Semiconductor media:
													--Solid-state non-volatile storage devices(flash memorizer):
0/0/0	0	0	0/0	0/0/0	0/0	0//0	0/0/	0/0/0	0/0			0/0/0	---Unrecorded
												0/0/0	---Recorded
0/0/0	0	0	0/0	0/0/0	0/0	0//0	0/0/	0/0/0	0/0		//	0/0/0	Solid State Nonvolatile Memory Device (Flash Memory) Containing Human Genetic Resources Information
0/0/0	0	0	0/0	0/0/0	0/0	0//0	0/0/	0/0/0	0/0		//	0/0/0	Solid State Nonvolatile Memory Device (Flash Memory) for Recording Radio, Film and Television Programs
0/0/0	0	0	0/0	0/0/0	0/0	0//0	0/0/	0/0/0	0/0		//	0/0/0	Recorded solid state nonvolatile memory devices (flash memory) processed abroad and returned to China
0/0/0	0	0	0/0	0/0/0	0/0	0//0	0/0/	0/0/0	0/0		//	0/0/0	Other recorded solid—state non—volatile memory devices (flash memory)
													--"Smart cards":
0/0/0	0	0	0/0	0/0/0	0/0	0//0	0/0/	0/0/0	0/0			0/0/0	---Unrecorded
0/0/0	0	0	0/0	0/0/0	0/0	0//0	0/0/	0/0/0	0/0			0/0/0	---Other
													--Other:
0/0/0	0	0	0/0	0/0/0	0/0	0//0	0/0/	0/0/0	0/0			0/0/0	---Unrecorded
													---Recorded
0/0/0	0	0	0/0	0/0/0	0/0	0//0	0/0/	0/0/0	0/0		//	0/0/0	Other Semiconductor Media Containing Information on Human Genetic Resources
0/0/0	0	0	0/0	0/0/0	0/0	0//0	0/0/	0/0/0	0/0		//	0/0/0	Other Semiconductor Media with Radio, Film and Television Programs
0/0/0	0	0	0/0	0/0/0	0/0	0//0	0/0/	0/0/0	0/0		//	0/0/0	Other recorded semiconductor media processed overseas and returned to China
0/0/0	0	0	0/0	0/0/0	0/0	0//0	0/0/	0/0/0	0/0		//	0/0/0	Other recorded semiconductor media
													-Other:
													---Gramophone recorols:
													----Recorded
0/0/0	8.4	3	0/0	0/0/0	0/0	0/0/0	0/0/	0/0/13.5	0/0		//	0/0/0	Record recording of radio, film and television programs
0/0/0	8.4	3	0/0	0/0/0	0/0	0/0/0	0/0/	0/0/13.5	0/0		//	0/0/0	Recorded Records Processed Overseas and Returned to China
0/0/0	8.4	3	0/0	0/0/0	0/0	0/0/0	0/0/	0/0/13.5	0/0		//	0/0/0	Other recorded records
0/0/0	0	0	0/0	0/0/0	0/0	0//0	0/0/	0/0/0	0/0			0/0/0	----Other
													---For the machines of heading No. 84.71:

税则号列	货品名称〔CIQ 扩展编码及品名—T2 表示见附表 2〕	最惠(%)	暂定税率	普通	增值/消费	出口退税	计量单位	监管条件/特殊证件	检验检疫	对美关税	亚太上/下
8523.8021	----未录制〔101 软、硬、光盘驱动器,102 磁带、磁盘〕	0		14	13/	13	张/千克	/		20	
8523.8029	----其他										
8523.8029 10	其他含人类遗传资源信息资料的品目 8471 所列机器用其他媒体〔999〕	0		14	13/	9,13	张/千克	V/		5	
8523.8029 90	其他品目 8471 所列机器用其他媒体(磁性、光学或半导体媒体除外)〔999〕	0		14	13/	9,13	张/千克	/		5	
	---其他:										
8523.8091	----未录制〔101 软、硬、光盘驱动器,102 磁带、磁盘〕	0		14	9/	13	张/千克	/		5	
8523.8099	----其他										
8523.8099 10	其他含人类遗传资源信息资料的媒体〔999〕	0		14	9/	9,13	张/千克	V/			
8523.8099 20	其他录有广播电影电视节目的媒体〔999〕	0		14	9/	9,13	张/千克	b/			
8523.8099 90	其他媒体(磁性、光学或半导体媒体除外)〔999〕	0		14	9/	9,13	张/千克	f/			
85.24	**平板显示模组,不论是否装有触摸屏:**										
	-不含驱动器或控制电路:										
8524.1100	--液晶的〔999〕	5		50	13/	13	个/千克	/		30	
8524.1200	--有机发光二极管的(OLED)〔999〕	8		40	13/	13	个/千克	/		33	
	--其他:										
8524.1910	---电视机用等离子显像组件〔101 Ⅰ类其它电视接收、发送装置及其零件,102 Ⅱ类其它电视接收、发送装置及其零件,103 Ⅲ类其它电视接收、发送装置及其零件〕	5/2.5		80	13/	13	个/千克	/		30	4/2
	---发光二极管的:										
8524.1921	----电视机用〔101 Ⅰ类其它电视接收、发送装置及其零件,102 Ⅱ类其它电视接收、发送装置及其零件,103 Ⅲ类其它电视接收、发送装置及其零件〕	5		80	13/	13	个/千克	/		30	3.3/3.3
8524.1929	----其他〔999〕	0		64	13/	13	个/千克	/		20	
8524.1990	---其他〔999〕	8		40	13/	13	个/千克	/		33	
	-其他:										
	--液晶的										
8524.9110	---专用于或主要用于税目 85.17 所列装置的〔999〕	0		16	13/	13	个/千克	/		25	
8524.9120	---专用于或主要用于税目 85.19、85.21、85.25、85.26 或 85.27 所列设备的										
8524.9120 10	非特种用途的电视摄像机、视频摄录一体机、数字照相机用液晶平板显示模组(含驱动器或控制电路,不论是否装有触摸屏)〔101 Ⅰ类家用型摄录一体机,102 Ⅱ类家用型摄录一体机,103 Ⅲ类家用型摄录一体机,104 Ⅰ类其它摄录放像装置及其零件,105 Ⅱ类其它摄录放像装置及其零件,106 Ⅲ类其它摄录放像装置及其零件〕	3.4/1.7	①	67	13/	13	个/千克	/		7	2.2/1.1
8524.9120 20	用于雷达设备及无线电导航设备用的液晶平板显示模组(含驱动器或控制电路,不论是否装有触摸屏(P))〔999〕	3.4/1.7		67	13/	13	个/千克	/			2.2/1.1
8524.9120 90	其他专用于或主要用于税目 85.19、85.21、85.25、85.26 或 85.27 所列设备的液晶模组(含驱动器或控制电路,不论是否装有触摸屏)〔999〕	3.4/1.7		67	13/	13	个/千克	/		8.4	2.2/1.1
8524.9130	---专用于或主要用于税目 85.35、85.36 或 85.37 所列装置的〔101 其它高压电器及其零件(高压电器及其零件),102 其它低压电器及其零件(低压电器及其零件)〕	7		50	13/	13	个/千克	/		32	
8524.9140	---专用于或主要用于税目 87.01 至 87.05 所列车辆的〔999〕	6		100	13/	13	个/千克	6/			5.4/5.4
8524.9190	---其他〔999〕	5		50	13/	13	个/千克	/		30	
	--有机发光二极管的(OLED):										
8524.9210	---专用于或主要用于税目 85.17 所列装置的〔999〕	0		16	13/	13	个/千克	/		25	
8524.9220	---专用于或主要用于税目 85.19、85.21、85.25、85.26 或 85.27 所列设备的										

① 1—6 月:2%

协定税率 %								RCEP		特惠税率 %			Article Description
东/冰/格	巴基斯坦	韩国	瑞士 上/下	哥/秘/柬	澳/毛	新西/坡/智	中国港/澳/台	东盟及马来/澳/韩	日/新	亚太2国	老/柬/缅	98/97/95	
0/0/0	0	0	0/0	0/0/0	0/0	0//0	0/0/	0/0/0	0/0			0/0/0	----Unrecorded
													----Other
0/0/0	0	0	0/0	0/0/0	0/0	0//0	0/0/	0/0/0	0/0		//	0/0/0	Other media used by other machines listed in heading 8471 containing information on human genetic resources
0/0/0	0	0	0/0	0/0/0	0/0	0//0	0/0/	0/0/0	0/0		//	0/0/0	Other media used by other machines listed in headings 8471
													---Other:
0/0/0	0	0	0/0	0/0/0	0/0	0//0	0/0/	0/0/0	0/0			0/0/0	----Unrecorded
													----Other
0/0/0	0	0	0/0	0/0/0	0/0	0//0	0/0/	0/0/0	0/0		//	0/0/0	Other media containing information on human genetic resources
0/0/0	0	0	0/0	0/0/0	0/0	0//0	0/0/	0/0/0	0/0		//	0/0/0	Other Media Recording Radio, Film and Television Programs
0/0/0	0	0	0/0	0/0/0	0/0	0//0	0/0/	0/0/0	0/0		//	0/0/0	Other media
													Flat panel display module, whether or not equipped with touch screen
													-—Without driver orcontrol circuit:
0/0/	0	5		//0	2.3/0	0//0	0/0/	4.5/4.5/5	5/4.5			0//	--Liquid crystal
0/0/0	4.2	7.2	1.2/1.2	0/0/0	0/0	0/0/0	0/0/	11.4/11.4/11.4	11.4/11.4			0/0/0	--Organic light emitting diode (OLED)
													--Other:
0/0/0	5.3	12	1.5/1.5	//0	0/0	0//0	0/0/	14.3/14.3/	/14.3			0//	---Plasma imaging module for television
													---Light emitting diode
0/0/	5.3		1.5/1.5	/0/0	0/0	0/0/0	0/0/	5/5/	/5			0/0/0	----For TV
0/0/0	0	0	0/0	0/0/0	0/0	0//0	0/0/	0/0/0	0/0			0/0/0	----Other
0/0/0	4.2	7.2	1.2/1.2	0/0/0	0/0	0/0/0	0/0/	11.4/11.4/11.4	11.4/11.4			0/0/0	---Other
													-Other:
													--Liquid crystal
0/0/0	0	0	0/0	0/0/0	0/0	0//0	0/0/	0/0/0	0/0			0/0/0	---Used exclusively or primarily for installations listed in heading 85.17
													---Dedicated or mainly used for equipment listed in heading 85.19, 85.21, 85.25, 85.26 or 85.27
0/0/0	4.4	4.7	0.9/0.9	0/0/0	0/0	0/0/0	0/0/0	0/0/1.4	1.4/0			0/0/0	Liquid crystal flat panel display module (including driver or control circuit, whether equipped with touch screen or not) for TV camera, video camera and digital camera for non special purposes
0/0/0	4.4	4.7	0.9/0.9	0/0/0	0/0	0/0/0	0/0/0	0/0/1.4	1.4/0			0/0/0	Liquid crystal flat panel display module for radar equipment and radio navigation equipment (including driver or control circuit, whether or not equipped with touch screen (P))
0/0/0	4.4	4.7	0.9/0.9	0/0/0	0/0	0/0/0	0/0/0	0/0/1.4	1.4/0			0/0/0	Other liquid crystal modules (including drivers or control circuits, whether or not equipped with touch screens) dedicated or mainly used for the equipment listed in heading 85.19, 85.21, 85.25, 85.26 or 85.27
0/0/0	4	0	2.8/2.8	0/0/0	0/4.2	0//0	0/0/0	0/0/0	6.4/0			0/0/0	---Used exclusively or primarily for installations listed in heading 85.35, 85.36 or 85.37
0/0/0	3.5	9	1/1	0/0/0	0/7.1	0/0/0	0/0/0	6/6/6	6/6			0/0/0	---Dedicated to or mainly used for trains under heading 87.01 to 87.05
0/0/	0	5		//0	2.3/0	0//0	0/0/	4.5/4.5/5	5/4.5			0//	---Other
													--Organic light emitting diode (OLED)
0/0/0	0	0	0/0	0/0/0	0/0	0//0	0/0/	0/0/0	0/0			0/0/0	---Used exclusively or primarily for installations listed in heading 85.17
													---Dedicated or mainly used for equipment listed in heading 85.19, 85.21, 85.25, 85.26 or 85.27

税则号列	货品名称〔CIQ扩展编码及品名—T2表示见附表2〕	最惠(%)	暂定税率	普通	增值/消费	出口退税	计量单位	监管条件/特殊证件	检验检疫	对美关税	亚太上/下
8524.9220 10	非特种用途的电视摄像机、视频摄录一体机、数字照相机用有机发光二极管平板显示模组(含驱动器或控制电路,不论是否装有触摸屏)〔101Ⅰ类家用型摄录一体机,102Ⅱ类家用型摄录一体机,103Ⅲ类家用型摄录一体机,104Ⅰ类其它摄录放像装置及其零件,105Ⅱ类其它摄录放像装置及其零件,106Ⅲ类其它摄录放像装置及其零件〕	3.4/1.7	①	67	13/	13	个/千克	/		7	2.2/1.1
8524.9220 20	用于雷达设备及无线电导航设备用的有机发光二极管平板显示模组(含驱动器或控制电路,不论是否装有触摸屏(P))〔999〕	3.4/1.7		67	13/	13	个/千克	/			2.2/1.1
8524.9220 90	其他专用于或主要用于税目85.19、85.21、85.25、85.26或85.27所列设备的有机发光二极管(OLED)模组(含驱动器或控制电路,不论是否装有触摸屏)〔999〕	3.4/1.7		67	13/	13	个/千克	/		8.4	2.2/1.1
8524.9230	---专用于或主要用于税目85.35、85.36或85.37所列装置的〔101其它高压电器及其零件(高压电器及其零件),102其它低压电器及其零件(低压电器及其零件)〕	7		50	13/	13	个/千克	/		32	
8524.9240	---专用于或主要用于税目87.01至87.05所列车辆的〔999〕	6		100	13/	13	个/千克	6/			5.4/5.4
8524.9250	---电视接收机用〔999〕	15	5	80	13/	13	个/千克	/		30	9.8/9.8
8524.9260	---专用于或主要用于税目85.28所列其他监视器的〔999〕	0		57	13/	13	个/千克	/		25	
8524.9290	---其他〔999〕	8		40	13/	13	个/千克	/		33	
	--其他:										
8524.9910	---电视机用等离子显像组件〔101Ⅰ类其它电视接收、发送装置及其零件,102Ⅱ类其它电视接收、发送装置及其零件,103Ⅲ类其它电视接收、发送装置及其零件〕	5/2.5		80	13/	13	个/千克	/		30	4/2
	---发光二极管的:										
8524.9921	----电视机用〔101Ⅰ类其它电视接收、发送装置及其零件,102Ⅱ类其它电视接收、发送装置及其零件,103Ⅲ类其它电视接收、发送装置及其零件〕	5		80	13/	13	个/千克	/		30	3.3/3.3
8524.9929	----其他〔999〕	0		64	13/	13	个/千克	/		20	
8524.9990	---其他〔999〕	8		40	13/	13	个/千克	/		33	
85.25	**无线电广播、电视发送设备,不论是否装有接收装置或声音的录制、重放装置;电视摄像机、数字照相机及视频摄录一体机:**										
8525.5000	-发送设备[T2]	0		30	13/	13	台/千克	O/		5	
	-装有接收装置的发送设备:										
8525.6010	---卫星地面站设备[T2]	0		14	13/	13	台/千克	O/		20	
8525.6090	---其他[T2]	0		30	13/	13	台/千克	/		5	
	-电视摄像机、数字照相机及视频摄录一体机:										
	--本章子目注释——所列高速设备 :										
8525.8110	---电视摄像机〔101Ⅰ类电视摄像机,102Ⅱ类电视摄像机,103Ⅲ类电视摄像机〕	0		17	13/	13	台/千克	/			0/0
8525.8120	---数字照相机〔999〕	0		17	13/	13	台/千克	/			
8525.8130	---视频摄录一体机〔101Ⅰ类电视摄像机,102Ⅱ类电视摄像机,103Ⅲ类电视摄像机,104Ⅰ类家用型摄录一体机,105Ⅱ类家用型摄录一体机,106Ⅲ类家用型摄录一体机〕	0		17	13/	13	台/千克	/		10	
	--其他,本章子目注释二所列抗辐射或耐辐射设备 :										
8525.8210	---电视摄像机										
8525.8210 10	抗辐射电视摄像机(能抗5×104戈瑞(硅)以上辐射而又不会降低使用质量)〔101Ⅰ类电视摄像机,102Ⅱ类电视摄像机,103Ⅲ类电视摄像机〕	0		17	13/	13	台/千克	3/			0/0
8525.8210 90	其他本章子目注释二所列抗辐射或耐辐射电视摄像机〔101Ⅰ类电视摄像机,102Ⅱ类电视摄像机,103Ⅲ类电视摄像机〕	0		17	13/	13	台/千克	/			0/0

① 1—6月:2%

协定税率 %								RCEP		特惠税率 %			Article Description
东/冰/格	巴基斯坦	韩国	瑞士 上/下	哥/秘/柬	澳/毛	新西/坡/智	中国港/澳/台	东盟及马来/澳/韩	日/新	亚太2国	老/柬/缅	98/97/95	
0/0/0	4.4	4.7	0.9/0.9	0/0/0	0/0	0/0/0	0/0/	0/0/1.4	1.4/0			0/0/0	Organic light emitting diode flat panel display module (including driver or control circuit, whether equipped with touch screen or not) for TV camera, video recorder and digital camera for non special purposes
0/0/0	4.4	4.7	0.9/0.9	0/0/0	0/0	0/0/0	0/0/	0/0/1.4	1.4/0			0/0/0	Organic light emitting diode flat panel display module for radar equipment and radio navigation equipment (including driver or control circuit, whether or not equipped with touch screen (P))
0/0/0	4.4	4.7	0.9/0.9	0/0/0	0/0	0/0/0	0/0/	0/0/1.4	1.4/0			0/0/0	Other organic light emitting diode (OLED) modules (including drivers or control circuits, whether or not equipped with touch screens) dedicated or mainly used for the equipment listed in heading 85.19, 85.21, 85.25, 85.26 or 85.27
0/0/0	4	0	2.8/2.8	0/0/0	0/4.2	0//0	0/0/0	0/0/0	6.4/0			0/0/0	---Used exclusively or primarily for installations listed in heading 85.35, 85.36 or 85.37
0/0/0	3.5	9	1/1	0/0/0	0/7.1	0/0/0	0/0/0	6/6/6	6/6			0/0/0	---Dedicated to or mainly used for trains under heading 87.01 to 87.05
0/0/	5.3		1.5/1.5	/0/0	/0	0/0/0	0/0/					0/0/0	---For TV receiver
0/0/0	0	0	0/0	0/0/0	0/0	0//0	0/0/	0/0/0	0/0			0/0/0	---Dedicated or mainly used for other monitors listed in heading 85.28
0/0/0	4.2	7.2	1.2/1.2	0/0/0	0/0	0/0/0	0/0/	11.4/11.4/11.4	11.4/11.4			0/0/0	---Other
													--Other
0/0/0	5.3	12	1.5/1.5	//0	0/0	0//0	0/0/	14.3/14.3/	/14.3			0//	---Plasma imaging module for television
													---Light emitting diode
0/0/	5.3		1.5/1.5	/0/0	0/0	0/0/0	0/0/	5/5/	/5			0/0/0	----For TV
0/0/0	0	0	0/0	0/0/0	0/0	0//0	0/0/	0/0/0	0/0			0/0/0	----Other
0/0/0	4.2	7.2	1.2/1.2	0/0/0	0/0	0/0/0	0/0/	11.4/11.4/11.4	11.4/11.4			0/0/0	---Other
													Transmission apparatus for radio-broadcasting or television, whether or not incorporating reception apparatus or sound recording or reproducing apparatus; television cameras; digital cameras and video camera recorders;
0/0/0	0	0	0/0	0/0/0	0/0	0//0	0/0/	0/0/0	0/0			0/0/0	-Transmission apparatus
													-Transmission apparatus incorporating reception apparatus:
0/0/0	0	0	0/0	0/0/0	0/0	0//0	0/0/	0/0/0	0/0			0/0/0	---Satellite earth station
0/0/0	0	0	0/0	0/0/0	0/0	0//0	0/0/	0/0/0	0/0			0/0/0	---Other
													-Television cameras, digital cameras and video camera recorders:
													--Notes to subheadings of this chapter — high speed equipment listed:
0/0/0	2		0/0	0/0/0	0/0	0/0/0	0/0/	0/0/9	9.1/0			0/0/0	---Television camera
0/0/0	0	0	0/0	0/0/0	0/0	0//0	0/0/	0/0/0	0/0			0/0/0	---Digital camera
0/0/0	0	0	0/0	0/0/0	0/0	0//0	0/0/	0/0/0	0/0			0/0/0	---Video camera recorders
													--Other radiation resistant or radiation resistant equipment listed in Note 2 of subheading of this chapter
													---Television camera
0/0/0	2		0/0	0/0/0	0/0	0/0/0	0/0/	0/0/9	9.1/0			0/0/0	Radiation resistant TV camera (5) × Radiation above 14 Gy (silicon) without reducing the service quality)
0/0/0	2		0/0	0/0/0	0/0	0/0/0	0/0/	0/0/9	9.1/0			0/0/0	Other radiation resistant or radiation resistant television cameras listed in Note 2 of subheading of this chapter

税则号列	货品名称〔CIQ 扩展编码及品名－T2 表示见附表 2〕	最惠(%)	暂定税率	普通	增值/消费	出口退税	计量单位	监管条件/特殊证件	检验检疫	对美关税	亚太上/下
8525.8220	---数字照相机〔999〕	0		17	13/	13	台/千克	/			
8525.8230	---视频摄录一体机〔101 Ⅰ类电视摄像机，102 Ⅱ类电视摄像机，103 Ⅲ类电视摄像机，104 Ⅰ类家用型摄录一体机，105 Ⅱ类家用型摄录一体机，106 Ⅲ类家用型摄录一体机〕	0		17	13/	13	台/千克	/		10	
	--其他，本章子目注释三所列夜视设备 ：										
8525.8310	---电视摄像机〔101 Ⅰ类电视摄像机，102 Ⅱ类电视摄像机，103 Ⅲ类电视摄像机〕	0		17	13/	13	台/千克	/			0/0
8525.8320	---数字照相机〔999〕	0		17	13/	13	台/千克	/			
8525.8330	---视频摄录一体机〔101 Ⅰ类电视摄像机，102 Ⅱ类电视摄像机，103 Ⅲ类电视摄像机，104 Ⅰ类家用型摄录一体机，105 Ⅱ类家用型摄录一体机，106 Ⅲ类家用型摄录一体机〕	0		17	13/	13	台/千克	/		10	
	--其他：										
	---电视摄像机：										
8525.8911	----其他，特种用途的〔101 Ⅰ类电视摄像机，102 Ⅱ类电视摄像机，103 Ⅲ类电视摄像机〕	0		17	13/	13	台/千克	/			0/0
8525.8912	----非特种用途的广播级〔101 Ⅰ类电视摄像机，102 Ⅱ类电视摄像机，103 Ⅲ类电视摄像机〕	0		130	13/	13	台/千克	/		25	0/0
8525.8919	----非特种用途的其他类型〔101 Ⅰ类电视摄像机，102 Ⅱ类电视摄像机，103 Ⅲ类电视摄像机〕	0		130	13/	13	台/千克	/		25	0/0
	---数字照相机：										
8525.8921	----其他，特种用途的〔999〕	0		17	13/	13	台/千克	/			
8525.8922	----非特种用途的单镜头反光型〔999〕	0		130	13/	13	台/千克	/		25	
8525.8923	----非特种用途的，其他可换镜头的〔999〕	0		130	13/	13	台/千克	/		25	
8525.8929	----非特种用途的其他类型〔999〕	0		130	13/	13	台/千克	/		25	
	---视频摄录一体机：										
8525.8931	----其他，特种用途的〔101 Ⅰ类电视摄像机，102 Ⅱ类电视摄像机，103 Ⅲ类电视摄像机，104 Ⅰ类家用型摄录一体机，105 Ⅱ类家用型摄录一体机，106 Ⅲ类家用型摄录一体机〕	0		17	13/	13	台/千克	/		10	
8525.8932	----非特种用途的广播级〔101 Ⅰ类电视摄像机，102 Ⅱ类电视摄像机，103 Ⅲ类电视摄像机〕	0		130	13/	13	台/千克	/		25	
8525.8933	----非特种用途的家用型〔101 Ⅰ类家用型摄录一体机，102 Ⅱ类家用型摄录一体机，103 Ⅲ类家用型摄录一体机〕	0		130	13/	13	台/千克	/		25	
8525.8939	----非特种用途的其他类型〔101 Ⅰ类电视摄像机，102 Ⅱ类电视摄像机，103 Ⅲ类电视摄像机〕	0		130	13/	13	台/千克	A/	LM	25	
85.26	**雷达设备、无线电导航设备及无线电遥控设备：**										
	-雷达设备：										
8526.1010	---导航用										
8526.1010 10	用于导弹、火箭等的导航雷达设备(用于弹道导弹、运载火箭、探空火箭、巡航导弹、无人驾驶航空飞行器的目标探测)〔999〕	0		8	13/	13	台/千克	3/			
8526.1010 90	其他导航用雷达设备〔999〕	0		8	13/	13	台/千克	/			
8526.1090	---其他										
8526.1090 10	飞机机载雷达(包括气象雷达，地形雷达和空中交通管制应答系统)〔999〕	0		14	13/	13	台/千克	/			
8526.1090 20	雷达生命探测仪〔999〕	0		14	13/	13	台/千克	O/		5	
8526.1090 30	用于导弹、火箭等的机载雷达设备(用于弹道导弹、运载火箭、探空火箭、巡航导弹、无人驾驶航空飞行器的目标探测)〔999〕	0		14	13/	13	台/千克	3/		5	
8526.1090 40	用于导弹、火箭等的其他雷达设备(用于弹道导弹、运载火箭、探空火箭、巡航导弹、无人驾驶航空飞行器的目标探测)〔999〕	0		14	13/	13	台/千克	3/		5	
8526.1090 90	其他雷达设备〔999〕	0		14	13/	13	台/千克	/		5	
	-其他：										
	--无线电导航设备：										
8526.9110	---机动车辆用〔999〕	0		8	13/	13	台/千克	/		5	
8526.9190	---其他										

① 完税价格 不高于 5000 美元/ 台，20.9%；完税价格 高于 5000 美元/台：3.0%＋7249.5 元/台

② 完税价格≤5000 美 元/台：21%；完税价格＞5000 美元/台：1.8%＋7776 元/台

协定税率 %								RCEP		特惠税率 %			Article Description
东/冰/格	巴基斯坦	韩国	瑞士上/下	哥/秘/柬	澳/毛	新西/坡/智	中国港/澳/台	东盟及马来/澳/韩	日/新	亚太2国	老/柬/缅	98/97/95	
0/0/0	0	0	0/0	0/0/0	0/0	0//0	0/0/	0/0/0	0/0			0/0/0	---Digital camera
0/0/0	0	0	0/0	0/0/0	0/0	0//0	0/0/	0/0/0	0/0			0/0/0	---Video camera recorders
													--Other radiation resistant or radiation resistant equipment listed in Note 3 of subheading of this chapter
0/0/0	2		0/0	0/0/0	0/0	0/0/0	0/0/	0/0/9	9.1/0			0/0/0	---Television camera
0/0/0	0	0	0/0	0/0/0	0/0	0//0	0/0/	0/0/0	0/0			0/0/0	---Digital camera
0/0/0	0	0	0/0	0/0/0	0/0	0//0	0/0/	0/0/0	0/0			0/0/0	---Video camera recorders
													--Other
													---Television camera
0/0/0	2		0/0	0/0/0	0/0	0/0/0	0/0/	0/0/9	9.1/0			0/0/0	----Other, special purpose
0/0/0	①		0/0	0/0/0	0/17.5	0/0/0	0/0/	31.5/31.5/33.3	31.8/31.5			0/0/0	----Non special purpose broadcast level
0/0/0	①	②	0/0	0/0/0	0/17.5	0/0/0	0/0/0	0/0/32.7	31.8/0			0/0/0	----Other types for non special purposes
													---Digital camera:
0/0/0	0	0	0/0	0/0/0	0/0	0//0	0/0/	0/0/0	0/0			0/0/0	----Other, special purpose
0/0/0	0	0	0/0	0/0/0	0/0	0//0	0/0/	0/0/0	0/0			0/0/0	----Single lens reflective type for non special purpose
0/0/0	0	0	0/0	0/0/0	0/0	0//0	0/0/	0/0/0	0/0			0/0/0	----Non special purpose, other interchangeable lens
0/0/0	0	0	0/0	0/0/0	0/0	0//0	0/0/	0/0/0	0/0			0/0/0	----Other types for non special purposes
													---Video camera recorders
0/0/0	0	0	0/0	0/0/0	0/0	0//0	0/0/	0/0/0	0/0			0/0/0	----Other, special purpose
0/0/0	0	0	0/0	0/0/0	0/0	0//0	0/0/	0/0/0	0/0			0/0/0	----Non special purpose broadcast level
0/0/0	0	0	0/0	0/0/0	0/0	0//0	0/0/	0/0/0	0/0			0/0/0	----Non special purpose household type
0/0/0	0	0	0/0	0/0/0	0/0	0//0	0/0/	0/0/0	0/0			0/0/0	----Other types for non special purposes
													Radar apparatus, radio navigational aid aparatus and radio remote control apparatus:
													-Radar apparatus:
													---For navigational aid
0/0/0	0	0.9	0/0	0/0/0	0/0	0//0	0/0/	0/1.8/1.8	0/1.8			0/0/0	Navigational radar equipments for missiles or rockets (for target detection of ballistic missiles, carrier rockets, sounding rockets)
0/0/0	0	0.9	0/0	0/0/0	0/0	0//0	0/0/	0/1.8/1.8	0/1.8			0/0/0	Other radar apparatus for navigational aid
													---Other
0/0/0	0	2.3	0/0	0/0/0	0/0	0//0	0/0/	0/0/4.5	0/0			0/0/0	Airborne radars (including meteorological radars, terrain following radars and air traffic control response system)
0/0/0	0	2.3	0/0	0/0/0	0/0	0//0	0/0/	0/0/4.5	0/0			0/0/0	Radar life detecting instrument
0/0/0	0	2.3	0/0	0/0/0	0/0	0//0	0/0/	0/0/4.5	0/0			0/0/0	Airborne radars for missiles and rockets (for ballistic missiles, carrier rockets and sounding rockets, etc. to detect targets)
0/0/0	0	2.3	0/0	0/0/0	0/0	0//0	0/0/	0/0/4.5	0/0			0/0/0	Other radars for missiles and rockets (for ballistic missiles, carrier rockets and sounding rockets, etc. to detect targets)
0/0/0	0	2.3	0/0	0/0/0	0/0	0//0	0/0/	0/0/4.5	0/0			0/0/0	Other radars
													-Other:
													--Radio navigational aid apparatus:
0/0/0	0	0	0/0	0/0/0	0/0	0//0	0/0/	0/0/0	0/0			0/0/0	---For motor vehicles
													---Other

税则号列	货品名称〔CIQ 扩展编码及品名－T2 表示见附表 2〕	最惠(%)	暂定税率	普通	增值/消费	出口退税	计量单位	监管条件/特殊证件	检验检疫	对美关税	亚太上/下
8526.9190 10	制导装置(使 300km 射程导弹达到≤10km 圆公算偏差)〔999〕	0		8	13/	13	台/千克	3/		5	
8526.9190 90	其他无线电导航设备〔999〕	0		8	13/	13	台/千克	/		5	
8526.9200	--无线电遥控设备〔999〕	0		14	13/	13	台/千克	O/		20	
85.27	**无线电广播接收设备,不论是否与声音的录制、重放装置或时钟组合在同一机壳内:**										
	-不需外接电源的无线电收音机:										
8527.1200	--袖珍盒式磁带收放机[T2]	0		130	13/	13	台/千克	/			
8527.1300	--其他收录(放)音组合机〔101:Ⅰ类收录(放)音组合机;102:Ⅱ类收录(放)音组合机;103:Ⅲ类收录(放)音组合机〕	0		130	13/	13	台/千克	/			
8527.1900	--其他〔101:Ⅰ类收音机,102:Ⅱ类收音机,103:Ⅲ类收音机〕	0		130	13/	13	台/千克	/		20	
	-需外接电源的汽车用无线电收音机:										
8527.2100	--收录(放)音组合机										
8527.2100 10	具备接收和转换数字广播数据系统信号功能需外接电源的汽车用收录(放)音组合机〔101:Ⅰ类收录(放)音组合机;102:Ⅱ类收录(放)音组合机;103:Ⅲ类收录(放)音组合机〕	0		130	13/	13	台/千克	/		5	
8527.2100 90	其他需外接电源汽车收录(放)音组合机[T2]	15		130	13/	13	台/千克	/		20	
8527.2900	--其他〔101:Ⅰ类收音机,102:Ⅱ类收音机,103:Ⅲ类收音机〕	0		130	13/	13	台/千克	/		5	
	-其他:										
8527.9100	--收录(放)音组合机[T2]	0		130	13/	13	台/千克	/	L	25	
8527.9200	--带时钟的收音机[T2]	0		130	13/	13	台/千克	/		25	
8527.9900	--其他〔101:Ⅰ类收音机,102:Ⅱ类收音机,103:Ⅲ类收音机〕	0		130	13/	13	台/千克	/		25	
85.28	**监视器及投影机,未装电视接收装置;电视接收装置,不论是否装有无线电收音装置或声音、图像的录制或重放装置:**										
	-阴极射线管监视器:										
8528.4200	--可直接连接且设计用于税目 84.71 的自动数据处理设备的[T2]	0		40	13/	13	台/千克	6/	L	20	
	--其他:										
8528.4910	---彩色的[T2]	0		130	13/	13	台/千克	6/		5	0/0
8528.4990	---单色的[T2]	0		100	13/	13	台/千克	6/		5	0/0
	-其他监视器:										
	--可直接连接且设计用于税目 84.71 的自动数据处理设备的:										
	---液晶的:										
8528.5211	----专用于或主要用于税目 84.71 的自动数据处理设备的〔999〕	0		40	13/	13	台/千克	/	L	10	
8528.5212	----其他,彩色的〔999〕	15		130	13/	13	台/千克	6/	L	40	9.8/9.8
8528.5219	----其他,单色的〔999〕	10		100	13/	13	台/千克	6/	L	20	6.5/6.5
	---其他:										
8528.5291	----专用于或主要用于税目 84.71 的自动数据处理设备的,彩色的〔999〕	0		40	13/	13	台/千克	/	L	25	
8528.5292	----其他,彩色的〔999〕	15		130	13/	13	台/千克	6/	L	25	9.8/9.8
8528.5299	----其他,单色的〔999〕	10		100	13/	13	台/千克	6/	L		6.5/6.5
	--其他:										
8528.5910	---彩色的										
8528.5910 10	车载液晶显示器〔999〕	20	10	130	13/	13	台/千克	6/		30	13/13
8528.5910 20	航空器用显示器〔999〕	20	1	130	13/	13	台/千克	6/		21	13/13
8528.5910 90	其他彩色的监视器[T2]	20		130	13/	13	台/千克	6/		40	13/13
8528.5990	---单色的[T2]	10		100	13/	13	台/千克	6/		35	6.5/6.5
	-投影机:										
	--可直接连接且设计用于税目 84.71 的自动数据处理设备的:										
8528.6210	---专用于或主要用于税目 84.71 的自动数据处理设备的										
8528.6210 10	专用或主要用于品目 8471 商品的彩色投影机〔999〕	0		14	13/	13	台/千克	/	L	20	
8528.6210 90	其他专用或主要用于品目 8471 商品的投影机〔999〕	0		14	13/	13	台/千克	/	L	20	
8528.6220	---其他,彩色的〔999〕	15		130	13/	13	台/千克	6/	L	40	9.8/9.8
8528.6290	---其他,单色的〔999〕	10		100	13/	13	台/千克	/	L		

协定税率 %								RCEP		特惠税率 %			Article Description
东/冰/格	巴基斯坦	韩国	瑞士上/下	哥/秘/柬	澳/毛	新西/坡/智	中国港/澳/台	东盟及马来/澳/韩	日/新	亚太2国	老/柬/缅	98/97/95	
0/0/0	0	0.4	0/0	0/0/0	0/0.9	0//0	0/0/	0/1.8/1.8	0/1.8			0/0/0	Guidance devices (making 300km-range misslies, circle probability or estimated chances deviation≤10km)
0/0/0	0	0.4	0/0	0/0/0	0/0.9	0//0	0/0/	0/1.8/1.8	0/1.8			0/0/0	Other radio navigational aid apparatus
0/0/0	0	1	0/0	0/0/0	0/0	0//0	0/0/	0/0/4.5	4.5/0			0/0/0	--Radio remote control apparatus
													Reception apparatus for radio-broadcasting, whether or not combined, in the same housing, with sound recording or reproducing apparatus or a clock:
													-Radio-broadcast receivers capable of operating without an external source of power:
0/0/0	16	9.3	0/0	0/0/0	0/0	0/0/0	0/0/	0/0/18	0/0			0/0/0	--Pocket-size radio cassette-players
0/0/0	8.4	3	0/0	0/0/0	0/0	0/0/0	0/0/	0/0/13.5	0/0			0/0/0	--Other apparatus combined with sound recording or reproducing apparatus
0/0/0	8.4	7	0/0	0/0/0	0/0	0/0/0	0/0/	0/0/13.5	0/0			0/0/0	--Other
													-Radio-broadcast receivers not capable of operating without an external source of power, of a kind used in motor vehicles:
													--Combined with sound recording or reproducing apparatus
0/0/0	8.4	7	1.5/1.5	0/0/0	0/0	0/0/0	0/0/	14/14.3/14	14.1/14.3			0/0/0	Vehicle mounted (released) sound combination machine for receiving and converting digital broadcast data system signal function requiring external power supply
0/0/0	8.4	7	1.5/1.5	0/0/0	0/0	0/0/0	0/0/	14/14.3/14	14.1/14.3			0/0/0	
0/0/0	8.4	7	0/0	0/0/0	0/0	0/0/0	0/0/	0/0/13.5	0/0			0/0/0	--Other
													-Other:
0/0/0	8.4	3	0/0	0/0/0	0/0	0/0/0	0/0/	0/0/13.5	0/0			0/0/0	--Combined with sound recording or reproducing apparatus
0/0/0	8.4	3	0/0	0/0/0	0/0	0/0/0	0/0/	0/0/13.5	0/0			0/0/0	--Not combined with sound recording or reproducing apparatus but combined with a clock
0/0/0	21.6	16.2	0/0	0/0/0	0/13.5	0/0/0	0/0/	0/0/25.2	0/0			0/0/0	--Other
													Monitors and projectors, not incorporatig television reception apparatus; reception apparatus for tele vision, whether or not incorporating radiobroad cast receivers or sound or video recordig or reproducing apparatus:
													-Cathode-ray tube monitors:
0/0/0	0	0	0/0	0/0/0	0/0	0//0	0/0/	0/0/0	0/0			0/0/0	--Capable of directly connecting to and designed for use with an auto matic data processing machine of heading 84.71
													--Other:
0/0/0	20.8	18	0/0	0/0/0	0/13.5	0/0/0	0/0/	0/0/28	0/0			0/0/0	---Colour
0/0/0	10.6	3.8	0/0	0/0/0	0/0	0/0/0	0/0/	0/0/17.1	0/0			0/0/0	---monochrone
													-Other monitors:
													--Capable of directly connecting tO and designed for use with an automatic data processing machine of heading 84.71:
													---0f LCD:
0/0/0	0	0	0/0	0/0/0	0/0	0//0	0/0/	0/0/0	0/0			0/0/0	----Of a kind solely or principally used in an automatic data processing system of heading 84.71
0/0/0	18.2	19.5		/0/0	0/18	0/0/0	0/0/	5/5/	/5			0/0/0	----Other, colour
0/0/0	10.6		1.9/1.9	0/0/0	0/0	0/0/0	0/0/	5/5/	/5			0/0/0	----Other, monochrome
													---Other:
0/0/0	0	0	0/0	0/0/0	0/0	0//0	0/0/	0/0/0	0/0			0/0/0	----Of a kind solely or principally used in an automatic data processing system of heading 84.71, colour
0/0/0	18.2	19.5		/0/0	0/18	0/0/0	0/0/	5/5/	/5			0/0/0	----Other, colour
0/0/0	10.6		1.9/1.9	0/0/0	0/0	0/0/0	0/0/	5/5/	/5			0/0/0	----Other, monochrome
													--Other:
													---Colour
0/0/0	18.2	19.5		/0/0	0/18	0/0/0	0/0/	5/5/	/5			0/0/0	LCD Monitors, specially used for Vehicle Navigator
0/0/0	18.2	19.5		/0/0	0/18	0/0/0	0/0/	5/5/	/5		//	0/0/0	Aircraft indicator
0/0/0	18.2	19.5		/0/0	0/18	0/0/0	0/0/	5/5/	/5			0/0/0	Other colors monitors
0/0/0	10.6		1.9/1.9	0/0/0	0/0	0/0/0	0/0/	5/5/	/5			0/0/0	---monochrome
													-Projectors:
													--Capable of directly connecting tO and designed for use with an automatic data processing machine of heading 84.71:
													----Of a kind solely or principally used in an auto matic data processing system of heading 84.71
0/0/0	0	0	0/0	0/0/0	0/0	0//0	0/0/	0/0/0	0/0			0/0/0	Specially used or mainly used for color projector of heading No.84.71
0/0/0	0	0	0/0	0/0/0	0/0	0//0	0/0/	0/0/0	0/0			0/0/0	Other used or mainly used for projector of heading No.84.71
0/0/0	17.9	19.5		0/0/0	0/18	0/0/0	0/0/	5/5/	15/5			0/0/0	---Other, colour
0/0/0	8.4		1.5/1.5	0/0/0	0/0	0/0/0	0/0/	5/5/	/5			0/0/0	---Other, monochrome

税则号列	货品名称〔CIQ 扩展编码及品名－T2 表示见附表 2〕	最惠(%)	暂定税率	普通	增值/消费	出口退税	计量单位	监管条件/特殊证件	检验检疫	对美关税	亚太上/下
	--其他:										
8528.6910	---彩色的[T2]	15		130	13/	13	台/千克	6/	L	40	9.8/9.8
8528.6990	---单色的[T2]	10		100	13/	13	台/千克	/	L	15	
	-电视接收装置,不论是否装有无线电收音装置或声音、图像的录制或重放装置:										
	--在设计上不带有视频显示器或屏幕的:										
8528.7110	---彩色卫星电视接收机[T2]	0		130	13/	13	台/千克	O/	L	20	0/0
8528.7180	---其他彩色的[T2]	0		130	13/	13	台/千克	/	L	25	0/0
8528.7190	---单色的[T2]	0		100	13/	13	台/千克	/			
	--其他,彩色的:										
	---阴极射线显像管的:										
8528.7211	----模拟电视接收机[T2]	10		130	13/	13	台/千克	6/	L		6.5/6.5
8528.7212	----数字电视接收机[T2]	10		130	13/	13	台/千克	6/	L		6.5/6.5
8528.7219	----其他[T2]	10		130	13/	13	台/千克	6/	L		6.5/6.5
	---液晶显示器的:										
8528.7221	----模拟电视接收机[T2]	15		130	13/	13	台/千克	/	L	40	10.5/10.5
8528.7222	----数字电视接收机[T2]	15		130	13/	13	台/千克	/	L	40	10.5/10.5
8528.7229	----其他[T2]	15		130	13/	13	台/千克	/	L	25	10.5/10.5
	---等离子显示器的:										
8528.7231	----模拟电视接收机[T2]	10		130	13/	13	台/千克	/	L		7/7
8528.7232	----数字电视接收机[T2]	15		130	13/	13	台/千克	/	L	25	10.5/10.5
8528.7239	----其他[T2]	15		130	13/	13	台/千克	/	L		10.5/10.5
	---其他:										
8528.7291	----模拟电视接收机[T2]	10		130	13/	13	台/千克	/	L		7/7
8528.7292	----数字电视接收机[T2]	15		130	13/	13	台/千克	/	L	40	10.5/10.5
8528.7299	----其他[T2]	15		130	13/	13	台/千克	/	L		10.5/10.5
8528.7300	-其他,单色的[T2]	7		100	13/	13	台/千克	6/			
85.29	**专用于或主要用于税目 85.24 至 85.28 所列装置或设备的零件:**										
	-各种天线或天线反射器及其零件:										
8529.1010	---雷达设备及无线电导航设备用〔999〕	0		8	13/	13	千克	/			
8529.1020	---无线电收音机及其组合机、电视接收机用[T2]	0		90	13/	13	千克	/		25	
8529.1090	---其他										
8529.1090 21	卫星电视接收用天线[T2]	0		20	13/	13	千克/个	O/		20	
8529.1090 29	其他无线广播电视用天线(税目 85.25 至 85.28 所列其他装置或设备的,包括天线反射器)[T2]	0		20	13/	13	千克/个	O/		20	
8529.1090 90	其他无线电设备天线及其零件(税目 85.25 至 85.28 所列其他装置或设备的,包括天线反射器)[T2]	0		20	13/	13	千克/个	/		20	
	-其他:										
8529.9010	---电视发送、差转设备及卫星电视地面接收转播设备用										
8529.9010 11	卫星电视接收用解码器[T2]	0		30	13/	13	千克/个	O/		20	
8529.9010 12	卫星电视接收用收视卡[T2]	0		30	13/	13	千克/个	O/		20	
8529.9010 13	卫星电视接收用器件板卡[T2]	0		30	13/	13	千克/个	O/		20	
8529.9010 14	卫星电视接收用专用零件[T2]	0		30	13/	13	千克/个	O/		20	
8529.9010 90	其他电视发送,差转等设备零件(包括其他卫星电视地面接收转播设备零件)[T2]	0		30	13/	13	千克/个	/		20	
8529.9020	---税目 85.24 所列设备用										
8529.9020 10	税目 85.24 所列设备用零件,用于雷达设备及无线电导航设备〔999〕	2.8/1.4		53	13/	13	千克/个	/			1.8/0.9
8529.9020 90	其他税目 85.24 所列设备用零件〔999〕	2.8/1.4		53	13/	13	千克/个	/		7.8	1.8/0.9
	---电视摄像机、视频摄录一体机及数字照相机用:										
8529.9041	----特种用途的[T2]	2.7/1.3		17	13/	13	千克	/		7.7	1.8/0.8
8529.9042	----非特种用途的取像模块〔101:Ⅰ类家用型摄录一体机;102:Ⅱ类家用型摄录一体机;103:Ⅲ类家用型摄录一体机;104:Ⅰ类其它摄录放像装置及其零件;105:Ⅱ类其它摄录放像装置及其零件;106:Ⅲ类其它摄录放像装置及其零件〕	4/2	①	100	13/	13	千克	/		28	2.6/1.3
8529.9049	----其他[T2]	4/2	②	100	13/	13	千克	/		27	3.6/1.8

① 1－6 月:3%

② 1－6 月:2%

协定税率 %								RCEP		特惠税率 %			Article Description
东/冰/格	巴基斯坦	韩国	瑞士 上/下	哥/秘/柬	澳/毛	新西/坡/智	中国港/澳/台	东盟及马来/澳/韩	日/新	亚太2国	老/柬/缅	98/97/95	
													--Other:
0/0/0	17.9	19.5		0/0/0	0/18	0/0/0	0/0/	5/5/	15/5			0/0/0	---Colour
0/0/0	8.4		1.5/1.5	0/0/0	0/0	0/0/0	0/0/	5/5/	/5			0/0/0	---Monochrome
													-Reception apparatus for television, whether or not incorporating radio-broadcast receivers or sound or video recording or reproducing apparatus:
													--Not designed to incorporate a video display or screen:
/0/0	16.8			0//0	0/15	0//0	0/0/	27/27/27	27.3/27			0/0/	---Colour satellite television receivers
0/0/	14.7			0//0	0/15	0/0/0	0/0/	0/0/27	27.3/0			0/0/	---Other colour
0/0/0	8.4	3	0/0	0/0/0	0/0	0/0/0	0/0/	0/0/13.5	13.6/0			0/0/0	---monochrome
													--Other, colour:
													---Of cathode-ray tube monitors:
/0/	14.7		10/10	0//0	0/18	0//0	0/0/					0/0/	----Analogue
/0/	14.7		10/10	0//0	14/18	0//0	0/0/					0/0/	----Digital
/0/	14.7		10/10	0//0	0/18	0//0	0/0/					0/0/	----Other
													---Of LCD:
5/0/	21			//0	0/18	0//0	0/0/					0/0/	----Analogue
5/0/	21	21		//0	14/18	0//0	0/0/					0/0/	----Digital
5/0/	21			//0	0/18	0//0	0/0/					0/0/	----Other
													---Of plasma:
5/0/	14.7			//0	0/18	0//0	0/0/					0/0/	----Analogue
5/0/	14.7			//0	14/18	0//0	0/0/					0/0/	----Digital
5/0/	14.7	21		//0	0/18	0//0	0/0/					0/0/	----Other
													---Other:
5/0/	14.7			0/0/0	0/18	0//0	0/0/					0/0/0	----Analogue
5/0/	14.7			//0	14/18	0//0	0/0/					0/0/	----Digital
5/0/	14.7			0//0	0/18	0//0	0/0/					0/0/	----Other
0/0/0	8.4	3	1.5/1.5	0/0/0	0/0	0/0/0	0/0/	0/0/13.5	13.6/0			0/0/0	--Other, monchrome
													Parts suitable for use solely or principally with the apparatus of headingsNo. 85. 24 to 85. 28:
													-Aerials and aerial reflectors of all kinds; parts suitable for use therewith:
0/0/0	0	0.3	0/0	0/0/0	0/0	0//0	0/0/	0/0/1.4	0/0			0/0/0	---For radar apparatus and radio navigational aid apparatus
0/0/0	0	0	0/0	0/0/0	0/0	0//0	0/0/	0/0/0	0/0			0/0/0	---For radio-broadcast receivers and their combinations, television receivers
													---Other
0/0/0	0	0	0/0	0/0/0	0/0	0//0	0/0/	0/1.8/0	0/1.8			0/0/0	Satellite TV receiving antenna
0/0/0	0	0	0/0	0/0/0	0/0	0//0	0/0/	0/1.8/0	0/1.8			0/0/0	Other radio broadcasting and television antenna(suitable for use solely or principally with the apparatus of heading No. 85. 25 to 85. 28, including antenna reflectors)
0/0/0	0	0	0/0	0/0/0	0/0	0//0	0/0/	0/1.8/0	0/1.8			0/0/0	Other radio antennas and parts (suitable for use solely or principally with the apparatus of heading No. 85. 25 to 85. 28, including antenna reflectors)
													-Other:
													---Of television transmission or translation apparatus, satellite television ground receiving and relaying apparatus
0/0/0	0	0	0/0	0/0/0	0/0	0//0	0/0/	0/0/0	0/0			0/0/0	Decoders for statellite TV recervers
0/0/0	0	0	0/0	0/0/0	0/0	0//0	0/0/	0/0/0	0/0			0/0/0	CA card for receiving satellite television
0/0/0	0	0	0/0	0/0/0	0/0	0//0	0/0/	0/0/0	0/0			0/0/0	CRD cards for receiving statellite TV
0/0/0	0	0	0/0	0/0/0	0/0	0//0	0/0/	0/0/0	0/0			0/0/0	Parts exclusive for receiving statellite TV signals
0/0/0	0	0	0/0	0/0/0	0/0	0//0	0/0/	0/0/0	0/0			0/0/0	Parts of other television tronsmission or translation apparatus (including parts of satellite television ground receiving and relaying apparatus)
													---For equipment listed in heading 85.24
0/0/0.3	2.7	4.1	0.7/0.7	1.8/0.9/0	0/0.7	0/0/0	0/0/	0/0/0	0/0			0/0/0	Parts for equipment listed in heading 85.24 for radar equipment and radio navigation equipment
0/0/0.3	2.7	4.1	0.7/0.7	1.8/0.9/0	0/0.7	0/0/0	0/0/	0/0/0	0/0			0/0/0	Parts for equipment listed in other tax heading 85.24
													---For TV camera, video recorder and digital camera:
0/0/0	2	5.2	0/0	0/0/0	0/0	0//0	0/0/	5/5/	/5			0/0/0	----Of special purpose
0/0/0	3.5	2.4	1.2/1.2	0/0/0	0/0	0/0/0	0/0/0	0/0/10.8	10.9/0			0/0/0	----Cameera modules without special pnrpose
0/0/0	3.5	5.6	1.2/1.2	0/0/0	0/0	0/0/0	0/0/0	11.2/11.4/11.2	11.3/11.4			0/0/0	----Other

税则号列	货品名称〔CIQ扩展编码及品名－T2表示见附表2〕	最惠(%)	暂定税率	普通	增值/消费	出口退税	计量单位	监管条件/特殊证件	检验检疫	对美关税	亚太上/下
8529.9050	---雷达设备及无线电导航设备用〔999〕	0.5/0.3		8	13/	13	千克	/			0.3/0.2
8529.9060	---无线电收音机及其组合机用[T2]	5/2.5		130	13/	13	千克	/		30	3.3/1.6
	---电视接收机用(高频调谐器除外)：										
8529.9081	----彩色电视接收机用[T2]	5/2.5		80	13/	13	千克	/		30	3.3/1.6
8529.9089	----其他[T2]	0		50	13/	13	千克	/		10	
8529.9090	---其他										
8529.9090 11	卫星电视接收用高频调谐器[T2]	0		57	13/	13	千克/个	O/		25	
8529.9090 90	税目85.25至85.28所列装置或设备其他零件〔999〕	0		57	13/	13	千克/个	/		25	
85.30	**铁道、电车道、道路或内河航道、停车场、港口或机场用的电气信号、安全或交通管理设备(税目86.08的货品除外)：**										
8530.1000	-铁道或电车道用的设备〔999〕	8		20	13/	13	个/千克	/			5.2/5.2
8530.8000	-其他设备〔999〕	8		20	13/	13	个/千克	/		28	
8530.9000	-零件〔999〕	6		20	13/	13	千克	/		26	
85.31	**电气音响或视觉信号装置(例如，电铃、电笛、显示板、防盗或防火报警器)，但税目85.12或85.30的货品除外：**										
8531.1000	-防盗或防火报警器及类似装置[T2]	10		40	13/	13	个/千克	A/	L	20	
8531.2000	-装有液晶装置(LCD)或发光二极管(LED)的显示板〔999〕	0		70	13/	13	个/千克	/		25	
	-其他装置：										
8531.8010	---蜂鸣器										
8531.8010 01	音量不超过110db的小型蜂鸣器〔999〕	10	7.5	70	13/	13	个/千克	/		32.5	
8531.8010 90	其他蜂鸣器〔999〕	10		70	13/	13	个/千克	/		35	
8531.8090	---其他										
8531.8090 10	飞机用频闪灯、警告组件	2.5/1.3	1	70	13/	13	个/千克	/		11	
8531.8090 90	其他电气音响或视觉信号装置	2.5/1.3		70	13/	13	个/千克	/		12.5	
	-零件：										
8531.9010	---防盗或防火报警器及类似装置用〔999〕	0		40	13/	13	千克	/		10	
8531.9090	---其他[T2]	0		70	13/	13	千克	/		20	
85.32	**固定、可变或可调(微调)电容器：**										
8532.1000	-固定电容器，用于50/60赫兹电路，其额定无功功率不低于0.5千瓦(电力电容器)〔999〕	0		20	13/	13	千克/千个	/		25	
	-其他固定电容器：										
	--钽电容器：										
8532.2110	---片式〔999〕	0		35	13/	13	千克/千个	/		25	
8532.2190	---其他〔999〕	0		35	13/	13	千克/千个	/		25	
	--铝电介电容器：										
8532.2210	---片式〔999〕	0		35	13/	13	千克/千个	/		25	
8532.2290	---其他〔999〕	0		35	13/	13	千克/千个	/		25	
8532.2300	--单层瓷介电容器〔999〕	0		35	13/	13	千克/千个	/		25	
	--多层瓷介电容器：										
8532.2410	---片式〔999〕	0		35	13/	13	千克/千个	/		25	
8532.2490	---其他〔999〕	0		35	13/	13	千克/千个	/		25	
	--纸介质或塑料介质电容器：										
8532.2510	---片式〔999〕	0		35	13/	13	千克/千个	/		25	
8532.2590	---其他〔999〕	0		35	13/	13	千克/千个	/		25	
8532.2900	--其他〔999〕	0		35	13/	13	千克/千个	/		25	
8532.3000	-可变或可调(微调)电容器〔999〕	0		35	13/	13	千克/千个	/		25	
	-零件：										
8532.9010	---税号8532.1000所列电容器用〔999〕	0		20	13/	13	千克	/		5	
8532.9090	---其他〔999〕	0		35	13/	13	千克	/		10	
85.33	**电阻器(包括变阻器及电位器)，但加热电阻器除外：**										
8533.1000	-固定碳质电阻器，合成或薄膜式〔999〕	0		50	13/	13	千克/千个	/		25	
	-其他固定电阻器：										
	--额定功率不超过20瓦：										
8533.2110	---片式〔999〕	0		50	13/	13	千克/千个	/		25	
8533.2190	---其他〔999〕	0		50	13/	13	千克/千个	/		25	
8533.2900	--其他〔999〕	0		50	13/	13	千克/千个	/		20	
	-线绕可变电阻器，包括变阻器及电位器：										
8533.3100	--额定功率不超过20瓦〔999〕	0		50	13/	13	千克/千个	/		25	
8533.3900	--其他〔999〕	0		50	13/	13	千克/千个	/		25	

协定税率 %								RCEP		特惠税率 %			Article Description
东/冰/格	巴基斯坦	韩国	瑞士上/下	哥/秘/柬	澳/毛	新西/坡/智	中国港/澳/台	东盟及马来/澳/韩	日/新	亚太2国	老/柬/缅	98/97/95	
0/0/0	0	0.3	0/0	0/0/0	0/0	0//0	0/0/	0/0/1.4	1.4/0			0/0/0	---Of radar apparatus and radio navigational aid apparatus
0/0/0	5.3	3	1.5/1.5	0/0/0	0/0	0/0/0	0/0/	0/0/13.5	13.6/0			0/0/0	---Of radio-broadcast receivers and their combinations
													---Of television receivers (Other than H. F tuners):
0/0/	5.3		1.5/1.5	/0/0	0/0	0/0/0	0/0/	5/5/	/5			0/0/0	----Of colour television receivers (other than plasma display modules or parts thereof, organic light emitting diode display screen)
0/0/0	0	0	0/0	0/0/0	0/0	0//0	0/0/	0/0/0	0/0			0/0/0	----Other
													---Other
0/0/0	0	0	0/0	0/0/0	0/0	0//0	0/0/	0/0/0	0/0			0/0/0	High-frequency tuners for satellite television
0/0/0	0	0	0/0	0/0/0	0/0	0//0	0/0/	0/0/0	0/0			0/0/0	Other parts of apparatus of headings No. 85. 25 ～ 85. 28
													Electrical signalling, safety or traffic control equipment for railways, tramways, roads, inland waterways, parking facilities, port installations or airfields (other than those of heading No. 86. 08):
0/0/0	2	2	0/0	0/0/0	0/0	0//0	0/0/	0/0/9	9.1/0			0/0/0	-Equipment for railways or tramways
0/0/0	2	1.6	0/0	0/0/0	0/0	0//0	0/0/	0/0/7.2	7.3/0			0/0/0	-Other equipment
0/0/0	2	1.6	0/0	0/0/0	0/0	0//0	0/0/	0/0/7.2	7.3/0			0/0/0	-Parts
													Electric sound or visual signalling apparatus (for example, bells, sirens, indicator panels, burglar or fire alarms), other than those of headingNos. 85. 12 or 85. 30:
0/0/0	2	2	0/0	0/0/0	0/0	0/0/0	0/0/	9/9/9	9.1/9			0/0/0	-Burglar or fire alarms and similar apparatus
0/0/0	0	0	0/0	0/0/0	0/0	0//0	0/0/	0/0/0	0/0			0/0/0	-Indicator panels incorporating liquid crystal devices (LCD) or light emitting diodes (LED)
													-Other apparatus:
													---Buzzers
0/0/0	8.4	7.5	1.5/1.5	0/0/0	0/0	0/0/0	0/0/	5/5/	/5			0/0/0	Small buzzers, volue<110dB
0/0/0	8.4	7.5	1.5/1.5	0/0/0	0/0	0/0/0	0/0/	5/5/	/5			0/0/0	Other buzzers
													---Other
0/0/0	2	2	0/0	0/0/0	0/0	0/0/0	0/0/	0/0/9	9.1/0		//	0/0/0	Strobe light and warning components for aircraft
0/0/0	2	2	0/0	0/0/0	0/0	0/0/0	0/0/	0/0/9	9.1/0		//	0/0/0	Other electrical audio or visual signaling devices
													-Parts:
0/0/0	0	0	0/0	0/0/0	0/0	0//0	0/0/	0/0/0	0/0			0/0/0	---Of burglar or fire alarms and similar apparatus
0/0/0	0	0	0/0	0/0/0	0/0	0//0	0/0/	0/0/0	0/0			0/0/0	---Other
													Electrical capacitors, fixed, variable or adjustable (preset):
0/0/0	0	0	0/0	0/0/0	0/0	0//0	0/0/	0/0/0	0/0			0/0/0	-Fixed capacitors designed for use in 50/60 Hz circuits and having a reactive power handling capacity of not less than 0. 5 kV (power capacitors)
													-Other fixed capacitors:
													--Tantalum:
0/0/0	0	0	0/0	0/0/0	0/0	0//0	0/0/	0/0/0	0/0			0/0/0	---Laminate
0/0/0	0	0	0/0	0/0/0	0/0	0//0	0/0/	0/0/0	0/0			0/0/0	---Other
													--Aluminium electrolytic:
0/0/0	0	0	0/0	0/0/0	0/0	0//0	0/0/	0/0/0	0/0			0/0/0	---Laminate
0/0/0	0	0	0/0	0/0/0	0/0	0//0	0/0/	0/0/0	0/0			0/0/0	---Other
0/0/0	0	0	0/0	0/0/0	0/0	0//0	0/0/	0/0/0	0/0			0/0/0	--Ceramic dielectric, single layer
													--Ceramic dielectric, multilayer:
0/0/0	0	0	0/0	0/0/0	0/0	0//0	0/0/	0/0/0	0/0			0/0/0	---Laminate
0/0/0	0	0	0/0	0/0/0	0/0	0//0	0/0/	0/0/0	0/0			0/0/0	---Other
													--Dielectric of paper or plastics:
0/0/0	0	0	0/0	0/0/0	0/0	0//0	0/0/	0/0/0	0/0			0/0/0	---Laminate
0/0/0	0	0	0/0	0/0/0	0/0	0//0	0/0/	0/0/0	0/0			0/0/0	---Other
0/0/0	0	0	0/0	0/0/0	0/0	0//0	0/0/	0/0/0	0/0			0/0/0	--Other
0/0/0	0	0	0/0	0/0/0	0/0	0//0	0/0/	0/0/0	0/0			0/0/0	-Variable or adjustable (pre-set) capacitors
													-Parts:
0/0/0	0	0	0/0	0/0/0	0/0	0//0	0/0/	0/0/0	0/0			0/0/0	---Of the capacitors of subheadingNo. 8532. 1000
0/0/0	0	0	0/0	0/0/0	0/0	0//0	0/0/	0/0/0	0/0			0/0/0	---Other
													Electrical resistors (including rheostats and potentiometers), other than heating resistors:
0/0/0	0	0	0/0	0/0/0	0/0	0//0	0/0/	0/0/0	0/0			0/0/0	-Fixed carbon resistors, composition or film types
													-Other fixed resistors:
													--For a power handling capacity not exceeding 20W:
0/0/0	0	0	0/0	0/0/0	0/0	0//0	0/0/	0/0/0	0/0			0/0/0	---Laminate
0/0/0	0	0	0/0	0/0/0	0/0	0//0	0/0/	0/0/0	0/0			0/0/0	---Other
0/0/0	0	0	0/0	0/0/0	0/0	0//0	0/0/	0/0/0	0/0			0/0/0	Other
													-Wirewound variable resistors, including rheostats and potentiometers:
0/0/0	0	0	0/0	0/0/0	0/0	0//0	0/0/	0/0/0	0/0			0/0/0	--For a power handling capacity not exceeding 20 W
0/0/0	0	0	0/0	0/0/0	0/0	0//0	0/0/	0/0/0	0/0			0/0/0	--Other

税则号列	货品名称〔CIQ 扩展编码及品名—T2 表示见附表 2〕	最惠(%)	暂定税率	普通	增值/消费	出口退税	计量单位	监管条件/特殊证件	检验检疫	对美关税	亚太上/下
8533.4000	-其他可变电阻器,包括变阻器及电位器〔999〕	0		50	13/	13	千克/千个	/		25	
8533.9000	-零件〔999〕	0		50	13/	13	千克	/		25	
85.34	**印刷电路:**										
8534.0010	---4 层以上的〔999〕	0		35	13/	13	块/千克	/		25	
8534.0090	---其他〔999〕	0		50	13/	13	块/千克	/		25	
85.35	**电路的开关、保护或连接用的电气装置(例如,开关、熔断器、避雷器、电压限幅器、电涌抑制器、插头及其他连接器、接线盒),用于电压超过 1000 伏的线路:**										
8535.1000	-熔断器〔999〕	10		50	13/	13	个/千克	A/	L	35	
	-自动断路器:										
8535.2100	--用于电压低于 72.5 千伏的线路:〔999〕	10		50	13/	13	个/千克	A/	L	35	
	--其他:										
8535.2910	---用于电压在 72.5 千伏以上,但不高于 220 千伏的线路〔999〕	10		50	13/	13	个/千克	/		35	
8535.2920	---用于电压高于 220 千伏,但不高于 750 千伏的线路〔999〕	10		50	13/	13	个/千克	/		35	
8535.2990	---其他〔999〕	10		50	13/	13	个/千克	/			
	-隔离开关及断续开关:										
8535.3010	---用于电压在 72.5 千伏以上,但不高于 220 千伏的线路										
8535.3010 10	72.5 千伏≤电压≤220 千伏的隔离开关及断续开关,含汞〔999〕	10		50	13/	13	个/千克	89/			8/8
8535.3010 90	其他 72.5 千伏≤电压≤220 千伏的隔离开关及断续开关〔999〕	10		50	13/	13	个/千克	/			8/8
8535.3020	---用于电压高于 220 千伏,但不高 750 千伏的线路										
8535.3020 10	220 千伏<电压≤750 千伏隔离开关及断续开关,含汞〔999〕	10		50	13/	13	个/千克	89/			
8535.3020 90	其他 220 千伏<电压≤750 千伏隔离开关及断续开关〔999〕	10		50	13/	13	个/千克	/			
8535.3090	---其他										
8535.3090 10	其他隔离开关及断续开关,含汞(用于电压超过 1000 伏的线路)〔999〕	10		50	13/	13	个/千克	89/		35	
8535.3090 90	其他隔离开关及断续开关(用于电压超过 1000 伏的线路)〔999〕	10		50	13/	13	个/千克	/	L	35	
8535.4000	-避雷器、电压限幅器及电涌抑制器〔999〕	10		50	13/	13	个/千克	/		35	
8535.9000	-其他										
8535.9000 10	触发式火花隙(阳极延迟时间≤15ms,阳极峰值额定电流≥500A)〔101 高压开关装置,102 其它高压电器及其零件〕	10		50	13/	13	千克	3/		30	6.5/6.5
8535.9000 20	具有快速开关功能的模件或组件(阳极峰值电压≥2kV;电流≥500A;接通时间为 1 微秒或更短)〔101 高压开关装置,102 其它高压电器及其零件〕	10		50	13/	13	千克	3/		30	6.5/6.5
8535.9000 30	受电弓〔101 高压开关装置,102 其它高压电器及其零件〕	10	5	50	13/	13	千克	/		25	6.5/6.5
8535.9000 40	250 千米/小时及以上高速动车组用高压电缆接头〔301 高压开关装置,302 其它高压电器及其零件〕	10	6	50	13/	13	千克	/		26	6.5/6.5
8535.9000 90	其他电压>1000 伏电路开关等电气装置〔101 高压开关装置,102 其它高压电器及其零件〕	10		50	13/	13	千克	/	L	30	6.5/6.5
85.36	**电路的开关、保护或连接用的电器装置(例如,开关、继电器、熔断器、电涌抑制器、插头、插座、灯座及其他连接器、接线盒),用于电压不超过 1000 伏的线路;光导纤维、光导纤维束或光缆用连接器:**										
8536.1000	-熔断器〔999〕	10		50	13/	13	个/千克	A/	L	35	
8536.2000	-自动断路器〔101 断路器,102 其它低压电器及其零件〕	9		50	13/	13	个/千克	A/	L	34	
8536.3000	-其他电路保护装置〔999〕	0		50	13/	13	个/千克	A/	L	25	
	-继电器:										
	--用于电压不超过 60 伏的线路:										
8536.4110	---用于电压不超过 36 伏的线路										
8536.4110 10	电压≤36 伏的继电器,含汞〔999〕	10		50	13/	13	个/千克	89/		35	
8536.4110 90	其他电压≤36 伏的继电器〔999〕	10		50	13/	13	个/千克	/		35	
8536.4190	---其他										
8536.4190 10	36 伏<电压≤60 伏的继电器,含汞	10		50	13/	13	个/千克	89/		35	
8536.4190 90	其他 36 伏<电压≤60 伏的继电器	10		50	13/	13	个/千克	/	L	35	
8536.4900	--其他										
8536.4900 10	电压大于 60 伏的继电器,含汞(用于电压不超过 1000 伏的线路)〔999〕	10		50	13/	13	个/千克	89/		35	

协定税率 %								RCEP		特惠税率 %			
东/冰/格	巴基斯坦	韩国	瑞士上/下	哥/秘/柬	澳/毛	新西/坡/智	中国港/澳/台	东盟及马来/澳/韩	日/新	亚太2国	老/柬/缅	98/97/95	Article Description
0/0/0	0	0	0/0	0/0/0	0/0	0//0	0/0/	0/0/0	0/0			0/0/0	-Other variable resistors, including rheostats and potentiometers
0/0/0	0	0	0/0	0/0/0	0/0	0//0	0/0/	0/0/0	0/0			0/0/0	-Parts
													Printed circuits:
0/0/0	0	0	0/0	0/0/0	0/0	0//0	0/0/	0/0/0	0/0			0/0/0	---Of more than 4 layers
0/0/0	0	0	0/0	0/0/0	0/0	0//0	0/0/	0/0/0	0/0			0/0/0	---Other
													Electrical apparatus for switching or protecting electrical circuits, or for making connections to or in electrical circuits (for example, switches, fuses, lightning arresters, voltage limiters, surge suppressors, plugs and other conneltors, junction boxes), for a voltage exceeding 1000 volts:
0/0/0	7.8	2.8	1.4/1.4	0/0/0	0/0	0/0/0	0/0/	0/0/12.6	12.7/0			0/0/0	-Fuses
													-Automatic circuit breakers:
0/0/0	7.8	2.8	0/0	0/0/0	0/0	0/0/0	0/0/	12.6/12.6/12.6	12.7/12.6			0/0/0	--For a voltage of less than 72.5 kV
													--Other:
0/0/0	3.5	2.8	0/0	0/0/0	0/0	0//0	0/0/	0/0/9	9.1/0			0/0/0	---For 72.5kV≤Voltage≤220kV
0/0/0	3.5	2.8	0/0	0/0/0	0/0	0//0	0/0/	0/0/9	9.1/0			0/0/0	---For 220kV≤Voltage≤750kV
0/0/0	2	2	0/0	0/0/0	0/0	0//0	0/0/	9.5/9.5/9.5	/9.5			0/0/0	---For Voltage>750kV
													-Isolating switches and make-and-break switches:
													---For 72.5kV≤Voltage≤220kV
0/0/0	2	2	2.5/2.5	0/0/0	0/0	0//0	0/0/	0/0/9	9.1/0		//	0/0/0	Isolating swithches and make－and－break switches for 72.5kV≤Voltages≤220 kV ,containing mercury
0/0/0	2	2	2.5/2.5	0/0/0	0/0	0//0	0/0/	0/0/9	9.1/0		//	0/0/0	Other Isolating swithches and make－and－break switches for 72.5kV≤Voltages≤220 kV ,containing mercury
													---For 220kV≤Voltage≤750kV
0/0/0	2	2	2.5/2.5	0/0/0	0/0	0//0	0/0/	0/0/9	9.1/0		//	0/0/0	Isolating swithches and make－and－break switches for 220kV<Voltages≤750 kV ,containing mercury
0/0/0	2	2	2.5/2.5	0/0/0	0/0	0//0	0/0/	0/0/9	9.1/0		//	0/0/0	Other Isolating swithches and make－and－break switches for 220kV<Voltages≤750 kV
													---Other
0/0/0	2	2	2.5/2.5	0/0/0	0/0	0//0	0/0/	0/0/9	9.1/0		//	0/0/0	Other Isolating swithches and make－and－break switches (for lines voltages over 1000V),containing mercury
0/0/0	2	2	2.5/2.5	0/0/0	0/0	0//0	0/0/	0/0/9	9.1/0		//	0/0/0	Other Isolating swithches and make－and－break switches (for lines voltages over 1000V)
0/0/0	14.4	3.6	1.8/1.8	0/0/0	0/0	0/0/0	0/0/	0/0/16.2	16.4/0			0/0/0	-Lightning arresters, voltage limiters and surge suppressors
													-Other
0/0/0	3.5	6	1/1	0/0/0	0/0	0/0/0	0/0/	9.5/9.5/	9.5/9.5			0/0/0	Triggered spark gap(time for delay of anode≤15ms, rating current of anode's peak value≥500A)
0/0/0	3.5	6	1/1	0/0/0	0/0	0/0/0	0/0/	9.5/9.5/	9.5/9.5			0/0/0	Module or groupware that can be speedily switched on or off (peak voltage value of anode≥2kV, current≥500A, time for switching on 1 ms)
0/0/0	3.5	6	1/1	0/0/0	0/0	0/0/0	0/0/	9.5/9.5/	9.5/9.5		//	0/0/0	Pantograph
0/0/0	3.5	6	1/1	0/0/0	0/0	0/0/0	0/0/	9.5/9.5/	9.5/9.5			0/0/0	High voltage cable joints for high－speed EMUs of 25 km / h and above
0/0/0	3.5	6	1/1	0/0/0	0/0	0/0/0	0/0/	9.5/9.5/	9.5/9.5			0/0/0	Other electrical apparatuses for switching or protecting electrical circuits, or for making connections to or in electrical circuits, for a voltage exceeding 1000 V)
													Electrical apparatus for switching or protecting electrical circuits, or for making connections to or in electricalcircuits (for example, switches, relays, fuses, surge suppressors, plugs, sockets, lamp-holders, and other connecltors junction boxes), for a voltage not exceeding 1000 volts; connectors for optical fibres. optical fibre bundles or cables:
0/0/0	3.5		1/1	0/0/0	0/0	0/0/0	0/0/0	9.5/9.5/	/9.5			0/0/0	-Fuses
0/0/0	2	0	0.9/0.9	0/0/0	0/0	0//0	0/0/	0/0/0	8.2/0			0/0/0	-Automatic circuit breakers
0/0/0	2	4.2	0/0	0/0/0	0/0	0//0	0/0/	0/0/8.1	8.2/0			0/0/0	-Other apparatus for protecting electrical circuits
													Relays:
													--For a voltage not exceeding 60 V:
													---For a voltage not exceeding 36V
0/0/0	3.5	4.6	0/0	0/0/0	0/0	0/0/0	0/0/	9.3/9.5/9.3	9.4/9.5		//	0/0/0	Relays with Voltages≤36 V, containing mercury
0/0/0	3.5	4.6	0/0	0/0/0	0/0	0/0/0	0/0/	9.3/9.5/9.3	9.4/9.5		//	0/0/0	Other relays with Voltages≤36 V
													---Other
0/0/0	2	6	0/0	0/0/0	0/0	0/0/0	0/0/	5/5/	/5		//	0/0/0	Relays with 36<Voltages≤60 V, containing mercury
0/0/0	2	6	0/0	0/0/0	0/0	0/0/0	0/0/	5/5/	/5		//	0/0/0	Other relays with 36<Voltages≤60 V
													--Other
0/0/0	3.5	4.6	0/0	0/0/0	0/0	0/0/0	0/0/	9.3/9.5/9.3	9.4/9.5		//	0/0/0	Relays over 60 V (for lines Voltages≤1000 V), containing mercury

税则号列	货品名称〔CIQ 扩展编码及品名—T2 表示见附表 2〕	最惠(%)	暂定税率	普通	增值/消费	出口退税	计量单位	监管条件/特殊证件	检验检疫	对美关税	亚太上/下
8536.4900 90	其他电压大于 60 伏的继电器(用于电压不超过 1000 伏的线路)〔999〕	10		50	13/	13	个/千克	/	L	35	
8536.5000	-其他开关										
8536.5000 10	电压≤1000 伏的其他开关,含汞〔999〕	0		50	13/	13	个/千克	89/		25	
8536.5000 90	其他电压≤1000 伏的其他开关〔999〕	0		50	13/	13	个/千克	/	L	25	
	-灯座、插头及插座:										
8536.6100	--灯座〔999〕	10		50	13/	13	个/千克	/		30	
8536.6900	--其他〔101 插头,102 插座,103 转换器〕	0		50	13/	13	个/千克	/	L	25	
8536.7000	-光导纤维、光导纤维束或光缆用连接器〔101 其它低压电器及其零件,102 路由器,103 光缆,104 光通信数字同步设备〕	8		30	13/	13	千克	/		23	
	-其他装置:										
	---接插件:										
8536.9011	----工作电压不超过 36 伏的〔999〕	0		50	13/	13	千克	/		25	
8536.9019	----其他〔999〕	0		50	13/	13	千克	A/	L	25	
8536.9090	---其他〔999〕	0		50	13/	13	千克	A/	L	20	
85.37	**用于电气控制或电力分配的盘、板、台、柜及其他基座,装有两个或多个税目 85.35 或 85.36 所列的装置,包括装有第九十章所列的仪器或装置,以及数控装置,但税目 85.17 的交换机除外:**										
	-用于电压不超过 1000 伏的线路:										
	---数控装置:										
8537.1011	----可编程序控制器										
8537.1011 01	机床用可编程序控制器(PLC)〔101 低压电器及其零件,102 集成电路,103 其它电子元器件〕	5	3	14	13/	13	个/千克	/			2.5/2.5
8537.1011 10	调节和编程控制器(8479899960 绕线机用)〔101 集成电路,102 其它电子元器件〕	5		14	13/	13	个/千克	3/			2.5/2.5
8537.1011 90	其他可编程控制器(用于电压不超过 1000 伏的线路)〔999〕	5		14	13/	13	个/千克	/			2.5/2.5
8537.1019	----其他										
8537.1019 01	机床用其他数控单元(包括单独进口的 CNC 操作单元)〔999〕	5	3	14	13/	13	个/千克	/		28	2.5/2.5
8537.1019 90	其他非机床用数控装置(用于电压不超过 1000 伏的线路)〔999〕	5		14	13/	13	个/千克	/		30	2.5/2.5
8537.1090	---其他										
8537.1090 01	电梯用控制柜及控制柜专用印刷电路板(电压不超过 1000 伏的线路)〔999〕	8	4	50	13/	13	个/千克	/		24	4/4
8537.1090 21	控制器[用于机器人或末端操纵装置(详见核两用清单)]〔999〕	8		50	13/	13	个/千克	3/		28	4/4
8537.1090 22	数字控制器(专用于编号 8479899959 电动式振动试验系统)〔999〕	8		50	13/	13	个/千克	3/			4/4
8537.1090 30	飞机用控制模块(电压不超过 1000 伏的线路)〔999〕	8	1	50	13/	13	个/千克	/		21	4/4
8537.1090 90	其他电力控制或分配的装置(电压不超过 1000 伏的线路)〔999〕	8		50	13/	13	个/千克	A/	L	28	4/4
	-用于电压超过 1000 伏的线路:										
8537.2010	---全封闭组合式高压开关装置,用于电压在 500 千伏及以上的线路〔101 高压开关装置,102 其它高压电器及其零件〕	8		30	13/	13	台/千克	/		33	4/4
8537.2090	---其他〔999〕	8		50	13/	13	千克	/		28	4/4
85.38	**专用于或主要用于税目 85.35、85.36 或 85.37 所列装置的零件:**										
	-税目 85.37 所列货品用的盘、板、台、柜及其他基座,但未装有关装置:										
8538.1010	---税号 8537.2010 所列货品用〔999〕	0		50	13/	13	千克	/		25	0/0
8538.1090	---其他〔999〕	0		50	13/	13	千克	/		20	0/0
8538.9000	-其他〔101 高压电器及其零件,102 低压电器及其零件〕	7		50	13/	13	千克	/	L	32	
85.39	**白炽灯泡、放电灯管,包括封闭式聚光灯及紫外线灯管或红外线灯泡;弧光灯;发光二极管(LED)光源:**										
8539.1000	-封闭式聚光灯〔999〕	8		45	13/	13	只/千克	/		13	
	-其他白炽灯泡,但不包括紫外线灯管或红外线灯泡:										
	--卤钨灯:										
8539.2110	---科研、医疗专用〔999〕	8		20	13/	13	只/千克	/		33	
8539.2120	---火车、航空器及船舶用〔999〕	8		20	13/	13	只/千克	/			

协定税率 %								RCEP		特惠税率 %			Article Description
东/冰/格	巴基斯坦	韩国	瑞士上/下	哥/秘/柬	澳/毛	新西/坡/智	中国港/澳/台	东盟及马来/澳/韩	日/新	亚太2国	老/柬/缅	98/97/95	
0/0/0	3.5	4.6	0/0	0/0/0	0/0	0/0/0	0/0/	9.3/9.5/9.3	9.4/9.5		//	0/0/0	Other relays over 60 V (for lines Voltages≤1000 V)
													-Other switches
0/0/0	0	0	0/0	0/0/0	0/0	0//0	0/0/	0/0/0	0/0		//	0/0/0	Other switches with voltages ≤ 1000 V, containing mercury
0/0/0	0	0	0/0	0/0/0	0/0	0//0	0/0/	0/0/0	0/0		//	0/0/0	Other switches with voltages ≤ 1000 V
													-Lamp-holders, plugs and sockets:
0/0/0	2	4.6	0/0	0/0/0	0/0	0/0/0	0/0/	9.3/9.5/9.3	9.4/9.5			0/0/0	--Lamp-holders
0/0/0	0	0	0/0	0/0/0	0/0	0//0	0/0/	0/0/0	0/0			0/0/0	--Other
0/0/0	2		0.8/0.8	0/0/0	0/0	0//0	0/0/	5/5/	/5			0/0/0	-Connectors for optical fibres, optical fibre bundles or cables
													-Other apparatus:
													---Connector:
0/0/0	0	0	0/0	0/0/0	0/0	0//0	0/0/	0/0/0	0/0			0/0/0	----For a voltage not exceeding 36 V
0/0/0	0	0	0/0	0/0/0	0/0	0//0	0/0/	0/0/0	0/0			0/0/0	----Other
0/0/0	0	0	0/0	0/0/0	0/0	0//0	0/0/	0/0/0	0/0			0/0/0	---Other
													Boards, panels, consoles, desks, cabinets and other bases, equipped with two or more apparatus of headingNo. 85.35 or 85.36, for electric control or the distribution of electricity, including those incorporating instruments or apparatus of Chapter 90, and numerical control apparatus, other than switching apparatus of headingNo. 85.17:
													-For a voltage not exceeding 1000 V:
													---Numerical control panels:
													----Programmable logic controuers(PLC)
0/0/0	0	2.5	0.5/0.5	0/0/0	0/0	0//0	0/0/0	4.8/4.8/	/4.8			0/0/0	Programmable logic controuers for machine tools
0/0/0	0	2.5	0.5/0.5	0/0/0	0/0	0//0	0/0/0	4.8/4.8/	/4.8			0/0/0	Adiusting and programming controllers for winding machine of subbeading No. 8479.899060
0/0/0	0	2.5	0.5/0.5	0/0/0	0/0	0//0	0/0/0	4.8/4.8/	/4.8			0/0/0	Other programming logic controllers (for the circuit with its voltage≤1000V)
													----Other
0/0/0	0	2.5	2.1/2.1	0/0/0	0/0	0//0	0/0/0	4.9/4.9/	/4.9			0/0/0	Other digital control units for machine tool (CNC operating unit with separate import)
0/0/0	0	2.5	2.1/2.1	0/0/0	0/0	0//0	0/0/0	4.9/4.9/	/4.9			0/0/0	Other digital controller not for machine tool(for a voltage≤1000V)
													---Other
0/0/0	0	3.9	3.5/3.5	0/0/0	0/0	0//0	0/0/	7.8/8/7.8	7.9/8			0/0/0	Control cabinet (electric cabinet) for elevators and circuit board for control cabinet(for the circuit with its voltage≤1000V)
0/0/0	0	3.9	3.5/3.5	0/0/0	0/0	0//0	0/0/	7.8/8/7.8	7.9/8			0/0/0	Controllers(use for roloots or end - operation devices, see the dual - purpose nuclear goods list for details)
0/0/0	0	3.9	3.5/3.5	0/0/0	0/0	0//0	0/0/	7.8/8/7.8	7.9/8			0/0/0	Digital controllers (only use of electric vibration test system subweading No. 8479.899959)
0/0/0	0	3.9	3.5/3.5	0/0/0	0/0	0//0	0/0/	7.8/8/7.8	7.9/8		//	0/0/0	Control module for aircraft (lines with voltage not exceeding 1000 V)
0/0/0	0	3.9	3.5/3.5	0/0/0	0/0	0//0	0/0/	7.8/8/7.8	7.9/8			0/0/0	Other power contorl or distribution devices (for the circuit with its voltage≤1000V)
													-For a voltage exceeding 1000 V:
0/0/0	0	3.9	2.1/2.1	0/0/0	0/0	0//0	0/0/	7.6/7.6/7.6	7.9/7.6			0/0/0	---Gas insulated switchgear, for a voltage of 500 kV or more
0/0/0	0	3.9	0/0	0/0/0	0/0	0//0	0/0/	7.8/8/7.8	7.9/8			0/0/0	---Other
													Parts suitable for use solely or principally with the apparatus of headingNo. 85.35, 85.36 or 85.37:
													-Boards, panels, consoles, desks, cabinets and other bases for the goods of headingNo. 85.37, not equipped with their apparatus:
0/0/0	0	1.6	0/0	0/0/0	0/0	0//0	0/0/	0/0/7.6	7.6/0			0/0/0	---For the goods of headingNo. 8537.2010
0/0/0	0	3.5	0/0	0/0/0	0/0	0//0	0/0/	6.3/6.3/6.7	6.4/6.3			0/0/0	---Other
0/0/0	4	0	2.8/2.8	0/0/0	0/4.2	0//0	0/0/0	0/0/0	6.4/0			0/0/0	-Other
													Electric filament or discharge lamps, including sealed beam lamp units and ultra-violet or infra-red lamps; arc-lamps; Light—emitting diode(LED) light source:
0/0/0	2	2	0/0	0/0/0	0/0	0//0	0/0/	0/0/9	9.1/0			0/0/0	-Sealed beam lamp units
													-Other filament lamps, excluding ultra-violet or infra-red lamps:
													--Tungsten halogen:
0/0/0	4	0	0/0	0/0/0	0/0	0//0	0/0/	0/0/0	7.3/0			0/0/0	---For scientific or medical uses only
0/0/0	2	1.6	0/0	0/0/0	0/0	0//0	0/0/	0/0/7.2	7.3/0			0/0/0	---For locomotives and rolling-stock, aircraft or ships

税则号列	货品名称〔CIQ 扩展编码及品名－T2 表示见附表 2〕	最惠(%)	暂定税率	普通	增值/消费	出口退税	计量单位	监管条件/特殊证件	检验检疫	对美关税	亚太上/下
8539.2130	---机动车辆用〔999〕	8		45	13/	13	只/千克	/		13	
8539.2190	---其他〔999〕	6		70	13/	13	只/千克	/			
	--其他灯，功率不超过 200 瓦，但额定电压超过 100 伏：										
8539.2210	---科研、医疗专用〔999〕	5		20	13/	13	只/千克	/		10	
8539.2290	---其他〔999〕	5		70	13/	13	只/千克	/		30	
	--其他：										
8539.2910	---科研、医疗专用〔999〕	5		20	13/	13	只/千克	/		25	4/4
8539.2920	---火车、航空器及船舶用〔999〕	5		20	13/	13	只/千克	/		10	
8539.2930	---机动车辆用〔999〕	5		45	13/	13	只/千克	/		10	
	---其他：										
8539.2991	----12 伏及以下的〔999〕	6		70	13/	13	只/千克	/		31	
8539.2999	----其他〔999〕	6		70	13/	13	只/千克	/		16	
	-放电灯管，但紫外线灯管除外：										
	--热阴极荧光灯：										
8539.3110	---科研、医疗专用〔999〕	8		20	13/	13	只/千克	/		18	6.4/6.4
8539.3120	---火车、航空器及船舶用〔999〕	8		20	13/	13	只/千克	/		13	
	---其他：										
8539.3191	----紧凑型										
8539.3191 10	紧凑型热阴极荧光灯（不超过 30 瓦、单支含汞量超过 5 毫克的）〔999〕	8		70	13/	13	只/千克	89/		28	
8539.3191 90	其他紧凑型热阴极荧光灯〔999〕	8		70	13/	13	只/千克	/		28	
8539.3199	----其他										
8539.3199 10	直管型热阴极荧光灯（低于 60 瓦、单支含汞量超过 5 毫克的直管型荧光灯（使用三基色荧光粉））〔999〕	8		70	13/	13	只/千克	89/		28	
8539.3199 20	直管型热阴极荧光灯（低于 40 瓦（含 40 瓦）、单支含汞量超过 10 毫克的直管型荧光灯（使用卤磷酸盐荧光粉））〔999〕	8		70	13/	13	只/千克	89/		28	
8539.3199 90	其他用途用其他热阴极荧光灯〔999〕	8		70	13/	13	只/千克	/		28	
	--汞或钠蒸汽灯；金属卤化物灯：										
8539.3230	---钠蒸气灯〔999〕	8		20	13/	13	只/千克	/		33	
8539.3240	---汞蒸气灯										
8539.3240 01	彩色投影机用的照明光源（汞蒸汽灯）〔999〕	8	3	20	13/	13	只/千克	/		28	
8539.3240 10	用于普通照明用途的高压汞灯〔999〕	8		20	13/	13	只/千克	89/		33	
8539.3240 90	其他汞蒸汽灯〔999〕	8		20	13/	13	只/千克	/		33	
8539.3290	---其他〔999〕	8		70	13/	13	只/千克	/		33	
	--其他：										
8539.3910	---科研、医疗专用〔999〕	8		20	13/	13	只/千克	/		18	6.4/6.4
8539.3920	---火车、航空器及船舶用〔999〕	8		20	13/	13	只/千克	/		13	
8539.3990	---其他										
8539.3990 11	用于电子显示的冷阴极管荧光灯（长度≤500 毫米的，单支含汞量超过 3.5 毫克；500 毫米＜长度≤1500 毫米的，单支含汞量超过 5 毫克；长度＞1500 毫米的，单支含汞量超过 13 毫克）〔999〕	0		70	13/	13	只/千克	89/		25	
8539.3990 19	其他用于平板显示器背光源的冷阴极管荧光灯〔999〕	0		70	13/	13	只/千克	/		25	
8539.3990 20	其他紧凑型冷阴极管荧光灯（不超过 30 瓦、单支含汞量超过 5 毫克的）〔999〕	0		70	13/	13	只/千克	89/		25	
8539.3990 30	其他直管型荧光灯（低于 60 瓦、单支含汞量超过 5 毫克的直管型荧光灯（使用三基色荧光粉））〔999〕	0		70	13/	13	只/千克	89/		25	
8539.3990 40	其他直管型荧光灯（低于 40 瓦（含 40 瓦）、单支含汞量超过 10 毫克的直管型荧光灯（使用卤磷酸盐荧光粉））〔999〕	0		70	13/	13	只/千克	89/		25	
8539.3990 50	用于电子显示的外置电极荧光灯（长度≤500 毫米的，单支含汞量超过 3.5 毫克；500 毫米＜长度≤1500 毫米的，单支含汞量超过 5 毫克；长度＞1500 毫米的，单支含汞量超过 13 毫克）〔999〕	0		70	13/	13	只/千克	89/		25	
8539.3990 90	其他用途的其他放电灯管〔999〕	8		70	13/	13	只/千克	/		33	
	-紫外线灯管或红外线灯泡；弧光灯：										
8539.4100	--弧光灯〔999〕	8		20	13/	13	只/千克	/		28	
8539.4900	--其他〔999〕	8		20	13/	13	只/千克	/			
	-发光二极管（LED）光源：										

协定税率 %								RCEP		特惠税率 %			Article Description
东/冰/格	巴基斯坦	韩国	瑞士上/下	哥/秘/柬	澳/毛	新西/坡/智	中国港/澳/台	东盟及马来/澳/韩	日/新	亚太2国	老/柬/缅	98/97/95	
0/0/0	3.5	6	0/0	0/0/0	0/0	0//0	0/0/	9.5/9.5/	/9.5			0/0/0	---For motor vehicles
0/0/0	8.4	2.1	1.1/1.1	0/0/0	0/0	0/0/0	0/0/	0/0/9.5	9.5/0			0/0/0	---Other
													--Other, of a power not exceeding 200 W and for a voltage exceeding 100 V:
0/0/0	3.5		1.1/1.1	0/0/0	0/0	0/0/0	0/0/	5/5/	/5			0/0/0	---For scientific or medical uses only
0/0/0	0	0	0/0	0/0/0	0/0	0//0	0/0/	0/0/0	0/0			0/0/0	---Other
													--Other:
0/0/0	0	0	0/0	0/0/0	0/0	0//0	0/0/	0/0/0	0/0			0/0/0	---For scientific or medical uses only
0/0/0	3.5	2.1	1.1/1.1	0/0/0	0/0	0/0/0	0/0/	0/0/9.5	9.5/0			0/0/0	---For locomotives and rolling-stock, aircraft or ships
0/0/0	0	2.3	0/0	0/0/0	0/0	0//0	0/0/	4.5/4.5/4.5	4.7/4.5			0/0/0	---For motor vehicles
													---Other:
0/0/0	4.2	2.4	1.2/1.2	0/0/0	0/0	0/0/0	0/0/	0/0/10.8	10.9/0			0/0/0	----Of a voltage 12 V or less
0/0/0	4.2	2.4	1.2/1.2	0/0/0	0/0	0/0/0	0/0/	0/0/10.8	10.9/0			0/0/0	----Other
													-Discharge lamps, other than ultra-violet lamps:
													--Fluorescent, hot cathode:
0/0/0	2		0/0	0/0/0	0/0	0//0	0/0/	5/5/	/5			0/0/0	---For scientific or medical uses only
0/0/0	2		0/0	0/0/0	0/0	0//0	0/0/	5/5/	/5			0/0/0	---For locomotives and rolling-stock, aircraft or ships
													---Other:
													----Compact type
0/0/0	4	0	0/0	0/0/0	0/0	0//0	0/0/	0/0/0	7.3/0		//	0/0/0	Compact hot cathode fluorescent lamp (not more than 30 watts, single mercury content more than 5 mg)
0/0/0	4	0	0/0	0/0/0	0/0	0//0	0/0/	0/0/0	7.3/0		//	0/0/0	Other compact hot cathode fluorescent lamps
													----Other
0/0/0	2	0	0/0	0/0/0	0/0	0//0	0/0/	0/0/0	7.3/0		//	0/0/0	Straight tube hot cathode fluorescent lamp (straight tube type fluorescent lamp with mercury content of more than 5mg and less than 60W, using trichromatic phosphor)
0/0/0	2	0	0/0	0/0/0	0/0	0//0	0/0/	0/0/0	7.3/0		//	0/0/0	Straight tube hot cathode fluorescent lamp (less than 40 watts (including 40 watts), single straight tube fluorescent lamp with mercury content more than 10 mg (using halo-phosphate phosphor))
0/0/0	2	0	0/0	0/0/0	0/0	0//0	0/0/	0/0/0	7.3/0		//	0/0/0	Other hot cathode fluorescent lamps for other uses
													--Mercury or sodium vapour lamps; metal halide lamps:
0/0/0	2	1.6	0/0	0/0/0	0/0	0//0	0/0/	0/0/7.2	7.3/0			0/0/0	---Sodium vapour lamps
													---Mercury vapour lamps
0/0/0	2	1.6	0/0	0/0/0	0/0	0//0	0/0/	7.2/7.2/7.2	7.3/7.2			0/0/0	Mercury vapor light for color LCD projectors
0/0/0	2	1.6	0/0	0/0/0	0/0	0//0	0/0/	7.2/7.2/7.2	7.3/7.2		//	0/0/0	High pressure mercury lamps for general lighting
0/0/0	2	1.6	0/0	0/0/0	0/0	0//0	0/0/	7.2/7.2/7.2	7.3/7.2			0/0/0	Other mercury vapor light
0/0/0	4	0	0/0	0/0/0	0/0	0//0	0/0/	0/0/0	7.3/0			0/0/0	---Other
													--Other:
0/0/0	2		0/0	0/0/0	0/0	0//0	0/0/	5/5/	/5			0/0/0	---For scientific or medical uses only
0/0/0	2		0/0	0/0/0	0/0	0//0	0/0/	5/5/	/5			0/0/0	---For locomotives and rolling-stock, aircraft or ships
													---Other
0/0/0	2	3.7	0/0	0/0/0	0/0	0//0	0/0/0	7.2/7.2/7.2	7.5/7.2		//	0/0/0	Cold cathode tube fluorescent lamp for electronic display (single tube with length ≤ 500mm contains more than 3.5mg of mercury; single tube with length < 1500mm contains more than 5mg of mercury; single tube with length > 1500mm contains more than 13mg of mercury)
0/0/0	2	3.7	0/0	0/0/0	0/0	0//0	0/0/0	7.2/7.2/7.2	7.5/7.2		//	0/0/0	Other CCT fluorescent lamps for flat panel display backlight
0/0/0	2	3.7	0/0	0/0/0	0/0	0//0	0/0/0	7.2/7.2/7.2	7.5/7.2		//	0/0/0	Other compact cold cathode tube fluorescent lamps (not exceeding 30 watts, single tube containing more than 5 mg of mercury)
0/0/0	2	3.7	0/0	0/0/0	0/0	0//0	0/0/0	7.2/7.2/7.2	7.5/7.2		//	0/0/0	Other straight tube fluorescent lamps (straight tube fluorescent lamps with mercury content less than 60 watts and single tube more than 5 mg (using trichromatic phosphor))
0/0/0	2	3.7	0/0	0/0/0	0/0	0//0	0/0/0	7.2/7.2/7.2	7.5/7.2		//	0/0/0	Other straight tube fluorescent lamps (less than 40 watts (including 40 watts), single straight tube fluorescent lamp with mercury content more than 10 mg (using halophosphate phosphor))
0/0/0	2	3.7	0/0	0/0/0	0/0	0//0	0/0/0	7.2/7.2/7.2	7.5/7.2		//	0/0/0	External electrode fluorescent lamp for electronic display (with mercury content of a single tube more than 3.5 mg for the length ≤ 500 mm; mercury content of a single tube more than 5 mg for the length < 500 mm; mercury content of a single tube more than 13 mg for the length > 1500 mm)
0/0/0	2	3.7	0/0	0/0/0	0/0	0//0	0/0/0	7.2/7.2/7.2	7.5/7.2			0/0/0	Other discharge lamps for other purposes
													-Ultraviolet or infrared lamps; arc-lamps:
0/0/0	2		0/0	0/0/0	0/0	0//0	0/0/	5/5/	/5			0/0/0	--Arc-lamps
0/0/0	2		0/0	0/0/0	0/0	0//0	0/0/	5/5/	/5			0/0/0	--Other
													-Light—emitting diode (LED) light source

税则号列	货品名称〔CIQ 扩展编码及品名－T2 表示见附表 2〕	最惠(%)	暂定税率	普通	增值/消费	出口退税	计量单位	监管条件/特殊证件	检验检疫	对美关税	亚太上/下
8539.5100	--发光二极管(LED)模块〔999〕	6		80	13/	13	个/千克	/		16	
	--发光二极管(LED)灯泡(管)：										
8539.5210	---发光二极管(LED)灯泡〔999〕	8		80	13/	13	只/千克	/		33	
8539.5220	---发光二极管(LED)灯管〔999〕	8		80	13/	13	只/千克	/		33	
	-零件：										
8539.9010	---发光二极管(LED)模块的〔999〕	8		70	13/	13	千克	/		28	
8539.9090	---其他〔999〕	8		20	13/	13	千克	/		33	
85.40	**热电子管、冷阴极管或光阴极管(例如,真空管或充气管、汞弧整流管、阴极射线管、电视摄像管)：**										
	-阴极射线电视显像管,包括视频监视器用阴极射线管：										
8540.1100	--彩色的〔999〕	8		40	13/	13	只/千克	6/			
8540.1200	--单色的〔999〕	8		40	13/	13	只/千克	6/		13	
	-电视摄像管;变像管及图像增强管;其他光阴极管：										
8540.2010	---电视摄像管〔999〕	8		35	13/	13	只/千克	/			
8540.2090	---其他										
8540.2090　10	电子条纹相机的条纹显像管〔999〕	8		17	13/	13	只/千克	/		33	
8540.2090　90	其他电视摄像管;其他变像管及图像增强管;其他光阴极管〔999〕	8		17	13/	13	只/千克	/		33	
	-单色的数据/图形显示管;彩色的数据/图形显示管,屏幕荧光点间距小于 0.4 毫米：										
8540.4010	---彩色的数据/图形显示管,屏幕荧光点间距小于 0.4 毫米〔999〕	8		17	13/	13	只/千克	6/			
8540.4020	---单色的数据/图形显示管〔999〕	8		17	13/	13	只/千克	6/		18	
	-其他阴极射线管：										
8540.6010	---雷达显示管〔999〕	6		14	13/	13	只/千克	/			3.9/3.9
8540.6090	---其他〔999〕	8		17	13/	13	只/千克	6/		28	
	-微波管(例如,磁控管、速调管、行波管、返波管),但不包括栅控管：										
8540.7100	--磁控管〔999〕	8		17	13/	13	只/千克	/		33	
	--其他：										
8540.7910	---速调管〔999〕	8		17	13/	13	只/千克	/			
8540.7990	---其他〔999〕	8		17	13/	13	只/千克	/		18	
	-其他管：										
8540.8100	--接收管或放大管〔999〕	8		17	13/	13	只/千克	/		28	
8540.8900	--其他										
8540.8900　10	光电倍增管(光电阴极面积大于 20 平方厘米,并且阳极脉冲上升时间小于 1 纳秒)〔999〕	8		17	13/	13	只/千克	3/		33	
8540.8900　90	其他电子管(包括光阴极管或汞弧整流管〔999〕	8		17	13/	13	只/千克	/		33	
	-零件：										
	--阴极射线管用：										
8540.9110	---电视显像管用〔999〕	6		40	13/	13	千克	/			
8540.9120	---雷达显示管用〔999〕	5		14	13/	13	千克	/			3.3/3.3
8540.9190	---其他〔999〕	8		17	13/	13	千克	/		13	
	--其他：										
8540.9910	---电视摄像管用〔999〕	8		35	13/	13	千克	/			5.2/5.2
8540.9990	---其他〔999〕	8		17	13/	13	千克	/		33	
85.41	**半导体器件(例如,二极管、晶体管,半导体基换能器);光敏半导体器件,包括不论是否装在组件内或组装成块的光电池;发光二极管(LED),不论是否与其他发光二极管(LED)组装;已装配的压电晶体：**										
8541.1000	-二极管,但光敏二极管或发光二极管除外〔999〕	0		30	13/	13	个/千克	/		25	
	-晶体管,但光敏晶体管除外：										
8541.2100	--耗散功率小于 1 瓦的〔999〕	0		30	13/	13	个/千克	/		25	
8541.2900	--其他〔999〕	0		30	13/	13	个/千克	/		25	
8541.3000	-半导体开关元件、两端交流开关元件及三端双向可控硅开关元件,但光敏器件除外〔999〕	0		30	13/	13	个/千克	/		25	

协定税率 %								RCEP		特惠税率 %			Article Description
东/冰/格	巴基斯坦	韩国	瑞士 上/下	哥/秘/柬	澳/毛	新西/坡/智	中国港/澳/台	东盟及马来/澳/韩	日/新	亚太2国	老/柬/缅	98/97/95	
0/0/0	0	0	0/0	0/0/0	0/0	0/0/0	0/0/	9/9/9	9.1/9			0/0/0	--Light emitting diode (LED) module
													--Light emitting diode (LED) bulb (tube)
0/0/0	0	0	0/0	0/0/0	0/0	0/0/0	0/0/	9/9/9	9.1/9			0/0/0	---Light emitting diode (LED) bulb
0/0/0	0	0	0/0	0/0/0	0/0	0/0/0	0/0/	9/9/9	9.1/9			0/0/0	---Light emitting diode (LED) tube
													-Parts:
0/0/0		9.3	2/2	0/0/0	0/0	0/0/0	0/0/	18.7/19/18.7	18.8/19			0/0/0	--Light emitting diode (LED) module
0/0/0	4		0/0	0/0/0	0/0	0//0	0/0/0	5/5/	/5			0/0/0	---Other
													Thermionic, cold cathode or photo-cathode valves and tubes (for example, vacuum or vapour or gas filled valves and tubes, mercury arc rectifying valves and tubes, cathode-ray tubes, television camera tubes):
													-Cathode-ray television picture tubes, including video monitor cathode-ray tubes:
0/0/0	4.2	5.6	1.2/1.2	0/0/0	0/0	0/0/0	0/0/	11.2/11.4/11.2	11.3/11.4			0/0/0	--Colour
0/0/0	8.4	3	1.5/1.5	0/0/0	0/0	0/0/0	0/0/	0/0/13.5	13.6/0			0/0/0	--Monochrome
													-Television camera tubes; image converters and intensifiers; other photo-cathode tubes:
0/0/0	4.2	2.4	1.2/1.2	0/0/0	0/0	0/0/0	0/0/	10.8/10.8/10.8	11.3/10.8			0/0/0	---Television camera tubes
													---Other
0/0/0	2	0	0/0	0/0/0	0/0	0//0	0/0/	0/0/0	7.3/0			0/0/0	Stripe kinescope of electronic stripe camera (striation kinescope tube specially used for Serial Number 9006.5900 40)
0/0/0	2	0	0/0	0/0/0	0/0	0//0	0/0/	0/0/0	7.3/0			0/0/0	Other television camera tubes, other image converter tube and image intensifier tubes, other photo cathode tubes
													-Data/graphic display tubes, monochrome; data/graphic displaytubes, colour, with a phosphor dot screen pitch smaller than 0.4mm
0/0/0	2	0	0/0	0/0/0	0/0	0//0	0/0/	0/0/0	7.3/0			0/0/0	---Data/graphic displaytubes, colour, with a phosphor dot screen pitch smaller than 4mm
0/0/0	2	0	0/0	0/0/0	0/0	0//0	0/0/	0/0/0	7.3/0			0/0/0	---Data/graphic display tubes, monochrome
													-Other cathode-ray tubes:
0/0/0	0	0	0/0	0/0/0	0/0	0//0	0/0/	0/0/0	0/0			0/0/0	---Radar display tubes
0/0/0	2	0	0/0	0/0/0	0/0	0//0	0/0/	0/0/0	7.3/0			0/0/0	---Other
													-Microwave tubes (for example, magnetrons, klystrons, travelling wave tubes, carcinotrons), excluding grid-controlled tubes:
0/0/0	2	3.7	0/0	0/0/0	0/0	0//0	0/0/	7.5/7.6/7.5	7.5/7.6			0/0/0	--Magnetrons
													--Other:
0/0/0	2	0	0/0	0/0/0	0/0	0//0	0/0/	0/0/0	7.3/0			0/0/0	---Klystrons
0/0/0	2	0	0/0	0/0/0	0/0	0//0	0/0/	0/0/0	7.3/0			0/0/0	---Other
													-Other valves and tubes:
0/0/0	2		0/0	0/0/0	0/0	0//0	0/0/	5/5/	/5			0/0/0	--Receiver or amplifier valves and tubes
													--Other
0/0/0	2	0	0/0	0/0/0	0/0	0//0	0/0/0	7.2/7.2/7.2	7.3/7.2			0/0/0	Electron-multiplier phototube (Photoelectric cathode area greater than 20 square centimeters, and the anode pulse rise time less than 1ns)
0/0/0	2	0	0/0	0/0/0	0/0	0//0	0/0/0	7.2/7.2/7.2	7.3/7.2			0/0/0	Other electron tube(including photo-cathode valves and mercury arc rectifying valves and tubes)
													-Parts:
													--Of cathode-ray tubes:
0/0/0	0	0	0/0	0/0/0	0/0	0//0	0/0/	0/0/0	0/0			0/0/0	---Of television picture tubes
0/0/0	0	0	0/0	0/0/0	0/0	0//0	0/0/	0/0/0	0/0			0/0/0	---Of radar display tubes
0/0/0	2		0/0	0/0/0	0/0	0//0	0/0/	5/5/	/5			0/0/0	---Other
													--Other:
0/0/0	2	0	0/0	0/0/0	0/0	0//0	0/0/	0/0/0	7.3/0			0/0/0	---Of television camera tubes
0/0/0	2		0/0	0/0/0	0/0	0//0	0/0/	5/5/	/5			0/0/0	---Other
													Semiconductor devices (e.g., diodes, transistors, semiconductor based transducers); photosensitive semiconductor devices, including photocells, whether or not installed in components or assembled into blocks; light emitting diodes (LEDs), whether or not assembled with other light emitting diodes (LEDs); assembled piezoelectric crystals:
0/0/0	0	0	0/0	0/0/0	0/0	0//0	0/0/	0/0/0	0/0			0/0/0	-Diodes, other than photosensitive or light emitting diodes
													-Transistors, other than photosensitive transistors:
0/0/0	0	0	0/0	0/0/0	0/0	0//0	0/0/	0/0/0	0/0			0/0/0	--With a dissipation rate of less than 1 W
0/0/0	0	0	0/0	0/0/0	0/0	0//0	0/0/	0/0/0	0/0			0/0/0	--Other
0/0/0	0	0	0/0	0/0/0	0/0	0//0	0/0/	0/0/0	0/0			0/0/0	-Thyristors, diacs and triacs, other than photosensitive devices

税则号列	货品名称〔CIQ 扩展编码及品名—T2 表示见附表 2〕	最惠(%)	暂定税率	普通	增值/消费	出口退税	计量单位	监管条件/特殊证件	检验检疫	对美关税	亚太上/下
	-光敏半导体器件,包括不论是否装在组件内或组装成块的光电池;发光二极管:										
8541.4100	--发光二极管(LED)〔999〕	0		30	13/	13	个/千克	/		25	
8541.4200	--未装在组件内或组装成块的光电池〔999〕	0		30	13/	13	个/千克	/		25	
8541.4300	--已装在组件内或组装成块的光电池〔999〕	0		30	13/	13	个/千克	/		25	
8541.4900	--其他〔999〕	0		30	13/	13	个/千克	/		25	
	-其他半导体器件:										
	--半导体基换能器:										
	---传感器:										
8541.5111	----检测湿度、气压及其组合指标的〔999〕	11		30	13/	13	个/千克	/		31	
8541.5112	----用于检测温度、电量、理化指标的;利用光学检 测其他指标的										
8541.5112 10	用于检测温度的半导体基传感器((P))〔999〕	0		31	13/	13	个/千克	/			0/0
8541.5112 90	用于检测电量、理化指标的半导体基传感器;利用光学检测其他指标的半导体基传感器〔999〕	0		31	13/	13	个/千克	/		10	0/0
8541.5113	----液体或气体的流量、液位、压力或其他变化量的〔999〕	0		17	13/	13	个/千克	/		10	
8541.5119	----其他〔999〕	2/1		17	13/	13	个/千克	/			1.3/0.7
	---执行器:										
8541.5121	----电动机〔999〕	9		35	13/	13	个/千克	/		34	5.9/5.9
8541.5129	----其他〔999〕	0		30	13/	13	个/千克	/		20	
8541.5130	---振荡器〔999〕	8		40	13/	13	个/千克	/		33	
8541.5140	---谐振器〔999〕	8		40	13/	13	个/千克	/		33	
8541.5900	--其他(8541.5000)〔999〕	0		30	13/	13	个/千克	/		20	
8541.6000	-已装配的压电晶体〔999〕	0		30	13/	13	个/千克	/		25	
8541.9000	-零件〔999〕	0		30	13/	13	千克	/		20	
85.42	**集成电路:**										
	-集成电路:										
	--处理器及控制器,不论是否带有存储器、转换器、逻辑电路、放大器、时钟及时序电路或其他电路:										
	---多元件集成电路:										
8542.3111	----具有变流功能的半导体模块										
8542.3111 10	多元件集成电路中的自动数据处理设备机器及组件、电讯设备用的具有变流动能的半导体模块〔999〕	0		30	13/	13	个/千克	/			
8542.3111 90	多元件集成电路中的其他具有变流功能的半导体模块〔999〕	0		30	13/	13	个/千克	/			
8542.3119	----其他										
8542.3119 10	安全芯片(不论是否带有存储器、转换器、逻辑电路、放大器、时钟及时序电路或其他电路)	0		46	13/	13	个/千克	3/			0/0
8542.3119 90	其他用作处理器及控制器的多元件集成电路(不论是否带有存储器、转换器、逻辑电路、放大器、时钟及时序电路或其他电路)	0		46	13/	13	个/千克	/			0/0
8542.3190	---其他										
8542.3190 10	安全芯片(不论是否带有存储器、转换器、逻辑电路、放大器、时钟及时序电路或其他电路)	0		24	13/	13	个/千克	3/			
8542.3190 90	其他用作处理器及控制器的集成电路(不论是否带有存储器、转换器、逻辑电路、放大器、时钟及时序电路或其他电路)	0		24	13/	13	个/千克	/			
	--存储器:										
8542.3210	---多元件集成电路〔999〕	0		45	13/	13	个/千克	/			0/0
8542.3290	---其他〔999〕	0		24	13/	13	个/千克	/			
	--放大器:										
8542.3310	---多元件集成电路〔999〕	0		45	13/	13	个/千克	/			0/0
8542.3390	---其他〔999〕	0		24	13/	13	个/千克	/			
	--其他:										
8542.3910	---多元件集成电路〔999〕	0		45	13/	13	个/千克	/			0/0
8542.3990	---其他〔999〕	0		24	13/	13	个/千克	/			
8542.9000	-零件〔999〕	0		30	13/	13	千克	/			

协定税率 %								RCEP		特惠税率 %			Article Description
东/冰/格	巴基斯坦	韩国	瑞士 上/下	哥/秘/柬	澳/毛	新西/坡/智	中国港/澳/台	东盟及马来/澳/韩	日/新	亚太2国	老/柬/缅	98/97/95	
													-Photosensitive semiconductor devices, including photovoltaic cells whether or not assembled in modules or made up into panels; light emitting diodes:
0/0/0	0	0	0/0	0/0/0	0/0	0//0	0/0/	0/0/0	0/0			0/0/0	--Light emitting diode (LED)
0/0/0	0	0	0/0	0/0/0	0/0	0//0	0/0/	0/0/0	0/0			0/0/0	--Photocells not installed in components or assembled into blocks
0/0/0	0	0	0/0	0/0/0	0/0	0//0	0/0/	0/0/0	0/0			0/0/0	--A photocell that has been installed in a module or assembled into a block
0/0/0	0	0	0/0	0/0/0	0/0	0//0	0/0/	0/0/0	0/0			0/0/0	--Other(8541.4090)
													-Other semiconductor devices:
													--Semiconductor based transducer:
													---Sensor:
0/0/0	3.5	6.6	1.1/1.1	0/0/0	0/0	0/0/0	0/0/	10.5/10.5/	/10.5			0/0/0	----Detection of humidity, air pressure and their combined indicators
													----Used to detect temperature, electric quantity and physical and chemical indexes; Using optics to detect other indicators
0/0/0	1.6	2.3	0/0	0/0/0	0/0	0//0	0/0/	0/0/0	0/0			0/0/0	Semiconductor based sensor for detecting temperature ((P))
0/0/0	1.6	2.3	0/0	0/0/0	0/0	0//0	0/0/	0/0/0	0/0			0/0/0	A semiconductor based sensor for detecting electric quantity and physical and chemical indexes; Semiconductor based sensor for optical detection of other indexes
0/0/0	0	0	0/0	0/0/0	0/0	0//0	0/0/	0/0/0	0/0			0/0/0	----Offlow,liquidlevel,pressureorotherchangesofliquid orgas
0//0	0	1	2/1	0/0/0	0/0	0//0	0/0/0	0/0/4.5	4.7/0			0/0/0	----Other
													---brake actuator:
0/0/0	3.5	4.2	0.9/0.9	0/0/0	0/0	0/0/0	0/0/0	8.4/8.6/8.4	8.4/8.6			0/0/0	----Motor
0/0/0	0	0	0/0	0/0/0	0/0	0//0	0/0/	0/0/0	0/0			0/0/0	----Other
0/0/0	4.2	7.2	1.2/1.2	0/0/0	0/0	0/0/0	0/0/	11.4/11.4/11.4	11.4/11.4			0/0/0	---Oscillator
0/0/0	4.2	7.2	1.2/1.2	0/0/0	0/0	0/0/0	0/0/	11.4/11.4/11.4	11.4/11.4			0/0/0	---Resonator
0/0/0	0	0	0/0	0/0/0	0/0	0//0	0/0/	0/0/0	0/0			0/0/0	--Other(8541.5000)
0/0/0	0	0	0/0	0/0/0	0/0	0//0	0/0/	0/0/0	0/0			0/0/0	-Mounted piezo-electric crystals
0/0/0	0	0	0/0	0/0/0	0/0	0//0	0/0/	0/0/0	0/0			0/0/0	-Parts
													Electronic integrated circuits:
													-Electronic integrated circuits:
													--Proceesors and controuers, whether or not combined with memories, converter, logic circuit, amplifier, clock and timing circuit or other circuit
													---Multi—component integrated circuits:
													----Semiconductor modules with converting function
0/0/0	3.5	0	0/0	0/0/0	0/0	0/0/0	0/0/	0/0/0	9.1/0			0/0/0	Automatic data processing equipment machine and assembly in multi element integrated circuit, semiconductor module with variable kinetic energy for telecommunication equipment
0/0/0	3.5	0	0/0	0/0/0	0/0	0/0/0	0/0/	0/0/0	9.1/0			0/0/0	Semiconductor module with variable current function in multi element integrated circuit
													----Other
0/0/0	0	2	0/0	0/0/0	0/0	0/0/0	0/0/	0/0/0	0/0		//	0/0/0	Safety chip (with or without memory, converter, logic circuit, amplifier, clock and time sequence circuit or other circuits)
0/0/0	0	2	0/0	0/0/0	0/0	0/0/0	0/0/	0/0/0	0/0		//	0/0/0	Other multicomponent integrated circuits (with or without memory, converter, logic circuit, amplifier, clock and time sequence circuit or other circuits) used as processors and controllers
													---Other
0/0/0	0	0	0/0	0/0/0	0/0	0//0	0/0/	0/0/0	0/0		//	0/0/0	Safety chip (with or without memory, converter, logic circuit, amplifier, clock and time sequence circuit or other circuits)
0/0/0	0	0	0/0	0/0/0	0/0	0//0	0/0/	0/0/0	0/0		//	0/0/0	Other integrated circuits used as processors and controllers (whether or not with memory, converters, logic circuits, amplifiers, clock and time sequence circuits or other circuits)
													--Memories
0/0/0	0	2	0/0	0/0/0	0/0	0/0/0	0/0/	0/0/0	0/0			0/0/0	Multi component integrated circuits
0/0/0	0	0	0/0	0/0/0	0/0	0//0	0/0/	0/0/0	0/0			0/0/0	---other
													--Amplifier
0/0/0	0	2	0/0	0/0/0	0/0	0/0/0	0/0/	0/0/0	0/0			0/0/0	---Multi-component integrated circuits
0/0/0	0	0	0/0	0/0/0	0/0	0//0	0/0/	0/0/0	0/0			0/0/0	---other
													--Other:
0/0/0	0	2	0/0	0/0/0	0/0	0/0/0	0/0/	0/0/0	0/0			0/0/0	---Multi-component integrated circuits
0/0/0	0	0	0/0	0/0/0	0/0	0//0	0/0/	0/0/0	0/0			0/0/0	---other
0/0/0	0	0	0/0	0/0/0	0/0	0//0	0/0/	0/0/0	0/0			0/0/0	-Parts

税则号列	货品名称〔CIQ 扩展编码及品名－T2 表示见附表 2〕	最惠(%)	暂定税率	普通	增值/消费	出口退税	计量单位	监管条件/特殊证件	检验检疫	对美关税	亚太上/下
85.43	**本章其他税目未列名的具有独立功能的电气设备及装置：**										
8543.1000	-粒子加速器										
8543.1000 10	脉冲电子加速器(峰值能量为 500 千电子伏或更高)〔999〕	5		11	13/	13	台/千克	3/		30	
8543.1000 20	中子发生器系统，包括中子管(真空下，利用静电加速来诱发氚-氚核反应)〔999〕	5		11	13/	13	台/千克	3/		30	
8543.1000 90	其他粒子加速器〔999〕	5		11	13/	13	台/千克	/		30	
	-信号发生器：										
8543.2010	---输出信号频率在 1500 兆赫兹以下的通用信号发生器〔999〕	3.8/1.9		80	13/	13	台/千克	/		13.8	
8543.2090	---其他										
8543.2090 10	高速脉冲发生器(脉冲上升时间小于 500ps)〔999〕	2/1		20	13/	13	台/千克	3/		22	
8543.2090 90	其他输出信号频率≥1500MHz 的通用信号发生器〔999〕	2/1		20	13/	13	台/千克	/		22	
8543.3000	-电镀、电解或电泳设备及装置										
8543.3000 10	电化学还原槽；锂汞齐电解槽(电化学还原槽为化学交换过程的铀浓缩设计的)〔999〕	0		35	13/	13	台/千克	3/		10	
8543.3000 20	产氟电解槽(每小时产 250 克以上)〔999〕	0		35	13/	13	台/千克	3/		10	
8543.3000 90	其他电镀、电解或电泳设备及装置〔999〕	0		35	13/	13	台/千克	/		10	
8543.4000	-电子烟及类似的个人电子雾化设备〔999〕	0		35	13/	13	台/千克	/		10	
	-其他设备及装置：										
8543.7091	----金属、矿藏探测器〔101 机电产品及其零件，102 电子测量分析设备及其零件〕	0		17	13/	13	台/千克	/		20	
8543.7092	----高、中频放大器〔999〕	0		17	13/	13	台/千克	/		5	
8543.7093	----电篱网激发器〔999〕	8		35	13/	13	台/千克	/		13	
8543.7099	----其他										
8543.7099 10	飞行数据记录器、报告器〔101 机电产品及其零件，102 电子测量分析设备及其零件〕	0		35	13/	13	台/千克	/			
8543.7099 20	无线广播电视用激励器(具有独立功能)〔101 机电产品及其零件，102 电视接收、发送装置及其零件〕	0		35	13/	13	台/千克	O/		10	
8543.7099 30	模/数转换器(能设计或改进成军用、或设计成抗辐射的)〔101 机电产品及其零件，102 调制解调器〕	0		35	13/	13	台/千克	3/		10	
8543.7099 40	质谱仪用的离子源(原子质量单位≥230，分辨率＞2/230)〔999〕	0		35	13/	13	台/千克	3/		10	
8543.7099 50	密码机、密码卡、密钥管理产品(不包括数字电视智能卡、蓝牙模块、用于知识产权保护的加密狗)〔101 电话密码机，102 传真密码机，103 其他密码机，104 密码卡〕	0		35	13/	13	台/千克	23/		10	
8543.7099 90	其他未列名的具有独立功能的电气设备及装置〔999〕	0		35	13/	9,13	台/千克	/		10	
	-零件：										
8543.9010	---粒子加速器用〔999〕	0		11	13/	13	千克	/		5	
	---信号发生器用：										
8543.9021	----输出信号频率在 1500 兆赫兹以下的通用信号发生器用〔999〕	0		80	13/	13	千克	/			
8543.9029	----其他〔999〕	0		20	13/	13	千克	/		10	
8543.9030	---金属、矿藏探测器用〔999〕	0		17	13/	13	千克	/		25	
8543.9040	---高、中频放大器用〔999〕	0		17	13/	13	千克	/		10	
8543.9090	---其他〔999〕	0		35	13/	13	千克	/		25	
85.44	**绝缘(包括漆包或阳极化处理)电线、电缆(包括同轴电缆)及其他绝缘电导体，不论是否有接头；由多根具有独立保护套的光纤组成的光缆，不论是否与电导体装配或装有接头：**										
	-绕组电线：										
8544.1100	--铜制〔999〕	10	8	70	13/	13	千克/米	/		28	6.5/6.5
8544.1900	--其他〔101 电线，102 其它电线电缆〕	10		70	13/	13	千克/米	/		30	
8544.2000	-同轴电缆及其他同轴电导体[T2]	10		20	13/	13	千克	/		20	6.5/6.5
	-车辆、航空器、船舶用点火布线组及其他布线组：										
8544.3020	---机动车辆用										
8544.3020 01	车辆用电控柴油机的线束〔999〕	10	5	20	13/	13	千克	/		10	

协定税率 %								RCEP		特惠税率 %			Article Description
东/冰/格	巴基斯坦	韩国	瑞士 上/下	哥/秘/柬	澳/毛	新西/坡/智	中国港/澳/台	东盟及马来/澳/韩	日/新	亚太2国	老/柬/缅	98/97/95	
													Electrical machines and apparatus, having individual functions, not specified or included elsewhere in this Chapter:
													-Particle accelerators
0/0/0	0	1	0/0	0/0/0	0/0	0//0	0/0/	0/0	4.5/0			0/0/0	Pulsed electron accelerators(peak value power≥500kEV)
0/0/0	0	1	0/0	0/0/0	0/0	0//0	0/0/	0/0	4.5/0			0/0/0	Neutron generator systems, including neutron tubes(in vacuum condition, induce the tritium-deuteron reaction through acceleration of static)
0/0/0	0	1	0/0	0/0/0	0/0	0//0	0/0/	0/0	4.5/0			0/0/0	Other particle accelerator
													-Signal generators:
0/0/0	8.4		1.5/1.5	0/0/0	0/0	0/0/0	0/0/0	13.5/13.5	13.6/13.5			0/0/0	---Universal signal generators, with a frequency range of less than 1500 MHz
													---Other
0/0/0	2	0	0/0	0/0/0	0/0	0//0	0/0/0	0/7.2	0/7.2			0/0/0	High - speed pulse generator(risetime of pulse <500ps)
0/0/0	2	0	0/0	0/0/0	0/0	0//0	0/0/0	0/7.2	0/7.2			0/0/0	Other versatile signal generators with the ouput signal frequency≥1500MHz
													-Machines and apparatus for electro-plating, electrolysis or electrophoresis
0/0/0	0	0	0/0	0/0/0	0/0	0//0	0/0/	0/0/0	0/0			0/0/0	Electrochemical lithium amalgam electrolysis cells reduction cells(specially designed for uranium concentration in chemical exchange process)
0/0/0	0	0	0/0	0/0/0	0/0	0//0	0/0/	0/0/0	0/0			0/0/0	Fluorine generating electrolytic cells(produce more than 250 g/h)
0/0/0	0	0	0/0	0/0/0	0/0	0//0	0/0/	0/0/0	0/0			0/0/0	Other machines and equipment for electro-plating, electrolysis or electrophoresis
0/0/0	0	0	0/0	0/0/0	0/0	0//0	0/0/	0/0/0	0/0			0/0/0	-Electronic cigarette and similar personal electronic atomization equipment
													-Other equipment and devices:
0/0/0	0	0	0/0	0/0/0	0/0	0//0	0/0/	0/0/0	0/0			0/0/0	----Metal or mine detectors
0/0/0	0	0	0/0	0/0/0	0/0	0//0	0/0/	0/0/0	0/0			0/0/0	----High or intermediate frequency amplifiers
0/0/0	2	2	0/0	0/0/0	0/0	0/0/0	0/0/	0/0/9	9.1/0			0/0/0	----Electric fence energizers
													----Other
0/0/0	0	0	0/0	0/0/0	0/0	0//0	0/0/	0/0/0	0/0			0/0/0	Flying data recorders and reporters
0/0/0	0	0	0/0	0/0/0	0/0	0//0	0/0/	0/0/0	0/0			0/0/0	Exciters for wireless television broadcasting(having independently functions)
0/0/0	0	0	0/0	0/0/0	0/0	0//0	0/0/	0/0/0	0/0			0/0/0	Analog/digital converters(capable of being designed or improved for military uses or being designed to resist radiation)
0/0/0	0	0	0/0	0/0/0	0/0	0//0	0/0/	0/0/0	0/0			0/0/0	Ion source for mass spectrogragh (atomic quality unit≥230, exculpation>2/230)
0/0/0	0	0	0/0	0/0/0	0/0	0//0	0/0/	0/0/0	0/0			0/0/0	Cipher, cipher card (not including the intelligent digital TV card, Bluetooth module, for intellectual property protection dongle)
0/0/0	0	0	0/0	0/0/0	0/0	0//0	0/0/	0/0/0	0/0			0/0/0	Other unisted electrical equipment and devices, having independently functions
													-Parts:
0/0/0	0	0	0/0	0/0/0	0/0	0//0	0/0/	0/0/0	0/0			0/0/0	---Of particle accelerators
													---Of signal generators:
0/0/0	0	0	0/0	0/0/0	0/0	0//0	0/0/	0/0/0	0/0			0/0/0	----Of the generators of subheading No. 8543. 2010
0/0/0	0	0	0/0	0/0/0	0/0	0//0	0/0/	0/0/0	0/0			0/0/0	----Other
0/0/0	0	0	0/0	0/0/0	0/0	0//0	0/0/	0/0/0	0/0			0/0/0	---Of metal or mine detectors
0/0/0	0	0	0/0	0/0/0	0/0	0//0	0/0/	0/0/0	0/0			0/0/0	---Of high or intermediate frequency amplifiers
0/0/0	0	0	0/0	0/0/0	0/0	0//0	0/0/	0/0/0	0/0			0/0/0	---Other
													Insulated (including enamelled or anodized) wire, cable(including co－axial cable) and other insulated electric conductors, whether or not fitted with connectors; optical fibre cables, made up of multiple individually sheathed fibres, whether or not assembled with electric conductors or fitted with connectors:
													-Winding wire:
0/0/0	2	4.6	1/1	0/0/0	0/0	0/0/0	0/0/0	9.3/9.5/9.3	9.4/9.5			0/0/0	--Of copper
0/0/0	16	12	2/2	0/0/0	0/0	0/0/0	0/0/	19/19/	/19			0/0/0	--Other
0/0/0	0	2	4/4	0/0/0	0/0	0/0/0	0/0/0	0/0/9	9.1/0			0/0/0	-Co-axial cable and other co-axial electric conductors
													-Ignition wiring sets and other wiring sets of a kind used in vehicles, aircraft or ships:
													---For motor vehicles
5/0/0	8	4.6	0/0	0/0/0	0/0	0//0	0/0/	9/9.8/	9.1/9.8			0/0/0	Wiring harness for electronic control diesel engines of vehicles

税则号列	货品名称〔CIQ 扩展编码及品名－T2 表示见附表 2〕	最惠(%)	暂定税率	普通	增值/消费	出口退税	计量单位	监管条件/特殊证件	检验检疫	对美关税	亚太上/下
8544.3020 90	机动车辆用其他点火布线组及其他布线组〔999〕	10		20	13/	13	千克	/		15	
8544.3090	---其他〔101 绞股线,102 电线,103 电缆,104 其它电线电缆〕	5		70	13/	13	千克	/		15	
	-其他电导体,额定电压不超过 1000 伏:										
	--有接头:										
	---额定电压不超过 80 伏:										
8544.4211	----电缆[T2]	0		20	13/	13	千克/米	/		25	
8544.4219	----其他[T2]	0		70	13/	13	千克	/		25	
	---额定电压超过 80 伏,但不超过 1000 伏:										
8544.4221	----电缆〔101 电线,102 电缆,103 其它电线电缆〕	0		20	13/	13	千克/米	A/	L	15	
8544.4229	----其他〔101 绞股线,102 电线,103 其它电线电缆〕	0		70	13/	13	千克	A/	L	25	
	--其他:										
	---额定电压不超过 80 伏:										
8544.4911	----电缆[T2]	0		20	13/	13	千克/米	/		15	
8544.4919	----其他[T2]	0		70	13/	13	千克	/		25	
	---额定电压超过 80 伏,但不超过 1000 伏:										
8544.4921	----电缆〔101 电缆,102 其它电线电缆〕	6		20	13/	13	千克/米	A/	L	21	3.9/3.9
8544.4929	----其他〔101 绞股线,102 电线,103 其它电线电缆〕	8		70	13/	13	千克	/		18	5.2/5.2
	-其他电导体,额定电压超过 1000 伏:										
	---电缆:										
8544.6012	----额定电压不超过 35 千伏										
8544.6012 10	250 千米/小时及以上高速动车组用高压电缆〔999〕	8	4	50	13/	13	千克/米	/		14	5.2/5.2
8544.6012 90	其他 1 千伏＜额定电压≤35 千伏的电缆〔999〕	8		50	13/	13	千克/米	/		18	5.2/5.2
8544.6013	----额定电压超过 35 千伏,但不超过 110 千伏〔999〕	8		20	13/	13	千克/米	/		33	5.2/5.2
8544.6014	----额定电压超过 110 千伏,但不超过 220 千伏〔999〕	8		20	13/	13	千克/米	/		28	5.2/5.2
8544.6019	----其他〔101 电缆,102 其它电线电缆〕	8		20	13/	13	千克/米	/		33	5.2/5.2
8544.6090	---其他										
8544.6090 01	额定电压≥500 千伏的气体绝缘金属封闭输电线[T2]	15	10	70	13/	13	千克	/		30	9.8/9.8
8544.6090 90	额定电压＞1 千伏的其他电导线[T2]	15		70	13/	13	千克	/		35	9.8/9.8
8544.7000	-光缆〔999〕	0		20	13/	13	千克/米	/		15	
85.45	**碳电极、碳刷、灯碳棒、电池碳棒及电气设备用的其他石墨或碳精制品,不论是否带金属:**										
	-碳电极:										
8545.1100	--炉用〔999〕	8		35	13/	0	千克	3/		33	
8545.1900	--其他										
8545.1900 10	燃料电池用碳电极片(不论是否带金属)〔999〕	10	5	35	13/	0	千克	3/		10	
8545.1900 90	其他碳电极(不论是否带金属)〔999〕	10		35	13/	0	千克	3/		15	
8545.2000	-碳刷〔999〕	10		35	13/	13	千克	/		35	
8545.9000	-其他〔999〕	10		35	13/	13	千克	3/		20	
85.46	**各种材料制的绝缘子:**										
8546.1000	-玻璃制〔999〕	10		35	13/	13	千克	/		35	
	-陶瓷制										
8546.2010	---输变电线路绝缘瓷套管〔999〕	6		35	13/	13	千克	/		31	
8546.2090	---其他										
8546.2090 01	输变电架空线路用长棒形瓷绝缘子瓷件(单支长度为 1～2 米,实芯)〔999〕	12	3	35	13/	13	千克	/		13	
8546.2090 90	其他陶瓷制绝缘子(包括非输变电线路绝缘瓷套管)〔999〕	12		35	13/	13	千克	/		22	
8546.9000	-其他〔999〕	10		35	13/	13	千克	/		35	
85.47	**电气机器、器具或设备用的绝缘零件,除了为装配需要而在模制时装入的小金属零件(例如,螺纹孔)以外,全部用绝缘材料制成,但税目 85.46 的绝缘子除外;内衬绝缘材料的贱金属制线路导管及其接头:**										
8547.1000	-陶瓷制绝缘零件〔999〕	7		35	13/	13	千克	/		17	
8547.2000	-塑料制绝缘零件〔999〕	7		35	13/	13	千克	/	L	27	
	-其他:										
8547.9010	---内衬绝缘材料的贱金属制线路导管及其接头〔999〕	7		50	13/	13	千克	/		12	

协定税率 %								RCEP		特惠税率 %			Article Description
东/冰/格	巴基斯坦	韩国	瑞士 上/下	哥/秘/柬	澳/毛	新西/坡/智	中国港/澳/台	东盟及马来/澳/韩	日/新	亚太2国	老/柬/缅	98/97/95	
5/0/0	8	4.6	0/0	0/0/0	0/0	0//0	0/0/	9/9.8/	9.1/9.8			0/0/0	Other ignition wiring sets and other wiring sets of a king used for motor vehicles
/0/0	4	2.3	0/0	0/0/0	0/0	0//0	0/0/					0/0/0	---Other
													-Other electric conductors, for a voltage not exceeding 1000 V:
													--Fitted with connectors:
													---For a voltage not exceeding 80 V:
0/0/0	0	0	0/0	0/0/0	0/0	0//0	0/0/	0/0/0	0/0			0/0/0	----Electric cable
0/0/0	0	0	0/0	0/0/0	0/0	0//0	0/0/	0/0/0	0/0			0/0/0	----Other
													---for a voltage exceeding 80V but not exceeding 1000 V:
0/0/0	0	0	0/0	0/0/0	0/0	0//0	0/0/	0/0/0	0/0			0/0/0	----Electric cable
0/0/0	0	0	0/0	0/0/0	0/0	0//0	0/0/	0/0/0	0/0			0/0/0	----Other
													--Other:
													---For a voltage not exceeding 80 V:
0/0/0	0	0	0/0	0/0/0	0/0	0//0	0/0/	0/0/0	0/0			0/0/0	----Electric cable
0/0/0	0	0	0/0	0/0/0	0/0	0//0	0/0/	0/0/0	0/0			0/0/0	----Other
													---For a voltage exceeding 80 V but not exceeding 1000 V:
0/0/0	0	3.9	0.6/0.6	0/0/0	0/0	0//0	0/0/	5/5/	/5			0/0/0	----Electric cable
0/0/0	0	0	1.2/1.2	0/0/0	0/0	0/0/0	0/0/0	0/0/0	11.3/0			0/0/0	----Other
													-Other electric conductors, for a voltage exceeding 1000 V:
													---Electric cable:
													----For a voltage not execedding 35 kV
0/0/0	0	2	1/1	0/0/0	0/0	0/0/0	0/0/	0/0/9	9.1/0			0/0/0	High voltage cables for high－speed EMUs of 25 km / h and above
0/0/0	0	2	1/1	0/0/0	0/0	0/0/0	0/0/	0/0/9	9.1/0			0/0/0	Other cables with 1 kV ＜ rated voltage ≤ 35 kV
0/0/0	2	1.6	0/0	0/0/0	0/0	0//0	0/0/	0/0/7.6	7.6/0			0/0/0	----For a voltage execedding 35 kV, but not execedding 110 kV
0/0/0	2	0	0/0	0/0/0	0/0	0//0	0/0/	0/0/0	7.6/0			0/0/0	----For a voltage execedding 110 kV, but not execedding 220 kV
0/0/0	2	5.4		0/0/0	0/0	0//0	0/0/	5/5/	/5			0/0/0	----Other
													---Other
0/0/0	14	12.6	0/0	0/0/0	0/0	0/0/0	0/0/	20/20/	20/20			0/0/0	Gas-insulated transmission electric wire, rated voltage ≥ 500kV
0/0/0	14	12.6	0/0	0/0/0	0/0	0/0/0	0/0/	20/20/	20/20			0/0/0	Other electric conductor with a rated voltage＞1kV
0/0/0	0	0	0/0	0/0/0	0/0	0//0	0/0/	0/0/0	0/0			0/0/0	-Optical fibre cables
													Carbon electrodes, carbon brushes, lamp carbons, battery carbons and other articles of graphite or other carbon, with or without metal, of a kind used for electrical purposes:
													-Carbon Electrodes:
0/0/0	2	1.6	0/0	0/0/0	0/0	0//0	0/0/	7.2/7.2/7.2	7.3/7.2			0/0/0	--Of a kind used for furnaces
													--Other
0/0/0	3.5	2.1	1.1/1.1	0/0/0	0/0	0/0/0	0/0/	0/0/9.5	9.5/0		//	0/0/0	Carbon electrodes for fuel cells (with or without metal)
0/0/0	3.5	2.1	1.1/1.1	0/0/0	0/0	0/0/0	0/0/	0/0/9.5	9.5/0		//	0/0/0	Other carbon electrodes (with or without metal)
0/0/0	3.5	2.1	1.1/1.1	0/0/0	0/0	0/0/0	0/0/	9.5/9.5/9.5	9.5/9.5			0/0/0	-Brushes
0/0/0	3.5	2.1	1.1/1.1	0/0/0	0/0	0/0/0	0/0/	9.5/9.5/9.5	9.5/9.5			0/0/0	-Other
													Electrical insulators of any material:
0/0/0	3.5	2.1	1.1/1.1	0/0/0	0/0	0/0/0	0/0/	0/0/9.5	9.5/0			0/0/0	-Of glass
													-electrical
0/0/0	0	1.2	0.6/0.6	0/0/0	0/0	0//0	0/0/	0/0/5.4	5.5/0			0/0/0	---Power transmission and converting ceramic bushings
													---Other
0/0/0	4.2	2.4	1.2/1.2	0/0/0	0/0	0/0/0	0/0/	0/0/10.8	10.9/0			0/0/0	Porcelain parts of long - rod porcelain insulators for electric transmission and transformation overhead lines (length of a single rod: 1～2m, solid)
0/0/0	4.2	2.4	1.2/1.2	0/0/0	0/0	0/0/0	0/0/	0/0/10.8	10.9/0			0/0/0	Other electrical insulators of ceramics (including not power transmission and transformation and converting ceramic bushings)
0/0/0	3.5	2	1/1	0/0/0	0/0	0/0/0	0/0/	9/9/9	9.1/9			0/0/0	-Other
													Insulating fittings for electrical machines, appliances or equipment, being fittings wholly of insulating material apart from any minor components of metal (for example, threaded sockets) incorporated during moulding solely for purposes of assembly, other than insulators of headingNo. 85. 46; electrical conduit tubing and joints therefor, of base metal lined with insulating material:
0/0/0	2	3.7	0.8/0.8	0/0/0	0/0	0//0	0/0/	7.5/7.6/7.5	7.5/7.6			0/0/0	-Insulating fittings of ceramics
0/0/0	2	3.7	0.8/0.8	0/0/0	0/0	0//0	0/0/	7.2/7.2/7.2	7.5/7.2			0/0/0	-Insulating fittings of plastics
													-Other:
0/0/0	2	2	0/0	0/0/0	0/0	0/0/0	0/0/	0/0/9	9.1/0			0/0/0	---Electrical conduit tubing and joints therefor, of base metal lined with insulating material

税则号列	货品名称〔CIQ 扩展编码及品名－T2 表示见附表 2〕	最惠(%)	暂定税率	普通	增值/消费	出口退税	计量单位	监管条件/特殊证件	检验检疫	对美关税	亚太上/下
8547.9090	---其他〔999〕	7		35	13/	13	千克	/	L	32	
85.48	**机器或设备的本章其他税目未列名的电气零件 :**										
8548.0000	机器或设备的本章其他税目未列名的电气零件										
8548.0000 01	电磁干扰滤波器〔101 其它机电产品及其零件,102 集成电路,103 其它电子元器件〕	8	1	40	13/	13	千克	/		26	
8548.0000 02	非电磁干扰滤波器〔999〕	8	1	40	13/	13	千克	/			
8548.0000 10	可调脉冲单模染料振荡器(平均输出功率＞lw 重复率＞1khz 脉宽＜100ns 可见光范围)〔999〕	8		40	13/	13	千克	3/		33	
8548.0000 20	可调脉冲染料激光放大器和振荡器(不包括单模震荡器)(平均输出功率＞30w 重复率＞1khz 脉宽＜100ns 可见光范围)〔999〕	8		40	13/	13	千克	3/		33	
8548.0000 30	触摸感应数据输入装置(即触摸屏)无显示的性能,安装于有显示屏的设备中,通过检测显示区域内触摸动作的发生及位置进行工作。触摸感应可通过电阻、静电电容、声学脉冲识别、红外光或其他触摸感应技术来获得〔999〕	0		40	13/	13	千克	/		25	
8548.0000 90	85 章其他编号未列名的电气零件〔999〕	8		40	13/	13	千克	/		33	
85.49	**电子电气废弃物及碎料:**										
	-原电池、原电池组及蓄电池的废物、废料;废原电池 、废原电池组及废蓄电池:										
8549.1100	--铅酸蓄电池的废物、废料;废铅酸蓄电池〔999〕	8		36	13/	13	千克	9/			
8549.1200	--其他,含铅、镉或汞的〔999〕	8		36	13/	13	千克	9/			
8549.1300	--按化学类型分拣且不含铅、镉或汞的〔999〕	8		36	13/	13	千克	9/			
8549.1400	--未分拣且不含铅、镉或汞的〔999〕	8		36	13/	13	千克	9/			
8549.1900	--其他〔999〕	8		36	13/	13	千克	9/			
	-主要用于回收贵金属的:										
8549.2100	--含有原电池、原电池组、蓄电池、汞开关、源于阴极射线管的玻璃或其他活化玻璃,或含有镉、汞、铅或多氯联苯(PCBs)的电气或电子元件〔999〕	5		31	13/	0	千克	9/			
8549.2900	--其他〔999〕	4		21	13/	0	千克	9/			
	-其他电气、电子组件及印刷电路板:										
8549.3100	--含有原电池、原电池组、蓄电池、汞开关、源于阴极射线管的玻璃或其他活化玻璃,或含有镉、汞、铅或多氯联苯(PCBs)的电气或电子元件〔999〕	8		40	13/	0	千克	9/			
8549.3900	--其他〔999〕	6.5		35	13/	0	千克	9/			
	-其他:										
8549.9100	--含有原电池、原电池组、蓄电池、汞开关、源于阴极射线管的玻璃或其他活化玻璃,或含有镉、汞、铅或多氯联苯(PCBs)的电气或电子元件〔999〕	8		40	13/	0	千克	9/			
8549.9900	--其他〔999〕	6.5		35	13/	0	千克	9/			

协定税率 %								RCEP		特惠税率 %			Article Description
东/冰/格	巴基斯坦	韩国	瑞士上/下	哥/秘/柬	澳/毛	新西/坡/智	中国港/澳/台	东盟及马来/澳/韩	日/新	亚太2国	老/柬/缅	98/97/95	
0/0/0	2	0	0/0	0/0/0	0/0	0//0	0/0/	7.2/7.2/7.2	7.3/7.2			0/0/0	---Other
													Electrical parts of machinery or equipment not listed in other tax items in this chapter
													Electrical parts of machinery or equipment not listed in other tax items in this chapter
0/0/0	4.2	7.2	1.2/1.2	0/0/0	0/0	0/0/0	0/0/	11.4/11.4/11.4	11.4/11.4			0/0/0	Electromagnetic interference filter
0/0/0	4.2	7.2	1.2/1.2	0/0/0	0/0	0/0/0	0/0/	11.4/11.4/11.4	11.4/11.4			0/0/0	Non electromagnetic interference filter
0/0/0	4.2	7.2	1.2/1.2	0/0/0	0/0	0/0/0	0/0/	11.4/11.4/11.4	11.4/11.4			0/0/0	Adjustable pulse single—mode dye oscillator (average output power > LW repetition rate > 1kHz pulse width < 1ns visible light range)
0/0/0	4.2	7.2	1.2/1.2	0/0/0	0/0	0/0/0	0/0/	11.4/11.4/11.4	11.4/11.4			0/0/0	Tunable pulsed dye laser amplifier and oscillator (excluding single—mode oscillator) (average output power > 3W, repetition rate > 1kHz, pulse width < 1ns, visible light range)
0/0/0	4.2	7.2	1.2/1.2	0/0/0	0/0	0/0/0	0/0/	11.4/11.4/11.4	11.4/11.4			0/0/0	The touch sensing data input device (i.e. touch screen) has no display performance. It is installed in the equipment with display screen and works by detecting the occurrence and position of touch action in the display area. Touch sensing can be obtained by resistance, electrostatic capacitance, acoustic pulse recognition, infrared light or other touch sensing technologies
0/0/0	4.2	7.2	1.2/1.2	0/0/0	0/0	0/0/0	0/0/	11.4/11.4/11.4	11.4/11.4			0/0/0	Other electrical parts not listed in Chapter 85
													Electronic and electrical waste and scrap
													-Waste and waste of primary battery, primary battery pack and battery; Waste primary battery, waste primary battery pack and waste battery
0/0/0	2	0	0/0	0/0/0	0/0	0//0	0/0/	0/0/0	7.3/0	4		0/0/0	--Wastes and wastes of lead—acid batteries; Waste lead—acid battery
0/0/0	2	0	0/0	0/0/0	0/0	0//0	0/0/	0/0/0	7.3/0	4		0/0/0	--Others, containing lead, cadmium or mercury
0/0/0	2	0	0/0	0/0/0	0/0	0//0	0/0/	0/0/0	7.3/0	4		0/0/0	--Sorted by chemical type and free of lead, cadmium or mercury
0/0/0	2	0	0/0	0/0/0	0/0	0//0	0/0/	0/0/0	7.3/0	4		0/0/0	--Unsorted and free of lead, cadmium or mercury
0/0/0	2	0	0/0	0/0/0	0/0	0//0	0/0/	0/0/0	7.3/0	4		0/0/0	--Other
													-It is mainly used to recover precious metals
0/0/0	1.2	0.2	0.1/0.1	0/0/0	0/0	0/0/0	0/0/	0/0/0	0/0			0/0/0	--Electrical or electronic components containing primary cells, primary battery packs, batteries, mercury switches, glass or other activated glass derived from cathode ray tubes, or containing cadmium, mercury, lead or polychlorinated biphenyls (PCBs)
0/0/0	1.2	0	0/0	0/0/0	0/0	0//0	0/0/	0/0/0	0/0			0/0/0	--Other
													-Other electrical and electronic components and printed circuit boards
0/0/0	3.3	0.8	0.4/0.4	0/0/0	0/0	0/0/0	0/0/	0/0/0	5.9/0			0/0/0	--Electrical or electronic components containing primary cells, primary battery packs, batteries, mercury switches, glass or other activated glass derived from cathode ray tubes, or containing cadmium, mercury, lead or polychlorinated biphenyls (PCBs)
0/0/0	2	0	0/0	0/0/0	0/0	0//0	0/0/	0/0/0	5.9/0			0/0/0	--Other
													-Other
0/0/0	3.3	0.8	0.4/0.4	0/0/0	0/0	0/0/0	0/0/	0/0/0	5.9/0			0/0/0	--Electrical or electronic components containing primary cells, primary battery packs, batteries, mercury switches, glass or other activated glass derived from cathode ray tubes, or containing cadmium, mercury, lead or polychlorinated biphenyls (PCBs)
0/0/0	2	0	0/0	0/0/0	0/0	0//0	0/0/	0/0/0	5.9/0			0/0/0	--Other

第十七类
车辆、航空器、船舶
及有关运输设备

注释：

一、本类不包括税目95.03或95.08的物品以及税目95.06的长雪橇、平底雪橇及类似品。

二、本类所称"零件"及"零件、附件"，不适用于下列货品，不论其是否确定为供本类货品使用：

(一)各种材料制的接头、垫圈或类似品(按其构成材料归类或归入税目84.84)或硫化橡胶(硬质橡胶除外)的其他制品(税目40.16)；

(二)第十五类注释二所规定的贱金属制通用零件(第十五类)或塑料制的类似品(第三十九章)；

(三)第八十二章的物品(工具)；

(四)税目83.06的物品；

(五)税目84.01至84.79的机器或装置及其零件，但供本类所列货品使用的散热器除外；税目84.81或84.82的物品及税目84.83的物品(这些物品是构成发动机或其他动力装置所必需的)；

(六)电机或电气设备(第八十五章)；

(七)第九十章的物品；

(八)第九十一章的物品；

(九)武器(第九十三章)；

(十)税目94.05的灯具、照明装置及其零件；

(十一)作为车辆零件的刷子(税目96.03)。

三、第八十六章至第八十八章所称"零件"或"附件"，不适用于那些非专用于或非主要用于这几章所列物品的零件、附件。同时符合这几章内两个或两个以上税目规定的零件、附件，应按其主要用途归入相应的税目。

四、在本类中：

(一)既可在道路上，又可在轨道上行驶的特殊构造的车辆，应归入第八十七章的相应税目；

(二)水陆两用的机动车辆，应归入第八十七章的相应税目；

(三)可兼作地面车辆使用的特殊构造的航空器，应归入第八十八章的相应税目。

五、气垫运输工具应按本类最相似的运输工具归类，其规定如下：

(一)在导轨上运行的(气垫火车)，归入第八十六章；

(二)在陆地行驶或水陆两用的，归入第八十七章；

(三)在水上航行的，不论能否在海滩或浮码头登陆及能否在冰上行驶，一律归入第八十九章。

气垫运输工具的零件、附件，应按照上述规定，与最相类似的运输工具的零件、附件一并归类。

气垫火车的导轨固定装置及附件应与铁道轨道固定装置及附件一并归类。气垫火车运行系统的信号、安全或交通管理设备应与铁路的信号、安全或交通管理设备一并归类。

第八十六章
铁道及电车道机车、车辆及其零件；铁道及电车道轨道固定装置及其零件、附件；各种机械(包括电动机械)交通信号设备

注释：

一、本章不包括：

(一)木制或混凝土制的铁道或电车道轨枕及气垫火车用的混凝土导轨(税目44.06或68.10)；

(二)税目73.02的铁道及电车道铺轨用钢铁材料；

(三)税目85.30的电气信号、安全或交通管理设备。

二、税目86.07主要适用于：

(一)轴、轮、行走机构、金属轮箍、轮圈、毂及轮子的其他零件；

(二)车架、底架、转向架；

(三)轴箱；制动装置；

(四)车辆缓冲器；钩或其他联结器及车厢走廊联结装置；

(五)车身。

三、除上述注释一另有规定的以外，税目86.08包括：

(一)已装配的轨道、转车台、站台缓冲器、量载规；

(二)铁道及电车道、道路、内河航道、停车场、港口或机场用的臂板信号机、机械信号盘、平交道口控制器、信号及道岔控制器及其他机械(包括电动机械)信号、安全或交通管理设备，不论是否装有电力照明装置。

税则号列	货品名称〔CIQ扩展编码及品名—T2表示见附表2〕	最惠(%)	暂定税率	普通	增值/消费	出口退税	计量单位	监管条件/特殊证件	检验检疫	对美关税	亚太上/下
86.01	**铁道电力机车，由外部电力或蓄电池驱动：**										
	-由外部电力驱动：										
	---直流电机驱动的：										
8601.1011	----微型机控制的〔999〕	3		11	13/	13	辆/千克	/			2/2
8601.1019	----其他〔999〕	3		11	13/	13	辆/千克	/			2/2
8601.1020	---交流电机驱动的〔999〕	3		11	13/	13	辆/千克	/			2/2
8601.1090	---其他〔999〕	3		11	13/	13	辆/千克	/			2/2
8601.2000	-由蓄电池驱动〔999〕	3		11	13/	13	辆/千克	/			

SECTION XVII
VEHICLES, AIRCRAFT, VESSELS AND ASSOCIATED TRANSPORT EQUIPMENT

Notes:

1. This Section does not cover articles of headingNo. 95.03 or 95.08, or bobsleighs, toboggans or the like of heading. 95.06.
2. The expressions "parts" and "parts and accessories" do not apply to the following articles, whether or not they are identifiable as for the goods of this Section:
   (a) Joints, washers or the like of any material (classified according to their constituent material or in headingNo. 84.84) or other articles of vulcanized rubber other than hard rubber (heading. 40.16);
   (b) Parts of general use, as defined in Note 2 to Section XV, of base metal (Section XV), or similar goods of plastics (Chapter 39);
   (c) Articles of Chapter 82 (tools);
   (d) Articles of headingNo. 83.06;
   (e) Machines or apparatus of headings No. 84.01 to 84.79, or parts thereof but except for goods listed in this kind of radiator; articles of heading. 84.81 or 84.82 or, provided they constitute integral parts of engines or motors, articles of heading-No. 84.83;
   (f) Electrical machinery or equipment (Chapter 85);
   (g) Articles of Chapter 90;
   (h) Articles of Chapter 91;
   (ij) Arms (Chapter 93);
   (k) Lamps or lighting fittings of headingNo. 94.05;
   (e) Brushes of a kind used as parts of vehicles (headingNo. 96.03).
3. References in Chapters 86 to 88 to "parts" or "accessories" do not apply to parts or accessories which are not suitable for use solely or principally with the articles of those Chapters. A part or accessory which answers to a description in two or more of the headings of those Chapters is to be classified under that heading which corresponds to the principal use of that part or accessory.
4. For the purposes of this Section:
   (a) Vehicles specially constructed to travel on both road and rail are classified under the appropriate heading of Chapter 87;
   (b) Amphibious motor vehicles are classified under the appropriate heading of Chapter 87;
   (c) Aircraft specially constructed so that they can also be used as road vehicles are classified under the appropriate heading of Chapter 88.
5. Air-cushion vehicles are to be classified within this Section with the vehicles to which they are most akin as follows:
   (a) In Chapter 86 if designed to travel on a guide-track (hovertrains);
   (b) In Chapter 87 if designed to travel over land or over both land and water;
   (c) In Chapter 89 if designed to travel over water, whether or not able to land on beaches or landingstages or also able to travel over ice.

   Parts and accessories of air-cushion vehicles are to be classified in the same way as those of vehicles of the heading in which the air-cushion vehicles are classified under the above provisions.

   Hovertrain track fixtures and fittings are to be classified as railway track fixtures and fittings, and signalling, safety or traffic control equipment for hovertrain transport systems as signalling, safety or traffic control equipment for railways.

Chapter 86
Railway or tramway locomotives, rolling-stock and parts thereof; railway or tramway track fixtures and fittings and parts thereof; mechanical (including electro-mechanical) traffic signalling equipment of all kinds

Notes:

1. This Chapter does not cover:
   (a) Railway or tramway sleepers of wood or of concrete, or concrete guide-track sections for hovertrain (heading No. 44.06 or 68.10);
   (b) Railway or tramway track construction material of iron or steel of heading No. 73.02;
   (c) Electrical signalling, safety of traffic control equipment of heading No. 85.30.
2. Heading No. 86.07 applies, *inter alia*, to:
   (a) Axles, wheels, wheel sets (running gear), metal tyres, hoops and hubs and other parts of wheels;
   (b) Frames, underframes, bogies and bissel-bogies;
   (c) Axle boxes; brake gear;
   (d) Buffers for rolling-stock; hooks and other coupling gear and corridor connections;
   (e) Coachwork.
3. Subject to the provisions of Note 1 above, headingNo. 86.08 applies, *inter alia*, to:
   (a) Assembled track, turntables, platform buffers, loading gauges;
   (b) Semaphores, mechanical signal discs, level crossing control gear, signal and point controls, and other mechanical (including electro-mechanical) signalling, safety or traffic control equipment, whether or not fitted with electric lighting, for railways, tramways, roads, inland waterways, parking facilities, port installations or airfields.

协定税率 %								RCEP		特惠税率 %			Article Description
东/冰/格	巴基斯坦	韩国	瑞士上/下	哥/秘/柬	澳/毛	新西/坡/智	中国港/澳/台	东盟及马来/澳/韩	日/新	亚太2国	老/柬/缅	98/97/95	
													Rail locomotives powered from an external source of electricity or by electric accumulators:
													-Powered from an external source of electricity:
													---Drived by DC motors:
0/0/0	0	0	0/0	0/0/0	0/0	0//0	0/0/	0/0/0	0/0			0/0/0	----Controlled by microprocessings
0/0/0	0	0	0/0	0/0/0	0/0	0//0	0/0/	0/0/0	0/0			0/0/0	----Other
0/0/0	0	0	0/0	0/0/0	0/0	0//0	0/0/	0/0/0	0/0			0/0/0	---Drived by AC motors
0/0/0	0	0	0/0	0/0/0	0/0	0//0	0/0/	0/0/0	0/0			0/0/0	---Other
0/0/0	0	0	0/0	0/0/0	0/0	0//0	0/0/	0/0/0	0/0			0/0/0	-Powered by electric accumulators

税则号列	货品名称〔CIQ 扩展编码及品名—T2 表示见附表 2〕	最惠(%)	暂定税率	普通	增值/消费	出口退税	计量单位	监管条件/特殊证件	检验检疫	对美关税	亚太上/下
86.02	**其他铁道机车;机车煤水车:**										
	-柴油电力机车:										
8602.1010	---微型机控制的〔999〕	3		11	13/	13	辆/千克	/			2/2
8602.1090	---其他〔999〕	3		11	13/	13	辆/千克	/		8	2/2
8602.9000	-其他〔999〕	3		11	13/	13	辆/千克	/			
86.03	**铁道及电车道用的机动客车、货车、敞车,但税目 86.04 的货品除外:**										
8603.1000	-由外部电力驱动〔999〕	3		11	13/	13	辆/千克	/			2/2
8603.9000	-其他〔999〕	3		11	13/	13	辆/千克	/			
86.04	**铁道及电车道用的维修或服务车,不论是否机动(例如,工场车、起重机车、道碴捣固车、轨道校正车、检验车及查道车):**										
	---检验车及查道车:										
8604.0011	----隧道限界检查车〔999〕	3		14	13/	13	辆/千克	/			2/2
8604.0012	----钢轨在线打磨列车〔999〕	3		14	13/	13	辆/千克	/		8	2/2
8604.0019	----其他〔999〕	5		14	13/	13	辆/千克	/			3.3/3.3
	---其他:										
8604.0091	----电气化接触网架线机(轨行式)〔999〕	5		20	13/	13	辆/千克	/			3.3/3.3
8604.0099	----其他〔999〕	5		20	13/	13	辆/千克	/			
86.05	**铁道及电车道用的非机动客车;行李车、邮政车和其他铁道及电车道用的非机动特殊用途车辆(税目 86.04 的货品除外):**										
8605.0010	---铁道客车〔999〕	5		14	13/	13	辆/千克	/			
8605.0090	---其他〔999〕	5		14	13/	13	辆/千克	/			
86.06	**铁道及电车道用的非机动有篷及无篷货车:**										
8606.1000	-油罐货车及类似车〔999〕	5		14	13/	13	辆/千克	/			
8606.3000	-自卸货车,但子目 8606.10 的货品除外〔999〕	5		14	13/	13	辆/千克	/			
	-其他:										
8606.9100	--带篷及封闭的〔999〕	5		14	13/	13	辆/千克	/			
8606.9200	--敞篷的,厢壁固定且高度超过 60 厘米〔999〕	5		14	13/	13	辆/千克	/			
8606.9900	--其他〔999〕	5		14	13/	13	辆/千克	/			
86.07	**铁道及电车道机车或其他车辆的零件:**										
	-转向架、轴、轮及其零件:										
8607.1100	--驾驶转向架〔999〕	3		11	13/	13	套/千克	/			
8607.1200	--其他转向架〔999〕	3		11	13/	13	套/千克	/		28	2/2
	--其他,包括零件:										
8607.1910	---轴〔999〕	3		11	13/	13	根/千克	/		28	
8607.1990	---其他〔999〕	3		11	13/	13	千克	/		28	
	-制动装置及其零件:										
8607.2100	--空气制动器及其零件〔999〕	3		11	13/	13	千克	/		28	
8607.2900	--其他〔999〕	3		11	13/	13	千克	/		13	
8607.3000	-钩、其他联结器、缓冲器及其零件〔999〕	3		11	13/	13	千克	/		28	
	-其他:										
8607.9100	--机车用〔999〕	3		11	13/	13	千克	/		28	
8607.9900	--其他〔999〕	3		11	13/	13	千克	/		23	
86.08	**铁道及电车道轨道固定装置及附件;供铁道、电车道、道路、内河航道、停车场、港口或机场用的机械(包括电动机械)信号、安全或交通管理设备;上述货品的零件:**										
8608.0010	---轨道自动计轴设备〔999〕	3		20	13/	13	千克/台	/			2/2
8608.0090	---其他〔999〕	4		20	13/	13	千克	/		29	
86.09	**集装箱(包括运输液体的集装箱),经特殊设计、装备适用于各种运输方式:**										
	---20 英尺的:										
8609.0011	----保温式〔101 新,102 旧〕	10		35	13/	13	个/千克	AB/	PQ		
8609.0012	----罐式〔101 新,102 旧〕	10		35	13/	13	个/千克	AB/	PQ	20	6.5/6.5
8609.0019	----其他〔101 新,102 旧〕	10		35	13/	13	个/千克	AB/	PQ	35	6.5/6.5
	---40 英尺的:										
8609.0021	----保温式的〔101 新,102 旧〕	10		35	13/	13	个/千克	AB/	PQ		
8609.0022	----罐式〔101 新,102 旧〕	10		35	13/	13	个/千克	AB/	PQ		
8609.0029	----其他〔101 新,102 旧〕	10		35	13/	13	个/千克	AB/	PQ		
8609.0030	---45、48、53 英尺的〔101 新,102 旧〕	10		35	13/	13	个/千克	AB/	PQ		
8609.0090	---其他〔101 新,102 旧〕	10		35	13/	13	个/千克	AB/	PQ	35	

协定税率 %								RCEP		特惠税率 %			Article Description
东/冰/格	巴基斯坦	韩国	瑞士上/下	哥/秘/柬	澳/毛	新西/坡/智	中国港/澳/台	东盟及马来/澳/韩	日/新	亚太2国	老/柬/缅	98/97/95	
													Other rail locomotives; locomotive tenders:
													-Diesel-electric locomotives:
0/0/0	0	0	0/0	0/0/0	0/0	0//0	0/0/	0/0/0	0/0			0/0/0	---Controled by microprocessings
0/0/0	0	0	0/0	0/0/0	0/0	0//0	0/0/	0/0/0	0/0			0/0/0	---Other
0/0/0	0	0	0/0	0/0/0	0/0	0//0	0/0/	0/0/0	0/0			0/0/0	-Other
													Self-propelled railway or tramway coaches, vans and trucks, other than those of headingNo. 86. 04:
0/0/0	0	0	0/0	0/0/0	0/0	0//0	0/0/	0/0/0	0/0			0/0/0	-Powered from an external source of electricity:
0/0/0	0	0	0/0	0/0/0	0/0	0//0	0/0/	0/0/0	0/0			0/0/0	-Other
													Railway or tramway maintenance or service vehicles, whether or not self-propelled (for example, workshops, cranes, ballast tampers, trackliners, testing coaches and track inspection vehicles):
													---Testing coaches and track inspection vehicles:
0/0/0	0	0	0/0	0/0/0	0/0	0//0	0/0/	0/0/0	0/0			0/0/0	----Inspection vehicles for tunnel clearance
0/0/0	0	0	0/0	0/0/0	0/0	0//0	0/0/	0/0/0	0/0			0/0/0	----Sanding vehicles for on-line rails
0/0/0	0	0	0/0	0/0/0	0/0	0//0	0/0/	0/0/0	0/0			0/0/0	----Other
													---Other:
0/0/0	0	0	0/0	0/0/0	0/0	0//0	0/0/	0/0/0	0/0			0/0/0	----Installing vehicles for suspension of contact wire (running on rails)
0/0/0	2	0	0/0	0/0/0	0/0	0//0	0/0/	0/0/0	6.4/0			0/0/0	----Other
													Railway or tramway passenger coaches, not self-propelled; luggage vans, post office coaches and other special purpose railway or tramway coaches, not self-propelled (excluding those of headingNo. 86. 04):
0/0/0	0	0	0/0	0/0/0	0/0	0//0	0/0/	0/0/0	0/0			0/0/0	---Railway passenger coaches
0/0/0	0	0	0/0	0/0/0	0/0	0//0	0/0/	0/0/0	0/0			0/0/0	---Other
													Railway or tramway goods vans and wagons, not self-propelled:
0/0/0	0	0	0/0	0/0/0	0/0	0//0	0/0/	0/0/0	0/0			0/0/0	-Tank wagons and the like
0/0/0	0	0	0/0	0/0/0	0/0	0//0	0/0/	0/0/0	0/0			0/0/0	-Self-discharging vans and wagons, other than those of subheadingNo. 8606. 1000
													-Other:
0/0/0	0	0	0/0	0/0/0	0/0	0//0	0/0/	0/0/0	0/0			0/0/0	--Covered and closed
0/0/0	0	0	0/0	0/0/0	0/0	0//0	0/0/	0/0/0	0/0			0/0/0	--Open, with non-removable sides of a hight exceeding 60 cm
0/0/0	0	0	0/0	0/0/0	0/0	0//0	0/0/	0/0/0	0/0			0/0/0	--Other
													Parts of railway or tramway locomotives or rolling-stock:
													-Bogies, bissel-bogies, axles and wheels, and parts thereof:
0/0/0	0	0	0/0	0/0/0	0/0	0//0	0/0/	0/0/0	0/0			0/0/0	--Driving bogies and bissel-bogies
0/0/0	0	0	0/0	0/0/0	0/0	0//0	0/0/	0/0/0	0/0			0/0/0	--Other bogies and bissel-bogies
													--Other, including parts:
0/0/0	0	0	0/0	0/0/0	0/0	0//0	0/0/	0/0/0	0/0			0/0/0	---Axles
0/0/0	0	0	0/0	0/0/0	0/0	0//0	0/0/	0/0/0	0/0			0/0/0	---Other
													-Brakes and parts thereof:
0/0/0	0	0	0/0	0/0/0	0/0	0//0	0/0/	0/2.7/0	0/2.7			0/0/0	--Air brakes and parts thereof
0/0/0	0	0	0/0	0/0/0	0/0	0//0	0/0/	0/0/0	0/0			0/0/0	--Other
0/0/0	0	0	0/0	0/0/0	0/0	0//0	0/0/	2.7/2.7/2.7	2.8/2.7			0/0/0	-Hooks and other coupling devices, buffers, and parts thereof
													-Other:
0/0/0	0	0	0/0	0/0/0	0/0	0//0	0/0/	0/2.7/0	0/2.7			0/0/0	--Of locomotives
0/0/0	0	0	0.3/0.3	0/0/0	0/0	0//0	0/0/	2.7/2.7/2.7	2.7/2.7			0/0/0	--Other
													Railway or tramway track fixtures and fittings; mechanical (including electro-mechanical) signalling, safety or traffic control equipment for railways, tramways, roads, inland waterways, parking facilities, port installations or airfields; parts of the foregoing:
0/0/0	0	0	0/0	0/0/0	0/0	0//0	0/0/	0/0/0	0/0			0/0/0	---Rail automatic axle counting equipments
0/0/0	0	0	0/0	0/0/0	0/0	0//0	0/0/	0/0/0	0/0			0/0/0	---Other
													Containers (including containers for the transport of fluids) specially designed and equipped for carriage by one or more modes of transport:
													---Of 20 feet:
0/0/0	3.5	2.1	1.1/1.1	0/0/0	0/0	0/0/0	0/0/	0/0/9.5	9.5/0			0/0/0	----Insulated
0/0/0	3.5	2.1	1.1/1.1	0/0/0	0/0	0/0/0	0/0/	0/0/9.5	9.5/0			0/0/0	----Tank type
0/0/0	3.5	2.1	1.1/1.1	0/0/0	0/0	0/0/0	0/0/	0/0/9.5	9.5/0			0/0/0	----Other
													---Of 40 feet:
0/0/0	3.5	2.1	1.1/1.1	0/0/0	0/0	0/0/0	0/0/	0/0/9.5	9.5/0			0/0/0	----Insulated
0/0/0	3.5	2.1	1.1/1.1	0/0/0	0/0	0/0/0	0/0/	0/0/9.5	9.5/0			0/0/0	----Tank type
0/0/0	3.5	2.1	1.1/1.1	0/0/0	0/0	0/0/0	0/0/	0/0/9.5	9.5/0			0/0/0	----Other
0/0/0	3.5	2.1	1.1/1.1	0/0/0	0/0	0/0/0	0/0/	0/0/9.5	9.5/0			0/0/0	---Of 45,48,53 feet
0/0/0	3.5	2.1	1.1/1.1	0/0/0	0/0	0/0/0	0/0/	0/0/9.5	9.5/0			0/0/0	---Other

第八十七章
车辆及其零件、附件，但铁道及电车道车辆除外

注释：

一、本章不包括仅可在钢轨上运行的铁道及电车道车辆。

二、本章所称"牵引车、拖拉机"，是指主要为牵引或推动其他车辆、器具或重物的车辆。除了上述主要用途以外，不论其是否还具有装运工具、种子、肥料或其他货品的辅助装置。

用于安装在税目87.01的牵引车或拖拉机上，作为可替换设备的机器或作业工具，即使与牵引车或拖拉机一同报验，不论是否已安装在车(机)上，仍应归入其各自相应的税目。

三、装有驾驶室的机动车辆底盘，应归入税目87.02至87.04，而不归入税目87.06。

四、税目87.12包括所有儿童两轮车。其他儿童脚踏车归入税目95.03。

子目注释：

子目8708.22包括：

(一)带框的前挡风玻璃、后窗及其他窗；

(二)装有加热器件或者其他电气或电子装置的前挡风玻璃、后窗及其他窗，不论是否带框。上述货品专用于或主要用于税目87.01至87.05的机动车辆。

税则号列	货品名称〔CIQ扩展编码及品名－T2表示见附表2〕	最惠(%)	暂定税率	普通	增值/消费	出口退税	计量单位	监管条件/特殊证件	检验检疫	对美关税	亚太上/下
87.01	**牵引车、拖拉机(税目87.09的牵引车除外)：**										
8701.1000	-单轴拖拉机〔999〕	9		20	9/	9	辆/千克	6/		14	
	-半挂车用的公路牵引车：										
8701.2100	--仅装有压燃式活塞内燃发动机(柴油或半柴油发动机)的车辆〔999〕	6		20	13/	13	辆/千克	46Axy/	LM	31	
8701.2200	--同时装有压燃式活塞内燃发动机(柴油或半柴油发动机)及驱动电动机的车辆〔999〕	6		20	13/	13	辆/千克	46Axy/	LM	31	
8701.2300	--同时装有点燃式活塞内燃发动机及驱动电动机的车辆〔999〕	6		20	13/	13	辆/千克	46Axy/	LM	31	
8701.2400	--仅装有驱动电动机的车辆〔999〕	6		20	13/	13	辆/千克	46Axy/	LM	31	
8701.2900	--其他〔999〕	6		20	13/	13	辆/千克	46Axy/	LM		
8701.3000	-履带式牵引车、拖拉机										
8701.3000 10	履带式拖拉机〔999〕	6		20	9/	9,13	辆/千克	6A/	M	31	
8701.3000 90	履带式牵引车〔999〕	6		20	13/	9,13	辆/千克	6A/	M	31	
	-其他，其发动机功率：										
	--不超过18千瓦：										
8701.9110	---拖拉机〔999〕	8		20	13/	9,13	辆/千克	6A/	LM	13	
8701.9190	---其他〔999〕	8		20	13/	9,13	辆/千克	6A/	LM	33	
	--超过18千瓦，但不超过37千瓦：										
8701.9210	---拖拉机〔999〕	8		20	13/	9,13	辆/千克	6A/	LM	13	
8701.9290	---其他〔999〕	8		20	13/	9,13	辆/千克	6A/	LM	33	
	--超过37千瓦，但不超过75千瓦：										
8701.9310	---拖拉机〔999〕	8		20	13/	9,13	辆/千克	6A/	M	13	
8701.9390	---其他〔999〕	8		20	13/	9,13	辆/千克	6A/	LM	33	
	--超过75千瓦，但不超过130千瓦：										
8701.9410	---拖拉机										
8701.9410 10	发动机功率超过110千瓦但不超过130千瓦的轮式拖拉机〔999〕	8	5	20	13/	9,13	辆/千克	6A/	M	10	
8701.9410 90	发动机功率超过75千瓦但不超过130千瓦的其他拖拉机〔999〕	8		20	13/	9,13	辆/千克	6A/	M	13	
8701.9490	---其他〔999〕	8		20	13/	9,13	辆/千克	6A/	LM	33	
	--超过130千瓦：										
8701.9510	---拖拉机										
8701.9510 10	发动机功率超过130千瓦的轮式拖拉机〔999〕	8	5	20	13/	9,13	辆/千克	6A/	M	10	
8701.9510 90	发动机功率超过130千瓦的其他拖拉机〔999〕	8		20	13/	9,13	辆/千克	6A/	M	13	
8701.9590	---其他〔999〕	8		20	13/	9,13	辆/千克	6A/	LM	33	
87.02	**客运机动车辆，10座及以上(包括驾驶座)：**										
	-仅装有压燃式活塞内燃发动机(柴油或半柴油发动机)的车辆：										
8702.1020	---机坪客车〔999〕	4		90	13/	13	辆/千克	6AO/	M		
	---其他：										
8702.1091	----30座及以上(大型客车)〔999〕	15		90	13/	13	辆/千克	46AOxy/	LM		
8702.1092	----20座及以上，但不超过29座										
8702.1092 10	20≤座≤23仅装有压燃式活塞内燃发动机(柴油或半柴油发动机)的客车〔999〕	15		230	13/5	13	辆/千克	46AOxy/	LM		
8702.1092 90	24≤座≤29仅装有压燃式活塞内燃发动机(柴油或半柴油发动机)的客车〔999〕	15		230	13/	13	辆/千克	46AOxy/	LM		
8702.1093	----10座及以上，但不超过19座〔999〕	15		230	13/5	13	辆/千克	46AOxy/	LM	20	

Chapter 87
Vehicles other than railway or tramway rolling-stock, and parts and accessories thereof

Notes:

1. This Chapter does not cover railway or tramway rolling-stock designed solely for running on rails.
2. For the purposes of this Chapter, "tractors" means vehicles constructed essentially for hauling or pushing another vehicle, appliance or load, whether or not they contain subsidiary provision for the transport, in connection with the main use of the tractor, of tools, seeds, fertilizers or other goods.
   Machines and working tools designed for fitting to tractors of headingNo. 87. 01 as interchangeable equipment remain classified in their respective headings even if presented with the tractor, and whether or not mounted on it.
3. Motor chassis fitted with cabs fall in headings No. 87. 02 to 87. 04, and not in headingNo. 87. 06.
4. HeadingNo. 87. 12 includes all children's bicycles. Other children's cycles fall in headingNo. 95. 03.

Subheading Note:

1. Subheading 8708.22 covers :
   (c) front windscreens (windshields), rear windows and other windows, framed; and
   (d) front windscreens (windshields), rear windows and other windows, whether or not framed, incorporating heating devices or other electrical or electronic devices, when suitable for use solely or principally with the motor vehicles of headings 87.01 to 87.05.".

协定税率 %								RCEP		特惠税率 %			Article Description
东/冰/格	巴基斯坦	韩国	瑞士上/下	哥/秘/柬	澳/毛	新西/坡/智	中国港/澳/台	东盟及马来/澳/韩	日/新	亚太2国	老/柬/缅	98/97/95	
													Tractors (other than tractors of h eading No. 87. 09):
0/0/0	2	1.8	0/0	0/0/0	0/0	0//0	0/0/	0/0/8.1	8.2/0			0/0/0	-Pedestrian controlled tractors
													-Road tractor for semi—trailer:
5/0/0	4.8	2.8	0/0	0//0	0/0	0//0	0/0/	5/5/	/5			0/0/	-- With only compression—ignition internal combustion piston engine (diesel or semi—diesel)
5/0/0	4.8	2.8	0/0	0//0	0/0	0//0	0/0/	5/5/	/5			0/0/	-- With both compression—ignition internal combustion piston engine (diesel or semi—diesel) and electric motor as motors for propulsion
5/0/0	4.8	2.8	0/0	0//0	0/0	0//0	0/0/	5/5/	/5			0/0/	-- With both spark—ignition internal combustion piston engine and electric motor as motors for propulsion
5/0/0	4.8	2.8	0/0	0//0	0/0	0//0	0/0/	5/5/	/5			0/0/	-- With only electric motor for propulsion
5/0/0	4.8	2.8	0/0	0//0	0/0	0//0	0/0/	5/5/	/5			0/0/	-- Other
													-Track-laying tractors
0/0/0	0	0	0/0	0/0/0	0/0	0//0	0/0/	0/0/0	0/0			0/0/0	Track-laying tractors
0/0/0	0	0	0/0	0/0/0	0/0	0//0	0/0/	0/0/0	0/0			0/0/0	Track-laying tractors
													-Other, of an engine power:
													--Not exceeding 18kW:
0/0/0	0	0	0/0	0/0/0	0/0	0//0	0/0/	0/0/0	7.3/0			0/0/0	---Tractors
0/0/0	2	0	0/0	0/0/0	0/0	0//0	0/0/	0/0/0	7.3/0			0/0/0	---other
													--Exceeding 18kW, but not exceeding 37kW:
0/0/0	0	0	0/0	0/0/0	0/0	0//0	0/0/	0/0/0	7.3/0			0/0/0	---Tractors
0/0/0	2	0	0/0	0/0/0	0/0	0//0	0/0/	0/0/0	7.3/0			0/0/0	---Other
													--Exceeding 37kW, but not exceeding 75kW:
0/0/0	0	0	0/0	0/0/0	0/0	0//0	0/0/	0/0/0	7.3/0			0/0/0	---Tractors
0/0/0	2	0	0/0	0/0/0	0/0	0//0	0/0/	0/0/0	7.3/0			0/0/0	---Other
													--Exceeding 75kW, but not exceeding 130kW:
													---Tractors
0/0/0	0	0	0/0	0/0/0	0/0	0//0	0/0/	0/0/0	7.3/0			0/0/0	Wheeled tractors, Engine power exceeding 110 kW but not exceeding 130 kw
0/0/0	0	0	0/0	0/0/0	0/0	0//0	0/0/	0/0/0	7.3/0			0/0/0	Other tractors, Engine power exceeding 75 kW but not exceeding 130 kw
0/0/0	2	0	0/0	0/0/0	0/0	0//0	0/0/	0/0/0	7.3/0			0/0/0	---Other
													--Exceeding 130kw:
													---Tractors
0/0/0	0	0	0/0	0/0/0	0/0	0//0	0/0/	0/0/0	7.3/0			0/0/0	Wheeled tractors, Engine power exceeding 130 kw
0/0/0	0	0	0/0	0/0/0	0/0	0//0	0/0/	0/0/0	7.3/0			0/0/0	Wheeled tractors, Engine power exceeding 130 kw
0/0/0	2	0	0/0	0/0/0	0/0	0//0	0/0/	0/0/0	7.3/0			0/0/0	---Other
													Motor vehicles for the transport of ten or more persons, including the driver:
													-With only compression-ignition internal combustion piston engine(diesel or semidiesel):
0/0/0	0	1.8	0/0	0/0/0	0/0	0//0	0/0/	3.6/3.6/3.6	3.6/3.6			0/0/0	---Buses for transport passengers at airport
													---Other:
/0/0		15		0//0	0/17.9	0//0	0/0/					0/0/	----With 30 seats or more
													----With 20 seats or more, but not exceeding 29 seats
/0/0		15		0//0	0/17.9	0//0	0/0/					0/0/	Passenger buses, 20-23 seats, with compression- ignition internal combustion piston engine(with diesel or semidiesel engine)
/0/0		15		0//0	0/17.9	0//0	0/0/					0/0/	Passenger buses, 21-29 seats, with compression- ignition internal combustion piston engine(diesel or semi-diesel)
/0/0		15		0//0	0/17.9	0//0	0/0/					0/0/	----With 10 Seats or more, but not exceeding 19 seats

税则号列	货品名称〔CIQ 扩展编码及品名－T2 表示见附表 2〕	最惠(%)	暂定税率	普通	增值/消费	出口退税	计量单位	监管条件/特殊证件	检验检疫	对美关税	亚太上/下
	-同时装有压燃式活塞内燃发动机(柴油或半柴油发动机)及驱动电动机的车辆:										
8702.2010	---机坪客车〔999〕	4		90	13/	13	辆/千克	6AO/	M		
	---其他:										
8702.2091	----30 座及以上(大型客车)〔999〕	15		90	13/	13	辆/千克	46AOxy/	LM		
8702.2092	----20 座及以上,但不超过 29 座										
8702.2092 10	20≤座≤23 同时装有压燃式活塞内燃发动机(柴油或半柴油发动机)及驱动电动机的客车〔999〕	15		230	13/5	13	辆/千克	46AOxy/	LM		
8702.2092 90	24≤座≤29 同时装有压燃式活塞内燃发动机(柴油或半柴油发动机)及驱动电动机的客车〔999〕	15		230	13/0	13	辆/千克	46AOxy/	LM		
8702.2093	----10 座及以上,但不超过 19 座〔999〕	15		230	13/5	13	辆/千克	46AOxy/	LM		
	-同时装有点燃式活塞内燃发动机及驱动电动机的车辆:										
8702.3010	---30 座及以上(大型客车)〔999〕	15		90	13/	13	辆/千克	46AOxy/	LM		
8702.3020	---20 座及以上,但不超过 29 座										
8702.3020 10	20≤座≤23 同时装有点燃式活塞内燃发动机及驱动电动机的客车〔999〕	15		230	13/5	13	辆/千克	46AOxy/	LM		
8702.3020 90	24≤座≤29 同时装有点燃式活塞内燃发动机及驱动电动机的客车〔999〕	15		230	13/0	13	辆/千克	46AOxy/	LM		
8702.3030	---10 座及以上,但不超过 19 座〔999〕	15		230	13/5	13	辆/千克	46AOxy/	LM		
	-仅装有驱动电动机的车辆:										
8702.4010	---30 座及以上(大型客车)										
8702.4010 10	纯电动机坪客车〔999〕	15	4	90	13/	13	辆/千克	6AO/	M		
8702.4010 90	其他 30 座及以上仅装有驱动电动机的大型客车〔999〕	15		90	13/	13	辆/千克	46AOxy/	M		
8702.4020	---20 座及以上,但不超过 29 座										
8702.4020 10	20≤座≤23 仅装有驱动电动机的客车〔999〕	15		230	13/5	13	辆/千克	46AOxy/	LM		
8702.4020 90	24≤座≤29 仅装有驱动电动机的客车〔999〕	15		230	13/0	13	辆/千克	46AOxy/	LM		
8702.4030	---10 座及以上,但不超过 19 座〔999〕	15		230	13/5	13	辆/千克	46AOxy/	LM		
	-其他:										
8702.9010	---30 座及以上(大型客车)〔999〕	15		90	13/	13	辆/千克	46AOxy/	LM		
8702.9020	---20 座及以上,但不超过 29 座										
8702.9020 01	20≤座≤23 装有非压燃式活塞内燃发动机的客车〔999〕	15		230	13/5	13	辆/千克	46AOxy/	LM		
8702.9020 90	24≤座≤29 装有非压燃式活塞内燃发动机的客车〔999〕	15		230	13/	13	辆/千克	46AOxy/	LM		
8702.9030	---10 座及以上,但不超过 19 座〔999〕	15		230	13/5	13	辆/千克	46AOxy/	LM		
87.03	**主要用于载人的机动车辆(税目 87.02 的货品除外),包括旅行小客车及赛车:**										
	-雪地行走专用车;高尔夫球车及类似车辆:										
	---高尔夫球车及类似车辆:										
8703.1011	----全地形车〔101 电动全地形车,102 内燃机动全地形车,103 混合动力全地形车,104 其他能源全地形车〕	15		150	13/	13	辆/千克	46xy/			
8703.1019	----其他〔999〕	15		150	13/	13	辆/千克	6/			
8703.1090	---其他〔999〕	15		150	13/	13	辆/千克	6/			
	-仅装有点燃式活塞内燃发动机的其他车辆:										
	--气缸容量(排气量)不超过 1000 毫升:										
8703.2130	---小轿车										
8703.2130 10	仅装有排量≤1 升的点燃式活塞内燃发动机的小轿车〔999〕	15		230	13/1	13	辆/千克	46AOxy/	LM		13.5/13.5
8703.2130 90	仅装有排量≤1 升的点燃式活塞内燃发动机小轿车的成套散件〔999〕	15		230	13/	13	辆/千克	46Oxy/			13.5/13.5
8703.2140	---越野生(4 轮驱动)										
8703.2140 10	仅装有排量≤1 升的点燃式活塞内燃发动机的越野车(4 轮驱动)〔999〕	15		230	13/1	13	辆/千克	46AOxy/	LM		13.5/13.5
8703.2140 90	仅装有排量≤1 升的点燃式活塞内燃发动机的越野车(4 轮驱动)的成套散件〔999〕	15		230	13/	13	辆/千克	46Oxy/			13.5/13.5
8703.2150	---9 座及以下的小客车										
8703.2150 10	仅装有排量≤1 升的点燃式活塞内燃发动机的小客车(9 座及以下)〔999〕	15		230	13/1	13	辆/千克	46AOxy/	LM		13.5/13.5

协定税率 %								RCEP		特惠税率 %			Article Description
东/冰/格	巴基斯坦	韩国	瑞士上/下	哥/秘/柬	澳/毛	新西/坡/智	中国港/澳/台	东盟及马来/澳/韩	日/新	亚太2国	老/柬/缅	98/97/95	
													--With both compression—ignition internal combustion piston engine(diesel or semi—diesel)and electric motor as motors for propulsion:
0/0/0	0	1.8	0/0	0/0/0	0/0	0//0	0/0/	3.6/3.6/3.6	3.6/3.6			0/0/0	---Buses for transport passengers at airport
													---Other:
/0/0		15		0//0	0/17.9	0//0	0/0/					0/0/	----With 30 seats or more
													----With 20 seats or more.but not exceeding 29 seats
/0/0		15		0//0	0/17.9	0//0	0/0/					0/0/	Passenger buses, 20-23 seats, with compression- ignition internal combustion piston engine(with diesel or semidiesel engine,with drive motor)
/0/0		15		0//0	0/17.9	0//0	0/0/					0/0/	
/0/0		15		0//	0/17.9	0//0	0/0/					0//	----With 10 seats or more.but not exceeding 19 seats
													-Vehicles equipped with positive ignition piston internal combustion engine and driving motor at the same time
5/0/0		15		0//0	0/17.9	0//0	0/0/					0/0/	---With 30 seats or more
													---With 20 seats or more.but not exceeding 29 seats
5/0/0		15		0//0	0/17.9	0//0	0/0/					0/0/	Passenger buses, 20-23 seats, with spark-ignition internal combustion reciprocating piston engine,with drive motor
5/0/0		15		0//0	0/17.9	0//0	0/0/					0/0/	Passenger buses, 24-29 seats, with spark-ignition internal combustion reciprocating piston engine,with drive motor
5/0/0		15		0/0/0	0/17.9	0//0	0/0/					0/0/0	---With 10 seats or more,but not exceeding 19 seats
													-With only electric motor for propulsion:
													---With 30 seats or more
5/0/0		15		0//0	0/17.9	0//0	0/0/				//	0/0/	Pure electric bus
5/0/0		15		0//0	0/17.9	0//0	0/0/				//	0/0/	Other large buses with 30 seats or more only equipped with drive motors
													---With 20 seats or more,but not exceeding 29 seats
5/0/0		15		0//0	0/17.9	0//0	0/0/					0/0/	Passenger buses,20-23 seats,with drive motor
5/0/0		15		0//0	0/17.9	0//0	0/0/					0/0/	Passenger buses,24-29 seats,with drive motor
5/0/0		15		0/0/0	0/17.9	0//0	0/0/					0/0/0	---With 10 seats or more,but not exceeding 19 seats
													-Other:
5/0/0		15		0//0	0/17.9	0//0	0/0/					0/0/	---With 30 seats or more
													---With 20 seats or more, but not exceeding 29 seats
5/0/0		15		0//0	0/17.9	0//0	0/0/					0/0/	Buses for transport passengers, with non-compression-ignition internal combustion piston engine,with 20～23 seats
5/0/0		15		0//0	0/17.9	0//0	0/0/					0/0/	Buses for transport passengers, with non-compression-ignition internal combustion piston engine,with 24～29 seats
5/0/0		15		0/0/0	0/17.9	0//0	0/0/					0/0/0	---With 10 seats or more, but not exceeding 19 seats
													Motor cars and other motor vehicles principally designed for the transport of persons (other than those of headingNo. 87.02), including station wagons and racing cars:
													-Vehicles specially designed for travelling on snow; golf cars and similar vehicles:
													---Golf cars and similar vehicles
0/0/0		15		0/0/0	0/17.9	0/0/0	0/0/	23.8/23.8/23.8	/23.8			0/0/0	----All terrain vehicle
0/0/0	20			0/0/0	0/17.9	0/0/0	0/0/	15/15/	/15			0/0/0	----Other
0/0/0				0/0/0	0/17.9	0/0/0	0/0/	15/15/	/15			0/0/0	---Other
													-Other vehicles with positive ignition piston internal combustion engines only:
													--Of a cylinder capacity not exceeding 1000 cc:
													---Saloon cars
/0/	22.5			0//	0/17.9	0//0	0/0/					0//	Saloon cars of cylinder capacity not exceeding 1L, with spark-ignition internal combustion eciprocating piston engine
/0/	22.5			0//	0/17.9	0//0	0/0/					0//	Complete parts of saloon cars with spark-ignition internal combustion reciprocating piston engine,cylinder capacity≤1L
													---Gross-country cars (4WD)
/0/	22.5			0//	0/17.9	0//0	0/0/					0//	Off-road vehicles(4WD) of cylinder capacity not exceeding 1L, with spark-ignition internal combustion eciprocating piston engine
/0/	22.5			0//	0/17.9	0//0	0/0/					0//	Complete parts of gross-country cars (4WD) with spark-ignition internal combustion reciprocating piston engine,cylinger capacity≤1L
													---Station wagons (with 9 seats or less)
/0/	22.5			0//	0/17.9	0//0	0/0/					0//	Station wagons(9 seats or less),of a cylinder capacity exceeding 1L, with spark-ignition internal combustion reciprocating piston engine

税则号列	货品名称〔CIQ 扩展编码及品名—T2 表示见附表 2〕	最惠(%)	暂定税率	普通	增值/消费	出口退税	计量单位	监管条件/特殊证件	检验检疫	对美关税	亚太上/下
8703.2150 90	仅装有排量≤1 升的点燃式活塞内燃发动机的小客车的成套散件(9 座及以下)〔999〕	15		230	13/	13	辆/千克	46Oxy/			13.5/13.5
8703.2190	---其他										
8703.2190 10	仅装有排量≤1 升的点燃式活塞内燃发动机的其他载人车辆〔999〕	15		230	13/1	13	辆/千克	46AOxy/	LM		13.5/13.5
8703.2190 90	仅装有排量≤1 升的点燃式活塞内燃发动机的其他载人车辆的成套散件〔999〕	15		230	13/	13	辆/千克	46Oxy/			13.5/13.5
	--气缸容量(排气量)超过 1000 毫升,但不超过 1500 毫升:										
8703.2230	---小轿车										
8703.2230 10	仅装有 1<排量≤1.5 升点燃式活塞内燃发动机小轿车〔999〕	15		230	13/3	13	辆/千克	46AOxy/	LM		13.5/13.5
8703.2230 90	仅装有 1<排量≤1.5 升点燃式活塞内燃发动机小轿车的成套散件〔999〕	15		230	13/	13	辆/千克	46Oxy/			13.5/13.5
8703.2240	---越野车(4 轮驱动)										
8703.2240 10	仅装有 1<排量≤1.5 升点燃式活塞内燃发动机四轮驱动越野车〔999〕	15		230	13/3	13	辆/千克	46AOxy/	LM		13.5/13.5
8703.2240 90	仅装有 1<排量≤1.5 升点燃式活塞内燃发动机四轮驱动越野车的成套散件〔999〕	15		230	13/	13	辆/千克	46Oxy/			13.5/13.5
8703.2250	---9 座及以下的小客车										
8703.2250 10	仅装有 1<排量≤1.5 升点燃式活塞内燃发动机小客车(≤9 座)〔999〕	15		230	13/3	13	辆/千克	46AOxy/	LM		13.5/13.5
8703.2250 90	仅装有 1<排量≤1.5 升点燃式活塞内燃发动机小客车的成套散件(≤9 座)〔999〕	15		230	13/	13	辆/千克	46Oxy/			13.5/13.5
8703.2290	---其他										
8703.2290 10	仅装有 1<排量≤1.5 升点燃式活塞内燃发动机其他载人车辆〔999〕	15		230	13/3	13	辆/千克	46AOxy/	LM		13.5/13.5
8703.2290 90	仅装有 1<排量≤1.5 升点燃式活塞内燃发动机其他载人车的成套散件〔999〕	15		230	13/	13	辆/千克	46Oxy/			13.5/13.5
	--气缸容量(排气量)超过 1500 毫升,但不超过 3000 毫升:										
	---气缸容量(排气量)超过 1500 毫升,但不超过 2000 毫升:										
8703.2341	----小轿车										
8703.2341 10	仅装有 1.5<排量≤2 升的点燃式活塞内燃发动机小轿车〔999〕	15		230	13/5	13	辆/千克	46AOxy/	LM		13.5/13.5
8703.2341 90	仅装有 1.5<排量≤2 升的点燃式活塞内燃发动机小轿车的成套散件〔999〕	15		230	13/	13	辆/千克	46Oxy/			13.5/13.5
8703.2342	----越野车(4 轮驱动)										
8703.2342 10	仅装有 1.5<排量≤2 升的点燃式活塞内燃发动机越野车(4 轮驱动)〔999〕	15		230	13/5	13	辆/千克	46AOxy/	LM		13.5/13.5
8703.2342 90	仅装有 1.5<排量≤2 升的点燃式活塞内燃发动机越野车的成套散件(4 轮驱动)〔999〕	15		230	13/	13	辆/千克	46Oxy/			13.5/13.5
8703.2343	----9 座及以下的小客车										
8703.2343 10	仅装有 1.5<排量≤2 升的点燃式活塞内燃发动机小客车(9 座及以下的)〔999〕	15		230	13/5	13	辆/千克	46AOxy/	LM		13.5/13.5
8703.2343 90	仅装有 1.5<排量≤2 升的点燃式活塞内燃发动机小客车的成套散件(9 座及以下的)〔999〕	15		230	13/	13	辆/千克	46Oxy/			13.5/13.5
8703.2349	----其他										
8703.2349 10	仅装有 1.5<排量≤2 升的点燃式活塞内燃发动机的其他载人车辆〔999〕	15		230	13/5	13	辆/千克	46AOxy/	LM		13.5/13.5

协定税率 %								RCEP		特惠税率 %			Article Description
东/冰/格	巴基斯坦	韩国	瑞士上/下	哥/秘/柬	澳/毛	新西/坡/智	中国港/澳/台	东盟及马来/澳/韩	日/新	亚太2国	老/柬/缅	98/97/95	
/0/	22.5			0//	0/17.9	0//0	0/0/					0//	Complete parts of station wagons (with 9 seats or less) with spark-ignition internal combustion reciprocating piston engine, cylinder capacity≤1L
													---Other
/0/	22.5			0//	0/17.9	0//0	0/0/					0//	Other passenger vehicles of a cylinder capacity exceeding 1L with spark-ignition internal combustion reciprocating piston engine
/0/	22.5			0//	0/17.9	0//0	0/0/					0//	Complete parts of other vehicles with spark-ignition internal combustion reciprocating piston engine, cylinder capacity≤1L
													--Of a cylinder capacity exceeding 1000ccc but not exceeding 1500cc:
													---Saloon cars
/0/	22.5	22.5		0//	0/17.9	0//0	0/0/					0//	Saloon cars of cylinder capacity exceeding 1L but not exceeding 1.5L, with spark-ignition internal combustion eciprocating piston engine
/0/	22.5	22.5		0//	0/17.9	0//0	0/0/					0//	Complete parts of saloon car with spark-igition internal combustion reciprocating piston engine, 1L<cylinder capacity≤1. 5L
													---Cross-country cars (4WD)
/0/	22.5			0//	0/17.9	0//0	0/0/					0//	Off-road vehicles (4WD) of cylinder capacity exceeding 1L but not exceeding 1.5L, with spark-ignition internal combustion eciprocating piston engine
/0/	22.5			0//	0/17.9	0//0	0/0/					0//	Complete parts of cross-country cars (4WD) with spark-ignition inernal combustion reciprocating piston engine, 1L<cylinder capacity≤1. 5L
													---Station wagons (with 9 seats or less)
/0/	22.5			0//	0/17.9	0//0	0/0/					0//	Station wagons(9 seats or less) of cylinder capacity exceeding 1L but not exceeding 1.5L, with spark-ignition internal combustion eciprocating piston engine
/0/	22.5			0//	0/17.9	0//0	0/0/					0//	Complete parts of station wagons (with 9seats or less) with spark-ignition internal combustion reciprocating piston engine, 1L<cylinder capacity≤1. 5L
													---Other
/0/	22.5			0//	0/17.9	0//0	0/0/					0//	Other passenger vehicles of cylinder capacity exceeding 1L but not exceeding 1.5L, with spark-ignition internal combustion eciprocating piston engine
/0/	22.5			0//	0/17.9	0//0	0/0/					0//	Complete parts of other vehicles with spark-ingition internal combustion reciprocating piston engine, 1L<cylinder capacity ≤1. 5L
													--Of a cylinder capacity exceeding 1500cc but not exceeding 3000cc:
													---Of a cylinder capacity exceeding 1500cc but not exceeding 2000cc:
													Saloon cars
/0/	22.5	22.5		0//	5/17.9	0//0	0/0/					0//	Saloon cars of cylinder capacity exceeding 1.5L but not exceeding 2L, with spark-ignition internal combustion eciprocating piston engine
/0/	22.5	22.5		0//	5/17.9	0//0	0/0/					0//	Complete parts of saloon cars with spark-ignition internal cmbustion reciprocating piston engine, 1. 5L<cylinder capacity≤2L
													----Cross-country cars (4WD)
/0/	22.5	22.5		0//	5/17.9	0//0	0/0/					0//	Off-road vehicles (4WD) of cylinder capacity exceeding 1.5L but not exceeding 2L, with spark-ignition internal combustion eciprocating piston engine
/0/	22.5	22.5		0//	5/17.9	0//0	0/0/					0//	Complete parts of cross-country cars (4WD) with spark-ignition internal combustion reciprocating piston engine, 1. 5L<cylinder capacity≤2L
													----Station wagons (with 9 seats or less)
/0/	22.5	22.5		0//	5/17.9	0//0	0/0/					0//	Station wagons(9 seats or less) of cylinder capacity exceeding 1.5L but not exceeding 2L, with spark-ignition internal combustion eciprocating piston engine
/0/	22.5	22.5		0//	5/17.9	0//0	0/0/					0//	Complete parts of station wagons (with 9 seats or less) with spark-ignition internal combustion reciprocating piston engine, 1. 5L<cylinder capacity≤2L
													----Other
/0/	22.5			0//	5/17.9	0//0	0/0/					0//	Other passenger vehicles of cylinder capacity exceeding 1.5L but not exceeding 2L, with spark-ignition internal combustion eciprocating piston engine

税则号列	货品名称〔CIQ 扩展编码及品名－T2 表示见附表 2〕	最惠(%)	暂定税率	普通	增值/消费	出口退税	计量单位	监管条件/特殊证件	检验检疫	对美关税	亚太上/下
8703.2349　90	仅装有 1.5＜排量≤2 升的点燃式活塞内燃发动机的其他载人车辆的成套散件〔999〕	15		230	13/	13	辆/千克	46Oxy/			13.5/13.5
	---气缸容量(排气量)超过 2000 毫升，但不超过 2500 毫升：										
8703.2351	----小轿车										
8703.2351　10	仅装有 2＜排量≤2.5 升的点燃式活塞内燃发动机小轿车〔999〕	15		230	13/9	13	辆/千克	46AOxy/	LM		13.5/13.5
8703.2351　90	仅装有 2＜排量≤2.5 升的点燃式活塞内燃发动机小轿车的成套散件〔999〕	15		230	13/	13	辆/千克	46Oxy/			13.5/13.5
8703.2352	----越野车(4 轮驱动)										
8703.2352　10	仅装有 2＜排量≤2.5 升的点燃式活塞内燃发动机越野车(4 轮驱动)〔999〕	15		230	13/9	13	辆/千克	46AOxy/	LM		13.5/13.5
8703.2352　90	仅装有 2＜排量≤2.5 升的点燃式活塞内燃发动机越野车的成套散件(4 轮驱动)〔999〕	15		230	13/	13	辆/千克	46Oxy/			13.5/13.5
8703.2353	----9 座及以下的小客车										
8703.2353　10	仅装有 2＜排量≤2.5 升的点燃式活塞内燃发动机小客车(9 座及以下的)〔999〕	15		230	13/9	13	辆/千克	46AOxy/	LM		13.5/13.5
8703.2353　90	仅装有 2＜排量≤2.5 升的点燃式活塞内燃发动机的小客车的成套散件(9 座及以下的)〔999〕	15		230	13/	13	辆/千克	46Oxy/			13.5/13.5
8703.2359	----其他										
8703.2359　10	仅装有 2＜排量≤2.5 升的点燃式活塞内燃发动机的其他载人车辆〔999〕	15		230	13/9	13	辆/千克	46AOxy/	LM		13.5/13.5
8703.2359　90	仅装有 2＜排量≤2.5 升的点燃式活塞内燃发动机的其他载人车辆的成套散件〔999〕	15		230	13/	13	辆/千克	46Oxy/			13.5/13.5
	---气缸容量(排气量)超过 2500 毫升，但不超过 3000 毫升：										
8703.2361	----小轿车										
8703.2361　10	仅装有 2.5＜排量≤3 升的点燃式活塞内燃发动机小轿车〔999〕	15		270	13/12	13	辆/千克	46AOxy/	ML		13.5/13.5
8703.2361　90	仅装有 2.5＜排量≤3 升的点燃式活塞内燃发动机小轿车的成套散件〔999〕	15		270	13/	13	辆/千克	46Oxy/			13.5/13.5
8703.2362	----越野车(4 轮驱动)										
8703.2362　10	仅装有 2.5＜排量≤3 升的点燃式活塞内燃发动机越野车(4 轮驱动)〔999〕	15		270	13/12	13	辆/千克	46AOxy/	ML		13.5/13.5
8703.2362　90	仅装有 2.5＜排量≤3 升的点燃式活塞内燃发动机越野车的成套散件(4 轮驱动)〔999〕	15		270	13/	13	辆/千克	46Oxy/			13.5/13.5
8703.2363	----9 座及以下的小客车										
8703.2363　10	仅装有 2.5＜排量≤3 升的点燃式活塞内燃发动机小客车(9 座及以下的)〔999〕	15		270	13/12	13	辆/千克	46AOxy/	ML		13.5/13.5
8703.2363　90	仅装有 2.5＜排量≤3 升的点燃式活塞内燃发动机小客车的成套散件(9 座及以下的)〔999〕	15		270	13/	13	辆/千克	46Oxy/			13.5/13.5
8703.2369	----其他										
8703.2369　10	仅装有 2.5＜排量≤3 升的点燃式活塞内燃发动机的其他载人车辆〔999〕	15		270	13/12	13	辆/千克	46AOxy/	ML		13.5/13.5
8703.2369　90	仅装有 2.5＜排量≤3 升的点燃式活塞内燃发动机的其他载人车辆的成套散件〔999〕	15		270	13/12	13	辆/千克	46Oxy/			13.5/13.5
	--气缸容量(排气量)超过 3000 毫升： ---气缸容量(排气量)超过 3000 毫升，但不超过 4000 毫升：										
8703.2411	----小轿车										

协定税率 %								RCEP		特惠税率 %			Article Description
东/冰/格	巴基斯坦	韩国	瑞士 上/下	哥/秘/柬	澳/毛	新西/坡/智	中国港/澳/台	东盟及马来/澳/韩	日/新	亚太2国	老/柬/缅	98/97/95	
/0/	22.5			0//	5/17.9	0//0	0/0/					0//	Complete parts of other motor vehicles principally designed for the transport of person's with spark-ignition internal combustion reciprocating piston engine, 1. 5L<cylinder capacity ≤2L
													---Of a culinder capacity exceeding 2000cc but not exceeding 2500cc:
													----Saloon cars
/0/	22.5	22.5		0//	5/17.9	0//0	0/0/					0//	Saloon cars of cylinder capacity exceeding 2L but not exceeding 2.5L, with spark-ignition internal combustion eciprocating piston engine
/0/	22.5	22.5		0//	5/17.9	0//0	0/0/					0//	Complete parts of saloon cars with spark-ignition internal combustion reciprocating piston engine, 2L<cylinder capacity ≤2. 5L
													----Cross-country cars (4WD)
/0/	22.5	22.5		0//	5/17.9	0//0	0/0/					0//	Off-road vehicles (4WD) of cylinder capacity exceeding 2L but not exceeding 2.5L, with spark-ignition internal combustion eciprocating piston engine
/0/	22.5	22.5		0//	5/17.9	0//0	0/0/					0//	Complete parts of crass-country cars (4WD) with spark-ignition internal combustion reciprocating piston engine, 2L<cylinder capacity≤2. 5L
													----Station wagons (with 9 seats or less)
/0/	22.5	22.5		0//	5/17.9	0//0	0/0/					0//	Station wagons (9 seats or less) of cylinder capacity exceeding 2L but not exceeding 2.5L, with spark-ignition internal combustion eciprocating piston engine
/0/	22.5	22.5		0//	5/17.9	0//0	0/0/					0//	Complete parts of station wagons (with 9 seats or less) with spark-ignition internal combustion reciprocating piston engine, 2L<cylinder capacity≤2. 5L
													----Other
/0/	22.5			0//	5/17.9	0//0	0/0/					0//	Other passenger vehicles of cylinder capacity exceeding 2L but not exceeding 2.5L, with spark-ignition internal combustion eciprocating piston engine
/0/	22.5			0//	5/17.9	0//0	0/0/					0//	Complete parts of other motor vehicles (with 9 seats or less) designed for transport of person's, with spark-ignition internal combustion reciprocating piston engine, 2L<cylinder capacity≤2. 5L
													---Of a cylinder capacity exceeding 2500cc but not exceeding 3000cc:
													----Saloon cars
/0/	22.5	22.5		0//	5/17.9	0//0	0/0/	15//	15/			0//	Saloon cars of cylinder capacity exceeding 2.5L but not exceeding 3L, with spark-ignition internal combustion eciprocating piston engine
/0/	22.5	22.5		0//	5/17.9	0//0	0/0/	15//	15/			0//	Complete parts of saloon cars with spark-ignition internal combustion reciprocating piston engine, 2. 5L<cylinder capacity≤3L
													----Cross-country cars (4WD)
0/0/	22.5			0//0	5/17.9	0/0/0	0/0/	15/15/	15/15			0//	Off-road vehicles (4WD) of cylinder capacity exceeding 2.5L but not exceeding 3L, with spark-ignition internal combustion eciprocating piston engine
0/0/	22.5			0//0	5/17.9	0/0/0	0/0/	15/15/	15/15			0//	Complete parts of cross-country cars (4WD) with spark-ignition internal combustion reciprocating piston engine, 2. 5L<cylinder capacity≤3L
													----Station wagons (with 9 seats or less)
0/0/	22.5	22.5		0//0	5/17.9	0/0/0	0/0/	15/15/	15/15			0//	Station wagons (9 seats or less) of cylinder capacity exceeding 2.5L but not exceeding 3L, with spark-ignition internal combustion eciprocating piston engine
0/0/	22.5	22.5		0//0	5/17.9	0/0/0	0/0/	15/15/	15/15			0//	Complete parts of station wagons (with 9 seats or less) with spark-ignition internal combustion reciporcating piston engine, 2. 5L<cylinder capacity≤3L
													----Other
0/0/	22.5			0//0	5/17.9	0/0/0	0/0/	15/15/	15/15			0//	Other passenger vehicles of cylinder capacity exceeding 2.5L but not exceeding 3L, with spark-ignition internal combustion eciprocating piston engine
0/0/	22.5			0//0	5/17.9	0/0/0	0/0/	15/15/	15/15			0//	Complete parts of other passenger vehicles of a cylinder capacity exceeding 2.5L but not exceeding 3L, with spark-ignition internal combustion reciprocating piston engine
													--Of a cylinder capacity exceeding 3000cc:
													---Of a cylinder capacity exceeding 3000cc but not exceeding 4000cc:
													----Saloon cars

税则号列	货品名称〔CIQ 扩展编码及品名－T2 表示见附表 2〕	最惠(%)	暂定税率	普通	增值/消费	出口退税	计量单位	监管条件/特殊证件	检验检疫	对美关税	亚太上/下
8703.2411 10	仅装有 3<排量≤4 升的点燃式活塞内燃发动机小轿车〔999〕	15		270	13/25	13	辆/千克	46AOxy/	LM		13.5/13.5
8703.2411 90	仅装有 3<排量≤4 升的点燃式活塞内燃发动机小轿车的成套散件〔999〕	15		270	13/	13	辆/千克	46Oxy/			13.5/13.5
8703.2412	----越野车(4 轮驱动)										
8703.2412 10	仅装有 3<排量≤4 升的点燃式活塞内燃发动机越野车(4 轮驱动)〔999〕	15		270	13/25	13	辆/千克	46AOxy/	LM		13.5/13.5
8703.2412 90	仅装有 3<排量≤4 升的点燃式活塞内燃发动机越野车的成套散件(4 轮驱动)〔999〕	15		270	13/	13	辆/千克	46Oxy/			13.5/13.5
8703.2413	----9 座及以下的小客车										
8703.2413 10	仅装有 3<排量≤4 升的点燃式活塞内燃发动机的小客车(9 座及以下的)〔999〕	15		270	13/25	13	辆/千克	46AOxy/	LM		13.5/13.5
8703.2413 90	仅装有 3<排量≤4 升的点燃式活塞内燃发动机的小客车的成套散件(9 座及以下的)〔999〕	15		270	13/	13	辆/千克	46Oxy/			13.5/13.5
8703.2419	----其他										
8703.2419 10	仅装有 3<排量≤4 升的点燃式活塞内燃发动机的其他载人车辆〔101 货车,102 其他汽车〕	15		270	13/25	13	辆/千克	46AOxy/	LM		13.5/13.5
8703.2419 90	仅装有 3<排量≤4 升的点燃式活塞内燃发动机的其他载人车辆的成套散件〔999〕	15		270	13/25	13	辆/千克	46Oxy/			13.5/13.5
	---气缸容量(排气量)超过 4000 毫升：										
8703.2421	----小轿车										
8703.2421 10	仅装有排气量>4 升的点燃式活塞内燃发动机小轿车〔999〕	15		270	13/40	13	辆/千克	46AOxy/	LM		13.5/13.5
8703.2421 90	仅装有排气量>4 升的点燃式活塞内燃发动机小轿车的成套散件〔999〕	15		270	13/	13	辆/千克	46Oxy/			13.5/13.5
8703.2422	----越野车(4 轮驱动)										
8703.2422 10	仅装有排气量>4 升的点燃式活塞内燃发动机越野车(4 轮驱动)〔999〕	15		270	13/40	13	辆/千克	46AOxy/	LM		13.5/13.5
8703.2422 90	仅装有排气量>4 升的点燃式活塞内燃发动机越野车的成套散件(4 轮驱动)〔999〕	15		270	13/	13	辆/千克	46Oxy/			13.5/13.5
8703.2423	----9 座及以下的小客车										
8703.2423 10	仅装有排气量>4 升的点燃式活塞内燃发动机的小客车(9 座及以下的)〔999〕	15		270	13/40	13	辆/千克	46AOxy/	LM		13.5/13.5
8703.2423 90	仅装有排气量>4 升的点燃式活塞内燃发动机的小客车的成套散件(9 座及以下的)〔999〕	15		270	13/	13	辆/千克	46Oxy/			13.5/13.5
8703.2429	----其他										
8703.2429 10	仅装有排气量>4 升的点燃式活塞内燃发动机的其他载人车辆〔999〕	15		270	13/40	13	辆/千克	46AOxy/	LM		13.5/13.5
8703.2429 90	仅装有排气量>4 升的点燃式活塞内燃发动机的其他载人车辆的成套散件〔999〕	15		270	13/40	13	辆/千克	46Oxy/			13.5/13.5
	-仅装有压燃式活塞内燃发动机(柴油或半柴油发动机)的其他车辆：										
	--气缸容量(排气量)不超过 1500 毫升：										
	---气缸容量(排气量)不超过 1000 毫升：										
8703.3111	----小轿车										
8703.3111 10	仅装有排气量≤1 升的压燃式活塞内燃发动机小轿车〔999〕	15		230	13/1	13	辆/千克	46AOxy/	LM		
8703.3111 90	仅装有排气量≤1 升的压燃式活塞内燃发动机小轿车的成套散件〔999〕	15		230	13/	13	辆/千克	46Oxy/			
8703.3119	----其他										
8703.3119 10	仅装有排气量≤1 升的压燃式活塞内燃发动机的其他载人车辆〔999〕	15		230	13/1	13	辆/千克	46AOxy/	LM		

协定税率 %								RCEP		特惠税率 %			Article Description
东/冰/格	巴基斯坦	韩国	瑞士上/下	哥/秘/柬	澳/毛	新西/坡/智	中国港/澳/台	东盟及马来/澳/韩	日/新	亚太2国	老/柬/缅	98/97/95	
/0/	22.5	22.5		0//0	5/17.9	0//0	0/0/	15//	15/			0/0/	Saloon cars of cylinder capacity exceeding 3L but not exceeding 4L, with spark-ignition internal combustion eciprocating piston engine
/0/	22.5	22.5		0//0	5/17.9	0//0	0/0/	15//	15/			0/0/	Complete parts of saloon cars with spark-ignition internal combustion reciprocating piston engine, 3L<cylinder capacity ≤4L
													----Cross-country cars (4WD)
/0/	22.5	22.5		0//0	5/17.9	0//0	0/0/	15//	15/			0/0/	Off-road vehicles (4WD) of cylinder capacity exceeding 3L but not exceeding 4L, with spark-ignition internal combustion eciprocating piston engine
/0/	22.5	22.5		0//0	5/17.9	0//0	0/0/	15//	15/			0/0/	Complete parts of crass-country cars (4WD) with spark-ignition internal combustion reciprocating piston engine, 3L<cylinder capacity≤4L
													----Station wagons (with 9 seats or less)
/0/	22.5			0//0	5/17.9	0//0	0/0/	15//	15/			0/0/	Station wagons (9 seats or less) of cylinder capacity exceeding 3L but not exceeding 4L, with spark-ignition internal combustion eciprocating piston engine
/0/	22.5			0//0	5/17.9	0//0	0/0/	15//	15/			0/0/	Complete parts of station wagons (with 9 seats or less) with spark-ignition internal combustion reciprocating piston engine, 3<cylinder capacity≤4L
													----Other
/0/	22.5			0//0	5/17.9	0//0	0/0/	15//	15/			0/0/	Other passenger vehicles of cylinder capacity exceeding 3L but not exceeding 4L, with spark-ignition internal combustion eciprocating piston engine
/0/	22.5			0//0	5/17.9	0//0	0/0/	15//	15/			0/0/	Complete parts of other passenger vehicles of a cylinder capacity exceeding 3L but not exceeding 4L, with spark-ignition internal combustion reciprocating piston engine
													---Of a cylinder capacity exceeding 4000cc:
													----Saloon cars
/0/	22.5	22.5		0//0	5/17.9	0//0	0/0/					0/0/	Saloon cars of cylinder capacity exceeding 4L, with spark-ignition internal combustion eciprocating piston engine
/0/	22.5	22.5		0//0	5/17.9	0//0	0/0/					0/0/	Complete parts of saloon cars with spork-ignition internal combustion reciprocating piston engine, cylinder capacity>4L
													----Cross-country cars (4WD)
/0/	22.5			0//0	5/17.9	0//0	0/0/					0/0/	Off-road vehicles (4WD) of cylinder capacity exceeding 4L, with spark-ignition internal combustion eciprocating piston engine
/0/	22.5			0//0	5/17.9	0//0	0/0/					0/0/	Complete parts of cross-country cars with spark-ignition internal combustion reciprocating piston engine, cylinder capacity>4L
													----Station wagons (with 9 seats or less)
/0/	22.5			0//0	5/17.9	0//0	0/0/					0/0/	Station wagons (9 seats or less) of cylinder capacity exceeding 4L, with spark-ignition internal combustion eciprocating piston engine
/0/	22.5			0//0	5/17.9	0//0	0/0/					0/0/	Complete parts of station wagons with spark-ignition internal combustion reciporcating piston engine, cylinder capacity>4L (with 9 seats or less)
													----Other
/0/	22.5			0//0	5/17.9	0//0	0/0/					0/0/	Other passenger vehicles of cylinder capacity exceeding 4L, with spark-ignition internal combustion eciprocating piston engine
/0/	22.5			0//0	5/17.9	0//0	0/0/					0/0/	Complete parts of other passenger vehicles of a cylinder capacity exceeding 4L, with spark-ignition internal combustion reciprocating piston engine
													-Other vehicles, with compression-ignition internal combustion piston engine (diesel or semi-diesel):
													--Of a cylinder capacity not exceedlirg 1500cc:
													---Of a cylinder capacity not exceeding 1000 cc:
													----Saloon cars
/0/0				0//0	5/17.9	0//0	0/0/					0/0/	Saloon cars of a cylinder capacity not exceeding 1L, with compression-ignition internal combustion reciprocating piston engine
/0/0				0//0	5/17.9	0//0	0/0/					0/0/	Complete parts of saloon cars with compression-ignition internal combustion piston engine, cylinder capacity≤1L
													----Other
0/0/0				0/0/0	5/17.9	0/0/0	0/0/	15/15/	/15			0/0/0	Other passenger cars of a cylinder capacity not exceeding 1L, with compression-ignition internal combustion reciprocating piston engine

税则号列	货品名称〔CIQ 扩展编码及品名—T2 表示见附表 2〕	最惠(%)	暂定税率	普通	增值/消费	出口退税	计量单位	监管条件/特殊证件	检验检疫	对美关税	亚太上/下
8703.3119 90	仅装有排气量≤1 升的压燃式活塞内燃发动机的其他载人车辆的成套散件〔999〕	15		230	13/	13	辆/千克	46Oxy/			
	---气缸容量(排气量)超过 1000 毫升,但不超过 1500 毫升:										
8703.3121	----小轿车										
8703.3121 10	仅装有 1 升<排气量≤1.5 升的压燃式活塞内燃发动机小轿车〔999〕	15		230	13/3	13	辆/千克	46AOxy/	LM		
8703.3121 90	仅装有 1 升<排气量≤1.5 升的压燃式活塞内燃发动机小轿车的成套散件〔999〕	15		230	13/	13	辆/千克	46Oxy/			
8703.3122	----越野车(4 轮驱动)										
8703.3122 10	仅装有 1 升<排气量≤1.5 升的压燃式活塞内燃发动机越野车(4 轮驱动)〔999〕	15		230	13/3	13	辆/千克	46AOxy/	LM		
8703.3122 90	仅装有 1 升<排气量≤1.5 升的压燃式活塞内燃发动机越野车的成套散件(4 轮驱动)〔999〕	15		230	13/	13	辆/千克	46Oxy/			
8703.3123	----9 座及以下的小客车										
8703.3123 10	仅装有 1 升<排气量≤1.5 升的压燃式活塞内燃发动机小客车(9 座及以下的)〔999〕	15		230	13/3	13	辆/千克	46AOxy/	LM		
8703.3123 90	仅装有 1 升<排气量≤1.5 升的压燃式活塞内燃发动机小客车的成套散件(9 座及以下的)〔999〕	15		230	13/	13	辆/千克	46Oxy/			
8703.3129	----其他										
8703.3129 10	仅装有 1 升<排气量≤1.5 升的压燃式活塞内燃发动机的其他载人车辆〔999〕	15		230	13/3	13	辆/千克	46AOxy/	LM		
8703.3129 90	仅装有 1 升<排气量≤1.5 升的装压燃式活塞内燃发动机的其他载人车辆的成套散件〔999〕	15		230	13/	13	辆/千克	46Oxy/			
	--气缸容量(排气量)超过 1500 毫升,但不超过 2500 毫升:										
	---气缸容量(排气量)超过 1500 毫升,但不超过 2000 毫升:										
8703.3211	----小轿车										
8703.3211 10	仅装有 1.5<排量≤2 升的压燃式活塞内燃发动机小轿车〔999〕	15		230	13/5	13	辆/千克	46AOxy/	LM		13.5/13.5
8703.3211 90	仅装有 1.5<排量≤2 升的压燃式活塞内燃发动机小轿车的成套散件〔999〕	15		230	13/	13	辆/千克	46Oxy/			13.5/13.5
8703.3212	----越野车(4 轮驱动)										
8703.3212 10	仅装有 1.5<排量≤2 升的压燃式活塞内燃发动机越野车(4 轮驱动)〔999〕	15		230	13/5	13	辆/千克	46AOxy/	LM		13.5/13.5
8703.3212 90	仅装有 1.5<排量≤2 升的压燃式活塞内燃发动机越野车的成套散件(4 轮驱动)〔999〕	15		230	13/	13	辆/千克	46Oxy/			13.5/13.5
8703.3213	----9 座及以下的小客车										
8703.3213 10	仅装有 1.5<排量≤2 升的装压燃式活塞内燃发动机小客车(9 座及以下的)〔999〕	15		230	13/5	13	辆/千克	46AOxy/	LM		13.5/13.5
8703.3213 90	仅装有 1.5<排量≤2 升的压燃式活塞内燃发动机小客车的成套散件(9 座及以下的)〔999〕	15		230	13/	13	辆/千克	46Oxy/			13.5/13.5
8703.3219	----其他										
8703.3219 10	仅装有 1.5<排量≤2 升的压燃式活塞内燃发动机的其他载人车辆〔999〕	15		230	13/5	13	辆/千克	46AOxy/	LM		13.5/13.5
8703.3219 90	仅装有 1.5<排量≤2 升的压燃式活塞内燃发动机的其他载人车辆的成套散件〔999〕	15		230	13/	13	辆/千克	46Oxy/			13.5/13.5
	---气缸容量(排气量)超过 2000 毫升,但不超过 2500 毫升:										
8703.3221	----小轿车										

协定税率 %								RCEP		特惠税率 %			Article Description
东/冰/格	巴基斯坦	韩国	瑞士上/下	哥/秘/柬	澳/毛	新西/坡/智	中国港/澳/台	东盟及马来/澳/韩	日/新	亚太2国	老/柬/缅	98/97/95	
0/0/0				0/0/0	5/17.9	0/0/0	0/0/	15/15/	/15			0/0/0	Complete parts of other moter vehicles designed for transport of person's with compression-ignition internal cmobustion piston engine, cylinder capaeity≤1L
													---Of a cylinder capacity exceeding 1000cc but not exceeding 1500cc:
													----Saloon cars
/0/0				0//	5/17.9	0//0	0/0/					0//	Saloon cars of a cylinder capacity exceeding 1L but not exceeding 1.5L, with compression-ignition internal combustion reciprocating piston engine
/0/0				0//	5/17.9	0//0	0/0/					0//	Complete parts of salotn cars with compression-ignition internal combustion piston engine, 1L<cylinder capacity≤1. 5L
													----Cross-country cars (4WD)
/0/0				0//	5/17.9	0//0	0/0/					0//	Off-road vehicles(4WD) of cylinder capacity exceeding 1L but not exceeding 1. 5L, with compression-ignition internal combustion reciprocating piston engine
/0/0				0//	5/17.9	0//0	0/0/					0//	Complete parts of cross-country cars(4WD) with compression-ignition internal combustion piston engine, 1L<cylinder ≤1. 5L
													----Station wagons (with 9 seats or less)
/0/0				0//	5/17.9	0//0	0/0/					0//	Station wagons(9 seats or less) of cylinder capacity exceeding 1L but not exceeding 1.5L, with compression-ignition internal combustion reciprocating piston engine
/0/0				0//	5/17.9	0//0	0/0/					0//	Complate parts of station wagons (with 9 seats or less) with compression-ignition internal combustion piston engine, 1L<cylinder capacity≤1. 5L
													----Other
0/0/0				0/0/0	5/17.9	0/0/0	0/0/	15/15/	/15			0/0/0	Other passenger vehicles of cylinder capacity exceeding 1L but not exceeding 1.5L, with compression-ignition internal combustion reciprocating piston engine
0/0/0				0/0/0	5/17.9	0/0/0	0/0/	15/15/	/15			0/0/0	Complete parts of other motor vehicles designed for the transport of person's with comperssion-ignition internal combustion piston engine, 1L<cylinder capacity≤1. 5L
													--Of a cylinder capaity exceeding 1500cc, but not exceeding 2500cc:
													---Of a cylinder capacity exceeding 1500cc, but not exceeding 2000cc:
													----Saloon cars
/0/0	22.5			0//	5/17.9	0//0	0/0/					0//	Saloon cars of a cylinder capacity exceeding 1.5L but not exceeding 2L, with compression-ignition internal combustion reciprocating piston engine
/0/0	22.5			0//	5/17.9	0//0	0/0/					0//	Complete parts of saloon cars with compression-ignition internal combustion piston engine, 1. 5L<cylinder capacity≤2L
													----Cross-country cars (4WD)
/0/0	22.5	22.5		0//	5/17.9	0//0	0/0/					0//	Off-road vehicles(4WD) of cylinder capacity exceeding 1.5L but not exceeding 2L, with compression-ignition internal combustion reciprocating piston engine
/0/0	22.5	22.5		0//	5/17.9	0//0	0/0/					0//	Complete parts of cross-country cars(4WD) with compression-ignition internal combustion piston engine, 1. 5L<cylinder capcity≤2L
													----Station wagons (with 9 seats or less)
/0/0	22.5	22.5		0//	5/17.9	0//0	0/0/					0//	Station wagons(9 seats or less) of cylinder capacity exceeding 1.5L but not exceeding 2L, with compression-ignition internal combustion reciprocating piston engine
/0/0	22.5	22.5		0//	5/17.9	0//0	0/0/					0//	Complete parts of station wagons with compression-ignition internel combustion piston engine, 1. 5L<cylinder capacity≤2L(with 9 seats or less)
													----Other
/0/0	22.5			0//	5/17.9	0//0	0/0/					0//	Other passenger vehicles of cylinder capacity exceeding 1.5L but not exceeding 2L, with compression-ignition internal combustion reciprocating piston engine
/0/0	22.5			0//	5/17.9	0//0	0/0/					0//	Complete parts of other motor vehicles principally designed for the transport of persons with compression-ignition internal combustion piston engine, 1. 5L<cylinder capacity ≤2L
													---Of a cylinder capacity exceeding 2000cc, but not exceeding 2500cc:
													----Saloon cars

税则号列	货品名称〔CIQ 扩展编码及品名－T2 表示见附表 2〕	最惠(%)	暂定税率	普通	增值/消费	出口退税	计量单位	监管条件/特殊证件	检验检疫	对美关税	亚太上/下
8703.3221 10	仅装有 2<排量≤2.5 升的压燃式活塞内燃发动机小轿车〔999〕	15		230	13/9	13	辆/千克	46AOxy/	LM		13.5/13.5
8703.3221 90	仅装有 2<排量≤2.5 升的燃式活塞内燃发动机小轿车的成套散件〔999〕	15		230	13/	13	辆/千克	46Oxy/			13.5/13.5
8703.3222	----越野车(4 轮驱动)										
8703.3222 10	仅装有 2<排量≤2.5 升的燃式活塞内燃发动机越野车(4 轮驱动)〔999〕	15		230	13/9	13	辆/千克	46AOxy/	LM		13.5/13.5
8703.3222 90	仅装有 2<排量≤2.5 升的燃式活塞内燃发动机越野车的成套散件(4 轮驱动)〔999〕	15		230	13/	13	辆/千克	46Oxy/			13.5/13.5
8703.3223	----9 座及以下的小客车										
8703.3223 10	仅装有 2<排量≤2.5 升的燃式活塞内燃发动机小客车(9 座及以下的)〔999〕	15		230	13/9	13	辆/千克	46AOxy/	LM		13.5/13.5
8703.3223 90	仅装有 2<排量≤2.5 升的压燃式活塞内燃发动机小客车的成套散件(9 座及以下的)〔999〕	15		230	13/	13	辆/千克	46Oxy/			13.5/13.5
8703.3229	----其他										
8703.3229 10	仅装有 2<排量≤2.5 升的压燃式活塞内燃发动机的其他载人车辆〔999〕	15		230	13/9	13	辆/千克	46AOxy/	LM		13.5/13.5
8703.3229 90	仅装有 2<排量≤2.5 升的压燃式活塞内燃发动机的其他载人车辆的成套散件〔999〕	15		230	13/	13	辆/千克	46Oxy/			13.5/13.5
	--气缸容量(排气量)超过 2500 毫升： ---气缸容量(排气量)超过 2500 毫升，但不超过 3000 毫升：										
8703.3311	----小轿车										
8703.3311 10	仅装有 2.5<排量≤3 升的压燃式活塞内燃发动机小轿车〔999〕	15		270	13/12	13	辆/千克	46AOxy/	LM		13.5/13.5
8703.3311 90	仅装有 2.5<排量≤3 升的压燃式活塞内燃发动机小轿车的成套散件〔999〕	15		270	13/	13	辆/千克	46Oxy/			13.5/13.5
8703.3312	----越野车(4 轮驱动)										
8703.3312 10	仅装有 2.5<排量≤3 升的压燃式活塞内燃发动机越野车(4 轮驱动)〔999〕	15		270	13/12	13	辆/千克	46AOxy/	LM		13.5/13.5
8703.3312 90	仅装有 2.5<排量≤3 升的压燃式活塞内燃发动机越野车的成套散件(4 轮驱动)〔999〕	15		270	13/	13	辆/千克	46Oxy/			13.5/13.5
8703.3313	----9 座及以下的小客车										
8703.3313 10	仅装有 2.5<排量≤3 升的压燃式活塞内燃发动机小客车(9 座及以下的)〔999〕	15		270	13/12	13	辆/千克	46AOxy/	LM		13.5/13.5
8703.3313 90	仅装有 2.5<排量≤3 升的压燃式活塞内燃发动机小客车的成套散件(9 座及以下的)〔999〕	15		270	13/	13	辆/千克	46Oxy/			13.5/13.5
8703.3319	----其他										
8703.3319 10	仅装有 2.5<排量≤3 升的压燃式活塞内燃发动机的其他载人车辆〔999〕	15		270	13/12	13	辆/千克	46AOxy/	LM		13.5/13.5
8703.3319 90	仅装有 2.5<排量≤3 升的压燃式活塞内燃发动机的其他载人车辆的成套散件〔999〕	15		270	13/12	13	辆/千克	46Oxy/			13.5/13.5
	---气缸容量(排气量)超过 3000 毫升，但不超过 4000 毫升：										
8703.3321	----小轿车										
8703.3321 10	仅装有 3<排量≤4 升的压燃式活塞内燃发动机小轿车〔999〕	15		270	13/25	13	辆/千克	46AOxy/	LM		13.5/13.5
8703.3321 90	仅装有 3<排量≤4 升的压燃式活塞内燃发动机小轿车的成套散件〔999〕	15		270	13/	13	辆/千克	46Oxy/			13.5/13.5
8703.3322	----越野车(4 轮驱动)										

协定税率 %								RCEP		特惠税率 %			Article Description
东/冰/格	巴基斯坦	韩国	瑞士上/下	哥/秘/柬	澳/毛	新西/坡/智	中国港/澳/台	东盟及马来/澳/韩	日/新	亚太2国	老/柬/缅	98/97/95	
/0/0	22.5			0//	5/17.9	0//0	0/0/					0//	Saloon cars of a cylinder capacity exceeding 2L but not exceeding 2.5L, with compression-ignition internal combustion reciprocating piston engine
/0/0	22.5			0//	5/17.9	0//0	0/0/					0//	Complete parts of saloon cars with compression -ignition internal combustion piston engine, 2L < cylinder capacity ≤ 2. 5L
													----Cross-country cars (4WD)
/0/0	22.5			0//	5/17.9	0//0	0/0/					0//	Off-road vehicles (4WD) of cylinder capacity exceeding 2L but not exceeding 2. 5L, with compression-ignition internal combustion reciprocating piston engine
/0/0	22.5			0//	5/17.9	0//0	0/0/					0//	Complete parts of cross-country cars (4WD) with compression-ignition internal combustion piston engine, 2L < cylinder capcity ≤ 2. 5L
													----Station wagons (with 9 seats or less)
/0/0	22.5	22.5		0//	5/17.9	0//0	0/0/					0//	Station wagons(9 seats or less) of cylinder capacity exceeding 2L but not exceeding 2.5L, with compression-ignition internal combustion reciprocating piston engine
/0/0	22.5	22.5		0//	5/17.9	0//0	0/0/					0//	Complete parts of station wagons with compression-ignition internel combustion piston engine, 2L < cylinder capacity ≤ 2. 5L(with 9 seats or less)
													----Other
/0/0	22.5			0//	5/17.9	0//0	0/0/					0//	Other passenger vehicles of cylinder capacity exceeding 2L but not exceeding 2. 5L, with compression-ignition internal combustion reciprocating piston engine
/0/0	22.5			0//	5/17.9	0//0	0/0/					0//	Complete parts of other motor vehicles designed for the transport of person's with compression-ignition internal combustion piston engine, 2L < cylinder capacity ≤ 2. 5L
													--Of a cyhinder capacity exceeding 2500cc:
													---Of a cylinder capacity exceeding 2500cc, but not exceeding 3000cc:
													----Saloon cars
0/0/0	22.5			0//0	5/17.9	0/0/0	0/0/	15/15/	/15			0//	Saloon cars of a cylinder capacity exceeding 2,5L but not exceeding 3L, with compression-ignition internal combustion reciprocating piston engine
0/0/0	22.5			0//0	5/17.9	0/0/0	0/0/	15/15/	/15			0//	Complete parts of saloon cars with compression -ignition internal combustion piston engine, 2. 5L < cylinder capacity ≤ 3L
													----Cross-country cars(4wd)
0/0/0	22.5	22.5		0//0	5/17.9	0/0/0	0/0/	15/15/	/15			0//	Off-road vehicles(4WD) of cylinder capacity exceeding 2,5L but not exceeding 3L, with compression-ignition internal combustion reciprocating piston engine
0/0/0	22.5	22.5		0//0	5/17.9	0/0/0	0/0/	15/15/	/15			0//	Complete parts of cross-country cars (4WD) with compression-ignition internal combustion piston engine, 2. 5L < cylinder capacity ≤ 3L
													Station wagons (with 9 seats or less)
0/0/0	22.5			0//0	5/17.9	0/0/0	0/0/	15/15/	/15			0//	Station wagons(9 seats or less) of cylinder capacity exceeding 2.5L but not exceeding 3L, with compression-ignition internal combustion reciprocating piston engine
0/0/0	22.5			0//0	5/17.9	0/0/0	0/0/	15/15/	/15			0//	Complate parts of station wagon (with 9 seats or less) with compression-ignition internal combustion piston engine, 2. 5L < cylinder capacity ≤ 3L
													----Other
0/0/0	22.5			0//0	5/17.9	0/0/0	0/0/	15/15/	/15			0//	Other passenger vehicles of cylinder capacity exceeding 2.5L but not exceeding 3L, with compression-ignition internal combustion reciprocating piston engine
0/0/0	22.5			0//0	5/17.9	0/0/0	0/0/	15/15/	/15			0//	Complete parts of other passenger vehicles of a cylinder capacity exceeding 2.5L but not exceeding 3L, with compression-ignition internal combustion reciprocating piston engine
													---Of a cylinder capacity exceeding 3000cc, but not exceeding 4000cc:
													----Saloon cars
0/0/0	22.5			0//0	5/17.9	0/0/0	0/0/	15/15/	/15			0/0/	Saloon cars of a cylinder capacity exceeding 3L but not exceeding 4L, with compression-ignition internal combustion reciprocating piston engine
0/0/0	22.5			0//0	5/17.9	0/0/0	0/0/	15/15/	/15			0/0/	Complate parts of station saloon cars with compression-ignition internal combustion piston egnine, 3L < cylinder capacity ≤ 4L
													----Cross-country cars (4WD)

税则号列	货品名称〔CIQ扩展编码及品名－T2表示见附表2〕	最惠(%)	暂定税率	普通	增值/消费	出口退税	计量单位	监管条件/特殊证件	检验检疫	对美关税	亚太上/下
8703.3322　10	仅装有3＜排量≤4升的压燃式活塞内燃发动机越野车(4轮驱动)〔999〕	15		270	13/25	13	辆/千克	46AOxy/	LM		13.5/13.5
8703.3322　90	仅装有3＜排量≤4升的压燃式活塞内燃发动机越野车的成套散件(4轮驱动)〔999〕	15		270	13/	13	辆/千克	46Oxy/			13.5/13.5
8703.3323	----9座及以下的小客车										
8703.3323　10	仅装有3＜排量≤4升的压燃式活塞内燃发动机小客车(9座及以下的)〔999〕	15		270	13/25	13	辆/千克	46AOxy/	LM		13.5/13.5
8703.3323　90	仅装有3＜排量≤4升的压燃式活塞内燃发动机小客车的成套散件(9座及以下的)〔999〕	15		270	13/	13	辆/千克	46Oxy/			13.5/13.5
8703.3329	----其他										
8703.3329　10	仅装有3＜排量≤4升的压燃式活塞内燃发动机的其他载人车辆〔999〕	15		270	13/25	13	辆/千克	46AOxy/	LM		13.5/13.5
8703.3329　90	仅装有3＜排量≤4升的压燃式活塞内燃发动机的其他载人车辆的成套散件〔999〕	15		270	13/25	13	辆/千克	46Oxy/			13.5/13.5
	---气缸容量(排气量)超过4000毫升：										
8703.3361	----小轿车										
8703.3361　10	仅装有排量＞4升的压燃式活塞内燃发动机小轿车〔999〕	15		270	13/40	13	辆/千克	46AOxy/	LM		13.5/13.5
8703.3361　90	仅装有排量＞4升的压燃式活塞内燃发动机小轿车的成套散件〔999〕	15		270	13/	13	辆/千克	46Oxy/			13.5/13.5
8703.3362	----越野车(4轮驱动)										
8703.3362　10	仅装有排量＞4升的压燃式活塞内燃发动机越野车(4轮驱动)〔999〕	15		270	13/40	13	辆/千克	46AOxy/	LM		13.5/13.5
8703.3362　90	仅装有排量＞4升的压燃式活塞内燃发动机越野车的成套散件(4轮驱动)〔999〕	15		270	13/	13	辆/千克	46Oxy/			13.5/13.5
8703.3363	----9座及以下的小客车										
8703.3363　10	仅装有排量＞4升的压燃式活塞内燃发动机小客车(9座及以下的)〔999〕	15		270	13/40	13	辆/千克	46AOxy/	LM		13.5/13.5
8703.3363　90	仅装有排量＞4升的压燃式活塞内燃发动机小客车的成套散件(9座及以下的)〔999〕	15		270	13/	13	辆/千克	46Oxy/			13.5/13.5
8703.3369	----其他										
8703.3369　10	仅装有排量＞4升的压燃式活塞内燃发动机其他载人车辆〔999〕	15		270	13/40	13	辆/千克	46AOxy/	LM		13.5/13.5
8703.3369　90	仅装有排量＞4升的压燃式活塞内燃发动机其他载人车辆的成套散件〔999〕	15		270	13/40	13	辆/千克	46Oxy/			13.5/13.5
	-同时装有点燃式活塞内燃发动机及驱动电动机的其他车辆，可通过接插外部电源进行充电的除外：										
	---气缸容量(排气量)不超过1000毫升：										
8703.4011	----小轿车										
8703.4011　10	同时装有点燃式活塞内燃发动机(排量≤1升)及驱动电动机的小轿车(可通过接插外部电源进行充电的除外)〔999〕	15		230	13/1	13	辆/千克	46AOxy/	LM		13.5/13.5
8703.4011　90	同时装有点燃式活塞内燃发动机(排量≤1升)及驱动电动机的小轿车的成套散件(可通过接插外部电源进行充电的除外)〔999〕	15		230	13/	13	辆/千克	46Oxy/			13.5/13.5
8703.4012	----越野车(4轮驱动)										
8703.4012　10	同时装有点燃式活塞内燃发动机(排量≤1升)及驱动电动机的越野车(4轮驱动)(可通过接插外部电源进行充电的除外)〔999〕	15		230	13/1	13	辆/千克	46AOxy/	LM		13.5/13.5

协定税率 %								RCEP		特惠税率 %			Article Description
东/冰/格	巴基斯坦	韩国	瑞士上/下	哥/秘/柬	澳/毛	新西/坡/智	中国港/澳/台	东盟及马来/澳/韩	日/新	亚太2国	老/柬/缅	98/97/95	
0/0/0	22.5			0//0	5/17.9	0/0/0	0/0/	15/15/	/15			0/0/	Off-road vehicles(4WD) of cylinder capacity exceeding 3L but not exceeding 4L, with compression-ignition internal combustion reciprocating piston engine
0/0/0	22.5			0//0	5/17.9	0/0/0	0/0/	15/15/	/15			0/0/	Complete parts of cross-country cars(4WD) with compression-ignition internal combustion piston engine, 3L<cylinder capacity≤4L
													----Station wagons (with 9 seats or less)
0/0/0	22.5			0//0	5/17.9	0/0/0	0/0/	15/15/	/15			0/0/	Station wagons(9 seats or less) of cylinder capacity exceeding 3L but not exceeding 4L, with compression-ignition internal combustion reciprocating piston engine
0/0/0	22.5			0//0	5/17.9	0/0/0	0/0/	15/15/	/15			0/0/	Complate parts of station wagons(with 9 seats or less) with compression-ignition internal combustion piston engine, 3L<cylinder capacity≤4L
													----Other
0/0/0	22.5			0//0	5/17.9	0/0/0	0/0/	15/15/	/15			0/0/	Other passenger vehicles of cylinder capacity exceeding 3L but not exceeding 4L, with compression-ignition internal combustion reciprocating piston engine
0/0/0	22.5			0//0	5/17.9	0/0/0	0/0/	15/15/	/15			0/0/	Complete parts of other passenger vehicles of a cylinder capacity exceeding 3L but not exceeding 4L, with compression-ignition internal combustion reciprocating piston engine
													---Of a cylinder capacity exceeding 4000cc:
													----Saloon cars
0/0/0	22.5			0//0	0/17.9	0/0/0	0/0/	15/15/	/15			0/0/	Saloon cars of a cylinder capacity exceeding 4L, with compression-ignition internal combustion reciprocating piston engine
0/0/0	22.5			0//0	0/17.9	0/0/0	0/0/	15/15/	/15			0/0/	Complete parts of saloon cars with compression -ignition internal combustion piston engine, cylinder capacity >4L
													----Cross-country cars (4WD)
0/0/0	22.5			0//0	0/17.9	0/0/0	0/0/	15/15/	/15			0/0/	Off-road vehicles(4WD) of cylinder capacity exceeding 4L, with compression-ignition internal combustion reciprocating piston engine
0/0/0	22.5			0//0	0/17.9	0/0/0	0/0/	15/15/	/15			0/0/	Complete parts of cross-country cars(4WD) with compression-ignition internal combustion piston engine, cylinder capacity>4L
													----Station wagons (with 9 seats or less)
0/0/0	22.5			0//0	0/17.9	0/0/0	0/0/	15/15/	/15			0/0/	Station wagons(9 seats or less) of cylinder capacity exceeding 4L, with compression-ignition internal combustion reciprocating piston engine
0/0/0	22.5			0//0	0/17.9	0/0/0	0/0/	15/15/	/15			0/0/	Complete parts of station wagons(with 9 seats or less) with compression-ignition internal combustion piston engine, cylinder capacity>4L
													----Other
0/0/0	22.5			0//0	0/17.9	0/0/0	0/0/	15/15/	/15			0/0/	Other passenger vehicles of cylinder capacity exceeding 4L, with compression-ignition internal combustion reciprocating piston engine
0/0/0	22.5			0//0	0/17.9	0/0/0	0/0/	15/15/	/15			0/0/	Complete parts of other passenger vehicles of a cylinder capacity exceeding 4L, with compression-ignition internal combustion reciprocating piston engine
													-Other vehicles equipped with positive ignition piston internal combustion engine and drive motor can be charged by connecting external power supply
													---Of a cylinder capacity exceeding 1000cc:
													----Saloon cars
/0/	22.5			0//	0/17.9	0//0	0/0/					0//	Saloon cars of cylinder capacity not exceeding 1L, with spark-ignition internal combustion eciprocating piston engine, with drive motor (Except for charging by external power supply)
/0/	22.5			0//	0/17.9	0//0	0/0/					0//	Complete parts of saloon cars of cylinder capacity not exceeding 1L, with spark-ignition internal combustion eciprocating piston engine, with drive motor (Except for charging by external
													----Cross-country cars(4WD)
/0/	22.5			0//	0/17.9	0//0	0/0/					0//	Off-road vehicles(4WD) of cylinder capacity not exceeding 1L, with spark-ignition internal combustion eciprocating piston engine, with drive motor (Except for charging by external power supply)

税则号列	货品名称〔CIQ 扩展编码及品名－T2 表示见附表 2〕	最惠(%)	暂定税率	普通	增值/消费	出口退税	计量单位	监管条件/特殊证件	检验检疫	对美关税	亚太上/下
8703.4012 90	同时装有点燃式活塞内燃发动机(排量≤1 升)及驱动电动机的越野车(4 轮驱动)的成套散件(可通过接插外部电源进行充电的除外)〔999〕	15		230	13/	13	辆/千克	46Oxy/			13.5/13.5
8703.4013	----9 座及以下的小客车										
8703.4013 10	同时装有点燃式活塞内燃发动机(排量≤1 升)及驱动电动机的小客车(9 座及以下,可通过接插外部电源进行充电的除外)〔999〕	15		230	13/1	13	辆/千克	46AOxy/	LM		13.5/13.5
8703.4013 90	同时装有点燃式活塞内燃发动机(排量≤1 升)及驱动电动机的小客车的成套散件(9 座及以下,可通过接插外部电源进行充电的除外)〔999〕	15		230	13/1	13	辆/千克	46Oxy/			13.5/13.5
8703.4019	----其他										
8703.4019 10	同时装有点燃式活塞内燃发动机(排量≤1 升)及驱动电动机的其他载人车辆(可通过接插外部电源进行充电的除外)〔999〕	15		230	13/1	13	辆/千克	46AOxy/	LM		13.5/13.5
8703.4019 90	同时装有点燃式活塞内燃发动机(排量≤1 升)及驱动电动机的其他载人车辆的成套散件(可通过接插外部电源进行充电的除外)〔999〕	15		230	13/1	13	辆/千克	46Oxy/			13.5/13.5
	---气缸容量(排气量)超过 1000 毫升,但不超过 1500 毫升:										
8703.4021	----小轿车										
8703.4021 10	同时装有点燃式活塞内燃发动机(1<排量≤1.5 升)及驱动电动机的小轿车(可通过接插外部电源进行充电的除外)〔999〕	15		230	13/3	13	辆/千克	46AOxy/	LM		13.5/13.5
8703.4021 90	同时装有点燃式活塞内燃发动机(1<排量≤1.5 升)及驱动电动机的小轿车的成套散件(可通过接插外部电源进行充电的除外)〔999〕	15		230	13/3	13	辆/千克	46Oxy/			13.5/13.5
8703.4022	----越野车(4 轮驱动)										
8703.4022 10	同时装有点燃式活塞内燃发动机(1<排量≤1.5 升)及驱动电动机的四轮驱动越野车(可通过接插外部电源进行充电的除外)〔999〕	15		230	13/3	13	辆/千克	46AOxy/	LM		13.5/13.5
8703.4022 90	同时装有点燃式活塞内燃发动机(1<排量≤1.5 升)及驱动电动机的四轮驱动越野车的成套散件(可通过接插外部电源进行充电的除外)〔999〕	15		230	13/3	13	辆/千克	46Oxy/			13.5/13.5
8703.4023	----9 座及以下的小客车										
8703.4023 10	同时装有点燃式活塞内燃发动机(1<排量≤1.5 升)及驱动电动机的小客车(9 座及以下,可通过接插外部电源进行充电的除外)〔999〕	15		230	13/3	13	辆/千克	46AOxy/	LM		13.5/13.5
8703.4023 90	同时装有点燃式活塞内燃发动机(1<排量≤1.5 升)及驱动电动机的小客车的成套散件(9 座及以下,可通过接插外部电源进行充电的除外)〔999〕	15		230	13/3	13	辆/千克	46Oxy/			13.5/13.5
8703.4029	----其他										
8703.4029 10	同时装有点燃式活塞内燃发动机(1<排量≤1.5 升)及驱动电动机的其他载人车辆(可通过接插外部电源进行充电的除外)〔999〕	15		230	13/3	13	辆/千克	46AOxy/	LM		13.5/13.5
8703.4029 90	同时装有点燃式活塞内燃发动机(1<排量≤1.5 升)及驱动电动机的其他载人车辆的成套散件(可通过接插外部电源进行充电的除外)〔999〕	15		230	13/3	13	辆/千克	46Oxy/			13.5/13.5
	---气缸容量(排气量)超过 1500 毫升,但不超过 2000 毫升:										
8703.4031	----小轿车										
8703.4031 10	同时装有点燃式活塞内燃发动机(1.5<排量≤2 升)及驱动电动机的小轿车(可通过接插外部电源进行充电的除外)〔999〕	15		230	13/5	13	辆/千克	46AOxy/	LM		13.5/13.5

协定税率 %								RCEP		特惠税率 %			Article Description
东/冰/格	巴基斯坦	韩国	瑞士 上/下	哥/秘/柬	澳/毛	新西/坡/智	中国港/澳/台	东盟及马来/澳/韩	日/新	亚太2国	老/柬/缅	98/97/95	
/0/	22.5			0//	0/17.9	0//0	0/0/					0//	Complete parts of off-road vehicles(4WD) of cylinder capacity not exceeding 1L, with spark-ignition internal combustion eciprocating piston engine, with drive motor (Except for charging by external
													----Station wagons(with 9 seats or less)
/0/	22.5			0//	0/17.9	0//0	0/0/					0//	Station wagons(9 seats or less) of cylinder capacity not exceeding 1L, with spark-ignition internal combustion eciprocating piston engine, with drive motor (Except for charging by external power supply)
/0/	22.5			0//	0/17.9	0//0	0/0/					0//	Complete parts of station wagons(9 seats or less) of cylinder capacity not exceeding 1L, with spark-ignition internal combustion eciprocating piston engine, with drive motor (Except for charging by external
													----Other
/0/	22.5			0//	0/17.9	0//0	0/0/					0//	Other passenger vehicles of cylinder capacity not exceeding 1L, with spark-ignition internal combustion eciprocating piston engine, with drive motor (Except for charging by external power supply)
/0/	22.5			0//	0/17.9	0//0	0/0/					0//	Complete parts of Other passenger vehicles of cylinder capacity not exceeding 1L, with spark-ignition internal combustion eciprocating piston engine, with drive motor (Except for charging by external
													---Of a cylinder capacity exceeding 1000cc, but not exceeding 1500cc:
													----Saloon cars
/0/	22.5	22.5		0//	0/17.9	0//0	0/0/					0//	Saloon cars of cylinder capacity exceeding 1L but not exceeding 1.5L, with spark-ignition internal combustion eciprocating piston engine, with drive motor (Except for charging by external power supply)
/0/	22.5	22.5		0//	0/17.9	0//0	0/0/					0//	Complete parts of saloon cars of cylinder capacity exceeding 1L but not exceeding 1.5L, with spark-ignition internal combustion eciprocating piston engine, with drive motor (Except for charging by external
													----Cross-country cars(4WD)
/0/	22.5			0//	0/17.9	0//0	0/0/					0//	Off-road vehicles (4WD) of cylinder capacity exceeding 1L but not exceeding 1.5L, with spark-ignition internal combustion eciprocating piston engine, with drive motor (Except for charging by external power supply)
/0/	22.5			0//	0/17.9	0//0	0/0/					0//	Complete parts of Off-road vehicles(4WD) of cylinder capacity exceeding 1L but not exceeding 1.5L, with spark-ignition internal combustion eciprocating piston engine, with drive motor (Except for charging by external
													----Station wagons(with 9 seats or less)
/0/	22.5			0//	0/17.9	0//0	0/0/					0//	Station wagons(9 seats or less) of cylinder capacity exceeding 1L but not exceeding 1.5L, with spark-ignition internal combustion eciprocating piston engine, with drive motor (Except for charging by external power supply)
/0/	22.5			0//	0/17.9	0//0	0/0/					0//	Complete parts of Station wagons(9 seats or less) of cylinder capacity exceeding 1L but not exceeding 1.5L, with spark-ignition internal combustion eciprocating piston engine, with drive motor (Except for charging by external
													----Other
/0/	22.5			0//	0/17.9	0//0	0/0/					0//	Other passenger vehicles of cylinder capacity exceeding 1L but not exceeding 1.5L, with spark-ignition internal combustion eciprocating piston engine, with drive motor (Except for charging by external power supply)
/0/	22.5			0//	0/17.9	0//0	0/0/					0//	Complete parts of Other passenger vehicles of cylinder capacity exceeding 1L but not exceeding 1.5L, with spark-ignition internal combustion eciprocating piston engine, with drive motor (Except for charging by external
													---Of a cylinder capacity exceeding 1500cc, but not exceeding 2000cc:
													----Saloon cars
/0/	22.5	22.5		0//	5/17.9	0//0	0/0/					0//	Saloon cars of cylinder capacity exceeding 1.5L but not exceeding 2L, with spark-ignition internal combustion eciprocating piston engine, with drive motor (Except for charging by external power supply)

税则号列	货品名称〔CIQ扩展编码及品名－T2表示见附表2〕	最惠(%)	暂定税率	普通	增值/消费	出口退税	计量单位	监管条件/特殊证件	检验检疫	对美关税	亚太上/下
8703.4031 90	同时装有点燃式活塞内燃发动机(1.5＜排量≤2升)及驱动电动机的小轿车的成套散件(可通过接插外部电源进行充电的除外)〔999〕	15		230	13/5	13	辆/千克	46Oxy/			13.5/13.5
8703.4032	----越野车(4轮驱动)										
8703.4032 10	同时装有点燃式活塞内燃发动机(1.5＜排量≤2升)及驱动电动机的四轮驱动越野车(可通过接插外部电源进行充电的除外)〔999〕	15		230	13/5	13	辆/千克	46AOxy/	LM		13.5/13.5
8703.4032 90	同时装有点燃式活塞内燃发动机(1.5＜排量≤2升)及驱动电动机的四轮驱动越野车的成套散件(可通过接插外部电源进行充电的除外)〔999〕	15		230	13/5	13	辆/千克	46Oxy/			13.5/13.5
8703.4033	----9座及以下的小客车										
8703.4033 10	同时装有点燃式活塞内燃发动机(1.5＜排量≤2升)及驱动电动机的小客车(9座及以下,可通过接插外部电源进行充电的除外)〔999〕	15		230	13/5	13	辆/千克	46AOxy/	LM		13.5/13.5
8703.4033 90	同时装有点燃式活塞内燃发动机(1.5＜排量≤2升)及驱动电动机的小客车的成套散件(9座及以下,可通过接插外部电源进行充电的除外)〔999〕	15		230	13/5	13	辆/千克	46Oxy/			13.5/13.5
8703.4039	----其他										
8703.4039 10	同时装有点燃式活塞内燃发动机(1.5＜排量≤2升)及驱动电动机的其他载人车辆(可通过接插外部电源进行充电的除外)〔999〕	15		230	13/5	13	辆/千克	46AOxy/	LM		13.5/13.5
8703.4039 90	同时装有点燃式活塞内燃发动机(1.5＜排量≤2升)及驱动电动机的其他载人车辆的成套散件(可通过接插外部电源进行充电的除外)〔999〕	15		230	13/5	13	辆/千克	46Oxy/			13.5/13.5
	---气缸容量(排气量)超过2000毫升,但不超过2500毫升:										
8703.4041	----小轿车										
8703.4041 10	同时装有点燃式活塞内燃发动机(2＜排量≤2.5升)及驱动电动机的小轿车(可通过接插外部电源进行充电的除外)〔999〕	15		230	13/9	13	辆/千克	46AOxy/	LM		13.5/13.5
8703.4041 90	同时装有点燃式活塞内燃发动机(2＜排量≤2.5升)及驱动电动机的小轿车的成套散件(可通过接插外部电源进行充电的除外)〔999〕	15		230	13/9	13	辆/千克	46Oxy/			13.5/13.5
8703.4042	----越野车(4轮驱动)										
8703.4042 10	同时装有点燃式活塞内燃发动机(2＜排量≤2.5升)及驱动电动机的四轮驱动越野车(可通过接插外部电源进行充电的除外)〔999〕	15		230	13/9	13	辆/千克	46AOxy/	LM		13.5/13.5
8703.4042 90	同时装有点燃式活塞内燃发动机(2＜排量≤2.5升)及驱动电动机的四轮驱动越野车的成套散件(可通过接插外部电源进行充电的除外)〔999〕	15		230	13/9	13	辆/千克	46Oxy/			13.5/13.5
8703.4043	----9座及以下的小客车										
8703.4043 10	同时装有点燃式活塞内燃发动机(2＜排量≤2.5升)及驱动电动机的小客车(9座及以下,可通过接插外部电源进行充电的除外)〔999〕	15		230	13/9	13	辆/千克	46AOxy/	LM		13.5/13.5
8703.4043 90	同时装有点燃式活塞内燃发动机(2＜排量≤2.5升)及驱动电动机的小客车的成套散件(9座及以下,可通过接插外部电源进行充电的除外)〔999〕	15		230	13/9	13	辆/千克	46Oxy/			13.5/13.5
8703.4049	----其他										
8703.4049 10	同时装有点燃式活塞内燃发动机(2＜排量≤2.5升)及驱动电动机的其他载人车辆(可通过接插外部电源进行充电的除外)〔999〕	15		230	13/9	13	辆/千克	46AOxy/	LM		13.5/13.5
8703.4049 90	同时装有点燃式活塞内燃发动机(2＜排量≤2.5升)及驱动电动机的其他载人车辆的成套散件(可通过接插外部电源进行充电的除外)〔999〕	15		230	13/9	13	辆/千克	46Oxy/			13.5/13.5

协定税率 %								RCEP		特惠税率 %			Article Description
东/冰/格	巴基斯坦	韩国	瑞士上/下	哥/秘/柬	澳/毛	新西/坡/智	中国港/澳/台	东盟及马来/澳/韩	日/新	亚太2国	老/柬/缅	98/97/95	
/0/	22.5	22.5		0//	5/17.9	0//0	0/0/					0//	Complete parts of saloon cars of cylinder capacity exceeding 1L but not exceeding 1.5L, with spark-ignition internal combustion eciprocating piston engine, with drive motor (Except for charging by external
													----Cross-country cars(4WD)
/0/	22.5	22.5		0//	5/17.9	0//0	0/0/					0//	Off-road vehicles(4WD) of cylinder capacity exceeding 1.5L but not exceeding 2L, with spark-ignition internal combustion eciprocating piston engine, with drive motor (Except for charging by external power supply)
/0/	22.5	22.5		0//	5/17.9	0//0	0/0/					0//	Complete parts of Off-road vehicles(4WD) of cylinder capacity exceeding 1L but not exceeding 1.5L, with spark-ignition internal combustion eciprocating piston engine, with drive motor (Except for charging by external
													----Station wagons(with 9 seats or less)
/0/	22.5	22.5		0//	5/17.9	0//0	0/0/					0//	Station wagons(9 seats or less) of cylinder capacity exceeding 1.5L but not exceeding 2L, with spark-ignition internal combustion eciprocating piston engine, with drive motor (Except for charging by external power supply)
/0/	22.5	22.5		0//	5/17.9	0//0	0/0/					0//	Complete parts of Station wagons(9 seats or less) of cylinder capacity exceeding 1L but not exceeding 1.5L, with spark-ignition internal combustion eciprocating piston engine, with drive motor (Except for charging by external
													----Other
/0/	22.5			0//	5/17.9	0//0	0/0/					0//	Other passenger vehicles of cylinder capacity exceeding 1.5L but not exceeding 2L, with spark-ignition internal combustion eciprocating piston engine, with drive motor (Except for charging by external power supply)
/0/	22.5			0//	5/17.9	0//0	0/0/					0//	Complete parts of Other passenger vehicles of cylinder capacity exceeding 1,5L but not exceeding 2L, with spark-ignition internal combustion eciprocating piston engine, with drive motor (Except for charging by external
													---Of a cylinder capacity exceeding 2000cc, but not exceeding 2500cc:
													----Saloon cars
/0/	22.5	22.5		0//	5/17.9	0//0	0/0/					0//	Saloon cars of cylinder capacity exceeding 2L but not exceeding 2.5L, with spark-ignition internal combustion eciprocating piston engine, with drive motor (Except for charging by external power supply)
/0/	22.5	22.5		0//	5/17.9	0//0	0/0/					0//	Complete parts of saloon cars of cylinder capacity exceeding 1L but not exceeding 1.5L, with spark-ignition internal combustion eciprocating piston engine, with drive motor (Except for charging by external
													----Cross-country cars(4WD)
/0/	22.5	22.5		0//	5/17.9	0//0	0/0/					0//	Off-road vehicles (4WD) of cylinder capacity exceeding 2L but not exceeding 2.5L, with spark-ignition internal combustion eciprocating piston engine, with drive motor (Except for charging by external power supply)
/0/	22.5	22.5		0//	5/17.9	0//0	0/0/					0//	Complete parts of Off-road vehicles(4WD) of cylinder capacity exceeding 1L but not exceeding 1.5L, with spark-ignition internal combustion eciprocating piston engine, with drive motor (Except for charging by external
													----Station wagons(with 9 seats or less)
/0/	22.5	22.5		0//	5/17.9	0//0	0/0/					0//	Station wagons(9 seats or less) of cylinder capacity exceeding 2L but not exceeding 2.5L, with spark-ignition internal combustion eciprocating piston engine, with drive motor (Except for charging by external power supply)
/0/	22.5	22.5		0//	5/17.9	0//0	0/0/					0//	Complete parts of Station wagons(9 seats or less) of cylinder capacity exceeding 1L but not exceeding 1.5L, with spark-ignition internal combustion eciprocating piston engine, with drive motor (Except for charging by external
													----Other
/0/	22.5			0//	5/17.9	0//0	0/0/					0//	Other passenger vehicles of cylinder capacity exceeding 2L but not exceeding 2.5L, with spark-ignition internal combustion eciprocating piston engine, with drive motor (Except for charging by external power supply)
/0/	22.5			0//	5/17.9	0//0	0/0/					0//	Complete parts of Other passenger vehicles of cylinder capacity exceeding 2L but not exceeding 2.5L, with spark-ignition internal combustion eciprocating piston engine, with drive motor (Except for charging by external

税则号列		货品名称〔CIQ 扩展编码及品名—T2 表示见附表 2〕	最惠(%)	暂定税率	普通	增值/消费	出口退税	计量单位	监管条件/特殊证件	检验检疫	对美关税	亚太上/下
		---气缸容量(排气量)超过 2500 毫升,但不超过 3000 毫升:										
8703.4051		----小轿车										
8703.4051	10	同时装有点燃式活塞内燃发动机(2.5<排量≤3 升)及驱动电动机的小轿车(可通过接插外部电源进行充电的除外)〔999〕	15		270	13/12	13	辆/千克	46AOxy/	ML		13.5/13.5
8703.4051	90	同时装有点燃式活塞内燃发动机(2.5<排量≤3 升)及驱动电动机的小轿车的成套散件(可通过接插外部电源进行充电的除外)〔999〕	15		270	13/12	13	辆/千克	46Oxy/			13.5/13.5
8703.4052		----越野车(4 轮驱动)										
8703.4052	10	同时装有点燃式活塞内燃发动机(2.5<排量≤3 升)及驱动电动机的四轮驱动越野车(可通过接插外部电源进行充电的除外)〔999〕	15		270	13/12	13	辆/千克	46AOxy/	ML		13.5/13.5
8703.4052	90	同时装有点燃式活塞内燃发动机(2.5<排量≤3 升)及驱动电动机的四轮驱动越野车的成套散件(可通过接插外部电源进行充电的除外)〔999〕	15		270	13/12	13	辆/千克	46Oxy/			13.5/13.5
8703.4053		----9 座及以下的小客车										
8703.4053	10	同时装有点燃式活塞内燃发动机(2.5<排量≤3 升)及驱动电动机的小客车(9 座及以下,可通过接插外部电源进行充电的除外)〔999〕	15		270	13/12	13	辆/千克	46AOxy/	ML		13.5/13.5
8703.4053	90	同时装有点燃式活塞内燃发动机(2.5<排量≤3 升)及驱动电动机的小客车的成套散件(9 座及以下,可通过接插外部电源进行充电的除外)〔999〕	15		270	13/12	13	辆/千克	46Oxy/			13.5/13.5
8703.4059		----其他										
8703.4059	10	同时装有点燃式活塞内燃发动机(2.5<排量≤3 升)及驱动电动机的其他载人车辆(可通过接插外部电源进行充电的除外)〔999〕	15		270	13/12	13	辆/千克	46AOxy/	ML		13.5/13.5
8703.4059	90	同时装有点燃式活塞内燃发动机(2.5<排量≤3 升)及驱动电动机的其他载人车辆的成套散件(可通过接插外部电源进行充电的除外)〔999〕	15		270	13/12	13	辆/千克	46Oxy/			13.5/13.5
		---气缸容量(排气量)超过 3000 毫升,但不超过 4000 毫升:										
8703.4061		----小轿车										
8703.4061	10	同时装有点燃式活塞内燃发动机(3<排量≤4 升)及驱动电动机的小轿车(可通过接插外部电源进行充电的除外)〔999〕	15		270	13/25	13	辆/千克	46AOxy/	LM		13.5/13.5
8703.4061	90	同时装有点燃式活塞内燃发动机(3<排量≤4 升)及驱动电动机的小轿车的成套散件(可通过接插外部电源进行充电的除外)〔999〕	15		270	13/25	13	辆/千克	46Oxy/			13.5/13.5
8703.4062		----越野车(4 轮驱动)										
8703.4062	10	同时装有点燃式活塞内燃发动机(3<排量≤4 升)及驱动电动机的四轮驱动越野车(可通过接插外部电源进行充电的除外)〔999〕	15		270	13/25	13	辆/千克	46AOxy/	LM		13.5/13.5
8703.4062	90	同时装有点燃式活塞内燃发动机(3<排量≤4 升)及驱动电动机的四轮驱动越野车的成套散件(可通过接插外部电源进行充电的除外)〔999〕	15		270	13/25	13	辆/千克	46Oxy/			13.5/13.5
8703.4063		----9 座及以下的小客车										
8703.4063	10	同时装有点燃式活塞内燃发动机(3<排量≤4 升)及驱动电动机的小客车(9 座及以下,可通过接插外部电源进行充电的除外)〔999〕	15		270	13/25	13	辆/千克	46AOxy/	LM		13.5/13.5
8703.4063	90	同时装有点燃式活塞内燃发动机(3<排量≤4 升)及驱动电动机的小客车的成套散件(9 座及以下,可通过接插外部电源进行充电的除外)〔999〕	15		270	13/25	13	辆/千克	46Oxy/			13.5/13.5
8703.4069		----其他										

协定税率 %								RCEP		特惠税率 %			
东/冰/格	巴基斯坦	韩国	瑞士上/下	哥/秘/柬	澳/毛	新西/坡/智	中国港/澳/台	东盟及马来/澳/韩	日/新	亚太2国	老/柬/缅	98/97/95	Article Description
													---Of a cylinder capacity exceeding 2500cc, but not exceeding32000cc:
													----Saloon cars
/0/	22.5	22.5		0//	5/17.9	0//0	0/0/	15//	15/			0//	Saloon cars of cylinder capacity exceeding 2.5L but not exceeding 3L, with spark-ignition internal combustion eciprocating piston engine, with drive motor (Except for charging by external power supply)
/0/	22.5	22.5		0//	5/17.9	0//0	0/0/	15//	15/			0//	Complete parts of saloon cars of cylinder capacity exceeding 1L but not exceeding 1.5L, with spark-ignition internal combustion eciprocating piston engine, with drive motor (Except for charging by external
													----Cross-country cars(4WD)
0/0/	22.5			0//0	5/17.9	0/0/0	0/0/	15/15/	15/15			0//	Off-road vehicles(4WD) of cylinder capacity exceeding 2.5L but not exceeding 3L, with spark-ignition internal combustion eciprocating piston engine, with drive motor (Except for charging by external power supply)
0/0/	22.5			0//0	5/17.9	0/0/0	0/0/	15/15/	15/15			0//	Complete parts of Off-road vehicles(4WD) of cylinder capacity exceeding 1L but not exceeding 1.5L, with spark-ignition internal combustion eciprocating piston engine, with drive motor (Except for charging by external
													----Station wagons(with 9 seats or less)
0/0/	22.5	22.5		0//0	5/17.9	0/0/0	0/0/	15/15/	15/15			0//	Station wagons(9 seats or less) of cylinder capacity exceeding 2.5L but not exceeding 3L, with spark-ignition internal combustion eciprocating piston engine, with drive motor (Except for charging by external power supply)
0/0/	22.5	22.5		0//0	5/17.9	0/0/0	0/0/	15/15/	15/15			0//	Complete parts of Station wagons(9 seats or less) of cylinder capacity exceeding 1L but not exceeding 1.5L, with spark-ignition internal combustion eciprocating piston engine, with drive motor (Except for charging by external
													----Other
0/0/	22.5			0//0	5/17.9	0/0/0	0/0/	15/15/	15/15			0//	Other passenger vehicles of cylinder capacity exceeding 2.5L but not exceeding 3L, with spark-ignition internal combustion eciprocating piston engine, with drive motor (Except for charging by external power supply)
0/0/	22.5			0//0	5/17.9	0/0/0	0/0/	15/15/	15/15			0//	Complete parts of Other passenger vehicles of cylinder capacity exceeding 2.5L but not exceeding 3L, with spark-ignition internal combustion eciprocating piston engine, with drive motor (Except for charging by external
													---Of a cylinder capacity exceeding 3000cc, but not exceeding 4000cc:
													----Saloon cars
/0/	22.5	22.5		0//0	5/17.9	0//0	0/0/	15//	15/			0/0/	Saloon cars of cylinder capacity exceeding 3L but not exceeding 4L, with spark-ignition internal combustion eciprocating piston engine, with drive motor (Except for charging by external power supply)
/0/	22.5	22.5		0//0	5/17.9	0//0	0/0/	15//	15/			0/0/	Complete parts of saloon cars of cylinder capacity exceeding 1L but not exceeding 1.5L, with spark-ignition internal combustion eciprocating piston engine, with drive motor (Except for charging by external
													----Cross-country cars(4WD)
/0/	22.5	22.5		0//0	5/17.9	0//0	0/0/	15//	15/			0/0/	Off-road vehicles(4WD) of cylinder capacity exceeding 3L but not exceeding 4L, with spark-ignition internal combustion eciprocating piston engine, with drive motor (Except for charging by external power supply)
/0/	22.5	22.5		0//0	5/17.9	0//0	0/0/	15//	15/			0/0/	Complete parts of Off-road vehicles(4WD) of cylinder capacity exceeding 1L but not exceeding 1.5L, with spark-ignition internal combustion eciprocating piston engine, with drive motor (Except for charging by external
													----Station wagons(with 9 seats or less)
/0/	22.5			0//0	5/17.9	0//0	0/0/	15//	15/			0/0/	Station wagons(9 seats or less) of cylinder capacity exceeding 3L but not exceeding 4L, with spark-ignition internal combustion eciprocating piston engine, with drive motor (Except for charging by external power supply)
/0/	22.5			0//0	5/17.9	0//0	0/0/	15//	15/			0/0/	Complete parts of Station wagons(9 seats or less) of cylinder capacity exceeding 1L but not exceeding 1.5L, with spark-ignition internal combustion eciprocating piston engine, with drive motor (Except for charging by external
													----Other

税则号列	货品名称〔CIQ 扩展编码及品名—T2 表示见附表 2〕	最惠(%)	暂定税率	普通	增值/消费	出口退税	计量单位	监管条件/特殊证件	检验检疫	对美关税	亚太上/下
8703.4069 10	同时装有点燃式活塞内燃发动机(3<排量≤4 升)及驱动电动机的其他载人车辆(可通过接插外部电源进行充电的除外)〔999〕	15		270	13/25	13	辆/千克	46AOxy/	LM		13.5/13.5
8703.4069 90	同时装有点燃式活塞内燃发动机(3<排量≤4 升)及驱动电动机的其他载人车辆的成套散件(可通过接插外部电源进行充电的除外)〔999〕	15		270	13/25	13	辆/千克	46Oxy/			13.5/13.5
	---气缸容量(排气量)超过 4000 毫升:										
8703.4071	----小轿车										
8703.4071 10	同时装有点燃式活塞内燃发动机(排量>4 升)及驱动电动机的小轿车(可通过接插外部电源进行充电的除外)〔999〕	15		270	13/40	13	辆/千克	46AOxy/	LM		13.5/13.5
8703.4071 90	同时装有点燃式活塞内燃发动机(排量>4 升)及驱动电动机的小轿车的成套散件(可通过接插外部电源进行充电的除外)〔999〕	15		270	13/40	13	辆/千克	46Oxy/			13.5/13.5
8703.4072	----越野车(4 轮驱动)										
8703.4072 10	同时装有点燃式活塞内燃发动机(排量>4 升)及驱动电动机的四轮驱动越野车(可通过接插外部电源进行充电的除外)〔999〕	15		270	13/40	13	辆/千克	46AOxy/	LM		13.5/13.5
8703.4072 90	同时装有点燃式活塞内燃发动机(排量>4 升)及驱动电动机的四轮驱动越野车的成套散件(可通过接插外部电源进行充电的除外)〔999〕	15		270	13/40	13	辆/千克	46Oxy/			13.5/13.5
8703.4073	----9 座及以下的小客车										
8703.4073 10	同时装有点燃式活塞内燃发动机(排量>4 升)及驱动电动机的小客车(9 座及以下,可通过接插外部电源进行充电的除外)〔999〕	15		270	13/40	13	辆/千克	46AOxy/	LM		13.5/13.5
8703.4073 90	同时装有点燃式活塞内燃发动机(排量>4 升)及驱动电动机的小客车的成套散件(9 座及以下,可通过接插外部电源进行充电的除外)〔999〕	15		270	13/40	13	辆/千克	46Oxy/			13.5/13.5
8703.4079	----其他										
8703.4079 10	同时装有点燃式活塞内燃发动机(排量>4 升)及驱动电动机的其他载人车辆(可通过接插外部电源进行充电的除外)〔999〕	15		270	13/40	13	辆/千克	46AOxy/	LM		13.5/13.5
8703.4079 90	同时装有点燃式活塞内燃发动机(排量>4 升)及驱动电动机的其他载人车辆的成套散件(可通过接插外部电源进行充电的除外)〔999〕	15		270	13/40	13	辆/千克	46Oxy/			13.5/13.5
	-同时装有压燃式活塞内燃发动机(柴油或半柴油发动机)及驱动电动机的其他车辆,可通过接插外部电源进行充电的除外:										
	---气缸容量(排气量)不超过 1000 毫升:										
8703.5011	----小轿车										
8703.5011 10	同时装有压燃式活塞内燃发动机(柴油或半柴油发动机,排量≤1 升)及驱动电动机的小轿车(可通过接插外部电源进行充电的除外)〔999〕	15		230	13/1	13	辆/千克	46AOxy/	LM		
8703.5011 90	同时装有压燃式活塞内燃发动机(柴油或半柴油发动机,排量≤1 升)及驱动电动机的小轿车的成套散件(可通过接插外部电源进行充电的除外)〔999〕	15		230	13/1	13	辆/千克	46Oxy/			
8703.5019	----其他										
8703.5019 10	同时装有压燃式活塞内燃发动机(柴油或半柴油发动机,排量≤1 升)及驱动电动机的其他载人车辆(可通过接插外部电源进行充电的除外)〔999〕	15		230	13/1	13	辆/千克	46AOxy/	LM		

协定税率 %								RCEP		特惠税率 %			Article Description
东/冰/格	巴基斯坦	韩国	瑞士 上/下	哥/秘/柬	澳/毛	新西/坡/智	中国港/澳/台	东盟及马来/澳/韩	日/新	亚太2国	老/柬/缅	98/97/95	
/0/	22.5			0//0	5/17.9	0//0	0/0/	15//	15/			0/0/	Other passenger vehicles of cylinder capacity exceeding 3L but not exceeding 4L, with spark-ignition internal combustion eciprocating piston engine, with drive motor (Except for charging by external power supply)
/0/	22.5			0//0	5/17.9	0//0	0/0/	15//	15/			0/0/	Complete parts of Other passenger vehicles of cylinder capacity exceeding 3L but not exceeding 4L, with spark-ignition internal combustion eciprocating piston engine, with drive motor (Except for charging by external
													---Of a cylinder capacity exceeding 4000cc:
													----Saloon cars
/0/	22.5	22.5		0//0	5/17.9	0//0	0/0/					0/0/	Saloon cars of cylinder capacity exceeding 4L, with spark-ignition internal combustion eciprocating piston engine, with drive motor (Except for charging by external power supply)
/0/	22.5	22.5		0//0	5/17.9	0//0	0/0/					0/0/	Complete parts of saloon cars of cylinder capacity exceeding 1L but not exceeding 1.5L, with spark-ignition internal combustion eciprocating piston engine, with drive motor (Except for charging by external
													----Cross-country cars(4WD)
/0/	22.5			0//0	5/17.9	0//0	0/0/					0/0/	Off-road vehicles(4WD) of cylinder capacity exceeding 4L, with spark-ignition internal combustion eciprocating piston engine, with drive motor (Except for charging by external power supply)
/0/	22.5			0//0	5/17.9	0//0	0/0/					0/0/	Complete parts of Off-road vehicles(4WD) of cylinder capacity exceeding 1L but not exceeding 1.5L, with spark-ignition internal combustion eciprocating piston engine, with drive motor (Except for charging by external
													----Station wagons(with 9 seats or less)
/0/	22.5			0//0	5/17.9	0//0	0/0/					0/0/	Station wagons(9 seats or less) of cylinder capacity exceeding 4L, with spark-ignition internal combustion eciprocating piston engine, with drive motor (Except for charging by external power supply)
/0/	22.5			0//0	5/17.9	0//0	0/0/					0/0/	Complete parts of Station wagons(9 seats or less) of cylinder capacity exceeding 1L but not exceeding 1.5L, with spark-ignition internal combustion eciprocating piston engine, with drive motor (Except for charging by external
													----Other
/0/	22.5			0//0	5/17.9	0//0	0/0/					0/0/	Other passenger vehicles of cylinder capacity exceeding 4L, with spark-ignition internal combustion eciprocating piston engine, with drive motor (Except for charging by external power supply)
/0/	22.5			0//0	5/17.9	0//0	0/0/					0/0/	Complete parts of other passenger vehicles of cylinder capacity exceeding 4L, with spark-ignition internal combustion eciprocating piston engine, with drive motor (Except for charging by external
													-Other vehicles, with both compression — ignition internal combustion piston engine(diesel or semi—diesel) and electric motor as motors for propulsion, other than those capable of being charged by plugging to external source ot electric power:
													---Of fl cylinder capacity not exceeding 1000cc:
													----Saloon cars
/0/0				0//0	5/17.9	0//0	0/0/					0/0/	Saloon cars of cylinder capacity cylinder not exceeding 1L, with compression-ignition internal combustion reciprocating piston engine(with diesel or semidiesel engine), with drive motor (Except for charging by external power supply)
/0/0				0//0	5/17.9	0//0	0/0/					0/0/	Complete parts of saloon cars of cylinder capacity cylinder not exceeding 1L, with compression-ignition internal combustion reciprocating piston engine(with diesel or semidiesel engine), with drive motor (Except for charging by external power supply)
													----other
0/0/0				0/0/0	5/17.9	0/0/0	0/0/	15/15/	/15			0/0/0	Other passenger vehicles of cylinder capacity cylinder not exceeding 1L, with compression-ignition internal combustion reciprocating piston engine(with diesel or semidiesel engine), with drive motor (Except for charging by external power supply)

税则号列	货品名称〔CIQ扩展编码及品名—T2表示见附表2〕	最惠(%)	暂定税率	普通	增值/消费	出口退税	计量单位	监管条件/特殊证件	检验检疫	对美关税	亚太上/下
8703.5019　90	同时装有压燃式活塞内燃发动机(柴油或半柴油发动机,排量≤1升)及驱动电动机的其他载人车辆的成套散件(可通过接插外部电源进行充电的除外)〔999〕	15		230	13/1	13	辆/千克	46Oxy/			
	---气缸容量(排气量)超过1000毫升,但不超过1500毫升:										
8703.5021	----小轿车										
8703.5021　10	同时装有压燃式活塞内燃发动机(柴油或半柴油发动机,1升<排量≤1.5升)及驱动电动机的小轿车(可通过接插外部电源进行充电的除外)〔999〕	15		230	13/3	13	辆/千克	46AOxy/	LM		
8703.5021　90	同时装有压燃式活塞内燃发动机(柴油或半柴油发动机,1升<排量≤1.5升)及驱动电动机的小轿车的成套散件(可通过接插外部电源进行充电的除外)〔999〕	15		230	13/3	13	辆/千克	46Oxy/			
8703.5022	----越野车(4轮驱动)										
8703.5022　10	同时装有压燃式活塞内燃发动机(柴油或半柴油发动机,1升<排量≤1.5升)及驱动电动机的四轮驱动越野车(可通过接插外部电源进行充电的除外)〔999〕	15		230	13/3	13	辆/千克	46AOxy/	LM		
8703.5022　90	同时装有压燃式活塞内燃发动机(柴油或半柴油发动机,1升<排量≤1.5升)及驱动电动机的四轮驱动越野车的成套散件(可通过接插外部电源进行充电的除外)〔999〕	15		230	13/3	13	辆/千克	46Oxy/			
8703.5023	----9座及以下的小客车										
8703.5023　10	同时装有压燃式活塞内燃发动机(柴油或半柴油发动机,1升<排量≤1.5升)及驱动电动机的小客车(9座及以下,可通过接插外部电源进行充电的除外)〔999〕	15		230	13/3	13	辆/千克	46AOxy/	LM		
8703.5023　90	同时装有压燃式活塞内燃发动机(柴油或半柴油发动机,1升<排量≤1.5升)及驱动电动机的小客车的成套散件(9座及以下,可通过接插外部电源进行充电的除外)〔999〕	15		230	13/3	13	辆/千克	46Oxy/			
8703.5029	----其他										
8703.5029　10	同时装有压燃式活塞内燃发动机(柴油或半柴油发动机,1升<排量≤1.5升)及驱动电动机的其他载人车辆(可通过接插外部电源进行充电的除外)〔999〕	15		230	13/3	13	辆/千克	46AOxy/	LM		
8703.5029　90	同时装有压燃式活塞内燃发动机(柴油或半柴油发动机,1升<排量≤1.5升)及驱动电动机的其他载人车辆的成套散件(可通过接插外部电源进行充电的除外)〔999〕	15		230	13/3	13	辆/千克	46Oxy/			
	---气缸容量(排气量)超过1500毫升,但不超过2000毫升:										
8703.5031	----小轿车										
8703.5031　10	同时装有压燃式活塞内燃发动机(柴油或半柴油发动机,1.5升<排量≤2升)及驱动电动机的小轿车(可通过接插外部电源进行充电的除外)〔999〕	15		230	13/5	13	辆/千克	46AOxy/	LM		13.5/13.5
8703.5031　90	同时装有压燃式活塞内燃发动机(柴油或半柴油发动机,1.5升<排量≤2升)及驱动电动机的小轿车的成套散件(可通过接插外部电源进行充电的除外)〔999〕	15		230	13/5	13	辆/千克	46Oxy/			13.5/13.5
8703.5032	----越野车(4轮驱动)										

协定税率 %								RCEP		特惠税率 %			Article Description
东/冰/格	巴基斯坦	韩国	瑞士上/下	哥/秘/柬	澳/毛	新西/坡/智	中国港/澳/台	东盟及马来/澳/韩	日/新	亚太2国	老/柬/缅	98/97/95	
0/0/0				0/0/0	5/17.9	0/0/0	0/0/	15/15/	/15			0/0/0	Complete parts ofOther passenger vehicles of cylinder capacity cylinder not exceeding 1L, with compression-ignition internal combustion reciprocating piston engine(with diesel or semidiesel engine), with drive motor (Except for charging by external power supply)
													---Of a cylinder capacity exceeding 1000cc, but not exceeding 1500cc:
													----Saloon cars
/0/0				0//	5/17.9	0//0	0/0/					0//	Saloon cars of cylinder capacity cylinder exceeding 1L but not exceeding 1.5L, with compression-ignition internal combustion reciprocating piston engine(with diesel or semidiesel engine), with drive motor (Except for charging by external power supply)
/0/0				0//	5/17.9	0//0	0/0/					0//	Complete parts of saloon cars of cylinder capacity cylinder exceeding 1L but not exceeding 1.5L, with compression-ignition internal combustion reciprocating piston engine(with diesel or semidiesel engine), with drive motor (Except for charging by external power supply)
													----Cross-country cars (4WD)
/0/0				0//	5/17.9	0//0	0/0/					0//	Off-road vehicles(4WD) of cylinder capacity cylinder exceeding 1L but not exceeding 1.5L, with compression-ignition internal combustion reciprocating piston engine(with diesel or semidiesel engine), with drive motor (Except for charging by external power supply)
/0/0				0//	5/17.9	0//0	0/0/					0//	Complete parts of off-road vehicles(4WD) of cylinder capacity cylinder exceeding 1L but not exceeding 1.5L, with compression-ignition internal combustion reciprocating piston engine(with diesel or semidiesel engine), with drive motor (Except for charging by external power supply)
													----Station wagcms(with 9 seats or less)
/0/0				0//	5/17.9	0//0	0/0/					0//	Station wagons(9 seats or less) of cylinder capacity cylinder exceeding 1L but not exceeding 1.5L, with compression-ignition internal combustion reciprocating piston engine (with diesel or semidiesel engine), with drive motor (Except for charging by external power supply)
/0/0				0//	5/17.9	0//0	0/0/					0//	Complete parts of station wagons(9 seats or less) of cylinder capacity cylinder exceeding 1L but not exceeding 1.5L, with compression-ignition internal combustion reciprocating piston engine(with diesel or semidiesel engine), with drive motor (Except for charging by external power supply)
													----Other
0/0/0				0/0/0	5/17.9	0/0/0	0/0/	15/15/	/15			0/0/0	Other passenger vehicles of cylinder capacity cylinder exceeding 1L but not exceeding 1.5L, with compression-ignition internal combustion reciprocating piston engine(with diesel or semidiesel engine), with drive motor (Except for charging by external power supply)
0/0/0				0/0/0	5/17.9	0/0/0	0/0/	15/15/	/15			0/0/0	Complete parts of other passenger vehicles of cylinder capacity cylinder exceeding 1L but not exceeding 1.5L, with compression-ignition internal combustion reciprocating piston engine(with diesel or semidiesel engine), with drive motor (Except for charging by external power supply)
													---Of a cylinder capacity exceeding 1500cc, but not exceeding 2000cc:
													----Saloon cars
/0/0	22.5			0//	5/17.9	0//0	0/0/					0//	Saloon cars of cylinder capacity cylinder exceeding 1.5L but not exceeding 2L, with compression-ignition internal combustion reciprocating piston engine(with diesel or semidiesel engine), with drive motor (Except for charging by external power supply)
/0/0	22.5			0//	5/17.9	0//0	0/0/					0//	Complete parts of saloon cars of cylinder capacity cylinder exceeding 1L but not exceeding 1.5L, with compression-ignition internal combustion reciprocating piston engine(with diesel or semidiesel engine), with drive motor (Except for charging by external power supply)
													----Cross-country cars (4WD)

税则号列	货品名称〔CIQ扩展编码及品名—T2表示见附表2〕	最惠(%)	暂定税率	普通	增值/消费	出口退税	计量单位	监管条件/特殊证件	检验检疫	对美关税	亚太上/下
8703.5032 10	同时装有压燃式活塞内燃发动机(柴油或半柴油发动机,1.5升<排量≤2升)及驱动电动机的四轮驱动越野车(可通过接插外部电源进行充电的除外)〔999〕	15		230	13/5	13	辆/千克	46AOxy/	LM		13.5/13.5
8703.5032 90	同时装有压燃式活塞内燃发动机(柴油或半柴油发动机,1.5升<排量≤2升)及驱动电动机的四轮驱动越野车的成套散件(可通过接插外部电源进行充电的除外)〔999〕	15		230	13/5	13	辆/千克	46Oxy/			13.5/13.5
8703.5033	----9座及以下的小客车										
8703.5033 10	同时装有压燃式活塞内燃发动机(柴油或半柴油发动机,1.5升<排量≤2升)及驱动电动机的小客车(9座及以下,可通过接插外部电源进行充电的除外)〔999〕	15		230	13/5	13	辆/千克	46AOxy/	LM		13.5/13.5
8703.5033 90	同时装有压燃式活塞内燃发动机(柴油或半柴油发动机,1.5升<排量≤2升)及驱动电动机的小客车的成套散件(9座及以下,可通过接插外部电源进行充电的除外)〔999〕	15		230	13/5	13	辆/千克	46Oxy/			13.5/13.5
8703.5039	----其他										
8703.5039 10	同时装有压燃式活塞内燃发动机(柴油或半柴油发动机,1.5升<排量≤2升)及驱动电动机的其他载人车辆(可通过接插外部电源进行充电的除外)〔999〕	15		230	13/5	13	辆/千克	46AOxy/	LM		13.5/13.5
8703.5039 90	同时装有压燃式活塞内燃发动机(柴油或半柴油发动机,1.5升<排量≤2升)及驱动电动机的其他载人车辆的成套散件(可通过接插外部电源进行充电的除外)〔999〕	15		230	13/5	13	辆/千克	46Oxy/			13.5/13.5
	---气缸容量(排气量)超过2000毫升,但不超过2500毫升:										
8703.5041	----小轿车										
8703.5041 10	同时装有压燃式活塞内燃发动机(柴油或半柴油发动机,2升<排量≤2.5升)及驱动电动机的小轿车(可通过接插外部电源进行充电的除外)〔999〕	15		230	13/9	13	辆/千克	46AOxy/	LM		13.5/13.5
8703.5041 90	同时装有压燃式活塞内燃发动机(柴油或半柴油发动机,2升<排量≤2.5升)及驱动电动机的小轿车的成套散件(可通过接插外部电源进行充电的除外)〔999〕	15		230	13/9	13	辆/千克	46Oxy/			13.5/13.5
8703.5042	----越野车(4轮驱动)										
8703.5042 10	同时装有压燃式活塞内燃发动机(柴油或半柴油发动机,2升<排量≤2.5升)及驱动电动机的四轮驱动越野车(可通过接插外部电源进行充电的除外)〔999〕	15		230	13/9	13	辆/千克	46AOxy/	LM		13.5/13.5
8703.5042 90	同时装有压燃式活塞内燃发动机(柴油或半柴油发动机,2升<排量≤2.5升)及驱动电动机的四轮驱动越野车的成套散件(可通过接插外部电源进行充电的除外)〔999〕	15		230	13/9	13	辆/千克	46Oxy/			13.5/13.5
8703.5043	----9座及以下的小客车										
8703.5043 10	同时装有压燃式活塞内燃发动机(柴油或半柴油发动机,2升<排量≤2.5升)及驱动电动机的小客车(9座及以下,可通过接插外部电源进行充电的除外)〔999〕	15		230	13/9	13	辆/千克	46AOxy/	LM		13.5/13.5
8703.5043 90	同时装有压燃式活塞内燃发动机(柴油或半柴油发动机,2升<排量≤2.5升)及驱动电动机的小客车的成套散件(9座及以下,可通过接插外部电源进行充电的除外)〔999〕	15		230	13/9	13	辆/千克	46Oxy/			13.5/13.5
8703.5049	----其他										

协定税率 %								RCEP		特惠税率 %			Article Description
东/冰/格	巴基斯坦	韩国	瑞士 上/下	哥/秘/柬	澳/毛	新西/坡/智	中国港/澳/台	东盟及马来/澳/韩	日/新	亚太2国	老/柬/缅	98/97/95	
/0/0	22.5	22.5		0//	5/17.9	0//0	0/0/					0//	Off-road vehicles(4WD) of cylinder capacity cylinder exceeding 1.5L but not exceeding 2L, with compression-ignition internal combustion reciprocating piston engine(with diesel or semidiesel engine), with drive motor (Except for charging by external power supply)
/0/0	22.5	22.5		0//	5/17.9	0//0	0/0/					0//	Complete parts of off-road vehicles(4WD) of cylinder capacity cylinder exceeding 1L but not exceeding 1.5L, with compression-ignition internal combustion reciprocating piston engine(with diesel or semidiesel engine), with drive motor (Except for charging by external power supply)
													----Station wagcms(with 9 seats or less)
/0/0	22.5	22.5		0//	5/17.9	0//0	0/0/					0//	Station wagons(9 seats or less) of cylinder capacity cylinder exceeding 1.5L but not exceeding 2L, with compression-ignition internal combustion reciprocating piston engine (with diesel or semidiesel engine), with drive motor (Except for charging by external power supply)
/0/0	22.5	22.5		0//	5/17.9	0//0	0/0/					0//	Complete parts of station wagons(9 seats or less) of cylinder capacity cylinder exceeding 1L but not exceeding 1.5L, with compression-ignition internal combustion reciprocating piston engine(with diesel or semidiesel engine), with drive motor (Except for charging by external power supply)
													----Other
/0/0	22.5			0//	5/17.9	0//0	0/0/					0//	Other passenger vehicles of cylinder capacity cylinder exceeding 1.5L but not exceeding 2L, with compression-ignition internal combustion reciprocating piston engine(with diesel or semidiesel engine), with drive motor (Except for charging by external power supply)
/0/0	22.5			0//	5/17.9	0//0	0/0/					0//	Complete parts of other passenger vehicles of cylinder capacity cylinder exceeding 1.5L but not exceeding 2L, with compression-ignition internal combustion reciprocating piston engine(with diesel or semidiesel engine), with drive motor (Except for charging by external power supply)
													---Of a cylinder capacity exceeding 2000cc, but not exceeding 2500cc:
													----Saloon cars
/0/0	22.5			0//	5/17.9	0//0	0/0/					0//	Saloon cars of cylinder capacity cylinder exceeding 2L but not exceeding 2.5L, with compression-ignition internal combustion reciprocating piston engine(with diesel or semidiesel engine), with drive motor (Except for charging by external power supply)
/0/0	22.5			0//	5/17.9	0//0	0/0/					0//	Complete parts of saloon cars of cylinder capacity cylinder exceeding 1L but not exceeding 1.5L, with compression-ignition internal combustion reciprocating piston engine(with diesel or semidiesel engine), with drive motor (Except for charging by external power supply)
													----Cross-country cars (4WD)
/0/0	22.5			0//	5/17.9	0//0	0/0/					0//	Off-road vehicles(4WD) of cylinder capacity cylinder exceeding 2L but not exceeding 2.5L, with compression-ignition internal combustion reciprocating piston engine(with diesel or semidiesel engine), with drive motor (Except for charging by external power supply)
/0/0	22.5			0//	5/17.9	0//0	0/0/					0//	Complete parts of off-road vehicles(4WD) of cylinder capacity cylinder exceeding 1L but not exceeding 1.5L, with compression-ignition internal combustion reciprocating piston engine(with diesel or semidiesel engine), with drive motor (Except for charging by external power supply)
													----Station wagcms(with 9 seats or less)
/0/0	22.5	22.5		0//	5/17.9	0//0	0/0/					0//	Station wagons(9 seats or less) of cylinder capacity cylinder exceeding 2L but not exceeding 2.5L, with compression-ignition internal combustion reciprocating piston engine (with diesel or semidiesel engine), with drive motor (Except for charging by external power supply)
/0/0	22.5	22.5		0//	5/17.9	0//0	0/0/					0//	Complete parts of station wagons(9 seats or less) of cylinder capacity cylinder exceeding 2L but not exceeding 2.5L, with compression-ignition internal combustion reciprocating piston engine(with diesel or semidiesel engine), with drive motor (Except for charging by external power supply)
													----Other

税则号列		货品名称〔CIQ 扩展编码及品名—T2 表示见附表 2〕	最惠(%)	暂定税率	普通	增值/消费	出口退税	计量单位	监管条件/特殊证件	检验检疫	对美关税	亚太上/下
8703.5049	10	同时装有压燃式活塞内燃发动机(柴油或半柴油发动机,2 升<排量≤2.5 升)及驱动电动机的其他载人车辆(可通过接插外部电源进行充电的除外)〔999〕	15		230	13/9	13	辆/千克	46AOxy/	LM		13.5/13.5
8703.5049	90	同时装有压燃式活塞内燃发动机(柴油或半柴油发动机,2 升<排量≤2.5 升)及驱动电动机的其他载人车辆的成套散件(可通过接插外部电源进行充电的除外)〔999〕	15		230	13/9	13	辆/千克	46Oxy/			13.5/13.5
		---气缸容量(排气量)超过 2500 毫升,但不超过 3000 毫升:										
8703.5051		----小轿车										
8703.5051	10	同时装有压燃式活塞内燃发动机(柴油或半柴油发动机,2.5 升<排量≤3 升)及驱动电动机的小轿车(可通过接插外部电源进行充电的除外)〔999〕	15		270	13/12	13	辆/千克	46AOxy/	LM		13.5/13.5
8703.5051	90	同时装有压燃式活塞内燃发动机(柴油或半柴油发动机,2.5 升<排量≤3 升)及驱动电动机的小轿车的成套散件(可通过接插外部电源进行充电的除外)〔999〕	15		270	13/12	13	辆/千克	46Oxy/			13.5/13.5
8703.5052		----越野车(4 轮驱动)										
8703.5052	10	同时装有压燃式活塞内燃发动机(柴油或半柴油发动机,2.5 升<排量≤3 升)及驱动电动机的四轮驱动越野车(可通过接插外部电源进行充电的除外)〔999〕	15		270	13/12	13	辆/千克	46AOxy/	LM		13.5/13.5
8703.5052	90	同时装有压燃式活塞内燃发动机(柴油或半柴油发动机,2.5 升<排量≤3 升)及驱动电动机的四轮驱动越野车的成套散件(可通过接插外部电源进行充电的除外)〔999〕	15		270	13/12	13	辆/千克	46Oxy/			13.5/13.5
8703.5053		----9 座及以下的小客车										
8703.5053	10	同时装有压燃式活塞内燃发动机(柴油或半柴油发动机,2.5 升<排量≤3 升)及驱动电动机的小客车(9 座及以下,可通过接插外部电源进行充电的除外)〔999〕	15		270	13/12	13	辆/千克	46AOxy/	LM		13.5/13.5
8703.5053	90	同时装有压燃式活塞内燃发动机(柴油或半柴油发动机,2.5 升<排量≤3 升)及驱动电动机的小客车的成套散件(9 座及以下,可通过接插外部电源进行充电的除外)〔999〕	15		270	13/12	13	辆/千克	46Oxy/			13.5/13.5
8703.5059		----其他										
8703.5059	10	同时装有压燃式活塞内燃发动机(柴油或半柴油发动机,2.5 升<排量≤3 升)及驱动电动机的其他载人车辆(可通过接插外部电源进行充电的除外)〔999〕	15		270	13/12	13	辆/千克	46AOxy/	LM		13.5/13.5
8703.5059	90	同时装有压燃式活塞内燃发动机(柴油或半柴油发动机,2.5 升<排量≤3 升)及驱动电动机的其他载人车辆的成套散件(可通过接插外部电源进行充电的除外)〔999〕	15		270	13/12	13	辆/千克	46Oxy/			13.5/13.5
		---气缸容量(排气量)超过 3000 毫升,但不超过 4000 毫升:										
8703.5061		----小轿车										
8703.5061	10	同时装有压燃式活塞内燃发动机(柴油或半柴油发动机,3 升<排量≤4 升)及驱动电动机的小轿车(可通过接插外部电源进行充电的除外)〔999〕	15		270	13/25	13	辆/千克	46AOxy/	LM		13.5/13.5

协定税率 %								RCEP		特惠税率 %			Article Description
东/冰/格	巴基斯坦	韩国	瑞士上/下	哥/秘/柬	澳/毛	新西/坡/智	中国港/澳/台	东盟及马来/澳/韩	日/新	亚太2国	老/柬/缅	98/97/95	
/0/0	22.5			0//	5/17.9	0//0	0/0/					0//	Other passenger vehicles of cylinder capacity cylinder exceeding 2L but not exceeding 2.5L, with compression-ignition internal combustion reciprocating piston engine(with diesel or semidiesel engine), with drive motor (Except for charging by external power supply)
/0/0	22.5			0//	5/17.9	0//0	0/0/					0//	Complete parts of other passenger vehicles of cylinder capacity cylinder exceeding 2L but not exceeding 2.5L, with compression-ignition internal combustion reciprocating piston engine(with diesel or semidiesel engine), with drive motor (Except for charging by external power supply)
													---Of a cylinder capacity exceeding 2500cc, but not exceeding 3000cc:
													----Saloon cars
0/0/0	22.5			0//0	5/17.9	0/0/0	0/0/	15/15/	/15			0//	Saloon cars of cylinder capacity cylinder exceeding 2.5L but not exceeding 3L, with compression-ignition internal combustion reciprocating piston engine(with diesel or semidiesel engine), with drive motor (Except for charging by external power supply)
0/0/0	22.5			0//0	5/17.9	0/0/0	0/0/	15/15/	/15			0//	Complete parts of saloon cars of cylinder capacity cylinder exceeding 2.5L but not exceeding 3L, with compression-ignition internal combustion reciprocating piston engine(with diesel or semidiesel engine), with drive motor (Except for charging by external power supply)
													----Cross-country cars (4WD)
0/0/0	22.5	22.5		0//0	5/17.9	0/0/0	0/0/	15/15/	/15			0//	Off-road vehicles(4WD) of cylinder capacity cylinder exceeding 2.5L but not exceeding 3L, with compression-ignition internal combustion reciprocating piston engine(with diesel or semidiesel engine), with drive motor (Except for charging by external power supply)
0/0/0	22.5	22.5		0//0	5/17.9	0/0/0	0/0/	15/15/	/15			0//	Complete parts of off-road vehicles(4WD) of cylinder capacity cylinder exceeding 2.5L but not exceeding 3L, with compression-ignition internal combustion reciprocating piston engine(with diesel or semidiesel engine), with drive motor (Except for charging by external power supply)
													----Station wagcms(with 9 seats or less)
0/0/0	22.5			0//0	5/17.9	0/0/0	0/0/	15/15/	/15			0//	Station wagons(9 seats or less) of cylinder capacity cylinder exceeding 2.5L but not exceeding 3L, with compression-ignition internal combustion reciprocating piston engine (with diesel or semidiesel engine), with drive motor (Except for charging by external power supply)
0/0/0	22.5			0//0	5/17.9	0/0/0	0/0/	15/15/	/15			0//	Complete parts of station wagons(9 seats or less) of cylinder capacity cylinder exceeding 2.5L but not exceeding 3L, with compression-ignition internal combustion reciprocating piston engine(with diesel or semidiesel engine), with drive motor (Except for charging by external power supply)
													----Other
0/0/0	22.5			0//0	5/17.9	0/0/0	0/0/	15/15/	/15			0//	Other passenger vehicles of cylinder capacity cylinder exceeding 2.5L but not exceeding 3L, with compression-ignition internal combustion reciprocating piston engine(with diesel or semidiesel engine), with drive motor (Except for charging by external power supply)
0/0/0	22.5			0//0	5/17.9	0/0/0	0/0/	15/15/	/15			0//	Complete parts of other passenger vehicles of cylinder capacity cylinder exceeding 2.5L but not exceeding 3L, with compression-ignition internal combustion reciprocating piston engine(with diesel or semidiesel engine), with drive motor (Except for charging by external power supply)
													---Of a cylinder capacity exceeding 3000cc, but not exceeding 4000cc:
													----Saloon cars
0/0/0	22.5			0//0	5/17.9	0/0/0	0/0/	15/15/	/15			0/0/	Saloon cars of cylinder capacity cylinder exceeding 3L but not exceeding 4L, with compression-ignition internal combustion reciprocating piston engine(with diesel or semidiesel engine), with drive motor (Except for charging by external power supply)

税则号列	货品名称〔CIQ 扩展编码及品名－T2 表示见附表 2〕	最惠(%)	暂定税率	普通	增值/消费	出口退税	计量单位	监管条件/特殊证件	检验检疫	对美关税	亚太上/下
8703.5061 90	同时装有压燃式活塞内燃发动机(柴油或半柴油发动机,3 升＜排量≤4 升)及驱动电动机的小轿车的成套散件(可通过接插外部电源进行充电的除外)〔999〕	15		270	13/25	13	辆/千克	46Oxy/			13.5/13.5
8703.5062	----越野车(4 轮驱动)										
8703.5062 10	同时装有压燃式活塞内燃发动机(柴油或半柴油发动机,3 升＜排量≤4 升)及驱动电动机的四轮驱动越野车(可通过接插外部电源进行充电的除外)〔999〕	15		270	13/25	13	辆/千克	46AOxy/	LM		13.5/13.5
8703.5062 90	同时装有压燃式活塞内燃发动机(柴油或半柴油发动机,3 升＜排量≤4 升)及驱动电动机的四轮驱动越野车的成套散件(可通过接插外部电源进行充电的除外)〔999〕	15		270	13/25	13	辆/千克	46Oxy/			13.5/13.5
8703.5063	----9 座及以下的小客车										
8703.5063 10	同时装有压燃式活塞内燃发动机(柴油或半柴油发动机,3 升＜排量≤4 升)及驱动电动机的小客车(9 座及以下,可通过接插外部电源进行充电的除外)〔999〕	15		270	13/25	13	辆/千克	46AOxy/	LM		13.5/13.5
8703.5063 90	同时装有压燃式活塞内燃发动机(柴油或半柴油发动机,3 升＜排量≤4 升)及驱动电动机的小客车的成套散件(9 座及以下,可通过接插外部电源进行充电的除外)〔999〕	15		270	13/25	13	辆/千克	46Oxy/			13.5/13.5
8703.5069	----其他										
8703.5069 10	同时装有压燃式活塞内燃发动机(柴油或半柴油发动机,3 升＜排量≤4 升)及驱动电动机的其他载人车辆(可通过接插外部电源进行充电的除外)〔999〕	15		270	13/25	13	辆/千克	46AOxy/	LM		13.5/13.5
8703.5069 90	同时装有压燃式活塞内燃发动机(柴油或半柴油发动机,3 升＜排量≤4 升)及驱动电动机的其他载人车辆的成套散件(可通过接插外部电源进行充电的除外)〔999〕	15		270	13/25	13	辆/千克	46Oxy/			13.5/13.5
	---气缸容量(排气量)超过 4000 毫升:										
8703.5071	----小轿车										
8703.5071 10	同时装有压燃式活塞内燃发动机(柴油或半柴油发动机,排量＞4 升)及驱动电动机的小轿车(可通过接插外部电源进行充电的除外)〔999〕	15		270	13/40	13	辆/千克	46AOxy/	LM		13.5/13.5
8703.5071 90	同时装有压燃式活塞内燃发动机(柴油或半柴油发动机,排量＞4 升)及驱动电动机的小轿车的成套散件(可通过接插外部电源进行充电的除外)〔999〕	15		270	13/40	13	辆/千克	46Oxy/			13.5/13.5
8703.5072	----越野车(4 轮驱动)										
8703.5072 10	同时装有压燃式活塞内燃发动机(柴油或半柴油发动机,排量＞4 升)及驱动电动机的四轮驱动越野车(可通过接插外部电源进行充电的除外)〔999〕	15		270	13/40	13	辆/千克	46AOxy/	LM		13.5/13.5
8703.5072 90	同时装有压燃式活塞内燃发动机(柴油或半柴油发动机,排量＞4 升)及驱动电动机的四轮驱动越野车的成套散件(可通过接插外部电源进行充电的除外)〔999〕	15		270	13/40	13	辆/千克	46Oxy/			13.5/13.5
8703.5073	----9 座及以下的小客车										
8703.5073 10	同时装有压燃式活塞内燃发动机(柴油或半柴油发动机,排量＞4 升)及驱动电动机的的小客车(9 座及以下,可通过接插外部电源进行充电的除外)〔999〕	15		270	13/40	13	辆/千克	46AOxy/	LM		13.5/13.5

协定税率 %								RCEP		特惠税率 %			Article Description
东/冰/格	巴基斯坦	韩国	瑞士上/下	哥/秘/柬	澳/毛	新西/坡/智	中国港/澳/台	东盟及马来/澳/韩	日/新	亚太2国	老/柬/缅	98/97/95	
0/0/0	22.5			0//0	5/17.9	0/0/0	0/0/	15/15/	/15			0/0/	Complete parts of saloon cars of cylinder capacity cylinder exceeding 3L but not exceeding 4L, with compression-ignition internal combustion reciprocating piston engine(with diesel or semidiesel engine), with drive motor (Except for charging by external power supply)
													----Cross-country cars (4WD)
0/0/0	22.5			0//0	5/17.9	0/0/0	0/0/	15/15/	/15			0/0/	Off-road vehicles(4WD) of cylinder capacity cylinder exceeding 3L but not exceeding 4L, with compression-ignition internal combustion reciprocating piston engine(with diesel or semidiesel engine), with drive motor (Except for charging by external power supply)
0/0/0	22.5			0//0	5/17.9	0/0/0	0/0/	15/15/	/15			0/0/	Complete parts of off-road vehicles(4WD) of cylinder capacity cylinder exceeding 3L but not exceeding 4L, with compression-ignition internal combustion reciprocating piston engine (with diesel or semidiesel engine), with drive motor (Except for charging by external power supply)
													----Station wagcms(with 9 seats or less)
0/0/0	22.5			0//0	5/17.9	0/0/0	0/0/	15/15/	/15			0/0/	Station wagons(9 seats or less) of cylinder capacity cylinder exceeding 3L but not exceeding 4L, with compression-ignition internal combustion reciprocating piston engine(with diesel or semidiesel engine), with drive motor (Except for charging by external power supply)
0/0/0	22.5			0//0	5/17.9	0/0/0	0/0/	15/15/	/15			0/0/	Complete parts of station wagons(9 seats or less) of cylinder capacity cylinder exceeding 3L but not exceeding 4L, with compression-ignition internal combustion reciprocating piston engine(with diesel or semidiesel engine), with drive motor (Except for charging by external power supply)
													----Other
0/0/0	22.5			0//0	5/17.9	0/0/0	0/0/	15/15/	/15			0/0/	Other passenger vehicles of cylinder capacity cylinder exceeding 3L but not exceeding 4L, with compression-ignition internal combustion reciprocating piston engine(with diesel or semidiesel engine), with drive motor (Except for charging by external power supply)
0/0/0	22.5			0//0	5/17.9	0/0/0	0/0/	15/15/	/15			0/0/	Complete parts of other passenger vehicles of cylinder capacity cylinder exceeding 3L but not exceeding 4L, with compression-ignition internal combustion reciprocating piston engine (with diesel or semidiesel engine), with drive motor (Except for charging by external power supply)
													---Of a cylinder capacity exceeding4000cc:
													----Saloon cars
0/0/0	22.5			0//0	0/17.9	0/0/0	0/0/	15/15/	/15			0/0/	Saloon cars of cylinder capacity cylinder exceeding 4L, with compression ignition internal combustion reciprocating piston engine(with diesel or semidiesel engine), with drive motor (Except for charging by external power supply)
0/0/0	22.5			0//0	0/17.9	0/0/0	0/0/	15/15/	/15			0/0/	Complete parts of saloon cars of cylinder capacity cylinder exceeding 3L but not exceeding 4L, with compression-ignition internal combustion reciprocating piston engine(with diesel or semidiesel engine), with drive motor (Except for charging by external power supply)
													----Cross-country cars (4WD)
0/0/0	22.5			0//0	0/17.9	0/0/0	0/0/	15/15/	/15			0/0/	Off-road vehicles(4WD) of cylinder capacity cylinder exceeding 4L, with compression-ignition internal combustion reciprocating piston engine(with diesel or semidiesel engine), with drive motor (Except for charging by external power supply)
0/0/0	22.5			0//0	0/17.9	0/0/0	0/0/	15/15/	/15			0/0/	Complete parts of off-road vehicles(4WD) of cylinder capacity cylinder exceeding 4L, with compression-ignition internal combustion reciprocating piston engine(with diesel or semidiesel engine), with drive motor (Except for charging by external power supply)
													----Station wagcms(with 9 seats or less)
0/0/0	22.5			0//0	0/17.9	0/0/0	0/0/	15/15/	/15			0/0/	Station wagons(9 seats or less) of cylinder capacity cylinder exceeding 4L, with compression-ignition internal combustion reciprocating piston engine(with diesel or semidiesel engine), with drive motor (Except for charging by external power supply)

税则号列	货品名称〔CIQ 扩展编码及品名－T2 表示见附表 2〕	最惠(%)	暂定税率	普通	增值/消费	出口退税	计量单位	监管条件/特殊证件	检验检疫	对美关税	亚太上/下
8703.5073 90	同时装有压燃式活塞内燃发动机(柴油或半柴油发动机,排量＞4 升)及驱动电动机的小客车的成套散件(9 座及以下,可通过接插外部电源进行充电的除外)〔999〕	15		270	13/40	13	辆/千克	46Oxy/			13.5/13.5
8703.5079	----其他										
8703.5079 10	同时装有压燃式活塞内燃发动机(柴油或半柴油发动机,排量＞4 升)及驱动电动机的的其他载人车辆(可通过接插外部电源进行充电的除外)〔999〕	15		270	13/40	13	辆/千克	46AOxy/	LM		13.5/13.5
8703.5079 90	同时装有压燃式活塞内燃发动机(柴油或半柴油发动机,排量＞4 升)及驱动电动机的的其他载人车辆的成套散件(可通过接插外部电源进行充电的除外)〔999〕	15		270	13/40	13	辆/千克	46Oxy/			13.5/13.5
	-同时装有点燃式活塞内燃发动机及驱动电动机 、可通过接插外部电源进行充电的其他车辆 :										
	---气缸容量(排气量)不超过 1000 毫升:										
8703.6011	----小轿车〔999〕	15		270	13/1	13	辆/千克	46AO/	LM		13.5/13.5
8703.6012	----越野车(4 轮驱动)〔999〕	15		270	13/1	13	辆/千克	46AO/	LM		13.5/13.5
8703.6013	----9 座及以下的小客车〔999〕	15		270	13/1	13	辆/千克	46AO/	LM		13.5/13.5
8703.6019	----其他〔999〕	15		270	13/1	13	辆/千克	46AO/	LM		13.5/13.5
	---气缸容量(排气量)超过 1000 毫升,但不超过 1500 毫升:										
8703.6021	----小轿车〔999〕	15		270	13/3	13	辆/千克	46AO/	LM		13.5/13.5
8703.6022	----越野车(4 轮驱动)〔999〕	15		270	13/3	13	辆/千克	46AO/	LM		13.5/13.5
8703.6023	----9 座及以下的小客车〔999〕	15		270	13/3	13	辆/千克	46AO/	LM		13.5/13.5
8703.6029	----其他〔999〕	15		270	13/3	13	辆/千克	46AO/	LM		13.5/13.5
	---气缸容量(排气量)超过 1500 毫升,但不超过 2000 毫升:										
8703.6031	----小轿车〔999〕	15		270	13/5	13	辆/千克	46AO/	LM		13.5/13.5
8703.6032	----越野车(4 轮驱动)〔999〕	15		270	13/5	13	辆/千克	46AO/	LM		13.5/13.5
8703.6033	----9 座及以下的小客车〔999〕	15		270	13/5	13	辆/千克	46AO/	LM		13.5/13.5
8703.6039	----其他〔999〕	15		270	13/5	13	辆/千克	46AO/	LM		13.5/13.5
	---气缸容量(排气量)超过 2000 毫升,但不超过 2500 毫升:										
8703.6041	----小轿车〔999〕	15		270	13/9	13	辆/千克	46AO/	LM		13.5/13.5
8703.6042	----越野车(4 轮驱动)〔999〕	15		270	13/9	13	辆/千克	46AO/	LM		13.5/13.5
8703.6043	----9 座及以下的小客车〔999〕	15		270	13/9	13	辆/千克	46AO/	LM		13.5/13.5
8703.6049	----其他〔999〕	15		270	13/9	13	辆/千克	46AO/	LM		13.5/13.5
	---气缸容量(排气量)超过 2500 毫升,但不超过 3000 毫升:										
8703.6051	----小轿车〔999〕	15		270	13/12	13	辆/千克	46AO/	LM		13.5/13.5
8703.6052	----越野车(4 轮驱动)〔999〕	15		270	13/12	13	辆/千克	46AO/	LM		13.5/13.5
8703.6053	----9 座及以下的小客车〔999〕	15		270	13/12	13	辆/千克	46AO/	LM		13.5/13.5
8703.6059	----其他〔999〕	15		270	13/12	13	辆/千克	46AO/	LM		13.5/13.5
	---气缸容量(排气量)超过 3000 毫升,但不超过 4000 毫升:										
8703.6061	----小轿车〔999〕	15		270	13/25	13	辆/千克	46AO/	LM		13.5/13.5
8703.6062	----越野车(4 轮驱动)〔999〕	15		270	13/25	13	辆/千克	46AO/	LM		13.5/13.5
8703.6063	----9 座及以下的小客车〔999〕	15		270	13/25	13	辆/千克	46AO/	LM		13.5/13.5
8703.6069	----其他〔999〕	15		270	13/25	13	辆/千克	46AO/	LM		13.5/13.5
	---气缸容量(排气量)超过 4000 毫升:										
8703.6071	----小轿车〔999〕	15		270	13/40	13	辆/千克	46AO/	LM		13.5/13.5
8703.6072	----越野车(4 轮驱动)〔999〕	15		270	13/40	13	辆/千克	46AO/	LM		13.5/13.5
8703.6073	----9 座及以下的小客车〔999〕	15		270	13/40	13	辆/千克	46AO/	LM		13.5/13.5
8703.6079	----其他〔999〕	15		270	13/40	13	辆/千克	46AO/	LM		13.5/13.5
	-同时装有压燃式活塞内燃发动机(柴油或半柴油发动机)及驱动电动机、可通过接插外部电源进行充电的其他车辆:										
	---气缸容量(排气量)不超过 1000 毫升:										
8703.7011	----小轿车〔999〕	15		270	13/1	13	辆/千克	46AO/	LM		13.5/13.5
8703.7012	----越野车(4 轮驱动)〔999〕	15		270	13/1	13	辆/千克	46AO/	LM		13.5/13.5
8703.7013	----9 座及以下的小客车〔999〕	15		270	13/1	13	辆/千克	46AO/	LM		13.5/13.5
8703.7019	----其他〔999〕	15		270	13/1	13	辆/千克	46AO/	LM		13.5/13.5
	---气缸容量(排气量)超过 1000 毫升,但不超过 1500 毫升:										
8703.7021	----小轿车〔999〕	15		270	13/3	13	辆/千克	46AO/	LM		13.5/13.5
8703.7022	----越野车(4 轮驱动)〔999〕	15		270	13/3	13	辆/千克	46AO/	LM		13.5/13.5
8703.7023	----9 座及以下的小客车〔999〕	15		270	13/3	13	辆/千克	46AO/	LM		13.5/13.5
8703.7029	----其他〔999〕	15		270	13/3	13	辆/千克	46AO/	LM		13.5/13.5
	---气缸容量(排气量)超过 1500 毫升,但不超过 2000 毫升:										
8703.7031	----小轿车〔999〕	15		270	13/5	13	辆/千克	46AO/	LM		13.5/13.5
8703.7032	----越野车(4 轮驱动)〔999〕	15		270	13/5	13	辆/千克	46AO/	LM		13.5/13.5
8703.7033	----9 座及以下的小客车〔999〕	15		270	13/5	13	辆/千克	46AO/	LM		13.5/13.5

协定税率 %								RCEP		特惠税率 %			Article Description
东/冰/格	巴基斯坦	韩国	瑞士上/下	哥/秘/柬	澳/毛	新西/坡/智	中国港/澳/台	东盟及马来/澳/韩	日/新	亚太2国	老/柬/缅	98/97/95	
0/0/0	22.5			0//0	0/17.9	0/0/0	0/0/	15/15/	/15			0/0/	Complete parts of station wagons(9 seats or less) of cylinder capacity cylinder exceeding 4L, with compression-ignition internal combustion reciprocating piston engine(with diesel or semidiesel engine), with drive motor (Except for charging by external power supply)
													----Other
0/0/0	22.5			0//0	0/17.9	0/0/0	0/0/	15/15/	/15			0/0/	Other passenger vehicles of cylinder capacity cylinder exceeding 3L but not exceeding 4L, with compression-ignition internal combustion reciprocating piston engine(with diesel or semidiesel engine), with drive motor (Except for charging by external power supply)
0/0/0	22.5			0//0	0/17.9	0/0/0	0/0/	15/15/	/15			0/0/	Complete parts of other passenger vehicles of cylinder capacity cylinder exceeding 4L, with compression-ignition internal combustion reciprocating piston engine(with diesel or semidiesel engine), with drive motor (Except for charging by external power supply)
													-Other vehicles equipped with positive ignition piston internal combustion engine and drive motor, which can be charged by plugging in external power supply
													---Of a cylinder capacity not exceeding 1000 cc:
/0/	22.5			0//	0/17.9	0//0	0/0/					0//	----Saloon cars
/0/	22.5			0//	0/17.9	0//0	0/0/					0//	----Cross－country cars(4WD)
/0/	22.5			0//	0/17.9	0//0	0/0/					0//	----Station wagcms(with 9 seats or less)
/0/	22.5			0//	0/17.9	0//0	0/0/					0//	----Other
													---Of a cylinder capacity 1000 cc, but not exceeding 1500 cc:
/0/	22.5			0//	0/17.9	0//0	0/0/					0//	----Saloon cars
/0/	22.5			0//	0/17.9	0//0	0/0/					0//	----Cross－country cars(4WD)
/0/	22.5			0//	0/17.9	0//0	0/0/					0//	----Station wagcms(with 9 seats or less)
/0/	22.5			0//	0/17.9	0//0	0/0/					0//	----Other
													---Of a cylinder capacity 1500 cc, but not exceeding 2000 cc:
/0/	22.5			0//	0/17.9	0//0	0/0/					0//	----Saloon cars
/0/	22.5			0//	0/17.9	0//0	0/0/					0//	----Cross－country cars(4WD)
/0/	22.5			0//	0/17.9	0//0	0/0/					0//	----Station wagcms(with 9 seats or less)
/0/	22.5			0//	0/17.9	0//0	0/0/					0//	----Other
													---Of a cylinder capacity 2000 cc, but not exceeding 2500 cc:
/0/	22.5			0//	0/17.9	0//0	0/0/					0//	----Saloon cars
/0/	22.5			0//	0/17.9	0//0	0/0/					0//	----Cross－country cars(4WD)
/0/	22.5			0//	0/17.9	0//0	0/0/					0//	----Station wagcms(with 9 seats or less)
/0/	22.5			0//	0/17.9	0//0	0/0/					0//	----Other"
													---Of a cylinder capacity 2500 cc, but not exceeding 3000 cc:
/0/	22.5			0//	0/17.9	0//0	0/0/	15//	15/			0//	----Saloon cars
/0/	22.5			0//	0/17.9	0//0	0/0/	15/15/	15/15			0//	----Cross－country cars(4WD)
/0/	22.5			0//	0/17.9	0//0	0/0/	15/15/	15/15			0//	----Station wagcms(with 9 seats or less)
/0/	22.5			0//	0/17.9	0//0	0/0/	15/15/	15/15			0//	Other
													---Of a cylinder capacity 3000 cc, but not exceeding 4000 cc:
/0/	22.5			0//	0/17.9	0//0	0/0/	15//	15/			0//	----Saloon cars
/0/	22.5			0//	0/17.9	0//0	0/0/	15//	15/			0//	----Cross－country cars(4WD)
/0/	22.5			0//	0/17.9	0//0	0/0/	15//	15/			0//	----Station wagcms(with 9 seats or less)
/0/	22.5			0//	0/17.9	0//0	0/0/	15//	15/			0//	----Other
													---Of a cylinder capacity exceeding 4000 cc:
/0/	22.5			0//	0/17.9	0//0	0/0/					0//	----Saloon cars
/0/	22.5			0//	0/17.9	0//0	0/0/					0//	----Cross－country cars(4WD)
/0/	22.5			0//	0/17.9	0//0	0/0/					0//	----Station wagcms(with 9 seats or less)
/0/	22.5			0//	0/17.9	0//0	0/0/					0//	----Other
													-Other vehicles equipped with compression ignition piston internal combustionengine (diesel or semi diesel engine) and drive motor, which can be charged byconnecting external power supply:
													---Of a cylinder capacity not exceeding 1000 cc:
0/0/0		22.5		0/0/0	0/17.9	0/0/0	0/0/					0/0/0	----Saloon cars
0/0/0		22.5		0/0/0	0/17.9	0/0/0	0/0/	15/15/	/15			0/0/0	----Cross－country cars(4WD)
0/0/0		22.5		0/0/0	0/17.9	0/0/0	0/0/	15/15/	/15			0/0/0	----Station wagcms(with 9 seats or less)
0/0/0		22.5		0/0/0	0/17.9	0/0/0	0/0/	15/15/	/15			0/0/0	----Other
													---Of a cylinder capacity 1000 cc, but not exceeding 1500 cc:
0/0/0		22.5		0/0/0	0/17.9	0/0/0	0/0/					0/0/0	----Saloon cars
0/0/0		22.5		0/0/0	0/17.9	0/0/0	0/0/					0/0/0	----Cross－country cars(4WD)
0/0/0		22.5		0/0/0	0/17.9	0/0/0	0/0/					0/0/0	----Station wagcms(with 9 seats or less)
0/0/0		22.5		0/0/0	0/17.9	0/0/0	0/0/	15/15/	/15			0/0/0	----Other
													---Of a cylinder capacity 1500 cc, but not exceeding 2000 cc:
0/0/0		22.5		0/0/0	0/17.9	0/0/0	0/0/					0/0/0	----Saloon cars
0/0/0		22.5		0/0/0	0/17.9	0/0/0	0/0/					0/0/0	----Cross－country cars(4WD)
0/0/0		22.5		0/0/0	0/17.9	0/0/0	0/0/					0/0/0	----Station wagcms(with 9 seats or less)

税则号列	货品名称〔CIQ扩展编码及品名－T2表示见附表2〕	最惠(%)	暂定税率	普通	增值/消费	出口退税	计量单位	监管条件/特殊证件	检验检疫	对美关税	亚太上/下
8703.7039	----其他〔999〕	15		270	13/5	13	辆/千克	46AO/	LM		13.5/13.5
	---气缸容量(排气量)超过2000毫升，但不超过2500毫升：										
8703.7041	----小轿车〔999〕	15		270	13/9	13	辆/千克	46AO/	LM		13.5/13.5
8703.7042	----越野车(4轮驱动)〔999〕	15		270	13/9	13	辆/千克	46AO/	LM		13.5/13.5
8703.7043	----9座及以下的小客车〔999〕	15		270	13/9	13	辆/千克	46AO/	LM		13.5/13.5
8703.7049	----其他〔999〕	15		270	13/9	13	辆/千克	46AO/	LM		13.5/13.5
	---气缸容量(排气量)超过2500毫升，但不超过3000毫升：										
8703.7051	----小轿车〔999〕	15		270	13/12	13	辆/千克	46AO/	LM		13.5/13.5
8703.7052	----越野车(4轮驱动)〔999〕	15		270	13/12	13	辆/千克	46AO/	LM		13.5/13.5
8703.7053	----9座及以下的小客车〔999〕	15		270	13/12	13	辆/千克	46AO/	LM		13.5/13.5
8703.7059	----其他〔999〕	15		270	13/12	13	辆/千克	46AO/	LM		13.5/13.5
	---气缸容量(排气量)超过3000毫升，但不超过4000毫升：										
8703.7061	----小轿车〔999〕	15		270	13/25	13	辆/千克	46AO/	LM		13.5/13.5
8703.7062	----越野车(4轮驱动)〔999〕	15		270	13/25	13	辆/千克	46AO/	LM		13.5/13.5
8703.7063	----9座及以下的小客车〔999〕	15		270	13/25	13	辆/千克	46AO/	LM		13.5/13.5
8703.7069	----其他〔999〕	15		270	13/25	13	辆/千克	46AO/	LM		13.5/13.5
	---气缸容量(排气量)超过4000毫升：										
8703.7071	----小轿车〔999〕	15		270	13/40	13	辆/千克	46AO/	LM		13.5/13.5
8703.7072	----越野车(4轮驱动)〔999〕	15		270	13/40	13	辆/千克	46AO/	LM		13.5/13.5
8703.7073	----9座及以下的小客车〔999〕	15		270	13/40	13	辆/千克	46AO/	LM		13.5/13.5
8703.7079	----其他〔999〕	15		270	13/40	13	辆/千克	46AO/	LM		13.5/13.5
8703.8000	-仅装有驱动电动机的其他车辆	15		270	13/	13	辆/千克	6AO	LM	/	13.5
8703.8000 10	旧的仅装有驱动电动机的其他载人车辆〔999〕	15		270	13/	13	辆/千克	46Axy/	M		13.5/13.5
8703.8000 90	其他仅装有驱动电动机的其他载人车辆〔999〕	15		270	13/	13	辆/千克	6AO/	LM		13.5/13.5
8703.9000	-其他										
8703.9000 21	其他型排气量≤1升的其他载人车辆〔999〕	15		270	13/1	13	辆/千克	46AOxy/	LM		13.5/13.5
8703.9000 22	其他型1升＜排气量≤1.5升的其他载人车辆〔999〕	15		270	13/3	13	辆/千克	46AOxy/	LM		13.5/13.5
8703.9000 23	其他型1.5升＜排气量≤2升的其他载人车辆〔999〕	15		270	13/5	13	辆/千克	46AOxy/	LM		13.5/13.5
8703.9000 24	其他型2升＜排气量≤2.5升的其他载人车辆〔999〕	15		270	13/9	13	辆/千克	46AOxy/	LM		13.5/13.5
8703.9000 25	其他型2.5升＜排气量≤3升的其他载人车辆〔999〕	15		270	13/12	13	辆/千克	46AOxy/	LM		13.5/13.5
8703.9000 26	其他型3升＜排气量≤4升的其他载人车辆〔999〕	15		270	13/25	13	辆/千克	46AOxy/	LM		13.5/13.5
8703.9000 27	其他型排气量＞4升的其他载人车辆〔999〕	15		270	13/40	13	辆/千克	46AOxy/	LM		13.5/13.5
8703.9000 29	其他无法区分排气量的载人车辆〔999〕	15		270	13/	13	辆/千克	6AO/	LM		13.5/13.5
8703.9000 90	8703.9000所列车辆的成套散件〔999〕	15		270	13/	13	辆/千克	6O/			13.5/13.5
87.04	**货运机动车辆：**										
	-非公路用自卸车：										
8704.1030	---电动轮货运自卸车〔999〕	6		20	13/	13	辆/千克	6A/	M		
8704.1090	---其他〔999〕	6		20	13/	13	辆/千克	6A/	M		
	-仅装有压燃式活塞内燃发动机(柴油或半柴油发动机)的其他货车：										
8704.2100	--车辆总重量不超过5吨〔999〕	15		70	13/	9,13	辆/千克	46AOxy/	LM		
	--车辆总重量超过5吨，但不超过20吨：										
8704.2230	---车辆总重量超过5吨，但小于14吨〔999〕	15		70	13/	13	辆/千克	46Axy/	LM		13.5/13.5
8704.2240	---车辆总重量在14吨及以上，但不超过20吨〔999〕	15		40	13/	13	辆/千克	46Axy/	LM		13.5/13.5
8704.2300	--车辆总重量超过20吨										
8704.2300 10	固井水泥车、压裂车、混砂车、连续油管车、液氮泵车用底盘(动力装置仅装有压燃式活塞内燃发动机，车辆总重量＞35吨，装驾驶室)〔999〕	15	10	40	13/	13	辆/千克	46AOxy/	LM		
8704.2300 20	起重≥55吨汽车起重机用底盘(动力装置仅装有压燃式活塞内燃发动机)〔999〕	15	8	40	13/	13	辆/千克	46AOxy/	LM		
8704.2300 30	车辆总重量≥31吨清障车专用底盘(动力装置仅装有压燃式活塞内燃发动机)〔999〕	15	10	40	13/	13	辆/千克	46AOxy/	LM		
8704.2300 90	柴油型的其他超重型货车(仅装有压燃式活塞内燃发动机，超重型指车辆总重量＞20吨)〔999〕	15		40	13/	13	辆/千克	46AOxy/	LM		
	-仅装有点燃式活塞内燃发动机的其他货车：										
8704.3100	--车辆总重量不超过5吨〔999〕	15		70	13/	13	辆/千克	46AOxy/	LM		
	--车辆总重量超过5吨：										
8704.3230	---车辆总重量超过5吨，但不超过8吨〔999〕	15		70	13/	13	辆/千克	46Axy/	LM		
8704.3240	---车辆总重量超过8吨〔999〕	15		70	13/	13	辆/千克	46Axy/	LM		

协定税率 %								RCEP		特惠税率 %			Article Description
东/冰/格	巴基斯坦	韩国	瑞士上/下	哥/秘/柬	澳/毛	新西/坡/智	中国港/澳/台	东盟及马来/澳/韩	日/新	亚太2国	老/柬/缅	98/97/95	
0/0/0		22.5		0/0/0	0/17.9	0/0/0	0/0/					0/0/0	----Other
													---Of a cylinder capacity 2000 cc, but not exceeding 2500 cc:
0/0/0		22.5		0/0/0	0/17.9	0/0/0	0/0/					0/0/0	----Saloon cars
0/0/0		22.5		0/0/0	0/17.9	0/0/0	0/0/					0/0/0	----Cross—country cars(4WD)
0/0/0		22.5		0/0/0	0/17.9	0/0/0	0/0/					0/0/0	----Station wagcms(with 9 seats or less)
0/0/0		22.5		0/0/0	0/17.9	0/0/0	0/0/					0/0/0	----Other
													---Of a cylinder capacity 2500 cc, but not exceeding 3000 cc:
0/0/0		22.5		0/0/0	0/17.9	0/0/0	0/0/	15/15/	/15			0/0/0	----Saloon cars
0/0/0		22.5		0/0/0	0/17.9	0/0/0	0/0/	15/15/	/15			0/0/0	----Cross—country cars(4WD)
0/0/0		22.5		0/0/0	0/17.9	0/0/0	0/0/	15/15/	/15			0/0/0	----Station wagcms(with 9 seats or less)
0/0/0		22.5		0/0/0	0/17.9	0/0/0	0/0/	15/15/	/15			0/0/0	----Other
													---Of a cylinder capacity 3000 cc, but not exceeding 4000 cc:
0/0/0		22.5		0/0/0	0/17.9	0/0/0	0/0/	15/15/	/15			0/0/0	----Saloon cars
0/0/0		22.5		0/0/0	0/17.9	0/0/0	0/0/	15/15/	/15			0/0/0	----Cross—country cars(4WD)
0/0/0		22.5		0/0/0	0/17.9	0/0/0	0/0/	15/15/	/15			0/0/0	----Station wagcms(with 9 seats or less)
0/0/0		22.5		0/0/0	0/17.9	0/0/0	0/0/	15/15/	/15			0/0/0	----Other
													---Of a cylinder capacity exceeding 4000 cc:
0/0/0		22.5		0/0/0	0/17.9	0/0/0	0/0/	15/15/	/15			0/0/0	----Saloon cars
0/0/0		22.5		0/0/0	0/17.9	0/0/0	0/0/	15/15/	/15			0/0/0	----Cross—country cars(4WD)
0/0/0		22.5		0/0/0	0/17.9	0/0/0	0/0/	15/15/	/15			0/0/0	----Station wagcms(with 9 seats or less)
0/0/0		22.5		0/0/0	0/17.9	0/0/0	0/0/	15/15/	/15			0/0/0	----Other
0/0/10	22.5	22.5		0	0	0	0/0/0	0/0/				0/0/	-With electric motor for propulSlon
0/0/0	22.5	22.5		0/0/0	0/17.9	0/0/0	0/0/	15/15/	15/15		//	0/0/0	Old other manned vehicles with drive motor only
0/0/0	22.5	22.5		0/0/0	0/17.9	0/0/0	0/0/	15/15/	15/15		//	0/0/0	Other manned vehicles with drive motor only
													-Other
0/0/0	22.5	22.5		0/0/0	0/17.9	0/0/0	0/0/	15/15/	15/15			0/0/0	Other motor vehicles designed for transport of person's, cylinder capacity ≤1L
0/0/0	22.5	22.5		0/0/0	0/17.9	0/0/0	0/0/	15/15/	15/15			0/0/0	Other motor vehicles designed for transport of person's, 1.5L<cylinder capacity ≤2L
0/0/0	22.5	22.5		0/0/0	0/17.9	0/0/0	0/0/	15/15/	15/15			0/0/0	Other motor vehicles designed for transport of person's, 2L <cylinder capacity ≤2.5L
0/0/0	22.5	22.5		0/0/0	0/17.9	0/0/0	0/0/	15/15/	15/15			0/0/0	Other motor vehicles designed for transport of person's, 2.5L<cylinder capacity ≤3L
0/0/0	22.5	22.5		0/0/0	0/17.9	0/0/0	0/0/	15/15/	15/15			0/0/0	Other motor vehicles designed for transport of person's, 3L <cylinder capacity ≤4L
0/0/0	22.5	22.5		0/0/0	0/17.9	0/0/0	0/0/	15/15/	15/15			0/0/0	Other motor vehicles designed for transport of person's, cylinder capacity >4L
0/0/0	22.5	22.5		0/0/0	0/17.9	0/0/0	0/0/	15/15/	15/15			0/0/0	Other motor vehicles designed for transport of person's, 1L <cylinder capacity ≤1.5L
0/0/0	22.5	22.5		0/0/0	0/17.9	0/0/0	0/0/	15/15/	15/15			0/0/0	Electronic vehicles and other passenger vehicles which can not distingguished cylinder capacity
0/0/0	22.5	22.5		0/0/0	0/17.9	0/0/0	0/0/	15/15/	15/15			0/0/0	Complete parts of passenger vehicles of subheading No.8703.9000
													Motor vehicles for the transport of goods:
													-Dumpers designed for off-highway use:
0/0/0	0	0	0/0	0/0/0	0/0	0//0	0/0/	5.4/5.4/5.4	5.6/5.4			0/0/0	---Electromobile dumpers for the transport of goods
0/0/0	0	0	0/0	0/0/0	0/0	0//0	0/0/	5.4/5.4/5.4	5.5/5.4			0/0/0	---Other
													-Other trucks equipped only with compression ignition piston internal combustion engines (diesel or semi diesel engines)
/0/0		15		0//0	0/17.9	0//0	0/0/					0/0/	--G. v. w. not exceeding 5 tons
													--G. v. w. exceeding 5 tons, but not exceeding 20 tons:
5/0/0	18	9.3	2/2	0/0/0	0/14.3	0//0	0/0/					0/0/0	---G. v. w. exceeding 5 tons, but notexceeding 14 tons
5/0/0	18	9.3	2/2	0/0/0	0/14.3	0//0	0/0/					0/0/0	---G. v. w. of 14 tons or more, but not exceeding 20 tons
													--G. v. w. exceeding 20 tons
5/0/0		7	1.5/1.5	0//0	0/0	0//0	0/0/					0/0/	Cementing truck, car, fracturing sand mixing truck, coiled tubing unit, liquid nitrogen pump vehicle chassis (gross vehicle weight > 35 tons, installed cab)
5/0/0		7	1.5/1.5	0//0	0/0	0//0	0/0/					0/0/	Chassis for crane lorries, lifting capacity≥55tons, with compression-ignition internal combustion piston engine
5/0/0		7	1.5/1.5	0//0	0/0	0//0	0/0/					0/0/	Special chassis for wreckers truck with total vehicle G. v. w≥31 tons
5/0/0		7	1.5/1.5	0//0	0/0	0//0	0/0/					0/0/	Other overweight truck, with compression-ignition internal combustion piston engine (diesel or semi-diesel, G. v. w>20 tons)
													-Other, only with spark-ignition internal combustion piston engine:
5/0/0		15		0//0	0/17.9	0//0	0/0/					0/0/	--G. v. w. not exceeding 5 tons
													--G. v. w. exceeding 5 tons:
5/0/0		9.3	2/2	0/0/0	0/14.3	0//0	0/0/					0/0/0	---G. v. w. exceeding 5 tons, but not exceeding 8 tons
5/0/0		9.3	2/2	0/0/0	0/14.3	0//0	0/0/					0/0/0	---G. v. w. exceeding 8 tons

税则号列	货品名称〔CIQ 扩展编码及品名—T2 表示见附表 2〕	最惠(%)	暂定税率	普通	增值/消费	出口退税	计量单位	监管条件/特殊证件	检验检疫	对美关税	亚太上/下
	-同时装有压燃式活塞内燃发动机（柴油或半柴油发动 机）及驱动电动机的其他货车：										
8704.4100	--车辆总重量不超过 5 吨〔999〕	15		70	13/	9,13	辆/千克	46AOxy/	LM		
	--车辆总重量超过 5 吨，但不超过 20 吨：										
8704.4210	---车辆总重量超过 5 吨，但小于 14 吨〔999〕	15		70	13/	13	辆/千克	46Axy/	LM		13.5/13.5
8704.4220	---车辆总重量在 14 吨及以上，但不超过 20 吨〔999〕	15		40	13/	13	辆/千克	46Axy/	LM		13.5/13.5
8704.4300	--车辆总重量超过 20 吨										
8704.4300 10	固井水泥车、压裂车、混砂车、连续油管车、液氮泵车用底盘（动力装置为同时装有压燃式活塞内燃发动机（柴油或半柴油发动机）及驱动电动机，车辆总重量＞35 吨，装驾驶室）〔999〕	15	10	40	13/	13	辆/千克	46AOxy/	LM		
8704.4300 20	起重≥55 吨汽车起重机用底盘（动力装置为同时装有压燃式活塞内燃发动机（柴油或半柴油发动机）及驱动电动机）〔999〕	15	8	40	13/	13	辆/千克	46AOxy/	LM		
8704.4300 30	车辆总重量≥31 吨清障车专用底盘（动力装置为同时装有压燃式活塞内燃发动机（柴油或半柴油发动机）及驱动电动机）〔999〕	15	10	40	13/	13	辆/千克	46AOxy/	LM		
8704.4300 90	同时装有压燃式活塞内燃发动机（柴油或半柴油发动机）及驱动电动机的其他货车，车辆总重量超过 20 吨〔999〕	15		40	13/	13	辆/千克	46AOxy/	LM		
	-同时装有点燃式活塞内燃发动机及驱动电动机的其他货车：										
8704.5100	--车辆总重量不超过 5 吨〔999〕	15		70	13/	13	辆/千克	46AOxy/	LM		
	--车辆总重量超过 5 吨：										
8704.5210	---车辆总重量超过 5 吨，但不超过 8 吨〔999〕	15		70	13/	13	辆/千克	46Axy/	LM		
8704.5220	---车辆总重量超过 8 吨〔999〕	15		70	13/	13	辆/千克	46Axy/	LM		
8704.6000	-仅装有驱动电动机的其他货车〔999〕	15		70	13/	13	辆/千克	46Axy/	LM		
8704.9000	-其他〔101 电动汽车，102 内燃机汽车，103 混合动力汽车，104 其他能源汽车〕	15		70	13/	13	辆/千克	46Axy/	LM		
87.05	**特殊用途的机动车辆（例如，抢修车、起重车、救火车、混凝土搅拌车、道路清洁车、喷洒车、流动工场车及流动放射线检查车），但主要用于载人或运货的车辆除外：**										
	-起重车：										
	---全路面起重车：										
8705.1021	----最大起重重量不超过 50 吨〔101 起重车，102 汽车起重机〕	15		30	13/	13	辆/千克	6A/	ML	40	
8705.1022	----最大起重量量超过 50 吨，但不超过 100 吨〔101 起重车，102 汽车起重机〕	10		30	13/	13	辆/千克	6A/	ML	35	
8705.1023	----最大起重重量超过 100 吨〔101 起重车，102 汽车起重机〕	10		30	13/	13	辆/千克	6A/	ML	35	
	---其他：										
8705.1091	----最大起重重量不超过 50 吨〔101 起重车，102 汽车起重机〕	15		30	13/	13	辆/千克	6A/	ML	40	
8705.1092	----最大起重重量超过 50 吨，但不超过 100 吨〔101 起重车，102 汽车起重机〕	10		30	13/	13	辆/千克	6A/	ML	35	
8705.1093	----最大起重重量超过 100 吨〔101 起重车，102 汽车起重机〕	10		30	13/	13	辆/千克	6A/	ML	35	
8705.2000	-钻探车〔999〕	12		17	13/	13	辆/千克	6A/	ML	17	
	-救火车：										
8705.3010	---装有云梯的救火车〔999〕	3		8	13/	13	辆/千克	6A/	M	8	
8705.3090	---其他〔999〕	3		8	13/	13	辆/千克	6A/	M	8	
8705.4000	-混凝土搅拌车〔999〕	15		35	13/	13	辆/千克	6A/	LM	20	13.5/13.5
	-其他：										
8705.9010	---无线电通信车〔999〕	9		35	13/	13	辆/千克	6A/	LM	14	8.1/8.1
8705.9020	---放射线检查车〔999〕	9		14	13/	13	辆/千克	6A/	ML	14	8.1/8.1
8705.9030	---环境监测车〔999〕	12		20	13/	13	辆/千克	6A/	ML	17	10.8/10.8
8705.9040	---医疗车〔999〕	12		30	13/	13	辆/千克	6A/	ML	17	10.8/10.8
	---电源车：										
8705.9051	----航空电源车（频率为 400 赫兹）〔999〕	12		30	13/	13	辆/千克	6/		17	10.8/10.8
8705.9059	----其他〔999〕	12		30	13/	13	辆/千克	6A/	ML	17	10.8/10.8
8705.9060	---飞机加油车、调温车、除冰车〔999〕	12		35	13/	13	辆/千克	6A/	M	17	10.8/10.8
8705.9070	---道路（包括跑道）扫雪车〔999〕	12		35	13/	13	辆/千克	6A/	LM	17	10.8/10.8
8705.9080	---石油测井车、压裂车、混沙车〔999〕	12		35	13/	13	辆/千克	6A/	LM	17	10.8/10.8
	---其他：										

协定税率 %								RCEP		特惠税率 %			Article Description
东/冰/格	巴基斯坦	韩国	瑞士上/下	哥/秘/柬	澳/毛	新西/坡/智	中国港/澳/台	东盟及马来/澳/韩	日/新	亚太2国	老/柬/缅	98/97/95	
													-Other trucks equipped with compression ignition pistoninternal combustion engine (diesel or semi diesel engine) anddrive motor:
/0/0		15		0//0	0/17.9	0//0	0/0/					0/0/	-- g.v.w. not exceeding 5 tonnes
													-- g.v.w. exceeding 5 tonnes but not exceeding 20 tonnes
5/0/0	18	9.3	2/2	0/0/0	0/14.3	0//0	0/0/					0/0/0	---g.v.w. exceeding 5 tonnes but not exceeding 14 tonnes
5/0/0	18	9.3	2/2	0/0/0	0/14.3	0//0	0/0/					0/0/0	---The total vehicle weight is 14 tons and above, but not more than 20 tons
													-- g.v.w. exceeding 20 tonnes
5/0/0		7	1.5/1.5	0//0	0/0	0//0	0/0/					0/0/	Chassis for cementing cement truck, fracturing truck, sand mixing truck, coiled tubing truck and liquid nitrogen pump truck (the power unit is equipped with compression ignition piston internal combustion engine (diesel or semi diesel engine) and driving motor at the same time, the total weight of the vehicle is > 35t, and the cab is installed)
5/0/0		7	1.5/1.5	0//0	0/0	0//0	0/0/					0/0/	Chassis for truck crane with lifting capacity ⩾ 55T (the power unit is equipped with compression ignition piston internal combustion engine (diesel or semi diesel engine) and drive motor)
5/0/0		7	1.5/1.5	0//0	0/0	0//0	0/0/					0/0/	Special chassis for obstacle removal vehicle with total vehicle weight ⩾ 31 tons (the power unit is equipped with compression ignition piston internal combustion engine (diesel or semi diesel engine) and drive motor)
5/0/0		7	1.5/1.5	0//0	0/0	0//0	0/0/					0/0/	Other trucks equipped with compression ignition piston internal combustion engine (diesel or semi diesel engine) and drive motor, with a total vehicle weight of more than 2 tons
													-Vehicles equipped with positive ignition piston internal combustion engine and driving motor at the same time
5/0/0		15		0//0	0/17.9	0//0	0/0/					0/0/	-- g.v.w. not exceeding 5 tonnes
													-- g.v.w. exceeding 5 tonnes
5/0/0		9.3	2/2	0/0/0	0/14.3	0//0	0/0/					0/0/0	-- g.v.w. exceeding 5 tonnes but not exceeding 8 tonnes
5/0/0		9.3	2/2	0/0/0	0/14.3	0//0	0/0/					0/0/0	-- g.v.w. exceeding 8 tonnes
0/0/0		15		0/0/0	0/17.9	0/0/0	0/0/	23.8/23.8/23.8	/23.8			0/0/0	-Other trucks equipped with drive motors only
0/0/0		15		0/0/0	0/17.9	0/0/0	0/0/	23.8/23.8/23.8	/23.8			0/0/0	-Other
													Special purpose motor vehicles, other than those principally designed for the transport of persons or goods (for example, breakdown lorries, crane lorries, fire fighting vehicles, concrete-mixer lorries, road sweeper lorries, spraying lorries, mobile workshops, mobile radiological units):
													-Crane lorries:
													---All-road crane lorries:
0/0/0	8.4	7	1.5/1.5	0/0/0	0/0	0/0/0	0/0/	13.5/13.5/13.5	14.1/13.5			0/0/0	----Of a maxium lifting capacity not more than 50tons
0/0/0	2	4.6	0/0	0/0/0	0/0	0/0/0	0/0/	9/9/9	9.1/9			0/0/0	----Of a maxium lifting capacity exceeding 50tons, but not exceeding 100tons
0/0/0	2	4.6	0/0	0/0/0	0/0	0/0/0	0/0/	9/9/9	9.1/9			0/0/0	----Of a maxium lifting capacity exceeding 100tons
													---Other:
0/0/0	8.4	7	1.5/1.5	0/0/0	0/0	0/0/0	0/0/	13.5/13.5/13.5	14.1/13.5			0/0/0	----Of a maxium lifting capacity not more than 50tons
0/0/0	2	4.6	0/0	0/0/0	0/0	0/0/0	0/0/	9/9/9	9.4/9			0/0/0	----Of a maxium lifting capacity exceeding 50tons, but not exceeding 100 tons
0/0/0	2	4.6	0/0	0/0/0	0/0	0/0/0	0/0/	9/9/9	9.1/9			0/0/0	----Of a maxium lifting capacity exceeding 100 tons
0/0/0	4.2	5.6	1.2/1.2	0/0/0	0/0	0/0/0	0/0/	10.8/10.8/10.8	11.3/10.8			0/0/0	-Mobile drilling derricks
													-Fire fighting vehicles:
0/0/0	0	1.4	0/0	0/0/0	0/0	0//0	0/0/	2.7/2.7/2.7	2.8/2.7			0/0/0	---Mounted with scaling ladder
0/0/0	0	1.4	0/0	0/0/0	0/0	0//0	0/0/	2.7/2.7/2.7	2.8/2.7			0/0/0	---Other
0/0/0	5.3	7	1.5/1.5	0/0/0	0/0	0/0/0	0/0/	13.5/13.5/13.5	14.1/13.5			0/0/0	-Concrete-mixer lorries
													-Other:
0/0/0	2	4.2	0/0	0/0/0	0/0	0/0/0	0/0/	8.1/8.1/8.1	8.2/8.1			0/0/0	---Radio communication vans
0/0/0	2	4.2	0/0	0/0/0	0/0	0//0	0/0/	8.1/8.1/8.1	8.2/8.1			0/0/0	---Mobile radiological units
0/0/0	3.5	5.6	1.2/1.2	0/0/0	0/0	0/0/0	0/0/	10.8/10.8/10.8	10.9/10.8			0/0/0	---Mobile environmental monitoring units
0/0/0	3.5	7.2	1.2/1.2	0/0/0	0/0	0/0/0	0/0/	11.4/11.4/	/11.4			0/0/0	Mobile clinics
													---Mobile electric generator sets:
0/0/0	3.5	5.6	1.2/1.2	0/0/0	0/0	0/0/0	0/0/	10.8/10.8/10.8	10.9/10.8			0/0/0	----Airplane charging vehicles (frequency 400Hz)
0/0/0	3.5	5.6	1.2/1.2	0/0/0	0/0	0/0/0	0/0/	10.8/10.8/10.8	10.9/10.8			0/0/0	----Other
0/0/0	3.5	5.6	1.2/1.2	0/0/0	0/0	0/0/0	0/0/	10.8/10.8/10.8	10.9/10.8			0/0/0	---Mobile vehicles for aircraft refuelling, air-conditioning or deicing
0/0/0	3.5	5.6	1.2/1.2	0/0/0	0/0	0/0/0	0/0/	10.8/10.8/10.8	10.9/10.8			0/0/0	---Snow sweep vehicles for cleansing streets or airfield runways
0/0/0	3.5	5.6	1.2/1.2	0/0/0	0/0	0/0/0	0/0/	10.8/10.8/10.8	10.9/10.8			0/0/0	---Petrolcum well logging trucks, fracturing unit trucks and mixing sand trucks
													---Other:

税则号列	货品名称〔CIQ扩展编码及品名－T2表示见附表2〕	最惠(%)	暂定税率	普通	增值/消费	出口退税	计量单位	监管条件/特殊证件	检验检疫	对美关税	亚太上/下
8705.9091	----混凝土泵车〔999〕	12		35	13/	13	辆/千克	6A/	LM	17	10.8/10.8
8705.9099	----其他										
8705.9099 01	跑道除冰车〔999〕	12	10	35	13/	13	辆/千克	6A/	M	15	10.8/10.8
8705.9099 30	用于导弹、火箭等的车辆(为弹道导弹、运载火箭等运输、装卸和发射而设计的)〔999〕	12		35	13/	13	辆/千克	36/		17	10.8/10.8
8705.9099 90	其他特殊用途的机动车辆(主要用于载人或运货的车辆除外)〔999〕	12		35	13/	13	辆/千克	6A/	LM	17	10.8/10.8
87.06	**装有发动机的机动车辆底盘,税目87.01至87.05所列车辆用:**										
8706.0010	---非公路用自卸车底盘〔999〕	6		14	13/	13	台/千克	6/			
	---货车底盘:										
8706.0021	----车辆总重量在14吨及以上的〔999〕	6		30	13/	13	台/千克	46AOxy/	ML		
8706.0022	----车辆总重量在14吨以下的〔999〕	6		45	13/	13	台/千克	46AOxy/	ML		
8706.0030	---大型客车底盘〔999〕	6		70	13/	13	台/千克	46Oxy/			
8706.0040	---汽车起重机底盘〔999〕	6		100	13/	13	台/千克	6AO/	ML		
8706.0090	---其他〔999〕	6		100	13/	13	台/千克	46AOxy/	ML		
87.07	**机动车辆的车身(包括驾驶室),税目87.01至87.05所列车辆用:**										
8707.1000	-税目87.03所列车辆用〔999〕	6		100	13/	13	台/千克	6/		31	
	-其他:										
8707.9010	---税号8702.1092、8702.1093、8702.9020及8702.9030所列车辆用〔999〕	6		70	13/	13	台/千克	6/		31	5.4/5.4
8707.9090	---其他〔999〕	6		70	13/	13	台/千克	6/		31	5.4/5.4
87.08	**机动车辆的零件、附件,税目87.01至87.05所列车辆用:**										
8708.1000	-缓冲器(保险杠)及其零件〔999〕	6		100	13/	13	千克	6/			5.8/5.8
	-车身(包括驾驶室)的其他零件、附件:										
8708.2100	--坐椅安全带〔999〕	6		100	13/	13	千克	6A/	LM		
	--本章子目注释一所列的前挡风玻璃、后窗及其他车窗:										
	---天窗:										
8708.2211	----电动的(8708.2941)〔999〕	6		100	13/	13	千克/套	6/	L		5.4/5.4
8708.2212	----手动的(8708.2942)〔999〕	6		100	13/	13	千克/套	6/	L		5.4/5.4
8708.2290	---其他〔999〕	6		100	13/	13	千克/套	6/	L		5.4/5.4
	--其他:										
8708.2930	---车窗玻璃升降器〔999〕	6		100	13/	13	千克	6/			5.4/5.4
	---其他车身覆盖件:										
8708.2951	----侧围〔999〕	6		100	13/	13	千克	6/			5.4/5.4
8708.2952	----车门〔999〕	6		100	13/	13	千克/个	6/			5.4/5.4
8708.2953	----发动机罩盖〔999〕	6		100	13/	13	千克	6/			5.4/5.4
8708.2954	----前围〔999〕	6		100	13/	13	千克	6/			5.4/5.4
8708.2955	----行李箱盖(或背门)〔999〕	6		100	13/	13	千克	6/			5.4/5.4
8708.2956	----后围〔999〕	6		100	13/	13	千克	6/			5.4/5.4
8708.2957	----翼子板(或叶子板)〔999〕	6		100	13/	13	千克	6/			5.4/5.4
8708.2959	----其他〔999〕	6		100	13/	13	千克	6/			5.4/5.4
8708.2990	---其他〔999〕	6		100	13/	13	千克	6/			5.4/5.4
	-制动器、助力制动器及其零件:										
8708.3010	---装在蹄片上的制动摩擦片〔999〕	6		100	13/	13	千克	6/	L		
	---防抱死制动系统(ABS):										
8708.3021	----税目87.01和税号8704.1030及8704.1090所列车辆用〔999〕	6		11	13/	13	千克	6/		11	5.4/5.4
8708.3029	----其他〔999〕	6		100	13/	13	千克	6/			5.4/5.4
	---其他:										
8708.3091	----税目87.01所列车辆用〔999〕	6		14	13/	13	千克	6/	L		5.4/5.4
8708.3092	----税号8702.1091及8702.9010所列车辆用〔999〕	6		70	13/	13	千克	6/	L		5.4/5.4
8708.3093	----税号8704.1030及8704.1090所列车辆用〔999〕	6		11	13/	13	千克	6/			5.4/5.4
8708.3094	----税号8704.2100、8704.2230、8704.3100及8704.3230所列车辆用〔999〕	6		45	13/	13	千克	6/	L		5.4/5.4
8708.3095	----税号8704.2240、8704.2300及8704.3240所列车辆用〔999〕	6		30	13/	13	千克	6/	L		5.4/5.4
8708.3096	----税目87.05所列车辆用〔999〕	6		100	13/	13	千克	6/	L		5.4/5.4
8708.3099	----其他车辆用										
8708.3099 11	纯电动或混合动力汽车用电动制动器(由制动器电子控制单元、踏板行程模拟器、制动执行器等组成)〔999〕	6	5	100	13/	13	千克/个	6/			5.4/5.4
8708.3099 19	其他机动车辆用制动器(包括助力制动器)〔999〕	6		100	13/	13	千克/个	6/			5.4/5.4

协定税率 %								RCEP		特惠税率 %			Article Description
东/冰/格	巴基斯坦	韩国	瑞士上/下	哥/秘/柬	澳/毛	新西/坡/智	中国港/澳/台	东盟及马来/澳/韩	日/新	亚太2国	老/柬/缅	98/97/95	
0/0/0	3.5	5.6	1.2/1.2	0/0/0	0/0	0/0/0	0/0/	11.2/11.4/11.2	11.3/11.4			0/0/0	----Concrete pump truck
													----Other
0/0/0	3.5	5.6	1.2/1.2	0/0/0	0/0	0/0/0	0/0/	11.2/11.4/11.2	11.3/11.4			0/0/0	Runway deicing vehicle
0/0/0	3.5	5.6	1.2/1.2	0/0/0	0/0	0/0/0	0/0/	11.2/11.4/11.2	11.3/11.4			0/0/0	Vehicles for carrying missiles or rockets (specially designed for transporting, handling and launching of ballistic missiles or carrier rockets)
0/0/0	3.5	5.6	1.2/1.2	0/0/0	0/0	0/0/0	0/0/	11.2/11.4/11.2	11.3/11.4			0/0/0	Other special purpose motor vehicles(other than those principally designed for the transport of person's or goods)
													Chassis fitted with engines, for the motor vehicles of headings No. 87. 01 to 87. 05:
0/0/0	2	3.7	0/0	0/0/0	0/5.7	0//0	0/0/	7.2/7.2/7.2	7.3/7.2			0/0/0	---For the subheading 8704.1030 or 8704.1090
													---For the vehicles of subheading 8704.2100 to 8704.9000:
5/0/0		4.6	0/0	0//0	0/7.1	0//0	0/0/					0/0/	----For vehicles g. v. w of 14tons or more
5/0/0		4.6	0/0	0/0/0	0/7.1	0//0	0/0/					0/0/0	----For vehicles g. v. w less than 14 tons
0/0/0		9.3	2/2	0//0	0/14.3	0/0/0	0/0/	18.7/19/18.7	18.8/19			0/0/	---For passenger motor vehicles with 30 seats or more
0/0/0		9.3	2/2	0/0/0	0/14.3	0/0/0	0/0/	18/18/18	18.8/18			0/0/0	---For crane lorries
0/0/0		4.6	0/0	0/0/0	0/7.1	0/0/0	0/0/	9.5/9.5/9.5	/9.5			0/0/0	---Other
													Bodies (including cabs), for the motor vehicles of headings No. 87. 01 to 87. 05:
0/0/0		4.6	0/0	0/0/0	0/7.1	0/0/0	0/0/	9.3/9.5/9.3	9.4/9.5			0/0/0	-For the vehicles of headingNo. 87. 03
													-Other:
0/0/0	3.5	4.6	0/0	0/0/0	0/7.1	0/0/0	0/0/	9/9/9	9.4/9			0/0/0	---For the vehicles of subheadingNo. 8702. 1092、8702. 1093、8702. 9020 or 8702. 9030
0/0/0	3.5	4.6	0/0	0/0/0	0/7.1	0/0/0	0/0/	9/9/9	9.4/9			0/0/0	---Other
													Parts and accessories of the motor vehicles of headings No. 87. 01 to 87. 05:
0/0/0	0	6	0/0	0/0/0	0/7.1	0/0/0	0/0/0	9.5/9.5/9.5	9.5/9.5			0/0/0	-Bumpers and parts thereof
													-Other parts and accessories of bodies (including cabs):
0/0/0	3.5	4.6	0/0	0/0/0	0/7.1	0/0/0	0/0/	9.3/9.5/9.3	9.4/9.5			0/0/0	--Safety seat belts
													--Windscreens, rearwindows and otherwindows listed in note 1of subheading of thischapter:
													---Skylight:
0/0/0	4	9	0/0	0/0/0	0/7.1	0/0/0	0/0/0	6/6/	/6			0/0/0	----Electric
0/0/0	2	4.6	0/0	0/0/0	0/7.1	0/0/0	0/0/0	9/9/9	9.4/9			0/0/0	----Hand—operated
0/0/0	2	6	0/0	0/0/0	0/7.1	0/0/0	0/0/0	9.5/9.5/9.5	9.5/9.5			0/0/0	---Other
													--Other:
5/0/0	6.3	4.6	0/0	0/0/0	0/7.1	0//0	0/0/0	9.5/9.5/	9.5/6			0/0/0	---Windowpane raiser
													---Other covered parts of bodies:
0/0/0	2	6	0/0	0/0/0	0/7.1	0/0/0	0/0/0	9.5/9.5/	9.5/9.5			0/0/0	----Side appearance of bodies
0/0/0	2	6	0/0	0/0/0	0/7.1	0/0/0	0/0/0	9.5/9.5/	9.5/9.5			0/0/0	----doors
0/0/0	2	6	0/0	0/0/0	0/7.1	0/0/0	0/0/0	9.5/9.5/	9.5/9.5			0/0/0	----Bonnets
0/0/0	2	6	0/0	0/0/0	0/7.1	0/0/0	0/0/0	9.5/9.5/	9.5/9.5			0/0/0	----Frontal appearance of bodies
0/0/0	2	6	0/0	0/0/0	0/7.1	0/0/0	0/0/0	9.5/9.5/	9.5/9.5			0/0/0	----Rear compartment covers(or rear door)
0/0/0	2	6	0/0	0/0/0	0/7.1	0/0/0	0/0/0	9.5/9.5/	9.5/9.5			0/0/0	----Rear appearance of bodies
0/0/0	4	6	0/0	0/0/0	0/7.1	0/0/0	0/0/0	9.5/9.5/	9.5/9.5			0/0/0	----Running-boards
0/0/0	2	6	0/0	0/0/0	0/7.1	0/0/0	0/0/0	9.5/9.5/9.5	9.5/9.5			0/0/0	----Other
0/0/0	3.5	9	1/1	0/0/0	0/7.1	0/0/0	0/0/0	6/6/6	6/6			0/0/0	---Other
													-Brakes and servo-brakes and parts thereof:
0/0/0	3.5	2	0/0	0/0/0	0/7.1	0/0/0	0/0/	0/0/9	9.1/0			0/0/0	---Mounted brake linings
													---Anti-skid brake system:
0/0/0	0	2.8	0/0	0/0/0	0/0	0//0	0/0/	5.4/5.4/5.4	5.6/5.4			0/0/0	----Of the rehicles of heading 87. 01、8704. 1030 and 8704. 1090
5/0/0	6.3	9	0/0	0/0/0	0/7.1	0//0	0/0/	6//	6/			0/0/0	----Other
													---Other:
0/0/0	0	2.8	0/0	0/0/0	0/0	0//0	0/0/	5.4/5.4/5.4	5.6/5.4			0/0/0	----Of the vehicles of heading No. 87. 01
5/0/0	6.3	6	0/0	0/0/0	0/7.1	0//0	0/0/	6//	6/			0/0/0	----Of the vehicles of subheading No. 8702. 1091 and 8702. 9010
0/0/0	0	2.8	0/0	0/0/0	0/0	0//0	0/0/	5.4/5.4/5.4	5.6/5.4			0/0/0	----Of the vehicles of subheading No. 8704. 1030 and 8704. 1090
5/0/0	6.3	6	0/0	0/0/0	0/7.1	0//0	0/0/	6//	6/			0/0/0	----Of the vehicles of subheading No. 8704. 2100, 8704. 2230, 8704. 3100 and 8704. 3230
0/0/0	4	2	0/0	0/0/0	0/7.1	0/0/0	0/0/	0/0/9	9.1/0			0/0/0	----Of the vehicles of subheading No. 8704. 2240, 8704. 2300 and 8704. 3240
0/0/0	2	4.6	0/0	0/0/0	0/7.1	0/0/0	0/0/	9/9/9	9.4/9			0/0/0	----Of the vehicles of heading No. 87. 05
													----Other
5/0/0	9	6	1/1	0/0/0	0/7.1	0//0	0/0/	6//	6/			0/0/0	Electric brake for pure electric or hybrid vehicles (electronic control unit,composed of a brake pedal travel simulator, the brake actuator etc.)
5/0/0	9	6	1/1	0/0/0	0/7.1	0//0	0/0/	6//	6/			0/0/0	Brakes of other vehicles (including booster brake)

税则号列	货品名称〔CIQ 扩展编码及品名－T2 表示见附表 2〕	最惠(%)	暂定税率	普通	增值/消费	出口退税	计量单位	监管条件/特殊证件	检验检疫	对美关税	亚太上/下
8708.3099 20	燃油汽车用电动制动器(由制动器电子控制单元、踏板行程模拟器、制动执行器等组成)〔999〕	6	5	100	13/	13	千克/个	6/			5.4/5.4
8708.3099 90	其他机动车辆用制动器(包括助力制动器)的零件〔999〕	6		100	13/	13	千克/个	6/	L		5.4/5.4
	-变速箱及其零件:										
8708.4010	---税目 87.01 所列车辆用										
8708.4010 10	发动机功率 65 千瓦及以上的动力换挡拖拉机用变速箱〔999〕	6	3	14	13/	13	个/千克	6/			
8708.4010 90	其他牵引车、拖拉机用变速箱及其零件〔999〕	6		14	13/	13	个/千克	6/			
8708.4020	---税号 8702.1091 及 8702.9010 所列车辆用〔999〕	6		70	13/	13	个/千克	6/			
8708.4030	---税号 8704.1030 及 8704.1090 所列车辆用										
8708.4030 01	扭矩＞1500Nm 非公路自卸车用变速箱〔999〕	6	3	11	13/	13	个/千克	6/			
8708.4030 90	其他非公路自卸车用变速箱及其零件〔999〕	6		11	13/	13	个/千克	6/			
8708.4040	---税号 8704.2100、8704.2230、8704.3100 及 8704.3230 所列车辆用〔999〕	6		45	13/	13	个/千克	6/			
8708.4050	---税号 8704.2240、8704.2300 及 8704.3240 所列车辆用〔999〕	6		30	13/	13	个/千克	6/			
8708.4060	---税目 87.05 所列车辆用〔999〕	6		100	13/	13	个/千克	6/			
	---其他:										
8708.4091	----税目 87.03 所列车辆用自动换挡变速箱及其零件										
8708.4091 10	税目 87.03 所列车辆用自动换挡变速箱的液力变矩器〔999〕	6	3	100	13/	13	个/千克	6/			
8708.4091 20	税目 87.03 所列车辆用自动换挡变速箱的铝阀芯〔999〕	6	3	100	13/	13	个/千克	6/			
8708.4091 91	税目 87.03 所列车辆用自动换挡变速箱〔999〕	6		100	13/	13	个/千克	6/			
8708.4091 99	其他税目 87.03 所列车辆用自动换挡变速箱的零件〔999〕	6		100	13/	13	个/千克	6/			
8708.4099	----其他										
8708.4099 10	其他未列名机动车辆用变速箱〔999〕	6		100	13/	13	个/千克	6/			
8708.4099 20	其他未列名机动车辆自动变速箱用液力变矩器〔999〕	6	3	100	13/	13	个/千克	6/			
8708.4099 30	其他未列名机动车辆自动变速箱用铝阀芯〔999〕	6	3	100	13/	13	个/千克	6/			
8708.4099 90	其他未列名机动车辆用变速箱的零件〔999〕	6		100	13/	13	个/千克	6/			
	-装有差速器的驱动桥及其零件,不论是否装有其他传动部件;非驱动桥及其零件:										
	---装有差速器的驱动桥及其零件,不论是否装有其他传动部件:										
8708.5071	----税目 87.01 所列车辆用										
8708.5071 10	发动机功率 65 千瓦及以上的动力换挡拖拉机用驱动桥(装有差速器的,不论是否装有其他传动件)〔999〕	6	3	14	13/	13	个/千克	6/			5.4/5.4
8708.5071 90	其他牵引车、拖拉机用驱动桥及其零件(装有差速器的,不论是否装有其他传动件)〔999〕	6		14	13/	13	个/千克	6/			5.4/5.4
8708.5072	----税号 8702.1091 及 8702.9010 所列车辆用										
8708.5072 01	轴荷≥10 吨的中后驱动桥的零件〔999〕	6		70	13/	13	个/千克	6/			5.4/5.4
8708.5072 91	其他大型客车用驱动桥(装有差速器的,不论是否装有其他传动件)〔999〕	6		70	13/	13	个/千克	6/			5.4/5.4
8708.5072 99	其他大型客车用驱动桥的零件(装有差速器的,不论是否装有其他传动件)〔999〕	6		70	13/	13	个/千克	6/			5.4/5.4
8708.5073	----税号 8704.1030 及 8704.1090 所列车辆用〔999〕	6		11	13/	13	个/千克	6/			5.4/5.4
8708.5074	----税号 8704.2100.8704.2230.8704.3100 及 8704.3230 所列车辆用										
8708.5074 10	柴、汽油型轻型货车用驱动桥(87042100,87042230,87043100,87043230 所列总重量≤14 吨车辆用,装差速器)〔999〕	6		45	13/	13	个/千克	6/			5.4/5.4
8708.5074 90	柴、汽油型轻型货车用驱动桥的零件(87042100,87042230,87043100,87043230 所列总重量≤14 吨车辆用,装差速器)〔999〕	6		45	13/	13	个/千克	6/			5.4/5.4
8708.5075	----税号 8704.2240、8704.2300 及 8704.3240 所列车辆用										

协定税率 %								RCEP		特惠税率 %			Article Description
东/冰/格	巴基斯坦	韩国	瑞士上/下	哥/秘/柬	澳/毛	新西/坡/智	中国港/澳/台	东盟及马来/澳/韩	日/新	亚太2国	老/柬/缅	98/97/95	
5/0/0	9	6	1/1	0/0/0	0/7.1	0//0	0/0/	6//	6/		//	0/0/0	Electric brake for Fuel vehicles (electronic control unit, composed of a brake pedal travel simulator, the brake actuator etc.)
5/0/0	9	6	1/1	0/0/0	0/7.1	0//0	0/0/	6//	6/			0/0/0	Parts of brakes for other motor vehicles (including servo-brakes)
													-Gear boxes and parts thereof:
													---Of the vehicles of heading of No. 87.01
0/0/0	0		0/0	0/0/0	0/0	0//0	0/0/0	5/5/	/5			0/0/0	Transmission gear box of engine power 65 kW and above for shift tractor
0/0/0	0		0/0	0/0/0	0/0	0//0	0/0/0	5/5/	/5			0/0/0	Transmission and other parts for drive-axles
5/0/0			0/0	0//0	0/7.1	0//0	0/0/0	6//	6/			0/0/	---Of the vehicles of subheading No. 8702.1091 and 8702.9010
													---Of the vehicles of subheading No. 8704.1030 and 8704.1090
0/0/0	0	4.8	0/0	0//0	0/0	0//0	0/0/0	5/5/	/5			0/0/	Gear boxes for off-highway dumpers use, troque>1500Nm
0/0/0	0	4.8	0/0	0//0	0/0	0//0	0/0/0	5/5/	/5			0/0/	Other gear boxes and parts for off-highway dumpers use
5/0/0			0/0	0//0	0/7.1	0//0	0/0/0	6//	6/			0/0/	---Of the vehicles of subheading No. 8704.2100, 8704.2230, 8704.3100 and 8704.3230
5/0/0			0/0	0//0	0/7.1	0//0	0/0/0	6//	6/			0/0/	---Of the vehicles of subheading No. 8704.2240, 8704.2300 and 8704.3240
0/0/0	3.5		0/0	0/0/0	0/7.1	0/0/0	0/0/0	6/6/	6/6			0/0/0	---Of the vehicles of heading No. 87.05
													---Other:
													----Automatic gearshift for saloon cars and parts thereof, of headings 87.03
5/0/0		8	0/0	0//0	0/7.1	0//0	0/0/	6//	6/		//	0/0/	Torque converter for automatic transmission of car
5/0/0		8	0/0	0//0	0/7.1	0//0	0/0/	6//	6/		//	0/0/	Aluminum valve element for automatic transmission of car
5/0/0		8	0/0	0//0	0/7.1	0//0	0/0/	6//	6/			0/0/	Other automatic gearshift for saloon cars
5/0/0		8	0/0	0//0	0/7.1	0//0	0/0/	6//	6/			0/0/	Parts of automatic gearshift for saloon cars
													----Other
0/0/0	0		0/0	0//0	0/7.1	0/0/0	0/0/0	6/6/	6/6			0/0/	Other gearboxes for other not else where specified vehicles
0/0/0	0		0/0	0//0	0/7.1	0/0/0	0/0/0	6/6/	6/6		//	0/0/	Torque converter for automatic transmission of other motor vehicles not listed
0/0/0	0		0/0	0//0	0/7.1	0/0/0	0/0/0	6/6/	6/6		//	0/0/	Aluminum valve element for automatic transmission of other motor vehicles not listed
0/0/0	0		0/0	0//0	0/7.1	0/0/0	0/0/0	6/6/	6/6			0/0/	Spare parts for gearboxes for other not elsewhere specified vehicles
													-Drive-axles with differential, whether or not provided with other transmission components and non-driving axles and parts thereof:
													---Drive-axles with differential and part thereof, whether or not provided with other transmission components:
													----Of the vehicles of heading No. 87.01
0/0/0	0	2.8	0/0	0/0/0	0/0	0//0	0/0/	5.4/5.4/5.4	5.6/5.4			0/0/0	Differential of engine power 65 kW and above for shift tractor
0/0/0	0	2.8	0/0	0/0/0	0/0	0//0	0/0/	5.4/5.4/5.4	5.6/5.4			0/0/0	Drive-axles with differential and parts there of the vehicles of heading No. 87.01, whether or not provided with other transmission components.
													----Of the vehicles of subheading No. 8702.1091 and 8702.9010
5/0/0	9	9	0/0	0/0/0	0/7.1	0//0	0/0/					0/0/0	Parts of middle and rear drive-axles and parts thereof, axle loading capacity≥10t
5/0/0	9	9	0/0	0/0/0	0/7.1	0//0	0/0/					0/0/0	Other drive-axles for other buses(with differential, whether or not provided with other transmission components)
5/0/0	9	9	0/0	0/0/0	0/7.1	0//0	0/0/					0/0/0	Parts of drive-axles with differential for other large buses (whether or not provided with other transmission components)
0/0/0	0	2.8	0/0	0/0/0	0/0	0//0	0/0/	5.4/5.4/5.4	5.6/5.4			0/0/0	----Of the vehicles of subheading No. 8704.1030 and 8704.1090
													----Of the vehicles of subheading No. 8704.2100, 8704.2230, 8704.3100 and 8704.3230
5/0/0	9	6	0/0	0/0/0	0/7.1	0//0	0/0/					0/0/0	Drive-axles for diesel oil and gasoline light trucks(used by ≤14 ton vehicles listed in 8707.2100, 2300, 3100 and 3230 and with differential gears)
5/0/0	9	6	0/0	0/0/0	0/7.1	0//0	0/0/					0/0/0	Parts of drive-axles for diesel oil and gasoline light trucks (used by ≤14 tons vehicles of subheading No. 8707.2100, 2300, 3100 and 3230 and with differential)
													----Of the vehicles of subheading No. 8704.2240, 8704.2300 and 8704.3240

税则号列	货品名称〔CIQ 扩展编码及品名－T2 表示见附表 2〕	最惠(%)	暂定税率	普通	增值/消费	出口退税	计量单位	监管条件/特殊证件	检验检疫	对美关税	亚太上/下
8708.5075 10	其他柴、汽油型重型货车用驱动桥(指编号 8704.2240,8704.2300 及 8704.3240 所列车辆用)〔999〕	6		30	13/	13	个/千克	6/			5.4/5.4
8708.5075 90	其他柴、汽油型重型货车用驱动桥的零件(指编号 87042240,87042300 及 87043240 所列车辆用)〔999〕	6		30	13/	13	个/千克	6/			5.4/5.4
8708.5076	----税目 87.05 所列车辆用										
8708.5076 10	特种车用驱动桥(指 8705 所列车辆用,装有差速器,不论是否装有其他传动件)〔999〕	6		100	13/	13	个/千克	6/			5.4/5.4
8708.5076 90	特种车用驱动桥的零件(指 87.05 所列车辆用,装有差速器,不论是否装有其他传动件)〔999〕	6		100	13/	13	个/千克	6/			5.4/5.4
8708.5079	----其他										
8708.5079 10	未列名机动车辆用驱动桥(装有差速器的,不论是否装有其他传动件)〔999〕	6		100	13/	13	个/千克	6/			5.4/5.4
8708.5079 90	未列名机动车辆用驱动桥的零件(装有差速器的,不论是否装有其他传动件)〔999〕	6		100	13/	13	个/千克	6/			5.4/5.4
	---非驱动桥及其零件:										
8708.5081	----税目 87.01 所列车辆用〔999〕	6		14	13/	13	千克	6/			
8708.5082	----税号 8702.1091 及 8702.9010 所列车辆用〔999〕	6		70	13/	13	千克	6/			
8708.5083	----税号 8704.1030 及 8704.1090 所列车辆用〔999〕	6		11	13/	13	千克	6/			
8708.5084	----税号 8704.2100、8704.2230、8704.3100 及 8704.3230 所列车辆用〔999〕	6		45	13/	13	千克	6/			
8708.5085	----税号号 8704.2240、8704.2300 及 8704.3240 所列车辆用〔999〕	6		30	13/	13	千克	6/			
8708.5086	----税目 87.05 所列车辆用〔999〕	6		100	13/	13	千克	6/		11	
8708.5089	----其他										
8708.5089 10	未列名机动车辆用非驱动桥〔999〕	6		100	13/	13	千克/个	6/			
8708.5089 90	未列名机动车辆用非驱动桥的零件〔999〕	6		100	13/	13	千克/个	6/			
	-车轮及其零件、附件:										
8708.7010	---税目 87.01 所列车辆用〔999〕	6		14	13/	13	千克	6/			
8708.7020	---税号 8702.1091 及 8702.9010 所列车辆用〔999〕	6		70	13/	13	千克	6/			
8708.7030	---税号 8704.1030 及 8704.1090 所列车辆用〔999〕	6		11	13/	13	千克	6/			
8708.7040	---税号 8704.2100、8704.2230、8704.3100 及 8704.3230 所列车辆用〔999〕	6		45	13/	13	千克	6/			
8708.7050	---税号 8704.2240、8704.2300 及 8704.3240 所列车辆用〔999〕	6		30	13/	13	千克	6/			
8708.7060	---税目 87.05 所列车辆用〔999〕	6		100	13/	13	千克	6/			
	---其他:										
8708.7091	----铝合金制的〔999〕	6		100	13/	13	千克	6A/	M		
8708.7099	----其他〔999〕	6		100	13/	13	千克	6/			
	-悬挂系统及其零件(包括减振器):										
8708.8010	---税目 87.03 所列车辆用〔999〕	6		100	13/	13	千克	6/			5.4/5.4
8708.8090	---其他〔999〕	6		100	13/	13	千克	6/			5.4/5.4
	-其他零件、附件:										
	--散热器及其零件:										
8708.9110	---水箱散热器〔999〕	6		100	13/	13	个/千克	6/			
8708.9120	---机油冷却器〔999〕	6		100	13/	13	个/千克	6/			
8708.9190	---其他〔999〕	6		100	13/	13	个/千克	6/			
8708.9200	--消声器(消音器)排气管及零件〔999〕	6		100	13/	13	千克	6/			
	--离合器及其零件:										
8708.9310	---税目 87.01 所列车辆用							6			
8708.9310 10	发动机功率 65 千瓦及以上的动力换挡拖拉机用离合器〔999〕	6	3	14	13/	13	千克	6/			
8708.9310 90	其他牵引车、拖拉机用离合器及其零件〔999〕	6		14	13/	13	千克	6/			
8708.9320	---税号 8702.1091 及 8702.9010 所列车辆用〔999〕	6		70	13/	13	千克	6/			
8708.9330	---税号 8704.1030 及 8704.1090 所列车辆用〔999〕	6		11	13/	13	千克	6/			
8708.9340	---税号 8704. 2100、8704. 2230、8704. 3100 及 8704.3230 所列车辆用〔999〕	6		45	13/	13	千克	6/			
8708.9350	---税号 8704.2240、8704.2300 及 8704.3240 所列车辆用〔999〕	6		30	13/	13	千克	6/			
8708.9360	---税目 87.05 所列车辆用〔999〕	6		100	13/	13	千克	6/			

协定税率 %								RCEP		特惠税率 %			
东/冰/格	巴基斯坦	韩国	瑞士上/下	哥/秘/柬	澳/毛	新西/坡/智	中国港/澳/台	东盟及马来/澳/韩	日/新	亚太2国	老/柬/缅	98/97/95	Article Description
5/0/0	9	6	0/0	0/0/0	0/7.1	0//0	0/0/					0/0/0	Drive-axles for other diesel oil and gasoline heavy trucks (referring to vehicles subheading No. 8704.2240,8704.2300 and 8704.3240)
5/0/0	9	6	0/0	0/0/0	0/7.1	0//0	0/0/					0/0/0	Parts of drive-axles bridges for other diesel oil and gasoline heavy trucks (referring to vehicles subheading No. 8704.2240,8704.2300 and 8704.3240)
													----Of the vehicles of heading No. 87.05
0/0/0	2	4.6	0/0	0/0/0	0/7.1	0/0/0	0/0/	9/9/9	9.4/9			0/0/0	Drive-axles for special vehicles(referring to vehicles of heading No. 8705, with differential, whether or not provided transmussion components)
0/0/0	2	4.6	0/0	0/0/0	0/7.1	0/0/0	0/0/	9/9/9	9.4/9			0/0/0	Parts of drive-axles for special vehicles(referring to vehicles of heading No. 87.05, with differential, whether or not provided transmussion components)
													----Other
5/0/0	9	9	4/4	0/0/0	0/7.1	0//0	0/0/	6//	6/			0/0/0	Drive-axles for unlisted motor vehicles (with differential, whether or not provided transmussion components)
5/0/0	9	9	4/4	0/0/0	0/7.1	0//0	0/0/	6//	6/			0/0/0	Parts of drive-axles of unlisted motor vehicles (with differential, whether or not provided transmussion components)
													---Non-driving axles and parts thereof:
0/0/0	5	2.8	0/0	0/0/0	0/0	0//0	0/0/	5.4/5.4/5.4	5.6/5.4			0/0/0	----Of the vehicles of heading No. 87.01
0/0/0	6.8	9	1.5/1.5	0/0/0	0/10.7	0/0/0	0/0/	14.3/14.3/	/14.3			0/0/0	----Of the vehicles of subheading No. 8702.1091 and 8702.9010
0/0/0	5	2.8	0/0	0/0/0	0/0	0//0	0/0/	5.4/5.4/5.4	5.6/5.4			0/0/0	----Of the vehicles of subheading No. 8704.1030 and 8704.1090
0/0/0	3.5	4.6	0/0	0/0/0	0/7.1	0/0/0	0/0/	9/9/9	9.4/9			0/0/0	----Of the vehicles of subheading No. 8704.2100,8704.2230, 8704.3100 and 8704.3230
0/0/0	4	4.6	0/0	0/0/0	0/7.1	0/0/0	0/0/	9.5/9.5/9.5	/9.5			0/0/0	----Of the vehicles of subheading No. 8704.2240, 8704.2300 and 8704.3240
0/0/0	2	4.6	0/0	0/0/0	0/7.1	0/0/0	0/0/	9/9/9	9.4/9			0/0/0	----Of the vehicles of heading No. 87.05
													----Other
0/0/0	3.5		0/0	0/0/0	0/7.1	0/0/0	0/0/	6/6/	6/6			0/0/0	Non-drive-axles for not specified motor vehicles
0/0/0	3.5		0/0	0/0/0	0/7.1	0/0/0	0/0/	6/6/	6/6			0/0/0	Parts of non-drive-axles for not specified motor vehicles
													-Road wheels and parts and accessories thereof:
0/0/0	5	2.8	0/0	0/0/0	0/0	0//0	0/0/0	5.4/5.4/5.4	5.6/5.4			0/0/0	---Of the vehicles of heading No. 87.01
0/0/0	3.5	4.6	0/0	0/0/0	0/7.1	0/0/0	0/0/0	9/9/9	9.4/9			0/0/0	---Of the vehicles of subheadings No. 8702.1091 and 8702.9010
0/0/0	5	2.8	0/0	0/0/0	0/0	0//0	0/0/0	5.4/5.4/5.4	5.6/5.4			0/0/0	---Of the vehicles of subheadings No. 8704.1030 and 8704.1090
0/0/0	3.5	2	0/0	0/0/0	0/7.1	0/0/0	0/0/0	0/0/9	9.1/0			0/0/0	---Of the vehicles of subheadings No. 8704.2100,8704.2230, 8704.3100 and 8704.3230
0/0/0	4	4.6	0/0	0/0/0	0/7.1	0/0/0	0/0/0	9/9/9	9.4/9			0/0/0	---Of the vehicles of subheadings No. 8704.2240, 8704.2300 and 8704.3240
0/0/0	2	4.6	0/0	0/0/0	0/7.1	0/0/0	0/0/0	9/9/9	9.4/9			0/0/0	---Of the vehicles of heading No. 87.05
													---Other:
0/0/0	0		0/0	0/0/0	0/7.1	0/0/0	0/0/0	6/6/	/6			0/0/0	----Of aluminium alloy
0/0/0	3.5		0/0	0/0/0	0/7.1	0/0/0	0/0/0	6/6/	/6			0/0/0	Other
													-Suspension systems and parts there of (in-cluding shock-absorbers):
0/0/0	0	2	0/0	0/0/0	0/7.1	0/0/0	0/0/	0/0/9	9.4/0			0/0/0	---Of the vehicles of heading No. 87.03
0/0/0	3.5	2	0/0	0/0/0	0/7.1	0/0/0	0/0/	0/0/9	9.1/0			0/0/0	---Other
													-Other parts and accessories:
													--Radiators and parts therof:
0/0/0	0	4.6	0/0	0/0/0	0/7.1	0/0/0	0/0/	9.3/9.5/9.3	9.4/9.5			0/0/0	---Water tank radiators
0/0/0	0	4.6	0/0	0/0/0	0/7.1	0/0/0	0/0/	9.3/9.5/9.3	9.4/9.5			0/0/0	---Oil coolers
0/0/0	0	4.6	0/0	0/0/0	0/7.1	0/0/0	0/0/	9.3/9.5/9.3	9.4/9.5			0/0/0	---Other
0/0/0	0		0/0	0/0/0	0/7.1	0/0/0	0/0/	6/6/	6/6			0/0/0	--Silencers (mufflers) and exhaust pipes, parts therof
													--Clutches and parts thereof:
													---Of the vehicles of heading No. 87.01
0/0/0	5	2.8	0/0	0/0/0	0/0	0//0	0/0/	5.4/5.4/5.4	5.6/5.4			0/0/0	Clutch of engine power 65 kW and above for shift tractor
0/0/0	5	2.8	0/0	0/0/0	0/0	0//0	0/0/	5.4/5.4/5.4	5.6/5.4			0/0/0	Drive-axles with Clutch and parts there of the vehicles of heading No. 87.01, whether or not provided with other transmission components.
0/0/0	3.5	6	0/0	0/0/0	0/7.1	0/0/0	0/0/	9.5/9.5/	/9.5			0/0/0	---Of the vehicles of subheadings No. 8702.1091 and 8702.9010
0/0/0	5	2.8	0/0	0/0/0	0/0	0//0	0/0/	5.4/5.4/5.4	5.6/5.4			0/0/0	---Of the vehicles of subheadings No. 8704.1030 and 8704.1090
0/0/0	3.5	4.6	0/0	0/0/0	0/7.1	0/0/0	0/0/	9.3/9.5/9.3	9.4/9.5			0/0/0	---Of the vehicles of subheadings No. 8704.2100 , 8704.2230, 8704.3100 and 8704.3230
0/0/0	2	6	0/0	0/0/0	0/7.1	0/0/0	0/0/	9.5/9.5/	/9.5			0/0/0	---Of the vehicles of subheadings No. 8704.2240, 8704.2300 and 8704.3240
0/0/0	2	6	0/0	0/0/0	0/7.1	0/0/0	0/0/	9.5/9.5/9.5	/9.5			0/0/0	---Of the vehicles of heading No. 87.05

税则号列	货品名称〔CIQ 扩展编码及品名—T2 表示见附表 2〕	最惠(%)	暂定税率	普通	增值/消费	出口退税	计量单位	监管条件/特殊证件	检验检疫	对美关税	亚太上/下
8708.9390	---其他〔999〕	6		100	13/	13	千克	6/			
	--转向盘、转向柱、转向器及其零件:										
8708.9410	---税目 87.01 所列车辆用〔999〕	6		14	13/	13	千克	6/			
8708.9420	---税号 8702.1091 及 8702.9010 所列车辆用										
8708.9420 01	座位≥30 的客车用转向器零件〔999〕	6		70	13/	13	千克	6/			
8708.9420 90	大型客车用其他转向盘、转向柱及其零件(包括转向器)〔999〕	6		70	13/	13	千克	6/			
8708.9430	---税号 8704.1030 及 8704.1090 所列车辆用〔999〕	6		11	13/	13	千克	6/			
8708.9440	---税号 8704.2100、8704.2230、8704.3100 及 8704.3230 所列车辆用〔999〕	6		45	13/	13	千克	6/			
8708.9450	---税号 8704.2240、8704.2300 及 8708.3240 所列车辆用										
8708.9450 01	总重≥14 吨柴油型货车转向器的零件〔999〕	6		30	13/	13	千克	6/			
8708.9450 90	其他重型货车用转向盘、转向柱、转向器及其零件(指编号 8704.2240、8704.2300 及 8704.3240 所列车辆用)〔999〕	6		30	13/	13	千克	6/			
8708.9460	---税目 87.05 所列车辆用转向器〔999〕	6		100	13/	13	千克	6/			
8708.9490	---其他										
8708.9490 01	采用电动转向系统的转向盘、转向柱、转向器及其零件〔999〕	6		100	13/	13	千克	6/			
8708.9490 90	其他未列名机动车辆用转向盘、转向柱及其零件(包括转向器)〔999〕	6		100	13/	13	千克	6/			
8708.9500	--带充气系统的安全气囊及其零件〔999〕	6		100	13/	13	千克	6/			5.4/5.4
	--其他:										
8708.9910	---税目 87.01 所列车辆用〔999〕	6		14	13/	13	千克	6/			
	---税号 8702.1091 及 8702.9010 所列车辆用:										
8708.9921	----车架〔999〕	6		70	13/	13	千克	6/			
8708.9929	----其他〔999〕	6		70	13/	13	千克	6/			
	---税号 8704.1030 及 8704.1090 所列车辆用:										
8708.9931	----车架〔999〕	6		11	13/	13	千克	6/			
8708.9939	----其他〔999〕	6	3	11	13/	13	千克	6/			
	---税号 8704.2100、8704.2230、8704.3100 及 8704.3230 所列车辆用:										
8708.9941	----车架〔999〕	6		45	13/	13	千克	6/			
8708.9949	----其他〔999〕	6		45	13/	13	千克	6/			
	---税号 8704.2240、8704.2300 及 8704.3240 所列车辆用:										
8708.9951	----车架〔999〕	6		30	13/	13	千克	6/			
8708.9959	----其他〔999〕	6		30	13/	13	千克	6/	L		
8708.9960	---税目 87.05 所列车辆用〔999〕	6		100	13/	13	千克	6/			
	---其他:										
8708.9991	----车架〔999〕	6		100	13/	13	千克/个	6/			
8708.9992	----传动轴〔999〕	6		100	13/	13	千克	6/			
8708.9999	----其他										
8708.9999 10	混合动力汽车动力传动装置及其零件(由发电机、电动机和动力分配装置等组成,税目 87.01 至 87.04 所列车辆用)〔999〕	6		100	13/	13	千克	6/			
8708.9999 90	机动车辆用未列名零件、附件(税目 87.01 至 87.04 所列车辆用)〔999〕	6		100	13/	13	千克	6/			
87.09	**短距离运输货物的机动车辆,未装有提升或搬运设备,用于工厂、仓库、码头或机场;火车站台上用的牵引车;上述车辆的零件:**										
	-车辆:										
	--电动的:										
8709.1110	---牵引车〔999〕	10		30	13/	13	辆/千克	6/		35	
8709.1190	---其他〔999〕	10		30	13/	13	辆/千克	6/		35	
	--其他:										
8709.1910	---牵引车〔999〕	10		30	13/	13	辆/千克	6/		35	
8709.1990	---其他〔999〕	10		30	13/	13	辆/千克	6/		35	
8709.9000	-零件〔999〕	8		17	13/	13	千克	6/		33	
87.10	**坦克及其他机动装甲战斗车辆,不论是否装有武器;上述车辆的零件:**										

协定税率 %								RCEP		特惠税率 %			Article Description
东/冰/格	巴基斯坦	韩国	瑞士 上/下	哥/秘/柬	澳/毛	新西/坡/智	中国港/澳/台	东盟及马来/澳/韩	日/新	亚太2国	老/柬/缅	98/97/95	
0/0/0	5		0/0	0/0/0	0/7.1	0/0/0	0/0/	6/6/6	6/6			0/0/0	---Other
													--Steering wheels, steering columns and steering boxes parts thereof:
0/0/0	0	2.8	0/0	0/0/0	0/0	0//0	0/0/	5.4/5.4/5.4	5.6/5.4			0/0/0	---Of the vehicles of heading No. 87. 01
													---Of the vehicles of subheadings No. 8702. 1091 and 8702. 9010
0/0/0	3.5	4.6	0/0	0/0/0	0/7.1	0/0/0	0/0/	9.3/9.5/	9.4/9.5			0/0/0	Parts of steering boxes for the buses with 30 seats or more
0/0/0	3.5	4.6	0/0	0/0/0	0/7.1	0/0/0	0/0/	9.3/9.5/	9.4/9.5			0/0/0	Other steering wheels, steering columns and parts thereof for large buses
0/0/0	0	2.8	0/0	0/0/0	0/0	0//0	0/0/	5.4/5.4/5.4	5.6/5.4			0/0/0	---Of the vehicles of subheadings No. 8704. 1030 and 8704. 1090
0/0/0	3.5	4.6	0/0	0/0/0	0/7.1	0/0/0	0/0/	6/6/	/6			0/0/0	---Of the vehicles of subheadings No. 8704. 2100, 8704. 2230, 8704. 3100 and 8704. 3230
													---Of the vehicles of subheadings No. 8704. 2240, 8704. 2300 and 8704. 3240
0/0/0	3.5	4.6	0/0	0/0/0	0/7.1	0/0/0	0/0/	9.3/9.5/9.3	9.4/9.5			0/0/0	Redirector components of diesel oil trucks whose weight≥14 tons
0/0/0	3.5	4.6	0/0	0/0/0	0/7.1	0/0/0	0/0/	9.3/9.5/9.3	9.4/9.5			0/0/0	Steering wheels, steering columns, steering boxes and parts thereof for the vehicles of subheading No. 8704. 2240, 8704. 2300 and 8704. 3240
0/0/0	3.5	4.6	0/0	0/0/0	0/7.1	0/0/0	0/0/	9/9/9	9.4/9			0/0/0	---Of the vehicles of heading No. 87. 05
													---Other
0/0/0	3.5		4/4	0/0/0	0/7.1	0/0/0	0/0/	6/6/	6/6			0/0/0	Steering wheels, steering columns, steering boxes and thereof parts, with electric power steering system
0/0/0	3.5		4/4	0/0/0	0/7.1	0/0/0	0/0/	6/6/	6/6			0/0/0	Steering wheels, steering columns, steering gears and thereof parts for other unlisted motor vehicles
5/0/0	9	9	0/0	0//0	0/7.1	0//0	0/0/	6//	6/			0/0/	--Safety air-bags with inflater system; parts thereof
													--Other:
0/0/0	0	1.2	0/0	0/0/0	0/0	0//0	0/0/	0/0/5.4	5.5/0			0/0/0	---Of the vehicles of heading No. 87. 01
													---Of the vehicles of subheadings No. 87 02. 1091 and 8702. 9010:
0/0/0	20	15		0/0/0	0/17.9	0/0/0	0/0/	22.5/23.8/23.3	22.7/23.8			0/0/0	----Frames
0/0/0	20	15		0/0/0	0/17.9	0/0/0	0/0/	23.8/23.8/	23.8/23.8			0/0/0	----Other
													---Of the vehicles of subheading No. 87 04. 1030 and 8704. 1090:
0/0/0	0	2.8	0/0	0/0/0	0/0	0//0	0/0/	5.4/5.4/5.4	5.6/5.4			0/0/0	----Frames
0/0/0	0	2.8	0/0	0/0/0	0/0	0//0	0/0/	5.4/5.4/5.4	5.6/5.4			0/0/0	----Other
													---Of the vehicles of subheadings No. 8704. 2100, 8704. 2230, 8704. 3100 and 8704. 3230:
0/0/0		15		0/0/0	0/17.9	0/0/0	0/0/	23.8/23.8/23.8	23.8/23.8			0/0/0	----Frames
0/0/0	0	15		0/0/0	0/17.9	0/0/0	0/0/	23.8/23.8/23.8	23.8/23.8			0/0/0	----Other
													---Of the vehicles of subheadings No. 8704. 2240, 8704. 2300 and 8704. 3240:
0/0/0	2	4.6	0/0	0/0/0	0/7.1	0/0/0	0/0/	9/9/9	9.4/9			0/0/0	----Frames
0/0/0	3.5	4.6	0/0	0/0/0	0/7.1	0/0/0	0/0/	9.3/9.5/9.3	9.4/9.5			0/0/0	----Other
0/0/0	8.4	3	1.5/1.5	0/0/0	0/10.7	0/0/0	0/0/	0/0/13.5	13.6/0			0/0/0	---Of the vehicles of heading No. 87. 05
													---Other:
0/0/0	3.5	4.6	0/0	0/0/0	0/7.1	0/0/0	0/0/0	9.3/9.5/9.3	9.4/9.5			0/0/0	----Frames
0/0/0	3.5	4.6	0/0	0/0/0	0/7.1	0/0/0	0/0/0	9.3/9.5/9.3	9.4/9.5			0/0/0	----Transmission shafts
													----Other
0/0/0	0	4.6	0/0	0/0/0	0/7.1	0/0/0	0/0/0	9.3/9.5/9.3	9.4/9.5			0/0/0	Transmission device of hybrid electric vehicle and part (made of generators, motor and power spilt device, of vehicles of subheading No. 87. 01 to 87. 04)
0/0/0	0	4.6	0/0	0/0/0	0/7.1	0/0/0	0/0/0	9.3/9.5/9.3	9.4/9.5			0/0/0	Parts and accessories of motor vehicles, not elsewhere specified or included (of the vehicles of subheading No. 87. 01 to 87. 04)
													Works trucks, self-propelled, not fitted with lifting or handling equipment, of the type used in factories, warehouses, dock areas or airports for short distance transport of goods; tractors of the type used on railway station platforms; parts of the foregoing vehicles:
													-Vehicles:
													--Electrical:
0/0/0	4	2	0/0	0/0/0	0/0	0/0/0	0/0/	0/0/9	9.1/0			0/0/0	---Tractors
0/0/0	4	2	0/0	0/0/0	0/0	0/0/0	0/0/	0/0/9	9.1/0			0/0/0	---Other
													--Other:
0/0/0	3.5	4.9	1.1/1.1	0/0/0	0/0	0/0/0	0/0/	10/10/10	/10			0/0/0	---Tractors
0/0/0	3.5	4.9	1.1/1.1	0/0/0	0/0	0/0/0	0/0/	10/10/10	/10			0/0/0	---Other
0/0/0	2	1.6	0/0	0/0/0	0/0	0//0	0/0/	0/0/7.6	7.6/0			0/0/0	-Parts
													Tanks and other armoured fighting vehicles, motorized, whether or not fitted with weapons, and parts of such vehicles:

税则号列	货品名称〔CIQ 扩展编码及品名－T2 表示见附表 2〕	最惠(%)	暂定税率	普通	增值/消费	出口退税	计量单位	监管条件/特殊证件	检验检疫	对美关税	亚太上/下
8710.0010	---整车〔999〕	15		100	13/	0	辆/千克	6/			
8710.0090	---零件〔999〕	15		100	13/	0	千克	6/			
87.11	**摩托车(包括机器脚踏两用车)及装有辅助发动机的脚踏车,不论有无边车;边车:**										
8711.1000	-装有活塞内燃发动机,气缸容量(排气量)不超过 50 毫升										
8711.1000 10	微马力摩托车及脚踏两用车(装有活塞发动机,微马力指排气量=50cc)〔999〕	45		150	13/	13	辆/千克	46Axy/	LM	70	
8711.1000 90	微马力摩托车及脚踏两用车(装有活塞发动机,微马力指排气量<50cc)〔999〕	45		150	13/	13	辆/千克	6A/	LM	70	
	-装有活塞内燃发动机,气缸容量(排气量)超过 50 毫升,但不超过 250 毫升										
8711.2010	---气缸容量超过 50 毫升,但不超过 100 毫升〔999〕	45		150	13/	13	辆/千克	46Axy/	LM	70	
8711.2020	---气缸容量超过 100 毫升,但不超过 125 毫升〔999〕	45		150	13/	13	辆/千克	46Axy/	LM	70	
8711.2030	---气缸容量超过 125 毫升,但不超过 150 毫升〔999〕	45		150	13/	13	辆/千克	46Axy/	LM	70	
8711.2040	---气缸容量超过 150 毫升,但不超过 200 毫升〔999〕	45		150	13/	13	辆/千克	46Axy/	LM	70	
8711.2050	---气缸容量超过 200 毫升,但不超过 250 毫升										
8711.2050 10	200<排量<250 毫升装有活塞内燃发动机摩托车及脚踏两用车〔999〕	45		150	13/	13	辆/千克	46Axy/	LM	70	
8711.2050 90	排量=250 毫升装有活塞内燃发动机摩托车及脚踏两用车〔101 自行车零配件,102 其它非机动脚踏车零配件,103 摩托车〕	45		150	13/3	13	辆/千克	46Axy/	LM	70	
	-装有活塞内燃发动机,气缸容量(排气量)超过 250 毫升,但不超过 500 毫升:										
8711.3010	---气缸容量(排气量)超过 250 毫升,但不超过 400 毫升〔999〕	45		150	13/10	13	辆/千克	46Axy/	LM	70	32.9/32.9
8711.3020	---气缸容量(排气量)超过 400 毫升,但不超过 500 毫升〔999〕	45		150	13/10	13	辆/千克	46Axy/	LM	70	32.9/32.9
8711.4000	-装有活塞内燃发动机,气缸容量(排气量)超过 500 毫升,但不超过 800 毫升〔999〕	40		150	13/10	13	辆/千克	46Axy/	LM	65	
8711.5000	-装有活塞内燃发动机,气缸容量(排气量)超过 800 毫升〔999〕	30		150	13/10	13	辆/千克	46Axy/	LM	55	
8711.6000	-装有驱动电动机的										
8711.6000 10	电动自行车(包括机器脚踏两用车;脚踏车)〔999〕	45		150	13/	13	辆/千克	6A/	ML	70	
8711.6000 90	其他装有电驱动电动机的摩托车〔999〕	45		150	13/	13	辆/千克	6A/	LM	70	
8711.9000	-其他										
8711.9000 10	其他排气量≤250 毫升摩托车及脚踏两用车〔999〕	45		150	13/3	13	辆/千克	6A/	LM	70	
8711.9000 20	其他排气量>250 毫升摩托车及脚踏两用车〔999〕	45		150	13/10	13	辆/千克	6A/	LM	70	
8711.9000 30	其他无法区分排气量的摩托车及脚踏两用车〔999〕	45		150	13/3	13	辆/千克	6A/	LM	70	
8711.9000 90	装有其他辅助发动机的脚踏车,边车〔999〕	45		150	13/	13	辆/千克	6A/	LM	70	
87.12	**自行车及其他非机动脚踏车(包括运货三轮脚踏车):**										
8712.0020	---竞赛型自行车〔999〕	7		130	13/	13	辆/千克	6/		32	4.9/4.9
8712.0030	---山地自行车〔999〕	7		130	13/	13	辆/千克	6/		32	4.9/4.9
	---越野自行车:										
8712.0041	----16、18 及 20 英寸〔10116、18 英寸越野自行车,10220 英寸越野自行车,103 其他越野自行车〕	7		130	13/	13	辆/千克	6/		32	4.9/4.9
8712.0049	----其他〔101:16、18 英寸越野自行车,102:20 英寸越野自行车,103:其他越野自行车,104:货运三轮脚踏车〕	7		130	13/	13	辆/千克	6/		32	4.9/4.9
	---其他自行车:										
8712.0081	----16 英寸及以下										
8712.0081 10	12～16 英寸的未列名自行车〔999〕	5		130	13/	13	辆/千克	6/	L	30	3.5/3.5
8712.0081 90	11 英寸及以下的未列名自行车〔999〕	5		130	13/	13	辆/千克	6/	L	30	3.5/3.5
8712.0089	----其他〔10112－16 英寸其它自行车,10211 英寸及以下其它自行车,103 其它自行车〕	5		130	13/	13	辆/千克	6/	L	30	3.5/3.5
8712.0090	---其他〔101:12－16 英寸其它自行车,102:11 英寸及以下其它自行车,103:其它自行车,104:货运三轮脚踏车,105:其他脚踏车〕	5		130	13/	13	辆/千克	6/	L	30	3.5/3.5

协定税率 %								RCEP		特惠税率 %			Article Description
东/冰/格	巴基斯坦	韩国	瑞士上/下	哥/秘/柬	澳/毛	新西/坡/智	中国港/澳/台	东盟及马来/澳/韩	日/新	亚太2国	老/柬/缅	98/97/95	
0/0/0	8.4	3	1.5/1.5	0/0/0	0/0	0/0/0	0/0/	0/0/13.5	13.6/0			0/0/0	---Assembled
0/0/0	8.4	3	1.5/1.5	0/0/0	0/0	0/0/0	0/0/	0/0/13.5	13.6/0			0/0/0	---Parts and accessories
													Motorcycles (including mopeds) and cycles fitted with an auxiliary motor, with or without side-cars; side-cars:
													-With internal combustion piston engine of a cylinder capacity not exceeding 50 cc
0/0/0	36	27	18.9/18.9	0/0/0	0/27	0/0/0	0/0/	42.8/42.8/42.8	/42.8			0/0/0	Micro horsepower motorcycles and mopeds (with reciprocating internal combustion piston engine, micro horsep ower cylinder capacity=50cc)
0/0/0	36	27	18.9/18.9	0/0/0	0/27	0/0/0	0/0/	42.8/42.8/42.8	/42.8			0/0/0	Micro horsepower motorcycles and mopeds (with reciprocating internal combustion piston engine, micro horsepower cylinder capacity<50cc)
													-With internal combustion piston engine of a cylinder capacity exceeding 50 cc, but not exceeding 250cc
0/0/0		27	18.9/18.9	0/0/0	0/27	0/0/0	0/0/	42.8/42.8/42.8	/42.8			0/0/0	---Of a cylinder capacity exceeding 50cc, but not exceeding 100cc
0/0/0		27	18.9/18.9	0/0/0	0/27	0/0/0	0/0/	42.8/42.8/42.8	/42.8			0/0/0	---Of a cylinder capacity exceeding 100cc but not exceeding 125cc
0/0/0		27	18.9/18.9	0/0/0	0/27	0/0/0	0/0/	42.8/42.8/42.8	/42.8			0/0/0	---Of a cylinder capacity exceeding 125cc but not exceeding 150cc
0/0/0		27	18.9/18.9	0//0	0/27	0/0/0	0/0/	42.8/42.8/42.8	/42.8			0/0/	---Of a cylinder capacity exceeding 150cc, but not exceeding 200cc
													---Of a cylinder capacity exceeding 200cc< but not exceeding 250cc
0/0/0		27	18.9/18.9	0//0	0/27	0/0/0	0/0/	42.8/42.8/42.8	/42.8			0/0/	200cc<displocement< 250cc loaded exhaust volume of reciprocating piston internal combustion engine for motorcycles and mopeds
0/0/0		27	18.9/18.9	0//0	0/27	0/0/0	0/0/	42.8/42.8/42.8	/42.8			0/0/	Displacement =250cc with reciprocating internal combustion piston engine for motorcycles and mopeds
													-With internal combustion piston engine of a cylinder capacity exceeding 250cc, but not exceeding 500cc:
0/0/0	32.8	27		0//0	0/27	0/0/0	0/0/	42.8/42.8/42.8	/42.8			0/0/	---Of a cylinder capacity exceeding 250cc, but not exceeding 400cc
0/0/0	32.8	27		0//0	0/27	0/0/0	0/0/	42.8/42.8/42.8	/42.8			0/0/	---Of a cylinder capacity exceeding 400cc, but not exceeding 500cc
0/0/0		24		0//0	0/24	0/0/0	0/0/	38/38/38	/38			0/0/	-With internal combustion piston engine of a cylinder capacity exceeding 500 cc, but not exceeding 800 cc
0/0/0		18		0//0	0/18	0/0/0	0/0/	28.5/28.5/28.5	28.6/28.5			0/0/	-With internal combustion piston engine of a cylinder capacity exceeding 800 cc
													-With electric motor for propulSlon
0/0/0				0//0	0/27	0/0/0	0/0/	5/5/	/5			0/0/	Electric bicycle and side-cars, and mopeds
0/0/0				0//0	0/27	0/0/0	0/0/	5/5/	/5			0/0/	Other motorcycle with electric drive motor
													-Other
0/0/0				0//0	0/27	0/0/0	0/0/	5/5/	/5			0/0/	Motorcycles and mopedes, of a cylinder capacity not exceeding 250m
0/0/0				0//0	0/27	0/0/0	0/0/	5/5/	/5			0/0/	Motorcycles and mopedes, of a cylinder capacity exceeding 250m
0/0/0				0//0	0/27	0/0/0	0/0/	5/5/	/5			0/0/	Motorcycles and mopedes, a cylinder capacity of its engine can not be distinguished
0/0/0				0//0	0/27	0/0/0	0/0/	5/5/	/5			0/0/	Mopeds and side-cars, fitted with an auxiliary motor
													Bicycles and other cycles (including delivery tricycles), not motorized:
0/0/0	3.5	2.6	1.3/1.3	0/0/0	0/0	0/0/0	0/0/0	0/0/11.7	11.8/0			0/0/0	---Racing bicycle
0/0/0	3.5	2.6	1.3/1.3	0/0/0	0/0	0/0/0	0/0/0	0/0/11.7	11.8/0			0/0/0	---Mountain bicycle
													---Cross-country bicycles:
0/0/0	3.5	2.6	1.3/1.3	0/0/0	0/0	0/0/0	0/0/0	0/0/11.7	11.8/0			0/0/0	----16inchs, 18inchs and 20inchs
0/0/0	3.5	2.6	1.3/1.3	0/0/0	0/0	0/0/0	0/0/0	0/0/11.7	11.8/0			0/0/0	----Other
													---Other cycles:
													----Not larger than 16inchs
0/0/0	3.5	2.6	1.3/1.3	0/0/0	0/0	0/0/0	0/0/0	0/0/11.7	11.8/0			0/0/0	Bicycles, 12inches～16inches, not elsewhere specified or included
0/0/0	3.5	2.6	1.3/1.3	0/0/0	0/0	0/0/0	0/0/0	0/0/11.7	11.8/0			0/0/0	Bicycles, 11inchs or less, not elsewhere specified or included
0/0/0	3.5	2.6	1.3/1.3	0/0/0	0/0	0/0/0	0/0/0	0/0/11.7	11.8/0			0/0/0	----Other
0/0/0	11.3		2.3/2.3	0/0/0	0/13.8	0/0/0	0/0/0	5/5/	/5			0/0/0	---Other

税则号列	货品名称〔CIQ 扩展编码及品名—T2 表示见附表 2〕	最惠(%)	暂定税率	普通	增值/消费	出口退税	计量单位	监管条件/特殊证件	检验检疫	对美关税	亚太 上/下
87.13	**残疾人用车,不论是否机动或其他机械驱动:**										
8713.1000	-非机械驱动〔999〕	5		20	0/	13	辆/千克	6/			
8713.9000	-其他〔999〕	4		20	0/	13	辆/千克	6/			
87.14	**零件、附件,税目 87.11 至 87.13 所列车辆用:**										
8714.1000	-摩托车(包括机器脚踏两用车)用										
8714.1000 01	星型轮及碟刹件〔999〕	15	10	100	13/	13	千克	6/		35	
8714.1000 10	摩托车架〔999〕	15		100	13/	13	千克	46xy/		40	
8714.1000 20	摩托车用防抱死制动系统(ABS)及其零件〔999〕	15	8	100	13/	13	千克	6/		33	
8714.1000 90	摩托车其他零件,附件(包括机动脚踏两用车的零件、附件)〔999〕	15		100	13/	13	千克	6/		40	
8714.2000	-残疾人车辆用〔101 其他车辆零部件,102 其它非机动脚踏车零配件〕	5		17	13/	13	千克	6/		30	
	-其他:										
8714.9100	--车架、轮叉及其零件〔101 自行车零配件,102 其它非机动脚踏车零配件〕	5		80	13/	13	千克	6/		30	
	--轮圈及辐条:										
8714.9210	---轮圈〔101 自行车零配件,102 其它非机动脚踏车零配件〕	5		80	13/	13	千克	6/		30	
8714.9290	---辐条〔101 自行车零配件,102 其它非机动脚踏车零配件〕	5		80	13/	13	千克	6/		30	
	--轮毂(倒轮制动毂及毂闸除外);飞轮、链轮:										
8714.9310	---轮毂〔101 自行车零配件,102 其它非机动脚踏车零配件〕	5		80	13/	13	千克	6/		30	
8714.9320	---飞轮〔101 自行车零配件,102 其它非机动脚踏车零配件〕	5		80	13/	13	千克	6/		30	
8714.9390	---其他〔101 自行车零配件,102 其它非机动脚踏车零配件〕	5		80	13/	13	千克	6/		30	
8714.9400	--制动器(包括倒轮制动毂及毂闸)及其零件〔101 自行车零配件,102 其它非机动脚踏车零配件〕	5		80	13/	13	千克	6/		30	
8714.9500	--鞍座〔101 自行车零配件,102 其它非机动脚踏车零配件〕	5		80	13/	13	千克/个	6/		30	
	--脚蹬、曲柄链轮及其零件:										
8714.9610	---脚蹬及其零件〔101 自行车零配件,102 其它非机动脚踏车零配件〕	5		80	13/	13	千克	6/		30	
8714.9620	---曲柄链轮及其零件〔101 自行车零配件,102 其它非机动脚踏车零配件〕	5		80	13/	13	千克	6/		30	
8714.9900	--其他〔101 自行车零配件,102 其它非机动脚踏车零配件〕	5		80	13/	13	千克	6/		30	3.5/3.5
87.15	**婴孩车及其零件:**										
8715.0000	婴孩车及其零件										
8715.0000 10	婴孩车〔101 婴儿推车,102 学步车〕	6		80	13/	13	千克	6A/	LM	31	
8715.0000 90	婴孩车零件〔999〕	6		80	13/	13	千克	6A/	LM	31	
87.16	**挂车及半挂车或其他非机械驱动车辆及其零件:**										
8716.1000	-供居住或野营用厢式挂车及半挂车〔999〕	10		35	13/	13	辆/千克	6A/	LM	35	
8716.2000	-农用自装或自卸式挂车及半挂车〔999〕	10		35	13/	9,13	辆/千克	6/		35	
	-其他货运挂车及半挂车:										
	--罐式挂车及半挂车:										
8716.3110	---油罐挂车及半挂车〔999〕	10		20	13/	13	辆/千克	6A/	ML	35	
8716.3190	---其他〔999〕	10		35	13/	13	辆/千克	6A/	ML	35	
	--其他:										
8716.3910	---货柜挂车及半挂车〔999〕	10		20	13/	13	辆/千克	6A/	ML	35	
8716.3990	---其他〔999〕	10		35	13/	13	辆/千克	6A/	ML	35	
8716.4000	-其他挂车及半挂车〔999〕	10		35	13/	13	辆/千克	6A/	ML	35	
8716.8000	-其他车辆〔999〕	10		80	13/	13	辆/千克	6/		35	
8716.9000	-零件〔999〕	10		35	13/	13	千克	6/		15	

协定税率 %								RCEP		特惠税率 %			Article Description
东/冰/格	巴基斯坦	韩国	瑞士上/下	哥/秘/柬	澳/毛	新西/坡/智	中国港/澳/台	东盟及马来/澳/韩	日/新	亚太2国	老/柬/缅	98/97/95	
													Carriages for disabled persons, whether or not motorised or otherwise mechanically propelled:
0/0/0	5	0	0/0	0/0/0	0/0	0//0	0/0/	0/0/0	0/0			0/0/0	-Not mechanically propelled
0/0/0	0	0.8	0/0	0/0/0	0/0	0//0	0/0/	0/0/3.6	3.6/0			0/0/0	-Other
													Parts and accessories of vehicles of headings No. 87.11 to 87.13:
													-Of motorcycles (including mopeds)
0/0/0	0	18		0/0/0	0/18	0/0/0	0/0/	28.5/28.5/	28.6/28.5			0/0/0	Star-shaped wheels and disc brakes
0/0/0	0	18		0/0/0	0/18	0/0/0	0/0/	28.5/28.5/	28.6/28.5			0/0/0	Frams of motorcycles
0/0/0	0	18		0/0/0	0/18	0/0/0	0/0/	28.5/28.5/	28.6/28.5		//	0/0/0	Motorcycles Anti lock braking system (ABS) and parts thereof
0/0/0	0	18		0/0/0	0/18	0/0/0	0/0/	28.5/28.5/	28.6/28.5			0/0/0	Other parts and accessories thereof, of motorcycles and mopeds
0/0/0	0	0	0/0	0/0/0	0/0	0//0	0/0/	0/0/0	0/0			0/0/0	-Of carriages for disabled persons
													-Other:
0/0/0	4.2	2.4	1.2/1.2	0/0/0	0/0	0/0/0	0/0/0	0/0/10.8	10.9/0			0/0/0	--Frames and forks, and parts thereof
													--Wheel rims and spokes:
0/0/0	4.8	2.4	1.2/1.2	0/0/0	0/0	0/0/0	0/0/0	0/0/10.8	10.9/0			0/0/0	---Wheel rims
0/0/0	4.2	2.4	1.2/1.2	0/0/0	0/0	0/0/0	0/0/0	0/0/10.8	10.9/0			0/0/0	---Spokes
													--Hubs, other than coaster braking hubs and hub brakes, and free-wheel, sprocket wheels:
0/0/0	4.2	2.4	1.2/1.2	0/0/0	0/0	0/0/0	0/0/0	0/0/10.8	10.9/0			0/0/0	---Hubs
0/0/0	4.2	2.4	1.2/1.2	0/0/0	0/0	0/0/0	0/0/0	10.8/10.8/10.8	10.9/10.8			0/0/0	---Free-wheel
0/0/0	4.2	2.4	1.2/1.2	0/0/0	0/0	0/0/0	0/0/0	0/0/10.8	10.9/0			0/0/0	---Other
0/0/0	4.8	2.4	1.2/1.2	0/0/0	0/0	0/0/0	0/0/0	10.8/10.8/10.8	10.9/10.8			0/0/0	--Brakes, including coaster braking hubs and hub brakes, and parts thereof
0/0/0	4.2	2.4	1.2/1.2	0/0/0	0/0	0/0/0	0/0/0	0/0/10.8	10.9/0			0/0/0	--Saddles
													--Pedals and crank-gear, and parts thereof:
0/0/0	4.2	2.4	1.2/1.2	0/0/0	0/0	0/0/0	0/0/0	0/0/10.8	10.9/0			0/0/0	---Pedals and parts thereof
0/0/0	4.8	2.4	1.2/1.2	0/0/0	0/0	0/0/0	0/0/0	10.8/10.8/10.8	10.9/10.8			0/0/0	---Crank-gear and parts thereof
0/0/0	0	2.4	1.2/1.2	0/0/0	0/0	0/0/0	0/0/0	0/0/10.8	10.9/0			0/0/0	--Other
													Baby carriages and parts thereof:
													Baby carriages and parts thereof
0/0/0	16	9.3	2/2	0/0/0	0/0	0/0/0	0/0/	18/18/18	18.8/18			0/0/0	Baby carriages
0/0/0	16	9.3	2/2	0/0/0	0/0	0/0/0	0/0/	18/18/18	18.8/18			0/0/0	Baby car parts
													Trailers and semi-trailers; other vehicles, not mechanically propelled; parts thereof:
0/0/0	2	4.6	0/0	0/0/0	0/0	0/0/0	0/0/	9/9/9	9.4/9			0/0/0	-Trailers and semi-trailers of the caravan type, for housing or camping
0/0/0	2	4.6	0/0	0/0/0	0/0	0//0	0/0/	9/9/9	9.4/9			0/0/0	-Self-loading or self-unloading trailers and semi-trailers for agricultural purposes
													-Other trailers and semi-trailers for the transport of goods:
													--Tanker trailers and tanker semi-trailers:
0/0/0	2	4.6	0/0	0/0/0	0/0	0/0/0	0/0/	9/9/9	9.1/9			0/0/0	---Oil tanker trailers and semi-trailers
0/0/0	2	2	0/0	0/0/0	0/0	0//0	0/0/	0/0/9	9.1/0			0/0/0	---Other
													--Other:
0/0/0	2	2	0/0	0/0/0	0/0	0//0	0/0/	0/0/9	9.1/0			0/0/0	---Van trailers and semi-trailers
0/0/0	2	2	0/0	0/0/0	0/0	0//0	0/0/	0/0/9	9.1/0			0/0/0	---Other
0/0/0	2	2	0/0	0/0/0	0/0	0//0	0/0/	0/0/9	9.1/0			0/0/0	-Other trailers and semi-trailers
0/0/0	3.5	2	0/0	0/0/0	0/0	0/0/0	0/0/	0/0/9	9.1/0			0/0/0	-Other vehicles
0/0/0	2	2	0/0	0/0/0	0/0	0/0/0	0/0/	0/0/9	9.1/0			0/0/0	-Parts

第八十八章
航空器、航天器及其零件

注释:

一、本章所称"无人驾驶航空器"是指除税目 88.01 的航空器以外,没有飞行员驾驶的任何航空器,它们可设计用于载物或安装永久性集成的数码相机或其他能在飞行中发挥实用功能的设备 。但"无人驾驶航空器"不包括专供娱乐用的飞行玩具(税目 95.03)。

一、子目注释:

一、子目 8802.11 至 8802.40 所称"空载重量",是指航空器在正常飞行状态下,除去机组人员、燃料及非永久性安装设备后的重量。

二、子目 8806.21 至 8806.24 及 8806.91 至 8806.94 所称"最大起飞重量",是指航空器在正常飞行状态下起飞时的最大重量,包括有效载荷、设备和燃料的重量。

税则号列	货品名称〔CIQ 扩展编码及品名—T2 表示见附表 2〕	最惠(%)	暂定税率	普通	增值/消费	出口退税	计量单位	监管条件/特殊证件	检验检疫	对美关税	亚太上/下
88.01	**气球及飞艇;滑翔机、悬挂滑翔机及其他无动力航空器:**										
8801.0010	---滑翔机及悬挂滑翔机:〔999〕	3		11	13/	13	架/千克	/		23	
8801.0090	---其他										
8801.0090 10	自然视距以外可控飞行的无人驾驶飞艇(在 30 分钟≤最大续航时间<1 小时,阵风≥46.3 千米/小时条件下具有起飞和稳定飞行能力;或者最大续航时间≥1 小时。)〔999〕	3		11	13/	13	架/千克	3/		23	
8801.0090 90	气球、其他飞艇及无动力航空器(滑翔机除外)〔999〕	3		11	13/	13	架/千克	/		23	
88.02	**其他航空器(例如,直升机、飞机),税目 88.06 的无人驾驶航空器除外;航天器(包括卫星)及其运载工具、亚轨道运载工具:**										
	-直升机:										
8802.1100	--空载重量不超过 2000 千克〔999〕	2		11	13/	13	架/千克	O/		7	1.3/1.3
	--空载重量超过 2000 千克:										
8802.1210	---空载重量超过 2000 千克,但不超过 7000 千克〔999〕	2		11	13/	13	架/千克	O/		12	1.3/1.3
8802.1220	---空载重量超过 7000 千克〔999〕	2		11	13/	13	架/千克	O/			1.3/1.3
8802.2000	-飞机及其他航空器,空载重量不超过 2000 千克〔101 直升机,102 航天器〕	5		11	13/	13	架/千克	O/		10	
8802.3000	-飞机及其他航空器,空载重量超过 2000 千克,但不超过 15000 千克〔101 飞机,102 航天器〕	4		11	13/	13	架/千克	O/		9	
	-飞机及其他航空器,空载重量超过 15000 千克:										
8802.4010	---空载重量超过 15000 千克,但不超过 45000 千克〔101 飞机,102 航天器〕	5		11	13/	13	架/千克	O/			3.5/3.5
8802.4020	---空载重量超过 45000 千克〔999〕	1		11	13/	13	架/千克	O/			0.7/0.7
8802.6000	-航天器(包括卫星)及其运载工具、亚轨道运载工具										
8802.6000 10	通信卫星〔999〕	0		11	13/	13	架/千克	/			
8802.6000 90	航天器(包括卫星,但通信卫星除外)及其运载工具(包括亚轨道运载工具)〔101 航天器,102 其它航空器〕	2		11	13/	13	架/千克	/			
88.04	**降落伞(包括可操纵降落伞及滑翔伞)、旋翼降落伞及其零件、附件:**										
8804.0000	降落伞(包括可操纵降落伞及滑翔伞)、旋翼降落伞及其零件、附件〔999〕	2		11	13/	13	千克	/		7	
88.05	**航空器的发射装置、甲板停机装置或类似装置和地面飞行训练器及其零件:**										
8805.1000	-航空器的发射装置及其零件;甲板停机装置或类似装置及其零件〔999〕	1.5		11	13/	13	千克	/		6.5	
	-地面飞行训练器及其零件:										
8805.2100	--空战模拟器及其零件〔999〕	0		11	13/	13	千克	/			
8805.2900	--其他〔999〕	0		11	13/	13	千克	O/			0/0
88.06	**无人驾驶航空器:**										
8806.1000	-设计用于旅客运输的〔101 直升机,102 飞机,103 航天器〕	3		11	13/	13	架/千克	O/			
	-其他,仅使用遥控飞行的:										
	--最大起飞重量不超过 250 克:										
8806.2110	---航拍无人机										
8806.2110 10	仅使用遥控飞行的最大起飞重量≤250 克的航拍无人机(用于特种用途的电视摄像或数字照相(P))〔999〕	0		99	13/	13	架/千克	/			
8806.2110 90	其他仅使用遥控飞行的最大起飞重量≤250 克的航拍无人机〔999〕	0		99	13/	13	架/千克	/		5	
8806.2190	---其他〔101 直升机,102 飞机,103 航天器〕	3.5		11	13/	13	架/千克	O/		8.5	

Chapter 88
Aircraft, spacecraft, and parts thereof

Note:

1. - For the purposes of this Chapter, the expression "unmanned aircraft" means any aircraft, other than those of heading 88.01, designed to be flown without a pilot on board. They may be designed to carry a payload or equipped with permanently integrated digital cameras or other equipment which would enable them to perform utilitarian functions during their flight. The expression "unmanned aircraft", however, does not cover flying toys, designed solely for amusement purposes (heading 95.03)."

Subheading Note:

For the purposes of subheadings Nos. 8802. 11 to Nos. 8802. 40, the expression "unladen weight" means the weight of the machine in normal flying order, excluding the weight of the crew and of fuel and equipment other than permanently fitted items of equipment.

2. — For the purposes of subheadings 8806.21 to 8806.24 and 8806.91 to 8806.94, the expression "maximum take—off weight" means the maximum weight of the machine in normal flying order, at take—off, including the weight of payload, equipment and fuel.".

协定税率 %								RCEP		特惠税率 %			Article Description
东/冰/格	巴基斯坦	韩国	瑞士上/下	哥/秘/柬	澳/毛	新西/坡/智	中国港/澳/台	东盟及马来/澳/韩	日/新	亚太2国	老/柬/缅	98/97/95	
													Balloons and dirigibles; gliders, hang gliders and other non-powered aircraft:
0/0/0	0	0	0/0	0/0/0	0/0	0//0	0/0/	0/0/0	0/0			0/0/0	---Cliders and hang gliders
													---Other
0/0/0	0	0	0/0	0/0/0	0/0	0//0	0/0/	0/0/0	0/0			0/0/0	Natural sights outside of controlled flight of unmanned airship, in 30 minutes or less maximum duration $<$ 1 hour, under the condition of wind acuity $\geqslant$46.3 kilometers per hour and stable flight take-off ability; Or a maximum duration for $\geqslant$1 hour or more
0/0/0	0	0	0/0	0/0/0	0/0	0//0	0/0/	0/0/0	0/0			0/0/0	Balloons and dirigibles; and other non-powered aircraft (excluding gliders)
													Other aircraft (for example, helicopters, aeroplanes),aircraft, except unman ned aircraft of heading 88.06 spacecraft (including satellites) and suborbital and spacecraft launch vehicles:
													-Helicopters:
0/0/0	0	0	0/0	0/0/0	0/0	0//0	0/0/	0/0/0	0/0			0/0/0	--Of an unladen weight not exceeding 2000kg
													--Of an unladen weight exceeding 2000kg:
0/0/0	0	0	0/0	0/0/0	0/0	0//0	0/0/	0/0/0	0/0			0/0/0	---Of an unladen weight exceeding 2000kg,but not exceeding 7000kg
0/0/0	0	0	0/0	0/0/0	0/0	0//0	0/0/	0/0/0	0/0			0/0/0	---Of an unladen weight exceeding 7000kg
0/0/0	0	1	0/0	0/0/0	0/0	0//0	0/0/	0/0/4.5	4.5/0			0/0/0	-Aeroplanes and other aircraft, of an unladen weight not exceeding 2000kg
0/0/0	0	0	0/0	0/0/0	0/0	0//0	0/0/	0/0/0	0/0			0/0/0	-Aeroplanes and other aircraft, of an unladen weight exceeding 2000kg,but not exceeding 15000kg
													-Aeroplanes and other aircraft, of an unladen weight exceeding 15000kg:
0/0/0	0	0	0/0	0/0/0	0/0	0//0	0/0/	0/0/0	0/0			0/0/0	---Of an unladen weight exceeding 15000kg,but not exceeding 45000kg
0/0/0	0	0	0/0	0/0/0	0/0	0//0	0/0/	0/0/0	0/0			0/0/0	---Of an unladen weight exceeding 45000kg
													-Spacecraft (including satellites) and suborbital and spacecraft launch vehicles
0/0/0	0	0	0/0	0/0/0	0/0	0//0	0/0/	0/0/0	0/0			0/0/0	Communication satellite
0/0/0	0	0	0/0	0/0/0	0/0	0//0	0/0/	0/0/0	0/0			0/0/0	Spacecraft(including satellites) and suborbital and spacecraft launch vehicles
													Parachutes (including dirigible parachutes and paragliders) and rotochutes; parts thereof and accessories thereto:
0/0/0	0	0	0/0	0/0/0	0/0	0//0	0/0/	0/0/0	0/0			0/0/0	Parachutes (including dirigible parachutes and paragliders) and rotochutes; parts thereof and accessories thereto
													Aircraft launching gear; deck-arrestor or similar gear; ground flying trainers; parts of the foregoing articles:
0/0/0	0	0	0/0	0/0/0	0/0	0//0	0/0/	0/0/0	0/0			0/0/0	-Aircraft launching gear and parts thereof; deck-arrestor or similar gear and parts thereof
													-Ground flying trainers and parts thereof:
0/0/0	0	0	0/0	0/0/0	0/0	0//0	0/0/	0/0/0	0/0			0/0/0	--Air combat simulators and parts thereof
0/0/0	0	0	0/0	0/0/0	0/0	0//0	0/0/	0/0/0	0/0			0/0/0	--Other
													Unmanned aircraft
0/0/0	0	0.1	0/0	0/0/0	0/0	0//0	0/0/	0/0/0	0/0			0/0/0	-- Designed for the carriage of passengers
													- Other, for remote—controlled flight only :
													--With maximum take—off weight not more than 250 g
													---camera drones
0/0/0	4	6	0/0	0/0/0	0/3.2	0/0/0	0/0/	0/0/0	0/0			0/0/0	Aerial photographing UAV with maximum takeoff weight $\leqslant$ 25g only using remote control flight (TV camera or digital camera (P) for special purposes)
0/0/0	4	6	0/0	0/0/0	0/3.2	0/0/0	0/0/	0/0/0	0/0			0/0/0	Other aerial photographing UAVs with maximum takeoff weight $\leqslant$ 25g only using remote control flight
0/0/0	0	0.5	0/0	0/0/0	0/0	0//0	0/0/	0/0/0	0/0			0/0/0	---Other

税则号列	货品名称〔CIQ 扩展编码及品名—T2 表示见附表 2〕	最惠(%)	暂定税率	普通	增值/消费	出口退税	计量单位	监管条件/特殊证件	检验检疫	对美关税	亚太上/下
	--最大起飞重量超过 250 克,但不超过 7 千克:										
8806.2210	---航拍无人机										
8806.2210 10	仅使用遥控飞行的 250 克＜最大起飞重量≤7 千克的航拍无人机(用于特种用途的电视摄像或数字照相(P))〔999〕	0		99	13/	13	架/千克	/			
8806.2210 90	其他仅使用遥控飞行的 250 克＜最大起飞重量≤7 千克的航拍无人机〔999〕	0		99	13/	13	架/千克	/		5	
8806.2290	---其他										
8806.2290 10	仅使用遥控飞行的 250 克＜最大起飞重量≤7 千克的其他无人驾驶航空器(两用物项和技术出口管制的)〔101 直升机,102 飞机,103 航天器〕	3.5		11	13/	13	架/千克	3O/		8.5	
8806.2290 90	仅使用遥控飞行的 250 克＜最大起飞重量≤7 千克的其他无人驾驶航空器〔101 直升机,102 飞机,103 航天器〕	3.5		11	13/	13	架/千克	O/		8.5	
	--最大起飞重量超过 7 千克,但不超过 25 千克:										
8806.2310	---航拍无人机										
8806.2310 10	仅使用遥控飞行的 7 千克＜最大起飞重量≤25 千克的航拍无人机(用于特种用途的电视摄像或数字照相(P))〔999〕	0		99	13/	13	架/千克	/			
8806.2310 90	其他仅使用遥控飞行的 7 千克＜最大起飞重量≤25 千克的航拍无人机〔999〕	0		99	13/	13	架/千克	/		5	
8806.2390	---其他										
8806.2390 10	仅使用遥控飞行的 7 千克＜最大起飞重量≤25 千克的其他无人驾驶航空器(两用物项和技术出口管制的)〔101 直升机,102 飞机,103 航天器〕	3.5		11	13/	13	架/千克	3O/		8.5	
8806.2390 90	仅使用遥控飞行的 7 千克＜最大起飞重量≤25 千克的其他无人驾驶航空器〔101 直升机,102 飞机,103 航天器〕	3.5		11	13/	13	架/千克	O/		8.5	
	--最大起飞重量超过 25 千克,但不超过 150 千克:										
8806.2410	---航拍无人机										
8806.2410 10	仅使用遥控飞行的 25 千克＜最大起飞重量≤150 千克的航拍无人机(用于特种用途的电视摄像或数字照相(P))〔999〕	0		99	13/	13	架/千克	/			
8806.2410 90	其他仅使用遥控飞行的 25 千克＜最大起飞重量≤150 千克的航拍无人机〔999〕	0		99	13/	13	架/千克	/		5	
8806.2490	---其他										
8806.2490 10	仅使用遥控飞行的 25 千克＜最大起飞重量≤150 千克的其他无人驾驶航空器(两用物项和技术出口管制的)〔101 直升机,102 飞机,103 航天器〕	3.5		11	13/	13	架/千克	3O/		8.5	
8806.2490 90	仅使用遥控飞行的 25 千克＜最大起飞重量≤150 千克的其他无人驾驶航空器〔101 直升机,102 飞机,103 航天器〕	3.5		11	13/	13	架/千克	O/		8.5	
	--其他:										
8806.2910	---航拍无人机										
8806.2910 10	仅使用遥控飞行的最大起飞重量＞150 千克的航拍无人机(用于特种用途的电视摄像或数字照相(P))〔999〕	0		99	13/	13	架/千克	/			
8806.2910 90	其他仅使用遥控飞行的最大起飞重量＞150 千克的航拍无人机〔999〕	0		99	13/	13	架/千克	/		5	
8806.2990	---其他										
8806.2990 10	仅使用遥控飞行的最大起飞重量＞150 千克的其他无人驾驶航空器(两用物项和技术出口管制的)〔101 直升机,102 飞机,103 航天器〕	3.5		11	13/	13	架/千克	3O/			
8806.2990 90	仅使用遥控飞行的最大起飞重量＞150 千克的其他无人驾驶航空器〔101 直升机,102 飞机,103 航天器〕	3.5		11	13/	13	架/千克	O/			
	-其他:										
	--最大起飞重量不超过 250 克:										
8806.9110	---航拍无人机										
8806.9110 10	其他最大起飞重量≤250 克的航拍无人机(用于特种用途的电视摄像或数字照相(P))〔999〕	0		99	13/	13	架/千克	/			
8806.9110 90	其他其他最大起飞重量≤250 克的航拍无人机〔999〕	0		99	13/	13	架/千克	/		5	
8806.9190	---其他〔101 直升机,102 飞机,103 航天器〕	3.5		11	13/	13	架/千克	O/		8.5	
	--最大起飞重量超过 250 克,但不超过 7 千克:										
8806.9210	---航拍无人机										
8806.9210 10	其他 250 克＜最大起飞重量≤7 千克的航拍无人机(用于特种用途的电视摄像或数字照相(P))〔999〕	0		99	13/	13	架/千克	/			
8806.9210 90	其他其他 250 克＜最大起飞重量≤7 千克的航拍无人机〔999〕	0		99	13/	13	架/千克	/		5	

协定税率 %								RCEP		特惠税率 %			Article Description
东/冰/格	巴基斯坦	韩国	瑞士上/下	哥/秘/柬	澳/毛	新西/坡/智	中国港/澳/台	东盟及马来/澳/韩	日/新	亚太2国	老/柬/缅	98/97/95	
													-- With maximum take—off weight more than 250 g but not more than 7 kg ---camera drones
0/0/0	4	6	0/0	0/0/0	0/3.2	0/0/0	0/0/	0/0/0	0/0			0/0/0	Only aerial UAVs with 25 g < maximum takeoff weight ≤ 7 kg flying by remote control (TV camera or digital camera for special purposes (P))
0/0/0	4	6	0/0	0/0/0	0/3.2	0/0/0	0/0/	0/0/0	0/0			0/0/0	Other aerial photographing UAVs with only remote control flight of 25g < maximum takeoff weight ≤ 7kg ---Other
0/0/0	0	0.5	0/0	0/0/0	0/0	0//0	0/0/	0/0/0	0/0			0/0/0	Other unmanned aerial vehicles (dual—use items and technologies subject to export control) using only remote control flight with a maximum take—off weight of 25 g < 7 kg
0/0/0	0	0.5	0/0	0/0/0	0/0	0//0	0/0/	0/0/0	0/0			0/0/0	Only other unmanned aerial vehicles with remote control flight of 25g < maximum takeoff weight ≤ 7kg --With maximum take—off weight more than 7 kg but not more than 25 kg ---camera drones
0/0/0	4	6	0/0	0/0/0	0/3.2	0/0/0	0/0/	0/0/0	0/0			0/0/0	Only aerial UAVs with 7 kg < maximum takeoff weight ≤ 25 kg flying by remote control (TV camera or digital camera for special purposes (P))
0/0/0	4	6	0/0	0/0/0	0/3.2	0/0/0	0/0/	0/0/0	0/0			0/0/0	Other aerial photographing UAVs with only remote control flight of 7 kg < maximum takeoff weight ≤ 25 kg --- Other
0/0/0	0	0.5	0/0	0/0/0	0/0	0//0	0/0/	0/0/0	0/0			0/0/0	Only other unmanned aerial vehicles (dual—use items and technologies subject to export control) with remote control flying of 7 kg < maximum takeoff weight ≤ 25 kg
0/0/0	0	0.5	0/0	0/0/0	0/0	0//0	0/0/	0/0/0	0/0			0/0/0	Only other unmanned aerial vehicles with remote control flight of 7 kg < maximum takeoff weight ≤ 25 kg --With maximum take—off weight more than 25 kg but not more than 150 kg ---camera drones
0/0/0	4	6	0/0	0/0/0	0/3.2	0/0/0	0/0/	0/0/0	0/0			0/0/0	Only aerial UAVs with 25 kg < maximum takeoff weight ≤ 15 kg flying by remote control (TV camera or digital camera for special purposes (P))
0/0/0	4	6	0/0	0/0/0	0/3.2	0/0/0	0/0/	0/0/0	0/0			0/0/0	Other aerial photographing UAVs that only use remote control flight, 25 kg < maximum takeoff weight ≤ 15 kg --- Other
0/0/0	0	0.5	0/0	0/0/0	0/0	0//0	0/0/	0/0/0	0/0			0/0/0	Only other unmanned aerial vehicles (dual—use items and technologies subject to export control) with 25 kg < maximum takeoff weight ≤ 15 kg in remote control flight
0/0/0	0	0.5	0/0	0/0/0	0/0	0//0	0/0/	0/0/0	0/0			0/0/0	Only other unmanned aerial vehicles with 25 kg < maximum takeoff weight ≤ 15 kg in remote control flight are used -- Other ---camera drones
0/0/0	4	6	0/0	0/0/0	0/3.2	0/0/0	0/0/	0/0/0	0/0			0/0/0	Aerial photographing UAV with a maximum takeoff weight of > 15 kg only using remote control flight (TV camera or digital camera (P) for special purposes)
0/0/0	4	6	0/0	0/0/0	0/3.2	0/0/0	0/0/	0/0/0	0/0			0/0/0	Other aerial photographing UAVs with a maximum takeoff weight of more than 15 kg only using remote control flight --- Other
0/0/0	0	0.1	0/0	0/0/0	0/0	0//0	0/0/	0/0/0	0/0			0/0/0	Other unmanned aerial vehicles (dual—use items and technologies subject to export control) using only remotely operated aircraft with a maximum takeoff weight > 15 kg
0/0/0	0	0.1	0/0	0/0/0	0/0	0//0	0/0/	0/0/0	0/0			0/0/0	Only other unmanned aerial vehicles with a maximum takeoff weight of more than 15 kg using remote control flight - Other --With maximum take—off weight not more than 250 g ---camera drones
0/0/0	4	6	0/0	0/0/0	0/3.2	0/0/0	0/0/	0/0/0	0/0			0/0/0	Other aerial photographing UAVs with maximum takeoff weight ≤ 25g (TV camera or digital camera (P) for special purposes)
0/0/0	4	6	0/0	0/0/0	0/3.2	0/0/0	0/0/	0/0/0	0/0			0/0/0	Other aerial UAVs with maximum takeoff weight ≤ 25g
0/0/0	0	0.5	0/0	0/0/0	0/0	0//0	0/0/	0/0/0	0/0			0/0/0	--- Other -- With maximum take—off weight more than 250 g but not more than 7 kg ---camera drones
0/0/0	4	6	0/0	0/0/0	0/3.2	0/0/0	0/0/	0/0/0	0/0			0/0/0	Other aerial UAVs with 25g < maximum takeoff weight ≤ 7kg (TV camera or digital camera for special purposes (P))
0/0/0	4	6	0/0	0/0/0	0/3.2	0/0/0	0/0/	0/0/0	0/0			0/0/0	Other aerial UAVs with 25g < maximum takeoff weight ≤ 7kg

税则号列	货品名称〔CIQ 扩展编码及品名—T2 表示见附表 2〕	最惠(%)	暂定税率	普通	增值/消费	出口退税	计量单位	监管条件/特殊证件	检验检疫	对美关税	亚太上/下
8806.9290	---其他										
8806.9290 10	250 克<最大起飞重量≤7 千克的其他无人驾驶航空器(两用物项和技术出口管制的)〔101 直升机,102 飞机,103 航天器〕	3.5		11	13/	13	架/千克	3O/		8.5	
8806.9290 90	250 克<最大起飞重量≤7 千克的其他无人驾驶航空器〔101 直升机,102 飞机,103 航天器〕	3.5		11	13/	13	架/千克	O/		8.5	
	--最大起飞重量超过 7 千克,但不超过 25 千克:										
8806.9310	---航拍无人机										
8806.9310 10	其他 7 千克<最大起飞重量≤25 千克的航拍无人机(用于特种用途的电视摄像或数字照相(P))〔999〕	0		99	13/	13	架/千克	/			
8806.9310 90	其他 7 千克<最大起飞重量≤25 千克的航拍无人机〔999〕	0		99	13/	13	架/千克	/		5	
8806.9390	---其他										
8806.9390 10	7 千克<最大起飞重量≤25 千克的其他无人驾驶航空器(两用物项和技术出口管制的)〔101 直升机,102 飞机,103 航天器〕	3.5		11	13/	13	架/千克	3O/		8.5	
8806.9390 90	7 千克<最大起飞重量≤25 千克的其他无人驾驶航空器〔101 直升机,102 飞机,103 航天器〕	3.5		11	13/	13	架/千克	O/		8.5	
	--最大起飞重量超过 25 千克,但不超过 150 千克:										
8806.9410	---航拍无人机										
8806.9410 10	其他 25 千克<最大起飞重量≤150 千克的航拍无人机(用于特种用途的电视摄像或数字照相(P))〔999〕	0		99	13/	13	架/千克	/			
8806.9410 90	其他 25 千克<最大起飞重量≤150 千克的航拍无人机〔999〕	0		99	13/	13	架/千克	/		5	
8806.9490	---其他										
8806.9490 10	25 千克<最大起飞重量≤150 千克的其他无人驾驶航空器(两用物项和技术出口管制的)〔101 直升机,102 飞机,103 航天器〕	3.5		11	13/	13	架/千克	3O/		8.5	
8806.9490 90	25 千克<最大起飞重量≤150 千克的其他无人驾驶航空器〔101 直升机,102 飞机,103 航天器〕	3.5		11	13/	13	架/千克	O/		8.5	
8806.9900	--其他										
8806.9900 10	最大起飞重量>150 千克的其他无人驾驶航空器(两用物项和技术出口管制的)〔101 直升机,102 飞机,103 航天器〕	3		11	13/	13	架/千克	3O/			
8806.9900 90	最大起飞重量>150 千克的其他无人驾驶航空器〔101 直升机,102 飞机,103 航天器〕	3		11	13/	13	架/千克	O/			
88.07	**税目 88.01、88.02 或 88.06 所列货品的零件:**										
8807.1000	-推进器、水平旋翼及其零件(8803.1000)〔999〕	1		11	13/	13	千克	/			
8807.2000	-起落架及其零件(8803.2000)〔999〕	1		11	13/	13	千克	/			
8807.3000	-飞机、直升机及无人驾驶航空器的其他零件(8803.3000)〔999〕	1		11	13/	13	千克	/			
8807.9000	-其他(8803.9000)										
8807.9000 10	两用物项管制的火箭及其零部件〔999〕	0		11	13/	13	千克	3/		5	
8807.9000 90	其他未列名的航空器、航天器零件(指税目 88.01 或 88.02 所列货品用的)〔999〕	0		11	13/	13	千克	/		5	

协定税率 %								RCEP		特惠税率 %			Article Description
东/冰/格	巴基斯坦	韩国	瑞士上/下	哥/秘/柬	澳/毛	新西/坡/智	中国港/澳/台	东盟及马来/澳/韩	日/新	亚太2国	老/柬/缅	98/97/95	
													--- Other
0/0/0	0	0.5	0/0	0/0/0	0/0	0//0	0/0/	0/0/0	0/0			0/0/0	Other unmanned aerial vehicles with 25g < maximum take-off weight ⩽ 7kg (dual—use items and technologies subject to export control)
0/0/0	0	0.5	0/0	0/0/0	0/0	0//0	0/0/	0/0/0	0/0			0/0/0	Other unmanned aerial vehicles with 25g < maximum take-off weight ⩽ 7kg
													--With maximum take—off weight more than 7 kg but not more than 25 kg
													---camera drones
0/0/0	4	6	0/0	0/0/0	0/3.2	0/0/0	0/0/	0/0/0	0/0			0/0/0	Other aerial UAVs with 7kg < maximum takeoff weight ⩽ 25kg (TV camera or digital camera for special purposes (P))
0/0/0	4	6	0/0	0/0/0	0/3.2	0/0/0	0/0/	0/0/0	0/0			0/0/0	Other aerial UAVs with 7kg < maximum takeoff weight ⩽ 25kg
													--- Other
0/0/0	0	0.5	0/0	0/0/0	0/0	0//0	0/0/	0/0/0	0/0			0/0/0	Other unmanned aerial vehicles with 7kg < maximum take-off weight ⩽ 25kg (dual—use items and technologies subject to export control)
0/0/0	0	0.5	0/0	0/0/0	0/0	0//0	0/0/	0/0/0	0/0			0/0/0	Other unmanned aerial vehicles with 7kg < maximum take-off weight ⩽ 25kg
													--With maximum take—off weight more than 25 kg but not more than 150 kg
													---camera drones
0/0/0	4	6	0/0	0/0/0	0/3.2	0/0/0	0/0/	0/0/0	0/0			0/0/0	Other aerial photographing UAVs with 25 kg < maximum takeoff weight ⩽ 15 kg (TV camera or digital camera for special purposes (P))
0/0/0	4	6	0/0	0/0/0	0/3.2	0/0/0	0/0/	0/0/0	0/0			0/0/0	Other aerial UAVs with 25 kg < maximum takeoff weight ⩽ 15 kg
													--- Other
0/0/0	0	0.5	0/0	0/0/0	0/0	0//0	0/0/	0/0/0	0/0			0/0/0	25 kg < maximum takeoff weight ⩽ 15 kg other unmanned aerial vehicles (dual—use items and technologies subject to export control)
0/0/0	0	0.5	0/0	0/0/0	0/0	0//0	0/0/	0/0/0	0/0			0/0/0	Other unmanned aerial vehicles with 25 kg < maximum takeoff weight ⩽ 15 kg
													-- Other
0/0/0	0	0.1	0/0	0/0/0	0/0	0//0	0/0/	0/0/0	0/0			0/0/0	Other unmanned aerial vehicles with a maximum takeoff weight > 15 kg (dual—use items and technologies subject to export control)
0/0/0	0	0.1	0/0	0/0/0	0/0	0//0	0/0/	0/0/0	0/0			0/0/0	Other unmanned aerial vehicles with maximum takeoff weight > 15 kg
													Parts of goods of heading 88.01, 88.02 or 88.06.
0/0/0	0	0	0/0	0/0/0	0/0	0//0	0/0/	0/0/0	0/0			0/0/0	- Propellers and rotors and parts thereof
0/0/0	0	0	0/0	0/0/0	0/0	0//0	0/0/	0/0/0	0/0			0/0/0	- Under—carriages and parts thereof
0/0/0	0	0	0/0	0/0/0	0/0	0//0	0/0/	0/0.9/0	0/0.9			0/0/0	- Other parts of airplanes, helicopters or unmanned aircraft
													- Other
0/0/0	0	0	0/0	0/0/0	0/0	0//0	0/0/	0/0/0	0/0			0/0/0	Rockets and their components for dual—use item control
0/0/0	0	0	0/0	0/0/0	0/0	0//0	0/0/	0/0/0	0/0			0/0/0	Other unlisted aircraft and spacecraft parts (for the goods listed in tariff item 88.1 or 88.2)

第八十九章
船舶及浮动结构体

注释：

已装配、未装配或已拆卸的船体、未完工或不完整的船舶以及未装配或已拆卸的完整船舶，如果不具有某种船舶的基本特征，应归入税目89.06。

税则号列	货品名称〔CIQ扩展编码及品名－T2表示见附表2〕	最惠(%)	暂定税率	普通	增值/消费	出口退税	计量单位	监管条件/特殊证件	检验检疫	对美关税	亚太上/下
89.01	**巡航船、游览船、渡船、货船、驳船及类似的客运或货运船舶：**										
	-巡航船、游览船及主要用于客运的类似船舶；各式渡船：										
8901.1010	---机动船舶										
8901.1010　10	高速客船(包括主要用于客运的类似船舶)〔999〕	5		14	13/	13	艘/千克	O/			
8901.1010　90	其他机动巡航船游览船及各式渡船(包括主要用于客运的类似船舶)〔999〕	5		14	13/	13	艘/千克	O/			
8901.1090	---非机动船舶〔999〕	8		30	13/	13	艘/千克	/			
	-液货船：										
	---成品油船：										
8901.2011	----载重量不超过10万吨〔999〕	9		14	13/	13	艘/千克	O/			
8901.2012	----载重量超过10万吨，但不超过30万吨〔999〕	9		14	13/	13	艘/千克	/			
8901.2013	----载重量超过30万吨〔999〕	6		14	13/	13	艘/千克	/			
	---原油船：										
8901.2021	----载重量不超过15万吨〔999〕	9		14	13/	13	艘/千克	O/			
8901.2022	----载重量超过15万吨，但不超过30万吨〔999〕	9		14	13/	13	艘/千克	/			
8901.2023	----载重量超过30万吨〔999〕	6		14	13/	13	艘/千克	/			
	---液化石油气船：										
8901.2031	----容积在20000立方米及以下〔999〕	9		14	13/	13	艘/千克	O/			
8901.2032	----容积在20000立方米以上〔999〕	6		14	13/	13	艘/千克	/			
	---液化天然气船：										
8901.2041	----容积在20000立方米及以下〔999〕	9		14	13/	13	艘/千克	/			
8901.2042	----容积在20000立方米以上〔999〕	6		14	13/	13	艘/千克	/			
8901.2090	---其他〔999〕	9		14	13/	13	艘/千克	O/			
8901.3000	-冷藏船，但子目8901.20的船舶除外〔999〕	9		14	13/	13	艘/千克	/			
	-其他货运船舶及其他客货兼运船舶：										
	---机动集装箱船：										
8901.9021	----可载标准集装箱在6000箱及以下〔999〕	9		14	13/	13	艘/千克	O/			
8901.9022	----可载标准集装箱在6000箱以上〔999〕	6		14	13/	13	艘/千克	/			
	---机动滚装船：										
8901.9031	----载重量在2万吨及以下〔999〕	9		14	13/	13	艘/千克	O/			
8901.9032	----载重量在2万吨以上的〔999〕	6		14	13/	13	艘/千克	/			
	---机动散货船：										
8901.9041	----载重量不超过15万吨〔999〕	9		14	13/	13	艘/千克	3O		/	
8901.9041　10	特殊民用物项管制的自航自卸式泥驳(具体商品描述详见相关公告)〔999〕	9		14	13/	13	艘/千克	3O/			
8901.9041　90	其他载重量不超过15万吨散货船〔999〕	9		14	13/	13	艘/千克	O/			
8901.9042	----载重量超过15万吨，但不超过30万吨〔999〕	9		14	13/	13	艘/千克	/			
8901.9043	----载重量超过30万吨〔999〕	9		14	13/	13	艘/千克	/			
8901.9050	---机动多用途船〔999〕	9		14	13/	13	艘/千克	/			
8901.9080	---其他机动船舶〔999〕	9		14	13/	13	艘/千克	O/			
8901.9090	---其他非机动船舶〔999〕	8		30	13/	13	艘/千克	O/			
89.02	**捕鱼船；加工船及其他加工保藏鱼类产品的船舶：**										
8902.0010	---机动船舶〔999〕	7		14	13/	13	艘/千克	O/			
8902.0090	---非机动船舶〔999〕	8		30	13/	9,13	艘/千克	/			
89.03	**娱乐或运动用快艇及其他船舶；划艇及轻舟：**										
	-充气船(包括刚性外壳的)：										
8903.1100	--装有或设计装有发动机，空载(净)重量(不包括发动机)不超过100千克〔999〕	10		30	13/	13	艘/千克	/		15	
8903.1200	--未设计装有发动机且空载(净)重量不超过100千克〔999〕	10		30	13/	13	艘/千克	/		15	
8903.1900	--其他〔999〕	10		30	13/	13	艘/千克	/		15	
	-帆船，充气船除外，不论是否装有辅助发动机：										
8903.2100	--长度不超过7.5米〔101客运船舶，102货运船舶，103客、货两用船舶〕	8		30	13/	13	艘/千克	/		33	
8903.2200	--长度超过7.5米但不超过24米										

Chapter 89
Ships, boats and floating structures

Note:

A hull, an unfinished or incomplete vessel, assembled, unassembled or disassembled, or a complete vessel unassembled or disassembled, is to be classified in heading No. 89. 06 if it does not have the essential character of a vessel of a particular kind.

协定税率 %								RCEP		特惠税率 %			Article Description
东/冰/格	巴基斯坦	韩国	瑞士上/下	哥/秘/柬	澳/毛	新西/坡/智	中国港/澳/台	东盟及马来/澳/韩	日/新	亚太2国	老/柬/缅	98/97/95	
													Cruise ships, excursion boats, ferry-boats, cargo ships, barges and similar vessels for the transport of persons or goods:
													-Cruise ships, excursion boats and similar vessels principally designed for the transport of persons; ferry-boats of all kinds:
													---Motor vessels
0/0/0	0	2.3	0/0	0/0/0	0/0	0/0/0	0/0/	4.5/4.5/4.5	4.7/4.5			0/0/0	High-speed passenger vessels (similar vessels principally designed for the transport of persons)
0/0/0	0	2.3	0/0	0/0/0	0/0	0/0/0	0/0/	4.5/4.5/4.5	4.7/4.5			0/0/0	Other cruise ships, excursion boats ferry-boats of all kinds (similar vessels principally designed for the transport of persons)
0/0/0	2	3.7	0/0	0/0/0	0/0	0//0	0/0/	7.2/7.2/7.2	7.3/7.2			0/0/0	---Other
													-Tankers:
													---Finished oil tankers:
5/0/0		4.2	0/0	0/0/0	0/0	0//0	0/0/	5/5/	/5			0/0/0	----Loading not exceeding 100000t
5/0/0		4.2	0/0	0/0/0	0/0	0//0	0/0/	5/5/	/5			0/0/0	----Loading exceeding 100000t, but not exceeding 300000t
5/0/0		2.8	0/0	0/0/0	0/0	0//0	0/0/	5/5/	/5			0/0/0	----Loading exceeding 300000t
													---Crude oil tankers:
5/0/0		4.2	0/0	0/0/0	0/0	0//0	0/0/	5/5/	/5			0/0/0	----Loading not exceeding 150000t
5/0/0		4.2	0/0	0/0/0	0/0	0//0	0/0/	5/5/	/5			0/0/0	----Loading exceeding 150000t, but not exceeding 300000t
5/0/0		2.8	0/0	0/0/0	0/0	0//0	0/0/	5/5/	/5			0/0/0	----Loading exceeding 300000t
													---Liquified petroleum gas carriers:
5/0/0		4.2	0/0	0/0/0	0/0	0//0	0/0/	5/5/	/5			0/0/0	----Volume with $20000m^3$ or less
5/0/0		2.8	0/0	0/0/0	0/0	0//0	0/0/	5/5/	/5			0/0/0	----Volume more than $20000m^3$
													---Liquified natural gas carriers:
5/0/0		4.2	0/0	0/0/0	0/0	0//0	0/0/	5/5/	/5			0/0/0	----Volume with $20000m^3$ or less
5/0/0		2.8	0/0	0/0/0	0/0	0//0	0/0/	5/5/	/5			0/0/0	----Volume more than $20000m^3$
5/0/0		4.2	0/0	0/0/0	0/0	0//0	0/0/	5/5/	/5			0/0/0	---Other
0/0/0	2	4.2	0/0	0/0/0	0/0	0/0/0	0/0/	8.1/8.1/8.1	8.4/8.1			0/0/0	-Refrigerated vessels, other than those of subheading No. 8901. 20
													-Other vessels for the transport of goods and other vessels for the transport of both persons and goods:
													---Motor container vessels:
5/0/0		4.2	0/0	0/0/0	0/0	0//0	0/0/	5/5/	/5			0/0/0	----Capable loading standard containers with 6000 or less
5/0/0		2.8	0/0	0/0/0	0/0	0//0	0/0/	5/5/	/5			0/0/0	----Capable loading standard containers more than 6000
													---Motor Ro-Ro carriers:
5/0/0		4.2	0/0	0/0/0	0/0	0//0	0/0/	5/5/	/5			0/0/0	----Loading with 20000t or less
5/0/0		2.8	0/0	0/0/0	0/0	0//0	0/0/	5/5/	/5			0/0/0	----Loading more than 20000t
													---Motor bulk carriers:
5/0/0		6	0	0	0	0	0//0	0/0/				0/0/	----Loading not exceeding 150000t
5/0/0		4.2	0/0	0/0/0	0/0	0//0	0/0/	5/5/	/5		//	0/0/0	Self propelled dump barge for special civil items control (see relevant announcement for specific commodity description)
5/0/0		4.2	0/0	0/0/0	0/0	0//0	0/0/	5/5/	/5		//	0/0/0	Other bulk carriers with a capacity of no more than 150000 tons
5/0/0		4.2	0/0	0/0/0	0/0	0//0	0/0/	5/5/	/5			0/0/0	----Loading exceeding 150000t, not exceeding 300000t
5/0/0		4.2	0/0	0/0/0	0/0	0//0	0/0/	5/5/	/5			0/0/0	----Loading exceeding 300000t
5/0/0		4.2	0/0	0/0/0	0/0	0//0	0/0/	5/5/	/5			0/0/0	---Multi-purposes motor vessels
0/0/0	2	4.2	0/0	0/0/0	0/0	0/0/0	0/0/	8.1/8.1/8.1	8.2/8.1			0/0/0	---Other motor vessels
0/0/0	2	3.7	0/0	0/0/0	0/0	0/0/0	0/0/	7.2/7.2/7.2	7.3/7.2			0/0/0	---Other non-motor vessels
													Fishing vessels; factory ships and other vessels for processing or preserving fishery products:
0/0/0	2	3.2	0/0	0/0/0	0/0	0/0/0	0/0/	6.3/6.3/6.3	6.6/6.3			0/0/0	---Motor vessels
0/0/0	2	3.7	0/0	0/0/0	0/0	0//0	0/0/	7.2/7.2/7.2	7.5/7.2			0/0/0	---Other
													Yachts and other vessels for pleasure or sports; rowing boats and canoes:
													- Inflatable (including rigid hull inflatable) boats:
0/0/0	2	4.6	0/0	0/0/0	0/0	0//0	0/0/	9/9/9	9.4/9			0/0/0	-- Fitted or designed to be fitted with a motor, unladen (net) weight (excluding the motor) not exceeding 100 kg
0/0/0	2	4.6	0/0	0/0/0	0/0	0//0	0/0/	9/9/9	9.4/9			0/0/0	-- Not designed for use with a motor and unladen (net) weight not exceeding 100 kg
0/0/0	2	4.6	0/0	0/0/0	0/0	0//0	0/0/	9/9/9	9.4/9			0/0/0	--Other
													- Sailboats, other than inflatable, with or without auxiliary motor:
0/0/0	2	3.7	0/0	0/0/0	0/0	0//0	0/0/	7.5/7.6/8	7.5/7.6			0/0/0	-- Of a length not exceeding 7.5 m
													-- Of a length exceeding 7.5 m but not exceeding 24 m

税则号列	货品名称〔CIQ 扩展编码及品名—T2 表示见附表 2〕	最惠(%)	暂定税率	普通	增值/消费	出口退税	计量单位	监管条件/特殊证件	检验检疫	对美关税	亚太上/下
8903.2200 10	长度超过 8 米,但不超过 24 米的机动帆船(娱乐或运动用,充气船除外)〔101 客运船舶,102 货运船舶,103 客、货两用船舶〕	8		30	13/10	13	艘/千克	/		33	
8903.2200 90	其他帆船,长度超过 7.5 米,但不超过 24 米(娱乐或运动用,充气船除外,不论是否装有辅助发动机)〔101 客运船舶,102 货运船舶,103 客、货两用船舶〕	8		30	13/	13	艘/千克	/		33	
8903.2300	--长度超过 24 米										
8903.2300 10	长度超过 24 米,但小于 90 米的机动帆船(娱乐或运动用,充气船除外,不论是否装有辅助发动机)〔101 客运船舶,102 货运船舶,103 客、货两用船舶〕	8		30	13/10	13	艘/千克	/		33	
8903.2300 90	长度超过 24 米的其他帆船(娱乐或运动用,充气船除外,不论是否装有辅助发动机)〔101 客运船舶,102 货运船舶,103 客、货两用船舶〕	8		30	13/	13	艘/千克	/		33	
	-汽艇,非充气的,但装有舷外发动机的除外:										
8903.3100	--长度不超过 7.5 米〔101 客运船舶,102 货运船舶,103 客、货两用船舶〕	10		30	13/	13	艘/千克	/		20	
8903.3200	--长度超过 7.5 米但不超过 24 米										
8903.3200 10	长度超过 8 米,但不超过 24 米的汽艇(娱乐或运动用,非充气的,但装有舷外发动机的除外)〔101 客运船舶,102 货运船舶,103 客、货两用船舶〕	10		30	13/10	13	艘/千克	/		20	
8903.3200 90	其他汽艇,长度超过 7.5 米,但不超过 8 米(娱乐或运动用,非充气的,但装有舷外发动机的除外)〔101 客运船舶,102 货运船舶,103 客、货两用船舶〕	10		30	13/	13	艘/千克	/		20	
8903.3300	--长度超过 24 米										
8903.3300 10	长度超过 24 米,但小于 90 米的汽艇(娱乐或运动用,非充气的,但装有舷外发动机的除外)〔101 客运船舶,102 货运船舶,103 客、货两用船舶〕	10		30	13/10	13	艘/千克	/		20	
8903.3300 90	长度大于等于 90 米的其他汽艇(娱乐或运动用,非充气的,但装有舷外发动机的除外)〔101 客运船舶,102 货运船舶,103 客、货两用船舶〕	10		30	13/	13	艘/千克	/		20	
	-其他:										
8903.9300	--长度不超过 7.5 米〔999〕	10		30	13/	13	艘/千克	/		35	
8903.9900	--其他										
8903.9900 10	8 米<长度<90 米的娱乐或运动用其他机动船舶或快艇〔101 客运船舶,102 其它船舶〕	10		30	13/10	13	艘/千克	/		35	
8903.9900 90	其他长度超过 7.5 米的娱乐或运动用船舶或快艇(包括划艇及轻舟)〔999〕	10		30	13/	13	艘/千克	/		35	
89.04	**拖轮及顶推船:**										
8904.0000	拖轮及顶推船〔999〕	9		14	13/	13	艘/千克	/			
89.05	**灯船、消防船、挖泥船、起重船及其他不以航行为主要功能的船舶;浮船坞;浮动或潜水式钻探或生产平台:**										
8905.1000	-挖泥船	3		11	13/	13	艘/千克	3		/	
8905.1000 10	耙吸式挖泥船、绞吸式挖泥船、斗式挖泥船、吸沙船〔999〕	3		11	13/	13	艘/千克	3/			
8905.1000 90	其他挖泥船〔999〕	3		11	13/	13	艘/千克	/			
8905.2000	-浮动或潜水式钻探或生产平台〔999〕	6		11	13/	13	座/千克	/		31	
	-其他:										
8905.9010	---浮船坞〔999〕	8		30	13/	13	个/千克	/			
8905.9090	---其他〔999〕	3		11	13/	13	个/千克	/		28	
89.06	**其他船舶,包括军舰及救生船,但划艇除外:**										
8906.1000	-军舰〔999〕	5		14	13/	13	艘/千克	/			
	-其他:										
8906.9010	---机动船舶〔999〕	5		14	13/	13	艘/千克	/		30	
8906.9020	---非机动船舶〔999〕	8		30	13/	0	艘/千克	/		33	
8906.9030	---未制成或不完整的船舶,包括船舶分段〔999〕	8		30	13/	0	艘/千克	/		33	
89.07	**其他浮动结构体(例如,筏、柜、潜水箱、浮码头、浮筒及航标):**										
8907.1000	-充气筏〔999〕	8		30	13/	13	艘/千克	/		18	
8907.9000	-其他〔999〕	8		30	13/	13	个/千克	/		28	
89.08	**供拆卸的船舶及其他浮动结构体:**										
8908.0000	供拆卸的船舶及其他浮动结构体〔999〕	3		11	13/	13	艘/千克	9AB/	PQ	28	

协定税率 %								RCEP		特惠税率 %			Article Description
东/冰/格	巴基斯坦	韩国	瑞士上/下	哥/秘/柬	澳/毛	新西/坡/智	中国港/澳/台	东盟及马来/澳/韩	日/新	亚太2国	老/柬/缅	98/97/95	
0/0/0	2	3.7	0/0	0/0/0	0/0	0//0	0/0/	7.5/7.6/8	7.5/7.6			0/0/0	Motor sailboats (other than inflatable boats) with a length of more than 8 meters but not more than 24 meters (for entertainment or sports)
0/0/0	2	3.7	0/0	0/0/0	0/0	0//0	0/0/	7.5/7.6/8	7.5/7.6			0/0/0	Other sailboats, exceeding 7.5 m but not exceeding 24 m in length (other than inflatable boats for entertainment or sports, whether or not equipped with auxiliary engines)
													-- Of a length exceeding 24 m
0/0/0	2	3.7	0/0	0/0/0	0/0	0//0	0/0/	7.5/7.6/8	7.5/7.6			0/0/0	Motor driven sailboats (other than inflatable boats for entertainment or sports, whether or not equipped with auxiliary engines) exceeding 24 meters but less than 9 meters in length
0/0/0	2	3.7	0/0	0/0/0	0/0	0//0	0/0/	7.5/7.6/8	7.5/7.6			0/0/0	Other sailboats (other than inflatable boats for recreational or sports purposes, whether or not equipped with auxiliary engines) exceeding 24 meters in length
													- Motorboats, other than inflatable, not including outboard motorboats :
0/0/0	3.5	4.9	1.1/1.1	0/0/0	0/0	0/0/0	0/0/	9.8/10/9.8	9.8/10			0/0/0	-- Of a length not exceeding 7.5 m
													-- Of a length exceeding 7.5 m but not exceeding 24 m
0/0/0	3.5	4.9	1.1/1.1	0/0/0	0/0	0/0/0	0/0/	9.8/10/9.8	9.8/10			0/0/0	Motor boats exceeding 8 m but not exceeding 24 m in length (for entertainment or sports, non inflatable, except those equipped with outboard engines)
0/0/0	3.5	4.9	1.1/1.1	0/0/0	0/0	0/0/0	0/0/	9.8/10/9.8	9.8/10			0/0/0	Other motor boats, exceeding 7.5 m but not exceeding 8 m in length (for entertainment or sports, non inflatable, except those equipped with outboard engines)
													-- Of a length exceeding 24 m
0/0/0	3.5	4.9	1.1/1.1	0/0/0	0/0	0/0/0	0/0/	9.8/10/9.8	9.8/10			0/0/0	Motor boats with a length of more than 24 meters but less than 9 meters (for entertainment or sports, non inflatable, except those equipped with outboard engines)
0/0/0	3.5	4.9	1.1/1.1	0/0/0	0/0	0/0/0	0/0/	9.8/10/9.8	9.8/10			0/0/0	Other motor boats (recreational or sports, non inflatable, except those equipped with outboard engines) with a length of 9 meters or more
													-Other
0/0/0	2		0/0	0/0/0	0/0	0//0	0/0/	5/5/	/5			0/0/0	-- Of a length not exceeding 7.5 m
													--Other
0/0/0	2		0/0	0/0/0	0/0	0//0	0/0/	5/5/	/5			0/0/0	Other motor ships or speedboats for entertainment or sports with a length of 8m < 90m
0/0/0	2		0/0	0/0/0	0/0	0//0	0/0/	5/5/	/5			0/0/0	Other recreational or sports ships or speedboats (including rowing boats and light boats) with a length of more than 7.5 meters
													Tugs and pusher craft:
0/0/0	2	4.2	0/0	0/0/0	0/0	0/0/0	0/0/	8.4/8.6/8.4	8.4/8.6			0/0/0	Tugs and pusher craft
													Light-vessels, fire-floats, dredgers, floating cranes, and other vessels the navigability of which is subsidiary to their main function; floating docks; floating or submersible drilling or roduction platforms:
0/0/0	0	2	0	0	0	0	0//0	0/0/				0/0/0	-Dredgers
0/0/0	0	1.4	0/0	0/0/0	0/0	0//0	0/0/	2.7/2.7/2.7	2.8/2.7		//	0/0/0	Drag suction dredger, cutter suction dredger, bucket dredger, sand suction dredger
0/0/0	0	1.4	0/0	0/0/0	0/0	0//0	0/0/	2.7/2.7/2.7	2.8/2.7		//	0/0/0	Other dredgers
0/0/0	0	2.8	0/0	0/0/0	0/0	0//0	0/0/	5.4/5.4/5.4	5.6/5.4			0/0/0	-Floating or submersible drilling or production platforms
													-Other:
5/0/0		3.7	0/0	0/0/0	0/0	0//0	0/0/	5/5/	/5			0/0/0	---Floating docks
0/0/0	0	1.4	0/0	0/0/0	0/0	0//0	0/0/	2.7/2.7/2.7	2.8/2.7			0/0/0	---Other
													Other vessels, including warships and lifeboats other than rowing boats:
0/0/0	0	2.3	0/0	0/0/0	0/0	0//0	0/0/	4.5/4.5/4.5	4.5/4.5			0/0/0	-Warships
													-Other:
0/0/0	0		0/0	0/0/0	0/0	0//0	0/0/	4.9/4.9/	/4.9			0/0/0	---Motor vessels
0/0/0	2	3.7	0/0	0/0/0	0/0	0//0	0/0/	7.2/7.2/7.2	7.5/7.2			0/0/0	---Not-motorized vessels
0/0/0	2	3.7	0/0	0/0/0	0/0	0//0	0/0/	7.5/7.6/7.5	7.5/7.6			0/0/0	---Unfinished or incomplete vessels, including subsections of vessels
													Other floating structures (for example, rafts, tanks, cofferdams, landing-stages, buoys and beacons):
0/0/0	2	3.7	0/0	0/0/0	0/0	0//0	0/0/	7.5/7.6/7.5	7.5/7.6			0/0/0	-Inflatable rafts
0/0/0	2	3.7	0/0	0/0/0	0/0	0//0	0/0/	7.5/7.6/7.5	7.5/7.6			0/0/0	-Other
													Vessels and other floating structures for breaking up:
0/0/0	0	1.4	0/0	0/0/0	0/0	0//0	0/0/	2.7/2.7/2.7	2.8/2.7			0/0/0	Vessels and other floating structures for breaking up

第十八类
光学、照相、电影、计量、检验、医疗或外科用仪器及设备、精密仪器及设备；钟表；乐器；上述物品的零件、附件

第九十章
光学、照相、电影、计量、检验、医疗或外科用仪器及设备、精密仪器及设备；上述物品的零件、附件

注释：

一、本章不包括：

(一)机器、设备或其他专门技术用途的硫化橡胶(硬质橡胶除外)制品（税目 40.16)、皮革或再生皮革制品(税目 42.05)或纺织材料制品(税目 59.11)；

(二)纺织材料制的承托带及其他承托物品，其承托器官的作用仅依靠自身的弹性(例如，孕妇用的承托带，用于胸部、腹部、关节或肌肉的承托绷带)(第十一类)；

(三)税目 69.03 的耐火材料制品；税目 69.09 的实验室、化学或其他专门技术用途的陶瓷器；

(四)税目 70.09 的未经光学加工的玻璃镜及税目 83.06 或第七十一章的非光学元件的贱金属或贵金属制的镜子；

(五)税目 70.07、70.08、70.11、70.14、70.15 或 70.17 的货品；

(六)第十五类注释二所规定的贱金属制通用零件（第十五类)或塑料制的类似品(第三十九章)；但专用于医疗、外科、牙科或兽医的植入物应归入税目 90.21

(七)税目 84.13 的装有计量装置的泵；计数和检验用的衡器或单独报验的天平砝码(税目 84.23)；升降、起重及搬运机械(税目 84.25 至 84.28)；纸张或纸板的各种切割机器（税目 84.41)；税目 84.66 的用于机床或水射流切割机上调整工件或工具的附件，包括具有读度用的光学装置的附件(例如，“光学”分度头)，但其本身主要是光学仪器的除外(例如，校直望远镜)；计算机器(税目 84.70)；税目 84.81 的阀门及其他装置；税目 84.86 的机器及装置(包括将电路图投影或绘制到感光半导体材料上的装置)；

(八)自行车或机动车辆用探照灯或聚光灯(税目 85.12)；税目 85.13 的手提式电灯；电影录音机、还音机及转录机(税目 85.19)；拾音头或录音头（税目 85.22)；电视摄像机、数字照相机视频摄录一体机(税目 85.25)；雷达设备、无线电导航设备或无线电遥控设备(税目 85.26)；光导纤维、光导纤维束或光缆用连接器(税目 85.36)；税目 85.37 的数控制装置；税目 85.39 的封闭式聚光灯；税目 85.44 的光缆；

(九)税目 94.05 的探照灯及聚光灯；

(十)第九十五章的物品；

(十一)税目 96.20 的独脚架、双脚架、三脚架及类似品；

(十二)容量的计量器具(按其构成的材料归类)；

(十三)卷轴、线轴及类似芯子(按其构成材料归类，例如，归入税目 39.23 或第十五类)。

二、除上述注释一另有规定的以外，本章各税目所列机器、设备、仪器或器具的零件、附件，应按下列规定归类：

(一)凡零件、附件本身已构成本章或第八十四章、第八十五章或第九十一章各税目(税目 84.87、85.48 或 90.33 除外)所包括的货品，应一律归入其相应的税目；

(二)其他零件、附件，如果专用于或主要用于某种或同一税目项下的多种机器、仪器或器具(包括税目 90.10、90.13 或 90.31 的机器、仪器或器具)，应归入相应机器、仪器或器具的税目；

(三)所有其他零件、附件均应归入税目 90.33。

三、第十六类注释三及四也适用于本章。

四、税目 90.05 不包括武器用望远镜瞄准具、潜艇或坦克上的潜望镜式望远镜及本章或第十六类的机器、设备、仪器或器具用的望远镜；这类望远镜瞄准具及望远镜应归入税目90.13。

五、计量或检验用的光学仪器、器具或机器，如果既可归入税目 90.13，又可归入税目 90.31，则应归入税目 90.31。

六、税目 90.21 所称“矫形器具”，是指下列用途的器具：

预防或矫正人体畸变；

生病、手术或受伤后人体部位的支撑或固定；

矫形器具包括用于矫正畸形的鞋及特种鞋垫，但需符合下列任一条件：

(一)定制的；

(二)成批生产的、单独报验，且不成双的、设计为左右两脚同样适用。

七、税目 90.32 仅适用于：

(一)液体或气体的流量、液位、压力或其他变化量的自动控制仪器及装置或温度自动控制装置，不论其是否依靠要被自动控制的因素所发生的不同的电现象来进行工作的，它们将被自控因素调到并保持在一设定值上，通过持续或定期测量实际值来保持稳定，修正偏差；

(二)电量自动调节器及自动控制非电量的仪器或装置，依靠要被控制的因素所发生的不同的电现象来进行工作，它们将被控制的因素调到并保持在一设定值上，通过持续或定期测量实际值来保持稳定，修正任何偏差。

SECTION XVIII

OPTICAL, PHOTOGRAPHIC, CINEMATOGRAPHIC, MEASURING, CHECKING, PRECISION, MEDICALOR SURGICAL INSTRUMENTS AND APPARATUS; CLOCKS AND WATCHES; MUSICAL INSTRUMENTS; PARTS AND ACCESSORIES THEREOF

Chapter 90

Optical, photographic, cinematographic, measuring, checking, precision, medical or surgical instruments and apparatus; parts and accessories thereof

Notes:

1. This Chapter does not cover:
   (a) Articles of a kind used in machines, appliances or for other technical uses, of vulcanized rubber other than hard rubber (heading No. 40.16), of leather or of composition leather (heading No. 42.05) or of textile material (heading No. 59.11);
   (b) Supporting belts or other support articles of textile material, whose intended effect on the organ to be supported or held derives solely from their elasticity (for example, maternity belts, thoracic support bandages, abdominal support bandages, supports for joints or muscles) (Section XI);
   (c) Refractory goods of heading No. 69.03; ceramic wares for laboratory, chemical or other technical uses, of heading No. 69.09;
   (d) Glass mirrors, not optically worked, of heading No. 70.09, or mirrors of base metal or of precious metal, not being optical elements (heading No. 83.06 or Chapter 71);
   (e) Goods of heading No. 70.07, 70.08, 70.11, 70.14, 70.15 or 70.17;
   (f) Parts of general use, as defined in Note 2 to Section XV, of base metal (Section XV) or similar goods of plastics (Chapter 39); however, articles specially designed for use exclusively in implants in medical, surgical, dental or veterinary sciences are to be classified in heading 90.21;".
   (g) Pumps incorporating measuring devices, of heading No. 84.13; weight-operated counting or checking machinery, or separately presented weights for balances (heading No. 84.23); lifting or handling machinery (headings No. 84.25 to 84.28); paper or paperboard cutting machines of all kinds (heading No. 84.41); fittings for adjusting work or tools on machine-tools or water iet iutting machine, of heading No. 84.66, including fittings with optical devices for reading the scale (for example, "optical" dividing heads) but not those which are in themselves essentially optical instruments (for example, alignment telescopes); calculating machines (heading No. 84.70); valves or other appliances of heading 84.81; machines and apparats (including opparatus for the projection or dralving of circuit pattern on sensitized semiconductor materials) of heading 84.86.
   (h) Searchlights or spotlights of a kind used for cycles or motor vehicles (heading No. 85.12); portable electric lamps of heading 85.13; cinematographic sound recording, reproducing or re-recording apparatus (heading No. 85.19); sound-heads (heading No. 85.22); television cameras digital cameras and video camera retorders(heading No. 85.25) radar apparatus, radio navigational aid apparatus or radio remote control apparatus(heading No. 85.26); conneltors for optical fibres optical fibre bundles or cables(heading 85.36); numerical control apparatus of heading No. 85.37; sealed beam lamp units of heading No. 85.39; optical fibre cables of heading No. 85.44;
   (ij) Searchlights or spotlights of heading No. 94.05;
   (k) Articles of Chapter 95;
   (l) unipod, bipod, tripod or the like of heading No.96.20;
   (m) Capacity measures, which are to be classified according to their constituent material;
   (n) Spools, reels or similar supports (which are to be classified according to their constituent material, for example, in heading No. 39.23 or Section XV).
2. Subject to Note 1 above, parts and accessories for machines, apparatus, instruments or articles of this Chapter are to be classified according to the following rules:
   (a) Parts and accessories which are goods included in any of the headings of this Chapter or of Chapter 84, 85 or 91 (other than heading No. 84.87, 87.48 or 90.33) are in all cases to be classified in their respective headings;
   (b) Other parts and accessories, if suitable for use solely or principally with a particular kind of machine, instrument or apparatus, or with a number of machines, instruments or apparatus of the same heading (including a machine, instrument or apparatus of heading No. 90.10, 90.13 or 90.31) are to be classified with the machines, instruments or apparatus of that kind;
   (c) All other parts and accessories are to be classified in heading No. 90.33.
3. The provisions of Notes 3 and 4 to Section III or XVI apply also to this Chapter.
4. Heading No. 90.05 does not apply to telescopic sights for fitting to arms, periscopic telescopes for fitting to submarines or tanks, or to telescopes for machines, appliances, instruments or apparatus of this Chapter of Section XVI; such telescopic sights and telescopes are to be classified in heading No. 90.13.
5. Measuring or checking optical instruments, appliances or machines which, but for this Note, could be classified both in heading No. 90.13 and in heading No. 90.31 are to be classified in heading No. 90.31.
6. For the purposes of heading No. 90.21, the expression "orthopaedic appliances" means appliances for:
   Preventing or correcting bodily deformities;
   Supporting or holding parts of the body following an illness, operation or injury.
   Orthopaedic appliances include footwear and special insoles designed to correct orthopaedic conditions, provided that they are either:
   (a) made to measure or
   (b) mass-produced, presented singly. and not in pairs and designed to fit either foot equally
7. Heading No. 90.32 applies only to:
   (a) Instruments and apparatus for automatically controlling the flow, level, pressure or other variables of liquids or gases, or for automatically controlling temperature, whether or not their operation depends on an electrical phenomenon which varies according to the factor to be automatically controlled; which are designed to bring this factor to, and maintain it at, a desired value, stabilised against disturbances, by constantly or periodically measuring its actual value;
   (b) Automatic regulators of electrical quantities, and instruments or apparatus for automatically controlling non-electrical quantities the operation of which depends on an electrical phenomenon varying according to the factor to be controlled, which are designed to bring this factor to, and maintain it at, a desired value, stabilised against disturbances, by constantly or periodically measuring its actual value.

税则号列	货品名称〔CIQ扩展编码及品名－T2表示见附表2〕	最惠(%)	暂定税率	普通	增值/消费	出口退税	计量单位	监管条件/特殊证件	检验检疫	对美关税	亚太上/下
90.01	**光导纤维及光导纤维束;光缆,但税目85.44的货品除外;偏振材料制的片及板;未装配的各种材料制透镜(包括隐形眼镜片)、棱镜、反射镜及其他光学元件,但未经光学加工的玻璃制上述元件除外:**										
9001.1000	-光导纤维、光导纤维束及光缆										
9001.1000 01	非色散位移单模光纤(G.652,包括G652A、G652B、G652C、G652D等)〔999〕	5		20	13/	13	千克	/		30	4.5/4.5
9001.1000 02	其他单模光纤〔999〕	5		20	13/	13	千克	/		30	4.5/4.5
9001.1000 90	光导纤维束、光缆及其他光导纤维(但品目8544的货品除外)〔999〕	5		20	13/	13	千克	/		30	4.5/4.5
9001.2000	-偏振材料制的片及板										
9001.2000 10	液晶投影仪用偏光板〔999〕	0		20	13/	13	千克	/		25	0/0
9001.2000 20	数字电影放映机用偏光板〔999〕	0		20	13/	13	千克	/		25	0/0
9001.2000 90	其他偏振材料制的片及板〔999〕	0		20	13/	13	千克	/		25	0/0
9001.3000	-隐形眼镜片〔999〕	7	6	70	13/	13	片/千克	/		26	
	-玻璃制眼镜片:										
9001.4010	---变色镜片〔999〕	7		90	13/	13	片/千克	/			
	---其他:										
9001.4091	----太阳镜片〔999〕	7		90	13/	13	片/千克	/			
9001.4099	----其他〔999〕	7		70	13/	13	片/千克	/		32	
	-其他材料制眼镜片:										
9001.5010	---变色镜片〔999〕	7		90	13/	13	片/千克	/		27	
	---其他:										
9001.5091	----太阳镜片〔999〕	7		90	13/	13	片/千克	/		32	
9001.5099	----其他〔999〕	7		70	13/	13	片/千克	/		32	
	-其他:										
9001.9010	---彩色滤光片〔999〕	2/1		20	13/	13	千克/片	/		22	1.3/0.7
9001.9090	---其他										
9001.9090 10	光通信用微光组件的光学元件(包括波长800-1700nm薄膜滤光片、自聚焦透镜、法拉第旋转片)〔999〕	2/1	①	20	13/	13	千克	/		21	1.3/0.7
9001.9090 20	微型镜片(激光视盘机激光收发装置用)〔999〕	2/1		20	13/	13	千克	/		22	1.3/0.7
9001.9090 30	非涅耳透镜投影屏(屏幕对角线≥80英寸,投射比≤0.26,增益比≥0.8,镜头间距≤100微米)〔999〕	2/1		20	13/	13	千克	/		22	1.3/0.7
9001.9090 40	液晶显示屏背光模组的光学元件(包括导光板、反射板、扩散片、增亮片)〔101计算机、辅助设备及其零件,102视听设备及其零件〕	2/1		20	13/	13	千克	/		22	1.3/0.7
9001.9090 50	液晶投影仪用偏光元件〔999〕	2/1		20	13/	13	千克	/		22	1.3/0.7
9001.9090 60	数字电影放映机用偏光元件〔999〕	2/1		20	13/	13	千克	/		22	1.3/0.7
9001.9090 90	税目90.01未列名的其他光学元件(未经光学加工的玻璃制元件除外)〔999〕	2/1		20	13/	13	千克	/		22	1.3/0.7
90.02	**已装配的各种材料制透镜、棱镜、反射镜及其他光学元件,作为仪器或装置的零件、配件,但未经光学加工的玻璃制上述元件除外:**										
	-物镜:										
	--照相机、投影仪、照片放大机及缩片机用:										
9002.1110	---税号9006.1010至9006.3000所列照相机用〔999〕	6		14	13/	13	千克/个	/			4.8/4.8
9002.1120	---缩微阅读机用〔999〕	6		14	13/	13	千克/个	/			3.9/3.9
	---其他照相机用:										
9002.1131	----单反相机镜头										
9002.1131 10	单反相机镜头(整机)〔999〕	6	3	80	13/	13	千克/个	/		28	
9002.1131 90	单反相机镜头的零件及附件〔999〕	6	3	80	13/	13	千克/个	/		28	
9002.1139	----其他〔999〕	6	3	80	13/	13	千克/个	/		28	
9002.1190	---其他										
9002.1190 10	彩色投影机和数字光处理器的镜头及镜头组件〔999〕	10	3	80	13/	13	千克/个	/		28	
9002.1190 90	其他投影仪等用物镜(包括照片放大机用物镜)〔999〕	10		80	13/	13	千克/个	/		35	
	--其他:										
9002.1910	---摄影机或放映机用〔999〕	3.8/1.9		40	13/	13	千克/个	/		28.8	

① 1－6月:1%

协定税率 %								RCEP		特惠税率 %			Article Description
东/冰/格	巴基斯坦	韩国	瑞士上/下	哥/秘/柬	澳/毛	新西/坡/智	中国港/澳/台	东盟及马来/澳/韩	日/新	亚太2国	老/柬/缅	98/97/95	
													Optical fibres and optical fibre bundles; optical fibre cables, other than those of heading No 85.44; sheets and plates of polarizing material; lenses (including contact lenses), prisms, mirrors and other optical elements, of any material, unmounted, other than such elements of glass not optically worked:
													-Optical fibres, optical fibre bundles and cables
0/0/0	0	4.5	0/0	0/0/0	0/0	0//0	0/0/	4.9/4.9/	/4.9			0/0/0	Dispersion-unshifted single-mode fibers (G.652 including G652A、G652B、G652C、G652D)
0/0/0	0	4.5	0/0	0/0/0	0/0	0//0	0/0/	4.9/4.9/	/4.9			0/0/0	Other single-mode fibers
0/0/0	0	4.5	0/0	0/0/0	0/0	0//0	0/0/	4.9/4.9/	/4.9			0/0/0	Optical fiber bundles, cables and other optical fibres (excluding the items under Heading No.85.44)
													-Sheets and plates of polarizing material
0/0/	2	1.6	0/0	0/0/0	0/0	0//0	0/0/	0/0/7.2	7.3/0			0/0/0	Polarizer for LCD rojector
0/0/	2	1.6	0/0	0/0/0	0/0	0//0	0/0/	0/0/7.2	7.3/0			0/0/0	Polarizer for digit film projector
0/0/	2	1.6	0/0	0/0/0	0/0	0//0	0/0/	0/0/7.2	7.3/0			0/0/0	Other sheets and plates of polarizing material
0/0/0	2	6	0/0	0/0/0	0/0	0/0/0	0/0/	9.5/9.5/	/9.5			0/0/0	-Contact lenses
													-Spectacle lenses of glass:
0/0/0	16	9.3	2/2	0/0/0	0/0	0/0/0	0/0/	18/18/18	18.8/18			0/0/0	---Photochromic
													---Other:
0/0/0	16	9.3	2/2	0/0/0	0/0	0/0/0	0/0/	18/18/18	18.8/18			0/0/0	----For sunglasses
0/0/0	16	9.3	2/2	0/0/0	0/0	0/0/0	0/0/	18/18/18	18.8/18			0/0/0	----Other
													-Spectacle lenses of other materials:
0/0/0	16	9.3	2/2	0/0/0	0/0	0/0/0	0/0/	18.7/19/18.7	18.8/19			0/0/0	---Photochromic
													---Other:
0/0/0	16	9.3	2/2	0/0/0	0/0	0/0/0	0/0/	18.7/19/18.7	18.8/19			0/0/0	----For sunglasses
0/0/0	16	4	2/2	0/0/0	0/0	0/0/0	0/0/	18/18/18	18.2/18			0/0/0	----Other
													-Other:
0/0/0	2	3.7	0/0	0/0/0	0/0	0//0	0/0/	0/0/7.2	7.3/0			0/0/0	---Color filter
													---Other
0/0/0	2	1.6	0.8/0.8	0/0/0	0/0	0//0	0/0/	0/0/7.2	7.3/0			0/0/0	Optical element optical components (including light wavelength of 800-1700nm thin film filter, self focusing lens, Faraday rotation piece)
0/0/0	2	1.6	0.8/0.8	0/0/0	0/0	0//0	0/0/	0/0/7.2	7.3/0			0/0/0	Micro lenses(VCD and laser transceiver device)
0/0/0	2	1.6	0.8/0.8	0/0/0	0/0	0//0	0/0/	0/0/7.2	7.3/0			0/0/0	The Fresnel lens projection screen (screen diagonal 80 inches or more, projection than 0.26 or less, gain more than 0.8 or higher, lens distance 100 microns or less)
0/0/0	2	1.6	0.8/0.8	0/0/0	0/0	0//0	0/0/	0/0/7.2	7.3/0			0/0/0	Optical element of LCD backlight module (including light guide plate, a reflecting plate, a diffusion piece, brightening sheet)
0/0/0	2	1.6	0.8/0.8	0/0/0	0/0	0//0	0/0/	0/0/7.2	7.3/0			0/0/0	LCD projector with polarized components
0/0/0	2	1.6	0.8/0.8	0/0/0	0/0	0//0	0/0/	0/0/7.2	7.3/0			0/0/0	Digital movie projector with polarized components
0/0/0	2	1.6	0.8/0.8	0/0/0	0/0	0//0	0/0/	0/0/7.2	7.3/0			0/0/0	Other optical elements, not specified or included elsewhere in the heading No. 9001(other than of glass made elements not optically processed)
													Lenses, prisms, mirrors and other optical elements, of any material, mounted, being parts of or fittings for instruments or apparatus, other than such elements of glass not optically worked:
													-Objective lenses:
													--For cameras, projectors or photographic enlargers or reducers:
0/0/0	2	0	0/0	0/0/0	0/0	0//0	0/0/	0/0/0	7.3/0			0/0/0	---For the photographic cameras of subheadings No. 9006.1010、9006.3000
0/0/0	2	0	0/0	0/0/0	0/0	0//0	0/0/	0/0/0	7.3/0			0/0/0	---For microfilm, microfiche or other microform readers
													---For other cameras:
													----Lens for single lens reftex cameras
0/0/0	8.4		1.5/1.5	0/0/0	0/0	0/0/0	0/0/	14.3/14.3/	7.5/14.3			0/0/0	SLR camera lens (machine)
0/0/0	8.4		1.5/1.5	0/0/0	0/0	0/0/0	0/0/	14.3/14.3/	7.5/14.3			0/0/0	Parts and accessories of SLR camera lens
0/0/0	8.4	3	1.5/1.5	0/0/0	0/0	0/0/0	0/0/	0/0/13.5	13.6/0			0/0/0	----Other
													---Other
0/0/0	8.4	7	1.5/1.5	0/0/0	0/0	0/0/0	0/0/0	14/14.3/14	14.1/14.3			0/0/0	Lenses and lens components for colour crystal projector and digital light processor
0/0/0	8.4	7	1.5/1.5	0/0/0	0/0	0/0/0	0/0/0	14/14.3/14	14.1/14.3			0/0/0	Other objective lenses for cameras, projectors (including lenses for photographic enlargers)
													--Other:
0/0/0	8.4	3	1.5/1.5	0/0/0	0/0	0/0/0	0/0/	0/0/13.5	13.6/0			0/0/0	---For cinematographic cameras or projectors

税则号列	货品名称〔CIQ扩展编码及品名－T2表示见附表2〕	最惠(%)	暂定税率	普通	增值/消费	出口退税	计量单位	监管条件/特殊证件	检验检疫	对美关税	亚太上/下
9002.1990	---其他										
9002.1990 10	摄像机、摄录一体机的镜头〔999〕	3.8/1.9	①	50	13/	13	千克/个	/		28	
9002.1990 20	手机、平板电脑用物镜(800万像素及以上)〔999〕	3.8/1.9		50	13/	13	千克/个	/		28.8	
9002.1990 90	税目90.02未列名的其他物镜〔999〕	3.8/1.9		50	13/	13	千克/个	/		28.8	
	-滤光镜：										
9002.2010	---照相机用	3.8/1.9		80	13/	13	千克/个	/		28.8	2.5/1.2
9002.2090	---其他〔999〕	3.8/1.9		40	13/	13	千克/个	/		13.8	2.5/1.2
	-其他：										
9002.9010	---照相机用										
9002.9010 10	照相机用带屈光度调节装置的目镜(但物镜，滤色镜除外)〔999〕	3.8/1.9		80	13/	13	千克/个	/		23.8	
9002.9010 90	其他照相机用未列名光学元件(但物镜、滤色镜除外)〔999〕	3.8/1.9		80	13/	13	千克/个	/		23.8	
9002.9090	---其他										
9002.9090 10	抗辐射镜头[能抗 5×10^4 戈瑞(硅)以上辐射而又不会降低使用质量]〔999〕	3.8/1.9		40	13/	13	千克/个	3/		23.8	
9002.9090 20	其他带屈光度调节装置的目镜〔999〕	3.8/1.9		40	13/	13	千克/个	/		23.8	
9002.9090 30	掩模版〔999〕	3.8/1.9		40	13/	13	千克/个	/		23.8	
9002.9090 90	其他光学仪器用未列名光学元件(但物镜，滤色镜除外)〔999〕	3.8/1.9		40	13/	13	千克/个	/		23.8	
90.03	**眼镜架及其零件：**										
	-眼镜架：										
9003.1100	--塑料制〔999〕	7		70	13/	13	千克/副	/		32	
	--其他材料制：										
9003.1910	---金属材料制〔999〕	7	6	70	13/	13	千克/副	/		31	
9003.1920	---天然材料制										
9003.1920 10	濒危动植物产品制眼镜架〔999〕	7		70	13/	0	千克/副	FE/			
9003.1920 90	其他天然材料制眼镜架〔999〕	7		70	13/	13	千克/副	/			
9003.1990	---其他〔999〕	7		70	13/	13	千克/副	/			
9003.9000	-零件〔999〕	6		70	13/	13	千克	/		31	
90.04	**矫正视力、保护眼睛或其他用途的眼镜、挡风镜及类似品：**										
9004.1000	-太阳镜〔999〕	7	6	100	13/	13	千克/副	/		16	
	-其他：										
9004.9010	---变色镜〔999〕	7		100	13/	13	千克/副	/		27	
9004.9090	---其他〔999〕	7		90	13/	13	千克/副	/		32	
90.05	**双筒望远镜、单筒望远镜、其他光学望远镜及其座架；其他天文仪器及其座架，但不包括射电天文仪器：**										
9005.1000	-双筒望远镜〔999〕	10		50	13/	13	个/千克	/		35	
	-其他仪器：										
9005.8010	---天文望远镜及其他天文仪器〔999〕	3		8	13/	13	台/千克	/		13	
9005.8090	---其他〔999〕	10		50	13/	13	台/千克	/		30	
	-零件、附件(包括座架)：										
9005.9010	---天文望远镜及其他天文仪器用〔999〕	2		8	13/	13	千克	/		7	1.6/1.6
9005.9090	---其他〔999〕	6		30	13/	13	千克	/		31	
90.06	**照相机(电影摄影机除外)；照相闪光灯装置及闪光灯泡，但税目85.39的放电灯泡除外：**										
9006.3000	-水下、航空测量或体内器官检查用的特种照相机；法庭或犯罪学用的比较照相机〔999〕	9		17	13/	13	台/千克	/		34	
9006.4000	-一次成像照相机〔999〕	5		70	13/	13	台/千克	/		30	
	-其他照相机：										
	--使用胶片宽度为35毫米：										
9006.5310	---通过镜头取景[单镜头反光式(SLR)]〔999〕	9		100	13/	13	台/千克	/			
9006.5390	---其他〔999〕	9		100	13/	13	台/千克	/		34	
	--其他：										
9006.5910	---激光照相排版设备〔999〕	9		35	13/	13	台/千克	/			

① 1－6月：3％

协定税率 %								RCEP		特惠税率 %			Article Description
东/冰/格	巴基斯坦	韩国	瑞士上/下	哥/秘/柬	澳/毛	新西/坡/智	中国港/澳/台	东盟及马来/澳/韩	日/新	亚太2国	老/柬/缅	98/97/95	
													---Other
0/0/0	8.4	7	1.5/1.5	0/0/0	0/0	0/0/0	0/0/0	0/0/13.5	13.6/0			0/0/0	Lenses for vidicon and amcorder
0/0/0	8.4	7	1.5/1.5	0/0/0	0/0	0/0/0	0/0/0	0/0/13.5	13.6/0			0/0/0	Mobile phone, tablet computer in an objective lens (8000000 pixels and above)
0/0/0	8.4	7	1.5/1.5	0/0/0	0/0	0/0/0	0/0/0	0/0/13.5	13.6/0			0/0/0	Other objective lenses not specified or included
													-Filters:
0/0/0	8.4	7	1.5/1.5	0/0/0	0/0	0/0/0	0/0/	13.5/13.5/13.5	13.6/13.5			0/0/0	---For cameras
0/0/0	8.4	7	1.5/1.5	0/0/0	0/0	0/0/0	0/0/	13.5/13.5/13.5	13.6/13.5			0/0/0	---Other
													-Other:
													---For cameras
0/0/0	8.4	7	1.5/1.5	0/0/0	0/0	0/0/0	0/0/0	0/0/13.5	13.6/0			0/0/0	Eyepiece with diopter adjustment device for camera(excluding objective lenses and filters)
0/0/0	8.4	7	1.5/1.5	0/0/0	0/0	0/0/0	0/0/0	0/0/13.5	13.6/0			0/0/0	Other optical elements for cameras (other than objective, filters)
													---Other
0/0/0	8.4	7	1.5/1.5	0/0/0	0/0	0/0/0	0/0/0	0/0/13.5	13.6/0			0/0/0	Radiation resistance lenses (capable of resisting radiance>5 $\times 10^4$ Gy (Si) and not lowering operation quality)
0/0/0	8.4	7	1.5/1.5	0/0/0	0/0	0/0/0	0/0/0	0/0/13.5	13.6/0			0/0/0	Other eyepiece with diopter adjustment device
0/0/0	8.4	7	1.5/1.5	0/0/0	0/0	0/0/0	0/0/0	0/0/13.5	13.6/0			0/0/0	Photomask
0/0/0	8.4	7	1.5/1.5	0/0/0	0/0	0/0/0	0/0/0	0/0/13.5	13.6/0			0/0/0	Other unlisted optial elements for optial instruments (other than objective lenses and filters)
													Frames and mountings for spectacles, goggles or the like, and parts thereof:
													-Frames and mountings:
0/0/0	14.4	3.6	1.8/1.8	0/0/0	0/0	0/0/0	0/0/	0/0/16.2	16.4/0			0/0/0	--Of plastics
													--Of other materials:
0/0/0	2	2	0/0	0/0/0	0/0	0//0	0/0/	0/0/9	9.1/0			0/0/0	---Of metal materials
													---Of natural materials
0/0/0	2	2	0/0	0/0/0	0/0	0//0	0/0/	0/0/9	9.1/0			0/0/0	Frames and mountings of product of endangered animals and plants
0/0/0	2	2	0/0	0/0/0	0/0	0//0	0/0/	0/0/9	9.1/0			0/0/0	Frames and mountings of other natural materials
0/0/0	2	2	0/0	0/0/0	0/0	0//0	0/0/	0/0/9	9.1/0			0/0/0	---Other
0/0/0	2	2	0/0	0/0/0	0/0	0//0	0/0/	0/0/9	9.1/0			0/0/0	-Parts
													Spectacles, goggles and the like, corrective, protective or other:
0/0/0	16	9.3	2/2	0/0/0	0/0	0/0/0	0/0/	18.7/19/18.7	18.8/19			0/0/0	-Sunglasses
													-Other:
0/0/0	9	3.2	1.6/1.6	0/0/0	0/0	0/0/0	0/0/	0/0/14.4	14.5/0			0/0/0	---Photochromic spectacles
0/0/0		4	2/2	0/0/0	0/0	0/0/0	0/0/	0/0/18	18.2/0			0/0/0	---Other
													Binoculars, monoculars, other optical telescopes, and mountings therefor; other astronomical instruments and mountings therefor, but not including instruments for radio-astronomy:
0/0/0	8.4	3	1.5/1.5	0/0/0	0/0	0/0/0	0/0/	0/0/13.5	13.6/0			0/0/0	-Binoculars
													-Other instruments:
0/0/0	0	0	0/0	0/0/0	0/0	0//0	0/0/	0/0/0	0/0			0/0/0	---Astronomical telescopes and other astronomical instruments
0/0/0	4.2	2.4	1.2/1.2	0/0/0	0/0	0/0/0	0/0/	0/0/10.8	10.9/0			0/0/0	---Other
													-Parts and accessories (including mountings):
0/0/0	0	0	0/0	0/0/0	0/0	0//0	0/0/	0/0/0	0/0			0/0/0	---Of instruments of subheading 9005.8010
0/0/0	2	0	0/0	0/0/0	0/0	0//0	0/0/	0/0/0	7.3/0			0/0/0	---Other
													Photographic (other than cinematographic) cameras; photographic fla-shlight apparatus and flashbulbs, other than discharge lamps of heading No. 85.39:
0/0/0	2		0/0	0/0/0	0/0	0//0	0/0/	5/5/	/5			0/0/0	-Cameras specially designed for underwater use, for aerial survey or for medical or surgical examination of internal organs; comparison cameras for forensic or criminological purposes
0/0/0	0	1	0/0	0/0/0	0/0	0//0	0/0/	0/0/4.5	4.5/0			0/0/0	-Instant print cameras
													-Other cameras:
													-- For roll film of a width of 35 mm.
0/0/0		15	9/9	0//0	0/15	0/0/0	0/0/	23.8/23.8/23.8	23.8/23.8			0/0/	---With a through the lens viewfinder (single lens reflex (SLR))
0/0/0		9.3	2/2	0/0/0	0/0	0/0/0	0/0/	18/18/18	18.8/18			0/0/0	---Other
													--Other
0/0/0	2	4.2	0/0	0/0/0	0/0	0/0/0	0/0/	8.1/8.1/8.1	8.4/8.1			0/0/0	---Laser photo typesetting equipment

税则号列	货品名称〔CIQ扩展编码及品名－T2表示见附表2〕	最惠(%)	暂定税率	普通	增值/消费	出口退税	计量单位	监管条件/特殊证件	检验检疫	对美关税	亚太上/下
	---制版照相机：										
9006.5921	----电子分色机〔999〕	9		20	13/	13	台/千克	/			
9006.5929	----其他〔999〕	9		20	13/	13	台/千克	/			
9006.5930	---通过镜头取景[单镜头反光式(SLR)]，使用胶片宽度小于35毫米〔999〕	9		100	13/	13	台/千克	/			
	---其他，使用胶片宽度小于35毫米：										
9006.5941	----缩微照相机，使用缩微胶卷、胶片或其他缩微品的(9006.5210)〔999〕	9		17	13/	13	台/千克	/		14	
9006.5949	----其他(9006.5290)〔999〕	9		100	13/	13	台/千克	/		14	
9006.5990	---其他										
	-照相闪光灯装置及闪光灯泡 ：										
9006.5990 10	分幅相机(记录速率超过每秒225000帧)〔999〕	9		100	13/	13	台/千克	3/			5.9/5.9
9006.5990 20	分幅相机(帧曝光时间为50纳秒或更短)〔999〕	9		100	13/	13	台/千克	3/			5.9/5.9
9006.5990 90	使用胶片宽＞35mm的其他照相机〔999〕	9		100	13/	13	架/千克	/			5.9/5.9
	-照相闪光灯装置及闪光灯泡：										
9006.6100	--放电式(电子式)闪光灯装置										
9006.6100 01	照相手机用闪光灯组件〔999〕	9	4	80	13/	13	个/千克	/		29	
9006.6100 02	照相机外置式电子闪光灯(闪光指数GN≥30，具有无线闪光功能，支持自动变焦)〔999〕	9		80	13/	13	个/千克	/		34	
9006.6100 90	其他放电式(电子式)闪光灯装置〔999〕	9		80	13/	13	个/千克	/		34	
	--其他：										
9006.6910	---闪光灯泡〔101 其它电光源及其零件，102 其他电子式光学仪器零件〕	9		80	13/	13	个/千克	/		34	
9006.6990	---其他〔999〕	9		80	13/	13	个/千克	/		29	
	-零件、附件：										
	--照相机用：										
9006.9110	---税号9006.3000、9006.5921、9006.5929所列照相机用〔999〕	8		17	13/	13	千克	/		18	5.2/5.2
9006.9120	---一次成像照相机用〔999〕	5		100	13/	13	千克	/		30	3.3/3.3
	---其他：										
9006.9191	----自动调焦组件〔999〕	8	6	100	13/	13	千克/套	/		31	5.2/5.2
9006.9192	----快门组件〔999〕	8	6	100	13/	13	千克/套	/		31	5.2/5.2
9006.9199	----其他〔999〕	8	6	100	13/	13	千克	/		26	5.2/5.2
9006.9900	--其他〔999〕	8		80	13/	13	千克	/		33	
90.07	**电影摄影机、放映机，不论是否带有声音的录制或重放装置：**										
	-摄影机：										
9007.1010	---高速摄影机〔999〕	12		40	13/	13	台/千克	/			
9007.1090	---其他〔999〕	12		40	13/	13	台/千克	/			
	-放映机：										
9007.2010	---数字式										
9007.2010 01	2K及以上分辨率的硬盘式数字电影放映机〔999〕	8		40	13/	13	台/千克	/			
9007.2010 90	其他数字式放映机〔999〕	8		40	13/	13	台/千克	/			
9007.2090	---其他〔999〕	8		40	13/	13	台/千克	/		33	5.2/5.2
	-零件、附件：										
9007.9100	--摄影机用〔999〕	8	5	40	13/	13	千克	/		15	
9007.9200	--放映机用										
9007.9200 10	2K及以上分辨率的硬盘式数字电影放映机用零附件〔999〕	8	3	40	13/	13	千克	/		13	
9007.9200 90	电影放映机(不包括2K及以上分辨率的硬盘式)用零附件〔999〕	8	5	40	13/	13	千克	/		15	
90.08	**影像投影仪，但电影用除外；照片(电影片除外)放大机及缩片机：**										
	-投影仪、放大机及缩片机：										
9008.5010	---幻灯机〔999〕	10		40	13/	13	台/千克	/			
9008.5020	---缩微胶卷、缩微胶片或其他缩微品的阅读机，不论是否可以进行复制〔101：Ⅰ类设备，102：Ⅱ类设备，103：其他类缩微阅读机设备〕	10		17	13/	13	台/千克	/		15	
	---其他影像投影仪：										
9008.5031	----正射投影仪〔101：Ⅰ类设备，102：Ⅱ类设备，103：其他类正射投影仪设备〕	12		40	13/	13	台/千克	/		17	
9008.5039	----其他〔101：有源式，Ⅰ类设备，102：有源式，Ⅱ类设备，103：有源式，其他类影像投影仪设备，104：机械式〕	12		40	13/	13	台/千克	/		22	
9008.5040	---照片(电影片除外)放大机及缩片机〔101：有源式，Ⅰ类设备，102：有源式，Ⅱ类设备，103：有源式，其他类照片(电影片除外)放大机及缩片机设备，104：机械式〕	12		80	13/	13	台/千克	/		22	

协定税率 %								RCEP		特惠税率 %			Article Description
东/冰/格	巴基斯坦	韩国	瑞士上/下	哥/秘/柬	澳/毛	新西/坡/智	中国港/澳/台	东盟及马来/澳/韩	日/新	亚太2国	老/柬/缅	98/97/95	
													---Cameras of a kind used for preparing printing plates or cylinders:
0/0/0	4.2	2.4	1.2/1.2	0/0/0	0/0	0/0/0	0/0/	0/0/10.8	10.9/0			0/0/0	----Electronic colour scanners
0/0/0	2	2	0/0	0/0/0	0/0	0//0	0/0/	0/0/9	9.1/0			0/0/0	----Other
0/0/0		15	9/9	0//0	0/15	0/0/0	0/0/	23.8/23.8/23.8	23.8/23.8			0/0/	---With a through the lens viewfinder (single lens reflex (SLR)),for roll film of a width less than 35 mm.
													---Other,for roll film of a width less than 35 mm.
0/0/0	2	0	0/0	0/0/0	0/0	0//0	0/0/	0/0/0	8.2/0			0/0/0	---Cameras of a kind used for recording documents on microfilm.microfiche or other microforms
0//0		15	9/9	0//0	0/15	0/0/0	0/0/	23.8/23.8/23.8	23.8/23.8			0/0/	----Other,
													---Other,
													-Photographic flashlight apparatus and flashbulbs
0/0/0		15		0//0	0/15	0/0/0	0/0/	23.8/23.8/23.8	/23.8			0/0/	Frame cameras (rate of recording>225000 frame/sec)
0/0/0		15		0//0	0/15	0/0/0	0/0/	23.8/23.8/23.8	/23.8			0/0/	Electromc (or electromc shutter) framing cameras(frane exposure time≤51 nanoseconds)
0/0/0		15		0//0	0/15	0/0/0	0/0/	23.8/23.8/23.8	/23.8			0/0/	Other cameras, for roll film of a width>35mm
													-Photographic flashlight apparatus and flashbulbs:
													--Discharge lamp ("electronic") flashlight apparatus
0/0/0		3.6	1.8/1.8	0/0/0	0/0	0/0/0	0/0/	16.2/16.2/16.2	16.4/16.2			0/0/0	Flashlight component for camera mobile phone
0/0/0		3.6	1.8/1.8	0/0/0	0/0	0/0/0	0/0/	16.2/16.2/16.2	16.4/16.2			0/0/0	Camera external electronic flash (flash index GN ≥ 30, with wireless flash function, support auto zoom)
0/0/0		3.6	1.8/1.8	0/0/0	0/0	0/0/0	0/0/	16.2/16.2/16.2	16.4/16.2			0/0/0	Other discharge lamp("electronic") flashlight apparatus
													--Other:
0/0/0	10.1	10.8	1.8/1.8	0/0/0	0/0	0/0/0	0/0/	17.1/17.1/	/17.1			0/0/0	---Flasbbulbs
0/0/0	10.1	3.6	1.8/1.8	0/0/0	0/0	0/0/0	0/0/	0/0/16.2	16.4/0			0/0/0	---Other
													-Parts and accessories:
													--For cameras:
0/0/0	2	1.6	0/0	0/0/0	0/0	0//0	0/0/	0/0/7.2	7.3/0	0		0/0/0	---For cameras of subheadings No.9006.3000,9006.5921 and 9006.5929
0/0/0	0	0	0/0	0/0/0	0/0	0//0	0/0/	0/0/0	0/0	0		0/0/0	---For instant print cameras
													---Other:
0/0/0	2	2	0/0	0/0/0	0/0	0/0/0	0/0/	0/0/9	9.1/0	0		0/0/0	----Automatic focal setting units
0/0/0	2	2	0/0	0/0/0	0/0	0/0/0	0/0/	0/0/9	9.1/0	0		0/0/0	----Shutter units
0/0/0	2	2	0/0	0/0/0	0/0	0/0/0	0/0/	0/0/9	9.1/0	0		0/0/0	----Other
0/0/0	4.2	2.4	1.2/1.2	0/0/0	0/0	0/0/0	0/0/	0/0/10.8	10.9/0			0/0/0	--Other
													Cinematographic cameras and projectors, whether or not incorporating sound recording or reproducing apparatus:
													-Cameras:
0/0/0	4.9	2.8	1.4/1.4	0/0/0	0/0	0/0/0	0/0/	0/0/12.6	12.7/0			0/0/0	---High speed cameras
0/0/0	7.8	2.8	1.4/1.4	0/0/0	0/0	0/0/0	0/0/	0/0/12.6	12.7/0			0/0/0	---Other
													-Projectors:
													---Digital
0/0/0	7.8	2.8	1.4/1.4	0/0/0	0/0	0/0/0	0/0/	0/0/12.6	12.7/0			0/0/0	Digital film projector ,resolution ≥2K,disk type
0/0/0	7.8	2.8	1.4/1.4	0/0/0	0/0	0/0/0	0/0/	0/0/12.6	12.7/0			0/0/0	Other digital projectors
0/0/0	7.8	2.8	1.4/1.4	0/0/0	0/0	0/0/0	0/0/	0/0/12.6	12.7/0			0/0/0	---Other
													-Parts and accessories:
0/0/0	2	1.6	0/0	0/0/0	0/0	0//0	0/0/	0/0/7.6	7.6/0			0/0/0	--For cameras
													--For projectors
0/0/0	2	0	0/0	0/0/0	0/0	0//0	0/0/	0/0/0	7.6/0			0/0/0	Parts and accessories of hard disk digit film projector with a resolution ratio of 2k or above
0/0/0	2	0	0/0	0/0/0	0/0	0//0	0/0/	0/0/0	7.6/0			0/0/0	Parts and accessories of film projector, excluding of a hard disk digit with a resolution ratio of 2k or above
													Image projectors, other than cinematographic; photographic (other than cinematographic) enlargers and reducers:
													-Image projectors、enlargers and reducers:
0/0/0	4.9	2.8	1.4/1.4	0/0/0	0/0	0/0/0	0/0/	0/0/12.6	12.7/0			0/0/0	---Slide projectors
0/0/0	2	2	0/0	0/0/0	0/0	0//0	0/0/	0/0/9	9.1/0			0/0/0	---Microfilm, microfiche or other microform readers, whether or not capable of producing copies
													---Other image projectors:
0/0/0			1.8/1.8	0/0/0	0/0	0/0/0	0/0/	5/5/	/5			0/0/0	----Orthographical projectors
0/0/0			1.8/1.8	0/0/0	0/0	0/0/0	0/0/	5/5/	/5			0/0/0	----Other
0/0/0		9.3	2/2	0/0/0	0/0	0/0/0	0/0/	18/18/18	18.8/18			0/0/0	---Photographic(other than cinematographic) enlargers and reducers

税则号列	货品名称〔CIQ 扩展编码及品名－T2 表示见附表 2〕	最惠(%)	暂定税率	普通	增值/消费	出口退税	计量单位	监管条件/特殊证件	检验检疫	对美关税	亚太上/下
	-零件、附件：										
9008.9010	---缩微阅读机用〔999〕	8		17	13/	13	千克	/			5.2/5.2
9008.9020	---照片放大机及缩片机用〔999〕	8		80	13/	13	千克	/			5.2/5.2
9008.9090	---其他〔999〕	8		40	13/	13	千克	/		28	
90.10	**本章其他税目未列名的照相(包括电影)洗印用装置及设备；负片显示器；银幕及其他投影屏幕：**										
	-照相(包括电影)胶卷或成卷感光纸的自动显影装置及设备或将已冲洗胶卷自动曝光到成卷感光纸上的装置及设备：										
9010.1010	---电影用〔999〕	12		40	13/	13	台/千克	/			7.8/7.8
9010.1020	---特种照相用〔999〕	8		20	13/	13	台/千克	/		33	5.2/5.2
	---其他：										
9010.1091	----彩色胶卷用〔999〕	12		100	13/	13	台/千克	/			
9010.1099	----其他〔999〕	12		100	13/	13	台/千克	/		37	
	-照相(包括电影)洗印用其他装置及设备；负片显示器：										
9010.5010	---负片显示器〔999〕	0		50	13/	13	台/千克	/		5	
	---其他：										
9010.5021	----电影用〔999〕	0		40	13/	13	台/千克	/			0/0
9010.5022	----特种照相用〔999〕	0		20	13/	13	台/千克	/		25	
9010.5029	----其他〔999〕	0		100	13/	13	台/千克	/		25	
9010.6000	-银幕及其他投影屏幕〔999〕	0		50	13/	13	个/千克	/		5	
	-零件、附件：										
9010.9010	---电影用〔999〕	0		40	13/	13	千克	/			
9010.9020	---特种照相用〔999〕	0		20	13/	13	千克	/		25	
9010.9090	---其他〔999〕	0		100	13/	13	千克	/		10	
90.11	**复式光学显微镜，包括用于显微照相、显微电影摄影及显微投影的：**										
9011.1000	-立体显微镜〔999〕	0		14	13/	13	台/千克	/		25	
9011.2000	-显微照相、显微电影摄影及显微投影用的其他显微镜〔999〕	0		14	13/	13	台/千克	/		20	
9011.8000	-其他显微镜										
9011.8000 10	高倍测量显微镜，放大倍数≥1000 倍，分辨率≤0.08 微米〔999〕	0		14	13/	13	台/千克	/		20	
9011.8000 90	其他显微镜〔999〕	0		14	13/	13	台/千克	/		20	
9011.9000	-零件、附件〔999〕	0		14	13/	13	千克	/		20	
90.12	**显微镜，但光学显微镜除外；衍射设备：**										
9012.1000	-显微镜，但光学显微镜除外；衍射设备〔999〕	0		14	13/	13	台/千克	/			
9012.9000	-零件、附件〔999〕	0		14	13/	13	千克	/			
90.13	**激光器，但激光二极管除外；本章其他税目未列名的光学仪器及器具：**										
9013.1000	-武器用望远镜瞄准具；潜望镜式望远镜；作为本章或第十六类的机器、设备、仪器或器具部件的望远镜										
9013.1000 10	设计用为本章或第十六类的机器、设备、仪器或器具部件的望远镜〔999〕	0		14	13/	13	个/千克	/		25	
9013.1000 90	武器用望远镜瞄准具及潜望镜式望远镜〔999〕	8		14	13/	13	个/千克	/		33	
9013.2000	-激光器，但激光二极管除外										
9013.2000 10	激光切割机用气体激光发生器、切割功率≥2 千瓦〔999〕	0		11	13/	13	个/千克	/			
9013.2000 20	AVLIS、MLIS 和 CRISLA 激光系统〔999〕	0		11	13/	13	个/千克	3/			
9013.2000 30	氩离子激光器(平均输出功率≥40瓦特、工作波长 400～515 纳米)〔999〕	0		11	13/	13	个/千克	3/			
9013.2000 40	紫翠玉激光器(带宽≤0.005 纳米，重复率＞125 赫兹，功率＞30 瓦特等)〔999〕	0		11	13/	13	个/千克	3/			
9013.2000 50	脉冲二氧化碳激光器(重复率＞250 赫兹，功率＞500 瓦，脉冲宽度＜200 纳秒等)〔999〕	0		11	13/	13	个/千克	3/			
9013.2000 60	脉冲受激准分子激光器(XeF、XeCl、KrF 型，重复率＞250赫兹，功率＞500 瓦等)〔999〕	0		11	13/	13	个/千克	3/			
9013.2000 70	铜蒸汽激光器(平均输出功率≥40 瓦特、工作波长 500～600 纳米)〔999〕	0		11	13/	13	个/千克	3/			
9013.2000 80	掺钕激光器(非玻璃激光器，两用物项管制商品)〔999〕	0		11	13/	13	个/千克	3/			

协定税率 %								RCEP		特惠税率 %			Article Description
东/冰/格	巴基斯坦	韩国	瑞士 上/下	哥/秘/柬	澳/毛	新西/坡/智	中国港/澳/台	东盟及马来/澳/韩	日/新	亚太2国	老/柬/缅	98/97/95	
													-Parts and accessories:
0/0/0	2	0	0/0	0/0/0	0/0	0//0	0/0/	0/0/0	7.3/0			0/0/0	---Of microfilm, microfiche or other microform readers
0/0/0	4.9	2.8	1.4/1.4	0/0/0	0/0	0/0/0	0/0/	0/0/12.6	12.7/0			0/0/0	---Of photographic enlargers and reducers
0/0/0	7.8	2.8	1.4/1.4	0/0/0	0/0	0/0/0	0/0/	0/0/12.6	12.7/0			0/0/0	---Other
													Apparatus and equipment for photographic (including cinematographic) laboratories, not specified or included elsewhere in this Chapter; negatoscopes; projection screens:
													-Apparatus and equipment for automatically developing photographic (including cinematographic) film or paper in rolls or for automatically exposing developed film to rolls of photographic paper:
0/0/0	4.9	2.8	1.4/1.4	0/0/0	0/0	0/0/0	0/0/	0/0/12.6	12.7/0			0/0/0	---Of a kind used in cinematographic film
0/0/0	2	0	0/0	0/0/0	0/0	0//0	0/0/	0/0/0	7.6/0			0/0/0	---Of a kind used in special photographic film or paper
													---Other:
0/0/0		15	10.5/10.5	0/0/0	0/15	0/0/0	0/0/	23.8/23.8/23.8	/23.8			0/0/0	----For the colour photographic film in rolls
0/0/0	8.4	9	1.5/1.5	0/0/0	0/0	0/0/0	0/0/	14.3/14.3/14.3	/14.3			0/0/0	----Other
													-Other apparatus and equipment for photographic (including cinematographic) laboratories; negatoscope:
0/0/0	4.9	2.8	0/0	0/0/0	0/0	0/0/0	0/0/	0/0/12.6	0/0			0/0/0	---Negatoscopes
													---Other:
0/0/0	7.8	2.8	0/0	0/0/0	0/0	0/0/0	0/0/	0/0/12.6	0/0			0/0/0	----Of a kind used in cinematographic film
0/0/0	2	1.6	0/0	0/0/0	0/0	0//0	0/0/	0/0/7.6	0/0			0/0/0	----Of a kind used in special photographic film or paper
0/0/0	9.5	3.4	0/0	0/0/0	0/0	0/0/0	0/0/	0/0/15.3	0/0			0/0/0	----Other
0/0/0	7.8	2.8	0/0	0/0/0	0/0	0/0/0	0/0/	0/0/12.6	12.7/0			0/0/0	-Projection screens
													-Parts and accessories:
0/0/0	0	0	0/0	0/0/0	0/0	0//0	0/0/	0/0/0	0/0			0/0/0	---Of a kind used in cinematographic film
0/0/0	0	0	0/0	0/0/0	0/0	0//0	0/0/	0/0/0	0/0			0/0/0	---Of a kind used in special photographic film or paper
0/0/0	0	0	0/0	0/0/0	0/0	0//0	0/0/	0/0/0	0/0			0/0/0	---Other
													Compound optical microscopes, including those for photomicrography, cinephotomi-crography or microprojection:
0/0/0	0	0	0/0	0/0/0	0/0	0//0	0/0/	0/0/0	0/0			0/0/0	-Stereoscopic microscopes
0/0/0	0	0	0/0	0/0/0	0/0	0//0	0/0/	0/0/0	0/0			0/0/0	-Other microscopes, for photomicrography, cinephotomicrography or microprojection
													-Other microscopes
0/0/0	2	1.4	0/0	0/0/0	0/0	0//0	0/0/	6.3/6.3/6.3	6.4/6.3			0/0/0	High expansion measuring microscopes, magnification factor ≥1000, resolution ratio≤0.08μ
0/0/0	2	1.4	0/0	0/0/0	0/0	0//0	0/0/	6.3/6.3/6.3	6.4/6.3			0/0/0	Other microscopes
0/0/0	0	0	0/0	0/0/0	0/0	0//0	0/0/	0/0/0	0/0			0/0/0	-Parts and accessories
													Microscopes other than optical microscopes; diffraction apparatus:
0/0/0	0	0	0/0	0/0/0	0/0	0//0	0/0/	0/0/0	0/0			0/0/0	-Microscopes other than optical microscopes and diffraction apparatus
0/0/0	0	0	0/0	0/0/0	0/0	0//0	0/0/	0/0/0	0/0			0/0/0	-Parts and accessories
													lasers, other than laser diodes; other optical appliances and instruments, not specified or included elsewhere in this Chapter:
													-Telescopic sights for fitting to arms; periscopes; telescopes designed to form parts of machines, appliances, instruments or apparatus of this Chapter or Section XVI
0/0/0	2	0	0/0	0/0/0	0/0	0//0	0/0/	0/0/0	7.3/0			0/0/0	Telescopes designed to form parts of machines, appliances, instruments or apparatus of this Chapter or Section X VI
0/0/0	2	0	0/0	0/0/0	0/0	0//0	0/0/	0/0/0	7.3/0			0/0/0	Parts and accessories of telescopic sights for fitting to arms, periscopes, telescopes
													-Lasers, other than laser diodes
0/0/0	0	1.2	0/0	0/0/0	0/0	0//0	0/0/	0/0/5.4	5.5/0			0/0/0	Gas laser generators for laser cutting machines, cutting power ≥ 2 kW
0/0/0	0	1.2	0/0	0/0/0	0/0	0//0	0/0/	0/0/5.4	5.5/0			0/0/0	AVLIS, MLIS, CRISLA laser systems
0/0/0	0	1.2	0/0	0/0/0	0/0	0//0	0/0/	0/0/5.4	5.5/0			0/0/0	Argon ion lasers (average output power ≥ 40W, working wavelength=400nm~515nm)
0/0/0	0	1.2	0/0	0/0/0	0/0	0//0	0/0/	0/0/5.4	5.5/0			0/0/0	Alexandrite lasers (bandwidth≤0.005nm, repetition rate>125Hz, power>30W)
0/0/0	0	1.2	0/0	0/0/0	0/0	0//0	0/0/	0/0/5.4	5.5/0			0/0/0	Pulsed carbon dioxide lasers (repetition rate>250Hz, power>500W, pules width<200ns)
0/0/0	0	1.2	0/0	0/0/0	0/0	0//0	0/0/	0/0/5.4	5.5/0			0/0/0	Pulsed excimer lasers (XeF、XeCl or KrF type, recurrent rate>250Hz, power>500W)
0/0/0	0	1.2	0/0	0/0/0	0/0	0//0	0/0/	0/0/5.4	5.5/0			0/0/0	Copper vapor lasers(average output power≥40W, working wavelength=500nm~600nm)
0/0/0	0	1.2	0/0	0/0/0	0/0	0//0	0/0/	0/0/5.4	5.5/0			0/0/0	Neodymium doped laser (not glass laser) (Dual-use items controlled commodity)

税则号列	货品名称〔CIQ 扩展编码及品名－T2 表示见附表 2〕	最惠(%)	暂定税率	普通	增值/消费	出口退税	计量单位	监管条件/特殊证件	检验检疫	对美关税	亚太上/下
9013.2000 91	用于 2.5GB/S 及以上 SDH、波分复用光传输设备的 980 纳米、1480 纳米的泵浦激光器〔999〕	0		11	13/	13	个/千克	/			
9013.2000 92	用于 2.5GB/S 及以上光通信设备的 850 纳米、1260～1625 纳米，且功率≤200 毫瓦的激光器(泵浦激光机除外)〔999〕	0		11	13/	13	个/千克	/			
9013.2000 99	其他激光器，但激光二极管除外〔999〕	0		11	13/	13	个/千克	/			
	-其他装置、仪器及器具：										
9013.8010	---放大镜〔999〕	12		50	13/	13	个/千克	/		37	7.8/7.8
9013.8020	---光学门眼〔999〕	12		50	13/	13	个/千克	/		22	7.8/7.8
9013.8090	---其他〔999〕	5		17	13/	13	个/千克	/		30	
	-零件、附件：										
9013.9010	---税号 9013.1000 及 9013.2000 所列货品用										
9013.9010 10	武器用望远镜瞄准器具或潜望镜式望远镜用零件及附件〔999〕	6		11	13/	13	千克	/		16	
9013.9010 90	激光器以及作为本章或第十六类的机器、设备、仪器或器具部件的望远镜用的零件及附件(武器用望远镜瞄准器具或潜望镜式望远镜用零件及附件除外)〔999〕	0		11	13/	13	千克	/			
9013.9090	---其他										
9013.9090 10	太阳能定日镜的零件〔999〕	0		17	13/	13	千克	/		25	
9013.9090 90	品目 90.13 所列其他货品的零附件〔999〕	0		17	13/	13	千克	/		25	
90.14	**定向罗盘；其他导航仪器及装置：**										
9014.1000	-定向罗盘〔999〕	0		8	13/	13	个/千克	/		20	
	-航空或航天导航仪器及装置(罗盘除外)：										
9014.2010	---自动驾驶仪										
9014.2010 10	无人航空飞行器的自动驾驶仪〔999〕	0		8	13/	13	个/千克	3/			0/0
9014.2010 90	其他自动驾驶仪〔999〕	0		8	13/	13	个/千克	/			0/0
9014.2090	---其他										
9014.2090 11	航空惯性导航仪〔999〕	0		8	13/	13	个/千克	3/			0/0
9014.2090 12	其他航天惯性导航仪(天文陀螺盘及其他利用天体或卫星进行导航的装置)〔999〕	0		8	13/	13	个/千克	3/			0/0
9014.2090 13	陀螺稳定平台〔999〕	0		8	13/	13	个/千克	3/			0/0
9014.2090 15	陀螺仪(额定漂移率小于 0.5 度/小时的陀螺仪)〔999〕	0		8	13/	13	个/千克	3/			0/0
9014.2090 16	专门设计的导航信息处理机(用于弹道导弹、运载火箭、探空火箭等的目标探测)〔999〕	0		8	13/	13	个/千克	3/			0/0
9014.2090 17	地形等高线绘制设备(用于弹道导弹、运载火箭、探空火箭、巡航导弹、无人驾驶航空飞行器的目标探测)〔999〕	0		8	13/	13	个/千克	3/			0/0
9014.2090 18	场景绘图及相关设备(用于弹道导弹、运载火箭、探空火箭等的目标探测)〔999〕	0		8	13/	13	个/千克	3/			0/0
9014.2090 90	其他航空或航天导航仪器及装置(但罗盘除外)〔999〕	0		8	13/	13	个/千克	/			0/0
9014.8000	-其他仪器及装置										
9014.8000 10	比例误差小于 0.25%的加速度表〔101 电子，102 机械〕	0		8	13/	13	个/千克	3/		10	
9014.8000 20	高度表(用于弹道导弹、运载火箭、探空火箭、巡航导弹、无人驾驶航空飞行器的目标探测)〔999〕	0		8	13/	13	个/千克	3/		10	
9014.8000 90	其他导航仪器及装置〔999〕	0		8	13/	13	个/千克	/		10	
	-零件、附件：										
9014.9010	---自动驾驶仪用〔999〕	0		8	13/	13	千克	/			
9014.9090	---其他〔999〕	0		8	13/	13	千克	/		5	
90.15	**大地测量(包括摄影测量)、水道测量、海洋、水文、气象或地球物理用仪器及装置，不包括罗盘；测距仪：**										
9015.1000	-测距仪〔101 电子，102 机械〕	0		14	13/	13	台/千克	/		25	
9015.2000	-经纬仪及视距仪〔999〕	0		14	13/	13	台/千克	/		25	
9015.3000	-水平仪〔999〕	9		14	13/	13	台/千克	/		34	
9015.4000	-摄影测量用仪器及装置〔999〕	0		14	13/	13	千克	/		25	
9015.8000	-其他仪器及装置										
9015.8000 10	机载或舰载重力仪(精度为 1 毫伽或更好、稳态记录时间至多为 2 分钟的)〔999〕	0		14	13/	13	台/千克	3/		5	0/0

协定税率 %								RCEP		特惠税率 %			Article Description
东/冰/格	巴基斯坦	韩国	瑞士 上/下	哥/秘/柬	澳/毛	新西/坡/智	中国港/澳/台	东盟及马来/澳/韩	日/新	亚太2国	老/柬/缅	98/97/95	
0/0/0	0	1.2	0/0	0/0/0	0/0	0//0	0/0/	0/0/5.4	5.5/0			0/0/0	980nm, 1480nm pump laser of SDH ≥ 2.5GB/s, optical transmission equipment for wave-divison multicomplexing
0/0/0	0	1.2	0/0	0/0/0	0/0	0//0	0/0/	0/0/5.4	5.5/0			0/0/0	For the 850 nm,1260～1625 nm and above 2.5GB/S optical communicationdevice,and the laser power less than 200 mW (excluding pumped laser machine)
0/0/0	0	1.2	0/0	0/0/0	0/0	0//0	0/0/	0/0/5.4	5.5/0			0/0/0	Other lasers, other than laser diodes
													-Other devices, appliances and instruments:
0/0/0	3.5	2.4	1.2/1.2	0/0/0	0/0	0/0/0	0/0/	0/0/10.8	10.9/0			0/0/0	---Hand magnifying glasses
0/0/0	3.5	2.4	1.2/1.2	0/0/0	0/0	0/0/0	0/0/	0/0/10.8	10.9/0			0/0/0	---Door eyes
0/0/	0		0/0	0/0/0	0/0	0//0	0/0/	4.9/4.9/	/4.9			0/0/0	---Other
													-Parts and accessories:
													---For goods of subhedding No. 9013.1000 and 9013.2000
0/0/0	0	1.2	0/0	0/0/0	0/0	0//0	0/0/	5.4/5.4/5.4	5.5/5.4			0/0/0	Parts and accessories of telescopic sights for fitting to arms, periscopes, telescopes designed to form parts of machines
0/0/0	0	1.2	0/0	0/0/0	0/0	0//0	0/0/	5.4/5.4/5.4	5.5/5.4			0/0/0	Parts and accessories of laser machines, equipment, instruments or apparatus components with the telescope , as well as this chapter or Section 16 (weapon with a telescope aimed at periscope telescope equipment or parts and accessories except)
													---Other
0/0/	2	8	0/0	0/0/0	0/0	0//0	0/0/	0/7.2/8	0/7.2			0/0/0	Solar heliostat parts
0/0/	2	8	0/0	0/0/0	0/0	0//0	0/0/	0/7.2/8	0/7.2			0/0/0	The 90.13 items listed parts and accessories of other goods
													Direction finding compasses; other navigational instruments and appliances:
0/0/0	0	0.9	0/0	0/0/0	0/0	0//0	0/0/	0/0/1.8	0/0			0/0/0	-Direction finding compasses
													-Instruments and appliances for aeronautical or space navigation (other than compasses):
													---Automatic pilot
0/0/0	0	0.9	0/0	0/0/0	0/0	0//0	0/0/	0/0/1.8	0/0			0/0/0	Automatic piolt for unmanned aircrafts
0/0/0	0	0.9	0/0	0/0/0	0/0	0//0	0/0/	0/0/1.8	0/0			0/0/0	Other navigatioral automatic pilot
													---Other
0/0/0	0	0	0/0	0/0/0	0/0	0//0	0/0/	0/0/0	0/0			0/0/0	Inertial navigation instruments for airplanes
0/0/0	0	0	0/0	0/0/0	0/0	0//0	0/0/	0/0/0	0/0			0/0/0	Other space inertial navigational instument(astronomical gyrocompass and astronomical or satellite navigational devices thereof)
0/0/0	0	0	0/0	0/0/0	0/0	0//0	0/0/	0/0/0	0/0			0/0/0	Gyro stabilized platforms
0/0/0	0	0	0/0	0/0/0	0/0	0//0	0/0/	0/0/0	0/0			0/0/0	Gyroscopes (rated drift rate<0.5 degree/h)
0/0/0	0	0	0/0	0/0/0	0/0	0//0	0/0/	0/0/0	0/0			0/0/0	Specially-designed navigation information processors (for target detection of ballistic missiles, carrier rockets or sounding rockets)
0/0/0	0	0	0/0	0/0/0	0/0	0//0	0/0/	0/0/0	0/0			0/0/0	Terrain contour mapping equipments for target detection of ballistic missiles, carrier rockets or sounding rockets
0/0/0	0	0	0/0	0/0/0	0/0	0//0	0/0/	0/0/0	0/0			0/0/0	Scene mapping cquipments and relative equipments (for target detection of ballistic missiles, carrier rockets or sounding rockets)
0/0/0	0	0	0/0	0/0/0	0/0	0//0	0/0/	0/0/0	0/0			0/0/0	Other instruments and appliances for aeronautical or space navigation (other than compasses)
													-Other instruments and appliances
0/0/0	0	0	0/0	0/0/0	0/0	0//0	0/0/	0/1.8/0	0/1.8			0/0/0	Accelerometers, proportion error<0.25%
0/0/0	0	0	0/0	0/0/0	0/0	0//0	0/0/	0/1.8/0	0/1.8			0/0/0	Altimeters (for target detection of ballistic missiles, carrier rockets or sounding rockets)
0/0/0	0	0	0/0	0/0/0	0/0	0//0	0/0/	0/1.8/0	0/1.8			0/0/0	Other navigational instruments and appliances
													-Parts and accessories:
0/0/0	0	0	0/0	0/0/0	0/0	0//0	0/0/	0/0/0	0/0			0/0/0	---For automatic pilot
0/0/0	0	0	0/0	0/0/0	0/0.8	0//0	0/0/	0/0/0	0/0			0/0/0	---Other
													Surveying (including photogrammetrical surveying), hydrographic, oceanographic, hydrological, meteorological or geophysical instruments and appliances, excluding compasses; rangefinders:
0/0/0	2	1.8	0/0	0/0/0	0/0	0//0	0/0/	0/0/8.1	8.2/0			0/0/0	-Rangefinders
0/0/0	2	0	0/0	0/0/0	0/0	0//0	0/0/	0/0/0	8.2/0			0/0/0	-Theodolites and tachymeters(tacheometers)
0/0/0	2	1.8	0/0	0/0/0	0/0	0//0	0/0/	0/0/8.1	8.2/0			0/0/0	-Levels
0/0/0	2	0	0/0	0/0/0	0/0	0//0	0/0/	0/0/0	8.2/0			0/0/0	-Photogrammetrical surveying instruments and appliances
													-Other instruments and appliances
0/0/0	0	1		0/0/0	0/0	0//0	0/0/	0/0/4.5	4.5/0			0/0/0	Air-borne or ship-borne gravimeters (accuracy 1 milligamma or more better, duration of static recording≤2 min)

税则号列	货品名称〔CIQ 扩展编码及品名－T2 表示见附表 2〕	最惠(%)	暂定税率	普通	增值/消费	出口退税	计量单位	监管条件/特殊证件	检验检疫	对美关税	亚太上/下
9015.8000 20	机载或舰载重力梯度仪(精度为 1 毫伽或更好、稳态记录时间至多为 2 分钟的)〔999〕	0		14	13/	13	台/千克	3/		5	0/0
9015.8000 90	其他测量仪器及装置〔101 电子,102 机械〕	0		14	13/	13	台/千克	/		5	0/0
9015.9000	-零件、附件										
9015.9000 10	用于机、舰载重力仪和重力梯度仪的部件〔999〕	0		14	13/	13	千克	3/		10	
9015.9000 90	其他税目 90.15 所列仪器及装置的零、附件〔101 电子,102 机械〕	0		14	13/	13	千克	/		10	
90.16	**感量为 50 毫克或更精密的天平,不论是否带有砝码:**										
9016.0010	---感量为 0.1 毫克或更精密的天平〔101 电子衡器,102 机械量具〕	9		14	13/	13	台/千克	/		29	
9016.0090	---其他〔101 电子衡器,102 机械量具〕	9		30	13/	13	台/千克	/		34	
90.17	**绘图、划线或数学计算仪器及器具(例如,绘图机、比例缩放仪、分度规、绘图工具、计算尺及盘式计算器);本章其他税目未列名的手用测量长度的器具(例如,量尺、量带、千分尺及卡尺):**										
9017.1000	-绘图台及绘图机,不论是否自动〔101 电子衡器,102 机械量具〕	8		20	13/	13	台/千克	/		18	
9017.2000	-其他绘图、划线或数学计算器具〔999〕	0		70	13/	13	个/千克	/		20	
9017.3000	-千分尺、卡尺及量规〔999〕	8		20	13/	13	个/千克	/		18	
9017.8000	-其他仪器及器具〔999〕	8		20	13/	13	个/千克	/		28	
9017.9000	-零件、附件〔999〕	0		20	13/	13	千克	/		25	
90.18	**医疗、外科、牙科或兽医用仪器及器具,包括闪烁扫描装置、其他电气医疗装置及视力检查仪器:**										
	-电气诊断装置(包括功能检查或生理参数检查用装置):										
9018.1100	--心电图记录仪〔999〕	0		17	13/	13	台/千克	6O/		5	
	--超声波扫描装置:										
9018.1210	---B 型超声波诊断仪〔999〕	1.8/0.9		35	13/	13	台/千克	6OA/	M	6.8	1.5/0.8
	---其他:										
9018.1291	----彩色超声波诊断仪										
9018.1291 10	彩色超声波诊断仪(整机)〔999〕	1.3/0.6		17	13/	13	台/千克	6OA/	M	6.3	1.2/0.5
9018.1291 90	彩色超声波诊断仪的零件及附件〔999〕	1.3/0.6		17	13/	13	台/千克	6/			1.2/0.5
9018.1299	----其他〔999〕	1.3/0.6		17	13/	13	台/千克	6A/	M	6.3	1.2/0.5
	--核磁共振成像装置:										
9018.1310	---成套装置〔999〕	1.6/0.8		17	13/	13	套/千克	6OA/	M	26.6	
9018.1390	---零件〔999〕	1.6/0.8		17	13/	13	个/千克	6/			
9018.1400	--闪烁摄影装置〔999〕	5		17	13/	13	台/千克	6A/	M	10	
	--其他:										
9018.1930	---病员监护仪										
9018.1930 10	病员监护仪(整机)〔999〕	0		17	13/	13	台/千克	6A/	M	25	0/0
9018.1930 90	病员监护仪的零件及附件〔999〕	0		17	13/	13	台/千克	6/		25	0/0
	---听力诊断装置:										
9018.1941	----听力计〔999〕	0		17	13/	13	台/千克	6A/	M	20	0/0
9018.1949	----其他〔999〕	0		17	13/	13	台/千克	6A/	M	10	0/0
9018.1990	---其他〔999〕	0		17	13/	13	台/千克	6A/	M	5	0/0
9018.2000	-紫外线及红外线装置〔101 诊断仪器及零部件,102 治疗仪器及零部件〕	0		17	13/	13	台/千克	6A/	M	10	
	-注射器、针、导管、插管及类似品:										
9018.3100	--注射器,不论是否装有针头[T2]	8		50	13/	13	个/千克	6A/	M	13	5.2/5.2
	--管状金属针头及缝合用针:										
9018.3210	---管状金属针头[T2]	8		50	13/	13	千克	6A/	M	33	5.2/5.2
9018.3220	---缝合用针〔999〕	4		17	13/	13	千克	6A/	M	9	2.6/2.6
9018.3900	--其他〔999〕	4		17	13/	13	个/千克	6A/	M	9	
	-牙科用其他仪器及器具:										
9018.4100	--牙钻机,不论是否与其他牙科设备组装在同一底座上〔999〕	4		17	13/	13	台/千克	6A/	M	29	
	--其他:										
9018.4910	---装有牙科设备的牙科用椅〔999〕	4		17	13/	13	台/千克	6A/	M	9	
9018.4990	---其他〔999〕	4		17	13/	13	台/千克	6A/	M	14	

协定税率 %								RCEP		特惠税率 %			Article Description
东/冰/格	巴基斯坦	韩国	瑞士上/下	哥/秘/柬	澳/毛	新西/坡/智	中国港/澳/台	东盟及马来/澳/韩	日/新	亚太2国	老/柬/缅	98/97/95	
0/0/0	0	1		0/0/0	0/0	0//0	0/0/	0/0/4.5	4.5/0			0/0/0	Air-borne or ship-borne gravity gradiometers (accuracy 1 milligamma or more better, duration of static recording≤2 min)
0/0/0	0	1		0/0/0	0/0	0//0	0/0/	0/0/4.5	4.5/0			0/0/0	Other instruments and appliances
													-Parts and accessories
0/0/0	0	1	0/0	0/0/0	0/0	0//0	0/0/	0/0/4.5	4.5/0			0/0/0	Parts and components of other geodetic measuring instruments and devices
0/0/0	0	1	0/0	0/0/0	0/0	0//0	0/0/	0/0/4.5	4.5/0			0/0/0	Other parts and accessoried of heading No.90.15
													Balances of a sensitivity of 50 mg or better, with or without weights:
0/0/0	2	1.8		0/0/0	0/0	0//0	0/0/	0/0/8.1	8.2/0			0/0/0	---Of a sensitivity of 0.1 mg or better
0/0/0	3.5	2.1	0/0	0/0/0	0/0	0/0/0	0/0/	0/0/9.5	9.5/0			0/0/0	---Other
													Drawing, marking-out or mathematical-calculating instruments (for example, drafting machines, pantographs, protractors, drawing sets, slide rules, disc calculators); instruments for measuring length, for use in the hand (for example, measuring rods and tapes, micrometers, callipers), not specified or included elsewhere in this Chapter:
0/0/0	2	1.6	0/0	0/0/0	0/0	0//0	0/0/	0/0/7.2	7.3/0			0/0/0	-Drafting tables and machines, whether or not automatic
0/0/0	0	0	0/0	0/0/0	0/0	0//0	0/0/	0/0/0	0/0			0/0/0	-Other drawing, marking-out or mathematical calculating instruments
0/0/0	4	1.6	0.8/0.8	0/0/0	0/0	0//0	0/0/	7.2/7.2/7.2	7.3/7.2			0/0/0	-Micrometers, callipers and gauges
0/0/0	2	0	0.8/0.8	0/0/0	0/0	0//0	0/0/	7.2/7.2/7.2	7.3/7.2			0/0/0	-Other instruments
0/0/0	0	0	0/0	0/0/0	0/0	0//0	0/0/	0/0/0	0/0			0/0/0	-Parts and accessories
													Instruments and appliances used in medical, surgical, dental or veterinary sciences, including scintigraphic apparatus, other electro-medical apparatus and sight-testing instruments:
													-Electro-diagnostic apparatus (including apparatus for functional exploratory examination or for checking physiological parameters):
0/0/0	0	0	0/0	0/0/0	0/0	0//0	0/0/	0/0/0	0/0			0/0/0	--Electro-cardiographs
													--Ultrasonic scanning apparatus:
0/0/0	0	3.2	0/0	0/0/0	0/0	0//0	0/0/	0/0/6.3	6.4/0			0/0/0	---B-ultrasonic diagnostic equipment
													---Other:
													----Chromoscope ultrasonic diagnostice-quipment
0/0/0	0	4.5	0/0	0/0/0	0/0	0//0	0/0/	0/0/4.5	4.5/0			0/0/0	Color ultrasonic diagnostic apparatus (machine)
0/0/0	0	4.5	0/0	0/0/0	0/0	0//0	0/0/	0/0/4.5	4.5/0			0/0/0	Parts and accessories of color ultrasonic diagnostic instrument
0/0/0	0	4.5	0/0	0/0/0	0/0	0//0	0/0/	0/0/4.5	4.5/0			0/0/0	----Other
													--Magnetic resonance imaging apparatus:
0/0/0	0	1.8	0/0	0/0/0	0/0	0//0	0/0/	0/0/3.6	3.6/0			0/0/0	---Complete equipments
0/0/0	0	1.8	0/0	0/0/0	0/0	0//0	0/0/	3.6/3.6/3.6	3.6/3.6			0/0/0	---Parts
0/0/0	0	2.3	0/0	0/0/0	0/0	0//0	0/0/	4.5/4.5/4.5	4.7/4.5			0/0/0	--Scintigraphic apparatus
													--Other:
													---Patient moniturs
0/0/0	0	0	0/0	0/0/0	0/0	0//0	0/0/	0/0/0	0/0			0/0/0	The patient monitor (machine)
0/0/0	0	0	0/0	0/0/0	0/0	0//0	0/0/	0/0/0	0/0			0/0/0	Parts and accessories of patient monitor
													---Hearing diagnostic apparatas:
0/0/0	0	0	0/0	0/0/0	0/0	0//0	0/0/	0/0/0	0/0			0/0/0	----Andiometer
0/0/0	0		0/0	0/0/0	0/0	0//0	0/0/	0/0/3.6	3.6/0			0/0/0	----Other
0/0/0	0	0	0/0	0/0/0	0/0	0//0	0/0/	0/3.6/0	0/3.6			0/0/0	---Other
0/0/0	0	0	0/0	0/0/0	0/0	0//0	0/0/	0/0/0	0/0			0/0/0	-Ultra-violet or infra-red ray apparatus
													-Syringes, needles, catheters, cannulae and the like:
0/0/0	0	1.6	0.8/0.8	0/0/0	0/0	0//0	0/0/	0/0/7.2	7.3/0			0/0/0	--Syringes, with or without needles
													--Tubular metal needles and needles for sutures:
0/0/0	0	1.6	0/0	0/0/0	0/0	0//0	0/0/	7.2/7.2/7.2	7.3/7.2			0/0/0	---Tubular metal needles
0/0/0	0	0	0/0	0/0/0	0/0	0//0	0/0/	0/0/0	0/0			0/0/0	---Needles for sutures
0/0/0	0	0	0.4/0.4	0/0/0	0/0	0//0	0/0/	0/0/0	3.8/0			0/0/0	--Other
													-Other instruments and appliances, used in dental sciences:
0/0/0	0	0	0/0	0/0/0	0/0	0//0	0/0/	0/0/0	0/0			0/0/0	--Dental drill engines, whether or not combined on a single base with other dental equipment
													--Other:
0/0/0	0	0.8	0.4/0.4	0/0/0	0/0	0//0	0/0/	0/0/3.6	3.6/0			0/0/0	---Dentists' chairs incorporating dental equipment
0/0/0	0	0	0.4/0.4	0/0/0	0/0	0//0	0/0/	0/0/0	3.6/0			0/0/0	---Other

税则号列		货品名称〔CIQ扩展编码及品名—T2表示见附表2〕	最惠(%)	暂定税率	普通	增值/消费	出口退税	计量单位	监管条件/特殊证件	检验检疫	对美关税	亚太上/下
9018.5000		-眼科用其他仪器及器具〔101诊断仪器及零部件,102治疗仪器及零部件〕	0		17	13/	13	千克	6A/	M	25	0/0
		-其他仪器及器具:										
9018.9010		---听诊器〔999〕	4		17	13/	13	个/千克	6/		9	2.6/2.6
9018.9020		---血压测量仪器及器具										
9018.9020	10	电血压测量仪器及器具〔999〕	0		17	13/	13	个/千克	6A/	M	20	2.6/2.6
9018.9020	20	含汞的非电子血压测量仪器及器具〔999〕	4		17	13/	13	个/千克	89/		24	2.6/2.6
9018.9020	90	其他血压测量仪器及器具〔999〕	4		17	13/	13	个/千克	6A/	M	24	2.6/2.6
9018.9030		---内窥镜										
9018.9030	10	内窥镜(整机)〔999〕	0		17	13/	13	台/千克	6A/	M	10	0/0
9018.9030	90	内窥镜的零件及附件〔999〕	0		17	13/	13	台/千克	6/			0/0
9018.9040		---肾脏透析设备(人工肾)〔999〕	0		17	13/	13	台/千克	6A/	M	5	0/0
9018.9050		---透热疗法设备〔999〕	0		17	13/	13	台/千克	6A/	M	5	0/0
9018.9060		---输血设备〔101一次性使用输血器,102血液透析、过滤设备,103一次性使用血路产品,104血泵,105其他输血设备〕	0		17	13/	13	台/千克	6A/	M	5	0/0
9018.9070		---麻醉设备										
9018.9070	10	电麻醉设备〔999〕	0		17	13/	13	台/千克	6A/	M	5	2.6/2.6
9018.9070	90	其他麻醉设备〔999〕	4		17	13/	13	台/千克	6A/	M	9	2.6/2.6
		---其他:										
9018.9091		----宫内节育器〔999〕	4		17	0/	0	个/千克	6A/	M	9	2/2
9018.9099		----其他										
9018.9099	11	电子的其他医疗、外科用仪器器具(整机)[T2]	0		17	13/	13	台/千克	6A/	M	25	2.6/2.6
9018.9099	12	医用可解脱弹簧圈(整机)〔999〕	4	1	17	13/	13	台/千克	6A/	M	26	2.6/2.6
9018.9099	13	颅内取栓支架(整机)〔999〕	4	2	17	13/	13	台/千克	6A/	M	27	2.6/2.6
9018.9099	19	其他医疗、外科或兽医用仪器器具(整机)[T2]	4		17	13/	13	台/千克	6A/	M	29	2.6/2.6
9018.9099	91	电子的其他医疗、外科用仪器器具的零件及附件[T2]	0		17	13/	13	台/千克	6A/	M	25	2.6/2.6
9018.9099	99	其他医疗、外科或兽医用仪器器具的零件及附件[T2]	4		17	13/	13	台/千克	6/		29	2.6/2.6
90.19		**机械疗法器具;按摩器具;心理功能测验装置;臭氧治疗器;氧气治疗器、喷雾治疗器、人工呼吸器及其他治疗用呼吸器具:**										
		-机械疗法器具;按摩器具;心理功能测验装置:										
9019.1010		---按摩器具[T2]	10		40	13/	13	台/千克	A/	M	35	
9019.1090		---其他[T2]	4		30	13/	13	台/千克	/		14	
		-臭氧治疗器、氧气治疗器、喷雾治疗器、人工呼吸器及其他治疗用呼吸器具:										
9019.2010		---有创呼吸机										
9019.2010	10	有创呼吸机(整机)((C))〔999〕	4		17	13/	13	台/千克	A/	M	14	
9019.2010	90	有创呼吸机的零件及附件((C))〔999〕	4		17	13/	13	台/千克	A/	M	14	
9019.2020		---无创呼吸机										
9019.2020	11	具有自动人机同步追踪功能或自动调节呼吸压力功能的无创呼吸机(整机)((P)(C))〔999〕	4		17	13/	13	台/千克	A/	M		
9019.2020	19	具有自动人机同步追踪功能或自动调节呼吸压力功能的无创呼吸机的零件及附件((P)(C))〔999〕	4		17	13/	13	台/千克	A/	M		
9019.2020	91	其他无创呼吸机(整机)((C))〔999〕	4		17	13/	13	台/千克	A/	M	14	
9019.2020	99	其他无创呼吸机的零件及附件((C))〔999〕	4		17	13/	13	台/千克	A/	M	14	
9019.2090		---其他〔999〕	4		17	13/	13	台/千克	A/	M	14	
90.20		**其他呼吸器具及防毒面具,但不包括既无机械零件又无可互换过滤器的防护面具:**										
9020.0000		其他呼吸器具及防毒面具(但不包括既无机械零件又无可互换过滤器的防护面具)〔999〕	8	4	30	13/	13	千克	/	L	9	
90.21		**矫形器具,包括支具、外科手术带、疝气带;夹板及其他骨折用具;人造的人体部分;助听器及为弥补生理缺陷或残疾而穿戴、携带或植入人体内的其他器具:**										
9021.1000		-矫形或骨折用器具										

协定税率 %								RCEP		特惠税率 %			Article Description
东/冰/格	巴基斯坦	韩国	瑞士上/下	哥/秘/柬	澳/毛	新西/坡/智	中国港/澳/台	东盟及马来/澳/韩	日/新	亚太2国	老/柬/缅	98/97/95	
0/0/0	0	2.6	0/0	0/0/0	0/0	0//0	0/0/	3.6/3.6/3.8	3.6/3.6			0/0/0	-Other ophthalmic instruments and appliances
													-Other instruments and appliances:
0/0/0	0	0	0/0	0/0/0	0/0	0//0	0/0/	0/0/0	0/0			0/0/0	---Stethoscopes
													---Sphygmomanometers and appliances
0/0/0	0	0	0/0	0/0/0	0/0	0//0	0/0/	0/0/0	0/0			0/0/0	Electronic Sphygmomanometers and appliances
0/0/0	0	0	0/0	0/0/0	0/0	0//0	0/0/	0/0/0	0/0		//	0/0/0	Non－electronic blood pressure measuring instruments and apparatus containing Mercury
0/0/0	0	0	0/0	0/0/0	0/0	0//0	0/0/	0/0/0	0/0			0/0/0	Other Sphygmomanometers and appliances
													---Endoscopes
0/0/0	0	0	0/0	0/0/0	0/0	0//0	0/0/	0/3.6/0	0/3.6			0/0/0	Endoscope (machine)
0/0/0	0	0	0/0	0/0/0	0/0	0//0	0/0/	0/3.6/0	0/3.6			0/0/0	Parts and accessories of endoscope mirror
0/0/0	0	0	0/0	0/0/0	0/0	0//0	0/0/	0/3.6/0	0/3.6			0/0/0	---Artificial kidney (dialysis) apparatus
0/0/0	0	0	0/0	0/0/0	0/0	0//0	0/0/	0/0/0	0/0			0/0/0	---Diathermy apparatus
0/0/0	0	0	0/0	0/0/0	0/0	0//0	0/0/	0/0/0	3.6/0			0/0/0	---Blood transfusion apparatus
													---Anaesthetic apparatus and instruments
0/0/0	0	0	0/0	0/0/0	0/0	0//0	0/0/	0/0/0	0/0			0/0/0	Electronic anaesthetic apparatus and instruments
0/0/0	0	0	0/0	0/0/0	0/0	0//0	0/0/	0/0/0	0/0			0/0/0	Other anaesthetic apparatus and instruments
													---Other:
0/0/0	0	0	0/0	0/0/0	0/0	0//0	0/0/	0/0/0	0/0			0/0/0	----Intrauterine device
													----Other
0/0/0	0	0	0.4/0.4	0/0/0	0/0	0//0	0/0/	0/0/0	3.6/0			0/0/0	Other medical and surgical instruments for electronic surgery (whole machine)
0/0/0	0	0	0.4/0.4	0/0/0	0/0	0//0	0/0/	0/0/0	3.6/0		//	0/0/0	Medical detachable spring coil(whole machine)
0/0/0	0	0	0.4/0.4	0/0/0	0/0	0//0	0/0/	0/0/0	3.6/0			0/0/0	Intracranial thrombectomy support (complete machine)
0/0/0	0	0	0.4/0.4	0/0/0	0/0	0//0	0/0/	0/0/0	3.6/0			0/0/0	Other instruments for medical, surgical, or veterinary medicine (whole machine)
0/0/0	0	0	0.4/0.4	0/0/0	0/0	0//0	0/0/	0/0/0	3.6/0			0/0/0	Parts and accessories of the other medical and surgical instruments of the electronics
0/0/0	0	0	0.4/0.4	0/0/0	0/0	0//0	0/0/	0/0/0	3.6/0			0/0/0	Other parts and accessories for medical, surgical or veterinary instruments
													Mechano-therapy appliances; massage apparatus; psychological aptitude-testing apparatus; ozone therapy, oxygen therapy, aerosol therapy, artificial respiration or other therapeutic respiration apparatus:
													-Mechano-therapy appliances; massage apparatus; psychological aptitude-testing apparatus:
0/0/0	8.4	3	1.5/1.5	0/0/0	0/0	0/0/0	0/0/	13.5/13.5/13.5	13.6/13.5			0/0/0	---Massage apparatus
0/0/0	0	0	0.4/0.4	0/0/0	0/0	0//0	0/0/	0/0/0	3.6/0			0/0/0	---Other
													- ozone therapyapparatus, oxygentherapy apparatus, spray therapyapparatus, artificialrespirator and othertherapeutic breathingapparatus:
													---Invasive ventilator
0/0/0	0	1.8	0.4/0.4	0/0/0	0/0	0//0	0/0/	3.6/3.6/3.6	3.8/3.6			0/0/0	Invasive ventilator (complete) ((c))
0/0/0	0	1.8	0.4/0.4	0/0/0	0/0	0//0	0/0/	3.6/3.6/3.6	3.8/3.6			0/0/0	Parts and accessories of invasive ventilator ((c))
													---Noninvasive ventilator
0/0/0	0	1.8	0.4/0.4	0/0/0	0/0	0//0	0/0/	3.6/3.6/3.6	3.8/3.6			0/0/0	Noninvasive ventilator with automatic man－machine synchronous tracking function or automatic adjustment of respiratory pressure (complete) ((P) (c))
0/0/0	0	1.8	0.4/0.4	0/0/0	0/0	0//0	0/0/	3.6/3.6/3.6	3.8/3.6			0/0/0	Parts and accessories of noninvasive ventilator with automatic man－machine synchronous tracking function or automatic adjustment of respiratory pressure ((P) (c))
0/0/0	0	1.8	0.4/0.4	0/0/0	0/0	0//0	0/0/	3.6/3.6/3.6	3.8/3.6			0/0/0	Other non－invasive respirators (complete) (c))
0/0/0	0	1.8	0.4/0.4	0/0/0	0/0	0//0	0/0/	3.6/3.6/3.6	3.8/3.6			0/0/0	Parts and accessories of other non－invasive respirators ((c))
0/0/0	0	1.8	0.4/0.4	0/0/0	0/0	0//0	0/0/	3.6/3.6/3.6	3.8/3.6			0/0/0	---Other
													Other breathing appliances and gas masks, excluding protective masks having neither mechanical parts nor replaceable filters:
0/0/0	2	1.6	0/0	0/0/0	0/0	0//0	0/0/	0/0/7.2	7.3/0			0/0/0	Other breathing appliances and gas masks, excluding protective masks having neither mechanical parts nor replaceable filters
													Orthopaedic appliances, including crutches, surgical belts and trusses; splints and other fracture appliances; artificial parts of the body; hearing aids and other appliances which are worn or carried, or implanted in the body, to compensate for a defect or disability:
													-Orthopaedic or fracture appliances

税则号列	货品名称〔CIQ扩展编码及品名－T2表示见附表2〕	最惠(%)	暂定税率	普通	增值/消费	出口退税	计量单位	监管条件/特殊证件	检验检疫	对美关税	亚太上/下
9021.1000 10	钢铁制自攻螺钉(不包括不锈钢紧固件),矫形或骨折用((F))〔999〕	4		57	13/	13	千克	/		9	
9021.1000 20	抗拉强度≥800兆帕,杆径>6mm的其他钢铁制螺钉及螺栓(不包括不锈钢紧固件),矫形或骨折用(不论是否带有螺母或垫圈,不包括方头螺钉、钩头螺钉、环头螺钉(F))〔999〕	4		57	13/	13	千克	/			
9021.1000 30	杆径>6mm的其他钢铁制螺钉及螺栓(不包括不锈钢紧固件),矫形或骨折用(不论是否带有螺母或垫圈(F))〔101 螺钉,102 螺栓〕	4		57	13/	13	千克	/		9	
9021.1000 40	钢铁制垫圈(不包括不锈钢紧固件),矫形或骨折用(不包括弹簧垫圈及其他防松垫圈(F))〔999〕	4		57	13/	13	千克	/		9	
9021.1000 50	矫形或骨折用钛管〔999〕	4		57	13/	13	千克	/			
9021.1000 90	其他矫形或骨折用器具(但不包括人造关节)〔101 人体接触的进入式医疗器具,102 与人体接触的非进入式医疗器具〕	4		57	13/	13	千克	/		9	
	-假牙及牙齿固定件:										
9021.2100	--假牙〔999〕	4		17	13/	13	千克	/		9	
9021.2900	--其他										
9021.2900 10	钢铁制自攻螺钉(不包括不锈钢紧固件),牙齿固定用((F))〔999〕	4	2	57	13/	13	千克	/			
9021.2900 20	抗拉强度≥800兆帕,杆径>6mm的其他钢铁制螺钉及螺栓(不包括不锈钢紧固件),牙齿固定用(不论是否带有螺母或垫圈,不包括方头螺钉、钩头螺钉、环头螺钉(F))〔999〕	4	2	57	13/	13	千克	/			
9021.2900 30	杆径>6mm的其他钢铁制螺钉及螺栓(不包括不锈钢紧固件),牙齿固定用(不论是否带有螺母或垫圈(F))〔101 螺钉,102 螺栓〕	4	2	57	13/	13	千克	/			
9021.2900 40	钢铁制垫圈(不包括不锈钢紧固件),牙齿固定用(不包括弹簧垫圈及其他防松垫圈(F))〔999〕	4	2	57	13/	13	千克	/			
9021.2900 90	其他牙齿固定件〔999〕	4	2	57	13/	13	千克	/			
	-其他人造的人体部分:										
9021.3100	--人造关节〔999〕	4	2	17	13/	13	千克/套	/			
9021.3900	--其他										
9021.3900 10	人工心脏瓣膜〔999〕	4	1	17	13/	13	千克	/			
9021.3900 90	其他人造的人体部分〔999〕	4		17	13/	13	千克	/			
9021.4000	-助听器,不包括零件、附件〔999〕	4	1	17	13/	13	个/千克	/			
9021.5000	-心脏起搏器,不包括零件、附件〔999〕	0		17	13/	13	个/千克	A/	M		0/0
	-其他:										
	---支架:										
9021.9011	----血管支架〔999〕	0		17	13/	13	千克/个	/			
9021.9019	----其他〔999〕	0		17	13/	13	千克/个	/			
9021.9090	---其他										
9021.9090 10	人工耳蜗植入装置〔999〕	0		17	13/	13	千克	/			
9021.9090 90	其他弥补生理缺陷、残疾用器具等(包括穿戴、携带或植入人体内的器具及零件)〔101 与人体接触的进入式医疗器具,102 与人体接触的非进入式医疗器具,103 其他医疗器具〕	0		17	13/	13	千克	/			
90.22	**X射线或α射线、β射线、γ射线或其他离子射线的应用设备,不论是否用于医疗、外科、牙科或兽医,包括射线照相及射线治疗设备,X射线管及其他X射线发生器、高压发生器、控制板及控制台、荧光屏、检查或治疗用的桌、椅及类似品:**										
	-X射线的应用设备,不论是否用于医疗、外科、牙科或兽医,包括射线照相或射线治疗设备:										
9022.1200	--X射线断层检查仪[T2]	1.3/0.7		11	13/	13	台/千克	6OA/	M	6.3	0.9/0.5
9022.1300	--其他,牙科用〔999〕	0		11	13/	13	台/千克	6OA/	M	20	
9022.1400	--其他,医疗、外科或兽医用										
9022.1400 10	医用直线加速器〔999〕	0		11	13/	13	台/千克	6OA/	M		
9022.1400 90	其他医疗或兽医用X射线应用设备〔999〕	0		11	13/	13	台/千克	6OA/	M	25	
	--其他:										
9022.1910	---低剂量X射线安全检查设备										

协定税率 %								RCEP		特惠税率 %			Article Description
东/冰/格	巴基斯坦	韩国	瑞士上/下	哥/秘/柬	澳/毛	新西/坡/智	中国港/澳/台	东盟及马来/澳/韩	日/新	亚太2国	老/柬/缅	98/97/95	
0/0/0	0	1.8	1.7/1.7	0/0/0	0/0	0/0/0	0/0/	0/0/0	0/0			0/0/0	Self tapping screws of iron and steel (excl. stainless steel fasteners), for orthopedics or fractures ((f))
0/0/0	0	1.8	1.7/1.7	0/0/0	0/0	0/0/0	0/0/	0/0/0	0/0			0/0/0	Other steel screws and bolts (excluding stainless steel fasteners) with tensile strength ⩾ 8 MPa and rod diameter > 6mm, for orthopedic or fracture (whether with or without nuts or washers, excluding square head screws, hook head screws and ring head screws (f))
0/0/0	0	1.8	1.7/1.7	0/0/0	0/0	0/0/0	0/0/	0/0/0	0/0			0/0/0	Other screws and bolts of iron and steel with rod diameter > 6mm (excluding stainless steel fasteners), for orthopedic or fracture (whether with nut or washer (f))
0/0/0	0	1.8	1.7/1.7	0/0/0	0/0	0/0/0	0/0/	0/0/0	0/0			0/0/0	Washers of iron and steel (excl. stainless steel fasteners), for orthopedics or fractures (excl. spring washers and other lock washers (f))
0/0/0	0	1.8	1.7/1.7	0/0/0	0/0	0/0/0	0/0/	0/0/0	0/0			0/0/0	Titanium tube for orthopedic or fracture
0/0/0	0	1.8	1.7/1.7	0/0/0	0/0	0/0/0	0/0/	0/0/0	0/0			0/0/0	Other orthopedic or fracture appliances (excluding artificial joints)
													-Artificial teeth and dental fittings:
0/0/0	0	0	0/0	0/0/0	0/0	0//0	0/0/	0/0/0	0/0			0/0/0	--Artificial teeth
													--Other
0/0/0	0	0	0.4/0.4	0/0/0	0/0	0/0/0	0/0/	0/0/0	0/0			0/0/0	Self tapping screws of iron and steel (excl. stainless steel fasteners), for tooth fixation ((f))
0/0/0	0	0	0.4/0.4	0/0/0	0/0	0/0/0	0/0/	0/0/0	0/0			0/0/0	Other steel screws and bolts (excluding stainless steel fasteners) with tensile strength ⩾ 8 MPa and rod diameter > 6mm for tooth fixation (whether with nuts or washers, excluding square head screws, hook head screws and ring head screws (f))
0/0/0	0	0	0.4/0.4	0/0/0	0/0	0/0/0	0/0/	0/0/0	0/0			0/0/0	Other steel screws and bolts (excluding stainless steel fasteners) with rod diameter > 6mm for tooth fixation (whether with nut or washer (f))
0/0/0	0	0	0.4/0.4	0/0/0	0/0	0/0/0	0/0/	0/0/0	0/0			0/0/0	Steel washers (excluding stainless steel fasteners), for tooth fixation (excluding spring washers and other lock washers (f))
0/0/0	0	0	0.4/0.4	0/0/0	0/0	0/0/0	0/0/	0/0/0	0/0			0/0/0	Other tooth fixings
													-Other artificial parts of the body:
0/0/0	0	0	0.4/0.4	0/0/0	0/0	0//0	0/0/0	0/0/0	3.6/0			0/0/0	--Artificial joints
													--Other
0/0/0	0	0.8	0/0	0/0/0	0/0	0//0	0/0/	3.6/3.6/3.6	3.6/3.6		//	0/0/0	Artificial heart valve
0/0/0	0	0.8	0/0	0/0/0	0/0	0//0	0/0/	3.6/3.6/3.6	3.6/3.6		//	0/0/0	Other artificial parts of the body
0/0/0	0	0	0.4/0.4	0/0/0	0/0	0//0	0/0/	0/0/0	3.6/0			0/0/0	-Hearing aids, excluding parts and accessories
0/0/0	0	0	0/0	0/0/0	0/0	0//0	0/0/	0/0/0	3.6/0			0/0/0	-Pacemakers for stimulating heart muscles, excluding parts and accessories
													-Other:
													---Stents:
0/0/0	0	0	0/0	0/0/0	0/0	0//0	0/0/	0/0/0	3.6/0			0/0/0	----Intravascular stents
0/0/0	0	0.8	0/0	0/0/0	0/0	0//0	0/0/	0/0/3.6	3.6/0			0/0/0	----Other
													---Other
0/0/0	0	0	0/0	0/0/0	0/0	0//0	0/0/	3.6/3.6/3.6	3.6/3.6			0/0/0	Cochlear implant devices
0/0/0	0	0	0/0	0/0/0	0/0	0//0	0/0/	3.6/3.6/3.6	3.6/3.6			0/0/0	Other appliances to compensate for a defect or disability (including appliances and parts which are worn or carried, or implanted in the body)
													Apparatus based on the use of X-rays or of alpha, beta, gamma or other ionising. radiations, whether or not for medical, surgical, dental or veterinary uses, including radiography or radiotherapy apparatus, X-ray tubes and other X-ray generators, high tension generators, control panels and desks, screens, examination or treatment tables, chairs and the like:
													-Apparatus based on the use of X-rays, whether or not for medical, surgical, dental or veterinary uses, including radiography or radiotherapy apparatus:
0/0/0	0	1.8	0/0	0/0/0	0/0	0//0	0/0/	0/0/3.6	3.6/0			0/0/0	--Computed tomography apparatus
0/0/0	0	0	0/0	0/0/0	0/0	0//0	0/0/	0/0/0	0/0			0/0/0	--Other, for dental uses
													--Other, for medical, surgical or veterinary uses
0/0/0	0	0	0/0	0/0/0	0/0	0//0	0/0/	0/3.6/0	0/3.6			0/0/0	Linear accelerators for medical use
0/0/0	0	0	0/0	0/0/0	0/0	0//0	0/0/	0/3.6/0	0/3.6			0/0/0	Other apparatus based on the use of X-rays, for medical or veterinary uses
													--For other uses:
													---Low dosage X-ray security inspecting equipment

税则号列	货品名称〔CIQ扩展编码及品名—T2表示见附表2〕	最惠(%)	暂定税率	普通	增值/消费	出口退税	计量单位	监管条件/特殊证件	检验检疫	对美关税	亚太上/下
9022.1910 10	采用X光机技术或X射线加速器技术的X射线安全检查设备(能量大于100千电子伏,不包括采用X射线交替双能加速器技术的第二代X射线安全检查设备)〔999〕	0		11	13/	13	台/千克	A/	M	5	
9022.1910 90	其他低剂量X射线安全检查设备〔999〕	0		11	13/	13	台/千克	A/	M	5	
9022.1920	---X射线无损探伤检测仪〔999〕	0		11	13/	13	台/千克	A/	M	20	
9022.1990	---其他										
9022.1990 10	X射线全自动燃料芯块检查台(专门设计或制造用于检验燃料芯块的最终尺寸和表面缺陷)〔999〕	0		11	13/	13	台/千克	3A/	M		
9022.1990 20	X射线晶圆制造厚度测量设备	0		11	13/	13	台/千克	A/	M		
9022.1990 90	其他X射线应用设备〔999〕	0		11	13/	13	台/千克	6A/	M		
	-α射线、β射线、γ射线或其他离子射线应用设备,不论是否用于医疗、外科、牙科或兽医,包括射线照相或射线治疗设备:										
	--医疗、外科、牙科或兽医用:										
9022.2110	---应用α射线、β射线、γ射线的(9022.2100)〔101 诊断仪器及零部件,102 治疗仪器及零部件〕	0		11	13/	13	台/千克	6A/	M	10	
9022.2190	---其他〔101 诊断仪器及零部件,102 治疗仪器及零部件〕	4		17	13/	13	台/千克	6A/	M	29	2.6/2.6
	--其他:										
9022.2910	---γ射线无损探伤检测仪〔999〕	0		11	13/	13	台/千克	A/	M		
9022.2990	---其他										
9022.2990 10	γ射线全自动燃料芯块检查台(专门设计或制造用于检验燃料芯块的最终尺寸和表面缺陷)〔999〕	0		11	13/	13	台/千克	3A/	M	5	
9022.2990 90	其他非医疗用α、β、γ射线设备〔999〕	0		11	13/	13	台/千克	/		5	
9022.3000	-X射线管〔999〕	0		11	13/	13	个/千克	A/	M		
	-其他,包括零件、附件:										
9022.9010	---X射线影像增强器〔999〕	0		11	13/	13	个/千克	AO/	M		
9022.9090	---其他										
9022.9090 20	闪光X射线发生器(峰值能量≥500千电子伏)〔999〕	4.5		14	13/	13	个/千克	3O/		29.5	
9022.9090 30	X射线断层检查仪专用探测器〔999〕	4.5	3	14	13/	13	个/千克	O/		28	
9022.9090 40	数字化X射线摄影系统平板探测器〔999〕	4.5	3	14	13/	13	个/千克	/		28	
9022.9090 50	应用除α、β、γ射线以外离子射线的医用设备的零件及附件(医疗、外科、牙科或兽医用)〔101 诊断仪器及零部件,102 治疗仪器及零部件〕	0		14	13/	13	台/千克	6A/	M	25	
9022.9090 60	其他射线发生器的零部件〔999〕	4.5	1	14	13/	13	个/千克	/		26	
9022.9090 70	X射线断层检查仪专用闪烁体、准直器〔999〕	4.5	3	14	13/	13	个/千克	/		28	
9022.9090 90	税目90.22所列其他设备及零件(包括高压发生器、控制板及控制台、荧光屏等)〔999〕	4.5		14	13/	13	个/千克	/		29.5	
90.23	**专供示范(例如,教学或展览)而无其他用途的仪器、装置及模型:**										
9023.0010	---教习头〔999〕	0		20	13/	13	千克	/		25	
9023.0090	---其他〔999〕	0		20	13/	13	千克	/		5	
90.24	**各种材料(例如,金属、木材、纺织材料、纸张、塑料)的硬度、强度、压缩性、弹性或其他机械性能的试验机器及器具:**										
	-金属材料的试验用机器及器具:										
9024.1010	---电子万能试验机〔999〕	0		20	13/	13	台/千克	/		10	0/0
9024.1020	---硬度计〔999〕	0		20	13/	13	台/千克	/		10	0/0
9024.1090	---其他〔999〕	0		20	13/	13	台/千克	/		5	0/0
9024.8000	-其他机器及器具〔999〕	1.3/0.6		20	13/	13	台/千克	/		6.3	
9024.9000	-零件、附件〔999〕	0		20	13/	13	千克	/		5	
90.25	**记录式或非记录式的液体比重计及类似的浮子式仪器、温度计、高温计、气压计、湿度计、干湿球湿度计及其组合装置:**										
	-温度计及高温计,未与其他仪器组合:										
9025.1100	--液体温度计,可直接读数										
9025.1100 10	含汞的可直接读数的非电子液体温度计〔999〕	4		40	13/	13	个/千克	89/		24	
9025.1100 90	其他可直接读数的液体温度计〔999〕	4		40	13/	13	个/千克	/		24	
	--其他:										
9025.1910	---工业用	2.8/1.4		20	13/	13	个/千克			/12.8,11.4	1.8/0.9
9025.1910 10	温度传感器〔101:电子温度计;102:温度计〕	0		20	13/	13	个/千克	/			0/0

协定税率 %								RCEP		特惠税率 %			Article Description
东/冰/格	巴基斯坦	韩国	瑞士上/下	哥/秘/柬	澳/毛	新西/坡/智	中国港/澳/台	东盟及马来/澳/韩	日/新	亚太2国	老/柬/缅	98/97/95	
0/0/0	0	1.8	0/0	0/0/0	0/0	0//0	0/0/	0/0/3.6	3.6/0			0/0/0	x-ray security inspection equipments adopting the technology of x-ray apparatuses or x-ray accelerat- ors (with energy higher than 100 kilo electron volt, excluding the second generation security inspection equipments adopting the technology of alternating dual-energy x-ray accelerators)
0/0/0	0	1.8	0/0	0/0/0	0/0	0//0	0/0/	0/0/3.6	3.6/0			0/0/0	Other low dosage X-ray security inspecting equipment
0/0/0	0		0/0	0/0/0	0/0	0//0	0/0/	0/0/3.6	3.6/0			0/0/0	---X-ray non-destructive testing appliances
													---Other
0/0/0	0		0/0	0/0/0	0/0	0//0	0/0/	0/0/3.6	3.6/0			0/0/0	X-ray fully-automatic fuel core exouiwins table(Specially designed or made to inspect final dimensions and superficial defects of fuel core)
0/0/0	0		0/0	0/0/0	0/0	0//0	0/0/	0/0/3.6	3.6/0		//	0/0/0	X—ray wafer thickness measuring equipment
0/0/0	0		0/0	0/0/0	0/0	0//0	0/0/	0/0/3.6	3.6/0			0/0/0	Other apparatus based on the use of X-rays
													-Apparatus based on the use of alpha, beta, gamma inoising or other radiations, whether or not for medical, surgical, dental or veterinary uses, including radiography or radiothe rapy apparatus:
													--For medical, surgical, dental or veterinary uese
0/0/0	0	0	0/0	0/0/0	0/0	0//0	0/0/	0/0/0	0/0			0/0/0	---application α Ray、β Ray、γ radial
0/0/0	0	0	0.4/0.4	0/0/0	0/0	0//0	0/0/	0/0/0	3.6/0			0/0/0	---Other,
													--Other,
0/0/0	4	0	0/0	0/0/0	0/0	0//0	0/0/	0/0/0	0/0			0/0/0	---γ-Ray non-destructivetesting appliances
													---Other
0/0/0	4	0	0/0	0/0/0	0/0	0//0	0/0/	0/0/0	0/0			0/0/0	γ-Ray fully-autornatic fuel core examiwins table(specially designed or made to inspect final dimensions and superficial defects of fuel core)
0/0/0	4	0	0/0	0/0/0	0/0	0//0	0/0/	0/0/0	0/0			0/0/0	Other α-rays、β-rays、γ-rays, not for medical uses
0/0/0	0	0.4	0/0	0/0/0	0/0	0//0	0/0/	1.8/1.8/1.8	1.8/1.8			0/0/0	-X-ray tubes
													-Other, including parts and accessories:
0/0/0	0	2.8	0/0	0/0/0	0/0	0//0	0/0/	0/5.4/5.4	0/5.4			0/0/0	---X-ray intensifiers
													---Other
0/0/0	0	1.4	0.5/0.5	0/0/0	0/0	0//0	0/0/	0/0/0	3.6/0			0/0/0	Flash X-ray generators (peak value power≥500keV)
0/0/0	0	1.4	0.5/0.5	0/0/0	0/0	0//0	0/0/	0/0/0	3.6/0			0/0/0	Detectors specified for X-ray tomography instruments
0/0/0	0	1.4	0.5/0.5	0/0/0	0/0	0//0	0/0/	0/0/0	3.6/0			0/0/0	Digital X ray photogrammetry system plate detector
0/0/0	0	1.4	0.5/0.5	0/0/0	0/0	0//0	0/0/	0/0/0	3.6/0			0/0/0	Application Division α、β、γ Parts and accessories of medical equipment other than ion rays (medical, surgical, dental or veterinary)
0/0/0	0	1.4	0.5/0.5	0/0/0	0/0	0//0	0/0/	0/0/0	3.6/0			0/0/0	Parts of other ray generators
0/0/0	0	1.4	0.5/0.5	0/0/0	0/0	0//0	0/0/	0/0/0	3.6/0			0/0/0	Special scintillator and collimator for X—ray tomography
0/0/0	0	1.4	0.5/0.5	0/0/0	0/0	0//0	0/0/	0/0/0	3.6/0			0/0/0	Other apparatus and its parts of heading 90.22, (including high voltage generators, control panels and console, screens)
													Instruments, apparatus and models, designed for demonstrational purposes (for example, in education or exhibitions), unsuitable for other uses:
0/0/0	4	0	0/0	0/0/0	0/0	0//0	0/0/	0/6.3/0	0/6.3			0/0/0	---Training mannequin
0/0/0	4	0	0/0	0/0/0	0/3.2	0//0	0/0/	0/6.3/0	0/6.3			0/0/0	---Other
													Machines and appliances for testing the hardness, strength, compressibility, elasticity or other mechanical properties of materials (for example, metals, wood, textiles, paper, plastics):
													-Machines and appliances for testing metals:
0/0/0	2	1.4	0/0	0/0/0	0/0	0//0	0/0/	0/0/6.3	6.4/0			0/0/0	---Electric multitesting machines
0/0/0	2	1.4	0/0	0/0/0	0/0	0//0	0/0/	0/0/6.3	6.4/0			0/0/0	---Machiness and applinances for testing hardness
0/0/0	4	4.5	0/0	0/0/0	0/0	0//0	0/0/	6.3/6.3/6.7	6.4/6.3			0/0/0	---Other
0/0/0	0	2.3	0/0	0/0/0	0/0	0//0	0/0/	4.5/4.5/4.5	4.5/4.5			0/0/0	-Other machines and appliances
0/0/0	0		0/0	0/0/0	0/0	0//0	0/0/	0/0/5.4	5.5/0			0/0/0	-Parts and accessories
													Hydrometers and similar floating instruments, thermometers and pyrometers, barometers, hygrometers and psychrometers, recording or not, and any combination of these instruments:
													-Thermometers and pyrometers, not combined with other instruments:
													--Liquid-filled, for direct reading
0/0/0	0	0	0/0	0/0/0	0/0	0//0	0/0/	0/0/0	0/0		//	0/0/0	Direct reading non—electronic liquid thermometers containing mercury
0/0/0	0	0	0/0	0/0/0	0/0	0//0	0/0/	0/0/0	0/0		//	0/0/0	Other liquid thermometers with direct reading
													--Other:
0/0/0	4	0	0	0	0	0	0//0	0/0/				0/0/0	---For technical use
0/0/0	2	0	0/0	0/0/0	0/0	0//0	0/0/	7.6/7.6/7.6	7.6/7.6		//	0/0/0	Temperature sensor

税则号列	货品名称〔CIQ 扩展编码及品名—T2 表示见附表 2〕	最惠(%)	暂定税率	普通	增值/消费	出口退税	计量单位	监管条件/特殊证件	检验检疫	对美关税	亚太上/下
9025.1910 20	其他含汞的非液体的工业用非电子温度计及高温计〔999〕	0		20	13/	13	个/千克	89/		10	0/0
9025.1910 90	其他非液体的工业用温度计及高温计〔101:电子温度计;102:温度计〕	0		20	13/	13	个/千克	/		10	0/0
9025.1990	---其他										
9025.1990 10	红外线人体测温仪〔999〕	0		80	13/	13	个/千克	/		10	0/0
9025.1990 20	其他含汞的非液体的非电子温度计及高温计〔999〕	0		80	13/	13	个/千克	89/		10	0/0
9025.1990 90	非液体的其他温度计,高温计〔101 电子温度计,102 温度计〕	0		80	13/	13	个/千克	/		10	0/0
9025.8000	-其他仪器										
9025.8000 10	含汞的非电子温度计和气压计〔999〕	11		30	13/	13	个/千克	89/		31	
9025.8000 90	其他温度计,比重计,湿度计等仪器〔101 温度计,102 比重计,103 湿度计,104 其他机械式仪表及其零件〕	11		30	13/	13	个/千克	/		31	
9025.9000	-零件、附件										
9025.9000 10	红外线测温仪传感器元件〔999〕	0		20	13/	13	千克/个	/		10	0/0
9025.9000 90	其他比重计、温度计等类似仪器的零件〔101 温度计零件,102 比重计零件,103 其他机械式仪表及其零件〕	0		20	13/	13	千克/个	/		10	0/0
90.26	**液体或气体的流量、液位、压力或其他变化量的测量或检验仪器及装置(例如,流量计、液位计、压力表、热量计),但不包括税目 90.14、90.15、90.28 或 90.32 的仪器及装置:**										
9026.1000	-测量、检验液体流量或液位的仪器及装置〔101 电子分析仪(电子测量仪),102 机械测量仪〕	0		17	13/	13	个/千克	/		10	
	-测量、检验压力的仪器及装置:										
9026.2010	---压力/差压变送器										
9026.2010 10	锰铜压力计(压力超过 10GPa)〔999〕	0		17	13/	13	个/千克	3/		10	
9026.2010 20	镱制成的压力计,流体动力学实验专用仪器仪表,测量压力超过 10GPa 的〔101 电子分析仪,102 机械分析仪〕	0		17	13/	13	个/千克	3/		10	
9026.2010 30	聚偏二氟乙烯/聚二氟乙烯制成的压力计(流体动力学实验专用仪器仪表,测量压力超过 10GPa 的)〔101 电子分析仪,102 机械分析仪〕	0		17	13/	13	个/千克	3/		10	
9026.2010 90	其他压力,差压变送器〔101 电子分析仪,102 机械分析仪〕	0		17	13/	13	个/千克	/		10	
9026.2090	---其他										
9026.2090 10	压力传感器(两用物项管制商品)〔101 电子分析仪,102 机械分析仪〕	0		17	13/	13	个/千克	3/		10	
9026.2090 20	含汞的非电子压力表〔999〕	0		17	13/	13	个/千克	89/		10	
9026.2090 90	其他测量、检验压力的仪器及装置〔101 电子测量仪(电子分析仪),102 机械测量仪(机械分析仪)〕	0		17	13/	13	个/千克	/		10	
	-其他仪器及装置:										
9026.8010	---测量气体流量的仪器及装置〔101 电子测量仪(电子分析仪),102 机械测量仪(机械分析仪)〕	0		17	13/	13	个/千克	/		10	
9026.8090	---其他〔101 电子分析仪,102 机械分析仪〕	0		17	13/	13	个/千克	/		10	
9026.9000	-零件、附件	0		17	13/	13	千克			/10	
9026.9000 10	液位仪用探棒〔101:电子分析仪;102:机械分析仪〕	0		17	13/	13	千克	/			
9026.9000 90	其他液体或气体的测量或检验仪器零件(主要是进行流量、液位、压力或其他变化量的测量或检验)〔101:电子分析仪;102:机械分析仪〕	0		17	13/	13	千克	/		10	
90.27	**理化分析仪器及装置(例如,偏振仪、折光仪、分光仪、气体或烟雾分析仪);测量或检验黏性、多孔性、膨胀性、表面张力及类似性能的仪器及装置;测量或检验热量、声量或光量的仪器及装置(包括曝光表);检镜切片机:**										
9027.1000	-气体或烟雾分析仪										
9027.1000 10	用于连续操作的气体检测器[可用于出口管制的化学品或有机化合物(含有磷、硫、氟或氯,其浓度低于 0.3mg/m³)的检测,或为检测受抑制的胆碱酯酶的活性而设计]〔101 电子分析仪,102 机械分析仪〕	1.8/0.9		17	13/	13	台/千克	3/			
9027.1000 90	其他气体或烟雾分析仪〔101 电子分析仪,102 机械分析仪〕	1.8/0.9		17	13/	13	台/千克	/		6.8	
	-色谱仪及电泳仪:										
	---色谱仪:										
9027.2011	----气相色谱仪〔999〕	0		17	13/	13	台/千克	/		5	
9027.2012	----液相色谱仪〔999〕	0		17	13/	13	台/千克	/		5	
9027.2019	----其他〔999〕	0		17	13/	13	台/千克	/		5	

协定税率 %								RCEP		特惠税率 %			Article Description
东/冰/格	巴基斯坦	韩国	瑞士上/下	哥/秘/柬	澳/毛	新西/坡/智	中国港/澳/台	东盟及马来/澳/韩	日/新	亚太2国	老/柬/缅	98/97/95	
0/0/0	2	0	0/0	0/0/0	0/0	0//0	0/0/	7.6/7.6/7.6	7.6/7.6		//	0/0/0	Other non—liquid industrial non electronic thermometers and pyrometers containing mercury
0/0/0	2	0	0/0	0/0/0	0/0	0//0	0/0/	7.6/7.6/7.6	7.6/7.6		//	0/0/0	Other non liquid industrial thermometers and pyrometers
													---Other
0/0/0	2	0	0/0	0/0/0	0/0	0//0	0/0/	0/0/0	7.6/0			0/0/0	Infrared body thermometer
0/0/0	2	0	0/0	0/0/0	0/0	0//0	0/0/	0/0/0	7.6/0		//	0/0/0	Other non—liquid non electronic thermometers and pyrometers containing mercury
0/0/0	2	0	0/0	0/0/0	0/0	0//0	0/0/	0/0/0	7.6/0			0/0/0	Other thermometers and pyrometers, non-liquid
													-Other instruments
0/0/0	3.5	6.6	1.1/1.1	0/0/0	0/0	0/0/0	0/0/	10.5/10.5/	/10.5		//	0/0/0	Non — electronic thermometers and barometers containing mercury
0/0/0	3.5	6.6	1.1/1.1	0/0/0	0/0	0/0/0	0/0/	10.5/10.5/	/10.5		//	0/0/0	Other thermometers, hydrometers, hygrometers, etc
													-Parts and accessories
0/0/0	2	0	0/0	0/0/0	0/4.8	0//0	0/0/	7.2/7.2/7.2	7.3/7.2			0/0/0	Sensor capacitor element of infrared thermo-meter
0/0/0	2	0	0/0	0/0/0	0/4.8	0//0	0/0/	7.2/7.2/7.2	7.3/7.2			0/0/0	Parts of other hydrometers, thermometers and similar instruments
													Instruments and apparatus for measuring or checking the flow, level, pressure or other variables of liquids or gases (for example, flow meters, level gauges, manometers, heat meters), excluding instruments and apparatus of heading No. 90.14, 90.15, 90.28 or 90.32:
0/0/0	0	0	0/0	0/0/0	0/0	0//0	0/0/	0/0/0	0/0			0/0/0	-For measuring or checking the flow or level of liquids
													-For measuring or checking pressure:
													---Pressure/differential pressure transducers
0/0/0	0	0	0/0	0/0/0	0/0	0//0	0/0/	0/0/0	0/0			0/0/0	Manganese-copper pressure gauges (pressure>10GPa)
0/0/0	0	0	0/0	0/0/0	0/0	0//0	0/0/	0/0/0	0/0			0/0/0	Made of ytterbium gauge(pressure>10GPa)
0/0/0	0	0	0/0	0/0/0	0/0	0//0	0/0/	0/0/0	0/0			0/0/0	Made of polyvinylidene fluoride pressure gauge(pressure>10GPa)
0/0/0	0	0	0/0	0/0/0	0/0	0//0	0/0/	0/0/0	0/0			0/0/0	Other pressure、differential pressure transducers
													---Other
0/0/0	0	0	0/0	0/0/0	0/0	0//0	0/0/	0/0/0	0/0			0/0/0	Pressure sensor(not glass laser)(Dual-use items controlled commodity)
0/0/0	0	0	0/0	0/0/0	0/0	0//0	0/0/	0/0/0	0/0		//	0/0/0	Non—electronic pressure gauge containing mercury
0/0/0	0	0	0/0	0/0/0	0/0	0//0	0/0/	0/0/0	0/0			0/0/0	Other instruments and equipment for measuring or checking pressure
													-Other instruments or apparatus:
0/0/0	0	0	0/0	0/0/0	0/0	0//0	0/0/	0/0/0	0/0			0/0/0	Instruments or apparatus for measuring the flow of gases
0/0/0	0	0	0/0	0/0/0	0/0	0//0	0/0/	0/0/0	0/0			0/0/0	---Other
												0/0/0	-Parts and accessories
0/0/0	0	0	0/0	0/0/0	0/0	0//0	0/0/	0/0/0	0/0		//	0/0/0	Probe for liquid level instrument
0/0/0	0	0	0/0	0/0/0	0/0	0//0	0/0/	0/0/0	0/0		//	0/0/0	Other liquid or gas measuring or testing instrument parts (mainly for measuring or testing flow, liquid level, pressure or other changes
													Instruments and apparatus for physical or chemical analysis (for example, polarimeters, refractometers, spectrometers, gas or smoke analysis apparatus); instruments and apparatus for measuring or checking viscosity, porosity, expansion, surface tension or the like; instruments and apparatus for measuring or checking quantities of heat, sound or light (including exposure meters); microtomes:
													-Gas or smoke analysis apparatus
0/0/0	2	3.2	0.7/0.7	0/0/0	0/0	0//0	0/0/	0/0/6.3	6.4/0			0/0/0	Used in continuously operating gas tester [for testing chemicals or organic compounds under export control (containing phosphor, sulfur, fluorine or chlorine with concentration lower than 0.3mg/m^3) or for testing the activity of cholinesterase under control]
0/0/0	2	3.2	0.7/0.7	0/0/0	0/0	0//0	0/0/	0/0/6.3	6.4/0			0/0/0	Other gas or smoke analysis apparatus
													-Chromatographs and electrophoresis instruments:
													---Chromatographs instruments:
0/0/0	0	0	0/0	0/0/0	0/0	0//0	0/0/	0/0/0	0/0			0/0/0	----Gas chromatographs instruments
0/0/0	0	0	0/0	0/0/0	0/0	0//0	0/0/	0/0/0	0/0			0/0/0	----Liquid chromatosraphs instruments
0/0/0	0	0	0/0	0/0/0	0/0	0//0	0/0/	0/0/0	0/0			0/0/0	----Other

税则号列	货品名称〔CIQ扩展编码及品名－T2表示见附表2〕	最惠(%)	暂定税率	普通	增值/消费	出口退税	计量单位	监管条件/特殊证件	检验检疫	对美关税	亚太上/下
9027.2020	---电泳仪〔999〕	0		17	13/	13	台/千克	/		5	
9027.3000	-使用光学射线(紫外线、可见光、红外线)的分光仪、分光光度计及摄谱仪	0		17	13/	13	台/千克			/10	
9027.3000 10	傅立叶红外光谱仪〔101:电子分析仪;102:机械分析仪〕	0		17	13/	13	台/千克	/			
9027.3000 20	近红外光谱仪〔101:电子分析仪;102:机械分析仪〕	0		17	13/	13	台/千克	/			
9027.3000 30	台式和手持拉曼光谱仪〔101:电子分析仪;102:机械分析仪〕	0		17	13/	13	台/千克	/			
9027.3000 90	其他分光仪、分光光度计及摄谱仪(使用光学射线(紫外线、可见光、红外线)的)〔101:电子分析仪;102:机械分析仪〕	0		17	13/	13	台/千克	/		10	
	-使用光学射线(紫外线、可见光、红外线)的其他仪器及装置:										
9027.5010	---基因测序仪〔101电子分析仪;102机械分析仪〕	0		17	13/	13	台/千克	6/			
9027.5090	---其他										
9027.5090 10	流式细胞仪〔101电子分析仪,102机械分析仪〕	0		17	13/	13	台/千克	6/			
9027.5090 90	其他使用光学射线的其他仪器及装置(光学射线是指紫外线、可见光、红外线)〔101电子分析仪,102机械分析仪〕	0		17	13/	13	台/千克	6/		5	
	-其他仪器及装置:										
	--质谱仪:										
9027.8110	---集成电路生产用氦质谱检漏台〔999〕	0		17	13/	13	台/千克	/			
9027.8120	---质谱联用仪〔999〕	0		17	13/	13	台/千克	/		5	
9027.8190	---其他										
9027.8190 10	两用物项管制的UF6质谱仪/离子源〔999〕	0		17	13/	13	台/千克	3/		5	
9027.8190 20	测大于230质量单位离子质谱仪(分辨率高于2/230)〔999〕	0		17	13/	13	台/千克	3/		5	
9027.8190 90	其他质谱仪〔999〕	0		17	13/	13	台/千克	/		5	
	--其他:										
9027.8910	---曝光表〔999〕	0		70	13/	13	个/千克	/		5	
9027.8990	---其他										
9027.8990 10	转矩流变仪〔101电子测量仪,102电子分析仪,103机械测量仪,104机械分析仪〕	0		17	13/	13	台/千克	6/			
9027.8990 90	其他理化分析仪器及装置(包括测量或检验粘性及类似性能的仪器及装置)〔101电子测量仪,102电子分析仪,103机械测量仪,104机械分析仪〕	0		17	13/	13	台/千克	6/		5	
9027.9000	-检镜切片机;零件、附件〔999〕	0		17	13/	13	千克	/		5	
90.28	**生产或供应气体、液体及电力用的计量仪表,包括它们的校准仪表:**										
	-气量计:										
9028.1010	---煤气表〔999〕	10		30	13/	13	个/千克	/		35	
9028.1090	---其他〔999〕	10		30	13/	13	个/千克	/		15	
	-液量计:										
9028.2010	---水表〔999〕	10		30	13/	13	个/千克	/		35	
9028.2090	---其他〔999〕	10		30	13/	13	个/千克	/		15	
	-电量计:										
	---电度表:										
9028.3011	----单相感应式〔999〕	0		30	13/	13	个/千克	/			
9028.3012	----三相感应式〔999〕	0		30	13/	13	个/千克	/			
9028.3013	----单相电子式(静止式)〔999〕	0		30	13/	13	个/千克	/		25	
9028.3014	----三相电子式(静止式)〔999〕	0		30	13/	13	个/千克	/		25	
9028.3019	----其他〔999〕	0		30	13/	13	个/千克	/			
9028.3090	---其他〔999〕	0		30	13/	13	个/千克	/		20	
	-零件、附件:										
9028.9010	---工业用〔101其他电子仪表,102其他机械式仪表及其零件〕	0		30	13/	13	千克	/		25	
9028.9090	---其他〔101其他电子仪表,102其他机械式仪表及其零件〕	0		50	13/	13	千克	/		20	
90.29	**转数计、产量计数器、车费计、里程计、步数计及类似仪表;速度计及转速表,税目90.14及90.15的仪表除外;频闪观测仪:**										
	-转数计、产量计数器、车费计、里程计、步数计及类似仪表:										
9029.1010	---转数计〔999〕	12		50	13/	13	个/千克	/		37	
9029.1020	---车费计、里程计〔101其他车辆零部件,102其他电子仪表〕	12		35	13/	13	个/千克	/		32	
9029.1090	---其他〔999〕	12		35	13/	13	个/千克	/		32	
	-速度计及转速表,频闪观测仪:										
9029.2010	---车辆用速度计〔999〕	10		35	13/	13	个/千克	/		15	
9029.2090	---其他〔999〕	10		35	13/	13	个/千克	/		30	
9029.9000	-零件、附件〔999〕	6		35	13/	13	千克	/		26	

协定税率 %								RCEP		特惠税率 %			Article Description
东/冰/格	巴基斯坦	韩国	瑞士上/下	哥/秘/柬	澳/毛	新西/坡/智	中国港/澳/台	东盟及马来/澳/韩	日/新	亚太2国	老/柬/缅	98/97/95	
0/0/0	0	0	0/0	0/0/0	0/0	0//0	0/0/	0/0/0	0/0			0/0/0	---Electrophoresis instruments
												0/0/0	-Spectrometers, spectrophotometers and spectrographs using optical radiations (UV, visible, IR)
0/0/0	0	0	0/0	0/0/0	0/0	0//0	0/0/	0/0/0	0/0		//	0/0/0	Fourier infrared spectrometer
0/0/0	0	0	0/0	0/0/0	0/0	0//0	0/0/	0/0/0	0/0		//	0/0/0	Near infrared spectrometer
0/0/0	0	0	0/0	0/0/0	0/0	0//0	0/0/	0/0/0	0/0		//	0/0/0	Desktop and handheld Raman spectrometers
0/0/0	0	0	0/0	0/0/0	0/0	0//0	0/0/	0/0/0	0/0		//	0/0/0	Other spectrometers, spectrophotometer and spectrograph (using optical rays (ultraviolet, visible, infrared)
													-Other instruments and apparatus using optical radiations (UV, visible, IR):
0/0/0	0	0	0/0	0/0/0	0/0	0//0	0/0/	0/0/0	0/0			0/0/0	---Gene sequencer
													---Other
0/0/0	0	0	0/0	0/0/0	0/0	0//0	0/0/	0/0/0	0/0		//	0/0/0	Flow cytometry
0/0/0	0	0	0/0	0/0/0	0/0	0//0	0/0/	0/0/0	0/0		//	0/0/0	Other instruments and devices using optical rays (optical rays refer to ultraviolet, visible and infrared rays)
													-Other instruments and apparatus:
													--Mass spectrograph:
0/0/0	0	0	0/0	0/0/0	0/0	0//0	0/0/	0/0/0	0/0			0/0/0	---Helium mass spectrometry leak detector for integrated circuit production
0/0/0	0	0	0/0	0/0/0	0/0	0//0	0/0/	0/0/0	0/0			0/0/0	--- Mass spectrometers
													---Other
0/0/0	0	0	0/0	0/0/0	0/0	0//0	0/0/	0/0/0	0/0			0/0/0	UF6 mass spectrometer / ion source for dual—use item control
0/0/0	0	0	0/0	0/0/0	0/0	0//0	0/0/	0/0/0	0/0			0/0/0	Mass spectrometer for measuring ions greater than 230 mass units (resolution higher than 2 / 230)
0/0/0	0	0	0/0	0/0/0	0/0	0//0	0/0/	0/0/0	0/0			0/0/0	Other mass spectrometers
													--Other:
0/0/0	7.8	2.8	0/0	0/0/0	0/0	0/0/0	0/0/	0/0/12.6	12.7/0			0/0/0	---Exposure meter
													---Other
0/0/0	0	0	0/0	0/0/0	0/0	0//0	0/0/	0/0/0	0/0			0/0/0	HAAKE Polylab OS
0/0/0	0	0	0/0	0/0/0	0/0	0//0	0/0/	0/0/0	0/0			0/0/0	Other physical and chemical analysis instruments and devices (including instruments and devices for measuring or checking viscosity and similar properties)
0/0/0	0	0	0/0	0/0/0	0/0	0//0	0/0/	0/0/0	0/0			0/0/0	-Microtomes; parts and accessories
													Gas, liquid or electricity supply or production meters, including calibrating meters therefor:
													-Gas meters:
0/0/0	2	2	0/0	0/0/0	0/0	0//0	0/0/	0/0/9	9.1/0			0/0/0	---Coal gas meters
0/0/0	2	2	0/0	0/0/0	0/0	0/0/0	0/0/	0/0/9	9.1/0			0/0/0	---Other
													-Liquid meters:
0/0/0	2	2	0/0	0/0/0	0/0	0/0/0	0/0/	0/0/9	9.1/0			0/0/0	---Water meters
0/0/0	2		0/0	0/0/0	0/0	0/0/0	0/0/	5/5/	/5			0/0/0	---Other
													-Electricity meters:
													---Watt-hour meter:
0/0/0	2	2	0/0	0/0/0	0/0	0//0	0/0/	0/0/9	0/0			0/0/0	----Single- phase inductions type
0/0/0	2	2	0/0	0/0/0	0/0	0//0	0/0/	0/0/9	0/0			0/0/0	----Threephase inductions type
0/0/0	2	2	0/0	0/0/0	0/0	0//0	0/0/	0/0/9	0/0			0/0/0	----Single-phase induction type(static)
0/0/0	2	2		0/0/0	0/0	0//0	0/0/	0/0/9	0/0			0/0/0	----Three-phase induction type(static)
0/0/0	2	6	0/0	0/0/0	0/0	0//0	0/0/	0/0/9.3	0/0			0/0/0	----Other
0/0/0	2	2	0/0	0/0/0	0/0	0/0/0	0/0/	0/0/9	0/0			0/0/0	---Other
													-Parts and accessories:
0/0/0	2	1.6	0/0	0/0/0	0/0	0//0	0/0/	0/0/7.6	0/0			0/0/0	---For technical use
0/0/0	2	0	0/0	0/0/0	0/0	0//0	0/0/	0/0/0	0/0			0/0/0	---Other
													Revolution counters, production counters, taximeters, mileometers, pedometers and the like; speed indicators and tachometers, other than those of heading No. 90. 14 or 90. 15; stroboscopes:
													-Revolution counters, production counters, taximeters, mileometers, pedometers and the like:
0/0/0	8.4	3	6/6	0/0/0	0/0	0/0/0	0/0/	0/0/13.5	13.6/0			0/0/0	---Revolution counters
0/0/0	8.4		1.5/1.5	0/0/0	0/0	0/0/0	0/0/	5/5/	/5			0/0/0	---Taximeters and mileometers
0/0/0	8.4		1.5/1.5	0/0/0	0/0	0/0/0	0/0/	5/5/	/5			0/0/0	---Other
													-Speed indicators and tachometers; stroboscopes:
0/0/0	4	6	0/0	0/0/0	0/0	0//0	0/0/	9.5/9.5/9.5	9.5/9.5			0/0/0	---Speed indicators for motor vehicles
0/0/0	3.5	2	0/0	0/0/0	0/0	0//0	0/0/	9/9/9	9.1/9			0/0/0	---Other
0/0/0	0		0.6/0.6	0/0/0	0/0	0//0	0/0/	5/5/	/5			0/0/0	-Parts and accessories

税则号列	货品名称〔CIQ 扩展编码及品名—T2 表示见附表 2〕	最惠(%)	暂定税率	普通	增值/消费	出口退税	计量单位	监管条件/特殊证件	检验检疫	对美关税	亚太上/下
90.30	**示波器、频谱分析仪及其他用于电量测量或检验的仪器和装置,但不包括税目 90.28 的各种仪表;α 射线、β 射线、γ 射线、X 射线、宇宙射线或其他离子射线的测量或检验仪器及装置:**										
9030.1000	-离子射线的测量或检验仪器及装置〔999〕	0		20	13/	13	台/千克	/			
	-示波器:										
9030.2010	---测试频率在 300 兆赫兹以下的通用示波器〔999〕	0		80	13/	13	台/千克	/		20	
9030.2090	---其他〔999〕	0		20	13/	13	台/千克	/		10	
	-检测电压、电流、电阻或功率(用于测试或检验半导体晶圆或器件用的除外)的其他仪器及装置:										
	--万用表,不带记录装置:										
9030.3110	---量程在五位半及以下的数字万用表〔999〕	0		130	13/	13	台/千克	/		5	
9030.3190	---其他〔999〕	0		20	13/	13	台/千克	/		10	
9030.3200	--万用表,带记录装置〔999〕	0		20	13/	13	台/千克	/		10	
	--其他,不带记录装置:										
9030.3310	---量程在五位半及以下的数字电流表、电压表〔999〕	3.8/1.9		130	13/	13	台/千克	/		23.8	
9030.3320	---电阻测试仪〔101 电子测量仪,102 机械测量仪〕	10		80	13/	13	台/千克	/		20	
9030.3390	---其他〔999〕	2.3/1.1		20	13/	13	台/千克	/		22.3	
9030.3900	--其他,带记录装置〔999〕	0		20	13/	13	台/千克	/		10	
	-通讯专用的其他仪器及装置(例如,串音测试器、增益测量仪、失真度表、噪声计):										
9030.4010	---测试频率在 12.4 千兆赫兹以下的数字式频率计〔999〕	0		80	13/	13	台/千克	/		10	
9030.4090	---其他〔101 其他行业成套设备,102 电子测量仪〕	0		20	13/	13	台/千克	/		5	
	-其他仪器及装置:										
9030.8200	--测试或检验半导体晶圆或器件(包括集成电路)用〔999〕	0		20	13/	13	台/千克	/			
	--其他,带有记录装置:										
9030.8410	---电感及电容测试仪〔999〕	0		80	13/	13	台/千克	/		25	
9030.8490	---其他〔999〕	0		20	13/	13	台/千克	/		10	
	--其他:										
9030.8910	---电感及电容测试仪〔999〕	0		80	13/	13	台/千克	/		10	
9030.8990	---其他										
9030.8990 10	中子探测和测量仪表(专用于测定核反应堆堆芯内中子通量的)〔999〕	0		20	13/	13	台/千克	3/		10	
9030.8990 90	其他电量的测量或检验仪器及装置(未装有记录装置的)〔999〕	0		20	13/	13	台/千克	/		10	
9030.9000	-零件、附件										
9030.9000 01	检测半导体晶片及器件的仪器零件(包括附件)〔999〕	0		17	13/	13	千克	/		10	
9030.9000 02	ITA 产品用的印刷电路组件(包括外接组件,如符合 PCMCIA 标准的卡)〔999〕	0		17	13/	13	千克	/		10	
9030.9000 10	用于声表面滤波器测试的测试头(频率带宽在 81GHZ 以上,且探针最小间距在周围排列下为 50 微米,阵列下为 180 微米)〔999〕	0		17	13/	13	千克	/			
9030.9000 90	税目 90.30 所属货品的零件及附件〔999〕	0		17	13/	13	千克	/		10	
90.31	**本章其他税目未列名的测量或检验仪器、器具及机器;轮廓投影仪:**										
9031.1000	-机械零件平衡试验机										
9031.1000 10	陀螺动态平衡测试仪〔999〕	0		17	13/	13	台/千克	3/		20	0/0
9031.1000 90	其他机械零件平衡试验机〔999〕	0		17	13/	13	台/千克	/		20	0/0
9031.2000	-试验台										
9031.2000 10	陀螺/马达运转试验台〔999〕	7		17	13/	13	台/千克	3/			
9031.2000 20	加速度表测试台〔999〕	7		17	13/	13	台/千克	3/			
9031.2000 30	试车台(能试推力>90kN 火箭发动机的或同时测量三个推力分量的)〔999〕	7		17	13/	13	台/千克	3/			

协定税率 %								RCEP		特惠税率 %			Article Description
东/冰/格	巴基斯坦	韩国	瑞士上/下	哥/秘/柬	澳/毛	新西/坡/智	中国港/澳/台	东盟及马来/澳/韩	日/新	亚太2国	老/柬/缅	98/97/95	
													Oscilloscopes, spectrum analysers and other instruments and apparatus for measuring or checking electrical quantities, excluding meters of heading No. 90.28; instruments and apparatus for measuring or detecting alpha, beta, gamma, X-ray, cosmic or other ionizing radiations:
0/0/0	0		0/0	0/0/0	0/0	0//0	0/0/	0/0/4.5	4.5/0			0/0/0	-Instruments and apparatus for measuring or detecting ionizing radiations
													-Oscilloscopes and oscillographs:
0/0/0	2	1.6	0/0	0/0/0	0/0	0/0/0	0/0/	0/0/7.2	0/0			0/0/0	---For general use, of test frequency less than 300 MHz
0/0/0	0	1	0/0	0/0/0	0/0	0//0	0/0/	0/4.5/4.5	0/4.5			0/0/0	---Other
													-Other instruments and apparatus, for measuring or checking voltage, current, resistance or power (other than those for measuring or checking semiconductor wafers or devices):
													--Multimeters without a recording device:
0/0/0	8.4	3	0/0	0/0/0	0/0	0/0/0	0/0/	0/0/13.5	0/0			0/0/0	---Digital, of measuring range of 5.5 or less
0/0/0	0	2.3	0/0	0/0/0	0/0	0//0	0/0/	0/0/4.5	0/0			0/0/0	---Other
0/0/0	2	1.6	0/0	0/0/0	0/0	0//0	0/0/	0/0/7.2	7.3/0			0/0/0	--Multimeters with a recording device
													--other without a recording device:
0/0/0	8.4	3	1.5/1.5	0/0/0	0/0	0/0/0	0/0/	0/0/13.5	13.6/0			0/0/0	---Digital ammeters or voltmeters. of measuing rang of 5.5or less
0/0/0	9		1.4/1.4	0/0/0	0/0	0/0/0	0/0/	5/5/	/5			0/0/0	---Resistnace measaring instruments
0/0/0	4		0.9/0.9	0/0/0	0/0	0//0	0/0/	5/5/	/5			0/0/0	---Other
0/0/0	2		0/0	0/0/0	0/0	0//0	0/0/	0/0/7.2	7.3/0			0/0/0	--Other with a recordins device
													-Other instruments and apparatus, specially designed for telecommunications (for example, cross-talk meters, gain measuring instruments, distortion factor meters, psophometers):
0/0/0	0	0	0/0	0/0/0	0/0	0//0	0/0/	0/0/0	0/0			0/0/0	---Digital frequency meters, of test frequency less than 12.4 GHz
0/0/0	0	0	0/0	0/0/0	0/0	0//0	0/0/	0/0/0	0/0			0/0/0	---Other
													-Other instruments and apparatus:
0/0/0	0	0	0/0	0/0/0	0/0	0//0	0/0/	0/0/0	0/0			0/0/0	--For measuring or checking semiconductor wafers or devices (including integrated circuits)
													--Other, with a recording device:
0/0/0	2		0/0	0/0/0	0/0	0/0/0	0/0/	9/9/9.5	9.1/9			0/0/0	---For measuring inductances or capacitances
0/0/0	2	3.7	0/0	0/0/0	0/0	0//0	0/0/	0/0/7.2	7.3/0			0/0/0	---Other
													--Other:
0/0/0	7.8		0/0	0/0/0	0/0	0/0/0	0/0/	0/0/12.6	12.7/0			0/0/0	---For measuring inductances or capacitances
													---Other
0/0/0	2		0/0	0/0/0	0/0	0//0	0/0/	0/0/7.2	7.3/0			0/0/0	Neutron detection and measurement instruments (used exclusively to measure the neutron flux of the reactor cores)
0/0/0	2		0/0	0/0/0	0/0	0//0	0/0/	0/0/7.2	7.3/0			0/0/0	Other instruments and apparatus for measuring or checking electrical quantities (without a recording device)
													-Parts and accessories
0/0/0	2	1.4	0/0	0/0/0	0/0	0//0	0/0/	0/0/6.3	6.4/0			0/0/0	Parts of instruments for measuring or checking semiconductor wafers or devices
0/0/0	2	1.4	0/0	0/0/0	0/0	0//0	0/0/	0/0/6.3	6.4/0			0/0/0	Printed circuit components for products falling within the ITA(including such components for external connections such as cards that conform to the PCMCLA standard)
0/0/0	2	1.4	0/0	0/0/0	0/0	0//0	0/0/	0/0/6.3	6.4/0		//	0/0/0	Test head for testing surface acoustic filter (frequency bandwidth is above 81ghz, and the minimum spacing of probes is 50 μm under surrounding arrangement and 180 μm under array)
0/0/0	2	1.4	0/0	0/0/0	0/0	0//0	0/0/	0/0/6.3	6.4/0			0/0/0	Parts and accessories of goods of heading 90.30
													Measuring or checking instruments, appliances and machines, not specified or included elsewhere in this Chapter; profile projectors:
													-Machines for balancing mechanical parts
0/0/0	2	0	0/0	0/0/0	0/0	0//0	0/0/	6.3/6.3/6.3	6.4/6.3			0/0/0	Gyro dynamic balancing testers
0/0/0	2	0	0/0	0/0/0	0/0	0//0	0/0/	6.3/6.3/6.3	6.4/6.3			0/0/0	Other machines for balancing mechanical parts
													-Test benches
0/0/0	2	3.2	2.9/2.9	0/0/0	0/0	0//0	0/0/	6.3/6.3/6.3	6.6/6.3			0/0/0	Gyro/motor running test-benches
0/0/0	2	3.2	2.9/2.9	0/0/0	0/0	0//0	0/0/	6.3/6.3/6.3	6.6/6.3			0/0/0	Accelerometer test-benches
0/0/0	2	3.2	2.9/2.9	0/0/0	0/0	0//0	0/0/	6.3/6.3/6.3	6.6/6.3			0/0/0	Testbed (capable of testing rocket engine with a thrust > 90kN or testing three individual thrust forces at the same time)

税则号列	货品名称〔CIQ 扩展编码及品名－T2 表示见附表 2〕	最惠(%)	暂定税率	普通	增值/消费	出口退税	计量单位	监管条件/特殊证件	检验检疫	对美关税	亚太上/下
9031.2000 40	惯性平台测试台(测试平台包括高精度离心机和转台)〔999〕	7		17	13/	13	台/千克	3/			
9031.2000 90	其他试验台〔999〕	7		17	13/	13	台/千克	/			
	-其他光学仪器及器具:										
9031.4100	--制造半导体器件(包括集成电路)时检验半导体晶圆、器件(包括集成电路)或检测光掩模或光栅用〔999〕	0		17	13/	13	台/千克	/			
	--其他:										
9031.4910	---轮廓投影仪〔999〕	0		20	13/	13	台/千克	/		25	
9031.4920	---光栅测量装置〔999〕	0		17	13/	13	台/千克	/		25	
9031.4990	---其他										
9031.4990 10	光盘质量在线检测仪及离线检测仪〔999〕	0		17	13/	13	台/千克	/		20	
9031.4990 90	其他光学测量或检验仪器和器具(第 90 章其他税目未列名的)〔999〕	0		17	13/	13	台/千克	/		20	
	-其他仪器、器具及机器:										
9031.8010	---光纤通信及光纤性能测试仪〔999〕	2/1		17	13/	13	台/千克	/			1.3/0.7
9031.8020	---坐标测量仪〔999〕	2/1		17	13/	13	台/千克	/		12	
	---无损探伤检测仪器(射线探伤仪除外):										
9031.8031	----超声波探伤检测仪〔999〕	2/1		17	13/	13	台/千克	/			1.3/0.7
9031.8032	----磁粉探伤检测仪〔999〕	2/1		17	13/	13	台/千克	/		12	1.3/0.7
9031.8033	----涡流探伤检测仪〔999〕	2/1		17	13/	13	台/千克	/		12	1.3/0.7
9031.8039	----其他〔999〕	2/1		17	13/	13	台/千克	/		12	1.3/0.7
9031.8090	---其他										
9031.8090 10	惯性测量单元测试仪〔999〕	2/1		17	13/	13	台/千克	3/			1.3/0.7
9031.8090 20	陀螺调谐测试仪〔999〕	2/1		17	13/	13	台/千克	3/			1.3/0.7
9031.8090 30	跑道摩擦系数测试仪〔999〕	2/1		17	13/	13	台/千克	/			1.3/0.7
9031.8090 40	音频生命探测仪〔999〕	2/1		17	13/	13	台/千克	/			1.3/0.7
9031.8090 50	音视频生命探测仪〔999〕	2/1		17	13/	13	台/千克	/			1.3/0.7
9031.8090 60	集成电路测试分选设备〔999〕	2/1		17	13/	13	台/千克	/			1.3/0.7
9031.8090 70	飞机发动机用电磁线性位移传感器〔999〕	2/1	①	17	13/	13	台/千克	/			1.3/0.7
9031.8090 90	其他测量、检验仪器、器具及机器(指第 90 章其他税目未列名的)〔101 电子测量仪,102 机械测量仪〕	2/1		17	13/	13	台/千克	/			1.3/0.7
9031.9000	-零件、附件										
9031.9000 20	惯性测量单元稳定元件加工夹具〔999〕	0		17	13/	13	千克	3/		10	
9031.9000 30	惯性平台平衡夹具〔999〕	0		17	13/	13	千克	3/		10	
9031.9000 90	编号 9031 的仪器及器具的其他零件(第 90 章其他编号未列名的)〔999〕	0		17	13/	13	千克	/		10	
90.32	**自动调节或控制仪器及装置:**										
9032.1000	-恒温器〔101 其它电子测量分析设备及其零件,102 其它机械测量分析设备及其零件〕	7		17	13/	13	台/千克	/		27	
9032.2000	-恒压器〔101 其它电子测量分析设备及其零件,102 其它机械测量分析设备及其零件〕	0		17	13/	13	台/千克	/		10	
	-其他仪器及装置:										
9032.8100	--液压或气压的〔999〕	0		17	13/	13	台/千克	/			0/0
	--其他:										
	---列车自动控制系统(ATC)车载设备:										
9032.8911	----列车自动防护系统(ATP)车载设备〔999〕	7		17	13/	13	台/千克	/		12	
9032.8912	----列车自动运行系统(ATO)车载设备〔999〕	7		17	13/	13	台/千克	/			
9032.8919	----其他〔999〕	7		17	13/	13	台/千克	/		12	
9032.8990	---其他										
9032.8990 10	具有可再生能源和智能电网应用的自动电压和电流调节器;非液压或气压的自动调控流量、液位和湿度的仪器(自动控制、调节装置)〔999〕	7	5	17	13/	13	台/千克	/			
9032.8990 20	超燃冲压喷气或组合循环发动机的燃烧调节装置(自动控制、调节装置)〔999〕	7		17	13/	13	台/千克	3/			

① 1－6 月:1%

协定税率 %								RCEP		特惠税率 %			Article Description
东/冰/格	巴基斯坦	韩国	瑞士上/下	哥/秘/柬	澳/毛	新西/坡/智	中国港/澳/台	东盟及马来/澳/韩	日/新	亚太2国	老/柬/缅	98/97/95	
0/0/0	2	3.2	2.9/2.9	0/0/0	0/0	0//0	0/0/	6.3/6.3/6.3	6.6/6.3			0/0/0	Inertial platform test-benches (including high-precision centrifuge and turntable)
0/0/0	2	3.2	2.9/2.9	0/0/0	0/0	0//0	0/0/	6.3/6.3/6.3	6.6/6.3			0/0/0	Other test benches
													-Other optical instruments and appliances:
0/0/0	0	0	0/0	0/0/0	0/0	0//0	0/0/	0/0/0	0/0			0/0/0	--For inspecting semiconduct (including integrated circuits) or wafers or devices or for inspecting photomasks or reticles used in manufacturing semiconductor devices (including integrated circuits):
													--Other:
0/0/0	2	4.6	0/0	0/0/0	0/0	0//0	0/0/	0/0/9	9.1/0			0/0/0	---Profile proiecters
0/0/0	0	0	0/0	0/0/0	0/0	0//0	0/0/	0/0/0	0/0			0/0/0	---Optical grating measuring device
													---Other
0/0/0	0	0	0/0	0/0/0	0/0	0//0	0/0/	0/0/0	0/0			0/0/0	Automatic inspection detectors (AID) for CD production
0/0/0	0	0	0/0	0/0/0	0/0	0//0	0/0/	0/0/0	0/0			0/0/0	Other measuring or checking optical instruments and appliances, not elsewhere specified or included in chapter 90
													-Other instruments, appliances and machines:
0/0/0	0	2.3	0/0	0/0/0	0/0	0//0	0/0/	4.5/4.5/4.5	4.5/4.5			0/0/0	---Optical telecommunication and optical fibre performance testing instruments
0/0/0	0	2.3	0/0	0/0/0	0/0	0//0	0/0/	4.5/4.5/4.5	4.5/4.5			0/0/0	---Coordinate measuring machine
													---Apparatus for exaninations, without damaging structure (other than apparatus for radiological examinations):
0/0/0	0	3.2	0/0	0/0/0	0/0	0//0	0/0/	0/0/4.5	4.5/0			0/0/0	----Apparatus for ultrasonic examinations
0/0/0	0	3.2	0/0	0/0/0	0/0	0//0	0/0/	0/0/4.5	4.5/0			0/0/0	----Apparatus for magnetic examinations
0/0/0	0	3.2	0/0	0/0/0	0/0	0//0	0/0/	0/0/4.5	4.5/0			0/0/0	----Apparatus for eddy examinations
0/0/0	0		0/0	0/0/0	0/0	0//0	0/0/	0/0/4.5	4.5/0			0/0/0	----Other
													---Other
0//0	0	1	2/1	0/0/0	0/0	0//0	0/0/0	0/0/4.5	4.7/0			0/0/0	Inertial measurement unit testers
0//0	0	1	2/1	0/0/0	0/0	0//0	0/0/0	0/0/4.5	4.7/0			0/0/0	Gyro tuning testers
0//0	0	1	2/1	0/0/0	0/0	0//0	0/0/0	0/0/4.5	4.7/0			0/0/0	Runway friction coefficient testers
0//0	0	1	2/1	0/0/0	0/0	0//0	0/0/0	0/0/4.5	4.7/0			0/0/0	Audio life detection instrument
0//0	0	1	2/1	0/0/0	0/0	0//0	0/0/0	0/0/4.5	4.7/0			0/0/0	Audio and video life detection instrument
0//0	0	1	2/1	0/0/0	0/0	0//0	0/0/0	0/0/4.5	4.7/0			0/0/0	Integrated circuit testing and sorting equipment
0//0	0	1	2/1	0/0/0	0/0	0//0	0/0/0	0/0/4.5	4.7/0		//	0/0/0	Electromagnetic linear displacement sensor for aircraft engine
0//0	0	1	2/1	0/0/0	0/0	0//0	0/0/0	0/0/4.5	4.7/0			0/0/0	Other measuring or checking instruments, appliances and machines (not elsewhere specified or included in Chapter 90)
													-Parts and accessories
0/0/0	0	0	0/0	0/0/0	0/0	0//0	0/0/	0/0/0	0/0			0/0/0	Processing clamps for stabling element of inertial measurement unit
0/0/0	0	0	0/0	0/0/0	0/0	0//0	0/0/	0/0/0	0/0			0/0/0	Inertial platform balancing clamps
0/0/0	0	0	0/0	0/0/0	0/0	0//0	0/0/	0/0/0	0/0			0/0/0	Other parts of instruments, appliances and machines of heading No. 90. 31, not elsewhere specified or included in chapter 90
													Automatic regulating or controlling instruments and apparatus:
0/0/0	2	0	0.7/0.7	0/0/0	0/0	0//0	0/0/	0/0/0	6.4/0			0/0/0	-Thermostats
0/0/0	2	1.4	0/0	0/0/0	0/0	0//0	0/0/	0/0/6.3	6.4/0			0/0/0	-Manostats
													-Other instruments and apparatus:
0/0/0	2	4.5	0/0	0/0/0	0/0	0//0	0/0/	6.3/6.3/6.7	6.4/6.3			0/0/0	--Hydraulic or pneumatic
													--Other:
													---Devices Automatic Train control system(ATC), installed on trains:
0/0/0	2	3.2		0/0/0	0/0	0//0	0/0/	6.3/6.3/6.3	6.6/6.3			0/0/0	----Devices Automatic Train protective system (ATP), installed on trains
0/0/0	2	3.2		0/0/0	0/0	0//0	0/0/	6.3/6.3/6.3	6.4/6.3			0/0/0	----Devices Automatic Train operation system (ATO), installed on trains
0/0/0	2	3.2		0/0/0	0/0	0//0	0/0/	6.3/6.3/6.3	6.4/6.3			0/0/0	----Other
													---Other
0/0/0	4	3.2		0/0/0	0/0	0//0	0/0/	6.3/6.3/6.3	6.6/6.3			0/0/0	With renewable energy and smart grid application of the automatic voltage and current regulator; instrument non hydraulic or pneumatic automatic control flow, liquid level and humidity(automatic control device)
0/0/0	4	3.2		0/0/0	0/0	0//0	0/0/	6.3/6.3/6.3	6.6/6.3			0/0/0	Combustion adjusting device for combined jet engine (automatic control and regulating devices)

税则号列	货品名称〔CIQ 扩展编码及品名－T2 表示见附表 2〕	最惠(%)	暂定税率	普通	增值/消费	出口退税	计量单位	监管条件/特殊证件	检验检疫	对美关税	亚太上/下
9032.8990 30	三坐标测量机用自动控制柜〔999〕	7	3	17	13/	13	台/千克	/			
9032.8990 40	飞机自动驾驶系统(包括自动驾驶、电子控制飞行、自动故障分析、警告系统配平系统及推力监控设备及其相关仪表)〔999〕	7	1	17	13/	13	台/千克	/			
9032.8990 50	机床用成套数控伺服装置(包括 CNC 操作单元,带有配套的伺服放大器和伺服电机)〔999〕	7	3	17	13/	13	台/千克	/			
9032.8990 60	电喷点火程序控制单元(自动控制、调节装置)〔999〕	7	3	17	13/	13	台/千克	/			
9032.8990 70	印刷机用成套数控伺服传动装置(包括运动控制器或可编程序自动控制器、人机界面单元,带有配套的伺服驱动器和伺服电机)〔999〕	7	3	17	13/	13	台/千克	/			
9032.8990 80	纯电动或混合动力汽车用电机控制器总成(自动控制、调节装置)〔999〕	7	4	17	13/	13	台/千克	/			
9032.8990 91	发动机气门正时控制(VTC)模块〔999〕	7	3	17	13/	13	台/千克	/			
9032.8990 99	其他自动调节或控制仪器及装置〔999〕	7		17	13/	13	台/千克	/			
9032.9000	-零件、附件										
9032.9000 01	飞机自动驾驶系统的零件(包括自动驾驶、电子控制飞行、自动故障分析、警告系统配平系统及推力监控设备及其相关仪表的零件)〔999〕	5	1	17	13/	13	千克	/			
9032.9000 10	飞机发动机燃油控制器用电路板〔999〕	5	1	17	13/	13	千克	/		11	
9032.9000 90	其他自动调节或控制仪器零件、附件〔999〕	5		17	13/	13	千克	/		15	
90.33	**第九十章所列机器、器具、仪器或装置用的本章其他税目未列名的零件、附件：**										
9033.0000	第九十章所列机器、器具、仪器或装置用的本章其他税目未列名的零件、附件										
9033.0000 10	用于 90 章环境产品的其他税目未列名的零件、附件:(太阳能定日镜、9015.80 的商品,90.26 的商品,90.27 的商品(9027.8011 和 9027.8091 除外),9031.49 的商品,测振仪,手振动仪,可再生能源和智能电网应用的自动电压和电流调节器,自动调控流量、液位和湿度的仪器)〔101 其它电子测量分析设备及其零件,102 其它机械测量分析设备及其零件〕	6	5	17	13/	13	千克	/		25	
9033.0000 90	第 90 章其他编号未列名零、附件(指第 90 章所列机器、器具、仪器或装置用)〔101 其它电子测量分析设备及其零件,102 其它机械测量分析设备及其零件〕	6		17	13/	13	千克	/		26	

协定税率 %								RCEP		特惠税率 %			Article Description
东/冰/格	巴基斯坦	韩国	瑞士上/下	哥/秘/柬	澳/毛	新西/坡/智	中国港/澳/台	东盟及马来/澳/韩	日/新	亚太2国	老/柬/缅	98/97/95	
0/0/0	4	3.2		0/0/0	0/0	0//0	0/0/	6.3/6.3/6.3	6.6/6.3			0/0/0	Automatic control cabinet with three coordinate measuring machine
0/0/0	4	3.2		0/0/0	0/0	0//0	0/0/	6.3/6.3/6.3	6.6/6.3			0/0/0	The aircraft autopilot system(including automatic driving, electronic control flight, automatic fault analysis and warning system trim system and thrust monitoring equipment and instrumentation)
0/0/0	4	3.2		0/0/0	0/0	0//0	0/0/	6.3/6.3/6.3	6.6/6.3			0/0/0	With complete sets of CNC servo device for machine tools(including CNC operating unit, with supporting servo amplifier and servo motor)
0/0/0	4	3.2		0/0/0	0/0	0//0	0/0/	6.3/6.3/6.3	6.6/6.3			0/0/0	EFI ignition program control unit(automatic control and regulation device)
0/0/0	4	3.2		0/0/0	0/0	0//0	0/0/	6.3/6.3/6.3	6.6/6.3			0/0/0	Printing machine with complete sets of numerical control servo drive device (including motion controller or automatic programmable controller, man-machine interface unit, servo drive and servo motor) that contains form a complete set
0/0/0	4	3.2		0/0/0	0/0	0//0	0/0/	6.3/6.3/6.3	6.6/6.3			0/0/0	Pure electric or hybrid cars with motor controller assembly, automatic control, adjusting device)
0/0/0	4	3.2		0/0/0	0/0	0//0	0/0/	6.3/6.3/6.3	6.6/6.3		//	0/0/0	Engine valve timing control (VTC) module
0/0/0	4	3.2		0/0/0	0/0	0//0	0/0/	6.3/6.3/6.3	6.6/6.3		//	0/0/0	Other automatic regulating or controlling instruments and devices
													-Parts and accessories
0/0/0	0	2.3	0.5/0.5	0/0/0	0/0	0//0	0/0/	4.5/4.5/4.5	4.7/4.5			0/0/0	Parts of automatic pilotting systems for aircraft(including instruments of automatic pilotting, electronic flight control, automatic failure analysis, warning systems balancing system and thrust monitoring equipment and in struments and meters)
0/0/0	0	2.3	0.5/0.5	0/0/0	0/0	0//0	0/0/	4.5/4.5/4.5	4.7/4.5		//	0/0/0	Circuit board for aircraft engine fuel controller
0/0/0	0	2.3	0.5/0.5	0/0/0	0/0	0//0	0/0/	4.5/4.5/4.5	4.7/4.5			0/0/0	Other parts and acessories of automatic regulating or controlling instruments
													Parts and accessories (not specified or included elsewhere in this Chapter) for machines, appliances, instruments or apparatus of Chapter 90:
													Parts and accessories (not specified or included elsewhere in this Chapter) for machines, appliances, instruments or apparatus of Chapter 90
0/0/0	4	0	0.6/0.6	0/0/0	0/0	0//0	0/0/	0/0/0	5.6/0			0/0/0	Chapter 90 environmental products used for the other items not listed parts, accessories: (solar heliostat, 9015.80, 90.26 of goods, the goods 90.27 (except 9027.8011 and 9027.8091), 9031.49 goods, vibration, hand vibration meter, renewable energy and smart grid applications of automatic voltage and current regulator, automatic regulation and control flow, liquid level instruments and humidity)
0/0/0	4	0	0.6/0.6	0/0/0	0/0	0//0	0/0/	0/0/0	5.6/0			0/0/0	Chapter 90 other number their zero, attachment (refer to chapter 90 listed machines, apparatus, instruments and devices)

第九十一章
钟表及其零件

注释：

一、本章不包括：

(一)钟表玻璃及钟锤(按其构成材料归类)；

(二)表链(根据不同情况，归入税目 71.13 或 71.17)；

(三)第十五类注释二所规定的贱金属制通用零件(第十五类)、塑料制的类似品(第三十九章)及贵金属或包贵金属制的类似品(一般归入税目 71.15)；但钟、表发条则应作为钟、表的零件归类(税目 91.14)；

(四)轴承滚珠(根据不同情况，归入税目 73.26 或 84.82)；

(五)税目 84.12 的物品，不需擒纵器可以工作的；

(六)滚珠轴承(税目 84.82)；

(七)第八十五章的物品，本身未组装在或未与其他零件组装在钟、表机芯内，也未组装成专用于或主要用于钟、表机芯零件的(第八十五章)。

二、税目 91.01 仅包括表壳完全以贵金属或包贵金属制的表，以及用贵金属或包贵金属与税目 71.01 至 71.04 的天然、养殖珍珠或宝石、半宝石(天然、合成或再造)合制的表。用贱金属上镶嵌贵金属制成表壳的表应归入税目 91.02。

三、本章所称"表芯"，是指由摆轮及游丝、石英晶体或其他能确定时间间隔的装置来进行调节的机构，并带有显示器或可装机械指示器的系统。表芯的厚度不超过 12 毫米，长、宽或直径不超过 50 毫米。

四、除注释一另有规定的以外，钟、表的机芯及其他零件，既适用于钟或表，又适用于其他物品(例如，精密仪器)的，均应归入本章。

税则号列	货品名称〔CIQ 扩展编码及品名－T2 表示见附表 2〕	最惠(%)	暂定税率	普通	增值/消费	出口退税	计量单位	监管条件/特殊证件	检验检疫	对美关税	亚太上/下
91.01	**手表、怀表及其他表，包括秒表，表壳用贵金属或包贵金属制成的：**										
	-电力驱动的手表，不论是否附有秒表装置：										
9101.1100	--仅有机械指示器的〔999〕	8		100	13/①	13	只/千克	/			5.2/5.2
	--其他：										
9101.1910	---仅有光电显示器的〔999〕	8		100	13/①	13	只/千克	/			
9101.1990	---其他〔999〕	8		100	13/①	13	只/千克	/			
	-其他手表，不论是否附有秒表装置：										
9101.2100	--自动上弦的										
9101.2100 10	含濒危动物皮自动上弦贵金属机械手表(表壳用贵金属或包贵金属制成的)〔999〕	8		80	13/①	0	只/千克	EF/			5.2/5.2
9101.2100 90	其他自动上弦贵金属机械手表(表壳用贵金属或包贵金属制成的)〔999〕	8		80	13/①	13	只/千克	/			5.2/5.2
9101.2900	--其他										
9101.2900 10	含濒危动物皮非自动上弦贵金属机械手表(表壳用贵金属或包贵金属制成的)〔999〕	8		80	13/①	0	只/千克	EF/			5.2/5.2
9101.2900 90	其他非自动上弦贵金属机械手表(表壳用贵金属或包贵金属制成的)〔999〕	8		80	13/①	13	只/千克	/			5.2/5.2
	-其他：										
9101.9100	--电力驱动的〔999〕	8		100	13/	13	只/千克	/			
9101.9900	--其他〔999〕	15		80	13/	13	只/千克	/			
91.02	**手表、怀表及其他表，包括秒表，但税目 91.01 的货品除外：**										
	-电力驱动的手表，不论是否附有秒表装置：										
9102.1100	--仅有机械指示器的〔999〕	10		100	13/①	13	只/千克	/		35	6.5/6.5
9102.1200	--仅有光电显示器的〔999〕	15		100	13/①	13	只/千克	/		40	
9102.1900	--其他〔999〕	8		100	13/①	13	只/千克	/		33	
	-其他手表，不论是否装有秒表装置：										
9102.2100	--自动上弦的										

① 进口关税完税价格在 10000 元人民币及以上时，税率为 20%

Chapter 91
Clocks and watches and parts thereof

Notes:

1. This Chapter does not cover:
   (a) Clock or watch glasses or weights (classified according to their constituent material);
   (b) Watch chains (heading No. 71. 13 or 71. 17, as the case may be);
   (c) Parts of general use defined in Note 2 to Section XV, of base metal (Section XV), or similar goods of plastics (Chapter 39) or of precious metal or metal clad with precious metal (generally heading No. 71. 15); clock or watch springs are, however, to be classified as clock or watch parts (heading No. 91. 14);
   (d) Bearing balls (heading No. 73. 26 or 84. 82, as the case may be);
   (e) Articles of heading No. 84. 12 constructed to work without an escapement;
   (f) Ball bearings (heading No. 84. 82);
   (g) Articles of Chapter 85, not yet assembled together or with other components into watch or clock movements or into articles suitable for use solely or principally as parts of such movements (Chapter 85).
2. Heading 91. 01 covers only watches with case wholly of precious metal or of metal clad with precious metal, or of the same materials combined with natural or cultured pearls, or precious or semiprecious stones (natural, synthetic or reconstructed) of headings 71. 01 to 71. 04. Watches with case of base metal inlaid with precious metal fall in heading 91. 02.
3. For the purposes of this Chapter, the expression "watch movements" means devices regulated by a balance-wheel and hairspring, quartz crystal or any other system capable of determining intervals of time, with a display or a system to which a mechanical display can be incorporated. Such watch movements shall not exceed 12 mm in thickness and 50 mm in width, length or diameter.
4. Except as provided in Note 1, movements and other parts suitable for use both in clocks or watches and in other articles (for example, precision instruments) are to be classified in this Chapter.

协定税率 %								RCEP		特惠税率 %			Article Description
东/冰/格	巴基斯坦	韩国	瑞士 上/下	哥/秘/柬	澳/毛	新西/坡/智	中国港/澳/台	东盟及马来/澳/韩	日/新	亚太2国	老/柬/缅	98/97/95	
													Wrist-watches, pocket-watches and other watches, including stop-watches, with case of precious metal or of metal clad with precious metal:
													-Wrist-watches, electrically operated whether or not incorporating a stop-watch facility:
0/0/0	3.5	2.2	4.6/4.6	0/0/0	0/0	0/0/0	0/0/	0/0/9.9	10/0		//	0/0/0	--With mechanical display only
													--Other:
0/0/0	9	3.2	1.6/1.6	0/0/0	0/0	0/0/0	0/0/	0/0/14.4	14.5/0			0/0/0	---With optoelectronic display only
0/0/0	8.4	3	6.3/6.3	0/0/0	0/0	0/0/0	0/0/	0/0/13.5	13.6/0			0/0/0	---Other
													-Other wrist-watches, whether or not incorporating a stop-watch facility:
													--Automatic winding
0/0/0	3.5	2.2	4.6/4.6	0/0/0	0/0	0/0/0	0/0/	0/0/9.9	10/0			0/0/0	Mechanical-watches of precious metal, containing endangered animals skins, automatic winding (with case of precious metal or of metal clad with precious metal)
0/0/0	3.5	2.2	4.6/4.6	0/0/0	0/0	0/0/0	0/0/	0/0/9.9	10/0			0/0/0	Other mechanical-watches of precious metal, automatic winding(with case of precious metal or of metal clad with precious metal)
													--Other
0/0/0	8.4	3	6.3/6.3	0/0/0	0/0	0/0/0	0/0/	0/0/13.5	13.6/0			0/0/0	Mechanical-watches of precious metal, containing endangered animals skins, non-automatic winding, (with case of precious metal or of metal clad with precious metal)
0/0/0	8.4	3	6.3/6.3	0/0/0	0/0	0/0/0	0/0/	0/0/13.5	13.6/0			0/0/0	Other mechanical-watches of precious metal, non-automatic winding, (with case of precious metal or metalclad with precious meta)
													-Other:
0/0/0	8.4	3	1.5/1.5	0/0/0	0/0	0/0/0	0/0/	0/0/13.5	13.6/0			0/0/0	--Electrically operated
0/0/0		9.3	8.4/8.4	0/0/0	0/0	0/0/0	0/0/	18/18/18	18.8/18			0/0/0	--Other
													Wrist-watches, pocket-watches and other watches, including stop-watches, other than those of heading No. 91. 01:
													-Wrist-watches, electrically operated, whether or not incorporating a stop-watch facility:
0/0/0	4.3	2.5	5.3/5.3	0/0/0	0/0	0/0/0	0/0/	11.3/11.3/11.3	11.4/11.3			0/0/0	--With mechanical display only
0/0/0		13.8	2.3/2.3	0/0/0	0/13.8	0/0/0	0/0/	21.9/21.9/21.9	/21.9			0/0/0	--With optoelectronic clisplay only
0/0/0	8.4	3	1.5/1.5	0/0/0	0/0	0/0/0	0/0/	13.5/13.5/13.5	13.6/13.5			0/0/0	--Other
													-Other wrist-watches, whether or not incorporating a stop-watch facility:
													--Automatic winding

税则号列	货品名称〔CIQ 扩展编码及品名－T2 表示见附表 2〕	最惠(%)	暂定税率	普通	增值/消费	出口退税	计量单位	监管条件/特殊证件	检验检疫	对美关税	亚太上/下
9102.2100 10	含濒危动物皮其他自动上弦的机械手表(用贵金属或包贵金属制壳的除外)〔999〕	11		80	13/①	0	只/千克	EF/		36	
9102.2100 90	其他自动上弦的机械手表(用贵金属或包贵金属制壳的除外)〔999〕	11		80	13/①	13	只/千克	/		36	
9102.2900	--其他										
9102.2900 10	含濒危动物皮其他非自动上弦机械手表(用贵金属或包贵金属制壳的除外)〔999〕	10		80	13/①	0	只/千克	EF/		35	
9102.2900 90	其他非自动上弦的机械手表(用贵金属或包贵金属制壳的除外)〔999〕	10		80	13/①	13	只/千克	/		35	
	-其他：										
9102.9100	--电力驱动的〔999〕	10		100	13/	13	只/千克	/		35	
9102.9900	--其他〔999〕	15		80	13/	13	只/千克	/			
91.03	**以表芯装成的钟，但不包括税目 91.04 的钟：**										
9103.1000	-电力驱动的〔999〕	15		100	13/	13	只/千克	/		25	
9103.9000	-其他〔999〕	15		100	13/	13	只/千克	/		40	
91.04	**仪表板钟及车辆、航空器、航天器或船舶用的类似钟：**										
9104.0000	仪表板钟及车辆、航空器、航天器或船舶用的类似钟〔999〕	10		100	13/	13	只/千克	/		35	
91.05	**其他钟：**										
	-闹钟：										
9105.1100	--电力驱动的〔999〕	15		100	13/	13	只/千克	/		40	
9105.1900	--其他〔999〕	10		100	13/	13	只/千克	/			
	-挂钟：										
9105.2100	--电力驱动的〔999〕	15		100	13/	13	只/千克	/		40	
9105.2900	--其他〔999〕	10		100	13/	13	只/千克	/		35	
	-其他：										
	--电力驱动的：										
9105.9110	---天文钟〔999〕	2		8	13/	13	只/千克	/			
9105.9190	---其他〔999〕	15		100	13/	13	只/千克	/		40	
9105.9900	--其他〔999〕	10		100	13/	13	只/千克	/		30	
91.06	**时间记录器以及测量、记录或指示时间间隔的装置，装有钟、表机芯或同步电动机的(例如，考勤钟、时刻记录器)：**										
9106.1000	-考勤钟、时刻记录器〔999〕	10		50	13/	13	只/千克	/		20	
9106.9000	-其他〔101 其他车辆零部件，102 其他钟表、计时器及零件〕	10		50	13/	13	只/千克	/		20	
91.07	**装有钟、表机芯或同步电动机的定时开关：**										
9107.0000	装有钟、表机芯或同步电动机的定时开关〔999〕	8		50	13/	13	个/千克	/		28	
91.08	**已组装的完整表芯：**										
	-电力驱动的：										
9108.1100	--仅有机械指示器或有可装机械指示器的装置的〔999〕	16	10	80	13/	13	只/千克	/			
9108.1200	--仅有光电显示器的〔999〕	16		80	13/	13	只/千克	/			
9108.1900	--其他〔999〕	16		80	13/	13	只/千克	/			10.4/10.4
9108.2000	-自动上弦的〔999〕	16		80	13/	13	只/千克	/			10.4/10.4
	-其他：										
9108.9010	---表面尺寸在 33.8 毫米及以下〔999〕	16		80	13/	13	只/千克	/			
9108.9090	---其他〔999〕	16		80	13/	13	只/千克	/			
91.09	**已组装的完整钟芯：**										
9109.1000	-电力驱动的〔999〕	16		100	13/	13	只/千克	/		41	
9109.9000	-其他〔999〕	16		100	13/	13	只/千克	/			
91.10	**未组装或部分组装的完整钟、表机芯(机芯套装件)；已组装的不完整钟、表机芯；未组装的不完整钟、表机芯：**										
	-表的：										
9110.1100	--未组装或部分组装的完整机芯(机芯套装件)〔999〕	16		80	13/	13	只/千克	/			

① 进口关税完税价格在 10000 元人民币及以上时，税率为 20%

协定税率 %								RCEP		特惠税率 %			Article Description
东/冰/格	巴基斯坦	韩国	瑞士 上/下	哥/秘/柬	澳/毛	新西/坡/智	中国港/澳/台	东盟及马来/澳/韩	日/新	亚太2国	老/柬/缅	98/97/95	
0/0/0	3.5	2.2	4.6/4.6	0/0/0	0/0	0/0/0	0/0/	9.9/9.9/9.9	10/9.9			0/0/0	Mechanical-watches, containing endangered animals skins, automatic winding(other than with case of precious metal or metal clad with precious metal)
0/0/0	3.5	2.2	4.6/4.6	0/0/0	0/0	0/0/0	0/0/	9.9/9.9/9.9	10/9.9			0/0/0	Other mechanical-watches, automatic winding (other than with case of precious metal or of metal clad with precious metal)
													--Other
0/0/0	8.4	3	6.3/6.3	0/0/0	0/0	0/0/0	0/0/	0/0/13.5	13.6/0			0/0/0	Othe mechanical-watches, containing endangered animals skins, non-automatic winding(other than with case of precious metal or of metal clad with precious metal)
0/0/0	8.4	3	6.3/6.3	0/0/0	0/0	0/0/0	0/0/	0/0/13.5	13.6/0			0/0/0	Other mechanical - watches, non-automatic winding, (other than with case of precious metal or metalclad with precious metal)
													-Other:
0/0/0	8.4	3	6.3/6.3	0/0/0	0/0	0/0/0	0/0/	0/0/13.5	13.6/0			0/0/0	--Electrically operated
0/0/0		9.3	8.4/8.4	0/0/0	0/0	0/0/0	0/0/	18/18/18	18.8/18			0/0/0	--Other
													Clocks with watch movements, excluding clocks of heading No. 91. 04:
0/0/0		13.8	9.7/9.7	0/0/0	0/13.8	0/0/0	0/0/	21.9/21.9/21.9	21.9/21.9			0/0/0	-Electrically operated
0/0/0		9.3	8.4/8.4	0/0/0	0/0	0/0/0	0/0/	18/18/18	18.8/18			0/0/0	-Other
													Instrument panel clocks and clocks of a similar type for vehicles, aircraft, spacecraft or vessels:
0/0/0	2	2	0/0	0/0/0	0/0	0//0	0/0/	0/0/9	9.1/0			0/0/0	Instrument panel clocks and clocks of a similar type for vehicles, aircraft, spacecraft or vessels
													Other clocks:
													-Alarm clocks:
0/0/0	18.4	13.8	9.7/9.7	0/0/0	0/13.8	0/0/0	0/0/	21.9/21.9/21.9	21.9/21.9			0/0/0	--Electrically operated
0/0/0	16	9.3	2/2	0/0/0	0/0	0/0/0	0/0/	18/18/18	18.8/18			0/0/0	--Other
													-Wall clocks:
0/0/0	18.4	13.8	2.3/2.3	0/0/0	0/13.8	0/0/0	0/0/	21.9/21.9/21.9	21.9/21.9			0/0/0	--Electrically operated
0/0/0		9.3	2/2	0/0/0	0/0	0/0/0	0/0/	18/18/18	18.8/18			0/0/0	--Other
													-Other:
													--Electrically operated:
0/0/0	0	0	0.3/0.3	0/0/0	0/0	0//0	0/0/	0/0/0	2.7/0			0/0/0	---Astronomical chronometer
0/0/0		13.8	2.3/2.3	0/0/0	0/13.8	0/0/0	0/0/	21.9/21.9/	21.9/21.9			0/0/0	---Other
0/0/0	9	3.2	6.7/6.7	0/0/0	0/0	0/0/0	0/0/	0/0/14.4	14.5/0			0/0/0	--Other
													Time of day recording apparatus and apparatus for measuring, recording or otherwise indicating intervals of time, with clock or watch movement or with synchronous motor (for example, time-registers, time-recorders):
0/0/0	9	3.2	1.6/1.6	0/0/0	0/0	0/0/0	0/0/	0/0/14.4	14.5/0			0/0/0	-Time-registers; time-recorders
0/0/0	9	3.2	6.7/6.7	0/0/0	0/0	0/0/0	0/0/	0/0/14.4	14.5/0			0/0/0	-Other
													Time switches with clock or watch movement or with synchronous motor:
0/0/0	4.2	2.4	1.2/1.2	0/0/0	0/0	0/0/0	0/0/	0/0/10.8	10.9/0			0/0/0	Time switches with clock or watch movement or with synchronous motor
													Watch movements, complete and assembled:
													-Electrically operated:
0/0/0	9	3.2	1.6/1.6	0/0/0	0/0	0/0/0	0/0/	15.2/15.2/15.2	/15.2			0/0/0	--With mechanical display only or with a device to which a mechanical display can be incorporated
0/0/0	9	3.2	6.7/6.7	0/0/0	0/0	0/0/0	0/0/	0/0/14.4	14.5/0			0/0/0	--With optoelectronic display only
0/0/0	5.6	3.2	6.7/6.7	0/0/0	0/0	0/0/0	0/0/	0/0/14.4	14.5/0			0/0/0	--Other
0/0/0	9	3.2	6.7/6.7	0/0/0	0/0	0/0/0	0/0/	5/5/	/5			0/0/0	-Automatic winding
													-Other:
0/0/0	9	3.2	6.7/6.7	0/0/0	0/0	0/0/0	0/0/	0/0/14.4	14.5/0			0/0/0	---Measuring 33. 8mm or less
0/0/0	9	3.2	6.7/6.7	0/0/0	0/0	0/0/0	0/0/	0/0/14.4	14.5/0			0/0/0	---Other
													Clock movements, complete and assembled:
0/0/0	9	3.2	1.6/1.6	0/0/0	0/0	0/0/0	0/0/	0/0/14.4	14.5/0			0/0/0	-Eletrically operated
0/0/0	9	3.2	1.6/1.6	0/0/0	0/0	0/0/0	0/0/	0/0/14.4	14.5/0			0/0/0	-Other
													Complete watch or clock movements, unassembled or partly assembled (movement sets); incomplete watch or clock movements, assembled; rough watch or clock movements:
													-Of watches:
0/0/0	9	3.2	6.7/6.7	0/0/0	0/0	0/0/0	0/0/	5/5/	/5			0/0/0	--Complete movements, unassembled or partly assembled (movement sets)

税则号列	货品名称〔CIQ 扩展编码及品名－T2 表示见附表 2〕	最惠(%)	暂定税率	普通	增值/消费	出口退税	计量单位	监管条件/特殊证件	检验检疫	对美关税	亚太上/下
9110.1200	--已组装的不完整表机芯〔999〕	16		70	13/	13	千克	/			
9110.1900	--未组装的不完整表机芯〔999〕	16		70	13/	13	千克	/			
	-其他：										
9110.9010	---未组装或部分组装的完整钟芯〔999〕	16		100	13/	13	千克/只	/			
9110.9090	---其他〔999〕	16		80	13/	13	千克	/			
91.11	**表壳及其零件：**										
9111.1000	-贵金属表壳或包贵金属表壳										
9111.1000 10	按重量计含金量在80%及以上的黄金表壳〔999〕	14		80	13/	0	只/千克	J/			
9111.1000 90	其他贵金属或包贵金属制的表壳〔999〕	14		80	13/	0,13	只/千克	/			
9111.2000	-贱金属表壳，不论是否镀金或镀银〔999〕	14		80	13/	13	只/千克	/			9.1/9.1
9111.8000	-其他表壳〔999〕	14		80	13/	13	只/千克	/			
9111.9000	-零件〔999〕	14		80	13/	0,13	千克	/			
91.12	**钟壳和本章所列其他货品的类似外壳及其零件：**										
9112.2000	-壳〔999〕	14		80	13/	13	只/千克	/		39	
9112.9000	-零件〔999〕	12		80	13/	13	千克	/			
91.13	**表带及其零件：**										
9113.1000	-贵金属或包贵金属制										
9113.1000 10	按重量计含金量在80%及以上的黄金表带〔999〕	20		130	13/	0	千克	J/			
9113.1000 90	其他贵金属或包贵金属制的表带及零件〔999〕	20		130	13/	0,13	千克	/			
9113.2000	-贱金属制，不论是否镀金或镀银〔999〕	14		100	13/	13	千克	/		39	
9113.9000	-其他										
9113.9000 10	濒危动物皮制的表带及其零件〔999〕	14		100	13/	0	千克	FE/		39	
9113.9000 90	其他非金属制的表带及其零件〔999〕	14		100	13/	13	千克	/		39	
91.14	**钟、表的其他零件：**										
9114.3000	-钟面或表面〔999〕	14		50	13/	13	千克	/			
9114.4000	-夹板及横担（过桥）〔999〕	14		50	13/	13	千克	/			9.1/9.1
	-其他：										
9114.9010	---宝石轴承〔999〕	14		50	13/	13	千克	/			
9114.9020	---发条，包括游丝〔999〕	14		50	13/	13	千克	/			
9114.9090	---其他〔999〕	14		70	13/	13	千克	/		39	

协定税率 %								RCEP		特惠税率 %			Article Description
东/冰/格	巴基斯坦	韩国	瑞士上/下	哥/秘/柬	澳/毛	新西/坡/智	中国港/澳/台	东盟及马来/澳/韩	日/新	亚太2国	老/柬/缅	98/97/95	
0/0/0	9	3.2	1.6/1.6	0/0/0	0/0	0/0/0	0/0/	0/0/14.4	14.5/0			0/0/0	--Incomplete movements, assembled
0/0/0	9	3.2	1.6/1.6	0/0/0	0/0	0/0/0	0/0/	0/0/14.4	14.5/0			0/0/0	--Rough movements
													-Other:
0/0/0	9	3.2	1.6/1.6	0/0/0	0/0	0/0/0	0/0/	0/0/14.4	14.5/0			0/0/0	---Complete movements, unassembled or partly assembled
0/0/0	9	3.2	1.6/1.6	0/0/0	0/0	0/0/0	0/0/	0/0/14.4	14.5/0			0/0/0	---Other
													Watch cases and parts thereof:
													-Cases of precious metal or of metal clad with precious metal
0/0/0	7.8	2.8	5.9/5.9	0/0/0	0/0	0/0/0	0/0/	0/0/12.6	12.7/0			0/0/0	Watch-cases of gold, containing 80% or more by weight of gold
0/0/0	7.8	2.8	5.9/5.9	0/0/0	0/0	0/0/0	0/0/	0/0/12.6	12.7/0			0/0/0	Other watch-cases of precious metal or of metal clad with precious metal
0/0/0	4.9	2.8	1.4/1.4	0/0/0	0/0	0/0/0	0/0/	0/0/12.6	12.7/0			0/0/0	-Cases of base metal, whether or not gold-plated silver-plated
0/0/0	7.8	2.8	1.4/1.4	0/0/0	0/0	0/0/0	0/0/	0/0/12.6	12.7/0			0/0/0	-Other cases
0/0/0	7.8	2.8	1.4/1.4	0/0/0	0/10	0/0/0	0/0/	0/0/12.6	12.7/0			0/0/0	-Parts
													Clock cases and cases of a similar type for other goods of this Chapter, and parts thereof:
0/0/0	7.8	2.8	1.4/1.4	0/0/0	0/0	0/0/0	0/0/	0/0/12.6	12.7/0			0/0/0	-Cases
0/0/0	4.2	2.4	1.2/1.2	0/0/0	0/0	0/0/0	0/0/	0/0/10.8	10.9/0			0/0/0	-Parts
													Watch straps, watch bands and watch bracelets, and parts thereof:
													-Of precious metal or of metal clad with pecious metal
0/0/0	16	9.3		0/0/0	0/0	0/0/0	0/0/	18/18/18	18.8/18			0/0/0	Gold watch straps, containing 80% or more of gold by weight of gold
0/0/0	16	9.3		0/0/0	0/0	0/0/0	0/0/	18/18/18	18.8/18			0/0/0	Other watch straps and parts thereof of precious metals or of metal clad with precious metal
0/0/0	7.8	2.8	1.4/1.4	0/0/0	0/0	0/0/0	0/0/	0/0/12.6	12.7/0			0/0/0	-Of base metal, whether or not gold- plated or silver-plated
													-Other
0/0/0	7.8	2.8	1.4/1.4	0/0/0	0/10	0/0/0	0/0/	0/0/12.6	12.7/0			0/0/0	Watch straps, watch bands and watch bracelets, and parts thereof, of endangered animals skins
0/0/0	7.8	2.8	1.4/1.4	0/0/0	0/10	0/0/0	0/0/	0/0/12.6	12.7/0			0/0/0	Other watch straps, watch bands and watch bracelets and parts thereof, of non-metal
													Other clock or watch parts:
0/0/0	7.8	2.8	5.9/5.9	0/0/0	0/10	0/0/0	0/0/	0/0/12.6	12.7/0			0/0/0	-Dials
0/0/0	7.8	2.8	1.4/1.4	0/0/0	0/0	0/0/0	0/0/	0/0/12.6	12.7/0			0/0/0	-Plates and bridges
													-Other:
0/0/0	4.9	2.8	1.4/1.4	0/0/0	0/0	0/0/0	0/0/	0/0/12.6	12.7/0			0/0/0	---Jewel bearings
0/0/0	4.9	2.8	1.4/1.4	0/0/0	0/0	0/0/0	0/0/	13.1/13.3/13.1	13.1/13.3			0/0/0	---Springs, including hair—springs
0/0/0	7.8	2.8	5.9/5.9	0/0/0	0/8.4	0/0/0	0/0/	5/5/	/5			0/0/0	---Other

第九十二章
乐器及其零件、附件

注释：

一、本章不包括：

（一）第十五类注释二所规定的贱金属制通用零件（第十五类）或塑料制的类似品（第三十九章）；

（二）第八十五章或第九十章的传声器、扩大器、扬声器、耳机、开关、频闪观测仪及其他附属仪器、器具或设备，虽用于本章物品但未与该物品组成一体或安装在同一机壳内；

（三）玩具乐器或器具（税目95.03）；

（四）清洁乐器用的刷子（税目96.03），或独脚架、双脚架、三脚架及类似品（税目96.20）；或

（五）收藏品或古物（税目97.05或97.06）。

二、用于演奏税目92.02、92.06所列乐器的弓、槌及类似品，如果与该乐器一同报验，数量合理，用途明确，应归入有关乐器的相应税目。

税目92.09的卡片、盘或卷，即使与乐器一同报验，也不视为该乐器的组成部分，而应作为单独报验的物品对待。

税则号列	货品名称〔CIQ扩展编码及品名一T2表示见附表2〕	最惠(%)	暂定税率	普通	增值/消费	出口退税	计量单位	监管条件/特殊证件	检验检疫	对美关税	亚太上/下
92.01	**钢琴，包括自动钢琴、拨弦古钢琴及其他键盘弦乐器：**										
9201.1000	-竖式钢琴〔999〕	10		70	13/	13	台/千克	/		35	
9201.2000	-大钢琴										
9201.2000 01	完税价格≥5万美元的大钢琴〔999〕	10	1	70	13/	13	台/千克	/		21	
9201.2000 90	其他大钢琴〔999〕	10		70	13/	13	台/千克	/		30	
9201.9000	-其他〔999〕	10		70	13/	13	台/千克	/		20	
92.02	**其他弦乐器（例如，吉他、小提琴、竖琴）：**										
9202.1000	-弓弦乐器										
9202.1000 11	完税价格≥1.5万美元的含濒危动物皮及濒危木的弓弦乐器〔999〕	10	1	70	13/	0	只/千克	FE/		26	
9202.1000 19	其他含濒危动物皮及濒危木的弓弦乐器〔999〕	10		70	13/	0	只/千克	FE/		35	
9202.1000 91	完税价格≥1.5万美元的不含野生动物皮弓弦乐器〔999〕	10	1	70	13/	13	只/千克	/		26	
9202.1000 99	其他弓弦乐器〔999〕	10		70	13/	13	只/千克	/		35	
9202.9000	-其他										
9202.9000 10	含濒危物种成分的其他弦乐器〔101吉他，102小提琴，103大提琴，104竖琴，105二胡，106其他弓弦乐器〕	10		70	13/	0	只/千克	FE/		20	
9202.9000 90	其他弦乐器〔101吉他，102小提琴，103大提琴，104竖琴，105二胡，106其他弓弦乐器〕	10		70	13/	13	只/千克	/		20	
92.05	**管乐器（例如，键盘管风琴、手风琴、单簧管、小号、风笛），但游艺场风琴及手摇风琴除外：**										
9205.1000	-铜管乐器										
9205.1000 01	完税价格≥2000美元的铜管乐器〔999〕	10	1	70	13/	13	只/千克	/		11	
9205.1000 90	其他铜管乐器〔999〕	10		70	13/	13	只/千克	/		20	
	-其他：										
9205.9010	---键盘管风琴；簧风琴及类似的游离金属簧片键盘乐器〔999〕	10		80	13/	13	只/千克	/		35	
9205.9020	---手风琴及类似乐器〔999〕	10		80	13/	13	只/千克	/		30	
9205.9030	---口琴〔999〕	10		80	13/	13	只/千克	/		35	
9205.9090	---其他										
9205.9090 01	完税价格≥1万美元的其他管乐器（但游艺场风琴及手摇风琴除外）〔999〕	10	1	70	13/	13	只/千克	/		26	
9205.9090 91	其他含濒危物种成分的管乐器（但游艺场风琴及手摇风琴除外）〔999〕	10		70	13/	0	只/千克	EF/		35	
9205.9090 99	其他管乐器（但游艺场风琴及手摇风琴除外）〔999〕	10		70	13/	13	只/千克	/		35	
92.06	**打击乐器（例如，鼓、木琴、钹、响板、响葫芦）：**										
9206.0000	打击乐器（例如，鼓、木琴、钹、响板、响葫芦）										
9206.0000 10	含濒危动物皮及濒危木的打击乐器（例如，鼓、木琴、钹、响板）〔101鼓，102钹，103锣，104木琴，105其他打击乐器〕	10		70	13/	0	只/千克	EF/		20	
9206.0000 90	其他打击乐器（例如，鼓、木琴、钹、响板）〔101鼓，102钹，103锣，104木琴，105其他打击乐器〕	10		70	13/	13	只/千克	/		20	

Chapter 92
Musical instruments; parts and accessories of such articles

Notes:

1. This Chapter does not cover:
   (a) Parts of general use, as defined in Note 2 to Section XV, of base metal (Section XV), or similar goods of plastics (Chapter 39);
   (b) Microphones, amplifiers, loudspeakers, headphones, switches, stroboscopes or other accessory instruments, apparatus or equipment of Chapter 85 or 90, for use with but not incorporated in or housed in the same cabinet as instruments of this Chapter;
   (c) Toy instruments or apparatus (heading No. 95.03);
   (d) Brushes for cleaning musical instruments (heading No. 96.03); or
   (e) Collectors' pieces or antiques (heading No. 97.05 or 97.06).
2. Bows and sticks and similar devices used in playing the musical instruments of headings No. 92.02 and 92.06 presented with such instruments in numbers normal thereto and clearly intended for use therewith, are to be classified in the same heading as the relative instruments.
   Cards, discs and rolls of heading No. 92.09 presented with an instrument are to be treated as separate articles and not as forming a part of such instrument.

协定税率 %								RCEP		特惠税率 %			Article Description
东/冰/格	巴基斯坦	韩国	瑞士上/下	哥/秘/柬	澳/毛	新西/坡/智	中国港/澳/台	东盟及马来/澳/韩	日/新	亚太2国	老/柬/缅	98/97/95	
													Pianos, including automatic pianos; harpsichords and other keyboard stringed instruments:
0/0/0	9.8	3.5	1.8/1.8	0/0/0	0/0	0/0/0	0/0/	0/0/15.8	15.9/0			0/0/0	-Upright pianos
													-Grand pianos
0/0/0	9.8	3.5	1.8/1.8	0/0/0	0/0	0/0/0	0/0/	15.8/15.8/15.8	15.9/15.8			0/0/0	Grand pianos, duty-paid price≥USD 50000/set
0/0/0	9.8	3.5	1.8/1.8	0/0/0	0/0	0/0/0	0/0/	15.8/15.8/15.8	15.9/15.8			0/0/0	Other grand pianos
0/0/0	9.8	3.5	1.8/1.8	0/0/0	0/0	0/0/0	0/0/	15.8/15.8/15.8	16.4/15.8			0/0/0	-Other
													Other string musical instruments (for example, guitars, violins, harps):
													-Played with a bow
0/0/0	9.8	0	1.8/1.8	0/0/0	0/0	0/0/0	0/0/	0/0/0	15.9/0			0/0/0	Played with a bow, duty-paid price≥USD 15000/set, containing endangered animals skins and endangered wood
0/0/0	9.8	0	1.8/1.8	0/0/0	0/0	0/0/0	0/0/	0/0/0	15.9/0			0/0/0	Other played with a bow, containing endangered animals skins and endangered wood
0/0/0	9.8	0	1.8/1.8	0/0/0	0/0	0/0/0	0/0/	0/0/0	15.9/0			0/0/0	Played with a bow, duty-paid price≥USD 15000/set, other than endangered animals skins
0/0/0	9.8	0	1.8/1.8	0/0/0	0/0	0/0/0	0/0/	0/0/0	15.9/0			0/0/0	Other played with a bow
													-Other
0/0/0	11.2	3.5	1.8/1.8	0/0/0	0/0	0/0/0	0/0/	0/0/15.8	15.9/0			0/0/0	Other played with a bow, containing endangered species composition
0/0/0	11.2	3.5	1.8/1.8	0/0/0	0/0	0/0/0	0/0/	0/0/15.8	15.9/0			0/0/0	Other string musical instruments
													Wind musical instruments (for example keyboard pipe organs、accordions、clarinets、trumpets、bag pipes) other than fairground or gans and mechanical street organs:
													-Brass wind instruments
0/0/0	9.8	0	1.8/1.8	0/0/0	0/0	0/0/0	0/0/	0/0/0	15.9/0			0/0/0	Brass-wind instruments, duty-paid price≥USD 2000/set
0/0/0	9.8	0	1.8/1.8	0/0/0	0/0	0/0/0	0/0/	0/0/0	15.9/0			0/0/0	Other brass-wind instruments
													-Other:
0/0/0	16	9.3	2/2	0/0/0	0/0	0/0/0	0/0/	18/18/18	18.8/18			0/0/0	---Keyboard pipe organs; harmoniums and similar keyboard instruments with free metal reeds
0/0/0	16.8	9.8	2.1/2.1	0/0/0	0/0	0/0/0	0/0/	18.9/18.9/18.9	19.7/18.9			0/0/0	---Accordions and similar instruments
0/0/0	16.8	9.8	2.1/2.1	0/0/0	0/0	0/0/0	0/0/	18.9/18.9/18.9	19.7/18.9			0/0/0	---mouth organs
													---Other
0/0/0	9.8	0	1.8/1.8	0/0/0	0/0	0/0/0	0/0/	0/0/0	15.9/0			0/0/0	Other brass-wind instruments, duty-paid price ≥USD 10000/set
0/0/0	9.8	0	1.8/1.8	0/0/0	0/0	0/0/0	0/0/	0/0/0	15.9/0			0/0/0	Other wind musical instruments, containing components of endangered animals, other than fairground organs and mechanical street organs:
0/0/0	9.8	0	1.8/1.8	0/0/0	0/0	0/0/0	0/0/	0/0/0	15.9/0			0/0/0	Other wind musical instruments, other than fairground organs and mechanical street organs:
													Percussion musical instruments (for example, drums, xylophones, cymbals, castanets, maracas):
													Percussion musical instruments (for example, drums, xylophones, cymbals, castanets, maracas)
0/0/0	11.2	3.5	1.8/1.8	0/0/0	0/0	0/0/0	0/0/	0/0/15.8	15.9/0			0/0/0	Percussion musical instruments (for example, drums, xylophones, cymbals, castanets, maracas) containing endangered animal skins and endangered wood
0/0/0	11.2	3.5	1.8/1.8	0/0/0	0/0	0/0/0	0/0/	0/0/15.8	15.9/0			0/0/0	Other percussion musical instruments (for example, drums, xylophones, cymbals, castanets, maracas)

税则号列	货品名称〔CIQ 扩展编码及品名—T2 表示见附表 2〕	最惠(%)	暂定税率	普通	增值/消费	出口退税	计量单位	监管条件/特殊证件	检验检疫	对美关税	亚太上/下
92.07	**通过电产生或扩大声音的乐器(例如,电风琴、电吉他、电手风琴):**										
9207.1000	-键盘乐器,但手风琴除外〔101 电子琴,102 电风琴,103 其他电声乐器〕	12		100	13/	13	只/千克	/	L	37	
9207.9000	-其他										
9207.9000 10	其他通过电产生或扩大声音的含濒危物种成分的乐器〔301 电吉他,302 其他电声乐器〕	12		100	13/	0	个/千克	EF/		22	
9207.9000 90	其他通过电产生或扩大声音的乐器〔301 电吉他,302 其他电声乐器〕	12		100	13/	13	个/千克	/		22	
92.08	**百音盒、游艺场风琴、手摇风琴、机械鸣禽、乐锯及本章其他税目未列名的其他乐器;各种媒诱音响器、哨子、号角、口吹音响信号器:**										
9208.1000	-百音盒〔999〕	10		80	13/	13	个/千克	/		30	
9208.9000	-其他〔999〕	10		80	13/	13	个/千克	/		35	
92.09	**乐器的零件(例如,百音盒的机械装置)、附件(例如,机械乐器用的卡片、盘及带卷);节拍器、音叉及各种定音管:**										
9209.3000	-乐器用的弦〔999〕	10		70	13/	13	千克	/		20	
	-其他:										
9209.9100	--钢琴的零件、附件										
9209.9100 10	钢琴含濒危物种成分的零件、附件〔301〕	10		70	13/	0	千克	EF/		35	
9209.9100 90	钢琴的其他零件、附件〔301〕	10		70	13/	13	千克	/		35	
9209.9200	--税目 92.02 所列乐器的零件、附件										
9209.9200 10	品目 92.02 所列乐器含濒危物种成分的零件、附件〔301〕	10		70	13/	0	千克	EF/		20	
9209.9200 90	品目 92.02 所列乐器的其他零件、附件〔301〕	10		70	13/	13	千克	/		20	
9209.9400	--税目 92.07 所列乐器的零件、附件										
9209.9400 10	品目 92.07 所列乐器含濒危物种成分的零件、附件〔301〕	10		70	13/	0	千克	EF/		35	
9209.9400 90	品目 92.07 所列乐器的其他零件、附件〔301〕	10		70	13/	13	千克	/		35	
	--其他:										
9209.9910	---节拍器、音叉及定音管〔999〕	10		70	13/	13	千克	/		35	
9209.9920	---百音盒的机械装置〔999〕	10		70	13/	13	千克	/		35	6.5/6.5
9209.9990	---其他〔999〕										
9209.9990 10	本章其他编号未列名的含濒危物种成分的乐器零件〔301〕	10		70	13/	0	千克	EF/		30	
9209.9990 90	本章其他编号未列名的其他乐器零件〔301〕	10		70	13/	13	千克	/		30	

协定税率 %								RCEP		特惠税率 %			Article Description
东/冰/格	巴基斯坦	韩国	瑞士上/下	哥/秘/柬	澳/毛	新西/坡/智	中国港/澳/台	东盟及马来/澳/韩	日/新	亚太2国	老/柬/缅	98/97/95	
													Musical instruments, the sound of which is produced or must be amplified electrically (for example, organs, guitars, accordions):
0/0/0	24		12/12	0/0/0	0/18	0/0/0	0/0/	12/12/	/12			0/0/0	-Keyboard instruments, other than accordions
													-Other
0/0/0	24		12/12	0/0/0	0/18	0/0/0	0/0/	12/12/	/12			0/0/0	Other musical instruments, the sound of which is produced or must be amplified electrically, containing components of endangered animals
0/0/0	24		12/12	0/0/0	0/18	0/0/0	0/0/	12/12/	/12			0/0/0	Other musical instruments, the sound of which is produced or must be amplified electrically
													Musical boxes, fairground organs, mechanical street organs, mechanical singing birds, musical saws and other musical instruments not falling within any other heading of this Chapter; decoy calls of all kinds; whistles, call horns and other mouth-blown sound signalling instruments:
0/0/0	17.6	13.2	2.2/2.2	0/0/0	0/13.2	0/0/0	0/0/	20.9/20.9/22	21/20.9			0/0/0	-Musical boxes
0/0/0		13.2	2.2/2.2	0/0/0	0/13.2	0/0/0	0/0/	20.9/20.9/22	21/20.9			0/0/0	-Other
													Parts (for example, mechanisms for musical boxes) and accessories (for example, cards, discs and rolls for mechanical instruments) of musical instruments; metronomes, tuning forks and pitch pipes of all kinds:
0/0/0	9.8	3.5	1.8/1.8	0/0/0	0/0	0/0/0	0/0/	0/0/15.8	15.9/0			0/0/0	-Musical instrument strings
													-Other:
													--Parts and accessories for pianos
0/0/0	9.8	3.5	1.8/1.8	0/0/0	0/0	0/0/0	0/0/	15.8/15.8/15.8	15.9/15.8			0/0/0	Piano Parts, Accessories with Endangered Species Components
0/0/0	9.8	3.5	1.8/1.8	0/0/0	0/0	0/0/0	0/0/	15.8/15.8/15.8	15.9/15.8			0/0/0	Other parts and accessories for piano
													--Parts and accessories for the musical instruments of heading No. 92.02
0/0/0	9.8	3.5	1.8/1.8	0/0/0	0/0	0/0/0	0/0/	0/0/15.8	15.9/0			0/0/0	Items listed in heading 92.02 contain parts and accessories containing endangered species
0/0/0	9.8	3.5	1.8/1.8	0/0/0	0/0	0/0/0	0/0/	0/0/15.8	15.9/0			0/0/0	Other parts and accessories of musical instruments listed in heading 92.02
													--Parts and accessories for the musical instruments of heading No. 92.07
0/0/0	9.8	8.1	1.8/1.8	0/0/0	0/0	0/0/0	0/0/	16.3/16.6/16.3	16.4/16.6			0/0/0	Items listed in heading 92.07 contain parts and accessories containing endangered species
0/0/0	9.8	8.1	1.8/1.8	0/0/0	0/0	0/0/0	0/0/	16.3/16.6/16.3	16.4/16.6			0/0/0	Other parts and accessories of musical instruments listed in heading 92.07
													--Other:
0/0/0	9.8	3.5	1.8/1.8	0/0/0	0/0	0/0/0	0/0/	0/0/15.8	15.9/0			0/0/0	Metsonomes tuning froks and pitch pipes
0/0/0	9.8	3.5	1.8/1.8	0/0/0	0/0	0/0/0	0/0/	0/0/15.8	15.9/0			0/0/0	---Mechanisms for musicol boxes
													---Other
0/0/0	9.8	3.5	1.8/1.8	0/0/0	0/0	0/0/0	0/0/	15.8/15.8/15.8	15.9/15.8			0/0/0	Unlisted musical instrument parts containing endangered species in this Chapter
0/0/0	9.8	3.5	1.8/1.8	0/0/0	0/0	0/0/0	0/0/	15.8/15.8/15.8	15.9/15.8			0/0/0	Other musical instrument parts not numbered in this chapter

第十九类
武器、弹药及其零件、附件

第九十三章
武器、弹药及其零件、附件

注释：

一、本章不包括：

(一)第三十六章的货品(例如，火帽、雷管、信号弹)；

(二)第十五类注释二所规定的贱金属制通用零件(第十五类)或塑料制的类似品(第三十九章)；

(三)装甲战斗车辆(税目 87.10)；

(四)武器用的望远镜瞄准具及其他光学装置(第九十章)，但安装在武器上或与武器一同报验以备安装在该武器上的除外；

(五)弓、箭、钝头击剑或玩具(第九十五章)；

(六)收藏品及古物(税目 97.05 或 97.06)。

二、税目 93.06 所称“零件”，不包括税目 85.26 的无线电设备及雷达设备。

税则号列	货品名称〔CIQ 扩展编码及品名—T2 表示见附表 2〕	最惠(%)	暂定税率	普通	增值/消费	出口退税	计量单位	监管条件/特殊证件	检验检疫	对美关税	亚太上/下
93.01	**军用武器，但左轮手枪、其他手枪及税目 93.07 的兵器除外：**										
	-火炮武器(例如，大炮、榴弹炮及迫击炮)：										
9301.1010	---自推进的〔999〕	13		80	13/	0	座/千克	/			
9301.1090	---其他〔999〕	13		80	13/	0	座/千克	/			
9301.2000	-火箭发射器；火焰喷射器；手榴弹发射器；鱼雷发射管及类似发射装置〔999〕	13		80	13/	0	个/千克	/			
9301.9000	-其他〔999〕	13		80	13/	0	支/千克	/			
93.02	**左轮手枪及其他手枪，但税目 93.03 或 93.04 的货品除外：**										
9302.0000	左轮手枪及其他手枪，但税目 93.03 或 93.04 的货品除外〔999〕	13		80	13/	0	支/千克	/			
93.03	**靠爆炸药发射的其他火器及类似装置(例如，运动用猎枪及步枪、前装枪、维利式信号枪及其他专为发射信号弹的装置、发射空包弹的左轮手枪和其他手枪、弩枪式无痛捕杀器、抛缆枪)：**										
9303.1000	-前装枪〔999〕	13		80	13/	13	支/千克	/			
9303.2000	-其他运动、狩猎或打靶用猎枪，包括组合式滑膛来复枪〔999〕	13		80	13/	13	支/千克	/			
9303.3000	-其他运动、狩猎或打靶用步枪〔999〕	13		80	13/	13	支/千克	/			
9303.9000	-其他〔999〕										
9303.9000 10	复核射孔器(已装配)〔999〕	13		80	13/	13	支/千克	k/		33	
9303.9000 90	其他火器及类似装置〔999〕	13		80	13/	13	支/千克	/		33	
93.04	**其他武器(例如，弹簧枪、气枪、气手枪、警棍)，但不包括税目 93.07 的货品：**										
9304.0000	其他武器(例如，弹簧枪、气枪、气手枪、警棍)，但不包括税目 93.07 的货品〔999〕	13		80	13/	13	支/千克	/		23	
93.05	**税目 93.01 至 93.04 所列物品的零件、附件：**										
9305.1000	-左轮手枪或其他手枪用〔999〕	13		80	13/	0,13	千克	/			
9305.2000	-税目 93.03 的猎枪或步枪用〔999〕	13		80	13/	0,13	千克	/			
	-其他：										
9305.9100	--税目 93.01 的军用武器用〔999〕	13		80	13/	0	千克	/			
9305.9900	--其他〔999〕	13		80	13/	0,13	千克	/		23	
93.06	**炸弹、手榴弹、鱼雷、地雷、水雷、导弹及类似武器及其零件；子弹、其他弹药和射弹及其零件，包括弹丸及弹垫：**										
	-猎枪子弹及其零件；气枪弹丸：										
9306.2100	--猎枪子弹〔999〕	13		80	13/	13	千克	/			
9306.2900	--其他〔999〕	13		80	13/	13	千克	/		23	
	-其他子弹及其零件：										
9306.3080	---铆接机或类似工具用及弩枪式无痛捕杀器用子弹及其零件〔999〕	13		80	13/	0,13	千克	/			
9306.3090	---其他〔999〕	13		80	13/	0,13	千克	/			
9306.9000	-其他										
9306.9000 10	两用物项管制的导弹及其零件(能把 500 千克以上有效载荷投掷到 300 千米以上的)〔999〕	13		80	13/	0	千克	3/			

SECTION XIX
ARMS AND AMMUNITION; PARTS AND ACCESSORIES THEREOF

Chapter 93
Arms and ammunition; parts and accessories thereof

Notes:

1. This Chapter does not cover:
   (a) Goods of Chapter 36 (for example, percussion caps, detonators, signalling flares);
   (b) Parts of general use, as defined in Note 2 to Section XV, of base metal (Section XV), or similar goods of plastics (Chapter 39);
   (c) Armoured fighting vehicles (heading No. 87.10);
   (d) Telescopic sights and other optical devices suitable for use with arms, unless mounted on a firearm or presented with the firearm on which they are designed to be mounted (Chapter 90);
   (e) Bows, arrows, fencing foils or toys (Chapter 95);
   (f) Collectors' pieces or antiques (heading No. 97.05 or 97.06).
2. In heading No. 93.06, the reference to "parts thereof" does not include radio or radar apparatus of heading No. 85.26.

协定税率 %								RCEP		特惠税率 %			Article Description
东/冰/格	巴基斯坦	韩国	瑞士上/下	哥/秘/柬	澳/毛	新西/坡/智	中国港/澳/台	东盟及马来/澳/韩	日/新	亚太2国	老/柬/缅	98/97/95	
													Military weapons, other than revolvers, pistols and the arms of heading No. 93.07:
													-Artillery weapons(for example, guns, howitzers and mortars):
0/0/0	4.6	2.6	1.3/1.3	0/0/0	0/0	0/0/0	0/0/	0/0/11.7	11.8/0			0/0/0	---Self-propelled
0/0/0	4.6	2.6	1.3/1.3	0/0/0	0/0	0/0/0	0/0/	0/0/11.7	11.8/0			0/0/0	---Other
0/0/0	4.6	2.6	1.3/1.3	0/0/0	0/0	0/0/0	0/0/	0/0/11.7	11.8/0			0/0/0	-Rocket launchers; flame-throwers; grenade launchers; torpedo tubes and similar projectors
0/0/0	4.6	2.6	1.3/1.3	0/0/0	0/0	0/0/0	0/0/	0/0/11.7	11.8/0			0/0/0	-Other
													Revolvers and pistols, other than those of heading 93.03 or 93.04:
0/0/0	4.6	2.6	1.3/1.3	0/0/0	0/0	0/0/0	0/0/	0/0/11.7	11.8/0			0/0/0	Revolvers and pistols, other than those of heading No. 93.03 or 93.04
													Other firearms and similar devices which operate by the firing of an explosive charge (for example, sporting shotguns and rifles, muzzle-loading firearms, Very pistols and other devices designed to project only signal flares, pistols and revolvers for firing blank ammunition, captive-bolt humane killers, linethrowing guns):
0/0/0	4.6	2.6	1.3/1.3	0/0/0	0/0	0/0/0	0/0/	0/0/11.7	11.8/0			0/0/0	-Muzzle-loading firearms
0/0/0	4.6	2.6	5.5/5.5	0/0/0	0/0	0/0/0	0/0/	0/0/11.7	11.8/0			0/0/0	-Other sporting, hunting or target shooting shotguns, including combination shotgunrifles
0/0/0	4.6	2.6	1.3/1.3	0/0/0	0/0	0/0/0	0/0/	0/0/11.7	11.8/0			0/0/0	-Other sporting, hunting or target shooting rifles
													-Other
0/0/0	4.6	2.6	1.3/1.3	0/0/0	0/0	0/0/0	0/0/	0/0/11.7	11.8/0		//	0/0/0	Review perforator (assembled)
0/0/0	4.6	2.6	1.3/1.3	0/0/0	0/0	0/0/0	0/0/	0/0/11.7	11.8/0		//	0/0/0	Other firearms and similar devices
													Other arms (for example, spring, air or gas guns and pistols, truncheons), excluding those of heading No. 93.07:
0/0/0	4.6	2.6		0/0/0	0/0	0/0/0	0/0/	0/0/11.7	11.8/0			0/0/0	Other arms (for example, spring, air or gas guns and pistols, truncheons), excluding those of heading No. 93.07
													Parts and accessories of articles of headings No. 93.01 to 93.04:
0/0/0	4.6	2.6	1.3/1.3	0/0/0	0/0	0/0/0	0/0/	0/0/11.7	11.8/0			0/0/0	-Of revolvers or pistols
0/0/0	4.6	2.6	1.3/1.3	0/0/0	0/0	0/0/0	0/0/	0/0/11.7	11.8/0			0/0/0	-Of shotguns or rifles of heading No. 93.03
													-Other:
0/0/0	4.6	2.6	1.3/1.3	0/0/0	0/0	0/0/0	0/0/	0/0/11.7	11.8/0			0/0/0	--Of military weapons of heading No. 93.01
0/0/0	4.6	2.6	1.3/1.3	0/0/0	0/0	0/0/0	0/0/	0/0/11.7	11.8/0			0/0/0	--Other
													Bombs, grenades, torpedoes, mines, missiles, and similar munitions of war and parts thereof; cartridges and other ammunition and projectiles and parts thereof, including shot and cartridge wads:
													-Shotgun cartridges and parts thereof; air gun pellets:
0/0/0	4.6	2.6	1.3/1.3	0/0/0	0/0	0/0/0	0/0/	0/0/11.7	11.8/0			0/0/0	--Cartridges
0/0/0	4.6	2.6	1.3/1.3	0/0/0	0/0	0/0/0	0/0/	0/0/11.7	11.8/0			0/0/0	--Other
													-Other cartridges and parts thereof:
0/0/0	4.6	2.6	1.3/1.3	0/0/0	0/0	0/0/0	0/0/	0/0/11.7	11.8/0			0/0/0	---Cartridges for riveting or similar tools or for captivebolt humane killers and parts thereof
0/0/0	4.6	2.6	1.3/1.3	0/0/0	0/0	0/0/0	0/0/	0/0/11.7	11.8/0			0/0/0	---Other
													-Other
0/0/0	4.6	2.6	1.3/1.3	0/0/0	0/0	0/0/0	0/0/	0/0/11.7	11.8/0			0/0/0	Missiles and parts thereof under contorol of sensitive item (capable of throwing an available load over 500kg beyond 300km)

税则号列		货品名称〔CIQ 扩展编码及品名一T2 表示见附表 2〕	最惠(%)	暂定税率	普通	增值/消费	出口退税	计量单位	监管条件/特殊证件	检验检疫	对美关税	亚太上/下
9306.9000	20	运载火箭(能把 500 千克以上有效载荷投掷到 300 千米以上的)〔999〕	13		80	13/	0	千克	3/			
9306.9000	30	探空火箭(能把 500 千克以上有效载荷投掷到 300 千米以上的)〔999〕	13		80	13/	0	千克	3/			
9306.9000	40	巡航导弹(能把 500 千克以上有效载荷投掷到 300 千米以上的)〔999〕	13		80	13/	0	千克	3/			
9306.9000	50	聚能射孔弹、聚能切割弹、高能气体压裂弹等油气井用射弹〔999〕	13		80	13/	13	千克	k/			
9306.9000	90	其他弹药和射弹及其零件(包括炸弹、手榴弹、鱼雷、地雷、水雷、导弹等)〔999〕	13		80	13/	0,13	千克	/			
93.07		**剑、短弯刀、刺刀、长矛和类似的武器及其零件;刀鞘、剑鞘:**										
9307.0010		---军用										
9307.0010	10	军用刀鞘、剑鞘、濒危动物制〔999〕	13		80	13/	0	千克/件	FE/		23	
9307.0010	90	其他军用剑、刀、长矛和类似的武器及其零件(包括刀鞘、剑鞘)〔999〕	13		80	13/	0	千克/件	/		23	
9307.0090		---其他										
9307.0090	10	其他濒危动物制的刀鞘、剑鞘〔999〕	13		80	13/	0	千克/件	FE/		23	
9307.0090	90	其他剑、刀、长矛和类似的武器及其零件(包括刀鞘、剑鞘)〔999〕	13		80	13/	13	千克/件	/		23	

协定税率 %								RCEP		特惠税率 %			Article Description
东/冰/格	巴基斯坦	韩国	瑞士上/下	哥/秘/柬	澳/毛	新西/坡/智	中国港/澳/台	东盟及马来/澳/韩	日/新	亚太2国	老/柬/缅	98/97/95	
0/0/0	4.6	2.6	1.3/1.3	0/0/0	0/0	0/0/0	0/0/	0/0/11.7	11.8/0			0/0/0	Carrier rockets (capable of throwing an available load over 500kg beyond 300km)
0/0/0	4.6	2.6	1.3/1.3	0/0/0	0/0	0/0/0	0/0/	0/0/11.7	11.8/0			0/0/0	Sounding rockets (capable of throwing an available load over 500kg beyond 300km)
0/0/0	4.6	2.6	1.3/1.3	0/0/0	0/0	0/0/0	0/0/	0/0/11.7	11.8/0			0/0/0	Cruise missiles (capable of throwing an available load over 500kg beyond 300km)
0/0/0	4.6	2.6	1.3/1.3	0/0/0	0/0	0/0/0	0/0/	0/0/11.7	11.8/0		//	0/0/0	Charge for oil and gas wells, such as shaped charge, shaped charge, high energy gas fracturing projectile, etc.
0/0/0	4.6	2.6	1.3/1.3	0/0/0	0/0	0/0/0	0/0/	0/0/11.7	11.8/0			0/0/0	Other ammunition and projectiles and parts thereof(including bombs, grenades, torpedoes, mines, missiles)
													Swords, cutlasses, bayonets, lances and similar arms and parts thereof and scabbards and sheaths therefor:
													---For military
0/0/0	4.6	2.6	1.3/1.3	0/0/0	0/0	0/0/0	0/0/	0/0/11.7	11.8/0			0/0/0	Scabbards and sheaths of endangered animals,for military
0/0/0	4.6	2.6	1.3/1.3	0/0/0	0/0	0/0/0	0/0/	0/0/11.7	11.8/0			0/0/0	Other swords, cutlasses, lances and similar arms and parts thereof(including scabbards and sheaths),for military
													---Other
0/0/0	4.6	2.6	1.3/1.3	0/0/0	0/0	0/0/0	0/0/	0/0/11.7	11.8/0			0/0/0	Scabbards and sheaths of endangered animals
0/0/0	4.6	2.6	1.3/1.3	0/0/0	0/0	0/0/0	0/0/	0/0/11.7	11.8/0			0/0/0	Other swords, cutlasses, lances and similar arms and parts thereof (including scabbards and sheaths)

第二十类
杂 项 制 品
第九十四章
家具;寝具、褥垫、弹簧床垫、软坐垫及类似的填充制品;未列名灯具及照明装置;发光标志、发光铭牌及类似品;活动房屋

注释:

一、本章不包括:

(一)第三十九章、第四十章或第六十三章的充气或充水的褥垫、枕头及坐垫;

(二)落地镜〔例如税目70.09的试衣镜(旋转镜)〕;

(三)第七十一章的物品;

(四)第十五类注释二所规定的贱金属制通用零件(第十五类)、塑料制的类似品(第三十九章)或税目83.03的保险箱;

(五)冷藏或冷冻设备专用的特制家具(税目84.18);缝纫机专用的特制家具(税目84.52);

(六)第八十五章的灯或光源及其零件;

(七)税目85.18、85.19、85.21或税目85.25至85.28所列装置专用的特制家具(应分别归入税目85.18、85.22或85.29);

(八)税目87.14的物品;

(九)装有税目90.18所列牙科用器具或漱口盂的牙科用椅(税目90.18);

(十)第九十一章的物品(例如,钟及钟壳);

(十一)玩具家具、玩具灯具或玩具照明装置(税目95.03)、台球桌或其他供游戏用的特制家具(税目95.04)、魔术用的特制家具或中国灯笼及类似的装饰品(灯串除外)(税目95.05);

(十二)独脚架、双脚架、三脚架及类似品(税目96.20)

二、税目94.01至94.03的物品(零件除外),只适用于落地式的物品。

对下列物品,即使是悬挂的、固定在墙壁上的或叠摞的,仍归入上述各税目:

(一)碗橱、书柜、其他架式家具(包括与将其固定于墙上的支撑物一同报验的单层搁架)及组合家具。

(二)坐具及床。

三、(一)税目94.01至94.03所列货品的零件,不包括玻璃(包括镜子)、大理石或其他石料以及第六十八章及第六十九章所列任何其他材料的片、块(不论是否切割成形,但未与其他零件组装);

(二)税目94.04的货品,如果单独报验,不能作为税目94.01、94.02或94.03所列货品的零件归类。

四、税目94.06所称"活动房屋",是指在工厂制成成品或制成部件并一同报验,供以后在有关地点上组装的房屋,例如,工地用房、办公室、学校、店铺、工作棚、车房或类似的建筑物。

活动房屋包括钢结构"模块建筑单元",它们通常具有标准集装箱的形状和尺寸,其内部已部分或者全部进行了预装配。这种模块建筑单元通常设计用于组装为永久的建筑物。

税则号列		货品名称〔CIQ扩展编码及品名－T2表示见附表2〕	最惠(%)	暂定税率	普通	增值/消费	出口退税	计量单位	监管条件/特殊证件	检验检疫	对美关税	亚太上/下
94.01		**坐具(包括能作床用的两用椅,但税目94.02的货品除外)及其零件:**										
9401.1000		-飞机用坐具〔999〕	0		100	13/	13	个/千克	/		20	
		-机动车辆用坐具:										
9401.2010		---皮革或再生皮革面的[T2]	6		100	13/	13	个/千克	/	L	11	
9401.2090		---其他〔101其他车辆零部件,102其他家具,103靠垫〕	6		100	13/	13	个/千克	/	L	11	
		-可调高度的转动坐具:										
9401.3100		--木制的										
9401.3100	10	濒危木制可调高度的转动坐具〔999〕	0		100	13/	0	个/千克	EF/		10	
9401.3100	90	其他木制可调高度的转动坐具〔999〕	0		100	13/	13	个/千克	/		10	
9401.3900		--其他〔999〕	0		100	13/	13	个/千克	/		10	
		-能做床用的两用椅,但庭园坐具或野营设备除外 :										
		--木制的:										
9401.4110		---皮革或再生皮革面的〔999〕	0		100	13/	13	个/千克	/		25	
9401.4190		---其他〔999〕	0		100	13/	13	个/千克	/		25	
		--其他:										
9401.4910		---皮革或再生皮革面的〔999〕	0		100	13/	13	个/千克	/	L	25	
9401.4990		---其他〔999〕	0		100	13/	13	个/千克	/	L	25	
		-藤、柳条、竹及类似材料制的坐具:										
9401.5200		--竹制的〔999〕	0		100	13/	13	个/千克	AB/	PQ	25	
9401.5300		--藤制的〔999〕	0		100	13/	13	个/千克	AB/	PQ	25	
9401.5900		--其他〔101柳及柳制品,102柳条及类似材料制的家具〕	0		100	13/	13	个/千克	AB/	PQ		
		-木框架的其他坐具:										
		--装软垫的:										

SECTION XX
MISCELLANEOUS MANUFACTURED ARTICLES
Chapter 94
Furniture; bedding, mattresses, mattress supports, cushions and similar stuffed furnishings; uminaires and lighting fittings, not elsewhere specified or included; illuminated signs, illuminated name-plates and the like; prefabricated buildings

Notes:

1. This Chapter does not cover:
   (a) Pneumatic or water mattresses, pillows or cushions, of Chapter 39, 40 or 63;
   (b) Mirrors designed for placing on the floor or ground (for example, cheval-glasses (swing-mirrors) of heading No. 70.09);
   (c) Articles of Chapter 71;
   (d) Parts of general use as defined in Note 2 to Section XV, of base metal (Section XV), or similar goods of plastics (Chapter 39), or safes of heading NO. 83.03;
   (e) Furniture specially designed as parts of refrigerating or freezing equipment of heading 84.18; furniture specially designed for sewing machines (heading NO. 84.52);
   (f) Lamps or lighting fittings of Chapter 85;
   (g) Furniture specially designed as parts of apparatus of heading No. 85.18 (heading No. 85.18), of headings No. 85.19 to 85.21 (heading 85.22) or of headings Nos. 85.25 to 85.28 (heading No. 85.29);
   (h) Articles of heading No. 87.14;
   (ij) Dentists' chairs incorporating dental appliances of heading 90.18 or dentists' spittoons (heading No. 90.18);
   (k) Articles of Chapter 91 (for example, clocks and clock cases);
   (l) Toy furniture or toy lamps or lighting fittings (heading No. 95.03), billiard tables or other furniture specially constructed for games (heading No. 95.04), furniture for conjuring tricks or decorations (other than electric garlands) such as Chinese lanterns (heading No. 95.05).
2. The articles (other than parts) referred to in headings No. 94.01 to 94.03 are to be classified in those headings only if they are designed for placing on the floor or ground.
   The following are, however, to be classified in the above-mentioned headings even if they are designed to be hung, to be fixed to the wall or to stand one on the other:
   (a) Cupboards, bookcases, other shelved furniture (including single shelves presented with supports for fixing them to the wall) and unit furniture
   (b) Seats and beds.
3. (a) In headings No. 94.01 to 94.03 references to parts of goods do not include references to sheets or slabs (whether or not cut to shape but not combined with other parts) of glass (including mirrors), marble or other stone or of any other material referred to in Chapter 68 and 69.
   (b) Goods described in heading No. 94.04, presented separately, are not to be classified in heading No. 94.01, 94.02 or 94.03 as parts of goods.
4. For the purposes of heading No. 94.06, the expression "prefabricated buildings" means buildings which are finished in the factory or put up as elements, presented together, to be assembled on site, such as housing or worksite accommodation, offices, schools, shops, sheds, garages or similar buildings.
   Prefabricated buildings include "modular building units" of steel, normally presented in the size and shape of a standard shipping container, but substantially or completely pre-fitted internally. Such modular building units are normally designed to be assembled together to form permanent buildings.

协定税率 %								RCEP		特惠税率 %			Article Description
东/冰/格	巴基斯坦	韩国	瑞士上/下	哥/秘/柬	澳/毛	新西/坡/智	中国港/澳/台	东盟及马来/澳/韩	日/新	亚太2国	老/柬/缅	98/97/95	
													Seats (other than those of heading No. 94.02), whether or not convertible into beds, and parts thereof:
0/0/0	0	0	0/0	0/0/0	0/0	0//0	0/0/	0/0/0	0/0			0/0/0	-Seats of a kind used for aircraft
													-Seats of a kind used for motor vehicles:
5/0/0	8	6	0/0	0/0/0	0/0	0//0	0/0/	9.8/9.8/	/9.8			0/0/0	---With outer surface of leather or composition leather
5/0/0	8	4.6	0/0	0/0/0	0/0	0//0	0/0/	9.8/9.8/	/9.8			0/0/0	---Other
													-Swivel seats with variable height adjustment
													--Of wood
0/0/0	0	0	0/0	0/0/0	0/0	0//0	0/0/	0/0/0	0/0			0/0/0	Rotating seat with adjustable height
0/0/0	0	0	0/0	0/0/0	0/0	0//0	0/0/	0/0/0	0/0			0/0/0	Other wooden rotating seats with adjustable height
0/0/0	0	0	0/0	0/0/0	0/0	0//0	0/0/	0/0/0	0/0			0/0/0	--Other,
													- Seats other than garden seats or camping equipment, convertible into beds :
													Of wood
0/0/0	0	0	0/0	0/0/0	0/0	0//0	0/0/	0/0/0	0/0			0/0/0	---With outer surface of leather or composition leather
0/0/0	0	0	0/0	0/0/0	0/0	0//0	0/0/	0/0/0	0/0			0/0/0	---Other,
													--Other,
0/0/0	0	0	0/0	0/0/0	0/0	0//0	0/0/	0/0/0	0/0			0/0/0	---With outer surface of leather or composition leather
0/0/0	0	0	0/0	0/0/0	0/0	0//0	0/0/	0/0/0	0/0			0/0/0	---Other,
													-Seats of cane, osier, bamboo or similar materials:
0/0/0	0	0	0/0	0/0/0	0/0	0//0	0/0/	0/0/0	0/0		0//	0/0/0	--Of bamboo
0/0/0	0	0	0/0	0/0/0	0/0	0//0	0/0/	0/0/0	0/0		0//	0/0/0	--Of rattan
0/0/0	0	0	0/0	0/0/0	0/0	0//0	0/0/	0/0/0	0/0		0//	0/0/0	--Other
													-Other seats, with wooden frames:
													--Upholstered:

税则号列	货品名称〔CIQ 扩展编码及品名－T2 表示见附表 2〕	最惠(%)	暂定税率	普通	增值/消费	出口退税	计量单位	监管条件/特殊证件	检验检疫	对美关税	亚太上/下
9401.6110	---皮革或再生皮革面的〔101 其他木制品,102 软体家具〕	0		100	13/	13	个/千克	AB/	PQ	25	
9401.6190	---其他〔101 其他木制品,102 软体家具〕	0		100	13/	13	个/千克	AB/	PQ	10	
9401.6900	--其他										
9401.6900 10	其他濒危木框架的坐具〔101 其他木制品,102 其他家具〕	0		100	13/	0	个/千克	ABEF/	PQ	25	
9401.6900 90	其他木框架的坐具(不包括编号 94011000－94015000 的坐具)〔101 其他木制品,102 其他家具〕	0		100	13/	13	个/千克	AB/	PQ	25	
	-金属框架的其他坐具:										
	--装软垫的:										
9401.7110	---皮革或再生皮革面的〔999〕	0		100	13/	13	个/千克	/		25	
9401.7190	---其他〔999〕	0		100	13/	13	个/千克	/		20	
9401.7900	--其他〔101 其他家具,102 其他体育竞技运动器具〕	0		100	13/	13	个/千克	/		20	
	-其他坐具:										
9401.8010	---石制的〔999〕	0		100	13/	13	个/千克	/		25	
9401.8090	---其他										
9401.8090 10	其他濒危木制坐具[T2]	0		100	13/	0	个/千克	EF/		5	
9401.8090 91	儿童用汽车安全坐椅〔999〕	0		100	13/	13	个/千克	A/	LM	5	
9401.8090 99	其他坐具〔101 其他家具,102 靠垫,103 其他日用纺织制品〕	0		100	13/	13	个/千克	/	L	5	
	-零件:										
9401.9100	--木制的										
9401.9100 10	座具的濒危木制零件〔999〕	0		100	13/	0	千克	EF/		5	
9401.9100 90	座具的其他木制零件〔101 其他车辆零部件,102 家具零件〕	0		100	13/	13	千克	/		5	
	--其他:										
9401.9910	---机动车辆用座椅调角器(9401.9011)〔101 其他车辆零部件,102 其他家具〕	6		100	13/	13	套/千克	/		11	
9401.9990	---其他〔101 其他车辆零部件,102 其他家具,103 不属于危险化学品的金属(非法检)〕	0		100	13/	13	千克	/	L	5	
94.02	**医疗、外科、牙科或兽医用家具(例如,手术台、检查台、带机械装置的病床、牙科用椅);有旋转、倾斜、升降装置的理发用椅及类似椅;上述物品的零件:**										
	-牙科、理发及类似用途的椅及其零件:										
9402.1010	---理发用椅及其零件〔999〕	0		100	13/	13	个/千克	/			
9402.1090	---其他〔999〕	0		30	13/	13	个/千克	/		10	
9402.9000	-其他〔999〕	0		30	13/	13	件/千克	/		10	
94.03	**其他家具及其零件:**										
9403.1000	-办公室用金属家具〔999〕	0		100	13/	13	件/千克	/		20	
9403.2000	-其他金属家具〔999〕	0		100	13/	13	件/千克	/		20	
9403.3000	-办公室用木家具										
9403.3000 10	濒危木制办公室用木家具〔101 其他木制品,102 木家具〕	0		100	13/	0	件/千克	ABFE/	PQ	20	
9403.3000 90	其他办公室用木家具〔101 其他木制品,102 木家具〕	0		100	13/	13	件/千克	AB/	MPQ	20	
9403.4000	-厨房用木家具										
9403.4000 10	濒危木制厨房用木家具〔101 其他木制品,102 木家具〕	0		100	13/	0	件/千克	ABFE/	PQ	25	
9403.4000 90	其他厨房用木家具〔101 其他木制品,102 木家具〕	0		100	13/	13	件/千克	AB/	MPQ	25	
	-卧室用木家具:										
9403.5010	---红木制										
9403.5010 10	卧室用濒危红木制家具〔101 其他木制品,102 木家具〕	0		100	13/	0	件/千克	ABFE/	PQ		
9403.5010 90	其他卧室用红木制家具〔101 其他木制品,102 木家具〕	0		100	13/	13	件/千克	AB/	PQ		
	---其他:										
9403.5091	----天然漆(大漆)漆木家具[T2]	0		100	13/	13	件/千克	AB/	MPQ	20	
9403.5099	----其他										
9403.5099 10	卧室用其他濒危木家具〔101 其他木制品,102 木家具〕	0		100	13/	0	件/千克	ABFE/	PQ	25	
9403.5099 90	卧室用其他木家具〔101:其他木制品;102:木家具;103:儿童用〕	0		100	13/	13	件/千克	AB/	MPQ	25	
	-其他木家具:										
9403.6010	---红木制										
9403.6010 10	濒危红木制其他家具(非卧室用)〔101 其他木制品,102 木家具〕	0		100	13/	0	件/千克	ABFE/	PQ	25	
9403.6010 90	其他红木制家具(非卧室用)〔101 其他木制品,102 木家具〕	0		100	13/	13	件/千克	AB/	PQ	25	
	---其他:										
9403.6091	----天然漆(大漆)漆木家具[T2]	0		100	13/	13	件/千克	AB/	MPQ	25	
9403.6099	----其他										
9403.6099 10	濒危木制其他家具(非卧室用)〔101:其他木制品;102:木家具〕	0		100	13/	0	件/千克	ABFE/	PQ	25	
9403.6099 90	其他木家具(非卧室用)〔101 其他木制品,102 木家具〕	0		100	13/	13	件/千克	AB/	PQ	25	
9403.7000	-塑料家具〔999〕	0		100	13/	13	件/千克	/		20	

协定税率 %								RCEP		特惠税率 %			Article Description
东/冰/格	巴基斯坦	韩国	瑞士上/下	哥/秘/柬	澳/毛	新西/坡/智	中国港/澳/台	东盟及马来/澳/韩	日/新	亚太2国	老/柬/缅	98/97/95	
0/0/0	0	0	0/0	0/0/0	0/0	0//0	0/0/	0/0/0	0/0			0/0/0	---With outer surface of leather or composition leather
0/0/0	0	0	0/0	0/0/0	0/0	0//0	0/0/	0/0/0	0/0			0/0/0	---Other
													--Other
0/0/0	0	0	0/0	0/0/0	0/0	0//0	0/0/	0/0/0	0/0			0/0/0	Other seats, with endangered wood frames
0/0/0	0	0	0/0	0/0/0	0/0	0//0	0/0/	0/0/0	0/0			0/0/0	Other seats, with wood frames (other than seats of No. 94011000～94015000)
													-Other seats, with metal frames:
													--Upholstered:
0/0/0	0	0	0/0	0/0/0	0/0	0//0	0/0/	0/0/0	0/0			0/0/0	---With outer surface of leather or composition leather
0/0/0	0	0	0/0	0/0/0	0/0	0//0	0/0/	0/0/0	0/0			0/0/0	---Other
0/0/0	0	0	0/0	0/0/0	0/0	0//0	0/0/	0/0/0	0/0			0/0/0	--Other
													-Other seats:
0/0/0	0	0	0/0	0/0/0	0/0	0//0	0/0/	0/0/0	0/0			0/0/0	---Of stone
													---Other
0/0/0	0	0	0/0	0/0/0	0/0	0//0	0/0/	0/0/0	0/0			0/0/0	Other seats of endangered wood
0/0/0	0	0	0/0	0/0/0	0/0	0//0	0/0/	0/0/0	0/0			0/0/0	Automobile safety seat for children
0/0/0	0	0	0/0	0/0/0	0/0	0//0	0/0/	0/0/0	0/0			0/0/0	Other seats
													-Parts:
													--Of wood
0/0/0	0	0	0/0	0/0/0	0/0	0//0	0/0/	0/0/0	0/0			0/0/0	Endangered wooden parts of seat
0/0/0	0	0	0/0	0/0/0	0/0	0//0	0/0/	0/0/0	0/0			0/0/0	Other wooden parts of seat
													--Other
5/0/0	8		0/0	0/0/0	0/0	0//0	0/0/					0/0/0	--Seat angle requlating devices of the motor Vehicles
0/0/0	0	0	0/0	0/0/0	0/0	0//0	0/0/	0/0/0	0/0			0/0/0	--Other
													Medical, surgical, dental or veterinary furniture (for example, operating tables, examination tables, hospital beds with mechanical fittings, dentists' chairs); barbers' chairs and similar chairs, having rotating as well as both reclining and elevating movements; parts of the foregoing articles:
													-Dentists', barbers' or similar chairs and parts thereof:
0/0/0	0	0	0/0	0/0/0	0/0	0//0	0/0/	0/0/0	0/0			0/0/0	---Barbers chairs and parts thereof
0/0/0	0	0	0/0	0/0/0	0/0	0//0	0/0/	0/0/0	0/0			0/0/0	---Other
0/0/0	0	0	0/0	0/0/0	0/0	0//0	0/0/	0/0/0	0/0			0/0/0	-Other
													Other furniture and parts thereof:
0/0/0	0	0	0/0	0/0/0	0/0	0//0	0/0/	0/0/0	0/0			0/0/0	-Metal furniture of a kind used in offices
0/0/0	0	0	0/0	0/0/0	0/0	0//0	0/0/	0/0/0	0/0			0/0/0	-Other metal furniture
													-Wooden furniture of a kind used in offices
0/0/0	0	0	0/0	0/0/0	0/0	0//0	0/0/	0/0/0	0/0		0/0/	0/0/0	Furniture of endangered wood, of a kind used in offices
0/0/0	0	0	0/0	0/0/0	0/0	0//0	0/0/	0/0/0	0/0		0/0/	0/0/0	Other wooden furniture of a kind used in offices
													-Wooden furniture of a kind used in the kitchen
0/0/0	0	0	0/0	0/0/0	0/0	0//0	0/0/	0/0/0	0/0		/0/	0/0/0	Furniture of endangered wood, of a kind used in the kitchen
0/0/0	0	0	0/0	0/0/0	0/0	0//0	0/0/	0/0/0	0/0		/0/	0/0/0	Other wooden furniture of a kind used in the kitchen
													-Wooden furniture of a kind used in the bedroom:
													---Of rose wood
0/0/0	0	0	0/0	0/0/0	0/0	0//0	0/0/	0/0/0	0/0		/0/	0/0/0	Furniture of endangered rose wood, of a kind used in the bedroom
0/0/0	0	0	0/0	0/0/0	0/0	0//0	0/0/	0/0/0	0/0		/0/	0/0/0	Other furniture of rose wood, of a kind used in the bedroom
													---Other:
0/0/0	0	0	0/0	0/0/0	0/0	0//0	0/0/	0/0/0	0/0		/0/	0/0/0	----Lacquer, lacquer wood furniture
													----Other
0/0/0	0	0	0/0	0/0/0	0/0	0//0	0/0/	0/0/0	0/0		/0/	0/0/0	Furniture of other endangered wood, of a kind used in the bedroom
0/0/0	0	0	0/0	0/0/0	0/0	0//0	0/0/	0/0/0	0/0		/0/	0/0/0	Furniture of other wood, of a kind used in the bedroom
													-Other wooden furniture:
													--Of rose wood
0/0/0	0	0	0/0	0/0/0	0/0	0//0	0/0/	0/0/0	0/0		/0/	0/0/0	Other furniture of rose endangered wood (other than use in the bedroom)
0/0/0	0	0	0/0	0/0/0	0/0	0//0	0/0/	0/0/0	0/0		/0/	0/0/0	Other furniture of rose wood (use in the bedroom)
													---Other:
0/0/0	0	0	0/0	0/0/0	0/0	0//0	0/0/	0/0/0	0/0		/0/	0/0/0	----Lacquer, lacquer wood furniture
													----Other
0/0/0	0	0	0/0	0/0/0	0/0	0//0	0/0/	0/0/0	0/0		/0/	0/0/0	Other furniture of endangered wood(other than use in the bedroom)
0/0/0	0	0	0/0	0/0/0	0/0	0//0	0/0/	0/0/0	0/0		/0/	0/0/0	Other furniture of wood(other than use in the bedroom)
0/0/0	0	0	0/0	0/0/0	0/0	0//0	0/0/	0/0/0	0/0			0/0/0	-Furniture of plastics

税则号列	货品名称〔CIQ 扩展编码及品名—T2 表示见附表 2〕	最惠(%)	暂定税率	普通	增值/消费	出口退税	计量单位	监管条件/特殊证件	检验检疫	对美关税	亚太上/下
	-其他材料制的家具,包括藤、柳条、竹或类似材料制的:										
9403.8200	--竹制的〔998:其他竹及竹制品;999:竹制或藤制家具〕	0		100	13/	13	件/千克	AB/	PQ		
9403.8300	--藤制的〔998:藤及藤制品;999:竹制或藤制家具〕	0		100	13/	13	件/千克	AB/	PQ		
	--其他:										
9403.8910	---柳条及类似材料制的[T2]	0		100	13/	13	件/千克	AB/	PQ		
9403.8920	---石制的〔999〕	0		100	13/	13	件/千克	/		25	
9403.8990	---其他〔999〕	0		100	13/	13	件/千克	/		25	
	-零件:										
9403.9100	--木制的										
9403.9100 10	品目 94.03 所列物品的濒危木制零件〔999〕	0		100	13/	0	千克	EF/		25	
9403.9100 90	品目 94.03 所列物品的其他木制零件〔999〕	0		100	13/	13	千克	/		25	
9403.9900	--其他〔999〕	0		100	13/	13	千克	/		25	
94.04	**弹簧床垫;寝具及类似用品,装有弹簧、内部用任何材料填充、衬垫或用海绵橡胶、泡沫塑料制成,不论是否包面(例如,褥垫、被子、羽绒被、靠垫、坐垫及枕头):**										
9404.1000	-弹簧床垫〔999〕	10		100	13/	13	个/千克	/		20	
	-褥垫:										
9404.2100	--海绵橡胶或泡沫塑料制,不论是否包面										
9404.2100 10	蔺草包面的垫子(单件面积大于 1 平方米,无论是否包边)〔101 蔺草及其制品,102 褥垫,103 靠垫〕	10		100	13/	13	个/千克	4ABxy/	PQ	30	
9404.2100 90	海绵橡胶或泡沫塑料制褥垫(不论是否包面)〔101 褥垫,102 靠垫〕	10		100	13/	13	个/千克	/		30	
9404.2900	--其他材料制〔999〕	10		100	13/	13	个/千克	/		35	6.5/6.5
	-睡袋:										
9404.3010	---羽毛或羽绒填充的										
9404.3010 10	濒危野禽羽毛或羽绒填充的睡袋〔999〕	10		130	13/	0	个/千克	FE/			
9404.3010 90	其他羽毛或羽绒填充的睡袋〔999〕	10		130	13/	13	个/千克	/			
9404.3090	---其他〔999〕	10		100	13/	13	个/千克	/		35	
	-被子(包括羽绒被)、床罩:										
9404.4010	---羽毛或羽绒填充的										
9404.4010 10	濒危鸟类羽绒或羽毛填充的被子、床罩〔101 被子,102 床单、床罩〕	10		130	13/	0	千克/件	EF/		35	
9404.4010 90	其他羽绒或羽毛填充的被子、床罩〔101 被子,102 床单、床罩〕	10		130	13/	13	千克/件	/		35	
9404.4020	---兽毛填充的										
9404.4020 10	濒危兽毛填充的被子、床罩〔101 被子,102 床单、床罩〕	10		130	13/	0	千克/件	EF/		35	
9404.4020 90	其他兽毛填充的被子、床罩〔101 被子,102 床单、床罩〕	10		130	13/	13	千克/件	/		35	
9404.4030	---丝棉填充的〔101 被子,102 床罩〕	10		130	13/	13	千克/件	/		35	
9404.4040	---化纤棉填充的〔101 被子,102 床单、床罩〕	10		130	13/	13	千克/件	/		30	
9404.4090	---其他〔101 被子,102 床单、床罩〕	10		130	13/	13	千克/件	/		30	
	-其他:										
9404.9010	---羽毛或羽绒填充的										
9404.9010 10	濒危鸟类羽绒或羽毛填充其他寝具及类似品〔101 褥垫,102 靠垫,103 日用纺织制品〕	10		130	13/	0	千克	EF/		35	
9404.9010 90	其他羽绒或羽毛填充的其他寝具及类似品〔101 褥垫,102 靠垫,103 日用纺织制品〕	10		130	13/	13	千克	/		35	
9404.9020	---兽毛填充的										
9404.9020 10	濒危兽毛填充的其他寝具及类似品〔999〕	10		130	13/	0	千克	EF/		35	
9404.9020 90	其他兽毛填充的其他寝具及类似品〔999〕	10		130	13/	13	千克	/		35	
9404.9030	---丝棉填充的〔999〕	10		130	13/	13	千克	/		35	
9404.9040	---化学纤维棉填充的[T2]	10		130	13/	13	千克	/		30	
9404.9090	---其他〔101 靠垫,102 其他日用纺织制品〕	10		130	13/	13	千克	/		30	
94.05	**其他税目未列名的灯具及照明装置,包括探照灯、聚光灯及其零件;装有固定光源的发光标志、发光铭牌及类似品,以及其他税目未列名的这些货品的零件:**										
	-枝形吊灯及天花板或墙壁上的其他电气照明装置 ,但不包括公共露天场所或街道上的电气照明装置 :										
9405.1100	--设计为仅使用发光二极管(LED)光源的〔999〕	5		80	13/	13	个/千克	/	L	25	
9405.1900	--其他〔101 吊灯,102 其它灯具及其零件〕	5		80	13/	13	个/千克	/	L	25	

协定税率 %								RCEP		特惠税率 %			Article Description
东/冰/格	巴基斯坦	韩国	瑞士上/下	哥/秘/柬	澳/毛	新西/坡/智	中国港/澳/台	东盟及马来/澳/韩	日/新	亚太2国	老/柬/缅	98/97/95	
													-Furniture of other materials, including cane, osier, bamboo or similar materials:
0/0/0	0	0	0/0	0/0/0	0/0	0//0	0/0/	0/0/0	0/0		/0/	0/0/0	--Of bamboo
0/0/0	0	0	0/0	0/0/0	0/0	0//0	0/0/	0/0/0	0/0		/0/	0/0/0	--Of rattan
													---Other:
0/0/0	0	0	0/0	0/0/0	0/0	0//0	0/0/	0/0/0	0/0		/0/	0/0/0	---Of osier or similar materials
0/0/0	0	0	0/0	0/0/0	0/0	0//0	0/0/	0/0/0	0/0			0/0/0	---Of stone
0/0/0	0	0	0/0	0/0/0	0/0	0//0	0/0/	0/0/0	0/0			0/0/0	---Other
													-Parts
													--Of wood
0/0/0	0	0	0/0	0/0/0	0/0	0//0	0/0/	0/0/0	0/0			0/0/0	Endangered wooden parts of articles of heading 94.3
0/0/0	0	0	0/0	0/0/0	0/0	0//0	0/0/	0/0/0	0/0			0/0/0	Other wooden parts of articles of heading 94.3
0/0/0	0	0	0/0	0/0/0	0/0	0//0	0/0/	0/0/0	0/0			0/0/0	--Other
													Mattress supports; articles of bedding and similar furnishing (for example, mattresses, quilts, eiderdowns, cushions, pouffes and pillows) fitted with springs or stuffed or internally fitted with any material or of cellular rubber or plastics, whether or not covered:
0/0/0	16	9.3	2/2	0/0/0	0/0	0/0/0	0/0/	18.7/19/18.7	18.8/19			0/0/0	-Mattress supports
													-Mattresses:
													--Of cellular rubber or plastics, whether or not covered
0/0/0	16	9.3	2/2	0/0/0	0/0	0/0/0	0/0/	18.7/19/18.7	18.8/19			0/0/0	Mattresses covered with rush (area of single piece > $1m^2$, whether or not edged)
0/0/0	16	9.3	2/2	0/0/0	0/0	0/0/0	0/0/	18.7/19/18.7	18.8/19			0/0/0	Mattresses of foam rubber or foamed plastics (whether or not covered)
0/0/0	0	9.3	2/2	0/0/0	0/0	0/0/0	0/0/	18.7/19/18.7	18.8/19			0/0/0	--Of other materials
													-Sleeping bags:
													---Stunffed with feathers or down
0/0/0	16	9.3	2/2	0/0/0	0/0	0/0/0	0/0/	18/18/18	18.8/18			0/0/0	Sleeping bags stuffed with feathers or down of endang ered wild birds
0/0/0	16	9.3	2/2	0/0/0	0/0	0/0/0	0/0/	18/18/18	18.8/18			0/0/0	Sleeping bags, stuffed with other feathers or down
0/0/0		9.3	2/2	0/0/0	0/0	0/0/0	0/0/	18/18/18	18.8/18			0/0/0	---Other
													-Quilt (includingduvet), bedspread:
													---Stuffed with feathers or down
0//0	0	9.3	2/2	0/0/0	0/0	0/0/0	0/0/	18/18/18	18.8/18			0/0/0	Quilts and bedspreads filled with down or feathers of endangered birds
0//0	0	9.3	2/2	0/0/0	0/0	0/0/0	0/0/	18/18/18	18.8/18			0/0/0	Other quilts and bedspreads filled with down or feathers
													---Stuffed with animal hair
0/0/0	0	9.3	2/2	0/0/0	0/0	0/0/0	0/0/	18.7/19/18.7	18.8/19			0/0/0	Quilts, bedspreads filled with endangered animal hair
0/0/0	0	9.3	2/2	0/0/0	0/0	0/0/0	0/0/	18.7/19/18.7	18.8/19			0/0/0	Quilts and bedspreads filled with other animal hair
0/0/0	0	9.3	2/2	0/0/0	0/0	0/0/0	0/0/	18/18/18	18.8/18			0/0/0	---Stuffed with silk wadding
0/0/0	0	9.3	2/2	0/0/0	0/0	0/0/0	0/0/	18.7/19/18.7	18.8/19			0/0/0	Stuffed with man made fibres
0/0/0	0	9.3	2/2	0/0/0	0/0	0/0/0	0/0/	18.7/19/18.7	18.8/19			0/0/0	---Other
													-Other
													---Stuffed with feathers or down
0//0	0	9.3	2/2	0/0/0	0/0	0/0/0	0/0/	18/18/18	18.8/18			0/0/0	Other articles of bedding and similar furnishing, stuffed with feathers of down of endangered wild birds
0//0	0	9.3	2/2	0/0/0	0/0	0/0/0	0/0/	18/18/18	18.8/18			0/0/0	Other articles of bedding and similar furnishing, stuffed with pther feathers of down
													---Stuffed with animal hair
0/0/0	0	9.3	2/2	0/0/0	0/0	0/0/0	0/0/	18.7/19/18.7	18.8/19			0/0/0	Articles of bedding, stuffed with endangered wild animal hair (including quilt and similar furnishing)
0/0/0	0	9.3	2/2	0/0/0	0/0	0/0/0	0/0/	18.7/19/18.7	18.8/19			0/0/0	Articles of bedding and similar furnishing, stuffed with other animal hair
0/0/0	0	9.3	2/2	0/0/0	0/0	0/0/0	0/0/	18/18/18	18.8/18			0/0/0	---Stuffed with silk wadding
0/0/0	0	9.3	2/2	0/0/0	0/0	0/0/0	0/0/	18.7/19/18.7	18.8/19			0/0/0	---Stuffed with man-made fibres
0/0/0	0	9.3	2/2	0/0/0	0/0	0/0/0	0/0/	18.7/19/18.7	18.8/19			0/0/0	---Other
													Lamps and lighting fittings including searchlights and spotlights and parts thereof, not elsewhere specified or included; illuminated signs, illuminated name-plates and the like, having apermanently fixed light source, andparts thereof not elsewhere specified or included:
													-- Chandeliers and other electric ceiling or wall lighting fittings, excluding those of a kind used for lighting public open spaces or thoroughfares :
0/0/0	2	2	0/0	0/0/0	0/0	0//0	0/0/	0/0/9	9.1/0			0/0/0	-- Designed for use solely with light-emitting diode (LED) light sources
0/0/0	2	2	0/0	0/0/0	0/0	0//0	0/0/	0/0/9	9.1/0			0/0/0	--Other

税则号列	货品名称〔CIQ 扩展编码及品名—T2 表示见附表 2〕	最惠(%)	暂定税率	普通	增值/消费	出口退税	计量单位	监管条件/特殊证件	检验检疫	对美关税	亚太上/下
	-电气的台灯、床头灯或落地灯：										
9405.2100	--设计为仅使用发光二极管(LED)光源的										
9405.2100 10	设计为仅使用发光二极管(LED)光源的含濒危物种成分的电气台灯、床头灯、落地灯〔999〕	10		80	13/	0	台/千克	EF/	L	35	
9405.2100 90	设计为仅使用发光二极管(LED)光源的其他电气台灯、床头灯、落地灯〔999〕	10		80	13/	13	台/千克	/	L	35	
9405.2900	--其他										
9405.2900 10	其他含濒危物种成分的电气台灯、床头灯、落地灯〔101 台灯，102 落地灯，103 其它灯具及其零件〕	10		80	13/	0	台/千克	EF/	L	35	
9405.2900 90	其他电气台灯、床头灯、落地灯〔999〕	10		80	13/	13	台/千克	/	L	35	
	-圣诞树用的灯串：										
9405.3100	--设计为仅使用发光二极管(LED)光源的〔999〕	8		100	13/	13	套/千克	/		33	
9405.3900	--其他〔999〕	8		100	13/	13	套/千克	/		33	
	-其他电气灯具及照明装置：										
9405.4100	--光伏的，且设计为仅使用发光二极管(LED)光源的〔999〕	8.5		73	13/	13	台/千克	/		18.5	
	--其他，设计为仅使用发光二极管(LED)光源的：										
9405.4210	---探照灯和聚光灯〔999〕	10		70	13/	13	台/千克	/		30	
9405.4290	---其他〔999〕	6		80	13/	13	千克	/		16	
	--其他：										
9405.4910	---探照灯和聚光灯〔101 探照灯，102 聚光灯具〕	10		70	13/	13	台/千克	/		30	
9405.4990	---其他〔999〕	6		80	13/	13	千克	/		16	
9405.5000	-非电气的灯具及照明装置〔999〕	10		80	13/	13	千克	/		35	
	-发光标志、发光铭牌及类似品：										
9405.6100	--设计为仅使用发光二极管(LED)光源的〔999〕	10		80	13/	13	千克	/	L	30	
9405.6900	--其他〔999〕	10		80	13/	13	千克	/	L	30	
	-零件：										
9405.9100	--玻璃制〔999〕	8		70	13/	13	千克	/		18	
9405.9200	--塑料制〔999〕	8		70	13/	13	千克	/		28	
9405.9900	--其他〔999〕	8		70	13/	13	千克	/		28	
94.06	**活动房屋：**										
9406.1000	-木制的〔999〕	8		70	13/	13	千克	AB/	PQ	28	5.2/5.2
9406.2000	-钢结构模块建筑单元〔999〕	8		70	13/	13	千克	/		33	5.2/5.2
9406.9000	-其他										
9406.9000 10	用动植物材料制作的活动房屋(木制的除外)〔999〕	8		70	13/	13	千克	AB/	PQ	33	5.2/5.2
9406.9000 20	带有风扇的高效空气粒子过滤单元(HEPA)的封闭洁净室〔999〕	8		70	13/	13	千克	3/		33	5.2/5.2
9406.9000 90	其他活动房屋〔999〕	8		70	13/	13	千克	/		33	5.2/5.2

协定税率 %								RCEP		特惠税率 %			Article Description
东/冰/格	巴基斯坦	韩国	瑞士上/下	哥/秘/柬	澳/毛	新西/坡/智	中国港/澳/台	东盟及马来/澳/韩	日/新	亚太2国	老/柬/缅	98/97/95	
													-Electrical desk lamp, bedsidelamp or floor lamp:
													-- Designed for use solely with light-emitting diode (LED) light sources
0/0/0	16	12	2/2	0/0/0	0/0	0/0/0	0/0/	19/19/	/19			0/0/0	Electric desk lamp, bedside lamp and floor lamp with endangered species components designed to use only light emitting diode (LED) light source
0/0/0	16	12	2/2	0/0/0	0/0	0/0/0	0/0/	19/19/	/19			0/0/0	Other electrical desk lamps, bedside lamps, floor lamps designed to use only light emitting diode (LED) light sources
													--Other
0/0/0	16	12	2/2	0/0/0	0/0	0/0/0	0/0/	19/19/	/19			0/0/0	Other electric desk lamps, bedside lamps and floor lamps containing endangered species
0/0/0	16	12	2/2	0/0/0	0/0	0/0/0	0/0/	19/19/	/19			0/0/0	Other electric desk lamps, bedside lamps, floor lamps
													- Lighting strings of a kind used for Christmas trees :
0/0/0	9	3.2	1.6/1.6	0/0/0	0/0	0/0/0	0/0/	0/0/14.4	14.5/0			0/0/0	-- Designed for use solely with light-emitting diode (LED) light sources
0/0/0	9	3.2	1.6/1.6	0/0/0	0/0	0/0/0	0/0/	0/0/14.4	14.5/0			0/0/0	--Other
													- Other electric luminaires and lighting fittings :
0/0/0	6.5	2.3	1.2/1.2	0/0/0	0/0	0/0/0	0/0/	0/0/9	9.1/0			0/0/0	-- Photovoltaic, designed for use solely with light—emitting diode (LED) light sources
													--Other, designed for use solely with light—emitting diode (LED) light sources
0/0/0	9.8	3.5	1.8/1.8	0/0/0	0/0	0/0/0	0/0/	0/0/15.8	15.9/0			0/0/0	---Searchlights and Spotlights
0/0/0	0	0	0/0	0/0/0	0/0	0/0/0	0/0/	9/9/9	9.1/9			0/0/0	---Other
													--Other
0/0/0	9.8	3.5	1.8/1.8	0/0/0	0/0	0/0/0	0/0/	0/0/15.8	15.9/0			0/0/0	---Searchlights and Spotlights
0/0/0	0	0	0/0	0/0/0	0/0	0/0/0	0/0/	9/9/9	9.1/9			0/0/0	---Other,
0/0/0		12	2/2	0/0/0	0/0	0/0/0	0/0/	19/19/	/19			0/0/0	-Non-electrical lamps and lighting fittings
													-Illuminated signs, illuminated name plates and the like
0/0/0	16	9.3	2/2	0/0/0	0/0	0/0/0	0/0/	18.7/19/18.7	18.8/19			0/0/0	-- Designed for use solely with light-emitting diode (LED) light sources
0/0/0	16	9.3	2/2	0/0/0	0/0	0/0/0	0/0/	18.7/19/18.7	18.8/19			0/0/0	--Other
													-Parts
0/0/0	16	12	2/2	0/0/0	0/0	0/0/0	0/0/	19/19/	/19			0/0/0	--Of glass
0/0/0	16	9.3	2/2	0/0/0	0/0	0/0/0	0/0/	18.7/19/18.7	18.8/19			0/0/0	--Of plastics
0/0/0		9.3	2/2	0/0/0	0/0	0/0/0	0/0/	18.7/19/18.7	18.8/19			0/0/0	--Other
													Prefabricated buildings:
0/0/0	2	2	0/0	0/0/0	0/0	0/0/0	0/0/	0/0/9	9.1/0			0/0/0	-Of wood
0/0/0	2	2	0/0	0/0/0	0/0	0/0/0	0/0/	0/0/9	9.1/0			0/0/0	- Modular building units, of steel
													-Other
0/0/0	2	2	0/0	0/0/0	0/0	0/0/0	0/0/	0/0/9	9.1/0			0/0/0	Prefabricated buildings of materials of animal or vegetable, excuding of wood
0/0/0	2	2	0/0	0/0/0	0/0	0/0/0	0/0/	0/0/9	9.1/0			0/0/0	Sealed clean room with fan, for filtering unit of high efficiency particulatc air(HEPA)
0/0/0	2	2	0/0	0/0/0	0/0	0/0/0	0/0/	0/0/9	9.1/0			0/0/0	Other prefabricated buildings

第九十五章
玩具、游戏品、运动用品及其零件、附件

注释：

一、本章不包括：

(一)蜡烛(税目34.06)；

(二)税目36.04的烟花、爆竹或其他烟火制品；

(三)已切成一定长度但未制成钓鱼线的纱线、单丝、绳、肠线及类似品(第三十九章、税目42.06或第十一类)；

(四)税目42.02、43.03或43.04的运动用袋或其他容器；

(五)第六十一章或第六十二章的纺织品制的化妆舞会服装；第六十一章或第六十二章的纺织品制的运动服装或特殊衣着(例如，击剑服或足球守门员球衣)，无论是否附带保护配件，例如，肘部、膝部或腹股沟部位的保护垫或填充物；

(六)第六十三章的纺织品制的旗帜及帆板或滑行车用帆；

(七)第六十四章的运动鞋靴(装有冰刀或滑轮的溜冰鞋除外)或第六十五章的运动用帽；

(八)手杖、鞭子、马鞭或类似品(税目66.02)及其零件(税目66.03)；

(九)税目70.18的未装配的玩偶或其他玩具用的玻璃假眼；

(十)第十五类注释二所规定的贱金属制通用零件(第十五类)或塑料制的类似货品(第三十九章)；

(十一)税目83.06的铃、钟、锣及类似品；

(十二)液体泵(税目84.13)、液体或气体的过滤、净化机器及装置(税目84.21)、电动机(税目85.01)、变压器(税目84.04)；录制声音或其他信息用的圆盘、磁带、固态非易失性数据存储器件、"智能卡"及其他媒体，不论是否已录制(税目85.23)；无线电遥控设备(税目85.26)或无绳红外线遥控器件(85.43)；

(十三)第十七类的运动用车辆(长雪橇、平底雪橇及类似品除外)；

(十四)儿童两轮车(税目87.12)；

(十五)无人驾驶航空器(税目88.06)；

(十六)运动用船艇，例如，轻舟、赛艇(第八十九章)及其桨、橹和类似品(木制的归入第四十四章)；

(十七)运动及户外游戏用的眼镜、护目镜及类似品(税目90.04)；

(十八)媒诱音响器及哨子(税目92.08)；

(十九)第九十三章的武器及其他物品；

(二十)各种灯串(税目94.05)；

(二十一)独脚架、双脚架、三脚架及类似品(税目96.20)；

(二十二)球拍线、帐篷或类似的野营用品、分指手套、连指手套和露指手套(按其构成材料归类)；

(二十三)餐具、厨房用具、盥洗用品、地毯及纺织材料制的其他铺地制品、服装、床上、餐桌、盥洗及厨房用织物制品及具有实用功能的类似货品(按其构成材料归类)。

二、本章包括天然或养殖珍珠、宝石或半宝石(天然、合成或再造)、贵金属或包贵金属只作为小零件的物品。

三、除上述注释一另有规定的以外，凡专用于或主要用于本章各税目所列物品的零件、附件，应与有关物品一并归类。

四、除上述注释一另有规定的以外，税目95.03主要适用于该税号所列的物品与一项或多项其他货品组合而成的物品，只要这些物品为零售包装，且组合后具有玩具的基本特征。这些组合物品不能视为归类总规则三(二)所指的成套货品，如果单独报验，应归入其他税号。

五、税目95.03不包括因其设计、形状或构成材料可确认为专供动物使用的物品，例如，"宠物玩具"(归入其相应的税目)。

六、税目95.08中：

(一)"游乐场乘骑游乐设施"是指主要目的为游乐或娱乐的装置、组合装置或设备，用于运载、传送、导引一人或多人越过或穿行某一固定或限 定的路径(包括水道)，或者特定区域，这些设施不包括通常安装在住宅 区或操场内的设备；

(二)"水上乐园娱乐设备"是指特征为特定的涉水区域且无设定路径的 装置、组合装置或设备。这些设备仅包括专为水上乐园设计的设备；

(三)"游乐场娱乐设备"是指凭借运气、力量或技巧来玩的游戏设备，通常需要操作员或服务员，可安装在永久性建筑物或独立的摊位，这些设备不包括税目95.04的设备。本税目不包括在本协调制度其他税目中列名更为具体的设备。

子目注释：

一、子目9504.50包括：

(一)在电视机、监视器或其他外部屏幕或表面上重放图像的视频游戏控制器；

(二)自带显示屏的视频游戏设备，不论是否便携式。

本子目不包括用硬币、钞票、银行卡、代币或任何其他支付方式使其工作的视频游戏控制器或设备(子目9504.30)

税则号列	货品名称〔CIQ扩展编码及品名—T2表示见附表2〕	最惠(%)	暂定税率	普通	增值/消费	出口退税	计量单位	监管条件/特殊证件	检验检疫	对美关税	亚太上/下
95.03	**三轮车、单脚滑行车、踏板车及类似的带轮玩具；玩偶车；玩偶；其他玩具；缩小(按比例缩小)的模型及类似的娱乐用模型，不论是否活动；各种智力玩具：**										
9503.0010	---三轮车、踏板车、踏板汽车和类似的带轮玩具；玩偶车〔101儿童三轮车，102儿童推车，103最大鞍座高度435mm—635mm范围内的儿童自行车，104儿童踏板车，105儿童玩偶车，106其他童车〕	0		80	13/	13	辆/千克	/	L	20	
	---玩偶，不论是否着装；玩具动物：										

Chapter 95
Toys, games and sports requisites; parts and accessories thereof

Notes:

1. This Chapter does not cover:
   (a) Candles (heading No. 34.06);
   (b) Fireworks or other pyrotechnic articles of heading No. 36.04;
   (c) Yarns, monofilament, cords or gut or the like for fishing, cut to length but not made up into fishing lines, of Chapter 39, heading No. 42.06 or Section XI;
   (d) Sports bags or other containers of heading No. 42.02, 43.03 or 43.04;
   (e) Fancy dress of textiles, of Chapter 6 1 or 62; sports clothing and special articles of apparel of textiles, of Chapter 61 or 62, whether or not in corporating incidentally protective components such as pads or padding in the elbow, knee or groin areas(for example, fencing clothing or soccer goalkeeper jerseys);
   (f) Textile flags or bunting, or sails for boats, sailboards or land craft, of Chapter 63;
   (g) Sports footwear (other than skating boots with ice or roller skates attached) of Chapter 64, or sports headgear of Chapter 65;
   (h) Walking-sticks, whips, riding-crops or the like (heading No. 66.02), or parts thereof (heading No. 66.03);
   (ij) Unmounted glass eyes for dolls or other toys, of heading No. 70.18;
   (k) Parts of general use, as defined in Note 2 to Section XV, of base metal (Section XV), or similar goods of plastics (Chapter 39);
   (l) Bells, gongs or the like of heading No. 83.06;
   (m) Pumps for liquids (heading No. 84.13), filtering or purifying machinery and apparatus for liquids or gases (heading No. 84.21), electric motors (heading No. 85.01), electric transformers (heading No. 85.04); discs, tapes, solid-state non-volatile storage devices, "smart cards" and other media for the recording of sound or of other phenomena, wheter or not recorded(heading 85.23), radio remote control appppratus (heading85.26) or cordless infrared remote control devices (heading85.43)
   (n) Sports vehicles (other than bobsleighs, toboggans and the like) of Section XVII;
   (o) Children's bicycles (heading No. 87.12);
   (p) Unmanned aircraft (heading 88.06);
   (q) Sports craft such as canoes and skiffs (Chapter 89), or their means of propulsion (Chapter 44 for such articles made of wood);
   (r) Spectacles, goggles or the like, for sports or outdoor games (heading No. 90.04);
   (s) Decoy calls or whistles (heading No. 92.08);
   (t) Arms or other articles of Chapter 93;
   (u) Electric garlands of all kinds (heading No. 94.05);
   (v) unipod, bipod, tripod or the like(heading No.96.20);
   (w) Racket strings, tents or other camping goods, or gloves, mittens and mitts (classified according to their constituent material). or

   (x) Tableware, kitchenware, toilet articles, carpetsand other textile floor coverings, apparel, bed linen, table linen, toilet linen, kitchen linen and similar articles having a utilitarian function(classified according to their constituent material).

2. This Chapter includes articles in which natural or cultured pearls, precious or semi-precious stones (natural, synthetic or reconstructed), precious metal or metal clad with precious metal constitute only minor consistuents.
3. Subject to Note 1 above, parts and accessories which are suitable for use solely or principally with articles of this Chapter are to be classified with those articles.
4. Subject to the provisions of Note 1 above, heading 95.03 applies, inter alia, to articles of this heading combined with one or more items, which cannot be considered as sets under the terms of Ceneral Interpretative Rule 3 (b), and which, if presented separately, would be classified in other headings, provided the articles are put up together for retail sale and the combinations have the essential character of toys.
5. Heading 95.03 does not cover articles which, on account of their design, shape or constituent material, are identifiable as intended exclusively for animals, for example, "pet toys"(classification in their own appropriate heading).
6. For the purposes of heading 95.08:
   (d) The expression "amusement park rides" means a device or combination of devices or equipment that carry, convey, or direct a person or persons over or through a fixed or restricted course, including watercourses, or within a defined area for the primary purposes of amusement or entertainment. Such rides may be combined within an amusement park, theme park, water park or fairground. These amusement park rides do not include equipment of a kind commonly installed in residences or playgrounds;
   (e) The expression "water park amusements" means a device or combination of devices or equipment that are characterized by a defined area involving water, with no purposes built path. Water park amusements only include equipment designed specifically for water parks; and
   (f) The expression "fairground amusements" means games of chance, strength or skill, which commonly employ an operator or attendant and may be installed in permanent buildings or independent concession stalls. Fairground amusements do not include equipment of heading 95.04. This heading does not include equipment more specifically classified elsewhere in the Nomenclature.".

Subheading Note:

1. Subheading 9504.50 covers:
   (a) Video game consoles from which the image is reproduced on a television receiver, a monitor or other external screen or surface;
   (b) Video game machines having a self-contained video screen, whether or not portable.
   This subheading does not cover video game consoles or machines operated by coins, banknotes, bank cards, tokens or by any other means of payment(subheading9504.30)

协定税率 %								RCEP		特惠税率 %			Article Description
东/冰/格	巴基斯坦	韩国	瑞士上/下	哥/秘/柬	澳/毛	新西/坡/智	中国港/澳/台	东盟及马来/澳/韩	日/新	亚太2国	老/柬/缅	98/97/95	
0/0/0	0	0	0/0	0/0/0	0/0	0//0	0/0/	0/0/0	0/0			0/0/0	**Tricycles, scooters, pedal cars and similar wheeled toys; dals carriages; dolls; Other toys; re duced-size("scale") models and similar recreational models working or not; puzzles of all kinds;** ---Tricycles, scooters, pedal cars and similar wheeled toys; doll's carriage ---Dolls, whether or not dressed; toy representing animals or non-human creatures;

税则号列	货品名称〔CIQ扩展编码及品名—T2表示见附表2〕	最惠(%)	暂定税率	普通	增值/消费	出口退税	计量单位	监管条件/特殊证件	检验检疫	对美关税	亚太上/下
9503.0021	----动物〔101 布绒玩具,102 竹木玩具,103 塑胶玩具,104 电玩具,105 软体造型玩具,106 弹射玩具,107 金属玩具〕	0		80	13/	13	个/千克	A/	LM	25	
9503.0029	----其他〔101 布绒玩具,102 竹木玩具,103 塑胶玩具,104 电玩具,105 纸制玩具,106 软体造型玩具,107 弹射玩具,108 金属玩具,109 玩具收藏品〕	0		80	13/	13	个/千克	A/	LM	25	
9503.0060	---智力玩具[101 布绒玩具,102 竹木玩具,103 塑胶玩具,104 电玩具,105 纸制玩具,106 类似文具玩具,107 软体造型玩具,108 金属玩具,109 玩具收藏品]	0		80	13/	13	套/千克	A/	LM	25	
	---其他玩具:										
9503.0083	----带动力装置的玩具及模型										
9503.0083 10	玩具无人机〔999〕	0		80	13/	13	套/千克	A/	LM	25	
9503.0083 90	带动力装置的玩具及模型〔301 布绒玩具,302 竹木玩具,303 塑胶玩具,304 电玩具,305 弹射玩具,306 金属玩具,307 其他未列名玩具,308 玩具收藏品〕	0		80	13/	13	套/千克	A/	LM	25	
9503.0089	----其他〔101 乘骑玩具,102 其他未列名玩具,103 玩具收藏品〕	0		80	13/	13	个/千克	A/	LM	25	
9503.0090	---零件、附件〔999〕	0		80	13/	13	千克	A/	LM	25	
95.04	**视频游戏控制器及设备,桌上或室内游戏用品,包括弹球机、台球、娱乐专用桌及保龄球自动球道设备,用硬币、钞票、银行卡、代币或任何其他支付方式使其工作的游乐机器:**										
9504.2000	-台球用品及附件										
9504.2000 10	濒危木制的台球用品及附件〔999〕	0		80	13/	0	千克	EF/		20	
9504.2000 90	其他台球用品及附件〔999〕	0		80	13/	13	千克	/		20	
	-用硬币、钞票、银行卡、代币及任何其他支付方式使其工作的其他游戏用品,但保龄球自动球道设备除外:										
9504.3010	---电子游戏机〔999〕	0		130	13/	13	台/千克	/		10	
9504.3090	---其他〔999〕	0		80	13/	13	台/千克	/			
9504.4000	--游戏纸牌〔999〕	0		80	13/	13	副/千克	/		10	
	-视频游戏控制器及设备,但子目 9504.30 的货品除外:										
9504.5020	---自带视频显示装置的视频游戏控制器及设备〔999〕	0		130	13/	13	台/千克	/			
9504.5030	---其他视频游戏控制器及设备〔999〕	0		130	13/	13	台/千克	/			
9504.5080	---零件及附件(9504.5011,9504.5091)〔999〕	0		130	13/	13	个/千克	/			
	-其他:										
9504.9010	---其他电子游戏机〔999〕	0		130	13/	13	台/千克	/			
	---保龄球自动球道设备及器具:										
9504.9021	----保龄球自动分瓶机〔999〕	0		80	13/	13	台/千克	/		10	
9504.9022	----保龄球〔999〕	0		80	13/	13	个/千克	/		10	
9504.9023	----保龄球瓶〔999〕	0		80	13/	13	个/千克	/		20	
9504.9029	----其他〔999〕	0		80	13/	13	台/千克	/		10	
9504.9030	---中国象棋、国际象棋、跳棋等棋类用品〔999〕	0		80	13/	13	副/千克	/		25	
9504.9040	---麻将及类似桌上游戏用品〔101:麻将;102:其他游戏器具〕	0		80	13/	13	副/千克	/		25	
9504.9090	---其他〔101 其它游戏机,102 游乐设备零件,103 其他游戏器具〕	0		80	13/	13	台/千克	/		20	
95.05	**节日(包括狂欢节)用品或其他娱乐用品,包括魔术道具及嬉戏品:**										
9505.1000	-圣诞节用品										
9505.1000 10	含动植物性材料的圣诞用品(不包括成套圣诞节灯具)〔101 木制工艺品,102 其他木制品,103 其他草及草制品,104 其他竹藤柳草类,105 含动物产品类〕	0		100	13/	13	千克	AB/	PQ	25	
9505.1000 90	其他圣诞节用品(不包括成套圣诞节灯具)〔101 含木制品,102 不含木制品〕	0		100	13/	13	千克	/		25	
9505.9000	-其他〔101 含木制品,102 不含木制品〕	0		100	13/	13	千克	/		10	
95.06	**一般的体育活动、体操、竞技及其他运动(包括乒乓球运动)或户外游戏用的本章其他税号未列名用品及设备;游泳池或戏水池:**										
	-滑雪屐及其他滑雪用具:										
9506.1100	--滑雪屐〔999〕	6	3	50	13/	13	双/千克	/		23	
9506.1200	--滑雪屐扣件(滑雪屐带)〔999〕	6	3	50	13/	13	千克	/		23	
9506.1900	--其他〔999〕	6	3	50	13/	13	千克	/		23	
	-滑水板、冲浪板、帆板及其他水上运动用具:										
9506.2100	--帆板〔999〕	6		50	13/	13	个/千克	/		31	
9506.2900	--其他〔999〕	6		50	13/	13	个/千克	/		16	
	-高尔夫球棍及其他高尔夫球用具:										

协定税率 %								RCEP		特惠税率 %			Article Description
东/冰/格	巴基斯坦	韩国	瑞士上/下	哥/秘/柬	澳/毛	新西/坡/智	中国港/澳/台	东盟及马来/澳/韩	日/新	亚太2国	老/柬/缅	98/97/95	
0/0/0	0	0	0/0	0/0/0	0/0	0//0	0/0/	0/0/0	0/0			0/0/0	----Animals
0/0/0	0	0	0/0	0/0/0	0/0	0//0	0/0/	0/0/0	0/0			0/0/0	----Other
0/0/0	0	0	0/0	0/0/0	0/0	0//0	0/0/	0/0/0	0/0			0/0/0	---Puzzles
													---Other toys:
													----Toys and models with power devices
0/0/0	0	0	0/0	0/0/0	0/0	0//0	0/0/	0/0/0	0/0			0/0/0	Toy UAV
0/0/0	0	0	0/0	0/0/0	0/0	0//0	0/0/	0/0/0	0/0			0/0/0	Toys and models with power devices
0/0/0	0	0	0/0	0/0/0	0/0	0//0	0/0/	0/0/0	0/0			0/0/0	----Other
0/0/0	0	0	0/0	0/0/0	0/0	0//0	0/0/	0/0/0	0/0			0/0/0	---Parts and accessories
													Vide game controlle, table or parlour games, in cluding pintables, billiards, special tables for casino games and automatic bowling alley equipment amusement machines operated by coins, bank notes, bank cards, tokens or by any other means of payment:
													-Articles and accessories for billiards of all kinds
0/0/0	0	0	0/0	0/0/0	0/0	0//0	0/0/	0/0/0	0/0			0/0/0	Articles and accessories for billiards of endangered wood
0/0/0	0	0	0/0	0/0/0	0/0	0//0	0/0/	0/0/0	0/0			0/0/0	Other articles and accessories for billiards of au kinds
													-Other games, operated by coins, banknotes bank cords, tokens or by other means of payment, other than automatic bowing alley equipment:
0/0/0	0	0	0/0	0/0/0	0/0	0//0	0/0/	0/0/0	0/0			0/0/0	---Video games
0/0/0	0	0	0/0	0/0/0	0/0	0//0	0/0/	0/0/0	0/0			0/0/0	---Other
0/0/0	0	0	0/0	0/0/0	0/0	0//0	0/0/	0/0/0	0/0			0/0/0	--Playing cards
													-Video game consoles or machines operated, other than heading 9504. 30:
0/0/0	0	0	0/0	0/0/0	0/0	0//0	0/0/	0/0/0	0/0			0/0/0	---Video game controller and equipment with video display device
0/0/0	0	0	0/0	0/0/0	0/0	0//0	0/0/	0/0/0	0/0			0/0/0	---Other video game controllers and devices
0/0/0	0	0	0/0	0/0/0	0/0	0//0	0/0/	0/0/0	0/0			0/0/0	---Parts and accessories
													-Other:
0/0/0	0	0	0/0	0/0/0	0/0	0//0	0/0/	0/0/0	0/0			0/0/0	---Other video games
													---Automatic bowling alley equipments and appliances:
0/0/0	0	0	0/0	0/0/0	0/0	0//0	0/0/	0/0/0	0/0			0/0/0	----Automatic bowling pin distributing machines
0/0/0	0	0	0/0	0/0/0	0/0	0//0	0/0/	0/0/0	0/0			0/0/0	----Bowling balls
0/0/0	0	0	0/0	0/0/0	0/0	0//0	0/0/	0/0/0	0/0			0/0/0	----Bowling pins
0/0/0	0	0	0/0	0/0/0	0/0	0//0	0/0/	0/0/0	0/0			0/0/0	----Other
0/0/0	0	0	0/0	0/0/0	0/0	0//0	0/0/	0/0/0	0/0			0/0/0	---Chess and other board games, including Chinese chess, international chess, Chinese cherkers and draughts
0/0/0	0	0	0/0	0/0/0	0/0	0//0	0/0/	0/0/0	0/0			0/0/0	---Mahjong and similiar table games
0/0/0	0	0	0/0	0/0/0	0/0	0//0	0/0/	0/0/0	0/0			0/0/0	---Other
													Festive, carnival or other entertainment articles, including conjuring tricks and novelty jokes:
													-Articles for Christmas festivities
0/0/0	0	0	0/0	0/0/0	0/0	0//0	0/0/	0/0/0	0/0			0/0/0	Articles for Christmas festivities containing animals or vegetable materials (other than lighting sets of a kind used for Christmas)
0/0/0	0	0	0/0	0/0/0	0/0	0//0	0/0/	0/0/0	0/0			0/0/0	Other articles for Christmas festivities (other than lighting sets of a kind used for Christmas)
0/0/0	0	0	0/0	0/0/0	0/0	0//0	0/0/	0/0/0	0/0			0/0/0	-Other
													Articles and equipment for general physical exercise, gymnastics, athletics, other sports (including table-tennis) or out door games, not specified or included elsewhere in this Chapter; swimming pools and paddling pools:
													-Snow-skis and other snow-ski equipment:
0//0	0	2.8	1.4/1.4	0/0/0	0/0	0/0/0	0/0/	0/0/12.6	12.7/0			0/0/0	--Skis
0/0/0	0	2.8	1.4/1.4	0/0/0	0/0	0/0/0	0/0/	0/0/12.6	12.7/0			0/0/0	--Ski-fastenings (ski-bindings)
0/0/0	0	2.8	1.4/1.4	0/0/0	0/0	0/0/0	0/0/	0/0/12.6	12.7/0			0/0/0	--Other
													-Water-skis, surf-boards, sailboards and other water-sport equipment:
0/0/0	0	2.4	1.2/1.2	0/0/0	0/0	0/0/0	0/0/	0/0/10.8	10.9/0			0/0/0	--Sailboards
0/0/0	0	2.8	1.4/1.4	0/0/0	0/0	0/0/0	0/0/	0/0/12.6	12.7/0			0/0/0	--Other
													-Golf clubs and other golf equipment:

税则号列	货品名称〔CIQ 扩展编码及品名—T2 表示见附表 2〕	最惠(%)	暂定税率	普通	增值/消费	出口退税	计量单位	监管条件/特殊证件	检验检疫	对美关税	亚太 上/下
9506.3100	--棍，全套〔999〕	6		50	13/10	13	根/千克	/		26	
9506.3200	--球〔999〕	6		50	13/10	13	个/千克	/		26	
9506.3900	--其他〔999〕	6		50	13/	13	千克	/		31	
	-乒乓球运动用品及器械：										
9506.4010	---乒乓球〔999〕	6		50	13/	13	百个/千克	/		31	
9506.4090	---其他〔999〕	6		50	13/	13	千克	/			
	-网球拍、羽毛球拍或类似的球拍，不论是否装弦：										
9506.5100	--草地网球拍，不论是否装弦〔999〕	6		50	13/	13	支/千克	/			
9506.5900	--其他〔999〕	6		50	13/	13	支/千克	/		31	
	-球，但高尔夫球及乒乓球除外：										
9506.6100	--草地网球〔999〕	6		50	13/	13	个/千克	/			
	--可充气的球：										
9506.6210	---篮球、足球、排球〔999〕	6		50	13/	13	个/千克	/		31	
9506.6290	---其他〔999〕	6		50	13/	13	个/千克	/		16	
9506.6900	--其他〔999〕	6		50	13/	13	个/千克	/		31	
	-溜冰鞋及旱冰鞋，包括装有冰刀的溜冰靴：										
9506.7010	---溜冰鞋〔999〕	6		50	13/	13	双/千克	/		26	3.9/3.9
9506.7020	---旱冰鞋〔999〕	6		50	13/	13	双/千克	/		26	3.9/3.9
	-其他：										
	---一般的体育活动、体操或竞技用品及设备：										
	---健身及康复器械：										
9506.9111	----跑步机										
9506.9111 10	跑步机(整机)〔101 电动跑步机，102 其他跑步机〕	6		50	13/	13	台/千克	/		16	
9506.9111 90	跑步机的零件及附件〔101 电动跑步机，102 其他跑步机〕	6		50	13/	13	台/千克	/		16	
9506.9119	----其他〔101 力量型训练器材，102 力量型训练长凳，103 曲柄踏板类训练器材，104 划船机，105 踏步机、台阶机和登山机，106 椭圆训练机，107 带固定飞轮和不带自由飞轮的练习自行车，108 其他健身器材〕	6		50	13/	13	千克	/		16	
9506.9190	---其他〔999〕	6		50	13/	13	千克	/		16	
	--其他：										
9506.9910	---滑板〔999〕	6		50	13/	13	个/千克	/		16	
9506.9990	---其他〔101 康复健身器械及其零件；102 其他体育竞技运动器具〕	6		50	13/	13	个/千克	/		16	
95.07	**钓鱼竿、钓鱼钩及其他钓鱼用品；捞鱼网、捕蝶网及类似网；囮子“鸟”(税目 92.08 或 97.05 的货品除外)以及类似的狩猎用品：**										
9507.1000	-钓鱼竿										
9507.1000 10	用植物性材料制作的钓鱼竿〔101 其他木制品，102 其他竹藤柳草类，103 钓鱼器具〕	6		80	13/	13	副/千克	AB/	PQ	31	
9507.1000 90	其他钓鱼竿〔999〕	6		80	13/	13	副/千克	/		31	
9507.2000	-钓鱼钩，不论有无系钩丝〔999〕	6		80	13/	13	千克	/		26	
9507.3000	-钓线轮〔999〕	6		80	13/	13	个/千克	/		31	
9507.9000	-其他〔999〕	6		80	13/	13	千克	/		16	3.9/3.9
95.08	**流动马戏团及流动动物园；游乐场乘骑游乐设施和水上乐园娱乐设备；游乐场娱乐设备，包括射击用靶；流动剧团：**										
9508.1000	-流动马戏团及流动动物园										
9508.1000 10	有濒危动物的流动马戏团(包括流动动物园)〔999〕	6		100	13/	0	千克	FEAB/	PQ		
9508.1000 90	其他流动马戏团及流动动物园〔999〕	6		100	13/	13	千克	AB/	PQ		
	-游乐场乘骑游乐设施和水上乐园娱乐设备 ：										
9508.2100	--过山车〔101 大型游乐设施，102 其他游戏器具〕	6		100	13/	13	千克	AB/	PQ	16	
9508.2200	--旋转木马，秋千和旋转平台〔101 大型游乐设施，102 其他游戏器具〕	6		100	13/	13	千克	AB/	PQ	16	
9508.2300	--碰碰车〔101 大型游乐设施，102 其他游戏器具〕	6		100	13/	13	千克	AB/	PQ	16	
9508.2400	--运动模拟器和移动剧场〔101 大型游乐设施，102 其他游戏器具〕	6		100	13/	13	千克	AB/	PQ	16	
9508.2500	--水上乘骑游乐设施〔101 大型游乐设施，102 其他游戏器具〕	6		100	13/	13	千克	AB/	PQ	16	
9508.2600	--水上乐园娱乐设备〔101 大型游乐设施，102 其他游戏器具〕	6		100	13/	13	千克	AB/	PQ	16	
9508.2900	--其他〔101 大型游乐设施，102 其他游戏器具〕	6		100	13/	13	千克	AB/	PQ	16	
9508.3000	-游乐场娱乐设备〔101 大型游乐设施，102 其他游戏器具〕	6		100	13/	13	千克	AB/	PQ	16	
9508.4000	-流动剧团〔101 大型游乐设施，102 其他游戏器具〕	6		100	13/	13	千克	AB/	PQ	16	

协定税率 %								RCEP		特惠税率 %			Article Description
东/冰/格	巴基斯坦	韩国	瑞士上/下	哥/秘/柬	澳/毛	新西/坡/智	中国港/澳/台	东盟及马来/澳/韩	日/新	亚太2国	老/柬/缅	98/97/95	
0//0	0	2.8	1.4/1.4	0/0/0	0/0	0/0/0	0/0/	12.6/12.6/12.6	12.7/12.6			0/0/0	--Clubs, complete
0/0/0	0	2.4	1.2/1.2	0/0/0	0/0	0/0/0	0/0/	0/0/10.8	10.9/0			0/0/0	--Balls
0//0	0	2.8	1.4/1.4	0/0/0	0/0	0/0/0	0/0/0	12.6/12.6/12.6	12.7/12.6			0/0/0	--Other
													-Articles and equipment for table-tennis:
0/0/0	0	2.4	1.2/1.2	0/0/0	0/0	0/0/0	0/0/	0/0/10.8	10.9/0			0/0/0	---Table-tennis balls
0/0/0	0	2.8	1.4/1.4	0/0/0	0/0	0/0/0	0/0/	0/0/12.6	12.7/0			0/0/0	---Other
													-Tennis, badminton or similar rackets, whether or not strung:
0/0/0	0	2.8	1.4/1.4	0/0/0	0/0	0/0/0	0/0/	0/0/12.6	12.7/0			0/0/0	--Lawn-tennis rackets, whether or not strung
0/0/0	0	2.8	1.4/1.4	0/0/0	0/0	0/0/0	0/0/	0/0/12.6	12.7/0			0/0/0	--Other
													-Balls, other than golf balls and tabletennis balls:
0/0/0	0	2.4	1.2/1.2	0/0/0	0/0	0/0/0	0/0/	0/0/10.8	10.9/0			0/0/0	--Lawn-tennis balls
													--Inflatable:
0/0/0	0	2.4	1.2/1.2	0/0/0	0/0	0/0/0	0/0/	0/0/10.8	10.9/0			0/0/0	---Basketballs, footballs or volleyballs
0/0/0	0	2.4	1.2/1.2	0/0/0	0/0	0/0/0	0/0/	0/0/10.8	10.9/0			0/0/0	---Other
0/0/0	0	2.4	1.2/1.2	0/0/0	0/0	0/0/0	0/0/	0/0/10.8	10.9/0			0/0/0	--Other
													-Ice skates and roller skates, including skating boots with skates attached:
0/0/0	0	2.8	1.4/1.4	0/0/0	0/0	0/0/0	0/0/	0/0/12.6	12.7/0			0/0/0	---Ice skates
0/0/0	0	2.8	1.4/1.4	0/0/0	0/0	0/0/0	0/0/	0/0/12.6	12.7/0			0/0/0	---Roller skates
													-Other:
													--Articles and equipment for general physical exercise, gymnastics or athletics:
													---Equipment for exercise and recovery:
													----Runing machines
0/0/0	0	2.4	1.2/1.2	0/0/0	0/0	0/0/0	0/0/0	0/0/10.8	10.9/0			0/0/0	The treadmill (machine)
0/0/0	0	2.4	1.2/1.2	0/0/0	0/0	0/0/0	0/0/0	0/0/10.8	10.9/0			0/0/0	Parts and accessories of treadmill
0/0/0	0	2.4	1.2/1.2	0/0/0	0/0	0/0/0	0/0/0	0/0/10.8	10.9/0			0/0/0	----Other
0/0/0	0	2.4	1.2/1.2	0/0/0	0/0	0/0/0	0/0/	0/0/10.8	10.9/0			0/0/0	---Other
													--Other:
0/0/0	0	2.4	1.2/1.2	0/0/0	0/0	0/0/0	0/0/	0/0/10.8	10.9/0			0/0/0	---Skateboards
0/0/0	0	2.4	0/0	0/0/0	0/0	0/0/0	0/0/	0/0/10.8	10.9/0			0/0/0	---Other
													Fishing rods, fish-hooks and other line fishing tackle; fish landing nets, butterfly nets and similar nets; decoy "birds" (other than those of heading 92.08 or 97.05) and similar hunting or shooting requisites:
													-Fishing rods
0//0	16.8		2.1/2.1	0/0/0	0/0	0/0/0	0/0/	6/6/	/6			0/0/0	Fishing rods of vegetable materials
0//0	16.8		2.1/2.1	0/0/0	0/0	0/0/0	0/0/	6/6/	/6			0/0/0	Other fishing rods
0//0	16.8	12.6	2.1/2.1	0/0/0	0/0	0/0/0	0/0/	20/20/	/20			0/0/0	-Fish-hooks, whether or not snelled
0//0	16.8	12.6	2.1/2.1	0/0/0	0/0	0/0/0	0/0/	20/20/	/20			0/0/0	-Fishing reels
0/0/0	15.1	12.6	2.1/2.1	0/0/0	0/12.6	0/0/0	0/0/	20/20/	/20			0/0/0	-Other
													Travelling circuses and travelling menageries; amusement park rides and water park amusements; fairground amusements, including shooting galleries; travelling theatres.
													-Travelling circuses and travelling menageries
0/0/0	8.4	3	1.5/1.5	0/0/0	0/0	0/0/0	0/0/	0/0/13.5	13.6/0			0/0/0	Travelling circuses and travelling menageries, having endangered animals
0/0/0	8.4	3	1.5/1.5	0/0/0	0/0	0/0/0	0/0/	0/0/13.5	13.6/0			0/0/0	Other travelling circuses and travelling menageries
													- Amusement park rides and water park amusements
0/0/0	9.6	3	1.5/1.5	0/0/0	0/0	0/0/0	0/0/	0/0/13.5	13.6/0			0/0/0	-- Roller coasters
0/0/0	9.6	3	1.5/1.5	0/0/0	0/0	0/0/0	0/0/	0/0/13.5	13.6/0			0/0/0	-- Carousels, swings and roundabouts
0/0/0	9.6	3	1.5/1.5	0/0/0	0/0	0/0/0	0/0/	0/0/13.5	13.6/0			0/0/0	-- Dodge'em cars
0/0/0	9.6	3	1.5/1.5	0/0/0	0/0	0/0/0	0/0/	0/0/13.5	13.6/0			0/0/0	-- Motion simulators and moving theatres
0/0/0	9.6	3	1.5/1.5	0/0/0	0/0	0/0/0	0/0/	0/0/13.5	13.6/0			0/0/0	-- Water rides
0/0/0	9.6	3	1.5/1.5	0/0/0	0/0	0/0/0	0/0/	0/0/13.5	13.6/0			0/0/0	-- Water park amusements
0/0/0	9.6	3	1.5/1.5	0/0/0	0/0	0/0/0	0/0/	0/0/13.5	13.6/0			0/0/0	-- Other
0/0/0	9.6	3	1.5/1.5	0/0/0	0/0	0/0/0	0/0/	0/0/13.5	13.6/0			0/0/0	- Fairground amusements
0/0/0	9.6	3	1.5/1.5	0/0/0	0/0	0/0/0	0/0/	0/0/13.5	13.6/0			0/0/0	- Travelling theatres

第九十六章
杂 项 制 品

注释：

一、本章不包括：

（一）化妆盥洗用笔（第三十三章）；

（二）第六十六章的制品（例如，伞或手杖的零件）；

（三）仿首饰（税目 71.17）；

（四）第十五类注释二所规定的贱金属制通用零件（第十五类）或塑料制的类似品（第三十九章）；

（五）第八十二章的利口器及其他物品，其柄或其他零件是雕刻或模塑材料制的；但税目 96.01 或 96.02 适用于单独报验的上述物品的柄或其他零件；

（六）第九十章的物品，例如，眼镜架（税目 90.03）、数学绘图笔（税目 90.17）、各种牙科、医疗、外科或兽医专用刷子（税目 90.18）；

（七）第九十一章的物品（例如，钟壳或表壳）；

（八）乐器及其零件、附件（第九十二章）；

（九）第九十三章的物品（武器及其零件）；

（十）第九十四章的物品（例如，家具、灯具及照明装置）；

（十一）第九十五章的物品（玩具、游戏品、运动用品）；

（十二）艺术品、收藏品及古物（第九十七章）。

二、税目 96.02 所称“植物质或矿物质雕刻材料”，是指：

（一）用于雕刻的硬种子、硬果核、硬果壳、坚果及类似植物材料（例如，象牙果及棕榈子）；

（二）琥珀、海泡石、粘聚琥珀、粘聚海泡石、黑玉及其矿物代用品。

三、税目 96.03 所称“制帚、制刷用成束、成簇的材料”，仅指未装配的成束、成簇的兽毛、植物纤维或其他材料。这些成束、成簇的材料无需分开即可安装在帚、刷之上，或只需经过简单加工（例如，将顶端修剪成形）即可安装的。

四、除税目 96.01 至 96.06 或 96.15 的货品以外，本章的物品还包括全部或部分用贵金属、包贵金属、天然或养殖珍珠、宝石或半宝石（天然、合成或再造）制成的物品。而且，税目 96.01 至 96.06 及 96.15 包括天然或养殖珍珠、宝石或半宝石（天然、合成或再造）、贵金属或包贵金属只作为小零件的物品。

税则号列	货品名称〔CIQ 扩展编码及品名—T2 表示见附表 2〕	最惠(%)	暂定税率	普通	增值/消费	出口退税	计量单位	监管条件/特殊证件	检验检疫	对美关税	亚太上/下
96.01	**已加工的兽牙、骨、龟壳、角、鹿角、珊瑚、珍珠母及其他动物质雕刻材料及其制品(包括模塑制品)：**										
9601.1000	-已加工的兽牙及其制品										
9601.1000 10	已加工的濒危兽牙及其制品[T2]	20		100	13/	0	千克	AFEB/	PQ		
9601.1000 90	其他已加工的兽牙及其制品[T2]	20		100	13/	13	千克	AB/	PQ		
9601.9000	-其他										
9601.9000 10	其他已加工濒危动物质雕刻料(包括其制品)〔101 含木制品的工艺品，102 不含木制品的工艺品〕	20		100	13/	0	千克	AFEB/	PQ	45	
9601.9000 20	牛角纽扣坯圆片(濒危动物制除外)〔101：含木制品的工艺品；102：不含木制品的工艺品〕	20	6	100	13/	13	千克	AB/	PQ	31	
9601.9000 90	其他已加工动物质雕刻料及其制品〔101 含木制品的工艺品，102 不含木制品的工艺品〕	20		100	13/	13	千克	AB/	PQ	45	
96.02	**已加工的植物质或矿物质雕刻材料及其制品；蜡、硬脂、天然树胶、天然树脂或塑型膏制成的模塑或雕刻制品以及其他税目未列名的模塑或雕刻制品；已加工的未硬化明胶(税目 35.03 的明胶除外)及未硬化明胶制品：**										
9602.0010	---装药用胶囊〔999〕	5		40	13/	13	千克	/		15	
9602.0090	---其他[T2]	12		100	13/	13	千克	AB/	PQ		
96.03	**帚、刷(包括作为机器、器具、车辆零件的刷)、非机动的手工操作地板清扫器、拖把及毛掸；供制帚、刷用的成束或成簇的材料；油漆块垫及滚筒；橡皮扫帚(橡皮辊除外)：**										
9603.1000	-用枝条或其他植物材料捆扎而成的帚及刷，不论是否有把〔101 其他竹及竹制品，102 棕及棕制品，103 扫帚〕	12		100	13/	13	把/千克	AB/	PQ	32	
	-牙刷、剃须刷、发刷、指甲刷、睫毛刷及其他人体化妆用刷，包括作为器具零件的上述刷：										
9603.2100	--牙刷，包括齿板刷〔101 牙刷，102 齿板刷〕	8		100	13/	13	把/千克	A/	M	28	
9603.2900	--其他										
9603.2900 10	濒危动物毛制剃须刷、发刷(包括睫毛刷等人体化妆刷)〔101 含木制品，102 不含木制品〕	6		100	13/	0	支/千克	FE/		26	3.9/3.9
9603.2900 90	其他剃须刷，发刷，睫毛刷等人体化妆刷(包括作为器具零件的子目 960329 所属的刷)〔101 含木制品，102 不含木制品〕	6		100	13/	13	支/千克	/		26	3.9/3.9

Chapter 96
Miscellaneous manufactured articles

Notes:

1. This Chapter does not cover:
   (a) Pencils for cosmetic or toilet uses (Chapter 33);
   (b) Articles of Chapter 66 (for example, parts of umbrellas or walking-sticks);
   (c) Imitation jewellery (heading No. 71.17);
   (d) Parts of general use, as defined in Note 2 to Section XV, of base metal (Section XV), or similar goods of plastics (Chapter 39);
   (e) Cutlery or other articles of Chapter 82 with handles or other parts of carving or moulding materials; heading No. 96.01 or 96.02 applies, however, to separately pressented handles or other parts of such articles;
   (f) Articles of Chapter 90 (for exampple, spectacle frames (heading No. 90.03), mathematical drawing pens (heading No. 90.17), brushes of a kind specialized for use in dentistry or for medical, surgical or veterinary purposes (heading No. 90.18);
   (g) Articles of Chapter 91 (for example, clock or watch cases);
   (h) Musical instruments or parts or accessories thereof (Chapter 92);
   (ij) Articles of Chapter 93 (arms and parts thereof);
   (k) Articles of Chapter 94 (for example, furniture, lamps and lighting fittings);
   (l) Articles of Chapter 95 (toys, games, sports requisites);
   (m) Works of art, collectors' pieces or antiques (Chapter 97).
2. In heading No. 96.02 the expression "vegetable or mineral carving material" means:
   (a) Hard seeds, pips, hulls and nuts and similar vegetable materials of a kind used for carving (for example, corozo and dom);
   (b) Amber, meerschaum, agglomerated amber and agglomerated meerschaum, jet and mineral substitutes for jet.
3. In heading No. 96.03 the expression "prepared knots and tufts for broom or brush making" applies only to unmounted knots and tufts of animal hair, vegetable fibre or other material, which are ready for incorporation without division in brooms or brushes, or which require only such further minor processes as trimming to shape at the top, to render them ready for such incorporation.
4. Articles of this Chapter, other than those of headings No. 96.01 to 96.06 or 96.15, remain classified in the Chapter whether or not composed wholly or partly of precious metal or metal clad with precious metal, of natural or cultured pearls, or precious or semiprecious stones (natural, synthetic or reconstructed). However, headings No. 96.01 to 96.06 and 96.15 include articles in which natural or cultured pearls, precious or semi-precious stones (natural, synthetic or reconstructed), precious metal or metal clad with precious metal constitute only minor constituents.

协定税率 %								RCEP		特惠税率 %			Article Description
东/冰/格	巴基斯坦	韩国	瑞士上/下	哥/秘/柬	澳/毛	新西/坡/智	中国港/澳/台	东盟及马来/澳/韩	日/新	亚太2国	老/柬/缅	98/97/95	
													Worked ivory, bone, tortoise-shell, horn, antlers, coral, mother-of-pearl and other animal carving material and articles of these materials (including articles obtained by moulding):
													-Worked ivory and articles of ivory
0/0/0	16	9.3	2/2	0/0/0	0/0	0/0/0	0/0/	18/18/18	18.2/18			0/0/0	Worked ivory and articles of ivory, of endangered animals
0/0/0	16	9.3	2/2	0/0/0	0/0	0/0/0	0/0/	18/18/18	18.2/18			0/0/0	Other worked ivory and articles of ivory
													-Other
0/0/0	16	9.3	2/2	0/0/0	0/0	0/0/0	0/0/	18.7/19/18.7	18.8/19			0/0/0	Other worked carving material and articles of these materials of endangered animals
0/0/0	16	9.3	2/2	0/0/0	0/0	0/0/0	0/0/	18.7/19/18.7	18.8/19		//	0/0/0	Fillet of horn button (except for endangered animals)
0/0/0	16	9.3	2/2	0/0/0	0/0	0/0/0	0/0/	18.7/19/18.7	18.8/19			0/0/0	Other worked animal carving material and articles of these materials
													Worked vegetable or mineral carving material and articles of these materials; moulded or carved articles of wax, of stearin, of natural gums or natural resins or of modelling pastes, and other moulded or carved articles, not elsewhere specified or included; worked, unhardened gelatin (except gelatin of heading No35.03) and articles of unhardened gelatin:
0/0/0	3.5	2.1	1.1/1.1	0/0/0	0/0	0/0/0	0/0/	0/0/9.5	9.5/0			0/0/0	---Pharmaceutical capsules
0/0/0	20	15	2.5/2.5	0/0/0	0/15	0/0/0	0/0/	23.8/23.8/23.8	23.8/23.8			0/0/0	---Other
													Brooms, brushes (including brushes constituting parts of machines, appliances or vehicles), hand-operated mechanical floor sweepers, not motorized, mops and feather dusters; prepared knots and tufts for broom or brush making; paint pads and rollers; squeegees (other than roller squeegees):
0/0/0	20	15	2.5/2.5	0/0/0	0/15	0/0/0	0/0/	23.8/23.8/23.8	23.8/23.8			0/0/0	-Brooms and brushes, consisting of twigs or other vegetable materials bound together, with or without handles
													-Tooth brushes, shaving brushes, hair brushes, nail brushes, eyelash brushes and other toilet brushes for use on the person, including such brushes constituting parts of appliances:
0/0/0	20	15	2.5/2.5	0/0/0	0/15	0/0/0	0/0/	23.8/23.8/	/23.8			0/0/0	--Tooth brushes, including dental-plate brushes
													--Other
0/0/0	5.3	3	1.5/1.5	0/0/0	0/0	0/0/0	0/0/	0/0/13.5	13.6/0			0/0/0	Shaving brushes, hair brushes(including eyelash brushes and other toilet brushes for use on the person) of wild animal hair
0/0/0	5.3	3	1.5/1.5	0/0/0	0/0	0/0/0	0/0/	0/0/13.5	13.6/0			0/0/0	Shaving brushes, hair brushes, eyelash brushes and other toilet brushes for use on the person(including parts and appliances of subheading No. 960329)

税则号列	货品名称〔CIQ 扩展编码及品名—T2 表示见附表 2〕	最惠(%)	暂定税率	普通	增值/消费	出口退税	计量单位	监管条件/特殊证件	检验检疫	对美关税	亚太上/下
	-画笔、毛笔及化妆用的类似笔：										
9603.3010	---画笔										
9603.3010 10	濒危动物毛制的画笔〔999〕	8		100	13/	0	支/千克	FE/		28	4.8/4.8
9603.3010 90	其他画笔〔999〕	8		100	13/	13	支/千克	/		28	4.8/4.8
9603.3020	---毛笔										
9603.3020 10	濒危动物毛制的毛笔〔999〕	8		100	13/	0	支/千克	FE/		28	5.2/5.2
9603.3020 90	其他毛笔〔999〕	8		100	13/	13	支/千克	/		28	5.2/5.2
9603.3090	---其他										
9603.3090 10	濒危动物毛制化妆用的类似笔〔999〕	6		100	13/	0	支/千克	FE/		26	3.9/3.9
9603.3090 90	其他化妆用的类似笔〔999〕	6		100	13/	13	支/千克	/		26	3.9/3.9
	-油漆刷、涂料刷、清漆刷及类似的刷(子目 9603.30 的货品除外)；油漆块垫及滚筒：										
	---漆刷及类似刷：										
9603.4011	----猪鬃制〔101 含木制品，102 不含木制品〕	6		100	13/	13	把/千克	/		26	
9603.4019	----其他〔101 含木制品，102 不含木制品〕	6		100	13/	13	把/千克	/		16	
9603.4020	---油漆块垫及滚筒〔101 含木制品，102 不含木制品〕	6		100	13/	13	个/千克	/		16	
	-其他作为机器、器具、车辆零件的刷：										
	---金属丝刷：										
9603.5011	----作为机器、器具零件的刷〔101：含木制品；102：不含木制品〕	8		50	13/	13	个/千克	/		28	
9603.5019	----其他〔101：其他车辆零部件；102：含木制品；103：不含木制品〕	8		100	13/	13	个/千克	/		33	
	---其他：										
9603.5091	----作为机器、器具零件的刷										
9603.5091 10	濒危动物毛制作为机器零件其他刷(包括器具零件的其他刷)〔101 含木制品，102 不含木制品〕	8		50	13/	0	个/千克	FE/		28	
9603.5091 90	其他作为机器、器具零件的其他刷〔101：含木制品；102：不含木制品〕	8		50	13/	13	个/千克	/		28	
9603.5099	----其他										
9603.5099 10	濒危动物毛制作为车辆零件的其他刷〔101 其他车辆零部件，102 含木制品，103 不含木制品〕	8		100	13/	0	个/千克	FE/		28	
9603.5099 90	其他作为车辆零件的其他刷[T2]	8		100	13/	13	个/千克	/		28	
	-其他：										
9603.9010	---羽毛掸										
9603.9010 10	濒危野禽羽毛掸〔999〕	6		130	13/	0	个/千克	AFEB/	PQ		3.9/3.9
9603.9010 90	其他羽毛掸〔999〕	6		130	13/	13	个/千克	AB/	PQ		3.9/3.9
9603.9090	---其他										
9603.9090 10	濒危动物毛、鬃、尾制其他帚，刷(包括拖把及其他毛掸)〔101 含木制品，102 不含木制品〕	6		100	13/	0	个/千克	AFEB/	PQ	26	
9603.9090 20	其他动植物材料制帚，刷，拖把等(包括动植物材料制非机动的手工操作地板清扫器、毛掸)〔101 其他木制品，102 其他竹及竹制品，103 棕及棕制品，104 扫帚，105 藁杆，106 其他竹藤柳草类〕	6		100	13/	13	个/千克	AB/	PQ	26	
9603.9090 90	其他材料制帚，刷，拖把及毛掸(包括其他材料制非机动的手工操作地板清扫器等)〔101 含木制品，102 不含木制品〕	6		100	13/	13	个/千克	/		26	
96.04	**手用粗筛、细筛：**										
9604.0000	手用粗筛、细筛〔101 含木制品，102 不含木制品〕	6		100	13/	13	个/千克	AB/	PQ	16	
96.05	**个人梳妆、缝纫或清洁鞋靴、衣服用的成套旅行用具：**										
9605.0000	个人梳妆、缝纫或清洁鞋靴、衣服用的成套旅行用具〔101 含木制品，102 不含木制品〕	6		100	13/	13	套/千克	/		26	
96.06	**纽扣、揿扣、纽扣芯及纽扣和揿扣的其他零件；纽扣坯：**										
9606.1000	-揿扣及其零件〔101 含木制品，102 不含木制品〕	6		100	13/	13	千克	/		31	
	-纽扣：										
9606.2100	--塑料制，未用纺织材料包裹〔101：含木制品；102：不含木制品〕	6		100	13/	13	千克	/		31	
9606.2200	--贱金属制，未用纺织材料包裹〔101：含木制品；102：不含木制品〕	6		100	13/	13	千克	/		31	
9606.2900	--其他										
9606.2900 10	含濒危动物成分的其他纽扣〔101：含木制品；102：不含木制品〕	6		100	13/	0	千克	FE/		31	
9606.2900 90	其他纽扣〔101：含木制品；102：不含木制品〕	6		100	13/	13	千克	/		31	

协定税率 %								RCEP		特惠税率 %			Article Description
东/冰/格	巴基斯坦	韩国	瑞士 上/下	哥/秘/柬	澳/毛	新西/坡/智	中国港/澳/台	东盟及马来/澳/韩	日/新	亚太2国	老/柬/缅	98/97/95	
													-Artists' brushes, writing brushes and similar brushes for the application of cosmetics:
													---Artists' brushes
0/0/0	10.5	15	2.5/2.5	0/0/0	0/15	0/0/0	0/0/	23.8/23.8/23.8	23.8/23.8			0/0/0	Artists' brushes of endangered animal hair
0/0/0	10.5	15	2.5/2.5	0/0/0	0/15	0/0/0	0/0/	23.8/23.8/23.8	23.8/23.8			0/0/0	Other artists' brushes
													---Writing brushes
0/0/0	12.6	9.3	2/2	0/0/0	0/0	0/0/0	0/0/	18/18/18	18.8/18			0/0/0	Writing brushes of endangered animal hair
0/0/0	12.6	9.3	2/2	0/0/0	0/0	0/0/0	0/0/	18/18/18	18.8/18			0/0/0	Other writing brushes
													---Other
0/0/0	15.8	15	2.5/2.5	0/0/0	0/15	0/0/0	0/0/	23.8/23.8/23.8	/23.8			0/0/0	Similar brushes for the application of cosmetics, of endangered animal hair
0/0/0	15.8	15	2.5/2.5	0/0/0	0/15	0/0/0	0/0/	23.8/23.8/23.8	/23.8			0/0/0	Other similar brushes for the application of cosmeties
													-Paint, distemper, varnish or similar brushes (other than brushes of subheading No. 9603. 30); paint pads and rollers:
													---Paint, distemper, varnish or similar brushes:
0/0/0	16	9.3	2/2	0/0/0	0/0	0/0/0	0/0/	18/18/18	18.8/18			0/0/0	----Of pigs', hogs' or boars' bristle
0/0/0	18.4	13.8	2.3/2.3	0/0/0	0/13.8	0/0/0	0/0/	21.9/21.9/21.9	21.9/21.9			0/0/0	----Other
0/0/0	18.4	13.8	2.3/2.3	0/0/0	0/13.8	0/0/0	0/0/	21.9/21.9/21.9	21.9/21.9			0/0/0	---Paint pads and rollers
													-Other brushes constituting parts of machines, appliances or vehicles:
													---Brushes of metal wire:
0/0/0	7.8	2.8	1.4/1.4	0/0/0	0/0	0/0/0	0/0/	0/0/12.6	12.7/0			0/0/0	----Constituting parts of machines or appliances
0/0/0	4.9	2.8	5.9/5.9	0/0/0	0/0	0/0/0	0/0/	0/0/12.6	12.7/0			0/0/0	----Other
													---Other:
													----Constituting parts of machines or appliances
0/0/0	7.8	2.8	1.4/1.4	0/0/0	0/0	0/0/0	0/0/	12.6/12.6/12.6	12.7/12.6			0/0/0	Other brushes constituting parts of machines or appliances, of endangered animal hair
0/0/0	7.8	2.8	1.4/1.4	0/0/0	0/0	0/0/0	0/0/	12.6/12.6/12.6	12.7/12.6			0/0/0	Other brushes constituting parts of machines or appliances
													----Other
0/0/0	4.9	2.8	1.4/1.4	0/0/0	0/0	0/0/0	0/0/	0/0/12.6	12.7/0			0/0/0	Other brushes constituting parts of vehicles, of endangered animal hair
0/0/0	4.9	2.8	1.4/1.4	0/0/0	0/0	0/0/0	0/0/	0/0/12.6	12.7/0			0/0/0	Other brushes constituting parts of vehicles
													-Other:
													---Feather dusters
0/0/0	13.2	9.8	2.1/2.1	0/0/0	0/0	0/0/0	0/0/	18.9/18.9/18.9	19.7/18.9			0/0/0	Feather dusters of endangered wild birds
0/0/0	13.2	9.8	2.1/2.1	0/0/0	0/0	0/0/0	0/0/	18.9/18.9/18.9	19.7/18.9			0/0/0	Other feather dusters
													---Other
0/0/0	12	3	1.5/1.5	0/0/0	0/0	0/0/0	0/0/	0/0/13.5	13.6/0			0/0/0	Other brooms, brushes (including mops, feather dusters), of hair, bristles or tails, of endangered animals
0/0/0	12	3	1.5/1.5	0/0/0	0/0	0/0/0	0/0/	0/0/13.5	13.6/0			0/0/0	Brooms, brushes, mops (including feather dusters, hand-operated mechanical floor sweepers, not motorized) of other animal or vegetable materials
0/0/0	12	3	1.5/1.5	0/0/0	0/0	0/0/0	0/0/	0/0/13.5	13.6/0			0/0/0	Brooms, brushes, mops and feather dusters(inclueling hand-operated mechanical floor sweepers, not motorized, of other materials)
													Hand sieves and hand riddles:
0/0/0	16.8	12.6	2.1/2.1	0/0/0	0/0	0/0/0	0/0/	20/20/20	20/20			0/0/0	Hand sieves and hand riddles
													Travel sets for personal toilet, sewing or shoe or clothes cleaning:
0/0/0	8.4	3	1.5/1.5	0/0/0	0/0	0/0/0	0/0/	0/0/13.5	13.6/0			0/0/0	Travel sets for personal toilet, sewing or shoe or clothes cleaning
													Buttons, press-fasteners, snap-fasteners and press-studs, button moulds and other parts of these articles; button blanks:
0/0/0	16.8	12.6	2.1/2.1	0/0/0	0/0	0/0/0	0/0/	20/20/	/20			0/0/0	-Press-fasteners, snap-fasteners and press-studs and parts thereof
													-Buttons:
0/0/0	16.8	12.6	2.1/2.1	0/0/0	0/0	0/0/0	0/0/0	20/20/	/20			0/0/0	--Of plastics, not covered with textile material
0/0/0	8.4	3	1.5/1.5	0/0/0	0/0	0/0/0	0/0/0	0/0/13.5	13.6/0			0/0/0	--Of base metal, not covered with textile material
													--Other
0/0/0	8.4	3	1.5/1.5	0/0/0	0/0	0/0/0	0/0/	0/0/13.5	13.6/0			0/0/0	Other buttons containing materials of endangered animals
0/0/0	8.4	3	1.5/1.5	0/0/0	0/0	0/0/0	0/0/	0/0/13.5	13.6/0			0/0/0	Other buttons

税则号列	货品名称〔CIQ 扩展编码及品名－T2 表示见附表 2〕	最惠(%)	暂定税率	普通	增值/消费	出口退税	计量单位	监管条件/特殊证件	检验检疫	对美关税	亚太上/下
9606.3000	-纽扣芯及纽扣的其他零件；纽扣坯〔101：含木制品；102：不含木制品〕	6		100	13/	13	千克	/		31	
96.07	**拉链及其零件：**										
	-拉链：										
9607.1100	--装有贱金属制齿的〔101 含木制品，102 不含木制品〕	6		130	13/	13	米/千克	/		31	
9607.1900	--其他〔101 含木制品，102 不含木制品〕	6		130	13/	13	米/千克	/		31	3.9/3.9
9607.2000	-零件〔101 含木制品，102 不含木制品〕	6		130	13/	13	千克	/		31	
96.08	**圆珠笔；毡尖和其他渗水式笔尖笔及唛头笔；自来水笔、铁笔型自来水笔及其他钢笔；蜡纸铁笔；活动铅笔；钢笔杆、铅笔套及类似的笔套；上述物品的零件(包括帽、夹)，但税目 96.09 的货品除外：**										
9608.1000	-圆珠笔〔999〕	8		80	13/	13	支/千克	/		28	5.2/5.2
9608.2000	-毡尖和其他渗水式笔尖笔及唛头笔〔101 彩笔，102 其他笔〕	12		80	13/	13	支/千克	/		32	
	-自来水笔、铁笔型自来水笔及其他钢笔：										
9608.3010	---墨汁画笔〔101 毛笔，102 其他笔〕	12		80	13/	13	支/千克	/		32	
9608.3020	---自来水笔〔999〕	12		80	13/	13	支/千克	/		32	
9608.3090	---其他〔999〕	12		80	13/	13	支/千克	/		32	
9608.4000	-活动铅笔〔999〕	12		80	13/	13	支/千克	/		32	
9608.5000	-由上述两个或多个子目所列物品组成的成套货品〔999〕	12		80	13/	13	套/千克	/		32	
9608.6000	-圆珠笔芯，由圆珠笔头和墨芯构成〔999〕	12		80	13/	13	支/千克	/		32	
	-其他：										
9608.9100	--钢笔头及笔尖粒〔999〕	8		70	13/	13	支/千克	/		28	
	--其他：										
9608.9910	---机器、仪器用笔〔999〕	8		40	13/	13	支/千克	/		18	
9608.9920	---蜡纸铁笔；钢笔杆、铅笔杆及类似的笔杆〔101 蜡纸铁笔，102 笔杆等〕	12		80	13/	13	支/千克	/		32	
9608.9990	---其他〔999〕	10		80	13/	13	千克	/		30	
96.09	**铅笔(税目 96.08 的铅笔除外)、颜色铅笔、铅笔芯、蜡笔、图画碳笔、书写或绘画用粉笔及裁缝划粉：**										
	-铅笔及颜色铅笔，笔芯包裹在外壳中：										
9609.1010	---铅笔〔999〕	12		80	13/	13	千克/百支	/		32	
9609.1020	---颜色铅笔〔999〕	12		80	13/	13	千克	/		32	
9609.2000	-铅笔芯，黑的或其他颜色的〔999〕	12		80	13/	13	千克	/		32	
9609.9000	-其他〔101 蜡笔，102 碳笔，103 粉笔〕	6		80	13/	13	千克	/		26	
96.10	**具有书写或绘画面的石板、黑板及类似板，不论是否镶框：**										
9610.0000	具有书写或绘画面的石板、黑板及类似板，不论是否镶框〔999〕	6		80	13/	13	千克	/		26	
96.11	**手用日期戳、封缄戳、编号戳及类似印戳(包括标签压印器)；手工操作的排字盘及带有排字盘的手印器：**										
9611.0000	手用日期戳、封缄戳、编号戳及类似印戳(包括标签压印器)；手工操作的排字盘及带有排字盘的手印器										
9611.0000 10	含濒危动物成分的手用日期戳(包括封缄戳及类似印戳)〔101 含木制品，102 不含木制品〕	8		80	13/	0	千克	FE/		33	
9611.0000 90	手用日期戳、封缄戳及类似印戳(包括编号戳、标签压印器；手工排字盘及带有字盘的手印器)〔101 含木制品，102 不含木制品〕	8		80	13/	13	千克	/		33	
96.12	**打字机色带或类似色带，已上油或经其他方法处理能着色的，不论是否装轴或装盒；印台，不论是否已加印油或带盒子：**										
9612.1000	-色带〔999〕	8		35	13/	13	个/千克	/		18	
9612.2000	-印台〔101 含木制品，102 不含木制品〕	10		100	13/	13	个/千克	/		20	
96.13	**香烟打火机和其他打火器(不论是机械的，还是电气的)及其零件，但打火石及打火机芯除外：**										
9613.1000	-袖珍气体打火机，一次性的〔999〕	10		130	13/	13	个/千克	B/	N		
9613.2000	-袖珍气体打火机，可充气的〔999〕	10		130	13/	13	个/千克	B/	N	35	
9613.8000	-其他打火器〔101 台式打火机，102 其它打火机(器)及其零件〕	10		130	13/	13	个/千克	B/	N	20	
9613.9000	-零件〔999〕	10		130	13/	13	千克	/		20	

协定税率 %								RCEP		特惠税率 %			Article Description
东/冰/格	巴基斯坦	韩国	瑞士上/下	哥/秘/柬	澳/毛	新西/坡/智	中国港/澳/台	东盟及马来/澳/韩	日/新	亚太2国	老/柬/缅	98/97/95	
0/0/0	8.4	3	1.5/1.5	0/0/0	0/0	0/0/0	0/0/	0/0/13.5	13.6/0			0/0/0	-Button moulds and other parts of buttons; button blanks
													Slide fasteners and parts thereof:
													-Slide fasteners:
0/0/0	16.8	12.6	2.1/2.1	0/0/0	0/0	0/0/0	0/0/	20/20/	/20			0/0/0	--Fitted with chain scoops of base metal
0/0/0	10.3	12.6	2.1/2.1	0/0/0	0/0	0/0/0	0/0/	20/20/20	20/20			0/0/0	--Other
0/0/0	16.8	12.6	2.1/2.1	0/0/0	0/0	0/0/0	0/0/	20/20/20	20/20			0/0/0	-Parts
													Ball point pens; felt tipped and other porous-tipped pens and markers; fountain pens, stylograph pens and other pens; duplicating stylos; propelling or sliding pencils; pen-holders, pencil-holders and similar holders; parts (including caps and clips) of the foregoing articles, other than those of heading No. 96.09:
0/0/0	5.3	3	1.5/1.5	0/0/0	0/0	0/0/0	0/0/	0/0/13.5	13.6/0			0/0/0	-Ball point pens
0/0/0	16.8	12.6	2.1/2.1	0/0/0	0/0	0/0/0	0/0/	20/20/	/20			0/0/0	-Felt tipped and other porous-tipped pens and markers
													-Fountain pens, stylograph pens and other pens:
0/0/0	16.8	9.8	2.1/2.1	0/0/0	0/0	0/0/0	0/0/	18.9/18.9/18.9	19.7/18.9			0/0/0	---Indian ink drawing pens
0/0/0	16.8	12.6	2.1/2.1	0/0/0	0/0	0/0/0	0/0/	20/20/20	/20			0/0/0	---Fountain pens
0/0/0	16.8	12.6	2.1/2.1	0/0/0	0/0	0/0/0	0/0/	20/20/20	20/20			0/0/0	---Other
0/0/0	16.8	12.6	2.1/2.1	0/0/0	0/0	0/0/0	0/0/	20/20/20	/20			0/0/0	-Propelling or sliding pencils
0/0/0	16.8	12.6	2.1/2.1	0/0/0	0/0	0/0/0	0/0/	20/20/20	20/20			0/0/0	-Sets of articles from two or more of the foregoing subheadings
0/0/0	16.8	12.6	2.1/2.1	0/0/0	0/0	0/0/0	0/0/	20/20/	/20			0/0/0	-Refills for ball point pens, comprising the ball point and ink-reservoir
													-Other:
0/0/0	4.2	2.4	1.2/1.2	0/0/0	0/0	0/0/0	0/0/	0/0/10.8	10.9/0			0/0/0	--Pen nibs and nib points
													--Other:
0/0/0	9.8	3.5	1.8/1.8	0/0/0	0/0	0/0/0	0/0/	0/0/15.8	15.9/0			0/0/0	---Of a kind used on machines or instruments
0/0/0	16.8	12.6	2.1/2.1	0/0/0	0/0	0/0/0	0/0/	20/20/20	20/20			0/0/0	---Duplicating stylos; pen-holders, pencil-holders and similar holders
0/0/0	16.8	12.6	0/0	0/0/0	0/0	0/0/0	0/0/	20/20/	/20			0/0/0	---Other
													Pencils (other than pencils of heading No. 96.08), crayons, pencil leads, pastels, drawing charcoals, writing or drawing chalks and tailors' chalks:
													-Pencils and crayons, with leads encased in a sheath:
0/0/0	16.8	12.6	2.1/2.1	0/0/0	0/0	0/0/0	0/0/	20/20/20	20/20			0/0/0	---Pencils
0/0/0	16.8	12.6	2.1/2.1	0/0/0	0/0	0/0/0	0/0/	20/20/20	/20			0/0/0	---Crayons
0/0/0	16.8	12.6	2.1/2.1	0/0/0	0/0	0/0/0	0/0/	20/20/	/20			0/0/0	-Pencil leads, black or coloured
0/0/0	8.4	3	1.5/1.5	0/0/0	0/9	0/0/0	0/0/	0/0/13.5	13.6/0			0/0/0	-Other
													Slates and boards, with writing or drawing surfaces, whether or not framed:
0/0/0	8.4	3	1.5/1.5	0/0/0	0/0	0/0/0	0/0/	0/0/13.5	13.6/0			0/0/0	Slates and boards, with writing or drawing surfaces, whether or not framed
													Date, sealing or numbering stamps, and the like (including devices for printing or embossing labels), designed for operating in the hand; hand-operated composing sticks and hand printing sets incorporating such composing sticks:
													Date, sealing or numbering stamps, and the like (including devices for printing or embossing labels), designed for operating in the hand; hand-operated composing sticks and hand printing sets incorporating such composing sticks
0/0/0	16.8	12.6	2.1/2.1	0/0/0	0/0	0/0/0	0/0/	20/20/	/20			0/0/0	Date, sealing, and the like, designed for operating in the hand, containing materials of endangered animals
0/0/0	16.8	12.6	2.1/2.1	0/0/0	0/0	0/0/0	0/0/	20/20/	/20			0/0/0	Other date, sealing or numbering stamps, and the like (including devices for printing or embossing labels), designed for operating in the hand; hand-operated composing sticks and hand printing sets incorporating such composing sticks
													Typewriter or similar ribbons, inked or otherwise prepared for giving impressions, whether or not on spools or in cartridges; ink-pads, whether or not inked, with or without boxes:
0/0/0	3.5	4.9	1.1/1.1	0/0/0	0/0	0/0/0	0/0/	9.8/10/9.8	9.8/10			0/0/0	-Inked ribbons
0/0/0	20	15	2.5/2.5	0/0/0	0/15	0/0/0	0/0/	23.8/23.8/23.8	23.8/23.8			0/0/0	-Ink-pads
													Cigarette lighters and other lighters, whether or not mechanical or electrical, and parts thereof other than flints and wicks:
0/0/0	20	15	2.5/2.5	0/0/0	0/15	0/0/0	0/0/	23.8/23.8/23.8	/23.8			0/0/0	-Pocket lighters, gas fuelled, non refillable
0/0/0	20	15	2.5/2.5	0/0/0	0/15	0/0/0	0/0/	23.8/23.8/23.8	23.8/23.8			0/0/0	-Pocket lighters, gas fuelled, refillable
0/0/0	20	15	2.5/2.5	0/0/0	0/15	0/0/0	0/0/	23.8/23.8/	/23.8			0/0/0	-Other lighters
0/0/0	20	15	2.5/2.5	0/0/0	0/15	0/0/0	0/0/	23.8/23.8/23.8	/23.8			0/0/0	-Parts

税则号列	货品名称〔CIQ 扩展编码及品名—T2 表示见附表 2〕	最惠(%)	暂定税率	普通	增值/消费	出口退税	计量单位	监管条件/特殊证件	检验检疫	对美关税	亚太上/下
96.14	**烟斗(包括烟斗头)和烟嘴及其零件:**										
9614.0010	---烟斗及烟斗头										
9614.0010 10	含濒危动物成分的烟斗及烟斗头(仅指野生哺乳类牙齿制产品)〔101 含木制品,102 不含木制品〕	10		130	13/	0	个/千克	ABEF/	PQ	35	
9614.0010 20	用植物性材料制作的烟斗及烟斗头〔101 其他木制品,102 含木制品,103 不含木制品〕	10		130	13/	13	个/千克	AB/	PQ	35	
9614.0010 90	其他烟斗及烟斗头〔101 含木制品,102 不含木制品〕	10		130	13/	13	个/千克	/		35	
9614.0090	---其他										
9614.0090 10	含濒危野生动物成分的烟嘴及其零件(仅指野生哺乳类牙齿制产品)〔101 含木制品,102 不含木制品〕	10		130	13/	0	千克	FE/		35	
9614.0090 90	其他烟嘴及其零件〔101 含木制品,102 不含木制品〕	10		130	13/	13	千克	/		35	
96.15	**梳子、发夹及类似品;发卡、卷发夹、卷发器或类似品及其零件,但税目 85.16 的货品除外:**										
	-梳子、发夹及类似品:										
9615.1100	--硬质橡胶或塑料制〔999〕	6		130	13/	13	千克	/		26	3.9/3.9
9615.1900	--其他										
9615.1900 10	含濒危动物成分的其他材料制梳子(包括角质发夹等,金属、塑料及家畜来源的产品除外)〔101 含木制品,102 不含木制品〕	6		130	13/	0	千克	FE/		26	
9615.1900 90	其他材料制梳子、发夹及类似品(硬质橡胶、塑料制的除外)〔101 含木制品,102 不含木制品〕	6		130	13/	13	千克	/		26	
9615.9000	-其他〔101 含木制品,102 不含木制品〕	6		130	13/	13	千克	/		26	3.9/3.9
96.16	**香水喷雾器或类似的化妆用喷雾器及其座架、喷头;粉扑及粉拍,施敷脂粉或化妆品用:**										
9616.1000	-香水喷雾器或类似的化妆用喷雾器及其座架、喷头〔101 含木制品,102 不含木制品〕	6		130	13/	13	千克	/		26	3.9/3.9
9616.2000	-粉扑及粉拍,施敷脂粉或化妆品用〔101 含木制品,102 不含木制品〕	6		130	13/	13	千克	/		26	3.9/3.9
96.17	**保温瓶和其他真空容器及其零件,但玻璃瓶胆除外:**										
	---保温瓶:										
9617.0011	----玻璃内胆制〔999〕	8		130	13/	13	个/千克	/		28	
9617.0019	----其他〔999〕	8		130	13/	13	个/千克	/		28	
9617.0090	---其他〔999〕	8		130	13/	13	千克/个	/		28	
96.18	**裁缝用人体模型及其他人体活动模型;橱窗装饰用的自动模型及其他活动陈列品:**										
9618.0000	裁缝用人体模型及其他人体活动模型;橱窗装饰用的自动模型及其他活动陈列品										
9618.0000 10	用植物性材料制作的人体模型〔999〕	10		80	13/	13	千克	AB/	PQ	30	
9618.0000 90	裁缝用其他人体模型(包括橱窗装饰用的自动模型及其他活动陈列品)〔101 含木制品,102 不含木制品〕	10		80	13/	13	千克	/		30	
96.19	**任何材料制的卫生巾(护垫)及卫生棉条、尿布及尿布衬里和类似品:**										
	---尿裤及尿布:										
9619.0011	----供婴儿使用的〔999〕	4	0	80	13/	13	千克	A/	M	10	
9619.0019	----其他〔999〕	4	0	80	13/	13	千克	A/	M	10	
9619.0020	---卫生巾(护垫)及卫生棉条〔999〕	4		80	13/	13	千克	A/	M	14	
9619.0090	---其他〔999〕	6		80	13/	13	千克	A/	M	16	3.9/3.9
96.20	**独脚架、双脚架、三脚架及类似品:**										
9620.0010	---专用于税目 85.19、85.21,子目 8525.8、9006.3、9006.5、9007.1 或 9007.2 所列设备的独脚架、双脚架、三脚架及类似品〔999〕	8		80	13/	13	千克	/		33	
9620.0090	---其他〔999〕	8		80	13/	13	千克	/		33	

协定税率 %								RCEP		特惠税率 %			Article Description
东/冰/格	巴基斯坦	韩国	瑞士 上/下	哥/秘/柬	澳/毛	新西/坡/智	中国港/澳/台	东盟及马来/澳/韩	日/新	亚太2国	老/柬/缅	98/97/95	
													Smoking pipes (including pipe bowls) and cigar or cigarette holders, and parts thereof:
													---Pipes and pipe bowls
0/0/0	20		2.5/2.5	0/0/0	0/15	0/0/0	0/0/	10/10/	/10			0/0/0	Smoking pipes (including pipe bowls) containing materials of endangered animals(only referring to products made of ivory of wild mammals)
0/0/0	20		2.5/2.5	0/0/0	0/15	0/0/0	0/0/	10/10/	/10			0/0/0	Smoking pipes and pipe bowls, of vegetable materials
0/0/0	20		2.5/2.5	0/0/0	0/15	0/0/0	0/0/	10/10/	/10			0/0/0	Other smoking pipes and pipe bowls
													---Other
0/0/0	20		2.5/2.5	0/0/0	0/15	0/0/0	0/0/	10/10/	/10			0/0/0	Cigar or cigarette holders, and parts thereof, containing endangered wild animal materials (only referring to products made of ivory of wild mammals)
0/0/0	20		2.5/2.5	0/0/0	0/15	0/0/0	0/0/	10/10/	/10			0/0/0	Other cigar or cigarette holders, and parts thereof
													Combs, hair-slides and the like; hairpins, curling pins, curling grips, hair-curlers and the like, other than those of heading No. 85. 16, and parts thereof:
													-Combs, hair-slides and the like:
0/0/0	10.1	3.6	1.8/1.8	0/0/0	0/0	0/0/0	0/0/	0/0/16.2	16.4/0			0/0/0	--Of hard rubber or plastics
													--Other
0/0/0	14.4	3.6	1.8/1.8	0/0/0	0/0	0/0/0	0/0/	0/0/16.2	16.4/0			0/0/0	Combs containing endangered animals materials (including hair-slides made of horns, but not including products made of metal, plastic or material of domestic animals)
0/0/0	14.4	3.6	1.8/1.8	0/0/0	0/0	0/0/0	0/0/	0/0/16.2	16.4/0			0/0/0	Combs, hair-slides and the like, of other materials(other than hard rubber or plastics materials)
0/0/0	10.1	3.6	1.8/1.8	0/0/0	0/0	0/0/0	0/0/	0/0/16.2	16.4/0			0/0/0	-Other
													Scent sprays and similar toilet sprays, and mounts and heads therefor; powderpuffs and pads for the application of cosmetics or toilet preparations:
0/0/0	10.1	3.6	1.8/1.8	0/0/0	0/0	0/0/0	0/0/	0/0/16.2	16.4/0			0/0/0	-Scent sprays and similar toilet sprays, and mounts and heads therefor
0/0/0	10.1	3.6	1.8/1.8	0/0/0	0/0	0/0/0	0/0/	0/0/16.2	16.4/0			0/0/0	-Powder-puffs and pads for the application of cosmetics or toilet preparations
													Vacuum flasks and other vacuum vessels, complete; parts thereof other than glass inners:
													---Vacuum flasks:
0/0/0	19.2	14.4	2.4/2.4	0/0/0	0/14.4	0/0/0	0/0/	22.8/22.8/22.8	/22.8			0/0/0	----Of glass internal liner
0/0/0	19.2	14.4	2.4/2.4	0/0/0	0/14.4	0/0/0	0/0/	22.8/22.8/22.8	/22.8			0/0/0	----Other
0/0/0	14.4	3.6	1.8/1.8	0/0/0	0/0	0/0/0	0/0/	0/0/16.2	16.4/0			0/0/0	---Other
													Tailors' dummies and other lay figures; automata and other animated displays used for shop window dressing:
													Tailors' dummies and other lay figures; automata and other animated displays used for shop window dressing
0/0/0	16.8	12.6	2.1/2.1	0/0/0	0/0	0/0/0	0/0/	20/20/	/20			0/0/0	Dummies of vegetable materials
0/0/0	16.8	12.6	2.1/2.1	0/0/0	0/0	0/0/0	0/0/	20/20/	/20			0/0/0	Tailors' other dummies (including automaton and other animated displays used for shop window dressing)
													Sanitary towels(Pads)and tampons, napkins (diapers), napkin liners and similar articles, of any material:
													---Diaper and napkin
0//0	0			//0	0/0	0//0	0/0/0	7.1/7.1/	/7.1			0/0/0	----Forbabies
0//0	0			//0	0/0	0//0	0/0/0	7.1/7.1/	/7.1			0/0/0	----Other
0/0/0	5.3	2	0/0	0/0/0	0/0	0//0	0/0/0	0/0/9	9.1/0			0/0/0	---Sanitary towels(Pads)and tampons
0/0/0	5.3	2.8	1.4/1.4	0/0/0	0/0	0/0/0	0/0/0	0/0/12.6	12.7/0			0/0/0	---Other
													Monopods, bipods, tripods and similar articles:
/0/0	0	0	0/0	0/0/0	0/0	0//	0/0/	0/0/0	7.3/0			0/0/0	---Monopod, bipod, tripod and similar articles specially used for equipment listed in heading 85.19, 85.21, subheading 8525.8, 9006.3, 9006.5, 9007.1 or 9007.2
/0/0	0	0	0/0	0/0/0	0/0	0//	0/0/	0/0/0	0/0			0/0/0	---Other

第二十一类
艺术品、收藏品及古物

第九十七章
艺术品、收藏品及古物

注释：

一、本章不包括：

(一)品目 49.07 的未经使用的邮票、印花税票，邮政信笺(印有邮票的纸品)及类似的票证；

(二)作舞台、摄影的布景及类似用途的已绘制画布(税目 59.07)，但可归入税目 97.06 的除外；

(三)天然或养殖珍珠、宝石或半宝石(税目 71.01 至 71.03)。

二、税目 97.01 不适用于成批生产的镶嵌画复制品 、铸造品及具有商业性质的传统工艺品，即使这些物品是由艺术家设计或创造的。

三、税目 97.02 所称"雕版画、印制画、石印画的原本"，是指以艺术家完全手工制作的单块或数块印版直接印制出来的黑白或彩色原本，不论艺术家使用何种方法或材料，但不包括使用机器或照相制版方法制作的。

四、税目 97.03 不适用于成批生产的复制品及具有商业性质的传统手工艺品，即使这些物品是艺术家设计或创造的。

五、(一)除上述注释一至四另有规定的以外，可归入本章各税目的物品，均应归入本章的相应税目而不归入本目录的其他税目；

(二)税目 97.06 不适用于可以归入本章其他各税目的物品。

六、已装框的油画、粉画及其他绘画、版画、拼贴画及类似装饰板，如果框架的种类及价值与作品相称，应与作品一并归类。如果框架的种类及价值与作品不相称，应分别归类。

税则号列	货品名称〔CIQ 扩展编码及品名—T2 表示见附表 2〕	最惠(%)	暂定税率	普通	增值/消费	出口退税	计量单位	监管条件/特殊证件	检验检疫	对美关税	亚太上/下
97.01	**油画、粉画及其他手绘画，但带有手工绘制及手工描饰的制品或税目 49.06 的图纸除外；拼贴画、镶嵌画及类似装饰板：**										
	-超过 100 年的：										
9701.2100	--油画、粉画及其他手绘画〔999〕	4	0	50	13/	0	幅/千克	/			
9701.2200	--镶嵌画										
9701.2200 10	含濒危动物成分的超过 100 年的镶嵌画(指一切源自濒危动物的产品)〔999〕	6	0	50	13/	0	幅/千克	ABFE/		10	
9701.2200 20	用其他动植物材料制作的超过 100 年的镶嵌画(指一切源自野生动物的产品)〔999〕	6	0	50	13/	0	幅/千克	AB/		10	
9701.2200 90	其他超过 100 年的镶嵌画〔999〕	6	0	50	13/	0	幅/千克	/		10	
9701.2900	--其他										
9701.2900 10	超过 100 年的含濒危动物成分的拼贴画(包括类似装饰板，指一切源自濒危动物的产品)〔999〕	6	0	50	13/	0	幅/千克	ABFE/	PQ	10	
9701.2900 20	超过 100 年的用其他动植物材料制作的拼贴画(包括类似装饰板，指一切源自野生动物的产品)〔999〕	6	0	50	13/	0	幅/千克	AB/	PQ	10	
9701.2900 90	超过 100 年的其他拼贴画及类似装饰板〔999〕	6	0	50	13/	0	幅/千克	/		10	
	-其他：										
	--油画、粉画及其他手绘画：										
	---原件：										
9701.9111	----唐卡〔999〕	6		50	13/	0	幅/千克	/			
9701.9119	----其他〔999〕	1		50	13/	0	幅/千克	/		21	
9701.9120	---复制品〔999〕	6		50	13/	0	幅/千克	/		16	
9701.9200	--镶嵌画										
9701.9200 10	含濒危动物成分的其他镶嵌画(指一切源自濒危动物的产品)〔999〕	6		50	13/	0	幅/千克	ABFE/	PQ	16	
9701.9200 20	用其他动植物材料制作的其他镶嵌画(指一切源自野生动物的产品)〔999〕	6		50	13/	0	幅/千克	AB/	PQ	16	
9701.9200 90	其他镶嵌画〔999〕	6		50	13/	0	幅/千克	/		16	
9701.9900	--其他										
9701.9900 10	含濒危动物成分的其他拼贴画(包括类似装饰板，指一切源自濒危动物的产品)〔999〕	6		50	13/	0	幅/千克	ABFE/	PQ	16	
9701.9900 20	用其他动植物材料制作的其他拼贴画(包括类似装饰板，指一切源自野生动物的产品)〔999〕	6		50	13/	0	幅/千克	AB/	PQ	16	
9701.9900 90	其他拼贴画及类似装饰板〔999〕	6		50	13/	0	幅/千克	/		16	
97.02	**雕版画、印制画、石印画的原本：**										
9702.1000	-超过 100 年的〔999〕	1		50	13/	0	幅/千克	/		11	
9702.9000	-其他〔999〕	1		50	13/	0	幅/千克	/		11	
97.03	**各种材料制的雕塑品原件：**										
9703.1000	-超过 100 年的										

SECTION XXI
WORKS OF ART, COLLECTORS' PIECES AND ANTIQUES

Chapter 97
Works of art, collectors' pieces and antiques

Notes:

1. This Chapter does not cover:
   (a) Unused postage or revenue stamps, postal stationery (stamped paper) or the like, of heading 49.07;
   (b) Theatrical scenery, studio back-cloths or the like, of painted canvas (heading No. 59.07) except if they may be classified in heading No. 97.06;
   (c) Pearls, natural or cultured, or precious or semi-precious stones (headings No. 71.01 to 71.03).
2. - Heading 97.01 does not apply to mosaics that are mass－produced reproductions, casts or works of conventional craftsmanship of a commercial character, even if these articles are designed or created by artists.
3. For the purposes of heading No. 97.02, the expression "original engravings, prints and lithographs" means impressions produced directly, in black and white or in colour, of one or of several plates wholly executed by hand by the artist, irrespective of the process or of the material employed by him, but not including any mechanical or photomechanical process.
4. Heading No. 97.03 does not apply to mass-produced reproductions or works of conventional craftsmanship of a commercial character, even if these articles are designed or created by artists.
5. (a) Subject to Notes 1 to 4 above, articles of this Chapter are to be classified in this Chapter and not in any other Chapter of the Nomenclature.
   (b) heading No. 97.06 does not apply to articles of the preceding headings of this Chapter.
6. Frames around paintings, drawings, pastels, collages or similar decorative plaques, engravings, prints or lithographs are to be classified with those articles, provided they are of a kind and of a value normal to those articles. Frames which are not of a kind or of a value normal to the articles referred to in this Note are to be classified separately.

协定税率 %								RCEP		特惠税率 %			Article Description
东/冰/格	巴基斯坦	韩国	瑞士上/下	哥/秘/柬	澳/毛	新西/坡/智	中国港/澳/台	东盟及马来/澳/韩	日/新	亚太2国	老/柬/缅	98/97/95	
													Paintings, drawings and pastels, executed entirely by hand, other than drawings of heading No. 49.06 and other than hand-painted or hand-decorated manufactured articles; collages mosaics and similar decorative plaques:
													- Of an age exceeding 100 years :
0/0/0	5.4	2.5	1.3/1.3	0/0/0	0/0	0/0/0	0/0/	0/0/10.8	10.9/0			0/0/0	-- Paintings, drawings and pastels
													-- Mosaics
0/0/0	7.8	2.8	1.4/1.4	0/0/0	0/0	0/0/0	0/0/	0/0/12.6	12.7/0			0/0/0	Mosaics containing endangered animals for more than 1 years (referring to all products derived from endangered animals)
0/0/0	7.8	2.8	1.4/1.4	0/0/0	0/0	0/0/0	0/0/	0/0/12.6	12.7/0			0/0/0	Mosaics made of other animal and plant materials for more than 1 years (referring to all products derived from wild animals)
0/0/0	7.8	2.8	1.4/1.4	0/0/0	0/0	0/0/0	0/0/	0/0/12.6	12.7/0			0/0/0	Other mosaics over 1 years old
													-- Other
0/0/0	7.8	2.8	1.4/1.4	0/0/0	0/0	0/0/0	0/0/	0/0/12.6	12.7/0			0/0/0	Collages containing endangered animals for more than 1 years (including similar decorative panels, referring to all products derived from endangered animals)
0/0/0	7.8	2.8	1.4/1.4	0/0/0	0/0	0/0/0	0/0/	0/0/12.6	12.7/0			0/0/0	Collages made of other animal and plant materials for more than 1 years (including similar decorative panels, referring to all products derived from wild animals)
0/0/0	7.8	2.8	1.4/1.4	0/0/0	0/0	0/0/0	0/0/	0/0/12.6	12.7/0			0/0/0	Other collages and similar decorative panels over 1 years
													- Other :
													-- Paintings, drawings and pastels
													---The originals:
0/0/0	4.2	2.4	1.2/1.2	0/0/0	0/0	0/0/0	0/0/	0/0/10.8	10.9/0			0/0/0	----Thangka
0/0/0	4.2	2.4	1/1	0/0/0	0/0	0/0/0	0/0/	0/0/10.8	10.9/0			0/0/0	----Other
0/0/0	7.8	2.8	1.4/1.4	0/0/0	0/0	0/0/0	0/0/	0/0/12.6	12.7/0			0/0/0	---Reproductions
													-- Mosaics
0/0/0	7.8	2.8	1.4/1.4	0/0/0	0/0	0/0/0	0/0/	0/0/12.6	12.7/0			0/0/0	Other mosaic paintings containing endangered animals (referring to all products derived from endangered animals)
0/0/0	7.8	2.8	1.4/1.4	0/0/0	0/0	0/0/0	0/0/	0/0/12.6	12.7/0			0/0/0	Other mosaic paintings made of other animal and plant materials (referring to all products derived from wild animals)
0/0/0	7.8	2.8	1.4/1.4	0/0/0	0/0	0/0/0	0/0/	0/0/12.6	12.7/0			0/0/0	Other mosaics
													-- Other
0/0/0	7.8	2.8	1.4/1.4	0/0/0	0/0	0/0/0	0/0/	0/0/12.6	12.7/0			0/0/0	Other collages containing endangered animals (including similar decorative panels, referring to all products derived from endangered animals)
0/0/0	7.8	2.8	1.4/1.4	0/0/0	0/0	0/0/0	0/0/	0/0/12.6	12.7/0			0/0/0	Other collages made of other animal and plant materials (including similar decorative panels, referring to all products derived from wild animals)
0/0/0	7.8	2.8	1.4/1.4	0/0/0	0/0	0/0/0	0/0/	0/0/12.6	12.7/0			0/0/0	Other collages and similar decorative panels
													Original engravings, prints and lithographs.
0/0/0	4.2	2.4	1/1	0/0/0	0/0	0/0/0	0/0/	0/0/10.8	10.9/0			0/0/0	- Of an age exceeding 100 years
0/0/0	4.2	2.4	1/1	0/0/0	0/0	0/0/0	0/0/	0/0/10.8	10.9/0			0/0/0	- Other
													Original sculpture and statuary, in any material.
													- Of an age exceeding 100 years

税则号列	货品名称〔CIQ扩展编码及品名—T2表示见附表2〕	最惠(%)	暂定税率	普通	增值/消费	出口退税	计量单位	监管条件/特殊证件	检验检疫	对美关税	亚太上/下
9703.1000 10	超过100年的濒危动植物材料制的雕塑品原件(指一切源自濒危动植物的产品)〔999〕	1		50	13/	0	件/千克	FE/		21	
9703.1000 90	超过100年的其他各种材料制的雕塑品原件〔999〕	1		50	13/	0	件/千克	/		21	
9703.9000	-其他										
9703.9000 10	其他濒危动植物材料制的雕塑品原件(指一切源自濒危动植物的产品)〔999〕	1		50	13/	0	件/千克	FE/		21	
9703.9000 90	其他各种材料制的雕塑品原件〔999〕	1		50	13/	0	件/千克	/		21	
97.04	**使用过或未使用过的邮票、印花税票、邮戳印记、首日封、邮政信笺(印有邮票的纸品)及类似品,但税目49.07的货品除外:**										
9704.0010	---邮票〔999〕	4		50	13/	0	千克	/		29	
9704.0090	---其他〔999〕	6		50	13/	0	千克	/			
97.05	**具有考古学、人种学、历史学、动物学、植物学、矿物学、解剖学、古生物学或钱币学意义的收集品及珍藏品:**										
9705.1000	-具有考古学、人种学或历史学意义的收集品及珍藏品										
9705.1000 10	具有考古学、人种学或历史学意义的含濒危动植物的收藏品〔101植物标本,102具有动物学、植物学、矿物学、解剖学、历史学、考古学、古生物学、人种学或钱币学意义的收集品及珍藏品〕	0		0	13/	0	千克	ABFE/	PQ	10	
9705.1000 20	具有考古学、人种学或历史学意义的含有人类遗传资源的组织标本、手术样本〔999〕	0		0	13/	0	千克	ABV/	VW	10	
9705.1000 90	其他具有考古学、人种学或历史学意义的的收藏品〔101植物标本,102具有动物学、植物学、矿物学、解剖学、历史学、考古学、古生物学、人种学或钱币学意义的收集品及珍藏品〕	0		0	13/	0	千克	AB/	PQ	10	
	-具有动物学、植物学、矿物学、解剖学或古生物学意义的收集品及珍藏品:										
9705.2100	--人类标本及其部分										
9705.2100 10	含有人类遗传资源的组织标本、手术样本〔401人类医学、生命科学研究用,402具有动物学、植物学、矿物学、解剖学、历史学、考古学、古生物学、人种学或钱币学意义的收集品及珍藏品〕	0		0	13/	0	千克	ABV/	VW	10	
9705.2100 90	其他人类标本及其部分〔401人类医学、生命科学研究用,402具有动物学、植物学、矿物学、解剖学、历史学、考古学、古生物学、人种学或钱币学意义的收集品及珍藏品〕	0		0	13/	0	千克	AB/	PQ	10	
9705.2200	--灭绝或濒危物种及其部分										
9705.2200 10	含濒危动植物的收藏品(具有动植物学意义的)〔101植物标本,102具有动物学、植物学、矿物学、解剖学、历史学、考古学、古生物学、人种学或钱币学意义的收集品及珍藏品〕	0		0	13/	0	千克	ABFE/	PQ	10	
9705.2200 20	古生物化石〔999〕	0		0	13/	0	千克	ABz/	PQ	10	
9705.2200 90	其他灭绝物种及其部分〔101植物标本,102具有动物学、植物学、矿物学、解剖学、历史学、考古学、古生物学、人种学或钱币学意义的收集品及珍藏品〕	0		0	13/	0	千克	AB/	PQ	10	
9705.2900	--其他										
9705.2900 10	其他古生物化石〔999〕	0		0	13/	0	千克	ABz/	PQ	10	
9705.2900 20	有矿物学研究价值、可供收集和珍藏的钟乳石〔999〕	0		0	13/	0	千克	ABu/	PQ	10	
9705.2900 90	其他具有动、植、矿物学意义的收藏品(还包括具有解剖、古生物学意义的收藏品)〔101植物标本,102具有动物学、植物学、矿物学、解剖学、历史学、考古学、古生物学、人种学或钱币学意义的收集品及珍藏品〕	0		0	13/	0	千克	AB/	PQ	10	
	-具有钱币学意义的收集品及珍藏品 :										
9705.3100	--超过100年的〔101植物标本,102具有动物学、植物学、矿物学、解剖学、历史学、考古学、古生物学、人种学或钱币学意义的收集品及珍藏品〕	0		0	13/	0	千克	AB/	PQ	10	
9705.3900	--其他〔101植物标本,102具有动物学、植物学、矿物学、解剖学、历史学、考古学、古生物学、人种学或钱币学意义的收集品及珍藏品〕	0		0	13/	0	千克	AB/	PQ	10	
97.06	**超过100年的古物:**										
9706.1000	-超过250年的										
9706.1000 10	超过250年的濒危动植古物(具收藏或文史价值的)〔101植物标本,102超过100年的古物〕	0		0	13/	0	件/千克	ABFE/	PQ	20	
9706.1000 90	其他超过250年的古物〔999〕	0		0	13/	0	件/千克	/		20	
9706.9000	-其他										
9706.9000 10	其他超过100年的濒危动植古物(具收藏或文史价值的)〔101植物标本,102超过100年的古物〕	0		0	13/	0	件/千克	ABFE/	PQ	20	
9706.9000 90	其他超过100年的古物〔999〕	0		0	13/	0	件/千克	/		20	

协定税率 %								RCEP		特惠税率 %			Article Description
东/冰/格	巴基斯坦	韩国	瑞士 上/下	哥/秘/柬	澳/毛	新西/坡/智	中国港/澳/台	东盟及马来/澳/韩	日/新	亚太2国	老/柬/缅	98/97/95	
0/0/0	4.8	2.4	1/1	0/0/0	0/7.2	0/0/0	0/0/	0/0/10.8	10.9/0			0/0/0	Original sculptures made of endangered animals and plants materials with more than 1 years (referring to all products derived from endangered animals and plants)
0/0/0	4.8	2.4	1/1	0/0/0	0/7.2	0/0/0	0/0/	0/0/10.8	10.9/0			0/0/0	Original sculptures made of various other materials for more than 1 years
													- Other
0/0/0	4.8	2.4	1/1	0/0/0	0/7.2	0/0/0	0/0/	0/0/10.8	10.9/0			0/0/0	Original sculptures made of other endangered animals and plants (referring to all products derived from endangered animals and plants)
0/0/0	4.8	2.4	1/1	0/0/0	0/7.2	0/0/0	0/0/	0/0/10.8	10.9/0			0/0/0	Original sculptures made of various other materials
													Used or unused postage or revenue stamps, stamp-postmarks, first-day covers, postal stationery (stamped paper), and the like, other than those of heading No. 49. 07:
0/0/0	2	0	0/0	0/0/0	0/0	0//0	0/0/	0/0/0	7.3/0			0/0/0	---Postage
0/0/0	4.9	2.8	1.4/1.4	0/0/0	0/0	0/0/0	0/0/	0/0/12.6	12.7/0			0/0/0	---Other
													Collections and collectors' pieces of archaeological, ethnographic, historical, zoological, botanical, mineralogical, anatomical, paleontological, or numismatic interest.
													- Collections and collectors' pieces of archaeological, ethnographic or historical interest
0/0/0	0	0	0/0	0/0/0	0/0	0//0	0/0/	0/0/0	0/0			0/0/0	A collection of endangered animals and plants of archaeological, ethnographic or historical significance
0/0/0	0	0	0/0	0/0/0	0/0	0//0	0/0/	0/0/0	0/0			0/0/0	Tissue samples and surgical samples containing human genetic resources with archaeological, ethnological or historical significance
0/0/0	0	0	0/0	0/0/0	0/0	0//0	0/0/	0/0/0	0/0			0/0/0	Other collections of archaeological, ethnographic or historical significance
													- Collections and collectors' pieces of zoological, botanical, mineralogical, anatomical or paleontological interest:
													-- Human specimens and parts thereof
0/0/0	0	0	0/0	0/0/0	0/0	0//0	0/0/	0/0/0	0/0			0/0/0	Tissue samples and surgical samples containing human genetic resources
0/0/0	0	0	0/0	0/0/0	0/0	0//0	0/0/	0/0/0	0/0			0/0/0	Other human specimens and parts thereof
													-- Extinct or endangered species and parts thereof
0/0/0	0	0	0/0	0/0/0	0/0	0//0	0/0/	0/0/0	0/0			0/0/0	Collections containing endangered animals and plants (of Zoological and Botanical Significance)
0/0/0	0	0	0/0	0/0/0	0/0	0//0	0/0/	0/0/0	0/0			0/0/0	Paleontological fossil
0/0/0	0	0	0/0	0/0/0	0/0	0//0	0/0/	0/0/0	0/0			0/0/0	Other extinct species and their parts
													-- Other
0/0/0	0	0	0/0	0/0/0	0/0	0//0	0/0/	0/0/0	0/0			0/0/0	Other paleontological fossils
0/0/0	0	0	0/0	0/0/0	0/0	0//0	0/0/	0/0/0	0/0			0/0/0	Stalactite with mineralogical research value for collection and collection
0/0/0	0	0	0/0	0/0/0	0/0	0//0	0/0/	0/0/0	0/0			0/0/0	Other collections with animal, plant and Mineralogical Significance (including collections with anatomical and paleontological significance)
													- Collections and collectors' pieces of numismatic interest:
0/0/0	0	0	0/0	0/0/0	0/0	0//0	0/0/	0/0/0	0/0			0/0/0	-- Of an age exceeding 100 years
0/0/0	0	0	0/0	0/0/0	0/0	0//0	0/0/	0/0/0	0/0			0/0/0	-- Other
													Antiques of an age exceeding 100 years.
													- Of an age exceeding 250 years
0/0/0	0	0	0/0	0/0/0	0/0	0//0	0/0/	0/0/0	0/0			0/0/0	Endangered animal and plant antiquities (with collection or cultural and historical value) over 25 years
0/0/0	0	0	0/0	0/0/0	0/0	0//0	0/0/	0/0/0	0/0			0/0/0	Other antiquities over 25 years old
													- Other
0/0/0	0	0	0/0	0/0/0	0/0	0//0	0/0/	0/0/0	0/0			0/0/0	Other endangered animal and plant antiquities over 1 years (with collection or cultural and historical value)
0/0/0	0	0	0/0	0/0/0	0/0	0//0	0/0/	0/0/0	0/0			0/0/0	Other antiquities over 1 years old

第二十二类
特殊交易品及未分类商品

第九十八章
特殊交易品及未分类商品

税则号列	货品名称〔CIQ 扩展编码及品名—T2 表示见附表 2〕	最惠(%)	暂定税率	普通	增值/消费	出口退税	计量单位	监管条件/特殊证件	检验检疫	对美关税	亚太上/下
98.01	**未分类商品**										
9801.0010	人民币 2000 元及以下的非税、非证进口商品〔999〕	0		0	0/	0	千克	/			
9801.0090	其他未分类商品[T2]	0		0	0/	9,13	千克	/			
9802.0010	流通中的人民币现钞(包括纸币及硬币)〔999〕	0		0	0/	0	千克	m/			
9802.0090	流通中的外币现钞(包括纸币及硬币)〔999〕	0		0	0/	0	千克	/			
98.03	**出口计算机软件(仅用于出口,不包括与产品固化或集成为一体的软件)**										
9803.0040	出口的定制型软件(不包括与产品固化或集成为一体的软件)〔999〕	0		0	0/	0	套	/			
9803.0050	出口的定制型检测报告、蓝图及类似品〔999〕	0		0	0/	0	件	/			

SECTION XXII
ARTICLES OF SPECIAL TRADE AND GOOD UNCLASSIFIED

Chapter 98
Articles of Special Trade and Good Unclassified

协定税率 %								RCEP		特惠税率 %			Article Description
东/冰/格	巴基斯坦	韩国	瑞士上/下	哥/秘/柬	澳/毛	新西/坡/智	中国港/澳/台	东盟及马来/澳/韩	日/新	亚太2国	老/柬/缅	98/97/95	
													Good unclassified
													Import goods exempted from the levy of customs duties and not subject to license control, value≤2000RMB
													Other unclassified commodities
													RMB cash in circulation (including notes and coins)
													Foreign currency notes in circulation (including notes and coins)
													Computer software, not including software hardwired or integrated in products
													Software exported (excluding software solidified or integrated with products)
													Test reports, blueprints and similar products for export

2

2022版中华人民共和国海关进出口商品规范申报目录

Index Catalogue on Essential Standard Data Required by China Customs for the Declaration of Import and Export Goods(2022)

进出口商品规范申报目录

商品编码	申报要素
0101	1.品名 2.是否改良种用 3.品种
0102	1.品名 2.是否改良种用
01031000	1.品名 2.是否改良种用
01039	1.品名 2.个体重量
0104	1.品名 2.是否改良种用
0105	1.品名 2.是否改良种用 3.个体重量
01061	1.品名 2.是否改良种用
0106201	1.品名 2.是否改良种用
01062020	1.品名 2.用途（食用）
01062090	1.品名
010631	1.品名 2.是否改良种用
010632	1.品名 2.是否改良种用
010633	1.品名 2.是否改良种用
01063910	1.品名 2.是否改良种用 3.如为信鸽请注明足环号
0106392	1.品名 2.用途（食用）
01063990	1.品名 2.如为信鸽请注明足环号
01064	1.品名 2.是否改良种用
01069	1.品名 2.是否改良种用
0201	1.品名 2.制作或保存方法（鲜、冷）3.加工方法（整头、半头带骨、去骨）4.牛肉部位（如眼肉、腱子肉等）5.包装规格 6.英文品名 7.品牌（中文或外文名称）8.厂号 9.级别（A 级、B 级等） 10.饲养方式（草饲、谷饲等）11.签约日期 12.加工程度（精修、粗修等）
0202	1.品名 2.制作或保存方法（冻）3.加工方法（整头、半头带骨、去骨）4.牛肉部位（如眼肉、腱子肉等）5.包装规格 6.英文品名 7.品牌（中文或外文名称）8.厂号 9 级别（A 级、B 级等） 10.饲养方式（草饲、谷饲等）11.签约日期 12.加工程度（精修、粗修等）
0203	1.品名 2.制作或保存方法（鲜、冷、冻）3.加工方法（整头、半头带骨、去骨）4.包装规格 5.厂号
0204	1.品名 2.制作或保存方法（鲜、冷、冻）3.加工方法（整头、半头带骨、去骨）4.包装规格 5.厂号
0205	1.品名 2.制作或保存方法（鲜、冷、冻）3.包装规格 4.厂号
0206	1.品名 2.制作或保存方法（鲜、冷、冻）3.种类（舌、肝、心管、板筋等）4.包装规格 5.厂号
02071100	1.品名 2.制作或保存方法（鲜、冷）3.加工方法（整只、带骨或去骨等）4.厂号 5.品牌（中文或外文名称）
02071200	1.品名 2.制作或保存方法（冻）3.加工方法（整只、带骨或去骨等）4.厂号 5.品牌（中文或外文名称）
020713	1.品名 2.制作或保存方法（鲜、冷）3.加工方法（带骨、去骨）4.厂号 5.品牌（中文或外文名称）
0207141	1.品名 2.制作或保存方法（冻）3.加工方法（带骨、去骨）4.厂号 5.品牌（中文或外文名称）
02071421	1.品名 2.制作或保存方法（冻）3.加工方法（带骨、去骨）4.厂号 5.品牌（中文或外文名称）
02071422	1.品名 2.制作或保存方法（冻）3.加工方法（带骨、去骨）4.厂号 5.品牌（中文或外文名称）6.规格（个体重量）
02071429	1.品名 2.制作或保存方法（冻）3.加工方法（带骨、去骨）4.种类（心、肝等）5.厂号 6.品牌（中文或外文名称）
02072400	1.品名 2.制作或保存方法（鲜、冷）3.加工方法（整只、带骨或去骨等）
02072500	1.品名 2.制作或保存方法（冻）3.加工方法（整只、带骨或去骨等）
02072600	1.品名 2.制作或保存方法（鲜、冷）3.加工方法（带骨、去骨）4.杂碎请列明具体种类
02072700	1.品名 2.制作或保存方法（冻）3.加工方法（带骨、去骨）4.杂碎请列明具体种类 5.厂号 6.品牌（中文或外文名称）7.英文品名
02074100	1.品名 2.制作或保存方法（鲜、冷）3.加工方法（整只）4.厂号
02074200	1.品名 2.制作或保存方法（冻）3.加工方法（整只）4.厂号
02074300	1.品名 2.制作或保存方法（鲜、冷）3.厂号
02074400	1.品名 2.制作或保存方法（鲜、冷）3.加工方法（带骨或去骨等）4.杂碎请列明具体种类 5.厂号
02074500	1.品名 2.制作或保存方法（冻）3.加工方法（带骨或去骨等）4.杂碎请列明具体种类 5.厂号
02075100	1.品名 2.制作或保存方法（鲜、冷）3.加工方法（整只）4.厂号
02075200	1.品名 2.制作或保存方法（冻）3.加工方法（整只）4.厂号
02075300	1.品名 2.制作或保存方法（鲜、冷）3.厂号
02075400	1.品名 2.制作或保存方法（鲜、冷）3.加工方法（带骨或去骨等）4.杂碎请列明具体种类 5.厂号
02075500	1.品名 2.制作或保存方法（冻）3.加工方法（带骨或去骨等）4.杂碎请列明具体种类 5.厂号
02076000	1.品名 2.制作或保存方法（鲜、冷、冻）3.加工方法（整只、带骨或去骨等）4.杂碎请列明具体种类 5.厂号
02081010	1.品名 2.制作或保存方法（鲜、冷）3.包装规格 4.厂号
02081020	1.品名 2.制作或保存方法（冻）3.包装规格 4.厂号
02081090	1.品名 2.制作或保存方法（鲜、冷、冻）3.杂碎请列明具体种类 4.用途（食用）5.包装规格 6.厂号
02083000	1.品名 2.制作或保存方法（鲜、冷、冻）3.杂碎请列明具体种类 4.用途（食用）5.包装规格 6.厂号
02084000	1.品名 2.制作或保存方法（鲜、冷、冻）3.杂碎请列明具体种类 4.用途（食用）5.包装规格 6.厂号
02085000	1.品名 2.制作或保存方法（鲜、冷、冻）3.杂碎请列明具体种类 4.用途（食用）5.包装规格 6.厂号
02086000	1.品名 2.制作或保存方法（鲜、冷、冻）3.杂碎请列明具体种类 4.用途（食用）5.包装规格 6.厂号
02089010	1.品名 2.制作或保存方法（鲜、冷、冻）3.杂碎请列明具体种类 4.用途（食用）5.包装规格 6.厂号
02089090	1.品名 2.制作或保存方法（鲜、冷、冻）3.杂碎请列明具体种类 4.用途（食用）5.包装规格 6.厂号
0209	1.品名 2.制作或保存方法（未炼制、未提取脂肪，干、熏、盐腌、盐渍等）3.厂号
02101	1.品名 2.部位（腿肉、腹肉等），是否带骨 3.制作或保存方法（干、熏、盐腌、盐渍等）4.加工方法（带骨、去骨）5.厂号
02102000	1.品名 2.制作或保存方法（干、熏、盐腌、盐渍等）3.厂号
02109100	1.品名 2.用途 3.制作或保存方法（干、熏、盐腌、盐渍等）4.杂碎请列明具体种类 5.厂号
02109200	1.品名 2.用途 3.制作或保存方法（干、熏、盐腌、盐渍等）4.杂碎请列明具体种类 5.厂号
02109300	1.品名 2.用途 3.制作或保存方法（干、熏、盐腌、盐渍等）4.杂碎请列明具体种类 5.厂号
02109900	1.品名 2.用途 3.制作或保存方法（干、熏、盐腌、盐渍等）4.杂碎请列明具体种类 5.厂号
03011	1.品名 2.用途（观赏用）3.状态（活）4.拉丁学名
03019110	1.品名 2.状态（活）3.是否为鱼苗 4.拉丁学名
03019190	1.品名 2.状态（活）3.拉丁学名
03019210	1.品名 2.状态（活）3.是否为鱼苗 4.拉丁学名
03019290	1.品名 2.状态（活）3.拉丁学名
03019310	1.品名 2.状态（活）3.是否为鱼苗 4.拉丁学名
03019390	1.品名 2.状态（活）3.拉丁学名
03019410	1.品名 2.状态（活）3.是否为鱼苗 4.拉丁学名
0301949	1.品名 2.状态（活）3.拉丁学名
03019510	1.品名 2.状态（活）3.是否为鱼苗 4.拉丁学名
03019590	1.品名 2.状态（活）3.拉丁学名
0301991	1.品名 2.状态（活）3.是否为鱼苗 4.拉丁学名
0301999	1.品名 2.状态（活）3.拉丁学名
03021	1.品名 2.制作或保存方法（鲜、冷）3.拉丁学名 4.个体重量[如 1000～2000 克/条（块）等]
03022	1.品名 2.制作或保存方法（鲜、冷）3.拉丁学名 4.个体重量[如 1000～2000 克/条（块）等]
03023	1.品名 2.制作或保存方法（鲜、冷）3.拉丁学名 4.个体重量[如 1000～2000 克/条（块）等]
03024	1.品名 2.制作或保存方法（鲜、冷）3.拉丁学名 4.个体重量[如 1000～2000 克/条（块）等]
03025	1.品名 2.制作或保存方法（鲜、冷）3.拉丁学名 4.个体重量[如 1000～2000 克/条（块）等]
03027	1.品名 2.制作或保存方法（鲜、冷）3.拉丁学名 4.个体重量[如 1000～2000 克/条（块）等]
03028	1.品名 2.制作或保存方法（鲜、冷）3.拉丁学名 4.个体重量[如 1000～2000 克/条（块）等]
03029	1.品名 2.制作或保存方法（鲜、冷）3.拉丁学名
03031	1.品名 2.制作或保存方法（冻）3.拉丁学名 4.个体重量[如 1000～2000 克/条（块）等]
03032	1.品名 2.制作或保存方法（冻）3.拉丁学名 4.个体重量[如 1000～2000 克/条（块）等]
03033	1.品名 2.制作或保存方法（冻）3.拉丁学名 4.个体重量[如 1000～2000 克/条（块）等]
03034	1.品名 2.制作或保存方法（冻）3.拉丁学名 4.个体重量[如 1000～2000 克/条（块）等]
03035	1.品名 2.制作或保存方法（冻）3.拉丁学名 4.个体重量[如 1000～2000 克/条（块）等]
03036	1.品名 2.制作或保存方法（冻）3.拉丁学名 4.个体重量[如 1000～2000 克/条（块）等]
03038100	1.品名 2.制作或保存方法（冻）3.拉丁学名 4.个体重量[如 1000～2000 克/条（块）等]
03038200	1.品名 2.制作或保存方法（冻）3.拉丁学名 4.个体重量[如 1000～2000 克/条（块）等]
03038300	1.品名 2.制作或保存方法（冻）3.拉丁学名 4.个体重量[如 1000～2000 克/条（块）等]
03038400	1.品名 2.制作或保存方法（冻）3.拉丁学名 4.个体重量[如 1000～2000 克/条（块）等]
03038910	1.品名 2.制作或保存方法（冻）3.拉丁学名 4.个体重量[如 1000～2000 克/条（块）等]5.捕捞方式
03038920	1.品名 2.制作或保存方法（冻）3.拉丁学名 4.个体重量[如 1000～2000 克/条（块）等]
03038930	1.品名 2.制作或保存方法（冻）3.拉丁学名 4.个体重量[如 1000～2000 克/条（块）等]
03038990	1.品名 2.制作或保存方法（冻）3.拉丁学名 4.个体重量[如 1000～2000 克/条（块）等]
03039	1.品名 2.制作或保存方法（冻）3.拉丁学名
03043	1.品名 2.制作或保存方法（鲜、冷）3.拉丁学名 4.个体重量[如 1000～2000 克/片（块）等]
03044	1.品名 2.制作或保存方法（鲜、冷）3.拉丁学名 4.个体重量[如 1000～2000 克/片（块）等]
03045	1.品名 2.制作或保存方法（鲜、冷）3.拉丁学名 4.个体重量[如 1000～2000 克/片（块）等]
03046100	1.品名 2.制作或保存方法（冻）3.拉丁学名 4.个体重量[如 1000～2000 克/片（块）等]
0304621	1.品名 2.制作或保存方法（冻）3.拉丁学名 4.个体重量[如 1000～2000 克/片（块）等]
03046290	1.品名 2.制作或保存方法（冻）3.拉丁学名 4.个体重量[如 1000～2000 克/片（块）等]5.是否带皮、刺、鳞、鳍
03046300	1.品名 2.制作或保存方法（冻）3.拉丁学名 4.个体重量[如 1000～2000 克/片（块）等]5.是否带皮、刺、鳞、鳍
03046900	1.品名 2.制作或保存方法（冻）3.拉丁学名 4.个体重量[如 1000～2000 克/片（块）等]5.是否带皮、刺、鳞、鳍
03047	1.品名 2.制作或保存方法（冻）3.拉丁学名 4.个体重量[如 1000～2000 克/片（块）等]5.是否带皮、刺、鳞、鳍
03048100	1.品名 2.制作或保存方法（冻）3.拉丁学名 4.个体重量[如 1000～2000 克/片（块）等]5.是否带皮、刺、鳞、鳍
03048200	1.品名 2.制作或保存方法（冻）3.拉丁学名 4.个体重量[如 1000 2000 克/片（块）等]5.是否带皮、刺、鳞、鳍
03048300	1.品名 2.制作或保存方法（冻）3.拉丁学名 4.个体重量[如 1000～2000 克/片（块）等]5.是否带皮、刺、鳞、鳍
03048400	1.品名 2.制作或保存方法（冻）3.拉丁学名 4.个体重量[如 1000～2000 克/片（块）等]

商品编码	申报要素
03048500	1.品名 2.制作或保存方法(冻)3.拉丁学名 4.个体重量[如 1000～2000 克/片(块)等]
03048600	1.品名 2.制作或保存方法(冻)3.拉丁学名 4.个体重量[如 1000～2000 克/片(块) 等]5.是否带皮、刺、鳞、鳍
03048700	1.品名 2.制作或保存方法(冻)3.拉丁学名 4.个体重量[如 1000～2000 克/片(块) 等]5.是否带皮、刺、鳞、鳍
03048800	1.品名 2.制作或保存方法(冻)3.拉丁学名 4.个体重量[如 1000～2000 克/片(块)等]
03048900	1.品名 2.制作或保存方法(冻)3.拉丁学名 4.个体重量[如 1000～2000 克/片(块) 等]5.是否带皮、刺、鳞、鳍
03049	1.品名 2.制作或保存方法(冻)3.拉丁学名 4.个体重量[如 1000～2000 克/片(块)等]
03052000	1.品名 2.制作或保存方法(干、熏、盐腌、盐渍)3.拉丁学名
03053	1.品名 2.制作或保存方法(干、盐腌、盐渍)3.拉丁学名
03054	1.品名 2.制作或保存方法(熏)3.拉丁学名
03055	1.品名 2.制作或保存方法(干)3.拉丁学名
03056	1.品名 2.制作或保存方法(盐腌、盐渍)3.拉丁学名
03057	1.品名 2.用途 3.拉丁学名
03061100	1.品名 2.制作或保存方法(冻)3.状态(带壳、去壳)4.拉丁学名 5.个体重量 6.包装规格
03061200	1.品名 2.制作或保存方法(冻)3.状态(带壳、去壳)4.拉丁学名 5.个体重量 6.包装规格
030614	1.品名 2.制作或保存方法(冻)3.状态(带壳、去壳)4.拉丁学名 5.个体重量 6.包装规格
03061500	1.品名 2.制作或保存方法(冻)3.状态(带壳、去壳)4.拉丁学名 5.个体重量 6.包装规格
030616	1.品名 2.制作或保存方法(冻)3.状态(带壳、去壳)4.拉丁学名 5.规格(如 41～50 个/磅)6.包装规格
030617	1.品名 2.制作或保存方法(冻)3.状态(带壳、去壳)4.拉丁学名 5.规格(如 41～50 个/磅)6.包装规格 7.品牌(中文或外文名称)
030619	1.品名 2.制作或保存方法(冻)
03063110	1.品名 2.是否为种苗 3.拉丁学名
03063190	1.品名 2.制作或保存方法(活、鲜、冷等)3.状态(带壳、去壳)4.拉丁学名 5.个体重量 6.包装规格
03063210	1.品名 2.是否为种苗 3.拉丁学名
03063290	1.品名 2.制作或保存方法(活、鲜、冷等)3.状态(带壳、去壳)4.拉丁学名 5.个体重量 6.包装规格 7.品牌(中文或外文名称)
03063310	1.品名 2.是否为种苗 3.拉丁学名
0306339	1.品名 2.制作或保存方法(活、鲜、冷等)3.状态(带壳、去壳)4.拉丁学名 5.个体重量 6.包装规格
03063410	1.品名 2.是否为种苗 3.拉丁学名
03063490	1.品名 2.制作或保存方法(活、鲜、冷等)3.状态(带壳、去壳)4.拉丁学名 5.个体重量 6.包装规格
03063510	1.品名 2.是否为种苗 3.拉丁学名
03063590	1.品名 2.制作或保存方法(活、鲜、冷等)3.状态(带壳、去壳)4.拉丁学名 5.个体重量 6.包装规格
03063610	1.品名 2.是否为种苗 3.拉丁学名
03063690	1.品名 2.制作或保存方法(活、鲜、冷等)3.拉丁学名 4.状态(是否全虾、去头、去肠线,去尾、带壳、去壳、裹面粉等)5.个体重量 6.包装规格
03063910	1.品名 2.是否为种苗
03063990	1.品名 2.制作或保存方法(活、鲜、冷等)
03069100	1.品名 2.制作或保存方法(干、盐腌、盐渍等)3.状态(带壳、去壳)4.拉丁学名 5.个体重量 6.包装规格
03069200	1.品名 2.制作或保存方法(干、盐腌、盐渍等)3.状态(带壳、去壳)4.拉丁学名
030693	1.品名 2.制作或保存方法(干、盐腌、盐渍等)3.状态(带壳、去壳)4.拉丁学名 5.个体重量 6.包装规格
03069400	1.品名 2.制作或保存方法(干、盐腌、盐渍等)3.状态(带壳、去壳)4.拉丁学名 5.个体重量 6.包装规格
030695	1.品名 2.制作或保存方法(干、盐腌、盐渍等)3.状态(带壳、去壳)4.拉丁学名 5.个体重量 6.包装规格
03069900	1.品名 2.制作或保存方法(干、盐腌、盐渍等)
03071110	1.品名 2.是否为种苗 3.拉丁学名
03071190	1.品名 2.制作或保存方法(活、鲜、冷)3.状态(带壳、去壳)4.拉丁学名 5.个体重量 6.包装规格 7.品牌(中文或外文名称)
03071200	1.品名 2.制作或保存方法(冻)3.状态(带壳、去壳)4.拉丁学名 5.个体重量 6.包装规格
03071900	1.品名 2.制作或保存方法(干、盐腌、盐渍等)3.状态(带壳、去壳)4.拉丁学名 5.个体重量 6.包装规格
03072110	1.品名 2.是否为种苗 3.拉丁学名
0307219	1.品名 2.制作或保存方法(活、鲜、冷)3.状态(带壳、去壳)4.拉丁学名 5.个体重量 6.包装规格
030722	1.品名 2.制作或保存方法(冻)3.状态(带壳、去壳)4.拉丁学名 5.个体重量 6.包装规格
030729	1.品名 2.制作或保存方法(干、盐腌、盐渍等)3.状态(带壳、去壳)4.拉丁学名 5.个体重量 6.包装规格
03073110	1.品名 2.是否为种苗 3.拉丁学名
03073190	1.品名 2.制作或保存方法(活、鲜、冷)3.状态(带壳、去壳)4.拉丁学名 5.个体重量 6.包装规格
03073200	1.品名 2.制作或保存方法(冻)3.状态(带壳、去壳)4.拉丁学名 5.个体重量 6.包装规格
03073900	1.品名 2.制作或保存方法(干、盐腌、盐渍等)3.状态(带壳、去壳)4.拉丁学名 5.个体重量 6.包装规格
03074210	1.品名 2.是否为种苗 3.拉丁学名
03074291	1.品名 2.制作或保存方法(活、鲜、冷)3.拉丁学名 4.个体重量 5.包装规格
03074299	1.品名 2.制作或保存方法(活、鲜、冷)3.拉丁学名
03074310	1.品名 2.制作或保存方法(冻)3.拉丁学名(规范到属)4.个体重量 5.包装规格
03074390	1.品名 2.制作或保存方法(冻)3.拉丁学名
03074910	1.品名 2.制作或保存方法(干、盐腌、盐渍等)3.拉丁学名 4.个体重量 5.包装规格
03074990	1.品名 2.制作或保存方法(干、盐腌、盐渍等)3.拉丁学名
03075100	1.品名 2.制作或保存方法(活、鲜、冷)3.拉丁学名 4.个体重量 5.包装规格
03075200	1.品名 2.制作或保存方法(冻)3.拉丁学名 4.个体重量 5.包装规格
03075900	1.品名 2.制作或保存方法(干、盐腌、盐渍等)3.拉丁学名 4.个体重量 5.包装规格
03076010	1.品名 2.是否为种苗 3.拉丁学名
03076090	1.品名 2.制作或保存方法(活、鲜、冷、冻、干、盐腌、盐渍等)3.拉丁学名 4.个体重量 5.包装规格
03077110	1.品名 2.是否为种苗 3.拉丁学名
0307719	1.品名 2.制作或保存方法(活、鲜、冷)3.拉丁学名
03077200	1.品名 2.制作或保存方法(冻)3.拉丁学名
03077900	1.品名 2.制作或保存方法(干、盐腌、盐渍等)3.拉丁学名
03078110	1.品名 2.是否为种苗 3.拉丁学名
03078190	1.品名 2.制作或保存方法(活、鲜、冷)3.拉丁学名
03078210	1.品名 2.是否为种苗 3.拉丁学名
03078290	1.品名 2.制作或保存方法(活、鲜、冷)3.拉丁学名
03078300	1.品名 2.制作或保存方法(冻)3.拉丁学名
03078400	1.品名 2.制作或保存方法(冻)3.拉丁学名
03078700	1.品名 2.制作或保存方法(干、盐腌、盐渍等)3.拉丁学名
03078800	1.品名 2.制作或保存方法(干、盐腌、盐渍等)3.拉丁学名
03079110	1.品名 2.是否为种苗 3.拉丁学名
03079190	1.品名 2.制作或保存方法(活、鲜、冷)3.拉丁学名
03079200	1.品名 2.制作或保存方法(冻)3.拉丁学名
03079900	1.品名 2.制作或保存方法(干、盐腌、盐渍等)3.拉丁学名
03081110	1.品名 2.种苗请注明个体长度、尾数/千克等 3.拉丁学名
03081190	1.品名 2.制作或保存方法(活、鲜、冷)3.拉丁学名
03081200	1.品名 2.制作或保存方法(冻)3.是否经水煮 4.拉丁学名 5.包装规格
03081900	1.品名 2.制作或保存方法(干、盐腌、盐渍等)3.是否经水煮 4.拉丁学名 5.包装规格
03082110	1.品名 2.种苗请注明个体长度、尾数/千克等 3.拉丁学名
03082190	1.品名 2.制作或保存方法(活、鲜、冷)3.拉丁学名
03082200	1.品名 2.制作或保存方法(冻)3.拉丁学名 4.包装规格
03082900	1.品名 2.制作或保存方法(干、盐腌、盐渍等)3.拉丁学名 4.包装规格
03083011	1.品名 2.种苗请注明个体长度、尾数/千克等 3.拉丁学名
03083019	1.品名 2.制作或保存方法(活、鲜、冷)3.拉丁学名
03083090	1.品名 2.制作或保存方法(冻、干、盐腌、盐渍等)3.拉丁学名 4.包装规格
03089011	1.品名 2.种苗请注明个体长度、尾数/千克等
03089012	1.品名 2.制作或保存方法(活、鲜、冷)
03089019	1.品名 2.制作或保存方法(活、鲜、冷)
03089090	1.品名 2.制作或保存方法(冻、干、盐腌、盐渍等)3.包装规格
03091000	1.品名 2.用途
03099000	1.品名 2.用途
0401	1.品名 2.制作或保存方法(未浓缩及未加糖或其他甜物质)3.脂肪含量(按重量计)4.成分含量 5.包装规格(如 1 升/盒)6.品牌(中文或外文名称)
0402	1.品名 2.制作或保存方法(浓缩、加糖或其他甜物质)3.外观(粉状、粒状等)4.脂肪含量(按重量计)5.成分含量 6.包装规格(如 25 千克/包)7.品牌(中文或外文名称)
04032	1.品名 2.加工方法(发酵、酸化、浓缩、加糖及其他甜物质、香料等)3.保存方法(常温、冷藏等)4.成分含量 5.发酵菌种 6.包装规格 7.品牌(中文或外文名称)
04039000	1.品名 2.加工方法(发酵、酸化、浓缩、加糖及其他甜物质、香料等)3.保存方法(常温、冷藏等)4.成分含量 5.包装规格 6.品牌(中文或外文名称)
04041000	1.品名 2.制作或保存方法(浓缩、加糖及其他甜物质)3.成分含量 4.品牌(中文或外文名称)
04049000	1.品名 2.成分含量
04051000	1.品名 2.成分含量(乳脂、乳的无脂固形物、水及其他成分含量)3.包装规格 4.品牌(中文或外文名称)
04052000	1.品名 2.成分含量 3.包装规格 4.品牌(中文或外文名称)
04059000	1.品名 2.成分含量 3.包装规格 4.品牌(中文或外文名称)
04061000	1.品名 2.制作或保存方法(未熟化、未固化等)3.成分含量 4.包装规格 5.品牌(中文或外文名称)
04062000	1.品名 2.制作方法(磨碎、粉化等)3.乳脂含量 4.包装规格 5.品牌(中文或外文名称)
04063000	1.品名 2.制作或保存方法(未熟化、未固化等)3.成分含量 4.包装规格 5.品牌(中文或外文名称)
04064000	1.品名 2.制作或保存方法(熟化、固化、磨碎或粉化等)3.成分含量 4.是否带蓝纹或娄地青霉生产的带有纹理 5.包装规格 6.品牌(中文或外文名称)
04069000	1.品名 2.制作或保存方法(熟化、固化、磨碎或粉化等)3.成分含量 4.包装规格 5.品牌(中文或外文名称)
04071	1.品名 2.是否孵化用受精禽蛋
04072	1.品名 2.制作或保存方法(鲜、带壳)
04079	1.品名 2.制作或保存方法(鲜、带壳、腌制、煮过)
0408	1.品名 2.制作或保存方法(鲜、冻、干、去壳、蒸、水煮、制成型等)
0409	1.品名 2.来源(天然)3.品牌(中文或外文名称)4.包装规格
04101000	1.品名 2.用途(食用)
04109010	1.品名 2.品种(燕子的品种)3.外形(燕盏或燕碎,燕条等)4.含水量
04109021	1.品名 2.制作或保存方法(鲜)3.品牌(中文或外文名称)
04109022	1.品名 2.制作或保存方法(鲜)3.外观(粉)4.品牌(中文或外文名称)
04109023	1.品名 2.外观(粉)3.品牌(中文或外文名称)
04109029	1.品名 2.品牌(中文或外文名称)
04109090	1.品名 2.用途(食用)
0501	1.品名 2.是否经加工
05021	1.品名
05029	1.品名 2.用途(制刷用)
0504001	1.品名 2.制作或保存方法(鲜、冷、冻、干、熏、盐腌、盐渍)
05040021	1.品名 2.制作或保存方法(冷、冻)3.品牌(中文或外文名称)
05040029	1.品名 2.制作或保存方法(鲜、冷、冻、干、熏、盐腌、盐渍)

商品编码	申报要素
05040090	1.品名 2.制作或保存方法(鲜、冷、冻、干、熏、盐腌、盐渍)
05051000	1.品名 2.用途 3.制作或保存方法(仅经洗涤、消毒或为了保藏而做过处理)4.含绒量(包含绒子和绒丝含量)5.羽毛长度 6.羽毛来源(鸭、鹅等)
05059	1.品名 2.用途 3.制作或保存方法(仅经洗涤、消毒或为了保藏而做过处理)
05061000	1.品名 2.处理方法(经酸处理等)
05069011	1.品名 2.成分 3.处理方法(未经加工或经脱脂等)4.外观(粉末)5.是否废料
05069019	1.品名 2.处理方法(未经加工或经脱脂等)
05069090	1.品名 2.处理方法(未经加工、经脱脂、脱胶等)
05071000	1.品名 2.处理方法(未经加工或经脱脂等)3.是否为粉末及废料
05079	1.品名 2.处理方法(未经加工或经脱脂等)3.是否为粉末及废料
05080010	1.品名 2.处理方法(未经加工或经脱脂等)3.是否为粉末及废料
05080090	1.品名 2.处理方法(未经加工或经脱脂等)3.是否为粉末及废料
0510	1.品名 2.制作或保存方法(鲜、冷、冻、干或用其他方法暂时保藏)
05111000	1.品名
05119111	1.品名
05119119	1.品名 2.用途
05119190	1.品名 2.用途
05119910	1.品名
05119920	1.品名
05119930	1.品名
05119940	1.品名
05119990	1.品名 2.用途
0601	1.品名 2.状态(休眠、生长、开花)3.种类(球茎、块茎、鳞茎、块根等)4.是否种用
06021000	1.品名 2.栽培方法(无根插枝、接穗等)
06022010	1.品名 2.是否种用
06022090	1.品名
06023010	1.品名 2.是否种用
06023090	1.品名
06024010	1.品名 2.是否种用
06024090	1.品名
06029010	1.品名
06029091	1.品名 2.是否种用
06029092	1.品名
06029093	1.品名
06029094	1.品名
06029095	1.品名
06029099	1.品名
0603	1.品名 2.用途(制花束或装饰用)3.制作或保存方法(鲜、干、染色、漂白、浸渍等)
0604	1.品名 2.用途(制花束或装饰用)3.是否带花及花蕾 4.制作或保存方法(鲜、干、染色、漂白、浸渍等)
0701	1.品名 2.制作或保存方法(鲜、冷)3.是否种用
0702	1.品名 2.制作或保存方法(鲜、冷)
07031	1.品名 2.制作或保存方法(鲜、冷)
07032010	1.品名 2.制作或保存方法(鲜、冷)
07032020	1.品名 2.制作或保存方法(鲜、冷)
07032090	1.品名 2.制作或保存方法(鲜、冷)
07039	1.品名 2.制作或保存方法(鲜、冷)
0704	1.品名 2.制作或保存方法(鲜、冷)
0705	1.品名 2.制作或保存方法(鲜、冷)
0706	1.品名 2.制作或保存方法(鲜、冷)
0707	1.品名 2.制作或保存方法(鲜、冷)
0708	1.品名 2.制作或保存方法(鲜、冷)
0709	1.品名 2.制作或保存方法(鲜、冷)
07101000	1.品名 2.制作或保存方法(冻)
07102	1.品名 2.制作或保存方法(冻)
07103000	1.品名 2.制作或保存方法(冻)
07104000	1.品名 2.制作或保存方法(冻)
07108	1.品名 2.制作或保存方法(冻)
07109000	1.品名 2.制作或保存方法(冻)
0711	1.品名 2.用途(是否适于直接食用)3.制作或保存方法(用盐水、二氧化硫气体、亚硫酸水或其他防腐 液)
0712	1.品名 2.制作或保存方法(干制,包括脱水、蒸干或冻干)
07131010	1.品名 2.制作或保存方法(干制且脱荚)3.是否种用
07131090	1.品名 2.制作或保存方法(干制且脱荚)3.品种(黄豌豆、青豌豆、白豌豆等)
07132010	1.品名 2.制作或保存方法(干制且脱荚)3.是否种用
07132090	1.品名 2.制作或保存方法(干制且脱荚)3.是否种用
07133110	1.品名 2.制作或保存方法(干制且脱荚)3.是否种用
07133190	1.品名 2.制作或保存方法(干制且脱荚)3.是否种用
07133210	1.品名 2.制作或保存方法(干制且脱荚)3.是否种用
07133290	1.品名 2.制作或保存方法(干制且脱荚)3.是否种用
07133310	1.品名 2.制作或保存方法(干制且脱荚)3.是否种用
07133390	1.品名 2.制作或保存方法(干制且脱荚)3.是否种用
07133400	1.品名 2.制作或保存方法(干制且脱荚)3.是否种用
07133500	1.品名 2.制作或保存方法(干制且脱荚)3.是否种用
07133900	1.品名 2.制作或保存方法(干制且脱荚)3.是否种用
07134010	1.品名 2.制作或保存方法(干制且脱荚)3.是否种用
07134090	1.品名 2.制作或保存方法(干制且脱荚)3.是否种用
07135010	1.品名 2.制作或保存方法(干制且脱荚)3.是否种用
07135090	1.品名 2.制作或保存方法(干制且脱荚)3.是否种用
07136010	1.品名 2.制作或保存方法(干制且脱荚)3.是否种用
07136090	1.品名 2.制作或保存方法(干制且脱荚)3.是否种用
07139010	1.品名 2.制作或保存方法(干制且脱荚)3.是否种用
07139090	1.品名 2.制作或保存方法(干制且脱荚)3.是否种用
07141010	1.品名 2.制作或保存方法(鲜、冷、冻、干)3.是否种用
07141020	1.品名 2.制作或保存方法(鲜、冷、冻、干)3.是否种用
07141030	1.品名 2.制作或保存方法(鲜、冷、冻、干)3.是否种用

商品编码	申报要素
07142011	1.品名 2.制作或保存方法(鲜、冷、冻、干)3.是否种用
07142019	1.品名 2.制作或保存方法(鲜、冷、冻、干)3.是否种用
07142020	1.品名 2.制作或保存方法(鲜、冷、冻、干)3.是否种用
07142030	1.品名 2.制作或保存方法(鲜、冷、冻、干)3.是否种用
07143000	1.品名 2.制作或保存方法(鲜、冷、冻、干)3.是否种用
07144000	1.品名 2.制作或保存方法(鲜、冷、冻、干)3.是否种用
07145000	1.品名 2.制作或保存方法(鲜、冷、冻、干)3.是否种用
07149010	1.品名 2.制作或保存方法(鲜、冷、冻、干)3.是否种用
07149021	1.品名 2.制作或保存方法(鲜、冷、冻、干)3.是否种用
07149029	1.品名 2.制作或保存方法(鲜、冷、冻、干)3.是否种用
07149090	1.品名 2.制作或保存方法(鲜、冷、冻、干)3.是否种用
08011100	1.品名 2.制作或保存方 法 3.加工方法(去内壳或未去内壳)4.是否种用 5.种类
08011200	1.品名 2.制作或保存方 法 3.加工方法(去内壳或未去内壳)4.是否种用 5.种类
080119	1.品名 2.制作或保存方 法 3.加工方法(去内壳或未去内壳)4.是否种用 5.种类
08012100	1.品名 2.制作或保存方 法 3.加工方法(去壳或未去壳)
08012200	1.品名 2.制作或保存方 法 3.加工方法(去壳或未去壳)
08013100	1.品名 2.制作或保存方法 3.加工方法(未去壳)
08013200	1.品名 2.制作或保存方法 3.加工方法(去壳)4.等级
08021100	1.品名 2.制作或保存方 法 3.加工方法(去壳或未去壳)
08021200	1.品名 2.制作或保存方 法 3.加工方法(去壳或未去壳)
08022	1.品名 2.制作或保存方 法 3.加工方法(去壳或未去壳)4.种类
08023	1.品名 2.制作或保存方 法 3.加工方法(去壳或未去壳)4.种类
08024	1.品名 2.制作或保存方 法 3.加工方法(去壳或未去壳)
08025	1.品名 2.制作或保存方 法 3.加工方法(去壳或未去壳)
08026	1.品名 2.制作或保存方 法 3.加工方法(去壳或未去壳)4.是否种用 5.签约日期
08026110	1.品名 2.制作或保存方 法 3.加工方法(去壳或未去壳)4.是否种用 5.签约日期
08026190	1.品名 2.制作或保存方 法 3.加工方法(去壳或未去壳)4.是否种用 5.签约日期
08026200	1.品名 2.制作或保存方 法 3.加工方法(去壳或未去壳)4.是否种用 5.签约日期
08027000	1.品名 2.制作或保存方 法 3.加工方法(去壳或未去壳)
08028000	1.品名 2.制作或保存方 法 3.加工方法(去壳或未去壳)
08029100	1.品名 2.制作或保存方法 3.加工方法(未去壳)
08029200	1.品名 2.制作或保存方法 3.加工方法(去壳)
080299	1.品名 2.制作或保存方 法 3.加工方法(去壳或未去壳)
0803	1.品名 2.制作或保存方法(鲜、干)3.干制方法(脱水、蒸干或冻干)4.种类(大香蕉、蕉仔、皇帝蕉等)5.等级(A 级、B 级、C 级等)6.品牌(中文或外文名称)7.注册厂商 8.每箱把数(如 9 把/箱)
08041000	1.品名 2.制作或保存方法(鲜、干)3.等级
08042000	1.品名 2.制作或保存方法(鲜、干)3.等级
08043000	1.品名 2.制作或保存方法(鲜、干)3.种类(如青菠萝、金菠萝等)4.等级 5.去除果冠请注明
08044000	1.品名 2.制作或保存方法(鲜、干)3.等级
08045010	1.品名 2.制作或保存方法(鲜、干)3.等级
08045020	1.品名 2.制作或保存方法(鲜、干)3.等级
08045030	1.品名 2.制作或保存方法(鲜、干)3.等级(如 4A、5A、统级等)4.种类(如油竹、花竹和沙竹等)5.品牌(中文或外文名称)6.注册厂商
08051000	1.品名 2.制作或保存方法(鲜、干)3.种类(脐橙、夏橙等)4.等级(如一级、二级等)5.品牌(中文或外文名称)6.注册厂商 7.每箱个数(如 30 个/箱)
08052	1.品名 2.制作或保存方法(鲜、干)3.种类 4.等级
08054000	1.品名 2.制作或保存方法(鲜、干)3.等级
08055000	1.品名 2.制作或保存方法(鲜、干)3.等级 4.品牌(中文或外文名称)
08059000	1.品名 2.制作或保存方法(鲜、干)3.等级
08061000	1.品名 2.制作或保存方法(鲜)3.种类 4.规格 5.品牌(中文或外文名称)
08062000	1.品名 2.制作或保存方法(干)3.等级 4.品牌(中文或外文名称)
08071100	1.品名 2.制作或保存方法(鲜)3.等级 4.品牌(中文或外文名称)
080719	1.品名 2.制作或保存方法(鲜)3.等级
08072000	1.品名 2.制作或保存方法(鲜)3.等级 4.品牌(中文或外文名称)
08081000	1.品名 2.制作或保存方法(鲜)3.种类(蛇果、加纳果、青苹果、富士等)4.等级 5.品牌(中文或外文名称)
08083	1.品名 2.制作或保存方法(鲜)3.等级
08084000	1.品名 2.制作或保存方法(鲜)3.等级
08091000	1.品名 2.制作或保存方法(鲜)3.等级
08092100	1.品名 2.制作或保存方法(鲜)3.等级
08092900	1.品名 2.制作或保存方法(鲜)3.等级 4.种类(如 Bing, Lambert, Van, Tu lare, Chelan, Tieton, Skeena 等)5.品牌(中文或外文名称)6.注册厂商 7.尺寸(按果径最大处以毫米为单位计算)
08093000	1.品名 2.制作或保存方法(鲜)3.等级
08094000	1.品名 2.制作或保存方法(鲜)3.等级
08101000	1.品名 2.制作或保存方法(鲜)3.等级
08102000	1.品名 2.制作或保存方法(鲜)3.等级
08103000	1.品名 2.制作或保存方法(鲜)3.等级
08104000	1.品名 2.制作或保存方法(鲜)3.等级 4.品牌(中文或外文名称)
08105000	1.品名 2.制作或保存方法(鲜)3.种类(如 Hayward, Hort16A, SunGold, Jintao, Sorelli, kiwiberry 等)4.等级
08106000	1.品名 2.制作或保存方法(鲜)3.等级(如一级等)4.种类(如金枕、干尧、青尼等)5.品牌(中文或外文名称)6.注册厂商
08107000	1.品名 2.制作或保存方法(鲜)3.等级
08109010	1.品名 2.制作或保存方法(鲜)3.等级
08109030	1.品名 2.制作或保存方法(鲜)3.等级
08109040	1.品名 2.制作或保存方法(鲜)3.等级
08109050	1.品名 2.制作或保存方法(鲜)3.等级
08109060	1.品名 2.制作或保存方法(鲜)3.等级
08109070	1.品名 2.制作或保存方法(鲜)3.等级
08109080	1.品名 2.制作或保存方法(鲜)3.等级 4.种类

商品编码	申报要素
08109090	1.品名 2.制作或保存方法(鲜)3.等级
08111000	1.品名 2.制作或保存方法(冻)
08112000	1.品名 2.制作或保存方法(冻)
08119010	1.品名 2.制作或保存方法(冻、未去壳)
08119090	1.品名 2.制作或保存方法(冻)
0812	1.品名 2.是否适于直接食用 3.制作或保存方法(用盐水、二氧化硫气体、亚硫酸水或其他防腐液)
08131000	1.品名 2.制作或保存方法(干)
08132000	1.品名 2.制作或保存方法(干)
08133000	1.品名 2.制作或保存方法(干)
08134010	1.品名 2.制作或保存方法(干)3.等级
08134020	1.品名 2.制作或保存方法(干)
08134030	1.品名 2.制作或保存方法(干)
08134040	1.品名 2.制作或保存方法(干)3.加工程度(去壳、未去壳)
08134090	1.品名 2.制作或保存方法(干)
08135000	1.品名 2.制作或保存方法(干)3.种类
0814	1.品名 2.制作或保存方法(鲜、冻、干,用盐水、亚硫酸水或其他防腐液暂时保藏的)
09011100	1.品名 2.制作或保存方法(豆、粉等,未焙炒且未浸除咖啡碱)3.品种 4.产区
09011200	1.品名 2.制作或保存方法(豆、粉等,未焙炒且已浸除咖啡碱)3.品种 4.产区
09012100	1.品名 2.制作或保存方法(豆、粉等,已焙炒且未浸除咖啡碱)3.品种 4.产区
09012200	1.品名 2.制作或保存方法(豆、粉等,已焙炒且已浸除咖啡碱)3.品种 4.产区
09019010	1.品名 2.种类(咖啡豆荚或豆皮)3.品种 4.产区
09019020	1.品名 2.成分 3.品种 4.产区
0902	1.品名 2.制作或保存方法(未发酵、半发酵、发酵)3.内包装每件净重 4.品牌(中文或外文名称)
0903	1.品名
09041	1.品名 2.制作和保存方法(未磨、已磨干、粉)
09042100	1.品名 2.制作和保存方法(未磨、已磨干、粉)
09042200	1.品名 2.制作和保存方法(未磨、已磨干、粉)
0905	1.品名 2.加工方法(未磨、已磨)
09061100	1.品名 2.加工方法(未磨、已磨)
09061900	1.品名 2.加工方法(未磨、已磨)
09062000	1.品名 2.加工方法(未磨、已磨)
0907	1.品名 2.加工方法(未磨、已磨)
09081	1.品名 2.加工方法(未磨、已磨)
09082	1.品名 2.加工方法(未磨、已磨)
09083	1.品名 2.加工方法(未磨、已磨)
0909	页蒿子杜松果:
09092	1.品名 2.加工方法(未磨、已磨)
09093	1.品名 2.加工方法(未磨、已磨)
09096	页蒿子或小茴香子杜松果:1.品名 2.加工方法(未磨、已磨)
09101	1.品名 2.加工方法(未磨、已磨)
09102000	1.品名
09103000	1.品名
09109	1.品名 2.成分含量
09109100	1.品名 2.成分含量
09109900	1.品名 2.成分含量
1001	1.品名 2.是否种用 3.是否硬粒 4.种类(白麦、红麦、冬麦、春麦)5.有无滞期费(无滞期费、滞期费未确定、滞期费已申报)
10021000	1.品名 2.是否种用 3.有无滞期费(无滞期费、滞期费未确定、滞期费已申报)
10029000	1.品名 2.是否种用 3.有无滞期费(无滞期费、滞期费未确定、滞期费已申报)
1003	1.品名 2.是否种用 3.蛋白含量 4.用途(酿酒、饲料等) 5.有无滞期费(无滞期费、滞期费未确定、滞期费已申报)
10041000	1.品名 2.是否种用 3.有无滞期费(无滞期费、滞期费未确定、滞期费已申报)
10049000	1.品名 2.是否种用 3.有无滞期费(无滞期费、滞期费未确定、滞期费已申报)
1005	1.品名 2.是否种用 3.转(非转)基因请注明 4.有无滞期费(无滞期费、滞期费未确定、滞期费已申报)
10061021	1.品名 2.种类 3.加工方法(去壳、未去壳)4.粒长 5.长宽比 6.包装规格 7.有无滞期费(无滞期费、滞期费未确定、滞期费已申报)
10061029	1.品名 2.种类 3.加工方法(去壳、未去壳)4.粒长 5.长宽比 6.包装规格 7.有无滞期费(无滞期费、滞期费未确定、滞期费已申报)
10061081	1.品名 2.种类 3.加工方法(去壳、未去壳)4.粒长 5.长宽比 6.包装规格 7.有无滞期费(无滞期费、滞期费未确定、滞期费已申报)
10061089	1.品名 2.种类 3.加工方法(去壳、未去壳)4.粒长 5.长宽比 6.包装规格 7.有无滞期费(无滞期费、滞期费未确定、滞期费已申报)
10062020	1.品名 2.种类 3.加工方法(去壳、未去壳)4.制作或保存方法(糙米)5.粒长 6.长宽比 7.包装规格 8.有无滞期费(无滞期费、滞期费未确定、滞期费已申报)
10062080	1.品名 2.种类 3.加工方法(去壳、未去壳)4.粒长 5.长宽比 6.包装规格 7.有无滞期费(无滞期费、滞期费未确定、滞期费已申报)
10063020	1.品名 2.种类 3.加工方法(去壳、未去壳)4.粒长 5.长宽比 6.包装规格 7.有无滞期费(无滞期费、滞期费未确定、滞期费已申报)
10063080	1.品名 2.种类 3.加工方法(去壳、未去壳)4.粒长 5.长宽比 6.包装规格 7.有无滞期费(无滞期费、滞期费未确定、滞期费已申报)
10064020	1.品名 2.种类 3.加工方法(去壳、未去壳)4.包装规格 5.有无滞期费(无滞期费、滞期费未确定、滞期费已申报)
10064080	1.品名 2.种类 3.加工方法(去壳、未去壳)4.包装规格 5.有无滞期费(无滞期费、滞期费未确定、滞期费已申报)
10071000	1.品名 2.用途(食用)3.是否种用 4.包装规格 5.有无滞期费(无滞期费、滞期费未确定、滞期费已申报)
10079000	1.品名 2.用途(食用)3.是否种用 4.包装规格 5.有无滞期费(无滞期费、滞期费未确定、滞期费已申报)
10081000	1.品名 2.是否种用 3.包装规格 4.有无滞期费(无滞期费、滞期费未确定、滞期费已申报)
10082100	1.品名 2.是否种用 3.包装规格 4.有无滞期费(无滞期费、滞期费未确定、滞期费已申报)
10082900	1.品名 2.是否种用 3.包装规格 4.有无滞期费(无滞期费、滞期费未确定、滞期费已申报)
10083000	1.品名 2.是否种用 3.包装规格 4.有无滞期费(无滞期费、滞期费未确定、滞期费已申报)
10084010	1.品名 2.是否种用 3.包装规格 4.有无滞期费(无滞期费、滞期费未确定、滞期费已申报)
10084090	1.品名 2.是否种用 3.包装规格 4.有无滞期费(无滞期费、滞期费未确定、滞期费已申报)
10085010	1.品名 2.是否种用 3.包装规格 4.有无滞期费(无滞期费、滞期费未确定、滞期费已申报)
10085090	1.品名 2.是否种用 3.包装规格 4.有无滞期费(无滞期费、滞期费未确定、滞期费已申报)
10086010	1.品名 2.是否种用 3.包装规格 4.有无滞期费(无滞期费、滞期费未确定、滞期费已申报)
10086090	1.品名 2.是否种用 3.包装规格 4.有无滞期费(无滞期费、滞期费未确定、滞期费已申报)
10089010	1.品名 2.是否种用 3.包装规格 4.有无滞期费(无滞期费、滞期费未确定、滞期费已申报)
10089090	1.品名 2.是否种用 3.包装规格 4.有无滞期费(无滞期费、滞期费未确定、滞期费已申报)
1101	1.品名 2.状态(细粉)
1102	1.品名 2.种类(玉米、长粒米等)3.状态(细粉)
1103	1.品名 2.种类(小麦、玉米、燕麦等)3.状态(粗粒、粗粉、团粒等)
1104	1.品名 2.种类(燕麦、大麦、小麦等)3.制作或保存方法(去壳、滚压、制片等)
1105	1.品名 2.状态(细粉、粗粉、粉末、粉片、颗粒及团粒)
11061000	1.品名 2.种类(豌豆、鹰嘴豆等)3.状态(细粉、粗粉、粉末)
11062000	1.品名 2.种类(豌豆、鹰嘴豆等)3.状态(细粉、粗粉、粉末)
11063000	1.品名 2.种类(豌豆、鹰嘴豆等)3.状态(细粉、粗粉、粉末)
1107	1.品名 2.制作或保存方法(未焙制、已焙制)
11081100	1.品名 2.种类(小麦淀粉)
11081200	1.品名 2.种类(玉米淀粉)
11081300	1.品名 2.种类(马铃薯淀粉)
11081400	1.品名 2.种类(木薯淀粉)
11081900	1.品名 2.种类(大米淀粉、竹芋淀粉等)
11082000	1.品名
1109	1.品名
12011000	1.品名 2.种类(黄大豆、黑大豆、青大豆等)3.是否种用 4.转(非转)基因请注明
1201901	1.品名 2.种类(黄大豆)3.转(非转)基因请注明 4.蛋白含量 5.油含量 6.签约日期 7.有无滞期费(无滞期费、滞期费未确定、滞期费已申报)
12019020	1.品名 2.种类(黑大豆)3.转(非转)基因请注明
12019030	1.品名 2.种类(青大豆)3.转(非转)基因请注明
12019090	1.品名 2.种类 3.转(非转)基因请注明
1202	1.品名 2.制作或保存方法(未去壳、去壳、未焙炒、未烹煮)3.是否种用
1203	1.品名 2.用途(榨油用)
1204	1.品名
12051010	1.品名 2.是否种用 3.芥子酸含量及所得固体成分每克葡萄糖苷酸(酯)含量 4.转(非转)基因请注明
12051090	1.品名 2.是否种用 3.芥子酸含量及所得固体成分每克葡萄糖苷酸(酯)含量 4.转(非转)基因请注明
12059	1.品名 2.是否种用 3.转(非转)基因请注明
12060010	1.品名 2.是否种用
12060090	1.品名 2.种类(食用型、油用型)3.油含量
12071	1.品名 2.是否种用
12072100	1.品名 2.是否种用
12072900	1.品名 2.是否种用
12073010	1.品名 2.是否种用
12073090	1.品名 2.是否种用
12074010	1.品名 2.是否种用
12074090	1.品名 2.是否种用
12075010	1.品名 2.是否种用
12075090	1.品名 2.是否种用
12076010	1.品名 2.是否种用
12076090	1.品名 2.种类(食用型、油用型)3.油含量
12077010	1.品名
12077091	1.品名
12077092	1.品名
12077099	1.品名
12079100	1.品名 2.是否种用
120799	1.品名 2.是否种用
1208	1.品名 2.状态(细粉、粗粉)
12091000	1.品名 2.用途(种植用)3.转(非转)基因请注明
12092100	1.品名 2.用途(种植用)
12092200	1.品名 2.用途(种植用)
12092300	1.品名 2.用途(种植用)
12092400	1.品名 2.用途(种植用)
12092500	1.品名 2.用途(种植用)
12092910	1.品名 2.用途(种植用)3.转(非转)基因请注明
12092990	1.品名 2.用途(种植用)
12093000	1.品名 2.用途(种植用)
12099100	1.品名 2.用途(种植用)
12099900	1.品名 2.用途(种植用)
1210	1.品名 2.制作或保存方法(鲜、干、未研磨、研磨、未制成团粒等)
1211201	1.品名 2.用途(作香料、药料、杀虫、杀菌等类似用途)3.制作或保存方法(鲜、干等)
1211202	1.品名 2.用途(作香料、药料、杀虫、杀菌等类似用途)3.制作或保存方法(鲜、干等)
12112091	1.品名 2.用途(作香料、药料、杀虫、杀菌等类似用途)3.制作或保存方法(鲜、干等)

商品编码	申报要素
12112092	1.品名 2.用途(作香料、药料、杀虫、杀菌等类似用途)3.制作或保存方法(鲜、干等)
12112099	1.品名 2.用途(作香料、药料、杀虫、杀菌等类似用途)3.制作或保存方法(鲜、干等)
12113000	1.品名 2.用途(作香料、药料、杀虫、杀菌等类似用途)3.制作或保存方法(鲜、干等)
12114000	1.品名 2.用途(作香料、药料、杀虫、杀菌等类似用途)3.制作或保存方法(鲜、干等)
12115000	1.品名 2.用途(作香料、药料、杀虫、杀菌等类似用途)3.制作或保存方法(鲜、干等)
12116000	1.品名 2.用途(作香料、药料、杀虫、杀菌等类似用途)3.制作或保存方法(鲜、干等)
12119011	1.品名 2.用途(作香料、药料、杀虫、杀菌等类似用途)3.制作或保存方法(鲜、干等)
12119012	1.品名 2.用途(作香料、药料、杀虫、杀菌等类似用途)3.制作或保存方法(鲜、干等)
12119013	1.品名 2.用途(作香料、药料、杀虫、杀菌等类似用途)3.制作或保存方法(鲜、干等)
12119014	1.品名 2.用途(作香料、药料、杀虫、杀菌等类似用途)3.制作或保存方法(鲜、干等)
12119015	1.品名 2.用途(作香料、药料、杀虫、杀菌等类似用途)3.制作或保存方法(鲜、干等)
12119016	1.品名 2.用途(作香料、药料、杀虫、杀菌等类似用途)3.制作或保存方法(鲜、干等)
12119017	1.品名 2.用途(作香料、药料、杀虫、杀菌等类似用途)3.制作或保存方法(鲜、干等)
12119018	1.品名 2.用途(作香料、药料、杀虫、杀菌等类似用途)3.制作或保存方法(鲜、干等)
12119019	1.品名 2.用途(作香料、药料、杀虫、杀菌等类似用途)3.制作或保存方法(鲜、干等)
12119021	1.品名 2.用途(作香料、药料、杀虫、杀菌等类似用途)3.制作或保存方法(鲜、干等)
12119022	1.品名 2.用途(作香料、药料、杀虫、杀菌等类似用途)3.制作或保存方法(鲜、干等)
12119023	1.品名 2.用途(作香料、药料、杀虫、杀菌等类似用途)3.制作或保存方法(鲜、干等)
12119024	1.品名 2.用途(作香料、药料、杀虫、杀菌等类似用途)3.制作或保存方法(鲜、干等)
12119025	1.品名 2.用途(作香料、药料、杀虫、杀菌等类似用途)3.制作或保存方法(鲜、干等)
12119026	1.品名 2.用途(作香料、药料、杀虫、杀菌等类似用途)3.制作或保存方法(鲜、干等)
12119027	1.品名 2.用途(作香料、药料、杀虫、杀菌等类似用途)3.制作或保存方法(鲜、干等)
12119028	1.品名 2.用途(作香料、药料、杀虫、杀菌等类似用途)3.制作或保存方法(鲜、干等)
12119029	1.品名 2.用途(作香料、药料、杀虫、杀菌等类似用途)3.制作或保存方法(鲜、干等)
12119031	1.品名 2.用途(作香料、药料、杀虫、杀菌等类似用途)3.制作或保存方法(鲜、干等)
12119032	1.品名 2.用途(作香料、药料、杀虫、杀菌等类似用途)3.制作或保存方法(鲜、干等)
12119033	1.品名 2.用途(作香料、药料、杀虫、杀菌等类似用途)3.制作或保存方法(鲜、干等)
12119034	1.品名 2.用途(作香料、药料、杀虫、杀菌等类似用途)3.制作或保存方法(鲜、干等)
12119035	1.品名 2.用途(作香料、药料、杀虫、杀菌等类似用途)3.制作或保存方法(鲜、干等)
12119036	1.品名 2.用途(作香料、药料、杀虫、杀菌等类似用途)3.制作或保存方法(鲜、干等)
12119037	1.品名 2.用途(作香料、药料、杀虫、杀菌等类似用途)3.制作或保存方法(鲜、干等)
12119038	1.品名 2.用途(作香料、药料、杀虫、杀菌等类似用途)3.制作或保存方法(鲜、干等)
12119039	1.品名 2.用途(作香料、药料、杀虫、杀菌等类似用途)3.制作或保存方法(鲜、干等)
12119050	1.品名 2.用途(作香料、药料、杀虫、杀菌等类似用途)3.制作或保存方法(鲜、干等)
1211909	1.品名 2.用途(作香料、药料、杀虫、杀菌等类似用途)3.制作或保存方法(鲜、干等)
121221	1.品名 2.制作或保存方法(鲜、冷、冻、干等)3.拉丁学名 4.是否适合供人食用
121229	1.品名 2.制作或保存方法(鲜、冷、冻、干等)3.拉丁学名 4.是否适合供人食用
12129100	1.品名 2.制作或保存方法(鲜、冷、冻等)
12129200	1.品名 2.制作或保存方法(鲜、冷、冻等)
12129300	1.品名 2.制作或保存方法(鲜、冷、冻等)
12129400	1.品名 2.制作或保存方法(鲜、冷、冻等)
12129911	1.品名 2.用途(主要供人食用)
12129912	1.品名 2.用途(主要供人食用)
12129919	1.品名 2.用途(主要供人食用)
12129993	1.品名 2.用途(主要供人食用)
12129994	1.品名 2.用途(主要供人食用)
12129996	1.品名 2.用途(主要供人食用)
12129999	1.品名 2.用途(主要供人食用)
1213	1.品名 2.制作或保存方法(切碎、碾磨、挤压等) 3.加工程度(未经处理)
12141000	1.品名 2.状态(粗粉及团粒等)
12149000	1.品名 2.原产于美国的苜蓿草请申报相对饲喂价值(RFV)
13012000	1.品名 2.用途(食品、饮料、制药等)
13019010	1.品名
13019020	1.品名
13019030	1.品名
13019040	1.品名
13019090	1.品名
13021100	1.品名 2.制作或保存方法(液汁、浸膏、粉末)
13021200	1.品名 2.制作或保存方法(液汁、浸膏、粉末)
13021300	1.品名 2.制作或保存方法(液汁、浸膏、粉末)3.有效成分含量(α 酸等)
13021400	1.品名 2.制作或保存方法(液汁、浸膏、粉末)
130219	1.品名 2.制作或保存方法(液汁、浸膏、粉末)
13022000	1.品名 2.用途(食品用、医药用)
13023100	1.品名 2.等级(食品级、医药级等)
13023200	1.品名 2.来源 3.黏度 4.级别(食用级、工业级)
13023911	1.品名 2.种类(卡帕胶、阿欧塔胶、莱姆达胶等)3.用途(乳品、肉类、水、糖果、果冻、甜品)
13023912	1.品名 2.用途
13023919	1.品名 2.用途
13023990	1.品名 2.来源 3.用途
14011000	1.品名 2.用途(主要作编结用)
14012000	1.品名 2.用途(主要作编结用)3.种类 4.加工程度(去皮或未去皮)5.直径 6.长度
14019	1.品名 2.用途(主要作编结用)
14042000	1.品名 2.纤维长度
14049010	1.品名 2.用途(主要供染料或鞣料用)
14049090	1.品名
1501	1.品名
1502	1.品名 2.加工方法 3.是否含瘦肉
1503	1.品名 2.加工程度(未经乳化、混合或其他方法制 作)
15041000	1.品名 2.成分含量 3.加工程度(未经化学改性)4.饲料用的鱼油、脂及其分离品请注明是否精炼 5.保健用鱼油请注明 DHA+EPA 浓度 6.品牌(中文或外文名称,无品牌请申报厂商)
15042000	1.品名 2.成分含量 3.加工程度(未经化学改性)4.饲料用的鱼油、脂及其分离品请注明是否精炼 5.保健用鱼油请注明 DHA+EPA 浓度 6.品牌(中文或外文名称,无品牌请申报厂商)
15043000	1.品名 2.成分含量 3.加工程度(未经化学改性)4.品牌(中文或外文名称,无品牌请申报厂商)
1505	1.品名
1506	1.品名 2.加工程度(未经化学改性)
1507	1.品名 2.加工方法(初榨、非初榨)3.加工程度(未经化学改性)
1508	1.品名 2.加工方法(初榨、非初榨)3.加工程度(未经化学改性)
1509	1.品名 2.加工方法(初榨、非初榨)3.加工程度(未经化学改性)4.用途 5.包装规格 6.品牌(中文或外文名 称)7.游离酸度(以油酸计)8.产区
1510	1.品名 2.加工程度(未经化学改性)3.加工方法(初榨、非初榨)4.包装规格 5.品牌(中文或外文名称)
15111000	1.品名 2.加工方法(初榨)3.加工程度(未经化学改性)
15119	1.品名 2.加工方法(精制)3.加工程度(未经化学改性)4.包装规格 5.品牌(中文或外文名称,无品牌请申报厂商)6.熔点
1512	1.品名 2.加工方法(初榨、非初榨)3.加工程度(未经化学改性)
1513	1.品名 2.加工方法(初榨、非初榨)3.加工程度(未经化学改性)
15141100	1.品名 2.加工方法(初榨)3.加工程度(未经化学改性)4.芥子酸含量
15141900	1.品名 2.加工方法(非初榨)3.加工程度(未经化学改性)4.芥子酸含量及所得固体成分每克葡萄糖苷酸(酯)含量
15149	1.品名 2.加工方法(初榨、非初榨)3.加工程度(未经化学改性)
15151	1.品名 2.加工方法(初榨、非初榨)3.加工程度(未经化学改性)
15152	1.品名 2.加工方法(初榨、非初榨)3.加工程度(未经化学改性)
15153000	1.品名 2.加工方法(初榨、非初榨)3.加工程度(未经化学改性)
15155000	1.品名 2.加工方法(初榨、非初榨)3.加工程度(未经化学改性)4.包装规格 5.品牌(中文或外文名称,无品牌请申报厂商)
15156000	1.品名 2.加工方法(初榨、非初榨)3.加工程度(未经化学改性)4.用途 5.成分含量 6.品牌(中文或外文名称,无品牌请申报厂商)
15159010	1.品名 2.加工方法(初榨、非初榨)3.加工程度(未经化学改性)4.用途
15159020	1.品名 2.加工方法(初榨、非初榨)3.加工程度(未经化学改性)4.用途
15159030	1.品名 2.加工方法(初榨、非初榨)3.加工程度(未经化学改性)4.用途
15159040	1.品名 2.加工方法(初榨、非初榨)3.加工程度(未经化学改性)4.用途
15159090	1.品名 2.加工方法(初榨、非初榨)3.加工程度(未经化学改性)4.用途 5.成分含量 6.品牌(中文或外文名称,无品牌请申报厂商)
1516	1.品名 2.加工方法(全部或部分氢化、相互酯化、再酯化或反油酸化)
15171000	1.品名 2.加工方法 3.加工原料(动物油脂、植物油脂、微生物油脂)4.品牌(中文或外文名称)
15179010	1.品名 2.成分含量 3.加工原料(豆油、菜子油、棕榈油、微生物油脂)4.品牌(中文或外文名称)
15179090	1.品名 2.成分含量 3.加工原料(动物油脂、植物油脂、微生物油脂)4.品牌(中文或外文名称)
1518	1.品名 2.成分含量 3.加工方法(经熟炼、氧化、脱水、硫化、吹制等)
1520	1.品名 2.成分含量
15211000	1.品名 2.成分
15219010	1.品名
15219090	1.品名
1522	1.品名 2.来源
16010010	1.品名 2.是否用天然肠衣做外包装 3.成分含量 4.包装规格 5.品牌(中文或外文名称)
16010020	1.品名 2.成分含量 3.包装规格 4.品牌(中文或外文名称)
16010030	1.品名 2.成分含量 3.包装规格 4.品牌(中文或外文名称)
16021000	1.品名 2.成分含量 3.包装规格 4.品牌(中文或外文名称)
16022000	1.品名 2.加工方法(煮、蒸、烤、煎、炸、炒等) 3.成分含量 4.包装规格 5.品牌(中文或外文名称)
16023100	1.品名 2.加工方法(煮、蒸、烤、煎、炸、炒等) 3.成分含量 4.包装规格 5.品牌(中文或外文名称)
16023210	1.品名 2.加工方法(煮、蒸、烤、煎、炸、炒等) 3.成分含量 4.包装规格 5.品牌(中文或外文名称)
1602329	1.品名 2.加工方法(煮、蒸、烤、煎、炸、炒等) 3.成分含量 4.包装规格 5.品牌(中文或外文名称)
16023910	1.品名 2.加工方法(煮、蒸、烤、煎、炸、炒等) 3.成分含量 4.包装规格 5.品牌(中文或外文名称)

商品编码	申报要素
1602399	1.品名 2.加工方法(煮、蒸、烤、煎、炸、炒等) 3.成分含量 4.包装规格 5.品牌(中文或外文名称)
16024100	1.品名 2.加工方法(煮、蒸、烤、煎、炸、炒等) 3.成分含量 4.包装规格 5.品牌(中文或外文名称)
16024200	1.品名 2.加工方法(煮、蒸、烤、煎、炸、炒等) 3.成分含量 4.包装规格 5.品牌(中文或外文名称)
16024910	1.品名 2.加工方法(煮、蒸、烤、煎、炸、炒等) 3.成分含量 4.包装规格 5.品牌(中文或外文名称)
16024990	1.品名 2.加工方法(煮、蒸、烤、煎、炸、炒等) 3.成分含量 4.包装规格 5.品牌(中文或外文名称)
16025010	1.品名 2.加工方法(煮、蒸、烤、煎、炸、炒等) 3.成分含量 4.包装规格 5.品牌(中文或外文名称)
16025090	1.品名 2.加工方法(煮、蒸、烤、煎、炸、炒等) 3.成分含量 4.包装规格 5.品牌(中文或外文名称)
16029010	1.品名 2.加工方法(煮、蒸、烤、煎、炸、炒等) 3.成分含量 4.包装规格 5.品牌(中文或外文名称)
16029090	1.品名 2.加工方法(煮、蒸、烤、煎、炸、炒等) 3.成分含量 4.包装规格 5.品牌(中文或外文名称)
1603	1.品名 2.加工方法(精、汁)3.包装规格
16041	1.品名 2.状态(整条或切块、非整条或切块)3.加工方法(烤、煎、炸等) 4.包装规格
16042	1.品名 2.状态(整条或切块、非整条或切块)3.加工方法(烤、煎、炸等) 4.包装规格
16043	1.品名 2.状态(整条或切块、非整条或切块)3.加工方法(烤、煎、炸等) 4.包装规格 5.品牌(中文或外文名称)
16051000	1.品名 2.加工方法(烤、煎、炸等)3.状态(去壳)4.包装规格
16052	1.品名 2.加工方法(烤、煎、炸等)3.状态(去壳)4.是否非密封包装 5.包装规格
16053000	1.品名 2.加工方法(烤、煎、炸等)3.状态(去壳)4.包装规格
16054	1.品名 2.加工方法(烤、煎、炸等)3.状态(去壳)4.包装规格
16055	1.品名 2.加工方法(烤、煎、炸等)3.包装规格
16056	1.品名 2.加工方法(烤、煎、炸等)3.包装规格
17011	1.品名 2.加工方法(未加香料或着色剂)3.按重量计干燥状态的糖含量对应的旋光度 4.品牌(中文或外文名称,无品牌请申报厂商)
17019100	1.品名 2.加工方法(加香料或着色剂)3.成分含量 4.品牌(中文或外文名称,无品牌请申报厂商)
170199	1.品名 2.成分含量 3.品牌(中文或外文名称,无品牌请申报厂商)
17021	1.品名 2.按重量计干燥无水乳糖的含量 3.品牌(中文或外文名称,无品牌请申报厂商)
17022000	1.品名 2.品牌(中文或外文名称,无品牌请申报厂商)
17023000	1.品名 2.按重量计干燥状态的果糖含量 3.用途(食用、医用)4.品牌(中文或外文名称,无品牌请申报厂商)
17024000	1.品名 2.按重量计干燥状态的果糖含量 3.品牌(中文或外文名称,无品牌请申报厂商)
17025000	1.品名 2.按重量计干燥状态的果糖含量 3.品牌(中文或外文名称,无品牌请申报厂商)
17026000	1.品名 2.种类(高果糖浆、高果糖晶体、低聚酯果糖等)3.按重量计干燥状态的果糖含量 4.用途(食用、医用)5.品牌(中文或外文名称,无品牌请申报厂商)
17029	1.品名 2.成分含量 3.品牌(中文或外文名称,无品牌请申报厂商)
1703	1.品名 2.原料 3.成分含量 4.品牌(中文或外文名称,无品牌请申报厂商)
1704	1.品名 2.成分含量 3.包装规格 4.品牌(中文或外文名称,无品牌请申报厂商)
1801	1.品名 2.加工方法(整颗或破碎的、生的或焙炒的)
1802	1.品名
1803	1.品名 2.是否脱脂(未脱脂、全部脱脂或部分脱脂)
1804	1.品名
1805	1.品名 2.加工方法(粉末状、未加糖或其他甜物质)3.可可脂含量 4.包装规格
18061000	1.品名 2.加工方法(粉末状、加糖或其他甜物质) 3.容器包装或内包装每件净重 4.成分含量 5.品牌(中文或外文名称)
18062000	1.品名 2.成分含量 3.形状(条状、块状等)4.容器包装或内包装每件净重 5.品牌(中文或外文名称)
18063	1.品名 2.成分含量 3.形状(条状、块状)4.容器包装或内包装每件净重 5.是否夹心 6.品牌(中文或外文名称)
18069000	1.品名 2.成分含量 3.容器包装或内包装每件净重 4.品牌(中文或外文名称)
19011	1.品名 2.成分含量 3.用途(供婴幼儿食用适用的年龄阶段)4.包装规格 5.品牌(中文或外文名称)
19012000	1.品名 2.成分含量 3.用途(供烘焙面包、糕饼等 用)4.包装规格
19019000	1.品名 2.成分含量 3.包装规格 4.品牌(中文或外文名称)
19021	1.品名 2.成分含量 3.加工方法(生的、未包馅或未经其他方法加工)4.是否速冻请注明
19022000	1.品名 2.成分含量 3.加工方法(包馅或经其他方法加工)
19023010	1.品名 2.成分含量
19023020	1.品名 2.成分含量
19023030	1.品名 2.种类(即食面条、快熟面条)3.成分含量 4.包装规格 5.品牌(中文或外文名称)
19023090	1.品名 2.成分含量 3.包装规格 4.品牌(中文或外文名称)
19024000	1.品名 2.成分含量
1903	1.品名 2.成分含量 3.包装规格
19041000	1.品名 2.加工方法(膨化或烘炒)3.成分含量 4.包装规格 5.品牌(中文或外文名称)
19042000	1.品名 2.加工方法(未烘炒、未烘炒与烘炒或膨化混合)3.成分含量 4.包装规格 5.品牌(中文或外文名称)
19043000	1.品名 2.加工方法(干、碾碎)3.成分含量 4.包装规格 5.品牌(中文或外文名称)
19049000	1.品名 2.加工方法(经过预煮或经其他方法制作) 3.成分含量 4.包装规格 5.品牌(中文或外文名称)
19051000	1.品名 2.成分含量 3.包装规格 4.品牌(中文或外文名称)
19052000	1.品名 2.成分含量 3.包装规格 4.品牌(中文或外文名称)
19053	1.品名 2.成分含量 3.包装规格 4.品牌(中文或外文名称)
19054000	1.品名 2.成分含量 3.包装规格 4.品牌(中文或外文名称)
19059000	1.品名 2.成分含量 3.加工方法(烘焙等)4.包装规格 5.品牌(中文或外文名称)
2001	1.品名 2.加工方法(用醋或醋酸制作或保藏)3.包装规格 4.品牌(中文或外文名称)
20021010	1.品名 2.加工方法(整个、切片等)3.成分含量 4.包装规格 5.品牌(中文或外文名称)
20021090	1.品名 2.加工方法(整个、切片等)3.成分含量 4.包装规格 5.品牌(中文或外文名称)
2002901	1.品名 2.包装规格(重量/罐)3.成分含量 4.品牌(中文或外文名称)
20029090	1.品名 2.加工方法(绞碎等)3.成分含量 4.包装规格
2003	1.品名 2.加工方法 3.成分含量 4.包装规格 5.品牌(中文或外文名称)
20041000	1.品名 2.加工方法 3.保存方法(冻等)4.成分含量 5.包装规格 6.品牌(中文或外文名称)
20049000	1.品名 2.加工方法 3.保存方法(冻等)4.成分含量 5.包装规格 6.品牌(中文或外文名称)
20051000	1.品名 2.加工方法 3.保存方法(未冷冻等)4.成分含量 5.包装规格 6.品牌(中文或外文名称)
20052000	1.品名 2.加工方法 3.保存方法(未冷冻等)4.成分含量 5.包装规格 6.品牌(中文或外文名称)
20054000	1.品名 2.加工方法 3.保存方法(未冷冻等)4.成分含量 5.包装规格 6.品牌(中文或外文名称)
200551	1.品名 2.加工方法 3.保存方法(未冷冻等)4.成分含量 5.是否脱荚 6.包装规格 7.品牌(中文或外文名称)
200559	1.品名 2.加工方法 3.保存方法(未冷冻等)4.成分含量 5.包装规格 6.品牌(中文或外文名称)
20056	1.品名 2.加工方法 3.保存方法(未冷冻等)4.成分含量 5.包装规格 6.品牌(中文或外文名称)
20057000	1.品名 2.加工方法 3.保存方法(未冷冻等)4.成分含量 5.包装规格 6.品牌(中文或外文名称)
20058000	1.品名 2.加工方法 3.保存方法(未冷冻等)4.成分含量 5.包装规格 6.品牌(中文或外文名称)
20059110	1.品名 2.加工方法 3.保存方法(未冷冻等)4.成分含量 5.包装规格 6.品牌(中文或外文名称)
20059190	1.品名 2.加工方法 3.保存方法(未冷冻等)4.成分含量 5.包装规格 6.品牌(中文或外文名称)
20059920	1.品名 2.加工方法 3.保存方法(未冷冻等)4.成分含量 5.包装规格 6.品牌(中文或外文名称)
20059940	1.品名 2.加工方法 3.保存方法(未冷冻等)4.成分含量 5.包装规格 6.品牌(中文或外文名称)
20059950	1.品名 2.加工方法 3.保存方法(未冷冻等)4.成分含量 5.包装规格 6.品牌(中文或外文名称)
20059960	1.品名 2.加工方法 3.保存方法(未冷冻等)4.成分含量 5.包装规格 6.品牌(中文或外文名称)
20059970	1.品名 2.加工方法 3.保存方法(未冷冻等)4.成分含量 5.包装规格 6.品牌(中文或外文名称)
2005999	1.品名 2.加工方法 3.保存方法(未冷冻等)4.成分含量 5.包装规格 6.品牌(中文或外文名称)
2006	1.品名 2.加工方法(沥干、糖渍、裹糖)3.成分含量 4.包装规格 5.品牌(中文或外文名称)
2007	1.品名 2.加工方法(烹煮)3.成分含量 4.包装规格 5.品牌(中文或外文名称)
20081	1.品名 2.加工方法(烹煮、炒、炸、糖泡、浸渍、渗透等)3.成分含量 4.包装规格 5.品牌(中文或外文名称)
20082	1.品名 2.加工方法(烹煮、炒、炸、糖泡、浸渍、渗透等)3.成分含量 4.包装规格 5.品牌(中文或外文名称)
20083	1.品名 2.加工方法(烹煮、炒、炸、糖泡、浸渍、渗透等)3.成分含量 4.包装规格 5.品牌(中文或外文名称)
20084	1.品名 2.加工方法(烹煮、炒、炸、糖泡、浸渍、渗透等)3.成分含量 4.包装规格 5.品牌(中文或外文名称)
20085000	1.品名 2.加工方法(烹煮、炒、炸、糖泡、浸渍、渗透等)3.成分含量 4.包装规格 5.品牌(中文或外文名称)
20086	1.品名 2.加工方法(烹煮、炒、炸、糖泡、浸渍、渗透等)3.成分含量 4.包装规格 5.品牌(中文或外文名称)
20087	1.品名 2.加工方法(烹煮、炒、炸、糖泡、浸渍、渗透等)3.成分含量 4.包装规格 5.品牌(中文或外文名称)
20088000	1.品名 2.加工方法(烹煮、炒、炸、糖泡、浸渍、渗透等)3.成分含量 4.包装规格 5.品牌(中文或外文名称)
20089100	1.品名 2.加工方法(烹煮、炒、炸、糖泡、浸渍、渗透等)3.成分含量 4.包装规格 5.品牌(中文或外文名称)
20089300	1.品名 2.加工方法(烹煮、炒、炸、糖泡、浸渍、渗透等)3.成分含量 4.包装规格 5.品牌(中文或外文名称)
20089700	1.品名 2.加工方法(烹煮、炒、炸、糖泡、浸渍、渗透等)3.成分含量 4.包装规格 5.品牌(中文或外文名称)
20089910	1.品名 2.加工方法(烹煮、炒、炸、糖泡、浸渍、渗透等)3.成分含量 4.包装规格 5.品牌(中文或外文名称)
20089920	1.品名 2.加工方法(烹煮、炒、炸、糖泡、浸渍、渗透等)3.成分含量 4.包装规格 5.品牌(中文或外文名称)
2008993	1.品名 2.加工方法(烹煮、炒、炸、糖泡、浸渍、渗透等)3.成分含量 4.包装规格 5.品牌(中文或外文名称)
20089940	1.品名 2.加工方法(烹煮、炒、炸、糖泡、浸渍、渗透等)3.成分含量 4.包装规格 5.品牌(中文或外文名称)
20089990	1.品名 2.加工方法(烹煮、炒、炸、糖泡、浸渍、渗透等)3.成分含量 4.包装规格 5.品牌(中文或外文名称)
2009	1.品名 2.成分含量 3.白利糖度值 4.浓缩果汁请注明浓缩倍数 5.加工方法(是否发酵、加酒精、冷冻、混合等)6.保存方法(储藏温度)7.包装规格 8.品牌(中文或外文名称)
2101	1.品名 2.成分含量 3.包装规格 4.品牌(中文或外文名称)
21021000	1.品名 2.是否活性酵母 3.包装规格 4.品牌(中文或外文名称)
21022000	1.品名 2.是否活性酵母 3.是否已死的单细胞微生物 4.包装规格 5.品牌(中文或外文名称)
21023000	1.品名 2.包装规格 3.品牌(中文或外文名称)
21031000	1.品名 2.成分含量 3.包装规格 4.品牌(中文或外文名称)

商品编码	申报要素
21032000	1.品名 2.成分含量 3.包装规格 4.品牌(中文或外文名称)
21033000	1.品名 2.成分含量 3.包装规格 4.品牌(中文或外文名称)
21039010	1.品名 2.成分含量 3.包装规格 4.品牌(中文或外文名称)
21039020	1.品名 2.成分含量(酒精含量、香料和各种配料含量及糖含量等)3.包装规格 4.品牌(中文或外文名称)
21039090	1.品名 2.成分含量 3.包装规格 4.品牌(中文或外文名称)
2104	1.品名 2.成分含量 3.包装规格 4.品牌(中文或外文名称)
2105	1.品名 2.包装规格 3.品牌(中文或外文名称)
21061000	1.品名 2.成分含量 3.包装规格 4.品牌(中文或外文名称)
21069010	1.品名 2.成分含量 3.包装规格 4.品牌(中文或外文名称)
21069020	1.品名 2.成分含量 3.包装规格 4.品牌(中文或外文名称)
21069030	1.品名 2.成分含量 3.包装规格 4.品牌(中文或外文名称)
21069040	1.品名 2.成分含量 3.是否可直接饮用 4.包装规格 5.品牌(中文或外文名称)
21069050	1.品名 2.成分含量 3.包装规格 4.品牌(中文或外文名称)
2106906	1.品名 2.成分含量 3.包装规格 4.品牌(中文或外文名称)
21069090	1.品名 2.成分含量 3.包装规格 4.品牌(中文或外文名称)
22011	1.品名 2.包装规格 3.品牌(中文或外文名称)4.生产日期
2201901	1.品名 2.加工方法(未加糖或其他甜物质及未加味)3.来源(天然)4.包装规格 5.品牌(中文或外文名称)6 生产日期
22019090	1.品名 2.加工方法(未加糖或其他甜物质及未加味)3.包装规格 4.品牌(中文或外文名称)5.生产日期
22021000	1.品名 2.加工方法(加糖、加味或其他甜物质)3.包装规格 4.品牌(中文或外文名称)5.生产日期
22029100	1.品名 2.成分含量(酒精浓度等)3.包装规格 4.品牌(中文或外文名称)5.生产日期
22029900	1.品名 2.成分 3.包装规格 4.品牌(中文或外文名称)5.生产日期
2203	1.品名(中文及外文名称)2.是否麦芽酿造 3.酒精浓度 4.麦芽浓度 5.包装规格 6.品牌(中文或外文名称);7.生产日期
22041000	1.品名(中文及外文名称)2.种类(汽酒)3.酒精浓度 4.级别 5.年份(没有年份的申报无年份)6.产区(中文及外文名称)7.酒庄名(中文及外文名称) 8.葡萄品种(中文及外文名称)9.包装规格 10.品牌(中文或外文名称)
22042	1.品名(中文及外文名称)2.进口方式(原液区内加工、原液区外加工、原瓶有品牌、国内贴品牌) 3.酒精浓度 4.级别 5.年份(没有年份的申报无年 份)6.产区(最小子产区中文及外文名称)7.酒庄名(中文及外文名称)8.葡萄品种(中文及外文名称)9.包装规格(包装规格×每项单位数、升/桶或升/集装箱罐)10.进口方式(原液区内加工、原液区外加工、原瓶有品牌、国内贴品牌)11.品牌(中文或外文名称)
22043000	1.品名(中文及外文名称)2.种类(酿酒葡萄汁)3.包装规格 4.品牌(中文或外文名称)
2205	1.品名(中文及外文名称)2.加工方法(鲜葡萄酿造、加植物或香料)3.包装规格 4.品牌(中文或外文名称)
22060010	1.品名(中文及外文名称)2.加工方法(发酵、混合)3.包装规格 4.品牌(中文或外文名称)
22060090	1.品名(中文及外文名称)2.成分含量 3.加工方法(发酵、混合)4.酒精浓度 5.包装规格 6.品牌(中文或外文名称)7.年份 8.级别
2207	1.品名(中文及外文名称)2.加工方法(未改性、改性)3.酒精浓度 4.品牌(中文或外文名称)
22082000	1.品名(中文及外文名称)2.原料 3.酒精浓度 4.进口方式(原液区内加工、原液区外加工、原瓶有品牌、国内贴品牌)5.包装规格(包装规格×每项单位数、升/桶或升/集装箱罐)6.品牌(中文或外文名称)7.级别 8.产区(最小子产区中文及外文名称)
22083000	1.品名(中文及外文名称)2.原料 3.酒精浓度 4.进口方式(原液区内加工、原液区外加工、原瓶有品牌、国内贴品牌)5.包装规格(包装规格×每项单位数、升/桶或升/集装箱罐)6.品牌(中文或外文名称)7.产区(最小子产区中文及外文名称)8.陈年年份 9.酒桶使用
22084000	1.品名(中文及外文名称)2.原料 3.酒精浓度 4.包装规格 5.品牌(中文或外文名称)
22085000	1.品名(中文及外文名称)2.原料 3.酒精浓度 4.包装规格 5.品牌(中文或外文名称)
22086000	1.品名(中文及外文名称)2.原料 3.酒精浓度 4.包装规格 5.品牌(中文或外文名称)
22087000	1.品名(中文及外文名称)2.原料 3.酒精浓度 4.进口方式(原液区内加工、原液区外加工、原瓶有品牌、国内贴品牌)5.包装规格(包装规格×每项单位数、升/桶或升/集装箱罐)6.品牌(中文或外文名称)
22089010	1.品名(中文及外文名称)2.原料 3.酒精浓度 4.包装规格 5.品牌(中文或外文名称)
22089020	1.品名 2.原料 3.酒精浓度 4.包装规格 5.品牌(中文或外文名称)
22089090	1.品名(中文及外文名称)2.原料 3.酒精浓度 4.包装规格 5.品牌(中文或外文名称)
2209	1.品名(中文及外文名称)2.醋酸浓度 3.包装规格 4.品牌(中文或外文名称)
23011	1.品名 2.用途(不适合供人食用)3.状态(渣粉、团粒)
23012010	1.品名 2.用途(不适合供人食用)3.状态(渣粉、团粒)4.成分含量(蛋白质含量等)5.种类(红、白鱼粉)
23012090	1.品名 2.用途(不适合供人食用)3.状态(渣粉、团粒)
2302	1.品名 2.种类(玉米的、小麦的等)
2303	1.品名 2.种类 3.是否配制
2304	1.品名 2.原料
2305	1.品名 2.原料
23061000	1.品名 2.原料
23062000	1.品名 2.原料
23063000	1.品名 2.原料
23064100	1.品名 2.原料 3.转(非转)基因请注明
23064900	1.品名 2.原料
23065000	1.品名 2.原料
23066000	1.品名 2.原料
23069000	1.品名 2.原料
2307	1.品名
2308	1.品名 2.用途(饲料用等)
23091	1.品名 2.成分含量 3.用途(狗食、猫食等)4.加工方法(配制的)5.包装规格 6.品牌(中文或外文名称)
23099010	1.品名 2.成分含量(须分别标明载体及活性物质) 3.加工方法(配制的)4.包装规格 5.品牌(中文或外文名称)
23099090	1.品名 2.成分含量 3.加工方法(配制的)4.包装规格 5.品牌(中文或外文名称)
24011	1.品名 2.加工方法(未去梗)
24012	1.品名 2.加工方法(去梗、部分去梗)
24013000	1.品名 2.是否废料
2402	1.品名 2.种类(卷烟、雪茄烟)3.来源(烟草制或烟草代用品制)4.品牌(中文或外文名称)5.型号或系列名称
24031	1.品名 2.用途(经燃烧吸用)
24039100	1.品名 2.加工方法(均化、再造)
24039900	1.品名 2.是否烟草精汁
24041	1.品名 2.成分(含烟草、再造烟草、尼古丁、烟草或尼古丁代用品等)3.用途(非经燃烧吸用)4.品牌(中文或外文名称)5.型号或系列名称
24049	1.品名 2.用途(人体摄入)3.品牌(中文或外文名称)4.型号或系列名称
25010011	1.品名 2.成分含量 3.包装规格 4.是否食用盐
25010019	1.品名 2.成分含量 3.包装规格 4.是否食用盐
25010020	1.品名 2.成分含量 3.包装规格
25010030	1.品名 2.成分含量 3.包装规格
2502	1.品名 2.加工方法(未焙烧)
2503	1.品名 2.加工工艺 3.状态(液态、固态、粉状、块状)4.成分含量 5.计价日期
2504	1.品名 2.外观(粉末、鳞片、块等)3.来源(是否天然)4.是否球化加工 5.石墨含量 6.细度指标(细度或鳞片大小)
2505	1.品名 2.来源(如海砂、湖砂或河砂等)
2506	1.品名 2.加工方法(天然状态、粗加修整、简单切割等)3.外观(颜色、形状)4.规格
2507	1.品名 2.成分含量 3.是否活化 4.用途 5.颜色 6.形状 7.加工方法(煅烧、未煅烧)8.白度 9.细度指标(细度或鳞片大小)
25081000	1.品名 2.是否活化 3.用途 4.蒙脱石含量
25083000	1.品名 2.是否活化 3.氧化铝含量 4.级别 5.含有添加剂、未含有改性添加剂请注明 6.改性、未改性请注明
25084000	1.品名 2.是否活化 3.氧化铝含量 4.级别 5.是否含有添加剂或改性
25085000	1.品名 2.种类 3.是否活化 4.用途
25086000	1.品名 2.种类 3.是否活化 4.用途
25087000	1.品名 2.种类 3.是否活化 4.用途
2509	1.品名
2510	1.品名 2.加工方法(是否碾磨及其他进一步加工) 3.种类(磷灰石、天然磷酸钙、天然磷酸铝钙及磷酸盐白垩)4.注明五氧化二磷含量
25111000	1.品名 2.加工方法 3.级别(钻井级、化工级、涂料级等)4.细度(目数)
25112000	1.品名 2.加工方法
2512	1.品名 2.是否活化 3.表观比重 4.品牌(中文或外文名称)5.种类 6.是否改性 7.二氧化硅含量
25131000	1.品名 2.加工方法(如天然原状、破碎)3.用途
25132000	1.品名 2.种类(刚玉岩、天然刚玉砂、天然石榴石、天然磨料等)
2514	1.品名 2.用途 3.加工方法(天然原状、粗加修整、锯、割等)4.形状
25151	1.品名 2.加工方法(天然原状、粗加修整、锯、割 等)3.外观(颜色形状)4.表观比重 5.体积或面积数量(立方米数或平方米数)6.花色品种的中文及英文名称 7.规格(长宽高)8.矿区名称
25152000	1.品名 2.加工方法(天然原状、粗加修整、锯、割 等)3.外观(颜色形状)4.除蜡石外要注明表观比重
25161	1.品名 2.加工方法(天然原状、粗加修整、锯、割 等)3.外观(颜色形状)4.体积或面积数量(立方米数或平方米数)5.花色品种的中文及英文名称 6.规格(长宽高)7.矿区名称
25162000	1.品名 2.加工方法(天然原状、粗加修整、锯、割 等)3.形状 4.体积或面积数量(立方米数或平方米数)5.花色品种的中文及英文名称 6.规格(长宽高)
25169000	1.品名 2.用途 3.加工方法(天然原状、粗加修整、锯、割等)4.形状
25171000	1.品名 2.用途 3.形状
25172000	1.品名 2.用途 3.来源(是否矿渣、浮渣、残渣等)
25173000	1.品名 2.用途
25174	1.品名
2518	1.品名 2.加工方法(夯混、是否煅烧或烧结、粗加修整、锯、割等)3.形状
2519	1.品名 2.加工方法 3.成分含量 4.粉状请注明细度,粒状请注明直径
2520	1.品名 2.用途(是否牙科用或其他用途)3.来源
2521	1.品名 2.用途
2522	1.品名
2523	1.品名 2.用途 3.品牌(中文或外文名称)4.厂家名称
2524	1.品名 2.是否青石棉 3.是否长纤维 4.型号
2525	1.品名 2.用途 3.形状
25261	1.品名 2.加工方法(天然原状、粗加修整、简单切 割)3.是否破碎
25262010	1.品名 2.加工方法(天然原状、粗加修整、简单切 割)3.是否破碎
25262020	1.品名 2.加工方法(天然原状、粗加修整、简单切 割)3.是否破碎 3.白度
25280010	1.品名
25280090	1.品名 2.成分含量
25291000	1.品名 2.外观(颜色形状)
25292	1.品名 2.外观(颜色形状)3.氟化钙含量
25293000	1.品名 2.外观(颜色形状)
25301010	1.品名 2.用途 3.加工方法(天然开采、简单破碎、磨粉、未膨胀等)4.形状 5.成分含量 6.白度
25301020	1.品名 2.用途 3.加工方法(天然开采、简单破碎、磨粉、未膨胀等)4.形状 5.成分含量
25302000	1.品名 2.用途 3.加工方法(天然开采、简单破碎、磨粉、未膨胀等)4.形状 5.成分含量
25309010	1.品名 2.用途 3.加工方法(天然开采、简单破碎、磨粉、未膨胀等)4.形状 5.成分含量
25309020	1.品名 2.用途 3.加工方法(天然开采、简单破碎、磨粉、未膨胀等)4.形状 5.成分含量
2530909	1.品名 2.用途 3.加工方法(天然开采、简单破碎、磨粉、未膨胀等)4.形状 5.成分含量

商品编码	申报要素
260111	1.品名 2.加工方法(破碎、磨碎、磁选、重力分离、浮选、筛选等)3.成分含量 4.平均粒度 5.来源(原产国及矿区名称)6.签约日期 7.计价日期 8.有无滞期费(无滞期费、滞期费未确定、滞期费已申报)
26011200	1.品名 2.加工方法(破碎、磨碎、磁选、重力分离、浮选、筛选等)3.成分含量 4.来源(原产国及矿区名称)5.签约日期 6.计价日期 7.有无滞期费(无滞期费、滞期费未确定、滞期费已申报)
26012000	1.品名 2.加工方法(破碎、磨碎、磁选、重力分离、浮选、筛选等)3.成分含量 4.来源(原产国及矿区名称)5.签约日期 6.计价日期 7.有无滞期费(无滞期费、滞期费未确定、滞期费已申报)
2602	1.品名 2.用途 3.加工方法(破碎、磨碎、磁选、重力分离、浮选、筛选等) 4.成分含量 5.来源(原产国及矿区名称)6.签约日期 7.计价日期 8.有无滞期费(无滞期费、滞期费未确定、滞期费已申报)
2603	1.品名 2.加工方法(破碎、磨碎、磁选、重力分离、浮选、筛选等)3.成分含量 4.含水率 5.来源(原产国及矿区名称)6.签约日期 7.计价日期 8.有无滞期费(无滞期费、滞期费未确定、滞期费已申报)
2604	1.品名 2.加工方法(破碎、磨碎、磁选、重力分离、浮选、筛选等)3.成分含量 4.来源(原产国及矿区名称)5.签约日期 6.计价日期 7.有无滞期费(无滞期费、滞期费未确定、滞期费已申报)
2605	1.品名 2.加工方法(破碎、磨碎、磁选、重力分离、浮选、筛选等)3.成分含量(申报主要伴生矿物元素含量)4.用途 5.来源(原产国及矿区名称)6.签约日期 7.计价日期 8.有无滞期费(无滞期费、滞期费未确定、滞期费已申报)
2606	1.品名 2.加工方法(破碎、磨碎、磁选、重力分离、浮选、筛选等)3.成分含量 4.来源(原产国及矿区名称)5.签约日期 6.计价日期 7.有无滞期费(无滞期费、滞期费未确定、滞期费已申报)
2607	1.品名 2.加工方法(破碎、磨碎、磁选、重力分离、浮选、筛选等)3.成分含量 4.来源(原产国及矿区名称)5.签约日期 6.计价日期 7.有无滞期费(无滞期费、滞期费未确定、滞期费已申报)
2608	1.品名 2.加工方法(破碎、磨碎、磁选、重力分离、浮选、筛选等)3.成分含量 4.来源(原产国及矿区名称)5.签约日期 6.计价日期 7.有无滞期费(无滞期费、滞期费未确定、滞期费已申报)
2609	1.品名 2.加工方法(破碎、磨碎、磁选、重力分离、浮选、筛选等)3.成分含量 4.来源(原产国及矿区名称)5.签约日期 6.计价日期 7.有无滞期费(无滞期费、滞期费未确定、滞期费已申报)
2610	1.品名 2.加工方法(破碎、磨碎、磁选、重力分离、浮选、筛选等)3.成分含量 4.来源(原产国及矿区名称)5.签约日期 6.计价日期 7.有无滞期费(无滞期费、滞期费未确定、滞期费已申报)
2611	1.品名 2.加工方法(破碎、磨碎、磁选、重力分离、浮选、筛选等)3.成分含量 4.来源(原产国及矿区名称)5.签约日期
26121000	1.品名 2.加工方法(破碎、磨碎、磁选、重力分离、浮选、筛选等)3.成分含量 4.种类(钛铀矿、水硅铀矿、沥青铀矿等)5.来源(原产国及矿区名称)6.签约日期 7.计价日期 8.有无滞期费(无滞期费、滞期费未确定、滞期费已申报)
26122000	1.品名 2.加工方法(破碎、磨碎、磁选、重力分离、浮选、筛选等)3.成分含量 4.种类(独居矿、钍石等)5.来源(原产国及矿区名称)6.签约日期 7.计价日期 8.有无滞期费(无滞期费、滞期费未确定、滞期费已申报)
2613	1.品名 2.加工方法(破碎、磨碎、磁选、重力分离、浮选、筛选等)3.成分含量 4.来源(原产国及矿区名称)5.签约日期 6.计价日期 7.有无滞期费(无滞期费、滞期费未确定、滞期费已申报)
2614	1.品名 2.加工方法(破碎、磨碎、磁选、重力分离、浮选、筛选等)3.成分含量 4.来源(原产国及矿区名称)5.签约日期 6.计价日期 7.有无滞期费(无滞期费、滞期费未确定、滞期费已申报)
26151000	1.品名 2.加工方法(破碎、磨碎、磁选、重力分离、浮选、筛选等)3.成分含量 4.粒度 5.来源(原产国及矿区名称)6.签约日期 7.计价日期 8.有无滞期费(无滞期费、滞期费未确定、滞期费已申报)
26159	1.品名 2.加工方法(破碎、磨碎、磁选、重力分离、浮选、筛选等)3.成分含量 4.来源(原产国及矿区名称)5.签约日期 6.计价日期 7.有无滞期费(无滞期费、滞期费未确定、滞期费已申报)
26161000	1.品名 2.加工方法(破碎、磨碎、磁选、重力分离、浮选、筛选等)3.外观(颜色、形状)4.成分含量 5.来源(原产国及矿区名称)6.签约日期 7.计价日期 8.有无滞期费(无滞期费、滞期费未确定、滞期费已申报)
26169000	1.品名 2.加工方法(破碎、磨碎、磁选、重力分离、浮选、筛选等)3.含水率 4.成分含量 5.黄金矿砂请申报粒度[货物通过 74 微米(或 200 目)标准筛的筛下物的量比]6.来源(原产国及矿区名称)7.签约日期 8.计价日期 9.有无滞期费(无滞期费、滞期费未确定、滞期费已申报)
2617	1.品名 2.加工方法(破碎、磨碎、磁选、重力分离、浮选、筛选等)3.成分含量 4.来源(原产国及矿区名称)5.签约日期 6.计价日期 7.有无滞期费(无滞期费、滞期费未确定、滞期费已申报)
2618	1.品名 2.用途 3.加工方法(破碎、磨碎、磁选、重力分离、浮选、筛选等) 4.形状 5.成分含量 6.来源
2619	1.品名 2.用途 3.加工方法(破碎、磨碎、磁选、重力分离、浮选、筛选等) 4.形状 5.成分含量 6.来源 7.计价日期 8.有无滞期费(无滞期费、滞期费未确定、滞期费已申报)
2620	1.品名 2.用途 3.加工方法(破碎、磨碎、磁选、重力分离、浮选、筛选等) 4.形状 5.成分含量 6.来源
2621	1.品名 2.用途 3.加工方法(破碎、磨碎、磁选、重力分离、浮选、筛选等) 4.形状 5.成分含量 6.来源
27011100	1.品名 2.挥发物含量(以干燥、无矿物质计)3.以潮湿、无矿物质计热值 4.收到基低位或高位热值 5.灰分 6.含硫量 7.含水量 8.签约日期 9.计价日期 10.有无滞期费(无滞期费、滞期费未确定、滞期费已申报)
27011210	1.品名 2.挥发物含量(以干燥、无矿物质计)3.以潮湿、无矿物质计热值和收到基低位或高位热值 4.胶质层最大厚度 5.黏结指数 6.灰分 7.含硫量 8.含水量 9.签约日期 10.计价日期 11.有无滞期费(无滞期费、滞期费未确定、滞期费已申报) 12.品种(按检验证明上的描述申报)
27011290	1.品名 2.挥发物含量(以干燥、无矿物质计)3.以潮湿、无矿物质计热值 4.收到基低位或高位热值 5.黏结指数 6.灰分 7.含硫量 8.含水量 9.签约日期 10.计价日期 11.有无滞期费(无滞期费、滞期费未确定、滞期费已申报)
27011900	1.品名 2.挥发物含量(以干燥、无矿物质计)3.以潮湿、无矿物质计热值 4.收到基低位或高位热值 5.灰分 6.含硫量 7.含水量 8.透光率 9.签约日期 10.计价日期 11.有无滞期费(无滞期费、滞期费未确定、滞期费已申报)
27012000	1.品名 2.外观 3.挥发物含量(以干燥、无矿物质 计)4.等级 5.以潮湿、无矿物质计热值 6.收到基低位或高位热值 7.灰分 8.含硫量 9.含水量 10.签约日期 11.计价日期 12.有无滞期费(无滞期费、滞期费未确定、滞期费已申报)
27021000	1.品名 2.外观 3.是否黑玉 4.挥发物含量(以干燥、无灰基计)5.以潮湿、无矿物质计热值 6.收到基低位或高位热值 7.透光率 8.含水量 9.签约日期 10.计价日期 11.有无滞期费(无滞期费、滞期费未确定、滞期费已申报)
27022000	1.品名 2.外观 3.是否黑玉 4.挥发物含量(以干燥、无灰基计)5.以潮湿、无矿物质计热值 6.收到基低位或高位热值 7.透光率 8.含水量 9.签约日期 10.计价日期 11.有无滞期费(无滞期费、滞期费未确定、滞期费已申报)
2703	1.品名 2.外观 3.来源 4.签约日期 5.计价日期
27040010	1.品名 2.来源 3.挥发物含量(以干燥、无矿物质计)4.气孔率 5.含磷量 6.灰分 7.粒度 8.含水量 9.含硫量 10.签约日期 11.计价日期
27040090	1.品名 2.来源 3.签约日期 4.计价日期
2705	1.品名 2.来源 3.签约日期 4.计价日期
2706	1.品名 2.外观 3.来源 4.成分含量 5.签约日期 6.计价日期
27071000	1.品名 2.成分含量 3.签约日期 4.计价日期 5.有无滞期费(无滞期费、滞期费未确定、滞期费已申报)
27072000	1.品名 2.成分含量 3.签约日期 4.计价日期 5.有无滞期费(无滞期费、滞期费未确定、滞期费已申报)
27073000	1.品名 2.成分含量 3.签约日期 4.计价日期 5.有无滞期费(无滞期费、滞期费未确定、滞期费已申报)
27074000	1.品名 2.成分含量(以美国标准实验方法 D86 为准,250℃时)3.结晶点 4.外观 5.签约日 期 6.计价日期 7.有无滞期费(无滞期费、滞期费未确定、滞期费已申报)
27075000	1.品名 2.成分含量(需用 HS/T 50 方法测得芳烃含量)3.按 ISO 3405 方法,温度在 250℃时以体积计的馏出量 4.馏程(初馏点温度及终馏点温度等) 5.200℃以下时蒸馏出的芳烃体积百分比 6.签约日期 7.计价日期 8.有无滞期费(无滞期费、滞期费未确定、滞期费已申报)9.品牌(中文或外文名称)10.型号
27079	1.品名 2.成分含量(需用 HS/T 50 方法测得芳烃含量)3.按 ISO 3405 方法,温度在 250℃时以体积计的馏出量 4.馏程(初馏点温度及终馏点温度等)5.签约日期 6.计价日期 7.有无滞期费(无滞期费、滞期费未确定、滞期费已申报)8.品牌(中文或外文名称)9.型号
2708	1.品名 2.外观 3.来源 4.签约日期 5.计价日期
2709	1.品名 2.种类 3.密度或 API 度 4.若为凝析油需注明 5.签约日期 6.计价日期 7.有无滞期费(无滞期费、滞期费未确定、滞期费已申报)8.品牌(中文或外文名称)9.型号
27101210	1.品名 2.馏程 3.含硫量 4.签约日期 5.计价日期 6.有无滞期费(无滞期费、滞期费未确定、滞期费已申报)7.品牌(中文或外文名称)8.型号
27101220	1.品名 2.馏程 3.签约日期 4.计价日期 5.有无滞期费(无滞期费、滞期费未确定、滞期费已申报)
27101230	1.品名 2.馏程 3.用途 4.品牌(中文或外文名称)5.型号 6.包装规格 7.签约日期 8.计价日期 9.有无滞期费(无滞期费、滞期费未确定、滞期费已申报)
27101291	1.品名 2.成分含量 3.签约日期 4.计价日期 5.有无滞期费(无滞期费、滞期费未确定、滞期费已申报)
27101299	1.品名 2.馏程 3.成分含量 4.签约日期 5.计价日期 6.有无滞期费(无滞期费、滞期费未确定、滞期费已申报)7.品牌(中文或外文名称)8.型号
2710191	1.品名 2.馏程 3.签约日期 4.计价日期 5.有无滞期费(无滞期费、滞期费未确定、滞期费已申报)6.品牌(中文或外文名称)7.型号
27101922	1.品名 2.馏程 3.运动黏度指标(50℃和 100℃)4.含硫量 5.水和沉淀物含 量 6.闪点(7 号燃料油注明开口闪点,其他注明闭口闪点)7.灰分 8.签约日期 9.计价日期 10.有无滞期费(无滞期费、滞期费未确定、滞期费已申报)
27101923	1.品名 2.馏程 3.含硫量 4.签约日期 5.计价日期 6.有无滞期费(无滞期费、滞期费未确定、滞期费已申报)
27101929	1.品名 2.馏程 3.签约日期 4.计价日期 5.有无滞期费(无滞期费、滞期费未确定、滞期费已申报)
27101991	1.品名 2.用途 3.从石油或沥青提取矿物油类的百分比含量 4.品牌(中文或外文名称)5.型号 6.包装规格 7.签约日期 8.计价日期 9.有无滞期费(无滞期费、滞期费未确定、滞期费已申报)
27101992	1.品名 2.用途 3.从石油或沥青提取矿物油类的百分比含量 4.品牌(中文或外文名称)5.型号 6.包装规格 7.签约日期 8.计价日期 9.有无滞期费(无滞期费、滞期费未确定、滞期费已申报)
27101993	1.品名 2.用途 3.品牌(中文或外文名称)4.型号 5.包装规格 6.签约日期 7.计价日期 8.有无滞期费(无滞期费、滞期费未确定、滞期费已申报)
27101994	1.品名 2.初馏点 3. 98%馏出温度 4.正构烷烃含 量 5.芳烃含量 6.包装规格 7.签约日期 8.计价日期 9.有无滞期费(无滞期费、滞期费未确定、滞期费已申报)
27101999	1.品名 2.成分含量 3.包装规格 4.签约日期 5.计价日期 6.有无滞期费(无滞期费、滞期费未确定、滞期费已申报) 7.品牌(中文或外文名称)8.型号
27102000	1.品名 2.用途 3.成分 4.从石油或沥青提取矿物油类的百分比含量 5.签约日期 6.计价日期 7.有无滞期费(无滞期费、滞期费未确定、滞期费已申报)
27109	1.品名 2.来源 3.签约日期 4.计价日期 5.有无滞期费(无滞期费、滞期费未确定、滞期费已申报)
27111100	1.品名 2.状态(液化)3.成分含量 4.加工方法(压力货、冷冻货等)5.签约日期 6.计价日期 7.有无滞期费(无滞期费、滞期费未确定、滞期费已申报) 8.百万英热值(MMBtu)
27111200	1.品名 2.状态(液化)3.成分含量 4.加工方法(压力货、冷冻货等)5.签约日期 6.计价日期 7.有无滞期费(无滞期费、滞期费未确定、滞期费已申报)
27111310	1.品名 2.状态(液化)3.成分含量 4.加工方法(压力货、冷冻货等)5.签约日期 6.计价日期 7.有无滞期费(无滞期费、滞期费未确定、滞期费已申报)
27111390	1.品名 2.状态(液化)3.成分含量 4.加工方法(压力货、冷冻货等)5.签约日期 6.计价日期 7.有无滞期费(无滞期费、滞期费未确定、滞期费已申报)

商品编码	申报要素
27111400	1.品名 2.状态(液化)3.成分含量 4.加工方法(压力货、冷冻货等)5.签约日期 6.计价日期 7.有无滞期费(无滞期费、滞期费未确定、滞期费已申报)
271119	1.品名 2.状态(液化)3.成分含量 4.加工方法(压力货、冷冻货等)5.签约日期 6.计价日期 7.有无滞期费(无滞期费、滞期费未确定、滞期费已申报)
27111910	1.品名 2.状态(液化)3.成分含量 4.加工方法(压力货、冷冻货等)5.签约日期 6.计价日期 7.有无滞期费(无滞期费、滞期费未确定、滞期费已申报)
27111990	1.品名 2.状态(液化)3.成分含量 4.加工方法(压力货、冷冻货等)5.签约日期 6.计价日期 7.有无滞期费(无滞期费、滞期费未确定、滞期费已申报)
27112100	1.品名 2.状态(气态)3.成分含量 4.包装容器容积 5.加工方法(压力货、冷冻货等)6.签约日期 7.计价日期 8.有无滞期费(无滞期费、滞期费未确定、滞期费已申报)9.百万英热值(MMBtu)
27112900	1.品名 2.状态(气态)3.成分含量 4.包装容器容积 5.加工方法(压力货、冷冻货等)6.签约日期 7.计价日期 8.有无滞期费(无滞期费、滞期费未确定、滞期费已申报)
27121000	1.品名 2.用途 3.是否零售包装
27122000	1.品名 2.加工方法 3.含油量
27129	1.品名 2.加工方法
271311	1.品名 2.用途 3.加工方法(是否煅烧)4.含硫量 5.灰分 6.种类(针状焦、弹丸焦、海绵焦、粉焦等)7.签约日期 8.计价日期 9.有无滞期费(无滞期费、滞期费未确定、滞期费已申报)
271312	1.品名 2.用途 3.加工方法(是否煅烧)4.含硫量 5.灰分 6.种类(针状焦、弹丸焦、海绵焦、粉焦等)7.签约日期 8.计价日期 9.有无滞期费(无滞期费、滞期费未确定、滞期费已申报)
27132000	1.品名 2.针入度 3.用途 4.加工方法 5.品牌(中文或外文名称)6.包装规 格 7.含蜡量 8.签约日期 9.计价日 期 10.有无滞期费(无滞期费、滞期费未确定、滞期费已申报)
27139000	1.品名 2.用途 3.加工方法 4.签约日期 5.计价日期 6.有无滞期费(无滞期费、滞期费未确定、滞期费已申报)
2714	1.品名 2.用途 3.加工方法 4.成分含量 5.签约日期 6.计价日期 7.有无滞期费(无滞期费、滞期费未确定、滞期费已申报)
2715	1.品名 2.用途 3.加工方法 4.成分含量 5.签约日期 6.计价日期 7.有无滞期费(无滞期费、滞期费未确定、滞期费已申报)
2716	1.品名
2801	1.品名 2.成分含量 3.包装规格 4.品牌(中文或外文名称)5.型号
2802	1.品名 2.成分含量 3.包装规格
2803	1.品名 2.来源 3.有无活性 4.成分含量 5.包装规格 6.型 号 7.品牌(中文或外文名称)
28041000	1.品名 2.成分含量
28042	1.品名 2.成分含量
28043000	1.品名 2.成分含量
28044000	1.品名 2.成分含量
28045000	1.品名 2.成分含量
2804611	1.品名 2.用途(用于电子工业等)3.加工方法(经掺杂等)4.成分含量 5.直径
28046120	1.品名 2.用途(用于电子工业等)3.加工方法(经掺杂等)4.成分含量 5.直径
28046190	1.品名 2.用途 3.加工方法(西门子法、硅烷热分解法等经掺杂 P 型、经掺杂 N 型,未经掺杂)4.成分含量 5.外观(多晶硅碎料、块料或锅底料、头尾料等)6.电阻率 7.是否需清洗 8.品牌(中文或外文名称)9.型号
28046900	1.品名 2.用途 3.加工方法(经掺杂等)4.成分含量 5.牌号
28047	1.品名 2.成分含量
28048000	1.品名 2.成分含量
28049	1.品名 2.用途(用于电子工业等)3.加工方法(经掺杂等)4.成分含量 5.包装规格
28051	1.品名 2.成分含量 3.包装规格
28053	1.品名 2.混合稀土应注明各组分含量 3.是否电池级的稀土金属、钪及钇 4.包装规格
28054000	1.品名 2.成分含量 3.包装规格
2806	1.品名 2.成分含量
2807	1.品名 2.成分含量
2808	1.品名 2.成分含量
2809	1.品名 2.成分含量
2810	1.品名 2.成分含量
281111	1.品名 2.成分含量 3.包装规格
28111200	1.品名 2.成分含量
281119	1.品名 2.成分含量
28112100	1.品名 2.成分含量
281122	1.品名 2.成分含量 3.品牌(中文或外文名称)4.外观 5.加工工艺 6.粒度 7.型号
28112900	1.品名 2.成分含量
2812	1.品名 2.成分含量
2813	1.品名 2.成分含量
2814	1.品名 2.氨含量
28151100	1.品名 2.成分含量 3.用途
28151200	1.品名 2.成分含量 3.用途 4.来源(是否从碱法或硫酸盐法制木浆时所剩残余产品中获得)
28152000	1.品名 2.成分含量 3.用途
28153000	1.品名 2.成分含量 3.用途
2816	1.品名 2.成分含量
2817	1.品名 2.成分含量
28181010	1.品名 2.成分含量 3.外观(颜色形状等)4.晶型 5.莫氏硬度
28181090	1.品名 2.成分含量 3.外观(颜色形状等)4.晶型
28182000	1.品名 2.外观(颜色形状等)3.成分含量 4.用途(冶金用或非冶金用)
28183000	1.品名 2.成分含量
28191000	1.品名 2.成分含量
28199000	1.品名 2.成分含量
2820	1.品名 2.成分含量
28211000	1.品名 2.成分含量
28212000	1.品名 2.铁按三氧化二铁计含量
2822	1.品名 2.成分含量
2823	1.品名 2.成分含量,是否与其他物质混合 3.是否经表面处理
2824	1.品名 2.成分含量
28251010	1.品名 2.水合肼含量
28251020	1.品名 2.成分含量
28251090	1.品名 2.成分含量
28252	1.品名 2.成分含量
28253	1.品名 2.成分含量
28254000	1.品名 2.成分含量
28255000	1.品名 2.成分含量
28256000	1.品名 2.成分含量
28257000	1.品名 2.成分含量
28258000	1.品名 2.成分含量
28259011	1.品名 2.成分含量
28259012	1.品名 2.外观(颜色形 状)3.粒度 4.成分含量
28259019	1.品名 2.成分含量
2825902	1.品名 2.成分含量
2825903	1.品名 2.成分含量
2825904	1.品名 2.成分含量
28259090	1.品名 2.成分含量
28261210	1.品名 2.氟质量分数 3.铝质量分数 4.烧减量 5.松装密度 6.成分含量
28261290	1.品名 2.成分含量
282619	1.品名 2.成分含量
28263000	1.品名 2.成分含量
28269	1.品名 2.成分含量
28271	1.品名 2.肥料用请注明 3.成分含量 4.外观(粉状、颗粒)
28272000	1.品名 2.成分含量
28273	1.品名 2.成分含量
28274	1.品名 2.成分含量
28275	1.品名 2.成分含量
28276000	1.品名 2.成分含量
2828	1.品名 2.成分含量
28291	1.品名 2.成分含量
28299000	1.品名 2.成分含量 3.如为高氯酸铵请注明粒度
2830	1.品名 2.成分含量
2831	1.品名 2.成分含量
2832	1.品名 2.成分含量
2833	1.品名 2.成分含量
28341000	1.品名 2.成分含量
283421	1.品名 2.肥料用请注明 3.成分含量
283429	1.品名 2.成分含量
28351000	1.品名 2.成分含量
28352200	1.品名 2.成分含量
28352400	1.品名 2.成分含量
28352510	1.品名 2.正磷酸氢钙请注明氟含量 3.用途(饲料 级)4.成分含量
28352520	1.品名 2.正磷酸氢钙请注明氟含量 3.用途(食品级)4.成分含量
28352590	1.品名 2.正磷酸氢钙请注明氟含量 3.用途 4.成分含量
28352600	1.品名 2.成分含量
283529	1.品名 2.成分含量
28353	1.品名 2.用途(饲料、食品等)3.成分含量
28362000	1.品名 2.成分含量
28363000	1.品名 2.成分含量
28364000	1.品名 2.成分含量
28365000	1.品名 2.成分含量 3.用途 4.品牌(中文或外文名称)
28366000	1.品名 2.成分含量
28369	1.品名 2.成分含量
2837	1.品名 2.成分含量 3.包装规格
2839	1.品名 2.成分含量
2840	1.品名 2.成分含量
28413000	1.品名 2.成分含量
28415000	1.品名 2.成分含量
28416	1.品名 2.成分含量
28417	1.品名 2.成分含量
28418010	1.品名 2.成分含量 3.含量(WO3 含量)
28418020	1.品名 2.成分含量
28418030	1.品名 2.成分含量
28418040	1.品名 2.成分含量 3.含量(WO3 含量)
28418090	1.品名 2.成分含量
28419000	1.品名 2.成分含量
2842	1.品名 2.成分含量 3.包装规格
2843	1.品名 2.成分含量 3.包装规格
2844	1.品名 2.成分含量
2845	1.品名 2.成分含量
28461	1.品名 2.成分含量
2846901	1.品名 2.成分含量
28469021	1.品名 2.成分含量
28469022	1.品名 2.成分含量
28469023	1.品名 2.成分含量
28469024	1.品名 2.成分含量
28469025	1.品名 2.成分含量
28469026	1.品名 2.成分含量
28469028	1.品名 2.成分含量
28469029	1.品名 2.成分含量
2846903	1.品名 2.成分含量
2846904	1.品名 2.成分含量
2846909	1.品名 2.成分含量
2847	1.品名 2.成分含量 3.包装规格
2849	1.品名 2.成分含量 3.品牌(中文或外文名称)4.型号 5.外观(颜色形状等)6.用途 7.碳化钨请注明粒度
2850	1.品名 2.成分含量

商品编码	申报要素
2852	1.品名 2.成分含量
28531000	1.品名 2.成分含量 3.包装规格
28539010	1.品名 2.是否饮用 3.成分含量 4.包装规格
28539030	1.品名 2.成分含量
28539040	1.品名 2.铜母合金请注明磷的重量百分比
28539050	1.品名 2.成分含量
28539090	1.品名 2.成分含量
2901	1.品名 2.成分含量 3.用途 4.用作气体燃料的应报明包装容器容积 5.签约日期 6.计价日期
29011000	1.品名 2.成分含量 3.用途 4.用作气体燃料的应报明包装容器容积
29012100	1.品名 2.成分含量 3.用途 4.用作气体燃料的应报明包装容器容积
29012200	1.品名 2.成分含量 3.用途 4.用作气体燃料的应报明包装容器容积 5.签约日期 6.计价日期
29012310	1.品名 2.成分含量 3.用途 4.用作气体燃料的应报明包装容器容积 5.签约日期 6.计价日期
29012320	1.品名 2.成分含量 3.用途 4.用作气体燃料的应报明包装容器容积
29012330	1.品名 2.成分含量 3.用途 4.用作气体燃料的应报明包装容器容积
290129	1.品名 2.成分含量 3.用途 4.用作气体燃料的应报明包装容器容积
29021100	1.品名 2.成分含量 3.用途 4.签约日期 5.计价日期
290219	1.品名 2.成分含量 3.用途
29022000	1.品名 2.成分含量 3.签约日期 4.计价日期
29023000	1.品名 2.成分含量 3.签约日期 4.计价日期
29024	1.品名 2.成分含量 3.签约日期 4.计价日期
29025000	1.品名 2.成分含量 3.签约日期 4.计价日期
29026000	1.品名 2.成分含量 3.签约日期 4.计价日期
29027000	1.品名 2.成分含量 3.签约日期 4.计价日期
29029010	1.品名 2.成分含量
29029020	1.品名 2.成分含量 3.结晶温度
29029030	1.品名 2.成分含量
29029040	1.品名 2.成分含量
29029050	1.品名 2.成分含量
29029090	1.品名 2.成分含量
29031	1.品名 2.成分含量 3.用途
29032100	1.品名 2.成分含量 3.用途 4.签约日期 5.计价日期
29032200	1.品名 2.成分含量 3.用途
29032300	1.品名 2.成分含量 3.用途
290329	1.品名 2.成分含量 3.用途
29034	1.品名 2.成分含量 3.用途
29035	1.品名 2.成分含量 3.用途
29036	1.品名 2.成分含量 3.用途
29037	1.品名 2.成分含量 3.用途
29038	1.品名 2.成分含量 3.用途
29039	1.品名 2.成分含量 3.用途
2904	1.品名 2.成分含量 3.用途
29051100	1.品名 2.成分含量 3.用途 4.包装规格 5.签约日期 6.计价日期
290512	1.品名 2.成分含量 3.用途 4.包装规格 5.签约日期 6.计价日期
29051300	1.品名 2.成分含量 3.用途 4.包装规格 5.签约日期 6.计价日期
29051410	1.品名 2.成分含量 3.用途 4.包装规格 5.签约日期 6.计价日期
29051420	1.品名 2.成分含量 3.用途 4.包装规格
29051430	1.品名 2.成分含量 3.用途 4.包装规格
29051610	1.品名 2.成分含量 3.用途 4.包装规格
29051690	1.品名 2.成分含量 3.用途 4.包装规格 5.签约日期 6.计价日期
29051700	1.品名 2.成分含量 3.用途 4.包装规格
29051910	1.品名 2.成分含量 3.用途 4.包装规格
29051990	1.品名 2.成分含量 3.用途 4.包装规格 5.签约日期 6.计价日期
29052	1.品名 2.成分含量 3.用途 4.包装规格
29053100	1.品名 2.成分含量 3.用途 4.包装规格 5.签约日期 6.计价日期
29053200	1.品名 2.成分含量 3.用途 4.包装规格 5.签约日期 6.计价日期
290539	1.品名 2.成分含量 3.用途 4.包装规格
29054100	1.品名 2.成分含量 3.用途 4.包装规格
29054200	1.品名 2.成分含量 3.用途 4.包装规格
29054300	1.品名 2.成分含量 3.用途 4.包装规格
29054400	1.品名 2.成分含量 3.用途 4.包装规格
29054500	1.品名 2.成分含量 3.用途 4.包装规格 5.签约日期 6.计价日期 7.丙三醇(甘油)请报明颜色及外观状态
290549	1.品名 2.成分含量 3.用途 4.包装规格
29055	1.品名 2.成分含量 3.用途 4.包装规格
2906	1.品名 2.成分含量 3.用途
29071110	1.品名 2.成分含量 3.用途 4.签约日期 5.计价日期
29071190	1.品名 2.成分含量 3.用途
290712	1.品名 2.成分含量 3.用途
290713	1.品名 2.成分含量 3.用途
290715	1.品名 2.成分含量 3.用途
290719	1.品名 2.成分含量 3.用途
29072100	1.品名 2.成分含量 3.用途
290722	1.品名 2.成分含量 3.用途
29072300	1.品名 2.成分含量 3.用途 4.签约日期 5.计价日期
290729	1.品名 2.成分含量 3.用途
2908	1.品名 2.成分含量 3.用途
29091100	1.品名 2.成分含量 3.用途
29091910	1.品名 2.成分含量 3.用途
29091990	1.品名 2.成分含量 3.用途 4.签约日期 5.计价日期
29092000	1.品名 2.成分含量 3.用途
29093	1.品名 2.成分含量 3.用途
29094100	1.品名 2.成分含量 3.用途 4.签约日期 5.计价日期
29094300	1.品名 2.成分含量 3.用途 4.签约日期 5.计价日期
29094400	1.品名 2.成分含量 3.用途
290949	1.品名 2.成分含量 3.用途
29095000	1.品名 2.成分含量 3.用途
29096000	1.品名 2.成分含量 3.用途
29101000	1.品名 2.成分含量 3.用途

商品编码	申报要素
29102000	1.品名 2.成分含量 3.用途 4.签约日期 5.计价日期
29103000	1.品名 2.成分含量 3.用途
29104000	1.品名 2.成分含量 3.用途
29105000	1.品名 2.成分含量 3.用途
29109000	1.品名 2.成分含量 3.用途
2911	1.品名 2.成分含量 3.用途
2912	1.品名 2.成分含量 3.用途 4.四聚甲醛报明外观
2913	1.品名 2.成分含量 3.用途
29141100	1.品名 2.成分含量 3.用途 4.签约日期 5.计价日期
29141200	1.品名 2.成分含量 3.用途
29141300	1.品名 2.成分含量 3.用途
29141900	1.品名 2.成分含量 3.用途
29142200	1.品名 2.成分含量 3.用途 4.签约日期 5.计价日期
29142300	1.品名 2.成分含量 3.用途
291429	1.品名 2.成分含量 3.用途
29143	1.品名 2.成分含量 3.用途
29144000	1.品名 2.成分含量 3.用途
29145	1.品名 2.成分含量 3.用途
29146	1.品名 2.成分含量 3.用途
29147	1.品名 2.成分含量 3.用途
29151	1.品名 2.成分含量 3.用途
29152111	1.品名 2.成分含量 3.用途
29152119	1.品名 2.成分含量 3.用途 4.签约日期 5.计价日期
29152190	1.品名 2.成分含量 3.用途
29152400	1.品名 2.成分含量 3.用途
291529	1.品名 2.成分含量 3.用途
29153	1.品名 2.成分含量 3.用途
29154000	1.品名 2.成分含量 3.用途
29155	1.品名 2.成分含量 3.用途
29156000	1.品名 2.成分含量 3.用途
29157	1.品名 2.成分含量 3.用途
29159000	1.品名 2.成分含量 3.用途
29161100	1.品名 2.成分含量 3.用途
29161210	1.品名 2.成分含量 3.用途
29161220	1.品名 2.成分含量 3.用途
29161230	1.品名 2.成分含量 3.用途
29161240	1.品名 2.成分含量 3.用途 4.外观(颜色、形状)5.签约日期 6.计价日期
29161290	1.品名 2.成分含量 3.用途
29161300	1.品名 2.成分含量 3.用途
29161400	1.品名 2.成分含量 3.用途 4.签约日期 5.计价日期
29161500	1.品名 2.成分含量 3.用途
29161600	1.品名 2.成分含量 3.用途
29161900	1.品名 2.成分含量 3.用途
29162	1.品名 2.成分含量 3.用途
29163	1.品名 2.成分含量 3.用途
29171	1.品名 2.成分含量 3.用途
29172	1.品名 2.成分含量 3.用途
29173200	1.品名 2.成分含量 3.用途
29173300	1.品名 2.成分含量 3.用途
291734	1.品名 2.成分含量 3.用途
29173500	1.品名 2.成分含量 3.用途
29173611	1.品名 2.成分含量 3.用途 4.对苯二甲酸请注明 4－CBA 值 5.对苯二甲酸请注明 P－TL 酸值 6.对苯二甲酸请注明色度 7.对苯二甲酸请注明水分 8.签约日期 9.计价日期
29173619	1.品名 2.成分含量 3.用途 4.对苯二甲酸请注明 4－CBA 值 5.对苯二甲酸请注明 P－TL 酸值 6.对苯二甲酸请注明色度 7.对苯二甲酸请注明水分
29173690	1.品名 2.成分含量 3.用途 4.对苯二甲酸请注明 4－CBA 值 5.对苯二甲酸请注明 P－TL 酸值 6.对苯二甲酸请注明色度 7.对苯二甲酸请注明水分
29173700	1.品名 2.成分含量 3.用途
29173910	1.品名 2.成分含量 3.用途 4.签约日期 5.计价日期
29173990	1.品名 2.成分含量 3.用途
2918	1.品名 2.成分含量 3.用途
2919	1.品名 2.成分含量 3.用途
2920	1.品名 2.成分含量 3.用途
2921	1.品名 2.成分含量 3.用途
2922	1.品名 2.成分含量 3.用途 4.包装规格
29231000	1.品名 2.成分含量 3.用途
29232000	1.品名 2.成分含量 3.用途
29233000	1.品名 2.成分含量 3.用途
29234000	1.品名 2.成分含量 3.用途
29239000	1.品名 2.成分含量 3.用途
2924	1.品名 2.成分含量 3.用途 4.包装规格
2925	1.品名 2.成分含量 3.用途
29261000	1.品名 2.成分含量 3.用途 4.签约日期 5.计价日期
29262000	1.品名 2.成分含量 3.用途
29263000	1.品名 2.成分含量 3.用途
29264000	1.品名 2.成分含量 3.用途
29269	1.品名 2.成分含量 3.用途
2927	1.品名 2.成分含量 3.用途
2928	1.品名 2.成分含量 3.用途
29291	1.品名 2.成分含量 3.用途
29299	1.品名 2.成分含量 3.用途
2930	1.品名 2.成分含量 3.用途
2931	1.品名 2.成分含量 3.用途
2932	1.品名 2.成分含量(对于成分较复杂、字节较长商品可用 CAS 号代替)3.用途
2933	1.品名 2.成分含量 3.用途 4.签约日期
29341	1.品名 2.成分含量 3.用途
29342000	1.品名 2.成分含量 3.用途
29343000	1.品名 2.成分含量 3.用途

商品编码	申报要素
29349100	1.品名 2.成分含量 3.用途
29349200	1.品名 2.成分含量 3.用途
29349910	1.品名 2.成分含量 3.用途
29349920	1.品名 2.成分含量 3.用途
29349930	1.品名 2.成分含量 3.用途
29349940	1.品名 2.成分含量 3.用途
29349950	1.品名 2.成分含量 3.用途
29349960	1.品名 2.成分含量 3.用途
29349990	1.品名 2.成分含量 3.用途
2935	1.品名 2.成分含量 3.用途
29362100	1.品名 2.成分含量 3.用途
29362200	1.品名 2.成分含量 3.用途
29362300	1.品名 2.成分含量 3.用途
29362400	1.品名 2.成分含量 3.用途
29362500	1.品名 2.成分含量 3.用途
29362600	1.品名 2.成分含量 3.用途
29362700	1.品名 2.成分含量 3.用途
29362800	1.品名 2.成分含量 3.用途
29362900	1.品名 2.成分含量 3.用途
29369	1.品名 2.成分含量 3.用途
29371100	1.品名 2.成分含量 3.用途
293712	1.品名 2.成分含量 3.用途
29371900	1.品名 2.成分含量 3.用途
29372	1.品名 2.成分含量 3.用途
29375000	1.品名 2.成分含量 3.用途
29379000	1.品名 2.成分含量 3.用途
2938	1.品名 2.成分含量 3.用途
2939	1.品名 2.成分含量 3.用途
29400010	1.品名 2.成分含量 3.用途
29400090	1.品名 2.成分含量 3.用途
2941	1.品名 2.用途(用于制口服、注射还是外用药)
2942	1.品名 2.成分含量 3.用途
30012000	1.品名 2.用途 3.加工工艺 4.品牌(中文或外文名称)5.型号
30019010	1.品名 2.用途 3.加工工艺 4.品牌(中文或外文名称)5.型号
30019090	1.品名 2.用途 3.加工工艺 4.品牌(中文或外文名称)5.型号
30021	1.品名 2.用途 3.加工工艺 4.是否配定剂量 5.是否零售包装 6.是否经国家药品监督管理部门批准注册请注明 7.如获得批准注册,请申报有效注册证号 8.品牌(中文或外文名称)9.型号 10.包装规格
30024	1.品名 2.用途 3.加工工艺 4.是否配定剂量 5.是否零售包装 6.是否经国家药品监督管理部门批准注册请注明 7.如获得批准注册,请申报有效注册证号 8.品牌(中文或外文名称)9.型号 10.包装规格
30025	1.品名 2.用途 3.加工工艺 4.是否配定剂量 5.是否零售包装 6.是否经国家药品监督管理部门批准注册请注明 7.如获得批准注册,请申报有效注册证号 8.品牌(中文或外文名称)9.型号 10.包装规格
30029040	1.品名 2.用途 3.加工工艺 4.是否配定剂量 5.是否零售包装 6.是否经国家药品监督管理部门批准注册请注明 7.如获得批准注册,请申报有效注册证号 8.品牌(中文或外文名称)9.型号 10.包装规格
30029090	1.品名 2.用途 3.加工工艺 4.是否配定剂量 5.是否零售包装 6.是否经国家药品监督管理部门批准注册请注明 7.如获得批准注册,请申报有效注册证号 8.品牌(中文或外文名称)9.型号 10.包装规格
3003	1.品名 2.用途 3.成分 4.是否配定剂量或零售包装 5.化学通用名 6.品牌(中文或外文名称)7.型号 8.包装规格
30041	1.品名 2.用途 3.成分 4.是否配定剂量或零售包装 5.化学通用名 6.是否经国家药品监督管理部门批准注册请注明 7.如获得批准注册,请申报有效注册证号 8.品牌(中文或外文名称)9.包装规格
30042	1.品名 2.用途 3.成分 4.是否配定剂量或零售包装 5.化学通用名 6.是否经国家药品监督管理部门批准注册请注明 7.如获得批准注册,请申报有效注册证号 8.品牌(中文或外文名称)9.包装规格
30043	1.品名 2.用途 3.成分 4.是否配定剂量或零售包装 5.化学通用名 6.是否经国家药品监督管理部门批准注册请注明 7.如获得批准注册,请申报有效注册证号 8.品牌(中文或外文名称)9.包装规格
30044	1.品名 2.用途 3.成分 4.是否配定剂量或零售包装 5.化学通用名 6.是否经国家药品监督管理部门批准注册请注明 7.如获得批准注册,请申报有效注册证号 8.品牌(中文或外文名称)9.包装规格
30045000	1.品名 2.用途 3.成分 4.是否配定剂量或零售包装 5.化学通用名 6.是否经国家药品监督管理部门批准注册请注明 7.如获得批准注册,请申报有效注册证号 8.品牌(中文或外文名称)9.包装规格
30046	1.品名 2.用途 3.成分 4.是否配定剂量或零售包装 5.化学通用名 6.是否经国家药品监督管理部门批准注册请注明 7.如获得批准注册,请申报有效注册证号 8.品牌(中文或外文名称)9.包装规格
30049010	1.品名 2.用途 3.成分 4.是否配定剂量或零售包装 5.化学通用名 6.是否经国家药品监督管理部门批准注册请注明 7.如获得批准注册,请申报有效注册证号 8.品牌(中文或外文名称)9.包装规格
30049020	1.品名 2.用途 3.成分 4.是否配定剂量或零售包装 5.化学通用名 6.是否经国家药品监督管理部门批准注册请注明 7.如获得批准注册,请申报有效注册证号 8.品牌(中文或外文名称)9.包装规格
30049051	1.品名 2.用途 3.成分 4.是否配定剂量或零售包装 5.化学通用名 6.是否经国家药品监督管理部门批准注册请注明 7.如获得批准注册,请申报有效注册证号 8.品牌(中文或外文名称)9.包装规格
30049052	1.品名 2.用途 3.成分 4.是否配定剂量或零售包装 5.化学通用名 6.是否经国家药品监督管理部门批准注册请注明 7.如获得批准注册,请申报有效注册证号 8.品牌(中文或外文名称)9.包装规格
30049053	1.品名 2.用途 3.成分 4.是否配定剂量或零售包装 5.化学通用名 6.是否经国家药品监督管理部门批准注册请注明 7.如获得批准注册,请申报有效注册证号 8.品牌(中文或外文名称)9.包装规格
30049054	1.品名 2.用途 3.成分 4.是否配定剂量或零售包装 5.化学通用名 6.是否经国家药品监督管理部门批准注册请注明 7.如获得批准注册,请申报有效注册证号 8.品牌(中文或外文名称)9.包装规格
30049055	1.品名 2.用途 3.成分 4.是否配定剂量或零售包装 5.化学通用名 6.是否经国家药品监督管理部门批准注册请注明 7.如获得批准注册,请申报有效注册证号 8.品牌(中文或外文名称)9.包装规格

商品编码	申报要素
30049059	1.品名 2.用途 3.成分 4.是否配定剂量或零售包装 5.化学通用名 6.是否经国家药品监督管理部门批准注册请注明 7.如获得批准注册,请申报有效注册证号 8.品牌(中文或外文名称)9.包装规格
30049090	1.品名 2.用途 3.成分 4.是否配定剂量或零售包装 5.化学通用名 6.是否经国家药品监督管理部门批准注册请注明 7.如获得批准注册,请申报有效注册证号 8.品牌(中文或外文名称)9.包装规格
3005	1.品名 2.用途 3.成分 4.是否经过药物浸涂或制成零售包装 5.品牌(中文或外文名称)6.型号 7.包装规格
30061000	1.品名 2.用途 3.品牌(中文或外文名称)4.型号 5.包装规格
30063000	1.品名 2.用途 3.成分 4.品牌(中文或外文名称)5.型号 6.包装规格
30064000	1.品名 2.用途 3.成分 4.品牌(中文或外文名称)5.型号 6.包装规格
30065000	1.品名 2.组成(指箱或包中的药品、器具等)3.品牌(中文或外文名称)4.型号
30066	1.品名 2.用途 3.成分 4.品牌(中文或外文名称)5.型号 6.包装规格
30067000	1.品名 2.用途 3.成分 4.品牌(中文或外文名称)5.型号 6.包装规格
30069100	1.品名 2.用途 3.品牌(中文或外文名称)4.型号
30069200	1.品名
30069300	1.品名 2.用途 3.品牌(中文或外文名称)4.型号
3101	1.品名 2.用途 3.加工工艺 4.包装规格 5.是否经过化学处理 6.是否与化学肥料混合 7.品牌(中文或外文名称)
3102	1.品名 2.包装规格 3.总氮含量 4.品牌(中文或外文名称)5.型号 6.成分含量
3103	1.品名 2.包装规格 3.总磷含量 4.品牌(中文或外文名称)5.型号
31042	1.品名 2.包装规格 3.按照重量计氯化钾含量 4.用途(是否肥料用)5.总钾含量(以氧化物计)6.品牌(中文或外文名称)7.型号
31043000	1.品名 2.包装规格 3.用途(是否肥料用)4.总钾含量(以氧化物计)5.品牌(中文或外文名称)6.型号
31049	1.品名 2.包装规格 3.用途(是否肥料用)4.总钾含量(以氧化物计)5.品牌(中文或外文名称)6.型号
3105	1.品名 2.成分含量 3.包装规格 4.总氮含量、总磷含量、总钾(以氧化物计)含量 5.品牌(中文或外文名称)6.型号
3201	1.品名 2.用途 3.加工工艺 4.品牌(中文或外文名称)5.型号
3202	1.品名 2.成分含量 3.品牌(中文或外文名称)4.包装规格
3203	1.品名 2.用途 3.加工工艺 4.包装规格 5.品牌(中文或外文名称)6.型号 7.成分含量
3204	1.品名 2.成分含量 3.用途 4.染料须报明种类(分散染料、酸性染料、碱性染料等)5.包装规格 6.品牌(中文或外文名称)7.型号
3205	1.品名 2.成分 3.品牌(中文或外文名称)4.型号
32061110	1.品名 2.成分含量 3.用途 4.型号 5.品牌(中文或外文名称)6.如果加入放射性盐,请注明放射性比度 7.签约日期
32061190	1.品名 2.成分含量 3.用途 4.包装规格 5.型号 6.品牌(中文或外文名称)7.如果加入放射性盐,请注明放射性比度
32061900	1.品名 2.成分含量 3.用途 4.包装规格 5.型号 6.品牌(中文或外文名称)7.如果加入放射性盐,请注明放射性比度
32062000	1.品名 2.成分含量 3.用途 4.包装规格 5.型号 6.品牌(中文或外文名称)7.如果加入放射性盐,请注明放射性比度
32064	1.品名 2.成分含量 3.用途 4.包装规格 5.型号 6.品牌(中文或外文名称)7.如果加入放射性盐,请注明放射性比度
32065000	1.品名 2.成分含量 3.用途 4.包装规格 5.型号 6.品牌(中文或外文名称)7.如果加入放射性盐,请注明放射性比度
3207	1.品名 2.用途 3.外观 4.成分含量 5.品牌(中文或外文名称)6.型号
3208	1.品名 2.成分含量 3.用途 4.分散于或溶于非水介质请注明 5.包装规格 6.品牌(中文或外文名称)7.型号
3209	1.品名 2.成分含量 3.用途 4.施工状态下挥发性有机物含量 5.品牌(中文或外文名称)6.型号
3210	1.品名 2.成分含量 3.用途 4.施工状态下挥发性有机物含量 5.品牌(中文或外文名称)6.型号
3211	1.品名 2.成分含量 3.用途 4.品牌(中文或外文名称)5.型号
32121000	1.品名 2.成分含量 3.用途 4.包装规格 5.外观(箔)6.品牌(中文或外文名称)7.规格 8.加工工艺
32129000	1.品名 2.成分含量 3.用途 4.包装规格 5.外观 6.品牌(中文或外文名称)
3213	1.品名 2.用途 3.品牌(中文或外文名称)4.型号 5.是否成套
3214	1.品名 2.成分含量 3.用途 4.施工状态下挥发性有机物含量 5.品牌(中文或外文名称)6.型号
32151	1.品名 2.用途(如子目 8443.31、8443.32 或 8443.39 所列设备用等)3.颜色 4.成分含量 5.是否具有曝光显影功能
32159	1.品名 2.用途 3.成分含量
3301	1.品名 2.用途 3.加工工艺 4.包装规格 5.品牌(中文或外文名称)6.型号 7.成分含量
33021	1.品名 2.成分 3.用途 4.酒精含量 5.品牌(中文或外文名称)6.型号 7.包装规格
33029000	1.品名 2.成分 3.用途 4.品牌(中文或外文名称)5.型号 6.包装规格
3303	1.品名 2.包装规格 3.品牌(中文或外文名称)
33041000	1.品名 2.用途 3.包装规格 4.品牌(中文或外文名称)
33042000	1.品名 2.用途 3.包装规格 4.品牌(中文或外文名称)5.色号
33043000	1.品名 2.用途 3.包装规格 4.品牌(中文或外文名称)
33049	1.品名 2.用途 3.包装规格 4.品牌(中文或外文名称)
3305	1.品名 2.用途 3.包装规格 4.品牌(中文或外文名称)5.型号(货号)
3306	1.品名 2.包装规格 3.品牌(中文或外文名称)4.型号(货号)
33071000	1.品名 2.用途 3.包装规格 4.品牌(中文或外文名称)5.型号(货号)
33072000	1.品名 2.用途 3.包装规格 4.品牌(中文或外文名称)5.型号(货号)
33073000	1.品名 2.用途 3.包装规格 4.品牌(中文或外文名称)5.型号(货号)
33074	1.品名 2.用途 3.包装规格 4.品牌(中文或外文名称)5.型号(货号)
33079000	1.品名 2.用途 3.包装规格 4.品牌(中文或外文名称)5.型号(货号)
34011100	1.品名 2.成分含量 3.外观 4.包装规格 5.品牌(中文或外文名称)6.型号
340119	1.品名 2.成分含量 3.外观 4.包装规格 5.品牌(中文或外文名称)
34012000	1.品名 2.成分含量 3.外观 4.包装规格 5.品牌(中文或外文名称)
34013000	1.品名 2.成分含量 3.外观 4.包装规格 5.品牌(中文或文名称)
34023	1.品名 2.种类(阴离子型)3.成分 4.品牌(中文或外文名称)5.型号
34024	1.品名 2.种类(阳离子型、非离子型等)3.成分 4.品牌(中文或外文名称)5.型号

商品编码	申报要素
34025	1.品名 2.用途 3.是否零售包装 4.成分 5.品牌(中文或外文名称)6.型号
34029000	1.品名 2.用途 3.是否零售包装 4.成分 5.品牌(中文或外文名称)6.型号
3403	1.品名 2.用途 3.成分含量 4.从石油或沥青提取矿物油类的百分比含量 5.品牌(中文或外文名称)6.型号
3404	1.品名 2.用途 3.成分 4.品牌(中文或外文名称)5.型号
3405	1.品名 2.用途 3.成分 4.品牌(中文或外文名称)5.型号
3406	1.品名 2.成分 3.品牌(中文或外文名称)4.型号
3407	1.品名 2.用途 3.外观 4.包装规格 5.成分含量 6.品牌(中文或外文名称)7.型号
35011000	1.品名 2.包装规格 3.品牌(中文或外文名称)4.型号 5.用途
35019000	1.品名 2.包装规格 3.品牌(中文或外文名称)4.型号 5.用途
35021	1.品名 2.用途 3.外观 4.成分含量
35022000	1.品名 2.用途 3.外观 4.成分含量
35029000	1.品名 2.用途 3.外观 4.成分含量
35030010	1.品名 2.用途 3.外观 4.包装规格
35030090	1.品名 2.用途 3.外观 4.包装规格
35040010	1.品名 2.用途 3.来源 4.包装规格 5.蛋白质含量
35040090	1.品名 2.用途 3.来源 4.包装规格 5.蛋白质含量
3505	1.品名 2.用途 3.还原糖含量 4.包装规格 5.品牌(中文或外文名称)6.型号
35061000	1.品名 2.用途 3.包装规格 4.成分含量 5.品牌(中文或外文名称)6.型号
35069110	1.品名 2.用途 3.包装规格 4.成分含量 5.品牌(中文或外文名称)6.型号
35069120	1.品名 2.用途 3.包装规格 4.成分含量 5.品牌(中文或外文名称)6.型号
35069190	1.品名 2.光学透明膜黏合剂和光固化液体黏合剂需注明英文品名 3.用途(如显示屏或触摸屏制造用等) 4.包装规格 5.遮光包装需注明 6.成分含量 7.光学透明膜黏合剂和光固化液体黏合剂需注明透光率 8.光学透明膜黏合剂需注明断差吸收能力 5.品牌(中文或外文名称)6.型号
35069900	1.品名 2.用途 3.包装规格 4.成分含量 5.品牌(中文或外文名称)6.型号
35071000	1.品名 2.用途 3.种类
35079	1.品名 2.用途 3.种类
3601	1.品名 2.成分
3602	1.品名 2.成分
3603	1.品名
3604	1.品名
3605	1.品名
36061000	1.品名 2.用途 3.包装容器的容积
3606901	1.品名 2.用途 3.外观
36069090	1.品名 2.用途 3.外观
3701	1.品名 2.用途 3.材质 4.是否成卷 5.是否一次成像 6.是否已曝光 7.规格尺寸(长×宽×厚度)8.品牌(中文或外文名称)9.型号 10.总面积(平方米)11.包装规格(张/盒)
3702	1.品名 2.用途 3.材质 4.是否成卷 5.是否一次成像 6.是否已曝光 7.规格尺寸(长×宽×厚度)8.品牌(中文或外文名称)9.型号 10.进口总面积(平方米),包括涂布和白边面积之和 11.包装规格(张/盒或平方米/卷)
3703	1.品名 2.用途 3.是否成卷 4.规格尺寸 5.是否已曝光 6.品牌(中文或外文名称)7.型号
3704	1.品名 2.用途 3.规格尺寸 4.材质(软片、硬片,纸、纸板、纺织物、胶等)4.是否已曝光 5.是否已冲洗 6.品牌(中文或外文名称)
3705	1.品名 2.用途 3.规格尺寸 4.材质(软片、硬片,纸、纸板、纺织物、胶等)4.是否已曝光 5.是否已冲洗 6.品牌(中文或外文名称)
3706	1.品名 2.用途 3.规格尺寸 4.材质(软片、硬片,纸、纸板、纺织物、胶等)4.是否已曝光 5.是否已冲洗 6.品牌(中文或外文名称)
37071000	1.品名 2.用途 3.包装规格 4.成分 5.是否含银 6.是否有感光作用 7.品牌(中文或外文名称)8.型号
37079	1.品名 2.用途 3.包装规格 4.成分 5.是否含银 6.品牌(中文或外文名称)7.型号
3801	1.品名 2.用途 3.状态 4.加工工艺 5.成分含量 6.品牌(中文或外文名称)7.型号
38021010	1.品名 2.用途 3.来源 4.包装规格 5.干品填充密度
38021090	1.品名 2.用途 3.来源 4.包装规格
38029000	1.品名 2.用途 3.来源 4.包装规格
3803	1.品名 2.用途
3804	1.品名
3805	1.品名 2.用途 3.成分含量
3806	1.品名 2.来源
3807	1.品名 2.用途
3808	1.品名 2.用途 3.成分含量 4.包装规格 5.品牌(中文或外文名称)6.型号
3809	1.品名 2.用途 3.成分 4.品牌(中文或外文名称)5.型号
3810	1.品名 2.用途 3.成分 4.品牌(中文或外文名称)5.型号
3811	1.品名 2.包装规格 3.用途 4.成分 5.品牌(中文或外文名称)6.型号
3812	1.品名 2.用途 3.成分 4.品牌(中文或外文名称)5.型号
3813	1.品名 2.用途 3.成分
3814	1.品名 2.用途 3.成分含量 4.品牌(中文或外文名称)5.型号
3815	1.品名 2.用途(如促进某某聚合物的聚合等)3.成分含量
3816	1.品名 2.用途 3.成分
3817	1.品名 2.用途 3.成分
3818001	1.品名 2.用途 3.外观 4.成分 5.直径 6.加工程度
38180090	1.品名 2.用途 3.外观 4.成分 5.加工程度
3819	1.品名 2.用途 3.成分 4.从石油或沥青提取矿物油类的百分比含量 5.品牌(中文或外文名称)6.型号
3820	1.品名 2.用途 3.成分 4.品牌(中文或外文名称)5.型号
3821	1.品名 2.用途 3.成分
3822	1.品名 2.用途 3.成分 4.是否血源筛查用诊断试剂 5.是否有衬背

商品编码	申报要素
3823	1.品名 2.成分含量 3.来源(动植物油脂等)4.加工程度(是否经过皂化、是否经过水解)5.品牌(中文或外文名称)6.型号
38241000	1.品名 2.用途 3.成分含量 4.品牌(中文或外文名称)5.型号
38243000	1.品名 2.用途 3.成分含量 4.品牌(中文或外文名称)5.型号
38244	1.品名 2.用途 3.成分含量 4.品牌(中文或外文名称)5.型号
38245000	1.品名 2.用途 3.成分含量 4.品牌(中文或外文名称)5.型号
38246000	1.品名 2.用途 3.来源 4.成分含量 5.品牌(中文或外文名称)6.型号
38248	1.品名 2.用途 3.成分含量 4.品牌(中文或外文名称)5.型号
38249	1.品名 2.用途 3.成分含量 4.包装规格 5.品牌(中文或外文名称)6.型号
3825	1.品名 2.用途 3.来源
3826	1.品名 2.用途 3.成分含量 4.从石油或沥青提取矿物油类的百分比含量
3827	1.品名 2.用途 3.成分含量
39011000	1.品名 2.外观(形状透明度颜色等)3.成分含量 4.单体单元的种类和比例 5.比重 6.底料来源(再生料、瓶片料、新料、副牌料)7.级别 8.品牌(中文或外文名称)9.型号 10.签约日期 11.用途
39012000	1.品名 2.外观(形状透明度颜色等)3.成分含量 4.单体单元的种类和比例 5.比重 6.底料来源(再生料、瓶片料、新料、副牌料)7.级别 8.品牌(中文或外文名称)9.型号 10.签约日期 11.用途
39013000	1.品名 2.外观(形状透明度颜色等)3.成分含量 4.单体单元的种类和比例 5.底料来源(再生料、瓶片料、新料、副牌料)6.级别 7.品牌(中文或外文名称)8.牌号或型号 9.签约日期 10.生产厂商 11.用途
39014	1.品名 2.外观(形状透明度颜色等)3.成分含量 4.单体单元的种类和比例 5.比重 6.底料来源(再生料、瓶片料、新料、副牌料)7.级别 8.品牌(中文或外文名称)9.型号 10.签约日期 11.用途
39019010	1.品名 2.外观(形状透明度颜色等)3.成分含量 4.单体单元的种类和比例 5.比重 6.底料来源(再生料、瓶片料、新料、副牌料)7.级别 8.品牌(中文或外文名称)9.型号 10.签约日期 11.用途
39019090	1.品名 2.外观(形状透明度颜色等)3.成分含量 4.单体单元的种类和比例 5.底料来源(再生料、瓶片料、新料、副牌料)6.级别 7.品牌(中文或外文名称)8.型号 9.签约日期 10.用途
3902	1.品名 2.外观(形状透明度颜色等)3.成分含量 4.单体单元的种类和比例 5.底料来源(再生料、瓶片料、新料、副牌料)6.级别 7.品牌(中文或外文名称)8.型号 9.签约日期 10.用途
39031	1.品名 2.外观(形状透明度颜色等)3.是否可发性 4.是否改性 5.成分含量 6.单体单元的种类和比例 7.底料来源(再生料、瓶片料、新料、副牌料)8.级别 9.品牌(中文或外文名称)10.型号 11.签约日期 12.用途
39032000	1.品名 2.外观(形状透明度颜色等)3.成分含量 4.单体单元的种类和比例 5.底料来源(再生料、瓶片料、新料、副牌料)6.品牌(中文或外文名称)7.型号 8.签约日期 9.用途
39033	1.品名 2.外观(形状透明度颜色等)3.成分含量 4.单体单元的种类和比例 5.是否改性 6.底料来源(再生料、瓶片料、新料、副牌料)7.级别 8.品牌(中文或外文名称)9.型号 10.签约日期 11.用途
39039000	1.品名 2.外观(形状透明度颜色等)3.成分含量 4.单体单元的种类和比例 5.底料来源(再生料、瓶片料、新料、副牌料)6.品牌(中文或外文名称)7.型号 8.签约日期 9.用途
39041	1.品名 2.外观(形状透明度颜色等)3.是否掺杂其他物质 4.成分含量 5.单体单元的种类和比例 6.底料来源(再生料、瓶片料、新料、副牌料)7.品牌(中文或外文名称)8.型号 9.签约日期 10.用途
39042	1.品名 2.外观(形状透明度颜色等)3.是否塑化 4.成分含量 5.单体单元的种类和比例 6.底料来源(再生料、瓶片料、新料、副牌料)7.品牌(中文或外文名称)8.型号 9.签约日期 10.用途
39043000	1.品名 2.外观(形状透明度颜色等)3.成分含量 4.单体单元的种类和比例 5.底料来源(再生料、瓶片料、新料、副牌料)6.品牌(中文或外文名称)7.型号 8.签约日期 9.用途
39044000	1.品名 2.外观(形状透明度颜色等)3.成分含量 4.单体单元的种类和比例 5.底料来源(再生料、瓶片料、新料、副牌料)6.品牌(中文或外文名称)7.型号 8.签约日期 9.用途
39045000	1.品名 2.外观(形状透明度颜色等)3.成分含量 4.单体单元的种类和比例 5.底料来源(再生料、瓶片料、新料、副牌料)6.品牌(中文或外文名称)7.型号 8.签约日期 9.用途
39046	1.品名 2.外观(形状透明度颜色等)3.成分含量 4.单体单元的种类和比例 5.底料来源(再生料、瓶片料、新料、副牌料)6.品牌(中文或外文名称)7.型号 8.签约日期 9.用途
39049000	1.品名 2.外观(形状透明度颜色等)3.成分含量 4.单体单元的种类和比例 5.底料来源(再生料、瓶片料、新料、副牌料)6.品牌(中文或外文名称)7.型号 8.签约日期 9.用途
3905	1.品名 2.外观(形状透明度颜色等)3.成分含量 4.单体单元的种类和比例 5.底料来源(再生料、瓶片料、新料、副牌料)6.品牌(中文或外文名称)7.型号 8.签约日期 9.用途
3906	1.品名 2.外观(形状透明度颜色等)3.成分含量 4.单体单元的种类和比例 5.底料来源(再生料、瓶片料、新料、副牌料)6.品牌(中文或外文名称)7.型号 8.签约日期 9.用途
39071	1.品名 2.外观(形状透明度颜色等)3.成分含量 4.单体单元的种类和比例 5.底料来源(再生料、瓶片料、新料、副牌料)6.品牌(中文或外文名称)7.型号 8.签约日期 9.用途
39072	1.品名 2.外观(形状透明度颜色等)3.成分含量 4.单体单元的种类和比例 5.聚乙二醇请注明相对分子质量 6.底料来源(再生料、瓶片料、新料、副牌料)7.品牌(中文或外文名称)8.型号 9.签约日期
39073000	1.品名 2.外观(形状透明度颜色等)3.成分含量及溴含量 4.底料来源(再生料、瓶片料、新料、副牌料)5.品牌(中文或外文名称)6.型号 7.签约日期
39074000	1.品名 2.外观(形状透明度颜色等)3.成分含量 4.底料来源(再生料、瓶片料、新料、副牌料)5.品牌(中文或外文名称)6.型号 7.签约日期
39075000	1.品名 2.外观(形状透明度颜色等)3.成分含量 4.单体单元的种类和比例 5.底料来源(再生料、瓶片料、新料、副牌料)6.品牌(中文或外文名称)7.型号 8.用途
39076	1.品名 2.外观(形状透明度颜色等)3.是否切片 4.成分含量 5.单体单元的种类和比例 6.粘数 7.底料来源(再生料、瓶片料、新料、副牌料)8.级别 9.品牌(中文或外文名称)10.型号 11.签约日期
39077000	1.品名 2.外观(形状透明度颜色等)3.成分含量 4.单体单元的种类和比例 5.底料来源(再生料、瓶片料、新料、副牌料)6.品牌(中文或外文名称)7.型号 8.签约日期 9.用途

商品编码	申报要素
39079100	1.品名 2.外观(形状透明度颜色等)3.是否饱和 4.成分含量 5.单体单元的种类和比例 6.底料来源(再生料、瓶片料、新料、副牌料)7.品牌(中文或外文名称)8.型号 9.签约日期
39079910	1.品名 2.外观(形状透明度颜色等)3.成分含量 4.单体单元的种类和比例 5.底料来源(再生料、瓶片料、新料、副牌料)6.品牌(中文或外文名称)7.型号 8.签约日期
3907999	1.品名 2.外观(形状透明度颜色等)3.成分含量 4.单体单元的种类和比例 5.底料来源(再生料、瓶片料、新料、副牌料)6.品牌(中文或外文名称)7.型号 8.签约日期
3908	1.品名 2.外观(形状透明度颜色等)3.是否切片 4.成分含量 5.单体单元的种类和比例 6.底料来源(再生料、瓶片料、新料、副牌料)7.级别 8.品牌(中文或外文名称)9.型号 10.签约日期 11.用途
3909	1.品名 2.外观(形状透明度颜色等)3.成分含量 4.单体单元的种类和比例 5.底料来源(再生料、瓶片料、新料、副牌料)6.品牌(中文或外文名称)7.型号 8.签约日期 9.用途
3910	1.品名 2.外观(形状颜色等)3.用途 4.是否溶于水 5.成分含量 6.底料来源(再生料、瓶片料、新料、副牌料)7.品牌(中文或外文名称)8.型号 9.签约日期
39111000	1.品名 2.外观(形状透明度颜色等)3.成分含量 4.底料来源(再生料、瓶片料、新料、副牌料)5.品牌(中文或外文名称)6.型号 7.签约日期 8.用途
39112000	1.品名 2.外观(形状透明度颜色等)3.成分含量 4.底料来源(再生料、瓶片料、新料、副牌料)5.品牌(中文或外文名称)6.型号 7.签约日期 8.用途
39119000	1.品名 2.外观(形状透明度颜色等)3.成分含量 4.单体单元的种类和比例 5.底料来源(再生料、瓶片料、新料、副牌料)6.品牌(中文或外文名称)7.型号 8.签约日期 9.用途
39121	1.品名 2.外观(形状透明度颜色等)3.是否塑化 4.成分含量 5.底料来源(再生料、瓶片料、新料、副牌料)6.品牌(中文或外文名称)7.型号 8.签约日期 9.用途
39122000	1.品名 2.外观(形状透明度颜色等)3.成分含量 4.底料来源(再生料、瓶片料、新料、副牌料)5.品牌(中文或外文名称)6.型号 7.签约日期 8.用途
39123	1.品名 2.外观(形状透明度颜色等)3.成分含量 4.底料来源(再生料、瓶片料、新料、副牌料)5.品牌(中文或外文名称)6.型号 7.签约日期 8.用途
39129000	1.品名 2.外观(形状透明度颜色等)3.成分含量 4.底料来源(再生料、瓶片料、新料、副牌料)5.品牌(中文或外文名称)6.型号 7.签约日期 8.用途
3913	1.品名 2.外观(形状透明度颜色等)3.成分含量 4.底料来源(再生料、瓶片料、新料、副牌料)5.品牌(中文或外文名称)6.型号 7.签约日期 8.用途
3914	1.品名 2.外观(形状颜色等)3.成分 4.底料来源(再生料、瓶片料、新料、副牌料)5.用途 6.品牌(中文或外文名称)7.型号 8.签约日期 9.级别 10.阴离子还是阳离子还是两性
39151000	1.品名 2.来源 3.成分 4.是否已经破坏性处理 5.如为成卷,需注明是否带有轴心
39152000	1.品名 2.来源 3.成分 4.是否已经破坏性处理 5.如为成卷,需注明是否带有轴心
39153000	1.品名 2.来源 3.成分 4.是否已经破坏性处理 5.如为成卷,需注明是否带有轴心
39159010	1.品名 2.来源 3.成分 4.是否已经破坏性处理 5.如为成卷,需注明是否带有轴心
39159090	1.品名 2.来源 3.成分 4.是否已经破坏性处理 5.如为成卷,需注明是否带有轴心
3916	1.品名 2.外观(单丝、条、杆、型材、异型材)3.成分含量 4.单丝请注明截面直径 5.品牌(中文或外文名称)6.型号 7.用途
39171000	1.品名 2.成分 3.用途 4.品牌(中文或外文名称)5.型号
39172	1.品名 2.成分(乙烯聚合物、丙烯聚合物、氯乙烯聚合物等)3.品牌(中文或外文名称)4.型号 5.用途
39173	1.品名 2.成分 3.是否装有附件 4.爆破压力 5.是否经加强或与其他材料合 制 6.种类(硬管、软管)7.品牌(中文或外文名称)8.型号 9.用途
39174000	1.品名 2.材质
3918	1.品名 2.材质 3.品牌(中文或外文名称)4.型号 5.用途
39191	1.品名 2.用途 3.外观(板、片、膜、箔、带、扁条)4.是否成卷 5.是否单面自粘 6.成分 7.规格尺寸 8.品牌(中文或外文名称)9.型号
39199010	1.品名 2.用途 3.外观(板、片、膜、箔、带、扁条)4.是否成卷 5.是否单面自粘 6.成分 7.规格尺寸 8.品牌(中文或外文名称)9.型号
39199090	1.品名 2.用途(如半导体晶圆制造用等)3.外观(板、片、膜、箔、带、扁条)4.是否成卷 5.是否单面自粘 6.成分 7.规格尺寸 8.若为半导体晶圆制造用需注明形状(如圆形等)9.品牌(中文或外文名称)10.型号
39201010	1.品名 2.用途 3.外观(颜色形状等)4.成分 5.规格尺寸 6.品牌(中文或外文名称,无品牌请申报厂商)7.型号 8.适用电池种类
39201090	1.品名 2.用途 3.外观(颜色形状等)4.成分 5.规格尺寸 6.品牌(中文或外文名称,无品牌请申报厂商)7.型号
39202	1.品名 2.用途 3.外观(颜色形状等)4.成分 5.规格尺寸 6.品牌(中文或外文名称,无品牌请申报厂商)7.型号 8.适用电池种类
39203000	1.品名 2.用途 3.外观(颜色形状等)4.成分 5.规格尺寸 6.品牌(中文或外文名称)7.型号
39204	1.品名 2.用途 3.外观(颜色形状等)4.成分 5.规格尺寸 6.PVC 制品请注明增塑剂含量 7.品牌(中文或外文名称)8.型号
39205	1.品名 2.用途 3.外观(颜色形状等)4.成分 5.规格尺寸 6.品牌(中文或外文名称)7.型号
39206	1.品名 2.用途 3.外观(颜色形状等)4.成分 5.规格尺寸 6.品牌(中文或外文名称)7.型号
39207	1.品名 2.用途 3.外观(颜色形状等)4.成分 5.规格尺寸 6.品牌(中文或外文名称)7.型号
39209	1.品名 2.用途 3.外观(颜色形状等)4.成分 5.规格尺寸 6.品牌(中文或外文名称)7.型号
3921	1.品名 2.成分 3.外观 4.是否与其他材料合制 5.泡沫塑料请注明 6.用途 7.规格尺寸 8.品牌(中文或外文名称)9.型号
3922	1.品名 2.用途 3.材质 4.品牌(中文或外文名称)5.型号

商品编码	申报要素
39231000	1.品名 2.用途(如半导体晶圆、掩模或光罩用等) 3.材质 4.半导体晶圆、掩模或光罩用需报是否具有特定形状或装置 5.半导体晶圆、掩模或光罩用需注明是否有 ROHS 认证 6.品牌(中文或外文名称)7.规格或型号
39232	1.品名 2.用途 3.材质 4.品牌(中文或外文名称)5.规格或型号
39233000	1.品名 2.用途 3.材质 4.品牌(中文或外文名称)5.规格或型号
39234000	1.品名 2.用途 3.材质 4.品牌(中文或外文名称)5.规格或型号
39235000	1.品名 2.用途 3.材质 4.品牌(中文或外文名称)5.规格或型号
39239000	1.品名 2.用途 3.材质 4.品牌(中文或外文名称)5.规格或型号
3924	1.品名 2.用途 3.材质 4.品牌(中文或外文名称)5.规格或型号
3925	1.品名 2.用途 3.塑料制囤、柜、罐、桶及类似容器请注明容积 4.材质 5.品牌(中文或外文名称)
3926	1.品名 2.用途 3.材质 4.品牌(中文或外文名称)5.规格或型号
40011000	1.品名 2.外观 3.包装规格 4.签约日期 5.干胶含量
40012100	1.品名 2.外观(板、片、带等)3.型号 4.包装规格 5.签约日期
40012200	1.品名 2.外观(板、片、带等)3.型号 4.包装规格 5.是否随附生产国主管当局出具的检验证书,并列明橡胶的等级、规格及检验结果 6.签约日期
40012900	1.品名 2.外观(板、片、带等)3.型号 4.包装规格 5.签约日期
40013000	1.品名 2.外观(板、片、带等)3.型号 4.包装规格 5.签约日期
400211	1.品名 2.用途 3.外观(板、片、带等)4.成分含量 5.签约日期 6.品牌(中文或外文名称)7.型号
400219	1.品名 2.用途 3.外观(板、片、带等)4.丁苯橡胶请注明是否充油、热塑 5.成分含量 6.签约日期 7.品牌(中文或外文名称)8.型号
40022	1.品名 2.外观(板、片、带等)3.成分含量 4.签约日期 5.品牌(中文或外文名称)6.型号
40023	1.品名 2.外观(板、片、带等)3.成分含量 4.签约日期 5.品牌(中文或外文名称)6.型号
40024	1.品名 2.外观(板、片、带等)3.成分含量 4.签约日期 5.品牌(中文或外文名称)6.型号
40025	1.品名 2.外观(板、片、带等)3.成分含量 4.签约日期 5.品牌(中文或外文名称)6.型号
40026	1.品名 2.外观(板、片、带等)3.成分含量 4.签约日期 5.品牌(中文或外文名称)6.型号
40027	1.品名 2.外观(板、片、带等)3.成分含量 4.签约日期 5.品牌(中文或外文名称)6.型号
40028000	1.品名 2.外观(板、片、带等)3.成分含量 4.签约日期 5.品牌(中文或外文名称)6.型号
40029	1.品名 2.外观(板、片、带等)3.成分含量 4.签约日期 5.品牌(中文或外文名称)6.型号
4003	1.品名 2.外观(板、片、带等)3.来源
4004	1.品名 2.外观(粉、粒 等)3.来源 4.水分 5.杂质 6.干胶含量
4005	1.品名 2.外观(板、片、带等)3.成分 4.签约日期 5.品牌(中文或外文名称)6.型号
4006	1.品名 2.用途 3.外观(板、片、带等)4.材质 5.品牌(中文或外文名称)6.型号
4007	1.品名 2.外观(板、片、带等)3.截面尺寸 4.材质 5.品牌(中文或外文名称)6.型号
4008	1.品名 2.外观(板、片、带等)3.是否海绵橡胶 4.规格尺寸 5.材质 6.品牌(中文或外文名称)7.型号
40091	1.品名 2.用途 3.外观(板、片、带等)4.材质构成(是否加强或与其他材料合制)5.是否装有附件 6.品牌(中文或外文名称)7.型号
40092	1.品名 2.用途 3.外观(板、片、带等)4.材质构成(是否加强或与其他材料合制)5.是否装有附件 6.品牌(中文或外文名称)7.型号
40093	1.品名 2.用途 3.外观(板、片、带等)4.材质构成(是否加强或与其他材料合制)5.是否装有附件 6.品牌(中文或外文名称)7.型号
40094	1.品名 2.用途 3.外观(板、片、带等)4.材质构成(是否加强或与其他材料合制)5.是否装有附件 6.品牌(中文或外文名称)7.型号
40101	1.品名 2.用途 3.外观 4.材质构成(有加强材料的也要注明其材质)5.品牌(中文或外文名称)6.型号
40103100	1.品名 2.用途 3.外观 4.材质 5.规格尺寸(外周长)6.截面形状 7.品牌(中文或外文名称)
40103200	1.品名 2.用途 3.外观 4.材质 5.规格尺寸(外周长)6.截面形状 7.品牌(中文或外文名称)
40103300	1.品名 2.用途 3.外观 4.材质 5.规格尺寸(外周长)6.截面形状 7.品牌(中文或外文名称)
40103400	1.品名 2.用途 3.外观 4.材质 5.规格尺寸(外周长)6.截面形状 7.品牌(中文或外文名称)
40103500	1.品名 2.用途 3.外观 4.材质 5.规格尺寸(外周长)6.品牌(中文或外文名称)
40103600	1.品名 2.用途 3.外观 4.材质 5.规格尺寸(外周长)6.品牌(中文或外文名称)
40103900	1.品名 2.用途 3.外观 4.材质 5.规格尺寸(外周长)6.传动带请填报截面形状 7.品牌(中文或外文名称)
40111000	1.品名 2.用途 3.型号 4.辋圈尺寸 5.断面宽度 6.胎面花纹 7 品牌(中文或外文名称)8.速度等级
40112000	1.品名 2.用途 3.型号 4.辋圈尺寸 5.断面宽度 6.品牌(中文或外文名称)
40113000	1.品名 2.用途 3.型号 4.辋圈尺寸 5.断面宽度 6.品牌(中文或外文名称)
40114000	1.品名 2.用途 3.型号 4.辋圈尺寸 5.断面宽度 6.品牌(中文或外文名称)
40115000	1.品名 2.用途 3.型号 4.辋圈尺寸 5.断面宽度 6.品牌(中文或外文名称)
40117	1.品名 2.用途 3.型号 4.辋圈尺寸 5.胎面花纹(人字型胎面或类似胎面等)6.断面宽度 7.品牌(中文或外文名称)
40118	1.品名 2.用途 3.型号 4.辋圈尺寸 5.胎面花纹(人字型胎面或类似胎面等)6.断面宽度 7.品牌(中文或外文名称)
40119	1.品名 2.用途 3.型号 4.辋圈尺寸 5.胎面花纹(人字型胎面或类似胎面等)6.断面宽度 7.品牌(中文或外文名称)
4012	1.品名 2.用途 3.是否实心 4.充气轮胎请注明翻新或旧的 5.品牌(中文或外文名称)6.型号
4013	1.品名 2.用途 3.品牌(中文或外文名称)

商品编码	申报要素
40141000	1.品名 2.用途 3.品牌(中文或外文名称)
40149000	1.品名 2.用途 3.品牌(中文或外文名称)
40151200	1.品名 2.用途(医疗、外科、牙科或兽医用)3.品牌(中文或外文名称)
40151900	1.品名 2.用途 3.品牌(中文或外文名称)4.成分(含胶率)5.规格型号(S、M、XL 等)
40159	1.品名 2.用途 3.品牌(中文或外文名称)
40161	1.品名 2.用途 3.是否海绵橡胶 4.材质 5.是否机器及仪器用 6.品牌(中文或外文名称)7.型号
40169100	1.品名 2.用途 3.是否海绵橡胶 4.材质 5.品牌(中文或外文名称)6.型号
40169200	1.品名 2.用途 3.是否海绵橡胶 4.材质 5.品牌(中文或外文名称)6.型号
401693	1.品名 2.用途 3.是否海绵橡胶 4.材质 5.是否机器及仪器用 6.品牌(中文或外文名称)7.型号
40169400	1.品名 2.用途 3.是否海绵橡胶 4.材质 5.品牌(中文或外文名称)6.型号
40169500	1.品名 2.用途 3.是否海绵橡胶 4.材质 5.品牌(中文或外文名称)6.型号
401699	1.品名 2.用途 3.是否海绵橡胶 4.材质 5.是否机器及仪器用 6.品牌(中文或外文名称)7.型号
4017	1.品名 2.外观 3.成分
4101201	1.品名 2.制作或保存方法(鲜、干、盐渍、石灰浸渍、浸酸)3.是否鞣制(未鞣制、退鞣处理)4.状态(整张/半张,是否去肉修边等)5.平均每张重量 6.种类(公牛、未育/已育母牛、奶牛、阉牛、小牛、马)7.产区(如澳大利亚维多利亚、新南威尔士等)8.等级(若为混装货,请注明各等级占比)9.生产商名称 10.签约日期 11.用途
41012020	1.品名 2.制作或保存方法(鲜、干、盐渍、石灰浸渍、浸酸)3.是否鞣制(未鞣制、退鞣处理)4.状态(整张/半张,是否去肉修边等)5.平均每张重量 6.种类(公牛、未育/已育母牛、奶牛、阉牛、小牛、马)7.产区(如澳大利亚维多利亚、新南威尔士等)8.等级(若为混装货,请注明各等级占比)9.生产商名称 10.签约日期 11.用途
41015	1.品名 2.制作或保存方法(鲜、干、盐渍、石灰浸渍、浸酸)3.是否鞣制(未鞣制、退鞣处理)4.状态(整张/半张,是否去肉修边等)5.平均每张重量 6.种类(公牛、未育/已育母牛、奶牛、阉牛、小牛、马)7.产区(如澳大利亚维多利亚、新南威尔士等)8.等级(若为混装货,请注明各等级占比)9.生产商名称 10.签约日期 11.用途
41019	1.品名 2.制作或保存方法(鲜、干、盐渍、石灰浸渍、浸酸)3.是否鞣制(未鞣制、退鞣处理)4.状态(整张/半张,是否去肉修边等)5.平均每张重量 6.种类(公牛、未育/已育母牛、奶牛、阉牛、小牛、马)7.产区(如澳大利亚维多利亚、新南威尔士等)8.等级(若为混装货,请注明各等级占比)9.生产商名称 10.签约日期 11.用途
4102	1.品名 2.制作或保存方法(鲜、干、盐渍、石灰浸渍、浸酸、未鞣制、退鞣处理)3.种类(羔羊、绵 羊)4.状态(带毛、不带毛)5.毛长(单位:英寸)6.张幅(单 位:平方英尺)7.等级(若为混装货,请注明各等级占比)8.用途(毛革一体、制革)9.生产商名称 10.签约日期
4103	1.品名 2.制作或保存方法(鲜、干、盐渍、石灰浸渍、浸酸、未鞣制、退鞣处理)3.种类(山羊、猪、爬行动物等)4.是否源于野生动 物 5.张幅(单位:平方英尺)6.重量(单位:磅)7.等级(若为混装货,请注明各等级占比) 8.生产商名称(英文全称)9.签约日期
4104	1.品名 2.鞣制方法(植鞣、铬鞣、油鞣等)3.状态(干、湿)4.鞣制后是否经进一步加工(是或否,如是请注明经何加工)5.种类(公牛、母牛、奶牛、阉牛、马) 6.是否源于野生动物 7.规格(厚度、平均尺寸及平均重量)8.品种 9.用途 10.级别(头层皮 TR1/2/3,二层皮 A/B/C/D 级)11.部位(整张、半张、背皮、颈肩、颈头、头颈等)12.是否经修边或裁剪 13.生产商名称(英文全称)14.签约日期
4105	1.品名 2.制作或保存方法(鞣制无毛)3.种类(羔羊、绵羊)4.状态(干、湿)5.是否源于野生动 物 6.规格(厚度、张幅)
4106	1.品名 2.制作或保存方法(鞣制无毛)3.种类(如爬行动物、小山羊)4.状态(干、湿)5.是否源于野生动 物 6.规格(厚度、张幅、张数)
410711	1.品名 2.制作或保存方法(表面是否涂覆、涂覆何种物质等)3.种类(牛、马)4.是否整张 5.状态(无毛全粒面未剖层、无毛粒面剖层)6.牛皮层数 7.规格(厚度、平均面积)8.颜色 9.用途(鞋面、箱包、鞋底、家具、汽车座椅、皮带等)
410712	1.品名 2.制作或保存方法(表面是否涂覆、涂覆何种物质等)3.种类(牛、马)4.是否整张 5.状态(无毛全粒面未剖层、无毛粒面剖层)6.牛皮层数 7.规格(厚度、平均面积)8.颜色 9.用途(鞋面、箱包、鞋底、家具、汽车座椅、皮带等)
41071910	1.品名 2.制作或保存方法(表面是否涂覆、涂覆何种物质等)3.种类(牛、马)4.是否整张 5.状态(无毛全粒面未剖层、无毛粒面剖层等)6.牛皮层数 7.用途(机器带用)8.规格(厚度、平均面积)9.颜色
41071990	1.品名 2.制作或保存方法(表面是否涂覆、涂覆何种物质等)3.种类(牛、马)4.是否整张 5.状态(无毛全粒面未剖层、无毛粒面剖层等)6.牛皮层数 7.规格(厚度、平均面积)8.颜色 9.用途(鞋面、箱包、鞋底、家具、汽车座椅、皮带等)
41079100	1.品名 2.制作或保存方法(表面是否涂覆、涂覆何种物质等)3.种类(牛、马)4.是否整张 5.状态(无毛全粒面未剖层、无毛粒面剖层)6.牛皮层数 7.规格(厚度、平均面积)8.颜色 9.用途(鞋面、箱包、鞋底、家具、汽车座椅、皮带等)
41079200	1.品名 2.制作或保存方法(表面是否涂覆、涂覆何种物质等)3.种类(牛、马)4.是否整张 5.状态(无毛全粒面未剖层、无毛粒面剖层)6.牛皮层数 7.规格(厚度、平均面积)8.颜色 9.用途(鞋面、箱包、鞋底、家具、汽车座椅、皮带等)
41079910	1.品名 2.制作或保存方法(表面是否涂覆、涂覆何种物质等)3.种类(牛、马)4.是否整张 5.状态(无毛全粒面未剖层、无毛粒面剖层等)6.牛皮层数 7.用途(机器带用)8.规格(厚度、平均面积)9.颜色
41079990	1.品名 2.制作或保存方法(表面是否涂覆、涂覆何种物质等)3.种类(牛、马)4.是否整张 5.状态(无毛全粒面未剖层、无毛粒面剖层等)6.牛皮层数 7.规格(厚度、平均面积)8.颜色 9.用途(鞋面、箱包、鞋底、家具、汽车座椅、皮带等)
4112	1.品名 2.种类 3.状态(无毛全粒面或无毛羊皮纸化等)4.规格(厚度及面积)5.颜色
4113	1.品名 2.制作或保存方法 3.状态(无毛全粒面等)4.规格(长/宽或面积)5.整张/背皮/腹皮等
4114	1.品名 2.制作或保存方法(漆皮、镀金属)3.规格(厚度)4.请注明平方英尺数/张
41151000	1.品名 2.制作或保存方法(再生)3.状态(块、张、条、卷、边角料、粉末)4.规格(厚度)
41152000	1.品名 2.状态(块、张、条、卷、边角料、粉末) 3.用途 4.是否经过筛选
4201	1.品名 2.材质 3.用途
420211	1.品名 2.种类(衣箱、提箱、小手袋等)3.表面材质及成分含量(皮革、再生皮革需具体到皮革种类)4.品牌(中文或外文名称)5.款号
420212	1.品名 2.种类(衣箱、提箱、小手袋等)3.表面材质及成分含量(塑料、纺织物等)4.品牌(中文或外文名称)5.款号
42021900	1.品名 2.种类(衣箱、提箱、小手袋等)3.表面材质及成分含量 4.品牌(中文或外文名称)5.款号
42022	1.品名 2.种类(手提包、晚宴包等)3.表面材质及成分含量(皮革、再生皮革、塑料、纺织物等)4.品牌(中文或外文名称)5.款号
42023	1.品名 2.种类(钱夹、钱包、手机套等)3.表面材质及成分含量(皮革、再生皮革、塑料、纺织物等)4.品牌(中文或外文名称)5.款号
42029	1.品名 2.种类(工具包、运动包等)3.表面材质及成分含量(皮革、再生皮革、塑料、纺织物等)4.品牌(中文或外文名称)5.款号
42031000	1.品名 2.表面材质及成分含量(皮革、再生皮革需具体到皮革种类)3.衣服种类 4.品牌(中文或外文名称)5.款号
42032	1.品名 2.用途(专供运动用、劳保用等)3.表面材质及成分含量(皮革、再生皮革需具体到皮革种类)
42033	1.品名 2.表面材质及成分含量(皮革、再生皮革需具体到皮革种类)3.品牌(中文或外文名称)4.款号
42034000	1.品名 2.表面材质及成分含量(皮革、再生皮革需具体到皮革种类)3.品牌(中文或外文名称)4.款号
42050010	1.品名 2.材质(皮革或再生皮革)
42050020	1.品名 2.用途(机械、技术用等)3.材质(皮革或再生皮革)
42050090	1.品名 2.用途 3.材质(皮革或再生皮革)4.品牌(中文或外文名称)
4206	1.品名
43011000	1.品名 2.状态(生毛皮)3.外观(整张、带头、尾、爪等)4.品种(深棕、黑十字等)5.性别(公、母)7.尺寸(50 号、40 号等)6.颜色 7.等级(以各拍卖会等级体系为准、残次皮需明确种类及等级)(中英文)8.是否来自拍卖会及拍卖日期、把号
43013000	1.品名 2.种类(中国羔羊、波斯羔羊等)3.状态(生毛皮)4.外观(整张、头、尾、爪等)
43016000	1.品名 2.种类(蓝狐、蓝霜狐皮等)3.状态(生毛皮)4.外观(整张、头、尾、爪等)5.尺寸(50 号、40 号等)6.颜色(深、浅)7.质量(世家皇冠、世家级)8.是否来自拍卖会及拍卖会日期
43018010	1.品名 2.种类(兔皮等)3.状态(生毛皮)4.外观(整张、头、尾、爪等)5.颜色(白色、黑色等)
43018090	1.品名 2.种类(中国羔羊、波斯羔羊、狐皮、兔皮 等)3.状态(生毛皮)4.外观(整张、头、尾、爪等)
43019	1.品名 2.种类(中国羔羊、波斯羔羊、狐皮、兔皮 等)3.状态(生毛皮)4.外观(整张、头、尾、爪等)
43021100	1.品名 2.制作或保存方法(鞣制未缝制或已缝制毛皮)3.外观(整张、带头、尾、爪等)4.重量、张数 5.品种(深棕、黑十字等)6.性别(公、母)7.尺寸(50 号、40 号等)8.颜色 9.等级(以各拍卖会等级体系为准、残次皮需明确种类及等级)(中英文)10.是否来自拍卖会及拍卖日期、把号
43021910	1.品名 2.种类(蓝狐、蓝霜狐皮等)3.制作或保存方法(鞣制未缝制或已缝制毛皮)4.外观(整张、头、尾、爪等)5.尺寸(50 号、40 号等)6.颜色(深、浅)7.质量(世家皇冠、世家级)8.是否来自拍卖会及拍卖会日期
43021920	1.品名 2.种类(兔皮等)3.制作或保存方法(鞣制未缝制或已缝制毛皮)4.外观(整张、头、尾、爪等)5.规格
43021930	1.品名 2.种类(中国羔羊、波斯羔羊等)3.制作或保存方法(鞣制未缝制或已缝制毛皮)4.外观(整张、头、尾、爪等)5.规格
43021990	1.品名 2.种类(中国羔羊、波斯羔羊、狐皮、兔皮等)3.制作或保存方法(鞣制未缝制或已缝制毛皮)4.外观(整张、头、尾、爪等)5.规格
43022000	1.品名 2.种类(中国羔羊、波斯羔羊、狐皮、兔皮等)3.制作或保存方法(鞣制未缝制或已缝制毛皮)4.外观(整张、头、尾、爪等)
43023	1.品名 2.种类(中国羔羊、波斯羔羊、狐皮、兔皮等)3.制作或保存方法(鞣制未缝制或已缝制毛皮)4.外观(整张、头、尾、爪等)5.规格
4303	1.品名 2.材质(里、外)3.衣服种类
4304	1.品名 2.材质(人造毛皮)
44011	1.品名 2.种类(中文、拉丁文属名、拉丁文种名) 3.外观(圆木段、块、枝、成捆或类似形状等)
44012	1.品名 2.种类(中文、拉丁文属名、拉丁文种名)3.规格 4.用途
44013100	1.品名 2.外观(棒)3.规格(直径×长度)
44013200	1.品名 2.外观(块)3.规格(最小截面尺寸)
44013900	1.品名 2.外观(片等类似形状)
44014	1.品名 2.外观(末、废料、碎片等)3.用途
44021000	1.品名 2.材质 3.是否活化
44022000	1.品名 2.材质 3.是否活化
44029000	1.品名 2.材质 3.是否活化 4.碳含量 5.挥发分
44031	1.品名 2.种类(中文、拉丁文属名、拉丁文种名) 3.加工方法(用油漆、着色剂等防腐剂处理等是否去皮、去边或粗锯成方等) 4.最小截面尺寸 5.长度 6.是否蓝 变 7.是否烘干 8.签约日期
44032	1.品名 2.种类(中文、拉丁文属名、拉丁文种名) 3.加工方法(是否去皮、去边或粗锯成方等)4.最小截面尺寸 5.长度 6.级别(锯材级、切片级等)7.是否蓝变 8.是否烘干 9.签约日期
44034	1.品名 2.种类(中文、拉丁文属名、拉丁文种名) 3.加工方法(是否去皮、去边或粗锯成方等)4.最小截面尺寸 5.长度 6.级别(锯材级、切片级等)7.是否蓝变 8.是否烘干 9.签约日期
44039	1.品名 2.种类(中文、拉丁文属名、拉丁文种名) 3.加工方法(是否去皮、去边或粗锯成方等)4.最小截面尺寸 5.长度 6.级别(锯材级、切片级等)7.是否蓝变 8.是否烘干 9.签约日期
4404	1.品名 2.种类(中文、拉丁文属名、拉丁文种名) 3.外观(棒状、条状等)4.加工方法(是否经纵锯、车圆、弯曲或其他方式加 工)
4405	1.品名 2.用途 3.如为木粉且单一材种注明中文、拉丁文属名及种名
4406	1.品名 2.加工方法(是否浸渍)3.规格(长×宽×高)4.种类(中文、拉丁文属名、拉丁文种名)

商品编码	申报要素
44071	1.品名 2.种类(中文、拉丁文属名、拉丁文种名) 3.规格(长度×宽度) 4.厚度(毫米)5.加工方法(是否经纵锯、纵切、刨切或旋切)6.等级 7.是否蓝变 8.是否净边 9.是否烘干 10.签约日期
44072	1.品名 2.种类(中文、拉丁文属名、拉丁文种名) 3.规格(长度×宽度) 4.厚度(毫米)5.等级 6.是否蓝变 7.是否净边 8.是否烘干 9.签约日期
44079100	1.品名 2.种类(中文、拉丁文属名、拉丁文种名) 3.规格(长度×宽度) 4.厚度(毫米)5.等级 6.是否蓝变 7.是否净边 8.是否烘干 9.签约日期
44079200	1.品名 2.种类(中文、拉丁文属名、拉丁文种名) 3.规格(长度×宽度) 4.厚度(毫米)5.等级 6.毛边板或直边板请注明 7.是否蓝变 8.是否净边 9.是否烘干 10.签约日期
44079300	1.品名 2.种类(中文、拉丁文属名、拉丁文种名) 3.规格(长度×宽度) 4.厚度(毫米)5.等级 6.是否蓝变 7.是否净边 8.是否烘干 9.签约日期
44079400	1.品名 2.种类(中文、拉丁文属名、拉丁文种名) 3.规格(长度×宽度) 4.厚度(毫米)5.等级 6.是否蓝变 7.是否净边 8.是否烘干 9.签约日期
44079500	1.品名 2.种类(中文、拉丁文属名、拉丁文种名) 3.规格(长度×宽度) 4.厚度(毫米)5.等级 6.是否蓝变 7.是否净边 8.是否烘干 9.签约日期
44079600	1.品名 2.种类(中文、拉丁文属名、拉丁文种名) 3.规格(长度×宽度) 4.厚度(毫米)5.等级 6.是否蓝变 7.是否净边 8.是否烘干 9.签约日期
44079700	1.品名 2.种类(中文、拉丁文属名、拉丁文种名) 3.规格(长度×宽度) 4.厚度(毫米)5.等级 6.是否蓝变 7.是否净边 8.是否烘干 9.签约日期
44079910	1.品名 2.种类(中文、拉丁文属名、拉丁文种名) 3.规格(长度×宽度) 4.厚度(毫米)5.等级 6.是否蓝变 7.是否净边 8.是否烘干 9.签约日期
44079920	1.品名 2.种类(中文、拉丁文属名、拉丁文种名) 3.规格(长度×宽度) 4.厚度(毫米)5.等级 6.是否蓝变 7.是否净边 8.是否烘干 9.签约日期
44079930	1.品名 2.种类(中文、拉丁文属名、拉丁文种名) 3.规格(长度×宽度) 4.厚度(毫米)5.等级 6.是否蓝变 7.是否净边 8.是否烘干 9.签约日期
44079980	1.品名 2.种类(中文、拉丁文属名、拉丁文种名) 3.规格(长度×宽度) 4.厚度(毫米)5.等级 6.是否蓝变 7.是否净边 8.是否烘干 9.签约日期
44079990	1.品名 2.种类(中文、拉丁文属名、拉丁文种名) 3.规格(长度×宽度) 4.厚度(毫米)5.等级 6.是否蓝变 7.是否净边 8.是否烘干 9.签约日期
4408	1.品名 2.用途(饰面用等)3.种类(中文、拉丁文属名、拉丁文种名)4.规格(长度×宽度)5.厚度(毫米)6.加工方法(纵锯、刨切、旋切等)7.请注明立方米数或平方米数
4409	1.品名 2.种类(中文、拉丁文属名、拉丁文种名) 3.外观(舌榫、槽榫、半槽榫等)4.规格(长度×宽度)5.厚度(毫米)6.加工方法
4410	1.品名 2.材质(木质或类似木质材料)3.请注明立方米数或平方米数
441112	1.品名 2.加工方法(是否经机械加工或盖面、干法、湿法等)3.密度(克/立方厘米)4.厚度(毫米)5.请注明是否辐射松制 6.请注明立方米数或平方米数
44111311	1.品名 2.加工方法(是否经机械加工或盖面、干法、湿法等)3.密度(克/立方厘米)4.厚度(毫米)5.请注明是否辐射松制 6.请注明立方米数或平方米数
44111319	1.品名 2.加工方法(是否经机械加工或盖面、干法、湿法等)3.密度(克/立方厘米)4.厚度(毫米) 5.请注明是否辐射松制 6.请注明立方米数或平方米数
4411132	1.品名 2.加工方法(是否经机械加工或盖面、干法、湿法等)3.密度(克/立方厘米)4.厚度(毫米)5.请注明是否辐射松制 6.请注明立方米数或平方米数
4411139	1.品名 2.加工方法(是否经机械加工或盖面、干法、湿法等)3.密度(克/立方厘米)4.厚度(毫米) 5.请注明是否辐射松制 6.请注明立方米数或平方米数
44111411	1.品名 2.加工方法(是否经机械加工或盖面、干法、湿法等)3.密度(克/立方厘米)4.厚度(毫米) 5.请注明是否辐射松制 6.请注明立方米数或平方米数
44111419	1.品名 2.加工方法(是否经机械加工或盖面、干法、湿法等)3.密度(克/立方厘米)4.厚度(毫米) 5.请注明是否辐射松制 6.请注明立方米数或平方米数
4411142	1.品名 2.加工方法(是否经机械加工或盖面、干法、湿法等)3.密度(克/立方厘米)4.厚度(毫米)5.请注明是否辐射松制 6.请注明立方米数或平方米数
4411149	1.品名 2.加工方法(是否经机械加工或盖面、干法、湿法等)3.密度(克/立方厘米)4.厚度(毫米) 5.请注明是否辐射松制 6.请注明立方米数或平方米数
44119	1.品名 2.加工方法(是否经机械加工或盖面、干法、湿法等)3.密度(克/立方厘米)4.请注明是否辐射松制 5.请注明立方米数或平方米数
4412	1.品名 2.每层材质及树种名称 3.最大的单层厚度 4.规格(长度×宽度)5.厚度(毫米)6.加工方法 7.请注明立方米数或平方米数
4413	1.品名 2.加工方法(压缩、浸渍等)3.外观(块、板、条、异型)
4414	1.品名 2.材质(木制)3.种类(如是单一材种注明中文、拉丁文属名及种名)
4415	1.品名 2.材质(木制)3.种类(如是单一材种注明中文、拉丁文属名及种名)4.用途
4416	1.品名 2.材质(木制)3.种类(如是单一材种注明中文、拉丁文属名及种名)
4417	1.品名 2.材质(木制)3.种类(如是单一材种注明中文、拉丁文属名及种名)
44181	1.品名 2.用途(建筑用)3.材质(木制等)4.种类(如是单一材种注明中文、拉丁文属名及种名)
44182	1.品名 2.用途(建筑用)3.材质(木制等)4.种类(如是单一材种注明中文、拉丁文属名及种名)5.规格
44183000	1.品名 2.材质(木制等)3.种类(如是单一材种注明中文、拉丁文属名及种名)4.类型(柱、梁)5.规格
44184000	1.品名 2.用途(建筑用)3.材质(木制等)4.种类(如是单一材种注明中文、拉丁文属名及种名)5.规格
44185000	1.品名 2.用途(建筑用)3.材质(木制等)4.种类(如是单一材种注明中文、拉丁文属名及种名)5.规格
44187	1.品名 2.加工方法(已装拼)3.材质(木制等)4.种类(如是单一材种注明中文、拉丁文属名及种名) 5.类型(马赛克地板、多层地板等)6.规格
44188	1.品名 2.用途(工程结构用)3.材质(木制等)4.种类(如是单一材种注明中文、拉丁文属名及种名)
44189	1.品名 2.用途(建筑用)3.材质(木制等)4.种类(如是单一材种注明中文、拉丁文属名及种名)
44191	1.品名 2.材质(竹制)3.是否是一次性产品 4.种类(如是单一材种注明中文、拉丁文属名及种名)
44192000	1.品名 2.材质(热带木制)3.种类(如是单一材种注明中文、拉丁文属名及种名)
44199010	1.品名 2.材质(木制等)3.是否是一次性产品 4.种类(如是单一材种注明中文、拉丁文属名及种名)5.小包装类别(塑料、纸制等)6.包含附件请注明附件名称
44199090	1.品名 2.材质(木制等)3.是否是一次性产品 4.种类(如是单一材种注明中文、拉丁文属名及种名)
4420	1.品名 2.材质(竹制、木制等)3.种类(如是单一材种注明中文、拉丁文属名及种名)4.用途
44211000	1.品名 2.材质(竹制、木制等)3.种类(如是单一材种注明中文、拉丁文属名及种名)
44212000	1.品名 2.材质(竹制、木制等)3.种类(如是单一材种注明中文、拉丁文属名及种名)
44219110	1.品名 2.材质(竹制)3.种类(如是单一材种注明中文、拉丁文属名及种名)4.是否是一次性产品 5.规格(长、宽、厚、直径等)
44219190	1.品名 2.材质(竹制)3.种类(如是单一材种注明中文、拉丁文属名及种名)4.是否为一次性制品
44219910	1.品名 2.材质(木制等)3.种类(如是单一材种注明中文、拉丁文属名及种名)4.是否是一次性产品 5.规格(长、宽、厚、直径等)6.用途
44219990	1.品名 2.材质(木制等)3.种类种类(如是单一材种注明中文、拉丁文属名及种名)4.是否为一次性制品 5.用途
45011000	1.品名 2.加工程度(未加工、简单加工等)
45019	1.品名 2.状态(碎的、粒状的或粉状的)3.是否为废料
4502	1.品名 2.加工方法(经除去表皮或粗切成方形等加工)3.外观(块、板、片或条状等)
4503	1.品名 2.规格 3.等级
4504	1.品名 2.外观(块、板、片等形状)
46012100	1.品名 2.材质(竹、藤、稻草等)3.用途
46012200	1.品名 2.材质(竹、藤、稻草等)
46012911	1.品名 2.材质(竹、藤、稻草等)3.单位面积
46012919	1.品名 2.材质(竹、藤、稻草等)
4601292	1.品名 2.材质(竹、藤、稻草等)
46012990	1.品名 2.材质(竹、藤、稻草等)
46019	1.品名 2.材质(竹、藤、稻草等)
4602	1.品名 2.材质(竹、藤、草、玉米皮、柳条等)3.植物材料制请注明 4.品牌(中文或外文名称)
4701	1.品名(机械木浆)2.品牌(中文或外文名称)3.签约日期
4702	1.品名(溶解级化学木浆)2.品牌(中文或外文名称)3.签约日期
4703	1.品名 2.材质(针叶木、非针叶木)3.加工方法(漂白、未漂白、半漂白)4.水分含量 5.品牌(中文或外文名称)6.签约日期 7.形状(卷筒或平板)
4704	1.品名 2.材质(针叶木、非针叶木)3.加工方法(漂白、未漂白、半漂白)4.水分含量 5.品牌(中文或外文名称)
4705	1.品名 2.加工方法(用机械和化学联合制浆法)3.水分含量 4.品牌(中文或外文名称)
47061000	1.品名 2.种类(棉短绒)3.用途(造纸或生产粘胶纤维等)4.粘度(具体数值或范围区间,单位为 dl/g)5.α纤维素含量(不溶级分,以 R18、硫酸盐法或亚硫酸盐法计) 6.725℃时灰分(申报具体百分比数值或范围区间)
47062000	1.品名 2.来源(从回收纸或纸板提取的)3.原料种类(如美废 13 号)
47063000	1.品名 2.来源(从回收纸或纸板提取的)3.用途(造纸或生产粘胶纤维等)4.粘度(具体数值或范围区间,单位为 dl/g) 5.α纤维素含量(不溶级分,以 R18、硫酸盐法或亚硫酸盐法计)6.725℃时灰分(申报具体百分比数值或范围区间)
47069	1.品名 2.材质(草浆等)3.加工方法(机械、化学、半化学)
47071000	1.品名 2.种类(未漂白废牛皮纸、废瓦楞纸)3.状态(废碎)4.产地标准及标号(美废、欧废、港废等)5.签约日期
47072000	1.品名 2.种类(漂白废牛皮纸、废报纸等)3.状态(废碎)4.产地标准及标号(美废、欧废、港废等)5.签约日期
47073000	1.品名 2.种类(未漂白废牛皮纸、废报纸等)3.状态(废碎)4.产地标准及标号(美废、欧废、港废等)5.签约日期
47079000	1.品名 2.种类(未漂白废牛皮纸、废报纸等)3.产地标准及标号(美废、欧废、港废等)4.签约日期
4801	1.品名 2.用途(书写、印刷等用)3.加工程度(未涂布、未染面等)4.规格(成条、成卷的宽度或成张的边长)5.每平方米克重 6.机械或化学一机械法制得的纤维含量 7.粗糙度 8.签约日期 9.品牌(中文或外文名称,无品牌请申报厂商)
48021	1.品名 2.用途 3.种类 4.加工程度(未涂布、未染面等)5.规格(成条、成卷的宽度或成张的边长)6.每平方米克重 7.签约日期 8.品牌(中文或外文名称,无品牌请申报厂商)
48022	1.品名 2.用途 3.种类 4.加工程度(未涂布、未染面等)5.规格(成条、成卷的宽度或成张的边长)6.每平方米克重 7.签约日期 8.品牌(中文或外文名称,无品牌请申报厂商)
48024000	1.品名 2.用途 3.种类 4.加工程度(未涂布、未染面等)5.规格(成条、成卷的宽度或成张的边长)6.每平方米克重 7.签约日期 8.品牌(中文或外文名称,无品牌请申报厂商)
48025	1.品名 2.用途(书写、印刷等用)3.种类 4.加工程度(未涂布、未染面等)5.规格(成条、成卷的宽度或成张的边长)6.每平方米克重 7.纤维种类和含量 8.签约日期 9.品牌(中文或外文名称,无品牌请申报厂商)
48026	1.品名 2.用途(书写、印刷等用)3.种类 4.加工程度(未涂布、未染面等)5.规格(成条、成卷的宽度或成张的边长)6.每平方米克重 7.纤维种类和含量 8.签约日期 9.品牌(中文或外文名称,无品牌请申报厂商)
4803	1.品名 2.种类(卫生纸、面巾纸等类似纸)3.规格(成条、成卷的宽度或成张的边长)4.签约日期 5.品牌(中文或外文名称,无品牌请申报厂商)
48041	1.品名 2.种类(牛皮挂面纸)3.加工程度(未漂白、漂白、未涂布)4.规格(成条、成卷的宽度或成张的边长)5.每平方米克重 6.纤维种类和含量 7.请注明耐破度、紧度、横向环压指数、横向耐折度 8.品牌(中文或外文名称)9.签约日期 10.厂商(中文或外文名称)

商品编码	申报要素
48042	1.品名 2.种类(袋用牛皮纸)3.加工程度(未漂白、漂白、未涂布)4.规格(成条、成卷的宽度或成张的边长)5.每平方米克重 6.纤维种类和含量 7.请注明耐破度、紧度、横向环压指数、横向耐折度 8.是否机器上光 9.品牌(中文或外文名称)10.签约日期
48043100	1.品名 2.种类 3.加工程度(未漂白、未涂布)4.规格(成条、成卷的宽度或成张的边长)5.每平方米克重 6.纤维种类和含量 7.请注明耐破度、紧度、横向环压指数、横向耐折度 8.品牌(中文或外文名称)9.签约日期
48043900	1.品名 2.种类(耐磨纸原纸等)3.加工程度(漂白、未涂布)4.规格(成条、成卷的宽度或成张的边长)5.每平方米克重 6.纤维种类和含量 7.品牌(中文或外文名称)8.签约日期
48044100	1.品名 2.种类 3.加工程度(未漂白、未涂布)4.规格(成条、成卷的宽度或成张的边长)5.每平方米克重 6.纤维种类和含量 7.请注明耐破度、紧度、横向环压指数、横向耐折度 8.品牌(中文或外文名称)9.签约日期
48044200	1.品名 2.种类 3.加工程度(本体均匀漂白、未涂 布)4.规格(成条、成卷的宽度或成张的边长)5.每平方米克重 6.纤维种类和含量 7.请注明耐破度、紧度、横向环压指数、横向耐折度 8.品牌(中文或外文名称)9.签约日期
48044900	1.品名 2.种类 3.加工程度(漂白、未涂布)4.规格(成条、成卷的宽度或成张的边长)5.每平方米克重 6.纤维种类和含量 7.请注明耐破度、紧度、横向环压指数、横向耐折度 8.品牌(中文或外文名称)9.签约日期
48045100	1.品名 2.种类 3.加工程度(未漂白、未涂布)4.规格(成条、成卷的宽度或成张的边长)5.每平方米克重 6.纤维种类和含量 7.请注明耐破度、紧度、横向环压指数、横向耐折度 8.品牌(中文或外文名称)9.签约日期
48045200	1.品名 2.种类 3.加工程度(本体均匀漂白、未涂 布)4.规格(成条、成卷的宽度或成张的边长)5.每平方米克重 6.纤维种类和含量 7.请注明耐破度、紧度、横向环压指数、横向耐折度 8.品牌(中文或外文名称)9.签约日期
48045900	1.品名 2.种类 3.加工程度(漂白、未涂布)4.规格(成条、成卷的宽度或成张的边长)5.每平方米克重 6.纤维种类和含量 7.请注明耐破度、紧度、横向环压指数、横向耐折度 8.品牌(中文或外文名称)9.签约日期
48051	1.品名 2.种类 3.加工程度(未涂布)4.规格(成条、成卷的宽度或成张的边长)5.每平方米克重 6.纤维种类和含量 7.签约日期 8.品牌(中文或外文名称,无品牌请申报厂商)
48052	1.品名 2.种类 3.加工程度(未涂布)4.规格(成条、成卷的宽度或成张的边长)5.每平方米克重 6.原料 7.强度(缪伦耐破指数)8.签约日期 9.品牌(中文或外文名称,无品牌请申报厂商)
48053000	1.品名 2.种类 3.加工程度(未涂布)4.规格(成条、成卷的宽度或成张的边长)5.每平方米克重 6.灰分含量 7.强度(缪伦耐破指数)8.签约日期 9.品牌(中文或外文名称,无品牌请申报厂商)
48054000	1.品名 2.种类 3.加工程度(未涂布)4.规格(成条、成卷的宽度或成张的边长)5.每平方米克重 6.签约日期 7.品牌(中文或外文名称,无品牌请申报厂商)
48055000	1.品名 2.种类 3.加工程度(未涂布)4.规格(成条、成卷的宽度或成张的边长)5.每平方米克重 6.签约日期 7.品牌(中文或外文名称,无品牌请申报厂商)
48059110	1.品名 2.种类 3.加工程度(未涂布)4.规格(成条、成卷的宽度或成张的边长)5.每平方米克重 6.签约日期 7.型 号 8.品牌(中文或外文名称,无品牌请申报厂商)
48059190	1.品名 2.种类 3.加工程度(未涂布)4.规格(成条、成卷的宽度或成张的边长)5.每平方米克重 6.签约日期 7.品牌(中文或外文名称,无品牌请申报厂商)
48059200	1.品名 2.种类 3.加工程度(未涂布)4.规格(成条、成卷的宽度或成张的边长)5.每平方米克重 6.签约日期 7.品牌(中文或外文名称,无品牌请申报厂商)
48059300	1.品名 2.种类 3.加工程度(未涂布)4.规格(成条、成卷的宽度或成张的边长)5.每平方米克重 6.签约日期 7.品牌(中文或外文名称,无品牌请申报厂商)
48061000	1.品名 2.种类 3.规格(成条、成卷的宽度或成张的边长)4.签约日期 5.品牌(中文或外文名称,无品牌请申报厂商)
48062000	1.品名 2.种类 3.规格(成条、成卷的宽度或成张的边长)4.签约日期 5.品牌(中文或外文名称,无品牌请申报厂商)
48063000	1.品名 2.种类 3.规格(成条、成卷的宽度或成张的边长)4.签约日期 5.品牌(中文或外文名称,无品牌请申报厂商)
48064000	1.品名 2.种类 3.规格(成卷的宽度或成张的边长)4.签约日期 5.品牌(中文或外文名称,无品牌请申报厂商)
4807	1.品名 2.加工方法(黏合多层)3.加工程度(未经表面涂布或未浸渍)4.规格(成条、成卷的宽度或成张的边长)5.签约日期 6.品牌(中文或外文名称,无品牌请申报厂商)
48081000	1.品名 2.种类(瓦楞纸、皱纹牛皮纸等)3.规格(成条、成卷的宽度或成张的边长)4.签约日期 5.品牌(中文或外文名称,无品牌请申报厂商)
48084000	1.品名 2.用途 3.种类 4.规格(成条、成卷的宽度或成张的边长)5.签约日期 6.品牌(中文或外文名称,无品牌请申报厂商)
48089000	1.品名 2.用途 3.种类 4.规格(成条、成卷的宽度或成张的边长)5.签约日期 6.品牌(中文或外文名称,无品牌请申报厂商)
48092000	1.品名 2.种类(自印复写纸)3.加工程度(涂布或浸渍)4.规格(成条、成卷的宽度或成张的边长)5.签约日期 6.品牌(中文或外文名称,无品牌请申报厂商)
48099000	1.品名 2.种类(复写纸、拷贝纸等)3.加工程度(涂布或浸渍)4.规格(成条、成卷的宽度或成张的边长)5.签约日期 6.品牌(中文或外文名称,无品牌请申报厂商)
48101	1.品名 2.用途(书写、印刷等)3.种类(牛皮纸、白板纸、铜版纸等)4.状态(成卷或张等)5.加工程度(单面或双面涂布无机物、漂白)6.规格(成条、成卷的宽度或成张的边 长)7.每平方米克重 8.纤维种类和含量 9.签约日期 10.品牌(中文或外文名称,无品牌请申报厂商)
48102	1.品名 2.用途(书写、印刷)3.种类(牛皮纸、白板纸、铜版纸等)4.状态(成卷或张等)5.加工程度(单面或双面涂布无机物、漂白)6.规格(成条、成卷的宽度或成张的边 长)7.每平方米克重 8.纤维种类和含量 9.签约日期 10.品牌(中文或外文名称,无品牌请申报厂商)

商品编码	申报要素
48103	1.品名 2.用途(包装等)3.种类(牛皮纸、白板纸、铜版纸等)4.状态(成卷或张等)5.加工程度(单面或双面涂布无机物、漂白)6.规格(成条、成卷的宽度或成张的边长)7.每平方米克重 8.纤维种类和含量 9.签约日期 10.品牌(中文或外文名称,无品牌请申报厂商)
48109	1.品名 2.用途(书写、印刷等)3.种类(牛皮纸、白板纸、铜版纸等)4.状态(成卷或张等)5.加工程度(单面或双面涂布无机物、漂白)6.规格(成条、成卷的宽度或成张的边 长)7.每平方米克重 8.纤维种类和含量 9.签约日期 10.品牌(中文或外文名称,无品牌请申报厂商)
4811	1.品名 2.种类 3.加工程度(涂布、浸渍、饰面、漂白等)4.形状(成卷或成张矩形等)5. 每平方米克重 6.品牌(中文或外文名称)7.型号
4812	1.品名 2.材质(纸浆制)3.外观(块、板、片)4.品牌(中文或外文名称,无品牌请申报厂商)
48131000	1.品名 2.规格(如成小本或管状、宽度)3.品牌(中文或外文名称,无品牌请申报厂商)
48132000	1.品名 2.规格(成卷、宽度)3.品牌(中文或外文名称,无品牌请申报厂商)
48139000	1.品名 2.规格(宽度等)3.品牌(中文或外文名称,无品牌请申报厂商)
48142000	1.品名 2.加工程度(用木粒或草粒、塑料、编结材料等饰面、涂面)3.品牌(中文或外文名称,无品牌请申报厂商)4.规格尺 寸 5.签约日期
48149000	1.品名 2.加工程度(用木粒或草粒、塑料、编结材料等饰面、涂面)3.是否为窗用透明纸 4.品牌(中文或外文名称,无品牌请申报厂商)5.规格尺寸 6.签约日期
48162000	1.品名 2.种类(自印复写纸、热敏转印纸等)3.规格(成条、成卷的宽度或成张的边长)4.品牌(中文或外文名称,无品牌请申报厂商)
48169010	1.品名 2.种类(自印复写纸、热敏转印纸等)3.规格(成条、成卷的宽度或成张的边长)4.品牌(中文或外文名称,无品牌请申报厂商)
48169090	1.品名 2.种类(复写纸、拷贝纸、转印纸、油印蜡纸、胶版纸等)3.规格(成条、成卷的宽度或成张的边长)4.品牌(中文或外文名称,无品牌请申报厂商)
4817	1.品名 2.材质(纸制)
4818	1.品名 2.用途(家庭、卫生、医院用等)3.材质(纸制)4.种类(卫生纸、纸台布等)5.规格(成条、成卷的宽度或成张的边长)
48191000	1.品名 2.材质(瓦楞纸或纸板制)
48192000	1.品名 2.材质
48193000	1.品名 2.材质 3.底宽长度
48194000	1.品名 2.材质 3.底宽长度
48195000	1.品名 2.材质
48196000	1.品名 2.材质
4820	1.品名 2.材质
4821	1.品名 2.材质 3.加工程度(印制、非印制)
48221000	1.品名 2.用途(纺织纱线用等)3.材质(纸制)
48229000	1.品名 2.用途 3.材质(纸制)
48232000	1.品名 2.材质(纸制)3.形状(圆形、三角形等)4.规格
48234000	1.品名 2.用途(已印制的自动记录器用等)3.材质(纸制)4.规格
48236100	1.品名 2.材质(竹浆纸制)3.种类(盘、碟、盆、杯等)4.规格
482369	1.品名 2.材质 3.种类(盘、碟、盆、杯等)4.规格
48237000	1.品名 2.加工方法(压制、模制)3.材质(纸浆制)4.规格
48239010	1.品名 2.用途 3.材质(以纸或纸板为底制成)4.规格
48239020	1.品名 2.材质(纸制)3.规格
48239030	1.品名 2.材质(纸制)3.规格
48239090	1.品名 2.材质(纸制)3.形状(圆形、三角形等)4.规格
4901	1.品名 2.种类(字典、百科全书等)3.状态(成册、单张)
4902	1.品名 2.出版周期(日刊、周刊等)
4903	1.品名 2.用途(儿童用)3.种类(图画书、绘画或涂色书)
4904	1.品名 2.种类(原稿或印本等)
49052000	1.品名 2.状态(成册)
49059000	1.品名
4906	1.品名(设计图纸原稿或手稿及其复制件)
49070010	1.品名 2.外观(新的)3.种类(小型张、四方联等)
49070020	1.品名 2.外观(新的)
49070030	1.品名 2.种类(证券、特许权等)
49070090	1.品名 2.种类(证券、特许权等)3.信息内容物种类(如软件、数据、互联网内容物或服务等)4.给予信息内容物使用权的种类(如存取、复制或密钥等)
4908	1.品名 2.加工方法(釉转印等)
4909	1.品名 2.加工方法(印刷或有图画等)
4910	1.品名
49111	1.品名 2.用途(有商业价值、无商业价值)
49119100	1.品名 2.用途(有商业价值、无商业价值等)
491199	1.品名 2.材质 3.用途(有商业价值、无商业价值等)4.印刷内容
5001	1.品名 2.用途(用于缫丝)3.种类
50020011	1.品名 2.种类(桑蚕厂丝)3.是否加捻
50020012	1.品名 2.种类(桑蚕土丝)3.是否加捻
50020013	1.品名 2.种类(桑蚕双宫丝)3.是否加捻
50020019	1.品名 2.种类 3.是否加捻
50020020	1.品名 2.种类(柞蚕丝)3.是否加捻
50020090	1.品名 2.种类 3.是否加捻
5003	1.品名 2.是否梳理
5004	1.品名 2.是否供零售用
5005	1.品名 2.种类(绢纺纱线等)3.是否供零售用 4.成分含量
5006	1.品名 2.种类(绢纺纱线、蚕胶丝、丝纱线、䌷纱线)3.是否供零售用 4.成分含量
5007	1.品名 2.种类(䌷丝、桑蚕丝、绢丝、柞蚕丝等)3.织造方法(机织)4.染整方法(漂白、未漂白、色织)5.成分含量 6.幅宽
51011100	1.品名 2.加工程度(含脂、脱脂、碳化等)3.剪羊毛请注明细度(微米数)4.剪羊毛请注明长度 5.剪羊毛请注明草杂含量
51011900	1.品名 2.加工程度(含脂、脱脂、碳化等)
51012100	1.品名 2.加工程度(未梳、含脂、脱脂、碳化等)3.剪羊毛请注明细度(微米数)4.剪羊毛请注明长度 5.剪羊毛请注明草杂含量
51012900	1.品名 2.加工程度(未梳、含脂、脱脂、碳化等)
51013000	1.品名 2.加工程度(未梳、含脂、脱脂、碳化等)
51021100	1.品名 2.种类(未梳理的兔毛、克什米尔山羊毛、山羊绒、骆驼毛)

商品编码	申报要素
51021910	1.品名 2.种类(未梳理的兔毛、克什米尔山羊毛、山羊绒、骆驼毛)
51021920	1.品名 2.种类(未梳理的兔毛、克什米尔山羊毛、山羊绒、骆驼毛)3.颜色 4.纤维长度 5.净绒率
51021930	1.品名 2.种类(未梳理的兔毛、克什米尔山羊毛、山羊绒、骆驼毛)
51021990	1.品名 2.种类(未梳理的兔毛、克什米尔山羊毛、山羊绒、骆驼毛)
51022000	1.品名 2.种类(未梳理的兔毛、克什米尔山羊毛、山羊绒、骆驼毛)
5103	1.品名 2.种类(羊毛落毛、动物细毛或粗毛废料)
5104	1.品名 2.种类(源于羊毛、动物粗、细毛等的回收纤维)
51051000	1.品名 2.种类(羊毛条、羊毛片毛、兔毛、克什米尔山羊毛)3.梳理方法(粗梳或精梳)
51052100	1.品名 2.种类(羊毛条、羊毛片毛、兔毛、克什米尔山羊毛)3.梳理方法(粗梳或精梳)
51052900	1.品名 2.种类(羊毛条、羊毛片毛、兔毛、克什米尔山羊毛)3.梳理方法(粗梳或精梳)4.其他精梳羊毛请注明支数 5.其他精梳羊毛请注明细度
51053	1.品名 2.种类(羊毛条、羊毛片毛、兔毛、克什米尔山羊毛)3.梳理方法(粗梳或精梳)
51054000	1.品名 2.种类(羊毛条、羊毛片毛、兔毛、克什米尔山羊毛)3.梳理方法(粗梳或精梳)
5106	1.品名 2.梳理方法(粗梳)3.是否供零售用 4.成分含量
5107	1.品名 2.梳理方法(精梳)3.是否供零售用 4.成分含量
5108	1.品名 2.梳理方式(精梳、粗梳)3.是否供零售用 4.成分含量
5109	1.品名 2.种类(羊毛等)3.是否供零售用 4.成分含量
5110	1.品名 2.种类(马毛等粗毛纱线)3.成分含量
5111	1.品名 2.种类(羊毛、驼马毛、美洲驼毛等)3.织造方法(机织)4.梳理方法(粗梳)5.成分含量 6.幅宽 7.每平方米克重
5112	1.品名 2.种类(羊毛、驼马毛、美洲驼毛等)3.织造方法(机织)4.梳理方法(精梳)5.成分含量 6.幅宽 7.每平方米克重
5113	1.品名 2.种类(马毛等)3.织造方法(机织) 4.成分含量 5.幅宽 6.每平方米克重
5201	1.品名 2.是否梳理 3.纤维长度 4.品级 5.转(非转)基因请注明
52021000	1.品名 2.来源(废棉线、回收纤维等)3.成分含量 4.颜色
52029100	1.品名 2.来源(废棉线、回收纤维等)3.成分含量
52029900	1.品名 2.来源(废棉线、回收纤维等)3.成分含量 4.棉种类(包括精落、抄斩、车肚、统破籽、回丝等)
5203	1.品名 2.是否梳理 3.纤维长度 4.转(非转)基因请注明
5204	1.品名 2.是否供零售用 3.成分含量 4.纱线细度 5.每只重量 6.是否上浆 7.终捻捻向
5205	1.品名 2.梳理方法(粗梳、精梳)3.纱线形态(单纱、股线或缆线)4.是否供零售用 5.成分含量 6.纱线细度 7.品牌(中文或外文名称)8.加工工艺(环锭纺、气流纺、赛络纺等)9.签约日期
5206	1.品名 2.梳理方法(粗梳、精梳)3.纱线形态(单纱、股线或缆线)4.是否供零售用 5.成分含量 6.纱线细度 7.品牌(中文或外文名称,无品牌请申报厂商)
5207	1.品名 2.是否供零售用 3.成分含量
5208	1.品名 2.织造方法(机织物)3.染整方法(漂白、未漂白、色织、染色、印花等)4.组织结构(平纹、三线或四线斜纹、四线双面斜纹或十字斜纹、其他斜 纹)5.成分含量 6.幅宽 7.每平方米克重 7.品牌(中文或外文名称)
5209	1.品名 2.织造方法(机织物)3.染整方法(漂白、未漂白、色织、染色、印花等)4.组织结构(平纹、粗斜纹、其他三线或四线斜纹、其他斜纹等)5.成分含量 6.幅宽 7.每平方米克重 8.品牌(中文或外文名称)
5210	1.品名 2.织造方法(机织物)3.染整方法(漂白、未漂白、色织、染色、印花等)4.组织结构(平纹、三线或四线斜纹、四线双面斜纹或十字斜纹、其他斜纹等)5.注明与其混纺的化纤是长丝还是短纤 6.成分含量 7.幅宽 8.每平方米克重 9.品牌(中文或外文名称)
5211	1.品名 2.织造方法(机织物)3.染整方法(漂白、未漂白、色织、染色、印花等)4.组织结构(平纹、粗斜纹、其他三线或四线斜纹、其他斜纹等)5.注明与其混纺的化纤是长丝还是短纤 6.成分含量 7.幅宽 8.每平方米克重 9.品牌(中文或外文名称)
5212	1.品名 2.织造方法(机织物)3.染整方法(漂白、未漂白、色织、染色、印花等)4.组织结构(平纹、斜纹等)5.成分含量 6.幅宽 7.每平方米克重 8.品牌(中文或外文名称)
53011000	1.品名 2.加工程度(生的、经沤制)
53012100	1.品名 2.加工程度(破开或打成)3.可纺支数 4.长度
53012900	1.品名 2.加工程度(栉梳等)
53013000	1.品名 2.是否为短纤或废麻 3.种类(二粗、机械短麻、落麻)
53021000	1.品名 2.加工程度(生的、沤制的)
53029000	1.品名 2.加工程度(生的、沤制的)3.是否为短纤或废麻
53031000	1.品名 2.种类(黄麻、洋麻、菽麻等)3.加工程度(未纺制的、生的或沤制的)
53039000	1.品名 2.种类(黄麻、洋麻、菽麻等)3.加工程度(未纺制的、生的或沤制的)4.是否为短纤或废麻
53050011	1.品名 2.种类(苎麻)3.加工程度(生的)
53050012	1.品名 2.种类(苎麻)3.加工程度(经加工但未纺制的)
53050013	1.品名 2.种类(苎麻)3.是否为短纤或废麻
53050019	1.品名 2.种类(苎麻)
53050020	1.品名 2.种类(蕉麻)3.加工程度(生的或经加工但未纺制的)
5305009	1.品名 2.种类(椰壳纤维、西沙尔麻等)3.是否为短纤或废麻 4.用途 5.加工程度(生的、经加工未纺制、梳理、机卷、棕绳等)6.签约日期
5306	1.品名 2.纱线形态(单纱、股线或缆线)3.纱线细度
5307	1.品名 2.种类(黄麻、洋麻、菽麻等)3.纱线形态(单纱、股线或缆线)4.纱线细度
53081000	1.品名 2.种类(椰壳纤维纱线)3.成分含量 4.纱线细度
53082000	1.品名 2.种类(大麻纱线)3.成分含量 4.纱线细度
5308901	1.品名 2.种类(苎麻纱线)3.染整方法(漂白、未漂白、色织)4.成分含量 5.纱线细度
5308909	1.品名 2.种类(纸纱线等)3.成分含量 4.纱线细度
5309	1.品名 2.织造方法(机 织)3.染整方法(漂白、未漂白、色织)4.成分含量 5.幅宽 6.每平方米克重
5310	1.品名 2.种类(黄麻、洋麻、菽麻等)3.织造方法(机织)4.染整工艺(漂白、未漂白、色织)5.成分含量 6.幅宽 7.每平方米克重
5311	1.品名 2.种类(黄麻、洋麻、菽麻等)3.织造方法(机织)4.染整工艺(漂白、未漂白、色织)5.成分含量 6.幅宽 7.每平方米克重
5401	1.品名 2.是否供零售用 3.纤维成分(聚酯等)4.每只重量 5.是否上浆 6.终捻捻向
54021	1.品名 2.种类(高强力纱或变形纱线等)3.纱线形态(单纱、股线或缆线) 4.是否供零售用 5.纤维成分(聚酰胺等)6.纱线细度
54022000	1.品名 2.种类(高强力纱或变形纱线等)3.纱线形态(单纱、股线或缆线) 4.是否供零售用 5.纤维成分(聚酯等)6.纱线细度
54023	1.品名 2.种类(高强力纱或变形纱线等)3.纱线形态(单纱、股线或缆线) 4.是否供零售用 5.纤维成分(聚酯等)6.纱线细度
540244	1.品名 2.种类(高强力纱或变形纱线等)3.纱线形态(单纱、股线或缆线) 4.高强纱请注明用途 5.是否供零售用 6.纤维成分(聚酯等)7.纱线细度 8.是否加捻(如加捻请注明捻度)
540245	1.品名 2.种类(高强力纱或变形纱线等)3.纱线形态(单纱、股线或缆线) 4.高强纱请注明用途 5.是否供零售用 6.纤维成分(聚酰胺等)7.纱线细度 8.是否加捻(如加捻请注明捻度)
54024600	1.品名 2.种类(高强力纱或变形纱线等)3.纱线形态(单纱、股线或缆线) 4.高强纱请注明用途 5.是否供零售用 6.纤维成分(聚酯等)7.纱线细度 8.是否加捻(如加捻请注明捻度)
54024700	1.品名 2.种类(高强力纱或变形纱线等)3.纱线形态(单纱、股线或缆线) 4.高强纱请注明用途 5.是否供零售用 6.纤维成分(聚酯等)7.纱线细度 8.是否加捻(如加捻请注明捻度)
54024800	1.品名 2.种类(高强力纱或变形纱线等)3.纱线形态(单纱、股线或缆线) 4.高强纱请注明用途 5.是否供零售用 6.纤维成分(聚丙烯)7.纱线细度 8.是否加捻(如加捻请注明捻度)
54024910	1.品名 2.种类(高强力纱或变形纱线等)3.纱线形态(单纱、股线或缆线) 4.高强纱请注明用途 5.是否供零售用 6.纤维成分(聚酯等)7.纱线细度 8.是否加捻(如加捻请注明捻度)9.断裂强度
54024990	1.品名 2.种类(高强力纱或变形纱线等)3.纱线形态(单纱、股线或缆线) 4.高强纱请注明用途 5.是否供零售用 6.纤维成分(聚酯等)7.纱线细度 8.是否加捻(如加捻请注明捻度)
540251	1.品名 2.种类(高强力纱或变形纱线等)3.纱线形态(单纱、股线或缆线) 4.是否供零售用 5.纤维成分(聚酰胺等)6.纱线细度 7.是否加捻(如加捻请注明捻度)
54025200	1.品名 2.种类(高强力纱或变形纱线等)3.纱线形态(单纱、股线或缆线) 4.是否供零售用 5.纤维成分(聚酯等)6.纱线细度 7.是否加捻(如加捻请注明捻度)
54025300	1.品名 2.种类(高强力纱或变形纱线等)3.纱线形态(单纱、股线或缆线) 4.是否供零售用 5.纤维成分(聚丙烯)6.纱线细度 7.是否加捻(如加捻请注明捻度)
54025920	1.品名 2.种类(高强力纱或变形纱线等)3.纱线形态(单纱、股线或缆线) 4.是否供零售用 5.纤维成分(聚乙烯)6.纱线细度 7.是否加捻(如加捻请注明捻度)8.断裂强度
54025990	1.品名 2.种类(高强力纱或变形纱线等)3.纱线形态(单纱、股线或缆线) 4.是否供零售用 5.纤维成分(聚酯等)6.纱线细度 7.是否加捻(如加捻请注明捻度)
54026	1.品名 2.种类(高强力纱或变形纱线等)3.纱线形态(单纱、股线或缆线) 4.是否供零售用 5.纤维成分(聚酯等)6.纱线细度
5403	1.品名 2.种类(高强力纱或变形纱线等)3.纱线形态(单纱、股线或缆线) 4.是否供零售用 5.纤维成分(如粘胶等)6.纱线细度 7.纱线捻度 8.高强力纱需注明断裂强度(单位:厘牛顿/特克斯)9.股数
5404	1.品名 2.种类(单丝、扁条等)3.纤维成分 4.单丝细度或扁条表观宽度
5405	1.品名 2.种类(单丝、扁条等)3.纤维成分 4.单丝细度或扁条表观宽度
5406	1.品名 2.是否供零售用 3.纤维成分
54071	1.品名 2.织造方法(机织、平行纱层叠黏合)3.染整方法(漂白、色织、染色等)4.组织结构(平纹、斜纹、缎纹等)5.成分含量 6.幅宽 7.每平方米克重 8.是否为高强力纱 9.品牌(中文或外文名称)
54072000	1.品名 2.织造方法(机织、平行纱层叠黏合)3.染整方法(漂白、色织、染色等)4.组织结构(平纹、斜纹、缎纹等)5.成分含量 6.幅宽 7.每平方米克重 8.品牌(中文或外文名称)
54073000	1.品名 2.织造方法(机织、平行纱层叠黏合)3.染整方法(漂白、色织、染色等)4.组织结构(平纹、斜纹、缎纹等)5.成分含量 6.幅宽 7.每平方米克重 8.品牌(中文或外文名称)
54074	1.品名 2.织造方法(机织、平行纱层叠黏合)3.染整方法(漂白、色织、染色等)4.组织结构(平纹、斜纹、缎纹等)5.成分含量 6.幅宽 7.每平方米克重 8.品牌(中文或外文名称)
54075	1.品名 2.织造方法(机织、平行纱层叠黏合)3.染整方法(漂白、色织、染色等)4.组织结构(平纹、斜纹、缎纹等)5.成分含量(聚酯变形长丝等成分及含量)6.幅宽 7.每平方米克重 8.品牌(中文或外文名称)
54076	1.品名 2.织造方法(机织、平行纱层叠黏合)3.染整方法(漂白、色织、染色等)4.组织结构(平纹、斜纹、缎纹等)5.成分含量(聚酯非变形长丝等成分及含量)6.幅宽 7.每平方米克重 8.品牌(中文或外文名称)
54077	1.品名 2.织造方法(机织、平行纱层叠黏合)3.染整方法(漂白、色织、染色等)4.组织结构(平纹、斜纹、缎纹等)5.合成纤维种类(长丝、短纤)6.成分含量 7.幅宽 8.每平方米克重 9.品牌(中文或外文名称)
54078	1.品名 2.织造方法(机织、平行纱层叠黏合)3.染整方法(漂白、色织、染色等)4.组织结构(平纹、斜纹、缎纹等)5.成分含量 6.幅宽 7.每平方米克重 8.品牌(中文或外文名称)
54079	1.品名 2.织造方法(机织、平行纱层叠黏合)3.染整方法(漂白、色织、染色等)4.组织结构(平纹、斜纹、缎纹等)5.成分含量 6.幅宽 7.每平方米克重 8.品牌(中文或外文名称)
5408	1.品名 2.织造方法(机织、平行纱层叠黏合)3.染整方法(漂白、色织、染色等)4.组织结构(平纹、斜纹、缎纹等)5.成分含量 6.幅宽 7.每平方米克重 8.品牌(中文或外文名称)
5501	1.品名 2.纤维成分 3.单丝细度 4.丝束长度 5.是否加捻(如加捻请注明捻 度)6.丝束总细度
5502	1.品名 2.纤维成分 3.单丝细度 4.丝束长度 5.是否加捻(如加捻请注明捻 度)6.丝束总细度
5503	1.品名 2.加工程度(未梳、未经纺前加工)3.纤维成分 4.长度 5.细度
5504	1.品名 2.加工程度(未梳、未经纺前加工)3.人造纤维种类 4.细度 5.长度
5505	1.品名 2.来源(落绵、废纱、回收纤维)3.纤维成分 4.颜色(白色、杂色等)
5506	1.品名 2.加工程度(已梳、经纺前加工)3.纤维成分
5507	1.品名 2.加工程度(已梳、经纺前加工)3.纤维成分

商品编码	申报要素
5508	1.品名 2.成分含量 3.纱线细度 4.每只重量 5.是否上浆 6.终捻捻向 7.是否供零售用
5509	1.品名 2.种类(单纱、股线、缆线)3.是否供零售用 4.成分含量 5.纱线细度 6.股线注明股数
5510	1.品名 2.种类(单纱、股线、缆线)3.是否供零售用 4.成分含量 5.纱线细度 6.股线注明股数
5511	1.品名 2.种类(单纱、股线、缆线)3.是否供零售用 4.成分含量 5.纱线细度
5512	1.品名 2.织造方法(机 织)3.染整方法(漂白、未漂白、色织、染色等)4.组织结构(平纹、斜纹、缎纹等)5.合成纤维种类(长丝、短纤)6.成分含量 7.幅宽 8.每平方米克重 9.品牌(中文或外文名称)
5513	1.品名 2.织造方法(机 织)3.染整方法(漂白、未漂白、色织、染色等)4.组织结构(平纹、三线或四线斜纹、四线双面斜纹或十字斜纹、其他斜纹等) 5.成分含量 6.幅宽 7.每平方米克重 8.品牌(中文或外文名称)
5514	1.品名 2.织造方法(机 织)3.染整方法(漂白、未漂白、色织、染色等)4.组织结构(平纹、三线或四线斜纹、四线双面斜纹或十字斜纹、其他斜纹等) 5.成分含量 6.幅宽 7.每平方米克重 8.品牌(中文或外文名称)
5515	1.品名 2.织造方法(机 织)3.染整方法(漂白、未漂白、色织、染色等)4.组织结构(平纹、斜纹、缎纹等)5.成分含量 6.幅宽 7.每平方米克重 8.品牌(中文或外文名称)
5516	1.品名 2.织造方法(机织)3.染整方法(漂白、未漂白、色织、染色等)4.组织结构(平纹、斜纹、缎纹等)5.成分含量 6.幅宽 7.每平方米克重 8.品牌(中文或外文名称)
56012	1.品名 2.纤维成分(如棉制)
56013000	1.品名 2.状态(纤维屑、球结)
5602	1.品名 2.加工方法(针刺缝编、涂布、浸渍、层压、包覆等)3.纤维成分含量
560311	1.品名 2.加工方法(水刺、纺粘、热风、针刺、湿法、熔喷、闪蒸、其他(需注明)3.处理工艺(涂布、浸渍、层压、包覆等)4.是否化学纤维长丝制 5.每平方米克重 6.成分含量 7.用途 8.品牌(中文或外文名称,无品牌请申报厂商)
560312	1.品名 2.加工方法(水刺、纺粘、热风、针刺、湿法、熔喷、闪蒸、其他(需注明)3.处理工艺(涂布、浸渍、层压、包覆等)4.是否化学纤维长丝制 5.每平方米克重 6.成分含量 7.用途 8.品牌(中文或外文名称,无品牌请申报厂商)
560313	1.品名 2.加工方法(水刺、纺粘、热风、针刺、湿法、熔喷、闪蒸、其他(需注明)3.处理工艺(涂布、浸渍、层压、包覆等)4.是否化学纤维长丝制 5.每平方米克重 6.成分含量 7.用途 8.品牌(中文或外文名称,无品牌请申报厂商)
56031410	1.品名 2.加工方法(水刺、纺粘、热风、针刺、湿法、熔喷、闪蒸、其他(需注明)3.处理工艺(涂布、浸渍、层压、包覆等)4.是否化学纤维长丝制 5.每平方米克重 6.成分含量 7.用途 8.品牌(中文或外文名称,无品牌请申报厂商)
56031490	1.品名 2.加工方法(水刺、纺粘、热风、针刺、湿法、熔喷、闪蒸、其他(需注明)3.处理工艺(涂布、浸渍、层压、包覆等)4.化学纤维长丝制应注明 5.每平方米克重 6.成分含量 7.用途 8.品牌(中文或外文名称,无品牌请申报厂商)或厂商(中文或外文名 称)
56039110	1.品名 2.加工方法(水刺、纺粘、热风、针刺、湿法、熔喷、闪蒸、其他(需注明)3.处理工艺(涂布、浸渍、层压、包覆等)4.每平方米克重 5.成分含量 6.用途 7.品牌(中文或外文名称,无品牌请申报厂商)
56039190	1.品名 2.加工方法(水刺、纺粘、热风、针刺、湿法、熔喷、闪蒸、其他(需注明)3.处理工艺(涂布、浸渍、层压、包覆等)4.每平方米克重 5.成分含量 6.用途 7.品牌(中文或外文名称,无品牌请申报厂商)
56039210	1.品名 2.加工方法(水刺、纺粘、热风、针刺、湿法、熔喷、闪蒸、其他(需注明)3.处理工艺(涂布、浸渍、层压、包覆等)4.每平方米克重 5.成分含量 6.用途 7.品牌(中文或外文名称,无品牌请申报厂商)
56039290	1.品名 2.加工方法(水刺、纺粘、热风、针刺、湿法、熔喷、闪蒸、其他(需注明)3.处理工艺(涂布、浸渍、层压、包覆等)4.每平方米克重 5.成分含量 6.用途 7.品牌(中文或外文名称,无品牌请申报厂商)
56039310	1.品名 2.加工方法(水刺、纺粘、热风、针刺、湿法、熔喷、闪蒸、其他(需注明)3.处理工艺(涂布、浸渍、层压、包覆等)4.每平方米克重 5.成分含量 6.用途 7.品牌(中文或外文名称,无品牌请申报厂商)
56039390	1.品名 2.加工方法(水刺、纺粘、热风、针刺、湿法、熔喷、闪蒸、其他(需注明)3.处理工艺(涂布、浸渍、层压、包覆等)4.每平方米克重 5.成分含量 6.用途 7.品牌(中文或外文名称,无品牌请申报厂商)
56039410	1.品名 2.加工方法(水刺、纺粘、热风、针刺、湿法、熔喷、闪蒸、其他(需注明)3.处理工艺(涂布、浸渍、层压、包覆等)4.每平方米克重 5.成分含量 6.用途 7.品牌(中文或外文名称,无品牌请申报厂商)
56039490	1.品名 2.加工方法(水刺、纺粘、热风、针刺、湿法、熔喷、闪蒸、其他(需注明)3.处理工艺(涂布、浸渍、层压、包覆等)4.每平方米克重 5.成分含量 6.用途 7.品牌(中文或外文名称,无品牌请申报厂商)
5604	1.品名 2.加工方法(浸渍、涂布或包覆等)3.内层材质 4.外层材质
5605	1.品名 2.含金属纱线 3.成分含量
5606	1.品名 2.种类(绳绒及粗松花线、纵行起圈纱线等)
56072100	1.品名 2.用途(包扎用等)3.纤维成分
56072900	1.品名 2.纤维成分
56074100	1.品名 2.用途(包扎用等)3.纤维成分
56074900	1.品名 2.纤维成分
56075000	1.品名 2.纤维成分
56079	1.品名 2.纤维成分
56081100	1.品名 2.用途(渔网、购物网等)3.纤维成分 4.成网方式(结制)
56081900	1.品名 2.用途(渔网、购物网等)3.纤维成分
56089000	1.品名 2.用途(渔网、购物网等)3.纤维成分
5609	1.品名 2.用途 3.纤维成分
5701	1.品名 2.织造方法(栽绒、手织等)3.纤维成分 4.规格尺寸
57021000	1.品名 2.织造方法(机织、手织等)3.纤维成分 4.规格尺寸
57022000	1.品名 2.织造方法(栽绒、手织等)3.纤维成分 4.规格尺寸
57023	1.品名 2.织造方法(栽绒、手织等)3.纤维成分 4.规格尺寸
57024	1.品名 2.织造方法(栽绒、手织等)3.纤维成分 4.规格尺寸
57025	1.品名 2.织造方法(栽绒、手织等)3.纤维成分 4.规格尺寸
57029	1.品名 2.织造方法(栽绒、手织等)3.纤维成分 4.规格尺寸

商品编码	申报要素
5703	1.品名 2.织造方法(簇 绒)3.纤维成分 4.固定方式(施胶、绒头固定方法等)5.规格尺寸
5704	1.品名 2.织造方法(毡呢)3.是否为铺地制品 4.纤维成分 5.规格尺寸(最大表面面积)
5705	1.品名 2.是否为铺地制 品 3.纤维成分 4.是否含有膨润土 5.规格尺寸 6.织造方法(无纺、黏绒、植绒、针织等)7.固定方式(施胶、涂层黏合等)
58011000	1.品名 2.织造方法(机织)3.幅宽 4.纤维成分
58012100	1.品名 2.织造方法(机织)3.起绒方式(经起绒、纬起绒或绳绒)4.幅宽 5.纤维成分
58012200	1.品名 2.织造方法(机织)3.割绒请注明 4.幅宽 5.纤维成分
58012300	1.品名 2.织造方法(机织)3.起绒方式(经起绒、纬起绒或绳绒)4.幅宽 5.纤维成分
58012600	1.品名 2.织造方法(机织)3.起绒方式(经起绒、纬起绒或绳绒)4.幅宽 5.纤维成分
58012710	1.品名 2.织造方法(机织)3.起绒方式(经起绒、纬起绒或绳绒)4.幅宽 5.纤维成分
58012720	1.品名 2.织造方法(机织)3.起绒方式(经起绒、纬起绒或绳绒)4.是否为割绒 5.幅宽 6.纤维成分
58013100	1.品名 2.织造方法(机织)3.起绒方式(经起绒、纬起绒或绳绒)4.幅宽 5.纤维成分
58013200	1.品名 2.织造方法(机织)3.起绒方式(经起绒、纬起绒或绳绒)4.是否为割绒 5.幅宽 6.纤维成分
58013300	1.品名 2.织造方法(机织)3.起绒方式(经起绒、纬起绒或绳绒)4.幅宽 5.纤维成分
58013600	1.品名 2.织造方法(机织)3.起绒方式(经起绒、纬起绒或绳绒)4.幅宽 5.纤维成分
58013710	1.品名 2.织造方法(机织)3.起绒方式(经起绒、纬起绒或绳绒)4.幅宽 5.纤维成分
58013720	1.品名 2.织造方法(机织)3.起绒方式(经起绒、纬起绒或绳绒)4.是否为割绒 5.幅宽 6.纤维成分
58019010	1.品名 2.织造方法(机织)3.幅宽 4.纤维成分
58019090	1.品名 2.织造方法(机织)3.起绒方式(经起绒、纬起绒或绳绒)4.幅宽 5.纤维成分
58021010	1.品名 2.织造方法(机织)3.起绒方式(簇绒或毛圈)4.是否漂白 5.幅宽 6.纤维成分
58021090	1.品名 2.织造方法(机织)3.起绒方式(簇绒或毛圈)4.幅宽 5.纤维成分
58022	1.品名 2.织造方法(机织)3.起绒方式(簇绒或毛圈)4.幅宽 5.纤维成分
58023	1.品名 2.织造方法(机织)3.起绒方式(簇绒或毛圈)4.幅宽 5.纤维成分
5803	1.品名 2.组织结构(纱罗)3.幅宽 4.纤维成分
5804	1.品名 2.种类(网眼、花边)3.织造方法(机制、手工制)4.幅宽 5.纤维成分
5805	1.品名 2.用途(装饰用)3.种类(手工针绣嵌花装饰毯等)4.幅宽 5.纤维成分
58061	1.品名 2.织造方法(机织)3.起绒方式(毛巾、绳绒等)4.成分含量 5.幅宽
58062000	1.品名 2.织造方法(机织)3.成分含量 4.幅宽
58063	1.品名 2.织造方法(机织)3.成分含量 4.幅宽
58064	1.品名 2.织造方法(机织)3.成分含量 4.幅宽
5807	1.品名 2.织造方法(机织、针织等)3.成分含量 4.刺绣请注明
5808	1.品名 2.规格(成匹)3.成分含量
5809	1.品名 2.用途(衣着、装饰等)3.织造方法(金属线或含金属纱线机织)4.成分含量
5810	1.品名 2.织造方法(刺绣)3.是否见底布 4.成分含量
5811	1.品名 2.表面成分含量 3.胎料材质
5901	1.品名 2.用途 3.处理材质 4.成分含量 5.处理工艺(涂布、浸渍、层压)
5902	1.品名 2.成分含量 3.是否高强力纱制 4.纱线细度 5.股 数 6.织物密度 7.幅宽 8.品牌(中文或外文名称)
59031010	1.品名 2.处理材质 3.成分含量 4.处理工艺(涂布、浸渍、层压)5.是否双面涂层或包覆
59031020	1.品名 2.处理材质 3.成分含量 4.处理工艺(涂布、浸渍、层压)5.是否双面涂层或包覆 6.聚氯乙烯塑料是否为泡沫塑料请注 明 7.织物是否仅起增强作用请注明
59031090	1.品名 2.处理材质 3.成分含量 4.处理工艺(涂布、浸渍、层压)5.是否双面涂层或包覆
59032010	1.品名 2.处理材质 3.成分含量 4.处理工艺(涂布、浸渍、层压)5.是否双面涂层或包覆
59032020	1.品名 2.处理材质 3.成分含量 4.处理工艺(涂布、浸渍、层压)5.是否双面涂层或包覆 6.聚氨酯塑料是否为泡沫塑料请注明 7.织物是否仅起增强作用请注明 8.其他塑料是否为泡沫塑料请注明
59032090	1.品名 2.处理材质 3.成分含量 4.处理工艺(涂布、浸渍、层压)5.是否双面涂层或包覆
59039	1.品名 2.处理材质 3.成分含量 4.处理工艺(涂布、浸渍、层压)5.是否双面涂层或包覆
5904	1.品名
5905	1.品名 2.是否糊墙用 3.是否为纸衬背 4.表面层纤维成分含量 5.幅宽
59061	1.品名 2.织造方法(机织、针织、钩编等)3.处理材质(橡胶)4.是否是胶粘带、绝缘带 5.幅宽
59069100	1.品名 2.织造方法(机织、针织、钩编等)3.处理材质(橡胶)4.幅宽
59069910	1.品名 2.织造方法(机织、针织、钩编等)3.处理材质(橡胶)4.是否是胶粘带、绝缘带 5.幅宽
59069990	1.品名 2.织造方法(机织、针织、钩编等)3.处理材质(橡胶)4.幅宽
59070010	1.品名 2.处理材质 3.是否为绝缘带
59070020	1.品名 2.是否为已绘制画布 3.处理材质
59070090	1.品名 2.处理材质
5908	1.品名 2.用途
5909	1.品名 2.纤维成分
5910	1.品名 2.纤维成分 3.厚度
59111	1.品名 2.用途 3.成分含量
59112000	1.品名 2.成分含量

商品编码	申报要素
59113	1.品名 2.用途 3.是否为环状或有连接装置的纺织物或毡呢 4.每平方米克重 5.成分含量
59114000	1.品名 2.用途 3.成分含量
59119000	1.品名 2.用途(如半导体晶圆制造用等)3.若为半导体晶圆制造用需注明是否为自粘式 4.若为半导体晶圆制造用需注是否为圆形 5.成分含量
60011000	1.品名 2.织造方法(针织或钩编)3.起绒方法(毛圈或长毛绒)4.幅宽 5.成分含量
60012	1.品名 2.织造方法(针织或钩编)3.起绒方法(毛圈或长毛绒)4.幅宽 5.成分含量
60019	1.品名 2.织造方法(针织或钩编)3.幅宽 4.成分含量 5.是否起绒
6002	1.品名 2.织造方法(针织或钩编)3.橡胶线含量 4.成分含量 5.幅宽 6.弹性纱线含量
6003	1.品名 2.织造方法(针织或钩编)3.成分含量 4.幅宽
6004	1.品名 2.织造方法(针织或钩编)3.橡胶线含量 4.成分含量 5.幅宽 6.弹性纱线含量
6005	1.品名 2.织造方法(经编针织)3.染整方法(色织、染色、漂白等)4.成分含量 5.幅宽
6006	1.品名 2.织造方法(针织或钩编)3.染整方法(色织、染色、漂白等)4.成分含量 5.幅宽
6101	1.品名 2.织造方法(针织或钩编)3.种类(大衣、短大衣、斗篷等)4.类别(男式)5.成分含量 6.品牌(中文或外文名称)7.货号
6102	1.品名 2.织造方法(针织或钩编)3.种类(大衣、短大衣、斗篷等)4.类别(女式)5.成分含量 6.品牌(中文或外文名称)7.货号
61031	1.品名 2.织造方法(针织或钩编)3.种类(西服套装)4.类别(男式)5.成分含量 6.品牌(中文或外文名称)7.货号 8.套装组成及数量
61032	1.品名 2.织造方法(针织或钩编)3.种类(便服套装)4.类别(男式)5.成分含量 6.品牌(中文或外文名称)7.货号 8.套装组成及数量
61033	1.品名 2.织造方法(针织或钩编)3.种类(上衣) 4.类别(男式)5.成分含量 6.是否全开襟 7.是否有拉链 8.品牌(中文或外文名称)9.货号
61034100	1.品名 2.织造方法(针织或钩编)3.种类(长裤、护胸背带工装裤、马裤、短裤等)4.类别(男式)5.成分含量 6.品牌(中文或外文名称)7.货号
61034200	1.品名 2.织造方法(针织或钩编)3.种类(长裤、护胸背带工装裤、马裤、短裤等)4.类别(男式)5.成分含量 6.品牌(中文或外文名称)7.货号
61034300	1.品名 2.织造方法(针织或钩编)3.种类(长裤、护胸背带工装裤、马裤、短裤等)4.类别(男式)5.成分含量 6.品牌(中文或外文名称)7.货号
61034900	1.品名 2.织造方法(针织或钩编)3.种类(长裤、护胸背带工装裤、马裤、短裤等)4.类别(男式)5.成分含量 6.品牌(中文或外文名称)7.货号
61041	1.品名 2.织造方法(针织或钩编)3.种类(西服套装)4.类别(女式)5.成分含量 6.品牌(中文或外文名称)7.货号 8.套装组成及数量
61042	1.品名 2.织造方法(针织或钩编)3.种类(便服套装)4.类别(女式)5.成分含量 6.品牌(中文或外文名称)7.货号 8.套装组成及数量
61043	1.品名 2.织造方法(针织或钩编)3.种类(上衣) 4.类别(女式)5.成分含量 6.是否全开襟 7.是否有拉链 8.品牌(中文或外文名称)9.货号
61044	1.品名 2.织造方法(针织或钩编)3.种类(连衣裙)4.类别(女式)5.成分含量 6.品牌(中文或外文名称)7.货号
61045	1.品名 2.织造方法(针织或钩编)3.种类(裙子、裙裤)4.类别(女式)5.成分含量 6.品牌(中文或外文名称)7.货号
61046100	1.品名 2.织造方法(针织或钩编)3.种类(长裤、护胸背带工装裤、马裤、短裤等)4.类别(女式)5.成分含量 6.品牌(中文或外文名称)7.货号
61046200	1.品名 2.织造方法(针织或钩编)3.种类(长裤、护胸背带工装裤、马裤、短裤等)4.类别(女式)5.成分含量 6.品牌(中文或外文名称)7.货号
61046300	1.品名 2.织造方法(针织或钩编)3.种类(长裤、护胸背带工装裤、马裤、短裤等)4.类别(女式)5.成分含量 6.品牌(中文或外文名称)7.货号
61046900	1.品名 2.织造方法(针织或钩编)3.种类(长裤、护胸背带工装裤、马裤、短裤等)4.类别(女式)5.成分含量 6.品牌(中文或外文名称)7.货号
61051000	1.品名 2.织造方法(针织或钩编)3.种类(衬衫、POLO 衫等)4.类别(男式)5.成分含量 6.品牌(中文或外文名称)7.货号
61052000	1.品名 2.织造方法(针织或钩编)3.种类(衬衫、POLO 衫等)4.类别(男式)5.成分含量 6.品牌(中文或外文名称)7.货号
61059000	1.品名 2.织造方法(针织或钩编)3.种类(衬衫、POLO 衫等)4.类别(男式)5.成分含量 6.品牌(中文或外文名称)7.货号
61061000	1.品名 2.织造方法(针织或钩编)3.种类(衬衫、POLO 衫等)4.类别(女式)5.成分含量 6.品牌(中文或外文名称)7.货号
61062000	1.品名 2.织造方法(针织或钩编)3.种类(衬衫、POLO 衫等)4.类别(女式)5.成分含量 6.品牌(中文或外文名称)7.货号
61069000	1.品名 2.织造方法(针织或钩编)3.种类(衬衫、POLO 衫等)4.类别(女式)5.成分含量 6.品牌(中文或外文名称)7.货号
6107	1.品名 2.织造方法(针织或钩编)3.种类(内裤、三角裤、长睡衣、睡衣裤、浴衣等)4.类别(男式)5.成分含量 6.品牌(中文或外文名称)7.货号
61081	1.品名 2.织造方法(针织或钩编)3.种类(长衬裙、衬裙)4.类别(女式)5.成分含量 6.品牌(中文或外文名称)7.货号
61082	1.品名 2.织造方法(针织或钩编)3.种类(三角裤、短衬裤)4.类别(女式)5.成分含量 6.品牌(中文或外文名称)7.货号
61083	1.品名 2.织造方法(针织或钩编)3.种类(睡衣、睡衣裤)4.类别(女式)5.成分含量 6.品牌(中文或外文名称)7.货号
61089	1.品名 2.织造方法(针织或钩编)3.种类(浴衣、晨衣等)4.类别(女式)5.成分含量 6.品牌(中文或外文名称)7.货号
6109	1.品名 2.织造方法(针织或钩编)3.类别(男式、女式、男女同款)4.是否有领 5.是否有扣 6.是否有拉链 7.成分含量 8.品牌(中文或外文名称)9.货号
61101	1.品名 2.织造方法(针织、钩编是否为起绒)3.类别(男式、女式)4.如为背心,请注明是否为外穿背心 5.成分含量 6.品牌(中文或外文名称)7.货号

商品编码	申报要素
61102000	1.品名 2.织造方法(针织、钩编是否为起绒)3.类别(男式、女式)4.如为背心,请注明是否为外穿背心 5.成分含量 6.品牌(中文或外文名称)7.货号
61103000	1.品名 2.织造方法(针织、钩编是否为起绒)3.类别(男式、女式)4.如为背心,请注明是否为外穿背心 5.成分含量 6.品牌(中文或外文名称)7.货号
61109	1.品名 2.织造方法(针织、钩编是否为起绒)3.类别(男式、女式)4.如为背心,请注明是否为外穿背心 5.成分含量 6.品牌(中文或外文名称)7.货号
6111	1.品名 2.织造方法(针织或钩编)3.种类(外衣、雨衣等)4.类别(婴儿)5.成分含量 6.尺寸(衣长及裤长)7.品牌(中文或外文名称)8.货号
6112	1.品名 2.织造方法(针织或钩编)3.种类(运动套装、运动装、滑雪服、游泳服)4.类别(男式、女式)5.成分含量 6.品牌(中文或外文名称)7.货号 8.套装组成及数量
6113	1.品名 2.织造方法(针织或钩编)3.处理材料(塑料、橡胶)4.品牌(中文或外文名称)5.货号
6114	1.品名 2.织造方法(针织或钩编)3.种类(连身衣、夏服、水洗服、无袖罩衫等)4.类别(男式、女式、儿童)5.成分含量 6.品牌(中文或外文名称)7.货号
61151000	1.品名 2.织造方法(针织或钩编)3.用途 4.品牌(中文或外文名称)5.货号
61152100	1.品名 2.织造方法(针织或钩编)3.种类(连裤袜、紧身裤袜)4.成分含量 5.单丝细度 6.品牌(中文或外文名称)7.货号
61152200	1.品名 2.织造方法(针织或钩编)3.种类(连裤袜、紧身裤袜)4.成分含量 5.单丝细度 6.品牌(中文或外文名称)7.货号
611529	1.品名 2.织造方法(针织或钩编)3.种类(连裤袜、紧身裤袜)4.成分含量 5.品牌(中文或外文名称)6.货号
61153000	1.品名 2.织造方法(针织或钩编)3.种类(长筒袜、中筒袜)4.类别(女式)5.成分含量 6.单丝细度 7.品牌(中文或外文名称)8.货号
61159400	1.品名 2.织造方法(针织或钩编)3.种类(短袜、里袜、袜套等)4.成分含量 5.单丝细度 6.品牌(中文或外文名称)7.货号
61159500	1.品名 2.织造方法(针织或钩编)3.种类(短袜、里袜、袜套等)4.成分含量 5.单丝细度 6.品牌(中文或外文名称)7.货号
61159600	1.品名 2.织造方法(针织或钩编)3.种类(短袜、里袜、袜套等)4.类别(男式、女式)5.成分含量 6.单丝细度 7.品牌(中文或外文名称)8.货号
61159900	1.品名 2.织造方法(针织或钩编)3.种类(短袜、里袜、袜套等)4.类别(男式、女式)5.成分含量 6.单丝细度 7.品牌(中文或外文名称)8.货号
61161000	1.品名 2.织造方法(针织或钩编)3.处理材料(塑料、橡胶)4.成分含量 5.品牌(中文或外文名称)6.货号
61169	1.品名 2.织造方法(针织或钩编)3.成分含量 4.品牌(中文或外文名称)5.货号
61171	1.品名 2.织造方法(针织或钩编)3.成分含量 4.品牌(中文或外文名称)5.货号
61178	1.品名 2.织造方法(针织或钩编)3.成分含量 4.品牌(中文或外文名称)
61179000	1.品名 2.织造方法(针织或钩编)3.成分含量
6201	1.品名 2.织造方法(机织等)3.种类(大衣、短大衣、斗篷等)4.类别(男式)5.面料成分含量 6.如有填充物,请注明成分含量 7.品牌(中文或外文名称)8.货号
6202	1.品名 2.织造方法(机织等)3.种类(大衣、短大衣、斗篷等)4.类别(女式)5.面料成分含量 6.如有填充物,请注明成分含量 7.品牌(中文或外文名称)8.货号
62031	1.品名 2.织造方法(机织等)3.种类(西服套装) 4.类别(男式)5.成分含量 6.品牌(中文或外文名称)7.货号 8.套装组成及数量
62032	1.品名 2.织造方法(机织等)3.种类(便服套装) 4.类别(男式)5.成分含量 6.品牌(中文或外文名称)7.货号 8.套装组成及数量
62033	1.品名 2.织造方法(机织等)3.种类(上衣)4.类别(男式)5.成分含量 6.是否全开襟 7.是否有拉链 8.品牌(中文或外文名称)9.货号
62034100	1.品名 2.织造方法(机织等)3.种类(长裤、护胸背带工装裤、马裤、短裤 等)4.类别(男式)5.成分含量 6.品牌(中文或外文名称)7.货号
62034210	1.品名 2.织造方法(机织等)3.种类(阿拉伯裤) 4.类别(男式)5.成分含量 6.品牌(中文或外文名称)7.货号
62034290	1.品名 2.织造方法(机织等)3.种类(长裤、护胸背带工装裤、马裤、短裤 等)4.类别(男式)5.成分含量 6.品牌(中文或外文名称)7.货号
62034310	1.品名 2.织造方法(机织等)3.种类(阿拉伯裤) 4.类别(男式)5.成分含量 6.品牌(中文或外文名称)7.货号
62034390	1.品名 2.织造方法(机织等)3.种类(长裤、护胸背带工装裤、马裤、短裤 等)4.类别(男式)5.成分含量 6.品牌(中文或外文名称)7.货号
62034910	1.品名 2.织造方法(机织等)3.种类(阿拉伯裤) 4.类别(男式)5.成分含量 6.品牌(中文或外文名称)7.货号
62034990	1.品名 2.织造方法(机织等)3.种类(长裤、护胸背带工装裤、马裤、短裤 等)4.类别(男式)5.成分含量 6.品牌(中文或外文名称)7.货号
62041	1.品名 2.织造方法(机织等)3.种类(西服套装) 4.类别(女式)5.成分含量 6.品牌(中文或外文名称)7.货号 8.套装组成及数量
62042	1.品名 2.织造方法(机织等)3.种类(便服套装) 4.类别(女式)5.成分含量 6.品牌(中文或外文名称)7.货号 8.套装组成及数量
62043	1.品名 2.织造方法(机织等)3.种类(上衣)4.类别(男式)5.成分含量 6.是否全开襟 7.是否有拉链 8.品牌(中文或外文名称)9.货号
62044	1.品名 2.织造方法(机织等)3.种类(连衣裙)4.类别(女式)5.成分含量 6.品牌(中文或外文名称)7.货号
62045	1.品名 2.织造方法(机织等)3.种类(裙子、裙裤)4.类别(女式)5.成分含量 6.品牌(中文或外文名称)7.货号
62046	1.品名 2.织造方法(机织等)3.种类(长裤、护胸背带工装裤、马裤、短裤 等)4.类别(女式)5.成分含量 6.品牌(中文或外文名称)7.货号
6205	1.品名 2.织造方法(机织等)3.种类(衬衫、POLO 衫等)4.类别(男式)5.成分含量 6.品牌(中文或外文名称)7.货号
6206	1.品名 2.织造方法(机织等)3.种类(衬衫、POLO 衫等)4.类别(女式)5.成分含量 6.品牌(中文或外文名称)7 货号
6207	1.品名 2.织造方法(机织等)3.种类(内衣背心、内裤、三角裤、长睡衣等)4.类别(男式)5.成分含量 6.品牌(中文或外文名称)7.货号
62081	1.品名 2.织造方法(机织等)3.种类(长衬裙、衬裙)4.类别(女式)5.成分含量 6.品牌(中文或外文名称)7.货号
62082	1.品名 2.织造方法(机织等)3.种类(睡衣、睡衣裤)4.类别(女式)5.成分含量 6.品牌(中文或外文名称)7.货号

商品编码	申报要素
62089	1.品名 2.织造方法(机织等)3.种类(内衣背心、三角裤、短衬裤等)4.类别(女式)5.成分含量 6.品牌(中文或外文名称)7.货号
6209	1.品名 2.织造方法(机织等)3.种类(外衣、雨衣等)4.类别(婴儿)5.成分含量 6.尺寸(衣长及裤长)7.品牌(中文或外文名称)8.货号
62101	1.品名 2.织造方法(无纺布、毡呢)3.种类(上衣、长裤、短裤、连体衣、分体衣等)4.类别(男式、女式)5.面料成分含量 6.品牌(中文或外文名称)7.货号
62102000	1.品名 2.织造方法(机织等)3.种类(大衣、雨衣、短大衣、斗篷等)4.类别(男式)5.处理材料(塑料、橡胶等)6.品牌(中文或外文名称)7.货号
62103000	1.品名 2.织造方法(机织等)3.种类(大衣、雨衣、短大衣、斗篷等)4.类别(女式)5.处理材料(塑料、橡胶等)6.品牌(中文或外文名称)7.货号
62104000	1.品名 2.织造方法(机织等)3.种类(上衣、长裤、短裤等)4.类别(男式)5.处理材料(塑料、橡胶等)6.品牌(中文或外文名称)7.货号
62105000	1.品名 2.织造方法(机织等)3.种类(上衣、长裤、短裤等)4.类别(女式)5.处理材料(塑料、橡胶等)6.品牌(中文或外文名称)7.货号
62111	1.品名 2.织造方法(机织等)3.种类(游泳服)4.类别(男式、女式、儿童)5.成分含量 6.品牌(中文或外文名称)7.货号 8.若为套装申报组成及数量
62112	1.品名 2.织造方法(机织等)3.种类(滑雪服)4.类别(男式、女式、儿童)5.成分含量 6.品牌(中文或外文名称)7.货号 8.若为套装申报组成及数量
62113	1.品名 2.织造方法(机织等)3.种类(连身衣、夏服、水洗服、无袖罩衫等)4.类别(男式)5.成分含量 6.品牌(中文或外文名称)7.货号 8.若为套装申报组成及数量 9.如为上衣类服装申报是否开襟 10.如为上衣类服装申报是否有拉链 11.如为上衣类服装申报是否有衬里或夹层
62114	1.品名 2.织造方法(机织等)3.种类(连身衣、夏服、水洗服、无袖罩衫等)4.类别(女式)5.成分含量 6.品牌(中文或外文名称)7.货号 8.若为套装申报组成及数量 9.如为上衣类服装申报是否开襟 10.如为上衣类服装申报是否有拉链 11.如为上衣类服装申报是否有衬里或夹层
62121	1.品名 2.种类(胸罩)3.成分含量 4.品牌(中文或外文名称)5.货号
62122	1.品名 2.种类(束腰带、腹带)3.成分含量 4.品牌(中文或外文名称)5.货号
62123	1.品名 2.种类(束腰胸衣)3.成分含量 4.品牌(中文或外文名称)5.货号
62129	1.品名 2.种类(吊裤带、吊袜带、束袜带等)3.成分含量 4.品牌(中文或外文名称)5.货号
6213	1.品名 2.织造方法(机织刺绣、非刺绣)3.成分含量 4.尺寸 5.品牌(中文或外文名称)6.货号
6214	1.品名 2.织造方法(机织等)3.成分含量 4.品牌(中文或外文名称)5.货号
6215	1.品名 2.织造方法(机织等)3.成分含量 4.品牌(中文或外文名称)5.货号
6216	1.品名 2.织造方法(机织等)3.是否浸渍(塑料或橡胶)4.是否为运动手套 5.成分含量 6.品牌(中文或外文名称)7.货号
6217	1.品名 2.成分含量 3.织造方法(机织等)4.品牌(中文或外文名称)5.货号
63011000	1.品名 2.种类(电暖毯)3.成分含量 4.品牌(中文或外文名称)
63012000	1.品名 2.种类(毯子、旅行毯等)3.成分含量 4.品牌(中文或外文名称)
63013000	1.品名 2.种类(毯子、旅行毯等)3.成分含量 4.品牌(中文或外文名称)
63014000	1.品名 2.种类(毯子、旅行毯等)3.成分含量 4.品牌(中文或外文名称)
63019000	1.品名 2.种类(毯子、旅行毯等)3.成分含量 4.品牌(中文或外文名称)
6302	1.品名 2.用途(床上用品、餐桌用品、盥洗用品、厨房用品)3.织造方法(针织或钩编、印花、机织、机织刺绣等)4.成分含量 5.品牌(中文或外文名称)
63031	1.品名 2.种类(窗帘、帘帷、帐幔、床帷)3.织造方法(针织、钩编、机织等)4.成分含量 5.品牌(中文或外文名称)
63039100	1.品名 2.种类(窗帘、帘帷、帐幔、床帷)3.织造方法(针织、钩编、机织等)4.成分含量 5.品牌(中文或外文名称)
63039200	1.品名 2.种类(窗帘、帘帷、帐幔、床帷)3.织造方法(针织、钩编、机织等)4.成分含量 5.品牌(中文或外文名称)
63039900	1.品名 2.种类(窗帘、帘帷、帐幔、床帷)3.织造方法(针织、钩编、机织等)4.成分含量 5.品牌(中文或外文名称)
63041	1.品名 2.织造方法(针织、钩编、机织、针织手工、钩编手工等)3.成分含量 4.品牌(中文或外文名称)
63042	1.品名 2.是否装饰用 3.织造方法(针织手工、针织等)4.成分含量 5.是否以本章子目注释一所列物质浸渍或涂层 6.品牌(中文或外文名称)
63049	1.品名 2.是否装饰用 3.织造方法(针织、钩编、非针织或非钩编、针织手工 等)4.成分含量 5.品牌(中文或外文名称)
6305	1.品名 2.用途(储运袋、茶包等)
6306	1.品名 2.种类(油苫布、天篷、遮阳篷、风帆、帐篷等)3.成分含量 4.品牌(中文或外文名称)
63071000	1.品名 2.成分含量 3.是否清洁剂浸渍、涂布或包覆 4.功能用途 5.品牌(中文或外文名称)
63072000	1.品名 2.成分含量 3.品牌(中文或外文名称)
63079	1.品名 2.成分含量 3.品牌(中文或外文名称)
6308	1.品名 2.是否为零售包 装 3.是否为制成品(制成品,非制成品)4.品牌(中文或外文名称)
6309	1.品名 2.是否为旧
6310	1.品名 2.是否经分拣 3.成分含量 4.颜色(如白色或杂色)5.新旧请注明
64011	1.品名 2.款式(装金属护头等)3.鞋面材料 4.鞋底材料 5.品牌(中文或外文名称)6.货号
64019	1.品名 2.款式(未过踝、过膝、过踝但未到膝)3.鞋面材料 4.鞋底材料 5.品牌(中文或外文名称)6.货号
64021	1.品名 2.款式(是否过踝)3.鞋面材料 4.鞋底材料 5.品牌(中文或外文名称)6.货号
64022000	1.品名 2.款式(人字拖 等)3.鞋面材料 4.鞋底材料 5.请注明是否栓塞方法制 6.品牌(中文或外文名称)7.货号
64029	1.品名 2.款式(是否过踝)3.鞋面材料 4.鞋底材料 5.品牌(中文或外文名称)6.货号
64031	1.品名 2.款式(滑雪靴、越野滑雪鞋靴、滑雪板靴 等)3.鞋面材料 4.鞋底材料 5.品牌(中文或外文名称)6.货号
64032000	1.品名 2.款式 3.鞋面材料 4.鞋底材料 5.品牌(中文或外文名称)6.货号
64034000	1.品名 2.款式(装金属护头等)3.鞋面材料 4.鞋底材料 5.品牌(中文或外文名称)6.货号
64035111	1.品名 2.款式(过踝但低于小腿)3.鞋面材料 4.鞋底材料 5.内底长度 6.品牌(中文或外文名称)7.货号
64035119	1.品名 2.款式(过踝但低于小腿)3.鞋面材料 4.鞋底材料 5.内底长度 6.品牌(中文或外文名称)7.货号
64035191	1.品名 2.款式(过踝不低于小腿)3.鞋面材料 4.鞋底材料 5.内底长度 6.品牌(中文或外文名称)7.货号
64035199	1.品名 2.款式(过踝不低于小腿)3.鞋面材料 4.鞋底材料 5.内底长度 6.品牌(中文或外文名称)7.货号
64035900	1.品名 2.款式(未过踝)3.鞋面材料 4.鞋底材料 5.内底长度 6.品牌(中文或外文名称)7.货号
64039111	1.品名 2.款式(过踝但低于小腿)3.鞋面材料 4.鞋底材料 5.内底长度 6.品牌(中文或外文名称)7.货号
64039119	1.品名 2.款式(过踝但低于小腿)3.鞋面材料 4.鞋底材料 5.内底长度 6.品牌(中文或外文名称)7.货号
64039191	1.品名 2.款式(过踝不低于小腿)3.鞋面材料 4.鞋底材料 5.内底长度 6.品牌(中文或外文名称)7.货号
64039199	1.品名 2.款式(过踝不低于小腿)3.鞋面材料 4.鞋底材料 5.内底长度 6.品牌(中文或外文名称)7.货号
64039900	1.品名 2.款式(未过踝)3.鞋面材料 4.鞋底材料 5.内底长度 6.品牌(中文或外文名称)7.货号
6404	1.品名 2.款式 3.鞋面材料 4.鞋底材料 5.品牌(中文或外文名称)6.货号
6405	1.品名 2.款式 3.鞋面材料 4.鞋底材料 5.品牌(中文或外文名称)6.货号
6406	1.品名 2.材质 3.加工程度(是否已成型)4.用途
6501	1.品名 2.材质(毡呢)3.品牌(中文或外文名称)
6502	1.品名 2.材质 3.制作工艺(编结、拼制)4.品牌(中文或外文名称)
6504	1.品名 2.制作工艺(编结、拼制)3.品牌(中文或外文名称)
65050010	1.品名 2.品牌(中文或外文名称)
65050020	1.品名 2.制作工艺(是否钩编)3.品牌(中文或外文名称)
65050091	1.品名 2.材质(毡呢)3.品牌(中文或外文名称)
65050099	1.品名 2.制作工艺(针织、机织等)3.品牌(中文或外文名称)
65061000	1.品名 2.材质 3.用途 4.是否带有能滤除生物因子滤器的面罩 5.品牌(中文或外文名称)
65069	1.品名 2.材质 3.品牌(中文或外文名称)
6507	1.品名 2.材质
6601	1.品名 2.种类或用途 3.手持请注明 4.品牌(中文或外文名称)
6602	1.品名 2.材质 3.品牌(中文或外文名称)
6603	1.品名 2.材质
6701	1.品名 2.羽毛、羽绒请注明加工程度(漂白、染色、卷曲等)
6702	1.品名 2.制作材料(塑料丝等)
6703	1.品名 2.加工程度(经梳理、稀疏、脱色等)3.制作材料 4.长度(英寸)
6704	1.品名 2.制作材料 3.如为人发制请申报长度(英寸)
6801	1.品名 2.种类(长方砌石、扁平石、路缘石)3.材质
6802	1.品名 2.用途 3.材质(大理石、花岗岩)4.加工程度(切、锯、抛光及是否石刻等)5.尺寸(最大表面积的最大边长)6.花色品种的中英文名称
6803	1.品名 2.加工程度 3.材质
68041000	1.品名 2.用途(碾磨或磨浆、磨光用等)3.材质(石料、黏聚合成料等)4.是否装支架
68042	1.品名 2.用途(碾磨或磨浆、磨光用等)3.材质(石料、黏聚合成料等)4.是否装支架 5.品牌(中文或外文名称)
68043010	1.品名 2.用途(碾磨或磨浆、磨光用等)3.材质(石料、黏聚合成料等)4.是否装支架
68043090	1.品名 2.用途(碾磨或磨浆、磨光用等)3.材质(石料、黏聚合成料等)4.是否装支架
6805	1.品名 2.基底材料 3.砂粒材质 4.是否有涂层(如有,请申报材质)5.品牌(中文或外文名称)6.型号 7.尺寸
68061	1.品名 2.材质(矿物纤维等)3.形状 4.含有石棉纤维的要注明其含量
68062000	1.品名 2.材质(页状蛭石、膨胀黏土、泡沫矿渣等)3.形状 4.含有石棉纤维的要注明其含量
68069000	1.品名 2.材质 3.形状 4.含有石棉纤维的要注明其含量
6807	1.品名 2.形状
6808	1.品名 2.种类(镶板、平板瓦、砖等)3.原料(稻草、刨花等)4.粘料(水泥、石膏等矿物性黏合材 料)
6809	1.品名 2.加工方法(是否装饰、经贴面或加强等) 3.是否未经装饰,仅用纸或纸板贴面或加强的 4.成分含量
6810	1.品名 2.用途(铁道用等)3.种类(砖、瓦、管及建筑构件钢筋混凝土板等)4.材料(水泥、混凝土、人造石)
6811	1.品名 2.种类(砖、瓦、管、板等)3.材料(石棉水泥、纤维素水泥等)
6812	1.品名 2.种类(纱线、机织物、服装、鞋帽、衬垫 等)3.材料(青石棉、其他石棉、石棉纤维)
6813	1.品名 2.材质 3.种类(片、卷、带、闸衬、闸垫、扇形等)
6814	1.品名 2.材质(云母)3.形状(板、片、带等)4.是否黏聚或复制的
68151100	1.品名 2.材质 3.品牌(中文或外文名称,无品牌请申报厂商)
68151200	1.品名 2.材质 3.品牌(中文或外文名称,无品牌请申报厂商)
68151310	1.品名 2.材质 3.品牌(中文或外文名称,无品牌请申报厂商)
68151390	1.品名 2.材质 3.碳纤维纱线请注明碳含量、比模量和比极限抗拉强度
68151900	1.品名 2.材质 3.品牌(中文或外文名称,无品牌请申报厂商)
68152000	1.品名 2.材质
68159	1.品名 2.材质
68159100	1.品名 2.材质
6901	1.品名 2.材质(硅质化石粉、硅藻土或类似硅土等)3.种类(砖、瓦等)
6902	1.品名 2.种类(耐火砖、瓦、块等)3.成分含量 4.耐火温度
6903	1.品名 2.种类(坩埚、支架、马弗罩等)3.成分含量 4.耐火温度
6904	1.品名 2.种类(建筑用砖、地面砖等)3.品牌(中文或外文名称)
69051000	1.品名 2.种类(屋顶瓦等)
69059000	1.品名 2.种类(烟囱罩等)
6906	1.品名 2.种类(套管、导管、槽管等)
690721	1.品名 2.种类(贴面砖、铺面砖等)3.尺寸(最大表面积的最大边长)4.按重量计吸水率 5.品牌(中文或外文名称)6.颜色

商品编码	申报要素
690722	1.品名 2.种类(贴面砖、铺面砖等)3.尺寸(最大表面积的最大边长)4.按重量计吸水率 5.品牌(中文或外文名称)6.颜色
690723	1.品名 2.种类(贴面砖、铺面砖等)3.尺寸(最大表面积的最大边长)4.按重量计吸水率 5.品牌(中文或外文名称)6.颜色
69073	1.品名 2.种类(马赛克等)3.尺寸(最大表面积的最大边长)4.按重量计吸水率 5.品牌(中文或外文名称)6.颜色
69074	1.品名 2.种类(饰面陶瓷等)3.尺寸(最大表面积的最大边长)4.按重量计吸水率 5.品牌(中文或外文名称)6.颜色
6909	1.品名 2.用途(实验室用、化学用、农业用等)3.种类(瓷制、陶制)4.莫氏硬度
69101000	1.品名 2.材质(瓷制)3.品牌(中文或外文名称)4.规格型号
69109000	1.品名 2.材质(陶制等)3.品牌(中文或外文名称)4.规格型号
6911101	1.品名 2.材质(瓷制、陶制)3.种类(餐具、厨房器具等)4.是否为骨瓷 5.品牌(中文或外文名称)
6911102	1.品名 2.材质(瓷制、陶制)3.种类(餐具、厨房器具等)4.品牌(中文或外文名称)
69119000	1.品名 2.材质(瓷制、陶制)3.种类(餐具、厨房器具等)4.品牌(中文或外文名称)
6912	1.品名 2.材质(瓷制、陶制)3.种类(餐具、厨房器具等)4.品牌(中文或外文名称)
6913	1.品名 2.材质(瓷制、陶制)3.用途
6914	1.品名 2.材质(瓷制、陶制)3.用途
7001	1.品名 2.用途 3.状态(废、碎、块料)4.外观(颜色)
70021000	1.品名 2.用途 3.直径
70022010	1.品名 2.用途(光导纤维预制棒等)3.直径 4.品牌(中文或外文名称)5.进口状态(芯棒或成品预制棒)6.种类(单模、多模、特种预制棒等)
70022090	1.品名 2.用途
700231	1.品名 2.用途(光导纤维用、光通信用等)3.材质(熔融石英、熔融硅石等)4.级别(波导级)5.外径
70023200	1.品名 2.用途(光导纤维用、光通信用等)3.材质(熔融石英、熔融硅石等)4.线膨胀系数 5.级别(波导级)6.外径
70023900	1.品名 2.用途(光导纤维用、光通信用等)3.材质(熔融石英、熔融硅石等)4.线膨胀系数 5.级别(波导级)6.外径
70031200	1.品名 2.用途 3.加工方法(整块着色、具有吸收层等)4.状态(是否夹丝)5.形状(板、片、型材、异型材)6.工艺(铸制或轧制)7.品牌(中文或外文名称,无品牌请申报厂商)8.型号 9.规格尺寸(长×宽×厚)
70031900	1.品名 2.用途 3.状态(是否夹丝)4.形状(板、片、型材、异型材)5.工艺(铸制或轧制)6.品牌(中文或外文名称,无品牌请申报厂商)7.型号 8.规格尺寸(长×宽×厚)
70032000	1.品名 2.用途 3.状态(是否夹丝)4.形状(板、片、型材、异型材)5.工艺(铸制或轧制)6.品牌(中文或外文名称,无品牌请申报厂商)7.型号 8.规格尺寸(长×宽×厚)
70033000	1.品名 2.用途 3.状态(是否夹丝)4.形状(板、片、型材、异型材)5.工艺(铸制或轧制)6.品牌(中文或外文名称,无品牌请申报厂商)7.型号 8.规格尺寸(长×宽×厚)
70042000	1.品名 2.用途 3.加工方法(整块着色、具有吸收层等)4.状态(是否经过表面加工)5.形状(板、片)6.工艺(拉制或吹制)
70049000	1.品名 2.用途 3.状态(是否经过表面加工)4.形状(板、片)5.工艺(拉制或吹制)
70051000	1.品名 2.用途 3.加工方法(具有吸收、反射或非反射层的)4.状态(是否夹丝)5.形状(板、片)6.工艺(浮法、表面研磨、抛光)
70052100	1.品名 2.用途 3.加工方法(整块着色、不透明、镶色等)4.状态(是否夹丝)5.形状(板、片)6.工艺(浮法、表面研磨、抛光)
70052900	1.品名 2.用途 3.状态(是否夹丝)4.形状(板、片)5.工艺(浮法、表面研磨、抛光)
70053000	1.品名 2.用途 3.状态(是否夹丝)4.形状(板、片)5.工艺(浮法、表面研磨、抛光)
7006	1.品名 2.用途 3.加工方法(经弯曲、磨边、镂刻、钻孔、涂珐琅等)4.状态(未用其他材料镶框或装配)5.形状(板、片、型材、异型材)6.如为液晶玻璃基板,需申报第几代 7.品牌(中文或外文名称,无品牌请申报厂商)8.型号 9.规格尺寸(长×宽×厚)
70071110	1.品名 2.用途(航空器、航天器、船舶等)3.加工方法(钢化、层压)4.品牌(中文或外文名称)
70071190	1.品名 2.用途(车辆等)3.加工方法(钢化、层压)4.品牌(中文或外文名称)
70071900	1.品名 2.用途 3.加工方法(钢化、层压)4.品牌(中文或外文名称)
70072110	1.品名 2.用途(航空器、航天器、船舶等)3.加工方法(钢化、层压)4.品牌(中文或外文名称)
70072190	1.品名 2.用途(车辆等)3.加工方法(钢化、层压)4.品牌(中文或外文名称)
70072900	1.品名 2.用途 3.加工方法(钢化、层压)4.品牌(中文或外文名称)
7008	1.品名 2.用途(隔温、隔音)3.类型(中空、真空等)4.层数 5.品牌(中文或外文名称)
70091000	1.品名 2.用途(车辆后视用等)3.加工方法(未经光学加工)
70099	1.品名 2.用途(车辆后视用等)3.加工方法(未经光学加工)4.是否镶框
70101000	1.品名 2.用途(用于运输或盛装货物)3.容积
70102000	1.品名 2.用途(用于运输或盛装货物)
70109	1.品名 2.用途(用于运输或盛装货物)3.容积
7011	1.品名 2.用途(制灯泡、阴极射线管等)3.加工方法(用荧光物质衬里、未封口、无配件等)
70131000	1.品名 2.用途(供餐桌、厨房、盥洗室、室内装饰用)3.材质(是否玻璃陶瓷制)4.器皿种类(杯等)5.工艺流程(手工、机械、半手工)
70132200	1.品名 2.用途(供餐桌、厨房、盥洗室、室内装饰用)3.是否铅晶质玻璃 4.器皿种类(杯等)5.平脚、高脚杯 6.规格 7.型号 8.品牌(中文或外文名称)9.工艺流程(手工、机械、半手工)
70132800	1.品名 2.用途(供餐桌、厨房、盥洗室、室内装饰用)3.是否铅晶质玻璃 4.器皿种类(杯等)5.平脚、高脚杯 6.规格 7.型号 8.品牌(中文或外文名称)9.工艺流程(手工、机械、半手工)
70133300	1.品名 2.用途(供餐桌、厨房、盥洗室、室内装饰用)3.是否铅晶质玻璃 4.器皿种类(杯等)5.平脚、高脚杯 6.规格 7.型号 8.品牌(中文或外文名称)9.工艺流程(手工、机械、半手工)
70133700	1.品名 2.用途(供餐桌、厨房、盥洗室、室内装饰用)3.是否铅晶质玻璃 4.器皿种类(杯等)5.平脚、高脚杯 6.规格 7.型号 8.品牌(中文或外文名称)9.工艺流程(手工、机械、半手工)
70134	1.品名 2.用途(供餐桌、厨房、盥洗室、室内装饰用)3.是否铅晶质玻璃 4.器皿种类(杯等)5.线膨胀系数 6.工艺流程(手工、机械、半手工)
70139	1.品名 2.用途(供餐桌、厨房、盥洗室、室内装饰用)3.是否铅晶质玻璃 4.器皿种类(杯等)5.工艺流程(手工、机械、半手工)
70140010	1.品名 2.用途(具体列明用于光学仪器名称)3.规格尺寸 4.是否经光学加工
70140090	1.品名 2.用途(是否用于光学仪器)3.规格尺寸 4.是否经光学加工
70151010	1.品名 2.用途(用于制造眼镜等)3.加工方法(未经光学加工)4.形状(弧面、弯曲、凹形、扇形等)5.元件种类(视力矫正玻璃毛坯等)6.特殊功能(变色等)
70151090	1.品名 2.用途(用于制造眼镜等)3.加工方法(未经光学加工)4.形状(弧面、弯曲、凹形、扇形等)5.元件种类(视力矫正玻璃毛坯等)
70159010	1.品名 2.用途(用于制造钟表等)3.加工方法(未经光学加工)4.形状(弧面、弯曲、凹形、扇形等)5.元件种类(视力矫正玻璃毛坯等)
70159020	1.品名 2.用途(用于制造眼镜等)3.加工方法(未经光学加工)4.形状(弧面、弯曲、凹形、扇形等)5.元件种类(视力矫正玻璃毛坯等)6.特殊功能(变色等)
70159090	1.品名 2.用途(用于制造眼镜等)3.加工方法(未经光学加工)4.形状(弧面、弯曲、凹形、扇形等)5.元件种类(视力矫正玻璃毛坯等)
7016	1.品名 2.用途(建筑铺面用)3.加工方法(压制、模制等)4.种类(马赛克,花饰铅条窗玻璃,铺面砖、块、片等)
7017	1.品名 2.用途(实验室、卫生、配药用)3.材质(熔融石英、熔融硅石)4.器皿种类(量筒等)5.线膨胀系数
7018	1.品名 2.用途(装饰用 等)3.加工方法(灯工方法等)4.玻璃球的直径 5.材质(钙钠玻璃、铅晶玻璃等)6.品牌(中文或外文名称)7.型号
70191	1.品名 2.材质(玻璃纤维制)3.种类(梳条、粗纱、纱线、短纤、毡等)4.长度
70196100	1.品名 2.材质(玻璃纤维制)3.织造方法(机织)4.纱线类型(粗纱)
70196200	1.品名 2.材质(玻璃纤维制)
70196310	1.品名 2.材质(玻璃纤维制)3.织造方法(机织) 4.纱线类型(细纱等)5.幅宽
70196320	1.品名 2.材质(玻璃纤维制)3.织造方法(机织) 4.纱线类型(细纱等)5.幅宽 6.每平方米克重 7.单纱细度 8.标称厚度
70196390	1.品名 2.材质(玻璃纤维制)3.织造方法(机织) 4.纱线类型(细纱等)5.幅宽 6.每平方米克重 7.单纱细度
701964	1.品名 2.材质(玻璃纤维制)3.织造方法(机织) 4.纱线类型(细纱等)5.幅宽
701965	1.品名 2.材质(玻璃纤维制)3.织造方法(机织) 4.纱线类型(粗纱等)5.幅宽
701966	1.品名 2.材质(玻璃纤维制)3.织造方法(机织) 4.纱线类型(粗纱等)5.幅宽
701969	1.品名 2.材质(玻璃纤维制)3.织造方法 4.幅宽
70197	1.品名 2.材质(玻璃纤维制)3.种类(毡、垫等)
70198	1.品名 2.材质(玻璃棉制)3.种类(纤维网、板等)
7019902	1.品名 2.用途 3.材质(玻璃纤维布浸胶)4.每平方米重量
7019909	1.品名 2.材质(玻璃纤维制)3.种类(纤维网、垫、板等)
70200011	1.品名 2.用途 3.材质(玻璃制)4.导电层材质、电阻值
70200012	1.品名 2.用途 3.材质(玻璃制)
70200013	1.品名 2.用途 3.材质(熔融石英或其他熔融硅石制)
70200019	1.品名 2.用途 3.材质(玻璃制)
70200091	1.品名 2.用途 3.材质(玻璃制)4.平整度
70200099	1.品名 2.用途 3.材质(玻璃制)4.平整度
7101101	1.品名 2.种类(黑珍珠等)3.加工程度(打孔、未加工等)4.状态(未成串、未镶嵌等)5.来源(天然)6.等级
71011091	1.品名 2.种类(黑珍珠等)3.加工程度(打孔、未加工等)4.状态(未成串、未镶嵌等)5.来源(天然)6.等级
71011099	1.品名 2.种类(黑珍珠等)3.加工程度(打孔、未加工等)4.状态(未成串、未镶嵌等)5.来源(天然)6.等级
71012110	1.品名 2.种类(黑珍珠等)3.加工程度(打孔、未加工等)4.状态(未成串、未镶嵌等)5.来源(养殖)6.等级
71012190	1.品名 2.种类(黑珍珠等)3.加工程度(打孔、未加工等)4.状态(未成串、未镶嵌等)5.来源(养殖)6.等级
71012210	1.品名 2.种类(黑珍珠等)3.加工程度(打孔、未加工等)4.状态(未成串、未镶嵌等)5.来源(养殖)6.等级
71012290	1.品名 2.种类(黑珍珠等)3.加工程度(打孔、未加工等)4.状态(未成串、未镶嵌等)5.来源(养殖)6.等级
71021000	1.品名 2.用途 3.加工程度(未加工,经简单锯开、劈开、粗磨等)4.来源(天然)
71022	1.品名 2.用途 3.加工程度(未加工,经简单锯开、劈开、粗磨等)4.来源(天然)
71023100	1.品名 2.用途 3.加工程度(未加工,经简单锯开、劈开、粗磨等)4.来源(天然)
71023900	1.品名 2.用途 3.加工程度(未加工,经简单锯开、劈开、粗磨等)4.来源(天然)5.数量规格(每批次钻石颗数,单个重量区间)6.形状(碎钻、圆钻、方钻、水滴钻等)7.颜色(无色、粉色、黄色等)8.销售商
71031000	1.品名 2.种类(红宝石、蓝宝石、祖母绿、翡翠等)3.加工程度和状态(未加工、经简单锯开、粗制成形、未成串、未镶嵌)4.来源(天然)5.等级 6.产区(软玉和硬玉需申报矿坑)7.矿物学名及英文名称 8.规格(单个直径、重量)9.化学成分 10.件数(缅甸公盘成交需申报玉石编号)11.颜色
71039100	1.品名 2.种类(水晶/紫晶、软玉/和田玉等)3.加工程度(未加工,经简单锯开、粗制成形、钻孔、打磨、热处理、充填等)4.状态(未成串、未镶嵌等)5.来源(天然)6.等级 7.矿物学名 8.规格 9.化学成分 10.颜色
71039910	1.品名 2.种类(水晶/紫晶、软玉/和田玉等)3.加工程度(未加工,经简单锯开、粗制成形、钻孔、打磨、热处理、充填等)4.状态(未成串、未镶嵌等)5.来源(天然)6.等级 7.矿物学名 8.规格 9.化学成分 10.颜色
71039920	1.品名 2.种类(水晶/紫晶、软玉/和田玉等)3.加工程度(未加工,经简单锯开、粗制成形、钻孔、打磨、热处理、充填等)4.状态(未成串、未镶嵌等)5.来源(天然)6.等级 7.矿物学名 8.规格 9.化学成分 10.颜色

商品编码	申报要素
71039930	1.品名 2.种类(水晶/紫晶、软玉/和田玉等)3.加工程度(未加工，经简单锯开、粗制成形、钻孔、打磨、热处理、充填等)4.状态(未成串、未镶嵌等)5.来源(天然)6.等级 7.矿物学名 8.规格 9.化学成分 10.颜色
71039940	1.品名 2.种类(水晶/紫晶、软玉/和田玉等)3.加工程度(未加工，经简单锯开、粗制成形、钻孔、打磨、热处理、充填等)4.状态(未成串、未镶嵌等)5.来源(天然)6.等级 7.矿物学名 8.规格 9.化学成分 10.颜色
71039990	1.品名 2.种类(红宝石、蓝宝石、祖母绿、翡翠等)3.加工程度(未加工，经简单锯开、粗制成形)4.状态(未成串、未镶嵌等)5.来源(天然)6.等级 7.矿物学名 8.规格 9.化学成分 10.颜色
7104	1.品名 2.用途 3.种类(压电石英等)4.加工程度(经简单锯开、粗制成形)5.状态(未成串、未镶嵌等)6.来源(合成、再造)
7105	1.品名 2.种类(压电石英等)3.来源(天然、合成、再造)
71061	1.品名 2.形状(粉末)3.材质(纯银、银合金、镀金、镀铂)4.加工程度(未锻造、半制成)5.纯度 6.平均粒径
71069	1.品名 2.形状(粉末)3.材质(纯银、银合金、镀金、镀铂)4.加工程度(未锻造、半制成)5.纯度
7107	1.品名 2.基底材质(铜等)
7108	1.品名 2.形状(粉末)3.材质(纯金、金合金、镀铂)4.纯度 5.加工程度(未锻造、半制成)6.货币用请注明用途
7109	1.品名 2.基底材质(铜、银等)
7110	1.品名 2.形状(粉末等)3.材质(铂、钯、铑、铱、锇、钌)4.加工程度(未锻造,板、片等)5.贵金属成分含量
7111	1.品名 2.基底材质(铜、银、金等)
7112	1.品名 2.状态(废碎料、灰)3.来源(由破碎含有贵金属的电路板而得等) 4.贵金属的成分含量
7113	1.品名 2.材质(铂、金、银等)3.加工方法(镶嵌钻石、镶嵌红宝石等包金、包银、镀金等)4.首饰种类(戒指等)5.贵金属成分含量 6.品牌(中文或外文名称)
7114	1.品名 2.种类(餐具等)3.材质(铂、金、银等)4.加工方法(包金、镀金等)5.贵金属成分含量
7115	1.品名 2.用途(工业用、实验室用等)3.种类(坩埚等)4.形状(格栅形状等)5.材质(铂等)6.贵金属成分含量
71161000	1.品名 2.种类(手镯等)3.材质(养殖珍珠、天然珍珠)
71162000	1.品名 2.种类(手镯等)3.材质(宝石、半宝石)
7117	1.品名 2.种类(袖扣、饰扣、手镯等)3.材质 4.是否镀贵金属 5.品牌(中文或外文名称)
7118	1.品名 2.用途(法定货币、非法定货币)3.材质(铜制等)4.成分含量
7201	1.品名 2.形状(锭、块等)3.材质(生铁、镜 铁)4.成分含量(铁、碳、铬、锰、磷、硅的含量)
72021	1.品名 2.材质(锰铁)3.成分含量(铁含量及合金元素的含量)4.碳含量
72022	1.品名 2.材质(硅铁)3.成分含量(铁含量及合金元素的含量)4.形状(块状、粉状等)5.计价日期 6.签约日期
72023000	1.品名 2.材质(锰铁、硅铁、铬铁、镍铁等)3.成分含量(铁含量及合金元素的含量)
72024	1.品名 2.材质(铬铁)3.成分含量(铁含量及合金元素的含量)4.计价日期 5.签约日期
72025000	1.品名 2.材质(锰铁、硅铁、铬铁、镍铁等)3.成分含量(铁含量及合金元素的含量)
72026000	1.品名 2.材质(锰铁、硅铁、铬铁、镍铁等)3.成分含量(铁含量及合金元素的含量)4.计价日期 5.签约日期
72027000	1.品名 2.材质(锰铁、硅铁、铬铁、镍铁等)3.成分含量(铁含量及合金元素的含量)
72028	1.品名 2.材质(锰铁、硅铁、铬铁、镍铁等)3.成分含量(铁含量及合金元素的含量)
72029100	1.品名 2.材质(锰铁、硅铁、铬铁、镍铁等)3.成分含量(铁含量及合金元素的含量)
720292	1.品名 2.材质(锰铁、硅铁、铬铁、镍铁等)3.成分含量(铁含量及合金元素的含量)
72029300	1.品名 2.材质(锰铁、硅铁、铬铁、镍铁等)3.成分含量(铁含量及合金元素的含量)
720299	1.品名 2.材质(锰铁、硅铁、铬铁、镍铁等)3.成分含量(铁含量及合金元素的含量)
7203	1.品名 2.形状(块、团、团粒等)3.来源(是直接从铁矿还原所得还是海绵铁产品)4.成分含量(铁、碳、合金元素、非合金元素的含量)
72041000	1.品名 2.用途(供再熔炼钢用)3.形状(废碎、切割、压缩成包或板、条状 等)4.材质(铸铁)5.来源(机械加工产生、由破碎何种钢铁制品而得)6.成分含量(所含金属总含量和各种金属名称及含量)7.牌号 8.规格(长宽厚或堆密度等)9.计价日期
72042100	1.品名 2.用途(供再熔炼钢用)3.形状(废碎、切割、压缩成包或板、条状 等)4.材质(不锈钢)5.来源(机械加工产生、由破碎何种钢铁制品而得)6.成分含量(所含金属总含量和各种金属名称及含量)7.钢号 8.牌号 9.规格(长宽厚或堆密度等)10.计价日期
72042900	1.品名 2.用途(供再熔炼钢用)3.形状(废碎、切割、压缩成包或板、条状 等)4.材质(硅电钢、高速钢等,取向性硅电钢请注明)5.来源(机械加工产生、由破碎何种钢铁制品而得)6.成分含量(所含金属总含量和各种金属名称及含量)7.钢号 8.牌号 9.规格(长宽厚或堆密度等) 10.计价日期
72043000	1.品名 2.用途(供再熔炼钢用)3.形状(废碎、切割、压缩成包或板、条状 等)4.材质(镀锡钢)5.来源(机械加工产生、由破碎何种钢铁制品而得)6.成分含量(所含金属总含量和各种金属名称及含量)7.钢号 8.牌号 9.规格(长宽厚或堆密度等)10.计价日期
72044100	1.品名 2.用途(供再熔炼钢用)3.形状(废碎、切割、压缩成包或板、条状 等)4.材质(非合金钢) 5.来源(机械加工产生、由破碎何种钢铁制品而得)6.成分含量(所含金属总含量和各种金属名称及含量)7.钢号 8.牌号 9.规格(长宽厚或堆密度等)10.计价日期
72044900	1.品名 2.用途(供再熔炼钢用)3.形状(废碎、切割、压缩成包或板、条状 等)4.材质(非合金钢)5.来源(机械加工产生、由破碎何种钢铁制品而得)6.成分含量(所含金属总含量和各种金属名称及含量)7.钢号 8.牌号 9.规格(长宽厚或堆密度等)10.计价日期
72045000	1.品名 2.用途(供再熔炼钢用)3.形状(废碎、切割、压缩成包或板、条状 等)4.材质(铸铁、合金钢、不锈钢等)5.来源(机械加工产生、由破碎何种钢铁制品而得)6.成分含量(所含金属总含量和各种金属名称及含量)7.钢号 8.牌号 9.规格(长宽厚或堆密度等)10.计价日期

商品编码	申报要素
72051000	1.品名 2.形状(颗粒、粉末)3.材质(生铁、镜铁、合金钢等)4.成分含量(铁、碳、合金元素、非合金元素的含量)5.粒度
72052100	1.品名 2.形状(颗粒、粉末)3.材质(生铁、镜铁、合金钢等)4.成分含量(铁、碳、合金元素、非合金元素的含量)5.粒度
720529	1.品名 2.形状(颗粒、粉末)3.材质(生铁、镜铁、合金钢等)4.成分含量(铁、碳、合金元素、非合金元素的含量)5.粒度
7206	1.品名 2.形状(方锭、其他初级形状等)3.材质(铁、非合金钢)4.成分含量(铁、碳、合金元素、非合金元素的含量)
72071100	1.品名 2.形状(大方坯、小方坯等)3.材质(铁、非合金钢)4.加工方法(初轧、粗锻等)5.成分含量(铁、碳、合金元素、非合金元素的含量)6.截面形状(正方形等)7.截面尺寸
72071200	1.品名 2.形状(大方坯、小方坯等)3.材质(铁、非合金钢)4.加工方法(初轧、粗锻等)5.成分含量(铁、碳、合金元素、非合金元素的含量)6.截面形状(正方形等)7.截面尺寸
72071900	1.品名 2.形状(大方坯、小方坯等)3.材质(铁、非合金钢)4.加工方法(初轧、粗锻等)5.成分含量(铁、碳、合金元素、非合金元素的含量)6.截面形状(正方形等)7.计价日期 8.签约日期
72072000	1.品名 2.形状(大方坯、小方坯等)3.材质(铁、非合金钢)4.加工方法(初轧、粗锻等)5.成分含量(铁、碳、合金元素、非合金元素的含量)6.截面形状(正方形等)
7208	1.品名 2.形状(平板、卷板)3.材质(铁、非合金钢)4.加工方法(热轧等)5.加工程度(是否酸洗，是否轧有花纹，是否包覆及镀层、涂层等)6.成分含量(铁、碳、合金元素、非合金元素的含量)7.规格(板材的厚度、宽度)8.屈服强度 9.钢号
7209	1.品名 2.形状(平板、卷板)3.材质(铁、非合金钢)4.加工方法(冷轧)5.加工程度(未包覆、未镀层、未涂层等)6.成分含量(铁、碳、合金元素、非合金元素的含量)7.规格(板材的厚度、宽度)8.技术参数(屈服强度)9.钢号
7210	1.品名 2.形状(平板、卷板)3.材质(铁、非合金钢)4.加工方法(经包覆、经镀层、经涂层)5.成分含量(铁、碳、合金元素、非合金元素的含量)6.规格(板材的厚度、宽度)7.涂层种类(锡、铅、电镀锌、涂锌等)8.钢号
7211	1.品名 2.形状(平板、卷板)3.材质(铁、非合金钢)4.加工方法(热轧、冷轧未包覆、未镀层、未涂层等)5.成分含量(铁、碳、合金元素、非合金元素的含量)6.规格(板材的厚度、宽度)7.钢号
7212	1.品名 2.形状(平板、卷板)3.材质(铁、非合金钢)4.加工方法(热轧、冷轧经包覆、经镀层、经涂层)5.成分含量(铁、碳、合金元素、非合金元素的含量)6.规格(板材的厚度、宽度)7.涂层种类(锡、铅、电镀锌、涂锌等)
72131000	1.品名 2.形状(条、杆)3.材质(铁、非合金钢)4.加工方法(热轧) 5.状态(不规则盘卷,带有凹痕、凸缘等)6.成分含量(合金元素、非合金元素的含量)7.规格(条、杆的直径)
72132000	1.品名 2.形状(条、杆)3.材质(易切削钢) 4.加工方法(热轧)5.状态(不规则盘卷、不带有凹痕、凸缘等)6.成分含量(合金元素、非合金元素的含量)7.规格(条、杆的直径)
72139	1.品名 2.形状(条、杆)3.材质(铁、非合金钢)4.加工方法(热轧) 5.状态(不规则盘卷)6.成分含量(合金元素、非合金元素的含量)7.截面形状 8.规格(圆形截面需报条、杆的直径)
72141000	1.品名 2.形状(条、杆)3.材质(铁、非合金钢)4.加工方法(锻造) 5.成分含量(合金元素、非合金元素的含量)6.规格(条、杆的直径)
72142000	1.品名 2.形状(条、杆)3.材质(铁、非合金钢)4.加工方法(热轧、热拉拔、热挤压)5.状态(带有轧制产生的变形或轧制后的扭曲)6.成分含量(合金元素、非合金元素的含量)7.规格(条、杆的直径)8.钢号
72143000	1.品名 2.形状(条、杆)3.材质(易切削钢) 4.加工方法(热轧、热拉拔、热挤压)5.成分含量(合金元素、非合金元素的含量)6.状态(不带有轧制产生的变形或轧制后的扭曲)7.规格(条、杆的直径)
72149	1.品名 2.形状(条、杆)3.材质(铁、非合金钢)4.加工方法(热轧、热拉拔、热挤压)5.成分含量(合金元素、非合金元素的含量)6.状态(不带有轧制产生的变形或轧制后的扭曲)7.规格(条、杆的直径)8.截面形状(正方形等)
7215	1.品名 2.形状(条、杆)3.材质(铁、非合金钢)4.加工方法(热加工、冷加工)5.加工程度 6.成分含量(铁、碳、合金元素、非合金元素的含量)7.规格(条、杆的直径)8.易切削钢请注明
7216	1.品名 2.形状(槽钢、角钢、工字钢、H 型钢等)3.材质(铁、非合金钢)4.加工方法(热轧、热拉拔、热挤压、冷加工、冷成形 等)5.加工程度(例如，打孔、冲孔、扭绞、涂层 等)6.成分含量(合金元素、非合金元素的含量)7.规格(型材的截面高度)
7217	1.品名 2.形状(丝)3.材质(铁、非合金钢)4.加工方法(镀层、涂层) 5.成分含量(铁、碳、合金元素、非合金元素的含量)6.镀或涂层种类(锌、铜等)7.状态(盘、卷等)
7218	1.品名 2.形状(方锭等) 3.材质(不锈钢) 4.截面形状(正方形等) 5.钢号
72191	1.品名 2.形状(卷板、平板等)3.材质(不锈钢) 4.加工方法(热轧、冷轧)5.加工程度(是否经酸洗)6.成分含量 7.规格(板材的厚度、宽度)8.钢号
72192	1.品名 2.形状(卷板、平板等)3.材质(不锈钢) 4.加工方法(热轧、冷轧)5.加工程度 6.成分含量 7.规格(板材的厚度、宽度)8.钢号
72193	1.品名 2.形状(卷板、平板等)3.材质(不锈钢) 4.加工方法(热轧、冷轧)5.加工程度 6.成分含量 7.规格(板材的厚度、宽度)8.钢号
72199000	1.品名 2.形状(卷板、平板等)3.材质(不锈钢) 4.加工方法(热轧、冷轧)5.加工程度 6.成分含量 7.规格(板材的厚度、宽度)8.钢号
7220	1.品名 2.形状(卷板、平板等)3.材质(不锈钢) 4.加工方法(热轧、冷轧)5.加工程度 6.成分含量(铁、碳、铬及合金元素、非合金元素的含量) 7.规格(板材的厚度、宽度)8.钢号
7221	1.品名 2.形状(条、杆)3.材质(不锈钢)4.加工方法(热轧)5.状态(不规则盘卷)6.成分含量(铁、碳、铬及合金元素、非合金元素的含量)7.钢号 8.直径
7222	1.品名 2.形状(条、杆、角材、型材、异型材)3.材质(不锈钢)4.加工方法(热轧、热拉拔、热挤压、冷成形、冷加工)5.成分含量(铁、碳、铬及合金元素、非合金元素的含量)6.截面形状(圆形、方形等)7.钢号
7223	1.品名 2.形状(丝)3.材质(不锈钢)4.加工方法(镀层、涂层)5.成分含量(铁、碳、铬及合金元素、非合金元素的含量)6.截面尺寸(圆形填直径，矩形填宽度厚度)7.钢号

商品编码	申报要素
72241000	1.品名 2.形状(方锭等)3.材质(硅锰钢等) 4.成分含量(铁、碳及合金元素、非合金元素的含量)5.钢号
72249	1.品名 2.形状(方锭等)3.材质(硅锰钢等) 4.成分含量(铁、碳及合金元素、非合金元素的含量)5.粗铸锻件坯请注明单件重量 6.钢号
72251	1.品名 2.形状(平板、卷材)3.材质(硅电钢、高速钢等,取向性硅电钢请注明)4.加工工艺(热轧、冷轧)5.成分含量(铁、碳、合金元素、非合金元素的含量)6.规格(板材的厚度、宽度)7.钢号 8.厂商(中文或外文名称)
72253000	1.品名 2.形状(平板、卷材)3.材质(硅电钢、高速钢等,取向性硅电钢请注明)4.加工工艺(热轧或冷轧)5.是否其他加工[无其他加工抛光、磨光或类似处理表面化学处 理包层或叠(迭)层工 艺镀层及涂层]6.成分含量(铁、碳、合金元素、非合金元素的含量)7.规格(板材的厚度、宽度)8.钢号
72254	1.品名 2.形状(平板、卷材)3.材质(硅电钢、高速钢等,取向性硅电钢请注明)4.是否其他加工[无其他加工抛光、磨光或类似处理表面化学处理包层或叠(迭)层工艺镀层及涂层]5.成分含量(铁、碳、合金元素、非合金元素的含量)6.规格(板材的厚度、宽度)7.钢号
72255000	1.品名 2.形状(平板、卷材)3.材质(硅电钢、高速钢等,取向性硅电钢请注明)4.加工工艺(热轧或冷轧)5.是否其他加工[无其他加工抛光、磨光或类似处理表面化学处 理包层或叠(迭)层工 艺镀层及涂层]6.成分含量(铁、碳、合金元素、非合金元素的含量)7.规格(板材的厚度、宽度)8.钢号
72259	1.品名 2.形状(平板、卷材)3.材质(硅电钢、高速钢等,取向性硅电钢请注明)4.加工方法(冷轧或热轧镀层、涂层等)5.成分含量(铁、碳、合金元素、非合金元素的含量) 6.规格(板材的厚度、宽 度)7.涂层种类(电镀锌、涂锌等)8.钢号
72261	1.品名 2.形状(平板、卷材)3.材质(硅电钢、高速钢等,取向性硅电钢请注明)4.加工方法(热轧、冷轧)5.成分含量(铁、碳、合金元素、非合金元素的含量)6.规格(板材的厚度、宽度)7.钢号 8.厂商(中文或外文名称)
72262000	1.品名 2.形状(平板、卷材)3.材质(硅电钢、高速钢等,取向性硅电钢请注明)4.加工方法(热轧、冷轧)5.成分含量(铁、碳、合金元素、非合金元素的含量)6.规格(板材的厚度、宽度)7.钢号
72269	1.品名 2.形状(平板、卷材)3.材质(硅电钢、高速钢等,取向性硅电钢请注明)4.加工方法(热轧或冷轧) 5.是否其他加工[无其他加工抛光、磨光或类似处理表面化学处 理包层或叠(迭)层工 艺镀层及涂层]6.成分含量(铁、碳、合金元素、非合金元素的含量)7.规格(板材的厚度、宽度) 8.涂层种类(电镀锌、涂锌等)9.钢号
7227	1.品名 2.形状(条、杆)3.材质(高速钢、硅锰钢等)4.加工方法(热轧)5.状态(不规则盘 卷)6.成分含量(铁、碳、合金元素、非合金元素的含量)7.钢号
72281000	1.品名 2.用途(适用场所或下游产品)3.形状(条、杆、角材、型材、异型材)4.材质(高速钢、硅锰钢等)5.加工方法(热轧、热拉拔、热挤压、冷成形、冷加工)6.成分含量(铁、碳、合金元素、非合金元素的含量)7.钢号
72282000	1.品名 2.用途(适用场所或下游产品)3.形状(条、杆、角材、型材、异型材)4.材质(高速钢、硅锰钢等)5.加工方法(热轧、热拉拔、热挤压、冷成形、冷加工)6.成分含量(铁、碳、合金元素、非合金元素的含量)7.钢号
72283	1.品名 2.用途(适用场所或下游产品)3.形状(条、杆、角材、型材、异型材)4.材质(高速钢、硅锰钢等)5.加工方法(热轧、热拉拔、热挤压、冷成形、冷加工)6.成分含量(铁、碳、合金元素、非合金元素的含量)7.钢号
72284000	1.品名 2.用途(适用场所或下游产品)3.形状(条、杆、角材、型材、异型材)4.材质(高速钢、硅锰钢等)5.加工方法(热轧、热拉拔、热挤压、冷成形、冷加工)6.成分含量(铁、碳、合金元素、非合金元素的含量)7.钢号
72285000	1.品名 2.用途(适用场所或下游产品)3.形状(条、杆、角材、型材、异型材)4.材质(高速钢、硅锰钢等)5.加工方法(热轧、热拉拔、热挤压、冷成形、冷加工)6.成分含量(铁、碳、合金元素、非合金元素的含量)7.钢号
72286000	1.品名 2.用途(适用场所或下游产品)3.形状(条、杆、角材、型材、异型材)4.材质(高速钢、硅锰钢等)5.加工方法(热轧、热拉拔、热挤压、冷成形、冷加工)6.成分含量(铁、碳、合金元素、非合金元素的含量)7.钢号
72287010	1.品名 2.用途(适用场所或下游产品)3.形状(条、杆、角材、型材、异型材)4.材质(高速钢、硅锰钢等)5.加工方法(热轧、热拉拔、热挤压、冷成形、冷加工)6.成分含量(铁、碳、合金元素、非合金元素的含量)7.空心钻钢需额外申报最大外形尺寸和最大内孔尺寸 8.钢号
72287090	1.品名 2.用途(适用场所或下游产品)3.形状(条、杆、角材、型材、异型材)4.材质(高速钢、硅锰钢等)5.加工方法(热轧、热拉拔、热挤压、冷成形、冷加工)6.成分含量(铁、碳、合金元素、非合金元素的含量)7.钢号
72288000	1.品名 2.用途(适用场所或下游产品)3.形状(条、杆、角材、型材、异型材)4.材质(高速钢、硅锰钢等)5.加工方法(热轧、热拉拔、热挤压、冷成形、冷加工)6.成分含量(铁、碳、合金元素、非合金元素的含量)7.空心钻钢需额外申报最大外形尺寸和最大内孔尺寸 8.钢号
7229	1.品名 2.形状(丝)3.材质(高速钢、硅锰钢等) 4.加工方法(镀层、涂层)5.成分含量(铁、碳、合金元素、非合金元素的含量)6.用途 7.钢号
7301	1.品名 2.形状(板桩,焊接的角材、型材、异型材)3.材质(铁、非合金钢、不锈钢、合金钢)4.加工方法(冷轧、热轧等)5 规格(截面尺寸)
7302	1.品名 2.用途(铁道及电车道铺轨用等) 3.材质(铁、非合金钢、不锈钢、合金钢)4.制品种类(钢轨、轨枕、岔道段体等)
7303	1.品名 2.规格(管的内径)3.形状(圆形截面管、空心异型材) 4.材质(铸铁)
73041	1.品名 2.规格(管的外 径)3.用途(锅炉用、石油或天然气钻探用等)4.形状(管、空心异型材) 5.材质(铁、非合金钢、不锈钢、合金钢)6.加工方法(冷拔、冷轧、热轧等)7.种类(无缝管)
730422	1.品名 2.规格(管的外 径)3.用途(锅炉用、石油或天然气钻探用等)4.形状(管、空心异型材) 5.材质(铁、非合金钢、不锈钢、合金钢)6.加工方法(冷拔、冷轧、热轧等)7.种类(无缝管)
730423	1.品名 2.规格(管的外 径)3.用途(锅炉用、石油或天然气钻探用等)4.形状(管、空心异型材) 5.材质(铁、非合金钢、不锈钢、合金钢)6.加工方法(冷拔、冷轧、热轧等)7.种类(无缝管)

商品编码	申报要素
73042400	1.品名 2.规格(管的外 径)3.用途(锅炉用、石油或天然气钻探用等)4.形状(管、空心异型材) 5.材质(铁、非合金钢、不锈钢、合金钢)6.加工方法(冷拔、冷轧、热轧等)7.种类(无缝管)
730429	1.品名 2.规格(管的外 径)3.用途(锅炉用、石油或天然气钻探用等)4.形状(管、空心异型材) 5.材质(铁、非合金钢、不锈钢、合金钢)6.加工方法(冷拔、冷轧、热轧等)7.种类(无缝管)8.屈服强度
73043	1.品名 2.规格(管的外 径)3.用途(锅炉用、石油或天然气钻探用等)4.形状(管、空心异型材) 5.材质(铁、非合金钢、不锈钢、合金钢)6.加工方法(冷拔、冷轧、热轧等)7.种类(无缝管)
73044	1.品名 2.规格(管的外 径)3.用途(锅炉用、石油或天然气钻探用等)4.形状(管、空心异型材) 5.材质(铁、非合金钢、不锈钢、合金钢)6.加工方法(冷拔、冷轧、热轧等)7.种类(无缝管)
73045	1.品名 2.规格(管的外 径)3.用途(锅炉用、石油或天然气钻探用等)4.形状(管、空心异型材) 5.材质(铁、非合金钢、不锈钢、合金钢)6.加工方法(冷拔、冷轧、热轧等)7.种类(无缝管)
73049000	1.品名 2.规格(管的外 径)3.用途(锅炉用、石油或天然气钻探用等)4.形状(管、空心异型材) 5.材质(铁、非合金钢、不锈钢、合金钢)6.加工方法(冷拔、冷轧、热轧等)7.种类(无缝管)
7305	1.品名 2.规格(管的外径)3.用途(石油或天然气管道用等)4.材质(铁、非合金钢、不锈钢、合金钢)5.种类(石油管道管等)6.加工方法(铆、纵向焊、埋弧焊)7.截面形状(圆形)
73061	1.品名 2.规格(圆管的外径、壁厚)3.用途(石油或天然气管道用等)4.材质(铁、非合金钢、不锈钢、合金钢)5.种类(焊接管等)6.加工方法(铆、纵向焊、埋弧焊)7.截面形状(圆形、方形或椭圆形等)
73062	1.品名 2.规格(圆管的外径、壁厚)3.用途(钻探石油及天然气用的套管等)4.材质(铁、非合金钢、不锈钢、合金钢)5.种类(焊接管等)6.加工方法(铆、纵向焊、埋弧焊)7.截面形状(圆形、方形或椭圆形等)
73063	1.品名 2.规格(圆管的外径、壁厚)3.用途 4.材质(铁、非合金钢、不锈钢、合金钢)5.种类(焊接管等)6.加工方法(铆、纵向焊、埋弧焊)7.截面形状(圆形、方形或椭圆形等)
73064000	1.品名 2.规格(圆管的外径、壁厚)3.用途 4.材质(铁、非合金钢、不锈钢、合金钢)5.种类(焊接管等)6.加工方法(铆、纵向焊、埋弧焊)7.截面形状(圆形、方形或椭圆形等)
73065000	1.品名 2.规格(圆管的外径、壁厚)3.用途 4.材质(铁、非合金钢、不锈钢、合金钢)5.种类(焊接管等)6.加工方法(铆、纵向焊、埋弧焊)7.截面形状(圆形、方形或椭圆形等)
73066	1.品名 2.规格(圆管的外径、壁厚)3.用途 4.材质(铁、非合金钢、不锈钢、合金钢)5.种类(焊接管等)6.加工方法(铆、纵向焊、埋弧焊)7.截面形状(圆形、方形或椭圆形等)
73069000	1.品名 2.规格(圆管的外径、壁厚)3.用途 4.材质(铁、非合金钢、不锈钢、合金钢)5.种类(焊接管等)6.加工方法(铆、纵向焊、埋弧焊)7.截面形状(圆形、方形或椭圆形等)
7307	1.品名 2.用途(用于管子之间连通)3.材质(无可锻性铸铁、可锻性铸铁、不锈钢、其他钢铁)4.种类(法兰、管套、十字接头、对焊件等)5.加工方法(铸造、锻造等)
73081000	1.品名 2.用途(支撑用等)3.材质 4.种类(桥梁体段等)
73082000	1.品名 2.用途(支撑用等)3.材质 4.种类(塔楼等)
73083000	1.品名 2.用途(支撑用等)3.材质 4.种类(门、窗等)
73084000	1.品名 2.用途(支撑用等)3.材质 4.种类(脚手架等)
73089000	1.品名 2.用途(支撑用等)3.材质 4.种类
7309	1.品名 2.用途(盛装液体用等)3.材质 4.种类(罐、桶等)5.规格(容积)6.是否装有机械或热力装置
73101000	1.品名 2.用途(盛装液体用等)3.材质 4.种类(罐、桶等)5.规格(容积)6.是否装有机械或热力装置
73102110	1.品名 2.用途(盛装液体用等)3.材质 4.种类(罐、桶等)5.加工方法(焊边接合、卷边接合等)6.规格(容积)7.是否装有机械或热力装置
73102190	1.品名 2.用途(盛装液体用等)3.材质 4.种类(罐、桶等)5.加工方法(焊边接合、卷边接合等)6.规格(容积)7.是否装有机械或热力装置
731029	1.品名 2.用途(盛装液体用等)3.材质 4.种类(罐、桶等)5.加工方法(焊边接合、卷边接合等)6.规格(容积)7.是否装有机械或热力装置
7311	1.品名 2.用途(压缩气体或液化气体用、零售包装用等)3.材质 4 种类(罐、桶等)
73121000	1.品名 2.材质 3.制品种类(绞股线、绳等)4.注明"非绝缘"
73129000	1.品名 2.材质 3.制品种类(吊索等)4.注明"非绝缘"
7313	1.品名 2.用途(围篱用)3.材质 4.种类(带刺钢铁丝、绞带、单股扁丝、松绞的双股丝)5.截面尺寸
7314	1.品名 2.用途(工业用 等)3.材质(铁、非合金钢、不锈钢、合金钢)4.种类(网、篱、格栅等) 5.加工方法(镀锌、涂锌、涂塑等)6.规格(网眼尺寸、丝的截面尺寸)
7315	1.品名 2.用途(自行车用、摩托车用等)3.材质 4.种类(铰接链、滚子链、日字环节链等)
7316	1.品名 2.材质 3.种类(钢铁锚、多爪锚等)
7317	1.品名 2.材质 3.种类(图钉、U 形钉、平头钉、波纹钉等)
73181100	1.品名 2.材质 3.螺钉种类(方头)4.品牌(中文或外文名称)5.型号 6.杆径
73181200	1.品名 2.材质 3.品牌(中文或外文名称)4.型号 5.杆径
73181300	1.品名 2.材质 3.品牌(中文或外文名称)4.型号 5.杆径
73181400	1.品名 2.材质 3.品牌(中文或外文名称)4.型号 5.杆径
73181510	1.品名 2.材质 3.抗拉强度 4.品牌(中文或外文名称)5.型号 6.杆径
73181500	1.品名 2.材质 3.抗拉强度 4.品牌(中文或外文名称)5.型号 6.杆径
73181600	1.品名 2.材质 3.品牌(中文或外文名称)4.型号
73181900	1.品名 2.材质 3.种类(螺钉、螺母、垫圈、铆钉、销等)4.品牌(中文或外文名称)5.型号
73182	1.品名 2.材质 3.品牌(中文或外文名称)4.型号
7319	1.品名 2.材质 3.种类(缝针、织补针、刺绣针、别针等)
7320	1.品名 2.用途(汽车用、铁道车辆用等)3.材质 4.种类(片簧、螺旋弹簧等)
7321	1.品名 2.材质 3.种类(煤油炉、煤气灶、烤肉架、烤炉等)4.原理(非电热)5.燃料种类(液体、固体、气体燃料)6.品牌(中文或外文名称)7.型号
7322	1.品名 2.用途(集中供暖用等)3.材质 4.种类(散热器、空气加热器、暖气分布器等)5.原理(非电热)6.是否装有电动风扇或鼓风机 7.品牌(中文或外文名称)

商品编码	申报要素
7323	1.品名 2.用途（厨房用、餐桌用等）3.材质（铁、非合金钢、不锈钢、合金钢）4.种类（水壶、煎锅等）5.加工方法（已搪瓷、未搪瓷）6.品牌（中文或外文名称）
7324	1.品名 2.用途（卫生间用等）3.材质（铁、非合金钢、不锈钢、合金钢）4.种类（脸盆、浴缸等）5.加工方法（已搪瓷、未搪瓷）6.品牌（中文或外文名称）
7325	1.品名 2.用途（工业用、非工业用、研磨机用等）3.材质（无可锻性铸铁等）4.种类（井盖、研磨球等）
7326	1.品名 2.用途（工业用、非工业用）3.材质 4.种类（捕鼠器、香烟盒等）5.加工方法（锻造、冲压 等，是否经进一步加工）
7401	1.品名 2.材质（铜锍、沉积铜）3.成分含量（铜化合物的含量）
7402	1.品名 2.成分含量（铜的含量及黄金含量）3.材质（锭状未精炼铜、其他未精炼铜）4.用途（电解精炼用等）5.计价日期 6.签约日期
740311	1.品名 2.形状（型材、线锭、坯段等）3.材质（精炼铜、黄铜、青铜、白铜等）4.加工方法（未锻轧等）5.成分含量（铜及合金元素的含量）6.计价日期 7.签约日期
74031200	1.品名 2.形状（型材、线锭、坯段等）3.材质（精炼铜、黄铜、青铜、白铜等）4.加工方法（未锻轧等）5.成分含量（铜及合金元素的含量）
74031300	1.品名 2.形状（型材、线锭、坯段等）3.材质（精炼铜、黄铜、青铜、白铜等）4.加工方法（未锻轧等）5.成分含量（铜及合金元素的含量）
74031900	1.品名 2.形状（型材、线锭、坯段等）3.材质（精炼铜、黄铜、青铜、白铜等）4.加工方法（未锻轧等）5.成分含量（铜及合金元素的含量）
74032	1.品名 2.形状（型材、线锭、坯段等）3.材质（精炼铜、黄铜、青铜、白铜等）4.加工方法（未锻轧等）5.成分含量（铜及合金元素的含量）
7404	1.品名 2.用途 3.材质（铜）4.状态（废、碎、管、板、线、棒、边角料 等）5.来源（生产加工产生的边角余料，拆解电线电缆、电器等）6.成分含量（总金属含量、铜含量及商品所含其他各种金属含量）7.回收率 8.计价日期 9.签约日期
7405	1.品名 2.用途（用作炼铜的添加剂）3.成分含量（铜、磷的含量）
7406	1.品名 2.用途（用作电镀基底、金属颜料等）3.形状（片状粉末、非片状粉 末）4.材质（精炼铜、黄铜、青铜、白铜等）5.成分含量（铜及合金元素的含量）6.粒度 7.牌号 8.型号
74071	1.品名 2.形状（条、杆、型材、异型材）3.材质（精炼铜、黄铜、青铜、白铜等）4.成分含量（铜及合金元素的含量）
74072111	1.品名 2.形状（条、杆、型材、异型材）3.材质（精炼铜、黄铜、青铜、白铜等）4.成分含量（铜及合金元素的含量）5.直线度
74072119	1.品名 2.形状（条、杆、型材、异型材）3.材质（精炼铜、黄铜、青铜、白铜等）4.成分含量（铜及合金元素的含量）
74072190	1.品名 2.形状（条、杆、型材、异型材）3.材质（精炼铜、黄铜、青铜、白铜等）4.成分含量（铜及合金元素的含量）
74072900	1.品名 2.形状（条、杆、型材、异型材）3.材质（精炼铜、黄铜、青铜、白铜等）4.成分含量（铜及合金元素的含量）
74081100	1.品名 2.形状（丝）3.材质（精炼铜、黄铜、青铜、白铜等）4.成分含量（铜及合金元素的含量）5.规格（丝的最大截面尺寸）6.牌号 7.型号
74081900	1.品名 2.形状（丝）3.材质（精炼铜、黄铜、青铜、白铜等）4.成分含量（铜及合金元素的含量）5.规格（丝的最大截面尺寸）6.含氧量 7.牌号 8.型号
74082	1.品名 2.形状（丝）3.材质（精炼铜、黄铜、青铜、白铜等）4.成分含量（铜及合金元素的含量）5.规格（丝的最大截面尺寸）6.牌号 7.型号
7409	1.品名 2.形状（板、片、带）3.材质（精炼铜、黄铜、青铜、白铜等）4.状态（盘卷、平板等）5.成分含量（铜及合金元素的含量）6.规格（长×宽×厚）7.含氧量 8.品牌（中文或外文名称，无品牌请申报厂商）9.牌号 10.型号
7410	1.品名 2.形状（箔）3.材质（精炼铜、黄铜、青铜、白铜等）4.状态（有无衬背）5.成分含量（铜及合金元素的各自含量）6.规格（整体厚度、铜箔厚度、长度、宽度）7.用途 8.品牌（中文或外文名称）9.牌号 10.种类（压延铜箔、电解铜箔，刚性覆铜板、柔性覆铜板）11.覆铜板的铜箔层数 12.覆铜板的基材材质（纸基、玻璃布基、复合基、环保型基 等）13.生产厂商
74111011	1.品名 2.材质（精炼铜、黄铜、青铜、白铜等）3.成分含量（铜及合金元素的含量）4.外径 5.有无螺纹或翅片 6.用途 7.品牌（中文或外文名称）8.牌号 9.型号
74111019	1.品名 2.材质（精炼铜、黄铜、青铜、白铜等）3.成分含量（铜及合金元素的含量）4.外径 5.有无螺纹或翅片 6.含氧量 7.用途 8.品牌（中文或外文名称）9.牌号 10.型号
74111020	1.品名 2.材质（精炼铜、黄铜、青铜、白铜等）3.成分含量（铜及合金元素的含量）4.外径 5.有无螺纹或翅片 6.用途 7.品牌（中文或外文名称）8.牌号 9.型号
74111090	1.品名 2.材质（精炼铜、黄铜、青铜、白铜等）3.成分含量（铜及合金元素的含量）4.外径 5.有无螺纹或翅片 6.用途 7.品牌（中文或外文名称）8.牌号 9.型号
74112	1.品名 2.材质（精炼铜、黄铜、青铜、白铜等）3.成分含量（铜及合金元素的含量）4.外径 5.有无螺纹或翅片 6.用途 7.品牌（中文或外文名称）8.牌号 9.型号
7412	1.品名 2.用途（用于管子之间连通）3.材质（精炼铜、黄铜、青铜、白铜等）4.种类（接头、肘管、管套）5.成分含量（铜及合金元素的含量）6.品牌（中文或外文名称）7.牌号 8.型号
7413	1.品名 2.材质（铜）3.种类（绞股线、缆、编带等）4.注明"非绝缘"5.品牌（中文或外文名称）6.牌号 7.型号
7415	1.品名 2.材质（铜）3.种类（图钉、U 形钉、螺钉、螺母、垫圈、铆钉等）4.品牌（中文或外文名称）5.型号
74181010	1.品名 2.用途（厨房用、餐桌用、卫生用等）3.材质（铜）4.种类（水壶、煎锅等）5.品牌（中文或外文名称）6.型号
74181020	1.品名 2.材质（铜）3.种类（煤油炉、煤气灶等）4.原理（非电热）5.品牌（中文或外文名称）6.型号
74181090	1.品名 2.用途（厨房用、餐桌用、卫生用等）3.材质（铜）4.种类（水壶、煎锅等）5.品牌（中文或外文名称）6.型号
74182000	1.品名 2.用途（厨房用、餐桌用、卫生用等）3.材质（铜）4.种类（水壶、煎锅等）5.品牌（中文或外文名称）6.型号
74192	1.品名 2.用途（工业用、非工业用）3.材质（铜）4.种类（链条、容器等）5.加工方法（锻造、冲压等）6.型号
74198010	1.品名 2.用途（工业用、非工业用）3.材质（铜）4.种类（链条、容器等）5.加工方法（锻造、冲压等）6.型号
74198020	1.品名 2.材质（铜）3.品牌（中文或外文名称）4.型号 5.用途

商品编码	申报要素
74198030	1.品名 2.材质（铜）3.种类 4.品牌（中文或外文名称）5.型号 6.用途
74198040	1.品名 2.材质（铜）3.种类（网、格栅、网眼铜板等）4.品牌（中文或外文名称）5.型号 6.用途
74198050	1.品名 2.材质（铜）3.种类 4.原理（非电热）5.品牌（中文或外文名称）6.型号 7.用途
7419809	1.品名 2.用途（工业用、非工业用）3.材质（铜）4.种类（链条、容器等）5.加工方法（锻造、冲压等）
75011000	1.品名 2.材质（镍锍、氧化镍烧结物等）3.来源 4.成分含量（镍化合物的含量）
75012	1.品名 2.材质（镍锍、氧化镍烧结物等）3.来源 4.成分含量（镍化合物的含量）5.计价日期
75021	1.品名 2.形状（锭、块等）3.材质（非合金镍、镍合金）4.加工方法（未锻轧）5.成分含量（例如，未锻轧非合金镍锭，含镍 99.986%，含钴 0.004%）6.计价日期 7.签约日期
75022000	1.品名 2.形状（锭、块等）3.材质（非合金镍、镍合金）4.加工方法（未锻轧）5.成分含量（例如，未锻轧非合金镍锭，含镍 99.986%，含钴 0.004%）
7503	1.品名 2.用途（供回收镍用）3.状态（废、碎）4.来源（非合金镍、镍合金的废碎料）5.成分含量（镍及合金元素的含量）
75040010	1.品名 2.形状（片状粉末、非片状粉末）3.材质（非合金镍、镍合金）4.成分含量（镍及合金元素的含量）5.粒度 6.计价日期 7.签约日期
75040020	1.品名 2.形状（片状粉末、非片状粉末）3.材质（非合金镍、镍合金）4.成分含量（镍及合金元素的含量）5.粒度
75051	1.品名 2.形状（条、杆、型材、异型材、丝）3.材质（非合金镍、镍合金）4.成分含量（镍及合金元素的含量）
75052	1.品名 2.形状（条、杆、型材、异型材、丝）3.材质（非合金镍、镍合金）4.成分含量（镍及合金元素的含量）5.丝的直径
7506	1.品名 2.形状（板、片、带、箔）3.材质（非合金镍、镍合金）4.成分含量（镍及合金元素的含量）5.规格（长×宽×厚）
7507	1.品名 2.材质（非合金镍、镍合金）3.种类（管、接头、肘管、管套等）4.成分含量（镍及合金元素的含量）
7508	1.品名 2.用途（电镀用、工业用、非工业用）3.材质（非合金镍、镍合金）4.种类（网、篱、格栅等）5.品牌（中文或外文名称）6.型号
7601	1.品名 2.形状（锭、块）3.材质（非合金铝、铝合金）4.加工方法（未锻轧或铸造、烧结等）5.成分含量（铝及合金元素的含量）6.计价日期 7.签约日期
7602	1.品名 2.用途 3.状态（碎、管、板、片、线、棒、边角料等）4.来源（生产加工产生的边角余料，拆解电线电缆、电器等）5.成分含量（总金属含量、铝含量及商品所含其他各种金属含量）6.回收率 7.计价日期 8.签约日期
7603	1.品名 2.形状（片状粉末、非片状粉末）3.材质（非合金铝、铝合金）4.成分含量（铝的含量）5.粒度 6.用途
7604	1.品名 2.形状（条、杆、型材、异型材）3.材质（非合金铝、铝合金）4.成分含量（铝及合金元素的含量）5.型材、异型材请注明是否空心 6.铝合金条、杆请注明截面周长 7.柱形实心体铝合金请注明 20℃时的极限抗拉强度 8.牌号
7605	1.品名 2.形状（丝）3.材质（非合金铝、铝合金）4.成分含量（铝及合金元素的含量）5.规格（丝的最大截面尺寸）
7606	1.品名 2.形状（矩形等）3.材质（非合金铝、铝合金）4.状态（板、片、带）5.成分含量（铝及合金元素的含量）6.规格（长×宽×厚）7.品牌（中文或外文名称）8.用途 9.牌号
7607	1.品名 2.形状（箔）3.材质（铝）4.状态（有无衬背、衬背材料）5.规格（长×宽×厚）6.加工方法（轧制等）7.加工程度（是否进一步加工）
76081000	1.品名 2.材质（非合金 铝）3.种类（管）4.成分含量（铝及合金元素的含量）5.管壁厚度 6.管壁外径 7.孔眼直径 8.管材长度
76082	1.品名 2.材质（铝合金）3.种类（管）4.成分含量（铝及合金元素的含量）5.管壁厚度 6.管壁外径 7.孔眼直径 8.管材长度
7609	1.品名 2.用途 3.材质（非合金铝、铝合金）4.种类（接头、肘管、管套）
76101000	1.品名 2.材质（铝）3.种类（门窗、门槛等）4.加工方法（铆接、栓接、钻孔、弯曲等）
76109000	1.品名 2.材质（铝）3.种类（塔楼、桥梁体段等）4.加工方法（铆接、栓接、钻孔、弯曲等）
7611	1.品名 2.用途（盛装液体用等）3.材质（铝）4.种类（罐、桶等）5.规格（容积）6.品牌（中文或外文名称）
76121000	1.品名 2.用途（盛装液体用等）3.材质（铝）4.种类（罐、桶等）5.规格（容积）6.品牌（中文或外文名称）
76129010	1.品名 2.用途（盛装液体用等）3.材质（铝）4.种类（罐、桶等）5.规格（容积）6.品牌（中文或外文名称）
76129090	1.品名 2.用途（盛装液体用等）3.材质（铝）4.种类（罐、桶等）5.规格（容积）6.品牌（中文或外文名称）
7613	1.品名 2.用途（盛装液体用等）3.材质（铝）4.种类（罐、桶等）5.规格（容积）6.品牌（中文或外文名称）
76141000	1.品名 2.材质（铝）3.种类（绞股线、缆、编带 等）4.状态（非绝缘）5.带钢芯请注明
76149000	1.品名 2.材质（铝）3.种类（绞股线、缆、编带 等）4.状态（非绝缘）5.带钢芯请注明
76151	1.品名 2.用途（厨房用、餐桌用等）3.材质（铝）4.种类（水壶、煎锅等）
76152000	1.品名 2.用途（卫生用 等）3.材质（铝）4.种类
7616	1.品名 2.用途（工业用、非工业用）3.材质（铝）4.种类（图钉、螺钉、布、网、篱等）
7801	1.品名 2.形状（锭、块）3.材质（精炼铅、铅合金）4.加工方法（未锻轧）5.成分含量（铅及合金元素的含量）6.计价日期 7.签约日期
7802	1.品名 2.用途（供回收铅用）3.材质（铅）4.状态（废、碎）5.来源（精炼铅、铅合金的废碎料）6.成分含量（铅的含量）
7804	1.品名 2.形状（板、片、带、箔、粉末及片状粉末）3.材质（铅）4.规格（板、箔的厚度）5.粒度
78060010	1.品名 2.形状（条、杆、型材、异型材、丝）3.材质（铅）
78060090	1.品名 2.用途（工业用、非工业用）3.材质（铅）4.种类（容器、铅坠等）
790111	1.品名 2.形状（锭、块）3.材质（非合金锌、锌合金）4.加工方法（未锻轧）5.成分含量（锌及合金元素的含量）6.计价日期 7.签约日期
79011200	1.品名 2.形状（锭、块）3.材质（非合金锌、锌合金）4.加工方法（未锻轧）5.成分含量（锌及合金元素的含量）
79012000	1.品名 2.形状（锭、块）3.材质（非合金锌、锌合金）4.加工方法（未锻轧）5.成分含量（锌及合金元素的含量）

商品编码	申报要素
7902	1.品名 2.用途(供回收锌用)3.状态(废、碎)4.来源(精炼锌、锌合金的废碎料)5.成分含量(锌的含量)
7903	1.品名 2.用途(用作硬质合金的黏合剂)3.形状(片状粉末、非片状粉末)4.材质(锌)5.成分含量(锌的含量)6.粒度
7904	1.品名 2.形状(条、杆、型材、异型材、丝)3.材质(锌)
7905	1.品名 2.形状(矩形等)3.材质(锌等)4.状态(板、片、带)5.成分含量(锌及合金元素的含量)6.规格(长×宽×厚)7.品牌(中文或外文名称)8.用途 9.加工程度(是否经表面处理剂处理、处理方法和所用材料)
7907	1.品名 2.用途 3.材质(锌、锌合金等)4.种类(管、接头、肘管、管套等)
8001	1.品名 2.形状(锭、块、粒)3.材质(非合金锡、锡合金)4.加工方法(未锻轧)5.成分含量(锡及合金元素的含量)6.计价日期 7.签约日期
8002	1.品名 2.用途(供回收锡用)3.状态(废、碎)4.来源(非合金锡、锡合金的废碎料)5.成分含量(锡的含量)
8003	1.品名 2.形状(条、杆、型材、异型材、丝)3.材质(锡)4.状态(是否带焊剂)
80070020	1.品名 2.形状(板、片、带)3.规格(长、宽、厚)4.材质(锡)5.状态(有无衬背、衬背材料)
80070030	1.品名 2.形状(箔、粉末)3.材质(锡)4.状态(有无衬背、衬背材料)5.规格(锡箔长×宽×厚)6.粉末粒度
80070040	1.品名 2.材质(锡)3.种类(接头、肘管、管套等)
80070090	1.品名 2.材质(锡)3.种类
81011000	1.品名 2.形状(粉末)3.材质(钨)4.成分含量(钨的含量)5.粉末请注明粒度
81019400	1.品名 2.形状(条、杆 等)3.材质(钨)4.加工方法(未锻轧、简单烧结等)
81019600	1.品名 2.形状(丝)3.材质(钨)
81019700	1.品名 2.用途(供回收钨用)3.材质(钨)4.状态(废、碎)5.来源
810199	1.品名 2.形状(条、杆、型材、异型材、板、片、带、箔)3.材质(钨、钨合金)4.加工方法(锻轧)5.用途 6.成分含量 7.每个重量 8.圆柱形请注明是否空心、内径
81021000	1.品名 2.形状(粉末)3.材质(钼)4.粉末请注明粒度
81029400	1.品名 2.形状(条、杆)3.材质(钼)4.加工方法(未锻轧、简单烧结等)
81029500	1.品名 2.形状(条、杆、型材、异型材、板、片、带、箔)3.材质(钼、钼合金)4.加工方法(锻轧)
81029600	1.品名 2.形状(丝)3.材质(钼)
81029700	1.品名 2.用途(供回收钼用)3.材质(钼)4.来源
81029900	1.品名 2.材质(钼)3.种类
81032	1.品名 2.形状(粉末、条、杆、型材、异型材、板、片、带、箔)3.材质(钽、钽合金)4.加工方法(锻轧、未锻轧、简单烧结等)5.状态(废、碎、非废碎)6.成分含量(钽的含量)7.粉末需申报松装密度
81033000	1.品名 2.形状(粉末、条、杆、型材、异型材、板、片、带、箔)3.材质(钽、钽合金)4.加工方法(锻轧、未锻轧、简单烧结等)5.状态(废、碎、非废碎)6.成分含量(钽的含量)
81039	1.品名 2.形状(粉末、条、杆、型材、异型材、板、片、带、箔)3.材质(钽、钽合金)4.加工方法(锻轧、未锻轧、简单烧结等)5.状态(废、废碎)6.成分含量(钽的含量)7.丝需申报直径
81041	1.品名 2.材质(镁)3.加工方法(未锻轧)4.成分含量(镁的含量)5.粉末请注明粒度
81042000	1.品名 2.用途(供回收镁用)3.状态(废、碎)4.来源
81043000	1.品名 2.形状(粉末等)3.材质(镁)4.来源(锉屑、车屑等)5.成分含量(镁的含量)6.粉末请注明粒度
81049	1.品名 2.材质(镁)3.加工方法(锻轧等)
81052010	1.品名 2.形状(粉末、颗粒等)3.材质(钴、钴合金、钴锍)4.状态(废、碎、非废碎)6.成分含量(钴:以干基钴为标准、水分含量、其他元素含量)7.计价日期 8.签约日期
81052020	1.品名 2.形状(粉末、颗粒等)3.材质(钴、钴合金、钴锍)4.状态(废、碎、非废碎)6.成分含量(钴:以干基钴为标准、水分含量、其他元素含量)
81052090	1.品名 2.形状(粉末、条、杆、型材、异型材、板、片、带、箔)3.材质(钴、钴合金、钴锍)4.加工方法(锻轧)5.状态(废、碎、非废碎)
81053000	1.品名 2.材质 3.状态(废、碎等)4.成分含量
81059000	1.品名 2.材质 3.成分含量
8106	1.品名 2.形状(粉末、条、杆、型材、异型材、板、片、带、箔)3.材质(铋、铋合金)4.加工方法(锻轧、未锻轧)5.状态(废、碎、非废碎)6.成分含量(铋的含量)
81082	1.品名 2.形状(粉末、杆等)3.材质(钛)4.加工方法(未锻轧)5.成分含量(钛的含量)6.粉末请注明粒度
81083000	1.品名 2.用途(供回收钛用)3.状态(废、碎)4.来源
81089	1.品名 2.形状(条、杆、型材、异型材、板、片、带、箔等)3.材质(钛)4.种类 5.加工方法 6.板、片、带、箔的厚度请注明
8109	1.品名 2.形状(粉末、条、杆、型材、异型材、板、片、带、箔)3.材质(锆、锆合金)4.加工方法(未锻轧等)5.状态(废、碎、非废碎)6.成分含量(锆的含量)7.粉末请注明粒度
8110	1.品名 2.形状(粉末、条、杆、型材、异型材、板、片、带、箔)3.材质(锑、锑合金)4.加工方法(未锻轧等)5.状态(废、碎、非废碎)6.成分含量(锑的含量)7.粉末请注明粒度
8111	1.品名 2.形状(粉末、条、杆、型材、异型材、板、片、带、箔)3.材质(锰、锰合金)4.加工方法(未锻轧、锻压、模压等)5.状态(废、碎、非废碎)6.成分含量(锰的含量)7.粉末请注明粒度
8112	1.品名 2.形状(粉末、条、杆、型材、异型材、板、片、带、箔)3.材质(铍、铬等贱金属及其合金) 4.加工方法(未锻轧等)5.状态(废、碎、非废碎)6.成分含量 7.粉末请注明粒度
8113	1.品名 2.材质(金属陶瓷)3.状态(废、碎、非废碎)
8201	1.品名 2.用途(砍伐用、修枝用等)3.材质(合金钢制等)4.种类(锹、铲、剪等)5.式样(单手操作等)6.品牌(中文或外文名称)
8202	1.品名 2.用途(加工金属用等)3.材质(合金钢制等)4.种类(手工锯、带锯片、圆锯片、直锯片等)5.带锯片、圆锯片带有钢制、金刚石制、氮化硼制工作部件请注明 6.品牌(中文或外文名称)
8203	1.品名 2.用途(锉木材用等)3.材质(合金钢制等)4.种类(锉、钳子、镊子等)5.品牌(中文或外文名称)
82041	1.品名 2.材质(合金钢制等)3.种类(扳手、扳钳、扳手套筒等)4.式样(固定的、可调的)5.品牌(中文或外文名称)
82042000	1.品名 2.材质(合金钢制等)3.种类(扳手、扳钳、扳手套筒等)4.品牌(中文或外文名称)
8205	1.品名 2.用途(家用等)3.材质(合金钢制等)4.种类(锤子、螺丝刀等)5.是否成套 6.品牌(中文或外文名称)
8206	1.品名 2.材质(合金钢制等)3.包含的种类(扳手、钳子、螺丝刀等)4.是否零售包装成套 5.品牌(中文或外文名称)
8207	1.品名 2.用途(钻探、铣削、锻压、镗孔用等)3.材质(合金钢制等)4.种类(锻模、铣刀等)5.是否带工作部件,若带有请注明材质(金属陶瓷、金刚石等)6.品牌(中文或外文名称)7.型号
82081	1.品名 2.用途(金属加工用)3.材质(不锈钢制等)4.种类(机器用刀片等)5.是否经镀层或涂层请注明 6.品牌(中文或外文名称)
82082000	1.品名 2.用途(木器加工用)3.材质(不锈钢制等)4.种类(机器用刀片等)5.品牌(中文或外文名称)
82083000	1.品名 2.用途(厨房器具、食品工业机器用等)3.材质(不锈钢制等)4.种类(机器用刀片等)5.品牌(中文或外文名称)
82084000	1.品名 2.用途(农业、园艺、林业机器用等)3.材质(不锈钢制等)4.种类(机器用刀片等)5.品牌(中文或外文名称)
82089000	1.品名 2.用途 3.材质(不锈钢制等)4.种类 5.品牌(中文或外文名称)
82090010	1.品名 2.用途(工具用)3.材质(金属陶瓷制)4.种类(板、杆、刀头等)5.是否装配 6.品牌(中文或外文名称)
82090021	1.品名 2.用途(工具用)3.材质(金属陶瓷制)4.种类(板、杆、刀头等)5.是否装配 6.晶粒度 7.品牌(中文或外文名称)
82090029	1.品名 2.用途(工具用)3.材质(金属陶瓷制)4.种类(板、杆、刀头等)5.是否装配 6.品牌(中文或外文名称)
82090030	1.品名 2.用途(工具用)3.材质(金属陶瓷制)4.种类(板、杆、刀头等)5.是否装配 6.品牌(中文或外文名称)
82090090	1.品名 2.用途(工具用)3.材质(金属陶瓷制)4.种类(板、杆、刀头等)5.是否装配 6.品牌(中文或外文名称)
8210	1.品名 2.用途(加工食品用等)3.材质(不锈钢制等)4.种类(绞肉机、榨汁机等)5.原理(手动)6.单件重量 7.品牌(中文或外文名称)
82111000	1.品名 2.材质(不锈钢制等)3.种类(餐刀、折叠刀等)4.式样(刃面固定、可换刃面)5.是否成套 6.品牌(中文或外文名称)
82119100	1.品名 2.材质(不锈钢制等)3.种类(餐刀)4.式样(刃面固定)5.品牌(中文或外文名称)
82119200	1.品名 2.材质(不锈钢制等)3.种类(折叠刀等) 4.式样(刃面固定)5.品牌(中文或外文名称)
82119300	1.品名 2.材质(不锈钢制等)3.种类(餐刀、折叠刀等)4.式样(可换刃面)5.品牌(中文或外文名称)
82119400	1.品名 2.材质(不锈钢制等)3.种类(刀片等)4.品牌(中文或外文名称)
82119500	1.品名 2.材质(不锈钢制等)3.种类(刀柄)4.品牌(中文或外文名称)
8212	1.品名 2.材质(不锈钢制等)3.种类(剃刀、安全刀片等)4.品牌(中文或外文名称)
8213	1.品名 2.用途(裁缝用等)3.材质(不锈钢制 等)4.种类(剪刀、剪刀片等)5.品牌(中文或外文名称)
82141000	1.品名 2.材质(不锈钢制等)3.种类(裁纸刀、铅笔刀等)4.品牌(中文或外文名称)
82142000	1.品名 2.材质(不锈钢制等)3.种类(指甲锉等)4.品牌(中文或外文名称)
82149000	1.品名 2.材质(不锈钢制等)3.种类(手动理发推剪、切菜刀等)4.品牌(中文或外文名称)
8215	1.品名 2.用途(餐桌、厨房用)3.材质(不锈钢制等)4.种类(餐叉、漏勺等)5.是否镀贵金属 6.是否成套 7.品牌(中文或外文名称)
83011000	1.品名 2.用途(机动车用、家具用等)3.材质(不锈钢制等)4.种类(钥匙锁、数码锁、电动锁、钥匙等)5.品牌(中文或外文名称)
83012	1.品名 2.用途(机动车用)3.材质(不锈钢制 等)4.种类(钥匙锁、数码锁、电动锁、钥匙等)5.品牌(中文或外文名称)
83013000	1.品名 2.用途(家具用)3.材质(不锈钢制等)4.种类(钥匙锁、数码锁、电动锁、钥匙等)5.品牌(中文或外文名称)
83014000	1.品名 2.用途 3.材质(不锈钢制等)4.种类(钥匙锁、数码锁、电动锁、钥匙等)5.品牌(中文或外文名称)
83015000	1.品名 2.用途(机动车用、家具用等)3.材质(不锈钢制等)4.种类(钥匙锁、数码锁、电动锁、钥匙等)5.品牌(中文或外文名称)
83016000	1.品名 2.用途(机动车用、家具用等)3.材质(不锈钢制等)4.种类(钥匙锁、数码锁、电动锁、钥匙等)5.品牌(中文或外文名称)
83017000	1.品名 2.用途(机动车用、家具用等)3.材质(不锈钢制等)4.种类(钥匙锁、数码锁、电动锁、钥匙等)5.品牌(中文或外文名称)
83021000	1.品名 2.用途(机动车用、家具用等)3.材质(不锈钢制等)4.品牌(中文或外文名称)
83022000	1.品名 2.用途(机动车用、家具用等)3.材质(不锈钢制等)4.直径 5.所装轮或胎的宽度 6.品牌(中文或外文名称)
83023000	1.品名 2.用途(机动车用、家具用等)3.材质(不锈钢制等)4.品牌(中文或外文名称)
83024	1.品名 2.用途(机动车用、家具用等)3.材质(不锈钢制等)4.品牌(中文或外文名称)
83025000	1.品名 2.用途(机动车用、家具用等)3.材质(不锈钢制等)4.品牌(中文或外文名称)
83026000	1.品名 2.用途(机动车用、家具用等)3.材质(不锈钢制等)4.品牌(中文或外文名称)
8303	1.品名 2.材质(不锈钢制等)3.种类(保险箱、保险柜、保险库的门等)4.品牌(中文或外文名称)
8304	1.品名 2.用途(办公室用)3.材质(不锈钢制 等)4.种类(档案柜、卡片索引柜、文件盘等)5.式样(非落地)6.品牌(中文或外文名称)
8305	1.品名 2.用途(办公室用、室内装饰或包装用)3.材质(不锈钢制等)4.种类(活页夹、宗卷夹、成条订书钉等)5.品牌(中文或外文名称)
8306	1.品名 2.材质(不锈钢制等)3.种类(铃、钟、锣、雕塑像、相框、画框等)4.是否镀贵金属 5.铃、钟、锣请注明非电动 6.品牌(中文或外文名称)
8307	1.品名 2.材质(钢铁制、其他贱金属制)3.种类(软管)4.品牌(中文或外文名称)
8308	1.品名 2.用途(用于衣服、提包上等)3.材质(不锈钢制等)4.种类(扣、钩、环、铆钉等)5.品牌(中文或外文名称)
8309	1.品名 2.形状(冠形、圆形等)3.材质(不锈钢制等)4.种类(塞子、盖子等)5.品牌(中文或外文名称)

商品编码	申报要素
8310	1.品名 2.用途(汽车用等)3.材质(不锈钢制、贱金属种类等)4.种类(标志、铭牌等)5.品牌(中文或外文名称)
8311	1.品名 2.用途(电弧焊用、气焊用、钎焊用等)3.材质(贱金属、硬质合金制)4.种类(电极、焊条、焊丝等)5.状态(以焊剂涂面、以焊剂为芯)6.品牌(中文或外文名称)
84011000	1.品名 2.用途 3.品牌(中文或外文名称)4.型号
84012000	1.品名 2.用途 3.品牌(中文或外文名称)4.型号
84013	1.品名 2.用途 3.品牌(中文或外文名称)4.型号
84014	1.品名 2.用途(适用于××品牌××机或通用于××机等)3.品牌(中文或外文名称)4.型号
84021	1.品名 2.用途 3.构造方式 4.蒸发量 5.品牌(中文或外文名称)6.型号
84022000	1.品名 2.用途 3.温度 4.品牌(中文或外文名称)5.型号
84029000	1.品名 2.用途 3.品牌(中文或外文名称)4.型号
84031010	1.品名 2.用途 3.品牌(中文或外文名称)4.型号 5.是否装有循环装置 6.功率 7.温度
84031090	1.品名 2.用途 3.品牌(中文或外文名称)4.型号 5.温度
84039000	1.品名 2.用途(适用于××品牌××机或通用于××机等)3.品牌(中文或外文名称)4.型号
84041	1.品名 2.用途 3.品牌(中文或外文名称)
84042000	1.品名 2.用途 3.品牌(中文或外文名称)
84049	1.品名 2.用途(适用于××品牌××机或通用于××机等)3.品牌(中文或外文名称)4.型号
84051000	1.品名 2.品牌(中文或外文名称)3.型号
84059000	1.品名 2.用途(适用于××品牌××机或通用于××机等)3.品牌(中文或外文名称)4.型号
84061000	1.品名 2.用途 3.品牌(中文或外文名称)4.型号 5.输出功率
84068	1.品名 2.用途 3.输出功率 4.品牌(中文或外文名称)5.型号
84069000	1.品名 2.用途(适用于××品牌××机或通用于××机等)3.品牌(中文或外文名称)4.型号
84071	1.品名 2.用途 3.输出功率 4.品牌(中文或外文名称)5.型号 6.燃料类型
84072100	1.品名 2.用途 3.发动机安装位置(舷外或舷内)4.品牌(中文或外文名称)5.型号 6.燃料类型 7.功率
84072900	1.品名 2.用途 3.发动机安装位置(舷外或舷内)4.品牌(中文或外文名称)5.型号 6.燃料类型 7.是否提供主动力 8.功率
84073100	1.品名 2.用途 3.排气量 4.成套散件或毛坯请注明 5.燃料类型 6.状态(成品、半成品、成套散件)7.生产件的通用零件编号后加注"/TY"8.成套散件装配后完整品的零部件的编号 9.品牌(中文或外文名称)10.型号 11.零部件完整编号并在前加注"S/""W/"或"WF/"之一(生产件填报"S/",品牌和适用的整车厂牌一致的维修件填报"W/",品牌和适用的整车厂牌不一致的维修件的填报"WF/")
84073200	1.品名 2.用途 3.排气量 4.成套散件或毛坯请注明 5.燃料类型 6.状态(成品、半成品、成套散件)7.生产件的通用零件编号后加注"/TY"8.成套散件装配后完整品的零部件的编号 9.品牌(中文或外文名称)10.型号 11.零部件完整编号并在前加注"S/""W/"或"WF/"之一(生产件填报"S/",品牌和适用的整车厂牌一致的维修件填报"W/",品牌和适用的整车厂牌不一致的维修件的填报"WF/")
84073300	1.品名 2.用途 3.排气量 4.成套散件或毛坯请注明 5.燃料类型 6.状态(成品、半成品、成套散件)7.生产件的通用零件编号后加注"/TY"8.成套散件装配后完整品的零部件的编号 9.品牌(中文及或外文名称)10.型号 11.零部件完整编号并在前加注"S/""W/"或"WF/"之一(生产件填报"S/",品牌和适用的整车厂牌一致的维修件填报"W/",品牌和适用的整车厂牌不一致的维修件的填报"WF/")
840734	1.品名 2.用途 3.排气量 4.成套散件或毛坯请注明 5.燃料类型 6.状态(成品、半成品、成套散件)7.生产件的通用零件编号后加注"/TY"8.成套散件装配后完整品的零部件的编号 9.品牌(中文或外文名称)10.型号 11.零部件完整编号并在前加注"S/""W/"或"WF/"之一(生产件填报"S/",品牌和适用的整车厂牌一致的维修件填报"W/",品牌和适用的整车厂牌不一致的维修件的填报"WF/")
84073410	1.品名 2.用途 3.排气量 4.成套散件或毛坯请注明 5.燃料类型 6.状态(成品、半成品、成套散件)7.生产件的通用零件编号后加注"/TY"8.成套散件装配后完整品的零部件的编号 9.品牌(中文或外文名称)10.型号 11.零部件完整编号并在前加注"S/""W/"或"WF/"之一(生产件填报"S/",品牌和适用的整车厂牌一致的维修件填报"W/",品牌和适用的整车厂牌不一致的维修件的填报"WF/")
84073420	1.品名 2.用途 3.排气量 4.成套散件或毛坯请注明 5.燃料类型 6.状态(成品、半成品、成套散件)7.生产件的通用零件编号后加注"/TY"8.成套散件装配后完整品的零部件的编号 9.品牌(中文或外文名称)10.型号 11.零部件完整编号并在前加注"S/""W/"或"WF/"之一(生产件填报"S/",品牌和适用的整车厂牌一致的维修件填报"W/",品牌和适用的整车厂牌不一致的维修件的填报"WF/")
84079	1.品名 2.用途 3.燃料类型 4.品牌(中文或外文名称)5.型号 6.转速
84081000	1.品名 2.用途 3.品牌(中文或外文名称)4.型号 5.输出功率
84082	1.品名 2.用途 3.输出功率 4.成套散件或毛坯请注明 5.生产件的通用零件编号后加注"/TY"6.成套散件装配后完整品的零部件的编号 7.品牌(中文或外文名称)8.型号 9.零部件完整编号并在前加注"S/""W/"或"WF/"之一(生产件填报"S/",品牌和适用的整车厂牌一致的维修件填报"W/",品牌和适用的整车厂牌不一致的维修件的填报"WF/")
84089	1.品名 2.用途 3.输出功率 4.品牌(中文或外文名称)5.型号 6.转速
84091000	1.品名 2.适用何种用途发动机(如飞机用、船舶用等)3.适用发动机的类型(点燃式/压燃式)4.品牌(中文或外文名称)5.零件号
840991	1.品名 2.适用何种用途发动机(如飞机用、船舶用等)3.适用发动机的类型(点燃式)4.品牌(中文或外文名称)5.零件号
84099910	1.品名 2.适用何种用途发动机(如飞机用、船舶用等)3.适用发动机的类型(压燃式)4.发动机输出功率 5.品牌(中文或外文名称)6.零件号
84099920	1.品名 2.适用何种用途发动机(如飞机用、船舶用等)3.适用发动机的类型(压燃式)4.发动机输出功率 5.品牌(中文或外文名称)6.零件号
8409999	1.品名 2.适用何种用途发动机(如飞机用、船舶用等)3.适用发动机类型(压燃式)4.发动机输出功率 5.品牌(中文或外文名称)6.零件号
84101100	1.品名 2.功率 3.品牌(中文或外文名称)4.型号
84101200	1.品名 2.功率 3.品牌(中文或外文名称)4.型号
841013	1.品名 2.功率 3.工作方式 4.品牌(中文或外文名称)5.型号
84109010	1.品名 2.品牌(中文或外文名称)3.原理 4.型号
84109090	1.品名 2.品牌(中文或外文名称)3.型号
84111	1.品名 2.原理 3.推力 4.品牌(中文或外文名称)5.型号
84112	1.品名 2.原理 3.功率 4.品牌(中文或外文名称)5.型号
84118	1.品名 2.原理 3.功率 4.品牌(中文或外文名称)5.型号
84119	1.品名 2.用途(适用于××品牌××机或通用于××机等)3.品牌(中文或外文名称)4.型号
84121	1.品名 2.用途 3.原理 4.品牌(中文或外文名称)5.型号
84122	1.品名 2.原理 3.用途 4.品牌(中文或外文名称)5.型号
84123	1.品名 2.原理 3.用途 4.品牌(中文及或外文名称) 5.型号
84128000	1.品名 2.原理 3.用途 4.品牌(中文或外文名称)5.型号
84129	1.品名 2.用途 3.品牌(中文或外文名称)4.型号
84131	1.品名 2.用途 3.是否装有或可装计量装置 4.品牌(中文或外文名称)5.型号
84132000	1.品名 2.是否手动 3.品牌(中文或外文名称)4.型号
84133	1.品名 2.用途(是否为活塞式内燃发动机用)3.适用发动机的输出功率 4.品牌(中文或外文名称)5.型号
84134000	1.品名 2.用途 3.品牌(中文或外文名称)4.型号
84135	1.品名 2.驱动方式(气动、电动、液压等)3.原理(往复式)4.用途 5.品牌(中文或外文名称)6.型号
84136	1.品名 2.驱动方式(气动、电动、液压等)3.原理(回转式)4.用途 5.品牌(中文或外文名称)6.型号
84137	1.品名 2.驱动方式(气动、电动、液压等)3.原理(离心式)4.转速 5.用途 6.品牌(中文或外文名称)7.型号
84138	1.品名 2.用途 3.品牌(中文或外文名称)4.型号 5.原理(柱塞式、齿轮式、螺杆式等)
84139	1.品名 2.用途(适用于××品牌××机或通用于××机等)3.品牌(中文或外文名称)4.型号
84141000	1.品名 2.用途(如半导体晶圆或平板显示屏制造用 等)3.品牌(中文或外文名称)4.型号 5.性能(抽气能力)
84142000	1.品名 2.是否手动或脚踏 3.品牌(中文或外文名称)4.型号
84143011	1.品名 2.用途 3.驱动方式 4.额定功率 5.品牌(中文或外文名称)6.型号
84143012	1.品名 2.用途 3.驱动方式 4.额定功率 5.品牌(中文或外文名称)6.型号
84143013	1.品名 2.用途 3.驱动方式 4.额定功率 5.品牌(中文或外文名称)6.型号
84143014	1.品名 2.用途 3.驱动方式 4.额定功率 5.品牌(中文或外文名称)6.型号
84143015	1.品名 2.用途 3.驱动方式 4.额定功率 5.品牌(中文或外文名称)6.型号
84143019	1.品名 2.用途 3.驱动方式 4.额定功率 5.品牌(中文或外文名称)6.型号
84143090	1.品名 2.用途 3.驱动方式 4.额定功率 5.品牌(中文或外文名称)6.型号
84144000	1.品名 2.用途 3.品牌(中文或外文名称)4.型号
841451	1.品名 2.类型(如吊扇、落地扇、壁扇等)3.输出功率 4.品牌(中文或外文名称)5.型号
84145910	1.品名 2.类型(如吊扇、落地扇、壁扇等)3.输出功率 4.品牌(中文或外文名称)5.型号
84145920	1.品名 2.类型(如吊扇、落地扇、壁扇等)3.输出功率 4.品牌(中文或外文名称)5.型号
84145930	1.品名 2.类型(如吊扇、落地扇、壁扇等)3.输出功率 4.品牌(中文或外文名称)5.型号
84145990	1.品名 2.用途(如微处理器、电信设备、自动数据处理设备或装置用等)3.类型(如吊扇、落地扇、壁扇等)4.输出功率 5.品牌(中文或外文名称)6.型号
84146010	1.品名 2.罩的平面最大边长 3.品牌(中文或外文名称)4.型号
84146090	1.品名 2.罩的平面最大边长 3.品牌(中文或外文名称)4.型号
84147	1.品名 2.罩的平面最大边长 3.品牌(中文或外文名称)4.型号
84148010	1.品名 2.用途 3.品牌(中文或外文名称)4.型号
84148020	1.品名 2.用途 3.品牌(中文或外文名称)4.型号
84148030	1.品名 2.用途 3.品牌(中文或外文名称)4.型号 5.压力比
8414804	1.品名 2.用途 3.品牌(中文或外文名称)4.型号
84148090	1.品名 2.用途 3.品牌(中文或外文名称)4.型号
84149	1.品名 2.用途(适用于××品牌××机或通用于××机等)3.品牌(中文或外文名称)4.型号 5.材质
84151010	1.品名 2.安装方式(窗式、壁式、置于天花板或地板上)3.是否为分体式 4.品牌(中文或外文名称)5.型号
8415102	1.品名 2.安装方式(窗式、壁式、置于天花板或地板上)3.是否为分体式 4.制冷量 5.品牌(中文或外文名称)6.型号
84152000	1.品名 2.用途 3.品牌(中文或外文名称)4.型号
841581	1.品名 2.是否装有制冷装置 3.是否装有冷热换向阀 4.制冷量 5.品牌(中文或外文名称)6.型号
841582	1.品名 2.是否装有制冷装置 3.是否装有冷热换向阀 4.制冷量 5.品牌(中文或外文名称)6.型号
84158300	1.品名 2.品牌(中文或外文名称)3.结构 4.型号
84159	1.品名 2.用途(适用于××品牌××机或通用于××机等)3.若为多元件集成电路需注明结构组成 4.适用机型制冷量(以"大卡/时"计)5.品牌(中文或外文名称)6.型号
84161000	1.品名 2.用途 3.燃料类型 4.品牌(中文或外文名称)5.型号
84162	1.品名 2.用途 3.燃料类型 4.品牌(中文或外文名称)5.型号
84163000	1.品名 2.用途 3.品牌(中文或外文名称)
84169000	1.品名 2.用途(适用于××品牌××机或通用于××机等)3.品牌(中文或外文名称)4.型号
84171000	1.品名 2.用途 3.加热方式 4.品牌(中文或外文名称)5.型号
84172000	1.品名 2.用途 3.加热方式 4.品牌(中文或外文名称)5.型号
84178	1.品名 2.用途 3.加热方式 4.品牌(中文或外文名称)5.型号
84179	1.品名 2.用途(适用于××品牌××机或通用于××机等)3.品牌(中文或外文名称)4.型号

商品编码	申报要素
84181010	1.品名 2.结构（冷藏—冷冻组合机）3.容积 4.品牌（中文或外文名称）5.型号
84181020	1.品名 2.结构（冷藏—冷冻组合机）3.容积 4.品牌（中文或外文名称）5.型号
84181030	1.品名 2.结构（冷藏—冷冻组合机）3.容积 4.品牌（中文或外文名称）5.型号
84182	1.品名 2.用途（是否家用）3.原理 4.容积 5.品牌（中文或外文名称）6.型号
84183010	1.品名 2.容积 3.最低制冷温度 4.是否柜式 5.品牌（中文或外文名称）6.型号
84183021	1.品名 2.容积 3.最低制冷温度 4.是否柜式 5.品牌（中文或外文名称）6.型号
84183029	1.品名 2.容积 3.最低制冷温度 4.是否柜式 5.品牌（中文或外文名称）6.型号
84184010	1.品名 2.结构（是否为立式）3.容积 4.最低制冷温度 5.品牌（中文或外文名称）6.型号
84184021	1.品名 2.结构（是否为立式）3.容积 4.最低制冷温度 5.品牌（中文或外文名称）6.型号
84184029	1.品名 2.结构（是否为立式）3.容积 4.最低制冷温度 5.品牌（中文或外文名称）6.型号
84185000	1.品名 2.用途 3.品牌（中文或外文名称）4.型号 5.容积 6.最低制冷温度
84186	1.品名 2.原理（是否为压缩式）3.品牌（中文或外文名称）4.型号
84189	1.品名 2.用途（适用于××品牌××机或通用于××机等）3.适用机型的制冷温度和容积 4.品牌（中文或外文名称）5.型号
84191	1.品名 2.原理 3.加热方式 4.用途 5.品牌（中文或外文名称）6.型号
84192000	1.品名 2.用途 3.品牌（中文或外文名称）4.型号
84193	1.品名 2.用途 3.干燥材质 4.品牌（中文或外文名称）5.型号
84194	1.品名 2.用途 3.品牌（中文或外文名称）4.型号 5.原理
84195000	1.品名 2.若为用氟聚合物制造的需注明 3.若为用氟聚合物制造的需注明入口管和出口管内径尺寸 4.用途 5.品牌（中文或外文名称）6.型号
8419601	1.品名 2.用途 3.制氧量 4.品牌（中文或外文名称）5.型号
84196090	1.品名 2.用途 3.品牌（中文或外文名称）4.型号
84198	1.品名 2.用途 3.品牌（中文或外文名称）4.型号
84199	1.品名 2.用途（适用于××品牌××机或通用于××机等）3.品牌（中文或外文名称）4.型号
84201000	1.品名 2.用途（如印刷电路板基板或印刷电路制造用等）3.品牌（中文或外文名称）4.型号
84209	1.品名 2.用途（适用于××品牌××机或通用于××机等）3.品牌（中文或外文名称）4.型号
84211100	1.品名 2.用途 3.原理 4.品牌（中文或外文名称）5.型号
84211210	1.品名 2.用途 3.原理 4.干衣量 5.品牌（中文或外文名称）6.型号
84211290	1.品名 2.用途 3.原理 4.干衣量 5.品牌（中文或外文名称）6.型号
84211910	1.品名 2.用途 3.原理 4.品牌（中文或外文名称）5.型号
84211920	1.品名 2.用途 3.原理 4.品牌（中文或外文名称）5.型号
84211990	1.品名 2.用途 3.原理 4.品牌（中文或外文名称）5.型号
84212110	1.品名 2.用途 3.品牌（中文或外文名称）4.型号 5.原理 6.单位时间水处理量
8421219	1.品名 2.用途 3.品牌（中文或外文名称）4.型号 5.原理 6.单位时间水处理量
84212200	1.品名 2.用途 3.原理 4.品牌（中文或外文名称）5.型号
84212300	1.品名 2.用途 3.原理 4.品牌（中文或外文名称）5.型号
842129	1.品名 2.用途 3.原理 4.若为用氟聚合物制造的需注明 5.氟聚合物制的需报过滤或净化介质的外观（膜等）及厚度 6.品牌（中文或外文名称）7.型号
84213100	1.品名 2.用途 3.原理 4.品牌（中文或外文名称）5.型号
84213200	1.品名 2.用途 3.原理 4.品牌（中文或外文名称）5.型号
84213910	1.品名 2.用途 3.原理 4.品牌（中文或外文名称）5.型号 6.额定功率（非电动的不需注明额定功率）
8421392	1.品名 2.用途 3.若为装备不锈钢外壳需注明 4.若为装备不锈钢外壳需注明入口管和出口管内径尺寸 5.原理 6.品牌（中文或外文名称）7.型号 8.额定功率（非电动的不需注明额定功率）
84213940	1.品名 2.用途 3.若为装备不锈钢外壳需注明 4.若为装备不锈钢外壳需注明入口管和出口管内径尺寸 5.原理 6.品牌（中文或外文名称）7.型号 8.额定功率（非电动的不需注明额定功率）
84213950	1.品名 2.用途 3.若为装备不锈钢外壳需注明 4.若为装备不锈钢外壳需注明入口管和出口管内径尺寸 5.原理 6.品牌（中文或外文名称）7.型号 8.额定功率（非电动的不需注明额定功率）
84213990	1.品名 2.用途 3.若为装备不锈钢外壳需注明 4.若为装备不锈钢外壳需注明入口管和出口管内径尺寸 5.原理 6.品牌（中文或外文名称）7.型号 8.额定功率（非电动的不需注明额定功率）
842191	1.品名 2.用途（适用于××品牌××机或通用于××机等）3.品牌（中文或外文名称）4.型号
84219910	1.品名 2.用途（适用于××品牌××机或通用于××机等）3.品牌（中文或外文名称）4.型号
84219990	1.品名 2.用途（适用于××品牌××机或通用于××机等）3.品牌（中文或外文名称）4.型号
84221	1.品名 2.品牌（中文或外文名称）3.型号
84222000	1.品名 2.用途 3.品牌（中文或外文名称）4.型号
84223010	1.品名 2.用途 3.品牌（中文或外文名称）4.型号
84223021	1.品名 2.用途 3.品牌（中文或外文名称）4.型号
84223029	1.品名 2.用途 3.品牌（中文或外文名称）4.型号
84223030	1.品名 2.用途 3.品牌（中文或外文名称）4.型号
84223090	1.品名 2.用途 3.品牌（中文或外文名称）4.型号
84224000	1.品名 2.用途 3.品牌（中文或外文名称）4.型号
84229	1.品名 2.用途（适用于××品牌××机或通用于××机等）3.品牌（中文或外文名称）4.型号
84231000	1.品名 2.用途 3.品牌（中文或外文名称）4.型号
84232	1.品名 2.用途 3.原理 4.品牌（中文或外文名称）5.型号
84233010	1.品名 2.用途 3.原理（如电子式称重等）4.品牌（中文或外文名称）5.型号
84233020	1.品名 2.用途 3.品牌（中文或外文名称）4.型号
84233030	1.品名 2.用途 3.原理（如电子式称重等）4.品牌（中文或外文名称）5.型号
84233090	1.品名 2.用途 3.原理（如电子式称重等）4.品牌（中文或外文名称）5.型号
84238110	1.品名 2.用途 3.原理 4.最大称量 5.品牌（中文或外文名称）6.型号
84238120	1.品名 2.用途 3.原理 4.最大称量 5.品牌（中文或外文名称）6.型号
84238190	1.品名 2.用途 3.原理（如电子式称重等）4.最大称量 5.品牌（中文或外文名称）6.型号
842382	1.品名 2.用途 3.原理（如电子式称重等）4.最大称量 5.品牌（中文或外文名称）6.型号
842389	1.品名 2.用途 3.原理（如电子式称重等）4.最大称量 5.品牌（中文或外文名称）6.型号
84239000	1.品名 2.用途（适用机型，如电子式称重衡器用等）3.品牌（中文或外文名称）4.型号
84241000	1.品名 2.用途 3.品牌（中文或外文名称）4.型号
84242000	1.品名 2.用途 3.品牌（中文或外文名称）4.喷射材料 5.型号
84243000	1.品名 2.喷射材料 3.用途 4.品牌（中文或外文名称）5.型号
84244	1.品名 2.用途 3.品牌（中文或外文名称）4.喷射材料 5.型号
84248200	1.品名 2.用途 3.品牌（中文或外文名称）4.喷射材料 5.型号
842489	1.品名 2.用途 3.品牌（中文或外文名称）4.喷射材料 5.型号
84248991	1.品名 2.用途 3.品牌（中文或外文名称）4.喷射材料 5.型号
84248999	1.品名 2.用途 3.品牌（中文或外文名称）4.喷射材料 5.型号
84249010	1.品名 2.用途（适用于××品牌××机或通用于××机等）3.品牌（中文或外文名称）4.型号
84249020	1.品名 2.用途（适用于××品牌××机或通用于××机等）3.品牌（中文或外文名称）4.型号
84249090	1.品名 2.用途（适用于××品牌××机或通用于××机等）3.品牌（中文或外文名称）4.型号
8425	1.品名 2.用途 3.驱动方式 4.品牌（中文或外文名称）5.型号 6.最大提升高度（距离）7.最大提升重量
8426	1.品名 2.用途 3.结构类型 4.品牌（中文或外文名称）5.型号
8427	1.品名 2.用途 3.推进方式 4.品牌（中文或外文名称）5.型号 6.最大提升高度（距离）7.最大提升重量
84281010	1.品名 2.用途 3.品牌（中文或外文名称）4.型号 5.提升速度 6.停层数 7.载重量
84281090	1.品名 2.用途 3.品牌（中文或外文名称）4.型号
84282000	1.品名 2.驱动方式 3.品牌（中文或外文名称）4.型号
84283	1.品名 2.用途 3.运送方式 4.工作构件类型（斗式、带式等）5.品牌（中文或外文名称）6.型号
84284000	1.品名 2.品牌（中文或外文名称）3.型号
84286	1.品名 2.用途 3.原理 4.结构类型 5.品牌（中文或外文名称）6.型号
84287000	1.品名 2.用途 3.品牌（中文或外文名称）4.型号
84289	1.品名 2.用途 3.品牌（中文或外文名称）4.型号
84291	1.品名 2.行走装置类型（轮胎式、履带式等）3.发动机输出功率 4.品牌（中文或外文名称）5.型号 6.型号 7.机身重量
84292	1.品名 2.是否自推进 3.发动机输出功率 4.品牌（中文或外文名称）5.型号
84293	1.品名 2.是否自推进 3.斗容量 4.品牌（中文或外文名称）5.型号
84294	1.品名 2.原理 3.是否自推进 4.机身重量 5.品牌（中文或外文名称）6.型号
84295100	1.品名 2.是否自推进 3.品牌（中文或外文名称）4.行走装置类型（轮胎式、履带式等）5.型号
8429521	1.品名 2.行走装置类型（轮胎式、履带式等）3.是否自推进 4.是否上部结构可旋转 360 度 5.品牌（中文或外文名称）6.型号 7.斗容量 8.功率 9.机身重量
84295290	1.品名 2.是否自推进 3.是否上部结构可旋转 360 度 4.品牌（中文或外文名称）5.行走装置类型（轮胎式、履带式等）6.型号
84295900	1.品名 2.是否自推进 3.品牌（中文或外文名称）4.行走装置类型（轮胎式、履带式等）5.是否自推进 6.型号 6.斗容量 7.功率 8.机重
84301000	1.品名 2.品牌（中文或外文名称）3.型号
84302000	1.品名 2.品牌（中文或外文名称）3.型号 4.是否自推进
84303	1.品名 2.是否自推进 3.品牌（中文或外文名称）4.型号
8430411	1.品名 2.用途 3.是否自推进 4.钻探深度 5.品牌（中文或外文名称）6.型号
84304121	1.品名 2.用途 3.是否自推进 4.钻探深度 5.品牌（中文或外文名称）6.型号
84304122	1.品名 2.用途 3.是否自推进 4.钻探深度 5.品牌（中文或外文名称）6.型号 7.机身号 8.钻头直径 9.机身重量
84304129	1.品名 2.用途 3.是否自推进 4.钻探深度 5.品牌（中文或外文名称）6.型号
84304190	1.品名 2.用途 3.是否自推进 4.钻探深度 5.品牌（中文或外文名称）6.型号
84304900	1.品名 2.用途 3.是否自推进 4.钻探深度 5.品牌（中文或外文名称）6.型号
84305	1.品名 2.用途 3.是否自推进 4.牙轮直径 5.品牌（中文或外文名称）6.型号
84306	1.品名 2.用途 3.是否自推进 4.钻筒直径 5.品牌（中文或外文名称）6.型号
8431	1.品名 2.用途（适用于××品牌××机或通用于××机等）3.如为破碎锤注明是否带有钎杆 4.品牌（中文或外文名称）5.型号
84321000	1.品名 2.用途 3.品牌（中文或外文名称）4.型号
84322	1.品名 2.用途 3.品牌（中文或外文名称）4.型号
84323	1.品名 2.用途 3.品牌（中文或外文名称）4.型号
84324	1.品名 2.用途 3.品牌（中文或外文名称）4.型号
84328	1.品名 2.用途 3.品牌（中文或外文名称）4.型号
84329000	1.品名 2.用途（适用于××品牌××机或通用于××机等）3.品牌（中文或外文名称）4.型号
84331	1.品名 2.用途 3.驱动方式 4.切割装置的旋转类型 5.品牌（中文或外文名称）6.型号
84332000	1.品名 2.用途 3.品牌（中文或外文名称）4.型号
84333000	1.品名 2.品牌（中文或外文名称）3.型号
84334000	1.品名 2.品牌（中文或外文名称）3.型号
84335100	1.品名 2.用途 3.品牌（中文或外文名称）4.型号 5.功率

商品编码	申报要素
84335200	1.品名 2.用途 3.品牌(中文或外文名称)4.型号
84335300	1.品名 2.用途 3.品牌(中文或外文名称)4.型号 5.功率
84335910	1.品名 2.用途 3.品牌(中文或外文名称)4.型号 5.功率
84335920	1.品名 2.用途 3.品牌(中文或外文名称)4.型号 5.功率
84335990	1.品名 2.用途 3.品牌(中文或外文名称)4.型号 5.功率
84336	1.品名 2.用途 3.品牌(中文或外文名称)4.型号
84339	1.品名 2.用途(适用于××品牌××机或通用于××机等)3.品牌(中文或外文名称)4.型号
84341000	1.品名 2.用途 3.品牌(中文或外文名称)4.型号
84342000	1.品名 2.用途 3.品牌(中文或外文名称)4.型号
84349000	1.品名 2.用途(适用于××品牌××机或通用于××机等)3.品牌(中文或外文名称)4.型号
84351000	1.品名 2.用途 3.品牌(中文或外文名称)4.型号
84359000	1.品名 2.用途(适用于××品牌××机或通用于××机等)3.品牌(中文或外文名称)4.型号
84361000	1.品名 2.用途 3.品牌(中文或外文名称)4.型号
84362	1.品名 2.用途 3.品牌(中文或外文名称)4.型号
84368000	1.品名 2.用途 3.品牌(中文或外文名称)4.型号
84369	1.品名 2.用途(适用于××品牌××机或通用于××机等)3.品牌(中文或外文名称)4.型号
84371	1.品名 2.用途 3.品牌(中文或外文名称)4.型号
84378000	1.品名 2.用途 3.品牌(中文或外文名称)4.型号
84379000	1.品名 2.用途(适用于××品牌××机或通用于××机等)3.品牌(中文或外文名称)4.型号
84381000	1.品名 2.用途 3.品牌(中文或外文名称)4.型号
84382000	1.品名 2.用途 3.品牌(中文或外文名称)4.型号
84383000	1.品名 2.用途 3.品牌(中文或外文名称)4.型号
84384000	1.品名 2.用途 3.品牌(中文或外文名称)4.型号
84385000	1.品名 2.用途 3.品牌(中文或外文名称)4.型号
84386000	1.品名 2.用途 3.品牌(中文或外文名称)4.型号
84388000	1.品名 2.用途 3.品牌(中文或外文名称)4.型号
84389000	1.品名 2.用途(适用于××品牌××机或通用于××机等)3.品牌(中文或外文名称)4.型号
84391000	1.品名 2.用途 3.品牌(中文或外文名称)4.型号
84392000	1.品名 2.用途 3.品牌(中文或外文名称)4.型号
84393000	1.品名 2.用途 3.品牌(中文或外文名称)4.型号
84399	1.品名 2.用途(适用于××品牌××机或通用于××机等)3.品牌(中文或外文名称)4.型号
84401	1.品名 2.用途 3.品牌(中文或外文名称)4.型号
84409000	1.品名 2.用途(适用于××品牌××机或通用于××机等)3.品牌(中文或外文名称)4.型号
84411000	1.品名 2.用途 3.品牌(中文或外文名称)4.型号
84412000	1.品名 2.用途 3.品牌(中文或外文名称)4.型号
84413	1.品名 2.用途 3.品牌(中文或外文名称)4.型号
84414000	1.品名 2.用途 3.品牌(中文或外文名称)4.型号
84418	1.品名 2.用途 3.品牌(中文或外文名称)4.型号
84419	1.品名 2.用途(适用于××品牌××机或通用于××机等)3.品牌(中文或外文名称)4.型号
84423	1.品名 2.用途 3.原理 4.品牌(中文或外文名称)5.型号
84424000	1.品名 2.用途(适用于××品牌××机或通用于××机等)3.品牌(中文或外文名称)4.型号
84425000	1.品名 2.用途 3.原理 4.品牌(中文或外文名称)5.型号
84431100	1.品名 2.用途 3.原理 4.进料方式 5.品牌(中文或外文名称)6.型号
84431200	1.品名 2.用途 3.原理 4.进料方式 5.品牌(中文或外文名称)6.型号
844313	1.品名 2.用途 3.原理 4.进料方式 5.品牌(中文或外文名称)6.型号 7.印刷速度 8.印刷方式
84431400	1.品名 2.用途 3.原理 4.进料方式 5.品牌(中文或外文名称)6.型号
84431500	1.品名 2.用途 3.原理 4.进料方式 5.品牌(中文或外文名称)6.型号
84431600	1.品名 2.用途 3.原理 4.进料方式 5.品牌(中文或外文名称)6.型号 7.线速度 8.幅宽
84431700	1.品名 2.用途 3.原理 4.进料方式 5.印刷速度 6.品牌(中文或外文名称)7.型号
844319	1.品名 2.用途 3.原理 4.进料方式 5.品牌(中文或外文名称)6.型号
844331	1.品名 2.原理 3.功能 4.品牌(中文或外文名称)5.型号
8443321	1.品名 2.用途(是否专用于税目 84.71 所列设备)3.原理 4.品牌(中文或外文名称)5.型号 6.打印幅宽 7.打印速度
8443322	1.品名 2.用途 3.原理 4.品牌(中文或外文名称)5.型号
84433290	1.品名 2.用途 3.原理 4.品牌(中文或外文名称)5.型号
8443391	1.品名 2.用途(是否专用于税目 84.71 所列设备)3.原理 4.品牌(中文或外文名称)5.型号
8443392	1.品名 2.用途(是否专用于税目 84.71 所列设备)3.原理 4.品牌(中文或外文名称)5.型号
8443393	1.品名 2.用途(是否专用于税目 84.71 所列设备)3.原理 4.品牌(中文或外文名称)5.型号
84433990	1.品名 2.用途(是否专用于税目 84.71 所列设备)3.原理 4.品牌(中文或外文名称)5.型号
84439	1.品名 2.用途(适用于××品牌××机或通用于××机等)3.品牌(中文或外文名称)4.型号
8444	1.品名 2.用途 3.品牌(中文或外文名称)4.型号
8445	1.品名 2.用途 3.原理 4.品牌(中文或外文名称)5.型号
8446	1.品名 2.用途 3.原理 4.织物宽度 5.品牌(中文或外文名称)6.型号
84471	1.品名 2.圆筒直径 3.品牌(中文或外文名称)4.型号
84472	1.品名 2.原理 3.品牌(中文或外文名称)4.型号 5.幅宽
84479	1.品名 2.原理 3.品牌(中文或外文名称)4.型号
8448	1.品名 2.用途(适用于××品牌××机或通用于××机等)3.品牌(中文或外文名称)4.型号
8449	1.品名 2.原理 3.品牌(中文或外文名称)4.型号
84501	1.品名 2.原理 3.是否全自动 4.干衣量 5.品牌(中文或外文名称)6.型号
84502	1.品名 2.原理 3.是否全自动 4.干衣量 5.品牌(中文或外文名称)6.型号

商品编码	申报要素
84509	1.品名 2.用途(适用于××品牌××机或通用于××机等)3.品牌(中文或外文名称)4.型号
84511000	1.品名 2.用途 3.品牌(中文或外文名称)4.型号 5.衣容量(千克)
84512	1.品名 2.用途 3.干衣量 4.品牌(中文或外文名称)5.型号
84513000	1.品名 2.用途 3.品牌(中文或外文名称)4.型号
84514000	1.品名 2.用途 3.品牌(中文或外文名称)4.型号
84515000	1.品名 2.用途 3.品牌(中文或外文名称)4.型号
84518000	1.品名 2.用途 3.品牌(中文或外文名称)4.型号
84519000	1.品名 2.用途(适用于××品牌××机或通用于××机等)3.品牌(中文或外文名称)4.型号
84521	1.品名 2.用途 3.是否手动 4.品牌(中文或外文名称)5.型号
84522	1.品名 2.用途 3.是否自动 4.品牌(中文或外文名称)5.型号
84523000	1.品名 2.用途 3.品牌(中文或外文名称)4.型号
84529	1.品名 2.用途(适用于××品牌××机或通用于××机等)3.品牌(中文或外文名称)4.型号
84531000	1.品名 2.用途 3.品牌(中文或外文名称)4.型号
84532000	1.品名 2.用途 3.品牌(中文或外文名称)4.型号
84538000	1.品名 2.用途 3.品牌(中文或外文名称)4.型号
84539000	1.品名 2.用途(适用于××品牌××机或通用于××机等)3.品牌(中文或外文名称)4.型号
84541000	1.品名 2.用途 3.品牌(中文或外文名称)4.型号
84542	1.品名 2.用途 3.品牌(中文或外文名称)4.型号
84543	1.品名 2.用途 3.品牌(中文或外文名称)4.型号
84549	1.品名 2.用途(适用于××品牌××机或通用于××机等)3.品牌(中文或外文名称)4.型号
84551	1.品名 2.用途 3.加工方式 4.品牌(中文或外文名称)5.型号
84552	1.品名 2.用途 3.加工方式 4.品牌(中文或外文名称)5.型号
84553000	1.品名 2.用途(适用于××品牌××机或通用于××机等)3.品牌(中文或外文名称)4.型号 5.规格(轧辊长度、辊身直径、辊颈直径)
84559000	1.品名 2.用途(适用于××品牌××机或通用于××机等)3.品牌(中文或外文名称)4.型号
84561	1.品名 2.功能 3.加工方式 4.品牌(中文或外文名称)5.型号
84562000	1.品名 2.功能 3.加工方式 4.品牌(中文或外文名称)5.型号
84563010	1.品名 2.控制方式 3.功能 4.加工方式 5.品牌(中文或外文名称)6.型号 7.功率 8.加工精度
84563090	1.品名 2.控制方式 3.功能 4.加工方式 5.品牌(中文或外文名称)6.型号 7.功率
84564	1.品名 2.功能 3.加工方式 4.品牌(中文或外文名称)5.型号
84565000	1.品名 2.功能 3.加工方式 4.品牌(中文或外文名称)5.型号
84569000	1.品名 2.功能 3.加工方式 4.品牌(中文或外文名称)5.型号
84571	1.品名 2.用途 3.功能(如金属钻、镗、铣等) 4.可加装刀库注明刀库容量及选配件 5.是否可自动换刀 6.品牌(中文或外文名称)7.型号
84572000	1.品名 2.用途 3.功能(如金属钻、镗、铣等) 4.加工工位数 5.动力头个数 6.品牌(中文或外文名称)7.型号
84573000	1.品名 2.用途 3.功能(如金属钻、镗、铣等) 4.加工工位数 5.动力头个数 6.品牌(中文或外文名称)7.型号
8458	1.品名 2.用途 3.控制方式 4.主轴方向(垂直或水平)5.品牌(中文或外文名称)6.型号
84591000	1.品名 2.用途 3.功能 4.动力头移动方式 5.品牌(中文或外文名称)6.控制方 式 7.型号 8.可加装刀库注明刀库容量及选配件
84592	1.品名 2.用途 3.功能 4.控制方式 5.品牌(中文或外文名称)6.型号
84593	1.品名 2.用途 3.功能 4.控制方式 5.品牌(中文或外文名称)6.型号
84594	1.品名 2.用途 3.功能 4.控制方式 5.品牌(中文或外文名称)6.型号
84595	1.品名 2.用途 3.功能 4.控制方式 5.是否为升降台式 6.品牌(中文或外文名称)7.型号
84596	1.品名 2.用途 3.功能 4.控制方式 5.是否为龙门式 6.品牌(中文或外文名称)7.型号
84597000	1.品名 2.用途 3.功能 4.品牌(中文或外文名称)5.控制方 式 6.型号
84601210	1.品名 2.用途 3.控制方式 4.坐标定位精度 5.品牌(中文或外文名称)6.型号
84601290	1.品名 2.用途 3.控制方式 4.坐标定位精度 5.品牌(中文或外文名称)6.型号
84601910	1.品名 2.用途 3.控制方式 4.坐标定位精度 5.品牌(中文或外文名称)6.型号
84601990	1.品名 2.用途 3.控制方式 4.坐标定位精度 5.品牌(中文或外文名称)6.型号
846022	1.品名 2.用途 3.控制方式 4.坐标定位精度 5.结构类型(内圆、外圆等)6.品牌(中文或外文名称)7.型号
8460231	1.品名 2.用途 3.控制方式 4.坐标定位精度 5.结构类型(内圆、外圆等)6.品牌(中文或外文名称)7.型号
846024	1.品名 2.用途 3.控制方式 4.坐标定位精度 5.结构类型(内圆、外圆等)6.品牌(中文或外文名称)7.型号
84602911	1.品名 2.用途 3.控制方式 4.坐标定位精度 5.结构类型(内圆、外圆等)6.品牌(中文或外文名称)7.型号
84602912	1.品名 2.用途 3.控制方式 4.坐标定位精度 5.结构类型(内圆、外圆等)6.品牌(中文或外文名称)7.型号
84602919	1.品名 2.用途 3.控制方式 4.坐标定位精度 5.结构类型(内圆、外圆等)6.品牌(中文或外文名称)7.型号
84602990	1.品名 2.用途 3.控制方式 4.坐标定位精度 5.结构类型(内圆、外圆等)6.品牌(中文或外文名称)7.型号
84603	1.品名 2.用途 3.控制方式 4.品牌(中文或外文名称)5.型号
84604	1.品名 2.用途 3.品牌(中文或外文名称)4.型号
84609010	1.品名 2.用途 3.品牌(中文或外文名称)4.型号
84609020	1.品名 2.用途 3.品牌(中文或外文名称)4.型号
84609090	1.品名 2.用途 3.品牌(中文或外文名称)4.型号
84612	1.品名 2.用途 3.功能 4.结构类型 5.品牌(中文或外文名称)6.型号
84613000	1.品名 2.用途 3.功能 4.结构类型 5.品牌(中文或外文名称)6.型号
84614	1.品名 2.用途 3.控制方式 4.功能 5.品牌(中文或外文名称)6.型号
84615000	1.品名 2.用途 3.功能 4.品牌(中文或外文名称)5.型号
84619	1.品名 2.用途 3.功能 4.结构类型 5.品牌(中文或外文名称)6.型号
84621	1.品名 2.用途 3.功能 4.控制方式 5.品牌(中文或外文名称)6.型号
84622	1.品名 2.用途 3.功能 4.控制方式 5.品牌(中文或外文名称)6.型号
84623	1.品名 2.用途 3.功能 4.控制方式 5.品牌(中文或外文名称)6.型号

商品编码	申报要素
84624	1.品名 2.用途 3.功能 4.控制方式 5.品牌(中文或外文名称)6.型号
84625	1.品名 2.用途 3.功能 4.控制方式 5.品牌(中文或外文名称)6.型号
84626	1.品名 2.用途 3.功能 4.控制方式 5.品牌(中文或外文名称)6.型号
84629	1.品名 2.用途 3.功能 4.控制方式 5.品牌(中文或外文名称)6.型号
8463	1.品名 2.用途 3.功能 4.品牌(中文或外文名称)5.型号
8464	1.品名 2.用途 3.功能 4.加工材料 5.品牌(中文或外文名称)6.型号
8465	1.品名 2.用途 3.功能 4.加工材料 5.品牌(中文或外文名称)6.型号
8466	1.品名 2.用途(适用于××品牌××机或通用于××机等)3.品牌(中文或外文名称)4.型号
84671	1.品名 2.驱动方式 3.是否为手提式 4.品牌(中文或外文名称)5.型号
84672	1.品名 2.驱动方式 3.是否为手提式 4.品牌(中文或外文名称)5.型号
84678	1.品名 2.驱动方式 3.是否为手提式 4.品牌(中文或外文名称)5.型号
84679	1.品名 2.用途(适用于××品牌××机或通用于××机等)3.品牌(中文或外文名称)4.型号
84681000	1.品名 2.原理 3.是否为手提式 4.品牌(中文或外文名称)5.型号
84682000	1.品名 2.原理 3.是否为手提式 4.品牌(中文或外文名称)5.型号
84688000	1.品名 2.原理 3.是否为手提式 4.品牌(中文或外文名称)5.型号
84689000	1.品名 2.用途(适用于××品牌××机或通用于××机等)3.品牌(中文或外文名称)4.型号
84701000	1.品名 2.是否需外接电源 3.品牌(中文或外文名称)4.型号
84702	1.品名 2.是否有打印装置 3.品牌(中文或外文名称)4.型号
84703000	1.品名 2.品牌(中文或外文名称)3.型号
84705	1.品名 2.用途 3.品牌(中文或外文名称)4.型号
84709000	1.品名 2.用途 3.品牌(中文或外文名称)4.型号
84713	1.品名 2.配置(系统组成部件)3.品牌(中文或外文名称)4.型号
84714110	1.品名 2.机型 3.配置(系统组成部件)4.品牌(中文或外文名称)5.型号 6.操作系统
84714120	1.品名 2.机型 3.配置(系统组成部件)4.品牌(中文或外文名称)5.型号 6.操作系统
84714140	1.品名 2.机型 3.配置(系统组成部件)4.品牌(中文或外文名称)5.型号 6.操作系统
84714190	1.品名 2.机型 3.配置(系统组成部件)4.品牌(中文或外文名称)5.型号 6.操作系统
84714910	1.品名 2.机型 3.配置(系统组成部件)4.是否以系统形式报验 5.品牌(中文或外文名称)6.型号 7.操作系统
84714920	1.品名 2.机型 3.配置(系统组成部件)4.是否以系统形式报验 5.品牌(中文或外文名称)6.型号 7.操作系统
84714940	1.品名 2.机型 3.配置(系统组成部件)4.是否以系统形式报验 5.品牌(中文或外文名称)6.型号 7.操作系统
84714991	1.品名 2.配置(例如,包括现场控制站、操作员站以及工程师站等)3.是否以系统形式报验 4.品牌(中文或外文名称)5.型号 6.操作系统
84714999	1.品名 2.配置(系统组成部件)3.是否以系统形式报验 4.品牌(中文或外文名称)5.型号 6.操作系统
84715010	1.品名 2.机型 3.配置(系统组成部件)4.品牌(中文或外文名称)5.型号 6.操作系统 7.用途
84715020	1.品名 2.机型 3.配置(系统组成部件)4.品牌(中文或外文名称)5.型号 6.操作系统 7.用途
84715040	1.品名 2.机型 3.配置(系统组成部件)4.品牌(中文或外文名称)5.型号 6.操作系统 7.用途
84715090	1.品名 2.机型 3.配置(系统组成部件)4.品牌(中文或外文名称)5.型号 6.操作系统 7.用途
84716040	1.品名 2.品牌(中文或外文名称)3.型号
84716050	1.品名 2.品牌(中文或外文名称)3.型号
84716060	1.品名 2.品牌(中文或外文名称)3.型号
84716071	1.品名 2.品牌(中文或外文名称)3.型号 4.连接方式(有线、无线)
84716072	1.品名 2.品牌(中文或外文名称)3.型号 4.连接方式(有线、无线)5.DPI(分辨率) 6.CPI(鼠标精度)
84716090	1.品名 2.品牌(中文或外文名称)3.型号
8471701	1.品名 2.品牌(中文或外文名称)3.型号 4.硬盘容量及缓存容 量 5.硬盘种类(固态硬盘、机械硬盘 等)
84717020	1.品名 2.品牌(中文或外文名称)3.型号
84717030	1.品名 2.品牌(中文或外文名称)3.型号 4.是否带有刻录功能 5.刻录速度
84717090	1.品名 2.品牌(中文或外文名称)3.型号
84718000	1.品名 2.品牌(中文或外文名称)3.型号
84719000	1.品名 2.品牌(中文或外文名称)3.型号
84721000	1.品名 2.用途 3.品牌(中文或外文名称)4.型号
84723	1.品名 2.用途 3.品牌(中文或外文名称)4.型号
84729010	1.品名 2.用途(存款、取款、存取款一体机等)3.品牌(中文或外文名称)4.型号 5.配置 6.安装方式(穿墙式等)
8472902	1.品名 2.用途 3.品牌(中文或外文名称)4.型号
84729030	1.品名 2.用途 3.品牌(中文或外文名称)4.型号
84729040	1.品名 2.用途 3.品牌(中文或外文名称)4.型号
84729050	1.品名 2.用途 3.品牌(中文或外文名称)4.型号
84729060	1.品名 2.用途 3.品牌(中文或外文名称)4.型号
84729090	1.品名 2.用途 3.品牌(中文或外文名称)4.型号
84732	1.品名 2.用途(适用于××品牌××机或通用于××机等)3.品牌(中文或外文名称)4.型号
84733010	1.品名 2.用途(适用于××品牌××机或通用于××机等)3.品牌(中文或外文名称)4.型号
84733090	1.品名 2.用途(适用于××品牌××机或通用于××机等)3.品牌(中文或外文名称)4.型号 5.如为内存条需申报容量
84734	1.品名 2.用途(适用于××品牌××机或通用于××机等)3.品牌(中文或外文名称)4.型号
84735000	1.品名 2.用途(适用于××品牌××机或通用于××机等)3.品牌(中文或外文名称)4.型号
84741000	1.品名 2.用途 3.品牌(中文或外文名称)4.型号
84742	1.品名 2.用途 3.原理 4.品牌(中文或外文名称)5.型号
84743	1.品名 2.用途 3.品牌(中文或外文名称)4.型号
84748	1.品名 2.用途 3.原理 4.品牌(中文或外文名称)5.型号
84749000	1.品名 2.用途(适用于××品牌××机或通用于××机等)3.品牌(中文或外文名称)4.型号
84751000	1.品名 2.用途 3.品牌(中文或外文名称)4.型号

商品编码	申报要素
84752	1.品名 2.用途 3.品牌(中文或外文名称)4.型号
84759000	1.品名 2.用途(适用于××品牌××机或通用于××机等)3.品牌(中文或外文名称)4.型号
84762	1.品名 2.供应商品种类 3.是否装有加热或制冷装置 4.品牌(中文或外文名称)5.型号
84768	1.品名 2.供应商品种类 3.是否装有加热或制冷装置 4.品牌(中文或外文名称)5.型号
84769000	1.品名 2.用途(适用于××品牌××机或通用于××机等)3.品牌(中文或外文名称)4.型号
84771010	1.品名 2.用途 3.功能 4.品牌(中文或外文名称)5.型号 6.合模力 7.螺杆直 径 8.注射容量 9.射出速度
84771090	1.品名 2.用途 3.功能 4.品牌(中文或外文名称)5.型号 6.合模力
84772	1.品名 2.用途 3.功能 4.品牌(中文或外文名称)5.型号
84773	1.品名 2.用途 3.功能 4.品牌(中文或外文名称)5.型号
84774	1.品名 2.用途 3.功能 4.品牌(中文或外文名称)5.型号
84775	1.品名 2.用途 3.功能 4.品牌(中文或外文名称)5.型号
84778000	1.品名 2.用途 3.品牌(中文或外文名称)4.型号
84779000	1.品名 2.用途(适用于××品牌××机或通用于××机等)3.品牌(中文或外文名称)4.型号
84781000	1.品名 2.用途 3.品牌(中文或外文名称)4.型号
84789000	1.品名 2.用途(适用于××品牌××机或通用于××机等)3.品牌(中文或外文名称)4.型号
84791	1.品名 2.用途 3.功能 4.品牌(中文或外文名称)5.型号
84792000	1.品名 2.用途 3.功能 4.品牌(中文或外文名称)5.型号
84793000	1.品名 2.用途 3.功能 4.品牌(中文或外文名称)5.型号
84794000	1.品名 2.用途 3.品牌(中文或外文名称)4.型号
84795	1.品名 2.用途 3.功能 4.品牌(中文或外文名称)5.型号
84796000	1.品名 2.用途 3.功能 4.品牌(中文或外文名称)5.型号
84797100	1.品名 2.用途 3.品牌(中文或外文名称)4.型号
84797900	1.品名 2.用途 3.品牌(中文或外文名称)4.型号
847981	1.品名 2.用途 3.功能 4.品牌(中文或外文名称)5.型号
84798200	1.品名 2.用途 3.功能 4.品牌(中文或外文名称)5.型号
84798310	1.品名 2.用途 3.功能 4.品牌(中文或外文名称)5.型号
84798390	1.品名 2.用途 3.功能 4.品牌(中文或外文名称)5.型号
84798910	1.品名 2.用途 3.功能 4.品牌(中文或外文名称)5.型号
84798920	1.品名 2.用途 3.功能 4.品牌(中文或外文名称)5.型号
84798940	1.品名 2.用途 3.功能 4.品牌(中文或外文名称)5.型号
84798950	1.品名 2.用途 3.功能 4.品牌(中文或外文名称)5.型号
8479896	1.品名 2.用途 3.功能 4.品牌(中文或外文名称)5.型号
8479899	1.品名 2.用途 3.功能 4.品牌(中文或外文名称)5.型号
84799	1.品名 2.用途(适用于××品牌××机或通用于××机等)3.品牌(中文或外文名称)4.型号
84801000	1.品名 2.用途 3.适用材料 4.品牌(中文或外文名称)5.型号 6.模具材质
84802000	1.品名 2.用途 3.适用材料 4.品牌(中文或外文名称)5.型号 6.模具材质
84803000	1.品名 2.用途 3.适用材料 4.品牌(中文或外文名称)5.型号 6.模具材质
84804	1.品名 2.用途 3.适用材料 4.品牌(中文或外文名称)5.型号 6.模具材质 7.原理
84805000	1.品名 2.用途 3.适用材料 4.品牌(中文或外文名称)5.型号 6.模具材质
84806000	1.品名 2.用途 3.适用材料 4.品牌(中文或外文名称)5.型号 6.模具材质
84807	1.品名 2.用途 3.适用材料 4.品牌(中文或外文名称)5.型号 6.模具材质 7.原理
84811000	1.品名 2.用途 3.品牌(中文或外文名称)4.型号
84812	1.品名 2.用途 3.品牌(中文或外文名称)4.型号
84813000	1.品名 2.用途 3.品牌(中文或外文名称)4.型号
84814000	1.品名 2.用途 3.品牌(中文或外文名称)4.型号
8481802	1.品名 2.用途 3.是否电磁式 4.品牌(中文或外文名称)5.型号
8481803	1.品名 2.用途 3.品牌(中文或外文名称)4.型号
84818040	1.品名 2.用途 3.品牌(中文或外文名称)4.型号
84818090	1.品名 2.用途 3.品牌(中文或外文名称)4.型号
84819010	1.品名 2.用途(适用于××品牌××机或通用于××机等)3.品牌(中文或外文名称)4.型号
84819090	1.品名 2.用途(适用于××品牌××机或通用于××机等)3.品牌(中文或外文名称)4.型号
84821	1.品名 2.结构类型 3.品牌(中文或外文名称)4.型号
84822000	1.品名 2.结构类型 3.品牌(中文或外文名称)4.型号
84823000	1.品名 2.结构类型 3.品牌(中文或外文名称)4.型号
84824000	1.品名 2.结构类型 3.滚柱直径、长度 4.品牌(中文或外文名称)5.型号
84825000	1.品名 2.结构类型 3.品牌(中文或外文名称)4.型号
84828000	1.品名 2.结构类型 3.品牌(中文或外文名称)4.型号
84829100	1.品名 2.用途(适用于××品牌××机或通用于××机等)3.如是滚珠请申报最大、最小及标称直径 4.品牌(中文或外文名称)5.型号
84829900	1.品名 2.用途(适用于××品牌××机或通用于××机等)3.品牌(中文或外文名称)4.型号
84831	1.品名 2.用途 3.品牌(中文或外文名称)4.型号
84832000	1.品名 2.注明是否装有滚珠或滚子轴承 3.用途 4.品牌(中文或外文名称)5.型号
84833000	1.品名 2.如为轴承座需注明是否带有滚珠或滚子轴 承 3.用途 4.品牌(中文或外文名称)5.型号
84834	1.品名 2.原理 3.用途 4.品牌(中文或外文名称)5.型号
84835000	1.品名 2.用途 3.品牌(中文或外文名称)4.型号
84836000	1.品名 2.用途 3.品牌(中文或外文名称)4.型号
84839000	1.品名 2.用途 3.品牌(中文或外文名称)4.型号
84841000	1.品名 2.组成材料(金属片与其他材料制、双层金属片制、多层金属片制)3.品牌(中文或外文名称)4.型号
84842000	1.品名 2.结构 3.品牌(中文或外文名称)4.型号
84849000	1.品名 2.各自构成材料 3.是否成套包装 4.品牌(中文或外文名称)5.型号

商品编码	申报要素
84851000	1.品名 2.用途 3.增材材质 4.品牌(中文或外文名称)5.型号
84852000	1.品名 2.用途 3.增材材质 4.品牌(中文或外文名称)5.型号
84853	1.品名 2.用途 3.增材材质 4.品牌(中文或外文名称)5.型号
84858010	1.品名 2.用途 3.增材材质 4.品牌(中文或外文名称)5.型号
84858020	1.品名 2.用途 3.增材材质 4.品牌(中文或外文名称)5.型号
84858090	1.品名 2.用途 3.增材材质 4.品牌(中文或外文名称)5.型号
84859	1.品名 2.用途(适用于××品牌××机或通用于××机等)3.品牌(中文或外文名称)4.型号
84861	1.品名 2.用途 3.功能 4.品牌(中文或外文名称)5.型号
84862	1.品名 2.用途 3.功能 4.品牌(中文或外文名称)5.型号
84863	1.品名 2.用途 3.功能 4.品牌(中文或外文名称)5.型号
84864	1.品名 2.用途 3.功能 4.品牌(中文或外文名称)5.型号
84869	1.品名 2.用途(适用于××品牌××机或通用于××机等)3.品牌(中文或外文名称)4.型号
8487	1.品名 2.用途(适用于××品牌××机或通用于××机等)3.品牌(中文或外文名称)4.型号
85011010	1.品名 2.用途 3.输出功率 4.品牌(中文或外文名称)5.型号
8501109	1.品名 2.用途 3.输出功率 4.机座尺寸 5.品牌(中文或外文名称)6.型号
85012000	1.品名 2.用途 3.是否为交直流两用 4.输出功率 5.品牌(中文或外文名称)6.型号
85013100	1.品名 2.是否为直流 3.输出功率 4.品牌(中文或外文名称)5.型号
85013200	1.品名 2.是否为直流 3.输出功率 4.品牌(中文或外文名称)5.型号
85013300	1.品名 2.是否为直流 3.输出功率 4.品牌(中文或外文名称)5.型号
85013400	1.品名 2.是否为直流 3.输出功率 4.品牌(中文或外文名称)5.型号
85014000	1.品名 2.是否为单相交流 3.输出功率 4.品牌(中文或外文名称)5.型号
85015100	1.品名 2.输出功率 3.是否为多相交流 4.品牌(中文或外文名称)5.型号
85015200	1.品名 2.输出功率 3.是否为多相交流 4.品牌(中文或外文名称)5.型号
85015300	1.品名 2.输出功率 3.是否为多相交流 4.品牌(中文或外文名称)5.型号
85016	1.品名 2.用途 3.是否为交流 4.输出功率 5.品牌(中文或外文名称)6.型号
85017100	1.品名 2.是否为直流 3.输出功率 4.是否为光伏发电机 5.品牌(中文或外文名称)6.型号
85017210	1.品名 2.是否为直流 3.输出功率 4.是否为光伏发电机 5.品牌(中文或外文名称)6.型号
85017220	1.品名 2.是否为直流 3.输出功率 4.是否为光伏发电机 5.品牌(中文或外文名称)6.型号
85017230	1.品名 2.是否为直流 3.输出功率 4.是否为光伏发电机 5.品牌(中文或外文名称)6.型号
85017240	1.品名 2.是否为直流 3.输出功率 4.是否为光伏发电机 5.品牌(中文或外文名称)6.型号
85018	1.品名 2.是否为交流 3.输出功率 4.是否为光伏发电机 5.品牌(中文或外文名称)6.型号
8502	1.品名 2.组成原动机类型 3.输出功率 4.品牌(中文或外文名称)5.型号
85030010	1.品名 2.用途(适用于××品牌××机或通用于××机等)3.品牌(中文或外文名称)4.型号
85030020	1.品名 2.用途(所适用整机的类型及输出功率)3.品牌(中文或外文名称)4.型号
85030030	1.品名 2.用途(适用于××品牌××机或通用于××机等)3.品牌(中文或外文名称)4.型号
85030090	1.品名 2.用途(所适用整机的类型及输出功率)3.品牌(中文或外文名称)4.型号
85041	1.品名 2.用途 3.品牌(中文或外文名称)4.型号
85042	1.品名 2.额定容量 3.是否为液体介质 4.品牌(中文或外文名称)5.型号
85043	1.品名 2.额定容量 3.是否为液体介质 4.品牌(中文或外文名称)5.型号
85044013	1.品名 2.用途 3.类型(交流稳压电源或直流稳压电源)4.额定输出功率 5.精度 6.品牌(中文或外文名称)7.型号
85044014	1.品名 2.用途 3.类型(交流稳压电源或直流稳压电源)4.额定输出功率 5.精度 6.品牌(中文或外文名称)7.型号
85044015	1.品名 2.用途 3.类型(交流稳压电源或直流稳压电源)4.额定输出功率 5.精度 6.品牌(中文或外文名称)7.型号
85044019	1.品名 2.用途 3.类型(交流稳压电源或直流稳压电源)4.额定输出功率 5.精度 6.品牌(中文或外文名称)7.型号
85044020	1.品名 2.功率 3.品牌(中文或外文名称)4.型号
85044030	1.品名 2.功率 3.品牌(中文或外文名称)4.型号
85044091	1.品名 2.用途 3.是否封装 4.品牌(中文或外文名称)5.型号
85044099	1.品名 2.用途 3.功率 4.品牌(中文或外文名称)5.型号
85045000	1.品名 2.用途 3.品牌(中文或外文名称)4.型号
85049	1.品名 2.用途(适用于××品牌××机或通用于××机等)3.品牌(中文或外文名称)4.型号
85051110	1.品名材质 3.品牌(中文或外文名称)4.型号
85051190	1.品名 2.材质 3.品牌(中文或外文名称)4.型号
85051900	1.品名 2.材质 3.品牌(中文或外文名称)4.型号
85052000	1.品名 2.用途 3.品牌(中文或外文名称)4.型号
85059010	1.品名 2.用途 3.原理 4.品牌(中文或外文名称)5.型号
85059090	1.品名 2.用途(如核磁共振成像装置用等)3.如不为零件需申报原理 4.品牌(中文或外文名称)5.型号
85061011	1.品名 2.用途 3.电池电解质(二氧化锰、氧化汞、氧化银、锂、锌空气等) 4.形状 5.品牌(中文或外文名称)6.型号 7.容量 8.是否含汞
85061012	1.品名 2.用途 3.电池电解质(二氧化锰、氧化汞、氧化银、锂、锌空气等)4.形状 5.品牌(中文或外文名称)6.型号 7.容量 8.是否含汞
85061019	1.品名 2.用途 3.电池电解质(二氧化锰、氧化汞、氧化银、锂、锌空气等)4.品牌(中文或外文名称)5.型号 6.容量 7.是否含汞
85061090	1.品名 2.用途 3.电池电解质(二氧化锰、氧化汞、氧化银、锂、锌空气等)4.品牌(中文或外文名称)5.型号 6.容量 7.是否含汞

商品编码	申报要素
85063000	1.品名 2.用途 3.电池电解质(二氧化锰、氧化汞、氧化银、锂、锌空气等)4.品牌(中文或外文名称)5.型号 6.容量 7.是否含汞
85064000	1.品名 2.用途 3.电池电解质(二氧化锰、氧化汞、氧化银、锂、锌空气等)4.品牌(中文或外文名称)5.型号 6.容量 7.是否含汞
85065000	1.品名 2.用途 3.电池电解质(二氧化锰、氧化汞、氧化银、锂、锌空气等)4.品牌(中文或外文名称)5.型号 6.容量 7.是否含汞
85066000	1.品名 2.用途 3.电池电解质(二氧化锰、氧化汞、氧化银、锂、锌空气等)4.品牌(中文或外文名称)5.型号 6.容量 7.是否含汞
85068000	1.品名 2.用途 3.电池电解质(二氧化锰、氧化汞、氧化银、锂、锌空气等)4.品牌(中文或外文名称)5.型号 6.容量 7.是否含汞
85069	1.品名 2.用途(适用原电池或原电池组类型)3.品牌(中文或外文名称)4.型号
85071000	1.品名 2.用途 3.电池电解质(铅酸、镍镉、镍铁、镍氢、锂离子等)4.品牌(中文或外文名称)5.型号 6.容量 7.是否含汞 8.额定电压
85072000	1.品名 2.用途 3.电池电解质(铅酸、镍镉、镍铁、镍氢、锂离子等)4.品牌(中文或外文名称)5.型号 6.容量 7.是否含汞 8.额定电压
85073000	1.品名 2.用途 3.电池电解质(铅酸、镍镉、镍铁、镍氢、锂离子等)4.品牌(中文或外文名称)5.型号 6.容量 7.是否含汞 8.额定电压
85075000	1.品名 2.用途 3.电池电解质(铅酸、镍镉、镍铁、镍氢、锂离子等)4.品牌(中文或外文名称)5.型号 6.容量 7.是否含汞 8.额定电压
85076000	1.品名 2.用途 3.电池电解质(铅酸、镍镉、镍铁、镍氢、锂离子等)4.品牌(中文或外文名称)5.型号 6.容量 7.是否含汞 8.额定电压
85078	1.品名 2.用途 3.电池电解质(铅酸、镍镉、镍铁、镍氢、锂离子等)4.品牌(中文或外文名称)5.型号 6.容量 7.是否含汞 8.额定电压
85079	1.品名 2.用途(适用于××品牌××机或通用于××机等)3.品牌(中文或外文名称)4.型号
85081	1.品名 2.驱动方式 3.集尘器容积 4.品牌(中文或外文名称)5.型号 6.功率
85086000	1.品名 2.驱动方式 3.品牌(中文或外文名称)4.型号
85087	1.品名 2.用途(适用于××品牌××机或通用于××机等)3.品牌(中文或外文名称)4.型号
85094	1.品名 2.用途(是否家 用)3.机身重量 4.功率 5.品牌(中文或外文名称)6.型号
85098010	1.品名 2.用途 3.机身重量 4.功率 5.品牌(中文或外文名称)6.型号
85098020	1.品名 2.用途 3.机身重量 4.功率 5.品牌(中文或外文名称)6.型号
85098090	1.品名 2.用途 3.机身重量 4.功率 5.品牌(中文或外文名称)6.型号
85099000	1.品名 2.用途(适用于××品牌××机或通用于××机等)3.品牌(中文或外文名称)4.型号
85101000	1.品名 2.品牌(中文或外文名称)3.型号
85102000	1.品名 2.品牌(中文或外文名称)3.型号
85103000	1.品名 2.品牌(中文或外文名称)3.型号
85109000	1.品名 2.用途(适用于××品牌××机或通用于××机等)3.品牌(中文或外文名称)4.型号
85111000	1.品名 2.用途 3.功能 4.生产件的通用零件编号后加注"/TY"5.成套散件装配后完整品的零部件的编号 6.品牌(中文或外文名称)7.型号 8.零部件完整编号并在前加注"S/""W/"或"WF/"之一(生产件填报"S/",品牌和适用的整车厂牌一致的维修件填报"W/",
85112	1.品名 2.用途 3.功能 4.品牌(中文或外文名称)5.型号
85113	1.品名 2.用途 3.功能 4.品牌(中文或外文名称)5.型号
85114010	1.品名 2.用途 3.功能 4.品牌(中文或外文名称)5.型号
8511409	1.品名 2.用途 3.功能 4.适用发动机的输出功率 5.品牌(中文或外文名称)6.型号
85115	1.品名 2.用途 3.功能 4.品牌(中文或外文名称)5.型号
85118000	1.品名 2.用途 3.功能 4.品牌(中文或外文名称)5.型号
85119	1.品名 2.用途(适用于××品牌××机或通用于××机等)3.品牌(中文或外文名称)4.型号
85121000	1.品名 2.用途 3.功能 4.品牌(中文或外文名称)5.型号
85122010	1.品名 2.用途 3.功能 4.生产件的通用零件编号后加注"/TY"5.成套散件装配后完整品的零部件的编号 6.品牌(中文或外文名称)7.型号 8.零部件完整编号并在前加注"S/""W/"或"WF/"之一(生产件填报"S/",品牌和适用的整车厂牌一致的维修件填报"W/ ",品牌和适用的整车厂牌不一致的维修件的填报"WF/")
85122090	1.品名 2.用途 3.功能 4.生产件的通用零件编号后加注"/TY"5.成套散件装配后完整品的零部件的编号 6.品牌(中文或外文名称)7.型号 8.零部件完整编号并在前加注"S/""W/"或"WF/"之一(生产件填报"S/",品牌和适用的整车厂牌一致的维修件填报"W/ ",品牌和适用的整车厂牌不一致的维修件的填报"WF/")
85123011	1.品名 2.用途 3.功能 4.生产件的通用零件编号后加注"/TY"5.成套散件装配后完整品的零部件的编号 6.品牌(中文或外文名称)7.型号 8.零部件完整编号并在前加注"S/""W/"或"WF/"之一(生产件填报"S/",品牌和适用的整车厂牌一致的维修件填报"W/ ",品牌和适用的整车厂牌不一致的维修件的填报"WF/")
85123012	1.品名 2.用途 3.功能 4.生产件的通用零件编号后加注"/TY"5.成套散件装配后完整品的零部件的编号 6.品牌(中文或外文名称)7.型号 8.零部件完整编号并在前加注"S/""W/"或"WF/"之一(生产件填报"S/",品牌和适用的整车厂牌一致的维修件填报"W/ ",品牌和适用的整车厂牌不一致的维修件的填报"WF/")
85123019	1.品名 2.用途 3.功能 4.生产件的通用零件编号后加注"/TY"5.成套散件装配后完整品的零部件的编号 6.品牌(中文或外文名称)7.型号 8.零部件完整编号并在前加注"S/""W/"或"WF/"之一(生产件填报"S/",品牌和适用的整车厂牌一致的维修件填报"W/ ",品牌和适用的整车厂牌不一致的维修件的填报"WF/")
85124000	1.品名 2.用途 3.功能 4.生产件的通用零件编号后加注"/TY"5.成套散件装配后完整品的零部件的编号 6.品牌(中文或外文名称)7.型号 8.零部件完整编号并在前加注"S/""W/"或"WF/"之一(生产件填报"S/",品牌和适用的整车厂牌一致的维修件填报"W/ ",品牌和适用的整车厂牌不一致的维修件的填报"WF/")
85129000	1.品名 2.用途(适用于××品牌××机或通用于××机等)3.功能 4.生产件的通用零件编号后加注"/TY"5.成套散件装配后完整品的零部件的编号 6.品牌(中文或外文名称)7.型号 8.零部件完整编号并在前加注"S/""W/"或"WF/"之一(生产件填报"S/",品牌和适用的整车厂牌一致的维修件填报"W/ ",品牌和适用的整车厂牌不一致的维修件的填报"WF/")
85131	1.品名 2.是否手提式 3.品牌(中文或外文名称)4.型号

商品编码	申报要素
85139	1.品名 2.用途(适用于××品牌××机或通用于××机等)3.品牌(中文或外文名称)4.型号
85141	1.品名 2.用途(工业用,实验室用)3.加热原理 4.品牌(中文或外文名称)5.型号
85142000	1.品名 2.用途(工业用,实验室用)3.加热原理 4.品牌(中文或外文名称)5.型号
85143	1.品名 2.用途(工业用,实验室用)3.加热原理 4.品牌(中文或外文名称)5.型号
85144000	1.品名 2.用途(工业用,实验室用)3.加热原理 4.品牌(中文或外文名称)5.型号
85149	1.品名 2.用途(适用于××品牌××机或通用于××机等)3.品牌(中文或外文名称)4.型号
85151100	1.品名 2.原理 3.焊接过程中是否使用钎料 4.品牌(中文或外文名称)5.型号
85151900	1.品名 2.原理 3.若为印刷电路组件制造用需注明 4.焊接过程中是否使用钎料 5.品牌(中文或外文名称)6.型号
85152120	1.品名 2.原理 3.是否为全自动或半自动 4.品牌(中文或外文名称)5.型号
85152191	1.品名 2.原理 3.是否为全自动或半自动 4.品牌(中文或外文名称)5.型号
85152199	1.品名 2.原理 3.是否为全自动或半自动 4.品牌(中文或外文名称)5.型号
85152900	1.品名 2.原理 3.是否为全自动或半自动 4.品牌(中文或外文名称)5.型号
85153120	1.品名 2.原理 3.是否为全自动或半自动 4.品牌(中文或外文名称)5.型号
85153191	1.品名 2.原理 3.是否为全自动或半自动 4.品牌(中文或外文名称)5.型号
85153199	1.品名 2.原理 3.是否为全自动或半自动 4.品牌(中文或外文名称)5.型号
85153900	1.品名 2.原理 3.是否为全自动或半自动 4.品牌(中文或外文名称)5.型号
85158010	1.品名 2.原理 3.品牌(中文或外文名称)4.型号
85158090	1.品名 2.原理 3.品牌(中文或外文名称)4.型号
85159000	1.品名 2.用途(适用于××品牌××机或通用于××机等)3.若为印刷电路组件制造用需注明 4.品牌(中文或外文名称)5.型号
85161010	1.品名 2.工作方式(储存式、即热式、浸入式等) 3.加热原理 4.品牌(中文或外文名称)5.型号 6.容量
85161020	1.品名 2.工作方式(储存式、即热式、浸入式等) 3.加热原理 4.品牌(中文或外文名称)5.型号
85161090	1.品名 2.工作方式(储存式、即热式、浸入式等)3.加热原理 4.品牌(中文或外文名称)5.型号
85162100	1.品名 2.用途 3.工作方式(储存式、辐射式、对流式等)4.品牌(中文或外文名称)5.型号
85162910	1.品名 2.用途 3.工作方式(储存式、辐射式、对流式等)4.品牌(中文或外文名称)5.型号
85162920	1.品名 2.用途 3.工作方式(储存式、辐射式、对流式等)4.品牌(中文或外文名称)5.型号
8516293	1.品名 2.用途 3.工作方式(储存式、辐射式、对流式等)4.品牌(中文或外文名称)5.型号
85163	1.品名 2.用途 3.加热原理 4.品牌(中文或外文名称)5.型号
85164000	1.品名 2.用途 3.加热原理 4.品牌(中文或外文名称)5.型号
85165000	1.品名 2.用途 3.加热原理 4.品牌(中文或外文名称)5.型号
85166	1.品名 2.用途 3.加热原理 4.品牌(中文或外文名称)5.型号
85167	1.品名 2.用途 3.加热原理 4.品牌(中文或外文名称)5.型号
85168000	1.品名 2.用途 3.品牌(中文或外文名称)4.型号
85169	1.品名 2.用途(适用于××品牌××机或通用于××机等)3.品牌(中文和外文名称)4.型号
85171100	1.品名 2.用途 3.适用网络种类(蜂窝网络、无线网络、有线网络、以太网等)4.品牌(中文或外文名称)5.型号 6.是否加密
85171300	1.品名 2.用途 3.适用网络种类(蜂窝网络、无线网络、有线网络、以太网等)4.品牌(中文或外文名称)5.型号 6.是否加密
85171410	1.品名 2.用途 3.适用网络种类(蜂窝网络、无线网络)4.品牌(中文或外文名称)5.型号 6.是否加密
85171420	1.品名 2.用途 3.适用网络种类(蜂窝网络、无线网络)4.品牌(中文或外文名称)5.型号 6.是否加密
85171490	1.品名 2.用途 3.适用网络种类(蜂窝网络、无线网络)4.品牌(中文或外文名称)5.型号 6.是否加密
85171800	1.品名 2.用途 3.适用网络种类(蜂窝网络、无线网络、有线网络、以太网等)4.品牌(中文或外文名称)5.型号 6.是否加密
851761	1.品名 2.用途 3.品牌(中文或外文名称)4.型号 5.是否加密
85176211	1.品名 2.用途 3.控制方式 4.处理信号的类型 5.型号
85176212	1.品名 2.用途 3.控制方式 4.处理信号的类型 5.型号
85176219	1.品名 2.用途 3.控制方式 4.处理信号的类型 5.型号
8517622	1.品名 2.用途 3.通讯方式 4.品牌(中文或外文名称)5.型号 6.是否加密
8517623	1.品名 2.用途 3.通讯方式 4.适用网络种类(蜂窝网络、有线网络、以太网 等)5.品牌(中文或外文名称)6.型号
85176292	1.品名 2.用途 3.功能 4.适用网络种类(蜂窝网络、有线网络、以太网等)5.品牌(中文或外文名称)6.型号
85176293	1.品名 2.用途 3.功能 4.适用网络种类(蜂窝网络、有线网络、以太网等)5.品牌(中文或外文名称)6.型号
85176294	1.品名 2.用途 3.功能 4.适用网络种类(蜂窝网络、有线网络、以太网等)5.品牌(中文或外文名称)6.型号
85176299	1.品名 2.用途 3.功能 4.适用网络种类(蜂窝网络、有线网络、以太网等)5.品牌(中文或外文名称)6.型号
851769	1.品名 2.用途 3.品牌(中文或外文名称)4.型号
85177100	1.品名 2.用途(适用于××品牌××机或通用于××机等)3.品牌(中文或外文名称)4.型号
85177910	1.品名 2.用途(适用于××品牌××机或通用于××机等)3.品牌(中文或外文名称)4.型号
85177920	1.品名 2.用途(适用于××品牌××机或通用于××机等)3.品牌(中文或外文名称)4.型号
85177930	1.品名 2.用途(适用于××品牌××机或通用于××机等)3.显示屏或显示模块请申报尺寸(英寸)4.显示屏或显示模块请申报种类(如LED、OLED 等)5.显示屏或显示模块请申报是否需要二次加工 6.品牌(中文或外文名称)7.型号
85177940	1.品名 2.用途(适用于××品牌××机或通用于××机等)3.品牌(中文或外文名称)4.型号
85177950	1.品名 2.用途(适用于××品牌××机或通用于××机等)3.品牌(中文或外文名称)4.型号
85177990	1.品名 2.用途(适用于××品牌××机或通用于××机等)3.品牌(中文或外文名称)4.型号
85181000	1.品名 2.品牌(中文或外文名称)3.型号
85182100	1.品名 2.结构类型(是否有箱体)3.用途 4.品牌(中文或外文名称)5.型号
85182200	1.品名 2.结构类型(是否有箱体)3.用途 4.品牌(中文或外文名称)5.型号 6.喇叭数量和尺寸
85182900	1.品名 2.结构类型(是否有箱体)3.用途 4.品牌(中文或外文名称)5.型号 6.喇叭尺寸
85183000	1.品名 2.品牌(中文或外文名称)3.型号
85184000	1.品名 2.品牌(中文或外文名称)3.型号
85185000	1.品名 2.组成部件 3.品牌(中文或外文名称)4.型号
85189000	1.品名 2.用途(适用于××品牌××机或通用于××机等)3.品牌(中文或外文名称)4.型号
85192000	1.品名 2.支付方式 3.品牌(中文或外文名称)4.型号
85193000	1.品名 2.品牌(中文或外文名称)3.型号
85198	1.品名 2.使用媒介 3.品牌(中文或外文名称)4.型号
85211	1.品名 2.用途 3.使用媒介 4.品牌(中文或外文名称)5.型号
85219	1.品名 2.使用媒介 3.类型 4.品牌(中文或外文名称)5.型号
8522	1.品名 2.用途(适用于××品牌××机或通用于××机等)3.品牌(中文或外文名称)4.型号
852321	1.品名 2.用途 3.是否录制 4.品牌(中文或外文名称)5.型号 6.录制内容类型
8523291	1.品名 2.用途 3.是否录制 4.品牌(中文或外文名称)5.型号 6.录制内容类型
8523292	1.品名 2.用途 3.是否录制 4.磁带宽度 5.品牌(中文或外文名称)6.型号 7.录制内容类型
85232990	1.品名 2.用途 3.是否录制 4.品牌(中文或外文名称)5.型号 6.录制内容类型
85234	1.品名 2.用途 3.是否录制 4.录制内容类型 5.品牌(中文或外文名称)6.型号 7.存储容量 8.读取速度
852351	1.品名 2.用途 3.是否录制 4.品牌(中文或外文名称)5.型号 6.容量
852352	1.品名 2.用途 3.是否录制 4.品牌(中文或外文名称)5.型号 6.是否加密 7.存储容量
852359	1.品名 2.用途 3.是否录制 4.品牌(中文或外文名称)5.型号
85238	1.品名 2.用途 3.是否录制 4.品牌(中文或外文名称)5.型号
85241100	1.品名 2.用途 3.平面显示模组类型(液晶)4.是否含驱动器或控制电路 5.尺寸 6.品牌(中文或外文名称)7.型号 8.配置(请注明配置显示驱动板、HDMI 接口、标记板、解码板、高频头、视频接口、触摸功能等)9.单片重量 10.是否已切割
85241200	1.品名 2.用途 3.平面显示模组类型(有机发光二极管)4.是否含驱动器或控制电路 5.尺寸 6.品牌(中文或外文名称)7.型号
852419	1.品名 2.用途 3.平面显示模组类型(等离子、发光二极管等)4.是否含驱动器或控制电路 5.尺寸 6.品牌(中文或外文名称)7.型号
85249110	1.品名 2.用途 3.平面显示模组类型(液晶)4.是否含驱动器或控制电路 5.是否需要二次加工 6.尺寸 7.品牌(中文或外文名称)8.型号
85249120	1.品名 2.用途 3.平面显示模组类型(液晶)4.是否含驱动器或控制电路 5.尺寸 6.品牌(中文或外文名称)7.型号
85249130	1.品名 2.用途 3.平面显示模组类型(液晶)4.是否含驱动器或控制电路 5.尺寸 6.品牌(中文或外文名称)7.型号
85249140	1.品名 2.用途 3.平面显示模组类型(液晶)4.是否含驱动器或控制电路 5.尺寸 6.品牌(中文或外文名称)7.型号
85249190	1.品名 2.用途 3.平面显示模组类型(液晶)4.是否含驱动器或控制电路 5.尺寸 6.品牌(中文或外文名称)7.型号
85249210	1.品名 2.用途 3.平面显示模组类型(有机发光二极管)4.是否含驱动器或控制电路 5.是否需要二次加工 6.尺寸 7.品牌(中文或外文名称)8.型号
85249220	1.品名 2.用途 3.平面显示模组类型(有机发光二极管)4.是否含驱动器或控制电路 5.尺寸 6.品牌(中文或外文名称)7.型号
85249230	1.品名 2.用途 3.平面显示模组类型(有机发光二极管)4.是否含驱动器或控制电路 5.尺寸 6.品牌(中文或外文名称)7.型号
85249240	1.品名 2.用途 3.平面显示模组类型(有机发光二极管)4.是否含驱动器或控制电路 5.尺寸 6.品牌(中文或外文名称)7.型号
85249250	1.品名 2.用途 3.平面显示模组类型(有机发光二极管)4.是否含驱动器或控制电路 5.尺寸 6.品牌(中文或外文名称)7.型号
85249260	1.品名 2.用途 3.平面显示模组类型(有机发光二极管)4.是否含驱动器或控制电路 5.尺寸 6.品牌(中文或外文名称)7.型号
85249290	1.品名 2.用途 3.平面显示模组类型(有机发光二极管)4.是否含驱动器或控制电路 5.尺寸 6.品牌(中文或外文名称)7.型号
852499	1.品名 2.用途 3.平面显示模组类型(等离子、发光二极管等)4.是否含驱动器或控制电路 5.尺寸 6.品牌(中文或外文名称)7.型号
85255000	1.品名 2.用途 3.品牌(中文或外文名称)4.型号
85256	1.品名 2.用途 3.结构组成 4.品牌(中文或外文名称)5.型号
85258110	1.品名 2.用途 3.是否可装内置存储装置 4.品牌(中文或外文名称)5.型号
85258120	1.品名 2.用途 3.是否可装内置存储装置 4.品牌(中文或外文名称)5.型号
85258130	1.品名 2.用途 3.是否可装内置存储装置 4.品牌(中文或外文名称)5.型号
852582	1.品名 2.用途 3.是否可装内置存储装置 4.品牌(中文或外文名称)5.型号
85258210	1.品名 2.用途 3.是否可装内置存储装置 4.品牌(中文或外文名称)5.型号
85258220	1.品名 2.用途 3.是否可装内置存储装置 4.品牌(中文或外文名称)5.型号

商品编码	申报要素
85258230	1.品名 2.用途 3.是否可装内置存储装置 4.品牌(中文或外文名称)5.型号
852583	1.品名 2.用途 3.是否可装内置存储装置 4.品牌(中文或外文名称)5.型号
85258310	1.品名 2.用途 3.是否可装内置存储装置 4.品牌(中文或外文名称)5.型号
85258320	1.品名 2.用途 3.是否可装内置存储装置 4.品牌(中文或外文名称)5.型号
85258330	1.品名 2.用途 3.是否可装内置存储装置 4.品牌(中文或外文名称)5.型号
85258911	1.品名 2.用途 3.是否可装内置存储装置 4.品牌(中文或外文名称)5.型号
85258912	1.品名 2.用途 3.是否可装内置存储装置 4.品牌(中文或外文名称)5.型号
85258919	1.品名 2.用途 3.高清摄像头报玻璃镜头层数 4.高清摄像头报接口类型(是否 USB2.0 以上接口)5.高清摄像头报硬件传感器像素 6.是否可装内置存储装置 7.品牌(中文或外文名称)8.型号
8525892	1.品名 2.用途 3.是否可装内置存储装置 4.品牌(中文或外文名称)5.型号
8525893	1.品名 2.用途 3.是否可装内置存储装置 4.品牌(中文或外文名称)5.型号
85261	1.品名 2.用途 3.品牌(中文或外文名称)4.型号
852691	1.品名 2.用途 3.品牌(中文或外文名称)4.型号
85269200	1.品名 2.用途 3.品牌(中文或外文名称)4.型号 5.控制距离
85271	1.品名 2.使用媒介(是否为盒式磁带)3.是否需外接电源 4.品牌(中文或外文名称)5.型号 6.外形尺寸
85272100	1.品名 2.用途 3.结构组成 4.具备接收和转换数字广播数据系统信号功能的需注明 5.品牌(中文或外文名称)6.型号
85272900	1.品名 2.用途 3.结构组成 4.品牌(中文或外文名称)5.型号
85279100	1.品名 2.用途 3.品牌(中文或外文名称)4.型号
85279200	1.品名 2.用途 3.品牌(中文或外文名称)4.型号
85279900	1.品名 2.用途 3.品牌(中文或外文名称)4.型号
85284200	1.品名 2.用途 3.显示原理 4.显示屏幕尺寸 5.接口类型(包括接口电路)6.品牌(中文或外文名称)7.型号
852849	1.品名 2.用途 3.显示原理 4.显示屏幕尺寸 5.品牌(中文或外文名称)6.型号
85285211	1.品名 2.用途 3.显示原理 4.显示屏幕尺寸 5.接口类型(包括接口电路) 6.构成(是否带标记板、解码板或高频头板等信号处理板)7.品牌(中文或外文名称)8.型号
85285212	1.品名 2.用途 3.显示原理 4.显示屏幕尺寸 5.接口类型(包括接口电路) 6.构成(是否带标记板、解码板或高频头板等信号处理板)7.品牌(中文或外文名称)8.型号
85285219	1.品名 2.用途 3.显示原理 4.显示屏幕尺寸 5.接口类型(包括接口电路) 6.构成(是否带标记板、解码板或高频头板等信号处理板)7.品牌(中文或外文名称)8.型号
85285291	1.品名 2.用途 3.显示原理 4.显示屏幕尺寸 5.接口类型(包括接口电路)6.品牌(中文或外文名称)7.型号
85285292	1.品名 2.用途 3.显示原理 4.显示屏幕尺寸 5.接口类型(包括接口电路)6.品牌(中文或外文名称)7.型号
85285299	1.品名 2.用途 3.显示原理 4.显示屏幕尺寸 5.接口类型(包括接口电路)6.品牌(中文或外文名称)7.型号
85285910	1.品名 2.用途 3.显示原理 4.显示屏幕尺寸 5.品牌(中文或外文名称)6.型号 7.最高分辨率
85285990	1.品名 2.用途 3.显示原理 4.显示屏幕尺寸 5.品牌(中文或外文名称)6.型号
85286210	1.品名 2.用途 3.显示原理 4.接口类型(包括接口电路)5.品牌(中文或外文名称)6.型号 7.亮度
85286220	1.品名 2.用途 3.显示原理 4.接口类型(包括接口电路)5.品牌(中文或外文名称)6.型号 7.亮度
85286290	1.品名 2.用途 3.显示原理 4.接口类型(包括接口电路)5.品牌(中文或外文名称)6.型号 7.亮度
852869	1.品名 2.用途 3.显示原理 4.接口类型(包括接口电路)5.品牌(中文或外文名称)6.型号 7.亮度
852871	1.品名 2.用途 3.是否带显示屏 4.品牌(中文或外文名称)5.型号
852872	1.品名 2.用途 3.显示原理 4.显示屏幕尺寸 5.品牌(中文或外文名称)6.型号
85287300	1.品名 2.用途 3.显示原理 4.显示屏幕尺寸 5.品牌(中文或外文名称)6.型号
85291010	1.品名 2.用途(适用于××品牌××机或通用于××机等)3.品牌(中文或外文名称)4.型号
85291020	1.品名 2.用途(适用于××品牌××机或通用于××机等)3.品牌(中文或外文名称)4.型号
85291090	1.品名 2.用途(适用于××品牌××机或通用于××机等)3.品牌(中文或外文名称)4.型号
85299010	1.品名 2.用途(适用于××品牌××机或通用于××机等)3.品牌(中文或外文名称)4.型号
85299020	1.品名 2.用途(适用于××品牌××机或通用于××机等)3.品牌(中文或外文名称)4.型号
85299041	1.品名 2.用途(适用于××品牌××机或通用于××机等)3.品牌(中文或外文名称)4.型号
85299042	1.品名 2.用途(适用于××品牌××机或通用于××机等)3.是否带有数字信号处理电路 4.品牌(中文或外文名称)5.型号
85299049	1.品名 2.用途(适用于××品牌××机或通用于××机等)3.品牌(中文或外文名称)4.型号
85299050	1.品名 2.用途(适用于××品牌××机或通用于××机等)3.品牌(中文或外文名称)4.型号
85299060	1.品名 2.用途(适用于××品牌××机或通用于××机等)3.品牌(中文或外文名称)4.型号
8529908	1.品名 2.用途(适用于××品牌××机或通用于××机等)3.品牌(中文或外文名称)4.型号
85299090	1.品名 2.用途(适用于××品牌××机或通用于××机等)3.品牌(中文或外文名称)4.型号
85301000	1.品名 2.用途 3.品牌(中文或外文名称)4.型号

商品编码	申报要素
85308000	1.品名 2.用途 3.品牌(中文或外文名称)4.型号
85309000	1.品名 2.用途(适用于××品牌××机或通用于××机等)3.品牌(中文或外文名称)4.型号
85311000	1.品名 2.用途 3.品牌(中文或外文名称)4.型号 5.工作原理
85312000	1.品名 2.用途 3.显示原理 4.品牌(中文或外文名称)5.型号 6.规格尺寸
85318010	1.品名 2.用途 3.音量 4.品牌(中文或外文名称)5.型号
85318090	1.品名 2.用途 3.品牌(中文或外文名称)4.型号
85319	1.品名 2.用途(适用于××品牌××机或通用于××机等)3.品牌(中文或外文名称)4.型号
85321000	1.品名 2.用途 3.额定无功功率 4.适用频率 5.品牌(中文或外文名称)6.型号
85322	1.品名 2.结构类型(单层、多层等和片式、非片式)3.介质类型 4.品牌(中文或外文名称)5.型号
85323000	1.品名 2.是否可变、可调 3.品牌(中文或外文名称)4.型号
85329	1.品名 2.用途(适用于××品牌××机或通用于××机等)3.品牌(中文或外文名称)4.型号
85331000	1.品名 2.结构类型 3.介质 4.品牌(中文或外文名称)5.型号
85332	1.品名 2 额定功率 3.结构类型(片式、线绕式等)4.品牌(中文或外文名称)5.型号
85333	1.品名 2 额定功率 3.结构类型(片式、线绕式等)4.品牌(中文或外文名称)5.型号
85334000	1.品名 2.品牌(中文或外文名称)3.型号
85339000	1.品名 2.用途(适用于××品牌××机或通用于××机等)3.品牌(中文或外文名称)4.型号
8534	1.品名 2.电路层数 3.是否不带有机械元件 4.是否不带有有源电气元件 5.品牌(中文或外文名称)6.型号
85351000	1.品名 2.用途 3.电压 4.品牌(中文或外文名称)5.型号
85352100	1.品名 2.用途 3.电压 4.品牌(中文或外文名称)5.型号
853529	1.品名 2.用途 3.电压 4.品牌(中文或外文名称)5.型号
85353010	1.品名 2.用途 3.电压 4.品牌(中文或外文名称)5.型号
85353020	1.品名 2.用途 3.电压 4.品牌(中文或外文名称)5.型号
85353090	1.品名 2.用途 3.电压 4.品牌(中文或外文名称)5.型号
85354000	1.品名 2.用途 3.电压 4.品牌(中文或外文名称)5.型号
85359000	1.品名 2.用途 3.电压 4.品牌(中文或外文名称)5.型号
85361000	1.品名 2.用途 3.电压 4.品牌(中文或外文名称)5.型号
85362000	1.品名 2.用途 3.电压 4.品牌(中文或外文名称)5.型号
85363000	1.品名 2.用途 3.电压 4.品牌(中文或外文名称)5.型号
85364110	1.品名 2.用途 3.电压 4.品牌(中文或外文名称)5.型号
85364190	1.品名 2.用途 3.电压 4.品牌(中文或外文名称)5.型号
85364900	1.品名 2.用途 3.电压 4.品牌(中文或外文名称)5.型号
85365000	1.品名 2.用途 3.电压 4.品牌(中文或外文名称)5.型号
85366100	1.品名 2.用途 3.电压 4.品牌(中文或外文名称)5.型号
85366900	1.品名 2.用途 3.电压 4.品牌(中文或外文名称)5.型号
85367000	1.品名 2.用途 3.品牌(中文或外文名称)4.型号
85369011	1.品名 2.用途 3.电压 4.品牌(中文或外文名称)5.型号
85369019	1.品名 2.用途 3.电压 4.品牌(中文或外文名称)5.型号
85369090	1.品名 2.用途 3.电压 4.品牌(中文或及外文名称)5.型号
85371011	1.品名 2.用途 3.原理 4.电压 5.品牌(中文或外文名称)6.型号
85371019	1.品名 2.用途 3.原理 4.电压 5.品牌(中文或外文名称)6.型号
85371090	1.品名 2.用途 3.原理 4.电压 5.品牌(中文或外文名称)6.型号
85372	1.品名 2.用途 3.原理 4.电压 5.品牌(中文或外文名称)6.型号
8538	1.品名 2.用途(适用于××品牌××机或通用于××机等)3.是否装有税目 85.35 或 85.36 所列装置 4.品牌(中文或外文名称)5.型号
85391000	1.品名 2.用途 3.类型 4.品牌(中文或外文名称)5.型号
853921	1.品名 2.用途 3.类型 4.品牌(中文或外文名称)5.型号
853922	1.品名 2.用途 3.类型 4.功率 5.额定电压 6.品牌(中文或外文名称)7.型号
853929	1.品名 2.用途 3.类型 4.功率 5.额定电压 6.品牌(中文或外文名称)7.型号
853931	1.品名 2.类型 3.品牌(中文或外文名称)4.型号
853932	1.品名 2.类型 3.品牌(中文或外文名称)4.型号
85393910	1.品名 2.类型 3.品牌(中文或外文名称)4.型号
85393920	1.品名 2.类型 3.品牌(中文或外文名称)4.型号
85393990	1.品名 2.类型 3.品牌(中文或外文名称)4.型号
85394	1.品名 2.类型 3.品牌(中文或外文名称)4.型号
85395	1.品名 2.类型 3.品牌(中文或外文名称)4.型号
85395100	1.品名 2.用途 3.品牌(中文或外文名称)4.型号
85399	1.品名 2.用途(适用于××品牌××机或通用于××机等)3.品牌(中文或外文名称)4.型号
85401	1.品名 2.原理 3.品牌(中文或外文名称)4.型号
85402	1.品名 2.用途 3.品牌(中文或外文名称)4.型号
85404010	1.品名 2.是否彩色 3.荧光点距 4.品牌(中文或外文名称)5.型号
85404020	1.品名 2.是否单色 3.荧光点距 4.品牌(中文或外文名称)5.型号
85406010	1.品名 2.用途 3.类型 4.品牌(中文或外文名称)5.型号
85406090	1.品名 2.用途 3.类型 4.品牌(中文或外文名称)5.型号
85407	1.品名 2.用途 3.类型 4.品牌(中文或外文名称)5.型号
85408	1.品名 2.用途 3.类型 4.品牌(中文或外文名称)5.型号
85409	1.品名 2.用途(适用于××品牌××机或通用于××机等)3.品牌(中文或外文名称)4.型号
85411000	1.品名 2.品牌(中文或外文名称)3.型号
85412	1.品名 2.耗散功率 3.品牌(中文或外文名称)4.型号
85413000	1.品名 2.是否由多个半导体元件构成 3.品牌(中文或外文名称)4.型号
85414100	1.品名 2.品牌(中文或外文名称)3.型号
85414200	1.品名 2.额定功率 3.品牌(中文或外文名称)4.型号 5.转换效率
85414300	1.品名 2.额定功率 3.品牌(中文或外文名称)4.型号 5.转换效率
85414900	1.品名 2.品牌(中文或外文名称)3.型号
85415111	1.品名 2.用途 3.功能 4.品牌(中文或外文名称)5.型号
85415121	1.品名 2.用途 3.功能 4.品牌(中文或外文名称)5.型号
85415129	1.品名 2.用途 3.功能 4.品牌(中文或外文名称)5.型号
85415130	1.品名 2.用途 3.功能 4.品牌(中文或外文名称)5.型号

商品编码	申报要素
85415140	1.品名 2.用途 3.功能 4.品牌(中文或外文名称)5.型号
85415900	1.品名 2.用途 3.功能 4.是否由多个半导体元件构成 5.品牌(中文或外文名称)6.型号
85416000	1.品名 2.是否已装配 3.品牌(中文或外文名称)4.型号
85419000	1.品名 2.用途(适用于××品牌××机或通用于××机等)3.品牌(中文或外文名称)4.型号
854231	1.品名 2.应用场景 3.功能 4.是否封装 5.是否切割 6.品牌(中文或外文名称)7.型号 8.是否量产(量产或非量产)
854232	1.品名 2.应用场景 3.功能 4.是否封装 5.是否切割 6.品牌(中文或外文名称)7.型号 8.是否量产(量产或非量产)9.容量
854233	1.品名 2.应用场景 3.功能 4.是否封装 5.是否切割 6.品牌(中文或外文名称)7.型号 8.是否量产(量产或非量产)
854239	1.品名 2.应用场景 3.功能 4.是否封装 5.是否切割 6.品牌(中文或外文名称)7.型号 8.是否量产(量产或非量产)
85429000	1.品名 2.用途(适用于××品牌××机或通用于××机等)3.品牌(中文或外文名称)4.型号
85431000	1.品名 2.用途 3.功能 4.品牌(中文或外文名称)5.型号
85432	1.品名 2.用途 3.功能 4.输出信号频率范围 5.品牌(中文或外文名称)6.型号
85433000	1.品名 2.用途 3.功能 4.品牌(中文或外文名称)5.型号
85434000	1.品名 2.功能 3.品牌(中文或外文名称)4.型号
85437091	1.品名 2.用途 3.功能 4.品牌(中文或外文名称)5.型号
85437092	1.品名 2.用途 3.功能 4.品牌(中文或外文名称)5.型号
85437093	1.品名 2.用途 3.功能 4.品牌(中文或外文名称)5.型号
85437099	1.品名 2.用途 3.功能 4.品牌(中文或外文名称)5.型号
85439	1.品名 2.用途(适用于××品牌××机或通用于××机等)3.品牌(中文或外文名称)4.型号
85441	1.品名 2.用途 3.材质 4.品牌(中文或外文名称)5.型号
85442000	1.品名 2.用途 3.结构类型(同轴、有接头等)4.品牌(中文或外文名称)5.型号
85443020	1.品名 2.用途 3.品牌(中文或外文名称)4.型号 5.额定电压
85443090	1.品名 2.用途 3.结构类型(有接头等)4.品牌(中文或外文名称)5.型号 6.额定电压
85444211	1.品名 2.用途 3.结构类型(是否有接头是否同轴电缆)4.品牌(中文或外文名称)5.型号 6.额定电压
85444219	1.品名 2.用途 3.结构类型(是否有接头是否同轴电导体)4.品牌(中文或外文名称)5.型号 6.额定电压
85444221	1.品名 2.用途 3.结构类型(是否有接头是否同轴电缆)4.品牌(中文或外文名称)5.型号 6.额定电压
85444229	1.品名 2.用途 3.结构类型(是否有接头是否同轴电导体)4.品牌(中文或外文名称)5.型号 6.额定电压
85444911	1.品名 2.用途 3.结构类型(是否有接头是否同轴电缆)4.品牌(中文或外文名称)5.型号 6.额定电压
85444919	1.品名 2.用途 3.结构类型(是否有接头是否同轴电导体)4.品牌(中文或外文名称)5.型号 6.额定电压
85444921	1.品名 2.用途 3.结构类型(是否有接头是否同轴电缆)4.品牌(中文或外文名称)5.型号 6.额定电压
85444929	1.品名 2.用途 3.结构类型(是否有接头是否同轴电导体)4.品牌(中文或外文名称)5.型号 6.额定电压
85446012	1.品名 2.用途 3.结构类型(有接头等)4.品牌(中文或外文名称)5.型号 6.额定电压
85446013	1.品名 2.用途 3.结构类型(有接头等)4.品牌(中文或外文名称)5.型号 6.额定电压
85446014	1.品名 2.用途 3.结构类型(有接头等)4.品牌(中文或外文名称)5.型号 6.额定电压
85446019	1.品名 2.用途 3.结构类型(有接头等)4.品牌(中文或外文名称)5.型号 6.额定电压
85446090	1.品名 2.用途 3.结构类型(有接头等)4.品牌(中文或外文名称)5.型号 6.额定电压
85447000	1.品名 2.是否每根光纤被覆 3.品牌(中文或外文名称)4.型号
8545	1.品名 2.用途 3.材质 4.品牌(中文或外文名称)5.型号
8546	1.品名 2.用途 3.材质 4.品牌(中文或外文名称)5.型号
8547	1.品名 2.用途 3.材质 4.品牌(中文或外文名称)5.型号
85480000	1.品名 2.用途 3.品牌(中文或外文名称)4.型号
85491	1.品名 2.来源
85492	1.品名 2.来源
85493	1.品名 2.来源
85499	1.品名 2.来源
8601	1.品名 2.用途 3.驱动装置类型 4.控制装置类型 5.品牌(中文或外文名称)6.型号
86021	1.品名 2.用途 3.驱动装置类型 4.控制装置类型 5.品牌(中文或外文名称)6.型号
86029000	1.品名 2.用途 3.驱动装置类型 4.品牌(中文或外文名称)5.型号
8603	1.品名 2.用途 3.驱动装置类型 4.品牌(中文或外文名称)5.型号
8604	1.品名 2.用途 3.类型 4.品牌(中文或外文名称)5.型号
8605	1.品名 2.用途 3.类型 4.品牌(中文或外文名称)5.型号
8606	1.品名 2.用途 3.类型 4.结构 5.品牌(中文或外文名称)6.型号
8607	1.品名 2.用途(适用于××品牌××车或通用于××机等)3.品牌(中文或外文名称)4.型号
8608	1.品名 2.用途 3.品牌(中文或外文名称)4.型号
8609	1.品名 2.类型(公路等)3.规格尺寸 4.品牌(中文或外文名称)
87011000	1.品名 2.品牌(中文或外文名称)3.型号
87012	1.品名 2.用途 3.品牌(中文或外文名称)4.型号
87013000	1.品名 2.结构类型 3.品牌(中文或外文名称)4.型号
87019	1.品名 2.结构类型 3.功率 4.用途 5.品牌(中文或外文名称)6.型号
87021020	1.品名 2.发动机类型(柴油、半柴油、汽油等)3.成套散件请注明 4.车辆的厂家品牌(中文或外文名称)5.车辆厂家备案的品牌或具体款式的名称 6.排气量(毫升)7.规格型号
8702109	1.品名 2.发动机类型(柴油、半柴油、汽油等)3.成套散件请注明 4.座位数 5.车辆的厂家品牌(中文或外文名称)6.车辆厂家备案的品牌或具体款式的名称 7.排气量(毫升)8.规格型号
87022010	1.品名 2.发动机类型(柴油及驱动电动机等)3.成套散件请注明 4.车辆的厂家品牌(中文或外文名称)5.车辆厂家备案的品牌或具体款式的名称 6.排气量(毫升)7.规格型号
8702209	1.品名 2.发动机类型(柴油及驱动电动机等)3.成套散件请注明 4.座位数 5.车辆的厂家品牌(中文或外文名称)6.车辆厂家备案的品牌或具体款式的名称 7.排气量(毫升)8.规格型号
87023	1.品名 2.发动机类型(汽油及驱动电动机等)3.成套散件请注明 4.座位数 5.车辆的厂家品牌(中文或外文名称)6.车辆厂家备案的品牌或具体款式的名称 7.排气量(毫升)8.规格型号
87024	1.品名 2.发动机类型(电动等)3.成套散件请注明 4.座位数 5.车辆的厂家品牌(中文或外文名称)6.车辆厂家备案的品牌或具体款式的名称 7.功率(千瓦)8.规格型号
87029	1.品名 2.发动机类型(柴油、半柴油、汽油等)3.成套散件请注明 4.座位数 5.车辆的厂家品牌(中文或外文名称)6.车辆厂家备案的品牌或具体款式的名称 7.排气量(毫升)8.规格型号
87031011	1.品名 2.发动机类型(柴油、半柴油、汽油等)3.成套散件请注明 4.座位数 5.车辆的厂家品牌(中文或外文名称)6.车辆厂家备案的品牌或具体款式的名称 7.排气量(毫升)8.型号
87031019	1.品名 2.发动机类型(柴油、半柴油、汽油等)3.成套散件请注明 4.排气量(毫升)5.车辆的厂家品牌(中文或外文名称)6.车辆厂家备案的品牌或具体款式的名称 7.型号
87031090	1.品名 2.发动机类型(柴油、半柴油、汽油等)3.成套散件请注明 4.排气量(毫升)5.车辆的厂家品牌(中文或外文名称)6.车辆厂家备案的品牌或具体款式的名称 7.型号
87032	1.品名 2.发动机类型(柴油、半柴油、汽油等)3.成套散件请注明 4.座位数 5.车辆的厂家品牌(中文或外文名称)6.车辆厂家备案的品牌或具体款式的名称 7.排气量(毫升)8.型号 9.是否中规车请注明(中规车、非中规 车)10.非中规车请注明原销售目的国车版、型(美规、欧规、加规、中东规等)
87033	1.品名 2.发动机类型(柴油、半柴油、汽油等)3.成套散件请注明 4.座位数 5.车辆的厂家品牌(中文或外文名称)6.车辆厂家备案的品牌或具体款式的名称 7.排气量(毫升)8.型号 9.是否中规车请注明(中规车、非中规 车)10.非中规车请注明原销售目的国车版、型(美规、欧规、加规、中东规等)
87034	1.品名 2.发动机类型(汽油及驱动电动机等)3.成套散件请注明 4.座位数 5.是否可通过接插外部电源进行充电 6.车辆的厂家品牌(中文或外文名称)7.车辆厂家备案的品牌或具体款式的名称 8.排气量(毫升)9.型号 10.是否中规车请注明(中规车、非中规 车)11.非中规车请注明原销售目的国车版、型(美规、欧规、加规、中东规等)
87035	1.品名 2.发动机类型(柴油及驱动电动机等)3.成套散件请注明 4.座位数 5.是否可通过接插外部电源进行充电 6.车辆的厂家品牌(中文或外文名称)7.车辆厂家备案的品牌或具体款式的名称 8.排气量(毫升)9.型号 10.是否中规车请注明(中规车、非中规 车)11.非中规车请注明原销售目的国车版、型(美规、欧规、加规、中东规等)
87036	1.品名 2.发动机类型(汽油及驱动电动机等)3.成套散件请注明 4.座位数 5.是否可通过接插外部电源进行充电 6.车辆的厂家品牌(中文或外文名称)7.车辆厂家备案的品牌或具体款式的名称 8.排气量(毫升)9.型号 10.是否中规车请注明(中规车、非中规 车)11.非中规车请注明原销售目的国车版、型(美规、欧规、加规、中东规等)
87037	1.品名 2.发动机类型(柴油及驱动电动机等)3.成套散件请注明 4.座位数 5.是否可通过接插外部电源进行充电 6.车辆的厂家品牌(中文或外文名称)7.车辆厂家备案的品牌或具体款式的名称 8.排气量(毫升)9.型号 10.是否中规车请注明(中规车、非中规 车)11.非中规车请注明原销售目的国车版、型(美规、欧规、加规、中东规等)
87038000	1.品名 2.发动机类型(电动等)3.成套散件请注明 4.座位数 5.车辆的厂家品牌(中文或外文名称)6.车辆厂家备案的品牌或具体款式的名称 7.功率(千瓦)8.型号 9.是否中规车请注明(中规车、非中规车)10.非中规车请注明原销售目的国车版、型(美规、欧规、加规、中东规等)
87039000	1.品名 2.发动机类型(柴油、半柴油、汽油等)3.成套散件请注明 4.座位数 5.车辆的厂家品牌(中文或外文名称)6.车辆厂家备案的品牌或具体款式的名称 7.排气量(毫升)8.型号 9.是否中规车请注明(中规车、非中规 车)10.非中规车请注明原销售目的国车版、型(美规、欧规、加规、中东规等)
87041030	1.品名 2.用途 3.是否为电动轮 4.车辆的厂家品牌(中文或外文名称)5.型号
87041090	1.品名 2.用途 3.是否为电动轮 4.发动机类型(柴油、半柴油、汽油等)5.车体长、宽、高(空载状 态)6.车辆总重 7.车辆的厂家品牌(中文或外文名称)8.型号
87042100	1.品名 2.发动机类型(柴油、半柴油、汽油等)3.车辆总重 4.整备质量 5.驾驶室座位排数 6.驾驶室座位数 7.载货重量 8.车辆的厂家品牌(中文或外文名称)9.型号 10.是否中规车请注明(中规车、非中规车)11.非中规车请注明原销售目的国车版、型(美规、欧规、加规、中东规等)
870422	1.品名 2.发动机类型(柴油、半柴油、汽油等)3.车辆总重 4.车辆的厂家品牌(中文或外文名称)5.型号 6.是否中规车请注明(中规车、非中规车)7.非中规车请注明原销售目的国车版、型(美规、欧规、加规、中东规等)
87042300	1.品名 2.发动机类型(柴油、半柴油、汽油等)3.车辆总重 4.车辆的厂家品牌(中文或外文名称)5.型号
87043100	1.品名 2.发动机类型(柴油、半柴油、汽油等)3.车辆总重 4.整备质量 5.驾驶室座位排数 6.驾驶室座位数 7.载货重量 8.车辆的厂家品牌(中文或外文名称)9.型号 10.是否中规车请注明(中规车、非中规车)11.非中规车请注明原销售目的国车版、型(美规、欧规、加规、中东规等)
870432	1.品名 2.发动机类型(柴油、半柴油、汽油等)3.车辆总重 4.车辆的厂家品牌(中文或外文名称)5.型号 6.是否中规车请注明(中规车、非中规车)7.非中规车请注明原销售目的国车版、型(美规、欧规、加规、中东规等)
87044	1.品名 2.发动机类型(柴油、半柴油、汽油等)3.车辆总重 4.车辆的厂家品牌(中文或外文名称)5.型号
87045	1.品名 2.发动机类型(柴油、半柴油、汽油等)3.车辆总重 4.车辆的厂家品牌(中文或外文名称)5.型号 6.是否中规车请注明(中规车、非中规车)7.非中规车请注明原销售目的国车版、型(美规、欧规、加规、中东规等)

商品编码	申报要素
87046000	1.品名 2.发动机类型(柴油、半柴油、汽油等)3.车辆总重 4.车辆的厂家品牌(中文或外文名称)5.型号 6.是否中规车请注明(中规车、非中规车)7.非中规车请注明原销售目的国车版、型(美规、欧规、加规、中东规等)
87049000	1.品名 2.发动机类型(柴油、半柴油、汽油等)3.车辆总重 4.车辆的厂家品牌(中文或外文名称)5.型号 6.是否中规车请注明(中规车、非中规车)7.非中规车请注明原销售目的国车版、型(美规、欧规、加规、中东规等)
87051	1.品名 2.作业范围(全路面等)3.最大起重重量 4.车辆的厂家品牌(中文或外文名称)5.型号
87052000	1.品名 2.用途 3.品牌(中文或外文名称)4.型号
87053	1.品名 2.固定安装配置 3.品牌(中文或外文名称)4.型号
87054000	1.品名 2.固定安装配置 3.品牌(中文或外文名称)4.型号
87059010	1.品名 2.用途 3.固定安装配置 4.车辆的厂家品牌(中文或外文名称)5.型号
87059020	1.品名 2.用途 3.固定安装配置 4.车辆的厂家品牌(中文或外文名称)5.型号
87059030	1.品名 2.用途 3.固定安装配置 4.车辆的厂家品牌(中文或外文名称)5.型号
87059040	1.品名 2.用途 3.固定安装配置 4.车辆的厂家品牌(中文或外文名称)5.型号
87059059	1.品名 2.用途 3.固定安装配置 4.车辆的厂家品牌(中文或外文名称)5.型号
87059060	1.品名 2.用途 3.固定安装配置 4.车辆的厂家品牌(中文或外文名称)5.型号
87059070	1.品名 2.用途 3.固定安装配置 4.车辆的厂家品牌(中文或外文名称)5.型号
87059080	1.品名 2.用途 3.固定安装配置 4.车辆的厂家品牌(中文或外文名称)5.型号
8705909	1.品名 2.用途 3.固定安装配置 4.车辆的厂家品牌(中文或外文名称)5.型号
87060010	1.品名 2.适用车型(适用于××品牌××车型)3.品牌(中文或外文名称)4.型号
8706002	1.品名 2.适用车型(适用于××品牌××车型)3.车辆总重量 4.是否带驾驶室 5.品牌(中文或外文名称)6.型号
87060030	1.品名 2.适用车型(适用于××品牌××车型)3.是否带驾驶室 4.品牌(中文或外文名称)5.型号
87060040	1.品名 2.适用车型(适用于××品牌××车型)3.是否带驾驶室 4.品牌(中文或外文名称)5.型号
87060090	1.品名 2.适用车型(适用于××品牌××车型)3.品牌(中文或外文名称)4.型号
8707	1.品名 2.适用车型(适用于××品牌××车型)3.品牌(中文或外文名称)4.型号
87081000	1.品名 2.成套散件或毛坯请注明 3.生产件的通用零件编号后加注"/TY"4.成套散件装配后完整品的零部件的编号 5.品牌(中文或外文名称)6.适用车型(适用于××品牌××车型)7.型号 8.零部件完整编号并在前加注"S/""W/"或"WF/"之一(生产件填报"S/",品牌和适用的整车厂牌一致的维修件填报"W/",品牌和适用的整车厂牌不一致的维修件的填报"WF/")
87082100	1.品名 2.成套散件或毛坯请注明 3.生产件的通用零件编号后加注"/TY"4.成套散件装配后完整品的零部件的编号 5.品牌(中文或外文名称)6.适用车型(适用于××品牌××车型)7.型号 8.零部件完整编号并在前加注"S/""W/"或"WF/"之一(生产件填报"S/",品牌和适用的整车厂牌一致的维修件填报"W/",品牌和适用的整车厂牌不一致的维修件的填报"WF/")
87082211	1.品名 2.成套散件或毛坯请注明 3.生产件的通用零件编号后加注"/TY"4.成套散件装配后完整品的零部件的编号 5.品牌(中文或外文名称)6.适用车型(适用于××品牌××车型)7.型号 8.零部件完整编号并在前加注"S/""W/"或"WF/"之一(生产件填报"S/",品牌和适用的整车厂牌一致的维修件填报"W/",品牌和适用的整车厂牌不一致的维修件的填报"WF/")
87082212	1.品名 2.品牌 3.适用车型(适用于××品牌××车型)4.型号
87082290	1.品名 2.品牌 3.适用车型(适用于××品牌××车型)4.型号
87082930	1.品名 2.成套散件或毛坯请注明 3.生产件的通用零件编号后加注"/TY"4.成套散件装配后完整品的零部件的编号 5.品牌(中文或外文名称)6.适用车型(适用于××品牌××车型)7.型号 8.零部件完整编号并在前加注"S/""W/"或"WF/"之一(生产件填报"S/",品牌和适用的整车厂牌一致的维修件填报"W/",品牌和适用的整车厂牌不一致的维修件的填报"WF/")
8708295	1.品名 2.品牌(中文或外文名称)3.适用车型(适用于××品牌××车型)4.型号
87082990	1.品名 2.品牌(中文或外文名称)3.适用车型(适用于××品牌××车型)4.型号
87083010	1.品名 2.适用车型(适用于××品牌××车型)3.成套散件或毛坯请注明 4.生产件的通用零件编号后加注"/TY"5.成套散件装配后完整品的零部件的编号 6.品牌(中文或外文名称)7.型号 8.零部件完整编号并在前加注"S/""W/"或"WF/"之一(生产件填报"S/",品牌和适用的整车厂牌一致的维修件填报"W/",品牌和适用的整车厂牌不一致的维修件的填报"WF/")
8708302	1.品名 2.适用车型(适用于××品牌××车型)3.成套散件或毛坯请注明 4.生产件的通用零件编号后加注"/TY"5.成套散件装配后完整品的零部件的编号 6.品牌(中文或外文名称)7.型号 8.零部件完整编号并在前加注"S/""W/"或"WF/"之一(生产件填报"S/",品牌和适用的整车厂牌一致的维修件填报"W/",品牌和适用的整车厂牌不一致的维修件的填报"WF/")
87083091	1.品名 2.适用车型(适用于××品牌××车型)3.成套散件或毛坯请注明 4.生产件的通用零件编号后加注"/TY"5.成套散件装配后完整品的零部件的编号 6.品牌(中文或外文名称)7.型号 8.零部件完整编号并在前加注"S/""W/"或"WF/"之一(生产件填报"S/",品牌和适用的整车厂牌一致的维修件填报"W/",品牌和适用的整车厂牌不一致的维修件的填报"WF/")
87083092	1.品名 2.适用车型(适用于××品牌××车型)3.成套散件或毛坯请注明 4.生产件的通用零件编号后加注"/TY"5.成套散件装配后完整品的零部件的编号 6.品牌(中文或外文名称)7.型号 8.零部件完整编号并在前加注"S/""W/"或"WF/"之一(生产件填报"S/",品牌和适用的整车厂牌一致的维修件填报"W/",品牌和适用的整车厂牌不一致的维修件的填报"WF/")
87083093	1.品名 2.适用车型(适用于××品牌××车型)3.成套散件或毛坯请注明 4.生产件的通用零件编号后加注"/TY"5.成套散件装配后完整品的零部件的编号 6.品牌(中文或外文名称)7.型号 8.零部件完整编号并在前加注"S/""W/"或"WF/"之一(生产件填报"S/",品牌和适用的整车厂牌一致的维修件填报"W/",品牌和适用的整车厂牌不一致的维修件的填报"WF/")
87083094	1.品名 2.适用车型(适用于××品牌××型号××排气量车)3.成套散件或毛坯请注明 4.生产件的通用零件编号后加注"/TY" 5.成套散件装配后完整品的零部件的编号 6.品牌(中文或外文名称)7.型号 8.零部件完整编号并在前加注"S/""W/"或"WF/"之一(生产件填报"S/",品牌和适用的整车厂牌一致的维修件填报"W/",品牌和适用的整车厂牌不一致的维修件的填报"WF/")
87083095	1.品名 2.适用车型(适用于××品牌××车型)3.成套散件或毛坯请注明 4.生产件的通用零件编号后加注"/TY"5.成套散件装配后完整品的零部件的编号 6.品牌(中文或外文名称)7.型号 8.零部件完整编号并在前加注"S/""W/"或"WF/"之一(生产件填报"S/",品牌和适用的整车厂牌一致的维修件填报"W/",品牌和适用的整车厂牌不一致的维修件的填报"WF/")
87083096	1.品名 2.适用车型(适用于××品牌××车型)3.成套散件或毛坯请注明 4.生产件的通用零件编号后加注"/TY"5.成套散件装配后完整品的零部件的编号 6.品牌(中文或外文名称)7.型号 8.零部件完整编号并在前加注"S/""W/"或"WF/"之一(生产件填报"S/",品牌和适用的整车厂牌一致的维修件填报"W/",品牌和适用的整车厂牌不一致的维修件的填报"WF/")
87083099	1.品名 2.适用车型(适用于××品牌××车型)3.成套散件或毛坯请注明 4.生产件的通用零件编号后加注"/TY"5.成套散件装配后完整品的零部件的编号 6.品牌(中文或外文名称)7.型号 8.零部件完整编号并在前加注"S/""W/"或"WF/"之一(生产件填报"S/",品牌和适用的整车厂牌一致的维修件填报"W/",品牌和适用的整车厂牌不一致的维修件的填报"WF/")
87084010	1.品名 2.适用车型(适用于××品牌××车型)3.成套散件或毛坯请注明 4.生产件的通用零件编号后加注"/TY"5.成套散件装配后完整品的零部件的编 号 6.是否为拖拉机用变速箱 7.拖拉机发动机的功率 8.是否动力换档式 9.品牌(中文或外文名称)10.型号 11.零部件完整编号并在前加注"S/""W/ "或"WF/"之一(生产件填报"S/",品牌和适用的整车厂牌一致的维修件填报" W/",品牌和适用的整车厂牌不一致的维修件的填报"WF/")
87084020	1.品名 2.适用车型(适用于××品牌××车型)3.成套散件或毛坯请注明 4.生产件的通用零件编号后加注"/TY"5.成套散件装配后完整品的零部件的编号 6.品牌(中文或外文名称)7.型号 8.零部件完整编号并在前加注"S/""W/"或"WF/"之一(生产件填报"S/",品牌和适用的整车厂牌一致的维修件填报"W/",品牌和适用的整车厂牌不一致的维修件的填报"WF/")9.座位数
87084030	1.品名 2.适用车型(适用于××品牌××车型)3.成套散件或毛坯请注明 4.生产件的通用零件编号后加注"/TY"5.成套散件装配后完整品的零部件的编号 6.品牌(中文或外文名称)7.扭矩 8.型号 9.零部件完整编号并在前加注"S/ ""W/"或"WF/"之一(生产件填报"S/",品牌和适用的整车厂牌一致的维修件填报"W/",品牌和适用的整车厂牌不一致的维修件的填报"WF/")
87084040	1.品名 2.适用车型(适用于××品牌××型号××排气量车型)3.成套散件或毛坯请注明 4.生产件的通用零件编号后加注"/TY "5.成套散件装配后完整品的零部件的编号 6.品牌(中文或外文名称)7.扭矩 8.型号 9.零部件完整编号并在前加注"S/ ""W/"或"WF/"之一(生产件填报"S/ ",品牌和适用的整车厂牌一致的维修件填报"W/",品牌和适用的整车厂牌不一致的维修件的填报"WF/")
87084050	1.品名 2.适用车型(适用于××品牌××型号××排气量车型)3.成套散件或毛坯请注明 4.生产件的通用零件编号后加注"/TY "5.成套散件装配后完整品的零部件的编号 6.品牌(中文或外文名称)7.扭矩 8.型号 9.零部件完整编号并在前加注"S/ ""W/"或"WF/"之一(生产件填报"S/ ",品牌和适用的整车厂牌一致的维修件填报"W/",品牌和适用的整车厂牌不一致的维修件的填报"WF/")
87084060	1.品名 2.适用车型(适用于××品牌××车型)3.成套散件或毛坯请注明 4.生产件的通用零件编号后加注"/TY"5.成套散件装配后完整品的零部件的编号 6.品牌(中文或外文名称)7.扭矩 8.型号 9.零部件完整编号并在前加注"S/ ""W/"或"WF/"之一(生产件填报"S/ ",品牌和适用的整车厂牌一致的维修件填报"W/",品牌和适用的整车厂牌不一致的维修件的填报"WF/")
8708409	1.品名 2.适用车型(适用于××品牌××型号××排气量车型)3.原理(是否为 6 档及 6 档以上)4.成套散件或毛坯请注明 5.生产件的通用零件编号后加注"/TY"6.成套散件装配后完整品的零部件的编号 7.变速箱类型(手动挡/自动挡/手自一体)8.品牌(中文或外文名称)9.扭矩 10.型号 11.零部件完整编号并在前加注"S/ ""W/"或"WF/"之一(生产件填报"S/ ",品牌和适用的整车厂牌一致的维修件填报"W/",品牌和适用的整车厂牌不一致的维修件的填报"WF/")
87085071	1.品名 2.适用车型(适用于××品牌××车型)3.驱动位置 4.轴荷 5.成套散件或毛坯请注明 6.生产件的通用零件编号后加注"/TY"7.成套散件装配后完整品的零部件的编号 8.是否为拖拉机用变速箱 9.拖拉机发动机的功率 10.是否动力换档式 11.品牌(中文或外文名称)12.型号 13.零部件完整编号并在前加注"S/""W/ "或"WF/"之一(生产件填报"S/",品牌和适用的整车厂牌一致的维修件填报" W/",品牌和适用的整车厂牌不一致的维修件的填报"WF/")
87085072	1.品名 2.适用车型(适用于××品牌××车型)3.驱动位置 4.轴荷 5.成套散件或毛坯请注明 6.生产件的通用零件编号后加注"/TY"7.成套散件装配后完整品的零部件的编号 8.品牌(中文或外文名称)9.型号 10.零部件完整编号并在前加注"S/""W/"或"WF/"之一(生产件填报"S/",品牌和适用的整车厂牌一致的维修件填报"W/",品牌和适用的整车厂牌不一致的维修件的填报"WF/")

商品编码	申报要素
87085073	1.品名 2.适用车型(适用于××品牌××车型)3.驱动位置 4.轴荷 5.成套散件或毛坯请注明 6.生产件的通用零件编号后加注"/TY"7.成套散件装配后完整品的零部件的编号 8.品牌(中文或外文名称)9.型号 10.零部件完整编号并在前加注"S/""W/"或"WF/"之一(生产件填报"S/",品牌和适用的整车厂牌一致的维修件填报"W/",品牌和适用的整车厂牌不一致的维修件的填报"WF/")
87085074	1.品名 2.适用车型(适用于××品牌××车型)3.驱动位置 4.成套散件或毛坯请注明 5.生产件的通用零件编号后加注"/TY" 6.成套散件装配后完整品的零部件的编号 7.品牌(中文或外文名称)8.型号 9.零部件完整编号并在前加注"S/""W/"或"WF/"之一(生产件填报"S/",品牌和适用的整车厂牌一致的维修件填报"W/",品牌和适用的整车厂牌不一致的维修件的填报"WF/")
87085075	1.品名 2.适用车型(适用于××品牌××型号××排气量车型)3.驱动位置 4.成套散件或毛坯请注明 5.生产件的通用零件编号后加注"/TY"6.成套散件装配后完整品的零部件的编号 7.品牌(中文或外文名称)8.型号 9.零部件完整编号并在前加注"S/""W/"或"WF/"之一(生产件填报"S/",品牌和适用的整车厂牌一致的维修件填报"W/",品牌和适用的整车厂牌不一致的维修件的填报"WF/")
87085076	1.品名 2.适用车型(适用于××品牌××车型)3.驱动位置 4.成套散件或毛坯请注明 5.生产件的通用零件编号后加注"/TY" 6.成套散件装配后完整品的零部件的编号 7.品牌(中文或外文名称)8.型号 9.零部件完整编号并在前加注"S/""W/"或"WF/"之一(生产件填报"S/",品牌和适用的整车厂牌一致的维修件填报"W/",品牌和适用的整车厂牌不一致的维修件的填报"WF/")
87085079	1.品名 2.适用车型(适用于××品牌××车型)3.成套散件或毛坯请注明 4.生产件的通用零件编号后加注"/TY"5.成套散件装配后完整品的零部件的编号 6.品牌(中文或外文名称)7.型号 8.零部件完整编号并在前加注"S/""W/"或"WF/"之一(生产件填报"S/",品牌和适用的整车厂牌一致的维修件填报"W/",品牌和适用的整车厂牌不一致的维修件的填报"WF/")
8708508	1.品名 2.适用车型(适用于××品牌××型号××排气量车型)3.成套散件或毛坯请注明 4.生产件的通用零件编号后加注"/TY "5.成套散件装配后完整品的零部件的编号 6.品牌(中文或外文名称)7.型号 8.零部件完整编号并在前加注"S/""W/"或"WF/"之一(生产件填报"S/",品牌和适用的整车厂牌一致的维修件填报"W/",品牌和适用的整车厂牌不一致的维修件的填报"WF/")
87087010	1.品名 2.材质 3.适用车型(适用于××品牌××车型)4.成套散件或毛坯请注明 5.生产件的通用零件编号后加注"/TY"6.成套散件装配后完整品的零部件的编号 7.车轮尺寸 8.品牌(中文或外文名称)9.型号 10.零部件完整编号并在前加注"S/""W/"或 "WF/"之一(生产件填报"S/",品牌和适用的整车厂牌一致的维修件填报"W/",品牌和适用的整车厂牌不一致的维修件的填报"WF/")
87087020	1.品名 2.材质 3.适用车型(适用于××品牌××车型)4.成套散件或毛坯请注明 5.生产件的通用零件编号后加注"/TY"6.成套散件装配后完整品的零部件的编号 7.车轮尺寸 8.品牌(中文或外文名称)9.型号 10.零部件完整编号并在前加注"S/""W/"或 "WF/"之一(生产件填报"S/",品牌和适用的整车厂牌一致的维修件填报"W/",品牌和适用的整车厂牌不一致的维修件的填报"WF/")
87087030	1.品名 2.材质 3.适用车型(适用于××品牌××车型)4.成套散件或毛坯请注明 5.生产件的通用零件编号后加注"/TY"6.成套散件装配后完整品的零部件的编号 7.车轮尺寸 8.品牌(中文或外文名称)9.型号 10.零部件完整编号并在前加注"S/""W/"或 "WF/"之一(生产件填报"S/",品牌和适用的整车厂牌一致的维修件填报"W/",品牌和适用的整车厂牌不一致的维修件的填报"WF/")
87087040	1.品名 2.材质 3.适用车型(适用于××品牌××车型)4.成套散件或毛坯请注明 5.生产件的通用零件编号后加注"/TY"6.成套散件装配后完整品的零部件的编号 7.车轮尺寸 8.品牌(中文或外文名称)9.型号 10.零部件完整编号并在前加注"S/""W/"或 "WF/"之一(生产件填报"S/",品牌和适用的整车厂牌一致的维修件填报"W/",品牌和适用的整车厂牌不一致的维修件的填报"WF/")
87087050	1.品名 2.材质 3.适用车型(适用于××品牌××车型)4.成套散件或毛坯请注明 5.生产件的通用零件编号后加注"/TY"6.成套散件装配后完整品的零部件的编号 7.车轮尺寸 8.品牌(中文或外文名称)9.型号 10.零部件完整编号并在前加注"S/""W/"或 "WF/"之一(生产件填报"S/",品牌和适用的整车厂牌一致的维修件填报"W/",品牌和适用的整车厂牌不一致的维修件的填报"WF/")
87087060	1.品名 2.材质 3.适用车型(适用于××品牌××车型)4.成套散件或毛坯请注明 5.生产件的通用零件编号后加注"/TY"6.成套散件装配后完整品的零部件的编号 7.车轮尺寸 8.品牌(中文或外文名称)9.型号 10.零部件完整编号并在前加注"S/""W/"或 "WF/"之一(生产件填报"S/",品牌和适用的整车厂牌一致的维修件填报"W/",品牌和适用的整车厂牌不一致的维修件的填报"WF/")
87087091	1.品名 2.材质 3.适用车型(适用于××品牌××车型)4.成套散件或毛坯请注明 5.生产件的通用零件编号后加注"/TY"6.成套散件装配后完整品的零部件的编号 7.车轮尺寸 8.品牌(中文或外文名称)9.型号 10.零部件完整编号并在前加注"S/""W/"或"WF/"之一(生产件填报"S/",品牌和适用的整车厂牌一致的维修件填报"W/",品牌和适用的整车厂牌不一致的维修件的填报"WF/")
87087099	1.品名 2.材质 3.适用车型(适用于××品牌××车型)4.成套散件或毛坯请注明 5.生产件的通用零件编号后加注"/TY"6.成套散件装配后完整品的零部件的编号 7.车轮尺寸 8.品牌(中文或外文名称)9.型号 10.零部件完整编号并在前加注"S/""W/"或 "WF/"之一(生产件填报"S/",品牌和适用的整车厂牌一致的维修件填报"W/",品牌和适用的整车厂牌不一致的维修件的填报"WF/")
87088	1.品名 2.适用车型(适用于××品牌××型号××排气量车型)3.成套散件或毛坯请注明 4.生产件的通用零件编号后加注"/TY "5.成套散件装配后完整品的零部件的编号 6.品牌(中文或外文名称)7.型号 8.零部件完整编号并在前加注"S/""W/"或"WF/"之一(生产件填报"S/",品牌和适用的整车厂牌一致的维修件填报"W/",品牌和适用的整车厂牌不一致的维修件的填报"WF/")

商品编码	申报要素
870891	1.品名 2.适用车型(适用于××品牌××车型)3.成套散件或毛坯请注明 4.生产件的通用零件编号后加注"/TY"5.成套散件装配后完整品的零部件的编号 6.品牌(中文或外文名称)7.型号 8.零部件完整编号并在前加注"S/""W/"或"WF/"之一(生产件填报"S/",品牌和适用的整车厂牌一致的维修件填报"W/",品牌和适用的整车厂牌不一致的维修件的填报"WF/")
87089200	1.品名 2.适用车型(适用于××品牌××车型)3.成套散件或毛坯请注明 4.生产件的通用零件编号后加注"/TY"5.成套散件装配后完整品的零部件的编号 6.品牌(中文或外文名称)7.型号 8.零部件完整编号并在前加注"S/""W/"或"WF/"之一(生产件填报"S/",品牌和适用的整车厂牌一致的维修件填报"W/",品牌和适用的整车厂牌不一致的维修件的填报"WF/")
870893	1.品名 2.适用车型(适用于××品牌××车型)3.成套散件或毛坯请注明 4.生产件的通用零件编号后加注"/TY"5.成套散件装配后完整品的零部件的编号 6.品牌(中文或外文名称)7.型号 8.零部件完整编号并在前加注"S/""W/"或"WF/"之一(生产件填报"S/",品牌和适用的整车厂牌一致的维修件填报"W/",品牌和适用的整车厂牌不一致的维修件的填报"WF/")
87089410	1.品名 2.适用车型(适用于××品牌××车型)3.成套散件或毛坯请注明 4.生产件的通用零件编号后加注"/TY"5.成套散件装配后完整品的零部件的编号 6.品牌(中文或外文名称)7.型号 8.零部件完整编号并在前加注"S/""W/"或"WF/"之一(生产件填报"S/",品牌和适用的整车厂牌一致的维修件填报"W/",品牌和适用的整车厂牌不一致的维修件的填报"WF/")
87089420	1.品名 2.适用车型(适用于××品牌××车型)3.成套散件或毛坯请注明 4.生产件的通用零件编号后加注"/TY"5.成套散件装配后完整品的零部件的编号 6.座位数 7.品牌(中文或外文名称)8.型号 9.零部件完整编号并在前加注"S/""W/"或"WF/"之一(生产件填报"S/",品牌和适用的整车厂牌一致的维修件填报"W/",品牌和适用的整车厂牌不一致的维修件的填报"WF/")
87089430	1.品名 2.适用车型(适用于××品牌××型号××排气量车型)3.成套散件或毛坯请注明 4.生产件的通用零件编号后加注"/TY "5.成套散件装配后完整品的零部件的编号 6.品牌(中文或外文名称)7.型号 8.零部件完整编号并在前加注"S/""W/"或"WF/"之一(生产件填报"S/",品牌和适用的整车厂牌一致的维修件填报"W/",品牌和适用的整车厂牌不一致的维修件的填报"WF/")
87089440	1.品名 2.适用车型(适用于××品牌××型号××排气量车型)3.成套散件或毛坯请注明 4.生产件的通用零件编号后加注"/TY "5.成套散件装配后完整品的零部件的编号 6.品牌(中文或外文名称)7.型号 8.零部件完整编号并在前加注"S/""W/"或"WF/"之一(生产件填报"S/",品牌和适用的整车厂牌一致的维修件填报"W/",品牌和适用的整车厂牌不一致的维修件的填报"WF/")
87089450	1.品名 2.适用车型(适用于××品牌××车型)3.成套散件或毛坯请注明 4.生产件的通用零件编号后加注"/TY"5.成套散件装配后完整品的零部件的编号 6.品牌(中文或外文名称)7.型号 8.零部件完整编号并在前加注"S/""W/"或"WF/"之一(生产件填报"S/",品牌和适用的整车厂牌一致的维修件填报"W/",品牌和适用的整车厂牌不一致的维修件的填报"WF/")
87089460	1.品名 2.适用车型(适用于××品牌××车型)3.成套散件或毛坯请注明 4.生产件的通用零件编号后加注"/TY"5.成套散件装配后完整品的零部件的编号 6.品牌(中文或外文名称)7.型号 8.零部件完整编号并在前加注"S/""W/"或"WF/"之一(生产件填报"S/",品牌和适用的整车厂牌一致的维修件填报"W/",品牌和适用的整车厂牌不一致的维修件的填报"WF/")
87089490	1.品名 2.适用车型(适用于××品牌××型号××排气量车型)3.成套散件或毛坯请注明 4.生产件的通用零件编号后加注"/TY "5.成套散件装配后完整品的零部件的编号 6.品牌(中文或外文名称)7.型号 8.零部件完整编号并在前加注"S/""W/"或"WF/"之一(生产件填报"S/",品牌和适用的整车厂牌一致的维修件填报"W/",品牌和适用的整车厂牌不一致的维修件的填报"WF/")
87089500	1.品名 2.适用车型(适用于××品牌××车型)3.成套散件或毛坯请注明 4.生产件的通用零件编号后加注"/TY"5.成套散件装配后完整品的零部件的编号 6.品牌(中文或外文名称)7.型号 8.零部件完整编号并在前加注"S/""W/"或"WF/"之一(生产件填报"S/",品牌和适用的整车厂牌一致的维修件填报"W/",品牌和适用的整车厂牌不一致的维修件的填报"WF/")
87089910	1.品名 2.适用车型(适用于××品牌××型号××排气量车型)3.品牌(中文或外文名称)4.型号
87089921	1.品名 2.适用车型(适用于××品牌××车型)3.成套散件或毛坯请注明 4.生产件的通用零件编号后加注"/TY"5.成套散件装配后完整品的零部件的编号 6.品牌(中文或外文名称)7.型号 8.零部件完整编号并在前加注"S/""W/"或"WF/"之一(生产件填报"S/",品牌和适用的整车厂牌一致的维修件填报"W/",品牌和适用的整车厂牌不一致的维修件的填报"WF/")
87089929	1.品名 2.适用车型(适用于××品牌××车型)3.座位数 4.品牌(中文或外文名称)5.型号
87089931	1.品名 2.适用车型(适用于××品牌××车型)3.成套散件或毛坯请注明 4.生产件的通用零件编号后加注"/TY"5.成套散件装配后完整品的零部件的编号 6.品牌(中文或外文名称)7.型号 8.零部件完整编号并在前加注"S/""W/"或"WF/"之一(生产件填报"S/",品牌和适用的整车厂牌一致的维修件填报"W/",品牌和适用的整车厂牌不一致的维修件的填报"WF/")
87089939	1.品名 2.适用车型(适用于××品牌××车型)3.品牌(中文或外文名称)4.型号
87089941	1.品名 2.适用车型(适用于××品牌××车型)3.成套散件或毛坯请注明 4.生产件的通用零件编号后加注"/TY"5.成套散件装配后完整品的零部件的编号 6.品牌(中文或外文名称)7.型号 8.零部件完整编号并在前加注"S/""W/"或"WF/"之一(生产件填报"S/",品牌和适用的整车厂牌一致的维修件填报"W/",品牌和适用的整车厂牌不一致的维修件的填报"WF/")
87089949	1.品名 2.适用车型(适用于××品牌××车型)3.品牌(中文或外文名称)4.型号

商品编码	申报要素
87089951	1.品名 2.适用车型(适用于××品牌××车型)3.成套散件或毛坯请注明 4.生产件的通用零件编号后加注"/TY"5.成套散件装配后完整品的零部件的编号 6.品牌(中文或外文名称)7.型号 8.零部件完整编号并在前加注"S/""W/"或"WF/"之一(生产件填报"S/",品牌和适用的整车厂牌一致的维修件填报"W/",品牌和适用的整车厂牌不一致的维修件的填报"WF/")
87089959	1.品名 2.适用车型(适用于××品牌××车型)3.品牌(中文或外文名称)4.型号
87089960	1.品名 2.适用车型(适用于××品牌××车型)3.品牌(中文或外文名称)4.型号
87089991	1.品名 2.适用车型(适用于××品牌××车型)3.成套散件或毛坯请注明 4.生产件的通用零件编号后加注"/TY"5.成套散件装配后完整品的零部件的编号 6.品牌(中文或外文名称)7.型号 8.零部件完整编号并在前加注"S/""W/"或"WF/"之一(生产件填报"S/",品牌和适用的整车厂牌一致的维修件填报"W/",品牌和适用的整车厂牌不一致的维修件的填报"WF/")
87089992	1.品名 2.适用车型(适用于××品牌××车型)3.品牌(中文或外文名称)4.型号
87089999	1.品名 2.适用车型(适用于××品牌××车型)3.品牌(中文或外文名称)4.型号
87091	1.品名 2.发动机类型 3.适用场所 4.品牌(中文或外文名称)5.型号 6.技术参数(最高时速、转弯半径等)
87099000	1.品名 2.用途(适用于××品牌××车或通用于××机等)3.品牌(中文或外文名称)4.型号
8710	1.品名 2.品牌(中文或外文名称)3.型号
87111000	1.品名 2.发动机类型 3.排气量 4.品牌(中文或外文名称)5.型号
87112	1.品名 2.发动机类型 3.排气量 4.品牌(中文或外文名称)5.型号
87113	1.品名 2.发动机类型 3.排气量 4.品牌(中文或外文名称)5.型号
87114000	1.品名 2.发动机类型 3.排气量 4.品牌(中文或外文名称)5.型号
87115000	1.品名 2.发动机类型 3.排气量 4.品牌(中文或外文名称)5.型号
87116000	1.品名 2.发动机类型 3.品牌(中文或外文名称)4.型号
87119000	1.品名 2.发动机类型 3.排气量 4.品牌(中文或外文名称)5.型号
87120020	1.品名 2.用途(竞赛型、山地型、越野型等)3.轮径 4.品牌(中文或外文名称)5.型号
87120030	1.品名 2.用途(竞赛型、山地型、越野型等)3.轮径 4.品牌(中文或外文名称)5.型号
8712004	1.品名 2.用途(竞赛型、山地型、越野型等)3.轮径 4.品牌(中文或外文名称)5.型号
8712008	1.品名 2.用途(竞赛型、山地型、越野型等)3.轮径 4.品牌(中文或外文名称)5.型号
87120090	1.品名 2.用途(竞赛型、山地型、越野型等)3.轮径 4.品牌(中文或外文名称)5.型号
8713	1.品名 2.用途 3.驱动方式 4.品牌(中文或外文名称)5.型号
8714	1.品名 2.用途(适用于××品牌××车或通用于××机等)3.品牌(中文或外文名称)4.型号
8715	1.品名 2.若为零件请注明适用车型 3.品牌(中文或外文名称)4.型号
87161000	1.品名 2.用途 3.类型 4.品牌(中文或外文名称)5.型号
87162000	1.品名 2.用途 3.类型 4.品牌(中文或外文名称)5.型号
87163	1.品名 2.用途 3.类型 4.品牌(中文或外文名称)5.型号
87164000	1.品名 2.品牌(中文或外文名称)3.型号
87168000	1.品名 2.品牌(中文或外文名称)3.型号
87169000	1.品名 2.用途(适用于××品牌××车或通用于××机等)3.品牌(中文或外文名称)4.型号
8801	1.品名 2.用途 3.品牌(中文或外文名称)4.型号
88021	1.品名 2.用途 3.类型 4.空载重量 5.品牌(中文或外文名称)6.型号
88022000	1.品名 2.用途 3.类型 4.空载重量 5.品牌(中文或外文名称)6.型号 7.公务机请注明 8.民航局注册号 9.飞机出厂序列号(S/N,即 SERIAL NUMBER)10.旧飞机请注明并申报飞机原生产日期
88023000	1.品名 2.用途 3.类型 4.空载重量 5.品牌(中文或外文名称)6.型号 7.公务机请注明 8.民航局注册号 9.飞机出厂序列号(S/N,即 SERIAL NUMBER)10.旧飞机请注明并申报飞机原生产日期
88024	1.品名 2.用途 3.类型 4.空载重量 5.品牌(中文或外文名称)6.型号 7.公务机请注明 8.民航局注册号 9.飞机出厂序列号(S/N,即 SERIAL NUMBER)10.旧飞机请注明并申报飞机原生产日期
88026000	1.品名 2.若为通信用需注明 3.品牌(中文或外文名称)4.型号
8804	1.品名 2.用途(适用于××品牌××机或通用于××机等)3.品牌(中文或外文名称)4.型号
8805	1.品名 2.用途(适用于××品牌××机或通用于××机等)3.品牌(中文或外文名称)4.型号
88061000	1.品名 2.用途 3.类型 4.空载重量 5.品牌(中文或外文名称)6.型号
88062	1.品名 2.用途 3.类型 4.最大起飞重量 5.品牌(中文或外文名称)6.型号
88069	1.品名 2.用途 3.类型 4.最大起飞重量 5.品牌(中文或外文名称)6.型号
8807	1.品名 2.用途(适用于××品牌××机或通用于××机等)3.品牌(中文或外文名称)4.型号
89011	1.品名 2.驱动方式 3.品牌(中文或外文名称)4.型号 5.最高时速
8901201	1.品名 2.用途 3.载重量 4.品牌(中文或外文名称)5.型号
8901202	1.品名 2.用途 3.载重量 4.品牌(中文或外文名称)5.型号
8901203	1.品名 2.用途 3.容积 4.品牌(中文或外文名称)5.型号
8901204	1.品名 2.用途 3.容积 4.品牌(中文或外文名称)5.型号
89012090	1.品名 2.用途 3.载重量 4.品牌(中文或外文名称)5.型号
89013000	1.品名 2.品牌(中文或外文名称)3.型号
8901902	1.品名 2.用途 3.可载标准集装箱数 4.品牌(中文或外文名称)5.型号
8901903	1.品名 2.用途 3.载重量 4.品牌(中文或外文名称)5.型号
8901904	1.品名 2.用途 3.载重量 4.品牌(中文或外文名称)5.型号
89019050	1.品名 2.用途 3.品牌(中文或外文名称)4.型号
89019080	1.品名 2.用途 3.品牌(中文或外文名称)4.型号
89019090	1.品名 2.用途 3.品牌(中文或外文名称)4.型号
8902	1.品名 2.用途 3.驱动方式 4.品牌(中文或外文名称)5.型号

商品编码	申报要素
89031	1.品名 2.用途 3.类型 4.发动机安装方式 5.船体长度 6.固定安装配置 7.品牌(中文或外文名称)8.型号
89032	1.品名 2.用途 3.类型 4.发动机安装方式 5.船体长度 6.品牌(中文或外文名称)7.型号 8.发动机品牌(中文及外文名称)、型号 9.发动机功率
89033	1.品名 2.用途 3.类型 4.发动机安装方式 5.船体长度 6.品牌(中文或外文名称)7.型号 8.发动机品牌(中文及外文名称)、型号 9.发动机功率
89039	1.品名 2.用途 3.类型 4.船体长度 5.固定安装配置 6.品牌(中文或外文名称)7.型号 8.发动机品牌(中文及外文名称)、型号 9.发动机功率
8904	1.品名 2.功能 3.品牌(中文或外文名称)4.型号
8905	1.品名 2.用途 3.品牌(中文或外文名称)4.型号
8907	1.品名 2.材质 3.品牌(中文或外文名称)4.型号
8908	1.品名 2.轻吨数(不包括非金属固定压载在内的空船重量)3.船型(如油轮、客船、驳船、集装箱船等)
90011000	1.品名 2.结构 3.用途 4.品牌(中文或外文名称)5.型号
90012000	1.品名 2.用途 3.材质 4.规格尺寸 5.加工程度(是否已经裁切成型)6.品牌(中文或外文名称)7.型号
90013000	1.品名 2.品牌(中文或外文名称)3.型号 4.材质 5.种类(软片或硬片)6.颜色 7.直径 8.使用周期(日抛、月抛等)9.度数(近视或远视度数,是否带散光度数)
90014	1.品名 2.材质 3.类型(变色等)4.品牌(中文或外文名称)5.型号
90015	1.品名 2.材质 3.类型(变色等)4.品牌(中文或外文名称)5.型号
90019010	1.品名 2.用途(适用于××品牌××机或通用于××机等)3.材质 4.品牌(中文或外文名称)5.型号
90019090	1.品名 2.用途(适用于××品牌××机或通用于××机等)3.材质 4.如为薄膜滤光片请申报波长 5.品牌(中文或外文名称)6.型号
9002	1.品名 2.用途(适用于××品牌××机或通用于××机等)3.是否已装配 4.品牌(中文或外文名称)5.型号
9003	1.品名 2.材质 3.品牌(中文或外文名称)4.型号
9004	1.品名 2.用途 3.类型(变色等)4.品牌(中文或外文名称)5.型号
90051000	1.品名 2.用途 3.是否双筒 4.品牌(中文或外文名称)5.型号
90058	1.品名 2.用途 3.品牌(中文或外文名称)4.型号
90059	1.品名 2.用途(适用于××品牌××机或通用于××机等)3.品牌(中文或外文名称)4.型号
90063000	1.品名 2.用途 3.原理 4.品牌(中文或外文名称)5.型号
90064000	1.品名 2.用途 3.原理 4.品牌(中文或外文名称)5.型号
900653	1.品名 2.用途 3.原理 4.胶片宽度 5.品牌(中文或外文名称)6.型号
90065910	1.品名 2.用途 3.原理 4.品牌(中文或外文名称)5.型号
9006592	1.品名 2.用途 3.原理 4.品牌(中文或外文名称)5.型号
90065930	1.品名 2.用途 3.原理 4.胶片宽度 5.品牌(中文或外文名称)6.型号
9006594	1.品名 2.用途 3.原理 4.胶片宽度 5.品牌(中文或外文名称)6.型号
90065990	1.品名 2.用途 3.原理 4.品牌(中文或外文名称)5.型号
90066	1.品名 2.用途 3.原理 4.品牌(中文或外文名称)5.型号
90069	1.品名 2.用途(适用于××品牌××机或通用于××机等)3.品牌(中文或外文名称)4.型号
90071	1.品名 2.用途 3.原理 4.胶片宽度 5.摄影速度 6.品牌(中文或外文名称)7.型号
90072	1.品名 2.用途 3.原理 4.品牌(中文或外文名称)5.型号
90079	1.品名 2.用途(适用于××品牌××机或通用于××机等)3.品牌(中文或外文名称)4.型号
90085010	1.品名 2.用途 3.品牌(中文或外文名称)4.型号
90085020	1.品名 2.用途 3.品牌(中文或外文名称)4.型号
9008503	1.品名 2.用途 3.原理 4.品牌(中文或外文名称)5.型号
90085040	1.品名 2.用途 3.品牌(中文或外文名称)4.型号
90089	1.品名 2.用途(适用于××品牌××机或通用于××机等)3.品牌(中文或外文名称)4.型号
90101	1.品名 2.用途 3.原理 4.品牌(中文或外文名称)5.型号
90105	1.品名 2.用途 3.原理 4.品牌(中文或外文名称)5.型号
90106000	1.品名 2.用途 3.品牌(中文或外文名称)4.型号
90109	1.品名 2.用途(适用于××品牌××机或通用于××机等)3.品牌(中文或外文名称)4.型号
90111000	1.品名 2.用途 3.原理 4.品牌(中文或外文名称)5.型号 6.倍数
90112000	1.品名 2.用途 3.原理 4.品牌(中文或外文名称)5.型号 6.倍数
90118000	1.品名 2.用途 3.原理 4.品牌(中文或外文名称)5.型号 6.倍数
90119000	1.品名 2.用途(适用于××品牌××机或通用于××机等)3.品牌(中文或外文名称)4.型号
90121000	1.品名 2.用途 3.原理 4.品牌(中文或外文名称)5.型号
90129000	1.品名 2.用途(适用于××品牌××机或通用于××机等)3.品牌(中文或外文名称)4.型号
90131000	1.品名 2.用途 3.品牌(中文或外文名称)4.型号
90132000	1.品名 2.用途 3.原理 4.品牌(中文或外文名称)5.型号
90138010	1.品名 2.原理 3.品牌(中文或外文名称)4.型号
90138020	1.品名 2.原理 3.品牌(中文或外文名称)4.型号
90138090	1.品名 2.用途 3.原理 4.品牌(中文或外文名称)5.型号
90139	1.品名 2.用途(适用于××品牌××机或通用于××机等)3.品牌(中文或外文名称)4.型号
90141000	1.品名 2.用途 3.原理 4.品牌(中文或外文名称)5.型号
90142	1.品名 2.用途 3.品牌(中文或外文名称)4.型号
90148000	1.品名 2.用途 3.原理 4.品牌(中文或外文名称)5.型号
90149	1.品名 2.用途(适用于××品牌××机或通用于××机等)3.品牌(中文或外文名称)4.型号
90151000	1.品名 2.用途 3.原理 4.品牌(中文或外文名称)5.型号
90152000	1.品名 2.用途 3.原理 4.品牌(中文或外文名称)5.型号
90153000	1.品名 2.用途 3.原理 4.品牌(中文或外文名称)5.型号
90154000	1.品名 2.用途 3.原理 4.品牌(中文或外文名称)5.型号
90158000	1.品名 2.用途 3.原理 4.品牌(中文或外文名称)5.型号
90159000	1.品名 2.用途(适用于××品牌××机或通用于××机等)3.品牌(中文或外文名称)4.型号

商品编码	申报要素
9016	1.品名 2.感量 3.品牌(中文或外文名称)4.型号
90171000	1.品名 2.用途 3.功能 4.品牌(中文或外文名称)5.型号
90172000	1.品名 2.用途 3.功能 4.是否手用 5.品牌(中文或外文名称)6.型号
90173000	1.品名 2.用途 3.功能 4.是否手用 5.品牌(中文或外文名称)6.型号
90178000	1.品名 2.用途 3.功能 4.品牌(中文或外文名称)5.型号
90179000	1.品名 2.用途(适用于××品牌××机或通用于××机等)3.品牌(中文或外文名称)4.型号
90181100	1.品名 2.用途 3.如为整机,请申报原理 4.品牌(中文或外文名称)5.型号 6.探头数量 7.如有医疗器械注册编号请申报注册编号
901812	1.品名 2.用途 3.如为整机,请申报原理 4.品牌(中文或外文名称)5.型号 6.探头数量 7.如有医疗器械注册编号请申报注册编号
90181310	1.品名 2.用途 3.如为整机,请申报原理 4.品牌(中文或外文名称)5.型号 6.探头数量 7.如有医疗器械注册编号请申报注册编号
90181390	1.品名 2.用途 3.如为整机,请申报原理 4.品牌(中文或外文名称)5.型号 6.探头数量 7.如有医疗器械注册编号请申报注册编号
90181400	1.品名 2.用途 3.如为整机,请申报原理 4.品牌(中文或外文名称)5.型号 6.探头数量 7.如有医疗器械注册编号请申报注册编号
901819	1.品名 2.用途 3.如为整机,请申报原理 4.品牌(中文或外文名称)5.型号 6.探头数量 7.如有医疗器械注册编号请申报注册编号
90182000	1.品名 2.用途 3.原理 4.品牌(中文或外文名称)5.型号 6.如有医疗器械注册编号请申报注册编号
90183100	1.品名 2.用途 3.品牌(中文或外文名称)4.型号 5.如有医疗器械注册编号请申报注册编号
901832	1.品名 2.用途 3.品牌(中文或外文名称)4.型号
90183900	1.品名 2.用途 3.组成或构成 4.品牌(中文或外文名称)5.型号 6.如有医疗器械注册编号请申报注册编号
90184100	1.品名 2.用途 3.品牌(中文或外文名称)4.型号 5.如有医疗器械注册编号请申报注册编号
90184910	1.品名 2.用途 3.品牌(中文或外文名称)4.型号 5.如有医疗器械注册编号请申报注册编号
90184990	1.品名 2.用途 3.原理 4.品牌(中文或外文名称)5.型号 6.如有医疗器械注册编号请申报注册编号
90185000	1.品名 2.用途 3.原理 4.品牌(中文或外文名称)5.型号 6.如有医疗器械注册编号请申报注册编号
90189010	1.品名 2.用途 3.品牌(中文或外文名称)4.型号 5.如有医疗器械注册编号请申报注册编号
90189020	1.品名 2.用途 3.原理 4.品牌(中文或外文名称)5.型号
90189030	1.品名 2.用途 3.品牌(中文或外文名称)4.型号 5.配置(如含三晶片摄像系统、监视器、冷光源等)6.如有医疗器械注册编号请申报注册编号
90189040	1.品名 2.用途 3.原理 4.品牌(中文或外文名称)5.如有医疗器械注册编号请申报注册编号
90189050	1.品名 2.用途 3.原理 4.品牌(中文或外文名称)5.如有医疗器械注册编号请申报注册编号
90189060	1.品名 2.用途 3.品牌(中文或外文名称)4.型号 5.如有医疗器械注册编号请申报注册编号
90189070	1.品名 2.用途 3.原理 4.品牌(中文或外文名称)5.型号 6.如有医疗器械注册编号请申报注册编号
9018909	1.品名 2.用途 3.原理 4.品牌(中文或外文名称)5.型号 6.如有医疗器械注册编号请申报注册编号
90191010	1.品名 2.用途 3.功能 4.品牌(中文或外文名称)5.型号 6.如有医疗器械注册编号请申报注册编号
90191090	1.品名 2.用途 3.功能 4.原理 5.品牌(中文或外文名称)6.型号 7.如有医疗器械注册编号请申报注册编号
90192	1.品名 2.用途 3.功能 4.品牌(中文或外文名称)5.型号 6.如有医疗器械注册编号请申报注册编号
9020	1.品名 2.用途 3.构成 4.有无机械零件或可互换过滤装置 5.品牌(中文或外文名称)6.型号 7.如有医疗器械注册编号请申报注册编号
90211000	1.品名 2.用途 3.品牌(中文或外文名称)4.材质 5.型号 6.技术参数 7.如有医疗器械注册编号请申报注册编号
90212	1.品名 2.品牌(中文或外文名称)3.材质 4.型号 5.如有医疗器械注册编号请申报注册编号
90213100	1.品名 2.用途 3.人造关节部位 4.品牌(中文或外文名称)5.材质 6.型号 7.如有医疗器械注册编号请申报注册编号
90213900	1.品名 2.用途 3.品牌(中文或外文名称)4.材质 5.型号 6.如有医疗器械注册编号请申报注册编号
90214000	1.品名
90215000	1.品名 2.材质
90219	1.品名 2.用途 3.原理 4.品牌(中文或外文名称)5.型号 6.如有医疗器械注册编号请申报注册编号
90221200	1.品名 2.用途 3.原理 4.品牌(中文或外文名称)5.型号 6.排数
90221300	1.品名 2.用途 3.原理 4.品牌(中文或外文名称)5.型号
90221400	1.品名 2.用途 3.原理 4.品牌(中文或外文名称)5.型号
902219	1.品名 2.用途 3.原理 4.品牌(中文或外文名称)5.型号
90222	1.品名 2.用途 3.原理 4.品牌(中文或外文名称)5.型号
90223000	1.品名 2.用途 3.原理 4.品牌(中文或外文名称)5.型号
90229010	1.品名 2.用途 3.原理 4.品牌(中文或外文名称)5.型号
90229090	1.品名 2.用途 3.原理 4.品牌(中文或外文名称)5.型号
9023	1.品名 2.用途 3.品牌(中文或外文名称)4.型号
90241	1.品名 2.功能 3.试验材料类型 4.品牌(中文或外文名称)5.型号
90248000	1.品名 2.功能 3.试验材料类型 4.品牌(中文或外文名称)5.型号
90249000	1.品名 2.用途(适用于××品牌××机或通用于××机等)3.品牌(中文或外文名称)4.型号
90251	1.品名 2.原理 3.是否可直接读数 4.品牌(中文或外文名称)5.型号
90258000	1.品名 2.原理 3.品牌(中文或外文名称)4.型号
90259000	1.品名 2.用途(适用于××品牌××机或通用于××机等)3.品牌(中文或外文名称)4.型号
90261000	1.品名 2.功能 3.检测对象 4.品牌(中文或外文名称)5.型号
90262	1.品名 2.功能 3.检测对象 4.品牌(中文或外文名称)5.型号
90268	1.品名 2.功能 3.检测对象 4.品牌(中文或外文名称)5.型号
90269000	1.品名 2.用途(适用于××品牌××机或通用于××机等)3.品牌(中文或外文名称)4.型号
90271000	1.品名 2.原理 3.功能 4.检测对象 5.品牌(中文或外文名称)6.型号
90272	1.品名 2.原理 3.功能 4.检测对象 5.品牌(中文或外文名称)6.型号
90273000	1.品名 2.原理 3.功能 4.检测对象 5.品牌(中文或外文名称)6.型号
90275	1.品名 2.原理 3.功能 4.检测对象 5.品牌(中文或外文名称)6.型号
90278	1.品名 2.原理 3.功能 4.检测对象 5.品牌(中文或外文名称)6.型号
90279000	1.品名 2.用途(适用于××品牌××机或通用于××机等)3.品牌(中文或外文名称)4.型号
90281	1.品名 2.用途 3.品牌(中文或外文名称)4.型号
90282	1.品名 2.用途 3.品牌(中文或外文名称)4.型号
90283	1.品名 2.用途 3.原理 4.品牌(中文或外文名称)5.型号
90289	1.品名 2.用途(适用于××品牌××机或通用于××机等)3.品牌(中文或外文名称)4.型号
90291	1.品名 2.用途 3.品牌(中文或外文名称)4.型号
90292	1.品名 2.用途 3.品牌(中文或外文名称)4.型号
90299000	1.品名 2.用途(适用于××品牌××机或通用于××机等)3.品牌(中文或外文名称)4.型号
90301000	1.品名 2.用途 3.功能 4.品牌(中文或外文名称)5.型号
90302	1.品名 2.用途 3.功能 4.频率 5.品牌(中文或外文名称)6.型号
903031	1.品名 2.用途 3.功能 4.量程 5.是否带记录装置 6.品牌(中文或外文名称)7.型号
90303200	1.品名 2.用途 3.功能 4.量程 5.是否带记录装置 6.品牌(中文或外文名称)7.型号
90303310	1.品名 2.用途 3.功能 4.量程 5.是否带记录装置 6.品牌(中文或外文名称)7.型号
90303320	1.品名 2.用途 3.功能 4.是否带记录装置 5.品牌(中文或外文名称)6.型号
90303390	1.品名 2.用途 3.功能 4.是否带记录装置 5.品牌(中文或外文名称)6.型号
90303900	1.品名 2.用途 3.功能 4.是否带记录装置 5.品牌(中文或外文名称)6.型号
90304	1.品名 2.用途 3.功能 4.测试频率 5.品牌(中文或外文名称)6.型号
90308200	1.品名 2.用途 3.功能 4.是否带记录装置 5.品牌(中文或外文名称)6.型号 7.测试结果显示内容(例如,电压值、电流值等)
903084	1.品名 2.用途 3.功能 4.是否带记录装置 5.品牌(中文或外文名称)6.型号
903089	1.品名 2.用途 3.功能 4.是否带记录装置 5.品牌(中文或外文名称)6.型号
90309000	1.品名 2.用途(适用于××品牌××机或通用于××机等)3.品牌(中文或外文名称)4.型号
90311000	1.品名 2.用途 3.功能 4.品牌(中文或外文名称)5.型号
90312000	1.品名 2.用途 3.功能 4.品牌(中文或外文名称)5.型号
90314	1.品名 2.用途 3.功能 4.品牌(中文或外文名称)5.型号
90318	1.品名 2.用途 3.原理 4.功能 5.品牌(中文或外文名称)6.型号
90319000	1.品名 2.用途(适用于××品牌××机或通用于××机等)3.品牌(中文或外文名称)4.型号
90321000	1.品名 2.用途 3.原理 4.功能 5.品牌(中文或外文名称)6.型号
90322000	1.品名 2.用途 3.原理 4.功能 5.品牌(中文或外文名称)6.型号
90328	1.品名 2.用途 3.原理 4.功能 5.品牌(中文或外文名称)6.型号
90329000	1.品名 2.用途(适用于××品牌××机或通用于××机等)3.品牌(中文或外文名称)4.型号
9033	1.品名 2.用途(适用于××品牌××机或通用于××机等)3.品牌(中文或外文名称)4.型号
9101	1.品名 2.外壳材质(贵金属或包贵金属制)3.驱动方式(电子、机械、自动、非自动)4.指示方式(指针、光电)5.品牌(中文或外文名称)6.型号
9102	1.品名 2.外壳材质(金属制等)3.驱动方式(电子、机械、自动、非自动)4.指示方式(指针、光电)5.品牌(中文或外文名称)6.型号
9103	1.品名 2.驱动方式(电子、机械、自动、非自动)3.品牌(中文或外文名称)4.型号
9104	1.品名 2.驱动方式(电子、机械、自动、非自动)3.品牌(中文或外文名称)4.型号
91051	1.品名 2.驱动方式(电子、机械、自动、非自动)3.品牌(中文或外文名称)4.型号
91052	1.品名 2.驱动方式(电子、机械、自动、非自动)3.品牌(中文或外文名称)4.型号
91059110	1.品名 2.用途(车辆、船舶等用)3.品牌(中文或外文名称)4.型号
91059190	1.品名 2.用途(闹钟、天文钟等)3.驱动方式(电子、机械)4.品牌(中文或外文名称)5.型号
91059900	1.品名 2.用途(闹钟、天文钟等)3.驱动方式(电子、机械)4.品牌(中文或外文名称)5.型号
91061000	1.品名 2.用途(闹钟、天文钟等)3.驱动方式(电子、机械)4.品牌(中文或外文名称)5.型号
91069000	1.品名 2.用途(闹钟、天文钟等)3.驱动方式(电子、机械)4.品牌(中文或外文名称)5.型号
9107	1.品名 2.用途(闹钟、天文钟等)3.驱动方式(电子、机械)4.品牌(中文或外文名称)5.型号
91081	1.品名 2.用途(闹钟、天文钟等)3.驱动方式(电子、机械)4.表面尺寸 5.指示方式 6.品牌(中文或外文名称)
91082000	1.品名 2.用途(闹钟、天文钟等)3.驱动方式(电子、机械)4.表面尺寸 5.指示方式 6.品牌(中文或外文名称)
91089010	1.品名 2.用途(考勤钟、停车记时表等)3.驱动方式(电子、机械)4.表面尺寸 5.品牌(中文或外文名称)
91089090	1.品名 2.表面尺寸
9109	1.品名 2.驱动方式(电子、机械、自动、非自动)
91101	1.品名 2.驱动方式(电子、机械、自动、非自动)
91109	1.品名 2.用途
91111000	1.品名 2.材质 3.贵金属含量 4.品牌(中文或外文名称)5.型号
91112000	1.品名 2.材质 3.品牌(中文或外文名称)4.型号
91118000	1.品名 2.材质 3.品牌(中文或外文名称)4.型号

商品编码	申报要素
91119000	1.品名 2.材质
9112	1.品名 2.用途
91131000	1.品名 2.材质(贵金属、贱金属等)3.贵金属含量 4.品牌(中文或外文名称)5.型号
91132000	1.品名 2.材质(贵金属、贱金属等)3.品牌(中文或外文名称)4.型号
91139000	1.品名 2.材质(贵金属、贱金属等)3.是否野生动物皮制 4.品牌(中文或外文名称)5.型号
91143000	1.品名 2.材质(贵金属、贱金属等)
91144000	1.品名 2.材质(贵金属、贱金属等)
91149010	1.品名 2.用途 3.材质
91149020	1.品名 2.用途 3.材质
91149090	1.品名 2.材质(贵金属、贱金属等)
9201	1.品名 2.产品编码 3.材质(象牙琴键、贵金属、贱金属等)4.种类(新旧、竖卧式、是否数码)5.品牌(中文或外文名称)6.型号 7.旧钢琴请申报生产年份
92021000	1.品名 2.是否为野生动物皮制 3.用途 4.型号 5.品牌(中文或外文名称)
92029000	1.品名 2.是否为野生动物皮制 3.用途 4.型号 5.品牌(中文或外文名称)6.竖琴请报琴弦数量
9205	1.品名 2.种类 3.品牌(中文或外文名称)4.型号
9206	1.品名 2.是否为野生动物皮制 3.用途 4.品牌(中文或外文名称)5.型号
92071000	1.品名 2.种类 3.品牌(中文或外文名称)4.型号
92079000	1.品名 2.种类 3.品牌(中文或外文名称)4.型号
92081000	1.品名 2.种类 3.品牌(中文或外文名称)
92089000	1.品名 2.品牌(中文或外文名称)
92093000	1.品名 2.用途(适用乐器类型)3.品牌(中文或外文名称)4.材质 5.型号
92099	1.品名 2.用途
9301	1.品名 2.驱动方式 3.型号
9302	1.品名 2.型号
9303	1.品名 2.型号
9304	1.品名 2.型号
9305	1.品名 2.型号
9306	1.品名 2.型号
9307	1.品名 2.用途
94011000	1.品名 2.用途 3.品牌(中文或外文名称)
94012	1.品名 2.用途(适用车 型)3.材质(骨架及覆面)4.品牌(中文或外文名称,无品牌请申报厂商)
94013	1.品名 2.用途 3.材质 4.是否可调节、可转动 5.品牌(中文或外文名称)
94014	1.品名 2.用途 3.材质 4.是否可做床用 5.品牌(中文或外文名称)
94015	1.品名 2.用途 3.材质 4.品牌(中文或外文名称)
94016110	1.品名 2.用途 3.座面的表面材质 4.框架材质(如为单一材质请申报木材中文及拉丁学名)5.是否装软垫 6.品牌(中文或外文名称)
94016190	1.品名 2.用途 3.表面材质 4.框架材质(如为单一材质请申报木材中文及拉丁学名)5.是否装软垫 6.品牌(中文或外文名称)
94016900	1.品名 2.用途 3.座面的表面材质 4.框架材质(如为单一材质请申报木材中文及拉丁学名)5.是否装软垫 6.品牌(中文或外文名称)
94017	1.品名 2.用途 3.座面的表面材质 4.框架材质 5.是否装软垫 6.品牌(中文或外文名称)
94018010	1.品名 2.用途 3.材质 4.品牌(中文或外文名称)
94018090	1.品名 2.用途 3.材质 4.品牌(中文或外文名称)
94019100	1.品名 2.用途(适用车型)3.材质
94019910	1.品名 2.用途(适用车型)3.材质
94019990	1.品名 2.用途(适用车型)3.材质
94021010	1.品名 2.用途 3.材质 4.品牌(中文或外文名称)
94021090	1.品名 2.用途 3.配置附属装置 4.是否带医疗用具 5.品牌(中文或外文名称)
94029000	1.品名 2.用途 3.配置附属装置 4.是否带医疗用具 5.品牌(中文或外文名称)
94031000	1.品名 2.材质 3.是否办公室用 4.品牌(中文或外文名称)5.规格
94032000	1.品名 2.用途 3.材质 4.品牌(中文或外文名称)5.规格
94033000	1.品名 2.材质(如为单一实木材质请申报木材中文及拉丁学名)3.是否办公室用 4.品牌(中文或外文名称)5.规格
94034000	1.品名 2.材质(如为单一实木材质请申报木材中文及拉丁学名)3.是否厨房用 4.品牌(中文或外文名称)5.规格
94035010	1.品名 2.材质(如为单一实木材质请申报木材中文及拉丁学名)3.是否卧室用 4.品牌(中文或外文名称)5.规格
9403509	1.品名 2.材质(如为单一实木材质请申报木材中文及拉丁学名)3.是否卧室用 4.品牌(中文或外文名称)5.规格
94036010	1.品名 2.用途 3.材质(如为单一实木材质请申报木材中文及拉丁学名)4.品牌(中文或外文名称)5.规格
94036091	1.品名 2.用途 3.材质(如为单一实木材质请申报木材中文及拉丁学名)4.品牌(中文或外文名称)5.规格
94036099	1.品名 2.用途 3.材质(如为单一实木材质请申报木材中文及拉丁学名)4.品牌(中文或外文名称)5.规格
94037000	1.品名 2.用途 3.材质 4.品牌(中文或外文名称)5.规格
94038	1.品名 2.用途 3.材质 4.品牌(中文或外文名称)5.规格
94039	1.品名 2.用途 3.材质 4.规格
94041000	1.品名 2.品牌(中文或外文名称)3.规格
94042	1.品名 2.材质 3.品牌(中文或外文名称)4.规格
94043	1.品名 2.材质(填充物)3.品牌(中文或外文名称)4.规格
94044	1.品名 2.材质(填充物)3.品牌(中文或外文名称)4.规格
94049	1.品名 2.材质(填充物)3.品牌(中文或外文名称)4.规格
94051	1.品名 2.用途 3.品牌(中文或外文名称)
94052	1.品名 2.材质 3.用途 4.品牌(中文或外文名称)
94053	1.品名 2.材质 3.用途 4.品牌(中文或外文名称)
94054100	1.品名 2.用途 3.品牌(中文或外文名称)
94054210	1.品名 2.用途 3.是否为真空灯泡请注明 4.是否为封闭式充气灯泡请注明 5.品牌(中文或外文名称)
94054290	1.品名 2.用途 3.品牌(中文或外文名称)
94054910	1.品名 2.用途 3.是否为真空灯泡请注明 4.是否为封闭式充气灯泡请注明 5.品牌(中文或外文名称)
94054990	1.品名 2.用途 3.品牌(中文或外文名称)
94055000	1.品名 2.材质 3.用途 4.品牌(中文或外文名称)
94056	1.品名 2.材质 3.用途 4.品牌(中文或外文名称)
94059	1.品名 2.材质 3.用途
9406	1.品名 2.材质 3.内部配置 4.规格(尺寸)
95030010	1.品名 2.用途 3.种类 4.品牌(中文或外文名称)
95030002	1.品名 2.用途 3.种类 4.品牌(中文或外文名称)
95030060	1.品名 2.用途 3.种类 4.品牌(中文或外文名称)
95030083	1.品名 2.用途 3.种类 4.是否带有动力装置 5.品牌(中文或外文名称)
95030089	1.品名 2.用途 3.种类 4.品牌(中文或外文名称)
95030090	1.品名 2.用途 3.种类 4.品牌(中文或外文名称)
95042000	1.品名 2.用途 3.品牌(中文或外文名称)
95043010	1.品名 2.用途 3.种类 4.品牌(中文或外文名称)
95043090	1.品名 2.用途 3.品牌(中文或外文名称)
95044000	1.品名 2.用途 3.品牌(中文或外文名称)
95045020	1.品名 2.用途 3.种类 4.是否与电视接收机配套使用 5.品牌(中文或外文名称)
95045030	1.品名 2.用途 3.种类 4.是否与电视接收机配套使用 5.品牌(中文或外文名称)
95045080	1.品名 2.用途 3.种类 4.是否与电视接收机配套使用 5.品牌(中文或外文名称)
95049010	1.品名 2.种类 3.品牌(中文或外文名称)
9504902	1.品名 2.种类 3.品牌(中文或外文名称)
95049030	1.品名 2.种类 3.品牌(中文或外文名称)
95049040	1.品名 2.种类 3.品牌(中文或外文名称)
95049090	1.品名 2.材质 3.品牌(中文或外文名称)
95051000	1.品名 2.用途 3.品牌(中文或外文名称)
95059000	1.品名 2.用途 3.品牌(中文或外文名称)
95061	1.品名 2.种类 3.品牌(中文或外文名称)4.型号
95062	1.品名 2.种类 3.品牌(中文或外文名称)4.型号
95063	1.品名 2.品牌(中文或外文名称)3.型号
95064	1.品名 2.品牌(中文或外文名称)3.型号
95065	1.品名 2.种类 3.品牌(中文或外文名称)4.型号
95066	1.品名 2.种类 3.品牌(中文或外文名称)4.型号
95067	1.品名 2.种类 3.品牌(中文或外文名称)4.型号
950691	1.品名 2.用途 3.种类 4.品牌(中文或外文名称)5.型号
950699	1.品名 2.材质 3.品牌(中文或外文名称)4.型号
95071000	1.品名 2.材质 3.品牌(中文或外文名称)4.型号
95072000	1.品名 2.品牌(中文或外文名称)3.型号
95073000	1.品名 2.品牌(中文或外文名称)3.型号
95079000	1.品名 2.用途 3.品牌(中文或外文名称)4.型号
9508	1.品名
96011000	1.品名 2.是否野生动物产品
96019000	1.品名 2.材质 3.加工工艺
96020010	1.品名
96020090	1.品名 2.材质 3.加工工艺
96031000	1.品名 2.用途 3.材质
96032100	1.品名 2.用途 3.材质
96032900	1.品名 2.用途 3.材质
96033	1.品名 2.用途 3.材质
96034	1.品名 2.用途 3.材质
96035	1.品名 2.用途(具体作为何种机器、器具零件,作 用)3.材质
96039	1.品名 2.用途 3.材质
9604	1.品名
9605	1.品名 2.组成(内装货品)
96061000	1.品名 2.材质 3.种类 4.是否用纺织材料包裹
96062	1.品名 2.材质 3.纺织材料包裹、非纺织材料包裹
96063000	1.品名 2 种类
9607	1.品名 2.材质 3.品牌(中文或外文名称)4.如为拉链应申报是否装有贱金属制咪牙齿
9608	1.品名 2.种类 3.品牌(中文或外文名称)4.型号
9609	1.品名 2.种类 3.品牌(中文或外文名称)4.型号
9610	1.品名 2.种类 3.品牌(中文或外文名称)
9611	1.品名 2.用途
9612	1.品名 2.材质 3.品牌(中文或外文名称)4.型号
9613	1.品名 2.种类 3.型号 4.品牌(中文或外文名称)
96140010	1.品名 2.材质 3.品牌(中文或外文名称)4.型号
96140090	1.品名 2.材质 3.品牌(中文或外文名称)
9615	1.品名 2.材质 3.品牌(中文或外文名称)
96161000	1.品名 2.用途
96162000	1.品名 2.用途 3.材质
9617	1.品名 2.内胆材质 3.品牌(中文或外文名称)4.型号
9618	1.品名 2.用途 3.材质
9619001	1.品名 2.用途(婴儿用、成人用等)3.品牌(中文或外文名称)4.系列 5.码数(型号)6.包装规格(每包所含片数) 7.每包重量(kg)
96190020	1.品名 2.品牌(中文或外文名称)3.系列 4.包装规格(每包所含片数)5.每包重量(kg)
96190090	1.品名 2.品牌(中文或外文名称)3.系列 4.包装规格(每包所含片数)5.每包重量(kg)
9620	1.品名 2.用途 3.品牌(中文或外文名称)
9701	1.品名 2.创作年份 3.尺寸大小
9702	1.品名 2.创作年份 3.尺寸大小 4.原作者姓名 5.作品名称
9703	1.品名 2.创作年份 3.尺寸大小 4.作者 5.作品名称
9704	1.品名 2.种类 3.指运国(地区)
9705	1.品名 2.种类 3.年代 4.是否野生动物产品
9706	1.品名 2.年代 3.是否野生动物产品

3

常用代码表

Common Codes List

监管证件代码表

监管证件代码	监管证件名称
#	零关税申请单
0	反制措施排除代码
1	进口许可证
2	两用物项和技术进口许可证
3	两用物项和技术出口许可证
4	出口许可证
5	纺织品临时出口许可证
6	旧机电产品禁止进口
7	自动进口许可证
8	禁止出口商品
9	禁止进口商品
@	准予担保通知书
A	检验检疫
B	电子底账
D	毛坯钻石进出境检验
E	濒危物种允许出口证明书
F	濒危物种允许进口证明书
G	两用物项和技术出口许可证(定向)
H	港澳 OPA 纺织品证明
I	麻醉药品精神药物进出口准许证
J	黄金及黄金制品进出口准许证
K	深加工结转申请表
L	药品进出口准许证
M	密码产品和设备进口许可证
O	自动进口许可证(新旧机电产品)
P	固体废物进口许可证
Q	进口药品通关单
R	进口兽药通关单
S	农药进出口登记管理放行通知单
T	提发货凭证
U	合法捕捞产品通关证明
V	人类遗传资源材料出口、出境证明
X	有毒化学品环境管理放行通知单
Y	原产地证明
Z	赴境外加工光盘进口备案证明
a	保税核注清单
b	进口广播电影电视节目带(片)提取单
c	内销征税联系单
d	援外项目任务通知函
e	关税配额外优惠税率进口棉花配额证
f	音像制品(成品)进口批准单
g	技术出口合同登记证
h	核增核扣表
i	技术出口许可证
k	民用爆炸物品进出口审批单
m	银行调运人民币现钞进出境证明
n	音像制品(版权引进)批准单
q	国别关税配额证明
r	预归类标志
s	适用 ITA 税率的商品用途认定证明
t	关税配额证明
v	自动进口许可证(加工贸易)
x	出口许可证(加工贸易)
y	出口许可证(边境小额贸易)
z	古生物化石出境批件

监管证件代码表综合说明

一、监管证件代码表结构

监管证件代码表由两部分组成,即监管证件代码和监管证件名称。例如:代码"1",为进口许可证,如果《税则》中某一商品编号后"监管条件"列注有"1"(即监管证件代码),则说明在一般贸易项下进口该种商品需申领进口许可证。

二、监管证件类别及监管证件代码、名称说明

(一)禁止进出口货物

禁止进出口货物是指商务部会同国务院其他有关部门依法制定、调整并公布禁止进/出口货物目录,以及其他法律、行政法规定禁止进/出口的货物,包括国家规定停止进口的商品、执行联合国安理会有关决议规定禁止进出口的商品等。其他法律、行政法规等规定禁止进出口的,从其规定。

1.代码"9"——禁止进口商品:指国务院授权商务部门会同有关部门,依照《中华人民共和国对外贸易法》等有关法律法规,制定、调整并公布的禁止进口货物目录所列商品及法律、法规等规定禁止进口的商品。商品编码后有此代码的商品禁止进口。

2.代码"8"——禁止出口商品:指国务院授权商务部门会同有关部门,依照《中华人民共和国对外贸易法》等有关法律法规,制定、调整并公布的禁止出口货物目录所列商品及法律、法规等规定禁止出口的商品。商品编码后有此代码的商品禁止出口。

3.代码"6"——旧机电产品禁止进口:商品编码后面有此代码的机电产品,其旧品禁止进口。

(二)进口许可证

进口许可证是指商务部及其授权发证机构依法对实行数量限制或其他限制的进口货物颁发准予进口的许可证件。对国家规定有数量限制的进口货物,实行配额管理;其他限制进口货物,实行许可证管理。实行进口许可证管理的货物为两大类,即环境保护部、商务部、海关总署令 2014 年第 26 号《消耗臭氧层物质进出口管理办法》规定的消耗臭氧层物质和商务部、海关总署、质检总局令 2008 年第 5 号《重点旧机电产品进口管理办法》规定的重点旧机电产品。具体管理目录详见年度《进口许可证管理货物目录》。

代码“1”——进口许可证：指商务部配额许可证事务局或其授权机关签发的进口许可证。

（三）出口许可证

出口许可证是指商务部授权发证机关依法对实行数量限制或其他限制的出口货物签发的准予出口的许可证件。国家规定有数量限制的限制出口货物，实行配额和招标管理；其他限制出口货物，实行许可证管理。具体管理目录详见年度《出口许可证管理货物目录》。

1.代码“4”——出口许可证：指商务部配额许可证事务局或其授权发证机构签发的出口许可证。

2.代码“x”——出口许可证(加工贸易)：适用于加工贸易方式下出口许可证管理的商品。

3.代码“y”——出口许可证(边境小额贸易)：适用于边境小额贸易项下需凭出口许可证办理有关手续的商品。

（四）两用物项和技术进口许可证

两用物项和技术进口许可证是指商务部及其授权发证机关签发的准予进口《两用物项和技术进口许可证管理目录》中商品的许可证件，包括监控化学品(含生产技术及专用设备)、易制毒化学品和放射性同位素、《商用密码进口许可清单》所列物项和技术。具体管理目录详见年度《两用物项和技术进出口许可证管理目录》之《两用物项和技术进口许可证管理目录》。进口放射性同位素需按《放射性同位素与射线装置安全和防护条例》和《两用物项和技术进出口许可证管理办法》有关规定，报生态环境部审批后，在商务部配额许可证事务局申领两用物项和技术进口许可证。

代码“2”——两用物项和技术进口许可证：指列入《两用物项和技术进口许可证管理目录》的商品，进口时由商务部签发两用物项和技术进口许可证。

（五）两用物项和技术出口许可证

两用物项和技术出口许可证是指商务部授权发证机关准予两用物项和技术出口签发的许可证件。其中，向缅甸、老挝、阿富汗等特定国家(地区)出口氯化铵等17种易制毒化学品为定向出口。纳入《两用物项和技术出口许可证管理目录》的两用物项和技术类别包括核、核两用品及相关技术、生物两用品及相关设备和技术、监控化学品(含生产技术及专用设备)、有关化学品及相关设备和技术、导弹及相关物项和技术、易制毒化学品、部分无人驾驶航空飞行器和高性能计算机、《商用密码出口管制清单》所列物项和技术、特殊民用物项(耙吸式挖泥船、绞吸式挖泥船、斗式挖泥船、吸砂船、自航自卸式泥驳)等两用物项和技术。受《中华人民共和国导弹及相关物项和技术出口管制条例》管制，用于民用航空用途的民用航空零部件出口按《民用航空零部件出口分类管理办法》实行许可证件分类管理制度。具体管理目录详见年度《两用物项和技术进出口许可证管理目录》之《两用物项和技术出口许可证管理目录》。

1.代码“3”——两用物项和技术出口许可证：根据商务部会同海关总署联合发布的《两用物项和技术进出口许可证管理办法》，由商务部授权的发证机构签发两用物项和技术出口许可证。

2.代码“G”——两用物项和技术出口许可证(定向)：指列入《向特定国家(地区)出口易制毒化学品管理目录》的商品，向特定国家出口时由商务部签发易制毒化学品定向出口许可证。

（六）自动进口许可证

自动进口许可证是指商务部授权发证机构依法对实行自动进口许可管理的货物颁发的准予进口的许可证件。其中，属加工贸易“自动进口许可证”管理的商品有原油和成品油。具体管理目录详见年度《自动进口许可管理货物目录》。

1.代码“7”——自动进口许可证：指部分进口商品实行自动进口许可管理，由商务部及其授权机构按职责分工签发自动进口许可证。

2.代码“O”——自动进口许可证(新旧机电产品)：根据《机电产品进口管理办法》和《机电产品进口自动许可实施办法》，进口实行自动进口许可管理的机电产品，进口单位应当在办理海关报关手续前，向商务部或地方外经贸主管机构、部门机电办申领自动进口许可证。

3.代码“v”——自动进口许可证(加工贸易)：适用于加工贸易方式下自动进口许可证管理的商品。

（七）入/出境检验检疫

入/出境检验检疫是指海关依法对列入《海关实施检验检疫的进出境商品目录》(简称《检验检疫法检目录》)，以及虽未列入《检验检疫法检目录》，但国家有关法律、行政法规明确规定海关实施检验检疫的进出境货物及特殊物品等实施检验检疫。

实行入境检验检疫管理的货物主要包括四类：列入《检验检疫法检目录》的进境货物、进口旧机电产品、进口捐赠的医疗器械，以及其他未列入《检验检疫法检目录》，但国家有关法律、行政法规规定实施检验检疫的入境货物及特殊物品等。

实行出境检验检疫管理的货物主要包括三类：列入《检验检疫法检目录》的出境货物、对外经济技术援助物资及人道主义紧急救灾援助物资，以及其他未列入《检验检疫法检目录》，但国家有关法律、行政法规规定实施检验检疫的出境货物及特殊物品等。

1.代码“A”——入境检验检疫：指海关根据《中华人民共和国进出口商品检验法》《中华人民共和国动植物检疫法》和《中华人民共和国食品安全法》等有关法律、法规，对列入《海关实施检验检疫的进出境商品目录》的进口商品实行入境检验检疫。

2.代码“B”——出境检验检疫(电子底账)：指海关根据《中华人民共和国进出口商品检验法》、《中华人民共和国动植物检疫法》和《中华人民共和国食品安全法》等有关法律、法规，对列入《海关实施检验检疫的进出境商品目录》的出口商品实行出境检验检疫。

3.代码“D”——毛坯钻石进出境检验：为履行我国国际义务，制止“冲突钻石”非法交易，海关总署等六部委联合发布2002年第132号公告，对毛坯钻石进出口实施金伯利进程国际证书制度，对进出境毛坯钻石实施检验。专指《金伯利进程国际证书制度》规定的毛坯钻石进出境检验。

（八）野生动植物进出口

野生动植物进出口证书是指对纳入《进出口野生动植物种商品目录》管理范围的野生动植物及其制品实施进/出口许可管理，国家濒管办及其授权办事处签发准予进/出口的许可证件。野生动植物进出口证书包括中华人民共和国濒危野生动植物种国际贸易公约允许进出口证明书(简称《公约证书》)、中华人民共和国海峡两岸野生动植物允许进出口证明书(简称《海峡两岸证书》)、中华人民共和国野生动植物允许进出口证明书(简称《非公约证书》)及非《进出口野生动植物种商品目录》物种证明(简称《物种证明》)。

《进出口野生动植物种商品目录》所列野生动植物或其产品以一般贸易、无偿捐赠、无偿提供、旅客携带、交换、邮寄及其他各种方式进出口的，海关均按规定进行监管。

野生动植物进出口证书适用范围及管理规则详见国家濒管办、海关总署公告2019年第2号。

“公约证书”适用于开展进出口属《濒危野生动植物种国际贸易公约》(简称《公约》)附录范围内野生动植物及其制品的活动(除与台湾地区之外)，包括常规版本和专用版本。其中，常规版本适用于开展一般情况下《公约》附录物种及其制品的进口、出口、再出口。专用版本适用于《公约》附录物种从海上引进、标本巡回展出、个人所有活体动物、乐器多次跨境转移、个人携带二胡等五种情形。

“海峡两岸证书”适用于中国大陆与台湾地区进出口属《公约》附录范围内野生动植物及其制品的活动，包括常规版本和专用版本。其中，常规版本适用于一般情况下《公约》附录野生动植物及其制品的进口、出口、再出口。专用版本适用于《公约》附录野生动植物及其制品的巡回展出、个人所有活体动物、乐器多次跨境转移、个人携带二胡等四种情形。

“非公约证书”适用于未被列入《公约》附录，但属国家重点保护的野生动植物及其制品的出口。

“中华人民共和国濒危物种进出口管理办公室非《进出口野生动植物种商品目录》物种证明”适用于上述三种情形之外但列入《进出口野生动植物种商品目录》的野生动植物及其制品的进出口。

具体管理目录详见《进出口野生动植物种商品目录》。

1.代码“E”——濒危物种允许出口证明书：指根据《中华人民共和国野生动物保护法》及相关法律法规，对列入《濒危野生动植物种国际贸易公约》及《国家重点保护野生动物名录》《国家重点保护野生植物名录》货物，出口时由国家濒危物种进出口管理办公室或其办事机构签发允许出口证明书。

2.代码“F”——濒危物种允许进口证明书：指根据《中华人民共和国野生动物保护法》及相关法律法规，对列入《濒危野生动植物种国际贸易公约》的货物，进口时由国家濒危物种进出口管理办公室或其办事机构签发允许进口证明书。

（九）麻醉药品精神药物进(出)口准许证

麻醉药品进出口准许证是指国家药品监督管理部门依法对连续使用后易使身体产生依赖性、能成瘾癖的麻醉药品实施进出口监督管理，签发准予麻醉药品进出口的许可证件。麻醉药品包括阿片类、可卡因类、大麻类、合成麻醉药类及其他易成瘾癖的药品、药用原植物及其制剂。具体管理目录详见《麻醉药品品种目录》。

精神药物进出口准许证是指国家药品监督管理部门依法对直接作用于中枢神经系统使之兴奋或抑制,连续使用能产生依赖性的精神药品实施进出口监督管理,签发准予精神药物进出口的许可证件。具体管理目录详见《精神药品品种目录》。

代码“I”——麻醉药品精神药物进(出)口准许证:根据《中华人民共和国药品管理法》和《麻醉药品和精神药品管理条例》等相关法律法规,国家对麻醉药品、精神药品进(出)口实行进(出)口准许证管理制度。

(十)黄金及黄金制品进出口准许证

黄金及黄金制品进出口准许证是指中国人民银行总行或其授权的中国人民银行分支机构依法对列入《黄金及黄金制品进出口管理商品目录》的进出口黄金及其制品实施监督管理并签发准予进出口的许可证件。进出口黄金及黄金制品范围详见《黄金及黄金制品进出口管理商品目录》。

代码“J”——黄金及黄金制品进出口准许证:指根据《中华人民共和国金银管理条例》及相关法律法规,对进出口黄金及其制品,由中国人民银行授权发证机构签发的准许进出境证件。

(十一)药品进出口准许证

药品进(出)口准许证是指国家药品监督管理部门授权机构依法对列入兴奋剂目录的蛋白同化制剂、肽类激素等供医疗使用及教学、科研需要的兴奋剂实施进出口管理,签发准予进出口的许可证件。兴奋剂是指兴奋剂目录所列的禁用物质,包括蛋白同化制剂品种、肽类激素品种、麻醉药品品种、刺激剂(含精神药品)品种、药品类易制毒化学品品种、医疗用毒性药品品种及其他品种兴奋剂。对兴奋剂目录中第七类“其他品种”,海关暂不按照兴奋剂实行管理。具体管理措施详见《蛋白同化制剂和肽类激素进出口管理办法》,具体管理目录详见兴奋剂目录公告。

代码“L”——药品进出口准许证:根据《中华人民共和国反兴奋剂条例》,国家药品监督管理部门依法对列入兴奋剂目录的蛋白同化制剂、肽类激素等供医疗使用的兴奋剂实施进出口管理,签发准予进出口的许可证件。

(十二)进口药品通关单

进口药品通关单是指国家药品监督管理局及其授权发证机关依法对进口药品实施监督管理所签发的准予药品进口的监管证件。列入“进口药品通关单”管理的药品是指用于预防、治疗、诊断人的疾病,有目的地调节人的生理机能并规定有适应症或者功能主治、用法和用量的物质,包括中药材、中药饮片、中成药、化学原料药及其制剂、抗生素、生化药品、放射性药品、血清、疫苗、血液制品和诊断药品等。2015 年 1 月 29 日《海关总署关于明确人体组织器官进口有关问题的通知》(署监函〔2015〕46 号)中,针对人供体角膜等人体组织器官进口报关手续过程中存在企业无法取得上述货物的“进口药品通关单”(Q 证)问题,允许以下四种情况免于验核“进口药品通关单”:(1)涉及我国人类遗传资源的国际合作项目中人类遗传资源材料的出口、出境,海关验核人类遗传资源管理办公室核发的出口、出境证明办理出口报关手续;(2)人体血液、组织器官进口时,应当办理入境检验检疫手续;(3)原国家食品药品监督管理总局已明确人体血液、组织器官进口不按照进口药品管理,上述货物进口时,海关可不再验核“进口药品通关单”;(4)军队医疗机构办理人体血液、组织器官进口报关手续的,海关验核军队卫生主管部门出具的相关进口批件,并按照上述要求办理进口手续。具体管理目录详见原国家食品药品监督管理总局、海关总署发布的《进口药品目录》。

代码“Q”——进口药品通关单:根据《中华人民共和国药品管理法》及相关法律法规,对列入《进口药品管理目录》的药品,国家药品监督管理局及其授权机构签发进口药品通关单。

(十三)进口兽药通关单

进口兽药通关单是指农业农村部或兽药进口口岸所在地省级人民政府兽医行政管理部门对列入《进口兽药管理目录》的进口兽药实施监督管理,签发准予进口的监管证件。兽药是指用于预防、治疗、诊断动物疾病或者有目的地调节动物生理机能的物质(含药物饲料添加剂),主要包括血清制品、疫苗、诊断制品、微生态制品、中药材、中成药、化学药品、抗生素、生化药品、放射性药品及外用杀虫剂、消毒剂等。

代码“R”——进口兽药通关单:根据《兽药管理条例》,农业农村部或兽药进口口岸所在地省级人民政府兽医行政管理部门对列入《进口兽药管理目录》的进口兽药实施监督管理,签发进口兽药通关单。

(十四)农药进出口登记管理放行通知单

农药进/出口登记管理放行通知单是指农业农村部及其授权发证机关依法对纳入《中华人民共和国进出口农药管理名录》范围的进出口农药实施登记管理签发的证明文件。农药是指用于预防、消灭或者控制危害农业、林业的病、虫、草和其他有害生物,以及有目的地调节植物、昆虫生长的化学合成或者来源于生物、其他天然物质的一种物质或者几种物质的混合物及其制剂。具体管理目录详见《进出口农药管理名录》。

代码“S”——农药进出口登记管理放行通知单:根据《农药管理条例》及有关法律法规,《中华人民共和国进出口农药管理名录》的商品进出口时,农业农村部授权机构签发农药进出口登记管理放行通知单。

(十五)银行调运人民币现钞进出境证明

银行调运人民币现钞进出境证明是指中国人民银行总行及其授权的分行依法对银行调运进出境在流通中使用的货币现钞实施监督管理,签发准予调运人民币进出境的证明文件。调运进出境的货币现钞是指在流通中使用的人民币,包括各种面额的纸币和硬币。

代码“m”——银行调运人民币现钞进出境证明:是指中国人民银行授权机构对商业银行跨境调运人民币现钞业务签发《银行调运人民币现钞进出境证明》。

(十六)有毒化学品进出口环境管理放行通知单

有毒化学品进出口环境管理放行通知单是指国家环境保护部门依法对纳入《中国严格限制进出口的有毒化学品目录》管理的化学品实施进出口环境管理,签发准予有关化学品进出口的许可证件。具体管理目录详见《中国严格限制进出口的有毒化学品目录》。

代码“X”——有毒化学品进出口环境管理放行通知单:指列入《中国严格限制进出口的有毒化学品目录》的进出口化学品,由生态环境部签发的放行通知单。

(十七)赴境外加工光盘进口备案证明

代码“Z”——赴境外加工光盘进口备案证明:境内出版单位出版的音像电子出版物赴境外加工光盘类产品(含黑胶唱片)并返回境内的,须向所在地省级新闻出版主管部门提供拟入境产品的内容进行备案。备案后,省级新闻出版主管部门开具“赴境外加工光盘进口备案证明”。

出版单位向海关办理赴境外加工并返回国内光盘类产品(商品编码为 8523499030 或 8523801120)进口报关纳税手续前,须申领“赴境外加工光盘进口备案证明”,海关按现行规定办理验放手续。

(十八)进口广播电影电视节目带(片)提取单

代码“b”——进口广播电影电视节目带(片)提取单:纳入《进口广播电影电视节目带(片)提取单》管理货物目录的商品进口时,国家电影局、国家广播电视总局按职责分工签发《进口广播电影电视节目带(片)提取单》。

(十九)音像制品(成品)进口批准单

代码“f”——音像制品(成品)进口批准单:纳入《音像制品(成品)进口批准单》管理货物目录的音像制品(成品)进口时,中央宣传部(新闻出版署)签发《音像制品(成品)进口批准单》。

(二十)音像制品(版权引进)批准单

代码“n”——音像制品(版权引进)批准单:是指中央宣传部(新闻出版署)对进口用于出版的音像制品母盘(带)等签发《音像制品(版权引进)批准单》。

(二十一)关税配额外优惠税率进口棉花配额证

代码“e”——关税配额外优惠税率进口棉花配额证:指对于一定数量的关税配额外报关进口的棉花,按“暂定优惠关税税率”征收进口关税,由国家发展改革委授权机构出具关税配额外优惠关税税率进口棉花配额证。

(二十二)国别关税配额证明

代码“q”——国别关税配额证明:进口原产于新西兰并享受协定税率的羊毛或毛条时,应单独向海关申报,并按照海关总署令第 175 号规定提交原产地证明文件和商务部及其授权机构签发的在备注栏注明“新西兰羊毛、毛条国别配额”字样的农产品进口关税配额证,该证简称“国别关税配额证明”。

(二十三)纺织品临时出口许可证

代码“5”——纺织品临时出口许可证:经营者在出口《输欧盟纺织品出口临时管理商品目录》(商务部、海关总署、质检总局 2005 年第103号公告)、《对美出口纺织品临时管理商品目录》(商务部、海关总署、质检总局2005年第87号、104号公告)、商务部2005年第49号公告及商务部、海关总署2004年第82号公告等文件所列货物前,应到当地发证机构办理相应的纺织品临时出口许可证件。商务部授权配额许可证事务局统一管理、指导全国各地方商务主管部门发证机构的纺织品临时出口许可证件的发证工作。

(二十四)合法捕捞产品通关证明

合法捕捞产品通关证明是农业农村部依据我国加入相关国际渔业组织的承诺规定,对纳入《实施合法捕捞证明的水产品清单》的部分水产品签发合法捕捞产品进口的通关证明。根据农业部、海关总署公告第1696号,对金枪鱼等4类水产品进口实施"合法捕捞产品通关证明"制度;根据农业部、海关总署公告第2146号,对从俄罗斯进口的狭鳕等水产品实施"合法捕捞产品通关证明"制度。

代码"U"——合法捕捞产品通关证明:进口"实施合法捕捞证明的水产品清单"所列的水产品,由农业农村部授权单位签发"合法捕捞产品通关证明"。

(二十五)民用爆炸物品进出口审批单

民用爆炸物品进/出口审批单是指国家民用爆破器材行业行政主管部门依法对民用爆破器材产品及生产所需的具有爆炸危险属性的原材料(含半成品)的进出口实行统一管理,签发准予进出口的批准文件。民用爆炸物品是指用于非军事目的、列入民用爆炸物品品名表的各类火药、炸药及其制品和雷管、导火索等点火、起爆器材。民用爆炸物品管理范围详见《民用爆炸物品进/出口审批单》管理货物目录。

代码"k"——民用爆炸物品进出口审批单:是指工业和信息化部依法对纳入《民用爆炸物品进/出口审批单》管理货物目录的进出口民用爆炸物品签发《民用爆炸物品进/出口审批单》。

(二十六)人类遗传资源材料出口、出境证明

代码"V"——人类遗传资源材料出口、出境证明:是指国家科技主管部门依法对含有人体基因组、基因及其产物的器官、组织、细胞、血液、制备物、重组脱氧核糖核酸(DNA)构建体等人类遗传材料及相关的信息资料出口、出境签发《人类遗传资源材料出口、出境证明》。

(二十七)技术出口许可证

技术出口许可证是指商务部授权发证机构依法对限制出口技术实施出口许可管理,签发准予出口的许可证件。技术出口是指从我国境内向我国境外,通过贸易、投资或者经济技术合作的方式转移技术的行为,包括专利权转让、专利申请权转让、专利实施许可、技术秘密转让、技术服务和其他方式的技术转移。技术出口分为禁止出口技术、限制出口技术和自由出口技术,具体目录详见《中国禁止出口限制出口技术目录》。凡出口列入《中国禁止出口限制出口技术目录》中限制出口技术的,应办理由国家对外贸易主管部门授权发证机构颁发的技术出口许可证。

代码"i"——技术出口许可证:是指商务部权发证机构依法对限制出口技术签发《技术出口许可证》。

(二十八)技术出口合同登记证

技术出口合同登记证是指商务部授权发证机构依法对自由出口技术实施合同登记管理,签发准予出口的许可证件。

代码"g"——技术出口合同登记证:是指商务部授权发证机构依法对属于自由出口技术签发《技术出口合同登记证》。

(二十九)援外项目任务通知函

代码"d"——援外项目任务通知函:商务部为加强对外援助物资项目的管理,对援外物资项目项下的物资出口签发《援外项目任务通知函》。

(三十)古生物化石出境批件

古生物化石是指地质时期形成并赋存于地层中的动物、植物等遗体化石或者遗迹化石。依据《古生物化石保护条例》《古生物化石管理办法》《古生物化石保护条例实施办法》对古生物化石实行出口/出境管理,因科学研究、教学、科普展览等,需将古生物化石运送出境的,由自然资源部发放出境证明。对临时入境、复带出境的古生物化石的查验、复验,由自然资源部指定的机构负责;查验、复验相符的,由自然资源部发放出境证明。其中规定:未命名的古生物化石不得出境。

重点保护古生物化石符合下列条件之一,经国务院自然资源主管部门批准,方可出境:(1)因科学研究需要与国外有关研究机构进行合作的;(2)因科学、文化交流需要在境外进行展览的。

一般保护古生物化石经所在地省、自治区、直辖市人民政府自然资源主管部门批准,方可出境。

代码"z"——古生物化石出境批件:是指自然资源部授权机构对古生物化石(参考海关商品编方9705000020)出境签发《古生物化石出境批件》。

(三十一)军品出口许可证

军品出口许可证是指国家军品出口主管部门依法对列入军品出口管理清单范围内的军品及纳入军品管理的货物出口实施监督管理,签发准予出口的许可证件。军品出口,是指用于军事目的的装备、专用生产设备及其他物资、技术和有关服务的贸易性出口。警用装备的出口适用《中华人民共和国军品出口管理条例》。军品出口管理清单内的军品包括轻武器,火炮及其他发射装置,弹药、地雷、水雷、炸弹、反坦克导弹及其他爆炸装置,坦克、装甲车辆及其他军用车辆,军事工程装备与设备,军用舰船及其专用装备与设备,军用航空飞行器及其专用装备与设备,火箭、导弹、军用卫星及其辅助设备,军用电子产品及火控、测距、光学、制导与控制装置,火炸药、推进剂、燃烧剂及相关化合物,军事训练设备,核、生、化武器防护装备与设备,后勤装备、物资及其他辅助军事装备,以及其他产品共十四大类。

三、监管证件填报要求

(一)在报关单"许可证号"栏目填写的监管证件种类

"许可证号"栏目填报以下由商务部及其授权发证机关签发的进(出)口货物许可证的监管证件代码。

1.进口许可证(监管证件代码"1");
2.两用物项和技术进口许可证(监管证件代码"2");
3.两用物项和技术出口许可证(监管证件代码"3");
4.出口许可证(监管证件代码"4");
5.两用物项和技术出口许可证(定向)(监管证件代码"G")
6.出口许可证(加工贸易)(监管证件代码"x");
7.出口许可证(边境小额贸易)(监管证件代码"y")。

(二)在报关单"随附单据"栏目填报的监管证件种类

除"许可证号"栏目填报的进(出)口许可证外的其他监管证件代码在报关单"随附单据"栏目填报。

1.自动进口许可证(监管证件代码"7");
2.入境检验检疫(监管证件代码"A");
3.出境检验检疫(电子底账)(监管证件代码"B");
4.毛坯钻石进出境检验(监管证件代码"D");
5.濒危物种允许出口证明书(监管证件代码"E");
6.濒危物种允许进口证明书(监管证件代码"F");
7.麻醉药品精神药物进(出)口准许证(监管证件代码"I");
8.黄金及黄金制品进出口准许证(监管证件代码"J");
9.药品进/出口准许证(蛋白同化制剂、肽类激素)(监管证件代码"L");
10.自动进口许可证(新旧机电产品)(监管证件代码"O");
11.进口药品通关单(监管证件代码"Q");
12.进口兽药通关单(监管证件代码"R");
13.农药进出口登记管理放行通知单(监管证件代码"S");
14.合法捕捞产品通关证明(监管证件代码"U");
15.人类遗传资源材料出口、出境证明(监管证件代码"V");
16.有毒化学品进出口环境管理放行通知单(监管证件代码"X");
17.赴境外加工光盘进口备案证明(监管证件代码"Z");
18.进口广播电影电视节目带(片)提取单(监管证件代码"b");
19.援外项目任务通知函(监管证件代码"d");
20.音像制品(成品)进口批准单(监管证件代码"f");
21.技术出口合同登记证(监管证件代码"g");
22.技术出口许可证(监管证件代码"i");
23.民用爆炸物品进出口审批单(监管证件代码"k");
24.银行调运人民币现钞进出境证明(监管证件代码"m");
25.音像制品(版权引进)批准单(监管证件代码"n");
26.自动进口许可证(加工贸易)(监管证件代码"v");
27.古生物化石出境批件(监管证件代码"z")。

(三)在报关单"备注"栏目填报的监管证件种类

H2010通关管理系统中海关暂未设置监管证件代码且属于监管证件管理的进出口货物,应在报关单"备注"栏填写批件类型及批件号,例如军品出口许可证等。

监管方式代码表

监管方式代码	监管方式简称	监管方式全称
0110	一般贸易	一般贸易
0130	易货贸易	易货贸易
0139	旅游购物商品	用于旅游者 5 万美元以下的出口小批量订货
0200	料件销毁	加工贸易料件、残次品(折料)销毁
0214	来料加工	来料加工装配贸易进口料件及加工出口货物
0245	来料料件内销	来料加工料件转内销
0255	来料深加工	来料深加工结转货物
0258	来料余料结转	来料加工余料结转
0265	来料料件复出	来料加工复运出境的原进口料件
0300	来料料件退换	来料加工料件退换
0314	加工专用油	国营贸易企业代理来料加工企业进口柴油
0320	不作价设备	加工贸易外商提供的不作价进口设备
0345	来料成品减免	来料加工成品凭征免税证明转减免税
0400	边角料销毁	加工贸易边角料、副产品(按状态)销毁
0420	加工贸易设备	加工贸易项下外商提供的进口设备
0444	保区进料成品	按成品征税的保税区进料加工成品转内销货物
0445	保区来料成品	按成品征税的保税区来料加工成品转内销货物
0446	加工设备内销	加工贸易免税进口设备转内销
0456	加工设备结转	加工贸易免税进口设备结转
0466	加工设备退运	加工贸易免税进口设备退运出境
0500	减免设备结转	用于监管年限内减免税设备的结转
0513	补偿贸易	补偿贸易
0544	保区进料料件	按料件征税的保税区进料加工成品转内销货物
0545	保区来料料件	按料件征税的保税区来料加工成品转内销货物
0615	进料对口	进料加工(对口合同)
0642	进料以产顶进	进料加工成品以产顶进
0644	进料料件内销	进料加工料件转内销
0654	进料深加工	进料深加工结转货物
0657	进料余料结转	进料加工余料结转
0664	进料料件复出	进料加工复运出境的原进口料件
0700	进料料件退换	进料加工料件退换
0715	进料非对口	进料加工(非对口合同)
0744	进料成品减免	进料加工成品凭征免税证明转减免税
0815	低值辅料	低值辅料
0844	进料边角料内销	进料加工项下边角料转内销
0845	来料边角料内销	来料加工项下边角料内销
0864	进料边角料复出	进料加工项下边角料复出口
0865	来料边角料复出	来料加工项下边角料复出口
1039	市场采购	市场采购
1139	国轮油物料	中国籍运输工具境内添加的保税油料、物料
1200	保税间货物	海关保税场所及保税区域之间往来的货物
1210	保税电商	保税跨境贸易电子商务
1215	保税工厂	保税工厂
1233	保税仓库货物	保税仓库进出境货物
1234	保税区仓储转口	保税区进出境仓储转口货物
1239	保税电商 A	保税跨境贸易电子商务 A
1300	修理物品	进出境修理物品
1371	保税维修	保税维修
1427	出料加工	出料加工
1500	租赁不满 1 年	租期不满 1 年的租赁贸易货物
1523	租赁贸易	租期在 1 年及以上的租赁贸易货物
1616	寄售代销	寄售、代销贸易
1741	免税品	免税品
1831	外汇商品	免税外汇商品
2025	合资合作设备	合资合作企业作为投资进口设备物品
2210	对外投资	对外投资
2225	外资设备物品	外资企业作为投资进口的设备物品
2439	常驻机构公用	外国常驻机构进口办公用品
2600	暂时进出货物	暂时进出口货物
2700	展览品	进出境展览品
2939	陈列样品	驻华商业机构不复运出口的进口陈列样品
3010	货样广告品	进出口的货样广告品
3039	货样广告品 B(已废止)	无经营权单位进出口的货样广告品
3100	无代价抵偿	无代价抵偿进出口货物
3339	其他进出口免费	其他进出口免费提供货物
3410	承包工程进口	对外承包工程进口物资
3422	对外承包出口	对外承包工程出口物资
3511	援助物资	国家和国际组织无偿援助物资
3611	无偿军援	无偿军援
3612	捐赠物资	进出口捐赠物资
3910	军事装备	军事装备
4019	边境小额	边境小额贸易(边民互市贸易除外)

监管方式代码	监管方式简称	监管方式全称
4039	对台小额	对台小额贸易
4139	对台小额商品交易市场	进入对台小额商品交易专用市场的货物
4200	驻外机构运回	我驻外机构运回旧公用物品
4239	驻外机构购进	我驻外机构境外购买运回国的公务用品
4400	来料成品退换	来料加工成品退换
4500	直接退运	直接退运
4539	进口溢误卸	进口溢卸、误卸货物
4561	退运货物	因质量不符、延误交货等原因退运进出境货物
4600	进料成品退换	进料成品退换
5000	料件进出区	料件进出海关特殊监管区域
5010	特殊区域研发货物	海关特殊监管区域与境外之间进出的研发货物
5014	区内来料加工	海关特殊监管区域与境外之间进出的来料加工货物
5015	区内进料加工货物	海关特殊监管区域与境外之间进出的进料加工货物
5033	区内仓储货物	加工区内仓储企业从境外进口的货物
5034	区内物流货物	海关特殊监管区域与境外之间进出的物流货物
5100	成品进出区	成品进出海关特殊监管区域
5200	区内边角调出	用于区内外非实际进出境货物
5300	设备进出区	设备及物资进出海关特殊监管区域
5335	境外设备进区	海关特殊监管区域从境外进口的设备及物资
5361	区内设备退运	海关特殊监管区域设备及物资退运境外
6033	物流中心进出境货物	保税物流中心与境外之间进出仓储货物
9500	特许权使用费后续征税	特许权使用费后续征税
9600	内贸货物跨境运输	内贸货物跨境运输
9610	电子商务	跨境贸易电子商务
9639	海关处理货物	海关变卖处理的超期未报货物、走私违规货物
9700	后续补税	无原始报关单的后续补税
9710	跨境电商 B2B 直接出口	跨境电子商务企业对企业直接出口
9739	其他贸易	其他贸易
9800	租赁征税	租赁期 1 年及以上的租赁贸易货物的租金
9810	跨境电商出口海外仓	跨境电子商务出口海外仓
9839	留赠转卖物品	外交机构转售境内或国际活动留赠放弃特批货物
9900	其他	其他

监管方式代码表说明

进出口货物海关监管方式(以下简称“监管方式”),即现行进出口货物报关单“监管方式”,是以国际贸易中进出口货物的交易方式为基础,结合海关对进出口货物的征税、统计及监管条件综合设定的海关对进出口货物的管理方式。

由于海关对不同监管方式下进出口货物的监管、征税、统计作业的要求不尽相同,因此为满足海关管理的要求,H2010 通关管理系统的监管方式代码采用四位数字结构,其中前两位是按海关监管要求和计算机管理需要划分的分类代码,后二位为海关统计代码。

一般贸易

一、定义与代码

一般贸易是指我国境内有进出口经营权的企业单边进口或单边出口的贸易。

本监管方式代码为“0110”,简称“一般贸易”。

二、适用范围

(一)本监管方式包括:

1.以正常交易方式成交的进出口货物。

2.贷款援助的进出口货物。

3.外商投资企业进口供加工内销产品的料件。

4.外商投资企业用国产原材料加工成品出口或采购产品出口。

5.供应外国籍船舶、飞机等运输工具的国产燃料、物料及零配件。

6.保税仓库进口供应给中国籍国际航行运输工具使用的燃料、物料等保税货物。

7.境内企业在境外投资以实物投资带出的设备、物资。

8.来料养殖、来料种植的进出口货物。

(二)本监管方式不适用:

1.进出口货样广告品,监管方式为“货样广告品”(3010)。

2.没有对外贸易经营资格的单位获准临时进出口货物,监管方式为“其他贸易”(9739)。

3.境外劳务合作项目,对方以实物产品抵偿我劳务人员工资所进口的货物(如钢材、木材、化肥、海产品等),对外承包工程期间在国外获取及在境外购买的设备、物资等,监管方式为“承包工程进口”(3410)。

易货贸易

一、定义与代码

易货贸易是指不通过货币媒介而直接用出口货物交换进口货物的贸易。

本监管方式代码为“0130”,简称“易货贸易”。

二、适用范围

本监管方式仅适用于易货贸易经营企业在核准的范围内易货贸易的进出口货物。

本监管方式不适用

(一)对台小额贸易中签订易货合同的贸易,监管方式为“对台小额”(4039)。

(二)边境小额贸易企业易货贸易进出口货物,监管方式为“边境小额”(4019)。

旅游购物商品

一、定义与代码

旅游购物商品是指境外旅游者用自带外汇购买的或委托境内企业托运出境 5 万美元以下的旅游商品或小批量订货。

本监管方式代码为“0139”,简称“旅游购物商品”。

二、适用范围

以下情况不适用本监管方式:

(一)出口 5 万美元以上旅游购物商品。出口旅游商品 5 万美元以上的,有进出口经营权的企业,按“一般贸易”(0110)申报出口,没有进出口经营权的企业,按“其他贸易”(9739)申报出口。

(二)入境旅游者(包括外籍运输工具服务人员)自带出境用外汇购买的旅游纪念品、工艺品、中药材和中成药,由出境地海关旅检部门按照规定限值、限量办理。

料件销毁、边角料销毁

一、定义与代码

(一)料件销毁,监管方式代码“0200”,全称“加工贸易料件、残次品(折料)销毁”,简称“料件销毁”。

(二)边角料销毁,监管方式代码“0400”,全称“加工贸易边角料、副产品(按状态)销毁”,简称“边角料销毁”。

二、适用范围

(一)料件销毁适用于加工贸易企业因故无法内销或者退运而作销毁处置且未因处置获得收入的料件、残次品,其中残次品应按单耗折成料件。

(二)边角料销毁适用于加工贸易企业因故无法内销或者退运而作销毁处置且未因处置获得收入的边角料、副产品。

来料加工

一、定义与代码

来料加工是指进口料件由境外企业提供，经营企业不需要付汇进口，按照境外企业的要求进行加工或者装配，只收取加工费，制成品由境外企业销售的经营活动。

本监管方式代码“0214”，简称：来料加工。

二、适用范围

（一）本监管方式包括：

1.来料加工项下进口的料件和加工出口的成品。

2.设立保税工厂的加工贸易企业来料加工进口料件和出口成品。

（二）本监管方式不适用的情况：

1.国营企业代理来料加工企业进口加工生产用柴油，监管方式为“加工专用油”（0314）。

2.由特定企业以加工贸易进口原油加工成品油，不返销出境，供应国内市场的，监管方式为“进料以产顶进”（0642）。

3.进口5000美元以下的78种列名辅料，监管方式为“低值辅料”（0815）。

加工贸易保税货物深加工结转

一、定义与代码

加工贸易保税货物深加工结转是指来料加工、进料加工经营企业将保税进口料件加工的产品不直接出口，在境内结转给另一个加工贸易企业再加工后复出口。

来料深加工结转货物监管方式代码“0255”，简称“来料深加工”。

进料深加工结转货物监管方式代码“0654”，简称“进料深加工”。

二、适用范围

（一）本监管方式适用：

1.非海关特殊监管区域加工贸易经营企业之间来料、进料深加工货物结转。

2.非海关特殊监管区域加工贸易经营企业转自海关特殊监管区域加工贸易经营企业加工的货物。

（二）本监管方式不适用：

1.保税区、保税物流园区等海关特殊监管区域之间结转的货物，监管方式为“保税间货物”（1200）。

2.出口加工区企业生产的产品结转至其他出口加工区或非海关特殊监管区域加工复出口，加工区企业转出、转入报关单监管方式为“成品进出区”（5100）。

3.经营企业进料加工产品转给享受减免税优惠的企业，监管方式为“进料成品转减免”（0744）。

加工贸易余料结转

加工贸易余料结转是指加工贸易企业在经营来料加工、进料加工的加工复出口业务过程中剩余的、可以继续用于加工制成品的加工贸易进口料件，结转到同一经营单位、同一加工企业、同样进口料件和同一加工监管方式的另一个加工贸易合同项下继续加工复出口。

来料余料结转监管方式代码“0258”，简称“来料余料结转”。

进料余料结转监管方式代码“0657”，简称“进料余料结转”。

加工贸易料件复出

一、定义与代码

加工贸易料件复出是指来料加工、进料加工进口的保税料件因品质、规格等原因退运，以及加工过程中产生的剩余料件、边角料、废料退运出境。

来料加工料件复出监管方式代码“0265”，简称“来料料件复出”。

来料加工边角料复出监管方式代码“0865”，简称“来料边角料复出”。

进料加工料件复出监管方式代码“0664”，简称“进料料件复出”。

进料加工边角料复出监管方式代码“0864”，简称“进料边角料复出”。

二、适用范围

（一）加工贸易料件复出适用：

1.来料加工、进料加工进口的保税料件因品质、规格等原因退运，以及加工过程中产生的剩余料件、边角料、废料退运出境。

2.经营企业因加工贸易出口产品售后服务需要，申请出口加工贸易手册项下进口的保税料件。

（二）本监管方式不适用：

加工贸易进口料件、剩余料件及边角料、废料复运出境后更换同类货物进口，监管方式为“来料料件退换”（0300）、“进料料件退换”（0700）。

加工贸易货物退换

一、定义与代码

（一）加工贸易料件退换

加工贸易料件退换是指来料、进料加工进口的保税料件因品质、规格等原因退运出境，更换料件复进口。

来料加工料件退换监管方式代码“0300”，简称“来料料件退换”。

进料加工料件退换监管方式代码“0700”，简称“进料料件退换”。

（二）加工贸易成品退换

加工贸易成品退换是指来料、进料加工出口的成品因品质、规格或其他原因退运进境，经加工、维修或更换同类商品复出口。

来料加工成品退换监管方式代码“4400”，简称“来料成品退换”。

进料加工成品退换监管方式代码“4600”，简称“进料成品退换”。

二、适用范围

该监管方式不适用于来料加工、进料加工过程中产生的剩余料件、边角料、废料退运出境，以及进口料件因品质、规格等原因退运出境且不再更换同类货物进境。

这几类货物分别适用以下监管方式：来料料件复出（0265）、来料边角料复出（0865）、进料料件复出（0664）、进料边角料复出（0864）。

加工贸易保税货物转内销

包括以下监管方式：来料料件内销（0245）、来料成品减免（0345）、进料料件内销（0644）、进料成品减免（0744）、进料边角料内销（0844）、来料边角料内销（0845）。

一、定义与代码

（一）加工贸易保税料件转内销是指经营企业来料、进料加工过程中产生的剩余料件或用剩余料件生产的制成品、半成品、残次品以及受灾保税货物，经批准转为国内销售，不再加工复出口，包括海关事后发现有关企业擅自转内销并准予补办进口手续的货物。

来料加工料件转内销监管方式代码“0245”，简称“来料料件内销”。

进料加工料件转内销监管方式代码“0644”，简称“进料料件内销”。

（二）加工贸易保税货物减免是指来料、进料加工成品在境内销售给凭征免税证明进口货物的企业。

来料加工成品转减免监管方式代码“0345”，简称“来料成品转减免”。

进料加工成品转减免监管方式代码“0744”，简称“进料成品转减免”。

（三）加工贸易边角料内销是指经批准在境内销售的来料、进料加工过程中有形损耗产生的、仍有商业价值的边角料，包括来料、进料加工副产品。

来料加工边角料转内销监管方式代码“0845”，简称“来料边角料内销”。

进料加工边角料转内销监管方式代码“0844”，简称“进料边角料内销”。

二、适用范围

（一）加工贸易保税货物内销监管方式适用于边角料、剩余料件、残次品、副产品和受灾保税货物。

1.边角料，是指加工贸易企业经营来料加工、进料加工业务，在海关核定的单耗内、加工过程中产生的、无法再用于加工该合同项下出口制成品的数量合理的废、碎及下脚料件。

2.剩余料件，是指加工贸易企业在经营业务过程中剩余的、可以继续用于加工制成品的加工贸易进口料件。

3.残次品，是指加工贸易企业经营来料加工、进料加工业务，在生产过程中产生的有严重缺陷或者达不到出口合同标准，无法复出口的制品（包括完成品和未完成品）。

4.副产品，是指加工贸易企业经营来料加工、进料加工业务，在加工生产出口合同规定的制成品（即主产品）过程中同时产生的且出口合同未规定应当复出口的一个或者一个以上的其他产品。

5.受灾保税货物，是指加工贸易企业经营业务过程中，因不可抗力原因或者其他经海关审核认可的正当理由造成灭失、短少、损毁等导致无法复出口的保税进口料件和制品。

（二）以下情况不适用加工贸易保税货物转内销的监管方式：

1.特定企业以加工贸易的方式进口原油炼制成品油，不返销出境而供应国内市场，监管方式为"进料以产顶进"（0642）。

2.保税区、出口加工区加工贸易转内销货物，监管方式为"保区进料料件"（0544）、"保区来料料件"（0545）。

3.企业擅自内销加工贸易保税货物，按走私或违规处理的。

加工专用油

加工专用油是指指定国营贸易企业代理来料加工企业进口来料加工生产用柴油。

本监管方式代码"0314"，简称"加工专用油"。

加工贸易设备

包括以下监管方式：不作价设备（0320）、加工贸易设备（0420）、加工设备内销（0446）、加工设备结转（0456）、加工设备退运（0466）。

一、定义与代码

（一）外商提供的加工贸易不作价设备是指境外企业与境内企业开展来料、进料加工业务，外商免费向境内加工贸易经营单位提供加工生产所需设备，境内经营单位不需支付外汇、不需用加工费或差价偿还。

外商提供的加工贸易不作价设备监管方式代码"0320"，简称"不作价设备"。

（二）加工贸易设备是指来料加工、进料加工贸易项下外商作价提供、不扣减企业投资总额的进口设备。

加工贸易设备监管方式代码"0420"，简称"加工贸易设备"。

（三）加工贸易设备转内销是指在海关监管期内的加工贸易免税进口设备经批准转售给境内非加工贸易企业。

加工贸易设备转内销监管方式代码"0446"，简称"加工设备内销"。

（四）加工贸易设备结转是指海关监管期内的加工贸易免税进口设备经批准转让给另一加工企业，或从本企业一本《加工贸易手册》结转入另一本《加工贸易手册》。

加工贸易设备结转监管方式代码"0456"，简称"加工设备结转"。

（五）加工贸易设备退运是指加工贸易免税进口设备退运出境。

加工贸易设备退运监管方式代码"0466"，简称"加工设备退运"。

二、适用范围

以下情况不适用本监管方式：

（一）暂时进口（期限在半年以内）加工贸易生产所需不作价设备（限模具、单台设备），按暂时进口货物办理。

（二）外商投资企业投资总额内资金进口的设备，监管方式"合资合作设备"（2025）、"外资设备物品"（2225）。

（三）外商投资企业自有资金（投资总额以外）进口设备，监管方式"一般贸易"（0110）。

（四）出口加工区的设备进口、退运及结转，分别适用"境外设备进区"（代码 5335）、"区内设备退运"（代码 5361）和"设备进出区"（代码 5300）。

监管年限内减免税设备结转

一、定义与代码

监管年限内减免税设备结转是指进口企业在减免税设备监管年限内转让给另一享受减免税待遇的企业。

本监管方式代码"0500"，简称"减免设备结转"。

二、适用范围

本监管方式不适用于加工贸易项下进口设备结转给另一加工贸易企业，监管方式为"加工设备结转"（0456）。

保税区加工贸易内销货物

保税区进料加工、来料加工的加工成品不复运出境，转为国内使用，按征税方式区分，适用以下监管方式：

一、区内加工企业来料、进料加工全部用境外运入料件加工的制成品销往非保税区，以及来料、进料加工内销制成品所含进口料件的品名、数量、价值难以区分的，按照制成品征税，监管方式为：

（一）按成品征税的保税区来料加工成品转内销货物，监管方式代码"0445"，简称"保区来料成品"。

（二）按成品征税的保税区进料加工成品转内销货物，监管方式代码"0444"，简称"保区进料成品"。

二、区内企业来料、进料加工用含有部分境外运入料件加工的制成品销往非保税区时，对其制成品按照所含进口料件征税，其监管方式为：

（一）按料件征税的保税区来料加工成品转内销货物，监管方式代码"0545"，简称"保区来料料件"。

（二）按料件征税的保税区进料加工成品转内销货物，监管方式代码"0544"，简称"保区进料料件"。

补偿贸易

一、定义与代码

补偿贸易是指由境外厂商提供或者利用国外出口信贷进口生产技术或设备，我方企业（包括外商投资企业）进行生产，以返销其产品的方式分期偿还对方技术、设备价款或贷款本息的交易方式。包括经经贸主管部门批准，使用该企业（包括企业联合体）所生产的其他产品返销给对方，进行间接补偿。

补偿贸易偿还对方技术、设备价款或贷款本息的方式一般有两种：

（一）产品出口先偿还设备价款，还清本息后再出口收汇。

（二）设备价款本息在每批出口货物价款中扣还一部分，直到还清为止。

本监管方式代码"0513"，简称"补偿贸易"。

二、适用范围

本监管方式包括补偿贸易中对方有偿或免费提供的机器设备、模具等。

本监管方式不包括：

（一）直接用国内产品同国外厂商交换设备、料件或成品，以货换货，监管方式为"易货贸易"（0130）。

（二）出口产品收取外汇，监管方式为"一般贸易"（0110）。

（三）在补偿贸易合同中同时订有来料加工合同的，来料加工合同部分，监管方式为"来料加工"（0214）。

进料加工贸易

一、定义与代码

进料加工贸易，是指进口料件由经营企业付汇进口，制成品由经营企业外销出口的经营活动。

进料加工贸易按照对外签约形式分为"进料加工非对口合同"和"进料加工对口合同"。

进料加工非对口合同是指我方有外贸进出口经营权的企业动用外汇购买进口原料、材料、元器件、零部件、配套件和包装物料（以下简称料件），加工成品或半成品再返销出口的交易形式。

本监管方式代码"0715"，简称"进料非对口"。

进料加工对口合同是指买卖双方分别签订进出口对口合同，料件进口时，我方先付料件款，加工成品出口时再向对方收取出口成品款项的交易形式，包括动用外汇的对口合同或不同客户的对口的联号合同以及对开信用证的对口合同。

本监管方式代码"0615"，简称"进料对口"。

境外客户为境内企业加工复出口产品提供进口 5000 美元及以下、数量零星的辅料或包装物料，以及数量合理直接用于服装生产车间的小型易耗性生产工具。

本监管方式代码"0815"，简称"低值辅料"。

二、适用范围

（一）本监管方式包括：

1.进料加工项下进口料件和加工出口产品。

2.设立保税工厂的加工贸易企业进料加工进口料件和出口成品。

（二）本监管方式不适用出口加工区加工贸易进出口货物，其监管方式为"区内进料加工货物"（5015）。

加工贸易成品油以产顶进

加工贸易成品油以产顶进是指特定企业以加工贸易形式进口原油，加工供国内市场的成品油。

本监管方式代码"0642"，简称"进料以产顶进"。

市场采购

一、定义与代码

市场采购贸易方式是指由符合条件的经营者在经国家商务主

管等部门认定的市场集聚区内采购的，单票报关单商品在15万（含15万）美元以下，并在采购地办理出口商品通关手续的贸易方式。

本监管方式代码“1039”，简称“市场采购”。

二、适用范围

以下出口商品不适用市场采购贸易方式：

（一）国家禁止、限制出口的商品；

（二）未在经认定的市场聚集区内采购的商品；

（三）未经市场采购商品认定体系确认的商品；

（四）使用现金结算的商品；

（五）贸易管制主管部门确定的不适用市场采购贸易方式的商品。

国轮油物料

一、定义与代码

国轮油物料指中国籍国际航行的运输工具在境内添加的保税仓库进口仓储的油料、物料。

本监管方式代码“1139”，简称“国轮油物料”。

二、适用范围

本监管方式适用于从保税仓库提取，供应航行国际航线的中国籍船舶、民用航空器等运输工具的进口燃料、物料及零配件等。

本监管方式不适用从设在非海关特殊监管区域的保税仓库提取，供应航行国际航线的外国籍船舶、飞机等运输工具的进口燃料、物料，监管方式为“保税仓库货物”（1233）。

保税区间及保税仓库间货物结转

一、定义与代码

保税区间及保税仓库间货物结转是指保税区、保税物流园区、出口加工区、出口监管仓库、保税仓库、保税物流中心（A、B型）等海关特殊监管区域、保税监管场所间往来的货物。

本监管方式代码“1200”，简称“保税间货物”。

二、适用范围

本监管方式不适用出口加工区间结转货物，不同出口加工区企业结转货物适用“成品进出区”（5100）和“料件进出区”（5000）。

网购保税

一、定义与代码

网购保税，监管方式代码“1210”，全称“跨境电子商务网购保税”，简称“网购保税”。

二、适用范围

本监管方式适用于境内个人或电子商务企业在经海关认可的电子商务平台实现跨境交易，并通过海关特殊监管区域或保税监管场所进出的电子商务零售进出境商品[（海关特殊监管区域、保税监管场所与境内区外（场所外）之间通过电子商务平台交易的零售进出口商品不适用该监管方式）]。

保税仓库进出境仓储、转口货物

一、定义与代码

保税仓库进出境仓储及转口货物，指从境外进口直接存入保税仓库、保税仓库出境的仓储、转口货物，以及出口监管仓库出境的货物。

本监管方式代码“1233”，简称“保税仓库货物”。

二、适用范围

（一）本监管方式适用于经批准设立的保税仓库进出境和出口监管仓库的出境货物。包括从保税仓库提取用于外国籍国际航行运输工具的物料。

（二）不适用本监管方式的情况：

1.保税仓库、出口监管仓库进口自用的货架、办公用品、管理用具、运输车辆、搬运、起重和包装设备以及改装用的机器等，其监管方式为“一般贸易”（0110）。

2.从保税仓库提取用于本国籍运输工具或用于维修境内设备的仓储货物，按进口申报，其监管方式为“一般贸易”（0110）。

3.保税仓库进境货物销往境内，按货物运出保税仓库的实际用途填报相应的监管方式。

4.境内存入出口监管仓库和出口监管仓库的退仓货物，分各种监管方式。

5.保税区、保税物流中心进出境仓储、转口货物，其监管方式分别为“保税区仓储转口”（1234）、“物流中心进出境货物”（6033）。

6.保税仓库货物出仓运往境内其他地方转为正式进口的，在仓库主管海关办结出仓报关手续，填制出口报关单，监管方式填写“1200”，进口报关单按实际进口监管方式填报。

7.保税仓库寄售维修零部件申请免税出仓的，进口报关单贸易方式应为“无代价抵偿货物”（“3100”）。

保税区进出境仓储、转口货物

一、定义与代码

保税区进出境仓储、转口货物是指从境外存入保税区、保税物流园区和从保税区、保税物流园区运出境的仓储、转口货物。

本监管方式代码为“1234”，简称“保税区仓储转口”。

二、适用范围

下列情况不适用本监管方式：

（一）保税区、保税物流园区除仓储、转口货物以外的其他进出境货物，按实际监管方式填报。

（二）从境内非海关特殊监管区域、保税监管场所运入保税区、保税物流园区的货物，按实际监管方式填报。

从境内非海关特殊监管区域、保税监管场所运人保税区、保税物流园区的货物退回境内，按实际监管方式填报。

（三）从保税区、保税物流园区运往境内非海关特殊监管区域、保税监管场所的货物，按实际监管方式填报。

网购保税A

一、定义与代码

网购保税A，监管方式代码“1239”，全称“跨境电子商务网购保税A”，简称“网购保税A”。

二、适用范围

本监管方式适用于境内电子商务企业通过海关特殊监管区域或保税物流中心（B型）一线进境的跨境电子商务零售进口商品。

寄售代销贸易

一、定义与代码

寄售代销贸易是指寄售人把货物运交事先约定的代销人，由代销人按照事先约定或根据寄售代销协议规定的条件，在当地市场代为销售，所得货款扣除代销人的佣金和其他费用后，按协议规定方式将余款付给寄售人的交易形式。寄售人与代销人之间不是买卖关系，而是委托关系，代销人对货物没有所有权。

本监管方式代码为“1616”，简称“寄售代销”。

二、适用范围

本监管方式包括寄售代销贸易进出口的货物及进口寄售货物的增发部分。

本监管方式不包括：

委托我驻港澳机构代销的鲜活商品，其监管方式应为“一般贸易”（0110）。

进出境修理物品

一、定义与代码

进出境修理物品是指进境或出境维护修理的货物、物品。

本监管方式代码“1300”，简称“修理物品”。

二、适用范围

本监管方式适用于各类进出境维修的货物，以及修理货物维修所用的原材料、零部件。

以下情况不适用本监管方式：

（一）按加工贸易保税货物管理的进境维修业务。

（二）加工贸易进口料件和出口成品进出境维修，分别适用来料料件退换（0300）、来料成品退换（4400）、进料料件退换（0700）、进料成品退换（4600）。

出料加工贸易

一、定义及代码

出料加工贸易是指境内企业将境内原辅料、零部件、元器件或半成品交由境外厂商按我方要求进行加工或装配，成品复运进口，我方支付加工费的交易方式。

本监管方式代码为“1427”，简称“出料加工”。

二、适用范围

本监管方式不包括：

（一）运往境外维修的货物，以及石化生产过程中所需催化剂需运至国外添加氢以增加活性后复运进境继续投入生产使用，不改变其物理和化学性质，未产生新的产品，监管方式为“修理物品”

(1300)。

(二)出料加工,原则上不改变原出口货物的物理形态。对完全改变原出口货物的物理形态如出口废钢进口钢材,出口废铝进口铝合金板材等,不属出料加工,应按一般贸易货物办理进出口手续。

租赁贸易

一、定义及代码

租赁贸易是指经营租赁业务的企业与外商签订国际租赁合同项下境内企业租赁进口或出租出口的货物。

赁期在1年及以上的进出口货物,监管方式代码为"1523",简称"租赁贸易"。

租赁期在1年及以上的进出口货物分期办理征税手续时,每期征税适用监管方式代码为"9800",简称"租赁征税"。

租赁期不满1年的进出口货物,监管方式代码为"1500",简称"租赁不满1年"。

二、适用范围

以下情况不适用本监管方式:

(一)经营租赁业务的企业进口自用的设备、办公用品,监管方式为"一般贸易"(0110)。

(二)加工贸易租赁进口的机器设备,监管方式应为"加工贸易设备"(0420)。

(三)补偿贸易租借进口的货物,其监管方式应为"补偿贸易"(0513)。

(四)"租赁贸易"(1523)期满复运出(进)口的货物,监管方式为"退运货物"(4561);"租赁不满1年"(1500)期满复运出(进)境的货物,监管方式为"租赁不满1年"(1500)。

免税品

一、定义及代码

免税品是指设在国际机场、港口、车站和过境口岸的免税品商店进口,按有关规定销售给办完出境手续的旅客的免税商品,供外国籍船员和我国远洋船员购买送货上船出售的免税商品,供外交人员购买的免税品,以及在我国际航机,国际班轮上向国际旅客出售的免税商品。

本监管方式代码"1741",简称"免税品"。

二、适用范围

(一)本监管方式适用于:

1.范围:进出境口岸免税店、运输工具免税店、市内免税店、外交人员免税店和供船免税店等五类免税店进口核定品种的免税品。

2.供应对象:办结出境手续的出境旅客、国际航行运输工具服务人员、外交人员。

(二)本监管方式不适用:

1.境内免税外汇商店销售给为我出国人员、华侨的免税外汇商品,监管方式为"外汇商品"(1831)。

2.经营免税品业务的单位进口的供维修使用的零部件、工具、展台、货架,监管方式为"一般贸易"(0110)。

3.免税品退运出境,监管方式为"其他"(9900)。

免税外汇商品

一、定义及代码

免税外汇商品是指由经批准的经营单位进口,销售专供人境的我国特定出国人员和驻华外交人员的免税外汇商品。

本监管方式代码"1831",简称"外汇商品"。

二、适用范围

(一)本监管方式适用:

1.免税外汇商品供应对象是指我国驻外外交机构人员、留学人员、访问学者、赴境外劳务人员、援外人员和远洋船员。

2.上述人员用结存外汇在境内免税外汇商品店购买限定品种的免税外汇商品。

3.专供外国驻华外交人员免税商品的特定公司进口的免税外汇商品。

(二)本监管方式不适用:

1.设在国际机场、港口、车站和过境口岸的免税品商店所进口的,按有关规定销售给办结出境手续的旅客的免税商品,供外国籍船员和我国远洋船员购买送货上船出售的免税商品,供外交人员购买的免税品,以及在我国际航机,国际班轮上向国际旅客出售的免税商品。监管方式为"免税品"(1741)。

2.经营免税外汇商品的单位进口供商品维修用的零部件、工具和商场自用的货架、手推车等。监管方式为"一般贸易"(0110)。

3.因故经批准转内销进口免税外汇商品,监管方式为"一般贸易"(0110)。

4.免税外汇商品退运出境,监管方式为"退运货物"(4561)。

外商投资企业作为投资进口的设备、物品

一、定义及代码

外商投资企业作为投资进口的设备、物品是指外商投资企业投资总额内的资金(包括中方投资)进口的机器设备、零部件和其他建厂(场)物料,安装、加固机器所需材料,以及进口本企业自用合理数量的交通工具、生产用车辆、办公用品(设备)(以下简称"设备物品")。

中外合资、合作企业进口设备、物品,监管方式代码"2025",简称"合资合作设备"。外商独资企业(以下简称"外资企业")进口设备、物品,监管方式代码为"2225",简称"外资设备物品"。

二、适用范围

(一)外商投资企业是指中外合资企业、中外合作企业、外商独资企业,包括华侨、港、澳、台同胞投资企业。

(二)"设备"是指外商投资企业在其投资总额内进口本企业自用的机器设备、零部件和其他物料[指建厂(场)以及安装、加固机器所需材料]及生产用车辆。

(三)"物品"是指外商投资企业进口自用合理数量的办公用品(设备)和交通工具。

(四)下列情况不适用本监管方式:

1.鼓励类和限制类外商投资企业、外商投资研究开发中心、先进技术型和产品出口型外商投资企业,以及符合中西部省、自治区、直辖市利用外资优势产业和优势项目目录的项目、企业自有资金(投资总额以外,具体是指企业储备基金、发展基金、折旧和税后利润),在原批准的生产经营范围内,对设备进行更新维修,进口国内不能生产或性能不能满足需要的自用设备及其配套的技术、配件、备件,监管方式为"一般贸易"(0110)。

2.外商投资企业经营来料加工、进料加工、租赁贸易等进口的设备物品,分别适用"不作价设备"(0320)、"加工贸易设备"(0420)、"租赁不满1年"(1500)、"租赁贸易"(1523)。

3.外国常驻机构进口自用合理数量的公用物品,监管方式为"常驻机构公用"(2439)。

4.没有实际进出境,在境内结转的减免税设备,监管方式为"减免设备结转"(0500)。

对外投资

一、定义与代码

对外投资,监管方式代码"2210",简称"对外投资"。

二、适用范围

本监管方式适用于境内企业在境外投资,以实物投资出口的设备、物资。

退运货物

一、定义及代码

退运货物是指原进出口货物因残损、短少、品质不良或者规格不符、延误交货或其他原因退运出、进境的货物。

本监管方式代码"4561",简称"退运货物"。

二、适用范围

(一)本监管方式适用以下监管方式进出口货物退运出进境:

代码	名称	代码	名称
0110	一般贸易	3339	其他进出口免费
0130	易货贸易	3410	承包工程进口
0139	旅游购物商品	3422	对外承包出口
1523	租赁贸易	3511	无偿援助
1616	寄售代销	3612	捐赠物资
2025	合资合作企业设备物品	4019	边境小额
2225	外资企业设备物品	4039	对台小额
1831	外汇免税商品	9739	其他贸易
3010	货样广告品		

(二)本监管方式不适用:

1.货物进境后、放行结关前退运的货物,监管方式为"直接退运"(4500)。

2.加工贸易进出口货物退运，监管方式为“来料料件退换”(0300)、“进料料件退换”(0700)、“来料成品退换”(4400)、“进料成品退换”(4600)。

3.加工贸易设备退运，监管方式为“加工设备退运”(0466)。

4.“租赁不满1年”(1500)、“免税品”(1741)退运出境，监管方式为“其他”(9900)。

5.出口加工区进口设备退运出境，监管方式为“区内设备退运”(5361)。

6.进出口无代价抵偿货物，被更换的原进口货物退运出境，监管方式为“其他”(9900)。

外国常驻机构进出境公用物品

一、定义及代码

外国常驻机构进出境公用物品是指境外(地区)企业、新闻机构、经贸机构、文化团体及其他境外(地区)法人经我国政府主管部门批准，在境内设立的常驻代表机构为开展公务活动所需进出境的物品。

本监管方式代码“2439”，简称“常驻机构公用”。

二、适用范围

(一)本监管方式包括常驻机构进境自用且数量合理的办公用机器设备、家具、文具、机动车辆等及复运出境的原进境的公用物品。

(二)本监管方式适用于以下机构：

1.外国企业和其他经济组织常驻机构。

2.外国民间经济贸易团体常驻机构。

3.外国常驻新闻机构。

4.其他外国常驻机构。

5.华侨、港澳同胞、台湾同胞经营的企业常驻机构。

(三)下列监管业务不适用本监管方式：

1.外国驻中国使馆、领馆，联合国及其专门机构，以及其他与中国政府签有协议的国际组织驻中国代表机构进出境物品填报“外国使领馆公私用物品进出境申报单”。

2.外国人员子女学校进出境物品，监管方式为“其他贸易”(9739)。

3.常驻机构人员进境自用的汽车，监管方式为“其他贸易”(9739)。

4.外国驻华使、领馆在我国内购运出境的货物，监管方式为“其他”(9900)。

5.暂时进出境的公用物品，监管方式为“暂时进出口”(2600)。

暂时进出境货物

一、定义及代码

暂时进出境货物是指经海关批准，暂时进出关境并且在规定的期限内复运出境、进境的货物。

本监管方式代码“2600”，简称“暂时进出货物”。

二、适用范围

(一)本监管方式包括：

1.文化、体育交流活动中使用的表演、比赛用品。

2.进行新闻报道或者摄制电影、电视节目使用的仪器、设备及用品。

3.开展科研、教学、医疗活动使用的仪器、设备及用品。

4.在本款第1至第3项所列活动中使用的交通工具及特种车辆。

5.货样。

6.慈善活动使用的仪器、设备及用品。

7.供安装、调试、检测、修理设备时使用的仪器及工具。

8.盛装货物的容器。

9.旅游用自驾交通工具及其用品。

10.工程施工中使用的设备、仪器及其用品。

11.海关批准的其他暂时进出境货物。

(二)以下情况不适用本监管方式：

1.进出境展览品，监管方式为“展览品”(2700)；

2.驻华商业机构不复运出口的进口陈列样品，监管方式为“陈列样品”(2939)；

3.对外承包工程出口物资，监管方式为“对外承包出口”(3422)；

4.进出境修理物品，监管方式为“修理物品”(1300)；

5.租赁贸易进出口货物，其监管方式为“租期不满1年”(1500)、“租赁贸易”(1523)；

6.企业使用旧钢瓶容器进口燃料、物料，按进口燃料、物料的监管方式申报，报关单“包装种类”栏目填报“旧钢瓶”。

7.从境外暂时进境的货物转入保税区、出口加工区等海关特殊监管区域和保税监管场所的，不属于复运出境。

8.用于装载海关监管货物的进出境集装箱。

9.享有外交特权和豁免的外国驻华机构或者人员暂时进出境物品。

进出境展览品

一、定义及代码

进出境展览品是指外国来华或我国为到国外举办经济、文化、科技等展览或参加博览会而进出口的展览品及展览品有关的宣传品、布置品、招待品、小卖品和其他物品。

本监管方式代码“2700”，简称“展览品”。

二、适用范围

(一)进出境展览品主要包括：

1.在展览会、交易会、会议及类似活动中展示或者使用的货物，包括：

(1)为了示范展览会展出机器或者器具所使用的货物；

(2)设置临时展台的建筑材料及装饰材料；

(3)宣传展示货物的电影片、幻灯片、录像带、录音带、说明书、广告、光盘、显示器材等。

2.上述所列活动中使用的交通工具及特种车辆。

3.其它经海关批准用于展示的进出境货物、物品。

(二)以下情况不适用本监管方式：

1.ATA单证册项下的暂准进出口展览品，持证人免填报关单。

2.不复运出(进)境而留在国内(外)销售的进出境展览品，按实际监管方式填报。

3.在商店或者其他营业场所以销售国外货物为目的而组织的非公共展览。

货样、广告品

一、定义及代码

货样广告品，监管方式代码“3010”，全称“进出口的货样广告品”，简称“货样广告品”。

二、适用范围

本监管方式适用于有进出口经营权的单位进出口货样广告品。暂时进出口的货样、广告品和驻华商业机构不复运出口的进口陈列样品不适用本监管方式。

无代价抵偿进出口货物

一、定义及代码

无代价抵偿货物是指进出口货物海关放行后，因残损、短少、品质不良或者规格不符原因，由进出口货物的发货人、承运人或保险公司免费补偿或更换的与原货物相同或者与合同规定相符的货物。

本监管方式代码“3100”，简称“无代价抵偿”。

二、适用范围

下列情况不适用本监管方式：

(一)来料加工、进料加工贸易进口料件和出口成品因残损、短少、品质不良或者规格不符原因，由进出口货物的发货人、承运人或保险公司免费补偿或更换的与原货物相同或者与合同规定相符的货物，分别适用具体列名的料件或成品退换的监管方式。

(二)与无代价抵偿进出口货物相关的原进出口货物退运出、进境，监管方式为“其他”(9900)。

其他免费提供的进出口货物

一、定义及代码

其他免费提供货物指除已具体列名的礼品、无偿援助和赠送物资、捐赠物资、无代价抵偿进口货物、国外免费提供的货样、广告品等及归入列名监管方式的免费提供货物以外，进出口其他免费提供的货物。

本监管方式代码“3339”，简称“其他进出口免费”。

二、适用范围

(一)本监管方式包括：

1.外商在经贸活动中赠送的物品。

2.外国人捐赠品。

3.驻外中资机构向国内单位赠送的物资。

4.经贸活动中，由外商免费提供的试车材料、消耗性物品等。

(二)下列情况不适用本监管方式：

1.保税仓库中由外商免费提供进口的机械设备、手工工具、运输工具、办公用品等，监管方式为“其他贸易”(9739)。

2.免税店由外商免费提供进口的货架、柜台、手推车等，监管方式为“其他贸易”(9739)。

3.来料加工、进料加工贸易项下外商免费提供的机械设备，监管方式为“不作价设备”(0320)。

4.国家和国际组织无偿援助物资，监管方式为“援助物资”(3511)。

5.捐赠物资，监管方式为“捐赠物资”(3612)。

6.无代价抵偿进出口货物，监管方式为“无代价抵偿”(3100)。

对外承包工程进出口物资

一、定义及代码

对外承包工程出口物资是指经商务部批准的有对外承包工程经营权的公司为承包国外建设工程和开展劳务合作等对外合作项目而出口的设备、物资。

承包工程出口物资监管方式代码“3422”，简称“对外承包出口”。

对外承包工程进口物资是指承包工程期间在国外获取的设备、物资，以及境外劳务合作项目对方以实物产品抵偿我劳务人员工资所进口的货物。

监管方式代码“3410”，简称“承包工程进口”。

二、适用范围

(一)本监管方式不包括我劳务人员带出的自用生活物资，监管方式为“其他”(9900)。

(二)援外成套项目出口的货物应根据无偿援助或贷款援助，监管方式代码分别选用“援助物资”(3511)或“一般贸易”(0110)。

(三)边境地区有对外经济技术合作经营权的企业与毗邻国家边境地区开展承包工程和劳务合作项下出口的工程设备、物资(包括在外购买及换回的)运回境内时，其监管方式代码为“边境小额”(4019)。

(四)承包工程结束后复运进境原从国内运出的承包工程项下的设备、物资，其监管方式为“退运货物”(4561)。

国家或国际组织无偿援助和赠送的物资

一、定义及代码

国家或国际组织无偿援助和赠送的物资是指我国根据两国政府间的协议或临时决定，对外提供无偿援助的物资、捐赠品，或我国政府、组织基于友好关系向对方国家政府、组织赠送的物资，以及我国政府、组织接受国际组织、外国政府、组织无偿援助、捐赠或赠送的物资。

本监管方式代码“3511”，简称“援助物资”。

二、适用范围

(一)有关名词：

外国政府，是指外国国家的中央政府。

国际组织，是指联合国各专门机构，以及长期与我国有合作关系的其他国际组织。

国际条约，是指依据《中华人民共和国缔结条约程序法》以“中华人民共和国”、“中华人民共和国政府”以及“中华人民共和国政府部门”名义同外国缔结协定或协议以及参加的国际条约。

(二)以下情况不适用本监管方式：

1.贷款援助的进出口货物(包括我方利用贷款或援助款项自行采购进口的货物)，监管方式为“一般贸易”(0110)。

2.来(出)访的团体和人员相互馈赠的礼品，监管方式为“其他”(9900)。

3.经济贸易往来关系赠送的物资，监管方式为“其他进出口免费”(3339)。

4.随援外物资一并出口或另外发运的批量出口的生活物资，应按照“其他贸易”(9739)报关。

5.以扶贫、慈善、救灾为目的，向我国境内或向境外捐赠的直接用于扶贫、救灾、兴办公益福利事业的物资，监管方式为“捐赠物资”(3612)。

进出口捐赠物资

一、定义及代码

进出口捐赠物资是指境外捐赠人以扶贫、慈善、救灾为目的，向我国境内捐赠的直接用于扶贫、救灾、兴办公益福利事业的物资，以及境内捐赠人以扶贫、慈善、救灾为目的，向境外捐赠的直接用于扶贫、救灾、兴办公益福利事业的物资。

本监管方式代码为“3612”，简称“捐赠物资”。

二、适用范围

(一)本监管方式适用范围：

1.捐赠人

(1)境外捐赠人包括华侨，港、澳、台同胞，外籍人，包括法人。

(2)境内捐赠人，包括法人。

2.扶贫、慈善公益性事业的物资

(1)新的衣服、被褥、鞋帽、帐篷、手套、睡袋、毛毯及其他维持基本生活的必需用品等。

(2)食品类及饮用品(调味品、水产品、水果、饮料、烟酒等除外)。

(3)医疗类，包括直接用于治疗特困患者疾病或贫困地区治疗地方病，以及基本医疗卫生、公共环境卫生所需的基本医疗药品、基本医疗器械、医疗书籍和资料。

(4)直接用于公共图书馆、公共博物馆、各类职业学校、高中、初中、小学、幼儿园教育的教学仪器、器材、图书、资料和一般学习用品。

(5)直接用于环境保护的专用仪器。

(6)经国务院批准的其他直接用于扶贫、慈善事业的物资。

3.受赠人和使用人

受赠人是指国务院有关部门和各省、自治区、直辖市人民政府，以及从事人道救助和发展扶贫、慈善事业为宗旨的全国性的社会团体。包括中国红十字会总会、全国妇女联合会、中国残疾人联合会、中华慈善总会、中国初级卫生保健基金会和宋庆龄基金会。

使用人(使用单位)是指捐赠物资的直接使用者或负责分配该捐赠物资的单位或个人。

(二)下列情况不适用本监管方式：

1.国家间、国际组织无偿援助和赠送的物资，监管方式为“援助物资”(3511)。

2.经贸往来中赠送的物品、外国人捐赠品、我驻外(包括驻港、澳)中资机构向国内单位赠送的物资等。监管方式为“其他进出口免费”(3339)。

边境小额贸易

一、定义及代码

边境小额贸易指我国沿陆地边境线经国家批准对外开放的边境县(旗)、边境城市辖区内(以下简称边境地区)，经批准有边境小额贸易经营权的企业，通过国家指定的陆地边境口岸，与毗邻国家边境地区的企业或其他贸易机构进行的贸易活动。

本监管方式代码“4019”，简称“边境小额”。

二、适用范围

(一)本监管方式包括：

1.边境地区有对外经济技术合作经营权的企业与我国毗邻国家边境地区以易货贸易、现汇贸易形式开展的边境小额贸易。

2.边境地区有对外经济技术合作经营权的企业与我国毗邻国家边境地区经济合作(工程承包、劳务输出)项下进出口物资及原出口工程设备、物资(包括在境外购买及换回的)运回境内。

(二)下列情况不适用本监管方式：

1.边民互市贸易(互市进口商品)，边民通过互市贸易进口的生活用品(列入边民互市进口商品不予免税清单的除外)，每人每日价值在人民币8000元以下的，免征进口关税和进口环节税，超过人民币8000元的，超出部分照章征税，监管方式为“其他贸易”(9739)。

2.未获准经营边境小额贸易的企业进出口货物。

3.对台湾居民同大陆对台小额贸易公司成交用台湾船只直接运进产自台湾的产品和运出大陆产品到台湾，监管方式为“对台小额”(4039)。

对台湾小额

一、定义及代码

对台湾小额贸易是指台湾地区居民与大陆经批准的企业依照有关规定进行的货物交易。

本监管方式代码“4039”，简称“对台小额”。

二、适用范围

本监管方式不适用于进入厦门大嶝对台小额商品交易市场的人员带出台湾产品，每人每日价值人民币6000元以下免征进口关税和进口环节税，超出部分照章征税，监管方式为“其他贸易”(9739)。

对台小额商品交易市场

一、定义及代码

对台小额商品交易市场是经国家批准设立,用于开展对台民间小额商品交易活动,并实行封闭管理的特定区域,以下简称"交易市场"。

本监管方式代码"4139",简称"对台小额商品交易市场"。

二、适用范围

本监管方式仅限于厦门大嶝对台小额商品交易市场。

下列情况不适用本监管方式:

(一)对台湾居民同大陆对台小额贸易公司成交用台湾船只直接运进产自台湾的产品和运出大陆产品到台湾,监管方式为"对台小额"(4039)。

(二)我国沿陆地边境线经国家批准对外开放的边境县(旗)、边境城市辖区内(以下简称边境地区)经批准有边境小额贸易经营权的企业,通过国家指定的陆地边境口岸,与毗邻国家边境地区的企业或其他贸易机构进行的贸易活动,监管方式为"边境小额"(4019)。

驻外机构运回旧公用物品

一、定义及代码

驻外机构运回旧公用物品是指我驻各国(地区)使、领馆,驻国外、港澳地区的经济、贸易机构,驻国际组织代表处等我驻外机构更新且闲置不用而运回或因机构撤销而运回的物品,包括临时出国展览团、考察团等运回的生产资料和公用物品。

本监管方式代码为"4200",简称"驻外机构运回"。

二、适用范围

本监管方式不适用暂时进出境公用物品。

直接退运货物

一、定义及代码

直接退运货物是指进口货物收发货人、原运输工具负责人或者其代理人(以下统称当事人)在有关货物进境后、办结海关放行手续前,因海关责令或有正当理由获准退运境外的货物。

本监管方式代码"4500",简称"直接退运"。

二、适用范围

(一)在货物进境后、办结海关放行手续前,有下列情形之一的,当事人可以向海关申请办理直接退运手续:

1.因国家贸易管理政策调整,收货人无法提供相关证件的;

2.属于错发、误卸或者溢卸货物,能够提供发货人或者承运人书面证明文书的;

3.收发货人双方协商一致同意退运,能够提供双方同意退运的书面证明文书的;

4.有关贸易发生纠纷,能够提供法院判决书、仲裁机构仲裁决定书或者无争议的有效货物所有权凭证的;

5.货物残损或者国家检验检疫不合格,能够提供国家检验检疫部门根据收货人申请而出具的相关检验证明文书的。

(二)在货物进境后、办结海关放行手续前,有下列情形之一依法应当退运的,由海关责令当事人将进口货物直接退运境外:

1.进口国家禁止进口的货物,经海关依法处理后的;

2.违反国家检验检疫政策法规,经国家检验检疫部门处理并且出具"检验检疫处理通知书"或者其他证明文书后的;

3.未经许可擅自进口属于限制进口的固体废物用作原料,经海关依法处理后的;

4.违反国家有关法律、行政法规,应当责令直接退运的其他情形。

(三)保税区、出口加工区及其他海关特殊监管区域和保税监管场所进口货物的直接退运。

(四)下列情况不适用本监管方式:

1.放行后的进口货物退运出境,其监管方式为"退运货物"(4561)。

2.进口转关货物在进境地海关放行后,当事人申请办理退运手续的,应当按照一般退运手续办理。

料件进出海关特殊监管区域

料件进出海关特殊监管区域适用于海关特殊监管区域内保税加工、保税物流或研发企业与境内(区外)之间进出的料件,包括此类料件在境内的退运、退换。

本监管方式代码"5000",简称"料件进出区"。

海关特殊监管区域与境外之间进出的研发货物

游关特殊监管区域与境外之间进出的研发货物适用于海关转殊监管区域内企业从境外购进的用于研发的料件、成品,或研发后将上述货物退回境外,但不包括企业自用或其他用途的设备。

本监管方式代码"5010",简称"特殊区域研发货物"。

海关特殊监管区域与境外之间进出的来料加工货物

海关特殊监管区域与境外之间进出的来料加工货物适用于海关特殊监管区域内企业在来料加工贸易业务项下的料件从境外进口及制成品出境。

本监管方式代码"5014",简称"区内来料加工"。

海关特殊监管区域与境外之间进出的进料加工货物

海关特殊监管区域与境外之间进出的进料加工货物适用于海关特殊监管区域区内企业在进料加工贸易业务项下的料件从境外进口及制成品出境。

本监管方式代码"5015",简称"区内进料加工货物"。

海关特殊监管区域与境外之间进出的物流货物

海关特殊监管区域与境外之间进出的物流货物适用于海关特殊监管区域内企业从境外运进或运往境外的仓储、分拨、配送、转口货物,包括流通领域的物流货物及供区内加工生产用的仓储货物。

本监管方式代码"5034",简称"区内物流货物"。

成品进出海关特殊监管区域

成品进出海关特殊监管区域适用于海关特殊监管区域内保税加工、保税物流或研发企业与境内(区外)之间进出的成品,包括此类成品在境内的退运、退换。

本监管方式代码"5100",简称"成品进出区"。

设备及物资进出海关特殊监管区域

设备及物资进出海关特殊监管区域适用于海关特殊监管区域内企业从境内(区外)购进的自用设备、物资,或将此类设备、物资销往区外,结转到同一海关特殊监管区域或另一海关特殊监管区域的企业,以及在境内的退运、退换。

本监管方式代码"5300",简称"设备进出区"。

海关特殊监管区域从境外进口的设备及物资

海关特殊监管区域从境外进口的设备及物资适用于海关特殊监管区域内企业从境外进口用于区内业务所需的设备、物资,以及区内企业和行政管理机构自用合理数量的办公用品等。

监管方式代码"5335",简称"境外设备进区"。

海关特殊监管区域设备及物资退运境外

海关特殊监管区域设备及物资退运境外适用于海关特殊监管区域内企业将监管方式代码"5335"项下的设备、物资退运境外。

本监管方式代码"5361",简称"区内设备退运"。

物流中心进出境货物

一、定义及代码

保税物流中心进出境仓储货物是指从境外直接存入保税物流中心(A、B型)和从保税物流中心(A、B型)运出境的仓储、转口货物。

本监管方式代码为"6033",简称"物流中心进出境货物"。

二、适用范围

(一)保税物流中心(A型)是指经海关批准,由中国境内企业法人经营,专门从事保税仓储物流业务的海关监管场所。

保税物流中心(A型)按照服务范围分为公用型物流中心和自用型物流中心。

1.公用型物流中心是指由专门从事仓储物流业务的中国境内企业法人经营,向社会提供保税仓储物流综合服务的海关监管场所。

2.自用型物流中心是指中国境内企业法人经营,仅向本企业或者本企业集团内部成员提供保税仓储物流服务的海关监管场所。

(二)保税物流中心(B型)(以下简称物流中心)是指经海关批准,由中国境内一家企业法人经营、多家企业进入并从事保税仓储物流业务的海关集中监管场所。

(三)下列情况不适用本监管方式:

1.从境内(海关特殊监管区域除外)运入保税物流中心(A、B型)货物和从保税物流中心(A、B型)提取运往境内的货物。

2.保税物流中心(A、B型)与保税区、出口加工区、保税物流园区、保税仓库、出口监管仓库及保税物流中心(A、B型)之间等海关特殊监管区域或保税监管场所之间往来的货物，监管方式填报为“保税间货物”(1200)。

3.保税仓库进出境仓储、转口货物，监管方式为“保税仓库货物”(1233)。

4.保税区、保税物流园区进出境仓储、转口货物，监管方式为“保税区仓储转口”(1234)。

内贸货物跨境运输

一、定义及代码

内贸货物跨境运输是指国内贸易货物由我国关境内一口岸启运，通过境外运至我国关境内另一口岸的业务，以下简称“跨境运输”。

本监管方式代码为“9600”，简称“内贸货物跨境运输”。

二、适用范围

经海关总署批准的进出境口岸、所经境外口岸、运输方式等实行跨境运输的货物。

跨境直购

一、定义及代码

跨境直购，监管方式代码“9610”，全称“跨境电子商务直购”，简称“跨境直购”。

二、适用范围

本监管方式适用于境内个人或电子商务企业通过电子商务交易平台实现交易，并采用“清单核放、汇总申报”模式办理通关手续的电子商务零售进出口商品(通过海关特殊监管区域或保税监管场所一线的电子商务零售进出口商品除外)。

海关处理货物

一、定义及代码

海关处理货物是指由海关提取变卖处理的超期未报关进口货物、误卸、溢卸货物、放弃进口货物，以及走私违规案件查处的货物。

本监管方式代码“9639”，简称“海关处理货物”。

二、适用范围

本监管方式适用以下定义的货物：

(一)超期未报关货物，是指进口货物的收货人自运输工具申报进境之日起超过3个月未向海关申报，由海关提取依法变卖处理的进口货物。

超期未报关货物还包括保税货物、暂时进口货物超过规定的期限3个月，未向海关办理复运出境或者其他有关手续，以及过境、转运和通运货物超过规定的期限3个月，未运输出境，由海关提取依法变卖处理。

(二)误卸、溢卸货物，是指未列入进境运输工具载货清单、运单申报进境的误卸或者溢卸的货物，运输工具负责人或进口货物收货人未向海关办理退运出境或申报进口手续，由海关提取依法变卖处理的进口货物。

(三)放弃进口货物，是指进口货物的收货人或其所有人声明放弃，由海关提取依法变卖处理的进口货物。

(四)超期未报关进口货物、误卸或者溢卸进口货物属于危险品或者鲜活、易腐、易烂、易失效、易变质、易变质等不宜长期保存的货物的，海关根据实际情况，提前提取依法变卖处理。

(五)进出境物品所有人声明放弃的物品，在海关规定期限内未办理海关手续或者无人认领的物品，以及无法投递又无法退回的进境邮递物品，由海关提取依法变卖处理。

(六)走私违法案件予以没收，由海关依法变卖处理的货物。

无原始报关单的后续补税

无原始报关单的后续补税是指无法获得原始报关单的后续退补税货物，包括调查、稽查补税及审价、归类等各种原因的后续退补税货物。

本监管方式代码“9700”，简称“后续补税”。

其他贸易

一、定义及代码

其他贸易是指除本章上述各节列名的监管方式以外，列入海关“其他贸易”统计的进出口货物。

本监管方式代码“9739”，简称“其他贸易”。

二、适用范围

(一)本监管方式适用：

1.我国境内经批准临时进出口货物的机关、团体、学校、企事业单位等进出口货物、物品。

2.外国驻华使、领馆在我国内购买货物出口。

3.外商投资企业外方常驻人员和外国驻华机构的常驻人员，以及持有长期居留证件和来华定居的引进专家等进口自用汽车。

4.进入厦门大嶝对台小额商品交易市场的人员带出台湾产品，每人每日价值人民币6000元以下免征进口关税和进口环节税，超出部分照章征税，监管方式为“其他贸易”。

5.外国企业常驻我国办事机构进口不复运出境的陈列用企业产品样品。

6.未列入运输工具进口载货清单、提(运)单、或多于进口载货清单、提(运)单所列数量的货物，运输工具负责人或溢卸货物的收货人申请办理进口溢卸货物。

(二)本监管方式不包括：

1.入境旅客在境内购买5万美元以内的旅游商品托运出境，监管方式为“旅游购物商品”(0139)。

2.本国籍运输工具在境内添加进口保税油、物料，监管方式为“国轮油物料”(1139)。

3.外国常驻机构进口办公用品，监管方式为“常驻机构公用”(2439)。

4.驻华商业机构进口不复运出口的陈列样品，监管方式为“陈列样品”(2939)。

5.对台湾小额贸易，监管方式为“对台小额”(4039)。

6.除援助、捐赠以外进出口其他免费提供的货物，监管方式为“其他进出口免费”(3339)。

7.我国驻外机构在境外购买的公务用品、机动车辆运回境内，监管方式为“驻外机构购进”(4239)。

8.海关拍卖处理超期未报货物、走私违规货物，监管方式为“海关处理货物”(9639)。

9.驻华外交机构转售境内非外交机构或个人，国际文体交流活动进口物品获准留赠或放弃，监管方式为“留赠转卖物品”(9839)。

留赠转卖物品

留赠转卖物品是指外国(地区)驻我国外交机构转售境内非外交机构或国际文体活动留赠、放弃的特批进口物品。

本监管方式代码“9839”，简称“留赠转卖物品”。

其他

一、定义及代码

指除已具体列名监管方式以外其他不列入海关统计的进出境货物、物品。

本监管方式代码“9900”，简称“其他”。

二、适用范围

(一)从货运渠道进出境的个人行李物品。

(二)中国驻外国使领馆出口公务或自用物品。

(三)在境内结转的进出口货物：

1.以出顶进货物，指经批准在国内以外汇向有关进出口公司购买出口商品顶替其应进口的同一商品。

2.供应国内外汇免税商店并收取外汇的出口商品。

3.经批准将来料加工、进料加工贸易项下加工的成品转为免税外汇商品。

4.经批准内销征税的进口免税品。

(四)边民互市贸易进出境货物。

(五)我国远洋渔业企业进口自捕水产品。

(六)国有文物收藏单位经国家文物局核准后，授受境外捐赠、归还和从境外追索的文物进口。

国有文物收藏单位系指经国家文物局审核批准从事文物收藏和研究的博物馆(院)、展览馆、研究所(院)等单位。

(七)与无代价抵偿进出口货物相关的原进口货物退运出境或原出口货物退运进境。

(八)我国各银行总行调运进出境的人民币现钞。

征免性质代码表

征免性质代码	征免性质简称	征免性质全称
101	一般征税	一般征税进出口货物
118	整车征税	构成整车特征的汽车零部件纳税
119	零部件征税	不构成整车特征的汽车零部件纳税
201	无偿援助	无偿援助进出口物资
299	其他法定	其他法定减免税进出口货物
301	特定区域	特定区域进口自用物资及出口货物
307	保税区	保税区进口自用物资
399	其他地区	其他执行特殊政策地区出口货物
401	科教用品	大专院校及科研机构进口科教用品
402	示范平台用品	
403	技术改造	企业技术改造进口货物
405	科技开发用品	科学研究、技术开发机构进口科技开发用品
406	重大项目	国家重大项目进口货物
407	动漫用品	动漫开发生产用品
408	重大技术装备	生产重大技术装备进口关键零部件及原材料
409	科技重大专项	科技重大专项进口关键设备、零部件和原材料
412	基础设施	通信、港口、铁路、公路、机场建设进口设备
413	残疾人	残疾人组织和企业进出口货物
417	远洋渔业	远洋渔业自捕水产品
418	国产化	国家定点生产小轿车和摄录机企业进口散件
419	整车特征	构成整车特征的汽车零部件进口
422	集成电路	集成电路生产企业进口货物
423	新型显示器件	新型显示器件生产企业进口物资
426	集成电路和软件企业进口设备	集成电路设计、先进封装测试、集成电路生产企业和软件企业进口设备
428	集成电路产业进口货物	集成电路生产企业、先进封装测试企业和关键原材料及零配件生产企业进口货物
491	零关税自用生产设备	海南零关税进口自用生产设备
492	零关税交通工具及游艇	海南零关税进口交通工具及游艇
493	零关税自用生产设备缴纳进口环节税	海南零关税进口自用生产设备并自愿缴纳进口环节增值税、消费税
494	零关税交通工具游艇缴纳进口环节税	海南零关税进口交通工具及游艇并自愿缴纳进口环节增值税、消费税
496	含进口料件加工增值货物	海南自由贸易港加工增值含进口料件货物内销免征关税
497	不含进口料件加工增值货物	海南自由贸易港加工增值不含进口料件货物内销免征关税
499	**ITA** 产品	非全税号信息技术产品
501	加工设备	加工贸易外商提供的不作价进口设备
502	来料加工	来料加工装配和补偿贸易进口料件及出口成品
503	进料加工	进料加工贸易进口料件及出口成品
506	边境小额	边境小额贸易进口货物
510	港澳 **OPA**	港澳在内地加工的纺织品获证出口
591	零关税原辅料	海南零关税原辅料进口
592	原辅料部分征税	海南零关税原辅料征收进口环节税
593	内外贸同船运输加注保税油	海南自由贸易港内外贸同船运输境内船舶加注保税油
594	内外贸同船运输加注本地生产燃料油	海南自由贸易港内外贸同船运输境内船舶加注本地生产燃料油
595	进出岛航班加注保税油全免	海南自由贸易港进出岛航班加注保税航油全免
596	进出岛航班加注保税油部分征税	海南自由贸易港进出岛航班加注保税航油自愿缴纳进口环节增值税
601	中外合资	中外合资经营企业进出口货物
602	中外合作	中外合作经营企业进出口货物
603	外资企业	外商独资企业进出口货物
605	勘探开发煤层气	勘探开发煤层气
606	海洋石油	勘探、开发海洋石油进口货物
608	陆上石油	勘探、开发陆上石油进口货物
609	贷款项目	利用贷款进口货物
610	海上应急救援	海上应急救援
611	贷款中标	国际金融组织贷款、外国政府贷款中标机电设备零部件
666	加征关税排除措施	加征关税排除措施
686	市场化组织采购排除措施	市场化组织采购排除措施
698	公益收藏	国有公益性收藏单位进口藏品
701	部分进口饲料	部分进口饲料、矿物质微量元素舔砖
702	中资“方便旗”船	回国登记中资“方便旗”船
703	航空公司进口飞机	国内航空公司进口的空载重量在 25 吨以上的飞机
704	花卉种子	花卉种子
705	科普事业	科普事业进口自用相关科普商品
706	租赁企业进口飞机	租赁企业进口空载重量在 25 吨以上的客货运飞机
707	博览会留购展品	博览会留购展品
708	替代种植农产品	替代种植进口农产品
789	鼓励项目	国家鼓励发展的内外资项目进口设备
799	自有资金	外商投资额度外利用自有资金进口设备、备件、配件
801	救灾捐赠	救灾捐赠进口物资
802	慈善捐赠	境外捐赠人无偿向我境内受赠人捐赠的直接用于慈善事业的免税进口物资
803	抗艾滋病药物	进口抗艾滋病病毒药物
811	种子种源	进口种子(苗)、种畜(禽)、鱼种(苗)和种用野生动植物种源

征免性质代码	征免性质简称	征免性质全称
815	野生动植物	进口种用野生动植物和军警用工作犬
818	中央储备粮油	中央储备粮油免征进口环节增值税政策
819	科教图书	进口科研教学用图书资料
888	航材减免	经核准的航空公司进口维修用航空器材
898	国批减免	国务院特准减免税的进出口货物
899	选择征税	选择征税
901	科研院所	科研院所进口科学研究、科技开发和教学用品
902	高等学校	高等学校进口科学研究、科技开发和教学用品
903	工程研究中心	国家工程研究中心进口科学研究、科技开发和教学用品
904	国家企业技术中心	国家企业技术中心进口科学研究、科技开发和教学用品
905	转制科研机构	转制科研机构进口科学研究、科技开发和教学用品
906	重点实验室	国家重点实验室及企业国家重点实验室进口科学研究、科技开发和教学用品
907	国家工程技术研究中心	国家工程技术研究中心进口科学研究、科技开发和教学用品
908	社会研发机构	社会研发机构进口科学研究、科技开发和教学用品
909	示范平台	国家中小企业公共服务示范平台(技术类)进口科学研究、科技开发和教学用品
910	外资研发中心	外资研发中心进口科学研究、科技开发和教学用品
911	出版物进口单位	出版物进口单位进口用于科研、教学的图书、文献、报刊及其他资料
912	国家实验室	国家实验室进口科学研究、科技开发和教学用品
913	国家产业创新中心	国家产业创新中心进口科学研究、科技开发和教学用品
915	国家制造业创新中心	国家制造业创新中心进口科学研究、科技开发和教学用品
916	国家技术创新中心	国家技术创新中心进口科学研究、科技开发和教学用品
917	公共图书馆	公共图书馆进口用于科研、教学的图书、文献、报刊及其他资料
918	国家临床医学研究中心	国家临床医学研究中心进口科学研究、科技开发和教学用品
919	党校(行政学院)	党校(行政学院)进口科学研究、科技开发和教学用品
921	大型客机研制物资	大型客机、大型客机发动机研制进口物资
922	进博会留购展品	进博会留购展品
926	服贸会留购展品	服贸会留购展品
927	进口钻石	自上海钻石交易所销往国内市场的毛坯钻石和成品钻石
928	三代核电	三代核电项目进口设备
930	疫情防控物资	新冠肺炎疫情防控进口物资
931	消博会留购展品	消博会留购展品
939	运动会	运动会
997	自贸协定	
998	内部暂定	享受内部暂定税率的进出口货物
999	例外减免	例外减免税进出口货物

征减免税方式代码表

征减免税方式代码	征减免税方式名称
1	照章征税
2	折半征税
3	全免
4	特案
5	征免性质
6	保证金
7	保函
8	折半补税
9	全额退税

运输方式代码表

运输方式代码	运输方式名称
0	非保税区
1	监管仓库
2	水路运输
3	铁路运输
4	公路运输
5	航空运输
6	邮件运输
7	保税区
8	保税仓库
9	其它运输
H	边境特殊海关作业区
T	综合实验区
W	物流中心
X	物流园区
Y	保税港区
Z	出口加工区
L	旅客携带
P	洋浦保税港区
S	特殊综合保税区
G	固定设施

关区代码表

关区代码	关区简称
0000	**海关总署**
0100	**北京关区**
0101	京机场关
0102	京监管处
0103	京关展览
0104	京西城关
0105	京会展关
0106	大兴机场
0107	机场库区
0108	京综合处
0109	机场旅检
0110	平谷海关
0111	京车站关
0112	京邮局关
0113	京中关村
0114	海淀海关
0115	京东城关
0116	大兴旅检
0117	亦庄海关
0118	京朝阳关
0119	通州海关
0121	京稽查处
0123	机场调技
0124	北京站
0125	西客站
0126	丰台海关
0127	京快件
0128	顺义海关
0129	天竺海关
0130	亦庄物流
0131	大兴综保
0200	**天津海关**
0201	津南开关
0202	新港海关
0203	塘沽海关
0204	东港海关
0205	津塘沽办
0206	津邮局关
0207	津机场办
0208	津保税区
0209	津蓟州关
0210	武清海关
0211	泰达综保
0212	津物流园
0213	东疆综保
0214	津滨综保
0215	津机快件
0216	津开物流
0217	津东疆关
0218	静海海关
0219	津北辰关
0220	津关税处
0221	津宁河关
0222	津大港关
0223	津临港关

关区代码	关区简称
0224	津南疆关
0225	津西青关
0226	津北塘关
0227	津河西关
0228	津东丽关
0229	津蓟物流
0230	津保税关
0400	**石家庄区**
0401	鹿泉海关
0402	秦皇岛关
0403	唐山海关
0404	廊坊海关
0405	保定海关
0406	邯郸海关
0407	秦综保区
0408	沧州海关
0409	廊坊综保
0410	石机场关
0411	张家口关
0412	曹妃甸关
0413	邢台海关
0414	曹综保区
0415	衡水海关
0416	石关快件
0417	承德海关
0418	石综保区
0419	武安物流
0420	京唐物流
0421	正定海关
0422	京唐港关
0423	雄安海关
0424	黄骅港关
0425	辛集物流
0426	北戴河关
0500	**太原关区**
0501	晋阳海关
0502	并机场关
0503	大同海关
0504	临汾海关
0505	方略物流
0506	太原综保
0507	运城海关
0508	晋城海关
0509	兰花物流
0510	太原邮件
0511	武宿海关
0512	长治海关
0513	阳泉海关
0514	朔州海关
0515	忻州海关
0516	大同保 B
0600	**满洲里关**
0601	海拉尔关
0602	额尔古纳
0603	满十八里

关区代码	关区简称
0604	赤峰海关
0605	通辽海关
0606	满哈沙特
0607	满室韦
0608	满互贸区
0609	满铁路
0610	满市区
0611	满机场
0612	阿尔山关
0613	赤峰物流
0614	额布都格
0615	满综保区
0616	满关邮办
0700	**呼特关区**
0701	赛罕海关
0702	二关铁路
0703	包头海关
0704	呼关邮办
0705	二关公路
0706	包头箱站
0707	额济纳关
0708	乌拉特关
0709	满达口岸
0710	东乌海关
0711	机场海关
0712	呼综保区
0713	鄂尔多斯
0714	集宁海关
0715	乌海海关
0716	鄂综保区
0717	包头保 B
0718	巴市保 B
0719	二关公直
0720	七苏保 B
0721	阿拉善关
0800	**沈阳关区**
0801	浑南海关
0802	锦州海关
0803	沈邮局关
0804	抚顺海关
0805	铁西海关
0806	辽阳海关
0807	沈机场关
0808	辽中海关
0809	沈快件
0810	葫芦岛关
0811	辽宁朝阳
0812	沈抚新区
0813	铁岭海关
0814	铁保(B 型)
0815	阜新海关
0816	锦港保 B
0900	**大连海关**
0901	大连港湾
0902	大连机场

关区代码	关区简称
0903	连开发区
0904	湾里综保
0905	北良港关
0906	连保税区
0907	连物流园
0908	连大窑湾
0909	连邮局关
0910	连窑综保
0911	长兴岛关
0912	大连快件
0915	庄河海关
0916	七贤岭关
0917	旅顺海关
0919	金石滩关
0930	丹东海关
0931	本溪海关
0932	丹太平湾
0940	营口海关
0941	盘锦海关
0942	盘港物流
0943	营口综保
0950	鲅鱼圈关
0951	营港物流
0953	仙人岛办
0960	大东港关
0980	鞍山海关
1500	**长春关区**
1501	绿园海关
1502	兴隆海关
1503	长白海关
1504	临江口岸
1505	图们海关
1506	通化海关
1507	珲春海关
1508	吉林海关
1509	延吉海关
1510	长春综保
1511	龙嘉机场
1512	松原海关
1513	白城海关
1514	白山海关
1515	图们车办
1516	通海关村
1517	珲长岭子
1518	吉关车办
1519	图们三合
1521	一汽场站
1522	长白山海关
1523	四平海关
1524	辽源海关
1525	图们桥办
1526	通集青石
1527	珲春圈河
1528	吉林物流
1529	延吉南坪

关区代码	关区简称
1531	兴隆铁路
1536	通集铁路
1537	珲沙坨子
1539	图开山屯
1546	通集公路
1547	珲综保区
1549	延古城里
1557	珲春车办
1559	延吉邮办
1567	珲综口岸
1569	延吉机办
1579	延关快件
1589	延吉保 B
1591	长邮海关
1593	长白邮办
1595	图们邮办
1596	通集邮办
1900	**哈尔滨区**
1901	哈尔滨关
1902	绥关铁路
1903	黑河海关
1904	同江海关
1905	佳木斯海关
1906	牡丹江关
1907	东宁海关
1908	逊克海关
1909	齐齐哈尔
1910	大庆海关
1911	密山海关
1912	虎林海关
1913	同江富锦
1914	抚远海关
1915	漠河海关
1916	萝北海关
1917	嘉荫海关
1918	饶河海关
1919	冰城香办
1920	哈开发区
1921	绥综保区
1922	冰城邮办
1923	哈关车办
1924	哈机场关
1925	绥关公路
1926	哈综保区
1927	哈综口岸
1928	绥综口岸
1929	牡保 B 型
1930	冰城海关
1931	鹤岗海关
1932	黑河保 B
1933	绥化海关
2200	**上海海关**
2201	浦江海关
2202	吴淞海关
2203	虹桥机场
2204	闵开发区
2205	车站海关

关区代码	关区简称
2206	邮局海关
2207	洋山海关
2208	宝山海关
2209	龙吴海关
2210	浦东海关
2211	卢湾监管
2212	奉贤海关
2213	莘庄海关
2214	漕河泾发
2215	西北物流
2216	浦机综保
2217	嘉定海关
2218	外高桥关
2219	沪杨浦关
2220	金山海关
2221	松江海关
2222	青浦海关
2223	沪科创关
2224	崇明海关
2225	外港海关
2226	贸易网点
2227	普陀区站
2228	沪会展关
2229	航交办
2230	沪徐汇关
2231	洋山市内
2232	嘉定综保
2233	浦东机场
2234	沪钻交所
2235	松江综 A
2236	洋山芦潮
2237	松江综 B
2238	青浦综保
2239	奉贤综保
2240	漕河泾综
2241	沪黄浦关
2242	沪业二处
2243	沪虹口关
2244	上海快件
2245	金桥综保
2246	外高桥综
2247	沪化工区
2248	洋山港区
2249	洋山特综
2250	沪空港办
2251	沪金桥办
2252	虹桥 B 保
2300	**南京海关**
2301	连云港关
2302	南通海关
2303	苏州海关
2304	无锡海关
2305	张家港关
2306	常州海关
2307	镇江海关
2308	新生圩关
2309	盐城海关

关区代码	关区简称
2310	扬州海关
2311	徐州海关
2312	江阴海关
2313	张保税区
2314	苏工业区
2315	淮安海关
2316	泰州海关
2317	禄口机场
2318	金陵江北
2319	如皋海关
2320	锡关机办
2321	常溧阳办
2322	镇丹阳办
2323	金陵海关
2324	常熟海关
2325	昆山海关
2326	吴江海关
2327	太仓海关
2328	苏吴中办
2329	启东海关
2330	泰泰兴办
2331	宜兴海关
2332	锡锡山办
2333	南通关办
2334	新沂保 B
2335	昆山加工
2336	苏园加工
2337	徐州综保
2338	苏关邮办
2339	南通加工
2340	无锡加工
2341	连关加工
2342	连赣榆办
2343	宁南加工
2344	苏高加工
2345	镇江加工
2346	连关综保
2347	苏园 B 区
2348	金港海关
2349	金陵邮办
2350	苏高物流
2351	金陵江宁
2352	宁空保 B
2353	常关出加
2354	扬关出加
2355	常熟出加
2356	吴江出加
2357	常关武办
2358	苏园保税
2359	吴中出加
2360	盐关港办
2361	淮关出加
2362	澄关物流
2363	靖江物流
2364	武进出加
2365	张保税港
2366	宿迁海关

关区代码	关区简称
2367	泰出加区
2368	苏高综保
2369	昆山综保
2370	连关物流
2371	盐机场办
2372	盐城综保
2373	淮安综保
2374	锡高综保
2375	靖江海关
2376	南通综保
2377	龙潭综保
2378	江宁综保
2379	苏相城办
2380	太仓综保
2381	苏园贸易
2382	苏虎丘办
2383	如东海关
2384	如皋物流
2385	泰州综保
2386	镇江综保
2387	常州综保
2388	武进综保
2389	常熟综保
2390	吴江综保
2391	徐州物流
2392	通海门办
2393	通海安办
2394	吴中综保
2395	大丰物流
2396	海安物流
2397	江阴综保
2398	扬州综保
2900	**杭州关区**
2901	钱综三处
2902	钱江海关
2903	温州海关
2904	舟山海关
2905	台州海关
2906	绍兴海关
2907	湖州海关
2908	嘉兴海关
2909	钱关下沙
2910	杭州机场
2911	钱关邮办
2912	钱关萧办
2915	丽水海关
2916	杭州快件
2917	衢州海关
2918	钱关余办
2919	钱关富办
2920	金华海关
2921	义乌海关
2922	金关永办
2923	义乌物流
2924	金义综保
2925	义乌综保
2927	义关机办

关区代码	关区简称
2928	杭关电商
2929	钱关建办
2931	温关邮办
2932	温经开关
2933	温关机办
2934	温关鳌办
2935	温关瑞办
2936	温关乐办
2937	温州物流
2938	温州综保
2941	嵊泗海关
2942	舟关金塘
2943	舟关综保
2951	台关临办
2952	台关温办
2953	台关玉办
2961	绍关虞办
2962	绍关诸办
2963	绍关新办
2964	绍兴综保
2971	湖关安办
2972	湖关德办
2973	德清保 B
2979	湖州保 B
2981	嘉关乍办
2982	嘉关善办
2983	嘉兴综保
2984	嘉关宁办
2985	嘉兴桐办
2986	嘉综 B 区
2991	杭州综保
2992	杭州物流
3100	**宁波关区**
3101	海曙海关
3102	镇海海关
3103	甬北城办
3104	北仑海关
3105	甬保税区
3106	大榭海关
3107	余姚海关
3108	慈溪海关
3109	甬机场关
3110	象山海关
3111	甬加工区
3112	甬物流区
3113	慈加工区
3114	鄞州海关
3115	栎社海关
3116	梅山港区
3117	梅山保税
3118	宁波快件
3119	甬邮局关
3120	镇海物流
3121	甬北港办
3122	甬北穿办
3123	甬江海关
3124	奉化海关
3125	宁海海关
3126	甬新区关
3300	**合肥海关**
3301	芜湖海关
3302	安庆海关
3303	马鞍山关
3304	黄山海关
3305	蚌埠海关
3306	铜陵海关
3307	阜阳海关
3308	池州海关
3309	滁州海关
3310	庐州海关
3311	新桥机场
3312	芜湖综保
3313	经开综保
3315	宣城海关
3316	蚌埠物流
3317	合肥综保
3318	淮南海关
3319	宿州海关
3320	合关快件
3321	安庆物流
3322	宣城物流
3323	空港物流
3324	马综保区
3325	六安海关
3326	淮北海关
3327	亳州海关
3328	铜陵物流
3500	**福州关区**
3501	马尾海关
3502	榕福清办
3503	宁德海关
3504	三明海关
3505	榕罗源办
3506	莆田海关
3507	长乐机场
3508	榕江阴港
3509	榕邮局办
3510	南平海关
3511	武夷山关
3512	黄岐监管
3513	榕快安办
3515	平潭港区
3516	平潭海关
3520	福州综保
3521	榕翔保 B
3522	福物流园
3523	榕江阴综
3700	**厦门关区**
3701	厦门海关
3702	泉刺桐办
3703	漳州海关
3704	东山海关
3705	泉石狮办
3706	龙岩海关
3707	泉泉港办
3708	海沧港区
3709	海沧保税
3710	高崎海关
3711	东渡海关
3712	海沧海关
3713	邮局海关
3714	象屿保税
3715	机场海关
3716	集同海关
3717	象屿综保
3718	泉综保区
3719	厦门加工
3720	厦门物流
3722	大嶝监管
3723	泉晋江办
3724	邮轮海关
3725	翔安海关
3726	泉陆地港
3727	古雷海关
3728	泉安溪办
3729	泉南安办
3730	厦五通办
3731	漳招银办
3732	泉州海关
3733	漳州保 B
3735	泉州保 B
3777	厦稽查处
3788	厦侦查局
4000	**南昌关区**
4001	赣江海关
4002	九江海关
4003	赣州海关
4004	景德镇关
4005	吉安海关
4006	昌北机场
4007	青山湖关
4008	龙南海关
4009	新余海关
4010	浔关区办
4011	洪关区办
4012	虔关区办
4013	上饶海关
4014	南昌物流
4015	吉井加工
4016	鹰潭海关
4017	赣州综保
4018	宜春海关
4019	南昌综保
4020	龙南物流
4021	萍乡海关
4022	抚州海关
4023	九江综保
4024	南昌快件
4025	南昌邮件
4026	吉井综保
4200	**青岛海关**
4201	烟台海关
4202	日照海关
4203	龙口海关
4204	威海海关
4205	济南海关
4206	潍坊海关
4207	淄博海关
4208	烟综保西
4209	荣成海关
4210	青保税区
4211	济宁海关
4212	泰安海关
4213	临沂海关
4214	青前湾港
4215	菏泽海关
4216	东营海关
4217	枣庄海关
4218	青开发区
4219	蓬莱海关
4220	青机场关
4221	烟机场办
4222	莱州海关
4223	青岛邮关
4224	烟关长办
4225	威海港办
4226	青聊城办
4227	青岛大港
4228	烟关快件
4229	德州海关
4230	前湾保税
4231	烟开发区
4232	日岚山办
4233	济机场办
4234	济加工区
4235	济邮局办
4236	荣龙眼办
4237	现场业务
4238	威邮局办
4239	潍诸城办
4240	青关快件
4241	烟综保东
4242	威综保北
4243	济曲阜办
4244	青滨州办
4245	烟台邮办
4246	青胶综保
4247	威机场办
4248	青莱芜办
4249	潍加工区
4250	青西综区
4251	淄博物流
4253	日照物流
4254	青岛物流
4255	潍寿光办
4256	威港快件
4257	临综保区
4258	前湾口岸

关区代码	关区简称
4259	黄关快件
4260	青港快件
4261	烟港快件
4262	威综保南
4263	海阳海关
4264	烟莱阳办
4265	胶州海关
4266	即墨海关
4267	烟招远办
4268	青董港关
4269	石港快件
4270	威文登办
4271	日照综保
4272	大港快件
4273	即墨综保
4274	烟福保 B
4275	烟芝罘办
4276	菏港保税
4277	青西保 B
4288	烟八角办
4300	**济南海关**
4301	泉城海关
4302	济机场关
4303	济综保区
4305	济邮局关
4306	章锦综保
4310	潍坊海关
4311	潍诸城办
4312	潍综保区
4313	潍寿光办
4315	诸城物流
4320	淄博海关
4321	淄博物流
4322	淄博综保
4330	泰安海关
4341	济机快件
4342	济邮快件
4350	东营海关
4351	东营综保
4360	聊城海关
4370	德州海关
4380	滨州海关
4381	滨州物流
4390	莱芜海关
4600	**郑州关区**
4601	金水海关
4602	洛阳海关
4603	南阳海关
4604	郑机场关
4605	郑邮局关
4606	郑车站关
4607	安阳海关
4608	新区海关
4609	商丘海关
4610	周口海关
4611	经开综保
4612	新郑海关

关区代码	关区简称
4613	郑州空港
4614	焦作海关
4615	三门峡关
4616	新乡海关
4617	信阳海关
4618	鹤壁海关
4619	德众物流
4620	郑航空港
4621	许昌海关
4622	南阳综保
4623	商丘物流
4624	漯河海关
4625	濮阳海关
4626	民权办
4627	民权保 B
4628	济源海关
4629	驻马店海关
4630	平顶山海关
4631	开封海关
4632	许昌保 B
4700	**武汉海关**
4701	宜昌海关
4702	荆州海关
4703	襄阳海关
4704	黄石海关
4705	汉阳海关
4706	宜三峡办
4707	鄂加工区
4708	现场一处
4709	武江物流
4710	武关货管
4711	武关快件
4712	武关机场
4713	邮局海关
4714	新港海关
4715	汉口海关
4716	十堰海关
4718	武昌海关
4719	东湖综保
4720	黄石物流
4721	仙桃海关
4722	东湖陆港
4723	宜昌物流
4724	襄阳物流
4725	空港综保
4726	新港综保
4727	荆门海关
4728	鄂州海关
4729	随州海关
4730	恩施海关
4731	经开综保
4732	仙桃物流
4733	荆门保 B
4734	宜昌综保
4900	**长沙关区**
4901	衡阳海关
4902	岳阳海关

关区代码	关区简称
4903	郴州海关
4904	常德海关
4905	星关霞办
4906	株洲海关
4907	韶山海关
4908	湘机场关
4909	株关醴办
4910	郴州综保
4911	永州海关
4913	金霞物流
4914	张家界关
4915	衡阳综保
4916	星沙海关
4917	湘潭综保
4918	星关浏办
4919	岳阳综保
4920	湘邮海关
4921	黄花综保
4922	株洲物流
4923	邵阳海关
4924	益阳海关
4925	怀化海关
4926	湘西海关
4927	星关铁运
4928	娄底海关
5000	**广东分署**
5100	**广州海关**
5101	内港新风
5102	越秀海关
5103	清远海关
5104	清远英德
5105	天河保税
5106	南沙散货
5107	肇庆大旺
5108	肇庆德庆
5109	海珠滘心
5110	南海海关
5111	南海官窑
5112	南海九江
5113	南海北村
5114	南海平洲
5115	荔湾海关
5116	南海业务
5117	桂江车场
5118	平洲旅检
5119	南海三山
5120	海珠海关
5121	内港芳村
5122	内港洲嘴
5123	内港四仓
5124	双东车场
5125	从化海关
5126	内港赤航
5130	广州萝岗
5131	花都海关
5132	花都码头
5133	穗知识城

关区代码	关区简称
5134	穗保税处
5135	天河海关
5136	穗统计处
5137	穗价格处
5138	高明食出
5139	穗监管处
5140	穗关税处
5141	广州机场
5142	民航快件
5143	广州车站
5144	穗机综保
5145	广州邮办
5146	穗关会展
5147	穗邮办监
5148	穗大郎站
5149	大铲海关
5150	顺德海关
5151	顺德保税
5152	顺德食出
5153	顺德车场
5154	北窖车场
5155	顺德旅检
5157	陈村车场
5158	顺德勒流
5160	番禺海关
5161	沙湾车场
5162	番禺旅检
5163	番禺货柜
5164	番禺船舶
5165	南沙保税
5166	南沙新港
5167	南沙货港
5168	南沙汽车
5169	南沙海关
5170	肇庆海关
5171	肇庆高要
5172	肇庆车场
5173	肇庆新港
5174	肇庆旅检
5175	肇庆码头
5176	肇庆四会
5177	肇庆三榕
5178	云浮海关
5179	罗定海关
5180	佛山海关
5181	高明海关
5182	佛山澜石
5183	三水码头
5184	佛山窖口
5185	佛山快件
5186	佛山保税
5187	佛山车场
5188	佛山火车
5189	佛山新港
5190	韶关海关
5191	韶关乐昌
5192	三水海关

关区代码	关区简称
5193	三水车场
5194	三水港
5195	审单中心
5196	云浮新港
5197	白云电商
5198	穗河源关
5199	穗技术处
5200	**黄埔关区**
5201	埔老港关
5202	埔新港关
5203	增城海关
5204	东莞海关
5205	太平海关
5206	惠州海关(作废)
5207	凤岗海关
5208	穗东海关
5209	埔东海关
5210	埔红海办
5211	河源海关
5212	新沙海关
5213	埔长安关
5214	常平海关
5216	沙田海关
5217	寮步车场
5218	江龙车场
5219	黄埔综保
5220	东莞物流
5221	埔荔城办
5222	清溪物流
5223	东莞邮办
5224	萝岗海关
5225	虎门综保
5300	**深圳海关**
5301	皇岗海关
5302	罗湖海关
5303	沙头角关
5304	蛇口海关
5305	福强海关
5306	笋岗海关
5307	南头海关
5308	龙岗海关
5309	布吉海关
5310	淡水办
5311	深关车站
5312	深监管处
5313	深调查局
5314	深关邮局
5315	惠东海关
5316	大鹏海关
5317	深机场关
5318	梅林海关
5319	同乐海关
5320	文锦渡关
5321	福田海关
5322	沙保税关
5323	深审单处
5324	深审价办

关区代码	关区简称
5325	深关税处
5326	深数统处
5327	深法规处
5328	深规范处
5329	深保税处
5330	盐保税关
5331	三门岛办
5332	深财务处
5333	深侦查局
5334	深稽查处
5335	深技术处
5336	深办公室
5337	大亚湾核
5338	惠州港关
5339	坪山海关
5340	沙湾海关
5341	深惠州关
5342	深红海办
5343	深盐物流
5344	惠石化办
5345	深圳湾关
5346	深机快件
5348	深关大铲
5349	前海港区
5350	大运通关
5351	前海保税
5352	梅沙海关
5353	西九龙关
5354	莲塘海关
5355	福中海关
5356	前海海关
5357	观澜海关
5358	西沥海关
5700	**拱北关区**
5701	拱稽查处
5710	闸口海关
5720	中山海关
5721	中山港
5724	中石岐办
5725	坦洲货场
5726	中山物流
5727	小榄港
5728	神湾港
5729	中山快件
5730	香洲海关
5740	湾仔海关
5741	湾仔船舶
5750	九洲海关
5760	拱白石办
5770	斗门海关
5771	斗井岸办
5772	斗平沙办
5780	高栏海关
5781	高综保区
5782	宏达码头
5788	大桥海关
5790	青茂海关

关区代码	关区简称
5791	拱跨工区
5792	拱保税区
5793	万山海关
5794	桂山中途
5795	横琴海关
5796	澳大校区
5798	拱关邮检
5799	南屏快件
6000	**汕头海关**
6001	汕关货一
6002	汕关货二
6003	汕关行邮
6004	潮汕机场
6006	汕关保税
6007	汕关业务
6008	濠江海关
6009	汕关邮包
6010	汕保物流
6011	揭阳海关
6012	普宁海关
6013	澄海海关
6014	广澳海关
6015	南澳海关
6016	濠江现场
6018	揭关惠来
6019	龙湖海关
6020	汕港海关
6021	潮州海关
6022	饶平海关
6023	饶平快件
6026	汕头综保
6028	潮阳海关
6031	汕尾海关
6032	海城海关
6033	尾关陆丰
6038	汕关快件
6041	梅州海关
6042	梅州兴宁
6046	梅州综保
6400	**海口关区**
6401	海口港
6402	三亚海关
6403	八所海关
6404	洋浦区关
6405	海保税区
6406	文昌海关
6407	美兰机场
6408	洋浦港
6409	海口综保
6410	马村港
6411	椰城海关
6412	三沙海关
6413	博鳌机场
6414	海空综保
6415	三亚B保
6700	**湛江关区**
6701	湛江海关

关区代码	关区简称
6702	茂名海关
6703	徐闻海关
6704	海东海关
6705	茂名水东
6706	湛江吴川
6707	廉江海关
6708	茂名高州
6709	茂名信宜
6710	东海岛关
6711	霞山海关
6712	霞海海关
6713	湛江机场
6714	湛江博贺
6715	湛江快件
6716	湛江物流
6717	湛江调顺
6718	湛江遂溪
6719	湛江综保
6800	**江门关区**
6810	江门海关
6811	高沙海关
6812	外海海关
6813	江门旅检
6815	外海电商
6816	江门车场
6817	江门保税
6820	新会海关
6821	新会港
6827	新会稽查
6830	台山海关
6831	台公益港
6837	台山稽查
6840	开平海关
6841	开平码头
6847	开平电商
6850	恩平海关
6851	恩平港
6857	恩平稽查
6860	鹤山海关
6861	鹤山码头
6866	南方电商
6867	鹤松电商
6870	阳江海关
6871	阳江港
6872	阳江车场
6877	阳江稽查
7200	**南宁关区**
7201	邕州海关
7202	北海海关
7203	梧州海关
7204	桂林海关
7205	柳州海关
7206	防城海关
7207	东兴海关
7208	凭祥海关
7209	贵港海关
7210	水口海关

关区代码	关区简称
7211	龙邦海关
7212	钦州海关
7213	桂林机办
7214	北海综保
7215	钦州综保
7216	南宁综保
7217	钦州港关
7218	玉林海关
7219	南凭综保
7220	友谊关
7221	邕机场关
7222	邕邮局关
7223	贺州海关
7224	河池海关
7225	爱店海关
7226	峒中海关
7227	防港保 B
7228	硕龙海关
7229	平孟海关
7230	柳州保 B
7231	梧州综保
7900	**成都关区**
7901	蓉青关
7902	蓉机双流
7903	蓉乐关
7904	蓉攀关
7905	蓉绵关
7906	蓉邮关
7907	蓉盐关
7908	蓉内关
7909	公路场站
7910	蓉机快件
7911	蓉泸关
7912	蓉戎关
7913	蓉南关
7914	蓉绵加工
7915	蓉锦关
7916	蓉锦西区
7917	蓉遂关
7918	蓉旌关
7919	蓉通关
7920	蓉机保 B
7921	蓉泸保 B
7922	蓉锦双流
7923	蓉戎保 B
7924	蓉青保 B
7925	蓉新关
7926	蓉利关
7927	蓉新物流
7928	蓉青综保
7929	蓉泸综保
7930	蓉戎综保
7931	蓉锦综保
7932	蓉绵综保
7933	蓉南保 B
7934	蓉賨关
8000	**重庆关区**
8001	重庆海关

关区代码	关区简称
8002	两江海关
8003	重庆机场
8004	重庆邮局
8005	万州海关
8006	渝州海关
8007	重庆水港
8008	渝加工区
8009	涪陵海关
8010	寸滩水港
8011	渝关快件
8012	两寸海关
8013	西永综保
8014	西永海关
8015	渝贸园区
8016	渝铁物流
8017	渝公物流
8018	黔江海关
8019	江津综保
8020	永川海关
8021	涪陵综保
8022	果园保 B
8023	万州综保
8024	永川综保
8300	**贵阳海关**
8301	筑城海关
8302	黔机场关
8303	遵义海关
8304	贵阳综保
8305	贵阳现场
8306	贵安综保
8307	贵安海关
8308	六盘水关
8309	遵义综保
8310	凯里海关
8311	毕节海关
8312	兴义海关
8313	铜仁海关
8600	**昆明关区**
8601	滇中海关
8602	畹町海关
8603	瑞丽海关
8604	章凤海关
8605	盈江海关
8606	孟连海关
8607	南伞海关
8608	孟定海关
8609	打洛海关
8610	腾冲海关
8611	沧源海关
8612	勐腊海关
8613	河口海关
8614	金水河关
8615	天保海关
8616	田蓬海关
8617	大理海关
8618	芒市海关
8619	腾驻隆阳
8620	昆明机场

关区代码	关区简称
8621	邮局海关
8622	西双版纳
8623	丽江海关
8624	思茅海关
8625	河口山腰
8626	怒江海关
8627	昆明高新
8628	昆明加工
8629	香格里拉
8631	勐康海关
8632	昆明快件
8633	红河综保
8634	昆明综保
8635	昆综口岸
8636	高新物流
8637	红综口岸
8638	磨憨快件
8639	机场电商
8640	腾俊物流
8641	都龙海关
8642	瑞驻姐告
8643	瑞驻弄岛
8644	孟驻临翔
8645	西驻关累
8646	蒙自海关
8647	曲靖海关
8648	玉溪海关
8649	磨憨铁路
8800	拉萨海关
8801	聂拉木关
8802	日喀则关
8803	狮泉河关
8804	机场海关
8805	八廓海关
8806	普兰海关
8807	亚东海关
8808	吉隆海关
8809	林芝海关
8810	拉萨综保
9000	**西安关区**
9001	关中海关
9002	咸阳机场
9003	宝鸡海关
9004	邮局海关
9005	关中综 A
9006	关中综 B
9007	西安综保
9008	高新综保
9009	车站海关
9010	延安海关
9011	渭南海关
9012	榆林海关
9013	西咸综保
9014	汉中海关
9015	商洛海关
9016	航空综保
9017	宝鸡综保
9018	杨凌综保

关区代码	关区简称
9400	**乌关区**
9401	乌昌公路
9402	霍尔果斯
9403	吐尔尕特
9404	阿拉山口
9405	塔城海关
9406	伊宁海关
9407	吉木乃关
9408	喀什海关
9409	红其拉甫
9410	阿勒泰关
9411	塔克什肯
9412	乌拉斯太
9413	哈密关
9414	红山嘴
9415	伊尔克什
9416	库尔勒关
9417	乌机场关
9418	乌加工区
9419	都拉塔关
9420	乌昌关
9421	霍中心 A
9422	石河子关
9423	山口综保
9424	喀什综保
9425	卡拉苏关
9426	奎屯物流
9427	中哈合作中心配套区
9428	乌邮局关
9429	乌综保区
9430	阿克苏关
9500	**兰州关区**
9501	金城海关
9502	酒泉海关
9503	中川机场
9504	武威物流
9505	天水海关
9506	金昌海关
9507	兰州综保
9508	敦煌机场
9509	平凉海关
9600	**银川海关**
9601	兴庆海关
9602	河东机场
9603	石嘴山关
9604	银川综保
9605	银关快件
9606	石嘴山物流
9607	中卫海关
9700	**西宁关区**
9701	西海海关
9702	青海物流
9703	西宁机场
9704	格尔木海关
9705	西宁综保
9900	**政法司**

国内地区代码表

地区代码	地区名称
11013	中关村国家自主创新示范区(东城园)
11019	东城区
11023	中关村国家自主创新示范区(西城园)
11029	西城区
11039	崇文区
11049	宣武区
11053	中关村国家自主创新示范区(朝阳园)
11059	朝阳区
11063	中关村国家自主创新示范区(丰台园)
11069	丰台区
11073	中关村国家自主创新示范区(石景山园)
11079	石景山
11083	中关村国家自主创新示范区(海淀园)
11089	海淀区其他
11093	中关村国家自主创新示范区(门头沟园)
11099	门头沟
11103	中关村国家自主创新示范区(房山园)
11109	房山
11113	中关村国家自主创新示范区(顺义园)
11115	北京天竺出口加工区
11116	北京天竺综合保税区
11119	顺义
11123	中关村国家自主创新示范区(昌平园)
11129	昌平
11132	北京经济技术开发区
11133	中关村国家自主创新示范区(大兴一亦庄园)
11136	北京大兴国际机场综合保税区(北京区域)
11139	大兴其他
1113W	北京亦庄保税物流中心
11143	中关村国家自主创新示范区(通州园)
11149	通县
11153	中关村国家自主创新示范区(怀柔园)
11159	怀柔
11163	中关村国家自主创新示范区(平谷园)
11169	平谷
11173	中关村国家自主创新示范区(延庆园)
11179	延庆
11183	中关村国家自主创新示范区(密云园)
11189	密云
11909	北京其他
12019	和平区
12029	河东区
12039	河西区
12043	天津新技术产业园区
12049	南开区其他
12059	河北区
12069	红桥区
12072	天津经济技术开发区
12074	天津港保税区
12075	天津出口加工区
12076	天津东疆、泰达综合保税区
12077	天津保税物流园
12079	滨海新区(塘沽其他)
1207W	天津经济技术开发区保税物流中心
12089	滨海新区(汉沽)
12099	滨海新区(大港)
12106	天津滨海新区综合保税区
12109	东丽区
12119	西青区
12129	津南区
12139	北辰区
12149	宁河县
12159	武清县
12169	静海县
12179	宝坻县
12189	蓟县
1218W	蓟州保税物流中心(B型)
12909	天津其他
13013	石家庄高新技术产业开发实验区
13016	石家庄综合保税区
13019	石家庄其他
1301W	辛集保税物流中心(B型)
13022	曹妃甸经济技术开发区
13026	曹妃甸综合保税区
13029	唐山
1302W	唐山港京唐港区保税物流中心(B型)
13032	秦皇岛经济技术开发区
13035	河北秦皇岛出口加工区
13036	秦皇岛综合保税区
13039	秦皇岛其他
13049	邯郸
13059	邢台
13063	保定高新技术产业开发区
13069	保定其他
1306N	雄安新区(保定)
13079	张家口
13089	承德
13099	沧州
1309N	雄安新区(沧州)
13102	廊坊经济技术开发区
13105	河北廊坊出口加工区
13106	廊坊综合保税区
13109	廊坊
13119	衡水
13129	武安
1312W	河北武安保税物流中心(B型)
1331N	河北雄安新区
13909	河北其他
14012	山西太原经济技术开发区
14013	太原高新技术产业开发区
14016	太原武宿综合保税区
14019	太原其他
14022	大同经济技术开发区
14029	大同
1402W	大同国际陆港保税物流中心(B型)
14039	阳泉
14043	长治高新技术产业开发区
14049	长治
14059	晋城
1405W	山西兰花保税物流中心(B型)
14069	朔州
14079	雁北
14089	忻州
14099	吕梁
14102	晋中经济技术开发区
14109	晋中
14119	临汾
1411W	山西方略保税物流中心
14129	运城
14139	古交
14909	山西其他
15015	内蒙古呼和浩特出口加工区
15016	呼和浩特综合保税区
15019	呼和浩特
15023	包头高新技术产业开发区
15029	包头其他
1502W	包头保税物流中心(B型)
15039	乌海
15049	赤峰
1504W	赤峰保税物流中心
15059	二连
15066	满洲里综合保税区
15069	满洲里
15079	呼伦贝尔盟
15089	哲里木盟
15099	兴安盟
15109	乌兰察布盟
1510W	七苏木保税物流中心(B型)
15119	巴彦淖尔市
1511W	巴彦淖尔市保税物流中心(B型)
15126	鄂尔多斯综合保税区
15129	伊克昭盟
15139	阿拉善盟
15149	锡林郭勒盟
15909	内蒙古其他
21012	沈阳经济技术开发区
21013	沈阳南湖科技开发区
21015	辽宁沈阳、张士出口加工区
21016	沈阳综合保税区
21019	沈阳其他
21022	大连经济技术开发区
21023	大连高新技术产业园区
21024	大连大窑湾保税区
21025	辽宁大连出口加工区
21026	大连大窑湾、湾里综合保税区
21027	大连保税物流园区
21029	大连其他
21033	鞍山高新技术产业开发区
21039	鞍山其他
21049	抚顺
21059	本溪
21069	丹东
21079	锦州

地区代码	地区名称
2107W	锦州港保税物流中心(B型)
21082	营口经济技术开发区
21086	营口综合保税区
21089	营口
2108W	营口港保税物流中心
21099	阜新
21109	辽阳
21119	盘锦
2111W	盘锦港保税物流中心(B型)
21129	铁岭
2112W	铁岭保税物流中心(B型)
21139	朝阳
21149	葫芦岛市
21159	瓦房店
21169	海城
21179	兴城
21189	铁法
21199	北票
21209	开源
21909	辽宁其他
22012	长春经济技术开发区
22013	长春南湖一南岭新技术产业园区
22016	长春兴隆综合保税区
22019	长春其他
22023	吉林高新技术产业开发区
22029	吉林其他
2202W	吉林市保税物流中心(B型)
22039	四平
22049	辽源
22059	通化
22069	白山
22075	吉林珲春出口加工区
22076	珲春综合保税区
22079	珲春
22089	图们
22099	白城
22109	延边
22119	公主岭
22129	梅河口
22139	集安
22149	桦甸
22159	九台
22169	蛟河
22179	松原
22189	延吉市
2218W	延吉国际空港经济开发区保税物流中心(B型)
22909	吉林其他
23012	哈尔滨经济技术开发区
23013	哈尔滨高技术开发区
23016	哈尔滨综合保税区
23019	哈尔滨其他
23029	齐齐哈尔
23039	鸡西
23049	鹤岗
23059	双鸭山
23063	大庆高新技术产业开发区
23069	大庆其他
23079	伊春
23089	佳木斯
23099	七台河
23109	牡丹江
2310W	牡丹江保税物流中心(B型)
23119	黑河
2311W	黑河保税物流中心(B型)
23126	绥芬河综合保税区
23129	绥芬河
23139	松花江
23142	绥化经济技术开发区
23149	绥化
23159	大兴安岭
23169	阿城
23179	同江
23189	富锦
23199	铁力
23209	密山
23909	黑龙江其他
31019	黄浦
31029	南市
31039	卢湾
31043	上海漕河泾新技术开发区
31049	徐汇其他
31052	上海经济技术开发区
31059	长宁
31069	静安
31079	普陀
3107W	上海西北物流园区保税物流中心
31089	闸北
31099	虹口
31109	杨浦
31112	上海闵行经济技术开发区
31113	上海浦江高科技园区
31115	上海漕河泾出口加工区
31116	漕河泾综合保税区
31119	闵行其他
3111W	虹桥商务区保税物流中心(B型)
31129	宝山
31145	上海嘉定出口加工区
31146	上海嘉定综合保税区
31149	嘉定
31159	川沙
31162	上海闵行经济技术开发区(临港新城)
31166	洋山保税港区
31169	南汇
31175	上海闵行出口加工区
31176	奉贤综合保税区
31179	奉贤
31185	上海松江出口加工区
31186	松江综合保税区
31189	松江
31199	金山
31205	上海青浦出口加工区
31206	青浦综合保税区
31209	青浦
31219	崇明
31222	上海浦东新区
31224	上海外高桥保税区
31225	上海金桥出口加工区南区
31226	上海外高桥、上海浦东机场或金桥综合保税区
31227	上海保税物流园区
31229	浦东其他
3122S	洋山特殊综合保税区
31909	上海其他
32013	南京浦口高新技术外向型开发区
32015	江苏南京出口加工区
32016	南京综合保税区
32019	南京其他
3201W	南京空港保税物流中心(B型)
32023	无锡高新技术产业开发区
32025	江苏无锡出口加工区
32026	无锡高新区综合保税区
32029	无锡其他
32036	徐州综合保税区
32039	徐州
3203W	徐州、新沂保税物流中心(B型)
32043	常州高新技术产业开发区
32045	江苏常州出口加工区
32046	常州综合保税区
32049	常州其他
32052	苏州工业园区
32053	苏州高新技术产业开发区
32055	江苏苏州工业园区加工区
32056	苏州工业园综合保税区、苏州高新综保区
32059	苏州其他
32062	南通经济技术开发区
32065	江苏南通出口加工区
32066	南通综合保税区
32069	南通其他
3206W	如皋港保税物流中心(B型)
32072	连云港经济技术开发区
32075	江苏连云港出口加工区
32076	连云港综合保税区
32079	连云港其他
3207W	连云港保税物流中心
32085	江苏省淮安出口加工区
32086	淮安综合保税区
32089	淮安市
32096	盐城综合保税区
32099	盐城
3209W	大丰港保税物流中心(B型)
32105	江苏扬州出口加工区
32106	扬州综合保税区
32109	扬州
32115	江苏镇江出口加工区
32116	镇江综合保税区
32119	镇江
32125	江苏泰州出口加工区
32126	泰州综合保税区
32129	泰州
3212W	靖江保税物流中心(B型)
32139	仪征
32145	江苏常熟出口加工区
32146	常熟综合保税区
32149	常熟
32154	江苏张家港保税区
32156	张家港保税港区
32157	张家港保税物流园
32159	张家港其他
32166	江阴综合保税区
32169	江阴
3216W	江阴保税物流中心
32179	宿迁
32189	丹阳
32199	东台
32209	兴化
32229	宜兴

地区代码	地区名称
32235	江苏昆山出口加工区
32236	昆山综合保税区
32239	昆山
32249	启东
32255	江苏吴江出口加工区
32256	吴江综合保税区
32259	吴江市
32266	太仓港综合保税区
32269	太仓市
3226W	太仓保税物流中心
32546	武进综合保税区
3256W	江苏海安保税物流中心(B型)
32909	江苏其他
33012	杭州经济技术开发区
33013	杭州高新技术产业开发区
33015	浙江杭州出口加工区
33016	杭州综合保税区
33019	杭州其他
33022	宁波经济技术开发区
33023	宁波高新技术产业开发区
33024	宁波北仑港保税区
33025	浙江宁波出口加工区
33026	宁波梅山、北仑港综合保税区
33027	宁波保税物流园
33029	宁波其他
3302W	宁波栎社保税物流中心
33032	温州经济技术开发区
33036	温州综合保税区
33039	温州其他
3303W	温州保税物流中心(B型)
33045	浙江嘉兴出口加工区
33046	嘉兴综合保税区
33049	嘉兴
33052	湖州经济技术开发区
33053	湖州莫干山高新技术产业开发区
33059	湖州
3305W	湖州及湖州德清物流中心(B型)
33066	绍兴综合保税区
33069	绍兴
33072	金华经济技术开发区
33076	金义综合保税区(一期)
33079	金华
33089	衢州
33096	舟山港综合保税区
33099	舟山
33109	丽水
33119	台州
33129	余姚
33139	海宁
33149	兰溪
33159	瑞安
33169	萧山
3316W	杭州保税物流中心
33179	江山
33186	义乌综合保税区
33189	义乌
3318W	义乌保税物流中心
33199	东阳
33202	宁波杭州湾经济技术开发区
33205	浙江慈溪出口加工区
33206	宁波前湾综合保税区
33209	慈溪
33219	奉化
33229	诸暨
33239	黄岩
3352W	宁波镇海保税物流中心(B型)
33909	浙江其他
34012	合肥经济技术开发区
34013	合肥科技工业园区
34015	安徽合肥出口加工区
34016	合肥或合肥经济技术开发区综合保税区
34019	合肥其他
3401W	合肥空港保税物流中心(B型)
34022	芜湖经济技术开发区
34023	芜湖高新技术产业开发区
34025	安徽芜湖出口加工区
34026	芜湖综合保税区
34029	芜湖其他
34033	蚌埠高新技术产业开发区
34039	蚌埠
3403W	蚌埠(皖北)保税物流中心
34042	安徽淮南经济技术开发区
34043	淮南高新技术产业开发区
34049	淮南
34052	马鞍山经济技术开发区
34053	马鞍山慈湖高新技术产业开发区
34056	马鞍山综合保税区
34059	马鞍山
34069	淮北
34072	铜陵经济技术开发区
34079	铜陵
3407W	铜陵(皖中南)保税物流中心(B型)
34082	安庆桐城经济技术开发区
34089	安庆
3408W	安庆(皖西南)保税物流中心(B型)
34099	黄山
34109	阜阳
34119	宿州
34122	滁州经济技术开发区
34129	滁州
34132	安徽六安经济技术开发区
34139	六安
34142	宣城宁国经济技术开发区
34149	宣城
3414W	安徽皖东南保税物流中心(B型)
34159	巢湖
34162	池州经济技术开发区
34169	池州
34179	亳州
34909	安徽其他
35012	福州经济技术开发区
35013	福州科技园区
35014	福建马尾保税区
35015	福建福州、福清出口加工区
35016	福州江阴港和福州综合保税区
35017	福州保税物流园区
35019	福州其他
3501W	翔福保税物流中心(B型)
35021	厦门特区
35023	厦门火炬高技术产业开发区
35024	厦门象屿保税区
35025	福建厦门出口加工区
35026	厦门海沧港、象屿综合保税区
35027	厦门象屿保税物流园
35029	厦门其他
3502W	厦门火炬(翔安)保税物流中心
35039	莆田
35049	三明
35055	福建泉州出口加工区
35056	泉州综合保税区
35059	泉州
35069	漳州
3506W	漳州台商投资区保税物流中心(B型)
35079	南平
35089	宁德
35099	龙岩
35109	永安
35119	石狮
3511W	泉州石湖港保税物流中心(B型)
35128	平潭综合试验区
35129	平潭
35909	福建其他
36012	南昌及南昌小蓝经济技术开发区
36013	南昌高新技术产业开发区
36015	江西南昌出口加工区
36016	南昌综合保税区
36019	南昌其他
3601W	南昌保税物流中心
36023	景德镇高新技术产业开发区
36029	景德镇
36032	萍乡经济技术开发区
36039	萍乡
36042	九江经济技术开发区
36043	九江共青城高新技术产业开发区
36045	江西九江出口加工区
36046	九江综合保税区
36049	九江
36053	新余高新技术产业开发区
36059	新余
36063	鹰潭高新技术产业开发区
36069	鹰潭
36072	赣州、龙南及瑞金经济技术开发区
36073	赣州高新技术产业开发区
36075	江西赣州出口加工区
36076	赣州综合保税区
36079	赣州
3607W	龙南保税物流中心(B型)
36082	宜春经济技术开发区
36083	宜春丰城高新技术产业开发区
36089	宜春
36092	上饶经济技术开发区
36099	上饶
36102	井冈山经济技术开发区
36103	吉安高新技术产业开发区
36105	井冈山出口加工区
36106	井冈山综合保税区
36109	吉安
36113	抚州高新技术产业开发区
36119	抚州
36129	瑞昌
36909	江西其他
37013	济南高技术产业开发区
37015	山东济南出口加工区
37016	济南或济南章锦综合保税区
37019	济南其他

地区代码	地区名称
37022	青岛经济技术开发区
37023	青岛高新技术产业开发区
37024	青岛保税区
37025	山东青岛出口加工区
37026	青岛前湾保税港区、青岛西海岸和胶州湾综合保税区
37027	青岛保税物流园
37029	青岛其他
3702W	青岛保税物流中心
37033	淄博高新技术产业开发区
37036	淄博综合保税区
37039	淄博
3703W	淄博保税物流中心
37049	枣庄
37056	东营综合保税区
37059	东营
37062	烟台经济技术开发区
37065	山东烟台出口加工区
37066	烟台综合保税区
37069	烟台其他
3706W	烟台福山回里保税物流中心(B型)
37073	潍坊高新技术产业开发区
37075	山东潍坊出口加工区
37076	潍坊综合保税区
37079	潍坊其他
37089	济宁
37099	泰安
37103	威海火炬高技术产业开发区
37105	山东威海出口加工区
37106	威海综合保税区北区
37109	威海其他
37112	日照经济技术开发区
37116	日照综合保税区
37119	日照
3711W	日照保税物流中心
37129	山东省滨州其他
3712W	鲁中运达保税物流中心
37139	德州
37149	聊城
37156	临沂综合保税区
37159	临沂
37169	菏泽
3716W	菏泽内陆港保税物流中心(B型)
37179	青州
37189	龙口
37199	曲阜
37209	莱芜
37219	新泰
37229	胶州
37239	诸城
3723W	青岛保税港区诸城功能区保税物流中心(B型)
37249	莱阳
37259	滕州
37266	威海综合保税区南区
37269	文登
37279	荣城
37286	青岛即墨综合保税区
37289	即墨
37299	平度
37909	山东其他
41012	郑州经济技术开发区
41013	郑州高新技术开发区
41015	河南郑州出口加工区
41016	郑州新郑、经开综合保税区
41018	郑州航空港经济综合实验区
41019	郑州其他
4101W	河南保税物流中心
41029	开封
41033	洛阳高新技术产业开发区
41039	洛阳其他
41049	平顶山
41059	安阳
41069	鹤壁
41079	新乡
41089	焦作
4108W	河南德众保税物流中心
41099	濮阳
41109	许昌
4110W	河南许昌保税物流中心(B型)
41119	漯河
41129	三门峡
41139	商丘
4113W	河南商丘、民权保税物流中心(B型)
41149	周口
41159	驻马店
41166	南阳卧龙综合保税区
41169	南阳
41179	信阳
41189	义马
41199	汝州
41209	济源
41219	禹州
41229	卫辉
41239	辉县
41249	泌阳
41909	河南其他
42012	武汉经济技术开发区
42013	武汉东湖新技术开发区
42015	湖北武汉出口加工区
42016	武汉东湖综合保税区
42019	武汉其他
4201W	武汉东西湖保税物流中心
42022	黄石经济技术开发区
42029	黄石
4202W	黄石棋盘洲保税物流中心
42039	十堰
42049	沙市
42056	宜昌综合保税区
42059	宜昌
4205W	宜昌三峡保税物流中心(B型)
42062	襄阳经济技术开发区
42063	襄阳高新技术产业开发区
42069	襄阳其他
4206W	襄阳保税物流中心(B型)
42079	鄂州
42089	荆门
4208W	荆门保税物流中心(B型)
42099	黄冈
42102	汉川经济技术开发区
42109	孝感
42119	咸宁
42122	荆州经济技术开发区
42129	荆州
42139	郧阳
42149	鄂西
42159	随州
42169	老河口
42172	枣阳经济技术开发区
42179	枣阳
42189	神农架
42199	仙桃市
4219W	仙桃保税物流中心(B型)
42209	潜江市
42219	天门市
42506	武汉新港空港
42909	湖北其他
43012	长沙经济技术开发区
43013	长沙科技开发区
43016	长沙黄花综合保税区
43019	长沙其他
4301W	长沙金霞保税物流中心
43023	株州高新技术产业开发区
43029	株州其他
4302W	株洲铜塘湾保税物流中心(B型)
43032	湘潭经济技术开发区
43033	湘潭高新技术产业开发区
43036	湘潭综合保税区
43039	湘潭
43043	衡阳高新技术产业开发区
43046	衡阳综合保税区
43049	衡阳
43059	邵阳
43062	岳阳经济技术开发区
43066	岳阳城陵矶综合保税区
43069	岳阳
43072	常德经济技术开发区
43073	常德高新技术产业开发区
43079	常德
43089	张家界
43093	益阳高新技术产业开发区
43099	益阳
43102	娄底经济技术开发区
43109	娄底
43113	郴州高新技术产业开发区
43115	湖南郴州出口加工区
43116	郴州综合保税区
43119	郴州
43129	永州
43133	怀化高新技术产业开发区
43139	怀化
43149	湘西
43159	醴陵
43169	湘乡
43179	耒阳
43189	汨罗
43199	津市
43202	浏阳经济技术开发区
43209	浏阳其他
43909	湖南其他
44012	广州经济技术开发区
44013	广州天河高新技术产业开发区
44014	广州保税区
44015	广东广州出口加工区
44016	广州白云机场、黄埔综合保税区
44017	广州保税物流园区
44019	广州其他

地区代码	地区名称
44029	韶关
44031	深圳特区
44033	深圳科技工业园
44034	福田盐田沙头角保税区
44035	广东深圳出口加工区
44036	深圳前海、坪山综合保税区
44037	深圳盐田保税物流园
44039	深圳其他
4403W	深圳机场保税物流中心
44041	珠海特区
44043	珠海高新技术产业开发区
44044	珠海保税区
44045	珠澳跨境工业区珠海园区
44046	珠海高栏港综合保税区
44048	珠海横琴新区
44049	珠海其他
44051	汕头特区
44054	汕头保税区
44056	汕头综合保税区
44059	汕头其他
4405W	汕头保税物流中心(B型)
44063	佛山高新技术产业开发区
44069	佛山其他
44079	江门
4407W	江门大广海湾保税物流中心(B型)
44082	湛江经济技术开发区
44083	湛江高新技术产业开发区
44086	湛江综合保税区
44089	湛江其他
4408W	湛江保税物流中心(B型)
44093	茂名高新技术产业开发区
44099	茂名
44129	肇庆
44133	惠州高新技术产业开发区
44139	惠州其他
44146	梅州综合保税区
44149	梅州
44159	汕尾
44169	河源
44179	阳江
44189	清远
44193	东莞松山湖高新技术产业开发区
44196	东莞虎门港综合保税区
44199	东莞
4419W	东莞保税物流中心
44203	中山火炬高技术产业开发区
44209	中山其他
4420W	中山保税物流中心
44219	潮州
44229	顺德
4422W	佛山国通保税物流中心(B型)
44235	广东南沙出口加工区
44236	广州南沙保税港区
44239	番禺
44249	揭阳
44289	南海
44299	云浮市
44306	广州南沙综合保税区
44309	南沙其他
44536	深圳盐田综合保税区(一期)
4469W	东莞清溪保税物流中心(B型)
44909	广东其他

地区代码	地区名称
45013	南宁高新技术产业开发区
45016	南宁综合保税区
45019	南宁其他
4501W	南宁保税物流中心
45029	柳州
4502W	柳州保税物流中心(B型)
45033	桂林高新技术产业开发区
45039	桂林其他
45049	梧州
45055	广西北海出口加工区
45056	北海综合保税区
45059	北海
45069	玉林
45079	百色
45089	河池
45096	钦州综合保税区
45099	钦州
45106	广西凭祥综合保税区
45109	凭祥
45119	东兴
45129	防城港市
4512W	防城港保税物流中心(B型)
45139	贵港市
45149	崇左
45159	来宾
45169	贺州
45909	广西其他
46011	海口
46013	海南国际科技园区
46014	海南海口保税区
46016	海口综合保税区及海口空港综合保税区
46021	三亚
4602W	海南三亚保税物流中心(B型)
46031	三沙
46041	五指山
46051	琼海
46061	儋州
46062	洋浦经济开发区
46066	洋浦保税港区
46071	文昌
46081	万宁
46091	东方
46101	定安
46111	屯昌
46121	澄迈
46131	临高
46141	白沙
46151	昌江
46161	乐东
46171	陵水
46181	保亭
46191	琼中
46901	海南其他
46902	海南洋浦经济技术开发区
46906	海南洋浦保税港区
50012	万州经济技术开发区
50016	重庆万州综合保税区
50019	万州区
50026	重庆涪陵综合保税区
50029	涪陵区
50039	渝中区
50049	大渡口区

地区代码	地区名称
50052	重庆两江新区江北区
50056	重庆两路寸滩综合保税区(水港)
50059	江北区
5005W	重庆果园保税物流中心(B型)
50066	重庆西永综合保税区
50069	沙坪坝区
5006W	重庆铁路保税物流中心
50073	重庆高新技术产业开发区
50079	九龙坡区
50082	重庆经济技术开发区
50089	南岸区
50092	重庆两江新区北碚区
50099	北碚区
50109	万盛区
50119	双桥区
50122	重庆两江新区渝北区
50125	重庆出口加工区
50126	重庆两路寸滩综合保税区(空港)
50129	渝北区
50139	巴南区
5013W	重庆南彭公路保税物流中心(B型)
50212	长寿经济技术开发区
50219	长寿县
50229	綦江区
50239	潼南县
50249	重庆市铜梁区
50259	大足区
50269	荣昌县
50279	重庆市璧山区
50289	梁平县
50299	城口县
50309	丰都县
50319	垫江县
50329	武隆县
50339	忠县
50349	开县
50359	云阳县
50369	奉节县
50379	巫山县
50389	巫溪县
50399	黔江
50409	石柱土家族自治县
50419	秀山土家族苗族自治县
50429	酉阳土家族苗族自治县
50439	彭水苗族土家族自治县
50816	重庆江津综合保税区
50819	江津区
50829	合川区
50836	重庆永川综合保税区
50839	永川区
50849	南川区
51012	成都经济技术开发区
51013	成都高新技术产业开发区
51015	四川成都出口加工区
51016	成都高新、国际铁路港或高新西园综合保税区
51019	成都其他
5101W	成都空港、天府新区成都片区保税物流中心
51039	自贡
51049	攀枝花
51053	泸州高新技术产业开发区

地区代码	地区名称
51056	泸州综合保税区
51059	泸州
5105W	泸州港保税物流中心(B型)
51069	德阳
51072	绵阳经济技术开发区
51073	绵阳高新技术产业开发区
51075	四川绵阳出口加工区
51076	绵阳综合保税区
51079	绵阳其他
51082	广元经济技术开发区
51089	广元
51099	遂宁
51109	内江
51113	乐山高新技术产业开发区
51119	乐山
51142	宜宾临港经济开发区
51146	宜宾综合保税区
51149	宜宾
5114W	宜宾港保税物流中心(B型)
51159	南充
5115W	南充保税物流中心(B型)
51169	达县
51179	雅安
51189	阿坝
51199	甘孜
51209	凉山
51229	广汉
51239	江油
51249	都江堰
51259	峨眉山
51269	资阳
51279	眉山
51289	广安
51299	巴中
5151W	成都铁路保税物流中心(B型)
51909	四川其他
52013	贵阳高新技术产业开发区
52016	贵阳综合保税区
52019	贵阳其他
52029	六盘水
52036	遵义综合保税区
52039	遵义
52049	铜仁
52059	黔西南
52069	毕节
52079	安顺
52089	黔东南
52099	黔南
52502	贵阳贵安新区
52506	贵安综合保税区
52909	贵州其他
53012	昆明经济技术开发区
53013	昆明高新技术产业开发区
53015	云南昆明出口加工区
53016	昆明综合保税区
53019	昆明其他
5301W	昆明高新保税物流中心(B型)
53029	东川
53039	昭通
53042	曲靖经济技术开发区
53049	曲靖
53059	楚雄
53069	玉溪
53072	云南省蒙自经济技术开发区
53076	云南红河综合保税区
53079	红河
53089	文山
53099	普洱
53109	西双版纳
53119	大理
53129	保山
53139	德宏
53149	丽江
53159	怒江
53169	迪庆
53179	临沧
53189	畹町
53199	瑞丽
53209	河口
5351W	腾俊国际陆港保税物流中心(B型)
53909	云南其他
54012	拉萨经济技术开发区
54016	拉萨综合保税区
54019	拉萨
54029	昌都
54039	山南
54049	日喀则
54059	那曲
54069	阿里
54079	林芝
54909	西藏其他
61012	陕西航天、陕西航空、西安市经济技术开发区
61013	西安新技术产业开发区
61015	陕西西安出口加工区
61016	西安、西安高新、西安航空基地和西安关中综合保税区
61019	西安其他
61029	铜川
61033	宝鸡高新技术产业开发区
61036	宝鸡综合保税区
61039	宝鸡其他
61043	杨凌农业高新技术产业示范区
61046	陕西西咸空港、杨凌综合保税区
61049	咸阳
6104W	陕西西咸保税物流中心
61059	渭南
61062	汉中经济技术开发区
61069	汉中
61079	安康
61089	商洛
61099	延安
61102	陕西榆林经济技术开发区
61109	榆林
61909	陕西其他
62013	兰州宁卧庄新技术产业开发区
62016	兰州新区综合保税区
62019	兰州其他
62029	嘉峪关
62039	金昌
62049	白银
62059	天水
62069	酒泉
62079	张掖
62089	武威
6208W	武威保税物流中心
62099	定西
62109	陇南
62119	平凉
62129	庆阳
62139	临夏
62149	甘南
62909	甘肃其他
63012	西宁经济技术开发区
63013	青海高新技术产业开发区
63016	西宁综合保税区
63019	西宁
63029	海东
6302W	青海曹家堡保税物流中心(B型)
63039	海北
63049	黄南
63059	海南
63069	果洛
63079	玉树
63082	格尔木昆仑经济技术开发区
63089	海西
63909	青海其他
64012	银川经济技术开发区
64016	银川综合保税区
64019	银川
64029	石嘴山
6402W	石嘴山保税物流中心(B型)
64039	吴中
64049	固原
64059	中卫
64909	宁夏其他
65012	乌鲁木齐经济技术开发区
65013	乌鲁木齐高新技术产业开发区
65015	新疆乌鲁木齐出口加工区
65016	乌鲁木齐综合保税区
65019	乌鲁木齐其他
65029	克拉玛依
65036	阿拉山口综合保税区
65039	博乐
65049	巴音
65059	阿克苏
65069	克孜
65076	喀什综合保税区
65079	喀什
65089	和田
65095	中哈霍尔果斯国际边境合作中心中方配套区(一期)
65096	霍尔果斯综合保税区
65099	伊宁
6509A	中哈霍尔果斯国际边境合作中心中方区域
6509W	奎屯保税物流中心
65109	塔城
65119	阿勒泰
65122	石河子经济技术开发区
65129	石河子
65219	吐鲁番
65229	哈密
65239	昌吉回族自治州
65909	新疆其他

港口代码表

请登录网址（https://www.i—tong.cn），或打开手机微信“扫一扫”，扫描下列二维码，按步骤操作，获取具体内容。

操作步骤：

第一步：登录上述网址或者扫码后，进入“易通网”注册界面，凭本书封面“扫码获取增值服务”标签涂层中的账号及密码，完成注册。（已经注册的直接登录“易通网”）

第二步：进入易通网首页，查询“易通助手”项下的常用代码表，找到“港口代码表”，点击查看或者直接下载，获取具体表格内容。

常用代码表

结汇方式代码表
计量单位代码表
港口航线代码表
监管方式与征免性质对照表
成交方式代码表
关区代码表
国内地区代码表
企业性质代码表
征免性质代码表
包装种类代码表
征免税方式代码表
港口代码表
UN编码
项目产业性质代码表
监管证件代码表
贸易方式代码表

Aruba	阿鲁巴	ABW000	查看
Carleton, Canada	卡尔顿（加拿大）	CAN075	查看
Santiago De Cuba, Cuba	圣地亚哥（古巴）	CUB117	查看
St.Nazaire, France	圣纳泽尔（法国）	FRA234	查看
Nauplia, Greece	纳夫普利亚（希腊）	GRC129	查看
Porto Empedocle, Italy	恩佩多克莱港（意大利）	ITA153	查看
Campeche, Mexico	坎佩切（墨西哥）	MEX009	查看
Calbayog, Philippines	甲描育（菲律宾）	PHL045	查看
Lomma, Sweden	卢马（瑞典）	SWE138	查看
Van Bc, United States	VAN BC (美国)	USA918	查看

‹ 1 2 3 4 5 6 ··· 427 › 前往 1 页 10条/页 共 4270 条

国内口岸代码表

请登录网址（https://www.i—tong.cn），或打开手机微信“扫一扫”，扫描下列二维码，按步骤操作，获取具体内容。

操作步骤：

第一步：登录上述网址或者扫码后，进入“易通网”注册界面，凭本书封面“扫码获取增值服务”标签涂层中的账号及密码，完成注册。（已经注册的直接登录“易通网”）

第二步：进入易通网首页，查询“易通助手”项下的常用代码表，找到“国内口岸代码表”，点击查看或者直接下载，获取具体表格内容。

常用代码表

国内地区代码表
企业性质代码表
征免性质代码表
包装种类代码表
征免税方式代码表
港口代码表
UN编码
项目产业性质代码表
监管证件代码表
贸易方式代码表
运输方式代码表
国别（地区）代码表
三字代码表
进口货物贸易协定代码表
用途代码表
国内口岸代码表

Beijing Pinggu Automobile Luga...	北京平谷国际陆港	110002	查看
Chizhou	池州	340801	查看
Zhanjiang Donghaidao Baogang...	湛江东海岛宝钢基地码头	440816	查看
Chongqing Jiangbei Internation...	重庆江北国际机场	500601	查看
Beijing Tianzhu Comprehensive ...	北京天竺综合保税区	110003	查看
Chuzhou	滁州	340901	查看

‹ 1 2 3 4 5 6 ··· 138 › 前往 1 页 10条/页 共 1376 条

UN 编码

请登录网址（https://www.i－tong.cn），或打开手机微信“扫一扫”，扫描下列二维码，按步骤操作，获取具体内容。

操作步骤：

第一步：登录上述网址或者扫码后，进入“易通网”注册界面，凭本书封面“扫码获取增值服务”标签涂层中的账号及密码，完成注册。（已经注册的直接登录“易通网”）

第二步：进入易通网首页，查询“易通助手”项下的常用代码表，找到“UN 编码”，点击查看或者直接下载，获取具体表格内容。

常用代码表

地区性质代码表
币制代码表
结汇方式代码表
计量单位代码表
港口航线代码表
监管方式与征免性质对照表
成交方式代码表
关区代码表
国内地区代码表
企业性质代码表
征免性质代码表
包装种类代码表
征免税方式代码表
港口代码表
UN编码
项目产业性质代码表

全部　请输入关键字　搜索

名称	编号	操作
氧氯化硒	2879	查看
2,4,6-三硝基苯酚铵[干的或含水<10%]	1900-01-04	查看
硝基磁漆	1139, 1263,1293	查看
溴	1744	查看
氰化亚铜(三)钠	2316	查看
灭多威乳剂[含量0.5%~30%]	2758, 2772, 2991, 2992, 3005, 3006	查看
次氯酸钙混合或水合物[含水量5.5%~10%],如:	2880	查看
环三次甲基三硝胺[含水≥15%]	1900-03-12	查看
过氯乙烯木器漆	1139, 1263,1293	查看
五氟化溴	1745	查看

随附单据

序号	单证名称	来源部门	具体明细
1	合同	进出口企业	
2	发票	进出口企业	
3	装箱单	进出口企业	
4	提/运单	进出口企业	
5	载货清单(舱单)	进出口企业	
6	代理报关委托协议(纸质)		
6	代理报关委托协议(电子)		
7	检验检疫证书	国内外官方机构/相关机构	1.兽医(卫生)证书 2.动物检疫证书 3.植物检疫证书 4.装运前检验证书 5.重量证书 6.TCK 检验证书(美国小麦) 7.熏蒸证书 8.放射性物质检测合格证明 9.木材发货检验码单 10.水果预检验证书 11.中转进境确认证明文件(经港澳地区中转入境水果) 12.检测报告
8	批准文件	海关(由海关总署签发的除纳入《监管证件表》目录的相关批准文件)	1.海关进口证明书 2.海关免税证明 3.免于办理强制性产品认证证明 4.进境动植物检疫许可证 5.进口车辆识别代码(VIN)校验报告单 6,境外捐赠机构登记和捐赠医疗器械备案材料 7.入/出境特殊物品卫生检疫审批单 8.进口食品接触产品备案书 9.型式试验合格证明(首次进口压力管道元件) 10.进口棉花境外供货企业登记证书(已登记的境外供货企业) 11.进口涂料备案书 12.同意调入函(植物繁殖材料) 13.实施金伯利进程国际证书制度注册登记证

检验检疫证件代码表

证件代码	证件名称	证件代码	证件名称
L	民用商品入境验证	R	进口食品卫生监督检验
M	进口商品检验	S	出口食品卫生监督检验
N	出口商品检验	V	进境卫生检疫
P	进境动植物、动植物产品检疫	W	出境卫生检疫
Q	出境动植物、动植物产品检疫		

特殊证件代码表

特殊监管证件代码	特殊监管证件说明	具体要求或发布单位
1	含甲苯、丙酮、丁酮、硫酸4种易制毒化学品之一且比例高于40%的货物应当办理《两用物项和技术进出口许可证》	海关总署关于明确易制毒化学品监管有关问题的通知 主要内容:为进一步规范易制毒化学品进出口监管,经研究并商商务部,现就易制毒化学品进出口许可证件管理有关要求明确如下:一、根据商务部公告2007年第23号,含甲苯、丙酮、丁酮、硫酸4种易制毒化学品之一且比例高于40%的货物应当办理《两用物项和技术进出口许可证》(以下简称"两用物项许可证")。含甲苯、丙酮、丁酮、硫酸4种易制毒化学品之一且比例高于40%的货物是指:(一)上述4种物项的单一成份含量超过40%的混合物;(二)上述4种物项的单一成份含量不超过40,但其总含量超过40%的混合物。上述易制毒化学品混合物进出口时,商务发证机构按照含量占比最高的物项核发两用物项许可证,许可证"商品名称"和"海关商品编号"栏目均按该物项填报,"规格型号"栏目则填报不同成份的品名简称及其含量。例如,含甲苯20%、丙酮30%、丁酮20%和硫酸10%的混合物办理两用物项许可证时,许可证商品名称栏目填写"丙酮",海关商品编号栏目填写"2914110000",规格型号栏目填写"丙30甲20丁20硫10"。海关在办理易制毒化学品混合物通关手续时,应要求进出口经营者按照货物实际商品名称及相应海关商品编号申报,验核两用物项许可证,并人工核扣许可证进出口数量。二、因加工贸易方式在境内产生的副产品属于易制毒化学品的货物,企业办理其内销手续时无须申领《两用物项和技术进口许可证》。三、含易制毒化学品的混合物办理深加工结转手续时,转入方企业无须提交《两用物项和技术进口许可证》。 施行时间:2012年8月6日。
2	其第二法定计量数量(计量单位为升)应统一按附件中给定公式,由第一法定数量(计量单位为千克)换算后向海关申报	中华人民共和国海关总署公告 2013年第10号 自2009年1月1日起,国家按照升(第二法定数量)对成品油计征进口环节消费税。海关总署陆续发布了2008年第99号公告、2009年第15号公告(已废止)和2010年第46号公告,对应税成品油商品的第二法定数量进行了规范。为确保海关统计数据的准确性,便于企业在办理各类海关手续中遵循统一标准,经研究,现就成品油的法定数量申报要求补充规定如下:一、进出口货物的收发货人及其代理人在向海关申报《中华人民共和国进出口税则》和《中华人民共和国海关统计商品目录》中商品品目"2710"项下商品时,其第二法定计量数量(计量单位为升)应统一按附件中给定公式,由第一法定数量(计量单位为千克)换算后向海关申报。二、第一法定数量未在合同等报关单随附单证及其他相关单证中直接列明的,应先按照实际密度及体积计算并申报第一法定数量,再换算第二法定数量。零售包装的成品油,其第一法定数量应为扣除零售包装后的液体部分重量。按照商业惯例成品油通常会含有一定数量的水份,申报第一法定数量时不应扣除含水量。三、本公告适用于进出口货物报关单、进出境货物备案清单等各类具有第二法定计量单位和法定数量栏目的海关单证的申报及修改。四、本公告内容自2013年4月1日起执行。 特此公告。 2013年3月8日
3	危险化学品目录(2015版) 凡列入《危险化学品目录(2015版)》的商品均应依法向海关申报。凡编码涉及危险化学品的商品,出口报关时应向海关申请电子底账,出口报关时应填写电子底账号;进口时应向海关申报"检验检疫名称"等信息。	特别提示:由于存在危险化学品和非危险化学品共用一个HS编码的情况,若不属于目录内货物且无检验检疫监管条件的,出口申报时可勾选"非危险化学品",请认真核对品名(参见易通网的《危险化学品商品编号和检验检疫名称对应表》)。 危险化学品属法定检验范围,现行《危险化学品目录》(2015版)中涉及危险化学品项目多达2828项,目前新一代通关管理系统仅凭《实施检验检疫的进出境商品目录》》的商品HS编码来区分是否需实施法定检验,由于海关税则的HS编码以及商品名称与《危险化学品目录》中的化学品名称尚未一一对应,法检目录外但在《危险化学品目录》(2015版)的危化品未进行监管条件设置,在向海关申报进出口过程中,对未进行监管条件设置的危险化学品的监管很大程度上依靠企业的主动申报,系统不能进行有效识别和风险判别,可能造成逃漏检风险。

企业产品许可类别代码表

类别代码	类别名称	强制级别	证书类别
000	企业产品许可类别		
100	通关司类		
101	检疫处理单位审批	D	98
102	实施绿色通道制度申请	D	99
103	直通放行申请		98,99
104	检疫处理人员审批		98,99
200	卫生司类		
203	出入境特殊物品卫生检疫审批	A	19,20
300	动植司类		
301	出境水果包装厂注册登记	B	21
302	出境水果果园注册登记	B	99
303	进境水果境外果园/包装厂注册登记	C	21
304	出境水生动物养殖场/包转场检验检疫注册登记	A	99
305	出口饲料和饲料添加剂生产、加工、存放企业注册登记	C	99
306	进口饲料和饲料添加剂生产企业注册登记	C	98
307	进境非食用动物产品生产、加工、存放企业注册登记	C	98
308	出境货物木质包装除害处理标识加施资格申请	B	99
309	出境种苗花卉生产经营企业注册登记	B	99
310	出境竹木草制品生产企业注册登记	C	99
311	出口植物产品生产、加工、存放企业注册登记	C	99
312	进境植物繁殖材料隔离检疫圃申请	C	98
315	供港澳陆生动物饲养场、中转场检验检疫注册	C	12
317	进出境动物指定隔离检疫场使用申请	C	98,99
318	出境动物及其非食用动物产品生产、加工、存放企业注册登记	C	99
319	进境栽培介质使用单位注册	C	98
320	进境动物遗传物质进口代理及使用单位备案	A	98
321	进境动物及动物产品国外生产单位注册	C	98
322	饲料进口企业备案	B	98
323	饲料出口企业备案	C	99
324	出境货物木质包装除害处理合格凭证	C	99
325	进境动植物检疫许可证	A	17
326	进境粮食加工储存单位注册	C	98
400	检验司类		
401	进出口商品免验	A	98,99
402	进口旧机电产品备案	C	39
404	出口产品型式试验	B	32
408	汽车预审备案	C	98
409	免于强制性认证特殊用途进口汽车检测处理程序车辆	C	98
410	免于办理强制性产品认证	C	40
411	强制性产品(CCC)认证	C	40
412	进口涂料备案	C	98
413	进口可用作原料的固体废物国内收货人注册登记	D	98
414	进口可用作原料的固体废物国外供货商注册登记	D	98
415	进出境集装箱场站登记	C	98,99
416	进口棉花境外供货商登记注册	B	98
417	出口玩具质量许可(注册登记)	A	11
418	对出口食品包装生产企业和进口食品包装的进口商实行备案	B	21
419	输美日用陶瓷生产厂认证	A	99
421	进出口商品检验鉴定机构许可	B	98,99
422	进口废物原料装运前检验证书	C	33
423	进口旧机电产品装运前检验证书	C	27
500	食品局类		
501	出口肉类产品养殖场备案	A	99
502	出口蛋禽养殖场备案	B	99
503	出口蜂产品养蜂基地备案	C	99
504	出口食品原料种植场备案	C	99
505	供港澳蔬菜生产加工企业备案	C	99
506	供港澳蔬菜种植基地备案	C	99
507	出口粮谷豆类生产加工企业注册登记	C	99
508	进口食品境外出口商代理商备案	C	98
509	进口食品进口商备案	C	98
510	进口肉类收货人备案	C	98
511	进口肉类存储冷库备案	C	98
512	出口加工用水产养殖场备案	A	99
513	进口水产品存储冷库备案	C	98
514	出口化妆品生产企业备案	C	99
515	进口化妆品收货人备案	C	98
516	进口化妆品产品备案	A	98
517	进口预包装食品标签备案	A	25
518	出口食品生产企业备案	A	15
519	进口食品境外生产企业注册	A	16
520	出口食品生产企业境外注册	A	14
522	水果冻肉预检验证书	C	98
523	进口化妆品产品套装备案	A	25
600	综合类		18
601	进口其他证书	D	98
602	出口其他证书	A	99
700	认监委类		
800	准入肉类名单		17
900	进口肉类名录		17

包装种类代码表

种类代码	种类名称
00	散装
01	裸装
22	纸制或纤维板制盒/箱
23	木制或竹藤等植物性材料制盒/箱
29	其他材料制盒/箱
32	纸制或纤维板制桶
33	木制或竹藤等植物性材料制桶
39	其他材料制桶
04	球状罐类
06	包/袋
92	再生木托
93	天然木托
98	植物性铺垫材料
99	其他包装

关联理由代码表

关联理由代码	关联理由名称
1	通关单超过有效期
2	换证凭单/条超过有效期
3	进口复出口
4	出口复进口
5	出境预检
6	登检换证
7	与其它报检批拼箱
8	保税出库
9	进口车辆换证
10	拼单

结汇方式代码表

结汇方式代码	结汇方式名称
1	信汇
2	电汇
3	票汇
4	付款交单
5	承兑交单
6	信用证
7	先出后结
8	先结后出
9	其他

用途代码表

用途代码	用途名称
01	外贸自营内销
02	特区内销
03	其它内销
04	企业自用
05	加工返销
06	借用
07	收保证金
08	免费提供
09	作价提供
10	货样,广告品
11	其它
13	以产顶进

货物属性代码表

属性代码	属性名称
11	3C 目录内
12	3C 目录外
13	无需办理 3C 认证
14	预包装
15	非预包装
16	转基因产品
17	非转基因产品
18	首次进出口
19	正常
20	废品
21	旧品
22	成套设备
23	带皮木材/板材
24	不带皮木材/板材
25	A 级特殊物品
26	B 级特殊物品
27	C 级特殊物品
28	D 级特殊物品
29	V/W 非特殊物品
30	市场采购

危包规格代码表

规格代码	规格名称	规格简称
1A1	钢制不可拆装桶顶圆桶	闭口钢桶
1A2	钢制可拆装桶顶圆桶	开口钢桶
1B1	铝制不可拆装桶顶圆桶	闭口铝桶
1B2	铝制可拆装桶顶圆桶	开口铝桶
1D	胶合板圆桶	胶板圆桶
1G	纤维圆桶	纤维圆桶
1H1	塑料不可拆装桶顶圆桶	闭口塑料圆桶
1H2	塑料可拆装桶顶圆桶	开口塑料圆桶
2C1	塞式木琵琶桶	木琵琶桶
2C2	非水密型木琵琶桶	木琵琶桶
3A1	钢制不可拆装罐顶罐	闭口钢罐
3A2	钢制可拆装罐顶罐	开口钢罐
3B1	铝制不可拆装罐顶罐	闭口铝罐
3B2	铝制可拆装罐顶罐	开口铝罐
3H1	塑料制不可拆装罐顶罐	闭口塑料罐
3H2	塑料制可拆装罐顶罐	开口塑料罐
4A	钢箱	钢箱
4B	铝箱	铝箱
4C1	大木箱	大木箱
4C2	箱壁防撒漏木箱	防漏木箱
4D	胶合板箱	胶合板箱
4F	再生木木箱	再生木木箱
4G	纤维板箱	纤维板箱
4H1	膨胀的塑料箱	塑料箱
4H2	硬质的塑料箱	塑料箱
5H	塑料编织袋	塑料编织袋
5H1	塑料编织无内衬或涂层的袋	塑料编织袋
5H2	塑料编织防撒漏的袋	塑料编织袋
5H3	塑料编织防水的袋	塑料编织袋
5H4	塑料薄膜袋	塑料薄膜袋
5L1	无内衬或涂层的纺织品编织袋	纺织品编织袋
5L2	纺织品防撒漏的纺织品编织袋	纺织品编织袋
5L3	纺织品防水的纺织品编织袋	纺织品编织袋
5M1	多层的纸袋	纸袋
5M2	多层防水纸袋	纸袋
6HA1	塑料容器在钢桶内复合包装	钢桶塑料复包
6HA2	塑料容器在钢条或钢皮箱内复合包装	钢皮箱塑料复包
6HB	塑料容器在铝桶内复合包装	铝桶塑料复包
5M1	多层的纸袋	纸袋
6HB2	塑料容器在铝条或铝皮箱内复合包装	铝皮箱塑料复包
6HC	塑料容器在木箱内复合包装	木箱塑料复包
6HD1	塑料容器在胶合板桶内复合包装	胶板桶塑料复包
6HD2	塑料容器在胶合板箱内复合包装	胶板箱塑料复包
6HG1	塑料容器在纤维桶内复合包装	纤维桶塑料复包
6HG2	塑料容器在纤维板箱内复合包装	纤维板箱塑料复包
6HH1	塑料容器在塑料桶内复合包装	塑料桶塑料复包
6HH2	塑料容器在硬塑料箱内复合包装	硬塑料箱复包
6PA1	玻璃、陶瓷、粗陶器在钢桶内复合包装	玻璃钢桶复包
6PA2	玻璃、陶瓷、粗陶器在钢条或钢皮箱内复合包装	玻璃陶瓷钢皮箱复包
6PB1	玻璃、陶瓷、粗陶器在铝桶内复合包装	玻璃陶瓷铝桶复包
6PB2	玻璃、陶瓷、粗陶器在铝条或铝皮箱内复合包装	玻璃陶瓷铝皮箱复包
6PC	玻璃、陶瓷、粗陶器在木箱内复合包装	玻璃陶瓷木箱复包
6PD1	玻璃、陶瓷、粗陶器在胶合板内复合包装	玻璃陶瓷胶板复包
6PD2	玻璃、陶瓷、粗陶器在柳条筐内复合包装	玻璃陶瓷柳条筐复包
6PG1	玻璃、陶瓷、粗陶器在纤维桶内复合包装	玻璃陶瓷纤维桶复包
6PG2	玻璃、陶瓷、粗陶器在纤维板箱内复合包装	玻璃陶瓷纤维板复包
6PH1	玻璃、陶瓷、粗陶器在膨胀塑料包装内复合包	玻璃陶瓷膨塑复包
6PH2	玻璃、陶瓷、粗陶器在硬塑料包装内复合包装	玻璃陶瓷硬塑复包

集装箱规格代码表

规格代码	规格名称
11	普通 2 * 标准箱(L)
12	冷藏 2 * 标准箱(L)
13	罐式 2 * 标准箱(L)
21	普通标准箱(S)
22	冷藏标准箱(S)
23	罐式标准箱(S)
31	其他标准箱(S)
32	其他 2 * 标准箱(L)

货币代码表

货币代码	货币符号	中文名称
110	HKD	港币
112	IDR	印度尼西亚卢比
116	JPY	日本元
121	MOP	澳门元
122	MYR	马来西亚林吉特
129	PHP	菲律宾比索
132	SGD	新加坡元
133	KRW	韩国圆
136	THB	泰国铢
142	CNY	人民币
143	TWD	新台币
300	EUR	欧元
302	DKK	丹麦克朗
303	GBP	英镑
326	NOK	挪威克朗
330	SEK	瑞典克朗
331	CHF	瑞士法郎
344	RUB	俄罗斯卢布
501	CAD	加拿大元
502	USD	美元
601	AUD	澳大利亚元
609	NZD	新西兰元

计量单位代码表

计量单位代码	计量单位名称
001	台
002	座
003	辆
004	艘
005	架
006	套
007	个
008	只
009	头
010	张
011	件
012	支
013	枝
014	根
015	条
016	把
017	块
018	卷
019	副
020	片
021	组
022	份
023	幅
025	双
026	对
027	棵
028	株
029	井
030	米
031	盘
032	平方米
033	立方米
034	筒
035	千克
036	克
037	盆
038	万个
039	具
040	百副
041	百支
042	百把

计量单位代码	计量单位名称
043	百个
044	百片
045	刀
046	疋
047	公担
048	扇
049	百枝
050	千只
051	千块
052	千盒
053	千枝
054	千个
055	亿支
056	亿个
057	万套
058	千张
059	万张
060	千伏安
061	千瓦
062	千瓦时
063	千升
067	英尺
070	吨
071	长吨
072	短吨
073	司马担
074	司马斤
075	斤
076	磅
077	担
078	英担
079	短担
080	两
081	市担
083	盎司
084	克拉
085	市尺
086	码
088	英寸
089	寸
095	升

计量单位代码	计量单位名称
096	毫升
097	英加仑
098	美加仑
099	立方英尺
101	立方尺
110	平方码
111	平方英尺
112	平方尺
115	英制马力
116	公制马力
118	令
120	箱
121	批
122	罐
123	桶
124	扎
125	包
126	箩
127	打
128	筐
129	罗
130	匹
131	册
132	本
133	发
134	枚
135	捆
136	袋
139	粒
140	盒
141	合
142	瓶
143	千支
144	万双
145	万粒
146	千粒
147	千米
148	千英尺
149	百万贝可
163	部
164	亿株
170	人份

成交方式代码表

成交方式代码	成交方式名称
1	CIF
2	C&F
3	FOB
4	C&I

成交方式代码	成交方式名称
5	市场价
6	垫仓
7	EXW

国别(地区)代码表

代码	中文国家(地区)名称	国际标准英文简称	英文国家(地区)名称	优惠/普通税率标记	船舶吨税优/普标记
101	阿富汗	AFG	Afghanistan	L	H
102	巴林	BHR	Bahrian	L	H
103	孟加拉国	BGD	Bangladesh	L	L
104	不丹	BTN	Bhutan	H	H
105	文莱	BRN	Brunei	L	H
106	缅甸	MMR	Myanmar	L	H
107	柬埔寨	KHM	Cambodia	L	H
108	塞浦路斯	CYP	Cyprus	L	L
109	朝鲜	PRK	Korea,DPR	L	L
110	中国香港	HKG	Hong Kong,China	L	L
111	印度	IND	India	L	L
112	印度尼西亚	IDN	Indonesia	L	L
113	伊朗	IRN	Iran	L	L
114	伊拉克	IRQ	Iraq	L	H
115	以色列	ISR	Israel	L	L
116	日本	JPN	Japan	L	L
117	约旦	JOR	Jordan	L	H

代码	中文国家(地区)名称	国际标准英文简称	英文国家(地区)名称	优惠/普通税率标记	船舶吨税优/普标记
118	科威特	KWT	Kuwait	L	H
119	老挝	LAO	Lao PDR	L	H
120	黎巴嫩	LBN	Lebanon	L	L
121	中国澳门	MAC	Macau,China	L	L
122	马来西亚	MYS	Malaysia	L	L
123	马尔代夫	MDV	Maldives	L	H
124	蒙古	MNG	Mongolia	L	L
125	尼泊尔联邦民主共和国	NPL	Nepal, FDR	L	H
126	阿曼	OMN	Oman	L	L
127	巴基斯坦	PAK	Pakistan	L	L
128	巴勒斯坦	PSE	Palestine	H	H
129	菲律宾	PHL	Philippines	L	L
130	卡塔尔	QAT	Qatar	L	H
131	沙特阿拉伯	SAU	Saudi Arabia	L	H
132	新加坡	SGP	Singapore	L	L
133	韩国	KOR	Korea, Rep.	L	L

代码	中文国家(地区)名称	国际标准英文简称	英文国家(地区)名称	优惠/普通税率标记	船舶吨税优/普标记
134	斯里兰卡	LKA	Sri Lanka	L	L
135	叙利亚	SYR	Syrian Arab Republic	L	H
136	泰国	THA	Thailand	L	L
137	土耳其	TUR	Turkey	L	L
138	阿联酋	ARE	United Arab Emirates	L	H
139	也门	YEM	Yemen	L	L
141	越南	VNM	Viet Nam	L	L
142	中国	CHN	China	L	L
143	中国台湾	TWN	Taiwan,China	L	H
144	东帝汶	TLS	Timor－Leste	L	H
145	哈萨克斯坦	KAZ	Kazakhstan	L	H
146	吉尔吉斯斯坦	KGZ	Kyrgyzstan	L	H
147	塔吉克斯坦	TJK	Tajikistan	L	H
148	土库曼斯坦	TKM	Turkmenistan	L	H
149	乌兹别克斯坦	UZB	Uzbekistan	L	H
199	亚洲其他国家(地区)		Oth. Asia nes		H
201	阿尔及利亚	DZA	Algeria	L	L
202	安哥拉	AGO	Angola	L	H
203	贝宁	BEN	Benin	L	H
204	博茨瓦纳	BWA	Botswana	L	H
205	布隆迪	BDI	Burundi	L	H
206	喀麦隆	CMR	Cameroon	L	H
207	加那利群岛		Canary Islands	H	H
208	佛得角	CPV	Cape Verde	L	H
209	中非	CAF	Central African Republic.	L	H
210	塞卜泰(休达)		Ceuta	H	H
211	乍得	TCD	Chad	L	H
212	科摩罗	COM	Comoros	H	H
213	刚果(布)	COG	Congo	L	L
214	吉布提	DJI	Djibouti	L	H
215	埃及	EGY	Egypt	L	L
216	赤道几内亚	GNQ	Equatorial Guinea	L	H
217	埃塞俄比亚	ETH	Ethiopia	L	L
218	加蓬	GAB	Gabon	L	H
219	冈比亚	GMB	Gambia	L	H
220	加纳	GHA	Ghana	L	L
221	几内亚	GIN	Guinea	L	H
222	几内亚比绍	GNB	Guinea－Bissau	L	H
223	科特迪瓦	CIV	Cote d'lvoire	L	H
224	肯尼亚	KEN	Kenya	L	L
225	利比里亚	LBR	Liberia	L	L
226	利比亚	LBY	Libyan Arab Jamahiriya	L	H
227	马达加斯加	MDG	Madagascar	L	H
228	马拉维	MWI	Malawi	L	H
229	马里	MLI	Mali	L	H
230	毛里塔尼亚	MRT	Mauritania	L	H
231	毛里求斯	MUS	Mauritius	L	H
232	摩洛哥	MAR	Morocco	L	L
233	莫桑比克	MOZ	Mozambique	L	H
234	纳米比亚	NAM	Namibia	L	H
235	尼日尔	NER	Niger	L	H
236	尼日利亚	NGA	Nigeria	L	H
237	留尼汪	REU	Reunion	H	H
238	卢旺达	RWA	Rwanda	L	H
239	圣多美和普林西比	STP	Sao Tome and Principe	H	H
240	塞内加尔	SEN	Senegal	L	H
241	塞舌尔	SYC	Seychelles	H	H
242	塞拉利昂	SLE	Sierra Leone	L	H
243	索马里	SOM	Somalia	L	H
244	南非	ZAF	South Africa	L	L
245	西撒哈拉	ESH	Western Sahara	H	H
246	苏丹	SDN	Sudan	L	L
247	坦桑尼亚	TZA	Tanzania	L	H
248	多哥	TGO	Togo	L	H
249	突尼斯	TUN	Tunisia	L	L
250	乌干达	UGA	Uganda	L	H
251	布基纳法索	BFA	Burkina Faso	L	H
252	刚果(金)	COD	Congo,DR	L	L
253	赞比亚	ZMB	Zambia	L	H
254	津巴布韦	ZWE	Zimbabwe	L	H
255	莱索托	LSO	Lesotho	L	H
256	梅利利亚		Melilla	H	H
257	斯威士兰	SWZ	Swaziland	L	H
258	厄立特里亚	ERI	Eritrea	L	H
259	马约特	MYT	Mayotte	L	H
260	南苏丹共和国		Republic of South Sudan	L	H
299	非洲其他国家(地区)		Oth. Afr. nes		H
301	比利时	BEL	Belgium	L	L
302	丹麦	DNK	Denmark	L	L
303	英国	GBR	United Kingdom	L	L
304	德国	DEU	Germany	L	L
305	法国	FRA	France	L	L
306	爱尔兰	IRL	Ireland	L	L
307	意大利	ITA	Italy	L	L
308	卢森堡	LUX	Luxembourg	L	L
309	荷兰	NLD	Netherlands	L	L
310	希腊	GRC	Greece	L	L
311	葡萄牙	PRT	Portugal	L	L
312	西班牙	ESP	Spain	L	L
313	阿尔巴尼亚	ALB	Albania	L	L
314	安道尔	AND	Andorra	H	H
315	奥地利	AUT	Austria	L	L
316	保加利亚	BGR	Bulgaria	L	L
318	芬兰	FIN	Finland	L	L
320	直布罗陀	GIB	Gibraltar	H	L
321	匈牙利	HUN	Hungary	L	L
322	冰岛	ISL	Iceland	L	H
323	列支敦士登	LIE	Liechtenstein	L	H
324	马耳他	MLT	Malta	L	L
325	摩纳哥	MCO	Monaco	L	H
326	挪威	NOR	Norway	L	L
327	波兰	POL	Poland	L	L
328	罗马尼亚	ROM	Romania	L	L
329	圣马力诺	SMR	San Marino	L	H
330	瑞典	SWE	Sweden	L	L
331	瑞士	CHE	Switzerland	L	H
334	爱沙尼亚	EST	Estonia	L	L
335	拉脱维亚	LVA	Latvia	L	L
336	立陶宛	LTU	Lithuania	L	L
337	格鲁吉亚	GEO	Georgia	L	L
338	亚美尼亚	ARM	Armenia	L	H
339	阿塞拜疆	AZE	Azerbai jan	L	H
340	白俄罗斯	BLR	Belarus	L	H
343	摩尔多瓦	MDA	Moldova	L	H
344	俄罗斯联邦	RUS	Russian Federation	L	L
347	乌克兰	UKR	Ukraine	L	L
349	塞尔维亚和黑山			H	H
350	斯洛文尼亚	SVN	Slovenia	L	L
351	克罗地亚	HRV	Croatia	L	L
352	捷克	CZE	Czech Republic	L	L
353	斯洛伐克	SVK	Slovakia	L	L
354	北马其顿共和国	MKD	Republic of North Macedonia	L	H
355	波黑	BIH	Bosnia and Hercegovina	L	H
356	梵蒂冈城国	VAT	Vatican City State	H	H
357	法罗群岛	FRO	Faroe Islands	L	H
358	塞尔维亚	SRB	Serbia	L	H
359	黑山	MNE	Montenegro	L	H
399	欧洲其他国家(地区)		Oth. Eur. nes		H
401	安提瓜和巴布达	ATG	Antigua & Barbuda	L	H
402	阿根廷	ARG	Argentina	L	L
403	阿鲁巴	ABW	Aruba	H	H
404	巴哈马	BHS	Bahamas	H	L
405	巴巴多斯	BRB	Barbados	L	H
406	伯利兹	BLZ	Belize	L	H

代码	中文国家(地区)名称	英文国家(地区)名称	英文国别名称	优惠/普通税率标记	船舶吨税优/普标记
408	多民族玻利维亚国	BOL	Estado Plurinacional de Bolivia	L	H
409	博内尔		Bonaire	H	H
410	巴西	BRA	Brazil	L	L
411	开曼群岛	CYM	Cayman Islands	H	L
412	智利	CHL	Chile	L	L
413	哥伦比亚	COL	Colombia	L	H
414	多米尼克	DMA	Dominica	L	H
415	哥斯达黎加	CRI	Costa Rica	L	H
416	古巴	CUB	Cuba	L	L
417	库腊索岛	CUW	Curacao	H	H
418	多米尼加共和国	DOM	Dominican Republic	L	H
419	厄瓜多尔	ECU	Ecuador	L	H
420	法属圭亚那	GUF	French Guiana	H	H
421	格林纳达	GRD	Grenada	L	H
422	瓜德罗普	GLP	Guadeloupe	H	H
423	危地马拉	GTM	Guatemala	L	H
424	圭亚那	GUY	Guyana	L	H
425	海地	HTI	Haiti	L	H
426	洪都拉斯	HND	Honduras	L	H
427	牙买加	JAM	Jamaica	L	H
428	马提尼克	MTQ	Martinique	H	H
429	墨西哥	MEX	Mexico	L	L
430	蒙特塞拉特	MSR	Montserrat	H	H
431	尼加拉瓜	NIC	Nicaragua	L	H
432	巴拿马	PAN	Panama	L	L
433	巴拉圭	PRY	Paraguay	L	H
434	秘鲁	PER	Peru	L	L
435	波多黎各	PRI	Puerto Rico	L	H
436	萨巴		Saba	H	H
437	圣卢西亚	LCA	Saint Lucia	L	H
438	圣马丁岛		Saint Martin Islands	H	H
439	圣文森特和格林纳丁斯	VCT	Saint Vincent and Grenadines	L	H
440	萨尔瓦多	SLV	El Salvador	L	H
441	苏里南	SUR	Suriname	L	H
442	特立尼达和多巴哥	TTO	Trinidad and Tobago	L	H
443	特克斯和凯科斯群岛	TCA	Turks and Caicos Islands	H	H
444	乌拉圭	URY	Uruguay	L	H
445	委内瑞拉	VEN	Venezuela	L	H
446	英属维尔京群岛	VGB	Virgin Islands, British	H	H
447	圣其茨和尼维斯	KNA	Saint Kitts and Nevis	L	H
448	圣皮埃尔和密克隆	SPM	Saint. Pierre and Miquelon	L	H
449	荷属安地列斯	ANT	Netherlands Antilles	H	H
499	拉丁美洲其他国家(地区)	BES	Oth. L.Amer. nes		H
501	加拿大	CAN	Canada	L	L
502	美国	USA	United States	L	L
503	格陵兰	GRL	Greenland	L	H
504	百慕大	BMU	Bermuda	H	L
599	北美洲其他国家(地区)		Oth. N.Amer. nes		H
601	澳大利亚	AUS	Australia	L	H
602	库克群岛	COK	Cook Islands	L	H
603	斐济	FJI	Fiji	L	H
604	盖比群岛		Gambier Islands	H	H
605	马克萨斯群岛		Marquesas Islands	H	H
606	瑙鲁	NRU	Nauru	H	H
607	新喀里多尼亚	NCL	New Caledonia	L	H
608	瓦努阿图	VUT	Vanuatu	L	H
609	新西兰	NZL	New Zealand	L	L
610	诺福克岛	NFK	Norfolk Island	H	H
611	巴布亚新几内亚	PNG	Papua New Guinea	L	H
612	社会群岛		Society Islands	H	H
613	所罗门群岛	SLB	Solomon Islands	L	H
614	汤加	TON	Tonga	L	H
615	土阿莫土群岛		Tuamotu Islands	H	H
616	土布艾群岛		Tubai Islands	H	H
617	萨摩亚	WSM	Samoa	L	H
618	基里巴斯	KIR	Kiribati	L	H
619	图瓦卢	TUV	Tuvalu	H	H
620	密克罗尼西亚联邦	FSM	Micronesia, Fs	L	H
621	马绍尔群岛	MHL	Marshall Islands	H	H
622	帕劳	PLW	Palau	H	H
623	法属波利尼西亚	PYF	French Polynesia	L	H
625	瓦利斯和浮图纳	WLF	Wallis and Futuna	L	H
699	大洋洲其他国家(地区)	MNP	Oth. Ocean. nes		H
701	国(地)别不详		Countries(reg.) unknown	H	H
702	联合国及机构和国际组织		UN and oth. int'l org.		
999	中性包装原产国别		Conutries of Neutral Package	H	H

地区性质代码表

地区性质代码	地区性质名称
1	经济特区
2	沿海开放城市
3	经济技术开发区
4	经济开放区
5	海南省
6	西藏自治区
7	广东省
8	福建省
9	北京市、新疆
A	保税工业区
B	新技术开发园区

企业性质代码表

企业性质代码	企业性质名称
1	国有
2	合作
3	合资
4	独资
5	集体
6	私营
7	个体工商户
8	报关
9	其他

4

中华人民共和国海关进口关税税率附表

（2022年1月1日起实施）

Import tariff attached table

（Enforced from January 1, 2022）

附表 1：

Attached table 1：

2022 年关税配额商品税目、税率表

（2022 年 1 月 1 日起实施）

In-Quota Interim Duty Rate on Imported Goods，2022

（Enforced from January 1，2022）

说明：2022 年在国家规定配额内的进口货物，按下表配额内的税率执行；超过配额数量的进口货物，执行税则当中的法定关税税率，即配额外税率。

Explanation：During 2022，according to the state regulations，goods imported within quota，will be processed using the In-Quota Duty Rate Schedule below；goods imported exceeding the quota amount，will be processed using Statutory Tariff Rate in the Tariff Schedule，that is，Out-Quota Tariff Rate.

序号 No.	货品名称 Description of Goods	税则号列 Tariff No.	2022 年进口税率(%) Import Duty Rate(%)					
			配额外税率 Out-Quota Duty Rate		配额内税率 In-Quota Duty Rate	国别关税配额税率		
			普通税率 Gen.	最惠国税率 M. F. N.		中国—新西兰(%)	中国—澳大利亚(%)	中国—毛里求斯
1	小麦	10011100	180	65	1			
		10011900	180	65	1			
		10019100	180	65	1			
		10019900	180	65	1			
		11010000	130	65	6			
		11031100	130	65	9			
		11032010	180	65	10			
2	玉米	10051000	180	20	1			
		10059000	180	65	1			
		11022000	130	40	9			
		11031300	130	65	9			
		11042300	180	65	10			
3	稻谷和大 米	10061021	180	65	1			
		10061029	180	65	1			
		10061081	180	65	1			
		10061089	180	65	1			
		10062020	180	65	1			
		10062080	180	65	1			
		10063020	180	65	1			
		10063080	180	65	1			
		10064020	180	10	1			
		10064080	180	10	1			
		11029021	130	40	9			
		11029029	130	40	9			
		11031931	70	10	9			
		11031939	70	10	9			
4	糖	17011200	125	50	15			15
		17011300	125	50	15			15
		17011400	125	50	15			15
		17019100	125	50	15			15
		17019910	125	50	15			15
		17019920	125	50	15			15
		17019990	125	50	15			15
5	羊毛	51011100	50	38	1	0	0	
		51011900	50	38	1	0	0	
		51012100	50	38	1	0	0	
		51012900	50	38	1	0	0	
		51013000	50	38	1	0	0	
		51031010	50	38	1	0	0	
6	毛条	51051000	50	38	3	0		
		51052100	50	38	3	0		
		51052900	50	38	3	0		
7	棉花	52010000	125	40[注 1]	1			
		52030000	125	40	1			
8	化肥	31021000	150	50	4[注 2]			
		31052000	150	50	4[注 3]			
		31053000	150	50	4[注 4]			

[注 1]：对配额外进口的一定数量棉花，适用滑准税形式暂定关税，具体方式如下：

1.当进口棉花完税价格高于或等于 14.000 元/千克时，按 0.280 元/千克计征从量税；

2.当进口棉花完税价格低于 14.000 元/千克时，暂定从价税率按下式计算：$Ri=9.0/Pi + 2.69\% \times Pi - 1$。对上式计算结果四舍五入保留 3 位小数。其中 Ri 为暂定从价税率，当按上式计算值高于 40%时，Ri 取值 40%；Pi 为关税完税价格，单位为元/千克。

[注 2、3、4]：进口暂定税率为 1%。

附表 2：CIQ 扩展编码及品名

HS 编码	CIQ 扩展品名
0106191010	101 斑马，102 犀，103 貘，104 其他野生奇蹄动物，105 鹿，106 长颈鹿，107 黄羊，108 河马，109 羚牛，110 羚羊，111 青羊（斑羚），112 叉角羚，113 骆马，114 美洲驼，115 角马，116 梅花鹿，117 马鹿，118 其他野生偶蹄动物，119 狐狸，120 貂，121 大熊猫，122 小熊猫，123 熊，124 水獭，125 果子狸，126 狮，127 虎，128 豹，129 貉，130 豺，131 狼，132 大灵猫，133 小灵猫，134 野狗，135 其他野生食肉动物，136 旱獭，137 松鼠，138 花鼠，139 麝鼠，140 海狸鼠，141 河狸，142 地鼠，143 豪猪，144 其他野生啮齿动物，145 猩猩，146 狒狒，147 山魈，148 其他野生灵长动物，149 象，150 刺猬，151 穿山甲，152 袋鼠，153 蝙蝠，154 其他野生哺乳动物
0106191090	101 其他饲养奇蹄动物，102 其他饲养偶蹄动物，103 伴侣犬，104 工作犬，105 其他用途犬，106 伴侣猫，107 其他用途猫，108 其他饲养食肉动物，109 大鼠，110 小鼠，111 豚鼠，112 其他饲养啮齿动物，113 其他饲养兔形目动物，114 其他饲养哺乳动物
0106199010	101 斑马，102 犀，103 貘，104 其他野生奇蹄动物，105 鹿，106 长颈鹿，107 黄羊，108 河马，109 羚牛，110 羚羊，111 青羊（斑羚），112 叉角羚，113 骆马，114 美洲驼，115 角马，116 梅花鹿，117 马鹿，118 其他野生偶蹄动物，119 狐狸，120 貂，121 大熊猫，122 小熊猫，123 熊，124 水獭，125 果子狸，126 狮，127 虎，128 豹，129 貉，130 豺，131 狼，132 大灵猫，133 小灵猫，134 野狗，135 其他野生食肉动物，136 旱獭，137 松鼠，138 花鼠，139 麝鼠，140 海狸鼠，141 河狸，142 地鼠，143 豪猪，144 其他野生啮齿动物，145 猩猩，146 狒狒，147 山魈，148 其他野生灵长动物，149 象，150 刺猬，151 穿山甲，152 袋鼠，153 蝙蝠，154 其他野生哺乳动物
0106199090	101 其他饲养奇蹄动物，102 其他饲养奇蹄动物，103 伴侣犬，104 工作犬，105 其他用途犬，106 伴侣猫，107 其他用途猫，108 其他饲养食肉动物，109 大鼠，110 小鼠，111 豚鼠，112 其他饲养啮齿动物，113 其他饲养兔形目动物，114 其他饲养哺乳动物
0106201900	101 乌龟，102 草龟，103 绿毛龟，104 鳖（甲鱼、团鱼），105 玳瑁，106 鳄龟，107 其他龟鳖，108 蛇，109 蜥蜴，110 鳄，111 壁虎，112 巨蜥，113 蟒，114 其他爬行动物
0106209090	101 乌龟，102 草龟，103 绿毛龟，104 鳖（甲鱼、团鱼），105 玳瑁，106 鳄龟，107 其他龟鳖，108 蛇，109 蜥蜴，110 鳄，111 壁虎，112 巨蜥，113 蟒，114 其他爬行动物
0106391010	101 鹌鹑，102 鹧鸪，103 孔雀，104 竹鸡，105 锦鸡，106 锦鸡，107 雉（山鸡），108 乌骨鸡，109 鸬鹚，110 鹈鹕，111 其他野生鸡形目禽鸟，112 天鹅，113 鸳鸯，114 野鸭，115 大雁，116 其他野生雁形目禽鸟，117 画眉，118 杜鹃（野生禽鸟），119 百灵，120 金丝鸟，121 相思鸟，122 鹤，123 鸵鸟，124 鸸鹋，125 朱鹮，126 火烈鸟，127 巨嘴鸟，128 厚嘴妥空，129 其他野生禽鸟
0106399010	101 鹌鹑，102 鹧鸪，103 孔雀，104 竹鸡，105 松鸡，106 锦鸡，107 雉（山鸡），108 乌骨鸡，109 鸬鹚，110 鹈鹕，111 其他野生鸡形目禽鸟，112 天鹅，113 鸳鸯，114 野鸭，115 大雁，116 其他野生雁形目禽鸟，117 画眉，118 杜鹃（野生禽鸟），119 百灵，120 金丝鸟，121 相思鸟，122 鹤，123 鸵鸟，124 鸸鹋，125 朱鹮，126 火烈鸟，127 鹰，128 巨嘴鸟，129 厚嘴妥空，130 其他野生禽鸟
0106901910	101 斑马，102 犀，103 貘，104 其他野生奇蹄动物，105 鹿，106 长颈鹿，107 黄羊，108 河马，109 羚牛，110 羚羊，111 青羊（斑羚），112 叉角羚，113 骆马，114 美洲驼，115 角马，116 梅花鹿，117 马鹿，118 其他野生偶蹄动物，119 狐狸，120 貂，121 大熊猫，122 小熊猫，123 熊，124 水獭，125 果子狸，126 狮，127 虎，128 豹，129 貉，130 豺，131 狼，132 大灵猫，133 小灵猫，134 野狗，135 其他野生食肉动物，136 旱獭，137 松鼠，138 花鼠，139 麝鼠，140 海狸鼠，141 河狸，142 地鼠，143 豪猪，144 其他野生啮齿动物，145 其他野生灵长动物，146 象，147 刺猬，148 穿山甲，149 袋鼠，150 蝙蝠，151 其他野生哺乳动物
0106901990	101 其他饲养奇蹄动物，102 其他饲养偶蹄动物，103 其他用途犬，104 其他用途猫，105 其他饲养食肉动物，106 大鼠，107 小鼠，108 豚鼠，109 其他饲养啮齿动物，110 其他饲养兔形目动物，111 其他饲养哺乳动物
0106909010	101 其他饲养奇蹄动物，102 其他饲养偶蹄动物，103 其他用途犬，104 其他用途猫，105 其他饲养食肉动物，106 大鼠，107 小鼠，108 豚鼠，109 其他饲养啮齿动物，110 其他饲养兔形目动物，111 其他饲养哺乳动物，112 斑马，113 犀，114 貘，115 其他野生奇蹄动物，117 鹿，118 长颈鹿，119 黄羊，120 河马，121 羚牛，122 羚羊，123 青羊（斑羚），124 叉角羚，125 骆马，126 美洲驼，127 角马，128 梅花鹿，129 马鹿，130 其他野生偶蹄动物，131 狐狸，132 貂，133 大熊猫，134 小熊猫，135 熊，136 水獭，137 果子狸，138 狮，139 虎，140 豹，141 貉，142 豺，143 狼，144 大灵猫，145 小灵猫，146 野狗，147 其他野生食肉动物，148 旱獭，149 松鼠，150 花鼠，151 麝鼠，152 海狸鼠，153 河狸，154 地鼠，155 豪猪，156 其他野生啮齿动物，157 其他野生灵长动物，158 象，159 刺猬，160 穿山甲，161 袋鼠，162 蝙蝠，163 其他野生哺乳动物，164 牛蛙，165 青蛙，166 金线蛙，167 棘胸蛙，168 其他蛙，169 大鲵（娃娃鱼），170 小鲵，171 蟾蜍，172 蝾螈，173 鱼螈，174 其他两栖动物，175 蚕，176 蟋蟀，177 蚱蜢，178 蝉，179 蝴蝶，180 其他昆虫（其他动物），181 禾虫，182 蜈蚣（其他动物），183 蝎（其他动物），184 蚯蚓（其他动物），185 其他本章动物
0106909090	101 其他饲养奇蹄动物，102 其他饲养偶蹄动物，103 伴侣犬，104 工作犬，105 其他用途犬，106 伴侣猫，107 其他用途猫，108 其他饲养食肉动物，109 大鼠，110 小鼠，111 豚鼠，112 其他饲养啮齿动物，113 其他饲养兔形目动物，114 其他饲养哺乳动物，115 牛蛙，116 青蛙，117 金线蛙，118 棘胸蛙，119 其他蛙，120 大鲵（娃娃鱼），121 小鲵，122 蟾蜍，123 蝾螈，124 鱼螈，125 其他两栖动物，126 蚕，127 蟋蟀，128 蚱蜢，129 蝉，130 蝴蝶，131 其他昆虫（其他动物），132 禾虫，133 蜈蚣（其他动物），134 蝎（其他动物），135 蚯蚓（其他动物），136 其他本章动物
0204500000	101 鲜的去骨山羊肉，102 鲜的带骨山羊肉，103 鲜的整头及半头山羊肉，104 冷藏去骨山羊肉，105 冷藏带骨山羊肉，106 冷藏整头及半头山羊肉，107 冻藏去骨山羊肉，108 冻藏带骨山羊肉，109 冻藏整头及半头山羊肉，110 鲜的去骨野羊肉，111 鲜的带骨野羊肉，112 鲜的整头及半头野羊肉，113 冷藏去骨野羊肉，114 冷藏带骨野羊肉，115 冻藏整头及半头野羊肉，116 冻藏去骨野羊肉，117 冻藏带骨野羊肉，118 冷藏整头及半头野羊肉，119 冷藏去骨山羊肉（6 月龄以下），120 冷藏带骨山羊肉（6 月龄以下），121 冷藏整头及半头山羊肉（6 月龄以下），122 冻藏去骨山羊肉（6 月龄以下），123 冻藏带骨山羊肉（6 月龄以下），124 冻藏整头及半头山羊肉（6 月龄以下）
0205000010	101 鲜的去骨野马肉，102 鲜的带骨野马肉，103 鲜的整头及半头野马肉，104 冷藏去骨野马肉，105 冷藏带骨野马肉，106 冷藏整头及半头野马肉，107 冻藏去骨野马肉，108 冻藏带骨野马肉，109 冻藏整头及半头野马肉，110 鲜的去骨野驴肉，111 鲜的带骨野驴肉，112 鲜的整头及半头野驴肉，113 冷藏去骨野驴肉，114 冷藏带骨野驴肉，115 冷藏整头及半头野驴肉，116 冻藏去骨野驴肉，117 冻藏带骨野驴肉，118 冻藏整头及半头野驴肉
0205000090	101 鲜的去骨马肉，102 鲜的带骨马肉，103 鲜的整头及半头马肉，104 冷藏去骨马肉，105 冷藏带骨马肉，106 冷藏整头及半头马肉，107 冻藏去骨马肉，108 冻藏带骨马肉，109 冻藏整头及半头马肉，110 鲜的去骨驴肉，111 鲜的带骨驴肉，112 鲜的整头及半头驴肉，113 冻藏去骨驴肉，114 冷藏带骨驴肉，115 冷藏整头及半头驴肉，116 冷藏去骨驴肉，117 冻藏带骨驴肉，118 冻藏整头及半头驴肉，119 鲜的去骨骡肉，120 鲜的带骨骡肉，121 鲜的整头及半头骡肉，122 冷藏去骨骡肉，123 冷藏带骨骡肉，124 冷藏整头及半头骡肉，125 冻藏去骨骡肉，126 冻藏带骨骡肉，127 冻藏整头及半头骡肉
0206100000	101 鲜的牛心，102 冷藏牛心，103 鲜的牛鞭，104 冷藏牛鞭，105 鲜的牛舌，106 冷藏牛舌，107 鲜的牛尾，108 冷藏牛尾，109 鲜的牛肝，110 冷藏牛肝，111 鲜的牛筋，112 冷藏牛筋，113 鲜的牛横膈膜，114 冷藏牛横膈膜，115 鲜的牛头及头块，116 冷藏的牛头及头块，117 鲜的牛食用皮，118 冷藏牛食用皮，119 鲜的牛肾，120 冷藏牛肾，121 鲜的牛脚，122 冷藏牛脚，123 鲜的其他牛杂碎，124 冷藏其他牛杂碎，125 鲜的野牛心，126 冷藏野牛心，，127 鲜的野牛舌，128 冷藏野牛舌，129 鲜的野牛尾，130 冷藏野牛尾，131 鲜的野牛肝，132 冷藏野牛肝，133 鲜的野牛筋，134 冷藏野牛筋，135 鲜的野牛横膈膜，136 冷藏野牛横膈膜，137 鲜的野牛头及头块，138 冷藏野牛头及头块，139 鲜的野牛食用皮，140 冷藏野牛食用皮，141 鲜的野牛肾，142 冷藏野牛肾，143 鲜的野牛脚，144 冷藏野牛脚，145 鲜的其他野牛杂碎，146 冷藏其他野牛杂碎，147 冷藏牛心（30 月龄以下），148 冷藏牛舌（30 月龄以下），149 冷藏牛尾（30 月龄以下），150 冷藏牛肝（30 月龄以下），151 冷藏牛筋（30 月龄以下），152 冷藏牛横膈膜（30 月龄以下），153 冷藏牛头及头块（冰鲜牛头（30 月龄以下）），154 冷藏牛头及头块（冰鲜牛唇（30 月龄以下）），155 冷藏牛肾（30 月龄以下），156 冷藏牛脚（冰鲜牛蹄（30 月龄以下）），157 冷藏其他牛杂碎（冰鲜牛骨（30 月龄以下）），158 冷藏牛唇，159 冷藏牛蹄，160 冷藏牛骨，161 冷藏牛胸腹隔膜，162 冷藏牛软骨，163 冷藏牛睾丸，164 冷藏牛心管，165 牛筋（30 月龄以下）

HS 编码	CIQ 扩展品名
0206290000	101 牛心，102 冻牛鞭，103 冻牛尾，104 冻牛筋，105 牛横膈膜，106 牛头及头块，107 牛食用皮，108 牛肾，109 牛脚，110 其他牛杂碎，111 野牛心，112 野牛尾，113 野牛筋，114 野牛横膈膜，115 野牛头及头块，116 野牛食用皮，117 野牛肾，118 野牛脚，119 其他野牛杂碎，121 牛心(30 月龄以下)，123 冻牛尾(30 月龄以下)，124 冻牛筋(30 月龄以下)，125 牛横膈膜(30 月龄以下)，126 牛头及头块(冷冻牛头肉(30 月龄以下))，127 牛头及头块(冷冻牛头肉)，128 牛头及头块(冷冻牛唇)，129 牛头及头块(冷冻牛唇(30 月龄以下))，130 牛肾(30 月龄以下)，131 牛脚(去除蹄匣)，132 其他牛杂碎(冷冻牛骨)，133 其他牛杂碎(冷冻牛骨(30 月龄以下))，134 其他牛杂碎(冷冻牛动脉管)，135 其他牛杂碎(冷冻牛心管)，136 其他牛杂碎(冷冻牛睾丸)，137 其他牛杂碎(冷冻牛食管)，138 其他牛杂碎(冷冻牛骨髓)，139 其他牛杂碎(冷冻牛软骨)，140 其他牛杂碎(冷冻牛软骨不含喉软骨)，149 冷冻牛胸腹隔膜，150 冷冻牛鞭(30 月龄以下)，151 冷冻牛蹄(去匣)(30 月龄以下)
0206300000	101 鲜的猪心，102 冷藏猪心，103 鲜的猪肝，104 冷藏猪肝，105 鲜的猪肺，106 冷藏猪肺，107 鲜的猪肾，108 冷藏猪肾，109 鲜的猪舌，110 冷藏猪舌，111 鲜的猪尾，112 冷藏猪尾，113 鲜的猪耳，114 冷藏猪耳，115 鲜的猪蹄，116 冷藏猪蹄，117 鲜的猪睾丸，118 冷藏猪睾丸，119 鲜的猪食用皮，120 冷藏猪食用皮，121 鲜的猪头及头块，122 冷藏猪头及头块，123 鲜的猪横膈膜，124 冷藏猪横膈膜，125 鲜的其他猪杂碎，126 冷藏其他猪杂碎，127 鲜的野猪心，128 冷藏野猪心，129 鲜的野猪肝，130 冷藏野猪肝，131 鲜的野猪肺，132 冷藏野猪肺，133 鲜的野猪肾，134 冷藏野猪肾，135 鲜的野猪舌，136 冷藏野猪舌，137 鲜的野猪尾，138 冷藏野猪尾，139 鲜的野猪耳，140 冷藏野猪耳，141 鲜的野猪蹄，142 冷藏野猪蹄，143 鲜的野猪全蹄，144 冷藏野猪全蹄，145 鲜的野猪睾丸，146 冷藏野猪睾丸，147 鲜的野猪食用皮，148 冷藏野猪食用皮 149 鲜的野猪头及头块，150 冷藏野猪头及头块，151 鲜的野猪横膈膜，152 冷藏野猪横膈膜，153 鲜的其他野猪杂碎，154 冷藏其他野猪杂碎，155 冷藏猪蹄(全蹄)，156 冷藏猪耳根，157 冷藏猪鼻，158 冷藏猪脸，159 冷藏猪唇，160 冷藏猪脚圈，161 冷藏猪下颚，162 冷藏猪心管，163 冷藏猪脚趾，164 冷藏猪皮，165 冷藏猪头，166 冷藏猪脑，167 冷藏猪气管，168 冷藏猪食管，169 冷藏猪软管，170 冷藏猪喉管，171 冷藏猪骨
0206490000	101 猪心，102 猪肺，103 猪肾，104 猪舌，105 猪尾，106 猪耳，107 猪蹄，109 猪睾丸，110 猪食用皮，111 猪头及头块，112 猪横膈膜，113 其他猪杂碎，114 野猪心，115 野猪肺，116 野猪肾，117 野猪舌，118 野猪尾，119 野猪耳，120 野猪蹄，121 野猪全蹄，122 野猪睾丸，123 野猪食用皮，124 野猪头及头块，125 野猪横膈膜，126 其他野猪杂碎，127 猪耳(不包括内耳)，128 猪耳(冷冻猪耳根)，129 猪蹄(全蹄)，130 猪蹄(冷冻猪脚圈)，131 猪蹄(冷冻猪脚趾)，132 猪头及头块)(冷冻猪脸)，133 猪头及头块(冷冻猪头)134 猪头及头块(不包括内耳)，135 猪头及头块(冷冻猪下颚)，136 猪头及头块(冷冻猪鼻)，137 猪头及头(冷冻猪唇)，138 其他猪杂碎(冷冻猪鞭)，139 其他猪杂碎(冷冻猪喉骨)，140 其他猪杂碎(冷冻猪气管)，141 其他猪杂碎(冷冻猪脑)，142 其他猪杂碎(冷冻猪食管)，143 其他猪杂碎(冷冻猪心管)，144 其他猪杂碎(冷冻猪软骨)，146 其他猪杂碎(冷冻猪骨)
0206800010	101 饲料用绵羊肠，102 饲料用绵羊真胃(绵羊肚)，103 饲料用绵羊瓣胃(绵羊百叶)，104 饲料用绵羊网胃，105 饲料用绵羊瘤胃，106 饲料用绵羊心，107 饲料用绵羊肝，108 饲料用绵羊肺，109 饲料用绵羊肾，110 饲料用其他绵羊杂碎，111 饲料用山羊肠，112 饲料用山羊真胃(山羊肚)，113 饲料用山羊瓣胃(山羊百叶)，114 饲料用山羊网胃，115 饲料用山羊瘤胃，116 饲料用山羊心，117 饲料用山羊肝，118 饲料用山羊肺，119 饲料用山羊肾，120 饲料用其他山羊杂碎，121 鲜的绵羊心，122 冷藏绵羊心，123 鲜的绵羊肝，124 冷藏绵羊肝，125 鲜的绵羊肺，126 冷藏绵羊肺，127 鲜的绵羊肾，128 冷藏绵羊肾，129 鲜的绵羊舌，130 冷藏绵羊舌，131 鲜的绵羊睾丸，132 冷藏绵羊睾丸，133 鲜的绵羊蹄，134 冷藏绵羊蹄，135 鲜的绵羊头及头块，136 冷藏绵羊头及头块，139 鲜的其他绵羊杂碎，140 冷藏其他绵羊杂碎，141 鲜的山羊心，142 冷藏山羊心，143 鲜的山羊肝，144 冷藏山羊肝，145 鲜的山羊肺，146 冷藏山羊肺，147 鲜的山羊肾，148 冷藏山羊肾，149 鲜的山羊舌，150 冷藏山羊舌，151 鲜的山羊睾丸，152 冷藏山羊睾丸，153 鲜的山羊蹄，154 冷藏山羊蹄，155 鲜的山羊头及头块，156 冷藏山羊头及头块，157 鲜的其他山羊杂碎，158 冷藏其他山羊杂碎，159 鲜的野山羊心，160 冷藏野山羊心，161 鲜的野山羊肝，162 冷藏野山羊肝，163 鲜的野山羊肺，164 冷藏野山羊肺，165 鲜的野山羊肾，166 冷藏野山羊肾，167 鲜的野山羊舌，168 冷藏野山羊舌，169 鲜的野山羊睾丸，170 冷藏野山羊睾丸，171 鲜的野山羊脚，172 冷藏野山羊脚，173 鲜的野山羊头及头块，174 冷藏野山羊头及头块，175 鲜的其他野山羊杂碎，176 冷藏其他野山羊杂碎，
0206800090	101 鲜的马心，102 冷藏马心，103 鲜的马肝，104 冷藏马肝，105 鲜的马肺，106 冷藏马肺，107 鲜的马肾，108 冷藏马肾，109 鲜的马舌，110 冷藏马舌，111 鲜的马睾丸，112 冷藏马睾丸，113 鲜的马脚，114 冷藏马脚，115 鲜的马头及头块，116 冷藏马头及头块，117 鲜的其他马杂碎，118 冷藏其他马杂碎，119 鲜的野马心，120 冷藏野马心，121 鲜的野马肝，122 冷藏野马肝，123 鲜的野马肺，124 冷藏野马肺，125 鲜的野马肾，126 冷藏野马肾，127 鲜的野马舌，128 冷藏野马舌，129 鲜的野马睾丸，130 冷藏野马睾丸，131 鲜的野马脚，132 冷藏野马脚，133 鲜的野马头及头块，134 冷藏野马头及头块，135 鲜的其他野马杂碎，136 冷藏其他野马杂碎，137 鲜的驴心，138 冷藏驴心，139 鲜的驴肝，140 冷藏驴肝，141 鲜的驴肺，142 冷藏驴肺，143 鲜的驴肾，144 冷藏驴肾，145 鲜的驴舌，146 冷藏驴舌，147 鲜的驴睾丸，148 冷藏驴睾丸，149 鲜的驴脚，150 冷藏驴脚，151 鲜的驴头及头块，152 冷藏驴头及头块，153 鲜的其他驴杂碎，154 冷藏其他驴杂碎，155 鲜的野驴心，156 冷藏野驴心 157 鲜的野驴肝 158 冷藏野驴肝，159 鲜的野驴肺，160 冷藏野驴肺，161 鲜的野驴肾，162 冷藏野驴肾，163 鲜的野驴舌，164 冷藏野驴舌，165 鲜的野驴睾丸，166 冷藏野驴睾丸，167 鲜的野驴脚，168 冷藏野驴脚，169 鲜的野驴头及头块，170 冷藏野驴头及头块，171 鲜的其他野驴杂碎，172 冷藏其他野驴杂碎，173 鲜的骡心，174 冷藏骡心，175 鲜的骡肝，176 冷藏骡肝，177 鲜的骡肺，178 冷藏骡肺，179 鲜的骡肾，180 冷藏骡肾，181 鲜的骡舌，182 冷藏骡舌，183 鲜的骡睾丸，184 冷藏骡睾丸，185 鲜的骡脚，186 冷藏骡脚，187 鲜的骡头及头块，188 冷藏骡头及头块，189 鲜的其他骡杂碎，190 冷藏其他骡杂碎
0206900010	101 饲料用绵羊肠，102 饲料用绵羊真胃(绵羊肚)，103 饲料用绵羊瓣胃(绵羊百叶)，104 饲料用绵羊网胃，105 饲料用绵羊瘤胃，106 饲料用绵羊心，107 饲料用绵羊肝，108 饲料用绵羊肺，109 饲料用绵羊肾，110 饲料用其他绵羊杂碎，111 饲料用山羊肠，112 饲料用山羊真胃(山羊肚)，113 饲料用山羊瓣胃(山羊百叶)，114 饲料用山羊网胃，115 饲料用山羊瘤胃，116 饲料用山羊心，117 饲料用山羊肝，118 饲料用山羊肺，119 饲料用山羊肾，120 饲料用其他山羊杂碎，121 绵羊心，122 绵羊肝，123 绵羊肺，124 绵羊肾，125 绵羊舌，126 绵羊睾丸 127 绵羊蹄，128 绵羊头及头块，129 其他绵羊杂碎，130 山羊心，131 山羊肝，132 山羊肺，133 山羊肾，134 山羊舌，135 山羊睾丸，136 山羊蹄，137 山羊头及头块，138 其他山羊杂碎，139 野羊心，140 野羊肝，141 野羊肺，142 野羊肾，143 野羊舌，144 野羊睾丸，145 野羊蹄，146 野羊头及头块，147 其他野羊杂碎，148 绵羊蹄(去除蹄匣)，149 绵羊头及头块(冷冻绵羊脸颊肉)，151 其他绵羊杂碎(冷冻绵羊鞭)，152 其他绵羊杂碎(冷冻绵羊横膈膜)，153 其他绵羊杂碎(冷冻绵羊筋)(不包括蹄筋)，154 其他绵羊杂碎(冷冻绵羊筋)，155 其他绵羊杂碎(冷冻绵羊板筋)，156 其他绵羊杂碎(冷冻绵羊尾)，157 其他绵羊杂碎(冷冻绵羊软骨不含喉/声带软骨)，158 其他绵羊杂碎(冷冻绵羊食管)，159 其他绵羊杂碎(冷冻绵羊动脉管)，160 其他绵羊杂碎(冷冻绵羊心管)，161 其他绵羊杂碎(冷冻绵羊骨)，162 其他绵羊杂碎(冷冻绵羊骨髓)，163 山羊蹄(去除蹄匣)，164 山羊头及头块(冷冻山羊脸颊肉)，165 其他山羊杂碎(冷冻山羊鞭)，166 其他山羊杂碎(冷冻山羊横膈膜)，167 其他山羊杂碎(冷冻山羊筋)(不包括蹄筋)，168 其他山羊杂碎(冷冻山羊筋)，169 其他山羊杂碎(冷冻山羊板筋)，170 其他山羊杂碎(冷冻山羊尾)，171 其他山羊杂碎(冷冻山羊软骨不含喉/声带软骨)，172 其他山羊杂碎(冷冻山羊食管)，173 其他山羊杂碎(冷冻山羊动脉管)，174 其他山羊杂碎(冷冻山羊心管)，175 其他山羊杂碎(冷冻山羊骨)，176 其他山羊杂碎(冷冻山羊骨髓)
0206900090	101 马心，102 马肝，103 马肺，104 马肾，105 马舌，106 马睾丸，107 马脚，108 马头及头块，109 其他马杂碎，110 野马心，111 野马肝，112 野马肺，113 野马肾，114 野马舌，115 野马睾丸，116 野马脚，117 野马头及头块，118 其他野马杂碎，119 驴心，120 驴肝，121 驴肺，122 驴肾，123 驴舌，124 驴睾丸，125 驴脚，126 驴头及头块，127 其他驴杂碎，128 野驴心，129 野驴肝，130 野驴肺，131 野驴肾，132 野驴舌，133 野驴睾丸，134 野驴脚，135 野驴头及头块，136 其他野驴杂碎，137 骡心，138 骡肝，139 骡肺，140 骡肾，141 骡舌，142 骡睾丸，143 骡脚，144 骡头及头块，145 其他骡杂碎，146 其他驴杂碎，驴皮
0207142990	101 冻的鸡肝，102 冻的其他鸡杂碎，103 冷冻鸡脖，104 冷冻鸡骨架，105 冷冻鸡冠，106 冷冻鸡肌腱，107 冷冻鸡脚骨，108 冷冻鸡皮，109 冷冻鸡肾，110 冷冻鸡心，111 冷冻其他鸡软骨，112 冷冻鸡头，113 冷冻鸡肉馅，114 冷冻鸡睾丸

HS 编码	CIQ 扩展品名
0207260000	101 鲜的带骨火鸡肉，不包括火鸡胸、火鸡腿，102 冷藏带骨火鸡肉，不包括火鸡胸、火鸡腿，103 鲜的其他火鸡肉，不包括火鸡胸、火鸡腿，104 冷藏其他火鸡肉，不包括火鸡胸、火鸡腿，105 鲜的火鸡胸、火鸡腿，106 冷藏的火鸡胸、火鸡腿，107 鲜的火鸡爪，108 冷藏火鸡爪，109 鲜的火鸡肫、胃，110 冷藏火鸡肫、胃，111 鲜的火鸡翼，不包括翼尖，112 冷藏火鸡翼，不包括翼尖，113 鲜的火鸡翼，包括翼尖，114 冷藏火鸡翼，包括翼尖，115 鲜的火鸡颈，116 冷藏火鸡颈，117 其他鲜的火鸡杂碎，118 其他冷藏火鸡杂碎，119 火鸡杂碎（冷藏火鸡翼尖，120 火鸡杂碎（冷藏火鸡肝），121 火鸡杂碎（冷藏火鸡脚骨），122 火鸡杂碎（冷藏火鸡软骨），123 火鸡杂碎（冷藏火鸡皮），124 火鸡杂碎（冷藏火鸡心），125 火鸡杂碎（冷藏火鸡肾）
0207270000	101 火鸡胸、火鸡腿，102 火鸡肫、火鸡胃，103 火鸡翼，不包括翼尖，104 火鸡爪，105 火鸡翼，包括翼尖，106 火鸡颈，107 其他火鸡肉（不包括火鸡胸、火鸡腿），108 带骨火鸡肉（不包括火鸡胸、火鸡腿），109 其他冻火鸡杂碎，110 其他冻火鸡杂碎（冷冻火鸡肾），111 火鸡杂碎（冷冻火鸡肝），112 火鸡杂碎（冷冻火鸡软骨），113 冷冻火鸡肉馅，114 火鸡杂碎（冷冻火鸡睾丸）
0207440000	101 鲜的鸭肉，102 冷藏鸭肉，103 鲜的鸭胸，104 冷藏鸭胸，105 鲜的鸭爪，106 冷藏鸭爪，107 鲜的鸭翼，不包括翼尖，108 冷藏鸭翼，不包括翼尖，109 鲜的鸭翼，包括翼尖，110 冷藏鸭翼，包括翼尖，111 鲜的鸭翼翼尖，112 冷藏鸭翼翼尖，113 鲜的鸭翼尖，114 冷藏鸭翼尖，115 鲜的鸭腿，116 冷藏鸭腿，117 鲜的鸭颈，118 冷藏鸭颈，119 鲜的鸭肫、胃，120 冷藏鸭肫、胃，121 鲜的其他鸭肉及杂碎，122 冷藏其他鸭肉及杂碎，123 冷藏鸭脚骨，124 冷藏鸭软骨，125 冷藏鸭皮，126 冷藏鸭心，127 冷藏鸭肾
0207450000	101 鸭肉，102 鸭胸，103 鸭爪，104 鸭翼，不包括翼尖，105 鸭翼，包括翼尖，106 鸭翼翼尖，107 鸭翼尖，108 鸭腿，109 鸭肝，110 鸭颈，111 鸭肫、胃，112 其他鸭肉及杂碎，113 冷冻鸭颈，114 冷冻鸭心，115 冷冻鸭肾，116 冷冻鸭肉馅，117 冷冻鸭舌
0207540000	101 鲜的鹅肉，102 冷藏鹅肉，103 鲜的鹅胸，104 冷藏鹅胸，105 鲜的鹅爪，106 冷藏鹅爪，107 鲜的鹅翼，不包括翼尖，108 冷藏鹅翼，不包括翼尖，109 鲜的鹅翼，包括翼尖，110 冷藏鹅翼，包括翼尖，111 鲜的鹅翼翼尖，112 冷藏鹅翼翼尖，113 鲜的鹅腿，114 冷藏鹅腿，115 鲜的鹅颈，116 冷藏鹅颈，117 鲜的其他鹅肉及杂碎，118 冷藏其他鹅肉及杂碎，119 冷藏鹅脚骨，120 冷藏鹅软骨，121 冷藏鹅皮，122 冷藏鹅心，123 冷藏鹅肾
0207550000	101 冻藏鹅肉，102 冻藏鹅胸，103 冻藏鹅爪，104 冻藏鹅翼，不包括翼尖，105 冻藏鹅鹅翼，包括翼尖，106 冻藏鹅翼翼尖，107 冻藏鹅腿，108 冻藏鹅肝，109 冻藏鹅颈，110 冻藏其它鹅肉及杂碎，111 冷冻鹅脚骨，112 冷冻鹅软骨，113 冷冻鹅心，114 冷冻鹅皮，115 冷冻鹅肾，116 冷冻鹅肉馅
0207600000	101 鲜的，饲养的，102 冷藏，饲养的，103 冻藏，饲养的，104 冷冻的整只珍珠鸡（不包括内脏及胃肠等消化道器官），105 冷冻的珍珠鸡肉（整的或块的，不包括冷冻珍珠鸡胸、冷冻珍珠鸡腿），106 冷冻未炼制珍珠鸡脂肪，107 冷冻珍珠鸡胸，108 冷冻珍珠鸡腿，109 冷冻珍珠鸡爪，110 冷冻珍珠鸡翼（不包括翼尖），111 冷冻珍珠鸡翼（包括翼尖），112 冷冻珍珠鸡翼尖，113 冷冻珍珠鸡肾，114 冷冻珍珠鸡颈，115 冷冻珍珠鸡软骨，116 冷冻珍珠鸡脚骨，117 冷冻珍珠鸡皮，118 冷冻珍珠鸡肝，119 冷冻珍珠鸡心，121 冷藏的整只珍珠鸡（不包括内脏及胃肠等消化道器官，122 冷藏珍珠鸡肉（整的或块的，不包括冰鲜珍珠鸡胸、冰鲜珍珠鸡腿），123 冷藏未炼制珍珠鸡脂肪，124 冷藏珍珠鸡胸，125 冷藏珍珠鸡腿，126 冷藏珍珠鸡爪，127 冷藏珍珠鸡翼（不包括翼尖），128 冷藏珍珠鸡翼（包括翼尖），129 冷藏珍珠鸡翼尖，130 冷藏珍珠鸡肾，131 冷藏珍珠鸡颈，132 冷藏珍珠鸡软骨，133 冷藏珍珠鸡脚骨，134 冰鲜珍珠鸡皮，135 冷藏珍珠鸡肝，136 冷藏珍珠鸡心，137 冷冻珍珠鸡骨，138 冷藏珍珠鸡骨，139 其他冷冻珍珠鸡杂碎，140 其他冷藏珍珠鸡杂碎
0208500000	101 鲜的蛇肉，102 冷藏蛇肉，103 冻藏蛇肉，104 鲜的鳄鱼肉，105 冷藏鳄鱼肉，106 冻藏鳄鱼肉，107 鲜的龟肉，108 冷藏龟肉，109 冻藏龟肉，110 鲜的甲鱼肉，111 冷藏甲鱼肉，112 冻藏甲鱼肉，113 鲜的其他饲养爬行动物肉及食用杂碎，114 冷藏其他饲养爬行动物肉及食用杂碎，115 冻藏其他饲养爬行动物肉及食用杂碎，116 鲜的其他野生爬行动物肉及食用杂碎，117 冷藏其他野生爬行动物肉及食用杂碎，118 冻藏其他野生爬行动物肉及食用杂碎
0208909010	101 未列出的鲜的野生奇蹄动物肉，102 未列出的冷藏野生奇蹄动物肉，103 未列出的冻藏野生奇蹄动物肉，104 鲜的野鹿肉，105 冷藏野鹿肉，106 冻藏野鹿肉，107 鲜的骆驼肉，108 冷藏骆驼肉，109 冻藏骆驼肉，110 未列出的鲜的野生偶蹄动物肉，111 未列出的冷藏野生偶蹄动物肉，112 未列出的冻藏野生偶蹄动物肉，113 鲜的山鸡肉，114 冷藏山鸡肉，115 冻藏山鸡肉，116 鲜的珍珠鸡肉，117 冷藏珍珠鸡肉，118 冻藏珍珠鸡肉，119 鲜的竹鸡肉，120 冷藏竹鸡肉，121 冻藏竹鸡肉，122 鲜的松鸡肉，123 冷藏松鸡肉，124 冻藏松鸡肉，125 鲜的沙鸡肉，126 冷藏沙鸡肉，127 冻藏沙鸡肉，128 鲜的石鸡肉，129 冷藏石鸡肉，130 冻藏石鸡肉，131 鲜的榛鸡肉，132 冷藏榛鸡肉，133 冻藏榛鸡肉，134 鲜的野鸭肉，135 冷藏野鸭肉，136 冻藏野鸭肉，137 鲜的野鹅肉，138 冷藏野鹅肉，139 冻藏野鹅肉，140 鲜的野鸽肉，141 冷藏野鸽肉，142 冻藏野鸽肉，143 鲜的鹌鹑肉，144 冷藏鹌鹑肉，145 冻藏鹌鹑肉，146 鲜的鹧鸪肉，147 冷藏鹧鸪肉，148 冻藏鹧鸪肉，149 鲜的麻雀肉，150 冷藏麻雀肉，151 冻藏麻雀肉，152 鲜的野生鸵鸟肉，153 冷藏野生鸵鸟肉，154 冻藏野生鸵鸟肉，155 未列出的鲜的野生禽鸟肉，156 未列出的冷藏野生禽鸟肉，157 未列出的冻藏野生禽鸟肉，158 鲜的熊肉，159 冷藏熊肉，160 冻藏熊肉，161 鲜的袋鼠肉，162 冷藏袋鼠肉，163 冻藏袋鼠肉，164 未列出其他的鲜的野生动物肉，165 未列出其他的冷藏野生动物肉，166 未列出其他的冻藏野生动物肉，167 鲜、冷的两栖类，168 冻的两栖类，169 鲜、冷的爬行类，170 冻的爬行类，171 鲜、冷的海洋哺乳动物，172 冻的海洋哺乳动物
0208909090	101 未列出的鲜的饲养奇蹄动物肉，103 未列出的冷藏饲养奇蹄动物肉，104 未列出的鲜的饲养奇蹄动物杂碎，106 未列出的冻藏饲养奇蹄动物杂碎，107 鲜的鹿肉，108 冷藏鹿肉，109 冻藏鹿肉，111 鲜的鹿心，112 冷藏鹿心，113 冻藏鹿心，114 鲜的鹿肝，115 冷藏鹿肝，116 冻藏鹿肝，117 鲜的鹿肺，118 冷藏鹿肺，119 冻藏鹿肺，120 鲜的鹿肾，121 冷藏鹿肾，122 冻藏鹿肾，123 鲜的鹿舌，124 冷藏鹿舌，125 冻藏鹿舌，126 鲜的鹿鞭，127 冷藏鹿鞭，128 冻藏鹿鞭，129 鲜的鹿睾丸，130 冷藏鹿睾丸，131 冻藏鹿睾丸，132 鲜的其他鹿杂碎，133 冷藏其他鹿杂碎，134 冻藏其他鹿杂碎，135 鲜的骆驼肉，136 冷藏骆驼肉，137 冻藏骆驼肉，138 鲜的骆驼杂碎，139 冷藏骆驼杂碎，140 冻藏骆驼杂碎，141 未列出的鲜的饲养偶蹄动物肉，142 未列出的冷藏饲养偶蹄动物肉，143 未列出的冻藏饲养偶蹄动物肉，144 未列出的鲜的饲养偶蹄动物杂碎，145 未列出的冷藏饲养偶蹄动物杂碎，146 未列出的冻藏饲养偶蹄动物杂碎，147 鲜的饲养鸵鸟肉，148 冷藏饲养鸵鸟肉，149 冻藏饲养鸵鸟肉，150 鲜的饲养鸵鸟杂碎，151 冷藏饲养鸵鸟杂碎，152 冻藏饲养鸵鸟杂碎，153 未列出的鲜的饲养禽鸟肉，154 未列出的冷藏饲养禽鸟肉，155 未列出的冻藏饲养禽鸟肉，156 未列出的鲜的饲养禽鸟杂碎，157 未列出的冷藏饲养禽鸟杂碎，158 未列出的冻藏饲养禽鸟杂碎，159 鲜的犬肉，160 冷藏犬肉，161 冻藏犬肉，162 鲜的犬杂碎，163 冷藏犬杂碎，164 冻藏犬杂碎，165 鲜的袋鼠肉，166 冷藏袋鼠肉，167 冻藏袋鼠肉，168 鲜的袋鼠杂碎，169 冷藏袋鼠杂碎，170 冻藏袋鼠杂碎，171 未列出的鲜的饲养动物肉，172 未列出的冻藏饲养动物肉，173 未列出的冷藏饲养动物肉，174 未列出的鲜的饲养动物杂碎，175 未列出的冷藏饲养动物杂碎，176 未列出的冻藏饲养动物杂碎，183 鲜的饲养牛蛙肉及食用杂碎，184 冷藏饲养牛蛙肉及食用杂碎，185 冻藏饲养牛蛙肉及食用杂碎，186 鲜的其他饲养两栖动物肉及杂碎，187 冷藏其他饲养两栖动物肉及杂碎，188 冻藏其他饲养两栖动物肉及杂碎，189 鲜的其他野生两栖动物肉及杂碎，190 冷藏其他野生两栖动物肉及杂碎，191 冻藏其他野生两栖动物肉及杂碎，192 未列出的鲜的饲养爬行动物肉及杂碎，193 未列出的冷藏饲养爬行动物肉及杂碎，194 未列出的冻藏饲养爬行动物肉及杂碎，195 未列出的鲜的野生爬行动物肉及杂碎，196 未列出的冷藏野生爬行动物肉及杂碎，197 未列出的冻藏野生爬行动物肉及杂碎，199 未列出的鲜的饲养海洋哺乳动物肉及杂碎，200 未列出的冷藏饲养海洋哺乳动物肉及杂碎，201 未列出的冻藏饲养海洋哺乳动物肉及杂碎，202 未列出的鲜的野生海洋哺乳动物肉及杂碎，203 未列出的冷藏野生海洋哺乳动物肉及杂碎，204 未列出的冻藏野生海洋哺乳动物肉及杂碎，205 冻藏其他鹿杂碎（冷冻鹿尾），206 冻藏其他鹿杂碎（冷冻鹿筋，不包括鹿蹄筋），207 冻藏其他鹿杂碎（冷冻鹿肌腱），

HS 编码	CIQ 扩展品名
0209100000	101 工业用肥猪肉(不带瘦肉),102 工业用猪油脂,103 饲料用肥猪肉(不带瘦肉),104 饲料用猪油脂,105 饲料用野生猪、牛、羊油脂,106 未炼制的鲜的食用纯肥猪肉,107 未炼制的冷藏食用纯肥猪肉,108 未炼制的冻藏食用纯肥猪肉,109 未炼制的干制食用纯肥猪肉,110 未炼制的熏制食用纯肥猪肉,111 未炼制的盐制食用纯肥猪肉,112 未炼制的鲜的食用猪脂肪,113 未炼制的冷藏食用猪脂肪,114 未炼制的冻藏食用猪脂肪,115 未炼制的干制食用猪脂肪,116 未炼制的熏制食用猪脂肪,117 未炼制的盐制食用猪脂肪,118 用其他方法提取的鲜的食用纯肥猪肉,119 用其他方法提取的冷藏食用纯肥猪肉,120 用其他方法提取的冻藏食用纯肥猪肉,121 用其他方法提取的干制食用纯肥猪肉,122 用其他方法提取的熏制食用纯肥猪肉,123 用其他方法提取的盐制食用纯肥猪肉,124 用其他方法提取的鲜的食用猪脂肪,125 用其他方法提取的冷藏食用猪脂肪,126 用其他方法提取的冻藏食用猪脂肪,127 用其他方法提取的干制食用猪脂肪,128 用其他方法提取的熏制食用猪脂肪,129 用其他方法提取的盐制食用猪脂肪,130 未炼制的冷藏食用猪脂肪(冰鲜未炼制猪脂肪(食用,不包括内脏脂肪)),131 未炼制的冻藏食用猪脂肪(冷冻未炼制猪脂肪(食用,不包括内脏脂肪))
0209900000	101 工业用禽油脂,102 饲料用禽油脂,103 未炼制的鲜的食用家禽脂肪,104 未炼制的冷藏食用家禽脂肪,105 未炼制的冻藏食用家禽脂肪,106 未炼制的干制食用家禽脂肪,107 未炼制的熏制食用家禽脂肪,108 未炼制的盐制食用家禽脂肪,109 用其他方法提取的鲜的食用家禽脂肪,110 用其他方法提取的冷藏食用家禽脂肪,111 用其他方法提取的冻藏食用家禽脂肪,112 用其他方法提取的干制食用家禽,脂肪,113 用其他方法提取的熏制食用家禽脂肪,114 用其他方法提取的盐制食用家禽脂肪,115 未炼制的冻藏食用家禽脂肪(冷冻未炼制鸡脂肪(食用,不包括内脏脂肪)),116 冷冻未炼制鸡脂肪,117 冷冻未炼制鸭脂肪,118 冷冻未炼制鹅脂肪,119 冷冻未炼制火鸡脂肪,120 冷藏未炼制鸡脂肪,121 冷藏未炼制鸭脂肪,122 冷藏未炼制鹅脂肪,123 冷藏未炼制火鸡脂肪
0301991990	101 草鱼,102 鳙鱼(胖头鱼),103 鲢鱼,104 青鱼,105 鲶鱼(鲇鱼),106 武昌鱼,107 大马哈鱼,108 黄鳝,109 泥鳅,110 鲫鱼,111 牛头鮰鱼,112 斑点叉尾鮰鱼,113 黄蜡鲳鱼(狮鼻鲳鱼参),114 多瑙哲罗鱼,115 其他淡水鱼,116 海鳗,117 鲽鱼,118 红鱼(似石首鱼),119 牙鲆鱼,120 石斑鱼,121 大鲮鲆鱼,122 带鱼,123 鳎鱼,124 鲑鱼,125 金枪鱼,126 鲱鱼,127 鲣鱼,128 沙丁鱼,129 黄鱼,130 鲨鱼,131 鲭鱼,132 鳀鱼,133 鳕鱼,134 鲳鱼,135 卡拉白鱼,136 其他海水鱼,137 金鱼,138 锦鲤,139 其他鱼,140 其他受精卵
0301999990	101 草鱼,102 鳙鱼(胖头鱼),103 鲢鱼,104 青鱼,105 淡水鲈鱼,106 鲶鱼(鲇鱼),107 武昌鱼,108 大马哈鱼,109 黄鳝,110 泥鳅,111 鲫鱼,112 鮰鱼,113 牛头鮰鱼,114 斑点叉尾鮰鱼,115 黄蜡鲳鱼(狮鼻鲳鱼参),116 罗非鱼,117 多瑙哲罗鱼,118 其他淡水鱼,119 海鳗,120 鲽鱼,121 红鱼(似石首鱼),122 牙鲆鱼,123 石斑鱼,124 大鲮鲆鱼,125 海水鲈鱼,126 带鱼,127 鳎鱼,128 鲑鱼,129 金枪鱼,130 鲱鱼,131 鲣鱼,132 沙丁鱼,133 黄鱼,134 鲨鱼,135 鲭鱼,136 鳀鱼,137 鳕鱼,138 鲳鱼,139 卡拉白鱼,140 其他海水鱼,141 金鱼,142 锦鲤,143 其他鱼
0302110000	101 养殖河鳟,102 养殖虹鳟,103 野生河鳟,104 野生虹鳟,105 克拉克大麻哈鱼,106 阿瓜大麻哈鱼,107 吉雨大麻哈鱼,108 亚利桑那大麻哈鱼,109 金腹大麻哈鱼
0302130000	101 养殖红大麻哈鱼,102 养殖细磷大麻哈鱼,103 养殖大麻哈鱼,104 养殖大鳞大麻哈鱼,105 养殖银大麻哈鱼,106 养殖马苏大麻哈鱼,107 养殖玫瑰大麻哈鱼,108 野生红大麻哈鱼,109 野生细磷大麻哈鱼,110 野生大麻哈鱼,111 野生大鳞大麻哈鱼,112 野生银大麻哈鱼,113 野生马苏大麻哈鱼,114 野生玫瑰大麻哈鱼
0302430000	101 饲料用沙丁鱼、黍鲱鱼,102 养殖沙丁鱼(沙丁鱼、沙瑙鱼属),103 养殖小沙丁鱼属,104 养殖黍鲱,105 养殖西鲱,106 野生沙丁鱼(沙丁鱼、沙瑙鱼属),107 野生小沙丁鱼属,108 野生黍鲱,109 野生西鲱
0302590000	101 饲料用其他海水鱼,102 犀鳕科,103 多丝真鳕科,104 鳕科,105 长尾鳕科,106 黑鳕科,107 无须鳕科,108 深海鳕科,109 南极鳕科
0302730000	101 饲料用其他海水鱼,102 养殖鲤属,103 养殖鲫属,104 养殖草鱼,105 养殖鲢属,106 养殖鲮属,107 养殖青鱼,108 养殖其他鲤科鱼(卡特拉鲃、野鲮属、哈氏纹唇鱼、何氏细须鲃、鲂属),109 野生鲤属,110 野生鲫属,111 野生草鱼,112 野生鲢属,113 野生鲮属,114 野生青鱼,115 野生其他鲤科鱼(卡特拉鲃、野鲮属、哈氏纹唇鱼、何氏细须鲃、鲂属))
0302899090	101 饲料用马面鱼,102 饲料用其他海水鱼,103 养殖石斑鱼,104 养殖鲥鱼,105 养殖鲷科,菱羊鲷除外(非生食),106 养殖鲷科,菱羊鲷除外(可能用于生食),107 养殖安康鱼(非生食),108 养殖安康鱼(可能用于生食),109 养殖海鲂,110 养殖鲆鱼,111 养殖鲽鱼,112 其他养殖鱼(非生食),113 其他养殖鱼(可能用于生食),114 黄狮鱼(非生食),115 黄狮鱼(可能用于生食),116 养殖海鲈鱼(非生食),117 养殖海鲈鱼(可能用于生食),118 野生石斑鱼,119 野生鲥鱼,120 野生鲷科,菱羊鲷除外,121 野生安康鱼,122 野生海鲂,123 野生鲆鱼,124 野生鲽鱼,125 海鲫鱼,126 金线鱼,127 马面鱼,128 马鲛鱼,129 野生海鲈鱼(非生食),130 野生海鲈鱼(可能用于生食),131 其他野生鱼(非生食),132 其他野生鱼(可能用于生食)
0302910010	101 鲜或冷养殖濒危鱼鱼肝,102 鲜或冷野生濒危鱼鱼肝,103 鲜或冷养殖濒危鱼鱼卵,104 鲜或冷野生濒危鱼鱼卵,105,鲜或冷养殖濒危鱼鱼精,106 鲜或冷野生濒危鱼鱼精
0302910090	101 其他鲜或冷养殖鱼鱼肝,102 其他鲜或冷野生鱼鱼肝,103 其他鲜或冷养殖鱼鱼精,104 其他鲜或冷野生鱼鱼精
0303120000	101 养殖细磷大麻哈鱼,102 养殖大麻哈鱼,103 养殖大鳞大麻哈鱼,104 养殖银大麻哈鱼,105 养殖马苏大麻哈鱼,106 养殖玫瑰大麻哈鱼,107 野生细磷大麻哈鱼,108 野生大麻哈鱼,109 野生大鳞大麻哈鱼,110 野生银大麻哈鱼,111 野生马苏大麻哈鱼,112 野生玫瑰大麻哈鱼
0303140000	101 养殖河鳟,102 养殖虹鳟,103 野生河鳟,104 野生虹鳟,105 克拉克大麻哈鱼,106 阿瓜大麻哈鱼,107 吉雨大麻哈鱼,108 亚利桑那大麻哈鱼,109 金腹大麻哈鱼
0303240000	101 饲料用其他海水鱼,102 养殖(鱼芒)鲶属,103 养殖胡鲶属,104 养殖真鮰属,105 野生(鱼芒)鲶属,106 野生胡鲶属,107 野生真鮰属
0303250000	101 饲料用其他海水鱼,102 养殖鲤属,103 养殖鲫属,104 养殖草鱼,105 养殖鲢属,106 养殖鲮属,107 养殖青鱼,108 养殖其他鲤科鱼(卡特拉鲃、野鲮属、哈氏纹唇鱼、何氏细须鲃、鲂属),109 野生鲤属,110 野生鲫属,111 野生草鱼,112 野生鲢属,113 野生鲮属,114 野生青鱼,115 野生其他鲤科鱼(卡特拉鲃、野鲮属、哈氏纹唇鱼、何氏细须鲃、鲂属)
0303390090	101 养殖鲽科,102 养殖鲆科,103 养殖舌鳎科,104 养殖鳎科,105 养殖菱鲆科,106 养殖刺鲆科,107 野生鲽科,108 野生鲆科,109 野生舌鳎科,110 野生鳎科,111 野生菱鲆科,112 野生刺鲆科
0303530000	101 饲料用沙丁鱼、黍鲱鱼,102 养殖沙丁鱼(沙丁鱼、沙瑙鱼属),103 养殖小沙丁鱼属,104 养殖黍鲱,105 养殖西鲱,106 野生沙丁鱼(沙丁鱼、沙瑙鱼属),107 野生小沙丁鱼属,108 野生黍鲱,109 野生西鲱
0303550000	101 饲料用其他海水鱼,102 养殖对称竹荚鱼,103 养殖新西兰竹荚鱼及竹荚鱼(竹荚鱼属),104 野生对称竹荚鱼,105 野生新西兰竹荚鱼及竹荚鱼(竹荚鱼属)
0303899090	101 饲料用马面鱼,102 饲料用其他海水鱼,103 养殖石斑鱼,104 养殖鲥鱼,105 养殖鲷科,106 养殖安康鱼,107 养殖海鲂,108 养殖鲆鱼,109 养殖鲽鱼,110 养殖红鱼,111 其他养殖鱼,112 野生石斑鱼,113 野生鲥鱼,114 野生鲷科,115 野生安康鱼,116 野生海鲂,117 野生鲆鱼,118 野生鲽鱼,119 野生红鱼,120 海鲫鱼,121 金线鱼,122 马面鱼,123 马鲛鱼,124 蓝圆鲹,999 其他野生鱼
0303910010	101 养殖冷冻鱼鱼肝,102 野生冷冻鱼鱼肝,103 养殖冷冻鱼鱼卵,104 野生冷冻鱼鱼卵,105 养殖冷冻鱼鱼精,106 野生冷冻鱼鱼精
0303910090	101 养殖冷冻鱼鱼肝,102 野生冷冻鱼鱼肝,103 养殖冷冻鱼鱼精,104 野生冷冻鱼鱼精
0304390090	101 养殖西鲤,102 养殖黑鲫,103 养殖草鱼,104 养殖鲢属,105 养殖鲮属,106 养殖青鱼,107 鳗鲡属,108 养殖黑鱼(鳢属),109 野生西鲤,110 野生黑鲫,111 野生草鱼,112 野生鲢属,113 野生鲮属,114 野生青鱼,115 其他野生鳗鱼(鳗鲡属),116 野生黑鱼(鳢属)
0304430000	101 养殖鲽科,102 养殖鲆科,103 养殖舌鳎科,104 养殖鳎科,105 养殖菱鲆科,106 养殖刺鲆科,107 野生鲽科,108 野生鲆科,109 野生舌鳎科,110 野生鳎科,111 野生菱鲆科,112 野生刺鲆科

HS 编码	CIQ 扩展品名
0304510090	101 鲜或冷的养殖罗非鱼(口孵非鲫属),102 鲜或冷的养殖鲶鱼(鱼芒)鲶属,103 鲜或冷的养殖胡鲶属,104 鲜或冷的养殖真鮰属,105 鲜或冷的养殖鲤属,106 鲜或冷的养殖鲫属,107 鲜或冷的养殖草鱼,108 鲜或冷的养殖鲢属,109 鲜或冷的养殖鲮属,110 鲜或冷的养殖青鱼,111 鲜或冷的养殖其他鳗鱼(鳗鲡属),112 鲜或冷的养殖尼罗河鲈鱼(尼罗尖吻鲈),113 鲜或冷的养殖黑鱼(醴属),114 鲜或冷的野生罗非鱼(口孵非鲫属),115 鲜或冷的野生鲶鱼(鱼芒)鲶属,116 鲜或冷的野生胡鲶属,117 鲜或冷的野生真鮰属,118 鲜或冷的野生鲤属,119 鲜或冷的野生鲫属,120 鲜或冷的野生草鱼,121 鲜或冷的野生鲢属,122 鲜或冷的野生鲮属,123 鲜或冷的野生青鱼,124 鲜或冷的野生其他鳗鱼(鳗鲡属),125 鲜或冷的野生尼罗河鲈鱼(尼罗尖吻鲈),126 鲜或冷的野生黑鱼(醴属),127 鲜或冷的养殖鲶属,128 鲜或冷的养殖其他鲤科鱼(卡特拉鲃、野鲮属、哈氏纹唇鱼、何氏细须鲃、鲂属),129 鲜或冷的野生鲶属,130 鲜或冷的野生其他鲤科鱼(卡特拉鲃、野鲮属、哈氏纹唇鱼、何氏细须鲃、鲂属)
0304530000	101 犀鳕科,102 多丝真鳕科,103 鳕科,104 长尾鳕科,105 黑鳕科,106 无须鳕科,107 深海鳕科,108 南极鳕科
0304590090	101 养殖石斑鱼,102 养殖鲥鱼,103 养殖鲷科(非生食),104 养殖鲷科(可能用于生食),105 养殖安康鱼,106 养殖海鲂,107 养殖鲆鱼,108 养殖其他鱼,109 野生鲷科(非生食),110 野生鲷科(可能用于生食),111 野生石斑鱼,112 野生鲥鱼,113 野生安康鱼,114 野生海鲂,115 野生鲆鱼,116 野生鲽鱼,117 海鲫鱼,118 金线鱼,119 马面鱼,120 马鲛鱼,121 野生其他鱼
0304629000	101 养殖(鱼芒)鲶属,102 养殖胡鲶属,103 养殖真鮰属,104 野生(鱼芒)鲶属,105 野生胡鲶属,106 野生真鮰属,107 养殖鲶属,108 野生鲶属
0304690090	101 冻的养殖鲤属,102 冻的养殖鲫属,103 冻的养殖草鱼,104 冻的养殖鲢属,105 冻的养殖鲮属,106 冻的养殖青鱼,107 冻的养殖其他鳗鱼(鳗鲡属),108 冻的养殖黑鱼(鳢属),109 冻的野生鲤属,110 冻的野生鲫属,111 冻的野生草鱼,112 冻的野生鲢属,113 冻的野生鲮属,114 冻的野生青鱼,115 冻的野生其他鳗鱼(鳗鲡属),116 冻的野生黑鱼(鳢属),117 冻的养殖其他鲤科鱼(卡特拉鲃、野鲮属、哈氏纹唇鱼、何氏细须鲃、鲂属),118 冻的野生其他鲤科鱼(卡特拉鲃、野鲮属、哈氏纹唇鱼、何氏细须鲃、鲂属)
0304810000	101 养殖大西洋鲑鱼(非生食),102 养殖大西洋鲑鱼(可能用于生食),103 养殖红大麻哈鱼,104 养殖细磷大麻哈鱼,105 养殖大麻哈鱼,106 养殖大鳞大麻哈鱼,107 养殖银大麻哈鱼,108 养殖马苏大麻哈鱼,109 养殖玫瑰大麻哈鱼,110 野生大西洋鲑鱼(非生食),111 野生大西洋鲑鱼(可能用于生食),112 野生红大麻哈鱼,113 野生细磷大麻哈鱼,114 野生大麻哈鱼,115 野生大鳞大麻哈鱼,116 野生银大麻哈鱼,117 野生马苏大麻哈鱼,118 野生玫瑰大麻哈鱼,119 多瑙哲罗鱼
0304820000	101 养殖河鳟,102 养殖虹鳟,103 野生河鳟,104 野生虹鳟,105 克拉克大麻哈鱼,106 阿瓜大麻哈鱼,107 吉雨大麻哈鱼鱼,108 亚利桑那大麻哈鱼,109 金腹大麻哈鱼
0304830000	101 养殖鲽科,102 养殖鲆科,103 养殖舌鳎科,104 养殖鳎科,105 养殖菱鲆科,106 养殖刺鲆科,107 野生鲽科,108 野生鲆科,109 野生舌鳎科,110 野生鳎科,111 野生菱鲆科,112 野生刺鲆科
0304930090	101 冻的养殖罗非鱼(口孵非鲫属),102 冻的养殖(鱼芒)鲶属,103 冻的养殖胡鲶属,104 冻的养殖真鮰属,105 冻的养殖鲤属,106 冻的养殖鲫属,107 冻的养殖草鱼,108 冻的养殖鲢属,109 冻的养殖鲮属,110 冻的养殖青鱼(鲤科鱼),111 冻的养殖其他鳗鱼(鳗鲡属),112 冻的养殖尼罗河鲈鱼(尼罗尖吻鲈),113 冻的养殖黑鱼(醴属),114 冻的野生罗非鱼(口孵非鲫属),115 冻的野生(鱼芒)鲶属,116 冻的野生胡鲶属,117 冻的野生真鮰属,118 冻的野生鲤属,119 冻的野生鲫属,120 冻的野生草鱼,121 冻的野生鲢属,122 冻的野生鲮属,123 冻的野生青鱼,124 冻的野生其他鳗鱼(鳗鲡属),125 冻的野生尼罗河鲈鱼(尼罗尖吻鲈),126 冻的野生黑鱼(鳢属),127 冻的养殖鲶属,128 冻的养殖其他鲤科鱼(卡特拉鲃、野鲮属、哈氏纹唇鱼、何氏细须鲃、鲂属),129 冻的野生鲶属,130 冻的野生其他鲤科鱼(卡特拉鲃、野鲮属、哈氏纹唇鱼、何氏细须鲃、鲂属)
0304990090	101 养殖石斑鱼,102 养殖鲥鱼,103 养殖鲷科,104 养殖安康鱼,105 养殖海鲂,106 养殖鲆鱼,107 养殖鲽鱼,108 养殖红鱼,109 养殖其他鱼,110 野生石斑鱼,111 野生鲥鱼,112 野生鲷科,113 野生安康鱼,114 野生海鲂,115 野生鲆鱼,116 野生鲽鱼,117 野生红鱼,118 海鲫鱼,119 金线鱼,120 马面鱼,121 马鲛鱼,122 野生其他鱼
0305200010	101 干制的养殖濒危鱼鱼肝,102 干制的野生濒危鱼鱼肝,103 干制的养殖濒危鱼鱼卵,104 干制的野生濒危鱼鱼卵,105 干制的养殖濒危鱼鱼精,106 干制的野生濒危鱼鱼精,107 熏制的养殖濒危鱼鱼肝,108 熏制的野生濒危鱼鱼肝,109 熏制的养殖濒危鱼鱼卵,110 熏制的野生濒危鱼鱼卵,111 熏制的养殖濒危鱼鱼精,112 熏制的野生濒危鱼鱼精,113 盐制的养殖濒危鱼鱼肝,114 盐制的野生濒危鱼鱼肝,115 盐制的养殖濒危鱼鱼卵,116 盐制的野生濒危鱼鱼卵,117 盐制的养殖濒危鱼鱼精,118 盐制的野生濒危鱼鱼精
0305200090	111 其他干制的养殖鱼鱼肝,112 其他干制的野生鱼鱼肝,113 其他干制的养殖鱼鱼卵,114 其他干制的野生鱼鱼卵,115 其他干制的养殖鱼鱼精,116 其他干制的野生鱼鱼精,117 其他熏制的养殖鱼鱼肝,118 其他熏制的野生鱼鱼肝,119 其他熏制的养殖鱼鱼卵,120 其他熏制的野生鱼鱼卵,121 其他熏制的养殖鱼鱼精,122 其他熏制的野生鱼鱼精,123 其他盐制的养殖鱼鱼肝,124 其他盐制的野生鱼鱼肝,125 其他盐制的养殖鱼鱼卵,126 其他盐制的野生鱼鱼卵,127 其他盐制的养殖鱼鱼精,128 其他盐制的野生鱼鱼精
0305320000	101 干制的犀鳕科,102 干制的多丝真鳕科,103 干制的鳕科,104 干制的长尾鳕科,105 干制的黑鳕科,106 干制的无须鳕科,107 干制的深海鳕科,108 干制的南极鳕科,109 盐腌或盐渍的犀鳕科,110 盐腌或盐渍的多丝真鳕科,111 盐腌或盐渍的鳕科,112 盐腌或盐渍的长尾鳕科,113 盐腌或盐渍的黑鳕科,114 盐腌或盐渍的无须鳕科,115 盐腌或盐渍的深海鳕科,116 盐腌或盐渍的南极鳕科
0305390090	101 干制的养殖石斑鱼,102 干制的养殖鲥鱼,103 干制的养殖鲷科,104 干制的养殖安康鱼,105 干制的养殖海鲂,106 干制的养殖鲆鱼,107 干制的养殖鲽鱼,108 干制的养殖红鱼,109 干制的养殖杂鱼,110 盐腌或盐渍的养殖石斑鱼,111 盐腌或盐渍的养殖鲥鱼,112 盐腌或盐渍的养殖鲷科,113 盐腌或盐渍的养殖安康鱼,114 盐腌或盐渍的养殖海鲂,115 盐腌或盐渍的养殖鲆鱼,116 盐腌或盐渍的养殖鲽鱼,117 盐腌或盐渍的养殖红鱼,118 盐腌或盐渍的养殖杂鱼,119 干制的野生石斑鱼,120 干制的野生鲥鱼,121 干制的野生鲷科,122 干制的野生安康鱼,123 干制的野生海鲂,124 干制的野生鲆鱼,125 干制的野生鲽鱼,126 干制的野生红鱼,127 干制的海鲫鱼,128 干制的金线鱼,129 干制的马面鱼,130 干制的马鲛鱼,131 干制的野生杂鱼,132 盐腌或盐渍的野生石斑鱼,133 盐腌或盐渍的野生鲥鱼,134 盐腌或盐渍的野生鲷科,135 盐腌或盐渍的野生安康鱼,136 盐腌或盐渍的野生海鲂,137 盐腌或盐渍的野生鲆鱼,138 盐腌或盐渍的野生鲽鱼,139 盐腌或盐渍的野生红鱼,140 盐腌或盐渍的海鲫鱼,141 盐腌或盐渍的金线鱼,142 盐腌或盐渍的马面鱼,143 盐腌或盐渍的马鲛鱼,144 盐腌或盐渍的野生杂鱼
0305420000	101 养殖大西洋鲱鱼,102 养殖太平洋鲱鱼,103 野生大西洋鲱鱼,104 野生太平洋鲱鱼
0305430000	101 养殖河鳟,102 养殖虹鳟,103 野生河鳟,104 野生虹鳟,105 克拉克大麻哈鱼,106 阿瓜大麻哈鱼,107 吉雨大麻哈鱼,108 亚利桑那大麻哈鱼,109 金腹大麻哈鱼
0305490090	101 熏制的养殖石斑鱼,102 熏制的养殖鲥鱼,103 熏制的养殖鲷科,104 熏制的养殖安康鱼,105 熏制的养殖海鲂,106 熏制的养殖鲆鱼,107 熏制的养殖鲽鱼,108 熏制的养殖红鱼,109 熏制的其他养殖鱼,110 熏制的野生石斑鱼,111 熏制的野生鲥鱼,112 熏制的野生鲷科,113 熏制的野生安康鱼,114 熏制的野生海鲂,115 熏制的野生鲆鱼,116 熏制的野生鲽鱼,117 熏制的野生红鱼,118 熏制的海鲫鱼,119 熏制的金线鱼,120 熏制的马面鱼,121 熏制的马鲛鱼,122 熏制的其他野生鱼
0305599090	101 干制的养殖石斑鱼,102 干制的养殖鲥鱼,103 干制的养殖鲷科,104 干制的养殖安康鱼,105 干制的养殖海鲂,106 干制的养殖鲆鱼,107 干制的养殖鲽鱼,108 干制的养殖红鱼,109 干制的养殖其他鱼,110 干制的野生石斑鱼,111 干制的野生鲥鱼,112 干制的野生鲷科,113 干制的野生安康鱼,114 干制的野生海鲂,115 干制的野生鲆鱼,116 干制的野生鲽鱼,117 干制的野生红鱼,118 干制的海鲫鱼,119 干制的金线鱼,120 干制的马面鱼,121 干制的马鲛鱼,122 干制的野生其他鱼
0305699090	101 盐腌或盐渍的养殖石斑鱼,102 盐腌或盐渍的养殖鲥鱼,103 盐腌或盐渍的养殖鲷科鱼,104 盐腌或盐渍的养殖安康鱼,105 盐腌或盐渍的养殖海鲂,106 盐腌或盐渍的养殖鲆鱼,107 盐腌或盐渍的养殖鲽鱼,108 盐腌或盐渍的养殖红鱼,109 盐腌或盐渍的养殖其他鱼,110 盐腌或盐渍的野生石斑鱼,111 盐腌或盐渍的野生鲥鱼,112 盐腌或盐渍的野生鲷科鱼,113 盐腌或盐渍的野生安康鱼,114 盐腌或盐渍的野生海鲂,115 盐腌或盐渍的野生鲆鱼,116 盐腌或盐渍的野生鲽鱼,117 盐腌或盐渍的野生红鱼,118 盐腌或盐渍的海鲫鱼,119 盐腌或盐渍的金线鱼,120 盐腌或盐渍的马面鱼,121 盐腌或盐渍的马鲛鱼,122 盐腌或盐渍的其他野生其他鱼

HS 编码	CIQ 扩展品名
0306149090	101 饲料用青蟹,102 饲料用其他海水蟹,103 饲料用淡水蟹,104 养殖花蟹,105 养殖软壳蟹,106 养殖老虎蟹,107 养殖青蟹,108 养殖中华绒螯蟹,109 养殖其他蟹,110 野生花蟹,111 野生软壳蟹,112 野生老虎蟹,113 野生青蟹,114 帝王蟹,115 雪蟹,116 毛蟹,117 面包蟹,118 棕蟹,119 蜘蛛蟹,120 野生其他蟹
0306319000	101 活龙虾,102 鲜或冷的带壳或去壳养殖岩礁虾,103 鲜或冷的带壳或去壳野生岩礁虾,104 鲜或冷的带壳或去壳养殖其他龙虾(真龙虾属、龙虾属、岩龙虾属),105 鲜或冷的带壳或去壳野生其他龙虾(真龙虾属、龙虾属、岩龙虾属)
0306339990	101 活的青蟹,102 活的其他海水蟹,103 饲料用青蟹,104 饲料用其他海水蟹,105 饲料用淡水蟹,106 鲜或冷的养殖青蟹,107 鲜或冷的野生青蟹,108 其他鲜或冷的带壳或去壳养殖蟹,109 其他鲜或冷的带壳或去壳野生蟹
0306359090	101 活的南美白对虾,102 活的斑节对虾,103 活的其他对虾,104 活的其他海水虾蟹,105 活的日本沼虾(青虾),106 活的罗氏沼虾(马来沼虾),107 活的其他淡水虾蟹,108 活的虾蛄,109 活的糠虾,110 活的其他甲壳动物
0306369090	101 其他养殖鲜或冷虾,102 其他野生鲜或冷虾,103 饲料用海水虾,104 饲料用淡水虾,105 活的南美白对虾,106 活的斑节对虾,107 活的其他对虾,108 活的其他海水虾蟹,109 活的日本沼虾(青虾),110 活的罗氏沼虾(马来沼虾),111 活的其他淡水虾蟹,112 活的虾蛄,113 活的糠虾,114 活的其他甲壳动物
0306391000	101 其他海水虾蟹,102 日本沼虾(青虾),103 罗氏沼虾(马来沼虾),104 中华小长臂虾,105 其他淡水虾蟹,106 虾蛄,107 糠虾,108 其他甲壳动物,109 鳖卵,110 龟卵
0306931000	101 养殖干制蟹类制品,102 野生干制蟹类制品,103 养殖盐腌及盐渍蟹类制品,104 野生盐腌及盐渍蟹类制品
0306932000	101 养殖干制蟹类制品,102 野生干制蟹类制品,103 养殖盐腌及盐渍蟹类制品,104 野生盐腌及盐渍蟹类制品
0306940000	101 养殖干制虾类制品,102 野生干制虾类制品,103 养殖盐腌及盐渍虾类制品,104 野生盐腌及盐渍虾类制品
0306959000	101 养殖干制虾类制品,102 野生干制虾类制品,103 养殖盐腌及盐渍虾类制品,104 野生盐腌及盐渍虾类制品
0306990000	101 干制的其他养殖甲壳动物,102 干制的其他野生甲壳动物,103 盐腌或盐渍的其他养殖甲壳动物,104 盐腌或盐渍的其他野生甲壳动物
0307429100	101 活的乌贼(墨鱼),102 活的鱿鱼,103 饲料用乌贼,104 饲料用鱿鱼,105 其他鲜、冷的养殖墨鱼(乌贼属、巨粒僧头乌贼、耳乌贼属),106 其他鲜、冷的野生墨鱼(乌贼属、巨粒僧头乌贼、耳乌贼属),107 其他鲜、冷的养殖鱿鱼(柔鱼属、枪乌贼属、双柔鱼属、拟乌贼属),108 其他鲜、冷的野生鱿鱼(柔鱼属、枪乌贼属、双柔鱼属、拟乌贼属)
0307429900	101 活的乌贼(墨鱼),102 活的鱿鱼,103 饲料用乌贼,104 饲料用鱿鱼,105 其他鲜、冷的养殖墨鱼,106 其他鲜、冷的野生墨鱼,107 其他鲜、冷的养殖鱿鱼,108 其他鲜、冷的野生鱿鱼
0307431000	101 冻的养殖墨鱼(乌贼属、巨粒僧头乌贼、耳乌贼属),102 冻的野生墨鱼(乌贼属、巨粒僧头乌贼、耳乌贼属),103 冻的养殖鱿鱼(柔鱼属、枪乌贼属、双柔鱼属、拟乌贼属),104 冻的野生鱿鱼(柔鱼属、枪乌贼属、双柔鱼属、拟乌贼属)
0307491000	101 干制的养殖墨鱼(乌贼属、巨粒僧头乌贼、耳乌贼属)102 干制的野生墨鱼(乌贼属、巨粒僧头乌贼、耳乌贼属)103 干制的养殖鱿鱼(柔鱼属、枪乌贼属、双柔鱼属、拟乌贼属),104 干制的野生鱿鱼(柔鱼属、枪乌贼属、双柔鱼属、拟乌贼属),105 盐制的养殖墨鱼(乌贼属、巨粒僧头乌贼、耳乌贼属),106 盐制的野生墨鱼(乌贼属、巨粒僧头乌贼、耳乌贼属),107 盐制的养殖鱿鱼(柔鱼属、枪乌贼属、双柔鱼属、拟乌贼属),108 盐制的野生鱿鱼(柔鱼属、枪乌贼属、双柔鱼属、拟乌贼属)
0307499000	101 其他干制的养殖墨鱼,102 其他干制的野生墨鱼,103 其他干制的养殖鱿鱼,104 其他干制的野生鱿鱼,105 其他盐制的养殖墨鱼,106 其他盐制的野生墨鱼,107 其他盐制的养殖鱿鱼,108 其他盐制的野生鱿鱼
0307609090	101 活的田螺,102 活的蜗牛,103 鲜、冷的养殖蜗牛及螺,104 鲜、冷的野生蜗牛及螺,105 冻的养殖蜗牛及螺,106 冻的野生蜗牛及螺,107 干的养殖蜗牛及螺,108 干的野生蜗牛及螺,109 盐腌或盐渍的养殖蜗牛及螺,110 盐腌或盐渍的野生蜗牛及螺
0307719100	104 活的其他海水贝,105 活的其他淡水贝,106 活的其他软体及其他水生无脊椎动物,107 鲜、冷的养殖蛤,108 鲜、冷的野生蛤
0307719990	101 鲜、冷的鸟蛤,102 鲜、冷的舟贝,103 非生食的鲜、冷的赤贝,104 可用于生食的鲜、冷的赤贝,105 鲜、冷的养殖缢蛏,106 活的文蛤,107 活的食用杂色蛤,108 活的紫石房蛤,109 活的毛蚶(赤贝)),110 活的泥蚶,111 活的缢蛏,112 活的其他鸟蛤及舟贝
0307720090	101 冻的其他养殖蛤,102 冻的其他野生蛤,103 冻的养殖鸟蛤,104 冻的野生鸟蛤,105 冻的养殖舟贝,106 冻的野生舟贝,107 冻的养殖缢蛏,108 冻的养殖扇贝,109 冻的野生扇贝,110 冻的野生北极贝,111 冻的养殖杂色蛤
0307790090	101 干制的其他养殖蛤,102 干制的其他野生蛤,103 干制的其他养殖鸟蛤,104 干制的其他野生鸟蛤,105 干制的其他养殖舟贝,106 干制的其他野生舟贝,107 盐制的其他养殖蛤,108 盐制的其他野生蛤,109 盐制的其他养殖鸟蛤,110 盐制的其他野生鸟蛤,111 盐制的其他养殖舟贝,112 盐制的其他野生舟贝
0307911090	101 毛蚶(赤贝),102 泥蚶,103 文蛤,104 杂色蛤苗,105 大竹蛏,106 缢蛏,107 紫石房蛤,108 海螺,109 象拔蚌,110 其他海水贝,111 河蚌,112 河蚬,113 其他淡水贝,117 其他软体及其他水生无脊椎动物
0307919090	101 活的软体动物,102 鲜、冷非生食的养殖北极贝,103 鲜、冷可用于生食的养殖北极贝,104 鲜、冷非生食的野生北极贝,105 鲜、冷可用于生食的野生北极贝,106 鲜、冷的其他养殖双壳贝类,107 鲜、冷的其他野生双壳贝类,108 鲜、冷的其他养殖单壳贝类,109 鲜、冷的其他野生单壳贝类,110 鲜、冷的养殖头足类,111 鲜、冷的其他野生头足类,112 鲜、冷的其他养殖软体动物,113 鲜、冷的其他野生软体动物,114 活的有害软体动物,115 活的海螺
0308901990	103 鲜或冷,104 鲜或冷的其他养殖棘皮类,105 鲜或冷的其他野生棘皮类,106 活的珊瑚虫,107 活的海鞘,108 活的食用海肠,110 活的其他食用水生无脊椎动物,112 活的其他种用观赏水生无脊椎动物
0308909010	111 其他冻的养殖濒危水生无脊椎动物,112 其他冻的野生濒危水生无脊椎动物,113 其他干制的养殖濒危水生无脊椎动物,114 其他干制的野生濒危水生无脊椎动物,115 其他盐制的养殖濒危水生无脊椎动物,116 其他盐制的野生濒危水生无脊椎动物
0308909090	105 其他冷冻的养殖棘皮类,106 其他冷冻的野生棘皮类,111 其他冻的养殖水生无脊椎动物,112 其他冻的野生水生无脊椎动物,113 其他干制的养殖水生无脊椎动物,114 其他干制的野生水生无脊椎动物,115 其他盐制的养殖水生无脊椎动物,116 其他盐制的野生水生无脊椎动物
0401200000	101 巴氏杀菌乳,102 超高温灭菌乳,103 保持灭菌乳,104 巴氏杀菌工艺调制乳,105 生乳,106 其他乳与乳制品,107 其他调制乳,108 灭菌工艺调制乳
0401400000	101 稀奶油,102 淡炼乳,103 加糖炼乳,104 调制淡炼乳,105 其他乳与乳制品
0401500000	101 稀奶油,102 奶油,103 无水奶油,104 淡炼乳,105 加糖炼乳,106 调制淡炼乳,107 其他乳与乳制品
0402210000	101 全脂乳粉,103 部分脱脂乳粉,104 儿童调制乳粉,105 其他乳与乳制品,106 孕产妇调制乳粉,107 其他调制乳粉
0402910000	101 巴氏杀菌工艺调制乳,102 稀奶油,103 奶油,104 无水奶油,105 其他奶油,106 淡炼乳,107 调制淡炼乳,108 其他炼乳,109 其他乳与乳制品,110 灭菌工艺调制乳,111 其他调制乳
0402990000	101 巴氏杀菌工艺调制乳,102 稀奶油,103 奶油,104 无水奶油,105 其他奶油,106 加糖炼乳,107 调制加糖炼乳,108 其他炼乳,109 其他乳与乳制品,110 灭菌工艺调制乳,111 其他调制乳
0407290090	101 食用鸭蛋,102 食用鹅蛋,103 食用鸽蛋,104 食用鹌鹑蛋,105 食用鹧鸪蛋,106 食用火鸡蛋,107 食用鸵鸟蛋,108 食用
0408990000	101 即食蛋沙律,102 其他食用蛋制品,103 全蛋液,104 蛋黄液,105 蛋白液,106 冰全蛋,107 冰蛋黄,108 冰蛋白
0502901910	101 野猪毛(鬃),102 野牛毛(绒),103 野羊毛(绒),104 獾毛,105 其他饲养奇蹄动物鬃毛,106 其他野生奇蹄动物鬃毛,107 其他饲养偶蹄动物鬃毛,108 其他野生偶蹄动物鬃毛,109 未列出的其他动物鬃毛
0502901990	101 牛毛,102 牦牛毛,103 水牛毛,104 绵羊毛,105 山羊毛,106 野猪毛(鬃),107 野牛毛(绒),108 野羊毛(绒),109 獾毛,110 其他饲养奇蹄动物鬃毛,111 其他野生奇蹄动物鬃毛,112 其他饲养偶蹄动物鬃毛,113 其他野生偶蹄动物鬃毛,114 未列出的其他动物鬃毛
0502902010	101 獾毛,102 其他饲养奇蹄动物鬃毛,103 其他野生奇蹄动物鬃毛,104 其他饲养偶蹄动物鬃毛,105 其他野生偶蹄动物鬃毛,106 未列出的其他动物鬃毛

HS 编码	CIQ 扩展品名
0502902090	101 獾毛,102 其他饲养奇蹄动物鬃毛,103 其他野生奇蹄动物鬃毛,104 其他饲养偶蹄动物鬃毛,105 其他野生偶蹄动物鬃毛,106 未列出的其他动物鬃毛
0504001900	101 鲜、冷、冻猪肠衣,102 干、熏的猪肠衣,103 鲜、冷、冻牛肠衣,104 干、熏、盐腌或腌渍的牛肠衣,105 鲜、冷、冻绵羊肠衣,106 干、熏的绵羊肠衣,107 鲜、冷、冻山羊肠衣,108 干、熏的山羊肠衣,109 鲜、冷、冻鹿肠衣,110 干、熏、盐腌或腌渍的鹿肠衣,111 鲜、冷、冻其他动物肠衣,112 干、熏、盐腌或腌渍的其他动物肠衣,113 干、熏、盐腌或腌渍的牛肠衣(牛肠衣(盐渍)),114 鲜、冷、冻山羊肠衣(山羊肠衣冷冻),115 鲜、冷、冻猪肠衣(猪肠衣(冷冻)),116 鲜、冷、冻绵羊肠衣(绵羊肠衣(冷冻)),152 干、熏的猪肠衣(猪肠衣(干制))
0504002900	101 鲜、冷、冻的猪胃、猪肚,102 干、熏、盐腌或盐渍的猪胃、猪肚,103 鲜、冷、冻的牛真胃,104 鲜、冷、冻的牛瓣胃、牛百叶,105 鲜、冷、冻的牛网胃,106 鲜、冷、冻的牛瘤胃,107 干、熏、盐腌或盐渍的牛真胃,108 干、熏、盐腌或盐渍的牛瓣胃、牛百叶,109 干、熏、盐腌或盐渍的牛网胃,110 干、熏、盐腌或盐渍的牛瘤胃,111 鲜、冷、冻的绵羊真胃,112 鲜、冷、冻的绵羊瓣胃、绵羊百叶,113 鲜、冷、冻的绵羊网胃,114 鲜、冷、冻的绵羊瘤胃,115 干、熏、盐腌或盐渍的绵羊真胃,116 干、熏、盐腌或盐渍的绵羊瓣胃、绵羊百叶,117 干、熏、盐腌或盐渍的绵羊网胃,118 干、熏、盐腌或盐渍的绵羊瘤胃,119 鲜、冷、冻的山羊真胃,120 鲜、冷、冻的山羊瓣胃、山羊百叶,121 鲜、冷、冻的山羊网胃,122 鲜、冷、冻的山羊瘤胃,123 干、熏、盐腌或盐渍的山羊真胃,124 干、熏、盐腌或盐渍的山羊瓣胃、山羊百叶,125 干、熏、盐腌或盐渍的山羊网胃,126 干、熏、盐腌或盐渍的山羊瘤胃,127 鲜、冷、冻的鹿真胃,128 鲜、冷、冻的鹿瓣胃、鹿百叶,129 鲜、冷、冻的鹿网胃,130 鲜、冷、冻的鹿瘤胃,131 干、熏、盐腌或盐渍的鹿真胃,132 干、熏、盐腌或盐渍的鹿瓣胃、鹿百叶,133 干、熏、盐腌或盐渍的鹿网胃,134 干、熏、盐腌或盐渍的鹿瘤胃,135 鲜、冷、冻的其他动物的胃,136 干、熏、盐腌或盐渍的其他动物的胃,137 鲜、冷、冻的猪胃、猪肚(冷冻猪胃),138 鲜、冷、冻的牛真胃(冷冻牛真胃),139 鲜、冷、冻的牛瓣胃、牛百叶(冰鲜牛瓣胃(30 月龄以下)),140 鲜、冷、冻的牛瓣胃、牛百叶(冷冻牛瓣胃),141 鲜、冷、冻的牛瓣胃、牛百叶,冷冻牛瓣胃(30 月龄以下),142 鲜、冷、冻的牛网胃(冷冻牛网胃),143 鲜、冷、冻的牛瘤胃(冷冻牛瘤胃),144 鲜、冷、冻的绵羊真胃(冷冻绵羊真胃),145 鲜、冷、冻的绵羊瓣胃、绵羊百叶(冷冻绵羊瓣胃),146 鲜、冷、冻的绵羊网胃(冷冻绵羊网胃),147 鲜、冷、冻的绵羊瘤胃(冷冻绵羊瘤胃),148 鲜、冷、冻的山羊真胃(冷冻山羊真胃),149 鲜、冷、冻的山羊瓣胃、山羊百叶(冷冻山羊瓣胃),150 鲜、冷、冻的山羊网胃(冷冻山羊网胃),151 鲜、冷、冻的山羊瘤胃(冷冻山羊瘤胃),152 冷藏猪胃,153 冷冻鸭胃,154 冷藏鸭胃,155 冷冻鹅胃,156 冷藏鹅胃,157 冷冻火鸡胃,158 冷藏火鸡胃,159 冷藏珍珠鸡胃,160 冷冻珍珠鸡胃,161 冷藏牛真胃,162 冷藏牛网胃,163 冷藏牛瘤胃
0504009000	101 鲜、冷、冻的猪肠,102 干、熏、盐腌或盐渍的猪肠,103 鲜、冷、冻的猪膀胱,104 干、熏、盐腌或盐渍的猪膀胱,105 鲜、冷、冻的牛肠,106 干、熏、盐腌或盐渍的牛肠,107 鲜、冷、冻的牛膀胱,108 干、熏、盐腌或盐渍的牛膀胱,109 鲜、冷、冻的绵羊肠,110 干、熏、盐腌或盐渍的绵羊肠,111 鲜、冷、冻的绵羊膀胱,112 干、熏、盐腌或盐渍的绵羊膀胱,113 鲜、冷、冻的山羊肠,114 干、熏、盐腌或盐渍的山羊肠,115 鲜、冷、冻的山羊膀胱,116 干、熏、盐腌或盐渍的山羊膀胱,117 鲜、冷、冻的鹿肠,118 干、熏、盐腌或盐渍的鹿肠,119 鲜、冷、冻的鹿膀胱,120 干、熏、盐腌或盐渍的鹿膀胱,121 鲜、冷、冻的其他动物肠,122 干、熏、盐腌或盐渍的其他动物肠,123 鲜、冷、冻的其他动物膀胱,124 干、熏、盐腌或盐渍的其他动物膀胱,125 冷藏牛肠,126 冷冻猪膀胱,127 冷藏猪膀胱,128 冷冻牛肠,129 冷藏猪肠,130 冷冻猪肠
0505901000	101 鸡毛,102 鸭毛,103 鸭绒,104 鹅毛,105 鹅绒,106 火鸡毛,107 其他禽鸟羽毛
0505909090	101 鸡毛,102(鸭毛)(未经加工鸭毛除外),103 鸭绒,104 鹅毛,105 鹅绒,106 火鸡毛,107 其他禽鸟羽毛,108 未经加工鸭毛
0506100000	101 猪骨,102 猪蹄壳,103 牛骨,104 牛蹄壳,105 含饲养偶蹄动物的杂骨、骨块、骨粒(工业用牛骨粒、羊骨粒、猪骨粒除外),106 其他饲养偶蹄动物骨、蹄、角,107 未列出的其他动物骨、蹄、角,108 工业用牛骨粒,109 工业用羊骨粒,110 工业用猪骨粒
0506901190	101 饲料用牛骨粉(骨成分 67%以上),102 饲料用羊骨粉(骨成分 67%以上),103 饲料用混合型饲养偶蹄动物骨粉
0506901990	101 饲料用猪骨粉(骨成分 67%以上),102 饲料用混合型饲养偶蹄动物骨粉,103 饲料用其他饲养偶蹄动物粉,104 饲料用野生偶蹄猪、牛、羊骨粉(骨成分 67%以上),105 饲料用其他动物骨粉(骨成份 67%以上),106 饲料用其他动物蹄粉,107 饲料用其他动物角粉,108 未列出的饲料用其他动物粉
0506909091	101 工业用牛软骨,102 工业用羊软骨,103 工业用猪软骨,104 工业用烘干鹿骨,105 工业用牛骨粒,106 工业用羊骨粒,107 工业用猪骨粒,999 未列出的其他动物骨、蹄、角
0506909099	101 工业用牛软骨,102 工业用羊软骨,103 工业用猪软骨,104 工业用烘干鹿骨,105 工业用牛骨粒,106 工业用羊骨粒,107 工业用猪骨粒,999 未列出的其他动物骨、蹄、角
0507100030	101 含饲养偶蹄动物的杂骨、骨块、骨粒,102 其他饲养偶蹄动物骨、蹄、角,103 其他野生偶蹄动物骨、蹄、角(河马牙除外),104 象牙,105 未列出的其他动物骨、蹄、角,106 河马牙
0507100090	101 含饲养偶蹄动物的杂骨、骨块、骨粒(工业用牛骨粒、羊骨粒、猪骨粒除外),102 其他饲养偶蹄动物骨、蹄、角,103 其他野生偶蹄动物骨、蹄、角,104 未列出的其他动物骨、蹄、角,105 工业用牛骨粒,106 工业用羊骨粒,107 工业用猪骨粒
0507902000	101 饲养鹿的鹿茸,102 非饲养鹿的鹿茸,103 药用鹿茸,104 药用马鹿茸
0507909010	101 饲养鹿的鹿角(工业用烘干鹿角除外),102 含饲养偶蹄动物的杂骨、骨块、骨粒,103 其他饲养偶蹄动物骨、蹄、角,104 非饲养鹿的鹿角(工业用烘干鹿角除外),105 其他野生偶蹄动物骨、蹄、角,106 未列出的其他动物骨、蹄、角,107 工业用烘干鹿角,201 药用水牛角,202 药用龟甲,203 药用鳖甲,204 药用鹿角
0507909090	101 猪蹄壳,102 牛蹄壳,103 牛角(工业用烘干牛角除外),104 饲养鹿的鹿角(工业用烘干鹿角除外),105 含饲养偶蹄动物的杂骨、骨块、骨粒(工业用牛骨粒、羊骨粒、猪骨粒除外),106 其他饲养偶蹄动物骨、蹄、角,107 非饲养鹿的鹿角(工业用烘干鹿角除外),108 其他野生偶蹄动物骨、蹄、角,109 未列出的其他动物骨、蹄、角,110 工业用牛骨粒,111 工业用羊骨粒,112 工业用猪骨粒,113 包括蹄、甲、爪及喙及其粉末和废料,114 工业用烘干牛角,201 药用水牛角,202 药用龟甲,203 药用鳖甲,204 药用鹿角
0508001090	101 药用瓦楞子,102 药用海螵蛸,103 药用蛤壳,104 药用石决明,105 药用牡蛎(壳),106 药用珍珠母,108 未列出的饲料用其他动物粉,109 未经加工虾蟹壳
0510001010	101 药用牛黄,102 药用人工牛黄,103 药用体外培育牛黄
0510009090	101 药用九香虫,102 药用虫白蜡,103 药用土鳖虫,104 药用蝉蜕,105 药用僵蚕,106 药用桑螵蛸,107 药用地龙,108 药用蜈蚣,109 药用全蝎,110 药用鸡内金,111 药用猪胆粉,112 药用哈蟆油,113 药用蛇蜕,114 药用水蛭,118 其他药用动物源性中药材
0511911190	101 鲈鱼卵,102 鲑鱼卵,103 鲟鱼卵,104 牙鲆鱼卵,105 虹鳟鱼卵,106 河豚鱼卵,107 大鲮鲆鱼卵,108 其他受精卵
0511991090	101 猪精液,102 绵羊精液,103 山羊精液,104 马精液,105 其他精液
0511992090	101 牛胚胎,102 猪胚胎,103 马胚胎,104 绵羊胚胎,105 山羊胚胎,106 其他胚胎
0511994010	101 马鬃毛(含马尾毛)(未经加工马(鬃)尾毛除外),102 其他饲养奇蹄动物鬃毛,103 野马鬃毛(含尾毛)(未经加工马(鬃)尾毛除外),104 其他野生奇蹄动物鬃毛,105 未经加工马(鬃)尾毛
0511994090	101 马鬃毛(含马尾毛)(未经加工马(鬃)尾毛除外,102 其他饲养奇蹄动物鬃毛,103 野马鬃毛(含尾毛),104 其他野生奇蹄动物鬃毛,105 未经加工马(鬃)尾毛
0511999010	101 其他动物卵细胞,102 其他动物繁殖材料,103 其他野生奇蹄动物鬃毛,104 其他野生偶蹄动物鬃毛,105 偶蹄动物标本,106 奇蹄动物标本,107 禽鸟标本,108 爬行动物标本,109 其他动物标本,110 动物尸体,120 未经加工马属动物(鬃)尾毛),121 未经加工鹿毛,122 未经加工负鼠毛

HS编码	CIQ扩展品名
0511999090	101 鳖卵，102 龟卵，103 蚕卵，104 牛卵细胞，105 猪卵细胞，106 绵羊卵细胞，107 山羊卵细胞，108 其他动物卵细胞，109 其他动物繁殖材料，110 其他昆虫（其他动物），111 其他饲养奇蹄动物鬃毛，112 其他饲养偶蹄动物鬃毛，113 其他禽鸟羽毛，114 蚕茧（未经加工的蚕茧除外），115 蚕蛹（未经加工的蚕蛹除外），116 其他蚕产品（不包含蚕丝等纺织原料），117 偶蹄动物标本，118 奇蹄动物标本，119 禽鸟标本，120 爬行动物标本，121 其他动物标本，122 动物尸体，131 药用穿山甲（鳞片），132 药用蛤蚧，133 药用蟾酥，134 药用金钱白花蛇，135 药用蕲蛇，136 药用乌梢蛇，137 宠物食品加工用动物副产品，138 未经加工的蚕茧，139 未经加工的蚕蛹，140 未经加工的长吐、滞头，141 未经加工的蜂巢，142 未经加工的蜂胶，143 未经加工马属动物（鬃）尾毛，144 未经加工鹿毛，145 未经加工负鼠毛
0601109199	101 球根海棠，102 其他观赏花木，103 洋葱（鳞球块根茎），104 蒜（种用），105 芋艿（种用），106 郁金香球茎，107 朱顶兰球茎，108 睡莲块根，109 水仙花球茎，110 其他鳞球块根茎
0601200099	101 洋葱（鳞球块根茎），102 蒜（种用），103 芋艿（种用），104 甘薯块茎，105 百合球茎，106 郁金香球茎，107 朱顶兰球茎，108 睡莲块根，109 水仙花球茎，110 其他鳞球块根茎
0602201000	101 芭蕉苗木，102 番石榴苗木，103 柑桔苗木，104 海棠苗木，105 胡桃苗木，106 梨苗木，107 李苗木，108 荔枝苗木，109 芒果苗木，110 葡萄苗木，111 苹果苗木，112 木瓜苗木，113 山核桃苗木，114 山楂苗木，115 柿苗木，116 香蕉苗木，117 杏苗木，118 椰子苗木，119 枇杷苗木，120 橄榄苗木，121 桃苗木，122 草莓苗木，123 樱桃苗木，124 甘蔗苗木，125 木莓苗木，126 其他果树苗木，127 其他组培苗
0602909110	101 春兰，102 君子兰，103 蝴蝶兰，104 惠兰，105 石槲兰，106 卡特利亚兰，107 舞女兰，108 兰花，109 其他组培苗，110 营养体
0602909191	101 其他林木苗木，102 其他观赏花木，103 其他组培苗，104 营养体
0602909199	101 白腊槭苗木，102 长叶松苗木，103 岛松苗木，104 其他松属苗木，105 黄檀苗木，106 柳苗木，107 榆苗木，108 杉属苗木，109 梧桐苗木，110 棕榈苗木，111 栎树苗木，112 槟榔苗木，113 其他林木苗木，114 牡丹，115 安祖花，116 其他观赏花木，117 其他组培苗，118 营养体
0602909991	101 其他观赏花木，102 其他盆景，103 组培苗，104 营养体
0602909999	101 长春花，102 复盆子，103 龙舌兰，104 水仙，105 黄杨，106 郁金香，107 茶花，108 春兰，109 君子兰，110 芦荟，111 含笑花，112 仙客来，113 万年青，114 牡丹，115 月季，116 惠兰，117 洋桔梗，118 天竺葵，119 唐菖蒲，120 一品红，121 非洲菊，122 满天星，123 安祖花，124 球根海棠，125 马蹄莲，126 石槲兰，127 卡特利亚兰，128 舞女兰，129 海枣，130 富贵竹，131 散尾葵，132 万寿菊，133 绿藤，134 姜花，135 年桔，136 草皮，137 其他观赏花木，138 三角枫盆景，139 五角枫盆景，140 鸡爪槭盆景，141 山茶花盆景，142 翠竹盆景，143 白花杜鹃盆景，144 金豆盆景，145 腊梅盆景，146 榕盆景，147 榆盆景，148 五针松盆景，149 罗汉松盆景，150 金钱松盆景，151 福建茶盆景，152 乌头叶蛇葡萄盆景，153 朱砂根盆景，154 紫金牛盆景，155 凌宵盆景，156 花孝顺竹盆景，157 凤尾竹盆景，158 黄杨盆景，159 锦鸡儿盆景，160 雪松属盆景，161 朴盆景，162 木桃盆景，163 代代盆景，164 佛手盆景，165 金桔盆景，166 其他盆景，167 花卉组培苗，168 马铃薯组培苗，169 葡萄苗组培苗，170 甘薯组培苗，171 苹果组培苗，172 水稻组培苗，173 其他组培苗，174 营养体，175 杜鹃切花，176 山茶花切花，177 月季切花，178 芍药切花，179 满天星切花，180 美人蕉切花，181 木兰花切花，182 樱花切花，183 牡丹切花，184 郁金香切花，185 杂草
0604901000	101 苔藓及地衣，102 苔藓（栽培介质），103 泥炭藓（栽培介质）
0709999090	101 魔芋，102 其他薯类，103 大白菜，104 小松菜，105 青梗菜，106 油菜，107 菜心，108 芥蓝，109 其他十字花科蔬菜，110 牛蒡，111 苦苣，112 茼蒿，113 其他菊科蔬菜，114 韭菜，115 荞头，116 百合，117 金针菜，118 其他百合科蔬菜，119 芫荽，120 结球茴香，121 其他伞形科蔬菜，122 其他茄科蔬菜，123 冬瓜，124 其他葫芦科蔬菜，125 黄秋葵，126 生姜，127 芡实，128 茭白，129 玉米笋，130 香椿芽，131 鱼腥草，132 食用大黄，133 马齿苋，134 苋菜，135 番杏，136 落葵，137 蕨菜，138 紫苏，139 薄荷，140 保鲜其他未列出蔬菜，141 欧芹，142 芜菁，143 茼蒿，144 西葫芦，145 苏子叶
0710809090	101 冷冻魔芋，102 冷冻其他薯类，103 冷冻萝卜，104 冷冻芜菁，105 冷冻山葵，106 冷冻大白菜，107 冷冻甘蓝，108 冷冻抱子甘蓝，109 冷冻羽衣甘蓝，110 冷冻小松菜，111 冷冻青梗菜，112 冷冻小白菜，113 冷冻油菜，114 冷冻菜心，115 冷冻芥蓝，116 冷冻青江菜，117 冷冻芥菜，118 冷冻花椰菜，119 冷冻西兰花，120 冷冻其他十字花科蔬菜，121 冷冻牛蒡，122 冷冻洋蓟，123 冷冻苦苣，124 冷冻菊苣，125 冷冻茼蒿，126 冷冻莴苣，127 冷冻生菜，128 冷冻其他菊科蔬菜，129 冷冻洋葱，130 冷冻大葱，131 冷冻青葱，132 冷冻韭葱，133 冷冻韭菜，134 冷冻荞头，135 冷冻百合，136 冷冻金针菜，137 冷冻芦笋，138 冷冻其他百合科蔬菜，139 冷冻胡萝卜，140 冷冻芹菜，141 冷冻芫荽，142 冷冻结球茴香，143 冷冻其他伞形科蔬菜，144 冷冻茄子，145 冷冻辣椒、甜椒，146 冷冻其他茄科蔬菜，147 冷冻黄瓜，148 冷冻南瓜，149 冷冻西葫芦，150 冷冻瓠瓜，151 冷冻苦瓜，152 冷冻冬瓜，153 冷冻丝瓜，154 冷冻其他葫芦科蔬菜，155 冷冻蚕豆，156 冷冻毛豆，157 冷冻四棱豆，158 冷冻豆苗，159 冷冻豆芽，160 冷冻银耳，161 冷冻木耳，162 冷冻蘑菇，163 冷冻金针菇，164 冷冻杏鲍菇，165 冷冻草菇、甜椒，166 冷冻猴头菇，167 冷冻姬菇，168 冷冻平菇，169 冷冻秀珍菇，170 冷冻口蘑，171 冷冻其他块菌，172 冷冻其他食用菌，173 冷冻黄秋葵，174 冷冻生姜，175 冷冻芡实，176 冷冻茭白，177 冷冻玉米笋，178 冷冻竹笋，179 冷冻香椿芽，180 冷冻鱼腥草，181 冷冻食用大黄，182 冷冻马齿苋，183 冷冻苋菜，184 冷冻番杏，185 冷冻落葵，186 冷冻蕨菜，187 冷冻紫苏，188 冷冻薄荷，189 冷冻油橄榄，190 冷冻其他未列出蔬菜
0711903900	101 腌渍萝卜，102 腌渍芜菁（包括大头菜），103 腌渍甘蓝（包菜、卷心菜），104 腌渍芥菜，105 腌渍洋葱，106 腌渍荞头，107 腌渍胡萝卜，108 腌渍茄子，109 腌渍豇豆，110 腌渍菜豆，111 腌渍其他豆科蔬菜，112 腌渍生姜，113 腌渍蕨菜，114 腌渍紫苏，115 腌渍其他包叶菜类蔬菜，116 腌渍其他小叶菜类蔬菜，117 腌渍其他根菜类蔬菜，118 腌渍其他果菜类蔬菜，119 盐渍其他瓜菜类蔬菜，120 腌渍其他未列出蔬菜
0711909000	101 腌渍萝卜，102 腌渍芜菁（包括大头菜），103 腌渍甘蓝（包菜、卷心菜），104 腌渍芥菜，105 腌渍洋葱，106 腌渍荞头，107 腌渍胡萝卜，108 腌渍茄子，109 腌渍豇豆，110 腌渍菜豆，111 腌渍其他豆科蔬菜，112 腌渍生姜，113 腌渍鱼腥草，114 腌渍食用大黄，115 腌渍马齿苋，116 腌渍蕨菜，117 腌渍紫苏，118 腌渍薄荷，119 腌渍其他未列出蔬菜
0712909990	102 脱水魔芋，103 脱水其他薯类，104 脱水萝卜，105 脱水甘蓝（包菜、卷心菜），106 脱水芥菜 107 脱水花椰菜（白花菜），108 脱水西兰花（绿花菜），109 脱水其他十字花科蔬菜，110 脱水牛蒡，111 脱水青葱，112 脱水芦笋，113 脱水胡萝卜，114 脱水芹菜，115 干甜椒，116 脱水南瓜，117 脱水西葫芦（笋瓜），118 脱水瓠瓜，119 脱水苦瓜，120 脱水甜玉米，121 脱水鱼腥草，122 脱水食用大黄，123 脱水马齿苋，124 脱水菠菜，125 脱水紫苏，126 脱水薄荷，127 脱水山野菜，128 脱水其他未列出蔬菜，129 马蹄叶，130 刺嫩芽，131 地瓜梗，132 蓖麻叶，133 甜墨角兰，134 莳萝的粉
0811909090	101 冷冻荔枝，102 冷冻菠萝，103 冷冻桃，104 冷冻草莓，105 冷冻苹果，106 冷冻梨，107 冷冻西瓜，108 冷冻樱桃，109 冷冻猕猴桃，110 冷冻龙眼，111 冷冻葡萄，112 冷冻榴莲，113 冷冻菠萝蜜，115 其他未列名冷冻坚果，116 冷冻蔓越莓，117 冷冻无花果，118 冷冻越橘，119 冷冻黑莓，120 冷冻木莓，121 冷冻穗醋栗，122 冷冻香蕉，123 冷冻柠檬，124 冷冻蓝莓，125 冷冻芒果，127 冷冻博伊森莓，128 冷冻番荔枝，129 冷冻番木瓜，130 冷冻石榴，999 其它冷冻植物产品
0813409090	101 药用芡实，102 药用薏米（薏苡仁），103 薏米，104 山楂干（其他工艺），105 其他干（坚）果）（其他工艺），106 桑葚干（其他工艺）107 其他蜜饯，108 菠萝蜜干（其他工艺），109 草莓干（其他工艺），110 橄榄干（其他工艺），111 哈密瓜干（其他工艺），112 蓝莓干（其他工艺），113 榴莲干（其他工艺），114 甜角（其他工艺），115 蔓越桔干果（其他工艺），116 蔓越莓干（其他工艺），117 玫瑰果干（其他工艺），118 樱桃干（其他工艺），119 猕猴桃干（其他工艺），120 木瓜干（其他工艺），121 酸角（其他工艺），122 蔷薇果干（其他工艺），123 桃干（其他工艺），124 甜瓜干（其他工艺），125 西西果干（其他工艺），126 罗望子干（其他工艺），127 提取（晒干的除外）、压榨、烹制、烘焙、冻干、脱水、裹糖屑、发酵、冷冻（经漂汤和杀青，并在－18 度以下冷冻）、浸酸、腌渍、炒制等工艺进行加工处理的
1207999900	101 未去壳油用花生，102 其他籽仁为皮或衣等包被的油籽，103 油用茶籽，104 油用大麻籽，105 油橄榄，106 油桐籽，107 油用橡子仁，108 葡萄籽，109 其他籽仁为坚硬外壳包被的油籽，110 去壳油用花生，111 油棕果、油棕仁，112 西豆，113 黑加仑籽，114 琉璃苣籽，115 苏籽，116 月见草籽，117 水飞蓟籽，118 奇亚籽

HS 编码	CIQ 扩展品名
1209299000	101 鸭茅属种子，102 苜蓿属种子，紫苜蓿种子除外，103 车轴草属种子，104 杂高粱种子，105 苏丹草种子，106 草革芦属种子，107 狼尾草属种子，108 梯牧草子
1209300090	101 地毯草种子，102 散尾葵种子，103 唐倡蒲种子，104 鸢尾种子，105 兔尾草种子，106 鹤望兰种子，107 其他花卉种子，108 海石竹种子，109 钻石花种子，110 黄花菜种子，111 矮文竹种子，112 天门冬种子，113 仙客来种子，114 报春花种子，115 欧洲报春种子，116 金鱼草种子，117 紫盆花种子，118 一串红种子，119 蓝花鼠尾草种子，120 罗勒种子，121 彩叶草种子，122 香蜂花种子，123 薄荷种子，124 迷迭香种子，125 紫苏种子，126 荆芥种子，127 大戟种子，128 宿根羽扇豆种子，129 多叶羽扇豆种子，130 羽扇豆种子，131 日中花种子，132 洋凤仙种子，133 新几内亚凤仙种子，134 非洲凤仙花种子，135 旱金莲种子，136 狼尾草种子，137 美洲矾根种子，138 小天蓝绣球种子，139 长春花种子，140 三色堇种子，141 角堇种子，142 堇菜种子，143 蜀葵种子，144 风铃草种子，145 桔梗种子，146 半边莲种子，147 假半边莲种子，148 百日菊种子，149 斑鸠菊种子，150 大滨菊种子，151 雏菊种子，152 春黄菊种子，153 翠菊种子，154 千日菊种子，155 大丽花种子，156 堆心菊种子，157 旱花种子，158 瓜叶菊种子，159 美兰菊种子，160 红花种子，161 大花藿香蓟种子，162 金缘叶金光菊种子，163 黑心金光菊种子，164 毛叶金光菊种子，165 大花金鸡菊种子，166 金盏花种子，167 甘野菊种子，168 甘菊种子，169 麦秆菊种子，170 天山蜡菊种子，171 硬叶蓝刺头种子，172 母菊种子，173 南非万寿菊种子，174 小黄菊种子，175 秋英种子，176 黄秋英种子，177 山牛蒡种子，178 蛇目菊种子，179 珠蓍种子，180 山矢车菊种子，181 松果菊种子，182 天人菊种子，183 万寿菊种子，184 孔雀草种子，185 向日葵种子，186 勋章菊种子，187 一点红种子，188 佩兰种子，189 紫松果菊种子，190 紫菀种子，191 高山紫菀种子，192 枪刀药种子，193 三花枪刀药种子，194 芦莉草种子，195 翼叶山牵牛种子，196 十字爵床种子，197 大岩桐种子，198 盐角草种子，199 红月见草种子，200 山桃草种子，201 紫芳草种子，202 洋桔梗种子，203 马利筋种子，204 块根马利筋种子，205 旅人蕉种子，206 细叶美女樱种子，207 美女樱种子，208 大花马齿苋种子，209 土人参种子，210 天竺葵种子，211 老鹳草种子，212 花毛茛种子，213 欧洲银莲花种子，214 耧斗菜种子，215 翠雀种子，216 乌头叶毛茛种子，217 飞燕草种子，218 黑种草种子，219 美人蕉种子，220 蝴蝶草种子，221 萼距花种子，222 平卧萼距花种子，223 繁星花种子，224 二裂叶委陵菜种子，225 碧冬茄种子，226 花烟草种子，227 蛾蝶花种子，228 小花矮牵牛种子，229 观赏辣椒种子，230 四季秋海棠种子，231 刺芹种子，232 野胡萝卜种子，233 大阿米芹种子，234 醉蝶花种子，235 紫罗兰种子，236 香雪球种子，237 羽衣甘蓝种子，238 金庭荠种子，239 屈曲花种子，240 诸葛菜种子，241 南庭芥种子，242 柱毛独行菜种子，243 桂竹香种子，244 鼠耳芥种子，245 石竹种子，246 康乃馨种子，247 须苞石竹种子，248 蓝灰石竹种子，249 麦仙翁种子，250 圆锥石头花种子，251 绒毛卷耳种子，252 瞿麦种子，253 春羽种子，254 龟背竹种子，255 千日红种子，256 羽状鸡冠花种子，257 鸡冠花种子，258 青葙种子，259 毛地黄种子，260 直立婆婆纳种子，261 婆婆纳种子，262 柳穿鱼种子，263 香彩雀种子，264 钓钟柳种子，265 毛蕊花种子，266 钓钟柳种子，267 腹水草种子，268 马蹄金种子，269 牵牛种子，270 冰岛罂粟种子，271 虞美人种子，272 花荵草种子，273 勿忘草种子，274 大叶滨紫草花种子，275 紫茉莉种子
1209910000	101 菜豆种子，102 番茄种子，103 葱种子，104 莴苣种子，105 萝卜种子，106 黄瓜种子，107 辣椒种子，108 白菜种子，109 菠菜种子，110 南瓜种子，111 茄子种子，112 西葫芦种子，113 甜菜种子，114 牛蒡种子，115 黄秋葵种子，116 芦笋种子，117 空心菜种子，118 苦瓜种子，119 韭菜种子，120 花椰菜种子，121 芹属种子，122 蕹菜种子，123 生菜种子，124 青瓜种子，125 非种用芥菜种子，126 芥兰种子，127 甘蓝种子，128 刺葵种子，129 豆薯种子，130 丝瓜种子，131 芫荽种子，132 刀豆种子，133 其他蔬菜种子，134 罗勒种子，135 紫苏种子，136 葫芦种子，137 瓠瓜种子，138 笋瓜种子，139 苦苣种子，140 菊苣种子，141 茼蒿种子，142 蓟属种子，143 青椒种子，144 茴香种子，145 胡萝卜种子，146 欧防风种子，147 鸭儿芹种子，148 青花菜种子，149 青菜种子，150 芜菁种子，151 油菜种子，152 菜苔种子，153 苋种子，154 刺苋种子，155 冬瓜种子，156 棱角丝瓜种子，157 藜种子，158 辣蓼种子，159 韭葱种子，160 洋葱种子，161 大葱种子，162 香葱种子，163 罗勒种子
1209990020	101 乔荆相思种子，102 银荆相思种子，103 红槭种子，104 糖槭种子，105 雪松种子，106 崖柏种子，107 珙桐种子，108 赤桉种子，109 黑核桃种子，110 班克松种子，111 黄花松种子，112 晚松种子，113 火炬松种子，114 西蒙得木种子，115 湿地松种子，116 黑木相思种子，117 其他林木种子，118 药用植物种子
1209990090	101 其他花卉种子，102 剪股颖属种子，103 早熟禾属种子，104 黍属种子，105 臂形草属种子，106 狗尾草属种子，107 笔花豆属种子，108 雀稗属种子，109 狗牙根种子，110 其他牧草种子，111 大麻种子，112 烟草种子，113 药用植物种子，114 糖类植物种子，115 种用甜菜，116 罂粟子，117 其他经济类植物种子，118 洋香瓜种子，119 梅子种子，120 其他瓜果种子
1211903999	101 药用玉竹，102 药用白芷，103 药用桔梗，104 药用高良姜，105 药用黄精，106 药用葛根，107 药用白茅根，108 药用芦根，109 药用薤白，110 药用白及，111 药用板蓝根，112 药用苍术，113 药用柴胡，114 药用赤芍，115 药用刺五加，116 药用丹参，117 药用地骨皮，118 药用地榆，119 药用独活，120 药用莪术，121 药用防风，122 药用附子，123 药用钩藤，124 药用骨碎补，125 药用何首乌，126 药用红景天，127 药用厚朴，129 药用麦冬(麦门冬)，130 药用牡丹皮，131 药用木通，132 药用牛膝，133 药用前胡，134 药用羌活，135 药用秦艽，136 药用青风藤，137 药用桑白皮，138 药用升麻，139 药用石菖蒲，140 药用太子参，141 药用天冬(天门冬)，142 药用土茯苓，143 药用威灵仙，144 药用五加皮，145 药用细辛，146 药用香附，147 药用续断(川断)，，148 药用玄参，149 药用延胡索(元胡)，150 药用远志，151 药用泽泻，152 药用知母，153 药用竹茹，154 药用茜草，155 药用巴戟天，156 药用木贼，157 药用首乌藤，158 药用桑枝，159 药用金银花，160 药用桑叶，161 药用荷叶，162 药用淡竹叶，163 药用紫苏，164 药用山银花，165 药用艾叶，166 药用杜仲叶，167 药用番泻叶，168 药用红花，169 药用厚朴花，170 药用芦荟，171 药用玫瑰花，172 药用木棉花，173 药用枇杷叶，174 药用蒲黄，175 药用辛夷，176 药用淫羊藿，177 药用银杏叶，178 药用佩兰，179 药用侧柏叶，180 药用泽兰，181 药用罗布麻，182 药用金荞麦，183 药用刀豆，184 药用山楂，185 药用木瓜，186 药用火麻仁，187 药用决明子，188 药用余甘子，189 药用佛手，190 药用沙棘，191 药用罗汉果，192 药用青果，193 药用栀子，194 药用砂仁，196 药用香橼，197 药用桑椹，198 药用橘红，199 药用橘皮或陈皮，200 药用莱菔子，201 药用紫苏子，202 药用酸枣仁，203 药用覆盆子，204 药用柏子仁，205 药用补骨脂，206 药用瓜蒌，207 药用诃子，208 药用芥子，209 药用连翘，210 药用牛蒡子，211 药用青皮，212 药用山茱萸，213 药用菟丝子，214 药用吴茱萸，215 药用五味子，216 药用夏枯草(球)，，217 药用亚麻子，218 药用郁李仁，219 药用枳壳，220 药用枳实，221 药用韭菜子，222 药用沙苑子，223 药用槐角，224 药用蒺藜，225 药用金樱子，226 药用女贞子，227 药用益智，228 药用灵芝，229 药用猪苓，230 药用薄荷，231 药用藿香，232 药用大蓟，233 药用墨旱莲，234 药用益母草，235 药用茵陈，236 药用马齿苋，237 药用小蓟，238 药用鱼腥草，239 药用香薷，240 药用蒲公英，241 药用车前草，242 药用鸡骨草，243 药用积雪草，244 药用金钱草，245 药用荆芥，248 药用片姜黄，251 药用车前子，276 食用橘红，285 食用藿香，289 食用香薷，290 食用蒲公英，291 食用夏枯草(球)，292 其他药用根和根茎类中药材，293 其他食用根和根茎类中药材，294 其他药用茎、皮类中药材，295 其他食用茎、皮类中药材，296 其他药用叶、花类中药材，297 其他食用叶、花类中药材，298 其他药用果实类中药材，299 其他食用果实类中药材，300，其他药用种子类中药材，301 其他食用种子类中药材，302 其他药用全草类中药材，303 其他食用全草类中药材，304 其他药用未列明类别中药材，305 其他食用未列明类别中药材，306 食用凉粉草，307 白头翁 PULSATILLAERADIX，308 北豆根 MENISPERMIRHIZOMA，309 槟榔 ARECAESEMEN，310 草豆蔻(草寇) ALPINIAEKATSUMADAISEMEN，311 穿山龙 DIOSCOREAENIPPONICAE，312 大腹皮(茯毛) ARECAEPERICARPIUM，313 防己 STEPHANIAETETRANDRAERADIX，314 黄藤 FIBRAUREAECAULIS，315 鸡血藤 SPATHOLOBCAULIS，316 老鹳草(玄草)，ERODIIHERBAGERANIIHERBA，317 莲须 NELUMBINISSTAMEN，318 马钱子 STRYCHNISEMEN，319 马钱子粉 STRYCHNISEMENPULVERATUM，320 蔓荆子 VITICISFRUCTUS，321 猫爪草 RANUNCULITERNATIRADIX，322 山豆根 SOPHORAETONKINENSISRADIXETRHIZOMA，323 水飞蓟 SILYBIFRUCTUS，324 松花粉 PINIPOLLEN，325 天仙子 HYOSCYAMISEMEN，326 西青果 CHEBULAEFRUCTUSIMMATURUS，327 仙茅 CURCULIGINISRHIZOMA，328 郁金 CURCUMAERADIX，329 重楼 PARIDISRHIZOMA，330 紫草 ARNEBIAERADIX，331 胡芦巴(葫芦巴) TRIGONELLAESEMEN，332 药用吐根，333 药用白鲜皮，334 药用弗朗鼠李皮
1212999990	101 瓜子，102 其他干(坚)果(其他工艺)，103 供制食品或医药用的植物产品，104 批准为新食品原料，105 干橡子仁(其他工艺)，106 海底椰干(其他工艺)，107 其他干(坚)果(提取(晒干的除外)、压榨、烹制、烘焙、冻干、脱水、裹糖屑、发酵、冷冻(经漂汤和杀青，并在－18 度以下冷冻)、浸酸、腌渍、炒制等工艺进行加工处理的)，108 凉粉草(其他工艺)，109 凉粉草(提取(晒干的除外)、压榨、烹制、烘焙、冻干、脱水、裹糖屑、发酵、冷冻(经漂汤和杀青，并在－18 度以下冷冻)、浸酸、腌渍、炒制等工艺进行加工处理的)

HS 编码	CIQ 扩展品名
1214900001	101 三叶草、驴喜豆等,不论是否制成团粒(其他饲草),102 三叶草、驴喜豆等,不论是否制成团粒(饲用其他淀粉)103 三叶草、驴喜豆等,不论是否制成团粒(饲用植物颗粒和植物粉),104 三叶草、驴喜豆等,不论是否制成团粒(其他植物饲料)
1214900002	101 三叶草、驴喜豆等,不论是否制成团粒(其他饲草,天然饲草除外),102 三叶草、驴喜豆等,不论是否制成团粒(饲用其他淀粉),103 三叶草、驴喜豆等,不论是否制成团粒(饲用植物颗粒和植物粉),104 三叶草、驴喜豆等,不论是否制成团粒(其他植物饲料),105 天然饲草
1302199099	101 供工业用的植物及植物提取物(包括液汁等),102 供制食品或医药用的植物提取物,103 批准为新食品原料,301 危险化学品,不用作食品添加剂,302 危险化学品,用作食品添加剂),303 其他化工品,不用作食品添加剂,304 其他化工品,用作食品添加剂
1502900000	101 工业用牛油脂,102 工业用羊油脂,103 工业用野生猪、牛、羊油脂,104 饲料用牛油脂,105 饲料用羊油脂,106 饲料用野生猪、牛、羊油脂,107 未炼制的食用牛脂肪,108 未炼制的食用羊脂肪,109 已炼制的食用牛油(脂),110 已炼制的食用羊油(脂),111 未炼制的食用牛脂肪(冰鲜未炼制牛脂肪(食用,不包括内脏脂肪),112 未炼制的食用牛脂肪(冰鲜未炼制牛脂肪(食用,不包括内脏脂肪,12 月龄以下),113 未炼制的食用牛脂肪(冰鲜未炼制牛脂肪(食用,不包括内脏脂肪,30 月龄以下)),114 未炼制的食用牛脂肪(冷冻未炼制牛脂肪(食用,不包括内脏脂肪)),115 未炼制的食用牛脂肪(冷冻未炼制牛脂肪(食用,不包括内脏脂肪,12 月龄以下)),116 未炼制的食用牛脂肪(冷冻未炼制牛脂肪(食用,不包括内脏脂肪,30 月龄以下)),117 未炼制的食用羊脂肪(冰鲜未炼制绵羊脂肪(食用,不包括内脏脂肪)),118 未炼制的食用羊脂肪(冰鲜未炼制山羊脂肪(食用,不包括内脏脂肪)),119 未炼制的食用羊脂肪(冷冻未炼制绵羊脂肪(食用,不包括内脏脂肪)),120 未炼制的食用羊脂肪(冷冻未炼制山羊脂肪(食用,不包括内脏脂肪)),121 冷冻未炼制绵羊羔羊脂肪(食用,不包括内脏脂肪),122(冷冻未炼制山羊羔羊脂肪(食用,不包括内脏脂肪)
1506000090	101 工业用其他饲养偶蹄动物油脂,102 工业用野生猪、牛、羊油脂,103 工业用其他野生偶蹄动物油脂,104 工业用马油脂,105 未列出的工业用其他动物油脂,106 饲料用其他饲养偶蹄动物油脂,107 饲料用其他野生偶蹄动物油脂,108 饲料用马油脂,109 未列出的饲料用其他动物油脂,110 未炼制的其他食用动物油(脂),111 已炼制的其他食用动物油(脂),113 养殖虾虾油,114 野生虾虾油,115 其他养殖水产动物油脂,116,其他野生水产动物油脂
1515909090	101 饲料添加剂,102 其他初榨植物食用油,103 食用茶油,104 其他食用植物油,301 属于危险化学品的食品添加剂,302 一般化学品,需申报仅用于工业用途不用于食品添加剂有检疫要求,303 易燃液体,需申报仅用于工业用途不用于食品添加剂有检疫要求,304 有检疫要求食品添加剂
1518000000	301 其他化工品,不用做食品添加剂,302 其他化工品,用做食品添加剂
1601001090	101 动物肉及杂碎,102 其他熟制禽肉制品,103 其他熟制畜肉制品,104 未列出的其他动物肉脏及杂碎制品
1601002090	101 动物肉及杂碎,102 其他熟制禽肉制品,103 其他熟制畜肉制品,104 其他养殖制作及保藏水产制品,105 其他野生制作及保藏水产制品,106 未列出的其他动物肉脏及杂碎制品
1602200010	101 动物肉及杂碎,102 其他熟制禽肉制品,103 其他熟制畜肉制品
1602200090	101 动物肉及杂碎,102 其他熟制禽肉制品,103 其他熟制畜肉制品
1602310000	101 火鸡肉及杂碎,102 热处理火鸡肉,103 其他热处理火鸡肉
1602329100	101 非热处理鸡肉,102 热处理鸡肉,103 其他热处理鸡肉
1602329200	101 非热处理鸡肉,102 热处理鸡肉,103 其他热处理鸡肉
1602329900	101 非热处理其他禽肉,102 热处理鸡肉,103 其他热处理鸡肉
1602391000	101 鸭肉罐头,102 鹅肉罐头,103 其他家禽肉及杂碎的罐头
1602399100	101 非热处理其他禽肉,102 热处理鸭肉,103 其他热处理鸭肉
1602399900	101 非热处理其他禽肉,102 热处理鹅肉,103 其他热处理鹅肉,104 其他熟制禽肉制品
1602420090	101 猪蹄,102 去骨熟制猪肉制品,103 带骨熟制猪肉制品,104 以上述产品为原料制成的熟制猪肉产品
1602909090	101 其他动物肉脏及杂碎,102 去骨熟制羊肉制品,103 带骨熟制羊肉制品,104 去骨熟制鹿肉制品,105 带骨熟制鹿肉制品,106 去骨熟制马肉制品,107 带骨熟制马肉制品,108 其他熟制禽肉制品,109 其他去骨熟制畜肉制品,110 其他带骨熟制畜肉制品
1604111000	101 养殖水产制品,102 野生水产制品,103 养殖鱼类罐头,104 野生鱼类罐头
1604130000	101 沙丁鱼水产制品,102 小沙丁鱼属水产制品,103 黍鲱水产制品,104 西鲱水产制品,105 沙丁鱼罐头,106 小沙丁鱼属罐头,107 黍鲱罐头,108 西鲱罐头
1604140000	101 金枪鱼水产制品,102 鲣鱼水产制品,103 狐鲣(狐鲣属)水产制品,104 金枪鱼罐头,105 鲣鱼罐头,106 狐鲣(狐鲣属)罐头
1604170010	103 养殖鱼类罐头,104 野生鱼类罐头,105 养殖花鳗鲡制成的烤鳗,106 野生花鳗鲡制成的烤鳗,107 养殖花鳗鲡制成的其他水产制品,108 野生花鳗鲡制成的其他水产制品
1604170020	103 养殖鱼类罐头,104 野生鱼类罐头,105 养殖欧洲鳗鲡制成的烤鳗,106 野生欧洲鳗鲡制成的烤鳗,107 养殖欧洲鳗鲡制成的其他水产制品,108 野生欧洲鳗鲡制成的其他水产制品
1604170090	103 养殖鱼类罐头,104 野生鱼类罐头,105 养殖日本鳗鲡制成的烤鳗,106 野生日本鳗鲡制成的烤鳗,107 养殖日本鳗鲡制成的其他水产制品,108 野生日本鳗鲡制成的其他水产制品,109 其他养殖鳗鲡制成的烤鳗,110 其他野生鳗鲡制成的烤鳗,111 其他养殖鳗鲡制成的其他水产制品,112 其他野生鳗鲡制成的其他水产制品
1604199090	101 养殖石斑鱼,102 养殖鲥鱼,103 养殖鲷科,104 养殖安康鱼,105 养殖海鲂,106 养殖鲆鱼,107 养殖鲽鱼,108 养殖红鱼,109 养殖鲈鱼,110 养殖黄鱼,111 养殖鲅鱼,112 其他养殖鱼,113 野生石斑鱼,114 野生鲥鱼,115 野生鲷科,116 野生安康鱼,117 野生海鲂,118 野生鲆鱼,119 野生鲽鱼,120 野生红鱼,121 海鲫鱼,122 金线鱼,123 马面鱼,124 野生鲅鱼,125 野生鲈鱼,126 野生黄鱼,127 马鲛鱼,128 带鱼,129 其他野生鱼,130 养殖石斑鱼罐头,131 养殖鲥鱼罐头,132 养殖鲷科罐头,133 养殖安康鱼罐头,134 养殖海鲂罐头,135 养殖鲆鱼罐头,136 养殖鲽鱼罐头,137 养殖红鱼罐头,138 其他养殖鱼罐头,139 野生石斑鱼罐头,140 野生鲥鱼罐头,141 野生鲷科罐头,142 野生安康鱼罐头,143 野生海鲂罐头,144 野生鲆鱼罐头,145 野生鲽鱼罐头,146 野生红鱼罐头,147 海鲫鱼罐头,148 金线鱼罐头,149 马面鱼罐头,150 马鲛鱼罐头,151 其他野生鱼罐头
1604201990	101 养殖石斑鱼,102 养殖鲥鱼,103 养殖鲷科,104 养殖安康鱼,105 养殖海鲂,106 养殖鲆鱼,107 养殖鲽鱼,108 养殖红鱼,109 其他养殖鱼,110 野生石斑鱼,111 野生鲥鱼,112 野生鲷科,113 野生安康鱼,114 野生海鲂,115 野生鲆鱼,116 野生鲽鱼,117 野生红鱼,118 海鲫鱼,119 金线鱼,120 马面鱼,121 马鲛鱼,122 其他野生鱼
1604209990	101 养殖石斑鱼,102 养殖鲥鱼,103 养殖鲷科,104 养殖安康鱼,105 养殖海鲂,106 养殖鲆鱼,107 养殖鲽鱼,108 养殖红鱼,109 其他养殖鱼,110 野生石斑鱼,111 野生鲥鱼,112 野生鲷科,113 野生安康鱼,114 野生海鲂,115 野生鲆鱼,116 野生鲽鱼,117 野生红鱼,118 海鲫鱼,119 金线鱼,120 马面鱼,121 马鲛鱼,122 其他野生鱼
1605401100	101 养殖水产制品,102 野生水产制品,103 养殖甲壳类罐头,104 野生甲壳类罐头
1605401900	101 养殖水产制品,102 野生水产制品,103 养殖甲壳类罐头,104 野生甲壳类罐头
1605409000	101 养殖水产制品,102 野生水产制品,103 养殖甲壳类罐头,104 野生甲壳类罐头
1605580010	101 野生水产制品,102 野生水产罐头
1605580090	101 野生水产制品,102 野生水产罐头
1605630000	101 养殖水产制品,102 野生水产制品,103 养殖水产罐头,104 野生水产罐头
1605690010	101 野生水产制品,102 野生水产罐头
1605690090	101 养殖水产制品,102 野生水产制品,103 养殖水产罐头,104 野生水产罐头

HS 编码	CIQ 扩展品名
1901900000	101 其他冷冻饮品，102 纯麦片，103 发酵豆制品，104 方便米、粉，105 通心粉，106 米粉，107 速食粮食产品，108 其他粮食制品，109 其他含肉速冻粮食制品，110 其他不含肉速冻粮食制品，111 其他不含馅速冻粮食制品，112 非发酵豆制品，113 婴幼儿谷类辅助食品，114 婴幼儿罐装辅助食品，115 特殊医学用途配方食品，116 灭菌工艺调制乳，117 其他调制乳，118 儿童调制乳粉，119 孕产妇调制乳粉，120 其他调制乳粉，121 淡炼乳，122 加糖炼乳，123 调制淡炼乳，124 调制加糖炼乳，125 其他炼乳，126 乳基婴儿配方乳粉基粉，127 乳基较大婴儿和幼儿配方乳粉基粉，128 其他乳与乳制品，129 巴氏杀菌工艺调制乳，130 其他纯谷物的冲调谷物制品，131 含其他原料的谷物类冲调谷物制品，132 淀粉质类冲调谷物制品，133 其他食糖
1904900000	101 其他粮食加工产品(食用)，102 膨化食品，103 其他糕点饼干，104 纯麦片，105 方便米、粉，106 速食粮食产品，107 其他粮食制品，108 其他含肉速冻粮食制品，109 其他不含肉速冻粮食制品，110 其他不含馅速冻粮食制品，111 其他纯谷物的冲调谷物制品，112 含其他原料的谷物类冲调谷物制品，113 淀粉质类冲调谷物制品
2005999100	101 荞头罐头，102 其他鳞茎类罐头，103 红焖大头菜罐头，104 其他芸苔属类罐头，105 香菜心罐头，106 雪菜罐头，107 橄榄菜罐头，108 其他叶菜类罐头，109 其他茄果类罐头，110 美味黄瓜罐头，111 苦瓜罐头，112 其他瓜类罐头，113 青刀豆罐头，114 芸豆罐头，115 红豆罐头，116 发酵豆类罐头，117 其他豆类罐头，118 其他茎类罐头，119 胡萝卜罐头，120 姜罐头，121 地瓜罐头，122 其他根茎类和薯芋类罐头，123 莲藕罐头，124 清水莲子罐头，125 其他水生类罐头，126 绿豆芽罐头，127 黄豆芽罐头，128 其他芽菜类罐头，129 其他多年生蔬菜罐头，130 玉米笋罐头，131 四鲜烤夫罐头，132 什锦蔬菜罐，133 其他蔬菜罐头
2008999000	101 苹果罐头，102 葡萄罐头，103 海棠罐头，104 干装苹果罐头，105 什锦水果罐头，106 马口铁什锦水果罐头，107 玻璃瓶什锦水果罐头，108 复合塑料袋什锦水果罐头，109 橄榄罐头，110 芒果罐头，111 双色罐头，112 枇杷罐头，113 杨梅罐头，114 猕猴桃罐头，115 番石榴罐头，116 番荔枝罐头，117 山楂罐头，118 李子罐头，119 榴莲罐头，120 其他瓜果类罐头，121 其他浆果和小型水果类罐头，122 其他核果类水果罐头，123 其他热带和亚热带水果罐头，124 其他未列名水果罐头，125 熟制葵花子，126 未列出的其他熟制坚果炒货，127 果脯，128 其他蜜饯，129 冷冻油炸甘薯
2103909000	101 食用茶油，102 食用芝麻油，103 食用植物调和油，104 海鲜酱，105 即食沙律酱，106 冰梅酱，107 柱侯酱，108 排骨酱，109 沙茶酱，110 沙爹酱，111 豆瓣酱，112 甜酸酱，113 黄豆酱，114 其他酱，115 酿造食醋，116 配制食醋，117 白米醋，118 添丁甜醋，119 苹果醋，120 大红浙醋，121 其他食醋，122 调味剂，123 鸡精，124 鲜味粉，125 鲜味膏，126 其他鲜味剂，127 混合调味品，128 豆豉，129 姜豉，130 沙姜粉，131 五香粉，132 调味汁，133 未列出的其他调味品，134 红豆馅，135 芝麻酱，136 榛子酱，137 扁桃仁酱，138 其他坚果及籽类的泥酱，139 水产调味品
2106100000	101 蛋白型固体饮料，102 具有保健食品批准文号，104 大豆蛋白，105 豌豆蛋白，106 特殊医学用途配方食品，107 蚕豆蛋白，108 其他豆类蛋白，109 小麦蛋白，110 燕麦蛋白，111 大米蛋白，112 玉米蛋白，113 其他谷类蛋白，114 花生蛋白，115 其他坚果及籽类蛋白，116 马铃薯蛋白，117 其他薯类蛋白，118 其他未列明植物蛋白，119 过瘤蛋白
2106909090	101 其他食用植物调和油，102 其他食用植物油，103 代用茶，104 其他茶叶及制品，105 其他乳与乳制品，106 即食坚果沙律，107 熟制坚果炒货，108 含乳饮料，109 植物蛋白饮料，110 蛋白型固体饮料，111 果香型固体饮料如菊花精、柠檬茶、果珍，112 果冻，115 未列出的其他饮料、冷冻饮品、咖啡、果冻，116 其他原酒，118 未列出的其他酒，119 冰片糖，120 糖浆，121 糖霜，122 胶基糖果，123 其他食糖，127 其他糖果，128 其他糖与糖果，巧克力与可可制品，129 发酵豆制品，130 红豆馅，131 即食通粉沙律 132 湿粉，133 湿面，134 速食粮食产品，135 其他粮食制品，136 含肉饺子，137 不含肉饺子，138 其他不含馅速冻粮食制品，139 其他蜜饯，140 具有保健食品批准文号，141 母乳营养补充剂，142 婴幼儿谷类辅助食品，143 婴幼儿罐装辅助食品，144 特殊医学用途配方食品，146 食用其他加工油脂，148 其他未列出的加工食品，149 燕窝制品，以燕窝为主要原料的食品，150 运动营养食品，151 孕产妇营养补充品，152 辅食营养补充品，153 非发酵豆制品，154 其他蛋白饮料，155 其他特殊用途饮料，156 植物饮料，157 其他酿酒原料，158 酵母制品(食品加工用酵母制品)(活性酵母)，159 酵母制品酵母制品(食品加工用酵母制品)(非活性酵母)，160 酵母制品酵母衍生制品(食品加工用酵母衍生制品)，161 酵母制品(食品加工用其他酵母产品)，162 酵母制品(食品加工用乳酸菌)，163 食品加工用乳酸菌产品，164 酵母制品(其他食品加工用菌种及其产品)，165 酵母制品(乳酸菌饮料)，166 大豆蛋白，167 豌豆蛋白，168 蚕豆蛋白，169 其他豆类蛋白，170 小麦蛋白，171 燕麦蛋白 172 大米蛋白，173 玉米蛋白，174 其他谷类蛋白，175 花生蛋白，176 其他坚果及籽类蛋白，177 马铃薯蛋白，178 其他薯类蛋白，179 其他植物蛋白，180 纯麦片，181 其他纯谷物的冲调谷物制品，182 含其他原料的谷物类冲调谷物制品，183 淀粉质类冲调谷物制品，184 保健食品原料，301 无检疫要求食品添加剂，
2201909000	101 饮用水(如矿泉水、纯净水等)，102 食用冰，103 其他冷冻饮品，104 未列出的其他饮料、冷冻饮品、咖啡、果冻，301 需申报仅用于工业用途不用于食品添加剂无检疫要求的化学品
2202100010	101 碳酸饮料，102 可直接饮用的蔬菜果汁类饮料，103 含乳饮料，104 植物蛋白饮料，105 茶饮料，106 运动饮料，108 具有保健食品批准文号，109 植物饮料，110 乳酸菌饮料
2202100090	101 碳酸饮料，102 可直接饮用的蔬菜果汁类饮料，103 含乳饮料，104 植物蛋白饮料，105 茶饮料，106 运动饮料，108 具有保健食品批准文号，109 植物饮料，110 乳酸菌饮料
2202990011	101 碳酸饮料，102 含乳饮料，103 植物蛋白饮料，104 茶饮料，105 运动饮料，106 其他软饮料，107 未列出的其他饮料、冷冻饮品、咖啡、果冻，108 具有保健食品批准文号，109 植物饮料，110 乳酸菌饮料
2202990019	101 碳酸饮料，102 含乳饮料，103 植物蛋白饮料，104 茶饮料，105 运动饮料，106 其他软饮料，107 未列出的其他饮料、冷冻饮品、咖啡、果冻，108 植物饮料，109 乳酸菌饮料
2202990099	101 碳酸饮料，102 含乳饮料，103 植物蛋白饮料，104 茶饮料，105 运动饮料，106 其他软饮料，107 蛋白型固体饮料，108 其他咖啡，109 未列出的其他饮料、冷冻饮品、咖啡、果冻，110 燕窝制品，以燕窝主要原料制成的饮料，111 乳酸菌饮料，112 植物饮料
2301101900	101 饲料用猪肉粉(肉成分 67%以上)，102 饲料用猪肉骨粉，103 饲料用猪血粉，104 饲料用鹿肉骨粉，105 饲料用鹿血粉，106 饲料用混合型饲养偶蹄动物肉骨粉，107 饲料用其他饲养偶蹄动物粉，108 饲料用野生偶蹄猪、牛、羊肉粉(肉成分 67%以上)，109 饲料用其他野生偶蹄动物粉，110 饲料用禽肉骨粉，111 饲料用禽血粉，112 饲料用其他动物肉粉(肉成份 67%以上)，113 饲料用其他动物肉骨粉，114 饲料用其他动物血粉
2309909000	101 饲料用乳粉、乳清粉，102 未列出的饲料用其他动物粉，103 添加剂预混合饲料，104 浓缩饲料，105 全价配合饲料，106 精料补充料，107 其他配制的动物饲料，108 其他宠物食品，109 饲用蛋粉
2501001900	101 饲料添加剂，102 矿盐，103 海盐，104 除海盐、矿盐外
2503000000	301 危险化学品，不用作食品添加剂，302 危险化学品，用作食品添加剂
2506100000	101 石英砂，102 石英粉，103 熔融石英砂，104 熔融石英粉，105 其他石英
2519909100	101 矿物源性饲料添加剂 102 氧化镁(包括轻质和重质)(无检疫要求食品添加剂)，103 氧化镁
2524901010	101 栽培介质，301 其他危险化学品
2524901090	101 栽培介质，301 其他危险化学品
2530102000	101 蛭石(栽培介质)，102 珍珠岩(栽培介质)，103 石材
2805199000	301 危险化学品，易于自燃的物质，302 危险化学品，遇水放出易燃气体的物质
2806100000	301 危险化学品，气体，302 危险化学品，不用作食品添加剂，303 危险化学品，用作食品添加剂
2811199090	301 危险化学品，气体，302 危险化学品，氧化性物质，303 危险化学品，毒性物质，304 危险化学品，腐蚀性物质，305 其他危险化学品，306 危险化学品，用作食品添加剂，307 其他化工品，不用作食品添加剂，308 其他化工品，用作食品添加剂
2811210000	301 危险化学品，不用作食品添加剂，302 危险化学品，用作食品添加剂，303 其他化工品，不用作食品添加剂，304 其他化工品，用作食品添加剂

HS编码	CIQ扩展品名
2825909000	301危险化学品，氧化性物质，302危险化学品，毒性物质，303危险化学品，腐蚀性物质，304其他危险化学品，305其他化工品，不用作食品添加剂，306其他化工品，用作食品添加剂
2827399000	101矿物源性饲料添加剂，301危险化学品，易于自燃的物质，302危险化学品，毒性物质，303危险化学品，腐蚀性物质，304危险化学品，杂项物质，305其他化工品，不用作食品添加剂，306其他化工品，用作食品添加剂
2827600000	101矿物源性饲料添加剂，301危险化学品，毒性物质，302危险化学品，腐蚀性物质，303其他化工品，不用作食品添加剂，304其他化工品，用作食品添加剂
2828900000	301危险化学品，氧化性物质，302危险化学品，腐蚀性物质，303其他化工产品
2831101000	301危险化学品，不用作食品添加剂，302危险化学品，用作食品添加剂
2832200000	301其他危险化学品，302其他化工品，不用作食品添加剂，303其他化工品，用作食品添加剂
2833299090	101矿物源性饲料添加剂，301危险化学品，毒性物质，302危险化学品，腐蚀性物质，303其他化工品，不用作食品添加剂，304其他化工品，用作食品添加剂
2834100000	301危险化学品，不用作食品添加剂，302危险化学品，用作食品添加剂，303其他化工产品
2835299000	101矿物源性饲料添加剂，301危险化学品，毒性物质，302其他化工品，不用作食品添加剂，303其他化工品，用作食品添加剂
2836500000	101矿物源性饲料添加剂，102碳酸钙(包括轻质和重质碳酸钙)，103生物碳酸钙，104活性钙，301需申报仅用于工业用途不用于食品添加剂无检疫要求的化学品
2836999000	101矿物源性饲料添加剂，301危险化学品，氧化性物质，302危险化学品，毒性物质，303其他化工品，不用作食品添加剂，304其他化工品，用作食品添加剂
2842100000	101矿物源性饲料添加剂，301其他危险化学品，需申报仅用于工业用途不用于食品添加剂无检疫要求，302无检疫要求食品添加剂，303一般化学品，需申报仅用于工业用途不用于食品添加剂无检疫要求，304属于危险化学品的食品添加剂
2842905000	301危险化学品，毒性物质，302危险化学品，杂项物质，303其他化工品，不用作食品添加剂，304其他化工品，用作食品添加剂
2842909090	101矿物源性饲料添加剂，301危险化学品，氧化性物质，302危险化学品，毒性物质，303其他化工品，不用作食品添加剂，304其他化工品，用作食品添加剂
2853909090	301危险化学品，气体，302危险化学品，易于自燃的物质，303危险化学品，遇水放出易燃气体的物质，304危险化学品，氧化性物质，305危险化学品，毒性物质，306危险化学品，腐蚀性物质，307危险化学品，杂项物质，308其他化工品
2903799090	301危险化学品，易燃液体，302危险化学品，毒性物质，303其他化工品
2903820010	301危险化学品，毒性物质，302其他化工产品
2905290000	301危险化学品，易燃液体，302危险化学品，毒性物质，303危险化学品，腐蚀性物质，304其他化工品，不用作食品添加剂，305其他化工品，用作食品添加剂
2905499000	1012－苯乙硫醇，102赤藓糖醇，1032，5－二甲基－3－呋喃硫醇，1042－丙硫醇，1052－甲基－1－丁硫醇，1062－戊基硫醇，1073－甲基－2－丁硫醇，1083－甲基丁基硫醇，1094－甲氧基－2－甲基－2－丁硫醇
2907121900	301危险化学品，不用作食品添加剂，302危险化学品，用作食品添加剂，303其他化工品
2907159000	301其他危险化学品，需申报仅用于工业用途不用于食品添加剂无检疫要求，302无检疫要求食品添加剂，303一般化学品，需申报仅用于工业用途不用于食品添加剂无检疫要求，304属于危险化学品的食品添加剂
2907299090	301危险化学品，302他化工品，不用作食品添加剂，303其他化工品，不用作食品添加剂
2912190090	301危险化学品，易燃液体，302危险化学品，毒性物质，303危险化学品，腐蚀性物质，304危险化学品，用作食品添加剂，305其他化工品，不用作食品添加剂，306其他化工品，用作食品添加剂
2915130000	301危险化学品，不用作食品添加剂，302危险化学品，用作食品添加剂，303其他化工品，不用作食品添加剂，304其他化工品，用作食品添加剂
2915219090	301腐蚀性物质，需申报仅用于工业用途不用于食品添加剂无检疫要求，302无检疫要求食品添加剂，303需申报仅用于工业用途不用于食品添加剂无检疫要求的化学品，304属于危险化学品的食品添加剂
2915299090	101饲料添加剂，301危险化学品，毒性物质，302其他化工品，不用作食品添加剂，303其他化工品，用作食品添加剂，305毒性物质和感染性物质，需申报仅用于工业用途不用于食品添加剂无检疫要求，306杂项物质，需申报仅用于工业用途不用于食品添加剂无检疫要求
2915390090	301危险化学品，易燃液体，302其他危险化学品，303危险化学品，用作食品添加剂，304其他化工品，不用作食品添加剂，305其他化工品，用作食品添加剂
2915509000	101饲料添加剂，301危险化学品，不用作食品添加剂，302危险化学品，用作食品添加剂，303其他化工品，不用作食品添加剂，304其他化工品，用作食品添加剂
2915900090	301危险化学品，气体，302危险化学品，易燃液体，303危险化学品，有机过氧化物，304危险化学品，毒性物质，305危险化学品，腐蚀性物质，306危险化学品，杂项物质，307其他危险化学品，308危险化学品，用作食品添加剂，309其他化工品，不用作食品添加剂，310其他化工品，用作食品添加剂
2916190090	101饲料添加剂，301危险化学品，爆炸品，302危险化学品，易燃液体，303危险化学品，有机过氧化物，304危险化学品，腐蚀性物质，305危险化学品，用作食品添加剂，306其他化工品，不用作食品添加剂，307其他化工品，用作食品添加剂
2916209090	301危险化学品，易燃固体，302其他化工品，不用作食品添加剂，303其他化工品，用作食品添加剂
2916310000	101饲料添加剂，301危险化学品，不用作食品添加剂，302危险化学品，用作食品添加剂，303其他化工品，不用作食品添加剂，304其他化工品，用作食品添加剂
2916399090	301危险化学品，爆炸品，302危险化学品，易燃固体，303危险化学品，有机过氧化物，304危险化学品，腐蚀性物质，305其他化工产品
2917209090	301其他危险化学品，需申报仅用于工业用途不用于食品添加剂无检疫要求，302无检疫要求食品添加剂，303一般化学品，需申报仅用于工业用途不用于食品添加剂无检疫要求，304属于危险化学品的食品添加剂
2918110000	101饲料添加剂，301危险化学品，易燃液体，302危险化学品，毒性物质，303其他化工品，不用作食品添加剂，304其他化工品，用作食品添加剂
2918300090	301危险化学品，腐蚀性物质，302其他化工品
2919900090	301危险化学品，毒性物质，302危险化学品，腐蚀性物质，303其他危险化学品，304其他化工品，不用作食品添加剂，305其他化工品，用作食品添加剂
2920900090	301危险化学品，爆炸品，302危险化学品，气体，303危险化学品，易燃液体，304危险化学品，有机过氧化物，305危险化学品，毒性物质，306危险化学品，腐蚀性物质，307危险化学品，杂项物质，308危险化学品，用作食品添加剂，309其他化工品，不用作食品添加剂，310其他化工品，用作食品添加剂
2922110001	301危险化学品，腐蚀性物质，302其他危险化学品，303其他化工产品
2922491990	101饲料添加剂，102天门冬氨酸钙(有检疫要求食品添加剂)，103L－丝氨酸(有检疫要求食品添加剂)，10410－十一烯酸烯丙酯(有检疫要求食品添加剂)，105dL－缬氨酸(有检疫要求食品添加剂)，106L－精氨酸(有检疫要求食品添加剂)，107l－组氨酸(有检疫要求食品添加剂)，108甘氨酸(有检疫要求食品添加剂)，109牛磺酸(2－氨基乙基磺酸)(有检疫要求食品添加剂)，110L－酪氨酸(有检疫要求食品添加剂)，301需申报仅用于工业用途不用于食品添加剂有检疫要求的化学品
2922499990	101饲料添加剂，301危险化学品，毒性物质，302其他化工产品
2923200000	101饲料添加剂，102保健食品，301改性大豆磷脂(无检疫要求食品添加剂)，302酶解大豆磷脂(无检疫要求食品添加剂)，303需申报仅用于工业用途不用于食品添加剂无检疫要求的化学品

HS 编码	CIQ 扩展品名
2927000090	301 危险化学品，爆炸品，302 危险化学品，易燃气体，303 危险化学品，易燃液体，304 危险化学品，易燃固体，305 其他危险化学品，306 其他化工产品
2928000090	301 危险化学品，爆炸品，302 危险化学品，易燃液体，303 危险化学品，易燃固体，304 危险化学品，毒性物质，305 危险化学品，杂项物质，306 其他危险化学品，307 其他化工产品
2930909099	301 危险化学品，爆炸品，302 危险化学品，气体，303 危险化学品，易燃液体，304 危险化学品，毒性物质，305 危险化学品，腐蚀性物质，306 危险化学品，杂项物质，307 其他危险化学品，308 其他化工产品
2934993090	101 医学或生命科学用途，401《人间传染的病原微生物名录》内一类病原微生物的核酸（两用物项管制遗传物质除外），402《人间传染的病原微生物名录》内二类病原微生物的核酸（两用物项管制遗传物质除外），403《人间传染的病原微生物名录》内三类病原微生物的核酸（两用物项管制遗传物质除外），404《人间传染的病原微生物名录》内四类病原微生物的核酸，405 新发传染病或名录外再现传染病病原微生物的核酸
2936240000	101 饲料添加剂，301 维生素 D2（无检疫要求食品添加剂），302 烟酸（无检疫要求食品添加剂），303 烟酰胺（无检疫要求食品添加剂），304 泛酸（无检疫要求食品添加剂），305 泛酸钙（无检疫要求食品添加剂），306 需申报仅用于工业用途不用于食品添加剂无检疫要求的化学品
2936270020	103 化工产品，301 抗坏血酸钙，302 抗坏血酸钠，303 需申报仅用于工业用途不用于食品添加剂无检疫要求的化学品
2936270030	301 无检疫要求食品添加剂，302 需申报仅用于工业用途不用于食品添加剂无检疫要求的化学品，999 其他化工产品
2936270090	101 饲料添加剂，102 化工产品，301 无检疫要求食品添加剂，302 需申报仅用于工业用途不用于食品添加剂无检疫要求的化学品
2936280000	101 饲料添加剂，102 保健食品，301 生育酚，302 维生素 E，303 天然维生素 E，304d－α 醋酸生育酚，305 需申报仅用于工业用途不用于食品添加剂无检疫要求的化学品
2939799091	301 无检疫要求食品添加剂，302 需申报仅用于工业用途不用于食品添加剂无检疫要求的化学品
2940001000	101 饲料添加剂，301 蔗糖脂肪酸酯（无检疫要求食品添加剂），302 乙酰磺胺酸钾（安赛蜜）（无检疫要求食品添加剂），303 蔗糖聚丙烯醚（无检疫要求食品添加剂），304 麦芽糖醇液（无检疫要求食品添加剂），d－核糖（无检疫要求食品添加剂），306d－木糖（无检疫要求食品添加剂），307（L－阿戊糖（无检疫要求食品添加剂），308（L－鼠李糖（无检疫要求食品添加剂），309 八乙酸蔗糖酯（无检疫要求食品添加剂）
2942000000	101 其他饲料添加剂，301 危险化学品，遇水放出易燃气体的物质，302 危险化学品，腐蚀性物质，303 其他危险化学品，304 其他化工产品
3001200090	101 动物白蛋白，102 动物球蛋白，103 动物纤维蛋白原，104 其他动物血清蛋白，105 动物培养器官，106 动物培养细胞，107 动物微生物培养培养基，108 其他动物器官、细胞、培养基，109 未列出的其他动物产品，110 其他化工产品，113 工业用牛胰腺，114 工业用猪胰腺，115 牛胆汁，116 牛胆粉、牛胆膏
3002120099	101 饲料用猪血粉，102 饲料用牛血粉，103 饲料用羊血粉，104 饲料用鹿血粉，105 饲料用禽血粉，106 饲料用其他动物血粉，107 饲料用其他饲养偶蹄动物粉，108 饲料用其他野生偶蹄动物粉，301 其他化工产品，402 临床采集，含《人间传染的病原微生物名录》内一类病原微生物，403 临床采集，含《人间传染的病原微生物名录》内二类病原微生物，404 临床采集，含《人间传染的病原微生物名录》内三类病原微生物，405 临床采集，含《人间传染的病原微生物名录》内四类病原微生物，406 临床采集，含新发传染病或名录外再现传染病病原微生物，407 临床采集，含寄生虫，408 临床采集，经过血液传播病原体筛查为阴性，409 商品化含《人间传染的病原微生物名录》内一类病原微生物，410 商品化含《人间传染的病原微生物名录》内二类病原微生物，411 商品化含《人间传染的病原微生物名录》内三类病原微生物，412 商品化含《人间传染的病原微生物名录》内四类病原微生物，413 商品化经过血液传播病原体筛查为阴性，414 临床用捐献配型的特殊血型血液的血份，415 按药品管理的人抗血清，416 其他人抗血清，417 其他人血份，418 用于人类医学、生命科学相关领域的多克隆抗体，419 按药品管理人血浆蛋白制品（白蛋白、球蛋白、纤维蛋白原）
3002493090	101 动检细菌，102 动检病毒，103 动检真菌，104 动检放线菌，105 动检螺旋体，106 动检立克次氏体，107 动检支原体，108 动检衣原体，109 动检菌种，110 动检毒种，111 其他动检微生物，112 动检寄生虫，113 植物细菌，114 植物病毒，201 食品加工用酵母制品（活性酵母），202 食品加工用酵母制品（非活性酵母），203 食品加工用酵母衍生制品，204 食品加工用其他酵母产品，205 食品加工用乳酸菌，206 食品加工用乳酸菌产品，207 其他食品加工用菌种及其产品，401 两用物项管制外的《人间传染的病原微生物名录》内第一类病毒，402 两用物项管制外的《人间传染的病原微生物名录》内第二类细菌，403 两用物项管制外的《人间传染的病原微生物名录》内第二类病毒（含 Prion），404 两用物项管制外的《人间传染的病原微生物名录》内第三类细菌，405 两用物项管制外的《人间传染的病原微生物名录》内第三类病毒（含 Prion），406《人间传染的病原微生物名录》内第四类病毒，407 新发传染病或名录外再现传染病细菌，408 新发传染病或名录外再现传染病病毒，409 非菌剂类环保微生物，410 经基因编辑的治疗人类疾病用细菌及病毒（环保微生物除外），411 经基因编辑的人类医学、生命科学研究用细菌及病毒（环保微生物除外），412 其他医学相关细菌及病毒，413 环保用微生物菌剂，414 环保用微生物菌剂样品
3002499090	101 非两物项管制其他动物毒素，102 其他动检微生物，401 人类医学、生命科学研究用其他毒素，402 人类医学、生命科学研究用其他类毒素，403《人间传染的病原微生物名录》内第二类真菌，404《人间传染的病原微生物名录》内第三类真菌，405《人间传染的病原微生物名录》内的放线菌，406《人间传染的病原微生物名录》内的衣原体，407《人间传染的病原微生物名录》内的支原体，408 两用物项外的《人间传染的病原微生物名录》内的立克次体，409《人间传染的病原微生物名录》内的螺旋体，410 新发传染病或名录外再现传染病真菌、放线菌、衣原体、支原体、立克次体、螺旋体，411 人类医学、生命科学研究用其他真菌、放线菌、衣原体、支原体、立克次体、螺旋体，412 治疗人类疾病用
3002590000	101 普通动物细胞，102SPF 级动物细胞，103 细胞库的动物细胞系，104 其他动物细胞，401 人源血细胞，402 临床用捐献配型的骨髓造血干细胞，403 临床用捐献配型的外周血造血干细胞，404 临床用捐献配型的脐带血造血干细胞，405 其他人源干细胞，406 国际知名保藏机构的人源细胞株（系），407 其他商品化的人源细胞株（系），408 经基因编辑的人源细胞（细胞株），409 其他培养的人源细胞，410 临床采集，含《人间传染的病原微生物名录》内一类病原微生物，411 临床采集，含《人间传染的病原微生物名录》内二类病原微生物，412 临床采集，含《人间传染的病原微生物名录》内三类病原微生物，413 临床采集，含《人间传染的病原微生物名录》内四类病原微生物，414 临床采集，含新发传染病或名录外再现传染病病原微生物，415 临床采集，含寄生虫，416 临床采集，经过血液传播病原体筛查为阴性，417 商品化含《人间传染的病原微生物名录》内一类病原微生物，418 商品化含《人间传染的病原微生物名录》内二类病原微生物，419 商品化含《人间传染的病原微生物名录》内三类病原微生物，420 商品化含《人间传染的病原微生物名录》内四类病原微生物，421 商品化经过血液传播病原体筛查为阴性
3002904010	101 动检细菌，102 动检病毒，103 动检真菌，104 动检放线菌，105 动检螺旋体，106 动检立克次氏体，107 动检支原体，108 动检衣原体，109 动检菌种，110 动检毒种，111 其他动检微生物，112 动检寄生虫，113 其他化工产品，401 两用物项管制目录内人及人兽共患病病原体的遗传物质和基因修饰生物体
3002904090	101 动检细菌，102 动检病毒，103 动检真菌，104 动检放线菌，105 动检螺旋体，106 动检立克次氏体，107 动检支原体，108 动检衣原体，109 动检菌种，110 动检毒种，111 其他动检微生物，112 动检寄生虫

HS 编码	CIQ 扩展品名
3002909001	401 临床采集，含《人间传染的病原微生物名录》内一类病原微生物的的人全血，402 临床采集，含《人间传染的病原微生物名录》内二类病原微生物的人全血，403 临床采集，含《人间传染的病原微生物名录》内三类病原微生物的人全血，404 临床采集，含《人间传染的病原微生物名录》内四类病原微生物的人全血，405 临床采集，含新发传染病或名录外再现传染病病原微生物的人全血，406 临床采集，含寄生虫的人全血，407 临床采集，经过血液传播病原体筛查为阴性的人全血，408 商品化含《人间传染的病原微生物名录》内一类病原微生物的的人全血，409 商品化含《人间传染的病原微生物名录》内二类病原微生物的人全血，410 商品化含《人间传染的病原微生物名录》内三类病原微生物的人全血，411 商品化含《人间传染的病原微生物名录》内四类病原微生物的人全血，412 商品化经过血液传播病原体筛查为阴性的人全血，413 临床用捐献配型的特殊血型血液，414 其他人血
3002909090	101 猪全血，102 马全血，103 兔全血，104 狗全血，105 其他动物全血，106 猪血浆，107 马血浆，108 兔血浆，109 狗血浆，110 其他动物血浆，111 胎牛血清，112 小(犊)牛血清，113 猪血清，114 马血清，115 兔血清，116 小鼠血清，117 其他动物血清，118 动检抗原，119 动检抗体，120 动检抗血清，121 动检补体，122 动检溶血素，123 动物球蛋白，124 动物纤维蛋白原，125 其他动物血清蛋白，126 其他动物性血液制品，127 动物微生物培养培养基，128 牛血清成品，129 牛血蛋白，130 牛血清白蛋白，131 动物体内诊断用试剂，132 非商品化动物体外诊断用试剂及试剂盒，133 商品化动物体外诊断用试剂及试剂盒
3203002000	301 其他危险化学品，需申报仅用于工业用途不用于食品添加剂无检疫要求，302 无检疫要求食品添加剂，303 一般化学品，需申报仅用于工业用途不用于食品添加剂无检疫要求，304 属于危险化学品的食品添加剂
3204110000	301 其他危险化学品，需申报仅用于工业用途不用于食品添加剂无检疫要求，302 无检疫要求食品添加剂，303 需申报仅用于工业用途不用于食品添加剂无检疫要求的化学品，304 一般化学品，需申报仅用于工业用途不用于食品添加剂无检疫要求，305 属于危险化学品的食品添加剂
3204120000	301 其他危险化学品，需申报仅用于工业用途不用于食品添加剂无检疫要求，302 无检疫要求食品添加剂，303 一般化学品，需申报仅用于工业用途不用于食品添加剂无检疫要求，304 属于危险化学品的食品添加剂
3204130000	301 其他危险化学品，需申报仅用于工业用途不用于食品添加剂无检疫要求，302 无检疫要求食品添加剂，303 需申报仅用于工业用途不用于食品添加剂无检疫要求的化学品，304 一般化学品，需申报仅用于工业用途不用于食品添加剂无检疫要求，305 属于危险化学品的食品添加剂
3204140000	301 其他危险化学品，需申报仅用于工业用途不用于食品添加剂无检疫要求，302 无检疫要求食品添加剂，303 一般化学品，需申报仅用于工业用途不用于食品添加剂无检疫要求，304 属于危险化学品的食品添加剂
3204199000	101 饲料添加剂，301 其他危险化学品，需申报仅用于工业用途不用于食品添加剂无检疫要求，302 无检疫要求食品添加剂，303 一般化学品，需申报仅用于工业用途不用于食品添加剂无检疫要求，304 属于危险化学品的食品添加剂
3208909010	301 属于危险化学品的涂料，302 不属于危险化学品的涂料
3301120000	111 面部香精油，112 发用香精精油，113 体用香精精油，301 危险化学品，不用作食品添加剂，302 危险化学品，用作食品添加剂，303 其他化工品，不用作食品添加剂，304 其他化工品，用作食品添加剂
3301130000	111 面部香精油，112 发用香精精油，113 体用香精精油，301 易燃液体，302 无检疫要求食品添加剂，303 无检疫要求的食品添加剂，304 属于危险化学品的食品添加剂
3301191000	111 面部香精油，112 发用香精精油，113 体用香精精油，301 易燃液体，302 无检疫要求食品添加剂，303 无检疫要求的食品添加剂，304 属于危险化学品的食品添加剂
3301250000	111 面部香精油，112 发用香精精油，113 体用香精精油，301 无检疫要求食品添加剂，302 需申报仅用于工业用途不用于食品添加剂无检疫要求的化学品
3301291000	111 面部香精油，112 发用香精精油，113 体用香精精油，999 易燃液体
3301309090	103 吐鲁香膏，104 晚香玉浸膏，105 香榧子壳浸膏，106 秘鲁香膏油，107 秘鲁香脂
3301901090	301 危险化学品，不用作食品添加剂，302 危险化学品，用作食品添加剂，303 其他化工品，不用作食品添加剂，304 其他化工品，用作食品添加剂
3302109001	301 危险化学品，用作食品添加剂，302 其他化工品，用作食品添加剂
3302109090	501 其他危险化学品，502 无检疫要求食品添加剂，503 无检疫要求的食品添加剂，504 属于危险化学品的食品添加剂
3303000010	101 液体香水、香氛，102 固体香膏(粉)，103 花露水、去痱水，301 危险化学品，易燃液体
3303000020	101 液体香水、香氛，102 固体香膏(粉)，103 花露水、去痱水，301 危险化学品，易燃液体
3304100011	101 防晒化妆品，102 婴幼儿驻留类肤用化妆品，103 成人口唇驻留类化妆品，104 成人口唇淋洗类化妆品，105 成人口唇膜类化妆品，106 成人口唇美容化妆品
3304100012	101 防晒化妆品，102 婴幼儿驻留类肤用化妆品，103 成人口唇驻留类化妆品，104 成人口唇淋洗类化妆品，105 成人口唇膜类化妆品，106 成人口唇美容化妆品
3304100091	101 防晒化妆品，102 婴幼儿驻留类肤用化妆品，103 成人口唇驻留类化妆品，104 成人口唇淋洗类化妆品，105 成人口唇膜类化妆品，106 成人口唇美容化妆品
3304100092	101 防晒化妆品，102 婴幼儿驻留类肤用化妆品，103 成人口唇驻留类化妆品，104 成人口唇淋洗类化妆品，105 成人口唇膜类化妆品，106 成人口唇美容化妆品
3304200011	101 美白化妆品，102 防晒化妆品，103 婴幼儿驻留类肤用化妆品，104 成人眼部驻留类化妆品，105 成人眼部淋洗类化妆品，106 成人眼部膜类化妆品，107 成人眼部美容化妆品
3304200012	101 美白化妆品，102 防晒化妆品，103 婴幼儿驻留类肤用化妆品，104 成人眼部驻留类化妆品，105 成人眼部淋洗类化妆品，106 成人眼部膜类化妆品，107 成人眼部美容化妆品
3304200091	101 美白化妆品，102 防晒化妆品，103 婴幼儿驻留类肤用化妆品，104 成人眼部驻留类化妆品，105 成人眼部淋洗类化妆品，106 成人眼部膜类化妆品，107 成人眼部美容化妆品
3304200092	101 美白化妆品，102 防晒化妆品，103 婴幼儿驻留类肤用化妆品，104 成人眼部驻留类化妆品，105 成人眼部淋洗类化妆品，106 成人眼部膜类化妆品，107 成人眼部美容化妆品
3304300001	101 成人指(趾)甲护理化妆品，102 成人指(趾)甲美容化妆品，103 婴幼儿指(趾)甲化妆品，301 危险化学品，易燃液体
3304300002	101 成人指(趾)甲护理化妆品，102 成人指(趾)甲美容化妆品，103 婴幼儿指(趾)甲化妆品，301 危险化学品，易燃液体
3304990021	201 婴幼儿驻留类肤用化妆品，202 婴幼儿淋洗类肤用化妆品，203 成人面部驻留类化妆品，204 成人面部淋洗类化妆品，205 成人面部膜类化妆品，206 成人眼部驻留类化妆品，207 成人口唇驻留类化妆品，208 成人眼部淋洗类化妆品，209 成人口唇淋洗类化妆品，210 成人体用驻留类化妆品，211 成人体用淋洗类化妆品，212 成人体用膜类化妆品，213 成人面部用美容化妆品，214 成人体用美容化妆品，215 成人睫毛用美容化妆品，216 成人眉用美容化妆品，217 婴幼儿美容化妆品，218 面部香精油，219 发用香精精油，220 体用香精精油，221 美白化妆品，222 防晒化妆品，223 美乳化妆品，224 健美化妆品，225 脱毛化妆品
3304990029	201 婴幼儿驻留类肤用化妆品，202 婴幼儿淋洗类肤用化妆品，203 成人面部驻留类化妆品，204 成人面部淋洗类化妆品，205 成人面部膜类化妆品，206 成人眼部驻留类化妆品，207 成人口唇驻留类化妆品，208 成人眼部淋洗类化妆品，209 成人口唇淋洗类化妆品，210 成人体用驻留类化妆品，211 成人体用淋洗类化妆品，212 成人体用膜类化妆品，213 成人面部用美容化妆品，214 成人体用美容化妆品，215 成人睫毛用美容化妆品，216 成人眉用美容化妆品，217 婴幼儿美容化妆品，218 面部香精油，219 发用香精精油，220 体用香精精油，221 美白化妆品，222 防晒化妆品，223 美乳化妆品，224 健美化妆品，225 脱毛化妆品

HS 编码	CIQ 扩展品名
3304990031	201 婴幼儿驻留类肤用化妆品，202 婴幼儿淋洗类肤用化妆品，203 成人面部驻留类化妆品，204 成人面部淋洗类化妆品，205 成人面部膜类化妆品，206 成人眼部驻留类化妆品，207 成人口唇驻留类化妆品，208 成人眼部淋洗类化妆品，209 成人口唇淋洗类化妆品，210 成人体用驻留类化妆品，211 成人体用淋洗类化妆品，212 成人体用膜类化妆品，213 成人面部用美容化妆品，214 成人体用美容化妆品，215 成人睫毛用美容化妆品，216 成人眉用美容化妆品，217 婴幼儿美容化妆品，218 面部香精油，219 发用香精精油，220 体用香精精油，221 美白化妆品，222 防晒化妆品，223 美乳化妆品，224 健美化妆品，225 脱毛化妆品
3304990039	201 婴幼儿驻留类肤用化妆品，202 婴幼儿淋洗类肤用化妆品，203 成人面部驻留类化妆品，204 成人面部淋洗类化妆品，205 成人面部膜类化妆品，206 成人眼部驻留类化妆品，207 成人口唇驻留类化妆品，208 成人眼部淋洗类化妆品，209 成人口唇淋洗类化妆品，210 成人体用驻留类化妆品，211 成人体用淋洗类化妆品，212 成人体用膜类化妆品，213 成人面部用美容化妆品，214 成人体用美容化妆品，215 成人睫毛用美容化妆品，216 成人眉用美容化妆品，217 婴幼儿美容化妆品，218 面部香精油，219 发用香精精油，220 体用香精精油，221 美白化妆品，222 防晒化妆品，223 美乳化妆品，224 健美化妆品，225 脱毛化妆品
3304990091	101 婴幼儿驻留类肤用化妆品，103 成人面部驻留类化妆品，104 成人体用驻留类化妆品，105 婴幼儿淋洗类肤用化妆品，106 成人面部淋洗类化妆品，107 成人口唇淋洗类化妆品，108 成人体用淋洗类化妆品，112 防晒化妆品，120 成人面部膜类化妆品，121 成人眼部驻留类化妆品，122 成人口唇驻留类化妆品，123 成人眼部淋洗类化妆品，124 成人体用膜类化妆品，125 面部香精油，126 发用香精精油，127 体用香精精油，128 美白化妆品
3304990099	101 婴幼儿驻留类肤用化妆品，103 成人面部驻留类化妆品，104 成人体用驻留类化妆品，105 婴幼儿淋洗类肤用化妆品，106 成人面部淋洗类化妆品，107 成人口唇淋洗类化妆品，108 成人体用淋洗类化妆品，112 防晒化妆品，120 成人面部膜类化妆品，121 成人眼部驻留类化妆品，122 成人口唇驻留类化妆品，123 成人眼部淋洗类化妆品，124 成人体用膜类化妆品，125 面部香精油，126 发用香精精油，127 体用香精精油，128 美白化妆品
3305900000	108 染发化妆品，109 育发化妆品，110 婴幼儿淋洗类发用化妆品，111 婴幼儿驻留类发用化妆品，112 成人淋洗类毛发用化妆品，113 成人驻留类毛发用化妆品
3504009000	101 保健食品，102 乳铁蛋白(无检疫要求食品添加剂)，103 需申报仅用于工业用途不用于食品添加剂无检疫要求的化学品，105 大豆蛋白，106 豌豆蛋白，107 蚕豆蛋白，108 其他豆类蛋白，109 小麦蛋白，110 燕麦蛋白，111 大米蛋白，112 玉米蛋白，113 其他谷类蛋白，114 花生蛋白，115 其他坚果及籽类蛋白，116 马铃薯蛋白，117 其他薯类蛋白，118 其他植物蛋白，119 浓缩牛奶蛋白，401 用于人类医学、生命科学相关领域，非用于治疗或预防疾病用
3506919090	301 危险化学品，易燃液体，302 其他化工品
3604100000	101 喷花类玩具烟花爆竹，102 旋转类玩具烟花爆竹，103 旋转升空类玩具烟花爆竹，104 火箭类玩具烟花爆竹，105 吐珠类玩具烟花爆竹，106 线香类玩具烟花爆竹，107 摩擦炮类玩具烟花爆竹，108 造型玩具类玩具烟花爆竹，109 地面礼花类玩具烟花爆竹，110 烟雾类玩具烟花爆竹，111 礼花弹类玩具烟花爆竹，112 玩具烟花爆竹组合，113 爆竹，114 喷花类大型烟花，115 旋转类大型烟花，116 火箭类大型烟花，117 吐珠类大型烟花，118 地面礼花类大型烟花，119 礼花弹类大型烟花，120 大型烟花组合
3814000000	301 危险化学品，易燃液体，302 危险化学品，毒性物质，303 其他化工品
3924100000	101 食品接触聚苯乙烯产品，102 食品接触聚乙烯产品，103 食品接触聚丙烯产品，104 食品接触聚氯乙烯产品，105 食品接触三聚氰胺一甲醛产品，106 食品接触丙烯腈一丁二烯一苯乙烯产品，107 食品接触丙烯腈一苯乙烯产品，108 食品接触不饱和聚酯树脂及其玻璃钢产品，109 食品接触对苯二甲酸乙二醇酯产品，110 食品接触尼龙产品，111 食品接触聚碳酸酯产品，112 食品接触聚偏二氯乙烯产品，113 食品接触聚甲基丙烯酸甲酯产品，114 食品接触聚甲基戊烯产品，115 食品接触复合塑料(仅指多种塑料材质复合)产品，116 食品接触其他塑料产品，117 食品用聚苯乙烯包装，118 食品用聚乙烯包装，119 食品用聚丙烯包装，120 食品用聚氯乙烯瓶盖垫片，121 食品用其他聚氯乙烯包装，122 食品用三聚氰胺一甲醛包装，123 食品用丙烯腈一丁二烯一苯乙烯包装，124 食品用丙烯腈一苯乙烯包装，125 食品用不饱和聚酯树脂及其玻璃钢包装，126 食品用对苯二甲酸乙二醇酯包装，127 食品用尼龙包装，128 食品用聚碳酸酯包装，129 食品用聚偏二氯乙烯包装，130 食品用聚甲基丙烯酸甲酯包装，131 食品用聚甲基戊烯包装，132 食品用复合塑料(仅指多种塑料材质复合)包装，133 食品用其他塑料包装，999 非食品用塑料容器用具
4301809010	101 斑马皮，102 野驴皮，103 其他野生奇蹄动物皮张，104 野猪皮，105 野羊皮，106 野骆驼皮，107 野鹿皮，108 其他野生偶蹄动物皮张，109 其他禽鸟皮，110 象皮，111 袋鼠皮，112 海豹皮，113 鳄鱼皮，114 蜥蜴皮，115 蛇皮，116 蟒蛇皮，117 未列出的其他动物皮张，118 艾鼬皮，119 臭鼬皮，120 短尾猫皮，121 负鼠皮，122 海狸皮，123 旱獭皮，124 貉子皮，125 浣熊皮，126 灰鼠皮，127 狼皮，128 猞猁皮，129 麝鼠皮，130 水獭皮，131 松鼠皮
4403499090	101 针叶原木，102 白柳桉原木及其他柳桉原木，103 羯布罗香木等原木，104 安哥拉香桃花心木等原木，105 其他非针叶原木
4407299099	101 加蓬榄木、非洲白梧桐等木厚板材，102 其他热带木木材，103 橡胶木方
4408391990	101 针叶木薄板，102 非针叶木薄板
4408901911	101 针叶木薄板，102 非针叶木薄板
4408901919	101 针叶木薄板，102 非针叶木薄板
4408901991	101 针叶木薄板，102 非针叶木薄板
4408901999	101 针叶木薄板，102 非针叶木薄板
4410909000	101 其他厚度超过 6 毫米的板材、方材、垫木，102 其他厚度小于或等于 6 毫米的薄板
4411121900	101 针叶木纤维板，102 非针叶木纤维板，103 其他纤维板
4411122900	101 针叶木纤维板，102 非针叶木纤维板，103 其他纤维板
4411129100	101 针叶木纤维板，102 非针叶木纤维板，103 其他纤维板
4411131100	101 针叶木纤维板，102 非针叶木纤维板，103 其他纤维板
4411131900	101 针叶木纤维板，102 非针叶木纤维板，103 其他纤维板
4411132900	101 针叶木纤维板，102 非针叶木纤维板，103 其他纤维板
4411139100	101 针叶木纤维板，102 非针叶木纤维板，103 其他纤维板
4411139900	101 针叶木纤维板，102 非针叶木纤维板，103 其他纤维板
4411142900	101 针叶木纤维板，102 非针叶木纤维板，103 其他纤维板
4411149900	101 针叶木纤维板，102 非针叶木纤维板，103 其他纤维板
4411921000	101 针叶木纤维板，102 非针叶木纤维板，103 其他纤维板
4411939000	101 针叶木纤维板，102 非针叶木纤维板，103 其他纤维板
4411942100	101 针叶木纤维板，102 非针叶木纤维板，103 其他纤维板
4415100020	101 针叶木木质包装，102 非针叶木木质包装
4415100090	101 针叶木木质包装，102 非针叶木木质包装，103 其他木质包装
4415209090	101 针叶木木质包装，102 非针叶木木质包装，103 其他木质包装
4416009090	101 其他木制品，102 针叶木木质包装，103 非针叶木木质包装
4419901000	101 木质餐具及厨房用具，102 食品接触木制产品
4823909000	101 其它纸及纸制品，102 食品接触原纸产品，103 食品接触复合纸产品(纸和塑料膜等其他材料复合)，104 食品接触上蜡纸产品，105 食品接触其他纸产品，106 食品用原纸包装，107 食品用复合纸包装(纸和塑料膜等其他材料复合)，108 食品用上蜡纸包装，109 食品用其他纸包装

HS 编码	CIQ 扩展品名
5102199010	101 未洗净其他野生奇蹄动物鬃毛,102 未洗净野牛毛(绒),103 未洗净其他野生偶蹄动物鬃毛,104 未洗净兔绒,105 未洗净未列出的其他动物鬃毛,106 洗净未列出的野生奇蹄动物鬃毛,107 洗净野牛毛(绒),108 洗净未列出的野生偶蹄动物鬃毛,109 洗净兔绒,110 洗净其他动物毛
5102199090	101 未洗净其他饲养奇蹄动物鬃毛,102 未洗净其他野生奇蹄动物鬃毛,103 未洗净牦牛绒,104 未洗净其他饲养偶蹄动物鬃毛,105 未洗净其他野生偶蹄动物鬃毛,106 未洗净兔绒,107 未洗净未列出的其他动物鬃毛,108 洗净未列出的饲养奇蹄动物鬃毛,109 洗净未列出的野生奇蹄动物鬃毛,110 洗净牦牛绒,111 洗净未列出的饲养偶蹄动物鬃毛,112 洗净未列出的野生偶蹄动物鬃毛,113 洗净兔绒,114 洗净其他动物毛
5102200010	101 未洗净其他野生奇蹄动物鬃毛,102 未洗净野牛毛(绒),103 未洗净其他野生偶蹄动物鬃毛,104 未洗净未列出的其他动物鬃毛,105 洗净未列出的野生奇蹄动物鬃毛,106 洗净未列出的野生偶蹄动物鬃毛,107 洗净未列出的其他动物鬃毛
5102200090	101 未洗净其他饲养奇蹄动物鬃毛,102 未洗净其他野生奇蹄动物鬃毛,103 未洗净其他饲养偶蹄动物鬃毛,104 未洗净野牛毛(绒),105 未洗净其他野生偶蹄动物鬃毛,106 未洗净未列出的其他动物鬃毛,107 洗净未列出的其他动物鬃毛
5103109010	101 未洗净其他野生奇蹄动物鬃毛,102 未洗净野牛毛(绒),103 未洗净其他野生偶蹄动物鬃毛,104 未洗净兔绒,105 未洗净未列出的其他动物鬃毛,106 洗净濒危野生动物细毛
8414512000	101 换气扇 I 类器具,102 换气扇 II 类器具,103 换气扇 III 类器具,104 换气扇 0I 类器具,105 换气扇 0 类器具,106 其它电扇及其零件 I 类器具,107 其它电扇及其零件 II 类器具,108 其它电扇及其零件 III 类器具,109 其它电扇及其零件 0I 类器具,110 其它电扇及其零件 0 类器具
8414513000	101 有旋转导风轮的风扇 I 类器具,102 有旋转导风轮的风扇 II 类器具,103 有旋转导风轮的风扇 III 类器具,104 有旋转导风轮的风扇 0I 类器具,105 有旋转导风轮的风扇 0 类器具
8414519900	101 其它电扇及其零件 I 类器具,102 其它电扇及其零件 II 类器具,103 其它电扇及其零件 III 类器具,104 其它电扇及其零件 0I 类器具,105 其它电扇及其零件 0 类器具
8414591000	101 吊扇 I 类器具,102 吊扇 II 类器具,103 吊扇 III 类器具,104 吊扇 0I 类器具,105 吊扇 0 类器具,106 其它电扇及其零件 I 类器具,107 其它电扇及其零件 II 类器具,108 其它电扇及其零件 III 类器具,109 其它电扇及其零件 0I 类器具,110 其它电扇及其零件 0 类器具
8414592000	101 换气扇 I 类器具,102 换气扇 II 类器具,103 换气扇 III 类器具,104 换气扇 0I 类器具,105 换气扇 0 类器具,106 其它电扇及其零件 I 类器具,107 其它电扇及其零件 II 类器具,108 其它电扇及其零件 III 类器具,109 其它电扇及其零件 0I 类器具,110 其它电扇及其零件 0 类器具
8414599091	101 台扇 I 类器具,102 台扇 II 类器具,103 台扇 III 类器具,104 台扇 0I 类器具,105 台扇 0 类器具,106 落地扇 I 类器具,107 落地扇 II 类器具,108 落地扇 III 类器具,109 落地扇 0I 类器具,110 落地扇 0 类器具,111 壁扇 I 类器具,112 壁扇 II 类器具,113 壁扇 III 类器具,114 壁扇 0I 类器具,115 壁扇 0 类器具,116 其它电扇及其零件 I 类器具,117 其它电扇及其零件 II 类器具,118 其它电扇及其零件 III 类器具,119 其它电扇及其零件 0I 类器具,120 其它电扇及其零件 0 类器具
8414599099	101 其它电扇及其零件 I 类器具,102 其它电扇及其零件 II 类器具,103 其它电扇及其零件 III 类器具,104 其它电扇及其零件 0I 类器具,105 其它电扇及其零件 0 类器具
8414909010	101 其它风机及其零件,102 其它电扇及其零件 I 类器具,103 其它电扇及其零件 II 类器具,104 其它电扇及其零件 III 类器具,105 其它电扇及其零件 0I 类器具,106 其它电扇及其零件 0 类器具,107 带有迷宫式密封装置往复式压缩机,108 其它空气压缩机(站)及零件,109 其它制冷设备用压缩机及其零件
8415200000	101 车用空气调节器 I 类器具,102 车用空气调节器 II 类器具,103 车用空气调节器 III 类器具,104 车用空气调节器 0I 类器具,105 车用空气调节器 0 类器具
8415811000	101 独立窗式空调调节器 I 类器具,102 独立窗式空调调节器 II 类器具,103 独立窗式空调调节器 III 类器具,104 独立窗式空调调节器 0I 类器具,105 独立窗式空调调节器 0 类器具,106 分体空调调节器 I 类器具,107 分体空调调节器 II 类器具,108 分体空调调节器 III 类器具,109 分体空调调节器 0I 类器具,110 分体空调调节器 0 类器具,111 其它空气调节装置及其零件 I 类器具,112 其它空气调节装置及其零件 II 类器具,113 其它空气调节装置及其零件 III 类器具,114 其它空气调节装置及其零件 0I 类器具,115 其它空气调节装置及其零件 0 类器具
8415812001	101 独立窗式空调调节器 I 类器具,102 独立窗式空调调节器 II 类器具,103 独立窗式空调调节器 III 类器具,104 独立窗式空调调节器 0I 类器具,105 独立窗式空调调节器 0 类器具,106 分体空调调节器 I 类器具,107 分体空调调节器 II 类器具,108 分体空调调节器 III 类器具,109 分体空调调节器 0I 类器具,110 分体空调调节器 0 类器具,111 其它空气调节装置及其零件 I 类器具,112 其它空气调节装置及其零件 II 类器具,113 其它空气调节装置及其零件 III 类器具,114 其它空气调节装置及其零件 0I 类器具,115 其它空气调节装置及其零件 0 类器具
8415812090	101 独立窗式空调调节器 I 类器具,102 独立窗式空调调节器 II 类器具,103 独立窗式空调调节器 III 类器具,104 独立窗式空调调节器 0I 类器具,105 独立窗式空调调节器 0 类器具,106 分体空调调节器 I 类器具,107 分体空调调节器 II 类器具,108 分体空调调节器 III 类器具,109 分体空调调节器 0I 类器具,110 分体空调调节器 0 类器具,111 其它空气调节装置及其零件 I 类器具,112 其它空气调节装置及其零件 II 类器具,113 其它空气调节装置及其零件 III 类器具,114 其它空气调节装置及其零件 0I 类器具,115 其它空气调节装置及其零件 0 类器具
8415821000	101 独立窗式空调调节器 I 类器具,102 独立窗式空调调节器 II 类器具,103 独立窗式空调调节器 III 类器具,104 独立窗式空调调节器 0I 类器具,105 独立窗式空调调节器 0 类器具,106 分体空调调节器 I 类器具,107 分体空调调节器 II 类器具,108 分体空调调节器 III 类器具,109 分体空调调节器 0I 类器具,110 分体空调调节器 0 类器具,111 其它空气调节装置及其零件 I 类器具,112 其它空气调节装置及其零件 II 类器具,113 其它空气调节装置及其零件 III 类器具,114 其它空气调节装置及其零件 0I 类器具,115 其它空气调节装置及其零件 0 类器具
8415822001	101 独立窗式空调调节器 I 类器具,102 独立窗式空调调节器 II 类器具,103 独立窗式空调调节器 III 类器具,104 独立窗式空调调节器 0I 类器具,105 独立窗式空调调节器 0 类器具,106 分体空调调节器 I 类器具,107 分体空调调节器 II 类器具,108 分体空调调节器 III 类器具,109 分体空调调节器 0I 类器具,110 分体空调调节器 0 类器具,111 其它空气调节装置及其零件 I 类器具,112 其它空气调节装置及其零件 II 类器具,113 其它空气调节装置及其零件 III 类器具,114 其它空气调节装置及其零件 0I 类器具,115 其它空气调节装置及其零件 0 类器具
8415822090	101 独立窗式空调调节器 I 类器具,102 独立窗式空调调节器 II 类器具,103 独立窗式空调调节器 III 类器具,104 独立窗式空调调节器 0I 类器具,105 独立窗式空调调节器 0 类器具,106 分体空调调节器 I 类器具,107 分体空调调节器 II 类器具,108 分体空调调节器 III 类器具,109 分体空调调节器 0I 类器具,110 分体空调调节器 0 类器具,111 其它空气调节装置及其零件 I 类器具,112 其它空气调节装置及其零件 II 类器具,113 其它空气调节装置及其零件 III 类器具,114 其它空气调节装置及其零件 0I 类器具,115 其它空气调节装置及其零件 0 类器具
8415830000	101 未装有制冷装置的空调器 I 类器具,102 未装有制冷装置的空调器 II 类器具,103 未装有制冷装置的空调器 III 类器具,104 未装有制冷装置的空调器 0I 类器具,105 未装有制冷装置的空调器 0 类器具
8418101000	101 冷藏冷冻组合机 I 类器具,102 冷藏冷冻组合机 II 类器具,103 冷藏冷冻组合机 III 类器具,104 冷藏冷冻组合机 0I 类器具,105 冷藏冷冻组合机 0 类器具
8418102000	101 冷藏冷冻组合机 I 类器具,102 冷藏冷冻组合机 II 类器具,103 冷藏冷冻组合机 III 类器具,104 冷藏冷冻组合机 0I 类器具,105 冷藏冷冻组合机 0 类器具

HS 编码	CIQ 扩展品名
8418103000	101 冷藏冷冻组合机 I 类器具，102 冷藏冷冻组合机 II 类器具，103 冷藏冷冻组合机 III 类器具，104 冷藏冷冻组合机 0I 类器具，105 冷藏冷冻组合机 0 类器具
8418211000	101 压缩式家用型冷藏箱 I 类器具，102 压缩式家用型冷藏箱 II 类器具，103 压缩式家用型冷藏箱 III 类器具，104 压缩式家用型冷藏箱 0I 类器具，105 压缩式家用型冷藏箱 0 类器具
8418212000	101 压缩式家用型冷藏箱 I 类器具，102 压缩式家用型冷藏箱 II 类器具，103 压缩式家用型冷藏箱 III 类器具，104 压缩式家用型冷藏箱 0I 类器具，105 压缩式家用型冷藏箱 0 类器具
8418213000	101 压缩式家用型冷藏箱 I 类器具，102 压缩式家用型冷藏箱 II 类器具，103 压缩式家用型冷藏箱 III 类器具，104 压缩式家用型冷藏箱 0I 类器具，105 压缩式家用型冷藏箱 0 类器具
8418292000	101 电气吸收式家用型冷藏箱 I 类器具，102 电气吸收式家用型冷藏箱 II 类器具，103 电气吸收式家用型冷藏箱 III 类器具，104 电气吸收式家用型冷藏箱 0I 类器具，105 电气吸收式家用型冷藏箱 0 类器具
8418500000	101 制冰机 I 类器具，102 制冰机 II 类器具，103 制冰机 III 类器具，104 制冰机 0I 类器具，105 制冰机 0 类器具，106 其它冷藏冷冻柜设备及其零件
8418699020	101 制冰机 I 类器具，102 制冰机 II 类器具，103 制冰机 III 类器具，104 制冰机 0 类器具，105 制冰机 0I 类器具，106 冰激凌机 I 类器具，107 冰激凌机 II 类器具，108 冰激凌机 III 类器具，109 冰激凌机 0 类器具，110 冰激凌机 0I 类器具
8421211000	101 非家用过滤及净化装置，102 家用型过滤或净化水的机器及装置 I 类器具，103 家用型过滤或净化水的机器及装置 II 类器具，104 家用型过滤或净化水的机器及装置 III 类器具，105 家用型过滤或净化水的机器及装置 0I 类器具，106 家用型过滤或净化水的机器及装置 0 类器具
8421220000	101 非家用过滤及净化装置，102 其它过滤及其喷射装置及其零件 I 类器具，103 其它过滤及其喷射装置及其零件 II 类器具，104 其它过滤及其喷射装置及其零件 III 类器具，105 其它过滤及其喷射装置及其零件 0I 类器具，106 其它过滤及其喷射装置及其零件 0 类器具
8421299090	101 非家用过滤及净化装置，102 其它过滤及其喷射装置及其零件 I 类器具，103 其他离心机及类似装置及其零件，104 其它过滤及其喷射装置及其零件 II 类器具，105 其它过滤及其喷射装置及其零件 III 类器具，106 其它过滤及其喷射装置及其零件 0I 类器具，107 其它过滤及其喷射装置及其零件 0 类器具
8421391000	101 其他离心机及类似装置及其零件，102 家用型气体过滤、净化机器及装置 I 类器具，103 家用型气体过滤、净化机器及装置 II 类器具，104 家用型气体过滤、净化机器及装置 III 类器具，105 家用型气体过滤、净化机器及装置 0I 类器具，106 家用型气体过滤、净化机器及装置 0 类器具
8422110000	101 洗碟机及其零件 I 类器具，102 洗碟机及其零件 II 类器具，103 洗碟机及其零件 III 类器具，104 洗碟机及其零件 0I 类器具，105 洗碟机及其零件 0 类器具
8422190000	101 洗碟机及其零件 I 类器具，102 洗碟机及其零件 II 类器具，103 洗碟机及其零件 III 类器具，104 洗碟机及其零件 0I 类器具，105 洗碟机及其零件 0 类器具
8422200000	101 其它食品加工机器及其零件，102 其它餐具清洗机及其零件 I 类器具，103 其它餐具清洗机及其零件 II 类器具，104 其它餐具清洗机及其零件 III 类器具，105 其它餐具清洗机及其零件 0I 类器具，106 其它餐具清洗机及其零件 0 类器具，107 其它大型家用及其类似用途电器及其零件 I 类器具，108 其它大型家用及其类似用途电器及其零件 II 类器具，109 其它大型家用及其类似用途电器及其零件 III 类器具，110 其它大型家用及其类似用途电器及其零件 0I 类器具，111 其它大型家用及其类似用途电器及其零件 0 类器具
8424891000	101 家用型喷射、喷雾机械器具 I 类器具，102 家用型喷射、喷雾机械器具 II 类器具，103 家用型喷射、喷雾机械器具 III 类器具，104 家用型喷射、喷雾机械器具 0I 类器具，105 家用型喷射、喷雾机械器具 0 类器具
8424899910	101 其它过滤及其喷射装置及其零件 I 类器具，102 其它过滤及其喷射装置及其零件 II 类器具，103 其它过滤及其喷射装置及其零件 III 类器具，104 其它过滤及其喷射装置及其零件 0I 类器具，105 其它过滤及其喷射装置及其零件 0 类器具
8424899990	101 其它过滤及其喷射装置及其零件 I 类器具，102 其它过滤及其喷射装置及其零件 II 类器具，103 其它过滤及其喷射装置及其零件 III 类器具，104 其它过滤及其喷射装置及其零件 0I 类器具，105 其它过滤及其喷射装置及其零件 0 类器具
8428399000	101 载货电梯、升降机，102 机械式停车设备及其它装卸、储运设备及其零件，103 其他装卸桥、提升、起重设备及零件
8450201100	101 洗衣机 I 类器具，102 洗衣机 II 类器具，103 洗衣机 III 类器具，104 洗衣机 0I 类器具，105 洗衣机 0 类器具
8450201200	101 洗衣机 I 类器具，102 洗衣机 II 类器具，103 洗衣机 III 类器具，104 洗衣机 0I 类器具，105 洗衣机 0 类器具
8451300000	101 印花机，102 纺织行业成套设备，103 熨烫机 I 类器具，104 熨烫机 II 类器具，105 熨烫机 III 类器具，106 熨烫机 0I 类器具，107 熨烫机 0 类器具
8451800001	101 其它印染机械及其零件，102 纺织行业成套设备，103 其它衣物处理设备及其零件 I 类器具，104 其它衣物处理设备及其零件 II 类器具，105 其它衣物处理设备及其零件 III 类器具，106 其它衣物处理设备及其零件 0I 类器具，107 其它衣物处理设备及其零件 0 类器具，108 其它大型家用及其类似用途电器及其零件 I 类器具，109 其它大型家用及其类似用途电器及其零件 II 类器具，110 其它大型家用及其类似用途电器及其零件 III 类器具，111 其它大型家用及其类似用途电器及其零件 0I 类器具，112 其它大型家用及其类似用途电器及其零件 0 类器具
8451800002	101 其它印染机械及其零件，102 纺织行业成套设备，103 其它衣物处理设备及其零件 I 类器具，104 其它衣物处理设备及其零件 II 类器具，105 其它衣物处理设备及其零件 III 类器具，106 其它衣物处理设备及其零件 0I 类器具，107 其它衣物处理设备及其零件 0 类器具，108 其它大型家用及其类似用途电器及其零件 I 类器具，109 其它大型家用及其类似用途电器及其零件 II 类器具，110 其它大型家用及其类似用途电器及其零件 III 类器具，111 其它大型家用及其类似用途电器及其零件 0I 类器具，112 其它大型家用及其类似用途电器及其零件 0 类器具
8451800003	101 其它印染机械及其零件，102 纺织行业成套设备，103 其它衣物处理设备及其零件 I 类器具，104 其它衣物处理设备及其零件 II 类器具，105 其它衣物处理设备及其零件 III 类器具，106 其它衣物处理设备及其零件 0I 类器具，107 其它衣物处理设备及其零件 0 类器具，108 其它大型家用及其类似用途电器及其零件 I 类器具，109 其它大型家用及其类似用途电器及其零件 II 类器具，110 其它大型家用及其类似用途电器及其零件 III 类器具，111 其它大型家用及其类似用途电器及其零件 0I 类器具，112 其它大型家用及其类似用途电器及其零件 0 类器具
8451800090	101 印花机，102 染色机，103 其它印染机械及其零件，104 纺织行业成套设备，105 其它衣物处理设备及其零件 I 类器具，106 其它衣物处理设备及其零件 II 类器具，107 其它衣物处理设备及其零件 III 类器具，108 其它衣物处理设备及其零件 0I 类器具，109 其它衣物处理设备及其零件 0 类器具，110 其它大型家用及其类似用途电器及其零件 I 类器具，111 其它大型家用及其类似用途电器及其零件 II 类器具，112 其它大型家用及其类似用途电器及其零件 III 类器具，113 其它大型家用及其类似用途电器及其零件 0I 类器具，114 其它大型家用及其类似用途电器及其零件 0 类器具
8456900000	101 电化学处理加工机床，102 火焰切割机，103 其它特种加工机床
8474201000	101 其它工程机械及其零件，102 建筑工业行业成套设备
8474202000	101 其它工程机械及其零件，102 建筑工业行业成套设备
8474209000	101 其它工程机械及其零件，102 建筑工业行业成套设备
8474802000	101 其它工程机械及其零件，102 建材行业成套设备，103 建筑工业行业成套设备，104 其他行业成套设备
8474809090	101 其它工程机械及其零件，102 建材行业成套设备，103 建筑工业行业成套设备，104 其他行业成套设备
8479600000	101 蒸发式空气冷却器 I 类器具，102 蒸发式空气冷却器 II 类器具，103 蒸发式空气冷却器 III 类器具，104 蒸发式空气冷却器 0I 类器具，105 蒸发式空气冷却器 0 类器具

HS 编码	CIQ 扩展品名
8479892000	101 空气增湿器及减湿器 I 类器具,102 空气增湿器及减湿器 II 类器具,103 空气增湿器及减湿器 III 类器具,104 空气增湿器及减湿器 0I 类器具,105 空气增湿器及减湿器 0 类器具
8479899200	101 机械行业成套设备,102 石油化工行业成套设备,103 铁路运输行业成套设备,104 交通行业成套设备,105 电子行业成套设备,106 通讯行业成套设备,107 电力行业成套设备,108 化工行业成套设备,109 石油天然气行业成套设备,110 冶金行业成套设备,111 纺织行业成套设备,112 轻工行业成套设备,113 建材行业成套设备,114 水利行业成套设备,115 兵工民品行业成套设备,116 劳动和劳动安全行业成套设备,117 公共安全行业成套设备,118 广播电影电视行业成套设备,119 船舶行业成套设备,120 环保行业成套设备,121 包装行业成套设备,122 煤炭行业成套设备,123 建筑工业行业成套设备,124 海洋行业成套设备,125 地质矿产行业成套设备,126 地震行业成套设备,127 印刷行业成套设备,128 其他行业成套设备
8479899990	101 机械行业成套设备,102 石油化工行业成套设备,103 铁路运输行业成套设备,104 交通行业成套设备,105 电子行业成套设备,106 通讯行业成套设备,107 电力行业成套设备,108 化工行业成套设备,109 石油天然气行业成套设备,110 冶金行业成套设备,111 纺织行业成套设备,112 轻工行业成套设备,113 建材行业成套设备,114 水利行业成套设备,115 兵工民品行业成套设备,116 劳动和劳动安全行业成套设备,117 公共安全行业成套设备,118 广播电影电视行业成套设备,119 船舶行业成套设备,120 环保行业成套设备,121 包装行业成套设备,122 煤炭行业成套设备,123 建筑工业行业成套设备,124 海洋行业成套设备,125 地质矿产行业成套设备,126 地震行业成套设备,127 印刷行业成套设备,128 其他行业成套设备
8479901000	101 船舶用零部件,102 船舶行业成套设备
8479909010	101 船舶用零部件,102 机械行业成套设备,103 电子行业成套设备,104 船舶行业成套设备,105 其他行业成套设备,106 其它过滤及其喷射装置及其零件 I 类器具,107 其它过滤及其喷射装置及其零件 II 类器具,108 其它过滤及其喷射装置及其零件 III 类器具,109 其它过滤及其喷射装置及其零件 0I 类器具,110 其它过滤及其喷射装置及其零件 0 类器具
8479909090	101 船舶用零部件,102 机械行业成套设备,103 电子行业成套设备,104 船舶行业成套设备,105 其他行业成套设备,106 其它过滤及其喷射装置及其零件
8480411000	101 机械行业成套设备,102 电子行业成套设备,103 轻工行业成套设备
8480412000	101 机械行业成套设备,102 电子行业成套设备,103 轻工行业成套设备
8480419000	101 机械行业成套设备,102 电子行业成套设备,103 轻工行业成套设备
8480490000	101 机械行业成套设备,102 电子行业成套设备,103 轻工行业成套设备
8480500000	101 轻工行业成套设备,102 其他行业成套设备
8480790090	101 机械行业成套设备,102 电子行业成套设备,103 轻工行业成套设备
8481802110	101 其它阀门及类似品(安全附件),102 其它阀门及类似品
8481802910	101 其它阀门及类似品(安全附件),102 其它阀门及类似品
8481804010	101 其它阀门及类似品(安全附件),102 其它阀门及类似品
8481804090	101 其它阀门及类似品(安全附件),102 其它阀门及类似品
8486204100	101 其它机床,102 电子行业成套设备
8486304100	101 电子行业成套设备,102 非家用过滤及净化装置
8486304900	101 其它机床,102 电子行业成套设备,103 非家用过滤及净化装置
8486403100	101 电子行业成套设备,102 机械式停车设备及其它装卸、储运设备及其零件
8486403900	101 起重机,102 机械式停车设备及其它装卸、储运设备及其零件,103 升降机,104 其他装卸桥、提升、起重设备及零件
8486901000	101 机械式停车设备及其它装卸、储运设备及其零件,102 其他装卸桥、提升、起重设备及零件
8504401300	101 Ⅰ类稳压电源,102 Ⅱ类稳压电源,103 Ⅲ类稳压电源
8504401400	101 Ⅰ类稳压电源,102 Ⅱ类稳压电源,103 Ⅲ类稳压电源
8504401500	101 Ⅰ类稳压电源,102 Ⅱ类稳压电源,103 Ⅲ类稳压电源
8504401920	101 Ⅰ类稳压电源,102 Ⅱ类稳压电源,103 Ⅲ类稳压电源
8504401930	101 Ⅰ类稳压电源,102 Ⅱ类稳压电源,103 Ⅲ类稳压电源
8504401940	101 Ⅰ类稳压电源,102 Ⅱ类稳压电源,103 Ⅲ类稳压电源
8504401990	101 Ⅰ类稳压电源,102 Ⅱ类稳压电源,103 Ⅲ类稳压电源
8506101110	101 锌一锰原电池及原电池组,102 碱性锌一锰原电池及原电池组,103 其他二氧化锰的原电池及原电池组
8506101190	101 锌一锰原电池及原电池组,102 碱性锌一锰原电池及原电池组,103 其他二氧化锰的原电池及原电池组
8506101210	101 锌一锰原电池及原电池组,102 碱性锌一锰原电池及原电池组,103 其他二氧化锰的原电池及原电池组
8506101290	101 锌一锰原电池及原电池组,102 碱性锌一锰原电池及原电池组,103 其他二氧化锰的原电池及原电池组
8506101910	101 锌一锰原电池及原电池组,102 碱性锌一锰原电池及原电池组,103 其他二氧化锰的原电池及原电池组,104 电池液(碱性的)
8506101990	101 锌一锰原电池及原电池组,102 碱性锌一锰原电池及原电池组,103 其他二氧化锰的原电池及原电池组,104 电池液(碱性的)
8507100000	101 起动用铅酸蓄电池,102 牵引用铅酸蓄电池,103 摩托车用铅酸蓄电池,104 固定型防酸式铅酸蓄电池,105 内燃机车用铅酸蓄电池,106 其他铅酸蓄电池,107 蓄电池(注有酸液)
8507200000	101 起动用铅酸蓄电池,102 牵引用铅酸蓄电池,103 摩托车用铅酸蓄电池,104 固定型防酸式铅酸蓄电池,105 内燃机车用铅酸蓄电池,106 其他铅酸蓄电池
8507500000	101 密封金属氢化物镍可充单体电池,102 其他镍氢蓄电池
8507600090	101 蜂窝电话用锂离子蓄电池,102 其他锂离子蓄电池
8507809010	101 其它蓄电池及其零件,102 注有碱液的,103 含氢氧化钾固体
8507809090	101 其它蓄电池及其零件,102 注有碱液的,103 含氢氧化钾固体
8508110000	101 真空吸尘器 I 类器具,102 真空吸尘器 II 类器具,103 真空吸尘器 III 类器具,104 真空吸尘器 0I 类器具,105 真空吸尘器 0 类器具
8508190000	101 真空吸尘器 I 类器具,102 真空吸尘器 II 类器具,103 真空吸尘器 III 类器具,104 真空吸尘器 0I 类器具,105 真空吸尘器 0 类器具
8508600000	101 真空吸尘器 I 类器具,102 真空吸尘器 II 类器具,103 真空吸尘器 III 类器具,104 真空吸尘器 0I 类器具,105 真空吸尘器 0 类器具
8509401000	101 食品研磨机,搅拌机及果、菜榨汁器 I 类器具,102 食品研磨机,搅拌机及果、菜榨汁器 II 类器具,103 食品研磨机,搅拌机及果、菜榨汁器 III 类器具,104 食品研磨机,搅拌机及果、菜榨汁器 0I 类器具,105 食品研磨机,搅拌机及果、菜榨汁器 0 类器具,106 豆浆机 I 类器具,107 豆浆机 II 类器具,108 豆浆机 III 类器具,109 豆浆机 0I 类器具,110 豆浆机 0 类器具
8509409000	101 食品研磨机,搅拌机及果、菜榨汁器 I 类器具,102 食品研磨机,搅拌机及果、菜榨汁器 II 类器具,103 食品研磨机,搅拌机及果、菜榨汁器 III 类器具,104 食品研磨机,搅拌机及果、菜榨汁器 0I 类器具,105 食品研磨机,搅拌机及果、菜榨汁器 0 类器具
8509801000	101 地板打蜡机 I 类器具,102 地板打蜡机 II 类器具,103 地板打蜡机 III 类器具,104 地板打蜡机 0I 类器具,105 地板打蜡机 0 类器具
8509802000	101 厨房废物处理器 I 类器具,102 厨房废物处理器 II 类器具,103 厨房废物处理器 III 类器具,104 厨房废物处理器 0I 类器具,105 厨房废物处理器 0 类器具
8509900000	101 其它电动器具及其零件,102 其它小型家用及类似用途电器及其零件
8510100000	101 电动剃须刀 I 类器具,102 电动剃须刀 II 类器具,103 电动剃须刀 III 类器具,104 电动剃须刀 0I 类器具,105 电动剃须刀 0 类器具
8510200000	101 电动毛发推剪 I 类器具,102 电动毛发推剪 II 类器具,103 电动毛发推剪 III 类器具,104 电动毛发推剪 0I 类器具,105 电动毛发推剪 0 类器具

HS 编码	CIQ 扩展品名
8510300000	101 电动脱毛机 I 类器具,102 电动脱毛机 II 类器具,103 电动脱毛机 III 类器具,104 电动脱毛机 0I 类器具,105 电动脱毛机 0 类器具
8511201000	101 航空器用零部件,102 船舶用零部件,103 铁道机车用零部件,104 其它发电机(组)及其零件
8511301000	101 航空器用零部件,102 船舶用零部件,103 铁道机车用零部件
8515809090	101 波峰焊设备,102 其它焊接设备及其零件
8516101000	101 电热水器 I 类器具,102 电热水器 II 类器具,103 电热水器 III 类器具,104 电热水器 0I 类器具,105 电热水器 0 类器具
8516102000	101 电热水器 I 类器具,102 电热水器 II 类器具,103 电热水器 III 类器具,104 电热水器 0I 类器具,105 电热水器 0 类器具
8516109000	101 电热水器 I 类器具,102 电热水器 II 类器具,103 电热水器 III 类器具,104 电热水器 0I 类器具,105 电热水器 0 类器具
8516210000	101 电气储存式散热器 I 类器具,102 电气储存式散热器 II 类器具,103 电气储存式散热器 III 类器具,104 电气储存式散热器 0I 类器具,105 电气储存式散热器 0 类器具
8516291000	101 其它电热器具及其零件 I 类器具,102 其它电热器具及其零件 II 类器具,103 其它电热器具及其零件 III 类器具,104 其它电热器具及其零件 0I 类器具,105 其它电热器具及其零件 0 类器具
8516292000	101 其它电热器具及其零件 I 类器具,102 其它电热器具及其零件 II 类器具,103 其它电热器具及其零件 III 类器具,104 其它电热器具及其零件 0I 类器具,105 其它电热器具及其零件 0 类器具,106 其它小型家用及类似用途电器及其零件 I 类器具,107 其它小型家用及类似用途电器及其零件 II 类器具,108 其它小型家用及类似用途电器及其零件 III 类器具,109 其它小型家用及类似用途电器及其零件 0I 类器具,110 其它小型家用及类似用途电器及其零件 0 类器具
8516293100	101 其它电热器具及其零件 I 类器具,102 其它电热器具及其零件 II 类器具,103 其它电热器具及其零件 III 类器具,104 其它电热器具及其零件 0I 类器具,105 其它电热器具及其零件 0 类器具,106 其它小型家用及类似用途电器及其零件 I 类器具,107 其它小型家用及类似用途电器及其零件 II 类器具,108 其它小型家用及类似用途电器及其零件 III 类器具,109 其它小型家用及类似用途电器及其零件 0I 类器具,110 其它小型家用及类似用途电器及其零件 0 类器具
8516293200	101 其它电热器具及其零件 I 类器具,102 其它电热器具及其零件 II 类器具,103 其它电热器具及其零件 III 类器具,104 其它电热器具及其零件 0I 类器具,105 其它电热器具及其零件 0 类器具,106 其它小型家用及类似用途电器及其零件 I 类器具,107 其它小型家用及类似用途电器及其零件 II 类器具,108 其它小型家用及类似用途电器及其零件 III 类器具,109 其它小型家用及类似用途电器及其零件 0I 类器具,110 其它小型家用及类似用途电器及其零件 0 类器具
8516293900	101 其它电热器具及其零件 I 类器具,102 其它电热器具及其零件 II 类器具,103 其它电热器具及其零件 III 类器具,104 其它电热器具及其零件 0I 类器具,105 其它电热器具及其零件 0 类器具,106 其它小型家用及类似用途电器及其零件 I 类器具,107 其它小型家用及类似用途电器及其零件 II 类器具,108 其它小型家用及类似用途电器及其零件 III 类器具,109 其它小型家用及类似用途电器及其零件 0I 类器具,110 其它小型家用及类似用途电器及其零件 0 类器具
8516299000	101 电气空间加热器 I 类器具,102 电气空间加热器 II 类器具,103 电气空间加热器 III 类器具,104 电气空间加热器 0I 类器具,105 电气空间加热器 0 类器具
8516310000	101 电吹风机 I 类器具,102 电吹风机 II 类器具,103 电吹风机 III 类器具,104 电吹风机 0I 类器具,105 电吹风机 0 类器具
8516320000	101 电热理发器具 I 类器具,102 电热理发器具 II 类器具,103 电热理发器具 III 类器具,104 电热理发器具 0I 类器具,105 电热理发器具 0 类器具,106 焗油机 I 类器具,107 焗油机 II 类器具,108 焗油机 III 类器具,109 焗油机 0I 类器具,110 焗油机 0 类器具
8516330000	101 电热干手器 I 类器具,102 电热干手器 II 类器具,103 电热干手器 III 类器具,104 电热干手器 0I 类器具,105 电热干手器 0 类器具
8516400000	101 电熨斗 I 类器具,102 电熨斗 II 类器具,103 电熨斗 III 类器具,104 电熨斗 0I 类器具,105 电熨斗 0 类器具
8516500000	101 微波炉 I 类器具,102 微波炉 II 类器具,103 微波炉 III 类器具,104 微波炉 0I 类器具,105 微波炉 0 类器具
8516601000	101 电磁炉 I 类器具,102 电磁炉 II 类器具,103 电磁炉 III 类器具,104 电磁炉 0I 类器具,105 电磁炉 0 类器具
8516603000	101 电饭锅 I 类器具,102 电饭锅 II 类器具,103 电饭锅 III 类器具,104 电饭锅 0I 类器具,105 电饭锅 0 类器具
8516604000	101 电炒锅 I 类器具,102 电炒锅 II 类器具,103 电炒锅 III 类器具,104 电炒锅 0I 类器具,105 电炒锅 0 类器具
8516605000	101 电热炉 I 类器具,102 电热炉 II 类器具,103 电热炉 III 类器具,104 电热炉 0I 类器具,105 电热炉 0 类器具
8516609000	101 电热炉 I 类器具,102 电热炉 II 类器具,103 电热炉 III 类器具,104 电热炉 0I 类器具,105 电热炉 0 类器具,106 光波炉 I 类器具,107 光波炉 II 类器具,108 光波炉 III 类器具,109 光波炉 0I 类器具,110 光波炉 0 类器具,111 油炸锅 I 类器具,112 油炸锅 II 类器具,113 油炸锅 III 类器具,114 油炸锅 0I 类器具,115 油炸锅 0 类器具
8516711000	101 电热咖啡壶或茶壶 I 类器具,102 电热咖啡壶或茶壶 II 类器具,103 电热咖啡壶或茶壶 III 类器具,104 电热咖啡壶或茶壶 0I 类器具,105 电热咖啡壶或茶壶 0 类器具
8516712000	101 电热咖啡壶或茶壶 I 类器具,102 电热咖啡壶或茶壶 II 类器具,103 电热咖啡壶或茶壶 III 类器具,104 电热咖啡壶或茶壶 0I 类器具,105 电热咖啡壶或茶壶 0 类器具
8516713000	101 电热咖啡壶或茶壶 I 类器具,102 电热咖啡壶或茶壶 II 类器具,103 电热咖啡壶或茶壶 III 类器具,104 电热咖啡壶或茶壶 0I 类器具,105 电热咖啡壶或茶壶 0 类器具
8516719000	101 电热咖啡壶或茶壶 I 类器具,102 电热咖啡壶或茶壶 II 类器具,103 电热咖啡壶或茶壶 III 类器具,104 电热咖啡壶或茶壶 0I 类器具,105 电热咖啡壶或茶壶 0 类器具,106 电热水壶 I 类器具,107 电热水壶 II 类器具,108 电热水壶 III 类器具,109 电热水壶 0I 类器具,110 电热水壶 0 类器具
8516721000	101 电热烤面包器 I 类器具,102 电热烤面包器 II 类器具,103 电热烤面包器 III 类器具,104 电热烤面包器 0I 类器具,105 电热烤面包器 0 类器具
8516722000	101 电热烤面包器 I 类器具,102 电热烤面包器 II 类器具,103 电热烤面包器 III 类器具,104 电热烤面包器 0I 类器具,105 电热烤面包器 0 类器具
8516729000	101 电热烤面包器 I 类器具,102 电热烤面包器 II 类器具,103 电热烤面包器 III 类器具,104 电热烤面包器 0I 类器具,105 电热烤面包器 0 类器具
8516791000	101 其它电热器具及其零件 I 类器具,102 其它电热器具及其零件 II 类器具,103 其它电热器具及其零件 III 类器具,104 其它电热器具及其零件 0I 类器具,105 其它电热器具及其零件 0 类器具,106 其它小型家用及类似用途电器及其零件 I 类器具,107 其它小型家用及类似用途电器及其零件 II 类器具,108 其它小型家用及类似用途电器及其零件 III 类器具,109 其它小型家用及类似用途电器及其零件 0I 类器具,110 其它小型家用及类似用途电器及其零件 0 类器具
8516800000	101 其它电热器具及其零件 I 类器具,102 其它电热器具及其零件 II 类器具,103 其它电热器具及其零件 III 类器具,104 其它电热器具及其零件 0I 类器具,105 其它电热器具及其零件 0 类器具
8517619000	101 不带附件及包装,102 包含附件及包装,103 其它通讯设备及其零件
8517621200	101 网络交换机,102 其它通讯设备及其零件
8517622910	101 光通信数字同步设备,102 其它通讯设备及其零件
8517622990	101 光通信数字同步设备,102 其它通讯设备及其零件
8517629400	101 Ⅰ类其它扬声器及其零件,102 Ⅱ类其它扬声器及其零件,103 Ⅲ类其它扬声器及其零件
8517691001	101 无线接收装置,102 无线寻呼机,103 其它通讯设备及其零件
8517691091	101 不带附件及包装,102 包含附件及包装
8517699000	101 其它办公机器及其零件,102 其它通讯设备及其零件
8518100001	101 Ⅰ类其它扬声器及其零件,102 Ⅱ类其它扬声器及其零件,103 Ⅲ类其它扬声器及其零件
8518100090	101 Ⅰ类其它扬声器及其零件,102 Ⅱ类其它扬声器及其零件,103 Ⅲ类其它扬声器及其零件

HS 编码	CIQ 扩展品名
8518210000	101Ⅰ类单喇叭音箱,102Ⅱ类单喇叭音箱,103Ⅲ类单喇叭音箱
8518220000	101Ⅰ类多喇叭音箱,102Ⅱ类多喇叭音箱,103Ⅲ类多喇叭音箱
8518290000	101Ⅰ类其它扬声器及其零件,102Ⅱ类其它扬声器及其零件,103Ⅲ类其它扬声器及其零件
8518300000	101Ⅰ类其它扬声器及其零件,102Ⅱ类其它扬声器及其零件,103Ⅲ类其它扬声器及其零件
8518400001	101Ⅰ类音频功率放大器,102Ⅱ类音频功率放大器,103Ⅲ类音频功率放大器
8518400090	101Ⅰ类音频功率放大器,102Ⅱ类音频功率放大器,103Ⅲ类音频功率放大器
8518500000	101Ⅰ类电气扩音机组,102Ⅱ类电气扩音机组,103Ⅲ类电气扩音机组
8518900001	101Ⅰ类其它扬声器及其零件,102Ⅱ类其它扬声器及其零件,103Ⅲ类其它扬声器及其零件,104Ⅰ类其它收录放音装置及其零件,105Ⅱ类其它收录放音装置及其零件,106Ⅲ类其它收录放音装置及其零件
8518900090	101Ⅰ类其它扬声器及其零件,102Ⅱ类其它扬声器及其零件,103Ⅲ类其它扬声器及其零件,104Ⅰ类其它收录放音装置及其零件,105Ⅱ类其它收录放音装置及其零件,106Ⅲ类其它收录放音装置及其零件
8519200090	101Ⅰ类录音机走带机构,102Ⅱ类录音机走带机构,103Ⅲ类录音机走带机构类,104Ⅰ类收音机,105Ⅱ类收音机,106Ⅲ类收音机,107Ⅰ类收录(放)音组合机,108Ⅱ类收录(放)音组合机,109Ⅲ类收录(放)音组合机,110Ⅰ类其它收录放音装置及其零件,111Ⅱ类其它收录放音装置及其零件,112Ⅲ类其它收录放音装置及其零件
8519300000	101Ⅰ类放音机,102Ⅱ类放音机,103Ⅲ类放音机,104Ⅰ类激光唱机,105Ⅱ类激光唱机,106Ⅲ类激光唱机
8519811100	101Ⅰ类放音机,102Ⅱ类放音机,103Ⅲ类放音机
8519811200	101Ⅰ类录音机,102Ⅱ类录音机,103Ⅲ类录音机
8519811900	101Ⅰ类录音机,102Ⅱ类录音机,103Ⅲ类录音机
8519812100	101Ⅰ类激光唱机,102Ⅱ类激光唱机,103Ⅲ类激光唱机
8519812910	101Ⅰ类录音机,102Ⅱ类录音机,103Ⅲ类录音机
8519812990	101Ⅰ类录音机,102Ⅱ类录音机,103Ⅲ类录音机
8519813900	101Ⅰ类录音机,102Ⅱ类录音机,103Ⅲ类录音机
8519891000	101Ⅰ类放音机,102Ⅱ类放音机,103Ⅲ类放音机
8519899000	101Ⅰ类录音机,102Ⅱ类录音机,103Ⅲ类录音机
8521101100	101Ⅰ类磁带录放像机,102Ⅱ类磁带录放像机,103Ⅲ类磁带录放像机
8521101900	101Ⅰ类磁带录放像机,102Ⅱ类磁带录放像机,103Ⅲ类磁带录放像机
8521102000	101Ⅰ类磁带录放像机,102Ⅱ类磁带录放像机,103Ⅲ类磁带录放像机
8521901110	101Ⅰ类激光视盘放像机,102Ⅱ类激光视盘放像机,103Ⅲ类激光视盘放像机
8521901190	101Ⅰ类激光视盘放像机,102Ⅱ类激光视盘放像机,103Ⅲ类激光视盘放像机
8521901210	101Ⅰ类激光视盘放像机,102Ⅱ类激光视盘放像机,103Ⅲ类激光视盘放像机
8521901290	101Ⅰ类激光视盘放像机,102Ⅱ类激光视盘放像机,103Ⅲ类激光视盘放像机
8521901910	101Ⅰ类激光视盘放像机,102Ⅱ类激光视盘放像机,103Ⅲ类激光视盘放像机
8521901990	101Ⅰ类激光视盘放像机,102Ⅱ类激光视盘放像机,103Ⅲ类激光视盘放像机
8521909090	101Ⅰ类其它摄录放像装置及其零件,102Ⅱ类其它摄录放像装置及其零件,103Ⅲ类其它摄录放像装置及其零件
8522100000	101Ⅰ类其它收录放音装置及其零件,102Ⅱ类其它收录放音装置及其零件,103Ⅲ类其它收录放音装置及其零件
8522901000	101Ⅰ类其它收录放音装置及其零件,102Ⅱ类其它收录放音装置及其零件,103Ⅲ类其它收录放音装置及其零件
8522902100	101Ⅰ类录音机走带机构,102Ⅱ类录音机走带机构,103Ⅲ类录音机走带机构
8522902200	101Ⅰ类其它收录放音装置及其零件,102Ⅱ类其它收录放音装置及其零件,103Ⅲ类其它收录放音装置及其零件
8522902300	101Ⅰ类其它收录放音装置及其零件,102Ⅱ类其它收录放音装置及其零件,103Ⅲ类其它收录放音装置及其零件
8522902900	101Ⅰ类其它收录放音装置及其零件,102Ⅱ类其它收录放音装置及其零件,103Ⅲ类其它收录放音装置及其零件
8522903190	101Ⅰ类其它收录放音装置及其零件,102Ⅱ类其它收录放音装置及其零件,103Ⅲ类其它收录放音装置及其零件
8522909100	101Ⅰ类其它收录放音装置及其零件,102Ⅱ类其它收录放音装置及其零件,103Ⅲ类其它收录放音装置及其零件
8522909900	101Ⅰ类其它收录放音装置及其零件,102Ⅱ类其它收录放音装置及其零件,103Ⅲ类其它收录放音装置及其零件
8523511000	101 其它计算机、辅助设备及其零件,102 磁带、磁盘
8523521000	101 软、硬、光盘驱动器,102 其它计算机、辅助设备及其零件,103 磁带、磁盘
8523529000	101 软、硬、光盘驱动器,102 其它计算机、辅助设备及其零件,103 磁带、磁盘
8525500000	101Ⅰ类其它电视接收、发送装置及其零件,102Ⅱ类其它电视接收、发送装置及其零件,103Ⅲ类其它电视接收、发送装置及其零件
8525601000	101Ⅰ类卫星电视接收机,102Ⅱ类卫星电视接收机,103Ⅲ类卫星电视接收机
8525609000	101Ⅰ类其它电视接收、发送装置及其零件,102Ⅱ类其它电视接收、发送装置及其零件,103Ⅲ类其它电视接收、发送装置及其零件
8527120000	101Ⅰ类放音机,102Ⅱ类放音机,103Ⅲ类放音机
8527210090	101Ⅰ类收录(放)音组合机,102Ⅱ类收录(放)音组合机,103Ⅲ类收录(放)音组合机
8527910000	101Ⅰ类收录(放)音组合机,102Ⅱ类收录(放)音组合机,103Ⅲ类收录(放)音组合机,104 其它收录放音装置及其零件
8527920000	101Ⅰ类其它收录放音装置及其零件,102Ⅱ类其它收录放音装置及其零件,103Ⅲ类其它收录放音装置及其零件,104 其它收录放音装置及其零件
8528420000	101 彩色视频监视器,102 黑白或其它单色视频监视器
8528491000	101Ⅰ类彩色视频监视器,102Ⅱ类彩色视频监视器,103Ⅲ类彩色视频监视器
8528499000	101Ⅰ类黑白或其它单色视频监视器,102Ⅱ类黑白或其它单色视频监视器,103Ⅲ类黑白或其它单色视频监视器
8528591090	101Ⅰ类彩色视频监视器,102Ⅱ类彩色视频监视器,103Ⅲ类彩色视频监视器
8528599000	101Ⅰ类黑白或其它单色视频监视器,102Ⅱ类黑白或其它单色视频监视器,103Ⅲ类黑白或其它单色视频监视器
8528691000	101Ⅰ类视频投影机,102Ⅱ类视频投影机,103Ⅲ类视频投影机
8528699000	101Ⅰ类视频投影机,102Ⅱ类视频投影机,103Ⅲ类视频投影机
8528711000	101Ⅰ类卫星电视接收机,102Ⅱ类卫星电视接收机,103Ⅲ类卫星电视接收机
8528718000	101Ⅰ类彩色电视机,102Ⅱ类彩色电视机,103Ⅲ类彩色电视机
8528719000	101Ⅰ类单色电视机,102Ⅱ类单色电视机,103Ⅲ类单色电视机
8528721100	101Ⅰ类彩色电视机,102Ⅱ类彩色电视机,103Ⅲ类彩色电视机
8528721200	101Ⅰ类彩色电视机,102Ⅱ类彩色电视机,103Ⅲ类彩色电视机
8528721900	101Ⅰ类彩色电视机,102Ⅱ类彩色电视机,103Ⅲ类彩色电视机
8528722100	101Ⅰ类彩色电视机,102Ⅱ类彩色电视机,103Ⅲ类彩色电视机
8528722200	101Ⅰ类彩色电视机,102Ⅱ类彩色电视机,103Ⅲ类彩色电视机
8528722900	101Ⅰ类彩色电视机,102Ⅱ类彩色电视机,103Ⅲ类彩色电视机
8528723100	101Ⅰ类彩色电视机,102Ⅱ类彩色电视机,103Ⅲ类彩色电视机
8528723200	101Ⅰ类彩色电视机,102Ⅱ类彩色电视机,103Ⅲ类彩色电视机

HS编码	CIQ扩展品名
8528723900	101Ⅰ类彩色电视机,102Ⅱ类彩色电视机,103Ⅲ类彩色电视机
8528729100	101Ⅰ类彩色电视机,102Ⅱ类彩色电视机,103Ⅲ类彩色电视机
8528729200	101Ⅰ类彩色电视机,102Ⅱ类彩色电视机,103Ⅲ类彩色电视机
8528729900	101Ⅰ类彩色电视机,102Ⅱ类彩色电视机,103Ⅲ类彩色电视机
8528730000	101Ⅰ类单色电视机,102Ⅱ类单色电视机,103Ⅲ类单色电视机
8529102000	101Ⅰ类其它收录放音装置及其零件,102Ⅱ类其它收录放音装置及其零件,103Ⅲ类其它收录放音装置及其零件,104Ⅰ类其它电视接收、发送装置及其零件,105Ⅱ类其它电视接收、发送装置及其零件,106Ⅲ类其它电视接收、发送装置及其零件
8529109021	101Ⅰ类其它电视接收、发送装置及其零件,102Ⅱ类其它电视接收、发送装置及其零件,103Ⅲ类其它电视接收、发送装置及其零件
8529109029	101Ⅰ类其它收录放音装置及其零件,102Ⅱ类其它收录放音装置及其零件,103Ⅲ类其它收录放音装置及其零件,104Ⅰ类其它电视接收、发送装置及其零件,105Ⅱ类其它电视接收、发送装置及其零件,106Ⅲ类其它电视接收、发送装置及其零件
8529109090	101Ⅰ类其它收录放音装置及其零件,102Ⅱ类其它收录放音装置及其零件,103Ⅲ类其它收录放音装置及其零件,104Ⅰ类其它电视接收、发送装置及其零件,105Ⅱ类其它电视接收、发送装置及其零件,106Ⅲ类其它电视接收、发送装置及其零件
8529901011	101Ⅰ类其它电视接收、发送装置及其零件,102Ⅱ类其它电视接收、发送装置及其零件,103Ⅲ类其它电视接收、发送装置及其零件
8529901012	101Ⅰ类其它电视接收、发送装置及其零件,102Ⅱ类其它电视接收、发送装置及其零件,103Ⅲ类其它电视接收、发送装置及其零件
8529901013	101Ⅰ类其它电视接收、发送装置及其零件,102Ⅱ类其它电视接收、发送装置及其零件,103Ⅲ类其它电视接收、发送装置及其零件
8529901014	101Ⅰ类其它电视接收、发送装置及其零件,102Ⅱ类其它电视接收、发送装置及其零件,103Ⅲ类其它电视接收、发送装置及其零件
8529901090	101Ⅰ类其它电视接收、发送装置及其零件,102Ⅱ类其它电视接收、发送装置及其零件,103Ⅲ类其它电视接收、发送装置及其零件
8529904100	101Ⅰ类其它摄录放像装置及其零件,102Ⅱ类其它摄录放像装置及其零件,103Ⅲ类其它摄录放像装置及其零件
8529904900	101Ⅰ类家用型摄录一体机,102Ⅱ类家用型摄录一体机,103Ⅲ类家用型摄录一体机,104Ⅰ类其它摄录放像装置及其零件,105Ⅱ类其它摄录放像装置及其零件,106Ⅲ类其它摄录放像装置及其零件
8529906000	101Ⅰ类其它收录放音装置及其零件,102Ⅱ类其它收录放音装置及其零件,103Ⅲ类其它收录放音装置及其零件
8529908100	101Ⅰ类其它电视接收、发送装置及其零件,102Ⅱ类其它电视接收、发送装置及其零件,103Ⅲ类其它电视接收、发送装置及其零件
8529908900	101Ⅰ类其它电视接收、发送装置及其零件,102Ⅱ类其它电视接收、发送装置及其零件,103Ⅲ类其它电视接收、发送装置及其零件
8529909011	101Ⅰ类其它电视接收、发送装置及其零件,102Ⅱ类其它电视接收、发送装置及其零件,103Ⅲ类其它电视接收、发送装置及其零件
8531100000	101防盗报警装置,102防火报警装置
8531909000	101可燃气体报警器,102有毒气体报警器,103其它视听设备及其零件
8544200000	101绞股线,102电缆,103同轴电缆,104其它电线电缆
8544421100	101电缆,102电脑连接线,103游戏机线,104其它电线电缆
8544421900	101绞股线,102电线,103电脑连接线,104游戏机线,105其它电线电缆
8544491100	101电缆,102电脑连接线,103游戏机线,104其它电线电缆
8544491900	101绞股线,102电线,103电脑连接线,104游戏机线,105其它电线电缆
8544609001	101绞股线,102电线,103其它电线电缆
8544609090	101绞股线,102电线,103其它电线电缆
9018310000	101一次性使用无菌注射器,102玻璃注射器,103预填充药剂及与药液配套的注射器,104胰岛素注射器,105兽医金属注射器,106兽医塑钢连续注射器,107一次性使用精密过滤输液器,108一次性使用重力(滴定管)式输液器,109一次性使用避光输液器,110一次性使用压力输液设备用输液器,111一次性使用吊瓶式和袋式输液器,112一次性使用流量设定微调式输液器,113其他注射器、输液器
9018321000	101一次性使用无菌注射针,102不锈钢注射针管,103一次性使用静脉输液针,104金属骨髓内针,105泪道探针,106一次性使用无菌牙科注射针,107一次性使用麻醉穿刺针,108其他管状金属针头
9018909911	101诊断仪器及零部件,102治疗仪器及零部件,103其他医疗仪器及零部件,104与人体接触的进入式医疗器具,105与人体接触的非进入式医疗器具,106其他医疗器具
9018909919	101诊断仪器及零部件,102治疗仪器及零部件,103其他医疗仪器及零部件,104与人体接触的进入式医疗器具,105与人体接触的非进入式医疗器具,106其他医疗器具
9018909991	101诊断仪器及零部件,102治疗仪器及零部件,103其他医疗仪器及零部件,104与人体接触的进入式医疗器具,105与人体接触的非进入式医疗器具,106其他医疗器具
9018909999	101诊断仪器及零部件,102治疗仪器及零部件,103其他医疗仪器及零部件,104与人体接触的进入式医疗器具,105与人体接触的非进入式医疗器具,106其他医疗器具
9019101000	101按摩垫I类器具,102按摩垫II类器具,103按摩垫III类器具,104按摩垫0I类器具,105按摩垫0类器具,106按摩椅I类器具,107按摩椅II类器具,108按摩椅III类器具,109按摩椅0I类器具,110按摩椅0类器具,111按摩床I类器具,112按摩床II类器具,113按摩床III类器具,114按摩床0I类器具,115按摩床0类器具,116其它按摩器具及其零件I类器具,117其它按摩器具及其零件II类器具,118其它按摩器具及其零件III类器具,119其它按摩器具及其零件0I类器具,120其它按摩器具及其零件0类器具
9019109000	101心理功能测验装置,102与人体接触的机械疗法器具,103其他机械疗法器具,104按摩垫I类器具,105按摩垫II类器具,106按摩垫III类器具,107按摩垫0I类器具,108按摩垫0类器具,109按摩椅I类器具,110按摩椅II类器具,111按摩椅III类器具,112按摩椅0I类器具,113按摩椅0类器具,114按摩床I类器具,115按摩床II类器具,116按摩床III类器具,117按摩床0I类器具,118按摩床0类器具,119其它按摩器具及其零件I类器具,120其它按摩器具及其零件II类器具,121其它按摩器具及其零件III类器具,122其它按摩器具及其零件0I类器具,123其它按摩器具及其零件0类器具
9401201000	101其他车辆零部件,102软体家具
9401809010	101其他家具,102靠垫,103其他日用纺织制品
9403509100	101其他木制品,102木家具,103儿童用
9403609100	101其他木制品,102木家具,103儿童用
9403891000	101柳及柳制品,102柳条及类似材料制的家具
9404904000	101褥垫,102靠垫,103其他日用纺织制品,104其他纺织制品
9601100010	101未列出的其他动物骨、蹄、角,102含木制品的工艺品,103不含木制品的工艺品
9601100090	101未列出的其他动物骨、蹄、角,102含木制品的工艺品,103不含木制品的工艺品
9603509990	101其他车辆零部件,102含木制品,103不含木制品
9801009000	101植物真菌,102植物线虫,103其他植物病原体,104杂草,105螨类,106多足虫类动物,107其他植物有害生物,108土壤,109科研用试剂和其它材料,110其他植物检疫类特殊物品,401含《人间传染的病原微生物名录》内一类病原微生物的人体体液、分泌物、排泄物(粪肥除外)),402含《人间传染的病原微生物名录》内二类病原微生物的人体体液、分泌物、排泄物(粪肥除外)),403含《人间传染的病原微生物名录》内三类病原微生物的人体体液、分泌物、排泄物(粪肥除外),404含《人间传染的病原微生物名录》内四类病原微生物的人体体液、分泌物、排泄物(粪肥除外),405含《人间传染的病原微生物名录》内含新发传染病或名录外再现传染病病原微生物的人体体液、分泌物、排泄物(粪肥除外),406含寄生虫的人体体液、分泌物、排泄物(粪肥除外),407活体人体寄生虫,408非活体寄生虫标本,999单项记录价值≤2000RMB的非税、证进口商品

附表 3： 2022 年进口商品从量、复合税税率表

税则号列	货品名称(简称)	2022 年最惠国税率	普通税率	对美关税(%)
02071200	整只,冻的鸡	1.3 元/千克	5.6 元/千克	1.3 元/千克+30
02071411	冻的的带骨鸡块	0.6 元/千克	4.2 元/千克	0.6 元/千克+30
02071419	冻的其他鸡块	0.7 元/千克	9.5 元/千克	0.7 元/千克+30
02071421	冻的鸡翼(不包括翼尖)	0.8 元/千克	8.1 元/千克	0.8 元/千克+30
02071422	鲜、冷、冻鸡爪	1 元/千克	3.2 元/千克	1 元/千克+30
02071429	冻的其他鸡杂碎	0.5 元/千克	3.2 元/千克	0.5 元/千克+30
05040021	冷和冻的鸡肫	1.3 元/千克	7.7 元/千克	1.3 元/千克+30
22030000	麦芽酿造的啤酒	0	7.5 元/升	0 元/升+25
27090000	石油原油及从沥青矿物提取的原油	0	85 元/吨	0 元/吨+2.5
37023190	彩色摄影用未曝光无齿孔彩色胶卷,宽度≤105 mm,用纸、纸板及纺织物以外任何材料制成	56 元/平方米	433 元/平方米	56 元/平方米+5
37023220	照相制版用未曝光涂卤化银液无齿孔胶卷,宽度≤105 mm,用纸、纸板及纺织物以外任何材料制成	4.5 元/平方米	104 元/平方米	
37023290	其他未曝光涂乳液无齿孔胶卷,宽度≤105 mm,用纸、纸板及纺织物以外任何材料制成	21 元/平方米	202 元/平方米	21 元/平方米+10
37023920	照相制版用未曝光未涂卤化银无齿孔感光胶卷,宽度≤105 mm,用纸、纸板及纺织物以外任何材料制成	12 元/平方米	104 元/平方米	12 元/平方米+7.5
37023990	其他未曝光未涂卤化银无齿孔感光胶卷,宽度≤105 m,用纸、纸板及纺织物以外任何材料制成	24 元/平方米	202 元/平方米	24 元/平方米+10
37024100	彩色摄影用未曝光无齿孔彩色胶卷,宽度＞610 mm,长度＞200m,用纸、纸板及纺织物以外任何材料制成	7.1 元/平方米	202 元/平方米	
37024221	印刷电路板制造用未曝光光致抗蚀干膜,宽度＞610 mm,长度＞200m,用纸、纸板及纺织物以外任何材料制成	0.6 元/平方米	110 元/平方米	0.6 元/平方米+25
37024229	照相制版用其他未曝光无齿孔胶卷 ,宽度＞610 mm,长度＞200m,用纸、纸板及纺织物以外任何材料制成	1.6 元/平方米	110 元/平方米	1 元/平方米+25
3702429201	未曝光红色或红外激光胶片	2.4 元/平方米	213 元/平方米	0.5 元/平方米+27.5
3702429290	其他未曝光红色或红外激光胶片	2.4 元/平方米	213 元/平方米	2.4 元/平方米+27.5
37024299	其他未曝光无齿孔宽长胶卷	7 元/平方米	213 元/平方米	7 元/平方米+30
37024321	照相制版用未曝光无齿孔激光照排片,宽度＞610 mm,长度≤200m,用纸、纸板及纺织物以外任何材料制成	0	104 元/平方米	
37024329	其他照相制版用未曝光无齿孔胶卷,宽度＞610 mm,长度≤200m,用纸、纸板及纺织物以外任何材料制成	3.7 元/平方米	104 元/平方米	3.7 元/平方米+12.5
37024390	其他用未曝光无齿孔胶卷,宽度 610 mm,长度≤200m,用纸、纸板及纺织物以外任何材料制成	17 元/平方米	202 元/平方米	17 元/平方米+10
37024421	照相制版用无齿孔未曝光激光照排片,105mm＜宽度≤610mm,用纸、纸板及纺织物以外任何材料制成	2.0 元/平方米	115 元/平方米	
37024422	印刷电路板制造用未曝光光致抗蚀干膜 ,105mm＜宽度≤610mm,用纸、纸板及纺织物以外任何材料制成	5 元/平方米	115 元/平方米	5 元/平方米+27.5
37024429	其他照相制版用无齿孔未曝光胶卷,105mm＜宽度≤610mm,用纸、纸板及纺织物以外任何材料制成	2.9 元/平方米	115 元/平方米	2.9 元/平方米+27.5
37024490	其他用无齿孔未曝光胶卷,105mm＜宽度≤610mm,用纸、纸板及纺织物以外任何材料制成	27 元/平方米	202 元/平方米	27 元/平方米+27.5
37025200	彩色摄影用未曝光彩色胶卷 ,宽度≤16 mm	91 元/平方米	433 元/平方米	91 元/平方米+5
37025300	幻灯片用未曝光彩色摄影胶卷,16 mm＜宽度≤35 mm,长度＜30m,用纸、纸板及纺织物以外任何材料制成	122.6 元/平方米	433 元/平方米	122.6 元/平方米+5
37025410	非幻灯片用未曝光彩色胶卷,宽度 35mm,长度≤2 m,用纸、纸板及纺织物以外任何材料制成	10 元/平方米	433 元/平方米	10 元/平方米+7.5
37025490	非幻灯片用彩色摄影用未曝光彩色胶卷,16 mm＜宽度＜35 mm,2 m＜长度≤30m,用纸、纸板及纺织物以外任何材料制成	24 元/平方米	433 元/平方米	
37025520	未曝光的彩色电影胶片,16mm＜ 宽度≤35mm, 长度＞30m,用纸、纸板及纺织物以外任何材料制成	8.7 元/平方米	232 元/平方米	8.7 元/平方米+10
37025590	未曝光彩色摄影用胶卷,16mm＜ 宽度≤35mm, 长度＞30m,用纸、纸板及纺织物以外任何材料制成,电影胶片除外	27 元/平方米	433 元/平方米	
37025620	未曝光的彩色电影胶片,宽度＞35mm,用纸、纸板及纺织物以外任何材料制成	13 元/平方米	232 元/平方米	13 元/平方米+10
37025690	未曝光的彩色摄影用胶卷,宽度＞35mm,用纸、纸板及纺织物以外任何材料制成,电影胶片除外	74 元/平方米	433 元/平方米	74 元/平方米+5
37029600	未曝光非彩色胶卷,宽度≤35mm,长度≤30m,用纸、纸板及纺织物以外任何材料制成	21 元/平方米	210 元/平方米	21 元/平方米+10
37029700	未曝光的非彩色胶卷, 宽度≤35mm, 长度＞30m,用纸、纸板及纺织物以外任何材料制成	9 元/平方米	210 元/平方米	9 元/平方米+10
37029800	未曝光的非彩色胶卷,宽度＞35mm,用纸、纸板及纺织物以外任何材料制成	10 元/平方米	210 元/平方米	

附表 4： **Attached table 4：**

进口反倾销、反补贴税清单 Import Antidumping and Countervailing Tariffs List

HS 编码	原产国名称	厂商中文名称	厂商英文名称	税种代码	税率	起始日期	截止日期
0207110000	巴西		SEARA ALIMENTOS LTDA	I	17.8%	2019/2/17	2024/2/16
0207110000	巴西		JBS AVES LTDA	I	17.8%	2019/2/17	2024/2/16
0207110000	巴西		SEARA COMERCIO DE ALIMENTOS LTDA	I	17.8%	2019/2/17	2024/2/16
0207110000	巴西		AGRICOLA JANDELLE S/A	I	17.8%	2019/2/17	2024/2/16
0207110000	巴西		BRF S.A.	I	25.8%	2019/2/17	2024/2/16
0207110000	巴西		C.Vale — Cooperativa Agroindustrial	I	32.4%	2019/2/17	2024/2/16
0207110000	巴西		Cooperativa Central Aurora Alimentos	I	20.2%	2019/2/17	2024/2/16
0207110000	巴西		LAR COOPERATIVA AGROINDUSTRIAL	I	20.2%	2019/2/17	2024/2/16
0207110000	巴西		Copacol — Cooperativa Agroindustrial Consolata	I	20.2%	2019/2/17	2024/2/16
0207110000	巴西		COOPAVEL COOPERATIVA AGROINDUSTRI-AL	I	20.2%	2019/2/17	2024/2/16
0207110000	巴西		Säo Salvador Alimentos S/A	I	20.2%	2019/2/17	2024/2/16
0207110000	巴西		RIVELLI ALIMENTOS S/A	I	20.2%	2019/2/17	2024/2/16
0207110000	巴西		GONCALVES & TORTOLA S/A	I	20.2%	2019/2/17	2024/2/16
0207110000	巴西		COOPERATIVA AGROINDUSTRIAL COPA-GRIL	I	20.2%	2019/2/17	2024/2/16
0207110000	巴西		VIBRA AGROINDUSTRIAL S/A	I	20.2%	2019/2/17	2024/2/16
0207110000	巴西		AGROSUL AGROAVICOLA INDUSTRIAL, S.A	I	20.2%	2019/2/17	2024/2/16
0207110000	巴西		KAEFER AGRO INDUSTRIAL LTDA	I	20.2%	2019/2/17	2024/2/16
0207110000	巴西		VOSSKO DO BRASIL ALIMENTOS CONGELA-DOS LTDA	I	20.2%	2019/2/17	2024/2/16
0207110000	巴西		AVENORTE AVICOLA CIANORTE LTDA.	I	20.2%	2019/2/17	2024/2/16
0207110000	巴西		ADORO S/A	I	20.2%	2019/2/17	2024/2/16
0207110000	巴西		BONASA ALIMENTOS SA	I	20.2%	2019/2/17	2024/2/16
0207110000	巴西		FLAMBOIÃ ALIMENTOS LTDA	I	20.2%	2019/2/17	2024/2/16
0207110000	巴西		FRIGORIFICO NOVA ARAÇÁ LTDA	I	20.2%	2019/2/17	2024/2/16
0207110000	巴西		RIO BRANCO ALIMENTOS S.A.	I	20.2%	2019/2/17	2024/2/16
0207110000	巴西		ZANCHETTA ALIMENTOS LTDA	I	20.2%	2019/2/17	2024/2/16
0207110000	巴西		AGRODANIELI INDÚSTRIA E COMÉRCIO LT-DA.	I	20.2%	2019/2/17	2024/2/16
0207110000	巴西		BELLO ALIMENTOS LTDA.	I	20.2%	2019/2/17	2024/2/16
0207110000	巴西		COASUL COOPERATIVA AGROINDUSTRIAL	I	20.2%	2019/2/17	2024/2/16
0207110000	巴西		COOPERATIVA LANGUIRU LTDA	I	20.2%	2019/2/17	2024/2/16
0207110000	巴西		All others	I	32.4%	2019/2/17	2024/2/16
0207110000	巴西		SHB COMERCIO E INDUSTRIA DE ALIMEN-TOS S.A.	I	25.8%	2019/2/17	2024/2/16
0207110000	巴西		COMPANHIA MINUANO DE ALIMENTOS	I	25.8%	2019/2/17	2024/2/16
0207110000	国(地)别不详的	国(地)别不详的		I	32.4%	2019/2/17	2024/2/16
0207120000	巴西		SEARA ALIMENTOS LTDA	I	17.8%	2019/2/17	2024/2/16
0207120000	巴西		JBS AVES LTDA	I	17.8%	2019/2/17	2024/2/16
0207120000	巴西		SEARA COMERCIO DE ALIMENTOS LTDA	I	17.8%	2019/2/17	2024/2/16
0207120000	巴西		AGRICOLA JANDELLE S/A	I	17.8%	2019/2/17	2024/2/16
0207120000	巴西		BRF S.A.	I	25.8%	2019/2/17	2024/2/16
0207120000	巴西		C.Vale — Cooperativa Agroindustrial	I	32.4%	2019/2/17	2024/2/16
0207120000	巴西		Cooperativa Central Aurora Alimentos	I	20.2%	2019/2/17	2024/2/16
0207120000	巴西		LAR COOPERATIVA AGROINDUSTRIAL	I	20.2%	2019/2/17	2024/2/16
0207120000	巴西		Copacol — Cooperativa Agroindustrial Consolata	I	20.2%	2019/2/17	2024/2/16
0207120000	巴西		COOPAVEL COOPERATIVA AGROINDUSTRI-AL	I	20.2%	2019/2/17	2024/2/16
0207120000	巴西		Säo Salvador Alimentos S/A	I	20.2%	2019/2/17	2024/2/16
0207120000	巴西		RIVELLI ALIMENTOS S/A	I	20.2%	2019/2/17	2024/2/16
0207120000	巴西		GONCALVES & TORTOLA S/A	I	20.2%	2019/2/17	2024/2/16
0207120000	巴西		COOPERATIVA AGROINDUSTRIAL COPA-GRIL	I	20.2%	2019/2/17	2024/2/16
0207120000	巴西		VIBRA AGROINDUSTRIAL S/A	I	20.2%	2019/2/17	2024/2/16
0207120000	巴西		AGROSUL AGROAVICOLA INDUSTRIAL, S.A	I	20.2%	2019/2/17	2024/2/16
0207120000	巴西		KAEFER AGRO INDUSTRIAL LTDA	I	20.2%	2019/2/17	2024/2/16
0207120000	巴西		VOSSKO DO BRASIL ALIMENTOS CONGELA-DOS LTDA	I	20.2%	2019/2/17	2024/2/16
0207120000	巴西		AVENORTE AVICOLA CIANORTE LTDA.	I	20.2%	2019/2/17	2024/2/16
0207120000	巴西		ADORO S/A	I	20.2%	2019/2/17	2024/2/16
0207120000	巴西		BONASA ALIMENTOS SA	I	20.2%	2019/2/17	2024/2/16
0207120000	巴西		FLAMBOIÃ ALIMENTOS LTDA	I	20.2%	2019/2/17	2024/2/16
0207120000	巴西		FRIGORIFICO NOVA ARAÇÁ LTDA	I	20.2%	2019/2/17	2024/2/16
0207120000	巴西		RIO BRANCO ALIMENTOS S.A.	I	20.2%	2019/2/17	2024/2/16
0207120000	巴西		ZANCHETTA ALIMENTOS LTDA	I	20.2%	2019/2/17	2024/2/16
0207120000	巴西		AGRODANIELI INDÚSTRIA E COMÉRCIO LT-DA.	I	20.2%	2019/2/17	2024/2/16
0207120000	巴西		BELLO ALIMENTOS LTDA.	I	20.2%	2019/2/17	2024/2/16
0207120000	巴西		COASUL COOPERATIVA AGROINDUSTRIAL	I	20.2%	2019/2/17	2024/2/16
0207120000	巴西		COOPERATIVA LANGUIRU LTDA	I	20.2%	2019/2/17	2024/2/16

HS编码	原产国名称	厂商中文名称	厂商英文名称	税种代码	税率	起始日期	截止日期
0207120000	巴西		All others	I	32.4%	2019/2/17	2024/2/16
0207120000	巴西		SHB COMERCIO E INDUSTRIA DE ALIMENTOS S.A.	I	25.8%	2019/2/17	2024/2/16
0207120000	巴西		COMPANHIA MINUANO DE ALIMENTOS	I	25.8%	2019/2/17	2024/2/16
0207120000	国(地)别不详的	国(地)别不详的		I	32.4%	2019/2/17	2024/2/16
0207131100	巴西		SEARA ALIMENTOS LTDA	I	17.8%	2019/2/17	2024/2/16
0207131100	巴西		JBS AVES LTDA	I	17.8%	2019/2/17	2024/2/16
0207131100	巴西		SEARA COMERCIO DE ALIMENTOS LTDA	I	17.8%	2019/2/17	2024/2/16
0207131100	巴西		AGRICOLA JANDELLE S/A	I	17.8%	2019/2/17	2024/2/16
0207131100	巴西		BRF S.A.	I	25.8%	2019/2/17	2024/2/16
0207131100	巴西		C.Vale — Cooperativa Agroindustrial	I	32.4%	2019/2/17	2024/2/16
0207131100	巴西		Cooperativa Central Aurora Alimentos	I	20.2%	2019/2/17	2024/2/16
0207131100	巴西		LAR COOPERATIVA AGROINDUSTRIAL	I	20.2%	2019/2/17	2024/2/16
0207131100	巴西		Copacol — Cooperativa Agroindustrial Consolata	I	20.2%	2019/2/17	2024/2/16
0207131100	巴西		COOPAVEL COOPERATIVA AGROINDUSTRIAL	I	20.2%	2019/2/17	2024/2/16
0207131100	巴西		São Salvador Alimentos S/A	I	20.2%	2019/2/17	2024/2/16
0207131100	巴西		RIVELLI ALIMENTOS S/A	I	20.2%	2019/2/17	2024/2/16
0207131100	巴西		GONCALVES & TORTOLA S/A	I	20.2%	2019/2/17	2024/2/16
0207131100	巴西		COOPERATIVA AGROINDUSTRIAL COPAGRIL	I	20.2%	2019/2/17	2024/2/16
0207131100	巴西		VIBRA AGROINDUSTRIAL S/A	I	20.2%	2019/2/17	2024/2/16
0207131100	巴西		AGROSUL AGROAVICOLA INDUSTRIAL, S.A	I	20.2%	2019/2/17	2024/2/16
0207131100	巴西		KAEFER AGRO INDUSTRIAL LTDA	I	20.2%	2019/2/17	2024/2/16
0207131100	巴西		VOSSKO DO BRASIL ALIMENTOS CONGELADOS LTDA	I	20.2%	2019/2/17	2024/2/16
0207131100	巴西		AVENORTE AVICOLA CIANORTE LTDA.	I	20.2%	2019/2/17	2024/2/16
0207131100	巴西		ADORO S/A	I	20.2%	2019/2/17	2024/2/16
0207131100	巴西		BONASA ALIMENTOS SA	I	20.2%	2019/2/17	2024/2/16
0207131100	巴西		FLAMBOIÃ ALIMENTOS LTDA	I	20.2%	2019/2/17	2024/2/16
0207131100	巴西		FRIGORIFICO NOVA ARAÇÁ LTDA	I	20.2%	2019/2/17	2024/2/16
0207131100	巴西		RIO BRANCO ALIMENTOS S.A.	I	20.2%	2019/2/17	2024/2/16
0207131100	巴西		ZANCHETTA ALIMENTOS LTDA	I	20.2%	2019/2/17	2024/2/16
0207131100	巴西		AGRODANIELI INDÚSTRIA E COMÉRCIO LTDA.	I	20.2%	2019/2/17	2024/2/16
0207131100	巴西		BELLO ALIMENTOS LTDA.	I	20.2%	2019/2/17	2024/2/16
0207131100	巴西		COASUL COOPERATIVA AGROINDUSTRIAL	I	20.2%	2019/2/17	2024/2/16
0207131100	巴西		COOPERATIVA LANGUIRU LTDA	I	20.2%	2019/2/17	2024/2/16
0207131100	巴西		All others	I	32.4%	2019/2/17	2024/2/16
0207131100	巴西		SHB COMERCIO E INDUSTRIA DE ALIMENTOS S.A.	I	25.8%	2019/2/17	2024/2/16
0207131100	巴西		COMPANHIA MINUANO DE ALIMENTOS	I	25.8%	2019/2/17	2024/2/16
0207131100	国(地)别不详的	国(地)别不详的		I	32.4%	2019/2/17	2024/2/16
0207131900	巴西		SEARA ALIMENTOS LTDA	I	17.8%	2019/2/17	2024/2/16
0207131900	巴西		JBS AVES LTDA	I	17.8%	2019/2/17	2024/2/16
0207131900	巴西		SEARA COMERCIO DE ALIMENTOS LTDA	I	17.8%	2019/2/17	2024/2/16
0207131900	巴西		AGRICOLA JANDELLE S/A	I	17.8%	2019/2/17	2024/2/16
0207131900	巴西		BRF S.A.	I	25.8%	2019/2/17	2024/2/16
0207131900	巴西		C.Vale — Cooperativa Agroindustrial	I	32.4%	2019/2/17	2024/2/16
0207131900	巴西		Cooperativa Central Aurora Alimentos	I	20.2%	2019/2/17	2024/2/16
0207131900	巴西		LAR COOPERATIVA AGROINDUSTRIAL	I	20.2%	2019/2/17	2024/2/16
0207131900	巴西		Copacol — Cooperativa Agroindustrial Consolata	I	20.2%	2019/2/17	2024/2/16
0207131900	巴西		COOPAVEL COOPERATIVA AGROINDUSTRIAL	I	20.2%	2019/2/17	2024/2/16
0207131900	巴西		São Salvador Alimentos S/A	I	20.2%	2019/2/17	2024/2/16
0207131900	巴西		RIVELLI ALIMENTOS S/A	I	20.2%	2019/2/17	2024/2/16
0207131900	巴西		GONCALVES & TORTOLA S/A	I	20.2%	2019/2/17	2024/2/16
0207131900	巴西		COOPERATIVA AGROINDUSTRIAL COPAGRIL	I	20.2%	2019/2/17	2024/2/16
0207131900	巴西		VIBRA AGROINDUSTRIAL S/A	I	20.2%	2019/2/17	2024/2/16
0207131900	巴西		AGROSUL AGROAVICOLA INDUSTRIAL, S.A	I	20.2%	2019/2/17	2024/2/16
0207131900	巴西		KAEFER AGRO INDUSTRIAL LTDA	I	20.2%	2019/2/17	2024/2/16
0207131900	巴西		VOSSKO DO BRASIL ALIMENTOS CONGELADOS LTDA	I	20.2%	2019/2/17	2024/2/16
0207131900	巴西		AVENORTE AVICOLA CIANORTE LTDA.	I	20.2%	2019/2/17	2024/2/16
0207131900	巴西		ADORO S/A	I	20.2%	2019/2/17	2024/2/16
0207131900	巴西		BONASA ALIMENTOS SA	I	20.2%	2019/2/17	2024/2/16
0207131900	巴西		FLAMBOIÃ ALIMENTOS LTDA	I	20.2%	2019/2/17	2024/2/16
0207131900	巴西		FRIGORIFICO NOVA ARAÇÁ LTDA	I	20.2%	2019/2/17	2024/2/16
0207131900	巴西		RIO BRANCO ALIMENTOS S.A.	I	20.2%	2019/2/17	2024/2/16
0207131900	巴西		ZANCHETTA ALIMENTOS LTDA	I	20.2%	2019/2/17	2024/2/16
0207131900	巴西		AGRODANIELI INDÚSTRIA E COMÉRCIO LTDA.	I	20.2%	2019/2/17	2024/2/16

HS 编码	原产国名称	厂商中文名称	厂商英文名称	税种代码	税率	起始日期	截止日期
0207131900	巴西		BELLO ALIMENTOS LTDA.	I	20.2%	2019/2/17	2024/2/16
0207131900	巴西		COASUL COOPERATIVA AGROINDUSTRIAL	I	20.2%	2019/2/17	2024/2/16
0207131900	巴西		COOPERATIVA LANGUIRU LTDA	I	20.2%	2019/2/17	2024/2/16
0207131900	巴西		All others	I	32.4%	2019/2/17	2024/2/16
0207131900	巴西		SHB COMERCIO E INDUSTRIA DE ALIMENTOS S.A.	I	25.8%	2019/2/17	2024/2/16
0207131900	巴西		COMPANHIA MINUANO DE ALIMENTOS	I	25.8%	2019/2/17	2024/2/16
0207131900	国(地)别不详的	国(地)别不详的		I	32.4%	2019/2/17	2024/2/16
0207132101	巴西		SEARA ALIMENTOS LTDA	I	17.8%	2019/2/17	2024/2/16
0207132101	巴西		JBS AVES LTDA	I	17.8%	2019/2/17	2024/2/16
0207132101	巴西		SEARA COMERCIO DE ALIMENTOS LTDA	I	17.8%	2019/2/17	2024/2/16
0207132101	巴西		AGRICOLA JANDELLE S/A	I	17.8%	2019/2/17	2024/2/16
0207132101	巴西		BRF S.A.	I	25.8%	2019/2/17	2024/2/16
0207132101	巴西		C.Vale — Cooperativa Agroindustrial	I	32.4%	2019/2/17	2024/2/16
0207132101	巴西		Cooperativa Central Aurora Alimentos	I	20.2%	2019/2/17	2024/2/16
0207132101	巴西		LAR COOPERATIVA AGROINDUSTRIAL	I	20.2%	2019/2/17	2024/2/16
0207132101	巴西		Copacol — Cooperativa Agroindustrial Consolata	I	20.2%	2019/2/17	2024/2/16
0207132101	巴西		COOPAVEL COOPERATIVA AGROINDUSTRIAL	I	20.2%	2019/2/17	2024/2/16
0207132101	巴西		São Salvador Alimentos S/A	I	20.2%	2019/2/17	2024/2/16
0207132101	巴西		RIVELLI ALIMENTOS S/A	I	20.2%	2019/2/17	2024/2/16
0207132101	巴西		GONCALVES & TORTOLA S/A	I	20.2%	2019/2/17	2024/2/16
0207132101	巴西		COOPERATIVA AGROINDUSTRIAL COPAGRIL	I	20.2%	2019/2/17	2024/2/16
0207132101	巴西		VIBRA AGROINDUSTRIAL S/A	I	20.2%	2019/2/17	2024/2/16
0207132101	巴西		AGROSUL AGROAVICOLA INDUSTRIAL, S.A	I	20.2%	2019/2/17	2024/2/16
0207132101	巴西		KAEFER AGRO INDUSTRIAL LTDA	I	20.2%	2019/2/17	2024/2/16
0207132101	巴西		VOSSKO DO BRASIL ALIMENTOS CONGELADOS LTDA	I	20.2%	2019/2/17	2024/2/16
0207132101	巴西		AVENORTE AVICOLA CIANORTE LTDA.	I	20.2%	2019/2/17	2024/2/16
0207132101	巴西		ADORO S/A	I	20.2%	2019/2/17	2024/2/16
0207132101	巴西		BONASA ALIMENTOS SA	I	20.2%	2019/2/17	2024/2/16
0207132101	巴西		FLAMBOIÃ ALIMENTOS LTDA	I	20.2%	2019/2/17	2024/2/16
0207132101	巴西		FRIGORIFICO NOVA ARAÇÁ LTDA	I	20.2%	2019/2/17	2024/2/16
0207132101	巴西		RIO BRANCO ALIMENTOS S.A.	I	20.2%	2019/2/17	2024/2/16
0207132101	巴西		ZANCHETTA ALIMENTOS LTDA	I	20.2%	2019/2/17	2024/2/16
0207132101	巴西		AGRODANIELI INDÚSTRIA E COMÉRCIO LTDA.	I	20.2%	2019/2/17	2024/2/16
0207132101	巴西		BELLO ALIMENTOS LTDA.	I	20.2%	2019/2/17	2024/2/16
0207132101	巴西		COASUL COOPERATIVA AGROINDUSTRIAL	I	20.2%	2019/2/17	2024/2/16
0207132101	巴西		COOPERATIVA LANGUIRU LTDA	I	20.2%	2019/2/17	2024/2/16
0207132101	巴西		All others	I	32.4%	2019/2/17	2024/2/16
0207132101	巴西		SHB COMERCIO E INDUSTRIA DE ALIMENTOS S.A.	I	25.8%	2019/2/17	2024/2/16
0207132101	巴西		COMPANHIA MINUANO DE ALIMENTOS	I	25.8%	2019/2/17	2024/2/16
0207132101	国(地)别不详的	国(地)别不详的		I	32.4%	2019/2/17	2024/2/16
0207132102	巴西		SEARA ALIMENTOS LTDA	I	17.8%	2019/2/17	2024/2/16
0207132102	巴西		JBS AVES LTDA	I	17.8%	2019/2/17	2024/2/16
0207132102	巴西		SEARA COMERCIO DE ALIMENTOS LTDA	I	17.8%	2019/2/17	2024/2/16
0207132102	巴西		AGRICOLA JANDELLE S/A	I	17.8%	2019/2/17	2024/2/16
0207132102	巴西		BRF S.A.	I	25.8%	2019/2/17	2024/2/16
0207132102	巴西		C.Vale — Cooperativa Agroindustrial	I	32.4%	2019/2/17	2024/2/16
0207132102	巴西		Cooperativa Central Aurora Alimentos	I	20.2%	2019/2/17	2024/2/16
0207132102	巴西		LAR COOPERATIVA AGROINDUSTRIAL	I	20.2%	2019/2/17	2024/2/16
0207132102	巴西		Copacol — Cooperativa Agroindustrial Consolata	I	20.2%	2019/2/17	2024/2/16
0207132102	巴西		COOPAVEL COOPERATIVA AGROINDUSTRIAL	I	20.2%	2019/2/17	2024/2/16
0207132102	巴西		São Salvador Alimentos S/A	I	20.2%	2019/2/17	2024/2/16
0207132102	巴西		RIVELLI ALIMENTOS S/A	I	20.2%	2019/2/17	2024/2/16
0207132102	巴西		GONCALVES & TORTOLA S/A	I	20.2%	2019/2/17	2024/2/16
0207132102	巴西		COOPERATIVA AGROINDUSTRIAL COPAGRIL	I	20.2%	2019/2/17	2024/2/16
0207132102	巴西		VIBRA AGROINDUSTRIAL S/A	I	20.2%	2019/2/17	2024/2/16
0207132102	巴西		AGROSUL AGROAVICOLA INDUSTRIAL, S.A	I	20.2%	2019/2/17	2024/2/16
0207132102	巴西		KAEFER AGRO INDUSTRIAL LTDA	I	20.2%	2019/2/17	2024/2/16
0207132102	巴西		VOSSKO DO BRASIL ALIMENTOS CONGELADOS LTDA	I	20.2%	2019/2/17	2024/2/16
0207132102	巴西		AVENORTE AVICOLA CIANORTE LTDA.	I	20.2%	2019/2/17	2024/2/16
0207132102	巴西		ADORO S/A	I	20.2%	2019/2/17	2024/2/16
0207132102	巴西		BONASA ALIMENTOS SA	I	20.2%	2019/2/17	2024/2/16
0207132102	巴西		FLAMBOIÃ ALIMENTOS LTDA	I	20.2%	2019/2/17	2024/2/16
0207132102	巴西		FRIGORIFICO NOVA ARAÇÁ LTDA	I	20.2%	2019/2/17	2024/2/16
0207132102	巴西		RIO BRANCO ALIMENTOS S.A.	I	20.2%	2019/2/17	2024/2/16

HS编码	原产国名称	厂商中文名称	厂商英文名称	税种代码	税率	起始日期	截止日期
0207132102	巴西		ZANCHETTA ALIMENTOS LTDA	I	20.2%	2019/2/17	2024/2/16
0207132102	巴西		AGRODANIELI INDÜSTRIA E COMÉRCIO LTDA.	I	20.2%	2019/2/17	2024/2/16
0207132102	巴西		BELLO ALIMENTOS LTDA.	I	20.2%	2019/2/17	2024/2/16
0207132102	巴西		COASUL COOPERATIVA AGROINDUSTRIAL	I	20.2%	2019/2/17	2024/2/16
0207132102	巴西		COOPERATIVA LANGUIRU LTDA	I	20.2%	2019/2/17	2024/2/16
0207132102	巴西		All others	I	32.4%	2019/2/17	2024/2/16
0207132102	巴西		SHB COMERCIO E INDUSTRIA DE ALIMENTOS S.A.	I	25.8%	2019/2/17	2024/2/16
0207132102	巴西		COMPANHIA MINUANO DE ALIMENTOS	I	25.8%	2019/2/17	2024/2/16
0207132102	国(地)别不详的	国(地)别不详的		I	32.4%	2019/2/17	2024/2/16
0207132103	巴西		SEARA ALIMENTOS LTDA	I	17.8%	2019/2/17	2024/2/16
0207132103	巴西		JBS AVES LTDA	I	17.8%	2019/2/17	2024/2/16
0207132103	巴西		SEARA COMERCIO DE ALIMENTOS LTDA	I	17.8%	2019/2/17	2024/2/16
0207132103	巴西		AGRICOLA JANDELLE S/A	I	17.8%	2019/2/17	2024/2/16
0207132103	巴西		BRF S.A.	I	25.8%	2019/2/17	2024/2/16
0207132103	巴西		C.Vale — Cooperativa Agroindustrial	I	32.4%	2019/2/17	2024/2/16
0207132103	巴西		Cooperativa Central Aurora Alimentos	I	20.2%	2019/2/17	2024/2/16
0207132103	巴西		LAR COOPERATIVA AGROINDUSTRIAL	I	20.2%	2019/2/17	2024/2/16
0207132103	巴西		Copacol — Cooperativa Agroindustrial Consolata	I	20.2%	2019/2/17	2024/2/16
0207132103	巴西		COOPAVEL COOPERATIVA AGROINDUSTRIAL	I	20.2%	2019/2/17	2024/2/16
0207132103	巴西		São Salvador Alimentos S/A	I	20.2%	2019/2/17	2024/2/16
0207132103	巴西		RIVELLI ALIMENTOS S/A	I	20.2%	2019/2/17	2024/2/16
0207132103	巴西		GONCALVES & TORTOLA S/A	I	20.2%	2019/2/17	2024/2/16
0207132103	巴西		COOPERATIVA AGROINDUSTRIAL COPAGRIL	I	20.2%	2019/2/17	2024/2/16
0207132103	巴西		VIBRA AGROINDUSTRIAL S/A	I	20.2%	2019/2/17	2024/2/16
0207132103	巴西		AGROSUL AGROAVICOLA INDUSTRIAL，S.A	I	20.2%	2019/2/17	2024/2/16
0207132103	巴西		KAEFER AGRO INDUSTRIAL LTDA	I	20.2%	2019/2/17	2024/2/16
0207132103	巴西		VOSSKO DO BRASIL ALIMENTOS CONGELADOS LTDA	I	20.2%	2019/2/17	2024/2/16
0207132103	巴西		AVENORTE AVICOLA CIANORTE LTDA.	I	20.2%	2019/2/17	2024/2/16
0207132103	巴西		ADORO S/A	I	20.2%	2019/2/17	2024/2/16
0207132103	巴西		BONASA ALIMENTOS SA	I	20.2%	2019/2/17	2024/2/16
0207132103	巴西		FLAMBOIÃ ALIMENTOS LTDA	I	20.2%	2019/2/17	2024/2/16
0207132103	巴西		FRIGORIFICO NOVA ARAÇÁ LTDA	I	20.2%	2019/2/17	2024/2/16
0207132103	巴西		RIO BRANCO ALIMENTOS S.A.	I	20.2%	2019/2/17	2024/2/16
0207132103	巴西		ZANCHETTA ALIMENTOS LTDA	I	20.2%	2019/2/17	2024/2/16
0207132103	巴西		AGRODANIELI INDÜSTRIA E COMÉRCIO LTDA.	I	20.2%	2019/2/17	2024/2/16
0207132103	巴西		BELLO ALIMENTOS LTDA.	I	20.2%	2019/2/17	2024/2/16
0207132103	巴西		COASUL COOPERATIVA AGROINDUSTRIAL	I	20.2%	2019/2/17	2024/2/16
0207132103	巴西		COOPERATIVA LANGUIRU LTDA	I	20.2%	2019/2/17	2024/2/16
0207132103	巴西		All others	I	32.4%	2019/2/17	2024/2/16
0207132103	巴西		SHB COMERCIO E INDUSTRIA DE ALIMENTOS S.A.	I	25.8%	2019/2/17	2024/2/16
0207132103	巴西		COMPANHIA MINUANO DE ALIMENTOS	I	25.8%	2019/2/17	2024/2/16
0207132103	国(地)别不详的	国(地)别不详的		I	32.4%	2019/2/17	2024/2/16
0207132104	巴西		SEARA ALIMENTOS LTDA	I	17.8%	2019/2/17	2024/2/16
0207132104	巴西		JBS AVES LTDA	I	17.8%	2019/2/17	2024/2/16
0207132104	巴西		SEARA COMERCIO DE ALIMENTOS LTDA	I	17.8%	2019/2/17	2024/2/16
0207132104	巴西		AGRICOLA JANDELLE S/A	I	17.8%	2019/2/17	2024/2/16
0207132104	巴西		BRF S.A.	I	25.8%	2019/2/17	2024/2/16
0207132104	巴西		C.Vale — Cooperativa Agroindustrial	I	32.4%	2019/2/17	2024/2/16
0207132104	巴西		Cooperativa Central Aurora Alimentos	I	20.2%	2019/2/17	2024/2/16
0207132104	巴西		LAR COOPERATIVA AGROINDUSTRIAL	I	20.2%	2019/2/17	2024/2/16
0207132104	巴西		Copacol — Cooperativa Agroindustrial Consolata	I	20.2%	2019/2/17	2024/2/16
0207132104	巴西		COOPAVEL COOPERATIVA AGROINDUSTRIAL	I	20.2%	2019/2/17	2024/2/16
0207132104	巴西		São Salvador Alimentos S/A	I	20.2%	2019/2/17	2024/2/16
0207132104	巴西		RIVELLI ALIMENTOS S/A	I	20.2%	2019/2/17	2024/2/16
0207132104	巴西		GONCALVES & TORTOLA S/A	I	20.2%	2019/2/17	2024/2/16
0207132104	巴西		COOPERATIVA AGROINDUSTRIAL COPAGRIL	I	20.2%	2019/2/17	2024/2/16
0207132104	巴西		VIBRA AGROINDUSTRIAL S/A	I	20.2%	2019/2/17	2024/2/16
0207132104	巴西		AGROSUL AGROAVICOLA INDUSTRIAL，S.A	I	20.2%	2019/2/17	2024/2/16
0207132104	巴西		KAEFER AGRO INDUSTRIAL LTDA	I	20.2%	2019/2/17	2024/2/16
0207132104	巴西		VOSSKO DO BRASIL ALIMENTOS CONGELADOS LTDA	I	20.2%	2019/2/17	2024/2/16
0207132104	巴西		AVENORTE AVICOLA CIANORTE LTDA.	I	20.2%	2019/2/17	2024/2/16
0207132104	巴西		ADORO S/A	I	20.2%	2019/2/17	2024/2/16
0207132104	巴西		BONASA ALIMENTOS SA	I	20.2%	2019/2/17	2024/2/16

HS编码	原产国名称	厂商中文名称	厂商英文名称	税种代码	税率	起始日期	截止日期
0207132104	巴西		FLAMBOIÃ ALIMENTOS LTDA	I	20.2%	2019/2/17	2024/2/16
0207132104	巴西		FRIGORIFICO NOVA ARAÇÁ LTDA	I	20.2%	2019/2/17	2024/2/16
0207132104	巴西		RIO BRANCO ALIMENTOS S.A.	I	20.2%	2019/2/17	2024/2/16
0207132104	巴西		ZANCHETTA ALIMENTOS LTDA	I	20.2%	2019/2/17	2024/2/16
0207132104	巴西		AGRODANIELI INDÚSTRIA E COMÉRCIO LTDA.	I	20.2%	2019/2/17	2024/2/16
0207132104	巴西		BELLO ALIMENTOS LTDA.	I	20.2%	2019/2/17	2024/2/16
0207132104	巴西		COASUL COOPERATIVA AGROINDUSTRIAL	I	20.2%	2019/2/17	2024/2/16
0207132104	巴西		COOPERATIVA LANGUIRU LTDA	I	20.2%	2019/2/17	2024/2/16
0207132104	巴西		All others	I	32.4%	2019/2/17	2024/2/16
0207132104	巴西		SHB COMERCIO E INDUSTRIA DE ALIMENTOS S.A.	I	25.8%	2019/2/17	2024/2/16
0207132104	巴西		COMPANHIA MINUANO DE ALIMENTOS	I	25.8%	2019/2/17	2024/2/16
0207132104	国(地)别不详的	国(地)别不详的		I	32.4%	2019/2/17	2024/2/16
0207132901	巴西		SEARA ALIMENTOS LTDA	I	17.8%	2019/2/17	2024/2/16
0207132901	巴西		JBS AVES LTDA	I	17.8%	2019/2/17	2024/2/16
0207132901	巴西		SEARA COMERCIO DE ALIMENTOS LTDA	I	17.8%	2019/2/17	2024/2/16
0207132901	巴西		AGRICOLA JANDELLE S/A	I	17.8%	2019/2/17	2024/2/16
0207132901	巴西		BRF S.A.	I	25.8%	2019/2/17	2024/2/16
0207132901	巴西		C.Vale — Cooperativa Agroindustrial	I	32.4%	2019/2/17	2024/2/16
0207132901	巴西		Cooperativa Central Aurora Alimentos	I	20.2%	2019/2/17	2024/2/16
0207132901	巴西		LAR COOPERATIVA AGROINDUSTRIAL	I	20.2%	2019/2/17	2024/2/16
0207132901	巴西		Copacol — Cooperativa Agroindustrial Consolata	I	20.2%	2019/2/17	2024/2/16
0207132901	巴西		COOPAVEL COOPERATIVA AGROINDUSTRIAL	I	20.2%	2019/2/17	2024/2/16
0207132901	巴西		São Salvador Alimentos S/A	I	20.2%	2019/2/17	2024/2/16
0207132901	巴西		RIVELLI ALIMENTOS S/A	I	20.2%	2019/2/17	2024/2/16
0207132901	巴西		GONCALVES & TORTOLA S/A	I	20.2%	2019/2/17	2024/2/16
0207132901	巴西		COOPERATIVA AGROINDUSTRIAL COPAGRIL	I	20.2%	2019/2/17	2024/2/16
0207132901	巴西		VIBRA AGROINDUSTRIAL S/A	I	20.2%	2019/2/17	2024/2/16
0207132901	巴西		AGROSUL AGROAVICOLA INDUSTRIAL, S.A	I	20.2%	2019/2/17	2024/2/16
0207132901	巴西		KAEFER AGRO INDUSTRIAL LTDA	I	20.2%	2019/2/17	2024/2/16
0207132901	巴西		VOSSKO DO BRASIL ALIMENTOS CONGELADOS LTDA	I	20.2%	2019/2/17	2024/2/16
0207132901	巴西		AVENORTE AVICOLA CIANORTE LTDA.	I	20.2%	2019/2/17	2024/2/16
0207132901	巴西		ADORO S/A	I	20.2%	2019/2/17	2024/2/16
0207132901	巴西		BONASA ALIMENTOS SA	I	20.2%	2019/2/17	2024/2/16
0207132901	巴西		FLAMBOIÃ ALIMENTOS LTDA	I	20.2%	2019/2/17	2024/2/16
0207132901	巴西		FRIGORIFICO NOVA ARAÇÁ LTDA	I	20.2%	2019/2/17	2024/2/16
0207132901	巴西		RIO BRANCO ALIMENTOS S.A.	I	20.2%	2019/2/17	2024/2/16
0207132901	巴西		ZANCHETTA ALIMENTOS LTDA	I	20.2%	2019/2/17	2024/2/16
0207132901	巴西		AGRODANIELI INDÚSTRIA E COMÉRCIO LTDA.	I	20.2%	2019/2/17	2024/2/16
0207132901	巴西		BELLO ALIMENTOS LTDA.	I	20.2%	2019/2/17	2024/2/16
0207132901	巴西		COASUL COOPERATIVA AGROINDUSTRIAL	I	20.2%	2019/2/17	2024/2/16
0207132901	巴西		COOPERATIVA LANGUIRU LTDA	I	20.2%	2019/2/17	2024/2/16
0207132901	巴西		All others	I	32.4%	2019/2/17	2024/2/16
0207132901	巴西		SHB COMERCIO E INDUSTRIA DE ALIMENTOS S.A.	I	25.8%	2019/2/17	2024/2/16
0207132901	巴西		COMPANHIA MINUANO DE ALIMENTOS	I	25.8%	2019/2/17	2024/2/16
0207132901	国(地)别不详的	国(地)别不详的		I	32.4%	2019/2/17	2024/2/16
0207132902	巴西		SEARA ALIMENTOS LTDA	I	17.8%	2019/2/17	2024/2/16
0207132902	巴西		JBS AVES LTDA	I	17.8%	2019/2/17	2024/2/16
0207132902	巴西		SEARA COMERCIO DE ALIMENTOS LTDA	I	17.8%	2019/2/17	2024/2/16
0207132902	巴西		AGRICOLA JANDELLE S/A	I	17.8%	2019/2/17	2024/2/16
0207132902	巴西		BRF S.A.	I	25.8%	2019/2/17	2024/2/16
0207132902	巴西		C.Vale — Cooperativa Agroindustrial	I	32.4%	2019/2/17	2024/2/16
0207132902	巴西		Cooperativa Central Aurora Alimentos	I	20.2%	2019/2/17	2024/2/16
0207132902	巴西		LAR COOPERATIVA AGROINDUSTRIAL	I	20.2%	2019/2/17	2024/2/16
0207132902	巴西		Copacol — Cooperativa Agroindustrial Consolata	I	20.2%	2019/2/17	2024/2/16
0207132902	巴西		COOPAVEL COOPERATIVA AGROINDUSTRIAL	I	20.2%	2019/2/17	2024/2/16
0207132902	巴西		São Salvador Alimentos S/A	I	20.2%	2019/2/17	2024/2/16
0207132902	巴西		RIVELLI ALIMENTOS S/A	I	20.2%	2019/2/17	2024/2/16
0207132902	巴西		GONCALVES & TORTOLA S/A	I	20.2%	2019/2/17	2024/2/16
0207132902	巴西		COOPERATIVA AGROINDUSTRIAL COPAGRIL	I	20.2%	2019/2/17	2024/2/16
0207132902	巴西		VIBRA AGROINDUSTRIAL S/A	I	20.2%	2019/2/17	2024/2/16
0207132902	巴西		AGROSUL AGROAVICOLA INDUSTRIAL, S.A	I	20.2%	2019/2/17	2024/2/16
0207132902	巴西		KAEFER AGRO INDUSTRIAL LTDA	I	20.2%	2019/2/17	2024/2/16
0207132902	巴西		VOSSKO DO BRASIL ALIMENTOS CONGELADOS LTDA	I	20.2%	2019/2/17	2024/2/16

HS编码	原产国名称	厂商中文名称	厂商英文名称	税种代码	税率	起始日期	截止日期
0207132902	巴西		AVENORTE AVICOLA CIANORTE LTDA.	I	20.2%	2019/2/17	2024/2/16
0207132902	巴西		ADORO S/A	I	20.2%	2019/2/17	2024/2/16
0207132902	巴西		BONASA ALIMENTOS SA	I	20.2%	2019/2/17	2024/2/16
0207132902	巴西		FLAMBOIÃ ALIMENTOS LTDA	I	20.2%	2019/2/17	2024/2/16
0207132902	巴西		FRIGORIFICO NOVA ARAÇÁ LTDA	I	20.2%	2019/2/17	2024/2/16
0207132902	巴西		RIO BRANCO ALIMENTOS S.A.	I	20.2%	2019/2/17	2024/2/16
0207132902	巴西		ZANCHETTA ALIMENTOS LTDA	I	20.2%	2019/2/17	2024/2/16
0207132902	巴西		AGRODANIELI INDÚSTRIA E COMÉRCIO LTDA.	I	20.2%	2019/2/17	2024/2/16
0207132902	巴西		BELLO ALIMENTOS LTDA.	I	20.2%	2019/2/17	2024/2/16
0207132902	巴西		COASUL COOPERATIVA AGROINDUSTRIAL	I	20.2%	2019/2/17	2024/2/16
0207132902	巴西		COOPERATIVA LANGUIRU LTDA	I	20.2%	2019/2/17	2024/2/16
0207132902	巴西		All others	I	32.4%	2019/2/17	2024/2/16
0207132902	巴西		SHB COMERCIO E INDUSTRIA DE ALIMENTOS S.A.	I	25.8%	2019/2/17	2024/2/16
0207132902	巴西		COMPANHIA MINUANO DE ALIMENTOS	I	25.8%	2019/2/17	2024/2/16
0207132902	国(地)别不详的	国(地)别不详的		I	32.4%	2019/2/17	2024/2/16
0207132990	巴西		SEARA ALIMENTOS LTDA	I	17.8%	2019/2/17	2024/2/16
0207132990	巴西		JBS AVES LTDA	I	17.8%	2019/2/17	2024/2/16
0207132990	巴西		SEARA COMERCIO DE ALIMENTOS LTDA	I	17.8%	2019/2/17	2024/2/16
0207132990	巴西		AGRICOLA JANDELLE S/A	I	17.8%	2019/2/17	2024/2/16
0207132990	巴西		BRF S.A.	I	25.8%	2019/2/17	2024/2/16
0207132990	巴西		C.Vale — Cooperativa Agroindustrial	I	32.4%	2019/2/17	2024/2/16
0207132990	巴西		Cooperativa Central Aurora Alimentos	I	20.2%	2019/2/17	2024/2/16
0207132990	巴西		LAR COOPERATIVA AGROINDUSTRIAL	I	20.2%	2019/2/17	2024/2/16
0207132990	巴西		Copacol — Cooperativa Agroindustrial Consolata	I	20.2%	2019/2/17	2024/2/16
0207132990	巴西		COOPAVEL COOPERATIVA AGROINDUSTRIAL	I	20.2%	2019/2/17	2024/2/16
0207132990	巴西		São Salvador Alimentos S/A	I	20.2%	2019/2/17	2024/2/16
0207132990	巴西		RIVELLI ALIMENTOS S/A	I	20.2%	2019/2/17	2024/2/16
0207132990	巴西		GONCALVES & TORTOLA S/A	I	20.2%	2019/2/17	2024/2/16
0207132990	巴西		COOPERATIVA AGROINDUSTRIAL COPAGRIL	I	20.2%	2019/2/17	2024/2/16
0207132990	巴西		VIBRA AGROINDUSTRIAL S/A	I	20.2%	2019/2/17	2024/2/16
0207132990	巴西		AGROSUL AGROAVICOLA INDUSTRIAL, S.A	I	20.2%	2019/2/17	2024/2/16
0207132990	巴西		KAEFER AGRO INDUSTRIAL LTDA	I	20.2%	2019/2/17	2024/2/16
0207132990	巴西		VOSSKO DO BRASIL ALIMENTOS CONGELADOS LTDA	I	20.2%	2019/2/17	2024/2/16
0207132990	巴西		AVENORTE AVICOLA CIANORTE LTDA.	I	20.2%	2019/2/17	2024/2/16
0207132990	巴西		ADORO S/A	I	20.2%	2019/2/17	2024/2/16
0207132990	巴西		BONASA ALIMENTOS SA	I	20.2%	2019/2/17	2024/2/16
0207132990	巴西		FLAMBOIÃ ALIMENTOS LTDA	I	20.2%	2019/2/17	2024/2/16
0207132990	巴西		FRIGORIFICO NOVA ARAÇÁ LTDA	I	20.2%	2019/2/17	2024/2/16
0207132990	巴西		RIO BRANCO ALIMENTOS S.A.	I	20.2%	2019/2/17	2024/2/16
0207132990	巴西		ZANCHETTA ALIMENTOS LTDA	I	20.2%	2019/2/17	2024/2/16
0207132990	巴西		AGRODANIELI INDÚSTRIA E COMÉRCIO LTDA.	I	20.2%	2019/2/17	2024/2/16
0207132990	巴西		BELLO ALIMENTOS LTDA.	I	20.2%	2019/2/17	2024/2/16
0207132990	巴西		COASUL COOPERATIVA AGROINDUSTRIAL	I	20.2%	2019/2/17	2024/2/16
0207132990	巴西		COOPERATIVA LANGUIRU LTDA	I	20.2%	2019/2/17	2024/2/16
0207132990	巴西		All others	I	32.4%	2019/2/17	2024/2/16
0207132990	巴西		SHB COMERCIO E INDUSTRIA DE ALIMENTOS S.A.	I	25.8%	2019/2/17	2024/2/16
0207132990	巴西		COMPANHIA MINUANO DE ALIMENTOS	I	25.8%	2019/2/17	2024/2/16
0207132990	国(地)别不详的	国(地)别不详的		I	32.4%	2019/2/17	2024/2/16
0207141100	巴西		SEARA ALIMENTOS LTDA	I	17.8%	2019/2/17	2024/2/16
0207141100	巴西		JBS AVES LTDA	I	17.8%	2019/2/17	2024/2/16
0207141100	巴西		SEARA COMERCIO DE ALIMENTOS LTDA	I	17.8%	2019/2/17	2024/2/16
0207141100	巴西		AGRICOLA JANDELLE S/A	I	17.8%	2019/2/17	2024/2/16
0207141100	巴西		BRF S.A.	I	25.8%	2019/2/17	2024/2/16
0207141100	巴西		C.Vale — Cooperativa Agroindustrial	I	32.4%	2019/2/17	2024/2/16
0207141100	巴西		Cooperativa Central Aurora Alimentos	I	20.2%	2019/2/17	2024/2/16
0207141100	巴西		LAR COOPERATIVA AGROINDUSTRIAL	I	20.2%	2019/2/17	2024/2/16
0207141100	巴西		Copacol — Cooperativa Agroindustrial Consolata	I	20.2%	2019/2/17	2024/2/16
0207141100	巴西		COOPAVEL COOPERATIVA AGROINDUSTRIAL	I	20.2%	2019/2/17	2024/2/16
0207141100	巴西		São Salvador Alimentos S/A	I	20.2%	2019/2/17	2024/2/16
0207141100	巴西		RIVELLI ALIMENTOS S/A	I	20.2%	2019/2/17	2024/2/16
0207141100	巴西		GONCALVES & TORTOLA S/A	I	20.2%	2019/2/17	2024/2/16
0207141100	巴西		COOPERATIVA AGROINDUSTRIAL COPAGRIL	I	20.2%	2019/2/17	2024/2/16
0207141100	巴西		VIBRA AGROINDUSTRIAL S/A	I	20.2%	2019/2/17	2024/2/16
0207141100	巴西		AGROSUL AGROAVICOLA INDUSTRIAL, S.A	I	20.2%	2019/2/17	2024/2/16

HS 编码	原产国名称	厂商中文名称	厂商英文名称	税种代码	税率	起始日期	截止日期
0207141100	巴西		KAEFER AGRO INDUSTRIAL LTDA	I	20.2%	2019/2/17	2024/2/16
0207141100	巴西		VOSSKO DO BRASIL ALIMENTOS CONGELADOS LTDA	I	20.2%	2019/2/17	2024/2/16
0207141100	巴西		AVENORTE AVICOLA CIANORTE LTDA.	I	20.2%	2019/2/17	2024/2/16
0207141100	巴西		ADORO S/A	I	20.2%	2019/2/17	2024/2/16
0207141100	巴西		BONASA ALIMENTOS SA	I	20.2%	2019/2/17	2024/2/16
0207141100	巴西		FLAMBOIÃ ALIMENTOS LTDA	I	20.2%	2019/2/17	2024/2/16
0207141100	巴西		FRIGORIFICO NOVA ARAÇÁ LTDA	I	20.2%	2019/2/17	2024/2/16
0207141100	巴西		RIO BRANCO ALIMENTOS S.A.	I	20.2%	2019/2/17	2024/2/16
0207141100	巴西		ZANCHETTA ALIMENTOS LTDA	I	20.2%	2019/2/17	2024/2/16
0207141100	巴西		AGRODANIELI INDÚSTRIA E COMÉRCIO LTDA.	I	20.2%	2019/2/17	2024/2/16
0207141100	巴西		BELLO ALIMENTOS LTDA.	I	20.2%	2019/2/17	2024/2/16
0207141100	巴西		COASUL COOPERATIVA AGROINDUSTRIAL	I	20.2%	2019/2/17	2024/2/16
0207141100	巴西		COOPERATIVA LANGUIRU LTDA	I	20.2%	2019/2/17	2024/2/16
0207141100	巴西		All others	I	32.4%	2019/2/17	2024/2/16
0207141100	巴西		SHB COMERCIO E INDUSTRIA DE ALIMENTOS S.A.	I	25.8%	2019/2/17	2024/2/16
0207141100	巴西		COMPANHIA MINUANO DE ALIMENTOS	I	25.8%	2019/2/17	2024/2/16
0207141100	国(地)别不详的	国(地)别不详的		I	32.4%	2019/2/17	2024/2/16
0207141900	巴西		SEARA ALIMENTOS LTDA	I	17.8%	2019/2/17	2024/2/16
0207141900	巴西		JBS AVES LTDA	I	17.8%	2019/2/17	2024/2/16
0207141900	巴西		SEARA COMERCIO DE ALIMENTOS LTDA	I	17.8%	2019/2/17	2024/2/16
0207141900	巴西		AGRICOLA JANDELLE S/A	I	17.8%	2019/2/17	2024/2/16
0207141900	巴西		BRF S.A.	I	25.8%	2019/2/17	2024/2/16
0207141900	巴西		C.Vale — Cooperativa Agroindustrial	I	32.4%	2019/2/17	2024/2/16
0207141900	巴西		Cooperativa Central Aurora Alimentos	I	20.2%	2019/2/17	2024/2/16
0207141900	巴西		LAR COOPERATIVA AGROINDUSTRIAL	I	20.2%	2019/2/17	2024/2/16
0207141900	巴西		Copacol — Cooperativa Agroindustrial Consolata	I	20.2%	2019/2/17	2024/2/16
0207141900	巴西		COOPAVEL COOPERATIVA AGROINDUSTRIAL	I	20.2%	2019/2/17	2024/2/16
0207141900	巴西		São Salvador Alimentos S/A	I	20.2%	2019/2/17	2024/2/16
0207141900	巴西		RIVELLI ALIMENTOS S/A	I	20.2%	2019/2/17	2024/2/16
0207141900	巴西		GONCALVES & TORTOLA S/A	I	20.2%	2019/2/17	2024/2/16
0207141900	巴西		COOPERATIVA AGROINDUSTRIAL COPAGRIL	I	20.2%	2019/2/17	2024/2/16
0207141900	巴西		VIBRA AGROINDUSTRIAL S/A	I	20.2%	2019/2/17	2024/2/16
0207141900	巴西		AGROSUL AGROAVICOLA INDUSTRIAL, S.A	I	20.2%	2019/2/17	2024/2/16
0207141900	巴西		KAEFER AGRO INDUSTRIAL LTDA	I	20.2%	2019/2/17	2024/2/16
0207141900	巴西		VOSSKO DO BRASIL ALIMENTOS CONGELADOS LTDA	I	20.2%	2019/2/17	2024/2/16
0207141900	巴西		AVENORTE AVICOLA CIANORTE LTDA.	I	20.2%	2019/2/17	2024/2/16
0207141900	巴西		ADORO S/A	I	20.2%	2019/2/17	2024/2/16
0207141900	巴西		BONASA ALIMENTOS SA	I	20.2%	2019/2/17	2024/2/16
0207141900	巴西		FLAMBOIÃ ALIMENTOS LTDA	I	20.2%	2019/2/17	2024/2/16
0207141900	巴西		FRIGORIFICO NOVA ARAÇÁ LTDA	I	20.2%	2019/2/17	2024/2/16
0207141900	巴西		RIO BRANCO ALIMENTOS S.A.	I	20.2%	2019/2/17	2024/2/16
0207141900	巴西		ZANCHETTA ALIMENTOS LTDA	I	20.2%	2019/2/17	2024/2/16
0207141900	巴西		AGRODANIELI INDÚSTRIA E COMÉRCIO LTDA.	I	20.2%	2019/2/17	2024/2/16
0207141900	巴西		BELLO ALIMENTOS LTDA.	I	20.2%	2019/2/17	2024/2/16
0207141900	巴西		COASUL COOPERATIVA AGROINDUSTRIAL	I	20.2%	2019/2/17	2024/2/16
0207141900	巴西		COOPERATIVA LANGUIRU LTDA	I	20.2%	2019/2/17	2024/2/16
0207141900	巴西		All others	I	32.4%	2019/2/17	2024/2/16
0207141900	巴西		SHB COMERCIO E INDUSTRIA DE ALIMENTOS S.A.	I	25.8%	2019/2/17	2024/2/16
0207141900	巴西		COMPANHIA MINUANO DE ALIMENTOS	I	25.8%	2019/2/17	2024/2/16
0207141900	国(地)别不详的	国(地)别不详的		I	32.4%	2019/2/17	2024/2/16
0207142101	巴西		SEARA ALIMENTOS LTDA	I	17.8%	2019/2/17	2024/2/16
0207142101	巴西		JBS AVES LTDA	I	17.8%	2019/2/17	2024/2/16
0207142101	巴西		SEARA COMERCIO DE ALIMENTOS LTDA	I	17.8%	2019/2/17	2024/2/16
0207142101	巴西		AGRICOLA JANDELLE S/A	I	17.8%	2019/2/17	2024/2/16
0207142101	巴西		BRF S.A.	I	25.8%	2019/2/17	2024/2/16
0207142101	巴西		C.Vale — Cooperativa Agroindustrial	I	32.4%	2019/2/17	2024/2/16
0207142101	巴西		Cooperativa Central Aurora Alimentos	I	20.2%	2019/2/17	2024/2/16
0207142101	巴西		LAR COOPERATIVA AGROINDUSTRIAL	I	20.2%	2019/2/17	2024/2/16
0207142101	巴西		Copacol — Cooperativa Agroindustrial Consolata	I	20.2%	2019/2/17	2024/2/16
0207142101	巴西		COOPAVEL COOPERATIVA AGROINDUSTRIAL	I	20.2%	2019/2/17	2024/2/16
0207142101	巴西		São Salvador Alimentos S/A	I	20.2%	2019/2/17	2024/2/16
0207142101	巴西		RIVELLI ALIMENTOS S/A	I	20.2%	2019/2/17	2024/2/16
0207142101	巴西		GONCALVES & TORTOLA S/A	I	20.2%	2019/2/17	2024/2/16
0207142101	巴西		COOPERATIVA AGROINDUSTRIAL COPAGRIL	I	20.2%	2019/2/17	2024/2/16

HS编码	原产国名称	厂商中文名称	厂商英文名称	税种代码	税率	起始日期	截止日期
0207142101	巴西		VIBRA AGROINDUSTRIAL S/A	I	20.2%	2019/2/17	2024/2/16
0207142101	巴西		AGROSUL AGROAVICOLA INDUSTRIAL, S.A	I	20.2%	2019/2/17	2024/2/16
0207142101	巴西		KAEFER AGRO INDUSTRIAL LTDA	I	20.2%	2019/2/17	2024/2/16
0207142101	巴西		VOSSKO DO BRASIL ALIMENTOS CONGELADOS LTDA	I	20.2%	2019/2/17	2024/2/16
0207142101	巴西		AVENORTE AVICOLA CIANORTE LTDA.	I	20.2%	2019/2/17	2024/2/16
0207142101	巴西		ADORO S/A	I	20.2%	2019/2/17	2024/2/16
0207142101	巴西		BONASA ALIMENTOS SA	I	20.2%	2019/2/17	2024/2/16
0207142101	巴西		FLAMBOIÃ ALIMENTOS LTDA	I	20.2%	2019/2/17	2024/2/16
0207142101	巴西		FRIGORIFICO NOVA ARAÇÁ LTDA	I	20.2%	2019/2/17	2024/2/16
0207142101	巴西		RIO BRANCO ALIMENTOS S.A.	I	20.2%	2019/2/17	2024/2/16
0207142101	巴西		ZANCHETTA ALIMENTOS LTDA	I	20.2%	2019/2/17	2024/2/16
0207142101	巴西		AGRODANIELI INDÚSTRIA E COMÉRCIO LTDA.	I	20.2%	2019/2/17	2024/2/16
0207142101	巴西		BELLO ALIMENTOS LTDA.	I	20.2%	2019/2/17	2024/2/16
0207142101	巴西		COASUL COOPERATIVA AGROINDUSTRIAL	I	20.2%	2019/2/17	2024/2/16
0207142101	巴西		COOPERATIVA LANGUIRU LTDA	I	20.2%	2019/2/17	2024/2/16
0207142101	巴西		All others	I	32.4%	2019/2/17	2024/2/16
0207142101	巴西		SHB COMERCIO E INDUSTRIA DE ALIMENTOS S.A.	I	25.8%	2019/2/17	2024/2/16
0207142101	巴西		COMPANHIA MINUANO DE ALIMENTOS	I	25.8%	2019/2/17	2024/2/16
0207142101	国(地)别不详的	国(地)别不详的		I	32.4%	2019/2/17	2024/2/16
0207142102	巴西		SEARA ALIMENTOS LTDA	I	17.8%	2019/2/17	2024/2/16
0207142102	巴西		JBS AVES LTDA	I	17.8%	2019/2/17	2024/2/16
0207142102	巴西		SEARA COMERCIO DE ALIMENTOS LTDA	I	17.8%	2019/2/17	2024/2/16
0207142102	巴西		AGRICOLA JANDELLE S/A	I	17.8%	2019/2/17	2024/2/16
0207142102	巴西		BRF S.A.	I	25.8%	2019/2/17	2024/2/16
0207142102	巴西		C.Vale — Cooperativa Agroindustrial	I	32.4%	2019/2/17	2024/2/16
0207142102	巴西		Cooperativa Central Aurora Alimentos	I	20.2%	2019/2/17	2024/2/16
0207142102	巴西		LAR COOPERATIVA AGROINDUSTRIAL	I	20.2%	2019/2/17	2024/2/16
0207142102	巴西		Copacol — Cooperativa Agroindustrial Consolata	I	20.2%	2019/2/17	2024/2/16
0207142102	巴西		COOPAVEL COOPERATIVA AGROINDUSTRIAL	I	20.2%	2019/2/17	2024/2/16
0207142102	巴西		São Salvador Alimentos S/A	I	20.2%	2019/2/17	2024/2/16
0207142102	巴西		RIVELLI ALIMENTOS S/A	I	20.2%	2019/2/17	2024/2/16
0207142102	巴西		GONCALVES & TORTOLA S/A	I	20.2%	2019/2/17	2024/2/16
0207142102	巴西		COOPERATIVA AGROINDUSTRIAL COPAGRIL	I	20.2%	2019/2/17	2024/2/16
0207142102	巴西		VIBRA AGROINDUSTRIAL S/A	I	20.2%	2019/2/17	2024/2/16
0207142102	巴西		AGROSUL AGROAVICOLA INDUSTRIAL, S.A	I	20.2%	2019/2/17	2024/2/16
0207142102	巴西		KAEFER AGRO INDUSTRIAL LTDA	I	20.2%	2019/2/17	2024/2/16
0207142102	巴西		VOSSKO DO BRASIL ALIMENTOS CONGELADOS LTDA	I	20.2%	2019/2/17	2024/2/16
0207142102	巴西		AVENORTE AVICOLA CIANORTE LTDA.	I	20.2%	2019/2/17	2024/2/16
0207142102	巴西		ADORO S/A	I	20.2%	2019/2/17	2024/2/16
0207142102	巴西		BONASA ALIMENTOS SA	I	20.2%	2019/2/17	2024/2/16
0207142102	巴西		FLAMBOIÃ ALIMENTOS LTDA	I	20.2%	2019/2/17	2024/2/16
0207142102	巴西		FRIGORIFICO NOVA ARAÇÁ LTDA	I	20.2%	2019/2/17	2024/2/16
0207142102	巴西		RIO BRANCO ALIMENTOS S.A.	I	20.2%	2019/2/17	2024/2/16
0207142102	巴西		ZANCHETTA ALIMENTOS LTDA	I	20.2%	2019/2/17	2024/2/16
0207142102	巴西		AGRODANIELI INDÚSTRIA E COMÉRCIO LTDA.	I	20.2%	2019/2/17	2024/2/16
0207142102	巴西		BELLO ALIMENTOS LTDA.	I	20.2%	2019/2/17	2024/2/16
0207142102	巴西		COASUL COOPERATIVA AGROINDUSTRIAL	I	20.2%	2019/2/17	2024/2/16
0207142102	巴西		COOPERATIVA LANGUIRU LTDA	I	20.2%	2019/2/17	2024/2/16
0207142102	巴西		All others	I	32.4%	2019/2/17	2024/2/16
0207142102	巴西		SHB COMERCIO E INDUSTRIA DE ALIMENTOS S.A.	I	25.8%	2019/2/17	2024/2/16
0207142102	巴西		COMPANHIA MINUANO DE ALIMENTOS	I	25.8%	2019/2/17	2024/2/16
0207142102	国(地)别不详的	国(地)别不详的		I	32.4%	2019/2/17	2024/2/16
0207142103	巴西		SEARA ALIMENTOS LTDA	I	17.8%	2019/2/17	2024/2/16
0207142103	巴西		JBS AVES LTDA	I	17.8%	2019/2/17	2024/2/16
0207142103	巴西		SEARA COMERCIO DE ALIMENTOS LTDA	I	17.8%	2019/2/17	2024/2/16
0207142103	巴西		AGRICOLA JANDELLE S/A	I	17.8%	2019/2/17	2024/2/16
0207142103	巴西		BRF S.A.	I	25.8%	2019/2/17	2024/2/16
0207142103	巴西		C.Vale — Cooperativa Agroindustrial	I	32.4%	2019/2/17	2024/2/16
0207142103	巴西		Cooperativa Central Aurora Alimentos	I	20.2%	2019/2/17	2024/2/16
0207142103	巴西		LAR COOPERATIVA AGROINDUSTRIAL	I	20.2%	2019/2/17	2024/2/16
0207142103	巴西		Copacol — Cooperativa Agroindustrial Consolata	I	20.2%	2019/2/17	2024/2/16
0207142103	巴西		COOPAVEL COOPERATIVA AGROINDUSTRIAL	I	20.2%	2019/2/17	2024/2/16
0207142103	巴西		São Salvador Alimentos S/A	I	20.2%	2019/2/17	2024/2/16
0207142103	巴西		RIVELLI ALIMENTOS S/A	I	20.2%	2019/2/17	2024/2/16

HS编码	原产国名称	厂商中文名称	厂商英文名称	税种代码	税率	起始日期	截止日期
0207142103	巴西		GONCALVES & TORTOLA S/A	I	20.2%	2019/2/17	2024/2/16
0207142103	巴西		COOPERATIVA AGROINDUSTRIAL COPAGRIL	I	20.2%	2019/2/17	2024/2/16
0207142103	巴西		VIBRA AGROINDUSTRIAL S/A	I	20.2%	2019/2/17	2024/2/16
0207142103	巴西		AGROSUL AGROAVICOLA INDUSTRIAL, S. A	I	20.2%	2019/2/17	2024/2/16
0207142103	巴西		KAEFER AGRO INDUSTRIAL LTDA	I	20.2%	2019/2/17	2024/2/16
0207142103	巴西		VOSSKO DO BRASIL ALIMENTOS CONGELADOS LTDA	I	20.2%	2019/2/17	2024/2/16
0207142103	巴西		AVENORTE AVICOLA CIANORTE LTDA.	I	20.2%	2019/2/17	2024/2/16
0207142103	巴西		ADORO S/A	I	20.2%	2019/2/17	2024/2/16
0207142103	巴西		BONASA ALIMENTOS SA	I	20.2%	2019/2/17	2024/2/16
0207142103	巴西		FLAMBOIÃ ALIMENTOS LTDA	I	20.2%	2019/2/17	2024/2/16
0207142103	巴西		FRIGORIFICO NOVA ARAÇÁ LTDA	I	20.2%	2019/2/17	2024/2/16
0207142103	巴西		RIO BRANCO ALIMENTOS S.A.	I	20.2%	2019/2/17	2024/2/16
0207142103	巴西		ZANCHETTA ALIMENTOS LTDA	I	20.2%	2019/2/17	2024/2/16
0207142103	巴西		AGRODANIELI INDÜSTRIA E COMÉRCIO LTDA.	I	20.2%	2019/2/17	2024/2/16
0207142103	巴西		BELLO ALIMENTOS LTDA.	I	20.2%	2019/2/17	2024/2/16
0207142103	巴西		COASUL COOPERATIVA AGROINDUSTRIAL	I	20.2%	2019/2/17	2024/2/16
0207142103	巴西		COOPERATIVA LANGUIRU LTDA	I	20.2%	2019/2/17	2024/2/16
0207142103	巴西		All others	I	32.4%	2019/2/17	2024/2/16
0207142103	巴西		SHB COMERCIO E INDUSTRIA DE ALIMENTOS S.A.	I	25.8%	2019/2/17	2024/2/16
0207142103	巴西		COMPANHIA MINUANO DE ALIMENTOS	I	25.8%	2019/2/17	2024/2/16
0207142103	国(地)别不详的	国(地)别不详的		I	32.4%	2019/2/17	2024/2/16
0207142104	巴西		SEARA ALIMENTOS LTDA	I	17.8%	2019/2/17	2024/2/16
0207142104	巴西		JBS AVES LTDA	I	17.8%	2019/2/17	2024/2/16
0207142104	巴西		SEARA COMERCIO DE ALIMENTOS LTDA	I	17.8%	2019/2/17	2024/2/16
0207142104	巴西		AGRICOLA JANDELLE S/A	I	17.8%	2019/2/17	2024/2/16
0207142104	巴西		BRF S.A.	I	25.8%	2019/2/17	2024/2/16
0207142104	巴西		C.Vale — Cooperativa Agroindustrial	I	32.4%	2019/2/17	2024/2/16
0207142104	巴西		Cooperativa Central Aurora Alimentos	I	20.2%	2019/2/17	2024/2/16
0207142104	巴西		LAR COOPERATIVA AGROINDUSTRIAL	I	20.2%	2019/2/17	2024/2/16
0207142104	巴西		Copacol — Cooperativa Agroindustrial Consolata	I	20.2%	2019/2/17	2024/2/16
0207142104	巴西		COOPAVEL COOPERATIVA AGROINDUSTRIAL	I	20.2%	2019/2/17	2024/2/16
0207142104	巴西		São Salvador Alimentos S/A	I	20.2%	2019/2/17	2024/2/16
0207142104	巴西		RIVELLI ALIMENTOS S/A	I	20.2%	2019/2/17	2024/2/16
0207142104	巴西		GONCALVES & TORTOLA S/A	I	20.2%	2019/2/17	2024/2/16
0207142104	巴西		COOPERATIVA AGROINDUSTRIAL COPAGRIL	I	20.2%	2019/2/17	2024/2/16
0207142104	巴西		VIBRA AGROINDUSTRIAL S/A	I	20.2%	2019/2/17	2024/2/16
0207142104	巴西		AGROSUL AGROAVICOLA INDUSTRIAL, S. A	I	20.2%	2019/2/17	2024/2/16
0207142104	巴西		KAEFER AGRO INDUSTRIAL LTDA	I	20.2%	2019/2/17	2024/2/16
0207142104	巴西		VOSSKO DO BRASIL ALIMENTOS CONGELADOS LTDA	I	20.2%	2019/2/17	2024/2/16
0207142104	巴西		AVENORTE AVICOLA CIANORTE LTDA.	I	20.2%	2019/2/17	2024/2/16
0207142104	巴西		ADORO S/A	I	20.2%	2019/2/17	2024/2/16
0207142104	巴西		BONASA ALIMENTOS SA	I	20.2%	2019/2/17	2024/2/16
0207142104	巴西		FLAMBOIÃ ALIMENTOS LTDA	I	20.2%	2019/2/17	2024/2/16
0207142104	巴西		FRIGORIFICO NOVA ARAÇÁ LTDA	I	20.2%	2019/2/17	2024/2/16
0207142104	巴西		RIO BRANCO ALIMENTOS S.A.	I	20.2%	2019/2/17	2024/2/16
0207142104	巴西		ZANCHETTA ALIMENTOS LTDA	I	20.2%	2019/2/17	2024/2/16
0207142104	巴西		AGRODANIELI INDÜSTRIA E COMÉRCIO LTDA.	I	20.2%	2019/2/17	2024/2/16
0207142104	巴西		BELLO ALIMENTOS LTDA.	I	20.2%	2019/2/17	2024/2/16
0207142104	巴西		COASUL COOPERATIVA AGROINDUSTRIAL	I	20.2%	2019/2/17	2024/2/16
0207142104	巴西		COOPERATIVA LANGUIRU LTDA	I	20.2%	2019/2/17	2024/2/16
0207142104	巴西		All others	I	32.4%	2019/2/17	2024/2/16
0207142104	巴西		SHB COMERCIO E INDUSTRIA DE ALIMENTOS S.A.	I	25.8%	2019/2/17	2024/2/16
0207142104	巴西		COMPANHIA MINUANO DE ALIMENTOS	I	25.8%	2019/2/17	2024/2/16
0207142104	国(地)别不详的	国(地)别不详的		I	32.4%	2019/2/17	2024/2/16
0207142200	巴西		SEARA ALIMENTOS LTDA	I	17.8%	2019/2/17	2024/2/16
0207142200	巴西		JBS AVES LTDA	I	17.8%	2019/2/17	2024/2/16
0207142200	巴西		SEARA COMERCIO DE ALIMENTOS LTDA	I	17.8%	2019/2/17	2024/2/16
0207142200	巴西		AGRICOLA JANDELLE S/A	I	17.8%	2019/2/17	2024/2/16
0207142200	巴西		BRF S.A.	I	25.8%	2019/2/17	2024/2/16
0207142200	巴西		C.Vale — Cooperativa Agroindustrial	I	32.4%	2019/2/17	2024/2/16
0207142200	巴西		Cooperativa Central Aurora Alimentos	I	20.2%	2019/2/17	2024/2/16
0207142200	巴西		LAR COOPERATIVA AGROINDUSTRIAL	I	20.2%	2019/2/17	2024/2/16
0207142200	巴西		Copacol — Cooperativa Agroindustrial Consolata	I	20.2%	2019/2/17	2024/2/16

HS编码	原产国名称	厂商中文名称	厂商英文名称	税种代码	税率	起始日期	截止日期
0207142200	巴西		COOPAVEL COOPERATIVA AGROINDUSTRIAL	I	20.2%	2019/2/17	2024/2/16
0207142200	巴西		São Salvador Alimentos S/A	I	20.2%	2019/2/17	2024/2/16
0207142200	巴西		RIVELLI ALIMENTOS S/A	I	20.2%	2019/2/17	2024/2/16
0207142200	巴西		GONCALVES & TORTOLA S/A	I	20.2%	2019/2/17	2024/2/16
0207142200	巴西		COOPERATIVA AGROINDUSTRIAL COPAGRIL	I	20.2%	2019/2/17	2024/2/16
0207142200	巴西		VIBRA AGROINDUSTRIAL S/A	I	20.2%	2019/2/17	2024/2/16
0207142200	巴西		AGROSUL AGROAVICOLA INDUSTRIAL, S.A	I	20.2%	2019/2/17	2024/2/16
0207142200	巴西		KAEFER AGRO INDUSTRIAL LTDA	I	20.2%	2019/2/17	2024/2/16
0207142200	巴西		VOSSKO DO BRASIL ALIMENTOS CONGELADOS LTDA	I	20.2%	2019/2/17	2024/2/16
0207142200	巴西		AVENORTE AVICOLA CIANORTE LTDA.	I	20.2%	2019/2/17	2024/2/16
0207142200	巴西		ADORO S/A	I	20.2%	2019/2/17	2024/2/16
0207142200	巴西		BONASA ALIMENTOS SA	I	20.2%	2019/2/17	2024/2/16
0207142200	巴西		FLAMBOIÃ ALIMENTOS LTDA	I	20.2%	2019/2/17	2024/2/16
0207142200	巴西		FRIGORIFICO NOVA ARAÇÁ LTDA	I	20.2%	2019/2/17	2024/2/16
0207142200	巴西		RIO BRANCO ALIMENTOS S.A.	I	20.2%	2019/2/17	2024/2/16
0207142200	巴西		ZANCHETTA ALIMENTOS LTDA	I	20.2%	2019/2/17	2024/2/16
0207142200	巴西		AGRODANIELI INDÚSTRIA E COMÉRCIO LTDA.	I	20.2%	2019/2/17	2024/2/16
0207142200	巴西		BELLO ALIMENTOS LTDA.	I	20.2%	2019/2/17	2024/2/16
0207142200	巴西		COASUL COOPERATIVA AGROINDUSTRIAL	I	20.2%	2019/2/17	2024/2/16
0207142200	巴西		COOPERATIVA LANGUIRU LTDA	I	20.2%	2019/2/17	2024/2/16
0207142200	巴西		All others	I	32.4%	2019/2/17	2024/2/16
0207142200	巴西		SHB COMERCIO E INDUSTRIA DE ALIMENTOS S.A.	I	25.8%	2019/2/17	2024/2/16
0207142200	巴西		COMPANHIA MINUANO DE ALIMENTOS	I	25.8%	2019/2/17	2024/2/16
0207142200	国(地)别不详的	国(地)别不详的		I	32.4%	2019/2/17	2024/2/16
0207142901	巴西		SEARA ALIMENTOS LTDA	I	17.8%	2019/2/17	2024/2/16
0207142901	巴西		JBS AVES LTDA	I	17.8%	2019/2/17	2024/2/16
0207142901	巴西		SEARA COMERCIO DE ALIMENTOS LTDA	I	17.8%	2019/2/17	2024/2/16
0207142901	巴西		AGRICOLA JANDELLE S/A	I	17.8%	2019/2/17	2024/2/16
0207142901	巴西		BRF S.A.	I	25.8%	2019/2/17	2024/2/16
0207142901	巴西		C.Vale — Cooperativa Agroindustrial	I	32.4%	2019/2/17	2024/2/16
0207142901	巴西		Cooperativa Central Aurora Alimentos	I	20.2%	2019/2/17	2024/2/16
0207142901	巴西		LAR COOPERATIVA AGROINDUSTRIAL	I	20.2%	2019/2/17	2024/2/16
0207142901	巴西		Copacol — Cooperativa Agroindustrial Consolata	I	20.2%	2019/2/17	2024/2/16
0207142901	巴西		COOPAVEL COOPERATIVA AGROINDUSTRIAL	I	20.2%	2019/2/17	2024/2/16
0207142901	巴西		São Salvador Alimentos S/A	I	20.2%	2019/2/17	2024/2/16
0207142901	巴西		RIVELLI ALIMENTOS S/A	I	20.2%	2019/2/17	2024/2/16
0207142901	巴西		GONCALVES & TORTOLA S/A	I	20.2%	2019/2/17	2024/2/16
0207142901	巴西		COOPERATIVA AGROINDUSTRIAL COPAGRIL	I	20.2%	2019/2/17	2024/2/16
0207142901	巴西		VIBRA AGROINDUSTRIAL S/A	I	20.2%	2019/2/17	2024/2/16
0207142901	巴西		AGROSUL AGROAVICOLA INDUSTRIAL, S.A	I	20.2%	2019/2/17	2024/2/16
0207142901	巴西		KAEFER AGRO INDUSTRIAL LTDA	I	20.2%	2019/2/17	2024/2/16
0207142901	巴西		VOSSKO DO BRASIL ALIMENTOS CONGELADOS LTDA	I	20.2%	2019/2/17	2024/2/16
0207142901	巴西		AVENORTE AVICOLA CIANORTE LTDA.	I	20.2%	2019/2/17	2024/2/16
0207142901	巴西		ADORO S/A	I	20.2%	2019/2/17	2024/2/16
0207142901	巴西		BONASA ALIMENTOS SA	I	20.2%	2019/2/17	2024/2/16
0207142901	巴西		FLAMBOIÃ ALIMENTOS LTDA	I	20.2%	2019/2/17	2024/2/16
0207142901	巴西		FRIGORIFICO NOVA ARAÇÁ LTDA	I	20.2%	2019/2/17	2024/2/16
0207142901	巴西		RIO BRANCO ALIMENTOS S.A.	I	20.2%	2019/2/17	2024/2/16
0207142901	巴西		ZANCHETTA ALIMENTOS LTDA	I	20.2%	2019/2/17	2024/2/16
0207142901	巴西		AGRODANIELI INDÚSTRIA E COMÉRCIO LTDA.	I	20.2%	2019/2/17	2024/2/16
0207142901	巴西		BELLO ALIMENTOS LTDA.	I	20.2%	2019/2/17	2024/2/16
0207142901	巴西		COASUL COOPERATIVA AGROINDUSTRIAL	I	20.2%	2019/2/17	2024/2/16
0207142901	巴西		COOPERATIVA LANGUIRU LTDA	I	20.2%	2019/2/17	2024/2/16
0207142901	巴西		All others	I	32.4%	2019/2/17	2024/2/16
0207142901	巴西		SHB COMERCIO E INDUSTRIA DE ALIMENTOS S.A.	I	25.8%	2019/2/17	2024/2/16
0207142901	巴西		COMPANHIA MINUANO DE ALIMENTOS	I	25.8%	2019/2/17	2024/2/16
0207142901	国(地)别不详的	国(地)别不详的		I	32.4%	2019/2/17	2024/2/16
0207142902	巴西		SEARA ALIMENTOS LTDA	I	17.8%	2019/2/17	2024/2/16
0207142902	巴西		JBS AVES LTDA	I	17.8%	2019/2/17	2024/2/16
0207142902	巴西		SEARA COMERCIO DE ALIMENTOS LTDA	I	17.8%	2019/2/17	2024/2/16
0207142902	巴西		AGRICOLA JANDELLE S/A	I	17.8%	2019/2/17	2024/2/16
0207142902	巴西		BRF S.A.	I	25.8%	2019/2/17	2024/2/16
0207142902	巴西		C.Vale — Cooperativa Agroindustrial	I	32.4%	2019/2/17	2024/2/16

HS编码	原产国名称	厂商中文名称	厂商英文名称	税种代码	税率	起始日期	截止日期
0207142902	巴西		Cooperativa Central Aurora Alimentos	I	20.2%	2019/2/17	2024/2/16
0207142902	巴西		LAR COOPERATIVA AGROINDUSTRIAL	I	20.2%	2019/2/17	2024/2/16
0207142902	巴西		Copacol — Cooperativa Agroindustrial Consolata	I	20.2%	2019/2/17	2024/2/16
0207142902	巴西		COOPAVEL COOPERATIVA AGROINDUSTRIAL	I	20.2%	2019/2/17	2024/2/16
0207142902	巴西		São Salvador Alimentos S/A	I	20.2%	2019/2/17	2024/2/16
0207142902	巴西		RIVELLI ALIMENTOS S/A	I	20.2%	2019/2/17	2024/2/16
0207142902	巴西		GONCALVES & TORTOLA S/A	I	20.2%	2019/2/17	2024/2/16
0207142902	巴西		COOPERATIVA AGROINDUSTRIAL COPAGRIL	I	20.2%	2019/2/17	2024/2/16
0207142902	巴西		VIBRA AGROINDUSTRIAL S/A	I	20.2%	2019/2/17	2024/2/16
0207142902	巴西		AGROSUL AGROAVICOLA INDUSTRIAL, S. A	I	20.2%	2019/2/17	2024/2/16
0207142902	巴西		KAEFER AGRO INDUSTRIAL LTDA	I	20.2%	2019/2/17	2024/2/16
0207142902	巴西		VOSSKO DO BRASIL ALIMENTOS CONGELADOS LTDA	I	20.2%	2019/2/17	2024/2/16
0207142902	巴西		AVENORTE AVICOLA CIANORTE LTDA.	I	20.2%	2019/2/17	2024/2/16
0207142902	巴西		ADORO S/A	I	20.2%	2019/2/17	2024/2/16
0207142902	巴西		BONASA ALIMENTOS SA	I	20.2%	2019/2/17	2024/2/16
0207142902	巴西		FLAMBOIÃ ALIMENTOS LTDA	I	20.2%	2019/2/17	2024/2/16
0207142902	巴西		FRIGORIFICO NOVA ARAÇÁ LTDA	I	20.2%	2019/2/17	2024/2/16
0207142902	巴西		RIO BRANCO ALIMENTOS S.A.	I	20.2%	2019/2/17	2024/2/16
0207142902	巴西		ZANCHETTA ALIMENTOS LTDA	I	20.2%	2019/2/17	2024/2/16
0207142902	巴西		AGRODANIELI INDÚSTRIA E COMÉRCIO LTDA.	I	20.2%	2019/2/17	2024/2/16
0207142902	巴西		BELLO ALIMENTOS LTDA.	I	20.2%	2019/2/17	2024/2/16
0207142902	巴西		COASUL COOPERATIVA AGROINDUSTRIAL	I	20.2%	2019/2/17	2024/2/16
0207142902	巴西		COOPERATIVA LANGUIRU LTDA	I	20.2%	2019/2/17	2024/2/16
0207142902	巴西		All others	I	32.4%	2019/2/17	2024/2/16
0207142902	巴西		SHB COMERCIO E INDUSTRIA DE ALIMENTOS S.A.	I	25.8%	2019/2/17	2024/2/16
0207142902	巴西		COMPANHIA MINUANO DE ALIMENTOS	I	25.8%	2019/2/17	2024/2/16
0207142902	国(地)别不详的	国(地)别不详的		I	32.4%	2019/2/17	2024/2/16
0207142990	巴西		SEARA ALIMENTOS LTDA	I	17.8%	2019/2/17	2024/2/16
0207142990	巴西		JBS AVES LTDA	I	17.8%	2019/2/17	2024/2/16
0207142990	巴西		SEARA COMERCIO DE ALIMENTOS LTDA	I	17.8%	2019/2/17	2024/2/16
0207142990	巴西		AGRICOLA JANDELLE S/A	I	17.8%	2019/2/17	2024/2/16
0207142990	巴西		BRF S.A.	I	25.8%	2019/2/17	2024/2/16
0207142990	巴西		C.Vale — Cooperativa Agroindustrial	I	32.4%	2019/2/17	2024/2/16
0207142990	巴西		Cooperativa Central Aurora Alimentos	I	20.2%	2019/2/17	2024/2/16
0207142990	巴西		LAR COOPERATIVA AGROINDUSTRIAL	I	20.2%	2019/2/17	2024/2/16
0207142990	巴西		Copacol — Cooperativa Agroindustrial Consolata	I	20.2%	2019/2/17	2024/2/16
0207142990	巴西		COOPAVEL COOPERATIVA AGROINDUSTRIAL	I	20.2%	2019/2/17	2024/2/16
0207142990	巴西		São Salvador Alimentos S/A	I	20.2%	2019/2/17	2024/2/16
0207142990	巴西		RIVELLI ALIMENTOS S/A	I	20.2%	2019/2/17	2024/2/16
0207142990	巴西		GONCALVES & TORTOLA S/A	I	20.2%	2019/2/17	2024/2/16
0207142990	巴西		COOPERATIVA AGROINDUSTRIAL COPA GRIL	I	20.2%	2019/2/17	2024/2/16
0207142990	巴西		VIBRA AGROINDUSTRIAL S/A	I	20.2%	2019/2/17	2024/2/16
0207142990	巴西		AGROSUL AGROAVICOLA INDUSTRIAL, S. A	I	20.2%	2019/2/17	2024/2/16
0207142990	巴西		KAEFER AGRO INDUSTRIAL LTDA	I	20.2%	2019/2/17	2024/2/16
0207142990	巴西		VOSSKO DO BRASIL ALIMENTOS CONGELADOS LTDA	I	20.2%	2019/2/17	2024/2/16
0207142990	巴西		AVENORTE AVICOLA CIANORTE LTDA.	I	20.2%	2019/2/17	2024/2/16
0207142990	巴西		ADORO S/A	I	20.2%	2019/2/17	2024/2/16
0207142990	巴西		BONASA ALIMENTOS SA	I	20.2%	2019/2/17	2024/2/16
0207142990	巴西		FLAMBOIÃ ALIMENTOS LTDA	I	20.2%	2019/2/17	2024/2/16
0207142990	巴西		FRIGORIFICO NOVA ARAÇÁ LTDA	I	20.2%	2019/2/17	2024/2/16
0207142990	巴西		RIO BRANCO ALIMENTOS S.A.	I	20.2%	2019/2/17	2024/2/16
0207142990	巴西		ZANCHETTA ALIMENTOS LTDA	I	20.2%	2019/2/17	2024/2/16
0207142990	巴西		AGRODANIELI INDÚSTRIA E COMÉRCIO LTDA.	I	20.2%	2019/2/17	2024/2/16
0207142990	巴西		BELLO ALIMENTOS LTDA.	I	20.2%	2019/2/17	2024/2/16
0207142990	巴西		COASUL COOPERATIVA AGROINDUSTRIAL	I	20.2%	2019/2/17	2024/2/16
0207142990	巴西		COOPERATIVA LANGUIRU LTDA	I	20.2%	2019/2/17	2024/2/16
0207142990	巴西		All others	I	32.4%	2019/2/17	2024/2/16
0207142990	巴西		SHB COMERCIO E INDUSTRIA DE ALIMENTOS S.A.	I	25.8%	2019/2/17	2024/2/16
0207142990	巴西		COMPANHIA MINUANO DE ALIMENTOS	I	25.8%	2019/2/17	2024/2/16
0207142990	国(地)别不详的	国(地)别不详的		I	32.4%	2019/2/17	2024/2/16
0504002100	巴西		SEARA ALIMENTOS LTDA	I	17.8%	2019/2/17	2024/2/16
0504002100	巴西		JBS AVES LTDA	I	17.8%	2019/2/17	2024/2/16
0504002100	巴西		SEARA COMERCIO DE ALIMENTOS LTDA	I	17.8%	2019/2/17	2024/2/16

HS 编码	原产国名称	厂商中文名称	厂商英文名称	税种代码	税率	起始日期	截止日期
0504002100	巴西		AGRICOLA JANDELLE S/A	I	17.8%	2019/2/17	2024/2/16
0504002100	巴西		BRF S.A.	I	25.8%	2019/2/17	2024/2/16
0504002100	巴西		C.Vale — Cooperativa Agroindustrial	I	32.4%	2019/2/17	2024/2/16
0504002100	巴西		Cooperativa Central Aurora Alimentos	I	20.2%	2019/2/17	2024/2/16
0504002100	巴西		LAR COOPERATIVA AGROINDUSTRIAL	I	20.2%	2019/2/17	2024/2/16
0504002100	巴西		Copacol — Cooperativa Agroindustrial Consolata	I	20.2%	2019/2/17	2024/2/16
0504002100	巴西		COOPAVEL COOPERATIVA AGROINDUSTRIAL	I	20.2%	2019/2/17	2024/2/16
0504002100	巴西		São Salvador Alimentos S/A	I	20.2%	2019/2/17	2024/2/16
0504002100	巴西		RIVELLI ALIMENTOS S/A	I	20.2%	2019/2/17	2024/2/16
0504002100	巴西		GONCALVES & TORTOLA S/A	I	20.2%	2019/2/17	2024/2/16
0504002100	巴西		COOPERATIVA AGROINDUSTRIAL COPAGRIL	I	20.2%	2019/2/17	2024/2/16
0504002100	巴西		VIBRA AGROINDUSTRIAL S/A	I	20.2%	2019/2/17	2024/2/16
0504002100	巴西		AGROSUL AGROAVICOLA INDUSTRIAL，S.A	I	20.2%	2019/2/17	2024/2/16
0504002100	巴西		KAEFER AGRO INDUSTRIAL LTDA	I	20.2%	2019/2/17	2024/2/16
0504002100	巴西		VOSSKO DO BRASIL ALIMENTOS CONGELADOS LTDA	I	20.2%	2019/2/17	2024/2/16
0504002100	巴西		AVENORTE AVICOLA CIANORTE LTDA.	I	20.2%	2019/2/17	2024/2/16
0504002100	巴西		ADORO S/A	I	20.2%	2019/2/17	2024/2/16
0504002100	巴西		BONASA ALIMENTOS SA	I	20.2%	2019/2/17	2024/2/16
0504002100	巴西		FLAMBOIÃ ALIMENTOS LTDA	I	20.2%	2019/2/17	2024/2/16
0504002100	巴西		FRIGORIFICO NOVA ARAÇÁ LTDA	I	20.2%	2019/2/17	2024/2/16
0504002100	巴西		RIO BRANCO ALIMENTOS S.A.	I	20.2%	2019/2/17	2024/2/16
0504002100	巴西		ZANCHETTA ALIMENTOS LTDA	I	20.2%	2019/2/17	2024/2/16
0504002100	巴西		AGRODANIELI INDÚSTRIA E COMÉRCIO LTDA.	I	20.2%	2019/2/17	2024/2/16
0504002100	巴西		BELLO ALIMENTOS LTDA.	I	20.2%	2019/2/17	2024/2/16
0504002100	巴西		COASUL COOPERATIVA AGROINDUSTRIAL	I	20.2%	2019/2/17	2024/2/16
0504002100	巴西		COOPERATIVA LANGUIRU LTDA	I	20.2%	2019/2/17	2024/2/16
0504002100	巴西		All others	I	32.4%	2019/2/17	2024/2/16
0504002100	巴西		SHB COMERCIO E INDUSTRIA DE ALIMENTOS S.A.	I	25.8%	2019/2/17	2024/2/16
0504002100	巴西		COMPANHIA MINUANO DE ALIMENTOS	I	25.8%	2019/2/17	2024/2/16
0504002100	国(地)别不详的	国(地)别不详的		I	32.4%	2019/2/17	2024/2/16
1003100000	澳大利亚	JW&JI麦克唐纳家族合伙	JW&JIMcdonald&Sons	I	73.6%	2020/5/19	2025/5/18
1003100000	澳大利亚	卡尔根诺米尼斯有限公司	KalganNomineesPty.Ltd.	I	73.6%	2020/5/19	2025/5/18
1003100000	澳大利亚	麦秆田公司	HaycroftEnterprises	I	73.6%	2020/5/19	2025/5/18
1003100000	澳大利亚	其他澳大利亚公司	AllOthers	I	73.6%	2020/5/19	2025/5/18
1003100000	澳大利亚	其他澳大利亚公司	All Others	J	6.9%	2020/5/19	2025/5/18
1003100000	澳大利亚	伊鲁卡信托	TheIlukaTrust	I	73.6%	2020/5/19	2025/5/18
1003100000	国(地)别不详的	国(地)别不详的		I	73.6%	2020/5/19	2025/5/18
1003100000	国(地)别不详的	国(地)别不详的		J	6.9%	2020/5/19	2025/5/18
1003900000	澳大利亚	JW&JI麦克唐纳家族合伙	JW&JIMcdonald&Sons	I	73.6%	2020/5/19	2025/5/18
1003900000	澳大利亚	卡尔根诺米尼斯有限公司	KalganNomineesPty.Ltd.	I	73.6%	2020/5/19	2025/5/18
1003900000	澳大利亚	麦秆田公司	HaycroftEnterprises	I	73.6%	2020/5/19	2025/5/18
1003900000	澳大利亚	其他澳大利亚公司	AllOthers	I	73.6%	2020/5/19	2025/5/18
1003900000	澳大利亚	其他澳大利亚公司	All Others	J	6.9%	2020/5/19	2025/5/18
1003900000	澳大利亚	伊鲁卡信托	TheIlukaTrust	I	73.6%	2020/5/19	2025/5/18
1003900000	国(地)别不详的	国(地)别不详的		I	73.6%	2020/5/19	2025/5/18
1003900000	国(地)别不详的	国(地)别不详的		J	6.9%	2020/5/19	2025/5/18
1108130000	欧盟	其他欧盟公司	All others	I	56.7%	2011/4/19	2024/2/5
1108130000	欧盟	其他欧盟公司	All Others	J	12.4%	2011/9/17	2022/9/15
1108130000	欧盟	德国艾维贝马铃薯淀粉工厂	Avebe Kartoffelstarkefabrik Prignitz/Wendland GmbH	I	12.6%	2011/4/19	2024/2/5
1108130000	欧盟	德国艾维贝马铃薯淀粉工厂	Avebe Kartoffelstarkefabrik Prignitz/Wendland GmbH	J	12.4%	2011/9/17	2022/9/15
1108130000	欧盟	法国罗盖特公司	ROQUETTE FRERES	I	56.7%	2011/4/19	2024/2/5
1108130000	欧盟	法国罗盖特公司	ROQUETTE FRERES	J	7.5%	2011/9/17	2022/9/15
1108130000	欧盟	艾维贝合作社公司	Coöperatie AVEBE U.A.	I	12.6%	2016/12/15	2024/2/5
1108130000	欧盟	艾维贝合作社公司	Coöperatie AVEBE U.A.	J	12.4%	2016/12/15	2022/9/15
1108130000	欧盟	皇家艾维贝合作社公司	Coöperatie Koninklijke Avebe U.A.	I	12.6%	2021/3/9	2024/2/5
1108130000	欧盟	皇家艾维贝合作社公司	Coöperatie Koninklijke Avebe U.A.	J	12.4%	2021/3/9	2022/9/15
1108130000	国(地)别不详	国(地)别不详的		I	56.7%	2011/4/19	2024/2/5
1108130000	国(地)别不详	国(地)别不详的		J	12.4%	2011/9/17	2022/9/15
2204210000	澳大利亚	富豪葡萄酒产业酒商有限公司	Treasury Wine Estates Vintners Limited	I	175.6%	2021/3/28	2026/3/27
2204210000	澳大利亚	卡塞拉酒业私人有限公司	Casella Wines Pty. Limited	I	170.9%	2021/3/28	2026/3/27
2204210000	澳大利亚	天鹅酿酒有限公司	Australia Swan Vintage Pty Ltd	I	116.2%	2021/3/28	2026/3/27
2204210000	澳大利亚	澳大利亚依恋森林酒庄	AUSTRALIA FARM AND LAND INVESTMENT PTY LTD	I	167.1%	2021/3/28	2026/3/27
2204210000	澳大利亚	澳大利亚誉加葡萄酒有限公司	Accolade Wines Australia Limited	I	167.1%	2021/3/28	2026/3/27
2204210000	澳大利亚	澳塔瓦酒庄	OCTTAVA WINES PTY LTD	I	167.1%	2021/3/28	2026/3/27

HS编码	原产国名称	厂商中文名称	厂商英文名称	税种代码	税率	起始日期	截止日期
2204210000	澳大利亚	澳洲佳酿集团	Australian Vintage Limited	I	167.1%	2021/3/28	2026/3/27
2204210000	澳大利亚	保乐力加酿酒师有限公司	Pernod Ricard Winemakers Pty Ltd	I	167.1%	2021/3/28	2026/3/27
2204210000	澳大利亚	博格丹投资有限公司	Bogdan Investments Pty Ltd	I	167.1%	2021/3/28	2026/3/27
2204210000	澳大利亚	布朗兄弟米拉瓦葡萄园有限公司	BROWN BROTHERS MILAWA VINEYARD PTY. LIMITED	I	167.1%	2021/3/28	2026/3/27
2204210000	澳大利亚	丹歌酒庄	AGREEN PTY LTD	I	167.1%	2021/3/28	2026/3/27
2204210000	澳大利亚	德灵酒庄	Dorrien Estate Winery Pty Ltd	I	167.1%	2021/3/28	2026/3/27
2204210000	澳大利亚	芬格富酒业集团	FERNGROVE VINEYARDS LTD	I	167.1%	2021/3/28	2026/3/27
2204210000	澳大利亚	福莱斯葡萄酒有限公司	(FOWLES WINE PTY LTD	I	167.1%	2021/3/28	2026/3/27
2204210000	澳大利亚	福润德酒业有限公司	FURUNDE WINE CO. PTY LTD	I	167.1%	2021/3/28	2026/3/27
2204210000	澳大利亚	歌浓葡萄酒有限责任公司	Kilikanoon Wines Pty Ltd	I	167.1%	2021/3/28	2026/3/27
2204210000	澳大利亚	红袋鼠葡萄酒有限公司	THE RED KANGAROO WINE COMPANY PTY. LTD.	I	167.1%	2021/3/28	2026/3/27
2204210000	澳大利亚	礼拜山酒庄	(Chapel Hill Winery Pty Ltd	I	167.1%	2021/3/28	2026/3/27
2204210000	澳大利亚	珀缇雅谷葡萄酒有限公司	Portia Valley Wines Pty Ltd	I	167.1%	2021/3/28	2026/3/27
2204210000	澳大利亚	绅士酒庄	ZILZIE WINES PTY LTD	I	167.1%	2021/3/28	2026/3/27
2204210000	澳大利亚	史密斯父子有限公司	S. SMITH & SON PTY. LIMITED	I	167.1%	2021/3/28	2026/3/27
2204210000	澳大利亚	泰勒飞力士	TERRA FELIX PTY. LTD.	I	167.1%	2021/3/28	2026/3/27
2204210000	澳大利亚	腾达堡	AUSTRALIAN FOOD & BEVERAGE GROUP PTY LTD	I	167.1%	2021/3/28	2026/3/27
2204210000	澳大利亚	温加拉葡萄酒集团有限公司	WINGARA WINE GROUP PTY. LTD.	I	167.1%	2021/3/28	2026/3/27
2204210000	澳大利亚	其他澳大利亚公司	All others	I	218.4%	2021/3/28	2026/3/27
2204210000	国(地)别不详	国(地)别不详		I	218.4%	2021/3/28	2026/3/27
2303300011	美国	TCE有限责任公司	TCE, LLC	I	50.0%	2017/12/20	2023/1/11
2303300011	美国	TCE有限责任公司	TCE, LLC	J	11.2%	2017/12/20	2023/1/11
2303300011	美国	阿格拉资源有限责任公司	AGRA RESOURCES, LLC	I	50.0%	2017/12/20	2023/1/11
2303300011	美国	阿格拉资源有限责任公司	AGRA RESOURCES, LLC	J	11.2%	2017/12/20	2023/1/11
2303300011	美国	阿奇尔丹尼斯米德兰公司	Archer—Daniels—Midland Company	I	49.8%	2017/12/20	2023/1/11
2303300011	美国	阿奇尔丹尼斯米德兰公司	Archer—Daniels—Midland Company	J	11.4%	2017/12/20	2023/1/11
2303300011	美国	埃尔克霍恩谷乙醇有限公司	Elkhorn Valley Ethanol, Limited Liability Company	I	49.8%	2017/12/20	2023/1/11
2303300011	美国	埃尔克霍恩谷乙醇有限公司	Elkhorn Valley Ethanol, Limited Liability Company	J	11.4%	2017/12/20	2023/1/11
2303300011	美国	爱国者可再生燃料有限责任公司	Patriot Renewable Fuels, LLC	I	49.8%	2017/12/20	2023/1/11
2303300011	美国	爱国者可再生燃料有限责任公司	Patriot Renewable Fuels, LLC	J	11.4%	2017/12/20	2023/1/11
2303300011	美国	爱荷华乙醇有限责任公司	IOWA ETHANOL, LLC	I	50.0%	2017/12/20	2023/1/11
2303300011	美国	爱荷华乙醇有限责任公司	IOWA ETHANOL, LLC	J	11.2%	2017/12/20	2023/1/11
2303300011	美国	安德森阿尔比恩乙醇公司	The Andersons Albion Ethanol LLC	I	49.8%	2017/12/20	2023/1/11
2303300011	美国	安德森阿尔比恩乙醇公司	The Andersons Albion Ethanol LLC	J	11.4%	2017/12/20	2023/1/11
2303300011	美国	安德森丹尼森乙醇公司	The Andersons Denison Ethanol LLC	I	49.8%	2017/12/20	2023/1/11
2303300011	美国	安德森丹尼森乙醇公司	The Andersons Denison Ethanol LLC	J	11.4%	2017/12/20	2023/1/11
2303300011	美国	安德森克里默思乙醇公司	The Andersons Clymers Ethanol LLC	I	49.8%	2017/12/20	2023/1/11
2303300011	美国	安德森克里默思乙醇公司	The Andersons Clymers Ethanol LLC	J	11.4%	2017/12/20	2023/1/11
2303300011	美国	安德森马拉松乙醇公司	The Andersons Marathon Ethanol LLC	I	49.8%	2017/12/20	2023/1/11
2303300011	美国	安德森马拉松乙醇公司	The Andersons Marathon Ethanol LLC	J	11.4%	2017/12/20	2023/1/11
2303300011	美国	北极光乙醇有限责任公司	NORTHERN LIGHTS ETHANOL, LLC	I	50.0%	2017/12/20	2023/1/11
2303300011	美国	北极光乙醇有限责任公司	NORTHERN LIGHTS ETHANOL, LLC	J	11.2%	2017/12/20	2023/1/11
2303300011	美国	北极星乙醇有限责任公司	NORTHSTAR ETHANOL, LLC	I	50.0%	2017/12/20	2023/1/11
2303300011	美国	北极星乙醇有限责任公司	NORTHSTAR ETHANOL, LLC	J	11.2%	2017/12/20	2023/1/11
2303300011	美国	博伊特生物精炼—北曼彻斯特有限责任公司	POET BIOREFINING — NORTH MANCHESTER, LLC	I	50.0%	2017/12/20	2023/1/11
2303300011	美国	博伊特生物精炼—北曼彻斯特有限责任公司	POET BIOREFINING — NORTH MANCHESTER, LLC	J	11.2%	2017/12/20	2023/1/11
2303300011	美国	博伊特生物精炼—波特兰有限责任公司	POET BIOREFINING — PORTLAND, LLC	I	50%	2017/12/20	2023/1/11
2303300011	美国	博伊特生物精炼—波特兰有限责任公司	POET BIOREFINING — PORTLAND, LLC	J	11.2%	2017/12/20	2023/1/11
2303300011	美国	博伊特生物精炼—福斯托里亚有限责任公司	POET BIOREFINING — FOSTORIA, LLC	I	50.0%	2017/12/20	2023/1/11
2303300011	美国	博伊特生物精炼—福斯托里亚有限责任公司	POET BIOREFINING — FOSTORIA, LLC	J	11.2%	2017/12/20	2023/1/11
2303300011	美国	博伊特生物精炼—克洛弗代尔有限责任公司	POET BIOREFINING — CLOVERDALE, LLC	I	50%	2017/12/20	2023/1/11
2303300011	美国	博伊特生物精炼—克洛弗代尔有限责任公司	POET BIOREFINING — CLOVERDALE, LLC	J	11.2%	2017/12/20	2023/1/11
2303300011	美国	博伊特生物精炼—利普西克有限责任公司	POET BIOREFINING — LEIPSIC, LLC	I	50%	2017/12/20	2023/1/11
2303300011	美国	博伊特生物精炼—利普西克有限责任公司	POET BIOREFINING — LEIPSIC, LLC	J	11.2%	2017/12/20	2023/1/11
2303300011	美国	博伊特生物精炼—马里昂有限责任公司	POET BIOREFINING — MARION, LLC	I	50%	2017/12/20	2023/1/11

HS编码	原产国名称	厂商中文名称	厂商英文名称	税种代码	税率	起始日期	截止日期
2303300011	美国	博伊特生物精炼－马里昂有限责任公司	POET BIOREFINING — MARION，LLC	J	11.2%	2017/12/20	2023/1/11
2303300011	美国	博伊特生物精炼－亚历山德里亚有限责任公司	POET BIOREFINING — ALEXANDRIA，LLC	I	50%	2017/12/20	2023/1/11
2303300011	美国	博伊特生物精炼－亚历山德里亚有限责任公司	POET BIOREFINING — ALEXANDRIA，LLC	J	11.2%	2017/12/20	2023/1/11
2303300011	美国	博伊特研究中心公司	POET RESEARCH CENTER，INC.	I	50%	2017/12/20	2023/1/11
2303300011	美国	博伊特研究中心公司	POET RESEARCH CENTER，INC.	J	11.2%	2017/12/20	2023/1/11
2303300011	美国	大草原乙醇有限责任公司	PRAIRIE ETHANOL，LLC	I	50.0%	2017/12/20	2023/1/11
2303300011	美国	大草原乙醇有限责任公司	PRAIRIE ETHANOL，LLC	J	11.2%	2017/12/20	2023/1/11
2303300011	美国	大河资源有限责任公司	Big River Resources，LLC	I	53.7%	2017/12/20	2023/1/11
2303300011	美国	大河资源有限责任公司	Big River Resources，LLC	J	11.2%	2017/12/20	2023/1/11
2303300011	美国	大平原乙醇有限责任公司	GREAT PLAINS ETHANOL，LLC	I	50.0%	2017/12/20	2023/1/11
2303300011	美国	大平原乙醇有限责任公司	GREAT PLAINS ETHANOL，LLC	J	11.2%	2017/12/20	2023/1/11
2303300011	美国	地平线乙醇有限责任公司	HORIZON ETHANOL，LLC	I	50.0%	2017/12/20	2023/1/11
2303300011	美国	地平线乙醇有限责任公司	HORIZON ETHANOL，LLC	J	11.2%	2017/12/20	2023/1/11
2303300011	美国	恩思乙醇有限责任公司	Ace Ethanol，LLC	I	49.8%	2017/12/20	2023/1/11
2303300011	美国	恩思乙醇有限责任公司	Ace Ethanol，LLC	J	11.4%	2017/12/20	2023/1/11
2303300011	美国	弗林特希尔斯资源有限合伙	Flint Hills Resources，LP	I	49.8%	2017/12/20	2023/1/11
2303300011	美国	弗林特希尔斯资源有限合伙	Flint Hills Resources，LP	J	11.4%	2017/12/20	2023/1/11
2303300011	美国	高峰乙醇有限责任公司	PINNACLE ETHANOL，LLC	I	50.0%	2017/12/20	2023/1/11
2303300011	美国	高峰乙醇有限责任公司	PINNACLE ETHANOL，LLC	J	11.2%	2017/12/20	2023/1/11
2303300011	美国	航行者乙醇有限责任公司	VOYAGER ETHANOL，LLC	I	50.0%	2017/12/20	2023/1/11
2303300011	美国	航行者乙醇有限责任公司	VOYAGER ETHANOL，LLC	J	11.2%	2017/12/20	2023/1/11
2303300011	美国	金谷能源有限责任公司	Golden Grain Energy，LLC	I	49.8%	2017/12/20	2023/1/11
2303300011	美国	金谷能源有限责任公司	Golden Grain Energy，LLC	J	11.4%	2017/12/20	2023/1/11
2303300011	美国	领先－玉米有限责任公司	PRO－CORN，LLC	I	50.0%	2017/12/20	2023/1/11
2303300011	美国	领先－玉米有限责任公司	PRO－CORN，LLC	J	11.2%	2017/12/20	2023/1/11
2303300011	美国	路易达孚大章克申有限公司	Louis Dreyfus Commodities Grand Junction LLC	I	49.8%	2017/12/20	2023/1/11
2303300011	美国	路易达孚大章克申有限公司	Louis Dreyfus Commodities Grand Junction LLC	J	11.4%	2017/12/20	2023/1/11
2303300011	美国	马奎斯能源(威斯康星)有限责任公司	Marquis Energy — Wisconsin，LLC	I	42.2%	2017/12/20	2023/1/11
2303300011	美国	马奎斯能源(威斯康星)有限责任公司	Marquis Energy — Wisconsin，LLC	J	11.6%	2017/12/20	2023/1/11
2303300011	美国	马奎斯能源有限责任公司	Marquis Energy LLC	I	42.2%	2017/12/20	2023/1/11
2303300011	美国	马奎斯能源有限责任公司	Marquis Energy LLC	J	11.6%	2017/12/20	2023/1/11
2303300011	美国	密苏里东北粮食有限责任公司	NORTHEAST MISSOURI GRAIN，LLC	I	50.0%	2017/12/20	2023/1/11
2303300011	美国	密苏里东北粮食有限责任公司	NORTHEAST MISSOURI GRAIN，LLC	J	11.2%	2017/12/20	2023/1/11
2303300011	美国	密苏里乙醇有限责任公司	MISSOURI ETHANOL，LLC	I	50.0%	2017/12/20	2023/1/11
2303300011	美国	密苏里乙醇有限责任公司	MISSOURI ETHANOL，LLC	J	11.2%	2017/12/20	2023/1/11
2303300011	美国	密歇根乙醇有限责任公司	MICHIGAN ETHANOL，LLC	I	50.0%	2017/12/20	2023/1/11
2303300011	美国	密歇根乙醇有限责任公司	MICHIGAN ETHANOL，LLC	J	11.2%	2017/12/20	2023/1/11
2303300011	美国	其他美国公司	All Others	I	53.7%	2017/12/20	2023/1/11
2303300011	美国	其他美国公司	All Others	J	12.0%	2017/12/20	2023/1/11
2303300011	美国	前沿乙醇有限责任公司	FRONTIER ETHANOL，LLC	I	50.0%	2017/12/20	2023/1/11
2303300011	美国	前沿乙醇有限责任公司	FRONTIER ETHANOL，LLC	J	11.2%	2017/12/20	2023/1/11
2303300011	美国	水獭溪乙醇有限责任公司	OTTER CREEK ETHANOL，LLC	I	50.0%	2017/12/20	2023/1/11
2303300011	美国	水獭溪乙醇有限责任公司	OTTER CREEK ETHANOL，LLC	J	11.2%	2017/12/20	2023/1/11
2303300011	美国	苏河乙醇有限责任公司	SIOUX RIVER ETHANOL，LLC	I	50.0%	2017/12/20	2023/1/11
2303300011	美国	苏河乙醇有限责任公司	SIOUX RIVER ETHANOL，LLC	J	11.2%	2017/12/20	2023/1/11
2303300011	美国	瓦莱罗可再生燃料有限责任公司	Valero Renewable Fuels Company，LLC	I	49.8%	2017/12/20	2023/1/11
2303300011	美国	瓦莱罗可再生燃料有限责任公司	Valero Renewable Fuels Company，LLC	J	11.4%	2017/12/20	2023/1/11
2303300011	美国	伊利诺斯河能源公司	Illinois River Energy，LLC	I	49.8%	2017/12/20	2023/1/11
2303300011	美国	伊利诺斯河能源公司	Illinois River Energy，LLC	J	11.4%	2017/12/20	2023/1/11
2303300011	美国	乙醇2000有限责任合伙	ETHANOL2000 LIMITED LIABILITY PARTNERSHIP	I	50.0%	2017/12/20	2023/1/11
2303300011	美国	乙醇2000有限责任合伙	ETHANOL2000 LIMITED LIABILITY PARTNERSHIP	J	11.2%	2017/12/20	2023/1/11
2303300011	美国	詹姆斯谷乙醇有限责任公司	JAMES VALLEY ETHANOL，LLC	I	50.0%	2017/12/20	2023/1/11
2303300011	美国	詹姆斯谷乙醇有限责任公司	JAMES VALLEY ETHANOL，LLC	J	11.2%	2017/12/20	2023/1/11
2303300011	美国	卓越能源有限责任公司	Absolute Energy，LLC	I	49.8%	2017/12/20	2023/1/11
2303300011	美国	卓越能源有限责任公司	Absolute Energy，LLC	J	11.4%	2017/12/20	2023/1/11
2303300011	国(地)别不详	国(地)别不详		I	53.7%	2017/12/20	2023/1/11
2303300011	国(地)别不详	国(地)别不详		J	11.4%	2017/12/20	2023/1/11
2303300019	美国	TCE有限责任公司	TCE，LLC	I	50.0%	2017/12/20	2023/1/11

HS 编码	原产国名称	厂商中文名称	厂商英文名称	税种代码	税率	起始日期	截止日期
2303300019	美国	TCE 有限责任公司	TCE, LLC	J	11.2%	2017/12/20	2023/1/11
2303300019	美国	阿格拉资源有限责任公司	AGRA RESOURCES, LLC	I	50.0%	2017/12/20	2023/1/11
2303300019	美国	阿格拉资源有限责任公司	AGRA RESOURCES, LLC	J	11.2%	2017/12/20	2023/1/11
2303300019	美国	阿奇尔丹尼斯米德兰公司	Archer－Daniels－Midland Company	I	49.8%	2017/12/20	2023/1/11
2303300019	美国	阿奇尔丹尼斯米德兰公司	Archer－Daniels－Midland Company	J	11.4%	2017/12/20	2023/1/11
2303300019	美国	埃尔克霍恩谷乙醇有限公司	Elkhorn Valley Ethanol, Limited Liability Company	I	49.8%	2017/12/20	2023/1/11
2303300019	美国	埃尔克霍恩谷乙醇有限公司	Elkhorn Valley Ethanol, Limited Liability Company	J	11.4%	2017/12/20	2023/1/11
2303300019	美国	爱国者可再生燃料有限责任公司	Patriot Renewable Fuels, LLC	I	49.8%	2017/12/20	2023/1/11
2303300019	美国	爱国者可再生燃料有限责任公司	Patriot Renewable Fuels, LLC	J	11.4%	2017/12/20	2023/1/11
2303300019	美国	爱荷华乙醇有限责任公司	IOWA ETHANOL, LLC	I	50.0%	2017/12/20	2023/1/11
2303300019	美国	爱荷华乙醇有限责任公司	IOWA ETHANOL, LLC	J	11.2%	2017/12/20	2023/1/11
2303300019	美国	安德森阿尔比恩乙醇公司	The Andersons Albion Ethanol LLC	I	49.8%	2017/12/20	2023/1/11
2303300019	美国	安德森阿尔比恩乙醇公司	The Andersons Albion Ethanol LLC	J	11.4%	2017/12/20	2023/1/11
2303300019	美国	安德森丹尼森乙醇公司	The Andersons Denison Ethanol LLC	I	49.8%	2017/12/20	2023/1/11
2303300019	美国	安德森丹尼森乙醇公司	The Andersons Denison Ethanol LLC	J	11.4%	2017/12/20	2023/1/11
2303300019	美国	安德森克里默思乙醇公司	The Andersons Clymers Ethanol LLC	I	49.8%	2017/12/20	2023/1/11
2303300019	美国	安德森克里默思乙醇公司	The Andersons Clymers Ethanol LLC	J	11.4%	2017/12/20	2023/1/11
2303300019	美国	安德森马拉松乙醇公司	The Andersons Marathon Ethanol LLC	I	49.8%	2017/12/20	2023/1/11
2303300019	美国	安德森马拉松乙醇公司	The Andersons Marathon Ethanol LLC	J	11.4%	2017/12/20	2023/1/11
2303300019	美国	北极光乙醇有限责任公司	NORTHERN LIGHTS ETHANOL, LLC	I	50.0%	2017/12/20	2023/1/11
2303300019	美国	北极光乙醇有限责任公司	NORTHERN LIGHTS ETHANOL, LLC	J	11.2%	2017/12/20	2023/1/11
2303300019	美国	北极星乙醇有限责任公司	NORTHSTAR ETHANOL, LLC	I	50.0%	2017/12/20	2023/1/11
2303300019	美国	北极星乙醇有限责任公司	NORTHSTAR ETHANOL, LLC	J	11.2%	2017/12/20	2023/1/11
2303300019	美国	博伊特生物精炼－北曼彻斯特有限责任公司	POET BIOREFINING － NORTH MANCHESTER, LLC	I	50.0%	2017/12/20	2023/1/11
2303300019	美国	博伊特生物精炼－北曼彻斯特有限责任公司	POET BIOREFINING － NORTH MANCHESTER, LLC	J	11.2%	2017/12/20	2023/1/11
2303300019	美国	博伊特生物精炼－波特兰有限责任公司	POET BIOREFINING － PORTLAND, LLC	I	50.0%	2017/12/20	2023/1/11
2303300019	美国	博伊特生物精炼－波特兰有限责任公司	POET BIOREFINING － PORTLAND, LLC	J	11.2%	2017/12/20	2023/1/11
2303300019	美国	博伊特生物精炼－福斯托里亚有限责任公司	POET BIOREFINING － FOSTORIA, LLC	I	50.0%	2017/12/20	2023/1/11
2303300019	美国	博伊特生物精炼－福斯托里亚有限责任公司	POET BIOREFINING － FOSTORIA, LLC	J	11.2%	2017/12/20	2023/1/11
2303300019	美国	博伊特生物精炼－克洛弗代尔有限责任公司	POET BIOREFINING － CLOVERDALE, LLC	I	50.0%	2017/12/20	2023/1/11
2303300019	美国	博伊特生物精炼－克洛弗代尔有限责任公司	POET BIOREFINING － CLOVERDALE, LLC	J	11.2%	2017/12/20	2023/1/11
2303300019	美国	博伊特生物精炼－利普西克有限责任公司	POET BIOREFINING － LEIPSIC, LLC	I	50.0%	2017/12/20	2023/1/11
2303300019	美国	博伊特生物精炼－利普西克有限责任公司	POET BIOREFINING － LEIPSIC, LLC	J	11.2%	2017/12/20	2023/1/11
2303300019	美国	博伊特生物精炼－马里昂有限责任公司	POET BIOREFINING － MARION, LLC	I	50.0%	2017/12/20	2023/1/11
2303300019	美国	博伊特生物精炼－马里昂有限责任公司	POET BIOREFINING MARION, LLC	J	11.2%	2017/12/20	2023/1/11
2303300019	美国	博伊特生物精炼－亚历山德里亚有限责任公司	POET BIOREFINING － ALEXANDRIA, LLC	I	50.0%	2017/12/20	2023/1/11
2303300019	美国	博伊特生物精炼－亚历山德里亚有限责任公司	POET BIOREFINING － ALEXANDRIA, LLC	J	11.2%	2017/12/20	2023/1/11
2303300019	美国	博伊特研究中心公司	POET RESEARCH CENTER, INC.	I	50.0%	2017/12/20	2023/1/11
2303300019	美国	博伊特研究中心公司	POET RESEARCH CENTER, INC.	J	11.2%	2017/12/20	2023/1/11
2303300019	美国	大草原乙醇有限责任公司	PRAIRIE ETHANOL, LLC	I	50.0%	2017/12/20	2023/1/11
2303300019	美国	大草原乙醇有限责任公司	PRAIRIE ETHANOL, LLC	J	11.2%	2017/12/20	2023/1/11
2303300019	美国	大河资源有限责任公司	Big River Resources, LLC	I	53.7%	2017/12/20	2023/1/11
2303300019	美国	大河资源有限责任公司	Big River Resources, LLC	J	11.2%	2017/12/20	2023/1/11
2303300019	美国	大平原乙醇有限责任公司	GREAT PLAINS ETHANOL, LLC	I	50.0%	2017/12/20	2023/1/11
2303300019	美国	大平原乙醇有限责任公司	GREAT PLAINS ETHANOL, LLC	J	11.2%	2017/12/20	2023/1/11
2303300019	美国	地平线乙醇有限责任公司	HORIZON ETHANOL, LLC	I	50.0%	2017/12/20	2023/1/11
2303300019	美国	地平线乙醇有限责任公司	HORIZON ETHANOL, LLC	J	11.2%	2017/12/20	2023/1/11
2303300019	美国	恩思乙醇有限责任公司	Ace Ethanol, LLC	I	49.8%	2017/12/20	2023/1/11
2303300019	美国	恩思乙醇有限责任公司	Ace Ethanol, LLC	J	11.4%	2017/12/20	2023/1/11
2303300019	美国	弗林特希尔斯资源有限合伙	Flint Hills Resources, LP	I	49.8%	2017/12/20	2023/1/11
2303300019	美国	弗林特希尔斯资源有限合伙	Flint Hills Resources, LP	J	11.4%	2017/12/20	2023/1/11
2303300019	美国	高峰乙醇有限责任公司	PINNACLE ETHANOL, LLC	I	50.0%	2017/12/20	2023/1/11
2303300019	美国	高峰乙醇有限责任公司	PINNACLE ETHANOL, LLC	J	11.2%	2017/12/20	2023/1/11
2303300019	美国	航行者乙醇有限责任公司	VOYAGER ETHANOL, LLC	I	50.0%	2017/12/20	2023/1/11
2303300019	美国	航行者乙醇有限责任公司	VOYAGER ETHANOL, LLC	J	11.2%	2017/12/20	2023/1/11

HS 编码	原产国名称	厂商中文名称	厂商英文名称	税种代码	税率	起始日期	截止日期
2303300019	美国	金谷能源有限责任公司	Golden Grain Energy, LLC	I	49.8%	2017/12/20	2023/1/11
2303300019	美国	金谷能源有限责任公司	Golden Grain Energy, LLC	J	11.4%	2017/12/20	2023/1/11
2303300019	美国	领先一玉米有限责任公司	PRO—CORN, LLC	I	50.0%	2017/12/20	2023/1/11
2303300019	美国	领先一玉米有限责任公司	PRO—CORN, LLC	J	11.2%	2017/12/20	2023/1/11
2303300019	美国	路易达孚大章克申有限公司	Louis Dreyfus Commodities Grand Junction LLC	I	49.8%	2017/12/20	2023/1/11
2303300019	美国	路易达孚大章克申有限公司	Louis Dreyfus Commodities Grand Junction LLC	J	11.4%	2017/12/20	2023/1/11
2303300019	美国	马奎斯能源（威斯康星）有限责任公司	Marquis Energy — Wisconsin, LLC	I	42.2%	2017/12/20	2023/1/11
2303300019	美国	马奎斯能源（威斯康星）有限责任公司	Marquis Energy — Wisconsin, LLC	J	11.6%	2017/12/20	2023/1/11
2303300019	美国	马奎斯能源有限责任公司	Marquis Energy LLC	I	42.2%	2017/12/20	2023/1/11
2303300019	美国	马奎斯能源有限责任公司	Marquis Energy LLC	J	11.6%	2017/12/20	2023/1/11
2303300019	美国	密苏里东北粮食有限责任公司	NORTHEAST MISSOURI GRAIN, LLC	I	50.0%	2017/12/20	2023/1/11
2303300019	美国	密苏里东北粮食有限责任公司	NORTHEAST MISSOURI GRAIN, LLC	J	11.2%	2017/12/20	2023/1/11
2303300019	美国	密苏里乙醇有限责任公司	MISSOURI ETHANOL, LLC	I	50.0%	2017/12/20	2023/1/11
2303300019	美国	密苏里乙醇有限责任公司	MISSOURI ETHANOL, LLC	J	11.2%	2017/12/20	2023/1/11
2303300019	美国	密歇根乙醇有限责任公司	MICHIGAN ETHANOL, LLC	I	50.0%	2017/12/20	2023/1/11
2303300019	美国	密歇根乙醇有限责任公司	MICHIGAN ETHANOL, LLC	J	11.2%	2017/12/20	2023/1/11
2303300019	美国	其他美国公司	All Others	I	53.7%	2017/12/20	2023/1/11
2303300019	美国	其他美国公司	All Others	J	12.0%	2017/12/20	2023/1/11
2303300019	美国	前沿乙醇有限责任公司	FRONTIER ETHANOL, LLC	I	50.0%	2017/12/20	2023/1/11
2303300019	美国	前沿乙醇有限责任公司	FRONTIER ETHANOL, LLC	J	11.2%	2017/12/20	2023/1/11
2303300019	美国	水獭溪乙醇有限责任公司	OTTER CREEK ETHANOL, LLC	I	50.0%	2017/12/20	2023/1/11
2303300019	美国	水獭溪乙醇有限责任公司	OTTER CREEK ETHANOL, LLC	J	11.2%	2017/12/20	2023/1/11
2303300019	美国	苏河乙醇有限责任公司	SIOUX RIVER ETHANOL, LLC	I	50.0%	2017/12/20	2023/1/11
2303300019	美国	苏河乙醇有限责任公司	SIOUX RIVER ETHANOL, LLC	J	11.2%	2017/12/20	2023/1/11
2303300019	美国	瓦莱罗可再生燃料有限责任公司	Valero Renewable Fuels Company, LLC	I	49.8%	2017/12/20	2023/1/11
2303300019	美国	瓦莱罗可再生燃料有限责任公司	Valero Renewable Fuels Company, LLC	J	11.4%	2017/12/20	2023/1/11
2303300019	美国	伊利诺斯河能源公司	Illinois River Energy, LLC	I	49.8%	2017/12/20	2023/1/11
2303300019	美国	伊利诺斯河能源公司	Illinois River Energy, LLC	J	11.4%	2017/12/20	2023/1/11
2303300019	美国	乙醇 2000 有限责任合伙	ETHANOL2000 LIMITED LIABILITY PARTNERSHIP	I	50.0%	2017/12/20	2023/1/11
2303300019	美国	乙醇 2000 有限责任合伙	ETHANOL2000 LIMITED LIABILITY PARTNERSHIP	J	11.2%	2017/12/20	2023/1/11
2303300019	美国	詹姆斯谷乙醇有限责任公司	JAMES VALLEY ETHANOL, LLC	I	50.0%	2017/12/20	2023/1/11
2303300019	美国	詹姆斯谷乙醇有限责任公司	JAMES VALLEY ETHANOL, LLC	J	11.2%	2017/12/20	2023/1/11
2303300019	美国	卓越能源有限责任公司	Absolute Energy, LLC	I	49.8%	2017/12/20	2023/1/11
2303300019	美国	卓越能源有限责任公司	Absolute Energy, LLC	J	11.4%	2017/12/20	2023/1/11
2303300019	国(地)别不详	国(地)别不详		I	53.7%	2017/12/20	2023/1/11
2303300019	国(地)别不详	国(地)别不详		J	11.4%	2017/12/20	2023/1/11
2303300090	美国	TCE 有限责任公司	TCE, LLC	I	50.0%	2017/1/12	2023/1/11
2303300090	美国	TCE 有限责任公司	TCE, LLC	J	11.2%	2017/1/12	2023/1/11
2303300090	美国	阿格拉资源有限责任公司	AGRA RESOURCES, LLC	I	50.0%	2017/1/12	2023/1/11
2303300090	美国	阿格拉资源有限责任公司	AGRA RESOURCES, LLC	J	11.2%	2017/1/12	2023/1/11
2303300090	美国	阿奇尔丹尼斯米德兰公司	Archer—Daniels—Midland Company	I	49.8%	2017/1/12	2023/1/11
2303300090	美国	阿奇尔丹尼斯米德兰公司	Archer—Daniels—Midland Company	J	11.4%	2017/1/12	2023/1/11
2303300090	美国	埃尔克霍恩谷乙醇有限公司	Elkhorn Valley Ethanol, Limited Liability Company	I	49.8%	2017/1/12	2023/1/11
2303300090	美国	埃尔克霍恩谷乙醇有限公司	Elkhorn Valley Ethanol, Limited Liability Company	J	11.4%	2017/1/12	2023/1/11
2303300090	美国	爱国者可再生燃料有限责任公司	Patriot Renewable Fuels, LLC	I	49.8%	2017/1/12	2023/1/11
2303300090	美国	爱国者可再生燃料有限责任公司	Patriot Renewable Fuels, LLC	J	11.4%	2017/1/12	2023/1/11
2303300090	美国	爱荷华乙醇有限责任公司	IOWA ETHANOL, LLC	I	50.0%	2017/1/12	2023/1/11
2303300090	美国	爱荷华乙醇有限责任公司	IOWA ETHANOL, LLC	J	11.2%	2017/1/12	2023/1/11
2303300090	美国	安德森阿尔比恩乙醇公司	The Andersons Albion Ethanol LLC	I	49.8%	2017/1/12	2023/1/11
2303300090	美国	安德森阿尔比恩乙醇公司	The Andersons Albion Ethanol LLC	J	11.4%	2017/1/12	2023/1/11
2303300090	美国	安德森丹尼森乙醇公司	The Andersons Denison Ethanol LLC	I	49.8%	2017/1/12	2023/1/11
2303300090	美国	安德森丹尼森乙醇公司	The Andersons Denison Ethanol LLC	J	11.4%	2017/1/12	2023/1/11
2303300090	美国	安德森克里默思乙醇公司	The Andersons Clymers Ethanol LLC	I	49.8%	2017/1/12	2023/1/11
2303300090	美国	安德森克里默思乙醇公司	The Andersons Clymers Ethanol LLC	J	11.4%	2017/1/12	2023/1/11
2303300090	美国	安德森马拉松乙醇公司	The Andersons Marathon Ethanol LLC	I	49.8%	2017/1/12	2023/1/11
2303300090	美国	安德森马拉松乙醇公司	The Andersons Marathon Ethanol LLC	J	11.4%	2017/1/12	2023/1/11
2303300090	美国	北极光乙醇有限责任公司	NORTHERN LIGHTS ETHANOL, LLC	I	50.0%	2017/1/12	2023/1/11
2303300090	美国	北极光乙醇有限责任公司	NORTHERN LIGHTS ETHANOL, LLC	J	11.2%	2017/1/12	2023/1/11
2303300090	美国	北极星乙醇有限责任公司	NORTHSTAR ETHANOL, LLC	I	50.0%	2017/1/12	2023/1/11

HS编码	原产国名称	厂商中文名称	厂商英文名称	税种代码	税率	起始日期	截止日期
2303300090	美国	北极星乙醇有限责任公司	NORTHSTAR ETHANOL, LLC	J	11.2%	2017/1/12	2023/1/11
2303300090	美国	博伊特生物精炼－北曼彻斯特有限责任公司	POET BIOREFINING — NORTH MANCHESTER, LLC	I	50.0%	2017/1/12	2023/1/11
2303300090	美国	博伊特生物精炼－北曼彻斯特有限责任公司	POET BIOREFINING — NORTH MANCHESTER, LLC	J	11.2%	2017/1/12	2023/1/11
2303300090	美国	博伊特生物精炼－波特兰有限责任公司	POET BIOREFINING — PORTLAND, LLC	I	50.0%	2017/1/12	2023/1/11
2303300090	美国	博伊特生物精炼－波特兰有限责任公司	POET BIOREFINING — PORTLAND, LLC	J	11.2%	2017/1/12	2023/1/11
2303300090	美国	博伊特生物精炼－福斯托里亚有限责任公司	POET BIOREFINING — FOSTORIA, LLC	I	50.0%	2017/1/12	2023/1/11
2303300090	美国	博伊特生物精炼－福斯托里亚有限责任公司	POET BIOREFINING — FOSTORIA, LLC	J	11.2%	2017/1/12	2023/1/11
2303300090	美国	博伊特生物精炼－克洛弗代尔有限责任公司	POET BIOREFINING — CLOVERDALE, LLC	I	50.0%	2017/1/12	2023/1/11
2303300090	美国	博伊特生物精炼－克洛弗代尔有限责任公司	POET BIOREFINING — CLOVERDALE, LLC	J	11.2%	2017/1/12	2023/1/11
2303300090	美国	博伊特生物精炼－利普西克有限责任公司	POET BIOREFINING — LEIPSIC, LLC	I	50.0%	2017/1/12	2023/1/11
2303300090	美国	博伊特生物精炼－利普西克有限责任公司	POET BIOREFINING — LEIPSIC, LLC	J	11.2%	2017/1/12	2023/1/11
2303300090	美国	博伊特生物精炼－马里昂有限责任公司	POET BIOREFINING — MARION, LLC	I	50.0%	2017/1/12	2023/1/11
2303300090	美国	博伊特生物精炼－马里昂有限责任公司	POET BIOREFINING — MARION, LLC	J	11.2%	2017/1/12	2023/1/11
2303300090	美国	博伊特生物精炼－亚历山德里亚有限责任公司	POET BIOREFINING — ALEXANDRIA, LLC	I	50.0%	2017/1/12	2023/1/11
2303300090	美国	博伊特生物精炼－亚历山德里亚有限责任公司	POET BIOREFINING — ALEXANDRIA, LLC	J	11.2%	2017/1/12	2023/1/11
2303300090	美国	博伊特研究中心公司	POET RESEARCH CENTER, INC.	I	50.0%	2017/1/12	2023/1/11
2303300090	美国	博伊特研究中心公司	POET RESEARCH CENTER, INC.	J	11.2%	2017/1/12	2023/1/11
2303300090	美国	大草原乙醇有限责任公司	PRAIRIE ETHANOL, LLC	I	50.0%	2017/1/12	2023/1/11
2303300090	美国	大草原乙醇有限责任公司	PRAIRIE ETHANOL, LLC	J	11.2%	2017/1/12	2023/1/11
2303300090	美国	大河资源有限责任公司	Big River Resources, LLC	I	53.7%	2017/1/12	2023/1/11
2303300090	美国	大河资源有限责任公司	Big River Resources, LLC	J	11.2%	2017/1/12	2023/1/11
2303300090	美国	大平原乙醇有限责任公司	GREAT PLAINS ETHANOL, LLC	I	50.0%	2017/1/12	2023/1/11
2303300090	美国	大平原乙醇有限责任公司	GREAT PLAINS ETHANOL, LLC	J	11.2%	2017/1/12	2023/1/11
2303300090	美国	地平线乙醇有限责任公司	HORIZON ETHANOL, LLC	I	50.0%	2017/1/12	2023/1/11
2303300090	美国	地平线乙醇有限责任公司	HORIZON ETHANOL, LLC	J	11.2%	2017/1/12	2023/1/11
2303300090	美国	恩思乙醇有限责任公司	Ace Ethanol, LLC	I	49.8%	2017/1/12	2023/1/11
2303300090	美国	恩思乙醇有限责任公司	Ace Ethanol, LLC	J	11.4%	2017/1/12	2023/1/11
2303300090	美国	弗林特希尔斯资源有限合伙	Flint Hills Resources, LP	I	49.8%	2017/1/12	2023/1/11
2303300090	美国	弗林特希尔斯资源有限合伙	Flint Hills Resources, LP	J	11.4%	2017/1/12	2023/1/11
2303300090	美国	高峰乙醇有限责任公司	PINNACLE ETHANOL, LLC	I	50.0%	2017/1/12	2023/1/11
2303300090	美国	高峰乙醇有限责任公司	PINNACLE ETHANOL, LLC	J	11.2%	2017/1/12	2023/1/11
2303300090	美国	航行者乙醇有限责任公司	VOYAGER ETHANOL, LLC	I	50.0%	2017/1/12	2023/1/11
2303300090	美国	航行者乙醇有限责任公司	VOYAGER ETHANOL, LLC	J	11.2%	2017/1/12	2023/1/11
2303300090	美国	金谷能源有限责任公司	Golden Grain Energy, LLC	I	49.8%	2017/1/12	2023/1/11
2303300090	美国	金谷能源有限责任公司	Golden Grain Energy, LLC	J	11.4%	2017/1/12	2023/1/11
2303300090	美国	领先－玉米有限责任公司	PRO—CORN, LLC	I	50.0%	2017/1/12	2023/1/11
2303300090	美国	领先－玉米有限责任公司	PRO—CORN, LLC	J	11.2%	2017/1/12	2023/1/11
2303300090	美国	路易达孚大章克申有限公司	Louis Dreyfus Commodities Grand Junction LLC	I	49.8%	2017/1/12	2023/1/11
2303300090	美国	路易达孚大章克申有限公司	Louis Dreyfus Commodities Grand Junction LLC	J	11.4%	2017/1/12	2023/1/11
2303300090	美国	马奎斯能源（威斯康星）有限责任公司	Marquis Energy — Wisconsin, LLC	I	42.2%	2017/1/12	2023/1/11
2303300090	美国	马奎斯能源（威斯康星）有限责任公司	Marquis Energy — Wisconsin, LLC	J	11.6%	2017/1/12	2023/1/11
2303300090	美国	马奎斯能源有限责任公司	Marquis Energy LLC	I	42.2%	2017/1/12	2023/1/11
2303300090	美国	马奎斯能源有限责任公司	Marquis Energy LLC	J	11.6%	2017/1/12	2023/1/11
2303300090	美国	密苏里东北粮食有限责任公司	NORTHEAST MISSOURI GRAIN, LLC	I	50.0%	2017/1/12	2023/1/11
2303300090	美国	密苏里东北粮食有限责任公司	NORTHEAST MISSOURI GRAIN, LLC	J	11.2%	2017/1/12	2023/1/11
2303300090	美国	密苏里乙醇有限责任公司	MISSOURI ETHANOL, LLC	I	50.0%	2017/1/12	2023/1/11
2303300090	美国	密苏里乙醇有限责任公司	MISSOURI ETHANOL, LLC	J	11.2%	2017/1/12	2023/1/11
2303300090	美国	密歇根乙醇有限责任公司	MICHIGAN ETHANOL, LLC	I	50.0%	2017/1/12	2023/1/11
2303300090	美国	密歇根乙醇有限责任公司	MICHIGAN ETHANOL, LLC	J	11.2%	2017/1/12	2023/1/11
2303300090	美国	其他美国公司	All Others	I	53.7%	2017/1/12	2023/1/11
2303300090	美国	其他美国公司	All Others	J	12.0%	2017/1/12	2023/1/11
2303300090	美国	前沿乙醇有限责任公司	FRONTIER ETHANOL, LLC	I	50.0%	2017/1/12	2023/1/11
2303300090	美国	前沿乙醇有限责任公司	FRONTIER ETHANOL, LLC	J	11.2%	2017/1/12	2023/1/11
2303300090	美国	水獭溪乙醇有限责任公司	OTTER CREEK ETHANOL, LLC	I	50.0%	2017/1/12	2023/1/11

HS 编码	原产国名称	厂商中文名称	厂商英文名称	税种代码	税率	起始日期	截止日期
2303300090	美国	水獭溪乙醇有限责任公司	OTTER CREEK ETHANOL，LLC	J	11.2%	2017/1/12	2023/1/11
2303300090	美国	苏河乙醇有限责任公司	SIOUX RIVER ETHANOL，LLC	I	50.0%	2017/1/12	2023/1/11
2303300090	美国	苏河乙醇有限责任公司	SIOUX RIVER ETHANOL，LLC	J	11.2%	2017/1/12	2023/1/11
2303300090	美国	瓦莱罗可再生燃料有限责任公司	Valero Renewable Fuels Company，LLC	I	49.8%	2017/1/12	2023/1/11
2303300090	美国	瓦莱罗可再生燃料有限责任公司	Valero Renewable Fuels Company，LLC	J	11.4%	2017/1/12	2023/1/11
2303300090	美国	伊利诺斯河能源公司	Illinois River Energy，LLC	I	49.8%	2017/1/12	2023/1/11
2303300090	美国	伊利诺斯河能源公司	Illinois River Energy，LLC	J	11.4%	2017/1/12	2023/1/11
2303300090	美国	乙醇 2000 有限责任合伙	ETHANOL2000 LIMITED LIABILITY PARTNERSHIP	I	50.0%	2017/1/12	2023/1/11
2303300090	美国	乙醇 2000 有限责任合伙	ETHANOL2000 LIMITED LIABILITY PARTNERSHIP	J	11.2%	2017/1/12	2023/1/11
2303300090	美国	詹姆斯谷乙醇有限责任公司	JAMES VALLEY ETHANOL，LLC	I	50.0%	2017/1/12	2023/1/11
2303300090	美国	詹姆斯谷乙醇有限责任公司	JAMES VALLEY ETHANOL，LLC	J	11.2%	2017/1/12	2023/1/11
2303300090	美国	卓越能源有限责任公司	Absolute Energy，LLC	I	49.8%	2017/1/12	2023/1/11
2303300090	美国	卓越能源有限责任公司	Absolute Energy，LLC	J	11.4%	2017/1/12	2023/1/11
2303300090	国(地)别不详	国(地)别不详		I	53.7%	2017/1/12	2023/1/11
2303300090	国(地)别不详	国(地)别不详		J	11.4%	2017/1/12	2023/1/11
2804619012	韩国		Innovation Silicon Co.，Ltd.	I	113.8%	2017/11/22	2025/1/19
2804619012	韩国		KCC Corp. and Korean Advanced Materials(KAM Corp)	I	113.8%	2017/11/22	2025/1/19
2804619012	韩国	OCI 株式会社	OCI Company Ltd.	I	4.4%	2017/11/22	2025/1/19
2804619012	韩国	SMP 株式会社	SMPLtd.	I	88.7%	2017/11/22	2025/1/19
2804619012	韩国	韩国硅业株式会社	Hankook Silicon Co.，Ltd.	I	9.5%	2017/11/22	2025/1/19
2804619012	韩国	韩华思路信株式会社	HANWHASOLUTIONSCORPORATION	I	8.9%	2020/6/5	2025/1/19
2804619012	韩国	其他韩国公司	All Others	I	88.7%	2017/11/22	2025/1/19
2804619012	韩国	熊津多晶硅有限公司	Woongjin Polysilicon Co.，Ltd.	I	113.8%	2017/11/22	2025/1/19
2804619012	美国		AE Polysilicon Corporation	I	57.0%	2020/1/20	2025/1/19
2804619012	美国		AE PolysiliconCorporation	J	2.1%	2014/1/20	2025/1/19
2804619012	美国	MEMC 帕萨迪纳有限公司	MEMC Pasadena，Inc.	I	53.6%	2014/1/20	2025/1/19
2804619012	美国	MEMC 帕萨迪纳有限公司	MEMCPasadena，Inc.	J	0.0%	2014/1/20	2025/1/19
2804619012	美国	REC 太阳能级硅有限责任公司	REC Solar Grade Silicon LLC	I	57%	2014/1/20	2025/1/19
2804619012	美国	REC 太阳能级硅有限责任公司	REC SolarGrade Silicon LLC	J	0.0%	2014/1/20	2025/1/19
2804619012	美国	REC 先进硅材料有限责任公司	REC Advanced Silicon Materials LLC	I	57.0%	2014/1/20	2025/1/19
2804619012	美国	REC 先进硅材料有限责任公司	REC Advanced Silicon Materials LLC	J	0.0%	2014/1/20	2025/1/19
2804619012	美国	赫姆洛克半导体公司	Hemlock Semiconductor Corporation	I	53.3%	2014/1/20	2025/1/19
2804619012	美国	赫姆洛克半导体公司	Hemlock Semiconductor Corporation	J	2.1%	2014/1/20	2025/1/19
2804619012	美国	其他美国公司	All Others	I	57.0%	2014/1/20	2025/1/19
2804619012	美国	其他美国公司	All Others	J	2.1%	2014/1/20	2025/1/19
2804619012	国(地)别不详	国(地)别不详		I	113.8%	2017/11/22	2025/1/19
2804619012	国(地)别不详	国(地)别不详		J	2.1%	2014/1/20	2025/1/19
2804619013	韩国		Innovation Silicon Co.，Ltd.	I	113.8%	2017/11/22	2025/1/19
2804619013	韩国		KCC Corp. and Korean Advanced Materials(KAM Corp)	I	113.8%	2017/11/22	2025/1/19
2804619013	韩国	OCI 株式会社	OCI Company Ltd.	I	4.4%	2017/11/22	2025/1/19
2804619013	韩国	SMP 株式会社	SMPLtd.	I	88.7%	2017/11/22	2025/1/19
2804619013	韩国	韩国硅业株式会社	Hankook Silicon Co.，Ltd.	I	9.5%	2017/11/22	2025/1/19
2804619013	韩国	韩华思路信株式会社	HANWHASOLUTIONSCORPORATION	I	8.9%	2020/6/5	2025/1/19
2804619013	韩国	其他韩国公司	All Others	I	88.7%	2017/11/22	2025/1/19
2804619013	韩国	熊津多晶硅有限公司	Woongjin Polysilicon Co.，Ltd.	I	113.8%	2017/11/22	2025/1/19
2804619013	美国		AE Polysilicon Corporation	I	57.0%	2020/1/20	2025/1/19
2804619013	美国		AE PolysiliconCorporation	J	2.1%	2014/1/20	2025/1/19
2804619013	美国	MEMC 帕萨迪纳有限公司	MEMC Pasadena，Inc.	I	53.6%	2014/1/20	2025/1/19
2804619013	美国	MEMC 帕萨迪纳有限公司	MEMCPasadena，Inc.	J	0.0%	2014/1/20	2025/1/19
2804619013	美国	REC 太阳能级硅有限责任公司	REC Solar Grade Silicon LLC	I	57%	2014/1/20	2025/1/19
2804619013	美国	REC 太阳能级硅有限责任公司	REC SolarGrade Silicon LLC	J	0.0%	2014/1/20	2025/1/19
2804619013	美国	REC 先进硅材料有限责任公司	REC Advanced Silicon Materials LLC	I	57%	2014/1/20	2025/1/19
2804619013	美国	REC 先进硅材料有限责任公司	REC Advanced Silicon Materials LLC	J	0%	2014/1/20	2025/1/19
2804619013	美国	赫姆洛克半导体公司	Hemlock Semiconductor Corporation	I	53.3%	2014/1/20	2025/1/19
2804619013	美国	赫姆洛克半导体公司	Hemlock Semiconductor Corporation	J	2.1%	2014/1/20	2025/1/19
2804619013	美国	其他美国公司	All Others	I	57.0%	2014/1/20	2025/1/19
2804619013	美国	其他美国公司	All Others	J	2.1%	2014/1/20	2025/1/19
2804619013	国(地)别不详	国(地)别不详		I	113.8%	2017/11/22	2025/1/19
2804619013	国(地)别不详	国(地)别不详		J	2.1%	2014/1/20	2025/1/19

HS 编码	原产国名称	厂商中文名称	厂商英文名称	税种代码	税率	起始日期	截止日期
2804619092	韩国		Innovation Silicon Co.,Ltd.	I	113.8%	2017/11/22	2025/1/19
2804619092	韩国		KCC Corp. and Korean Advanced Materials(KAM Corp)	I	113.8%	2017/11/22	2025/1/19
2804619092	韩国	OCI 株式会社	OCI Company Ltd.	I	4.4%	2017/11/22	2025/1/19
2804619092	韩国	SMP 株式会社	SMPLtd.	I	88.7%	2017/11/22	2025/1/19
2804619092	韩国	韩国硅业株式会社	Hankook Silicon Co.,Ltd.	I	9.5%	2017/11/22	2025/1/19
2804619092	韩国	韩华思路信株式会社	HANWHASOLUTIONSCORPORATION	I	8.9%	2020/6/5	2025/1/19
2804619092	韩国	其他韩国公司	All Others	I	88.7%	2017/11/22	2025/1/19
2804619092	韩国	熊津多晶硅有限公司	Woongjin Polysilicon Co.,Ltd.	I	113.8%	2017/11/22	2025/1/19
2804619092	美国		AE Polysilicon Corporation	I	57.0%	2020/1/20	2025/1/19
2804619092	美国		AE PolysiliconCorporation	J	2.1%	2014/1/20	2025/1/19
2804619092	美国	MEMC 帕萨迪纳有限公司	MEMC Pasadena,Inc.	I	53.6%	2014/1/20	2025/1/19
2804619092	美国	MEMC 帕萨迪纳有限公司	MEMCPasadena,Inc.	J	0.0%	2014/1/20	2025/1/19
2804619092	美国	REC 太阳能级硅有限责任公司	REC Solar Grade Silicon LLC	I	57%	2014/1/20	2025/1/19
2804619092	美国	REC 太阳能级硅有限责任公司	REC SolarGrade Silicon LLC	J	0.0%	2014/1/20	2025/1/19
2804619092	美国	REC 先进硅材料有限责任公司	REC Advanced Silicon Materials LLC	I	57%	2014/1/20	2025/1/19
2804619092	美国	REC 先进硅材料有限责任公司	REC Advanced Silicon Materials LLC	J	0.0%	2014/1/20	2025/1/19
2804619092	美国	赫姆洛克半导体公司	Hemlock Semiconductor Corporation	I	53.3%	2014/1/20	2025/1/19
2804619092	美国	赫姆洛克半导体公司	Hemlock Semiconductor Corporation	J	2.1%	2014/1/20	2025/1/19
2804619092	美国	其他美国公司	All Others	I	57%	2014/1/20	2025/1/19
2804619092	美国	其他美国公司	All Others	J	2.1%	2014/1/20	2025/1/19
2804619092	国(地)别不详	国(地)别不详		I	113.8%	2017/11/22	2025/1/19
2804619092	国(地)别不详	国(地)别不详		J	2.1%	2014/1/20	2025/1/19
2804619093	韩国		Innovation Silicon Co.,Ltd.	I	113.8%	2017/11/22	2025/1/19
2804619093	韩国		KCC Corp. and Korean Advanced Materials(KAM Corp)	I	113.8%	2017/11/22	2025/1/19
2804619093	韩国	OCI 株式会社	OCI Company Ltd.	I	4.4%	2017/11/22	2025/1/19
2804619093	韩国	SMP 株式会社	SMPLtd.	I	88.7%	2017/11/22	2025/1/19
2804619093	韩国	韩国硅业株式会社	Hankook Silicon Co.,Ltd.	I	9.5%	2017/11/22	2025/1/19
2804619093	韩国	韩华思路信株式会社	HANWHASOLUTIONSCORPORATION	I	8.9%	2020/6/5	2025/1/19
2804619093	韩国	其他韩国公司	All Others	I	88.7%	2017/11/22	2025/1/19
2804619093	韩国	熊津多晶硅有限公司	Woongjin Polysilicon Co.,Ltd.	I	113.8%	2017/11/22	2025/1/19
2804619093	美国		AE Polysilicon Corporation	I	57.0%	2020/1/20	2025/1/19
2804619093	美国		AE PolysiliconCorporation	J	2.1%	2014/1/20	2025/1/19
2804619093	美国	MEMC 帕萨迪纳有限公司	MEMC Pasadena,Inc.	I	53.6%	2014/1/20	2025/1/19
2804619093	美国	MEMC 帕萨迪纳有限公司	MEMCPasadena,Inc.	J	0.0%	2014/1/20	2025/1/19
2804619093	美国	REC 太阳能级硅有限责任公司	REC Solar Grade Silicon LLC	I	57.0%	2014/1/20	2025/1/19
2804619093	美国	REC 太阳能级硅有限责任公司	REC SolarGrade Silicon LLC	J	0.0%	2014/1/20	2025/1/19
2804619093	美国	REC 先进硅材料有限责任公司	REC Advanced Silicon Materials LLC	I	57.0%	2014/1/20	2025/1/19
2804619093	美国	REC 先进硅材料有限责任公司	REC Advanced Silicon Materials LLC	J	0.0%	2014/1/20	2025/1/19
2804619093	美国	赫姆洛克半导体公司	Hemlock Semiconductor Corporation	I	53.3%	2014/1/20	2025/1/19
2804619093	美国	赫姆洛克半导体公司	Hemlock Semiconductor Corporation	J	2.1%	2014/1/20	2025/1/19
2804619093	美国	其他美国公司	All Others	I	57.0%	2014/1/20	2025/1/19
2804619093	美国	其他美国公司	All Others	J	2.1%	2014/1/20	2025/1/19
2804619093	国(地)别不详	国(地)别不详		I	113.8%	2017/11/22	2025/1/19
2804619093	国(地)别不详	国(地)别不详		J	2.1%	2014/1/20	2025/1/19
2811199010	美国	艾菲纳化工有限公司	IofinaChemical,Inc.	I	123.4%	2018/10/16	2023/10/15
2811199010	美国	其他美国公司	AllOthers	I	123.4%	2018/10/16	2023/10/15
2811199010	日本	其他日本公司	AllOthers	I	41.1%	2018/10/16	2023/10/15
2811199010	国(地)别不详的	国(地)别不详的		I	123.4%	2018/10/16	2023/10/15
2902500000	韩国	韩华道达尔株式会社	HANWHATOTALPETROCHEMICALCO.,LTD.	I	6.2%	2018/6/23	2023/6/22
2902500000	韩国	丽川 NCC 株式会社	YeochunNCCCo.,Ltd	I	6.2%	2018/6/23	2023/6/22
2902500000	韩国	乐天化学株式会社	LOTTECHEMICALCORPORATION	I	7.5%	2018/6/23	2023/6/22
2902500000	韩国	(株)LG 化学	LGChem,Ltd	I	6.6%	2018/6/23	2023/6/22
2902500000	韩国	SK 综合化学株式会社	SKglobalchemicalCo.,Ltd	I	6.6%	2018/6/23	2023/6/22
2902500000	韩国	其他韩国公司	AllOthers	I	7.5%	2018/6/23	2023/6/22
2902500000	台湾	台湾化学纤维股份有限公司	HANWHATOTALPETROCHEMICALCO.,LTD.	I	3.8%	2018/6/23	2023/6/22
2902500000	台湾	其他台湾地区公司	AllOthers	I	4.2%	2018/6/23	2023/6/22
2902500000	美国	利安德化学品公司	LyondellChemicalCompany	I	13.9%	2018/6/23	2023/6/22
2902500000	美国	美国华美苯乙烯公司	WestlakeStyreneLL	I	13.7%	2018/6/23	2023/6/22
2902500000	美国	英力士苯领美国有限责任公司	INEOS Styrolution America LLC	I	13.9%	2018/6/23	2023/6/22
2902500000	美国	美洲苯乙烯公司	AmericasStyrenicsLLC	I	13.9%	2018/6/23	2023/6/22
2902500000	美国	其他美国公司	AllOthers	I	55.7%	2018/6/23	2023/6/22
2902500000	国(别)地详	国(别)地详		I	55.7%	2018/6/23	2023/6/22

HS 编码	原产国名称	厂商中文名称	厂商英文名称	税种代码	税率	起始日期	截止日期
2903230000	欧盟	陶氏德国设施有限公司	Dow Deutschland Anlagengesellschaft mbH	I	27.6%	2014/5/31	2025/5/30
2903230000	欧盟	法国苏威公司	SOLVAY BENVIC EUROPE－FRANCE S.A.S.	I	27.6%	2014/5/31	2025/5/30
2903230000	欧盟	其他欧盟公司	All Others	I	27.6%	2014/5/31	2025/5/30
2903230000	美国	西方化学公司	Occidental Chemical Corporation	I	71.8%	2014/5/31	2025/5/30
2903230000	美国	埃克塞尔公司	Axiall Corporation	I	71.8%	2014/5/31	2025/5/30
2903230000	美国	陶氏化学公司	The Dow Chemical Company	I	71.8%	2014/5/31	2025/5/30
2903230000	美国	美国 PPG 工业公司	PPG Industries	I	71.8%	2014/5/31	2025/5/30
2903230000	美国	其他美国公司	All Others	I	71.8%	2014/5/31	2025/5/30
2903230000	国(地)别不详	国(地)别不详		I	71.8%	2014/5/31	2025/5/30
2903911000	日本	其他日本公司	All Others	I	70.4%	2019/1/23	2024/1/22
2903911000	印度	印度的公司		I	31.9%	2019/1/23	2024/1/22
2903911000	日本	株式会社吴羽	KUREHACORPORATION	I	70.4 %	2019/1/23	2024/1/22
2903911000	国(地)别不详	国(地)别不详		I	70.4 %	2019/1/23	2024/1/22
2905121000	美国	QQ 化学公司	QQ Chemicals Corporation	I	267.4%	2020/11/8	2025/11/17
2905121000	美国	QQ 化学公司	QQ Chemicals Corporation	J	34.2%	2020/11/8	2025/11/17
2905121000	美国	其他美国公司	AllOthers	I	267.4%	2020/11/8	2025/11/17
2905121000	美国	其他美国公司	AllOthers	J	37.7%	2020/11/8	2025/11/17
2905121000	美国	陶氏化学公司	TheDowChemicalCompany	I	254.4%	2020/11/8	2025/11/17
2905121000	美国	陶氏化学公司	TheDowChemicalCompany	J	37.7%	2020/11/8	2025/11/17
2905121000	国(地)别不详	国(地)别不详		I	267.4%	2020/11/8	2025/11/17
2905121000	国(地)别不详	国(地)别不详		J	37.7%	2020/11/8	2025/11/17
2905130000	台湾	塑胶工业股份有限公司	FORMOSA PLASTICS CORPORATION	I	6.0%	2018/12/29	2023/12/28
2905130000	台湾	其他台湾地区公司	All Others	I	56.1%	2018/12/29	2023/12/28
2905130000	马来西亚	国油石化衍生公司/马石化营销(纳闽)有限公司	PETRONAS CHEMICALS DERIVATIVES SDN BHD)/(PETRONAS CHEMICALS MARKETING(LABUAN) LTD)	I	12.7%	2018/12/29	2023/12/28
2905130000	马来西亚	巴斯夫马来西亚国油化学私人有限公司	BASF PETRONAS Chemicals Sdn Bhd	I	26.7%	2018/12/29	2023/12/28
2905130000	马来西亚	奥伯帝莫马来西亚化学公司	Optimal Chemicals Sdn Bhd	I	26.7%	2018/12/29	2023/12/28
2905130000	马来西亚	其他马来西亚公司	All Others	I	26.7%	2018/12/29	2023/12/28
2905130000	美国	欧季亚公司	OXEA CORPORATION	I	52.2%	2018/12/29	2023/12/28
2905130000	美国	伊士曼化学公司	Eastman Chemical Company	I	139.3%	2018/12/29	2023/12/28
2905130000	美国	道化学公司	The Dow Chemical Company	I	139.3%	2018/12/29	2023/12/28
2905130000	美国	巴斯夫公司	BASF Corporation	I	139.3%	2018/12/29	2023/12/28
2905130000	美国	其他美国公司	All Others	I	139.3%	2018/12/29	2023/12/28
2905130000	国(地)别不详	国(地)别不详的	All Others	I	139.3%	2018/12/29	2023/12/28
2907111000	美国	英力士美国公司	INEOSAmericasLLC	I	287.2%	2019/9/6	2024/9/5
2907111000	美国	美国兰科运营有限责任公司	BlueCubeOperationsLLC	I	244.3%	2019/9/6	2024/9/5
2907111000	美国	其他美国公司	AllOthers	I	287.2%	2019/9/6	2024/9/5
2907111000	欧盟	其他欧盟公司	All Others	I	30.4%	2019/9/6	2024/9/5
2907111000	韩国	锦湖 P&B 化学株式会社	KUMHOP&BCHEMICALS,INC.	I	12.5%	2019/9/6	2024/9/5
2907111000	韩国	(株)LG 化学	LGCHEM,LTD.	I	12.6%	2019/9/6	2024/9/5
2907111000	韩国	其他韩国公司	AllOthers	I	23.7%	2019/9/6	2024/9/5
2907111000	日本	三井化学株式会社	MitsuiChemicals,Inc.	I	19.3%	2019/9/6	2024/9/5
2907111000	日本	其他日本公司	AllOthers	I	27.0%	2019/9/6	2024/9/5
2907111000	泰国	PTT 苯酚有限公司	PTTPhenolCompanyLimited	I	10.6%	2019/9/6	2024/9/5
2907111000	泰国	其他泰国公司	AllOthers	I	28.6%	2019/9/6	2024/9/5
2907111000	国(地)别不详	国(地)别不详		I	287.2%	2019/9/6	2024/9/5
2907121100	美国	北美沙索化学有限公司	Sasol Chemicals North America LLC	I	131.7%	2021/1/15	2026/1/14
2907121100	美国	美国沙索化学有限公司	Sasol Chemicals USA LLC	I	131.7%	2021/1/15	2026/1/14
2907121100	美国	其他美国公司	All Others	I	131.7%	2021/1/15	2026/1/14
2907121100	欧盟	朗盛德国有限责任公司	LANXESS Deutschland GmbH	I	27.9%	2021/1/15	2026/1/14
2907121100	欧盟	其他欧盟公司	All Others	I	49.5%	2021/1/15	2026/1/14
2907121100	日本	三井化学株式会社	Mitsui Chemicals, Inc.	I	54.8%	2021/1/15	2026/1/14
2907121100	日本	本州化学工业株式会社	Honshu Chemical Industry Co., Ltd.	I	54.8%	2021/1/15	2026/1/14
2907121100	日本	其他日本公司	All Others	I	54.8%	2021/1/15	2026/1/14
2907121100	国(地)别不详	国(地)别不详		I	131.7%	2021/1/15	2026/1/14
2907131000	台湾	和益化学工业股份有限公司	Formosan Union Chemical Corporation	I	6.87%	2007/3/29	2024/3/28
2907131000	台湾	其他台湾地区公司	All Others	I	20.38%	2007/3/29	2024/3/28
2907131000	台湾	中国人造纤维股份有限公司	China Man－Made Fiber Corporation	I	4.08%	2007/3/29	2024/3/28
2907131000	印度	其他印度公司	All Others	I	20.38%	2007/3/29	2024/3/28
2907131000	印度	印度十拿－赫蒂利亚有限公司	SI GROUP－INDIA LIMITED	I	12.22%	2007/3/29	2024/3/28
2907131000	国(地)别不详	国(地)别不详		I	20.38%	2007/3/29	2024/3/28
2907210001	日本	三井化学株式会社	Mitsui Chemicals,INC.	I	40.5%	2019/3/23	2024/3/22
2907210001	日本	住友化学株式会社	Sumitomo Chemical Company,Limited	I	40.5%	2019/3/23	2024/3/22
2907210001	日本	其他日本公司	All others	I	40.5%	2019/3/23	2024/3/22
2907210001	美国	茵蒂斯派克化学公司	INDSPEC Chemical Corporation	I	30.1%	2019/3/23	2024/3/22
2907210001	美国	其他美国公司	All others	I	30.1%	2019/3/23	2024/3/22
2907210001	国(地)别不详	国(地)别不详		I	40.5%	2019/3/23	2024/3/22
2907230001	韩国	其他韩国公司	All Others	I	37.1%	2007/8/30	2024/8/29

HS 编码	原产国名称	厂商中文名称	厂商英文名称	税种代码	税率	起始日期	截止日期
2907230001	日本	其他日本公司	All Others	I	37.1%	2007/8/30	2024/8/29
2907230001	台湾	其他台湾地区公司	All Others	I	37.1%	2007/8/30	2024/8/29
2907230001	新加坡	其他新加坡公司	All Others	I	37.1%	2007/8/30	2024/8/29
2907230001	新加坡	三井酚类新加坡公司	MITSUI PHENOLS SINGAPORE PTE. LTD.	I	5.0%	2007/8/30	2024/8/29
2907230001	台湾	信昌化学工业股份有限公司	Taiwan Prosperity Chemical Corporation	I	5.3%	2007/8/30	2024/8/29
2907230001	韩国	锦湖 P&B 化学株式会社	KUMHO P&B CHEMICALS, INC.	I	5.8%	2007/8/30	2024/8/29
2907230001	台湾	南亚塑胶工业股份有限公司	Nan Ya Plastics Corporation	I	6.0%	2007/8/30	2024/8/29
2907230001	台湾	长春人造树脂厂股份有限公司	CHANG CHUN PLASTICS CO., LTD.	I	6.0%	2007/8/30	2024/8/29
2907230001	日本	三井化学株式会社	Mitsui Chemicals, Inc.	I	6.1%	2007/8/30	2024/8/29
2907230001	日本	三菱化学株式会社	Mitsubishi Chemical Corporation	I	7.9%	2007/8/30	2024/8/29
2907230001	韩国	(株)LG 化学	LG Chem, Ltd.	I	4.7%	2009/12/15	2024/8/29
2907230001	泰国	其他泰国公司	All Others	I	31.0%	2018/3/6	2023/3/5
2907230001	泰国	PTT 苯酚有限公司	PTT Phenol Company Limited	I	9.7%	2018/3/6	2023/3/5
2907230001	国(地)别不详	国(地)别不详的		I	37.1%	2008/1/1	2024/8/29
2909430000	美国	伊士曼化工公司	Eastman Chemical Company	I	46.9%	2018/4/12	2024/1/27
2909430000	美国	陶氏化学公司	The Dow Chemical Company	I	75.5%	2018/4/12	2024/1/27
2909430000	美国	益科斯达化工产品有限公司	Equistar Chemicals, LP	I	37.5%	2018/4/12	2024/1/27
2909430000	欧盟	沙索德国有限责任公司	Sasol Germany GmbH	I	10.8%	2018/4/12	2024/1/27
2909430000	欧盟	沙索溶剂德国有限责任公司	Sasol Solvents Germany GmbH	I	10.8%	2018/4/12	2024/1/27
2909430000	欧盟	英力士化学拉瓦拉有限公司	INEOS Chemicals Lavera SAS	I	43.5%	2018/4/12	2024/1/27
2909430000	欧盟	巴斯夫欧洲公司	BASF SE	I	18.8%	2018/4/12	2024/1/27
2909430000	欧盟	其他欧盟公司	All others	I	43.5%	2018/4/12	2024/1/27
2909430000	美国	其他美国公司	All others	I	75.5%	2018/4/12	2024/1/27
2909430000	国(地)别不详	国(地)别不详		I	75.5%	2018/4/12	2024/1/27
2909440010	美国	陶氏化学公司	The Dow Chemical Company	I	57.4%	2022/1/11	2027/1/10
2909440010	美国	其他美国公司	All Others	I	65.3%	2022/1/11	2027/1/10
2909440010	国(地)别不详	国(地)别不详		I	65.3%	2022/1/11	2027/1/10
2909499010	美国	陶氏化学公司	The Dow Chemical Company	I	57.4%	2022/1/11	2027/1/10
2909499010	美国	其他美国公司	All Others	I	65.3%	2022/1/11	2027/1/10
2909499010	国(地)别不详	国(地)别不详		I	65.3%	2022/1/11	2027/1/10
2912499010	印度		BHARAT RASAYAN LIMITED	I	56.4%	2018/6/8	2023/6/7
2912499010	印度	赫曼尼工业有限公司	Hemani Industries Limited	I	36.4%	2018/6/8	2023/6/7
2912499010	印度	古吉拉特杀虫剂有限公司	Gujarat Insecticides Limited	I	52.0%	2018/6/8	2023/6/7
2912499010	印度	其他印度公司	All Others	I	56.9%	2018/6/8	2023/6/7
2912499010	国(别)地不详	国(别)地不详		I	56.9%	2018/6/8	2023/6/7
2914110000	日本	三菱化学株式会社	MITSUBISHI CHEMICAL CORPORATION	I	12.1%	2008/6/9	2025/6/7
2914110000	日本	其他日本公司	All Others	I	51.6%	2008/6/9	2025/6/7
2914110000	日本	三井化学株式会社	Mitsui Chemicals, Inc.	I	7.2%	2008/6/9	2025/6/7
2914110000	韩国	(株)LG 化学	LG Chem, Ltd.	I	5.0%	2008/6/9	2025/6/7
2914110000	韩国	其他韩国公司	All Others	I	51.6%	2008/6/9	2025/6/7
2914110000	新加坡	其他新加坡公司	All Others	I	51.6%	2008/6/9	2025/6/7
2914110000	台湾	其他台湾地区公司	All Others	I	51.6%	2008/6/9	2025/6/7
2914110000	台湾	台湾化学纤维股份有限公司	FORMOSA CHEMICALS&FIBRE CORPORATION	I	6.2%	2008/6/9	2025/6/7
2914110000	台湾	信昌化学工业股份有限公司	Taiwan Prosperity Chemical Corporation	I	6.5%	2008/6/9	2025/6/7
2914110000	台湾	台湾长春人造树脂厂股份有限公司	CHANG CHUN PLASTICS CO., LTD.	I	9.4%	2008/6/9	2025/6/7
2914110000	新加坡	三井酚类新加坡公司	MITSUI PHENOLS SINGAPORE PTE. LTD.	I	6.7%	2008/6/9	2025/6/7
2914110000	韩国	锦湖 P&B 化学株式会社	KUMHO P&B CHEMICALS, INC.	I	4.3%	2010/9/10	2025/6/7
2914110000	国(地)别不详	国(地)别不详		I	51.6%	2008/6/9	2025/6/7
2914130000	韩国	锦湖 P&B 化学株式会社	KUMHOP&BCHEMICALS,INC.	I	18.5%	2018/3/20	2023/3/19
2914130000	韩国	其他韩国公司	AllOthers	I	32.3%	2018/3/20	2023/3/19
2914130000	日本	三井化学株式会社	MitsuiChemicals,Inc.	I	45.0%	2018/3/20	2023/3/19
2914130000	日本	三菱化学株式会社	MitsubishiChemicalCorporation	I	47.80%	2018/3/20	2023/3/19
2914130000	日本	其他日本公司	AllOthers	I	190.40%	2018/3/20	2023/3/19
2914130000	南非	沙索南非有限公司	SasolSouthAfrica(Pty)Ltd.	I	15.90%	2018/3/20	2023/3/19
2914130000	南非	其他南非公司	AllOthers	I	34.1%	2018/3/20	2023/3/19
2914130000	国(地)别不详	国(地)别不详		I	190.4%	2018/3/20	2023/3/19
2921420020	印度	阿迪工业有限公司	AartiIndustries Limited	I	31.4%	2018/2/13	2023/2/12
2921420020	印度	阿迪工业有限公司	AartiIndustries Limited	I	21.2%	2018/2/13	2023/2/12
2921420020	印度	其他印度公司	All Others	I	49.9%	2018/2/13	2023/2/12
2921420020	印度	其他印度公司	All Others	I	166.8%	2018/2/13	2023/2/12
2921420020	国(地)别不详	国(地)别不详		I	49.9%	2018/2/13	2023/2/12
2921420020	国(地)别不详	国(地)别不详		I	166.8%	2018/2/13	2023/2/12
2921430001	欧盟	朗盛德国有限责任公司	LANXESS Deutschland GmbH	I	19.6%	2013/6/28	2024/6/27
2921430001	欧盟	其他欧盟公司	ALL Others	I	36.9%	2013/6/28	2024/6/27
2921430001	国(地)别不详	国(地)别不详		I	36.9%	2013/6/28	2024/6/27
2921430020	欧盟	朗盛德国有限责任公司	LANXESSDeutschlandGmbH	I	19.6%	2013/6/28	2024/6/27

HS编码	原产国名称	厂商中文名称	厂商英文名称	税种代码	税率	起始日期	截止日期
2921430020	欧盟	其他欧盟公司	ALLOthers	I	36.9%	2013/6/28	2024/6/27
2921430020	国(地)别不详	国(地)别不详		I	36.9%	2013/6/28	2024/6/27
2922110001	美国	陶氏化学公司	TheDowChemicalCompany	I	76.0%	2018/10/30	2023/10/29
2922110001	美国	英力士美国公司	INEOSAmericasLLC	I	97.1%	2018/10/30	2023/10/29
2922110001	美国	亨斯迈石化有限公司	HuntsmanPetrochemicalLLC	I	97.1%	2018/10/30	2023/10/29
2922110001	美国	其他美国公司	AllOthers	I	97.1%	2018/10/30	2023/10/29
2922110001	马来西亚	国油石化衍生公司/马石化营销(纳闽)有限公司	PETRONAS CHEMICALS DERIVATIVES SDN-BHD/PETRONAS CHEMICALS MARKETING (LABUAN)LTD	I	18.3%	2018/10/30	2023/10/29
2922110001	马来西亚	其他马来西亚公司	AllOthers	I	20.3%	2018/10/30	2023/10/29
2922110001	沙特阿拉伯	沙特基础工业公司	SaudiBasicIndustriesCorporation	I	10.1%	2018/10/30	2023/10/29
2922110001	沙特阿拉伯	其他沙特阿拉伯公司	AllOthers	I	27.9%	2018/10/30	2023/10/29
2922110001	泰国	TOC乙二醇有限公司	TOCGLYCOLCOMPANYLIMITED	I	37.6%	2018/10/30	2023/10/29
2922110001	泰国	其他泰国公司	AllOthers	I	37.6%	2018/10/30	2023/10/29
2922110001		国(地)别不详的		I	97.1%	2018/10/30	2023/10/29
2922120001	美国	陶氏化学公司	TheDowChemicalCompany	I	76.0%	2018/10/30	2023/10/29
2922120001	美国	英力士美国公司	INEOSAmericasLLC	I	97.1%	2018/10/30	2023/10/29
2922120001	美国	亨斯迈石化有限公司	HuntsmanPetrochemicalLLC	I	97.1%	2018/10/30	2023/10/29
2922120001	美国	其他美国公司	AllOthers	I	97.1%	2018/10/30	2023/10/29
2922120001	马来西亚	国油石化衍生公司/马石化营销(纳闽)有限公司	PETRONAS CHEMICALS DERIVATIVES SDN-BHD/PETRONAS CHEMICALS MARKETING (LABUAN)LTD	I	18.3%	2018/10/30	2023/10/29
2922120001	马来西亚	其他马来西亚公司	AllOthers	I	20.3%	2018/10/30	2023/10/29
2922120001	沙特阿拉伯	沙特基础工业公司	SaudiBasicIndustriesCorporation	I	10.1%	2018/10/30	2023/10/29
2922120001	沙特阿拉伯	其他沙特阿拉伯公司	AllOthers	I	27.9%	2018/10/30	2023/10/29
2922120001	泰国	TOC乙二醇有限公司	TOCGLYCOLCOMPANYLIMITED	I	37.6%	2018/10/30	2023/10/29
2922120001	泰国	其他泰国公司	AllOthers	I	37.6%	2018/10/30	2023/10/29
2922120001	国(地)别不详的	国(地)别不详的		I	97.1%	2018/10/30	2023/10/29
2922150000	美国	陶氏化学公司	TheDowChemicalCompany	I	76.0%	2018/10/30	2023/10/29
2922150000	美国	英力士美国公司	INEOSAmericasLLC	I	97.1%	2018/10/30	2023/10/29
2922150000	美国	亨斯迈石化有限公司	HuntsmanPetrochemicalLLC	I	97.1%	2018/10/30	2023/10/29
2922150000	美国	其他美国公司	AllOthers	I	97.1%	2018/10/30	2023/10/29
2922150000	马来西亚	国油石化衍生公司/马石化营销(纳闽)有限公司	PETRONAS CHEMICALS DERIVATIVES SDN-BHD/PETRONAS CHEMICALS MARKETING (LABUAN)LTD	I	18.3%	2018/10/30	2023/10/29
2922150000	马来西亚	其他马来西亚公司	AllOthers	I	20.3%	2018/10/30	2023/10/29
2922150000	沙特阿拉伯	沙特基础工业公司	SaudiBasicIndustriesCorporation	I	10.1%	2018/10/30	2023/10/29
2922150000	沙特阿拉伯	其他沙特阿拉伯公司	AllOthers	I	27.9%	2018/10/30	2023/10/29
2922150000	泰国	TOC乙二醇有限公司	TOCGLYCOLCOMPANYLIMITED	I	37.6%	2018/10/30	2023/10/29
2922150000	泰国	其他泰国公司	AllOthers	I	37.6%	2018/10/30	2023/10/29
2922150000	国(地)别不详的	国(地)别不详的		I	97.1%	2018/10/30	2023/10/29
2933710000	美国	巴斯夫美国公司	BASF Corporation	I	2.5%	2011/10/22	2022/10/21
2933710000	欧盟	宇部化学欧洲有限公司	UBE CHEMICAL EUROPE,S.A	I	2.6%	2011/10/22	2022/10/21
2933710000	美国	其他美国公司	All Others	I	24.2%	2011/10/22	2022/10/21
2933710000	欧盟	其他欧盟公司	All Others	I	25.5%	2011/10/22	2022/10/21
2933710000	欧盟	巴斯夫安特卫普公司	BASF ANTWERPEN N.V.	I	3.1%	2011/10/22	2022/10/21
2933710000	欧盟	道默有限公司	DOMO Caproleuna GmbH	I	3.2%	2011/10/22	2022/10/21
2933710000	欧盟	朗盛比利时公司	LANXESS NV	I	3.4%	2011/10/22	2022/10/21
2933710000	欧盟	波兰普瓦维股份公司	Zaklady Azotowe "Pulawy" S.A.	I	4.4%	2011/10/22	2022/10/21
2933710000	欧盟	波兰阿佐提塔诺股份公司	Zaklady Azotowe w Tarnowie—Moscicach S.A.	I	4.9%	2011/10/22	2022/10/21
2933710000	美国	Fibrant有限责任公司	Fibrant, LLC	I	2.2%	2016/3/12	2022/10/21
2933710000	欧盟	Fibrant公司	Fibrant B.V.	I	2.3%	2016/3/12	2022/10/21
2933710000	美国	艾德凡斯树脂和化学品责任有限公司	AdvanSix Resins & Chemicals LLC	I	3.6%	2018/6/9	2022/10/21
2933710000	国(地)别不详的	国(地)别不详的		I	25.5%	2011/10/22	2022/10/21
3703101000	欧盟	柯达有限公司	Kodak Limited	I	19.4%	2012/3/23	2023/3/22
3703101000	欧盟	富士胶片制造(欧洲)有限公司	FUJIFILM Manufacturing Europe B.V.	I	23.5%	2016/6/29	2023/3/22
3703101000	欧盟	其他欧盟公司	All Others	I	19.4%	2012/3/23	2023/3/22
3703101000	美国	富士胶片制造(美国)有限公司	FUJIFILM Manufacturing U.S.A., Inc.	I	23.6%	2016/6/29	2023/3/22
3703101000	美国	其他美国公司	All Others	I	28.8%	2012/3/23	2023/3/22
3703101000	日本	日本公司		I	28.8%	2012/3/23	2023/3/22
3703101000	国(别)地不详	国(别)地不详		I	28.8%	2012/3/23	2023/3/22
3703201000	欧盟	柯达有限公司	Kodak Limited	I	19.4%	2012/3/23	2023/3/22
3703201000	欧盟	富士胶片制造(欧洲)有限公司	FUJIFILM Manufacturing Europe B.V.	I	23.5%	2016/6/29	2023/3/22
3703201000	欧盟	其他欧盟公司	All Others	I	19.4%	2012/3/23	2023/3/22
3703201000	美国	富士胶片制造(美国)有限公司	FUJIFILM Manufacturing U.S.A., Inc.	I	23.6%	2016/6/29	2023/3/22
3703201000	美国	其他美国公司	All Others	I	28.8%	2012/3/23	2023/3/22
3703201000	日本	日本公司		I	28.8%	2012/3/23	2023/3/22
3703201000	国(别)地不详	国(别)地不详		I	28.8%	2012/3/23	2023/3/22
3703901000	欧盟	柯达有限公司	Kodak Limited	I	19.4%	2012/3/23	2023/3/22

HS 编码	原产国名称	厂商中文名称	厂商英文名称	税种代码	税率	起始日期	截止日期
3703901000	欧盟	富士胶片制造(欧洲)有限公司	FUJIFILM Manufacturing Europe B.V.	I	23.5%	2016/6/29	2023/3/22
3703901000	欧盟	其他欧盟公司	All Others	I	19.4%	2012/3/23	2023/3/22
3703901000	美国	富士胶片制造(美国)有限公司	FUJIFILM Manufacturing U.S.A., Inc.	I	23.6%	2016/6/29	2023/3/22
3703901000	美国	其他美国公司	All Others	I	28.8%	2012/3/23	2023/3/22
3703901000	日本	日本公司		I	28.8%	2012/3/23	2023/3/22
3703901000	国(别)地不详	国(别)地不详		I	28.8%	2012/3/23	2023/3/22
3904500010	日本	株式会社吴羽	KUREHA CORPORATION	I	47.1%	2017/4/20	2999/12/31
3904500010	日本	旭化成株式会社	ASAHI KASEI CHEMICALS CORP.	I	47.1%	2017/4/20	2999/12/31
3904500010	日本	其他日本公司	All Others	I	47.1%	2017/4/20	2999/12/31
3904500010	国(地)别不详	国(地)别不详		I	47.1%	2017/4/20	2999/12/31
3907101010	韩国	韩国工程塑料株式会社	KOREA ENGINEERING PLASTICS CO., LTD	I	30.0%	2017/10/24	2022/10/23
3907101010	韩国	(株)可隆塑胶股份有限公司	KOLON PLASTICS, INC.	I	6.2%	2017/10/24	2022/10/23
3907101010	韩国	其他韩国公司	All Others	I	30.4%	2017/10/24	2022/10/23
3907101010	泰国	泰国聚甲醛有限公司	THAI POLYACETAL CO., LTD	I	18.5%	2017/10/24	2022/10/23
3907101010	泰国	其他泰国公司	All Others	I	34.9%	2017/10/24	2022/10/23
3907101010	马来西亚	宝理塑料(亚太)公司	PolyplasticsAsiaPacificSdn.Bhd	I	8.0%	2017/10/24	2022/10/23
3907101010	马来西亚	其他马来西亚公司	AllOthers	I	9.5%	2017/10/24	2022/10/23
3907101010	国(地)别不详	国(地)别不详		I	34.9%	2017/10/24	2022/10/23
3907109010	韩国	韩国工程塑料株式会社	KOREAENGINEERINGPLASTICSCO., LTD	I	30.0%	2017/10/24	2022/10/23
3907109010	韩国	(株)可隆塑胶股份有限公司	KOLONPLASTICS, INC。	I	6.2%	2017/10/24	2022/10/23
3907109010	韩国	其他韩国公司	All Others	I	30.4%	2017/10/24	2022/10/23
3907109010	泰国	泰国聚甲醛有限公司	THAI POLYACETAL CO., LTD.	I	18.5%	2017/10/24	2022/10/23
3907109010	泰国	其他泰国公司	All Others	I	34.9%	2017/10/24	2022/10/23
3907109010	马来西亚	宝理塑料(亚太)公司	PolyplasticsAsiaPacificSdn.Bhd.	I	8.0%	2017/10/24	2022/10/23
3907109010	马来西亚	其他马来西亚公司	All Others	I	9.5%	2017/10/24	2022/10/23
3907109010	国(地)别不详	国(地)别不详		I	34.9%	2017/10/24	2022/10/23
3907299010	美国	沙特基础工业创新塑料美国有限公司	SABIC Innovative Plastics US LLC	I	17.3%	2022/1/7	2027/1/6
3907299010	美国	沙特基础工业创新塑料美国有限公司	SABIC Innovative Plastics US LLC	J	0.9%	2022/1/7	2027/1/6
3907299010	美国	其他美国公司	All others	I	48.6%	2022/1/7	2027/1/6
3907299010	美国	其他美国公司	All others	J	0.9%	2022/1/7	2027/1/6
3907299010	国(地)别不详	国(地)别不详		I	48.6%	2022/1/7	2027/1/6
3907299010	国(地)别不详	国(地)别不详		J	0.9%	2022/1/7	2027/1/6
3908101101	美国	英威达有限责任公司	INVISTA S.A R.L.	I	25.2%	2020/10/13	2026/10/12
3908101101	美国	奥升德功能材料有限公司	Ascend Performance Materials LLC	I	31.4%	2020/10/13	2026/10/12
3908101101	美国	其他美国公司	All others	I	37.5%	2020/10/13	2026/10/12
3908101101	国(地)别不详	国(地)别不详		I	37.5%	2020/10/13	2026/10/12
3908101200	俄罗斯	其他俄罗斯公司	All Others	I	23.9%	2011/1/1	2999/12/31
3908101200	欧盟	其他欧盟公司	All Others	I	23.9%	2011/1/1	2999/12/31
3908101200	台湾	其他台湾地区公司	All Others	I	23.9%	2011/1/1	2999/12/31
3908101200	美国	巴斯夫美国公司	BASF Corporation.	I	29.3%	2011/1/1	2999/12/31
3908101200	台湾	台湾化学纤维股份有限公司	FORMOSA CHEMICALS&FIBER CORPORATION	I	4.0%	2011/1/1	2999/12/31
3908101200	台湾	华隆股份有限公司	HUALON CORPORATION	I	4.2%	2011/1/1	2999/12/31
3908101200	台湾	集盛实业股份有限公司	Zig sheng Industrial Co., Ltd.	I	4.2%	2011/1/1	2999/12/31
3908101200	台湾	太洋尼龙股份有限公司	Tai-Young Nylon Co., Ltd	I	4.2%	2011/1/1	2999/12/31
3908101200	台湾	展颂股份有限公司	CHAIN YARN CO., LTD.	I	4.2%	2011/1/1	2999/12/31
3908101200	台湾	中国石油化学工业开发股份有限公司	China Petrochemical Development Corporation	I	4.2%	2011/1/1	2999/12/31
3908101200	台湾	力鹏企业股份有限公司	Li Peng Enterprise Co., Ltd.	I	4.3%	2011/1/1	2999/12/31
3908101200	欧盟	巴斯夫安特卫普公司	BASF ANTWERPEN N.V.	I	8.0%	2011/1/1	2999/12/31
3908101200	欧盟	巴斯夫欧洲公司	BASF SE	I	8.2%	2011/1/1	2999/12/31
3908101200	欧盟	道默有限公司	DOMO Caproleuna GmbH	I	8.2%	2011/1/1	2999/12/31
3908101200	欧盟	帝斯曼工程材料公司	DSMEngineeringMaterialsB.V.	I	8.2%	2020/7/17	2999/12/31
3908101200	欧盟	波兰阿佐提塔诺股份公司	Zaklady Azotowe w Tarnowie-Moscicach, S.A.	I	9.7%	2011/1/1	2999/12/31
3908101200	美国	其他美国公司	All Others	I	96.5%	2011/1/1	2999/12/31
3908101200	俄罗斯	古比雪夫氮公众股份有限公司	Public Joint Stock Company"KuibyshevAzot	I	5.9%	2017/3/16	2999/12/31
3908101200	欧盟	朗盛德国有限公司	LANXESS Deutschland GmbH	I	8.2%	2017/7/21	2999/12/31
3908101200	欧盟	朗盛比利时有限公司	LANXESS N.V.	I	8.2%	2017/7/21	2999/12/31
3908101200	美国	艾德凡斯树脂和化学品责任有限公司	AdvanSix Resins & Chemicals LLC	I	36.2%	2018/6/9	2999/12/31
3908101200	国(地)别不详	国(地)别不详		I	96.5%	2018/6/9	2999/12/31
3911900004	日本	东丽株式会社	Toray Industries, Inc.	I	26.9%	2020/12/1	2025/11/30
3911900004	日本	DIC 株式会社	DIC Corporation	I	27.3%	2020/12/1	2025/11/30
3911900004	日本	宝理塑料株式会社	POLYPLASTICS CO., LTD.	I	25.2%	2020/12/1	2025/11/30
3911900004	日本	东曹株式会社	Tosoh Corporation	I	25.6%	2020/12/1	2025/11/30
3911900004	日本	出光狮王塑料株式会社	Lion Idemitsu Composites Co., LTD.)	I	69.1%	2021/10/29	2025/11/30
3911900004	日本	出光复合材料株式会社	IDEMITSU FINE COMPOSITES CO., LTD.	I	33.6%	2021/10/29	2025/11/30
3911900004	日本	住友电木株式会社	Sumitomo Bakelite Co., Ltd.	I	34.5%	2020/12/1	2025/11/30

HS 编码	原产国名称	厂商中文名称	厂商英文名称	税种代码	税率	起始日期	截止日期
3911900004	日本	其他日本公司	All Others	I	69.1%	2020/12/1	2025/11/30
3911900004	美国	苏威特种聚合物美国有限公司	Solvay Specialty Polymers USA，LLC	I	214.1%	2020/12/1	2025/11/30
3911900004	美国	富特朗实业有限公司	Fortron Industries LLC	I	220.9%	2020/12/1	2025/11/30
3911900004	美国	其他美国公司	All Others	I	220.9%	2020/12/1	2025/11/30
3911900004	韩国	东丽尖端素材株式会社	Toray Advanced Materials Korea Inc.	I	26.4%	2020/12/1	2025/11/30
3911900004	韩国	SK 化工株式会社	SK Chemicals Co.，Ltd.	I	32.7%	2020/12/1	2025/11/30
3911900004	韩国	其他韩国公司	All Others	I	46.8%	2020/12/1	2025/11/30
3911900004	马来西亚	宝理塑料(亚太)公司	Polyplastics Asia Pacific Sdn. Bhd.	I	23.3%	2020/12/1	2025/11/30
3911900004	马来西亚	迪爱生复合物(马来西亚)有限公司	DIC Compounds(Malaysia) Sdn. Bhd.	I	40.5%	2020/12/1	2025/11/30
3911900004	马来西亚	其他马来西亚公司	All Others	I	40.5%	2020/12/1	2025/11/30
3911900004	国(地)别不详	国(地)别不详		I	220.9%	2020/12/1	2025/11/30
4002391000	美国	埃克森美孚公司	ExxonMobilChemicalLimited	I	75.5%	2018/8/20	2023/8/19
4002391000	美国	其他美国公司	AllOthers	I	75.5%	2018/8/20	2023/8/19
4002391000	欧盟	埃克森美孚化工有限公司	ExxonMobilChemicalLimited	I	71.9%	2018/8/20	2023/8/19
4002391000	欧盟	阿朗新科比利时有限公司	ARLANXEOBelgiumNV	I	27.4%	2018/8/20	2023/8/19
4002391000	欧盟	其他欧盟公司	AllOthers	I	71.9%	2018/8/20	2023/8/19
4002391000	新加坡	阿朗新科新加坡私人有限公司	ARLANXEOSINGAPOREPTE.LTD	I	23.1%	2018/8/20	2023/8/19
4002391000	新加坡	其他新加坡公司	AllOthers	I	45.2%	2018/8/20	2023/8/19
4002391000	国(地)别不详的	国(地)别不详的		I	75.5%	2018/8/20	2023/8/19
4002399000	美国	埃克森美孚公司	ExxonMobilCorporation	I	75.5%	2018/8/20	2023/8/19
4002399000	美国	埃克森美孚公司	ExxonMobilCorporation	T	66.5%	2018/4/20	2999/12/31
4002399000	美国	其他美国公司	AllOthers	I	75.5%	2018/8/20	2023/8/19
4002399000	美国	其他美国公司	AllOthers	T	66.5%	2018/4/20	2999/12/31
4002399000	欧盟	埃克森美孚化工有限公司	ExxonMobilChemicalLimited	I	71.9%	2018/8/20	2023/8/19
4002399000	欧盟	埃克森美孚化工有限公司	ExxonMobilChemicalLimited	T	63.7%	2018/4/20	2999/12/31
4002399000	欧盟	阿朗新科比利时有限公司	ARLANXEOBelgiumNV	I	27.4%	2018/8/20	2023/8/19
4002399000	欧盟	阿朗新科比利时有限公司	ARLANXEOBelgiumNV	T	30.9%	2018/4/20	2999/12/31
4002399000	欧盟	其他欧盟公司	AllOthers	I	71.9%	2018/8/20	2023/8/19
4002399000	欧盟	其他欧盟公司	AllOthers	T	63.7%	2018/4/20	2999/12/31
4002399000	新加坡	阿朗新科新加坡私人有限公司	ARLANXEOSINGAPOREPTE.LTD.	I	23.1%	2018/8/20	2023/8/19
4002399000	新加坡	阿朗新科新加坡私人有限公司	ARLANXEOSINGAPOREPTE.LTD.	T	26.0%	2018/4/20	2999/12/31
4002399000	新加坡	其他新加坡公司	AllOthers	I	45.2%	2018/8/20	2023/8/19
4002399000	新加坡	其他新加坡公司	AllOthers	T	66.5%	2018/4/20	2999/12/31
4002399000	国(地)别不详的	国(地)别不详的		I	75.5%	2018/8/20	2023/8/19
4002399000	国(地)别不详	国(地)别不详		T	66.5%	2018/4/20	2999/12/31
4002491000	美国	所有美国公司		I	151.0%	2005/5/10	2022/5/9
4002491000	欧盟	其他欧盟公司	All Others	I	151.0%	2005/5/10	2022/5/9
4002491000	欧盟	埃尼橡胶法国有限公司	Polimeri Europa Elastomeres France S.A.	I	53.0%	2005/5/10	2022/5/9
4002491000	日本	日本东曹株式会社	TOSOH CORPORATION	I	10.2%	2010/8/28	2022/5/9
4002491000	日本	昭和电工株式会社	SHOWA DENKO K.K	I	20.8%	2010/8/28	2022/5/9
4002491000	日本	其他日本公司	AllOthers	I	43.9%	2010/8/28	2022/5/9
4002491000	日本	日本电化株式会社	DenkaCompanyLimited	I	20.8%	2015/12/25	2022/5/9
4002491000	欧盟	阿朗新科德国有限公司	ARLANXEO Deutschland GmbH	I	11.0%	2016/11/9	2022/5/9
4002491000	国(地)别不详	国(地)别不详的		I	151.0%	2008/1/1	2022/5/9
4002499000	美国	所有美国公司		I	151.0%	2005/5/10	2022/5/9
4002499000	欧盟	其他欧盟公司	AllOthers	I	151.0%	2005/5/10	2022/5/9
4002499000	欧盟	埃尼橡胶法国有限公司	Polimeri Europa Elastomeres France S.A.	I	53.0%	2005/5/10	2022/5/9
4002499000	日本	日本东曹株式会社	TOSOH CORPORATION	I	10.2%	2010/8/28	2022/5/9
4002499000	日本	昭和电工株式会社	SHOWA DENKO K.K	I	20.8%	2010/8/28	2022/5/9
4002499000	日本	其他日本公司		I	43.9%	2010/8/28	2022/5/9
4002499000	日本	日本电化株式会社	DenkaCompanyLimited	I	20.8%	2015/12/25	2022/5/9
4002499000	欧盟	阿朗新科德国有限公司	ARLANXEO Deutschland GmbH	I	11.0%	2016/11/9	2022/5/9
4002499000	国(地)别不详	国(地)别不详		I	151.0%	2008/1/1	2022/5/9
4002591000	韩国	锦湖石油化学株式会社	KUMHOPETROCHEMICALCO.,LTD.	I	12.0%	2018/11/9	2023/11/8
4002591000	韩国	(株)LG 化学	LGCHEM,LTD.	I	15.0%	2018/11/9	2023/11/8
4002591000	韩国	其他韩国公司	AllOthers	I	37.3%	2018/11/9	2023/11/8
4002591000	日本	日本瑞翁株式会社	ZeonCorporation	I	28.1%	2018/11/9	2023/11/8
4002591000	日本	JSR 株式会社	JSRCorporation	I	16.0%	2018/11/9	2023/11/8
4002591000	日本	其他日本公司	AllOthers	I	56.4%	2018/11/9	2023/11/8
4002591000	国(地)别不详	国(地)别不详		I	56.4%	2018/11/9	2023/11/8
4002599000	韩国	锦湖石油化学株式会社	KUMHOPETROCHEMICALCO.,LTD.	I	12.0%	2018/11/9	2023/11/8
4002599000	韩国	(株)LG 化学：	LGCHEM,LTD.	I	15.0%	2018/11/9	2023/11/8
4002599000	韩国	其他韩国公司	AllOthers	I	37.3%	2018/11/9	2023/11/8
4002599000	日本	日本瑞翁株式会社	ZeonCorporation	I	28.1%	2018/11/9	2023/11/8
4002599000	日本	JSR 株式会社	JSRCorporation	I	16.0%	2018/11/9	2023/11/8
4002599000	日本	其他日本公司	AllOthers	I	56.4%	2018/11/9	2023/11/8
4002599000	国(地)别不详	国(地)别不详		I	56.4%	2018/11/9	2023/11/8
4002701000	韩国	锦湖 POLYCHEM 株式会社	KUMHO POLYCHEM Co.,Ltd.	I	12.5%	2020/12/20	2025/12/19

HS编码	原产国名称	厂商中文名称	厂商英文名称	税种代码	税率	起始日期	截止日期
4002701000	韩国	乐天玮萨黎司弹性体有限公司	Lotte Versalis Elastomers Co.,Ltd.	I	21.1%	2020/12/20	2025/12/19
4002701000	韩国	其他韩国公司	All Others	I	24.5%	2020/12/20	2025/12/19
4002701000	美国	陶氏化学公司	The Dow Chemical Company	I	222.0%	2020/12/20	2025/12/19
4002701000	美国	埃克森美孚公司	Exxon Mobil Corporation	I	214.9%	2020/12/20	2025/12/19
4002701000	美国	阿朗新科美国有限公司	ARLANXEO USA LLC	I	219.8%	2020/12/20	2025/12/19
4002701000	美国	美国狮子弹性体有限公司	Lion Copolymer Geismar,LLC	I	219.8%	2020/12/20	2025/12/19
4002701000	美国	其他美国公司	All Others	I	222.0%	2020/12/20	2025/12/19
4002701000	欧盟	阿朗新科荷兰有限公司	ARLANXEO Netherlands B.V.	I	18.1%	2020/12/20	2025/12/19
4002701000	欧盟	埃克森美孚化工法国公司	ExxonMobil Chemical France (ExxonMobil Chemical France Société par Actions Simplifiée)	I	14.7%	2020/12/20	2025/12/19
4002701000	欧盟	意大利玮萨黎司有限公司	Versalis S.p.A.	I	16.5%	2020/12/20	2025/12/19
4002701000	欧盟	其他欧盟公司	All Others	I	31.7%	2020/12/20	2025/12/19
4002701000	国(地)别不详	国(地)别不详		I	222.0%	2020/12/20	2025/12/19
4002709000	韩国	锦湖 POLYCHEM 株式会社	KUMHO POLYCHEM Co.,Ltd.	I	12.5%	2020/12/20	2025/12/19
4002709000	韩国	乐天玮萨黎司弹性体有限公司	Lotte Versalis Elastomers Co.,Ltd.	I	21.1%	2020/12/20	2025/12/19
4002709000	韩国	其他韩国公司	All Others	I	24.5%	2020/12/20	2025/12/19
4002709000	美国	陶氏化学公司	The Dow Chemical Company	I	222.0%	2020/12/20	2025/12/19
4002709000	美国	埃克森美孚公司	Exxon Mobil Corporation	I	214.9%	2020/12/20	2025/12/19
4002709000	美国	阿朗新科美国有限公司	ARLANXEO USA LLC	I	219.8%	2020/12/20	2025/12/19
4002709000	美国	美国狮子弹性体有限公司	Lion Copolymer Geismar,LLC	I	219.8%	2020/12/20	2025/12/19
4002709000	美国	其他美国公司	All Others	I	222.0%	2020/12/20	2025/12/19
4002709000	欧盟	阿朗新科荷兰有限公司	ARLANXEO Netherlands B.V.	I	18.1%	2020/12/20	2025/12/19
4002709000	欧盟	埃克森美孚化工法国公司	ExxonMobil Chemical France (ExxonMobil Chemical France Société par Actions Simplifiée)	I	14.7%	2020/12/20	2025/12/19
4002709000	欧盟	意大利玮萨黎司有限公司	Versalis S.p.A.	I	16.5%	2020/12/20	2025/12/19
4002709000	欧盟	其他欧盟公司	All Others	I	31.7%	2020/12/20	2025/12/19
4002709000	国(地)别不详	国(地)别不详		I	222.0%	2020/12/20	2025/12/19
4804210000	美国	开思通牛皮纸公司	Kapstone Kraft Paper Corporation	I	14.9%	2016/4/10	2999/12/31
4804210000	美国	其他美国公司	All Others	I	14.9%	2016/4/10	2999/12/31
4804210000	欧盟	毕瑞瑞典公司	BillerudKorsnäsSweden AB	I	23.5%	2016/4/10	2999/12/31
4804210000	欧盟	蒙迪斯坦博利斯基有限公司	MondiStambolijski EAD	I	29.0%	2016/4/10	2999/12/31
4804210000	欧盟	毕瑞芬兰公司	BillerudKorsnäsFinland Oy	I	26.2%	2016/4/10	2999/12/31
4804210000	欧盟	蒙迪弗兰特沙赫有限公司	Mondi Frantschach GmbH	I	26.2%	2016/4/10	2999/12/31
4804210000	欧盟	蒙迪斯特缇股份公司	Mondi Steti a.s.	I	26.2%	2016/4/10	2999/12/31
4804210000	欧盟	蒙迪狄娜股份公司	Mondi Dynäs Aktiebolag	I	26.2%	2016/4/10	2999/12/31
4804210000	欧盟	其他欧盟公司	All Others	I	29.0%	2016/4/10	2999/12/31
4804210000	日本	王子制纸株式会社	Oji Paper Co., Ltd.	I	20.5%	2016/4/10	2999/12/31
4804210000	日本	王子 Materia 株式会社	Oji Materia Co., Ltd.	I	20.5%	2016/4/10	2999/12/31
4804210000	日本	中越纸浆工业株式会社	Chuetsu Pulp & Paper Co., Ltd.	I	20.5%	2016/4/10	2999/12/31
4804210000	日本	大王制纸株式会社		I	20.5%	2016/4/10	2999/12/31
4804210000	日本	日本制纸株式会社	Nippon Paper Industries Co., Ltd.	I	20.5%	2016/4/10	2999/12/31
4804210000	日本	其他日本公司	All Others	I	20.5%	2016/4/10	2999/12/31
4804210000	国(地)别不详	国(地)别不详		I	29.0%	2016/4/10	2999/12/31
4804310020	美国	开思通牛皮纸公司	Kapstone Kraft Paper Corporation	I	14.9%	2016/4/10	2999/12/31
4804310020	美国	其他美国公司	All Others	I	14.9%	2016/4/10	2999/12/31
4804310020	欧盟	蒙迪斯坦博利斯基有限公司	MondiStambolijski EAD	I	29.0%	2016/4/10	2999/12/31
4804310020	欧盟	毕瑞瑞典公司	BillerudKorsnäsSweden AB	I	23.5%	2016/4/10	2999/12/31
4804310020	欧盟	毕瑞芬兰公司	BillerudKorsnäsFinland Oy	I	26.2%	2016/4/10	2999/12/31
4804310020	欧盟	蒙迪弗兰特沙赫有限公司	Mondi Frantschach GmbH	I	26.2%	2016/4/10	2999/12/31
4804310020	欧盟	蒙迪斯特缇股份公司	Mondi Steti a.s.	I	26.2%	2016/4/10	2999/12/31
4804310020	欧盟	蒙迪狄娜股份公司	Mondi Dynäs Aktiebolag	I	26.2%	2016/4/10	2999/12/31
4804310020	欧盟	其他欧盟公司	All Others	I	29.0%	2016/4/10	2999/12/31
4804310020	日本	王子制纸株式会社	Oji Paper Co., Ltd.	I	20.5%	2016/4/10	2999/12/31
4804310020	日本	王子 Materia 株式会社	Oji Materia Co., Ltd.	I	20.5%	2016/4/10	2999/12/31
4804310020	日本	中越纸浆工业株式会社	Chuetsu Pulp & Paper Co., Ltd.	I	20.5%	2016/4/10	2999/12/31
4804310020	日本	大王制纸株式会社		I	20.5%	2016/4/10	2999/12/31
4804310020	日本	日本制纸株式会社	Nippon Paper Industries Co., Ltd.	I	20.5%	2016/4/10	2999/12/31
4804310020	日本	其他日本公司	All Others	I	20.5%	2016/4/10	2999/12/31
4804310020	国(地)别不详	国(地)别不详		I	29.0%	2016/4/10	2999/12/31
4805911000	日本	大福制纸株式会社	Daifuku Seishi Co., Ltd.	I	15.0%	2007/4/18	2024/4/17
4805911000	日本	其他日本公司	All Others	I	40.83%	2007/4/18	2024/4/17
4805911000	日本	日本高度纸工业株式会社	NIPPON KODOSHI CORPORATION	I	22.0%	2007/4/18	2024/4/17
4805911000	国(地)别不详	国(地)别不详的		I	40.83%	2008/1/1	2024/4/17
5501300010	日本	日本依克丝兰工业株式会社	JAPAN EXLAN CO., LTD	I	16.1%	2016/7/14	2999/12/31
5501300010	日本	东丽株式会社	Toray Industries, Inc.	I	16.0%	2016/7/14	2999/12/31
5501300010	日本	其他日本公司	All Others	I	16.1%	2016/7/14	2999/12/31
5501300010	韩国	泰光产业株式会社	TAEKWANG INDUSTRIAL CO., LTD.	I	8.6%	2018/11/7	2999/12/31
5501300010	韩国	其他韩国公司	All Others	I	21.7%	2018/11/7	2999/12/31

HS编码	原产国名称	厂商中文名称	厂商英文名称	税种代码	税率	起始日期	截止日期
5501300010	土耳其	阿克萨丙烯酸化学工业公司	Aksa Akrilik Kimya Sanayii A.Ş.	I	8.2%	2016/7/14	2999/12/31
5501300010	土耳其	其他土耳其公司	All Others	I	16.1%	2016/7/14	2999/12/31
5501300010	日本	三菱化学株式会社	Mitsubishi Chemical Corporation	I	15.8%	2017/8/5	2999/12/31
5501300010	国(地)别不详	国(地)别不详		I	21.7%	2016/7/14	2999/12/31
5503300010	日本	日本依克丝兰工业株式会社	JAPAN EXLAN CO., LTD	I	16.1%	2016/7/14	2999/12/31
5503300010	日本	东丽株式会社	Toray Industries, Inc.	I	16.0%	2016/7/14	2999/12/31
5503300010	日本	其他日本公司	All Others	I	16.1%	2016/7/14	2999/12/31
5503300010	韩国	泰光产业株式会社	TAEKWANG INDUSTRIAL CO., LTD.	I	8.6%	2018/11/7	2999/12/31
5503300010	韩国	其他韩国公司	All Others	I	21.7%	2018/11/7	2999/12/31
5503300010	土耳其	阿克萨丙烯酸化学工业公司	Aksa Akrilik Kimya Sanayii A.Ş.	I	8.2%	2016/7/14	2999/12/31
5503300010	土耳其	其他土耳其公司	All Others	I	16.1%	2016/7/14	2999/12/31
5503300010	日本	三菱化学株式会社	三菱化学株式会社	I	15.8%	2017/8/5	2999/12/31
5503300010	国(地)别不详	国(地)别不详		I	21.7%	2016/7/14	2999/12/31
5506300010	日本	日本依克丝兰工业株式会社	JAPAN EXLAN CO., LTD	I	16.1%	2016/7/14	2999/12/31
5506300010	日本	东丽株式会社	Toray Industries, Inc.	I	16.0%	2016/7/14	2999/12/31
5506300010	日本	其他日本公司	All Others	I	16.1%	2016/7/14	2999/12/31
5506300010	韩国	泰光产业株式会社	TAEKWANG INDUSTRIAL CO., LTD.	I	8.6%	2018/11/7	2999/12/31
5506300010	韩国	其他韩国公司	All Others	I	21.7%	2018/11/7	2999/12/31
5506300010	土耳其	阿克萨丙烯酸化学工业公司	Aksa Akrilik Kimya Sanayii A.Ş.	I	8.2%	2016/7/14	2999/12/31
5506300010	土耳其	其他土耳其公司	All Others	I	16.1%	2016/7/14	2999/12/31
5506300010	日本	三菱化学株式会社	Mitsubishi Chemical Corporation	I	15.8%	2017/8/5	2999/12/31
5506300010	国(地)别不详	国(地)别不详		I	21.7%	2016/7/14	2999/12/31
7002201010	日本	信越化学株式会社	Shin－Etsu Chemical Co.,Ltd.	I	17.0%	2020/9/26	2023/7/10
7002201010	日本	住友电气工业株式会社	Sumitomo Electric Industries, Ltd.	I	31.2%	2020/9/26	2023/7/10
7002201010	日本	株式会社藤仓	Fujikura Ltd.	I	14.4%	2020/9/26	2023/7/10
7002201010	日本	古河电气工业株式会社	Furukawa Electric Co., Ltd.	I	31.2%	2020/9/26	2023/7/10
7002201010	日本	其他日本公司	ALL Others	I	31.2%	2020/9/26	2023/7/10
7002201010	美国	康宁公司	Corning Incorporated	I	41.7%	2020/9/26	2023/7/10
7002201010	美国	OFS－费特有限责任公司	OFS Fitel, LLC.	I	17.4%	2020/9/26	2023/7/10
7002201010	美国	其他美国公司	ALL Others	I	41.7%	2020/9/26	2023/7/10
7002201010	国(地)别不详	国(地)别不详		I	41.7%	2020/9/26	2023/7/10
7218910000	欧盟	其他欧盟公司	AllOthers	I	43.0%	2019/7/23	2024/7/22
7218910000	日本	日本冶金工业株式会社	NIPPONYAKINKOGYOCO.,LTD	I	18.1%	2019/7/23	2024/7/22
7218910000	日本	其他日本公司	AllOthers	I	29.0%	2019/7/23	2024/7/22
7218910000	韩国	株式会社 POSCO	POSCO	I	23.1%	2019/7/23	2024/7/22
7218910000	韩国	其他韩国公司	AllOthers	I	103.1%	2019/7/23	2024/7/22
7218910000	印度尼西亚	印度尼西亚公司		I	20.2%	2019/7/23	2024/7/22
7218910000	国(地)别不详	国(地)别不详		I	103.1%	2019/7/23	2024/7/22
7218990090	欧盟	其他欧盟公司	AllOthers	I	43.0%	2019/12/21	2024/7/22
7218990090	日本	日本冶金工业株式会社	NIPPONYAKINKOGYOCO.,LTD	I	18.1%	2019/12/21	2024/7/22
7218990090	日本	其他日本公司	AllOthers	I	29.0%	2019/12/21	2024/7/22
7218990090	韩国	株式会社 POSCO	POSCO	I	23.1%	2019/12/21	2024/7/22
7218990090	韩国	其他韩国公司	AllOthers	I	103.1%	2019/12/21	2024/7/22
7218990090	印度尼西亚	印度尼西亚公司		I	20.2%	2019/12/21	2024/7/22
7218990090	国(地)别不详	国(地)别不详		I	103.1%	2019/12/21	2024/7/22
7219110000	欧盟	其他欧盟公司	AllOthers	I	43.0%	2019/7/23	2024/7/22
7219110000	日本	日本冶金工业株式会社	NIPPONYAKINKOGYOCO.,LTD	I	18.1%	2019/7/23	2024/7/22
7219110000	日本	其他日本公司	AllOthers	I	29.0%	2019/7/23	2024/7/22
7219110000	韩国	株式会社 POSCO	POSCO	I	23.1%	2019/7/23	2024/7/22
7219110000	韩国	其他韩国公司	AllOthers	I	103.1%	2019/7/23	2024/7/22
7219110000	印度尼西亚	印度尼西亚公司		I	20.2%	2019/7/23	2024/7/22
7219110000	国(地)别不详	国(地)别不详		I	103.1%	2019/7/23	2024/7/22
7219121000	欧盟	其他欧盟公司	AllOthers	I	43.0%	2021/1/1	2024/7/22
7219121000	日本	日本冶金工业株式会社	NIPPONYAKINKOGYOCO.,LTD	I	18.1%	2021/1/1	2024/7/22
7219121000	日本	其他日本公司	AllOthers	I	29.0%	2021/1/1	2024/7/22
7219121000	韩国	株式会社 POSCO	POSCO	I	23.1%	2021/1/1	2024/7/22
7219121000	韩国	其他韩国公司	AllOthers	I	103.1%	2021/1/1	2024/7/22
7219121000	印度尼西亚	印度尼西亚公司		I	20.2%	2021/1/1	2024/7/22
7219121000	国(地)别不详	国(地)别不详		I	103.1%	2021/1/1	2024/7/22
7219129000	欧盟	其他欧盟公司	AllOthers	I	43.0%	2021/1/1	2024/7/22
7219129000	日本	日本冶金工业株式会社	NIPPONYAKINKOGYOCO.,LTD	I	18.1%	2021/1/1	2024/7/22
7219129000	日本	其他日本公司	AllOthers	I	29.0%	2021/1/1	2024/7/22
7219129000	韩国	株式会社 POSCO	POSCO	I	23.1%	2021/1/1	2024/7/22
7219129000	韩国	其他韩国公司	AllOthers	I	103.1%	2021/1/1	2024/7/22
7219129000	印度尼西亚	印度尼西亚公司		I	20.2%	2021/1/1	2024/7/22
7219129000	国(地)别不详	国(地)别不详		I	103.1%	2021/1/1	2024/7/22
7219131200	欧盟	其他欧盟公司		I	43.0%	2019/7/23	2024/7/22
7219131200	日本	日本冶金工业株式会社	NIPPONYAKINKOGYOCO.,LTD	I	18.1%	2019/7/23	2024/7/22
7219131200	日本	其他日本公司	AllOthers	I	29.0%	2019/7/23	2024/7/22
7219131200	韩国	株式会社 POSCO	POSCO	I	23.1%	2019/7/23	2024/7/22

HS 编码	原产国名称	厂商中文名称	厂商英文名称	税种代码	税率	起始日期	截止日期
7219131200	韩国	其他韩国公司	AllOthers	I	103.1%	2019/7/23	2024/7/22
7219131200	印度尼西亚	印度尼西亚公司		I	20.2%	2019/7/23	2024/7/22
7219131200	国(地)别不详	国(地)别不详		I	103.1%	2019/7/23	2024/7/22
7219131900	欧盟	其他欧盟公司	AllOthers	I	43.0%	2019/7/23	2024/7/22
7219131900	日本	日本冶金工业株式会社	NIPPONYAKINKOGYOCO.,LTD	I	18.1%	2019/7/23	2024/7/22
7219131900	日本	其他日本公司	AllOthers	I	29.0%	2019/7/23	2024/7/22
7219131900	韩国	株式会社 POSCO	POSCO	I	23.1%	2019/7/23	2024/7/22
7219131900	韩国	其他韩国公司	AllOthers	I	103.1%	2019/7/23	2024/7/22
7219131900	印度尼西亚	印度尼西亚公司		I	20.2%	2019/7/23	2024/7/22
7219131900	国(地)别不详	国(地)别不详		I	103.1%	2019/7/23	2024/7/22
7219132200	欧盟	其他欧盟公司	AllOthers	I	43.0%	2019/7/23	2024/7/22
7219132200	日本	日本冶金工业株式会社	NIPPONYAKINKOGYOCO.,LTD	I	18.1%	2019/7/23	2024/7/22
7219132200	日本	其他日本公司	AllOthers	I	29.0%	2019/7/23	2024/7/22
7219132200	韩国	株式会社 POSCO	POSCO	I	23.1%	2019/7/23	2024/7/22
7219132200	韩国	其他韩国公司	AllOthers	I	103.1%	2019/7/23	2024/7/22
7219132200	印度尼西亚	印度尼西亚公司		I	20.2%	2019/7/23	2024/7/22
7219132200	国(地)别不详	国(地)别不详		I	103.1%	2019/7/23	2024/7/22
7219132900	欧盟	其他欧盟公司	AllOthers	I	43.0%	2019/7/23	2024/7/22
7219132900	日本	日本冶金工业株式会社	NIPPONYAKINKOGYOCO.,LTD	I	18.1%	2019/7/23	2024/7/22
7219132900	日本	其他日本公司	AllOthers	I	29.0%	2019/7/23	2024/7/22
7219132900	韩国	株式会社 POSCO	POSCO	I	23.1%	2019/7/23	2024/7/22
7219132900	韩国	其他韩国公司	AllOthers	I	103.1%	2019/7/23	2024/7/22
7219132900	印度尼西亚	印度尼西亚公司		I	20.2%	2019/7/23	2024/7/22
7219132900	国(地)别不详	国(地)别不详		I	103.1%	2019/7/23	2024/7/22
7219141200	欧盟	其他欧盟公司	AllOthers	I	43.0%	2019/7/23	2024/7/22
7219141200	日本	日本冶金工业株式会社	NIPPONYAKINKOGYOCO.,LTD	I	18.1%	2019/7/23	2024/7/22
7219141200	日本	其他日本公司	AllOthers	I	29.0%	2019/7/23	2024/7/22
7219141200	韩国	株式会社 POSCO	POSCO	I	23.1%	2019/7/23	2024/7/22
7219141200	韩国	其他韩国公司	AllOthers	I	103.1%	2019/7/23	2024/7/22
7219141200	印度尼西亚	印度尼西亚公司		I	20.2%	2019/7/23	2024/7/22
7219141200	国(地)别不详	国(地)别不详		I	103.1%	2019/7/23	2024/7/22
7219141900	欧盟	其他欧盟公司	AllOthers	I	43.0%	2019/7/23	2024/7/22
7219141900	日本	日本冶金工业株式会社	NIPPONYAKINKOGYOCO.,LTD	I	18.1%	2019/7/23	2024/7/22
7219141900	日本	其他日本公司	AllOthers	I	29.0%	2019/7/23	2024/7/22
7219141900	韩国	株式会社 POSCO	POSCO	I	23.1%	2019/7/23	2024/7/22
7219141900	韩国	其他韩国公司	AllOthers	I	103.1%	2019/7/23	2024/7/22
7219141900	印度尼西亚	印度尼西亚公司		I	20.2%	2019/7/23	2024/7/22
7219141900	国(地)别不详	国(地)别不详		I	103.1%	2019/7/23	2024/7/22
7219142200	欧盟	其他欧盟公司	AllOthers	I	43.0%	2019/7/23	2024/7/22
7219142200	日本	日本冶金工业株式会社	NIPPONYAKINKOGYOCO.,LTD	I	18.1%	2019/7/23	2024/7/22
7219142200	日本	其他日本公司	AllOthers	I	29.0%	2019/7/23	2024/7/22
7219142200	韩国	株式会社 POSCO	POSCO	I	23.1%	2019/7/23	2024/7/22
7219142200	韩国	其他韩国公司	AllOthers	I	103.1%	2019/7/23	2024/7/22
7219142200	印度尼西亚	印度尼西亚公司		I	20.2%	2019/7/23	2024/7/22
7219142200	国(地)别不详	国(地)别不详		I	103.1%	2019/7/23	2024/7/22
7219142900	欧盟	其他欧盟公司	AllOthers	I	43.0%	2019/7/23	2024/7/22
7219142900	日本	日本冶金工业株式会社	NIPPONYAKINKOGYOCO.,LTD	I	18.1%	2019/7/23	2024/7/22
7219142900	日本	其他日本公司	AllOthers	I	29.0%	2019/7/23	2024/7/22
7219142900	韩国	株式会社 POSCO	POSCO	I	23.1%	2019/7/23	2024/7/22
7219142900	韩国	其他韩国公司	AllOthers	I	103.1%	2019/7/23	2024/7/22
7219142900	印度尼西亚	印度尼西亚公司		I	20.2%	2019/7/23	2024/7/22
7219142900	国(地)别不详	国(地)别不详		I	103.1%	2019/7/23	2024/7/22
7219210000	欧盟	其他欧盟公司	AllOthers	I	43.0%	2019/7/23	2024/7/22
7219210000	日本	日本冶金工业株式会社	NIPPONYAKINKOGYOCO.,LTD	I	18.1%	2019/7/23	2024/7/22
7219210000	日本	其他日本公司	AllOthers	I	29.0%	2019/7/23	2024/7/22
7219210000	韩国	株式会社 POSCO	POSCO	I	23.1%	2019/7/23	2024/7/22
7219210000	韩国	其他韩国公司	AllOthers	I	103.1%	2019/7/23	2024/7/22
7219210000	印度尼西亚	印度尼西亚公司		I	20.2%	2019/7/23	2024/7/22
7219210000	国(地)别不详	国(地)别不详		I	103.1%	2019/7/23	2024/7/22
7219220000	欧盟	其他欧盟公司	AllOthers	I	43.0%	2019/7/23	2024/7/22
7219220000	日本	日本冶金工业株式会社	NIPPONYAKINKOGYOCO.,LTD	I	18.1%	2019/7/23	2024/7/22
7219220000	日本	其他日本公司	AllOthers	I	29.0%	2019/7/23	2024/7/22
7219220000	韩国	株式会社 POSCO	POSCO	I	23.1%	2019/7/23	2024/7/22
7219220000	韩国	其他韩国公司	AllOthers	I	103.1%	2019/7/23	2024/7/22
7219220000	印度尼西亚	印度尼西亚公司		I	20.2%	2019/7/23	2024/7/22
7219220000	国(地)别不详	国(地)别不详		I	103.1%	2019/7/23	2024/7/22
7219230000	欧盟	其他欧盟公司	AllOthers	I	43.0%	2019/7/23	2024/7/22
7219230000	日本	日本冶金工业株式会社	NIPPONYAKINKOGYOCO.,LTD	I	18.1%	2019/7/23	2024/7/22
7219230000	日本	其他日本公司	AllOthers	I	29.0%	2019/7/23	2024/7/22
7219230000	韩国	株式会社 POSCO	POSCO	I	23.1%	2019/7/23	2024/7/22
7219230000	韩国	其他韩国公司	AllOthers	I	103.1%	2019/7/23	2024/7/22
7219230000	印度尼西亚	印度尼西亚公司		I	20.2%	2019/7/23	2024/7/22
7219230000	国(地)别不详	国(地)别不详		I	103.1%	2019/7/23	2024/7/22
7219241000	欧盟	其他欧盟公司	AllOthers	I	43.0%	2019/7/23	2024/7/22
7219241000	日本	日本冶金工业株式会社	NIPPONYAKINKOGYOCO.,LTD	I	18.1%	2019/7/23	2024/7/22

HS编码	原产国名称	厂商中文名称	厂商英文名称	税种代码	税率	起始日期	截止日期
7219241000	日本	其他日本公司	AllOthers	I	29.0%	2019/7/23	2024/7/22
7219241000	韩国	株式会社 POSCO	POSCO	I	23.1%	2019/7/23	2024/7/22
7219241000	韩国	其他韩国公司	AllOthers	I	103.1%	2019/7/23	2024/7/22
7219241000	印度尼西亚	印度尼西亚公司		I	20.2%	2019/7/23	2024/7/22
7219241000	国(地)别不详	国(地)别不详		I	103.1%	2019/7/23	2024/7/22
7219242000	欧盟	其他欧盟公司	AllOthers	I	43.0%	2019/7/23	2024/7/22
7219242000	日本	日本冶金工业株式会社	NIPPONYAKINKOGYOCO.,LTD	I	18.1%	2019/7/23	2024/7/22
7219242000	日本	其他日本公司	AllOthers	I	29.0%	2019/7/23	2024/7/22
7219242000	韩国	株式会社 POSCO	POSCO	I	23.1%	2019/7/23	2024/7/22
7219242000	韩国	其他韩国公司	AllOthers	I	103.1%	2019/7/23	2024/7/22
7219242000	印度尼西亚	印度尼西亚公司		I	20.2%	2019/7/23	2024/7/22
7219242000	国(地)别不详	国(地)别不详		I	103.1%	2019/7/23	2024/7/22
7219243000	欧盟	其他欧盟公司	AllOthers	I	43.0%	2019/7/23	2024/7/22
7219243000	日本	日本冶金工业株式会社	NIPPONYAKINKOGYOCO.,LTD	I	18.1%	2019/7/23	2024/7/22
7219243000	日本	其他日本公司	AllOthers	I	29.0%	2019/7/23	2024/7/22
7219243000	韩国	株式会社 POSCO	POSCO	I	23.1%	2019/7/23	2024/7/22
7219243000	韩国	其他韩国公司	AllOthers	I	103.1%	2019/7/23	2024/7/22
7219243000	印度尼西亚	印度尼西亚公司		I	20.2%	2019/7/23	2024/7/22
7219243000	国(地)别不详	国(地)别不详		I	103.1%	2019/7/23	2024/7/22
7220110000	欧盟	其他欧盟公司	AllOthers	I	43.0%	2019/7/23	2024/7/22
7220110000	日本	日本冶金工业株式会社	NIPPONYAKINKOGYOCO.,LTD	I	18.1%	2019/7/23	2024/7/22
7220110000	日本	其他日本公司	AllOthers	I	29.0%	2019/7/23	2024/7/22
7220110000	韩国	株式会社 POSCO	POSCO	I	23.1%	2019/7/23	2024/7/22
7220110000	韩国	其他韩国公司	AllOthers	I	103.1%	2019/7/23	2024/7/22
7220110000	印度尼西亚	印度尼西亚公司		I	20.2%	2019/7/23	2024/7/22
7220110000	国(地)别不详	国(地)别不详		I	103.1%	2019/7/23	2024/7/22
7220120000	欧盟	其他欧盟公司	AllOthers	I	43.0%	2019/7/23	2024/7/22
7220120000	日本	日本冶金工业株式会社	NIPPONYAKINKOGYOCO.,LTD	I	18.1%	2019/7/23	2024/7/22
7220120000	日本	其他日本公司	AllOthers	I	29.0%	2019/7/23	2024/7/22
7220120000	韩国	株式会社 POSCO	POSCO	I	23.1%	2019/7/23	2024/7/22
7220120000	韩国	其他韩国公司	AllOthers	I	103.1%	2019/7/23	2024/7/22
7220120000	印度尼西亚	印度尼西亚公司		I	20.2%	2019/7/23	2024/7/22
7220120000	国(地)别不详	国(地)别不详		I	103.1%	2019/7/23	2024/7/22
7225110000	日本	JFE 钢铁株式会社	JFE Steel Corporation	I	39.0%	2016/7/23	2999/12/31
7225110000	日本	新日铁住金株式会社	Nippon Steel & Sumitomo Metal Corporation	I	45.7%	2016/7/22	2999/12/31
7225110000	日本	其他日本公司	All Others	I	45.7%	2016/7/23	2999/12/31
7225110000	韩国	株式会社 POSCO	POSCO	I	37.3%	2016/7/23	2999/12/31
7225110000	韩国	其他韩国公司	All Others	I	37.3%	2016/7/23	2999/12/31
7225110000	欧盟	其他欧盟公司	AllOthers	I	46.3%	2016/7/23	2999/12/31
7225110000	国(地)别不详	国(地)别不详		I	46.3%	2016/7/23	2999/12/31
7226110000	日本	JFE 钢铁株式会社	JFE Steel Corporation	I	39.0%	2016/7/23	2999/12/31
7226110000	日本	新日铁住金株式会社	Nippon Steel & Sumitomo Metal Corporation	I	45.7%	2016/7/23	2999/12/31
7226110000	日本	其他日本公司	All Others	I	45.7%	2016/7/23	2999/12/31
7226110000	韩国	株式会社 POSCO	POSCO	I	37.3%	2016/7/23	2999/12/31
7226110000	韩国	其他韩国公司	All Others	I	37.3%	2016/7/23	2999/12/31
7226110000	欧盟	其他欧盟公司	AllOthers	I	46.3%	2016/7/23	2999/12/31
7226110000	国(地)别不详	国(地)别不详		I	46.3%	2016/7/23	2999/12/31
7304511001	欧盟	瓦卢瑞克德国公司	Vallourec Deutschland GmbH	I	57.9%	2019/6/14	2025/5/9
7304511001	欧盟	瓦卢瑞克法国钢管公司	VALLOUREC TUBES FRANCE	I	57.9%	2019/6/14	2025/5/9
7304511001	欧盟	意大利 IBF 公司	IBF S.P.A.	I	60.8%	2019/6/14	2025/5/9
7304511001	欧盟	其他欧盟公司	All others	I	60.8%	2019/6/14	2025/5/9
7304511001	美国	美国威曼高登锻造有限公司	Wyman—Gordon Forgings,Inc.	I	101.0%	2019/6/14	2025/5/9
7304511001	美国	其他美国公司	All others	I	147.8%	2019/6/14	2025/5/9
7304511001	国(地)别不详	国(地)别不详		I	147.8%	2019/6/14	2025/5/9
7304519001	欧盟	瓦卢瑞克德国公司	Vallourec Deutschland GmbH	I	57.9%	2019/6/14	2025/5/9
7304519001	欧盟	瓦卢瑞克法国钢管公司	VALLOUREC TUBES FRANCE	I	57.9%	2019/6/14	2025/5/9
7304519001	欧盟	意大利 IBF 公司	IBF S.P.A.	I	60.8%	2019/6/14	2025/5/9
7304519001	欧盟	其他欧盟公司	All others	I	60.8%	2019/6/14	2025/5/9
7304519001	美国	美国威曼高登锻造有限公司	Wyman—Gordon Forgings,Inc.	I	101.0%	2019/6/14	2025/5/9
7304519001	美国	其他美国公司	All others	I	147.8%	2019/6/14	2025/5/9
7304519001	国(地)别不详	国(地)别不详		I	147.8%	2019/6/14	2025/5/9
7304591001	欧盟	瓦卢瑞克德国公司	Vallourec Deutschland GmbH	I	57.9%	2019/6/14	2025/5/9
7304591001	欧盟	瓦卢瑞克法国钢管公司	VALLOUREC TUBES FRANCE	I	57.9%	2019/6/14	2025/5/9
7304591001	欧盟	意大利 IBF 公司	IBF S.P.A.	I	60.8%	2019/6/14	2025/5/9
7304591001	欧盟	其他欧盟公司	All others	I	60.8%	2019/6/14	2025/5/9
7304591001	美国	美国威曼高登锻造有限公司	Wyman—Gordon Forgings,Inc.	I	101.0%	2019/6/14	2025/5/9
7304591001	美国	其他美国公司	All others	I	147.8%	2019/6/14	2025/5/9
7304591001	国(地)别不详	国(地)别不详		I	147.8%	2019/6/14	2025/5/9
7304599001	欧盟	瓦卢瑞克德国公司	Vallourec Deutschland GmbH	I	57.9%	2019/6/14	2025/5/9
7304599001	欧盟	瓦卢瑞克法国钢管公司	VALLOUREC TUBES FRANCE	I	57.9%	2019/6/14	2025/5/9
7304599001	欧盟	意大利 IBF 公司	IBF S.P.A.	I	60.8%	2019/6/14	2025/5/9
7304599001	欧盟	其他欧盟公司	All others	I	60.8%	2019/6/14	2025/5/9

HS编码	原产国名称	厂商中文名称	厂商英文名称	税种代码	税率	起始日期	截止日期
7304599001	美国	美国威曼高登锻造有限公司	Wyman－Gordon Forgings,Inc.	I	101.0%	2019/6/14	2025/5/9
7304599001	美国	其他美国公司	All others	I	147.8%	2019/6/14	2025/5/9
7304599001	国(地)别不详	国(地)别不详		I	147.8%	2019/6/14	2025/5/9
7318120001	欧盟	其他欧盟公司	All Others	I	26.0%	2016/6/29	2999/12/31
7318120001	欧盟	卡马克斯有限两合公司	KAMAX GmbH & Co.KG	I	6.1%	2016/6/29	2999/12/31
7318120001	欧盟	皇家内德史罗夫控股有限公司	Koninklijke Nedschroef Holding B.V.	I	5.5%	2017/9/20	2999/12/31
7318120001	欧盟	内德史罗夫阿尔特纳有限公司	Nedschroef Altena GmbH	I	5.5%	2017/9/20	2999/12/31
7318120001	欧盟	内德史罗夫福罗劳顿有限公司	Nedschroef Fraulautern GmbH	I	5.5%	2017/9/20	2999/12/31
7318120001	欧盟	内德史罗夫海尔蒙德有限公司	Nedschroef Helmond B.V.	I	5.5%	2017/9/20	2999/12/31
7318120001	欧盟	内德史罗夫巴塞罗那有限公司	Nedschroef Barcelona SAU	I	5.5%	2017/9/20	2999/12/31
7318120001	欧盟	内德史罗夫贝京根有限公司	Nedschroef Beckingen GmbH	I	5.5%	2017/9/20	2999/12/31
7318120001	国(地)别不详	国(地)别不详		I	26.0%	2016/6/29	2999/12/31
7318140001	欧盟	其他欧盟公司	All Others	I	26.0%	2016/6/29	2999/12/31
7318140001	欧盟	卡马克斯有限两合公司	KAMAX GmbH & Co.KG	I	6.1%	2016/6/29	2999/12/31
7318140001	欧盟	皇家内德史罗夫控股有限公司	Koninklijke Nedschroef Holding B.V.	I	5.5%	2017/9/20	2999/12/31
7318140001	欧盟	内德史罗夫阿尔特纳有限公司	Nedschroef Altena GmbH	I	5.5%	2017/9/20	2999/12/31
7318140001	欧盟	内德史罗夫福罗劳顿有限公司	Nedschroef Fraulautern GmbH	I	5.5%	2017/9/20	2999/12/31
7318140001	欧盟	内德史罗夫海尔蒙德有限公司	Nedschroef Helmond B.V.	I	5.5%	2017/9/20	2999/12/31
7318140001	欧盟	内德史罗夫贝京根有限公司	Nedschroef Beckingen GmbH	I	5.5%	2017/9/20	2999/12/31
7318140001	欧盟	内德史罗夫巴塞罗那有限公司	Nedschroef Barcelona SAU	I	5.5%	2017/9/20	2999/12/31
7318140001	国(地)别不详	国(地)别不详		I	26.0%	2016/6/29	2999/12/31
7318151001	欧盟	其他欧盟公司	All Others	I	26.0%	2016/6/29	2999/12/31
7318151001	欧盟	卡马克斯有限两合公司	KAMAX GmbH & Co.KG	I	6.1%	2016/6/29	2999/12/31
7318151001	欧盟	皇家内德史罗夫控股有限公司	Koninklijke Nedschroef Holding B.V.	I	5.5%	2017/9/20	2999/12/31
7318151001	欧盟	内德史罗夫阿尔特纳有限公司	Nedschroef Altena GmbH	I	5.5%	2017/9/20	2999/12/31
7318151001	欧盟	内德史罗夫福罗劳顿有限公司	Nedschroef Fraulautern GmbH	I	5.5%	2017/9/20	2999/12/31
7318151001	欧盟	内德史罗夫海尔蒙德有限公司	Nedschroef Helmond B.V.	I	5.5%	2017/9/20	2999/12/31
7318151001	欧盟	内德史罗夫巴塞罗那有限公司	Nedschroef Barcelona SAU	I	5.5%	2017/9/20	2999/12/31
7318151001	欧盟	内德史罗夫贝京根有限公司	Nedschroef Beckingen GmbH	I	5.5%	2017/9/20	2999/12/31
7318151001	国(地)别不详	国(地)别不详		I	26.0%	2016/6/29	2999/12/31
7318159001	欧盟	其他欧盟公司	All Others	I	26.0%	2016/6/29	2999/12/31
7318159001	欧盟	卡马克斯有限两合公司	KAMAX GmbH & Co.KG	I	6.1%	2016/6/29	2999/12/31
7318159001	欧盟	皇家内德史罗夫控股有限公司	Koninklijke Nedschroef Holding B.V.	I	5.5%	2017/9/20	2999/12/31
7318159001	欧盟	内德史罗夫阿尔特纳有限公司	Nedschroef Altena GmbH	I	5.5%	2017/9/20	2999/12/31
7318159001	欧盟	内德史罗夫福罗劳顿有限公司	Nedschroef Fraulautern GmbH	I	5.5%	2017/9/20	2999/12/31
7318159001	欧盟	内德史罗夫海尔蒙德有限公司	Nedschroef Helmond B.V.	I	5.5%	2017/9/20	2999/12/31
7318159001	欧盟	内德史罗夫巴塞罗那有限公司	Nedschroef Barcelona SAU	I	5.5%	2017/9/20	2999/12/31
7318159001	欧盟	内德史罗夫贝京根有限公司	Nedschroef Beckingen GmbH	I	5.5%	2017/9/20	2999/12/31
7318159001	国(地)别不详	国(地)别不详		I	26.0%	2016/6/29	2999/12/31
7318210001	欧盟	其他欧盟公司	All Others	I	26.0%	2016/6/29	2022/6/27
7318210001	欧盟	卡马克斯有限两合公司	KAMAX GmbH & Co.KG	I	6.1%	2016/6/29	2999/12/31
7318210001	欧盟	皇家内德史罗夫控股有限公司	Koninklijke Nedschroef Holding B.V.	I	5.5%	2017/9/20	2999/12/31
7318210001	欧盟	内德史罗夫阿尔特纳有限公司	Nedschroef Altena GmbH	I	5.5%	2017/9/20	2999/12/31
7318210001	欧盟	内德史罗夫福罗劳顿有限公司	Nedschroef Fraulautern GmbH	I	5.5%	2017/9/20	2022/6/27
7318210001	欧盟	内德史罗夫海尔蒙德有限公司	Nedschroef Helmond B.V.	I	5.5%	2017/9/20	2999/12/31
7318210001	欧盟	内德史罗夫巴塞罗那有限公司	Nedschroef Barcelona SAU	I	5.5%	2017/9/20	2999/12/31

HS编码	原产国名称	厂商中文名称	厂商英文名称	税种代码	税率	起始日期	截止日期
7318210001	欧盟	内德史罗夫贝京根有限公司	Nedschroef Beckingen GmbH	I	5.5%	2017/9/20	2999/12/31
7318210001	国(地)别不详	国(地)别不详		I	26.0%	2016/6/29	2022/6/27
7318220001	欧盟	其他欧盟公司	All Others	I	26.0%	2016/6/29	2999/12/31
7318220001	欧盟	卡马克斯有限两合公司	KAMAX GmbH & Co.KG	I	6.1%	2016/6/29	2999/12/31
7318220001	欧盟	皇家内德史罗夫控股有限公司	Koninklijke Nedschroef Holding B.V.	I	5.5%	2017/9/20	2999/12/31
7318220001	欧盟	内德史罗夫阿尔特纳有限公司	(Nedschroef Altena GmbH)	I	5.5%	2017/9/20	2022/6/27
7318220001	欧盟	内德史罗夫福罗劳顿有限公司	Nedschroef Fraulautern GmbH	I	5.5%	2017/9/20	2999/12/31
7318220001	欧盟	内德史罗夫海尔蒙德有限公司	Nedschroef Helmond B.V.	I	5.5%	2017/9/20	2999/12/31
7318220001	欧盟	内德史罗夫巴塞罗那有限公司	Nedschroef Barcelona SAU	I	5.5%	2017/9/20	2999/12/31
7318220001	欧盟	内德史罗夫贝京根有限公司	Nedschroef Beckingen GmbH	I	5.5%	2017/9/20	2022/6/27
7318220001	国(地)别不详	国(地)别不详		I	26.0%	2016/6/29	2999/12/31
9001100001	美国	德拉克通信美国公司	Draka Communications Americas, Inc.	I	78.2%	2011/4/22	2022/4/21
9001100001	美国	康宁公司	Corning Incorporated	I	37.9%	2011/4/22	2022/4/21
9001100001	美国	美国 OFS－费特有限责任公司	OFS Fitel, LLC	I	33.3%	2011/4/22	2022/4/21
9001100001	美国	其他美国公司	All Others	I	78.2%	2011/4/22	2022/4/21
9001100001	欧盟	丹麦 OFS－费特有限责任公司	OFS Fitel Denmark ApS	I	29.1%	2011/4/22	2022/4/21
9001100001	欧盟	德拉克通信法国集团公司	Draka Comteq France SAS	I	12.9%	2011/4/22	2022/4/21
9001100001	欧盟	德拉克通信纤维有限公司	Draka Comteq Fibre B.V.	I	12.9%	2011/4/22	2022/4/21
9001100001	欧盟	菲布里奥蒂切苏德有限责任公司	Fibre Ottiche Sud －F.O.S.S.r.l.	I	24.7%	2011/4/22	2022/4/21
9001100001	欧盟	其他欧盟公司	All Others	I	29.1%	2011/4/22	2022/4/21
9001100001	印度	斯德雷特科技有限公司	Sterlite Technologies Limited	I	7.4%	2014/8/14	2025/8/13
9001100001	印度	贝拉古河光纤有限公司	Birla Furukawa Fibre Optics Limited	I	11.4%	2014/8/14	2025/8/13
9001100001	印度	康宁技术印度有限公司	Corning Technologies India Private Limited	I	24.5%	2014/8/14	2025/8/13
9001100001	印度	阿克什光纤有限公司	AkshOptifibre Limited	I	30.6%	2014/8/14	2025/8/13
9001100001	印度	其他印度公司	All Others	I	24.5%	2014/8/14	2025/8/13
9001100001	印度	菲诺莱克斯电缆有限公司	Finolex Cables Limited	I	30.6%	2014/8/14	2025/8/13
9001100001	国(地)别不详	国(地)别不详		I	78.2%	2014/8/14	2025/8/13
9001100001	日本	所有日本公司	All others	I	46.0%	2017/1/1	2022/12/31
9001100001	韩国	韩国LS电线株式会社	LS Cable&System Ltd.	I	9.1%	2017/1/1	2022/12/31
9001100001	韩国	韩国大韩光通信株式会社	TAIHAN Fiberoptics Co., LTD.	I	7.9%	2017/1/1	2022/12/31
9001100001	韩国	其他韩国公司	All others	I	46.0%	2017/1/1	2022/12/31
9001100002	印度	斯德雷特科技有限公司	STERLITE TECHNOLOGIES LIMITED	I	7.4%	2014/8/14	2025/8/13
9001100002	印度	贝拉古河光纤有限公司	Birla Furukawa Fibre Optics Limited	I	11.4%	2014/8/14	2025/8/13
9001100002	印度	康宁技术印度有限公司	Corning Technologies India Private Limited	I	24.5%	2014/8/14	2025/8/13
9001100002	印度	阿克什光纤有限公司	AkshOptifibre Limited	I	30.6%	2014/8/14	2025/8/13
9001100002	印度	菲诺莱克斯电缆有限公司	Finolex Cables Limited	I	30.6%	2014/8/14	2025/8/13
9001100002	印度	其他印度公司	All Others	I	24.5%	2014/8/14	2025/8/13
9001100002	国(地)别不详	国(地)别不详		I	30.6%	2014/8/14	2025/8/13
9021100010	欧盟	其他欧盟公司	All Others	I	26.0%	2022/1/1	2999/12/31
9021100010	欧盟	卡马克斯有限两合公司	KAMAX GmbH & Co.KG	I	6.1%	2022/1/1	2999/12/31
9021100010	欧盟	皇家内德史罗夫控股有限公司	Koninklijke Nedschroef Holding B.V.	I	5.5%	2022/1/1	2999/12/31
9021100010	欧盟	内德史罗夫阿尔特纳有限公司	Nedschroef Altena GmbH	I	5.5%	2022/1/1	2999/12/31
9021100010	欧盟	内德史罗夫福罗劳顿有限公司	Nedschroef Fraulautern GmbH	I	5.5%	2022/1/1	2999/12/31
9021100010	欧盟	内德史罗夫海尔蒙德有限公司	Nedschroef Helmond B.V.	I	5.5%	2022/1/1	2999/12/31
9021100010	欧盟	内德史罗夫贝京根有限公司	Nedschroef Beckingen GmbH	I	5.5%	2022/1/1	2999/12/31
9021100010	欧盟	内德史罗夫巴塞罗那有限公司	Nedschroef Barcelona SAU	I	5.5%	2022/1/1	2999/12/31
9021100010	国(地)别不详	国(地)别不详		I	26.0%	2022/1/1	2999/12/31
9021100020	欧盟	其他欧盟公司	All Others	I	26.0%	2022/1/1	2999/12/31
9021100020	欧盟	卡马克斯有限两合公司	KAMAX GmbH & Co.KG	I	6.1%	2022/1/1	2999/12/31
9021100020	欧盟	皇家内德史罗夫控股有限公司	Koninklijke Nedschroef Holding B.V.	I	5.5%	2022/1/1	2999/12/31
9021100020	欧盟	内德史罗夫阿尔特纳有限公司	Nedschroef Altena GmbH	I	5.5%	2022/1/1	2999/12/31
9021100020	欧盟	内德史罗夫福罗劳顿有限公司	Nedschroef Fraulautern GmbH	I	5.5%	2022/1/1	2999/12/31
9021100020	欧盟	内德史罗夫海尔蒙德有限公司	Nedschroef Helmond B.V.	I	5.5%	2022/1/1	2999/12/31
9021100020	欧盟	内德史罗夫贝京根有限公司	Nedschroef Beckingen GmbH	I	5.5%	2022/1/1	2999/12/31

HS编码	原产国名称	厂商中文名称	厂商英文名称	税种代码	税率	起始日期	截止日期
9021100020	欧盟	内德史罗夫巴塞罗那有限公司	Nedschroef Barcelona SAU	I	5.5%	2022/1/1	2999/12/31
9021100020	国(地)别不详	国(地)别不详		I	26.0%	2022/1/1	2999/12/31
9021100030	欧盟	其他欧盟公司	All Others	I	26.0%	2022/1/1	2999/12/31
9021100030	欧盟	卡马克斯有限两合公司	KAMAX GmbH & Co.KG	I	6.1%	2022/1/1	2999/12/31
9021100030	欧盟	皇家内德史罗夫控股有限公司	Koninklijke Nedschroef Holding B.V.	I	5.5%	2022/1/1	2999/12/31
9021100030	欧盟	内德史罗夫阿尔特纳有限公司	Nedschroef Altena GmbH	I	5.5%	2022/1/1	2999/12/31
9021100030	欧盟	内德史罗夫福罗劳顿有限公司	Nedschroef Fraulautern GmbH	I	5.5%	2022/1/1	2999/12/31
9021100030	欧盟	内德史罗夫海尔蒙德有限公司	Nedschroef Helmond B.V.	I	5.5%	2022/1/1	2999/12/31
9021100030	欧盟	内德史罗夫贝京根有限公司	Nedschroef Beckingen GmbH	I	5.5%	2022/1/1	2999/12/31
9021100030	欧盟	内德史罗夫巴塞罗那有限公司	Nedschroef Barcelona SAU	I	5.5%	2022/1/1	2999/12/31
9021100030	国(地)别不详	国(地)别不详		I	26.0%	2022/1/1	2999/12/31
9021100040	欧盟	其他欧盟公司	All Others	I	26.0%	2022/1/1	2999/12/31
9021100040	欧盟	卡马克斯有限两合公司	KAMAX GmbH & Co.KG	I	6.1%	2022/1/1	2999/12/31
9021100040	欧盟	皇家内德史罗夫控股有限公司	Koninklijke Nedschroef Holding B.V.	I	5.5%	2022/1/1	2999/12/31
9021100040	欧盟	内德史罗夫阿尔特纳有限公司	Nedschroef Altena GmbH	I	5.5%	2022/1/1	2999/12/31
9021100040	欧盟	内德史罗夫福罗劳顿有限公司	Nedschroef Fraulautern GmbH	I	5.5%	2022/1/1	2999/12/31
9021100040	欧盟	内德史罗夫海尔蒙德有限公司	Nedschroef Helmond B.V.	I	5.5%	2022/1/1	2999/12/31
9021100040	欧盟	内德史罗夫贝京根有限公司	Nedschroef Beckingen GmbH	I	5.5%	2022/1/1	2999/12/31
9021100040	欧盟	内德史罗夫巴塞罗那有限公司	Nedschroef Barcelona SAU	I	5.5%	2022/1/1	2999/12/31
9021100040	国(地)别不详	国(地)别不详		I	26.0%	2022/1/1	2999/12/31
9021290010	欧盟	其他欧盟公司	All Others	I	26.0%	2022/1/1	2999/12/31
9021290010	欧盟	卡马克斯有限两合公司	KAMAX GmbH & Co.KG	I	6.1%	2022/1/1	2999/12/31
9021290010	欧盟	皇家内德史罗夫控股有限公司	Koninklijke Nedschroef Holding B.V.	I	5.5%	2022/1/1	2999/12/31
9021290010	欧盟	内德史罗夫阿尔特纳有限公司	Nedschroef Altena GmbH	I	5.5%	2022/1/1	2999/12/31
9021290010	欧盟	内德史罗夫福罗劳顿有限公司	Nedschroef Fraulautern GmbH	I	5.5%	2022/1/1	2999/12/31
9021290010	欧盟	内德史罗夫海尔蒙德有限公司	Nedschroef Helmond B.V.	I	5.5%	2022/1/1	2999/12/31
9021290010	欧盟	内德史罗夫贝京根有限公司	Nedschroef Beckingen GmbH	I	5.5%	2022/1/1	2999/12/31
9021290010	欧盟	内德史罗夫巴塞罗那有限公司	Nedschroef Barcelona SAU	I	5.5%	2022/1/1	2999/12/31
9021290010	国(地)别不详	国(地)别不详		I	26.0%	2022/1/1	2999/12/31
9021290020	欧盟	其他欧盟公司	All Others	I	26.0%	2022/1/1	2999/12/31
9021290020	欧盟	卡马克斯有限两合公司	KAMAX GmbH & Co.KG	I	6.1%	2022/1/1	2999/12/31
9021290020	欧盟	皇家内德史罗夫控股有限公司	Koninklijke Nedschroef Holding B.V.	I	5.5%	2022/1/1	2999/12/31
9021290020	欧盟	内德史罗夫阿尔特纳有限公司	Nedschroef Altena GmbH	I	5.5%	2022/1/1	2999/12/31
9021290020	欧盟	内德史罗夫福罗劳顿有限公司	Nedschroef Fraulautern GmbH	I	5.5%	2022/1/1	2999/12/31
9021290020	欧盟	内德史罗夫海尔蒙德有限公司	Nedschroef Helmond B.V.	I	5.5%	2022/1/1	2999/12/31
9021290020	欧盟	内德史罗夫贝京根有限公司	Nedschroef Beckingen GmbH	I	5.5%	2022/1/1	2999/12/31
9021290020	欧盟	内德史罗夫巴塞罗那有限公司	Nedschroef Barcelona SAU	I	5.5%	2022/1/1	2999/12/31
9021290020	国(地)别不详	国(地)别不详		I	26.0%	2022/1/1	2999/12/31
9021290030	欧盟	其他欧盟公司	All Others	I	26.0%	2022/1/1	2999/12/31
9021290030	欧盟	卡马克斯有限两合公司	KAMAX GmbH & Co.KG	I	6.1%	2022/1/1	2999/12/31
9021290030	欧盟	皇家内德史罗夫控股有限公司	Koninklijke Nedschroef Holding B.V.	I	5.5%	2022/1/1	2999/12/31
9021290030	欧盟	内德史罗夫阿尔特纳有限公司	Nedschroef Altena GmbH	I	5.5%	2022/1/1	2999/12/31
9021290030	欧盟	内德史罗夫福罗劳顿有限公司	Nedschroef Fraulautern GmbH	I	5.5%	2022/1/1	2999/12/31
9021290030	欧盟	内德史罗夫海尔蒙德有限公司	Nedschroef Helmond B.V.	I	5.5%	2022/1/1	2999/12/31
9021290030	欧盟	内德史罗夫贝京根有限公司	Nedschroef Beckingen GmbH	I	5.5%	2022/1/1	2999/12/31

HS编码	原产国名称	厂商中文名称	厂商英文名称	税种代码	税率	起始日期	截止日期
9021290030	欧盟	内德史罗夫巴塞罗那有限公司	Nedschroef Barcelona SAU	I	5.5%	2022/1/1	2999/12/31
9021290030	国(地)别不详	国(地)别不详		I	26.0%	2022/1/1	2999/12/31
9021290040	欧盟	其他欧盟公司	All Others	I	26.0%	2022/1/1	2999/12/31
9021290040	欧盟	卡马克斯有限两合公司	KAMAX GmbH & Co.KG	I	6.1%	2022/1/1	2999/12/31
9021290040	欧盟	皇家内德史罗夫控股有限公司	Koninklijke Nedschroef Holding B.V.	I	5.5%	2022/1/1	2999/12/31
9021290040	欧盟	内德史罗夫阿尔特纳有限公司	Nedschroef Altena GmbH	I	5.5%	2022/1/1	2999/12/31
9021290040	欧盟	内德史罗夫福罗劳顿有限公司	Nedschroef Fraulautern GmbH	I	5.5%	2022/1/1	2999/12/31
9021290040	欧盟	内德史罗夫海尔蒙德有限公司	Nedschroef Helmond B.V.	I	5.5%	2022/1/1	2999/12/31
9021290040	欧盟	内德史罗夫贝京根有限公司	Nedschroef Beckingen GmbH	I	5.5%	2022/1/1	2999/12/31
9021290040	欧盟	内德史罗夫巴塞罗那有限公司	Nedschroef Barcelona SAU	I	5.5%	2022/1/1	2999/12/31
9021290040	国(地)别不详	国(地)别不详		I	26.0%	2022/1/1	2999/12/31

附表5：　中华人民共和国进境物品进口税税率表

税目序号	物品名称	税率(%)
1	书报、刊物、教育用影视资料；计算机、视频摄录一体机、数字照相机等信息技术产品；食品、饮料；金银；家具；玩具，游戏品、节日或其他娱乐用品；药品①	13
2	运动用品(不含高尔夫球及球具)、钓鱼用品；纺织品及其制成品；电视摄像机及其他电器用具；自行车；税目1、3中未包含的其他商品	20
3②	烟、酒；贵重首饰及珠宝玉石；高尔夫球及球具；高档手表；高档化妆品	50

注：①对国家规定减按3%征收进口环节增值税的进口药品，按照货物税率征税。

②税目3所列商品的具体范围与消费税征收范围一致。

附表6：　中华人民共和国进境物品归类表

税号	物品类别	范围	税率
01000000	食品、饮料、药品	食品：包括乳制品、糖制品、调味品，人参、高丽参、红参、奶粉及其他保健品、补品等；饮料：包括矿泉水、汽水，咖啡、茶，其他无酒精饮料。药品：包括中药酒等。	13%
		国家规定减按3%征收进口环节增值税的进口药品①。	3%
02000000	酒	包括啤酒、葡萄酒(香槟酒)、黄酒、果酒、清酒、米酒、白兰地、威士忌、伏特加、朗姆酒、金酒、白酒、保健酒、鸡尾酒、利口酒、龙舌兰、柯迪尔酒、梅子酒等用粮食、水果等含淀粉或糖的物质发酵或配制而制成的含乙醇的酒精饮料。	50%
03000000	烟	包括卷烟、雪茄烟、再造烟草、均化烟草、其他烟草及烟草代用品的制品，烟丝、斗烟、水烟、烟末等。	50%
04000000	纺织品及其制成品	衣着：包括外衣、外裤、内衣裤、衬衫/T恤衫、其他衣着等； 配饰：包括帽子、丝巾、头巾、围巾、领带、腰带、手套、袜子、手帕等； 家纺用品：包括毛毯、被子、枕头、床罩、睡袋、幔帐等； 其他：包括毛巾、浴巾、桌布、窗帘、地毯等。	20%
05000000	皮革服装及配饰	包括各式皮革服装及皮质配饰。	20%
06000000	箱包及鞋靴	箱：包括各种材质的箱子； 挎包、背包、提包：包括各种材质的挎包、背包、提包； 钱包、钥匙包：包括各种材质的钱包、钥匙包、卡片包； 其他：包括化妆包、包装袋(盒、箱)等。 鞋靴：包括皮鞋、皮靴、运动鞋、其他鞋靴等。	20%
07000000	表、钟及其配件、附件	高档手表：完税价格在人民币10000元及以上的手表。	50%
		表：包括高档手表外其他各种表； 钟：包括座钟、挂钟、台钟、落地钟等； 配件附件：包括各种表、钟的配件、附件。	20%

① 对国家规定减按3%征收进口环节增值税的进口药品，按照货物税率征税。抗癌药品、罕见病药品定义及范围详见《关于抗癌药品增值税政策的通知》(财税〔2018〕47号)《关于罕见病药品增值税政策的通知》(财税〔2019〕24号)。

税号	物品类别	范围	税率
08000000	金银、贵重首饰及珠宝玉石	贵重首饰及珠宝玉石(不含钻石):包括天然或养殖珍珠、宝石或半宝石(不含钻石),用天然或养殖珍珠、宝石或半宝石(不含钻石)制成的物品,以贱金属为底的非镶嵌钻石的包贵金属首饰。	50%
		钻石及钻石首饰。	20%
		金银:包括金、银、铂等贵金属及包贵金属,贵金属及包贵金属制的首饰(以贱金属为底的非镶嵌钻石的包贵金属首饰除外)、金银器和其他制品。	13%
09000000	化妆品、洗护用品	化妆品:包括芳香类化妆品、唇用化妆品、眼用化妆品、指(趾)甲化妆品、粉状化妆品和特殊功能类化妆品等。 芳香类化妆品:香水和花露水; 唇用化妆品:唇膏、唇彩、唇线笔等; 眼用化妆品:睫毛膏(液、油)、眼线笔(液)、眉笔、眼影、眼睑膏等; 指(趾)甲化妆品:洗甲(趾)液、去指(趾)甲油、指(趾)甲油、指(趾)甲膏等; 粉状化妆品:粉底、粉饼、扑面粉、胭脂(粉)、腮红(粉)等; 其他美容品或化妆品:用于消除皱纹、美化唇型的皮内注射美容制品。	50%或20%
		洗护用品:包括清洁用品、护肤用品、护发用品和其他洗护用品。 清洁用品:洗面奶(乳、皂)、洁面霜(露、蜜、粉、啫喱)、卸妆水(乳、膏、液、油)、鼻贴膜、去黑头膏(液)、剃须膏(泡沫)、磨砂膏、按摩膏、去角质膏(粉),牙膏、牙粉、牙线、漱口水,香皂、浴液、洗手液; 护肤用品:化妆水(含爽肤水、柔肤水、紧肤水、护肤水、收缩水)、须后水、面霜、眼霜、日霜、晚霜、冷霜、防晒霜(油)、晒黑油、祛斑霜、护肤膏(霜、露、乳液、喷雾)、隔离霜、面膜、面膜膏(粉)、眼膜、颈膜、护手霜、润唇膏,痱子粉、爽身粉、皮肤护理软膏; 护发用品:洗/护发液、发乳、发油、发蜡、焗油膏、发胶、发泥、定型水(啫喱、摩丝)、烫发剂、染发剂; 其他用品:丰(美、健)乳霜、纤体霜(膏)、健美霜、紧致霜、除臭露(剂)、精油、防蚊液等。	50%或20%
10000000	家用医疗、保健及美容器材	医疗器材:包括呼吸器具、矫形器具、夹板及其他骨折用具,血糖计、血糖试纸、电动洗眼器、红外线耳探热针、空气制氧机、治疗用雾化机、电动血压计、病人用拐杖、病人用轮椅等及上述物品的配件、附件; 保健器材:包括按摩床、按摩椅等及上述物品的配件、附件; 美容器材:包括蒸汽仪、喷雾器、化妆/美容专用工具等及上述物品的配件、附件。	20%
11000000	厨卫用具及小家电	厨房用具:包括各种材料制的餐具、刀具、炊具、灶具,锅、壶、杯、盘、碗、筷子、勺、铲、餐刀、餐叉、切菜刀、案板、削皮刀、绞肉机、食品研磨机、搅拌器、净水器、煤气灶、煤气点火器等;电饭煲、微波炉、电磁炉、抽油烟机、消毒碗柜、家用洗碗机、电烤箱、面包机、豆浆机、酸奶机、榨汁机、咖啡机、制冰机、饮水机、食品调理机、煮蛋器等厨房用具及配件、附件; 卫生用具、洁具:包括热水器、水龙头、淋浴用具、座便器及配件、附件等。 小家电:包括灯具、风扇、电暖器、电热毯、电熨斗、电吹风机、电动剃须刀、电动毛发推剪器、增湿机、除湿机、增除湿一体机、空气清新机、家用吸尘器、扫地机器人、地板打蜡机、电动剪草机等电器及上述物品的配件、附件等。	
		电话机等信息技术产品:包括固定电话机、手持移动电话机、可视电话机、寻呼机等。	
12000000	家具	包括各种材料制的沙发、组合式家具、柜、橱、台、桌、椅、书架、床、床垫、坐具等。	13%
13000000	空调及其配件、附件	包括空气调节器及其配件、附件等。	20%
14000000	电冰箱及其配件、附件	包括各式电冰箱、冰柜、红酒柜及其配件、附件等。	20%
15000000	洗衣设备及其配件、附件	包括波轮式洗衣机、滚筒式洗衣机、干衣机/烘干机、脱水机、家用地毯洗涤机等及上述物品的配件、附件。	20%
16000000	电视机及其配件、附件	包括各式电视机、电视收音联合机、电视收音录音联合机、电视录像联合机等及上述物品的配件、附件。	20%
17000000	摄影(像)设备及其配件、附件	包括电视摄像机、照相机(数字照相机除外)、照相制版机、放大机,胶卷、胶片、感光纸、镜箱、闪光灯、滤色镜、测光表、曝光表、遮光罩、水下摄影罩、半身镜、接镜环、取景器、自拍器、洗像盒、显影罐等。	
		视频摄录一体机、数字照相机、存储卡等信息技术产品。	

税号	物品类别	范围	税率
18000000	影音设备及其配件、附件	包括录音笔、录音机、收音机、MP3 播放机、MP4 播放机、收录音机、数码录放音器、电唱机、激光电唱机、放像机、录像机、激光视盘机、(单)功能座、音箱、自动伴唱机、卡拉 OK 混音器等及上述物品的配件、附件。	
		耳机及耳塞机,磁盘、磁带、光学媒体、半导体媒体以及其他影音类信息技术产品。	
19000000	计算机及其外围设备	包括个人计算机及其存储、输入、输出设备和附件、零部件。	13%
20000000	书报、刊物及其他各类印刷品	包括书报、刊物及其他各类印刷品。	13%
21000000	教育用影视资料	包括教育专用的电影片,幻灯片,原版录音带、录像带、磁盘、磁带、光学媒体、半导体媒体、唱片,地球仪、解剖模型、人体骨骼模型、教育用示意牌等。	13%
22000000	文具用品、玩具、游戏品、节日或其他娱乐用品	文具用品:包括各种书写用具及材料、照像簿、集邮簿、印刷日历、月历、放大镜、望远镜、绘图用颜料、装订用具、誊写钢板等各种文具用品。	
		文具类信息技术产品:电子计算器、电子字典、记事簿、电子(纸)书。 玩具:包括三轮车、单脚滑行车、踏板车及类似的带轮玩具;玩偶车;玩偶;缩小(按比例缩小)的模型及类似娱乐用模型;智力玩具等及上述物品的零件及附件。 游戏品(视频游戏控制器及设备、桌上或室内游戏用品):包括电子游戏机和视频游戏控制器、扑克牌、中国象棋、国际象棋、跳棋等棋类用品、麻将及类似桌上游戏用品等,及其上述游戏的零件、附件。 节日或其他娱乐用品:包括圣诞节、狂欢节等节日用品、魔术道具及嬉戏品等。	
23000000	邮票、艺术品、收藏品	包括中国大陆及境外各种邮票、小型张、纪念封等,纪念币,以及艺术品、收藏品。	20%
24000000	乐器	包括各种键盘类、弓弦类、拨弦类、打击类、管乐类等乐器及节拍器、音叉、定音器等器具及上述乐器的配件、附件。	20%
25000000	运动用品、钓鱼用品	高尔夫球及球具:包括高尔夫球杆和高尔夫球。	
		除高尔夫球以外各种球类,各种健身器具、航空和航海模型、钓鱼用品等,一般体育活动、体操、竞技、游泳、滑冰、滑雪及其他户内外活动用具及其配件、附件。	
26000000	自行车	包括不带发动机、电动机的自行车、三轮脚踏车、婴孩车及其他非机动脚踏车,及上述物品的配件、附件。	20%
27000000	其他物品	其他不能归入上述类别的物品。	20%

附表 7: 中华人民共和国进境物品完税价格表

税号	品名及规格	单位	完税价格(人民币:元)	税率
01000000	**食品、饮料、药品**			
01010000	**-食品**			
01010400	--参	千克	2000	13%
01010700	--奶粉	千克	200	13%
01010800	--调味品	千克	200	13%
01019900	--其他食品	件、千克	另行确定	13%
01020000	**-饮料**			
01020100	--茶叶	千克	200	13%
01020200	--咖啡	千克	200	13%
01029900	--其他饮料	千克	另行确定	13%
01030000	**-药品**			
01030100	--抗癌药品	件	另行确定	3%
01030200	--中药酒	瓶	另行确定	13%
01030300	--罕见病药品	件	另行确定	3%
01039900	--其他药品	件	另行确定	13%
02000000	**酒**			
02010000	**-啤酒**			
02010100	--12 度以下(不含 12 度)	瓶(不超过 750 毫升)	5	50%
02010200	--12 度至 22 度(不含 22 度)	瓶(不超过 750 毫升)	10	50%
02020000	**-葡萄酒**			
02020100	--12 度以下(不含 12 度)	瓶(不超过 750 毫升)	100	50%
02020200	--12 度至 22 度(含 22 度)	瓶(不超过 750 毫升)	200	50%
02030000	**-清酒**			
02030100	--12 度以下(不含 12 度)	瓶(不超过 750 毫升)	30	50%
02030200	--12 度至 22 度(不含 22 度)	瓶(不超过 750 毫升)	50	50%
02030300	--22 度及以上	瓶(不超过 750 毫升)	80	50%
02040000	**-白兰地**	瓶(不超过 750 毫升)	500	50%
02050000	**-威士忌**	瓶(不超过 750 毫升)	300	50%

税号	品名及规格	单位	完税价格（人民币：元）	税率
02060000	**-伏特加**	瓶（不超过 750 毫升）	100	50%
02070000	**-白酒**	瓶（不超过 750 毫升）	300	50%
02990000	**-其他酒**	瓶（不超过 750 毫升）	另行确定	50%
03000000	**烟**			
03010000	**-卷烟**	支	0.5	50%
03020000	**-雪茄烟**	支	10	50%
03030000	**-烟丝**	克	0.5	50%
03990000	**-其他烟**	克、支	另行确定	50%
04000000	**纺织品及其制成品**			
04010000	**-衣着**			
04010100	--外衣	件	300	20%
04010200	--外裤	条	200	20%
04010300	--内衣裤	条/件	100	20%
04010400	--衬衫/T 恤衫	件	200	20%
04019900	--其他衣着	件	另行确定	20%
04020000	**-配饰**			
04020100	--帽子	件	100	20%
04020200	--丝巾、头巾、围巾	条	100	20%
04020300	--领带	条	100	20%
04020400	--腰带	条	100	20%
04020500	--手套	双	100	20%
04029900	--其他配饰	件	另行确定	20%
04030000	**-家纺用品**			
04030100	--毛毯、被子、床罩、睡袋	床、件	400	20%
04030200	--枕头、床单、毛巾被、被套	条、件	100	20%
04030300	--地毯	平方米	200	20%
04030400	--窗帘	千克	100	20%
04039900	--其他家纺用品	件	另行确定	20%
04990000	**-其他纺织品及其制成品**	件	另行确定	20%
05000000	**皮革服装及配饰**			
05010000	**-皮革服装**			
05010100	--裘皮衣	件	另行确定	20%
05010200	--皮大衣	件	2000	20%
05010300	--皮上衣	件	1500	20%
05010400	--皮背心	件	1000	20%
05010500	--皮裤	件	1000	20%
05010600	--皮裙	件	1000	20%
05019900	--其他皮革服装	件	另行确定	20%
05020000	**-皮革配饰**			
05020100	--皮帽	件	200	20%
05020200	--皮带	条	100	20%
05020300	--皮手套	双	100	20%
05029900	--其他皮革配饰	件	另行确定	20%
05990000	**-其他皮革制品（箱包和鞋靴除外）**	件	另行确定	20%
06000000	**箱包和鞋靴**			
06010000	**-箱包**			
06010100	--箱	个	500	20%
06010200	--挎包、背包、提包	个	另行确定	20%
06010300	--钱包、钥匙包	个	100	20%
06019900	--其他箱包	个	另行确定	20%
06020000	**-鞋靴**			
06020100	--皮鞋	双	300	20%
06020200	--皮靴	双	400	20%
06020300	--运动鞋	双	200	20%
06029900	--其他鞋靴	双	另行确定	20%
07000000	**表、钟及其配件、附件**			
07010000	**-表**			
07010100	高档手表（审定价格在人民币 10000 元及以上）	块	另行确定	50%
07010200	--其他表			
07010210	---石英表（电子表）	块	200	20%
07010220	---机械表	块	500	20%
07010290	---其他表	块	另行确定	20%
07020000	**-钟**			
07020100	--座钟、挂钟、台钟	个、台	200	20%
07020200	--落地钟	台	600	20%
07029900	--其他钟	台	另行确定	20%

税号	品名及规格	单位	完税价格(人民币:元)	税率
07030000	**-钟表配件、附件**	件	另行确定	20%
08000000	**金银、贵重首饰及珠宝玉石**			
08010000	**-金银**	件	另行确定	13%
08020000	**-贵重首饰及珠宝玉石**			
08020100	--钻石及钻石首饰	件	另行确定	20%
08020200	--贵重首饰及珠宝玉石	件	另行确定	50%
09000000	**化妆品、洗护用品**			
09010000	**-化妆品**			
09010100	--芳香类化妆品			
09010110	---香水及花露水			
09010111	----香水及花露水	瓶	300	完税价格≥10 元/毫升(克)的,税率为 50%
09010112	----香水及花露水	瓶	300	完税价格<10 元/毫升(克)的,税率为 20%
09010200	--唇用化妆品			
09010210	---唇膏、唇彩			
09010211	----唇膏、唇彩	支	150	完税价格≥10 元/毫升(克)的,税率为 50%
09010212	----唇膏、唇彩	支	150	完税价格<10 元/毫升(克)的,税率为 20%
09010220	---唇线笔			
09010221	----唇线笔	支	100	完税价格≥10 元/毫升(克)的,税率为 50%
09010222	----唇线笔	支	100	完税价格<10 元/毫升(克)的,税率为 20%
09010290	---其他唇用化妆品			
09010291	----其他唇用化妆品	件	另行确定	完税价格≥10 元/毫升(克)或完税价格≥15 元/片(张)的,税率为 50%
09010299	----其他唇用化妆品	件	另行确定	完税价格<10 元/毫升(克),完税价格<15 元/片(张)的,税率为 20%
09010300	--眼用化妆品			
09010310	---睫毛膏(液、油)			
09010311	----睫毛膏(液、油)	支	100	完税价格≥10 元/毫升(克)的,税率为 50%
09010312	----睫毛膏(液、油)	支	100	完税价格<10 元/毫升(克)的,税率为 20%
09010320	---眼线笔(液)			
09010321	----眼线笔(液)	支	100	完税价格≥10 元/毫升(克)的,税率为 50%
09010322	----眼线笔(液)	支	100	完税价格<10 元/毫升(克)的,税率为 20%
09010330	---眉笔(眉粉)			
09010331	----眉笔(眉粉)	支	100	完税价格≥10 元/毫升(克)的,税率为 50%
09010332	----眉笔(眉粉)	支	100	完税价格<10 元/毫升(克)的,税率为 20%
09010340	---眼影			
09010341	----眼影	盒	100	完税价格≥10 元/毫升(克)的,税率为 50%
09010342	----眼影	盒	100	完税价格<10 元/毫升(克)的,税率为 20%
09010390	---其他眼用化妆品			
09010391	----其他眼用化妆品	件	另行确定	完税价格≥10 元/毫升(克)或完税价格≥15 元/片(张)的,税率为 50%
09010392	----其他眼用化妆品	件	另行确定	完税价格<10 元/毫升(克),完税价格<15 元/片(张)的,税率为 20%
09010400	--指(趾)甲化妆品			
09010410	---洗甲(趾)液			
09010411	----洗甲(趾)液	支	50	完税价格≥10 元/毫升(克)的,税率为 50%
09010412	----洗甲(趾)液	支	50	完税价格<10 元/毫升(克)的,税率为 20%
09010420	---指(趾)甲油			
09010421	----指(趾)甲油	支	20	完税价格≥10 元/毫升(克)的,税率为 50%

税号	品名及规格	单位	完税价格（人民币:元）	税率
09010422	----指(趾)甲油	支	20	完税价格＜10 元/毫升(克)的,税率为 20%
09010490	---其他指(趾)甲化妆品			
09010491	----其他指(趾)甲化妆品	件	另行确定	完税价格≥10 元/毫升(克)或完税价格≥15 元/片(张)的,税率为 50%
09010492	----其他指(趾)甲化妆品	件	另行确定	完税价格＜10 元/毫升(克),完税价格＜15 元/片(张)的,税率为 20%
09010500	--粉状化妆品			
09010510	---粉底及粉底液			
09010511	----粉底及粉底液	盒、支	200	完税价格≥10 元/克的,税率为 50%
09010512	----粉底及粉底液	盒、支	200	完税价格＜10 元/克的,税率为 20%
09010520	---粉饼			
09010521	----粉饼	盒	150	完税价格≥10 元/克的,税率为 50%
09010522	----粉饼	盒	150	完税价格＜10 元/克的,税率为 20%
09010530	---扑面粉			
09010531	----扑面粉	盒	150	完税价格≥10 元/克的,税率为 50%
09010532	----扑面粉	盒	150	完税价格＜10 元/克的,税率为 20%
09010540	---胭脂(粉)、腮红(粉)			
09010541	----胭脂(粉)、腮红(粉)	盒、支	100	完税价格≥10 元/克的,税率为 50%
09010542	----胭脂(粉)、腮红(粉)	盒、支	100	完税价格＜10 元/克的,税率为 20%
09010590	---其他粉状化妆品			
09010591	----其他粉状化妆品	件	另行确定	完税价格≥10 元/克的,税率为 50%
09010592	----其他粉状化妆品	件	另行确定	完税价格＜10 元/克的,税率为 20%
09010600	--其他美容品或化妆品			
09010610	---其他美容品或化妆品	件、套	另行确定	完税价格≥10 元/毫升(克)或完税价格≥15 元/片(张)的,税率为 50%
09010620	---其他美容品或化妆品	件、套	另行确定	完税价格＜10 元/毫升(克),完税价格＜15 元/片(张)的,税率为 20%
09020000	**-洗护用品**			
09020100	--清洁用品			
09020110	---洗面奶、洁面霜	支、瓶	100	20%
09020120	---卸妆水	支、瓶	150	20%
09020190	---其他清洁用品	件、套	另行确定	20%
09020200	--护肤用品			
09020210	---化妆水			
09020211	----化妆水	支、瓶	150	完税价格≥10 元/毫升(克)的,税率为 50%
09020212	----化妆水	支、瓶	150	完税价格＜10 元/毫升(克)的,税率为 20%
09020220	---眼霜			
09020221	----眼霜	支、瓶	200	完税价格≥10 元/毫升(克)的,税率为 50%
09020222	----眼霜	支、瓶	200	完税价格＜10 元/毫升(克)的,税率为 20%
09020230	---面霜及乳液			
09020231	----面霜及乳液	支、瓶	200	完税价格≥10 元/毫升(克)的,税率为 50%
09020232	----面霜及乳液	支、瓶	200	完税价格＜10 元/毫升(克)的,税率为 20%
09020240	---精华液(素)			
09020241	----精华液(素)	支、瓶	300	完税价格≥10 元/毫升(克)的,税率为 50%
09020242	----精华液(素)	支、瓶	300	完税价格＜10 元/毫升(克)的,税率为 20%
09020250	---防晒霜(露、乳液)			
09020251	----防晒霜(露、乳液)	支	150	完税价格≥10 元/毫升(克)的,税率为 50%
09020252	----防晒霜(露、乳液)	支	150	完税价格＜10 元/毫升(克)的,税率为 20%
09020260	---面膜			
09020261	----面膜	张、瓶	20	完税价格≥10 元/毫升(克)或完税价格≥15 元/片(张)的,税率为 50%
09020262	----面膜	张、瓶	20	完税价格＜10 元/毫升(克),完税价格＜15 元/片(张)的,税率为 20%
09020270	---润唇膏			

税号	品名及规格	单位	完税价格 (人民币:元)	税率
09020271	----润唇膏	支	20	完税价格≥10 元/毫升(克)的,税率为 50%
09020272	----润唇膏	支	20	完税价格<10 元/毫升(克)的,税率为 20%
09020280	---护手霜			
09020281	----护手霜	支、瓶	50	完税价格≥10 元/毫升(克)的,税率为 50%
09020282	----护手霜	支、瓶	50	完税价格<10 元/毫升(克)的,税率为 20%
09020290	---其他护肤用品			
09020291	----其他护肤用品	件、套	另行确定	完税价格≥10 元/毫升(克)或完税价格≥15 元/片(张)的,税率为 50%
09020292	----其他护肤用品	件、套	另行确定	完税价格<10 元/毫升(克),完税价格<15 元/片(张)的,税率为 20%
09020300	--护发用品			
09020310	---洗/护发液	支、瓶	30	20%
09020390	---其他护发用品	件、套	另行确定	20%
09029900	--其他清洁护理品	件、套	另行确定	20%
10000000	**家用医疗、保健及美容器材**			
10010000	**-家用医疗器材**			
10010100	--血糖计	个	500	20%
10010200	--血糖试纸	张	5	20%
10010300	--红外线耳探热针	个	200	20%
10010400	--家用雾化机	台	2000	20%
10010500	--血压计	个	500	20%
10019900	--其他家用医疗器材	件	另行确定	20%
10020000	**-家用保健器材**			
10020100	--按摩床	张	10000	20%
10020200	--按摩椅	张	5000	20%
10029900	--其他家用保健器材	件	另行确定	20%
10030000	**-家用美容器材**			
10030100	--蒸汽仪	台	200	20%
10030200	--喷雾器	台	400	20%
10039900	--其他家用美容器材	台	另行确定	20%
11000000	**厨卫用具及小家电**			
11010000	**-厨房用具**			
11010100	--餐具/刀具	个、把	20	20%
11010200	--炊具	件	100	20%
11010300	--灶具	件	1000	20%
11010400	--净水器(含过滤芯)	个	500	20%
11010500	--净水器过滤芯	个	200	20%
11011100	--电饭煲	个	500	20%
11011200	--微波炉	台	600	20%
11011300	--电磁炉	台	800	20%
11011400	--抽油烟机	台	1000	20%
11011500	--家用洗碗机	台	1500	20%
11011600	--电动榨汁机	台	100	20%
11011700	--咖啡机	台	4000	20%
11019900	--其他厨房用具	件、个	另行确定	20%
11020000	**-卫生用具、洁具**			
11020100	--热水器	台	1000	20%
11021120	--电吹风机	个	200	20%
11021130	--电动剃须刀	个	200	20%
11020400	--电动牙刷	个	200	20%
11029900	--其他卫生间用具	件、个	另行确定	20%
11030000	**-小家电**			
11030100	--电话机			
11030110	---普通电话机	台	200	13%
11030120	---手持移动电话机			
11030121	----键盘式手持移动电话机	台	1000	13%
11030122	----触屏式手持移动电话机	台	另行确定	13%
11030130	---电话传真机	台	1000	13%
11030140	---可视电话机	台	1000	13%
11030150	---电话机配件、附件	件	另行确定	13%
11030190	---其他电话机	台	另行确定	13%
11031200	--电风扇	台	400	20%
11031300	--电熨斗	台	200	20%

税号	品名及规格	单位	完税价格（人民币:元）	税率
11031400	--电暖器	台	400	20%
11031500	--增/除湿机、增除湿一体机	台	1500	20%
11031600	--空气清新机	台	1000	20%
11031700	--吸尘器	台	500	20%
11031800	--地板打蜡机	台	500	20%
11031900	--电动剪草机	台	2000	20%
11032000	--电缝纫机、编织机	台	2000	20%
11032100	--灯具	台、件	另行确定	20%
11039900	--其他小家电			
11039910	--其他家电类信息技术产品	件、个	另行确定	13%
11039990	--其他小家电	件、个	另行确定	20%
12000000	**家具**			
12010000	**-实木家具**	件	另行确定	13%
12020000	**-皮质家具**	件	1000	13%
12030000	**-藤、竹质家具**	件	600	13%
12990000	**-其他家具**	件	另行确定	13%
13000000	**空调及其配件、附件**			
13010000	**-空调**			
13010100	--1 匹及以下	台	2000	20%
13010200	--1 匹以上 2 匹以下(含 2 匹)	台	4000	20%
13010300	--2 匹以上 3 匹以下(含 3 匹)	台	6000	20%
13010400	--3 匹以上	台	另行确定	20%
13020000	**-空调配件、附件**	个	另行确定	20%
13990000	**-其他空调**	台	另行确定	20%
14000000	**电冰箱及其配件、附件**			
14010000	**-电冰箱、冰柜**			
14010100	--100 公升及以下	台	1000	20%
14010200	--101—200 公升	台	2000	20%
14010300	--201—250 公升	台	3000	20%
14010400	--251—300 公升	台	5000	20%
14010500	--301—400 公升	台	10000	20%
14010600	--401—500 公升	台	15000	20%
14010700	--501 公升及以上	台	另行确定	20%
14020000	**-红酒柜**			
14020100	--12 瓶及以下	台	1000	20%
14020200	--13—18 瓶	台	2000	20%
14020300	--19—45 瓶	台	3000	20%
14020400	--46—75 瓶	台	4000	20%
14020500	--76—120 瓶	台	5000	20%
14020600	--121 瓶及以上	台	另行确定	20%
14030000	**-电冰箱配件、附件**	件	另行确定	20%
14990000	**-其他电冰箱**	台	另行确定	20%
15000000	**洗衣设备及其配件、附件**			
15010000	**-洗衣机**			
15010100	--波轮式	台	1000	20%
15010200	--滚筒式	台	3000	20%
15020000	**-干衣机/烘干机**	台	2000	20%
15030000	**-洗衣设备配件、附件**	件	另行确定	20%
15990000	**-其他洗衣设备**	台	另行确定	20%
16000000	**电视机及其配件、附件**			
16010000	**-电视机**			
16010100	--22 英寸及以下	台	1000	20%
16010200	--23 英寸至 32 英寸	台	2000	20%
16010300	--33 英寸至 39 英寸	台	4000	20%
16010400	--40 英寸至 42 英寸	台	6000	20%
16010500	--43 英寸至 45 英寸	台	8000	20%
16010600	--46 英寸至 49 英寸	台	10000	20%
16010700	--50 英寸至 54 英寸	台	20000	20%
16010800	--55 英寸至 59 英寸	台	30000	20%
16010900	--60 英寸至 64 英寸	台	35000	20%
16011000	--65 英寸以上	台	另行确定	20%
16020000	**-电视机配件、附件**	件、个	另行确定	20%
16990000	**-其他电视机**	台	另行确定	20%
17000000	**摄影(像)设备及其配件、附件**			
17010000	**-照相机**			
17010100	--数字照相机			
17010110	----一体式数字照相机	台	2000	13%

税号	品名及规格	单位	完税价格（人民币:元）	税率
17010120	---镜头可拆卸式数字照相机			
17010121	----可拆卸式数字照相机机身	台	5000	13%
17010122	----可拆卸式数码照相机镜头	个	2000	20%
17010200	--照相机(非数字照相机)			
17010210	---反光式胶片照相机	台	5000	20%
17010220	---一次成像照相机	台	1000	20%
17010290	---其他照相机	台	另行确定	20%
17020000	**-摄像机**			
17020100	--电视摄像机	台	另行确定	20%
17020200	--视频摄录一体机	台	4000	13%
17029900	--其他摄像机	台	另行确定	20%
17030000	**-其他摄影(像)设备**			
17030100	--其他摄影(像)类信息技术产品	台、件	另行确定	13%
17030200	--其他摄影(像)设备	台、件	另行确定	20%
17990000	**-摄影(像)设备配件、附件**			
17990100	--数码存储卡			
17990110	---存储容量 8G 及以下	个	50	13%
17990120	---存储容量 8G 以上	个	200	13%
17990200	--闪光灯	个	500	20%
17990300	--支架	个	300	20%
17990400	--胶卷	个	20	20%
17999900	--其他摄影(像)设备配件、附件	件	另行确定	20%
18000000	**影音设备及其配件、附件**			
18010000	**-便携式影音设备**			
18010100	--录音笔	台	200	20%
18010200	--录音机	台	200	20%
18010300	--收音机	台	200	20%
18010400	--MP3 播放器(音频多媒体播放器)	台	100	20%
18010500	--MP4 播放器(视频多媒体播放器)	台	500	20%
18019900	--其他便携式影音设备	台	另行确定	20%
18020000	**-音响设备**			
18020100	--电唱机(含便携式激光唱机)	台	500	20%
18020200	--放像机	台	500	20%
18020300	--录像机	台	800	20%
18020400	--激光视盘机(LD、VCD、DVD 等)	台	500	20%
18020500	--(单)功能座(功放、调谐、均衡等)	台	1000	20%
18020600	--音箱	个	1000	20%
18020700	--便携式收音、录音、激光唱盘一体机	台	1000	20%
18029900	--其他音响设备	件	另行确定	20%
18030000	**-影音设备配件、附件**			
18030100	--耳机及耳塞机	副	50	13%
18030200	--磁盘	盘	30	13%
18030300	--磁带			
18030310	---重放声音或图像信息的磁带	盘	50	20%
18030320	---其他磁带	盘	10	13%
18030400	--半导体媒体	张	30	13%
18030500	--唱片			
18030510	---已录制唱片	张	50	20%
18030520	---其他唱片	张	50	13%
18030600	--光学媒体	张	另行确定	13%
18039900	--其他影音设备配件、附件	个、件	另行确定	20%
18990000	**-其他影音设备**			
18990100	--其他影音类信息技术产品	台、件	另行确定	13%
18990200	--其他影音设备	个、台	另行确定	20%
19000000	**计算机及其外围设备**			
19010000	**-计算机**			
19010100	--台式个人计算机主机	台	2000	13%
19010200	--主机、显示器一体机	台	3000	13%
19010300	--笔记本电脑(含平板电脑、掌上电脑、上网本等)			
19010310	---键盘式笔记本电脑	台	2000	13%
19010320	---触屏式笔记本电脑	台	另行确定	13%
19010400	--计算机配件			
19010410	---主板	块	500	13%
19010420	---中央处理器(CPU)	个	500	13%
19010430	---内存条			
19010431	----4G 及以下	条	200	13%

税号	品名及规格	单位	完税价格（人民币：元）	税率
19010432	----4G 以上	条	300	13%
19010440	---功能卡	块	300	13%
19010490	---其他计算机配件	块、个	另行确定	13%
19019900	--其他计算机	台	另行确定	13%
19020000	**-计算机外围设备**			
19020100	--鼠标	个	50	13%
19020200	--键盘	个	80	13%
19020300	--音箱	个	50	13%
19020400	--显示器			
19020410	---液晶显示器			
19020411	----19 英寸及以下	台	800	13%
19020412	----19 英寸以上，24 英寸及以下	台	1200	13%
19020413	----24 英寸以上	台	另行确定	13%
19020420	---显像管(CRT)显示器			
19020421	----17 英寸及以下	台	300	13%
19020422	----17 英寸以上	台	500	13%
19020490	---其他显示器	台	另行确定	13%
19020500	--打印机			
19020510	---激光打印机			
19020511	----黑白激光打印机	台	1000	13%
19020512	----彩色激光打印机	台	3000	13%
19020520	---喷墨打印机	台	500	13%
19020530	---针式打印机	台	1000	13%
19020540	---多功能一体打印机			
19020541	----喷墨多功能一体打印机	台	600	13%
19020542	----激光多功能一体打印机	台	1500	13%
19020590	---其他打印机	台	另行确定	13%
19020600	--扫描仪	台	1000	13%
19020700	--视频投影仪	台	5000	13%
19020800	--驱动器			
19020810	---CD	台	100	13%
19020820	---DVD	台	200	13%
19020890	---其他驱动器	台	另行确定	13%
19020900	--存储器			
19020910	---硬盘/移动硬盘			
19020911	----1T 及以下	个	300	13%
19020912	----1T 以上 2T 以下(含 2T)	个	500	13%
19020913	----2T 以上	个	另行确定	13%
19020920	---U 盘	个	50	13%
19020990	---其他存储器	个、盒	另行确定	13%
19029900	--其他计算机外围设备	台	另行确定	13%
20000000	**书报、刊物及其他各类印刷品**	本、套	另行确定	13%
21000000	**教育用影视资料**			
21010000	**-幻灯片**	片	10	13%
21020000	**-录音带**	盘	10	13%
21030000	**-录像带**	盘	50	13%
21990000	**-其他教育专用影视资料**	件	另行确定	13%
22000000	**文具用品、玩具、游戏品、节日或其他娱乐用品**			
22010000	**-文具用品**			
22010100	--电子计算器	个	200	13%
22010200	--电子字典/记事簿	个	300	13%
22010300	--电子(纸)书	台	800	13%
22010400	--笔	支	50	20%
22019900	--其他文具用品	件	另行确定	20%
22020000	**-玩具**			
22020100	--带轮玩具			
22020110	---单脚滑行车、踏板车	个	100	13%
22020190	---其他带轮玩具	个	另行确定	13%
22020200	--玩偶	个	100	13%
22020300	--缩小(按比例缩小)的模型及类似娱乐用模型	套	300	13%
22020400	--智力玩具	套	100	13%
22020500	--玩具乐器	个	100	13%
22029900	--其他玩具	件	另行确定	13%
22030000	**-游戏品**			
22030100	--游戏机			
22030110	---便携式游戏机	台	1000	13%
22030120	---电脑游戏机	台	2000	13%

税号	品名及规格	单位	完税价格（人民币:元）	税率
22030130	---其他游戏机	台	另行确定	13%
22030190	---游戏机配件、附件			
22030191	----游戏碟、盘、卡	张、个	60	13%
22030192	----游戏机遥控器、控制器	个	200	13%
22030199	----其他游戏机配件、附件	件	另行确定	13%
22030200	--桌上或室内游戏用品			
22030210	---纸牌游戏用品	套	50	13%
22030220	---棋类产品	套	50	13%
22030290	---其他桌上或室内游戏用品	件、套	另行确定	13%
22030900	--游戏品的配件、附件	件	另行确定	13%
22040000	**-节日或其他娱乐用品**			
22040100	--节日用品			
22040110	---节日装饰品	件	30	13%
22040120	---圣诞节传统用品	件	50	13%
22040130	---化装舞会及类似场合用品	件	20	13%
22040190	---其他节日用品	件	另行确定	13%
22040200	--魔术道具及嬉戏品	件	另行确定	13%
22040900	--其他娱乐用品	件	另行确定	13%
23000000	**邮票、艺术品、收藏品**			
23010000	**-邮票**			
23010100	--中国邮票、小型张、纪念封	张	另行确定	20%
23010200	--港澳台、外国邮票	张	5	20%
23010300	--港澳台、外国小型张、纪念封	张	10	20%
23020000	**-艺术品、收藏品**	件	另行确定	20%
24000000	**乐器**			
24010000	**-钢琴**			
24010100	--三角钢琴	架	90000	20%
24010200	--立式钢琴	架	15000	20%
24010300	--电子钢琴	架	5000	20%
24019900	--其他钢琴	架	另行确定	20%
24020000	**-电子琴**			
24020100	--49 键以下	台	800	20%
24020200	--49 键及以上	台	3000	20%
24030000	**-萨克斯**	把	10000	20%
24040000	**-电子吉他**	把	2000	20%
24050000	**-数码小提琴**	把	5000	20%
24060000	**-长、短笛**	支	5000	20%
24070000	**-单簧管**	支	4000	20%
24080000	**-双簧管**	支	10000	20%
24090000	**-古筝**	架	2000	20%
24990000	**-其他乐器**	件	另行确定	20%
25000000	**运动用品、钓鱼用品**			
25010000	**-高尔夫球及球具**			
25010100	--球杆	根	1000	50%
25010200	--球	个	20	50%
25019900	--其他高尔夫球具	件	另行确定	50%
25020000	**-运动器具**			
25020100	--网球拍	个	500	20%
25020200	--羽毛球拍	个	300	20%
25029900	--其他运动器具	件	另行确定	20%
25030000	**-多功能健身器具**			
25030100	--跑步机	件	2000	20%
25030200	--健身车	件	1000	20%
25030300	--综合训练器	件	3000	20%
25039900	--其他多功能健身器具	件	另行确定	20%
25040000	**-钓鱼用品**	件	另行确定	20%
25990000	**-其他运动用品**	件	另行确定	20%
26000000	**自行车**			
26010000	**-自行车**	辆	500	20%
26020000	**-三轮车**	辆	500	20%
26030000	**-婴孩车**	辆	200	20%
26090000	**-自行车配件、附件**	件	另行确定	20%
27000000	**其他物品**	件	另行确定	20%

备注:对 **02000000** 税号项下的各类酒，单瓶容量超出 **750** 毫升的，每满 **750** 毫升按照 **1** 瓶计征税赋，超出部分不足 **750** 毫升的不予计算。

5

中华人民共和国海关出口税则

（2022 年 1 月 1 日起实施）

Customs Export Tariff of the People's Republic of China

(Enforced from January 1,2022)

注释：

出口税则也采用《商品名称及编码协调制度》目录，进口税则的归类总规则同样适用于出口税则。

出口商品税率表

序号	EX①	税则号列	商品名称(简称)	出口税率(%)	2022年暂定税率(%)
1		03019210	鳗鱼苗	20	
2		05061000	经酸处理的骨胶原及骨	40	
3		05069011	含牛羊成分的骨粉及骨废料	40	
4		05069019	其他骨粉及骨废料	40	
5		05069090	其他骨及角柱	40	
6	ex	05069090	已脱胶骨、角柱	40	0
7		26070000	铅矿砂及其精矿	30	
8		26080000	锌矿砂及其精矿	30	
9	ex	26080000	灰色饲料氧化锌(氧化锌 ZnO 含量大于 80%)	30	0
10		26090000	锡矿砂及其精矿	50	20
11		26110000	钨矿砂及其精矿	20	
12		26159010	水合钽铌原料(钽铌富集物)	30	
13		26159090	其他铌钽钒矿砂及其精矿	30	
14		26171010	生锑(锑精矿,选矿产品)	20	
15		28047010	黄磷(白磷)	20	
16		28047090	其他磷	20	
17	ex	28269090	氟钽酸钾	30	
18		29022000	苯	40	0
19		41039011	经逆鞣处理的山羊板皮	20	
20		41039019	未经逆鞣处理的山羊板皮	20	
21		72011000	非合金生铁,含磷量小于或等于 0.5%	20	
22		72012000	非合金生铁,含磷量>0.5%	20	
23		72015000	合金生铁、镜铁	20	
24		72021100	锰铁,含碳量>2%	20	
25		72021900	锰铁,含碳量≤2%	20	
26		72022100	硅铁,含硅量>55%	25	
27		72022900	硅铁,含硅量≤55%	25	
28		72023000	硅锰铁	20	
29		72024100	铬铁,含碳量>4%	40	
30		72024900	铬铁,含碳量≤4%	40	
31		72041000	铸铁废碎料	40	
32		72042100	不锈钢废碎料	40	
33		72042900	其他合金钢废碎料	40	
34		72043000	镀锡钢铁废碎料	40	
35		72044100	机械加工中产生的废料	40	
36		72044900	其他钢铁废碎料	40	
37		72045000	供再熔的碎料钢铁锭	40	
38		74020000	未精炼铜、电解精炼用铜阳极	30	
39	ex	74031111	高纯阴极铜(铜含量不低于 99.9999%)	30	0
40	ex	74031111	高纯阴极铜(铜含量高于 99.9935%,但低于 99.9999%)	30	5
41		74031119	其他阴极精炼铜	30	10
42		74031190	精炼铜阴极型材	30	10
43		74031200	精炼铜的线锭	30	10
44		74031300	精炼铜的坯段	30	10
45		74031900	其他未锻轧的精炼铜	30	10
46		74032100	未锻轧的铜锌合金(黄铜)	30	5
47		74032200	未锻轧的铜锡合金(青铜)	30	5
48		74032900	其他未锻轧的铜合金(税目 7405 的铜母合金除外)	30	5
49		74040000	铜废碎料	30	15
50		74071010	铬锆铜制条、杆及型材及异型材	30	0
51		74071090	其他精炼铜条、杆及型材及异型材	30	0
52		74072111	直线度不大于 0.5 毫米/米铜锌合金条、杆	30	0
53		74072119	其他铜锌合金条、杆	30	0
54		74072190	其他黄铜条、杆及型材及异型材	30	0
55		74072900	其他铜合金条杆、型材及异型材	30	0

序号	EX[1]	税则号列	商品名称(简称)	出口税率(%)	2022年暂定税率(%)
56		74081100	最大截面尺寸>6mm的精炼铜丝	30	0
57		74081900	截面尺寸≤6mm的精炼铜丝	30	0
58		74082100	黄铜丝	30	0
59		74082210	铜镍锌铅合金(加铅德银)丝	30	0
60		74082290	其他白铜丝或德银(铜镍锌合金)丝	30	0
61		74082900	其他铜合金丝	30	0
62		74091110	含氧量不超过10PPM,厚度超过0.15mm的盘卷精炼铜板、片、带	30	0
63		74091190	厚度超过0.15mm的其他盘卷精炼铜板、片、带	30	0
64		74091900	其他精炼铜板、片、带	30	0
65		74092100	成卷的黄铜板、片、带	30	0
66		74092900	其他黄铜板、片、带	30	0
67		74093100	成卷的青铜板、片、带	30	0
68		74093900	其他青铜板、片、带	30	0
69		74094000	白铜或德银制板、片、带	30	0
70		74099000	其他铜合金板、片、带	30	0
71		75021010	按重量计镍、钴总量在99.99%及以上的,但钴含量不超过0.005%的非合金镍	40	5
72		75021090	其他非合金镍	40	15
73		75022000	未锻轧镍合金	40	15
74		75089010	电镀用镍阳极	40	15
75		76011010	按重量计含铝量在99.95%及以上的未锻轧非铝合金	30	0
76		76011090	其他未锻轧非铝合金	30	15
77	ex	76012000	碱金属含量(Na+K+Ca)<10ppm,氢含量<0.12ml/100gAl的低碱精炼铝合金	30	0
78	ex	76012000	其他未锻轧铝合金	30	15
79		76020000	铝废碎料	30	15
80		76041090	非合金铝型材及异形材	20	0
81		76042100	铝合金制空心异型材	20	0
82		76041010	非合金铝条、杆	20	0
83		76042910	铝合金条、杆	20	0
84		76042990	铝合金型材及异形材	20	0
85		76051100	纯铝制的粗丝	20	0
86		76051900	纯铝制的细丝	20	0
87		76052100	铝合金制的粗丝	20	0
88		76052900	铝合金制的细丝	20	0
89		76061121	0.3mm≤厚度<0.36mm的非合金铝与塑料复合的矩形板片带	20	0
90		76061129	其他0.3mm≤厚度<0.36mm的非合金铝制矩形铝板片带	20	0
91		76061191	0.28mm≤厚度≤0.35mm的铝合金制矩形铝板片带	20	0
92		76061199	纯铝制矩形的其他板、片及带	20	0
93		76061220	厚度<0.28mm的铝合金制矩形铝板片带	20	0
94		76061230	0.28mm≤厚度≤0.35mm的铝合金制矩形铝板片带	20	0
95		76061251	0.35mm<厚度≤4mm的铝合金与塑料复合的矩形板片带	20	0
96		76061259	其他0.35mm<厚度≤4mm的铝合金制矩形铝板片带	20	0
97		76061290	厚度>4mm的铝合金制矩形铝板片带	20	0
98		76069100	纯铝制非矩形的板、片及带	20	0
99		76069200	铝合金制非矩形的板、片及带	20	0
100		79011110	按重量计含锌量在99.995%及以上的未锻轧锌	20	0
101		79011190	含锌量不小于99.99%,并小于99.995%的未锻轧锌	20	5
102		79011200	含锌量<99.99%的未锻轧锌	20	15
103		79012000	未锻轧锌合金	20	0
104		81101010	未锻轧锑	20	5
105		81101020	锑粉末	20	
106		81102000	锑废碎料	20	

注①"ex"表示实施暂定税率的商品应在该税则号列范围内,以具体商品描述为准。

注②除标注ex的税则号列外,商品名称仅供参考,具体商品范围以《中华人民共和国进出口税则》中 的税则号列对应的商品范围为准。

6

中华人民共和国进出口关税税款计算方法

Calculation methods for Import and Export Tax of the People's Republic of China

本书所列计算方法是根据《中华人民共和国关税条例》、《中华人民共和国增值税暂行条例》及《中华人民共和国消费税暂行条例》编制的。

为便于使用，现将有关问题说明如下：

一、所称进口税包括进口关税、进口环节增值税(简称增值税)、进口环节消费税(简称消费税)，其中消费税仅对少数商品征收；出口税只含出口关税一项。

二、关税税率分为优惠关税税率和普通关税税率。凡原产地属于世贸组织成员或与我国签定有互惠双边贸易协定的国家或地区进口的商品，其进口关税税率使用优惠关税税率，否则使用普通关税税率。

三、税款计算公式

$$\text{进口关税税额}=\text{到岸价格}\times\text{进口关税税率}$$

$$\text{出口关税税额}=\frac{\text{离岸价格}}{1+\text{出口税税率}}\times\text{出口关税税率}$$

$$\text{增值税税额}=(\text{到岸价}+\text{进口关税额}+\text{消费税额})\times\text{增值税税率}$$

$$\text{从价消费税税额}=\left(\frac{\text{到岸价}+\text{关税额}}{1-\text{消费税税率}}\right)\times\text{消费税税率}$$

$$\text{从量消费税税额}=\text{应征消费税的商品数量}\times\text{消费税单位税额}$$

其中，从量消费税商品计量单位的换算标准(按体积净重计)如下：

啤酒 1 吨=988 升

黄酒 1 吨=962 升

汽油 1 吨=1388 升

柴油 1 吨=1176 升

$$\text{进口税额}=\text{进口关税}+\text{增值税}+\text{消费税}$$

$$=\left(\frac{\text{进口关税率}+\text{消费税率}+\text{增值税率}+\text{进口关税率}\times\text{增值税率}}{1-\text{消费税税率}}\right)\times\text{到岸价}$$

$$=\text{常数}\times\text{到岸价}$$

四、为便于计算进口税额，本书编制了《进口税计税系数表》，其使用方法如下：

(一)"系数表 1"适用于应征消费税税率不为 0 税率的商品。鉴于此类商品法定增值税率均为 17%，因此在本书中查出该商品的关税税率和消费税税率后，在"表 1"内找出这两个税率交叉栏内的常数，用进口货物的到岸价乘以该常数，即为应纳进口税额。

(二)"系数表 2"适用于消费税税率为 0 的进口商品。首先在本书中查出该商品的关税税率和增值税税率，然后在"表 2"内找出这两个税率的交叉栏内的常数，用进口货物的到岸价乘以该常数即为应纳进口税额。

五、对适用于暂定税率的商品，关税税率应用暂定关税税率。

The Calculation methods in this book is compiled in accordance with Regulations on Customs Tariff of the People's Republic of China, Provisional Regulations on Value-added Tax of the People's Republic of China and Provisional Regulations on Consumption Tax of the People's Republic of China.

For the convenience of usage, relevant explanations are listed below:

1. Import tax we mean consists of import customs duty (ICD), value-added tax (VAT), and consumption tax (CT) among which CT is levied on a few items of goods. Export tax consists of only export customs duty (ECD).

2. Import customs duty rates we mean fall into general duty rates and preferential duty rates. The preferential duty rates apply to goods originally produced or manufactured in countries with which the People's Republic of China has concluded trading agreement. Otherewise, the general duty rates will be applied.

3. Calculation formulae for tax collection

$$\text{ICD}=\text{CIF value}\times\text{ICD rate}$$

$$\text{ECD}=\frac{\text{FOB value}}{1+\text{ECD rate}}\times\text{ECD rate}$$

$$\text{VAT}=(\text{CIF value}+\text{ICD}+\text{CT})\times\text{VAT rate}$$

$$\textit{Ad Valorem CT}=\left(\frac{\text{CIF value}+\text{ICD}}{1-\text{CT rate}}\right)\times\text{CT rate}$$

$$\text{Specific CT}=\text{Quantity of goods}\times\text{unit CT rate}$$

Note: The following is the conversion table of measurements of goods on which specific consumption tax is levied (net bulk)

Beer	1ton=988 litres
Millet wine	1 ton=962 litres
Gasoline	1 ton=1388 litres
Diesel	1 ton=1176 litres

$$\text{Total Import Tax}=\text{ICD}+\text{VAT}+\text{CT}$$

$$=\left(\frac{\text{ICD rate}+\text{CT rate}+\text{VAT rate}+\text{ICD rate}\times\text{VAT rate}}{1-\text{CT rate}}\right)\times\text{CIF value}$$

$$=\text{Coefficient}\times\text{CIF value}$$

4. To facilitate easy calculation, we compiled tables of import tax coefficients for reference. The following are the exemplary usage methods:

(1) The Table of Import Tax Coefficient (Consumption Taxes Applicable) applies to goods on which the consumption tax is levied. In viewof the statutory VAT rate is 17% for all goods in this table, the user may first find the duty rate and consumption tax rate of a particular type of goods in the table, then find the coefficient where those two rates meet in the table. The import tax payable equals the coefficient times the CIF value.

(2) The Table of Import Tax Cofficients (Consumption Taxes Not Applicable) applies to goods on which no consumption tax is levied. The user may first find the duty rate and VAT rate of a particular type of goods in the table, then find the coefficient where those two rates meet in the table. The total import tax is the coefficient times the CIF value.

5. As far as goods on which Interim Duty Rate is appliable, ICD rate is no other than Interim Duty Rate.

表 1　进口关税与进口环节代征税(消费税)计税常数表

Table of import tariff and import tax (Consumption tax and value added tax)

	关税率	不同消费税税率对应常数										
		1%	3%	5%	9%	10%	12%	15%	20%	25%	30%	40%
增值税13%	0.0%	14.141%	16.495%	18.947%	24.176%	25.556%	28.409%	32.941%	41.250%	50.667%	61.429%	88.333%
	1.0%	15.283%	17.660%	20.137%	25.418%	26.811%	29.693%	34.271%	42.663%	52.173%	63.043%	90.217%
	2.0%	16.424%	18.825%	21.326%	26.659%	28.067%	30.977%	35.600%	44.075%	53.680%	64.657%	92.100%
	3.0%	17.566%	19.990%	22.516%	27.901%	29.322%	32.261%	36.929%	45.488%	55.187%	66.271%	93.983%
	5.0%	19.848%	22.320%	24.895%	30.385%	31.833%	34.830%	39.588%	48.313%	58.200%	69.500%	97.750%
	6.5%	21.561%	24.067%	26.679%	32.247%	33.717%	36.756%	41.582%	50.431%	60.460%	71.921%	100.575%
	8.0%	23.273%	25.814%	28.463%	34.110%	35.600%	38.682%	43.576%	52.550%	62.720%	74.343%	103.400%
	10.0%	25.556%	28.144%	30.842%	36.593%	38.111%	41.250%	46.235%	55.375%	65.733%	77.571%	107.167%
	11.0%	26.697%	29.309%	32.032%	37.835%	39.367%	42.534%	47.565%	56.788%	67.240%	79.186%	109.050%
	12.5%	28.409%	31.057%	33.816%	39.698%	41.250%	44.460%	49.559%	58.906%	69.500%	81.607%	111.875%
	15.0%	31.263%	33.969%	36.789%	42.802%	44.389%	47.670%	52.882%	62.438%	73.267%	85.643%	116.583%
	16.0%	32.404%	35.134%	37.979%	44.044%	45.644%	48.955%	54.212%	63.850%	74.773%	87.257%	118.467%
	23.0%	40.394%	43.289%	46.305%	52.736%	54.433%	57.943%	63.518%	73.738%	85.320%	98.557%	131.650%
	80.0%	105.455%	109.691%	114.105%	123.516%	126.000%	131.136%	139.294%	154.250%	171.200%	190.571%	239.000%
	100.0%	128.283%	132.990%	137.895%	148.352%	151.111%	156.818%	165.882%	182.500%	201.333%	222.857%	276.667%
	150.0%	185.354%	191.237%	197.368%	210.440%	213.889%	221.023%	232.353%	253.125%	276.667%	303.571%	370.833%

注：

1.所列常数均已包括增值税在内。

2.常数计算公式为：

$$常数=\frac{进口关税税率+消费税税率+增值税税率+进口关税税率\times增值税税率}{1-消费税税率}$$

表 2　进口关税与进口环节代征税(增值税)计税常数表

Table of Import Tariff and Import Tax(Value added Tax)

关税税率	不同增值税税率对应常数		关税税率	不同增值税税率对应常数		关税税率	不同增值税税率对应常数	
	9%	13%		9%	13%		9%	13%
0.0%	9.00%	13.00%	2.0%	11.18%	15.26%	3.5%	12.82%	16.96%
0.4%	9.44%	13.45%	2.1%	11.29%	15.37%	3.8%	13.14%	17.29%
0.5%	9.55%	13.57%	2.3%	11.51%	15.60%	4.0%	13.36%	17.52%
0.8%	9.87%	13.90%	2.5%	11.73%	15.83%	4.2%	13.58%	17.75%
1.0%	10.09%	14.13%	2.6%	11.83%	15.94%	4.3%	13.69%	17.86%
1.1%	10.20%	14.24%	2.7%	11.94%	16.05%	4.4%	13.80%	17.97%
1.3%	10.42%	14.47%	3.0%	12.27%	16.39%	4.5%	13.91%	18.09%
1.5%	10.64%	14.70%	3.1%	12.38%	16.50%	4.7%	14.12%	18.31%
1.7%	10.85%	14.92%	3.2%	12.49%	16.62%	4.8%	14.23%	18.42%
1.8%	10.96%	15.03%	3.3%	12.60%	16.73%	5.0%	14.45%	18.65%
1.9%	11.07%	15.15%	3.4%	12.71%	16.84%	5.3%	14.78%	18.99%

关税税率	不同增值税税率对应常数	
	9%	13%
5.4%	14.89%	19.10%
5.5%	15.00%	19.22%
5.6%	15.10%	19.33%
5.8%	15.32%	19.55%
6.0%	15.54%	19.78%
6.1%	15.65%	19.89%
6.3%	15.87%	20.12%
6.5%	16.09%	20.35%
6.7%	16.30%	20.57%
6.8%	16.41%	20.68%
7.0%	16.63%	20.91%
7.5%	17.18%	21.48%
7.9%	17.61%	21.93%
8.0%	17.72%	22.04%
8.3%	18.05%	22.38%
8.4%	18.16%	22.49%
8.5%	18.27%	22.61%
8.8%	18.59%	22.94%
9.0%	18.81%	23.17%
9.3%	19.14%	23.51%
9.4%	19.25%	23.62%
9.5%	19.36%	23.74%
9.7%	19.57%	23.96%
10.0%	19.90%	24.30%
10.5%	20.45%	24.87%
11.0%	20.99%	25.43%
11.3%	21.32%	25.77%
11.7%	21.75%	26.22%
12.0%	22.08%	26.56%
12.5%	22.63%	27.13%
12.6%	22.73%	27.24%

关税税率	不同增值税税率对应常数	
	9%	13%
12.8%	22.95%	27.46%
13.0%	23.17%	27.69%
13.1%	23.28%	27.80%
13.5%	23.72%	28.26%
13.8%	24.04%	28.59%
14.0%	24.26%	28.82%
14.3%	24.59%	29.16%
14.4%	24.70%	29.27%
15.0%	25.35%	29.95%
15.6%	26.00%	30.63%
16.0%	26.44%	31.08%
16.5%	26.99%	31.65%
17.0%	27.53%	32.21%
17.5%	28.08%	32.78%
18.0%	28.62%	33.34%
18.8%	29.49%	34.24%
19.0%	29.71%	34.47%
19.3%	30.04%	34.81%
20.0%	30.80%	35.60%
21.0%	31.89%	36.73%
21.9%	32.87%	37.75%
22.0%	32.98%	37.86%
22.5%	33.53%	38.43%
23.0%	34.07%	38.99%
23.3%	34.40%	39.33%
24.0%	35.16%	40.12%
24.5%	35.71%	40.69%
25.0%	36.25%	41.25%
26.3%	37.67%	42.72%
27.0%	38.43%	43.51%
28.0%	39.52%	44.64%
29.0%	40.61%	45.77%

关税税率	不同增值税税率对应常数	
	9%	13%
29.2%	40.83%	46.00%
30.0%	41.70%	46.90%
32.0%	43.88%	49.16%
35.0%	47.15%	52.55%
36.0%	48.24%	53.68%
38.0%	50.42%	55.94%
40.0%	52.60%	58.20%
45.0%	58.05%	63.85%
46.0%	59.14%	64.98%
50.0%	63.50%	69.50%
57.0%	71.13%	77.41%
60.0%	74.40%	80.80%
63.0%	77.67%	84.19%
65.0%	79.85%	86.45%
70.0%	85.30%	92.10%
75.0%	90.75%	97.75%
80.0%	96.20%	103.40%
85.0%	101.65%	109.05%
90.0%	107.10%	114.70%
100.0%	118.00%	126.00%
110.0%	128.90%	137.30%
114.0%	133.26%	141.82%
125.0%	145.25%	154.25%
130.0%	150.70%	159.90%
150.0%	172.50%	182.50%
160.0%	183.40%	193.80%
170.0%	194.30%	205.10%
180.0%	205.20%	216.40%
190.0%	216.10%	227.70%
230.0%	259.70%	272.90%
270.0%	303.30%	318.10%

计量单位换算表
Conversion Table

面(地)积换算

公制		英美制			
平方米	平方厘米	平方码	平方英尺	平方英寸	平方尺
1	10000	1.1960	10.7639	1550	9
0.0001	1	0.00012	0.00108	0.155	0.0009
0.8361	8361	1	9	1296	7.525
0.0929	929	0.1111	1	144	0.836
0.00065	6.45	0.00077	0.00694	1	0.0058
0.111	1111	0.133	1.196	172.2	1

长度换算

公制		中国市制	英美制		
米	厘米	尺	码	英尺	英寸
1	100	3	1.094	3.2808	39.37
0.01	1	0.03	0.01094	0.03281	0.3937
0.3333	33.33	1	0.3646	1.094	13.123
0.9144	91.44	2.743	1	3	36
0.3048	30.48	0.9144	0.3334	1	12
0.0254	2.54	0.0762	0.0278	0.833	1

1 米=100 厘米=1000 毫米

重量换算(一)

公制	英制	美制	港制
公吨	长吨	短吨	司马担
1	0.9842	1.1023	16.535
1.016	1	1.12	16.8
0.9072	0.8929	1	15
0.05	0.04921	0.0551	0.8267
0.0508	0.05	0.056	0.8402
0.0605	0.0594	0.0667	1

港制 1 司马担=100 司马斤
公制 1 公吨=10 公担
英制 1 长吨=20 英担(CWT)
1 英担=50.8024 千克
美制 1 短吨=20 短担(CWT)
1 短担=100 磅=45.36 千克

公制	中国市制	英美制
千克	斤	磅
1000	2000	2204.6
1016	2032	2242
907	1814	2000
50	100	110.23
50.8	101.6	112
60.48	120.96	133.33
1	2	2.2046
0.5	1	1.1023
0.4536	0.9072	1

重量换算(二)

公制		英美制常衡		英美制金衡或药衡		中国市制
千克	克	磅	唡	磅	唡	两
1	1000	2.2046	35.2736	2.697	31.1507	20
0.001	1	0.0022	0.03527	0.00268	0.0321	0.02
0.4536	453.59	1	16	1.2153	14.5833	9.072
0.02835	28.35	0.0625	1	0.07595	0.9114	0.567
0.3732	373.24	0.82286	13.1657	1	12	7.465
0.0311	31.10	0.06857	1.0971	0.08333	1	0.622
0.05	50	0.1102	1.76368	0.13396	1.6075	1

宝石:1 克拉=0.2 克　　　1 金衡=155.5 克拉

容(体)积换算(一)

公制	中国市制	英制	美制
升	升	英加仑	美加仑
1	1	0.22	0.264
4.546	4.546	1	1.201
3.785	3.785	0.833	1

1000 升=1 立方米　　1 升=1000 毫升=1000 立方厘米(c.c.)

英制 1 加仑=277.42 立方英寸　　英制 1 加仑=231 立方英寸

容(体)积换算(二)

公制		英美制			中国市制
立方米	立方厘米	立方码	立方英尺	立方英寸	立方尺
1	1000000	1.303	35.3147	61024	27
0.000001	1	0.0000013	0.00004	0.06102	0.000027
0.7636	764555	1	27	46656	20.643
0.02832	28317	0.037	1	1728	0.7646
0.000016	16.387	0.00002	0.00058	1	0.00044
0.037	37037	0.0484	1.308	2260	1

木材体积单位换算

板(Board Foot Measure,BFM)

指厚一英寸、面积一平方英尺的木材

板材的换算:100 板=2.36 立方米

原木的换算:100 板=5 立方米(近似值)

功率换算

1 千瓦(kW)=1.34 英制马力(hp)=2.36 公制马力(hp)

1 英制马力=0.746 千瓦(kW)

1 公制马力=0.735 千瓦(kW)

1 千伏安(kVA)$=\frac{千瓦(kW)}{0.80}$

粮谷重量容积换算

品名	1 公吨折合蒲式耳	1 蒲式耳折合	
		磅	千克
小麦、大豆	36.743	60	27.216
玉米	39.368	56	25.402
大麦(英制)	44.092	50	22.68
大麦(美制)	45.931	48	21.773

1 英制蒲式耳(1.0321 美制蒲式耳)合 36.3677 升。

石(原)油重量、容积换算

国别	1 公吨折合			
	千升	美制桶	英制加仑	美制加仑
贡国、印度尼西亚	1.18	7.4	259.1	310.6
伊朗、沙特阿拉伯	1.19	7.49	261.8	314.5
日本	1.11	6.99	244.5	293.3
英国、科威特	1.16	7.31	255.8	306.7
委内瑞拉	1.09	6.84	239.2	287.4

注:世界平均比重的原油通常以 1 公吨=7.35 桶(每桶为 42 美制加仑)或 1174 升计。

常用度量衡英文名称和简写

名称	英文名称	简写	名称	英文名称	简写
克	gram	g.	码	yard	yd.
千克	kilogram	kg.	英尺	foot	ft.
公担	quintal	q.	英寸	inch	in
公吨	metric ton	m.t.	平方米	square metre	sq.m.
长吨	long ton	l.t.	平方英尺	square foot	sq.ft
短吨	short ton	sh.t.	平方码	square yard	sq.yd
英担	hundredweight	cwt.	立方米	cubic metre	cu.m.
美担	hundredweight	cwt.	立方英尺	cubic toor	cu.ft.
磅	pound	lb.	升	litre	l.
唡(常衡)	ounce	oz.	毫升	millilitre	ml.
(金衡)	ounce	oz.t	加仑	gallon	gal.
司马担	picul		蒲式耳	bushel	bu.
米	metre	m.	克拉	carat	car.
公里	kilomere	km.	马力	horse power	hp.
厘米	centimetre	cm.	千瓦	kilowatt	kw.
毫米	millimetre	mm.	公吨度	metric ton unit	m.t.u.